S0-BXN-098

Periodical Title Abbreviations: By Title

ISSN 0737-7843

Periodical Title Abbreviations: By Title

Covering: Periodical Title Abbreviations, Database Abbreviations, and Selected Monograph Abbreviations in Science, the Social Sciences, the Humanities, Law, Medicine, Religion, Library Science, Engineering, Education, Business, Art, and Many Other Fields

ELEVENTH EDITION

Volume 2

Editor,
LELAND G. ALKIRE, JR
Reference Librarian,
Eastern Washington University

Associate Editor,
Cheryl Westerman-Alkire

DETROIT • NEW YORK • TORONTO • LONDON

Editor: **Leland G. Alkire Jr.**

Associate Editor: Cheryl Westerman-Alkire

Gale Research Staff

Editor: Regie A. Carlton

Production Director: Mary Beth Trimper
Production Assistant: Shanna Heilveil
Graphic Services Supervisor: Barbara Yarrow
Macintosh Artist: Mikal Ansari

Manager, Technical Support Services: Theresa A. Rocklin
Program Design: Sheila Printup

Library of Congress Catalog Card Number 84-640700
ISBN 0-7876-1213-8
ISSN 0737-7843
Printed in the United States of America

Contents

Gale's publications in the acronyms and abbreviations field include:

***Acronyms, Initialisms & Abbreviations Dictionary* series:**

Acronyms, Initialisms & Abbreviations Dictionary (Volume 1). A guide to acronyms, initialisms, abbreviations, and similar contractions, arranged alphabetically by abbreviation.

Acronyms, Initialisms & Abbreviations Dictionary Supplement (Volume 2). An interedition supplement in which terms are arranged alphabetically both by abbreviation and by meaning.

Reverse Acronyms, Initialisms & Abbreviations Dictionary (Volume 3). A companion to Volume 1 in which terms are arranged alphabetically by meaning of the acronym, initialism, or abbreviation.

***Acronyms, Initialisms & Abbreviations Dictionary* Subject Guide series:**

Computer & Telecommunications Acronyms (Volume 1). A guide to acronyms, initialisms, abbreviations, and similar contractions used in the field of computers and telecommunications in which terms are arranged alphabetically and by meaning.

Business Acronyms (Volume 2). A guide to business-oriented acronyms, initialisms, abbreviations, and similar contractions in which terms are arranged alphabetically both by abbreviation and by meaning.

***International Acronyms, Initialisms & Abbreviations Dictionary* series:**

International Acronyms, Initialisms & Abbreviations Dictionary (Volume 1). A guide to foreign and international acronyms, initialisms, abbreviations, and similar contractions, arranged alphabetically by abbreviation.

Reverse International Acronyms, Initialisms & Abbreviations Dictionary (Volume 2). A companion to Volume 1, in which terms are arranged alphabetically by meaning of the acronym, initialism, or abbreviation.

***Periodical Title Abbreviations* series:**

Periodical Title Abbreviations: By Abbreviation (Volume 1). A guide to abbreviations commonly used for periodical titles, arranged alphabetically by abbreviation.

Periodical Title Abbreviations: By Title (Volume 2). A guide to abbreviations commonly used for periodical titles, arranged alphabetically by title.

New Periodical Title Abbreviations (Volume 3). An interedition supplement in which terms are arranged alphabetically both by abbreviation and by title.

Highlights

Over 175,000 Total Entries
15,400 New Abbreviations
Broad Coverage
Arrangement by Title

Periodical Title Abbreviations: By Title (PTA-T) is Volume 2 of a three-volume collection of periodical titles. Serving as a companion volume to *Periodical Title Abbreviations: By Abbreviation (PTA-A)*, it contains essentially the same 175,000 entries, but arranges them in alphabetical order by title, rather than by abbreviation (Volume 3, *New Periodical Title Abbreviations*, will consist of an interedition supplement to the main volumes).

Scope of Coverage

PTA-T enables indexers, abstracters, authors, and bibliographers to determine if and how a given periodical title has been previously abbreviated. It is intended to be used neither as an authority file nor as a standard for periodical abbreviations, but merely as a record of the myriad ways in which commonly used indexing and abstracting services abbreviate periodical titles.

Introduction

Prior to 1981, each edition of *Periodical Title Abbreviations* (*PTA*) consisted of a single volume that described the multitudinous ways in which periodical titles are abbreviated. This was done by means of a simple alphabetical arrangement of such abbreviations, each of which followed by its respective full title.

For over a decade, *Periodical Title Abbreviations* attempted to meet the needs of academic, public and special libraries for quick translations of cryptic periodical citations, as well as similar needs among scholars, scientific researchers, and those generally associated with the information sciences. During this period, *PTA* made no attempt to prescribe short-form usage, nor has any authoritativeness been suggested since. Moreover, any effort at prescribing how a given periodical ought to be abbreviated seemed doomed from the start, for though standards already had been formulated by such bodies as the American National Standards Institute, they had not been widely accepted beyond the sciences.

Then, as now, the range of opinions expressed by indexers and abstracters regarding this important bibliographic problem ranged from a stony "no periodical abbreviations under any circumstances" to detached replies that scholars who use such specialized services will, of course, be able to determine the meaning involved. For those of us who labored over *Periodical Title Abbreviations*, the ideal of uniformly constructed abbreviations was overriden by the certain knowledge that such agreement among indexers was as yet a distant hope.

Purpose and Scope

The decision to produce the By Title volume of *Periodical Title Abbreviations* was motivated by the same assumptions as those that led to the creation of the original edition, now entitled *Periodical Title Abbreviations: By Abbreviation*. Like *PTA-A*, the By Title volume is intended only as a record of things as they are, not as they "should" be.

However, while identification and translation without comment remain the underlying principles of both volumes, an element that allows for prescriptiveness has emerged with the By Title volume. Now it is possible for an indexer, abstracter, researcher, author, or bibliographer to determine quickly if and how a given periodical title has been previously abbreviated. This leads to the hope that if a given title has been previously abbreviated in six different ways, an individual might see the wisdom of employing one of the existing abbreviations for that title rather than creating a seventh and redundant form.

In those instances where indexers, abstracters, or others see the need for new abbreviations, those of us whose daily lives are confounded by casually created abridgments will applaud their using some uniform system such as the *American Standard for Periodical Title Abbreviations*.

The list of major sources for the *PTA* series follows the User's Guide. No claim can be made for all-inclusiveness in *PTA-T*, nor for final authoritativeness, but if the present volume serves to restrain needless creation of new shortforms, then it will have served its users and others who are governed by such constructions.

For discussions of the full range of difficulties associated with periodical abbreviations, the reader is directed to the introduction to Volume 1 (*PTA: By Abbreviation*) and to the following publications:

Kinney, Mary R., *the Abbreviated Citation-A Bibliographic Problem*, Association of College and Research Libraries Monographs, Number 28, Chicago, American Library Association, 1967.

Alkire, Leland G., "The Initial Problem," *Serials Librarian*, vol. 2, summer 1978: 401-404.

(Excerpts from "The Initial Problem" follow this introduction.)

Discrepancies Among Titles

It should be noted with regard to discrepancies among seemingly related titles that the source indexes, abstracts, and bibliographies are not always clear about which of several publications is being cited. Reflecting both the strengths and weaknesses of these sources, entries in *PTA-T* will sometimes indicate the place of publication, but often will not. When such added information appears, it serves more precisely to identify a given title; but with those titles that frequently change city, or even country, of publication, some confusion can be expected to remain.

Entries for titles that progressively enlarge or change in word order can also be expected to create occasional questions, but users should keep in mind that the broad span of time encompassed by *PTA-T* makes such variations inevitable.

As with *PTA-A*, this volume is intended to be used in concert with such standard serial sources of fuller bibliographic information as the *List of Serials Union*, *New Serials Titles*, *Ulrich's International Periodicals Directory*, and *the British Union Catalogue of Periodicals*.

Available in Electronic Format

PTA-T is available for licensing on magnetic tape or diskette in a fielded format. Either the complete database or a custom selection of entries may be ordered. The database is available for internal data processing and nonpublishing purposes only. For more information, call 1-800-877-GALE.

Acknowledgments

A hearty thanks to the many individuals attached to Eastern Washington University for their aid and encouragement.

A special acknowledgment to David J. Jones for contribution of terms from his book, *Australian Periodical Title Abbreviations*.

Finally, a salute to the Classifications and Definitions Department of Gale Research for their unstinting tact, patience, and understanding as well as their considerable editorial efforts in bringing this volume into print.

Suggestions for New Material

As in the past, the users of *Periodical title Abbreviations* series remain a valuable source in the identification of abbreviations not yet included in the *PTA* system. Users wishing to suggest new entries may do so by mailing a photocopy of the suggested entries (i.e., the key to abbreviations in an index, abstract, or book), along with a complete bibliographic citation to the publication from which the pages were copied, to:

Leland G. Alkire Jr.
Mailstop 84
Eastern Washington University
Cheney, WA 99004
E-mail address: lalkire@ewu.edu

Excerpts from "The Initial Problem"*

In a July 1960 letter to *Science magazine,* a somewhat mournful plea was raised by one J.B. Sykes, in favor of "more sparing use of abbreviations when citing references to periodicals." He rightly saw that abbreviated titles often create some difficulty for the user.

In the years since Sykes' complaint, abbreviated periodical citations have proliferated in a way that has exceeded the expectations of even the most pessimistic of observers. Despite organized and sustained efforts, both before and after 1960, either to abandon outright the use of abbreviated citations or, failing this, to adopt a standardized system of abbreviated periodical titles, we are presently faced with a greater diversity than ever before.

Observers of language, such as George Orwell, Jacques Barzun, and Steven Leacock, have variously lamented, railed, and poked fun as abbreviated forms. But the battle has been a losing one. In government, business, and academe, an element of gamesmanship has long dictated that those "in-the-know" should speak in direct, if sometimes barbaric sounding terms, such as NASA, NATO, and ICSU. Further, in a kind of variant of punning, we are surrounded by a buzzing swarm of acronyms which not only identifies their users as the cognoscenti, but which also implies an element of one-upmanship. Some, like CORE and NOW, are clever as apt, but what was once bright and chic begins to wear thin through overuse. Yet in spite of what, in some quarters, has become a cautionary approach to the short-form phenomenon, it must be admitted that both the acronym and the abbreviation serve as time and space savers in these information-heavy times.

The real trouble with short-form usage lies in the tendency of abbreviated forms to duplicate one another. When we encounter a reference to an organization called AID, we must ask: Does it refer to the Agency for International Development or the Americans of Italian Descent? When such multimeaning abbreviations are used without accompanying definitions or in contexts that leave one in doubt, the result is often a breakdown in basic communication.

Small specialized professional groups are perhaps the greatest purveyors of this sort of noncommunication. Imagine, for a moment, a nonlibrarian, or even a librarian who has been away from the profession for a time, picking up a recent library publication and attempting to negotiate the foaming rapids of OCLC, CONSER, MULS, ISSN, and AACR. They will scarcely find themselves paddling in familiar waters. Indeed, some would ask if we are not entering a time when professional subspecialists will be *decreasingly* able to decipher one another's abb pro jarg (abbreviated professional jargon).

Whatever future may await us as librarians, as researchers, and as users of the English language, one thing is clear: The concern of J.B. Sykes in 1960 regarding the problem of abbreviated periodical titles haunts us in ways that are increasingly troublesome. When a reference, periodicals, or interlibrary loan librarian encounters a citation in which the title has been reduced to an abbreviation, AM for example, where does he or she turn? *Acta Musicologia*, *Atlantic Monthly*, *Americas*, or any of the eleven journals to which this abbreviation is commonly applied, all represent logical choices. To use another even more disconcerting example, the abbreviation MHM can mean either *Maryland History Magazine* or *Michigan History Magazine*, depending on the source of the citation. The list of such competitors could be extended indefinitely since tens of thousands of periodicals are currently employed by indexing and abstracting services, as well as by scholarly journals and bibliographies. Many of these publications, as must be obvious by now, employ periodical title abbreviations without regard to how such forms are used elsewhere. This disorderly situation is further compounded by the assumptions of scholars, students, and other users that a given abbreviation is not only unique, but that it is part of a generally acknowledged language, which others, particularly librarians, will immediately recognize. Often, because of experience, intuition, and the subject of the article in question, a little detective work will reveal the full title. Yet this work takes time, and inevitably, after a number of such requests, the librarian will draw a blank, particularly when a patron is uncertain as to the origin of the citation.

Attempts to bring order to this disarray have been numerous, if only partially successful, but one can hope, if orderly access to periodical information is seen as a desirable end, that the current proliferation of systems of abbreviation will one day be rationalized and reduced to a single, understandable system.

In the meantime, a few of us continue to recall that moment in the Apollo 12 Moon Mission when Ground Control discovered that a minor equipment failure was caused by something called the Digital Uplink Assembly. When the controllers radioed up that the fault lay in the DUA, the response from the crew of the Apollo 12 was: "What's a DUA?"

---

*Excerpted by permission of Haworth Press, Serials Librarian, vol. 2, summer 1978: 401-404.

User's Guide

The entries in *PTA-T* are arranged alphabetically by title. If a particular title has more than one abbreviation representing it, the various choices are then subarranged alphabetically by abbreviation, as they are in Volume 1 (*PTA-A*). Neither ampersands, articles, conjunctions, nor prepositions are considered in the alphabetizing; hyphenated terms in titles are treated as separate words. Entries may contain the following elements:

1) Complete title

2) Explanation of acronym within title

3) Place of publication

4) Sponsoring organization or Publisher

5) Translation

6) Abbreviated title

1) **2)** **3)**

> Boletim Tecnico. PETROBRAS [*Petroleo Brasileiro SA*] [*Technical Bulletin. PETROBRAS*] [*Centro de Pesquisas e Desenvolvimento*] [*Rio De Janeiro, Brazil*] — **Bol Tec PETROBRAS**

4) **5)** **6)**

The completeness of an entry is dependent upon both the nature of the term and the amount of information provided by the source. If additional information becomes available during future research, an entry will be revised.

Major Sources of Abbreviations Contained in Periodical Title Abbreviations Series

Abstract Bulletin of the Institute of Paper Chemistry
ACTFL (American Council on the Teaching of Foreign Languages) Annual Bibliography on Books and Articles on Pedagogy in Foreign Languages
Alternative Press Index
American Journal of Archaeology
American-German Review
American Literature Abstracts
Annee-Philologique
Annual Bibliography of English Language and Literature
Applied Science and Technology Index
Art Index
Arts and Humanities Citation Index
Bibliographic Index
Bibliography of Asian Studies
Bibliography of Corn
Bibliography and Index of Geology
Bibliography of North American Geology
Bibliography of Wheat
Biology Index
Biological and Agricultural Index
Serial Sources for the BIOSIS Data Base
Book Review Digest
Book Review Index
British Education Index
British Technology Index
Business Education Index
Business Periodicals Index
Canadian Periodicals Index
Catholic Periodicals Index
Chicorel Index to Mental Health Books Reviews
Christian Periodicals Index
Classified Shakespeare Bibliography
Combined Retrospective Index to Book Reviews in Scholarly Journals
Cumulated Index Medicus
Cumulative Index to Nursing and Allied Health Literature
Current Book Review Citations
Current Index to Statistics
DSH (Deafness, Speech, and Hearing) Abstracts
Education Index
Elsevier Book Series Abbreviations
Engineering Index
English Language Notes
ELH (English Literary History)
Film Literature Index
Forestry Abstracts
French Periodical Index
Geological Literature of North America, 1785-1918
Germanic Review
Harvard Guide to American History
Hospital Literature Index
Humanities Index
IMM (Institute of Mining and Metallurgy) Abstracts
Index of American Periodical Verse
Index Catalogue of Medical and Veterinary Zoology
Index Chemicus
Index to Economic Articles
Index to Legal Periodicals
Index to Little Magazines
Index to Periodicals by and about Negroes
Index to Religious Periodical Literature
Index to Science Fiction Magazines
Industrial Arts Index
INIS (International Nuclear Information System) Authority List for Journal Titles
INSPEC (Information Service for Physics, Electrotechnology, and Control)
Insurance Periodicals Index
International Bibliography of Social Sciences: Anthropology
International Bibliography of Social Sciences: Political Science
International Bibliography of Social Sciences: Sociology
International Index
International Nursing Index
Journal of Aesthetics and Art Criticism
Journal of American Folklore
Journal of English and Germanic Philology
Keats-Shelley Journal
Library and Information Science Abstracts
Library Literature
Mathematical Reviews
Metals Abstracts. Annual Index
Modern Humanities Research Association. Annual Bibliography of English Language and Literature
Modern Language Quarterly
Modern Philology
Music Index
Music Therapy Index
New Grove Dictionary of Music and Musicians
New Periodicals Index
Nineteenth Century Reader's Guide
Philological Quarterly
Philosopher's Index
Physikalische Berichte
PMLA (Publications of the Modern Language Association of America) Bibliography
Poetry Explication
Poole's Index to Periodical Literature
Popular Periodical Index
Predicasts. Source Directory
Progress of Medieval and Renaissance Studies in the United States and Canada
Quarterly Journal of Speech
Reader's Guide to Periodicals
Revue d'Histoire Ecclesiastique

Romanic Review
Scandinavian Studies
Science Citation Index
Science Fiction Book Review Index
Selective Bibliography of Shakespeare (McManaway and Roberts)
Shakespeare Quarterly
Social Science Citation Index
Social Sciences Index
Soils and Fertilizers
Southern Folklore Quarterly
Speech Monographs
Studies in Philology
Surface and Vacuum Physics Index
Topicator
Ulrich's International Periodicals Directory
Victorian Studies
Writings on American History
Yearbook of Comparative and General Literature
Year's Work in English Studies
Year's Work in Modern Language Studies

A

A and R. Analysis and Research (Japan) — A and R (JP)

A Bakony Termeszettudomanyi Kutatasanak Eredmenyei. Resultationes Investigationis Rerum Naturalium Montium Bakony — Bakony Termeszettud Kutatas Eredm

A Bekes Megyei Muzeumok Koezlemenyei — Bekes Koezl

A Budapesti Magyar Kiralyi Allami Vetoemagvizsgalo Allomas Evi Muekoedese — Budapesti Magyar Kir Allami Vetoem Allomas Evi Muek

A Defesa Nacional (Rio de Janeiro) — Defesa Nac Rio

A la Luz — AZ

A Magyar Allami Foeldtani Intezet evi Jelentesei/Annual Report. Hungarian Geological Institute — Magyar Allami Foeldt Intez Evi Jel

A Magyar Gyuemoelcz — Magyar Gyuem

A Magyar Kiralyi Allami Foeldtani Intezet Evi Jelentesei — Magyar Kir Allami Foeldt Intez Evi Jel

A Magyar Kiralyi Koezponti Szoeleszeti Kiserleti Allomas es Ampelologiai Intezet Evkoenyve. Annales. Institut Ampelologique Royal Hongrois — Magyar Kir Koezp Szoelesz Kiserl Allomas Ampelol Intez Evk

A Magyar Tudomanyos Akademia Biologiai es Agrartudomanyi Osztalyanak Koezlemenyei — Magyar Tud Akad Biol Agrartud Oszt Koezlem

A Magyar Tudomanyos Akademia Evkoenyvei — Magyar Tud Akad Evk

A. Merritt's Fantasy Magazine — AMF

A Mora Ferenc Muzeum Evkoenyve/Jahrbuch des Ferenc Mora Museums/Les Les Annales. Musee Ferenc Mora [*Szeged, Hungary*] — Mora Ferenc Muz Evk

A Pecsi Pedagogiai Foeiskola Evkoenyve — Pecsi Pedagog Foeisk Evk

A Povoa de Varzim — APV

A Szekely Nemzeti Muzeum Ertesitoeje — A Szekely Nemz Muz

A Szekely Nemzeti Muzeum Ertesitoeje — A Szekely Nemz Muz Ertes

A Terra Portuguesa — ATP

A Travers le Monde, Tour du Monde — AM

A Vanguarda. Semanario Republicano Federal — AV

A Voz da Verdade — VV

A. W. Dimock Lectures. New York State College of Agriculture and Life Sciences. Department of Plant Pathology — AW Dimock Lect NY State Coll Agric Life Sci Dep Plant Pathol

A1 Applications in Natural Resource Management — A1 Appl Nat Resour Manage

AAAM [*American Association for Automotive Medicine*] **Quarterly Journal** — AAAM Q Jnl

AABO [*Aabo Akademi, Domkyrkotorget*] **Akademi. Aarsskrift** — AABO Akad Aarssk

AACC (American Association of Cereal Chemists) Monograph — AACC (Am Assoc Cereal Chem) Monogr

AACC [*American Association of Cereal Chemists*] **Transactions** — AACC Trans

AACE (American Association of Cost Engineers) Bulletin — AACE (Am Assoc Cost Eng) Bull

AACE [*American Association of Cost Engineers*] **Transactions** — AAE

Aachener Beitraege zur Komparatistik — ABK

Aachener Kunstblaetter — Aach Kbl

Aachener Kuntsblaetter — Aachen Kuntsbl

AACLA [*Association of American Chambers of Commerce in Latin America*] **Outlook** — AACCLA Outl

AACOBS [*Australian Advisory Council on Bibliographical Services*] **Annual Report** — AACOBS Ann Rep

AADE [*American Association of Dental Editors*] **Journal** — AADE J

AAEC [*Australian Atomic Energy Commission*] **Nuclear News** — AAEC Nucl News

AAEC [*Australian Atomic Energy Commission*] **Nuclear News (Australia)** — AAEC Nucl News (AU)

AAESDA [*Association of Architects, Engineers, Surveyors, and Draughtsmen of Australia*] **Bulletin** — AAESDA Bul

AAG Bijdragen. Afdeling Agrarische Geschiedenis van de Landbouwhochgeschool te Wageningen — AAG Bijdr Afd Agrar Gesch Landbouwhochgeschool Wageningen

AAMA [*American Apparel Manufacturers Association*] **Technical Advisory Committee. Bulletin** — AAMA Tech Adv Com Bull

AAMA [*American Apparel Manufacturers Association*] **Technical Advisory Committee. Research Paper** — AAMA Tech Adv Comm Res Pap

AAMA [*American Apparel Manufacturers Association*] **Washington Letter** — AAMA Wash Let

AAMI [*Association for the Advancement of Medical Instrumentation*] **Technology Assessment Report** — AAMI Technol Assess Rep

AANA [*American Association of Nurse Anesthetists*] **Journal** — AANA J

AANNT [*American Association of Nephrology Nurses and Technicians*] **Journal** — AANNT

Aanwinsten van de Centrale Bibliotheek [*Brussels*] — AAN

AAPA [*Australian Asphalt Pavement Association*] **Newsletter** — AAPA Newsl

AAPG (American Association of Petroleum Geologists) Bulletin — AAPG (Am Assoc Pet Geol) Bull

AAPG [*American Association of Petroleum Geologists*] **Bulletin** — AAPG Bull

AAPG [*American Association of Petroleum Geologists*] **Memoir** — AAPG Mem

AAPG [*American Association of Petroleum Geologists*] **Studies in Geology** — AAPG Stud Geol

AARB [*Australian Road Research Board*] **Research Report ARR** — AARB Res Rep ARR

Aarboeger foer Nordisk Oldkyndighed og Historie — AaNo

Aarboeger foer Nordisk Oldkyndighed og Historie — ANOH

Aarbog for Aarhusstift — AS

Aarbog for det Danske Post- og Telegrafvaesen — Aarb d PT

Aarbog for Frederiksborg Amts Historiske Samfund — Aarbog Frederiksborg Amts Hist Samfd

Aarbog for Historisk Samfund for Soro Amt — Aarb So A

Aarboger foer Nordisk Oldkyndighed og Historie — Aarb

Aarboger for Nordisk Oldkyndighed og Historie — Aarb n O

Aarboger udg af Historish Samfund for Aarhus Stift — Aarb Aarh St

Aarbok foer Universitetet i Bergen. Matematisk-Naturvitenskapelig Serie — Aarbok Univ Bergen Mat-Naturvitensk Ser

Aardappelstudiecentrum voor de Kleinhandel — Aardappelstudiecentrum Kleinhandel

Aarhus Universitet. Laboratoriet foer Fysisk Geografi Skrifter — Aarhus Univ Lab Fys Geogr Skr

Aarhus University 50th Anniversary Symposium. Proceedings — Aarhus Univ 50th Anniv Symp Proc

AARN [*Alberta Association of Registered Nurses*] **News Letter** — AARN News Lett

AARN [*Alberta Association of Registered Nurses*] **Newsletter** — AARN Newsl

Aarsberetning fra Foreningen til Norske Fortidsminders Bevaring — Aarsberetn Foren Norske Fortidsmind Bevar

Aarsberetning fra Foreningen til Norske Fortidsminders Bevaring — NFMB

Aarsberetning Institut foer Sterilitetsforskning Kongelige Veterinaer og Landbohoejskole — Aarsberet Inst Sterilitetsforsk K Vet Landbohoejsk

Aarsbok. Jernkontoret — Aarsb Jernkontoret

Aarsbok. Kungl Vetenskaps-Societeten i Uppsala — Aarsb K Vetensk Soc Uppsala

Aarsbok-Vuosikirja. Societas Scientiarum Fennica — Aarsb Vuosik Soc Sci Fenn

Aarsskrift den Kongelige Veterinaer og Landbohoejskole (Denmark) — Aarsskr K Vet Landbohoejsk (DK)

Aarsskrift/Yearbook/Annuaire/Jahrbuch. Copenhagen Veterinaer og Landbohoejskole — Aarsskr Yearb Annu Jahrb Copenh Vet Landbohojsk

Aarstiderne — Aarst

AAS (American Astronautical Society) Science and Technology Series — AAS (Am Astronaut Soc) Sci Technol Ser

AAS [*American Astronomical Society*] **Photo-Bulletin** — AAS Photo-Bull

AAS [*American Astronautical Society*] **Science and Technology Series** — AAS Sci Technol Ser

AASL [*American Association of School Librarians*] **School Library Media Quarterly** — AASL SLMQ

AASRC [*American Association of Small Research Companies*] **Newsletter** — AASRC Newsl

AATCC (American Association of Textile Chemists and Colorists) Symposium. Coated Fabrics Update — AATCC Symp Coated Fabr Update

AATCC (American Association of Textile Chemists and Colorists) Textile Printing Symposium — AATCC Text Print Symp

AATCC [*American Association of Textile Chemists and Colorists*] **National Technical Conference. Book of Papers** — AATCC Nat Tech Conf Book Pap

AATCC [*American Association of Textile Chemists and Colorists*] **Symposium. Flock Technology** — AATCC Symp Flock Technol

AATCC [*American Association of Textile Chemists and Colorists*] **Symposium. Textile Industry and the Environment** — AATCC Symp Text Ind Environ

AAV (Association of Avian Veterinarians) Today — AAV Today

AAVSO [*American Association of Variable Star Observers*] **Circular** — AAVSO Circ

AAZPA (American Association of Zoological Parks and Aquariums) Annual Proceedings — AAZPA (Am Assoc Zool Parks Aquariums) Annu Proc

AAZPA (American Association of Zoological Parks and Aquariums) National Conference — AAZPA (Am Assoc Zool Parks Aquariums) Natl Conf

AAZPA [*American Association of Zoological Parks and Aquariums*] **Annual Proceedings** — PACNDF

AAZPA [*American Association of Zoological Parks and Aquariums*] **National Conference** — ANCPDF

AB Bookman's Weekly — AB

AB Bookman's Weekly — AB Bkman's W

ABA. Asociacion de Bibliotecarios de Antioquia (Medellin) — ABA Asoc Bibl Antioq Medellin

ABA [*American Bankers Association*] **Banking Journal** — ABA Bank J

ABA [*American Bankers Association*] **Banking Journal** — ABA Banking J
ABA [*American Bankers Association*] **Banking Journal** — Banking
ABA [*American Bankers Association*] **Banking Journal** — BNK
ABA [*American Banking Association*] **Journal** — GABA
Abaco — Aba
Abacus [*Australia*] — ABA
Abacus — ABC
Abakterielle, Artikulaere, und Periartikulaere Entzuendungen — Abak Artikulaere Periartikulaere Entzuendungen
ABB Review — ABB Rev
Abba Hushi Files [*Haifa*] — AHF
Abbrennstumpf- und Reibschweissen mit Verwandten Verfahren. Vortraege der Internationalen DVS-Tagung — Abbrennstumpf Reib Verw Verfahren Vortr Int DVS Tag
ABCA [*American Business Communication Association*] **Bulletin** — ABCA Bul
Abdominal Imaging — Abdom Imaging
Abdominal Surgery — Abdom Surg
A'Beckett's Reserved and Equity Judgements (New South Wales) — A'B RJ (NSW)
A'Beckett's Reserved Judgements [*Port Phillip*] — A'B Res Judgm
A'Beckett's Reserved Judgements [*Port Phillip*] [*Australia*] — A'Beck Res
A'Beckett's Reserved Judgements — A'Beck Res Judgm
A'Beckett's Reserved Judgements [*Port Phillip*] — A'Beckett
A'Beckett's Reserved Judgements [*New South Wales*] — RED
A'Beckett's Reserved Judgements [*New South Wales*] — Res & Eq Judg
A'Beckett's Reserved Judgements (New South Wales) — A'Beck RJ (NSW)
A'Beckett's Reserved Judgements (Port Phillip) — A'B RJPP
A'Beckett's Reserved Judgements (Port Phillip) — A'Beck RJ (PP)
A'Beckett's Reserved Judgements (Victoria) — A'Beck Judg (Vic)
A'Beckett's Reserved Judgements (Victoria) — A'Beck Judg (Vict)
Abeille de France [*Later, Abeille de France et l'Apiculteur*] — Abeille Fr
Abeille de France et l'Apiculteur — Abeill Fr Apicul
Abeille de France et l'Apiculteur — Abeille Fr Apic
Abeille Medicale (Paris) — Abeille Med (Paris)
Aberdeen Press and Journal — APJ
Aberdeen University. Journal — AUJ
Aberdeen University. Review — Aberdeen Univ Rev
Aberdeen University. Review — AUR
Aberdeen University. Studies — Aberdeen Univ Stu
Aberdeen University. Studies — AVUSAV
Aberystwyth Studies — A St
Abfallstoffe als Duenger. Moeglichkeiten und Grenzen. Vortraege zum Generalthema des VDLUFA-Kongresses — Abfallst Duenger Vortr Generalthema VDLUFA Kongr
Abfallwirtschaft an der Technischen Universitaet Berlin — Abfallwirtsch Tech Univ Berlin
Abfallwirtschaftliche Loesungen auf Kreisebene. Abfalltechnisches Kolloquium — Abfallwirtsch Loesungen Kreisebene Abfalltech Kolloq
Abhandlung. Naturhistorische Gesellschaft Nuernberg — Abh Naturhist Ges Nuernberg
Abhandlung. Naturhistorische Gesellschaft Nuernberg — ANGNDT
Abhandlungen. Abteilung fuer Phytomorphogenese der Timiriaseff. Instituts fuer Biologie — Abh Abt Phytomorphogenese
Abhandlungen. Akademie der Wissenschaften der DDR. Abteilung Mathematik, Naturwissenschaften, Technik — AAWTD2
Abhandlungen. Akademie der Wissenschaften der DDR. Abteilung Mathematik, Naturwissenschaften, Technik — Abh Akad Wiss DDR Abt Math Naturwiss Tech
Abhandlungen. Akademie der Wissenschaften der DDR. Abteilung Mathematik, Naturwissenschaften, Technik. 1978 [*Berlin*] — Abh Akad Wiss DDR Abt Math Naturwiss Tech 1978
Abhandlungen. Akademie der Wissenschaften der DDR. Abteilung Mathematik, Naturwissenschaften, Technik. 1979 [*Goettingen*] — Abh Akad Wiss DDR Abt Math Naturwiss Tech 1979
Abhandlungen. Akademie der Wissenschaften der DDR. Abteilung Mathematik, Naturwissenschaften, Technik. 1981 — Abh Akad Wiss DDR Abt Math Naturwiss Tech 1981
Abhandlungen. Akademie der Wissenschaften in Goettingen — AAG
Abhandlungen. Akademie der Wissenschaften in Goettingen — AAWG
Abhandlungen. Akademie der Wissenschaften in Goettingen. Mathematisch-Physikalische Klasse — Abh Akad Wiss Goettingen Math-Phys Kl
Abhandlungen. Akademie der Wissenschaften in Goettingen. Mathematisch-Physikalische Klasse [*Germany*] — Abh Akad Wiss Goettingen Math-Physik Kl
Abhandlungen. Akademie der Wissenschaften in Goettingen. Mathematisch-Physikalische Klasse. Beitraege zum Internationalen Geophysikalischen Jahr — AMBIB
Abhandlungen. Akademie der Wissenschaften in Goettingen. Philologisch-Historische Klasse — AAWGPh
Abhandlungen. Akademie der Wissenschaften in Mainz. Geistes- und Sozialwissenschaftliche Klasse — AAWM
Abhandlungen. Akademie der Wissenschaften in Prag — APA
Abhandlungen. Akademie der Wissenschaften und der Literatur in Mainz [*Wiesbaden*] — AAMZ
Abhandlungen. Akademie der Wissenschaften und der Literatur in Mainz. Geistes- und Sozialwissenschaftliche Klasse — AAWL
Abhandlungen. Akademie der Wissenschaften und der Literatur in Mainz. Mathematisch-Naturwissenschaftliche Klasse — Abhandl Akad Wiss Lit Mainz Math Naturwiss Kl
Abhandlungen. Arbeitsgemeinschaft fuer Tier- und Pflanzengeographische Heimatforschung im Saarland — Abh Arbgem Tier- u Pflageogr
Abhandlungen aus dem Gebiet der Auslandskunde. Reihe C. Naturwissenschaften — Abh Geb Auslandsk
Abhandlungen aus dem Gebiete der Geburtshilfe und Gynaekologie — Abh Geburtsh
Abhandlungen aus dem Gebiete der Naturwissenschaften Herausgegeben von dem Naturwissenschaftlichen Verein in Hamburg — Abh Naturw Ver Hamburg
Abhandlungen aus dem Gesamtgebiete der Hygiene — Abh Gesamtgeb Hyg
Abhandlungen aus dem Gesamtgebiete der Medizin — Abhandl Gesamtgeb Med
Abhandlungen aus dem Kaiser-Wilhelm-Institut fuer Eisenforschung zu Duesseldorf — Abh Kaiser Wilhelm Inst Eisenforsch Duesseldorf
Abhandlungen aus dem Kaiser-Wilhelm-Institut fuer Physikalische Chemie und Elektrochemie — Abh Kaiser Wilhelm Inst Phys Chem Elektrochem
Abhandlungen aus dem Landesmuseum der Provinz Westfalen. Museum fuer Naturkunde — Abh Landesmus Prov Westfalen Mus Naturk
Abhandlungen aus dem Mathematischen Seminar der Universitaet (Hamburg) — Abh Math Sem Univ (Hamburg)
Abhandlungen aus der Abteilung fuer Phytomorphogenese des Timiriaseff-Instituts fuer Biologie am Zentralen Exekutivkomitee der USSR — Abh Abt Phytomorphogenese Timiriaseff Inst Biol
Abhandlungen aus der Geschichte der Veterinaermedizin — Abhandl Gesch Veterinaermed
Abhandlungen aus der Kinderheilkunde und Ihren Grenzgebieten — Abh Kinderheilkd Ihren Grenzgeb
Abhandlungen aus der Naturgeschichte, Praktischen Arzneykunst und Chirurgie, aus den Schriften der Haarlemer und anderer Hollaendischen Gesellschaften — Abh Naturg
Abhandlungen aus Ethik und Moral — A Et M
Abhandlungen. Bayerische Akademie der Wissenschaften [*Munich*] — ABA
Abhandlungen. Bayerische Akademie der Wissenschaften — AbhBAW
Abhandlungen. Bayerische Akademie der Wissenschaften. Mathematisch-Naturwissenschaftliche Abteilung — Abhandl Bayer Akad Wiss Math Naturwiss Abt
Abhandlungen. Bayerische Akademie der Wissenschaften. Mathematisch-Naturwissenschaftliche Klasse — Abh Bayer Akad Wiss Math-Naturwiss Kl
Abhandlungen. Bayerische Akademie der Wissenschaften. Mathematisch-Physikalische Klasse — Abhandl Bayer Akad Wiss Math Phys Kl
Abhandlungen. Bayerische Akademie der Wissenschaften. Philosophisch-Historische Abteilung — Abhandl Bayer Akad Wiss Phil Hist Abt
Abhandlungen. Bayerische Akademie der Wissenschaften. Philosophisch-Historische Klasse — ABAW
Abhandlungen. Bayerische Akademie der Wissenschaften. Philosophisch-Philologische und Historische Klasse — Abhandl Bayer Akad Wiss Phil Philol Hist Kl
Abhandlungen (Berlin) — Abh (Berlin)
Abhandlungen. Braunschweigische Wissenschaftliche Gesellschaft — Abh Braunschw Wiss Ges
Abhandlungen. Braunschweigische Wissenschaftliche Gesellschaft — Abh Braunschweig Wiss Gesellsch
Abhandlungen. Braunschweigische Wissenschaftliche Gesellschaft — Abhandl Braunschweig Wiss Ges
Abhandlungen. Braunschweigische Wissenschaftliche Gesellschaft — ABWGA
Abhandlungen. Braunschweigische Wissenschaftliche Gesellschaft — ABWGAZ
Abhandlungen der Academie der Wissenschaften zu Berlin — AAWB
Abhandlungen der Akademie der Wissenschaften der DDR — Abh Akad Wiss DDR
Abhandlungen der Akademie der Wissenschaften in Goettingen. Mathematisch-Physika — Abh Akad Wiss Goettingen Math Phys Kl Folge 3
Abhandlungen der Akademie der Wissenschaften zu Goettingen — Abh Goett
Abhandlungen der Akademie der Wissenschaften zu Goettingen — Goett Abh
Abhandlungen der Bayerischen Akademie der Wissenschaften — Abh Bay Ak Wiss
Abhandlungen der Bayerischen Akademie der Wissenschaften — Abh Bayer Ak
Abhandlungen der Bayerischen Akademie der Wissenschaften — Abh Bayer Akad Wiss
Abhandlungen der Bayerischen Akademie der Wissenschaften — Abh Bayr
Abhandlungen der Bayerischen Akademie der Wissenschaften — Abh Muench
Abhandlungen der Bayerischen Akademie der Wissenschaften. Mathematisch-Naturwissenschaftliche Abteilung — Abh Bayer Akad Wiss Math Naturwiss Abt
Abhandlungen der Bayerischen Akademie der Wissenschaften. Mathematisch-Naturwissenschaftliche Klasse (Muenchen) — Abh Akad Wiss Muenchen
Abhandlungen der Bayerischen Akademie der Wissenschaften. Mathematisch-Physikalische Klasse — Abh Bayer Akad Wiss Math Phys Kl
Abhandlungen der Bayerischen Akademie der Wissenschaften (Muenchen) — Abh Muenchen
Abhandlungen der Bayerischen Akademie der Wissenschaften. Philosophisch-Historische Abteilung — ABAWPH
Abhandlungen der Bayerischen Akademie der Wissenschaften. Philosophisch-Philologische Klasse — ABAWPP
Abhandlungen der Bayerischen Benedictiner-Akademie — ABBA
Abhandlungen der Boehmischen Gesellschaft der Wissenschaften, nebst der Geschichte derselben — Abh Boehm Ges
Abhandlungen der Chursaechsischen Weinbaugesellschaft — Abh Chursaechs Weinbauges
Abhandlungen der Deutschen — AAB
Abhandlungen der Deutschen Akademie der Wissenschaften in Prag — ADAWP
Abhandlungen der Deutschen Akademie der Wissenschaften in Prag. Philosophisch-Historische Klasse — ADAWPPH
Abhandlungen der Deutschen Akademie der Wissenschaften zu Berlin — Abh Berl
Abhandlungen der Deutschen Akademie der Wissenschaften zu Berlin — Abh Berl Akad
Abhandlungen der Deutschen Akademie der Wissenschaften zu Berlin — Abh Deut Akad Wiss Berlin
Abhandlungen der Deutschen Akademie der Wissenschaften zu Berlin — Abhdl Berlin

Abhandlungen der Deutschen Akademie der Wissenschaften zu Berlin. Klasse fuer Chemie, Geologie, und Biologie — Abh Deutsch Akad Wiss Berlin Kl Chem

Abhandlungen der Deutschen Akademie der Wissenschaften zu Berlin. Klasse fuer Mathematik und Allgemeine Naturwissenschaften — Abh Dtsch Akad Wiss Berlin

Abhandlungen der Deutschen Akademie der Wissenschaften zu Berlin. Klasse fuer Medizinische Wissenschaften — Abh Dtsch Akad Wiss Berlin Kl Med Wiss

Abhandlungen der Deutschen Akademie der Wissenschaften zu Berlin. Mathematisch-Naturwissenschaftliche Klasse — Abh Dtsch Akad Wiss Berlin Math Naturwiss Kl

Abhandlungen der Deutschen Gesellschaft der Wissenschaften und Kuenste in Prag. Mathematisch-Naturwissenschaftliche Klasse — Abh Deutsch Ges Wiss Prag Math Naturwiss Kl

Abhandlungen der Geistes- und Socialwissenschaftlichen Klasse. Akademie der Wissenschaften und der Literatur in Mainz — Abh Akad Mainz

Abhandlungen der Geistes- und Socialwissenschaftlichen Klasse. Akademie der Wissenschaften und der Literatur in Mainz — Abh Mainz

Abhandlungen der Geistes- und Socialwissenschaftlichen Klasse. Akademie der Wissenschaften und der Literatur in Mainz — AGSA Mz

Abhandlungen der Geologischen Bundesanstalt (Austria) — Abh Geol Bundesanst (Austria)

Abhandlungen der Geologischen Landesanstalt (DDR) — Abh Geol Landesanst DDR

Abhandlungen der Gesellschaft der Kuenste und Wissenschaften in Batavia — Abh Ges Kuenste Batavia

Abhandlungen der Gesellschaft der Wissenschaften zu Goettingen — Abh Ges Wiss Goettg

Abhandlungen der Gesellschaft der Wissenschaften zu Goettingen. Mathematisch-Physikalische Klasse — Abh Ges Wiss Goettingen Math Phys Kl

Abhandlungen der Hallischen Naturforschenden Gesellschaft — Abh Hallischen Naturf Ges

Abhandlungen der Heidelberger Akademie der Wissenschaften — Abh Heidelb Akad Wiss

Abhandlungen der Heidelberger Akademie der Wissenschaften. Philosophisch-Historische Klasse — Abh Heid

Abhandlungen der Heidelberger Akademie der Wissenschaften. Philosophisch-Historische Klasse — Abh Heidelb Ak

Abhandlungen der Heidelberger Akademie der Wissenschaften. Philosophisch-Historische Klasse — Abh Heidelberg

Abhandlungen der Heidelberger Akademie der Wissenschaften. Philosophisch-Historische Klasse — Abhandl Heidelb Akad

Abhandlungen der Heidelberger Akademie der Wissenschaften. Philosophisch-Historische Klasse — Heid Ak Abh

Abhandlungen der Heidelberger Akademie der Wissenschaften. Stiftung Heinrich Lanz. Mathematisch-Naturwissenschaftliche Klasse — Abh Heidelberger Akad Wiss Math Naturwiss Kl

Abhandlungen der Herder-Gesellschaft und des Herder Instituts zu Riga — Abhandl Herder-Ges Herder Inst

Abhandlungen der Hessischen Geologischen Landesanstalt — Abh HGLA

Abhandlungen der K. Gesellschaft der Wissenschaften zu Goettingen. Mathematisch-Physikalische Klasse — Abh K Ges Wiss Goettingen Math Phys Kl

Abhandlungen der Koeniglich Bayerischen Akademie der Wissenschaften. Mathematisch-Physikalische Klasse — Abh Akad Wiss Muenchen

Abhandlungen der Koeniglich Bayerischen Akademie der Wissenschaften. Mathematisch-Physikalische Klasse — Abh K Bayer Ak Wiss M Ph Kl Muench

Abhandlungen der Koeniglich Boehmischen Gesellschaft der Wissenschaften (Prag) — PragerAbh

Abhandlungen der Koeniglich Preussischen Akademie der Wissenschaften. Physikalisch-Mathematische Classe — Abh Koenigl Preuss Akad Wiss Phys Math Cl

Abhandlungen der Koeniglichen Akademie der Wissenschaften in Berlin — Abh Acad Berl

Abhandlungen der Koeniglichen Akademie der Wissenschaften in Berlin — Abh Phys Kl Koenigl Akad Wiss Berlin

Abhandlungen der Koeniglichen Akademie der Wissenschaften in Berlin — Abh Phys Math Kl Koenigl Akad Wiss Berlin

Abhandlungen der Koeniglichen Akademie der Wissenschaften in Berlin — Berlin Abhandl

Abhandlungen der Koeniglichen Boehmischen Gesellschaft der Wissenschaften — Abh K Boehm Ges Wiss M N Cl

Abhandlungen der Koeniglichen Gesellschaft der Wissenschaften, Goettingen. Mathematisch-Physikalische Klasse — Abh Koenigl Ges Wiss Goettingen Math Phys Kl

Abhandlungen der Koeniglichen Gesellschaft der Wissenschaften zu Goettingen — Abh Ges Wiss Goett

Abhandlungen der Koeniglichen Gesellschaft der Wissenschaften zu Goettingen — Abhandl K Gesell Wiss Goettingen

Abhandlungen der Kungliga. Gesellschaft der Wissenschaften zu Goettingen — Gott Abh

Abhandlungen der Kurfuerstlich-Mainzischen Akademie Nuetzlicher Wissenschaften zu Erfurt/Nova Acta Academiae Electoralis Moguntinae Scientiar Utilium Quae Erfurti Est — Abh Kurfuerstl Mainz Akad Nuetzl Wiss Erfurt

Abhandlungen der Kurfuerstlich-Mainzischen Akademie Nuetzlicher Wissenschaften zu Erfurt/Nova Acta Academiae Electoralis Moguntinae Scientiarum Utilium quae Erfurti Est — Nova Acta Acad Mogunt Sci Util Erfurti

Abhandlungen der Mathematisch-Naturwissenschaftlichen Klasse. Akademie der Wissenschaften und der Literatur. Mainz — Abh Math Naturwiss Kl Akad Wiss Lit Mainz

Abhandlungen der Mathematisch-Physikalischen Classe der Koeniglich Bayerischen Akademie der Wissenschaften — Abh Akad Muench

Abhandlungen der Mathematisch-Physikalischen Classe der Koeniglich Bayerischen Akademie der Wissenschaften — Abh Bayer Akad Wiss

Abhandlungen der Mathematisch-Physikalischen Classe der Koeniglich Bayerischen Akademie der Wissenschaften (Muenchen) — Abh Akad Wiss Muenchen

Abhandlungen der Mathematisch-Physikalischen Classe der Koeniglich Bayerischen Akademie der Wissenschaften (Muenchen) — Abh Math Phys Abt Akad Wiss Muenchen

Abhandlungen der Mathematisch-Physikalischen Klasse der Koeniglich Bayerischen Akademie der Wissenschaften. Muenchen — Abh Akad Muenchen

Abhandlungen der Mathematisch-Physischen Classe der Koeniglich Saechsischen Gesellschaft der Wissenschaften — Abh Math Phys Kl Koenigl Saechs Ges Wiss

Abhandlungen der Mathematisch-Physischen Classe der Koeniglich Saechsischen Gesellschaft der Wissenschaften — Abh Saechs Ges Wiss

Abhandlungen der Medizinischen Fakultaet der Sun Yatsen-Universitaet Canton [*A publication*] — Abhandl Med Fak Sun Yatsen-Univ Canton

Abhandlungen der Naturforschenden Gesellschaft. Halle — Abh Natf Ges Halle

Abhandlungen der Naturforschenden Gesellschaft in Zuerich — Abh Naturf Ges Zuerich

Abhandlungen der Naturforschenden Gesellschaft zu Goerlitz — Abhandl Naturforsch Ges Goerlitz

Abhandlungen der Naturhistorischen Gesellschaft zu Nuernberg — Abh Naturhist Ges Nuernb

Abhandlungen der Naturhistorischen Gesellschaft zu Nuernberg — Abhandl Naturhist Ges Nuernberg

Abhandlungen der Naturhistorischen Gesellschaft zu Nuernberg — Nuernberg Abhandl

Abhandlungen der Naturwissenschaftlichen Gesellschaft Saxonia zu Gross- und Neuschoenau — Abh Naturwiss Ges Saxonia Gross Neuschoenau

Abhandlungen der Philologisch-Historische Klasse der Saechsischen Akademie der Wissenschaften — Abh Saech Ges Wiss

Abhandlungen der Philologisch-Historische Klasse der Saechsischen Akademie der Wissenschaften — Abh Saechs

Abhandlungen der Philologisch-Historische Klasse der Saechsischen Akademie der Wissenschaften — Abh Saechs Akad Phil

Abhandlungen der Philologisch-Historische Klasse der Saechsischen Akademie der Wissenschaften — ASWG

Abhandlungen der Philologisch-Historische Klasse der Saechsischen Akademie der Wissenschaften (Leipzig) — Abh Leipz

Abhandlungen der Philologisch-Historische Klasse der Saechsischen Akademie der Wissenschaften (Leipzig) — Abh Leipzig

Abhandlungen der Philologisch-Historische Klasse der Saechsischen Akademie der Wissenschaften (Leipzig) — Abhdl Leipzig

Abhandlungen der Philosophischen-Historischen Klasse. Akademie der Wissenschaften — AAWB

Abhandlungen der Physikalischen Klasse der Koeniglichen Akademie der Wissenschaften zu Berlin — Abh Koenigl Akad Wiss Berlin

Abhandlungen der Physikalisch-Mathematischen Klasse der Koeniglichen Akademie der Wissenschaften zu Berlin — Abh Koenigl Akad Wiss Berlin

Abhandlungen der Preussischen Akademie der Wissenschaften. Physikalisch-Mathematische Klasse — Abh Preuss Akad Wiss Phys Math

Abhandlungen der Preussischen Geologischen Landesanstalt — Abh Preuss Geol Landesanst

Abhandlungen der Saechsischen Akademie der Wissenschaften zu Leipzig. Mathematisch-Naturwissenschaftliche Klasse — Abh Saechs Ges Wiss Leipzig

Abhandlungen der Schlesischen Gesellschaft fuer Vaterlaendische Cultur. Abtheilung fuer Naturwissenschaften und Medicin — Abh Schles Gesell

Abhandlungen des Archaeologischepigraphischen Seminars der Universitaet Wien — AAES

Abhandlungen des Deutschen Archaeologischen Instituts. Kairo — ADIK

Abhandlungen des Deutschen Kaelte und Klimatechnischen Vereins — Abh Dtsch Kaelte Klimatech Ver

Abhandlungen des Deutschen Naturwissenschaftlich-Medizinischen Vereins fuer Boehmen "Lotos" — Abh Dt Naturw Med Ver Boehm

Abhandlungen des Forschungsinstituts fuer Flugfahrtmaterialien. Moscow — Abh Forschungsinst Flugfahrtmater Moscow

Abhandlungen des Geologischen Dienstes Berlin — Abh Geol Dienstes Berlin

Abhandlungen des Hessischen Landesamtes fuer Bodenforschung — Abh Hess Landesamtes Bodenforsch

Abhandlungen des Internationalen Keramischen Kongresses — Abh Int Keram Kongr

Abhandlungen des Landwirtshaftlichen Instituts in Omsk — Abh Landwirtsch Inst Omsk

Abhandlungen des Naturwissenschaftlichen Vereines fuer Sachsen und Thueringen in Halle — Abh Naturwiss Vereines Sachsen Halle

Abhandlungen des Naturwissenschaftlichen Vereins zu Magdeburg — Abh Naturwiss Vereins Magdeburg

Abhandlungen des Reichsstelle fuer Bodenforschung (Germany) — Abh Reichsstelle Bodenforsch (Ger)

Abhandlungen des Vereins fuer Forstwissenschaftliche Ausbildung — Abh Vereins Forstwiss Ausbild

Abhandlungen des Vereins fuer Naturwissenschaftliche Erforschung des Niederrheins — Abh Vereins Naturwiss Erforsch Niederrheins

Abhandlungen. Deutsche Akademie der Wissenschaften zu Berlin — Abh Dtsch Akad Wiss Berl

Abhandlungen. Deutsche Akademie der Wissenschaften zu Berlin — AbhAkWiss Berlin

Abhandlungen. Deutsche Akademie der Wissenschaften zu Berlin. Klasse fuer Bergbau, Huettenwesen, und Montangeologie — Abh Dtsch Akad Wiss Berlin Kl Bergbau Huettenwes Montangeol

Abhandlungen. Deutsche Akademie der Wissenschaften zu Berlin. Klasse fuer Chemie, Geologie, und Biologie — Abh Dtsch Akad Wiss Berl Kl Chem Geol Biol
Abhandlungen. Deutsche Akademie der Wissenschaften zu Berlin. Klasse fuer Chemie, Geologie, und Biologie — Abh Dtsch Akad Wiss Berlin Kl Chem Geol Biol
Abhandlungen. Deutsche Akademie der Wissenschaften zu Berlin. Klasse fuer Mathematik, Physik, und Technik — Abh Deut Akad Wiss Berlin Kl Math
Abhandlungen. Deutsche Akademie der Wissenschaften zu Berlin. Klasse fuer Mathematik, Physik, und Technik — Abh Deutsch Akad Wiss Berlin Kl Math Phys Tech
Abhandlungen. Deutsche Akademie der Wissenschaften zu Berlin. Klasse fuer Mathematik, Physik, und Technik [*Germany*] — Abh Dtsch Akad Wiss Berlin Kl Math Phys Tech
Abhandlungen. Deutsche Akademie der Wissenschaften zu Berlin. Klasse fuer Mathematik, Physik, und Technik — Abhandl Deut Akad Wiss Kl Math Phys Tech
Abhandlungen. Deutsche Akademie der Wissenschaften zu Berlin. Klasse fuer Mathematik und Allgemeine Naturwissenschaften — Abh Dtsch Akad Wiss Berlin Kl Math Allg Naturwiss
Abhandlungen. Deutsche Akademie der Wissenschaften zu Berlin. Klasse fuer Medizin — Abh Dtsch Akad Wiss Berl Kl Med
Abhandlungen. Deutsche Akademie der Wissenschaften zu Berlin. Klasse fuer Medizin — Abh Dtsch Akad Wiss Berlin Kl Med
Abhandlungen. Deutsche Akademie der Wissenschaften zu Berlin. Klasse fuer Medizin — ADWMA
Abhandlungen. Deutsche Akademie der Wissenschaften zu Berlin. Klasse fuer Sprachen, Literatur, und Kunst — ADAW
Abhandlungen. Deutsche Akademie der Wissenschaften zu Berlin. Mathematisch-Naturwissenschaftliche Klasse — Abh Dtsch Akad Wiss Berlin Math-Naturwiss Kl
Abhandlungen. Deutsche Akademie der Wissenschaften zu Berlin. Mathematisch-Naturwissenschaftliche Klasse — Abhandl Deut Akad Wiss Math Naturwiss Kl
Abhandlungen. Deutsche Akademie der Wissenschaften zu Berlin. Philosophisch-Historische Klasse — Abhandl Deut Akad Wiss Phil Hist Kl
Abhandlungen. Deutsche Orient-Gesellschaft — ADOG
Abhandlungen. Deutschen Akademie der Wissenschaften zu Berlin — AAWSAU
Abhandlungen. Deutscher Kaeltetechnische Verein — Abh Dtsch Kaeltetech Ver
Abhandlungen. Deutscher Palaestina-Verein — ADPV
Abhandlungen. Deutsches Archaeologisches Institut [*Cairo*] — ADAI
Abhandlungen einer Privatgesellschaft in Boehmen, zur Aufnahme der Mathematik, der Vaterlaendischen Geschichte, und der Naturgeschichte — Abh Privatges Boehmen
Abhandlungen einer Privatgesellschaft von Naturforschern und Oekonomen in Oberheutschland — Abh Privatges Naturf Oberdeutschl
Abhandlungen fuer die Kunde des Morgenlandes — Abh Kunde Morgenl
Abhandlungen fuer die Kunde des Morgenlandes [*Herausgegeben von der Deutschen Gesellschaft*] — Abhandl Kunde Morgenlandes
Abhandlungen fuer die Kunde des Morgenlandes — AbhKM
Abhandlungen fuer die Kunde des Morgenlandes — AbKM
Abhandlungen fuer die Kunde des Morgenlandes — AKM
Abhandlungen. Gebiet der Hirnforschung und Verhaltensphysiologie — Abh Geb Hirnforsch Verhaltensphysiol
Abhandlungen. Gebiet der Hirnforschung und Verhaltensphysiologie — AGHVA6
Abhandlungen. Gebiet der Naturwissenschaften — Abhandl Geb Naturwiss
Abhandlungen. Geologischer Dienst [*Berlin*] — AGDBAS
Abhandlungen. Geologischer Dienst (Berlin) — Abh Geol Dienstes (Berl)
Abhandlungen. Geologisches Landesamt in Baden Wuerttemberg — Abh Geol Landesamtes Baden Wuerttemb
Abhandlungen. Gesellschaft der Wissenschaften zu Goettingen — AbhGWG
Abhandlungen. Gesellschaft der Wissenschaften zu Goettingen — AGW
Abhandlungen. Gesellschaft der Wissenschaften zu Goettingen — AGWG
Abhandlungen. Gesellschaft der Wissenschaften zu Goettingen. Philosophisch-Historische Klasse — AGG
Abhandlungen. Heidelberger Akademie der Wissenschaften — AHAW
Abhandlungen. Heidelberger Akademie der Wissenschaften. Philosophisch-Historische Klasse — AHAWPK
Abhandlungen Herausgegeben vom Naturwissenschaftlichen Verein zu Bremen — Abhandl Naturwiss Ver Bremen
Abhandlungen Herausgegeben vom Naturwissenschaftlichen Vereine zu Bremen — Abhandl Naturw Ver Bremen
Abhandlungen Herausgegeben von der Senckenbergischen Naturforschenden Gesellschaft — Abh Senckenb Naturf Ges
Abhandlungen Herausgegeben von der Senkenbergischen Naturforschenden Gesellschaft (Frankfurt) — Abh Senkenb Ges Frankfurt
Abhandlungen. Institut fuer Hochspannungstechnik und Elektrische Anlagen [*West Germany*] — Abh Inst Hochspannungstech Elektr Anlagen
Abhandlungen. Institut fuer Hochspannungstechnik und Elektrische Anlagen — Abh Inst Hochspannungstechnik Elektr Anlagen
Abhandlungen. Institut fuer Metallhuettenwesen und Elektrometallurgie der Technischen Hochschule (Aachen) — Abh Inst Metallhuettenwes Elektrometall Tech Hochsch Aachen
Abhandlungen. Koenigliche Gesellschaft der Wissenschaften zu Goettingen. Mathematisch-Physikalische Klasse — Abhandl Ges Wiss Goettingen Math Phys Kl
Abhandlungen. Koenigliche Gesellschaft der Wissenschaften zu Goettingen. Philologisch-Historische Klasse — Abhandl Ges Wiss Goettingen Philol Hist Kl
Abhandlungen. Koenigliche Preussische Akademie der Wissenschaften zu Berlin [*A publication*] — AKAW
Abhandlungen. Koenigliche Saechsische Gesellschaft der Wissenschaften — AbKSGW
Abhandlungen. Koenigliche Saechsische Gesellschaft der Wissenschaften — ASG
Abhandlungen. Koeniglichen Akademie der Wissenschaften in Berlin — Abh Koenigl Akad Wiss Berlin
Abhandlungen. Koeniglichen Boehmischen Gesellschaft der Wissenschaften — Abh Koenigl Boehm Ges Wiss
Abhandlungen. Landesmuseum der Provinz Westfalen. Museum fuer Naturkunde — Abh Landes Prov Westfalon Mus Naturkd
Abhandlungen. Landesmuseum der Provinz Westfalen. Museum fuer Naturkunde — ALWNAO
Abhandlungen. Landesmuseum fuer Naturkunde zu Muenster in Westfalen — Abh Landesmus Naturkd Muenster Westfalen
Abhandlungen. Mathematisch-Physische Klasse der Saechsischen Akademie der Wissenschaften — Abh Math-Phys Kl Saechs Akad Wiss
Abhandlungen. Meteorologischer Dienst der Deutschen Demokratischen Republik — Abh Meteorol Dienstes DDR
Abhandlungen. Naturwissenschaftlicher Verein in Hamburg — Abh Naturwiss Ver Hamb
Abhandlungen. Naturwissenschaftlicher Verein in Hamburg — ANVHEJ
Abhandlungen. Naturwissenschaftlicher Verein zu Bremen — Abh Naturw Ver Bremen
Abhandlungen. Naturwissenschaftlicher Verein zu Bremen — Abh Naturwiss Ver Bremen
Abhandlungen. Naturwissenschaftlicher Verein zu Bremen — ANVBAV
Abhandlungen Oekonomischen, Technologischen, Naturwissenschaftlichen und Vermischten Inhalts — Abh Oekon Inhalts
Abhandlungen. Philologisch-Historische Klasse. Koenigliche Saechsische Gesellschaft der Wissenschaften — ASGW
Abhandlungen. Philosophisch-Historische Klasse der Saechsischen Gesellschaft [*A publication*] — ASG
Abhandlungen. Preussische Akademie der Wissenschaften — APAW
Abhandlungen. Preussische Akademie der Wissenschaften. Mathematisch-Naturwissenschaftliche Klasse — Abh Preuss Akad Wiss Math Naturwiss Kl
Abhandlungen. Preussische Akademie der Wissenschaften. Mathematisch-Naturwissenschaftliche Klasse — Abhandl Preuss Akad Wiss Math Naturwiss Kl
Abhandlungen. Preussische Akademie der Wissenschaften. Philosophisch-Historische Klasse — Abhandl Preuss Akad Wiss Phil Hist Kl
Abhandlungen. Preussische Akademie der Wissenschaften. Physikalisch-Mathematische Klasse — Abh Preuss Akad Wiss Phys Math Kl
Abhandlungen. Preussische Akademie der Wissenschaften. Physikalisch-Mathematische Klasse — Abhandl Preuss Akad Wiss Phys Math Kl
Abhandlungen. Rheinisch-Westfaelische Akademie der Wissenschaften — Abh Rheinisch-Westfael Akad Wiss
Abhandlungen. Rheinisch-Westfaelische Akademie der Wissenschaften — ARAWDK
Abhandlungen. Saechsische Akademie der Wissenschaften. Philologisch-Historische Klasse — Abhandl Saechs Akad Wiss Philol Hist Kl
Abhandlungen. Saechsische Akademie der Wissenschaften zu Leipzig — ASAWL
Abhandlungen. Saechsische Akademie der Wissenschaften zu Leipzig. Mathematisch-Naturwissenschaftliche Klasse — Abh Saechs Akad Wiss Leipzig Math Naturwiss Kl
Abhandlungen. Saechsische Akademie der Wissenschaften zu Leipzig. Mathematisch-Naturwissenschaftliche Klasse — Abh Saechs Akad Wiss Leipzig Math-Natur Kl
Abhandlungen. Saechsische Akademie der Wissenschaften zu Leipzig. Philosophisch-Historische Klasse — ASAW
Abhandlungen. Saechsische Akademie der Wissenschaften zu Leipzig. Philosophisch-Historische Klasse — ASAWL PHK
Abhandlungen. Saechsische Gesellschaft der Wissenschaften. Philologisch-Historische Klasse — Abhandl Saechs Ges Wiss Philol Hist Kl
Abhandlungen. Saechsische Gesellschaft der Wissenschaften zu Leipzig — L Abh
Abhandlungen. Schlesische Gesellschaft fuer Vaterlaendische Cultur. Geisteswissenschaftliche Reihe — Abhandl Schlesischen Ges Vaterlaend Cult Geisteswiss Reihe
Abhandlungen. Senckenbergische Naturforschende Gesellschaft — Abh Senckenb Naturforsch Ges
Abhandlungen. Senckenbergische Naturforschende Gesellschaft — ASNGA7
Abhandlungen. Staatliches Museum fuer Mineralogie und Geologie zu Dresden — Abh Staatl Mus Mineral Geol Dresden
Abhandlungen ueber die Pathophysiologie der Regulationen — Abh Pathophysiol Regul
Abhandlungen und Beobachtungen Durch Die Oekonomische Gesellschaft zu Bern Gesammelt — Abh Beob Oekon Ges Bern
Abhandlungen und Bericht des Vereins fuer Naturkunde zu Kassel — Abh Ber Vereins Naturk Kassel
Abhandlungen und Berichte aus dem Museum fuer Naturkunde und Vorgeschichte in Magdeburg — Abh Ber Mus Nat U Heimatk Naturk Vorgesch Magdeburg
Abhandlungen und Berichte aus dem Museum fuer Naturkunde und Vorgeschichte in Magdeburg — Abh Ber Mus Naturk Magdeburg
Abhandlungen und Berichte des Deutschen Museums — Abhandlung Ber Deut Mus
Abhandlungen und Berichte des Museums fuer Natur- und Heimatkunde zu Magdeburg — AbhBMM
Abhandlungen und Berichte des Staatlichen Musems fuer Voelkerkunde Dresden — Abh u Ber Staatl Mus f Voelkerkde Dresden
Abhandlungen und Berichte des Vereins fuer Naturkunde zu Cassel — Abhandl Ber Ver Naturk
Abhandlungen und Berichte des Zoologisch- Antropologisch- Ethnologischen Museums. Dresden — ABZoMD
Abhandlungen und Berichte. Deutsches Museum [*Germany*] — Abh Ber Dtsch Mus

Abhandlungen und Berichte. Deutsches Museum — Abhandl Ber Deut Mus
Abhandlungen und Berichte. Naturkundemuseums Goerlitz [*Germany*] — Abh Ber Naturkundemus Goerlitz
Abhandlungen und Berichte. Naturkundemuseums Goerlitz — ABNGAO
Abhandlungen und Berichte. Naturwissenschaftliche Gesellschaft Bayreuth — Abh Ber Naturwiss Ges Bayreuth
Abhandlungen und Berichte. Staatlichen Museum fuer Mineralogie und Geologie (Dresden) — Abh Ber St Mus Miner Geol (Dresden)
Abhandlungen und Berichte. Staatlichen Museum fuer Voelkerkunde Dresden [*Forschungsstelle*] — Abh Ber Staat Mus Volk Dres
Abhandlungen und Monatliche Mittheilungen aus dem Gesammtgebiete der Naturwissenschaften — Abh Monatl Mitth Gesammtgeb Naturwiss
Abhandlungen und Sitzungsberichte der Physikalisch-Medizinischen Gesellschaft. Wuerzburg — APhMGW
Abhandlungen und Verhandlungen. Naturwissenschaftlicher Verein in Hamburg — Abh Verh Naturwiss Ver Hamb
Abhandlungen und Verhandlungen. Naturwissenschaftlicher Verein in Hamburg — Abh Verh Naturwiss Ver Hamburg
Abhandlungen und Vortraege. Deutsches Bibel-Archiv — ADBA
Abhandlungen. Wissenschaftliches Forschungsinstitut fuer Konservenindustrie. Plovdiv — Abh Wiss Forschungsinst Konservenind Plovdiv
Abhandlungen. Zoologisch-Botanischen Gesellschaft in Wien — Abh Zool-Bot Ges Wien
Abhandlungen zum Christlich-Juedischen Dialog — ACJD
Abhandlungen zur Evangelischen Theologie — AET
Abhandlungen zur Evangelischen Theologie [*Bonn*] — AETh
Abhandlungen zur Geschichte der Mathematischen Wissenschaften mit Einschluss Ihrer Anwendungen — Abh zu Gesch d Math
Abhandlungen zur Geschichte der Mathematischen Wissenschaften mit Einschluss Ihrer Anwendungen — Abhandl Gesch Math Wiss
Abhandlungen zur Geschichte der Medizin und der Naturwissenschaften — Abh Gesch Med Naturwiss
Abhandlungen zur Geschichte der Naturwissenschaften und der Medizin — Abh zu Gesch d Med
Abhandlungen zur Geschichte der Naturwissenschaften und der Medizin — Abhandl Gesch Naturwiss Med
Abhandlungen zur Kunst, Musik, und Literaturwissenschaft — AKML
Abhandlungen zur Landeskunde der Provinz Westpreussen — Abh Landesk Prov Westpreussen
Abhandlungen zur Naturgeschichte, Chemie, Anatomie, Medicin und Physik, aus den Schriften des Instituts der Kuenste und Wissenschaften zu Bologna — Abh Naturgesch Chem
Abhandlungen zur Naturgeschichte der Thiere und Pflanzen, Welche Ehemals der Koeniglich Franzoesischen Akademie der Wissenschaften Vorgetragen Wurden — Abh Naturgesch Thiere Pflanzen
Abhandlungen zur Philosophie, Psychologie, und Paedagogik — APPP
Abhandlungen zur Philosophie und Ihrer Geschichte — Abh Philos Ges
Abhandlungen zur Philosophie und Paedagogik — AP Pd
Abhandlungen zur Theologie des Alten und Neuen Testaments — Abh Th ANT
Abhandlungen zur Theologie des Alten und Neuen Testaments — AbhTANT
Abhandlungen zur Theologie des Alten und Neuen Testaments [*Zurich*] — ATANT
Abhandlungen zur Theologie des Alten und Neuen Testaments [*Zurich*] — AThANT
Abhandlungen zur Theoretischen Biologie — Abhandl Theor Biol
Abhandlunggen der Koeniglich Preussischen Akademie der Wissenschaften. Physikalisch-Mathematische Classe — Abh Preuss Akad Wiss
Abhandlunggen der Koeniglich Preussischen Akademie der Wissenschaften. Physikalisch-Mathematische Classe (Berlin) — Abh Akad Wiss Berlin Phys
ABIA. Associacao Brasileira das Industrias da Alimentacao — ABIA Assoc Bras Ind Aliment
ABIA [*Associacao Brasileira das Industrias da Alimentacao*] **SAPRO Boletim Informativo** [*Setor de Alimentos Calorico-Proteicos*] — ABIA SAPRO Bol Inf
Abidjan Universite. Annales. Sciences — Abidjan Univ Ann Sci
Abinger Chronicle — AC
Ablauf- und Planungsforschung — Ablauf-Planungsforsch
Ablex Series in Artificial Intelligence — Ablex Ser Artif Intell
ABM (Associacao Brasileria de Metais) Boletim — ABM Bol
ABM (Associacao Brasileria de Metais) Congresso Anual — ABM Congr Anu
ABM [*Associacao Brasileira de Metais*] **Noticiario** — ABM Not
ABM [*Australian Board of Missions*] **Review** — ABM Rev
ABM [*Australian Board of Missions*] **Review** — ABMR
ABN [*Algemene Bank Nederland*] **Economic Review** — ABN Review
Abogado Cristiano — Abo C
Aboriginal Affairs Information Paper — Aborig Aff Info Paper
Aboriginal Child at School — Aborig Child Sch
Aboriginal History — AH
Aboriginal Law Bulletin — Aborig LB
Aboriginal Law Bulletin — ALB
Aboriginal News — Abor N
Aboriginal Quarterly — Aboriginal Q
Aboriginal-Islander-Message — AIM
Abortion Law Reporter — Abortion Law Rep
About Arts and Crafts. Department of Indian and Northern Affairs — AAAC
About Distance Education — About Distance Educ
Above the Ground Review — Ab G R
Abracadabra. Association of British Columbia Drama Educators — ABRA
Abraham Lincoln Quarterly — ALQ
Abrasive and Cleaning Methods — Abrasive Clean Methods
Abrasive Engineering — Abrasiv Eng
Abrasive Engineering — Abrasive Eng
Abrasive Engineering Society. Magazine — Abrasive Eng Soc Mag
Abrege des Transactions Philosophiques. Societe Royale de Londres. Huitieme Partie. Matiere Medicale et Pharmacie — Abr Trans Philos Soc Roy Londres Pt 8 Matiere Med
Abridged Biography and Genealogy Master Index — ABGMI
Abridged Index Medicus — ABIM
Abridged Index Medicus — Abr Index Med
Abridged Index Medicus — AbrIMed
Abridged Index Medicus — AIM
Abridged Readers' Guide to Periodical Literature — Abr Read Guide
Abridged Reader's Guide to Periodical Literature — Abr RG
Abridged Reader's Guide to Periodical Literature — ARG
Abridged Scientific Publications — Abr Sci Pubs
Abridged Scientific Publications from the Kodak Research Laboratories — Abr Sci Publ Kodak Res Lab
Abridged Weekly Weather Report for Canberra — Abridg Wkly Weath Rep Canb
Abridgments of Specification Patents for Inventions (Great Britain) — Abridg (Brit) Pat
Abr-nahrain [*Leiden, Netherlands*] — Abrn
Abruzzo — Ab
Absalon — Abs
Absatzwirtschaft — ABS
Absatzwirtschaft; Zeitschrift fuer Marketing — ABB
Abside — ABs
Abside — AE
Absorption, Distribution, Transformation, and Excretion of Drugs — Absorpt Distrib Transform Excretion Drugs
Absorption Spectra in the Ultraviolet and Visible Region — Absorpt Spectra Ultraviolet Visible Reg
Abstract and Applied Analysis — Abstr Appl Anal
Abstract Bulletin. Institute of Paper Chemistry — ABIPC
Abstract Bulletin. Institute of Paper Chemistry — ABPCA
Abstract Bulletin. Institute of Paper Chemistry — Abs Bull Inst Paper Chem
Abstract Bulletin. Institute of Paper Chemistry — Abstr Bull Inst Pap Chem
Abstract Bulletin. Institute of Paper Chemistry — Abstr Bull Inst Paper Chem
Abstract Collection. European Neurosciences Meeting — Abstr Collect Eur Neurosci Meet
Abstract Journal in Earthquake Engineering — Abstr J Earthq Eng
Abstract Journal in Earthquake Engineering — AJEED
Abstract Journal. Informatics (English Translation) — Abstr J Inf Engl Transl
Abstract Journal Informations (Moscow) — Abstr J Inf (Moscow)
Abstract Journal. Scientific and Technical Information (Moscow) — Abstr J Sci Tech Inf Moscow
Abstract of Proceedings. Royal Society of New South Wales — Abstr Proc R Soc NSW
Abstract. Proceedings. Association of American Geologists and Naturalists — Abstr Proc Assoc Amer Geol Naturalists
Abstracta Botanica — Abstr Bot
Abstracta Iranica — Abstr Iran
Abstracta Islamica — Ab Isl
Abstracts and Proceedings Series. CIP — Abstr Proc Ser CIP
Abstracts Bulletin. Geological Survey of South Australia — Abstr Bull Geol Surv S Aust
Abstracts. Centre for the Study of Islam and Christian-Muslim Relations — Abst CSICMR
Abstracts. Congress of Heterocyclic Chemistry — Abstr Congr Heterocycl Chem
Abstracts. Congress of the European Society for Experimental Surgery — Abstr Congr Eur Soc Exp Surg
Abstracts. Congress of the Polish Phthisiopneumonological Society — Abstr Congr Pol Phthisiopneumonol Soc
Abstracts. European Society for Surgical Research. Congress — Abstr Eur Soc Surg Res Congr
Abstracts for Social Workers — AbSocWk
Abstracts for Social Workers — Abstr Soc Work
Abstracts for Social Workers — Absts Soc Workers
Abstracts for Social Workers — ASW
Abstracts. Geological Society of America — Abstr Geol Soc Am
Abstracts in Anthropology — AA
Abstracts in Anthropology — AbAn
Abstracts in Anthropology — Abstr Anthropol
Abstracts in Biocommerce [*Biocommerce Data Ltd.*] [*England*] [*Information service or system*] — ABC
Abstracts. Institute of Petroleum — Abstr Inst Pet
Abstracts. International Congress of Gastroenterology — Abstr Int Congr Gastroenterol
Abstracts Journal. Chemical Reaction Documentation Service — Abstr J Chem React Doc Serv
Abstracts. London Shellac Research Bureau — Abstr London Shellac Res Bur
Abstracts. Meeting of the Weed Society of America — Abstr Meet Weed Soc Am
Abstracts. Meeting of the Weed Society of America — Abstr Mtg Weed Soc Amer
Abstracts. National Congress of the Italian Society of Marine Biology — Abstr Natl Congr Ital Soc Mar Biol
Abstracts of Air and Water Conservation Literature — Abstr Air Water Conserv Lit
Abstracts of Bacteriology — Abstr Bacteriol
Abstracts of Bulgarian Scientific Literature — Abstr Bulg Scient Lit
Abstracts of Bulgarian Scientific Literature. Agriculture and Forestry, Veterinary Medicine — Abstr Bulg Sci Lit Agric For Vet Med
Abstracts of Bulgarian Scientific Literature. Biology and Biochemistry — Abstr Bulg Sci Lit Biol Biochem
Abstracts of Bulgarian Scientific Literature. Biology and Medicine — Abstr Bulg Sci Lit Biol Med
Abstracts of Bulgarian Scientific Literature. Chemistry — Abstr Bulg Sci Lit Chem

Abstracts of Bulgarian Scientific Literature. Chemistry and Chemical Technology — Abstr Bulg Sci Lit Chem Chem Technol
Abstracts of Bulgarian Scientific Literature. Geology and Geography — Abstr Bulg Sci Lit Geol Geogr
Abstracts of Bulgarian Scientific Literature. Geosciences — Abstr Bulg Sci Lit Geosci
Abstracts of Bulgarian Scientific Literature. Mathematical and Physical Sciences — Abstracts Bulgar Sci Lit Math Phys Sci
Abstracts of Bulgarian Scientific Literature. Mathematics, Physics, Astronomy, Geophysics, Geodesy — Abstr Bulg Sci Lit Math Phys Astron Geophys Geod
Abstracts of Bulgarian Scientific Literature. Medicine — Abstr Bulg Sci Lit Med
Abstracts of Bulgarian Scientific Literature, Medicine, and Physical Culture — Abstr Bulg Sci Lit Med Phys Cult
Abstracts of Bulgarian Scientific Literature. Series A. Plant Breeding and Forest Economy — Abstr Bulg Sci Lit Ser A Plant Breed For Econ
Abstracts of Bulgarian Scientific Medical Literature — Abstr Bulg Sci Med Lit
Abstracts of Computer Literature — Abstr Comput Lit
Abstracts of Conference Papers. Triennial Conference. European Association for Potato Research — Abstr Conf Pap Trienn Conf Eur Assoc Potato Res
Abstracts of Current Literature. Aerospace Medical Association — Abstr Curr Lit Aerosp Med Assoc
Abstracts of Doctoral Dissertations. Ohio State University — Abstr Doct Diss Ohio St Univ
Abstracts of English Studies — AbEnSt
Abstracts of English Studies — Abstr Engl Stud
Abstracts of English Studies — AES
Abstracts of Entomology — Abstr Entomol
Abstracts of Folklore Studies — AbFolkSt
Abstracts of Folklore Studies — AbFS
Abstracts of Folklore Studies — Abstr Folk Stud
Abstracts of Geochronology and Isotope Geology — Abstr Geochronology Isot Geol
Abstracts of Health Care Management Studies — Abstr Health Care Manage Stud
Abstracts of Hospital Management Studies — Abstr Hosp Manage Stud
Abstracts of Hospital Management Studies — Abstr Hospit Manage Stud
Abstracts of Hospital Management Studies — AHMS
Abstracts of Hungarian Economic Literature — AHL
Abstracts of Instructional Materials in Vocational and Technical Education [*ERIC*] — AIM
Abstracts of Japanese Chemical Literature. Complete — Abstr Jpn Chem Lit Complete
Abstracts of Japanese Literature in Forest Genetics and Related Fields — Abstr Jap Lit Forest Genet
Abstracts of Japanese Medicine — Abstr Jpn Med
Abstracts of Military Bibliography — AbMilt
Abstracts of Military Bibliography — Abstr Mil Bibl
Abstracts of Military Bibliography — Abstr Mil Bibliogr
Abstracts of Military Bibliography — AMB
Abstracts of Mycology — Abstr Mycol
Abstracts of New World Archaeology — Abstr New World Archaeol
Abstracts of North American Geology — Abstr N Amer Geol
Abstracts of North American Geology — Abstr North Am Geol
Abstracts of Papers Accepted for Presentation. International Conference on Atomic Spectroscopy — Abstr Pap Int Conf At Sptrosc
Abstracts of Papers. American Chemical Society — Abs Pap ACS
Abstracts of Papers. American Chemical Society — Abstr Pap Am Chem Soc
Abstracts of Papers. Congress of Heterocyclic Chemistry — Abstr Pap Congr Heterocycl Chem
Abstracts of Papers. International Conference on the Physics of Electronic and Atomic Collisions — Abstr Pap Int Conf Phys Electron At Collisions
Abstracts of Papers. Joint Conference. Chemical Institute of Canada and American Chemical Society — Abstr Pap Jt Conf Chem Inst Can Am Chem Soc
Abstracts of Papers. Journal of the Japanese Society of Internal Medicine [*A publication*] — Abstr Pap J Jpn Soc Intern Med
Abstracts of Papers. Meeting of the American Chemical Society — Abstr Mtg ACS
Abstracts of Papers Presented at the Annual Meeting. American Society of Range Management — Abstr Pap Presented Ann Meet Am Soc Range Mange
Abstracts of Papers Presented at the Annual Meeting. Korean Surgical Society — Abstr Pap Presented Annu Meet Korean Surg Soc
Abstracts of Papers Presented at the Scientific Poultry Conference — Abstr Pap Sci Poult Conf
Abstracts of Papers Presented. Scandinavian Congress of Internal Medicine — Abstr Pap Scand Congr Intern Med
Abstracts of Papers Presented to the American Mathematical Society — Abstracts Amer Math Soc
Abstracts of Papers Read. Brighton and Sussex Natural History and Philosophical Society — Abstr Pap Brighton Sussex Nat Hist Soc
Abstracts of Papers. Society of American Foresters Meeting — Abstr Pap Soc Amer For
Abstracts of Papers Submitted. Annual Convention. Utah Academy of Sciences — Abstr Pap Utah Acad Sci
Abstracts of Papers Submitted. Lunar and Planetary Science Conference — Abstr Pap Lunar Planet Sci Conf
Abstracts of Photographic Science and Engineering Literature — AbPhoto
Abstracts of Photographic Science and Engineering Literature — Abstr Photogr Sci Eng Lit
Abstracts of Popular Culture — Abstr Pop Cult
Abstracts of Proceedings. Cornell Nutrition Conference for Feed Manufacturers — Abstr Proc Cornell Nutr Conf Feed Manuf
Abstracts of Proceedings. Royal Society of New South Wales — Abstr Proc Soc NSW
Abstracts of Published Papers and List of Translations. Commonwealth Scientific and Industrial Research Organisation (Australia) — Abstr Publ Pap List Transl CSIRO (Aust)
Abstracts of Refining Literature — Abstr Refin Lit
Abstracts of Research and Related Materials in Vocational and Technical Education — AbVoc
Abstracts of Research and Related Materials in Vocational and Technical Education — ARM
Abstracts of Research in Pastoral Care and Counseling — Abstr Res Pastor Care Couns
Abstracts of Researches. Tobacco, Salt, Camphor — Abstr Res Tob Salt Camphor
Abstracts of Romanian Scientific and Technical Literature — Abstr Rom Sci Tech Lit
Abstracts of Romanian Technical Literature — Abstr Rom Tech Lit
Abstracts of Selected Solar Energy Technology [*Japan*] — ASSET
Abstracts of Soviet Medicine — Abstr Sov Med
Abstracts of Soviet Medicine. Part A. Basic Medical Sciences — Abstr Sov Med Part A
Abstracts of Soviet Medicine. Part B. Clinical Medicine — Abstr Sov Med Part B
Abstracts of Technical Papers. Water Pollution Control Federation — Abstr Tech Pap Water Pollut Control Fed
Abstracts of the Annual Meeting. American Society for Microbiology — Abstr Annu Meet Am Soc Microbiol
Abstracts of the Papers Communicated to the Royal Society (London) — Abstr Pap Commun R Soc (London)
Abstracts of the Papers. Pacific Science Congress — Abstr Pap Pac Sci Congr
Abstracts of the Papers Printed in the Philosophical Transactions of the Royal Society (London) — Abstr Pap Printed Philos Trans R Soc (London)
Abstracts of the Proceedings. Chemical Society of London — Abstr Proc Chem Soc London
Abstracts of the Proceedings. Linnean Society of New South Wales — Abstr Proc Linn Soc NSW
Abstracts of Uppsala Dissertations. Faculty of Medicine — Abstr Uppsala Diss Fac Med
Abstracts of Uppsala Dissertations. Faculty of Pharmacy — Abstr Uppsala Diss Fac Pharm
Abstracts of Uppsala Dissertations. Faculty of Science — Abstr Uppsala Diss Fac Sci
Abstracts of Uppsala Dissertations in Medicine — Abstr Uppsala Diss Med
Abstracts of Uppsala Dissertations in Science — Abstr Uppsala Diss Sci
Abstracts of Working Papers in Economics [*Database*] — AWPE
Abstracts of World Medicine — Abstr Wld Med
Abstracts of World Medicine — Abstr World Med
Abstracts on Crime and Juvenile Delinquency — Abstr Crime Juv Del
Abstracts on Criminology and Penology — Abs Crim Pen
Abstracts on Criminology and Penology — Abstr Crim & Pen
Abstracts on Criminology and Penology — Abstr Criminol Penol
Abstracts on Criminology and Penology — CrimAb
Abstracts on Health Effects of Environmental Pollutants — Abstr Health Eff Environ Pollut
Abstracts on Health Effects of Environmental Pollutants — Abstr Health Environ Pollutants
Abstracts on Hygiene — Abstr Hyg
Abstracts on Hygiene and Communicable Diseases — Abstr Hyg Commun Dis
Abstracts on Police Science — Abstr Police Sci
Abstracts on Rural Development in the Tropics [*Database*] — RURAL
Abstracts on Tropical Agriculture — Abstr Trop Agri
Abstracts on Tropical Agriculture — Abstr Trop Agric
Abstracts on Tropical Agriculture [*Information service or system*] — ATA
Abstracts on Tropical Agriculture — DOA
Abstracts. Reports of the Geological Survey of Western Australia — Abstr Rep Geol Surv West Austr
Abstracts. Symposium on Nonbenzenoid Aromatic Compounds and Symposium on Structural Organic Chemistry — Abstr Symp Nonbenzenoid Aromat Compd Symp Struct Org Chem
Abstracts with Programs. Geological Society of America — Abstr Programs Geol Soc Am
Abteilung fuer Mineralogie am Landesmuseum Joanneum. Mitteilungen — Abt Mineral Landesmus Joanneum Mitt
Abteilung fuer Mineralogie am Landesmuseum Joanneum. Mitteilungsblatt — Abt Mineral Landesmus Joanneum Mitteilungsbl
Abteilung fuer Zoologie und Botanik am Landesmuseum Joanneum (Graz) Mitteilungsblatt — Abt Zool Bot Landesmus Joanneum Graz Mitteilungsbl
Abteilung fuer Zoologie und Botanik am Landesmuseum Joanneum, Graz. Mitteilungsheft — Abt Zool Bot Landesmus Joanneum Graz Mitteilungsh
Abtrennung von Feststoffen aus dem Abwasser. Siedlungswasserwirtschaftliches Kolloquium — Abtrennung Festst Abwasser Siedlungswasserwirtsch Kolloq
ABU [*Asian Broadcasting Union*] **Technical Review** — ABU Tech Rev
Abwassertechnik mit Abfalltechnik — Abwassertech Abfalltech
Abwassertechnische Vereinigung, Dokumentation, und Schriftenreihe aus Wissenschaft und Praxis — Abwassertech Ver Dok Schriftenr Wiss Prax
Abwassertechnische Vereinigung. Technisch-Wissenschaftliche Schriftenreihe — Abwassertech Ver Tech Wiss Schriftenr
AC [*Asbestos and Cement*]. The Fibrecement Review — AC
Academia Agriculturae ac Technicae Olstenensis. Acta Agricultura — Acad Agric Tech Olstenensis Acta Agric
Academia Agriculturae ac Technicae Olstenensis. Acta Protectio Aquarum et Piscatoria — Acad Agric Tech Olstenensis Acta Prot Aquarum Piscatoria
Academia Agriculturae ac Technicae Olstenensis. Acta Technologia Alimentorum — Acad Agric Tech Olstenensis Acta Technol Aliment
Academia Boliviana de Ciencias Economicas. Revista — Acad Boliviana Ciencias Econs R
Academia Brasileira de Ciencias. Anais — Acad Brasileira Cienc Anais

Academia (Chile) — AAC
Academia de Ciencias de Cuba. Informe Cientifico-Tecnico — Acad Cienc Cuba Inf Cient Tec
Academia de Ciencias de Cuba. Instituto de Geologia. Actas — Acad Cienc Cuba Inst Geol Actas
Academia de Ciencias de Cuba. Instituto de Geologia. Serie Geologica — Acad Cienc Cuba Inst Geol Ser Geol
Academia de Ciencias de Cuba. Instituto de Geologia y Paleontologia. Publicacion Especial — Acad Cienc Cuba Inst Geol Paleontol Publ Espec
Academia de Ciencias de Cuba. Serie Biologica — Acad Cienc Cuba Ser Biol
Academia de Ciencias do Estado de Sao Paulo. Publicacao — Acad Cienc Estado Sao Paulo Publ
Academia de Ciencias Exactas, Fisicas, y Naturales de Madrid. Memorias. Serie de Ciencias Fisico-Quimicas — Acad Cienc Exactas Fis Nat Madrid Mem Ser Cienc Fis Quim
Academia de Ciencias Exactas, Fisicas, y Naturales de Madrid. Memorias. Serie de Ciencias Naturales — Acad Cienc Exactas Fis Nat Madrid Mem Ser Cienc Natur
Academia de Ciencias Medicas de Cataluna y Baleares — Acad Cienc Med Cataluna Baleares
Academia de Ciencias Medicas, Fisicas, y Naturales de la Habana. Anales — Acad Cienc Med Fis y Naturales Habana Anales
Academia de Ciencias Medicas, Fisicas, y Naturales de la Habana. Annales — Ac Cienc Med Habana An
Academia de Ciencias y Artes de Barcelona. Memorias — Acad Cienc Artes Barc
Academia de Ciencias y Artes de Barcelona. Memorias — Acad Cienc Artes Barcelona Mem
Academia de Stiinte Agricole si Silvice. Buletinul Informativ — Acad Stiinte Agric Silvice Bul Inf
Academia Galega de Ciencias. Boletin — Acad Galega Cienc Bol
Academia Galega de Ciencias. Revista — Acad Galega Cienc Rev
Academia Mexicana de Ciencias Exactas, Fisicas, y Naturales. Anuario — Ac Mex Cienc An
Academia Nacional de Ciencias Exactas, Fisicas, y Naturales. Monografias — Acad Nac Cienc Exactas Fis Nat Monogr
Academia Nacional de Ciencias. Memorias y Revista — Acad Nac Cienc Mem Rev
Academia Nacional de Ciencias. Miscelanea (Cordoba) — Acad Nac Cienc Misc (Cordoba)
Academia Nacional de Medicina. Boletim (Brazil) — Acad Nac Med Bol (Braz)
Academia Peruana de Cirugia — Acad Peru Cir
Academia Republicii Populare Romane. Buletin Stiintific. Seria A. Matematica, Fizica, Chimie, Geologie, Geografie, Biologie. Stiinte Tehnice si Agricole — Acad Repub Pop Rom Bul Stiint A
Academia Republicii Populare Romane. Buletin Stiintific. Seria B. Stiinte Medicale — Acad Repub Pop Rom Bul Stiint B
Academia Republicii Populare Romine. Buletin Stiintific. Sectia de Biologie si Stiinte Agricole — Acad Repub Pop Rom Bul Stiint Sect Biol Stiinte Agric
Academia Republicii Populare Romine. Buletin Stiintific. Sectia de Geologie si Geografie — Acad Repub Pop Rom Bul Stiint Sect Geol Geogr
Academia Republicii Populare Romine. Buletin Stiintific. Sectia de Stiinte Matematice si Fizice — Acad Repub Pop Rom Bul Stiint Sect Stiinte Mat Fiz
Academia Republicii Populare Romine. Buletin Stiintific. Sectia de Stiinte Medicale — Acad Repub Pop Rom Bul Stiint Sect Stiinte Med
Academia Republicii Populare Romine. Buletin Stiintific. Sectiunea de Stiinte Tehnice si Chimice — Acad Repub Pop Rom Bul Stiint Sect Stiinte Teh Chim
Academia Republicii Populare Romine. Buletin Stiintific. Seria A [*Romania*] — Acad Repub Pop Rom Bul Stiint A
Academia Republicii Populare Romine. Buletin Stiintific. Seria Matematica, Fizica, Chimie — Acad Repub Pop Rom Bul Stiint Ser Mat Fiz Chim
Academia Republicii Populare Romine. Buletin Stiintific. Seria. Stiinte Medicale — Acad Repub Pop Rom Bul Stiint Ser Stiinte Med
Academia Republicii Populare Romine. Central de Cercetari Metalurgice. Studii si Cercertari de Metalurgie — Acad Repub Pop Rom Cent Cercet Metal Stud Cercet Metal
Academia Republicii Populare Romine. Centrul de Cercetari Metalurgice. Studii si Cercetari de Metalurgie — Acad Repub Pop Rom Cen Cercet Metal Stud Cercet Metal
Academia Republicii Populare Romine Filiala (Cluj). Studii si Cercetari de Agronomie — Acad Repub Pop Rom Fil (Cluj) Stud Cercet Agron
Academia Republicii Populare Romine Filiala (Cluj). Studii si Cercetari de Biologie — Acad Repub Pop Rom Fil (Cluj) Stud Cercet Biol
Academia Republicii Populare Romine Filiala (Cluj). Studii si Cercetari de Chimie — Acad Repub Pop Rom Fil (Cluj) Stud Cercet Chim
Academia Republicii Populare Romine Filiala (Cluj). Studii si Cercetari de Geologie, Geografie — Acad Repub Pop Rom Fil (Cluj) Stud Cercet Geol Geogr
Academia Republicii Populare Romine Filiala (Cluj). Studii si Cercetari de Matematica si Fizica — Acad Repub Pop Rom Fil (Cluj) Stud Cercet Mat Fiz
Academia Republicii Populare Romine Filiala (Cluj). Studii si Cercetari de Medicina — Acad Repub Pop Rom Fil (Cluj) Stud Cercet Med
Academia Republicii Populare Romine Filiala (Cluj). Studii si Cercetari Stiintifice — Acad Repub Pop Rom Fil (Cluj) Stud Cercet Stiint
Academia Republicii Populare Romine Filiala (Cluj). Studii si Cercetari Stiintifice. Seria 1. Stiinte Matematice, Fizice, Chimice, si Tehnice — Acad Repub Pop Rom Fil (Cluj) Stud Cercet Stiint Ser 1
Academia Republicii Populare Romine Filiala (Cluj). Studii si Cercetari Stiintifice. Seria 2. Stiinte Biologice, Agricole, si Medicale — Acad Repub Pop Rom Fil (Cluj) Stud Cercet Stiint Ser 2
Academia Republicii Populare Romine Filiala (Iasi). Studii si Cercetari Stiintifice. Chimie — Acad Repub Pop Rom Fil (Iasi) Stud Cercet Stiint Chim
Academia Republicii Populare Romine Filiala (Iasi). Studii si Cercetari Stiintifice. Medicina — Acad Repub Pop Rom Fil (Iasi) Stud Cercet Stiint Med
Academia Republicii Populare Romine Filiala (Iasi). Studii si Cercetari Stiintifice. Seria 1. Stiinte Matematice, Fizice, Chimice, si Tehnice — Acad Repub Pop Rom Fil Iasi Stud Cercet Stiint Ser 1
Academia Republicii Populare Romine Filiala (Iasi). Studii si Cercetari Stiintifice. Seria 2. Stiinte Biologice, Medicale, si Agricole — Acad Repub Pop Rom Fil (Iasi) Stud Cercet Stiint Ser 2
Academia Republicii Populare Romine. Institutul de Biochimie. Studii si Cercetari de Biochimie [*Romania*] — Acad Repub Pop Rom Stud Cercet Biochim
Academia Republicii Populare Romine. Institutul de Energetica. Studii si Cercetari de Mecanica Aplicata — Acad Repub Pop Rom Stud Cercet Mec Apl
Academia Republicii Populare Romine. Institutul de Energetica. Studii si Cercetari Energetica — Acad Repub Pop Rom Stud Cercet Energ
Academia Republicii Populare Romine. Institutul de Energetica. Studii si Cercetari Energetica. Serie A. Energetica Generala si Electroenergetica — Acad Repub Pop Rom Stud Cercet Energ Ser A
Academia Republicii Populare Romine. Institutul de Energetica. Studii si Cercetari Energetica. Serie B. Termoenergetica si Utilizarea Energetica a Combustibililor — Acad Repub Pop Rom Stud Cercet Energ Ser B
Academia Republicii Populare Romine. Institutul de Fizica Atomica Reports — Acad Repub Pop Rom Inst Fiz At Rep
Academia Republicii Populare Romine. Institutul de Fizica Atomica si Institutul de Fizica. Studii si Cercetari de Fizica [*Romania*] — Acad Repub Pop Rom Stud Cercet Fiz
Academia Republicii Populare Romine. Institutul de Fizica Atomica si Institutul de Fizica. Studii si Cercetari de Fizica — ARFAA
Academia Republicii Populare Romine. Institutul de Fiziologie Normala si Patologica Dr. D. Danielolpolu. Studii si Cercetari de Fiziologie [*Romania*] — Acad Repub Pop Rom Stud Cercet Fiziol
Academia Republicii Populare Romine. Institutul de Medicina Interna. Studii si Cercetari de Medicina Interna — Acad Repub Pop Rom Stud Cercet Med Interna
Academia Republicii Populare Romine. Studii si Cercetari de Biologie. Seria Biologie Animala — Acad Repub Pop Rom Stud Cercet Biol Ser Biol Anim
Academia Republicii Populare Romine. Studii si Cercetari de Biologie. Seria Biologie Vegetala — Acad Repub Pop Rom Stud Cercet Biol Ser Biol Veg
Academia Republicii Populare Romine. Studii si Cercetari de Chimice — Acad Repub Pop Rom Stud Cercet Chim
Academia Republicii Populare Romine. Studii si Cercetari de Geologie — Acad Repub Pop Rom Stud Cercet Geol
Academia Republicii Populare Romine. Studii si Cercetari Stiintifice. Seria Stiinte Medicina — Acad Repub Pop Rom Stud Cercet Stiint Ser Stiint Med
Academia Republicii Populare Romine. Studii si Cercetari Stiintifice. Seria Stiinte Medicina — Acad Repub Pop Rom Stud Cercet Stiint Ser Stiinte Med
Academia Republicii Socialiste Romania. Memoriile. Sectei de Stiinte Istorice — ARSR Mem Sect Stiint Ist
Academia Republicii Socialiste Romania. Memoriile Sectiilor Stiintifice — Acad Repub Soc Rom Mem Sect Stiint
Academia Romana. Memoriile Sectiunei Stiintifice — Acad Romana Mem Sect Sti
Academia Scientiarum et Artium Slovenica. Classis 3. Mathematica, Physica, Technica. Dissertationes. Series A. Methematica, Physica, Chemica — Acad Sci Artium Slov Cl 3 Math Phys Tech Diss Ser A
Academia Scientiarum Fennicae. Annales. Series A-III (Geologica-Geographica) — Acad Sci Fenn Ann Ser A-III Geol-Geogr
Academia Scientiarum Hungarica. Acta Antiqua — Acad Scient Hung Act Ant
Academia Scientiarum Hungarica. Acta Botanica — Acad Scient Hung Act Bot
Academia Scientiarum Hungarica. Acta Geodaetica, Geophysica, et Montanistica — Acad Scient Hung Acta Geod Geophys Montan
Academia Scientiarum Hungarica. Acta Historica — Acad Scient Hung Acta Hist
Academia Scientiarum Hungarica. Acta Litteraria — Acad Scient Hung Acta Lit
Academia Scientiarum Hungarica. Acta Microbiologica — Acad Scient Hung Acta Microbiol
Academia Scientiarum Hungarica. Acta Oeconomica — Acad Scient Hung Acta Oecon
Academia Sinica. Institute of Botany. Annual Report — Acad Sin Inst Bot Annu Rep
Academia Sinica. Institute of Vertebrate Palaeontology and Palaeoanthropology. Memoir — Acad Sin Inst Vertebr Palaeontol Palaeoanthropol Mem
Academia Sinica. Institute of Zoology. Monograph Series — Acad Sin Inst Zool Monogr Ser
Academia Sinica. Memoirs. Institute of Chemistry — Acad Sin Mem Inst Chem
Academia Sinica. Memoirs. National Research Institute of Chemistry — Acad Sin Mem Natl Res Inst Chem
Academia Sinica. Nanjing Institute of Geology and Palaeontology. Memoirs — Acad Sin Nanjing Inst Geol Palaeontol Mem
Academiae Scientiarum Fennicae. Annales. Mathematica — Ann Acad Sci Fenn Math
Academiae Scientiarum Fennicae. Annales. Mathematica. Dissertationes — Ann Acad Sci Fenn Math Diss
Academic Associates Newsletter — Acad Assoc Newsl
Academic Emergency Medicine — Acad Emerg Med
Academic Journal of Guangdong College of Pharmacy — Acad J Guangdong Coll Pharm
Academic Journal of Guangdong Medical and Pharmaceutical College — Acad J Guangdong Med Pharm Coll
Academic Medicine — Acad Med
Academic Radiology — Acad Radiol
Academic Reports. Faculty of Engineering. Tokyo Institute of Polytechnics — Acad Rep Fac Eng Tokyo Inst Polytech
Academic Science USSR — Acad Sci USSR
Academic Therapy — Acad Ther
Academic Therapy — Acad Therapy

Academie and Societe Lorraines des Sciences. Bulletin — Acad Soc Lorraines Sci Bull
Academie d'Agriculture de France. Comptes Rendus des Seances — Acad Ag France Compt Rend
Academie d'Agriculture de France. Comptes Rendus des Seances — Acad Ag France Comptes Rendus
Academie d'Agriculture de France. Comptes Rendus des Seances — Acad Agric Fr CR Seances
Academie des Inscriptions et Belles-Lettres. Comptes Rendus — Acad Inscript CR
Academie des Inscriptions et Belles-Lettres. Comptes Rendus des Seances — AIBL
Academie des Inscriptions et Belles-Lettres. Comptes Rendus des Seances — AIBLCr
Academie des Inscriptions et Belles-Lettres. Comptes Rendus des Seances [*Paris*] — CAIL
Academie des Inscriptions et Belles-Lettres. Fondation Eugene Piot. Monuments et Memoires [*Paris*] — Monuments Piot
Academie des Inscriptions et Belles-Lettres. Memoires [*Paris*] — Acad d Inscrip Memoires
Academie des Inscriptions et Belles-Lettres. Memoires (Paris) — Acad d Inscr (Paris) Mem
Academie des Inscriptions et Belles-Lettres. Memoires Presentes par Divers Savants — AIB
Academie des Inscriptions et Belles-Lettres. Memoires Presentes par Divers Savants (Paris) — Acad Inscr (Paris) Mem Div Savants
Academie des Inscriptions et Belles-Lettres. Monuments et Memoires [*Paris*] [*A publication*] — Acad d Inscr Mon et Mem
Academie des Inscriptions et Belles-Lettres. Monuments et Memoires (Paris) [*A publication*] — Acad d Inscr (Paris) Mon et Mem
Academie des Sciences Agricoles et Forestieres. Bulletin (Bucharest) — Acad Sci Agric For Bull (Bucharest)
Academie des Sciences, Arts et Belles-Lettres de Dijon. Seance Publique — Dijon Seances Acad
Academie des Sciences, Belles-Lettres, et Arts de Besancon. Proces-Verbaux et Memoires — ABes
Academie des Sciences Coloniales. Comptes Rendus des Seances — Acad Sci Colon CR Seanc
Academie des Sciences. Comptes Rendus des Seances. Supplement aux Series 1-2-3 — Acad Sci CR Seances Suppl Ser 123
Academie des Sciences. Comptes Rendus Hebdomadaires des Seances. Serie D. Sciences Naturelles [*Paris*] — CR Hebd Acad Sci Ser D
Academie des Sciences. Comptes Rendus. Serie 2. Mecanique, Physique, Chimie, Sciences de l'Univers, Sciences de la Terre — Acad Sci CR Ser 2
Academie des Sciences. Comptes Rendus. Serie 3. Sciences de la Vie — Acad Sci CR Ser 3
Academie des Sciences. Comptes Rendus. Serie Generale. La Vie des Sciences — Acad Sci CR Ser Gen Vie Sci
Academie des Sciences de Cracovie. Bulletin International — ASCBull
Academie des Sciences de Cracovie. Bulletin. Sciences Mathematiques et Naturelles — Acad D Sci De Cracovie Bul Sci Math Et Nat
Academie des Sciences d'Outre-Mer — ASOM
Academie des Sciences. Inscriptions et Belles-Lettres de Toulouse. Memoires — Acad Sci Inscriptions B L Toulouse Mem
Academie des Sciences, Inscriptions, et Belles-Lettres de Toulouse. Memoires — Acad Sci Toulouse Mem
Academie des Sciences Morales et Politiques (Paris). Memoires — Acad d Sci Mor et Pol (Paris) Mem
Academie des Sciences (Paris). Comptes Rendus — Ac Sc (Paris) C R
Academie des Sciences (Paris). Comptes Rendus Hebdomadaires des Seances. Serie B. Sciences Physiques — Acad Sci (Paris) CR Ser B
Academie des Sciences (Paris). Comptes Rendus Hebdomadaires des Seances. Serie C. Sciences Chimiques — Acad Sci (Paris) CR Ser C
Academie des Sciences (Paris). Comptes Rendus Hebdomadaires des Seances. Serie D. Sciences Naturelles — Acad Sci (Paris) CR Ser D
Academie des Sciences (Paris). Memoires — Acad d Sci (Paris) Mem
Academie des Sciences (Paris). Memoires Presentes par Divers Savants — Acad d Sci (Paris) Mem Div Savants
Academie et Societe Lorraines des Sciences — Acad Soc Lorraines Sci
Academie Europeenne d'Allergologie et Immunologie Clinique. Comptes Rendus de la Reunion Annuelle — Acad Eur Allergol Immunol Clin CR Reun Annu
Academie Imperiale des Sciences, Belles-Lettres, et Arts de Lyon. Classe des Sciences. Memoires — Ac Imp Lyon Cl Sc Mem
Academie Nationale de Medecine. Paris. Bulletin — Acad Natl Med Paris Bull
Academie Polonaise des Sciences. Bulletin. Serie des Sciences de la Terre [*A publication*] — Acad Pol Sci Bull Ser Sci Terre
Academie Polonaise des Sciences. Bulletin. Serie des Sciences Mathematiques [*A publication*] — Bull Acad Polon Sci Ser Sci Math
Academie Polonaise des Sciences. Bulletin. Serie des Sciences Physiques et Astronomiques — Acad Pol Sci Bull Ser Sci Phys Astron
Academie Polonaise des Sciences. Bulletin. Serie des Sciences Physiques et Astronomiques [*Warsaw*] — Bull Acad Polon Sci Ser Sci Phys Astronom
Academie Polonaise des Sciences. Bulletin. Serie des Sciences Techniques — Acad Pol Sci Bul Ser Sci Tech
Academie Polonaise des Sciences et des Lettres. Centre Polonais de Recherches Scientifiques de Paris. Bulletin — Bull Acad Polon Paris
Academie Roumaine. Bulletin de la Section Historique — Bull Roum
Academie Royale d'Archeologie de Belgique. Annales — ARABAn
Academie Royale d'Archeologie de Belgique. Bulletin — ARABBull
Academie Royale de Belgique — ABM
Academie Royale de Belgique. Annuaire — Acad R Belg Annu
Academie Royale de Belgique. Bulletin — Ac Belg B
Academie Royale de Belgique. Bulletin. Classe des Beaux-Arts — Acad Sci Belg Bul Cl Beaux-Arts
Academie Royale de Belgique. Bulletin. Classe des Beaux-Arts — BCBA
Academie Royale de Belgique. Bulletin. Classe des Lettres et des Sciences Morales et Politiques — Acad Sci Belg Bul Cl Lett
Academie Royale de Belgique. Bulletin. Classe des Lettres et des Sciences Morales et Politiques — ARB
Academie Royale de Belgique. Bulletin. Classe des Lettres et des Sciences Morales et Politiques — ARBBCL
Academie Royale de Belgique. Bulletin. Classe des Lettres et des Sciences Morales et Politiques — BAB
Academie Royale de Belgique. Bulletin. Classe des Lettres et des Sciences Morales et Politiques — BCLSMP
Academie Royale de Belgique. Bulletin. Classe des Lettres et des Sciences Morales et Politiques et Classe des Beaux-Arts — ARBDull
Academie Royale de Belgique. Bulletin. Classe des Sciences — Acad R Belg Bull Cl Sci
Academie Royale de Belgique. Bulletin. Classe des Sciences — Acad Roy Belg Bull Cl Sci
Academie Royale de Belgique. Bulletin. Classe des Sciences — Acad Sci Belg Bul Cl Sci
Academie Royale de Belgique. Classe des Sciences. Collection in Octavo. Memoires — Acad R Belg Cl Sci Collect Octavo Mem
Academie Royale de Belgique. Classe des Sciences. Collection in Quarto. Memoires — Acad R Belg Cl Sci Collect Quarto Mem
Academie Royale de Belgique. Classe des Sciences. Memoires — Acad R Belg Cl Sci Mem
Academie Royale de Belgique. Classe des Sciences. Memoires. Collection in 8 — Acad R Belg Cl Sci Mem Collect 8
Academie Royale de Belgique. Classe des Sciences. Memoires. Collection in Octavo — Acad Roy Belg Cl Sci Mem Coll in-8
Academie Royale de Belgique. Classe des Sciences. Memoires. Collection in Octavo — Acad Roy Belg Cl Sci Mem Collect 8o
Academie Royale de Belgique. Memoires. Classe des Lettres et des Sciences Morales et Politiques. Collection in Octavo — Acad Sci Belg Mem 8 Cl Lett
Academie Royale de Belgique. Memoires. Classe des Sciences. Collection in 8 — Acad R Belg Mem Cl Sci Collect 8
Academie Royale de Belgique. Memoires. Classe des Sciences. Collection in Octavo — Acad R Belg Mem Cl Sci Collect Octavo
Academie Royale de Belgique. Memoires. Classe des Sciences. Collection in Octavo — Acad Sci Belg Mem 8 Cl Sci
Academie Royale de Belgique. Memoires. Classe des Sciences. Collection in Quarto — Acad R Belg Mem Cl Sci Collect Quarto
Academie Royale de Langue et de Litterature Francaise de Belgique. Bulletin — AcLLB
Academie Royale de Medecine de Belgique. Bulletin — Acad R Med Belg Bull
Academie Royale de Medecine de Belgique. Bulletin — Acad Roy De Med De Belg Bul
Academie Royale de Medecine de Belgique. Bulletin et Memoires — Acad R Med Belg Bull Mem
Academie Royale de Medecine de Belgique. Memoires — Acad R Med Belg Mem
Academie Royale des Sciences. Belles-Lettres et Arts de Bordeaux. Seance Publique — Acad Roy Sci Bordeaux Seance Publique
Academie Royale des Sciences Coloniales (Brussels). Bulletin des Seances [*Belgium*] — Acad R Sci Colon (Brussels) Bull Seances
Academie Royale des Sciences Coloniales (Brussels). Classe des Sciences Naturelles et Medicales. Memoires. Collection in Octavo — Acad R Sci Colon (Brussels) Cl Sci Nat Med Mem Collect
Academie Royale des Sciences, des Lettres, et des Beaux-Arts de Belgique. Classe des Sciences. Bulletin — Acad R Sci Lett B-Arts Belg Cl Sci Bull
Academie Royale des Sciences, des Lettres, et des Beaux-Arts de Belgique. Memoires 4. Classe des Lettres — Acad d Sci d Belgique Mem 4 Cl d Lett
Academie Royale des Sciences, des Lettres, et des Beaux-Arts de Belgique. Memoires 4. Classe des Sciences — Acad d Sci d Belgique Mem 4 Cl d Sci
Academie Royale des Sciences, des Lettres, et des Beaux-Arts de Belgique. Memoires 8. Classe des Lettres — Acad d Sci d Belgique Mem 8 Cl d Lett
Academie Royale des Sciences, des Lettres, et des Beaux-Arts de Belgique. Memoires 8. Classe des Sciences — Acad d Sci d Belgique Mem 8 Cl d Sci
Academie Royale des Sciences d'Outre-Mer (Brussels). Bulletin des Seances — Acad R Sci Outre-Mer (Brussels) Bull Seances
Academie Royale des Sciences d'Outre-Mer. Bulletin des Seances — Acad R Sci Outre-Mer Bull
Academie Royale des Sciences d'Outre-Mer. Bulletin des Seances — Acad Roy Sci O-Mer B
Academie Royale des Sciences d'Outre-Mer. Bulletin des Seances — Acad Roy Sci Outre-Mer Bul Seances
Academie Royale des Sciences d'Outre-Mer. Classe des Sciences Techniques. Memoires in 8 (Brussels) — Acad Roy Sci Outre Mer Cl Sci Tech Mem 8 Brussels
Academie Serbe des Sciences et des Arts. Bulletin. Classe des Sciences Mathematiques et Naturelles. Sciences Naturelles — Acad Serbe Sci Arts Bull Cl Sci Math Nat Sci Nat
Academie Serbe des Sciences et des Arts. Bulletin. Classe des Sciences Medicales — Acad Serbe Sci Arts Bull Cl Sci Med
Academie Serbe des Sciences et des Arts. Classe des Sciences Mathematiques et Naturelles (Glas) — Acad Serb Sci Arts Classe Sci Math Nat (Glas)
Academie Serbe des Sciences et des Arts. Classe des Sciences Medicales. Glas — Acad Serbe Sci Arts Cl Sci Med Glas
Academie Serbe des Sciences et des Arts (Glas). Classe des Sciences Techniques — Acad Serbe Sci et Arts (Glas) Cl Sci Tech
Academie Spectrum. Berliner Journal fuer den Wissenschaftler — Acad Spectrum
Academie Tcheque des Sciences. Bulletin International. Classe des Sciences Mathematiques et Naturelles, et de la Medecine — Acad Tcheque Sci Bull Int Cl Sci Math Nat Med

Academy [*London*] — Ac
[*The*] **Academy** — Acad
Academy and Literature — Acad
Academy Bookman — Acad Bookman
Academy Law Review [*Kerala, India*] — Acad L Rev
Academy of American Franciscan History. Bibliography Series — AAFHB
Academy of American Franciscan History. Monograph Series — AAFHM
Academy of Management. Journal — Acad Manage J
Academy of Management. Journal — Acad Mangt J
Academy of Management. Journal — Acad Mgt J
Academy of Management. Journal — Academy of Mgmt Jrnl
Academy of Management. Journal — Acdmy Mgt J
Academy of Management. Journal — AMA
Academy of Management. Journal — AMJ
Academy of Management. Review — Acad Manage Rev
Academy of Management. Review — Acad Mgt R
Academy of Management. Review — Academy of Mgmt Review
Academy of Management. Review — Acdmy Mgt R
Academy of Management. Review — AMR
Academy of Marketing Science. Journal — Acad Marketing Science J
Academy of Marketing Science. Journal — AMK
Academy of Marketing Science. Journal — AMS
Academy of Medicine of New Jersey. Bulletin — Acad Med NJ Bull
Academy of Motion Picture Arts and Sciences. Bulletin — Acad Bul
Academy of Natural Sciences. Journal — Acad of Nat Sci Jour
Academy of Natural Sciences of Philadelphia. Contributions. Department of Limnology — Acad Nat Sci Philadelphia Contrib Dep Limnol
Academy of Natural Sciences of Philadelphia. Journal — Ac N Sc Phila J
Academy of Natural Sciences of Philadelphia. Mineralogical and Geological Section. Proceedings — Ac N Sc Phila Min G Sec Pr
Academy of Natural Sciences of Philadelphia Monographs — Acad Nat Sci Phila Mon
Academy of Natural Sciences of Philadelphia Monographs — Acad Nat Sci Phila Monog
Academy of Natural Sciences of Philadelphia. Proceedings — Ac N Sc Phila Pr
Academy of Natural Sciences of Philadelphia. Proceedings — Acad Natur Sci Phila Proc
Academy of Natural Sciences of Philadelphia. Special Publication — Acad Nat Sci Philadelphia Spec Pub
Academy of Political Science. Proceedings — Acad Pol Sci Proc
Academy of Political Science. Proceedings — GAPP
Academy of Science and Letters of Sioux City, Iowa. Proceedings — Ac Sc Sioux City Pr
Academy of Science of Kansas City. Transactions — Ac Sc Kansas City Tr
Academy of Science of St. Louis. Transactions — Ac Sc St L Tr
Academy of Science of St. Louis. Transactions — Acad Sci St Louis Trans
Academy of Sciences of the Lithuanian SSR. Mathematical Transactions — Acad Sci Lith SSR Math Trans
Academy of Sciences of the USSR. Mathematical Notes — Acad Sci USSR Math Notes
Academy Papers. American Academy of Physical Education — Acad Pap
Academy Papers. American Academy of Physical Education. Meeting — Acad Pap Am Acad Phys Ed Meet
Academy Proceedings in Engineering Sciences — Acad Proc Eng Sci
Academy Review — Acad Rev
Academy Review. California Academy of Periodontology — Acad Rev Calif Acad Periodontol
Academy. Rumanian People's Republic. Institute of Atomic Physics Report — Acad Rum Peoples Repub Inst At Phys Rep
Academy (Syracuse) — Acad (Syr)
Acarologia — Acarol
Acarology Newsletter — Acarol Newsl
Acarology. Proceedings. International Congress of Acarology — Acarol Proc Int Congr Acarol
Accademia dei Fisiocritici in Siena. Atti — Accad Fisiocrit Siena Atti
Accademia delle Scienze di Bologna. Memorie — ASB
Accademia delle Scienze di Torino. Memorie. Classe di Scienze Fisiche, Matematiche, e Naturali. Serie 5 — Mem Accad Sci Torino Cl Sci Fis Mat Natur 5
Accademia delle Scienze Fisiche e Matematiche. Rendiconto — Accad Sci Fis e Mat Rend
Accademia delle Scienze. Istituto di Bologna. Classe di Scienze Fisiche. Atti. Memorie — Accad Sci Ist Bologna Cl Sci Fis Atti Mem
Accademia di Acricoltura Scienze e Lettere di Verona. Atti e Memorie — Accad Agric Sci Lett Verona Atti Mem
Accademia di Mantova. Atti e Memorie — AMan
Accademia e Biblioteche d'Italia — ABI
Accademia e Biblioteche d'Italia — Accad Bibl Ital
Accademia e Biblioteche d'Italia — Accad Bibliot d'Italia
Accademia e Biblioteche d'Italia — Accad e Bibl Italia
Accademia Gioenia de Scienze Naturali in Catania. Bollettino delle Sedute — Ac Gioenia Sc Nat Catania B
Accademia Gioenia di Scienze Naturali in Catania. Atti — Accad Gioenia Sci Nat Catania Atti
Accademia Italiana della Vite e del Vino (Siena). Atti — Accad Ital Vite Vino (Siena) Atti
Accademia Italiana di Scienze Forestali. Annali — Accad Ital Sci For Ann
Accademia Ligure di Scienze e Lettere. Genoa. Atti — Accad Ligure Sci Lett Genoa Atti
Accademia Medica — Accad Med
Accademia Medica Lombarda. Atti — Accad Med Lomb Atti
Accademia Nazionale dei Lincei [*Rome*] — ANL
Accademia Nazionale dei Lincei. Atti. Classe di Scienze Fisiche, Matematiche, e Naturali. Rendiconti — Accad Naz Lincei Atti Cl Sci Fis Mat Nat Rend
Accademia Nazionale dei Lincei. Atti. Memorie. Classe di Scienze Fisiche, Matematiche, e Naturali. Sezione 1a — Accad Naz Lincei Atti Mem Cl Sci Fis Mat Nat Sez 1a
Accademia Nazionale dei Lincei. Atti. Memorie. Classe di Scienze Fisiche, Matematiche, e Naturali. Sezione 2a — Accad Naz Lincei Atti Mem Cl Sci Fis Mat Nat Sez 2a
Accademia Nazionale dei Lincei. Atti. Memorie. Classe di Scienze Fisiche, Matematiche, e Naturali. Sezione 3 — Accad Naz Lincei Atti Mem Cl Sci Fis Mat Nat Sez 3
Accademia Nazionale dei Lincei. Corso Estivo di Chimica — Accad Naz Lincei Corso Estivo Chim
Accademia Nazionale dei Lincei. Memorie — ANLM
Accademia Nazionale dei Lincei. Quaderno — Accad Naz Lincei Quad
Accademia Nazionale dei Lincei. Rendiconti. Classe di Scienze Morali, Storiche, e Filologiche — ANLMSF
Accademia Nazionale dei XL. Rendiconti. Serie 4 — Rend Accad Naz XL 4
Accademia Nazionale dei XL. Rendiconti. Serie 5 — Rend Accad Naz XL 5
Accademia Nazionale di Lincei. Rendiconti della Classe di Scienze Fisische, Matematiche e Naturali — Accad Naz Lincei Rendic Cl Fis Mat Nat
Accademia Nazionale di Scienze, Lettere, ed Arti (Modena). Atti e Memorie — Accad Naz Sci Lett Arti (Modena) Atti Mem
Accademia Nazionale Italiana di Entomologia. Atti. Rendiconti — Accad Naz Ital Entomol Atti Rend
Accademia Patavina di Scienze, Lettere, ed Arti. Atti e Memorie [*Padua*] — Accad Patavina Sci Lett Arti Atti Mem
Accademia Patavina di Scienze, Lettere, ed Arti. Collana Accademica — Accad Pata Sci Lett Arti Collana Accad
Accademia Pontaniana. Atti — Accad Pontaniana Atti
Accademia Pugliese delle Scienze. Atti e Relazioni. Parte 2. Classe di Scienze Fisiche, Mediche, e Naturali — Accad Pugliese Sci Att Relaz Parte 2
Accademia. Scienze di Siena detta de' Fisiocritici. Atti — Accad Sci Siena Fisiocrit Atti
Accademia Virgiliana di Mantova. Atti e Memorie — Accad Virgiliana Mantova Atti Mem
Accademie e Biblioteche d'Italia. Annali. Direzione Generale. Accademie e Biblioteche — Ac Bibl
Accao Regional — AR
Accelerator Dosimetry and Experience. Proceedings. International Conference on Accelerator Dosimetry and Experiences — Accel Dosim Exper Proc Int Conf Accel Dosim Exper
Accelerator Instrumentation. Annual Workshop — Accel Instrum Annu Workshop
Accelerators and Storage Rings — Accel Storage Rings
Accent — ACC
Accent on Information [*Database*] — AOI
Accent on Worship, Music, and the Arts — AC
Access Index to Little Magazines — Access Index Little Mag
Access Video [*Australia*] — Access V
Accessible Housing Bulletin — Acces Hous Bul
Accessory and Garage Equipment — Acc Gar Equip
Acciaio Inossidabile — Acciaio Inossid
Accident Analysis and Prevention — Accid Anal Prev
Accident Analysis and Prevention — Accident Anal Prev
Accident Analysis and Prevention (Elmsford, New York) — Accid Anal Prev (Elmsford NY)
Accident/Incident Reporting System [*Database*] — AIRS
Accident Prevention Bulletin — Accident Prevention Bul
Accidents Chromosomiques de la Reproduction. Compte-Rendu du Colloque — Accid Chromosomiques Reprod R Colloq
Accion Agraria (Cuzco) — Accion Agrar Cuzco
Accion Cientifica International — Acc Cient Int
Accion Farmaceutica — Accion Farm
Accion Medica (Argentina) — Acc Med (A)
Accion Medica (Bolivia) — Acc Med (B)
Accion Medica (Mexico) — Acc Med (M)
Accomplishments in Oncology — Accomp Oncol
Accountancy — ACC
Accountancy (England) — ACE
Accountancy Law Reports. Commerce Clearing House — Accountancy L Rep CCH
Accountant [*London*] — ACC
Accountant — ACT
Accountantadviseur — MEA
Accountants and Secretaries' Educational Journal — Accountants and Secretaries' Educ J
Accountants and Secretaries' Educational Journal — Accts Sec Educ J
Accountants Digest — Account Dig
Accountants' Index. Supplement — Account Index Suppl
Accountants' Journal — Account J
Accountants' Journal — Acct
Accountant's Magazine — Account Mag
Accountant's Magazine — ACM
Accounting and Business Research — ABR
Accounting and Business Research — ACB
Accounting and Business Research — Acc Bus Res
Accounting and Business Research — Account Bus Res
Accounting and Business Research — Accounting and Bus Research
Accounting and Business Research — Acct & Bus Res
Accounting and Data Processing Abstracts — ADPA
Accounting and Finance — Account Fin
Accounting and Finance [*Australia*] — ACF
Accounting and Finance — ATF
Accounting Forum — ACF
Accounting, Organizations, and Society — AOS
Accounting Research — Acc Res
Accounting Research — Account Res

Accounting Review — Acc Review
Accounting Review — Account R
Accounting Review — Account Rev
Accounting Review — Accounting R
Accounting Review — Acct R
Accounting Review — Acctg Rev
Accounting Review — Accting R
Accounting Review — ACR
Accounting Review — AR
Accounts of Chemical Research — Acc Chem Re
Accounts of Chemical Research — Acc Chem Res
Accounts of Chemical Research — Acct Chem Res
Accreditation and Quality Assurance. Journal for Quality, Comparability, and Relability in Chemical Measurement — Accredit Qual Assur
Accumulative Veterinary Index — Accumu Vet Index
ACD [*Association of Canadian Distillers*] **Bulletin** — ACD Bull
ACE [*Agricultural Communication in Education*] **Newsletter** — ACE News
ACEA [*Australian Council for Educational Administration*] **Bulletin** — ACEA Bull
ACEC [*Ateliers de Constructions Electriques de Charleroi*] **Reviews** — ACEC Rev
Acero y Energia — Ac Energ
Acero y Energia — Acero Energ
Acero y Energia. Numero Especial — Acero Energ Numero Espec
ACES [*Association for Comparative Economic Studies*] **Bulletin** — ACES Bul
ACES [*Australian Council for Educational Standards*] **Review** — ACES Rev
Acetylen in Wissenschaft und Industrie — Acetylen Wiss Ind
Acetylene — Acet
Acetylene Journal — Acet J
Acetylene Journal — Acetylene J
Acetylene Lighting and Welding Journal — Acet Light Weld J
Acetylene Welding — Acet Weld
Acetylene-Gas Journal — Acetylene Gas J
Acetylsalicylic Acid. New Uses for an Old Drug. Proceedings. Canadian Conference on Acetylsalicylic Acid. New Uses for an Old Drug — Acetylsalicylic Acid New Uses Old Drug Proc Can Conf
ACFAS. Association Canadienne Francaise pour l'Avancement des Sciences — ACFAS Assoc Can Fr Av Sci
ACH Models in Chemistry — ACH Models Chem
Achats et Entretien du Materiel Industriel [*France*] — Achats Entret Mater Ind
Achats et Entretien du Materiel Industriel — Achats et Entretien Mater Ind
ACHEMA [*Ausstellungs- Tegung fuer Chemisches Apparatewesen*] **Jahrbuch** — ACHEMA Jahr
Achimoowin. James Smith Reserve [*Saskatchewan, Canada*] — AC
ACHPER Healthy Lifestyles Journal — ACHPER Healthy Life J
Acht Arbeiten ueber Fluessige Kristalle Fluessigkristall-Konferenz Sozialistischer Laender — Acht Arb Fluess Krist Fluessigkrist Konf Soz Laender
ACI (American Concrete Institute) Materials Journal — ACI Mater J
ACI (American Concrete Institute) Proceedings — ACI Proc
ACI (American Concrete Institute) Publication — ACI Publ
ACI [*American Concrete Institute*] **Journal** — ACI J
ACIAR (Australian Centre for International Agricultural Research) Proceedings Series — ACIAR Proc Ser
Acid Magazine — Acid Mag
Acid Open Hearth Research Association. Bulletin — Acid Open Hearth Res Assoc Bull
Acid Sulphate Soils. Proceedings. International Symposium on Acid Sulphate Soils — Acid Sulphate Soils Proc Int Symp
Acidic Precipitation in Ontario Study — Acidic Precip Ont Study
Acidic Proteins of the Nucleus — Acidic Proteins Nucl
Acidification Research. Evaluation and Policy Applications. Proceedings. International Conference. Maastricht — Acidif Res Eval Policy Appl Proc Int Conf M
Aciers Speciaux — Aciers Spec
Aciers Speciaux — ACSPD
Aciers Speciaux — ACSPDI
Aciers Speciaux a Usinabilite Amelioree. Journees Metallurgiques Hispano-Francaises — Aciers Spec Usinabilite Amelior Jour Metall Hisp Fr
Aciers Speciaux et Leurs Emplois — Aciers Spec Leurs Emplois
Aciers Speciaux, Metaux, et Alliages — Aciers Spec Met Alliages
Acier-Stahl-Steel — ASSTA
ACL-MIT Press Series in Natural Language Processing — ACL MIT Press Ser Nat Lang Process
ACLS [*American Council of Learned Societies*] **Newsletter** — ACLS Newsl
ACM (Arquivos Catarinenses de Medicina) Edicao Cultural — ACM (Arq Catarinenses Med) Ed Cult
ACM Distinguished Dissertations — ACM Disting Diss
ACM Doctoral Dissertation Awards — ACM Doctor Diss Awards
ACM [*Association for Computing Machinery*] **Guide to Computing Literature** — ACM Guide Comput Lit
ACM [*Association for Computing Machinery*] **National Conference Proceedings** — ACM Proc
ACM [*Association for Computing Machinery*] **Transactions** — ACM Trans
ACM [*Association for Computing Machinery*] **Transactions on Computer Systems** — ACM Trans Comp
ACM [*Association for Computing Machinery*] **Transactions on Computer Systems** — ACM Trans Comput Syst
ACM [*Association for Computing Machinery*] **Transactions on Database Systems** — ACM Trans Database Syst
ACM [*Association for Computing Machinery*] **Transactions on Database Systems** — ACM Trans Database Systems
ACM [*Association for Computing Machinery*] **Transactions on Database Systems** — Database Sys
ACM [*Association for Computing Machinery*] **Transactions on Graphics** — ACM Trans Graphics
ACM [*Association for Computing Machinery*] **Transactions on Information Systems** — ACM T Inf S
ACM [*Association for Computing Machinery*] **Transactions on Mathematical Software** — ACM Trans Math Softw
ACM [*Association for Computing Machinery*] **Transactions on Mathematical Software** — ACM Trans Math Software
ACM [*Association for Computing Machinery*] **Transactions on Office Information Systems** — ACM Trans Off Inf Syst
ACM [*Association for Computing Machinery*] **Transactions on Office Information Systems** — ACM Trans OIS
ACM [*Association for Computing Machinery*] **Transactions on Programming Languages and Systems** — ACM Trans Program Lang Syst
ACM [*Association for Computing Machinery*] **Transactions on Programming Languages and Systems** — ATPSD
ACOG [*American College of Obstetricians and Gynecologists*] **Information** [*Database*] — ACOG Info
Acoreana — Acor
ACOSS [*Australian Council of Social Service*] **Quarterly** — ACOSS Q
Acoustical Holography — Acoust Hologr
Acoustical Imaging — Acoust Imaging
Acoustical Society of America. Journal — Acoust Soc Am J
Acoustical Society of America. Journal — Acoustical Soc Am
Acoustics Abstracts — Acoust Abstr
Acoustics Abstracts — Acoustics Abs
Acoustics and Noise Control in Canada — Acoust and Noise Control Can
Acoustics and Noise Control in Canada — Acoust Noise Control Can
Acoustics and Ultrasonics Abstracts — Acoust Ultrason Abstr
Acoustics Bulletin — Acoust Bull
Acoustics Letters — Acoust Lett
ACP. Applied Cardiopulmonary Pathophysiology — ACP Appl Cardiopulm Pathophysiol
ACP [American College of Physicians] Journal Club — ACP J Club
ACPC [*Australian Crime Prevention Council*] **Forum** — ACPC For
ACPTC (Association of College Professors of Textiles and Clothing) Proceedings. Combined Central, Eastern, and Western Regional Meetings — ACPTC Proc Comb Cent East West Reg Meet
Acqua Aria — AQARD
Acqua Industriale [*Italy*] — Acqua Ind
Acqua Industriale. Inquinamento — Acqua Ind Inquinamento
Acquired Immune Deficiency Syndrome Research — Acquired Immune Defic Syndr Res
Acquisition/Divestiture Weekly Report — Acq Divest
Acquisitions en Chirurgie Infantile — Acquis Chir Infant
Acquisitions Medicales Recentes — Acquis Med Recent
Acquisitions Monthly — Acq Month
Acres Australia — Acres Aust
ACRL [*Association of College and Research Libraries*] **College and Research Libraries** — ACRL C & RL
Acrolein (American Edition) — Acrolein Am Ed
Acropole. Revue du Monde Hellenique — Acr
Acros Organics Acta — Acros Org Acta
Across the Board — Across the Bd
Across the Board — CFB
Across the Board — Conf Brd
Across the Board. Conference Board (New York) — Across Board (NY)
Acrylic Fiber Technology and Applications — Acrylic Fiber Technol Appl
ACS (American Chemical Society) Organic Coatings and Applied Polymer Science. Proceedings — ACS Org Coat Appl Polym Sci Proc
ACS (American Chemical Society) Organic Coatings and Plastics Chemistry — ACS Org Coat Plast Chem
ACS [*American Chemical Society*] **Directory of Graduate Research** [*Database*] — ACS DGRF
ACS [*American Chemical Society*] **Division of Polymeric Materials Science and Engineering. Proceedings** — ACS Div Polym Mater Sci Eng Proc
ACS [*American Chemical Society*] **Monograph** — ACS Monogr
ACS [*American Chemical Society*] **Single Article Announcement** — ACS Single Art Announce
ACS [*American Chemical Society*] **Symposium Series** — ACS Symp S
ACS [*American Chemical Society*] **Symposium Series** — ACS Symp Ser
ACS Symposium Series. American Chemical Society — ACS Symp Ser Am Chem Soc
ACST [*Alaska Council on Science and Technology*] **Notes** — ACSTN
ACT [*American College Testing Program*] **Monograph Series** — ACT Monogr Ser
ACT [*Australian Capital Territory*] **Papers on Education** — ACT Pap Educ
ACT [*American College Testing Program*] **Special Report Series** — ACT Spec Rep Ser
ACT [*Australian Capital Territory*] **Teachers Federation. Teacher** — ACT Teach
Acta Academiae Aboensis — AAA
Acta Academiae Aboensis — AAAbo
Acta Academiae Aboensis — Acta Acad Aboensis
Acta Academiae Aboensis. Humaniora — Acta Abo
Acta Academiae Aboensis. Humaniora — Acta Ac Abo
Acta Academiae Aboensis. Serie A. Humaniora — AA Abo H
Acta Academiae Aboensis. Series A. Humaniora — AAA Hum
Acta Academiae Aboensis. Series A. Humaniora — AAAH
Acta Academiae Aboensis. Series A. Humaniora — AAASAH
Acta Academiae Aboensis. Series B. Mathematica et Physica — Acta Acad Abo Ser B
Acta Academiae Aboensis. Series B. Mathematica et Physica. Matematik Naturvetenskaper Teknik — Acta Acad Abo Ser B Math Phys Mat Naturvetensk Tek
Acta Academiae Agriculturae ac Technicae Olstenensis. Protectio Aquarum et Piscatoria — Acta Acad Agric Tech Olstenensis Prot Aquarum Piscatoria
Acta Academiae Agriculturae ac Technicae Olstenensis. Veterinaria — Acta Acad Agric Tech Olstenensis Vet

Acta Academiae Catholicae Suecanae — AACS
Acta Academiae Electoralis Moguntinae Scientiarum Utilium Quae Erfordiae Est — Acta Acad Elect Mogunt Sci Util Erfordiae
Acta Academiae Internationalis Historiae Medicinae — Acta Acad Int Hist Med
Acta Academiae Medicinae Hebei — Acta Acad Med Hebei
Acta Academiae Medicinae Nanjing — Acta Acad Med Nanjing
Acta Academiae Medicinae Primae Shanghai — Acta Acad Med Primae Shanghai
Acta Academiae Medicinae Shanghai — Acta Acad Med Shanghai
Acta Academiae Medicinae Sichuan — Acta Acad Med Sichuan
Acta Academiae Medicinae Sinicae — Acta Acad Med Sinicae
Acta Academiae Medicinae Wuhan — Acta Acad Med Wuhan
Acta Academiae Medicinae Wuhan (Chinese Edition) — Acta Acad Med Wuhan Chin Ed
Acta Academiae Paedagogicae in Civitate Pecs. Seria 6. Mathematica-Physica-Chemica-Technica — Acta Acad Paedagog Civitate Pecs Ser 6 Math-Phys-Chem-Tech
Acta Academiae Paedagogicae Jyvaskylaensis — AAPJ
Acta Academiae Paedagogicae Szegediensis — Acta Acad Paedagog Szeged
Acta Academiae Polytechnicae Pollack Mihaly Pecs — Acta Acad Polytech Pollack Mihaly Pecs
Acta Academiae Regiae Scientiarum Upsaliensis — Acta Acad Regiae Sci Ups
Acta Academiae Scientiarum Imperialis Petropolitanae [*St. Petersburg*] — Act Acad Sci Petrop
Acta Academiae Scientiarum Imperialis Petropolitanae — Acta Acad Sci Imp Petrop
Acta Academiae Scientiarum Naturalium Moravosilesiacae — Acta Acad Sci Nat Moravosilesiacae
Acta Academiae Scientiarum Polonae — Acta Acad Sci Pol
Acta Academiae Scientiarum Taurinensis — Acta Acad Sci Taurinensis
Acta Academiae Scientiarum Taurinensis. Classe di Scienze Fisiche, Matematiche, e Naturali — Acta Acad Sci Taurinensis Cl Sci Fis Mat Nat
Acta Academiae Scientiarum Upsaliensis — AASU
Acta Academiae Velehradensis — A Ac Vel
Acta Academiae Velehradensis — AAV
Acta Academiae Velehradensis — Acta Vel
Acta Academica. Reeks A — Acta Acad Reeks A
Acta Academica. Reeks B — Acta Acad Reeks B
Acta Academica. Reeks C — Acta Acad Reeks C
Acta Acustica — Acta Acust
Acta ad Archaeologiam et Artium Historiam Pertinentia — AAAH
Acta ad Archaeologiam et Artium Historiam Pertinentia [*Oslo*] — Acta A Art Hist
Acta ad Archaeologiam et Artium Historiam Pertinentia [*Oslo*] — Acta Arch Art Hist Pert
Acta ad Res Naturae Estonicae Perscrutandas. 1 Ser. Geologica, Chemica, et Physica — Acta Res Nat Est Perscrutandas 1 Ser
Acta ad Res Naturae Estonicae Perscrutandas. 2 Ser. Biologica — Acta Res Nat Est Perscrutandas 2 Ser
Acta Adriatica — Acta Adriat
Acta Agralia Fennica — Acta Agral Fenn
Acta Agraria — Acta Agrar
Acta Agraria et Silvestria — Acta Agrar Silvestria
Acta Agraria et Silvestria. Seria Rolnicza — Acta Agrar Silvestria Ser Roln
Acta Agraria et Silvestria. Series Agraria — Acta Agrar Silv Ser Agrar
Acta Agraria et Silvestria. Series Agraria — Acta Agrar Silvestria Ser Agrar
Acta Agraria et Silvestria. Series Rolnictwo — Acta Agr Silv Ser Roln
Acta Agraria et Silvestria. Series Silvestris — Acta Agrar Silv Ser Silv
Acta Agraria et Silvestria. Series Silvestris — Acta Agrar Silvestria Ser Silvestris
Acta Agraria et Silvestria. Series Zootechnia — AASZBW
Acta Agraria et Silvestria. Series Zootechnia — Acta Agrar Silvestria Ser Zootech
Acta Agriculturae Nucleatae Sinica — Acta Agric Nucleatae Sin
Acta Agriculturae Scandinavica — AASC
Acta Agriculturae Scandinavica — AASCAU
Acta Agriculturae Scandinavica — Acta Agr Scand
Acta Agriculturae Scandinavica — Acta Agric Scand
Acta Agriculturae Scandinavica. Section A. Animal Science — Acta Agric Scand Sect A
Acta Agriculturae Scandinavica. Section B. Soil and Plant Science — Acta Agric Scand Sect B
Acta Agriculturae Scandinavica. Supplementum — AASNAT
Acta Agriculturae Scandinavica. Supplementum — Acta Agric Scand Suppl
Acta Agriculturae Scandinavica. Supplementum — Suppl Acta Agric Scand
Acta Agriculturae Sinica — Acta Agr Sinica
Acta Agriculturae Sinica — Acta Agric Sin
Acta Agriculturae Sinica — NUNGAS
Acta Agriculturae Suecana — AASAAO
Acta Agriculturae Suecana — Acta Agric Suec
Acta Agriculturae Suecana — Acta Agric Suecana
Acta Agriculturae Universitatis Pekinensis — Acta Agric Univ Pekinensis
Acta Agrobotanica — AAGWAU
Acta Agrobotanica — Acta Agrobot
Acta Agronomica [*Palmira*] — ACAGAY
Acta Agronomica — Acta Agron
Acta Agronomica. Academiae Scientiarum Hungaricae — AASHAB
Acta Agronomica. Academiae Scientiarum Hungaricae [*Budapest*] — Act Agron H
Acta Agronomica. Academiae Scientiarum Hungaricae [*Budapest*] — Acta Agron Acad Sci Hung
Acta Agronomica. Academiae Scientiarum Hungaricae [*Budapest*] — Acta Agron Hung
Acta Agronomica. Academiae Scientiarum Hungaricae (Budapest) — Acta Agron (Budapest)
Acta Agronomica Hungarica — Acta Agron Hung
Acta Agronomica (Palmira) — Acta Agron (Palmira)
Acta Albertina — Acta Albert
Acta Albertina Ratisbonensia — AARAAJ
Acta Alimentaria — ACALDI
Acta Alimentaria — Acta Aliment
Acta Alimentaria. Academiae Scientiarum Hungaricae — Acta Aliment Acad Sci Hung
Acta Alimentaria Polonica — AAPODK
Acta Alimentaria Polonica — Acta Aliment Pol
Acta Allergologica — ACALAF
Acta Allergologica — Act Allerg
Acta Allergologica — Acta Allerg
Acta Allergologica — Acta Allergol
Acta Allergologica. Supplementum — AALSA9
Acta Allergologica. Supplementum — Acta Allergol Suppl
Acta Amazonica — AAMZAZ
Acta Americana — Acta Am
Acta Americana. Inter-American Society of Anthropology and Geography — Acta Amer
Acta Anaesthesiologica — ACAEA
Acta Anaesthesiologica [*Padua*] — ACAEAS
Acta Anaesthesiologica — Acta Anaesth
Acta Anaesthesiologica — Acta Anaesthesiol
Acta Anaesthesiologica Belgica — AABEAJ
Acta Anaesthesiologica Belgica — Acta Anaesthesiol Belg
Acta Anaesthesiologica Hellenica — Acta Anaesthesiol Hell
Acta Anaesthesiologica Italica — AANIBO
Acta Anaesthesiologica Italica — Acta Anaesthesiol Ital
Acta Anaesthesiologica (Padova) — Acta Anaesthesiol (Padova)
Acta Anaesthesiologica (Padua) — Acta Anaesthesiol (Padua)
Acta Anaesthesiologica Scandinavica — AANEAB
Acta Anaesthesiologica Scandinavica — Act Anae Sc
Acta Anaesthesiologica Scandinavica — Acta Anaesth Scandinav
Acta Anaesthesiologica Scandinavica — Acta Anaesthes Scand
Acta Anaesthesiologica Scandinavica — Acta Anaesthesiol Scand
Acta Anaesthesiologica Scandinavica. Supplementum — AASXAP
Acta Anaesthesiologica Scandinavica. Supplementum — Acta Anaesthesiol Scand Suppl
Acta Anaesthesiologica Sinica — Acta Anaesthesiol Sin
Acta Anatomica — ACATA5
Acta Anatomica — Act Anatom
Acta Anatomica — Acta Anat
Acta Anatomica (Basel) — Acta Anat (Basel)
Acta Anatomica Nipponica — Acta Anat Nippon
Acta Anatomica Nipponica — KAIZAN
Acta Anatomica Sinica — Acta Anat Sin
Acta Anatomica Sinica — CPHPA5
Acta Anatomica. Supplement. Bibliotheca Anatomica — Acta Anat Suppl Bibl Anat
Acta Anatomica. Supplementum — AANSAJ
Acta Anatomica. Supplementum — Acta Anat Suppl
Acta Anthropobiologica — Acta Anthr Biol
Acta Anthropogenetica — ACANDO
Acta Anthropogenetica — Acta Anthropog
Acta Anthropogenetica — Acta Anthropogen
Acta Anthropogenetica — Acta Anthropogenet
Acta Anthropologica (Mexico) — Acta Anthr (Mex)
Acta Anthropologica (Mexico City) — Acta Anthrop Mex
Acta Antiqua [*Budapest*] — AAn
Acta Antiqua Academiae Scientiarum Hungaricae — A Ant Hung
Acta Antiqua. Academiae Scientiarum Hungaricae — A Antiqua Acad Sci Hung
Acta Antiqua. Academiae Scientiarum Hungaricae — AAASH
Acta Antiqua. Academiae Scientiarum Hungaricae — AAH
Acta Antiqua. Academiae Scientiarum Hungaricae — AAnt
Acta Antiqua. Academiae Scientiarum Hungaricae — AAntHung
Acta Antiqua. Academiae Scientiarum Hungaricae [*Budapest*] — AcAn
Acta Antiqua. Academiae Scientiarum Hungaricae — Act Antiq H
Acta Antiqua. Academiae Scientiarum Hungaricae — Acta Ant H
Acta Antiqua et Archaeologica — Acta Ant
Acta Antiqua et Archaeologica — Acta Ant Arch
Acta Antiqua Hungarica — ActAntHung
Acta Antiqua. Magyar Tudomanyos Akademia — Acta Antiq Magyar Tud Akad
Acta Antique Academiae Scientiarum Hungaricae — A Ant H
Acta Antique Academiae Scientiarum Hungaricae — AAAH
Acta Antique Academiae Scientiarum Hungaricae — Acta Acad Hung
Acta Antique Academiae Scientiarum Hungaricae — Acta Ant Ac Hung
Acta Antique Academiae Scientiarum Hungaricae — Acta Ant Hung
Acta Apostolicae Sedis [*Cittal del Vaticano*] — AAS
Acta Apostolicae Sedis — Acta Apost Sedis
Acta Apostolicae Sedis (Cittal del Vaticano) — AASV
Acta Apostolorum Apocrypha — AAA
Acta Applicandae Mathematicae — Acta Appl Math
Acta Arachnologica — AACHBY
Acta Arachnologica — Acta Arachnol
Acta Archaeologia Sinica — Acta Archaeol Sin
Acta Archaeologica — AA
Acta Archaeologica — AArch
Acta Archaeologica — Ac Ar
Acta Archaeologica [*Copenhagen*] — Ac Arch
Acta Archaeologica — Act Archaeo
Acta Archaeologica — Acta A
Acta Archaeologica [*Copenhagen*] — Acta Ar
Acta Archaeologica — Acta Arch
Acta Archaeologica Academiae Scientiarum Hungaricae — A A Hung
Acta Archaeologica. Academiae Scientiarum Hungaricae — A Arch Acad Sci Hung
Acta Archaeologica Academiae Scientiarum Hungaricae — AAA
Acta Archaeologica. Academiae Scientiarum Hungaricae — AArchHung

Acta Archaeologica Academiae Scientiarum Hungaricae — AArH
Acta Archaeologica. Academiae Scientiarum Hungaricae — ACGCBJ
Acta Archaeologica Academiae Scientiarum Hungaricae — Acta A Acad Hung
Acta Archaeologica. Academiae Scientiarum Hungaricae — Acta Archaeol Acad Sci Hung
Acta Archaeologica Academiae Scientiarum Hungaricae [*Budapest*] — Acta Archaeol Hung
Acta Archaeologica Academiae Scientiarum Hungaricae (Budapest) — Acta Arch (Bp)
Acta Archaeologica Academiae Scientiarum Hungaricae (Budapest) — Acta Arch Budapest
Acta Archaeologica/Arheoloski Vestnik. Slovenska Akademija — AArchSlov
Acta Archaeologica (Budapest) — Acta Archaeol (Budapest)
Acta Archaeologica Carpathica [*Crakow*] — A Arch Carpathica
Acta Archaeologica Carpathica [*Krakow*] — AAC
Acta Archaeologica Carpathica [*Krakow*] — Acta A Carp
Acta Archaeologica Carpathica — Acta Arch Carp
Acta Archaeologica Carpathica [*Krakow*] — Acta Arch Carpathica
Acta Archaeologica (Copenhagen) — AAC
Acta Archaeologica (Copenhagen) — Act Arch (Copenhagen)
Acta Archaeologica (Kobenhaven) — Acta Arch Kobenhaven
Acta Archaeologica (Kobenhavn) — Acta Archaeol (Kobenhavn)
Acta Archaeologica (Ljubljana) — Ac Arch (Ljub)
Acta Archaeologica Lodziensia — A Arch Lodziensia
Acta Archaeologica Lundensia — Acta Arch Lund
Acta Archaeologica Storica [*Copenhagen*] — A Arch Stor
Acta Arctica — ACAR
Acta Arctica — ACARCZ
Acta Arctica — Acta Arct
Acta Argentina de Fisiologia y Fisiopatologia — Acta Argent Fisiol Fisiopatol
Acta Arithmetica — Act Arith
Acta Arithmetica — Acta Arith
Acta Asiatica — Ac As
Acta Asiatica — Acta As
Acta Asiatica — Acta Asiat
Acta Asiatica — ActaA
Acta Astronautica — Act Astron
Acta Astronautica — Acta Astronaut
Acta Astronomica — Acta Astron
Acta Astronomica Sinica — Acta Astron Sin
Acta Astronomica Sinica [*People's Republic of China*] — Acta Astron Sinica
Acta Astronomica Sinica — Acta Astronom Sinica
Acta Astrophysica Sinica — Acta Astrophys Sinica
Acta Audiologica y Foniatrica Hispano-Americana — Acta Audiol Foniat Hispano-Amer
Acta Automatica Sinica — Acta Autom Sin
Acta Automatica Sinica [*People's Republic of China*] — Acta Automat Sinica
Acta Baltica — AB
Acta Baltica — AcB
Acta Baltica — Acta Balt
Acta Baltico-Slavica — ABalt-Slav
Acta Baltico-Slavica — ABS
Acta Belgica de Arte Medicinali et Pharmaceutica Militari — Acta Belg Arte Med Pharm Mil
Acta Belgica. Medica Physica — Acta Belg Med Phys
Acta Biochemica et Biophysica Sinica/Sheng Wu Hua Yu Sheng Wu Li Hsueeh Pao — Acta Biochem Biophys Sin
Acta Biochimica — Acta Biochim
Acta Biochimica et Biophysica — Acta Biochim Biophys
Acta Biochimica et Biophysica. Academiae Scientiarum Hungaricae — ABBPA
Acta Biochimica et Biophysica. Academiae Scientiarum Hungaricae — Act Bioch H
Acta Biochimica et Biophysica. Academiae Scientiarum Hungaricae — Acta Biochim Biophys Acad Sci Hung
Acta Biochimica et Biophysica. Academiae Scientiarum Hungaricae — Acta Biochim Biophys Hung
Acta Biochimica et Biophysica Sinica — Acta Biochim Biophys Sin
Acta Biochimica et Biophysica Sinica — Acta Biochim Biophys Sinica
Acta Biochimica Iranica — Act Bio Ira
Acta Biochimica Iranica — Acta Biochim Iran
Acta Biochimica Polonica — Act Bioch P
Acta Biochimica Polonica — Acta Biochim Pol
Acta Biochimica Polonica — Acta Biochim Polon
Acta Biochimica Polonica (Translation) — Acta Biochim Pol (Trans)
Acta Biochimica Sinica — Acta Biochim Sin
Acta Biologiae et Medicinae Experimentalis — Acta Biol Med Exp
Acta Biologiae Experimentalis — Acta Biol Exp
Acta Biologiae Experimentalis. Polish Academy of Sciences — Acta Biol Exp Pol Acad Sci
Acta Biologiae Experimentalis Sinica — Acta Biol Exp Sin
Acta Biologiae Experimentalis Sinica — Acta Biol Exper Sinica
Acta Biologiae Experimentalis (Warsaw) — Acta Biol Exp (Warsaw)
Acta Biologica — Acta Biol
Acta Biologica. Academiae Scientiarum Hungaricae — Act Biol H
Acta Biologica. Academiae Scientiarum Hungaricae — Acta Biol Acad Sci Hung
Acta Biologica. Academiae Scientiarum Hungaricae — Acta Biol Hung
Acta Biologica. Academiae Scientiarum Hungaricae (Budapest) — Acta Biol (Budapest)
Acta Biologica. Academiae Scientiarum Hungaricae. Supplementum — Acta Biol Acad Sci Hung Suppl
Acta Biologica. Acta Litterarum ac Scientiarum. Sectio A (Szeged 1928-37) — Acta Biol Szeged 1928-37
Acta Biologica Cracoviensia. Series Botanica — Act Bio C B
Acta Biologica Cracoviensia. Series Botanica — Acta Biol Cracov Ser Bot
Acta Biologica Cracoviensia. Series Zoologia — Act Bio C Z
Acta Biologica Cracoviensia. Series Zoologia — Acta Biol Cracov Ser Zool
Acta Biologica Debrecina — Acta Biol Debrecina
Acta Biologica et Medica — Acta Biol Med
Acta Biologica et Medica (Gdansk) — Acta Biol Med (Gdansk)
Acta Biologica et Medica Germanica — ABMGA
Acta Biologica et Medica Germanica — Act Bio Med
Acta Biologica et Medica Germanica — Acta Biol Med Ger
Acta Biologica et Medica Germanica. Supplementband — Acta Biol Med Ger Suppl
Acta Biologica Hungarica — Acta Biol Hung
Acta Biologica Iugoslavica. Serija B — Acta Biol Iugosl Ser B
Acta Biologica Iugoslavica. Serija B. Mikrobiologija — Acta Biol Iugosl Ser B Mikrobiol
Acta Biologica Iugoslavica. Serija C — Acta Biol Iugosl Ser C
Acta Biologica Iugoslavica. Serija C. Iugoslavica Physiologica et Pharmacologica Acta — Acta Biol Iugosl Ser C Iugosl Physiol Pharmacol Acta
Acta Biologica Iugoslavica. Serija D. Ekologija — Acta Biol Iugosl Ser D Eko
Acta Biologica Iugoslavica. Serija E. Ichthyologia — Acta Biol Iugosl Ser E Ichthyol
Acta Biologica Iugoslavica. Serija F. Genetika — Acta Biol Iugosl Ser F
Acta Biologica Iugoslavica. Serija G. Biosistematika — Acta Biol Iugosl Ser G Biosistem
Acta Biologica Katowice — Acta Biol Katowice
Acta Biologica Latvica — Acta Biol Latv
Acta Biologica Paranaense — ACBPAW
Acta Biologica Paranaense — Acta Biol Parana
Acta Biologica (Szeged) — Acta Biol (Szeged)
Acta Biologica (Trent, Italy) — Acta Biol (Trent Italy)
Acta Biologica Venezuelica — ABVEAO
Acta Biologica Venezuelica — Acta Biol Venez
Acta Bio-Medica de l'Ateneo Parmense — Acta Bio-Med Ateneo Parmense
Acta Bioquimica Clinica Latinoamericana — ABCLDL
Acta Bioquimica Clinica Latinoamericana — Acta Bioquim Clin Latinoam
Acta Biotechnologica — ACBTDD
Acta Biotechnologica — Acta Biotech
Acta Biotechnologica — Acta Biotechnol
Acta Biotheoretica — ABIOAN
Acta Biotheoretica [*Leiden*] — Acta Biotheor
Acta Biotheoretica Dordrecht — Acta Biotheor
Acta Biotheoretica (Leiden) — Acta Biotheor (Leiden)
Acta Borealia — ACBO
Acta Borealia. A. Scientia — ABOAAB
Acta Borealia. A. Scientia — Acta Borealia A Sci
Acta Borealia. B. Humaniora — ABOA
Acta Botanica — Acta Bot
Acta Botanica. Academiae Scientiarum Hungaricae — ABOHAW
Acta Botanica. Academiae Scientiarum Hungaricae — Acta Bot Acad Sci Hung
Acta Botanica Academiae Scientiarum Hungaricae — Acta Bot Acad Sci Hungar
Acta Botanica. Academiae Scientiarum Hungaricae — Acta Bot Hung
Acta Botanica. Academiae Scientiarum Hungaricae (Budapest) — Acta Bot (Budapest)
Acta Botanica Barcinonensia — ABBADH
Acta Botanica Barcinonensia — Acta Bot Barc
Acta Botanica Bohemica — Act Bot Bohem
Acta Botanica Bohemica — Acta Bot Bohem
Acta Botanica Colombiana — Acta Bot Colomb
Acta Botanica Colombiana — MUTSAF
Acta Botanica Croatica — ABCRA2
Acta Botanica Croatica — Acta Bot Croat
Acta Botanica Cubana — ABCUDE
Acta Botanica Cubana — Acta Bot Cubana
Acta Botanica Fennica — ABFE
Acta Botanica Fennica — ABFEAC
Acta Botanica Fennica — Act Bot Fenn
Acta Botanica Fennica — Acta Bot Fenn
Acta Botanica Horti Bucurestiensis — Acta Bot Horti Bucur
Acta Botanica Horti Bucurestiensis — LGBBA3
Acta Botanica Hungarica — ABOHE2
Acta Botanica Hungarica — Acta Bot Hung
Acta Botanica Indica — ABOIB
Acta Botanica Indica — Acta Bot Indica
Acta Botanica Indica (India) — Acta Bot Indica (IN)
Acta Botanica Instituti Botanici. Universitatis Zagrebensis — ABBZAL
Acta Botanica Instituti Botanici. Universitatis Zagrebensis — Acta Bot Inst Bot Univ Zagreb
Acta Botanica Instituti Botanici Universitatis Zagrebiensis. Izvesta Botanickog Zavoda Kr Sveucilista u Zagrebu — Izv Bot Zavoda Kr Sveucilista U Zagrebu
Acta Botanica Islandica — ABIS
Acta Botanica Islandica — ABTIBR
Acta Botanica Islandica — Acta Bot Isl
Acta Botanica Malacitana — ABMAE5
Acta Botanica Malacitana — Acta Bot Malacitana
Acta Botanica Neerlandica — ABNRAN
Acta Botanica Neerlandica — Act Bot Nee
Acta Botanica Neerlandica — Acta Bot Neerl
Acta Botanica Neerlandica — Acta Bot Neerland
Acta Botanica Neerlandica. Supplement — Acta Bot Neerl Suppl
Acta Botanica Sinica — Acta Bot Sin
Acta Botanica Sinica — Acta Bot Sinica
Acta Botanica Sinica — CHWHAY
Acta Botanica Sinica (English Translation) — Acta Bot Sin (Engl Transl)
Acta Botanica Slovaca. Academiae Scientiarum Slovacae. Series B. Physiologica, Pathophysiologica — ABSPDB

Acta Botanica Slovaca Academiae Scientiarum Slovacae. Series B. Physiologica, Pathophysiologica — Acta Bot Slovaca Acad Sci Slovacae Ser B
Acta Botanica Taiwanica — Acta Bot Taiwan
Acta Botanica Taiwanica. Science Reports. National Taiwan University. Chih Wu Hsueh Pao — Act Bot Taiw Rep
Acta Botanica Taiwanica. Science Reports. National Taiwan University. Chih Wu Hsueh Pao — Chih Wu Hsueeh Pao
Acta Botanica Venezuelica — ABOVA6
Acta Botanica Venezuelica — Acta Bot Venez
Acta Botanica Yunnanica — Acta Bot Yunnanica
Acta Botanica Yunnanica — YCWCDP
Acta Brevia Neerlandica de Physiologia, Pharmacologia, Microbiologia — Acta Brev Neerl Physiol
Acta Brevia Neerlandica de Physiologia, Pharmacologia, Microbiologia — Acta Brevia Neerl Physiol Pharmacol Microbiol
Acta Brevia Sinensia — Acta Brev Sin
Acta Brevia Sinensia — Acta Brev Sinensia
Acta Brevia Sinensia — Acta Brevia Sin
Acta Cancerologica — Acta Cancerol
Acta Cancerologica — ATCCBG
Acta Cardiologica — A Card
Acta Cardiologica [*Bruxelles*] — ACCAA
Acta Cardiologica (Bruxelles) — Acta Cardiol (Brux)
Acta Cardiologica. Supplementum [*Bruxelles*] — Acta Cardiol Suppl
Acta Cartographica — Act Cart
Acta Chemica — Acta Chem
Acta Chemica et Physica — Acta Chem Phys
Acta Chemica Fennica [*Finland*] — Acta Chem Fenn
Acta Chemica, Mineralogica, et Physica — Acta Chem Mineral Phys
Acta Chemica, Mineralogica, et Physica — Acta Chem Mineralog Phys
Acta Chemica Scandinavica — A Chem Scand
Acta Chemica Scandinavica — Acta Chem Scand
Acta Chemica Scandinavica (Denmark) — Acta Chem Scand (DK)
Acta Chemica Scandinavica. Series A. Physical and Inorganic Chemistry — Act Chem A
Acta Chemica Scandinavica. Series A. Physical and Inorganic Chemistry — Acta Chem Scand Ser A
Acta Chemica Scandinavica. Series A. Physical and Inorganic Chemistry — Acta Chem Scand Ser A Phys Inorg Chem
Acta Chemica Scandinavica. Series B. Organic Chemistry and Biochemistry — Act Chem B
Acta Chemica Scandinavica. Series B. Organic Chemistry and Biochemistry — Acta Chem Scand (B)
Acta Chemica Scandinavica. Series B. Organic Chemistry and Biochemistry — Acta Chem Scand Ser B
Acta Chemica Scandinavica. Series B. Organic Chemistry and Biochemistry — Acta Chem Scand Ser B Org Chem Biochem
Acta Chimica. Academiae Scientiarum Hungaricae — Act Chim H
Acta Chimica. Academiae Scientiarum Hungaricae — Acta Chim Acad Sci Hung
Acta Chimica Hungarica — Acta Chim Hung
Acta Chimica. Societatis Scientiarum Lodziensis — Acta Chim Soc Sci Lodz
Acta Chirurgiae Maxillo-Facialis — Acta Chir Maxillo-Facialis
Acta Chirurgiae, Orthopaedicae, et Traumatologiae Cechoslovaca — Acta Chir Orthop Traumatol Cech
Acta Chirurgiae Plasticae — A Chir Plast
Acta Chirurgiae Plasticae [*Czechoslovakia*] — Acta Chir Plast
Acta Chirurgiae Plasticae (Prague) — Acta Chir Plast (Prague)
Acta Chirurgica. Academiae Scientiarum Hungaricae — ACAHA
Acta Chirurgica. Academiae Scientiarum Hungaricae — Act Chir H
Acta Chirurgica. Academiae Scientiarum Hungaricae — Acta Chir Acad Sci Hung
Acta Chirurgica Austriaca — Acta Chir Austriaca
Acta Chirurgica Austriaca. Supplement — Acta Chir Austriaca Suppl
Acta Chirurgica Belgica — A Chir Belg
Acta Chirurgica Belgica — Act Chir B
Acta Chirurgica Belgica — Acta Chir Belg
Acta Chirurgica Belgica. Supplement — Acta Chir Belg Suppl
Acta Chirurgica (Budapest) — Acta Chir (Budapest)
Acta Chirurgica Hellenica — Acta Chir Hell
Acta Chirurgica Hungarica — Acta Chir Hung
Acta Chirurgica Italica — A Chir It
Acta Chirurgica Italica — Acta Chir Ital
Acta Chirurgica Iugoslavica — Acta Chir Iugosl
Acta Chirurgica Jugoslavica — A Chir Jug
Acta Chirurgica Scandinavica — A Chir Scand
Acta Chirurgica Scandinavica — Act Chir Sc
Acta Chirurgica Scandinavica — Acta Chir Scand
Acta Chirurgica Scandinavica — Acta Chir Scandinav
Acta Chirurgica Scandinavica. Supplementum — Acta Chir Scand Suppl
Acta Ciencia Indica — ACIDB
Acta Ciencia Indica — ACIDBW
Acta Ciencia Indica — Acta Ci Indica
Acta Ciencia Indica — Acta Cienc Indica
Acta Ciencia Indica (India) — Acta Cienc Indica (IN)
Acta Ciencia Indica. Mathematics — Acta Cienc Indica Math
Acta Ciencia Indica. Physica — Acta Cienc Indica Physica
Acta Ciencia Indica. Physics — Acta Cienc Indica Phys
Acta Ciencia Indica. Series Chemistry — Acta Cienc Indica Chem
Acta Ciencia Indica. Series Chemistry [*India*] — Acta Cienc Indica Ser Chem
Acta Ciencia Indica. Series Mathematics [*India*] — Acta Cienc Indica Ser Math
Acta Cientifica — Acta Cient
Acta Cientifica Compostelana — ACCCA
Acta Cientifica Compostelana — Acta Ci Compostelana
Acta Cientifica Compostelana — Acta Cient Compostelana
Acta Cientifica Potosina — Acta Cient Potos
Acta Cientifica Potosina — Acta Cient Potosina
Acta Cientifica Venezolana — Act Cient V
Acta Cientifica Venezolana — Acta Cient Venez
Acta Cientifica Venezolana. Asociacion Venezolana para el Avance de la Ciencia — Acta Ci Venezolana
Acta Cientifica Venezolana. Asociacion Venezolana para el Avance de la Ciencia — Acta Cient Venezolana
Acta Cientifica Venezolana. Suplemento [*Venezuela*] — Acta Cient Venez Supl
Acta Cientifica Venezolana. Suplemento — ACVSA
Acta Cirurgica Brasileira — Acta Cir Bras
Acta Classica — ACl
Acta Classica — Acta Cl
Acta Classica. Universitatis Scientiarum Debreceniensis — ACD
Acta Classica. Universitatis Scientiarum Debreceniensis — Acta Cl Debrecen
Acta Classica. Universitatis Scientiarum Debreceniensis — Acta Class Debr
Acta Classica. Universitatis Scientiarum Debreceniensis — Acta Class Debrecen
Acta Classica. Universitatis Scientiarum Debreceniensis — ACUD
Acta Classica. Universitatis Scientiarum Debreceniensis — ACUSD
Acta Classica. Verhandelinge van die Klassieke Vereniging van Suid-Afrika — AClass
Acta Clinica Belgica — Act Clin B
Acta Clinica Belgica — Acta Clin Belg
Acta Clinica Belgica. Supplementum — Acta Clin Belg Suppl
Acta Clinica Odontologica — Acta Clin Odontol
Acta Comeniana — ACo
Acta Comeniana — ACom
Acta Concilii Constanciensis — AC Con
Acta Conciliorum et Epistolae Decretales — ACED
Acta Conciliorum Oecumenicorum — ACO
Acta Congressus Internationalis Historiae Pharmaciae — Acta Congr Int Hist Pharm
Acta Conventus Medicinae Internae Hungarici — Acta Conv Med Intern Hung
Acta Criminologiae Medicinae Legalis Japonica — Acta Criminol Med Leg Jpn
Acta Crystallographica — Acta Cryst
Acta Crystallographica — Acta Crystallogr
Acta Crystallographica. Section A — Act Cryst A
Acta Crystallographica. Section A — Acta Crystallogr A
Acta Crystallographica. Section A. Crystal Physics, Diffraction, Theoretical and General Crystallography — ACACB
Acta Crystallographica. Section A. Crystal Physics, Diffraction, Theoretical and General Crystallography — Acta Cryst Sect A
Acta Crystallographica. Section A. Crystal Physics, Diffraction, Theoretical and General Crystallography [*Denmark*] — Acta Crystallogr Sect A
Acta Crystallographica. Section A. Crystal Physics, Diffraction, Theoretical, and General Crystallography — Acta Crystallogr Sect A Cryst Phys
Acta Crystallographica. Section A. Foundations of Crystallography — Acta Crystallogr A
Acta Crystallographica. Section A. Foundations of Crystallography — Acta Crystallogr Sect A Found
Acta Crystallographica. Section A. Foundations of Crystallography — Acta Crystallogr Sect A Found Crystallogr
Acta Crystallographica. Section A. Fundamentals of Crystallography — Acta Crystallogr Sect A Fundam Crystallogr
Acta Crystallographica. Section B — Act Cryst B
Acta Crystallographica. Section B — Acta Crystallogr B
Acta Crystallographica. Section B. Structural Crystallography and Crystal Chemistry — ACBCA
Acta Crystallographica. Section B. Structural Crystallography and Crystal Chemistry [*Denmark*] — Acta Crystallogr Sect B
Acta Crystallographica. Section B. Structural Crystallography and Crystal Chemistry — Acta Crystallogr Sect B Struct Crystallogr Cryst Chem
Acta Crystallographica. Section B. Structural Science — Acta Crystallogr B
Acta Crystallographica. Section B. Structural Science — Acta Crystallogr Sect B Struct Sci
Acta Crystallographica. Section B. Structural Science and Crystal Chemistry — Acta Crystallogr Sect B Struct
Acta Crystallographica. Section C. Crystal Structure Communications — Acta Crystallogr C
Acta Crystallographica. Section C. Crystal Structure Communications — Acta Crystallogr Sect C
Acta Crystallographica. Section C. Crystal Structure Communications — Acta Crystallogr Sect C Cryst
Acta Crystallographica. Section C. Crystal Structure Communications — Acta Crystallogr Sect C Cryst Struct Commun
Acta Cuyana de Ingenieria — Acta Cuyana Ing
Acta Cybernetica — Acta Cybernet
Acta Cytologica — Act Cytol
Acta Cytologica — Acta Cytol
Acta Cytologica — ACYTA
Acta Cytologica (Baltimore) — Acta Cytol (Baltimore)
Acta Davosiana — Acta Davos
Acta Dendrobiologica — Acta Dendrobiol
Acta der Internationalen Vereinigung fuer Krebsbekaempfung — Acta Int Ver Krebsbekaempf
Acta Dermatologica — A Derm
Acta Dermatologica [*Japan*] — Acta Dermatol
Acta Dermatologica [*Kyoto*]. English Edition — ADMLBF
Acta Dermatologica/Hifuka Kiyo [*Kyoto, Japan*] — Acta Derm
Acta Dermatologica (Kyoto) (English Edition) — Acta Dermatol (Kyoto) (Engl Ed)
Acta Dermatologica-Kyoto (Japanese Edition) — Acta Dermatol Kyoto (Jpn Ed)
Acta Dermato-Venereologica — Act Der-Ven
Acta Dermato-Venereologica — Acta Dermat Vener
Acta Dermato-Venereologica — Acta Dermato-Venereol

Acta Dermato-Venereologica — Acta Derm-Venereol
Acta Dermato-Venereologica (Stockholm) — Acta Derm-Venereol (Stockh)
Acta Dermato-Venereologica. Supplementum — Acta Dermato-Venereol Suppl
Acta Dermato-Venereologica. Supplementum [*Stockholm*] — Acta Derm-Venereol Suppl
Acta Dermato-Venereologica. Supplementum (Stockholm) — Acta Derm-Venereol Suppl (Stockh)
Acta Dermatovenerologica Iugoslavica — Acta Dermatovenerol Iugosl
Acta Diabetologica [*Berlin*] — Acta Diabetol
Acta Diabetologica Latina — Act Diabet
Acta Diabetologica Latina — Acta Diabetol Lat
Acta Ecclesiastica — Ac Ec
Acta Ecclesiastica — Acta Eccl
Acta Ecologica — Acta Ecol
Acta Electronica — A Electr
Acta Electronica — Acta Electron
Acta Electronica Sinica — Acta Electron Sin
Acta Embryologiae et Morphologiae Experimentalis — A Embr Morph Exp
Acta Embryologiae et Morphologiae Experimentalis — Acta Embryol Morphol Exp
Acta Embryologiae et Morphologiae Experimentalis — Acta Embryol Morphol Exptl
Acta Embryologiae et Morphologiae Experimentalis — AEMXA
Acta Embryologiae et Morphologiae Experimentalis. New Series — Acta Embryol Morphol Exp New Ser
Acta Embryologiae Experimentalis [*Acta Embryologiae et Morphologiae Experimentalis*] [*Palermo*] [*Later,*] — Acta Embryol Exp
Acta Embryologiae Experimentalis [*Later, Acta Embryologiae et Morphologiae Experimentalis*] **(Palermo)** — Acta Embryol Exp (Palermo)
Acta Endocrinologica — Act Endocr
Acta Endocrinologica — Acta Endocrinol
Acta Endocrinologica Congress. Advance Abstracts — Acta Endocrinol Congr Adv Abstr
Acta Endocrinologica (Copenhagen) — Acta Endocrinol (Copenh)
Acta Endocrinologica Cubana — Acta Endocrinol Cubana
Acta Endocrinologica et Gynaecologica Hispanolusitana — A End Gyn
Acta Endocrinologica Iberica — A End Ib
Acta Endocrinologica Panamericana — Acta Endocrinol Panam
Acta Endocrinologica. Supplementum [*Copenhagen*] — Acta Endocrinol Suppl
Acta Endocrinologica. Supplementum (Copenhagen) — Acta Endocrinol Suppl (Copenh)
Acta Energiae Solaris Sinica — Acta Energ Sol Sin
Acta Energiae Solaris Sinica [*People's Republic of China*] — Acta Energ Solaris Sin
Acta Entomologica — Acta Ent
Acta Entomologica Bohemoslovaca — Act Ent Boh
Acta Entomologica Bohemoslovaca — Acta Ent Bohemoslov
Acta Entomologica Bohemoslovaca — Acta Entomol Bohemoslov
Acta Entomologica Fennica — ACEF
Acta Entomologica Fennica — Acta Ent Fenn
Acta Entomologica Fennica — Acta Entomol Fenn
Acta Entomologica Jugoslavica — Acta Ent Jugosl
Acta Entomologica Jugoslavica — Acta Entomol Jugosl
Acta Entomologica Lituanica — Acta Ent Litu
Acta Entomologica Lituanica — Acta Entomol Litu
Acta Entomologica. Musei Nationalis Pragae — Acta Entomol Mus Natl Pragae
Acta Entomologica. Musei Nationalis (Prague) — Acta Ent Mus Natn (Prague)
Acta Entomologica. Musei Nationalis (Prague) — Acta Ent (Prag)
Acta Entomologica Sinica — Acta Ent Sin
Acta Entomologica Sinica — Acta Entomol Sin
Acta Entomologica Sinica — Acta Entomol Sinica
Acta Environmentalica Universitatis Comenianae — Acta Environ Univ Comenianae
Acta Eruditorum — Acta Erud
Acta Eruditorum — Acta Erudit
Acta Eruditorum Anno 1682-1731 Publicata. Supplement. Actorum Eruditorum quae Lipsiae Publicantur — AErS
Acta et Commentationes Imperialis Universitatis Jurjevensis — Acta Commentat Imp Univ Jurjev
Acta et Commentationes Universitatis Dorpatensis — Acta Comment Univ Dorp
Acta et Commentationes Universitatis Dorpatensis — AUD
Acta et Commentationes Universitatis Tartuensis — Acta Commentat Univ Tartu
Acta et Commentationes Universitatis Tartuensis. A. Mathematica, Physica, Medica/Esti Vabariigi Tartu Ulikooli Toimetused — Esti Vabariigi Tartu Ulik Toimet
Acta et Commentationes Universitatis Tartuensis Dorpatensis A — Acta Commentat Univ Tartu Dorpat A
Acta et Commentationes Universitatis Tartuensis Dorpatensis. C — Acta Commentat Univ Tartu Dorpat C
Acta et Decreta Capitulorum Generalium Ordinis Praemonstratensis — AD Praem
Acta et Decreta Sacrorum Conciliorum Recentiorum — ADSCR
Acta et Diplomata Graeca Medii Aevi — MM
Acta et Diplomata Graeca Medii Aevi Sacra et Profana Collecta — ADGMA
Acta et Documenta Concilio Oecumenico Vaticano II Apparando — ADCOV
Acta Ethnographica — A Eth
Acta Ethnographica — AcEt
Acta Ethnographica — Act Ethnogr
Acta Ethnographica — AE
Acta Ethnographica. Academiae Scientiarum Hungaricae — Act Ethn H
Acta Ethnographica. Academiae Scientiarum Hungaricae — Acta Ethnog Hung
Acta Ethnographica. Academiae Scientiarum Hungaricae — Acta Ethnogr Acad Sci Hung
Acta Ethnographica. Academiae Scientiarum Hungaricae — Acta Ethnogr Hung
Acta Ethnographica. Academiae Scientiarum Hungaricae — AEASH
Acta Ethnographica. Academiae Scientiarum Hungaricae — AEH
Acta Ethnographica (Budapest) — Acta Ethnogr (Budapest)
Acta Ethnographica. Magyar Tudomanyos Akademia (Hungary) — A Ethn (Hung)
Acta Ethnographica. Magyar Tudomanyos Akademia (Hungary) — Acta Ethn (Hung)
Acta Ethnologica — Acta Ethn
Acta Ethnologica et Linguistica — AEL
Acta Ethnologica Slovaca — Acta Ethnol Slov
Acta Europaea Fertilitatis — Acta Eur Fertil
Acta Facultatis Medicae Fluminensis — Acta Fac Med Fluminensis
Acta Facultatis Medicae Universitatis Brunensis — Acta Fac Med Univ Brun
Acta Facultatis Paedagogicae Ostraviensis. Series A. Matematika, Fyzika — Acta Fac Paedagog Ostrav Ser A Mat Fyz
Acta Facultatis Paedagogicae Ostraviensis. Series E — Acta Fac Paedagog Ostra Ser E
Acta Facultatis Paedagogicae Ostraviensis. Series E — Acta Fac Paedagog Ostrav Ser E
Acta Facultatis Pharmaceuticae Bohemoslovenicae — Acta Fac Pharm Bohemoslov
Acta Facultatis Pharmaceuticae Brunensis et Bratislavensis — Acta Fac Pharm Brun Bratisl
Acta Facultatis Pharmaceuticae Universitatis Comenianae — Acta Fac Pharm Univ Comenianae
Acta Facultatis Pharmaceuticae Universitatis Comenianae — AFPCAG
Acta Facultatis Rerum Naturalium Universitatis Comenianae. Anthropologica — Acta Fac Rerum Nat Univ Comenianae Anthropol
Acta Facultatis Rerum Naturalium Universitatis Comenianae. Anthropologica — AFNABZ
Acta Facultatis Rerum Naturalium Universitatis Comenianae. Astronomia et Geophysica — Acta Fac Rerum Nat Univ Comenianae Astron Geophys
Acta Facultatis Rerum Naturalium Universitatis Comenianae. Botanica — Acta Fac Rerum Nat Univ Comenianae Bot
Acta Facultatis Rerum Naturalium Universitatis Comenianae. Botanica — AFNBA3
Acta Facultatis Rerum Naturalium Universitatis Comenianae. Chimia — Acta Fac Rerum Nat Univ Comenianae Chim
Acta Facultatis Rerum Naturalium Universitatis Comenianae. Chimia — AFRCA
Acta Facultatis Rerum Naturalium Universitatis Comenianae. Formatio et Protectio Naturae — Acta Fac Rerum Nat Univ Comenianae Form Prot Nat
Acta Facultatis Rerum Naturalium Universitatis Comenianae. Formatio et Protectio Naturae (Czechoslovakia) — Acta Fac Rerum Nat Univ Comenianae Form Prot Nat (CS)
Acta Facultatis Rerum Naturalium Universitatis Comenianae. Genetica — Acta Fac Rerum Nat Univ Comenianae Genet
Acta Facultatis Rerum Naturalium Universitatis Comenianae. Genetica — AFNGAI
Acta Facultatis Rerum Naturalium Universitatis Comenianae. Mathematica — Acta Fac Rerum Natur Univ Comenian Math
Acta Facultatis Rerum Naturalium Universitatis Comenianae. Microbiologia — Acta Fac Rerum Nat Univ Comenianae Microbiol
Acta Facultatis Rerum Naturalium Universitatis Comenianae. Microbiologia — AFCMCH
Acta Facultatis Rerum Naturalium Universitatis Comenianae. Physica — Acta Fac Rerum Nat Univ Comenianae Phys
Acta Facultatis Rerum Naturalium Universitatis Comenianae. Physica — AFRNA
Acta Facultatis Rerum Naturalium Universitatis Comenianae. Physiologia Plantarum — Acta Fac Rerum Nat Univ Comenianae Physiol Plant
Acta Facultatis Rerum Naturalium Universitatis Comenianae. Physiologia Plantarum — AFPPCN
Acta Facultatis Rerum Naturalium Universitatis Comenianae. Zoologia — Acta Fac Rerum Nat Univ Comenianae Zool
Acta Facultatis Rerum Naturalium Universitatis Comenianae. Zoologia — AFNZA7
Acta Farmaceutica Bonaerense — Acta Farm Bonaerense
Acta Farmaceutica Bonaerense — AFBODJ
Acta Faunistica Entomologica. Musei Nationalis Pragae — Acta Faun Entomol Mus Natl Pragae
Acta Faunistica Entomologica. Musei Nationalis Pragae — AFAEBG
Acta Forestalia Fennica — Act For Fenn
Acta Forestalia Fennica — Acta For Fenn
Acta Forestalia Fennica — AFRFAZ
Acta Fratrum Arvalium — AFA
Acta F.R.N. Universitatis Comenianae. Physiologia Plantarum — Acta FRN Univ Comenianae Physiol Plant
Acta Fytotechnica — ACFYAB
Acta Fytotechnica — Acta Fytotech
Acta Fytotechnica. Universitatis Agriculturae (Nitra) — Acta Fytotech Univ Agric (Nitra)
Acta Gastro-Enterologica Belgica — Act Gastr B
Acta Gastro-Enterologica Belgica — Acta Gastro-Enterol Belg
Acta Gastro-Enterologica Belgica — AGEBAX
Acta Gastroenterologica Boliviana — Acta Gastroenterol Boliv
Acta Gastroenterologica Latinoamericana — Acta Gastroenterol Latinoam
Acta Gastroenterologica Latinoamericana — AGLTBL
Acta Genetica et Statistica Medica — Acta Genet Stat Med
Acta Genetica et Statistica Medica — AGSMAY
Acta Genetica Sinica — Acta Genet Sin
Acta Genetica Sinica — ICHPCG
Acta Geneticae, Medicae, et Gemellologiae — Act Genet M
Acta Geneticae, Medicae, et Gemellologiae — Acta Genet Med Gemellol
Acta Geneticae, Medicae, et Gemellologiae — AGMGAK
Acta Geobotanica Barcinonensia — Acta Geobot Barc
Acta Geobotanica Barcinonensia — AGBAAF

Acta Geobotanica Hungarica — Acta Geobot Hung
Acta Geodaetica, Geophysica, et Montanistica — Act Geod Geophys et Montan
Acta Geodaetica, Geophysica, et Montanistica — Acta Geod Geophys Montan
Acta Geodaetica, Geophysica, et Montanistica [*Hungary*] — Acta Geod Geophys Montanistica
Acta Geodetica et Cartographica Sinica — Acta Geodet et Cartogr Sinica
Acta Geographica — AcGe
Acta Geographica [*France*] — Act Geogr
Acta Geographica — Acta Geogr
Acta Geographica Lodziensia — Acta Geogr Lodz
Acta Geographica Lodziensia — SAGLBQ
Acta Geographica Sinica — Acta Geogr Sinica
Acta Geographica Universitatis Lodziensis — Acta Geogr Univ Lodz
Acta Geologica. Academiae Scientiarum Hungaricae — Acta Geol Acad Sci Hung
Acta Geologica. Academiae Scientiarum Hungaricae — Acta Geol Hung
Acta Geologica. Academiae Scientiarum Hungaricae — AGAHAV
Acta Geologica Alpina — Acta Geol Alp
Acta Geologica et Geographica. Universitatis Comenianae. Geologica — Acta Geol Geogr Univ Comenianae Geol
Acta Geologica et Geographica. Universitatis Comenianae. Geologica — AGGCA
Acta Geologica Hispanica — ACGHAX
Acta Geologica Hispanica — Acta Geol Hisp
Acta Geologica Hispanica — Acta Geol Hispan
Acta Geologica Hungarica — AGHUE7
Acta Geologica Leopoldensia — Acta Geol Leopold
Acta Geologica Lilloana — Acta Geol Lilloana
Acta Geologica Lilloana — AGELAT
Acta Geologica Polonica — Acta Geol Pol
Acta Geologica Polonica — AGLPA8
Acta Geologica Sinica — Acta Geol Sin
Acta Geologica Sinica — Acta Geol Sinica
Acta Geologica Sinica — TCHPAX
Acta Geologica Sinica (English Translation) — Acta Geol Sin (Engl Transl)
Acta Geologica Sinica-English Edition — Act Geo S-E
Acta Geologica Taiwanica — Acta Geol Taiwan
Acta Geologica Taiwanica — Acta Geol Taiwanica
Acta Geologica Taiwanica — SRTUAW
Acta Geologica (Trent, Italy) — Acta Geol Trent Italy
Acta Geologica Universitatis Comenianae — Acta Geol Univ Comenianae
Acta Geophysica Polonica — Acta Geophys Pol
Acta Geophysica Polonica — Acta Geophys Polonica
Acta Geophysica Sinica — Acta Geophys Sin
Acta Germanica [*Capetown*] — ActaG
Acta Germanica zur Sprache und Dichtung Deutschlands — AGSD
Acta Gerontologica — Acta Gerontol
Acta Gerontologica — AGERAD
Acta Gerontologica Belgica — Acta Gerontol Belg
Acta Gerontologica et Geriatrica Belgica — Acta Gerontol Geriatr Belg
Acta Gerontologica et Geriatrica Belgica — AGGBBA
Acta Gerontologica Japonica — Acta Gerontol Jpn
Acta Gerontologica Japonica — YCKKAK
Acta Ginecologica — ACGLAB
Acta Ginecologica — Acta Ginecol
Acta Ginecologica (Madrid) — Acta Ginecol (Madr)
Acta Gynaecologica et Obstetrica Hispano Lusitana — Act Gynaecol Obstet Hisp Lusit
Acta Gynaecologica et Obstetrica Hispano Lusitana [*Portugal*] — Acta Gynaecol Obstet Hispano Lusitana
Acta Gynecologica Scandinavica — Acta Gynecol Scand
Acta Gynecologica Scandinavica. Supplement — Acta Gynecol Scand Suppl
Acta Haematologica [*Basel*] — ACHAAH
Acta Haematologica — Act Haemat
Acta Haematologica — Acta Haemat
Acta Haematologica — Acta Haematol
Acta Haematologica (Basel) — Acta Haematol (Basel)
Acta Haematologica Japonica — Acta Haematol Jpn
Acta Haematologica Japonica — NKGZAE
Acta Haematologica Polonica — Acta Haematol Pol
Acta Haematologica Polonica — AHPLBO
Acta Helvetica, Physico-Mathematico-Anatomico-Botanico-Medica — Acta Helv Phys Math
Acta Helvetica Physico-Mathematico-Botanico-Medica — Acta Helvet
Acta Hepato-Gastroenterologica [*Stuttgart/New York*] — Act Hep-Gas
Acta Hepato-Gastroenterologica [*Stuttgart/New York*] — Acta Hepato-Gastroenterol
Acta Hepato-Gastroenterologica — AHGSBY
Acta Hepato-Gastroenterologica (Stuttgart/New York) — Acta Hepato-Gastroenterol (Stuttg)
Acta Hepatologica — Acta Hepatol
Acta Hepatologica Japonica — Acta Hepatol Jpn
Acta Hepato-Splenologica — Acta Hepatosplen
Acta Hepato-Splenologica [*Germany*] — Acta Hepato-Splenol
Acta Herpetologica Japonica — Acta Herpetol Jpn
Acta Histochemica — Act Histoch
Acta Histochemica — Acta Histochem
Acta Histochemica — AHISA9
Acta Histochemica et Cytochemica — ACHCBO
Acta Histochemica et Cytochemica — Act Hist Cy
Acta Histochemica et Cytochemica — Acta Histochem Cytochem
Acta Histochemica (Jena) — Acta Histochem (Jena)
Acta Histochemica. Supplementband — Acta Histochem Suppl
Acta Histochemica. Supplementband [*Jena*] — Acta Histochem Supplementb
Acta Histochemica. Supplementband — AHSUA
Acta Histochemica. Supplementband (Jena) — Acta Histochem Suppl (Jena)
Acta Historiae Artium. Academiae Scientiarum Hungaricae — Act Hist Ar
Acta Historiae Artium. Magyar Tudomanyos Akademia [*Budapest*] — Acta HA
Acta Historiae Artium. Magyar Tudomanyos Akademia [*Budapest*] — AHA
Acta Historiae Artium. Magyar Tudomanyos Akademia (Hungary) — Acta Hist Art (Hung)
Acta Historiae Neerlandica — AHN
Acta Historiae Rerum Naturalium Nec Non Technicarum — Acta Hist Rerum Natur Nec Non Tech
Acta Historiae Rerum Naturalium nec non Technicarum — Acta Hist Rerum Natur Tech
Acta Historica — AcHi
Acta Historica. Academiae Scientiarum Hungaricae — A HistHung
Acta Historica. Academiae Scientiarum Hungaricae — Act Hist H
Acta Historica Bruxellensia — Act Hist Brux
Acta Historica Leopoldina — ACHLAG
Acta Historica Leopoldina — Acta Hist Leopold
Acta Historica Leopoldina — Acta Hist Leopoldina
Acta Historica. Magyar Tudomanyos Akademia (Hungary) — Acta Hist (Hung)
Acta Historica Medicinae Pharmaciae Veterinae — Acta Hist Med Pharm Vet
Acta Historica Scientiarum, Naturalium, et Medicinalium [*Odense*] — Acta Hist Sci Nat Med
Acta Historica Scientiarum, Naturalium, et Medicinalium — AHSMA7
Acta Historica Scientiarum, Naturalium, et Medicinalium (Odense) — Acta Hist Sci Nat Med (Odense)
Acta Historica. Societas Academica Dacoromana — Acta Hist
Acta Historica. Societatis Academica Dacoromana [*Rome*] — Acta Hist Dac
Acta Horti Bergiani — AHOBAM
Acta Horti Botanici Tadshikistanici — Acta Horti Bot Tadshik
Acta Horti Botanici Universitatis Latviensis — Act Hort Bot Univ Latv
Acta Horti Botanici Universitatis Latviensis — Act Hort Bot Univ Latviensis
Acta Horti Botanici Universitatis. Schriften des Botanischen Gartens der Universitaet. Universitaetes Botaniska Darza Rakst — Schriften Bot Gart Univ
Acta Horti Botanici Universitatis. Schriften des Botanischen Gartens der Universitaet. Universitates Botaniska Darza Raksti — Acta Horti Bot Univ
Acta Horti Gothoburgensis. Meddelanden fran Goeteborgs Botaniska Traedgard — Acta Hort Gotoburg
Acta Horti Gothoburgensis. Meddelanden fran Goeteborgs Botaniska Traedgard — Acta Horti Gothoburg
Acta Horti Gothoburgensis. Meddelanden fran Goeteborgs Botaniska Traedgard — Medd Goeteborgs Bot Traedg
Acta Horti Gothoburgensis. Meddelanden fran Goeteborgs Botaniska Traedgard — Meddel Goeteborgs Bot Trad
Acta Horti Gothoburgensis. Meddelanden fran Goeteborgs Botaniska Traedgard — Meddel Goeteborgs Bot Traedg
Acta Horti Gotoburgensis — ACGBAF
Acta Horti Gotoburgensis — Acta Horti Gotob
Acta Horti Gotoburgensis — Acta Horti Gotoburg
Acta Horticulturae — Acta Hort
Acta Horticulturae — Acta Hortic
Acta Horticulturae — AHORA
Acta Horticulturae Sinica — Acta Hortic Sin
Acta Horticulturae (The Hague) — Acta Hortic (The Hague)
Acta Horticulturalia [*Peking*] — Acta Hort
Acta Horticulturalia [*Peking*] — YUHPAA
Acta Horticulturalia (Beijing) — Acta Horti Beijing
Acta Horticulturalia (Peking) — Acta Hortic (Peking)
Acta Horticulturalia Sinica. Chinese Horticultural Society — Acta Hort Sin
Acta Hospitalia — Acta Hosp
Acta Humanistica et Scientifica. Universitatis Sangio Kyotiensis — Acta Humanistica Sci Univ Sangio Kyotiensis
Acta Humanistica et Scientifica. Universitatis Sangio Kyotiensis. Natural Science Series — Acta Human Sci Univ Sangio Kyotien Natur Sci Ser
Acta Humboldtiana. Series Geographica et Ethnographica — Acta Humboldtiana Ser Geog et Ethnograph
Acta Humboldtiana. Series Geologica et Palaeontologica — Acta Humboldt Ser Geol Palaeontol
Acta Hydrobiologica — Acta Hydrobiol
Acta Hydrobiologica — AHBPAX
Acta Hydrobiologica Sinica — Act Hydrobiol Sin
Acta Hydrobiologica Sinica [*People's Republic of China*] — Acta Hydrobiol Sin
Acta Hydrobiologica Sinica/Shui Sheng Sheng Wu Hsueeh Chi K'an (Peking) — Acta Hydrobiol Sin Peking
Acta Hydrochimica et Hydrobiologica [*Germany*] — Acta Hydrochim Hydrobiol
Acta Hydrochimica et Hydrobiologica — AHCBAU
Acta Hydrophysica [*Germany*] — Acta Hydrophys
Acta Hydrophysica (Deutsche Akademie der Wissenschaften zu Berlin. Zentralinstitut Physik der Erde. Selbstaendige Abteilung Physikalische Hydrographie) — Acta Hydrophys (Berl)
Acta Hygienica Epidemiologica et Microbiologica — Acta Hyg Epidemiol Microbiol
Acta Hymenopterologica (Tokyo) — Acta Hymenopt (Tokyo)
Acta Iberica Radiologica-Cancerologica — Acta Iber Radiol-Cancerol
Acta Ichthyologica et Piscatoria — Acta Ichthyol Piscatoria
Acta Ichthyologica et Piscatoria — AIPSCJ
Acta IMEKO. Proceedings of the International Measurement Conference — Acta IMEKO Proc Int Meas Conf
Acta Informatica — Acta Inf
Acta Informatica — Acta Inform
Acta Informatica — Acta Informat
Acta. Institut d'Anesthesiologie — A Inst Anesth
Acta. Institut d'Anesthesiologie — Acta Inst Anesthesiol
Acta. Institut d'Anesthesiologie — ATIAA5
Acta Instituti Anatomici Universitatis Helsinkiensis — A Inst Anat Univ Hels

Acta Instituti Botanici. Academia Scientiarum URSS. Series 6. Introductio Plantarum et Viridaria — Acta Inst Bot Acad Sci URSS Ser 6
Acta Instituti Botanici Academiae Scientiarum Slovacae. Series B. Physiologica, Pathophysiologica — Acta Inst Bot Acad Sci Slovacae Ser B
Acta Instituti et Horti Botanici Tartuensis — Acta Inst Hort Bot Tartu
Acta Instituti et Musei Zoologici Universitatis Atheniensis — Acta Inst Mus Zool Univ Athen
Acta Instituti Forestalis Zvolenensis — Acta Inst For Zvolenensis
Acta Instituti Forestalis Zvolenensis — AIFZAM
Acta Instituti Forestalis Zvolenensis. Vyskumny Ustav Lesneho Hospodarstva — Acta Inst For Zvolenensis Vysk Ustav Lesn Hospod
Acta Instituti Psychologici Universitatis Zagrabiensis — Acta Inst Psychol Univ Zagrabiensis
Acta Instituti Romani Finlandiae — Acta IRF
Acta Instituti Romani Finlandiae — AIRF
Acta Instituti Romani Finlandiae — IRF
Acta. International Scientific Congress on the Volcano of Thera — Acta Int Sci Congr Volcano Thera
Acta. International Union against Cancer — Acta Int Union Cancer
Acta Iranica — AI
Acta Isotopica — Acta Isot
Acta Japonica Medicinae Tropicalis — Act Jpn Med Trop
Acta Juridica. Academiae Scientiarum Hungaricae — Acta Jur Acad Sci Hung
Acta Juridica. Academiae Scientiarum Hungaricae — Acta Juridica
Acta Juridica. Academiae Scientiarum Hungaricae — Acta Juridica Acad Sci Hungaricae
Acta Juridica (Budapest) — Acta Jur (Budapest)
Acta Juridica (Cape Town) — Acta Jur (Cape Town)
Acta Jutlandica — Acta Jutl
Acta Krausi. Cuaderno del Instituto Nacional de Microbiologia (Buenos Aires) — Acta Krausi Cuad Inst Nac Microbiol (B Aires)
Acta Krausi. Cuaderno del Instituto Nacional de Microbiologia (Buenos Aires) — Acta Krausi Cuad Inst Nac Microbiol (Buenos Aires)
Acta Lapponica Fenniae — ALFE
Acta Latgalica — ActaL
Acta Leidensia — Acta Leiden
Acta Leidensia. Edita Cura et Sumptibus Medicinae Tropicae. Mededeelingen uit het Instituut voor Tropische Geneeskunde — Meded Inst Trop Geneesk
Acta Leidensia. Instituut voor Tropische Geneeskunde — Acta Leiden Inst Trop Geneeskd
Acta Leprologica — Acta Leprol
Acta Leprologica (Geneve) — Acta Leprol (Geneve)
Acta Limnologica — Acta Limnol
Acta Limnologica Indica — Acta Limnol Indica
Acta Linguistica — AcL
Acta Linguistica — AcLg
Acta Linguistica — AcLi
Acta Linguistica — Acta Ling
Acta Linguistica — Acta Linguist
Acta Linguistica — AL
Acta Linguistica. Academiae Scientiarum Hungaricae — Acta Linguist Hung
Acta Linguistica. Academiae Scientiarum Hungaricae — ActLingH
Acta Linguistica. Academiae Scientiarum Hungaricae — ALASH
Acta Linguistica. Academiae Scientiarum Hungaricae — ALH
Acta Linguistica. Academiae Scientiarum Hungaricae — ALingHung
Acta Linguistica Hafniensia — ALH
Acta Linguistica Hafniensia — ALHa
Acta Linguistica. Magyar Tudomanyos Akademia (Budapest, Hungary) — Acta Ling (Bud)
Acta Literaria (Concepcion, Chile) — ALCC
Acta Literaria et Scientiarum Sueciae — Acta Lit Et Scient Suec
Acta Literaria Universitatis Hafniensis — Acta Lit Univ Hafn
Acta Litteraria. Academiae Scientiarum Hungaricae — Acta Lit Hung
Acta Litteraria. Academiae Scientiarum Hungaricae — ActLitH
Acta Litteraria Academiae Scientiarum Hungaricae — ALit
Acta Litteraria. Academiae Scientiarum Hungaricae — ALitASH
Acta Litteraria. Academiae Scientiarum Hungaricae — ALitH
Acta Litteraria (Altenburg) — Acta Litt Altenburg
Acta Litteraria. Magyar Tudomanyos Akademia [*Budapest*] — Acta Litt
Acta Litteraria. Magyar Tudomanyos Akademia (Budapest, Hungary) — Acta Litt (Hung)
Acta Litterarum ac Scientiarum Regiae Universitatis Hungaricae Francisco-Josephinae. Sectio Scientiarum Naturalium — Acta Litt Sci Regiae Univ Hung Francisco Josephinae Sect Sci
Acta Litterarum Scientiarum Regiae Universitatis Hungaricae Francisco-Josephinae. Sectio Medicorum — Act Litt Sci Regiae Univ Hung Francisco-Josephinae Sect Med
ACTA [*Art Craft Teachers Association*] **Magazine** — ACTA Mag
Acta Manilana. Series A — Acta Manilana Ser A
Acta Manilana. Series A. Natural and Applied Sciences — Acta Manilana A
Acta Manilana. Series A. Natural and Applied Sciences — Acta Manilana Ser A Nat Appl Sci
Acta Manilana. Series A. Natural and Applied Sciences — AMNIB
Acta Martyrum et Sanctorum — AMS
Acta Marxistica-Leninistica — Acta Marx-Lenin
Acta Materiae Compositae Sinica — Acta Mater Compos Sin
Acta Materialia — Acta Mater
Acta Mathematica — Act Math
Acta Mathematica — Acta Math
Acta Mathematica. Academiae Scientiarum Hungaricae — Act Math H
Acta Mathematica. Academiae Scientiarum Hungaricae — Acta Math Acad Sci Hungar
Acta Mathematica et Informatica Universitatis Ostraviensis — Acta Math Inform Univ Ostraviensis
Acta Mathematica Hungarica — Acta Math Hungar
Acta Mathematica Scientia — Acta Math Sci
Acta Mathematica Sinica — Acta Math Sin
Acta Mathematica Sinica — Acta Math Sinica
Acta Mathematica Sinica. New Series — Acta Math Sinica NS
Acta Mathematica. Universitatis Comenianae — Acta Math Univ Comenian
Acta Mathematica Vietnamica — Acta Math Vietnam
Acta Mathematicae Applicatae Sinica — Acta Math Appl Sin
Acta Mathematicae Applicatae Sinica — Acta Math Appl Sinica
Acta Mechanica — Act Mechan
Acta Mechanica — Acta Mech
Acta Mechanica Sinica [*People's Republic of China*] — Acta Mech Sin
Acta Mechanica Sinica — Acta Mech Sinica
Acta Mechanica Sinica (Chinese Edition) — Acta Mech Sin (Chin Ed)
Acta Mechanica Solida Sinica — Acta Mech Solida Sin
Acta Medica. Academiae Scientiarum Hungaricae — A Med Sci Hung
Acta Medica. Academiae Scientiarum Hungaricae — Act Med H
Acta Medica. Academiae Scientiarum Hungaricae — Acta Med Acad Sci Hung
Acta Medica Austriaca — Acta Med Austriaca
Acta Medica Austriaca — AMAUBB
Acta Medica Austriaca. Supplement — Acta Med Austriaca Suppl
Acta Medica Auxologica (Milan) — Acta Med Auxol (Milan)
Acta Medica (Budapest) — Acta Med Budapest
Acta Medica Bulgarica — Acta Med Bulg
Acta Medica Bulgarica — AMB
Acta Medica Chirurgica Brasiliense — Acta Med Chir Bras
Acta Medica Colombiana — Acta Med Colomb
Acta Medica Costarricense — A Med Cost
Acta Medica Costarricense — Acta Med Costarric
Acta Medica Croatica [*Zagreb*] — Acta Med Croatica
Acta Medica de Tenerife — Acta Med Tenerife
Acta Medica de Tenerife — AMTFAQ
Acta Medica et Biologica — A Med Biol
Acta Medica et Biologica — Acta Med Biol
Acta Medica et Biologica (Niigata) — Acta Med Biol Niigata
Acta Medica et Biologica (Niigata) — AMBNA
Acta Medica et Philosophica Hafniensia — Act Med Philos Hafniensia
Acta Medica et Philosophica Hafniensia — Acta Med Phil Havn
Acta Medica (Fukuoka) — Acta Med (Fukuoka)
Acta Medica Hidalguense — Acta Med Hidalg
Acta Medica Hokkaidonensia — Acta Med Hokkaidonensia
Acta Medica Hondurena — Acta Med Hondur
Acta Medica Hungarica — Acta Med Hung
Acta Medica Instituti Superioris Medici (Sofia) — Acta Med Inst Super Med (Sofia)
Acta Medica Iranica — A Med Ir
Acta Medica Iranica — Acta Med Iran
Acta Medica Italica di Malattie Infettive e Parassitarie — Acta Med Ital Mal Infett Parassit
Acta Medica Italica di Medicina Tropicale e Subtropicale e di Gastroenterologia — Acta Med Ital Med Trop Subtrop
Acta Medica Italica di Medicina Tropicale e Subtropicale e di Gastroenterologia — Acta Med Ital Med Trop Subtrop Gastroenterol
Acta Medica Iugoslavica — Acta Med Iugosl
Acta Medica Iugoslavica — AMIUA
Acta Medica Iugoslavica (English Translation) — Acta Med Iugosl (Eng Transl)
Acta Medica Medianae — Acta Med Medianae
Acta Medica (Mexico) — Acta Med (Mex)
Acta Medica (Mexico City) — Acta Med Mexico City
Acta Medica Nagasakiensia — A Med Nag
Acta Medica Nagasakiensia — Acta Med Nagasaki
Acta Medica Okayama — Acta Med Okayama
Acta Medica Orientalia — A Med Or
Acta Medica Orientalia — Acta Med Orient
Acta Medica Orientalia — AMO
Acta Medica Patavina — A Med Pat
Acta Medica Patavina — Acta Med Pat
Acta Medica Patavina — Acta Med Pata
Acta Medica Peruana — Acta Med Peru
Acta Medica Philippina — A Med Phil
Acta Medica Philippina — Acta Med Philipp
Acta Medica Philippina — AMPIAF
Acta Medica Polona — Acta Med Pol
Acta Medica Polona — AMDPAA
Acta Medica Polona — AMP
Acta Medica Portuguesa — Acta Med Port
Acta Medica (Rio De Janeiro) — Acta Med (Rio De Janeiro)
Acta Medica Romana — Acta Med Rom
Acta Medica Romana — Acta Med Roman
Acta Medica Romana — Acta Med Romana
Acta Medica Romana — AMROBA
Acta Medica Scandinavica — A Med Scand
Acta Medica Scandinavica — Act Med Sc
Acta Medica Scandinavica — Acta Med Scand
Acta Medica Scandinavica — Acta Med Scandinav
Acta Medica Scandinavica — AMSVAZ
Acta Medica Scandinavica. Supplementum — Acta Med Scand Suppl
Acta Medica Scandinavica. Supplementum — AMSSAQ
Acta Medica Scandinavica Symposium Series — Acta Med Scand Symp Ser
Acta Medica Turcica — Acta Med Turc
Acta Medica Turcica — AMTUA3
Acta Medica Turcica. Supplementum — Acta Med Turc Suppl
Acta Medica Turcica. Supplementum — AMSUBX
Acta Medica Universitatis Kagoshimaensis — A Med Univ Kag
Acta Medica Universitatis Kagoshimaensis — Acta Med Univ Kagoshima
Acta Medica Universitatis Kagoshimaensis — AMUKAC

Acta Medica URSS [*Union des Republiques Socialistes Sovietiques*] — Acta Med URSS
Acta Medica Venezolana — A Med Ven
Acta Medica Venezolana — ACMVA3
Acta Medica Venezolana — Acta Med Venez
Acta Medica Veterinaria — Acta Med Vet
Acta Medica Veterinaria [*Naples*] — AMVEAX
Acta Medica Veterinaria (Madrid) — Acta Med Vet (Madr)
Acta Medica Vietnamica — A Med Vietn
Acta Medica Vietnamica — Acta Med Vietnam
Acta Medica Vietnamica — AMVIAB
Acta Medicae Historiae Patavina — A Med Hist Pat
Acta Medicae Historiae Patavina — Acta Med Hist Pat
Acta Medicae Historiae Patavina — Acta Med Hist Patav
Acta Medicinae Legalis et Socialis [*Liege*] — Acta Med Leg Soc
Acta Medicinae Legalis et Socialis (Liege) — Acta Med Leg Soc (Liege)
Acta Medicinae Okayama — A Med Ok
Acta Medicinae Okayama — Act Med Oka
Acta Medicinalia in Keijo — Acta Med Keijo
Acta Medicorum Berolinensium in Incrementum Artis et Scientiarum Collecta et Digesta — Acta Med Berol
Acta Medicorum Suecicorum — Acta Med Suec
Acta Medicotechnica — Acta Medicotech
Acta Metallurgica — Act Metall
Acta Metallurgica — Acta Metall
Acta Metallurgica et Materialia — Acta Metall Mater
Acta Metallurgica Sinica — Acta Met Sin
Acta Metallurgica Sinica — Acta Metall Sin
Acta Metallurgica Sinica. English Letters — Acta Metall Sin Engl Lett
Acta Meteorologica Sinica — A Met Sin
Acta Meteorologica Sinica — Acta Meteorol Sin
Acta Mexicana de Ciencia y Tecnologia — Acta Mex Cienc y Tecnol
Acta Mexicana de Ciencia y Tecnologia — Acta Mexicana Ci Tecn
Acta Mexicana de Ciencia y Tecnologia — AMXCB
Acta Mexicana de Ciencia y Tecnologia. Instituto Politecnico Nacional — Acta Mexicana Cienc Tecn
Acta Microbiologia Sinica — Act Microbiol Sin
Acta Microbiologica — Acta Microbiol
Acta Microbiologica. Academiae Scientiarum Hungaricae — A Micr Acad Sci Hung
Acta Microbiologica. Academiae Scientiarum Hungaricae — Act Micro H
Acta Microbiologica. Academiae Scientiarum Hungaricae — Acta Microbiol Acad Sci Hung
Acta Microbiologica. Academiae Scientiarum Hungaricae — AMAHA5
Acta Microbiologica Bulgarica — Acta Microbiol Bulg
Acta Microbiologica Bulgarica — AMBUDI
Acta Microbiologica et Immunologica Hungarica — Acta Microbiol Immunol Hung
Acta Microbiologica Hellenica — Acta Microbiol Hell
Acta Microbiologica Hellenica — AMBHAA
Acta Microbiologica Hungarica — Acta Microbiol Hung
Acta Microbiologica Hungarica — AMHUEF
Acta Microbiologica Polonica — Acta Microbiol Pol
Acta Microbiologica Polonica — Acta Microbiol Polon
Acta Microbiologica Polonica — AMPOAX
Acta Microbiologica Polonica. Series A. Microbiologia Generalis — Act Mic P A
Acta Microbiologica Polonica. Series A. Microbiologia Generalis — Acta Microbiol Pol Ser A
Acta Microbiologica Polonica. Series A. Microbiologia Generalis — Acta Microbiol Pol Ser A Microbiol Gen
Acta Microbiologica Polonica. Series A. Microbiologia Generalis — AMIGB
Acta Microbiologica Polonica. Series B. Microbiologia Applicata — Act Mic P B
Acta Microbiologica Polonica. Series B. Microbiologia Applicata — Acta Microbiol Pol Ser B
Acta Microbiologica Polonica. Series B. Microbiologia Applicata — Acta Microbiol Pol Ser B Microbiol Appl
Acta Microbiologica Polonica. Series B. Microbiologia Applicata — AMBBB
Acta Microbiologica Sinica — Acta Microbiol Sin
Acta Microbiologica Sinica — Acta Microbiol Sinica
Acta Microbiologica Sinica — WSHPA8
Acta Microbiologica Sinica (English Translation) — Acta Microbiol Sin Engl Transl
Acta Microbiologica, Virologica, et Immunologica — Acta Microbiol Virol Immunol
Acta Microbiologica, Virologica, et Immunologica — AMVIDE
Acta Microbiologica, Virologica, et Immunologica (Sofiia) — Acta Microbiol Virol Immunol (Sofiia)
Acta Mineralogica Sinica — Acta Mineral Sin
Acta Mineralogica-Petrographica — Acta Mineral-Petrogr
Acta Mineralogica-Petrographica (Acta Universitatis Szegediensis) — Acta Mineral-Petrogr (Szeged)
Acta Montana — Acta Mont
Acta Montana. Series AB. Geodynamics and Fuel, Carbon, Mineral Processing — Acta Mont Ser AB
Acta Montana. Series B. Fuel, Carbon, Mineral Processing — Acta Mont Ser B
Acta Moravske Muzeum — Acta Moravs Muz
Acta Morphologica [*Sofia*] — ACMODJ
Acta Morphologica. Academiae Scientiarum Hungaricae — Act Morph H
Acta Morphologica. Academiae Scientiarum Hungaricae — Acta Morphol Acad Sci Hung
Acta Morphologica. Academiae Scientiarum Hungaricae — AMSHAR
Acta Morphologica. Academiae Scientiarum Hungaricae. Supplementum — Acta Morphol Acad Sci Hung Suppl
Acta Morphologica Hungarica — Acta Morphol Hung
Acta Morphologica Hungarica — AMHUDE
Acta Morphologica Neerlando-Scandinavica — Act Morph N
Acta Morphologica Neerlando-Scandinavica — Acta Morphol Neerl-Scand
Acta Morphologica Neerlando-Scandinavica — AMNSAZ
Acta Morphologica (Sofia) — Acta Morphol (Sofia)
Acta Mozartiana — AcMoz
Acta Mozartiana — Act Mozart
Acta Musei et Horti Botanici Bohemiae Borealis. Historia Naturalis — Acta Mus Horti Bot Bohemiae Borealis Hist Nat
Acta Musei Historiae Naturalis — Acta Mus Hist Nat
Acta Musei Macedonici. Scientiarum Naturalium — Acta Mus Maced Sci Nat
Acta Musei Macedonici. Scientiarum Naturalium — Acta Mus Macedonici Sci Nat
Acta Musei Macedonici. Scientiarum Naturalium — AMMSBV
Acta Musei Moraviae — Acta Mus Morav
Acta Musei Moraviae. Scientiae Naturales — Acta Mus Morav Sci Nat
Acta Musei Moraviae. Scientiae Naturales — Acta Mus Morav Sci Natur
Acta Musei Moraviae. Scientiae Sociales — Acta Mus Morav Sci Soc
Acta Musei Napocensis — A Mus Napocensis
Acta Musei Napocensis — Acta Mus Nap
Acta Musei Napocensis — Acta Mus Napoca
Acta Musei Napocensis — Acta Mus Napocensis
Acta Musei Napocensis [*Cluj*] — AMN
Acta Musei Nationalis Pragae. Series B. Historia Naturalis — Acta Mus Natl Pragae Ser B
Acta Musei Nationalis Pragae. Series B. Historia Naturalis — Acta Mus Natl Pragae Ser B Hist Nat
Acta Musei Nationalis Pragae. Series B. Historia Naturalis — SNMPAM
Acta Musei Pardubicensis — Acta Mus Pardubic
Acta Musei Porolissensis — A Mus Porol
Acta Musei Silesiae. Series A. Scientiae Naturales — Acta Mus Silesiae Ser A Sci Nat
Acta Musicologica — A Mus
Acta Musicologica — Ac M
Acta Musicologica — AcMu
Acta Musicologica — AcMus
Acta Musicologica — Act Music
Acta Musicologica — Acta
Acta Musicologica — Acta Mus
Acta Musicologica — Acta Music
Acta Musicologica — AM
Acta Musicologica Fennica — Acta Musicolog Fenn
Acta Mycologica — ACMYAC
Acta Mycologica — Acta Mycol
Acta Mycologica Sinica — Acta Mycol Sin
Acta Naturalia de l'Ateneo Parmense — Acta Nat Ateneo Parmense
Acta Naturalia de l'Ateneo Parmense — ANPMD3
Acta Naturalia Islandica — ACNI
Acta Naturalia Islandica — Acta Nat Isl
Acta Naturalia Islandica — ANIRAE
Acta Neerlandica Morphologiae Normalis et Pathologicae — Acta Neerl Morphol Norm Pathol
Acta Neerlandica Morphologiae Normalis et Pathologicae — AN Morph
Acta Neonatologica Japonica — Acta Neonatol Jpn
Acta Neophilologica — AN
Acta Neurobiologiae Experimentalis — Act Neurob
Acta Neurobiologiae Experimentalis — Acta Neurobiol Exp
Acta Neurobiologiae Experimentalis — ANEXA
Acta Neurobiologiae Experimentalis [*Warsaw*] — ANEXAC
Acta Neurobiologiae Experimentalis. Supplementum — Acta Neurobiol Exp Suppl
Acta Neurobiologiae Experimentalis. Supplementum — ANEXBD
Acta Neurobiologiae Experimentalis (Warsaw) — Acta Neurobiol Exp (Warsaw)
Acta Neurobiologiae Experimentalis (Warszawa) — Acta Neurobiol Exp (Warsz)
Acta Neurochirurgica — ACNUA5
Acta Neurochirurgica — Act Neuroch
Acta Neurochirurgica — Acta Neurochir
Acta Neurochirurgica. Supplementum [*Wien*] — Acta Neurochir Suppl
Acta Neurochirurgica. Supplementum — ANCSBM
Acta Neurochirurgica. Supplementum (Wien) — Acta Neurochir Suppl (Wien)
Acta Neurochirurgica (Wien) — Acta Neurochir (Wien)
Acta Neurologica [*Naples*] — ACNLAC
Acta Neurologica — Acta Neurol
Acta Neurologica Belgica — Acta Neurol Belg
Acta Neurologica Belgica — ANUBBR
Acta Neurologica et Psychiatrica Belgica — Acta Neurol Psychiatr Belg
Acta Neurologica et Psychiatrica Belgica — ANP
Acta Neurologica et Psychiatrica Belgica — ANPBA
Acta Neurologica et Psychiatrica Belgica — ANPBAZ
Acta Neurologica Latinoamericana — Acta Neurol Latinoam
Acta Neurologica Latinoamericana — Acta Neurol Latinoamer
Acta Neurologica Latinoamericana — ANLAAC
Acta Neurologica (Naples) — Acta Neurol (Naples)
Acta Neurologica (Napoli) — Acta Neurol (Napoli)
Acta Neurologica. Quaderni — Acta Neurol Quad
Acta Neurologica Scandinavica — Act Neur Sc
Acta Neurologica Scandinavica — Acta Neurol Scand
Acta Neurologica Scandinavica — ANRSAS
Acta Neurologica Scandinavica. Supplementum — Acta Neurol Scand Suppl
Acta Neurologica Scandinavica. Supplementum — ANSLA
Acta Neuropathologica — Act Neurop
Acta Neuropathologica — Acta Neuropathol
Acta Neuropathologica — ANPTAL
Acta Neuropathologica (Berlin) — Acta Neuropathol (Berl)
Acta Neuropathologica. Supplementum [*Berlin*] — Acta Neuropathol Suppl
Acta Neuropathologica. Supplementum — ANLSBX
Acta Neuropathologica. Supplementum (Berlin) — Acta Neuropathol Suppl (Berl)
Acta Neuropsiquiatrica Argentina — Acta Neuropsiquiat Argent

Acta Neurovegetativa — ACNEAP
Acta Neurovegetativa — Acta Neuroveg
Acta Neurovegetativa. Supplementum — Acta Neuroveg Suppl
Acta Nipponica Medicinae Tropicalis — Acta Nipp Med Trop
Acta Nipponica Medicinae Tropicalis — Acta Nippon Med Trop
Acta Numismatica — Acta Num
Acta Numismatica — ANum
Acta Nuntiaturae Gallicae — ANG
Acta Nutrimenta Sinica — Acta Nutr Sin
Acta Obstetrica et Gynaecologica Japonica — Acta Obstet Gynaecol Jpn
Acta Obstetrica et Gynaecologica Japonica [*English Edition*] — AOGLAR
Acta Obstetrica et Gynaecologica Japonica [*Japanese Edition*] — NISFAY
Acta Obstetrica et Gynaecologica Japonica (English Edition) — Acta Obstet Gynaecol Jpn (Engl Ed)
Acta Obstetrica et Gynaecologica Japonica (Japanese Edition) — Acta Obstet Gynaecol Jpn (Jpn Ed)
Acta Obstetrica et Gynecologica Scandinavica — Act Obst Sc
Acta Obstetrica et Gynecologica Scandinavica — Acta Obst Gynec Scandinav
Acta Obstetrica et Gynecologica Scandinavica — Acta Obstet Gynecol Scand
Acta Obstetrica et Gynecologica Scandinavica — AOGSAE
Acta Obstetrica et Gynecologica Scandinavica. Supplement — Acta Obstet Gynecol Scand Suppl
Acta Obstetrica et Gynecologica Scandinavica. Supplement — AGSSAI
Acta Obstetrica y Ginecologica Hispano-Lusitana — Acta Obstet Ginecol Hisp-Lusit
Acta Obstetrica y Ginecologica Hispano-Lusitana. Suplemento — Acta Obstet Ginecol Hisp-Lusit Supl
Acta Oceanographica Taiwanica — Acta Oceanogr Taiwan
Acta Oceanographica Taiwanica — AOTADS
Acta Odontologica — Acta Odont
Acta Odontologica Latinoamericana — Acta Odontol Latinoam
Acta Odontologica Latinoamericana — AOLAEN
Acta Odontologica Pediatrica — Acta Odontol Pediatr
Acta Odontologica Scandinavica — Act Odon Sc
Acta Odontologica Scandinavica — Acta Odontol Scand
Acta Odontologica Scandinavica — AOSCA
Acta Odontologica Scandinavica. Supplementum — Acta Odontol Scand Suppl
Acta Odontologica Venezolana — Acta Odontol Venez
Acta Odontologica Venezolana — AOVEBE
Acta Oecologica. Oecologia Applicata — Acta Oecol Oecol Appl
Acta Oecologica. Oecologia Applicata — AOSADN
Acta Oecologica. Oecologia Generalis — Acta Oecol Oecol Gen
Acta Oecologica. Oecologia Generalis — AOSGD7
Acta Oecologica. Oecologia Plantarum — AOSPDY
Acta Oecologica. Oecologica Plantarum — Acta Oecol Oecol Plant
Acta Oecologica. Serie 1. Oecologia Generalis — Acta Oecol Ser 1
Acta Oecologica. Serie 2. Oecologia Applicata — Acta Oecol Ser 2
Acta Oecologica. Serie 3. Oecologia Plantarum — Acta Oecol Ser 3
Acta Oeconomica [*Budapest*] — ACO
Acta Oeconomica [*Budapest*] — Act Oecon
Acta Oeconomica [*Budapest*] — Acta Oecon
Acta Oeconomica. Academiae Scientiarum Hungaricae — Acta Oeconomica
Acta of Jinan University. Natural Sciences Edition — Acta Jinan Univ Nat Sci Ed
Acta of Kirin Medical University — Acta Kirin Med Univ
Acta Oncologica [*Madrid*] — Acta Oncol
Acta Oncologica — AONCAZ
Acta Oncologica Brasileira — Acta Oncol Bras
Acta Oncologica Brasileira — AOBRDN
Acta Oncologica (Madrid) — Acta Oncol (Madr)
Acta Operativo-Oeconomica — Acta Oper-Oecon
Acta Ophtalmologica — Acta Opht
Acta Ophthalmologica — ACOPAT
Acta Ophthalmologica — Acta Ophth
Acta Ophthalmologica — Acta Ophthalmol
Acta Ophthalmologica (Copenhagen) — Acta Ophthalmol (Copenh)
Acta Ophthalmologica Iugoslavica — Acta Ophthalmol Iugosl
Acta Ophthalmologica Iugoslavica — AOPIBU
Acta Ophthalmologica (Kobenhavn) — Act Ophth (K)
Acta Ophthalmologica Polonica — Acta Ophthalmol Pol
Acta Ophthalmologica Scandinavica [*Hvidovre*] — Acta Ophthalmol Scand
Acta Ophthalmologica Scandinavica. Supplement [*Copenhagen*] — Acta Ophthalmol Scand Suppl
Acta Ophthalmologica. Supplementum [*Kobenhavn*] — Acta Ophthalmol Suppl
Acta Ophthalmologica. Supplementum — AOPSAP
Acta Ophthalmologica. Supplementum (Copenhagen) — Acta Ophthalmol Suppl (Copenh)
Acta Optica Sinica — Acta Opt Sin
Acta Orientalia — AcOr
Acta Orientalia — Acta O
Acta Orientalia — Acta Or
Acta Orientalia — Acta Orient
Acta Orientalia [*Copenhagen*] — ActOr
Acta Orientalia — AO
Acta Orientalia [*Budapest*] — AOB
Acta Orientalia — AODNS
Acta Orientalia. Academiae Scientiarum Hungaricae [*Budapest*] — AcOr(B)
Acta Orientalia. Academiae Scientiarum Hungaricae — Acta Orient Acad Sci Hungar
Acta Orientalia. Academiae Scientiarum Hungaricae [*Budapest*] — ActOrHung
Acta Orientalia. Academiae Scientiarum Hungaricae — AOASH
Acta Orientalia. Academiae Scientiarum Hungaricae — AOH
Acta Orientalia. Academiae Scientiarum Hungaricae — AOrientHung
Acta Orientalia. Academiae Scientiarum Hungaricae (Budapest) — Acta Or (B)
Acta Orientalia (Copenhagen) — AcOr(K)
Acta Orientalia (Hungary) — Ac Or (H)
Acta Orientalia (Leiden) — AcOr(L)
Acta Orientalia. Magyar Tudomanyos Akademia [*Budapest*] — Ac OB
Acta Orientalia. Magyar Tudomanyos Akademia (Hungary) — Acta Orient (Hung)
Acta Orientalia Neerlandica — AON
Acta Orientalia. Societatis Orientales. Danica, Finlandica, Norvegica, Suecica [*Copenhagen*] — Ac O
Acta Ornithologica — Acta Ornith
Acta Ornithologica [*Warsaw*] — AORNAK
Acta Ornithologica [*Warsaw*] [*English translation*] — AORNBD
Acta Ornithologica (English Translation) — Acta Ornithol (Engl Transl)
Acta Ornithologica (Warsaw) — Acta Ornithol (Warsaw)
Acta Ornithologica (Warsaw) (English Translation) — Acta Ornithol (Warsaw) (Engl Transl)
Acta Orthopaedica Belgica — Acta Orthop Belg
Acta Orthopaedica Belgica — AOBEAF
Acta Orthopaedica Scandinavica — Act Orth Sc
Acta Orthopaedica Scandinavica — Acta Orthop
Acta Orthopaedica Scandinavica — Acta Orthop Scand
Acta Orthopaedica Scandinavica — Acta Orthop Scandinav
Acta Orthopaedica Scandinavica — AOSAAK
Acta Orthopaedica Scandinavica. Supplementum — Acta Orthop Scand Suppl
Acta Orthopaedica Scandinavica. Supplementum — AOSUAC
Acta Oto-Laryngologica — Act Oto-Lar
Acta Oto-Laryngologica — Acta Oto-Laryng
Acta Oto-Laryngologica — Acta Oto-Laryngol
Acta Oto-Laryngologica — AOLAA
Acta Otolaryngologica (Stockholm) — Acta Otolaryngol (Stockh)
Acta Otolaryngologica. Supplement (Stockholm) — Acta Otolaryngol Suppl (Stockh)
Acta Oto-Laryngologica. Supplementum — Acta Oto-Laryngol Suppl
Acta Oto-Laryngologica. Supplementum — AOLSA5
Acta Oto-Rhino-Laryngologica Belgica — Acta ORL Belg
Acta Oto-Rhino-Laryngologica Belgica — Acta Oto-Rhino-Lar Belg
Acta Oto-Rhino-Laryngologica Belgica — Acta Oto-Rhino-Laryngol Belg
Acta Oto-Rhino-Laryngologica Belgica — AORLA
Acta Otorhinolaryngologica Italica — Acta Otorhinolaryngol Ital
Acta Oto-Rino-Laringologica Espanola — Acta ORL Espan
Acta Oto-Rino-Laringologica Espanola — Acta Oto-Rino-Laringol Esp
Acta Oto-Rino-Laringologica Ibero-Americana — Acta Oto-Rino-Laringol Ibero-Am
Acta Oto-Rino-Laringologica Ibero-Americana — AORIA
Acta Otorrinolaringologica Espanola — Acta Otorrinolaringol Esp
Acta Paediatrica — A Paed
Acta Paediatrica — Acta Paediat
Acta Paediatrica — Acta Paediatr
Acta Paediatrica. Academiae Scientiarum Hungaricae — Act Paed H
Acta Paediatrica. Academiae Scientiarum Hungaricae — Acta Paed Hung
Acta Paediatrica. Academiae Scientiarum Hungaricae — Acta Paediatr Acad Sci Hung
Acta Paediatrica Belgica — A Paed Belg
Acta Paediatrica Belgica — Acta Paediatr Belg
Acta Paediatrica (Budapest) — Acta Paediatr (Budapest)
Acta Paediatrica Hungarica — Acta Paediatr Hung
Acta Paediatrica Japonica — Acta Paediatr Jpn
Acta Paediatrica Japonica (Overseas Edition) — Acta Paediatr Jpn (Overseas Ed)
Acta Paediatrica Latina — A Paed Lat
Acta Paediatrica Latina — Acta Paed Lat
Acta Paediatrica Latina — Acta Paediatr Lat
Acta Paediatrica Scandinavica — Act Paed Sc
Acta Paediatrica Scandinavica — Acta Paediat Scandinav
Acta Paediatrica Scandinavica — Acta Paediatr Scand
Acta Paediatrica Scandinavica. Supplementum — Acta Paediatr Scand Suppl
Acta Paediatrica Sinica — Acta Paediatr Sin
Acta Paediatrica (Stockholm) — Acta Paediatr (Stockholm)
Acta Paediatrica. Supplement — Acta Paediatr Suppl
Acta Paediatrica (Uppsala) — Acta Paediat (Uppsala)
Acta Paedopsychiatrica — ACPDA
Acta Paedopsychiatrica — Act Paedops
Acta Paedopsychiatrica — Acta Paedopsychiat
Acta Paedopsychiatrica — Acta Paedopsychiatr
Acta Paedopsychiatrica (Basel) — Acta Paedopsychiatr (Basel)
Acta Palaeobotanica — Acta Palaeobot
Acta Palaeontologica Polonica — Acta Palaeontol Pol
Acta Palaeontologica Polonica — Acta Palaeontol Polon
Acta Palaeontologica Sinica — Acta Palaeontol Sin
Acta Palaeontologica Sinica/Ku Sheng Wu Hsueh Pao — Acta Palaeont Sin
Acta Paracelsica — Acta Paracels
Acta Parasitologica Iugoslavica — Acta Parasitol Iugosl
Acta Parasitologica Lithuanica — Acta Parasitol Lith
Acta Parasitologica Lituanica — Acta Parasitol Litu
Acta Parasitologica Polonica — A Par Pol
Acta Parasitologica Polonica — Acta Parasitol Pol
Acta Pathologica et Microbiologica Scandinavica — Acta Path
Acta Pathologica et Microbiologica Scandinavica — Acta Path Microbiol Scandinav
Acta Pathologica et Microbiologica Scandinavica — Acta Pathol Microbiol Scand
Acta Pathologica et Microbiologica Scandinavica — APMIAL
Acta Pathologica et Microbiologica Scandinavica. Section A — Act Pat S A
Acta Pathologica et Microbiologica Scandinavica. Section A — Acta Pathol Microbiol Scand (A)
Acta Pathologica et Microbiologica Scandinavica. Section A — Acta Pathol Microbiol Scand Sect A
Acta Pathologica et Microbiologica Scandinavica. Section A. Pathology — Acta Pathol Microbiol Scand Sect A Pathol

Acta Pathologica et Microbiologica Scandinavica. Section A. Pathology — Acta Pathol Microbiol Sect A
Acta Pathologica et Microbiologica Scandinavica. Section A. Pathology — AMBPBZ
Acta Pathologica et Microbiologica Scandinavica. Section A. Supplement — Acta Pathol Microbiol Scand Sect A Suppl
Acta Pathologica et Microbiologica Scandinavica. Section B — Act Pat S B
Acta Pathologica et Microbiologica Scandinavica. Section B — Acta Pathol Microbiol Scand (B)
Acta Pathologica et Microbiologica Scandinavica. Section B — Acta Pathol Microbiol Scand Sect B
Acta Pathologica et Microbiologica Scandinavica. Section B. Microbiology — Acta Pathol Microbiol Scand Sect B Microbiol
Acta Pathologica et Microbiologica Scandinavica. Section B. Microbiology — APBMDF
Acta Pathologica et Microbiologica Scandinavica. Section B. Microbiology and Immunology — Acta Pathol Microbiol Scand Sect B Microbiol Immunol
Acta Pathologica et Microbiologica Scandinavica. Section B. Microbiology and Immunology — APMIBM
Acta Pathologica et Microbiologica Scandinavica. Section B. Supplement — Acta Pathol Microbiol Scand Sect B Suppl
Acta Pathologica et Microbiologica Scandinavica. Section C — Act Pat S C
Acta Pathologica et Microbiologica Scandinavica. Section C — Acta Pathol Microbiol Scand (C)
Acta Pathologica et Microbiologica Scandinavica. Section C — Acta Pathol Microbiol Scand Sect C
Acta Pathologica et Microbiologica Scandinavica. Section C. Immunology — Acta Pathol Microbiol Scand Sect C Immunol
Acta Pathologica et Microbiologica Scandinavica. Section C. Immunology — APSCD2
Acta Pathologica et Microbiologica Scandinavica. Section C. Supplement — Acta Pathol Microbiol Scand Sect C Suppl
Acta Pathologica et Microbiologica Scandinavica. Supplementum — Acta Pathol Microbiol Scand Suppl
Acta Pathologica et Microbiologica Scandinavica. Supplementum — APMUAN
Acta Pathologica Japonica — A Path Jap
Acta Pathologica Japonica — Act Pat Jap
Acta Pathologica Japonica — Acta Pathol Jpn
Acta Pathologica, Microbiologica, et Immunologica Scandinavica — Acta Pathol Microbiol Immunol Scand
Acta Pathologica, Microbiologica, et Immunologica Scandinavica — APMIS
Acta Pathologica, Microbiologica, et Immunologica Scandinavica. Section A — Acta Pathol Microbiol Immunol Scand Sect A
Acta Pathologica, Microbiologica, et Immunologica Scandinavica. Section A. Pathology — Acta Pathol Microbiol Immunol Scand
Acta Pathologica, Microbiologica, et Immunologica Scandinavica. Section A. Pathology — Acta Pathol Microbiol Immunol Scand Sect A Pathol
Acta Pathologica, Microbiologica, et Immunologica Scandinavica. Section A. Supplement — Acta Pathol Microbiol Immunol Scand
Acta Pathologica, Microbiologica, et Immunologica Scandinavica. Section A. Supplement — Acta Pathol Microbiol Immunol Scand Sect A Suppl
Acta Pathologica, Microbiologica, et Immunologica Scandinavica. Section B. Microbiology — Acta Pathol Microbiol Immunol Scand
Acta Pathologica, Microbiologica, et Immunologica Scandinavica. Section B. Microbiology — Acta Pathol Microbiol Immunol Scand Sect B
Acta Pathologica, Microbiologica, et Immunologica Scandinavica. Section B. Microbiology — Acta Pathol Microbiol Immunol Scand Sect B Microbiol
Acta Pathologica, Microbiologica, et Immunologica Scandinavica. Section C. Immunology — Acta Pathol Microbiol Immunol Scand
Acta Pathologica, Microbiologica, et Immunologica Scandinavica. Section C. Immunology — Acta Pathol Microbiol Immunol Scand Sect C Immunol
Acta Pathologica, Microbiologica, et Immunologica Scandinavica. Section C. Immunology. Supplementum — Acta Pathol Microbiol Immunol Scand Sect C Immunol Suppl
Acta Pathologica, Microbiologica, et Immunologica Scandinavica. Section C. Supplement — Acta Pathol Microbiol Immunol Scand Sect C Suppl
Acta Pathologica, Microbiologica, et Immunologica Scandinavica. Supplement — Acta Pathol Microbiol Immunol Scand Suppl
Acta Pediatrica Espanola — Acta Ped Esp
Acta Pediatrica Espanola — Acta Pediatr Esp
Acta Pedologica Sinica — Act Pedol Sin
Acta Pedologica Sinica — Acta Pedol Sin
Acta Pedologica Sinica — Acta Pedol Sinica
Acta Pedologica Sinica — TJHPAE
Acta Petrolei Sinica — Acta Pet Sin
Acta Petrolei Sinica. Petroleum Processing Section — Acta Pet Sin Pet Process Sect
Acta Petrologica et Mineralogica — Acta Petrol Mineral
Acta Petrologica, Mineralogica, et Analytica — Acta Petrol Mineral Anal
Acta Phaenologica — Acta Phaenol
Acta Pharmaceutica — Acta Pharm
Acta Pharmaceutica Fennica — Acta Pharm Fenn
Acta Pharmaceutica Hungarica — A Pharm Hung
Acta Pharmaceutica Hungarica — Acta Pharm Hung
Acta Pharmaceutica Hungarica — APHGAO
Acta Pharmaceutica Internationalia — A Pharm Int
Acta Pharmaceutica Internationalia — Acta Pharm Int
Acta Pharmaceutica Iugoslavica — Acta Pharm Iugosl
Acta Pharmaceutica Jugoslavica — Acta Pharm Jugosl
Acta Pharmaceutica Jugoslavica — Acta Pharmaceut Jugoslav
Acta Pharmaceutica Jugoslavica — APJUA8
Acta Pharmaceutica Nordica — Act Pharm N
Acta Pharmaceutica Nordica — Acta Pharm Nord
Acta Pharmaceutica Sinica — Acta Pharm Sin
Acta Pharmaceutica Sinica [*People's Republic of China*] — Acta Pharm Sinica
Acta Pharmaceutica Sinica — YHHPAL
Acta Pharmaceutica Suecica — Act Pharm S
Acta Pharmaceutica Suecica — Acta Pharm Suec
Acta Pharmaceutica Suecica — APSXAS
Acta Pharmaceutica Technologica — Acta Pharm Technol
Acta Pharmaceutica Technologica — APTEDD
Acta Pharmaceutica Technologica. Supplement — Acta Pharm Technol Suppl
Acta Pharmaceutica Turcica — Acta Pharm Turc
Acta Pharmaceutica (Zagreb) — Acta Pharm Zagreb
Acta Pharmaciae Historica. Academie Internationale d'Histoire de la Pharmacie — Acta Pharm Hist
Acta Pharmacologica et Toxicologica — Act Pharm T
Acta Pharmacologica et Toxicologica — Acta Pharm Tox
Acta Pharmacologica et Toxicologica — Acta Pharmac Tox
Acta Pharmacologica et Toxicologica — Acta Pharmacol
Acta Pharmacologica et Toxicologica — Acta Pharmacol Toxicol
Acta Pharmacologica et Toxicologica — APTOA6
Acta Pharmacologica et Toxicologica (Copenhagen) — Acta Pharmacol Toxicol (Copenh)
Acta Pharmacologica et Toxicologica. Supplementum — Acta Pharmacol Toxicol Suppl
Acta Pharmacologica et Toxicologica. Supplementum — APTSAI
Acta Pharmacologica Sinica — Act Phar Si
Acta Pharmacologica Sinica — Acta Pharmacol Sin
Acta Pharmacologica Sinica — CYLPDN
Acta Philologica Scandinavica — A Ph Sc
Acta Philologica Scandinavica — Acta Phil
Acta Philologica Scandinavica — Acta Philol Scand
Acta Philologica Scandinavica — APS
Acta Philologica Scandinavica. Tidsskrift foer Nordisk Sprogforskning — APhS
Acta Philologica. Societas Academica Dacoromana [*Rome*] — Acta Phil Soc Dac
Acta Philologica. Societas Academica Dacoromana — Acta Philol
Acta Philologica. Societas Academica Dacoromana — APh
Acta Philologica. Societas Academica Dacoromana — APhD
Acta Philosophica et Theologica. Societas Academica Dacoromana — Acta Philos Theol
Acta Philosophica Fennica — Acta Phil Fennica
Acta Philosophica Fennica — Acta Philos Fenn
Acta Philosophica Fennica [*Elsevier Book Series*] — APF
Acta Photonica Sinica — Acta Photonica Sin
Acta Physica. Academiae Scientiarum Hungaricae — Act Phys H
Acta Physica. Academiae Scientiarum Hungaricae — Acta Phys Acad Sci Hung
Acta Physica. Academiae Scientiarum Hungaricae — Acta Phys Acad Sci Hungar
Acta Physica Academiae Scientiarum Hungaricae. Supplement — Acta Phys Acad Sci Hung Suppl
Acta Physica Austriaca — Act Phys Au
Acta Physica Austriaca — Acta Phys Austriaca
Acta Physica Austriaca. Supplementum — Acta Phys Austriaca Suppl
Acta Physica et Chemica — Act Phys Ch
Acta Physica et Chemica — Acta Phys Chem
Acta Physica et Chemica — AUSHAF
Acta Physica et Chemica. Nova Series. Acta Universitatis Szegediensis — Acta Phys Chem Univ Szeged
Acta Physica et Chimica (Debrecina) [*Hungary*] — Acta Phys Chim (Debrecina)
Acta Physica et Chimica (Debrecina) — APDBA
Acta Physica Hungarica — Acta Phys Hung
Acta Physica Hungarica New Series. Heavy Ion Physics — Acta Phys Hung New Ser Heavy Ion Phys
Acta Physica Polonica — A Phys Pol
Acta Physica Polonica — Acta Phys Pol
Acta Physica Polonica. Series A — Act Phy P A
Acta Physica Polonica. Series A — Acta Phys Pol A
Acta Physica Polonica. Series A — Acta Phys Pol Ser A
Acta Physica Polonica. Series A [*Warsaw*] — Acta Phys Polon A
Acta Physica Polonica. Series B — Act Phy P B
Acta Physica Polonica. Series B — Acta Phys Pol B
Acta Physica Polonica. Series B — Acta Phys Pol Ser B
Acta Physica Polonica. Series B — Acta Phys Polon B
Acta Physica Sinica — Acta Phys Sin
Acta Physica Sinica — Acta Phys Sinica
Acta Physica Sinica. Abstracts — Acta Phy Sin Abstr
Acta Physica Sinica Abstracts — Acta Phys Sin Abstr
Acta Physica Slovaca — Acta Phys Slov
Acta Physica Slovaca — Acta Phys Slovaca
Acta Physica Slovaca — APSVC
Acta Physica Temperaturae Humilis Sinica — Acta Phys Temp Humilis Sin
Acta Physica Universitatis Comenianae — Acta Phys Univ Comenianae
Acta Physico-Chimica Sinica — Acta Phys Chim Sin
Acta Physicochimica URSS — Acta Physicochim URSS
Acta Physico-Medica Academiae Caesareae Leopoldino-Franciscanae Naturae Curiosorum Exhibentia Ephemerides Sive Observationes Historias et Experimenta — Act Phys Med Acad Nat Cur
Acta Physico-Medica Academiae Caesareae Leopoldino-Franciscanae Naturae Curiosorum Exhibentia Ephemerides Sive Observationes Historias et Experimenta — Act Phys Med Acad Nat Curios
Acta Physiochimica — Acta Physiochim
Acta Physiologiae Plantarum — Acta Physiol Plant
Acta Physiologica. Academiae Scientiarum Hungaricae — Act Physl H
Acta Physiologica. Academiae Scientiarum Hungaricae — Acta Physiol Acad Sci Hung
Acta Physiologica. Academiae Scientiarum Hungaricae — Acta Physiol Hung
Acta Physiologica. Academiae Scientiarum Hungaricae — APACAB
Acta Physiologica et Pharmacologica — APPBD
Acta Physiologica et Pharmacologica Bulgarica — Acta Physiol Pharmacol Bulg

Acta Physiologica et Pharmacologica Bulgarica — APPBDI
Acta Physiologica et Pharmacologica Latinoamericana — Acta Physiol Pharmacol Latinoam
Acta Physiologica et Pharmacologica Latinoamericana — APPLEF
Acta Physiologica et Pharmacologica Neerlandica — Acta Physiol Pharmac Neerl
Acta Physiologica et Pharmacologica Neerlandica — Acta Physiol Pharmacol Neerl
Acta Physiologica Hungarica — Acta Physiol Hung
Acta Physiologica Hungarica — APHHDU
Acta Physiologica Latino Americana — Act Physl L
Acta Physiologica Latino Americana — Acta Physiol Lat Am
Acta Physiologica Latino Americana. Suplemento — Acta Physiol Lat Am (Supl)
Acta Physiologica Latinoamericana [*Argentina*] — Acta Physiol Latinoam
Acta Physiologica Latinoamericana — Acta Physiol Latinoamer
Acta Physiologica Latinoamericana — APLTAF
Acta Physiologica, Pharmacologica, et Therapeutica Latinoamericana — Acta Physiol Pharmacol Ther Latinoam
Acta Physiologica Polonica — A Phys Pol
Acta Physiologica Polonica — Act Physl P
Acta Physiologica Polonica — Acta Physiol Pol
Acta Physiologica Polonica (English Translation) — Acta Physiol Pol (Engl Transl)
Acta Physiologica Polonica. Suplement [*Poland*] — Acta Physiol Pol Supl
Acta Physiologica Polonica (Translation) — Acta Physiol Pol (Transl)
Acta Physiologica Scandinavica — A Phys Scand
Acta Physiologica Scandinavica — Act Physl S
Acta Physiologica Scandinavica — Acta Physiol Scand
Acta Physiologica Scandinavica — Acta Physiologica Scandinav
Acta Physiologica Scandinavica — APSCA
Acta Physiologica Scandinavica. Supplementum — Acta Physiol Scand Suppl
Acta Physiologica Sinica — Acta Physiol Sin
Acta Phytochimica — Acta Phytochim
Acta Phytogeographica Suecica — Acta Phytogeogr Suec
Acta Phytomedica — Acta Phytomed
Acta Phytopathologica — Acta Phytopathol
Acta Phytopathologica. Academiae Scientiarum Hungaricae — Acta Phytopathol Acad Sci Hung
Acta Phytopathologica (Budapest) — Acta Phytopathol (Budapest)
Acta Phytopathologica Sinica — Acta Phytopathol Sin
Acta Phytopathologica Sinica — Acta Phytopathol Sinica
Acta Phytopathologica Sinica Translation Bulletin/Chi Wu Ping Li Hsueh I P'ao — Acta Phytopathol Sin Transl Bull
Acta Phytopathologica Sinica Translation Bulletin/Chi Wu Ping Li Hsueh I P'ao — Act Phytopath Sin Transl Bull
Acta Phytophylacica Sinica — Acta Phytophyl Sinica
Acta Phytophylacica Sinica — Acta Phytophylacica Sin
Acta Phytophysiologica Sinica — Acta Phytophysiol Sinica
Acta Phytophysiologica Sinica — Acta Phytophysiologica Sin
Acta Phytotaxonomica Barcinonensia — Acta Phytotaxon Barc
Acta Phytotaxonomica et Geobotanica — Acta Phytotaxon Geobot
Acta Phytotaxonomica et Geobotanica/Shokubutsu Bunrui Chiri — Shokubutsu Bunrui Chiri
Acta Phytotaxonomica et Geobotanica/Shokubutsu Bunrui Chiri (Kyoto) — Acta Phytotax Geobot Kyoto
Acta Phytotaxonomica Sinica — Acta Phytotaxon Sin
Acta Phytotaxonomica Sinica/Chih Wu Fen Lei Hsueh Pao — Act Phytotax Sin
Acta Phytotherapeutica — A Phytother
Acta Phytotherapeutica — Acta Phytother
Acta Phytotherapeutica — Acta Phytotherap
Acta Politecnica Mexicana — Acta Politec Mex
Acta Politica — Acta Polit
Acta Politica (Helsinki) — Acta Polit Helsinki
Acta Poloniae Historica — AcP
Acta Poloniae Historica — Act Pol His
Acta Poloniae Historica — APH
Acta Poloniae Maritima — Acta Pol Mar
Acta Poloniae Pharmaceutica — Act Pol Ph
Acta Poloniae Pharmaceutica — Acta Pol Pharm
Acta Poloniae Pharmaceutica (English Translation) — Acta Pol Pharm (Engl Transl)
Acta Poloniae Pharmaceutica (English Translation) — Acta Pol Pharm (Transl)
Acta Polymerica [*Germany*] — Acta Polym
Acta Polymerica Sinica — Acta Polym Sin
Acta Polytechnica — A Polytechn
Acta Polytechnica 1. Stavebni (Prague) — Acta Polytech 1 (Prague)
Acta Polytechnica 2. Strojni — Acta Polytech 2
Acta Polytechnica. Ceske Vysoke Uceni Technicke v Prace III — Acta Polytech Ceske Vys Uceni Tech v Pr III
Acta Polytechnica. Chemistry Including Metallurgy Series [*Sweden*] — Acta Polytech Chem Incl Metall Ser
Acta Polytechnica. Chemistry Including Metallurgy Series — APOCA
Acta Polytechnica. Mechanical Engineering Series — Acta Polytech Mech Eng Ser
Acta Polytechnica. Physics Including Nucleonics Series — Acta Polytech Phys Incl Nucleon Ser
Acta Polytechnica. Prace CVUT v Praze — Acta Polytech Prace CVUT
Acta Polytechnica. Prace CVUT v Praze. Series IV. Technicko-Teoreticka — Acta Polytech Prace CVUT Praze Ser IV Tech Teoret
Acta Polytechnica. Rada 1. Stavebni — Acta Polytech Rada 1 Stavebni
Acta Polytechnica. Rada 2. Strojni — Acta Polytech Rada 2 Strojni
Acta Polytechnica. Rada 3. Elektrotechnicka (Prague) — Acta Polytech Rada 3 Prague
Acta Polytechnica. Rada 4. Technicko-Teoreticka (Prague) — Acta Polytech Rada 4 Prague
Acta Polytechnica. Rada III. Elektrotechnicka — Acta Polytech Rada III Elektrotech
Acta Polytechnica. Rada IV. Technicko-Teoreticka — Acta Polytech Rada IV Tech-Teor
Acta Polytechnica. Rada IV. Technicko-Teoreticka (Prague) — Acta Polytech IV (Prague)
Acta Polytechnica Scandinavica — Acta Polytech Scand
Acta Polytechnica Scandinavica. Applied Physics Series [*Finland*] — Acta Polytech Scand Appl Phys Ser
Acta Polytechnica Scandinavica. Chemical Technology and Metallurgy Series — Acta Polytech Scand Chem Technol Metall Ser
Acta Polytechnica Scandinavica. Chemical Technology Series — Acta Polytech Scand Chem Technol Ser
Acta Polytechnica Scandinavica. Chemistry Including Metallurgy Series — Acta Polytech Scand Chem Incl Metall Ser
Acta Polytechnica Scandinavica. Chemistry Including Metallurgy Series — Acta Polytech Scandinavica Chem Incl Met Series
Acta Polytechnica Scandinavica. Chemistry Series — Act Poly Ch
Acta Polytechnica Scandinavica. Civil Engineering and Building Construction Series — Act Poly Ci
Acta Polytechnica Scandinavica. Civil Engineering and Building Construction Series [*Sweden*] — Acta Polytech Scand Civ Eng Build Constr Ser
Acta Polytechnica Scandinavica. Civil Engineering and Building Construction Series — Acta Polytech Scand Civ Eng Build Constru Ser
Acta Polytechnica Scandinavica. Electrical Engineering Series — Act Poly El
Acta Polytechnica Scandinavica. Electrical Engineering Series — Acta Polytech Scand Elec Eng Ser
Acta Polytechnica Scandinavica. Electrical Series — Acta Polytech Scand Electr Ser
Acta Polytechnica Scandinavica. Mathematics and Computer Science Series — Acta Polytech Scand Math Comput Sci Ser
Acta Polytechnica Scandinavica. Mathematics and Computing Machinery Series — Act Poly Ma
Acta Polytechnica Scandinavica. Mathematics and Computing Machinery Series — Acta Polytech Scand Math and Comput Mach Ser
Acta Polytechnica Scandinavica. Mathematics and Computing Machinery Series [*Finland*] — Acta Polytech Scand Math Comput Mach Ser
Acta Polytechnica Scandinavica. Mathematics Computing and Management in Engineering Series — Acta Polytech Scand Math Comput Engrg Ser
Acta Polytechnica Scandinavica. Mechanical Engineering Series — Act Poly Me
Acta Polytechnica Scandinavica. Mechanical Engineering Series — Acta Polytech Scand Mech Eng Ser
Acta Polytechnica Scandinavica. Physics Including Nucleonics Series — Act Poly Ph
Acta Polytechnica Scandinavica. Physics Including Nucleonics Series — Acta Polytech Scand Phys Incl Nucl Ser
Acta Polytechnica Scandinavica. Physics Including Nucleonics Series [*Finland*] [*A publication*] — Acta Polytech Scand Phys Incl Nucleon Ser
Acta Polytechnica Scandinavica. Physics Including Nucleonics Series — Acta Polytech Scand Phys Nucl Ser
Acta Polytechnica. Series III — Acta Polytech III
Acta Pontificia. Academia Scientiarum — Acta Pontif Acad Sci
Acta Pontificii Instituti Biblici — Acta Pont Inst Bibl
Acta Praehistorica — Acta Praehist
Acta Praehistorica et Archaeologica [*Berlin*] — Acta Pr Hist A
Acta Praehistorica et Archaeologica — Acta Praehist Archaeol
Acta Praehistorica et Archaeologica — Acta Praehist et Arch
Acta Praehistorica et Archaeologica — Acta Praehist et Archaeol
Acta Praehistorica et Archaeologica — APA
Acta Primae et Secundae Academiae Medicinae Shanghai — Acta Primae Secundae Acad Med Shanghai
Acta pro Fauna et Flora Universali. Ser 2. Botanica — Acta Fauna Fl Universali Ser 2 Bot
Acta Pro Fauna et Flora Universali. Serie 2. Botanica [*Bucharest*] — Act Faun Fl Un Bot
Acta Protozoologica — Acta Protozool
Acta Psiquiatrica y Psicologica (Argentina) — Acta Psiquiatr Psicol (Argent)
Acta Psiquiatrica y Psicologica de America Latina — Act Psiq Ps
Acta Psiquiatrica y Psicologica de America Latina — Acta Psiquiatr Psicol Am Lat
Acta Psiquiatrica y Psicologica de America Latina — APQPA
Acta Psychiatrica Belgica — Acta Psychiat Belg
Acta Psychiatrica Belgica — Acta Psychiatr Belg
Acta Psychiatrica et Neurologica — Acta Psych
Acta Psychiatrica et Neurologica — Acta Psychiatr Neurol
Acta Psychiatrica et Neurologica Scandinavica — Acta Psychiat Scand
Acta Psychiatrica et Neurologica Scandinavica — Acta Psychiatr Neurol Scand
Acta Psychiatrica et Neurologica Scandinavica. Supplementum — Acta Psychiatr Neurol Scand Suppl
Acta Psychiatrica Scandinavica — Act Psyc Sc
Acta Psychiatrica Scandinavica — Acta Psych Scand
Acta Psychiatrica Scandinavica [*Denmark*] — Acta Psychiat Scand
Acta Psychiatrica Scandinavica — Acta Psychiat Scandinav
Acta Psychiatrica Scandinavica — Acta Psychiatr Scand
Acta Psychiatrica Scandinavica — APYSA9
Acta Psychiatrica Scandinavica. Supplementum [*Denmark*] — Acta Psychiat Scand Suppl
Acta Psychiatrica Scandinavica. Supplementum — Acta Psychiatr Scand Suppl
Acta Psychiatrica Scandinavica. Supplementum — ASSUA6
Acta Psychologica — AcPs
Acta Psychologica [*Amsterdam*] — Act Psychol
Acta Psychologica [*Amsterdam*] — Acta Psychol
Acta Psychologica [*Amsterdam*] — APsych
Acta Psychologica (Amsterdam) — Acta Psychol (Amst)
Acta Psychologica (Amsterdam) — APSOA

Acta Psychologica Fennica — Acta Psychol Fenn
Acta Psychologica Gothoburgensia — Acta Psychol Gothoburg
Acta Psychologica Sinica [*Hsin-Li Hsueh-Pao*] — APS
Acta Psychologica Taiwanica — Act Psych T
Acta Psychologica Taiwanica — Acta Psychol Taiwan
Acta Psychologica Taiwanica — Acta PT
Acta Psychologica Taiwanica — APSTCI
Acta Psychologica Taiwanica — APT
Acta Psychotherapeutica et Psychosomatica — Acta Psychother Psychosom
Acta Psychotherapeutica et Psychosomatica — APYTA
Acta Psychotherapeutica, Psychosomatica, et Orthopaedagogica — Acta Psychother Psychosom Orthopaedagog
Acta Psychotherapeutica, Psychosomatica, et Orthopaedagogica — Acta Psychotherap Psychosom Orthopaedagog
Acta Radiobotanica et Genetica [*Japan*] — Acta Radiobot Genet
Acta Radiobotanica et Genetica — ARBGB9
Acta Radiobotanica et Genetica. Bulletin. Institute of Radiation Breeding — Acta Radiobotanica Genet Bull Inst Radiat Breed
Acta Radiologica — ACRAAX
Acta Radiologica — Acta Radiol
Acta Radiologica. Diagnosis — ACRDA
Acta Radiologica Interamericana — Acta Radiol Interam
Acta Radiologica. Oncology — Acta Radiol Oncol
Acta Radiologica. Oncology — AROBDR
Acta Radiologica. Oncology, Radiation Therapy, Physics, and Biology [*Stockholm*] — Acta Radiol Oncol Radiat Ther Phys Biol
Acta Radiologica. Oncology, Radiation Therapy, Physics, and Biology — Acta Radiol Oncol Radiat Therapy Phys and Biol
Acta Radiologica. Oncology, Radiation Therapy, Physics, and Biology — ARONDT
Acta Radiologica. Series One. Diagnosis [*Stockholm*] — Act Rad Dgn
Acta Radiologica. Series One. Diagnosis [*Stockholm*] — Acta Radiol Diagn
Acta Radiologica. Series One. Diagnosis (Stockholm) — Acta Radiol Diagn (Stockh)
Acta Radiologica. Series Two. Oncology, Radiation, Physics, and Biology [*Stockholm*] — Acta Radiol Oncol Radiat Phys Biol
Acta Radiologica (Stockholm) — Acta Radiol (Stockh)
Acta Radiologica. Supplementum [*Stockholm*] — Acta Radiol Suppl
Acta Radiologica. Supplementum — ARASA5
Acta Radiologica. Supplementum (Stockholm) — Acta Radiol Suppl (Stockh)
Acta Radiologica. Therapy, Physics, Biology [*Later, Acta Radiologica. Series Two. Oncology, Radiation, Physics, and Biology (Stockholm)*] — Act Rad TPB
Acta Radiologica. Therapy, Physics, Biology [*Later, Acta Radiologica. Series Two. Oncology, Radiation, Physics, and Biology (Stockholm)*] — Acta Radiol Ther Phys Biol
Acta Radiologica. Therapy, Physics, Biology [*Later, Acta Radiologica. Series Two. Oncology, Radiation, Physics, and Biology*] — ATHBA
Acta Radiologica. Therapy, Physics, Biology [*Later, Acta Radiologica. Series Two. Oncology, Radiation, Physics, and Biology*] — ATHBA3
Acta Radiologica. Therapy, Physics, Biology (Stockholm) [*Later, Acta Radiologica. Series Two. Oncology, Radiation, Physics, and Biology (Stockholm)*] — Acta Radiol Ther (Stockh)
Acta Regia; An Abstract of Rymer's Foedera — Act Reg
Acta Regia Societatis Physiographicae Lundensis — Acta Regia Soc Physiogr Lund
Acta Regiae Societatis Scientiarum et Litterarum Gothoburgensis. Zoologica — Acta Regiae Soc Sci Litt Gothob Zool
Acta Regiae Societatis Scientiarum et Litterarum Gothoburgensis. Zoologica — ARSZAE
Acta Rei Cretariae Romanae Fautorum — Acta RCF
Acta Rei Cretariae Romanae Fautorum — Acta RCRF
Acta Reproductiva Turcica — Acta Reprod Turc
Acta Reproductiva Turcica — ARTUD7
Acta Rerum Naturalium. Musei Nationalis Slovaci Bratislava — Acta Rerum Nat Mus Nat Slov Bratisl
Acta Rerum Naturalium. Musei Nationalis Slovaci Bratislava — ZSNMAS
Acta Reumatologica — Acta Reumatol
Acta Rheumatologica Scandinavica — Acta Rheum Scandinav
Acta Rheumatologica Scandinavica — Acta Rheumat Scand
Acta Rheumatologica Scandinavica — Acta Rheumatol Scand
Acta Rheumatologica Scandinavica — ARSCAD
Acta Rheumatologica Scandinavica. Supplementum — Acta Rheumatol Scand Suppl
Acta Rheumatologica Scandinavica. Supplementum — ARSSAR
Acta Rhumatologica — ACRHDN
Acta Rhumatologica — Acta Rhumatol
Acta Rhumatologica Belgica — Acta Rhumatol Belg
Acta Sagittariana — Acta Sag
Acta Salmanticensia — ASal
Acta Salmanticensia. Serie de Ciencias — Acta Salmant Cien
Acta Salmanticensia. Serie de Ciencias — Acta Salmant Ser Cienc
Acta Salmanticensia. Serie de Ciencias — Acta Salmanticensia Ser Cienc
Acta Salmanticensia. Serie de Ciencias — ASALAP
Acta Salmanticensia. Serie de Medicina — Acta Salmant Ser Med
Acta Salmanticensia. Serie de Medicina — Acta Salmanticensia Ser Med
Acta Salmanticensia. Serie de Medicina — ASSMBH
Acta Salmanticensia. Serie Filosofia y Letras — Acta Salmanticensia Ser Filos Letra
Acta Sanctae Sedis [*Rome*] — ASS
Acta Sanctorum — A S Boll
Acta Sanctorum — AASS
Acta Sanctorum — Acta SS
Acta Sanctorum Quotquot Toto Orbe Coluntur, Vel a Catholicis Scriptoribus Celebrantur — Acta Sanctorum
Acta Scaenographica — Acta Scaenograph
Acta Scholae Medicinalis Universitatis Imperialis (Kioto) — Acta Sch Med Univ Imp (Kioto)
Acta Scholae Medicinalis Universitatis in Gifu [*Japan*] — Acta Sch Med Gifu
Acta Scholae Medicinalis Universitatis in Gifu — Acta Sch Med Univ Gifu
Acta Scholae Medicinalis Universitatis in Kioto — Acta Sch Med Univ Kioto
Acta Scholae Medicinalis Universitatis in Kioto — ASMUAA
Acta Scientia Sinica — Acta Sci Sin
Acta Scientia Sinica/Chung Kuo K'o Hsueh — Act Sci Sin
Acta Scientiae Circumstantiae — Acta Sci Circumstantiae
Acta Scientiarum Litterarumque. Schedae Chemicae. Universitas Iagellonica — Acta Sci Litt Schedae Chem Univ Iagellon
Acta Scientiarum Litterarumque. Schedae Physicae. Universitas Iagellonica — Acta Sci Litt Schedae Phys Univ Iagellon
Acta Scientiarum Mathematicarum — Act Sci Mat
Acta Scientiarum Mathematicarum et Naturalium Universitatis Kolozsvar — Acta Sci Math Nat Univ Kolozsvar
Acta Scientiarum Mathematicarum (Szeged) — Acta Sci Math (Szeged)
Acta Scientiarum Naturalium. Academiae Scientiarum Bohemoslovacae [*Brno*] — PPUCA4
Acta Scientiarum Naturalium. Academiae Scientiarum Bohemoslovacae (Brno) — Acta Sci Nat Acad Sci Bohemoslov (Brno)
Acta Scientiarum Naturalium. Kirin University Journal. Natural Science — Acta Sci Nat Kirin Univ J Nat Sci
Acta Scientiarum Naturalium. Northeastern China People's University Journal. Natural Science — Acta Sci Nat Northeast China Peoples Univ J Nat Sci
Acta Scientiarum Naturalium. Universitatis Amoiensis — Acta Sci Nat Univ Amoi
Acta Scientiarum Naturalium Universitatis Amoiensis — Acta Sci Natur Univ Amoien
Acta Scientiarum Naturalium Universitatis Jilinensis — Acta Sci Natur Univ Jilin
Acta Scientiarum Naturalium. Universitatis Normalis Hunanensis — Acta Sci Nat Univ Norm Hunanensis
Acta Scientiarum Naturalium Universitatis Normalis Hunanensis — Acta Sci Natur Univ Norm Hunan
Acta Scientiarum Naturalium. Universitatis Pekinensis [*People's Republic of China*] — Acta Sci Nat Univ Pekin
Acta Scientiarum Naturalium. Universitatis Pekinensis — Acta Sci Natur Univ Pekinensis
Acta Scientiarum Naturalium Universitatis Sunyatseni — Act Sci Nat Univ Sunyatseni
Acta Scientiarum Naturalium Universitatis Sunyatseni — Acta Sci Natur Univ Sunyatseni
Acta Scientiarum Naturalium. Universitatis Sunyatseni (Zhongshandaxue Xuebao) [*A publication*] — Acta Sci Nat Univ Sunyatseni (Zhongshandaxue Xuebao)
Acta Scientiarum Naturalium. Universitatis Szechuanensis [*People's Republic of China*] — Acta Sci Nat Univ Szechuan
Acta Scientiarum Naturalium Universitatis Szechuanensis/Seu ch'uan Ta Hsueh Hsueh Pao, Tzu Jan K'o Hsueh — Seu Chuan Ta Hsueh Pao Tzu Jan Ko Hsueh
Acta Scientiarum Naturalium Universitatis Wuhanensis — Act Sci Nat Univ Wuhan
Acta Scientiarum Socialium. Societas Academica Dacoromana — Acta Sci Soc
Acta Scientiarum Vietnamicarum — Acta Sci Vietnam
Acta Sedimentologica Sinica — Acta Sedimentol Sin
Acta Seismologica Sinica [*People's Republic of China*] — Acta Seismol Sin
Acta Seminarii Neotestamentici Upsaliensis [*Uppsala*] — ASNU
Acta Semiotica et Linguistica — A S e L
Acta Sericologica — Acta Sericol
Acta Sericologica et Entomologica — Acta Sericol Entomol
Acta Silicata Sinica — Acta Silic Sin
Acta Societatis Botanicorum Poloniae — Acta Soc Bot Pol
Acta Societatis Botanicorum Poloniae — Acta Soc Bot Polon
Acta Societatis Botanicorum Poloniae. Publications. Societe Botanique de Pologne — Act Soc Bot Polon
Acta Societatis Botanicorum Poloniae. Publications. Societe Botanique de Pologne — Acta Soc Bot Poloniae
Acta Societatis Entomologicae Cechosloveniae — Acta Soc Entomol Cech
Acta Societatis Entomologicae Jugoslavensis — Acta Soc Ent Jugosl
Acta Societatis Entomologicae Serbo-Croato-Slovenae — Acta Soc Ent Serbo Cro Slov
Acta Societatis Humaniorum Litterarum Lundensis — ASLL
Acta Societatis Jablonovianae — Acta Soc Jablonov
Acta Societatis Linguisticae Upsaliensis — ASLU
Acta Societatis Medicorum Fennicae Duodecim — Acta Soc Med Fenn Duodecim
Acta Societatis Medicorum Fennicae Duodecim. Serie A — Acta Soc Med Fenn Duodecim Ser A
Acta Societatis Medicorum Fennicae Duodecim. Serie B — Acta Soc Med Fenn Duodecim Ser B
Acta Societatis Medicorum Upsaliensis — Acta Soc Med Ups
Acta Societatis Medicorum Upsaliensis — Acta Soc Med Upsal
Acta Societatis Medicorum Upsaliensis. Supplementum — Acta Soc Med Ups Suppl
Acta Societatis Ophthalmologicae Japonicae — Acta Soc Ophthalmol Jpn
Acta Societatis Paediatricae Hellenicae — Acta Soc Paed Hell
Acta Societatis Pathologicae Japonicae — Acta Soc Path Jap
Acta Societatis Philologae Lipsiensis — Acta Soc Phil Lips
Acta Societatis Physiologicae Scandinavicae — Acta Physiol Scand
Acta Societatis pro Fauna et Flora — ASFF
Acta Societatis pro Fauna et Flora Fennica — Acta Soc Fauna Flora Fenn
Acta Societatis Regiae Scientiarum Indo-Neerlandicae — Act Soc R Sc Indo Neerl
Acta Societatis Regiae Scientiarum Indo-Neerlandicae — Acta Soc Reg Sci Indo Neerl

Acta Societatis Regiae Scientiarum Indo-Neerlandicae. Verhandelingen der Natuurkundige Vereeniging in Nederlandsch-Indiee — Acta Soc Regiae Sci Indo Neerl
Acta Societatis Regiae Scientiarum Upsaliensis — Act Soc R Sc Upsal
Acta Societatis Regiae Scientiarum Upsaliensis — Act Upsal
Acta Societatis Scientiarum Fennica. Series B. Opera Biologica — Opera Biol
Acta Societatis Scientiarum Fennicae — Acta Soc Scient Fennicae
Acta Societatis Scientiarum Fennicae — ASSF
Acta Societatis Scientiarum Fennicae. Series B — Acta Soc Sci Fenn Ser B
Acta Societatis Scientiarum Naturalium Moravicae — Acta Soc Sci Natur Moravicae
Acta Societatis Zoologicae Cechoslovenicae — Acta Soc Zool Cechosl
Acta Sociologica — Act Sociol
Acta Sociologica — Acta Soc
Acta Sociologica — Acta Sociol
Acta Sociologica — PASO
Acta Socio-Medica Scandinavica — Acta Sociomed Scand
Acta Stereologica — Acta Stereol
Acta Stomatologica Belgica — Acta Stomatol Belg
Acta Stomatologica Belgica — ASBEB
Acta Stomatologica Croatica — Acta Stomatol Croat
Acta Stomatologica Patavina — Acta Stom Pat
Acta Sud Americana de Quimica — Acta Sud Am Quim
Acta Suplemento — Acta Supl
Acta Symposii de Evolutione Insectorum — Acta Symp Evolut Insect
Acta Technica. Academiae Scientiarum Hungaricae — Act Techn H
Acta Technica. Academiae Scientiarum Hungaricae — Acta Tech Acad Sci Hung
Acta Technica (Budapest) — Acta Tech (Budap)
Acta Technica. CSAV [*Ceskoslovenska Akademie Ved*] — Acta Tech CSAV
Acta Technica Gedanensia — Acta Techn Gedan
Acta Technica Hungarica — Acta Tech Hung
Acta Technica Hungarica — Acta Techn Hung
Acta Technica (Prague) — Acta Tech (Prague)
Acta Technica. Univerza v Ljubljani. Tehniska Fakulteta. Series Chimica — Acta Tech Univ Ljubljani Teh Fak Ser Chim
Acta Technologica Agriculturae [*Brno*]. A. Facultas Agronomica — Acta Tech Agric
Acta Teilhardiana — Acta Teilhard
Acta Theologica Danica — ATD
Acta Theologica Danica [*Copenhagen*] — AThD
Acta Therapeutica — Acta Ther
Acta Theriologica — Acta Theriol
Acta Theriologica Sinica — Acta Theriol Sin
Acta Toxicologica et Therapeutica — Acta Toxicol Ther
Acta Tropica — A Trop
Acta Tropica — Acta Trop
Acta Tropica (Basel) — Acta Trop (Basel)
Acta Tropica. Supplementum — Acta Trop Suppl
Acta Tuberculosea Belgica — Acta Tuberc Belg
Acta Tuberculosea et Pneumologica Belgica — Acta Tuberc Pneumol Belg
Acta Tuberculosea et Pneumologica Scandinavica — Acta Tuberc Pneumol Scand
Acta Tuberculosea et Pneumologica Scandinavica. Supplementum — Acta Tuberc Pneumol Scand Suppl
Acta Tuberculosea Japonica — Acta Tuberc Jpn
Acta Tuberculosea Scandinavica — Acta Tub
Acta Tuberculosea Scandinavica — Acta Tuberc Scand
Acta Tuberculosea Scandinavica. Supplementum — Acta Tuberc Scand Suppl
Acta Unio Internationalis Contra Cancrum — Acta Unio Int Cancrum
Acta Unio Internationalis Contra Cancrum — Acta Unio Int Contra Cancrum
Acta Universitatis Agriculturae (Brno). Facultas Agronomica — Acta Univ Agric (Brno) Fac Agron
Acta Universitatis Agriculturae (Brno). Facultas Silviculturae — Acta Univ Agric (Brno) Fac Silvic
Acta Universitatis Agriculturae (Brno). Facultas Silviculturae. Series C — Acta Univ Agr (Brno)
Acta Universitatis Agriculturae (Brno). Facultas Silviculturae. Series C — Acta Univ Agric Ser C (Brno)
Acta Universitatis Agriculturae (Brno). Facultas Veterinaria — Acta Univ Agric (Brno) Fac Vet
Acta Universitatis Agriculturae et Silviculturae. Brno. Rada B. Spisy Veterinarni — Acta Univ Agric Silvic Brno Rada B
Acta Universitatis Agriculturae et Silviculturae. Brno. Rada C. Spisy Fakulty Lesnicke — Acta Univ Agric Silvic Brno Rada C
Acta Universitatis Agriculturae. Facultas Agroeconomica. Rada D. Spisy Fakulty Provozne Ekonomicke — Acta Univ Agric Fac Agroecon Rada D Spisy Fak Provozne Ekon
Acta Universitatis Agriculturae. Facultas Agronomica — Acta Univ Agric Fac Agron
Acta Universitatis Agriculturae. Facultas Silviculturae — Acta Univ Agric Fac Silvic
Acta Universitatis Agriculturae. Facultas Silviculturae. Series C — AUAFA
Acta Universitatis Agriculturae. Facultas Veterinaria — Acta Univ Agric Fac Vet
Acta Universitatis Agriculturae. Facultas Veterinaria (Brno) — Acta Univ Agric Fac Vet Brno
Acta Universitatis Agriculturae. Facultas Veterinaria. Rada B — Acta Univ Agric Fac Vet Rada B
Acta Universitatis Bergensis. Series Mathematica. Rerumque Naturalium — Acta Univ Bergen Ser Math Rerumque Nat
Acta Universitatis Bergensis. Series Medica — Acta Univ Bergen Ser Med
Acta Universitatis Bergensis. Series Medica. Nova Series — Acta Univ Bergen Ser Med Nova Ser
Acta Universitatis Carolinae — AUC
Acta Universitatis Carolinae. Biologica — Acta Univ Carol Biol
Acta Universitatis Carolinae. Geographica — Acta Univ Carol Geogr
Acta Universitatis Carolinae. Geographica — AUCG-B
Acta Universitatis Carolinae. Geologica — Acta Univ Carol Geol
Acta Universitatis Carolinae. Geologica — Acta Univ Carolinae Geol
Acta Universitatis Carolinae. Geologica. Monographia — Acta Univ Carol Geol Monogr
Acta Universitatis Carolinae. Geologica. Supplementum — Acta Univ Carol Geol Suppl
Acta Universitatis Carolinae. Historia — Acta Univ Carol Hist
Acta Universitatis Carolinae. Mathematica et Physica — Acta Univ Carol Math Phys
Acta Universitatis Carolinae. Mathematica et Physica — Acta Univ Carolin Math Phys
Acta Universitatis Carolinae. Mathematica et Physica — Acta Univ Carolinae Math et Phys
Acta Universitatis Carolinae. Medica — Acta Univ Carol Med
Acta Universitatis Carolinae. Medica. Monographia — Acta Univ Carol Med Monogr
Acta Universitatis Carolinae. Medica. Monographia — AUCMB
Acta Universitatis Carolinae. Medica. Monographia (Praha) — Acta Univ Carol Med Monogr (Praha)
Acta Universitatis Carolinae. Medica (Praha) — Acta Univ Carol Med (Praha)
Acta Universitatis Carolinae. Medica. Supplementum [*Czechoslovakia*] — Acta Univ Carol Med Suppl
Acta Universitatis Carolinae. Philologica — AUC Ph
Acta Universitatis Carolinae Pragensis — AUCP
Acta Universitatis Debreceniensis de Ludovico Kossuth Nominatae — Acta Univ Debrecen Ludovico Kossuth Nominatae
Acta Universitatis Debreceniensis de Ludovico Kossuth Nominatae. Series 2. Biologica — Acta Univ Debrecen Ludovico Kossuth Nominatae Ser 2
Acta Universitatis Debreceniensis de Ludovico Kossuth Nominatae. Series Biologica — Acta Univ Debrec
Acta Universitatis Debreceniensis de Ludovico Kossuth Nominatae. Series Biologica — Acta Univ Debrecen Ludovico Kossuth Nominatae Ser Biol
Acta Universitatis Debreceniensis de Ludovico Kossuth Nominatae. Series Physica et Chimica — Acta Univ Debrecen Ludovico Kossuth Nominatae Ser Phys Chim
Acta Universitatis Futanensis. Scientiarum Naturalium — Acta Univ Futan Sci Nat
Acta Universitatis Gothoburgensis — Acta Univ Gothoburgensis
Acta Universitatis Gothoburgensis / Goeteborgs Universitets Arsskrift — Ac UG
Acta Universitatis Gothoburgensis/Goeteborgs Universitets Arsskrift — AUG
Acta Universitatis Gothoburgensis / Goeteborgs Universitets Arsskrift — GHA
Acta Universitatis Latviensis — Acta Univ Latv
Acta Universitatis Latviensis — Acta Univ Latviensis
Acta Universitatis Latviensis — AUL
Acta Universitatis Latviensis. Chemicorum Ordinis Series — Acta Univ Latv Chem Ordinis Ser
Acta Universitatis Latviensis. Mathematicorum et Physicorum Ordinis Series — Acta Univ Latv Math Phys Ordinis Ser
Acta Universitatis Latviensis. Medicorum Ordinis Series — Acta Univ Latv Med Ordinis Ser
Acta Universitatis Lodziensis — Acta Univ Lodz
Acta Universitatis Lodziensis. Folia Chimica — Acta Univ Lodz Folia Chim
Acta Universitatis Lodziensis Folia Mathematica — Acta Univ Lodz Folia Math
Acta Universitatis Lodziensis Folia Philosophica — Acta Univ Lodz Folia Philos
Acta Universitatis Lodziensis. Folia Physica — Acta Univ Lodz Folia Phys
Acta Universitatis Lodziensis. Seria 2. Nauki Matematyczno-Przyrodnicze — Acta Univ Lodz Ser 2
Acta Universitatis Lodziensis. Seria 2. Nauki Matematyczno-Przyrodnicze — Acta Univ Lodz Ser 2 Nauk Mat-Przyr
Acta Universitatis Lundensis — Acta Lund
Acta Universitatis Lundensis — AL
Acta Universitatis Lundensis — AUL
Acta Universitatis Lundensis — LUA
Acta Universitatis Lundensis. Lunds Universitets Arsskrift. Afdelningen foer Mathematik och Naturvetenskap — Act Un Lund
Acta Universitatis Lundensis. Lunds Universitets Arsskrift. Afdelningen foer Mathematik och Naturvetenskap — Lunds Univ Arsskr
Acta Universitatis Lundensis. Lunds Universitets Arsskrift. Afdelningen foer Mathematik och Naturvetenskap. Kongl Fysiografiska Saellskapets i Lund Handlingar. Ny Foeljd — Kongl Fysiogr Saellsk Lund Handl NF
Acta Universitatis Lundensis. Lunds Universitets Arsskrift. Afdelningen foer Mathematik och Naturvetenskap. Kongliga Fysiografiska Saellskapets i Lund Handlingar — Kongl Fysiogr Saellsk Handl
Acta Universitatis Lundensis. Lunds Universitets Arsskrift. Afdelningen foer Mathematik och Naturvetenskap. Ny Foeljd. Andra Afdelningen. Medicin Sam Matematiska och Naturvetenskapliga Aemnen — Lunds Univ Arsskr NF Andra Afd Med
Acta Universitatis Lundensis. Sectio 2. Medica, Mathematica, Scientiae Rerum Naturalium — Acta Univ Lund Sect 2
Acta Universitatis Lundensis. Sectio II. Scientiae Rerum Naturalium Medica, Mathematica — Acta Univ Lund Sect II Med Math Sci Rerum Nat
Acta Universitatis Medicinae Tongji (Chinese Edition) — Acta Univ Med Tongji (Chin Ed)
Acta Universitatis Medicinalis Secondae Shanghai — Acta Univ Med Secondae Shanghai
Acta Universitatis Nankinensis Scientiarum Naturalium/Nan Ching Ta Hsueh Hsueh Pao — Nan Ching Ta Hsueeh Hsueeh Pao
Acta Universitatis Nicolai Copernici. Biologia — Acta Univ Nicolai Copernici Biol
Acta Universitatis Nicolai Copernici. Geografia — Acta Univ Nicolai Copernici Geogr
Acta Universitatis Nicolai Copernici, Nauki Matematyczno-Przyrodnicze — Acta Univ Nicolai Copernici Nauki Mat Przyr

Acta Universitatis Nicolai Copernici. Prace Limnologiczne — Acta Univ Nicolai Copernici Pr Limnol
Acta Universitatis Ouluensis. Series A. Scientiae Rerum Naturalium — Acta Univ Oulu Ser A Sci Rerum Natur
Acta Universitatis Ouluensis. Series A. Scientiae Rerum Naturalium — AUOASRN
Acta Universitatis Ouluensis. Series A. Scientiae Rerum Naturalium. Biochemica — Acta Univ Ouluensis Ser A Sci Rerum Nat Biochem
Acta Universitatis Ouluensis. Series A. Scientiae Rerum Naturalium. Biologica [*A publication*] — Acta Univ Ouluensis Ser A Sci Rerum Nat Biol
Acta Universitatis Ouluensis. Series A. Scientiae Rerum Naturalium. Geologica [*A publication*] — Acta Univ Ouluensis Ser A
Acta Universitatis Ouluensis. Series A. Scientiae Rerum Naturalium. Mathematica — Acta Univ Oulu Ser A Sci Rerum Natur Math
Acta Universitatis Ouluensis. Series C. Technica — Acta Univ Ouluensis Ser C
Acta Universitatis Ouluensis. Series D. Medica — Acta Univ Ouluensis Ser D Med
Acta Universitatis Palackianae. Facultatis Medicae — Acta Univ Palack Fac Med
Acta Universitatis Palackianae Olomucensis — Acta Univ Palacki Olomuc
Acta Universitatis Palackianae Olomucensis — AUPO
Acta Universitatis Palackianae Olomucensis. Facultas Philosophica. Philologica — AUO-Ph
Acta Universitatis Palackianae Olomucensis. Facultas Rerum Naturalium — Acta Univ Palacki Olomuc Fac Rerum Nat
Acta Universitatis Palackianae Olomucensis. Facultas Rerum Naturalium. Biologica — Acta Univ Palacki Olomuc Fac Rerum Nat Biol
Acta Universitatis Palackianae Olomucensis. Facultas Rerum Naturalium. Chemica — Acta Univ Palacki Olomuc Fac Rerum Nat Chem
Acta Universitatis Palackianae Olomucensis. Facultas Rerum Naturalium. Mathematica — Acta Univ Palack Olomuc Fac Rerum Natur Math
Acta Universitatis Palackianae Olomucensis. Facultas Rerum Naturalium. Mathematica — Acta Univ Palacki Olomuc Fac Rerum Nat Math
Acta Universitatis Palackianae Olomucensis. Facultas Rerum Naturalium. Physica — Acta Univ Palacki Olomuc Fac Rerum Nat Phys
Acta Universitatis Palackianae Olomucensis. Facultas Rerum Naturalium. Series 2. Biologica — Acta Univ Palack Olomuc Fac Rerum Nat Ser 2 Biol
Acta Universitatis Palackianae Olomucensis. Facultas Scientiarum — Acta Univ Palacki Olomuc Fac Sci
Acta Universitatis Palackianae Olomucensis. Facultatis Medicae — Acta Univ Palacki Olomuc Fac Med
Acta Universitatis Palackianae Olomucensis. Facultatis Medicae. Supplementum — Acta Univ Palacki Olomuc Fac Med Suppl
Acta Universitatis Palackianae Olomucensis Historica [*Prague*] — AUPO
Acta Universitatis Palackianae Olomucensis. Facultas Rerum Naturalium. Geologica — Acta Univ Palack Olumuc Fac Rerum Nat Geol
Acta Universitatis Stockholmiensis. Stockholm Contributions in Geology — Acta Univ Stockh Stockholm Contrib Geol
Acta Universitatis Szegediensis. Acta Biologica — Acta Univ Szeged Acta Biol
Acta Universitatis Szegediensis. Acta Germanica et Romanica — AUS AG & R
Acta Universitatis Szegediensis. Acta Mineralogica-Petrographica — Acta Univ Szeged Acta Mineral Petrogr
Acta Universitatis Szegediensis. Acta Physica et Chemica — Acta Univ Szeged Acta Phys et Chem
Acta Universitatis Szegediensis de Attila Jozsef Nominatae. Papers in English and American Studies — AUS-PEAS
Acta Universitatis Szegediensis de Attila Jozsef Nominatae. Sectio: Acta Historiae Litterarum Hungaricarum — AUS AHLH
Acta Universitatis Szegediensis de Attila Jozsef Nominatae. Sectio: Ethnographica et Linguistica — AUS E & L
Acta Universitatis Szegediensis. Pars Biologica Scientiarum Naturalium. Acta Biologica — Acta Univ Szeged Pars Biol Sci Nat Acta Biol
Acta Universitatis Szegediensis. Pars Physica et Chemica Scientiarum Naturalium. Acta Physica et Chemica — Acta Univ Szeged Pars Phys Chem Sci Nat Acta Phys Chem
Acta Universitatis Szegediensis. Sectio Scientiarum Naturalium. Acta Chemica et Physica — Acta Univ Szeged Sect Sci Nat Acta Chem Phys
Acta Universitatis Szegediensis. Sectio Scientiarum Naturalium. Acta Chemica, Mineralogica, et Physica — Acta Univ Szeged Sect Sci Nat Acta Chem Mineral Phys
Acta Universitatis Szegediensis. Sectio Scientiarum Naturalium. Acta Mineralogica, Petrographica — Acta Univ Szeged Sect Sci Nat Acta Mineral Petrogr
Acta Universitatis Szegediensis. Sectio Scientiarum Naturalium. Pars Botanica — Acta Univ Szeged Sect Sci Nat Pars Bot
Acta Universitatis Tamperensis. Serie B — Acta Univ Tampere Ser B
Acta Universitatis Tamperensis. Series A — Acta Univ Tamper Ser A
Acta Universitatis Tsinghuanensis — Acta Univ Tsinghuan
Acta Universitatis Upsaliensis — Acta Univ Ups
Acta Universitatis Upsaliensis — AUBG
Acta Universitatis Upsaliensis. Abstracts of Uppsala Dissertations. Faculty of Medicine — Acta Univ Ups Abstr Uppsala Diss Fac Med
Acta Universitatis Upsaliensis. Abstracts of Uppsala Dissertations. Faculty of Pharmacy — Acta Univ Ups Abstr Uppsala Diss Fac Pharm
Acta Universitatis Upsaliensis. Abstracts of Uppsala Dissertations. Faculty of Science — Acta Univ Upsal Abstr Upps Diss Fac Sci
Acta Universitatis Upsaliensis. Abstracts of Uppsala Dissertations. Faculty of Science — Acta Univ Upsal Abstr Uppsala Diss Fac Sci
Acta Universitatis Upsaliensis. Abstracts of Uppsala Dissertations. Faculty of Science — ACUU
Acta Universitatis Upsaliensis. Abstracts of Uppsala Dissertations in Medicine [*Sweden*] — Acta Univ Ups Abstr Upps Diss Med
Acta Universitatis Upsaliensis. Abstracts of Uppsala Dissertations in Science — Acta Univ Ups Abstr Upps Diss Sci
Acta Universitatis Upsaliensis. Abstracts of Uppsala Dissertations in Science [*Sweden*] — Acta Univ Ups Abstr Uppsala Diss Sci
Acta Universitatis Upsaliensis. Acta Societatis Linguisticae Upsaliensis — AUUASLU
Acta Universitatis Upsaliensis. Historia Litterarum — AUUHL
Acta Universitatis Upsaliensis. Nova Acta Regiae Societatis Scientiarum Upsaliensis. Series VC — Acta Univ Ups Nova Acta Regiae Soc Sci Up Ser VC
Acta Universitatis Upsaliensis. Nova Acta Regiae Societatis Scientiarum Upsaliensis. Series VC — Acta Univ Ups Nova Acta Regiae Soc Sci Ups Ser VC
Acta Universitatis Upsaliensis. Nova Acta Regiae Societatis Scientiarum Upsaliensis. Series VC — AUUNBA
Acta Universitatis Upsaliensis. Skrifter Roerande Uppsala Universitet. C. Organisation och Historia. Acta Universitatis Upsaliensis — Acta Univ Upsaliensis Skr Uppsala Univ C Organ Hist
Acta Universitatis Upsaliensis. Studia Anglistica Upsaliensia — AUUSAU
Acta Universitatis Upsaliensis. Studia Ethnologica Upsaliensia — AUUSEU
Acta Universitatis Upsaliensis. Studia Germanistica Upsaliensia — AUUSGU
Acta Universitatis Upsaliensis. Studia Romanica Upsaliensia — AUUSRU
Acta Universitatis Upsaliensis. Symbolae Botanicae Upsalienses — Acta Univ Ups Symb Bot Ups
Acta Universitatis Upsaliensis. Symbolae Botanicae Upsalienses — AUUUDX
Acta Universitatis Voronegiensis — Acta Univ Voroneg
Acta Universitatis Wratislaviensis — Acta Univ Wratislav
Acta Universitatis Wratislaviensis [*Poland*] — Acta Univ Wratislaviensis
Acta Universitatis Wratislaviensis — AUW
Acta Universitatis Wratislaviensis. Matematyka, Fizyka, Astronomia — Acta Univ Wratislav Mat Fiz Astron
Acta Universitatis Wratislaviensis. Matematyka, Fizyka, Astronomia — AWMFAR
Acta Universitatis Wratislaviensis. Prace Geologiczno-Mineralogiczne — Acta Univ Wratislav Pr Geol Mineral
Acta Universitatis Wratislaviensis. Prace Zoologiczne [*Poland*] — Acta Univ Wratislav Pr Zool
Acta Urologica Belgica — Acta Urol Belg
Acta Urologica Belgica — AUBEAN
Acta Urologica Japonica — Acta Urol Jpn
Acta Urologica Japonica — HIKYAJ
Acta Valachica. Studii si Materiale de Istorie a Culturii — Valachica
Acta Venezolana — Acta Venez
Acta Vertebratica — Acta Vertebr
Acta Vertebratica — AVRTAJ
Acta Veterinaria — ACVTA
Acta Veterinaria [*Brno*] — ACVTB9
Acta Veterinaria. Academiae Scientiarum Hungaricae — Act Vet H
Acta Veterinaria. Academiae Scientiarum Hungaricae — Acta Vet Acad Sci Hung
Acta Veterinaria. Academiae Scientiarum Hungaricae — AVASAX
Acta Veterinaria (Belgrade) — Acta Vet (Belgr)
Acta Veterinaria (Belgrade) — Acta Vet Belgrade
Acta Veterinaria (Beograd) [*Yugoslavia*] — Acta Vet (Beogr)
Acta Veterinaria (Brno) — Acta Vet (Brno)
Acta Veterinaria (Brno). Supplementum — Acta Vet (Brno) Suppl
Acta Veterinaria (Budapest) — Acta Vet Budapest
Acta Veterinaria et Zootechnica Sinica — Acta Vet Zootech Sin
Acta Veterinaria et Zootechnica Sinica — CMHPAI
Acta Veterinaria Hungarica — Acta Vet Hung
Acta Veterinaria Hungarica — AVHUEA
Acta Veterinaria Japonica — Acta Vet Jap
Acta Veterinaria Scandinavica — Act Vet Sc
Acta Veterinaria Scandinavica — Acta Vet Scand
Acta Veterinaria Scandinavica — AVSCA7
Acta Veterinaria Scandinavica. Supplementum — Acta Vet Scand Suppl
Acta Veterinaria Scandinavica. Supplementum — AVSPAC
Acta Virologica [*English Edition*] — Act Virolog
Acta Virologica — Acta Virol
Acta Virologica [*Prague*] [*English Edition*] — AVIRA2
Acta Virologica (English Edition) — Acta Virol (Engl Ed)
Acta Virologica (Prague) — Acta Virol (Prague)
Acta Virologica (Prague) (English Edition) — Acta Virol (Prague) (Engl Ed)
Acta Virologica (Praha) — Acta Virol (Praha)
Acta Vitaminologica [*Later, Acta Vitaminologica et Enzymologica*] — Acta Vitaminol
Acta Vitaminologica [*Later, Acta Vitaminologica et Enzymological*] — ACVIA9
Acta Vitaminologica et Enzymologica [*Milano*] — Act Vit Enz
Acta Vitaminologica et Enzymologica [*Milano*] — Acta Vitaminol Enzymol
Acta Vitaminologica et Enzymologica — AVEZA6
Acta Vitaminologica et Enzymologica (Milano) — Acta Vitaminol Enzymol (Milano)
Acta y Memorias. Sociedad Espanola de Antropologia, Etnografia, y Prehistoria [*Madrid*] — Acta Mem Soc Esp Antr
Acta y Memorias. Sociedad Espanola de Antropologia, Etnografia, y Prehistoria [*Madrid*] — AMSE Antr
Acta y Memorias. Sociedad Espanola de Antropologia, Etnografia, y Prehistoria. [*Madrid*] — AMSEAP
Acta Zoologica — Acta Zool
Acta Zoologica [*Stockholm*] — AZOSAT
Acta Zoologica. Academiae Scientiarum Hungaricae — Act Zool H
Acta Zoologica. Academiae Scientiarum Hungaricae — Acta Zool Acad Sci Hung
Acta Zoologica. Academiae Scientiarum Hungaricae — Acta Zool Hung
Acta Zoologica. Academiae Scientiarum Hungaricae — AZSHAG
Acta Zoologica Bulgarica — Acta Zool Bulg
Acta Zoologica Bulgarica — AZBUD7
Acta Zoologica Colombiana — Acta Zool Colomb
Acta Zoologica Colombiana — LZNAAN
Acta Zoologica Cracoviensia — Acta Zool Cracov
Acta Zoologica Cracoviensia — AZCRAY

Acta Zoologica Cracoviensia [*English Translation*] — AZOCAF
Acta Zoologica Cracoviensia (English Translation) — Acta Zool Cracov (Engl Transl)
Acta Zoologica et Oecologica. Universitatis Lodziensis — Acta Zool Oecol Univ Lodz
Acta Zoologica et Pathologica Antverpiensia — Acta Zool Pathol Antverp
Acta Zoologica et Pathologica Antverpiensia — Acta Zool Pathol Antverpiensia
Acta Zoologica Fennica — Acta Zool Fenn
Acta Zoologica Fennica — AZFEAA
Acta Zoologica Hungarica — Acta Zoo Hung
Acta Zoologica Hungarica — AZI IUE4
Acta Zoologica Lilloana — Acta Zool Lilloana
Acta Zoologica Lilloana — AZOLA8
Acta Zoologica Mexicana — Acta Zool Mex
Acta Zoologica Mexicana — AZMXAY
Acta Zoologica Mexicana. Nueva Serie — Acta Zool Mex Nueva Ser
Acta Zoologica Sinica — Acta Zool Sin
Acta Zoologica (Stockholm) — Acta Zool (Stockh)
Acta Zoologica Taiwanica — Acta Zool Taiw
Acta Zootaxonomica Sinica — Acta Zootaxonomica Sin
Acta Zootechnica — Acta Zootech
Acta Zootechnica — ACZOAD
Acta Zootechnica. Universitatis Agriculturae (Nitra) — Acta Zootech Univ Agric (Nitra)
Actas Abreviadas de Academia General de Ciencias, Bellas-Letras y Nobles Artes — Actas Abr Acad Gen Ci
Actas. Academia Nacional de Ciencias de Cordoba — Act Acad Cienc Cordoba
Actas. Academia Nacional de Ciencias de Cordoba — Actas Acad Nac Cienc Cordoba
Actas. Academia Nacional de Ciencias Exactas, Fisicas, y Naturales de Lima [*A publication*] — Actas Acad Nac Cienc Exact Fis Natur Lima
Actas Bioquimicas — Actas Bioquim
Actas Ciba — Act Ci
Actas. Clinica Yodice — Actas Clin Yodice
Actas. Coloquio Internacional de Estudos Luso-Brasileiros — ACELB
Actas. Conferencia Internacional sobre la Utilizacion de la Energia Atomica con Fines Pacificos — Actas Conf Int Util Energ At Fines Pac
Actas. Congreso Geologico Argentino — Actas Cong Geol Argent
Actas. Congreso Internacional de Americanistas — ACIAm
Actas. Congreso Internacional de Historia de la Medicina — Actas Int Congr Hist Med
Actas. Congreso Internacional de Historia dos Descobrimentos — Actas Congr Int Hist Descobrimentos
Actas. Congreso Mundial de Psiquiatria — Actas Congr Mund Psiquiatr
Actas. Congreso Mundial de Veterinaria — Actas Congr Mund Vet
Actas. Congreso Mundial sobre Contaminacion del Aire — Actas Congr Mund Contam Aire
Actas. Congresso da Uniao Fitopatologica Mediterranea — Actas Congr Uniao Fitopatol Mediterr
Actas del Congreso Internacional de Geoquimica Organica — Actas Congr Int Geoquim Org
Actas Dermosifiliograficas — Actas Dermosifiliogr
Actas do Coloquio de Estudos Etnograficos Dr. Jose Leite de Vasconcelos — ACEELV
Actas do Coloquio Internacional de Estudos Luso-Brasileiros — ACIELB
Actas do Encontro Nacional de Catalise Basica e Aplicada (Industrial e Ambiental) — Actas Encontro Nac Catal Basica Apl Ind Ambiental
Actas. Jornadas Argentinas de Toxicologia Analitica — Actas Jorn Argent Toxicol Anal
Actas Jornadas Forestales — Actas Jornadas For
Actas Jornadas Geologicas Argentinas — Actas Jornadas Geol Argent
Actas Luso-Espanolas de Neurologia, Psiquiatria, y Ciencias Afines — Actas Luso-Esp Neurol Psiquiatr
Actas Luso-Espanolas de Neurologia, Psiquiatria, y Ciencias Afines — Actas-Luso Esp Neurol Psiquiatr Cienc Afines
Actas. Primera Reunion de Toponimia Pirenaica — ATopPir
Actas Procesales del Derecho Vivo — Derecho Vivo
Actas. Reunion Argentina de la Ciencia del Suelo — Actas Reun Argent Cienc Suelo
Actas. Reunion del Grupo de Trabajo del Cuaternario — Actas Reun Grupo Trab Cuat
Actas. Reunion Internacional sobre los Efectos Primarios de las Radiaciones en Quimica y Biologia — Actas Reun Int Efectos Primarios Radiaciones Quim Biol
Actas. Reunion Nacional el Cuaternario en Medios Semiaridos — Actas Reun Nac Cuat Medios Semiaridos
Actas. Simposio Iberoamericano de Catalise — Actas Simp Iberoam Catal
Actas Urologicas Espanolas — Actas Urol Esp
Actas y Memorias Conferencia Mundial de la Energia — Actas Mem Conf Mund Energ
Actas y Memorias. Congreso de Naturalistas Espanoles — Actas Mem Congr Nat Esp
Actas y Memorias. Congreso Internacional de Linguistica Romanica — AMCILR
Actas y Memorias. Sociedad Economica de los Amigos del Pais de la Provincia de Segovia — Actas Mem Soc Econ Amigos Pais Prov Segovia
Actas y Memorias. Sociedad Espanola de Antropologia, Etnografia, y Prehistoria — AMSEAEP
Acta-Scripta Metallurgica. Conference — Acta Scr Metall Conf
Acta-Scripta Metallurgica. Proceedings Series — Acta Scr Metall Proc Ser
Actes. Academie Nationale des Sciences, Belles-Lettres, et Arts de Bordeaux — AA Bordeaux
Actes. Colloque International — Actes Colloq Int
Actes. Colloque International. Institut pour l'Etude de la Renaissance et de l'Humanisme. Universite Libre de Bruxelles — Act Colloq Int Inst Etud Renaissance Hum
Actes. Colloque International. Soudage et Fusion par Faisceaux d'Electrons — Actes Colloq Int Soudage Fusion Faisceaux Electrons
Actes. Congres Benelux d'Histoire des Sciences — Act Congr Benelux Hist Sci
Actes. Congres Ceramique International — Actes Congr Ceram Int
Actes. Congres de la Federation International des Associations d'Etudes Classiques — ACEC
Actes. Congres International Ceramique — Actes Congr Int Ceram
Actes. Congres International d'Archeologie Chretienne/Atti. Congresso Internaztionale di Archeoogia Cristiana — ACIAC
Actes. Congres International de Catalyse — Actes Congr Int Catal
Actes. Congres International de Geochimie Organique — Actes Congr Int Geochim Org
Actes. Congres International de Numismatique — CIN
Actes. Congres International des Etudes Byzantines — Act Congr Int Etud Byzantines
Actes. Congres International des Orientalistes — ACIO
Actes. Congres International des Orientalistes — ACO
Actes. Congres International des Sciences Anthropologiques et Ethnologiques [*A publication*] — ACAE
Actes. Congres International d'Histoire des Sciences — Act Congr Int Hist Sci
Actes. Congres International d'Histoire des Sciences — Actes Congr Int Hist Sci
Actes. Congres International du Froid — Actes Congr Int Froid
Actes. Congres International. Societe Francaise de Radioprotection — Actes Congr Int Soc Fr Radioprot
Actes. Congres International. Union Internationale de Philosophie des Sciences — Act Congr Int Phil Sci
Actes. Congres Mondial Scientifique du Tabac — Actes Congr Mond Sci Tab
Actes. Congres Mondial. Societe Internationale pour l'Etude des Corps Gras — Actes Congr Mond Soc Int Etude Corps Gras
Actes. Congres National des Societes Savantes — Actes Cong Nat Soc Savant
Actes. Congres National des Societes Savantes. Section de Philologie et d'Historie — Actes CNS Sav
Actes. Congres National des Societes Savantes. Section des Sciences — Actes Congr Natl Soc Savantes Sect Sci
Actes. Congresso Internazionale di Archeologia Classica — Act CIAC
Actes de Chilander — A Chil
Actes de Colloques. Centre National pour l'Exploitations des Oceans (France) — Actes Colloq Cent Natl Exploit Oceans Fr
Actes de Dionysiou — A Dion
Actes de Kutlumus — A Kut
Actes de la Recherche en Sciences Sociales — Actes Rech Sci Soc
Actes de Philothee — A Phil
Actes de Xenophon — A Xen
Actes de Xeropotamou — A Xer
Actes de Zographou — A Zog
Actes d'Esphigmenou — A Esph
Actes du Congres International des Orientalistes — Atti Cong Or
Actes du Congresso Internazionale di Archeologia Classica — ACIA Cl
Actes du Museum d'Histoire Naturelle — Actes Mus Hist Nat
Actes du Pantocrator — A Pant
Actes du Protaton — A Prot
Actes du Xe Congres International d'Etudes Byzantines — Actes Xe Congr Internat Et Byzant
Actes et Colloques — Act Coll
Actes et Comptes Rendus de l'Association Colonies-Sciences — Actes C R Assoc Colon Sci
Actes et Conferences. Societe des Etudes Juives — Actes Confer Soc Et Juiv
Actes et Memoires. Congres International de Langue et Litterature du Midi de la France — AMCIM
Actes et Memoires. Congres International de Toponymie — AMCIT
Actes et Memoires. Congres International des Sciences Onomastiques — AMCISO
Actes. Institut National Genevois — Actes Inst Natl Genevois
Actes Juridiques Susiens — AJS
Actes. Museum d'Histoire Naturelle de Rouen — Act Mus Hist Natur Rouen
Actes/Rapports. Congres International de Numismatique — ACIN
Actes. Seminaire de Physiologie Comparee — Actes Semin Physiol Comp
Actes. Societe Helvetique des Sciences Naturelles — Actes Soc Helv Sci Nat
Actes. Societe Helvetique des Sciences Naturelles. Partie Scientifique — Actes Soc Helv Sci Nat Parte Sci
Actes. Societe Jurassienne d'Emulation — ASJE
Actes. Societe Linneenne de Bordeaux — Act Soc Linn Bordeaux
Actes. Societe Linneenne de Bordeaux — Actes Linn Soc Bord
Actes. Societe Linneenne de Bordeaux — Actes Soc Linn Bordeaux
Actes. Societe Linneenne de Bordeaux. Serie A — Actes Soc Linn Bordeaux Ser A
Actes. Societe Medicale des Hopitaux de Paris — Actes Soc Med Hop Paris
Actes. Societe Philologique — Actes Soc Philol
Actes. Symposium International des Sciences Physiques et Mathematiques dans la Premiere Moitie du 17e Siecle — Act Symp Int Sci Phys Math 17 Siecle
Actes. Symposium International sur les Ombelliferes — Actes Symp Int Ombelliferes
ACTH Related Peptides — ACTH Relat Pept
Actinides and Lanthanides. Reviews — Actinides Lanthanides Rev
Actinides. Electronic Structure and Related Properties — Actinides Electron Struct Relat Prop
Actinides Reviews — Actinides Rev
Actinometry and Atmospheric Optics. Reports. Interdepartmental Symposium on Actinometry and Atmospheric Optics — Actinometry Atmos Opt Rep Interdep Symp Actinometry Atmos Opt
Actinomycetes and Related Organisms — Actinomycetes Relat Org

Action [*Tunis*] — Act
Action Adaptation — Action Adap
Action for Better Education Newsletter — ABE News
Action for Development — Act Develop
Action Information — Action Info
Action Medicale — Action Med
Action Nationale — Act Nat
Action Nationale — Action Nat
Action Nationale — ActN
Action on Ageing. Proceedings of a Symposium — Action Ageing Proc Symp
Action Pharmaceutique — Act Pharm
Action Universitaire — Action Univ
Action, Use, and Natural Occurrence of Microbial Inhibitors in Food Proceedings — Action Use Nat Occurrence Microb Inhib Food Proc
Actions Chimiques et Biologiques des Radiations — Actions Chim Biol Radiat
Activated Sludge Process Control Series — Act Sludge Process Control Ser
Activation of Macrophages Proceedings. Workshop Conference Hoechst — Act Macrophages Proc Workshop Conf Hoechst
Active Systems (Great Britain) — Act Syst (GB)
Actividad Economica — Actividad Econ
Actividades Petroleras — Activ Petrol
Activitas Nervosa Superior [*Praha*] — ACNSA
Activitas Nervosa Superior — Act Nerv Super
Activitas Nervosa Superior [*Praha*] — Activ Nerv
Activitas Nervosa Superior [*Czechoslovakia*] — Activ Nerv Super
Activitas Nervosa Superior (Praha) — Act Nerv Super (Praha)
Activitatea Muzeelor — Act Muz
Activites. Port Autonome de Marseille — Activ Port Auto Marseille
Activities, Adaptation, and Aging — AAAA
Activities, Adaptation, and Aging — Act Adapt Aging
Activities Report. R & D Associates — Act Rep R & D Assoc
Activities Report. R & D Associates. Research and Development Associates for Military Food and Packaging Systems — Act Rep R & D Assoc Res Dev Assoc Mil Food Packag Syst
Activities Report. Research and Development Associates for Military Food and Packaging Systems — Act Rep Res Dev Assoc Mil Food Packag Syst
Activities Report. Research and Development Associates for Military Food and Packaging Systems, Incorporated — Act Rep Res Dev Assoc Mil Food Packag Syst Inc
Activity Bulletin for Teachers in Secondary Schools — Activity Bul
Activity Report of Reactor Physics Division — Act Rep React Phys Div
Activity-Driven CNS Changes in Learning and Development — Act Driven CNS Changes Learn Dev
Actos Universitarios. Universidad Nacional de La Plata — Act Univ La Plata
Acts and Joint Resolutions of the State of Iowa — Iowa Acts
Acts and Joint Resolutions. South Carolina — SC Acts
Acts and Resolves of Rhode Island and Providence Plantations — RI Acts & Resolves
Acts. Indiana — Ind Acts
Acts of Alabama — Ala Acts
Acts of Manitoba — Man Acts
Acts of New Brunswick — NB Acts
Acts of Prince Edward Island [*Canada*] — PEI Acts
Acts of the General Assembly of the Commonwealth of Virginia — Va Acts
Acts of the Legislature of West Virginia — W Va Acts
Acts, Resolves, and Consitutional Resolutions of the State of Maine — Me Acts
ACTU [*Australian Council of Trade Unions*] **Bulletin** — ACTU Bul
Actual (Merida, Venezuela) — ALM
Actual Specifying Engineer — Actual Specif Eng
Actualidad Bibliografica de Filosofia y Teologia — AB
Actualidad Medica — A Medica
Actualidad Medica — Act Med
Actualidad Medica — Actual Med
Actualidad Medica Peruana — Act Med Per
Actualidad Pediatrica — Act Ped
Actualidad Pediatrica (Granada) — Actual Pediatr (Granada)
Actualidades Biologicas — Actual Biol
Actualidades Biologicas (Lisbon) — Actual Biol Lisbon
Actualidades de la Ingenieria Agronomica — Actual Ing Agron
Actualidades Medicas — Actual Med
Actualidades (Venezuela) — AV
Actualite Automobile — Actual Auto
Actualite Chimique — Actual Chim
Actualite Chimique Canadienne — Actual Chim Can
Actualite Chimique et Industrielle — Actual Chim Ind
Actualite, Combustibles, Energie — ACOED
Actualite, Combustibles, Energie [*France*] — Actual Combust Energ
Actualite de la Formation Permanente — Actual Formation Perm
Actualite Dentaire — Act Dent
Actualite Economique — A Econ
Actualite Economique — Act Ec
Actualite Economique — Actu Econ
Actualite Economique — Actual Econ
Actualite Economique — Actualite Econ
Actualite Economique. Societe Canadienne de Science Economique — Actual Econ Soc Can Sci Econ
Actualite en Chine Populaire — Actual Chine Popul
Actualite Juridique — Act Jur
Actualite Juridique — Actual Jur
Actualite Juridique. Droit Administratif. Revue Mensuelle — AJDA
Actualite Legislative Dalloz [*France*] — ALD
Actualite Medicale — Actual Med
Actualite Religieuse dans le Monde — Actual Rel Mo
Actualite Therapeutique — Actual Ther
Actualites Agronomiques — Actual Agron
Actualites Agronomiques. Serie B — Actual Agron Ser B
Actualites Anatomo-Pathologiques — Act An-Path
Actualites Biochimiques — Act Biochim
Actualites Biochimiques — Actual Biochim
Actualites Biologiques (Paris) — Actual Biol (Paris)
Actualites Botaniques — Actual Bot
Actualites Cardiologiques et Angeiologiques Internationales — Act Card
Actualites de Biochimie Marine — Actual Biochim Mar
Actualites de Chimie Analytique, Organique, Pharmaceutique, et Bromatologique — Actual Chim Anal Org Pharm Bromatol
Actualites de Chimie Therapeutique — Actual Chim Ther
Actualites de Clinique Therapeutique — Act Clin Ther
Actualites de l'Hotel-Dieu — Actual Hotel-Dieu
Actualites de Physiologie Pathologique — Actual Physiol Pathol
Actualites d'Outre-Mer — Act O-Mer
Actualites Endocrinologiques — Actual Endocrinol
Actualites Endocrinologiques (Paris) — Actual Endocrinol (Paris)
Actualites et Culture Veterinaires — Act Cult Vet
Actualites Gynecologiques — Act Gyn
Actualites Gynecologiques — Actual Gynecol
Actualites Hematologiques — Act Hem
Actualites Hematologiques — Actual Hemat
Actualites Hematologiques — Actual Hematol
Actualites Hepato-Gastro-Enterologiques de l'Hotel-Dieu [*France*] — Actual Hepato-Gastro-Enterol Hotel-Dieu
Actualites Industrielles Lorraines — Actual Industr Lorraines
Actualites Marines — Actual Mar
Actualites Mathematiques — Actualites Math
Actualites Medico-Chirurgicales (Marseille) — Actual Med-Chir (Mars)
Actualites Nephrologiques. Hopital Necker — Actual Nephrol H Necker
Actualites Nephrologiques. Hopital Necker — Actual Nephrol Hop Necker
Actualites Neurophysiologiques — Act Neuro-Phys
Actualites Neurophysiologiques [*Paris*] — Actual Neurophysiol
Actualites Neurophysiologiques — ANUOA
Actualites Neurophysiologiques (Paris) — Actual Neurophysiol (Paris)
Actualites Odontostomatologiques [*Paris*] — Actual Odontostomatol
Actualites Pedagogiques — Actual Pedagog
Actualites Pharmacologiques — ACPMA
Actualites Pharmacologiques — Actual Pharm
Actualites Pharmacologiques — Actual Pharmacol
Actualites Pharmacologiques (Paris) — Actual Pharmacol (Paris)
Actualites Protozoologiques — Actual Protozool
Actualites Psychiatriques — Actual Psychiatr
Actualites Scientifiques et Industrielles — Actual Sci Ind
Actualites Scientifiques et Industrielles — Actualites Sci Indust
Actualites Scientifiques et Techniques — Actual Sci Techn
Actuarial Database — ACT
Actuarial Note — Actuar Note
Actuel Developpement — Actuel Dev
Actuel Developpement — Actuel Develop
Actuelle Gerontologie — Actuelle Gerontol
Actuelles des Droits de la Personne — Actuel Dr Person
Acupuncture and Electro-Therapeutics Research — Acupunct Electro-Ther Res
Acustica — ACUSA
Acustica — Acust
Acustica. Akustische Beihefte — Acustica Akust Beih
Acustica, United with Acta Acustica — Acust Acta Acust
Acute Care — ACUCDN
Acute Care Journal. International Society on Biotelemetry — Acute Care
Acute Diarrhoea in Childhood Symposium — Acute Diarrhoea Child Symp
Acute Fluid Replacement in the Therapy of Shock. Proceedings. Conference — Acute Fluid Replacement Ther Shock Pro Conf
Acute Leukemias. Pharmacokinetics and Management of Relapsed and Refractory Disease — Acute Leuk
Ad Astra — GADS
Ad Forum — ADF
Ad Nova Acta Eruditorum. Quae Lipsiae Publicantur. Supplementa — Nova Acta Erud Suppl
Ad Novas. Norwegian Geographical Studies — ANNGS
AD (Publication) (American Society of Mechanical Engineers, Aerospace Division) — AD Publ Am Soc Mech Eng Aerosp Div
Adabietsunaslik va Tilsunaslik Masalalari/Voprosy Literaturovedenija i Jazykoznanija (Taskent) — ATMTas
Adalbert Stifter Institut des Landes Oberoesterreich. Vierteljahresschrift — ASILO
ADAM [*Arts, Drama, Architecture, Music*] **International Review** — ADAM Int R
ADAM [*Arts, Drama, Architecture, Music*] **International Review** — AIR
Adam Mickiewicz University. Institute of Chemistry. Seria Chemia — Adam Mickiewicz Univ Inst Chem Ser Chem
Adansonia — Adans
Adansonia — ADNSA6
Adansonia. New Series — Adansonia NS
Adaptation to Environment. Essays on the Physiology of Marine Animals — Adapt Environ Essays Physiol Mar Anim
Adaptatsii Pingvinov — Adapt Pingvinov
Adapted Physical Activity Quarterly — Adapted P Act Q
Adaptivnye Osobennosti i Evolyutsiya Ptits Plenarnye Doklady Vsesoyuznoi Ornitologicheskoi Konferentsii — Adapt Osob Evol Ptits Plenarnye Dokl Vses Ornitol Konf
Adaptivnye Sistemy Avtomaticheskogo Upravleniya — Adapt Sist Avtom Upr
ADAS [*Agricultural Development and Advisory Service*] **Quarterly Review** — ADAS Q Rev
ADAS [*Agricultural Development and Advisory Service*] **Quarterly Review (Great Britain)** — ADAS Q Rev (GB)

Adate. Association pour le Developpement de l'Audio-visuel et de la Technologieen Education — Adate Assoc Dev Audio Vis Tech Ed
Addictive Behaviors — ADBED9
Addictive Behaviors — Addict Behav
Addictive Diseases — Addict Dis
Addictive Diseases — ADDIDV
Addis Ababa University. Bulletin. Geophysical Observatory — Addis Ababa Univ Bull Geophys Obs
Addison-Wesley Series in Computer Science and Information Processing — Addison-Wesley Ser Comput Sci Inform Process
Addison-Wesley Studies in Nonlinearity — Addison Wesley Stud Nonlinearity
Additional Series. Royal Botanic Gardens — Additional Ser Roy Bot
Additive fuer Schmierstoffe — Addit Schmierst
Additives for Rubber and Plastics. Papers Presented at the Meeting of the Chemical Marketing Research Association — Addit Rubber Plast Pap Meet
ADDLIS [*Alcoholism and Drug Dependence Librarians and Information Services*] **News** — ADDLIS N
Addresses and Proceedings. Ontario Soil and Crop Improvement Association — Address Proc Ontario Soil Crop Impr Ass
Addresses and Proceedings. Saskatchewan University Farm and Home Week — Address Proc Saskatchewan Univ Farm Home Week
Adelaide Children's Hospital. Records — Adelaide Children's Hosp Records
Adelaide. City. Municipal Year Book — City Adelaide Munic Yb
Adelaide Law Reports — Ad L R
Adelaide Law Review — Adel L Rev
Adelaide Law Review — Adel Law R
Adelaide Law Review — Adel Law Rev
Adelaide Law Review — Adel LR
Adelaide Law Review — Adelaide L Rev
Adelaide Law Review — Adelaide Law Rev
Adelaide Law Review — Adelaide LR
Adelaide Law Review — ALR
Adelaide Stock and Station Journal — Adel Stock and Station J
Adelaide University Graduates Union. Gazette — Adel Univ Grad Gaz
Adelaide University Graduates Union. Monthly Newsletter and Gazette — Adel Univ Grad Union Gaz
Adelaide University. Magazine — Adel Univ Mag
Adelaide University. Magazine — AUM
Adelphi — Ad
Adelphi — Adel
Adelphi Papers — Adelphi P
Adenine Arabinoside; an Antiviral Agent. Symposium — Adenine Arabinoside Antiviral Agent Symp
Adequacy of Dialysis. Proceedings of a Conference — Adequacy Dial Pro Conf
Adevarul Literar — ADL
ADFA [*Alcohol and Drug Foundation, Australia*] **Audio Visual Catalogue** — ADFA Aud Vis Cat
Adformatie. Weekblad voor Reclame en Marketing — ADT
Adgeziya Rasplavov — Adgez Rasplavov
Adgeziya Rasplavov i Paika Materialov — Adgez Rasplavov Paika Mater
Adhaesion — Adhaes
Adhaesion. Kleben and Dichten — Adhaes Kleben Dichten
Adherent — ADH
Adhesion and Adhesives [*Japan*] — Adhes Adhes
Adhesion and Adhesives (Kyoto) — Adhes Adhes Kyoto
Adhesion and Adsorption of Polymers — Adhes Adsorpt Polym
Adhesion Society. Proceedings of the Seventeenth Annual Meeting and the Symposium on Particle Adhesion — Adhes Soc Proc Seventeenth Annu Meet Symp Part Adhes
Adhesive and Sealant Council. Journal — Adhes Sealant Counc J
Adhesives Age — Adhes Age
Adhesives Age — Adhesives
Adhesives Age Directory — Adhesive D
Adhesives and Resins — Adhes Res
Adhesives and Resins — Adhes Resins
Adhesives and Sealants — Adhes Sealants
Adhesives Technology Annual — Adhes Tech Ann
Adipose Child Medical and Psychological Aspects. International Symposium — Adipose Child Int Symp
Adipose Tissue. Regulation and Metabolic Functions — Adipose Tissue Regul Metab Funct
Adipositas im Kindesalter Symposium — Adipositas Kindesalter Symp
Adipositas, Kreislauf, Anorektika. Vortraege des Symposions — Adipositas Kreislauf Anorektika Vortr Symp
Adjuvant Therapy of Cancer — ATCCEJ
Adjuvant Therapy of Cancer. Proceedings of the International Conference — Adjuvant Ther Cancer
Adjuvant Therapy of Cancer. Proceedings of the International Conference — Adjuvant Ther Cancer Proc Int Conf
Adler Museum Bulletin — Adler Mus Bull
ADL-Nachrichten — ADL-Nachr
ADM [*Asociacion Dental Mexicana*] **Revista** [*Mexico*] — ADM Rev
ADM. Revista de la Asociacion Dental Mexicana — ADM Rev Asoc Dent Mex
Admap — A
Administracao Centralizada Balancos — Admin Cent Bal
Administracion, Desarrollo, Integracion — Admin Desarr Integ
Administracion y Desarrollo — Adm y Desarr
Administrateur Hospitalier — Admin Hosp
Administratief Lexicon — Adm Lex
Administratief Lexicon — AL
Administration — Admin
Administration and Policy in Mental Health — Adm Policy Ment Health
Administration and Society — Adm and Soc
Administration and Society — Adm Socie
Administration and Society — Admin and Society
Administration and Society — ADS
Administration in Mental Health — Adm Ment He
Administration in Mental Health — Adm Ment Health
Administration in Mental Health — Admin Ment Hlth
Administration in Social Work — Adm Soc Work
Administration in Social Work — ASW
Administration Laboratory Project File [*Database*] — ALP
Administrativ Tidsskrift — Adm Tss
Administrative Change — Adm Change
Administrative Digest — Admin Dig
Administrative Law — Admin Law
Administrative Law Decisions. Australian — ALD
Administrative Law Decisions. Notes — ALN
Administrative Law Review — Ad L Rev
Administrative Law Review — Ad Law Rev
Administrative Law Review — Ad LR
Administrative Law Review — Adm L Rev
Administrative Law Review — Adm Law R
Administrative Law Review — Adm LR
Administrative Law Review — ALR
Administrative Law Review — IALR
Administrative Law Second. Pike and Fischer — Admin L 2d P & F
Administrative Management — A/M
Administrative Management — Adm Manage
Administrative Management — Adm Mgmt
Administrative Management — Adm Mgt
Administrative Management — Admin Manage
Administrative Management — Admin Mgmt
Administrative Notes. Information Dissemination. US Superintendent of Document s. Library Programs Service — Admin Note
Administrative Radiology — Adm Radiol
Administrative Rules and Regulations of the Government of Guam — Guam Admin R & Regs
Administrative Rules of Montana — Mont Admin R
Administrative Rules of South Dakota — SD Admin R
Administrative Rules of the State of Utah — Utah Admin R
Administrative Science Quarterly — Adm Sci
Administrative Science Quarterly — Adm Sci Q
Administrative Science Quarterly — Adm Sci Qua
Administrative Science Quarterly — Admin Sci Q
Administrative Science Quarterly — Admin Science Q
Administrative Science Quarterly — ASQ
Administrative Science Review — Admin Sci R
Administrative Staff College of India. Journal of Management — Admin Staff Col India J Man
Administrator. Manitoba Association of Principals — Admin Man
Administrators' Bulletin — Adm Bull
Administrator's Collection — Admin Collect
Administrator's Notebook — Adm Notebk
Admiralty Marine Science Publication — Admiralty Mar Sci Publ
Admixtures for Concrete. Improvement of Properties. Proceedings. International Symposium — Admixtures Concr Proc Int Symp
Adolescence — ADOL
Adolescence — ADOLA
Adolescence — Adoles
Adolescence — GADL
Adolescent Medicine — Adol Med
Adolescent Medicine State of the Arts Reviews — Adolesc Med State Arts Rev
Adolescent Mental Health Abstracts — Adolesc Ment Health Abstr
Adolescent Psychiatry — Adolesc Psychiatry
Adolescent Psychiatry — ADPSDJ
Adriamycin-Symposium — Adriamycin-Symp
Adriatic Meeting on Particle Physics — Adriat Meet Part Phys
Adsorbtsiya i Adsorbenty — Adsorbts Adsorbenty
Adsorbtsiya i Poristost. Trudy Vsesoyuznoi Konferentsii po Teoreticheskim Voprosam Adsorbtsii — Adsorbts Poristost Tr Vses Konf Teor Vopr Adsorbts
Adsorbtsiya i Poristost Trudy Vsesoyuznoi Konferentsii po Teoreticheskim Voprosam Adsorbtsii — Adsorbtsiya Poristost Tr Vses Konf Teor Vopr Adsorbtsii
Adsorption News — Adsorpt News
Adult Diseases [*Japan*] — Adult Dis
Adult Education — Adult Ed
Adult Education — Adult Educ
Adult Education — AE
Adult Education and the Library — Adult Ed and Lib
Adult Education Bulletin — Adult Ed Bul
Adult Education Journal — Adult Ed J
Adult Education Journal — AEJ
Adult Education Quarterly — Adult Educ Q
Adult Education-Washington — Adult Ed-W
Adult Leadership — A Lead
Adult Leadership — Adult Lead
Adult Learning — IADL
Adult Probation — A Prob
Advance Abstracts of Contributions on Fisheries and Aquatic Sciences in India — Adv Abstr Contrib Fish Aquat Sci India
Advance Abstracts of Contributions on Fisheries and Aquatic Sciences in India — AFQSB2
Advance Bibliography of Contents: Political Science and Government — ABC Pol Sci
Advance California Appellate Reports — ACA
Advance California Reports — AC
Advance Data — Adv Data
Advance Data — ADVSDF
Advance Data from Vital and Health Statistics — Advance Data

Advance Guard — AG
Advance in Education — Adv Ed
Advance Legislative Service to the General Statutes of North Carolina — NC Adv Legis
Advance of Phycology in Japan — Adv Phycol Japan
Advance Proceedings. Fluid Power Testing Symposium — Adv Proc Fluid Power Test Symp
Advance Release of Data for the Statistical Year Book of the Electric Utility Industry — Elec Data
Advance. Washington State University. College of Agriculture Research Center — Adv Wash State Univ Coll Agric Res Cent
Advanced and Next-Generation Satellites — Adv Next Gener Satell
Advanced Animal Breeder — Adv Anim Breed
Advanced Anthracite Technology and Research. Proceedings of the Conference [*A publication*] — Adv Anthracite Technol Res Proc Conf
Advanced Ceramic Materials — Adv Ceram Mat
Advanced Ceramic Processing and Technology — Adv Ceram Process Technol
Advanced Ceramics. Proceedings. International Symposium — Adv Ceram Proc Int Symp
Advanced Composite Materials — Adv Compos Mater
Advanced Composite Materials. New Materials, Applications, Processing, Evaluation, and Databases. Proceedings. France-Japan Seminar on Composite Materials — Adv Compos Mater Proc Fr Jpn Semin Compos Mater
Advanced Computational Methods for Boundary and Interior Layers — Adv Comput Methods Bound Inter Layers
Advanced Course in Astrophysics — Adv Course Astrophys
Advanced Course in Industrial Toxicology. Papers — Adv Course Ind Toxicol Pap
Advanced Course. Swiss Society of Astronomy and Astrophysics — Adv Course Swiss Soc Astron Astrophys
Advanced Cryogenics — Adv Cryog
Advanced Drug Delivery Reviews — Adv Drug Delivery Rev
Advanced Energy Conversion [*England*] — Adv Energy Convers
Advanced Engineering Mathematics — Adv Engrg Math
Advanced Fiber Communications Technologies — Adv Fiber Commun Technol
Advanced Fibrous Reinforced Composites — Adv Fibrous Reinf Compos
Advanced Heat Transfer in Manufacturing and Processing of New Materials — Adv Heat Transfer Manuf Process New Mater
Advanced Hematology — Adv Hematol
Advanced Lectures in Mathematics — Adv Lectures Math
Advanced Management — Adv Manag
Advanced Management — Adv Mgmt
Advanced Management Journal — Adv Manage J
Advanced Management Journal — Adv Mgmt J
Advanced Management Journal — Advan Manage J
Advanced Management Journal — Advanced Mgmt Jrnl
Advanced Management Journal — Advanced Mgt
Advanced Management Journal — Advanced Mgt J
Advanced Management Journal — AMJ
Advanced Management-Office Executive — Advanced Mgt-Office Exec
Advanced Manufacturing Technology [*Database*] — AMT
Advanced Materials and Processes — Adv Mater Processes
Advanced Materials for Optics and Electronics — Adv Mater Opt Electron
Advanced Materials Research (Zug, Switzerland) — Adv Mater Res Zug Switz
Advanced Materials (Weinheim) — Adv Mater Weinh
Advanced Medicine — Adv Med
Advanced Medicine Symposium — Adv Med Symp
Advanced Methods in Protein Sequence Determination — Adv Methods Protein Sequence Determination
Advanced Optical Manufacturing and Testing — Adv Opt Manuf Test
Advanced Performance Materials — Adv Perform Mater
Advanced Quantitative Techniques in the Social Sciences — Adv Quant Tech Soc Sci
Advanced Reactors. Physics, Design, and Economics. Proceedings. International Conference — Adv React Phys Des Econ Proc Int Conf
Advanced Religious Studies — Adv Rel St
Advanced Religious Studies — ARS
Advanced Research Projects. Agency Workshop on Needs of the Department of Defense for Catalysis — Adv Res Proj Agency Workshop Needs Dep Def Catal
Advanced Semiconductor Epitaxial Growth Processes and Lateral and Vertical Fabrication — Adv Semicond Epitaxial Growth Processes Lateral Vert Fabr
Advanced Series in Agricultural Sciences — Adv Ser Agric Sci
Advanced Series in Agricultural Sciences — ASASDF
Advanced Series in Astrophysics and Cosmology — Adv Ser Astrophys Cosmol
Advanced Series in Dynamical Systems — Adv Ser Dynam Systems
Advanced Series in Electrical and Computer Engineering — Adv Ser Electr Comput Engrg
Advanced Series in Management — Adv Ser Management
Advanced Series in Mathematical Physics — Adv Ser Math Phys
Advanced Series in Nonlinear Dynamics — Adv Ser Nonlinear Dynam
Advanced Series in Physical Chemistry — Adv Ser Phys Chem
Advanced Series on Circuits and Systems — Adv Ser Circuits Systems
Advanced Series on Complex Systems — Adv Ser Complex Systems
Advanced Series on Theoretical Physical Science — Adv Ser Theoret Phys Sci
Advanced Solar Energy Technology Newsletter — Adv Sol En Tech Newsl
Advanced Studies in Contemporary Mathematics — Adv Stud Contemp Math
Advanced Studies in Pure Mathematics — Adv Stud Pure Math
Advanced Studies in Pure Mathematics [*Elsevier Book Series*] — ASPM
Advanced Studies in Theoretical and Applied Econometrics — Adv Stud Theoret Appl Econometrics
Advanced Study Institute Book — Adv Stud Inst Book
Advanced Surface Engineering — Adv Surf Eng
Advanced Techniques for Integrated Circuit Processing — Adv Tech Integr Circuit Process
Advanced Techniques for Material Investigation and Fabrication — Adv Tech Mater Invest Fabr
Advanced Techniques in Biological Electron Microscopy — Adv Tech Biol Electron Microsc
Advanced Technology Libraries — Adv Tech Lib
Advanced Technology Libraries — Adv Technol Libr
Advanced Textbooks in Economics — Adv Textbooks Econom
Advanced Textbooks in Economics [*Amsterdam*] — Advanced Textbooks in Econom
Advanced Textbooks in Economics [*Elsevier Book Series*] — ATE
Advanced Texts in Econometrics — Adv Texts Econometrics
Advanced Therapeutics — Adv Ther
Advanced Vehicle News — Adv Vehicle News
Advanced Waste Treatment Research Publication — Adv Waste Treat Res Publ
Advancement of Science — Ad Sci
Advancement of Science — ADSCAH
Advancement of Science — Adv of Science
Advancement of Science — Adv Sci
Advancement of Science — Advance Sci
Advancement of Science — Advancement Sci
Advancement of Science — Advmt Sci
Advancement of Science (London) — Advmt Sci (Lond)
Advancement of Science. Report. British Association for the Advancement of Science — Advancem Sci
Advances and Technical Standards in Neurosurgery — Adv Tech Stand Neurosurg
Advances in Acarology — ADACAT
Advances in Acarology — Adv Acarol
Advances in Activation Analysis — ADAYAR
Advances in Activation Analysis — Adv Act Anal
Advances in Adhesives and Sealants Technology. Conference Papers — Adv Adhes Sealants Technol Conf Pap
Advances in Aerobiology. Proceedings. International Conference on Aerobiology — Adv Aerobiol Proc Int Conf Aerobiol
Advances in Aerosol Physics — Adv Aerosol Phys
Advances in Aerosol Physics (English Translation) — Adv Aerosol Phys Engl Transl
Advances in Agricultural Biotechnology — Adv Agric Biotech
Advances in Agricultural Biotechnology — Adv Agric Biotechnol
Advances in Agricultural Technology. AAT-W. United States Department of Agriculture. Science and Education Administration. Western Region — Adv Agric Technol AAT W US Dep Agric Sci Educ Adm West Reg
Advances in Agronomy — ADAGA7
Advances in Agronomy — Adv Agron
Advances in Agronomy — Advan Agron
Advances in Agronomy — Advances Agron
Advances in Agronomy and Crop Science — AACSE2
Advances in Agronomy and Crop Science — Adv Agron Crop Sci
Advances in Alcohol and Substance Abuse — AASA
Advances in Alcohol and Substance Abuse — AASADR
Advances in Alcohol and Substance Abuse — Adv Alcohol & Subst Abuse
Advances in Alcohol and Substance Abuse — Adv Alcohol Subst Abuse
Advances in Alicyclic Chemistry — Adv Alicyclic Chem
Advances in Analytical Chemistry and Instrumentation — AACIA2
Advances in Analytical Chemistry and Instrumentation — Adv Anal Chem Instrum
Advances in Analytical Toxicology — Adv Anal Toxicol
Advances in Anatomy, Embryology, and Cell Biology — Adv Anat Embryol Cell Biol
Advances in Anatomy, Embryology, and Cell Biology — EAENA3
Advances in Andrology — Adv Androl
Advances in Animal Physiology and Animal Nutrition — Adv Anim Physiol Anim Nutr
Advances in Animal Physiology and Animal Nutrition — FTPTAG
Advances in Antimicrobial and Antineoplastic Chemotherapy — AAACCA
Advances in Antimicrobial and Antineoplastic Chemotherapy — Adv Antimicrob Antineoplast Chemother
Advances in Applied Clifford Algebras — Adv Appl Clifford Algebras
Advances in Applied Mathematics — Adv Appl Ma
Advances in Applied Mathematics — Adv Appl Math
Advances in Applied Mechanics — Adv Appl Mech
Advances in Applied Mechanics — Adv in Appl Mech
Advances in Applied Mechanics — Advan Appl Mech
Advances in Applied Mechanics — Advances in Appl Mech
Advances in Applied Mechanics. Supplement — Adv Appl Mech Suppl
Advances in Applied Microbiology — ADAMAP
Advances in Applied Microbiology — Adv Appl Microb
Advances in Applied Microbiology — Adv Appl Microbiol
Advances in Applied Probability — Adv Ap Pr
Advances in Applied Probability — Adv Appl P
Advances in Applied Probability [*England*] — Adv Appl Prob
Advances in Applied Probability — Adv Appl Probab
Advances in Applied Probability — Advan Appl Probab
Advances in Applied Probability — Advances in Appl Probability
Advances in Applied Statistics — Adv Appl Statist
Advances in Aquatic Microbiology — AAPBBD
Advances in Aquatic Microbiology — Adv Aquat Microbiol
Advances in Archaeological Method and Theory — A Meth Th
Advances in Archaeological Method and Theory — Adv Archaeol Method Theory
Advances in Archaeological Method and Theory — Advan Archaeol Method Theory
Advances in Artificial Hip and Knee Joint Technology — Adv Artif Hip Knee Jt Technol
Advances in Astronomy and Astrophysics — Adv Astron Astrophys
Advances in Asymmetric Synthesis — Adv Asymmetric Synth

Advances in Atomic and Molecular Physics — Adv At Mol Phys
Advances in Atomic Spectroscopy — Adv At Spectrosc
Advances in Audiology — ADAUEJ
Advances in Audiology — Adv Audiol
Advances in Automated Analysis. Technicon International Congress — Adv Autom Anal Technicon Int Congr
Advances in Behavioral Biology — ADBBBW
Advances in Behavioral Biology — Adv Behav Biol
Advances in Behavioral Pharmacology — Adv Behav Pharmacol
Advances in Behaviour Research and Therapy — ABRTDI
Advances in Behaviour Research and Therapy — Adv Behav Res Ther
Advances in Beta-Adrenergic Blocking Therapy. Sotalol Proceedings. International Symposium — Adv Beta-Adrenergic Blocking Ther Sotalol Proc Int Symp
Advances in Bile Acid Research. Bile Acid Meeting — Adv Bile Acid Res Bile Acid Meet
Advances in Biochemical Engineering — ADBEA6
Advances in Biochemical Engineering — Adv Biochem Eng
Advances in Biochemical Engineering/Biotechnology — Adv Biochem Eng/Biotechnol
Advances in Biochemical Pharmacology — Adv Biochem Pharmacol
Advances in Biochemical Psychopharmacology — Adv Biochem Psychopharmacol
Advances in Biochemistry and Biophysics [*People's Republic of China*] — Adv Biochem Biophys
Advances in Bioengineering — Adv Bioeng
Advances in Bioengineering and Instrumentation — Adv Bioeng Instrum
Advances in Biological and Medical Physics — Adv Biol Med Phys
Advances in Biological Psychiatry — Adv Biol Psychiatry
Advances in Biological Waste Treatment. Proceedings. Conference on Biological Waste Treatment — Adv Biol Waste Treat Proc Conf
Advances in Biology (Berlin) — Adv Biol Berlin
Advances in Biology of the Skin — Adv Biol Skin
Advances in Biomaterials — Adv Biomater
Advances in Biomedical Alcohol Research. Congress. International Society for Biomedical Research on Alcoholism — Adv Biomed Alcohol Res Congr Int Soc Biomed Res Alcohol
Advances in Biomedical Engineering — ABEGB
Advances in Biomedical Engineering — ABEGBE
Advances in Biomedical Engineering — Adv Biomed Eng
Advances in Biomedical Engineering and Medical Physics — Adv Biomed Eng Med Phys
Advances in Biomolecular Simulations. Joint International Conference of IBM and Division de Chimie Physique — Adv Biomol Simul Jt Int Conf IBM Div Chim Phys
Advances in Biophysical Chemistry — Adv Biophys Chem
Advances in Biophysics [*Tokyo*] — Adv Biophys
Advances in Biosciences (Muzaffarnagar, India) — Adv Biosci Muzaffarnagar India
Advances in Biotechnological Processes — Adv Biotech Processes
Advances in Biotechnological Processes — Adv Biotechnol Processes
Advances in Blood Grouping — Adv Blood Grouping
Advances in Botanical Research — Adv Bot Res
Advances in Bryology — Adv Bryol
Advances in Cancer Chemotherapy — Adv Cancer Chemother
Advances in Cancer Control. Innovations and Research. Proceedings. Annual Meeting — Adv Cancer Control Proc Annu Meet
Advances in Cancer Research — Adv Cancer Res
Advances in Cancer Research — Advances Cancer Res
Advances in Carbene Chemistry — Adv Carbene Chem
Advances in Carbohydrate Analysis — Adv Carbohydr Anal
Advances in Carbohydrate Chemistry [*Later, Advances in Carbohydrate Chemistry and Biochemistry*] — Adv Carbohydr Chem
Advances in Carbohydrate Chemistry [*Later, Advances in Carbohydrate Chemistry and Biochemistry*] — Advances Carbohyd Chem
Advances in Carbohydrate Chemistry and Biochemistry — Adv Carbohyd Chem
Advances in Carbohydrate Chemistry and Biochemistry — Adv Carbohydr Chem Biochem
Advances in Carboyhydrate Chemistry — Advan Carbohyd Chem
Advances in Carboyhydrate Chemistry and Biochemistry — Advan Carbohyd Chem Biochem
Advances in Cardiac Surgery — Adv Card Surg
Advances in Cardiology — Adv Cardiol
Advances in Cardiopulmonary Diseases — Adv Cardiopulm Dis
Advances in Cardiovascular Physics — Adv Cardiovasc Phys
Advances in Catalysis and Related Subjects — Adv Catal
Advances in Catalysis. Science and Technology. Proceedings. National Symposium on Catalysis — Adv Catal Proc Natl Symp Catal
Advances in Catalytic Processes — Adv Catal Processes
Advances in Cell and Molecular Biology — Adv Cell Mol Biol
Advances in Cell Biology — Adv Cell Biol
Advances in Cell Culture — ADC
Advances in Cell Culture — Adv Cell Cult
Advances in Cellular Neurobiology — ADCND7
Advances in Cellular Neurobiology — Adv Cell Neurobiol
Advances in Cement Research — Adv Cem Res
Advances in Cementitious Materials — Adv Cem Mater
Advances in Cereal Science and Technology — ACSTDU
Advances in Cereal Science and Technology — Adv Cereal Sci Technol
Advances in Chemical Diagnosis and Treatment of Metabolic Disorders — Adv Chem Diagn Treat Metab Disord
Advances in Chemical Engineering — Adv Chem Eng
Advances in Chemical Engineering — Advan Chem Eng
Advances in Chemical Physics — ADCPAA
Advances in Chemical Physics — Adv Chem Phys
Advances in Chemistry — Adv Chem
Advances in Chemistry and Chemical Application (Kyoto) — Adv Chem Chem Appl (Kyoto)
Advances in Chemistry Series — ADCSAJ
Advances in Chemistry Series — Adv Chem Se
Advances in Chemistry Series — Adv Chem Ser
Advances in Chemistry Series — Advan Chem Ser
Advances in Chemistry Series — Advances in Chem Ser
Advances in Chemoreception — Adv Chemoreception
Advances in Chemotherapy — ADCMAZ
Advances in Chemotherapy — Adv Chemother
Advances in Chemotherapy — Advances Chemother
Advances in Child Development and Behavior — ADCDA8
Advances in Child Development and Behavior — Adv Child Dev Behav
Advances in Chitin Science — Adv Chitin Sci
Advances in Chromatography — ADCYA3
Advances in Chromatography — Adv Chromatogr
Advances in Chromatography (New York) — Adv Chromatogr (NY)
Advances in Cladistics — ADCLDZ
Advances in Cladistics — Adv Cladistics
Advances in Classical Trajectory Methods — Adv Classical Trajectory Methods
Advances in Clinical Cardiology — Adv Clin Cardiol
Advances in Clinical Chemistry — ACLCA9
Advances in Clinical Chemistry — Adv Clin Chem
Advances in Clinical Chemistry — Advan Clin Chem
Advances in Clinical Enzymology — ACENEB
Advances in Clinical Enzymology — Adv Clin Enzymol
Advances in Clinical Nutrition. Proceedings. International Symposium — Adv Clin Nutr Proc Int Symp
Advances in Clinical Pharmacology — ACLPDH
Advances in Clinical Pharmacology — Adv Clin Pharmacol
Advances in Clinical Pharmacology — AVCPAY
Advances in CNS Drug-Receptor Interactions — Adv CNS Drug Recept Interact
Advances in Coal Utilization Technology. Symposium Papers — Adv Coal Util Technol Symp Pap
Advances in Colloid and Interface Science — Adv Coll In
Advances in Colloid and Interface Science — Adv Coll Inter Sci
Advances in Colloid and Interface Science — Adv Colloid and Interface Sci
Advances in Colloid and Interface Science — Adv Colloid Interface Sci
Advances in Colloid Science — Adv Colloid Sci
Advances in Colloid Science — Advances Colloid Sci
Advances in Color Chemistry Series — Adv Color Chem Ser
Advances in Comparative Leukemia Research. Proceedings. International Symposium on Comparative Research on Leukemia and Related Diseases — Adv Comp Leuk Res Proc Int Symp
Advances in Comparative Physiology and Biochemistry — ACPBAQ
Advances in Comparative Physiology and Biochemistry — Adv Comp Physiol Biochem
Advances in Composite Materials. Proceedings. International Conference on Composite Materials — Adv Compos Mater Proc Int Conf
Advances in Computational Economics — Adv Comput Econom
Advances in Computational Mathematics — Adv Comput Math
Advances in Computer Security Management — Adv Comp Sec Man
Advances in Computers — Adv Comp
Advances in Computers — Adv Comput
Advances in Consumer Research Proceedings — AIC
Advances in Continuous Processing in the Non-Ferrous Metals Industry. Edited Proceedings. BNF [*British Non-Ferrous*] **International Conference** — Adv Contin Process Non-Ferrous Met Ind Ed Proc BNF Int Conf
Advances in Contraception — ADCOEB
Advances in Contraception — Adv Contracept
Advances in Contraceptive Delivery Systems [*Kiawah Island, South Carolina*] — Adv Contracept Deliv Syst
Advances in Contraceptive Delivery Systems — Adv Contracept Delivery Syst
Advances in Control Systems — Adv Control Syst
Advances in Control Systems and Signal Processing — Adv Control Systems Signal Process
Advances in Corrosion Science and Technology — Adv Corr Sci Technol
Advances in Corrosion Science and Technology — Adv Corros Sci Technol
Advances in Cryogenic Engineering — Adv Cryog Eng
Advances in Cryogenic Engineering — Advan Cryog Eng
Advances in Crystallography and Crystal Growth. Proceedings. Indo-Soviet Symposium on Crystal Growth — Adv Crystallogr Cryst Growth Proc Indo Sov Symp Cryst Growth
Advances in Cyclic Nucleotide and Protein Phosphorylation Research — ACNREY
Advances in Cyclic Nucleotide and Protein Phosphorylation Research — Adv Cyclic Nucleotide Protein Phosphorylation Res
Advances in Cyclic Nucleotide Research — ACNRCW
Advances in Cyclic Nucleotide Research — Adv Cyclic Nucleotide Res
Advances in Cycloaddition — Adv Cycloaddit
Advances in Cytopharmacology — ADCYB4
Advances in Cytopharmacology — Adv Cytopharmacol
Advances in Dendritic Macromolecules — Adv Dendritic Macromol
Advances in Dental Research — Adv Dent Res
Advances in Dermatology — Adv Dermatol
Advances in Desalination. Proceedings. National Symposium on Desalination — Adv Desalin Proc Nat Symp Desalin
Advances in Desert and Arid Land Technology and Development — Adv Desert Arid Land Technol Dev
Advances in Developmental and Behavioral Pediatrics — ADBPE9
Advances in Developmental Biochemistry — Adv Dev Biochem
Advances in Developmental Biology — Adv Dev Biol
Advances in Developmental Psychology — Adv Dev Psychol
Advances in Diesel Particulate Control — Adv Diesel Part Control

Advances in Differential Equations — Adv Differential Equations
Advances in Discrete Mathematics and Computer Science — Adv Discrete Math Comput Sci
Advances in Disease Prevention — AIDP
Advances in DNA Sequence Specific Agents — Adv DNA Sequence Specific Agents
Advances in Drug Research — ADRRAN
Advances in Drug Research — Adv Drug Res
Advances in Drying — Adv Drying
Advances in Earth and Planetary Sciences — Adv Earth and Planet Sci
Advances in Earth and Planetary Sciences — Adv Earth Planet Sci
Advances in Earth-Oriented Applications of Space Technology [*Later, Earth-Oriented Applications of Space Technology*] — Adv Earth Oriented Appl Space Technol
Advances in Earth-Oriented Applications of Space Technology [*Later, Earth-Oriented Applications of Space Technology*] — AEOTD
Advances in Ecological Research — Adv Ecol Res
Advances in Ecological Research — Advances Ecol Res
Advances in Ecological Research — AELRAY
Advances in Econometrics — Adv Econometrics
Advances in Economic Botany — Adv Econ Bot
Advances in Economic Botany — AEBOED
Advances in Electrochemistry and Electrochemical Engineering — Adv Electrochem Electrochem Eng
Advances in Electrochemistry and Electrochemical Engineering — AEEEA
Advances in Electron Transfer Chemistry — Adv Electron Transfer Chem
Advances in Electron Tube Techniques — Adv Electron Tube Tech
Advances in Electronic Circuit Packaging — Adv Electron Circuit Packag
Advances in Electronics — Adv Electron
Advances in Electronics and Electron Physics — Adv Electron Electron Phys
Advances in Electronics and Electron Physics — Advan Electron and Electron Phys
Advances in Electronics and Electron Physics. Supplement — Adv Electron Electron Phys Suppl
Advances in Electrophoresis — Adv Electrophor
Advances in Endocrinology and Metabolism — Adv Endocrinol Metab
Advances in Endogenous and Exogenous Opioids. Proceedings. International Narcotic Research Conference — Adv Endog Exog Opioids Proc Int Narc Res Conf
Advances in Energy Systems and Technology — Adv Energy Syst Technol
Advances in Engineering Science. Annual Meeting. Society of Engineering Science — Adv Eng Sci Annu Meet Soc Eng Sci
Advances in Engineering Software — Adv Eng Sof
Advances in Engineering Software — Adv Eng Software
Advances in Engineering Software — Adv Engng Software
Advances in Enhanced Heat Transfer. National Heat Transfer Conference — Adv Enhanced Heat Transfer Nat Heat Transfer Conf
Advances in Environmental Science and Engineering — Adv Environ Sci Eng
Advances in Environmental Science and Technology — Adv Environ Sci Technol
Advances in Environmental Science and Technology — AESTC
Advances in Environmental Science (Beijing) — Adv Environ Sci Beijing
Advances in Environmental Sciences — Adv Envir Sci
Advances in Environmental Sciences — Adv Environ Sci
Advances in Enzyme Regulation — Adv Enzyme Regul
Advances in Enzyme Regulation — AEZRA
Advances in Enzymology — Adv Enzym
Advances in Enzymology — Adv Enzymol
Advances in Enzymology and Related Areas of Molecular Biology — Adv Enzymol Relat Areas Mol Biol
Advances in Enzymology and Related Areas of Molecular Biology — AERAA
Advances in Enzymology and Related Subjects of Biochemistry [*Later, Advances in Enzymology and Related Areas of Molecular Biology*] — Adv Enzymol Relat Subj Biochem
Advances in Ephemeroptera Biology. Proceedings. International Conference on Ephemeroptera — Adv Ephemeroptera Biol Proc Int Conf
Advances in Epileptology — Adv Epileptol
Advances in Epitaxy and Endotaxy. Selected Chemical Problems — Adv Epitaxy Endotaxy Sel Chem Probl
Advances in Ethology — Adv Ethol
Advances in Experimental Medicine and Biology — Adv Exp Med Biol
Advances in Experimental Medicine and Biology — AEMBA
Advances in Experimental Social Psychology — Adv Exp Soc Psychol
Advances in Exploration Geophysics — Adv Explor Geophys
Advances in Extractive Metallurgy. International Symposium — Adv Extr Metall Int Symp
Advances in Fatigue Lifetime Predictive Techniques — Adv Fatigue Lifetime Predict Tech
Advances in Fertility Control — Adv Fertil Control
Advances in Fertility Research — Adv Fert Res
Advances in Fertility Research — Adv Fertil Res
Advances in Filtration and Separation Technology — Adv Filtr Sep Technol
Advances in Financial Planning and Forecasting — AFPAP
Advances in Fire Retardants — Adv Fire Retardants
Advances in Fisheries Oceanography — Adv Fish Oceanogr
Advances in Fluid Mechanics — Adv Fluid Mech
Advances in Fluidized Systems — Adv Fluid Syst
Advances in Fluorine Chemistry — ADFCA
Advances in Fluorine Chemistry — ADFCAK
Advances in Fluorine Chemistry — Adv Fluorine Chem
Advances in Fluorine Research and Dental Caries Prevention — Adv Fluorine Res Dent Caries Prev
Advances in Fluorine Research and Dental Caries Prevention — AFDCAO
Advances in Food and Nutrition Research — Adv Food Nutr Res
Advances in Food Research — Adv Food Res
Advances in Food Research — AFREA
Advances in Food Research. Supplement — Adv Food Res Suppl
Advances in Forensic Haemogenetics — Adv Forensic Haemogenet
Advances in Fracture Research. Proceedings. International Conference on Fracture — Adv Fract Res Proc Int Conf Fract
Advances in Free Radical Biology and Medicine — Adv Free Radical Biol Med
Advances in Free Radical Chemistry — Adv Free Radical Chem
Advances in Fuzzy Systems. Applications and Theory — Adv Fuzzy Systems Appl Theory
Advances in Gas Chromatography. Proceedings. International Symposium — Adv Gas Chromatogr
Advances in Gene Technology. Molecular Biology of Development. Proceedings. Miami Winter Symposium — Adv Gene Technol Mol Biol Dev Proc Miami Winter Symp
Advances in Gene Technology. Molecular Biology of the Endocrine System. Proceedings. Miami Winter Symposium — Adv Gene Technol Mol Biol Endocr Syst Proc Miami Winter Symp
Advances in General and Cellular Pharmacology — Adv Gen Cell Pharmacol
Advances in Genetics — ADGEA
Advances in Genetics — Adv Genet
Advances in Genetics — Adv Genetic
Advances in Genetics — Advan Genet
Advances in Genetics, Development, and Evolution of Drosophila. Proceedings. European Drosophila Research Conference — Adv Genet Dev Evol Drosophila Proc Eur Drosophila Res Conf
Advances in Genome Biology — Adv Genome Biol
Advances in Geophysics — ADGOA
Advances in Geophysics — Adv Geophys
Advances in Geophysics — Advan Geophys
Advances in Geophysics — Advances Geophys
Advances in Gerontological Research — Adv Gerontol Res
Advances in Gerontological Research — AGNRAO
Advances in Glass Technology. Technical Papers. International Congress on Glass — Adv Glass Technol Tech Pap Int Congr Glass
Advances in Graphite Furnace Atomic Absorption Spectrometry. Eastern Analytical Symposium — Adv Graphite Furn At Absorpt Spectrom East Anal Symp
Advances in Heat Pipe Technology. Proceedings. International Heat Pipe Conference — Adv Heat Pipe Technol Proc Int Heat Pipe Conf
Advances in Heat Transfer — Adv Heat Transfer
Advances in Heat Transfer — AHTRA
Advances in Heterocyclic Chemistry — Adv Heterocycl Chem
Advances in High Pressure Research [*England*] — Adv High Pressure Res
Advances in High Pressure Research [*England*] — AHPRB
Advances in High Temperature Chemistry — Adv High Temp Chem
Advances in High Temperature Chemistry — AHTCB
Advances in High Temperature Chemistry — AHTCBH
Advances in Holography — Adv Hologr
Advances in Horticultural Science — Adv Hortic Sci
Advances in Host Defense Mechanisms — Adv Host Def Mech
Advances in Human Fertility and Reproductive Endocrinology — Adv Hum Fertil Reprod Endocrinol
Advances in Human Genetics — ADHGA
Advances in Human Genetics — Adv Hum Gen
Advances in Human Genetics — Adv Hum Genet
Advances in Human Nutrition — Adv Hum Nutr
Advances in Human Psychopharmacology — Adv Hum Psychopharmacol
Advances in Hydrodynamics — Adv in Hydrodyn
Advances in Hydrogen Energy — Adv Hydrogen Energy
Advances in Hydroscience — ADHYA
Advances in Hydroscience — Adv Hydrosci
Advances in Hydroscience — Adv Hydroscience
Advances in Hydroscience — Advances Hydrosci
Advances in Hydrozoan Biology — Adv Hydrozoan Biol
Advances in Hyperbolic Partial Differential Equations — Adv Hyperbolic Partial Differential Equations
Advances in Image Pickup and Display — Adv Image Pickup Disp
Advances in Immunity and Cancer Therapy — Adv Immun Cancer Ther
Advances in Immunobiology. Blood Cell Antigens and Bone Marrow Transplantation. Proceedings. Annual Scientific Symposium — Adv Immunobiol Blood Cell Antigens Bone Marrow Transplant
Advances in Immunology — ADIMA
Advances in Immunology — Adv Immunol
Advances in Immunology — Advances Immun
Advances in Inflammation Research — Adv Inflammation Res
Advances in Information Systems Science — Adv Inf Syst Sci
Advances in Infrared and Raman Spectroscopy — Adv Infrared Raman Spectrosc
Advances in Inorganic and Bioinorganic Mechanisms — Adv Inorg Bioinorg Mech
Advances in Inorganic Biochemistry — Adv Inorg Biochem
Advances in Inorganic Biochemistry [*Elsevier Book Series*] — AIB
Advances in Inorganic Chemistry — Adv Inorg Chem
Advances in Inorganic Chemistry and Radiochemistry — Adv Inorg Chem Radiochem
Advances in Inorganic Chemistry and Radiochemistry — AICRA
Advances in Insect Physiology — Adv Insect Physiol
Advances in Instrumentation — Adv Instrum
Advances in Instrumentation — AVINB
Advances in Internal Medicine — Adv Intern Med
Advances in Internal Medicine — Advances Int Med
Advances in Internal Medicine — AIMNA
Advances in Internal Medicine and Pediatrics — Adv Intern Med Pediatr
Advances in International Maternal and Child Health — Adv Int Mat Child Health
Advances in Invertebrate Reproduction — Adv Invertebr Reprod

Advances in Laboratory Automation Robotics — Adv Lab Autom Rob
Advances in Laser Spectroscopy — Adv Laser Spectros
Advances in Lectin Research — Adv Lectin Res
Advances in Legume Systematics — Adv Legume Syst
Advances in Limnology — Adv Limnol
Advances in Lipid Research — Adv Lipid Res
Advances in Lipid Research — ALPDA
Advances in Lipobiology — Adv Lipobiol
Advances in Liquid Crystals — Adv Liq Cryst
Advances in Liquid Crystals — ALCRD7
Advances in Localized Corrosion. Proceedings. International Conference on Localized Corrosion — Adv Localized Corros Proc Int Conf
Advances in Low-Temperature Plasma Chemistry, Technology, Applications — Adv Low Temp Plasma Chem Technol Appl
Advances in Macromolecular Chemistry — Adv Macromol Chem
Advances in Magnetic Resonance — Adv Magn Reson
Advances in Management Studies — Adv Manage Stud
Advances in Management Studies — AMS
Advances in Marine Biology — Adv Mar Bio
Advances in Marine Biology — Adv Mar Biol
Advances in Marine Biology — AMBYAR
Advances in Mass Spectrometry — Adv Mass Spectrom
Advances in Mass Spectrometry — AMSPA
Advances in Mass Spectrometry in Biochemistry and Medicine. Proceedings. International Symposium on Mass Spectrometry in Biochemistry and Medicine — Adv Mass Spectrom Biochem Med Proc Int Symp Mass Spectrom
Advances in Materials Research — ADMRB
Advances in Materials Research — Adv Mater Res
Advances in Math (Beijing) — Adv in Math Beijing
Advances in Mathematical Sciences and Applications — Adv Math Sci Appl
Advances in Mathematics — Adv in Math
Advances in Mathematics — Adv Math
Advances in Mathematics (China) — Adv in Math China
Advances in Mathematics. Supplementary Studies — Advances in Math Suppl Studies
Advances in Measurement of Soil Physical Properties. Bringing Theory into Practice. Proceedings. Symposium — Adv Meas Soil Phys Prop Bringing Theory Pract Proc Symp
Advances in Meat Research — Adv Meat Res
Advances in Mechanics — Adv in Mech
Advances in Medical Oncology. Research and Education. Proceedings. International Cancer Congress — Adv Med Oncol Res Educ Proc Int Cancer Congr
Advances in Medical Physics. Symposium Papers. International Conference on Medical Physics — Adv Med Phys Symp Pap Int Conf
Advances in Medicinal Plant Research. Plenary Lectures. International Congress on Medicinal Plant Research — Adv Med Plant Res Plenary Lect Int Congr
Advances in Medicine. Proceedings. International Congress of Internal Medicine — Adv Med Proc Int Congr Intern Med
Advances in Membrane Fluidity — Adv Membr Fluid
Advances in Membrane Technology for Better Dairy Products. Abstracts of Papers presented at the IDF Symposium — Adv Membr Technol Better Dairy Prod Abstr Pap IDF Symp
Advances in Mental Science — Adv Ment Sci
Advances in Metabolic Disorders — Adv Metab Disord
Advances in Metabolic Disorders — AMTDA
Advances in Metabolic Disorders. Supplement — ADMDBP
Advances in Metabolic Disorders. Supplement — Adv Metab Disord Suppl
Advances in Metal-Organic Chemistry — Adv Met Org Chem
Advances in Metals in Medicine — Adv Met Med
Advances in Microbial Ecology — Adv Microb Ecol
Advances in Microbial Ecology — AMIED5
Advances in Microbial Engineering. Proceedings. International Symposium — Adv Microb Eng Proc Int Symp
Advances in Microbial Physiology — Adv Microb Physiol
Advances in Microbial Physiology [*England*] — Adv Microbial Physiol
Advances in Microbial Physiology — AMPIB
Advances in Microbiology of the Sea — ADMSB2
Advances in Microbiology of the Sea — Adv Microbiol Sea
Advances in Microcirculation — Adv Microcirc
Advances in Microcirculation — ADVMBT
Advances in Microwaves — ADMIA
Advances in Microwaves — Adv Microwaves
Advances in Modern Biology — Adv Mod Biol
Advances in Modern Biology (Moscow) — Adv Mod Biol (Moscow)
Advances in Modern Environmental Toxicology — Adv Mod Environ Toxicol
Advances in Modern Environmental Toxicology — AETODY
Advances in Modern Environmental Toxicology — AMET
Advances in Modern Genetics — Adv Mod Gen
Advances in Modern Nutrition — Adv Mod Nutr
Advances in Modern Nutrition — AMNUDA
Advances in Modern Toxicology — Adv Mod Toxicol
Advances in Modern Toxicology — AMTODM
Advances in Molecular and Cellular Immunology — Adv Mol Cell Immunol
Advances in Molecular Electronic Structure Theory — Adv Mol Electron Struct Theory
Advances in Molecular Genetics — Adv Mol Genet
Advances in Molecular Genetics of Plant-Microbe Interactions. Proceedings. International Symposium — Adv Mol Genet Plant Microbe Interact Proc Int Symp
Advances in Molecular Modeling — Adv Mol Model
Advances in Molecular Relaxation and Interaction Processes — Adv Mol Relax Interact Processes
Advances in Molecular Relaxation and Interaction Processes — Adv Mol Relaxation and Interaction Processes
Advances in Molecular Relaxation and Interaction Processes [*Netherlands*] — Adv Mol Relaxation Interact Processes
Advances in Molecular Relaxation and Interaction Processes — AMRPDF
Advances in Molecular Relaxation Processes [*Later, Advances in Molecular Relaxation and Interaction Processes*] — Adv Mol Rel
Advances in Molecular Relaxation Processes [*Later, Advances in Molecular Relaxation and Interaction Processes*] — Adv Mol Relax Processes
Advances in Molecular Relaxation Processes [*Later, Advances in Molecular Relaxation and Interaction Processes*] — Adv Mol Relaxation Processes
Advances in Molecular Relaxation Processes [*Later, Advances in Molecular Relaxation and Interaction Processes*] — Advan Mol Relaxation Processes
Advances in Molecular Spectroscopy. Proceedings. International Meeting on Molecular Spectroscopy — Adv Mol Spectrosc Proc Int Meet
Advances in Molecular Structure Research — Adv Mol Struct Res
Advances in Molten Salt Chemistry — Adv Molten Salt Chem
Advances in Molten Salt Chemistry [*Elsevier Book Series*] — AMSC
Advances in Molten Salt Chemistry — AMSCC
Advances in Morphogenesis — ADMOA
Advances in Morphogenesis — Adv Morphog
Advances in Morphogensis — Advances Morphogen
Advances in Multi-Photon Processes and Spectroscopy — Adv Multi-Photon Processes Spectrosc
Advances in Mutagenesis Research — Adv Mutagen Res
Advances in Myocardiology — Adv Myocardiol
Advances in Nephrology — Adv Nephrol
Advances in Nephrology — ANGYBQ
Advances in Nephrology. Necker Hospital — Adv Nephrol Necker Hosp
Advances in Neural Science — Adv Neural Sci
Advances in Neuroblastoma Research 3. Proceedings. Symposium on Advances in Neuroblastoma Research — Adv Neuroblastoma Res 3 Proc Symp
Advances in Neurochemistry — ADNEDZ
Advances in Neurochemistry — Adv Neurochem
Advances in Neurochemistry. Proceedings. All-Union Conference on Neurochemistry — Adv Neurochem Proc All-Union Conf Neurochem
Advances in Neurogerontology — Adv Neurogerontol
Advances in Neuroimmunology — Adv Neuroimmunol
Advances in Neuroimmunology — Adv Neuroimmunology
Advances in Neurological Sciences — Adv Neurol Sci
Advances in Neurological Sciences — SKNSAF
Advances in Neurology — ADNRA3
Advances in Neurology — Adv Neurol
Advances in Neuroscience — Adv Neurosci
Advances in Neurosurgery — Adv Neurosurg
Advances in Neurosurgery — AVNSBV
Advances in Nitrogen Heterocycles — Adv Nitrogen Heterocycles
Advances in Nonlinear Optics — Adv Nonlinear Opt
Advances in Nuclear Physics — Adv Nucl Phys
Advances in Nuclear Physics — ANUPB
Advances in Nuclear Quadrupole Resonance [*England*] — Adv Nucl Quadrupole Reson
Advances in Nuclear Science and Technology — Adv Nucl Sci Technol
Advances in Nuclear Science and Technology — ANUTA
Advances in Numerical Analysis — Adv Numer Anal
Advances in Numerical Computation Series — Adv Numer Comput Ser
Advances in Numerical Methods for Large Sparse Sets of Linear Equations — Adv Numer Methods Large Sparse Sets Linear Equations
Advances in Nursing Science — Adv Nurs Sci
Advances in Nursing Science — ANS
Advances in Nutritional Research — Adv Nutr Res
Advances in Nutritional Research — ANURD9
Advances in Obstetrics and Gynaecology — FGGYAV
Advances in Obstetrics and Gynaecology (Basel) — Adv Obstet Gynaecol (Basel)
Advances in Obstetrics and Gynecology — Adv Obstet
Advances in Obstetrics and Gynecology — AOGYA
Advances in Obstetrics and Gynecology (Baltimore) — Adv Obstet Gynecol (Baltimore)
Advances in Obstetrics and Gynecology (Osaka) [*Japan*] — Adv Obstet Gynecol (Osaka)
Advances in Ophthalmic, Plastic, and Reconstructive Surgery — Adv Ophthalmic Plast Reconstr Surg
Advances in Ophthalmology — Adv Ophthal
Advances in Ophthalmology [*Netherlands*] — Adv Ophthalmol
Advances in Ophthalmology — AVOMBI
Advances in Optical and Electron Microscopy — Adv Opt Electron Microsc
Advances in Optical and Electron Microscopy — AOEMAK
Advances in Optical Information Processing V — Adv Opt Inf Process V
Advances in Oral Biology — Adv Oral Biol
Advances in Oral Biology — AORBA
Advances in Oral Biology — AORBAI
Advances in Organic Chemistry — ADOCA
Advances in Organic Chemistry. Methods and Results — Adv Org Chem
Advances in Organic Chemistry. Methods and Results — Adv Org Chem Methods Results
Advances in Organic Coatings Science and Technology Series — Adv Org Coat Sci Technol Ser
Advances in Organic Geochemistry. Proceedings. International Congress — Adv Org Geochem Proc Int Congr
Advances in Organic Geochemistry. Proceedings. International Meeting — Adv Org Geochem Proc Int Meet
Advances in Organobromine Chemistry — Adv Organobromine Chem
Advances in Organometallic Chemistry — Adv Organomet Chem

Advances in Organometallic Chemistry — Adv Organometal Chem
Advances in Organometallic Chemistry — AOMCA
Advances in Organometallics. Proceedings. Indo-Soviet Symposium on Organometallic Chemistry — Adv Organomet Proc Indo Sov Symp Organomet Chem
Advances in Oto-Rhino-Laryngology — ADORB
Advances in Oto-Rhino-Laryngology — Adv Oto-Rhino-Laryngol
Advances in Oxygenated Processes — Adv Oxygenated Processes
Advances in Pain Research and Therapy — Adv Pain Res Ther
Advances in Parallel Computing — Adv Parallel Comput
Advances in Parasitology — ADPRA
Advances in Parasitology — Adv Parasitol
Advances in Partial Differential Equations — Adv Partial Differential Equations
Advances in Particle Physics — ADPPB
Advances in Particle Physics — Adv Part Phys
Advances in Particle Physics — Adv Particle Phys
Advances in Pathobiology — ADPADX
Advances in Pathobiology — Adv Pathobiol
Advances in Pediatric Infectious Diseases — Adv Pediatr Infect Dis
Advances in Pediatrics — ADPEA
Advances in Pediatrics — Adv Pediatr
Advances in Pediatrics — Advances Pediat
Advances in Perinatal Medicine — Adv Perinat Med
Advances in Perinatal Thyroidology — Adv Perinat Thyroidol
Advances in Peritoneal Dialysis — Adv Perit Dial
Advances in Pest Control Research — Adv Pest Control Res
Advances in Pest Control Research — APCRAW
Advances in Petroleum Chemistry and Refining — Adv Pet Chem Refin
Advances in Petroleum Chemistry and Refining — Adv Petrol Chem Refin
Advances in Petroleum Geochemistry — Adv Pet Geochem
Advances in Petroleum Recovery and Upgrading Technology Conference — Adv Pet Recovery Upgrading Technol Conf
Advances in Pharmaceutical Sciences — Adv Pharm Sci
Advances in Pharmaceutical Sciences — APHMA8
Advances in Pharmaceutical Sciences (Tokyo) — Adv Pharm Sci (Tokyo)
Advances in Pharmacology [*Later, Advances in Pharmacology and Chemotherapy*] — Adv Pharmacol
Advances in Pharmacology — Advances Pharmacol
Advances in Pharmacology [*Later, Advances in Pharmacology and Chemotherapy*] — ADVPA3
Advances in Pharmacology and Chemotherapy — Adv Pharmacol Chemother
Advances in Pharmacology and Chemotherapy — AVPCA
Advances in Pharmacology and Therapeutics. Proceedings. International Congress of Pharmacology — Adv Pharmacol Ther Proc Int Congr
Advances in Pharmacotherapy — ADPHDK
Advances in Pharmacotherapy — Adv Pharmacother
Advances in Photochemistry — ADPCA
Advances in Photochemistry — Adv Photochem
Advances in Photosynthesis — Adv Photosynth
Advances in Photosynthesis Research. Proceedings. International Congress on Photosynthesis — Adv Photosynth Res Proc Int Congr Photosynth
Advances in Physical Geochemistry — Adv Phys Geochem
Advances in Physical Organic Chemistry — Adv Phys Org Chem
Advances in Physical Organic Chemistry — APORA
Advances in Physical Sciences — Adv Phy Sci
Advances in Physical Sciences — Advances Phys Sci
Advances in Physical Sciences (USSR) — Adv Phys Sci (USSR)
Advances in Physics — Adv in Phys
Advances in Physics — Adv Phys
Advances in Physics — Adv Physics
Advances in Physics — Advan Phys
Advances in Physiological Sciences. Proceedings. International Congress of Physiological Sciences — Adv Physiol Sci Proc Int Congr
Advances in Pigment Cell Research. Proceedings. Symposia and Lectures. International Pigment Cell Conference — Adv Pigm Cell Res Proc Symp Lect Int Pigm Cell Conf
Advances in Pineal Research — Adv Pineal Res
Advances in Planned Parenthood — Adv Plann Parent
Advances in Planned Parenthood — Adv Planned Parent
Advances in Planned Parenthood — ADVPB4
Advances in Plant Morphology — Adv Pl Morph
Advances in Plant Nutrition — Adv Plant Nutr
Advances in Plant Pathology — Adv Plant Pathol
Advances in Plant Sciences Series — Adv Plant Sci Ser
Advances in Plasma Physics — Adv Plasma Phys
Advances in Plasma Physics — APLPB
Advances in Plastic and Reconstructive Surgery — Adv Plast Reconstr Surg
Advances in Plastic and Reconstructive Surgery — APRSEC
Advances in Plastics Technology — Adv Plast Technol
Advances in Polarography. Proceedings. International Congress — Adv Polarogr Proc Int Congr
Advances in Political Science — Adv Pol Sci
Advances in Pollen-Spore Research — Adv Pollen-Spore Res
Advances in Pollen-Spore Research — APSRDD
Advances in Polyamine Research — Adv Polyamine Res
Advances in Polyamine Research — APLRDC
Advances in Polymer Science — Adv Polym Sci
Advances in Polymer Science — Adv Polymer Sci
Advances in Polymer Science — APSID
Advances in Polymer Science/Fortschritte der Hochpolymeren-Forschung — Advan Polymer Sci Fortschr Hochpolym-Forsch
Advances in Polymer Technology — Adv Polym Technol
Advances in Polymer Technology. National Conference — Adv Polym Technol Natl Conf
Advances in Preconcentration and Dehydration of Foods. Symposium — Adv Preconc Dehydr Foods Symp
Advances in Primatology — Adv Primatol
Advances in Printing Science and Technology — Adv Print Sci Technol
Advances in Printing Science and Technology — Adv Printing Sci
Advances in Probability and Related Topics — Adv Probab Related Topics
Advances in Probability Theory — Adv Probab Theory
Advances in Process Analysis and Development in the Forest Products Industry — Adv Process Anal Dev For Prod Ind
Advances in Processing and Utilization of Forest Products — Adv Process Util For Prod
Advances in Prostaglandin and Thromboxane Research — Adv Prostaglandin Thromboxane Res
Advances in Prostaglandin and Thromboxane Research — APTRDI
Advances in Prostaglandin, Thromboxane, and Leukotriene Research — Adv Prostaglandin Thromboxane Leukot
Advances in Prostaglandin, Thromboxane, and Leukotriene Research — Adv Prostaglandin Thromboxane Leukot Res
Advances in Prostaglandin, Thromboxane, and Leukotriene Research — Adv Prostaglandin Thromboxane Leukotriene Res
Advances in Prostaglandin, Thromboxane, and Leukotriene Research — ATLRD6
Advances in Protein Chemistry — Adv Protein Chem
Advances in Protein Chemistry — Advances Protein Chem
Advances in Protein Chemistry — APCHA
Advances in Protein Phosphatases — Adv Protein Phosphatases
Advances in Protoplast Research. Proceedings. International Protoplast Symposium — Adv Protoplast Res Proc Int Protoplast Symp
Advances in Protozoological Research. Proceedings. International Conference of Hungary on Protozoology — Adv Protozool Res Proc Int Conf Hung Protozool
Advances in Psychoanalysis Theory, Research, and Practice — Adv Psychoanal Theory Res Pract
Advances in Psychoanalysis Theory, Research, and Practice — APTPED
Advances in Psychobiology — Adv Psychobiol
Advances in Psychobiology — AVPBC
Advances in Psychobiology — AVPBCP
Advances in Psychology — Adv Psych
Advances in Psychology [*Elsevier Book Series*] — AIP
Advances in Psychosomatic Medicine — Adv Psy Med
Advances in Psychosomatic Medicine — Adv Psychosom Med
Advances in Psychosomatic Medicine — FPMMAK
Advances in Quantum Chemistry — Adv Quantum Chem
Advances in Quantum Electronics — ADQEA
Advances in Quantum Electronics — Adv Quantum Electron
Advances in Radiation Biology — Adv Radiat Biol
Advances in Radiation Biology — ARDBA
Advances in Radiation Chemistry — Adv Radiat Chem
Advances in Radiation Chemistry — ARDCB
Advances in Radiation Research, Biology, and Medicine — Adv Radia Res Biol Med
Advances in Raman Spectroscopy — Adv Raman Spectrosc
Advances in Regulation of Cell Growth — Adv Regul Cell Growth
Advances in Renal Replacement Therapy — Adv Ren Replace Ther
Advances in Reproductive Endocrinology — Adv Reprod Endocrinol
Advances in Reproductive Physiology — ADRPB
Advances in Reproductive Physiology — ADRPBI
Advances in Reproductive Physiology — Adv R Physl
Advances in Reproductive Physiology — Adv Reprod Physiol
Advances in Research and Technology of Seeds — Adv Res Technol Seeds
Advances in Research on Neurodegeneration — Adv Res Neurodegener
Advances in Resist Technology and Processing — Adv Resist Technol Process
Advances in Robotics — Adv Robot
Advances in Science and Technology (Faenza, Italy) — Adv Sci Technol Faenza Italy
Advances in Science and Technology in the USSR. Mathematics and Mechanics Series — Adv Sci Tech USSR Math Mech Ser
Advances in Science and Technology in the USSR. Physics Series — Adv Sci Tech USSR Phys Ser
Advances in Seafood Biochemistry. Composition and Quality. Papers. American Chemical Society Annual Meeting — Adv Seafood Biochem Pap Am Chem Soc Annu Meet
Advances in Second Messenger and Phosphoprotein Research — Adv Second Messenger Phosphoprotein Res
Advances in Sex Hormone Research — Adv Sex Horm Res
Advances in Shock Research — Adv Shock Res
Advances in Silicon Chemistry — Adv Silicon Chem
Advances in Sleep Research — Adv Sleep Res
Advances in Sleep Research — AVSRCK
Advances in Small Animal Practice — Adv Small Anim Pract
Advances in Socio-Dental Research — Adv Sociodent Res
Advances in Soil Organic Matter Research. The Impact on Agriculture and the Environment — Adv Soil Org Matter Res Impact Agric Environ
Advances in Soil Science — Adv Soil Sci
Advances in Solar Energy — Adv Sol Energy
Advances in Solid State Physics — Adv Solid State Phys
Advances in Solid-State Chemistry — Adv Solid-State Chem
Advances in Space Biology and Medicine — Adv Space Biol Med
Advances in Space Exploration — Adv Space Explor
Advances in Space Research — Adv Space Res
Advances in Space Research — ASRSD
Advances in Space Research. Proceedings. Inter-American Symposium on Space Research — Adv Space Res Proc Inter Am Symp Space Res
Advances in Space Science — Adv Space Sci
Advances in Space Science and Technology — Adv Spa Sci

Advances in Space Science and Technology — Adv Space Sci Technol
Advances in Space Science and Technology — AVSTA
Advances in Spectroscopy — Adv Spectros
Advances in Spectroscopy — Adv Spectrosc
Advances in Spectroscopy — ASPEA
Advances in Spectroscopy (Chichester, United Kingdom) — Adv Spectrosc (Chichester UK)
Advances in Stereoencephalotomy — Adv Stereoencephalotomy
Advances in Steroid Analysis '90. Proceedings. Symposium on the Analysis of Steroids — Adv Steroid Anal 90 Proc Symp Anal Steroids
Advances in Steroid Biochemistry and Pharmacology — Adv Steroid Biochem
Advances in Steroid Biochemistry and Pharmacology — Adv Steroid Biochem Pharmacol
Advances in Strain in Organic Chemistry — Adv Strain Org Chem
Advances in Strawberry Production — Adv Strawberry Prod
Advances in Structural Biology — Adv Struct Biol
Advances in Structural Composites — Adv Struct Compos
Advances in Structure Research by Diffraction Methods — Adv Struct Res Diffr Methods
Advances in Structure Research by Diffraction Methods [*United States-Germany*] — ASDMA
Advances in Superconductivity III. Proceedings. International Symposium on Superconductivity — Adv Supercond III Proc Int Symp Supercond
Advances in Supramolecular Chemistry — Adv Supramol Chem
Advances in Surface and Thin Film Diffraction. Symposium — Adv Surf Thin Film Diffr Symp
Advances in Surface Coating Technology [*England*] — Adv Surf Coat Technol
Advances in Surgery — ADSUA
Advances in Surgery — Adv Surg
Advances in Surgery — Advances Surg
Advances in Teratology — ADTEAS
Advances in Teratology — Adv Teratol
Advances in Test Measurement — Adv Test Meas
Advances in Textile Processing — Adv Textile Process
Advances in Thanatology — Advan Thanatol
Advances in the Analytical Methodology of Leaf and Smoke. Symposium. Tobacco Chemist's Research Conference — Adv Anal Methodol Leaf Smoke Symp Tob Chem Res Conf
Advances in the Astronautical Sciences — ADASA9
Advances in the Astronautical Sciences — Adv Astronaut Sci
Advances in the Astronautical Sciences — Advan Astronaut Sci
Advances in the Biology of Disease — Adv Biol Dis
Advances in the Biosciences — Adv Biosci
Advances in the Biosciences — AVBIB
Advances in the Biosciences (Oxford) — Adv Biosci (Oxford)
Advances in the Drug Therapy of Mental Illness. Based on the Proceedings of a Symposium — Adv Drug Ther Ment Illness Proc Symp
Advances in the Engineering of the Smoke Curing Process. Proceedings. International Session — Adv Eng Smoke Curing Process Proc Int Sess
Advances in the Fusion of Glass. Proceedings. International Conference — Adv Fusion Glass Pro Int Conf
Advances in the Fusion of Glass. Proceedings. International Conference on Advances in the Fusion of Glass — Adv Fusion Glass Proc Int Conf
Advances in the Management of Cardiovascular Disease — Adv Manage Cardiovas Dis
Advances in the Management of Clinical Heart Disease — Adv Man Clin Heart Dis
Advances in the Mathematical Sciences — Adv Math Sci
Advances in the Mechanics and Physics of Surfaces — Adv Mech Phys Surf
Advances in the Study of Behavior — Adv Study Behav
Advances in the Study of Birth Defects — Adv Stud Birth Def
Advances in the Study of Birth Defects — Adv Study Birth Defects
Advances in the Synthesis and Reactivity of Solids — Adv Synth React Solids
Advances in the Understanding and Treatment of Asthma — Adv Understanding Treat Asthma
Advances in Theoretical Physics — Adv Theor Phys
Advances in Theoretical Physics — ATHPB
Advances in Therapy — Adv Ther
Advances in Thermal Conductivity. Papers. International Conference. Thermal Conductivity — Adv Therm Conduct Pap Int Conf Thermal Conduct
Advances in Thermal Engineering — Adv Therm Eng
Advances in Thermodynamics — Adv Thermodyn
Advances in Tracer Methodology — Adv Tracer Methodol
Advances in Tracer Methodology — ATM
Advances in Tracer Methodology — ATRMA
Advances in Transition Metal Coordination Chemistry — Adv Transition Met Coord Chem
Advances in Transport Processes — Adv Transp Processes
Advances in Tuberculosis Research — Adv Tuberc Res
Advances in Tumor Prevention, Detection, and Characterization — Adv Tumour Prev Detect Charact
Advances in Tumor Prevention, Detection, and Characterization [*Elsevier Book Series*] — ATPDC
Advances in Tunnelling Technology and Subsurface Use — ATTUD
Advances in Urethane Science and Technology — Adv Urethane Sci Technol
Advances in Vegetation Science — Adv Veg Sci
Advances in Veterinary Medicine (Berlin) — Adv Vet Med (Berl)
Advances in Veterinary Science [*Later, Advances in Veterinary Science and Comparative Medicine*] — Adv Vet Sci
Advances in Veterinary Science [*Later, Advances in Veterinary Science and Comparative Medicine*] — ADVSA
Advances in Veterinary Science and Comparative Medicine — Adv Vet Sci Comp Med
Advances in Veterinary Science and Comparative Medicine — AVSCB
Advances in Viral Oncology — Adv Viral Oncol
Advances in Virus Research — Adv Virus Res
Advances in Virus Research — Advan Virus Res
Advances in Waste Treatment Research — Adv Waste Treat Res
Advances in Water Resources [*England*] — Adv Water Resour
Advances in Welding Metallurgy — Adv Weld Metall
Advances in Welding Processes. International Conference — Adv Weld Processes
Advances in Welding Processes. International Conference — Adv Weld Processes Int Conf
Advances in Working Capital Management — AWCM
Advances in World Archaeology — Adv World Archaeol
Advances in X-Ray Analysis — Adv X-Ray Anal
Advances in X-Ray Chemical Analysis (Japan) — Adv X Ray Chem Anal (Jpn)
Advancing Frontiers of Plant Sciences — Adv Front Pl Sci
Advancing Frontiers of Plant Sciences — Adv Front Plant Sci
Advancing Frontiers of Plant Sciences — Adv Frontiers Plant Sci
Advancing Frontiers of Plant Sciences — Advan Front Plant Sci
Advancing Frontiers of Plant Sciences — Advanc Front Plant Sci
Advancing Frontiers of Plant Sciences — Advancing Frontiers Plant Sci
Advancing Frontiers of Plant Sciences — Advg Front Pl Sci
Advancing Technologies — Adv Technol
Adventures in Experimental Physics — Adventures Exp Phys
Adventures in Travel [*Database*] — AIT
Adverse Drug Reaction Bulletin — Adverse Drug React Bull
Adverse Drug Reactions and Acute Poisoning Reviews — Adverse Drug React Acute Poisoning Rev
Adverse Drug Reactions and Toxicological Reviews — Adverse Drug React Toxicol Rev
Adverse Effects of Environmental Chemicals and Psychotropic Drugs — Adverse Eff Environ Chem Psychotropic Drugs
Advertised Computer Technologies [*Database*] — ACT
Advertising Age — AA
Advertising Age — Ad Age
Advertising Age — ADA
Advertising Age — Adv Age
Advertising Age — Advert Age
Advertising Age Europe — AAE
Advertising Age Europe — Ad Age Eur
Advertising Agency Magazine — Adv Agency Mag
Advertising and Graphic Arts Techniques — Ad Techniq
Advertising and Marketing Intelligence [*Database*] — AMI
Advertising and Sales Promotion — ASP
Advertising and Selling — Adv & Sell
Advertising Business — Advert Bus
Advertising/Communications Times — ACT
Advertising Compliance Service — Ad Compl
Advertising Compliance Service. Special Report — Ad Compli S
Advertising News — AN
Advertising News of New York [*Later, Adweek*] — Anny
Advertising Photography in Chicago — Adv Photo Chic
Advertising Quarterly — Advert Q
Advertising World — Ad World
Advertising World — ADV
Advertising World — Advert World
Advisory Council for Scientific and Industrial Research (Canada). Annual Report — Advis CSIR (Can) Annu Rep
Advisory Group for Aerospace Research and Development — Advis Group Aerosp Res Dev
Advisory Group Meeting on Modification of Radiosensitivity of Biological Systems — Advis Group Meet Modif Radiosensitivity Biol Syst
Advisory Group Meeting on Tumour Localization with Radioactive Agents — Advis Group Meet Tumour Localization Radioact Agents
Advisory Leaflet. British Beekeepers Association — Advis Leafl Br Beekprs Ass
Advisory Leaflet. Ministry of Agriculture, Fisheries, and Food (Great Britain) — Adv Leafl Min Agr Fish Food (Gt Brit)
Advisory Leaflet. Queensland Department of Agriculture — Advis Leafl Qd Dep Agric
Advisory Leaflet. Queensland Department of Agriculture and Stock. Division of Plant Industry — Adv Leafl Queensland Dept Agr Stock Div Plant Ind
Advisory Leaflet. Queensland Department of Forestry — Adv Leafl Dep For Qd
Advisory Leaflet. Queensland Department of Forestry — Advis Leafl Dep For Queensl
Advisory Leaflet. West of Scotland Agricultural College — Adv Leafl W Scot Agr Coll
Advisory Leaflet. West of Scotland Agricultural College — Advis Leafl W Scotl Agric Coll
Advisory Service Leaflet. Timber Research and Development Association — Ad Serv Leafl Timb Res Developm Ass
Advocacy Now — Adv N
Advocate of Science and Annals of Natural History — Adv Sci Ann Nat Hist
Advocate. The National Gay and Lesbian News Magazine — IADV
Advocatenblad — A Bl
Advocatenblad — AB
Advocatenblad — Adv
Advocatenblad — Advbl
Advocates Quarterly — Adv Q
Advocates Quarterly — Advocates Q
Advocates Society. Journal — Advocates Soc J
Adweek Directory of Advertising. Midwestern Edition — Adweek MWD
Adweek Directory of Advertising. Southeastern Edition — Adweek SED
Adweek Directory of Advertising. Southwestern Edition — Adweek SWD
Adweek Directory of Advertising. Western Edition — Adweek WD
Adweek/Eastern Edition — Adweek E
Adweek/Midwest Edition — Adweek MW
Adweek/National Marketing Edition — Adweek Ntl

Adweek/New England Advertising Week — Adweek NE
Adweek/Southeast Edition — Adweek SE
Adweek/Southwest Advertising News — Adweek SAN
Adweek/Southwest Edition — Adweek S W
Adweek. Special Report — Adweek Spl
Adweek/Western Edition — Adweek W
Adweek's Marketing Week — Market Week
Adyar Library Bulletin — AdLB
Adyar Library Bulletin — ALB
Ad'yuvanty v Vaktsinno Syvorotochnom Dele — Ad'yuvanty Vaktsinno Syvorot Dele
AE and RS. Pennsylvania State University. Agricultural Experiment Station. Department of Agricultural Economics and Rural Sociology — AE RS PA State Univ Agr Sta Dept Agr Econ Rural Sociol
AE. Clemson Agricultural Experiment Station — AE Clemson Agr Exp Sta
AE. Delaware Agricultural Experiment Station. Department of Agricultural Economics — AE Del Agr Exp Stat Dept Agr Econ
AE. Department of Agricultural Economics and Rural Sociology. South Carolina Agricultural Experiment Station. Clemson University — AE Dep Agric Econ Rural Social SC Agric Exp Stn Clemson Univ
AE Information Series. University of North Carolina. State College of Agriculture and Engineering. Department of Agricultural Economics — AE Inform Ser Univ NC State Coll Agr Eng Dept Agr Econ
AE. Michigan State University of Agriculture and Applied Science. Extension Division. Agricultural Economics Department — AE Mich State Univ Agr Appl Sci Ext Div Agr Econ Dept
AE. Oklahoma State University. Department of Agricultural Economics — AE Okla State Univ Dep Agric Econ
AE Paper. Oklahoma State University. Cooperative Extension Service — AE Pap Okla State Univ Coop Ext Serv
AE Research. Department of Agricultural Economics, Cornell University. Agricultural Experiment Station — AE Res Dep Agric Econ Cornell Univ Agric Exp Stn
AE Research. New York State College of Agriculture. Department of Agricultural Economics — AE Res NY State Coll Agr Dept Agr Econ
AE. South Carolina Agricultural Experiment Station. Clemson University — AE SC Agric Exp Stn Clemson Univ
AE. University of Illinois. College of Agriculture. Experiment Station. Cooperative Extension Service — AE Univ Ill Coll Agr Exp Sta Coop Ext Serv
AE. University of Illinois. Department of Agricultural Economics — AE Univ Ill Dep Agric Econ
AEA Information Series. Louisiana Agricultural Experiment Station — AEA Inf Ser LA Agric Exp Stn
AEC Informations [*France*] — AEC Inf
AEC [*National Adult Education Clearinghouse*] **Newsletter** — AEC Newsl
AEC [*US Atomic Energy Commission*] **Symposium Series** — AEC Symp Ser
AEC. University of Kentucky. Cooperative Extension Service — AEC Univ Ky Coop Ext Serv
AECL [*Atomic Energy of Canada Limited*] **Research and Development in Engineering** — AECL Res & Dev Eng
AEDS [*Association for Educational Data Systems*] **Journal** — AEDS J
AEDS [*Association for Educational Data Systems*] **Journal** — AEDS Jrnl
AEDS [*Association for Educational Data Systems*] **Monitor** — AEDS Mon
AEDS [*Association for Educational Data Systems*] **Monitor** — AEDS Monit
AEES. University of Kentucky. Cooperative Extension Service — AEES Univ Ky Coop Ext Serv
AEG [*Allgemeine Elektrizitaets-Gesellschaft*] **Kernreaktoren** — AEG Kernreakt
AEG [*Allgemeine Elektrizitaets-Gesellschaft*] **Progress** [*Germany*] — AEG Prog
AEG [*Allgemeine Elektrizitaets-Gesellschaft*] **- Telefunken Progress** — AEG Telefunken Prog
AEG [*Allgemeine Elektrizitaets-Gesellschaft*] **- Telefunken Progress** — AEG-Telefunken Progr
Aegean Earth Sciences — Aegean Earth Sci
Aegyptiaca Helvetica — Aeg Helv
Aegyptica Christiana — Aeg Christ
Aegyptische Urkunden aus den Staatlichen Museen zu Berlin — Aeg U
Aegyptische Urkunden aus den Staatlichen Museen zu Berlin. Griechische Urkunden — Aeg UG
Aegyptische Zeitschrift — AeZ
Aegyptologische Abhandlungen — AA
Aegyptologische Abhandlungen [*Wiesbaden*] — AeA
Aegyptologische Abhandlungen [*Wiesbaden*] — AeAb
Aegyptologische Abhandlungen — Ag Abh
Aegyptologische Forschungen [*Glueckstadt*] — AeF
Aegyptologische Forschungen — Aeg Forsch
Aegyptologische Forschungen — Aegyptol Forschgn
Aegyptologische Forschungen — AF
Aegyptologische Forschungen [*Glueckstadt*] — AgFo
Aegyptologische Studien [*Berlin*] — AeS
Aegyptus — Ae
Aegyptus — Aeg
Aegyptus: Rivista Italiana di Egittologia e di Papirologia — Aeg
Aegyptus. Serie Scientifica — AegS
Aehrodinamika Razrezhennykh Gazov — Aehrodin Razrezh Gazov
AEI (American Enterprise Institute) Foreign Policy and Defense Review — AEI (Am Enterprise Inst) For Policy and Defense R
AEI [*American Enterprise Institute*] **Economist** — AEE
AEI [*American Enterprise Institute*] **Economist** — AEI Econom
AEI [*American Enterprise Institute*] **Economist** — AFO
AEI [*Associated Electrical Industries*] **Engineering** [*England*] — AEI Eng
AEI [*Associated Electrical Industries*] **Engineering Review** — AEI Eng Rev
AEI [*American Enterprise Institute for Public Policy Research*] **Foreign Policy and Defense Review** — AEI For Pol Def Rev
AEI [*American Enterprise Institute for Public Policy Research*] **Hoover Policy Studies** — AEI Hoover Pol Stud
AEN. Department of Agricultural Engineering. University of Kentucky — AEN Dep Agric Eng Univ KY
Aequationes Mathematicae — Aequ Math
Aequatoria — Aeq
Aere Perennius. Verslagen en Mededelinged uit Het Medisch-Encyclopaedisch Instituut van Vrije Universiteit — Aere Perennius
Aerftliga Aemnesomsaettningsrubbningar. Symposium — Aerftliga Aemnesomsaettningsrubbningar Symp
Aerial Archaeology — Aer Arch
Aerial Archaeology — Aerial Archaeol
Aero Digest — Aero Dig
Aero Mundial — Aero Mund
Aero Research Aircraft Bulletin — Aero Res Aircr Bull
Aero Research Technical Notes — Aero Res Tech Notes
Aero Revue — Aero Rev
Aero/Space Engineering — Aero/Space Eng
AERO [*Alternative Energy Resources Organization*] **Sun-Times** — AERO Sun-T
Aerodinamika Razrezhennykh Gazov [*Former USSR*] — Aerodin Razrezh Gazov
Aerodrome and Ground Aids — AGA
Aerodynamic Phenomena in Stellar Atmospheres. Symposium on Cosmical Gas Dynamics — Aerodyn Phenom Stellar Atmos Symp Cosmical Gas Dyn
Aerodynamics Note — Aerodyn Note
Aerodynamics Report (Australia). Aeronautics Research Laboratories — Aerodyn Rep (Aust) Aeronaut Res Lab
Aerodynamics Technical Memorandum — Aerodyn Techn Mem
Aerofizicheskie Issledovaniya — AEISDP
Aerofizicheskie Issledovaniya — Aerofiz Issled
Aerologist — Aerol
Aeromedica Acta — AEACA2
Aeromedica Acta — Aeromed Acta
Aeromedical Reviews — Aeromed Rev
Aerometric Information Retrieval System [*Database*] — AIRS
Aeromodeller — Aeromod
Aeronautic Review — Aeron Rev
Aeronautica — Aeron
Aeronautical and Astronautical News Letter — Aeronaut Astronaut News Lett
Aeronautical Engineering Review — Aero Eng R
Aeronautical Engineering Review — Aeronaut Eng Rev
Aeronautical Information Circular — AIC
Aeronautical Information Publication [*FAA*] — AIP
Aeronautical Journal — Aero J
Aeronautical Journal — Aeron J
Aeronautical Journal — Aeronaut J
Aeronautical Quarterly [*London*] — Aero Quart
Aeronautical Quarterly — Aeron Q
Aeronautical Quarterly — Aeronaut Q
Aeronautical Research Laboratories. Department of Defence. Australia. Reports — Aeronaut Res Lab Dep Def Aust Rep
Aeronautical Research Report — Aeron Res Rep
Aeronautical World — Aeron Wld
Aeronautique — Aeron
Aeronautique et l'Astronautique — Aeronaut Astronaut
Aeronomica Acta. A — Aeron Acta A
Aeroplane and Astronautics — Aeropl Astron
Aero-Revue Suisse — Aero Rev Suisse
Aerosol Age — AAA
Aerosol Age — Aeros Age
Aerosol Age — Aerosl Age
Aerosol Bulletin — Aeros Bull
Aerosol e Cosmeticos — Aerosol Cosmet
Aerosol News — Aeros Ne
Aerosol Report — Aerosol Rep
Aerosol Review 1982 — Aerosol 82
Aerosol Science [*England*] — Aerosol Sci
Aerosol Science and Technology — Aerosol Sci Technol
Aerosol Science and Technology — ASTYD
Aerosol Spray Report — Aerosol Spray Rep
Aerospace America — Aero Amer
Aerospace and Defence Review — Aerosp and Def Rev
Aerospace and Environmental Medicine — Aerosp Environ Med
Aerospace Canada — Aerosp Can
Aerospace Corporation Report — Aerosp Corp Rep
Aerospace Daily — Aerosp Dly
Aerospace/Defense Markets and Technology — Aero Def Mark Technol
Aerospace Engineering — Aero Eng
Aerospace Engineering — Aerosp Eng
Aerospace Facts and Figures — Aero F & F
Aerospace Historian — Aerospace Hist
Aerospace Information Digest — AID
Aerospace Intelligence — Aerosp Intel
Aerospace Intelligence — AI
Aerospace Medical Association. Preprints. Annual Scientific Meeting — Aerosp Med Assoc Prepr Annu Sci Meet
Aerospace Medical Research Laboratory. Technical Report — Aerosp Med Res Lab Tech Rep
Aerospace Medicine — AEMEA
Aerospace Medicine — AEMEAY
Aerospace Medicine — Aerosp Med
Aerospace Medicine — Aerospace Med
Aerospace Medicine and Biology — Aerosp Med Biol
Aerospace Report — Aerosp Rep
Aerospace Research Laboratories (US). Reports — Aerosp Res Lab (US) Rep
Aerospace Safety — Aero Safe
Aerospace Technology — Aerosp Technol
Aerospace Technology — Aerospace Tech

Aerospace Technology — AETEB
Aerospace Washington — Aerosp Wash
Aerotechnica Missili e Spazio — Aerotec Missili Spazio
Aerotechnique — Aerotechn
Aerotecnica — Aerot
Aerzteblatt fuer Baden-Wuerttemberg — Aerztebl Baden-Wuerttemb
Aerzteblatt Rheinland-Pfalz — Aerztebl Rheinl Pfalz
Aerztliche Forschung — Aerztl Forsch
Aerztliche Fortbildungskurse der Zuercher Kantonalen Liga Gegen die Tuberkulose in Arosa — Aerztl Fortbildungskurse Zuer Kanton Liga Tuberk Arosa
Aerztliche Fortbildungskurse der Zuercher Kantonalen Liga Gegen die Tuberkulose in Arosa — Aerztl Fortbildungskurse Zuercher Kanton Liga Tuberk Arosa
Aerztliche Jugendkunde — AEJUAX
Aerztliche Jugendkunde — Aerztl Jugendkd
Aerztliche Kosmetologie — Aerztl Kosmetol
Aerztliche Laboratorium — AELAAH
Aerztliche Laboratorium — Aerztl Lab
Aerztliche Monatshefte fuer Berufliche Fortbildung — Aerztl Monatsh Berufliche Fortbild
Aerztliche Monatshefte fuer Berufliche Fortbildung — ARZMAA
Aerztliche Nachrichten — Aerztl Nachr
Aerztliche Praxis — Aerztl Praxis
Aerztliche Psychologie — Aerztl Psychol
Aerztliche Rundschau — Aerztl Rundsch
Aerztliche Sachverstaendigen-Zeitung — Aerzt Sachverstztg
Aerztliche Sachverstaendigen-Zeitung — AS Zg
Aerztliche Sammeblaetter — Aerztl S Bl
Aerztliche Standeszeitung — Aerztl Stand Ztg
Aerztliche Vierteljahrsrundschau — Aerztl Vierteljrdsch
Aerztliche Wochenschrift — Aerztl Wochenschr
Aerztliche Wochenschrift — ARZWA6
AES [*American Electroplaters' Society*] **International Pulse Plating Symposium. Papers** — AES Int Pulse Plat Symp Pap
AES [*American Electroplaters' Society*] **Research Report** — AES Res Rep
Aesop Institute Newsletter — Aesop Inst Newsl
Aesthetic Plastic Surgery — Aesthetic Plast Surg
Aesthetics — AE
Aesthetische Medizin [*Germany*] — Aesthet Med
Aetherische Oele, Riechstoffe, Parfuemerien, Essenzen, und Aromen — Aetherische Oele Riechst Parfuem Essenzen Aromen
AEU. Asia Electronics United — AEUNA
AEU [*American Ethical Union*] **Reports** — AEU Rep
AEU-Archiv fuer Elektronik und Uebertragungstechnik — AEU-Arch El
AEU-Archiv fuer Elektronik und Uebertragungstechnik — AEU-Arch Elektron Uebertragungstech
Aevum — Ae
Aevum — Aev
Aevum Christianum — AeC
Aevum Christianum. Salzburger Beitraege zur Religions- und Geistesgeschichte des Abendlandes — Ae Ch Salz
AFA [*Aborigines' Friends' Association*] **Annual Report** — AFAA Rept
Afar between Continental and Oceanic Rifting. Proceedings of an International Symposium — Afar Cont Oceanic Rifting Proc Int Symp
Afdeling Informatica — Afd Inform
Afdeling Mathematische Besliskunde [*Amsterdam*] — Afd Math Beslisk
Afdeling Mathematische Statistiek [*Amsterdam*] — Afd Math Statist
Afdeling Numerieke Wiskunde — Afd Numer Wisk
Afdeling Toegepaste Wiskunde — Afd Toegepaste Wisk
Afdeling Zuivere Wiskunde — Afd Zuiv Wisk
Affari Esteri — Aff Est
Affari Sociali Internazionali — Aff Soc Int
Affarsvarlden — Affarsvarld
Affinity Techniques. Enzyme Purification. Part B — Affinity Tech Enzyme Purif Part B
Affirmative Action Compliance Manual for Federal Contractors. Bureau of National Affairs — Aff Action Compl Man BNA
Affirmative Action Coordinating Center. Newsletter — AACC News
Affirmative Action Planning Guide [*Database*] — AAPG
Affirmative Action Register — AAR
Affleck's Southern Rural Almanac and Plantation and Garden Calendar — Afflecks S Rural Alman
Afghan Geological and Mineral Survey. Bulletin — Afghan Geol Miner Surv Bull
Afghanistan Journal — Afghanistan J
Afhandlingar i Fysik, Kemi, och Mineralogi — Afh Fys Kemi Mineral
Afhandlinger. Norske Videnskaps-Akademi i Oslo — ANVA
AFI [*American Film Institute*] **Education Newsletter** — AFI Ed News
AFIPS [*American Federation of Information Processing Societies*] **Conference Proceedings** — AFIPS Conf Proc
AFIPS [*American Federation of Information Processing Societies*] **National Computer Conference and Exposition. Conference Proceedings** — AFIPS Nat Comput Conf Expo Conf Proc
AFIPS [*American Federation of Information Processing Societies*] **Washington Report** — AFIPS Washington Rep
AFL-CIO [*American Federation of Labor and Congress of Industrial Organizations*] **American Federationist** — AFL-CIO Am Fed
AFN [*Alaska Federation of Natives*] **Newsletter** — AFNN
Africa [Italy] — Af
Africa. An International Business, Economic, and Political Monthly — Africa An Int Business Econ Polit Mon
Africa. An International Business, Economic, and Political Monthly — ALG
Africa Confidential — AFR
Africa Contemporary Record — Afr Contemporary Rec
Africa Development. A Quarterly Journal. Council for the Development of Economic and Social Research in Africa — Africa Dev
Africa Digest — Afr Dig
Africa Economic Digest — AED
Africa. Fouilles. Monuments et Collections Archeologiques en Tunisie — Africa
Africa Guide — Afr G
Africa in Soviet Studies. Annual — Afr Sov Stud
Africa Index. Africa Bibliographic Centre Secretariat — Afr Ind Afr Bib Cent Sec
Africa Insight — Afr Insight
Africa Institute. Bulletin — Afr Inst B
Africa Institute. Bulletin — Afr Inst Bull
Africa International — Afr Int
Africa. International African Institute — Africa IAI
Africa Italiana [*Naples*] — Afri It
Africa Italiana — AfrIt
Africa Italiana — AI
Africa Italiana. Rivista de Storia e d'Arte — Afri I
Africa Italiana. Rivista de Storia e d'Arte — Afri It Stor Arte
Africa Italiana. Rivista de Storia e d'Arte — Africa Ital
Africa Italiana. Rivista de Storia e d'Arte — Africa Italiana Riv
Africa. Journal of the International African Institute — Afr J Int Afr Inst
Africa (London) — AfricaL
Africa Now — Afr Now
Africa Perspective — Afr Perspect
Africa Pulse — Afr Pulse
Africa Quarterly — AfQ
Africa Quarterly — Afr Q
Africa Quarterly — Afr Quart
Africa Quarterly — AQ
Africa Report — Afr Rep
Africa Report — Afr Report
Africa Report — Africa R
Africa Report — Africa Rep
Africa Report — Africa Rept
Africa Report — AR
Africa Report — GAFR
Africa Research Bulletin Series — Afr Res Bull
Africa Research Bulletin. Series A. Political — Afr Res Bul Ser A Pol
Africa. Revista Espanola de Colonizacion — AFR
Africa Seminar. Collected Papers — Afr Sem Coll Pap
Africa South — Afr South
Africa Theological Journal — Afr Th J
Africa Theological Journal — Africa Th J
Africa Today — Afr Today
Africa Today — Africa T
Africa Today — AfT
Africa Today — AT
Africa Today — GATO
Africa Woman — Afr Wom
Africaine Ouest Journal de Pharmacologie et Recherche Drogue — Afr Ouest J Pharmacol Rech Drogue
Africa-Middle East Petroleum Directory — Afr Mid East Pet Dir
African Abstracts — AA
African Abstracts — Afr Abstr
African Abstracts — AfrAb
African Administrative Studies — African Admin Studies
African Affairs — Afr Aff
African Affairs — Afr Affairs
African Affairs — AfrA
African Affairs — AfrAf
African Affairs — Afric Affairs
African Affairs — PAAF
African Architect — Afr Arch
African Arts — Afr Art
African Arts [*Los Angeles*] — Afr Arts
African Arts [*Los Angeles*] — AfrA
African Arts — PAAR
African Beekeeping — Afr Beekeep
African Bibliographic Center Current Reading List Series — Afr Bibl Cent Curr Reading List Ser
African Book Publishing Record — ABPR
African Book Publishing Record — Afr Bk Publishing Rec
African Business — AB
African Business — Afr Business
African Business — African Bus
African Business — AGC
African Business and Chamber of Commerce Review — Afr Bus Chamber Commer Rev
African Communist — Afr Communist
African Construction, Building, Civil Engineering, Land Development — AFP
African Defence Journal — Afric Df Jl
African Development — Afr Dev
African Development — Afr Develop
African Ecclesial Review — AFER
African Economic History — Afr Econ H
African Economic History — Afr Econ Hist
African Economic History — African Econ Hist
African Engineering — Afr Eng
African Environment — Afr Environ
African Environment — AFRE
African Environment. Environmental Studies and Regional Planning Bulletin. Supplement. Occasional Papers Series — Afr Environment Suppl
African Forum — Afr Forum
African Forum: A Quarterly Journal of Contemporary Affairs — AForum
African Forum (New York) — Afr Forum NY

African Historian — Afr Historian
African Historian (Ibadan) — Afr Historian I
African Historian. Journal. Historical Society. University of Ife — Afr Historian
African Historical Studies — Afr Hist Stud
African Historical Studies — AfrHS
African Historical Studies — AHS
African Industries — Afr Ind
African Insurance Record — Afr Insur Rec
African Journal of Agricultural Sciences — Afr J Agric Sci
African Journal of Clinical and Experimental Immunology — Afr J Clin Exp Immunol
African Journal of Clinical and Experimental Immunology — AJCIDY
African Journal of Ecology — Afr J Ecol
African Journal of Ecology — AJOEDE
African Journal of Educational Research — African J Ednl Research
African Journal of Medical Sciences [*Later, African Journal of Medicine and Medical Sciences*] — AFMSBG
African Journal of Medical Sciences [*Later, African Journal of Medicine and Medical Sciences*] — Afr J Med Sci
African Journal of Medicine and Medical Sciences — Afr J Med Med Sci
African Journal of Medicine and Medical Sciences — AJMSDC
African Journal of Mycology and Biotechnology — Afr J Mycol Biotechnol
African Journal of Pharmacy and Pharmaceutical Sciences — Afr J Pharm Pharm Sci
African Journal of Psychiatry — Afr J Psychiatr
African Journal of Science and Technology. Series A. Technology — Afr J Sci Technol Ser A
African Journal of Science and Technology. Series B. Science — Afr J Sci Technol Ser B
African Journal of Tropical Hydrobiology and Fisheries — Afr J Trop Hydrobiol Fish
African Journal of Tropical Hydrobiology and Fisheries — AJTHBC
African Journal of Tropical Hydrobiology and Fisheries. Special Issue — Afr J Trop Hydrobiol Fish Spec Issue
African Journal of Tropical Hydrobiology and Fisheries. Special Issue — AJTSBB
African Labour News — Afr Lab N
African Language Review — Afr Language Rev
African Language Review — AfrLRev
African Language Studies — Afr Lang Stud
African Language Studies — Afr Language Stud
African Language Studies — AfrLS
African Language Studies — ALS
African Languages/Langues Africaines — Afr Languages
African Languages/Langues Africaines — AL/LA
African Law Digest — Afr L Digest
African Law Digest — ALD
African Law Studies — Afr L Stud
African Law Studies — Afr Law Stud
African Law Studies — African LS
African Literature Association. Bulletin — Afr Lit Assoc Bul
African Literature Association Newsletter — Afr Lit Ass Newsl
African Literature Association. Newsletter — Afr Lit Assoc Newsl
African Literature Today — AFLT
African Literature Today — Afr Lit Tod
African Literature Today — Afr Lit Today
African Literature Today — Afric Lit Today
African Literature Today — ALT
African Manual on Mining — Afr Man Min
African Monthly [*Grahamstown*] — Af Mo
African Music — Af Mus
African Music — Afr Mus
African Music — Afr Music
African Music — AfricanM
African Newsletter — Afr Ne Lett
African Notes — Afr Notes
African Notes [*Ibadan*] — AfrN
African Notes (Ibadan) — Afr Notes I
African Perspectives — Afr Perspectives
African Religious Research — Afr Relig Res
African Religious Research — Afr Religious Res
African Research and Documentation — Afr Res Doc
African Research and Documentation — Afr Res Docum
African Review — Afr R
African Review — African R
African Review — African Rev
African Rural Economy Paper — Afr Rural Econ Pap
African Scholar — AfrSch
African Social Research — Afr Soc Res
African Social Research — AfriS
African Social Security Series — Afr Soc Secur Ser
African Social Security Series — Afr Soc Security Ser
African Soils — Afr Soils
African Studies — Afr St
African Studies — Afr Stud
African Studies — Afric Stud
African Studies — African Stud
African Studies [*Johannesburg*] — AfrS
African Studies Bulletin — Afr Stud B
African Studies Bulletin — Afr Stud Bull
African Studies Bulletin — African Stud Bul
African Studies Bulletin — ASB
African Studies Newsletter — Afr Stud Newsl
African Studies Review — Afr Stud R
African Studies Review — Afr Stud Rev
African Studies Review — Afric Stud R
African Studies Review — African Stud R
African Studies Review — African Studies R
African Studies Review — AfriSt
African Studies Review — AfrSR
African Studies Review — PASR
African Sugar and Cotton Journal — Afr Sug Cott J
African Trade Review — AFE
African Trade Review — Afr T Rev
African Trade Review — ATR
African Urban Notes — Afr Urban Notes
African Violet — Afr Violet
African Violet Magazine — Afr Violet Mag
African Wild Life — Afr Wild Life
African Wildlife — Afr Wildl
African Wildlife — AFWLAA
African Women — Afr Women
African Writers Series — Afr WS
Africana — AFRIAA
Africana Bulletin [*Warsaw*] — AfB
Africana Bulletin — Afr B
Africana Bulletin — Afr Bull
Africana Bulletin [*Warszawa*] — Africana B
Africana Bulletin — Africana Bull
Africana Bulletin — AfrnB
Africana Journal — Africana J
Africana Library Journal — Africana Lib J
Africana Library Journal — Africana Libr J
Africana Library Journal — AfrLJ
Africana Linguistica — Afr Ling
Africana Linguistica [*Tervuren*] — AfrL
Africana Marburgensia — Africana Marburg
Africana Marburgensia — AfrM
Africana Notes and News — Afr Notes News
Africana Research Bulletin — Africana Res B
Africana Research Bulletin — ARB
Africana Society of Pretoria. Yearbook — Afr Soc Pretoria Yearb
African-American Chamber of Commerce News — Afr Am Chamber Comm News
Africa-Tervuren — Afr Tervuren
Africa-Tervuren — Afr-T
Afrika Heute — Afr Heute
Afrika Matematika. The First Pan-African Mathematical Journal — Afrika Mat
Afrika Natuurlewe — Afr Natuurlewe
Afrika Post — Afr Post
Afrika Spectrum — Afr Spectrum
Afrika Spectrum — ALR
Afrika und Ubersee — Afr u Ubersee
Afrika und Uebersee — Afr Uebersee
Afrika und Uebersee — Afr und Ueb
Afrika und Uebersee — AU
Afrika und Uebersee — AuU
Afrika-Wirtschaft — Afr-Wirtsch
Afrique Agriculture — AAg
Afrique Agriculture — Afr Agric
Afrique Contemporaine — Afr Contemp
Afrique Contemporaine — Afr Contemporaine
Afrique Contemporaine [*Paris*] — Afrique Contemp
Afrique Contemporaine — AfrqC
Afrique Equatoriale. Haut Commissariat de la Republique. Bulletin de la Direction des Mines et de la Geologie — Afr Equat Haut Commis Repub Bull Dir Mines Geol
Afrique et Langage — Afr et Langage
Afrique et l'Asie [*Later, Afrique et l'Asie Modernes*] — Af A
Afrique et l'Asie [*Later, Afrique et l'Asie Modernes*] — Afr et As
Afrique et l'Asie Modernes — Afr Asie
Afrique et l'Asie Modernes — Afr Asie Mod
Afrique et l'Asie Modernes — Afr et Asie Mod
Afrique et l'Asie Modernes — Afr et Asie Modernes
Afrique Francaise — Afr Franc
Afrique Francaise Chirurgicale — Afr Fr Chir
Afrique Industrie — AI
Afrique Industrie Infrastructures — Afr Industr Infrastruct
Afrique Industrie Infrastructures — Afr Industrie Infrastructures
Afrique Industrie Infrastructures — AWO
Afrique Litteraire et Artistique — Afr Litt Artist
Afrique Litteraire et Artistique — Afr Litter et Artist
Afrique Litteraire et Artistique — Afrique Lit et Artistique
Afrique Litteraire et Artistique — ALA
Afrique Medicale — AFMEB8
Afrique Medicale — Afr Med
Afrique Nouvelle — AN
Afro-American Studies — AfrAm S
Afro-American Studies — Afr-Am Stud
Afro-Asian and World Affairs — AAWA
Afro-Asian and World Affairs — Afro-Asian and W Aff
Afro-Asian Economic Review — Afro Asian Econ Rev
Afro-Asian Journal of Ophthalmology — Afro-Asian J Ophtalmol
Afro-Asian Theatre Bulletin — AATB
Afro-Asian Writings — AAW
Afroasiatic Linguistics — Af L
Afroasiatic Linguistics — Afroasiatic Ling
Afro-Hispanic Review — AHR
AFS [*American Foundrymen's Society*] **Cast Metals Research Journal** — AFS Cast Met Res J

AFS [*American Foundrymen's Society*] **International Cast Metals Journal** — AFS Int Cast Met J
AFS [*American Foundrymen's Society*] **Research Reports** — AFS Res Rep
Aftenposten — AFPT
After Dark — AD
AFZ. (Allgemeine Fischwirtschaftszeitung) — AFZ (Allg Fischwirtschaftsztg)
Ag Bits. Computers in Agriculture. Cooperative Extension. University of California — Ag Bits Comput Agric Coop Ext Univ Calif
Ag Chem and Commercial Fertilizer [*Later, Farm Chemicals*] — ACCFC
Ag Chem and Commercial Fertilizer [*Later, Farm Chemicals*] — Ag Chem Commer Fert
Ag Consultant and Fieldman — Ag Consult Fieldman
AG. North Carolina Agricultural Extension Service. North Carolina State University — AG NC Agric Ext Serv NC State Univ
Ag Statistics. North Dakota Crop and Livestock Reporting Service. Agricultural Experiment Station — Ag Stat ND Crop Livest Rep Serv Agric Exp Stn
AGA [*American Gas Association*] **Plastic Pipe Symposium** — AGA Plast Pipe Symp
Against the Current — Current
AGARD [*Advisory Group for Aerospace Research and Development*] **Advisory Report** — AAARBK
AGARD [*Advisory Group for Aerospace Research and Development*] **Advisory Report** [*A publication*] — AGARD Adv Rep
AGARD [*Advisory Group for Aerospace Research and Development*] **Advisory Report** [*A publication*] — AGARD Advis Rep
AGARD [*Advisory Group for Aeronautical Research and Development*] **AG Document** — AGARD AG Doc
AGARD [*Advisory Group for Aerospace Research and Development*] **Agardograph** — AGAGAS
AGARD [*Advisory Group for Aerospace Research and Development*] **Agardograph** — AGARD Agardogr
AGARD [*Advisory Group for Aerospace Research and Development*] **Annual Meeting** — AGARD Annu Meet
AGARD [*Advisory Group for Aerospace Research and Development*] **Conference Proceedings** — AGARD Conf Proc
AGARD [*Advisory Group for Aerospace Research and Development*] **Conference Proceedings** — AGARD CP
AGARD [*Advisory Group for Aeronautical Research and Development*] **Conference Proceedings** — AGCPA
AGARD [*Advisory Group for Aerospace Research and Development*] **Conference Proceedings** — AGCPAV
AGARD [*Advisory Group for Aerospace Research and Development*] **Lecture Series** — AGARD Lect Ser
AGARD [*Advisory Group for Aerospace Research and Development*] **Manual** — AGARD Man
AGARD [*Advisory Group for Aerospace Research and Development*] **(North Atlantic Treaty Organization)** — AGARD (NATO)
AGARD [*Advisory Group for Aerospace Research and Development*] **Report** — AGARD Rep
AGARD [*Advisory Group for Aerospace Research and Development*] **Specification** — AGARD Specif
AgBiotech Bulletin — AgBiotech Bull
Age and Ageing — GAAG
Age and Ageing Science. Annuals — Age & Ageing
Age and Ageing. Supplement — Age Ageing Suppl
[*The*] **Age. Large Print Weekly** — LPW
Age Literary Supplement — Age Lit Supp
Age Nouveau — Age Nouv
Age Nouveau — AgN
Age Nouveau — AN
Age Nucleaire — Age Nucl
Age of Independence — Age Indep
Aged and High Risk Surgical Patient. Medical, Surgical, and Anesthetic Management — Aged High Risk Surg Patient Med Surg Anesth Manage
Aged Care and Services Review — Aged Care Serv Rev
Agefi — AG
Ageing and Society — PANS
Ageing of Fish. Proceedings. International Symposium — Ageing Fish Proc Int Symp
Agence Economique et Financiere — AGEFI
Agence Europe — AE
Agence Spatiale Europeenne. Brochure ESA [*European Space Agency*] — Agence Spat Eur Brochure ESA
Agence Spatiale Europeenne. Bulletin — Agence Spat Eur Bull
Agence Spatiale Europeenne. ESA STR — Agence Spat Eur ESA STR
Agence Spatiale Europeenne. Revue Scientifique et Technique — Agence Spat Eur Rev Sci Tech
Agency Sales — AGS
Agency Sales Magazine — AGE
Agenda de l'Agriculteur et du Vigneron — Agenda Agric Vigneron
Agents and Actions — Agent Actio
Agents and Actions. Supplement — Agents Actions Suppl
Agenutemagen. Indians of New Brunswick [*Canada*] — AGTG
Agenzia Economica Finanziaria — AEF
Agerpres Information Bulletin — AP Inf B
AgExporter. United States Department of Agriculture. Foreign Agricultural Service — AgExporter US Dep Agric Foreign Agric Serv
AGF [*Arbeitsgemeinschaft der Grossforschungseinrichtungen*] **Mitteilungen** — AGF Mitt
Agfa Kinetechnische Mitteilungen — Agfa Kinetech Mitt
Aggiornamenti Clinico Terapeutici — Aggiorn Clinico Ter
Aggiornamenti in Ematologia — Aggiorn Ematol
Aggiornamenti Sociali — Aggiorn Soc
Aggiornamenti sulle Malattie da Infezione [*Italy*] — Aggiorn Mal Infez
Aggiornamento Pediatrico — Aggiorn Pediatr
Agglomeration — Agglom
Agglomeration. International Symposium — Agglom Int Symp
Aggregate Resources Inventory Paper. Ontario Geological Survey — Aggregate Resour Inventory Pap Ontario Geol Surv
Aggressive Behavior — Aggressive Behav
Aging — GAGE
Aging and Human Development — Aging Hum Dev
Aging and Leisure Living — Aging Leis Living
Aging and Work — AGW
Aging Gametes, Their Biology and Pathology. Proceedings. International Symposium on Aging Gametes — Aging Gametes Proc Int Symp
Aging, Immunology, and Infectious Disease — Aging Immunol Infect Dis
Aging News — Aging N
Agitation dans l'Industrie Chimique. Symposium International de Genie Chimique — Agitation Ind Chim Symp Int Genie Chim
Aglow — AGL
AGMANZ News. Art Galleries and Museums Association of New Zealand — AGMANZ News
Agnes Karll-Schwester. Der Krankenpfleger — Agnes Karll Schwest Krankenpfleger
Agni Review — Agni
Agora. Informatics in a Changing World — Agora Inf Changing World
Agora Mathematica [*Paris*] — Agora Math
Agora-Documentaire [*Database*] — ADOC
Agora-Economie [*Database*] — AECO
Agora-English [*Database*] — AFPE
Agora-General [*Database*] — AGRA
Agora-Sports [*Database*] — ASPO
AGR. Akten der Gesellschaft fuer Griechische und Hellenistische Rechtesgechichte — AGR
AGR. University of Kentucky. Cooperative Extension Service — AGR Univ KY Coop Ext Serv
Agra Europe — Ag Europe
Agra University. Bulletin — Agra Univ Bul
Agra University. Journal of Research [*India*] — Agra Univ J Res
Agra University. Journal of Research — AUJR
Agra University. Journal of Research Science — Agra Univ J Res Sci
Agra University Journal of Research Science — Agra Univ Jour Res Sci
Agrarische Rundschau — Agrar Rundsch
Agrarpolitische Revue — Agrarpolit Rev
Agrartoerteneti Szemle — Agrartoert Szle
Agrartoerteneti Szemle — Agrartort Szemle
Agrartudomany — Agrartud
Agrartudomanyi Egyetem Agrarkozgazdasagi Karanak Kiadvanyai — Agrartud Egy Agrarkozgazd Kar Kiad
Agrartudomanyi Egyetem Agronomiai Kar Kiadvanyai. Editions. Faculty of Agronomy. University of Agricultural Sciences — Ed Fac Agron Univ Agric Sci
Agrartudomanyi Egyetem Agronomiai Karanak Kiadvanyai — Agrartud Egy Agron Kar Kiad
Agrartudomanyi Egyetem Allattenyesztesi Karanak Koezlemenyei (Goedoelloe) — Agrartud Egy Allattenyesz Karanak Kozl (Godollo)
Agrartudomanyi Egyetem Kert- es Szoeloegazdasagtudomanyi Karanak Evkoenyve. Annales Sectionis Horti- et Viticulturae Universitatis Scientiae Agriculturae — Agrartud Egyet Kert Szoeloegazdasagtud Karanak Evk
Agrartudomanyi Egyetem Kert-es Szologazdasagtudomanyi Karanak Evkonyve — Agrartud Egy Kert Szologazdasagtud Karanak Evk
Agrartudomanyi Egyetem Kert-es Szologazdasagtudomanyi Karanak Koezlemenyei — Agrartud Egy Kert Szologazdasagtud Karanak Kozl
Agrartudomanyi Egyetem Koezlemenyei (Goedoelloe) — Agrartud Egy Kozl (Godollo)
Agrartudomanyi Egyetem Mezoegazdasagi Gepeszmernoki Karanak Koezlemenyei — Agrartud Egy Mezogazd Gepeszmern Karanak Kozl
Agrartudomanyi Egyetem Mezoegazdasagi Karanak Evkonyve — Agrartud Egy Mezogazd Karanak Evk
Agrartudomanyi Egyetem Mezoegazdasagtudomanyi Karanak Koezlemenyei [*Hungary*] — Agrartud Egy Mezogazdasagtud Karanak Kozl
Agrartudomanyi Egyetem Mezoegazdasagtudomanyi Karanak Koezlemenyei (Goedoelloe) — Agrartud Egyet Mezoegtud Kar Koezl (Goedoelloe)
Agrartudomanyi Egyetem Mezoegazdasagtudomanyi Karanak Koezlemenyei (Goedoelloe) — Agrartud Egyetem Mezoegazdasagtud Kar Koezlem (Goedoelloe)
Agrartudomanyi Egyetem Tudomanyos Tajekoztatoja [*Hungary*] — Agrartud Egy Tud Tajek
Agrartudomanyi Egyetem Tudomanyos Tajekoztatoja (Goedoelloe) — Agrartud Egyetem Tud Tajekoz (Goedoelloe)
Agrartudomanyi Foiskola Tudomanyos Koezlemenyei (Debrecen) — Agrartud Foisk Tud Koezlem (Debrecen)
Agrartudomanyi Foiskola Tudomanyos Ulesszakanak Eloadasai Debreceni — Agrartud Foisk Tud Ulesszakanak Eloadasai Debreceni
Agrartudomanyi Koezlemenyek — Agrartud Kozl
Agrartudomanyi Szemle — Agrartud Sz
Agrarwirtschaft — AGR
Agrarwirtschaft — Agrarwirt
Agrarwirtschaft — Agrarwirts
Agrarwirtschaft — Agrawirts
Agrarwirtschaft und Agrarsoziologie [*Economie et Sociologie Rurales*] — Agrarwirt und Agrarsoziol
Agregation de Mathematiques — Agreg Math
Agregation Plaquettaire. Rapports presentes au Congres Francais de Medecine — Agregation Plaquettaire Rapp Congr Fr Med
Agressologie — Agressolog
Agressologie — AGSOA
Agri Hortique Genetica — Agr Hor Gen

Agri Hortique Genetica — Agri Hort Genet
Agri Marketing — Agri Mktg
AGRI/MECH Report. Economic Commission for Europe — AGRI/MECH Rep Econ Comm Eur
Agri-Afrique — Agri Afr
Agribusiness Decision — Agribus Decis
Agribusiness Information — AGBIZ
AgriBusiness News for Kentucky. University of Kentucky. Cooperative Exension Service — AgricBus News Ky Univ Ky Coop Ext Serv
Agribusiness Worldwide — Agribus W
Agrichemical Age — AGCACM
Agrichemical Age — Agrichem Age
Agrichemical West — Agrichem W
Agricoltore Bresciano — Agr Bresciano
Agricoltore Ferrarese — Agr Ferrarese
Agricoltura Coloniale — Agric Colon
Agricoltura della Spezia — Agr Spezia
Agricoltura delle Venezie — Agr Venezie
Agricoltura delle Venezie [*Italy*] — Agric Venezie
Agricoltura d'Italia [*Rome*] — Agr Ital
Agricoltura Italiana [*Pisa*] — AGIPAR
Agricoltura Italiana (Pisa) — AGIPA
Agricoltura Italiana (Pisa) — Agric Ital (Pisa)
Agricoltura Italiana (Pisa) — Agricoltura Ital (Pisa)
Agricoltura Italiana (Rome) — Agric Ital (Rome)
Agricoltura Milanese — Agr Milanese
Agricoltura Napoletana — Agr Napoletana
Agricoltura Nuova — Agric Nuova
Agricoltura Pugliese — Agric Pugliese
Agriculteurs de France — AGCFAZ
Agriculteurs de France — Agric Fr
Agricultor Costarricense — Agric Costarricense
Agricultor Mexicano y Hogar — Agric Mexicano
Agricultor Salvadoreno. Ministerio de Agricultura y Ganaderia — Agric Salvadoreno
Agricultura — Agr
Agricultura de Hoje — Agric Hoje
Agricultura de las Americas — Agr Amer
Agricultura de las Americas — Agric Am
Agricultura de las Americas — Agricultura Am
Agricultura de las Americas (Kansas City) — Agric Amer Kansas City
Agricultura em Sao Paulo — Agr Sao Paulo
Agricultura em Sao Paulo — Agric Sao Paulo
Agricultura en Chiriqui — Agric Chiriqui
Agricultura en El Salvador — Agric El Salv
Agricultura en El Salvador — Agric El Salvador
Agricultura en El Salvador — ASLVA8
Agricultura Experimental — Agric Exp
Agricultura (Heverlee) — AGRIAH
Agricultura (Lisboa) — AGLAAV
Agricultura (Lisboa) — Agr (Lisboa)
Agricultura (Santo Domingo) — Agr (Santo Domingo)
Agricultura Sinica — Agric Sin
Agricultura Tecnica — Agr Tec
Agricultura Tecnica — Agricultura Tec
Agricultura Tecnica [*Santiago*] — AGTCA9
Agricultura Tecnica. Chile. Direccion General de Agricultura — Agric Tecn
Agricultura Tecnica en Mexico — Agr Tec Mex
Agricultura Tecnica en Mexico — Agric Tec Mex
Agricultura Tecnica en Mexico — Agricultura Tec Mex
Agricultura Tecnica en Mexico — ATMXAQ
Agricultura Tecnica (Santiago) — Agric Tec (Santiago)
Agricultura Tropical — Agr Trop
Agricultura Tropical — Agric Trop
Agricultura Tropical — Agricultura Trop
Agricultura Tropical — AGTBA6
Agricultura Venezolana — Agric Venez
Agricultura Venezolana — AGVEAP
Agricultura y Ganaderia — AGGAA6
Agricultura y Ganaderia — Agr Ganad
Agricultura y Ganaderia — Agric Ganad
Agricultura y Sociedad — Agric Y Soc
Agriculturae Conspectus Scientificus — Agric Conspectus Sci
Agriculturae Conspectus Scientificus — PJZSAZ
Agricultural Administration — AGA
Agricultural Administration — Agric Adm
Agricultural Administration and Extension — Agric Adm Ext
Agricultural Ammonia News — Agr Ammonia News
Agricultural and Biological Chemistry [*Tokyo*] — Agr Biol Ch
Agricultural and Biological Chemistry [*Tokyo*] — Agr Biol Chem
Agricultural and Biological Chemistry [*Tokyo*] — Agric & Biol Chem
Agricultural and Biological Chemistry [*Tokyo*] — Agric Biol Chem
Agricultural and Credit Outlook — Ag & Cr Outlk
Agricultural and Food Chemistry — Agric Fd Chemy
Agricultural and Food Science in Finland — Agric Food Sci Finl
Agricultural and Forest Meteorology — AFMEEB
Agricultural and Forest Meteorology — Agric For Meteorol
Agricultural and Horticultural Engineering Abstracts — Agric Hort Engng Abstr
Agricultural and Veterinary Chemicals — Agr Vet Chem
Agricultural and Veterinary Chemicals — Agric Vet Chem
Agricultural Aviation — Agr Aviation
Agricultural Aviation — Agric Aviat
Agricultural Banking and Finance — Agr Banking Finan
Agricultural Biotechnology News — Agric Biotechnol News
Agricultural Bulletin. Canterbury Chamber of Commerce — Agr Bull Canterbury Chamber Commer
Agricultural Bulletin. Federated Malay States — Agric Bull Fed Malay States
Agricultural Bulletin. Oregon Department of Agriculture — Agr Bull Oreg Dept Agr
Agricultural Bulletin. Saga University — Agr Bull Saga Univ
Agricultural Bulletin. Saga University — Agric Bull Saga Univ
Agricultural Bureau of New South Wales. State Congress — Agric Bur NSW State Congr
Agricultural Chemicals — Ag Chem
Agricultural Chemicals — Ag Chemicals
Agricultural Chemicals — AGCHA7
Agricultural Chemicals — Agr Chem
Agricultural Chemicals — Agric Chem
Agricultural Commodities Data Base — AGDATA
Agricultural Communications Research Report — Agric Commun Res Rep
Agricultural Digest — Ag Digest
Agricultural Economics and Farm Management Occasional Paper. Department of Agriculture. University of Queensland — Agric Econ Fm Mgmt Occ Pap Dep Agric Qd Univ
Agricultural Economics Bulletin for Africa — Agric Econ B Afr
Agricultural Economics Bulletin for Africa — Agric Econ Bull for Afr
Agricultural Economics Bulletin. New South Wales. Division of Marketing and Economic Services — Agric Econ Bull NSW Div Mark Econ Serv
Agricultural Economics Extension Series. University of Kentucky. Cooperative Extension Service — Agric Econ Ext Ser Univ KY Coop Ext Serv
Agricultural Economics Information Series. University of Maryland. Cooperative Extension Service — Agr Econ Inform Ser Univ MD Coop Ext Serv
Agricultural Economics. Journal. International Association of Agricultural Economics — Agric Econ J Int Assoc Agric Econ
Agricultural Economics Mimeo. Michigan State University of Agriculture and Applied Science. Cooperative Extension Service — Agr Econ Mimeo Mich State Univ Agr Appl Sci Coop Ext Serv
Agricultural Economics Mimeo Report. Florida Agricultural Experiment Station — Agr Econ Mimeo Rep Fla Agr Exp Sta
Agricultural Economics Pamphlet. South Dakota Agricultural Experiment Station [*A publication*] — Agr Econ Pam S Dak Agr Exp Sta
Agricultural Economics Report. Department of Agricultural Economics. Michigan State University — Agric Econ Rep Dep Agric Econ Mich State Univ
Agricultural Economics Report. Kansas Agricultural Experiment Station — Agr Econ Rep Kans Agr Exp Sta
Agricultural Economics Report. Michigan State University. Department of Agricultural Economics — Agric Econ Rep Mich State Univ Dep Agric Econ
Agricultural Economics Report. Michigan State University of Agriculture and Applied Science. Cooperative Extension Service — Agr Econ Rep Mich State Univ Agr Appl Sci Coop Ext Serv
Agricultural Economics Report. North Dakota Agricultural Experiment Station — Agr Econ Rep N Dak Agr Exp Sta
Agricultural Economics Research — Ag Econ Res
Agricultural Economics Research — AGER
Agricultural Economics Research — Agr Econ Re
Agricultural Economics Research — Agr Econ Res
Agricultural Economics Research — Agric Econ Res
Agricultural Economics Research — Agric Econ Research
Agricultural Economics Research Report. Mississippi Agricultural and Forestry Experiment Station — Agric Econ Res Rep Miss Agric For Exp Sta
Agricultural Economics Research. United States Department of Agriculture. Economic Research Service — Agric Econ Res US Dep Agric Econ Res Serv
Agricultural Economist — Agric Econ
Agricultural Education — Agric Educ
Agricultural Education Magazine — Ag Ed
Agricultural Education Magazine — Agr Educ Ma
Agricultural Education Magazine — Agric Educ Mag
Agricultural Electricity Institute. Report — Agric Electr Inst Rep
Agricultural Engineer — Agric Engn
Agricultural Engineer (London) — Agric Eng (Lond)
Agricultural Engineering [*St. Joseph, MI*] — Ag Eng
Agricultural Engineering — AGENAZ
Agricultural Engineering [*St. Joseph, MI*] — Agr Eng
Agricultural Engineering — Agric Eng
Agricultural Engineering [*St. Joseph, MI*] — Agric Engin
Agricultural Engineering (Australia) — Agric Eng (Aust)
Agricultural Engineering (Australia) — Agric Engng (Aust)
Agricultural Engineering Extension Bulletin. New York State College of Agriculture. Department of Agricultural Engineering — Agr Eng Ext Bull NY State Coll Agr Dept Agr Eng
Agricultural Engineering Journal — Agric Eng J
Agricultural Engineering (South Africa) — Agric Eng (S Afr)
Agricultural Engineering (St. Joseph, MI) — Agric Eng (St Joseph Mich)
Agricultural Engineers Yearbook — Agric Eng Yearb
Agricultural Enterprise Studies in England and Wales Economic Report — Agric Enterp Stud Engl Wales Econ Rep
Agricultural Experiment Station. Agricultural College of Colorado. Bulletin — Agric Exp Sta Agric Coll Colorado Bull
Agricultural Experiment Station. Alabama Polytechnic Institute. Progress Report Series — Agric Exp Stn Ala Polytech Inst Prog Rep Ser
Agricultural Experiment Station at Arkansas Industrial University. Bulletin — Agric Exp Sta Arkansas Industr Univ Bull
Agricultural Experiment Station. University of Alaska. Bulletin — AESUAB
Agricultural Experiment Station. University of Alaska. Technical Bulletin — AESUATB
Agricultural Experiment Station. University of Vermont. Bulletin — Agric Exp Stn Univ VT Bull
Agricultural Experiment Station. University of Vermont. Bulletin — VAEBAI

Agricultural Finance Outlook — Agric Fin Out
Agricultural Finance Review — Agric Fin R
Agricultural Finance Review — Agric Fin Rev
Agricultural Finance Review — Agric Financ Rev
Agricultural Finance Review. United States Department of Agriculture. Economics, Statistics, and Cooperative Service — Agric Financ Rev US Dep Agric Econ Stat Coop Serv
Agricultural Gazette of Canada — Ag Gaz of Canada
Agricultural Gazette of Canada — Agric Gaz Can
Agricultural Gazette of Canada — Agric Gaz Canada
Agricultural Gazette of New South Wales — Ag Gaz NSW
Agricultural Gazette of New South Wales — Ag Gaz of New South Wales
Agricultural Gazette of New South Wales — AGNSAR
Agricultural Gazette of New South Wales — Agr Gaz NSW
Agricultural Gazette of New South Wales — Agric Gaz NSW
Agricultural Gazette of Tasmania — Agric Gaz Tasm
Agricultural History — Ag H
Agricultural History — Ag Hist
Agricultural History — Agr Hist
Agricultural History — Agric Hist
Agricultural History — AH
Agricultural History — PAGH
Agricultural History Review — Ag Hist R
Agricultural History Review — Agr Hist Rev
Agricultural History Review — Agric Hist R
Agricultural History Review — Agric Hist Rev
Agricultural Index — Agric Index
Agricultural, Insecticide, and Fungicide Association. News — AIF News
Agricultural Institute Review — Agr Inst Rev
Agricultural Institute Review — Agric Inst Rev
Agricultural Journal and Mining Record. Maritzburg — Agric J & Mining Rec Maritzburg
Agricultural Journal (Bridgetown, Barbados) — Agric J (Bridgetown Barbados)
Agricultural Journal (Cape Town) — Agric J (Cape Town)
Agricultural Journal. Department of Agriculture. Fiji Islands — Agric J Dep Agric Fiji Isl
Agricultural Journal. Department of Agriculture. Fiji Islands — AJAFAC
Agricultural Journal. Department of Agriculture (Suva, Fiji) — Agric J Dep Agric (Fiji)
Agricultural Journal. Department of Agriculture (Suva, Fiji) — Agric J (Suva Fiji)
Agricultural Journal. Department of Agriculture (Victoria, British Columbia) [*A publication*] — Agric J Dept Agric (Victoria BC)
Agricultural Journal. Department of Science and Agriculture (Barbados) — Agric J Barbados
Agricultural Journal. Kusunoki Society. Kusunoki Noho — Agric J Kusunoki Soc
Agricultural Journal of British Columbia — Ag J of British Columbia
Agricultural Journal of British Columbia — Agric J British Columbia
Agricultural Journal of British Guiana — Agric J Br Gui
Agricultural Journal of British Guiana — Agric J Br Guiana
Agricultural Journal of Egypt — Ag J of Egypt
Agricultural Journal of Egypt — Agric J Egypt
Agricultural Journal of India — Ag J of India
Agricultural Journal of India — Agric J India
Agricultural Journal of South Africa — Agric J S Afr
Agricultural Journal of the Cape Of Good Hope — Agric J Cape GH
Agricultural Journal of the Union of South Africa — Agric J Union S Afr
Agricultural Land. Our Disappearing Heritage. Symposium — Agric Land Our Disappearing Heritage Symp
Agricultural Law Journal — Agr LJ
Agricultural Leaders Digest — Agr Leaders Dig
Agricultural Literature of Czechoslovakia — Agric Lit Czech
Agricultural Machinery Journal — Agric Mach J
Agricultural Magazine. Kuo Li Pei Ching Nung Yeh Chuan Men Hsueeh Hsiao Tsa Chih — Agric Mag
Agricultural Marketing (Nagpur) — Agr Market (Nagpur)
Agricultural Marketing (Washington, DC) — Agr Market (Washington DC)
Agricultural Marketing (Washington, DC) — Agric Mark (Washington)
Agricultural Mechanization — Agr Mech
Agricultural Mechanization in Asia [*Japan*] — Agric Mech Asia
Agricultural Mechanization in Asia [*Japan*] — AMA
Agricultural Merchant — Agr Merchant
Agricultural Meteorology — AGMYA6
Agricultural Meteorology — Agr Meteor
Agricultural Meteorology — Agr Meteorol
Agricultural Meteorology — Agric Met
Agricultural Meteorology — Agric Meteorol
Agricultural Monographs. US Department of Agriculture — Agric Monogr USDA
Agricultural News (Barbados) — Agric News (Barbados)
Agricultural News Letter. E. I. Du Pont De Nemours and Company — Agric News Lett E I Du Pont De Nemours Co
Agricultural Newsletter — Ag NL
Agricultural Newsletter — Agr Newslett
Agricultural Newsletter (Manila) — Agric Newsl (Manila)
Agricultural Outlook — Ag Outlook
Agricultural Outlook — Agric Outl
Agricultural Outlook — Agric Outlook
Agricultural Outlook AO. US Department of Agriculture. Economic Research Service — Agric Outlook AO US Dep Agric Econ Res Serv
Agricultural Policy Review — Agr Policy Rev
Agricultural Progress — AGPGAZ
Agricultural Progress — Agr Prog
Agricultural Progress — Agr Progr
Agricultural Progress — Agric Prog
Agricultural Record [*South Australia*] — AGRED8
Agricultural Record — Agric Rec
Agricultural Record (South Australia) — Agric Rec (S Aust)
Agricultural Record. South Australia Department of Agriculture — Agric Rec South Aust Dep Agric
Agricultural Refineries. A Bridge from Farm to Industry — Agric Refin Bridge Farm Ind
Agricultural Research — Ag Res
Agricultural Research — Agr Res
Agricultural Research [*Washington, DC*] — AGREA5
Agricultural Research — Agric Res
Agricultural Research — AGYRA
Agricultural Research [*New Delhi*] — AGYRAB
Agricultural Research — ARES
Agricultural Research — GAGR
Agricultural Research [*Kurashiki*] — NOGKAV
Agricultural Research Corporation (Gezira). Technical Bulletin — Agric Res Corp (Gezira) Tech Bull
Agricultural Research Corporation [*Gezira*]. Technical Bulletin — ARTBCH
Agricultural Research Council. Food Research Institute [*Norwich*]. Annual Report — AFOAA5
Agricultural Research Council. Food Research Institute (Norwich). Annual Report — Agric Res Counc Food Res Inst (Norwich) Annu Rep
Agricultural Research Council (Great Britain). Letcombe Laboratory. Annual Report — Agric Res Counc (GB) Letcombe Lab Annu Rep
Agricultural Research Council (Great Britain). Radiobiological Laboratory — Agric Res Counc (GB) Radiobiol Lab
Agricultural Research Council (Great Britain). Radiobiological Laboratory. ARCRL — Agric Res Counc (GB) Radiobiol Lab ARCRL
Agricultural Research Council. Meat Research Institute [*Bristol*]. Annual Report — AGLABW
Agricultural Research Council. Meat Research Institute [*Bristol*]. Biennial Report — BARIDN
Agricultural Research Council. Meat Research Institute. Biennial Report (Bristol) — Agric Res Counc Meat Res Inst Bien Rep (Bristol)
Agricultural Research Council. Meat Research Institute (Bristol). Annual Report — Agric Res Counc Meat Res Inst (Bristol) Annu Rep
Agricultural Research Council. Meat Research Institute (Bristol). Memorandum — Agric Res Counc Meat Res Inst (Bristol) Memo
Agricultural Research Council. Meat Research Institute [*Bristol*]. Memorandum — AMRMC5
Agricultural Research Council. Radiobiology Laboratory Report [*United Kingdom*] — ARCRL Rep
Agricultural Research Council. Report — Agric Res Counc Rep
Agricultural Research Council. Soil Survey of England and Wales. Technical Monograph — Agric Res Counc Soil Surv Tech Monogr
Agricultural Research for Development — Agric Res Dev
Agricultural Research Guyana — Agric Res Guyana
Agricultural Research Guyana — ARGUC9
Agricultural Research in Kansas. Kansas Agricultural Experiment Station — Agric Res Kans Kans Agric Exp Stn
Agricultural Research (India) — Agr Res (India)
Agricultural Research Institute Ukiriguru. Progress Report — Agric Res Inst Ukiriguru Prog Rep
Agricultural Research Institute Ukiriguru. Progress Report — PRAUD9
Agricultural Research Journal of Kerala — Agr Res J Kerala
Agricultural Research Journal of Kerala — Agric Res J Kerala
Agricultural Research Journal of Kerala — ARJKAQ
Agricultural Research (Kurashiki) — Agric Res (Kurashiki)
Agricultural Research Manual. US Department of Agriculture. Science and Education Administration — Agric Res Man US Dep Agric Sci Educ Adm
Agricultural Research (New Delhi) — Agric Res (New Delhi)
Agricultural Research News Notes [*Lima*] — AGNNAC
Agricultural Research News Notes (Lima) — Agric Res News Notes (Lima)
Agricultural Research Organization. Department of Forestry. Ilanot Leaflet — Agric Res Organ Dep For Ilanot Leaf
Agricultural Research Organization. Division of Forestry. Ilanot Leaflet — Agric Res Organ Div For Ilanot Leafl
Agricultural Research Organization. Division of Forestry. Ilanot Leaflet — ARFLBA
Agricultural Research Organization. Division of Forestry. Ilanot Leaflet — LARFEN
Agricultural Research Organization. Pamphlet (Bet-Dagan) — Agric Res Organ Pam (Bet-Dagan)
Agricultural Research Organization. Preliminary Report (Bet-Dagan) — Agric Res Organ Prelim Rep (Bet-Dagan)
Agricultural Research Organization. Preliminary Report (Bet-Dagan) — PRAODP
Agricultural Research Organization. Volcani Center. Special Publication — Agric Res Organ Volcani Cent Spec Publ
Agricultural Research (Pretoria) — Agr Res (Pretoria)
Agricultural Research Reports [*Wageningen*] — VLONAB
Agricultural Research Reports (Wageningen) — Agric Res Rep (Wageningen)
Agricultural Research Reports (Wageningen) (Verslagen van Landbouwkundige Onderzoekingen) — Agric Res Rep (Wageningen) (Versl Landbouwk Onderz)
Agricultural Research Review [*Cairo*] — Agr Res Rev
Agricultural Research Review — Agric Res Rev
Agricultural Research Review — AGRRA
Agricultural Research Review [*Cairo*] — AGRRAA
Agricultural Research Review (Cairo) — Agric Res Rev (Cairo)
Agricultural Research. Seoul National University — Agri Res Seoul Nat Univ
Agricultural Research. Seoul National University — Agric Res Seoul Natl Univ
Agricultural Research. Seoul National University — NYSTDL
Agricultural Research (Taipei) — Agric Res Taipei
Agricultural Research. United States Department of Agriculture. Research Service — Agric Res US Dep Agric Res Serv

Agricultural Research. US Department of Agriculture. Agricultural Research Service — Agric Res US Dep Agric Agric Res Serv
Agricultural Research (Washington, DC) — Agr Res (Washington DC)
Agricultural Research (Washington, DC) — Agric Res (Wash DC)
Agricultural Review — Ag R
Agricultural Science [*Jogjakarta*] — ILPEAG
Agricultural Science [*Sofia*] — SENAAL
Agricultural Science Bulletin — Agric Sci Bull
Agricultural Science Digest — Agric Sci Dig
Agricultural Science Digest — ASDIDY
Agricultural Science in Finland — Agric Sci Finl
Agricultural Science in South Africa. Agroplantae — Agric Sci S Afr Agroplantae
Agricultural Science (Jogjakarta) — Agric Sci (Jogjakarta)
Agricultural Science Journal — Ag Sci J
Agricultural Science. National University of Peiping/Nung Hsueeh Yueeh K'an (Peiping) — Agric Sci Peiping
Agricultural Science Review — Ag Sci R
Agricultural Science Review — Agr Sci Rev
Agricultural Science Review — Agric Sci R
Agricultural Science Review — Agric Sci Rev
Agricultural Science Review. Cooperative State Research Service. US Department of Agriculture — Agric Sci Rev Coop State Res Serv US Dep Agric
Agricultural Science Review. Cooperative State Research Service. US Department of Agriculture — ASRWA7
Agricultural Science (Sofia) — Agric Sci (Sofia)
Agricultural Services Bulletin. Food and Agriculture Organization of the United Nations — Agric Serv Bull FAO
Agricultural Situation [*Later, Farmline Magazine*] — Ag Situation
Agricultural Situation [*Later, Farmline Magazine*] — Agr Situation
Agricultural Situation [*Later, Farmline Magazine*] — Agric Situa
Agricultural Situation in India — Agr Sit Ind
Agricultural Situation in India — Agr Situation India
Agricultural Situation in India — Agric Situation India
Agricultural Statistics — Ag Stat
Agricultural Statistics. North Dakota Crop and Livestock Reporting Service — Agr Statist N Dak Crop Livestock Rep Serv
Agricultural Supply Industry — Ag Sply Ind
Agricultural Systems — Agric Syst
Agricultural Systems — AGSYD5
Agricultural Technologist — Agric Technol
Agricultural University (Wageningen). Papers — Agric Univ (Wageningen) Pap
Agricultural University (Wageningen). Papers — AUWPET
Agricultural Wastes — Agr Wastes
Agricultural Wastes [*England*] — Agric Wastes
Agricultural Water Management — Agric Water Manage
Agricultural Water Management — AWMADF
Agricultural Weather Research Series — Agric Weather Res Ser
Agricultural World/Nogyo Sekai — Agric World
Agricultural Zoology Reviews — Agric Zool Rev
Agricultural-Energy Transportation Digest — Agric-Energy Transp Dig
Agriculture — Agric
Agriculture Abroad — Agr Abroad
Agriculture Abroad — Agric Abroad
Agriculture Algerienne — Agr Alger
Agriculture Algerienne [*Algeria*] — Agric Alger
Agriculture and Agro-Industries Journal — Agric Agroind J
Agriculture and Animal Husbandry — Agr Anim Husb
Agriculture and Animal Husbandry — Agric Anim Hub
Agriculture and Environment — AGEND4
Agriculture and Environment — Agric Environ
Agriculture and Food Chemistry. Journal — Ag Food Jl
Agriculture and Forestry Bulletin — AFBUD3
Agriculture and Forestry Bulletin — Agric For Bull
Agriculture and Forestry Bulletin. University of Alberta — AFBU
Agriculture and Forestry News/Nung Lin T'ung Hsin — Agric Forest News
Agriculture and Horticulture — Agr Hort
Agriculture and Horticulture [*Japan*] — Agric Hort
Agriculture and Livestock in India — Ag & Livestock India
Agriculture and Livestock in India — Agr Livestock India
Agriculture and Livestock in India — Agric Livestock India
Agriculture and Resources Quarterly — Agric Resour Q
Agriculture Asia — Agr Asia
Agriculture Asia — Agric Asia
Agriculture at OSU. Oklahoma State University. Agricultural Experiment Station — Agric OSU Okla State Univ Agric Exp Stn
Agriculture Bulletin — Agric Bull
Agriculture Bulletin. University of Alberta [*Later, Agriculture and Forestry Bulletin*] — AGBA
Agriculture Canada. Annual Report — Agric Can Annu Rep
Agriculture Canada. Monograph — Agric Can Monogr
Agriculture Canada. Rapport Annuel — Agric Can Rapp Annu
Agriculture Canada. Research Branch Report — Agric Can Res Branch Rep
Agriculture Canada. Weed Survey Series — Agric Can Weed Surv Ser
Agriculture Circular. United States Department of Agriculture — Agric Circ US Dep Agric
Agriculture. Corporation des Agronomes de la Province de Quebec (Montreal) — Agriculture Montreal
Agriculture Decisions — Agri Dec
Agriculture, Ecosystems, and Environment — AEENDO
Agriculture, Ecosystems, and Environment — Agric Ecosyst & Environ
Agriculture, Ecosystems, and Environment — Agric Ecosystems Environ
Agriculture Fact Sheet. US Department of Agriculture — Agric Fact Sh US Dep Agric
Agriculture, Food, and Nutrition Service. Publications — FNS
Agriculture (Great Britain). Ministry of Agriculture, Fisheries, and Food — Agr (Gt Brit)
Agriculture Handbook. United States Department of Agriculture — Agric Handb US Dep Agric
Agriculture Handbook. United States Department of Agriculture. Agricultural Research Service — Agric Handb US Dep Agric Agric Res Serv
Agriculture Handbook. United States Department of Agriculture. Combined Forest Pest Research and Development Program — Agric Handb US Dep Agric Comb For Pest Res Dev Program
Agriculture in Aomori. Aomori Nogyo. Aomori Prefecture Agricultural Improvement Association — Agric Aomori
Agriculture in Hokkaido [*Japan*] — Agric Hokkaido
Agriculture in Hokkaido. Hokuno — Agric Hokkaido Hokuno
Agriculture in Hokkaido/Nogyo Hokkaido — Agric Hokkaido Nogyo Hokkaido
Agriculture in Israel — Agr Israel
Agriculture in Northern Ireland — Agr N Ireland
Agriculture in Northern Ireland — Agriculture in Ire
Agriculture in the Americas — Ag Am
Agriculture in the Americas — Agr Am
Agriculture in the Americas — Agric Am
Agriculture in Yamaguchi/Nogyo Yamaguchi — Agric Yamaguchi
Agriculture Index — Agri Ind
Agriculture Information Bulletin. United States Department of Agriculture — Agr Inform Bull USDA
Agriculture Information Bulletin. United States Department of Agriculture — Agric Inf Bull US Dep Agric
Agriculture Information Bulletin. United States Department of Agriculture — Agric Inform Bull US Dep Agric
Agriculture Institute Review — Ag Inst R
Agriculture International — AGINEP
Agriculture International — Agric Int
Agriculture International — Agric Intnl
Agriculture (Journal of the Ministry of Agriculture) — J Ministry Ag
Agriculture (London) — AGRLAQ
Agriculture (Montreal) — Agr (Montreal)
Agriculture North [*Canada*] — AGNO
Agriculture of Gifu Prefecture/Gifu-ken No Nogyo — Agric Gifu Prefect
Agriculture Pakistan — Agr Pakistan
Agriculture Pakistan — Agric Pak
Agriculture Pakistan — Agric Pakistan
Agriculture Pakistan — Agriculture Pakist
Agriculture Pakistan — AGRPA4
Agriculture (Paris) — AGPAAH
Agriculture (Paris) — Agr (Paris)
Agriculture Pratique — AGPQAV
Agriculture Pratique — Agr Prat
Agriculture Pratique [*France*] — Agric Prat
Agriculture Pratique des Pays Chauds. Bulletin du Jardin Colonial et des Jardins d'Essai des Colonies Francaises — Agric Prat Pays Chauds
Agriculture Propagation. Gojo Noyu. Miyagi Prefecture Propagation Association — Agric Propag
Agriculture Review — Agric Rev
Agriculture Romande — Agr Romande
Agriculture Romande — Agric Romande
Agriculture, Rural Development, and Related Agencies Appropriations for Hearings — Agric Rural Dev Relat Agencies Appropriations Hearings
Agriculture Statistical Yearbook and Agriculture Sample [*Amman*] — ASY
Agriculture. The Journal. Ministry of Agriculture (London) — Agriculture London
Agriculture. Toward 2000 — Agric 2000
Agridata Network Review. Agricultural Education Edition — Agrid New Rev Agri Ed Ed
Agridata Network Review. Canadian Edition — Agrid Net Rev Can Ed
Agridata Network Review. Communicator Edition — Agrid Net Rev Com Ed
Agridata Network Review. Dairy Net Edition — Agrid Net Rev Dairy Net Ed
Agridata Network Review. Financial Edition Agrid Net Rev Fin Ed
Agridata Network Review. Government/University Edition — Agrid Net Rev Gov Univ Ed
Agridata Network Review. Producer Edition — Agrid Net Rev Prod Ed
Agridata Network Review. Telco Edition — Agrid Net Rev Telco Ed
Agridata Network Review. Western Livestock Edition — Agrid Net Rev West Livest Ed
Agrikultura (Nitre) — AGZPAA
Agri-Markets Data Service [*Database*] — AMDS
Agrimed Research Programme. The Enrichment of Wine in the European Community — Agrimed Res Programme Enrich Wine Eur Community
Agriscene (Australia) — Agriscene (Aust)
AgriScience — AgriScience
Agrisul — ASULAN
Agro Food Industry Hi-Tech — Agro Food Ind Hi Tech
Agro Industries — Agro Inds
Agro Sur — UCASBJ
Agro-Alimentaire — Agro Al
Agroanimalia — AROABM
Agrobiologiya — AGRBAU
Agrobiologiya — Agrobiol
Agroborealis — AGBO
Agroborealis — AGBOBO
Agroborealis. Alaska Agricultural and Forestry Experiment Station. University of Alaska. Fairbanks — Agroborealis Alaska Agric For Exp Stn Univ Alaska Fairbanks
Agroborealis. Alaska Agricultural Experiment Station (Fairbanks) — Agroborealis Alaska Agric Exp Stn (Fairbanks)
Agrobotanika — Agrobot
Agrochem Courier — Agrochem Cour
Agrochemia [*Bratislava*] — Agrochem

Agrochemia (Bratislava) — AGROB2
Agrochemophysica — AGPYAL
Agrochemophysica — Agrochem
Agrochimica — AGRCAX
Agrochimica — Agrochim
Agrochimica. Pisa Universita. Istituto di Chimica Agraria — Agrochim
Agrociencia — AGCCBR
Agrociencia. Serie A — AGCNCR
Agrociencia. Serie A — Agrocienc Ser A
Agrociencia. Serie C — AGRCCZ
Agrociencia. Serie C — Agrocienc Ser C
Agro-Ecological Atlas of Cereal Growing in Europe [*Elsevier Book Series*] — AEA
Agro-Ecosystems — AECODH
Agro-Ecosystems — Agro-Ecosyst
Agroforestry Review — Agrof Rev
Agrogeologisia Julkaisuja — Agrogeol Julk
Agrohemija — AGHJA4
Agrokemia es Talajtan — Agrokem Talajtan
Agrokemia es Talajtan — AKTLAU
Agrokemia es Talajtan. Supplement — Agrokem Talajtan Suppl
Agrokemia es Talajtan. Supplement — AGTSAN
Agrokhimicheskaya Kharakteristika Osnovnykh Tipov Pochv SSSR — Agrokhim Kharakt Osnovn Tipov Pochv SSSR
Agrokhimicheskaya Kharakteristika Pochv BSSR — Agrokhim Kharakt Pochv BSSR
Agrokhimiya — AGKYAU
Agrokhimiya — Agrokhim
Agrokhimiya i Gruntoznaustvo — Agrokhim Gruntoznst
Agrokhimiya i Pochvovedenie (Kharkov) — Agrokhim Pochvoved Kharkov
Agronomia [*Monterrey, Mexico*] — AGMOAA
Agronomia [*Caracas*] — AGNMBA
Agronomia [*Rio De Janeiro*] — AGRJAK
Agronomia [*Manizales*] — AGRMBU
Agronomia [*La Molina*] — ARNCAM
Agronomia Angolana — Agron Angol
Agronomia Angolana — Agron Angolana
Agronomia Angolana — Agronomia Angol
Agronomia Angolana — ARAOAR
Agronomia Costarricense — AGCODV
Agronomia Costarricense — Agron Costarric
Agronomia (Lima) — Agron (Lima)
Agronomia Lusitana — AGLUAN
Agronomia Lusitana — Agron Lusit
Agronomia Lusitana [*Portugal*] — Agron Lusitana
Agronomia Lusitana — Agronomia Lusit
Agronomia (Manizales) — Agron (Manizales)
Agronomia Mocambicana — Agron Mocambicana
Agronomia Mocambicana — AMOCBR
Agronomia (Monterrey, Mexico) — Agron (Mexico)
Agronomia Sul Rio Grandense — Agron Sul Rio Grandense
Agronomia Sulriograndense — Agron Sulriogr
Agronomia Sulriograndense — Agron Sulriograndense
Agronomia Sulriograndense — AGSLAV
Agronomia Tropical [*Maracay, Venezuela*] — Agron Trop
Agronomia Tropical (Maracaibo) — Agron Trop Maracaibo
Agronomia Tropical (Maracay, Venezuela) — Agron Trop (Maracay)
Agronomia Tropical (Maracay, Venezuela) — ATMVAK
Agronomia Tropical. Revista del Instituto Nacional de Agricultura — Agronomia Trop
Agronomia Tropical (Venezuela) — ATV
Agronomia y Veterinaria — Agron Vet
Agronomia y Veterinaria — AVBAAI
Agronomic Data. Washington State University. College of Agricultural Research Center — Agron Data Wash State Univ Coll Agric Res Cent
Agronomic Research for Food. Papers Presented at the Annual Meeting of the American Society of Agronomy — Agron Res Food Pap Annu Meet Am Soc Agron
Agronomico [*Campinas*] — AGRNAW
Agronomie [*Paris*] — AGRNDZ
Agronomie Coloniale. Bulletin Mensuel. Institut National d'Agronomie de la France d'Outre-Mer — Agron Colon
Agronomie Tropicale — Agron Trop
Agronomie Tropicale (Paris) — Agron Trop (Paris)
Agronomie Tropicale. Serie Agronomie Generale. Etudes Scientifiques [*Paris*] — Agron Trop Agron Gen Etud Sci
Agronomie Tropicale. Serie Agronomie Generale. Etudes Scientifiques — Agron Trop Ser Agron Gen Etud Sci
Agronomie Tropicale. Serie Agronomie Generale. Etudes Scientifiques — ATAEBC
Agronomie Tropicale. Serie Agronomie Generale. Etudes Techniques [*Paris*] — Agron Trop Agron Gen Etude Tech
Agronomie Tropicale. Serie Agronomie Generale. Etudes Techniques — Agron Trop Ser Agron Gen Etud Tech
Agronomie Tropicale. Serie Agronomie Generale. Etudes Techniques — AGTOAB
Agronomie Tropicale. Serie Riz et Riziculture et Cultures Vivrieres Tropicales — Agron Trop Riz Rizic Cult Vivrieres Trop
Agronomie Tropicale. Serie Riz et Riziculture et Cultures Vivrieres Tropicales — Agron Trop Ser Riz Rizic Cult Vivrieres Trop
Agronomie Tropicale. Serie Riz et Riziculture et Cultures Vivrieres Tropicales — ATNMAW
Agronomie Tropicale. Supplement — Agron Trop Suppl
Agronomisch-Historisch Jaarboek — Agron Hist Jaarb
Agronomist. Cooperative Extension Service. University of Maryland — Agron Coop Ext Serv Univ Md
Agronomists and Food. Contributions and Challenges. Papers Presented at the Annual Meeting. American Society of Agronomy — Agron Food Contrib Challenges Pap Annu Meet Am Soc Agron
Agronomski Glasnik — AGGLA5
Agronomski Glasnik — Agron Glas
Agronomski Glasnik — Agron Glasn
Agronomy — Agron
Agronomy — AGRYAV
Agronomy Abstracts — Agron Abstr
Agronomy and Soils Research Series. Clemson Agricultural Experiment Station — Agron Soils Res Ser Clemson Agr Exp Sta
Agronomy Branch Report (South Australia Department of Agriculture and Fisheries) — Agron Branch Rep (South Aust Dep Agric Fish)
Agronomy Department Series. Ohio Agricultural Experiment Station — Agron Dept Ser Ohio Agr Exp Sta
Agronomy Handbook — Agron Handb
Agronomy Journal — AGJOAT
Agronomy Journal — Agron J
Agronomy. Mimeograph Circular. North Dakota Agricultural Experiment Station — Agron Mimeogr Circ N Dak Agr Exp Sta
Agronomy Notes. University of Kentucky. College of Agriculture. Cooperative Extension Service — Agron Note Univ Ky Coll Agric Coop Ext Serv
Agronomy Pamphlet. South Dakota Agricultural Experiment Station — Agron Pam S Dak Agr Exp Sta
Agronomy Research Report AG. Agricultural Experiment Stations. University of Florida — Agron Res Rep AG Agric Exp Stn Univ Fla
Agronomy Research Report. Louisiana State University and Agricultural and Mechanical College. Department of Agronomy — Agron Res Rep LA State Univ Agric Mech Coll Dep Agron
Agronomy Society of New Zealand. Special Publication — Agron Soc NZ Spec Publ
Agronomy Society of New Zealand. Special Publication — SPAZD9
Agronomy Views. University of Nebraska. College of Agriculture and Home Economics. Extension Service — Agron Views Univ Nebr Coll Agr Home Econ Ext Serv
Agroplantae — AGPLAG
Agros (Lisboa) — Agros (Lisb)
Agrotecnia — ATEHA6
Agrotecnia (Madrid) — Agrotec (Madrid)
Agrotekhnika Providnikh Kul'tur — Agrotekh Provid Kul'tur
Agrotekhnika Vozdelyvaniya Ovoshchei i Gribov Shampin'onov — Agrotekh Vozdelyvaniya Ovoshchei Gribov Shampinonov
Agrupacion de Cooperativas Farmaceuticas — ACOFAR
Agua y Energia — Agua Energ
Aguedal — Agued
Aguia. Orgao da Renascenca Portuguesa — AORP
Agway Cooperator — Agway Coop
AHA [*American Hospital Association*] **Hospital Technology Alerts** — AHA Hosp Tech Alert
AHA [*American Hospital Association*] **Hospital Technology Series** — AHA Hosp Tech Ser
AHBAI [*American Health and Beauty Aids Institute*] **News** — AHBAI N
Ahmadu Bello University. Kano. Abdullahi Bayero College. Department of English and European Languages. Occasional Papers — Ahmadu Bello Univ Abdullahi Bayero Coll Dep Engl Eur Language
Ahora (Dominican Republic) — ARD
Ahrenlese des Georgikons — Ahrenlese Georgikons
Ahrokhimiia i Hruntoznavstvo — Ahrokhimiia Hruntozn
Ahrokhimiia i Hruntoznavstvo Respublikanskii Mizhvidomchyi Tematichnyi Zbirnyk — AGGRBO
Ahrokhimiia i Hruntoznavstvo Respublikanskii Mizhvidomchyi Tematichnyi Zbirnyk — Ahrokhim Hruntozn Resp Mizhvid Temat Zb
AIA [*American Institute of Architects*] **Journal** — AIA J
AIA [*American Institute of Architects*] **Journal** — AIA Jnl
AIAA [*American Institute of Aeronautics and Astronautics*] **Bulletin** — AIAA Bull
AIAA [*American Institute of Aeronautics and Astronautics*] **Journal** — AIAA J
AIAA [*American Institute of Aeronautics and Astronautics*] **Monographs** — AIAA Monogr
AIAA [*American Institute of Aeronautics and Astronautics*] **Paper** — AIAA Pap
AIAA [*American Institute of Aeronautics and Astronautics*] **Student Journal** — AIAA Stud J
AIAS [*Australian Institute of Aboriginal Studies*] **Newsletter** — AIAS Newslett
AIAW [*Association for Intercollegiate Athletics for Women*] **Handbook-Directory** — AIAW Handbk Dir
AIBDA Boletin Especial. Associacion Interamericana de Bibliotecarios y Documentalistas Agricolas — AIBDA Bol Espec
AIBS [*American Institute of Biological Sciences*] **Bulletin** — AIBS Bull
AIBS [*American Institute of Biological Sciences*] **Newsletter** — AIBS Newsl
AIC [*American Institute of Cooperation*] **Newsletter** — AIC Newsl
AICA [*Australasian Institute of Cost Accountants*] **Bulletin** — AICA Bull
AIChE (American Institute of Chemical Engineers) Equipment Testing Procedure. Evaporators — AIChE Equip Test Proced Evaporators
AIChE [*American Institute of Chemical Engineers*] **Annual Meeting. Preprints** — AIChE Annu Meet Prepr
AIChE [*American Institute of Chemical Engineers*] **Annual Meeting. Program Abstracts** — AIChE Annu Meet Program Abstr
AIChE [*American Institute of Chemical Engineers*] **Journal** — AIChEJ
AIChE [*American Institute of Chemical Engineers*] **Monograph Series** — AIChE Monogr Ser
AIChE [*American Institute of Chemical Engineers*] **National (or Annual) Meeting. Preprints** — AIChE Natl (or Annu) Meet Prepr
AIChE [*American Institute of Chemical Engineers*] **Papers** — AIChE Pap
AIChE [*American Institute of Chemical Engineers*] **Symposium Series** — ACSSCQ

AIChE [*American Institute of Chemical Engineers*] **Symposium Series** — AIChE Symp Ser
AICHE [*American Institute of Chemical Engineers*] **Workshop Series** — AICHE Workshp Ser
Aichi Cancer Center Research Institute. Annual Report — AHCCAX
Aichi Cancer Center Research Institute. Annual Report — Aichi Cancer Cent Res Inst Annu Rep
Aichi Daigaku Bungaku Ronso — Ai Daig Bung R
Aichi Gakugei Daigaku Kenkyu Hokoku [*Bulletin of the Aichi Gakugei University: Cultural Sciences*] — ACGKH
Aichi Journal of Experimental Medicine — Aichi J Exp Med
Aichi University of Education. Research Report. Natural Sciences [*Japan*] — Aichi Univ Educ Res Rep Nat Sci
Aichi-Gakuin Daigaku Shigakkai-Shi [*Aichi Gakuin Journal of Dental Science*] — AGDSAB
Aichi-Gakuin Daigaku Shigakkai-Shi [*Aichi-Gakuin Journal of Dental Science*] — Aichi Gakuin
Aichi-Gakuin Journal of Dental Science — Aichi-Gakuin J Dent Sci
Aichi-Ken Shokuhin Shikenshi Nempo — AKSKBN
AICPA [*American Institute of Certified Public Accountants*] **Washington Report** — AICPA Wash Rep
AID [*Agency for International Development*] **Research and Development Abstracts** — AID Res Dev Abstr
AIDC (American Industrial Development Council) Journal — AIDC (Am Ind Development Council) J
AIDS Clinical Review — AIDS Clin Rev
AIDS Education and Prevention — AIDS Educ Prev
AIDS [*Acquired Immune Deficiency Syndrome*] **Quarterly Bibliography from all Fields of Periodical Literature** — AIDS Quart Bibl Per Lit
AIDS [*Acquired Immune Deficiency Syndrome*] **Research** — AIDS Res
AIDS Research [*Acquired Immune Deficiency Syndrome*] — AIREEN
AIDS Research and Human Retroviruses — AIDS Res Hum Retroviruses
AIDS [*Acquired Immune Deficiency Syndrome*] **Research and Therapy** — AIDS Res Ther
AIDS Research Reviews — AIDS Res Rev
AIFM (Associazione Italiana Finiture del Metalli) Galvanotecnica and Nuove Finiture — AIFM Galvanotec Nuove Finiture
AIIE [*American Institute of Industrial Engineers*] **Transactions** — AIIE Trans
AIJ [*Australasian Insurance Journal*] **Manual of Australasian Life Assurance** — AIJ Man AustAs Life Assur
AIMM (Australasian Institute of Mining and Metallurgy) Bulletin — AIMM Bull
AIN [*Association of Interpretive Naturalists*] **News** — AIN N
Ain Shams Medical Journal — AIMJA9
Ain Shams Medical Journal — Ain Shams Med J
Ain Shams Science Bulletin — Ain Shams Sci Bull
Ain Shams Science Bulletin. Part A — Ain Shams Sci Bull Part A
Ain Shams University. Faculty of Agriculture. Bulletin — Ain Shams Univ Fac Agric Bull
Ain Shams University. Faculty of Agriculture. Research Bulletin — Ain Shams Univ Fac Agric Res Bull
Ain Shams University. Faculty of Agriculture. Research Bulletin — RBAADT
Aiolika Grammata — AiolikaG
AIP [*American Institute of Physics*] **Conference Proceedings** — AIP Conf Proc
AIP [*American Institute of Physics*] **Conference Proceedings. Particles and Fields Subseries** — AIP Conf Proc Part Fields Subser
AIPE [*American Institute of Plant Engineers*] **Newsletter** — AIPE Newsl
Air and Waste Management Association. Annual Meeting. Proceedings — Air Waste Manage Assoc Annu Meet Proc
Air and Water Pollution — Air Water Pollut
Air and Water Pollution — AWPOA
Air and Water Pollution — AWPOAZ
AIR. Archives of Interamerican Rheumatology — AIR Arch Interam Rheumatol
AIR. Archives of Interamerican Rheumatology — Arch Interamerican Rheumatol
Air, Atmospheric Chemistry, and Air Pollution. Seminar — Air Atmos Chem Air Pollut Semin
Air Cargo Magazine — Air Carg Mag
Air Carrier Financial Statistics — Air Car Fin Stat
Air Classics Quarterly Review — Air Clas Quart Rev
Air Classification of Solid Wastes — Air Classif Solid Wastes
Air Cleaning [*Japan*] — Air Clean
Air Commerce Bulletin — Air Commerce Bul
Air Conditioning and Oil Heat — Air Cond Oil Heat
Air Conditioning and Refrigeration News — Air Cond & Refrig N
Air Conditioning, Heating, and Refrigeration News — Air Cond Heat & Refrig N
Air Conditioning, Heating, and Refrigeration News — Air Cond Heat Refrig News
Air Conditioning, Heating, and Refrigeration News — Air Cond N
Air Conditioning, Heating, and Ventilating — ACHVA
Air Conditioning, Heating, and Ventilating — Air CHV
Air Conditioning, Heating, and Ventilating — Air Cond Heat & Ven
Air Conditioning, Heating, and Ventilating — Air Cond Heat Vent
Air Defense Artillery Magazine — Air D Arty
Air Engineering — Air Eng
Air et Cosmos. Hebdomadaire de l'Actualite Aerospatiale et des Techniques Avancees — AIR
Air et Cosmos. Special 1000 — Air Cos S
Air Force and Space Digest — AF/SD
Air Force Civil Engineer — AFCE
Air Force Civil Engineer — Air F Civ Eng
Air Force Civil Engineer — Air Force Civ Eng
Air Force Civil Engineer — Air Force Civil Eng
Air Force Comptroller — AIR
Air Force Comptroller — Air F Comp
Air Force Driver Magazine — AFDM
Air Force Engineering and Services Quarterly — AFEQD
Air Force Engineering and Services Quarterly [*United States*] — Air Force Eng Serv Q
Air Force Engineering and Services Quarterly — Air Force Eng Serv Quart
Air Force JAG [*Judge Advocate General*] **Law Review** [*Air Force Law Review*] [*Later,*] — AF JAG L Rev
Air Force Journal of Logistics — Air F J Log
Air Force Law Review — AF L R
Air Force Law Review — AF Law Rev
Air Force Law Review — AFL Rev
Air Force Law Review — Air Force Law R
Air Force Magazine — Air F Mgz
Air Force Screen Magazine — AFSM
Air Industriel — Air Ind
Air International — Air Int
Air Knife Coating. Seminar Notes. Technical Association. Pulp and Paper Industry — Air Knife Coat Semin Notes Tech Assoc Pulp Pap Ind
Air Law — Air L
Air Law Review — Air L Rev
Air Law Review — Air LR
Air Line Employee — Air Line Emp
Air Navigation Order — ANO
Air. Papers Based on Symposia — Air Pap Symp
Air Pollution — Air Pollut
Air Pollution Abstracts — AirPolAb
Air Pollution and Cancer in Man. Proceedings of the Hanover International Carcinogenesis Meeting — Air Pollut Cancer Man Proc Hanover Int Carcinog Meet
Air Pollution and Ecosystems. Proceedings. International Symposium — Air Pollut Ecosyst Proc Int Symp
Air Pollution Control — Air Pollut Control
Air Pollution Control and Design Handbook — Air Pollut Control Des Handb
Air Pollution Control and Industrial Energy Production — Air Pollut Control Ind Energy Prod
Air Pollution Control Association. Annual Meeting. Papers — Air Pollut Control Assoc Annu Meet Pap
Air Pollution Control Association. Journal — Air Poll Cont Assn J
Air Pollution Control Association. Journal — Air Poll Control Assn J
Air Pollution Control Association. Journal — Air Pollut Assoc J
Air Pollution Control Association. Journal — J Air Pollut Contr A
Air Pollution Control Conference — Air Pollut Control Conf
Air Pollution Control District. County of Los Angeles. Annual Report — Air Pollut Control Dist Cty Los Angeles Annu Rep
Air Pollution Control in Transport Engines. Symposium — Air Pollut Control Transp Engines Symp
Air Pollution Control Office. Publication. AP Series [*United States*] — Air Pollut Control Off US Publ AP Ser
Air Pollution Effects on Plant Growth. Symposium — Air Pollut Eff Plant Growth Symp
Air Pollution Foundation. Report — Air Pollut Found Rep
Air Pollution Modeling and Its Application — Air Pollut Model Its Appl
Air Pollution News [*Japan*] — Air Pollut News
Air Pollution. Proceedings. European Congress on the Influence of Air Pollution on Plants and Animals — Air Pollut Proc Eur Congr
Air Pollution Symposium on Low Pollution Power Systems Development — Air Pollut Symp Low Pollut Power Syst Dev
Air Pollution Technical Information Center File [*Database*] — APTIC
Air Pollution Technical Report — Air Pollut Tech Rep
Air Pollution Titles — Air Pollut Titles
Air Progress — IAIR
Air Progress Aviation Rev — Air Prog Aviat Rev
Air Quality and Environmental Factors — Air Qual Environ Factors
Air Quality and Smoke from Urban and Forest Fires. Proceedings of the International Symposium — Air Qual Smoke Urban For Fires Proc Int Symp
Air Quality Control Digest — Air Qual Cont Dig
Air Quality Control in the Printing Industry — Air Qual Control Print Ind
Air Quality in Minnestoa — Air Qual Minn
Air Quality Instrumentation — Air Qual Instrum
Air Quality Monographs — Air Qual Monogr
Air Reservist — Air Reserv
Air Reservist — AIRR
Air Safety Journal — Air Saf J
Air Safety Law and Technology — Air Saf Law Technol
Air Sampling Instruments for Evaluation of Atmospheric Contaminants — Air Sampling Instrum Eval Atmos Contam
Air Transport Interchange — Air Trans Interch
Air Transport World — Air Trans W
Air Transport World — Air Transp World
Air Transport World — ATW
Air Transportation Research Information Service [*Database*] — ATRIS
Air University. Library. Index to Military Periodicals — Air Univ Libr Index Mil Period
Air University. Library. Index to Military Periodicals — AirUnLibI
Air University. Review — Air Un Rev
Air University. Review — Air Univ R
Air University. Review — Air Univ Rev
Air University. Review. US Air Force — AF/AUR
Air/Water Pollution Report [*Database*] — A/WPR
Air/Water Pollution Report — Air/Water Poll Rept
Air Wonder Stories — AW
Air Wonder Stories — AWS
Airconditioning and Refrigeration Business — Aircond Refrig Bus
Aircraft Accident/Incident Reporting System [*Database*] — ADREP
Aircraft and Missiles — Aircr Missiles
Aircraft Engineering — Airc Engng
Aircraft Engineering — Aircr Eng

Aircraft Engineering — Aircraft
Aircraft Production — Aircr Prod
Air-Espace Techniques — Air-Espace Tech
Airline and Travel Food Service — Airline Trav Food Serv
Airline Quarterly — Airline Q
Airport Advisory — Airport Adv
Airport Characteristics Data Bank [*Database*] — ACDB
Airport Forum News Services — APC
Airports International — Airports Int
Airways Operations Instructions — AOI
Airworthiness Advisory Circular — AAC
AIS [*Australian Iron and Steel*] **Technical Society. Bulletin** — AIS Technical Soc Bul
AIT. Architektur Innenarchitektur Technischer Ausbau — AIT
AJAS: Australasian Journal of American Studies — AJAS
Ajia Bunka [*Asian Culture*] — ABK
Ajia Keizai. Journal of the Institute of Developing Economics — Ajia Keizai
Ajia Nogyo — AJNOD5
AJNR. American Journal of Neuroradiology — AAJNDL
AJNR. American Journal of Neuroradiology — AJNR
AJNR. American Journal of Neuroradiology — AJNR Am J Neuroradiol
Ajour Industril-Teknikk [*Norway*] — Ajour Ind-Tek
AJR. American Journal of Roentgenology — AAJRD
AJR. American Journal of Roentgenology — AJR
AJR. American Journal of Roentgenology — AJR Am J Roentgenol
AJR. American Journal of Roentgenology — AJROAM
AJRI. American Journal of Reproductive Immunology — AAJID
AJRI. American Journal of Reproductive Immunology — AAJID6
AJRI. American Journal of Reproductive Immunology — AJRI Am J Reprod Immunol
AJRIM. American Journal of Reproductive Immunology and Microbiology — AJRIM Am J Reprod Immunol Microbiol
AJRIM. American Journal of Reproductive Immunology and Microbiology — AJRMEK
Ajurnarmat. Inuit Cultural Institute — AJNT
Akademia Ekonomiczna imienia Oskara Langego we Wroclawiu. Prace Naukowe — Akad Ekon im Oskara Langego Wroclawiu Pr Nauk
Akademia Ekonomiczna w Poznaniu Zeszyty Naukowe — Akad Ekon Poznaniu Zesz Nauk
Akademia Ekonomiczna w Poznaniu Zeszyty Naukowe. Seria 2. Prace Habilitacyjne i Doktorskie — Akad Ekon Poznaniu Zesz Nauk Ser 2
Akademia Gorniczo-Hutnicza Imienia Stanislawa Staszica w Krakowie Zeszyty Naukowe Geologia — Akad Gorniczo-Hutnicza St Staszica Krakow Zesz Nauk Geol
Akademia Gorniczo-Hutnicza Imienia Stanislawa Staszica w Krakowie Zeszyty Naukowe Geologia — ZNAGDF
Akademia Medyczna imeni Juliana Marchlewskiego w Bialymstoku. Roczniki — Akad Med im Juliana Marchlewskiego Bialymstoku Rocz
Akademia Nauk SSSR Institut Nefti Trudy — Akad Nauk SSSR Inst Nefti Trud
Akademia Nauk Ukrainskoi RSR. Institut Teploenergetiki. Zbirnik Prats [*Ukrainian SSR*] — Akad Nauk Ukr RSR Inst Teploenerg Zb Pr
Akademia Rolnicza w Szczecinie. Rozprawy — Akad Roln Szczecinie Rozpr
Akademia Rolnicza w Warszawie. Zeszyty Naukowe. Lesnictwo — Akad Roln Warzawie Zesz Nauk Lesn
Akademia Rolnicza w Warszawie Zeszyty Naukowe Ogrodnictwo — Akad Roln Warszawie Zesz Nauk Ogrod
Akademia Rolnicza w Warszawie. Zeszyty Naukowe. Rolnictwo — Akad Roln Warszawie Zesz Nauk Roln
Akademia Rolnicza we Wroclawiu Zeszyty Naukowe Melioracja — Akad Roln Wroclawiu Zesz Nauk Melior
Akademia Rolnicza we Wroclawiu Zeszyty Naukowe Zootechnika — Akad Roln Wroclawiu Zesz Nauk Zootech
Akademiceskija Izvestija — Akad Izv
Akademie der Landwirtschaftswissenschaften. Tagungsbericht — Akad Landwirtschaftswiss Tagungsber
Akademie der Wissenschaften. Berlin. Institut fuer Orientforschung. Mitteilungen — MIO
Akademie der Wissenschaften der DDR. Abhandlungen. Abteilung Mathematik, Naturwissenschaften, Technik — Akad Wiss DDR Abh Abt Math Naturwiss Tech
Akademie der Wissenschaften der DDR. Abteilung Mathematik, Naturwissenschaften, Technik. Abhandlungen — Akad Wiss DDR Abt Math Naturwiss Tech Abh
Akademie der Wissenschaften der DDR. Forschungsbereich Geo- und Kosmoswissenschaften. Veroeffentlichungen — Akad Wiss DDR Forschungsbereich Geo Kosmoswiss Veroeff
Akademie der Wissenschaften der DDR. Zentralinstitut fuer Isotopen- und Strahlenforschung. Mitteilungen — Akad Wiss DDR Zentralinst Isot Strahlenforsch Mitt
Akademie der Wissenschaften der DDR. Zentralinstitut fuer Physik der Erde. Veroeffentlichungen — Akad Wiss DDR Zentralinst Phys Erde Veroeff
Akademie der Wissenschaften in Goettingen. Mathematisch-Physikalische Klasse. Abhandlungen. Folge 3 — Akad Wiss Goettingen Math Phys Kl Abh Folge 3
Akademie der Wissenschaften in Goettingen. Nachrichten. Mathematisch-Physikalische Klasse — Akad Wiss Gottingen Nachr Math-Physikal Kl
Akademie der Wissenschaften in Goettingen. Philologisch-Historische Klasse — AWG Phk
Akademie der Wissenschaften in Muenchen. Abhandlungen — AWMAbh
Akademie der Wissenschaften in Muenchen. Philosophisch-Historische Klasse. Sitzungsberichte — AWMSb
Akademie der Wissenschaften in Wien — Akad d Wissenschaften in Wien
Akademie der Wissenschaften in Wien. Philosophisch-Historische Klasse. Denkschriften — Akad d Wiss Denksch Philos-Hist Kl
Akademie der Wissenschaften in Wien. Philosophisch-Historische Klasse. Sitzungsberichte — Akad d Wiss Sitzungsb Philos-Hist Kl
Akademie der Wissenschaften in Wien. Sitzungsberichte — AWWSb
Akademie der Wissenschaften und der Literatur. Abhandlungen der Geistes- und Sozialwissenschaftlichen Klasse — Abhandl Akad Wiss Lit Geistes Sozialwiss Kl
Akademie der Wissenschaften und der Literatur. Abhandlungen der Geistes- und Sozialwissenschaftlichen Klasse (Mainz) — Abh Akad Wiss Lit Mainz
Akademie der Wissenschaften und der Literatur. Abhandlungen der Mathematisch-Naturwissenschaftlichen Klasse — Akad Wiss Abh Math Naturwiss Kl
Akademie der Wissenschaften und der Literatur in Mainz. Abhandlungen der Geistes- und Sozialwissenschaftlichen Klasse — AWLM AGSK
Akademie der Wissenschaften und der Literatur in Mainz. Abhandlungen der Geistes- und Sozialwissenschaftlichen Klasse — AWLMGS
Akademie der Wissenschaften und der Literatur in Mainz. Abhandlungen der Mathematisch-Naturwissenschaftlichen Klasse — Akad Wiss Lit Abh Math-Naturwiss Kl (Mainz)
Akademie der Wissenschaften und der Literatur in Mainz. Abhandlungen der Mathematisch-Naturwissenschaftlichen Klasse — Akad Wiss Lit Mainz Abh Math-Natur Kl
Akademie der Wissenschaften und der Literatur in Mainz. Abhandlungen der Mathematisch-Naturwissenschaftlichen Klasse — Akad Wiss Lit Mainz Abh Math-Naturwiss Kl
Akademie der Wissenschaften und der Literatur in Mainz. Abhandlungen der Mathematisch-Naturwissenschaftlichen Klasse — AWLMA9
Akademie der Wissenschaften und der Literatur in Mainz. Abhandlungen der Mathematisch-Naturwissenschaftlichen Klasse (Wiesbaden) — Akad Wiss Lit Mainz Math-Naturwiss Kl Abh
Akademie der Wissenschaften und der Literatur in Mainz. Jahrbuch (Wiesbaden) — Akad Wiss Lit Mainz Jahrb
Akademie der Wissenschaften und der Literatur in Mainz. Klasse der Literatur — AWLML
Akademie der Wissenschaften und der Literatur in Mainz. Mathematisch-Naturwissenschaftliche Klasse. Mikrofauna des Meeresbodens — AWMMAE
Akademie der Wissenschaften und der Literatur in Mainz. Mathematisch-Naturwissenschaftliche Klasse. Research in Molecular Biology — Akad Wiss Lit Mainz Math Naturwiss Kl Res Mol Biol
Akademie der Wissenschaften zu Berlin. Forschungsbericht — Akad Wiss Berlin Forschungsber
Akademiia Nauk SSSR. Doklady. Izvestiia. Seriia Geologicheskaia — Akad Nauk SSSR Doklady Izvestiia Ser Geol
Akademiia Nauk SSSR. Institut Etnografii. Kratkie Soobshcheniia — ANIEK
Akademiia Nauk SSSR. Institut Narodov Azii. Kratkie Soobshcheniia [*Moscow*] — KS
Akademiia Nauk SSSR. Institut Vostokovedeniia. Kratkie Soobshcheniia — ANIVK
Akademija Istorii Material'noj Kul'tury — AIMK
Akademija Nauk Armjanskoi SSR. Doklady — Akad Nauk Armjan SSR Dokl
Akademija Nauk Armjanskoi SSR. Istorija Estest'voznanija i Tehniki v Armenii — Istor Estestvoznan Tehn Armen
Akademija Nauk Azerbaidzanskoi SSR. Doklady — Akad Nauk Azerbaidzan SSR Dokl
Akademija Nauk BSSR. Institut Tehniceskoi Kibernetiki. Vycislitel'naja Tehnika v Masinostroenii — Vycisl Tehn v Masinostroen
Akademija Nauk Gruzinskoi SSR. Trudy Tbilisskogo Matematiceskogo Instituta Imeni A. M. Razmadze — Akad Nauk Gruzin SSR Trudy Tbiliss Mat Inst Razmadze
Akademija Nauk Kazahskoi SSR. Trudy Astrofiziceskogo Instituta — Akad Nauk Kazah SSR Trudy Astrofiz Inst
Akademija Nauk Kazahskoi SSR. Trudy Instituta Matematiki i Mehaniki — Akad Nauk Kazah SSR Trudy Inst Mat i Meh
Akademija Nauk Latviiskoi SSR. Institut Elektroniki i Vyceslitel'noi Tehniki. Problemy Slucainogo Poiska — Problemy Slucain Poiska
Akademija Nauk Latviiskoi SSR. Institut Mehaniki Polimerov. Mehanika Polimerov — Mehanika Polimerov
Akademija Nauk Latviiskoi SSR. Magnitnaja Gidrodinamika — Magnit Gidrodinamika
Akademija Nauk SSSR — ANSSSR
Akademija Nauk SSSR. Akusticeskii Zurnal — Akust Z
Akademija Nauk SSSR. Astronomiceskii Zurnal — Astronom Z
Akademija Nauk SSSR. Avtomatika i Telemehanika [*Moscow*] — Avtomat i Telemeh
Akademija Nauk SSSR i Akademija Pedagogiceskih Nauk SSSR. Kvant — Kvant
Akademija Nauk SSSR i Moskovskoe Matematiceskoe Obscestvo. Uspehi Matematiceskih Nauk — Uspehi Mat Nauk
Akademija Nauk SSSR. Radiotehnika i Elektronika — Radiotehn i Elektron
Akademija Nauk SSSR. Sibirskoe Otdelenie. Institut Matematiki. Optimizacija — Optimizacija
Akademija Nauk SSSR. Sibirskoe Otdelenie. Institut Matematiki. Vycislitel'nye Sistemy. Sbornik Trudov — Vycisl Sistemy
Akademija Nauk SSSR. Sibirskoe Otdelenie. Vycislitelnyi Centr. Preprint [*Novosibirsk*] — Akad Nauk SSSR Sibirsk Otdel Vycisl Centr Preprint
Akademija Nauk SSSR. Trudy Jakutskogo Filiala. Serija Fiziceskaja — Akad Nauk SSSR Trudy Jakutsk Filial Ser Fiz
Akademija Nauk SSSR. Uspehi Fiziceskih Nauk — Uspehi Fiz Nauk
Akademija Nauk Ukrainskoi RSR. Institut Elektrotehniki Avtomatika [*Kiev*] — Avtomatika
Akademija Nauk Ukrainskoi SSR. Doklady. Serija A. Fiziko-Matematiceskie i Tehniceskie Nauki — Dokl Akad Nauk Ukrain SSR Ser A
Akademija Nauk Ukrainskoi SSR L'vovskii Filial Matematiceskoi Fiziki Instituta Matematiki. Matematiceskie Metody i Fiziko-Mehaniceskie Polja — Mat Metody i Fiz-Meh Polja

Akademija Nauk Ukrainskoi SSR. Otdelenie Matematiki. Mehaniki i Kibernetiki. Prikladnaja Mehanika — Prikl Meh
Akademija Nauk UzSSR. Karakalpakskii Filial. Vestnik — Vestnik Karakalpak Fil Akad Nauk UzSSR
Akademija Nauka i Umjetnosti Bosne i Hercegovine. Radovi Odjeljenje Prirodnih i Matematickih Nauka — Akad Nauka Umjet Bosne Hercegov Rad Odjelj Prirod Mat Nauka
Akademija Nauka i Umjetnosti Bosne i Hercegovine. Radovi Odjeljenje Tehnickih Nauka — Akad Nauka i Umjet Bosne i Hercegov Rad Odjelj Tehn Nauka
Akademija Nauka i Umjetnosti Bosne i Hercegovine. Radovi Odjeljenje Tehnickih Nauka — Akad Nauka Umjet Bosne Hercegov Rad Odjelj Tehn Nauka
Akademische Blaetter — AkBl
Akademische Monatsblaetter — Akad Mbll
Akademische Rundschau — Akad Rundschau
Akademische Rundschau — AkR
Akademischer Verein fuer Juedische Geschichte und Literatur — AJGV
Akademiska Dzive — ADz
Akademiya Nauk Armenii. Doklady — Akad Nauk Arm Dokl
Akademiya Nauk Armenii. Doklady — Akad Nauk Armenii Dokl
Akademiya Nauk Armyanskoi SSR. Izvestiya. Seriya Matematika — Akad Nauk Armyan SSR Izv Ser Mat
Akademiya Nauk Armyanskoi SSR. Izvestiya. Seriya Mekhanika — Akad Nauk Armyan SSR Izv Ser Mek
Akademiya Nauk Armyanskoy SSR. Doklady — Akad Nauk Arm SSR Dokl
Akademiya Nauk Azerbaydzhanskoy SSR. Doklady — Akad Nauk Azerb SSR Dokl
Akademiya Nauk Azerbaydzhanskoy SSR. Izvestiya. Seriya Nauk o Zemle — Akad Nauk Azerb SSR Izv Ser Nauk Zemle
Akademiya Nauk Belarusskoi SSR. Doklady — Akad Nauk Belarus SSR Dok
Akademiya Nauk BSSR. Doklady — Akad Nauk BSSR Dokl
Akademiya Nauk Gruzii. Izvestiya. Seriya Khimicheskaya — Akad Nauk Gruz Izv Ser Khim
Akademiya Nauk Gruzii. Soobshcheniya — Akad Nauk Gruz Soobshch
Akademiya Nauk Gruzii. Soobshcheniya — Soobshch Akad Nauk Gruzii
Akademiya Nauk Gruzinskoi SSR. Institut Geofiziki. Trudy — Akad Nauk Gruz SSR Inst Geofiz Tr
Akademiya Nauk Gruzinskoy SSR. Geologicheskiy Institut. Trudy — Akad Nauk Gruz SSR Geol Inst Tr
Akademiya Nauk Gruzinskoy SSR. Institut Neorganicheskoi Khimii i Elektrokhimii Sbornik — Akad Nauk Gruz SSR Inst Neorg Khim Elektrokhim Sb
Akademiya Nauk Gruzinskoy SSR. Soobshcheniya — Akad Nauk Gruz SSR Soobshch
Akademiya Nauk Kazakhskoi SSR. Izvestiya. Seriya Fiziko-Matematicheskaya — Akad Nauk Kazak SSR Izv Ser Fiz Mat
Akademiya Nauk Kazakhskoy SSR. Institut Geologicheskikh Nauk. Trudy — Akad Nauk Kaz SSR Inst Geol Nauk Tr
Akademiya Nauk Kazakhskoy SSR. Izvestiya. Seriya Geologicheskaya — Akad Nauk Kaz SSR Izv Ser Geol
Akademiya Nauk Kazakhskoy SSR. Trudy Astrofizicheskogo Instituta — Akad Nauk Kazakh SSR Trudy Astrofiz Inst
Akademiya Nauk Latviskoi SSR. Izvestiya. Seriya Khimicheskaya — Akad Nauk Latvi SSR Izv Ser Khim
Akademiya Nauk Respubliki Armeniya. Izvestiya. Mekhanika — Izv Akad Nauk Respub Armeniya Mekh
Akademiya Nauk Respubliki Kazakhstan. Trudy Astrofizicheskogo Instituta — Akad Nauk Respub Kazakhstan Trudy Astrofiz Inst
Akademiya Nauk Respubliki Moldova. Izvestiya. Fizika i Tekhnika — Izv Akad Nauk Respub Moldova Fiz Tekhn
Akademiya Nauk Respubliki Moldova. Izvestiya. Matematika — Izv Akad Nauk Respub Moldova Mat
Akademiya Nauk SSSR. Avtomatika i Telemekhanika — Avtomat i Telemekh
Akademiya Nauk SSSR. Byulleten Instituta Teoreticheskoi Astronomii — Byull Inst Teoret Astronom
Akademiya Nauk SSSR. Doklady — Akad Nauk SSSR Dokl
Akademiya Nauk SSSR. Funktsional'nyi Analiz i ego Prilozheniya — Funktsional Anal i Prilozhen
Akademiya Nauk SSSR. Geologicheskiy Institut. Trudy — Akad Nauk SSSR Geol Inst Tr
Akademiya Nauk SSSR. Geologicheskiy Institut. Trudy — Akad Nauk SSSR Geol Inst Trudy
Akademiya Nauk SSSR. Geomorfologicheskaya Komissiya. Plenum. Materialy — Akad Nauk SSSR Geomorfol Kom Plenum Mater
Akademiya Nauk SSSR. Institut Nauchnoi i Tekhnicheskoi Informatsii. Referativnyi Zhurnal. Tekhnicheskaya Kibernetika — RZh Tekhn Kibernet
Akademiya Nauk SSSR. Institut Nauchnoi Informatsii. Referativnyi Zhurnal. Avtomatika. Telemekhanika i Vychislitel'naya Tekhnika — RZh Avtomat Telemekh i Vychisl Tekhn
Akademiya Nauk SSSR. Institut Nauchnoi Informatsii. Referativnyi Zhurnal. Matematika — RZh Mat
Akademiya Nauk SSSR. Institut Prikladnoi Matematiki. Preprint — Akad Nauk SSSR Inst Prikl Mat Preprint
Akademiya Nauk SSSR. Izvestiya. Seriya Fizicheskaya — Akad Nauk SSSR Izv Ser Fiz
Akademiya Nauk SSSR. Izvestiya. Seriya Geograficheskaya — Akad Nauk SSSR Izv Ser Geogr
Akademiya Nauk SSSR. Izvestiya. Seriya Geologicheskaya — Akad Nauk SSSR Izv Ser Geol
Akademiya Nauk SSSR. Komi Filial. Institut Geologii. Trudy — Akad Nauk SSSR Komi Fil Inst Geol Tr
Akademiya Nauk SSSR. Komissiya po Izucheniyu Chetvertichnogo Perioda. Byulleten — Akad Nauk SSSR Kom Izuch Chetvertich Perioda Byull
Akademiya Nauk SSSR. Kommissiya po Opredeleniyu Absolyutnogo Vozrasta Geologicheskikh Formatsiy. Trudy — Akad Nauk SSSR Kom Opred Absol Vozrasta Geol Form Tr
Akademiya Nauk SSSR. Metallofizika — Akad Nauk SSSR Metallofizka
Akademiya Nauk SSSR Mezhduvedomstvennoyy Geofizicheskiy Komitet pri Presidiume Geofizicheskiy Byulleten — Akad Nauk SSSR Mezhduvedomstv Geofiz Kom Geofiz Byull
Akademiya Nauk SSSR. Okeanograficheskaya Kommissiya. Trudy — Akad Nauk SSSR Okeanogr Kom Tr
Akademiya Nauk SSSR. Paleontologicheskiy Institut Trudy — Akad Nauk SSSR Paleontol Inst Tr
Akademiya Nauk SSSR. Sibirskoe Otdelenie. Institut Geologii i Geofiziki. Trudy — Akad Nauk SSSR Sib Otd Inst Geol Geofiz Tr
Akademiya Nauk SSSR. Sibirskoe Otdelenie. Limnologicheskiy Institut. Trudy Novosibirsk — Akad Nauk SSSR Sib Otd Limnol Inst Tr
Akademiya Nauk SSSR. Sibirskoe Otdelenie. Sibirskii Matematicheskii Zhurnal — Sibirsk Mat Zh
Akademiya Nauk SSSR. Sibirskoe Otdelenie. Vychislitelnyi Tsentr. Chislennye Metody Mekhaniki Sploshnoi Sredy — Chisl Metody Mekh Sploshn Sredy
Akademiya Nauk SSSR. Sibirskoe Otdelenie. Vychislitelnyi Tsentr. Preprint — Akad Nauk SSSR Sibirsk Otdel Vychisl Tsentr Preprint
Akademiya Nauk SSSR. Ural'skii Filial. Trudy Instituta Khimii — Akad Nauk SSSR Ural Fil Tr Inst Khim
Akademiya Nauk SSSR. Ural'skiy Nauchnyi Tsentr. Institut Geologii i Geokhimii. Trudy — Akad Nauk SSSR Ural Nauchn Tsentr Inst Geol Geokhim Tr
Akademiya Nauk SSSR. Vestnik — Akad Nauk SSSR Vestn
Akademiya Nauk SSSR. Vsesoyuznyi Institut Nauchnoi i Tekhnicheskoi Informatsii. Voprosy Informatsionnoi Teorii i Praktiki — Voprosy Informatsion Teorii i Praktiki
Akademiya Nauk SSSR. Yadernaya Fizika — Yadernaya Fiz
Akademiya Nauk Tadzhikskoy SSR. Doklady — Akad Nauk Tadzh SSR Dokl
Akademiya Nauk Tadzhikskoy SSR. Otdeleniye Fiziko-Matematicheskikh i Geologo-Khimicheskikh Nauk. Izvestiya — Akad Nauk Tadzh SSR Otd Fiz-Mat Geol-Khim Nauk Izv
Akademiya Nauk Turkmenskoy SSR. Izvestiya. Seriya Fiziko-Tekhnicheskikh. Khimicheskikh i Geologicheskikh Nauk — Akad Nauk Turkm SSR Izv Ser Fiz-Tekh Khim Geol Nauk
Akademiya Nauk Ukrainskoi SSR. Institut Gidromekhaniki. Gidromekhanika — Gidromekh
Akademiya Nauk Ukrainskoi SSR. Institut Kibernetiki. Kibernetika i Vychislitelnaya Tekhnika — Kibernet i Vychisl Tekhn
Akademiya Nauk Ukrainskoi SSR. Institut Matematiki. Matematicheskaya Fizika — Mat Fiz
Akademiya Nauk Ukrainskoi SSR. Institut Matematiki. Preprint — Akad Nauk Ukrain SSR Inst Mat Preprint
Akademiya Nauk Ukrainskoi SSR. Institut Matematiki. Ukrainskii Matematicheskii Zhurnal — Ukrain Mat Zh
Akademiya Nauk Ukrainskoi SSR. Institut Prikladnoi Matematikii, Mekhaniki. Mekhanika Tverdogo Tela — Mekh Tverd Tela
Akademiya Nauk Ukrainskoi SSR. Metallofizika — Akad Nauk Ukr SSR Metallofiz
Akademiya Nauk Ukrainskoi SSR. Otdelenie Fiziki. Ukrainskii Fizicheskii Zhurnal — Ukrain Fiz Zh
Akademiya Nauk Ukrainskoi SSR. Otdelenie Matematiki. Mekhaniki i Kibernetiki. Prikladnaya Mekhanika — Prikl Mekh
Akademiya Nauk Ukrainskoi SSR. Seriya Metallofizika [*Ukrainian SSR*] — Akad Nauk Ukr SSR Ser Metallofiz
Akademiya Nauk Ukrainskoy RSR. Dopovidi. Seriya B. Geologiya, Geofizika, Khimiya, ta Biologiya — Akad Nauk Ukr RSR Dopov Ser B
Akademiya Nauk Uzbekskoi SSR. Trudy Ordena Trudovogo Krasnogo Znameni Instituta Kibernetiki s Vychislitel'nym Tsentrom. Voprosy Vychislitel'noi i Prikladnoi Matematiki — Voprosy Vychisl i Prikl Mat
Akademiya Sel'skokhozyaistvennykh Nauk. Institut Agropochvovedeniya. Trudy Leningradskoi Laboratorii — Akad Skh Nauk Inst Agropochvoved Tr Leningr Lab
Akhboroti Akademiyai Fankhoi RSS Tochikiston Shu-Bai Fankhoi Biologi — Akhboroti Akad Fankhoi RSS Tochikiston Shu-Bai Fankhoi Biol
Akhboroti Akademiyai Fankhoi RSS Tochikiston Shu-Bai Fankhoi Biologi — ITOBAO
Akita Central Hospital. Medical Journal — Akita Cent Hosp Med J
Akita Journal — Akita J
Akita-Kenkritsu Chuo Byoin Igaku Zasshi [*Akita Central Hospital. Medical Journal*] — AKCBA
Akita-Kenkritsu Chuo Byoin Igaku Zasshi [*Akita Central Hospital. Medical Journal*] — AKCBAH
Akita-Kenkritsu Nogyo Tanki Daigaku Kenkyu Hokoku — AKNKDY
Akkadica [*Brussels*] — Akkad
Akkadisches Handwoerterbuch — AHW
Ak-Kitab al-Misri [*Cairo*] — AKAM
AKM Series in Theoretical Computer Science — AKM Ser Theoret Comput Sci
Akron Beacon Journal [*United States*] — Akron Beaco
Akron Business and Economic Review — ABE
Akron Business and Economic Review — Akron Bus & Econ R
Akron Business and Economic Review [*United States*] — Akron Bus and Econ Rev
Akron Law Review [*United States*] — Akr LR
Akron Law Review — Akron L Rev
Akta Grodshie i Ziemskie — AGZ
Akten Betreffende Cooperatieve Verenigingen — NSV
Akten Betreffende Naamloze Vennootschappen — NSN
Akten des Internationalen Amerikanisten-Kongresses — AIAK
Akten des Internationalen Leiniz Kongresses — Akten Int Leibniz Kongr
Akten des Internationalen Orientalisten-Kongresses — AIOK
Akten des IX. Internationalen Byzantinistenkongresses. Titel Griechisch — Akten IX Internat Byzantinistenkongr

Akten des XI. Internationalen Byzantinistenkongresses — Akten XI Internat Byzantinistenkongr
Aktiebolaget Atomenergi (Stockholm). Rapport — Ab Atomenergi (Stockholm) Rapp
Aktiebolaget Atomenergi (Stockholm). Rapport AE — Ab Atomenergi (Stockholm) AE
Aktiebolaget Atomenergi (Stockholm). Rapport AE — AKATAR
Aktivatsionnyi Analiz Biologicheskikh Ob'ektov — Akt Anal Biol Obektov
Aktivatsionnyi Analiz v Narodnom Khozyaistve — Akt Anal Nar Khoz
Aktoj de Internacia Scienca Akademio Comenius — Aktoj Int Sci Akad Comenius
Aktualne Problemy Informacji i Dokumentacji — Akt Probl Inf Dokum
Aktualne Problemy Informacji i Dokumentacji — Aktual Probl Inf & Dok
Aktualne Problemy Informacji i Dokumentacji — Aktual Probl Inf Dok
Aktualne Problemy Informacji i Dokumentacji — APDKA
Aktual'ni Pitannya Virazkovoi Khvorobi — Akt Pitan Virazko Khvorob
Aktual'nye Problemy Biologii Sinezelenykh Vodoroslei — Aktual Probl Biol Sinezelenykh Vodoroslei
Aktual'nye Problemy Farmakologii i Farmatsii, Vsesoyuznaya Nauchnaya Konferentsiya — Aktual Probl Farmakol Farm Vses Nauchn Konf
Aktual'nye Problemy Klinicheskoi i Teoreticheskoi Meditsiny — Aktual Probl Klin Teor Med
Aktual'nye Problemy Onkologii i Meditsinskoi Radiologii [*Belorussian SSR*] — Aktual Probl Onkol Med Radiol
Aktual'nye Problemy Professional'noi Patologii Respublikanskoi Mezhvedomstvennyi Sbornik — Aktual Probl Prof Patol Resp Mezhved Sb
Aktual'nye Problemy Razvitiya Ptitsevodstva — Aktual Probl Razvit Ptitsevod
Aktual'nye Problemy Svarki Tsvetnykh Metallov. Doklady Vsesoyuznoi Konferentsii — Aktual Probl Svarki Tsvetn Met Dokl Vses Konf
Aktual'nye Voprosy Biologii i Pochvovedeniya — Aktual Vopr Biol Pochvoved
Aktual'nye Voprosy Dermatologii i Venerologii — Aktual Vopr Dermatol Venerol
Aktual'nye Voprosy Eksperimental'noi i Klinicheskoi Meditsiny — Aktual Vopr Eksp Klin Med
Aktual'nye Voprosy Epidemiologii — Aktual Vopr Epidemiol
Aktual'nye Voprosy Farmatsii — Aktual Vopr Farm
Aktual'nye Voprosy Fiziki Tverdogo Tela — Aktual Vopr Fiz Tverd Tela
Aktual'nye Voprosy Gastroenterologii — Aktual Vopr Gastroenterol
Aktual'nye Voprosy Gastroenterologii — AVGADC
Aktual'nye Voprosy Ginekologii — Aktual Vopr Ginekol
Aktual'nye Voprosy Khimioterapii Zlokachestvennykh Opukholei — Aktual Vopr Khimioter Zlokach Opukholei
Aktual'nye Voprosy Kriobiologii i Kriomeditsiny, Materialy Simpoziuma — Aktual Vopr Kriobiol Kriomed Mater Simp
Aktual'nye Voprosy Oftal'mologii — Aktual Vopr Oftal
Aktual'nye Voprosy Oftal'mologii — Aktual Vopr Oftal'mol
Aktual'nye Voprosy Patologii Pecheni — Aktual Vopr Patol Pecheni
Aktual'nye Voprosy Polucheniya Fosfora i Soedinenii na Ego Osnove — Aktual Vopr Poluch Fosfora Soedin Ego Osn
Aktual'nye Voprosy Sanitarnoi Mikrobiologii — Aktual Vopr Sanit Mikrobiol
Aktual'nye Voprosy Sovremennoi Biokhimii — Aktual Vopr Sovrem Biokhim
Aktual'nye Voprosy Sovremennoi Onkologii — Aktual Vopr Sovrem Onkol
Aktual'nye Voprosy Sovremennoi Petrografii — Aktual Vopr Sovrem Petrogr
Aktual'nye Voprosy Teoreticheskoi i Klinicheskoi Meditsiny — Aktual Vopr Teor Klin Med
Aktuelle Dermatologie — AKDEDY
Aktuelle Dermatologie — Aktuel Dermatol
Aktuelle Fragen der Psychiatrie und Neurologie [*Switzerland*] — Aktuel Fragen Psychiat Neurol
Aktuelle Fragen der Psychiatrie und Neurologie — Aktuel Fragen Psychiatr Neurol
Aktuelle Fragen der Psychiatrie und Neurologie — BPNSAX
Aktuelle Fragen der Psychotherapie — Aktuel Fragen Psychother
Aktuelle Fragen der Psychotherapie — TPPYAL
Aktuelle Gerontologie — AKGRAH
Aktuelle Gerontologie — Aktuel Gerontol
Aktuelle Gerontologie — Aktuelle Gerontol
Aktuelle Neurologie — AKNUAR
Aktuelle Neurologie — Aktuel Neurol
Aktuelle Neurologie — Aktuelle Neurol
Aktuelle Otorhinolaryngologie — Aktuel Otorhinolaryngol
Aktuelle Probleme der Intensivmedizin — Aktuel Probl Intensivmed
Aktuelle Probleme der Landwirtschaftlichen Forschung. Seminar ueber Salmonellen in Futtermitteln, Futtermittelbewertung — Aktuel Probl Landwirtsch Forsch Semin
Aktuelle Probleme der Phoniatrie und Logopaedie — Aktuel Probl Phoniatr Logop
Aktuelle Probleme der Phoniatrie und Logopaedie — FOPHAD
Aktuelle Probleme der Polymer-Physik — Aktuel Probl Polym-Phys
Aktuelle Probleme in Chirurgie und Orthopadie — Aktuelle Probl Chir Orthop
Aktuelle Probleme in Chirurgie und Orthopaedie — Aktuel Probl Chir Orthop
Aktuelle Probleme in der Angiologie — Aktuel Probl Angiol
Aktuelle Probleme in der Chirurgie [*Later, Aktuelle Probleme in Chirurgie und Orthopaedie*] — Aktuel Probl Chir
Aktuelle Probleme in der Klinischen Biochemie — Aktuel Probl Klin Biochem
Aktuelle Probleme in der Psychiatrie, Neurologie, Neurochirurgie — Aktuel Probl Psych Neurol Neurochir
Aktuelle Radiologie — Aktuelle Radiol
Aktuelle Rheumatologie — AKRHDB
Aktuelle Rheumatologie [*Germany*] — Aktuel Rheumatol
Aktuelle Rheumatologie — Aktuelle Rheumatol
Aktuelle Traumatologie — AKTRAE
Aktuelle Traumatologie — Aktuel Traumatol
Aktuelle Traumatologie — Aktuelle Traumatol
Aktuelle Urologie — Aktuel Urol
Aktuelle Urologie — Aktuelle Urol
Aktuellt fran Lantbrukshogskolan — Aktuellt Lantbrukshogs
Aktuellt Och Historisk — Aktuellt Och Hist
Aktuelt Landbruksdepartementet. Opplysningstjeneste (Norway) — Aktuelt Landbruksdep Opplysningstjeneste (Norw)
Akusherstvo i Ginekologiia (Moskva) — Akush Ginekol (Mosk)
Akusherstvo i Ginekologiia (Sofiia) — Akush Ginekol (Sofiia)
Akusherstvo i Ginekologiya — AKGIA
Akusherstvo i Ginekologiya [*Moscow*] — AKGIAO
Akusherstvo i Ginekologiya (Kiev) — Akush Ginekol (Kiev)
Akusherstvo i Ginekologiya (Moscow) — Akush Ginekol (Mosc)
Akusherstvo i Ginekologiya (Moscow) — Akush Ginekol (Moscow)
Akusherstvo i Ginekologiya (Sofia) [*Bulgaria*] — Akush Ginekol (Sofia)
Akusticheskii Zhurnal — Akust Zh
Akusticheskii Zhurnal — AKZHA
Akustika i Ul'trazvukovaya Tekhnika — Akust Ul'trazvuk Tekh
Akustische Beihefte [*Switzerland*] — Akust Beih
Akustische Zeitschrift — Akust Z
Akvarium es Terrarium — Akvar Terrar
Akvarium i Komnatnye Rastenija — Akvar Komnatn Rast
Akwesasne Notes — Akw Notes
Akwesasne Notes — AKWS
Akzente — Akz
Al Ahram [*Cairo*] — AA
Al. Culukidzis Sahelobis Khutnaisis Sahelmcipho Pedagogiuri Institutis Sromebi — Al Culukidzis Sahelob Khutnaisi Sahelmc Ped Inst Srom
Al Markazi. Central Bank of Oman — ALM
Ala Breve — AL
ALA [*American Latvian Association*] **Zurnals** — ALAZ
Alabama Academy of Science. Journal — Ala Acad Sci Jour
Alabama Administrative Code — Ala Admin Code
Alabama Agribusiness — Ala Agribus
Alabama Agribusiness. Auburn University. Alabama Cooperative Extension Service — Ala Agribusiness Auburn Univ Ala Coop Ext Serv
Alabama. Agricultural Experiment Station. Alabama Polytechnic Institute. Bulletin — Ala Agric Exp Stn Ala Polytech Inst Bull
Alabama Agricultural Experiment Station. Alabama Polytechnic Institute. Circular — Alabama Agric Exp Sta Alabama Polytechn Inst Circ
Alabama. Agricultural Experiment Station. Annual Report — Ala Agric Exp Stn Annu Rep
Alabama. Agricultural Experiment Station. Auburn University. Agronomy and Soils Departmental Series — Ala Agric Exp Stn Auburn Univ Agron Soils Dep Ser
Alabama. Agricultural Experiment Station. Auburn University. Agronomy and Soils Departmental Series — DSASDE
Alabama. Agricultural Experiment Station. Auburn University. Bulletin — Ala Agric Exp Stn Auburn Univ Bull
Alabama. Agricultural Experiment Station. Auburn University. Department of Agronomy and Soils. Departmental Series — Ala Agric Exp Stn Auburn Univ Dep Agron & Soils Dep Ser
Alabama. Agricultural Experiment Station. Auburn University. Forestry Departmental Series — AEFDAU
Alabama. Agricultural Experiment Station. Auburn University. Forestry Departmental Series — Ala Agric Exp Stn Auburn Univ For Dep Ser
Alabama. Agricultural Experiment Station. Auburn University. Leaflet — Ala Agric Exp Stn Auburn Univ Leafl
Alabama. Agricultural Experiment Station. Auburn University. Progress Report — Ala Agric Exp Stn Auburn Univ Prog Rep
Alabama. Agricultural Experiment Station. Auburn University. Progress Report Series — Ala Agric Exp Stn Auburn Univ Prog Rep Ser
Alabama. Agricultural Experiment Station. Bulletin — Ala Agric Exp Stn Bull
Alabama. Agricultural Experiment Station. Bulletin (Auburn University) — Ala Agric Exp Stn Bull (Auburn Univ)
Alabama. Agricultural Experiment Station. Bulletin (Auburn University) — BAEAD2
Alabama. Agricultural Experiment Station. Circular — Ala Agric Exp Stn Cir
Alabama Agricultural Experiment Station. Horticulture Series — Alabama Agric Exp Sta Hort Ser
Alabama. Agricultural Experiment Station. Leaflet — Ala Agric Exp Stn Leafl
Alabama. Agricultural Experiment Station. Leaflet (Auburn University) — Ala Agric Exp Stn Leafl (Auburn Univ)
Alabama. Agricultural Experiment Station. Leaflet (Auburn University) — LAEADA
Alabama. Agricultural Experiment Station. Progress Report Series — Ala Agric Exp Stn Prog Rep Ser
Alabama. Agricultural Experiment Station. Progress Report Series (Auburn University) — AAERA5
Alabama. Agricultural Experiment Station. Progress Report Series (Auburn University) — Ala Agric Exp Stn Prog Rep Ser (Auburn Univ)
Alabama. Agricultural Experiment Station. Progress Report Series (Auburn University) — PRASD3
Alabama. Agricultural Experiment Station. Publications — Ala Ag Exp
Alabama Appellate Court Reports — Ala App
Alabama Bar Bulletin — Ala Bar Bull
Alabama Business — Ala Bus
Alabama Business and Economic Reports — Ala Bus and Econ Repts
Alabama Conservation — Ala Conserv
Alabama Conservation — ALCNAQ
Alabama Corn Variety Report — Ala Corn Variety Rep
Alabama Department of Industrial Relations. Annual Planning — Ala Dept Ind Rel Ann Plan
Alabama Forests — Ala For
Alabama. Geological Society. Bulletin — Alabama Geol Soc Bull
Alabama. Geological Survey — Ala G S
Alabama. Geological Survey and State Oil and Gas Board. Annual Reports — Ala Geol Survey and State Oil and Gas Board Ann Repts
Alabama. Geological Survey. Atlas Series — Ala Geol Surv Atlas Ser

Alabama. Geological Survey. Bulletin — Ala Geol Surv Bull
Alabama. Geological Survey. Circular — Ala Geol Surv Circ
Alabama. Geological Survey. County Report — Ala Geol Surv Cty Rep
Alabama. Geological Survey. Geo-Petro Notes — Ala Geol Surv Geo-Petro Notes
Alabama. Geological Survey. Information Series — Ala Geol Surv Inf Ser
Alabama. Geological Survey. Information Series — Alabama Geol Survey Inf Ser
Alabama. Geological Survey. Map — Ala Geol Surv Map
Alabama. Geological Survey. Map — Alabama Geol Survey Map
Alabama. Geological Survey. Special Report — Ala Geol Surv Spec Rep
Alabama Historian — Ala Hist
Alabama Historical Quarterly — Ala Hist Q
Alabama Historical Quarterly — AlaHQ
Alabama Historical Society. Transactions — Ala His S
Alabama Industrial and Scientific Society. Proceedings — Ala Ind Sc Soc Pr
Alabama Journal of Medical Sciences — AJOMA
Alabama Journal of Medical Sciences — AJOMAZ
Alabama Journal of Medical Sciences — Ala J Med Sci
Alabama Law Journal — Ala LJ
Alabama Law Review — Ala L Rev
Alabama Law Review — Ala Law R
Alabama Law Review — Ala LR
Alabama Law Review — Alabama L Rev
Alabama Law Review — LR
Alabama Lawyer — Ala Law
Alabama Lawyer — Law
Alabama Librarian — Ala Libn
Alabama Linguistic and Philological Series — ALPS
Alabama Marine Resources Bulletin — Ala Mar Res Bull
Alabama Marine Resources. Bulletin — Ala Mar Resour Bull
Alabama Marine Resources. Bulletin — AMRBB5
Alabama Medical and Surgical Age — Ala Med Surg Age
Alabama Medical Journal — Ala Med J
Alabama Medicine — Ala Med
Alabama Nurse — Ala Nurse
Alabama Planning Resource Checklist — Ala Plann Res Checkl
Alabama Polytechnic Institute. Engineering Experiment Station. Engineering Bulletin — Ala Polytech Inst Eng Exp Stn Eng Bull
Alabama Reports — Ala
Alabama Resources Information System [*Database*] — ARIS
Alabama Review — Ala R
Alabama Review — Ala Rev
Alabama Review — AR
Alabama State Bar Association. Proceedings — Ala State Bar Assn Proc
Alabama State Highway Department. Bulletin — Ala State Highway Dept Bul
Alabama Trucker — Ala Truck
Al-Abhath — Ab
Al-Abhath [*Beirut, Lebanon*] — Abh
Alacran Azul — AA
ALADI [*Asociacion Latinoamericana de Integracion*] **Newsletter** — ALADI Newsl
Alaendsk Odling. Arsbok — Alaendsk Odling
ALAFO [*Asociacion Latino Americana de Facultades de Odontologia*] **Revista** — ALAFO R
Alalakh Tablets — AIT
Alalakh Tablets — AT
Al-Alam al-Arabi [*Cairo*] — AAA
Al-Andalus — Al-An
Al-Andalus — And
Alandsk Odling: Arsbok — AO
Alaska — ALAS
Alaska — IALK
Alaska Administrative Code — Alaska Admin Code
Alaska Administrative Journal — Alaska Admin Jnl
Alaska. Agricultural Experiment Station. Bulletin — Alaska Agric Exp Stn Bull
Alaska. Agricultural Experiment Station. Circular — Alaska Agric Exp Stn Circ
Alaska. Agricultural Experiment Station. Publications — Alaska Ag Exp
Alaska Agricultural Experiment Stations. Annual Report — Alaska Agric Exp Sta Annual Rep
Alaska Anthropological Association. Newsletter — AAAN
Alaska Bar Brief — Alaska Bar Br
Alaska Bar Brief — Alaska BB
Alaska Business and Development — Alaska Bus and Development
Alaska Business and Industry — Alaska Bus Ind
Alaska Business and Industry [*Supersedes Alaska Industry*] — ALBI
Alaska Business Newsletter — ALBU
Alaska Climate Center. News and Review — ACCNR
Alaska Conservation Review — ALCR
Alaska Construction and Oil — ACAO
Alaska Construction and Oil — ACOID
Alaska Construction and Oil — Alaska Constr Oil
Alaska Cooperative Wildlife Research Unit — ACWR
Alaska Department of Fish and Game. Annual Report — Alaska Dept Fish Game Ann Rep
Alaska Department of Fish and Game. Commercial Operators — Alaska Dept Fish Game Com Opp
Alaska. Department of Fish and Game. Information Leaflet — AFGIL
Alaska. Department of Fish and Game. Project Progress Reports on Bears — AFGPRB
Alaska. Department of Fish and Game. Project Progress Reports on Caribou — AFGPRC
Alaska. Department of Fish and Game. Project Progress Reports on Deer — AFGPRD
Alaska. Department of Fish and Game. Project Progress Reports on Moose — AFGPRM
Alaska. Department of Fish and Game. Project Progress Reports on Mountain Goats — AFGPRG
Alaska. Department of Fish and Game. Project Progress Reports on Sheep — AFGPRS
Alaska. Department of Fish and Game. Project Progress Reports on Wildlife — AFGPRWQ
Alaska. Department of Fish and Game. Research Reports — AFGRR
Alaska. Department of Fish and Game. Sport Fish Division. Anadromous Fish Studies — AFS
Alaska. Department of Fish and Game. Sport Fish Division. Federal Aid in Fish Restoration Studies — AFR
Alaska. Department of Fish and Game. Subsistence Division. Technical Paper — AFGSDTP
Alaska. Department of Fish and Game. Wildlife Technical Bulletin — AFGWTB
Alaska. Department of Fisheries. Research Report — ADFRAV
Alaska. Department of Fisheries. Research Report — Alaska Dep Fish Res Rep
Alaska. Department of Mines. Report of the Commissioner of Mines. Biennium — Alaska Dept Mines Rept Commissioner Mines Bienn
Alaska. Department of Natural Resources. Division of Geological and Geophysical Surveys. Information Circular — ANRGGSIC
Alaska. Department of Natural Resources. Division of Geological and Geophysical Surveys. Special Report — ANRGGSSR
Alaska. Department of Natural Resources. Division of Mines and Geology — ANRM
Alaska. Department of Natural Resources. Division of Mines and Geology. Geochemical Report — Alaska Div Mines and Geology Geochem Rept
Alaska. Department of Natural Resources. Division of Mines and Geology. Geologic Report — Alaska Div Mines and Geology Geol Rept
Alaska. Department of Natural Resources. Division of Mines and Minerals. Report — Alaska Dept Nat Resour Div Mines Miner Rep
Alaska. Division of Geological and Geophysical Surveys. Geochemical Report — Alaska Div Geol Geophys Surv Geochem Rep
Alaska. Division of Geological and Geophysical Surveys. Geologic Report — Alaska Div Geol Geophys Surv Geol Rep
Alaska. Division of Geological Survey. Geochemical Report — Alaska Div Geol Surv Geochem Rep
Alaska. Division of Mines and Geology. Geochemical Report — Alaska Div Mines Geol Geochem Rep
Alaska. Division of Mines and Geology. Geologic Report — Alaska Div Mines Geol Geol Rep
Alaska. Division of Mines and Geology. Report — Alaska Div Mines Geol Rep
Alaska. Division of Mines and Minerals. Information Circular. Report — Alaska Div Mines and Minerals Inf Circ Rept
Alaska. Division of Mines and Minerals. Report — Alaska Div Mines Miner Rep
Alaska Earthlines/Tidelines. Alaska Geographic Society — ALES
Alaska Economic Report — AE
Alaska Economic Trends — Alaska Econ Trends
Alaska Economic Trends — ALET
Alaska Education News — ALED
Alaska Education News — ALEN
Alaska Farm Magazine [*Superseded by Alaska Farm and Garden*] — ALFM
Alaska Fish Tales and Game Trails — AFGT
Alaska Geographic — ALGE
Alaska Geographic — ALGED
Alaska History — ALHY
Alaska History News — ALHN
Alaska History Series — ALHI
Alaska in Perspective — ALIP
Alaska Industry — Alaska Ind
Alaska Industry — ALIN
Alaska Industry — ALSIB
Alaska Journal — ALAJ
Alaska Journal — AlasJ
Alaska Journal — Alaska J
Alaska Journal of Commerce and Pacific Rim Reporter — AJ
Alaska Law Journal — Alaska LJ
Alaska Law Review — ALLR
Alaska Medicine — Alaska Med
Alaska Medicine — ALMD
Alaska Medicine — ALMDB
Alaska Mines and Geology — ALMG
Alaska Mining and Minerals — ALMM
Alaska Music Educator — AK
Alaska Native Magazine [*Formerly, Alaska Native News*] — ALNN
Alaska Native Management Report — ANMR
Alaska Native News — Alaska Nat N
Alaska Native News — ALNN
Alaska Nurse — ALNU
Alaska Offshore — ALOF
Alaska Oil and Gas Conservation Commission. Statistical Report — Alaska Oil Gas Conserv Com Stat Rep
Alaska Oil and Gas News — AOGN
Alaska Oil and Industry News — Alaska Oil Ind N
Alaska Outer Continental Shelf Socioeconomic Studies Program. Special Reports [*A publication*] — AOCSSSR
Alaska Outer Continental Shelf Socioeconomic Studies Program. Technical Reports — AOCSSTR
Alaska Petroleum and Industrial Directory — Alaska Pet Ind Dir
Alaska Public Affairs Journal — APAJ
Alaska Quarterly Review — Alaska Q Rev
Alaska Region Report. United States Department of Agriculture. Forest Service — Alaska Reg Rep US Dep Agric For Serv
Alaska Review of Business and Economic Conditions — Alaska Rev Bus Econ Cond
Alaska Review of Social and Economic Conditions — Alaska R Social and Econ Conditions
Alaska Science Conference — Alaska Sci Conf

Alaska Science Conference. Proceedings — Alaska Sci Conf Proc
Alaska Seas and Coast — ALSC
Alaska Series Special Reports for Management — ASSRFM
Alaska Session Laws — Alaska Sess Laws
Alaska Statutes — Alaska Stat
Alaska Tidelines — ALTL
Alaska Today — ALAT
Alaska University. Anthropological Papers — Alaska Univ Anthrop Pa
Alaska University. Geophysical Institute. Report — Alaska Univ Geophys Inst Rep
Alaska University. School of Mines Publication. Bulletin — Alaska Univ School Mines Pub Bull
Alaska Wildlife Watcher's Report — AWWR
Alaskan Arctic Tundra Proceedings. Anniversary Celebration. Naval Arctic Research Laboratory — Alaskan Arct Tundra Proc Anniv Celebration Nav Arct Res Lab
Alaskan Philatelist — ALPH
Alaskana — ALSK
Alaskana Book Series — ALBS
Alaska's Wildlife — AKWL
Alauda. Revue Internationale d'Ornithologie — Alauda Rev Int Ornithol
Al-Azhar Journal of Microbiology — Al Azhar J Microbiol
Al-Azhar Journal of Pharmaceutical Sciences — Al Azhar J Pharm Sci
Alba de America. Revista Literaria — ADA
Alba Regia. Annales Musei Stephani Regis — Alb R
Albania — Alb
Albany Felt Guidelines — Albany Felt Guide
Albany Institute. Proceedings — Albany Inst Pr
Albany Institute. Transactions — Albany Inst Tr
Albany International Weekly News Digest — Albany News Dig
Albany Law Journal — Alb Law J
Albany Law Review — Alb L Rev
Albany Law Review — Albany L R
Albany Law Review — Albany L Rev
Albany Law Review — Alby LR
Al-Bathah [*Cairo*] — ABC
Alberta Business — ALB
Alberta Business — Alberta Bs
Alberta Business Index — Alberta Bus Ind
Alberta Business Journal — ALBJ
Alberta Business Journal. Chamber of Resources — Alberta Bus J
Alberta Case Locator [*Database*] — ACL
Alberta Conservationist — ALCO
Alberta Counselletter — Alta Counsltr
Alberta Counsellor — Alta Couns
Alberta. Department of Lands and Forests. Annual Report — Alberta Dep Lands For Annu Rep
Alberta. Department of Mines and Minerals. Mines Division. Annual Report — Alberta Dept Mines and Minerals Mines Div Ann Rept
Alberta Diver — Alberta Div
Alberta Energy — Alberta En
Alberta English — Alta Engl
Alberta English Notes — Alberta Eng N
Alberta Folklore Quarterly — AFQ
Alberta Gazette — Alberta Gaz
Alberta Gazette — ALGAB
Alberta Greenhouse Newsletter — Alberta Green Nl
Alberta. Historic Sites Service. Occasional Papers [*Canada*] — AHSSOP
Alberta Historical Review — AlbH
Alberta Historical Review — Alta Hist R
Alberta History — Alberta His
Alberta History — Alta Hist
Alberta Hog Journal — Alberta Hog J
Alberta Horticulturist. Alberta Horticultural Association — Alberta Hort
Alberta Journal of Educational Research — AJER
Alberta Journal of Educational Research — Alber J Edu
Alberta Journal of Educational Research — Alberta J Educ Res
Alberta Land Use Planning Data Bank — LANDUP
Alberta Lands and Forests. Annual Report — Alberta Lands For Annu Rep
Alberta Lands and Forests. Annual Report — ALFOAA
Alberta Law Quarterly — Alberta LQ
Alberta Law Reports — Alb LR
Alberta Law Reports — ALR
Alberta Law Reports — Alta
Alberta Law Reports — Alta LR
Alberta Law Reports (Canada) — Alberta L (Can)
Alberta Law Reports, Second Series — Alta LR (2d)
Alberta Law Review — Alb LR
Alberta Law Review — Alberta L R
Alberta Law Review — Alberta L Rev
Alberta Law Review — Alta L Rev
Alberta Learning Resources Journal — Alta Learn Res J
Alberta Legislation Information [*Database*] — ALI
Alberta. Legislature Library. Annual Report — Alberta Leg Lib An Rep
Alberta Library Association. Bulletin — Alta Libr Ass Bull
Alberta Medical Bulletin — Alberta Med Bull
Alberta Modern Language Journal — Alberta M L J
Alberta Modern Language Journal — Alta Mod Lang J
Alberta Motorist — Alberta Mot
Alberta Native News — ABNN
Alberta Naturalist — ALBN
Alberta North — ALNO
Alberta Oil Sands Environmental Research Program — AOSERP
Alberta Oil Sands Index [*Database*] — AOSI
Alberta Oil Sands Technology and Research Authority. Journal of Research — Alberta Oil Sands Technol Res Auth J Res
Alberta Pay and Benefits — Alberta Pay Ben
Alberta Perspective — Alta Pers
Alberta Petroleum Incentives Program — Alberta Pet Incent Prog
Alberta Provincial Museum. Natural History. Occasional Paper [*Canada*] — APMNHOP
Alberta Reports [*Information service or system*] — Alta Report
Alberta Reports [*Information service or system*] — AR
Alberta Research. Annual Report — Alberta Res Annu Rep
Alberta Research Council. Bulletin — Alberta Res Counc Bull
Alberta Research Council. Bulletin — Alberta Research Council Bull
Alberta Research Council. Information Series — Alberta Res Counc Inf Ser
Alberta Research Council. Information Series — Alberta Research Council Inf Ser
Alberta Research Council. Memoir — Alberta Research Council Mem
Alberta Research Council. Mimeographed Circular — Alberta Research Council Mimeo Circ
Alberta Research Council. Preliminary Report — Alberta Research Council Prelim Rept
Alberta Research Council. Preliminary Soil Survey Report — Alberta Research Council Prelim Soil Survey Rept
Alberta Research Council. Report — Alberta Res Counc Rep
Alberta Research Council. Report — Alberta Research Council Rept
Alberta Research. Economic Geology Report — Alberta Res Econ Geol Rep
Alberta Research. Information Series — Alberta Res Inf Ser
Alberta Research. Report — Alberta Res Rep
Alberta Science Education Journal — Alta Sci Ed J
Alberta Science Teacher — Alta Sci Teach
Alberta Series Report — Alberta Ser Rep
Alberta Society of Petroleum Geologists. Annual Field Conference. Guidebook — Alberta Soc Pet Geol Annu Field Conf Guideb
Alberta Society of Petroleum Geologists. Bulletin — Alberta Soc Pet Geol Bull
Alberta Society of Petroleum Geologists. Journal — ASPG J
Alberta Society of Petroleum Geologists. Journal. News Bulletin — Alberta Soc Petroleum Geologists Jour News Bull
Alberta Statistical Information System [*Database*] — ASIST
Alberta Teachers Association. Newsletter — ATA Newsletter
Alberta Transportation — Alberta Trans
Alberta. University. Department of Chemistry. Division of Theoretical Chemistry. Technical Report — Alberta Univ Dep Chem Div Theor Chem Tech Rep
Alberta University. Department of Civil Engineering. Structural Engineering Reports — Alberta Univ Dept Civil Eng Struct Eng Rep
Alberta Wilderness Association. Newsletter — Alberta Wild Assoc Nl
Albertan Geographer [*Canada*] — ABGE
Albertan Geographer — Albert Geogr
Alberta's Western Living — Alberta West Liv
Albertina Studien — Alb Stud
Albia Christiana — AC
Albiswerk-Berichte — Albiswerk-Ber
Albrecht Von Graefe's Archiv fuer Klinische und Experimentelle Ophthalmologie — A Graefe's A
Albrecht von Graefes Archiv fuer Klinische und Experimentelle Ophthalmologie — Albrecht Graefes Arch Klin Exp Ophthalmol
Albrecht Von Graefe's Archiv fuer Klinische und Experimentelle Ophthalmologie [*Germany*] — Albrecht Von Graefe's Arch Klin Exp Ophthalmol
Albrecht Von Graefe's Archiv fuer Ophthalmologie — Albrecht V Graefe's Arch Ophthal
Albrecht Von Graefe's Archiv fuer Ophthalmologie — Albrecht Von Graefe's Arch Ophthalmol
Albrecht Von Graefe's Archive for Clinical and Experimental Ophthalmology — AKOGAO
Albrecht Von Graefe's Archive for Clinical and Experimental Ophthalmology — Albrecht Von Graefe's Arch Clin Exp Ophthalmol
Albrecht-Thaer-Archiv — Albrecht Thaer Arch
Albrecht-Thaer-Archiv — ATHAA
Albright-Knox Art Gallery. Notes — Albright-Knox Gal Notes
Album Acoriano — AA
Album of Dated Latin Inscriptions — ADLI
Album of Dated Latin Inscriptions — Am Ac Rome
Album van Natuurmonumenten van Nederlandsch-Indiee — Album Natuurmonum Ned Indiee
Albumin Structure, Function, and Uses — Albumin Struct Funct Uses
Albuquerque Journal — Albuquer Jl
Alcan News — Alcan N
Alcantara — Alc
Alcheringa (Association of Australasian Palaeontologists) — Alcheringa (Assoc Australas Palaeontol)
Alco Products Review — Alco Prod Rev
ALCOA [*Aluminum Company of America*] **Research Laboratories. Technical Paper** — ALCOA Res Lab Tech Pap
Alcohol and Abnormal Protein Biosynthesis — Alcohol Abnorm Protein Biosynth
Alcohol and Alcoholism — Alcoh Alcoh
Alcohol and Alcoholism — Alcohol Alcohol
Alcohol and Alcoholism. Supplement — Alcohol Alcohol Suppl
Alcohol and Aldehyde Metabolizing Systems. Papers. International Symposium on Alcohol and Aldehyde Metabolizing Systems — Alcohol Aldehyde Metab Syst Pap Int Symp
Alcohol and Drug News — ADN
Alcohol and Drug Research — Alcohol Drug Res
Alcohol Clinical Update — Alcohol Clin Update
Alcohol Health and Research World — AHRW
Alcohol Health and Research World — Alcoh Health & Res W
Alcohol Health and Research World — Alcohol Health Res World

Alcohol Health and Research World — GAHR
Alcohol Health and Research World. National Institute on Alcohol Abuse and Alcoholism — Alcohol Health Res World Natl Inst Alcohol Abuse Alcohol
Alcohol in History — Alcoh Hist
Alcohol Intoxication and Withdrawal. Experimental Studies. Papers. Symposium — Alcohol Intox Withdrawal Pap Symp
Alcohol, Tobacco, and Firearms Summary Statistics. US Internal Revenue Service — IRS Alcohl
Alcoholic Liver Pathology. Proceedings. Liver Pathology Section. International Symposia. Alcohol and Drug Research — Alcohol Liver Pathol Proc Int Symp Alcohol Drug Res
Alcoholism and Alcohol Education — AAED
Alcoholism Clinical and Experimental Research — Alcohol Clin Exp Res
Alcoholism Digest — Alcohol Dig
Alcoholism. The National Magazine — ATNM
Alcor — ALC
Alcuin Club. Collections — ACC
Aldosterone. A Symposium — Aldosterone Symp
Alealoides — Aleal
Alemannisches Jahrbuch — ALJ
Alentejo Historico, Artistico, e Monumental — AHAM
Alexander Blain Hospital. Bulletin — Alexander Blain Hosp Bull
Alexander Turnbull Library. Bulletin — Alexander Turnbull Libr Bull
Alexandria Dental Journal — Alex Dent J
Alexandria Journal of Agricultural Research — Alex J Agric Res
Alexandria Journal of Agricultural Research — Alexandria J Agr Res
Alexandria Journal of Agricultural Research — Alexandria J Agric Res
Alexandria Medical Journal — Alexandria Med J
Alexandria University. Bulletin of the Faculty of Science — Alexandria Univ Bull Fac Sci
Alexandrian Erotic Fragments and Other Greek Papyri — AEFGP
Alexanor; Revue des Lepidopteristes Francais — Alexanor Rev Lepid Fr
Alfaatih University. Bulletin of the Faculty of Engineering — Alfaatih Univ Bull Fac Eng
Alfoeld: Irodalmi es Muvelodesi Folyoirat — Alfold
Alfred Benson Symposium — Alfred Benson Symp
Alfred Hospital. Clinical Reports — Alfr Hosp Clin Rep
Alfred P. Sloan Foundation. Report — Alfred P Sloan Found Rep
Alfred University. New York State. College of Ceramics. Monthly Report — Alfred Univ NY State Coll Ceram Mon Rep
Algebra and Logic — Alg Log
Algebra Berichte — Algebra Ber
Algebra Colloquium — Algebra Colloq
Algebra, Logic, and Applications — Algebra Logic Appl
Algebra y Analysis, Vectorial, y Tensorial — Algebra Anal Vectorial Tensor
Algebras, Groups, and Geometrics — Algebras Groups Geom
Algemeen Dagblad — ADB
Algemeen Fiscaal Tijdschrift — AFT
Algemeen Fiscaal Tijdschrift — Alg Fisc Tijdsch
Algemeen Handelblad — AH
Algemeen Hollandsch Landbouwblad. Officieel Orgaan van de Hollandsche Maatschappij van Landbouw — Alg Holl Landbouwbl
Algemeen Magazijn van Wetenschap, Konst, en Smaak — Alg Mag Wetensch
Algemeen Nederlands Tijdschrift voor Wijsbegeerte — ANTW
Algemeen Nederlands Tijdschrift voor Wijsbegeerte en Psychologie — ANTsW
Algemeen Nederlandsch Politieweekblad — ANP
Algemeen Politieblad van het Koninkrijk der Nederlanden — AP
Algemeen Politieblad van het Koninkrijk der Nederlanden — APB
Algemeen Proefstation der Algemeene Vereniging van Rubberplanters ter Oostkust van Sumatra. Vlugschrift — Alg Proefstn Alg Ver Rubberplant Oostkust Sumatra Vlugschr
Algemeen Rijksambtenaren Reglement — ARAR
Algemeen Weekblad voor Christendom en Cultuur — AWC
Algemeen Zuivelblad — Alg Zuivelbl
Algemeen-Zuivel-en Melkhygienisch Weekblad — Alg Zuivel Melkhyg Weekbl
Algemene Practische Rechtverzameling — Alg Pract Rechtverz
Algemene Practische Rechtverzameling — APR
Algemene Practische Rechtverzameling — APRV
Algeria. Service Geologique. Bulletin — Alger Serv Geol Bull
Algerie Agricole — Alger Agric
Algerie Medicale — Alger Med
Algerie Medicale [*Algeria*] — Algerie Med
Algodon Boletin de la Camara Algodonera del Peru — Algodon Bol Cam Algodonera Peru
Algodon Mexicano — Algodon Mex
Algodonero Boletin — Algodonero Bol
Algol — ALG
Algol Bulletin — Algol Bull
Algological Studies — Algol Stud
Algorithms and Combinatorics — Algorithms Combin
Algorithms and Combinatorics. Study and Research Texts — Algorithms Combin Study Res Texts
Algorithms for Chemical Computations. A Symposium — Algorithms Chem Comput Symp
Algoritmy i Algoritmiceskie Jazyki — Algoritmy i Algoritm Jazyki
Algot Holmbergs Arsbok — Algot Holmbergs Arsb
ALI-ABA [*American Law Institute - American Bar Association*] **Course Materials Journal** — ALI
ALI-ABA [*American Law Institute - American Bar Association*] **Course Materials Journal** — ALI ABA
ALI-ABA [*American Law Institute - American Bar Association*] **Course Materials Journal** — ALI-ABA Course Mat J
Alicyclic Chemistry — Alicyclic Chem
[*The*] **Alien Critic** — TAC
Alienist and Neurologist — Alienist Neurol
Aligarh Bulletin of Mathematics — Aligarh Bull Math
Aligarh. Institute of Islamic Studies. Bulletin — AIIS
Aligarh Journal of English Studies — AJES
Aligarh Journal of Statistics — Aligarh J Statist
Aligarh Muslim University Publications. Zoological Series — Aligarh Muslim Univ Publ Zool Ser
Alighieri — AL
Alighieri. Rassegna Bibliografica Dantesca — Aligh Ras Bib Dante
Alimenta — ALMTB
Alimentacion Latinoamericana — Aliment Latinoam
Alimentaria — ALMNEC
Alimentary Pharmacology and Therapeutics — Aliment Pharmacol Ther
Alimentation au Quebec — Aliment Quebec
Alimentation et la Vie — Aliment Vie
Alimentation et Travail. Symposium International — Aliment Trav Symp Int
Alimentation Moderne. Revue de la Conserve — RCA
Alimentazione Animale — Aliment Anim
Alimentazione Italiana — Aliment Ital
Alimentazione Nutrizione Metabolismo — Aliment Nutr Metab
Alimentos e Nutricao — Aliment Nutr
Alimentos y Nutricion Animal — Aliment Nutr Anim
Aliments et l'Alimentation — Aliments Aliment
Aliphatic, Alicyclic, and Saturated Heterocyclic Chemistry — AASHCD
Aliphatic, Alicyclic, and Saturated Heterocyclic Chemistry — Aliphatic Alicyclic Saturated Heterocycl Chem
Aliphatic and Related Natural Product Chemistry — Aliphatic Relat Nat Prod Chem
Aliphatic Chemistry — ALCYAP
Aliphatic Chemistry — Aliphatic Chem
Al-Islam. Singapore — Islam S
Alkalis in Blast Furnaces. Proceedings. Symposium on "Alkalis in Blast Furnaces. State of the Art" — Alkalis Blast Furn Proc Symp
Alkalmazott Matematikai Lapok — Alkalmaz Mat Lapok
Alkaloidal Clinic — Alkaloidal Clin
Alkaloids Chemistry and Physiology — Alkaloids Chem Physiol
Al-Khalij Al-Arabi — AAJBDJ
Al-Kitab [*Cairo*] — AK
Alkmaars Jaarboekje — AJ
Alkohol Industrie — Alkohol Ind
Alkohol Industrie. Wissenschaftliche Technische Brennereibeilage — Alkohol Ind Wiss Tech Brennereibeil
All about Business in Hawaii — All Hawaii
All Africa Conference of Churches. Bulletin — AACCB
All England Law Reports — AELR
All England Law Reports — All Eng
All England Law Reports — All ER
All India Congress Committee. Economic Review — AICCER
All India Oriental Conference. Proceedings and Transactions — AIOC
All India Reporter — AIR
All India Reporter — All Ind Rep
All India Reporter — All India Rptr
All India Symposium on Radioactivity and Metrology of Radionuclides. Proceedings — All India Symp Radioact Metrol Radionuclides Proc
All Pakistan Legal Decisions — All Pak Leg Dec
All Pakistan Legal Decisions — All Pak Legal Dec
All Pakistan Science Conference. Proceedings — All Pak Sci Conf Proc
All the Year Round — All the Year
Alla Bottega — AllaB
Allahabad Farmer — Allahabad Fmr
Allahabad Law Journal — ALJ
Allahabad Law Journal — Alla LJ
Allahabad Law Journal — Allahabad LJ
Allahabad University Studies — Allahabad Univ Studies
All-Alaska Weekly — AW
Allam- es Jogtudomany — Allam- es Jogtud
Allami Gazdasag — All Gazdasag
Allan Hancock Foundation. Occasional Papers [*New Series*] — OPAFD7
Allan Hancock Foundation. Occasional Papers (New Series) — Allan Hancock Found Occas Pap (New Ser)
Allan Hancock Foundation. Publications. Occasional Paper — AHFPAJ
Allan Hancock Foundation. Publications. Occasional Paper — Allan Hancock Found Publ Occas Pap
Allan Hancock Foundation. Publications. Occasional Paper — Allan Hancock Found Pubs Occasional Paper
Allan Hancock Foundation. Technical Reports — Allan Hancock Found Tech Rep
Allan Hancock Foundation. Technical Reports — TAHFDQ
Allan Hancock Monographs in Marine Biology — Allan Hancock Monogr Mar Biol
Allan Hancock Monographs in Marine Biology — ALMMB6
Allatgyogyaszati Oltoanyagellenorzo Intezet Evkonyve — Allatgyogy Oltoanyagellenorzo Intez Evk
Allatorvosi Koezloeny — Allatorv Koezl
Allatorvosi Lapok — Allat Lapok
Allatorvosi Lapok — Allatorv Lapok
Allattani Kozlemenyek — Allattani Kozl
Allattani Kozlemenyek — ALLKAS
Allattenyesztes [*Animal Breeding*] — ALTZAB
Allattenyesztes/Animal Breeding — Allattenyesz Anim Breed
Allattenyesztes es Takarmanyozas [*Animal Breeding and Feeding*] — Allattenyesz Takarmanyozas
Allattenyesztes es Takarmanyozas [*Animal Breeding and Feeding*] — ATAKDW
Allattenyesztesi Kutatointezet Evkoenyve — Allatteny Kutatointez Evk
Allattenyesztestani Tanszek — Allatteny
ALLC [*Association for Literary and Linguistic Computing*] **Bulletin** — ALLC Bull
ALLC [*Association for Literary and Linguistic Computing*] **Bulletin** — ALLCB
ALLC [*Association for Literary and Linguistic Computing*] **Journal** — ALLC J

All-Canada Weekly Summaries [*Database*] — ACWS
Allegheny Ludlum Horizons — Allegheny Ludlum Horiz
Allemagnes d'Aujourd'hui — Allem Aujourd
Allergic Disease and Therapy — Allerg Dis Ther
Allergie et Immunologie [*Paris*] — ALGIBW
Allergie et Immunologie (Paris) — Allerg Immunol (Paris)
Allergie und Asthma — ALASA
Allergie und Asthma — ALASAV
Allergie und Asthma — Allerg Asthma
Allergie und Asthmaforschung — Allerg Asthmaforsch
Allergie und Immunologie — ALIMC
Allergie und Immunologie [*Leipzig*] — ALIMCL
Allergie und Immunologie — Allerg Immunol
Allergie und Immunologie (Leipzig) — Allerg Immunol (Leipz)
Allergnaedigst Privilegierte Realzeitung der Wissenschaften, Kuenste, und der Commercien — Allergnaed Privileg Realzeitung Wiss
Allergnaedigst-Privilegirte Anzeigen aus Saemmtlich-Kaiserlich-Koeniglichen Erblaendern — Allergnaed Privileg Anz Saemmtl KK Erblaendern
Allergologia et Immunopathologia — AGIMBJ
Allergologia et Immunopathologia [*Madrid*] — Allergol Immunopathol
Allergologia et Immunopathologia (Madrid) — Allergol Immunopathol (Madr)
Allergologia et Immunopathologia. Supplementum — Allergol Immunopathol Suppl
Allergologie — ALLRDI
Allergology International — Allergol Int
Allergology. Proceedings. Congress. International Association of Allergology — Allergol Proc Congr Int Assoc Allergol
Allergy [*Copenhagen*] — LLRGDY
Allergy '74. Proceedings of the European Congress of Allergology and Clinical Immunology — Allergy 74 Proc Eur Congr Allergol Clin Immunol
Allergy Abstracts — Allerg Abstr
Allergy and Asthma Proceedings — Allergy Asthma Proc
Allergy Proceedings — Allergy Proc
Allergy Relief Newsletter — Allerg Relief Newsl
Allergy Shot — Allerg S
Allertonia — LLRTD5
Allevamenti e Veterinaria — Allevamenti Vet
Alley Music — Alley Mus
Allgemeine Berg- und Huettenmaennische Zeitung — Allgem Berg- u Huettenm Ztg
Allgemeine Berg- und Huettenmaennische Zeitung — Allgem Berg Zeitung
Allgemeine Bibliothek der Biblischen Literatur — ABBL
Allgemeine Bibliothek der Neuesten Deutschen Theologischen Literatur — ABTL
Allgemeine Botanische Zeitschrift — Allg Bot Z
Allgemeine Botanische Zeitschrift fuer Systematik, Floristik, Pflanzengeographie — Allg Bot Z Syst
Allgemeine Botanische Zeitung. Abteilung B. Morphologie und Geobotanik — Allg Bot Ztg Abt B
Allgemeine Brauer- und Hopfenzeitung — Allg Brau Hopfenztg
Allgemeine Deutsche Bibliothek — Allg Deutsche Biblioth
Allgemeine Deutsche Biographie — ADB
Allgemeine Deutsche Imkerzeitung — Allg Dt Imkerztg
Allgemeine Deutsche Imkerzeitung — Allg Dtsch Imkerztg
Allgemeine Deutsche Naturhistorische Zeitung — Allg Deutsche Naturh Ztg
Allgemeine Deutsche Naturhistorische Zeitung — Allg Deutsche Naturhist Zeitung
Allgemeine Enzyklopaedie der Wissenschaften und Kuenste — AEWK
Allgemeine Evangelisch-Lutherische Kirchenzeitung [*Luthardt*] — AELK
Allgemeine Evangelisch-Lutherische Kirchenzeitung [*Luthardt*] — AELKZ
Allgemeine Fischerei-Zeitung — ALFZA9
Allgemeine Fischereizeitung — Allg Fischereiztg
Allgemeine Fischerei-Zeitung — Allg Fisch-Ztg
Allgemeine Fischwirtschaftszeitung — Allg Fischwirtschaftsztg
Allgemeine Forst- und Holzwirtschaftliche Zeitung — AFHZAB
Allgemeine Forst- und Holzwirtschaftliche Zeitung — Allg Forst Holzwirtsch Zeit
Allgemeine Forst- und Holzwirtschaftliche Zeitung — Allg Forst Holzwirtsch Ztg
Allgemeine Forst- und Jagdzeitung — AFJZA
Allgemeine Forst- und Jagdzeitung — Allg Forst Jagdztg
Allgemeine Forst- und Jagdzeitung — Allg Forst- u Jagdztg
Allgemeine Forst- und Jagd-Zeitung (Vienna) — Allg Forst Jagd Zeitung Vienna
Allgemeine Forstzeitschrift — AFZSA
Allgemeine Forstzeitschrift — Allg Forstz
Allgemeine Forstzeitschrift — Allg Forstzeitschr
Allgemeine Forstzeitung — A Fo
Allgemeine Forstzeitung — AFZTA
Allgemeine Forstzeitung — Allg Forstztg
Allgemeine Geographische Ephemeriden — Allg Geogr Ephem
Allgemeine Gerber Zeitung — Allg Gerber Ztg
Allgemeine Historie der Reisen zu Wasser und zu Lande oder Sammlung von Reisebeschreibungen — Allg Hist Reisen
Allgemeine Homoeopathische Zeitung — AHZ
Allgemeine Imkerkalender — Allg Imkerkal
Allgemeine Lederindustrie Zeitung — Allg Lederind Ztg
Allgemeine Literatur-Zeitung — Allg Lit Zeitung
Allgemeine Medizinische Zentralzeitung — AMCZg
Allgemeine Militaer-Zeitung — Allg Militztg
Allgemeine Missions-Studien — Allg Missions Stud
Allgemeine Musikalische Zeitung — Allg Mus Zeitung
Allgemeine Musikalische Zeitung — AMZ
Allgemeine Musikzeitung — AMz
Allgemeine Nordische Annalen der Chemie fuer die Freunde der Naturkunde und Arzneiwissenschaft — Allg Nord Ann Chem Freunde Naturkd Arzneiwiss
Allgemeine Oel- und Fett-Zeitung [*Germany*] — Allg Oel-Fett-Ztg
Allgemeine Oesterreichische Chemiker und Techniker-Zeitung [*Austria*] — Allg Oesterr Chem Tech-Ztg
Allgemeine Oesterreichische Gerichtszeitung — Allg Oester Gerichtsztg
Allgemeine Oesterreichische Zeitschrift fuer den Landwirth, Forstmann, und Gaertner — Allg Oesterr Z Landwirth
Allgemeine Papier-Rundschau — Alg Pap-Rund
Allgemeine Papier-Rundschau — Allg Pap Rundsch
Allgemeine Papier-Rundschau — Allg Papier-Rundschau
Allgemeine Photographische Zeitung — Allg Photogr Ztg
Allgemeine Rundschau — Allg Rundsch
Allgemeine Rundschau — ARsch
Allgemeine Sport-Zeitung — ASZ
Allgemeine Textil-Zeitschrift — Allg Text Z
Allgemeine Textil-Zeitschrift und Textil-Ring — Allg Text Z Text Ring
Allgemeine Thueringische Gartenzeitung — Allg Thuering Gartenzeitung
Allgemeine Tonindustrie Zeitung — Allg Tonind Ztg
Allgemeine Treuhandstelle fuer die Juedische Auswanderung — ALTREU
Allgemeine und Praktische Chemie — Allg Prakt Chem
Allgemeine und Praktische Chemie — APKCA
Allgemeine Waermetechnik [*Germany*] — Allg Waermetech
Allgemeine Waermetechnik — AWTEA
Allgemeine Wiener Medizinische Zeitung — Allg Wien M Ztg
Allgemeine Wiener Medizinische Zeitung — Allg Wien Med Ztg
Allgemeine Wochenzeitung der Juden in Deutschland — AW
Allgemeine Wochenzeitung der Juden in Deutschland — AWJ
Allgemeine Wochenzeitung der Juden in Deutschland — AWJD
Allgemeine Zeitschrift fuer Bierbrauerei und Malzfabrikation — Allg Z Bierbrau Malzfabr
Allgemeine Zeitschrift fuer Entomologie — Allg Z Ent
Allgemeine Zeitschrift fuer Psychiatrie — Allg Z Psychiat
Allgemeine Zeitschrift fuer Psychiatrie und Ihre Grenzgebiete — Allg Z Psychiatr Ihre Grenzgeb
Allgemeine Zeitschrift fuer Psychiatrie und Psychischgerichtliche Medicin — Allg Zeits F Psychiat
Allgemeine Zeitschrift fuer Psychiatrie und Psychisch-Gerichtliche Medizin — Allg Ztschr Psychiat
Allgemeine Zeitung (Augsburg) — AZA
Allgemeine Zeitung des Judentums — AZDJ
Allgemeine Zeitung des Judentums — AZJ
Allgemeine Zellforschung und Mikroskopische Anatomie — Allg Zellforsch Mikrosk Anat
Allgemeine Zionistische Organisation — AZO
Allgemeiner Litterarischer Anzeiger, oder Annalen der Gesammten Litteratur fuer die Geschwinde Bekanntmachung Verschiedener Nachrichten aus d Gebiete der Gelehrsamkeit und Kunst — Allg Litt Anz
Allgemeiner Rabbiner-Verband — ARV
Allgemeines Archiv fuer die Geschichtskunde des Preussischen Staates — Ledeburs Arch
Allgemeines Archiv fuer die Geschichtskunde des Preussischen Staates (V. Ledebur, Editor) — V Ledeburs Arch
Allgemeines Forst- und Jagd-Archiv — Allg Forst Jagd Arch
Allgemeines Journal der Chemie — Allg J Chem
Allgemeines Literaturblatt — AL
Allgemeines Literaturblatt — ALB
Allgemeines Oeconomisches Forst-Magazin — Allg Oecon Forst Mag
Allgemeines Repertorium der Literatur — Allg Repert Lit
Allgemeines Statistisches Archiv — Allg Stat Arch
Allgemeines Statistisches Archiv — Allg Statis Arch
Allgemeines Statistisches Archiv — Allg Statist Arch
Allgemeines Statistisches Archiv — Allgemein Statist Arch
Allgemeines Statistisches Archiv — ALSAA
Allgemeines Teutsches Garten-Magazin oder Gemeinnuetzige Beitraege fuer alle Theile des Praktischen Gartenwesens — Allg Teutsch Gart Mag
Alliance Industrielle — ALIDA
Alliance Industrielle — Alliance Ind
Alliance Journal — AJ
Alliance/l'Alliance. Voice of Metis and Non-Status Indians of Quebec [*Canada*] — ALLI
Alliance Record — Alliance Recd
Alliance Review [*New York*] — AR
Alliance Teacher — Alliance Teach
Alliance Witness — AW
Allianz Berichte fuer Betriebstechnik und Schadenverhuetung — Allianz Ber Betriebstech Schadenverhuetung
Allied Health and Behavioral Sciences — Allied Health & Behav Sci
Allied Industrial Worker — Allied Ind Wkr
Allied Irish Bank Review — Allied Irish Bank R
Allied Veterinarian — Allied Vet
All-India Institute of Mental Health. Transactions — All-India Inst Ment Health Trans
Allionia [*Turin*] — ALLIAM
Allis-Chalmers Electrical Review — Allis-Chalmers Electr Rev
Allis-Chalmers Engineering Review — ACERB
Allis-Chalmers Engineering Review — Allis-Chalmers Eng Rev
Allison Research and Engineering — Allison Res Eng
Allmaenna Journalen — Allmaenna J
Allmaenna Svenska Elektriska Aktiebolaget. Research — Allm Sven Elektr Ab Res
Allmaenna Svenska Laekartidningen — Allm Sven Laekartidn
Allmaenna Svenska Utsaedesaktiebolaget Svaloef — Allmaenna Svenska Utsaedesaktiebol Svaloef
Allmaenna Svenska Utsaedesfoereningens Tidskrift — Allmaenna Svenska Utsaedesfoeren Tidskr
Alloy Casting Bulletin — Alloy Cast Bull
Alloy Digest — ALDGA

Alloy Digest — Alloy Dig
Alloy Metals Review — Alloy Met Rev
Allpanchis. Instituto de Pastoral Andina — IPA/A
All-State Sales Tax Reporter. Commerce Clearing House — All St Sales Tax Rep CCH
Alluminio e Nuova Metallurgia — Allum Nuova Met
Alluminio e Nuova Metallurgia [*Italy*] — Allum Nuova Metall
Alluminio e Nuova Metallurgia — ANOMA
Allwedd y Tannau — All T
Alma Cubana — AC
Alma Mater — AM
Alma Mater Philippina — Alma Mater Philipp
Alma Nova. Revista Mensal Ilustrada — ANRMI
Alma-Atinskii Gosudarstvennyi Pedagogiceskii Institut Imeni Abaja. Ucenye Zapiski — Alma-Atin Gos Ped Inst Ucen Zap
Al-Machriq [*Beyrouth*] — Mach
Almanac of Seapower — Sea Pwr A
Almanacco dei Bibliotecari Italiani — Alman Bibliot Italiani
Almanacco Letterario Bompiani — ALB
Almanach Chasse et Peche — Alm Chas Pec
Almanach de Brioude e son Arrondisement — Al Brioude
Almanach de Carlsbad, ou Melanges Medicaux, Scientifiques et Litteraires, Relatifs a ces Thermes et au Pays — Alman Carlsbad
Almanach de la Physique Instructive et Amusante — Alman Phys Instruct Amusante
Almanach der Koeniglich-Bayerischen Akademie der Wissenschaften — Alman Koenigl Bayer Akad Wiss
Almanach der Oesterreichischen Forschung — Alm Oesterr Forsch
Almanach der Psychoanalyse — A d P
Almanach des Lettres — AlL
Almanach des Vedettes — Alm Ved
Almanach du Crime — Alm Cr
Almanach fuer Literatur und Theologie — Alm Lit Theo
Almanach. Oesterreichische Akademie der Wissenschaften — AlmOAW
Almanak Agricola Brasileiro — Almanak Agric Brasil
Almanak van het Utrechtsche Landbouw-Genootschap — Alman Utrechtsche Landb Genootsch
Almanak voor Notariaat en Registratie — Alm NR
Al'manakh Ukraiens'koho Narodnoho Soiuzu — AUNS
Almanaque Cafetero — Alman Cafetero
Almanaque Cientifico — Alman Ci
Almanaque d'Ovar — AO
Al-Masarra. Al-Macarrat — Mas
Almeida Garrett. Homenagem do Club Fenianos Portuenses — AGHCFP
Al-Mujtama al-Jadid [*Cairo*] — AMAJ
Al-Mustami Al-Arabi [*Cairo*] — MA
Al-Mustansiriya University. Review [*Baghdad*] — MUR
Alon Hahevra Hanumismatit le'Israel — AHHI
Alon. Internal Quarterly of the Israel Numismatic Society — AISIN
Alpenlaendische Bienenzeitung — Alpenlaend Bienenztg
Alpes Orientales — Alpes Orient
Alpha-Fetoprotein and Hepatoma. Japanese Cancer Association. Symposium on Alpha-Fetoprotein and Hepatoma — Alpha-Fetoprotein Hepatoma Jpn Cancer Assn Symp
Alpha-Foeto-Proteine Compte Rendu. Conference Internationale — Alpha-Foeto-Proteine C R Conf Int
Alpine Journal — Alpine J
Alpine Journal — APJL
Al-Qantara. Revista de Estudios Arabes — Qantara
ALRA [*American Land Resource Association*] **Bulletin** — ALRA Bull
ALSA [*American Legal Studies Association*] **Forum** — ALSA F
Alsace-Lorraine. Service de la Carte Geologique. Memoires [*Strasbourg*] — Alsace-Lorraine Serv Carte Geol Mem
Alt- und Neuindische Studien [*Wiesbaden*] — Alt-Neuindische Stud
Alta Direccion — Alta Dir
Alta Frequenza — ALFRA
Alta Frequenza — Alta Freq
Alta Frequenza. Supplemento — Alta Freq Suppl
Altajskij Sbornik — Altajsk Sborn
Altalanos Nyelveszeti Tanulmanyok — ANT
Altbabylonische Briefe — ABr
Altbabylonische Briefe in Umschrift — ABBU
Altbaeyerische Monatsschrift — Altbayer Monatsschr
Altdeutsche Textbibliothek — AdTb
Altdeutsche Textbibliothek — ATB
Altdeutsche Textbibliothek. Ergaenzungsreihe — ADTBE
Alte Orient — AIO
Alte Orient — Alt Or
Alte Orient — Alte Or
Alte Orient — AO
Alte Orient Beihefte — Alte Orient Beih
Alte und Moderne Kunst — AlMK
Alte und Moderne Kunst. Oesterreichische Fachzeitschrift des Marktes fuer Antiquitaeten, Bilder, Kunstgegenstaende Alter, und Moderner Kunst — Alte Mod Kunst
Alten Sprachen — A Spr
Alten Sprachen — Alt Spr
Alten Sprachen — AS
Alter Orient — ALOR
Alter Orient und Altes Testament — AOAT
Alter Orient und Altes Testament. Sonderreihe — AOATS
Alternate Energy Magazine — Alternate Energy Mag
Alternate Futures — Altern
Alternate Routes — Alt Routes
Alternativas (Chile) — Altern (Chile)
Alternativas (Santiago) — AS
Alternative/Appropriate Technology Index — A T Index
Alternative Criminology Journal — ACJ
Alternative Culture and Institutions — Alt C I
Alternative Energy — Alt En
Alternative Energy Sources — Altern Energy Sources
Alternative Energy Sources. An International Compendium. Proceedings. Miami International Conference — Altern Energy Sources Proc Miami Int Conf
Alternative Energy Trends and Forecasts — Alt Energy
Alternative Features — Alt Ftr
Alternative Fuels Emissions and Technology — Altern Fuels Emiss Technol
Alternative Futures — Altern Fut
Alternative Higher Education — Altern High Ed
Alternative Media — Alt Media
Alternative Medicine — Alter Med
Alternative Medicine — ALTMEA
Alternative Methods in Toxicology — Altern Methods Toxicol
Alternative Methods in Toxicology — AMTOEN
Alternative Methods in Toxicology and the Life Sciences — Altern Methods Toxicol Life Sci
Alternative Pink Pages. Australasian Plant Pathology — APP
Alternative Press Index — Alt Press Ind
Alternative Press Index — Altern Press Index
Alternative Press Index — API
Alternative Press, Libraries, Journalism — Alt Pr J
Alternative Sources of Energy — Alt Energy
Alternative Sweeteners [*Monograph*] — Altern Sweeteners
Alternative Technologies for Power Production — Alternative Technol Power Prod
Alternative Therapies in Health and Medicine — Altern Ther Health Med
Alternatives — Alternat
Alternatives — Alternatv
Alternatives — ALTRD
Alternatives — IALT
Alternatives. Journal of the Friends of the Earth [*Canada*] — AJFE
Alternatives Non-Violentes — Alternat Non-Violentes
Alternatives. Perspectives on Society and Environment [*Canada*] — APSE
Alternatives to Laboratory Animals — ATLA
Alternatives to Laboratory Animals. ATLA — Alternatives Lab Anim ATLA
Alternstheorien Zellkern Membranen Giessener Symposion ueber Experimentelle Gerontologie — Alternstheorien Memb Giessener Symp Exp Gerontol
Altertuemer von Pergamon — AvP
Altertum [*Berlin*] — Alt
Altes Haus - Modern [*Germany*] — Altes Haus-Mod
Altfraenkische Chronik — Afr Ch
Alt-Franken — A Fr
Altfranzoesische Bibliothek — Altfranz Bibl
Althaus Modernisierung [*Germany*] — Althaus Mod
Altitute. Revista da Federacao dos Municipios da Beira-Serra — ARFMBS
Altnuernberger Landschaft. Mitteilungen — ANL
Alto Minho — AM
Altona, Hamburg, Wandsbek — AHW
Altorientalische Bibliothek — AOB
Altorientalische Denkmaeler im Vorderasiatischen Museum zu Berlin — AOD
Altorientalische Forschungen [*Berlin*] — Alt Fors
Altorientalische Forschungen [*Berlin*] — Alt Or F
Altorientalische Forschungen — AOF
Altorientalische Texte und Bilder zum Alten Testament — AOB
Altorientalische Texte und Untersuchungen — AOTU
Altorientalische Texte und Untersuchungen [*Leiden*] — ATU
Altorientalische Texte zum Alten Testament — AOT
Altorientalischer Kommentar zum Alten Testament — AOKAT
Altpreussische Forschungen — Altpreuss Forsch
Altpreussische Forschungen — APrF
Altpreussische Monatschrift — APMS
Altpreussische Monatsschrift — APrM
Altro Polo — AIP
Altschlesien — Asch
Altschlesische Blaetter — Altschles Bl
Altschul Symposia Series — Altschul Symp Ser
Altsprachliche Unterricht — AU
Alttestamentliche Abhandlungen — AA
Alttestamentliche Abhandlungen [*Muenster*] — ATA
Alt-Thueringen — Alt Thuer
Aluminium — Alum
Aluminium — ALUMA
Aluminium Courier — Alumin Cour
Aluminium World — Alum Wld
Aluminium World — Alumin Wld
Aluminum Abstracts — Alum Abstr
Aluminum and Magnesium — Alum Magnesium
Aluminum and Magnesium for Automotive Applications. Proceedings of a Symposium — Alum Magnesium Automot Appl Proc Symp
Aluminum and Non-Ferrous Metals News — Alum Non Ferrous Met News
Aluminum and The Non-Ferrous Review — Alum Non Ferrous Rev
Aluminum Archiv — Alum Arch
Aluminum Availability - Market Economy Countries. Bureau of Mines Information Circular — BMIC 8917
Aluminum Company of America. Research Laboratories. Technical Paper — Alum Co Am Res Lab Tech Pap
Aluminum Finishing Society of Kinki. Journal — Alum Finish Soc Kinki J
Aluminum News Letter — Alum News Lett
Aluminum Ranshofen Mitteilungen — Alum Ranshofen Mitt
Aluminum Research Laboratories. Technical Paper — Alum Res Lab Tech Pap

Aluminum Review — Alum Rev
Aluminum Statistical Review — Alum Stat
Aluminum Suisse — Alum Suisse
Aluminum Transformation Technology and Applications. Proceedings. International Symposium — Alum Transform Technol Appl Proc Int Symp
Aluminum World and Brass and Copper Industries — Alum World Brass Copper Ind
Alumnae Association. Women's Medical College of Pennsylvania. Report. Proceedings — Alumnae Assn Womens Med Coll Pa Rpt Proc
Alumnae Magazine — Alumnae Mag
Alumnae Magazine. Johns Hopkins Hospital. School of Nursing. Alumnae Association (Baltimore) — Alumnae Mag (Baltimore)
Alumni Association. University of British Columbia. Chronicle — UBC Alumni Chronicle
Alumni Bulletin. School of Dentistry. Indiana University — Alumni Bull Sch Dent Indiana Univ
Alumni Bulletin. University of Michigan. School of Dentistry — Alumni Bull Univ Mich Sch Dent
Alumni Bulletin. University of Virginia — Alumni Bull Univ Virginia
Alumni Gazette. College of William and Mary — Alumni Gaz Coll William
Alumni Magazine — Alumni Mag
Alumni Magazine. Columbia University - Presbyterian Hospital. School of Nursing. Alumni Association — Alumni Mag Columbia Univ Presbyt Hosp Sch Nurs
Alumni Magazine. Columbia University-Presbyterian Hospital. School of Nursing Alumni Association (New York) — Alumni Mag (NY)
Al-Urwa (Bombay) — AUB
Aluta. Muzeul Judetean — Alu
Alyuminievye Splavy. Sbornik Statei [*Former USSR*] — Alyum Splavy Sb Statei
ALZA Conference Series — ALZA Conf Ser
ALZA Conference Series — ALZAAY
Alzeyer Geschichtsblaetter — A Gb
Alzheimer Disease and Associated Disorders — Alzheimer Dis Assoc Disord
Alzheimer's Disease. Lessons from Cell Biology [*monograph*] — Alzheimers Dis Lessons Cell Biol
Alzheimer's Disease. New Treatment Strategies — Alzheimers Dis
Alzheimer's Research — Alzheimers Res
AM + R. Angewandte Elektronik. Mess und Regeltechnik — AM + R Angew Elektron Mess Regeltech
AM + R. Angewandte Mess- und Regeltechnik — AM + R Angew Mess Regeltech
AMA [*American Medical Association*] **Archives of Dermatology** — AMA Arch Dermatol
AMA [*American Medical Association*] **Archives of Dermatology and Syphilology** — AMA Arch Dermatol Syphilol
AMA [*American Medical Association*] **Archives of General Psychiatry** — AMA Arch Gen Psychiatry
AMA [*American Medical Association*] **Archives of Industrial Health** — AMA Arch Ind Health
AMA [*American Medical Association*] **Archives of Industrial Health** — AMIHA
AMA [*American Medical Association*] **Archives of Industrial Hygiene and Occupational Medicine** — AMA Arch Ind Hyg Occup Med
AMA [*American Medical Association*] **Archives of Internal Medicine** — AMA Archs Internal Med
AMA [*American Medical Association*] **Journal of Diseases of Children** — AMA J Dis Child
Amakusa Marine Biological Laboratory. Contributions — Amakusa Mar Biol Lab Contr
Amalgamated Engineering Union. Monthly Journal — AEU Mon J
Amalgamated Engineering Union. Monthly Journal — AEUMJ
Amalgamated Engineering Union. Monthly Journal — Amal Engr Union MJ
Amaru (Revista Literaria) — AU
Amateur Builder's Manual — Amat Build Man
Amateur Cine World — Amat Cine World
Amateur Entomologist — Amat Ent
Amateur Gardener and Gardeners Chronicle — Amateur Gard Gard Chron
Amateur Gardening, for the Lovers and Cultivators of Flowers and Fruits (Springfield) — Amateur Gard Springfield
Amateur Geologist — Amat Geol
Amateur Photographer — Amat Photogr
Amatores Herbarii/Shokubutsu Shumi — Amatores Herb
Amazing Detective Tales — AD
Amazing Detective Tales — ADT
Amazing Science Stories — ASS
Amazing Stories — AMZ
Amazing Stories. Annual — AA
Amazing Stories. Annual — AMA
Amazing Stories. Quarterly — AMQ
Amazing Stories. Quarterly — AQ
Amazing Stories. Quarterly Reissue — AMR
Amazing Stories. Science Fiction Novels — AMN
Amazonia Colombiana Americanista — Amazon Col Am
Amazonia Peruana. Centro Amazonico de Antropologia y Aplicacion Practica. Departamento de Documentacion y Publicaciones — CAAAP/AP
Amazoniana — AMAZAP
AMB. Revista da Associacao Medica Brasileira — AMB
Ambas Americas. Revista de Educacion, Bibliografia, i Agricultura — Ambas Amer
Ambio. Special Report — Ambio Spec Rep
Ambio. Special Report — AOSRB4
Ambito Cuaderno Literario — ACL
Ambtenaar — AMR
Ambulance Bulletin — Ambulance Bull
Ambulance Journal — Ambulance J
Amcham Journal (Manila) — ACJ
AMD Symposia Series (American Society of Mechanical Engineers) — AMD Symp Ser (Am Soc Mech Eng)
AMDEL [*Australian Mineral Development Laboratories*] **Bulletin** — AMDEL Bul
AMDEL [*Australian Mineral Development Laboratories*] **Bulletin** — AMDEL Bull
AME [*African Methodist Episcopal*] **Zion Quarterly Review** — AME Zion QR
Ameghiniana — AMGHB2
Amenagement du Territoire et Developpement Regional — Amenag Territ Develop Region
Amenagement du Territoire et Droit Foncier — Amenage Territ Droit Foncier
Amenagement et Nature — Amenag et Nature
Amended Specification (United Kingdom) — Amended Specif (UK)
Amerasia Journal — Amerasia J
America — A
America — AM
America — AMRIB
America — GAME
America Clinica — Am Clin
America. History and Life [*Database*] — AHL
America. History and Life — Am Hist Life
America. History and Life — AmerH
America. History and Life. Part A. Article Abstracts and Citations — Am Hist Life Part A
America. History and Life. Part B. Index to Book Reviews — Am Hist Life Part B
America. History and Life. Part C. American History Bibliography, Books, Articles, and Dissertations — Am Hist Life Part C
America. History and Life. Part D. Annual Index — Am Hist Life Part D
America. History and Life. Supplement — Am Hist Life Suppl
America Indigena — AI
America Indigena — Am Ind
America Indigena — Am Indigena
America Indigena — Amer Indig
America Indigena — AmerI
America Indigena. Instituto Indigenista Interamericano — III/AI
America Kenkyu — Amer Kenkyu
America Latina — AL
America Latina — ALat
America Latina — Am Lat
America Latina — Amer Lat
America Latina. Academia de Ciencias de la Union de Republicas Sovieticas Socialistas — URSS/AL
America Latina Informe de Mercados — ALIM
America Latina Informe Economico — ALIE
America Latina Informe Politico — ALIP
America Latina Union Sovietica — Amer Lat Un Sov
America (Quito) — Am (Quito)
America. Quito — AmericaQ
America. Revista de la Asociacion de Escritores y Artistas Americanos — AEA
Americal Society of Mechanical Engineers. Fuels and Combustion Technologies Division. Publication. FACT — Am Soc Mech Eng Fuels Combust Technol Div Publ FACT
American — Amer
American Academy in Rome. Memoirs — Am Acad Rome Mem
American Academy in Rome. Papers and Monographs — PAAR
American Academy of Actuaries. Journal — Am Acad Actuar Jnl
American Academy of Arts and Sciences. Memoirs — Am Acad Arts & Sci Mem
American Academy of Arts and Sciences. Memoirs — Amer Acad Arts & Sci Mem
American Academy of Arts and Sciences. Proceedings — Am Acad Arts & Sci Proc
American Academy of Arts and Sciences. Proceedings — Amer Acad of Arts and Sciences Proc
American Academy of Child Psychiatry. Journal — Am Acad Child Psychiat J
American Academy of Ophthalmology and Otolaryngology. Transactions — Am Acad Opthalmol Otolaryngol Trans
American Academy of Ophthalmology and Otolaryngology. Transactions. Section on Ophthalmology — Am Acad Ophthalmol Otolaryngol Trans Sect Ophthalmol
American Academy of Ophthalmology and Otolaryngology. Transactions. Section on Otolaryngology — Am Acad Ophthalmol Otolaryngol Trans Sect Otolaryngol
American Academy of Optometry Series — Am Acad Optom Ser
American Academy of Orthopaedic Surgeons. Symposium on Osteoarthritis — Am Acad Orthop Surg Symp Osteoarthritis
American Academy of Orthopedic Surgery. Instructional Course Lectures — Am Acad Orthop Surg Lectures
American Academy of Physicians' Assistants. Journal — PA J
American Academy of Political and Social Science. Annals — AAPSSA
American Academy of Political and Social Science. Annals — Am Acad Pol & Soc Sci Ann
American Academy of Political and Social Science. Annals — APSS
American Academy of Political and Social Science. Monographs — AAPSS Mg
American Academy of Psychoanalysis. Journal — Am Acad Psychoanal J
American Academy of Religion. Journal — Am Acad Relig J
American Agent and Broker — Am Ag Br
American Almanac — Am Alma
American Alpine Journal — AAJ
American Alpine Journal — Am Alpine Jour
American Alpine Journal — AMAJ
American Alpine News — Am Alpine N
American Animal Hospital Association. Bulletin — Am An Hosp Assoc Bul
American Annals of Education — Am Annals Educ
American Annals of the Deaf — AA
American Annals of the Deaf — Am Ann Deaf
American Annals of the Deaf — Am Annals Deaf
American Annals of the Deaf — ANDFA

American Annual — AmA
American Annual of Photography — Amer Ann Phot
American Annual of Photography — Amer Annual Phot
American Annual Register — Ann Reg
American Anthropological Association. Memoirs — AAAM
American Anthropological Association. Newsletter — Am Anthro Assoc Newsl
American Anthropologist — A ANTH
American Anthropologist — AA
American Anthropologist — AAn
American Anthropologist — AAnthr
American Anthropologist — Am An
American Anthropologist — Am Ant
American Anthropologist — Am Anth
American Anthropologist — Am Anthro
American Anthropologist — Am Anthrop
American Anthropologist — Am Anthropol
American Anthropologist — AmA
American Anthropologist — Amer Anthr
American Anthropologist — Amer Anthropol
American Anthropologist — Amer Anthropologist
American Anthropologist — GAAN
American Anthropologist. American Anthropological Association — AAA/AA
American Antiquarian — Am Antiq
American Antiquarian and Oriental Journal — AAOJ
American Antiquarian Society. Proceedings — AAS
American Antiquarian Society. Proceedings — Am Antiq Soc Proc
American Antiquarian Society. Proceedings — Amer Antiq Soc Proc
American Antiquarian Society. Proceedings. Annual Meeting — Amer Antiq Soc Proc Annual Meeting
American Antiques — Am Antiques
American Antiquity — AA
American Antiquity — AANTA
American Antiquity — AAY
American Antiquity — Am Ant
American Antiquity — Am Antiq
American Antiquity — Am Antiquit
American Antiquity — AMA
American Antiquity — Amer Antiq
American Antiquity — Amer Antiquity
American Antiquity — PAMA
American Antiquity. Society for American Archaeology — SAA/AA
American Aquarist — Amer Aquar
American Arab Affairs — AAA
American Arab Affairs — Am Arab Affairs
American Archaeological Expedition to Syria. Publication — AAES
American Architect — Am Arch
American Architect and Building News — Am Arch
American Archives of Rehabilitation Therapy — Am Arch Rehabil Ther
American Archives of Rehabilitation Therapy — Amer Arch Rehab Ther
American Archivist — A Arch
American Archivist — AA
American Archivist — Am Archiv
American Archivist — Am Archivis
American Archivist — Am Archivist
American Archivist — AmA
American Archivist — Amer Arch
American Archivist — Amer Archivist
American Archivist — ANA
American Art Journal — Am Art J
American Art Journal — Amer Art J
American Art Review — Am Art Rev
American Artist — AArt
American Artist — Am Artist
American Artist — GAAR
American Association for Respiratory Therapy. Times — AARTimes
American Association for State and Local History. Bulletin — Am Assoc State Local Hist Bull
American Association for the Advancement of Science. Abstracts of Papers. National Meeting — Am Assoc Adv Sci Abstr Pap Natl Meet
American Association for the Advancement of Science. Bulletin — AAAS Bull
American Association for the Advancement of Science. Committee on Desert and Arid Zones Research. Contribution — Am Assoc Adv Sci Comm Desert Arid Zones Res Contrib
American Association for the Advancement of Science. Proceedings — Am Assn Adv Sci Proc
American Association for the Advancement of Science. Proceedings. Memoirs — Am As Pr Mem
American Association for the Advancement of Science. Publication — AAAS Publication
American Association for the Advancement of Science. Publication — Am Assoc Adv Sci Publ
American Association for the Advancement of Science. Selected Symposia Series — AAAS Sel Sympos Ser
American Association for the Advancement of Science. Selected Symposia Series — AAAS Selected Symposia Series
American Association for the Advancement of Science. Symposium — Am Assoc Adv Sci Symp
American Association of Architectural Bibliographers. Papers — American Assoc Arch Bib
American Association of Cereal Chemists. Monograph Series — Am Assoc Cereal Chem Monogr Ser
American Association of Colleges for Teacher Education. Yearbook — Am Assn Col Teach Educ Yrbk
American Association of Collegiate Registrars. Journal — Am Assn Coll Reg J
American Association of Cost Engineers. Bulletin — AACE Bull
American Association of Industrial Nurses. Journal — Am Assoc Ind Nurses J
American Association of Museums. Proceedings — Am As Museums Pr
American Association of Occupational Health Nurses. Journal — AAOHN J
American Association of Pathologists and Bacteriologists. Symposium Monographs — Am Assoc Pathol Bacteriol Symp Mono
American Association of Petroleum Geologists. Bulletin — AAPG
American Association of Petroleum Geologists. Bulletin — AAPGB
American Association of Petroleum Geologists. Bulletin — Am As Petroleum G B
American Association of Petroleum Geologists. Bulletin — Am Assn Pet Geol Bul
American Association of Petroleum Geologists. Bulletin — Am Assn Pet Geologists Bull
American Association of Petroleum Geologists. Bulletin — Am Assoc Pet Geol Bull
American Association of Petroleum Geologists. Bulletin — Amer Assoc Pet Geol Bull
American Association of Petroleum Geologists. Continuing Education — AAPG Continuing Education
American Association of Petroleum Geologists. Explorer — AAPG Explorer
American Association of Petroleum Geologists. Memoir — AAPG Memoir
American Association of Petroleum Geologists. Memoir — Am Assoc Pet Geol Mem
American Association of Petroleum Geologists. Memoir — Am Assoc Petroleum Geologists Mem
American Association of Petroleum Geologists. Pacific Section. Correlation Section — Am Assoc Petroleum Geologists Pacific Sec Correlation Sec
American Association of Petroleum Geologists. Reprint Series — Am Assoc Pet Geol Repr Ser
American Association of Petroleum Geologists. Studies in Geology — Am Assoc Pet Geol Study Geol
American Association of Retired Persons. News Bulletin — Am Assoc Ret Per News Bul
American Association of School Administrators. Official Report — Am Assn Sch Adm Off Rep
American Association of Small Research Companies. News — Am Assoc Sm Res Comp N
American Association of Stratigraphic Palynologists. Contribution Series — Am Assoc Stratigr Palynol Contrib Ser
American Association of Teachers of French. National Bulletin — AATFNB
American Association of Teachers of Slavic and East European Languages. Bulletin — AATSEEL Bull
American Association of Teachers of Slavic and East European Languages. Journal — AATSEEL Jour
American Association of Textile Chemists and Colorists. National Technical Conference. Book of Papers — Am Assoc Text Chem Color Natl Tech Conf Book Pap
American Association of University Professors. Bulletin — AAUP Bul
American Association of University Professors. Bulletin — AAUP Bull
American Association of University Professors. Bulletin — AAUPB
American Association of University Professors. Bulletin — Am Assn Univ Prof B
American Association of University Professors. Bulletin — Am Assoc Univ Prof Bull
American Association of University Women. Journal — Am Assn Univ Women J
American Association of Veterinary Laboratory Diagnosticians. Proceedings of Annual Meeting — Am Assoc Vet Lab Diagn Proc Annu Meet
American Association of Zoo Veterinarians. Annual Proceedings — Am Assoc Zoo Vet Annu Proc
American Astronautical Society. Publications. Science and Technology — Am Astronaut Soc Publ Sci Technol
American Astronautical Society. Science and Technology Series — Am Astronaut Soc Sci Technol Ser
American Astronomical Society. Bulletin — AASBA
American Astronomical Society. Bulletin — Am Astron Soc Bull
American Astronomical Society. Photo Bulletin — Am Astron Soc Photo Bull
American Aviation — Am Aviation
American Aviation Historical Society. Journal — Amer Avia Hist Soc Jnl
American Baby — Am Baby
American Baby — IABY
American Baby for Expectant and New Parents — Am Baby
American Baby for Expectant and New Parents — Am Baby Expectant New Parents
American Baker — Amer Baker
American Banker — Am Bank
American Banker Directory of US Banking Executives — Am Bank Dir US Bank Exec
American Bankers Association. Bank Compliance — Am Bank Assoc Bank Comp
American Bankers Association. Banking Journal — Am Bank Assoc Bank Jnl
American Bankers Association. Banking Literature Index — Bank Lit Index
American Bankers' Association. Journal — Am Bankers Assn J
American Bankruptcy Law Journal — Am Ban LJ
American Bankruptcy Law Journal — Am Bankr L J
American Bankruptcy Law Journal — Am Bankrupt
American Baptist Flag — ABF
American Baptist Quarterly — Am B Q
American Baptist Quarterly — Am Bapt Q
American Bar Association. Antitrust Law Journal — ABA Antitrust L J
American Bar Association. Comparative Law Bureau. Annual Bulletin — ABA Comp L Bull
American Bar Association. Journal — ABA J
American Bar Association. Journal — ABA Jo
American Bar Association. Journal — ABA Jour
American Bar Association. Journal — Am Bar A J
American Bar Association. Journal — Am Bar Ass J

American Bar Association. Journal — Am Bar Assn J
American Bar Association. Journal — Am Bar Asso Jour
American Bar Association. Journal — Am Bar Assoc J
American Bar Association Journal — Amer Bar Assoc J
American Bar Association. Section of Antitrust Law — ABA Sect Antitrust L
American Bar Association. Section of Criminal Law — ABA Sect Crim L
American Bar Association. Section of Insurance, Negligence, and Compensation Law — ABA Sect Ins N & CL
American Bar Association. Section of International and Comparative Law. Bulletin — ABA Sect Int & Comp L Bull
American Bar Association. Section of Labor Relations Law — ABA Sect Lab Rel L
American Bar Association. Section of Mineral and Natural Resources Law — ABA Sect M & NRL
American Bar Association. Section of Real Property, Probate, and Trust Law. Proceedings — ABA Sect Real Prop L
American Bar Foundation. Research Journal — ABF Res J
American Bar Foundation. Research Journal — ABF Research J
American Bar Foundation. Research Journal — Am B Found Res J
American Bar Foundation. Research Journal — Am Bar Found Res J
American Bar News — Am Bar N
American Bee Journal — ABJOA
American Bee Journal — Am Bee J
American Bee Journal — Amer Bee J
American Beekeeping Federation. Newsletter — Am Beekeep Fed Newsl
American Behavioral Scientist — ABHSA
American Behavioral Scientist — ABS
American Behavioral Scientist — Am Behav Sci
American Behavioral Scientist — Am Behavioral Sci
American Behavioral Scientist — Am Behavioral Scientist
American Behavioral Scientist — Amer Behav Sci
American Behavioral Scientist — Amer Behav Scientist
American Behavioral Scientist — PAMB
American Benedictine Review — A Ben R
American Benedictine Review — ABR
American Benedictine Review — Am Benedictine Rev
American Benedictine Review [*St. Paul, MN*] — AmBenR
American Benedictine Review — AmBR
American Biblical Repository — Am Bib Repos
American Bibliopolist — Am Bibliop
American Biology Teacher — ABITA
American Biology Teacher — Am Biol Tea
American Biology Teacher — Am Biol Teach
American Biology Teacher — AMBT
American Biology Teacher — Amer Biol Teacher
American Biology Teacher — PABT
American Biotechnology Laboratory — Am Biotechnol Lab
American Birds — Am Birds
American Book Collector — ABC
American Book Collector — Am Bk Collec
American Book Collector — Am Bk Collector
American Book Collector — Amer Book Coll
American Book Publishing Record — Am Book Publ Recd
American Book Publishing Record — Amer Bk Pub Rec
American Book Publishing Record — BPR
American Book Review — ABR
American Book Review — Am Book Rev
American Book Review — AMR
American Bookman — AB
American Botanist Devoted to Economic and Ecological Botany (Binghamton) — Amer Bot Binghamton
American Botanist (San Diego) — Amer Bot San Diego
American Bottler — Am Bottler
American Brahms Society Newsletter — ABSN
American Breeders Association Report — Amer Breed Assoc Rep
American Brewer — Am Brew
American Brewer — Amer Brewer
American Brewer's Review — Am Brew Rev
American Builder — Am Bld
American Bureau of Geography. Bulletin — Am Bur Geog B
American Bus Association. Report — Am Bus Assoc Rep
American Business — Am Bsns
American Business — Am Business
American Business Education — Am Bsns Ed
American Business Education Yearbook — Am Bsns Ed Yrbk
American Business Law Journal — ABL
American Business Law Journal — Am Bus L J
American Business Law Journal — Am Bus Law
American Business Law Journal — Am Bus Law J
American Business Law Journal — American Business Law Jrnl
American Butter and Cheese Review — Am Butter R
American Camellia Yearbook [*American Camellia Society*] — Am Camellia Yearb
American Camellia Yearbook (American Camellia Society) — Am Camellia Yearb (Am Camellia Soc)
American Carbonator and Bottler — Am Carbonator Bottler
American Catholic Historical Society of Philadelphia. Records — ACHSP
American Catholic Historical Researches — ACHR
American Catholic Historical Society. Records — ACHS
American Catholic Historical Society. Records — ACHSR
American Catholic Historical Society. Records — Am Cath His Rec
American Catholic Historical Society. Records [*Philadelphia*] — Am Cath His S
American Catholic Historical Society. Records — AmCathHS
American Catholic Philosophical Association. Proceedings — ACPAP
American Catholic Quarterly — ACQ
American Catholic Quarterly Review — ACQR
American Catholic Quarterly Review — Am Cath Q
American Catholic Sociological Review — ACSR
American Catholic Sociological Review — Am Cath Sociol Rev
American Cattle Producer — Am Cattle Prod
American Cattle Producer — Amer Cattle Prod
American Ceramic Society. Bulletin — ACSBA
American Ceramic Society. Bulletin — Am Cer Soc Bul
American Ceramic Society. Bulletin — Am Ceram S
American Ceramic Society. Bulletin — Am Ceram Soc Bull
American Ceramic Society. Bulletin — Amer Ceram Soc Bull
American Ceramic Society. Bulletin — Ceramic S B
American Ceramic Society. Fall Meeting. Materials and Equipment. Whitewares Division. Proceedings — Am Ceram Soc Fall Meet Mater Equip Whitewares Div Proc
American Ceramic Society. Journal — Am Cer Soc J
American Ceramic Society. Journal — Am Ceramic Soc Jour
American Chamber of Commerce in Japan. Journal — AJJ
American Chamber of Commerce in Japan. Journal — Am Chamber Commer Japan J
American Chemical Journal — A Ch J
American Chemical Journal — Am Chem J
American Chemical Society. Division of Environmental Chemistry. Preprints — ACS Div Environ Chem Prepr
American Chemical Society. Division of Environmental Chemistry. Preprints — Am Chem Soc Div Environ Chem Prepr
American Chemical Society. Division of Fuel Chemistry. Preprints — ACS Div Fuel Chem Prepr
American Chemical Society. Division of Fuel Chemistry. Preprints — Am Chem Soc Div Fuel Chem Prepr
American Chemical Society. Division of Fuel Chemistry. Preprints — Am Chem Soc Div Fuel Prepr
American Chemical Society. Division of Fuel Chemistry. Preprints — Amer Chem Soc Div Fuel Chem Prepr
American Chemical Society. Division of Fuel Chemistry. Preprints of Papers — Am Chem Soc Div Fuel Chem Prepr Pap
American Chemical Society. Division of Gas and Fuel Chemistry. Preprints — Am Chem Soc Div Gas Fuel Chem
American Chemical Society. Division of Gas and Fuel Chemistry. Preprints — Am Chem Soc Div Gas Fuel Chem Prepr
American Chemical Society Division of Nuclear Chemistry and Technology Symposium on Exotic Nuclear Spectroscopy — Am Chem Soc Div Nucl Chem Technol Symp Exot Nucl Spectrosc
American Chemical Society. Division of Organic Coatings and Plastics Chemistry. Papers — Am Chem Soc Div Org Coat Plast Chem Pap
American Chemical Society. Division of Organic Coatings and Plastics Chemistry. Papers Presented at the Meeting — Am Chem Soc Div Org Coat Plast Chem Pap Meet
American Chemical Society. Division of Organic Coatings and Plastics Chemistry. Preprints — Amer Chem Soc Div Org Coatings Plast Chem Prepr
American Chemical Society. Division of Petroleum Chemistry. General Papers. Preprints — Am Chem Soc Div Pet Chem Gen
American Chemical Society. Division of Petroleum Chemistry. General Papers. Preprints — Am Chem Soc Div Pet Chem Gen Pap Prepr
American Chemical Society. Division of Petroleum Chemistry. Preprints — ACS Div Pet Chem Prepr
American Chemical Society. Division of Petroleum Chemistry. Preprints — Am Chem Soc Div Pet Chem Prepr
American Chemical Society. Division of Petroleum Chemistry. Preprints — Am Chem Soc Div Petr Chem Prepr
American Chemical Society. Division of Petroleum Chemistry. Preprints — Amer Chem Soc Div Petrol Chem Prepr
American Chemical Society. Division of Petroleum Chemistry. Symposia — Am Chem Soc Div Pet Chem Symp
American Chemical Society. Division of Polymer Chemistry. Preprints — Am Chem Soc Div Polym Chem Prepr
American Chemical Society. Division of Water, Air, and Waste Chemistry. General Papers — Am Chem Soc Div Water Air Waste Chem Gen Pap
American Chemical Society. Division of Water, Air, and Waste Chemistry. General Papers — Amer Chem Soc Div Water Air Waste Chem Gen Pap
American Chemical Society. Joint Conference with the Chemical Institute of Canada. Abstracts of Papers — Am Chem Soc Jt Conf Chem Inst Can Abstr Pap
American Chemical Society. Journal — Am Chem Soc J
American Chemical Society. Monograph — Am Chem Soc Mon
American Chemical Society. National Meeting. Abstracts of Papers — ACS Natl Meet Abstr Pap
American Chemical Society. Petroleum Chemistry Division. Preprints — Amer Chem Soc Petrol Chem Div Preprints
American Chemical Society. Report. Annual Meeting. Corporation Associates — Am Chem Soc Rep Annu Meet Corp Assoc
American Chemical Society. Rubber Division. Symposia — Am Chem Soc Rubber Div Symp
American Chemical Society Symposium — Am Chem Soc Symp
American Chemical Society Symposium on Chemical Pretreatment of Nuclear Waste for Disposal — Am Chem Soc Symp Chem Pretreat Nucl Waste Disposal
American Chemical Society Symposium on Enzyme Mimetic and Related Polymers — Amer Chem Soc Symp Enzyme Mimetic Relat Polym
American Chemical Society Symposium on Polymers from Biotechnology — Amer Chem Soc Symp Polym Biotechnol
American Chemical Society Symposium on Progress in Biomedical Polymers — Amer Chem Soc Symp Prog Biomed Polym
American Chemical Society. Symposium Series — Am Chem Soc Symp Ser
American Chemist — Am Chem
American Child — Am Child

American Childhood — Am Childh
American Chiropractic Association. Journal of Chiropractic — ACA J Chiropr
American Chiropractor — Am Chiro
American Choral Review — ACR
American Choral Review — Am Choral R
American Choral Review — AMCR
American Choral Review — Amer Choral R
American Christmas Tree Growers' Journal — Am Christmas Tree Grow J
American Christmas Tree Journal — Am Christmas Tree J
American Chrysanthemum Annual — Amer Chrysanthemum Annual
American Church Monthly — Am Church Mo
American Church Quarterly — ACQ
American Church Quarterly [*New York*] — AmChQ
American Church Review — Am Church R
American Church Review — American Church R
American Cinematographer — Am Cin
American Cinematographer — Am Cinem
American Cinematographer — Am Cinematgr
American Cinematographer — Am Cinematog
American Cinematographer — Amer Cinematogr
American City — AC
American City — Am City
American City — AMCIA
American City — Amer City
American City and County — Am City Cty
American City and County — GACY
American City (City Edition) — Am City (C ed)
American City (Town and Country Edition) — Am City (T & C ed)
American Civil Law Journal — Am Civ LJ
American Classic Screen — Amer Classic Screen
American Classical Review — ACR
American Classical Review — American Cl R
American Climatological and Clinical Association. Transactions — Am Climatol Assn Trans
American Clinical and Climatological Association. Transactions — Am Clin Climatol Assoc Trans
American Clinical Products Review — ACPR
American Collector — Am Coll
American College of Cardiology. Extended Learning — ACCEL
American College of Physicians. Bulletin — Am Coll Physicians Bull
American College of Physicians. Observer — Am Coll Physicians Obs
American College of Toxicology. Journal — Am Col Toxicol J
American College Testing. Research Reports — ACT Res Rep
American Committee for Irish Studies. Newsletter — ACIS Newsletter
American Comparative Literature Association. Newsletter — ACLAN
American Composers Alliance. Bulletin — ACA
American Concrete Institute. Journal — Am Concr Inst J
American Concrete Institute. Journal — Am Concrete Inst J
American Concrete Institute. Monograph — Am Concr Inst Monogr
American Concrete Institute. Monograph — Amer Concr Inst Monogr
American Concrete Institute. Publication SP — Am Concr Inst Publ SP
American Concrete Institute. Special Publication — Am Concr Inst SP
American Concrete Institute. Standards — Amer Concr Inst Stand
American Consular Bulletin — Am Cons B
American Consular Bulletin — Am Consul Bul
American Contractor — Am Contract
American Cooperation — Am Coop
American Co-Operative Journal — Am Co-Op J
American Corporation — Amer Corp
American Corrective Therapy Journal — Am Correct Ther J
American Corrective Therapy Journal — Amer Correct Ther J
American Cosmetics and Perfumery — Am Cosmet Perfum
American Cosmetics and Perfumery — Am Perfume
American Council for Judaism. Issues — Am Counc Jud Issues
American Council of Learned Societies. Newsletter — ACLSN
American Council on Consumer Interest. Proceedings — ACI
American Council on Consumer Interest. Proceedings — Am Counc Cons Int Proc
American Craft — Am Craft
American Craft — GACR
American Creamery and Poultry Produce Review — Am Creamery
American Criminal Law Quarterly — Am Crim L Q
American Criminal Law Review — Am Crim L Rev
American Criminal Law Review — Am Crim Law
American Criminal Law Review — Am Crim LR
American Criminal Law Review — IACL
American Crystallographic Association. Polycrystal Book Service. Transactions [*A publication*] — Am Cryst Assoc Trans
American Cyanamid Company. Mineral Dressing Notes — Am Cyanamid Co Miner Dressing Notes
American Cyanamid Company. Technical Bulletin — Am Cyanamid Co Tech Bull
American Daffodil Yearbook — Am Daffodil Yearb
American Dairy Products Review — Am Dairy Prod R
American Dairy Review — ADARA
American Dairy Review — Am Dairy R
American Dairy Review — Am Dairy Rev
American Dairy Review — Amer Dairy Rev
American Demographics — ADE
American Demographics — Am Demogr
American Demographics — Am Demographics
American Demographics — AMD
American Demographics — Amer Demogr
American Dental Surgeon — Am Dent Surg
American Dialect Dictionary — ADD
American Dialog — AmD
American Dietetic Association. Journal — Am Dietet Assn J
American Documentation — AD
American Documentation — Am Doc
American Documentation — Amer Doc
American Documentation Institute Microfilm [*Library of Congress, Washington, DC*] — ADIM
American Drop Forger — Am Drop Forger
American Druggist — Am Drug
American Druggist — Am Druggist
American Druggist — Amer Drug
American Druggist — Amer Druggist
American Druggist and Pharmaceutical Record — Am Drug Pharm Rec
American Druggist Merchandising — Am Druggist Merch
American Druggists Circular and Chemical Gazette — Am Drug Circ Chem Gaz
American Drycleaner — Am Drycleaner
American Dyestuff Reporter — ADREA
American Dyestuff Reporter — Am Dye Rep
American Dyestuff Reporter — Am Dyest Rep
American Dyestuff Reporter — Am Dyestuf
American Dyestuff Reporter — Am Dyestuff Reptr
American Dyestuff Reporter — Amer Dyestuff Rep
American Dyestuff Reporter — Amer Dyestuff Reporter
American Ecclesiastical Review — A Ec R
American Ecclesiastical Review — AER
American Ecclesiastical Review — Am Eccles Rev
American Ecclesiastical Review — Am ER
American Eclectic — Am Ecl
American Economic Association. Bulletin — Am Econ Assn Bul
American Economic Association. Publications — Am Econ Assn Publ
American Economic Association. Publications — Am Econ Assoc
American Economic Association. Publications — Am Econ Assoc Publ
American Economic Association Publications — Amer Econ Assoc Publ
American Economic Development Council. Conference Notes — Am Econ Dev Counc Conf Notes
American Economic Review — AER
American Economic Review — AERNA
American Economic Review — Am Ec R
American Economic Review — Am Ec Rev
American Economic Review — Am Econ R
American Economic Review — Am Econ Rev
American Economic Review — Am ER
American Economic Review — Amer Econ R
American Economic Review — Amer Econ Rev
American Economic Review. American Economic Association — AEA/AER
American Economic Review. Papers and Proceedings — Am Econ R Pa & Proc
American Economic Review. Supplement — AERS
American Economist — AEC
American Economist — Am Econ
American Economist — Am Economist
American Economist — AME
American Economist — Amer Economist
American Education — A Ed
American Education — Am Educ
American Education — AMED
American Educational Research Journal — AERJ
American Educational Research Journal — Am Ed Res J
American Educational Research Journal — Am Educ Res
American Egg and Poultry Review — Am Egg & Poultry R
American Electrochemical Society. Transactions — Am Electrochem Soc Trans
American Electroplaters and Surface Finishers Society. Annual Technical Conference. Proceedings — Am Electroplat Surf Finish Soc Annu Tech Conf Proc
American Electroplaters' Society. Annual Technical Conference — Am Electroplat Soc Ann Tech Conf
American Electroplaters' Society. Coatings for Solar Collectors Symposium. Proceedings — Am Electroplat Soc Coat Sol Collect Symp Proc
American Electroplaters' Society. Continuous Strip Plating Symposium — Am Electroplat Soc Contin Strip Plat Symp
American Electroplaters' Society. Decorative Plating Symposium — Am Electroplat Soc Decor Plat Symp
American Electroplaters' Society. Electroless Plating Symposium — Am Electroplat Soc Electroless Plat Symp
American Electroplaters' Society. International Pulse Plating Symposium. Papers — Am Electroplat Soc Int Pulse Plat Symp Pap
American Electroplaters' Society. Plating in the Electronics Industry — Am Electroplat Soc Plat Electron Ind
American Electroplaters' Society. Research Report — Am Electroplat Soc Res Rep
American Enameler — Am Enameler
American Engineer — Am Eng
American Engineer — Amer Eng
American Ensemble — AE
American Ensemble — Am Ens
American Enterprise — IAEN
American Enterprise Institute for Public Policy Research. AEI Forums — AEI Forums
American Enterprise Institute for Public Policy Research. National Energy Study — Am Enterp Inst Public Policy Res Natl Energy Study
American Entomological Society. Transactions — Am Entomol Soc Trans
American Entomologist — Amer Entomol
American Environmental Laboratory — Am Environ Lab
American Ephemeris and Nautical Almanac — AENA
American Ephemeris and Nautical Almanac — Am Ephem
American Ethnological Society. Bulletin of the Proceedings — AES
American Ethnological Society. Monographs — AESM

American Ethnological Society Monographs — Am Ethnol Soc Monogr
American Ethnological Society. Newsletter — AESNL
American Ethnological Society. Proceedings — AES Pr
American Ethnological Society. Publications — AESP
American Ethnologist — Am Ethnol
American Ethnologist — Amer Ethnol
American Ethnologist — Amer Ethnologist
American Ethnologist — PAET
American Ethnologist. American Ethnological Society — AES/AE
American Ethnologist (Washington, D.C.) — AEW
American Examiner — Am Ex
American Export Marketer — Am Exp Mark
American Exporter — Am Exporter
American Fabrics — AF
American Fabrics — Am Fabrics
American Fabrics and Fashions — Am Fabric Fashion
American Family — Am Fam
American Family Physician — AFPYA
American Family Physician — AFPYB
American Family Physician — Am Fam Phys
American Family Physician — Am Fam Physician
American Family Physician — IAFP
American Family Physician - GP — Am Fam Physician GP
American Farm Bureau Federation. Weekly News Letter — Am Farm Bur Feder W News Letter
American Farm Bureau Federation. Weekly News Letter — Am Farm Bur N L
American Farriers' Journal — Am Farriers J
American Federal Tax Reports. Second Series. Prentice-Hall — AFTR 2d P-H
American Federation of Information Processing Societies. Conference Proceedings. Fall and Spring Joint Computer Conferences — AFIPS Conf Proc Fall Spring Jt Comput Conf
American Federation of Information Processing Societies. Conference Proceedings. Fall Joint Computer Conference — AFIPS Conf Proc Fall Jt Comput Conf
American Federation of Information Processing Societies. Conference Proceedings. Spring Joint Computer Conference — AFIPS Conf Proc Spring Jt Comput Conf
American Federation of Information Processing Societies. National Computer Conference and Exposition. Conference Proceedings — AFIPS Natl Comp Conf Expo Conf Proc
American Federation of Teachers. Convention Proceedings — Am Fed Teach Conv Proc
American Federationist — Am Fed
American Federationist — Am Federationist
American Federationist — Amer Feder
American Feed Manufacturers Association. Nutrition Council. Proceedings — Am Feed Manuf Assoc Nutr Counc Proc
American Feed Manufacturers Association. Proceedings. Meeting of the Nutrition Council — Am Feed Manuf Assoc Proc Meet Nutr Counc
American Fencing — Am Fencing
American Fern Journal — Am Fern J
American Fern Journal — Amer Fern J
American Fertilizer and Allied Chemicals — Am Fert
American Fertilizer and Allied Chemicals — Am Fert Allied Chem
American Film — Am Film
American Film — Amer F
American Film — American F
American Film — GAFI
American Fisheries Society. Fish Culture Section. Publication — Am Fish Soc Fish Cult Sect Publ
American Fisheries Society. Monograph — Am Fish Soc Monogr
American Fisheries Society. Special Publication — Am Fish Soc Spec Publ
American Fisheries Society. Transactions — Am Fish Soc Trans
American Fisheries Society. Transactions — Am Fisheries Soc Trans
American Fitness — AM Fit
American Flint — Am Flint
American Florist — Am Flor
American Folklore Newsletter — Am Folk Newsl
American Folklore Society. Newsletter — Am Folk Soc Newsl
American Foreign Service Journal — AFSJ
American Foreign Service Journal — Am For Serv Jour
American Forests — AF
American Forests — Am For
American Forests — Am Forests
American Forests — Amer Forests
American Forests — AMFO
American Forests — AMFOA
American Forests — PAMF
American Forests and Forest Life — Amer Forests Forest Life
American Foundation for the Blind. Research Bulletin — AFB Res Bull
American Foundation for the Blind. Research Bulletin — AFBRB
American Foundation for the Blind. Research Bulletin — Am Found Blind Res Bull
American Foundation for the Blind. Research Series — Am Found Blind Res Ser
American Foundation for the Study of Man. Publications — Am Found Study Man Publ
American Foundryman — Am Foundryman
American Foundrymen's Society. Research Reports — Am Foundrymens Soc Res Rep
American Fox and Fur Farmer — Am Fox and Fur Farmer
American Fruit Grower — Am Fruit Grow
American Fruit Grower — Am Fruit Grower
American Fruit Grower — AMFGAR
American Fruit Grower Magazine — Am Fruit Grow Mag
American Fruits — Amer Fruits
American Game Bulletin. American Game Protective Association — Am Game Bull Am Game Protect Ass
American Gardener's Magazine and Register of Useful Discoveries and Improvements in Horticulture and Rural Affairs — Amer Gard Mag
American Gas Association. Abstracts — Am Gas Assoc Abstr
American Gas Association. Annual Report — Am Gas Assoc Annu Rep
American Gas Association. Bulletin of Abstracts — Am Gas Assoc Bull Abstr
American Gas Association. Laboratories. Research Bulletins, Research Reports — AGA Lab Res Bull Res Rep
American Gas Association. Monthly — AGA
American Gas Association. Monthly — AGA Mon
American Gas Association. Monthly — AGAMA
American Gas Association. Monthly — Am Gas As M
American Gas Association. Monthly — Am Gas Ass Mon
American Gas Association. Monthly — Am Gas Assoc Mon
American Gas Association. Monthly — Amer Gas Ass Mon
American Gas Association. Operating Section. Proceedings — AGA Oper Sec Proc
American Gas Association. Operating Section. Proceedings — Am Gas Assoc Oper Sect Proc
American Gas Association. Operating Section. Proceedings — Amer Gas Ass Oper Sect Proc
American Gas Association. Preprints — Am Gas Assoc Prepr
American Gas Association. Proceedings — Am Gas Assoc Proc
American Gas Engineering Journal — Am Gas Eng J
American Gas Institute. Abstracts — Am Gas Inst Abstr
American Gas Institute. Bulletin of Abstracts — Am Gas Inst Bull Abstr
American Gas Journal — Am Gas J
American Gas Journal — Am Gas Jrl
American Gas Journal — Amer Gas J
American Gas Light Journal — Am Gas Light J
American Gear Manufacturers Association. Standards — Amer Gear Mfr Ass Stand
American Gem Market System [*Database*] — AGMS
American Genealogist — Am Geneal
American Geographical and Statistical Society. Journal — Am Geog Stat Soc J
American Geographical Society. Bulletin — Am Geog Soc Bul
American Geographical Society. Bulletin. Journal — Am Geog Soc B J
American Geographical Society. Journal — Am Geog Soc Jour
American Geographical Society. Special Publication — Am Geog Soc Special Pub
American Geological Association. Bulletin — Am G As B
American Geological Institute. Report — Am Geol Inst Rept
American Geological Institute. Reprint Series — Am Geol Inst Repr Ser
American Geologist — Am G
American Geologist — Am Geol
American Geophysical Union. Antarctic Research Series — Am Geophys Union Antarct Res Ser
American Geophysical Union. Transactions — Am Geophys Union Trans
American Gladiolus Society Official Review — Amer Gladiolus Soc Off Rev
American Glass Review — AGLRA
American Glass Review — Am Glass Rev
American Group Psychotherapy Association. Monograph Series — Am Group Psychother Assoc Monogr Ser
American Group Psychotherapy Association. Monograph Series — MSAAEQ
American Guild of Organists. Quarterly — AGO
American Gynecological Society. Transactions — Am Gynecol Soc Trans
American Handel Society Newsletter — AHSN
American Harp Journal — AHJ
American Harp Journal — Am Harp J
American Health — Am Health
American Health — AMHE
American Health — GAMH
American Health Care Association. Journal — Am Health Care Assoc J
American Heart Association. Monograph — AHMOAH
American Heart Association. Monograph — Am Heart Assoc Monogr
American Heart Journal — AHJOA
American Heart Journal — Am Heart J
American Hebrew — Am Heb
American Herb Grower — Amer Herb Grower
American Heritage — AH
American Heritage — Am Her
American Heritage — Am Herit
American Heritage — Am Heritage
American Heritage — AmH
American Heritage — GAHE
American Heritage Dictionary — AHD
American Highways — Am Highw
American Highways — Amer Highways
[*The*] **American Hispanist** — TAH
American Hispanist (Indiana) — AHI
American Historical Association. Annual Report — Am Hist Assn Ann Rep
American Historical Association. Annual Report — Am Hist Assn Ann Rpt
American Historical Association. Newsletter — AHA Newsletter
American Historical Association. Reports — Am Hist Assn Rept
American Historical Magazine [*New York*] — Am Hist M
American Historical Record — Am Hist Rec
American Historical Register — Am Hist Reg
American Historical Review — A H Rev
American Historical Review — AH
American Historical Review — AHR
American Historical Review — Am His R
American Historical Review — Am Hist R
American Historical Review — Am Hist Rev
American Historical Review — Amer Hist Rev

American Historical Review — AmHR
American Historical Review — GHRV
American History Illustrated — Am Hist Ill
American History Illustrated — Am Hist Illus
American History Illustrated — AmHy
American History Illustrated — GAHI
American Home — Am Home
American Homes and Gardens — Am Homes
American Horologist and Jeweler — Am Horo Jewel
American Horologist and Jeweler — Am Horol Jeweler
American Horticultural Magazine — Am Hort Mag
American Horticultural Magazine — Amer Hort Mag
American Horticultural Society Gardeners Forum — Amer Hort Soc Gard Forum
American Horticulturist — Am Hort
American Horticulturist — Am Hortic
American Hospital Association. Publications — AHA Publ
American Hosta Society. Newsletter — Am Hosta Soc Newsl
American Humanities Index — AHI
American Humanities Index — Am Humanit Index
American Humor — A Humor
American Humor — Amer Hum
American Hunter — GAHU
American Imago — AI
American Imago — Am Im
American Imago — Am Imago
American Imago — Amer Imago
American Imago — AMIAA
American Imago — IAIM
American Import/Export Bulletin — Am Import Export Bul
American Import/Export Bulletin — Am Import/Export Bull
American Import Export Bulletin — Amer Imp Exp Bul
American Import/Export Management — AEX
American Import/Export Management — Am Import/Export Manage
American Import/Export Management — Am Import/Export Mgt
American Import Export Management — Amer Imp Exp Man
American in Britain — Am Brit
American Indian and Alaska Native Mental Health Research — Am Indian Alsk Native Ment Health Res
American Indian and Alaska Native Mental Health Research Monograph Series — Am Indian Alsk Native Ment Health Res Monogr Ser
American Indian Art Magazine — Am Indian Art Mag
American Indian Basketry Magazine — Am Ind Bas Mag
American Indian Basketry Magazine — AMIB
American Indian Crafts and Culture — AICC
American Indian Index — Am Indian Index
American Indian Journal — Am Indian J
American Indian Journal — Amer Ind J
American Indian Law Review — Am Ind LR
American Indian Law Review — Am Indian L Rev
American Indian Quarterly — AIQ
American Indian Quarterly — GAIQ
American Industrial Hygiene Association. Journal — AIHAA
American Industrial Hygiene Association. Journal — AIHAAP
American Industrial Hygiene Association. Journal — Am Ind Hyg
American Industrial Hygiene Association. Journal — Am Ind Hyg Ass J
American Industrial Hygiene Association. Journal — Am Ind Hyg Assn J
American Industrial Hygiene Association. Journal — Am Ind Hyg Assoc J
American Industrial Hygiene Association. Journal — Am Ind Hygiene Assn J
American Industrial Hygiene Association. Journal — Am Indust Hyg A J
American Industrial Hygiene Association Journal — Amer Ind Hyg Assoc J
American Industrial Hygiene Association. Journal — Amer Industr Hyg Assoc J
American Industrial Hygiene Association. Quarterly — Am Ind Hyg Assoc Q
American Industrial Hygiene Association. Quarterly — Am Indust Hyg A Quart
American Industries — Am Ind
American Inkmaker — AIM
American Inkmaker — Am Ink
American Inkmaker — Am Inkmaker
American Inkmaker — Amer Inkmaker
American Inkmaker — AMIKA
American Institute for Conservation. Journal — Am Inst Conserv J
American Institute for Yemen Studies Newsletter — AIYS News
American Institute of Aeronautics and Astronautics. Journal — AIAA Journal
American Institute of Aeronautics and Astronautics. Monographs — Am Inst Aeronaut Astronaut Monogr
American Institute of Aeronautics and Astronautics. Paper — Am Inst Aeronaut Astronaut Pap
American Institute of Architects. International Directory — Am Inst Arch Int Dir
American Institute of Architects. Journal — Am Inst Arch J
American Institute of Architects. Journal — Am Inst Archit J
American Institute of Architects. Quarterly Bulletin — Am Inst Archit Q Bull
American Institute of Banking. Bulletin — Am Inst Bank Bul
American Institute of Biological Sciences — Am Inst Biol Sci
American Institute of Biological Sciences. Bulletin — Am Inst Biol Sci Bull
American Institute of Biological Sciences. Publications — Am Inst Biol Sci Publ
American Institute of Biological Sciences. Symposia — Am Inst Biol Sci Symp
American Institute of Chemical Engineers. Journal — AIChE Journal
American Institute of Chemical Engineers. Monograph Series — AIChE Monograph Series
American Institute of Chemical Engineers. National Heat Transfer Conference. Preprints. AIChE Paper — Am Inst Chem Eng Natl Heat Transfer Conf Prepr AIChE Pap
American Institute of Chemical Engineers. National Meeting. Program Abstracts [*A publication*] — A I Ch E Natl Meet Program Abstr
American Institute of Chemical Engineers. Paper — Am Inst Chem Eng Pap
American Institute of Chemical Engineers. Symposium Series — AIChE Symp Series
American Institute of Chemical Engineers. Symposium Series — Am Inst Chem Eng Symp Ser
American Institute of Criminal Law and Criminology. Journal — Am Instit Crim Law and Criminol Jour
American Institute of Dental Medicine. Annual Meeting — Am Inst Dent Med Annu Meet
American Institute of Electrical Engineers. Proceedings — AIEE Proc
American Institute of Industrial Engineers. Detroit Chapter. Proceedings of the Annual Conference — AIDPA
American Institute of Industrial Engineers. Detroit Chapter. Proceedings of the Annual Conference — Am Inst Ind Eng Detroit Chapter Proc Annu Conf
American Institute of Industrial Engineers. Industrial Engineering — AIIE Ind Engng
American Institute of Industrial Engineers. Transactions — AIIE Transactions
American Institute of Instruction — Am Inst of Instruc
American Institute of Metals. Journal — Am Inst Met J
American Institute of Metals. Transactions — Am Inst Met Trans
American Institute of Mining and Metallurgical Engineers. Contributions — Am Inst Min Metall Eng Contrib
American Institute of Mining and Metallurgical Engineers. Institute of Metals Division. Special Report Series — Am Inst Min Metall Eng Inst Met Div Spec Rep Ser
American Institute of Mining and Metallurgical Engineers. Technical Publications — Am Inst Min Metall Eng Tech Publ
American Institute of Mining Engineers. Transactions. Bulletin — Am I M Eng Tr B
American Institute of Mining, Metallurgical, and Petroleum Engineers. Annual Meeting. Proceedings of Sessions — Am Inst Min Metall Pet Eng Annu Meet Proc Sess
American Institute of Mining, Metallurgical, and Petroleum Engineers. Annual Meeting. Proceedings of Sessions. Light Metals — Am Inst Min Metall Pet Eng Annu Meet Proc Sess Light Met
American Institute of Mining, Metallurgical, and Petroleum Engineers. Institute of Metals Division. Special Report Series — Am Inst Min Metall Petr Eng Inst Met Div Spec Rep Ser
American Institute of Mining, Metallurgical, and Petroleum Engineers. Minnesota Section. Annual Meeting — Am Inst Min Metall Pet Eng Minn Sect Annu Meet
American Institute of Mining, Metallurgical, and Petroleum Engineers. Minnesota Section. Proceedings. Annual Meeting — Am Inst Min Metall Pet Eng Minn Sect Proc Annu Meet
American Institute of Mining, Metallurgical, and Petroleum Engineers. Proceedings. Annual Minerals Symposium — AIME Proc Annu Miner Symp
American Institute of Mining, Metallurgical, and Petroleum Engineers. Society of Mining Engineers of AIME. Transactions — Am Inst Min Metall Pet Eng Soc Min Eng AIME Trans
American Institute of Mining, Metallurgical, and Petroleum Engineers. Transactions — AIME Trans
American Institute of Mining, Metallurgical, and Petroleum Engineers. Transactions — Am Inst Min Metall Pet Eng Trans
American Institute of Oral Biology. Annual Meeting — Am Inst Oral Biol Annu Meet
American Institute of Physics. Conference Proceedings — AIP Conference Proceedings
American Institute of Physics. Conference Proceedings — Am Inst Phys Conf Proc
American Institute of Physics. Conference Proceedings — APCPCS
American Institute of Physics. Information Program Newsletter — AIP Inf Progm Newsl
American Institute of Physics. Soviet Journal of Nuclear Physics — Soviet J Nuclear Phys
American Institute of Physics Translation Series — Amer Inst Phys Transl Ser
American Institute of Planners. Journal — Am Inst Plan
American Institute of Planners. Journal — Am Inst Plan J
American Institute of Planners. Journal — Am Inst Plann J
American Institute of Planners. Journal — Am Inst Planners J
American Institute of Planners. Journal — American Inst Planners Jnl
American Institute of Planners. Papers — Am Inst Plann Pap
American Institute of Plant Engineers. Journal — Am Inst Plant Eng J
American Institute of Professional Geologists. California Section. Annual Meeting. Proceedings — Am Inst Prof Geol Calif Sect Annu Meet Proc
American Institute of Refrigeration. Proceedings — Am Inst Refrig Proc
American Institute of the History of Pharmacy. Publication — Am Inst Hist Pharm Publ
American Intelligence Journal — Am Int J
American Intra-Ocular Implant Society. Journal — Am Intra Ocul Implant Soc J
American Irish Historical Society. Journal — Am Irish His S J
American Iron and Steel Institute. Annual Statistical Report — AISI Rpt
American Iron and Steel Institute. Contributions to the Metallurgy of Steel — Amer Iron Steel Inst Contrib Met Steel
American Iron and Steel Institute. Regional Technical Meetings. Addresses — Amer Iron Steel Inst Reg Tech Meetings Addresses
American Iron and Steel Institute. Steel Products Manual — AISI Steel Prod Man
American Iron and Steel Institute. Steel Research for Construction. Bulletin — Amer Iron Steel Steel Res Constr Bull
American Jewish Archives — AJA
American Jewish Archives — Am Jew Arch
American Jewish Archives — Am Jew Archs
American Jewish Archives — Am Jewish A
American Jewish Archives — AmJA
American Jewish Congress. News — Am Jew Congr News
American Jewish Historical Quarterly — AJHQ

American Jewish Historical Quarterly — Am Jew Hist Q
American Jewish Historical Quarterly — Am Jewish H
American Jewish Historical Quarterly — Amer Jew Hist Quart
American Jewish Historical Quarterly — AmJH
American Jewish Historical Society. Publications — AJHS
American Jewish Historical Society. Publications — Am Jew His
American Jewish Historical Society. Publications — Am Jew Hist Soc Publ
American Jewish History — AJH
American Jewish History — Am Jew H
American Jewish History — Am Jew Hist
American Jewish History — PAJH
American Jewish Yearbook — AJY
American Jewish Yearbook — AJYB
American Jewish Yearbook — Am Jew Yb
American Jewish Yearbook — Am Jew Yr Bk
American Jewish Yearbook — Amer Jew Yearb
American Journal of Acupuncture — AJAPB9
American Journal of Acupuncture — Am J Acupunct
American Journal of Agricultural Economics — AJA
American Journal of Agricultural Economics — AJAE
American Journal of Agricultural Economics — AJAEB
American Journal of Agricultural Economics — Am J Ag Econ
American Journal of Agricultural Economics — Am J Agr Ec
American Journal of Agricultural Economics — Am J Agr Econ
American Journal of Agricultural Economics — Am J Agric Econ
American Journal of Agricultural Economics — Amer J Agr Econ
American Journal of Agricultural Economics — Amer J Agric Econ
American Journal of Agriculture and Science — Am J Agr
American Journal of Alcohol and Drug Abuse — AJDA
American Journal of Alternative Agriculture — Am J Alternative Agric
American Journal of Anatomy — AJANA
American Journal of Anatomy — AJANA2
American Journal of Anatomy — Am J Anat
American Journal of Ancient History — Am J Anc Hist
American Journal of Arabic Studies — Am J Arab St
American Journal of Archaeology — A J Arch
American Journal of Archaeology — AJ Archaeol
American Journal of Archaeology — AJA
American Journal of Archaeology — AJAr
American Journal of Archaeology — Am J
American Journal of Archaeology — Am J Archae
American Journal of Archaeology — Am J Archaeol
American Journal of Archaeology — Am J of Arch
American Journal of Archaeology — Am Jnl Archae
American Journal of Archaeology — Am Journ Arch
American Journal of Archaeology — Am Journ Archaeol
American Journal of Archaeology — Am Journal Arch
American Journal of Archaeology — Amer J Archaeol
American Journal of Archaeology — Amer Journ Arch
American Journal of Archaeology — PAJA
American Journal of Art Therapy — AJATA
American Journal of Art Therapy — Am J Art Th
American Journal of Art Therapy — Am J Art Ther
American Journal of Art Therapy — Amer J Art Ther
American Journal of Botany — AJBOA
American Journal of Botany — AJBOAA
American Journal of Botany — Am J Bot
American Journal of Botany — Amer J Bot
American Journal of Botany — IABO
American Journal of Cancer — Am J Canc
American Journal of Cancer — Am J Cancer
American Journal of Cardiac Imaging — Am J Card Imaging
American Journal of Cardiology — AJCDA
American Journal of Cardiology — AJCDAG
American Journal of Cardiology — Am J Card
American Journal of Cardiology — Am J Cardiol
American Journal of Cardiology — Amer J Cardiol
American Journal of Cardiovascular Pathology — Am J Cardiovasc Pathol
American Journal of Chinese Medicine — AJCMBA
American Journal of Chinese Medicine — Am J Chin Med
American Journal of Chinese Medicine — Am J Chinese Med
American Journal of Chinese Medicine — Amer J Chinese Medicine
American Journal of Clinical Assessment — Am J Clin Assess
American Journal of Clinical Biofeedback — AJCBDD
American Journal of Clinical Biofeedback — Am J Clin Biofeedback
American Journal of Clinical Hypnosis — AJHNA3
American Journal of Clinical Hypnosis — Am J Clin Hypn
American Journal of Clinical Hypnosis — Am J Clin Hypnosis
American Journal of Clinical Hypnosis — Amer J Clin Hypnosis
American Journal of Clinical Medicine — Am J Clin Med
American Journal of Clinical Nutrition — AJCNA
American Journal of Clinical Nutrition — AJCNAC
American Journal of Clinical Nutrition — Am J Clin N
American Journal of Clinical Nutrition — Am J Clin Nutr
American Journal of Clinical Nutrition — Am J Clin Nutrition
American Journal of Clinical Nutrition — Amer J Clin Nutr
American Journal of Clinical Oncology — AJCOD
American Journal of Clinical Oncology — AJCODI
American Journal of Clinical Oncology — Am J Clin Oncol
American Journal of Clinical Pathology — AJCPA
American Journal of Clinical Pathology — AJCPAI
American Journal of Clinical Pathology — Am J Clin P
American Journal of Clinical Pathology — Am J Clin Path
American Journal of Clinical Pathology — Am J Clin Pathol
American Journal of Clinical Pathology — Amer J Clin Pathol
American Journal of Community Psychology — Am J Community Psychol
American Journal of Community Psychology — IJCP
American Journal of Comparative Law — AJCL
American Journal of Comparative Law — Am J Comp L
American Journal of Comparative Law — Am J Comp Law
American Journal of Comparative Law — Am J Compar Law
American Journal of Comparative Law — Am J Comparative Law
American Journal of Comparative Law — Amer J Comp L
American Journal of Comparative Law — Amer J Comp Law
American Journal of Computational Linguistics — Am J Comput Ling
American Journal of Conchology — Am J Conch
American Journal of Contact Dermatitis — Am J Contact Dermat
American Journal of Correction — Am J Corr
American Journal of Correction — Am J Correction
American Journal of Criminal Law — Am J Crim L
American Journal of Critical Care — Am J Crit Care
American Journal of Dental Science — Am J Dent Sci
American Journal of Dermatology and Genito-Urinary Diseases — Am J Dermat Gen Urin Dis
American Journal of Dermatology and Genito-Urinary Diseases — Amer J Dermatol Genito Urin Dis
American Journal of Dermatopathology — Am J Dermatopathol
American Journal of Digestive Diseases [*Later, Digestive Diseases and Sciences*] [*A publication*] — AJDDA
American Journal of Digestive Diseases [*Later, Digestive Diseases and Sciences*] [*A publication*] — AJDDAL
American Journal of Digestive Diseases [*Later, Digestive Diseases and Sciences*] [*A publication*] — Am J Dig Di
American Journal of Digestive Diseases [*Later, Digestive Diseases and Sciences*] [*A publication*] — Am J Dig Dis
American Journal of Digestive Diseases — Am J Digest Dis
American Journal of Digestive Diseases [*Later, Digestive Diseases and Sciences*] [*A publication*] — Amer J Digest Dis
American Journal of Digestive Diseases and Nutrition — Am J Dig Dis Nutr
American Journal of Digestive Diseases and Nutrition — Amer J Digestive Dis Nutr
American Journal of Diseases of Children — AJDC
American Journal of Diseases of Children — AJDCA
American Journal of Diseases of Children — AJDCAI
American Journal of Diseases of Children — Am J Dis Ch
American Journal of Diseases of Children — Am J Dis Child
American Journal of Diseases of Children — Amer J Dis Child
American Journal of Drug and Alcohol Abuse — AJDABD
American Journal of Drug and Alcohol Abuse — Am J Drug Alcohol Abuse
American Journal of Economics and Sociology — AES
American Journal of Economics and Sociology [*New York*] — AJE
American Journal of Economics and Sociology [*New York*] — AJES
American Journal of Economics and Sociology [*New York*] — AJESA
American Journal of Economics and Sociology [*New York*] — Am J Econ
American Journal of Economics and Sociology [*New York*] — Am J Econ S
American Journal of Economics and Sociology — Am J Econ Soc
American Journal of Economics and Sociology [*New York*] — Am J Econ Sociol
American Journal of Economics and Sociology [*New York*] — Am Jnl Econ & Soc
American Journal of Economics and Sociology [*New York*] — Am Jour Econ Sociol
American Journal of Economics and Sociology [*New York*] — Amer J Econ & Soc
American Journal of Economics and Sociology [*New York*] — Amer J Econ Sociol
American Journal of Economics and Sociology — American Jrnl of Economics and Sociology
American Journal of Economics and Sociology — ASO
American Journal of Economics and Sociology (New York) — Am J Econ Sociol (New York)
American Journal of Education — AJE
American Journal of Education — Am J Educ
American Journal of EEG Technology — AJETA6
American Journal of EEG Technology — Am J EEG Technol
American Journal of Emergency Medicine — Am J Emerg Med
American Journal of Enology — Am J Enol
American Journal of Enology and Viticulture — AJEV
American Journal of Enology and Viticulture — AJEVAC
American Journal of Enology and Viticulture — Am J Enol V
American Journal of Enology and Viticulture — Am J Enol Viti
American Journal of Enology and Viticulture — Am J Enol Vitic
American Journal of Epidemiology — AJEPA
American Journal of Epidemiology — AJEPAS
American Journal of Epidemiology — Am J Epidem
American Journal of Epidemiology — Am J Epidemiol
American Journal of Family Therapy — PAJF
American Journal of Forensic Medicine and Pathology — Am J Forensic Med Pathol
American Journal of Gastroenterology — AJGAA
American Journal of Gastroenterology — AJGAAR
American Journal of Gastroenterology — Am J Gastro
American Journal of Gastroenterology — Am J Gastroenterol
American Journal of Geriatric Psychiatry — Am J Geriatr Psychiatry
American Journal of Health Behavior, Education, & Promotion — AM J Health Beh
American Journal of Health Planning — Am J Health Plann
American Journal of Health Promotion — AM J Health Promotion
American Journal of Health-System Pharmacy — Am J Health Syst Pharm
American Journal of Hematology — AJHED
American Journal of Hematology — AJHEDD

American Journal of Hematology — Am J Hematol
American Journal of Horticulture and Florist's Companion — Amer J Hort Florists Companion
American Journal of Hospice Care — Am J Hosp Care
American Journal of Hospital Pharmacy — AJHPA
American Journal of Hospital Pharmacy — AJHPA9
American Journal of Hospital Pharmacy — Am J Hosp P
American Journal of Hospital Pharmacy — Am J Hosp Pharm
American Journal of Hospital Pharmacy — Amer J Hosp Pharm
American Journal of Human Biology — Am J Hum Biol
American Journal of Human Genetics — AJHGA
American Journal of Human Genetics — AJHGAG
American Journal of Human Genetics — Am J Hu Gen
American Journal of Human Genetics — Am J Hum Genet
American Journal of Human Genetics — Am J Hum Gntcs
American Journal of Human Genetics — Am J Human Genet
American Journal of Human Genetics — Amer J Hum Genet
American Journal of Human Genetics — Amer J Hum Genetics
American Journal of Hygiene — AJHYA2
American Journal of Hygiene — Am J Hyg
American Journal of Hygiene — Amer J Hyg
American Journal of Hygiene. Monographic Series — Am J Hyg Monogr Ser
American Journal of Hypertension — Am J Hypertens
American Journal of Individual Psychology — Am J Ind Psych
American Journal of Industrial Medicine — AJIMD8
American Journal of Industrial Medicine — Am J Ind Med
American Journal of Infection Control — AJICDC
American Journal of Infection Control — Am J Inf Con
American Journal of Infection Control — Am J Infect Control
American Journal of Insanity — Am J Insan
American Journal of International Law — A J I Law
American Journal of International Law — AJIL
American Journal of International Law — AJINB
American Journal of International Law — Am J Int L
American Journal of International Law — Am J Int Law
American Journal of International Law — Am J Internat Law
American Journal of International Law — Am J Int'l L
American Journal of International Law — Am Jour Internatl Law
American Journal of International Law — Amer J Int Law
American Journal of International Law — Amer J Internat Law
American Journal of International Law — Amer J Int'l L
American Journal of International Law — GJIL
American Journal of International Law. Proceedings — Am J Int Law Proc
American Journal of International Law. Supplement — Am J Int L Supp
American Journal of Intravenous Therapy [*Later, American Journal of Intravenous Therapy and Clinical Nutrition*] — Am J IV Ther
American Journal of Intravenous Therapy [*Later, American Journal of Intravenous Therapy and Clinical Nutrition*] — Am J IV Therapy
American Journal of Intravenous Therapy and Clinical Nutrition — Am J IV Clin Nutr
American Journal of Intravenous Therapy and Clinical Nutrition — Am J IV Ther Clin Nutr
American Journal of Jurisprudence — Am J Jur
American Journal of Jurisprudence — Am J Juris
American Journal of Jurisprudence — Am J Jurispr
American Journal of Jurisprudence — Am J Jurisprud
American Journal of Jurisprudence — Amer J Juris
American Journal of Kidney Diseases — AJKDD
American Journal of Kidney Diseases — Am J Kidney
American Journal of Kidney Diseases — Am J Kidney Dis
American Journal of Knee Surgery — Am J Knee Surg
American Journal of Law and Medicine — AJLMDN
American Journal of Law and Medicine — Am J Law Med
American Journal of Law and Medicine — Am JL and M
American Journal of Law and Medicine — Am JL & Med
American Journal of Law and Medicine — ILNM
American Journal of Legal History — AJLH
American Journal of Legal History — Am J Leg Hist
American Journal of Legal History — Am J Legal Hist
American Journal of Legal History — Am JLH
American Journal of Legal History — Am Jour Legal Hist
American Journal of Legal History — Amer J Leg Hist
American Journal of Legal History — AmJL
American Journal of Maternal Child Nursing — MCN
American Journal of Mathematical and Management Sciences — Am J Math Manage Sci
American Journal of Mathematical and Management Sciences — Amer J Math Management Sci
American Journal of Mathematics — AJMAA
American Journal of Mathematics — Am J Math
American Journal of Mathematics — Amer J Math
American Journal of Medical Electronics — Am J Med Electron
American Journal of Medical Electronics — AMELA3
American Journal of Medical Genetics — AJMGDA
American Journal of Medical Genetics — Am J Med Genet
American Journal of Medical Genetics — Amer J Med Genet
American Journal of Medical Genetics. Supplement — Am J Med Genet Suppl
American Journal of Medical Jurisprudence — Am J Med Jurispr
American Journal of Medical Quality — Am J Med Qual
American Journal of Medical Technology — AJMTA
American Journal of Medical Technology — AJMTAC
American Journal of Medical Technology — Am J Med Te
American Journal of Medical Technology — Am J Med Technol
American Journal of Medicine — AJMEA
American Journal of Medicine — AJMEAZ
American Journal of Medicine — Am J Med
American Journal of Mental Deficiency — AJMD
American Journal of Mental Deficiency — AJMDA
American Journal of Mental Deficiency — AJMDAW
American Journal of Mental Deficiency — Am J Men Deficiency
American Journal of Mental Deficiency — Am J Ment D
American Journal of Mental Deficiency — Am J Ment Defic
American Journal of Mental Deficiency — Am J Ment Deficiency
American Journal of Mental Deficiency — Am J Mental Deficiency
American Journal of Mental Deficiency — Amer J Ment Defic
American Journal of Mental Diseases — Am J Ment Dis
American Journal of Mental Retardation — Am J Ment Retard
American Journal of Microscopy and Popular Science (New York) — Am J Micr (NY)
American Journal of Mining — Amer J Mining
American Journal of Nephrology — AJNED9
American Journal of Nephrology — Am J Nephr
American Journal of Nephrology — Am J Nephrol
American Journal of Neuropathy — Am J Neurop
American Journal of Numismatics — AJN
American Journal of Numismatics — AJNum
American Journal of Numismatics — Am Jnl Numis
American Journal of Numismatics — Am Journ Num
American Journal of Nursing — AJNUA
American Journal of Nursing — Am J Nurs
American Journal of Nursing — Am J Nursing
American Journal of Nursing — Amer J Nursing
American Journal of Nursing — AMJN
American Journal of Nursing — GJON
American Journal of Obstetrics and Diseases of Woman and Children [*New York*] — Am J Obst
American Journal of Obstetrics and Diseases of Women and Children (New York) — Am J Obst NY
American Journal of Obstetrics and Gynecology — AJOGA
American Journal of Obstetrics and Gynecology — AJOGAH
American Journal of Obstetrics and Gynecology — Am J Obst G
American Journal of Obstetrics and Gynecology — Am J Obst Gynec
American Journal of Obstetrics and Gynecology — Am J Obstet Gynecol
American Journal of Obstetrics and Gynecology — Amer J Obstet Gyn
American Journal of Occupational Therapy — AJOT
American Journal of Occupational Therapy — AJOTA
American Journal of Occupational Therapy — AJOTAM
American Journal of Occupational Therapy — Am J Occu T
American Journal of Occupational Therapy — Am J Occup Ther
American Journal of Occupational Therapy — Am J Occup Therapy
American Journal of Ophthalmology — AJOPA
American Journal of Ophthalmology — AJOPAA
American Journal of Ophthalmology — Am J Ophth
American Journal of Ophthalmology — Am J Ophthal
American Journal of Ophthalmology — Am J Ophthalmol
American Journal of Ophthalmology — Amer J Ophthalmol
American Journal of Optometry — AJOYA
American Journal of Optometry and Archives of American Academy of Optometry [*Later, American Journal of Optometry and Physiological Optics*] — AJOAAX
American Journal of Optometry and Archives of American Academy of Optometry [*Later, American Journal of Optometry and Physiological Optics*] — Am J Optom and Arch Am Acad Optom
American Journal of Optometry and Archives of American Academy of Optometry [*Later, American Journal of Optometry and Physiological Optics*] — Am J Optom Arch Am Acad Optom
American Journal of Optometry and Archives of American Academy of Optometry [*Later, American Journal of Optometry and Physiological Optics*] — Amer J Optom and Arch Amer Acad Optom
American Journal of Optometry and Physiological Optics — Am J Optom
American Journal of Optometry and Physiological Optics — Am J Optom Physiol Opt
American Journal of Optometry and Physiological Optics — Amer J Optom Physiol Opt
American Journal of Optometry and Physiological Optics — AOPOCF
American Journal of Orthodontics — AJOHA
American Journal of Orthodontics — AJOHAK
American Journal of Orthodontics — Am J Orthod
American Journal of Orthodontics and Dentofacial Orthopedics — Am J Orthod Dentofacial Orthop
American Journal of Orthodontics and Oral Surgery [*Later, American Journal of Orthodontics*] — AJOOA7
American Journal of Orthodontics and Oral Surgery [*Later, American Journal of Orthodontics*] — Am J Orthod Oral Surg
American Journal of Orthodontics and Oral Surgery [*Later, American Journal of Orthodontics*]. Oral Surgery — Am J Orthod Oral Surg Oral Surg
American Journal of Orthopedic Surgery — Am J Orth Surg
American Journal of Orthopedics — Am J Orth
American Journal of Orthopedics — Am J Orthop
American Journal of Orthopsychiatry — AJOPs
American Journal of Orthopsychiatry — AJORA
American Journal of Orthopsychiatry — AJORAG
American Journal of Orthopsychiatry — Am J Orth Psych
American Journal of Orthopsychiatry — Am J Orthop
American Journal of Orthopsychiatry — Am J Orthopsych
American Journal of Orthopsychiatry — Am J Orthopsychiat
American Journal of Orthopsychiatry — Am J Orthopsychiatr
American Journal of Orthopsychiatry — Am J Orthopsychiatry
American Journal of Orthopsychiatry — Amer J Orthopsychiat
American Journal of Orthopsychiatry — GJOO

American Journal of Otolaryngology — Am J Otolaryngol
American Journal of Otology — AJOTBN
American Journal of Otology — Am J Otol
American Journal of Pathology — AJPAA
American Journal of Pathology — AJPAA4
American Journal of Pathology — Am J Path
American Journal of Pathology — Am J Pathol
American Journal of Pathology — Amer J Pathol
American Journal of Pediatric Hematology/Oncology — Am J Pediatr Hematol Oncol
American Journal of Perinatology — AJPEEK
American Journal of Perinatology — Am J Perinatol
American Journal of Pharmaceutical Education — AJPDA
American Journal of Pharmaceutical Education — AJPDAD
American Journal of Pharmaceutical Education — Am J Phar E
American Journal of Pharmaceutical Education — Am J Pharm Educ
American Journal of Pharmacy — AJP
American Journal of Pharmacy — Am J Pharm
American Journal of Pharmacy — Am Jl Ph
American Journal of Pharmacy — Amer J Pharm
American Journal of Pharmacy and the Sciences Supporting Public Health [*Later, American Journal of Pharmacy*] — AJPRA
American Journal of Pharmacy and the Sciences Supporting Public Health [*Later, American Journal of Pharmacy*] — AJPRAL
American Journal of Pharmacy and the Sciences Supporting Public Health [*Later, American Journal of Pharmacy*] — Am J Pharm
American Journal of Pharmacy and the Sciences Supporting Public Health [*Later, American Journal of Pharmacy*] — Am J Pharm Sci Supporting Public Health
American Journal of Pharmacy and the Sciences Supporting Public Health [*Later, American Journal of Pharmacy*] — APSHDH
American Journal of Philology — AJ
American Journal of Philology — AJP
American Journal of Philology — AJPh
American Journal of Philology — AJPhil
American Journal of Philology — Am J Phil
American Journal of Philology — Am J Philol
American Journal of Philology — Am Jnl Philol
American Journal of Philology — Am Journ of Ph
American Journal of Philology — Am Journ Phil
American Journal of Philology — Amer J Philo
American Journal of Philology — Amer J Philol
American Journal of Philology [*Baltimore*] — Amer Journ Philol
American Journal of Philology — American J Ph
American Journal of Philology [*Baltimore*] — AmJPh
American Journal of Philology — PAJP
American Journal of Photography — Am J Photogr
American Journal of Physical Anthropology — AJPA
American Journal of Physical Anthropology — AJPNA
American Journal of Physical Anthropology — AJPNA9
American Journal of Physical Anthropology — Am J P Anth
American Journal of Physical Anthropology — Am J Phys Anthr
American Journal of Physical Anthropology — Am J Phys Anthro
American Journal of Physical Anthropology — Am J Phys Anthrop
American Journal of Physical Anthropology — Am J Phys Anthropol
American Journal of Physical Anthropology — Am Jour Phys Anthropol
American Journal of Physical Anthropology — Am JPA
American Journal of Physical Anthropology — Amer J Phys Anthrop
American Journal of Physical Anthropology — Amer J Phys Anthropol
American Journal of Physical Anthropology — IPHA
American Journal of Physical Anthropology. New Series — Am J Phys Anthrop ns
American Journal of Physical Medicine — AJPBA
American Journal of Physical Medicine — AJPBA7
American Journal of Physical Medicine — Am J Phys M
American Journal of Physical Medicine — Am J Phys Med
American Journal of Physical Medicine — Amer J Phys Med
American Journal of Physical Medicine and Rehabilitation — Am J Phys Med Rehabil
American Journal of Physics — AJPIA
American Journal of Physics — Am J Phys
American Journal of Physics — Am J Physics
American Journal of Physics — Amer J of Phys
American Journal of Physics — Amer J Phys
American Journal of Physics — IAJP
American Journal of Physiologic Imaging — Am J Physiol Imag
American Journal of Physiologic Imaging — Am J Physiol Imaging
American Journal of Physiology — AJPHA
American Journal of Physiology — AJPHAP
American Journal of Physiology — Am J Physiol
American Journal of Physiology — Am J Physl
American Journal of Physiology — Amer J Physiol
American Journal of Physiology. Cell Physiology — AJCPD
American Journal of Physiology. Cell Physiology — Am J Physiol Cell Physiol
American Journal of Physiology. Endocrinology and Metabolism — Am J Physiol Endocrinol Metab
American Journal of Physiology. Endocrinology, Metabolism, and Gastrointestinal Physiology — AJPED
American Journal of Physiology. Endocrinology, Metabolism, and Gastrointestinal Physiology — Am J Physiol Endocrinol Metab Gastrointest Physiol
American Journal of Physiology. Gastrointestinal and Liver Physiology — Am J Physiol Gastrointest Liver Physiol
American Journal of Physiology. Heart and Circulatory Physiology — AJPPD
American Journal of Physiology. Heart and Circulatory Physiology — Am J Physiol Heart Circ Physiol
American Journal of Physiology. Regulatory, Integrative, and Comparative Physiology — Am J Physiol Regul Integr Comp Physiol
American Journal of Physiology. Renal, Fluid, and Electrolyte Physiology — AJRFD
American Journal of Physiology. Renal, Fluid, and Electrolyte Physiology — Am J Physiol Renal Fluid Electrolyte Physiol
American Journal of Political Science — Am J Pol Sc
American Journal of Political Science — Am J Pol Sci
American Journal of Political Science — Amer J Polit Sci
American Journal of Political Science — GJPS
American Journal of Politics — Am J Pol
American Journal of Politics — Am Jour Pol
American Journal of Practical Nursing — Am J Pract Nurs
American Journal of Preventive Medicine — AJPMEA
American Journal of Preventive Medicine — Am J Prev Med
American Journal of Primatology — AJPTDU
American Journal of Primatology — Am J Primatol
American Journal of Proctology [*Later, American Journal of Proctology, Gastroenterology, and Colon and Rectal Surgery*] — AJPOA
American Journal of Proctology [*Later, American Journal of Proctology, Gastroenterology, and Colon and Rectal Surgery*] — AJPOAC
American Journal of Proctology [*Later, American Journal of Proctology, Gastroenterology, and Colon and Rectal Surgery*] Am J Proct
American Journal of Proctology [*Later, American Journal of Proctology, Gastroenterology, and Colon and Rectal Surgery*] — Am J Proctol
American Journal of Proctology, Gastroenterology, and Colon and Rectal Surgery — Am J Proctol Gastroenterol Colon Rectal Surg
American Journal of Proctology, Gastroenterology, and Colon and Rectal Surgery (Georgetown) — Am J Proctol Gastroenterol Colon Rectal Surg (Georgetown)
American Journal of Progressive Therapeutics — Am J Progr Ther
American Journal of Psychiatry — AJPSA
American Journal of Psychiatry — AJPSAO
American Journal of Psychiatry — AJPsy
American Journal of Psychiatry — Am J Psych
American Journal of Psychiatry — Am J Psychi
American Journal of Psychiatry — Am J Psychiat
American Journal of Psychiatry — Am J Psychiatr
American Journal of Psychiatry — Am J Psychiatry
American Journal of Psychiatry — Am Jour Psychiatry
American Journal of Psychiatry — Amer J Psychiat
American Journal of Psychiatry — Amer J Psychiatry
American Journal of Psychiatry — GPSI
American Journal of Psychoanalysis — AJP
American Journal of Psychoanalysis — AJPYA8
American Journal of Psychoanalysis — Am J Psycha
American Journal of Psychoanalysis — Am J Psychoanal
American Journal of Psychoanalysis — Amer J Psychoanal
American Journal of Psychoanalysis — PAJO
American Journal of Psychology — A J Psy
American Journal of Psychology — AJ Psychol
American Journal of Psychology — AJPCA
American Journal of Psychology — AJPCAA
American Journal of Psychology — AJPs
American Journal of Psychology — AJPsych
American Journal of Psychology — Am J Psycho
American Journal of Psychology — Am J Psychol
American Journal of Psychology — Amer J Psychol
American Journal of Psychology — Amer Jour Psych
American Journal of Psychology — GPSO
American Journal of Psychotherapy — AJPst
American Journal of Psychotherapy — AJPTAR
American Journal of Psychotherapy — Am J Psychoth
American Journal of Psychotherapy — Am J Psychother
American Journal of Psychotherapy — Am J Psycht
American Journal of Psychotherapy — Amer J Psychother
American Journal of Psychotherapy — Amer J Psychotherap
American Journal of Psychotherapy — IPST
American Journal of Public Health — AJHEA
American Journal of Public Health — AJHEAA
American Journal of Public Health — AJPH
American Journal of Public Health — Am J Pub He
American Journal of Public Health — Am J Pub Health
American Journal of Public Health — Am J Publ Heal
American Journal of Public Health — Am J Public Health
American Journal of Public Health — GAPH
American Journal of Public Health and the Nation's Health [*Later, American Journal of Public Health*] — AJPEA
American Journal of Public Health and the Nation's Health [*Later, American Journal of Public Health*] — Am J Pub Health
American Journal of Public Health and the Nation's Health [*Later, American Journal of Public Health*] — Am J Public Health Nation's Health
American Journal of Public Health. Supplement — Am J Public Health Suppl
American Journal of Reproductive Immunology — AJRI
American Journal of Reproductive Immunology — Am J Reprod Im
American Journal of Reproductive Immunology — Am J Reprod Immunol
American Journal of Reproductive Immunology — Amer Jnl Reprod Immun
American Journal of Reproductive Immunology and Microbiology — Am J Reprod Immunol Microbiol
American Journal of Respiratory and Critical Care Medicine — Am J Respir Crit Care Med
American Journal of Respiratory Cell and Molecular Biology — Am J Respir Cell Mol Biol

American Journal of Rhinology — Am J Rhinol
American Journal of Roentgenology — AJROA
American Journal of Roentgenology — Am J Roentg
American Journal of Roentgenology — Am J Roentgenol
American Journal of Roentgenology — Amer J Roentg
American Journal of Roentgenology — Amer J Roentgenol
American Journal of Roentgenology and Radium Therapy [*Later, American Journal of Roentgenology*] — AJRTA
American Journal of Roentgenology and Radium Therapy [*Later, American Journal of Roentgenology*] — Am J Roentgenol Radium Ther
American Journal of Roentgenology, Radium Therapy, and Nuclear Medicine [*Later, American Journal of Roentgenology*] — AJRRA
American Journal of Roentgenology, Radium Therapy, and Nuclear Medicine [*Later, American Journal of Roentgenology*] — AJRRAV
American Journal of Roentgenology, Radium Therapy, and Nuclear Medicine [*Later, American Journal of Roentgenology*] — Am J Roentgenol
American Journal of Roentgenology, Radium Therapy, and Nuclear Medicine [*Later, American Journal of Roentgenology*] — Am J Roentgenol Radium Ther Nucl Med
American Journal of Rural Health — Amer Jnl Rural Health
American Journal of School Hygiene — Am J School Hygiene
American Journal of Science — AJS
American Journal of Science — AJSCA
American Journal of Science — AJSCAP
American Journal of Science — AJSci
American Journal of Science — Am J Sci
American Journal of Science — Amer J Sci
American Journal of Science — IAJS
American Journal of Science and Arts — Am J Sc and Arts
American Journal of Science and Arts — Am J Sci Arts
American Journal of Science and Arts — Amer J Sci Arts
American Journal of Science. Radiocarbon Supplement — Am J Sci Radiocarbon Suppl
American Journal of Science. Radiocarbon Supplement — Amer J Sci Radiocarbon Suppl
American Journal of Semiotics — AJS
American Journal of Semitic Languages — Amer J Semitic Lang
American Journal of Semitic Languages and Literature — Amer Journ Sem Lang
American Journal of Semitic Languages and Literatures — AJSemL
American Journal of Semitic Languages and Literatures — AJSL
American Journal of Semitic Languages and Literatures [*Chicago, IL*] — AJSLL
American Journal of Semitic Languages and Literatures — Am J Sem Lang
American Journal of Semitic Languages and Literatures — Am Journ Sem Lang
American Journal of Small Business — AJSBD
American Journal of Small Business — Am J Small Bus
American Journal of Small Business — American Jrnl of Small Business
American Journal of Small Business — ASB
American Journal of Small Business — Jl Small Bus
American Journal of Social Psychiatry — Am J Soc Psychiatr
American Journal of Social Science — Am J Soc Sci
American Journal of Social Science — Am Soc Sci J
American Journal of Sociology — AJ Soc
American Journal of Sociology — AJS
American Journal of Sociology — AJSOA
American Journal of Sociology — Am J Soc
American Journal of Sociology — Am J Socio
American Journal of Sociology — Am J Sociol
American Journal of Sociology — Am Jnl Soc
American Journal of Sociology — Am Jour Sociol
American Journal of Sociology — Am JS
American Journal of Sociology — Amer J Sociol
American Journal of Sociology — GAJS
American Journal of Sports Medicine — AJSMD
American Journal of Sports Medicine — Am J Sports Med
American Journal of Stomatology — Am J Stomat
American Journal of Surgery — AJSUA
American Journal of Surgery — AJSUAB
American Journal of Surgery — Am J Surg
American Journal of Surgery and Gynecology — Amer J Surg
American Journal of Surgical Pathology — AJSPDX
American Journal of Surgical Pathology — Am J Surg Pathol
American Journal of Syphilis — Am J Syph
American Journal of Syphilis and Neurology — Am J Syph Neurol
American Journal of Syphilis, Gonorrhea, and Venereal Diseases — Am J Syph Gonorrhea Vener Dis
American Journal of the Medical Sciences — AJMSA
American Journal of the Medical Sciences — AJMSA9
American Journal of the Medical Sciences — Am J Med Sc
American Journal of the Medical Sciences — Am J Med Sci
American Journal of the Medical Sciences — Am JM Sc
American Journal of the Medical Sciences — Amer J Med Sci
American Journal of Theology — AJT
American Journal of Theology — AJTh
American Journal of Theology — Am J Theol
American Journal of Theology — AmJTh
American Journal of Theology and Philosophy — Am J Th Ph
American Journal of Theology and Philosophy — Amer J Theol Phil
American Journal of Therapeutics and Clinical Reports — AJTRDA
American Journal of Therapeutics and Clinical Reports — Am J Ther Clin Rep
American Journal of Trial Advocacy — Am J Trial Ad
American Journal of Trial Advocacy — Am J Trial Advocacy
American Journal of Tropical Diseases and Preventive Medicine — Amer J Trop Dis Prev Med
American Journal of Tropical Diseases and Preventive Medicine (New Orleans) [*A publication*] — Am J Trop Dis (New Orleans)
American Journal of Tropical Medicine [*Later, American Journal of Tropical Medicine and Hygiene*] — Am J Trop Med
American Journal of Tropical Medicine and Hygiene — AJTHA
American Journal of Tropical Medicine and Hygiene — AJTHAB
American Journal of Tropical Medicine and Hygiene — Am J Trop M
American Journal of Tropical Medicine and Hygiene — Am J Trop Med Hyg
American Journal of Tropical Medicine and Hygiene — Am Trop Med
American Journal of Tropical Medicine and Hygiene — Amer J Trop Med Hyg
American Journal of Tropical Medicine (Baltimore) — Am Jour Trop Med Baltimore
American Journal of Veterinary Medicine — Am J Vet Med
American Journal of Veterinary Research — AJVRA
American Journal of Veterinary Research — AJVRAH
American Journal of Veterinary Research — Am J Vet Re
American Journal of Veterinary Research — Am J Vet Res
American Journal of Veterinary Research — Amer J Vet Res
American Journal of Veterinary Science — Am J Vet Sci
American Journal on Addictions — Am J Addict
American Judicature Society. Journal — Am Jud Soc
American Jurist and Law Magazine — Am Jurist
American Labor Legislation Review — Am Lab Leg Rev
American Labor Legislation Review — Am Labor Leg R
American Labor Legislation Review — Am Labor Legis Rev
American Laboratory [*Fairfield, Connecticut*] — ALBYBL
American Laboratory — Am Lab
American Laboratory (Boston) — Am Lab (Boston)
American Laboratory (Fairfield, Connecticut) — Am Lab (Fairfield Conn)
American Land — Am Land
American Landrace — Am Landrace
American Laundry Digest — Am Laund Dig
American Laundry Digest — Am Laundry Dig
American Law Institute. Proceedings — ALI Proc
American Law Journal — ALJ
American Law Journal — Am Law J
American Law Journal — Am LJ
American Law Journal. New Series — ALJNS
American Law Journal. New Series — Am Law J NS
American Law Journal. New Series — Am LJNS
American Law Journal (Ohio) [*or Okey*] — Am LJ (O)
American Law Journal. Old Series — Am LJ OS
American Law Magazine — ALM
American Law Magazine — Am Law Mag
American Law Magazine — Am LM
American Law Register and Review — Am Law Reg R
American Law Review — AL Rev
American Law Review — Am L Rev
American Law Review — Am Law R
American Law Review — Am Law Rev
American Law Review — Amer Law Rev
American Lawyer — Am Law
American Lawyer — Am Lawy
American Lawyer — Am Lawyer
American Lawyer — Amer Law
American Lawyer — Amer Lawy
American Leather Chemists Association. Journal — Am Leather Chem Assoc J
American Lecture Series — Am Lect Ser
American Lecture Series — AMLSBQ
American Legion Magazine — Am Leg Mag
American Legion Magazine — Am Legion M
American Legion Magazine — GALE
American Libraries [*Chicago*] — A Lib
American Libraries — AL
American Libraries — ALA
American Libraries [*Chicago*] — Am Lib
American Libraries [*Chicago*] — Am Libr
American Libraries [*Chicago*] — Am Libs
American Libraries — IALI
American Libraries (Chicago) — Am Libr (Chicago)
American Library Association. Adult Services Division. Joint Committee on Library Service to Labor Groups. Library Service to Labor Newsletter — ALA Lib Serv to Labor News
American Library Association. Association of Hospital and Institution Libraries. Book Guide — ALA Hosp Bk Guide
American Library Association. Booklist — Booklist
American Library Association. Bulletin — ALA Bul
American Library Association. Bulletin — Am Lib Assn Bul
American Library Association. Intellectual Freedom Committee. Newsletter — ALA Intellectual Freedom Newsl
American Library Association. Library Periodicals Round Table. Newsletter — ALA Lib Period Round Table Newsl
American Library Association. Reference Services Division. Reference Quarterly — ALA Ref Serv Div
American Library Association. Washington Newsletter — ALA Wash Newsl
American Library Directory [*Database*] — ALD
American Library Scholarship — Am L S
American Liszt Society Journal — ALSJ
American Liszt Society. Journal — Amer Liszt Soc J
American Literary Magazine — Am Lit M
American Literary Realism, 1870-1910 — ALR
American Literary Realism, 1870-1910 — Am Lit Real
American Literary Realism, 1870-1910 — Am Lit Realism
American Literature — AL
American Literature — Amer Lit

American Literature — AmLit
American Literature — GAML
American Literature Abstracts — AmerLitAb
American Literature, English Literature, and World Literature in English — ALELWLE
American Littoral Society. Special Publication — ALSPAA
American Littoral Society. Special Publication — Am Littoral Soc Spec Publ
American Livestock Journal — Am Livestock J
American Livestock Journal — Amer Livestock J
American Logger and Lumberman — Am Log Lumber
American Logger and Lumberman — Am Logger Lumberman
American Lumberman — Am Lumberman
American Lung Association. Bulletin — ALAB
American Lung Association. Bulletin — ALBLB
American Lung Association. Bulletin — Am Lung Assoc Bull
American Lutheran — Am Luth
American Lutherie — AL
American Lutherie — Am Lutherie
American Machinist — AM
American Machinist — Am Mach
American Machinist — Am Machin
American Machinist — Amer Mach
American Machinist/Metalworking Manufacturing — Am Mach/Metalwork Manuf
American Magazine — Am M
American Magazine — Am Mag
American Magazine of Art — Am M Art
American Magazine of Art — Am Mag Art
American Magazine of Civics — Am M Civics
American Magazine (Springfield, Ohio) — AMS
American Malacological Bulletin — Am Malacol Bull
American Malacological Bulletin — AMBUEJ
American Malacological Union. Annual Report — Am Malacolog Union Ann Rept
American Malacological Union. Bulletin [*Later, American Malacological Bulletin*] — Am Malacol Union Bull
American Malacological Union, Incorporated. Annual Report — Am Malacol Union Inc Annu Rep
American Malacological Union, Incorporated. Annual Report — ARMUA3
American Malacological Union, Incorporated. Bulletin [*Later, American Malacological Bulletin*] — Am Malacol Union Inc Bull
American Malacological Union, Incorporated. Bulletin [*Later, American Malacological Bulletin*] — AMUBBK
American Management Association. Survey Report — Am Management Assn Survey Rpt
American Management Associations. Research Study — Amer Manage Ass Res Stud
American Management Review — Am Management R
American Manufacturer — Am Manuf
American Marine Engineer — Am Marine Engineer
American Maritime Cases — Am Mar Cas
American Maritime Cases — MC
American Marketing Association. Proceedings — AMA
American Mathematical Monthly — Am Math M
American Mathematical Monthly — Am Math Mo
American Mathematical Monthly — Am Math Mon
American Mathematical Monthly — Amer Math Mon
American Mathematical Monthly — Amer Math Monthly
American Mathematical Monthly — AMMYA
American Mathematical Monthly — AMMYAE
American Mathematical Monthly — IAMM
American Mathematical Society. Bulletin — Am Math Soc Bul
American Mathematical Society. Colloquium Publications — Amer Math Soc Colloq Publ
American Mathematical Society. Memoirs — Am Math Soc Mem
American Mathematical Society. Memoirs — Am Math Soc Memoirs
American Mathematical Society. Translations — Amer Math Soc Transl
American Meat Institute. Foundation Bulletin — Am Meat Inst Found Bull
American Meat Institute. Foundation Circular — Am Meat Inst Found Circ
American Mechanic's Magazine — Amer Mech Mag
American Medical Association. Congress on Environmental Health — Am Med Assoc Congr Environ Health
American Medical Association. Journal — Am Med Assn J
American Medical Association. Transactions — Am Med Assn Trans
American Medical Association's Cost Effectiveness Plan — Am Med Assoc Cost Effect Pl
American Medical News — Am Med News
American Medical News Impact — Am Med News Impact
American Medical Weekly — Am Med W
American Medicine — Am Med
American Medicine — Amer Med
American Medico-Psychological Association. Proceedings — Am Med Psychol Assn Proc
American Men and Women of Science — AMWS
American Mercury — AM
American Mercury — Am Mer
American Mercury — Am Mercury
American Mercury — AmM
American Mercury — AmMerc
American Messianic Jew — Am Mess Jew
American Metal Market — Am Met Mark
American Metal Market — Am Mtl Mkt
American Metal Market — AMMKA
American Metal Market. Metalworking News Edition — Am Met Mark Metalwork News Ed
American Meteorological Journal — Am Meteorological J
American Meteorological Society. Bulletin — Am Met Soc Bull
American Meteorological Society. Bulletin — Am Meteorol Soc Bull
American Methodist Magazine — Am Meth M
American Microscopical Society. Proceedings — Am Micro Soc Pr
American Microscopical Society. Transactions — Am Micros Soc Trans
American Midland Naturalist — Am Midl Nat
American Midland Naturalist — Am Midl Natur
American Midland Naturalist — Am Midland Natural
American Midland Naturalist — Amer Midl Nat
American Midland Naturalist — AMNAA
American Midland Naturalist — AMNAAF
American Midland Naturalist — PAMN
American Midland Naturalist. Devoted to Natural History. Primarily that of the Prairie States — Amer Midl Naturalist
American Milk Review — Am Milk R
American Milk Review — Am Milk Rev
American Milk Review and Milk Plant Monthly — Am Milk Rev Milk Plant Mon
American Miller — Am Miller
American Miller and Processor — Am Miller Process
American Miller and Processor — Amer Miller Process
American Miller and Processor — AMPEA3
American Mineralogical Journal — Am Miner J
American Mineralogical Journal — Am Mineral J
American Mineralogist — Am Min
American Mineralogist — Am Miner
American Mineralogist — Am Mineral
American Mineralogist — Am Mineralogist
American Mineralogist — Amer Mineral
American Mineralogist — AMMIA
American Mining Congress. Journal — Am M Cong
American Mining Congress. Journal — Am Min Congr J
American Mining Congress. Proceedings — Am Min Congr Proc
American Mining Congress. Session Papers — Am Min Congr Sess Pap
American Monthly Magazine — Am Mo M
American Monthly Review — Am Mo R
American Mosquito Control Association. Bulletin — Am Mosq Control Assoc Bull
American Mosquito Control Association. Journal — Am Mosq Control Assoc
American Motorcyclist — AM
American Ms Magazine — Am Ms Mag
American Museum Journal — Am Mus J
American Museum Journal — Am Museum J
American Museum Journal — Amer Mus J
American Museum Novitates — Am Mus Novit
American Museum Novitates — Am Mus Novitates
American Museum Novitates — AMUNAL
American Museum of Natural History — AMNH
American Museum of Natural History. Bulletin — Am Mus Nat History Bull
American Museum of Natural History Bulletin — Amer Mus Nat Hist Bull
American Museum of Natural History. Bulletin. Memoirs — Am Mus N H B Mem
American Museum of Natural History. Bulletin. Science Guide. Special Publication — Am Mus Nat History Bull Sci Guide Special Pub
American Music — AM
American Music — Am Mus
American Music — GAMM
American Music Center. Newsletter — AMC
American Music Center Newsletter — AMCN
American Music Export Buyers Guide — Am Mus Exp Buy G
American Music Research Center Journal — Am Mus Res
American Music Research Center Journal — AMRCJ
American Music Teacher — Am Mus Tcr
American Music Teacher — Am Mus Teach
American Music Teacher — AMUTA
American Music Teacher Magazine — AMT
American Musical Digest — Am Mus Dgt
American Musical Instrument Society. Journal — Amer M Instrument Soc J
American Musical Instrument Society. Journal — AMIS J
American Musical Instrument Society. Newsletter — AMIS N
American Musicological Society. Journal — Am Musicol Soc J
American Musicological Society. Journal — AMS
American Musicological Society. Journal — AMS Jl
American Musicological Society. Journal — AMSJ
American Musicological Society Newsletter — AMSN
American National Red Cross. Annual Scientific Symposium — Am Natl Red Cross Annu Sci Symp
American National Red Cross. Annual Symposium — Am Natl Red Cross Annu Symp
American National Standards Institute. Standards — Am Natl Stand Inst Stand
American Native Press — Am Nat Pr
American Naturalist — Am Nat
American Naturalist — Am Natural
American Naturalist — Am Naturalist
American Naturalist — Amer Nat
American Naturalist — Amer Natur
American Naturalist — AMNTA
American Naturalist — AMNTA4
American Naturalist — IANA
American Naturalist. A Popular Illustrated Magazine of Natural History — Amer Naturalist
American Neptune — Am Nep
American Neptune — Am Neptune
American Neptune — Amer Neptune
American Newspaper Publishers Association. Newsprint Statistics — ANPA Stat
American Notes and Queries — Am N & Q
American Notes and Queries — Am Note Que
American Notes and Queries — Am Notes & Queries

American Notes and Queries — Amer Notes Quer
American Notes and Queries — ANQ
American Nuclear Society. Conference on Atomic and Nuclear Methods in Fossil Fuel Energy Research — Am Nucl Soc Conf At Nucl Methods Fossil Fuel Energy Res
American Nuclear Society/European Nuclear Society Topical Meeting. Thermal Reactor Safety — Am Nucl Soc Eur Nucl Soc Top Meet Therm React Saf
American Nuclear Society. International Topical Meeting — Am Nucl Soc Int Top Meet
American Nuclear Society. National Meeting Papers — Am Nucl Soc Natl Meet Pap
American Nuclear Society. National Topical Meeting — Am Nucl Soc Natl Top Meet
American Nuclear Society. National Topical Meeting on Advances in Reactor Physics. Proceedings — Am Nucl Soc Top Meet Adv React Phys Proc
American Nuclear Society. Proceedings. Pacific Basin Conference on Nuclear Power Development and the Fuel Cycle — Am Nucl Soc Proc Pac Basin Conf Nucl Power Dev Fuel Cycle
American Nuclear Society Topical Meeting. Irradiation Experimentation in Fast Reactors — Am Nucl Soc Top Meet Irradiat Exp Fast React
American Nuclear Society Topical Meeting on Gas-Cooled Reactors. HTGR and GCFBR — Am Nucl Soc Top Meet Gas-Cooled React HTGR GCFBR
American Nuclear Society. Topical Meeting on Light Water Reactor Fuel Performance — Am Nucl Soc Top Meet Light Water React Fuel Perform
American Nuclear Society. Transactions — Am Nucl Soc Trans
American Numismatic Society. Centennial Publication — ANS Cent Pub
American Numismatic Society. Centennial Publication — ANS Cent
American Numismatic Society. Centennial Publication — ANSCP
American Numismatic Society. Museum Notes — Am Num Soc Mus Notes
American Numismatic Society. Museum Notes — ANSMN
American Numismatic Society. Museum Notes — ANSMusN
American Numismatic Society. Museum Notes — ANSN
American Numismatic Society. Numismatic Notes and Monographs — ANSNNM
American Numismatic Society. Numismatic Studies — ANSNS
American Nurse — Am Nurse
American Nurseryman — Am Nurseryman
American Nurseryman — Amer Nurserym
American Nurseryman and the National Nurseryman — Am Nurseryman Natl Nurseryman
American Nurses' Association. Nursing Research Conferences — ANA Nurs Res Conf
American Nurses' Association. Publications — ANA Publ
American Nut Journal — Am Nut J
American Oil and Gas Reporter — Amer Oil Gas Reporter
American Oil Chemists' Society. Journal — Am Oil Chem Soc J
American Oil Chemists' Society. Journal — Am Oil Chemists Soc J
American Oil Chemists' Society. Monograph — Am Oil Chem Soc Monogr
American Ophthalmological Society. Transactions — Am Ophthal Soc Trans
American Opinion — Am Opinion
American Opinion — Amer O
American Opthalmological Society. Journal — Am Ophthal Soc J
American Optometric Association. Journal — Am Optom Assoc J
American Optometric Association. Journal — Am Optomet Assoc J
American Orchid Society. Bulletin — Am Orch Soc B
American Orchid Society. Bulletin — Am Orchid Soc Bull
American Orchid Society. Bulletin — AOSBAN
American Orchid Society. Yearbook — Am Orch Soc Yb
American Organist — Am Org
American Organist — AO
American Oriental Series — Amer Orient Ser
American Oriental Series — AOS
American Oriental Society. Journal — Am Orient Soc J
American Oriental Society. Journal — Am Oriental Soc J
American Oriental Society. Journal — Amer Oriental Soc Jour
American Oriental Society. Journal — AOS
American Ornithology — Am Orn
American Orthopsychiatric Association. Papers Presented. Annual Convention — Am Orthopsych Assoc Pap
American Orthoptic Journal — Am Orth J
American Orthoptic Journal — Am Orthopt J
American Orthoptic Journal — AOJTAW
American Osteopathic Association. Journal — Am Osteopath Assoc J
American Oxonian — AmOx
American Oxonian — AO
American Paint and Coatings Journal — Am Paint
American Paint and Coatings Journal — Am Paint Coat J
American Paint and Coatings Journal — APJ
American Paint and Varnish Manufacturers' Association. Scientific Section. Circulars — Am Paint Varn Mmanuf Assoc Sci Sect Circ
American Paint Journal [*Later, American Paint and Coatings Journal*] — Am Paint J
American Painter and Decorator — Am Painter Decor
American Painting Contractor — Am Paint Contract
American Painting Contractor — APACB
American Paper Converter — Am Pap Converter
American Paper Industry — Am Pap Ind
American Paper Industry — Am Paper Ind
American Paper Industry — Amer Pap Ind
American Paper Industry — APPIB
American Paper Institute. Food Additives Reference Manual — API Food Add Ref
American Paper Institute. Monthly Statistical Summary — API Statist Sum
American Paper Institute. Newsprint Division. Bulletin — API Newsprint Bull
American Paper Institute. Wood Pulp Statistics — API Wood Pulp Statist
American Paper Merchant — Am Pap Merchant
American Paper Merchant — Am Paper Merch
American Peace Directory — Am Peace Dir
American Peanut Research and Education Association. Journal — Am Peanut Res Educ Assoc J
American Peanut Research and Education Association. Proceedings — Am Peanut Res Educ Assoc Proc
American Peanut Research and Education Society. Proceedings — Am Peanut Res Educ Soc Proc
American Pecan Journal — Amer Pecan J
American Pediatric Society. Transactions — Am Pediat Soc Trans
American Peony Society Bulletin — Amer Peony Soc Bull
American People/Link [*Database*] — PLINK
American Peptide Symposium — Am Pept Symp
American Perfumer — Am Perfum
American Perfumer and Aromatics — Am Perfum Aromat
American Perfumer and Aromatics — Am Perfumer & Aromatics
American Perfumer and Aromatics — Am Perfumer Arom
American Perfumer and Cosmetics — Am Perfum Cosmet
American Perfumer and Cosmetics — Am Perfumer
American Perfumer and Essential Oil Review — Am Perfum Essent Oil Rev
American Perfumer and Essential Oil Review — Am Perfum Esst Oil Rev
American Perfumer and Essential Oil Review — Am Perfumer Ess Oil Rev
American Perfumer, Cosmetics, Toilet Preparations — Am Perfum Cosmet Toilet Prep
American Perspective — Am Perspect
American Perspective (Washington, DC) — APW
American Petroleum Institute. Abstracts of Refining Literature — Am Pet Inst Abstr Refin Lit
American Petroleum Institute. Bulletin — Am Pet Inst Bul
American Petroleum Institute. Division of Production, Drilling, and Production Practice. Papers — Amer Petrol Inst Div Prod Drilling Prod Pract Pap
American Petroleum Institute. Division of Refining. Proceedings — Am Pet Inst Div Refin Proc
American Petroleum Institute. Drilling and Production Practice — Am Petroleum Inst Drilling and Production Practice
American Petroleum Institute. Medical Research Publications — API Med Res Publ
American Petroleum Institute. Proceedings — Am Pet Inst Proc
American Petroleum Institute. Publication — Am Pet Inst Publ
American Petroleum Institute. Publication — API Publ
American Petroleum Institute. Quarterly — Am Pet Inst Q
American Petroleum Institute. Quarterly — Am Petr Inst Quart
American Petroleum Institute. Refining Department. Midyear Meeting. Preprints [*A publication*] — API Refining Dep Midyear Meet Prepr
American Petroleum Institute. Refining Department. Proceedings — Am Pet Inst Refin Dep Proc
American Petroleum Institute. Refining Department. Proceedings — Am Pet Inst Refin Dept Proc
American Petroleum Institute. Standards — Amer Petrol Inst Stand
American Petroleum Institute. Statistical Bulletin — Am Pet Inst Stat Bull
American Petroleum Institute. Technical Abstracts — Am Pet Inst Tech Abstr
American Petroleum Institute. Weekly Statistical Bulletin — Am Petr Inst Wkly Stat Bull
American Pharmaceutical Association. Journal — Am Pharm Assoc J
American Pharmacy — Am Pharm
American Pharmacy — AMPH
American Pharmacy — AMPHDF
American Philological Association. Transactions — APAT
American Philosophical Quarterly — Am Philos Q
American Philosophical Quarterly — Amer Phil Quart
American Philosophical Quarterly — APQ
American Philosophical Quarterly — PAPQ
American Philosophical Quarterly. Monograph Series — Amer Philos Quart Monograph Ser
American Philosophical Society. Library Bulletin — Am Philos Soc Lib Bull
American Philosophical Society. Memoirs — Am Philos Soc Mem
American Philosophical Society. Proceedings — Am Philos Soc Proc
American Philosophical Society. Proceedings — Amer Philos Soc Proc
American Philosophical Society. Proceedings — APS
American Philosophical Society. Transactions — Am Philos Soc Trans
American Philosophical Society. Transactions — Amer Philos Soc Trans
American Philosophical Society. Yearbook — Am Philos Soc YB
American Philosophical Society. Yearbook — Am Philos Soc Yearbook
American Photo — IAPH
American Photo Engraver — Am Photo Engraver
American Photographer — Amer Photogr
American Photography — Am Phot
American Photography — Am Photog
American Photography — Am Photogr
American Photography — Amer Phot
American Physical Education Association. Research Quarterly — Am Phys Ed Assn Res Q
American Physical Education Review — Am Phys Educ R
American Physical Society. Bulletin — Am Phys Soc Bull
American Physical Society. Division of Particles and Fields. Annual Meeting — Am Phys Soc Div Part Fields Annu Meet
American Physical Society. Topical Conference on Shock Waves in Condensed Matter — Am Phys Soc Top Conf Shock Waves Condens Matter
American Physics Teacher — Am Phys Teach
American Physics Teacher — Amer Phys Teacher
American Physiological Society. Methods in Physiology Series — Am Physiol Soc Methods Physiol Ser
American Phytopathological Society. Monograph — Am Phytopathol Soc Monogr
American Phytopathological Society. Monograph — APYMAP

American Phytopathological Society. Proceedings — Am Phytopathol Soc Proc
American Planning and Civic Planning — Am Planning
American Planning Association. Journal — Am Plan Assn J
American Planning Association. Journal — Am Plann Assoc J
American Planning Association. Journal — American Planning Assocn Jnl
American Poetry — IAPO
American Poetry Review — Am Poet Rev
American Poetry Review — Am Poetry
American Poetry Review — Amer Po R
American Poetry Review — APR
American Poetry Review — PAPR
American Poinsettia Society Newsletter — Amer Poinsettia Soc Newslett
American Political Science Association. Proceedings — Am Pol Sci Assn Proc
American Political Science Review — Am Pol Sc Rev
American Political Science Review [*Baltimore*] — Am Pol Sci
American Political Science Review — Am Pol Sci R
American Political Science Review — Am Pol Sci Rev
American Political Science Review — Am Pol Science R
American Political Science Review — Am Pol Science Rev
American Political Science Review — Am Poli Sci
American Political Science Review — Am Polit Sci R
American Political Science Review — Amer Polit Sci R
American Political Science Review — Amer Polit Sci Rev
American Political Science Review — APSR
American Political Science Review — GAPS
American Political Science Review. American Political Science Association — APSA/R
American Politics Quarterly — Am Pol Q
American Politics Quarterly — Am Polit Q
American Politics Quarterly — Am Politics Q
American Politics Quarterly — Amer Polit Quart
American Pomological Society. Proceedings — Am Pom Soc Pro
American Pomology (Ames) — Amer Pomol Ames
American Postal Worker — Am Postal Wkr
American Potato Journal — Am Pot J
American Potato Journal — Am Potato J
American Potato Journal — APOJA
American Potato Journal — APOJAY
American Poultry Advocate — Am P Advocate
American Poultry Journal — Am P J
American Poultry Journal — Am Poultry J
American Power Conference. Proceedings — Am Power Conf Proc
American Practitioner — Am Pract
American Practitioner — Am Practitioner
American Practitioner and Digest of Treatment — Am Pract Dig Treat
American Practitioner and Digest of Treatment — Am Pract Digest Treat
American Practitioner and Digest of Treatment — APDTA9
American Prefaces — Am Prefs
American Premiere — Amer Prem
American Presbyterian Review — Am Presb R
American Pressman — Am Pressman
American Pressman Reports — Am Pressman Rept
American Printer — Am Print
American Printer and Lithographer [*Later, American Printer*] — Am Printer Lithogr
American Printer and Lithographer [*Later, American Printer*] — Am Prnt Lith
American Printer and Lithographer [*Later, American Printer*] — Am Ptr & Lith
American Printing House for the Blind - Central Automated Resource List [*Database*] — APH-CARL
American Prison Association. Proceedings — Am Prison Assn Proc
American Produce Review — Am Prod R
American Professional Pharmacist — Am Prof Pharm
American Psychiatric Association. Mental Hospital Service. Monograph Series — Am Psychiatr Assoc Ment Hosp Serv Monogr Ser
American Psycho/Info Exchange [*Database*] — AMPIE
American Psychoanalytic Association. Journal — Am Psychoana Assn J
American Psychoanalytic Association. Journal — Am Psychoanal Assn J
American Psychoanalytic Association. Journal. Monograph Series — Am Psychoanal Assoc J Monogr Ser
American Psychological Association. Proceedings — Am Psychol Assn Proc
American Psychological Association. Proceedings of the Annual Convention — AMPCB
American Psychologist — A Psy
American Psychologist — Am P
American Psychologist — Am Psychol
American Psychologist — Am Psychologist
American Psychologist — Amer Psychol
American Psychologist — AMPSA
American Psychologist — AMPSAB
American Psychologist — AP
American Psychologist — APs
American Psychologist — GAMP
American Psychopathological Association. Proceedings — PAPAA4
American Psychopathological Association. Proceedings. Annual Meeting — Am Psychopathol Assoc Proc Annu Meet
American Public Health Association. Public Health Education. Section Newsletter — APHA
American Public Health Association. Reports — Am Pub Health Ass Rep
American Public Health Association. Yearbook — Am Public Health Assoc Yearb
American Public Works Association. Yearbook — Am Public Works Assoc Yearb
American Pulpwood Association. Legislative Bulletin — APA Legisl Bull
American Pulpwood Association. Monthly Pulpwood Summary — APA Pulpwood Sum
American Pulpwood Association. Pulpwood Highlights — APA Pulpwood Highl
American Pulpwood Association. Pulpwood Statistics — APA Pulpwood Statist
American Pulpwood Association. Safety Alert — APA Safety Alert
American Pulpwood Association. Technical Papers — APA Tech Papers
American Pulpwood Association. Technical Release — APA Tech Release
American Quarterly — Am Q
American Quarterly — Am Quar
American Quarterly — Am Quart
American Quarterly — Amer Quart
American Quarterly — AQ
American Quarterly — PAQT
American Quarterly Journal of Agriculture and Science — Am Q J Agr
American Quarterly Journal of Agriculture and Science — Amer Quart J Agric Sci
American Quarterly Microscopical Journal — Am Q Micro J
American Quarterly Observer — Am Q Obs
American Quarterly of Roentgenology — Am Q Roentgenol
American Quarterly on the Soviet Union — Am Q Sov Union
American Quarterly Register — Am Q Reg
American Quarterly Review [*1827-1837*] — Am Q
American Rabbit Journal — Am Rabbit J
American Rabbit Journal — ARBJAH
American Railway Engineering and Maintenance-of-Way Association. Proceedings. Annual Convention — Am Railw Eng Maint Way Assoc Proc Annu Conv
American Railway Engineering Association. Bulletin — Am Railw Eng Assoc Bull
American Railway Engineering Association. Bulletin — ARWBA
American Railway Engineering Association. Proceedings — Am Railw Eng Assoc Proc
American Railway Engineering Association. Technical Conference Proceedings — Am Railw Eng Assoc Tech Conf Proc
American Real Estate and Urban Economics Association. Journal — Am Real Estate & Urb Econ Assn J
American Record Guide — Am Rec G
American Record Guide — Am Rec Guide
American Record Guide — Am Record Gd
American Record Guide — AR
American Record Guide — ARG
American Record Guide — IARG
American Recorder — Am Recorder
American Recorder — Amer Recorder
American Recorder — AR
American Red Angus — Am Red Angus
American Reference Books Annual — Am Ref Bk Ann
American Reference Books Annual — ARBA
American Refractories Institute. Information Circular — Am Refract Inst Inf Circ
American Refractories Institute. Technical Bulletin — Am Refract Inst Tech Bull
American Rehabilitation — Am Rehabil
American Rehabilitation — Amer Rehab
American Rehabilitation Nursing Journal — ARN J
American Repertory of Arts, Sciences, and Manufactures — Amer Repert Arts Sci Manufactures
American Research Center in Egypt/Catalogs — Amer Res Center Egypt Cat
American Research Center in Egypt Newsletter — ARCE News
American Review [*Formerly, New American Review*] — Am R
American Review [*Formerly, New American Review*] — Am Rev
American Review — Amer R
American Review [*Formerly, New American Review*] — AR
American Review of Public Administration — Am R Public Admin
American Review of Public Administration — MPA
American Review of Public Administration — MRP
American Review of Respiratory Disease — Am R Resp D
American Review of Respiratory Disease — Am Rev Resp Dis
American Review of Respiratory Disease — Am Rev Respir Dis
American Review of Respiratory Disease — ARDSB
American Review of Respiratory Disease — ARDSBL
American Review of Respiratory Disease — ARRDA
American Review of Respiratory Diseases — Am Rev Respir Dis
American Review of Reviews — ARR
American Review of Science, Art, Inventions — Amer Rev Sci
American Review of Soviet Medicine — Am Rev Sov Med
American Review of Tuberculosis — Am R Tuberc
American Review of Tuberculosis — Am Rev Tuberc
American Review of Tuberculosis — Amer Rev Tuberc
American Review of Tuberculosis and Pulmonary Diseases — Am Rev Tub
American Review of Tuberculosis and Pulmonary Diseases — Am Rev Tuberc Pulm Dis
American Review of Tuberculosis and Pulmonary Diseases — ARTPA
American Review of Tuberculosis and Pulmonary Diseases — ARTPAN
American Review on the Soviet Union — Am Rev Sov Union
American Rheumatism Association Medical Information System [*Database*] — ARAMIS
American Rifleman — GARI
American Rocket Society. Journal — ARSJ
American Rocket Society. Paper — Am Rocket Soc Pap
American Rose Annual — Am Rose Annu
American Rose Annual — Amer Rose Annual
American Rose Quarterly — Amer Rose Quart
American Salesman — AMN
American Salesman — AMS
American Samoa Administrative Code — Am Samoa Admin Code
American Samoa Code Annotated — Am Samoa Code Ann
American Samoa Reports — Am Samoa
American Scandinavian Review — Am Scand Rev
American Scenic and Historic Preservation Society. Annual Report — Am Scenic and Historic Preservation Soc An Rp
American Scholar — Am Sch

American Scholar — Am Schol
American Scholar — Am Scholar
American Scholar — Amer Sch
American Scholar — Amer Scholar
American Scholar — AmS
American Scholar — AS
American Scholar — ASc
American Scholar — ASch
American Scholar — ASCOA
American Scholar — GTAS
American Scholar (Washington, D.C.) — ASW
American School and University — Am Sch & Univ
American School and University — ASU
American School and University — ASUNB
American School and University — IASU
American School Board Journal — Am Sch Bd J
American School Board Journal — Am Sch Board J
American School Board Journal — Am Sch Brd J
American School Board Journal — Am School Bd J
American Schools of Oriental Research. Bulletin — Am Sch Orient Res Bul
American Schools of Oriental Research. Bulletin — ASOR Bul
American Schools of Oriental Research. Newsletter — ASOR
American Schools of Oriental Research. Publications of the Jerusalem School. Archaeology — ASOR PJSA
American Sciences Press Series in Mathematical and Management Sciences — Amer Sci Press Ser Math Management Sci
American Scientist — Am Sci
American Scientist — Am Scient
American Scientist — Am Scientist
American Scientist — Amer Sci
American Scientist — Amer Scient
American Scientist — AMSCA
American Scientist — AMSCAC
American Scientist — ASci
American Scientist — IASC
American Secondary Education — Am Sec Educ
American Section. International Solar Energy Society. Proceedings. Annual Meeting — Am Sect Int Sol Energy Soc Proc Annu Meet
American Sephardi — Am Seph
American Sheep Breeder and Wool Grower — Am Sheep B & W
American Shipper — Am Shipp
American Showcase — Am Show
American Silk Grower and Agriculturist — Amer Silk Grower Agric
American Silk Grower and Farmer's Manual — Amer Silk Grower Farmers Manual
American Silk Journal — Am Silk J
American Silk Rayon Journal — Am Silk Rayon J
American Slavic and East European Review — Am Sl
American Slavic and East European Review — Am Slavic R
American Slavic and East European Review — Amer Slav East Eur Rev
American Slavic and East European Review — Amer Slavic East Europe Rev
American Slavic and East European Review — ASEER
American Slavic Review — ASR
American Society for Abrasive Methods. National Technical Conference. Proceedings — Am Soc Abrasive Methods Natl Tech Conf Proc
American Society for Abrasive Methods. National Technical Conference. Proceedings — Amer Soc Abrasive Method Nat Tech Conf Proc
American Society for Composites. Technical Conference. Proceedings — Am Soc Compos Tech Conf Proc
American Society for Engineering Education. Computers in Education Division. Transactions — Am Soc Eng Educ COED Trans
American Society for Engineering Education. Computers in Education Division. Transactions — Am Soc Eng Educ Comput Educ Div Trans
American Society for Geriatric Dentistry. Journal — ASGJA
American Society for Horticultural Science. Journal — Am Soc Hort Sci J
American Society for Horticultural Science. Tropical Region. Proceedings — Am Soc Hortic Sci Trop Reg Proc
American Society for Information Science. Journal — Am Soc Inf Sci J
American Society for Information Science. Proceedings — Am Soc Inf Sci Proc
American Society for Information Science. Proceedings. Annual Meeting — Am Soc Inf Sci Proc Annu Meet
American Society for Information Science. Proceedings of the ASIS Annual Meeting — Am Soc Inf Sci Proc ASIS Annu Meet
American Society for Metals. Materials/Metalworking. Technology Series — Am Soc Met Mater Metalwork Technol Ser
American Society for Metals. Technical Report System — Am Soc Met Tech Rep Syst
American Society for Metals. Transactions Quarterly — Am Soc Met Trans Q
American Society for Microbiology. Eastern Pennsylvania Branch. Annual Symposium. Proceedings — Am Soc Microbiol East Pa Branch Annu Symp Proc
American Society for Microbiology. Eastern Pennsylvania Branch. Symposia — Am Soc Microbiol East Penn Br Symp
American Society for Microbiology. News — ASM News
American Society for Municipal Improvements. Proceedings — Am Soc Munic Imp
American Society for Municipal Improvements. Proceedings — Am Soc Munic Improv Proc
American Society for Nondestructive Testing. National Fall Conference — Am Soc Nondestr Test Natl Fall Conf
American Society for Psychical Research. Journal — Am Soc Psych Res J
American Society for Psychical Research. Journal — Am Soc Psychical Res J
American Society for Quality Control. Annual Technical Conference. Transactions — Amer Soc Quality Contr Tech Conf Trans
American Society for Quality Control. Chemical Division. Transactions — Am Soc Qual Control Chem Div Trans
American Society for Testing and Materials. Annual Book of ASTM Standards — Am Soc Test Mater Annu Book ASTM Stand
American Society for Testing and Materials. Book of ASTM Standards — Am Soc Test Mater ASTM Stand
American Society for Testing and Materials. Book of ASTM Standards — Am Soc Test Mater Book ASTM Stand
American Society for Testing and Materials. Book of ASTM Standards — ASTM Book ASTM Stand
American Society for Testing and Materials. Book of ASTM Standards with Related Material — Am Soc Test Mater Book ASTM Stand Relat Mater
American Society for Testing and Materials. Book of ASTM Tentative Standards — Am Soc Test Mater Book ASTM Tentative Stand
American Society for Testing and Materials. Bulletin — ASTM Bul
American Society for Testing and Materials. Data Series — Am Soc Test Mater Data Ser
American Society for Testing and Materials. Geotechnical Testing Journal — ASTM Geotechnical Testing Journal
American Society for Testing and Materials. Meeting. Preprints — ASTM Meet Prepr
American Society for Testing and Materials. Proceedings — Am Soc Test Mater Proc
American Society for Testing and Materials. Special Technical Publication — Am Soc Test Mater Spec Tech Publ
American Society for Testing and Materials. Special Technical Publication — Am Soc Testing and Materials Spec Tech Pub
American Society for Testing and Materials. Special Technical Publication — Am Soc Testing Materials Special Tech Pub
American Society for Testing and Materials. Special Technical Publication — ASTM Special Technical Publication
American Society for Testing and Materials. Symposium on Consistency — Am Soc Test Mater Symp Consistency
American Society for Testing and Materials. Symposium on Plastics — Am Soc Test Mater Symp Plast
American Society of Agricultural Engineers. Microfiche Collection — Am Soc Agric Eng Microfiche Collect
American Society of Agricultural Engineers. Paper — Am Soc Agric Eng Pap
American Society of Agricultural Engineers. Publication — Am Soc Agric Eng Publ
American Society of Agricultural Engineers. Transactions — Am Soc Ag Eng
American Society of Agricultural Engineers. Transactions — ASAE Trans
American Society of Agronomy. Journal — Am Soc Agron J
American Society of Agronomy. Special Publication — Am Soc Agron Spec Publ
American Society of Anesthesiologists. Newsletter — ASA Newsletter
American Society of Animal Production. Record of Proceedings. Annual Meeting — Am Soc Anim Prod Rec Proc Annu Meet
American Society of Animal Science. Western Section. Proceedings — Am Soc Anim Sci West Sect Proc
American Society of Animal Science. Western Section. Proceedings. Annual Meeting — Am Soc Anim Sci West Sect Proc Annu Meet
American Society of Artificial Internal Organs. Journal — Am Soc Artif Intern Organs J
American Society of Artificial Internal Organs. Transactions — Am Soc Artif Intern Organs Trans
American Society of Brewing Chemists. Proceedings — Am Soc Brew Chem Proc
American Society of Church History. Papers — Am Soc Church Hist Papers
American Society of Civil Engineers. City Planning Division. Journal — Am Soc Civ Eng City Plann Div J
American Society of Civil Engineers. Environmental Engineering Division. Journal — Am Soc Civ Eng Environ Eng Div J
American Society of Civil Engineers. Hydraulics Division. Annual Specialty Conference. Proceedings — Am Soc Civ Eng Hydraul Div Annu Spec Conf Proc
American Society of Civil Engineers. Journal. Energy Division — Am Soc Civ Eng J Energy Div
American Society of Civil Engineers. Journal of Urban Planning — Am Soc Civil Engrs Urb Plann
American Society of Civil Engineers. Journal. Structural Division — Am Soc Civ E J Struct Div
American Society of Civil Engineers. Proceedings — Am Soc C E Proc
American Society of Civil Engineers. Proceedings — Am Soc Civil Eng Proc
American Society of Civil Engineers. Proceedings. Engineering Issues. Journal of Professional Activities — Am Soc Civ Eng Proc Eng Issues J Prof Act
American Society of Civil Engineers. Proceedings. Journal. Construction Division — Am Soc Civil Engrs Constr
American Society of Civil Engineers. Proceedings. Journal. Geotechnical Division — Am Soc Civil Engrs Geotech
American Society of Civil Engineers. Proceedings. Journal. Geotechnical Engineering Division — Am Soc Civil Eng Proc J Geotech Eng Div
American Society of Civil Engineers. Proceedings. Journal. Hydraulics Division — Am Soc Civ Eng Proc J Hydraul Div
American Society of Civil Engineers. Proceedings. Journal. Hydraulics Division — Am Soc Civil Engineers Proc Jour Hydraulics Div
American Society of Civil Engineers. Proceedings. Journal. Irrigation and Drainage Division — Am Soc Civ Eng Proc J Irrig Drain Div
American Society of Civil Engineers. Proceedings. Journal of Transportation Engineering — Am Soc Civil Engrs Transpn
American Society of Civil Engineers. Proceedings. Journal. Sanitary Engineering Division — Am Soc Civil Engineers Proc Jour Sanitary Eng Div
American Society of Civil Engineers. Proceedings. Journal. Structural Division — Am Soc Civil Engineers Proc Jour Structural Div

American Society of Civil Engineers. Proceedings. Journal. Structural Division — Am Soc Civil Engrs Struct
American Society of Civil Engineers. Proceedings. Journal. Surveying and Mapping Division — Am Soc Civil Engineers Proc Jour Surveying and Mapping Div
American Society of Civil Engineers. Proceedings. Transportation Engineering Journal — Am Soc Civ Eng Proc Transp Eng J
American Society of Civil Engineers. Proceedings. Transportation Engineering Journal — ASCE Proc Transp Eng J
American Society of Civil Engineers. Transactions — Am Soc Civ Eng Trans
American Society of Civil Engineers. Transactions — Am Soc Civil Engineers Trans
American Society of Civil Engineers. Transportation Engineering Journal — Am Soc Civ E Transp Eng J
American Society of Civil Engineers. Waterway, Port, Coastal, and Ocean Division — Am Soc Civ E J Waterway Port Div
American Society of Clinical Pathologists. Summary Report — Am Soc Clin Pathol Sum Rep
American Society of Heating and Ventilating Engineers. Guide — Am Soc Heat Vent Eng Guide
American Society of Heating, Refrigerating, and Air-Conditioning Engineers. ASHRAE Handbook and Product Directory — Am Soc Heat Refrig Air Cond Eng ASHRAE Handb Prod Dir
American Society of Heating, Refrigerating, and Air-Conditioning Engineers. Bulletin — ASHRAE B
American Society of Heating, Refrigerating, and Air-Conditioning Engineers. Handbook of Fundamentals — ASHRAE Handb Fundam
American Society of Heating, Refrigerating, and Air-Conditioning Engineers. Journal — Am Soc Heat Refrig Air Cond Eng J
American Society of Heating, Refrigerating, and Air-Conditioning Engineers. Journal — ASHRAE J
American Society of Heating, Refrigerating, and Air-Conditioning Engineers. Journal — ASHRAE Jol
American Society of Heating, Refrigerating, and Air-Conditioning Engineers. Transactions — Am Soc Heat Refrig Air Cond Eng Trans
American Society of Heating, Refrigerating, and Air-Conditioning Engineers. Transactions — ASHRAE Trans
American Society of Hypertension Symposium Series — Amer Soc Hypertens Symp Ser
American Society of International Law. Proceedings — Am Soc Int L Proc
American Society of International Law. Proceedings — Am Soc Int Law Proc
American Society of International Law. Proceedings — Am Soc Int'l L Proc
American Society of Limnology and Oceanography. Special Symposium — Am Soc Limnol Oceangr Spec Symp
American Society of Limnology and Oceanography. Special Symposium — Am Soc Limnol Oceanogr Spec Symp
American Society of Limnology and Oceanography. Special Symposium — ASLOBM
American Society of Lubrication Engineers. Special Publication — Am Soc Lubr Eng Spec Publ
American Society of Lubrication Engineers. Technical Preprints — Am Soc Lubr Eng Tech Prepr
American Society of Lubrication Engineers. Transactions — Am Soc Lubr Eng Trans
American Society of Mechanical Engineers. Aerospace Division. Publication AD — Am Soc Mech Eng Aerosp Div Publ AD
American Society of Mechanical Engineers and Metal Properties Council. Publication MPC — Am Soc Mech Eng Met Prop Counc Publ MPC
American Society of Mechanical Engineers. Applied Mechanics Division (AMD) — Am Soc Mech Eng Appl Mech Div (AMD)
American Society of Mechanical Engineers. Applied Mechanics Division. Applied Mechanics Symposia Series — Am Soc Mech Eng Appl Mech Div Appl Mech Symp Ser
American Society of Mechanical Engineers. Boiler and Pressure Vessel Code — ASME Boiler Pressure Vessel Code
American Society of Mechanical Engineers. Cavitation and Polyphase Flow Forum — Am Soc Mech Eng Cavitation Polyphase Flow Forum
American Society of Mechanical Engineers. Florida Section. Citrus Engineering Conference. Transactions — Am Soc Mech Eng Fla Sect Citrus Eng Conf Trans
American Society of Mechanical Engineers. Fluids Engineering Division. Publication FED — Am Soc Mech Eng Fluids Eng Div Publ FED
American Society of Mechanical Engineers. Heat Transfer Division. Publication HTD — Am Soc Mech Eng Heat Transfer Div Publ HTD
American Society of Mechanical Engineers. Internal Combustion Engine Division. Publication. ICE — Amer Soc Mech Eng Intern Combust Engine Div Publ ICE
American Society of Mechanical Engineers. Japan Society of Mechanical Engineers. Thermal Engineering Joint Conference. Proceedings — Am Soc Mech Eng Jpn Soc Mech Eng Therm Eng Jt Conf Proc
American Society of Mechanical Engineers. New Mexico Section. Proceedings. Annual ASME Symposium — Am Soc Mech Eng NM Sect Proc Annu ASME Symp
American Society of Mechanical Engineers. Papers — Am Soc Mech Eng Pap
American Society of Mechanical Engineers. Papers — ASME Pap
American Society of Mechanical Engineers. Papers — ASME Paper
American Society of Mechanical Engineers. Performance Test Codes — ASME Perform Test Codes
American Society of Mechanical Engineers. Pressure Vessels and Piping Division. Publication PVP — Am Soc Mech Eng Pressure Vessels Piping Div Publ PVP
American Society of Mechanical Engineers. Pressure Vessels and Piping Division. Publication PVP — Am Soc Mech Eng Pressure Vessels Piping Div PVP
American Society of Mechanical Engineers. Pressure Vessels and Piping Division. Publication PVP-PB — Am Soc Mech Eng Pressure Vessels Piping Div Publ PVP-PB
American Society of Mechanical Engineers. Pressure Vessels and Piping Division. Technical Report. PVP — Am Soc Mech Eng Pressure Vessels
American Society of Mechanical Engineers. Production Engineering Division. Publication PED — Am Soc Mech Eng Prod Eng Div Publ PED
American Society of Mechanical Engineers. Transactions — Am Soc Mechanical Engineers Trans
American Society of Mechanical Engineers. Transactions — ASME Trans
American Society of Mechanical Engineers. Transactions. Series F — ASME Trans Ser F
American Society of Mechanical Engineers. Transactions. Series I. — ASME Trans Ser I
American Society of Mechanical Engineers. Winter Annual Meeting — Am Soc Mech Eng Winter Annu Meet
American Society of Municipal Engineers. International Association of Public Works Officials. Yearbook — Am Soc Munic Eng Int Assoc Public Works Off Yearb
American Society of Municipal Engineers. Official Proceedings — Am Soc Munic Eng Off Proc
American Society of Naval Engineers. Journal — Am Soc Naval Eng J
American Society of Naval Engineers. Journal — Naval Engrs J
American Society of Photogrammetry. Annual Meeting. Proceedings — Am Soc Photogramm Annu Meet Proc
American Society of Photogrammetry. Fall Convention. Proceedings — Am Soc Photogramm Fall Conv Proc
American Society of Plastic and Reconstructive Surgeons. Educational Foundation. Proceedings of the Symposium — Am Soc Plast Reconstr Surg Educ Found Proc Symp
American Society of Psychosomatic Dentistry and Medicine. Journal — JPDMB
American Society of Refrigerating Engineers. Journal — Am Soc Refrig Eng J
American Society of Safety Engineers. Journal — Am Soc Safety Eng J
American Society of the Legion of Honor. Magazine — ASLH
American Society of the Legion of Honor. Magazine — ASLHM
American Society of Tool and Manufacturing Engineers. ASTME/ASM Western Metal and Tool Conference — ASTME/ASM West Metal Tool Conf
American Society of Tool and Manufacturing Engineers. ASTME Collected Papers — ASTME Collect Papers
American Society of Tool and Manufacturing Engineers. Creative Manufacturing Seminars. Technical Papers — ASTME Creative Mfg Semin Tech Papers
American Society of Tropical Medicine. Papers — Am Soc Trop Med Papers
American Society of University Composers. Proceedings — ASUC
American Society of Veterinary Clinical Pathologists. Bulletin — Am Soc Vet Clin Pathol Bull
American Society of Zoologists. Proceedings — Am Soc Zool Proc
American Sociological Review — A Soc R
American Sociological Review — Am Soc R
American Sociological Review — Am Soc Rev
American Sociological Review — Am Socio Rev
American Sociological Review — Am Sociol R
American Sociological Review — Am Sociol Rev
American Sociological Review — Am Sociological R
American Sociological Review — Amer Sociol R
American Sociological Review — Amer Sociol Rev
American Sociological Review — ASR
American Sociological Review — GASR
American Sociological Review. American Sociological Association — ASA/ASR
American Sociological Society. Papers and Proceedings — Am Sociol Soc Pap Proc
American Sociological Society. Publications — Am Sociol S
American Sociologist — Am Soc
American Sociologist — Am Sociol
American Sociologist — Am Sociologist
American Sociologist — Amer Sociol
American Sociologist — Amer Sociologist
American Spectator — Am Spect
American Spectator — Am Spectator
American Spectator — GASP
American Speech — Am Sp
American Speech — Am Speech
American Speech — Amer Sp
American Speech — AmS
American Speech — AS
American Speech — PASP
American Statistical Association. Journal — Am Stat Assn J
American Statistical Association. Journal — Am Statist Assn J
American Statistical Association. Proceedings of Business and Economic Statistics Section — ASA Pro Bu Ec
American Statistical Association. Proceedings of Social Statistics Section — ASA Pro So St
American Statistical Association. Proceedings of Statistical Computing Section — ASA Pro St Cp
American Statistical Association. Publications — Am Statist Assn Publ
American Statistical Association. Quarterly Publications — Am Stat Assoc Quar Publ
American Statistical Association. Quarterly Publications — Am Statis Assn
American Statistician — Am Stat
American Statistician — Am Statistician
American Statistician — Am Statistn
American Statistician — Amer Stat
American Statistician — Amer Statist
American Statistician — AST
American Statistics Index — Am Stat Index

American Statistics Index — Amer Stat Ind
American Statistics Index [*Database*] — ASI
American Stock Exchange Guide. Commerce Clearing House — Am Stock Ex Guide CCH
American Stockman — Am Stockman
American Stomatologist — Am Stomat
American String Teacher — AS
American String Teacher — AST
American Student Dental Association. News — ASDA News
American Studies — Am Stud
American Studies — Amer Stud
American Studies — AmerS
American Studies — AmS
American Studies — AmSt
American Studies — ASS
American Studies — PASU
American Studies in Papyrology — Am St P
American Studies in Papyrology — ASP
American Studies in Papyrology — ASPap
American Studies in Scandinavia — Am Stud Sc
American Studies International — Am Stud Int
American Studies International — ASInt
American Studies International — PASI
American Sugar Industry — Am Sugar Ind
American Surgeon — Am Surg
American Surgeon — Am Surgeon
American Surgeon — AMSUA
American Surgeon — AMSUAW
American Surgical Association. Transactions — Am Surg Assn Trans
American Suzuki Journal — Am Suzuki J
American Suzuki Journal — ASJ
American Swedish Historical Foundation. Yearbook — ASHFY
American Swedish Historical Foundation. Yearbook — ASHY
American Swedish Monthly — ASM
American Swimming — AM Swim
American Symphony Orchestra League. Newsletter — ASOL
American Taxpayers' Quarterly — Am Taxp Q
American Teacher — Am Tcr
American Teacher — Am Teach
American Telephone Journal — Am Teleph J
American Themis — Am Themis
American Theological Library Association. Newsletter — Am Theol Lib Assn Newsl
American Theological Library Association. Proceedings — ATLA Pro
American Thresherman — Am Thresherman
American Tomato Yearbook — Am Tom Yb
American Transcendental Quarterly — Am Transcen
American Transcendental Quarterly — AmTQ
American Transcendental Quarterly — ATQ
American Traveler — Am Trav
American Trial Lawyers Journal — Am Trial Law J
American Trial Lawyers Journal — ATL L J
American Trust Review of the Pacific — Am Trust Rev Pacific
American Tung News — Am Tung News
American Tung Oil Topics — Am Tung Oil Top
American Universities Field Staff Reports. Africa. Central and Southern Africa Series — Amer Univ Fieldstaff Rep Africa Cent Sth Afr Ser
American Universities Field Staff Reports. Africa. West Africa Series — Amer Univ Fieldstaff Rep Africa W Afr Ser
American Universities Field Staff. Reports. Asia — Am Univ Field Staff Rep Asia
American Universities Field Staff. Reports. East Asia Series — AUFS EA
American Universities Field Staff. Reports. North America — Am Univ Field Staff Rep North Am
American Universities Field Staff. Reports Series — AUFSRS
American Universities Field Staff. Reports. South America — Am Univ Field Staff Rep South Am
American Universities Field Staff. Reports. South Asia Series — AUFS SA
American Universities Field Staff. Reports. Southeast Asia Series — AUFS SEA
American University Law Review — Am U L Rev
American University Law Review — Am ULR
American University Law Review — Am Univ L Rev
American University Law Review — Amer Univ L Rev
American University Law Review — AULR
American University of Beirut. Faculty of Agricultural Sciences. Publication — Am Univ Beirut Fac Agric Sci Publ
American University Studies. Series V. Philosophy — Amer Univ Stud Ser V Philos
American Vegetable Grower — Am Veg Grow
American Vegetable Grower — Am Veg Grower
American Vegetable Grower — Amer Veg Grower
American Vegetable Grower and Greenhouse Grower — Am Veg Grow Greenhouse Grow
American Veterinary Medical Association. Journal — Am Vet Med Assn J
American Veterinary Medical Association. Proceedings — Am Vet Med Assn Proc
American Veterinary Medical Association. Scientific Proceedings of the Annual Meeting — Am Vet Med Assoc Sci Proc Annu Meet
American Veterinary Medical Association. Scientific Proceedings of the Annual Meeting — AVPMAM
American Veterinary Review — Am Vet Rev
American Vinegar Industry — Am Vinegar Ind
American Vinegar Industry and Fruit Products Journal — Am Vinegar Ind Fruit Prod J
American Visions — GAMV
American Vocational Journal — Am Voc J
American Water Resources Association. Proceedings Series — Am Water Resour Assoc Proc Ser
American Water Resources Association. Symposium. Proceedings — Am Water Resour Assoc Symp Proc
American Water Resources Association. Technical Publication Series. TPS-85-1 — Am Water Resour Assoc Tech Publ Ser TPS-85-1
American Water Resources Association. Technical Publication Series. TPS-85-2 — Am Water Resour Assoc Tech Publ Ser TPS-85-2
American Water Works Association. Annual Conference. Proceedings — Am Water Works Assoc Annu Conf Proc
American Water Works Association. Disinfection Seminar. Proceedings — Am Water Works Assoc Disinfect Semin Proc
American Water Works Association. Journal — Am Water Works Assn J
American Water Works Association. Journal — Am Water Works Assoc J
American Water Works Association. Journal — JAWWA5
American Water Works Association. Journal. Southeastern Section — Am Water Works Assoc Jour Southeastern Sec
American Water Works Association. Ontario Section. Proceedings. Annual Conference — Am Water Works Assoc Ont Sect Proc Annu Conf
American Water Works Association. Seminar on Water Treatment Waste Disposal. Proceedings — Am Water Works Assoc Semin Water Treat Waste Disposal Proc
American Water Works Association. Technology Conference Proceedings — Am Water Works Assoc Technol Conf Proc
American Welding Society. Journal — Am Weld Soc J
American Welding Society. Publication — Am Weld Soc Publ
American Welding Society. Publication AWS A.58-76 — Am Weld Soc Publ AWS A.58-76
American Welding Society. Standards — Amer Welding Soc Stand
American West — Am West
American West — Amer West
American West — AW
American Whig Review — Am Whig R
American Wine and Liquor Journal — Am Wine Liquor J
American Wine Society. Journal — Am Wine Soc J
American Women Composers Newsletter — AWCN
American Wood-Preservers' Association. Proceedings. Annual Meeting — Am Wood Preserv Assoc Proc Annu Meet
American Woods. United States Forest Service — Amer Woods US For Serv
American Wool and Cotton Reporter — Am Wool Cotton Rep
American Wool, Cotton, and Financial Reporter — Am Wool Cotton Financ Rep
American Year Review — AYR
American Zinc Institute. Journal — Am Zinc Inst J
American Zionist Federation. News and Views — Am Zion Fed News Views
American Zoologist — Am Zool
American Zoologist — Am Zoolog
American Zoologist — Am Zoologist
American Zoologist — Amer Zool
American Zoologist — AMZOA
American Zoologist — AMZOAF
American Zoologist — PAZO
Americana — Am
Americana — GAMR
Americana Annual — Am Ann
Americana Illustrated — Am Ill
Americana Norvegica — AN
Americana-Austriaca. Beitraege zur Amerikakunde — AAus
American-German Review — AGR
American-Scandinavian Review — Am Scand R
American-Scandinavian Review — ASR
American-Soviet Science Society. Science Bulletin — Am Sov Sci Soc Sci Bull
Americas — AAU
Americas — Am
Americas — AMRIA
[*The*] **Americas: A Quarterly Review of Inter-American Cultural History** — AM
[*The*] **Americas: A Quarterly Review of Inter-American Cultural History** — AmF
[*The*] **Americas: A Quarterly Review of Inter-American Cultural History** — AMS
[*The*] **Americas: A Quarterly Review of Inter-American Cultural History** — TAm
[*The*] **Americas. Academy of American Franciscan History** — AAFH/TAM
Americas (English Edition) — GAMS
Americas (Espanol) — AMSE
Americas. Organizacion de los Estados Americanos (Washington, DC) — Am OEA Span Wash
Americas. Organization of American States — Am OAS
Americas Review (Texas) — ART
America's Textiles — Am Text
America's Textiles — Am Textil
America's Textiles International — Am Text Int
America's Textiles. Knitter/Apparel Edition — Am Textil Knit Ap Ed
America's Textiles Reporter — Am Text Rep
America's Textiles Reporter/Bulletin Edition — Am Text Rep Bull Ed
America's Textiles Reporter/Bulletin Edition — Textil Rep
Americas (Washington, DC) — Ams Wash
Americn Scandinavian Review — Am Sca R
Amerikastudien [*American Studies*] — Amerikastud
Amerikastudien [*American Studies*] — Amst
Amerindian — AMIN
Amerique Francaise — AF
Amersand's Entertainment Guide — Ampersand Ent Gd
Amer-Scandinavian Review — AMSR
Ames Laboratory. Bulletin Series — Ames Lab Bull Ser
AMEX-Canada — AMEX
Amherst Papyri — P Amh
AMHS [*American Material Handling Society*] **Journal** — AMHSJ
AMI [*Institute fuer Arzneimittel*]-**Berichte** — AMI Ber

Ami des Champs. Societe Philomathique de Bordeaux — Ami Champs
Ami des Jardins — Ami Jard
Amico dell'Arte Cristiana — AAC
Amicus — Ami
AMINCO [*American Instrument Company*] **Laboratory News** — AMINCO Lab News
Amine Fluorescence Histochemistry. Scandinavia-Japan Seminar — Amine Fluores Histochem Scand Jpn Seminar
Amino Acid and Nucleic Acid — HATAA4
Amino Acid Transport and Uric Acid Transport Symposium — Amino Acid Transp Uric Acid Transp Symp
Amino Acids and Peptides — Amino Acids Pept
Amino Acids in Animal Husbandry. International Symposium. Reports — Amino Acids Anim Husb Int Symp Rep
Amino Acids, Peptide, and Protein Abstracts — AAPP Abstr
Amino Acids, Peptide, and Protein Abstracts — Amino Acids Pept Prot Abstr
Amino Acids, Peptides, and Proteins — Amino Acids Pept Proteins
Amino-Acids, Peptides, and Proteins — Am Ac Pep Prot
Aminokisloty v Zhivotnovodstve Mezhdunarodnyi Simpozium. Doklady — Aminokisloty Zhivotnovod Mezhdunar Simp Dokl
Aminosaeuren in Tierzucht. Internationales Symposium. Vortraege — Aminosaeuren Tierz Int Symp Vortr
Amis du Film et de la Television — AMIS
Amitie Charles Peguy. Feuillets Mensels — Am Ch P
Amitie Charles Peguy. Feuillets Mensuels — ACPFM
Amities France-Israel — AFI
AMMOHOUSE [*Ammunition House*] **Bulletin** — AMMOHOUSE Bull
AMMOHOUSE [*Ammunition House*] **Bulletin** — AMOBAN
Ammonia Plant Safety and Related Facilities — Ammonia Plant Saf
Amor de Libro — AdL
Amor de Libro — ALi
Amor de Libro — Am Li
Amor de Libro — AmL
Amorphous and Liquid Materials — Amorphous Liq Mater
Amorphous and Liquid Semiconductors — Amorphous Liq Semicond
Amorphous and Liquid Semiconductors. Proceedings. International Conference — Amorphous Liq Semicond Proc Int Conf
Amorphous Magnetism. Proceedings. International Symposium on Amorphous Magnetism — Amorphous Magn Proc Int Symp
Amorphous Materials. Modeling of Structure and Properties. Proceedings. Symposium — Amorphous Mater Model Struct Prop Proc Symp
Amorphous Materials. Papers Presented. International Conference on the Physics of Non-Crystalline Solids — Amorphous Mater Pap Int Conf Phys Non Cryst Solids
Amorphous Metals and Semiconductors. Proceedings. International Workshop — Amorphous Met Semicond Proc Int Workshop
Amorphous Semiconductors — Amorphous Semicond
Amorphous Semiconductors. Proceedings. International Conference — Amorphous Semicond Proc Int Conf
Amoxycillin (BRL 2333) Papers. International Symposium — Amoxycillin (BRL 2333) Pap Int Symp
AMP [*Australian Mutual Provident Society*] **News and Views** — AMP News
Ampere International Summer School on Magnetic Resonance in Chemistry and Biology — Ampere Int Summer Sch Magn Reson Chem Biol
Ampere International Summer School. Proceedings — Ampere Int Summer Sch Proc
Amphibia-Reptilia — Amphib Reptilia
Amphibia-Reptilia — AMREEH
AMPI (Association of Medical Physicists of India) Medical Physics Bulletin — AMPI (Assoc Med Phys India) Med Phys Bull
Ampurias — Amp
AMRC [*Australian Meat Research Committee*] **Review** — AMRC Rev
AMRC Review (Australian Meat Research Committee) — AMRC Rev Aust Meat Res Comm
AMSAC [*American Society of African Culture*] **Newsletter** — AMSAC
Amstblatt der Stadt Wien — Amtsbl Wien
Amstelodamum — Amstel
Amsterdam Classics in Linguistics — A Cl L
Amsterdam Classics in Linguistics — ACL
Amsterdam Studies in the Theory and History of Linguistic Science — SHL
Amsterdam Studies in the Theory and History of Linguistic Science. Series III. Studies in the History of Linguistics — SHL-3
Amsterdam Studies in the Theory and History of Linguistic Science. Series IV. Current Issues in Linguistic Theory — Amst St IV
Amsterdam Studies in the Theory and History of Linguistic Science. Series IV. Current Issues in Linguistic Theory — CILT
Amsterdam Studies in the Theory and History of Linguistic Science. Series V. Library and Information Sources in Linguistics — LISL
Amsterdamer Beitraege zur Aelteren Germanistik — ABaeG
Amsterdamer Beitraege zur Aelteren Germanistik — ABAG
Amsterdamer Beitraege zur Alteren Germanistik — ABG
Amsterdamer Beitraege zur Neueren Germanistik — ABNG
Amsterdamer Publikationen zur Sprache und Literatur — APSL
Amsterdams Sociologisch Tijdschrift — Amsterdams Sociol Tijds
Amtliche Berichte aus den Koeniglichen Kunstsammlungen — Amtl Ber Kgl Kunsts
Amtliche Berichte. Koenigliche Kunstsammlungen [*Berlin*] — ABKK
Amtliche Berichte. Koenigliche Kunstsammlungen — Amtl Ber
Amtliche Berichte. Preussische Kunstsammlunge [*Berlin*] — ABPK
Amtliche Nachrichten des Reichsversicherungsamts — Amtl Nachr Reichsversichgsamt
Amtliche Sammlung der Bundesgesetze und Verordnungen der Schweizerischen Eidgenoessenschaft — AS
Amtliche Veterinaernachrichten — Amt Vet Nachr
Amtliche Zeitung. Deutscher Fleischer-Verband — Amtl Ztg Deutsch Fleischer-Verbandes
Amtlicher Bericht der Versammlung Deutscher Naturforscher und Aerzte — Amtl Ber Versamml Dtsch Naturforsch Aerzte
Amtlicher Bericht ueber die Versammlung Deutscher Naturforscher und Aerzte — Amtl Ber Versamml Deutsch Naturf Aerzte
Amtlicher Bericht ueber die Verwaltung der Sammlungen des Westpreussischen Provinzialmuseums [*Danzig*] — Amtl Ber Verw Smlgg Westpr Prov Mus
Amts- und Mitteilungsblatt. Bundesanstalt fuer Materialpruefung — Amts-Mitteilungsbl Bundesanst Materialpruef
Amts- und Mitteilungsblatt. Bundesanstalt fuer Materialpruefung (Berlin) — Amts Mitteilungsbl Bundesanst Materialpruef (Berlin)
Amts- und Mitteilungsblatt der Bundesanstalt fuer Materialforschung und -Pruefung — Amts Mitteilungsbl Bundesanst Materialforsch Pruef
Amtsblatt. Bayerisches Staatsministerium fuer Landesentwicklung und Umweltfragen — ABSUD
Amtsblatt. Bayerisches Staatsministerium fuer Landesentwicklung und Umweltfragen — Amtsbl Bayer Staatsminist Landesentwickl Umweltfragen
Amtsblatt der Evangelischen Kirche in Deutschland — ABl EKD
Amtsblatt des Bayerischen Staatsministeriums fuer Unterricht und Kultus — KMBl
Amtsblatt. Europaeische Gemeinschaften — Amtsbl Eur Gem
Amurskii Sbornik — Amur Sb
Amyloid and Amyloidosis. International Symposium on Amyloidosis — Amyloid Amyloidosis Int Symp Amyloidoisis
Amyloid and Amyloidosis. Proceedings. International Symposium on Amyloidosis — Amyloid Amyloidosis Proc Int Symp
Amyloidosis. EARS [*European Amyloidosis Research Symposium*]. Proceedings. European Amyloidosis Research Symposium — Amyloidosis EARS Proc Eur Amyloidosis Res Symp
Amyloidosis. Proceedings. International Symposium on Amyloidosis. The Disease Complex — Amyloidosis Proc Int Symp Amyloidosis Dis Complex
Amyloidosis. Proceedings of the Sigrid Juselius Foundation Symposium — Amyloidosis Proc Sigrid Juselius Found Symp
Amyotrophic Lateral Sclerosis Recent Research Trends. Conference on Research Trends in Amyotrophic Lateral Sclerosis — Amyotrophic Lateral Scler Conf
An American Wood — Am Wood
An Leabharlann — An Leab
An Leabharlann. Library Association of Ireland — An Leab Ir
ANA [*American Nurses' Association*] **Clinical Conferences** — ANA Clin Conf
ANA [*American Nurses' Association*] **Clinical Session** — ANA Clin Sess
Anadolu Arastirmalari — Anadolu Aras
Anadolu Arastirmalari — AnAr
Anadolu Arastirmalari. Jahrbuch fuer Kleinasiatische Forschung — Anadolu Aras Jahrb Klein Forsch
Anadolu Arastirmalari. Jahrbuch fuer Kleinasiatische Forschung — JKF
Anaerobes and Anaerobic Infections. Symposia. International Congress of Microbiology — Anaerobes Anaerobic Infect Symp Int Congr Microbiol
Anaerobic Bacteria. Role in Disease. International Conference on Anaerobic Bacteria — Anaerobic Bact Role Dis Int Conf
Anaerobic Digestion. Proceedings. International Symposium on Anaerobic Digestion — Anaerobic Dig Proc Int Symp
Anaesthesia — Anaesth
Anaesthesia — ANASA
Anaesthesia and Intensive Care — AINCBS
Anaesthesia and Intensive Care — Anaesth Intensive Care
Anaesthesia and Intensive Care — Anesth Intensive Care
Anaesthesia and Pharmacology, with a Special Section on Professional Hazards — Anaesth Pharmacol Spec Sect Prof Hazards
Anaesthesia, Resuscitation, and Intensive Therapy — Anaesth Resusc Intensive Ther
Anaesthesia Safety for All. Proceedings. World Congress of Anaesthesiologists — Anaesth Proc World Congr Anaesthesiol
Anaesthesie im Alter. Bericht. Symposium. Anaesthesie und Intensivtherapie — Anaesth Alter Ber Symp
Anaesthesie, Intensivtherapie, Notfallmedizin — Anaesth Intensivther Notfallmed
Anaesthesie, Intensivtherapie, Notfallmedizin — Anasth Intensivther Notfallmed
Anaesthesiologia es Intenziv Therapia — Anaesthesiol Intenziv Ther
Anaesthesiologica Sinica — Anaesthesiol Sin
Anaesthesiologica Sinica — Anaesthesiolo Sin
Anaesthesiologie und Intensivmedizin — Anaesthesiol Intensivmed
Anaesthesiologie und Intensivmedizin — ANIMD2
Anaesthesiologie und Intensivmedizin (Berlin) — Anaesthesiol Intensivmed (Berlin)
Anaesthesiologie und Intensivmedizin (Erlangen, Federal Republic of Germany) — Anaesthesiol Intensivmed (Erlangen Fed Repub Ger)
Anaesthesiologie und Reanimation. Zeitschrift fuer Anaesthesie, Intensivtherapie, und Dringliche Medizinische Hilfe — Anaesthesiol Reanim
Anaesthesiologie und Wiederbelebung — Anaesthesiol Wiederbeleb
Anaesthesiologie und Wiederbelebung — Anaesthesiol Wiederbelebung
Anaesthesiologie und Wiederbelebung — ANWIAN
Anaesthesiologische Informationen — Anaesthesiol Inf
Anaesthesiologische und Intensivmedizinische Praxis — Anaesthesiol Intensivmed Prax
Anaesthesiologische und Intensivmedizinische Praxis — Anasthesiol Intensivmed Prax
Anaesthesiology and Intensive Care Medicine — Anaesthesiol Intensive Care Med
Anaesthesiology and Intensive Care Medicine — ANIMD2
Anaesthesiology and Resuscitation — Anaesthesiol Resusc
Anaesthesiology and Resuscitation — Anaesthesiol Resuscitation
Anaesthesiology. Proceedings of the World Congress of Anaesthesiologists — Anaesthesiol Proc World Congr Anaesthesiol
Anaesthesiology. Proceedings of the World Congress of Anaesthesiology — Anaesthesiol Proc World Congr

Anaesthesist — Anaesth
Anaesthesist — ANATAE
Anais — An
Anais. Academia Brasileira de Ciencias — AABCAD
Anais. Academia Brasileira de Ciencias — An Ac Brasi
Anais. Academia Brasileira de Ciencias — An Acad Bras Cienc
Anais. Academia Brasileira de Ciencias — An Acad Brasil Ci
Anais. Academia Brasileira de Ciencias — An Acad Brasil Cienc
Anais. Academia Brasileira de Ciencias — Anais Acad Bras Cienc
Anais. Academia Portuguesa da Historia — AAPH
Anais. Academia Portuguesa da Historia — An Acad Port Hist
Anais. Associacao Brasileira de Quimica — An Assoc Bras Quim
Anais. Associacao Quimica do Brasil — An Assoc Quim Bras
Anais Azevedos — An Azevedos
Anais Azevedos — ANAZAW
Anais. Biblioteca Nacional [*Rio De Janeiro*] — ABN
Anais. Bibliotecas e Arquivos de Portugal — ABAP
Anais Botanicos. Herbario "Barbosa Rodrigues" — ABHRAR
Anais Botanicos. Herbario "Barbosa Rodrigues" — An Bot Herb "Barbosa Rodrigues"
Anais Brasileiros de Dermatologia — ABDEB3
Anais Brasileiros de Dermatologia — An Bras Dermatol
Anais Brasileiros de Dermatologia e Sifilografia — ABDSAA
Anais Brasileiros de Dermatologia e Sifilografia — An Bras Dermatol Sifilogr
Anais Brasileiros de Ginecologia — An Bras Gin
Anais Brasileiros de Ginecologia [*Brazil*] — An Bras Ginecol
Anais Brasileiros de Ginecologia. Sociedade Brasileira de Ginecologia — Anais Brasil Ginecol
Anais. Conferencia de Fisico-Quimica Organica — An Conf Fis Quim Org
Anais. Congresso Brasiliero de Ceramica e III Iberoamericano de Ceramica, Vidrios, y Refractarios — An Congr Bras Ceram III Iberoam Ceram Vidrios Refract
Anais. Congresso Estadual de Quimica Technologica — An Congr Estadual Quim Technol
Anais. Congresso Latino-Americano de Engenharia e Equipamentos para as Industrias de Petroleo e Petroquimica — An Congr Lat Am Eng Equip Ind Pet Petroquim
Anais. Congresso Latino-Americano de Zoologia — ACLZAA
Anais. Congresso Latino-Americano de Zoologia — An Cong Lat-Am Zool
Anais. Congresso Nacional. Sociedade Botanica do Brasil — ABOBAE
Anais. Congresso Nacional. Sociedade Botanica do Brasil — An Cong Nac Soc Bot Bras
Anais. Congresso Panamericano de Engenharia de Minas e Geologia — An Congr Panam Eng Minas Geol
Anais da Academia Brasileira da Ciencias (Rio de Janeiro) — An Acad Bras Cien Rio
Anais da Academia Politecnica do Porto — AAPP
Anais da Sociedade Brasileira de Filosofia (Rio de Janeiro) — An Soc Bras Filos Rio
Anais da Sociedade de Biologia de Pernambuco — Anais Soc Biol Pernambuco
Anais da Universidade do Brasil (Rio de Janeiro) — An Univ Bras Rio
Anais de Farmacia e Quimica — An Farm Quim
Anais de Farmacia e Quimica de Sao Paulo — AFQSAZ
Anais de Farmacia e Quimica de Sao Paulo — An Farm Quim Sao Paulo
Anais de Historia — An Hist
Anais de Microbiologia — An Micr
Anais de Microbiologia — An Microbiol
Anais de Microbiologia (Rio De Janeiro) — An Microbiol (Rio De J)
Anais do Instituto Superior de Agronomia. Universidade Tecnica de Lisboa — An Inst Super Agron Univ Tec Lisboa
Anais do Municipio de Faro — AMF
Anais. Encontro Nacional de Fisica de Reatores e Termoidraulica — An Encontro Nac Fis Reatores Termoidraulica
Anais. Escola de Agronomia e Veterinaria. Universidade Federal de Goias — An Esc Agron Vet Univ Fed Goias
Anais. Escola Nacional de Saude Publica e de Medicina Tropical — An Esc Nac Saude Publica Med Trop
Anais. Escola Nacional de Saude Publica e de Medicina Tropical — ENSABO
Anais. Escola Nacional de Saude Publica e de Medicina Tropical (Lisbon) — An Esc Nac Saude Publica Med Trop (Lisbon)
Anais. Escola Superior de Agricultura "Luiz De Queiroz" — An Esc Super Agr "Luiz De Queiroz"
Anais. Escola Superior de Agricultura Luiz de Queiroz — An Esc Super Agric Luiz de Queiroz
Anais. Escola Superior de Agricultura "Luiz De Queiroz" — Anais Esc Sup Agric "Luiz Queiroz"
Anais. Escola Superior de Agricultura "Luiz De Queiroz." Universidade de Sao Paulo — AESQAW
Anais. Escola Superior de Agricultura "Luiz De Queiroz." Universidade de Sao Paulo — An Esc Super Agric "Luiz De Queiroz" Univ Sao Paulo
Anais. Escola Superior de Medicina Veterinaria [*Lisbon*] — ASMVAD
Anais. Escola Superior de Medicina Veterinaria (Lisbon) — An Esc Super Med Vet (Lisb)
Anais. Escola Superior de Quimica. Universidade do Recife — An Esc Super Quim Univ Recife
Anais. Faculdade de Ciencias. Universidade do Porto — AFPOAI
Anais. Faculdade de Ciencias. Universidade do Porto — An Fac Ci Univ Porto
Anais. Faculdade de Ciencias. Universidade do Porto — An Fac Cienc Univ Porto
Anais. Faculdade de Ciencias. Universidade do Porto — Anais Fac Cienc Porto
Anais. Faculdade de Farmacia do Porto — AFFPA5
Anais. Faculdade de Farmacia do Porto — An Fac Farm Porto
Anais. Faculdade de Farmacia e Odontologia. Universidade de Sao Paulo — AFFSAE
Anais. Faculdade de Farmacia e Odontologia. Universidade de Sao Paulo — An Fac Farm Odontol Univ Sao Paulo
Anais. Faculdade de Farmacia. Universidade do Recife — An Fac Farm Univ Recife
Anais. Faculdade de Farmacia. Universidade Federal de Pernambuco — An Fac Farm Univ Fed Pernambuco
Anais. Faculdade de Medicina. Bahia. Universidade da Bahia — An Fac Med Bahia Univ Bahia
Anais. Faculdade de Medicina de Porto Alegre — AFAMA5
Anais. Faculdade de Medicina de Porto Alegre — An Fac Med Porto Alegre
Anais. Faculdade de Medicina e Cirurgia — Anais Fac Med
Anais. Faculdade de Medicina. Universidade de Sao Paulo — AFMDA4
Anais. Faculdade de Medicina. Universidade de Sao Paulo — An Fac Med Univ Sao Paulo
Anais. Faculdade de Medicina. Universidade do Parana [*Curitiba*] — AMIPAZ
Anais. Faculdade de Medicina. Universidade do Parana (Curitiba) — An Fac Med Univ Parana (Curitiba)
Anais. Faculdade de Medicina. Universidade do Recife — AMURAX
Anais. Faculdade de Medicina. Universidade do Recife — An Fac Med Univ Recife
Anais. Faculdade de Medicina. Universidade Federal de Minas Gerais [*Belo Horizonte*] — AFMMAV
Anais. Faculdade de Medicina. Universidade Federal de Minas Gerais (Belo Horizonte) — An Fac Med Univ Fed Minas Gerais (Belo Horizonte)
Anais. Faculdade de Medicina. Universidade Federal de Pernambuco — AFUPBD
Anais. Faculdade de Medicina. Universidade Federal de Pernambuco — An Fac Med Univ Fed Pernambuco
Anais. Faculdade de Odontologia. Universidade Federal de Pernambuco — An Fac Odontol Univ Fed Pernambuco
Anais. Faculdade de Odontologia. Universidade Federal do Rio De Janeiro — An Fac Odontol Univ Fed Rio De J
Anais. Faculdade de Sciencias do Porto — Anais Fac Sci Porto
Anais. II Congresso Latino-Americano de Zoologia — Anais II Congr Latin-Amer Zool
Anais. Instituto de Higiene e Medicina Tropical — AIHTDH
Anais. Instituto de Higiene e Medicina Tropical [*Lisbon*] — An Inst Hig Med Trop
Anais. Instituto de Higiene e Medicina Tropical (Lisbon) — An Inst Hig Med Trop (Lisb)
Anais. Instituto de Medicina Tropical [*Lisbon*] — AIMTA5
Anais. Instituto de Medicina Tropical [*Lisbon*] — An Inst Med Trop
Anais. Instituto de Medicina Tropical (Lisbon) — An Inst Med Trop (Lisb)
Anais. Instituto de Medicina Tropical. Lisbon — An Inst Med Trop Lisbon
Anais. Instituto do Vinho do Porto — AIVP
Anais. Instituto do Vinho do Porto — An Inst Vinho Porto
Anais. Instituto Pinheiros — An Inst Pinheiros
Anais. Instituto Superior de Agronomia — AISA
Anais. Instituto Superior de Agronomia (Lisboa) — An Inst Agron (Lisboa)
Anais. Instituto Superior de Agronomia (Lisboa) — An Inst Super Agron (Lisboa)
Anais. Instituto Superior de Agronomia. Universidade Tecnica de Lisboa — An Inst Super Agron Univ Tec Lisb
Anais. Instituto Superior de Agronomia. Universidade Tecnica de Lisboa — Anais Inst Sup Agron Lisboa
Anais. Instituto Superior de Agronomia. Universidade Tecnica de Lisboa — Anais Inst Sup Agron Univ Tec Lisb
Anais. Junta de Investigacoes do Ultramar — An Junta Invest Ultramar
Anais. Junta de Investigacoes do Ultramar (Portugal) — An Junta Invest Ultramar (Port)
Anais. Ministerio do Ultramar. Junta de Investigacoes do Ultramar (Portugal) — An Minist Ultramar Junta Invest Ultramar Port
Anais. Municipio de Faro — An Mun Faro
Anais Paranaenses de Tuberculose e Doencas Toracicas — An Parana Tuber Doencas Torac
Anais Paulistas de Medicina e Cirurgia — An Paul Med Cir
Anais Paulistas de Medicina e Cirurgia — APMCA3
Anais Paulistas de Medicina e Cirurgia. Suplemento — An Paul Med Cir Supl
Anais. Reuniao de Fitossanitarisatas do Brasil — An Reun Fitossanit Bras
Anais. Reuniao de Fitossanitarisatas do Brasil — An Reuniao Fitossanit Brasil
Anais. Reuniao de Fitossanitarisatas do Brasil — RFBABQ
Anais. Santa Casa de Santos — An St Casa Santos
Anais. Seminario Brasileiro de Herbicidas e Ervas Daninhas — An Seminar Brasil Herbic Ervas Danin
Anais. Simposio Anual da ACIESP (Academia de Ciencias do Estado de Sao Paulo) — An Simp Anu ACIESP
Anais. Simposio Brasileiro de Eletroquimica e Eletroanalitica — An Simp Bras Eletroquim Eletroanal
Anais. Simposio de Quimica do Vale do Rio Doce — An Simp Quim Vale Rio Doce
Anais. Simposio Internacional sobre Tecnologia dos Alcoois como Combustivel — An Simp Int Tecnol Alcoois Combust
Anais. Sociedade Botanica do Brasil — An Soc Bot Bras
Anais. Sociedade de Biologia de Pernambuco — An Soc Biol Pernambuco
Anais. Sociedade de Biologia de Pernambuco — ANBPA7
Anais. Sociedade de Medicina de Pernambuco — AMPBAS
Anais. Sociedade de Medicina de Pernambuco — An Soc Med Pern
Anais. Sociedade de Medicina de Pernambuco — An Soc Med Pernambuco
Anais. Sociedade Entomologica do Brasil — An Soc Entomol Bras
Anais. Sociedade Entomologica do Brasil — Anais Soc Ent Brasil
Anais. Sociedade Entomologica do Brasil — ASENBI
Analabs, Incorporated. Research Notes — Analabs Res Notes
Anale. Institutul Central de Cercetari Agricole. Sectiei de Economice Agricole (Bucharest) — An Inst Cent Cercet Agr Sect Econ Agr (Bucharest)
Anale. Institutul Central de Cercetari Agricole. Sectiei de Pedologie — Anal Inst Cent Cerc Agric Sect Pedol

Anale. Institutul Central de Cercetari Agricole. Sectiei de Protectia Plantelor — An Inst Cent Cercet Agr Sect Prot Plant
Anale. Institutul Central de Cercetari Agricole. Seria B. Porumbul Dublu Hibrid — An Inst Cent Cercet Agric Ser B
Anale. Institutul Central de Cercetari Agricole. Series A (Bucharest) — An Inst Cent Cercet Agr Ser A (Bucharest)
Anale. Institutul Central de Cercetari Agricole. Series B (Bucharest) — An Inst Cent Cercet Agr Ser B (Bucharest)
Anale. Institutul Central de Cercetari Agricole. Series C (Bucharest) — An Inst Cent Cercet Agr Ser C (Bucharest)
Anale. Institutul de Cercetari pentru Cultura Cartofului si Sfeclei de Zahar (Brasov). Cartoful — An Inst Cercet Cul Cartofului Sfeclei Zahar (Brasov) Cartofu
Anale. Statiunea Centrala de Apicultura si Sericultura — Anale Stat Cent Apic Seri
Anale. Universitatea din Craiova. Seria Matematica, Fizica, Chimie, Electrotehnica — An Mat Fiz Chim Electroteh Univ Craiova
Anale. Universitatea din Craiova. Seria Matematica, Fizica, Chimie, Electrotehnica — An Univ Craiova Ser Mat Fiz Chim Electroteh
Analecta Aegyptiaca — A Aeg
Analecta Aegyptiaca — AAe
Analecta Aegyptiaca [*Copenhagen*] — AnAeg
Analecta Ambrosiana — AAmb
Analecta Anselmiana — AAns
Analecta Augustiniana — AAug
Analecta Augustiniana — Anal Aug
Analecta Biblica [*Rome*] — AB
Analecta Biblica — An Bi
Analecta Biblica [*Rome*] — An Bib
Analecta Biblica — An Bibl
Analecta Boerhaaviana — Analecta Boer
Analecta Bollandiana — AB
Analecta Bollandiana — An B
Analecta Bollandiana — Anal Boll
Analecta Bollandiana — Anal Bolland
Analecta Bollandiana — AnBol
Analecta Bollandiana [*Brussels*] — AnBoll
Analecta Calsanctiana — Anac
Analecta Cartusiana — A Car
Analecta Cisterciensia — AC
Analecta Cisterciensia — ACi
Analecta Cisterciensia — ACist
Analecta Cisterciensia — An Cist
Analecta Cisterciensia — Anal Cist
Analecta Cracoviana [*Cracow*] — AnCracov
Analecta Farmacia Gerundense — Analecta Farm Gerund
Analecta Franciscana — Anal Fran
Analecta Franciscana — Anal Franc
Analecta Franciscana — Anal Francisc
Analecta Geologica — Analecta Geol
Analecta Gregoriana — Anal Greg
Analecta Hibernica — Anal Hib
Analecta Husserliana. Yearbook of Phenomenological Research — Anal Hus Yb
Analecta Hymnica Medii Aevi — AH
Analecta Linguistica — Anal Ling
Analecta Lovanensia — AnLov
Analecta Lovaniensia Biblica et Orientalia — ALBO
Analecta Malacitana — A Mal
Analecta Mediaevalia Namurcensia — AMN
Analecta Monastica — AMon
Analecta Monastica — Anal Mon
Analecta Montserratensia — AMontserr
Analecta Montserratensia — AMt
Analecta Montserratensia — Anal Mont
Analecta Ordinis Carmelitarum Discalceatorum — An OCD
Analecta Ordinis Sancti Basilii Magni — Analecta Ord S Bas Magni
Analecta Ordinis Sancti Basilii Magni — Ann OSBM
Analecta Ordinis Sancti Basilii Magni — AOSBM
Analecta Orientalia — Anal O
Analecta Orientalia — Anal Or
Analecta Orientalia — AOR
Analecta Orientalia. Commentationes Scientificae de Rebus Orientis Antiqui. Pontificium Institutum Biblicum [*Rome*] — AnOr
Analecta Praemonstratensia — Anal Praem
Analecta Praemonstratensia — AnPraem
Analecta Praemonstratensia — AP
Analecta Praemonstratensia — APr
Analecta Praemonstratensia — APraem
Analecta Romana Instituti Danici — An Rom
Analecta Romana Instituti Danici — Anal Rom
Analecta Romana Instituti Danici — ARID
Analecta Sacra Tarraconensia — A S Tarr
Analecta Sacra Tarraconensia [*Barcelona*] — AnSATarrac
Analecta Sacra Tarraconensia — AnST
Analecta Sacra Tarraconensia [*Barcelona*] — AnSTar
Analecta Sacra Tarraconensia — AST
Analecta Sacra Tarraconensia. Annuari de la Biblioteca Balmes — Anal Sacra Tarraconensia
Analecta Sacra Tarraconensia. Revista de Ciencias Historico-Eclesiasticas — Anal Sacr Tarrac
Analecta Sacra Tarraconensia. Revista de Ciencias Historico-Eclesiasticas — AT
Analecta Sacri Ordinis Cisterciensis — An O Cist
Analecta Sacri Ordinis Cisterciensis [*Roma*] — ASOC
Analecta Sacri Ordinis Fratrum Praedicatorum — AnFP
Analecta Tarraconensia — AT
Analecta Veterinaria — Analecta Vet
Analecta Veterinaria — ANVTAH
Analecten zur Belustigung, Belehrung, und Unterhaltung fuer Leser aus Allen Staenden — Analecten Belust
Analectes. Ordre de Premontre — AOP
Analectes pour Servir a l'Histoire Ecclesiastique de la Belgique — AHEB
Analectes pour Servir a l'Histoire Ecclesiastique de la Belgique — Analectes Hist Eccl Belg
Analectic Magazine — Anal M
Analectic Magazine — Analectic M
Analele Academiei Republicii Populare Romane — Analele Acad Republ Populare Romane
Analele Academiei Republicii Populare Romine — An Acad Repub Pop Rom
Analele Academiei Republicii Populare Romine. Memoriile. Seria B. Sectiunea de Stiinte Medicale — An Acad Repub Pop Rom Mem Ser B
Analele. Academiei Republicii Socialiste Romania — An Acad Repub Soc Rom
Analele. Academiei Romane — An Ac R
Analele. Academiei Romane — An Acad Rom
Analele. Academiei Romane — Anal Acad Rom
Analele Dobrogei — A Dobr
Analele Dobrogei — An D
Analele Dobrogei — An Dobr
Analele. Institutul Central de Cercetari Agricole. Sectiei de Pedologie — An Inst Cent Cercet Agric Sect Pedol
Analele. Institutul Central de Cercetari Agricole. Sectiei de Protectia Plantelor — An Inst Cent Cercet Agric Sect Prot Plant
Analele Institutului de Cercetari Agronomice — An Inst Cercet Agron
Analele. Institutului de Cercetari Agronomice. Academia Republicii Populare Romine — Anal Inst Cerc Agron
Analele Institutului de Cercetari Agronomice al Romaniei — An Inst Cercet Agron Rom
Analele Institutului de Cercetari Agronomice. Seria A. Agroclimatologie, Pedologie, Agrochimie si Imbunatatiri Funciare — An Inst Cercet Agron Ser A
Analele Institutului de Cercetari Agronomice. Seria C. Fiziolgie, Genetica, Ameliorare, Protectia Plantelor si Tehnologie Agricola — An Inst Cercet Agron Ser C
Analele. Institutului de Cercetari pentru Cereale si Plante Tehnice-Fundulea — An Inst Cercet Cereale Plante Teh-Fundulea
Analele. Institutului de Cercetari pentru Cereale si Plante Tehnice-Fundulea [*Romania*] — An Inst Cercet pentru Cereale Plante Teh-Fundulea
Analele. Institutului de Cercetari pentru Cereale si Plante Tehnice-Fundulea — Anal Inst Cerc pentru Cereale Pl Tehn-Fundulea
Analele. Institutului de Cercetari pentru Cereale si Plante Tehnice-Fundulea. Seria A — An Inst Cercet pentru Cereale Plante Teh-Fundulea Ser A
Analele. Institutului de Cercetari pentru Cereale si Plante Tehnice-Fundulea. Seria B — An Inst Cercet pentru Cereale Plante Teh-Fundulea Ser B
Analele. Institutului de Cercetari pentru Cereale si Plante Tehnice-Fundulea. Seria C — An Inst Cercet pentru Cereale Plante Teh-Fundulea Ser C
Analele. Institutului de Cercetari pentru Imbunatatiri Funciare si Pedologie. Seria Hidrotehnica — An Inst Cercet Imbunatatiri Funciare Pedol Ser Hidroteh
Analele. Institutului de Cercetari pentru Imbunatatiri Funciare si Pedologie. Seria Pedologie — An Inst Cercet Imbunatatiri Funciare Pedol Ser Pedol
Analele. Institutului de Cercetari pentru Pedologie si Agrochimie — An Inst Cercet Pedol Agrochim
Analele Institutului de Cercetari pentru Pedologie si Agrochimie. Academia de Stiinte Agricole si Silvice — An Inst Cercet Pedol Agrochim Acad Stiinte Agric Silvice
Analele. Institutului de Cercetari pentru Protectia Plantelor — An Inst Cercet Prot Plant
Analele. Institutului de Cercetari pentru Protectia Plantelor — Anal Inst Cerc Prot Plantelor
Analele. Institutului de Cercetari pentru Protectia Plantelor. Academia de Stiinte. Agricole si Silvice — An Inst Cercet Prot Plant Acad Stiinte Agric Silvice
Analele. Institutului de Cercetari pentru Protectia Plantelor. Institutul Central de Cercetari Agricole (Bucharest) — An Inst Cercet Prot Plant Inst Cent Cercet Agric (Bucharest)
Analele Institutului de Cercetari si Experimentatie Forestiera — Analele Inst Cercet Exp Forest
Analele. Institutului de Cercetari. Zootehnice — Anal Inst Cerc Zooteh
Analele. Institutului de Cercetari. Zootehnice (Bucharest) — An Inst Cercet Zooteh (Bucharest)
Analele. Institutului de Studii si Cercetari Pedologice — An Inst Stud Cercet Pedol
Analele Institutului de Studii si Cercetari Pedologice. Academia de Stiinte Agricole si Silvice — An Inst Stud Cercet Pedol Acad Stiinte Agric Silvice
Analele Institutului National Zootehnic al Romaniei — An Inst Natl Zooteh Rom
Analele Minelor din Romania — An Minelor Rom
Analele Observatorului Astronomic si Meteorologic — An Obs Astr Met
Analele Romano-Sovietice — ARS
Analele Romino-Sovietice — An Rom Sov
Analele. Sectiei de Pedologie. Institutul Central de Cercetari Agricole — An Sect Pedol Inst Cent Cercet Agric
Analele. Sectiei de Protectia Plantelor. Institutul Central de Cercetari Agricole (Bucharest) — An Sect Prot Plant Inst Cent Cercet Agric (Bucharest)
Analele Stiintifice ale Universitatii Al. I. Cuza din Iasi. Sectiunea 1. Matematica, Fizica, Chimie — ACIFA
Analele Stiintifice ale Universitatii Al. I. Cuza din Iasi. Sectiunea 1. Matematica, Fizica, Chimie [*Romania*] — An Stiint Univ Al I Cuza Iasi Sect 1
Analele Stiintifice ale Universitatii Al. I. Cuza din Iasi. Sectiunea 1a. Matematica [*Romania*] — An Stiint Univ Al I Cuza Iasi Sect 1a
Analele Stiintifice ale Universitatii Al. I. Cuza din Iasi. Sectiunea 1a. Matematica — AUZMA

Analele Stiintifice ale Universitatii Al. I. Cuza din Iasi. Sectiunea 1b. Fizica [*Romania*] — An Stiint Univ Al I Cuza Iasi Sect 1b
Analele Stiintifice ale Universitatii Al. I. Cuza din Iasi. Sectiunea 1b. Fizica — AUZFA
Analele Stiintifice ale Universitatii Al. I. Cuza din Iasi. Sectiunea 1b. Fizica. Seria Noua — An Sti Univ Al I Cuza Iasi Sect 1b Fiz
Analele Stiintifice ale Universitatii Al. I. Cuza din Iasi. Sectiunea 1b. Fizica. Seria Noua — An Stiint Univ Al I Cuza Iasi Sect 1b Fiz N S
Analele Stiintifice ale Universitatii Al. I. Cuza din Iasi. Sectiunea 1c. Chimie [*Romania*] — An Stiint Univ Al I Cuza Iasi Sect 1c
Analele Stiintifice ale Universitatii Al. I. Cuza din Iasi. Sectiunea 1c. Chimie — Anal Stiint Univ Cuza Iasi Chim
Analele Stiintifice ale Universitatii Al. I. Cuza din Iasi. Sectiunea 1c. Chimie — AUZCA
Analele Stiintifice ale Universitatii Al. I. Cuza din Iasi. Sectiunea 2. Biologie, Geologie, Geografie — An Stiint Univ Al I Cuza Iasi Sect 2 Biol Geol Geogr
Analele Stiintifice ale Universitatii Al. I. Cuza din Iasi. Sectiunea 2. Stiinte Naturale — An Stiint Univ Al I Cuza Iasi Sect 2
Analele Stiintifice ale Universitatii Al I Cuza din Iasi. Sectiunea 2. Stiinte Naturale — An Stiint Univ Al I Cuza Iasi Sect 2 Stiinte Nat
Analele Stiintifice ale Universitatii Al. I. Cuza din Iasi. Sectiunea 2a. Biologie [*Romania*] — An Stiint Univ Al I Cuza Iasi Sect 2a
Analele Stiintifice ale Universitatii Al. I. Cuza din Iasi. Sectiunea 2a. Biologie — An Stiint Univ Al I Cuza Iasi Sect 2a Biol
Analele Stiintifice ale Universitatii Al. I. Cuza din Iasi. Sectiunea 2a. Biologie — AUIBA
Analele Stiintifice ale Universitatii Al. I. Cuza din Iasi. Sectiunea 2b. Geologie — An Stiint Univ Al I Cuza Iasi Sect 2b
Analele Stiintifice ale Universitatii Al. I. Cuza din Iasi. Sectiunea 2c. Geografie — An Stiint Univ Al I Cuza Iasi Sect 2c
Analele Stiintifice ale Universitatii Al. I. Cuza din Iasi. Seria Noua. Sectiunea 1. Matematica — An Sti Univ Al I Cuza Iasi Sect 1 Mat
Analele Stiintifice ale Universitatii Al. I. Cuza din Iasi. Seria Noua. Sectiunea 1a. Matematica — An Stiint Univ Al I Cuza Iasi Sect 1a Mat
Analele Stiintifice ale Universitatii Al. I. Cuza din Iasi. Seria Noua. Sectiunea 1a. Matematica — An Stiint Univ Al I Cuza Iasi Sect 1a Mat NS
Analele Stiintifice ale Universitatii Al. I. Cuza din Iasi. Seria Noua. Sectiunea 3e (Stiinte Sociale). Lingvistica — AnUILingv
Analele Stiintifice ale Universitatii Al. I. Cuza din Iasi. Serie Noua. Sectiunea 3f. Literatura — AnUILit
Analele Stiintifice ale Universitatii Al. I. Cuza din Iasi. Stiinte Naturale. Biologia [*Romania*] — An Stiint Univ Al I Cuza Iasi Stiinte Nat Biol
Analele Stiintifice ale Universitatii (Iasi) — ASUI
Analele Stiintifice. Universitatii Ovidius Constanta — An Stiint Univ Ovidius Constanta Ser Mat
Analele. Universitatii Al. I. Cuza (Iasi) — AUI
Analele. Universitatii Bucuresti — AUB
Analele. Universitatii Bucuresti. Biologie Animala — ABBACG
Analele. Universitatii Bucuresti. Biologie Animala — An Univ Bucur Biol
Analele. Universitatii Bucuresti. Biologie Animala — An Univ Bucur Biol Anim
Analele Universitatii Bucuresti. Biologie Animala — An Univ Bucuresti Biol Anim
Analele. Universitatii Bucuresti. Biologie Animala — Anal Univ Buc Biol Anim
Analele. Universitatii Bucuresti. Biologie Vegetala — An Univ Bucur Biol Veg
Analele Universitatii Bucuresti. Biologie Vegetala — An Univ Bucuresti Biol Veg
Analele. Universitatii Bucuresti. Chimie — An Univ Bucur Chim
Analele. Universitatii Bucuresti. Chimie — AUBCB
Analele. Universitatii Bucuresti. Chimie — AUBCBI
Analele. Universitatii Bucuresti. Fizica — ABFZA
Analele. Universitatii Bucuresti. Fizica — An Univ Bucur Fiz
Analele. Universitatii Bucuresti. Fizica — An Univ Bucuresti Fiz
Analele. Universitatii Bucuresti. Geografie — An Univ Bucuresti Geogr
Analele. Universitatii Bucuresti. Geologie — ABGLA
Analele. Universitatii Bucuresti. Geologie — An Univ Bucur Geol
Analele. Universitatii Bucuresti. Geologie — An Univ Bucuresti Geol
Analele. Universitatii Bucuresti. Limba Literara — AUB-LLR
Analele. Universitatii Bucuresti. Limba si Literatura Romana — AUBLL
Analele. Universitatii Bucuresti. Limbi Clasice si Orientale — AUB-LCO
Analele. Universitatii Bucuresti. Limbi Germanice — AnUBLG
Analele. Universitatii Bucuresti. Limbi Germanice — AUB-LG
Analele. Universitatii Bucuresti. Limbi Romanice — AUBLR
Analele. Universitatii Bucuresti. Literatura Universala Comparata — AnUBLUC
Analele. Universitatii Bucuresti. Literatura Universala Comparata — AUB-LUC
Analele. Universitatii Bucuresti. Matematica — An Univ Bucuresti Mat
Analele. Universitatii Bucuresti. Matematica-Mecanica — ABMMC
Analele. Universitatii Bucuresti. Matematica-Mecanica — An Univ Bucur Mat Mec
Analele. Universitatii Bucuresti. Matematica-Mecanica — An Univ Bucuresti Mat Mec
Analele Universitatii Bucuresti. Seria. Biologie — An Univ Bucuresti Biol
Analele. Universitatii Bucuresti. Seria Matematica — An Univ Bucuresti Ser Mat
Analele. Universitatii Bucuresti. Seria Stiintele Naturii — An Univ Bucuresti Ser Stiint Nat
Analele. Universitatii Bucuresti. Seria Stiintele Naturii. Biologie — An Univ Bucuresti Ser Stiint Nat Biol
Analele. Universitatii Bucuresti. Seria Stiintele Naturii. Biologie — Anal Univ Buc Ser Stiint Nat Biol
Analele. Universitatii Bucuresti. Seria Stiintele Naturii. Chimie — An Univ Bucur Ser Stiint Nat Chim
Analele. Universitatii Bucuresti. Seria Stiintele Naturii. Chimie — An Univ Bucuresti Ser Stiint Nat Chim
Analele. Universitatii Bucuresti. Seria Stiintele Naturii. Fizica [*Romania*] — An Univ Bucuresti Ser Stiint Nat Fiz
Analele. Universitatii Bucuresti. Seria Stiintele Naturii. Fizica — ASFZA
Analele. Universitatii Bucuresti. Seria Stiintele Naturii. Geologie, Geografie — An Univ Bucuresti Ser Stiint Nat Geol Geogr
Analele Universitatii Bucuresti. Seria Stiintele Naturii. Matematica-Mecanica — An Univ Bucuresti Ser Stiint Nat Mat Mec
Analele. Universitatii Bucuresti. Seria Stiintele Naturii. Matematica-Mecanica — An Univ Bucuresti Seria Stiint Nat Mat Mec
Analele Universitatii Bucuresti. Stiinte Sociale. Istorie — AUB Ist
Analele. Universitatii Bucuresti. Stiinte Sociale. Seria Istorie — Anal Univ Bucuresti
Analele. Universitatii Bucuresti. Stiintele Naturii — An Univ Bucur Stiint Nat
Analele. Universitatii Bucuresti. Stiintele Naturii — An Univ Bucuresti Sti Natur
Analele. Universitatii Bucuresti. Stiintele Naturii — An Univ Bucuresti Stiint Nat
Analele. Universitatii C. I. Parhon — Anal Univ C I Parhon
Analele. Universitatii C. I. Parhon. Seria Stiintele Naturii — An Univ C I Parhon Ser Stiint Nat
Analele Universitatii din Craiova. Biologie, Agronomie, Horticultura — An Univ Craiova Biol Agron Hortic
Analele. Universitatii din Craiova. Biologie Stiinte. Agricole. Seria A 3a — An Univ Craiova Biol Stiinte Agric Ser A 3a
Analele. Universitatii din Craiova. Matematica. Fizica-Chimie — An Univ Craiova Mat Fiz-Chim
Analele. Universitatii din Craiova. Seria 3a. Stiinte Agricole — An Univ Craiova Ser 3
Analele. Universitatii din Craiova. Seria Biologie Medicina Stiinte Agricole [*A publication*] — An Univ Craiova Ser Biol Med Stiinte Agr
Analele Universitatii din Craiova. Seria. Biologie, Medicina, Stiinte Agricole — An Univ Craiova Ser Biol Med Stiinte Agric
Analele Universitatii din Craiova. Seria Chimie — An Univ Craiova Ser Chim
Analele. Universitatii din Craiova. Seria Istorie, Geografie, Filologie — Anal Univ Craiova
Analele Universitatii din Craiova. Seria. Matematica Fizica-Chimie — An Univ Craiova Ser Mat Fiz Chim
Analele. Universitatii din Galati. Fascicula 6. Tehnologia si Chimia Produselor Alimentare — An Univ Galati Fasc 6
Analele. Universitatii din Galati. Fascicula 9. Metalurgie si Cocsochimie — An Univ Galati Fasc 9
Analele Universitatii din Galati. Metalurgie — An Univ Galati Metal
Analele. Universitatii din Timisoara. Seria Stiinte Filologice — AnUTFil
Analele. Universitatii din Timisoara. Seria Stiinte Filologice — AUT
Analele Universitatii din Timisoara. Seria Stiinte Fizice — An Univ Timisoara Ser Stiint Fiz
Analele. Universitatii din Timisoara. Seria Stiinte Fizice-Chimice — An Univ Timisoara Ser Sti Fiz-Chim
Analele. Universitatii din Timisoara. Seria Stiinte Fizice-Chimice — An Univ Timisoara Ser Stiint Fiz-Chim
Analele. Universitatii din Timisoara. Seria Stiinte Fizice-Chimice — An Univ Timisoara Ser Stiinte Fiz Chim
Analele. Universitatii din Timisoara. Seria Stiinte Fizice-Chimice — An Univ Timisoara Stiinte Fiz Chim
Analele. Universitatii din Timisoara. Seria Stiinte Matematice — An Univ Timisoara Ser Sti Mat
Analele. Universitatii din Timisoara. Seria Stiinte Matematice — An Univ Timisoara Ser Stiint Mat
Analele. Universitatii din Timisoara. Seria Stiinte Matematice-Fizice [*Romania*] — An Univ Timisoara Ser Stiinte Mat-Fiz
Analele Universitatii din Timisoara. Stiinte Fizice — An Univ Timisoara Stiinte Fiz
Analele. Universitatii Ovidius Constanta. Seria Matematica — An Univ Ovidius Constanta Ser Mat
Anales. Academia Argentina de Geografia (Buenos Aires) — An Acad Arg Geogr BA
Anales. Academia Chilena de Ciencias Naturales — ACNAAD
Anales. Academia Chilena de Ciencias Naturales — An Acad Chil Cienc Nat
Anales. Academia Chilena de Ciencias Naturales — Anales Acad Chilena Ci Nat
Anales. Academia de Biologia. Universidad Catolica de Chile — An Acad Biol Univ Catol Chile
Anales. Academia de Ciencias Medicas, Fisicas, y Naturales de La Habana — An Acad Cienc Med Fis Nat Habana
Anales. Academia de Ciencias Medicas, Fisicas, y Naturales (Habana) — An Acad Cien Med Fis Nat Hav
Anales. Academia de Ciencias Morales y Politicas — AACMP
Anales. Academia de la Historia de Cuba — AAHC
Anales. Academia de la Historia de Cuba (Habana) — An Acad Hist Cuba Hav
Anales Academia Geografia e Historia de Guatemala — AAG
Anales. Academia Matritense del Notariado — A Acad Matritense Notariado
Anales. Academia Nacional de Artes y Letras — AANAL
Anales. Academia Nacional de Ciencias Exactas, Fisicas, y Naturales [*Argentina*] — An Acad Nac Cienc Exactas Fis Nat
Anales. Academia Nacional de Ciencias Exactas, Fisicas, y Naturales — Anal Acad Nac Cienc Exactas Fis Nat
Anales. Academia Nacional de Ciencias Exactas, Fisicas, y Naturales de Buenos Aires — ACFBAA
Anales. Academia Nacional de Ciencias Exactas, Fisicas, y Naturales de Buenos Aires — An Acad Nac Cienc Exactas Fis Nat B Aires
Anales. Academia Nacional de Ciencias Exactas, Fisicas, y Naturales de Buenos Aires — An Acad Nac Cienc Exactas Fis Nat Buenos Aires
Anales. Academia Nacional de Ciencias Exactas, Fisicas, y Naturales de Buenos Aires — Anales Acad Nac Ci Exact Buenos Aires
Anales. Academia Nacional de Farmacia — An Acad Nac Farm
Anales. Administracion Nacional de Bosques. Ministerio de Agricultura y Ganaderia (Republica Argentina) — An Adm Nac Bosques Minist Agric Ganad (Repub Argent)
Anales Agronomicos — An Agron
Anales (Argentina). Direccion Nacional de Geologia y Mineria — An (Argent) Dir Nac Geol Min
Anales. Asociacion de Quimica y Farmacia del Uruguay — An As Quim Farm Urug

Anales. Asociacion de Quimica y Farmacia del Uruguay — An Asoc Quim Farm Urug
Anales. Asociacion Espanola Para el Progreso de la Ciencias — Anales Asoc Esp Progr Ci
Anales. Asociacion Espanola para el Progreso de las Ciencias — A Asoc Espan Progr Ci
Anales. Asociacion Espanola para el Progreso de las Ciencias — AAEPC
Anales. Asociacion Espanola para el Progreso de las Ciencias — An Asoc Esp Prog Cienc
Anales. Asociacion Quimica [*Argentina*] — An As Quim
Anales. Asociacion Quimica (Argentina) — An Asoc Quim (Argent)
Anales. Asociacion Quimica Argentina (Buenos Aires) — An Asoc Quim Arg BA
Anales. Ateneo de Clinica Quirurgica — An Ateneo Clin Quir
Anales. Casa de Salud Valdecilla [*Santander*] — ACSVAX
Anales. Casa de Salud Valdecilla — An Casa Salud Valdecilla
Anales. Casa de Salud Valdecilla (Santander) — An Casa Salud Valdecilla (Santander)
Anales. Catedra de Patologia y Clinica de la Tuberculosis. Universidad de Buenos Aires — An Catedra de Patol Clin Tuberc Univ B Aires
Anales. Catedra de Patologia y Clinica de la Tuberculosis. Universidad de Buenos Aires — APTGAG
Anales. Catedra de Tisioneumonologia — ACTIE3
Anales. Catedra de Tisioneumonologia — An Catedra Tisioneumonol
Anales. Catedra Francisco Suarez — A Catedra F Suarez
Anales. Catedra Francisco Suarez — ACFS
Anales. Catedra Francisco Suarez — An Cated Suarez
Anales. Centro de Cultura Valenciana — A Centro Cult Valenciana
Anales. Centro de Cultura Valenciana — ACCV
Anales. Centro de Investigacion y Desarrollo en Tecnologia de Pinturas — An Cent Invest Desarrollo Tecnol Pint
Anales. Centro de Investigaciones Tisiologicas — An Cent Invest Tisiol
Anales Cervantinos — AC
Anales Cervantinos — ACer
Anales Cerventinos. CSIC (Consejo Superior de Investigaciones Cientificas) — A Cerventinos
Anales Chilenos de Historia de la Medicina — An Chilenos Hist Med
Anales. CIDEPINT [*Centro de Investigacion y Desarrollo en Tecnologia de Pinturas*] — An CIDEPINT
Anales Cientificos — An Cient
Anales Cientificos (La Molina) — An Cient (La Molina)
Anales Cientificos (Lima) — An Cient (Lima)
Anales Cientificos. UNA (Universidad Nacional Agraria) — An Cient UNA (Univ Nac Agrar)
Anales. Circa Medico Argentino — An Circ Med Argent
Anales Climatologicos. Servicio Meteorologico Nacional [*Argentina*] — An Clim
Anales. Colegio Nacional del Medicos Militares (Mexico City) — An Col Nac Med Mil (Mexico City)
Anales. Comision de Investigaciones Cientificas. Provincia de Buenos Aires — An Com Invest Cient Prov Buenos Aires
Anales. Congreso Nacional de Medicina Veterinaria y Zootecnia — An Congr Nac Med Vet Zootec
Anales. Congreso Nacional de Metalurgia — An Congr Nac Metal
Anales. Congreso Panamericano di Ingenieria de Minas y Geologia — An Congr Panam Ing Minas Geol
Anales de Anatomia — An Anat
Anales de Antropologia — A Antropol
Anales de Antropologia — AAntr
Anales de Antropologia. Instituto de Investigaciones Historicas. Universidad Nacional Autonoma (Mexico) — An Antrop Mex
Anales de Arqueologia y Etnologia — An Arqueol Etnol
Anales de Ars Medici — An Ars Med
Anales de Bromatologia — An Bromat
Anales de Bromatologia — An Bromatol
Anales de Bromatologia — ANBRAD
Anales de Ciencias — An Cienc
Anales de Ciencias, Agricultura, Comercio, y Artes — ACACA
Anales de Ciencias Humanas — Anal Cienc Hum
Anales de Ciencias Naturales — An Cienc Natur
Anales de Ciencias Naturales — Anales Ci Nat
Anales de Ciencias Naturales. Instituto Jose de Acosta — Anales Ci Nat Inst Jose De Acosta
Anales de Cirugia [*Rosario*] — ANCIAP
Anales de Cirugia (Rosario) — An Cir (Rosario)
Anales de Economia. CSIC (Consejo Superior de Investigaciones Cientificas) — A Economia
Anales de Economia y Estadistica (Bogota) — An Econ Estad Bogota
Anales de Edafologia y Agrobiologia — AEDAAB
Anales de Edafologia y Agrobiologia — An Edafol Agrobiol
Anales de Edafologia y Fisiologia Vegetal — AEFVAG
Anales de Edafologia y Fisiologia Vegetal — An Edafol Fisiol Veg
Anales de Farmacia Hospitalaria — AFHOAC
Anales de Farmacia Hospitalaria — An Farm Hosp
Anales de Farmacia y Bioquimica (Buenos Aires) — An Farm Bioquim (Buenos Aires)
Anales de Filologia Clasica [*Buenos Aires*] — AFC
Anales de Fisica — An Fis
Anales de Fisica — An Fisica
Anales de Fisica. Monografias — An Fis Monogr
Anales de Fisica. Serie A — An Fis Ser A
Anales de Fisica. Serie B — An Fis Ser B
Anales de Fisica y Quimica — An Fis Quim
Anales de Historea Antigua y Medieval — AHAM
Anales de Historia Antigua y Medieval — A His Antigua Medieval
Anales de Ingenieria — An Ing
Anales de Investigacion Textil — An Invest Text
Anales de Investigaciones Agronomicas — An Invest Agron
Anales de Jurisprudencia [*Mexico*] — Anales Jur
Anales de la Instruccion Primaria. Consejo Nacional de Ensenanza Primaria y Normal (Montevideo) — An Instr Prim Monte
Anales de la Literatura Espanola Contemporanea — ALEC
Anales de la Narrativa Espanola Contemporanea — ANP
Anales de la Universidad — AnU
Anales de Lactologia y Quimica Agricola (Zaragoza) — An Lactol Quim Agric (Zaragoza)
Anales de Legislacion Argentina — ADLA
Anales de Literatura Hispanoamericana — ALHisp
Anales de Mecanica y Electricidad — AMEMA
Anales de Mecanica y Electricidad — An Mec Elect
Anales de Mecanica y Electricidad [*Spain*] — An Mec Electr
Anales de Medicina — An Med
Anales de Medicina. Academia de Ciencias Medicas de Cataluna y Baleares — An Med Acad Cienc Med Cataluna Baleares
Anales de Medicina. Cirugia — An Med Cir
Anales de Medicina. Especialidades — An Med Espec
Anales de Medicina Interna — An Med Interna
Anales de Medicina (Lima) — An Med (Lima)
Anales de Medicina. Medicina — An Med Med
Anales de Medicina Publica [*Argentina*] — An Med Publ
Anales de Medicina. Seccion de Medicina [*Spain*] — An Med Sec Med
Anales de Medicina (Sevilla) — An Med (Sevilla)
Anales de Medicina y Cirugia de Barcelona — A Med Cirugia
Anales de Parques Nacionales [*Buenos Aires*] — APNDAB
Anales de Parques Nacionales (Buenos Aires) — An Parques Nac (B Aires)
Anales de Pediatria — An Pediat
Anales de Quimica — An Quim
Anales de Quimica — An Quimica
Anales de Quimica — ANQUBU
Anales de Quimica International Edition — An Quim Int Ed
Anales de Quimica. Serie A. Quimica Fisica y Quimica Tecnica — An Quim A-Fis Tec
Anales de Quimica. Serie B. Quimica Inorganica y Quimica Analitica — An Quim Ser B
Anales de Quimica. Serie B. Quimica Inorganica y Quimica Analytica — An Quim B Inorg Anal
Anales de Quimica. Serie C. Quimica Organica y Bioquimica — An Quim C Org Bioquim
Anales de Quimica. Serie C. Quimica Organica y Bioquimica — An Quim Ser C
Anales de Quimica. Serie C. Quimica Organica y Bioquimica — An Quim Ser C Quim Org Bioquim
Anales de Quimica. Serie C. Quimica Organica y Bioquimica — AQSBD6
Anales de Quimica y Farmacia — An Quim Farm
Anales de Sociedad Cientifica Argentina — Anales Soc Ci Argent
Anales del Desarrollo — ADESAT
Anales del Desarrollo — An Desarrollo
Anales del Desarrollo (Granada, Spain) — An Desarrollo (Granada Spain)
Anales del INIA (Instituto Nacional de Investigaciones Agrarias). Serie. Techologia Agraria (Spain) — An INIA Ser Techol Agrar
Anales del Instituto de Edafologia. Ecologia y Fisiologia Vegetal — An Inst Edafol Ecol Fisiol Veg
Anales del Instituto Medico Nacional — An Inst Med Nac
Anales. Direccion General de Oficinas Quimica Nacionales (Argentina) — An Dir Gen Of Quim Nac (Argent)
Anales. Direccion General de Oficinas Quimica Nacionales (Argentina) — An Dir Gen Of Quim Nac (Argentina)
Anales. Direccion Nacional de Quimica (Argentina) — An Dir Nac Quim (Argent)
Anales. Direccion Nacional de Quimica (Argentina) — An Dir Nac Quim (Argentina)
Anales. Dispensario Publico Nacional para Enfermedades del Aparato Digestivo (Argentina) — An Dispensario Publico Nac Enferm Apar Dig (Argent)
Anales. Dispensario Publico Nacional para Enfermedades del Aparato Digestivo (Argentina) — An Dispensario Publico Nac Enferm Apar Dig (Argentina)
Anales. Escuela de Farmacia. Facultad de Ciencias Medicas. Universidad Nacional Mayor de San Marcos — An Esc Farm Fac Cienc Med Univ Nac Mayor San Marcos
Anales. Escuela de Quimica y Farmacia y Bioquimica. Universidad de Concepcion — AEQBDE
Anales. Escuela de Quimica y Farmacia y Bioquimica. Universidad de Concepcion — An Esc Quim Farm Bioquim Univ Concepcion
Anales. Escuela Nacional de Ciencias Biologicas [*Mexico*] — AENBAU
Anales. Escuela Nacional de Ciencias Biologicas — An Escuela Nac Cienc Biol
Anales. Escuela Nacional de Ciencias Biologicas (Mexico) — An Esc Nac Cienc Biol (Mex)
Anales. Escuela Nacional de Ciencias Biologicas (Mexico) — An Escuela Nac Cien Biol Mex
Anales. Escuela Nacional de Ciencias Biologicas (Mexico City) — An Esc Nac Cienc Biol (Mexico City)
Anales Espanoles de Odontoestomatologia — AEODA7
Anales Espanoles de Odontoestomatologia — An Esp Odontoestomatol
Anales Espanoles de Pediatria — An Esp Pediatr
Anales. Estacion Experimental de Aula Dei [*Zaragoza*] — AEECAM
Anales. Estacion Experimental de Aula Dei — An Estac Exp Aula Dei
Anales. Estacion Experimental de Aula Dei — Anales Estac Exp Aula Dei
Anales. Estacion Experimental de Aula Dei. Consejo Superior de Investigaciones Cientificas — An Estac Exp Aula Dei Cons Super Invest Cient
Anales. Estacion Experimental de Aula Dei (Zaragoza) — An Estac Exp Aula Dei (Zaragoza)
Anales. Facultad de Ciencias Fisicas y Matematicas. Universidad de Concepcion — An Fac Cienc Fis Mat Univ Concepcion

Anales. Facultad de Ciencias Juridicas y Sociales. Universidad de La Plata — An Fac Cien Jur Soc La Plata
Anales. Facultad de Ciencias Medicas (Asuncion) — An Fac Cien Med Asuncion
Anales. Facultad de Ciencias Naturales y Museo. Universidad Nacional. La Plata. Seccion Botanica — Anales Fac Ci Nat Mus Univ Nac La Plata Secc Bot
Anales. Facultad de Ciencias Quimicas y Farmacologicas. Universidad de Chile — AFCCDM
Anales. Facultad de Farmacia y Bioquimica. Universidad Nacional Mayor de San Marcos — An Fac Farm Bioquim Univ Nac Mayor San Marcos
Anales. Facultad de Farmacia y Bioquimica. Universidad Nacional Mayor de San Marcos de Lima — AFBMAA
Anales. Facultad de Farmacia y Bioquimica. Universidad Nacional Mayor de San Marcos de Lima — An Fac Farm Bioquim Univ Nac Mayor San Marcos Lima
Anales. Facultad de Ingenieria. Universidad de Concepcion — An Fac Ing Univ Concepcion
Anales. Facultad de Medicina. Universidad de la Republica [*Montevideo*] — AFMEA7
Anales. Facultad de Medicina. Universidad de la Republica (Montevideo) — An Fac Med (Montevideo)
Anales. Facultad de Medicina. Universidad de la Republica (Montevideo) — An Fac Med Univ Repub (Montev)
Anales. Facultad de Medicina. Universidad de la Republica Oriental del Uruguay — An Fac Med Univ Repub Orient Urug
Anales. Facultad de Medicina. Universidad Nacional Mayor de San Marcos de Lima [*Peru*] — AFMUAL
Anales. Facultad de Medicina. Universidad Nacional Mayor de San Marcos de Lima — An Fac Med Lima
Anales. Facultad de Medicina. Universidad Nacional Mayor de San Marcos de Lima — An Fac Med Univ Nac Mayor San Marcos Lima
Anales. Facultad de Medicina. Universidad Nacional Mayor de San Marcos de Lima (Peru) — An Fac Med Univ Nac Mayor San Marcos Lima (Peru)
Anales. Facultad de Odontologia. Universidad de la Republica [*Uruguay*] — An Fac Odontol Univ Repub Urug
Anales. Facultad de Odontologia. Universidad de la Republica [*Uruguay*] — UFOAAL
Anales. Facultad de Quimica. Universidad de la Republica Oriental del Uruguay — An Fac Quim Univ Repub Orient Urug
Anales. Facultad de Quimica y Farmacia. Universidad de Chile — AFQFAU
Anales. Facultad de Quimica y Farmacia. Universidad de Chile [*Santiago*] — An Fac Quim Farm Univ Chile
Anales. Facultad de Quimica y Farmacia. Universidad de Chile (Santiago) — An Fac Quim Farm (Santiago)
Anales. Facultad de Quimica y Farmacia. Universidad de Concepcion — AFQFBV
Anales. Facultad de Quimica y Farmacia. Universidad de Concepcion — An Fac Quim Farm Univ Concepcion
Anales. Facultad de Quimica y Farmacia. Universidad de la Republica Oriental del Uruguay — An Fac Quim Farm Univ Repub Orient Urug
Anales. Facultad de Veterinaria de Leon — AFVLA5
Anales. Facultad de Veterinaria de Leon — An Fac Vet Leon
Anales. Facultad de Veterinaria del Uruguay — AFVUBX
Anales. Facultad de Veterinaria del Uruguay — An Fac Vet Urug
Anales. Facultad de Veterinaria. Instituto de Investigaciones Veterinaria de Madrid — An Fac Vet Inst Invest Vet Madrid
Anales. Facultad de Veterinaria. Universidad de Madrid. Instituto de Investigaciones Veterinarias — An Fac Vet Univ Madrid Inst Invest Vet
Anales. Facultad de Veterinaria. Universidad de Zaragoza — An Fac Vet Univ Zaragoza
Anales Galdosianos — AG
Anales Galdosianos — AGald
Anales Graficos (Buenos Aires) — An Graf BA
Anales. Hospital de la Santa Cruz y San Pablo — AHOSA5
Anales. Hospital de la Santa Cruz y San Pablo — An Hosp St Cruz San Pablo
Anales. Hospital Militar Central. Lima — An Hosp Mil Cent Lima
Anales. Hospital Militar Central (Lima, Peru) — An Hosp Mil Cent (Lima Peru)
Anales Ilustrados. Colegio Oficial de Medicina. Provincia de Lerida — An Ilus Col Of Med Prov Lerida
Anales. INIA (Instituto Nacional de Investigaciones Agrarias). Serie. Proteccion Vegetal (Spain) — An INIA Ser Prot Veg
Anales. INIA [*Instituto Nacional de Investigaciones Agrarias*]. Serie. Agricola (Spain) — An INIA Ser Agric Spain
Anales. INIA [*Instituto Nacional de Investigaciones Agrarias*]. Serie. General (Spain) — An INIA Ser Gen (Spain)
Anales. INIA [*Instituto Nacional de Investigaciones Agrarias*]. Serie. Produccion Vegetal [*Spain*] — An INIA Ser Prod Veg
Anales. INIA [*Instituto Nacional de Investigaciones Agrarias*]. Serie. Recursos Naturales [*Spain*] — An INIA Ser Recur Nat
Anales. Instituto Botanico A. J. Cavanilles — An Inst Bot A J Cavanilles
Anales. Instituto Botanico A. J. Cavanilles (Madrid) — An Inst Bot A J Cavanilles (Madrid)
Anales. Instituto Corachan [*Spain*] — An Inst Corachan
Anales. Instituto de Arte Americano e Investigaciones Esteticas (Buenos Aires) — An Inst Art Am Invest Estet BA
Anales. Instituto de Biologia (Mexico) — An Inst Biol Mex
Anales. Instituto de Biologia. Universidad Nacional Autonoma de Mexico — An Inst Biol (Mexico)
Anales. Instituto de Biologia. Universidad Nacional Autonoma de Mexico — An Inst Biol Univ Mex
Anales. Instituto de Biologia. Universidad Nacional Autonoma de Mexico — An Inst Biol Univ Nac Auton Mex
Anales. Instituto de Biologia. Universidad Nacional Autonoma de Mexico. Serie Biologia Experimental — An Inst Biol Univ Nac Auton Mex Ser Biol Exp
Anales. Instituto de Biologia. Universidad Nacional Autonoma de Mexico. Serie Botanica — An Inst Biol Univ Nac Auton Mex Ser Bot
Anales. Instituto de Biologia. Universidad Nacional Autonoma de Mexico. Serie Botanica — Anales Inst Biol UNAM Ser Bot
Anales. Instituto de Biologia. Universidad Nacional Autonoma de Mexico. Serie Ciencias del Mar y Limnologia — An Inst Biol Univ Nac Auton Mex Ser Cienc Mar Limnol
Anales. Instituto de Biologia. Universidad Nacional Autonoma de Mexico. Serie Zoologia — An Inst Biol Univ Nac Auton Mex Ser Zool
Anales. Instituto de Biologia. Universidad Nacional Autonoma de Mexico. Serie Zoologia — Anales Inst Biol UNAM Ser Zool
Anales. Instituto de Biologia. Universidad Nacional de Mexico — Anales Inst Biol Univ Nac Mexico
Anales. Instituto de Edafologia, Ecologia, y Fisiologia Vegetal — Anales Inst Edafol
Anales. Instituto de Estudios Gerundenses — AIEG
Anales. Instituto de Estudios Gerundenses. CSIC (Consejo Superior de Investigaciones Cientificas) — A Inst Est Gerundenses
Anales. Instituto de Estudios Madrilenos — AIEM
Anales. Instituto de Estudios Madrilenos — An Inst Estud Madrilenos
Anales. Instituto de Estudios Madrilenos — Anae
Anales. Instituto de Etnografia Americana. Universidad Nacional de Cuyo — AIEC
Anales. Instituto de Farmacologia Espanola — AIFAAF
Anales. Instituto de Farmacologia Espanola — An Inst Farmac Esp
Anales. Instituto de Farmacologia Espanola — An Inst Farmacol Esp
Anales. Instituto de Geofisica. Universidad Nacional Autonoma de Mexico — AIGMA
Anales. Instituto de Geofisica. Universidad Nacional Autonoma de Mexico — An Inst Geofis UNAM
Anales. Instituto de Geofisica. Universidad Nacional Autonoma de Mexico — An Inst Geofis Univ Nac Auton Mex
Anales. Instituto de Geologia. Universidad Nacional Autonoma de Mexico — An Inst Geol Univ Nac Auton Mex
Anales. Instituto de Geologia. Universidad Nacional Autonoma de Mexico — UAMGAS
Anales. Instituto de Investigaciones Cientificas — Anales Inst Invest Ci
Anales. Instituto de Investigaciones Cientificas (Monterrey) — An Inst Invest Cientif Monterrey
Anales. Instituto de Investigaciones Cientificas. Universidad de Nuevo Leon [*A publication*] — An Inst Invest Cient Univ Nuevo Leon
Anales. Instituto de Investigaciones Cientificas y Tecnologicas. Universidad Nacional del Litoral — An Inst Invest Cient Tecnol Univ Nac Litoral
Anales. Instituto de Investigaciones Esteticas — AIIE
Anales. Instituto de Investigaciones Esteticas — IIE/A
Anales. Instituto de Investigaciones Esteticas (Mexico) — An Inst Invest Estet Mex
Anales. Instituto de Investigaciones Marinas de Punta de Betin — AIIBD2
Anales. Instituto de Investigaciones Marinas de Punta de Betin — An Inst Invest Mar Punta Betin
Anales. Instituto de Investigaciones Odontologicas. Universidad del Zulia (Maracaibo) — An Inst Invest Odontol (Maracaibo)
Anales. Instituto de Investigaciones Veterinarias — AIVMAT
Anales. Instituto de Investigaciones Veterinarias — An Inst Invest Vet
Anales. Instituto de Investigaciones Veterinarias (Madrid) — An Inst Invest Vet (Madrid)
Anales. Instituto de la Patagonia — An Inst Patagonia
Anales. Instituto de Linguistica. Universidad Nacional de Cuyo — AIL
Anales. Instituto de Linguistica. Universidad Nacional de Cuyo — AILC
Anales. Instituto de Literaturas Clasicas — AILC
Anales. Instituto de Matematicas. Universidad Nacional Autonoma de Mexico — An Inst Mat Univ Nac Autonoma Mexico
Anales. Instituto de Medicina Experimental Angel H. Roffo — An Inst Med Exp Angel H Roffo
Anales. Instituto de Medicina Experimental de Valencia — An Inst Med Exp Valencia
Anales. Instituto de Medicina Regional — AIMRAX
Anales. Instituto de Medicina Regional — An Inst Med Reg
Anales. Instituto de Oncologia "Angel H. Roffo" — An Inst Oncol Angel H Roffo
Anales. Instituto de Oncologia "Angel H. Roffo" (Buenos Aires) — An Inst Oncol Angel H Roffo (B Aires)
Anales. Instituto de Psicologia [*Buenos Aires*] — An Inst Psicol
Anales. Instituto Espanol de Edafologia, Ecologia, y Fisiologia Vegetal — An Inst Esp Edafol Ecol Fisiol Veg
Anales. Instituto Etnico Nacional [*Argentina*] — AIEN
Anales. Instituto Fitotecnico de Santa Catalina — Anales Inst Fitotecn Santa Catalina
Anales. Instituto Forestal de Investigaciones y Experiencias [*Madrid*] — IFIEA7
Anales. Instituto Forestal de Investigaciones y Experiencias (Madrid) — An Inst For Invest Exper (Madr)
Anales. Instituto Geologico de Mexico — An Inst Geol Mex
Anales. Instituto Medico Nacional (Mexico) — An Inst Med Nac (Mexico)
Anales. Instituto Municipal de Higiene de Zaragoza — An Inst Mun Hig Zaragoza
Anales. Instituto Municipal de Higiene de Zaragoza — An Inst Munic Hig Z
Anales. Instituto Municipal de Higiene de Zaragoza — An Inst Munic Hig Zaragoza
Anales. Instituto Nacional de Antropologia e Historia — AIAHAB
Anales. Instituto Nacional de Antropologia e Historia — AINAH
Anales. Instituto Nacional de Antropologia e Historia — An Inst Antrop Hist
Anales. Instituto Nacional de Antropologia e Historia — An Inst Nac Antropol Hist
Anales. Instituto Nacional de Antropologia e Historia — Anales Inst Nac Antropol
Anales. Instituto Nacional de Antropologia e Historia — AnINA

Anales. Instituto Nacional de Antropologia e Historia (Mexico) — An Inst Nac Antrop Hist Mex
Anales. Instituto Nacional de Investigaciones Agrarias. Serie Agricola — AIAADR
Anales. Instituto Nacional de Investigaciones Agrarias. Serie Agricola — An Inst Nac Invest Agrar Ser Agric
Anales. Instituto Nacional de Investigaciones Agrarias. Serie Ganadera — An Inst Nac Invest Agrar Ser Ganad
Anales. Instituto Nacional de Investigaciones Agrarias. Serie Ganadera — ANIGDI
Anales. Instituto Nacional de Investigaciones Agrarias. Serie General — AINGA5
Anales. Instituto Nacional de Investigaciones Agrarias. Serie General — An Inst Nac Invest Agrar Ser Gen
Anales. Instituto Nacional de Investigaciones Agrarias. Serie. General (Spain) — An Inst Nac Invest Agrar Ser Gen Spain
Anales. Instituto Nacional de Investigaciones Agrarias. Serie Higiene y Sanidad Animal — AIHADS
Anales. Instituto Nacional de Investigaciones Agrarias. Serie Higiene y Sanidad Animal — An Inst Nac Invest Agrar Ser Hig Sanid Anim
Anales. Instituto Nacional de Investigaciones Agrarias. Serie Produccion Animal — AIPACX
Anales. Instituto Nacional de Investigaciones Agrarias. Serie Produccion Animal — An Inst Nac Invest Agrar Ser Prod Anim
Anales. Instituto Nacional de Investigaciones Agrarias. Serie. Produccion Animal (Spain) — An Inst Nac Invest Agrar Ser Prod Anim (Spain)
Anales. Instituto Nacional de Investigaciones Agrarias. Serie Produccion Vegetal — AIPVCS
Anales. Instituto Nacional de Investigaciones Agrarias. Serie Produccion Vegetal — An Inst Nac Invest Agrar Ser Prod Veg
Anales. Instituto Nacional de Investigaciones Agrarias. Serie Proteccion Vegetal — An Inst Nac Invest Agrar Ser Prot Veg
Anales. Instituto Nacional de Investigaciones Agrarias. Serie Proteccion Vegetal — APTVAR
Anales. Instituto Nacional de Investigaciones Agrarias. Serie Recursos Naturales — An Inst Nac Invest Agrar Ser Recur Nat
Anales. Instituto Nacional de Investigaciones Agrarias. Serie Recursos Naturales — ASRNDH
Anales. Instituto Nacional de Investigaciones Agrarias. Serie Tecnologia Agraria — AITADK
Anales. Instituto Nacional de Investigaciones Agrarias. Serie Tecnologia Agraria — An Inst Nac Invest Agrar Ser Tecnol Agrar
Anales. Instituto Nacional de Investigaciones Agrarias. Serie. Tecnologia Agraria (Spain) — An Inst Nac Invest Agrar Ser Technol Agrar Spain
Anales. Instituto Nacional de Investigaciones Agrarias (Spain). Serie Produccion Animal — An Inst Nac Invest Agrar (Spain) Ser Prod Anim
Anales. Instituto Nacional de Investigaciones Agrarias (Spain). Serie Produccion Vegetal — An Inst Nac Invest Agrar (Spain) Ser Prod Veg
Anales. Instituto Nacional de Investigaciones Agrarias (Spain). Serie Proteccion Vegetal — An Insti Nac Invest Agrar (Spain) Ser Prot Veg
Anales. Instituto Nacional de Investigaciones Agrarias (Spain). Serie Recursos Naturales — An Inst Nac Invest Agrar (Spain) Ser Recur Nat
Anales. Instituto Nacional de Investigaciones Agronomicas (Madrid) — An Inst Nac Invest Agron (Madr)
Anales. Instituto Nacional de Investigaciones Agronomicas (Spain) — An Inst Nac Invest Agron (Spain)
Anales. Instituto Nacional de Microbiologia (Buenos Aires) — An Inst Nac Microbiol (B Aires)
Anales. Instituto Radio Quirurgico de Guipuzcoa — An Inst Radio Quir Guipuzcoa
Anales. Jardin Botanico de Madrid — An Jard Bot Madrid
Anales. Jardin Botanico de Madrid — Anales Jard Bot Madrid
Anales Jornadas Geologicas Argentinas — An Jorn Geol Argent
Anales Juridico-Socialies (Santiago) — An Jur Soc Santiago
Anales. Laboratorio de Ensayo de Materiales e Investigaciones Tecnologicas. Provincia de Buenos Aires — An Lab Ensayo Mater Invest Tecnol Prov Buenos Aires
Anales Medicoquirurgicos — An Med Quir
Anales Medicos. Asociacion Medica. Hospital Americano-Britanico Cowdray — An Med Assoc Med Hosp Am Br Cowdray
Anales Mexicanos de Ciencias — An Mex Cienc
Anales Mexicanos de Ciencias, Literatura, Mineria, Agricultura, Artes, Industria y Comercio en la Republica Mexicana — Anales Mex Ci
Anales. Museo Argentino de Ciencias Naturales Bernardino Rivadavia — An Mus Argent Cienc Nat Bernardino Rivadavia
Anales. Museo de Historia Natural de Valparaiso — An Mus Hist Nat Valparaiso
Anales. Museo Nacional David J. Gusman (San Salvador) — An Mus Nac Guzman S Salvador
Anales. Museo Nacional David J. Guzman — An Mus Nac David J Guzman
Anales. Museo Nacional David J. Guzman — ANDGAO
Anales. Museo Nacional de Historia Natural de Montevideo — AMHNAO
Anales. Museo Nacional de Historia Natural de Montevideo — An Mus Nac Hist Nat Montev
Anales. Museo Nacional de Historia y Etnografia (Mexico) — An Mus Nac Arqueol Hist Etnogr Mex
Anales. Museo Nacional de Montevideo — Anales Mus Nac Montevideo
Anales. Museo Nahuel Huapi. Ministerio de Obras Publicas de la Nacion. Administracion General de Parques Nacionales y Turismo — Anales Mus Nahuel Huapi
Anales Otorrinolaringologicos Ibero-Americanos — An ORL Ibero-Amer
Anales Otorrinolaringologicos Iberoamericanos — An Otorrinolariingol Ibero Am
Anales Otorrinolaringologicos Ibero-Americanos — An Otorrinolaringol Iber-Am
Anales Otorrinolaringologicos Ibero-Americanos — AOIAA4
Anales. Oviedo Universidad. Facultad de Veterinaria (Leon) — An Oviedo Univ Fac Vet (Leon)
Anales. Programa Academico de Medicina. Universidad Nacional Mayor de San Marcos (Lima) — An Programa Acad Med Univ Nac Mayor San Marcos (Lima)
Anales. Provincia Franciscana del Santo Evangelio de Mexico — An Prov Francis S Evan Mex
Anales. Real Academia de Ciencias Medicas, Fisicas, y Naturales de la Habana — An R Acad Cienc Med Fis Nat Habana
Anales. Real Academia de Ciencias Morales y Politicas — A Acad Ci Mor Pol
Anales. Real Academia de Farmacia — A Acad Farmacia
Anales. Real Academia de Farmacia — An R Acad Farm
Anales. Real Academia de Farmacia — ARAFAY
Anales. Real Academia de Farmacia. Instituto de Espana — An Real Acad Farm
Anales. Real Academia de Farmacia (Madrid) — An Acad Farm (Madrid)
Anales. Real Academia de Medicina y Cirugia de Valladolid — An R Acad Med Cir Valladolid
Anales. Real Academia Nacional de Medicina [*Spain*] — ARANA
Anales. Real Academia Nacional de Medicina [*Madrid*] — ARANAO
Anales. Real Academia Nacional de Medicina (Madrid) — An R Acad Nac Med (Madr)
Anales. Real Academia Nacional de Medicina (Madrid) — An R Acad Nacl Med (Madr)
Anales. Real Academia Nacional de Medicina (Spain) — An R Acad Nac Med Spain
Anales. Real Sociedad Espanola de Fisica y Quimica — An R Soc Esp Fis Quim
Anales. Real Sociedad Espanola de Fisica y Quimica. Serie A — An R Soc Esp Fis y Quim A
Anales. Real Sociedad Espanola de Fisica y Quimica. Serie A. Fisica [*Spain*] [*A publication*] — An R Soc Esp Fis Quim Ser A
Anales. Real Sociedad Espanola de Fisica y Quimica. Serie A. Fisica — ARSFA
Anales. Real Sociedad Espanola de Fisica y Quimica. Serie B. Quimica — An R Soc Esp Fis Quim Ser B
Anales. Real Sociedad Espanola de Fisica y Quimica. Serie B. Quimica [*A publication*] — An R Soc Esp Fis Quim Ser B Quim
Anales. Real Sociedad Espanola de Fisica y Quimica. Serie B. Quimica — ARSQA
Anales. Real Sociedad Espanola de Fisica y Quimica. Serie B. Quimica — ARSQAL
Anales. Reale Academia de Medicina — An R Acad Med
Anales. Seccion de Ciencias. Colegio Universitario de Gerona. Universidad Autonoma de Barcelona — An Secc Cienc Col Univ Gerona Univ Auton Barcelona
Anales. Seccion de Ciencias. Colegio Universitario de Gerona. Universidad Autonoma de Barcelona — ASCGD
Anales. Serie Produccion Animal. Instituto Nacional de Investigaciones Agrarias — An Ser Prod Anim Inst Nac Invest Agrar
Anales. Servicio Geologico Nacional de El Salvador. Boletin — An Serv Geol Nac El Salvador Bol
Anales. Servico Geologico Nacional de El Salvador. Boletin — An Serv Geol Nac Salvador Bol
Anales. Sociedad Cientifica Argentina — An Soc Cient Argent
Anales. Sociedad Cientifica Argentina — ASCAA
Anales. Sociedad Cientifica Argentina (Buenos Aires) — An Soc Cientif Arg BA
Anales. Sociedad Cientifica Argentina. Seccion Santa Fe — An Soc Cient Argent Sec S Fe
Anales. Sociedad Cientifica Argentina. Seccion Santa Fe — An Soc Cient Argent Secc St Fe
Anales. Sociedad Cientifica de Santa Fe — An Soc Cient S Fe
Anales. Sociedad Cientifica de Santa Fe — An Soc Cient St Fe
Anales. Sociedad de Biologia de Bogota — An Soc Biol Bogota
Anales. Sociedad de Geografia e Historia — An Soc Geogr Hist
Anales. Sociedad de Geografia e Historia — ASGH
Anales. Sociedad de Geografia e Historia — ASGHA9
Anales. Sociedad de Geografia e Historia de Guatemala — An Soc Geogr Hist Guat
Anales. Sociedad de Geografia e Historia de Guatemala — An Soc Geogr Hist Guatem
Anales. Sociedad de Geografia e Historia de Guatemala — ASGHG
Anales. Sociedad Espanola de Fisica y Quimica [*Spain*] — An Soc Esp Fis Quim
Anales. Sociedad Espanola de Fisica y Quimica — An Soc Espan Fis Quim
Anales. Sociedad Espanola de Hidrologia Medica — An Soc Esp Hidrol Med
Anales. Sociedad Humboldt — Anales Soc Humboldt
Anales. Sociedad Medico-Quirurgica del Guayas — AMGYAI
Anales. Sociedad Medico-Quirurgica del Guayas — An Soc Med-Quir Guayas
Anales. Sociedad Mexicana de Historia de la Ciencia de la Tecnologia — An Soc Mex Hist Cienc Tecnol
Anales. Sociedad Mexicana de Historia de la Ciencia y de la Tecnologia — An Soc Mex Hist Cienc Tecn
Anales. Sociedad Mexicana de Oftalmologia — An Soc Mex Oftalmol
Anales. Sociedad Mexicana de Oftalmologia — ASMOAQ
Anales. Sociedad Mexicana de Otorrinolaringologia — AMOTA9
Anales. Sociedad Mexicana de Otorrinolaringologia — An Soc Mex Otorinolaringol
Anales. Sociedad Mexicana de Otorrinolaringologia y Broncoesofagologia — An Soc Mex Otorrinolaringol Broncoesofagol
Anales. Sociedad Peruana de Historia de la Medicina — An Soc Peruana Hist Med
Anales. Sociedad Quimica Argentina — An Soc Quim Argent
Anales. Sociedad Rural Argentina — An Soc Rur Argent
Anales. Sociedad Rural Argentina — An Soc Rural Argent
Anales. Sociedad Veterinaria de Zootecnia — An Soc Vet Zootec
Anales. Universidad Catolica de Valparaiso — An Univ Catol Valparaiso
Anales. Universidad Central de Venezuela (Caracas) — An Univ Cent Caracas
Anales. Universidad Central del Ecuador — An Univ Cent Ecuador
Anales. Universidad Central del Ecuador — Anales Univ Centr Ecuador
Anales. Universidad Central del Ecuador — AUCE

Anales. Universidad Central del Ecuador (Quito) — An Univ Cent Quito
Anales. Universidad de Barcelona — An Univ Barcelona
Anales. Universidad de Chile — An Univ Chile
Anales. Universidad de Chile — AUC
Anales. Universidad de Chile (Santiago) — An Univ Chile Santiago
Anales. Universidad de Cuenca — An Univ Cuenca
Anales. Universidad de Guayaquil — AUG
Anales. Universidad de la Patagonia San Juan Bosco. Ciencias Geologicas — An Univ Patagonia San Juan Bosco Cienc Geol
Anales. Universidad de Madrid — An Univ Madrid
Anales. Universidad de Murcia — A Univ Murcia
Anales. Universidad de Murcia — An Univ Murcia
Anales. Universidad de Murcia — AUM
Anales. Universidad de Murcia. Ciencias — An Univ Murcia Cienc
Anales. Universidad de Narino (Pasto, Colombia) — An Univ Narino Pasto
Anales. Universidad de Santo Domingo — An Univ St Domingo
Anales. Universidad de Santo Domingo (Santo Domingo) — An Univ S Dom C Trujillo S Domingo
Anales. Universidad de Valencia — AUV
Anales. Universidad del Norte (Antofagasta) — An Univ Norte Antofagasta
Anales. Universidad del Norte (Chile) — An Univ Norte (Chile)
Anales. Universidad Hispalense — A Univ Hisp
Anales. Universidad Hispalense — An Hisp
Anales. Universidad Hispalense — An Univ Hisp
Anales. Universidad Hispalense — An Univ Hispalense
Anales. Universidad Hispalense — AUH
Anales. Universidad Hispalense — AUHisp
Anales. Universidad Hispalense. Serie de Ciencias — An Univ Hisp Ser Cienc
Anales. Universidad Hispalense. Serie de Ciencias — An Univ Hispalense Ser Cienc
Anales. Universidad Hispalense. Serie Medicina — An Univ Hisp Ser Med
Anales. Universidad Hispalense. Serie Veterinaria — An Univ Hisp Ser Vet
Anales. Universidad Hispalense. Serie Veterinaria — Anal Univ Hisp Ser Vet
Anales. Universidad Mayor de San Marcos (Lima) — An Univ S Marcos Lima
Anales. Universidad Nacional — Anales Univ Nac
Anales. Universidad Nacional de La Plata. Instituto del Museo. Seccion B. Paleobotanica — Anales Univ Nac La Plata Secc B Paleobot
Anales y Boletin. Museos de Arte de Barcelona — A B Mus Arte Barcelona
Anali Filoloskog Fakulteta [*Belgrade*] — AFF
Anali Filoloskog Fakulteta Beogradskog Univerziteta — AnaliFF
Anali Historijskog Instituta u Dubrovniku — An Dubrovnik
Anali Historijskog Instituta u Dubrovniku — An Hist Inst Dubrovniku
Anali Klinicke Bolnice Dr. M. Stojanovic — An Klin Boln Dr M Stojanovic
Anali Klinicke Bolnice Dr. M. Stojanovic. Suplement — An Klin Boln Dr M Stojanovic Supl
Anali za Sumarstvo (Zagreb) — An Sumar (Zagreb)
Analise Conjuntural da Economia Nordestina — Analise Conjuntural Econ Nordestina
Analise Social — Anal Soc
Analiticheskaya Khimiya Neorganicheskikh Soedinenij — Anal Khim Neorg Soedin
Analiticheskie Metody pri Geokhimicheskikh Issledovaniyakh. Materialy Geokhimicheskoi Konferentsii — Anal Metody Geokhim Issled Mater Geokhim Konf
Analiticheskii Kontrol Proizvodstva v Azotnoi Promyshlennosti — Anal Kontrol Proizvod Azotn Promsti
Analiz i Tekhnologiya Blagorodnykh Metallov. Trudy Soveshchaniya po Khimii, Analizu, i Tekhnologii Blagorodnykh Metallov — Anal Tekhnol Blagorodn Met Tr Soveshch
Analiz Prichin Avarii i Povrezhdenii Stroitel'nykh Konstruktsii — Anal Prichin Avarii Povrezhdenii Stroit Konstr
Analiz Prichin Avarii Stroitel'nykh Konstruktsii — Anal Prichin Avarii Stroit Konstr
Analiz Rud Tsvetnykh Metallov i Produktov Ikh Pererabotki — Anal Rud Tsvetn Met Prod Ikh Pererab
Analiza Moderna si Aplicatii — Anal Modern Apl
Analiza Systemowa i jej Zastosowania — Anal Syst Zastos
Analog Science Fiction — ASF
Analog Science Fiction-Science Fact — IASF
Analogovaya i Analogo-Tsifrovaya Vychislitel'naya Tekhnika — Analogovaya Analogo-Tsifrovaya Vychisl Tekh
Analusis — ANLSCY
Analyse des Plantes et Problemes des Engrais Mineraux. Colloque — Anal Plant Probl Engrais Miner Colloq
Analyse et Prevision — ALPVB
Analyse et Prevision — Anal et Previs
Analyse et Prevision — Anal Previs
Analyse et Prevision — Anal Prevision
Analyse Financiere — Anal Financ
Analyse Structurale des Amplitudes de Collision Les Houches. June Institute — Anal Struct Amplitudes Collision Les Houches June Inst
Analysen und Berichte aus Gesellschaftswissenschaften [*Germany*] — Anal Ber Gesellschaftswiss
Analysen und Prognosen ueber die Welt von Morgen — Anal Progn
Analysen und Prognosen ueber die Welt von Morgen [*Germany*] — Anal Progn Welt Morgen
Analyser og Problemer — AOP
Analyses of Hazardous Substances in Biological Materials — Anal Hazard Subst Biol Mater
Analyses. Revue Technique Merlin Gerin — Anal Rev Tech Merlin Gerin
Analysis and Application of Rare Earth Materials. NATO [*North Atlantic Treaty Organization*] **Advanced Study Institute** — Anal Appl Rare Earth Mater NATO Adv Study Inst
Analysis and Characterization of Oils, Fats, and Fat Products — Anal Charact Oils Fats Fat Prod
Analysis and Characterization of Oils, Fats, and Fat Products — AOFFA4
Analysis and Intervention in Developmental Disabilities — AIDDDH
Analysis and Intervention in Developmental Disabilities — Anal Intervention Dev Disabil
Analysis and Research (Tokyo) — Anal Res (Tokyo)
Analysis and Simulation of Biochemical Systems — Anal Simul Biochem Syst
Analysis by Gas Chromatography of Biochemicals — Anal Gas Chromatogr Biochem
Analysis Division. Proceedings. Annual ISA Analysis Division Symposium — Anal Div
Analysis Instrumentation — Anal Instrum
Analysis Instrumentation (Research Triangle Park, North Carolina) — Anal Instrum (Research Triangle Park NC)
Analysis Mathematica — Anal Math
Analysis of Clinical Specimens — Anal Clin Specimen
Analysis of Drugs and Metabolites by Gas Chromatography. Mass Spectrometry [*A publication*] — Anal Drugs Metab Gas Chromatogr Mass Spectrom
Analysis of Intrauterine Contraception. Proceedings. International Conference on Intrauterine Contraception — Anal Intrauterine Contracept Proc Int Conf
Analysis of Organic Materials — Anal Org Mater
Analysis of Organic Micropollutants in Water. Proceedings. European Symposium — Anal Org Micropollut Water Proc Eur Symp
Analysis of Petroleum for Trace Metals. A Symposium — Anal Pet Trace Met Symp
Analysis of Propellants and Explosives. Chemical and Physical Methods. International Annual Conference of ICT — Anal Propellants Explos Chem Phys Methods Int Annu Conf ICT
Analysis of Structural Composite Materials — Anal Struct Compos Mater
Analysis of Temperate Forest Ecosystems — Anal Temperate For Ecosyst
Analysis of the Timber Situation in the United States 1952-2030 [*An*] — Timber Sit
Analyst — Anal
Analyst (London) — ANALA
Analysts Journal — Analysts J
Analytica Chimica Acta — ACACA
Analytica Chimica Acta — Anal Chim Ac
Analytica Chimica Acta — Anal Chim Acta
Analytica Chimica Acta — Anal Chimica Acta
Analytica Chimica Acta — Analyt Chim
Analytical Abstracts — Anal Abstr
Analytical Abstracts — Analyt Abs
Analytical Abstracts — Analyt Abstr
Analytical Abstracts Online — AA
Analytical Advances — Anal Adv
Analytical and Enumerative Bibliography — AEB
Analytical and Enumerative Bibliography — Anal Enum Bibliog
Analytical and Preparative Isotachophoresis. Proceedings. International Symposium on Isotachophoresis — Anal Prep Isotachophoresis Proc Int Symp Isotachophoresis
Analytical and Quantitative Cytology — A Q C
Analytical and Quantitative Cytology — Anal Quant Cytol
Analytical and Quantitative Cytology — AQCYDT
Analytical and Quantitative Cytology and Histology — Anal Quant Cytol Histol
Analytical and Quantitative Cytology and Histology — AQCHED
Analytical and Quantitative Methods in Microscopy — Anal Quant Methods Microsc
Analytical Aspects of Drug Testing — Anal Aspects Drug Test
Analytical Aspects of Environmental Chemistry — Anal Aspects Environ Chem
Analytical Atomic Spectroscopy — Anal At Spectrosc
Analytical Biochemistry — Anal Biochem
Analytical Biochemistry — Analyt Bioc
Analytical Biochemistry — Analyt Biochem
Analytical Biochemistry — Analytical Biochem
Analytical Biochemistry — ANBCA
Analytical Biochemistry of Insects — Anal Biochem Insects
Analytical Calorimetry — ANACAD4
Analytical Calorimetry — Anal Calorim
Analytical Calorimetry — Anal Calorimetry
Analytical Cellular Pathology — Anal Cell Pathol
Analytical Chemistry — An Chem
Analytical Chemistry — Anal Chem
Analytical Chemistry — Analyt Chem
Analytical Chemistry — ANCHA
Analytical Chemistry (Changchung, People's Republic of China) — Anal Chem (Changchung People's Repub China)
Analytical Chemistry in Memory of Professor Anders Ringbom — Analytical Chem
Analytical Chemistry in Nuclear Fuel Reprocessing. Proceedings. ORNL [*Oak Ridge National Laboratory*] **Conference on Analytical Chemistry in Energy Technology** — Anal Chem Nucl Fuel Reprocess Proc ORNL Conf
Analytical Chemistry in Nuclear Technology. Proceedings. Conference on Analytical Chemistry in Energy Technology — Anal Chem Nucl Technol Proc Conf Anal Chem Energy Technol
Analytical Chemistry Instrumentation. Proceedings. Conference on Analytical Chemistry in Energy Technology — Anal Chem Instrum Proc Conf Anal Chem Energy Technol
Analytical Chemistry of Nitrogen and Its Compounds — Anal Chem Nitrogen Its Compd
Analytical Chemistry of Nuclear Fuels. Proceedings of the Panel — Anal Chem Nucl Fuels Proc Panel
Analytical Chemistry of Phosphorus Compounds — Anal Chem Phosphorus Compd
Analytical Chemistry of Sulfur and Its Compounds — Anal Chem Sulfur Its Compd

Analytical Chemistry of Synthetic Dyes — Anal Chem Synth Dyes
Analytical Chemistry Symposia Series [*Elsevier Book Series*] — ACSS
Analytical Chemistry Symposia Series — ACSSDR
Analytical Chemistry Symposia Series — Anal Chem Symp Ser
Analytical Communications — Anal Commun
Analytical Instrumentation — ANINE6
Analytical Instrumentation (New York) — Anal Instrum (NY)
Analytical Instruments and Computers — Anal Instrum Comput
Analytical Instruments and Computers — Analytic Instrum Comput
Analytical Instruments (Tokyo) — Anal Instrum (Tokyo)
Analytical Laboratory — Anal Lab
Analytical Laser Spectroscopy — Anal Laser Spectrosc
Analytical Letters — Anal Lett
Analytical Letters — Anal Letter
Analytical Letters — Anal Letters
Analytical Letters — ANALB
Analytical Letters — Analyt Lett
Analytical Letters. Part A. Chemical Analysis — Anal Lett Part A
Analytical Methods Applied to Air Pollution Measurements — Anal Methods Appl Air Pollut Meas
Analytical Methods for Pesticides and Plant Growth Regulators — Anal Methods Pestic Plant Growth Regul
Analytical Methods for Pesticides, Plant Growth Regulators, and Food Additives — Anal Methods Pestic Plant Growth Regul Food Addit
Analytical Microbiology Methods. Chromatography and Mass Spectrometry — Anal Microbiol Methods
Analytical News. Perkin-Elmer Limited — Anal News Perkin Elmer Ltd
Analytical Proceedings — Anal Proc
Analytical Proceedings — Analyt Proc
Analytical Proceedings — ANPRDI
Analytical Proceedings (London) — Anal Proc (London)
Analytical Proceedings. Royal Society of Chemistry [*United Kingdom*] — Anal Proc R Soc Chem
Analytical Profiles of Drug Substances — Anal Profiles Drug Subst
Analytical Pyrolysis — Anal Pyrolysis
Analytical Pyrolysis. Proceedings of the International Symposium on Analytical Pyrolysis — Anal Pyrolysis Proc Int Symp
Analytical Review. Or History of Literature, Domestic and Foreign, on an Enlarged Plan — Analytical Rev
Analytical Science and Technology — Anal Sci Technol
Analytical Sciences — Anal Sci
Analytical Sciences Monographs — Anal Sci Monogr
Analytical Sciences Monographs — ASMODT
Analytical Spectroscopy Library — Anal Spectrosc Libr
Analytical Spectroscopy. Proceedings. Conference on Analytical Chemistry in Energy Technology — Anal Spectrosc Proc Conf Anal Chem Energy Technol
Analytical Spectroscopy Series — Anal Spectrosc Ser
Analytical Tables of Foreign Trade. Section D — Analyt Tables For Trade Sect D
Analytical Techniques — Anal Tech
Analytical Techniques in Environmental Chemistry. Proceedings. International Congress — Anal Tech Environ Chem Proc Int Congr
Analytical Techniques in the Determination of Air Pollutants. Symposium — Anal Tech Determ Air Pollut Symp
Analytik in der Kosmetik. Moeglichkeiten, Grenzen, Bewertung, DGK-Symposium — Anal Kosmet DGK Symp
Analytiker-Taschenbuch — Anal Taschenb
Analytische Psychologie — Anal Psychol
Analytische Psychologie — ANAPC4
Analytische Schnellverfahren im Betrieb. Vortraege beim Metallurgischen Seminar — Anal Schnellverfahren Betr Vortr Metall Semin
Anaqueles (San Salvador) — Anaquel S Salvador
Anarchism — Anarch
ANARE (Australian National Antarctic Research Expeditions) Research Notes — ANARE (Aust Natl Antarct Res Exped) Res Notes
ANARE [*Australian National Antarctic Research Expeditions*] **Data Reports** — ANARE Data Rep
ANARE [*Australian National Antarctic Research Expeditions*] **Data Reports. Series B** — ANARE Data Rep Ser B
ANARE [*Australian National Antarctic Research Expeditions*] **Data Reports. Series C** — ANARE Data Rep Ser C
ANARE [*Australian National Antarctic Research Expeditions*] **Interim Reports** — ANARE Interim Rep
ANARE [*Australian National Antarctic Research Expeditions*] **Interim Reports. Series A** — AAXRAW
ANARE [*Australian National Antarctic Research Expeditions*] **Interim Reports. Series A** — ANARE Interim Rep Ser A
ANARE [*Australian National Antarctic Research Expeditions*] **News** — ANAREN
ANARE [*Australian National Antarctic Research Expeditions*] **Report** — ANARE Rep
ANARE [*Australian National Antarctic Research Expeditions*] **Report** — ANRPEN
ANARE [*Australian National Antarctic Research Expeditions*] **Report. Series B** — ANARE Rep Ser B
ANARE [*Australian National Antarctic Research Expeditions*] **Report. Series C** — ANARE Rep Ser C
ANARE [*Australian National Antarctic Research Expeditions*] **Scientific Reports** [*A publication*] — ANARE Sci Rep
ANARE [*Australian National Antarctic Research Expeditions*] **Scientific Reports. Series A-IV. Publications** — ANARE Sci Rep Ser A IV Publ
ANARE [*Australian National Antarctic Research Expeditions*] **Scientific Reports. Series B-I. Zoology** — ANARE Sci Rep Ser B I Zool
ANARE [*Australian National Antarctic Research Expeditions*] **Scientific Reports. Series B-IV. Medical Science** — ANARE Sci Rep Ser B IV Med Sci
Anasthesiologie, Intensivmedizin, Notfallmedizin, Schmerztherapie — Anasthesiol Intensivmed Notfallmed Schmerzther
Anatolian Studies — A St
Anatolian Studies — Anat Stud
Anatolian Studies — Anatolian Stud
Anatolian Studies — AnatS
Anatolian Studies [*London*] — AnatSt
Anatolian Studies — Ant St
Anatolian Studies — AS
Anatolian Studies. Journal of the British Institute of Archaeology at Ankara [*London*] — AnSt
Anatolian Studies. Journal of the British Institute of Archaeology at Ankara [*London*] — AnStud
Anatolische Personennamensippen — APS
Anatomia Clinica — Anat Clin
Anatomia e Chirurgia — Anat Chir
Anatomia, Histologia, Embryologia — AHEMA
Anatomia, Histologia, Embryologia — Anat Histol Embryol
Anatomia, Histologia, Embryologia. Zentralblatt fuer Veterinaermedizin. Reihe C — Anat His Em
Anatomical Record — Anat Rec
Anatomical Record — ANREA
Anatomical Record. Supplement — Anat Rec Suppl
Anatomische Gesellschaft. Jena. Verhandlungen — Anat Gesell Jena Verhandl
Anatomische Gesellschaft. Verhandlungen — Anat Ges Verh
Anatomische Hefte — An H
Anatomische Hefte — Anat H
Anatomische Hefte. Abteilung 2 — Anat Hefte Abt 2
Anatomische und Entwicklungsgeschichtliche Monographien — Anat Entw Gesch Monogr
Anatomischer Anzeiger — An A
Anatomischer Anzeiger. Ergaenzungsheft — Anat Anz Ergaenzungsh
Anatomischer Anzeiger; Zentralblatt fuer die Gesamte Wissenschaftliche Anatomie — ANANA
Anatomischer Anzeiger; Zentralblatt fuer die Gesamte Wissenschaftliche Anatomie — Anat Anz
Anatomiske Skrifter — Anat Skr
Anatomy and Embryology — Anat Embryo
Anatomy and Embryology [*Germany*] — Anat Embryol
Anatomy and Embryology — ANEMD
Anatomy and Embryology — ANEMDG
Anatomy and Embryology (Berlin) — Anat Embryol (Berl)
Anatomy, Anthropology, Embryology, and Histology — Anat Anthropol Embryol Histol
Anbar Abstracts (Accounting and Data) — Anbar Abs (Account Data)
Anbar Abstracts (Marketing and Distribution) — Anbar Abs (Mktng Distr)
Anbar Abstracts (Personnel and Training) — Anbar Abs (Personn Trng)
Anbar Abstracts (Top Management) — Anbar Abs (Top Mgmt)
Anbar Abstracts (Work Study) — Anbar Abs (Wk Study)
Anbar Management Services Joint Index — Anbar Mgmt Serv
Anchor Review — Anchor Rev
Anchorage Daily News [*United States*] — Anchorag DN
Ancien Pays de Looz — APL
Anciennes Religions Orientales — ARO
Ancient Christian Writers [*Westminster, MD*] — ACW
Ancient Culture and Society — ACS
Ancient Egypt — AE
Ancient Egypt — AEg
Ancient Egypt — AncEg
Ancient Egypt and the East — AEE
Ancient Egyptian Materials and Industries — AEMI
Ancient Egyptian Onomastica — AEO
Ancient Gaza — AG
Ancient India — AI
Ancient India — AIASI
Ancient India — Anc Ind
Ancient Monuments Society. Transactions — Ancient Monuments Soc Trans
Ancient Monuments Society. Transactions — T Anc Monum
Ancient Near East — ANE
Ancient Near East in Pictures Relating to the Old Testament — ANEP
Ancient Near Eastern Texts Relating to the Old Testament — ANET
Ancient Peoples and Places — APP
Ancient Philosophy — Ancient Phil
Ancient Records of Assyria and Babylonia — ARA
Ancient Records of Egypt — ARE
Ancient Roman Statutes — ARS
Ancient Society — Anc Soc
Ancient Society [*Leuven*] — AnSoc
Ancient Technology to Modern Science — Ancient Technol Mod Sci
Ancient World — Anc W
Ancient World — Anc World
ANCOLD [*Australian National Committee on Large Dams*] **Bulletin** — ANCOLD Bull
ANCSA News. Alaska Native Claims Settlement Act. Bureau of Land Management — ANCS
Andean Group Regional Report — ARR
Andean Quarterly (Santiago) — Andean Quart Santiago
Andean Report — Andean Rpt
Andelsbladet — Andb
Andere Sinema — Sinema
Anderseniana — And
Anderson Localization. Proceedings. Taniguchi International Symposium — Anderson Localization Proc Taniguchi Int Symp
Andhra Agricultural Journal — Andhra Agr J
Andhra Agricultural Journal — Andhra Agric J
Andhra Historical Research Society. Journal — AHRS
Andhra Pradesh Ground Water Department. District Series — Andhra Pradesh Ground Water Dep Dist Ser

Andhra Pradesh Ground Water Department. Research Series — Andhra Pradesh Ground Water Dep Res Ser
Andhra Weekly Reporter [*India*] — An WR
Andhra Weekly Reporter [*India*] — And WR
Andhra Weekly Reporter [*India*] — Andh WR
Andhra Weekly Reporter [*India*] — Andhra WR
Andover Newton Bulletin — ANB
Andover Newton Quarterly — AndNewQ
Andover Newton Quarterly [*Newton, MA*] — AndNewtQ
Andover Newton Quarterly — ANQ
Andover Review — And R
Andover Review — Andover R
Andrews University. Monographs — AUM
Andrews University. Seminary Studies — An U S S
Andrews University. Seminary Studies — AndrUnSS
Andrews University. Seminary Studies — AUSem St
Andrews University. Seminary Studies — AUSS
Androgens and Antiandrogens. Papers Presented at the International Symposium on Androgens and Antiandrogens — Androgens Antiandrogens Pap Int Symp
Androgens in Normal and Pathological Conditions. Proceedings. Symposium on Steroid Hormones — Androgens Norm Pathol Cond Proc Symp Steroid Horm
Andrologie — ANDLA
Anecdota Atheniensia et Alia — AA
Anecdota Graeca — AG
Anecdota Graeca — An Bekk
Anecdota Graeca — An Gr
Anecdota Graeca — Anecd Graec
Anecdota Graeca e Codices. Manuscriptis Bibliothecae Regiae Parisienses — An Par
Anecdota Graeca e Codices. Manuscriptis Bibliothecae Regiae Parisienses — Anec Gr Paris
Anecdota Graeca e Codices. Manuscriptis Bibliothecae Regiae Parisienses — AP
Anecdota Graeca e Codices. Manuscriptis Bibliothecarum Oxoniensium — AG
Anecdota Graeca e Codices. Manuscriptis Bibliothecarum Oxoniensium — Anecd Graec Oxon
Anecdota Graeca e Codices. Manuscriptis Bibliothecarum Oxoniensium — Anecd Ox
Anecdota Graeca e Codices. Manuscriptis Bibliothecarum Oxoniensium — AO
Anecdota Medica Graeca — Anecd Med Graec
Anecdota Oxonensia — A Ox
Anecdota quae ex Ambrosianae Bibliothecae Codicibus — AABC
Anecdota Varia Graeca et Latina — Anecd Stud
Anejos de Estudios Filologicos — AEF
Anesteziologiya i Reanimatologiya — Anesteziol Reanimatol
Anestezja i Reanimacja — Anest Reanim
Anestezja i Reanimacja. Intensywna Terapia — Anest Reanim Intensywna Ter
Anestezjologia, Intensywna Terapia — Anestezjol Intensywna Ter
Anesthesia Abstracts — Anesth Abstr
Anesthesia and Analgesia [*Cleveland*] — Anesth Anal
Anesthesia and Analgesia [*Baltimore*] — Anesth Analg
Anesthesia and Analgesia (Cleveland) — AACRA
Anesthesia and Analgesia (Cleveland) — Anesth Analg (Cleve)
Anesthesia and Analgesia (New York) — Anesth Analg (NY)
Anesthesia and Neurosurgery — Anesth Neurosurg
Anesthesia Progress — Anesth Prog
Anesthesia Progress in Dentistry — Anesth Prog Dent
Anesthesie, Analgesie, Reanimation [*Paris*] — AAREA
Anesthesie, Analgesie, Reanimation [*Paris*] — Anesth An R
Anesthesie, Analgesie, Reanimation [*Paris*] — Anesth Analg Reanim
Anesthesie, Analgesie, Reanimation (Paris) — Anesth Analg (Paris)
Anesthesie-Reanimation et Perinatologie. Journees d'Information Post-Universitaire — Anesth Reanim Perinat Journ Inf Post Univ
Anesthesiologie et Reanimation — Anesthesiol Reanim
Anesthesiology — ANESA
Anesthesiology — Anesthesiol
Anesthesiology Clinics of North America — Anesthesiol Clin North Am
Angeiologie — AGLOA
Angela Luisa — Ang L
Angelicum [*Rome*] — Ang
Angelo-Welsh Review — Ango Wels Rev
Angestellten-Versicherung — Angest Versich
Angewandte Botanik — Ang Bot
Angewandte Botanik — Angew Bot
Angewandte Chemie — Angew Chem
Angewandte Chemie. Ausgabe A. Wissenschaftlicher Teil — Angew Chem Ausg A
Angewandte Chemie. Ausgabe B. Technisch-Wirtschaftlicher-Teil — Angew Chem Ausg B
Angewandte Chemie. Beilage — Angew Chem Beil
Angewandte Chemie. International Edition in English — Angew Chem Int Ed Engl
Angewandte Chemie. International Edition in English — Angew Chem Intern Ed
Angewandte Chemie. International Edition in English. Supplement — Angew Chem Int Ed Engl Suppl
Angewandte Chromatographie — Angew Chromatogr
Angewandte Elektrochemie. Tagungsband. Ulmer Elektrochemische Tage — Angew Elektrochem Tagungsband Ulmer Elektrochem Tage
Angewandte Elektronik — Angew Elektron
Angewandte Elektronik. Mess und Regeltechnik — AEMRC7
Angewandte Elektronik. Mess und Regeltechnik — Angew Elektron Mess & Regeltech
Angewandte Informatik/Applied Informatics — Angew Inf
Angewandte Informatik/Applied Informatics — Angew Inf Appl Inf
Angewandte Informatik/Applied Informatics — Angew Infor
Angewandte Informatik/Applied Informatics — AWIFA
Angewandte Kosmetik — Angew Kosmet
Angewandte Makromolekulare Chemie — Angew Makro
Angewandte Makromolekulare Chemie — Angew Makromol Chem
Angewandte Makromolekulare Chemie — ANMCB
Angewandte Mathematik — Angew Math
Angewandte Meteorologie — Angew Met
Angewandte Meteorologie — Angew Meteorol
Angewandte Ornithologie — Angew Ornithol
Angewandte Parasitologie — Ang Paras
Angewandte Parasitologie — Angew Parasit
Angewandte Parasitologie — Angew Parasitol
Angewandte Parasitologie — AWPAA
Angewandte Pflanzensoziologie — Angew Pflanzensoziol
Angewandte Statistik und Oekonometrie — Angew Statist Oekon
Angewandte Statistik und Okonometrie — Angew Statist Okonometrie
Angewandte Systemanalyse [*Germany*] — Angew Systemanal
Angewandte Systemanalyse. Theorie und Praxis — Angew Systemanal
Angewandte UV-Spektroskopie — Angew UV Spektrosk
Angiologia — Angiol
Angiologia — ANGOA
Angiologica — ANGLA
Angiologisches Symposion — Angiol Symp
Angiologisches Symposion (Kitzbuehel) — Angiol Symp (Kitzbuehel)
Angiology — ANGIA
Angle Orthodontist — Angl Orthod
Angle Orthodontist — Angle Orthod
Angle Orthodontist — ANORA
Anglesey Historical Society Transactions — Anglesey Hist Soc Trans
Anglia — Agl
Anglia — Ang
Anglia Beiblatt — Ang Bbl
Anglia Beiblatt — Angl Bei
Anglia Beiblatt — AnglB
Anglia. Zeitschrift fuer Englische Philologie — Angl
Anglica Germanica — AG
Anglican Church of Canada. Journal of Proceedings. Incorporated Synod of the Diocese of Ottawa — ACCJ Proc Inc Synod Ottawa
Anglican Journal — ANJO
Anglican Messenger — ANGM
Anglican Review — Anglican R
Anglican Theological Review — Ang Theol Rev
Anglican Theological Review — Angl Th R
Anglican Theological Review [*Evanston, IL/Sewanee, TN*] — AnglTR
Anglican Theological Review — AThR
Anglican Theological Review — ATR
Anglistik und Amerikanistik — AuA
Anglistik und Englischunterricht — A und E
Anglistische Forschungen — AF
Anglistische Forschungen — Angl F
Anglistisches Seminar — AS
Anglo Batarian Society. Proceedings — Anglo Bat Soc Proc
Anglo Irish Studies — Anglo Ir Stud
Anglo-American Forum — AAF
Anglo-American Law Review — AALR
Anglo-American Law Review — An-Am LR
Anglo-American Law Review — Anglo-Am L Rev
Anglo-American Law Review — Anglo-Am Law Rev
Anglo-American Law Review — Anglo-Am LR
Anglo-American Magazine — AA
Anglo-American Magazine — Anglo Am M
Anglo-French Review — AFR
Anglo-German Medical Review — AMRWA
Anglo-German Medical Review — Anglo-Ger Med Rev
Anglo-German Review — AglGr
Anglo-Jewish Archives — AJA
Anglo-Norman Text Society — Anglo Norman Text Soc
Anglo-Norman Texts — ANT
Anglosaxon England — Anglosax En
Anglo-Saxon England — Anglo-Saxon Engl
Anglo-Saxon England — ASE
Anglo-Saxon Poetic Records — ASPR
Anglo-Spanish Quarterly Review — Anglo-Sp Q Rev
Anglo-Welsh Review — Anglo-Welsh
Anglo-Welsh Review — AWR
Angola. Servicos de Geologia e Minas. Boletim — Angola Serv Geol Minas Bol
Angora Goat and Mohair Journal — Angora Goat Mohair J
Angus Wildlife Review — Angus Wildl Rev
Anhaltische Gartenbau-Zeitung. Mit Beruecksichtigung der Landwirthschaft — Anhalt Gartenbau Zeitung
Anhaltische Geschichtsblaetter — AGB
Anharmonic Lattices, Structural Transitions, and Melting — Anharmonic Lattices Struct Transitions Melting
Anilinfarben-Industrie — Anilinfarben Ind
Anilinokrasochnaya Promyshlennost — Anilinokras Promst
Anima e Pensiero — AeP
Anima e Pensiero — APen
Animal and Human Health — Anim Hum Health
Animal Behavior — Anim Behav
Animal Behavior Abstracts — Anim Behav Abstr
Animal Behavior Monographs — ANBMAW
Animal Behavior Monographs — Anim Behav Monogr
Animal Behaviour — AnB

Animal Behaviour — ANBEA
Animal Behaviour — Animal Behav
Animal Behaviour — IANB
Animal Blood Groups and Biochemical Genetics — ABBGB
Animal Blood Groups and Biochemical Genetics — Anim Blood Groups Biochem Genet
Animal Blood Groups and Biochemical Genetics (Supplement) — Anim Blood Groups Biochem Genet (Suppl)
Animal Breeding — Anim Breed
Animal Breeding Abstracts — Anim Breed Abstr
Animal Breeding and Feeding — Anim Breed Feed
Animal Cell Biotechnology — Anim Cell Biotechnol
Animal Damage Control ADC. Purdue University Cooperative Extension Service — Anim Damage Control ADC Purdue Univ Coop Ext Serv
Animal de Compagnie — Anim Compagnie
Animal Feed Science and Technology — AFSTDH
Animal Feed Science and Technology — Anim Feed S
Animal Feed Science and Technology [*Netherlands*] — Anim Feed Sci Technol
Animal Genetics — Anim Genet
Animal Genetics and Evolution. Selected Papers. International Congress of Genetics. — Anim Genet Evol Sel Pap Int Congr Gen
Animal Health — ANHEA4
Animal Health — Anim Health
Animal Health — Anim Hlth
Animal Health International — Anim Hlth Int
Animal Health International Directory — Anim Hlth Int Dir
Animal Health VY. Purdue University Cooperative Extension Service — Anim Health VY Purdue Univ Coop Ext Serv
Animal Health Yearbook — Anim Hlth Yb
Animal Husbandry — Anim Husb
Animal Husbandry and Agricultural Journal — Anim Husb Agric J
Animal Husbandry and Veterinary Medicine — Anim Husb Vet Med
Animal Husbandry Mimeograph Series. Florida Agricultural Experiment Station — Anim Husb Mimeogr Ser Fla Agr Exp Sta
Animal Husbandry (Tokyo) — Anim Husb (Tokyo)
Animal Industry Today — Anim Ind Today
Animal International. World Society for the Protection of Animals — Anim Int World Soc Prot Anim
Animal Kingdom — Anim Kingdom
Animal Kingdom — ANKIAV
Animal Learning and Behavior — ALBVA
Animal Learning and Behavior — Anim Lear B
Animal Learning and Behavior — Anim Learn Behav
Animal Learning and Behavior — PALB
Animal Models of Human Disease — Anim Models Hum Dis
Animal Models of Thrombosis and Hemorrhagic Diseases — Anim Models Thromb Hemorrhagic Dis
Animal Nutrition and Health — Anim Nutr Health
Animal Nutrition and Health — ANUHAA
Animal Nutrition Research Council. Proceedings of the Annual Meeting — Anim Nutr Res Counc Proc Annu Meet
Animal Pharm World Animal Health News — APH
Animal, Plant, and Microbial Toxins. Proceedings of the International Symposium on Animal, Plant, and Microbial Toxins — Anim Plant Microb Toxins Proc Int Symp M
Animal Production — Anim Prod
Animal Production — Anim Produc
Animal Production — Animal Prod
Animal Production — ANIPA
Animal Quarantine — Anim Quar
Animal Regulation Studies — Anim Regul Stud
Animal Regulation Studies — ARESDS
Animal Reproduction Science — Anim Reprod Sci
Animal Research Laboratories Technical Paper. Australia Commonwealth Scientific and Industrial Research Organisation — Anim Res Lab Tech Pap Aust CSIRO
Animal Rights Law Reporter — Anim Rights L Rep
Animal Science — Ani Sci
Animal Science — Anim Sci
Animal Science [*Sofia*] — ZHVNAS
Animal Science and Technology — Anim Sci Technol
Animal Science Journal of Pakistan — Anim Sci J Pak
Animal Science Mimeograph Circular. Louisiana State University. Agricultural Experiment Station — AS Mimeogr Circ LA State Univ Agr Exp Sta
Animal Science Mimeograph Report. Florida Agricultural Experiment Station — Anim Sci Mimeogr Rep Fla Agr Exp Sta
Animal Science Mimeograph Series. Ohio State Agricultural Experiment Station — Anim Sci Mimeogr Ser Ohio State Agr Exp Sta
Animal Science Papers and Reports — Anim Sci Pap Rep
Animal Science Research Report — Anim Sci Res Rep
Animal Science (Sofia) — Anim Sci (Sofia)
Animal Sciences P. Poultry. Purdue University. Cooperative Extension Service — Animal Sci P Poult Purdue Univ Coop Ext Serv
Animal Sciences (Pretoria) — Anim Sci (Pretoria)
Animal Technology — Anim Technol
Animal Technology — ANTEDX
Animal Technology. Journal. Institute of Animal Technology — Anim Technol J Inst Anim Technol
Animal Virology — Anim Virol
Animal Welfare Institute Quarterly — Anim Welfare Inst Q
Animals [*London*] — AIWHAJ
Animals — GANS
Animals Agenda — IAAG
Animals Canada — Anim Can
Animals Defender and Anti-Vivisectionist — Anim Def Anti-Viv
Anionic Surfactants Chemical Analysis — Anionic Surfactants Chem Anal
Anisotropy Effects in Superconductors. Proceedings of an International Discussion Meeting. Atominstitut der Oesterreichischen Universitaeten — Anisotropy Eff Supercond Proc Int Discuss Meet
Anjou Historique — AH
Ankara Arkeoloji Muzesinde Bulunan Bogazkoy Tableteri [*Istanbul*] — ABoT
Ankara Nuclear Research and Training Center. Technical Journal — Ankara Nucl Res Train Cent Tech J
Ankara Nuclear Research Center. Technical Journal — Ankara Nucl Res Cent Tech J
Ankara Universitesi Dil ve Tarih-Cografya Fakultesi. Dergisi — AnkUDerg
Ankara Universitesi Dil ve Tarih-Cografya Fakultesi. Dergisi [*Ankara*] — AUDTCF
Ankara Universitesi Dil ve Tarih-Cografya Fakultesi. Yayinlari — AUDTCFY
Ankara Universitesi dis Hekimligi Fakultesi Dergisi — Ankara Univ Hekim Fak Derg
Ankara Universitesi Eczacilik Fakultesi Mecmuasi — Ankara Univ Eczacilik Fak Mecm
Ankara Universitesi. Tip Fakultesi. Mecmuasi — Ankara Univ Tip Fak Mecm
Ankara Universitesi. Tip Fakultesi. Mecmuasi — AUTFAE
Ankara Universitesi. Tip Fakultesi. Mecmuasi. Supplementum — AFKMAL
Ankara Universitesi. Tip Fakultesi. Mecmuasi. Supplementum — Ankara Univ Tip Fak Mecm Suppl
Ankara Universitesi. Veteriner Fakultesi. Dergisi — Ankara Univ Vet Fak Derg
Ankara Universitesi. Veteriner Fakultesi. Dergisi — VTFDA
Ankara Universitesi. Ziraat Fakultesi. Yayinlari — Ankara Univ Ziraat Fak Yayin
Ankara Universitesi Ziraat Fakultesi Yilligi — Ankara Univ Ziraat Fak Yilligi
Ankara University. Faculty of Agriculture. Publications — Ankara Univ Fac Agric Publ
ANL EES (Argonne National Laboratory. Energy and Environmental Systems Division) TM — ANL EES TM Argonne Natl Lab Energy Environ Syst Div
ANL FPP [*Argonne National Laboratory. Fusion Power Program*] **Technical Memorandum** — ANL FPP Tech Mem
ANL HEP [*Argonne National Laboratory. High Energy Physics*] **CP** — ANL HEP CP
ANL. United States Argonne National Laboratory. Report — ANL US Argonne Natl Lab Rep
Anleitungen Bienenzuechter — Anleit Bienenzuechter
Anmeldelser i Paedagogiske Tidsskrifter — Anmeld Paedagog Tidsskr
Ann Arbor News — AAN
Ann Arbor Observer — Ann Arbor Obs
Ann Arbor Review — AAR
Ann Arbor Sun — Arbor Sun
ANNA [*American Nephrology Nurses Association*] **Journal** — ANNA J
Annaes. Academia Brasileira de Ciencias — Ann Acad Bras Cienc
Annaes. Academia Brasileira de Sciencias — Ann Acad Brasil Sci
Annaes. Academia Nacional de Medicina do Rio de Janeiro — Ann Acad Nac Med Rio De Janeiro
Annaes Brasileiros de Gynecologia — Ann Bras Gynecol
Annaes da Sociedade Literaria Portuense [*Porto*] — Annaes Soc Lit Port
Annaes das Sciencias, das Artes, e das Letras. Por Huma Sociedade de Portuguezes Residentes em Paris — Ann Sci Soc Portug Paris
Annaes de Bibliographia Portugueza — ABP
Annaes de Sciencias Naturaes — Ann Sci Nat
Annaes de Sciencias Naturaes (Oporto) — Ann Sci Nat Oporto
Annaes. Faculdade de Medicina. Universidade de Sao Paulo — Ann Fac Med Univ Sao Paulo
Annaes. Sociedade de Biologia de Pernambuco — Ann Soc Biol Pernambuco
Annaes. Sociedade de Pharmacia e Chimica de Sao Paulo — Ann Soc Pharm Chim Sao Paulo
Annaes. Sociedade de Pharmacia e Quimica de Sao Paulo — Ann Soc Pharm Quim Sao Paulo
An-Nahar Arab Report — ANAR
An-Nahar Arab Report and Memo — An-Nahar Arab Rept and Memo
Annale. Natalse Museum — ANMUA9
Annale. Natalse Museum — Ann Natal Mus
Annale. Universita di Padova. Facolta di Economia e Commercio in Verona — Ann Univ Padova
Annale. Universiteit van Stellenbosch. Reeks B — Ann Univ Stellenbosch Reeks B
Annale. Universiteit van Stellenbosch. Serie A — Ann Univ Stellenbosch Ser A
Annale. Universiteit van Stellenbosch. Serie A1. Geologie — Ann Univ Stellenbosch Ser A1
Annale. Universiteit van Stellenbosch. Serie A2. Soologie — Ann Univ Stellenbosch Ser A2
Annale. Universiteit van Stellenbosch. Serie A-3. Landbouwetenskappe — Ann Univ Stellenbosch Ser A 3 Landbouwet
Annale. Universiteit van Stellenbosch. Serie A-3. Landbouwetenskappe — AUSAEW
Annale. Universiteit van Stellenbosch. Serie A4. Bosbou — Ann Univ Stellenbosch Ser A4
Annale. Universiteit van Stellenbosch. Serie A-4. Bosbou — AUSBDY
Annale. Universiteit van Stellenbosch. Serie A-II. Soologie — Ann Univ Stellenbosch Ser A II Sool
Annale. Universiteit van Stellenbosch. Serie A-III. Landbouwetenskappe — Ann Univ Stellenbosch Ser A III Landbou
Annale. Universiteit van Stellenbosch. Serie B — Ann Univ Stellenbosch Ser B
Annale van die Geologiese Opname (South Africa) — Ann Geol Opname (S Afr)
Annale van Geologiese Opname. Republiek van Suid-Afrika — Ann Geol Opname Repub S Afr
Annalen aller Verhandlungen und Arbeiten der Oeconomisch-Patriotischen Societaet des Fuerstenthumes Schweidnitz — Ann Verh Arbeiten Oecon Patriot Soc Fuerstenth Schweidnitz
Annalen Belg Vereniging voor Hospitaalgeschiedenis — Ann Belg Ver Hosp
Annalen der Badischen Gerichte — Ann Bad Gerichte

Annalen der Blumisterei fuer Gartenbesitzer, Kunstgaertner, Samenhaendler, und Blumenfreunde — Ann Blumisterei Gartenbesitz
Annalen der Chemie [*Justus Liebigs*] — Ann Chem
Annalen der Chemie (Justus Liebigs) — Ann Chem (Justus Liebigs)
Annalen der Erd-, Voelker- und Staatenkunde — Ann Erd Voelker Staatenk
Annalen der Forst- und Jagd-Wissenschaft — Ann Forst Jagd Wiss
Annalen der Gaertnerey. Nebst Einem Allgemeinen Intelligenzblatt fuer Garten- und Blumen-Freunde — Ann Gaertnerey
Annalen der Gemeinwirtschaft — ANX
Annalen der Gesammten Litteratur — Ann Gesammten Litt
Annalen der Gesammten Medicin als Wissenschaft und als Kunst, zur Beurtheilung ihrer Neuesten Erfindungen, Theorien, Systeme und Heilmethoden — Ann Gesammten Med
Annalen der Grossherzoglich Badischen Gerichte — ABadG
Annalen der Historischen Verein fuer den Niederrhein — Anah
Annalen der Hydrographie und Maritimen Meteorologie — Ann Hydrogr
Annalen der Hydrographie und Maritimen Meteorologie (Berlin) — AHB
Annalen der Koeniglichen Landwirtschaftlichen Hochschule Schwedens — Ann K Landwirtsch Hochsch Schwed
Annalen der Mecklenburgischen Landwirthschaftsgesellschaft — Ann Mecklenburg Landwirthschaftsges
Annalen der Meteorologie — A Met
Annalen der Mijnen van Belgie — Ann Mijnen Belg
Annalen der Natur- und Kulturphilosophie — Ann Natur Kulturphil
Annalen der Naturgeschichte — Ann Naturgesch
Annalen der Naturphilosophie — Ann N Ph
Annalen der Naturphilosophie — Ann Naturphil
Annalen der Pharmacie (Lemgo, Germany) — Ann Pharm (Lemgo Germany)
Annalen der Philosophie und Philosophischen Kritik — A Ph Ph K
Annalen der Philosophie und Philosophischen Kritik — AP
Annalen der Physik — Ann Physik
Annalen der Physik — ANPYA
Annalen der Physik (Germany) — Ann Phys (Germ)
Annalen der Physik (Leipzig) — Ann Phys (Leipzig)
Annalen der Physik und Chemie — An Physik
Annalen der Physik und Chemie — Ann Phys Chem
Annalen der Physik und Physikalischen Chemie — Ann Phys Phys Chem
Annalen der Tschechoslowakischen Akademie der Landwirtschaft — Ann Tschech Akad Landwirtsch
Annalen der Vereeniging tot het Hevordering van de Beoefening der Wetenschap Onder de Katholieken in Nederland — AVBWKN
Annalen des Deutschen Reiches — Ann Dt Reich
Annalen des Historischen Vereins fuer den Niederrhein — AHNRH
Annalen des Historischen Vereins fuer den Niederrhein — AHVNR
Annalen des Historischen Vereins fuer den Niederrhein — AHVNRh
Annalen des Historischen Vereins fuer den Niederrhein — AVN
Annalen des Naturhistorischen Hofmuseums — Ann Naturhist Hofmus
Annalen des Naturhistorischen Museums in Wien — ANMWAF
Annalen des Naturhistorischen Museums in Wien — Ann Naturhist Mus Wien
Annalen des Naturhistorischen Museums in Wien — Annln Naturh Mus Wien
Annalen des Naturhistorischen Museums in Wien. Serie A. fuer Mineralogie und Petrographie, Geologie und Palaentologie, Anthropologie und Praehistorie — Ann Naturhist Mus Wien Ser A
Annalen des Naturhistorischen Museums in Wien. Serie B. Botanik und Zoologie — Ann Naturhist Mus Wien Ser B Bot Zool
Annalen des Naturhistorischen Museums in Wien. Serie C. Jahresberichte — Ann Naturhist Mus Wien Ser C Jahresber
Annalen des Vereins fuer Nassauische Altertumskunde und Geschichtsforschung — AVNAG
Annalen des Vereins fuer Nassauische Altertumskunde und Geschichtsforschung — AVNAKGF
Annalen fuer das Gesamte Hebammenwesen — Ann Ges Hebammw
Annalen fuer die Landwirthschaft und das Landwirthschafts-Recht — Ann Landw Landw Recht
Annalen fuer Soziale Politik und Gesetzgebung — Ann Soz P
Annalen Landwirtschaftlichen Hochschule Schwedens — Ann Landwirtsch Hochsch Schwed
Annalen. Staedtische Allgemeine Krankenhaeuser zu Muenchen — Ann Staedt Allg Krankenhaeuser Muenchen
Annalen van de Belgische Vereniging voor Stralingsbescherming — Ann Belg Ver Stralingsbescherming
Annalen van de Geschied- en Oud-Heidkundige Kring van Ronse — A Ronse
Annalen van de Oudheidkundige Kring van het Land van Waas — Ann Oudheidk Kring Land Waas
Annalen van de Oudheidkundige Kring van het Land van Waas — AOKW
Annalen van het Koninklijk Museum van Belgisch Congo. Reeks in 8 Geologische Wetenschappen — Ann K Mus Belg Congo Reeks 8 Geol Wet
Annalen van het Thijmgenootschap — AnnThijm
Annalen van het Thijmgenootschap [*Utrecht*] — AnThijm
Annalen van het Thijmgenootschap — AThijmG
Annales — Ann
Annales Academiae Horti- et Viticulturae — Ann Acad Horti Vitic
Annales Academiae Jenensis — Ann Acad Jenensis
Annales Academiae Lugduno-Batavae — Ann Acad Lugduno Batavae
Annales Academiae Medicae Bialostocensis — Ann Acad Med Bialostoc
Annales Academiae Medicae Gedanensis — AAMGBD
Annales Academiae Medicae Gedanensis — Ann Acad Med Gedanensis
Annales Academiae Medicae Lodzensis — Ann Acad Med Lodz
Annales Academiae Medicae Lodzensis. Suplement — Ann Acad Med Lodz Supl
Annales Academiae Medicae Stetinensis — Ann Acad Med Stetin
Annales Academiae Medicae Stetinensis — RPMKAA
Annales Academiae Medicae Stetinensis. Suplement — AAMSDH
Annales Academiae Medicae Stetinensis. Suplement — Ann Acad Med Stetin Supl
Annales Academiae Regiae Scientiarum Upsaliensis — Ann Acad Reg Sci Upsal
Annales Academiae Regiae Scientiarum Upsaliensis — Ann Acad Regiae Sci Ups
Annales Academiae Regiae Scientiarum Upsaliensis — ARUPAS
Annales Academiae Scientarum Fennicae. Series A — Ann Acad Sci Fenn Ser A
Annales Academiae Scientiarum Fennicae — A Acad Sci Fenn
Annales Academiae Scientiarum Fennicae — AASF
Annales Academiae Scientiarum Fennicae — Ann Ac Fenn
Annales Academiae Scientiarum Fennicae — Ann Acad Sci Fen
Annales Academiae Scientiarum Fennicae. Serie B — Ann Acad Sci Fennicae
Annales. Academiae Scientiarum Fennicae. Series A 3. Geologica-Geographica — Ann Acad Sci Fenn Ser A 3 Geol
Annales. Academiae Scientiarum Fennicae. Series A 5. Medica — Ann Acad Sci Fenn Ser A 5 Medica
Annales Academiae Scientiarum Fennicae. Series A-I (Mathematica) — Ann Acad Sci Fenn A I
Annales Academiae Scientiarum Fennicae. Series A-I (Mathematica) — Ann Acad Sci Fenn Ser A I
Annales Academiae Scientiarum Fennicae. Series A-I (Mathematica) — Ann Acad Sci Fenn Ser A I (Math)
Annales Academiae Scientiarum Fennicae. Series A-I (Mathematica). Dissertationes — Ann Acad Sci Fenn Ser AI (Math) Dissertationes
Annales Academiae Scientiarum Fennicae. Series A-I (Mathematica-Physica) — Ann Acad Sci Fenn Ser AI (Math Phy)
Annales Academiae Scientiarum Fennicae. Series A-II (Chemica) — AAFCAX
Annales Academiae Scientiarum Fennicae. Series A-II (Chemica) — Ann Acad Sci Fenn A II
Annales Academiae Scientiarum Fennicae. Series A-II (Chemica) — Ann Acad Sci Fenn Ser A II
Annales Academiae Scientiarum Fennicae. Series A-II (Chemica) — Ann Acad Sci Fenn Ser A II (Chem)
Annales Academiae Scientiarum Fennicae. Series A-III (Geologica-Geographica) — AAFGAB
Annales Academiae Scientiarum Fennicae. Series A-III (Geologica-Geographica) [*A publication*] — Ann Acad Sci Fenn Ser A III
Annales Academiae Scientiarum Fennicae. Series A-III (Geologica-Geographica) — Ann Acad Sci Fenn Ser A III (Geol Geogr)
Annales Academiae Scientiarum Fennicae. Series A-IV (Biologica) — AAFBA
Annales Academiae Scientiarum Fennicae. Series A-IV (Biologica) — AAFBAU
Annales Academiae Scientiarum Fennicae. Series A-IV (Biologica) — Ann Acad Sci Fenn (Biol)
Annales Academiae Scientiarum Fennicae. Series A-IV (Biologica) — Ann Acad Sci Fenn Ser A IV
Annales Academiae Scientiarum Fennicae. Series A-IV (Biologica) — Ann Acad Sci Fenn Ser A IV (Biol)
Annales Academiae Scientiarum Fennicae. Series A-V (Medica) — AAFMBU
Annales Academiae Scientiarum Fennicae. Series A-V (Medica) — AFMAA
Annales Academiae Scientiarum Fennicae. Series A-V (Medica) — Ann Acad Sci Fenn (Med)
Annales Academiae Scientiarum Fennicae. Series A-V (Medica) — Ann Acad Sci Fenn Ser A V
Annales Academiae Scientiarum Fennicae. Series A-V (Medica) — Ann Acad Sci Fenn Ser A V (Med)
Annales Academiae Scientiarum Fennicae. Series A-V (Medica-Anthropologica) — AFMAAT
Annales Academiae Scientiarum Fennicae. Series A-V (Medica-Anthropologica) — Ann Acad Sci Fenn Ser A V (Med-Anthropol)
Annales Academiae Scientiarum Fennicae. Series A-VI (Physica) — AAFPA
Annales Academiae Scientiarum Fennicae. Series A-VI (Physica) — Ann Acad Sci Fenn A VI
Annales Academiae Scientiarum Fennicae. Series A-VI (Physica) — Ann Acad Sci Fenn Ser A VI
Annales Academiae Scientiarum Fennicae. Series A-VI (Physica) — Ann Acad Sci Fenn Ser A VI (Phys)
Annales Academici (The Hague and Leiden) — Ann Acad The Hague Leiden
Annales. Academie de Macon — AAM
Annales. Academie des Sciences Coloniales — Ann Acad Sci Colon
Annales. Academie des Sciences de Russie — AAR
Annales. Academie des Sciences Techniques a Varsovie — Ann Acad Sci Tech Varsovie
Annales. Academie Royale d'Agriculture de Suede — Ann Acad R Agric Suede
Annales. Academie Royale d'Agriculture et de Sylviculture de Suede — Ann Acad R Agric Sylvic Suede
Annales. Academie Royale d'Agriculture et de Sylviculture de Suede. Supplement — Ann Acad R Agric Sylvic Suede Suppl
Annales. Academie Royale d'Archeologie de Belgique — AAAB
Annales. Academie Royale d'Archeologie de Belgique — AABAn
Annales. Academie Royale d'Archeologie de Belgique — AARAB
Annales Academie Scientiarum Fennicae. Serie A. Suomalaisen Tiedeakatemian Toimtuksia — Ann Acad Sci Fenn Ser A
Annales. ACFAS [*Association Canadienne Francaise pour l'Avancement des Sciences*] — AACFAR
Annales. ACFAS [*Association Canadienne Francaise pour l'Avancement des Sciences*] — Ann ACFAS
Annales Africaines — A Afr
Annales Africaines — A Afric
Annales Africaines — Annales Afr
Annales Agriculturae Fenniae — ANAFA6
Annales Agriculturae Fenniae — Ann Agr Fenn
Annales Agriculturae Fenniae — Ann Agric Fenn
Annales Agriculturae Fenniae — Annls Agric Fenn
Annales Agriculturae Fenniae — Annls Agric Fenniae
Annales Agriculturae Fenniae. Maatalouden Tutkimuskeskuksen Aikakauskirja/ Journal. Agricultural Research Centre — Ann Agric Fenniae
Annales Agriculturae Fenniae. Seria Agrogeologia, -Chimica, et -Physica [*Finland*] — Ann Agric Fenn Ser Agrogeol -Chim -Phys

Annales Agriculturae Fenniae. Supplementum — Ann Agric Fenn Suppl
Annales Agriculturae Fenniae. Supplementum — Suppl Annls Agric Fenn
Annales Agronomiques — ANAGA
Annales Agronomiques — Ann Agron
Annales Agronomiques — Annls Agron
Annales Agronomiques. Hors-Serie [*France*] — Ann Agron Hors-Ser
Annales Agronomiques. Ministere de l'Agriculture — Ann Agron Minist Agric
Annales Agronomiques (Paris) — Ann Agron (Paris)
Annales Algeriennes de Chirurgie — Ann Alger Chir
Annales Algeriennes de Geographie — Ann Algeriennes Geogr
Annales. Amelioration des Plantes. Institut National de la Recherche Agronomique — Ann Amelior Pl
Annales Archeologiques — Ann Arch
Annales Archeologiques Arabes de Syrie — AAAS
Annales Archeologiques Arabes Syriennes — A A Syr
Annales Archeologiques Arabes Syriennes — A Arch Ar Syr
Annales Archeologiques Arabes Syriennes — AAAS
Annales Archeologiques Arabes Syriennes — Ann A Syr
Annales Archeologiques Arabes Syriennes — Ann AAS
Annales Archeologiques Arabes Syriennes — Annales Arch Syrie
Annales Archeologiques de Syrie — AArchSyr
Annales Archeologiques de Syrie [*Damascus*] — AAS
Annales Archeologiques de Syrie — AASy
Annales Archeologiques de Syrie [*Damascus*] — AnArchSyr
Annales Archeologiques de Syrie — Ann Archeol Syrie
Annales Archeologiques Syrie — Ann Arch Syr
Annales. Association Belge de Radioprotection — ABVSD
Annales. Association Belge de Radioprotection [*Belgium*] — Ann Assoc Belge Radioprot
Annales. Association Canadienne-Francaise pour l'Avancement des Sciences — Ann Assoc Can Fr Av Sci
Annales. Association des Anciens Etudiants. Faculte de Droit. Universite de Louvain — ADUL
Annales. Association Internationale pour le Calcul Analogique — Ann Ass Int Calcul Analogique
Annales. Association Internationale pour le Calcul Analogique — Ann Assoc Int Calcul Analogique
Annales. Association Philomatique Vogeso-Rhenane, Faisant Suite a la Flore d'Alsace de F. Kirschleger — Ann Assoc Philom Vogeso Rhenane
Annales Belges de Medecine Militaire — Ann Belg Med Mil
Annales. Belgische Vereniging voor Tropische Geneeskunde — Ann Belg Ver Trop Geneeskd
Annales. Belgische Vereniging voor Tropische Geneeskunde — ASBMAX
Annales. Belgische Verenigingen voor Tropische Geneeskunde voor Parasitologie en voor Menselijke en Dierlijke Mycologie — AMTPBN
Annales. Belgische Verenigingen voor Tropische Geneeskunde voor Parasitologie en voor Menselijke en Dierlijke Mycologie — Ann Belg Ver Trop Geneeskd Parasitol Mensel Dierl Mycol
Annales Biologicae Universitatum Hungariae. A Magyar Tudomanyegyejetenek Biologiai Intezeteinek Evkoenyve — Ann Biol Univ Hungariae
Annales Biologiques — ABCXA
Annales Biologiques — ANBI
Annales Biologiques — Ann Biol
Annales Biologiques (Copenhagen) — Ann Biol (Copenhagen)
Annales Bogoriensis — Ann Bogor
Annales Botanicae Systematicae — Ann Bot Syst
Annales Botanici Fennici — ABOF
Annales Botanici Fennici — ABOFA
Annales Botanici Fennici — Ann Bot Fenn
Annales Botanici Societatis Zoologicae Botanicae Fennicae "Vanamo" — Ann Bot Soc Zool Bot Fenn "Vanamo"
Annales Bryologici. A Yearbook Devoted to the Study of Mosses and Hepatics — Ann Bryol
Annales Camaldulenses Ordinis Sancti Benedicti — ACOSB
Annales Canonicorum Regularium S. Augustini — ACRSA
Annales. Centre de Recherches Agronomiques de Bambey au Senegal — Ann Cent Rech Agron Bambey Senegal
Annales. Centre de Recherches Agronomiques de Bambey au Senegal — Annls Cent Rech Agron Bambey
Annales. Centre d'Enseignement Superieur de Brazzaville — Ann Cent Enseign Super Brazzaville
Annales. Centre d'Etude des Religions — ACER
Annales. Centre d'Etude des Religions [*Brussels*] — AnCEtRel
Annales. Centre d'Etude sur l'Evolution de l'Homme et de la Nature — Ann Centre Etude Evol HommeNat
Annales. Centre Universitaire de Nice — ACUN
Annales. Centre Universitaire Mediterraneen de Nice — ACUM
Annales. Cercle Archeologique de Mons — A Mons
Annales. Cercle Archeologique de Mons — ACAM
Annales. Cercle Archeologique de Mons — Ann Cerc Archeol Mons
Annales. Cercle Archeologique d'Enghien — A Enghien
Annales. Cercle Archeologique d'Enghien — ACAE
Annales. Cercle Archeologique d'Enghien — Ann Cerc Archeol Enghien
Annales. Cercle Archeologique d'Enghien — Ann Cercle Archeol Enghien
Annales. Cercle Archeologique du Canton de Soignies — A Soignies
Annales. Cercle Archeologique du Canton de Soignies — ACACS
Annales. Cercle Archeologique du Canton de Soignies — Ann Cerc Archeol Canton Soignies
Annales. Cercle Archeologique du Canton de Soignies — ASS Ph
Annales. Cercle Archeologique du Pays de Waes — AAW
Annales. Cercle Archeologique du Pays de Waes — ACAPW
Annales. Cercle Archeologique et Folklorique de la Louviere et du Centre — A Louviere
Annales. Cercle Archeologique et Folklorique de la Louviere et du Centre — Ann Rep MFA
Annales. Cercle Archeologique et Historique d'Audenaerde — Audenaerde
Annales. Cercle Hutois des Sciences et Beaux-Arts — ACHSB
Annales. Cercle Hutois des Sciences et Beaux-Arts. Huy — A Huy
Annales. Chambre Centrale des Poids et Mesures — Ann Chambre Cent Poids Mes
Annales Chimiques (Athens). Section A — Ann Chim Athens A
Annales Chirurgiae et Gynaecologiae — Ann Chir Gynaecol
Annales Chirurgiae et Gynaecologiae Fenniae — ACGYA
Annales Chirurgiae et Gynaecologiae Fenniae [*Helsinki*] — Ann Chir Gy
Annales Chirurgiae et Gynaecologiae Fenniae [*Helsinki*] — Ann Chir Gynaecol
Annales Chirurgiae et Gynaecologiae Fenniae [*Helsinki*] — Ann Chir Gynaecol Fenn
Annales Chirurgiae et Gynaecologiae Fenniae. Supplementum — ACGSA
Annales Chirurgiae et Gynaecologiae Fenniae. Supplementum [*Helsinki*] — Ann Chir Gynaecol Fenn Suppl
Annales Chirurgiae et Gynaecologiae Fenniae. Supplementum [*Helsinki*] — Ann Chir Gynaecol Suppl
Annales Chirurgiae et Gynaecologiae. Supplementum — Ann Chir Gynaecol Suppl
Annales Chopin — A Ch
Annales Chopin — An Chopin
Annales Cisalpines d'Histoire Sociale — Ann Cisalp Hist Soc
Annales. College International pour l'Etude Scientifique des Techniques de Production Mecanique — Ann Coll Int Etude Sci Tech Prod Mec
Annales. College Royal des Medecins et Chirurgiens du Canada — Ann Coll R Med Chir Can
Annales Collegii Medici Antwerpiensis — Ann Coll Med Antwerp
Annales. Comite Flamand de France — ACFF
Annales. Congregation de la Mission — ACM
Annales. Congres de la Federation Archeologique et Historique de Belgique [*A publication*] — Ann Congr Federation Archeol Hist Belg
Annales Cryptogamici et Phytopathologici — Ann Cryptogam Phytopathol
Annales. Dakar Universite. Faculte des Sciences — Ann Dakar Univ Fac Sci
Annales d'Anatomie Pathologique — ANAPA
Annales d'Anatomie Pathologique [*Paris*] — Ann Anat Pathol
Annales d'Anatomie Pathologique et d'Anatomie Normale. Medico Chirurgicale [*A publication*] — Ann Anat Pathol Anat Norm Med Chir
Annales d'Anatomie Pathologique (Paris) — Ann Anat Pathol (Paris)
Annales d'Astrophysique [*France*] — Ann Astrophys
Annales d'Astrophysique. Supplement — Ann Astrophys Suppl
Annales de Bibliographie Theologique — ABT
Annales de Bibliographie Theologique — ABTh
Annales de Biochimie Clinique du Quebec — Ann Biochim Clin Que
Annales de Biologie — Annls Biol
Annales de Biologie Animale, Biochimie, et Biophysique — ABABA
Annales de Biologie Animale, Biochimie, et Biophysique — Ann Biol An
Annales de Biologie Animale, Biochimie, et Biophysique — Ann Biol Anim Biochim Biophys
Annales de Biologie Animale, Biochimie, et Biophysique — Annls Biol Anim Biochim Biophys
Annales de Biologie Clinique — ABCLA
Annales de Biologie Clinique [*Paris*] — Ann Biol Cl
Annales de Biologie Clinique (Paris) — Ann Biol Clin (Paris)
Annales de Biologie Lacustre — Ann Biol Lacustre
Annales de Bourgogne — A Bourgogne
Annales de Bourgogne — ABourg
Annales de Bourgogne — AnB
Annales de Bourgogne — Ann Bourgogne
Annales de Bourgogne — Ann de Bourgogne
Annales de Bourgogne — AnnBourg
Annales de Bretagne [*Later, Annales de Bretagne et des Pays de l'Ouest*] — ABret
Annales de Bretagne [*Later, Annales de Bretagne et des Pays de l'Ouest*] — AnBr
Annales de Bretagne [*Later, Annales de Bretagne et des Pays de l'Ouest*] — AnBret
Annales de Bretagne [*Later, Annales de Bretagne et des Pays de l'Ouest*] — Ann Bret
Annales de Bretagne [*Later, Annales de Bretagne et des Pays de l'Ouest*] — Ann de Bret
Annales de Bretagne et des Pays de l'Ouest — ABr
Annales de Bretagne et des Pays de l'Ouest — Ann Bretagne
Annales de Bretagne et des Pays de l'Ouest — Ann Bretagne Pays Ouest
Annales de Bromatologia — An Brom
Annales de Cardiologie et d'Angeiologie — ACAAB
Annales de Cardiologie et d'Angeiologie — Ann Card An
Annales de Cardiologie et d'Angeiologie — Ann Cardiol Angeiol
Annales de Chimie — A Ch
Annales de Chimie Analytique — Ann Chim Anal
Annales de Chimie Analytique et de Chimie Applique et Revue de Chimie Analytique Reunies — Ann Chim Anal Chim Appl
Annales de Chimie Analytique et Revue de Chimie Analytique Reunies — Ann Chim Anal Rev Chim Anal Reunies
Annales de Chimie et de Physique — Ann Chim Phys
Annales de Chimie (Istanbul) — Ann Chim (Istanbul)
Annales de Chimie (Paris) — ANCPA
Annales de Chimie (Paris, France) — Ann Chim (Fr)
Annales de Chimie (Paris, France) — Ann Chim (Paris)
Annales de Chirurgie — ANCHB
Annales de Chirurgie — Ann Chir
Annales de Chirurgie de la Main — ACHMDM
Annales de Chirurgie de la Main — Ann Chir Main
Annales de Chirurgie de la Main et du Membre Superieur — Ann Chir Main Memb Super
Annales de Chirurgie Infantile — ANIFA
Annales de Chirurgie Infantile — Ann Chir In

Annales de Chirurgie Infantile — Ann Chir Infant
Annales de Chirurgie (Paris) — Ann Chir (Paris)
Annales de Chirurgie Plastique — Ann Chir Pl
Annales de Chirurgie Plastique — Ann Chir Plast
Annales de Chirurgie Plastique — APLSA
Annales de Chirurgie Plastique et Esthetique — ACESEQ
Annales de Chirurgie Plastique et Esthetique — Ann Chir Plast Esthet
Annales de Chirurgie Plastique et Esthetique — Ann Chir Plast Esthetique
Annales de Chirurgie. Semaine des Hopitaux [*France*] — Ann Chir Sem Hop
Annales de Chirurgie Thoracique et Cardio-Vasculaire — ACSSBP
Annales de Chirurgie Thoracique et Cardio-Vasculaire — Ann Chir Thorac Cardio-Vasc
Annales de Cryptogamie Exotique — Ann Cryptog Exot
Annales de Cryptogamie Exotique — Ann Cryptogam Exot
Annales de Demographie Historique — Ann Dem Hist
Annales de Demographie Historique — Ann Demogr Hist
Annales de Dermatologie et de Syphiligraphie [*Later, Annales de Dermatologie et de Venereologie*] — ADSPA
Annales de Dermatologie et de Syphiligraphie [*Later, Annales de Dermatologie et de Venereologie*] — Ann Der Syp
Annales de Dermatologie et de Syphiligraphie [*Later, Annales de Dermatologie et de Venereologie*] — Ann Dermatol Syphiligr
Annales de Dermatologie et de Venereologie — ADVED7
Annales de Dermatologie et de Venereologie — Ann Dermatol Venereol
Annales de Droit — A Dr
Annales de Droit — Ann Dr
Annales de Droit et de Sciences Politiques — ADSP
Annales de Droit et de Sciences Politiques — An D S P
Annales de Droit et de Sciences Politiques — Ann Dr et Sc Polit
Annales de Droit et de Sciences Politiques — Ann Dr Sc Polit
Annales de Droit et de Sciences Politiques. Revue Trimestrielle [*Brussels*] [*A publication*] — Ann Dr Sc Pol
Annales de Droit International Medical — Ann de Droit Internat Med
Annales de Droit International Medical — Ann Droit Int Med
Annales de Droit. Revue Trimestrielle de Droit Belge — Ann de Droit
Annales de Gastroenterologie et d'Hepatologie — AGHPB
Annales de Gastroenterologie et d'Hepatologie — Ann Gastro
Annales de Gastroenterologie et d'Hepatologie — Ann Gastroenterol Hepatol
Annales de Gembloux — Ann Gembloux
Annales de Gembloux — Annls Gembloux
Annales de Genetique — AGTQA
Annales de Genetique — Ann Genet
Annales de Genetique et de Selection Animale — Ann Genet Sel Anim
Annales de Genetique. Museum National d'Histoire Naturelle — Ann Genet
Annales de Geographie — A Geogr
Annales de Geographie — AG
Annales de Geographie — An Geog
Annales de Geographie — ANGE-A
Annales de Geographie — Ann Geog
Annales de Geographie — Ann Geogr
Annales de Geographie — Annales De Geog
Annales de Geologie et de Paleontologie — An G Paleont
Annales de Geophysique — AGEPA
Annales de Geophysique — Ann Geophy
Annales de Geophysique — Ann Geophys
Annales de Haute-Provence — A H Prov
Annales de Kinesitherapie — ANKIDY
Annales de Kinesitherapie — Ann Kinesither
Annales de la Brasserie et de la Distillerie — Ann Brass Distill
Annales de la Medicine Physiologique [*Paris*] — Annales Med Physiol
Annales de la Mission de N.-D. de Sion en Terre Sainte (1877-1912) — AMNDS
Annales de la Nutrition et de l'Alimentation — ANAIA
Annales de la Nutrition et de l'Alimentation — Ann Nutr Al
Annales de la Nutrition et de l'Alimentation — Ann Nutr Aliment
Annales de la Nutrition et de l'Alimentation — Annls Nutr Aliment
Annales de la Nutrition et de l'Alimentation/Annals of Nutrition and Food — Ann Nutr Aliment Ann Nutr Food
Annales de la Philosophie Chretienne — AnPC
Annales de la Philosophie Chretienne — APC
Annales de la Propagation de la Foi — APF
Annales de la Propagation de la Foi (Lyons) — APFL
Annales de la Propriete Industrielle, Artistique, et Litteraire — Ann Prop Ind
Annales de la Propriete Industrielle, Artistique, et Litteraire — Ann Propr Ind
Annales de la Recherche Forestiere au Maroc — Ann Rech For Maroc
Annales de la Science Agronomique — Ann Sci Agron
Annales de la Science Agronomique Francaise et Etrangere — Ann Sci Agron Fr
Annales de la Science Agronomique Francaise et Etrangere — Ann Sci Agron Fr Etrang
Annales de l'Abeille — Ann Abeille
Annales de l'Abeille [*Paris*] — ANNAAM
Annales de l'Abeille — Annls Abeille
Annales de l'Amelioration des Plantes — AAPLA
Annales de l'Amelioration des Plantes [*Paris*] — AAPLA8
Annales de l'Amelioration des Plantes [*Paris*] — Ann A Plant
Annales de l'Amelioration des Plantes [*Paris*] — Ann Amelior Plantes
Annales de l'Amelioration des Plantes — Annls Amel Pl
Annales de l'Amelioration des Plantes. Institut National de la Recherche Agronomique. Serie B — Ann Amelior Plantes Inst Nat Rech Agron Ser B
Annales de l'Amelioration des Plantes (Paris) — Ann Amelior Plant (Paris)
Annales de l'Anesthesiologie Francaise — AANFA
Annales de l'Anesthesiologie Francaise — Ann Anesthesiol Fr
Annales de l'Economie Publique, Sociale, et Cooperative — A Econ Publ Soc Coop
Annales de l'Est — AE
Annales de l'Est — An Est
Annales de l'Est — Ann Est
Annales de l'Est et du Nord — AEN
Annales de l'Est et du Nord — AnE
Annales de l'Est et du Nord — AnEN
Annales de l'Est. Memoires — A Est M
Annales de l'Est Nancy — A Est
Annales de l'Extreme Orient et de l'Afrique — AEOA
Annales de l'Horticulture en Belgique — Ann Hort Belgique
Annales de Limnologie — ANLIB
Annales de Limnologie — Ann Limnol
Annales de l'Institut Henri Poincare. Analyse Non Lineaire — Ann Inst H Poincare Anal Non Lineaire
Annales de l'Institut Henri Poincare. Physique Theorique — Ann Inst H Poincare Phys Theor
Annales de l'Institut Henri Poincare. Probabilites et Statistique — Ann Inst H Poincare Probab Statist
Annales de Medecine Belge et Etrangere — Ann de Med Belge
Annales de Medecine de Reims — ANMRC2
Annales de Medecine de Reims — Ann Med Reims
Annales de Medecine de Reims-Champagne-Ardennes — Ann Med Reims-Champagne-Ardennes
Annales de Medecine et Chirurgie Infantiles — Ann Med et Chir Inf
Annales de Medecine et de Pharmacie Coloniales — Ann Med et Pharm Colon
Annales de Medecine et de Pharmacie Coloniales — Annls Med Pharm Colon
Annales de Medecine et de Pharmacie de Reims — AMPRB9
Annales de Medecine et de Pharmacie de Reims — Ann Med Pharm Reims
Annales de Medecine Interne — AMDIB
Annales de Medecine Interne — AMDIBO
Annales de Medecine Interne — Ann Med In
Annales de Medecine Interne — Ann Med Intern
Annales de Medecine Interne — Ann Med Interne
Annales de Medecine Legale — AMILAN
Annales de Medecine Legale — Ann Med Leg
Annales de Medecine Legale, Criminologie, Police Scientifique, et Toxicologie [*A publication*] — Ann Med Leg Criminol Police Toxicol
Annales de Medecine Legale de Criminologie, Police Scientifique, Medecine Sociale, et Toxicologie — Ann Med Leg Criminol Police Sci Med Soc Toxicol
Annales de Medecine Legale et de Criminologie — Ann Med Leg Criminol
Annales de Medecine (Paris) — Ann Med (Paris)
Annales de Medecine Veterinaire — AMVRA
Annales de Medecine Veterinaire — AMVRA4
Annales de Medecine Veterinaire — Ann Med Vet
Annales de Medecine Veterinaire — Ann Med Veterin
Annales de Medecine Veterinaire — Annls Med Vet
Annales de Microbiologie — ANMBC
Annales de Microbiologie [*Paris*] — ANMBCM
Annales de Microbiologie [*Institut Pasteur*] [*Paris*] — Ann Microb
Annales de Microbiologie (Paris) — Ann Microbiol (Paris)
Annales de Normandie — A d Normandie
Annales de Normandie — A Norm
Annales de Normandie — AnN
Annales de Normandie — Ann Normandie
Annales de Normandie — AnnNorm
Annales de Normandie; Revue Trimestrielle d'Etudes Regionales — A Normandie
Annales de Paleontologie — An Paleont
Annales de Paleontologie — Ann Paleontol
Annales de Paleontologie Invertebre — Ann Paleontol Invertebr
Annales de Paleontologie Invertebre — Ann Paleontol Invertebre
Annales de Paleontologie Vertebre — Ann Paleontol Vertebr
Annales de Paleontologie Vertebres-Invertebres — Ann Paleontol Vertebr Invertebr
Annales de Parasitologie Humaine et Comparee — Ann Parasit
Annales de Parasitologie Humaine et Comparee — Ann Parasitol
Annales de Parasitologie Humaine et Comparee — Ann Parasitol Hum Comp
Annales de Parasitologie Humaine et Comparee — APHCA
Annales de Pathologie — Ann Pathol
Annales de Pediatrie [*Paris*] — Ann Pediatr
Annales de Pediatrie — APSHA
Annales de Pediatrie (Paris) — Ann Pediatr (Paris)
Annales de Physiologie et de Physicochimie Biologique — Ann Phys Phys Chim
Annales de Physiologie et de Physicochimie Biologique — Ann Physiol Physicochim Biol
Annales de Physiologie Vegetale [*Bruxelles*] — Ann Physiol Veg
Annales de Physiologie Vegetale [*Paris*] — APVGAQ
Annales de Physiologie Vegetale (Bruxelles) — Annls Physiol Veg (Brux)
Annales de Physiologie Vegetale (Paris) — Ann Physiol Veg (Paris)
Annales de Physiologie Vegetale (Paris) — Annls Physiol Veg (Paris)
Annales de Physiologie Vegetale. Universite de Bruxelles — Ann Physiol Veg Univ Brux
Annales de Physiologie Vegetale. Universite de Bruxelles — Ann Physiol Veg Univ Bruxelles
Annales de Physiologie Vegetale. Universite de Bruxelles — APVBAB
Annales de Physique — Ann Phys
Annales de Physique [*Paris*] — Ann Physiq
Annales de Physique — ANPHA
Annales de Physique Biologique et Medicale — Ann Phys Bi
Annales de Physique Biologique et Medicale — Ann Phys Biol Med
Annales de Physique Biologique et Medicale — APBMBD
Annales de Physique (Les Ulis) — Ann Phys Les Ulis
Annales de Physique (Les Ulis). Colloque — Ann Phys Les Ulis Colloq
Annales de Physique (Paris) — Ann Phys (Paris)
Annales de Phytopathologie — Ann Phytopath

Annales de Phytopathologie — Ann Phytopathol
Annales de Phytopathologie — ANPTBM
Annales de Protistologie — Ann Protist
Annales de Radioelectricite [*France*] — Ann Radioelectr
Annales de Radiologie — ANLRAT
Annales de Radiologie — Ann Radiol
Annales de Radiologie. Medecine Nucleaire [*France*] — Ann Radiol Med Nucl
Annales de Radiologie. Medecine Nucleaire — ARMND
Annales de Radiologie Medecine Nucleaire-Revue d'Imagerie Medicale — Ann Radiol Med Nucl Rev Imag Med
Annales de Readaptation et de Medecine Physique — Ann Readapt Med Phys
Annales de Readaptation et de Medecine Physique — Ann Readaptation Med Phys
Annales de Readaptation et de Medecine Physique — ARMPEQ
Annales de Recherches Veterinaires — Ann Rech Vet
Annales de Recherches Veterinaires [*Annals of Veterinary Research*] — ARCVBP
Annales de Recherches Veterinaires/Annals of Veterinary Research — Ann Rech Vet Ann Vet Res
Annales de Saint-Louis des Francais — ASLF
Annales de Speleologie — Ann Speleol
Annales de Technologie Agricole [*Paris*] — Ann Tec Agr
Annales de Technologie Agricole — Ann Tech Agric
Annales de Technologie Agricole [*Paris*] — Ann Technol Agr
Annales de Technologie Agricole [*Paris*] — ATAPAA
Annales de Technologie Agricole (Paris) — Ann Technol Agric (Paris)
Annales de Virologie — Ann Virol
Annales de Virologie [*Paris*] — ANVIDL
Annales de Virologie (Paris) — Ann Virol (Paris)
Annales de Zoologie - Ecologie Animale — Ann Zool Ecol Anim
Annales de Zoologie - Ecologie Animale — Annls Zool Ecol Anim
Annales de Zoologie - Ecologie Animale — AZEAAR
Annales de Zootechnie — Ann Zootech
Annales de Zootechnie — Annls Zootech
Annales de Zootechnie [*Paris*] — AZOOAH
Annales de Zootechnie. Institut National de la Recherche Agronomique — Ann Zootech Inst Nat Rech Agron
Annales de Zootechnie (Paris) — Ann Zootech (Paris)
Annales de Zymologie — Ann Zymol
Annales d'Economie Collective — Ann Econom Coll
Annales d'Economie et de Sociologie Rurales — Ann Econ So
Annales d'Economie et de Statistique — Ann Econom Statist
Annales d'Economie Politique — A Econ Polit
Annales d'Embryologie et de Morphogenese — AEMMBP
Annales d'Embryologie et de Morphogenese — Ann Embryol Morphog
Annales d'Endocrinologie — ANENAG
Annales d'Endocrinologie [*Paris*] — Ann Endocr
Annales d'Endocrinologie [*Paris*] — Ann Endocrinol
Annales d'Endocrinologie — Annls Endocr
Annales d'Endocrinologie (Paris) — Ann Endocrinol (Paris)
Annales der Meteorologie — Ann Meteorol
Annales der Physik. 7 Folge — Ann Physik (7)
Annales des Composites — Ann Compos
Annales des Epiphyties [*Paris*] — AEPIAR
Annales des Epiphyties [*Paris*] — Ann Epiphyt
Annales des Epiphyties et de Phytogenetique — AEPHAO
Annales des Epiphyties et de Phytogenetique [*Paris*] — Ann Epiphyt Phytogenet
Annales des Epiphyties et de Phytogenetique [*Paris*] — Annls Epiphyt
Annales des Epiphyties (Paris) — Ann Epiphyt (Paris)
Annales des Falsifications — Ann Falsif
Annales des Falsifications et de l'Expertise Chimique [*Annales des Falsifications et de l'Expertise Chimique et Toxicologique*] [*France*] [*Later,*] — Ann Fals Expert Chim
Annales des Falsifications et de l'Expertise Chimique [*Later, Annales des Falsifications et de l'Expertise Chimique et Toxicologique*] — Ann Falsif Expert Chim
Annales des Falsifications et de l'Expertise Chimique [*Later, Annales des Falsifications et de l'Expertise Chimique et Toxicologique*] — Ann Falsif Expertise Chim
Annales des Falsifications et de l'Expertise Chimique [*Later, Annales des Falsifications et de l'Expertise Chimique et Toxicologique*] — Annls Falsif Expert Chim
Annales des Falsifications et de l'Expertise Chimique et Toxicologique — Ann Falsif Expert Chim Toxicol
Annales des Falsifications et des Fraudes [*Later, Annales des Falsifications et de l'Expertise Chimique*] — Ann Falsif Fraudes
Annales des Fermentations — Ann Ferment
Annales des Mines [*Paris*] — An Mines
Annales des Mines — Ann Min
Annales des Mines [*Paris*] — Ann Mines
Annales des Mines de Belgique — A Mines Belg
Annales des Mines de Belgique — An M Belgique
Annales des Mines de Belgique — Ann Mines Belg
Annales des Mines de Belgique — Annls Mines Belg
Annales des Mines de Roumanie — Ann Mines Roum
Annales des Mines. Documentation — Ann Mines Doc
Annales des Mines et de la Geologie. Tunisia — Ann Mines Geol Tunis
Annales des Mines et de la Geologie (Tunisia) — Ann Mines Geol (Tunisia)
Annales des Mines et de la Geologie. Tunisia. Serie 3. Hydrogeologie — Ann Mines Geol Tunis Ser 3
Annales des Mines et des Carburants. Documentation — Ann Mines Carbur Doc
Annales des Mines et des Carburants. Memoires — Ann Mines Carbur Mem
Annales des Mines et des Carburants. Partie Technique — Ann Mines Carbur Partie Tech
Annales des Mines. Memoires — Ann Mines Mem
Annales des Mines (Paris) — Annls Mines (Paris)
Annales des Mines. Partie Administrative — Ann Mines Partie Adm
Annales des Pays Nivernais — A Nivernais
Annales des Pays Nivernais — APN
Annales des Ponts et Chaussees — Ann Ponts Chaussees
Annales des Sciences Commerciales et Economiques — An Com
Annales des Sciences Commerciales et Economiques — ASC
Annales des Sciences Economiques Appliquees — A Sci Econ Appl
Annales des Sciences Economiques Appliquees — Ann Sc Econ Appliq
Annales des Sciences Economiques Appliquees — Ann Sci Econ Appl
Annales des Sciences Economiques Appliquees — Ann Sciences Econs Appliquees
Annales des Sciences Economiques Appliquees — ASE
Annales des Sciences Forestieres — Ann Sci For
Annales des Sciences Forestieres [*Paris*] — ANSFAS
Annales des Sciences Forestieres (Paris) — Ann Sci For (Paris)
Annales des Sciences Geologiques — An Sc Geol
Annales des Sciences Mathematiques du Quebec — Ann Sci Math Quebec
Annales des Sciences Naturelles — Ann Sc Nat
Annales des Sciences Naturelles. A. Botanique — Ann Sci Nat Bot
Annales des Sciences Naturelles. A. Botanique — Annls Sci Nat A Bot
Annales des Sciences Naturelles. B. Zoologie — Ann Sci Nat Zool
Annales des Sciences Naturelles. Botanique et Biologie Vegetale — Ann Sci Nat Bot Biol Veg
Annales des Sciences Naturelles. Botanique et Biologie Vegetale — Ann Sci Natur Bot Biol Veg
Annales des Sciences Naturelles. Botanique et Biologie Vegetale — ASNVAI
Annales des Sciences Naturelles (Paris) — ASNP
Annales des Sciences Naturelles. Zoologie — An Sc Nat Zool
Annales des Sciences Naturelles. Zoologie — Ann Sc Nat Zool
Annales des Sciences Naturelles. Zoologie et Biologie Animale — Ann Sci Nat Zool Biol Anim
Annales des Sciences Naturelles. Zoologie et Biologie Animale — ASNBAQ
Annales des Telecommunications — A Telecom
Annales des Telecommunications — Ann Telecom
Annales des Telecommunications — Ann Telecomm
Annales des Telecommunications — Ann Telecommun
Annales des Travaux Agricoles Scientifiques — Ann Trav Agr Sci
Annales des Travaux Publics de Belgique — An Trav Pub Belgique
Annales des Travaux Publics de Belgique — Ann Trav Publics Belg
Annales des Voyages — AV
Annales des Voyages, de la Geographie, et de l'Histoire — Ann Voyages
Annales des Voyages de la Geographie et de l'Histoire — AVGH
Annales d'Esthetique — Ann Esth
Annales d'Ethiopie — A Et
Annales d'Ethiopie — AE
Annales d'Ethiopie [*Paris/Addis-Ababa*] — AnEth
Annales d'Ethiopie — Ann Ethiopie
Annales d'Ethiopie — AnnEth
Annales d'Etudes Internationales — A Et Int
Annales d'Etudes Internationales — An Etud Int
Annales d'Histochimie — ANHIAG
Annales d'Histochimie — Ann Histoch
Annales d'Histochimie — Ann Histochim
Annales d'Histochimie — Annls Histochim
Annales d'Histoire Economique — AHE
Annales d'Histoire Economique et Sociale — AHES
Annales d'Histoire Economique et Sociale — Ann HES
Annales d'Histoire Sociale — AHS
Annales d'Histoire Sociale — AHSoc
Annales d'Horticulture et de Botanique ou Flore des Jardins du Royaume des Pays-Bas — Ann Hort Bot
Annales d'Hydrobiologie — AHYBB5
Annales d'Hydrobiologie — Ann Hydrob
Annales d'Hydrobiologie — Ann Hydrobiol
Annales d'Hygiene de Langue Francaise. Medecine et Nutrition — AHLFAJ
Annales d'Hygiene de Langue Francaise. Medecine et Nutrition — Ann Hyg Lang Fr Med Nutr
Annales d'Hygiene et de Medecine Coloniales — Ann Hyg et Med Colon
Annales d'Hygiene et de Medecine Coloniales — Annales D Hyg Et De Med Col
Annales d'Hygiene Publique et de Medecine Legale — Ann Hyg Pub et Med Legale
Annales d'Hygiene Publique et de Medecine Legale — Ann Hyg Publique Med Leg
Annales d'Hygiene Publique. Industrielle et Sociale — Ann Hyg Publique Ind Soc
Annales d'Immunologie — ANIMC
Annales d'Immunologie — Ann Immunol
Annales d'Immunologie (Paris) — Ann Immunol (Paris)
Annales Direction des Etudes et de l'Equipement. Service d'Exploitation Industrielle des Tabacs et des Allumettes — Annls SEITA
Annales. Direction des Etudes et de l'Equipement. Service d'Exploitation Industrielle des Tabacs et des Allumettes. Section 1 — ADEEAL
Annales. Direction des Etudes et de l'Equipement. Service d'Exploitation Industrielle des Tabacs et des Allumettes. Section 1 — Ann Dir Etud Equip Ser Exploit Ind Tab Allumettes Sec 1
Annales. Direction des Etudes et de l'Equipement. Service d'Exploitation Industrielle des Tabacs et des Allumettes. Section 2 — ADEEBM
Annales. Direction des Etudes et de l'Equipement. Service d'Exploitation Industrielle des Tabacs et des Allumettes. Section 2 — Ann Dir Etud Equip Serv Exploit Ind Tab Allumettes Sec 2
Annales d'Oculistique [*Paris*] — Ann Ocul
Annales d'Oculistique [*Paris*] — Ann Oculist
Annales d'Oculistique (Paris) — Ann Ocul (Paris)
Annales d'Oto-Laryngologie [*Later, Annales d'Oto-Laryngologie et de Chirurgie Cervico-Faciale*] — Ann Oto-Laryngol

Annales d'Oto-Laryngologie et de Chirurgie Cervico-Faciale — Ann Oto-Lar
Annales d'Oto-Laryngologie et de Chirurgie Cervico-Faciale — Ann Otolaryng
Annales d'Oto-Laryngologie et de Chirurgie Cervico-Faciale — Ann Oto-Laryngol Chir Cervico-Fac
Annales d'Oto-Laryngologie et de Chirurgie Cervico-Faciale — AOCCA
Annales du Centre d'Enseignement Superieur de Brazzaville — Ann Cent Enseignement Sup Brazzaville
Annales du Commerce Exterieur — ACE
Annales du Genie Chimique — Ann Genie Chimie
Annales du Marche Commun; Revue Bimestrielle pour l'Information et l'Harmonisation du Commerce et de l'Industrie — ALQ
Annales du Midi — A Midi
Annales du Midi; Revue de la France Meridionale — A d M
Annales du Midi; Revue de la France Meridionale [*Toulouse*] — AM
Annales du Midi; Revue de la France Meridionale [*Toulouse*] — AMid
Annales du Midi; Revue de la France Meridionale [*Toulouse*] — AnM
Annales du Midi; Revue de la France Meridionale [*Toulouse*] — Ann Midi
Annales du Midi. Revue de la France Meridionale — Annal Mid
Annales du Museum National d'Histoire Naturelle — Ann Mus Natl Hist Nat
Annales du Notariat et de l'Enregistrement — ANE
Annales du Notariat et de l'Enregistrement — Ann Not
Annales du Notariat et de l'Enregistrement — Ann Not Enr
Annales du Secteur du Platine et des Autres Metaux Precieux. Institut de Chimie Generale — Ann Sect Platine Autres Met Precieux Inst Chim Gen
Annales du Service Botanique et Agronomique. Direction Generale de l'Agriculture — Ann Serv Bot Direct Gen Agric
Annales du Service des Antiquites [*Kairo*] — Annales Service Antiqu
Annales du Tabac. Section 1 — Ann Tab Sec 1
Annales du Tabac. Section 2 — Ann Tab Sect 2
Annales du Tabac. Section 2 — ATSED2
Annales. Durban Museum — Ann Durban Mus
Annales d'Urologie — Ann Urol
Annales d'Urologie — AUROAV
Annales Ecclesiastici a Christo Nato ad Annum 1198 — AECN
Annales. Ecole des Hautes-Etudes de Gand — AEHEG
Annales. Ecole des Sciences. Universite d'Abidjan — Ann Ec Sci Univ Abidjan
Annales. Ecole Nationale d'Agriculture d'Alger — Ann Ec Natl Agric Alger
Annales. Ecole Nationale d'Agriculture d'Alger — Ann Ecole Nat Agr Alger
Annales. Ecole Nationale d'Agriculture de Montpellier — Ann Ec Natl Agric Montpellier
Annales. Ecole Nationale d'Agriculture de Rennes — Ann Ecole Natl Agric Rennes
Annales. Ecole Nationale des Eaux et Forets et de la Station de Recherches et Experiences Forestieres — Ann Ec Natl Eaux For Stn Rech Exper For
Annales. Ecole Nationale Superieure Agronomique — Ann Ecole Nat Super Agron
Annales. Ecole Nationale Superieure Agronomique de Toulouse — Ann Ecole Natl Super Agron Toulouse
Annales. Ecole Nationale Superieure Agronomique (Montpellier) — Ann Ec Natl Super Agron (Montpellier)
Annales. Ecole Nationale Superieure de Geologie Appliquee et de Prospection Miniere. Universite de Nancy — Ann Ec Natl Super Geol Appl Prospect Min Univ Nancy
Annales. Ecole Nationale Superieure de Mecanique (Nantes) — Ann Ecole Nat Sup Mec (Nantes)
Annales. Ecole Royale Superieure d'Agriculture de la Suede — Ann Ec R Super Agric Suede
Annales. Ecole Superieure d'Agriculture de la Suede — Ann Ec Super Agric Suede
Annales. Ecole Superieure des Mines de l'Oural a Ekatherinebourg — Ann Ec Super Mines Oural Ekatherinebourg
Annales. Ecole Superieure des Sciences. Institut des Hautes Etudes (Dakar) — Ann Ec Super Sci Inst Hautes Etud (Dakar)
Annales. Economies, Societes, Civilisations — A Ec Soc Civ
Annales: Economies, Societes, Civilisations — AESC
Annales. Economies, Societes, Civilisations — AnESC
Annales: Economies, Societes, Civilisations — Ann Econ Soc Civ
Annales: Economies, Societes, Civilisations — Ann Econ Soc Civilis
Annales. Economies, Societes, Civilisations — Ann ESC
Annales. Economies, Societes, Civilisations — Annales Econ
Annales: Economies, Societes, Civilisations — Annales-ESC
Annales. Economies, Societes, Civillizations — Ann Econ Soc Civiliations
Annales Economiques (Clermont) — A Econ (Clermont)
Annales Entomologici Fennici — AENF
Annales Entomologici Fennici — AETFA4
Annales Entomologici Fennici — Ann Ent Fenn
Annales Entomologici Fennici — Ann Entomol Fenn
Annales et Bulletin. Societe de Medecine d'Anvers — Ann Bull Soc Med Anvers
Annales et Bulletin. Societe de Medecine de Gand — Ann Bull Soc Med Gand
Annales et Bulletin. Societe Royale de Medecine de Gand — Ann Bull Soc R Med Gand
Annales et Bulletin. Societe Royale des Sciences Medicales et Naturelles de Bruxelles — Ann Bull Soc R Sci Med Nat Bruxelles
Annales et Bulletin. Societe Royale des Sciences Medicales et Naturelles de Bruxelles — Annales Bull Soc Sc Med Nat
Annales Europeennes de Physique Vegetale et d'Economie Publique — Ann Eur Phys Veg Econ Publique
Annales. Faculdade de Medicina de Sao Paulo — Ann Fac Med S Paulo
Annales Facultatis Agronomicae Universitatis Scientiae Agriculturae — Ann Fac Agron Univ Sci Agric
Annales. Faculte de Droit de Liege — A Fac Dr Liege
Annales. Faculte de Droit de Liege — AFDL
Annales. Faculte de Droit de Liege [*Liege, Belgium*] — Ann de la Fac de Droit de Liege
Annales. Faculte de Droit de Liege — Ann Dr Liege
Annales. Faculte de Droit de Liege — Ann Fac Dr L
Annales. Faculte de Droit de Liege — Ann Fac Liege
Annales. Faculte de Droit de Lyon — A Fac Dr Lyon
Annales. Faculte de Droit d'Istanbul [*Istanbul, Turkey*] — Ann de la Fac de Droit d'Istanbul
Annales. Faculte de Droit d'Istanbul — Ann Fac Istanbul
Annales. Faculte de Droit et de Science Politique (Clermont) — A Fac Dr Sci Polit (Clermont)
Annales. Faculte de droit et des Sciences Economiques (Sceaux) — A Fac Dr Sci Econ Sceaux
Annales. Faculte de Droit. Universite Nationale du Zaire — Ann Fac Droit Univ Natn Zaire
Annales. Faculte de Medecine et de Pharmacie. Universite Nationale du Zaire — Ann Fac Med Pharm Univ Natl Zaire
Annales. Faculte des Lettres d'Aix — AFLA
Annales. Faculte des Lettres d'Aix-En-Provence — ALA
Annales. Faculte des Lettres de Besancon — ALB
Annales. Faculte des Lettres de Bordeaux. Bulletin Hispanique — AFLB Hisp
Annales. Faculte des Lettres de Bordeaux. Revue d'Etudes Anciennes — AFLBor
Annales. Faculte des Lettres de Toulouse — ALT
Annales. Faculte des Lettres et des Sciences Humaines. Universite Aix-Marseilles — AFLA
Annales. Faculte des Lettres et des Sciences Humaines. Universite Aix-Marseilles — ALA
Annales. Faculte des Lettres et Sciences Humaines d'Aix — Ann Fac Lett Sci Humaines Aix
Annales. Faculte des Lettres et Sciences Humaines de l'Universite de Dakar — AFLD
Annales. Faculte des Lettres et Sciences Humaines de Nice — AFLNice
Annales. Faculte des Lettres et Sciences Humaines de Yaounde — AFLSHY
Annales. Faculte des Lettres et Sciences Humaines de Yaounde — Ann Fac Lett et Sci Hum
Annales. Faculte des Lettres et Sciences Humaines. Universite de Dakar — Ann Fac Lettres et Sci Hum Univ Dakar
Annales. Faculte des Lettres. Universite de Bordeaux — AFLUB
Annales. Faculte des Sciences de Marseille — Ann Fac Sci Mars
Annales. Faculte des Sciences de Marseille — Ann Fac Sci Marseille
Annales. Faculte des Sciences de Marseille — Annls Fac Sci Marseille
Annales. Faculte des Sciences de Toulouse. Mathematiques — Ann Fac Sci Toulouse Math
Annales. Faculte des Sciences du Cameroun — Ann Fac Sci Cameroun
Annales. Faculte des Sciences. Section Biologie. Chimie et Sciences de la Terre. Universite de Kinshasa — Ann Fac Sci Sect Biol Chim Sci Terre Univ Kinshasa
Annales. Faculte des Sciences. Section Biologie, Chimie, et Sciences de la Terre (Universite Nationale du Zaire) — Ann Fac Sci Sect Biol Chim Sci Terre (Univ Natl Zaire)
Annales. Faculte des Sciences. Universite de Clermont — Ann Fac Sci Univ Clermont
Annales. Faculte des Sciences. Universite de Clermont. Serie Biologie Animale — Ann Fac Sci Univ Clermont Ser Biol Anim
Annales. Faculte des Sciences. Universite de Dakar — Ann Fac Sci Univ Dakar
Annales. Faculte des Sciences. Universite de Saigon — Ann Fac Sci Univ Saigon
Annales. Faculte des Sciences. Universite de Toulouse — Ann Fac Sci Univ Toulouse
Annales. Faculte des Sciences. Universite de Toulouse pour les Sciences Mathematiques et les Sciences Physiques — Ann Fac Sci Univ Toulouse Sci Math Sci Phys
Annales. Faculte des Sciences. Universite de Yaounde — Ann Fac Sci Yaounde
Annales. Faculte des Sciences. Universite de Yaounde. Serie 3. Biologie-Biochimie — Ann Fac Sci Univ Yaounde Ser 3
Annales. Faculte des Sciences. Universite Nationale du Zaire (Kinshasa). Section Mathematique-Physique — Ann Fac Sci Univ Nat Zaire (Kinshasa) Sect Math-Phys
Annales. Federation Archeologique et Historique de Belgique — Ann FA Belg
Annales. Fondation Louis de Broglie [*France*] — Ann Fond Louis Broglie
Annales. Fondation Louis de Broglie — Ann Fond Louis de Broglie
Annales. Fondation Oceanographique Ricard. Vie Marine — Ann Fond Oceanogr Ricard Vie Mar
Annales Fonds Maeterlinck — AFM
Annales Forestales (Zagreb) — Ann For (Zagreb)
Annales Francaises d'Anesthesie et de Reanimation — Ann Fr Anesth Reanim
Annales Francaises de Chronometrie — Ann Fr Chronom
Annales Francaises de Chronometrie et de Micromecanique [*Later, Annales Francaises des Microtechniques et de Chronolmetrie*] — Ann Fr Chronom Micromec
Annales Francaises des Microtechniques et de Chronometrie — Ann Fr Microtech et Chronom
Annales. Francuski Institut. Zagreb — A I Fr Zagreb
Annales. Francuski Institut. Zagreb — AIFZ
Annales Fribourgeoises — A Fribourg
Annales Geologiques de la Peninsule Balkanique — Ann Geol Peninsule Balk
Annales Geologiques de la Peninsule Balkanique — GABPAG
Annales Geologiques de Madagascar — Ann Geol Madagascar
Annales Geologiques des Pays Helleniques — Ann Geol Pays Hell
Annales Geologiques. Service des Mines [*Madagascar*] — AGMMA4
Annales Geologiques. Service des Mines (Madagascar) — Ann Geol Serv Mines (Madagascar)
Annales Geophysicae — AG
Annales Geophysicae — ANGED
Annales Geophysicae (Gauthier-Villars) — Ann Geophys Gauthier Villars
Annales Geophysicae. Series A. Upper Atmosphere and Space Sciences — Ann Geophys Ser A

Annales Geophysicae. Series B. Terrestrial and Planetary Physics — Ann Geophys Ser B
Annales Guebhard — AGUEAK
Annales Guebhard — Ann Guebhard
Annales Guebhard Severine — Ann Guebhard Severine
Annales. Hebert et Haug — Ann Hebert Haug
Annales Historico-Naturales. Musei Nationalis Hungarici — AHMHAU
Annales Historico-Naturales. Musei Nationalis Hungarici — Ann Hist-Nat Mus Natl Hung
Annales Historico-Naturales. Musei Nationalis Hungarici. Pars Zoologica — Ann Hist Natur Mus Nat Hung Pars Zool
Annales Historico-Naturales Musei Nationalis Hungarici/ Termeszettudomanyi Muzeum Evkonyve — Ann Hist Nat Mus Natl Hung Termeszettud Muz Evk
Annales Historiques de la Revolution Francaise — AHRF
Annales Historiques de la Revolution Francaise — AnHRF
Annales Historiques de la Revolution Francaise — Ann Hist R
Annales Historiques de la Revolution Francaise — Ann Hist Revol Franc
Annales Homeopathiques Francaises — AHPFA5
Annales Homeopathiques Francaises — Ann Homeopath Fr
Annales. Hospital de la Santa Cruz y San Pablo — Ann Hosp St Cruz San Pablo
Annales. Hospital General de Catalunya — Ann Hosp Gen Catalunya
Annales. Hydrographie und Maritimen Meteorologie — Ann Hydrogr Marit Meteorol
Annales Hydrographiques — Ann Hydrogr
Annales. IHP Physique Theorique — Ann IHP Phys Theor
Annales Immunologiae Hungaricae — AIMHA3
Annales Immunologiae Hungaricae — Ann Immunol Hung
Annales. INSEE [*Institut National de la Statistique et des Etudes Economiques*] — Ann INSEE
Annales. Institut Agricole et Services de Recherche et d'Experimentation Agricoles de l'Algerie — Ann Inst Agric Serv Rech Exp Agric Alger
Annales. Institut Agricole et Services de Recherche et d'Experimentation Agricoles de l'Algerie — Annls Inst Agric Alger
Annales. Institut Agronomique de Moscow — Ann Inst Agron Moscow
Annales. Institut Archeologique du Luxembourg — AIA Lux
Annales. Institut Archeologique du Luxembourg — AIAL
Annales. Institut Archeologique du Luxembourg — Ann Inst Arch Luxembourg
Annales. Institut Archeologique du Luxembourg — Ann Inst Archeol Luxemb
Annales. Institut Archeologique du Luxembourg — Ann Lux
Annales. Institut Belge du Petrole — Ann Inst Belge Petrol
Annales. Institut Botanico-Geologique Colonial de Marseille — Ann Inst Bot Geol Colon Marseille
Annales. Institut Central Ampelologique Royal Hongrois — Ann Inst Cent Ampelol R Hong
Annales. Institut d'Analyse Physico-Chemique (Leningrad) — Ann Inst Anal Phys Chim Leningrad
Annales. Institut de Philosophie — AIPH
Annales. Institut de Physique du Globe. Universite de Paris et Bureau Central de Magnetisme Terrestre — Ann Inst Phys Globe Univ Paris Bur Cent Magn Terr
Annales. Institut de Recherches d'Ameliorations Foncieres et de la Science du Sol. Serie Ameliorations Foncieres — Ann Inst Rech Amelior Foncieres Sci Sol Ser Amelior Fonciere
Annales. Institut de Recherches d'Ameliorations Foncieres et de la Science du Sol. Serie Hydrotechnique — Ann Inst Rech Amelior Foncieres Sci Sol Ser Hydrotech
Annales. Institut de Recherches d'Ameliorations Foncieres et de la Science du Sol. Serie Science du Sol — Ann Inst Rech Amelior Foncieres Sci Sol Ser Sci Sol
Annales. Institut de Recherches Zootechniques de Roumanie — Ann Inst Rech Zootech Roum
Annales. Institut des Mines a Leningrade — Ann Inst Mines Leningrade
Annales. Institut d'Etudes du Travail et de la Securite Sociale — A Inst Et Trav Secur Soc
Annales. Institut d'Etudes Occidentes — AnnIEOc
Annales. Institut d'Etudes Occitanes — AIEO
Annales. Institut d'Etudes Orientales [*Alger*] — AIEO
Annales. Institut d'Etudes Orientales. Faculte des Lettres d'Alger — AnnIEO
Annales. Institut d'Etudes Orientales. Faculte des Lettres. Universite d'Alger — Ann Inst Et Orient
Annales. Institut d'Etudes Orientales. Universite d'Alger — Ann Inst Etud Orient Univ Alger
Annales. Institut d'Hydrologie et de Climatologie — Ann Inst Hydrol Climatol
Annales. Institut du Petrole (Belgium) — AIBPD
Annales. Institut Experimental du Tabac de Bergerac — AIETAX
Annales. Institut Experimental du Tabac de Bergerac — Ann Inst Exp Tabac Bergerac
Annales. Institut Fourier — Ann I Four
Annales. Institut Fourier — Ann Inst Fourier
Annales. Institut Fourier (Grenoble) — Ann Inst Fourier (Grenoble)
Annales. Institut Fourier. Universite de Grenoble — AIFUA
Annales. Institut Fourier. Universite de Grenoble [*France*] — Ann Inst Fourier Univ Grenoble
Annales. Institut Francais de Zagreb — AIF
Annales. Institut Francais de Zagreb — Ann Ifr Z
Annales. Institut Francais de Zagreb — Ann Inst Franc Zagreb
Annales. Institut Geologique de Hongrie — Ann Inst Geol Hong
Annales. Institut Henri Poincare — Ann Inst Henri Poincare
Annales. Institut Henri Poincare. Physique Theorique — Ann Inst Henri Poincare Phys Theor
Annales. Institut Henri Poincare. Section A — Ann Inst H Poincare Sect A
Annales. Institut Henri Poincare. Section A. Physique Theorique — AHPAA
Annales. Institut Henri Poincare. Section A. Physique Theorique — Ann I Hen A
Annales. Institut Henri Poincare. Section A. Physique Theorique — Ann Inst Henri Poincare A
Annales. Institut Henri Poincare. Section A. Physique Theorique — Ann Inst Henri Poincare Sect A
Annales. Institut Henri Poincare. Section A. Physique Theorique — Ann Inst Poincare Sect A
Annales. Institut Henri Poincare. Section A. Physique Theorique. Nouvelle Serie — Ann Inst H Poincare Sect A NS
Annales. Institut Henri Poincare. Section B — Ann Inst H Poincare Sect B
Annales. Institut Henri Poincare. Section B. Calcul des Probabilites et Statistique — AHPBA
Annales. Institut Henri Poincare. Section B. Calcul des Probabilites et Statistique — Ann I Hen B
Annales. Institut Henri Poincare. Section B. Calcul des Probabilites et Statistique — Ann Inst Henri Poincare B
Annales. Institut Henri Poincare. Section B. Calcul des Probabilites et Statistique [*France*] — Ann Inst Henri Poincare Sect B
Annales. Institut Henri Poincare. Section B. Calcul des Probabilites et Statistique — Ann Inst Poincare Sect B
Annales. Institut Henri Poincare. Section B. Nouvelle Serie — Ann Inst H Poincare Sect B NS
Annales. Institut Kondakov/Seminarium Kondakovianum — Ann Inst Kondakov
Annales. Institut Michel Pacha — AIMPCT
Annales. Institut Michel Pacha — Ann Inst Michel Pacha
Annales. Institut National Agronomique — AIAQA4
Annales. Institut National Agronomique [*Paris*] — Ann Inst Nat Agron
Annales. Institut National Agronomique [*Paris*] — Ann Inst Natl Agron
Annales. Institut National Agronomique (Paris) — Annls Inst Natn Agron (Paris)
Annales. Institut National de la Recherche Agronomique de Tunisie — Ann Inst Natl Rech A
Annales. Institut National de la Recherche Agronomique de Tunisie — Ann Inst Natl Rech Agron Tunis
Annales. Institut National de la Recherche Agronomique de Tunisie — Annls Inst Natn Rech Agron Tunisie
Annales. Institut National de la Recherche Agronomique. Serie A. Annales Agronomiques — Ann Inst Natl Rech Agron Ser A
Annales. Institut National de la Recherche Agronomique. Serie A Bis. Annales de Physiologie Vegetale — Ann Inst Natl Rech Agron Ser A Bis Ann Physiol Veg
Annales. Institut National de la Recherche Agronomique. Serie B. Annales de l'Amelioration des Plantes — Ann Inst Natl Rech Agron Ser B
Annales. Institut National de la Recherche Agronomique. Serie C. Annales des Epiphyties — AIRCAD
Annales. Institut National de la Recherche Agronomique. Serie C. Annales des Epiphyties — Ann Inst Natl Rech Agron Ser C
Annales. Institut National de la Recherche Agronomique. Serie C. Annales des Epiphyties — Ann Inst Natl Rech Agron Ser C Ann Epiphyt
Annales. Institut National de la Recherche Agronomique. Serie C. Bis — Ann Inst Natl Rech Agron Ser C Bis
Annales. Institut National de la Recherche Agronomique. Serie C Bis. Annales de l'Abeille — Ann Inst Natl Rech Agron Ser C Bis Ann Abeille
Annales. Institut National de la Recherche Agronomique. Serie D. Annales de Zootechnie — Ann Inst Natl Rech Agron Ser D
Annales. Institut National de la Recherche Agronomique. Serie D. Annales de Zootechnie — Ann Inst Natl Rech Agron Ser D Ann Zootech
Annales. Institut National de la Recherche Agronomique. Serie E. Annales de Technologie Agricole — Ann Inst Natl Rech Agron Ser E
Annales. Institut National de la Recherche Agronomique. Serie E. Annales de Technologie Agricole — Ann Inst Natl Rech Agron Ser E Ann Technol Agric
Annales. Institut National de Recherches Forestieres de Tunisie — Ann Inst Nat Rech For Tunis
Annales. Institut Oceanographique — Ann I Ocean
Annales. Institut Oceanographique — Ann Inst Oceanogr
Annales. Institut Oceanographique (Paris) — Ann Inst Oceanogr (Paris)
Annales. Institut Oriental. Universite d'Alger — AIOUAlger
Annales. Institut Pasteur [*Paris*] — AIPAA
Annales. Institut Pasteur — Ann Inst Pasteur
Annales. Institut Pasteur — Annls Inst Past
Annales. Institut Pasteur de Lille — AIPLA
Annales. Institut Pasteur de Lille — Ann Inst Pasteur Lille
Annales. Institut Pasteur. Immunologie — Ann Inst Pasteur Immun
Annales. Institut Pasteur. Immunologie — Ann Inst Pasteur Immunol
Annales. Institut Pasteur. Microbiologie — Ann Inst Pasteur Microb
Annales. Institut Pasteur. Microbiologie — Ann Inst Pasteur Microbiol
Annales. Institut Pasteur (Paris) — Ann Inst Pasteur (Paris)
Annales. Institut Pasteur (Paris) — Annls Inst Pasteur (Paris)
Annales. Institut Pasteur. Virologie — Ann Inst Pasteur Virol
Annales. Institut Phytopathologique Benaki — Ann Inst Phytopathol Benaki
Annales. Institut Phytopathologique Benaki — Annls Inst Phytopath Benaki
Annales. Institut Polytechnique de l'Oural — Ann Inst Polytech Oural
Annales. Institut Superieur de Philosophie — AISP
Annales. Institut Superieur de Philosophie. Universite Catholique de Louvain — Ann Inst Super Phil Univ Cath Louvain
Annales. Institut Technique du Batiment et des Travaux Publics — AITBA
Annales. Institut Technique du Batiment et des Travaux Publics — Ann Inst Tech Batim Trav Publics
Annales Instituti Agronomici Centralis Experimentalis — Ann Inst Agron Cent Exp
Annales. Instituti Biologici [*Tihany*]. Hungaricae Academiae Scientiarum — AIBGAD
Annales. Instituti Biologici Pervestigandae Hungarici — Ann Inst Biol Pervestigandae Hung
Annales. Instituti Biologici (Tihany). Hungaricae Academiae Scientiarum — Ann Inst Biol (Tihany) Hung
Annales. Instituti Biologici (Tihany). Hungaricae Academiae Scientiarum — Ann Inst Biol (Tihany) Hung Acad Sci
Annales. Instituti Geologici Publici Hungarici — Ann Inst Geol Publ Hung

Annales. Instituti Geologici Publici Hungarici — MGFIAL
Annales Instituti Protectionis Plantarum Hungarici — Ann Inst Prot Plant Hung
Annales. Instituto de Medicina Experimental. Universidad Nacional de Buenos Aires — Ann Inst Med Exp Univ Nac Buenos Aires
Annales Institutorum — Ann Inst
Annales Institutorum Quae in Urbe Erecta Sunt — AInst
Annales Institutorum Quae Provehendis Humanioribus Disciplinis Artibusque Colendis a Variis in Urbe Erecta Sunt Nationibus — Annales Institutorum
Annales Internationales de Criminologie — A Int Criminol
Annales Internationales de Criminologie — Ann Internat Criminologie
Annales Internationales de Criminologie — Annales Int'l de Crimin
Annales Islamologiques — An Isl
Annales. Laboratoire de Recherche des Musees de France — ALMF
Annales Latini Montium Arvernorum. Bulletin du Groupe d'Etudes Latines. Universite de Clermont — ALMArv
Annales Litteraires. Universite de Besancon — Ann Univ Besancon
Annales Maritimes et Coloniales — Ann Marit Colon
Annales Marocaines de Sociologie — Ann Marocaines de Sociologie
Annales Mathematicae Silesianae — Ann Math Sil
Annales Mathematiques Blaise Pascal — Ann Math Blaise Pascal
Annales Medicales Belges — Ann Med Belges
Annales Medicales de Nancy — AMNYAJ
Annales Medicales de Nancy — Ann Med Nancy
Annales Medicales de Nancy et de l'Est — AMNADI
Annales Medicales de Nancy et de l'Est — Ann Med Nancy Est
Annales Medicinae Experimentalis et Biologiae Fenniae — AMEBA
Annales Medicinae Experimentalis et Biologiae Fenniae — Ann Med Exp Biol Fenn
Annales Medicinae Experimentalis et Biologiae Fenniae. Supplementum — Ann Med Exp Biol Fenn Suppl
Annales Medicinae Internae Fenniae — AMFNAE
Annales Medicinae Internae Fenniae — Ann Med Intern Fenn
Annales Medicinae Internae Fenniae. Supplementum — Ann Med Intern Fenn Suppl
Annales Medicinae Militaris Fenniae — Ann Med Mil Fenn
Annales Medicinae Militaris Fenniae — SOAIAG
Annales Medico-Chirurgicales du Hainaut — Ann Med Chir Hainaut
Annales Medico-Psychologiques — AM-Ps
Annales Medico-Psychologiques — AMPYA
Annales Medico-Psychologiques — AMPYAT
Annales Medico-Psychologiques — Ann Med-Psy
Annales Medico-Psychologiques — Ann Med-Psychol
Annales Medico-Psychologiques — Annales Med Psychol
Annales. Musee Colonial de Marseille — AMCMAU
Annales. Musee Colonial de Marseille — Ann Mus Colon Mars
Annales. Musee Guimet — AMG
Annales. Musee Guimet — Ann Mus Guimet
Annales. Musee Guimet. Bibliotheque d'Etudes — Ann Mus Guimet Bibl Etud
Annales. Musee Royal de l'Afrique Centrale — AMRAC
Annales. Musee Royal de l'Afrique Centrale — AnnMAfrC
Annales. Musee Royal de l'Afrique Centrale. Serie in Octavo — Annls Mus R Afr Cent Ser 8vo
Annales. Musee Royal de l'Afrique Centrale. Serie in Octavo. Sciences Geologiques [*Tervuren*] — Ann Mus R Afr Cent Ser 8 Sci Geol
Annales. Musee Royal de l'Afrique Centrale. Serie in Quarto. Zoologie — Ann Mus R Afr Cent Ser Quarto Zool
Annales. Musee Royal du Congo Belge. Linguistique — AnnMCB-L
Annales. Musee Royal du Congo Belge. Serie in Octavo. Sciences Geologiques — Ann Mus R Congo Belge Ser 8o Sci Geol
Annales Musei Goulandris — AMUGAY
Annales Musei Goulandris — Ann Mus Goulandris
Annales. Museum d'Histoire Naturelle de Nice — Ann Mus Hist Nat Nice
Annales. Museum Francisceum — Ann Mus Francisc
Annales Musicologiques — AMu
Annales Musicologiques — Ann M
Annales Mycologici. Editi in Notitiam Scientiae Mycologicae Universalis — Ann Mycol
Annales Nestle (France) — Ann Nestle (Fr)
Annales. Observatoire de Besancon — Ann Obs Besancon
Annales. Observatoire National d'Athenes — Ann Obs Nat
Annales Odonto-Stomatologiques — Ann Odonto-Stomatol
Annales. Office National des Combustibles Liquides (France) — Ann Off Natl Combust Liq (France)
Annales Paderewski — APad
Annales Paediatriae Fenniae [*Finland*] — Ann Paediatr Fenn
Annales Paediatriae Fenniae. Supplementum — Ann Paediatr Fenn Suppl
Annales Paediatrica. Supplementum — Ann Paediatr Suppl
Annales Paediatrici — Ann Paediatr
Annales Paediatrici. International Review of Pediatrics — Ann Paediatr Int Rev Pediatr
Annales Paediatrici Japonici — Ann Paed Jap
Annales Paediatrici Japonici — Ann Paediat Jpn
Annales Paediatrici Japonici. Kioto Universitatis — Ann Pediatr Jpn Kioto Univ
Annales Parlementaires. Chambre de Representants — Ann P C
Annales Parlementaires. Senat — Ann P S
Annales Paulistas de Medicina e Cirurgia — Ann Paulist Med e Cirurg
Annales Pharmaceutici [*Poznan*] — APMCB4
Annales Pharmaceutici (Poznan) — Ann Pharm (Poznan)
Annales Pharmaceutiques Belges — Ann Pharm Belg
Annales Pharmaceutiques Francaises — Ann Pharm F
Annales Pharmaceutiques Francaises — Ann Pharm Fr
Annales Pharmaceutiques Francaises — Annls Pharm Fr
Annales Pharmaceutiques Francaises — APFRAD
Annales Politiques et Litteraires — Ann Pol et Litt
Annales Politiques et Litteraires — Ann Polit Litt
Annales Politiques et Litteraires — Annales Polit Et Litt
Annales Politiques et Litteraires — APL
Annales Polonici Mathematici — Ann Pol Math
Annales Polonici Mathematici — Ann Polon Math
Annales. Prince de Ligne — APL
Annales pro Experimentis Foresticis — Ann Exp For
Annales Publiees par la Faculte des Lettres de Toulouse — AFLT
Annales Publiees par la Faculte des Lettres et Sciences Humaines de Toulouse [*Via Domitia*] — AFLToul
Annales. Revue Mensuelle de Lettres Francaises — An
Annales. Science Agronomique Francaise et Etrangere — Ann Sci Agron Franc Etrangere
Annales Scientifiques de Franche Comte — Ann Sci Franche Comte
Annales Scientifiques de l'Universite de Clermont-Ferrand II. Probabilites et Applications — Ann Sci Univ Clermont Ferrand II Probab Appl
Annales Scientifiques de l'Universite de Franche-Comte Besancon. Mathematiques. 4eme Serie — Ann Sci Univ Franche Comte Besancon Math 4
Annales Scientifiques. Ecole Normale Superieure — Ann Sci Ec
Annales Scientifiques. Ecole Normale Superieure — Ann Sci Ecole Norm Sup
Annales Scientifiques, Litteraires, et Industrielles de l'Auvergne — Ann Sci Auvergne
Annales Scientifiques Textiles Belges — Ann Sci Text Belg
Annales Scientifiques. Universite de Besancon — Ann Sci Univ Bes
Annales Scientifiques. Universite de Besancon — Ann Sci Univ Besancon
Annales Scientifiques. Universite de Besancon. Biologie Animale — Ann Sci Univ Besancon Biol Anim
Annales Scientifiques. Universite de Besancon. Biologie Animale — AUBADE
Annales Scientifiques. Universite de Besancon. Biologie Vegetale — Ann Sci Univ Besancon Biol Veg
Annales Scientifiques. Universite de Besancon. Biologie Vegetale — ASUVDM
Annales Scientifiques. Universite de Besancon. Botanique — Ann Sci Univ Besancon Bot
Annales Scientifiques. Universite de Besancon. Botanique — ASBOA5
Annales Scientifiques. Universite de Besancon. Chimie — Ann Sci Univ Besancon Chim
Annales Scientifiques. Universite de Besancon. Climatologie — Ann Sci Univ Besancon Climatol
Annales Scientifiques. Universite de Besancon. Geologie — Ann Sci Univ Besancon Geol
Annales Scientifiques. Universite de Besancon. Geologie — ASBGAF
Annales Scientifiques. Universite de Besancon. Hydrographie — Ann Sci Univ Besancon Hydrogr
Annales Scientifiques. Universite de Besancon. Mathematiques — Ann Sci Univ Besancon Math
Annales Scientifiques. Universite de Besancon. Mathematiques. 3e Serie — Ann Sci Univ Besancon Math 3
Annales Scientifiques. Universite de Besancon. Mecanique et Physique Theorique — Ann Sci Univ Besancon Mec Phys Theor
Annales Scientifiques. Universite de Besancon. Medecine — Ann Sci Univ Besancon Med
Annales Scientifiques. Universite de Besancon. Medecine — ASBEA9
Annales Scientifiques. Universite de Besancon. Meteorologie — Ann Sci Univ Besancon Meteorol
Annales Scientifiques. Universite de Besancon. Physiologie et Biologie Animale — Ann Sci Univ Besancon Physiol Biol Anim
Annales Scientifiques. Universite de Besancon. Physiologie et Biologie Animale — ASPBB3
Annales Scientifiques. Universite de Besancon. Physique — Ann Sci Univ Besancon Phys
Annales Scientifiques. Universite de Besancon. Zoologie — Ann Sci Univ Besancon Zool
Annales Scientifiques. Universite de Besancon. Zoologie — ASZOAN
Annales Scientifiques. Universite de Besancon. Zoologie et Physiologie — Ann Sci Univ Besancon Zool Physiol
Annales Scientifiques. Universite de Besancon. Zoologie et Physiologie — ASBZA4
Annales Scientifiques. Universite de Besancon. Zoologie, Physiologie, et Biologie Animale — Ann Sci Univ Besancon Zool Physiol Biol Anim
Annales Scientifiques. Universite de Clermont — Ann Sci Univ Clermont
Annales Scientifiques. Universite de Clermont. Serie Mathematique — Ann Sci Univ Clermont Math
Annales Scientifiques. Universite de Clermont-Ferrand 2 — Ann Sci Univ Clermont Ferrand 2
Annales Scientifiques. Universite de Clermont-Ferrand. II. Mathematiques — Ann Sci Univ Clermont-Ferrand II Math
Annales Scientifiques. Universite de Jassy — Ann Sci Univ Jassy
Annales Scientifiques. Universite de Jassy — Annls Scient Univ Jassy
Annales Scientifiques. Universite de Jassy. Section 1. Mathematiques, Physique, Chimie — Ann Sci Univ Jass Sect 1
Annales Scientifiques. Universite de Jassy. Section 1. Mathematiques, Physique, Chimie — Ann Sci Univ Jassy Sect 1
Annales Scientifiques. Universite de Jassy. Section 2. Sciences Naturelles — Ann Sci Univ Jassy Sect 2
Annales Scientifiques. Universite de Reims et ARERS [*Association Regionale pour l'Etude et la Recherche Scientifiques*] — Ann Sci Univ Reims ARERS
Annales Scientifiques. Universite de Reims et ARERS (Association Regionale pour l'Etude et la Recherche Scientifiques) — Ann Sci Univ Reims ARERS (Assoc Reg Etude Rech Sci)
Annales. Section Dendrologique. Societe Botanique de Pologne — Ann Sect Dendrol Soc Bot Pol
Annales Sectionis Horti et Viticulturae Universitatis Scientiae Agriculturae — Ann Sect Horti Vitic Univ Sci Agric
Annales. Seminario de Metafisica — Ann Seminar Metaf
Annales. Service Archeologique de l'Iran — ASAI
Annales. Service Botanique de Tunisie — Ann Serv Bot Tunis

Annales. Service Botanique et Agronomique de Tunisie — Ann Serv Bot Agron Tunis
Annales. Service Botanique et Agronomique. Direction Generale de l'Agriculture de Tunisie — Ann Serv Bot Agron Dir Gen Agric Tunis
Annales. Service Botanique et Agronomique. Direction Generale de l'Agriculture Tunisie — Ann Serv Bot Tunisie
Annales. Service des Antiquites de l'Egypt — Ann du Serv
Annales. Service des Antiquites de l'Egypt — Ann du Service des Ant
Annales. Service des Antiquites de l'Egypt — Ann SA Eg
Annales. Service des Antiquites de l'Egypt — Ann Serv Ant Eg
Annales. Service des Antiquites de l'Egypt — Annales
Annales. Service des Antiquites de l'Egypt — AS
Annales. Service des Antiquites de l'Egypt — ASA
Annales. Service des Antiquites de l'Egypt. Supplement — Ann Serv Suppl
Annales. Service des Antiquites de l'Egypte — Ann SAE
Annales. Service des Antiquites de l'Egypte — Ann Serv
Annales. Service des Antiquites de l'Egypte — Ann Serv Ant
Annales. Service des Antiquites de l'Egypte — Ann Serv Antiqu
Annales. Service des Antiquites de l'Egypte — Ann Service des Ant
Annales. Service des Antiquites de l'Egypte — ANSAE
Annales. Service des Antiquites de l'Egypte — ASAE
Annales. Service des Mines. Comite Special du Katanga — Ann Serv Mines Com Spec Katanga
Annales Silesiae — AnnS
Annales. Societa Retorumantscha — AnnSR
Annales. Societa Retorumantscha — ASR
Annales. Societatis Belgicae Pharmaceuticae — Ann Soc Belg Pharm
Annales Societatis Doctrinae Studentium Academiae Medicae Silesiensis — Ann Soc Doctrinae Stud Acad Med Silesiensis
Annales Societatis Litterarum Estonicae in America — Annls Soc Lit Eston Am
Annales Societatis Litterarum Estonicae in Svecia — Ann Soc Litt Estonicae
Annales Societatis Mathematicae Polonae. Series IV. Fundamenta Informaticae — Ann Soc Math Pol Ser IV Fundam Inf
Annales Societatis Rebus Naturae Investigandis in Universitate Tartuensi Constitutae — Ann Soc Rebus Nat Invest Univ Tartu Const
Annales Societatis Scientiarum Faeroensis — Ann Soc Sci Faeroe
Annales Societatis Tartu — Annls Soc Tartu
Annales. Societe Archeologique de l'Arrondissement de Nivelles — ASAAN
Annales. Societe Archeologique de Namur — A Namur
Annales. Societe Archeologique de Namur — A Soc Arch Namur
Annales. Societe Archeologique de Namur — Ann Soc Arch Namur
Annales. Societe Archeologique de Namur — ASAN
Annales. Societe Belge de Medecine Tropicale — Ann Soc Belg Med Trop
Annales. Societe Belge de Medecine Tropicale — Ann Soc Belge Med Trop
Annales. Societe Belge de Medecine Tropicale — Annls Soc Belge Med Trop
Annales. Societe Belge de Neurologie — Ann Soc Belge Neurol
Annales. Societe Belge d'Histoire des Hopitaux — Ann Soc Belg Hist Hop
Annales. Societe Belge pour l'Etude du Petrole, de Ses Derives, et Succedanes — Ann Soc Belge Etude Pet Ses Deriv Succedanes
Annales. Societe d'Archeologie de Bruxelles — AnAB
Annales. Societe d'Archeologie de Bruxelles — ASAB
Annales. Societe d'Archeologie d'Histoire et de Folklore de Nivelles et du Brabant Wallon — A Nivelles
Annales. Societe de Medecine d'Anvers — Ann Soc Med Anvers
Annales. Societe de Medecine Legale de Belgique — Ann Soc Med Leg Belg
Annales. Societe de Science et Litterature de Cannes — Ann Soc Sci Litt Cannes
Annales. Societe de Sciences Naturelles de Bruges — Ann Soc Sci Med Nat Bruges
Annales. Societe d'Emulation, Agriculture, Sciences, Lettres, et Arts de l'Ain — Ann Soc Emul Ain
Annales. Societe d'Emulation de Bruges [*Handelingen van het Genootschap voor Geschiedenis te Bruges*] — Ann Soc Emulation Bruges
Annales. Societe d'Emulation de Bruges — ASEB
Annales. Societe d'Emulation pour l'Etude de l'Histoire et des Antiquites de Flandre — ASEF
Annales. Societe des Brasseurs pour l'Enseignement Professionel — Ann Soc Brass Enseign Prof
Annales. Societe des Lettres, Sciences, et Arts des Alpes-Maritimes (Nice) — A (Nice)
Annales. Societe des Sciences, Belles-Lettres, et Arts d'Orleans — An Soc Sci Orleans
Annales. Societe des Sciences Medicales et Naturelles de Bruxelles — Ann Soc Sci Med Bruxelles
Annales. Societe des Sciences Naturelles de la Charente-Maritime — Ann Soc Sci Nat Charente-Marit
Annales. Societe des Sciences Naturelles et d'Archeologie de Toulon et du Var — A Toulon
Annales. Societe d'Histoire et d'Archeologie de Gand — AHAG
Annales. Societe d'Histoire et d'Archeologie de Gand — ASHAG
Annales. Societe d'Histoire et d'Archeologie de l'Arrondisement de Saint-Malo — A St Malo
Annales. Societe d'Horticulture de la Haute-Garonne — Ann Soc Hort Haute Garonne
Annales. Societe d'Hydrologie Medicale de Paris — Ann Soc Hydr Med
Annales. Societe Entomologique de France — Ann Soc Ent
Annales. Societe Entomologique de France — Ann Soc Entomol Fr
Annales. Societe Entomologique de France — Annls Soc Ent Fr
Annales. Societe Entomologique du Quebec — AETQA
Annales. Societe Entomologique du Quebec — Ann Soc Entomol Que
Annales. Societe Geologique de Belgique — Ann Soc Geol Belg
Annales. Societe Geologique de Belgique — Ann Soc Geol Belgique
Annales. Societe Geologique de Belgique. Bulletin — Ann Soc Geol Belg Bull
Annales. Societe Geologique de Belgique. Bulletin. Supplement — Ann Soc Geol Belg Bull Suppl
Annales. Societe Geologique de Belgique. Memoires — Ann Soc Geol Belg Mem
Annales. Societe Geologique de Pologne — Ann Soc Geol Pol
Annales. Societe Geologique du Nord — Ann Soc Geol Nord
Annales. Societe Historique et Archeologique de l'Arrondissement de Saint-Malo — Ann Soc Hist Archeol Arrondissement Saint Malo
Annales. Societe Historique et Archeologique de Tournai — ASHAT
Annales. Societe Jean-Jacques Rousseau — AJJR
Annales. Societe Jean-Jacques Rousseau — Annales J J Rousseau
Annales. Societe J.J. Rousseau — ASR
Annales. Societe Lineenne de Lyon — Ann Soc Lin Lyon
Annales. Societe Linneenne de Lyon — Ann Soc Linn Lyon
Annales. Societe Linneenne du Departement de Maine-et-Loire — Ann Soc Linn Dep Maine et Loire
Annales. Societe Medico-Chirurgicale de Bruges — Ann Soc Med-Chir Bruges
Annales. Societe Nationale de l'Horticulture de France — Ann Soc Nat Hort Fr
Annales. Societe Polonaise de Mathematique — Ann Soc Pol Math
Annales. Societe Royale d'Archeologie de Bruxelles — Ann Arch Brux
Annales. Societe Royale d'Archeologie de Bruxelles — Ann Soc Roy Arch Bruxelles
Annales. Societe Royale d'Archeologie de Bruxelles — Ann SRA Brux
Annales. Societe Royale d'Archeologie de Bruxelles — ASRAB
Annales. Societe Royale des Sciences Medicales et Naturelles de Bruxelles — An Soc R Sci Med Nat Bruxelles
Annales. Societe Royale des Sciences Medicales et Naturelles de Bruxelles — Ann Soc R Sci Med Nat Bruxelles
Annales. Societe Royale des Sciences Medicales et Naturelles de Bruxelles — Ann Soc Roy Sci Med
Annales. Societe Royale d'Histoire et d'Archeologie de Tournai — ASRHAT
Annales. Societe Royale Zoologique de Belgique — Ann Soc R Zool Belg
Annales. Societe Royale Zoologique de Belgique — Ann Soc Zool Belg
Annales. Societe Royale Zoologique de Belgique — Annls Soc R Zool Belg
Annales. Societe Scientifique de Bruxelles — Ann Soc Sci Bruxelles
Annales. Societe Scientifique de Bruxelles. Section Sciences Economiques — ASB
Annales. Societe Scientifique de Bruxelles. Serie 1 — Ann Brux 1
Annales. Societe Scientifique de Bruxelles. Serie 1 — Ann Soc Sci Brux Ser 1
Annales. Societe Scientifique de Bruxelles. Serie 1 — Ann Soc Sci Bruxelles Ser 1
Annales. Societe Scientifique de Bruxelles. Serie 2. Sciences Naturelles et Medicales — Ann Soc Sci Bruxelles Ser 2
Annales. Societe Scientifique de Bruxelles. Serie 3. Sciences Economiques — Ann Soc Sci Bruxelles Ser 3
Annales. Societe Scientifique de Bruxelles. Serie A. Sciences Mathematiques — Ann Soc Sci Bruxelles Ser A
Annales. Societe Scientifique de Bruxelles. Serie B. Sciences Physiques et Naturelles — Ann Soc Scient Bruxelles S B Sc Phys Nat
Annales. Societe Scientifique de Bruxelles. Serie C. Sciences Medicales — Ann Soc Scient Bruxelles S C Sci Med
Annales. Societe Scientifique Litteraire de Cannes et de l'Arrondissement de Grasse — A Soc Sci Litt Cannes
Annales. Societe Suisse de Zoologie et du Museum d'Histoire Naturelle de Geneve — Ann Soc Suisse Zool Mus Hist Nat Geneve
Annales. Societes Belges de Medecine Tropicale, de Parasitologie, et de Mycologie — Ann Soc Belg Med Trop Parasitol Mycol
Annales Sociologiques — ASoc
Annales Sociologiques (Paris) — ASP
Annales. Station Biologique de Besse-En-Chandesse — Ann Stn Biol Besse-En-Chandesse
Annales. Station Centrale d'Hydrobiologie Appliquee — Ann Stat Centr Hydrobiol Appl
Annales. Station Centrale d'Hydrobiologie Appliquee — Ann Stn Cent Hydrobiol Appl
Annales. Station Federale de Recherches Forestieres. Zurich — Ann Stn Fed Rech For Zurich
Annales. Station Oceanographique de Salammbo — Ann Stat Oceanogr Salammbo
Annales Thijmgenootschap — Ann Thijmgenoot
Annales Universitatis Budapestiensis de Rolando Eotvos Nominatae. Sectio Philosophia et Sociologia — A Univ Sci Budapest Sect Philos Sociol
Annales Universitatis Fennicae Aboensis — Ann Univ Fenn Abo
Annales Universitatis Mariae Curie-Sklodowska — A Univ M Curie-Sklodowska
Annales Universitatis Mariae Curie-Sklodowska — Ann UMCS
Annales Universitatis Mariae Curie-Sklodowska — Annls Univ Mariae Curie-Sklodowska
Annales Universitatis Mariae Curie-Sklodowska — AnUMC
Annales Universitatis Mariae Curie-Sklodowska. Roczniki Universytetu Marii Curie-Sklodowskiej. Sect 3. Biologia — Ann Univ Mariae Curie Sklodowska Sect 3 Biol
Annales Universitatis Mariae Curie-Sklodowska. Sectio A. Mathematica — Ann Univ Mariae Curie-Sklodowska Sect A
Annales. Universitatis Mariae Curie-Sklodowska. Sectio AA. Chemia — Ann Univ Mariae Curie-Sklodowska
Annales Universitatis Mariae Curie-Sklodowska. Sectio AA. Physica et Chemia — ACFCAD
Annales Universitatis Mariae Curie-Sklodowska. Sectio AA. Physica et Chemia [*A publication*] — Ann Univ M Curie-Sklodowska Sect AA
Annales. Universitatis Mariae Curie-Sklodowska. Sectio AA. Physica et Chemia — Ann Univ Mariae Curie Sklodowska Sect AA Phys Chem
Annales Universitatis Mariae Curie-Sklodowska. Sectio AA. Physica et Chemia [*A publication*] — Ann Univ Mariae Curie-Sklodowska Sect AA
Annales. Universitatis Mariae Curie-Sklodowska. Sectio AA. Physics and Chemistry — Ann Univ Mariae Curie-Sklodowska
Annales Universitatis Mariae Curie-Sklodowska. Sectio AAA (Physica) — Ann Univ M Curie-Sklodowska Sect AAA (Phys)

Annales Universitatis Mariae Curie-Sklodowska. Sectio AAA. Physica — Ann Univ Mariae Curie Sklodowska Sect AAA Phys
Annales. Universitatis Mariae Curie-Sklodowska. Sectio AAA. Physica — Ann Univ Mariae Curie-Sklodowska
Annales Universitatis Mariae Curie-Sklodowska. Sectio AAA (Physica) [*Poland*] — Ann Univ Mariae Curie-Sklodowska Sect AAA
Annales Universitatis Mariae Curie-Sklodowska. Sectio B. Geographia, Geologia, Mineralogia, et Petrographia — Ann Univ Mariae Curie-Sklodowska Sect B
Annales Universitatis Mariae Curie-Sklodowska. Sectio C. Biologia — Ann Univ M Curie-Sklodowska Sect C
Annales Universitatis Mariae Curie-Sklodowska. Sectio C. Biologia — Ann Univ Mariae Curie-Sklodowska Sect C
Annales Universitatis Mariae Curie-Sklodowska. Sectio C. Biologia — Ann Univ Mariae Curie-Sklodowska Sect C Biol
Annales Universitatis Mariae Curie-Sklodowska. Sectio C. Biologia. Supplementum — Ann Univ Mariae Curie-Sklodowska Sect C Suppl
Annales Universitatis Mariae Curie-Sklodowska. Sectio D. Medicina — Ann Univ M Curie-Sklodowska Sect D
Annales Universitatis Mariae Curie-Sklodowska. Sectio D. Medicina — Ann Univ Mariae Curie-Sklodowska Med
Annales Universitatis Mariae Curie-Sklodowska. Sectio D. Medicina — Ann Univ Mariae Curie-Sklodowska Sect D
Annales Universitatis Mariae Curie-Sklodowska. Sectio D. Medicina — Ann Univ Mariae Curie-Sklodowska Sect D Med
Annales Universitatis Mariae Curie-Sklodowska. Sectio D. Medicina — AUMKA
Annales Universitatis Mariae Curie-Sklodowska. Sectio DD. Medicina Veterinaria — Ann Univ Mariae Curie-Sklodowska Sect DD
Annales Universitatis Mariae Curie-Sklodowska. Sectio DD. Medicina Veterinaria — Ann Univ Mariae Curie-Sklodowska Sect DD Med Vet
Annales Universitatis Mariae Curie-Sklodowska. Sectio E. Agricultura — Ann Univ Mariae Curie-Sklodowska Sect E
Annales Universitatis Mariae Curie-Sklodowska. Sectio E. Agricultura — Ann Univ Mariae Curie-Sklodowska Sect E Agric
Annales Universitatis Mariae Curie-Sklodowska. Sectio E. Agricultura. Supplementum — Ann Univ Mariae Curie-Sklodowska Sect E Suppl
Annales Universitatis Mariae Curie-Sklodowska. Sectio EE. Agraria — Ann Univ Mariae Curie-Sklodowska Sect EE
Annales Universitatis Mariae Curie-Sklodowska. Sectio F. Nauki Filozoficzne i Humanistyczne — AUMCS
Annales Universitatis Mariae Curie-Sklodowska. Sectio Oeconomica — A Univ M Curie-Sklodowska Oecon
Annales Universitatis Saraviensis — AUS
Annales Universitatis Saraviensis. Mathematisch-Naturwissenschaftliche Fakultaet — Ann Univ Sarav Math-Natur Fak
Annales Universitatis Saraviensis. Medizin — Ann Univ Sarav Med
Annales Universitatis Saraviensis. Medizin — Ann Univ Saraviensis Med
Annales Universitatis Saraviensis. Naturwissenschaften — Ann Univ Sara Naturwiss
Annales Universitatis Saraviensis. Naturwissenschaften — Ann Univ Saraviensis Naturwiss
Annales Universitatis Saraviensis. Philosophie — Ann Univ Saraviensis Phil
Annales Universitatis Saraviensis. Philosophie- Lettres — AnnUS
Annales Universitatis Saraviensis (Reihe). Mathematisch-Naturwissenschaftliche Fakultaet — Ann Univ Sara Math Naturwiss Fak
Annales Universitatis Saraviensis (Reihe). Mathematisch-Naturwissenschaftliche Fakultaet — Ann Univ Sarav (Reihe) Math-Naturwiss Fak
Annales Universitatis Saraviensis. Scientia — Ann Univ Sara Sci
Annales. Universitatis Saraviensis. Scientia — Ann Univ Sarav Sci
Annales Universitatis Saraviensis. Scientia — Ann Univ Saraviensis Sci
Annales Universitatis Saraviensis. Series Mathematicae — Ann Univ Sarav Ser Math
Annales Universitatis Saraviensis. Wissenschaften — Ann Univ Saraviensis Wiss
Annales Universitatis Saraviensis. Wissenschaften/Sciences — Ann Univ Sarav Wiss Sci
Annales Universitatis Scientiarum Budapestensis — Ann Univ Bp
Annales Universitatis Scientiarum Budapestensis de Rolando Eoetvoes Nominatae — AUB
Annales Universitatis Scientiarum Budapestensis de Rolando Eoetvoes Nominatae. Sectio Biologica — ABEBA
Annales Universitatis Scientiarum Budapestensis de Rolando Eoetvoes Nominatae. Sectio Biologica — Ann Univ Sci Budap Rolando Eotvos Nominatae Sect Biol
Annales Universitatis Scientiarum Budapestensis de Rolando Eoetvoes Nominatae. Sectio Chimica — Ann Univ Sci Budap Rolando Eotvos Nominatae Sect Chim
Annales Universitatis Scientiarum Budapestensis de Rolando Eoetvoes Nominatae. Sectio Chimica — Ann Univ Sci Budapest Rolando Eotvos Nominatae Sect Chim
Annales Universitatis Scientiarum Budapestensis de Rolando Eoetvoes Nominatae. Sectio Classica — Ann Un Bud
Annales Universitatis Scientiarum Budapestensis de Rolando Eoetvoes Nominatae. Sectio Computatorica — Ann Univ Sci Budapest Sect Comput
Annales Universitatis Scientiarum Budapestensis de Rolando Eoetvoes Nominatae. Sectio Geographica — A Univ Sci Budapest Sect Geogr
Annales Universitatis Scientiarum Budapestensis de Rolando Eoetvoes Nominatae. Sectio Geologica — Ann Univ Sci Budap Rolando Eotvos Nominatae Sect Geol
Annales Universitatis Scientiarum Budapestensis de Rolando Eoetvoes Nominatae. Sectio Mathematica — Ann Univ Sci Budapest Eotvos Sect Math
Annales Universitatis Scientiarum Budapestensis de Rolando Eoetvoes Nominatae. Sectio Philologica — AUBud
Annales Universitatis Scientiarum Budapestinenses — Ann Univ Budapest
Annales. Universitatis Scientiarum Budapestinenses de Rolando Eoetvoes Nominatae — Ann Eoetvoes
Annales. Universitatis Scientiarum Budapestinenses de Rolando Eoetvoes Nominatae — Annales Univ Budapest
Annales. Universitatis Scientiarum Budapestinenses de Rolando Eoetvoes Nominatae — AUB
Annales Universitatis Scientiarum Budapestinensis de Rolando Eotvoes Nominatae. Sectio Biologica — Ann Univ Sci Budapest Rolando Eotvoes Sect Biol
Annales Universitatis Turkuensis — AUT
Annales Universitatis Turkuensis. Series A — Ann Univ Turku Ser A
Annales Universitatis Turkuensis. Series A-I. Astronomica-Chemica-Physica-Mathematica — Ann Univ Turku Ser A I
Annales Universitatis Turkuensis. Series A-I. Astronomica-Chemica-Physica-Mathematica — AUTUA
Annales Universitatis Turkuensis. Series A-II. Biologica-Geographica — Ann Univ Turk Ser A II Biol-Geogr
Annales Universitatis Turkuensis. Series A-II. Biologica-Geographica — Ann Univ Turku Ser A II
Annales Universitatis Turkuensis. Series A-II. Biologica-Geographica-Geologica — Ann Univ Turk Ser A II Biol-Geogr-Geol
Annales. Universitatis Turkuensis. Series A-II. Biologica-Geographica-Geologica — ATYBAK
Annales Universitatis Turkuensis. Series D. Medica-Odontologica — Ann Univ Turku Ser D
Annales. Universite d'Abidjan — AdUA
Annales. Universite d'Abidjan — Ann Univ Abidjan
Annales. Universite d'Abidjan — As U A
Annales. Universite d'Abidjan. Ethnosociologie — A Univ Abidjan Ethnosociologie
Annales. Universite d'Abidjan. Histoire — A Univ Abidjan Histoire
Annales. Universite d'Abidjan. Lettres — A Univ Abidjan Lettres
Annales. Universite d'Abidjan. Linguistique — A Univ Abidjan Linguist
Annales. Universite d'Abidjan. Medecine — Ann Univ Abidjan Med
Annales. Universite d'Abidjan. Serie A. Droit — A Univ Abidjan Ser A Dr
Annales. Universite d'Abidjan. Serie B. Medecine — Ann Univ Abidjan Ser B Med
Annales. Universite d'Abidjan. Serie B. Medecine — AUAMCA
Annales. Universite d'Abidjan. Serie C. Sciences — ABJCAQ
Annales. Universite d'Abidjan. Serie C. Sciences — Ann Univ Abidjan Ser C Sci
Annales. Universite d'Abidjan. Serie E. Ecologie — Ann Univ Abidjan Ser E Ecol
Annales. Universite d'Abidjan. Serie E. Ecologie — AUAEAI
Annales. Universite d'Abidjan. Serie G. Geographie — Ann Univ Abidjan Ser G
Annales. Universite d'Ankara — Ann Univ Ankara
Annales. Universite de Besancon — AUB
Annales. Universite de Brazzaville — A d U B
Annales. Universite de Brazzaville — AdUB
Annales. Universite de Brazzaville — Ann Univ Brazzaville
Annales. Universite de Brazzaville. Serie C. Sciences — ABSCD6
Annales. Universite de Brazzaville. Serie C. Sciences — Ann Univ Brazzaville Ser C
Annales. Universite de Brazzaville. Serie C. Sciences — Ann Univ Brazzaville Ser C Sci
Annales. Universite de Grenoble — Ann Univ Grenoble
Annales. Universite de Grenoble — AnUG
Annales. Universite de Grenoble — AUG
Annales. Universite de Lyon — AnUL
Annales. Universite de Lyon — AUL
Annales. Universite de Lyon. 3e Serie. Lettres — Ann Univ Lyon 3e Ser Lett
Annales. Universite de Lyon. Fascicule Special — Ann Univ Lyon Fasc Spec
Annales. Universite de Lyon. Nouvelle Serie 2. Droit. Lettres — Ann Univ Lyon Nouv Ser 2
Annales. Universite de Lyon. Sciences. Medecine — Ann Univ Lyon Sci Med
Annales. Universite de Lyon. Sciences. Section A. Sciences Mathematiques et Astronomie — Ann Univ Lyon Sci Sect A
Annales. Universite de Lyon. Sciences. Section B. Sciences Physiques et Chimiques — Ann Univ Lyon Sci Sect B
Annales. Universite de Lyon. Sciences. Section C. Sciences Naturelles — Ann Univ Lyon Sci Sect C
Annales. Universite de Madagascar — Ann Univ Madag
Annales. Universite de Madagascar. Faculte de Droit et des Sciences Economiques — Ann Univ Madagascar Fac Droit et Sci Econ
Annales. Universite de Madagascar. Serie de Droit et des Sciences Economiques — A Univ Madagascar Ser Dr Sci Econ
Annales. Universite de Madagascar. Serie Lettres et Sciences Humaines — Ann Univ Madagascar Ser Lett et Sci Hum
Annales. Universite de Madagascar. Serie Sciences de la Nature et Mathematiques — Ann Univ Madagascar Ser Sci Nat Math
Annales. Universite de Madagascar. Serie Sciences de la Nature et Mathematiques — Ann Univ Madagascar Ser Sci Nature Math
Annales. Universite de Montpellier. Supplement Scientifique. Serie Botanique — Ann Univ Montp Suppl Sci Ser Bot
Annales. Universite de Paris — Ann Paris
Annales. Universite de Paris — Ann Univ Paris
Annales. Universite de Paris — AnnUP
Annales. Universite de Paris — AUP
Annales. Universite de Provence. Geologie Mediterraneenne — Ann Univ Provence Geol Mediterr
Annales. Universite des Sciences Sociales de Toulouse — A Univ Sci Soc Toulouse
Annales. Universite et ARERS [*Association Regionale pour l'Etude et la Recherche Scientifiques*] — Ann Univ ARERS
Annales. Universite et ARERS [*Association Regional pour l'Etude et la Recherche Scientifiques*] — AUNAB4

Annales. Universite et de l'Association Regionale pour l'Etude et la Recherche Scientifiques — Ann Univ Assoc Reg Etude Rech Sci
Annales. Universite Jean Moulin — A Univ Jean Moulin
Annales. Universites de Belgique — Ann Univ Belgique
Annales. Uniwersytet Marii Curie-Sklodowskiej. Sectio C. Biologia — Ann Uniw Marii Curie-Sklodowskiej Sect C Biol
Annales. Uniwersytet Marii Curie-Sklodowskiej. Sectio E. Agricultura — Ann Uniw Marii Curie Sklodowskiej Sect E Agric
Annales Valaisannes — AV
Annales Zoologica Fennici — AZOF
Annales Zoologici [*Warsaw*] — AZOGAR
Annales Zoologici Fennici — Ann Zool Fenn
Annales Zoologici Fennici — Annls Zool Fennici
Annales Zoologici Fennici — AZOFAO
Annales Zoologici. Societatis Zoologicae-Botanicae Fennicae "Vanamo" — Ann Zool Soc Zool-Bot Fenn "Vanamo"
Annales Zoologici. Societatis Zoologicae-Botanicae Fennicae "Vanamo" — AZZFAB
Annales Zoologici (Warsaw) — Ann Zool (Warsaw)
Annales-Conferencia — AC
Annali. Accademia di Agricoltura (Torino) — Anali Accad Agric (Torino)
Annali. Accademia di Agricoltura (Torino) — Ann Accad Agric (Torino)
Annali. Accademia Italiana di Scienze Forestali — A Acc Ital Sci For
Annali. Accademia Italiana di Scienze Forestali — ANLIA2
Annali. Accademia Italiana di Scienze Forestali — Ann Accad Ital Sci For
Annali. Accademia Nazionale di Agricoltura (Bologna) — Annali Accad Naz Agric (Bologna)
Annali Benacensi — Ann Benac
Annali Biologia Normale e Pathologica — Ann Biol Norm Pathol
Annali. Cattedra Petrarchesca. Reale Accademia Petrarca di Lettere, Arti, e Scienze. Arezzo — Ann Cattedra Petrarchesca
Annali Civili del Regno Delle Due Sicilie — Ann Civili Regno Due Sicilie
Annali dei Lavori Pubblici — Ann Lav Pubblici
Annali del Buon Pastore (Vienna) — ABPV
Annali del Liceo Classico Garibaldi di Palermo — ALCGP
Annali del Mezzogiorno — A Mezzogiorno
Annali della Fondazione Luigi Einaudi — Ann Fond Luigi Einaudi
Annali della Pubblica Istruzione — A Pubbl Istr
Annali della Pubblica Istruzione — API
Annali della Sanita Pubblica — ADSAAB
Annali della Sanita Pubblica — Ann Sanita Pubblica
Annali della Sanita Pubblica. Supplemento — Ann Sanita Pubblica Suppl
Annali della Sperimentazione Agraria — Ann Sper Agr
Annali della Sperimentazione Agraria — Ann Sper Agrar
Annali della Sperimentazione Agraria — Annali Sper Agr
Annali delle Universita Toscane — Annali d Univ Toscane
Annali delle'Istituto Sperimentale per l'Olivicoltura. Numero Speciale — Ann Ist Sper Olivic Numero Spec
Annali dell'Istituto Sperimentale per la Elaiotecnica — Ann Ist Sper Elaiotec
Annali dell'Isturzione Media — AIM
Annali di Agricoltura. Italy. Ministerio d'Agricoltura, Industria e Commercio (Rome) — Ann Agric Rome
Annali di Botanica (Genoa) — Ann Bot Genoa
Annali di Botanica (Rome) — Ann Bot (Rome)
Annali di Ca'Foscari. Serie Orientale — ACDF
Annali di Chimica — Ann Chim
Annali di Chimica Applicata [*Italy*] — Ann Chim Appl
Annali di Chimica Applicata — Annali Chim Appl
Annali di Chimica Applicata alla Farmacia ed alla Medicina — Ann Chim Appl Farm
Annali di Chimica Applicata alla Medicina Cioe alla Farmacia — Ann Chim Appl Med
Annali di Chimica Farmaceutica — Ann Chim Farm
Annali di Chimica (Rome) — Ann Chim (Rome)
Annali di Clinica Medica e di Medicina Sperimentale — Ann Clin Med Med Sper
Annali di Farmacoterapia e Chimica — Ann Farmacot Chim
Annali di Fisica — Ann Fis
Annali di Fitopatologia — Ann Fitopatol
Annali di Geofisica — Ann Geofis
Annali di Geofisica — Annali Geofisica
Annali di Laringologia, Otologia, Rinologia, Faringologia — Ann Laringol Otol Rinol Faringol
Annali di Laringologia, Otologia, Rinologia, Laringologia — Ann Laringol
Annali di Laringologia, Otologia, Rinologia, Laringologia — Ann Laringol Otol Rinol Laringol
Annali di Matematica Pura ed Applicata — Ann Mat Pura Appl
Annali di Medicina Navale — AMDNA4
Annali di Medicina Navale — Ann Med Nav
Annali di Medicina Navale e Coloniale — Ann Med Nav e Colon
Annali di Medicina Navale e Tropicale — Ann Med Nav Trop
Annali di Medicina Straniera — Ann Med Straniera
Annali di Merceol Siciliana — Ann Merceol Sicil
Annali di Microbiologia — ANMCAN
Annali di Microbiologia — Ann Microbiol
Annali di Microbiologia ed Enzimologia — AMEZAB
Annali di Microbiologia ed Enzimologia — Ann Microbiol Enzimol
Annali di Microbiologia ed Enzimologia — Annali Microbiol
Annali di Microbiologia (Milan) — Ann Microbiol (Milan)
Annali di Neurologia — Ann Neur
Annali di Neuropsichiatria e Psicoanalisi — Ann Neur Psich Psic
Annali di Neuropsichiatria e Psicoanalisi — Ann Neuropsichiatr Psicoanal
Annali di Nevrologia — Ann Nevrol
Annali di Oftalmologia e Clinica Oculistica — Ann Oftalmol Clin Ocul
Annali di Ostetricia e Ginecologia [*Italy*] — Ann Ostet Ginecol
Annali di Ostetricia, Ginecologia, Medicina Perinatale — Ann Ostet Ginecol Med Perinat
Annali di Ostetricia, Ginecologia, Medicina Perinatale — AOGMA
Annali di Ottalmologia — Ann Ottalmol
Annali di Ottalmologia e Clinica Oculistica — Ann Ottalmol Clin Ocul
Annali di Ottalmologia e Clinica Oculistica — Ann Ottalmol Clin Oculist
Annali di Radiologia Diagnostica — Ann Rad Diagn
Annali di Radiologia Diagnostica — Ann Radiol Diagn
Annali di Radiologia Diagnostica — ARDAAY
Annali di Radiologia e Fisica Medica — Ann Radiol Fis Med
Annali di Radioprotezione — Ann Radiopro
Annali di Scienze e Lettere — Ann Sci Lett
Annali di Sociologia (Milano) — A Sociol (Milano)
Annali di Stomatologia — Ann Stom
Annali di Stomatologia [*Roma*] — Ann Stomatol
Annali di Stomatologia — ASTOAR
Annali di Stomatologia e Clinica Odontoiatrica — Ann Stomatol Clin Odontoiatr
Annali di Stomatologia. Istituto Superiore di Odontoiatria G. Eastman — Ann Stomatol Ist Super Odontoiatr G Eastman
Annali di Stomatologia (Roma) — Ann Stomatol (Roma)
Annali di Storia del Diritto — Ann St Dir
Annali di Storia del Diritto — ASD
Annali di Storia Naturale — Ann Storia Nat
Annali di Studi Giuridici e Socio-Economici sui Servizii Sanitari Nazionale e Regionale — Annal Stud Giurid Socio Econ Serv Sanit Naz Reg
Annali d'Igiene — Ann Ig
Annali d'Igiene e Microbiologia — Ann Ig Microbiol
Annali d'Igiene. Sperimentali — Ann Ig Sper
Annali d'Igiene. Sperimentali — Annali Ig Sper
Annali. Facolta di Agraria (Bari) — A Fac Agrar (Bari)
Annali. Facolta di Agraria di Portici. Reale Universita di Napoli — Annali Fac Agr Portici
Annali. Facolta di Agraria di Portici. Regia Universita di Napoli — Ann Fac Agrar Portici Regia Univ Napoli
Annali. Facolta di Agraria (Milano) — A Fac Agrar (Milano)
Annali. Facolta di Agraria (Perugia) — Ann Fac Agr (Perugia)
Annali. Facolta di Agraria. Regia Universita di Pisa — Ann Fac Agrar Regia Univ Pisa
Annali. Facolta di Agraria. Universita Cattolica del Sacro Cuore — Ann Fac Agrar Univ Catt Sacro Cuore
Annali. Facolta di Agraria. Universita Cattolica del Sacro Cuore (Milan) — Ann Fac Agr Univ Cattol Sacro Cuore (Milan)
Annali. Facolta di Agraria. Universita degli Studi di Milano — Ann Fac Agrar Univ Studi Milano
Annali. Facolta di Agraria. Universita degli Studi di Perugia — Ann Fac Agr Univ Studii Perugia
Annali. Facolta di Agraria. Universita degli Studi di Perugia — Ann Fac Agrar Univ Stud Perugia
Annali. Facolta di Agraria. Universita degli Studi di Perugia — Annali Fac Agr Univ Perugia
Annali. Facolta di Agraria. Universita di Bari — Ann Fac Agrar Univ Bari
Annali. Facolta di Agraria. Universita di Bari — Annali Fac Agr Univ Bari
Annali. Facolta di Agraria. Universita di Milano — Annali Fac Agr Univ Milano
Annali. Facolta di Agraria. Universita di Pisa — Ann Fac Agr Univ Pisa
Annali. Facolta di Agraria. Universita di Pisa — Ann Fac Agrar Univ Pisa
Annali. Facolta di Economia e Commercio (Palermo) — A Fac Econ Com (Palermo)
Annali. Facolta di Economia e Commercio. Universita degli Studi di Messina — Ann Fac Econ Commer Univ Studi Mesina
Annali. Facolta di Economia e Commercio. Universita di Bari — Ann Fac Econ Commer Univ Bari
Annali. Facolta di Letter Filosofia e Magistero. Universita di Cagliari — Ann Fac Lett Fil Magist Univ Cagliari
Annali. Facolta di Lettere di Lecce — AFLL
Annali. Facolta di Lettere e Filosofia — Ann Fac Lett Filosof
Annali. Facolta di Lettere e Filosofia (Perugia) — AFLPer
Annali. Facolta di Lettere e Filosofia. Universita degli Studi di Perugia [*A publication*] — Ann Perugia
Annali. Facolta di Lettere e Filosofia. Universita di Bari — AFLB
Annali. Facolta di Lettere e Filosofia. Universita di Bari — AFLFB
Annali. Facolta di Lettere e Filosofia. Universita di Bari — Ann Bari
Annali. Facolta di Lettere e Filosofia. Universita di Macerata — AFLFUM
Annali. Facolta di Lettere e Filosofia. Universita di Macerata — AFLM
Annali. Facolta di Lettere e Filosofia. Universita di Napoli — AFLN
Annali. Facolta di Lettere e Filosofia. Universita di Napoli — Ann Nap Filos
Annali. Facolta di Lettere e Filosofia. Universita di Napoli — AUN
Annali. Facolta di Lettere e Filosofia. Universita di Padova — AFL Pad
Annali. Facolta di Lettere e Filosofia. Universita di Padova — Ann Fac Lett Filos Univ Padova
Annali. Facolta di Lettere e Filosofia. Universita di Perugia — AFLFP
Annali. Facolta di Lettere e Magistero. Universita di Napoli — Ann Nap
Annali. Facolta di Lettere, Filosofia, e Magistero. Universita di Cagliari — AFLC
Annali. Facolta di Lettere, Filosofia, e Magistero. Universita di Cagliari — Ann Cagliari
Annali. Facolta di Lettere, Filosofia, e Magistero. Universita di Cagliari — Ann Fac Lettere Univ Cagliari
Annali. Facolta di Lettere, Filosofia, e Magistero. Universita di Cagliari — AUCal
Annali. Facolta di Lettere Filosofia. Universita di Napoli — Ann Fac Lett Fil Univ Napoli
Annali. Facolta di Lettere. Universita di Cagliari — AFL Cagl
Annali. Facolta di Lingue e Litterature Straniere di Ca'Foscari — ACF
Annali. Facolta di Magistero. Universita di Bari — AFMB
Annali. Facolta di Magistero. Universita di Bari — AFMUB
Annali. Facolta di Magistero. Universita di Lecce — AFML

Annali. Facolta di Magistero. Universita di Lecce — Ann Lecce Mag
Annali. Facolta di Magistero. Universita di Palermo — AFMag
Annali. Facolta di Magistero. Universita di Palermo — AFMP
Annali. Facolta di Magistero. Universita di Palermo — Ann Pal
Annali. Facolta di Medicina e Chirurgia — Ann Fac Med Chirurg
Annali. Facolta di Medicina e Chirurgia. Universita degli Studi di Perugia che Pubblicano gli Atti della Accademia Anatomico-Chirurgica — Ann Fac Med Chir Univ Studi Perugia Atti Accad Anat Chir
Annali. Facolta di Medicina Veterinaria di Pisa. Universita degli Studi di Pisa — Ann Fac Med Vet Pisa Univ Studi Pisa
Annali. Facolta di Medicina Veterinaria di Torino — AMVTA
Annali. Facolta di Medicina Veterinaria di Torino — Ann Fac Med Vet Torino
Annali. Facolta di Medicina Veterinaria. Universita degli Studi di Pisa — Ann Fac Med Vet Univ Studi Pisa
Annali. Facolta di Medicina Veterinaria. Universita di Pisa — AFMVB
Annali. Facolta di Medicina Veterinaria. Universita di Pisa [*Italy*] — Ann Fac Med Vet Univ Pisa
Annali. Facolta di Medicina Veterinaria. Universita di Torino — Ann Fac Med Vet Univ Torino
Annali. Facolta di Scienze Agrarie. Universita degli Studi di Napoli — Annali Fac Sci Agr Univ Napoli
Annali. Facolta di Scienze Agrarie. Universita degli Studi di Napoli (Portici) — Ann Fac Sci Agr Univ Stud Napoli (Portici)
Annali. Facolta di Scienze Agrarie. Universita degli Studi di Napoli (Portici) — Ann Fac Sci Agrar Napoli (Portici)
Annali. Facolta di Scienze Agrarie. Universita degli Studi di Napoli (Portici) — Ann Fac Sci Agrar Univ Studi Napoli (Portici)
Annali. Facolta di Scienze Agrarie. Universita degli Studi di Torino — Ann Fac Sci Agrar Univ Studi Torino
Annali. Facolta di Scienze Agrarie. Universita degli Studi di Torino — Annali Fac Sci Agr Univ Torino
Annali. Facolta di Scienze Agrarie. Universita di Napoli. Serie 3 — Ann Fac Sci Agr Univ Napoli Ser 3
Annali. Facolta di Scienze Agrarie. Universita di Palermo — Ann Fac Sci Agrar Univ Palermo
Annali. Facolta di Scienze Agrarie. Universita di Torino — Ann Fac Sci Agr Univ Torino
Annali. Facolta di Scienze Politica (Genova) — A Fac Sci Polit (Genova)
Annali. Facolta di Scienze Poltiche ed Economia e Commercio. Universita degli Studi di Perugia. NS — Ann Fac Sci Polit Univ Studi Perugia NS
Annali. Fondazione Giangiacomo Feltrinelli — A Fond G Feltrinelli
Annali Fondazione Italiana per Storia Amministrativa — AniF
Annali. Fondazione Luigi Einaudi — A Fond L Einaudi
Annali Idrografici. Institute Idrografica della Regia Marina — Ann Idrogr
Annali Idrologici — Ann Idrol
Annali Idrologici — Annali Idrol
Annali Instituta Imeni N. P. Kondakova — Ann Inst Kond
Annali. Instituto di Corrispondenza Archeologica — AICA
Annali. Instituto di Corrispondenza Archeologica — Ann d Inst
Annali. Instituto di Corrispondenza Archeologica — Ann Inst
Annali. Instituto di Corrispondenza Archeologica — Annales dell'Inst Arch
Annali. Instituto di Corrispondenza Archeologica — Annali dell'Inst Arch
Annali Isnardi — Ann Isnardi
Annali Isnardi di Auxologia Normale e Patologica — Ann Isnardi Auxol Norm Patol
Annali. Istituto Carlo Forlanini — Ann Ist Carlo Forlanini
Annali. Istituto Carlo Forlanini — Annali Ist Carlo Forlanini
Annali. Istituto di Corrispondenza Archeologica — Adl
Annali. Istituto di Studi Danteschi — AISD
Annali. Istituto di Studi Europei Alcide de Gasperi — Ann Ist Stud Eur Alc Gasp
Annali. Istituto e Museo di Storia della Scienza di Firenze — Ann Ist Mus Stor
Annali. Istituto e Museo di Storia della Scienze di Firenze — Ann Ist Mus Stor Sci Firenze
Annali. Istituto Italiano di Numismatica — All Num
Annali. Istituto Italiano di Numismatica — AIIN
Annali. Istituto Italiano di Numismatica — Ann Ist It Num
Annali. Istituto Italiano di Numismatica — Ann Ist Num
Annali. Istituto Italiano di Numismatica — Annli Ist Numismatica
Annali. Istituto Italiano per gli Studi Storici — AIIS
Annali. Istituto Orientale di Napoli — Ann Ist Orient Napoli
Annali. Istituto Sperimentale Agronomico — Ann Ist Sper Agron
Annali. Istituto Sperimentale per il Tabacco — AISTD4
Annali. Istituto Sperimentale per il Tabacco — Ann Ist Sper Tab
Annali. Istituto Sperimentale per la Cerealicoltura — Ann Ist Sper Cereal
Annali. Istituto Sperimentale per la Cerealicoltura — Ann Ist Sper Cerealic
Annali. Istituto Sperimentale per la Floricoltura — Ann Ist Sper Flori
Annali. Istituto Sperimentale per la Floricoltura — Ann Ist Sper Floric
Annali. Istituto Sperimentale per la Floricoltura — Ann Ist Sper Floricolt
Annali. Istituto Sperimentale per la Frutticoltura — AIFCBM
Annali. Istituto Sperimentale per la Frutticoltura — Ann Ist Sper Fruttic
Annali. Istituto Sperimentale per la Frutticoltura — Ann Ist Sper Frutticolt
Annali. Istituto Sperimentale per la Nutrizione delle Piante — Ann Ist Sper Nutr Piante
Annali. Istituto Sperimentale per la Nutrizione delle Piante — ASNPBZ
Annali. Istituto Sperimentale per la Selvicoltura — Ann Ist Sper Selvi
Annali. Istituto Sperimentale per la Selvicoltura — Ann Ist Sper Selvic
Annali. Istituto Sperimentale per la Selvicoltura — ASSVB
Annali. Istituto Sperimentale per la Valorizzazione Tecnologica (Milan) — Ann Ist Sper Valorizzazione Tecnol (Milan)
Annali. Istituto Sperimentale per la Viticoltura (Conegliano, Italy) — Ann Ist Sper Vitic (Conegliano Italy)
Annali. Istituto Sperimentale per la Zoologia Agraria — AIZAAD
Annali. Istituto Sperimentale per la Zoologia Agraria — Ann Ist Sper Zool Agrar
Annali. Istituto Sperimentale per la Zoologia Agraria — Annali Ist Sper Zool Agr
Annali. Istituto Sperimentale per la Zootecnia — AISZAJ
Annali. Istituto Sperimentale per la Zootecnia — Ann Ist Sper Zootec
Annali. Istituto Sperimentale per l'Agrumicoltura — Ann Ist Sper Agrumic
Annali. Istituto Sperimentale per l'Assestamento Forestale e per l'Alpicoltura — Ann Ist Sper Asses For Alpic
Annali. Istituto Sperimentale per l'Assestamento Forestale e per l'Apicoltura — Ann Ist Sper Assestamento For Apic
Annali. Istituto Sperimentale per le Colture Foraggere — Ann Ist Sper Colt Foraggere
Annali. Istituto Sperimentale per le Colture Industriali — Ann Ist Sper Colt Ind
Annali. Istituto Sperimentale per l'Enologia (Asti) — Ann Ist Sper Enol (Asti)
Annali. Istituto Sperimentale per lo Studio e la Difesa del Suolo — Ann Ist Sper Stud Dif Suolo
Annali. Istituto Sperimentale per lo Studio e la Difesa del Suolo — ASDSAR
Annali. Istituto Sperimentale Zootecnico di Roma — Ann Ist Sper Zootec Roma
Annali. Istituto Storico Italo-Germanico in Trento — Ann Ist Stor Italo Germ Trento
Annali. Istituto Superiore di Sanita — AISSAW
Annali. Istituto Superiore di Sanita — Ann Ist Super Sanita
Annali. Istituto Superiore di Scienze e Lettere di Santa Chiera (Napoli) — AISLN
Annali. Istituto Universitario. Napoli. Sezione Romanza — AIUN SR
Annali. Istituto Universitario Orientale (Napoli) — AION
Annali. Istituto Universitario Orientale (Napoli) — AI(U)ON
Annali. Istituto Universitario Orientale (Napoli) — Ann Or (Napoli)
Annali. Istituto Universitario Orientale (Napoli) — AnnION
Annali. Istituto Universitario Orientale. Sezione Germanica [*Napoli*] — AIUO
Annali. Istituto Universitario Orientale. Sezione Germanica (Napoli) — AION-G
Annali. Istituto Universitario Orientale. Sezione Germanica (Napoli) — AION-SG
Annali. Istituto Universitario Orientale. Sezione Linguistica [*Napoli*] — AION Ling
Annali. Istituto Universitario Orientale. Sezione Linguistica (Napoli) — AION-L
Annali. Istituto Universitario Orientale. Sezione Linguistica (Napoli) — AION-SL
Annali. Istituto Universitario Orientale. Sezione Orientale (Napoli) — AION-O
Annali. Istituto Universitario Orientale. Sezione Orientale (Napoli) — AION-SO
Annali. Istituto Universitario Orientale. Sezione Romanza (Napoli) — AION-R
Annali. Istituto Universitario Orientale. Sezione Romanza (Napoli) — AION-SR
Annali. Istituto Universitario Orientale. Sezione Slava (Napoli) — AION-S
Annali. Istituto Universitario Orientale. Sezione Slava (Napoli) — AION-SS
Annali Italiani di Chirurgia — AICHAL
Annali Italiani di Chirurgia — Ann Ital Chir
Annali Italiani di Dermatologia Clinica e Sperimentale — ADRCAC
Annali Italiani di Dermatologia Clinica e Sperimentale — Ann Ital Dermatol Clin Sper
Annali Italiani di Dermatologia e Sifilologia — Ann Ital Dermatol Sifilol
Annali Italiani di Medicina Interna — Ann Ital Med Int
Annali Italiani di Pediatria — Ann Ital Pediatr
Annali Lateranensi — AL
Annali Lateranensi — AnnLat
Annali. Liceo Classico G. Garibaldi di Palermo — ALGP
Annali Manzoniani — AM
Annali Medici di Sondalo — Ann Med Sondalo
Annali Medici (Milan) — Ann Med (Milan)
Annali. Museo Civico di Storia Naturale Genova — Ann Mus Civ Stor Nat Genova
Annali. Museo Civico di Storia Naturale "Giacomo Doria" — AMGDAN
Annali. Museo Civico di Storia Naturale "Giacomo Doria" — Ann Mus Civ Stor Nat "Giacomo Doria"
Annali. Museo Civico di Storia Naturale "Giacomo Doria" — Annali Mus Civ Stor Nat Giacomo Doria
Annali. Museo Civico di Storia Naturali Giacomo Doria. Supplemento — Ann Mus Civ Stor Nat Giacomo Doria Suppl
Annali. Ospedale Maria Vittoria di Torino — Ann Osp Maria Vittoria Torino
Annali. Osservatorio Astronomico. Universita di Torino — Ann Osserv Astron Torino
Annali. Osservatorio Vesuviano — Ann Oss Vesuviano
Annali. Pisa Universita. Facolta di Agraria — Ann Pisa Univ Fac Agrar
Annali. Pontificio Museo Missionario Etnologico — Ann Pontificio Mus Mission Etnol
Annali. Pontificio Museo Missionario Etnologico (Vatican) — Ann Pontif Mus Miss Etnol (Vatican)
Annali. Pontifico Museo Missionario Ethnologico gia Lateranensi [*Roma*] — A Pontif Mus Miss Etnol
Annali. Reale Accademia d'Agricoltura di Torino — Ann R Accad Agric Torino
Annali. Reale Osservatorio Vesuviano — Ann R Oss Vesuviano
Annali. Reale Scuola Superiore di Agricoltura di Portici — Ann Reale Scuola Super Agric Portici
Annali. Reale Stazione Chimico-Agraria Sperimentale di Roma — Annali Staz Chim-Agr Sper Roma
Annali. Reale Stazione Sperimentale di Agrumicoltura e Frutticoltura in Acireale — Ann Sta Sperim Agrumicoltura
Annali. Reale Universita di Genova — Ann Univ Genova
Annali. Regia Scuola Superiore di Agricoltura in Portici — Ann Regia Sc Super Agric Portici
Annali. Regia Scuola Superiore di Agricoltura (Portici) — Ann Regia Super Agric (Portici)
Annali. Regio Istituto Superiore Agrario di Portici — Ann Regio Ist Super Agrar Portici
Annali Schiapparelli — Ann Schiapparelli
Annali Sclavo — Ann Sclavo
Annali Sclavo Monograph — Annal Sclavo Monogr
Annali. Scuola Normale Superiore — Ann Scu Norm Sup
Annali. Scuola Normale Superiore de Pisa — Ann Scu Norm Super Pisa
Annali. Scuola Normale Superiore di Pisa — Ann Pisa
Annali. Scuola Normale Superiore di Pisa — Ann Sc Norm Super Pisa
Annali. Scuola Normale Superiore di Pisa — ASN

Annali. Scuola Normale Superiore di Pisa — ASNP
Annali. Scuola Normale Superiore di Pisa — ASNSP
Annali. Scuola Normale Superiore di Pisa. Classe di Lettere e Filosofia — A Scuol Pisa
Annali. Scuola Normale Superiore di Pisa. Classe di Lettere e Filosofia — Ann R Scu Norm Sup Pisa
Annali. Scuola Normale Superiore di Pisa. Classe di Lettere e Filosofia — Ann Sc Pisa
Annali. Scuola Normale Superiore di Pisa. Classe di Lettere e Filosofia — Ann Scuola Pisa
Annali. Scuola Normale Superiore di Pisa. Classe di Lettere e Filosofia — ANSP
Annali. Scuola Normale Superiore di Pisa. Classe di Scienze — Ann Scuola Norm Sup Pisa Cl Sci
Annali. Scuola Normale Superiore di Pisa. Classe di Scienze. Serie IV — Ann Scuola Norm Sup Pisa Cl Sci 4
Annali. Scuola Normale Superiore di Pisa. Scienze, Fisiche, e Matematiche — Ann Sc Norm Super Pisa Sci Fis Mat
Annali. Scuola Normale Superiore di Pisa. Scienze, Fisiche, e Matematiche — Ann Scuola Norm Sup Pisa Sci Fis Mat
Annali. Seminario di Studi del Mondo Classico. Sezione di Archeologia e Storia Antica [*Napoli*] — Ann A Stor Ant
Annali. Seminario di Studi dell'Europa Orientale. Sezione Linguistico-Filogica. Istituto Universitario Orientale — Ann Sem Stud Eur Orient Sez Ling Filol Ist Univ Orient
Annali. Seminario Giuridico di Palermo — ASGP
Annali. Sezione Linguistica. Istituto Universitario Orientale — Ann Sez Ling
Annali. Societa degli Ingegneri e degli Architetti Italiani — Ann Soc Ingeg
Annali. Stazione Chimico-Agraria Sperimentale di Roma — Ann Stn Chim Agrar Sper Roma
Annali. Stazione Chimico-Agraria Sperimentale di Roma. Serie 3 — Ann Sta Chim-Agr Sper Roma Ser 3
Annali. Stazione Chimico-Agraria Sperimentale di Roma. Serie 3. Pubblicazione — Ann Stn Chim-Agrar Sper Roma Ser 3 Pubbl
Annali. Stazione Sperimentale Agrario di Modena — An Staz Sper Agr M
Annali. Stazione Sperimentale di Risicoltura e delle Colture Irrigue. Vercelli — Annali Staz Sper Risicolt Vercelli
Annali Triestini — AnnTriest
Annali Triestini a Cura. Universita di Trieste. Sezione II. Scienze ed Ingegneria — Ann Triest Cura Univ Trieste Sez II
Annali. Universita di Ferrara — Ann Univ Ferrara
Annali. Universita di Ferrara. Nuova Serie. Sezione XX. Biologia — Ann Univ Ferrara Nuova Ser Sez XX Biol
Annali. Universita di Ferrara. Nuova Serie. Sezione XX. Biologia — AUFBE4
Annali. Universita di Ferrara. Nuovo Serie. Sezione IX. Scienze Geologiche e Paleontologiche — Ann Univ Ferrara Sez IX
Annali. Universita di Ferrara. Nuovo Serie. Sezione VII — Ann Univ Ferrara Sez VII NS
Annali. Universita di Ferrara. Nuovo Serie. Sezione VII. Scienze Matematiche — Ann Univ Ferrara Sez VII
Annali. Universita di Ferrara. Sezione 5. Chimica Pura ed Applicata — Ann Univ Ferrara Sez 5
Annali. Universita di Ferrara. Sezione 6. Fisiologia e Chimica Biologica — Ann Univ Ferrara Sez 6
Annali. Universita di Ferrara. Sezione 9. Scienze Geologiche e Mineralogiche — Ann Univ Ferrara Sez 9 Sci Geol Mineral
Annali. Universita di Ferrara. Sezione 11. Farmacologia e Terapia — Ann Univ Ferrara Sez 11
Annali. Universita di Ferrara. Sezione I. Ecologia — ANFEBT
Annali. Universita di Ferrara. Sezione I. Ecologia — Ann Univ Ferrara Sez I Ecol
Annali. Universita di Ferrara. Sezione III. Biologia Animale — Ann Univ Ferrara Sez III Biol Anim
Annali. Universita di Ferrara. Sezione III. Biologia Animale — FUABBV
Annali. Universita di Ferrara. Sezione IV. Botanica — Ann Univ Ferrara Sez IV Bot
Annali. Universita di Ferrara. Sezione IV. Botanica — FEUBAI
Annali. Universita di Ferrara. Sezione IV. Fisiologia e Chimica Biologica — Ann Univ Ferrara Sez IV
Annali. Universita di Ferrara. Sezione IX. Scienze Geologiche e Mineralogiche — Ann Univ Ferrara Sez IX Sci Geol Mineral
Annali. Universita di Ferrara. Sezione IX. Scienze Geologiche e Paleontologiche — AFGPAA
Annali. Universita di Ferrara. Sezione IX. Scienze Geologiche e Paleontologiche — Ann Univ Ferrara Sez IX Sci Geol Paleontol
Annali. Universita di Ferrara. Sezione V. Chimica Pura ed Applicata — Ann Univ Ferrara Sez V
Annali. Universita di Ferrara. Sezione V. Chimica Pura ed Applicata. Supplemento — Ann Univ Ferrara Sez V Suppl
Annali. Universita di Ferrara. Sezione VI. Fisiologia e Chimica Biologica — Ann Univ Ferrara Sez VI Fisiol Chim Biol
Annali. Universita di Ferrara. Sezione VI. Fisiologia e Chimica Biologica — FUAFA8
Annali. Universita di Ferrara. Sezione XI. Farmacologia e Terapia — Ann Univ Ferrara Sez XI
Annali. Universita di Ferrara. Sezione XI. Farmacologia e Terapia — Ann Univ Ferrara Sez XI Farmacol Ter
Annali. Universita di Ferrara. Sezione XIII. Anatomia Comparata — Ann Univ Ferrara Sez XIII Anat Comp
Annali. Universita di Lecce — AUL
Annali. Universita di Lecce. Facolta di Lettere e Filosofia e di Magistero — Ann Lecce
Annali. Universita Toscane — Ann Univ Toscane
Annali. Universita Toscane — Annali Univ Tosc
Annali. Universita Toscane — AUT
Annali. Villaggio Sanatoriale di Sondalo — Ann Villaggio Sanat Sondalo
Annalis. Historico-Naturales Musei Nationalis Hungarici — Annls Hist-Nat Mus Natn Hung
Annals. Academy of Medicine (Singapore) — AAMSC
Annals. Academy of Medicine (Singapore) — Ann Acad Med (Singapore)
Annals. Agricultural Experiment Station. Government General of Chosen — Ann Agric Exp Stn Gov Gen Chosen
Annals. American Academy of Political and Social Science — A Amer Acad Polit Soc Sci
Annals. American Academy of Political and Social Science — AAA
Annals. American Academy of Political and Social Science — AAAPS
Annals. American Academy of Political and Social Science — AAAPSS
Annals. American Academy of Political and Social Science — AAPS
Annals. American Academy of Political and Social Science — AAYPA
Annals. American Academy of Political and Social Science — An Am Acad Pol Soc Sci
Annals. American Academy of Political and Social Science — Ann Am Acad
Annals. American Academy of Political and Social Science — Ann Am Acad Pol Sci
Annals. American Academy of Political and Social Science — Ann Am Acad Poli Soc Sci
Annals. American Academy of Political and Social Science — Ann Am Poli
Annals. American Academy of Political and Social Science — Ann Amer Acad Polit Soc Sci
Annals. American Academy of Political and Social Science — Annals
Annals. American Academy of Political and Social Science — Annals Am Acad
Annals. American Academy of Political and Social Science — APS
Annals. American Academy of Political and Social Science — GANP
Annals. American Academy of Political and Social Science (Philadelphia) — An Am Acad Pol Soc Sc Phila
Annals. American Academy of Political and Social Science (Philadelphia) — Ann Am Acad Pol Soc Sci (Philadelphia)
Annals. American Academy of Political and Social Sciences — Ann Am Acad Polit Social Sci
Annals. American Academy of Political and Social Sciences — Annt
Annals. American Conference of Governmental Industrial Hygienists — Ann Am Conf Gov Ind Hyg
Annals and Magazine of Natural History — AMNHA2
Annals and Magazine of Natural History — An Mag N H
Annals and Magazine of Natural History — AnMNH
Annals and Magazine of Natural History — Ann and Mag Nat Hist
Annals and Magazine of Natural History — Ann Mag Nat Hist
Annals and Magazine of Natural History — Ann Mag Natur Hist
Annals and Magazine of Natural History — Annals and Mag Nat History
Annals. Anricultural Experiment Station. Government General of Chosen/Noji Shikenjo Iho — Ann Agric Exp Sta Gov Gen Chosen
Annals. Association of American Geographers — A Assoc Amer Geogr
Annals. Association of American Geographers — AAAG
Annals. Association of American Geographers — Ann As Am G
Annals. Association of American Geographers — Ann Ass Am Geogr
Annals. Association of American Geographers — Ann Ass Amer Geogr
Annals. Association of American Geographers — Ann Ass Amer Geographers
Annals. Association of American Geographers — Ann Assn Am Geog
Annals. Association of American Geographers — Ann Assoc Am Geogr
Annals. Association of American Geographers — Ann Assoc Amer Geogr
Annals. Association of American Geographers — PAAG
Annals. Australian College of Dental Surgeons — Ann Aust Coll Dent Surg
Annals. Bhandarkar Oriental Research Institute — A Bhandarkar Or Res Inst
Annals. Bhandarkar Oriental Research Institute — ABORI
Annals. Bhandarkar Oriental Research Institute — An Bhand Or Res Inst
Annals. Bhandarkar Oriental Research Institute — AnnBhl
Annals. Botanical Society of Canada — Ann Bot Soc Canada
Annals. Cape Provincial Museums — Ann Cape Prov Mus
Annals. Cape Provincial Museums. Human Sciences — Ann Cape Prov Mus Hum Sci
Annals. Cape Provincial Museums. Natural History — Ann Cape Prov Mus Nat Hist
Annals. Carnegie Museum — Ann Carnegie Mus
Annals. College of Medicine [*Mosul*] — ACMMBB
Annals. College of Medicine (Mosul) — Ann Coll Med (Mosul)
Annals. Czechoslovak Academy of Agriculture — Ann Czech Acad Agric
Annals. Entomological Society of America — AESAA
Annals. Entomological Society of America — Ann Ent S A
Annals. Entomological Society of America — Ann Ent Soc Am
Annals. Entomological Society of America — Ann Entom Soc Am
Annals. Entomological Society of America — Ann Entomol Soc Am
Annals. Entomological Society of Quebec — AETQA3
Annals. Entomological Society of Quebec — Ann Ent Soc Queb
Annals. Entomological Society of Quebec — Ann Entomol Soc Que
Annals. Food Technology and Chemistry — Ann Food Technol Chem
Annals. Geological Survey — Ann Geol Surv
Annals. Geological Survey of Egypt — Ann Geol Surv Egypt
Annals. Geological Survey of South Africa — Ann Geol Surv S Afr
Annals. Hebrew Union College — Ann Heb Union Coll
Annals. High Performance Paper Society. Japan — Ann High Perform Pap Soc Jpn
Annals. Hungarian Geological Institute — Ann Hung Geol Inst
Annals. ICRP [*International Commission on Radiological Protection*] — ANICD6
Annals. ICRP [*International Commission on Radiological Protection*] — Ann ICRP
Annals. Indian Academy of Medical Sciences — AIADAX
Annals. Indian Academy of Medical Sciences — Ann Indian Acad Med Sci
Annals. Institute of Child Health [*Calcutta*] — AICHDO
Annals. Institute of Child Health (Calcutta) — Ann Inst Child Health (Calcutta)
Annals. Institute of Comparative Studies of Culture — A Inst Comp Stud Cult
Annals. Institute of Social Sciences (Tokyo) — Inst Social Science (Tokyo) Annals

Annals. Institute of Statistical Mathematics — Ann In St Ma
Annals. Institute of Statistical Mathematics — Ann I Stat
Annals. Institute of Statistical Mathematics — Ann Inst Statist Math
Annals. International Commission of Radiological Protection — Ann Inter Comm Radiol Prot
Annals. Israel Physical Society — Ann Isr Phys Soc
Annals. Israel Physical Society — Ann Israel Phys Soc
Annals. Jack Kerouac School of Disembodied Poetics — Ann J Kerou
Annals. Japan Association for Philosophy of Science — Ann Japan Assoc Philos Sci
Annals. Japan Association for Philosophy of Science — Ann Jpn Assoc Philos Sci
Annals. Japan Association for Philosophy of Science — JPYABL
Annals. Kurashiki Central Hospital — Ann Kurashiki Cent Hosp
Annals. Kurashiki Central Hospital — KCBNAY
Annals. Lyceum of Natural History (New York) — Ann Lyceum Nat Hist (NY)
Annals. Medical Section. Polish Academy of Sciences — ALMPB
Annals. Medical Section. Polish Academy of Sciences — ALMPBF
Annals. Medical Section. Polish Academy of Sciences — Ann Med Sect Pol Acad Sci
Annals. Medical University. Bialystok, Poland — Ann Med Univ Bialyst Pol
Annals. Medicina Academia de Ciencies Mediques de Catalunya i de Balears — Ann Med Acad Cienc Med Catalunya Balears
Annals. Medicina Academia de Ciencies Mediques de Catalunya i de Balears — ANMEDW
Annals. Missouri Botanical Garden — AMBGA7
Annals. Missouri Botanical Garden — Ann MO Bot
Annals. Missouri Botanical Garden — Ann MO Bot Gard
Annals. Missouri Botanical Garden — Ann MO Bot Gdn
Annals. Missouri Historical and Philosophical Society — Ann Missouri Hist Soc
Annals. Natal Museum — Ann Natal Mus
Annals. National Academy of Medical Sciences [*India*] — ANAIDI
Annals. National Academy of Medical Sciences — Ann Natl Acad Med Sci
Annals. National Academy of Medical Sciences (India) — Ann Natl Acad Med Sci (India)
Annals. New York Academy of Sciences — Ann New York Acad Sc
Annals. New York Academy of Sciences — Ann New York Acad Sci
Annals. New York Academy of Sciences — Ann NY Ac Sci
Annals. New York Academy of Sciences — Ann NY Acad
Annals. New York Academy of Sciences — Ann NY Acad Sci
Annals. New York Academy of Sciences — ANYAA
Annals. New York Academy of Sciences — ANYAA9
Annals. New York Academy of Sciences — ANYAS
Annals of Agricultural Science [*Cairo*] — AAGSAI
Annals of Agricultural Science (Cairo) — Ann Agric Sci (Cairo)
Annals of Agricultural Science (Moshtohor) — Ann Agric Sci (Moshtohor)
Annals of Agricultural Science. University of A'in Shams — Ann Agric Sci Univ A'in Shams
Annals of Air and Space Law — A Air Space Law
Annals of Air and Space Law — Annals Air and Space
Annals of Air and Space Law — Annals Air and Space L
Annals of Allergy — ANAEA3
Annals of Allergy — Ann Allergy
Annals of Allergy, Asthma, and Immunology — Ann Allergy Asthma Immunol
Annals of American Geographers — AAG
Annals of Applied Biology — AABIAV
Annals of Applied Biology — Ann Ap Biol
Annals of Applied Biology — Ann App Biol
Annals of Applied Biology — Ann Appl Biol
Annals of Applied Biology. Supplement — Ann Appl Biol Suppl
Annals of Applied Nematology — Ann Appl Nematol
Annals of Applied Probability — Ann Appl Probab
Annals of Archaeology and Anthropology [*Liverpool*] — AAA
Annals of Archaeology and Anthropology — AArchAnthr
Annals of Archaeology and Anthropology — Annals of A A
Annals of Archaeology and Anthropology (Liverpool) — Ann Arch Anthr Liverpool
Annals of Archaeology and Anthropology (Liverpool) — Ann Liv
Annals of Archaeology and Anthropology (Liverpool) — Liv Ann
Annals of Archaeology and Anthropology (Liverpool) — Liverpool AAA
Annals of Archaeology. University of Liverpool — AAL
Annals of Arid Zone — ANAZBX
Annals of Arid Zone — Ann Arid Zone
Annals of Assurance Sciences. Proceedings of Reliability and Maintainability Conference — Ann Assur Sci Proc Reliab Maint Conf
Annals of Behavioral Medicine — ABMEEH
Annals of Behavioral Medicine — Ann Behav Med
Annals of Biochemistry and Experimental Medicine [*Calcutta and New Delhi*] — Ann Biochem Exp Med
Annals of Biochemistry and Experimental Medicine (Calcutta and New Delhi) — Ann Biochem Exp Med (Calcutta)
Annals of Biology (Ludhiana) — Ann Biol (Ludhiana)
Annals of Biomedical Engineering — ABMEC
Annals of Biomedical Engineering — Ann Biomed
Annals of Biomedical Engineering — Ann Biomed Eng
Annals of Botany — ANBOA
Annals of Botany — Ann Bot
Annals of Botany (London) — Ann Bot (London)
Annals of Clinical and Laboratory Science — ACLSC
Annals of Clinical and Laboratory Science — Ann Clin Lab Sci
Annals of Clinical Biochemistry — ACBOBU
Annals of Clinical Biochemistry — Ann Clin Biochem
Annals of Clinical Medicine — Ann Clin Med
Annals of Clinical Psychiatry — Ann Clin Psychiatry
Annals of Clinical Research — ACLRBL
Annals of Clinical Research — Ann Clin R
Annals of Clinical Research — Ann Clin Res
Annals of Clinical Research. Supplement — ACSUB
Annals of Clinical Research. Supplement — Ann Clin Res Suppl
Annals of Community-Oriented Education — ACOE
Annals of Community-Oriented Education — Ann Comm Orient Educ
Annals of Dentistry — Ann Dent
Annals of Development — Ann Dev
Annals of Differential Equations — Ann Differential Equations
Annals of Discrete Mathematics [*Elsevier Book Series*] — ADM
Annals of Discrete Mathematics — Ann Discrete Math
Annals of Economic and Social Measurement — A Econ Soc Measurement
Annals of Economic and Social Measurement — Ann Econ Sm
Annals of Emergency Medicine — AEMED3
Annals of Emergency Medicine — Ann Emerg Med
Annals of Epidemiology — Ann Epidemiol
Annals of Eugenics — Ann Eugen
Annals of Family Studies — A Family Stud
Annals of General Practice — Ann Gen Pract
Annals of General Practice — Annals Gen Pract
Annals of General Practice — Annals General Prac
Annals of General Practice — Annals of Gen Prac
Annals of Geomorphology — Ann Geomorphol
Annals of Glaciology — ANGL
Annals of Glaciology — Ann Glaciol
Annals of Global Analysis and Geometry — Ann Global Anal Geom
Annals of Gynaecology and Pediatry — Ann Gynaec Pediat
Annals of Hematology — Ann Hematol
Annals of Human Biology — AHUBBJ
Annals of Human Biology — Ann Hum Bio
Annals of Human Biology — Ann Hum Biol
Annals of Human Genetics — ANHGAA
Annals of Human Genetics — Ann Hum Gen
Annals of Human Genetics — Ann Hum Genet
Annals of Human Genetics — Ann Human Genetics
Annals of Immunology — AIMLBG
Annals of Internal Medicine — AIMEA
Annals of Internal Medicine — Ann Int Med
Annals of Internal Medicine — Ann Intern Med
Annals of International Studies — Annals Internat Studies
Annals of Iowa — AI
Annals of Iowa — Ala
Annals of Iowa — AnIowa
Annals of Iowa — Ann IA
Annals of Iowa — Ann Iowa
Annals of Iowa — AnnI
Annals of Kentucky Natural History — AKNHAM
Annals of Kentucky Natural History — Ann KY Nat Hist
Annals of Kentucky Natural History — Annals KY Nat History
Annals of Library Science — Annals Lib Sci
Annals of Library Science and Documentation — Ann Libr Sci
Annals of Library Science and Documentation — Ann Libr Sci Docum
Annals of Life Insurance Medicine — Ann Life Ins Med
Annals of Mathematical Logic — Ann Math Logic
Annals of Mathematical Logic — Annals Math Log
Annals of Mathematical Statistics — Ann Math Stat
Annals of Mathematics — Ann Math
Annals of Mathematics and Artificial Intelligence — Ann Math Artificial Intelligence
Annals of Mathematics. Second Series — Ann of Math (2)
Annals of Mathematics. Studies — Ann of Math Stud
Annals of Mathematics. Studies — Ann of Math Studies
Annals of Medical History — Ann Med Hist
Annals of Medicine — Ann Med
Annals of Medicine (Hagerstown, Maryland) — Ann Med (Hagerstown Maryland)
Annals of Medicine (Helsinki) — Ann Med Helsinki
Annals of Neurology — Ann Neurol
Annals of Nuclear Energy — ANENDJ
Annals of Nuclear Energy — Ann Nuc Eng
Annals of Nuclear Energy — Ann Nucl Energy
Annals of Nuclear Medicine — Ann Nucl Med
Annals of Nuclear Science and Engineering — Ann Nucl Sci and Eng
Annals of Nuclear Science and Engineering — Ann Nucl Sci Eng
Annals of Nuclear Science and Engineering — Ann Nucl Sci Engng
Annals of Numerical Mathematics — Ann Numer Math
Annals of Nutrition and Metabolism — Ann Nutr Metab
Annals of Occupational Hygiene — Ann Occup Hyg
Annals of Occupational Hygiene — Annals Occup Hyg
Annals of Occupational Hygiene — AOHYA
Annals of Occupational Hygiene. Supplement — AOHSA
Annals of Oncology — Ann Oncol
Annals of Ophthalmology — Ann Ophth
Annals of Ophthalmology — Ann Ophthal
Annals of Ophthalmology — Ann Ophthalmol
Annals of Ophthalmology and Otology — Ann Ophth Otol
Annals of Ophthalmology and Otology — Ann Ophthalmol Otol
Annals of Ophthalmology and Otology — Annals Ophthal Otol
Annals of Oriental Research — An Or Res
Annals of Oriental Research — AOR
Annals of Oriental Research. University of Madras — Ann OR
Annals of Otology, Rhinology, and Laryngology — Ann O
Annals of Otology, Rhinology, and Laryngology — Ann Ot
Annals of Otology, Rhinology, and Laryngology — Ann Oto Rhinol Laryngol
Annals of Otology, Rhinology, and Laryngology — Ann Otol Rh
Annals of Otology, Rhinology, and Laryngology — Ann Otol Rhin Laryng

Annals of Otology, Rhinology, and Laryngology — Ann Otol Rhinol Laryngol
Annals of Otology, Rhinology, and Laryngology — Annals Otol Rhinol Laryngol
Annals of Otology, Rhinology, and Laryngology — AORHA
Annals of Otology, Rhinology, and Laryngology. Supplement — Ann Otol Rhinol Laryngol Suppl
Annals of Oto-Rino-Laryngologica Ibero-Americana — AOIAA
Annals of Pharmacotherapy — Ann Pharmacother
Annals of Pharmacy and Practical Chemistry — Ann Pharm Pract Chem
Annals of Philosophy — Ann Phil
Annals of Philosophy — Ann Philos
Annals of Philosophy, Natural History, Chemistry, Literature, Agriculture, and the Mechanical and Fine Arts — Ann Philos Nat Hist
Annals of Physical Medicine — Ann Phys Med
Annals of Physical Medicine — APMDA6
Annals of Physics [*New York*] — Ann Phys
Annals of Physics [*New York*] — Ann Physics
Annals of Physics (New York) — Ann Phys (New York)
Annals of Physiological Anthropology — Ann Physiol Anthropol
Annals of Physiological Anthropology — APANEE
Annals of Plastic Surgery — Ann Plast Surg
Annals of Plastic Surgery — APCSD4
Annals of Poznan Agricultural University — Ann Poznan Agric Univ
Annals of Probability — Anls Prob
Annals of Probability — Ann Probab
Annals of Probability — Ann Probability
Annals of Probability — AOP
Annals of Public and Cooperative Economy — ACE
Annals of Public and Cooperative Economy [*Formerly, Annals of Collective Economy*] [*A publication*] — Ann Public and Coop Econ
Annals of Public and Cooperative Economy — Annals Public and Coop Economy
Annals of Public and Cooperative Economy [*Formerly, Annals of Collective Economy*] [*A publication*] — APCE
Annals of Pure and Applied Logic — Ann Pur App
Annals of Pure and Applied Logic — Ann Pure Appl Logic
Annals of Regional Science — AARS
Annals of Regional Science — ARSC
Annals of Roentgenology — Ann Roentg
Annals of Saudi Medicine — Ann Saudi Med
Annals of Science — Ann of Sci
Annals of Science [*London*] — Ann Sci
Annals of Science — AnnS
Annals of Science — ANNSA8
Annals of Science [*London*] — ASc
Annals of Science (Cleveland) — An Sc (Cleveland)
Annals of Science. Kanazawa University — Ann Sci Kanazawa Univ
Annals of Science. Kanazawa University — KRSHB3
Annals of Science. Kanazawa University. Part 2. Biology-Geology — Ann Sci Kanazawa Univ Part 2 Biol-Geol
Annals of Science. Kanazawa University. Part 2. Biology-Geology — KDSRA2
Annals of Science (London) — Ann Sci (Lond)
Annals of Sports Medicine — Ann Sports Med
Annals of Statistics — Anls Stat
Annals of Statistics — Ann Statist
Annals of Statistics — AOS
Annals of Statistics — ASTSC
Annals of Surgery — Ann Surg
Annals of Surgery — ANSUA5
Annals of Surgical Oncology — Ann Surg Oncol
Annals of Systems Research — Ann Syst Res
Annals of Systems Research — Ann Systems Res
Annals of the CIRP — Ann CIRP
Annals of the History of Computing — Ann Hist Comput
Annals of the International Geophysical Year — Ann Int Geophys Year
Annals of the International Society of Dynamic Games — Ann Internat Soc Dynam Games
Annals of the IQSY [*International Quiet Sun Year*] — AIQSA
Annals of the IQSY [*International Quiet Sun Year*] — Ann IQSY
Annals of the Medical University. Bialystok, Poland — Ann Med Univ Bialystok Pol
Annals of the Propagation of the Faith — AP Faith
Annals of the Rheumatic Diseases — Ann Rheum D
Annals of the Rheumatic Diseases — Ann Rheum Dis
Annals of the Rheumatic Diseases — Ann Rheumat Dis
Annals of the Rheumatic Diseases — APDIAO
Annals of the University [*Grenoble*] — AU
Annals of the University of Craiova. Chemistry Series — Ann Univ Craiova Chem Ser
Annals of Thoracic Surgery — Ann Thor Surg
Annals of Thoracic Surgery — Ann Thorac
Annals of Thoracic Surgery — Ann Thorac Surg
Annals of Thoracic Surgery — Ann Thoracic Surg
Annals of Thoracic Surgery — ATHSAK
Annals of Tropical Medicine and Parasitology — Ann Trop M
Annals of Tropical Medicine and Parasitology — Ann Trop Med
Annals of Tropical Medicine and Parasitology — Ann Trop Med Paras
Annals of Tropical Medicine and Parasitology — Ann Trop Med Parasitol
Annals of Tropical Medicine and Parasitology — ATMPA2
Annals of Tropical Paediatrics — Ann Trop Paediatr
Annals of Tropical Paediatrics — ATPAD9
Annals of Tropical Research — Ann Trop Res
Annals of Tropical Research — ATREDV
Annals of Tuberculosis — Ann Tuberc
Annals of Vascular Surgery — Ann Vasc Surg
Annals of Veterinary Research — Ann Vet Res
Annals of War — Ann War
Annals of Western Medicine and Surgery. Los Angeles County Medical Association — Ann Western Med Surg
Annals of Wyoming — Ann Wyo
Annals of Wyoming — AW
Annals of Zoology — Ann Zool
Annals of Zoology [*Agra*] — AZLGAC
Annals of Zoology (Agra) — Ann Zool (Agra)
Annals. Oklahoma Academy of Science — Ann Okla Acad Sci
Annals. Philippine Chinese Historical Association — An Phil Chin Hist Asso
Annals. Phytopathological Society of Japan — Ann Phytopathol Soc Jap
Annals. Phytopathological Society of Japan — Ann Phytopathol Soc Jpn
Annals. Phytopathological Society of Japan — NSBGAM
Annals. Polish Roman Catholic Church Union Archives and Museum — Ann Pol Rom Cath Church Union
Annals. Research Institute for Land Reclamation and Soil Science. Hydrotechnics Series — Ann Res Inst Land Reclam Soil Sci Hydrotech Ser
Annals. Research Institute for Land Reclamation and Soil Science. Land Reclamation Series — Ann Res Inst Land Reclam Soil Sci Land Reclam Ser
Annals. Research Institute for Land Reclamation and Soil Science. Soil Science Series — Ann Res Inst Land Reclam Soil Sci Soil Sci Ser
Annals. Research Institute for Microbial Diseases — Ann Res Inst Micr Dis
Annals. Research Institute for Plant Protection. Central Research Institute for Agriculture. Bucharest — Ann Res Inst Plant Prot Cent Res Inst Agric Bucharest
Annals. Research Institute of Environmental Medicine. Nagoya University — Ann Res Inst Environ Med Nagoya Univ
Annals. Research Institute of Epidemiology and Microbiology — Ann Res Inst Epidemiol Microbiol
Annals. Research Institute of Epidemiology and Microbiology — TNEMBJ
Annals. Royal Agricultural College of Sweden — Ann R Agric Coll Swed
Annals. Royal Australasian College of Dental Surgeons — Ann R Australas Coll Dent Surg
Annals. Royal Botanic Garden (Calcutta) — Ann Roy Bot Gard Calcutta
Annals. Royal Botanic Garden (Peradeniya) — Ann Roy Bot Gard Peradeniya
Annals. Royal College of Physicians and Surgeons of Canada — Ann R Coll Physicians Surg Can
Annals. Royal College of Physicians and Surgeons of Canada — RYPAAO
Annals. Royal College of Surgeons of England — Ann R Coll Surg Eng
Annals. Royal College of Surgeons of England — Ann R Coll Surg Engl
Annals. Royal College of Surgeons of England — Ann RC Surg
Annals. Royal College of Surgeons of England — Ann Roy Coll Surg
Annals. Royal College of Surgeons of England — ARCSA
Annals. South Africa Museum — Ann S Afr Mus
Annals. South African Museum — ASAMAS
Annals. Tadzhik Astronomical Observatory (Dushanbe, USSR) — Ann Tadzh Astron Obs Dushanbe USSR
Annals. Technical Association of Man-Made Fiber Paper. Japan — Ann Tech Assoc Man Made Fiber Paper Jpn
Annals. Tokyo Astronomical Observatory — Ann Tokyo Astron Obs
Annals. Transvaal Museum — Ann Transv Mus
Annals. Transvaal Museum — Ann Transvaal Mus
Annals. Transvaal Museum — Ann Tvl Mus
Annals. Transvaal Museum — ATVMA4
Annals. Ukrainian Academy of Arts and Sciences in the United States — Ann Ukrain Acad US
Annals. Ukrainian Academy of Arts and Sciences in the US — Ann Ukr Acad Arts Sci US
Annals. Ukrainian Academy of Arts and Sciences in the US — AnnUA
Annals. Ukrainian Academy of Arts and Sciences in the US — AUA
Annals. Ukrainian Academy of Arts and Sciences in the US — AUASAQ
Annals. University of Craiova. Seria. Matematica, Fizica, Chimie, Electrotehnica — Ann Univ Craiova Ser Mat Fiz Chim Electroteh
Annals. University of Craiova. Series. Biology, Medicine, Agricultural Science — Ann Univ Craiova Ser Biol Med Agric Sci
Annals. Warsaw Agricultural University. SGGW-AR [*Szkola Glowna Gospodarstwa Wiejskiego - Akademia Rolnicza*]. Animal Science — Ann Warsaw Agric Univ SGGW-AR Anim Sci
Annals. Warsaw Agricultural University SGGW-AR [*Szkola Glowna Gospodarstwa Weijskiego-Akademia Rolnicza*]. Forestry and Wood Technology — Ann Warsaw Agric Univ SGGW AR For Wood Technol
Annals. Warsaw Agricultural University SGGW-AR (Szkola Glowna Gospodarstwa Weijskiego-Akademia Rolnicza). Horticulture — Ann Warsaw Agric Univ SGGW AR Hortic
Annals. Warsaw Agricultural University SGGW-AR (Szkola Glowna Gospodarstwa Weijskiego-Akademia Rolnicza). Land Reclamation — Ann Warsaw Agric Univ SGGW AR Land Reclam
Annals. Warsaw Agricultural University SGGW-AR [*Szkola Glowna Gospodarstwa Weijskiego-Akademia Rolnicza*]. Veterinary Medicine — Ann Warsaw Agric Univ SGGW AR Vet Med
Annals. White Russian Agricultural Institute — Ann White Russ Agric Inst
Annals. Zimbabwe Geological Survey — Ann Zimbabwe Geol Surv
Annaly Biologii. Moskovskoe Obscestvo Ispytatelej Prirody. Sekcijo Istorii Estestvoznanija (Moscow) — Ann Biol Moscow
Annaly Instituta Imeni N.P. Kondakova — AIK
Annaly Instituta imeni N.P. Kondakova — S Kond
Annaly Instituta imeni N.P. Kondakova — Sem Kondakov
Annaly Instituta imeni N.P. Kondakova — SK
Annaly Nauchno-Issledovatel'skogo Instituta Melioratsii i Pochvovedeniya. Seriya Melioratsiya — Ann Nauchno Issled Inst Melior Pochvoved Ser Melior
Annaly Nauchno-Issledovatel'skogo Instituta Melioratsii i Pochvovedeniya. Seriya Pochvovedenie — Ann Nauchno Issled Inst Melior Pochvoved Ser Pochvoved
Annaly Sel'skokhozyaistvennykh Nauk — Ann Skh Nauk
Annaly Sel'skokhozyaistvennykh Nauk. Seriya C. Sel'skokhozyaistvennaya Tekhnika — Ann Skh Nauk Ser C

Annaly Sel'skokhozyaistvennykh Nauk. Seriya E. Zashchita Rastenii — Ann Skh Nauk Ser E
Annamalai University. Agricultural Research Annual — Annamalai Univ Agric Res Annu
Anneau d'Or. Cahiers de Spiritualite Familiale — An Or
Annee Africaine — Annee Afr
Annee Agricole — Annee Agr
Annee Balzacienne — A Balzac
Annee Balzacienne — ABa
Annee Biologique — ANBLAT
Annee Biologique — Annee Biol
Annee Biologique (Paris) — Annee Biol (Paris)
Annee Canonique — ACan
Annee Cardiologique Internationale — Annee Cardiol Int
Annee Dominicaine — A Dom
Annee Endocrinologique — AENDA2
Annee Endocrinologique — Annee Endocrinol
Annee Epigraphique — AE
Annee Epigraphique — AEpigr
Annee Epigraphique — Ann Epigr
Annee Epigraphique — Annee Ep
Annee Epigraphique. Revue des Publications Epigraphiques Relatives a l'Antiquite Romaine — A Ep
Annee Epigraphique. Revue des Publications Epigraphiques Relatives a l'Antiquite Romaine — An Ep
Annee Epigraphique. Revue des Publications Epigraphiques Relatives a l'Antiquite Romaine — Annee Epig
Annee Epigraphique. Revue des Publications Epigraphiques Relatives a l'Antiquite Romaine — Annee Epigr
Annee Geophysique Internationale — Annee Geophys Int
Annee Medicale — Annee Med
Annee Obstetricale — Ann Obstet
Annee Pedagogique — Annee Pedagog
Annee Pediatrique — Ann Ped
Annee Philologique — AP
Annee Philologique — APh
Annee Philosophique — Annee Phil
Annee Politique, Economique, et Cooperative — Ann Polit Econ Coop
Annee Politique et Economique — A Pol Econ
Annee Politique et Economique — Ann Pol et Econ
Annee Politique et Economique — Annee Polit Econ
Annee Propedeutique — AnP
Annee Psychologique — Ann Psychol
Annee Psychologique — Annee Psychol
Annee Psychologique — AnnPsych
Annee Psychologique — ANPQA
Annee Sociologique — Ann Sociol
Annee Sociologique — Annee Sociol
Annee Sociologique — ASoc
Annee Theologique Augustinienne [*Paris*] — A Th
Annee Theologique Augustinienne — Ann Theol
Annee Theologique Augustinienne — ATA
Annee Theologique Augustinienne — AThAug
Annee Therapeutique — Ann Ther
Annee Therapeutique et Clinique en Ophtalmologie — Annee Ther Clin Ophtalmol
Annees. Academie des Sciences, Belles-Lettres, et Arts de Besancon — Annees Acad Sci Besancon
Annexe au Bulletin. Institut International de Froid — Annexe Bull Inst Int Froid
Anniversary Bulletin. Chuo University — Anniv Bull Chuo Univ
Annales. Societe Scientifique et Litteraire de Cannes et de l'Arrondissement de Grasse — ASCG
Annnual Report. Welsh Plant Breeding Station (Aberystwyth, Wales) — Annu Rep Welsh Plant Breed Stn (Aberystwyth Wales)
Annotated Bibliography. Animal/Human Series. Commonwealth Bureau of Animal Health — Annot Bibliogr Anim/Hum Ser Commonw Bur Anim Health
Annotated Bibliography. Commonwealth Bureau of Nutrition — Annot Bibliogr Commonw Bur Nutr
Annotated Bibliography. Commonwealth Bureau of Pastures and Field Crops — Annot Bibliogr Commonw Bur Pastures Field Crops
Annotated Bibliography. Commonwealth Bureau of Soils — Annot Bibliogr Commonw Bur Soils
Annotated Bibliography. Commonwealth Forestry Bureau (Oxford) — Bibliogr For Bur (Oxf)
Annotated Bibliography of Economic Geology — Annot Bibliogr Econ Geol
Annotated Bibliography of Economic Geology — Annot Bibliography of Econ Geology
Annotated Bibliography of Medical Mycology — Annot Bibliogr Med Myc
Annotated Bibliography. The Occurrence and Biological Effects of Fluorine Compounds. Supplement — Annot Bibliogr Occurrence Biol Eff Fluorine Compd Suppl
Annotated Code of Maryland — Md Ann Code
Annotated Code of Maryland — Md Code Ann
Annotated Laws of Massachusetts (Lawyers' Co-Op) — Mass Ann Laws (Law Co-Op)
Annotated Legal Forms Magazine — Ann Leg Forms Mag
Annotationes Zoologicae et Botanicae — Annot Zool Bot
Annotationes Zoologicae et Botanicae — AZBTAZ
Annotationes Zoologicae et Botanicae (Bratislava) — Annotness Zool Bot (Bratislava)
Annotationes Zoologicae Japonenses — Annot Zool Jap
Annotationes Zoologicae Japonenses — Annot Zool Japon
Annotationes Zoologicae Japonenses — Annot Zool Jpn
Annotationes Zoologicae Japonenses — Annotness Zool Jap
Annotationes Zoologicae Japonenses — AZOJA2
Annotatsii Dokladov. Seminar Instituta Prikladnoj Matematiki. Tbilisskij Universitet — Annot Dokl Semin Inst Prikl Mat Tbilis Univ
Annotatsii Dokladov. Soveshchanie po Yadernoi Spektroskopii i Teorii Yadra — Annot Dokl Soveshch Yad Spektrosk Teor Yadra
Annuaire. Academie de Medecine Valko Tchervenkov — Annu Acad Med Valko Tchervenkov
Annuaire. Academie Real de Belgique — AAB
Annuaire. Academie Real des Sciences, des Lettres, et des Beaux-Arts de Belgique — AASB
Annuaire. Academie Royale de Belgique — AARB
Annuaire. Academie Royale de Belgique — AnnAB
Annuaire. Academie Royale de Belgique — Annu Acad Roy Belg
Annuaire. Academie Royale des Sciences d'Outre Mer — Annu Acad R Sci Outre Mer
Annuaire. Academie Royale des Sciences d'Outre-Mer (Brussels) — Annu Acad R Sci Outre Mer Brussels
Annuaire. Academie Royale des Sciences et Belles-Lettres de Bruxelles — Annuaire Acad Roy Sci Bruxelles
Annuaire. Academie Rurale. Sofia. Faculte d'Agronomie — Annu Acad Rurale Sofia Fac Agron
Annuaire. Academie Rurale. Sofia. Faculte Forestiere — Annu Acad Rurale Sofia Fac For
Annuaire Administratif et Judiciaire de Belgique — An Ad
Annuaire Agricole de la Suisse — Annu Agric Suisse
Annuaire Agricole de la Suisse — LJSCAA
Annuaire. Association des Auditeurs et Anciens Auditeurs de l'Academie de Droit International a La Haye — AAAA
Annuaire. Association pour l'Encouragement des Etudes Grecques en France — AAEG
Annuaire. Association pour l'Encouragement des Etudes Grecques en France — AEG
Annuaire. Biologie. Faculte des Sciences Naturelles. Universite Kiril. Metodij (Skopje) — Annu Biol Fac Sci Nat Univ Kiril Metodij (Skopje)
Annuaire. Bureau de Longitudes (Paris) — Annu Bur Longitudes (Paris)
Annuaire. College de France — ACF
Annuaire. College de France — Ann Coll
Annuaire. Comite d'Etat pour la Geologie (Romania) — Annu Com Etat Geol (Rom)
Annuaire. Comite Geologique (Romania) — Annu Com Geol Rom
Annuaire. Conservatoire du Jardin Botaniques de Geneve — Annuaire Conserv Jard Bot Geneve
Annuaire. Corporation Professionnelle des Comptables Generaux Licencies du Quebec — Ann Corp Prof Comp Gen Lic Quebec
Annuaire de Biologie. Faculte des Sciences Naturelles. Universite Kiril. Metodij [*Skopje*] — GZABA8
Annuaire de Chimie — Annu Chim
Annuaire de Droit Maritime et Aerien — A Dr Marit Aer
Annuaire de Droit Maritime et Aerien — Annu Dr Marit Aer
Annuaire de l'Afrique du Nord — Annu Afr N
Annuaire de l'Afrique du Nord — Annu Afr Nord
Annuaire de l'Afrique et du Moyen Orient — Annu Afr Moyen Orient
Annuaire de Legislation Francaise et Etrangere — Ann Leg Fr Etr
Annuaire de l'Horticulture Belge — Annuaire Hort Belge
Annuaire de l'Universite de Sofia St. Kliment Ohridski. Faculte de Mathematiques — Annuaire Univ Sofia Fac Math Inform
Annuaire de l'URSS et des Pays Socialistes Europeens — Annu URSS
Annuaire de Statistique Industrielle (France) — Fr Ind
Annuaire des Agrumes. Annuaire de l'Arboriculture Fruitiere — Annuaire Agrumes
Annuaire des Archives Israelites — AnAI
Annuaire des Archives Israelites (de France) — AnnAIF
Annuaire des Auditeurs et Anciens Auditeurs. Academie de Droit International de la Haye — Annu A A A
Annuaire des Membres. Association Internationale de Pedagogie Universitaire — Ann Mem Assoc Int Pedagog Univ
Annuaire des Pays de l'Ocean Indien — Annu Pays Ocean Indien
Annuaire des Sciences Historiques — Annuaire Sci Hist
Annuaire d'Histoire Liegeoise — AHL
Annuaire d'Histoire Liegeoise — AnnHL
Annuaire du Loisir de l'Est du Quebec — Ann Loisir Est Quebec
Annuaire du Monde Musulman — AMM
Annuaire du Tiers-Monde — Annu Tiers-Monde
Annuaire. Ecole Pratique des Hautes Etudes — AEPHE
Annuaire. Ecole Pratique des Hautes Etudes — Ann Ec Pr
Annuaire. Ecole Pratique des Hautes Etudes. IV Section. Sciences Philologiques et Historiques — AEHE IV Sect
Annuaire. Ecole Pratique des Hautes Etudes. IV Section. Sciences Philologiques et Historiques — AEPHEH
Annuaire. Ecole Pratique des Hautes Etudes. IV Section. Sciences Philologiques et Historiques — Ann EPH Et
Annuaire. Ecole Pratique des Hautes Etudes, IVeme Section — Ann Ec Prat HEt
Annuaire. Ecole Pratique des Hautes Etudes. Section des Sciences Historiques et Philologiques — AEPHEHP
Annuaire. Ecole Pratique des Hautes Etudes. Section des Sciences Religieuses — AEPHER
Annuaire. Ecole Pratique des Hautes Etudes. V Section. Sciences Religeuses — An HE Sc Rel
Annuaire. Ecole Pratique des Hautes Etudes. V Section. Sciences Religieuses — AEPHERV
Annuaire. Ecole Pratique des Hautes Etudes. V Section. Sciences Religieuses — Ann Ec Pr
Annuaire. Ecole Superieure de Chimie Technologique. Sofia — Annu Ec Super Chim Technol Sofia
Annuaire. Ecole Superieure des Mines et de Geologie. Sofia — Annu Ec Super Mines Geol Sofia

Annuaire. Ecoles Superieures. Mechanique Technique — Annu Ec Super Mech Tech
Annuaire. Ecoles Techniques Superieures. Mechanique Appliquee — Annu Ec Tech Super Mech Appl
Annuaire. Ecoles Techniques Superieures. Physique — Annu Ec Tech Super Phys
Annuaire et Memoires. Comite d'Etudes Historiques et Scientifiques de l'Afrique Occidentale Francaise — AAOF
Annuaire et Regles de Jeu. Association Canadienne de Volley-Ball — Ann Reg Assoc Can Vol Ball
Annuaire Europeen — AE
Annuaire Europeen — Ann Eur
Annuaire Europeen — Annu Europ
Annuaire. Faculte d' Agriculture et de Sylviculture. Universite de Skopje. Agriculture — Annu Fac Agric Sylvic Univ Skopje Agric
Annuaire. Faculte d'Agriculture et de Sylviculture. Universite de Skopje — Annu Fac Agric Univ Skopje
Annuaire. Faculte d'Agriculture et de Sylviculture. Universite de Skopje. Pomologie — Annu Fac Agric Sylvi Univ Skopje Pomol
Annuaire. Faculte d'Agriculture et de Sylviculture. Universite de Skopje. Sylviculture — Annu Fac Agric Sylvic Univ Skopje Sylvic
Annuaire. Faculte d'Agriculture et de Sylviculture. Universite de Skopje. Viticulture — Annu Fac Agric Sylvi Univ Skopje Viti
Annuaire. Faculte d'Agriculture et de Sylviculture. Universite de Skopje. Zootechnie — Annu Fac Agric Sylvi Univ Skopje Zootech
Annuaire. Faculte d'Agriculture. Universite de Skopje — Annu Fac Agric Univ Skopje
Annuaire. Faculte de Biologie. Universite Kiril et Metodij-Skopje — Annu Fac Biol Univ Kiril Metodij Skopje
Annuaire. Faculte de Sylviculture. Universite de Skopje — Annu Fac Sylvic Univ Skopje
Annuaire. Faculte des Sciences Naturelles. Universite Kiril et Metodij (Skopje). Biologie — Annu Fac Sci Nat Univ Kiril Metodij (Skopje) Biol
Annuaire. Faculte des Sciences Naturelles. Universite Kiril et Metodij (Skopje). Mathematique, Physique, et Chimie — Annu Fac Sci Nat Univ Kiril Metodij (Skopje) Math Phys Chim
Annuaire. Federation Historique de Lorraine — AFHL
Annuaire Francais de Droit International — AFDI
Annuaire Francais de Droit International — Annu Franc de Droit Internat
Annuaire Francais de Droit International — Annu Franc Dr Int
Annuaire Francais de Droit International — Annuaire Francais Droit Int
Annuaire Francais de Droit International — Annuar Fr Dr Int
Annuaire Francais des Droits de l'Homme — Annu Franc Dr Homme
Annuaire Geologique et Mineralogique de la Russie — Annu Geol Mineral Russ
Annuaire. Institut d'Architecture et de Genie Civil-Sofia — Annu Inst Archit Genie Civ Sofia
Annuaire. Institut de Droit International — AIDI
Annuaire. Institut de Droit International — Ann Inst Dr Int
Annuaire. Institut de Droit International — Annu de l'Inst de Droit Internat
Annuaire. Institut de Geologie et de Geophysique (Romania) — Annu Inst Geol Geophys (Rom)
Annuaire. Institut de Mecanique Appliquee et d'Electrotechnique. Sofia — Annu Inst Mec Appl Electrotech Sofia
Annuaire. Institut de Philologie et d'Histoire Orientales [*Bruxelles*] — AIPhO
Annuaire. Institut de Philologie et d'Histoire Orientales et Slaves — A I Ph
Annuaire. Institut de Philologie et d'Histoire Orientales et Slaves — A I Ph Or
Annuaire. Institut de Philologie et d'Histoire Orientales et Slaves [*Bruxelles*] — AIPhOS
Annuaire. Institut de Philologie et d'Histoire Orientales et Slaves — AIPO
Annuaire. Institut de Philologie et d'Histoire Orientales et Slaves [*Bruxelles*] — AIPS
Annuaire. Institut de Philologie et d'Histoire Orientales et Slaves — Ann Inst Phil Hist Orient
Annuaire. Institut de Philologie et d'Histoire Orientales et Slaves — Ann Phil Hist
Annuaire. Institut de Philologie et d'Histoire Orientales et Slaves — Ann Phil Hist Orient
Annuaire. Institut de Philologie et d'Histoire Orientales et Slaves — Annu Inst Philol Hist Orient Slav
Annuaire. Institut de Philologie et d'Histoire Orientales et Slaves. Universite Libre de Bruxelles — Annu Inst Philol Hist Orient
Annuaire. Institut du Genie Civil. Sofia — Annu Inst Genie Civ Sofia
Annuaire. Institut Europeen de Securite Sociale — Annu Inst Europ Secur Soc
Annuaire. Institut Geologique de Roumanie — Annu Inst Geol Roum
Annuaire. Institut Minier et Geologique. Sofia — Annu Inst Min Geol Sofia
Annuaire. Institut Superieure de Genie Civil. Sofia — Annu Inst Super Genie Civ Sofia
Annuaire International de la Fonction Publique — Annu Int Fonction Publ
Annuaire. Musee d'Histoire de la Religion et de l'Atheisme — AMHR
Annuaire. Musee Greco-Romain d'Alexandrie — Ann Mus Alex
Annuaire. Musee Greco-Romain d'Alexandrie — Ann Mus Gr Rd Alex
Annuaire. Musee National Archeologique (Plovdiv) — AMNP
Annuaire. Musee National Archeologique (Plovdiv) — Ann Mus Nat Arch (Plovdiv)
Annuaire. Musees Royaux des Beaux-Arts de Belgique — AMBB
Annuaire. Musees Royaux des Beaux-Arts de Belgique — AMRB
Annuaire. Museum National d'Histoire Naturelle — ANHNAV
Annuaire. Museum National d'Histoire Naturelle — Annu Mus Natl Hist Nat
Annuaire. Observatoire Royale de Belgique. Deuxieme Serie. Annuaire Meteorologique — Annu Observ Belg Annu Meteorol
Annuaire Officiel. Academie de Medecine Veterinaire du Quebec — Ann Off Acad Med Vet Quebec
Annuaire. Ordre Souverain Militaire de Malte — Annu Ordre Souverain Mil Malte
Annuaire Roumain d'Anthropologie — Annu Roum Anthropol
Annuaire Roumain d'Anthropologie — ARNAAG
Annuaire Sanitaire International — Ann Sanit Int
Annuaire Sciences de l'Homme — Ann Sci Hom
Annuaire Seismique — Ann Seism
Annuaire. Societe Belge d'Astronomie — Ann Soc Belge Astr
Annuaire. Societe Chimique de France — Ann Soc Chim Fr
Annuaire. Societe de l'Histoire de Sundgovienne — Annu Soc Hist Sundgovienne
Annuaire. Societe d'Emulation de la Vendee — An SEV
Annuaire. Societe d'Emulation de la Vendee — SEV
Annuaire. Societe des Amis. Bibliotheque de Selestat — An Selestat
Annuaire. Societe des Etudes Juives — ASEJ
Annuaire. Societe d'Histoire des Regions de Thann-Guebwiller — An Thann
Annuaire. Societe d'Histoire du Val et de la Ville de Munster — An Munster
Annuaire. Societe d'Histoire du Val et de la Ville de Munster — Annu Soc Hist Val et Ville Munster
Annuaire. Societe d'Histoire et d'Archeologie de la Lorraine — An Lorraine
Annuaire. Societe d'Histoire et d'Archeologie de la Lorraine — Ann Hist A Lor
Annuaire. Societe d'Histoire et d'Archeologie de la Lorraine — ASAL
Annuaire. Societe d'Histoire et d'Archeologie de la Lorraine — ASHAL
Annuaire. Societe d'Histoire Sundgovienne — ASHS
Annuaire. Societe Francaise de Numismatique [*Paris*] — ASFN
Annuaire. Societe Francaise de Numismatique et d'Archeologie — Annuaire Soc Franc Numism
Annuaire. Societe Francaise d'Economie Alpestre — Ann Soc Fr Econ Alp
Annuaire. Societe Helvetique des Sciences Naturelles. Partie Scientifique — Annu Soc Helv Sci Nat Partie Sci
Annuaire. Societe Helvetique des Sciences Naturelles. Partie Scientifique — JSNTDC
Annuaire. Societe Historique et Literaire de Colmar — An Colmar
Annuaire. Societe Royal d'Archeologie de Bruxelles — Annu Soc Arch Bruxelles
Annuaire. Societe Royale Belge du Dahlia — Annuaire Soc Roy Belge Dahlia
Annuaire. Societe Suisse de Philosophie — ASSPh
Annuaire Statistique de la Belgique — Ann Stat Belg
Annuaire Statistique de la Belgique — Belg Stat A
Annuaire Statistique de la France — Fr Stat A
Annuaire Statistique de la Securite Sociale — Ann Stat Sec Soc
Annuaire Statistique de la Tunisie — Ann Stat Tunisie
Annuaire Statistique de la Tunisie — Ann Statist Tun
Annuaire Suisse de Science Politique — Annu Suisse Sci Polit
Annuaire. Universite de Sofia. Faculte d'Agronomie — Annu Univ Sofia Fac Agron
Annuaire. Universite de Sofia. Faculte d'Agronomie et de Sylviculture — Annu Univ Sofia Fac Agron Sylvic
Annuaire. Universite de Sofia. Faculte de Biologie — Annu Univ Sofia Fac Biol
Annuaire. Universite de Sofia. Faculte de Biologie, Geologie, et Geographie — Annu Univ Sofia Fac Biol Geol Geogr
Annuaire. Universite de Sofia. Faculte de Mathematiques — Annuaire Univ Sofia Fac
Annuaire. Universite de Sofia. Faculte de Mathematiques et Mecanique [*A publication*] — Annuaire Univ Sofia Fac Math Mec
Annuaire. Universite de Sofia. Faculte de Physique — Annu Univ Sofia Fac Phys
Annuaire. Universite de Sofia. Faculte de Physique — Annuaire Univ Sofia Fac Phys
Annuaire. Universite de Sofia. Faculte de Sylviculture — Annu Univ Sofia Fac Sylvic
Annuaire. Universite de Sofia. Faculte des Lettres — AUS
Annuaire. Universite de Sofia. Faculte des Sciences — Annu Univ Sofia Fac Sci
Annuaire. Universite de Sofia. Faculte des Sciences Physiques et Mathematiques — Annu Univ Sofia Fac Sci Phys Math
Annuaire. Universite de Sofia. Faculte Physico-Mathematique — Annu Univ Sofia Fac Phys Math
Annuaire. Universite de Sofia. Kliment Ochridski-Faculte de Biologie — Annu Univ Sofia Kliment Ochridski-Fac Biol
Annuaire. Universite de Sofia Kliment Ohridski. Faculte de Geologie et Geographie — Annu Univ Sofia Kliment Ohridski Fac Geol Geogr
Annuaire. Universite de Sofia Kliment Ohridski. Faculte de Mathematiques et Mecanique — Annu Univ Sofia Kliment Ohridski Fac Math Mec
Annuaire. Universite de Sofia Kliment Ohridski. Physique et Technologie des Semiconducteurs — Annu Univ Sofia Kliment Ohridski Phys Technol Semicond
Annuaire. Universite Royale Veterinaire et Agronomique (Copenhagen) — Annu Univ R Vet Agron Copenhagen
Annuaire-Bulletin. Societe de l'Histoire de France — ABSHF
Annuaire-Bulletin. Societe de l'Histoire de France — Annuaire Bull Soc Hist Fr
Annuaire-Bulletin. Societe d'Histoire de France — Annu Bull Soc Hist France
Annual Abstracts of Statistics [*Baghdad*] — AAS
Annual Aid Review — Ann Aid Rev
Annual Air Pollution Control Conference — Annu Air Pollut Control Conf
Annual. American Institute of Cooperation — Annu Amer Inst Coop
Annual. American Schools of Oriental Research — AASO
Annual. American Schools of Oriental Research — AASOR
Annual and Research Report. University of British Columbia. Faculty of Agricultural Sciences — Ann Res Rep Univ Br Col Agri Sci
Annual Arkansas Water Works and Pollution Control Conference and Short School. Proceedings — Annu Arkansas Water Works Pollut Control Conf Short Sch Proc
Annual. Bar-Ilan University Studies in Judaica and Humanities — Ann Bar-Il
Annual Battery Conference on Applications and Advances — Annu Battery Conf Appl Adv
Annual Bibliography. Modern Humanities Research Association — Annu Bibliogr Mod Humanit Res Assoc
Annual Bibliography of English Language and Literature — ABELL
Annual Bibliography of English Language and Literature — Annu Bibliogr Engl Lang Lit
Annual Bibliography of Indian Archaeology — ABIA

Annual Biochemical Engineering Symposium. Proceedings — Annu Biochem Eng Symp Proc
Annual Biology Colloquium — Annu Biol Colloq
Annual Biology Colloquium — PABCA8
Annual Biology Colloquium. Oregon State College — A Biol Colloq Ore St Coll
Annual Biology Division Research Conference — Annu Biol Div Res Conf
Annual Birth Defects Institute Symposium — Annu Birth Defects Inst Symp
Annual Book of ASTM [*American Society for Testing and Materials*] **Standards** — Annu Book ASTM Stand
Annual. Brewers Association Japan — Annu Brew Assoc Jpn
Annual. British School at Athens — ABS
Annual. British School at Athens — ABSA
Annual. British School at Athens — Ann Br Sch Ath
Annual. British School at Athens — Ann Br Sch Athens
Annual. British School at Athens — Annu Brit Sch Athens
Annual. British School at Athens — Annu Brit School Athens
Annual. British School at Athens — Annual Br Sc Athens
Annual. British School of Archaeology at Athens — A Br Sch Archeol Athens
Annual. British School of Archaeology at Athens — Ann B S Arch Ath
Annual Bulletin. Department of Agriculture. Northern Rhodesia — Annu Bull Dep Agric North Rhod
Annual Bulletin. International Dairy Federation — Annu Bull Int Dairy Fed
Annual Bulletin. International Dairy Federation — IDABA
Annual Bulletin of Horticultural Technological Society/Engei Gijutsu Kondankai Nenpo — Annual Bull Hort Technol Soc
Annual Bulletin of the Electric Statistics for Europe — ABEEA
Annual Bulletin. Societe Jersiaise — Annu Bull Soc Jersiaise
Annual Business Survey. Men's Store Operating Experiences — Ann Bus Surv Mens Store Op Exp
Annual Byzantine Studies Conference. Abstracts of Papers — Ann Byz Conf
Annual Clinical Congress. American College of Surgeons — Annu Clin Congr Am Coll Surg
Annual Clinical Symposium — Annu Clin Symp
Annual Conference and Seminar on Quality Control. Society of Photographic Scientists and Engineers. Summaries of Papers — Annu Conf Semin Qual Control Soc Photogr Sci Eng Summ Pap
Annual Conference. Australasian Corrosion Association — Annu Conf Australas Corros Assoc
Annual Conference. Australasian Institute of Metals — Annu Conf Australas Inst Met
Annual Conference. Australasian Institute of Mining and Metallurgy. Preprint of Papers — Annu Conf Australas Inst Min Metall Prepr Pap
Annual Conference. Australian Institute of Metals [*Later, Annual Conference. Australasian Institute of Metals*] — Annu Conf Aust Inst Met
Annual Conference. Aviation and Astronautics — Annu Conf Aviat Astronaut
Annual Conference. British Columbia Water and Waste Association. Proceedings [*A publication*] — Annu Conf B C Water Waste Assoc Proc
Annual Conference. California Mosquito and Vector Control Association. Proceedings and Papers — Annu Conf Calif Mosq Vector Control Assoc Proc Pap
Annual Conference. Cellular Plastics Division. Society. Plastics Industry — Annu Conf Cell Plast Div Soc Plast Ind
Annual Conference. European Physical Society. Condensed Matter Division — Annu Conf Eur Phys Soc Condens Matter Div
Annual Conference. Hungarian Physiological Society — Annu Conf Hung Physiol Soc
Annual Conference in Wastes Engineering. University of Minnesota. Center for Continuation Study — Annu Conf Wastes Eng Univ Minn Cent Contin Study
Annual Conference. International District Heating Association. Official Proceedings — Annu Conf Int Dist Heat Assoc Off Proc
Annual Conference. International Iron and Steel Institute. Report of Proceedings — Annu Conf Int Iron Steel Inst Rep Proc
Annual Conference. International Nuclear Target Development Society. Proceedings — Annu Conf Int Nucl Target Dev Soc Proc
Annual Conference. Manitoba Agronomists — Annu Conf Manit Agron
Annual Conference. Microbeam Analysis Society. Proceedings — Annu Conf Microbeam Anal Soc Proc
Annual Conference. National Water Supply Improvement Association. Technical Proceedings — Annu Conf Natl Water Supply Improv Assoc Tech Proc
Annual Conference of Alcoholism — Annu Conf Alcohol
Annual Conference of Health Inspectors of New South Wales — Ann Conf Health Inspectors NSW
Annual Conference of Health Inspectors of New South Wales — Health Inspectors Conf
Annual Conference of Metallurgists of CIM — Annu Conf Metall CIM
Annual Conference of Metallurgists. Proceedings — Annu Conf Metall Proc
Annual Conference on Adhesion and Adhesives — Annu Conf Adhes Adhes
Annual Conference on Environmental Toxicology — Annu Conf Environ Toxicol
Annual Conference on Glass Problems — Annu Conf Glass Prob
Annual Conference on Glass Problems. Collected Papers — Annu Conf Glass Prob Collect Pap
Annual Conference on Materials for Coal Conversion and Utilization. Proceedings — ACMPD
Annual Conference on Materials for Coal Conversion and Utilization. Proceedings — Annu Conf Mater Coal Convers Utiliz Proc
Annual Conference on Physical Electronics. Topical Conference. American Physical Society — Annu Conf Phys Electron Top Conf Am Phys Soc
Annual Conference on Protein Metabolism. Proceedings — Annu Conf Protein Metab Proc
Annual Conference on Research in Medical Education — Ann Conf Res Med Ed
Annual Conference on Research in Medical Education — Annu Conf Res Med Educ
Annual Conference on the Kidney — Annu Conf Kidney
Annual Conference on the Restoration of Coastal Vegetation in Florida. Proceedings — Annu Conf Restor Coastal Veg Fla Proc
Annual Conference. Ontario Petroleum Institute. Proceedings — Annu Conf Ont Pet Inst Proc
Annual Conference Proceedings. American Production and Inventory Control Society — Ann Conf Proc Am Prod Inv Cont Soc
Annual Conference Proceedings. American Water Works Association — Annu Conf Proc Am Water Works Associ
Annual Conference Proceedings. Theme Sessions. Roads and Transportation Association of Canada — Ann Conf Proc Theme Ses Road Transp Assoc Can
Annual Conference Proceedings. Travel Research Association — Ann Conf Proc Trav Res Assoc
Annual Conference. Soil Mechanics and Foundation Engineering — Annu Conf Soil Mech Found Eng
Annual Conference. SPI Reinforced Plastics/Composites Institute. Proceedings — Annu Conf SPI Reinf Plast Compos Inst Proc
Annual Conference. Steel Castings Research and Trade Association. Papers — Annu Conf Steel Cast Res Trade Assoc Pap
Annual Conference. Steel Foundry Practice. Discussion — Annu Conf Steel Foundry Pract Discuss
Annual Conference. Steel Foundry Practice. Papers — Annu Conf Steel Foundry Pract Pap
Annual Conference. Textile Institute (Manchester, England) — Annu Conf Text Inst (Manchester Engl)
Annual Connector Symposium. Proceedings — Annu Connector Symp Proc
Annual Consumer Expenditures Survey (Supplement to Drug Topics) — Drug Topic A
Annual Convention Proceedings. Washington Association of Wheat Growers — Annu Conv Proc Wash Ass Wheat Growers
Annual. Department of Antiquities. Jordan — A A Jord
Annual. Department of Antiquities (Jordan) — Ann D A (J)
Annual. Department of Antiquities of Jordan — ADAJ
Annual. Department of Antiquities of Jordan — Annual Dep Jordan
Annual. Department of Antiquities of Jordon — AAJ
Annual. Department of Antiquities of Jordon — Ann Ant Jord
Annual Department Seminar. University of Singapore. Department of Chemistry — Annu Dep Semin Univ Singapore Dep Chem
Annual Dog Watch — Ann Dog Watch
Annual Dry Bean Conference. Proceedings — Annu Dry Bean Conf Proc
Annual Economic Report. Nebraska — Ann Econ Rep Nebraska
Annual Economic Report. South African Reserve Bank — S Afr AR
Annual Editions. Readings in Anthropology — Ann Ed Read Anthro
Annual Editions. Readings in Education — Ann Ed Read Educ
Annual Editions. Readings in Health — Ann Ed Read H
Annual Editions. Readings in Marriage and Family — Ann Ed Read Mar Fam
Annual Editions. Readings in Sociology — Ann Ed Read Soc
Annual Egyptological Bibliography — A Eg B
Annual Egyptological Bibliography — AEB
Annual Egyptological Bibliography [*Leiden*] — AnEgB
Annual Egyptological Bibliography — Ann Eg Bibl
Annual Egyptological Bibliography — Ann Egypt Bib
Annual Energy Outlook — A Energy O
Annual Energy Review — A Energy R
Annual Engineering Conference. Conference Papers — Annu Eng Conf Conf Pap
Annual Engineering Conference. Institution of Engineers of Australia. Papers — Annu Eng Conf Inst Eng Aust Pap
Annual Environmental Engineering and Science Conference. Proceedings — Annu Environ Eng Sci Conf Proc
Annual Financial Report and Report of Operations. Public Employees' Retirement System. California — Ann Finan Rep Rep Op Pub Emp Ret Sys Calif
Annual Financial Report. City of Baltimore, Maryland — Ann Fin Rep Baltimore
Annual Financial Report. State of Michigan — Ann Finan Rep Michigan
Annual Financial Report. State of Oregon — Ann Finan Rep Oregon
Annual Forestry Symposium — Annu For Symp
Annual Frequency Control Symposium — Annu Freq Control Symp
Annual Frequency Control Symposium. Proceedings — Annu Freq Control Symp Proc
Annual. Gas Compressor Institute — Annu Gas Compressor Inst
Annual. Gas Measurement Institute — Annu Gas Meas Inst
Annual. Hebrew Union College — Annu Hebrew Union Coll
Annual. Higher Institute of Mining and Geology (Sofia) — Annu Higher Inst Min Geol (Sofia)
Annual Highway Geology Symposium. Proceedings — Annu Highway Geol Symp Proc
Annual History Journal — Anu Hist J
Annual Houston Neurological Scientific Symposium — Annu Houston Neurol Sci Symp
Annual IEEE Semiconductor Thermal Measurement and Management Symposium — Annu IEEE Semicond Therm Meas Manage Symp
Annual Index to Popular Music Record Reviews — Annu Index Pop Music Rec Rev
Annual Industrial Air and Water Pollution/Contamination Control Seminar. Book of Proceedings — Annu Ind Air Water Pollut Contam Control Semin Book Proc
Annual Industrial Air Pollution/Contamination Control Seminar. Book of Proceedings — Annu Ind Air Pollut Contam Control Semin Book Proc
Annual Industrial Air Pollution Control Seminar. Book of Proceedings — Annu Ind Air Pollut Control Semin Book Proc
Annual Industrial Water and Waste Conference. Pre-Printed Papers — Annu Ind Water Waste Conf Pre Printed Pap
Annual Information Meeting. Heavy Section Steel Technology Program — Annu Inf Meet Heavy Sect Steel Technol Program

Annual Institute on Securities Law and Regulations. Proceedings — Ann Inst Sec Law Reg Proc
Annual International Bulk Solids Conference. Papers and Discussions — Annu Int Bulk Solids Conf Pap Discuss
Annual International Conference. Canadian Nuclear Association — Annu Int Conf Can Nucl Assoc
Annual International Conference. Canadian Nuclear Association. Proceedings — Annu Int Conf Can Nucl Assoc Proc
Annual International Electronics Packaging Conference — Annu Int Electron Packag Conf
Annual Iowa Manpower Planning Report — Ann Iowa Manpower Pl Rep
Annual. Japanese Biblical Institute — AJBI
Annual Joint AIEE-IRE Conference on Electronics in Nucleonics and Medicine. Papers — Annu Jt AIEE IRE Conf Electron Nucleon Med Pap
Annual Journal. Institution of Engineers — Annu J Inst Eng
Annual Journal of Dietetic Software — Annu J Diet Software
Annual Karcher Symposium — Annu Karcher Symp
Annual Law Digest — Ann Law Dig
Annual Law Register of the United States — Ann Law Reg
Annual Law Review — Annual Law R
Annual. Leeds University Oriental Society — ALOS
Annual. Leeds University Oriental Society [*Leiden*] — An Leeds UOS
Annual. Leeds University Oriental Society [*Leiden*] — AnLeeds
Annual. Leeds University Oriental Society — Ann Leeds Un Or Soc
Annual Legal Bibliography — Annu Leg Bibliogr
Annual Legal Bibliography. Harvard University. Law School Library — Ann Leg Bib Harvard
Annual Lightwood Research Conference. Proceedings — Annu Lightwood Res Conf Proc
Annual Lightwood Research Conference. Proceedings — PALCDR
Annual LL — ALL
Annual Marine Coatings Conference. Proceedings — Annu Mar Coat Conf Proc
Annual McGraw-Hill Survey. Investment in Employee Safety and Health — McGraw ESH
Annual Meat Science Institute. Proceedings — Annu Meat Sci Inst Proc
Annual Medical-Scientific Conference. National Alcoholism Forum — Annu Med Sci Conf Natl Alcohol Forum
Annual Medicinal Chemistry Symposium — Annu Med Chem Symp
Annual Meeting. American College of Nutrition — Annu Meet Am Coll Nutr
Annual Meeting. American Institute of Dental Medicine — Annu Meet Am Inst Dent Med
Annual Meeting. American Institute of Mining, Metallurgical, and Petroleum Engineeers — Annu Meet Am Inst Min Metall Pet Eng
Annual Meeting. American Institute of Oral Biology — Annu Meet Am Inst Oral Biol
Annual Meeting. American Psychopathological Association — Annu Meet Am Psychopathol Assoc
Annual Meeting and Exhibition. Air and Waste Management Association — Annu Meet Exhib Air Waste Manage Assoc
Annual Meeting. Biomass Energy Institute — Annu Meet Biomass Energy Inst
Annual Meeting. Canadian College of Neuropsychopharmacology — Annu Meet Can Coll Neuropsychopharmacol
Annual Meeting. Corporation Associates. American Chemical Society — Annu Meet Corp Assoc Am Chem Soc
Annual Meeting. Electron Microscopy Society of America — Annu Meet Electron Microsc Soc Am
Annual Meeting. Entomological Society of America — A Meet Ent Soc Am
Annual Meeting. European Bone Marrow Transplantation Group — Annu Meet Eur Bone Marrow Transplant Group
Annual Meeting. European Environmental Mutagen Society — Annu Meet Eur Environ Mutagen Soc
Annual Meeting. Federation of American Societies for Environmental Biology — Annu Meet Fed Am Soc Environ Biol
Annual Meeting. Federation of Analytical Chemistry and Spectroscopy Societies. Papers — Annu Meet Fed Anal Chem Spectrosc Soc Pap
Annual Meeting. Information Council on Fabric Flammability. Proceedings — Annu Meet Inf Counc Fabr Flammability Proc
Annual Meeting. International Foundation for Biochemical Endocrinology — Annu Meet Int Found Biochem Endocrinol
Annual Meeting. International Society for Experimental Hematology — Annu Meet Int Soc Exp Hematol
Annual Meeting. International Society for Heart Research — Annu Meet Int Soc Heart Res
Annual Meeting. International Water Conference — AMICD
Annual Meeting. International Water Conference — Annu Meet Int Water Conf
Annual Meeting. Inter-Society Cytology Council. Transactions — Annu Meet Inter Soc Cytol Counc Trans
Annual Meeting. Kansas State Horticultural Society — A Meet Kans St Hort Soc
Annual Meeting. Marine Technology Society — Annu Meet Mar Technol Soc
Annual Meeting. Meteoritical Society — Annu Meet Meteorit Soc
Annual Meeting. Microbeam Analysis Society — Annu Meet Microbeam Anal Soc
Annual Meeting. Minnesota Section. AIME [*American Institute of Mining, Metallurgical, and Petroleum Engineers*]. Proceedings — Annu Meet Minn Sect AIME Proc
Annual Meeting. National Council on Radiation Protection and Measurements — Annu Meet Natl Counc Radiat Prot Meas
Annual Meeting. National Mastitis Council — Annu Meet Natl Mastitis Counc
Annual Meeting. National Mastitis Council, Inc. — Annu Meet Natl Mastitis Counc Inc
Annual Meeting. New Jersey Mosquito Control Association. Proceedings — Annu Meet NJ Mosq Control Assoc Proc
Annual Meeting of the International Society of Blood Purification — Annu Meet Int Soc Blood Purif
Annual Meeting on Modern Approaches to New Vaccines — Annu Meet Mod Approaches New Vaccines
Annual Meeting. Pan American Biodeterioration Society — Annu Meet Pan Am Biodeterior Soc
Annual Meeting Preprint. Technical Association. Pulp and Paper Industry — Annu Meet Prepr Tech Assoc Pulp Pap Ind
Annual Meeting Proceedings. International Institute of Synthetic Rubber Producers — Annu Meet Proc Int Inst Synth Rubber Prod
Annual Meeting. Scandinavian Society for Immunology. Abstracts of Papers — Annu Meet Scand Soc Immunol Abstr Pap
Annual Meeting. Society of Engineering Science. Proceedings — Annu Meet Soc Eng Sci Proc
Annual Meeting. Technical Association. Pulp and Paper Industry — Annu Meet Tech Assoc Pulp Pap Ind
Annual Meeting. Technical Section. Canadian Pulp and Paper Association. Preprints of Papers — Annu Meet Tech Sect Can Pulp Pap Assoc Prepr Pap
Annual Meeting-Proceedings. American Society of Photogrammetry — Annu Meet Proc Am Soc Photogramm
Annual Minerals Symposium Proceedings [*American Institute of Mining, Metallurgical, and Petroleum Engineers*] — Annu Miner Symp Proc
Annual Mining Symposium — Annu Min Symp
Annual Mining Symposium. Proceedings — Annu Min Symp Proc
Annual National Conference on Radiation Control — Annu Natl Conf Radiat Control
Annual National Conference. Plastics and Rubber Institute — Annu Natl Conf Plast Rubber Inst
Annual National Conference. PRI [*Plastics and Rubber Institute*] — Annu Natl Conf PRI
Annual National Information Retrieval Colloquium — Annu Natl Inf Retr Colloq
Annual New England (Northeast) Bioengineering Conference. Proceedings — Annu N Engl (Northeast) Bioeng Conf Proc
Annual North Carolina Cattlemen's Conference — Annu NC Cattlemens Conf
Annual Northeastern Regional Antipollution Conference — Annu Northeast Reg Antipollu Conf
Annual. Notre Dame Estate Planning Institute — Ann Notre Dame Est Plan Inst
Annual NSF [*National Science Foundation*] **Trace Contaminants Conference** — Annu NSF Trace Contam Conf
Annual Nuclear Medicine Seminar — Annu Nucl Med Semin
Annual Number. National Academy of Sciences. India — Annu Number Natl Acad Sci India
Annual Oak Ridge National Laboratory Life Science Symposium — Annu Oak Ridge Natl Lab Life Sci Symp
Annual of Advertising, Editorial Art, and Design — Ann Adv Ed Art Des
Annual of Animal Psychology — AAPYAD
Annual of Animal Psychology — Ann Anim Ps
Annual of Animal Psychology — Annu Anim Psychol
Annual of Armenian Linguistics — AArmL
Annual of Industrial Property Law — Ann Ind Prop L
Annual of Industrial Property Law — Ann Indus Prop L
Annual of Psychoanalysis — Annu Psychoanal
Annual of Psychoanalysis — APSACT
Annual of Urdu Studies — AnUS
Annual Office Salaries Directory — Ann Off Sal Dir
Annual Offshore Technology Conference. Proceedings — Annu Offshore Technol Conf Proc
Annual Oil and Gas Statistics — Ann Oil Gas Stat
Annual Pacific Technical Conference. Technical Papers. Society of Plastics Engineers — Annu Pac Tech Conf Tech Pap Soc Plast Eng
Annual. Palestine Exploration Fund — APEF
Annual. Peking Biological Science Association/Pe Ching Sheng Wu K'o Hsueh Hsueh Hui Nien Pao — Annual Peking Biol Sci Assoc
Annual Pfizer Research Conference. Proceedings — Annu Pfizer Res Conf Proc
Annual Pipeline Operation and Maintenance Institute — Annu Pipeline Oper Maint Inst
Annual Pittsburgh Conference on Modeling and Simulation — Annu Pittsburgh Conf Model Simul
Annual Planning Information. Anniston SMSA [*Standard Metropolitan Statistical Area*] — Ann Plan Info Anniston SMSA
Annual Planning Information for Connecticut — Ann Plan Info Connecticut
Annual Planning Information for Manpower Planners. New York SMSA (Standard Metropolitan Statistical Area) — Ann Plan Info SMSA New York
Annual Planning Information for Manpower Planners. Syracuse SMSA (Standard Metropolitan Statistical Area) — Ann Plan Info SMSA Syracuse
Annual Planning Information. Macon, Georgia SMSA (Standard Metropolitan Statistical Area) — Ann Plan Info Macon Georgia SMSA
Annual Planning Information. Modesto SMSA (Standard Metropolitan Statistical Area) — Ann Plan Info Modesto SMSA
Annual Planning Information Report. Daytona Beach SMSA (Standard Metropolitan Statistical Area) — Ann Plan Info Rep Daytona Beach SMSA
Annual Planning Information. Salinas-Seaside-Monterey SMSA (Standard Metropolitan Statistical Area) — Ann Plan Info Salinas Seaside Monterey SMSA
Annual Planning Information. State of Hawaii and Honolulu SMSA [*Standard Metropolitan Statistical Area*] — Ann Plan Info Hawaii SMSA
Annual Planning Information. State of Iowa — Ann Plan Info Iowa
Annual Planning Report. District of Columbia — Ann Plan Rep DC
Annual Planning Report. Lexington SMSA (Standard Metropolitan Statistical Area) — Ann Plan Rep Lexington SMSA
Annual Planning Report. Spokane SMSA (Standard Metropolitan Statistical Area) Washington — Ann Plan Rep Spokane SMSA
Annual Pollution Control Conference. Water and Wastewater Equipment Manufacturers Association — Annu Pollut Control Conf Water Wastewater Equip Manuf Assoc
Annual Poultry Market Review — Ann Poul Mark Rev
Annual Power Distribution Conference. Proceedings [*United States*] — APDPD
Annual Precise Time and Time Interval (PTTI) Applications and Planning Meeting — Annu Precise Time Time Interval PTTI Appl Plann Meet

Annual Priestley Lectures — Annu Priestley Lect
Annual Proceedings. American Association of Zoo Veterinarians — Annu Proc Am Assoc Zoo Vet
Annual Proceedings. Arizona Water Symposium — Annu Proc Ariz Water Symp
Annual Proceedings. Associated Scientific and Technical Societies of South Africa — Annu Proc Assoc Sci & Tech Soc S Afr
Annual Proceedings. Electron Microscopy Society of America — A Proc Electron Microsc Soc Am
Annual Proceedings. Gifu College of Pharmacy — A Proc Gifu Coll Pharm
Annual Proceedings. Gifu College of Pharmacy — Annu Proc Gifu Coll Pharm
Annual Proceedings. Gifu Pharmaceutical University — Annu Proc Gifu Pharm Univ
Annual Proceedings. Phytochemical Society — Annu Proc Phytochem Soc
Annual Proceedings. Phytochemical Society — APPHCZ
Annual Proceedings. Phytochemical Society of Europe — Annu Proc Phytochem Soc Eur
Annual Proceedings. Reliability Physics (Symposium) — Annu Proc Reliab Phys (Symp)
Annual Proceedings. Technical Sessions. American Electroplaters' Society — Annu Proc Tech Sess Am Electroplat Soc
Annual Procurement and Federal Assistance Report — Ann Proc Fed Assis Rep
Annual Professional Day for Chemistry Teachers — Annu Prof Day Chem Teach
Annual Progress in Child Psychiatry and Child Development — Annu Prog Child Psychiatry Chil Dev
Annual Progress in Child Psychiatry and Child Development — APCCBM
Annual Progress Report. Geological Survey of Western Australia — Annu Prog Rep Geol Surv West Aust
Annual Progress Report. Geological Survey. Western Australia — Ann Prog Rep Geol Surv West Austr
Annual Progress Report. Louisiana Agricultural Experiment Station — Annu Prog Rep La Agric Exp Stn
Annual Progress Report. National Foundation for Cancer Research [*US*] — Ann Prog Rep Nat Found Cancer Res
Annual Progress Report. Oak Ridge National Laboratory. Physics Division — Annu Prog Rep Oak Ridge Natl Lab Phys Div
Annual Progress Report of Research Center for Superconducting Materials and Electronics. Osaka University — Annu Prog Rep Res Cent Supercond Mater Electron Osaka Univ
Annual Progress Report. Pakistan Forest Institute. Peshawar — Ann Prog Rep Pak For Inst Pesh
Annual Progress Report. SEATO [*Southeast Asia Treaty Organization*] **Medical Research Laboratories** — Annu Prog Rep SEATO Med Res Lab
Annual Progress Report. SEATO [*Southeast Asia Treaty Organization*] **Medical Research Laboratories** — APRSCA
Annual Progress Report. Southeast Research Station. Louisiana Agricultural Experiment Station — Annu Prog Rep Southeast Res Stn La Agric Exp Stn
Annual Progress Report. Southeast South Dakota Agricultural Experiment Station. South Dakota State University — Annu Prog Rep Southeast SD Agric Exp Stn SD State Univ
Annual Progress Report. Tokai Works — Annu Prog Rep Tokai Works
Annual Public Water Supply Engineers' Conference. Proceedings — Annu Public Water Supply Eng Conf Proc
Annual Purdue Air Quality Conference. Proceedings — Ann Purdue Air Qual Conf Proc
Annual Purdue Air Quality Conference. Proceedings — Annu Purdue Air Qual Conf Proc
Annual Rainfall, Australia [*Australia Commonwealth Bureau of Meteorology*] — Ann Rainf Aust
Annual Reliability Physics Symposium. Proceedings — Annu Reliab Phys Symp Proc
Annual Remote Sensing of Earth Resources Conference. Technical Papers — Annu Remote Sens Earth Resour Conf Tech Pap
Annual Report. Acclimatisation Society of Victoria — Annual Rep Acclim Soc Victoria
Annual Report. Administrative Office. Courts of Georgia — Ann Rep Adm Off Court Georgia
Annual Report. Agricultural and Horticultural Research Station. Long Ashton, Bristol — Annu Rep Agric Hortic Res Stn Long Ashton Bristol
Annual Report. Agricultural Chemical Inspection Station (Japan) — Annu Rep Agric Chem Insp Stn Jpn
Annual Report. Agricultural Experiment Station. Alabama Polytechnic Institute (Alabama) — Annu Rep Agric Exp Stn Ala Polytech Inst Ala
Annual Report. Agricultural Experiment Station (Nebraska) — Annu Rep Agric Exp Stn (Nebr)
Annual Report. Agricultural Experiment Station. University of Maryland — Annu Rep Agric Exp Stn Univ MD
Annual Report. Agricultural Research Council. Letcombe Laboratory — Annu Rep Agric Res Counc Letcombe Lab
Annual Report. Agricultural Research Institute of Northern Ireland — Annu Rep Agric Res Inst North Irel
Annual Report. Air Pollution Control District. County of Los Angeles — Annu Rep Air Pollut Control Dist Cty Los Angeles
Annual Report. Air Resources Atmospheric Turbulence and Diffusion Laboratory [*A publication*] — Annu Rep Air Resour Atmos Turbul Diffus Lab
Annual Report. Akita Prefectural Institute of Public Health — Annu Rep Akita Prefect Inst Public Health
Annual Report. Alabama Agricultural Experiment Station — Annu Rep Ala Agr Exp Sta
Annual Report. Alberta Disaster Services — Ann Rep Alberta Dis Serv
Annual Report. Alberta Health Occupations Board — Ann Rep Alberta Health Occ Bd
Annual Report. Alberta Home Mortgage Corporation — Ann Rep Alberta Home Mort Corp
Annual Report. Alberta Housing Corp. — Ann Rep Alberta Hous Corp
Annual Report AMDEL [*Australian Mineral Development Laboratories*] [*Frewville*] [*A publication*] — Annu Rep AMDEL
Annual Report. American Bible Society — ARBS
Annual Report. American Congregational Association — RACA
Annual Report. American Gas Association — Annu Rep Am Gas Assoc
Annual Report. American Historical Association — Annu Rep Amer Hist Ass
Annual Report. American Historical Association — RAHA
Annual Report. American Institute of Physics — Annu Rep Am Inst Phys
Annual Report. American Jewish Committee — RAJC
Annual Report. American Judicature Society — Ann Rep Am Jud Soc
Annual Report and Accounts. All India Management Association — Ann Rep Acc India Man Assoc
Annual Report and Accounts. Cornish Chamber of Mines — Annu Rep Acc Cornish Chamber Mines
Annual Report and Accounts. London Transport Executive — Ann Rep Acc Lond Transp Ex
Annual Report and Balance Sheet. Bank Markazi. Iran — Ann Rep Bal Sh B Markazi Iran
Annual Report and Directory of Oklahoma Libraries — Ann Rep Dir Oklahoma Lib
Annual Report and Farm Facts — Ann Rep Farm Facts
Annual Report and Financial Statements. Institute of Corn and Agricultural Merchants — Annu Rep Finan Statements Inst Corn Agr Merchants
Annual Report and Proceedings. Belfast Naturalists' Field Club — Annual Rep Proc Belfast Naturalists Field Club
Annual Report and Review of Operations (Port of Melbourne) — Ann Rep Rev Op (Port Melbourne)
Annual Report and Statement of Accounts. New Zealand Milk Board — Ann Rep Stat Acc NZ Milk B
Annual Report and Transactions. Worcester (Massachusetts) Agricultural Society — Annual Rep Trans Worcester Agric Soc
Annual Report and Yearbook. Advertising Research Foundation — Ann Rep Yearb Adv Res Found
Annual Report. Anti-dumping Tribunal — Ann Rep Anti Dump Trib
Annual Report. Archaeological Department of India — ARADI
Annual Report. Archaeological Survey of India — Annu Rep Archaeol Surv India
Annual Report. Argonne National Laboratory. Division of Biological and Medical Research — Ann Rep Argonne Nat Lab Div Bio Med Res
Annual Report. Arkansas Agricultural Experiment Station at Arkansas Industrial University — Annual Rep Arkansas Agric Exp Sta Arkansas Industr Univ
Annual Report. Arkansas Housing Development Agency — Ann Rep Arkansas Hous Dev Agen
Annual Report. Asahi Glass Foundation for Contributions to Industrial Technology — Annu Rep Asahi Glass Found Contrib Ind Technol
Annual Report. Association Internationale des Botanistes. (Jena) — Annual Rep Assoc Int Bot Jena
Annual Report. Atlanta Regional Commission — Ann Rep Atlanta Reg Com
Annual Report. Australian Atomic Energy Commission — Annu Rep Aust At Energy Comm
Annual Report. Bank of Ceylon — Ann Rep Bank Ceylon
Annual Report. Bean Improvement Cooperative — Annu Rep Bean Improv Coop
Annual Report. Birmingham Natural History and Microscopical Society — Annual Rep Birmingham Nat Hist Microscop Soc
Annual Report. Birmingham Natural History and Philosophical Society — Annual Rep Birmingham Nat Hist Philos Soc
Annual Report. Board of Greenkeeping Research — Annu Rep Board Greenkeeping Res
Annual Report. Board of Management. Royal Adelaide Hospital — Ann Rep Manag Adel Hosp
Annual Report. Board of Regents of the Smithsonian Institution — ARBRSI
Annual Report. British Columbia. Minister of Mines and Petroleum Resources — Annu Rep BC Minist Mines Pet Resour
Annual Report. British Non Ferrous Metals Research Association — Annu Rep Br Non Ferrous Met Res Assoc
Annual Report. Brooklyn Museum — Ann Rep Brooklyn
Annual Report. Bureau de Recherches Geologiques et Minieres [*Paris*] — Annu Rep Bur Rec Geol Min
Annual Report. Bureau of Mines and Geo-Sciences (Philippines) — Annu Rep Bur Mines (Philipp)
Annual Report. California Avocado Assocation — Annual Rep Calif Avocado Assoc
Annual Report. California Institute of Technology — Annual Rep Calif Inst Technol
Annual Report. California. Office of Administrative Law — Ann Rep Calif Adm Law
Annual Report. California Public Broadcasting Commission — Ann Rep Calif Pub Broadc Com
Annual Report. California Water Resources Center — Annu Rep Calif Water Resour Cent
Annual Report. Canada. Board of Grain Commissioners. Grain Research Laboratory — Annu Rep Can Board Grain Comm Grain Res lab
Annual Report. Canada Department of Fisheries and Oceans. Newfoundland Region — Ann Rep Can Dept Fish Oceans Newfoundland Reg
Annual Report. Canadian Seed Growers Association — Annu Rep Can Seed Growers Ass .
Annual Report. Cancer Research Institute. Kanazawa University — Annu Rep Cancer Res Inst Kanazawa Univ
Annual Report. Cancer Research Institute. Kanazawa University — KCRAB8
Annual Report. Carnegie Institution of Washington. Department of Plant Biology — Annu Rep Carnegie Inst Wash Dep Plant Biol
Annual Report. Catholic Record Society — RCRS
Annual Report. Center for Adult Diseases [*Osaka*] — ARADAS
Annual Report. Center for Adult Diseases (Osaka) — Ann Rep Cent Adult Dis (Osaka)

Annual Report. Center for Adult Diseases (Osaka) — Annu Rep Cent Adult Dis (Osaka)
Annual Report. Central and Regional Arecanut Research Stations — Annu Rep Cent Reg Arecanut Res Stn
Annual Report. Central and Regional Arecanut Research Stations — CARCBE
Annual Report. Central Hygiene Experiment Station/Chung-Yang Wei-Shong Shih-Yen So Nein Pao — Annual Rep Centr Hyg Exp Sta
Annual Report. Centre for Resource Studies [*Kingston, Ontario*] — Annu Rep Centre Resour Stud
Annual Report. Ceramic Engineering Research Laboratory. Nagoya Institute of Technology — Annu Rep Ceram Eng Res Lab Nagoya Inst Technol
Annual Report. Ceramics Research Laboratory. Nagoya Institute of Technology — Annu Rep Ceram Res Lab Nagoya Inst Technol
Annual Report. Chamber of Mines Precambrian Research Unit. University of Cape Town — Annu Rep Chamber Mines Precambrian Res Unit
Annual Report. Chiba Prefectural Laboratory of Water Pollution — Annu Rep Chiba Prefect Lab Water Pollut
Annual Report. Civil Service Commission. Toronto — Ann Rep Civ Serv Com Toronto
Annual Report. Clemson Agricultural Experiment Station — Annu Rep Clemson Agr Exp Sta
Annual Report. Cocoa Research Institute (Tafo, Ghana) — Ann Rep Cocoa Res Inst (Tafo Ghana)
Annual Report. Cocoa Research Institute (Tafo, Ghana) — Annu Rep Cocoa Res Inst Tafo Ghana
Annual Report. Coffee Research Station. Lyamungu — Annual Rep Coffee Res Sta Lyamungu
Annual Report. Colorado Agricultural Experiment Station — Annu Rep Colo Agric Exp Stn
Annual Report. Committee on Corporations — Ann Rep Com Corp
Annual Report. Committee on Scientific Freedom and Responsibility — Ann Rep Com Sci Fr Resp
Annual Report. Commonwealth Scientific and Industrial Research Organisation. Marine Biochemistry Unit — Annu Rep CSIRO Mar Biochem Unit
Annual Report. Commonwealth Scientific and Industrial Research Organisation. Plant Industry — Annu Rep CSIRO Plant Ind
Annual Report. Commonwealth Scientific and Industrial Research Organization (Australia) — Annu Rep CSIRO Aust
Annual Report. Conference on Electrical Insulation and Dielectric Phenomena [*A publication*] — Annu Rep Conf Electr Insul Dielectr Phenom
Annual Report. Cornish Mining Development Association — Annu Rep Cornish Min Dev Ass
Annual Report. Council for Mineral Technology [*Randburg*] — Annu Rep Counc Miner Technol
Annual Report. Council. Royal Institution of South Wales with Appendix of Original Papers on Scientific Subjects — Annual Rep Council Roy Inst S Wales
Annual Report. CSIR [*Council for Scientific and Industrial Research*] — Annu Rep CSIR
Annual Report. Cultural and Social Centre for the Asian and Pacific Region — Ann Rep Cult Soc Cent Asian Pac Reg
Annual Report. Daiichi College of Pharmaceutical Sciences — Annu Rep Daiichi Coll Pharm Sci
Annual Report. Dante Society — Ann Rep DS
Annual Report. Dante Society — Annu Rep Dante Soc
Annual Report. Dante Society — ARDS
Annual Report. Department for Community Welfare. Western Australia — Ann Rep Dept Com Wel West Aust
Annual Report. Department of Agriculture and Stock. Queensland — Annu Rep Dep Agric Stock Queensl
Annual Report. Department of Agriculture. New South Wales — Annu Rep Dep Agr NSW
Annual Report. Department of Atomic Energy. Government of India — Annu Rep Dep At Energy Gov India
Annual Report. Department of Employment and Labour Relations. Queensland — Ann Rep Dept Emp Lab Rel Queensland
Annual Report. Department of Environment (India) — Ann Rep Dept Env (India)
Annual Report. Department of Fisheries. Prince Edward Island — Ann Rep Dept Fish Pr Ed Isl
Annual Report. Department of Health [*New Zealand*] — Ann Rep Dep Hlth NZ
Annual Report. Department of Labour and Industry (Western Australia) — Ann Rep Dept Lab Ind (West Aust)
Annual Report. Department of Mineral Resources (New South Wales) — Annu Rep Dep Miner Resour (NSW)
Annual Report. Department of Minerals and Energy (Victoria) [*Melbourne*] — Annu Rep Dep Miner Energy (Victoria)
Annual Report. Department of Mines and Energy (South Australia) — Annu Rep Dep Mines Energy (South Aust)
Annual Report. Department of Mines (Western Australia) — Annu Rep Dep Mines (West Aust)
Annual Report. Department of Public Works. Nova Scotia — Ann Rep Dept Pub Wk Nova Scotia
Annual Report. Department of Science and Agriculture (Barbados) — Annu Rep Dep Sci Agric Barbados
Annual Report. Department of Social Services. Charlottetown — Ann Rep Dept Soc Serv Charlottetown
Annual Report. Director. Department of Antiquities. Cyprus — Ann Rep Cypr
Annual Report. Director. Department of Antiquities. Cyprus — ARDC
Annual Report. Director. Department of Antiquities. Cyprus — RDAC
Annual Report. Director of Research. Philippine Sugar Association — Annu Rep Dir Res Philipp Sugar Assoc
Annual Report. Director of Sea Fisheries (South Africa) — Ann Rep Dir Sea Fish (S Africa)
Annual Report. Director of the Civilian Conservation Corps (US) — Ann Rep Dir Civ Cons Corp (US)
Annual Report. East African Agriculture and Forestry Research Organization — Annu Rep E Afr Agr Forest Res Organ
Annual Report. East African Railways Corp. — Ann Rep East Afr Rail Corp
Annual Report. East Malling Research Station — Rep E Malling Res Stn
Annual Report. East Malling Research Station (Kent) — Annu Rep East Malling Res Stn (Kent)
Annual Report. Economic Faculty. Tohoku University. Sendai — An Rep Econ Fac Tohoku Univ Sendai
Annual Report. Economic Poisons. Agricultural Experiment Station. University of Arizona. Special Bulletin — Annual Rep Econ Poisons Agric Exp Sta Univ Arizona Spec Bull
Annual Report. Employment Security Commission of New Mexico — Ann Rep Emp Sec Com New Mexico
Annual Report. Energy, Mines, and Resources (Canada) — Annu Rep Energy Mines Resour (Can)
Annual Report. Engineering Research Institute. Faculty of Engineering. University of Tokyo — Annu Rep Eng Res Inst Fac Eng Univ Tokyo
Annual Report. Engineering Research Institute. Tokyo University — Annu Rep Eng Res Inst Tokyo Univ
Annual Report. Engineering Research Institute. University of Tokyo — Annu Rep Eng Res Inst Univ Tokyo
Annual Report. Entomological Society of Ontario — Annu Rep Entomol Soc Ont
Annual Report. Environmental Pollution Research Center. Fukui Prefecture — Annu Rep Environ Pollut Res Cent Fukui Prefect
Annual Report. Environmental Pollution Research Center of Ibaraki-Ken — Annu Rep Environ Pollut Res Cent Ibaraki-Ken
Annual Report. Environmental Radioactivity Research Institute of Miyagi — Annu Rep Environ Radioact Res Inst Miyagi
Annual Report. Faculty of Education. Gunma University — Annu Rep Fac Educ Gunma Univ
Annual Report. Faculty of Education. Gunma University. Art and Technology Series — Annu Fac Educ Gunma Univ Art Technol Ser
Annual Report. Faculty of Education. Gunma University. Art and Technology Series — Annu Rep Fac Educ Gunma Univ Art Technol Ser
Annual Report. Faculty of Education. Gunma University. Art and Technology Series — GDKYA7
Annual Report. Faculty of Education. Gunma University. Art, Technology, Health, and Physical Education and Science of Human Living Series — GDKKD2
Annual Report. Faculty of Education. Iwate University — Annu Rep Fac Educ Iwate Univ
Annual Report. Faculty of Education. University of Iwate — Annu Rep Fac Educ Univ Iwate
Annual Report. Faculty of Education. University of Iwate — Annual Rep Fac Ed Univ Iwate
Annual Report. Faculty of Education. University of Iwate — IDKKBM
Annual Report. Faculty of Pharmaceutical Sciences. Nagoya City University — Annu Rep Fac Pharm Sci Nagoya City Univ
Annual Report. Faculty of Pharmaceutical Sciences. Nagoya City University — NSDYAI
Annual Report. Faculty of Pharmacy and Pharmaceutical Sciences. Fukuyama University — Annu Rep Fac Pharm Pharm Sci Fukuyama Univ
Annual Report. Faculty of Pharmacy. Kanazawa University — Annu Rep Fac Pharm Kanazawa Univ
Annual Report. Farmers Union Grain Terminal Association — Annu Rep Farmers Union Grain Terminal Ass
Annual Report. Federal Energy Administration — Ann Rep Fed En Adm
Annual Report. Florida Cooperative Extension Service — Annu Rep Fla Coop Ext Serv
Annual Report. Florida University. Agricultural Experiment Station — Annu Rep Fla Univ Agr Exp Sta
Annual Report. Fogg Art Museum — Ann Fogg
Annual Report. Fogg Art Museum [*Harvard University*] — Ann Rep Fogg Art Mus
Annual Report. Fogg Art Museum — Ann Rept Fogg
Annual Report. Food Research Institute. Aichi Prefecture — Annu Rep Food Res Inst Aichi Prefect
Annual Report. Freshwater Biological Association — Annu Rep Freshwater Biol Assoc
Annual Report. Fruit Growers' Association of Ontario — Annual Rep Fruit Growers Assoc Ontario
Annual Report. Fukuoka City Hygienic Laboratory — Annu Rep Fukuoka City Hyg Lab
Annual Report. Fukuoka City Institute of Public Health — Annu Rep Fukuoka City Inst Public Health
Annual Report. Gakugei Faculty. Iwate University/Iwate Daigaku. Gakugeigakubu Kenkyu Nempo — Annual Rep Gakugei Fac Iwate Univ
Annual Report. Geological Survey and Mines Department (Swaziland) — Annu Rep Geol Surv Mines Dep (Swaziland)
Annual Report. Geological Survey Department. British Territories in Borneo — Annu Rep Geol Surv Dep Br Territ Borneo
Annual Report. Geological Survey Department (Cyprus) — Annu Rep Geol Surv Dep (Cyprus)
Annual Report. Geological Survey Department (Malawi) — Annu Rep Geol Surv Dep (Malawi)
Annual Report. Geological Survey Division (Nigeria) — Annu Rep Geol Surv Div (Niger)
Annual Report. Geological Survey. Federation of Nigeria — Annu Rep Geol Surv Fed Niger
Annual Report. Geological Survey (Iowa) — Annu Rep Geol Surv Iowa
Annual Report. Geological Survey (New Hebrides) — Annu Rep Geol Surv (New Hebrides)
Annual Report. Geological Survey of Malaysia — Annu Rep Geol Surv Malays
Annual Report. Geological Survey of Malaysia — Annu Rep Geol Surv Malaysia

Annual Report. Geological Survey. Western Australia — Annu Rep Geol Surv West Aust
Annual Report. Geophysical Commission (Norway) — Annu Rep Geophys Comm (Norw)
Annual Report. Gohei Tanabe Co. — Annu Rep Gohei Tanabe Co
Annual Report. Government of the Provinces of Prince Edward Island. Department of Industry and Commerce — Ann Rep Pr Ed Isl Dept Ind Com
Annual Report. Gunma Institute of Public Health — Annu Rep Gunma Inst Public Health
Annual Report. Gunma Institute of Public Health and Gunma Research Center for Environmental Science — Annu Rep Gunma Inst Public Health Gunma Res Cent Environ Sci
Annual Report. Gunma Prefectural Institute of Public Health and Environmental Sciences — Annu Rep Gunma Prefect Inst Public Health Environ Sci
Annual Report. Gunmaken Industrial Research Laboratory — Annu Rep Gunmaken Ind Res Lab
Annual Report. Halifax Infirmary — Ann Rep Hal Inf
Annual Report. Hawaii Bicentennial Commission — Ann Rep Hawaii Bicent Com
Annual Report. Health and Medical Services of the State of Queensland — Ann Rep Hlth Med Serv
Annual Report. Henry Luce Foundation — Ann Rep Henry Luce Found
Annual Report. Hiroshima City Institute of Public Health — Annu Rep Hiroshima City Inst Public Health
Annual Report. Hiroshima Fisheries Experimental Station — Annu Rep Hiroshima Fish Exp Stn
Annual Report. Hokkaido Branch. Forestry and Forest Products Research Institute — Annu Rep Hokkaido Branch For For Prod Res Inst
Annual Report. Hokkaido Branch. Forestry and Forest Products Research Institute — RSHNDI
Annual Report. Hokkaido Branch. Government Forest Experiment Station — Annu Rep Hokkaido Branch Gov For Exp Stn
Annual Report. Hokkaido Branch. Government Forest Experiment Station — NRSHB2
Annual Report. Hokkaido Branch. Government Forest Experiment Station — Rep Forest Exp Stn Hokkaido
Annual Report. Hokusei Gakuin Junior College — Annu Rep Hokusei Gakuin Jr Coll
Annual Report. Hormel Institute. University of Minnesota — Annu Rep Hormel Inst Univ Minn
Annual Report. Hoshi College of Pharmacy — Annu Rep Hoshi Coll Pharm
Annual Report. Hydroscience and Geotechnology Laboratory. Faculty of Engineering. Saitama University — Annu Rep Hydrosci Geotechnol Lab Fac Eng Saitama Univ
Annual Report. Hygienic Laboratory of Okayama Prefecture — Annu Rep Hyg Lab Okayama Prefect
Annual Report. Illinois Agricultural Experiment Station — Annual Rep Illinois Agric Exp Sta
Annual Report. Illinois Society of Engineers — Annu Rep Ill Soc Eng
Annual Report. Indian Tea Association. Tocklai Experimental Station — Annu Rep Indian Tea Assoc Tocklai Exp Stn
Annual Report. Indiana Agricultural Experiment Station — Annu Rep Ind Agric Exp Stn
Annual Report. Institute for Fermentation (Osaka) — AFOSAP
Annual Report. Institute for Fermentation (Osaka) — Annu Rep Inst Ferment (Osaka)
Annual Report. Institute for Nuclear Study. University of Tokyo — Annu Rep Inst Nucl Stud Univ Tokyo
Annual Report. Institute for Virus Research [*Kyoto*] — Ann Rep Inst Vir Res
Annual Report. Institute for Virus Research. Kyoto University — Annu Rep Inst Virus Res Kyoto Univ
Annual Report. Institute for Virus Research. Kyoto University — ARIVAK
Annual Report. Institute of Archaeology [*London*] — ARIA
Annual Report. Institute of Archaeology. University of London — RIAUL
Annual Report. Institute of Endocrinology. Gunma University — Annu Rep Inst Endocrinol Gunma Univ
Annual Report. Institute of Environmental Pollution and Public Health. Oita Prefecture — Annu Rep Inst Environ Pollut Public Health Oita Pref
Annual Report. Institute of Food Microbiology. Chiba University — Annu Rep Inst Food Microbiol Chiba Univ
Annual Report. Institute of Food Microbiology. Chiba University — CDFKAW
Annual Report. Institute of Geological Sciences — Ann Rep Inst Geol Sci
Annual Report. Institute of Geoscience. University of Tsukuba — Annu Rep Inst Geosci Univ Tsukuba
Annual Report. Institute of Marine Engineers — Annu Rep Inst Mar Eng
Annual Report. Institute of Medical and Veterinary Science — Annu Rep Inst Med Vet Sci
Annual Report. Institute of Microbiology. Rutgers University — Annual Rep Inst Microbiol Rutgers Univ
Annual Report. Institute of Phonetics. University of Copenhagen — ARIPUC
Annual Report. Institute of Physics. Academia Sinica — Annu Rep Inst Phys Acad Sin
Annual Report. Institute of Physics. Academia Sinica — RIPSD3
Annual Report. Institute of Sciences and Technology. Meiji University — Annu Rep Inst Sci Technol Meiji Univ
Annual Report. Institute of Sociology — Annu Rep Inst Sociol
Annual Report. Interdisciplinary Research Institute of Environmental Sciences — Annu Rep Interdiscip Res Inst Environ Sci
Annual Report. International Association of Milk Sanitarians — Annu Rep Int Assoc Milk Sanit
Annual Report. International Crop Improvement Association — Annu Rep Int Crop Impr Ass
Annual Report. International Telecommunications Satellite Organization — Ann Rep Int Telecom Sat Org
Annual Report. International Tin Research Council — Annu Rep Int Tin Res Counc
Annual Report. Iowa Agriculture and Home Economics Experiment Station — Annu Rep Iowa Agric Home Econ Exp Stn
Annual Report. Iowa Energy Policy Council — Ann Rep Iowa En Pol Counc
Annual Report. Iowa Engineering Society — Annu Rep Iowa Eng Soc
Annual Report. Iowa Environmental Quality Commission — Ann Rep Iowa Env Qual Com
Annual Report. Iowa Geological Survey — Annu Rep Iowa Geol Surv
Annual Report. Itsuu Laboratory — Annu Rep Itsuu Lab
Annual Report. Iwate Medical University School of Liberal Arts and Sciences — Annu Rep Iwate Med Univ Sch Lib Arts Sci
Annual Report. Iwate Prefectural Institute of Public Health — Annu Rep Iwate Prefect Inst Public Health
Annual Report. Japanese Association for Radiation Research on Polymers — Annu Rep Jpn Assoc Radiat Res Polym
Annual Report. Japanese Association for Tuberculosis — Annu Rep Jpn Assoc Tuberc
Annual Report. Japanese Research Society for Synthetic Detergents — Annu Rep Jpn Res Soc Synth Deterg
Annual Report. Japanese Society for Tuberculosis — Annu Rep Jpn Soc Tuber
Annual Report. John Innes Horticultural Institution — Annu Rep John Innes Hortic Inst
Annual Report. Kawasaki Research Institute for Environmental Protection — Annu Rep Kawasaki Res Inst Environ Prot
Annual Report. Kentucky. Agricultural Experiment Station — Annu Rep Ky Agric Exp Stn
Annual Report. Kinki University. Atomic Energy Research Institute — KDGNBX
Annual Report. Kumamoto Livestock Experiment Station — Annu Rep Kumamoto Livest Exp Stn
Annual Report. Kyoritsu College of Pharmacy — Annu Rep Kyoritsu Coll Pharm
Annual Report. Kyoritsu College of Pharmacy — KYDKAJ
Annual Report. Kyoto City Environmental Monitoring and Research Center — Annu Rep Kyoto City Environ Monit Res Cent
Annual Report. Kyoto Prefectural Institute of Hygienic and Environmental Sciences — Annu Rep Kyoto Prefect Inst Hyg Environ Sci
Annual Report. Laboratory. Kyoto Prefectural Pharmaceutical Association — Annu Rep Lab Kyoto Prefect Pharm Assoc
Annual Report. Laboratory of Algology [*Trebon*] — LKAAAN
Annual Report. Laboratory of Algology (Trebon) — Annu Rep Lab Algol (Trebon)
Annual Report. Laboratory of Experimental Algology and Department of Applied Algology [*Trebon*] — LXAAAC
Annual Report. Laboratory of Experimental Algology and Department of Applied Algology (Trebon) — Annu Rep Lab Exp Algol Dep Appl Algol (Trebon)
Annual Report. Laboratory of Public Health. Hiroshima Prefecture — Annu Rep Lab Public Health Hiroshima Prefect
Annual Report. Laguna Marine Laboratory — Annual Rep Laguna Mar Lab
Annual Report. Library Council of Philadelphia — Annu Rep Libr Counc Phila
Annual Report. Liverpool Marine Biological Station on Puffin Island — Annual Rep Liverpool Mar Biol Sta Puffin Island
Annual Report. MAFES. Mississippi Agricultural and Forestry Experiment Station — Annu Rep MAFES Miss Agric For Exp St
Annual Report. Maine Advisory Council on Vocational Education — Ann Rep Maine Adv Counc Voc Ed
Annual Report. Maine State Board of Registration for Professional Engineers — Ann Rep Maine St Bd Reg Prof Eng
Annual Report. Manitoba Department of Economic Development and Tourism — Ann Rep Manitoba Dept Econ Dev Tour
Annual Report. Manitoba Lotteries Commission — Ann Rep Manitoba Lot Com
Annual Report. Maryland Agricultural Experiment Station — Annu Rep Md Agric Exp Stn
Annual Report. Mass Transit Division. Department of Transportation. State of Oregon — Ann Rep Mass Tran Div Dept Transp Oregon
Annual Report. Mauritius Sugar Industry Research Institute — Annu Rep Mauritius Sugar Ind Res Inst
Annual Report. Medical Research Council of Nigeria — Ann Rep Med Res Counc Nigeria
Annual Report. Medical Research Institute. Tokyo Medical and Dental University — Annu Rep Med Res Inst Tokyo Med Dent Univ
Annual Report. Medical Research Society for Mining and Smelting Industries — Annu Rep Med Res Soc Min Smelting Ind
Annual Report. Meiji Seika Company — Annu Rep Meiji Seika Co
Annual Report. Michigan Academy of Science, Arts, and Letters — Annual Rep Michigan Acad Sci
Annual Report. Michigan State Horticultural Society — Annu Rep Mich State Hortic Soc
Annual Report. Michigan State Horticultural Society — Annual Rep Michigan State Hort Soc
Annual Report. Mie Prefectural Institute of Public Health — Annu Rep Mie Prefect Inst Public Health
Annual Report. Milk Control Board of Manitoba — Ann Rep Milk Cont Bd Manitoba
Annual Report. Mineral Resources Department (Fiji) — Annu Rep Miner Resour Dep (Fiji)
Annual Report. Mineral Resources Division (Fiji) — Ann Rep Min Res Div (Fiji)
Annual Report. Mineral Resources Division (Manitoba) — Annu Rep Miner Resour Div (Manitoba)
Annual Report. Mines Service (Cyprus) — Annu Rep Mines Serv (Cyprus)
Annual Report. Minister of Mines and Petroleum Resources. British Columbia — Annu Rep Minist Mines Pet Resour BC
Annual Report. Minnesota Mississippi Headwaters Board — Ann Rep Minnestoa Mississippi Head Bd
Annual Report. Minnesota State Horticultural Society — Annu Rep Minn State Hortic Soc

Annual Report. Minnesota State Horticultural Society — Annual Rep Minnesota State Hort Soc
Annual Report. Mississippi Medicaid Commission — Ann Rep Mississippi Medicaid Com
Annual Report. Mississippi State University. Agricultural Experiment Station — Annu Rep Miss State Univ Agr Exp Sta
Annual Report. Missouri River Basin Commission — Ann Rep Missouri Riv Basin Com
Annual Report. Missouri Water and Sewerage Conference — Annu Rep Mo Water Sewerage Conf
Annual Report. Miyagi Prefectural Institute of Public Health and Environment — Annu Rep Miyagi Prefect Inst Public Health Environ
Annual Report. Miyazaki Prefectural Institute for Public Health and Environment — Annu Rep Miyazaki Prefect Inst Public Health Environ
Annual Report. Montreal Horticultural Society and Fruit Growers Association. Province of Quebec — Annual Rep Montreal Hort Soc
Annual Report. Museum of Fine Arts [*Boston*] — MFA AR
Annual Report. Nagasaki Prefectural Institute of Public Health and Environmental Sciences — Annu Rep Nagasaki Prefect Inst Public Health Environ Sci
Annual Report. Nagoya City Health Research Institute — Annu Rep Nagoya City Health Res Inst
Annual Report. Nagoya Fertilizer and Feed Inspection Station. Fertilizer Section/Nagoya Hishiryo Kensajo Jigyo Hokoku Hiryo No Bu — Annual Rep Nagoya Fertilizer Inspect Sta Fertilizer Sect
Annual Report. National Archives and Records Centre. Singapore — Ann Rep Nat Arc Rec Cent Singapore
Annual Report. National Archives of India — RNAI
Annual Report. National Industrial Research Institute [*South Korea*] — Annu Rep Natl Ind Res Inst
Annual Report. National Institute for Animal Industry. Ministry of Agriculture and Forestry (Japan) — A Rep Natn Inst Anim Ind (Japan)
Annual Report. National Institute of Genetics — Annu Rep Natl Inst Genet
Annual Report. National Institute of Genetics — Annual Rep Natl Inst Genet
Annual Report. National Institute of Genetics [*English Edition*] [*Japan*] — NIGAB
Annual Report. National Institute of Genetics (Japan) — Annu Rep Nat Inst Genet (Jap)
Annual Report. National Institute of Nutrition — Annu Rep Natl Inst Nutr
Annual Report. National Institute of Nutrition — ARNNA
Annual Report. National Institute of Nutrition (Japan) — Annu Rep Natl Inst Nutr (Jpn)
Annual Report. National Institute of Nutrition (Tokyo) — Annu Rep Natl Inst Nutr (Tokyo)
Annual Report. National Research Council of Canada — Ann Rep Nat Res Counc Can
Annual Report. National Science Foundation — Annual Rep Natl Sci Found
Annual Report. National Vegetable Research Station (Wellesbourne, England) — Annu Rep Nat Veg Res Stn (Wellesbourne Eng)
Annual Report. National Vegetable Research Station. Wellesbourne, England — Annu Rep Natl Veg Res Stn Wellesbourne Engl
Annual Report. National Veterinary Assay Laboratory — Annu Rep Natl Vet Assay Lab
Annual Report. National Veterinary Assay Laboratory — DIKNAA
Annual Report. National Veterinary Assay Laboratory (Japan) — Annu Rep Natl Vet Assay Lab (Jpn)
Annual Report. Natural History Society of New Brunswick — Annual Rep Nat Hist Soc New Brunswick
Annual Report. Natural Products Research Institute. Seoul National University — STSODQ
Annual Report. Natural Science Research Institute. Yonsei University — ARNYA
Annual Report. Nebraska Grain Improvement Association — Annu Rep Nebr Grain Impr Ass
Annual Report. Nebraska Wheat Commission — Annu Rep Nebr Wheat Comm
Annual Report. Netherlands Institute for Sea Research — Annu Rep Neth Inst Sea Res
Annual Report. New Jersey Department of Labor and Industry — Ann Rep New Jersey Dept Lab Ind
Annual Report. New Jersey Department of Transportation — Ann Rep New Jersey Dept Transp
Annual Report. New Mexico Agricultural Experiment Station — Annu Rep N Mex Agr Exp Sta
Annual Report. New York State Agricultural Experiment Station — Annu Rep NY State Agric Exp Stn
Annual Report. New York State Association of Dairy and Milk Inspectors — Annu Rep NY State Assoc Dairy Milk Insp
Annual Report. New York State Association of Milk and Food Sanitarians — Annu Rep NY State Assoc Milk Food Sanit
Annual Report. Nigeria Cocoa Research Institute — Annu Rep Nigeria Cocoa Res Inst
Annual Report. Nigeria Cocoa Research Institute — CRINBJ
Annual Report. Nigerian Institute for Oceanography and Marine Research — ARIQD8
Annual Report. Nigerian Institute for Oceanography and Marine Research (Lagos) — Annu Rep Nigerian Inst Oceanogr Mar Res (Lagos)
Annual Report. Northern Nut Growers Association — Annu Rep North Nut Grow Assoc
Annual Report. Noto Marine Laboratory — Annu Rep Noto Mar Lab
Annual Report. Noto Marine Laboratory — KDRNBK
Annual Report. Noto Marine Laboratory. Faculty of Science. University of Kanazawa — Annual Rep Noto Mar Lab
Annual Report. Nova Scotia Department of Labour — Ann Rep Nova Scotia Dept Lab
Annual Report. Nova Scotia Fruit Growers' Association — Annu Rep NS Fruit Grow Assoc
Annual Report of Asahikawa Medical College — Annual Rep Asahikawa Med College
Annual Report of Biological Works. Faculty of Science. Osaka University — Annu Rep Biol Works Fac Sci Osaka Univ
Annual Report of Biological Works. Faculty of Science. Osaka University — ARBWAM
Annual Report of Gunma Prefectural Industrial Technology Research Laboratory — Annu Rep Gunma Prefect Ind Technol Res Lab
Annual Report of Hydrogen Isotope Research Center. Toyama University — Annu Rep Hydrogen Isot Res Cent Toyama Univ
Annual Report of Hydrographical Observations. Fusan Fishery Experiment Station — Annual Rep Hydrogr Observ
Annual Report of Kagawa Prefecture Environmental Research Center — Annu Rep Kagawa Prefect Environ Res Cent
Annual Report of Natural Science and Home Economics. Kinjo Gakuin College — Annu Rep Natur Sci Home Econ Kinjo Gakuin Coll
Annual Report of Progress. Georgia Department of Mines, Mining, and Geology — Ann Rep Prog Georgia Dept MMG
Annual Report of Scientific Works. Faculty of Science. Osaka University [*Japan*] — Annu Rep Sci Works Fac Sci Osaka Univ
Annual Report of Studies. Doshisha Women's College of Liberal Arts — Annu Rep Stud Doshisha Women's Coll Lib Arts
Annual Report of Studies in Animal Nutrition and Allied Sciences. Rowett Research Institute — Annu Rep Stud Anim Nutr Allied Sci Rowett Res Inst
Annual Report of Studies. Jissen Women's University. Natural and Domestic Sciences — Annu Rep Stud Jissen Womens Univ Nat Domest Sci
Annual Report of Takamine Laboratory — Annu Rep Takamine Lab
Annual Report of the Director. Department of Terrestrial Magnetism. Carnegie Institution — Annu Rep Dir Dep Terr Magn Carnegie Inst
Annual Report of the Researches. Mishima College of Humanities and Sciences. Nihon University — Annu Rep Res Mishima Coll Human Sci Nihon Univ
Annual Report of the Researches. Mishima College of Humanities and Sciences. Nihon University. Natural Sciences — Annu Rep Res Mishima Coll Human Sci Nihon Univ Nat Sci
Annual Report of the Science of Living. Osaka City University — Annu Rep Sci Living Osaka City Univ
Annual Report of Vegetables and Flowers Research Works in Japan/Sosai Kaki Shiken Kenkyu Nenpo — Annual Rep Veg Fl Res Works Japan
Annual Report. Ohio Conference on Water Purification — Annu Rep Ohio Conf Water Purif
Annual Report. Ohio State Forestry Bureau — Annual Rep Ohio State Forest Bur
Annual Report. Ohio State Horticultural Society — Annu Rep Ohio State Hortic
Annual Report. Oil Palm Research Station — Annual Rep Oil Palm Res Sta
Annual Report. Okayama Prefectural Institute for Environmental Science and Public Health — Annu Rep Okayama Prefect Inst Environ Sci Public Health
Annual Report. Okayama Prefectural Research Center of Environment and Public Health — Annu Rep Okayama Prefect Res Cent Environ Public Health
Annual Report. Okinawa Prefectural Institute of Public Health — Annu Rep Okinawa Prefect Inst Public Health
Annual Report. Oklahoma Agricultural Experiment Station — Annu Rep Okla Agric Exp Stn
Annual Report on Animal Nutrition and Allied Sciences. Rowett Research Institute — Annu Rep Anim Nutr Allied Sci Rowett Res Inst
Annual Report on Cacao Research. Imperial College of Tropical Agriculture. St. Augustine. Trinidad — Annu Rep Cacao Res Imp Coll Trop Agric St Augustine Trinidad
Annual Report on Cacao Research. University of the West Indies — Annu Rep Cacao Res Univ West Indies
Annual Report on Cacao Research. University of the West Indies — ARCRBD
Annual Report on Energy Research, Development, and Demonstration. International Energy Agency — AREDD
Annual Report on Exchange Arrangements and Exchange Restrictions — AREAER
Annual Report on Geophysical Research in Norway — Annu Rep Geophys Res Norw
Annual Report on High-Tech Materials — Ann Rep High Tech Mat
Annual Report on Industrial Robots — Ann Rep Ind Robots
Annual Report on Mines. Department of Mines. Nova Scotia — Annu Rep Mines Dep Mines NS
Annual Report on Mines. Nova Scotia Department of Mines — Annu Rep Mines NS Dep Mines
Annual Report on Research and Technical Work. Department of Agriculture for Northern Ireland — Annu Rep Res Tech Work Dep Agric North Irel
Annual Report on Research and Technical Work. Department of Agriculture for Northern Ireland — ARTID5
Annual Report on Research and Technical Work. Ministry of Agriculture for Northern Ireland — A Rep Res Tech Wk Minist Agric Nth Ire
Annual Report on Stress — Annu Rep Stress
Annual Report on the Noxious, Beneficial, and Other Insects of the State of Missouri — Annual Rep Insects Missouri
Annual Report on the Progress of Rubber Technology — Annu Rep Prog Rubber Technol
Annual Report. Ontario Department of Mines — Ann Rep Ont Dep Mines
Annual Report. Oregon Horticultural Society — Annu Rep Oreg Hortic Soc
Annual Report. Oregon State Horticultural Society — Annu Rep Oreg State Hort Soc
Annual Report. Organization of the Petroleum Exporting Countries — AOPCD
Annual Report. Orient Hospital — Annu Rep Orient Hosp
Annual Report. Orient Hospital (Beirut) — Annu Rep Orient Hosp (Beirut)
Annual Report. Osaka Prefectural Radiation Research Institute — Annu Rep Osaka Prefect Radiat Res
Annual Report. Osaka Prefectural Radiation Research Institute — Annu Rep Osaka Prefect Radiat Res Inst

Annual Report. Pakistan Central Jute Committee — Annu Rep Pak Cent Jute Comm
Annual Report. Pasteur Institute of Southern India — Ann Rep Past Ins SI
Annual Report. Peanut Collaborative Research Support Program. CRSP — Annu Rep Peanut Collab Res Support Program CRSP
Annual Report. Peterborough Natural History, Scientific, and Archaeological Society — Annu Rep Peterborough Natur Hist Sci Archaeol Soc
Annual Report PETROBRAS [*Petroleo Brasileiro SA*] [*Rio De Janeiro*] — Annu Rep PETROBRAS
Annual Report. Philippine Sugar Association — Annu Rep Philipp Sugar Assoc
Annual Report. Prefectural University of Mie. Section 2. Natural Science — Annu Rep Prefect Univ Mie Sect 2
Annual Report. Production of Ammonia Using Coal as a Source of Hydrogen — Annu Rep Prod Ammonia Using Coal Source Hydrogen
Annual Report. Public Health Division. Pharmaceutical Society of Japan — Annu Rep Public Health Div Pharm Soc Jpn
Annual Report. Punjab Irrigation Research Institute — Annu Rep Punjab Irrig Res Inst
Annual Report. Quebec Society for the Protection of Plants — Annu Rep Que Soc Prot Plants
Annual Report. Quebec Society for the Protection of Plants — Annual Rep Quebec Soc Protect Pl
Annual Report. Queensland Department of Mines — Annu Rep Queensland Dep Mines
Annual Report. Radiation Center of Osaka Prefecture — Annu Rep Radiat Cent Osaka Prefect
Annual Report. Radiation Center of Osaka Prefecture — ARROAA
Annual Report. Record Research. East African Agriculture and Forestry Research Organisation — A Rep Rec Res
Annual Report. Research Activities. IPCR [*Institute of Physical and Chemical Research*] — Annu Rep Res Act IPCR
Annual Report. Research Department. Coffee Board (India) — Annu Rep Res Dep Coffee Board India
Annual Report. Research Division. Sudan. Ministry of Agriculture — Annu Rep Res Div Sudan Minist Agric
Annual Report. Research Institute for Chemical Fibers. Japan — Annu Rep Res Inst Chem Fibers Jpn
Annual Report. Research Institute for Chemobiodynamics. Chiba University — Annu Rep Res Inst Chemobiodyn Chiba Univ
Annual Report. Research Institute for Chemobiodynamics. Chiba University — CDSKAT
Annual Report. Research Institute for Organic Synthetic Chemistry — Annu Rep Res Inst Org Synth Chem
Annual Report. Research Institute for Wakan-Yaku Toyama Medical and Pharmaceutical University — Annu Rep Res Inst Wakan-Yaku Toyama Med Pharm Univ
Annual Report. Research Institute for Wakan-Yaku Toyama Medical and Pharmaceutical University — WKNDDH
Annual Report. Research Institute of Environmental Medicine. Nagoya University — Annu Rep Res Inst Environ Med Nagoya Univ
Annual Report. Research Institute of Environmental Medicine. Nagoya University [*English Edition*] — ARINAU
Annual Report. Research Institute of Environmental Medicine. Nagoya University (English Edition) — Annu Rep Res Inst Environ Med Nagoya Univ (Engl Ed)
Annual Report. Research Institute of Environmental Medicine. Nagoya University (Japanese Edition) — Annu Rep Res Inst Environ Med Nagoya Univ Jpn Ed
Annual Report. Research Institute of Physics (Sweden) — Annu Rep Res Inst Phys Swed
Annual Report. Research Institute of Tuberculosis. Kanazawa University [*Japan*] — Annu Rep Res Inst Tuberc Kanazawa Univ
Annual Report. Research Laboratory of Ground Failure. Niigata University. Faculty of Science — Annu Rep Res Lab Ground Failure Niigata Univ Fac Sci
Annual Report. Royal Society of South Australia — Annual Rep Roy Soc South Australia
Annual Report. Rubber Research Institute of Malaya — Annu Rep Rubber Res Inst Malaya
Annual Report. Sado Marine Biological Station. Niigata University — Annu Rep Sado Mar Biol Stn Niigata Univ
Annual Report. Sado Marine Biological Station. Niigata University — SRJKAK
Annual Report. Sankyo Research Laboratories — Annu Rep Sankyo Res Lab
Annual Report. Sankyo Research Laboratories — SKKNAJ
Annual Report. Santa Barbara Botanic Garden — Annual Rep Santa Barbara Bot Gard
Annual Report. Saranac Laboratory for the Study of Tuberculosis — Annu Rep Saranac Lab Stud Tuberc
Annual Report. Saskatchewan Energy and Mines — Annu Rep Saskatchewan Energy Mines
Annual Report. Scientific Research Council of Jamaica — Annu Rep Sci Res Counc Jamaica
Annual Report. Scottish Plant Breeding Station — Annual Rep Scott Pl Breed Sta
Annual Report. SEAFDEC Aquaculture Department — Annu Rep SEAFDEC Aquacult Dep
Annual Report. Secretary of the State Horticultural Society of Michigan — Annu Rep Secr State Hortic Soc Mich
Annual Report. Secretary. State Pomological Society of Michigan — Annu Rep Secr State Pomol Soc Mich
Annual Report. Seed Testing Laboratory/Shubyo Kensa Nenpo — Annual Rep Seed Test Lab
Annual Report. Shionogi Research Laboratory — Annu Rep Shionogi Res Lab
Annual Report. Shionogi Research Laboratory — SKNEA7
Annual Report. Shizuoka Public Health Laboratory [*Japan*] — Annu Rep Shizuoka Public Health Lab
Annual Report. Showa College of Pharmaceutical Sciences — Annu Rep Showa Coll Pharm Sci
Annual Report. Shropshire and North Wales Natural History and Antiquarian Society — Annual Rep Shropshire Nat Hist Soc
Annual Report. Smithsonian Institution — Ann Rep Smith Inst
Annual Report. Smithsonian Institution — Annu Rep Smiths Inst
Annual Report. Society for Libyan Studies — Ann Rep Soc Libyan Stud
Annual Report. Society for Libyan Studies — Annu Rep Soc Libyan Stud
Annual Report. Society for Libyan Studies [*London*] — AR Libyan Studies
Annual Report. Society for Libyan Studies [*London*] — SLS
Annual Report. Society for the Promotion of Construction Engineering — Annu Rep Soc Promot Constr Eng
Annual Report. Society of Plant Protection of North Japan — Annu Rep Soc Plant Prot N Jap
Annual Report. Society of Plant Protection of North Japan — Annu Rep Soc Plant Prot North Jpn
Annual Report. Society of Yamaguchi Industrial Health — Annu Rep Soc Yamaguchi Ind Health
Annual Report. South African Institute for Medical Research — Ann Rep S Afr Inst Med Res
Annual Report. Southern California Coastal Water Research Project — Annu Rep South Calif Coastal Water Res Proj
Annual Report. State Agricultural Experiment Station — Annual Rep State Agric Exp Sta
Annual Report. Storrs School Agricultural Experiment Station — Annual Rep Storrs School Agric Exp Sta
Annual Report. Sudan. Ministry of Agriculture — Annu Rep Sudan Minist Agric
Annual Report. Sudan. Ministry of Agriculture. Agricultural Research Division — Annu Rep Sudan Minist Agric Agric Res Div
Annual Report. Takeda Research Laboratories — Annu Rep Takeda Res Lab
Annual Report. Takeda Research Laboratories — TDKNAF
Annual Report. Tanabe Seiyaku Company Limited [*Japan*] — Annu Rep Tanabe Seiyaku Co Ltd
Annual Report to the Governor. Kansas Wheat Commission — Annu Rep Governor Kans Wheat Comm
Annual Report. Tobacco Institute of Puerto Rico — Annu Rep Tob Inst PR
Annual Report. Tobacco Research Institute — Annu Rep Tob Res Inst
Annual Report. Tobacco Research Institute (Taiwan) — Rep Tob Res Inst (Taiwan)
Annual Report. Tobacco Research Institute. Taiwan Tobacco and Wine Monopoly Bureau — Annu Rep Tob Res Inst Taiwan Tob & Wine Monop Bur
Annual Report. Tobacco Research Institute. Taiwan Tobacco and Wine Monopoly Bureau — TSYKDE
Annual Report. Tohoku College of Pharmacy — Annu Rep Tohoku Coll Pharm
Annual Report. Tohoku College of Pharmacy — TYKNAQ
Annual Report. Tokushima Prefectural Institute of Public Health and Environmental Sciences — Annu Rep Tokushima Prefect Inst Public Health Environ Sci
Annual Report. Tokyo College of Pharmacy — Annu Rep Tokyo Coll Pharm
Annual Report. Tokyo College of Pharmacy — TYDNAP
Annual Report. Tokyo Metropolitan Laboratories for Medical Sciences — Annu Rep Tokyo Metrop Labs Med Sci
Annual Report. Tokyo Metropolitan Research Institute for Environmental Protection — Annu Rep Tokyo Metrop Res Inst Environ Prot
Annual Report. Tokyo Metropolitan Research Institute for Environmental Protection. English Translation — Annu Rep Tokyo Metrop Res Inst Environ Prot Engl Transl
Annual Report. Tokyo Metropolitan Research Institute for Environmental Protection. Japanese Edition — Annu Rep Tokyo Metrop Res Inst Environ Prot Jpn Ed
Annual Report. Tokyo Metropolitan Research Laboratory of Public Health — A Rep Tokyo Metropol Res Lab Publ Hlth
Annual Report. Tokyo Metropolitan Research Laboratory of Public Health — Annu Rep Tokyo Metrop Res Lab Public Health
Annual Report. Tokyo University of Agriculture and Technology — Ann Rept Tokyo Univ Agr Technol
Annual Report. Tokyo University of Agriculture and Technology — Annu Rep Tokyo Univ Agric Technol
Annual Report. Tokyo University of Agriculture and Technology — RTATD8
Annual Report. Tokyo-to Laboratories for Medical Science — Annu Rep Tokyo to Lab Med Sci
Annual Report. Torry Research Station (Aberdeen, UK) — Annu Rep Torry Res Stn (Aberdeen UK)
Annual Report. Toyama Institute of Health — Annu Rep Toyama Inst Health
Annual Report. Tritium Research Center. Toyama University — Annu Rep Tritium Res Cent Toyama Univ
Annual Report. United Dental Hospital of Sydney. Institute of Dental Research — Annu Rep United Dent Hosp Sydney Inst Dent Res
Annual Report. United Fruit Company. Medical Department — Ann Rep United Fruit Co Med Dept
Annual Report. United States National Advisory Committee for Aeronautics — Ann Rep NACA
Annual Report. University of Delaware. College of Agricultural Sciences. Agricultural Experiment Station and Cooperative Extension Service — Annu Rep Univ Del Coll Agric Sci Agric Exp Stn Coop Ext Serv
Annual Report. University of Georgia. College of Agriculture. Experiment Stations — Annu Rep Univ GA Coll Agr Exp Sta
Annual Report. University of Minnesota. Hormel Institute — Annu Rep Univ Minn Hormel Inst
Annual Report. US Crude Oil and Natural Gas Reserves — Annu Rep US Crude Oil Nat Gas Reserves
Annual Report. US Regional Pasture Research Laboratory — Annual Rep US Regional Pasture Res Lab
Annual Report. Vegetable Growers Association of America — Annu Rep Veg Growers Ass Amer

Annual Report. Vegetable Growers Association of America — Annu Rep Veg Growers Assoc Am
Annual Report. Wakayama Prefectural Institute of Public Health — Annu Rep Wakayama Prefect Inst Public Health
Annual Report. Warwickshire Natural History and Archaeological Society — Annual Rep Warwickshire Nat Hist Soc
Annual Report. Welsh Plant Breeding Station. University College of Wales (Aberystwyth) — Annu Rep Welsh Plant Breed Stn Univ Coll Wales (Aberystwyth)
Annual Report. Western Australia. Department of Mines — Annu Rep West Aust Dep Mines
Annual Report. Worcester Art Museum — Ann Worc Art Mus
Annual Report. Wrapper and Hookah Tobacco Research Station — Annual Rep Wrapper Hookah Tobacco Res Sta
Annual Report. Wye College. University of London. Department of Hop Research — Annu Rep Wye Coll Univ London Dep Hop Res
Annual Report. Yakult Institute for Microbiological Research — Annu Rep Yakult Inst Microbiol Res
Annual Report. Yamaguchi Prefectural Environmental Pollution Research Center — Annu Rep Yamaguchi Prefect Environ Pollut Res Cent
Annual Report. Yokohama City Institute of Health — Annu Rep Yokohama City Inst Health
Annual Report. Yorkshire Philosophical Society — Ann Rep Yorkshire Phil Soc
Annual Reports. Chemical Laboratory. American Medical Association — Annu Rep Chem Lab Am Med Assoc
Annual Reports. Chemical Society. Section A. Physical and Inorganic Chemistry [*A publication*] — Annu Rep Chem Soc Sect A Phys Inorg Chem
Annual Reports. Conference on Electrical Insulation — Annu Rep Conf Electr Insul
Annual Reports. Faculty of Pharmaceutical Sciences. Tokushima University — Annu Rep Fac Pharm Sci Tokushima Univ
Annual Reports. Faculty of Pharmaceutical Sciences. Tokushima University — TDYKA8
Annual Reports in Inorganic and General Syntheses — Ann Rep Inorg Gen Synth
Annual Reports in Inorganic and General Syntheses — Annu Rep Inorg Gen Synth
Annual Reports in Medicinal Chemistry — Ann Rep Med Chem
Annual Reports in Medicinal Chemistry — Annu Rep Med Chem
Annual Reports in Medicinal Chemistry — ARMCBI
Annual Reports. Institute of Population Problems — Annu Rep Inst Popul Probl
Annual Reports. Institute of Population Problems — JMKNA2
Annual Reports. Kagoshima Prefectural Institute of Environmental Science — Annu Rep Kagoshima Prefect Inst Environ Sci
Annual Reports. Kinki University Atomic Energy Research Institute — Annu Rep Kinki Univ At Energy Res Inst
Annual Reports. Kurashiki Central Hospital — Annu Rep Kurashiki Cent Hosp
Annual Reports. National Research Institute of Chinese Medicine (Taiwan) — Annu Rep Natl Res Inst Chin Med Taiwan
Annual Reports. Natural Products Research Institute. Seoul National University — Annu Rep Nat Prod Res Inst Seoul Natl Univ
Annual Reports of Papua — Annual Rep Papua
Annual Reports of Studies [*Kyoto*] — AnRS
Annual Reports on Analytical Atomic Spectroscopy — Annu Rep Anal At Spectrosc
Annual Reports on Analytical Atomic Spectroscopy — ARASC7
Annual Reports on Fermentation Processes — Ann Rep Ferm Proc
Annual Reports on Fermentation Processes — Annu Rep Ferment Process
Annual Reports on Fermentation Processes — Annu Rep Ferment Processes
Annual Reports on NMR Spectroscopy — Annu Rep NMR Spectrosc
Annual Reports on the Progress of Chemistry — Ann Rept Progr Chem
Annual Reports on the Progress of Chemistry [*England*] — Annu Rep Prog Chem
Annual Reports on the Progress of Chemistry. Section A. General, Physical, and Inorganic Chemistry — Ann Rp Ch A
Annual Reports on the Progress of Chemistry. Section A. General, Physical, and Inorganic Chemistry — Annu Rep Prog Chem Sect A
Annual Reports on the Progress of Chemistry. Section A. General, Physical, and Inorganic Chemistry [*England*] — Annu Rep Prog Chem Sect A Gen Phys Inorg Chem
Annual Reports on the Progress of Chemistry. Section A. General, Physical, and Inorganic Chemistry — CSAAA
Annual Reports on the Progress of Chemistry. Section A. Inorganic Chemistry — Annu Rep Prog Chem Sect A Inorg Chem
Annual Reports on the Progress of Chemistry. Section A. Inorganic Chemistry — APCCDO
Annual Reports on the Progress of Chemistry. Section B. Organic Chemistry — Ann Rp Ch B
Annual Reports on the Progress of Chemistry. Section B. Organic Chemistry — Annu Rep Prog Chem Sect B
Annual Reports on the Progress of Chemistry. Section B. Organic Chemistry — Annu Rep Prog Chem Sect B Org Chem
Annual Reports on the Progress of Chemistry. Section B. Organic Chemistry — CACBB
Annual Reports on the Progress of Chemistry. Section B. Organic Chemistry — CACBB4
Annual Reports on the Progress of Chemistry. Section C. Physical Chemistry [*A publication*] — ACPCD
Annual Reports on the Progress of Chemistry. Section C. Physical Chemistry [*A publication*] — ACPCDW
Annual Reports on the Progress of Chemistry. Section C. Physical Chemistry [*A publication*] — Ann Rep Prog Chem Sect C Phys Chem
Annual Reports on the Progress of Chemistry. Section C. Physical Chemistry [*England*] — Annu Rep Prog Chem Sect C
Annual Reports on the Progress of Chemistry. Section C. Physical Chemistry — Annu Rep Prog Chem Sect C Phys Chem
Annual Reports. Proceedings. Barrow Naturalists' Field Club and Literary and Scientific Association — Annual Rep Proc Barrow Naturalists Field Club
Annual Reports. Research Reactor Institute. Kyoto University — Annu Rep Res React Inst Kyoto Univ
Annual Reports. Research Reactor Institute. Kyoto University — Annu Rep Res Reactor Inst Kyoto Univ
Annual Reports. Research Reactor Institute. Kyoto University — KURAAV
Annual Reports. Royal Society of Chemistry. Section B. Inorganic Chemistry — Annu Rep R Soc Chem Sect B
Annual Reports. Royal Society of Chemistry. Section C. Physical Chemistry — Annu Rep R Soc Chem Sect C
Annual Reports. State Board of Health of Massachusetts to the Legislature — Rep Bd Health Mass
Annual Reports. Takamatsu Technical College — Annu Rep Takamatsu Tech Coll
Annual Reports. Worcester Natural History Society — Annual Rep Worcester Nat Hist Soc
Annual Research Conference. Bureau of Biological Research. Rutgers University — Annu Res Conf Bur Biol Res Rutgers Univ
Annual Research Report. Red River Valley Agricultural Experiment Station — Ann Res Rep Red River Valley Agric Exp Stn
Annual Research Report. Red River Valley Agricultural Experiment Station — Annu Res Rep Red River Valley Agric Exp Stn
Annual Research Reviews. Angina Pectoris — Annu Res Rev Angina Pectoris
Annual Research Reviews. Angina Pectoris — ANPEDD
Annual Research Reviews. Anti-Diuretic Hormone — ADIHDJ
Annual Research Reviews. Anti-Diuretic Hormone — Annu Res Rev Anti-Diuretic Horm
Annual Research Reviews. Biofeedback — Annu Res Rev Biofeedback
Annual Research Reviews. Biofeedback — BIOFDL
Annual Research Reviews. Duodenal Ulcer — Annu Res Rev Duodenal Ulcer
Annual Research Reviews. Duodenal Ulcer — DUULD5
Annual Research Reviews. Effects of Psychotherapy — Annu Res Rev Eff Psychother
Annual Research Reviews. Effects of Psychotherapy — EFPSD9
Annual Research Reviews. Hodgkin's Disease and the Lymphomas — Annu Res Rev Hodgkin's Dis Lymphomas
Annual Research Reviews. Hodgkin's Disease and the Lymphomas — HDLYDQ
Annual Research Reviews. Hormones and Aggression — Annu Res Rev Horm & Aggression
Annual Research Reviews. Hormones and Aggression — HOAGDS
Annual Research Reviews. Hypothalamic Releasing Factors — Annu Res Rev Hypothal Releasing Factors
Annual Research Reviews. Hypothalamic Releasing Factors — HRFADM
Annual Research Reviews. Intrauterine Contraception — Annu Res Rev Intrauterine Contracept
Annual Research Reviews. Intrauterine Contraception — ICONDC
Annual Research Reviews. Oral Contraceptives — Annu Res Rev Oral Contracept
Annual Research Reviews. Oral Contraceptives — ORCODO
Annual Research Reviews. Peripheral Metabolism and Action of Thyroid Hormones [*A publication*] — Annu Res Rev Peripher Metab Action Thyroid Horm
Annual Research Reviews. Peripheral Metabolism and Action of Thyroid Hormones — PMAHD3
Annual Research Reviews. Physiological and Pathological Aspects of Prolactin Secretion — Annu Res Rev Physiol Pathol Aspects Prolactin Secretion
Annual Research Reviews. Physiological and Pathological Aspects of Prolactin Secretion — PPSED3
Annual Research Reviews. Pineal — Annu Res Rev Pineal
Annual Research Reviews. Pineal — PINEDV
Annual Research Reviews. Prolactin — Annu Res Rev Prolactin
Annual Research Reviews. Prolactin — PROLDI
Annual Research Reviews. Prostaglandins and the Gut — Annu Res Rev Prostaglandins Gut
Annual Research Reviews. Prostaglandins and the Gut — PGGUDU
Annual Research Reviews. Proteins of Animal Cell Plasma Membranes — Annu Res Rev Proteins Anim Cell Plasma Membr
Annual Research Reviews. Proteins of Animal Cell Plasma Membranes — PCPMDN
Annual Research Reviews. Regulation of Growth Hormone Secretion — Annu Res Rev Regul Growth Horm Secretion
Annual Research Reviews. Regulation of Growth Hormone Secretion — RGHSDH
Annual Research Reviews. Renal Prostaglandins — Annu Res Rev Renal Prostaglandins
Annual Research Reviews. Renal Prostaglandins — RPRODG
Annual Research Reviews. Renin — Annu Res Rev Renin
Annual Research Reviews. Renin — RENID3
Annual Research Reviews. Rheumatoid Arthritis and Related Conditions — Annu Res Rev Rheum Arthritis Relat Cond
Annual Research Reviews. Rheumatoid Arthritis and Related Conditions — RACND3
Annual Research Reviews. Somatostatin — Annu Res Rev Somatostatin
Annual Research Reviews. Somatostatin — SMTSDS
Annual Research Reviews. Sphingolipidoses and Allied Disorders — Annu Res Rev Sphingolipidoses Allied Disord
Annual Research Reviews. Sphingolipidoses and Allied Disorders — SADID4
Annual Research Reviews. Substance P — Annu Res Rev Subst P
Annual Research Reviews. Substance P — SUBPDJ

Annual Research Reviews. Ultrastructural Pathology of Human Tumors — Annu Res Rev Ultrastruct Pathol Hum Tumors
Annual Research Reviews. Ultrastructural Pathology of Human Tumors — UPHTDE
Annual Research Reviews. Vitamin-Trace Mineral-Protein Interactions — Annu Res Rev Vitam Trace Miner Protein Interact
Annual Research Reviews. Vitamin-Trace Mineral-Protein Interactions — VTMIDB
Annual Review. Academy of Natural Sciences of Philadelphia — Ann Rev Acad Nat Sci Philad
Annual Review and History of Literature — Annual Rev Hist Lit
Annual Review. Australian Mineral Industry — Ann Rev Austr Min Ind
Annual Review in Automatic Programming — Annu Rev Autom Program
Annual Review. Institute of Plasma Physics. Nagoya University — Annu Rev Inst Plasma Phys Nagoya
Annual Review. Institute of Plasma Physics. Nagoya University — Annu Rev Inst Plasma Phys Nagoya Univ
Annual Review of Analytical Chemistry — Ann Rev Analyt Chem
Annual Review of Anthropology — Ann R Anthr
Annual Review of Anthropology — Annu Rev Anthropol
Annual Review of Anthropology — ARAPCW
Annual Review of Applied Linguistics — ARAL
Annual Review of Astronomy and Astrophysics — Ann R Astro
Annual Review of Astronomy and Astrophysics — Annu Rev Astron Astrophys
Annual Review of Astronomy and Astrophysics — ARAA
Annual Review of Astronomy and Astrophysics — ARAAA
Annual Review of Behavior Therapy Theory and Practice — Annu Rev Behav Ther Theory Pract
Annual Review of Behavior Therapy Theory and Practice — ARBPD4
Annual Review of Biochemical and Allied Research in India — Annu Rev Biochem Allied Res India
Annual Review of Biochemical and Allied Research in India — ARBRA7
Annual Review of Biochemistry — A Rev Biochem
Annual Review of Biochemistry — Ann R Bioch
Annual Review of Biochemistry — Ann Rev Biochem
Annual Review of Biochemistry — Annu Rev Biochem
Annual Review of Biochemistry — ARBOA
Annual Review of Biochemistry — ARBOAW
Annual Review of Biophysics and Bioengineering — ABPBBK
Annual Review of Biophysics and Bioengineering — Ann R Bioph
Annual Review of Biophysics and Bioengineering — Annu Rev Biophys Bioeng
Annual Review of Biophysics and Biomolecular Structure — Annu Rev Biophys Biomol Struct
Annual Review of Biophysics and Biophysical Chemistry — Annu Rev Biophys Biophys Chem
Annual Review of Biophysics and Biophysical Chemistry — ARBCEY
Annual Review of Cell and Developmental Biology — Annu Rev Cell Dev Biol
Annual Review of Cell Biology — Annu Rev Cell Biol
Annual Review of Cell Biology — ARCBE2
Annual Review of Chemotherapy and Physiatrics of Cancer — Annu Rev Chemother Physiatr Cancer
Annual Review of Chronopharmacology — Annu Rev Chronopharmacol
Annual Review of Chronopharmacology — ANRCEI
Annual Review of Clinical Biochemistry — Annu Rev Clin Biochem
Annual Review of Earth and Planetary Sciences — Ann R Earth
Annual Review of Earth and Planetary Sciences — Annu Rev Earth Planet Sci
Annual Review of Ecology and Systematics — A Rev Ecol Syst
Annual Review of Ecology and Systematics — Ann R Ecol
Annual Review of Ecology and Systematics — Ann Rev Ecol
Annual Review of Ecology and Systematics — Ann Rev Ecol Sys
Annual Review of Ecology and Systematics — Annu Rev Ecol Syst
Annual Review of Ecology and Systematics — ARECB
Annual Review of Ecology and Systematics — ARECBC
Annual Review of Energy — Annu Rev Energy
Annual Review of Energy — AREND
Annual Review of Entomology — A Rev Ent
Annual Review of Entomology — Ann R Entom
Annual Review of Entomology — Ann Rev Ent
Annual Review of Entomology — Ann Rev Entomol
Annual Review of Entomology — Annu Rev Entomol
Annual Review of Entomology — ARENA
Annual Review of Entomology — ARENAA
Annual Review of Fluid Mechanics — Ann R Fluid
Annual Review of Fluid Mechanics — Annu Rev Fluid Mech
Annual Review of Fluid Mechanics — ARVFA
Annual Review of Fluid Mechanics — ARVFA3
Annual Review of Food Technology — Annu Rev Food Technol
Annual Review of Food Technology [*Mysore*] — ARFTAX
Annual Review of Food Technology (Mysore) — Annu Rev Food Technol (Mysore)
Annual Review of Genetics — A Rev Genet
Annual Review of Genetics — Ann R Genet
Annual Review of Genetics — Ann Rev Gen
Annual Review of Genetics — Annu Rev Genet
Annual Review of Genetics — ARVGB
Annual Review of Genetics — ARVGB7
Annual Review of Gerontology and Geriatrics — ARGG
Annual Review of Heat Transfer — Annu Rev Heat Transfer
Annual Review of Immunology — Annu Rev Immunol
Annual Review of Immunology — ARIMDU
Annual Review of Information Science and Technology — Ann R Infor
Annual Review of Information Science and Technology [*Encyclopedia Britannica*] — Annu Rev Inf Sci Technol
Annual Review of Information Science and Technology — ARISBC
Annual Review of Jazz Studies — Ann Rev Jazz Studies
Annual Review of Jazz Studies — Jazz Studies
Annual Review of Materials Science — Ann R Mater
Annual Review of Materials Science — Annu Rev Mater Sci
Annual Review of Medicine — Ann R Med
Annual Review of Medicine — Ann Rev Med
Annual Review of Medicine — Annu Rev Med
Annual Review of Medicine — ARMCA
Annual Review of Medicine — ARMCAH
Annual Review of Microbiology — A Rev Microbiol
Annual Review of Microbiology — Ann R Micro
Annual Review of Microbiology — Ann Rev Microbiol
Annual Review of Microbiology — Annu Rev Microbiol
Annual Review of Microbiology — ARMIA
Annual Review of Microbiology — ARMIAZ
Annual Review of Neuroscience — Annu Rev Neurosci
Annual Review of Neuroscience — ARNSD5
Annual Review of Nuclear and Particle Science — Annu Rev Nucl Part Sci
Annual Review of Nuclear and Particle Science — ANUSDC
Annual Review of Nuclear and Particle Science — ARPSD
Annual Review of Nuclear Science [*Later, Annual Review of Nuclear and Particle Science*] — Ann R Nucl
Annual Review of Nuclear Science [*Later, Annual Review of Nuclear and Particle Science*] — Ann Rev Nucl Sci
Annual Review of Nuclear Science [*Later, Annual Review of Nuclear and Particle Science*] — Ann Rev Nuclear Sci
Annual Review of Nuclear Science [*Later, Annual Review of Nuclear and Particle Science*] — Annu Rev Nucl Sci
Annual Review of Nuclear Science [*Later, Annual Review of Nuclear and Particle Science*] — ARNUA
Annual Review of Nuclear Science [*Later, Annual Review of Nuclear and Particle Science*] — ARNUA8
Annual Review of Numerical Fluid Mechanics and Heat Transfer — Annu Rev Numer Fluid Mech Heat Transfer
Annual Review of Nursing Research — Annu Rev Nurs Res
Annual Review of Nutrition — Annu Rev Nutr
Annual Review of Nutrition — ARNTD8
Annual Review of Petroleum Technology (London) — Annu Rev Pet Technol (London)
Annual Review of Pharmacology [*Later, Annual Review of Pharmacology and Toxicology*] — Ann R Pharm
Annual Review of Pharmacology [*Later, Annual Review of Pharmacology and Toxicology*] — Ann Rev Pharm
Annual Review of Pharmacology [*Later, Annual Review of Pharmacology and Toxicology*] — Ann Rev Pharmacol
Annual Review of Pharmacology [*Later, Annual Review of Pharmacology and Toxicology*] — Annu Rev Pharmacol
Annual Review of Pharmacology — Annual Rev Pharmacol
Annual Review of Pharmacology [*Later, Annual Review of Pharmacology and Toxicology*] — ARVPA
Annual Review of Pharmacology [*Later, Annual Review of Pharmacology and Toxicology*] — ARVPAX
Annual Review of Pharmacology and Toxicology — A Rev Pharmac Toxic
Annual Review of Pharmacology and Toxicology — Annu Rev Pharm Tox
Annual Review of Pharmacology and Toxicology — Annu Rev Pharmacol Toxicol
Annual Review of Pharmacology and Toxicology — ARPTD
Annual Review of Pharmacology and Toxicology — ARPTDI
Annual Review of Photochemistry — Annu Rev Photochem
Annual Review of Physical Chemistry — Ann R Ph Ch
Annual Review of Physical Chemistry — Ann Rev Phys Chem
Annual Review of Physical Chemistry — Annu Rev Phys Chem
Annual Review of Physical Chemistry — ARPLA
Annual Review of Physiology — Ann R Physl
Annual Review of Physiology — Ann Rev Physiol
Annual Review of Physiology — Annu Rev Physiol
Annual Review of Physiology — Annual Rev Physiol
Annual Review of Physiology — ARPHA
Annual Review of Physiology — ARPHAD
Annual Review of Phytopathology — A Rev Phytopath
Annual Review of Phytopathology — Ann R Phyto
Annual Review of Phytopathology — Ann Rev Phytopath
Annual Review of Phytopathology — Annu Rev Phytopathol
Annual Review of Phytopathology — Annual Rev Phytopathol
Annual Review of Phytopathology — APPYA
Annual Review of Phytopathology — APPYAG
Annual Review of Plant Physiology — A Rev Pl Physiol
Annual Review of Plant Physiology — Ann R Plant
Annual Review of Plant Physiology — Ann Rev Plant Physiol
Annual Review of Plant Physiology — Annu Rev Plant Physiol
Annual Review of Plant Physiology — ARPPA
Annual Review of Plant Physiology — ARPPA3
Annual Review of Plant Physiology and Plant Molecular Biology — Annu Rev Plant Physiol Plant Mol Biol
Annual Review of Progress in Applied Computational Electromagnetics — Annu Rev Prog Appl Comput Electromagn
Annual Review of Psychology — A Rev Psychol
Annual Review of Psychology — Ann R Psych
Annual Review of Psychology — Annu Rev Psychol
Annual Review of Psychology — ARPSA
Annual Review of Psychology — ARPSAC
Annual Review of Psychology — GRSI
Annual Review of Public Health — Annu Rev Public Health
Annual Review of Public Health — AREHDT
Annual Review of Public Health — ARPH
Annual Review of Rehabilitation — Annu Rev Rehabil

Annual Review of Rehabilitation — ARREEI
Annual Review of Sociology — Ann R Sociol
Annual Review of Sociology — Annu Rev Sociol
Annual Review of Sociology — ARVSDB
Annual Review of Sociology — GRSS
Annual Review of the Chemical Industry, 1981. Economic Commission for Europe — ECE Chem
Annual Review of the Schizophrenic Syndrome — Annu Rev Schizophr Syndr
Annual Review of the Schizophrenic Syndrome — SZCSAV
Annual Review of the Social Sciences of Religion — A R Soc Sci Rel
Annual Review. Residential Care Association — Annual R Residential Care Assoc
Annual Review. Rubber Research Institute of Sri Lanka — Annu Rev Rubber Res Inst Sri Lanka
Annual Reviews of Computational Physics — Annu Rev Comput Phys
Annual Reviews of Computational Physics — Annual Rev Comput Phys
Annual Reviews of Industrial and Engineering Chemistry — Annu Rev Ind Eng Chem
Annual Reviews of Plant Sciences — ALSSDM
Annual Reviews of Plant Sciences — Annu Rev Plant Sci
Annual Romantic Bibliography — Annu Romant Bibliogr
Annual Sanitary Report of the Province of Assam — Ann San Rep Prov Assam
Annual Scientific Meeting. Aerospace Medical Association — Annu Sci Meet Aerosp Med Assoc
Annual Scientific Papers. Higher Medical Institute. Varna — Annu Sci Pap Higher Med Inst Varna
Annual Scientific Papers. Medical Academy. Faculty of Medicine. Varna — Annu Sci Pap Med Acad Fac Med Varna
Annual Seminar on Theoretical Physics. Proceedings — Annu Semin Theor Phys Proc
Annual Simulation Symposium (Record of Proceedings) — Annu Simul Symp (Rec Proc)
Annual Southwestern IEEE [*Institute of Electrical and Electronics Engineering*] **Conference and Exhibition. Record** — Annu Southwest IEEE Conf Exhib Rec
Annual Statistical Summary. Michigan. Geological Survey Division — Annu Stat Summ Mich Geol Surv Div
Annual Statistical Summary. Michigan Geological Survey Division — MGSDA
Annual Survey of African Law — Annu Surv of Afr L
Annual Survey of African Law — ASAL
Annual Survey of American Chemistry. National Research Council — Annu Surv Am Chem Nat Res Counc
Annual Survey of American Law — An Sur Am L
Annual Survey of American Law — Ann Surv Am L
Annual Survey of American Law — Ann Survey Am L
Annual Survey of American Law — Annu Surv of Amer L
Annual Survey of American Law — ASAL
Annual Survey of American Law — IASA
Annual Survey of Colleges [*Database*] — ASC
Annual Survey of Commonwealth Law — Ann Surv Comm L
Annual Survey of Commonwealth Law — Ann Surv Commonw L
Annual Survey of Commonwealth Law — ASCL
Annual Survey of English Law — ASEL
Annual Survey of Indian Law — Annu Surv of Indian L
Annual Survey of Indian Law — ASIL
Annual Survey of Law — Ann Surv Law
Annual Survey of Law — Ann Surv of Law
Annual Survey of Law — ASL
Annual Survey of Manufacturers. AS-1. General Statistics for Industry Groups and Industries — ASM-1
Annual Survey of Manufacturers. AS-2. Value of Product Shipments — ASM-2
Annual Survey of Manufacturers. M81AS-4. Expenditures for Plant and Equipment — ASM M81AS-4
Annual Survey of Manufacturers. M81AS-5. Orgin of Exports of Manufactured Products — ASM M81AS-5
Annual Survey of Manufactures [*Database*] — ASM
Annual Survey of Massachusetts Law — Ann Surv Mass L
Annual Survey of Massachusetts Law — Ann Surv Mass Law
Annual Survey of Organometallic Chemistry — Annu Surv Organomet Chem
Annual Survey of Photochemistry — Annu Surv Photochem
Annual Survey of Research in Pharmacy — Annual Surv Res Pharm
Annual Survey of South African Law — Ann Surv SAL
Annual Survey of South African Law — Annu Surv of South Afr L
Annual Survey of South African Law — ASSAL
Annual. Swedish Theological Institute — ASTI
Annual Symposium. American College of Cardiology — Annu Symp Am Coll Cardiol
Annual Symposium. East African Academy. Proceedings — Annu Symp East Afr Acad Proc
Annual Symposium. Eastern Pennsylvania Branch, American Society for Microbiology. Proceedings — Annu Symp East PA Branch Am Soc Microbiol Proc
Annual Symposium in Botany — Annu Symp Bot
Annual Symposium in Plant Physiology — Annu Symp Plant Physiol
Annual Symposium. International College of Applied Nutrition — Annu Symp Int Coll Appl Nutr
Annual Symposium on Biomathematics and Computer Science in the Life Sciences. Abstracts — Annu Symp Biomath Comput Sci Life Sci Abstr
Annual Symposium on Biomathematics and Computer Science in the Life Sciences. Abstracts — SBCABE
Annual Symposium on Foundations of Computer Science (Proceedings) — Annu Symp Found Comput Sci (Proc)
Annual Symposium on Fundamental Cancer Research. Proceedings — Annu Symp Fundam Cancer Res Proc
Annual Symposium on Instrumentation for the Process Industries. Proceedings — Annu Symp Instrum Process Ind Proc
Annual Symposium on Microlithography — Annu Symp Microlithogr
Annual Symposium on Nursing Faculty Practice — Annu Symp Nurs Fac Pract
Annual Symposium on Photomask Technology — Annu Symp Photomask Technol
Annual Symposium on Photomask Technology and Management — Annu Symp Photomask Technol Manage
Annual Symposium on Radio and Space Sciences. Invited Special Articles — Annu Symp Radio Space Sci Invited Spec Artic
Annual Symposium on the Scientific Basis of Medicine — Annu Symp Sci Basis Med
Annual Symposium on Uranium and Precious Metals — Annu Symp Uranlum Precious Met
Annual Symposium. SSIEM (Society for the Study of Inborn Errors of Metabolism) — Annu Symp SSIEM
Annual Systems and Processing Salaries Report — Ann Sys Process Sal Rep
Annual Technical and Management Conference. Reinforced Plastics Division. Society of the Plastics Industry — Annu Tech Manage Conf Reinf Plast Div Soc Plast Ind
Annual Technical Conference. American Electroplaters' Society — Annu Tech Conf Am Electroplat Soc
Annual Technical Conference. American Electroplaters' Society — ATCSD
Annual Technical Conference Proceedings. Irrigation Association — Annu Tech Conf Proc Irrig Assoc
Annual Technical Conference Proceedings. Society of Vacuum Coaters — Annu Tech Conf Proc Soc Vac Coaters
Annual Technical Conference Proceedings. Sprinkler Irrigation Association — Annu Tech Conf Proc Sprinkler Irrig Assoc
Annual Technical Conference. Society of Plastics Engineers — Annu Tech Conf Soc Plast Eng
Annual Technical Conference Transactions. American Society for Quality Control — Annu Tech Conf Trans Am Soc Qual Control
Annual Technical Meeting. Petroleum Society of CIM. Preprints — Annu Tech Meet Pet Soc CIM Prepr
Annual Technical Symposium. SPIE. (Society of Photo-Optical Instrumentation Engineers) Proceedings — Annu Tech Symp SPIE Proc
Annual Tennessee Air Quality Report. State and Local — Ann Tenn Air Qual Rep St Loc
Annual Testis Workshop — Annu Testis Workshop
Annual Texas Conference. Utilization of Atomic Energy — Annu Tex Conf Util At Energy
Annual UMR-DNR [*University of Missouri, Rolla - Department of Natural Resources*] **Conference on Energy. Proceedings** — Annu UMR-DNR Conf Energy Proc
Annual UMR-DNR [*University of Missouri, Rolla - Department of Natural Resources*] **Conference on Energy. Proceedings** — AUCPD
Annual UMR-MEC [*University of Missouri, Rolla-Missouri Energy Council*] **Conference on Energy. Proceedings** — Annu UMR-MEC Conf Energy Proc
Annual Uranium Seminar. Proceedings — Annu Uranium Semin Proc
Annual Visiting Lecture Series. College of Pharmacy. University of Texas — Annu Visit Lect Ser Coll Pharm Univ Tex
Annual Volume. Institute of Marine Engineers — Annu Vol Inst Mar Eng
Annual Western Plastics for Tooling Conference — Annu West Plast Tool Conf
Annual Winter Conference on Brain Research — Annu Winter Conf Brain Res
Annual Workshop. Chemistry and Biochemistry of Herbicides — Annu Workshop Chem Biochem Herbic
Annual Workshop for Pesticide Residue Analysts (Western Canada) — Annu Workshop Pestic Residue Anal (West Can)
Annual World Conference on Magnesium. Proceedings — Annu World Conf Magnesium Proc
Annuale Mediaevale — AM
Annuale Mediaevale — AnM
Annuale Mediaevale — Ann Med
Annuale Mediaevale — Ann Mediaev
Annuals. Research Institute of Environmental Medicine. Nagoya University — Annu Res Inst Environ Med Nagoya Univ
Annuario. Accademia delle Scienze di Torino — Ann Ac Torino
Annuario. Accademia Etrusca di Cortona — AAEC
Annuario. Accademia Etrusca di Cortona — Ann Ac Etr
Annuario. Accademia Etrusca di Cortona — Annuario Ac Etr
Annuario. Accademia Etrusca di Cortona — Annuario Acc Etr Cortona
Annuario Accademico. Regia Universita degli Studi de Siena — Annu Accad Univ Stud
Annuario. Associazione Ottica Italiana — Annu Ass Ott Ital
Annuario Astronomico. Osservatorio Astronomico. Universita di Torino — Annu Astron Osserv
Annuario Chimico Italiano — Annuario Chim Ital
Annuario di Diritto Comparato e di Studi Legislativi — Ann Dir Comp
Annuario di Politica Internazionale — Annu Polit Int
Annuario di Statistica Agraria (Italy) — (Italy) Agr
Annuario di Studi Ebraici — ASE
Annuario di Studi Ebraici. Collegio Rabbinico Italiano [*Rome*] — AnStEbr
Annuario. Istituto di Sperimentazione per la Chimica Agraria in Torino — Annu Ist Sper Chim Agrar Torino
Annuario. Istituto Giapponese di Cultura in Roma — AIGC
Annuario. Liceo Ginnasio G. Mameli — ALGGM
Annuario. Liceo Ginnasio Statale G. Palmieri — ALGP
Annuario. Pontificia Accademia delle Scienze — Annu Pontif Accad Sci
Annuario. Reale Accademia d'Italia — Annu Accad Ital
Annuario. Reale Accademia d'Italia — Annu R Accad Ital
Annuario. Reale Accademia d'Italia — ARAI
Annuario. Reale Scuola Archeologica di Atene — ASAA
Annuario. Reale Scuola Superiore di Agricoltura di Portici — Annuario Reale Scuola Super Agric Portici
Annuario. Reale Universita di Modena — Annu Univ Modena
Annuario. Regia Scuola Archeologica Italiana di Atene — ARSIA

Annuario. Scuola Archeologica di Atene e delle Missioni Italiani in Oriente — Ann d R Scuol Arch Aten Miss Ital Oriente
Annuario. Scuola Archeologica di Atene e delle Missioni Italiani in Oriente — Ann Sc At
Annuario. Scuola Archeologica di Atene e delle Missioni Italiani in Oriente — Annuar Scuola Arch Atene
Annuario. Scuola Archeologica di Atene e delle Missioni Italiani in Oriente — Annuario Sc Archeol Atene
Annuario. Scuola Archeologica di Atene e delle Missioni Italiani in Oriente — ASA
Annuario. Scuola Archeologica di Atene e delle Missioni Italiani in Oriente — ASAIO
Annuario. Scuola Archeologica di Atene e Missioni Italiane in Oriente — A S Atene
Annuario. Scuola Archeologica di Atene e Missioni Italiane in Oriente — Ann Scu Archeol Atene
Annuario. Scuola Archeologica di Atene e Missioni Italiani in Oriente — Ann Sc At
Annuario. Scuola Archeologica di Atene e Missioni Italiani in Oriente — Annuario At
Annuario Statistico Italiano — Italy Ann
Annuario. Stazione Chimico-Agraria Sperimentale di Torino — Annu Sta Chim-Agr Sper Torino
Annuario. Stazione Sperimentale Agraria di Torino — Annu Stn Sper Agrar Torino
Annuario. Universita Cattolica del Sacro Cuore — AUCC
Annuarium des Roomsch-Katholieke Studenten in Nederland — ARKSN
Annuarium Historiae Conciliorum — AHC
Annuarium van de Apologetische Vereeniging (Petrus Canisius) — AAVPC
Ano Cultural Espanol — Ano Cult Esp
Anodes for Electrowinning. Proceedings. Sessions held at the AIME Annual Meeting — Anodes Electrowinning Proc Sess AIME Annu Meet
Anodic Behavior of Metals and Semiconductors Series — Anodic Behav Met Semicond Ser
Anodnaya Zashchita Metallov. Doklady Mezhvuzovskoi Konferentsii — Anodnaya Zashch Met Dokl Mezhvuz Konf
Anomalous Nuclear Effects in Deuterium/Solid Systems — Anomalous Nucl Eff Deuterium Solid Syst
Anorexia Nervosa. Multidisciplinary Conference of Anorexia Nervosa — Anorexia Nerv Multidisciplinary Conf
Anorganische und Allgemeine Chemie in Einzeldarstellungen — Anorg Allg Chem Einzel
Anotaciones Pediatricas [*Colombia*] — Anot Pediatr
ANPA/RI [*American Newspaper Publishers Association. Research Institute*] **Bulletin** — ANPA/RI Bull
ANPHI [*Academy of Nursing of the Philippines*] **Papers** — ANPHI Pap
ANPI. Dossier Technique — ANPI Dossier Tech
ANQ — IANQ
Anritsu Technical Bulletin — Anritsu Tech Bull
ANS. Advances in Nursing Science — ANS Adv Nurs Sci
ANS Topical Meeting. Gas-Cooled Reactors. HTGR (High-Temperature Gas-Cooled Reactor) and GCFBR (Gas-Cooled Fast Breeder Reactor) — ANS Top Meet Gas Cooled React HTGR GCFBR
ANSA (Antibiotik Ve Ilac Hammaddeleri Sanayii AS) Tip Bulteni — ANSA Tip Bul
ANSI [*American National Standards Institute*] **Reporter** — ANRTB
ANSI [*American National Standards Institute*] **Reporter** — ANSI Reptr
ANSI [*American National Standards Institute*] **Standards** — ANSI Stand
ANSI [*American National Standards Institute*] **Standards Action** — ANSDB
ANSI [*American National Standards Institute*] **Standards Action** — ANSI Std Action
Antaeus — PANT
Antaios — Ant
Antara Financial and Economic News [*Jakarta*] — FEN
Antarctic — ANTA
Antarctic Geological Map Series [*Tokyo*] — Antarct Geol Map Ser
Antarctic Geology. Proceedings. International Symposium on Antarctic Geology — Antarct Geol Proc Int Symp
Antarctic Geoscience. Symposium on Antarctic Geology and Geophysics — Antarct Geosci Symp Antarct Geol Geophys
Antarctic Journal of the United States — AJUS
Antarctic Journal of the United States — Antar Jour US
Antarctic Journal of the United States — Antarct J US
Antarctic Journal of the United States — Antarctic J
Antarctic Journal. United States — Antarc J US
Antarctic Meteorite Bibliography [*Database*] — AMB
Antarctic Nutrient Cycles and Food Webs. SCAR (Scientific Committee on Antarctic Research) Symposium on Antarctic Biology — Antarct Nutr Cycles Food Webs SCAR Symp Antarct Biol
Antarctic Record [*Japan*] — ANTAR
Antarctic Record — Antarct Rec
Antarctic Record [*New Zealand*] — ANTR
Antarctic Record (Tokyo) — Antarct Rec (Tokyo)
Antarctic Research Series — Antarct Res Ser
Antarctic Research Series — ANTRS
Antarctic Science — ANS
Antarctic Science — ANSC
Antarktika Doklady Komissii — Antarktika Doklady Kom
Antennas and Propagation Society. International Symposium — Antennas Propag Soc Int Symp
Antennas and Propagation Society. International Symposium — IAPSB
Anthologia Graeca — AG
Anthologia Graeca — Anth Graec
Anthologia Lyrica Graeca — Anth Lyr
Anthologia Lyrica Graeca — Anth Lyr Graec
Anthologia Lyrica Graeca — Anth Lyr Graeca
Anthologia Palatina — Anthol Palatina
Anthologica Annua. Publicaciones. Instituto Espanol de Estudios Eclesiasticos — Anthol Annua
Anthologica. Archivio di Sintesi Dermatologica — Anthol Arch Sint Dermatol
Anthologica Medica Dermatologica — Anthol Med Dermatol
Anthologica Medica Santoriana — Anthol Med Santoriana
Anthracite Conference of Lehigh University — Anthracite Conf Lehigh Univ
Anthropologia Hungarica — Anthr H
Anthropologia Hungarica — Anthr Hung
Anthropologiai Koezlemenyek [*Budapest*] — Anthr K
Anthropologiai Koezlemenyek — Anthr Kozl
Anthropologiai Koezlemenyek — Anthropol Koezlem
Anthropologiai Koezlemenyek — Anthropol Kozl
Anthropologiai Koezlemenyek (Hungary) — Anth (Hung)
Anthropologica — ANTH
Anthropologica — Anthrplgica
Anthropological Forum — Ant F
Anthropological Forum — Anthro Forum
Anthropological Forum — Anthropol Forum
Anthropological Index — Anthro I
Anthropological Index — Anthropol Index
Anthropological Index — Antrol
Anthropological Index to Current Periodicals in the Library of the Royal Anthropological Institute — AICP
Anthropological Institute. Journal — Anthrop J
Anthropological Journal of Canada — Anthr J Can
Anthropological Linguistics — AnL
Anthropological Linguistics — AnthL
Anthropological Linguistics — Anthr Ling
Anthropological Linguistics — Anthro Ling
Anthropological Linguistics — Anthrop Ling
Anthropological Linguistics — Anthrop Linguistics
Anthropological Linguistics — Anthropol Ling
Anthropological Linguistics; a Publication of the Archives of the Languages of the World. Indiana University. Anthropology Department — IU/AL
Anthropological Literature — Anthropol Lit
Anthropological Papers [*Smithsonian Institution*] — AP
Anthropological Papers. American Museum of Natural History — Anthr Pap
Anthropological Papers. American Museum of Natural History — Anthropol Pap Am Mus Nat Hist
Anthropological Papers. American Museum of Natural History — Anthropol Pap Amer Mus Nat Hist
Anthropological Papers. American Museum of Natural History — APAM
Anthropological Papers. American Museum of Natural History — APAMNH
Anthropological Papers. Museum of Anthropology. University of Michigan — Anthr P Mic
Anthropological Papers. Museum of Anthropology. University of Michigan — Anthropol Pap Mus Anthropol Univ Mich
Anthropological Papers. University of Alaska — APUA
Anthropological Quarterly — AnQu
Anthropological Quarterly — ANQU-A
Anthropological Quarterly — Anth Quart
Anthropological Quarterly — AnthQ
Anthropological Quarterly — Anthr Q
Anthropological Quarterly — Anthr Quart
Anthropological Quarterly — Anthrop Q
Anthropological Quarterly — Anthropol Quart
Anthropological Quarterly — GAQT
Anthropological Quarterly. Catholic University of America. Catholic Anthropological Conference — CUA/AQ
Anthropological Records. University of California — Anthropol Rec Univ Calif
Anthropological Report of Papua — Anthr Rep Pap
Anthropological Review — Anthrop R
Anthropological Review — Anthropol R
Anthropological Society of Bombay. Journal — AnSB
Anthropological Society of London. Memoirs — Anthropol Soc Lond Mem
Anthropologie [*Paris*] — L Anthrop
Anthropologie. Casopis Venovany Fysicke Anthropologii (Prague) — Anthropol (Pr)
Anthropologie (Hamburg) — Anthropol (H)
Anthropologie Marovske Muzeum — Anthropol MM
Anthropologie. Marovske Muzeum (Brno) — Anthropol(Brno)
Anthropologie (Paris) — Anthropol (P)
Anthropologie (Paris) — Anthropol(Paris)
Anthropologische Gesellschaft in Wien. Mitteilungen — Anthrop Gesell Wien Mitt
Anthropologische Gesellschaft in Wien. Mitteilungen — Anthropol Gesell In Wien Mitt
Anthropologische Gesellschaft in Wien. Sitzungsberichte — Anthropol Gesell In Wien Sitzungsb
Anthropologischer Anzeiger — Anthro Anz
Anthropologischer Anzeiger — Anthropol Anz
Anthropology Tomorrow — AT
Anthropology-UCLA — Anthr-UCLA
Anthroponymica Suecana — ASu
Anthropos — An
Anthropos — Ant
Anthropos — Anthr
Anthropos — Athr
Anthropos Internationale Zeitschrift fuer Voelker- und Sprachenkunde — Anthropos
Anti Nuclear — Anti Nk
Antibakterielle Chemotherapie in der Urologie. Norddeutsche Therapiegespraeche — Antibakt Chemother Urol Norddtsch Therapiegespraeche

Antibiotic Medicine — Antibiot Med
Antibiotic Medicine and Clinical Therapy — AMCTAH
Antibiotic Medicine and Clinical Therapy — Antibio Med Clin Ther
Antibiotic Medicine and Clinical Therapy — Antibiotic Med Clin Therapy
Antibiotic Medicine and Clinical Therapy (London) — Antibiot Med Clin Ther (London)
Antibiotic Medicine and Clinical Therapy (New York) — Antibiot Med Clin Ther (NY)
Antibiotica [*Bilingual Edition*] — ATIBA8
Antibiotica et Chemotherapia — Antibiot Chemother
Antibiotics [*Berlin*] — ANTBDO
Antibiotics and Chemotherapy — Antibiot and Chemother
Antibiotics and Chemotherapy — Antibiotics Chemother
Antibiotics and Chemotherapy (Basel) — Antibiot Chemother (Basel)
Antibiotics and Chemotherapy (Moscow) — Antibiot Chemother (Moscow)
Antibiotics and Chemotherapy (Osaka) — Antibiot Chemother Osaka
Antibiotics and Chemotherapy (Washington, DC) — Antibiot Chemother (Wash DC)
Antibiotics and Medical Biotechnology — AMBIEH
Antibiotics and Medical Biotechnology — Antibiot Med Biotechnol
Antibiotics and Other Secondary Metabolites. Biosynthesis and Production — Antibiot Other Second Metab Biosynth Prod
Antibiotics Annual — Antibiot Annu
Antibiotics Annual — Antibiot Annual
Antibiotics Monographs — Antibiot Monogr
Antibiotics, Vitamins, and Hormones — Antibiot Vitam Horm
Antibiotiki [*Moscow*] — ANTBAL
Antibiotiki — Antibiot
Antibiotiki i Khimioterapiya — Antib Khim
Antibiotiki i Khimioterapiya — Antibiot Khimioter
Antibiotiki i Meditsinskaya Biotekhnologiya — AMBIEH
Antibiotiki i Meditsinskaya Biotekhnologiya — Antibiot Med Biotekhnol
Antibiotiki Respublikanskii Mezhvedomstvennyi Sbornik — ANBKAQ
Antibiotiki Respublikanskii Mezhvedomstvennyi Sbornik — Antibiot Resp Mezhved Sb
Antibodies in Human Diagnosis and Therapy — Antibodies Hum Diagn Ther
Antibody, Immunoconjugates, and Radiopharmaceuticals — Antibody Immunoconjugates Radiopharm
Anti-Cancer Drug Design — Anti-Cancer Drug Des
Anticancer Research — Anticancer Res
Anticancer Research — ANTRD
Anticancer Research — ANTRD4
Antichita Altoadriatiche — AAAd
Antichita Classica e Cristiana — AClCr
Antichita Pisane — Ant Pis
Antichnaia Drevnost'i Srednie Veka [*Sverdlovsk*] — ADSV
Antichnyi Mir i Arkheologiia [*Saratov*] — AMA
Antichthon. Journal of the Australian Society for Classical Studies — Ant
Anti-Corrosion Methods and Materials — Anti-Corr Meth Mat
Anti-Corrosion Methods and Materials — Anti-Corros
Anti-Corrosion Methods and Materials — Anti-Corros Methods Mater
Anti-Corrosion Methods and Materials — Anti-Corrosion
Anti-Corrosion Methods and Materials — Anti-Corrosion Meth & Mat
Anti-Corrosion Methods and Materials — Anti-Corrosion Methods Mats
Antidepressant Drugs. Proceedings. International Symposium — Antidepressant Drugs Proc Int Symp
Antifungal Compounds — Antifungal Compd
Antigonish Review — AnR
Antigonish Review — Antigon Rev
Antigonish Review — AntigR
Antiinflammatory Agents. Chemistry and Pharmacology — Antiinflammatory Agents Chem Pharmacol
Antik Tanalmanyok [*Budapest*] — An Tan
Antik Tanulmanyok — AT
Antike [*Berlin und Leipzig*] — A
Antike — Ant
Antike, Alte Sprachen und Deutsche Bildung — AntAS
Antike Denkmaeler — Ant Denk
Antike Denkmaeler. Kaiserliches Deutsches Archaeologisches Institut — AD
Antike Denkmaeler. Kaiserliches Deutsches Archaeologisches Institut — Ant Denkm
Antike Gemmen in Deutschen Sammlungen — AGD
Antike Gemmen in Deutschen Sammlungen — AGDS
Antike Inschriften aus Jugoslavien — AIJ
Antike Kunst — AK
Antike Kunst — AnKu
Antike Kunst — Ant Kunst
Antike Kunst — AntK
Antike Muenzen und Geschnittene Steine — AMUGS
Antike Muenzen und Geschnittene Steine [*Berlin*] — Antike Mus Ges St
Antike Plastik — Ant Pl
Antike Plastik — AntP
Antike und Abendland — A & A
Antike und Abendland — Ant Ab
Antike und Abendland — Antike Aben
Antike und Abendland — Antike Abendl
Antike und Abendland — Au A
Antike und Christentum — A Ch
Antike und Christentum — AC
Antike und Christentum — Ant Chr
Antike und Christentum — Au C
Antike und Christentum — AuChr
Antike Welt [*Kuesnacht-Zuerich*] — AntWelt
Antike Welt — AW
Antiken Gemmen des Kunsthistorischen Museums in Wien — AGKMW
Antiken Muenzen Nord-Griechenlands — AMNG
Antiken Sarkophagreliefs — ASR
Antiken Sarkophagreliefs — SKR
Antikvarisk Tidskrift foer Sverige — Ant Tidskr
Antikvarisk Tidskrift foer Sverige — Antikv Tidskr Sverige
Antilliaans Juristenblad — AJ
Antilliaans Juristenblad — AJB
Antilliaanse Nieuwsbrief — AN
Antilliaanse Nieuwsbrief. Tweewekelijkse Uitgave van het Kabinet van de Gevolmachtigde Minister van de Nederlandse Antillen — ANT
Anti-Locust Bulletin — Anti-Locust Bull
Anti-Locust Memoir — Anti-Locust Mem
Anti-Locust Research Centre [*Later, Centre for Overseas Pest Research*] **Report** — Anti-Locust Res Cent Rep
Antimicrobial Agents and Chemotherapy — AMACC
Antimicrobial Agents and Chemotherapy — AMACCQ
Antimicrobial Agents and Chemotherapy — Antim Ag Ch
Antimicrobial Agents and Chemotherapy — Antimicrob Agents Chemother
Antimicrobial Agents Annual — Antimicrob Agents Annu
Antimicrobic Newsletter — Antimicrob Newsl
Antincendio — ANTIB
Antineoplastic and Immunosuppressive Agents — Antineoplast Immunosuppr Agents
Antineoplastische Chemotherapie — Antineoplast Chemother
Antinopolis Papyri — P Antin
Antioch Review — AnR
Antioch Review — Ant R
Antioch Review — Antioch R
Antioch Review — Antioch Rev
Antioch Review — AR
Antioch Review — PANR
Antioquia Medica — ANMDAQ
Antioquia Medica — Antioquia Med
Antioxidants in Therapy and Preventive Medicine — Antioxid Ther Prev Med
Antiproton-Nucleon and Antiproton-Nucleus Interactions — Antiproton Nucleon Antiproton Nucl Interact
Antiquarian Book Monthly Review — ABMR
Antiquarian Bookman — AB
Antiquarian Bookman — Ant Bk
Antiquarian Bookman — Antiq Bkman
Antiquarian Horological Society. Monograph — AHSM
Antiquarian Horology — Antiq Horol
Antiquarian Horology — Antiq Horology
Antiquarian Horology and the Proceedings of the Antiquarian Horological Society — Antiq Horology
Antiquaries Journal [*London*] — AJ
Antiquaries Journal — Antiq J
Antiquaries Journal — Antiq Jnl
Antiquaries Journal — Antiq Journ
Antiquaries Journal — Antiqu Journal
Antiquaries Journal — Antiquar J
Antiquaries Journal — Antiquaries J
Antiquaries Journal — Antiquaries Jnl
Antiquaries Journal — AntJ
Antiquaries Journal. Society of Antiquaries of London — Ant Journ
Antiquarische Gesellschaft in Zuerich. Mitteilungen — Antiq Gesell in Zuerich Mitt
Antiquary — Ant
Antiquary, Jewitt's — Antiquary
Antiquary (New Series) — Antiq (n s)
Antique Engines — Antique Eng
Antiques — Antiq
Antiques and Collecting Hobbies — GACH
Antiques in South Africa — Antiq S Afr
Antiques Journal — Antiques J
Antiquitaeten Rundschau — Antiq Rund
Antiquitaeten-Rundschau — AR
Antiquitas Hungarica — Ant H
Antiquitas Hungarica — AntHung
Antiquitas Hungarica — Antiqu Hung
Antiquitaten Rundschau — Antiquit Rundsch
Antiquite Classique — AC
Antiquite Classique — ACl
Antiquite Classique — An Cl
Antiquite Classique — Ant Cl
Antiquite Classique [*Brussels*] — Ant Class
Antiquite Classique — AntC
Antiquite Classique [*Brussels*] — Antiq Cl
Antiquite Classique — Antiq Class
Antiquite Classique — Antiqu Class
Antiquite Classique — Antiquite Cl
Antiquite Classique [*Brussels*] — L Ant Clas
Antiquite Classique [*Brussels*] — L'Ant Cl
Antiquites Africaines — Ant Afr
Antiquites Africaines — Antiq Afr
Antiquites Africaines — Antiqu Africaines
Antiquites Africaines — Antiquites Afr
Antiquites Nationales [*St.-Germain-En-Laye*] — Ant Nat
Antiquites Nationales — Antiq Nat
Antiquites Nationales — Antiqu Nationales
Antiquities of Athens — Ant Ath
Antiquities of Sunderland — Antiq Sunderland
Antiquity — A
Antiquity [*Gloucester*] — Ant
Antiquity — Antiq

Antiquity — Atqy
Antiquity — GANQ
Antiquity. A Quarterly Review of Archaeology. Antiquity Trust — AT/A
Antiquity and Survival — A and S
Antiquity and Survival — AaS
Antiquity and Survival [*The Hague*] — AnSur
Antiquity and Survival [*The Hague*] — AntSurv
Antiquity and Survival [*The Hague and Jerusalem*] — AS
Antisense and Nucleic Acid Drug Development — Antisense Nucleic Acid Drug Dev
Antisense Research and Development — Antisense Res Dev
Anti-Slavery Reporter and Aborigines' Friend — Anti Slav Rep Abor Friend
Antitrust and Trade Regulation Report [*Bureau of National Affairs*] — Antitrust & Trade Reg Rep
Antitrust and Trade Regulation Report [*Bureau of National Affairs*] — ATRR
Antitrust and Trade Regulation Report. Bureau of National Affairs — Antitrust & Trade Reg Rep BNA
Antitrust Bulletin — ANB
Antitrust Bulletin — Antitrust B
Antitrust Bulletin — Antitrust Bull
Antitrust Law and Economics Review — ALE
Antitrust Law and Economics Review — Antitr L and Ec R
Antitrust Law and Economics Review — Antitrust L & Econ Rev
Antitrust Law and Economics Review — Antitrust Law and Econ R
Antitrust Law and Economics Review — Antitrust Law Econ Rev
Antitrust Law Journal — Antitr LJ
Antitrust Law Journal — Antitrust LJ
Antitrust Law Symposium — Antitr Law Symp
Antitrust Law Symposium — Antitrust L Sym
Antitrust Newsletter — Antitrust Newsl
Antitumor Studies on Nitrocaphane (AT-1258) — Antitumor Stud Nitrocaphane (AT-1258)
Antiviral Research — Antiviral Res
Antiviral Research — AR
Antiviral Research — ARSRDR
Antiviral Therapy — Antiviral Ther
Antonianum — An
Antonianum — Anton
Antonianum Periodicum Trimetre Editumcura Professorum Pontificii Athenaei Antoniani de Urbe — Antonianum
Antonie Van Leeuwenhoek Journal of Microbiology — ANLEDR
Antonie van Leeuwenhoek Journal of Microbiology — Antonie Leeuwenhoek J Microbiol
Antonie Van Leeuwenhoek Journal of Microbiology and Serology [*Later, Antonie Van Leeuwenhoek Journal of Microbiology*] — A Van Leeuw
Antonie Van Leeuwenhoek Journal of Microbiology and Serology [*Later, Antonie Van Leeuwenhoek Journal of Microbiology*] — ALJMAO
Antonie Van Leeuwenhoek Journal of Microbiology and Serology [*Later, Antonie Van Leeuwenhoek Journal of Microbiology*] — Antonie Van Leewenhoek J Microbiol Serol
Antonie van Leeuwenhoek Nederlandsch Tijdschrift voor Hygiene, Microbiologie, en Serologie. Netherlands Society of Microbiology — Antonie Van Leeuwenhoek Ned Tijdschr Hyg
Antonio Tomas Pires. Livro de Homenagem — ATPLH
Antropoligia e Historia — Antrop Hist
Antropologia e Historia de Guatemala — AHG
Antropologia e Historia de Guatemala — Antrop Hist Guat
Antropologia (Santiago) — Antrop Santiago
Antropologia y Etnologia. CSIC (Consejo Superior de Investigaciones Cientificas) — Antrop Y Etnol
Antropologica — Antropologi
Antropologica [*Caracas*] — ATGAAT
Antropologica. Fundacion La Salle de Ciencias Naturales. Instituto Caribe de Antropologia y Sociologia — FSCN/A
Antropologica La Salle (Caracas) — Antrop Caracas
Antropologicky Archiv — ANOAAR
Antropologicky Archiv — Antropol Arch
Antwerpen; Tijdschrift der Stad Antwerpen — Antwerpen Tijdschr
Antwerpiensia — Antw
Antwerpsch Archievenblad — AA
Antybiotyki w Badaniu Procesow Biochemicznych — Antybiot Badaniu Procesow Biochem
ANU [*Australian National University*] **Historical Journal** — ANU Hist J
ANU [*Australian National University*] **Historical Journal** — ANU Hist Jnl
Anuar de Lingvistica si Istorie Literara — ALIL
Anuari. Institut d'Estudis Catalans — Anu Inst Est Catalans
Anuari. Institut d'Estudis Catalans. Seccio Historico-Arqueologica [*Barcelona*] — Anuari Inst
Anuari. Institut d'Estudis Catalans. Seccio Historico-Arqueologica — Anuari Inst Cat
Anuari. Oficina Romanica — AOR
Anuario. Academia Mexicana de Ciencias Exactas, Fisicas, y Naturales — Anuario Acad Mex Ci Exact
Anuario. Asociacion Francisco de Vitoria — AAFV
Anuario. Asociacion Francisco de Vitoria — Anu Asoc Francisco de Vitoria
Anuario Bago de Investigaciones Cientificas — Anu Bago Invest Cient
Anuario Bibliografico Cubano — AnBC
Anuario Brasileiro de Economia Florestal — Anu Bras Econ Florestal
Anuario Brasileiro de Economia Florestal — Anuario Brasil Econ Florest
Anuario Brasileiro de Economia Florestal. Instituto Nacional de Pinho — Anu Bras Econ Flor Inst Nac Pinho
Anuario Brasileiro de Odontologia — Anu Bras Odontol
Anuario. Centro de Edafologia y Biologia Aplicada de Salamanca — Anu Cent Edafol Biol Apl Salamanca
Anuario. Centro de Edafologia y Biologia Aplicada del CSIC (Centro de Edafologia y Biologia Aplicada) — Anu Cent Edafol Biol Apl CSIC
Anuario Centroamericano — ACA
Anuario Climatologico de Portugal — An Clim Port
Anuario Colombiano — AC
Anuario Colombiano de Historia Social y de la Cultura — ACHS
Anuario Colombiano de Historia Social y de la Cultura (Bogota) — Anuar Col Hist Soc Cult Bogota
Anuario. Comision Impulsora y Coordinadora de la Investigacion Cientifica — Anuario Comis Impuls Invest Ci
Anuario. Cuerpo Facultativo de Archiveros, Bibliotecarios, y Arqueologos [*Madrid*] — A Cuerp Fac
Anuario. Cuerpo Facultativo de Archiveros, Bibliotecarios, y Arqueologos [*Madrid*] — ACFA
Anuario da Literatura Brasileira — ALBr
Anuario de Biblioteconomia y Archivonomia (Mexico) — Anuar Bibliotec Archivon Mex
Anuario de Comercio Exterior de Mexico. Banco Nacional de Comercio Exterior — An Com Ext Mex Banco Nac Com Ext
Anuario de Derecho Penal y Ciencias Penales. Instituto Nacional de Estudios Juridicos — Anu Derecho Penal Ci Penales
Anuario de Derecho. Universidad de Panama — Anu Der Univ Panama
Anuario de Estudios Americanos — AnuE
Anuario de Estudios Americanos. Consejo Superior de Investigaciones Cientificas y Universidad de Sevilla, Escuela de Estudios Hispano-Americanos — EEHA/AEA
Anuario de Estudios Americanos. Escuela de Estudios Hispanoamericanos — Anu Est Am
Anuario de Estudios Americanos (Sevilla) — Anuar Estud Am Sevilla
Anuario de Estudios Atlanticos — AEA
Anuario de Estudios Atlanticos — Anu Estud Atl
Anuario de Estudios Centroamericanos — AEC
Anuario de Estudios Centroamericanos — Anuario Estud Centroam
Anuario de Estudios Medievales — AEM
Anuario de Filologia — AnuarioF
Anuario de Filologia. Facultad de Humanidades y Educacion (Maracaibo) — Anuar Filol Maracaibo
Anuario de Filosofia del Derecho — Anu de Filos del Derecho
Anuario de Geografia (Mexico) — Anuar Geogr Mex
Anuario de Historia de Derecho Espanol. Instituto Nacional de Estudios Juridicos. Ministerio de Justicia y CSIC (Consejo Superior de Investigaciones Cientificas) — Anu Hist Derecho Espan
Anuario de Historia del Derecho Espanol [*Madrid*] — AHD Esp
Anuario de Historia (Mexico) — Anuar Hist Mex
Anuario de la Economica Mexicana/Mexican Economy Annual — An Econ Mex Mex Econ
Anuario de la Historia del Derecho Espanol — AHDE
Anuario de la Historia del Derecho Espanol — An Hist Der
Anuario de Letras — AdL
Anuario de Letras. M — ALetM
Anuario de Letras (Mexico) — Anuar Letr Mex
Anuario de Prehistoria Madrilena — APM
Anuario de Psicologia (Guatemala) — Anuar Psicol Guat
Anuario. Departamento de Ingles [*Barcelona*] — ADI
Anuario do Distrito de Viana do Castelo — ADVC
Anuario Ecuatoriano de Derecho Internacional — Anu Ecuator Der Int
Anuario. Escuela de Biblioteconomia y Archivos (Caracas) — Anuar Escuela Bibl Arch Caracas
Anuario Estadistico de la Mineria Mexicana — Anu Estad Min Mex
Anuario Estadistico de Los Andes. Venezuela — An Estad Andes Venez
Anuario Estatistico Parana — An Estat Parana
Anuario. Facultad de Derecho — Anu Fac Der
Anuario. Facultad de Derecho — AYA
Anuario. Facultad de Derecho. Universidad de Los Andes — AFD
Anuario Filosofico — Anu Filosof
Anuario Hidrologico. Servicio Nacional de Meteorologia e Hidrologia — Anuario Hidrol
Anuario Indigenista — Anu Indig
Anuario Indigenista (Mexico) — Anuar Indig Mex
Anuario. Institut de'Estudios Catalans — AIEC
Anuario. Instituto de Antropologia e Historia (Caracas) — Anuar Inst Antrop Hist Caracas
Anuario. Instituto de Ciencias Penales y Criminologicas — Anu Inst Cienc Pen Criminol
Anuario. Instituto de Orientacion y Asistencia Tecnica del Oeste — AIOOD3
Anuario. Instituto de Orientacion y Asistencia Tecnica del Oeste — Anu Inst Orientac Asist Tec Oeste
Anuario. Instituto de Orientacion y Asistencia Tecnica del Oeste. Centro de Edafologia y Biologia Aplicada del CSIC — Anu Inst Orientac Asist Tec Oeste Cent Edafol Biol Apl CSIC
Anuario. Inter-American Institute for Musical Research (New Orleans) — Anuar Inter Am Inst Music Res New Orleans
Anuario Martiano — AMart
Anuario Mineral Brasileiro [*Brazil*] — Anu Miner Bras
Anuario Mineral Brasileiro — Anu Miner Brasil
Anuario Musical — An M
Anuario Musical — Anu Mus
Anuario Musical. Instituto Espanol de Musicologia. CSIC (Consejo Superior de Investigaciones Cientificas) — Anu Music
Anuario para o Estudo das Tradicoes Populares Portuguesas — AETPP
Anuario. Provincia de Caracas. Sociedad Economica de Amigos del Pais — Anuario Prov Caracas Soc Econ Amigos Pais
Anuario. Sociedad Folklorico de Mexico — ASFM
Anuario. Sociedade Broteriana — Anu Soc Broteriana
Anuario. Sociedade Broteriana — ASBRAE

Anuario Tecnico. Instituto de Pesquisas Zootecnicas "Francisco Osorio" — Anu Tec Inst Pesqui Zootec "Francisco Osorio"
Anuario Tecnico. Instituto de Pesquisas Zootecnicas "Francisco Osorio" — ATIAD8
Anuario Universidad de Los Andes — AUA
Anuarul Comisiunii Monumentelor Istorice. Sectia pentru Transilvania — ACM
Anuarul Comisiunii Monumentelor Istorice. Sectia Pentru Transilvania — ACM Tr
Anuarul Comisiunii Monumentelor Istorice. Sectia Pentru Transilvania — ACMI
Anuarul Comisiunii Monumentelor Istorice. Sectia Pentru Transilvania — ACMT
Anuarul Comisiunii Monumentelor Istorice. Sectia Pentru Transilvania — An Com Mon Trans
Anuarul. Comitetului de Stat al Geologiei. Republica Socialista Romania — Anu Com Stat Geol Repub Soc Rom
Anuarul Comitetului de Stat al Geologiei (Romania) — Anu Com Stat Geol (Rom)
Anuarul Comitetului Geologic (Romania) — Anu Com Geol Rom
Anuarul. Institutul de Studii Clasice — AICS
Anuarul. Institutul de Studii Clasice. Universitate din Cluj — Anu Inst Stud Cl
Anuarul Institutului de Istorie si Arheologie [*Cluj*] — AII Ar
Anuarul Institutului de Istorie si Arheologie [*Iasi*] — AIIA
Anuarul Institutului de Istorie si Arheologie [*Cluj*] — AIIC
Anuarul. Institutului de Istorie si Arheologie — Anu Inst Istor Arheologie
Anuarul Institutului de Istorie si Arheologie — Anul
Anuarul Institutului de Istorie si Arheologie (Cluj) — AIIAC
Anuarul. Institutului de Istorie si Arheologie (Cluj-Napoca) — An Inst (Cluj)
Anuarul. Institutului de Istorie si Arheologie (Cluj-Napoca) — An Inst Ist Arh (Cluj)
Anuarul Institutului de Istorie si Arheologie (Iasi) — AIIAI
Anuarul Institutului de Istorie si Arheologie (Iasi) — An Inst (Iasi)
Anuarul. Institutului de Patologie si Igiena Animala — Anu Inst Patol Ig Anim
Anuarul. Institutului de Patologie si Igiena Animala [*Bucuresti*] — APIGAT
Anuarul. Institutului de Patologie si Igiena Animala (Bucuresti) — Anu Inst Patol Ig Anim (Bucur)
Anuarul Institutului de Seruri si Vaccinuri Pasteur. Bucuresti — Anu Inst Seruri Vaccinuri Pasteur Bucuresti
Anuarul Institutului de Studii Classice [*Cluj*] — AISC
Anuarul Institutului de Studii Classice (Cluj) — A I St Cl
Anuarul Institutului de Studii Classice (Cluj) — An Inst Cluj
Anuarul. Institutului Geologic al Romaniei — AIGR
Anuarul. Institutului Geologic (Romania) — Anu Inst Geol (Rom)
Anuarul. Observatorului din Bucuresti — An Obs Buc
Anuarul. Universitatea Cluj — AUC
Anwendung von Isotopen in der Organischen Chemie und Biochemie — AISOBL
Anwendung von Isotopen in der Organischen Chemie und Biochemie — Anwend Isot Org Chem Biochem
ANZ [*Australia and New Zealand*] **Bank. Quarterly** — ANZ Bank Q
ANZ [*Australia and New Zealand*] **Bank. Quarterly Survey** — ANZ Quart Surv
ANZ [*Australia and New Zealand*] **Bank. Quarterly Survey** [*A publication*] — ANZ Sur
ANZ [*Australia and New Zealand*] **Bank. Quarterly Survey** [*A publication*] — ANZQ
ANZ [*Australia and New Zealand*] **Bank. Quarterly Survey** [*A publication*] — ANZQ Survey
ANZATVH [*Australian and New Zealand Association of Teachers of the Visually Handicapped*] **Newsletter** — ANZATVH Newsl
Anzeige von den Samlungen einer Privatgesellschaft in der Oberlausiz — Anz Saml Privatges Oberlausiz
Anzeigen der Churfuerstlichen Saechsischen Leipziger Oekonomischen Societaet — Anz Churfuerstl Saechs Leipziger Oekon Soc
Anzeigen der Koeniglich-Saechsischen Leipziger Oekonomischen Societaet — Anz Koenigl Saechs Leipziger Oekon Soc
Anzeigen der Kurfuerstlich Saechsischen Oberlausizischen Gesellschaft der Wissenschaften — Anz Kurfuerstl Saechs Oberlausiz Ges Wiss
Anzeigen der Oberlausitzischen Gesellschaft der Wissenschaften zu Goerlitz — Anz Oberlausitz Ges Wiss Goerlitz
Anzeiger. Akademie der Wissenschaften [*Vienna*] — AAW
Anzeiger. Akademie der Wissenschaften in Wien. Mathematisch-Naturwissenschaftliche Klasse — Anz Akad Wiss Wien Math Naturwiss Kl
Anzeiger. Akademie der Wissenschaften (Wien) — Anz (Wien)
Anzeiger der Akademie der Wissenschaften in Wien. Philosophisch-Historische Klasse — AAWWPH
Anzeiger der Akademie der Wissenschaften. Krakow — Anz Akad Wiss Krakow
Anzeiger der Akademie der Wissenschaften Wien — Anz Akad Wiss Wien
Anzeiger der Kaiserlichen Akademie der Wissenschaften in Wien. Mathematisch-Naturwissenschaftliche Klasse — Anz Kais Akad Wiss Wien Math Naturwiss Kl
Anzeiger der Oesterreichischen Akademie der Wissenschaften — Anz Oesterr Akad Wiss
Anzeiger der Oesterreichischen Akademie der Wissenschaften. Philosophisch-Historische Klasse — Anz OAW
Anzeiger der Oesterreichischen Akademie der Wissenschaften. Philosophisch-Historische Klasse — Anz Oe Ak
Anzeiger der Oesterreichischen Akademie der Wissenschaften. Philosophisch-Historische Klasse — Anz Oester Akad Wiss Phil Hist Kl
Anzeiger der Oesterreichischen Akademie der Wissenschaften. Philosophisch-Historische Klasse — Anz Oesterr Akad Wiss Phil Hist Klasse
Anzeiger der Oesterreichischen Akademie der Wissenschaften. Philosophisch-Historische Klasse (Wien) — Anz Ak (Wien)
Anzeiger der Oesterreichischen Akademie der Wissenschaften. Philosophisch-Historische Klasse (Wien) — Anz Akad (Wien)
Anzeiger der Oesterreichischen Akademie der Wissenschaften. Philosophisch-Historische Klasse (Wien) — Anz (Wien)
Anzeiger der Oesterreichischen Akademie der Wissenschaften. Philosophisch-Historische Klasse (Wien) — Anzeiger (Wien)
Anzeiger des Germanischen Nationalmuseums — Anz Germ Nationalmus
Anzeiger des Schlesischen Landesmuseums in Troppau — Anz Schles Landesmus Troppau
Anzeiger fuer Deutsches Altertum — Anz Dt Altert
Anzeiger fuer Deutsches Altertum — Anz f D Altert
Anzeiger fuer Deutsches Altertum und Deutsche Literatur — ADA
Anzeiger fuer die Altertumswissenschaft [*Innsbruck*] — AAW
Anzeiger fuer die Altertumswissenschaft — Anz Alt
Anzeiger fuer die Altertumswissenschaft — Anz Altertumsw
Anzeiger fuer die Altertumswissenschaft — Anz Altertumswiss
Anzeiger fuer die Altertumswissenschaft [*Innsbruck*] — AnzAltW
Anzeiger fuer die Altertumswissenschaft [*Innsbruck*] — AnzAW
Anzeiger fuer die Altertumswissenschaft. Herausgegeben von der Oesterreichischen Humanistischen Gesellschaft — AAHG
Anzeiger fuer Elsaessische Altertumskunde — AEAK
Anzeiger fuer Indogermanische Sprach- und Altertumskunde — AIdgSp
Anzeiger fuer Indogermanische Sprach- und Altertumskunde — AIF
Anzeiger fuer Ingenieure und Techniker — Anz Ing Tech
Anzeiger fuer Kunde der Deutschen Vorzeit — AKDV
Anzeiger fuer Maschinenwesen — Anz Maschinenwes
Anzeiger fuer Schaedlingskunde — Anz Schaedlingskd
Anzeiger fuer Schaedlingskunde, Pflanzen- und Umweltschutz [*Germany*] — Anz Schaedlingskd Pflanz- Umweltschutz
Anzeiger fuer Schaedlingskunde, Pflanzen- und Umweltschutz — Anz Schaedlingskd Pflanzen- und Umweltschutz
Anzeiger fuer Schaedlingskunde, Pflanzenschutz, Umweltschutz — Anz Schaedlingskd Pflanz
Anzeiger fuer Schaedlingskunde, Pflanzenschutz, Umweltschutz — Anz Schaedlingskd Pflanzenschutz Umweltschutz
Anzeiger fuer Schaedlingskunde und Pflanzenschutz [*Later, Anzeiger fuer Schaedlingskunde, Pflanzenschutz, Umweltschutz*] — Anz Schaedlingskd Pflanzenschutz
Anzeiger fuer Schweizerische Altertumskunde — Anz f Schw AK
Anzeiger fuer Schweizerische Altertumskunde — Anz Schw Alt
Anzeiger fuer Schweizerische Altertumskunde — Anz Schweiz
Anzeiger fuer Schweizerische Altertumskunde — Anz Schweiz AK
Anzeiger fuer Schweizerische Altertumskunde — Anz Schweiz Alt
Anzeiger fuer Schweizerische Altertumskunde — Anz Schweiz Altkde
Anzeiger fuer Schweizerische Altertumskunde — ASA
Anzeiger fuer Schweizerische Altertumskunde — ASAK
Anzeiger fuer Schweizerische Geschichte — Anz Schweiz Gesch
Anzeiger fuer Slavische Philologie — Anz Slav Philol
Anzeiger. Germanisches Nationalmuseum — AGN
Anzeiger. Germanisches Nationalmuseum — AGNM
Anzeiger. Germanisches Nationalmuseum — Anz Ger Nazionalmus
Anzeiger. Germanisches Nationalmuseum — Anz Germ Nat Mus
Anzeiger. Kaiserliche Akademie der Wissenschaften [*Wien*] — AKAW
Anzeiger. Oesterreichische Akademie der Wissenschaften [*Wien*]. Mathematisch-Naturwissenschaftliche Klasse — Anz Oesterr Akad Wiss Math Naturwiss Kl
Anzeiger. Oesterreichische Akademie der Wissenschaften. Mathematisch-Naturwissenschaftliche Klasse — Anz Osterr Akad Wiss Math-Naturwiss Kl
Anzeiger. Oesterreichische Akademie der Wissenschaften. Mathematisch-Naturwissenschaftliche Klasse — OSAWA8
Anzeiger. Oesterreichische Akademie der Wissenschaften [*Wien*]. Philosophisch-Historische Klasse — AOAW
Anzeiger. Oesterreichische Akademie der Wissenschaften (Wien) — Anz (Wien)
Anzeiger. Oesterreichische Akademie der Wissenschaften (Wien). Philosophisch-Historische Klasse — AAWW
Anzeiger. Ornithologische Gesellschaft in Bayern — Anz Orn Ges Bayern
Anzeiger. Ornithologische Gesellschaft in Bayern — Anz Ornithol Ges Bayern
Anzeiger. Ornithologische Gesellschaft in Bayern — AOGBAV
ANZHES [*Australian and New Zealand History of Education Society*] **Journal** — ANZHESJ
AOCS Monograph — AOMOD
Aomori Journal of Medicine — Aomori J Med
Aomori Kenritsu Chuo Byoin Ishi — AKCIB5
Aontas Review — Aontas Rev
AOPA [*Aircraft Owners and Pilots Association*] **General Aviation National Report** — AOPA Gen Aviat Natl Rep
AOPA [*Aircraft Owners' and Pilots' Association*] **Monthly Magazine** — AOPA Mo Mag
AOSTRA (Alberta Oil Sands Technology and Research Authority) Journal of Research — AOSTRA J Res
Aoyama Journal of General Education — Aoyama J Gen Educ
Aoyama Keizai Ronshu — AKR
APAIS. Australian Public Affairs Information Service — APAIS Aust Public Affairs Inf Serv
APA-PSIEP [*American Psychological Association-Project on Scientific Information Exchange in Psychology*] **Report** — APA-PSIEP Rep
Aparato Respiratorio y Tuberculosis — Apar Respir Tuberc
Aparatura Naukowa i Dydaktyczna — AANDD
Aparatura Naukowa i Dydaktyczna — Apar Nauk Dydakt
Apatitovye Proyavleniya Severnogo Kavkaza — Apatitovye Proyavleniya Sev Kavk
APAVE. Revue Technique du Groupement des Associations de Proprietaires d'Appareils a Vapeur et Electriques — APAVE
APC Review. Australian Parents Council — APC Review
APCA [*Air Pollution Control Association*] **Abstracts** — APCA Abstr
APCA [*Air Pollution Control Association*] **Annual Meeting. Proceedings** — APCA Annu Meet Proc
APCA [*Air Pollution Control Association*] **Journal** — APCA J
APCOM 77. Papers Presented at the International Symposium on the Application of Computers and Operations Research in the Mineral Industries — APCOM 77 Pap Int Symp Appl Comput Oper Res Miner Ind

APE [*Amalgamated Power Engineering Ltd.*] **Engineering** — APE Eng
APE [*Amalgamated Power Engineering Ltd.*] **Engineering** — APE Engng
APEA [*Australian Petroleum Exploration Association*] **Journal** — APEA J
Apeiron Journal for Ancient Philosophy and Science — Apeir
Aperature — PAPE
Apercus sur l'Economie Tchecoslovaque — Apercus Econ Tchecosl
APHIS 81. US Department of Agriculture. Animal and Plant Health Inspection Service — APHIS 81 US Dep Agric Anim Plant Health Inspect
APHIS 91. US Department of Agriculture. Animal and Plant Health Inspection Service — APHIS 91 US Dep Agric Anim Plant Health Inspect
API (American Petroleum Institute) Monograph Series — API Monogr Ser
API [*American Petroleum Institute*] **Weekly Statistical Bulletin** [*Database*] — WSB
Apiary Circular. British Columbia Department of Agriculture — Apiary Circ BC Dep Agric
Apiary Circular (Victoria) — Apiary Circ (Victoria)
APIC Studies in Data Processing — APIC Stud Data Processing
Apicoltore d'Italia — Apic Ital
Apicoltore d'Italia — Apicolt Ital
Apicoltore Moderno — Apic Mod
Apicoltore Moderno — Apicolt Mod
Apiculteur Algerien — Apicult Alger
Apiculteur d'Alsace et de Lorraine — Apicult Als-Lorr
Apiculteur Nord-Africain — Apicult Nord-Afr
Apicultor Americano — Apic Am
Apicultor Americano — Apicult Am
Apicultura Argentina — Apic Argent
Apicultura in Romania — Apic Rom
Apicultura Venezolana — Apic Venezol
Apicultural Abstracts [*Database*] — AA
Apicultural Abstracts [*Information service or system*] — Apic Abstr
Apicultural Abstracts — Apicult Abstr
Apiculture Francaise — Apic Fr
Apiculture in Western Australia — Apic W Aust
Apiculture Newsletter. Plant Industry Division. Alberta Department of Agriculture — Apic Newsl Pl Ind Div Alberta Dep Agric
Apiculture Nouvelle — Apic Nouv
APIJ. Australian Planning Institute. Journal — APIJ
APIOS Report — APIOS Rep
APL [*Applied Physics Laboratory*] **Technical Digest** — APL Tech Dig
APLA (American Patent Law Association). Quarterly Journal — Am Pat LQJ
APLA [*American Patent Law Association*] **Quarterly Journal** — APLA QJ
Aplikace Matematiky — Apl Mat
APMIS. Acta Pathologica, Microbiologica, et Immunologica Scandinavica — APMIS
APMIS. Acta Pathologica, Microbiologica, et Immunologica Scandinavica — APMIS Acta Pathol Microbiol Immunol Scand
APMIS [Acta Pathologica, Microbiologica, et Immunologica Scandinavica] Supplement — APMIS Suppl
APO. The Australian Post Office Magazine — APO
APOA [*Arctic Petroleum Operators Association*] **Reports** — APOAR
APOA [*Arctic Petroleum Operators Association*] **Review** — APOA
Apocalyptic Literature — ApLit
Apollo — Apo
Apologetische Blaetter — Ap Bl
Apoptosis in Immunology — Apoptosis Immunol
Aportaciones Matematicas — Aportaciones Mat
Aportaciones Matematicas. Comunicaciones — Aportaciones Mat Comun
Aportaciones Matematicas. Notas de Investigacion — Aportaciones Mat Notas Investigacion
Aportaciones Matematicas. Textos — Aportaciones Mat Textos
Apostolado Laico — Ap Laic
Apostolado Sacerdotal — AS
Apothekerpraktikant und Pharmazeutisch-Technischer Assistent — Apothekerprakt Pharm Tech Assist
Apotheker-Zeitung — Apoth Ztg
Apothekerzeitung — ApZg
Apotheker-Zeitung (Hanslian Edition) — Apoth Ztg (Hanslian Ed)
APP. Australasian Plant Pathology — APP Australas Plant Pathol
APP. Australasian Plant Pathology — Australas Plant Pathol
Appalachia Magazine — Appalachia Mag
Appalachian Business Review — APB
Appalachian Geological Society. Bulletin — Appalachian Geol Soc Bull
Appalachian Journal — Appal J
Appalachian Journal — Appalach J
Appalachian News Service — Appl News
Appaloosa News — Appaloosa N
Apparatura i Metody Rentgenovskogo Analiza [*Former USSR*] — App Metody Rentgenovskogo Anal
Apparatura i Metody Rentgenovskogo Analiza — Appar Metody Rentgenovskogo Anal
Apparaty i Mashiny Kislorodnykh i Kriogennykh Ustanovok — Appar Mash Kislorodn Kriog Ustanovok
Apparecchiature Idrauliche e Pneumatiche — Apparecch Idraul Pneum
Apparel International — Apparel Int
Apparel World — App World
Appeal Cases. District of Columbia — App DC
Appellate Court Administration Review — App Court Ad Rev
Appellate Decisions (Massachusetts) — Mass App Dec
Appellate Division Advance Sheets (Massachusetts) — Mass App Div Adv Sh
Appellate Division Reports [*New York*] — A D
Appellate Division Reports (Massachusetts) — Mass App Div
Appellate Division Reports. Second Series [*New York*] — A D 2d
Appendices on Provisional Nomenclature Symbols, Terminology, and Conventions. International Union of Pure and Applied Chemistry — Append Provis Nomencl Symb Terminol Conv IUPAC
Appenzellische Jahrbuecher — Ap J
Appenzellische Jahrbuecher — Ap Jahr
Appita Journal — Appita J
APPITA. Journal of the Australian and New Zealand Pulp and Paper Industry Technical Association — APPITA
Apple Educators' Newsletter — Apple Educ Newsl
Apple Research Digest. Washington Department of Agriculture — Apple Res Digest
Applesauce — Applesauc
Appleton's Journal — Appleton
Appleton's Magazine — Appleton M
Appliance Manufacturer — Appl Mfr
Appliance Manufacturer — Appliance Manuf
Appliance Retailing — App Ret
Applicable Algebra in Engineering, Communication, and Computing — Appl Algebra Engrg Comm Comput
Applicable Analysis — App Anal
Applicable Analysis — Appl Anal
Applicable Analysis — Applic Anal
Applicable Analysis — Applicable Anal
Applicable Mathematics Series — Appl Math Ser
Application for a Patent (South Africa) — Appl Pat S Afr
Application for a Patent under International Arrangements (South Africa) — Appl Pat Int Arrange S Afr
Application Notes. JASCO [*Japan Spectroscopic Co.*] — Appl Notes JASCO
Application of Admixtures in Concrete — Appl Admixtures Concr
Application of Atomic Energy in Agriculture — Appl At Energy Agric
Application of Charge Density Research to Chemistry and Drug Design — Appl Charge Density Res Chem Drug Des
Application of Chemical Engineering to the Treatment of Sewage and Industrial Liquid Effluents. Symposium — Appl Chem Eng Treat Sewage Ind Liq Effluents Symp
Application of Computer Methods in the Mineral Industry. Proceedings of the International Symposium — ACMIC
Application of Computers and Mathematics in the Mineral Industry — APCOM
Application of Herbicides in Oil Crops Plantings — Appl Herbic Oil Crops Plant
Application of High Magnetic Fields in Semiconductor Physics. Lectures Presented at the International Conference — Appl High Mag Fields Semicond Phys Lect Int Conf
Application of Isotope Techniques in Hydrology and Hydraulics — Appl Isot Tech Hydrol Hydraul
Application of Metrological Laser Methods in Machines and Systems — Appl Metrol Laser Methods Mach Syst
Application of Optical Instrumentation in Medicine — Appl Opt Instrum Med
Application of Physical Sciences to Food Research, Processing, Preservation. Proceedings. Conference — Appl Phys Sci Food Res Process Preserv Proc Conf
Application of Physico-Chemical Methods in the Chemical Analysis. Proceedings. Conference — Appl Phys Chem Methods Chem Anal Proc Conf
Application of Plasma Source Mass Spectrometry. Selected Papers. International Conference on Plasma Source Mass Spectrometry — Appl Plasma Source Mass Spectrom Sel Pap Int Conf
Application of Science and Medicine to Sport. Papers Presented. Annual Meeting. Canadian Association of Sports Sciences — Appl Sci Med Sport Pap Annu Meet Can Assoc Sports Sci
Application of Solar Energy. Proceedings of the Southeastern Conference on Application of Solar Energy. 1st — Appl Sol Energ Proc Southeast Conf 1st
Applicationes Mathematicae (Warsaw) — Appl Math Warsaw
Applications and Industry — Appl Ind
Applications of Artificial Intelligence — Appl Artif Intell
Applications of Automation Technology to Fatigue and Fracture Testing — Appl Autom Technol Fatigue Fract Test
Applications of Biochemical Systems in Organic Chemistry — Appl Biochem Syst Org Chem
Applications of Commercial Oxygen to Water and Wastewater Systems — Appl Commer Oxygen Water Wastewater Syst
Applications of Communications Theory — Appl Commun Theory
Applications of Cryogenic Technology — Appl Cryog Technol
Applications of Digital Image Processing — Appl Digital Image Process
Applications of Electronic Structure Theory — Appl Electron Struct Theory
Applications of Mathematics — Appl Math
Applications of Mathematics — Applications Math
Applications of Modern Technology in Business — Appl Modern Tech Business
Applications of Moessbauer Spectroscopy — Appl Moessbauer Spectrosc
Applications of New Mass Spectrometry Techniques in Pesticide Chemistry — Appl New Mass Spectrom Tech Pestic Chem
Applications of Optical Holography. International Conference — Appl Opt Hologr Int Conf
Applications of Photochemistry in Probing Biological Targets — Appl Photochem Probing Biol Targets
Applications of Polymer Concrete — Appl Polym Concr
Applications of Polymer Emulsions — Appl Polym Emulsions
Applications of Polymer Spectroscopy [*monograph*] — Appl Polym Spectrosc
Applications of Polymers. Proceedings. American Chemical Society Symposium Honoring O.A. Battista on Applied Polymer Science — Appl Polym Proc Am Chem Soc Symp O A Battista Appl Polym Sci
Applications of Surface Science — Appl Surf Sci
Applications of Synchrotron Radiation [*Monograph*] — Appl Synchrotron Radiat
Applications of the Newer Techniques of Analysis — Appl Newer Tech Anal
Applications of Thermodynamics to Metallurgical Processes. [*A*] **Short Course.** — Appl Thermodyn Metall Processes Short Course
Applications of X-Ray Topographic Methods to Materials Science. Proceedings. France-USA Seminar — Appl X Ray Topogr Methods Mater Sci Proc Fr USA Semin

Applications Research Technical Report. Beckman Instruments, Inc. — Appl Res Tech Rep Beckman Instrum Inc
Applied Acoustics — AACOB
Applied Acoustics — Appl Acoust
Applied Agricultural Research — Appl Agric Res
Applied and Computational Harmonic Analysis. Time-Frequency and Time-Scale Analysis. Wavelets, Numerical Algorithms, and Applications — Appl Comput Harmon Anal
Applied and Engineering Mathematics Series — Appl Engrg Math Ser
Applied and Environmental Microbiology — App Environ Microbiol
Applied and Environmental Microbiology — Appl Envir Microbiol
Applied and Environmental Microbiology — Appl Environ Microbiol
Applied and Fundamental Aspects of Plant Cell Tissue and Organ Culture — Appl Fundam Aspects Plant Cell Tissue Organ Cult
Applied and Theoretical Electrophoresis — Appl Theor Electrophor
Applied Animal Behaviour Science — Appl Anim Behav Sci
Applied Animal Ethology — Appl Anim Ethol
Applied Animal Ethology — Appl Anim Ethology
Applied Anthropology — Appl Anthrop
Applied Artificial Intelligence Reporter — A A Intignc
Applied Atomic Spectroscopy — Appl At Spectrosc
Applied Atomics — APATB
Applied Atomics [*England*] — Appl At
Applied Biocatalysis — Appl Biocatal
Applied Biochemistry and Bioengineering — Appl Biochem Bioeng
Applied Biochemistry and Biotechnology — ABB
Applied Biochemistry and Biotechnology — ABIBD
Applied Biochemistry and Biotechnology — Appl Biochem Biotechnol
Applied Biochemistry and Microbiology — Appl Biochem Micr
Applied Biochemistry and Microbiology — Appl Biochem Microbiol
Applied Biochemistry and Microbiology (English Translation of Prikladnaya Biokhimiya i Mikrobiologiya) — Appl Biochem Microbiol (Engl Transl Prikl Biokhim Mikrobiol)
Applied Biochemistry and Microbiology (Moscow) — Appl Biochem Microbiol Moscow
Applied Botany — Appl Bot
Applied Cardiology — Appl Cardiol
Applied Cardiopulmonary Pathophysiology — Appl Cardiopulm Pathophysiol
Applied Catalysis — APCAD
Applied Catalysis — Appl Catal
Applied Catalysis. B. Environmental — Appl Catal B
Applied Categorical Structures — Appl Categ Structures
Applied Chemistry at Protein Interfaces. Symposium — Appl Chem Protein Interfaces Symp
Applied Christianity — AC
Applied Chromatography — Appl Chromatogr
Applied Composite Materials — Appl Compos Mater
Applied Discrete Mathematics and Theoretical Computer Science — Appl Discrete Math Theoret Comput Sci
Applied Earth Science — Appl Earth Sci
Applied Economics [*United Kingdom*] — APE
Applied Economics — App Econ
Applied Economics — Appl Econ
Applied Economics — Applied Econ
Applied Electrical Phenomena — Appl Electr Phenom
Applied Electrical Phenomena (English Translation) — Appl Electr Phenom (Engl Transl)
Applied Electronics Annual — Appl El Ann
Applied Energy — APEND
Applied Energy — Appl Energy
Applied Entomology and Zoology — Appl Ent Zool
Applied Entomology and Zoology — Appl Entomol Zool
Applied Ergonomics — AERGB
Applied Ergonomics — Appl Ergon
Applied Ergonomics — Appl Ergonomics
Applied Genetics News — AGN
Applied Geochemistry — Appl Geochem
Applied Geochemistry. Supplement — Appl Geochem Suppl
Applied Geomechanics — App Geomech
Applied Human Science — Appl Human Sci
Applied Hydraulics — Appl Hydraul
Applied Immunohistochemistry — Appl Immunohistochem
Applied Industrial Hygiene — Appl Ind Hyg
Applied Information Technology — Appl Inform Tech
Applied Language Studies — Appl Lang Stud
Applied Laser Spectroscopy — Appl Laser Spectrosc
Applied Materials Research [*England*] — Appl Mater Res
Applied Mathematical Modelling — Appl Math Model
Applied Mathematical Modelling — Appl Math Modelling
Applied Mathematical Sciences — Appl Math Sci
Applied Mathematics. A Journal of Chinese Universities. Series B — Appl Math J Chinese Univ Ser B
Applied Mathematics and Computation — AMHCB
Applied Mathematics and Computation — APMCC5
Applied Mathematics and Computation — Appl Math and Comput
Applied Mathematics and Computation — Appl Math Comput
Applied Mathematics and Computation (New York) — Appl Math Comput (New York)
Applied Mathematics and Computer Science — Appl Math Comput Sci
Applied Mathematics and Engineering Science Texts — Appl Math Engrg Sci Texts
Applied Mathematics and Mathematical Computation — Appl Math Math Comput
Applied Mathematics and Mechanics — App Math & Mech
Applied Mathematics and Mechanics — Appl Math and Mech
Applied Mathematics and Mechanics — Appl Math Mech
Applied Mathematics and Mechanics (English Edition) — Appl Math Mech (English Ed)
Applied Mathematics and Optimization — AMOMB
Applied Mathematics and Optimization — Appl Math and Optimiz
Applied Mathematics and Optimization — Appl Math O
Applied Mathematics and Optimization — Appl Math Optim
Applied Mathematics Letters — Appl Math Lett
Applied Mathematics Notes — Appl Math Notes
Applied Mathematics Series — App Math Ser
Applied Mechanics — Appl Mech
Applied Mechanics Division. Symposia Series (American Society of Mechanical Engineers) — Appl Mech Div Symp Ser (Am Soc Mech Eng)
Applied Mechanics. Proceedings. International Congress of Applied Mechanics — Appl Mech Proc Int Congr
Applied Mechanics Reviews — AMR
Applied Mechanics Reviews — ApMec
Applied Mechanics Reviews — Appl Mech Rev
Applied Mechanics Symposia Series — Appl Mech Symp Ser
Applied Methods in Oncology [*Elsevier Book Series*] — AMO
Applied Methods in Oncology — Appl Methods Oncol
Applied Microbiology [*Later, Applied & Environmental Microbiology*] — APMBAY
Applied Microbiology [*Later, Applied and Environmental Microbiology*] — ApMicrobiol
Applied Microbiology [*Later, Applied and Environmental Microbiology*] — App Microbiol
Applied Microbiology [*Later, Applied and Environmental Microbiology*] — Appl Microb
Applied Microbiology [*Later, Applied and Environmental Microbiology*] — Appl Microbiol
Applied Microbiology and Biotechnology — Appl Microbiol Biotechnol
Applied Microbiology and Biotechnology — EJABDD
Applied Microbiology (Sofia) — Appl Microbiol Sofia
Applied Mineralogy. Proceedings. International Congress on Applied Mineralogy in the Minerals Industry — Appl Mineral Proc Int Congr Appl Mineral Miner Ind
Applied Mineralogy. Technische Mineralogie — Appl Mineral
Applied Neurophysiology — ANPHCL
Applied Neurophysiology — Appl Neurop
Applied Neurophysiology — Appl Neurophysiol
Applied Nuclear Radiochemistry — Appl Nucl Radiochem
Applied Numerical Mathematics — Appl Num M
Applied Numerical Mathematics — Appl Numer Math
Applied Nursing Research — Appl Nurs Res
Applied Nutrition — Appl Nutr
Applied Ocean Research — Appl Ocean Res
Applied Optics — Ap Optics
Applied Optics — App Op
Applied Optics — App Opt
Applied Optics — App Optics
Applied Optics — Appl Opt
Applied Optics — Appl Optics
Applied Optics. Supplement — Appl Opt Suppl
Applied Optimization — Appl Optim
Applied Organometallic Chemistry — Appl Organomet Chem
Applied Ornithology — ANORBB
Applied Ornithology — Appl Ornithol
Applied Parasitology — Appl Parasitol
Applied Pathology — Appl Pathol
Applied Pathology — APTHDM
Applied Pharmacokinetics [*Monograph*] — Appl Pharmacokinet
Applied Philosophy — Applied Phil
Applied Physics — APHYC
Applied Physics — App Phys
Applied Physics — Appl Phys
Applied Physics A. Materials Science and Processing — Appl Phys A Mater Sci Process
Applied Physics A. Solids and Surfaces — Appl Phys A Solids Surf
Applied Physics. A. Solids and Surfaces — Appl Phys A Solids Surfaces
Applied Physics and Engineering — Appl Phys Eng
Applied Physics. B. Photophysics amd Laser Chemistry — Appl Phys B Photophys Laser Chem
Applied Physics Communications — APCOD
Applied Physics Communications — Appl Phys Comm
Applied Physics Communications — Appl Phys Commun
Applied Physics Laboratory. Johns Hopkins University. Special Report — APL JHU SR
Applied Physics Letters — Appl Phys L
Applied Physics Letters — Appl Phys Lett
Applied Physics (London) — Appl Phys (London)
Applied Physics. Part A. Solids and Surfaces — Appl Phys A
Applied Physics. Part A. Solids and Surfaces [*Germany*] — Appl Phys Part A
Applied Physics. Part B. Photophysics and Laser Chemistry — APPCD
Applied Physics. Part B. Photophysics and Laser Chemistry — Appl Phys B
Applied Physics. Part B. Photophysics and Laser Chemistry [*Germany*] — Appl Phys Part B
Applied Physics Quarterly — Appl Phys Q
Applied Plant Science/Toegepaste Plantwetenskap — Appl Plant Sci Toegepaste Plantwetenskap
Applied Plastics — Appl Plast
Applied Plastics and Reinforced Plastics Review — Appl Plast Reinf Plast Rev
Applied Polymer Symposia — Appl Polym Symp
Applied Probability. Complete Author and Subject Index. Journal of Applied Probability and Advances in Applied Probability — Appl Probab Index
Applied Probability. Series of the Applied Probability Trust — Appl Probab Ser Appl Probab Trust

Applied Protein Chemistry [*Monograph*] — Appl Protein Chem
Applied Psycholinguistics — Appl Psycholinguist
Applied Psycholinguistics — APPSDZ
Applied Psychological Measurement — APMEDC
Applied Psychological Measurement — Appl Psychol Meas
Applied Psychology Monographs — Appl Psych Monogr
Applied Radiation and Isotopes — Appl Radiat Isot
Applied Radiology — Appl Radiol
Applied Radiology — Applied Radiol
Applied Radiology — ARDYA4
Applied Radiology and Nuclear Medicine [*Later, Applied Radiology*] — Appl Radiol Nucl Med
Applied Radiology and Nuclear Medicine [*Later, Applied Radiology*] — ARNMDL
Applied Research and Practice on Municipal and Industrial Waste — Appl Res Pract Munic Ind Waste
Applied Research in Mental Retardation — Appl Res Ment Retard
Applied Research in Mental Retardation — ARMREW
Applied Rheology — Appl Rheol
Applied Science — Applied Sc
Applied Science and Technology Index — A S & T Ind
Applied Science and Technology Index — Appl Sci Technol Index
Applied Science and Technology Index — AST
Applied Science and Technology Index — ASTI
Applied Science in the Casting of Metals [*Monograph*] — Appl Sci Cast Met
Applied Sciences and Development — Appl Sci Dev
Applied Scientific Research — Appl Sci Re
Applied Scientific Research — Appl Sci Res
Applied Scientific Research — Appld Sci Res
Applied Scientific Research Corporation of Thailand. Annual Report — Appl Sci Res Corp Thail Annu Rep
Applied Scientific Research Corporation of Thailand. Annual Report — ATHABZ
Applied Scientific Research Corporation of Thailand. Miscellaneous Investigation — Appl Sci Res Corp Thailand Misc Invest
Applied Scientific Research. Section A. Mechanics, Heat, Chemical Engineering, Mathematical Methods [*Netherlands*] — Appl Sci Res Sect A
Applied Scientific Research. Section B. Electrophysics, Acoustics, Optics, Mathematical Methods [*Netherlands*] — Appl Sci Res Sect B
Applied Scientific Research (The Hague) — Appl Sci Res (The Hague)
Applied Social Sciences Index and Abstracts — ASSIA
Applied Solar Energy — Appl Sol Energy
Applied Solar Energy (English Translation) — Appl Solar Energy (Engl Transl)
Applied Solid State Science — Appl Solid State Sci
Applied Solid State Science. Supplement — Appl Solid State Sci Suppl
Applied Spectroscopy — Appl Spect
Applied Spectroscopy — Appl Spectr
Applied Spectroscopy — Appl Spectrosc
Applied Spectroscopy — Appl Spectry
Applied Spectroscopy — APSPA4
Applied Spectroscopy Reviews — Appl Sp Rev
Applied Spectroscopy Reviews — Appl Spectrosc Rev
Applied Statistics — Appl Stat
Applied Statistics — Appl Stats
Applied Statistics — APSTA
Applied Statistics — AS
Applied Statistics. Proceedings of Conference at Dalhousie University — P Ap St Dalho
Applied Stochastic Models and Data Analysis — Appl Stochastic Models Data Anal
Applied Superconductivity [*Monograph*] — Appl Supercond
Applied Superconductivity Conference — Appl Supercond Conf
Applied Surface Chemistry (Tainan, Taiwan) — Appl Surf Chem Tainan Taiwan
Applied Therapeutics — Appl Ther
Applied Thermal Engineering. Design, Processes, Equipment, Economics — Appl Therm Eng
Applied Toxicology of Petroleum Hydrocarbons — Appl Toxicol Pet Hydrocarbons
Applied Tumor Immunology. Proceedings. International Symposium — Appl Tumor Immunol Proc Int Symp
Applied UV Spectroscopy — Appl UV Spectrosc
Appointment of Agents. Excise [*Database*] — AAE
Apports de la Science au Developpement de l'Industrie Textile. Conference Conjointe — Apports Sci Dev Ind Text Conf Conjointe
Appraisal. Children's Science Books — ACSB
Appraisal Institute. Magazine — AIM
Appraisal Journal — APJ
Appraisal Journal — Appraisal J
Appraisal Journal — Appraisal Jrnl
Appraisal of Halogenated Fire Extinguishing Agents. Proceedings. Symposium — Appraisal Halogenated Fire Extinguishing Agents Proc Symp
Appraisal Review Journal — App Rev J
Appraisal. Science Books for Young People — ASBYP
Apprentissage et Socialisation — App et Soc
Apprentissage et Socialisation — Apprent Social
Appretur Zeitung — Appretur Ztg
Approach — APP
Approaches to Automotive Emissions Control. Symposium — Approaches Automot Emiss Control Symp
Approaches to Planning and Design of Health Care Facilities in Developing Areas — Approaches Plann Des Health Care Facil Dev Areas
Approaches to the Cell Biology of Neurons — Approaches Cell Biol Neurons
Approaches to the Genetic Analysis of Mammalian Cells. Michigan Conference on Genetics — Approaches Genet Anal Mamm Cells Mich Conf Genet
Approdo Letterario — ApL
Appropriate Technology — Approp Technol
Appropriate Technology [*England*] — Appropriate Technol
Appropriate Technology — ATCYA
Approved Rx Drug Products — App Rx Dr Prod
Approximation and Optimization — Approx Optim
Approximation Theory and its Applications — Approx Theory Appl
APR. Allgemeine Papier-Rundschau — APR Allg Pap Rundsch
APRG [*Air Pollution Research Group*] **(South Africa. Council for Scientific and Industrial Research)** — APRG S Afr CSIR
April — Ap
APRO [*Aerial Phenomena Research Organization*] **Bulletin** — APRO Bull
Aptechnoe Delo — APDEAW
Aptechnoe Delo — Aptechn Delo
Apulum. Acta Musei Apulensis — Apulum
Apuntes Forestales Tropicales. Instituto de Dasonomia Tropical — Apuntes Forest Trop
Apuntes (Peru) — ASP
Apuntes. Universidad del Pacifica. Centro de Investigacion [*Lima*] — UP/A
AQEIC (Asociacion Quimica Espanola de la Industria del Cuero) Boletin Tecnico — AQEIC Bol Tec
Aqua Fennica — AQFEDI
Aqua Fennica — Aqua Fenn
Aqua Scientific and Technical Review — Aqua Sci Tech Rev
Aqua Terra — AQTEAH
Aquaculture — AQCLAL
Aquaculture and Fisheries Management — AFMAEX
Aquaculture and Fisheries Management — Aquacult Fish Manage
Aquaculture Department. Southeast Asian Fisheries Development Center. Quarterly Research Report — Aquacult Dep Southeast Asian Fish Dev Cent Q Res Rep
Aquaculture Engineering — Aquacult Eng
Aquaculture Magazine — Aquaculture Mag
Aquaculture Nutrition — Aquacult Nutr
Aqualine Abstracts — Aqualine Abstr
Aquarien Magazin — AQMAA4
Aquarien Magazin — Aquarien Mag
Aquarien Terrarien — AQTEBI
Aquarien- und Terrarien-Zeitschrift — Aquarien Terrar Z
Aquarium [*Wuppertal*] — AQRMAV
Aquarium Journal — AQJOAV
Aquarium Journal — Aquar J
Aquarium Journal — Aquarium J
Aquarium News (Brooklyn) — Aquar News Brooklyn
Aquarium Newsletter — Aquar Newslett
Aquarium Review. British Aquarists' Association — Aquar Rev
Aquarium Systems — Aquarium Syst
Aquatic Biology Abstracts — Aqua Biol Ab
Aquatic Botany — AQBODS
Aquatic Botany — Aquat Bot
Aquatic Ecological Chemistry — Aquat Ecol Chem
Aquatic Geochemistry — Aquat Geochem
Aquatic Information Retrieval [*Database*] — AQUIRE
Aquatic Insects — AQIND
Aquatic Insects — AQINDQ
Aquatic Insects — Aquat Insec
Aquatic Insects — Aquat Insects
Aquatic Mammals — AQMAD7
Aquatic Mammals — Aquat Mamm
Aquatic Microbial Ecology. Proceedings of the Conference — Aquat Microbiol Ecol Proc
Aquatic Microbiology — Aquat Microbiol
Aquatic Oligochaete Biology. Proceedings. International Symposium — Aquat Oligochaete Biol Proc Int Symp
Aquatic Sciences — Aquat Sci
Aquatic Sciences and Fisheries Abstracts — Aqua Sci & Fish Abstr
Aquatic Sciences and Fisheries Abstracts [*United Nations (already exists in GUS II database)*] [*Information service or system*] — ASFA
Aquatic Sciences and Fisheries Abstracts. Part I. Biological Sciences and Living Resources — Aquat Sci Fish Abst Part I
Aquatic Sciences and Fisheries Abstracts. Part II. Ocean Technology, Policy, and Non-Living Resources — Aquat Sci Fish Abst Part II
Aquatic Toxicology — AQTOD
Aquatic Toxicology — Aquat Toxicol
Aquatic Toxicology (Amsterdam) — Aquat Toxicol (Amst)
Aquatic Toxicology and Environmental Fate. 9th Volume. Symposium — Aquat Toxicol Environ Fate 9th Vol Symp
Aquatic Toxicology and Hazard Evaluation. Proceedings. Annual Symposium on Aquatic Toxicology — Aquat Toxicol Hazard Eval Proc Annu Symp Aquat Toxicol
Aquatic Toxicology (New York) — Aquat Toxicol (NY)
Aquatic Weed Control Society. Proceedings — Aquat Weed Control Soc Proc
Aquatic Weeds in South East Asia. Proceedings of a Regional Seminar on Noxious Aquatic Vegetation — Aquat Weeds South East Asia Proc Reg Semin Noxious Aquat Veg
Aqueous Biphasic Separations. Biomolecules to Metal Ions. Proceedings of an American Chemical Society Symposium on Aqueous Biphasic Separations — Aqueous Biphasic Sep Proc Am Chem Soc Symp
Aqueous Polymeric Coatings for Pharmaceutical Dosage Forms — Aqueous Polym Coat Pharm Dosage Forms
Aqueous Powder Coatings and Powder Electropaints — Aqueous Powder Coat Powder Electropaints
Aqueous Solubility Database — SOLUB
Aqueous-Environmental Chemistry of Metals [*Monograph*] — Aqueous Environ Chem Met
Aqui y Ahora la Juventud — Aqui Ahora Juv

Aquifer Restoration and Ground Water Rehabilitation — Aquifer Restor Ground Water Rehab
Aquileia Nostra — AN
Aquileia Nostra — Aquil Nost
Aquileia Nostra. Bollettino. Associazione Nazionale per Aquileia — Aqui N
Aquilo Serie Botanica — Aquilo Ser Bot
Aquilo Serie Zoologica — AQSZ
Aquilo Serie Zoologica — Aquilo Ser Zool
Aquinas Law Journal — Aqu Law J
Arab and International Lubricating Oil Industry. Arab Lubricating Oils Seminar — Arab Int Lubr Oil Ind Arab Lubr Oils Semin
Arab Commercial Law Review — Arab Com Law Rev
Arab Community Centre News — Arab Com Cent N
Arab Culture Series — ACS
Arab Economist — AE
Arab Economist — AEC
Arab Energy. Prospects to 2000 — Arab Enrgy
Arab Film and Television Center News — Arab F & TV
Arab Gulf Journal — Arab Gulf J
Arab Gulf Journal of Scientific Research — Arab Gulf J Sci Res
Arab Gulf Journal of Scientific Research. A. Mathematical and Physical Sciences — Arab Gulf J Sci Res A Math Phys Sci
Arab Journal of Mathematical Sciences — Arab J Math Sci
[*The*] **Arab Journal of Mathematics** — Arab J Math
Arab Journal of Nuclear Sciences and Applications — AJNAD
Arab Journal of Nuclear Sciences and Applications — Arab J Nucl Sci Appl
Arab Metallurgical News [*Algeria*] — Arab Metall News
Arab Mining Journal — Arab Min J
Arab News Bulletin [*London*] — ANB
Arab News Bulletin (Washington) — ANBW
Arab Press Bulletin — Arab Press Bull
Arab Regional Conference on Sulphur and Its Usages in the Arab World — Arab Reg Conf Sulphur Its Usages Arab World
Arab Science Congress. Papers — Arab Sci Congr Pap
Arab Studies Quarterly — Arab Stud Quart
Arab Studies Quarterly — Arab Studies Q
Arab Times — ARBTM
Arab Veterinary Medical Association. Journal — Arab Vet Med Assoc J
Arab World — ArabW
Arabian Journal for Science and Engineering — Arabian J Sci and Eng
Arabian Journal for Science and Engineering — Arabian J Sci Eng
Arabian Journal for Science and Engineering — Arabian J Sci Engrg
Arabian Studies — Arab Stud
Arabian Transport — Arab Trans
Arabic Sciences and Philosophy — Arabic Sci Philos
Arabic Translation Series — ATS
Arabica Revue de Etudes Arabes — Arab
Arabidopsis Information Service — Arabidopsis Inf Serv
Arachidonic Acid Metabolism and Tumor Initiation [*monograph*] — Arachidonic Acid Metab Tumor Initiation
Arachidonic Acid Metabolism and Tumor Promotion [*Monograph*] — Arachidonic Acid Metab Tumor Promot
Arachno Entomologia Lekarska — Arachno Entomol Lek
ARAMCO [*Arabian American Oil Company*] **World Magazine** — ARA
ARAMCO [*Arabian American Oil Company*] **World Magazine** — ARAMCO W
ARAMCO [*Arabian American Oil Company*] **World Magazine** — ARAMCO World M
Araneta Journal of Agriculture — Araneta J Agric
Araneta Research Journal — Araneta Res J
Araucaria — ARA
Araucaria de Chile — ACh
Araucariana. Serie Botanica — Araucariana Ser Bot
Araucariana. Serie Geociencias — Araucariana Ser Geocienc
Araucariana. Serie Zoologia — Araucariana Ser Zool
Arbeidervern — ARBDD
Arbeidsblad — Abl
Arbeidsblad — Arb
Arbeit und Gesundheit — Arb Gesund
Arbeit und Leistung [*Germany*] — Arb Leist
Arbeit und Recht — Arbeit U Recht
Arbeit und Sozialpolitik — Arbeit und Sozialpol
Arbeit und Wirtschaft — Arbeit und Wirt
Arbeiten. Anatomisches Institut — Arb Anat Inst
Arbeiten. Anatomisches Institut. Kaiserlich Japanischen Universitaet zu Sendai — Arb Anat Inst Kais Jpn Univ Sendai
Arbeiten aus Anglistik und Amerikanistik — Ar A A
Arbeiten aus dem Gebiet der Experimentellen Biologie — Arbeiten Exp Biol
Arbeiten aus dem Gebiete des Futterbaues — Arb Futterbau
Arbeiten aus dem Gebiete des Futterbaues — Arb Gebiete Futterbaues
Arbeiten aus dem Geologisch-Palaeontologischen Institut der Universitaet Stuttgart — AGPIC9
Arbeiten aus dem Geologisch-Palaeontologischen Institut der Universitaet Stuttgart — Arb Geol Palaeontol Inst Univ Stuttgart
Arbeiten aus dem Institut fuer Allgemeine Botanik der Universitaet Zuerich — Arbeiten Inst Allg Bot Univ Zuerich
Arbeiten aus dem Institut fuer Experimentelle Therapie — ArbIeTh
Arbeiten aus dem Institut fuer Experimentelle Therapie zu Frankfurt am Main — Arb Inst Exp Ther Frankfurt am Main
Arbeiten aus dem Institut fuer Geologie und Palaeontologie an der Universitaet Stuttgart — Arb Inst Geol Palaeontol Univ Stuttgart
Arbeiten aus dem Institut fuer Palaeobotanik und Petrographie der Brennsteine — Arbeiten Inst Palaeobot
Arbeiten aus dem Koeniglichen Botanischen Garten zu Breslau — Arbeiten Koenigl Bot Gart Breslau
Arbeiten aus dem Neurologischen Institut der Universitaet Wien — AnIW
Arbeiten aus dem Orientalischen Seminar der Universitaet Giessen — AOSG
Arbeiten aus dem Paul-Ehrlich-Institut. Bundesamt fuer Sera und Impfstoffe. Langen — Arb Paul Ehrlich Inst Bundesamt Sera Impfst Langen
Arbeiten aus dem Paul-Ehrlich-Institut. Bundesamt fuer Sera und Impfstoffe zu Frankfurt am Main — Arb Paul Ehrlich Inst Bundesamt Sera Impfstoffe Frankf AM
Arbeiten aus dem Reichsgesundheitsamt — Arb Reichsgesdhtsamt
Arbeiten aus dem Staatsinstitut fuer Experimentelle Therapie und dem Georg-Speyer-Hans zu Frankfurt am Main — Arb Staatsinst Exp Ther Georg Speyer Haus Frankfurt am Main
Arbeiten aus der Biologischen Meeresstation in Stalin — Arb Biol Meeresstation Stalin
Arbeiten aus der Biologischen Reichsanstalt fuer Land- und Forstwirtschaft. Berlin-Dahlem — Arb Biol Reichsanst Land Forstwirtsch Berlin Dahlem
Arbeiten aus der Medizinischen Fakultaet Okayama — Arb Med Fak Okayama
Arbeiten aus der Medizinischen Universitaet Okayama — Arb Med Univ Okayama
Arbeiten aus der Niedersaechsischen Staats- und Universitaetsbibliothek [*Goettingen*] — Arbeiten Niedersaechs Staats- u Universitaetsbibl
Arbeiten. Biologischen Reichsanstalt fuer Land- und Forstwirtschaft (Berlin) — Arb Biol Reichanst Land Forstw (Berlin)
Arbeiten. Botanischen Instituts in Wurzburg — Arb Bot Inst Wurz
Arbeiten der Deutschen Gesellschaft fuer Zuechtungskunde — ADGZ
Arbeiten der Deutschen Landwirtschafts-Gesellschaft — ADLG
Arbeiten der Deutschen Landwirtschafts-Gesellschaft — Arbeiten Deutsch Landw Ges
Arbeiten der Gelehrten Gesellschaft zur Erforschung Weissrutheniens — Arb Gelehrten Ges Erforsch Weissruthen
Arbeiten der Gory-Goretzkschen Gelehrten Gesellschaft — Arb Gory Goretzkschen Gelehrten Ges
Arbeiten der Kaiserlichen Biologischen Anstalt fuer Land und Forstwirtschaft — Arb Kais Biol Anst Land Forstwirtsch
Arbeiten der Ost-Sibirischen Staats-Universitaet — Arb Ost Sib Staats Univ
Arbeiten der W. W. Kujbyschews Staats Universitaet in Tomsk — Arb W W Kujbyschews Staats Univ Tomsk
Arbeiten der Wissenschaftlichen Forschungs-Sektion der Leningrader Gouvernements Abteilung des Arbeitsschutzes — Arb Wiss Forsch Sekt Leningr Gouv Abt Arbeitsschutzes
Arbeiten des Allrussischen Instituts fuer Experimentelle Medizin — Arb Allruss Inst Exp Med
Arbeiten des Allrussischen Mendelejew-Kongresses fuer Theoretische und Angewandte Chemie — Arb Allruss Mendelejew Kongr Theor Angew Chem
Arbeiten des Allrussischen Zentralen Wissenschaftlichen Fett-Forschungsinstituts — Arb Allruss Zent Wiss Fett Forschungsinst
Arbeiten des Archangelsk'schen Wissenschaftlichen Forschungsinstitut fuer Algen — Arb Archang Wiss Forschungsinst Algen
Arbeiten des Botanischen Instituts in Wuerzburg — Arbeiten Bot Inst Wuerzburg
Arbeiten des Instituts fuer Geschichte der Medizin an der Universitaet Leipzig — Arb Inst Gesch Med Univ Leipzig
Arbeiten des Laboratoriums zur Untersuchung von Eiweiss und des Eiweissstoffwechsels im Organismus — Arb Lab Unters Eiweiss Eiweissstoffwechsels Org
Arbeiten des Leningrader Instituts fuer Gewerbehygiene und Sicherheitstechnik — Arb Leningr Inst Gewerbehyg Sicherheitstech
Arbeiten des Milchwirtschaftlichen Instituts zu Wologda — Arb Milchwirtsch Inst Wologda
Arbeiten des Staatlichen Wissenschaftlichen Forschungsinstituts fuer Flugzeugwerkstoffe. Moscow — Arb Staatl Wiss Forschungsinst Flugzeugwerkstoffe Moscow
Arbeiten des Ungarischen Biologischen Forschungsinstitutes — Arb Ung Biol Forschungsinst
Arbeiten des Wissenschaftlichen Samoilow-Institut fuer Duengemittel und Insektofungicide. Moscow — Arb Wiss Samoilow Inst Duengem Insektofungic Moscow
Arbeiten des Zentralen Staatlichen Wissenschaftlichen Forschungsinstituts fuer Nichteisenmetalle — Arb Zent Staatl Wiss Forschungsinst Nichteisenmet
Arbeiten. Deutsche Landwirtschafts-Gesellschaft — Arb Deut Landwirt Ges
Arbeiten. Dritte Abteilung des Anatomischen Institutes der Kaiserlichen Universitaet Kyoto. Serie A. Untersuchungen ueber das Periphere Nervensystem — Arb Dritten Abt Anat Inst Kais Univ Kyoto Ser A
Arbeiten. Dritte Abteilung des Anatomischen Institutes der Kaiserlichen Universitaet Kyoto. Serie C. Experimentelle Tuberkuloseforschung — Arb Dritten Abt Anat Inst Kais Univ Kyoto Ser C
Arbeiten. Dritte Abteilung des Anatomischen Institutes der Kaiserlichen Universitaet Kyoto. Serie D. Lymphatologie — Arb Dritten Abt Anat Inst Kais Univ Kyoto Ser D
Arbeiten einer Vereinigten Gesellschaft in der Oberlausitz zu den Geschichten und der Gelahrtheit Ueberhaupt Gehoerende — Arbeiten Vereinigten Ges Oberlausitz
Arbeiten. Paul-Ehrlich-Institut — Arb Paul-Ehrlich-Inst
Arbeiten. Paul-Ehrlich-Institut, Georg-Speyer-Haus, und Ferdinand-Blum-Institut — Arb Paul Ehrlich Inst Georg Speyer Haus Ferdinand Blum Inst
Arbeiten ueber Physiologische und Angewandte Entomologie aus Berlin Dahlem [*A publication*] — Arb Physiol Angew Entomol Berlin Dahlem
Arbeiten und Berichte. Arbeitsgemeinschaft Katholischer Homiletiker Deutschlands — AAKHD
Arbeiten und Berichte. Sueddeutsche Versuchs und Forschungsanstalt fuer Milchwirtschaft — Arb Ber Sueddtsch Ver Forschungsanst Milchwirtsch
Arbeiten und Texte zur Slavistik — ATS
Arbeiten. Universitaet Hohenheim (Landwirtschaftliche Hochschule) — Arb Univ Hohenheim (Landwirtsch Hochsch)
Arbeiten zur Angewandten Statistik — Arbeiten Angew Statist
Arbeiten zur Bayerisch-Oesterreichischen Dialektgeografie — ABOD
Arbeiten zur Deutschen Philologie — ADPh

Arbeiten zur Geschichte des Antiken Judentums und des Urchristentums — AGAJU
Arbeiten zur Geschichte des Antiken Judentums und des Urchristentums — AGJU
Arbeiten zur Geschichte des Antiken Judentums und des Urchristentums [*Leiden*] — ArbGeschAntJudUrchr
Arbeiten zur Geschichte des Spaetjudentums und Urchristentums — AGSU
Arbeiten zur Kirchengeschichte — AKG
Arbeiten zur Literatur und Geschichte des Hellenistischen Judentums — ALGHJ
Arbeiten zur NT Textforschung — ANTF
Arbeiten zur Reinischen Landeskunde [*Germany*] — Arb Reinischen Landeskunde
Arbeiten zur Romanische Philologie — Arb z Roman Philol
Arbeiten zur Romanischen Philologie — ARP
Arbeiten zur Theologie [*Stuttgart/Berlin-Ost*] — ArbT
Arbeiten zur Theologie [*Stuttgart*] — ATh
Arbeiten zur Theologie [*Stuttgart/Berlin*] — AZTh
Arbeiter Teater Farband — ARTEF
Arbeitnehmerverdienste im Ausland — Arbeitneh Aus
Arbeits- und Forschungsberichte zur Saechsischen Bodendenkmalpflege — Arb F Ber Saechs
Arbeits- und Forschungsberichte zur Saechsischen Bodenkmalpflege — AFB
Arbeits- und Forschungsberichte zur Saechsischen Bodenkmalpflege — Arbeits u Forschber Sachsen
Arbeitsamt — AA
Arbeitsberichte des Instituts fuer Mathematische Maschinen und Datenverarbeitung (Informatik) — Arbeitsber Inst Math Masch Datenverarb Inform
Arbeitsberichte des Rechenzentrums [*Bochum*] — Arbeitsber Rechenzentrum
Arbeitsberichte. Instituts fuer Mathematische Maschinen und Datenverarbeitung. Band 14 — Arbeitsber Inst Math Masch Datenverarb Band 14
Arbeitsberichte. Instituts fuer Mathematische Maschinen und Datenverarbeitung. Band 15 — Arbeitsber Inst Math Masch Datenverarb Band 15
Arbeitsberichte Psychologische Methoden — Arbeitsber Psych Methoden
Arbeitsblaetter fuer Restauratoren — Arb Bl Rest
Arbeitsblaetter fuer Restauratoren — Arbeitsbl Restauraturen
Arbeitsgemeinschaft Deutscher Verfolgten-Organisationen — ADV
Arbeitsgemeinschaft fuer Forschung des Landes Nordrhein-Westfalen [*West Germany*] — Arbeitsgem-Forsch Landes Nordrh-Westfalen
Arbeitsgemeinschaft fuer Forschung des Landes Nordrhein-Westfalen. Geisteswissenschaften — AFLNW
Arbeitsgemeinschaft fuer Forschung des Landes Nordrhein-Westfalen. Geisteswissenschaften — AFNG
Arbeitsgemeinschaft fuer Pharmazeutische Verfahrenstechnik. Paperback APV — Arbeitsgem Pharm Verfahrenstech Paperback APV
Arbeitsgemeinschaft Getreideforschung. Veroeffentlichungen — Arbeitsgem Getreideforsch Veroeff
Arbeitsgemeinschaft Kartoffelforschung. Veroeffentlichungen — Arbeitsgem Kartoffelforsch Veroeff
Arbeitsgemeinschaft Rheinwasserwerke. Bericht — Arbeitsgem Rheinwasserwerke Ber
Arbeitsgemeinschaft Vorderer Orient — AGVO
Arbeitsmedizin, Sozialmedizin, Arbeitshygiene [*Later, Arbeitsmedizin, Sozialmedizin, Praeventivmedizin*] — Arbeitsmed Sozialmed Arbeitshyg
Arbeitsmedizin, Sozialmedizin, Praeventivmedizin — Arbeitsmed Sozialmed Praeventivmed
Arbeitsmedizinische Probleme des Dienstleistungsgewerbes — Arbeitsmed Probl Dienstleistungsgewerbes
Arbeitsmedizinisches Kolloquium Bericht ueber die Jahrestagung der Deutschen Gesellschaft fuer Arbeitsmedizin — Arbeitsmed Kolloq Ber Jahrestag Dtsh Ges Arbeitsmed
Arbeitspapiere zur Politischen Soziologie — Arbeitspapiere Pol Soziol
Arbeitsschutz bei der Anwendung Chemischer Technologien — Arbeitsschutz Anwend Chem Technol
Arbeitstagung Mengen- und Spurenelemente — Arbeitstag Mengen Spurenelem
Arbeitstagung ueber Extraterrestrische Biophysik und Biologie und Raumfahrtmedizin. Tagungsbericht — Arbeitstag Extraterr Biophys Biol Raumfahrtmed Tagungsber
Arbeitstagung ueber Physiologie und Pathophysiologie der Prostata — Arbeitstag Physiol Pathophysiol Prostata
Arbeitstechniken der Pharmazeutischen Industrie — Arbeitstech Pharm Ind
Arbejder. Universitet. Botanisk Have — Arbejder Univ Bot Have
Arbejderhojskolen — Arbh
Arbejdsmaendenes Fagblad — Arbm F
Arbetslivcentrum Dokumentationsenkenten [*Database*] — ALCDOK
Arbitration Journal — Ar J
Arbitration Journal — ARB
Arbitration Journal — Arb J
Arbitration Journal — Arbit J
Arbitration Journal — Arbitr J
Arbitration Journal — Arbitrat J
Arbitration Journal — Arbitration J
Arbitration Journal — Arbitration Jrnl
Arbitration Journal. Institute of Arbitrators — Arb J of the Inst of Arbitrators
Arbitration Journal (New Series) — Arb J (NS)
Arbitration Journal (Old Series) — Arb J (OS)
Arbitrazni Praxe — ARPRD
Arbitron Radio Summary Data [*Database*] — ARB
Arbog foer Dansk Skolehistorie — Arbog Dan Skokehist
Arbog-Danmarks Geologiske Undersoegelse [*Denmark*] — Arbog Dan Geol Unders
Arbok det Norske Videnskapsakademi — ArNVA
Arbok fuer Universitetet i Bergen. Matematisk-Naturvitenskapelig Serie — Arb U B Mat
Arbok fuer Universitetet i Bergen. Matematisk-Naturvitenskapelig Serie — ARBMA
Arbok fuer Universitetet i Bergen. Matematisk-Naturvitenskapelig Serie — Arbok Univ Bergen Mat-Natur Ser
Arbok fuer Universitetet i Bergen. Matematisk-Naturvitenskapelig Serie — Arbok Univ Bergen Mat-Naturvitensk Ser
Arbok fuer Universitetet i Bergen. Medisinsk Serie — Arbok Univ Bergen Med Ser
Arbok. Norske Videnskaps-Akademi i Oslo — Arbok Norske Vidensk Akad Oslo
Arbok Universitetet i Bergen. Naturvitenskapelig Rekke — Arbok Univ Bergen Naturvitensk Rekke
Arbok Universitetets Oldsaksamling — AUO
Arbok Universitetets Oldsaksamling (Oslo) — Univ Oldsaksaml Arbok (Oslo)
Arbol de Fuego — AdF
Arbol de Fuego — AF
Arbol de Letras — AdL
Arbor — AR
Arbor — Arb
Arbor Ciencia, Pensamiento y Cultura — Arb
Arbor Scientiarum. Beitraege Wissenschaftsgeschichte. Reihe C. Bibliographien [*A publication*] — Arbor Scientiarum Beitraege Wissenschaftsgeschichte Reihe C
Arboretum Bulletin. Arboretum Foundation (Seattle). University of Washington [*A publication*] — Arbor Bull Arbor Found (Seattle) Univ Wash
Arboretum Bulletin. Associates. Morris Arboretum — Arbor Bull Assoc
Arboretum Bulletin. Associates of the Morris Arboretum — Arbor Bull Assoc Morris Arbor
Arboretum Kornickie — Arbor Kornickie
Arboretum Leaves — Arbor Leaves
Arboretum Society Bulletin — Arbor Soc Bull
Arboricultural Association. Journal — Arbor Ass J
Arboricultural Journal — Arboric J
Arboricultural Society of South Africa — Arboric Soc South Africa
Arboriculture Fruitiere — Arboric Fruit
Arboriculture Fruitiere — Arboricult Fruit
Arbovirus Research in Australia. Proceedings. Symposium — Arbovirus Res Aust Proc Symp
Arc Furnace Meeting. Papers — Arc Furn Meet Pap
ARC [*Agricultural Research Council*] **Research Review (United Kingdom)** — ARC Res Rev (UK)
Arcadia [*Berlin*] — Arc
Arcadia, Accademia Letteraria Italiana. Atti e Memorie — AALIAM
Arcadia Zeitschrift fuer Vergleichende Literaturwissenschaft — Arcad
Arcana of Science and Art — Arcana Sci Art
Archaean Geochemistry — Archaean Geochem
Archaeoastronomy. Bulletin. Center for Archaeoastronomy — Archaeoastronomy Bull Cent Archaeoastron
Archaeoastronomy. Journal. Center for Archaeoastronomy — Archaeoastronomy J Cent Archaeoastron
Archaeoastronomy Supplement. Journal for the History of Astronomy — Archaeoastron
Archaeographie. Archaeologie und Elektronische Datenverarbeitung — Archaeographie
Archaeologia [*London*] — Ar
Archaeologia — ARCH
Archaeologia — Archaeol
Archaeologia Aeliana — A Ael
Archaeologia Aeliana — ArA
Archaeologia Aeliana — Arch Ael
Archaeologia Aeliana. Series 5 — Archaeol Aeliana 5 Ser
Archaeologia Austriaca — Arch Austr
Archaeologia Austriaca — Archaeol Austr
Archaeologia Austriaca — Archaeol Austriaca
Archaeologia Belgica — Arch Belg
Archaeologia Belgica — Archaeol Belgica
Archaeologia Cambrenses — A Cambr
Archaeologia Cambrenses — Arch Cam
Archaeologia Cambrensis — AC
Archaeologia Cambrensis — Arch Camb
Archaeologia Cambrensis — Arch Cambrensis
Archaeologia Cambrensis — Archaeol Cambrensis
Archaeologia Cambrensis. Journal. Cambrian Archaeological Association — Archaeol Cambr
Archaeologia Cantiana — Arch Cant
Archaeologia Cantiana — Archaeol Cantiana
Archaeologia Cantiana. Transactions of the Kent Archaeological Society — Arch Cantiana
Archaeologia Classica — AC
Archaeologia Geographica — Arch Geogr
Archaeologia Geographica. Beitraege zur Vergleichenden Geographisch-Kartographischen Methode in der Urgeschichtsforschung — A Geo
Archaeologia Helvetica — Arch Helv
Archaeologia Homerica — Arch Hom
Archaeologia Hungarica — Arch Hung
Archaeologia Iugoslavica — ArchIug
Archaeologia Jugoslavica — A Jug
Archaeologia Jugoslavica — Arch Jug
Archaeologia Jugoslavica — Arch Jugoslavica
Archaeologia Oxoniensis — Arch Oxon
Archaeologia Polona — A Pol
Archaeologia Polona — A Polona
Archaeologia Polona — AP
Archaeologia Polona — Arch Polon

Archaeologia Polona — Arch Polona
Archaeologia Polona — Archaeol Polona
Archaeologia Scotia — Arch Scot
Archaeologia Viva [*Paris*] — Arch Viva
Archaeologiai Ertesito — AErt
Archaeologiai Ertesito — Arch Ert
Archaeologiai Ertesitoe [*Budapest*] — Arch Ertes
Archaeologiai Ertesitoe [*Budapest*] — Arch Ertesitoe
Archaeologiai Koezlemenyek — AK
Archaeologiai Koezlemenyek — Arch K
Archaeologiai Koezlemenyek — Arch Koezl
Archaeologiai Koezlemenyek — Arch Koezlemenyek
Archaeologica Aeliana — Arch Aeliana
Archaeologica Lundensia. Investigationes de Antiquitibus urbis Lundae — Archaeol Lund
Archaeological Bibliography for Great Britain and Ireland — Arch Bib G Brit
Archaeological Chemistry. [*A*] Symposium — Archaeol Chem Symp
Archaeological Geology — Archaeol Geol
Archaeological Journal — AJ
Archaeological Journal — Arch J
Archaeological Journal [*London*] — Arch Journ
Archaeological Journal — Archaeol J
Archaeological Journal — Archaeological Jnl
Archaeological Journal (London) — Archaeol J (London)
Archaeological News — A News
Archaeological News — Arch N
Archaeological News — Arch News
Archaeological News — Archaeol News
Archaeological News Letter — ANL
Archaeological News Letter — Arch NL
Archaeological Report Comprising the Recent Work of the Egypt Exploration Fund and the Progress of Egyptology [*London*] — ARp
Archaeological Report (London) — A Rep (London)
Archaeological Reports — AR
Archaeological Reports [*London*] — Arch Rep
Archaeological Reports [*London*] — Arch Reports
Archaeological Reports — Archaeol Rep
Archaeological Review [*Bristol, England*] — AR
Archaeological Review — Archaeol Rev
Archaeological Sites Data Base — AZSITE
Archaeological Survey of Alberta. Occasional Papers — Archaeol Surv Alberta Occas Pap
Archaeological Survey of Alberta. Occasional Papers — ASAOP
Archaeological Survey of Alberta. Occasional Papers — OPAAER
Archaeological Survey of Egypt — ASE
Archaeologie Austriaca — A Austr
Archaeologie Austriaca — AAU
Archaeologie Austriaca — Ar Au
Archaeologie Austriaca — Arch A
Archaeologie Austriaca — Arch Austriaca
Archaeologie der Schweiz. Mitteilungsblatt der Schweizerischen Gesellschaft fuer Ur- und Fruehgeschichte — A Schw
Archaeologie des Schweiz — Arch S
Archaeologie des Schweiz — AS
Archaeologie und Naturwissenschaften — A Natur Wiss
Archaeologie und Naturwissenschaften — Arch Naturw
Archaeologische Bibliographie [*Berlin*] — AB
Archaeologische Bibliographie — Archaeol Biblio
Archaeologische Bibliographie — ArchBg
Archaeologische Forschungen [*Berlin*] — AF
Archaeologische Fuehrer der Schweiz — Ar F Schweiz
Archaeologische Informationen — Arch Inf
Archaeologische Mitteilungen aus Iran — AMI
Archaeologische Mitteilungen aus Iran — AMIran
Archaeologische Mitteilungen aus Iran [*Berlin*] — Arch Mitt Iran
Archaeologische Mitteilungen aus Iran. Neue Folge [*Berlin*] — ArchMIran
Archaeologische Mitteilungen aus Nordwestdeutschland — A M Nordwest D
Archaeologische Nachrichten aus Baden — A Nachr Bad
Archaeologische Nachrichten aus Baden — ANB
Archaeologische Nachrichten aus Baden — Arch Nachr Baden
Archaeologische Veroeffentlichungen. Deutsches Archaeologisches Institut Cairo — AV
Archaeologische Zeitung [*Berlin*] — Arch Zeit
Archaeologische Zeitung [*Berlin*] — Archaeol Zeitung
Archaeologische Zeitung — Archaeol Ztg
Archaeologische Zeitung [*Berlin*] — Archaeolog Zeitung
Archaeologische Zeitung — ArchZtg
Archaeologische Zeitung — AZ
Archaeologisch-Epigraphische Mitteilungen aus Oesterreich [*Ungarn*] — AEM
Archaeologisch-Epigraphische Mitteilungen aus Oesterreich — AEMOe
Archaeologisch-Epigraphische Mitteilungen aus Oesterreich-Ungarn — Archaeol Epigr Mitt
Archaeologisch-Epigraphische Mittheilungen aus Oesterreich-Ungarn — AEMO
Archaeologisch-Epigraphische Mittheilungen aus Oesterreich-Ungarn — AEMOU
Archaeologisch-Epigraphische Mittheilungen aus Oesterreich-Ungarn — Arch Ep Mitt
Archaeologisch-Epigraphische Mittheilungen aus Oesterreich-Ungarn — Arch Epigr Mitt Oesterreich
Archaeologisch-Epigraphische Mittheilungen aus Oesterreich-Ungarn — Archepigr Mitt
Archaeologischer Anzeiger — AA
Archaeologischer Anzeiger [*Berlin*] — ArchAnz
Archaeologischer Anzeiger [*Berlin*] — Jahrb Anz
Archaeologischer Anzeiger. Beiblatt zum Jahrbuch des Kaiserlich Deutschen Archaeologischen Instituts — AAJDAI
Archaeologischer Anzeiger (Berlin) — A AnZ B
Archaeologischer Anzeiger (Berlin) — Anzeiger Berlin
Archaeologischer Anzeiger zur Archaeologischen Zeitung — AAAZ
Archaeologischer Anzeiger zur Archaeologischen Zeitung — AANZ
Archaeologisches Intelligenzblatt zur Allgemeinen Literatur Zeitung — Arch Intelligenzblatt
Archaeologisches Korrespondenzblatt — A KorrBl
Archaeologisches Korrespondenzblatt — AKB
Archaeologisches Korrespondenzblatt — Arch Korr
Archaeologisches Korrespondenzblatt — Arch Korrbl
Archaeologisches Korrespondenzblatt — Arch Korrespondenzbl
Archaeologisches Korrespondenzblatt — Archaeol Korrespbl
Archaeologisch-Historische Bijdragen — AHB
Archaeology [*Cambridge, MA*] — Arch
Archaeology — GARC
Archaeology and Physical Anthropology in Oceania — APAO
Archaeology and Physical Anthropology in Oceania [*Later, Archaeology in Oceania*] — APAOBE
Archaeology and Physical Anthropology in Oceania [*Later, Archaeology in Oceania*] — Archaeol Phy Anthrop Oceania
Archaeology and Physical Anthropology in Oceania [*Later, Archaeology in Oceania*] — Archaeol Phys Anthropol Oceania
Archaeology. Archaeological Institute of America — AIA/A
Archaeology in Britain — Archaeol Brit
Archaeology in Oceania — AOCEDN
Archaeology in Oceania — Archaeol Oceania
Archaeology of Crete — AC
Archaeometry — Archaeometr
Archaiologika Analekta ex Athenon — AAA
Archaiologika Analekta ex Athenon — Arch An Ath
Archaiologika Analekta ex Athenon — Arch Analekta
Archaiologika Analekta ex Athenon — Athens Ann Arch
Archaiologike Ephemeris — AE
Archaiologike Ephemeris — Arch Eph
Archaiologike Ephemeris — Arch Ephem
Archaiologike Ephemeris — Arch Ephemeris
Archaiologike Ephemeris — Archaiol Ephem
Archaiologike Ephemeris — Eph
Archaiologike Ephemeris — Ephem
Archaiologikon Deltion — A Delt
Archaiologikon Deltion — AD
Archaiologikon Deltion — Arch Delt
Archaiologikon Deltion — Arch Deltion
Archaiologikon Deltion — Delt
Archaiologikon Deltion — Deltion
Arche — Ar
Archeia tes Pharmakeutikes (Athens) — APKTAA
Archeia tes Pharmakeutikes (Athens) — Arch Pharm (Athens)
Archeion Ekklesiastikes Historias — Arch Ekkl Hist
Archeion Ekklesiastiku kai Kanoniku Dikaiu — AEKD
Archeion Euboikon Meleton — A Eub M
Archeion Euboikon Meleton — AEM
Archeion Iatrikon Epistemon — Arch Iatr Epistem
Archeion Latrikon Epistemon — Arch Latr Epistem
Archeion Pontou — AP
Archeion Pontou — Arch Pont
Archeion Pontou — Arch Pontou
Archeion Pontou — ArcP
Archeion Thessalikon Meleton — A Th M
Archeion Thessalikon Meleton — Arch Tess
Archeion Thessalikon Meleton — Arch Thess Mel
Archeion Thrakes — ArchT
Archeion ton Byzantinon Mnemeion tes Hellados — ABME
Archeion ton Byzantinon Mnemeion tes Hellados — ABMH
Archeion ton Byzantinon Mnemeion tes Hellados — Arch B M
Archeion ton Byzantinon Mnemeion tes Hellados — Arch Byz Mnem
Archeion tou Thrakikou Laographikou kai Glossikou Thesaurou — ATLGT
Archeocivilisation [*Paris*] — Archeocivil
Archeolgrafo Triestino — Arch Triest
Archeolgrafo Triestino — Archeogr Triest
Archeolgrafo Triestino — AT
Archeolgrafo Triestino — ATriest
Archeologia [*Torun*] — Ar
Archeologia [*Paris*] — Ar
Archeologia [*Rome*] — Ar
Archeologia Classica — Arch Cl
Archeologia Classica [*Rome*] — Arch Classica
Archeologia Classica — ArchClass
Archeologia (Paris) — Ar (P)
Archeologia (Paris) — Arch (P)
Archeologia (Paris) — Arch (Paris)
Archeologia Polski — A Pol
Archeologia Polski — A Polski
Archeologia Polski — AP
Archeologia Polski — Arch Pol
Archeologia Polski — Arch Polski
Archeologia Polski — Archeol Pol
Archeologia. Rocznik Instytutu Historii Kultury Materialnej Polskiej Akademii Nauk (Warszawa) — Archeologia (Warzawa)
Archeologia (Rome) — Arch R
Archeologia (Torun) — Arch (T)
Archeologia. Tresors des Ages (Paris) — Archeologia (Paris)
Archeologia Veneta — A Ven

Archeologia Viva — A Viva
Archeologiceskij Sbornik Gosudarstvennyj Ordena Lenina Ermitaz — A Sbor
Archeologicke Rozhledy — A Rozhl
Archeologicke Rozhledy — Arch Rozhledy
Archeologicke Rozhledy — Archeol Rozhl
Archeologicke Studijni Materialy — ASM
Archeologie Armoricaine — ArchArm
Archeologie. Centre National de Recherches Archeologiques en Belgique — Ar
Archeologie. Centre National de Recherches Archeologiques en Belgique — Arch Belg
Archeologie Medievale [*Caen*] — A Mediev
Archeologie Quebec — Arch Quebec
Archeologie (Sofia) — Arch (Sofia)
Archeologija. Akademija Nauk Ukrains'koi RSR. Institut Archeologii (Kiev) — Archeologija (Kiev)
Archeologija. Organ na Archeologiceskija Institut i Muzej pri B'lgarskata Akademija na Naukite (Sofia) — Archeologija (Sof)
Archeologike Rozhledy — AR
Archeologike Rozhledy — Ar Roz
Archeologike Rozhledy — Arch Roz
Archeologike Rozhledy — Arch Rozhl
Archery World — Archery Wld
Archief van Sociale Geneeskunde en Hygiene en Tijdschrift voor Pathologie en Physiologie van den Arbeid — Arch Soc Geneeskd Hyg Tijdschr Pathol Physiol Arb
Archief voor de Geschiedenis der Oude Hollandsche Zending — AGOHZ
Archief voor de Geschiedenis van de Katholieke Kerk in Nederland — AGKKN
Archief voor de Geschiedenis van het Aartsbisdom Utrecht — AGAU
Archief voor de Geschiedenis van het Aartsbisdom Utrecht — Arch G Utrecht
Archief voor de Java Suikerindustrie — Arch Java Suikerindustr
Archief voor de Koffiecultuur in Nederlandsch-Indie — Arch Koffiecult Ned Indie
Archief voor de Rubbercultuur — Arch Rubbercult
Archief voor de Suikerindustrie in Nederland en Nederlandsch-Indie — Arch Suikerind Ned Ned Indie
Archief voor de Suikerindustrie in Nederland en Nederlandsch-Indie — Arch Suikerindustr Ned Ned Indie
Archief voor de Suikerindustrie in Nederlandsch-Indie — Arch Suikerind Ned Indie
Archief voor de Theecultuur — Arch Theecult
Archief voor de Theecultuur in Nederlandsch-Indie — Arch Theecult Ned Indie
Archief voor den Landbouw der Bergstreken in Nederlandsch-Indie — Arch Landb Bergstreken Ned Indie
Archief voor Nederlandsch Kerkgeschiedenis — Archief Nederld Kerkgesch
Archiginnasio — Archig
Archimedes Workshop on Molecular Solids under Pressure — Archimedes Workshop Mol Solids Pressure
Architect and Builder — Archit Build
Architect and Builder [*South Africa*] — Archt & Bldr
Architect and Engineer — Arch & Eng
Architect and Engineer — Archit Eng
Architect and Engineer of California and the Pacific Coast — Arch Eng Calif Pac Coast
Architect and Surveyor — Archit Surv
Architect and Surveyor — Archt & Surveyor
Architects' and Builders' Magazine [*New York*] — Arch & BM
Architects Forum — Archts Forum
Architects' Journal — AJ
Architects' Journal — Arch J
Architects' Journal — Archit J
Architects' Journal — Architects J
Architects' Journal — Archts Jnl
Architects News — Archits News
Architects News — Archts News
Architects' Trade Journal — Archts Trade Jnl
Architect's Yearbook — Arch Yr
Architect's Yearbook — Arch Yrbk
Architectura. Zeitschrift fuer Geschichte der Baukunst — Arch Z Ges
Architectural Aluminum Industry. Annual Statistical Review — Arch Alum
Architectural and Archaeological Society of Durham and Northumberland. Transactions — Archit Archaeol Soc Durham Northumberl Trans
Architectural Association. Annual Review — Archl Assocn Annual Review
Architectural Association. Quarterly — AAQ
Architectural Association. Quarterly — AAQU-A
Architectural Association. Quarterly — Archit Assoc Q
Architectural Bulletin — Archtl Bull
Architectural Design — ACLD-A
Architectural Design — AD
Architectural Design — Arch Des
Architectural Design — Archit Des
Architectural Design — Archtl Design
Architectural Digest — AD
Architectural Digest — Archit Dig
Architectural Digest — GARD
Architectural Education — Arch Ed
Architectural Forum — AF
Architectural Forum — Arch Forum
Architectural Forum — Archit Forum
Architectural Forum (Dublin) — Archtl Forum (Dublin)
Architectural History — Archit Hist
Architectural History — Architect Hist
Architectural History — Archtl History
Architectural Journal — Archtl Jnl
Architectural Magazine. Egyptian Association of Architects — Archtl Magazine Egyptian Assocn of Archts
Architectural Metals — Archit Met
Architectural Monographs — Archit Mono
Architectural Monographs — Archtl Monographs
Architectural Periodicals Index — Archit Per Ind
Architectural Periodicals Index — Archit Period Index
Architectural Preservation — Archtl Preservation
Architectural Psychology Newsletter — Archtl Psychology Newsletter
Architectural Record — ACUR-A
Architectural Record — Arch Rec
Architectural Record — Archit Rec
Architectural Record — Archtl Record
Architectural Record — ARD
Architectural Record — GARR
Architectural Review — AARV-A
Architectural Review — AR
Architectural Review — Arch R
Architectural Review — Arch Rev
Architectural Review — Archit R
Architectural Review — Archit Rev
Architectural Review — Architect Rev
Architectural Review — Archtl Review
Architectural Review (Chearn, England) — ARC
Architectural Science Review — Arch Sci Rev
Architectural Science Review — Arch Science R
Architectural Science Review — Archit Sci Rev
Architectural Science Review — Archt Sci Rev
Architectural Science Review — Archtl Science Review
Architectural Technology — Arch Tech
Architecture and Arts — Arch & Arts
Architecture and Building — Arch & B
Architecture and Building — Arch & Bldg
Architecture and Urbanism — A & U
Architecture Australia — Archit Aust
Architecture Australia — Archre Australia
Architecture, Building, Structural Engineering — Arch Build Eng
Architecture Canada — Arch Can
Architecture Concept — Arch Concept
Architecture Concept [*Canada*] — Archit Concept
Architecture d'Aujourd'hui — Arch Aujourd'hui
Architecture d'Aujourd'hui — Arch d'Aujourd'hui
Architecture d'Aujourd'hui — Archit Auj
Architecture d'Aujourd'hui — Archit Aujourd
Architecture d'Aujourd'hui — Archit d'Aujourd'hui
Architecture d'Aujourd'hui — ARDH-A
Architecture East Midlands — Archre East Midlands
Architecture et Comportement/Architecture and Behavior — Architecture & Comportement/Archre & Behavior
Architecture from Scandinavia — Archre from Scandinavia
Architecture in Australia [*Later, Architecture Australia*] — Arch
Architecture in Australia [*Later, Architecture Australia*] — Arch in Aust
Architecture in Australia [*Later, Architecture Australia*] — Archit
Architecture in Australia [*Later, Architecture Australia*] — Archit in Aust
Architecture in Australia [*Later, Architecture Australia*] — Archre in Australia
Architecture in Greece — Archre in Greece
Architecture in Ireland — Archre in Ireland
Architecture in Israel — Archre in Israel
Architecture, Mouvement, Continuite — ARMC
Architecture Nebraska — Archre Nebr
Architecture Plus — Archit Plus
Architecture South Africa — Archre SA
Architecture Today — Arch Today
Architecture West Midlands — Archre West Midlands
Architecture-Batiment-Construction — Arch-Bat-Constr
Architectures and Algorithms for Digital Image Processing — Archit Algorithms Digital Image Process
Architekt — Arch
Architektur und Wohnwelt [*Germany*] — Archit Wohnwelt
Architektur und Wohnwelt — ARCWD
Architektura — ARKT-B
Architektura a Urbanizmus — ARCU
Architettura Cronache e Storia — Archit Cronache Storia
Architettura e Arti Decorative. Rivista d'Arte e di Storia — Arch Arti Dec
Archiv aller Buergerlichen Wissenschaften zum Nutzen und Vergnuegen wie auch zum Selbstunterricht in Reiferen Jahren — Arch Aller Buergerl Wiss
Archiv der Agriculturchemie fuer Denkende Landwirthe — Arch Agriculturchem Denkende Landwirthe
Archiv der Deutschen Dominikaner — ADD
Archiv der Deutschen Seewarte — AD SW
Archiv der Elektrischen Uebertragung — Arch Elek Uebertragung
Archiv der Elektrischen Uebertragung — Arch Elektr Uebertrag
Archiv der Gegenwart — AdG
Archiv der Julius Klaus-Stiftung fuer Vererbungsforschung, Sozialanthropologie, und Rassenhygiene — AJKSAX
Archiv der Julius Klaus-Stiftung fuer Vererbungsforschung, Sozialanthropologie, und Rassenhygiene — Arch Julius Klaus Stiftung Vererbungsf
Archiv der Julius Klaus-Stiftung fuer Vererbungsforschung, Sozialanthropologie, und Rassenhygiene — Arch Julius Klaus-Stift Vererbforsch
Archiv der Mathematik — Arch Math
Archiv der Mathematik (Basel) — Arch Math (Basel)
Archiv der Naturwissenschaftlichen Landesdurchforschung von Boehmen — Arch Natw Ldsdurchforsch Boehmen
Archiv der Pharmacie des Apotheker-Vereins im Noerdlichen Teutschland — Arch Pharm Apotheker Vereins Noerdl Teutschl

Archiv der Pharmacie. Eine Zeitschrift des Apotheker-Vereins im Noerdlichen Teutschland (Berlin) — Arch Pharm Berlin
Archiv der Pharmazie — A Pharm
Archiv der Pharmazie — Arch Pharm
Archiv der Pharmazie [*Weinheim, Germany*] — ARPMAS
Archiv der Pharmazie und Berichte der Deutschen Pharmazeutischen Gesellschaft — APBDAJ
Archiv der Pharmazie und Berichte der Deutschen Pharmazeutischen Gesellschaft — Arch Pharm Ber Dtsch Pharm Ges
Archiv der Pharmazie und Berichte der Deutschen Pharmazeutischen Gesellschaft (Berlin) — Arch Pharm (Berl)
Archiv der Pharmazie (Weinheim) — Arch Pharm (Weinheim)
Archiv der Pharmazie (Weinheim, Germany) — Arch Pharm (Weinheim Ger)
Archiv der Teutschen Landwirthschaft — Arch Teutsch Landw
Archiv des Apotheker Vereins im Noerdlichen Deutschland — Arch Apoth Ver Noerd Deutschl
Archiv des Badewesens — Arch Badewes
Archiv des Garten- und Blumenbau-Vereins fuer Hamburg, Altona, und deren Umgegenden — Arch Garten Blumenbau Vereins Hamburg
Archiv des Historischen Vereins des Kantons Bern — Ar Berne
Archiv des Historischen Vereins von Mainfranken — AHVMF
Archiv des Historischen Vereins von Unterfranken und Aschaffenburg — AHVUA
Archiv des Historischen Vereins von Unterfranken und Aschaffenburg — Arch Hist Ver Unterfranken
Archiv des Oeffentlichen Rechts — Arch Oeff Recht
Archiv des Oeffentlichen Rechts — Arch Oeff Rechts
Archiv des Oeffentlichen Rechts — Archiv Off Rechts
Archiv des Vereins fuer Siebenbuergische Landeskunde — Arch Vereins Siebenbuerg Landesk
Archiv des Vereins fuer Siebenbuergische Landeskunde — AVsL
Archiv des Vereins fuer Siebenbuergische Landeskunde — AVSLK
Archiv des Voelkerrechts — Arch Voelkerrechts
Archiv des Voelkerrechts — Archiv Volkerrechts
Archiv foer Matematik og Naturvidenskab [*Norway*] — Arch Mat Naturvidensk
Archiv foer Pharmaci og Chemi — APCEAR
Archiv foer Pharmaci og Chemi — Arch Pharm Chem
Archiv foer Pharmaci og Chemi. Scientific Edition — Arch Pharm Chem Sci Ed
Archiv foer Pharmaci og Chemi. Scientific Edition — AVPCCS
Archiv for Pharmaci og Chemi — A Ph Ch
Archiv. Freunde der Naturgeschichte in Mecklenburg — Arch Freunde Naturgesch Mecklenburg
Archiv fuer Acker- und Pflanzenbau und Bodenkunde — AAPBCE
Archiv fuer Acker- und Pflanzenbau und Bodenkunde — Arch Acker-Pflanzenbau Bodenkd
Archiv fuer Aegyptische Archaeologie — A Ae A
Archiv fuer Aegyptische Archaeologie — A Aeg Arch
Archiv fuer Aegyptische Archaeologie — Arch Aeg Arch
Archiv fuer Alte und Neue Kirchengeschichte — AANKG
Archiv fuer Anatomie, Physiologie, und Wissenschaftliche Medicin — Arch Anat Physiol Wiss Med
Archiv fuer Anatomie, Physiologie, und Wissenschaftliche Medizin — Arch Anat Phys Wiss Med
Archiv fuer Anatomie, Physiologie, und Wissenschaftliche Medizin — Arch Anat Physiol
Archiv fuer Anatomie und Physiologie. Anatomische Abteilung — Arch Anat Physiol Anat Abt
Archiv fuer Anatomie und Physiologie. Physiologische Abteilung — Arch Anat Physiol Physiol Abt
Archiv fuer Anthropologie — AA
Archiv fuer Anthropologie — AAn
Archiv fuer Anthropologie — AAnth
Archiv fuer Anthropologie — Arch Anthrop
Archiv fuer Anthropologie — Archiv F Anthropol
Archiv fuer Anthropologie und Voelkerforschung — AAVF
Archiv fuer Anthropologie und Voelkerforschung — Archiv Anthrop
Archiv fuer Anthropologie, Voelkerforschung, und Kolonialen Kulturwandel — Arch f Anthr
Archiv fuer Arzneitherapie — Arch Arzneither
Archiv fuer Augenheilkunde — AfAh
Archiv fuer Augenheilkunde — Arch Augen
Archiv fuer Augenheilkunde — Arch Augenheilk
Archiv fuer Augenheilkunde — Arch Augenheilkd
Archiv fuer Augenheilkunde — Arch Aughlkde
Archiv fuer Begriffsgeschichte — ABG
Archiv fuer Begriffsgeschichte [*Bonn*] — ArBegriffsg
Archiv fuer Begriffsgeschichte — Arch Begriff
Archiv fuer Begriffs-Geschichte — Arch Begriffs Gesch
Archiv fuer Begriffsgeschichte — Arch f Begriffsgeschichte
Archiv fuer Bergbau und Huettenwesen — Arch Bergbau
Archiv fuer Bienenkunde — ARBKAK
Archiv fuer Bienenkunde — Arch Bienenk
Archiv fuer Bienenkunde — Arch Bienenkd
Archiv fuer Bodenfruchtbarkeit und Pflanzenproduktion — Arch Bodenfruchtbarkeit Pflanzenprod
Archiv fuer Celtische Lexikographie — Arch Celt Lexikogr
Archiv fuer Chemie und Meteorologie — Arch Chem Meteorol
Archiv fuer Chemie und Mikroskopie — Arch Chem Mikrosk
Archiv fuer Christliche Kunst — AchrK
Archiv fuer Christliche Kunst — ACK
Archiv fuer das Eisenhuettenwesen — Arch Eisenh
Archiv fuer das Eisenhuettenwesen — Arch Eisenhuettenwes
Archiv fuer das Eisenhuettenwesen [*Germany*] — Arch Eisenhuttenwesen
Archiv fuer das Post- und Fernmeldewesen — Arch Post und Fernmeldewes
Archiv fuer das Post- und Fernmeldewesen — Archiv Post U Fernmeldewesen
Archiv fuer das Studium der Neueren Sprachen — A
Archiv fuer das Studium der Neueren Sprachen — ANS
Archiv fuer das Studium der Neueren Sprachen und Literaturen — A Stn Spr
Archiv fuer das Studium der Neueren Sprachen und Literaturen — Archiv
Archiv fuer das Studium der Neueren Sprachen und Literaturen — Archiv f Stud
Archiv fuer das Studium der Neueren Sprachen und Literaturen — ASNS
Archiv fuer das Studium der Neueren Sprachen und Literaturen — ASNSL
Archiv fuer das Studium der Neuren Sprachen und Literaturen — ASSL
Archiv fuer das Studium Deutscher Kolonialsprachen — Archiv F D Stud D Kolonialsp
Archiv fuer den Menschen und Buerger in Allen Verhaeltnissen — Arch Menschen Buerger
Archiv fuer der Studium der Neuren Sprachen und Literaturen — Arch f d Stud d Neur Spr u Lit
Archiv fuer der Studium der Neuren Sprachen und Literaturen — Arch f d Studium d Neur Spr u Lit
Archiv fuer Dermatologie und Syphilis — Arch Dermat u Syph
Archiv fuer Dermatologie und Syphilis — Archiv F Dermat U Syph
Archiv fuer Dermatologische Forschung — ADMFAU
Archiv fuer Dermatologische Forschung — Arch Derm F
Archiv fuer Dermatologische Forschung — Arch Dermatol Forsch
Archiv fuer Deutsche Postgeschichte — ADP
Archiv fuer die Gesamte Naturlehre — Arch Gesamte Naturl
Archiv fuer die Gesamte Physiologie des Menschen und der Tiere [*Pfluegers*] — AGPPAS
Archiv fuer die Gesamte Physiologie des Menschen und der Tiere (Pfluegers) — Arch Gesamte Physiol Mens Tiere (Pfluegers)
Archiv fuer die Gesamte Psychologie — AGEPB
Archiv fuer die Gesamte Psychologie — APsyc
Archiv fuer die Gesamte Virusforschung — AGVIA3
Archiv fuer die Gesamte Virusforschung — Arch Gesamte Virusforsch
Archiv fuer die Gesamte Waermetechnik — Arch Gesamte Waermetech
Archiv fuer die Geschichte der Mathematik, der Naturwissenschaften und der Technik — Arch Gesch Math
Archiv fuer die Geschichte der Naturwissenschaften und der Technik. Berliner Gesellschaft fuer Geschichte der Naturwissenschaften und Medizin — Arch Gesch Naturwiss Tech
Archiv fuer die Naturkunde Estlands. 1 Serie Geologica, Chemica, et Physics — Arch Naturkd Estlands 1 Ser
Archiv fuer die Naturkunde Liv-, Ehst- und Kurlands. 1 Serie. Biologische Naturkunde — Arch Naturkd Liv Ehst Kurlands 2 Ser
Archiv fuer die Naturkunde Liv-, Ehst- und Kurlands. Serie 2. Biologische Naturkunde — Arch Naturk Liv Ehst Kurlands Ser 2 Biol Naturk
Archiv fuer die Naturkunde Liv-, Est-, und Kurlands — ANLKB
Archiv fuer die Naturkunde Liv-, Est-, und Kurlands [*Estonian SSR*] — Arch Naturkd Liv- Est- Kurlands
Archiv fuer die Naturkunde Ostbaltikums. 2 Serie. Biologische Naturkunde — Arch Naturkd Ostbaltikums 2 Ser
Archiv fuer die Naturwissenschaftliche Landesdurchforschung von Boehmen — Arch Naturwiss Landesdurchf Boehmen
Archiv fuer die Neuesten Entdeckungen aus der Urwelt — Arch Neuesten Entdeck Urwelt
Archiv fuer die Pharmacie und Aerztliche Naturkunde — Arch Pharm Aerztl Naturk
Archiv fuer die Physiologie — Arch Physiol
Archiv fuer die Zivilistische Praxis — Ziv A
Archiv fuer die Zivilistische Praxis — Ziv Pr
Archiv fuer Diplomatik — AD
Archiv fuer Diplomatik — AfD
Archiv fuer Diplomatik — Arch Diplomatik
Archiv fuer Diplomatik, Schriftgeschichte, Siegel- und Wappenkunde — A Dipl
Archiv fuer Druck und Papier — Arch Druck Pap
Archiv fuer Eisenbahntechnik — Arch Eisenbahntech
Archiv fuer Eisenbahnwesen — AfEis
Archiv fuer Elektronik und Uebertragungstechnik — AEU
Archiv fuer Elektronik und Uebertragungstechnik — Arch Elek Ubertr
Archiv fuer Elektronik und Uebertragungstechnik — Arch Elektron Uebertragungstech
Archiv fuer Elektronik und Uebertragungstechnik — Arch Elektron und Uebertragungstech
Archiv fuer Elektrotechnik [*Berlin*] — Arch Elektr
Archiv fuer Elektrotechnik (Berlin) — Arch Elektrotech (Berlin)
Archiv fuer Elsaessische Kirchengeschichte — AEKG
Archiv fuer Energiewirtschaft — Arch Energiewirtsch
Archiv fuer Entwicklungsmechanik der Organismen — Arch Entwicklungsmech Org
Archiv fuer Entwicklungsmechanik der Organismen — Arch Entwmech Org
Archiv fuer Entwicklungsmechanik der Organismen (Wilhelm Roux) — Arch Entwicklungsmech Org (Wilhelm Roux)
Archiv fuer Erzbergbau, Erzaufbereitung, Metallhuettenwesen — Arch Erzbergbau Erzaufbereit Metallhuettenwes
Archiv fuer Evangelisches Kirchenrecht — A Ev KR
Archiv fuer Exakte Wirtschaftsforschung — AeW
Archiv fuer Experimentelle Pathologie und Pharmakologie — Arch Exp Path Pharmak
Archiv fuer Experimentelle Pathologie und Pharmakologie — Arch Exp Pathol
Archiv fuer Experimentelle Pathologie und Pharmakologie — Arch Exp Pathol Pharmakol
Archiv fuer Experimentelle Veterinaermedizin — Arch Exp Ve
Archiv fuer Experimentelle Veterinaermedizin — Arch Exp Veterinaermed
Archiv fuer Experimentelle Veterinaermedizin — Arch Exp Vetmed
Archiv fuer Experimentelle Veterinaermedizin — AXVMA
Archiv fuer Experimentelle Veterinaermedizin — AXVMAW
Archiv fuer Experimentelle Zellforschung Besonders Gewebezuechtung — Arch Exp Zellforsch Besonders Gewebezuecht

Archiv fuer Experimentelle Zellforschung Besonders Gewebezuechtung — Archiv Exp Zellforsch Besonders Gewebezuecht
Archiv fuer Fischereiwissenschaft — Arch Fisch
Archiv fuer Fischereiwissenschaft — Arch Fischereiwiss
Archiv fuer Fischereiwissenschaft — AVFSAO
Archiv fuer Fischereiwissenschaft. Beiheft — Arch Fischereiwiss Beih
Archiv fuer Forstwesen — Arch Forstw
Archiv fuer Forstwesen — Arch Forstwes
Archiv fuer Forstwesen — Arch Forstwesen
Archiv fuer Frankfurts Geschichte und Kunst — AFGK
Archiv fuer Frauenkunde und Konstitutionsforschung — AFKo
Archiv fuer Frauenkunde und Konstitutionsforschung — Arch Frauenkde Konstitutforsch
Archiv fuer Gartenbau — Arch Gartenb
Archiv fuer Gartenbau — Arch Gartenbau
Archiv fuer Gefluegelkunde [*Archives of Poultry Science*] — AGEFAB
Archiv fuer Gefluegelkunde — Arch Gefluegelk
Archiv fuer Gefluegelkunde — Arch Gefluegelkd
Archiv fuer Gefluegelkunde/European Poultry Science/Revue de Science Avicole Europeenne — Arch Geflugelkd Eur Poult Sci Rev Sci Avicole Eur
Archiv fuer Gefluegelzucht und Kleintierkunde — Arch Gefluegelz Kleintierk
Archiv fuer Gefluegelzucht und Kleintierkunde — Arch Gefluegelzucht Kleintierk
Archiv fuer Genetik — AGNKA3
Archiv fuer Genetik [*Zurich*] — Arch Genet
Archiv fuer Geographie, Historie, Staats- und Kriegskunst — Arch Geogr
Archiv fuer Geschichte der Dioezese Linz — Arch Gesch Dioez Linz
Archiv fuer Geschichte der Mathematik, der Naturwissenschaften, und der Technik — Arch Gesch Math Naturwiss Techn
Archiv fuer Geschichte der Medizin — Arch Gesch Med
Archiv fuer Geschichte der Medizin und der Naturwissenschafter. Sudhoff's — Arch Gesch Med Naturwiss Sudhoffs
Archiv fuer Geschichte der Naturwissenschaften und Technik — Arch Gesch Natwiss
Archiv fuer Geschichte der Philosophie — A G Philos
Archiv fuer Geschichte der Philosophie — AGP
Archiv fuer Geschichte der Philosophie — AGPh
Archiv fuer Geschichte der Philosophie — Arch f G d Philos
Archiv fuer Geschichte der Philosophie — Arch f G Philos
Archiv fuer Geschichte der Philosophie — Arch f Gesch d Philos
Archiv fuer Geschichte der Philosophie — Arch f Gesch der Philos
Archiv fuer Geschichte der Philosophie — Arch Gesch
Archiv fuer Geschichte der Philosophie — Arch Gesch Phil
Archiv fuer Geschichte der Philosophie — Archiv Philos
Archiv fuer Geschichte der Philosophie — ArGP
Archiv fuer Geschichte des Buchwesens — ADGB
Archiv fuer Geschichte des Buchwesens — AGB
Archiv fuer Geschichte des Buchwesens — Archiv Gesch Buchw
Archiv fuer Geschichte des Buchwesens — Archiv Gesch Buchwes
Archiv fuer Geschichte des Hochstifts Augsburg — AGHA
Archiv fuer Geschichte, Statistik, Literatur, und Kunst — Arch Gesch
Archiv fuer Geschichte von Oberfranken — AGO
Archiv fuer Geschichte von Oberfranken — Arch Gesch Oberfranken
Archiv fuer Geschwulstforschung — Arch Geschw
Archiv fuer Geschwulstforschung — Arch Geschwulstforsch
Archiv fuer Geschwulstforschung — ARGEAR
Archiv fuer Gewerbepathologie und Gewerbehygiene — AGGHAR
Archiv fuer Gewerbepathologie und Gewerbehygiene — Arch Gewerbepathol Gewerbehyg
Archiv fuer Gewerbliche Rechtspflege — Arch Gewerbl Rechtspflege
Archiv fuer Gynaekologie — Arch Gynaekol
Archiv fuer Gynaekologie — ARGYAJ
Archiv fuer Gynaekologie. Deutsche Gesellschaft fuer Gynaekologie — Arch Gyn
Archiv fuer Hessische Geschichte und Altertumskunde — AHGA
Archiv fuer Hessische Geschichte und Altertumskunde — AHGAK
Archiv fuer Hessische Geschichte und Altertumskunde — Arch Hess Gesch Altertumskde
Archiv fuer Hydrobiologie — Arch Hydrob
Archiv fuer Hydrobiologie — Arch Hydrobiol
Archiv fuer Hydrobiologie. Beiheft — Arch Hydrobiol Beih
Archiv fuer Hydrobiologie. Supplementband — Arch Hydrobiol Suppl
Archiv fuer Hydrobiologie. Supplementband — Arch Hydrobiol Supplementb
Archiv fuer Hydrobiologie und Planktonkunde — Arch Hydrobiol Planktonk
Archiv fuer Hydrobiologie und Planktonkunde — Arch Hydrobiol u Planktonkunde
Archiv fuer Hygiene — Arch Hyg
Archiv fuer Hygiene und Bakteriologie — Arch Hyg Bakt
Archiv fuer Hygiene und Bakteriologie — Arch Hyg Bakteriol
Archiv fuer Innere Medizin — Arch Inn Med
Archiv fuer Japanische Chirurgie — Arch Jpn Chir
Archiv fuer Japanische Chirurgie — NIGHAE
Archiv fuer Katholisches Kirchenrecht — A kath KR
Archiv fuer Katholisches Kirchenrecht — AKK
Archiv fuer Katholisches Kirchenrecht — AKKR
Archiv fuer Keilschriftforschung — AfK
Archiv fuer Keilschriftforschung — Arch Keilschrforsch
Archiv fuer Keilschriftforschung — ArKF
Archiv fuer Kinderheilkunde — Arch Kinderh
Archiv fuer Kinderheilkunde — Arch Kinderheilkd
Archiv fuer Kinderheilkunde — ARKIAP
Archiv fuer Kinderheilkunde. Beihefte — Arch Kinderheilkd Beih
Archiv fuer Klinische Chirurgie — Arch Klin Chir
Archiv fuer Klinische Chirurgie. Langenbecks — AKCVA
Archiv fuer Klinische Chirurgie. Langenbecks [*Germany*] — Arch Klin Chir Langenbecks
Archiv fuer Klinische Medizin — AKMEA8
Archiv fuer Klinische Medizin — Arch Klin Med
Archiv fuer Klinische und Experimentelle Dermatologie — AKEDAX
Archiv fuer Klinische und Experimentelle Dermatologie — Arch Klin Exp Dermatol
Archiv fuer Klinische und Experimentelle Ohren-, Nasen-, und Kehlkopfheilkunde — AKONA
Archiv fuer Klinische und Experimentelle Ohren-, Nasen-, und Kehlkopfheilkunde — AKONAB
Archiv fuer Klinische und Experimentelle Ohren-, Nasen-, und Kehlkopfheilkunde — Arch Klin Exp Ohren- Nasen- Kehlkopfheilkd
Archiv fuer Klinische und Experimentelle Ophtalmologie — Arch Klin Exp Ophtalmol
Archiv fuer Kommunalwissenschaften — Arch Kommunalwiss
Archiv fuer Kommunalwissenschaften — Archiv Kommunalwiss
Archiv fuer Kreislaufforschung — AKBZAG
Archiv fuer Kreislaufforschung — Arch Kreislaufforsch
Archiv fuer Kriminalanthropolgie und Kriminalistik — Arch Krim Anthr
Archiv fuer Kriminalanthropologie und Kriminalistik — Archiv F Kriminalanthropol
Archiv fuer Kriminologie — Arch Kriminol
Archiv fuer Kriminologie — ARKRAI
Archiv fuer Kulturgeschichte [*Cologne/Graz*] — AfK
Archiv fuer Kulturgeschichte — AK
Archiv fuer Kulturgeschichte — AKG
Archiv fuer Kulturgeschichte [*Weimar*] — AKultG
Archiv fuer Kulturgeschichte — Arch Kulturgesch
Archiv fuer Kulturgeschichte — ArchK
Archiv fuer Kulturgeschichte — ArfK
Archiv fuer Kulturgeschichte — ArKulturg
Archiv fuer Kunstgeschichte — Arch Kunstgesch
Archiv fuer Lagerstaettenforschung — Arch Lagerstaettenforsch
Archiv fuer Lagerstaettenforschung der Geologischen Bundesanstalt — Arch Lagerstattenforsch Geol Bundesanst
Archiv fuer Lagerstaettenforschung in den Ostalpen — Arch Lagerstaettenforsch Ostalpen
Archiv fuer Landtechnik — Arch Landtech
Archiv fuer Landtechnik — ARLAB
Archiv fuer Laryngologie — Arch Laryngol
Archiv fuer Lateinische Lexicographie und Grammatik — A Lex
Archiv fuer Lateinische Lexicographie und Grammatik — Arch f Lat Lex
Archiv fuer Lateinische Lexicographie und Grammatik — Arch Lat Lex
Archiv fuer Lateinische Lexicographie und Grammatik — Archiv f Lat Lex
Archiv fuer Lateinische Lexicographie und Grammatik — Archiv fuer Latein Lexik
Archiv fuer Lateinische Lexikographie und Grammatik [*Munich/Leipzig*] — ALL
Archiv fuer Lateinische Lexikographie und Grammatik — ALLG
Archiv fuer Lebensmittel-Hygiene — Arch Lebensm Hyg
Archiv fuer Lebensmittelhygiene — Arch Lebensmittelhyg
Archiv fuer Literatur und Kirchengeschichte des Mittelalters — ALKM
Archiv fuer Literatur- und Kirchengeschichte des Mittelalters — ALKMA
Archiv fuer Literatur und Volksdichtung — ALV
Archiv fuer Literatur und Volksdichtung — ArchLit
Archiv fuer Literaturgeschichte — ALG
Archiv fuer Literaturgeschichte — Arch Litgesch
Archiv fuer Liturgiewissenschaft — ALW
Archiv fuer Liturgiewissenschaft — Ar Lw
Archiv fuer Liturgiewissenschaft — Arch Liturg
Archiv fuer Liturgiewissenschaft [*Regensburg*] — ArchLitg
Archiv fuer Mathematische Logik und Grundlagenforschung — Arch Math Log
Archiv fuer Mathematische Logik und Grundlagenforschung [*Stuttgart*] — Arch Math Logik Grundlag
Archiv fuer Mathematische Logik und Grundlagenforschung — Arch Math Logik Grundlagenforsch
Archiv fuer Mathematische Logik und Grundlagenforschung — Arch Math Logik und Grundlagenforsch
Archiv fuer Mathematische Versicherungswissenschaft — AMV
Archiv fuer Metallkunde [*Germany*] — Arch Metallkd
Archiv fuer Meteorologie, Geophysik, und Bioklimatologie. Serie A — AMGGA
Archiv fuer Meteorologie, Geophysik, und Bioklimatologie. Serie A — Arch Meteorol Geophys Bioklimatol Ser A
Archiv fuer Meteorologie, Geophysik, und Bioklimatologie. Serie A — Arch MGB A
Archiv fuer Meteorologie, Geophysik, und Bioklimatologie. Serie A. Meteorologie und Geophysik — Arch Met Geophys Bioklim Ser A Meteorologie und Geophysik
Archiv fuer Meteorologie, Geophysik, und Bioklimatologie. Serie A. Meteorologie und Geophysik — Archiv Meteorologie Geophysik u Bioklimatolgie Ser A
Archiv fuer Meteorologie, Geophysik, und Bioklimatologie. Serie B — AMGBA
Archiv fuer Meteorologie, Geophysik, und Bioklimatologie. Serie B — Arch Met Geophys Bioklimatologie Ser B
Archiv fuer Meteorologie, Geophysik, und Bioklimatologie. Serie B — Arch Meteorol Geophys Bioklimatol Ser B
Archiv fuer Meteorologie, Geophysik, und Bioklimatologie. Serie B — Arch MGB B
Archiv fuer Mikrobiologie — Arch Mikrobiol
Archiv fuer Mikroskopische Anatomie — Arch Mikr Anat
Archiv fuer Mikroskopische Anatomie und Entwicklungsmechanik — Arch Mikrosk Anat Entwicklungsmech
Archiv fuer Mikroskopische Anatomie und Entwicklungsmechanik — Arch Mikrosk Anat Entwmech
Archiv fuer Mineralogie, Geognosie, Bergbau, und Huettenkunde — Arch Miner
Archiv fuer Mittelrheinische Kirchengeschichte — AMrhKG
Archiv fuer Molluskenkunde — AMollK

Archiv fuer Molluskenkunde — Arch Molluskenkd
Archiv fuer Musikforschung — A Mf
Archiv fuer Musikforschung — AfMf
Archiv fuer Musikwissenschaft — AfM
Archiv fuer Musikwissenschaft — AfMw
Archiv fuer Musikwissenschaft — AMW
Archiv fuer Musikwissenschaft — Arch Mus
Archiv fuer Musikwissenschaft — Arch Musik
Archiv fuer Musikwissenschaft — Archiv fuer Mus
Archiv fuer Naturgeschichte — AfNg
Archiv fuer Naturgeschichte — Arch Naturg
Archiv fuer Naturgeschichte — Arch Naturgesch
Archiv fuer Naturgeschichte (Berlin) — Arch Naturg (Berlin)
Archiv fuer Naturschutz und Landschaftsforschung — Arch Naturschutz Landschaftsforsch
Archiv fuer Naturschutz und Landschaftsforschung — ARNLBG
Archiv fuer Naturschutz und Landschaftsforschung. Deutsche Akademie der Landwirtschaftswissenschaften zu Berlin — Arch Naturschutz Landschaftsf
Archiv fuer Oesterreichische Geschichte — AOe
Archiv fuer Oesterreichische Geschichte — AOEG
Archiv fuer Oesterreichische Geschichte — AOG
Archiv fuer Oesterreichische Geschichte — Arch Oesterr Gesch
Archiv fuer Oesterreichische Geschichte — Archiv f Oesterr Geschichte
Archiv fuer Oesterreichische Geschichte — Archiv Oesterr Gesch
Archiv fuer Ohren-, Nasen-, und Kehlkopfheilkunde [*Germany*] — Arch Ohren- Nasen- Kehlkopfheilkd
Archiv fuer Ohren-, Nasen-, und Kehlkopfheilkunde — Arch Ohr-Nas Kehlkopfheilk
Archiv fuer Ohrenheilkunde — Arch Ohrenh
Archiv fuer Ophthalmologie. Albrecht von Graefes — Arch Ophthalmol Albrecht von Graefes
Archiv fuer Optik — Arch Opt
Archiv fuer Orientforschung — AFO
Archiv fuer Orientforschung [*Berlin*] — AfOF
Archiv fuer Orientforschung — AK
Archiv fuer Orientforschung — AOF
Archiv fuer Orientforschung — Ar Or
Archiv fuer Orientforschung — Arch f Orientfors
Archiv fuer Orientforschung — Arch Orient
Archiv fuer Orientforschung — Archiv Orientforsch
Archiv fuer Orientforschung [*Graz, Austria*] — ArchOF
Archiv fuer Orientforschung (Berlin) — AfOFB
Archiv fuer Orthopaedie, Mechanotherapie, und Unfallchirurgie — Arch Orthop Mechanother Unfallchir
Archiv fuer Orthopaedische und Unfall-Chirurgie — AOUNAZ
Archiv fuer Orthopaedische und Unfall-Chirurgie — Arch Orthop
Archiv fuer Orthopaedische und Unfall-Chirurgie — Arch Orthop Unfall-Chir
Archiv fuer Paedagogik — A f Paed
Archiv fuer Papyrusforschung [*Leipzig*] — AfP
Archiv fuer Papyrusforschung — AfPap
Archiv fuer Papyrusforschung — Ar Pf
Archiv fuer Papyrusforschung — Arch P
Archiv fuer Papyrusforschung [*Leipzig*] — ArPapF
Archiv fuer Papyrusforschung und Verwandte Gebiete — AP
Archiv fuer Papyrusforschung und Verwandte Gebiete — APF
Archiv fuer Papyrusforschung und Verwandte Gebiete — Ar Pap
Archiv fuer Papyrusforschung und Verwandte Gebiete — Arch f Pap
Archiv fuer Papyrusforschung und Verwandte Gebiete — Arch fuer Pap
Archiv fuer Papyrusforschung und Verwandte Gebiete — Arch Papyrusf
Archiv fuer Papyrusforschung und Verwandte Gebiete — Arch PF
Archiv fuer Papyrusforschung und Verwandte Gebiete — Archiv Pap
Archiv fuer Pathologische Anatomie und Physiologie und fuer Klinische Medizin — Arch Path Anat
Archiv fuer Pathologische Anatomie und Physiologie und Klinische Medizin — Archiv F Pathol Anat
Archiv fuer Pflanzenbau — Arch Pflanzenbau
Archiv fuer Pflanzenbau. Abt. A der Wissenschaftliches Archiv fuer Landwirtschaft — Arch Pflanzenbau Abt A Wiss Arch Landwirtsch
Archiv fuer Pflanzenschutz — Arch Pflanzenschutz
Archiv fuer Pflanzenschutz — Arch Pflsch
Archiv fuer Pflanzenschutz — Arch Pflschutz
Archiv fuer Pflanzenschutz — AVPZAR
Archiv fuer Pharmakologie. Naunyn-Schmiedebergs [*Archiv fuer Pharmakologie und Experimentelle Pathologie. Naunyn-Schmiedebergs*] [*Germany*] [*Formerly,*] — Arch Pharmakol Naunyn-Schmiedebergs
Archiv fuer Pharmakologie und Experimentelle Pathologie. Naunyn-Schmiedebergs [*Archiv fuer Pharmakologie. Naunyn-Schmiedebergs*] [*Germany*] [*Later,*] — Arch Pharmakol Exp Pathol
Archiv fuer Philosophie — A f Ph
Archiv fuer Philosophie — A Ph
Archiv fuer Philosophie — ArchivPhilos
Archiv fuer Physikalische Therapie — APTKAS
Archiv fuer Physikalische Therapie — Arch Phys Ther
Archiv fuer Physiologie — Arch Physiol
Archiv fuer Physiologische und Pathologische Chemie und Mikroskopie (Von J. F. Heller) — Hellers Arch
Archiv fuer Phytopathologie und Pflanzenschutz — Arch Phytopath Pflschutz
Archiv fuer Phytopathologie und Pflanzenschutz — Arch Phytopathol Pflanzenschutz
Archiv fuer Politik und Geschichte — APG
Archiv fuer Postgeschichte in Bayern — A Pg B
Archiv fuer Protistenkunde — APRKAI
Archiv fuer Protistenkunde — Arch f Prot
Archiv fuer Protistenkunde — Arch Protistenk
Archiv fuer Protistenkunde. Protozoen-Algen-Pilze — Arch Protistenkd
Archiv fuer Psychiatrie und Nervenheilkunde — Arch Psychiatr
Archiv fuer Psychiatrie und Nervenkrankheiten — AfPsN
Archiv fuer Psychiatrie und Nervenkrankheiten — APNVAV
Archiv fuer Psychiatrie und Nervenkrankheiten — Arch Psychi
Archiv fuer Psychiatrie und Nervenkrankheiten — Arch Psychiat Nervenkr
Archiv fuer Psychiatrie und Nervenkrankheiten — Arch Psychiatr Nervenkr
Archiv fuer Psychiatrie und Nervenkrankheiten — Arch Psychiatr Nervenkrankh
Archiv fuer Psychologie — Arch Psych
Archiv fuer Psychologie (Frankfurt Am Main) — Arch Psychol (Frankf)
Archiv fuer Rassen- und Gesellschafts-Biologie Einschliessend Rassen- und Gesellschaftshygiene — Arch Rass- u Gec Biol
Archiv fuer Rechts- und Sozialphilosophie — Arch Rechts Soz
Archiv fuer Rechts- und Sozialphilosophie — Arch Rechts Sozialphil
Archiv fuer Rechts- und Sozialphilosophie — Archiv Rechts u Soz-Philos
Archiv fuer Rechts- und Sozialphilosophie — ARSP
Archiv fuer Rechts- und Soziaphilosophie — ArRS
Archiv fuer Rechts- und Wirtschaftsphilosophie — ARPh
Archiv fuer Rechts- und Wirtschaftsphilosophie — ARWP
Archiv fuer Rechtspflege in Sachsen. Thueringen und Anhalt — Arch Rechtspfl Sachs
Archiv fuer Reformationgeschichte — ArfR
Archiv fuer Reformationsgeschichte — AR
Archiv fuer Reformationsgeschichte — Arch Reformationsgesch
Archiv fuer Reformationsgeschichte — Archiv
Archiv fuer Reformationsgeschichte — ARG
Archiv fuer Reformationsgeschichte [*Guetersloh*] — ArRefg
Archiv fuer Reformationsgeschichte. Texte und Untersuchungen — AFR
Archiv fuer Reformationsgeschichte. Texte und Untersuchungen — AFTU
Archiv fuer Reformationsgeschichte. Texte und Untersuchungen — ARGTU
Archiv fuer Reformationsgeschichte. Texte und Untersuchungen — ARTU
Archiv fuer Religionspsychologie — ARPs
Archiv fuer Religionswissenschaft — A Re
Archiv fuer Religionswissenschaft — A Rel
Archiv fuer Religionswissenschaft — Arch f Rw
Archiv fuer Religionswissenschaft — Arch Rel Wiss
Archiv fuer Religionswissenschaft — Arch Relig
Archiv fuer Religionswissenschaft — Arch Religionsw
Archiv fuer Religionswissenschaft — Archiv F Religionswis
Archiv fuer Religionswissenschaft — Archiv Rel
Archiv fuer Religionswissenschaft — ArchRW
Archiv fuer Religionswissenschaft [*Leipzig/Berlin*] — ArRW
Archiv fuer Religionswissenschaft — ARW
Archiv fuer Schiffs- und Tropen-Hygiene — Archiv F Schiffs U Tropen Hyg
Archiv fuer Schiffs-und Tropen-Hygiene — Arch Schiffs-u Tropen-Hyg
Archiv fuer Schlesische Kirchengeschichte — Arch Schlesische Kirchengesch
Archiv fuer Schlesische Kirchengeschichte — ASKG
Archiv fuer Schriftkunde — Arch Schriftkde
Archiv fuer Schriftkunde — ArSK
Archiv fuer Sippenforschung und alle Verwandten Gebiete — Arch Sippenforsch
Archiv fuer Slavische Philologie — ASP
Archiv fuer Soziale Gesetzgebung und Statistik — ASGS
Archiv fuer Soziale Hygiene — ASozHy
Archiv fuer Sozialgeschichte — Arch Sozialgesch
Archiv fuer Sozialgeschichte — Archiv Soz Gesch
Archiv fuer Sozialwissenschaft und Sozialpolitik — A Sw Sp
Archiv fuer Systematische Philosophie — ASPh
Archiv fuer Technisches Messen — Arch Tech Mess
Archiv fuer Technisches Messen und Industrielle Messtechnik — Arch Tech Mess Ind Messtech
Archiv fuer Technisches Messen und Industrielle Messtechnik — Arch Tech Mess und Ind Messtech
Archiv fuer Technisches Messen und Messtechnische Praxis — Arch Tech Mess Messtech Prax
Archiv fuer Technisches Messen und Messtechnische Praxis — Arch Tech Mess und Messtech Prax
Archiv fuer Theatergeschichte — AThG
Archiv fuer Tieraerztliche Fortbildung — Arch Tieraerztl Fortbild
Archiv fuer Tierernaehrung [*Archives of Animal Nutrition*] — Arch Tierernaehr
Archiv fuer Tierernaehrung [*Archives of Animal Nutrition*] — ARTIA2
Archiv fuer Tierernaehrung/Archives of Animal Nutrition — Arch Tierernahr Arch Anim Nutr
Archiv fuer Tierernaehrung und Tierzucht. Abteilung B der Wissenschaftliches Archiv fuer Landwirtschaft — Arch Tierernaehr Tierz Abt B Wiss Arch Landwirtsch
Archiv fuer Tierzucht [*Germany*] — Arch Tierz
Archiv fuer Toxikologie [*Later, Archives of Toxicology*] — Arch Toxikol
Archiv fuer Toxikologie. Supplement — Arch Toxikol Suppl
Archiv fuer Urkundenforschung — ACC
Archiv fuer Urkundenforschung — AfU
Archiv fuer Urkundenforschung — Arch Urkdforsch
Archiv fuer Urkundenforschung — Arch Urkundenforsch
Archiv fuer Urkundenforschung — Archiv Urk
Archiv fuer Urkundenforschung — AUF
Archiv fuer Verdauungs-Krankheiten — Arch Verdau Kr
Archiv fuer Verdauungs-Krankheiten — Arch Verdau Krankh
Archiv fuer Verdauungs-Krankheiten mit Einschluss der Stoffwechselpathologie und der Diatetik — Arch Verdau Kr Stoffwechselpathol Diaet
Archiv fuer Verdauungs-Krankheiten mit Einschluss der Stoffwechselpathologie und der Diatetik — Arch Verdauungskr
Archiv fuer Verdauungs-Krankheiten Stoffwechselpathologie und Diaetetik — Arch Verdau Krankh Stoffwechselpathol Diaet
Archiv fuer Vergleichende Phonetik — Arch Vergl Phonetik
Archiv fuer Voelkerkunde — Ar Vk
Archiv fuer Voelkerkunde — Arch Voelkerk

Archiv fuer Voelkerkunde — Arch Voelkerkunde
Archiv fuer Voelkerkunde — Archiv Voelkerk
Archiv fuer Voelkerkunde — ArchV
Archiv fuer Voelkerkunde Museum fuer Voelkerkunde in Wien und von Verein Freunde der Voelkerkunde — MVW/AV
Archiv fuer Volkswohlfahrt — Arch Volkswohlfahrt
Archiv fuer Waermewirtschaft — Arch Waermewirtsch
Archiv fuer Waermewirtschaft und Dampfkesselwesen [*Germany*] — Arch Waermewirtsch Dampfkesselwes
Archiv fuer Welt-, Erd- und Staatenkunde und Ihre Hilfswissenschaften und Litteratur — Arch Welt Erd Staatenk
Archiv fuer Wissenschaftliche Botanik — Arch Wiss Bot
Archiv fuer Wissenschaftliche Erforschung des Alten Testaments [*Halle*] — AWAT
Archiv fuer Wissenschaftliche Kunde von Russland — Arch Wiss Kde Russland
Archiv fuer Wissenschaftliche Kunde von Russland — Arch Wiss Kunde Russland
Archiv fuer Wissenschaftliche Photographie — Arch Wiss Phot
Archiv fuer Wissenschaftliche und Praktische Tierheilkunde — Arch Wiss Prakt Tierheilkd
Archiv fuer Wissenschaftliche und Praktische Tierheilkunde — Arch Wissensch u Prakt Tierh
Archiv fuer Zellforschung — Arch Zellforsch
Archiv fuer Zivilistische Praxis — Arch Ziv Prax
Archiv fuer Zuechtungsforschung — Arch Zuechtungsforsch
Archiv Gemeinnuetziger Physischer und Medizinischer Kenntnisse — Arch Gemeinnuetz Phys Med Kenntn
Archiv Mecklenburgischer Naturforscher — Arch Mecklenburg Naturf
Archiv Orientalni — AO
Archiv Orientalni — AOR
Archiv Orientalni — Ar Or
Archiv Orientalni — Archiv Or
Archiv Orientalni [*Prague*] — ArchOr
Archiv Orientalni — ArchOrient
Archiv Orientalni — ArO
Archiv Patologii — AP
Archiv pro Prirodovedecky Vyzkum Cech — Arch Prir Vyzk Cech
Archiv pro Prirodovedecky Vyzkum Cech (Praha) — Arch Prirod Vyzk Cech Prag
Archiv Skandinavischer Beitraege zur Naturgeschichte — Arch Skand Beitr Naturgesch
Archiv und Atlas der Normalen und Pathologischen Anatomie in Typischen Roentgenbildern — Arch Atlas Norm Pathol Anat Roentgenbild
Archiv zur Klaerung der Wuenschelrutenfrage — Arch Klaerung Wuenschelrutenfrage
Archiva Biologia Hungarica — Arch Biol Hung
Archiva Medica Belgica — Arch Med Belg
Archiva Veterinaria — Arch Vet
Archiva Veterinaria [*Bucharest*] — ARVEBZ
Archiva Veterinaria (Bucharest) — Arch Vet (Buchar)
Archivalische Zeitschrift — Archival Z
Archivalische Zeitschrift — AZ
Archive [*Quezon City*] — Ar
Archive for History of Exact Sciences [*Berlin*] — AHES
Archive for History of Exact Sciences — Arch Hist E
Archive for History of Exact Sciences — Arch Hist Exact Sci
Archive for History of Exact Sciences — Arch History Exact Sci
Archive for Mathematical Logic — Arch Math Logic
Archive for Rational Mechanics and Analysis — Arch R Mech
Archive for Rational Mechanics and Analysis — Arch Ration Mech Anal
Archive for Rational Mechanics and Analysis — Arch Ration Mech and Anal
Archive for Rational Mechanics and Analysis — Arch Rational Mech Anal
Archive for Reformation History — Arch Reformation Hist
Archive of Aurelius Isidorus in the Egyptian Museum, Cairo, and the University of Michigan — P Cair Isidor
[*The*] **Archive (Philippines)** — ArchiveP
Archives — Arh
Archives Alsaciennes d'Histoire de l'Art — AAHA
Archives and Manuscripts — A & M
Archives and Manuscripts — Arch & Manus
Archives and Manuscripts — Arch and Manuscripts
Archives and Manuscripts — Arch Manuscr
Archives and Manuscripts — Archi & Manu
Archives and Manuscripts — Archives and Mss
Archives Balkaniques de Medecine. Chirurgie et Leurs Specialites — Arch Balkaniques Med Chir Spec
Archives Belges — ABelges
Archives Belges de Dermatologie — ABDMAQ
Archives Belges de Dermatologie — Arch Belg Dermatol
Archives Belges de Dermatologie et de Syphiligraphie — ABBSAY
Archives Belges de Dermatologie et de Syphiligraphie — Arch Belg Dermatol Syphiligr
Archives Belges de Dermatologie et de Syphiligraphie — Arch Belges Dermatol Syphiligr
Archives Belges de Medecine Legale — Arch Med Leg
Archives Belges de Medecine Sociale et d'Hygiene et Revue de Pathologie et de Physiologie du Travail — Arch Belg Med Soc Hyg Rev Pathol Physiol Trav
Archives Belges de Medecine Sociale, Hygiene, Medecine du Travail, et Medecine Legale — ABMHAM
Archives Belges de Medecine Sociale, Hygiene, Medecine du Travail, et Medecine Legale — Arch Belg Med Soc
Archives Belges de Medecine Sociale, Hygiene, Medecine du Travail, et Medecine Legale — Arch Belg Med Soc Hyg Med Trav Med Leg
Archives Belges de Medecine Sociale, Hygiene, Medecine du Travail, et Medecine Legale (Belgium) — Arch Belges Med Soc Hyg Med Trav Med Leg (Belgium)
Archives Belges. Medecine Sociale, Hygiene, Medecine du Travail, Medecine Legale — Arch Belg
Archives, Bibliotheques, Collections, Documentation — ABCD
Archives, Bibliotheques, et Musees de Belgique [*Later, Archives et Bibliotheques de Belgique*] — ABMB
Archives, Bibliotheques, et Musees de Belgique [*Later, Archives et Bibliotheques de Belgique*] — Arch Bibl et Mus
Archives Biographiques Contemporaines — Arch Biogr Contemp
Archives. California Chiropractic Association — Arch Cal Chiro
Archives Cliniques de Bordeaux — Arch Clin Bordeaux
Archives Concernant l'Histoire, les Langues, la Geographie, l'Ethnographie, etles Arts de l'Asie Orientale — Arch Hist Lang Geogr Ethnogr Arts Asie Orient
Archives d'Anatomie, d'Histologie, et d'Embryologie — AAHEAF
Archives d'Anatomie, d'Histologie, et d'Embryologie — Arch Anat Histol Embryol
Archives d'Anatomie, d'Histologie, et d'Embryologie; Normales et Experimentales — Arch Anat Histol Embryol Norm Exp
Archives d'Anatomie, d'Histologie, et d'Embryologie (Strasbourg) — Arch Anat Histol Embryol (Strasb)
Archives d'Anatomie et de Cytologie Pathologiques — AACPDQ
Archives d'Anatomie et de Cytologie Pathologiques — Arch Anat Cytol Pathol
Archives d'Anatomie Microscopique — Archs Anat Microsc
Archives d'Anatomie Microscopique et de Morphologie Experimentale — AAMMAU
Archives d'Anatomie Microscopique et de Morphologie Experimentale — Arch Anat M
Archives d'Anatomie Microscopique et de Morphologie Experimentale — Arch Anat Microsc Morphol Exp
Archives d'Anatomie Microscopique et de Morphologie Experimentale — Arch Anat Microscop Morphol Exp
Archives d'Anatomie Microscopique et de Morphologie Experimentale — Archs Anat Microsc Morph Exp
Archives d'Anatomie Pathologique [*Paris*] — AAPSAT
Archives d'Anatomie Pathologique (Paris) — Arch Anat Pathol (Paris)
Archives d'Anatomie Pathologique. Semaine des Hopitaux [*France*] — Arch Anat Pathol Sem Hop
Archives d'Anthropologie Criminelle, de Medecine Legale, et de Psychologie Normale et Pathologique — Arch Anthropol Criminelle
Archives de Biochimie et Cosmetologie — Arch Biochim Cosmetol
Archives de Biologie [*Archives of Biology*] — ABILAE
Archives de Biologie [*Liege*] — Arch Biol
Archives de Biologie (Liege) [*Belgium*] — Archs Biol (Liege)
Archives de Biologie (Paris) — Arch Biol Paris
Archives de Botanique. Bulletin Mensuel — Arch Bot Bull Mens
Archives de Botanique. Memoires — Arch Bot Mem
Archives de Botanique (Paris) — Arch Bot Paris
Archives de Chimie — Archiv Chim
Archives de Chimie et de Pharmacie (Warsaw) — Arch Chim Pharm Warsaw
Archives de Chimie et de Pharmacie (Zagreb) — Arch Chim Pharm (Zagreb)
Archives de Folklore — A Folk
Archives de Folklore — Arch Folk
Archives de Folklore. Universite Laval (Quebec) — AFLQ
Archives de la Flore de France et d'Allemagne — Arch Fl France Allemagne
Archives de l'Art Francais — AAF
Archives de l'Eglise d'Alsace — AEAl
Archives de l'Eglise d'Alsace — AEAls
Archives de l'Histoire des Sciences — Arch Hist Sci
Archives de l'Orient Chretien — AO Chr
Archives de l'Orient Chretien — AOC
Archives de l'Orient Chretien — APL
Archives de l'Orient Latin — AOL
Archives de l'Orient Latin — Arch Or Lat
Archives de Macanique Appliquee — Arch Mec Appl
Archives de Medecine des Enfants — Arch Med Enf
Archives de Medecine des Enfants — Arch Med Enfants
Archives de Medecine et Pharmacie Navales — Arch Med Pharm Nav
Archives de Medecine Experimentale et d'Anatomie Pathologique — Arch Med Exper et Anat Path
Archives de Medecine Generale et Tropicale — Arch Med Gen Trop
Archives de Medecine Navale — AMNP
Archives de Medecine Navale — Arch Med Nav
Archives de Medecine Navale — Arch Med Navale
Archives de Medecine Navale — Archives De Med Nav
Archives de Medecine (Sarajevo) — Arch Med (Sarajevo)
Archives de Medecine Sociale et d'Hygiene et Revue de Pathologie et de Physiologie du Travail — Arch Med Soc Hyg Rev Pathol Physiol Trav
Archives de Mineralogie. Societe des Sciences et des Lettres de Varsovie — Arch Mineral Soc Sci Varsovie
Archives de Parasitologie — Arch Parasitol
Archives de Parasitologie (Paris) — Arch Parasitol (Paris)
Archives de Pediatrie — Arch Pediatr
Archives de Pharmacie (Paris) — Arch Pharm (Paris)
Archives de Philologie. Academie Polonaise des Sciences et des Lettres — APhAP
Archives de Philosophie — AP
Archives de Philosophie — APhilos
Archives de Philosophie — Ar Ph
Archives de Philosophie — Arch Phil
Archives de Philosophie — Arch Philos
Archives de Philosophie — Archives Philos
Archives de Philosophie du Droit — Arch Phil Dr
Archives de Philosophie du Droit — Archiv Philos Dr
Archives de Philosophie (Paris) — Arch Phil Paris
Archives de Physique Biologique — Arch Phys Biol

Archives de Physique Biologique et de Chimie Physique des Corps Organises [*A publication*] — Arch Phys Biol Chim Phys Corps Organ
Archives de Plasmologie Generale — Arch Plasmol Gen
Archives de Politique Criminelle — Arch Pol Criminelle
Archives de Saint Jean-Prodrome sur le Mont Menecee — A Prod
Archives de Science Avicole — Arch Sci Avic
Archives de Science Avicole — Arch Sci Avicole
Archives de Sciences Sociales de la Cooperation et du Developpement — Arch Sci Soc Coop Dev
Archives de Sciences Sociales des Relgions — Arch Sci Soc Relig
Archives de Sciences Sociales des Religions — Arch SS Rel
Archives de Sciences Sociales des Religions — Archiv Sci Soc Rel
Archives de Sciences Sociales des Religions — Archiv Sci Soc Relig
Archives de Sciences Sociales des Religions — Archives Sci Sociales Relig
Archives de Sciences Sociales des Religions — Archs Sci Soc Religions
Archives de Sciences Sociales des Religions — ASSR
Archives de Sociologie des Religions — Ar SR
Archives de Sociologie des Religions — Arch Sociol Relig
Archives de Sociologie des Religions — Archiv Soc Rel
Archives de Sociologie des Religions — Archives Sociol Relig
Archives de Sociologie des Religions [*Paris*] — ArSocRel
Archives de Sociologie des Religions — ASR
Archives de Zoologie Experimentale et Generale — Arch Zool Exp Gen
Archives de Zoologie Experimentale et Generale — Arch Zool Exper et Gen
Archives de Zoologie Experimentale et Generale — Archs Zool Exp Gen
Archives de Zoologie Experimentale et Generale — AZEGAB
Archives de Zoologie Experimentale et Generale. Notes et Revue — Arch Zool Exp Gen Notes Rev
Archives de Zoologie Experimentale et Generale. Notes et Revue — AZXNAP
Archives Dermato-Syphiligraphiques. Clinique de l'Hopital Saint Louis — Arch Dermato Syphiligr Clin Hop Saint Louis
Archives des Lettres Modernes — ALM
Archives des Maladies de l'Appareil Digestif et des Maladies de la Nutrition — Arch Mal Appar Dig Mal Nutr
Archives des Maladies du Coeur, des Vaisseaux, et du Sang — Arch Mal Coeur Vaiss Sang
Archives des Maladies du Coeur, des Vaisseaux, et du Sang — Archives D Mal Du Coeur
Archives des Maladies du Coeur et des Vaisseaux — Arch Mal C
Archives des Maladies du Coeur et des Vaisseaux — Arch Mal Coeur
Archives des Maladies du Coeur et des Vaisseaux — Arch Mal Coeur Vaiss
Archives des Maladies Professionnelles de Medecine du Travail et de Securite Sociale — AMPMA
Archives des Maladies Professionnelles de Medecine du Travail et de Securite Sociale — Arch Mal Pr
Archives des Maladies Professionnelles de Medecine du Travail et de Securite Sociale — Arch Mal Prof
Archives des Maladies Professionnelles de Medecine du Travail et de Securite Sociale — Arch Mal Prof Med Trav Secur Soc
Archives des Maladies Professionnelles, Hygiene, et Toxicologie Industrielles — Arch Mal Prof Hyg Toxicol Ind
Archives des Missions Scientifiques et Litteraires — Ad M
Archives des Missions Scientifiques et Litteraires — AMSL
Archives des Missions Scientifiques et Litteraires — Arch Miss
Archives des Missions Scientifiques et Litteraires — Arch Missions Sci Litt
Archives des Missions Scientifiques et Litteraires — Archiv Mis
Archives des Missions Scientifiques et Litteraires — Archives Missions Scientif
Archives des Recherches Agronomiques et Pastorales au Vietnam — AAPVA4
Archives des Recherches Agronomiques et Pastorales au Vietnam — Arch Rech Agron Pastorales Vietnam
Archives des Sciences — Arch Sci
Archives des Sciences — Archives Sci
Archives des Sciences Biologiques (Belgrade) — Arch Sci Biol (Belgrade)
Archives des Sciences Biologiques (French Edition) — Arch Sci Biol Fr Ed
Archives des Sciences Biologiques (USSR) — Arch Sci Biol (USSR)
Archives des Sciences et Compte Rendu Seances de la Societe — Arch Sci C R Seances Soc
Archives des Sciences (Geneva) — Arch Sci (Geneva)
Archives des Sciences (Geneva) — ASGVAH
Archives des Sciences Physiologiques — Arch Sci Ph
Archives des Sciences Physiologiques — Arch Sci Physiol
Archives des Sciences Physiologiques — Archs Sci Physiol
Archives des Sciences Physiologiques — ASPHAK
Archives des Sciences Physiques et Naturelles — Arch Sc Phys Nat
Archives des Sciences Physiques et Naturelles. Supplement a la Bibliotheque Universelle — Arch Sci Phys Nat
Archives des Sciences. Societe de Physique et d'Histoire Naturelle de Geneve — Arch Sci Soc Phys Hist Nat Geneve
Archives d'Histoire Doctrinal et Litteraire [*Paris*] — AHDL
Archives d'Histoire Doctrinale et Litteraire du Moyen Age — AHD
Archives d'Histoire Doctrinale et Litteraire du Moyen-Age — AHDLMA
Archives d'Histoire Doctrinale et Litteraire du Moyen-Age — AHMA
Archives d'Histoire Doctrinale et Litteraire du Moyen-Age — Arch Hist Doctrinale Litt Moyen Age
Archives d'Histoire Dominicaine — AHD
Archives d'Histoire Dominicaine — Arch Hist Dom
Archives d'Histoire du Droit Oriental — AHDO
Archives d'Histoire du Droit Oriental — Arch Hist D O
Archives d'Histoire du Droit Oriental — Arch Hist Droit Oriental
Archives d'Histoire du Droit Oriental — Archiv Hist Dr Or
Archives d'Histoire du Droit Oriental — Archiv Hist Dr Orient
Archives d'Histoire Naturelle — Arch Hist Nat
Archives Diplomatiques et Consulaires — Archiv Diplom Consul
Archives d'Ophtalmologie — Arch Ophtal
Archives d'Ophtalmologie — Arch Ophtalmol
Archives d'Ophtalmologie — AROPDZ
Archives d'Ophtalmologie et Revue Generale d'Ophtalmologie — Arch Ophtalmol Rev Gen Ophtalmol
Archives d'Ophtalmologie et Revue Generale d'Ophtalmologie — AROHA8
Archives d'Ophtalmologie et Revue Generale d'Ophtalmologie (Paris) — Arch Ophtalmol (Paris)
Archives d'Ophtalmologie (Paris) — Arch Opht (Paris)
Archives du Museum d'Histoire Naturelle — Arch Mus Hist Nat
Archives et Bibliotheques — Aeb
Archives et Bibliotheques de Belgique — ABB
Archives et Bibliotheques de Belgique — Arch Bibl
Archives et Bibliotheques de Belgique — Archives & Bibl
Archives et Bibliotheques de Belgique — Archs et Biblioths Belgique
Archives Europeennes de Sociologie — AES
Archives Europeennes de Sociologie — Arch Eur So
Archives Europeennes de Sociologie — Arch Eur Sociol
Archives Europeennes de Sociologie — Archiv Eur Sociol
Archives Europeennes de Sociologie — Archiv Europ Sociol
Archives Europeennes de Sociologie — Archives Eur Sociol
Archives Europeennes de Sociologie — Archs Eur Sociologie
Archives Europeennes de Sociologie — ArES
Archives for Dermatological Research — ADRED
Archives for Dermatological Research — ADREDL
Archives for Dermatological Research — Arch Derm R
Archives for Dermatological Research — Arch Dermatol Res
Archives for Meteorology, Geophysics, and Bioclimatology. Series B. Theoretical and Applied Climatology — Arch Meteorol Geophys Bioclimatol Ser B Theor Appl Climatol
Archives Francaises de Pediatrie — AFPEAM
Archives Francaises de Pediatrie — Arch Fr Ped
Archives Francaises de Pediatrie — Arch Fr Pediatr
Archives Francaises des Maladies de l'Appareil Digestif — AMADBS
Archives Francaises des Maladies de l'Appareil Digestif — Arch Fr Mal
Archives Francaises des Maladies de l'Appareil Digestif — Arch Fr Mal App Dig
Archives Francaises des Maladies de l'Appareil Digestif — Arch Fr Mal Appar Dig
Archives Francaises des Maladies de l'Appareil Digestif. Supplement — Arch Fr Mal Appar Dig Suppl
Archives Generales de Medecine — Arch Gen Med
Archives Geologiques du Vietnam — Arch Geol Vietnam
Archives Geologiques du Vietnam — VNAGA2
Archives Heraldiques Suisses — AHS
Archives Heraldiques Suisses. Annuaire — Arch Herald Suisses
Archives Historique du Department de la Gironde — AHG
Archives Historiques du Departement de la Gironde — ADG
Archives Hospitalieres — Arch Hosp
Archives Hospitalieres et Revue de Science et Sante Reunies — Archi Hosp Rev Sci Sante Reunies
Archives. Institut de Botanique. Universite de Liege — Arch Inst Bot Univ Liege
Archives. Institut de Paleontologie Humaine — AIPH
Archives. Institut de Paleontologie Humaine — Archiv Inst Paleont Hum Mem
Archives. Institut d'Hessarek — Arch Inst Hessarek
Archives. Institut d'Hessarek (Institut Razi) — Arch Inst Hessarek (Inst Razi)
Archives. Institut du Radium. Universite de Paris et de la Fondation Curie. Radiophysiologie et Radiotherapie — Arch Inst Radium Univ Paris Fond Curie Radiophysiol Radiothe
Archives. Institut Grand-Ducal de Luxembourg — Archs Inst Gr-Duc Luxemb
Archives. Institut Grand-Ducal de Luxembourg. Section des Sciences Naturelles, Physiques, et Mathematiques — Arch Inst Grand Ducal Luxemb Sect Sci Nat Phys Math
Archives. Institut Grand-Ducal de Luxembourg. Section des Sciences Naturelles, Physiques, et Mathematiques — Arch Inst Grand-Ducal Luxemb Sect Sci
Archives. Institut Pasteur d'Algerie — Arch Inst Past Alg
Archives. Institut Pasteur d'Algerie — Arch Inst Pasteur Alger
Archives. Institut Pasteur d'Algerie — Arch Inst Pasteur Algerie
Archives. Institut Pasteur de la Guyane et du Territoire de l'Inini — Archs Inst Past Guy
Archives. Institut Pasteur de la Guyane Francaise et du Territoire de l'Inini — Archs Inst Past Guy Ter L In
Archives. Institut Pasteur de la Martinique — Archs Inst Past Mart
Archives. Institut Pasteur de Madagascar — Arch Inst Pasteur Madagascar
Archives. Institut Pasteur de Tananarive — Arch Inst Pasteur Tananarive
Archives. Institut Pasteur de Tunis — APTUA
Archives. Institut Pasteur de Tunis — Arch Inst Past Tunis
Archives. Institut Pasteur de Tunis — Arch Inst Pasteur Tunis
Archives. Institut Pasteur Hellenique — Arch Inst Pasteur Hell
Archives. Institut Prophylactique — Arch Inst Prophyl
Archives. Institut Razi — Arch Inst Razi
Archives. Institut Royal de Bacteriologie Camara Pestana — Arch Inst R Bacteriol Camara Pestana
Archives. Instituts Pasteur de l'Afrique du Nord — Arch Inst Pasteur Afrique N
Archives. Instituts Pasteur de l'Afrique du Nord — Arch Inst Pasteur Afrique Nord
Archives. Instituts Pasteur de l'Afrique du Nord — Archs Insts Pasteur Afr N
Archives. Instituts Pasteur d'Indochine — Arch Inst Pasteur Indochine
Archives Internationales Claude Bernard — Arch Int Claude Bernard
Archives Internationales de Chirurgie — Arch Int Chir
Archives Internationales de Laryngologie, d'Otologie, de Rhinologie et de Bronchooesophagoscopie — Arch Int Laryngol
Archives Internationales de Medecine Experimentale — Arch Int Med Exp
Archives Internationales de Neurologie — Arch Int Neur
Archives Internationales de Neurologie — Arch Int Neurol
Archives Internationales de Pharmacodynamie et de Therapie — AIPTAK
Archives Internationales de Pharmacodynamie et de Therapie — Arch I Phar

Archives Internationales de Pharmacodynamie et de Therapie — Arch Int Pharmacodyn Ther
Archives Internationales de Pharmacodynamie et de Therapie — Archs Int Pharmacodyn Ther
Archives Internationales de Physiologie — Arch Int Physiol
Archives Internationales de Physiologie — Archs Int Physiol
Archives Internationales de Physiologie, de Biochimie, et de Biophysique — Arch Int Physiol Biochim Biophys
Archives Internationales de Physiologie et de Biochimie — AIPBAY
Archives Internationales de Physiologie et de Biochimie — Arch I Phys
Archives Internationales de Physiologie et de Biochimie — Arch Int Physiol Biochim
Archives Internationales de Physiologie et de Biochimie — Archs Int Physiol Biochim
Archives Internationales de Sciologie de la Cooperation [*Paris*] — Arch Int Sociol Coop
Archives Internationales de Sociologie de la Cooperation et du Developpement — Archiv Int Sociol Coop Develop
Archives Internationales d'Histoire des Idees — AIHI
Archives Internationales d'Histoire des Sciences — AIHS
Archives Internationales d'Histoire des Sciences — AIHSAB
Archives Internationales d'Histoire des Sciences — Arch Int Hist Sci
Archives Internationales d'Histoire des Sciences — Arch Internat Hist Sci
Archives Internationales d'Histoire des Sciences [*Paris*] — Arch Internat Histoire Sci
Archives Israelites de France [*Paris*] — AI
Archives Italiennes de Biologie — AIBLA
Archives Italiennes de Biologie — AIBLAS
Archives Italiennes de Biologie — Arch It Bio
Archives Italiennes de Biologie — Arch Ital Biol
Archives Italiennes de Biologie — Archives Ital De Biol
Archives Juives — AJu
Archives Juives. Cahiers de la Commission des Archives Juives — Arch Juives
Archives. Kohno Clinical Medicine Research Institute — Arch Kohno Clin Med Res Inst
Archives Medicales — Arch Med
Archives Medicales d'Angers — Arch Med Angers
Archives Medicales de Normandie — Arch Med Normandie
Archives Medico-Chirurgicales de l'Appareil Respiratoire — Arch Med Chir Appar Respir
Archives Medico-Chirurgicales de l'Appareil Respiratoire — Arch Med Chir Appareil Resp
Archives Medico-Chirurgicales de Normandie — Archs Med-Chir Normandie
Archives. Missions Scientifiques et Litteraires — Archiv Miss
Archives. Musee Teyler — Arch Mus Teyler
Archives. Museum d'Histoire Naturelle de Lyon — Arch Mus Hist Nat Lyon
Archives. Museum National d'Histoire Naturelle — AMHNP
Archives. Museum National d'Histoire Naturelle (Paris) — Arch Mus Natl Hist Nat (Paris)
Archives Neerlandaises de Phonetique Experimentale — Arch Neerl Phon Exp
Archives Neerlandaises de Phonetique Experimentale — ArchNPhonExp
Archives Neerlandaises de Physiologie — Arch Neerl Physiol
Archives Neerlandaises de Zoologie — ANZOAM
Archives Neerlandaises de Zoologie — Arch Neerl Zool
Archives Neerlandaises de Zoologie — Archs Neerl Zool
Archives Neerlandaises des Sciences Exactes et Naturelles — Arch Neerl Sci Exact Nat
Archives Neerlandaises des Sciences Exactes et Naturelles [*Netherlands*] — Arch Neerl Sci Exactes Nat
Archives Neerlandaises des Sciences Exactes et Naturelles. Serie 3A. Sciences Exactes — Arch Neerl Sci Exactes Nat Ser 3A
Archives Neerlandaises des Sciences Exactes et Naturelles. Serie 3B. Sciences Naturelles — Arch Neerl Sci Exactes Nat Ser 3B
Archives Neerlandaises des Sciences Exactes et Naturelles. Serie 4A. Physica — Arch Neerl Sci Exactes Nat Ser 4A
Archives Neerlandaises des Sciences Exactes et Naturelles. Serie 4B. Archives Neerlandaises de Zoologie — Arch Neerl Sci Exactes Nat Ser 4B
Archives of Acoustics — ARACC
Archives of Acoustics — Arch Acoust
Archives of Agronomy and Soil Science — Arch Agron Soil Sci
Archives of AIDS Research — Arch Aids Res
Archives of American Art. Journal — Arch Am Art
Archives of Andrology — ARANDR
Archives of Andrology (New York) — Arch Androl (New York)
Archives of Animal Nutrition — Arch Anim Nutr
Archives of Antibiotics — Arch Antibiot
Archives of Asian Art — AAA
Archives of Asian Art — Archiv As Art
Archives of Biochemistry — Arch Biochem
Archives of Biochemistry — Archs Biochem
Archives of Biochemistry and Biophysics — ABBIA4
Archives of Biochemistry and Biophysics — Arch Bioch
Archives of Biochemistry and Biophysics — Arch Biochem
Archives of Biochemistry and Biophysics — Arch Biochem Biophys
Archives of Biochemistry and Biophysics — Archs Biochem Biophys
Archives of Biochemistry and Biophysics. Supplement — Arch Biochem Biophys Suppl
Archives of Biological Sciences [*English Translation of Arhiv Bioloskih Nauka*] — ABLSAG
Archives of Biological Sciences — Arch Biol Sci
Archives of Biological Sciences (Belgrade) — Arch Biol Sci (Belgrade)
Archives of Biological Sciences (English Translation of Arhiv Bioloskih Nauka) — Arch Biol Sci (Engl Transl)
Archives of Biological Sciences (English Translation of Arhiv Bioloskih Nauka) — Arch Biol Sci (Engl Transl Arh Biol Nauka)
Archives of Biology — Arch Biol
Archives of Child Health — Arch Child Health
Archives of Comparative Medicine and Surgery — Arch Comp Med Surg
Archives of Computational Methods in Engineering. State of the Art Reviews — Arch Comput Methods Engrg
Archives of Control Sciences — Arch Control Sci
Archives of Dermatology — Arch Dermat
Archives of Dermatology — Arch Dermatol
Archives of Dermatology — Archs Derm
Archives of Dermatology and Syphilology [*Chicago*] — Arch Dermatol Syphilol
Archives of Dermatology and Syphilology — Archives Dermat Syph
Archives of Dermatology and Syphilology (Chicago) — Arch Dermat and Syph (Chicago)
Archives of Diagnosis — Arch Diagn
Archives of Disease in Childhood — Arch Dis Ch
Archives of Disease in Childhood — Arch Dis Child
Archives of Disease in Childhood — Arch Dis Childhood
Archives of Disease in Childhood. Fetal and Neonatal Edition — Arch Dis Child Fetal Neonatal Ed
Archives of Environmental Contamination and Toxicology [*Germany*] — AECTC
Archives of Environmental Contamination and Toxicology — Arch Environ Contam Toxicol
Archives of Environmental Contamination and Toxicology — Archs Envir Contam Toxic
Archives of Environmental Health — AEHLA
Archives of Environmental Health — Arch Env He
Archives of Environmental Health — Arch Envir Health
Archives of Environmental Health — Arch Environ Health
Archives of Environmental Health — Arch Environ Hlth
Archives of Environmental Health — Archives Environ Health
Archives of Environmental Health — Archives Environ Hlth
Archives of Environmental Health — Archs Envir Hlth
Archives of Environmental Protection — Arch Environ Prot
Archives of Family Medicine — Arch Fam Med
Archives of Gastroenterology — Arch Gastroenterol
Archives of Gastroenterology — ARQGAF
Archives of General Psychiatry — Arch G Psyc
Archives of General Psychiatry — Arch Gen Psychiat
Archives of General Psychiatry — Arch Gen Psychiatr
Archives of General Psychiatry — Arch Gen Psychiatry
Archives of General Psychiatry — Archives Gen Psychiat
Archives of General Psychiatry — ARGPA
Archives of General Psychiatry — ARGPAQ
Archives of Gerontology and Geriatrics — AGGEDL
Archives of Gerontology and Geriatrics — Arch Gerontol Geriatr
Archives of Gynecology — ARCGDG
Archives of Gynecology — Arch Gynecol
Archives of Gynecology and Obstetrics — Arch Gynecol Obstet
Archives of Histology and Cytology — Arch Histol Cytol
Archives of Hygiene (Athens) — Arch Hyg (Athens)
Archives of Industrial Health — Arch Ind Hlth
Archives of Industrial Health — Arch Indust Health
Archives of Industrial Health — Arch Industr Hlth
Archives of Industrial Hygiene and Occupational Medicine — Arch Ind Hyg Occup Med
Archives of Industrial Hygiene and Occupational Medicine — Archives Ind Hyg & Occup Med
Archives of Industrial Hygiene and Toxicology — Arch Ind Hyg Toxicol
Archives of Insect Biochemistry and Physiology — Arch Insect Biochem Physiol
Archives of Interamerican Rheumatology — AIARA
Archives of Interamerican Rheumatology [*Brazil*] — Arch Interam Rheumatol
Archives of Internal Medicine — AIMDAP
Archives of Internal Medicine — Arch In Med
Archives of Internal Medicine — Arch Int Med
Archives of Internal Medicine — Arch Intern Med
Archives of Internal Medicine — Archs Intern Med
Archives of Internal Medicine (Moscow) — Arch Intern Med Moscow
Archives of Laryngology — Arch Laryngol
Archives of Maryland — Arch Maryland
Archives of Mass Spectral Data — Arch Mass Spectral Data
Archives of Meat, Fish, and Dairy Science — Arch Meat Fish Dairy Sci
Archives of Mechanics [*Archiwum Mechaniki Stosowanej*] — Arch Mech
Archives of Mechanics [*Archiwum Mechaniki Stosowanej*] — AVMHB
Archives of Mechanics (Archiwum Mechaniki Stosowanej) — Arch Mech (Arch Mech Stosow)
Archives of Medical Hydrology — Arch Med Hydrol
Archives of Medical Research — Arch Med Res
Archives of Metallurgy — Arch Metall
Archives of Microbiology — Arch Microb
Archives of Microbiology — Arch Microbiol
Archives of Natural History — ANHIDJ
Archives of Natural History — Arch Nat Hist
Archives of Natural History — Arch Natur Hist
Archives of Neurology — Arch Neurol
Archives of Neurology — Archives Neurol
Archives of Neurology — ARNEA
Archives of Neurology — ARNEAS
Archives of Neurology and Psychiatry — ANPSAI
Archives of Neurology and Psychiatry — Arch Neurol Psychiat
Archives of Neurology and Psychiatry — Arch Neurol Psychiatry
Archives of Neurology and Psychopathology — Arch Neurol Psychopathol
Archives of Neurology (Chicago) — Arch Neurol (Chicago)
Archives of Ophthalmology [*Chicago*] — Arch Ophth
Archives of Ophthalmology [*Chicago*] — Arch Ophthalmol
Archives of Ophthalmology — Archives Ophthal

Archives of Ophthalmology — AROPAW
Archives of Ophthalmology (Chicago) — Arch Ophthalmol Chicago
Archives of Oral Biology — AOBIAR
Archives of Oral Biology — Arch Oral B
Archives of Oral Biology — Arch Oral Biol
Archives of Orthopaedic and Traumatic Surgery — AOTSDE
Archives of Orthopaedic and Traumatic Surgery — Arch Orthop Trauma Surg
Archives of Otolaryngology — Arch Otolar
Archives of Otolaryngology — Arch Otolaryng
Archives of Otolaryngology — Arch Otolaryngol
Archives of Otolaryngology — AROTA
Archives of Otolaryngology — AROTAA
Archives of Otolaryngology and Head and Neck Surgery — AONSEJ
Archives of Otolaryngology and Head and Neck Surgery — Arch Otolaryngol Head and Neck Surg
Archives of Otolaryngology and Head and Neck Surgery — Arch Otolaryngol Head Neck Surg
Archives of Otology — Arch Otol
Archives of Oto-Rhino-Laryngology — AORLCG
Archives of Oto-Rhino-Laryngology — Arch Oto-R
Archives of Oto-Rhino-Laryngology — Arch Oto-Rhino-Laryngol
Archives of Oto-Rhino-Laryngology. Supplement — Arch Otorhinolaryngol Suppl
Archives of Pathology [*Later, Archives of Pathology and Laboratory Medicine*] — Arch Path
Archives of Pathology [*Later, Archives of Pathology and Laboratory Medicine*] — Arch Pathol
Archives of Pathology — Archs Path
Archives of Pathology [*Later, Archives of Pathology and Laboratory Medicine*] — ARPAAQ
Archives of Pathology and Laboratory Medicine — APLMAS
Archives of Pathology and Laboratory Medicine — Arch Path and Lab Med
Archives of Pathology and Laboratory Medicine — Arch Pathol Lab Med
Archives of Pediatrics [*New York*] — Arch of Ped
Archives of Pediatrics — Arch Pediat
Archives of Pediatrics — Arch Pediatr
Archives of Pediatrics — Archives Pediat
Archives of Pediatrics — ARPEA4
Archives of Pediatrics and Adolescent Medicine — Arch Pediatr Adolesc Med
Archives of Pharmacal Research [*Seoul*] — APHRDQ
Archives of Pharmacal Research — Arch Pharmacal Res
Archives of Pharmacal Research (Seoul) — Arch Pharmacal Res (Seoul)
Archives of Pharmacology — Arch Pharmacol
Archives of Physical Medicine — Arch Phys Med
Archives of Physical Medicine and Rehabilitation — APMHAI
Archives of Physical Medicine and Rehabilitation — APMR
Archives of Physical Medicine and Rehabilitation — Arch Phys M
Archives of Physical Medicine and Rehabilitation — Arch Phys Med
Archives of Physical Medicine and Rehabilitation — Arch Phys Med Rehab
Archives of Physical Medicine and Rehabilitation — Arch Phys Med Rehabil
Archives of Physical Therapy, X-Ray, Radium — Arch Phys Ther X Ray Radium
Archives of Physiology and Biochemistry — Arch Physiol Biochem
Archives of Podiatric Medicine and Foot Surgery — APMSDK
Archives of Podiatric Medicine and Foot Surgery — Arch Podiatr Med Foot Surg
Archives of Poultry Science — Arch Poult Sci
Archives of Practical Pharmacy [*Japan*] — Arch Pract Pharm
Archives of Practical Pharmacy — YAKUA2
Archives of Psychiatric Nursing — Arch Psychiatr Nurs
Archives of Psychiatry and Neurological Sciences — Arch Psychiatry Neurol Sci
Archives of Psychology — Archives Psychol
Archives of Research on Industrial Carcinogenesis — ARCAEX
Archives of Research on Industrial Carcinogenesis — Arch Res Ind Carcinog
Archives of Rubber Cultivation — Arch Rubber Cultiv
Archives of Rubber Cultivation — Arch Rubber Cultivation
Archives of Rubber Cultivation [*Bogor*] — ARUCAN
Archives of Rubber Cultivation (Bogor) — Arch Rubber Cultiv (Bogor)
Archives of Science and Transactions. Orleans County Society of Natural Sciences — Arch Sci Trans Orleans County Soc Nat Sci
Archives of Science. Orleans County Society of Natural Sciences. Transactions — Archives of Science Orleans Co Soc N Sc Tr
Archives of Sexual Behavior — Arch Sex Be
Archives of Sexual Behavior — Arch Sex Behav
Archives of Sexual Behavior — Archiv Sex Behav
Archives of Sexual Behavior — ASXBA8
Archives of Sexual Behavior — PASB
Archives of Surgery — Arch Surg
Archives of Surgery — ARSUAX
Archives of Tea Cultivation — Arch Tea Cultiv
Archives of Thermodynamics and Combustion — Arch Thermodyn Combust
Archives of Toxicology [*Berlin*] — Arch Toxic
Archives of Toxicology [*Berlin*] — Arch Toxicol
Archives of Toxicology/Archiv fuer Toxikologie — ARTODN
Archives of Toxicology (Berlin) — Arch Toxicol (Berl)
Archives of Toxicology. Supplement [*Berlin*] — Arch Toxicol Suppl
Archives of Toxicology. Supplement — ATSUDG
Archives of Virology — Arch Virol
Archives of Virology — Archs Virol
Archives of Virology — ARVID
Archives of Virology — ARVIDF
Archives of Virology. Supplementum — Arch Virol Suppl
Archives of Zoological Museum. Moscow State University — Arch Zool Mus Moscow State Univ
Archives. Office du Niger — AONGAD
Archives. Office du Niger — Arch Off Niger
Archives Orientales de Medecine et de Chirurgie — Arch Orient Med Chir
Archives Portugaises des Sciences Biologigues — APSBAU
Archives Portugaises des Sciences Biologiques — Arch Port Sci Biol
Archives Provinciales de Chirurgie — Arch Prov Chir
Archives Roumaines de Pathologie Experimentale et de Microbiologie — APEMAR
Archives Roumaines de Pathologie Experimentale et de Microbiologie — Arch Roum Pathol Exp Microbiol
Archives Royales de Mari — AR de M
Archives Royales de Mari — ARM
Archives Royales de Mari. Textes Administratives — ARMT
Archives Royales de Mari. Transcriptions et Traductions [*Paris*] — ARMT
Archives. Section des Sciences Naturelles, Physiques, et Mathematiques. Institut Grand-Ducal de Luxembourg — Arch Sect Sci Nat Phys Math Inst Grand Ducal Luxem
Archives Serbes de Medecine Generale — Arch Serbes Med Gen
Archives. Service de Sante de l'Armee Belge — Arch Serv Sante Armee Belge
Archives Slaves de Biologie — Arch Slaves Biol
Archives. Societe Francaise de Chirurgie Plastique et Reconstructive — Arch Soc Fr Chir Plast Reconstr
Archives Suisses d'Anthropologie Generale — Arch Suisses Anthrop
Archives Suisses d'Anthropologie Generale — Arch Suisses Anthropol Gen
Archives Suisses d'Anthropologie Generale — Archiv Suisses Anthropol Gen
Archives Suisses d'Anthropologie Generale — Archives Suisses Anthrop Gen
Archives Suisses d'Anthropologie Generale — Archs Suisses Anthrop Gen
Archives Suisses d'Anthropologie Generale — ASAG
Archives Suisses d'Anthropologie Generale — ASAPA3
Archives Suisses de Neurologie, Neurochirurgie, et de Psychiatrie — Arch Suisses Neurol Neurochir Psychiatr
Archives Suisses de Neurologie, Neurochirurgie, et de Psychiatrie/Archivio Svizzero di Neurologia, Neurochirurgia, e Psichiatria — SANNAW
Archives Suisses des Traditions Populaires — ASTP
Archives. Union Medicale Balkanique — Arch Union Med Balk
Archives. Union Medicale Balkanique — Archs Un Med Balkan
Archives. Union Medicale Balkanique — AUBKA7
Archives. Union Medicale Balkanique. Bulletin. Union Medicale Balkanique — Arch Union Med Balk Bull Union Med Balk
Archives Yearbook for South African History — Arch Yearb S Afr Hist
Archivi (Rome) — ArR
Archivii di Dermatologia Sperimentale — Arch Dermatol Sper
Archivii Italiani di Laringologia — AILAAB
Archivii Italiani di Laringologia — Arch Ital Laringol
Archivio — Ar
Archivio — Arch
Archivio. Alto Adige — AAA
Archivio. Alto Adige — AAAd
Archivio Bibliographico. Bibliotheca da Universidade de Coimbra — ABUC
Archivio Botanico — Arch Bot
Archivio Botanico e Biogeografico Italiano — Arch Bot Biogeogr Ital
Archivio Botanico (Forli) — Arch Bot Forli
Archivio Botanico per la Sistematica, Fitogeografic, e Genetica. Storia e Sperimentale. Bulletino. Istituto Botanico. Reale Universita di Modena — Arch Bot Sist
Archivio Dati Italiani di Geologia [*Database*] — ADIGE
Archivio "De Vecchi" per l'Anatomia Patologica e la Medicina Clinica — Arch De Vecchi Anat Patol
Archivio "De Vecchi" per l'Anatomia Patologica e la Medicina Clinica [*Italy*] — Arch De Vecchi Anat Patol Med Clin
Archivio "De Vecchi" per l'Anatomia Patologica e la Medicina Clinica — AVAPA
Archivio del Ricambio — Arch Ricam
Archivio della Corrispondenza degli Scienziati Italiani — Arch Corrisp Sci Italiani
Archivio della Societa Romana di Storia Patria — AdSR
Archivio. Deputazione Romana di Storia Patria — Arch Dep Rom
Archivio. Deputazione Romana di Storia Patria — Arch DRSP
Archivio. Deputazione Romana di Storia Patria — Arch Soc Rom
Archivio di Antropologia Criminale, Psichiatria, e Medicina Legale — Arch Antropol Crim Psichiatr Med Leg
Archivio di Chirurgia del Torace — Arch Chir Torace
Archivio di Chirurgia Ortopedica e di Medicina — Arch Chir Ortop Med
Archivio di Chirurgia Toracica e Cardiovascolare — Arch Chir Torac Cardiovasc
Archivio di Diritto Ecclesiastico — ADE
Archivio di Diritto Ecclesiastico. Monografie — ADEM
Archivio di Farmacologia Sperimentale e Scienze Affini — Arch Farmacol Sper Sci Affini
Archivio di Farmacologia Sperimentale e Scienze Affini — Arch Farmcol Sperim Sci Affini
Archivio di Filosofia — AF
Archivio di Filosofia — AFilos
Archivio di Filosofia — Ar Fi
Archivio di Filosofia — Ar Fil
Archivio di Filosofia — Arch Filosof
Archivio di Filosofia — ArF
Archivio di Fisiologia [*Firenze*] — Arch di Fisiol
Archivio di Fisiologia — Arch Fisiol
Archivio di Fisiologia — ARFIA
Archivio di Fisiologia — ARFIAY
Archivio di Logica e Filosofia della Matematica — Arch Logica Filos Mat
Archivio di Medicina Interna — Arch Med Interna
Archivio di Oceanografia e Limnologia — AOLVA
Archivio di Oceanografia e Limnologia — AOLVAE
Archivio di Oceanografia e Limnologia — Arch Oceanogr Limnol
Archivio di Ortopedia [*Archivio di Ortopedia e Reumatologia*] [*Italy*] [*Later,*] — Arch Ortop
Archivio di Ortopedia [*Later, Archivio di Ortopedia e Reumatologia*] — ARORA
Archivio di Ortopedia e Reumatologia — AOREDU
Archivio di Ortopedia e Reumatologia — Arch Ortop Reumatol

Archivio di Ostetricia e Ginecologia — AOGNAX
Archivio di Ostetricia e Ginecologia — Arch Ostet Ginecol
Archivio di Ottalmologia — Arch Ottalmol
Archivio di Patologia e Clinica Medica — APCMA
Archivio di Patologia e Clinica Medica — APCMAH
Archivio di Patologia e Clinica Medica — Arch Patol Clin Med
Archivio di Patologia e Clinica Medica — Arch Patol e Clin Med
Archivio di Patologia e Clinica Medica — Archo Patol Clin Med
Archivio di Psichiatria — Arch Psichiatr
Archivio di Psichiatria — Archivio Di Psichiat
Archivio di Psicologia, Neurologia, e Psichiatria — APNPA
Archivio di Psicologia, Neurologia, e Psichiatria — APNPAD
Archivio di Psicologia, Neurologia, e Psichiatria — Arch Psicol Neurol Psichiatr
Archivio di Radiologia — Arch Radiol
Archivio di Radiologia (Napoli) — Arch Radiol (Napoli)
Archivio di Scienze Biologiche [*Bologna*] — Arch Sci Biol
Archivio di Scienze Biologiche [*Bologna*] — ASBIA
Archivio di Scienze Biologiche — ASBIAL
Archivio di Scienze Biologiche (Naples) — Arch Sci Biol Naples
Archivio di Scienze del Lavoro — Arch Sci Lav
Archivio di Stato di Venezia — ASV
Archivio di Storia della Filosofia — ASF
Archivio di Storia della Scienza — Arch Storia Sci
Archivio di Storia della Scienza — ASSc
Archivio di Tisiologia e delle Malattie dell'Apparato Respiratorio [*Italy*] — Arch Tisiol Mal App Resp
Archivio di Tisiologia e delle Malattie dell'Apparato Respiratorio — Arch Tisiol Mal Appar Respir
Archivio "E. Maragliano" di Patologia e Clinica — AMPCA
Archivio e Maragliano di Patologia e Clinica — AMPCAV
Archivio "E. Maragliano" di Patologia e Clinica — Arch "E Maragliano" Patol Clin
Archivio e Maragliano di Patologia e Clinica — Arch Maragliano Patol Clin
Archivio e Rassegna Italiana di Ottalmologia — Arch Rass Ital Ottalmol
Archivio ed Atti. Societa Italiana di Chirurgia — Arch ed Atti Soc Ital Chir
Archivio ed Atti. Societa Medico-Chirurgica di Messina — Arch Atti Soc Med Chir Messina
Archivio Giuridico — Arch Giur
Archivio Glottologico Italiano — A G It
Archivio Glottologico Italiano [*Torino*] — AGI
Archivio Glottologico Italiano — Arch Gl It
Archivio Glottologico Italiano — Arch Glot Ital
Archivio Glottologico Italiano — Arch Glotl It
Archivio Glottologico Italiano [*Florence*] — ArGlottIt
Archivio Internazionale di Etnografia e Preistoria — Arch Int Etnogr Preist
Archivio Internazionale di Etnografia e Preistoria — Archivio Internaz Etnogr Preist
Archivio. Istituti Ospedalieri Santa Corona — Arch Ist Osp St Corona
Archivio. Istituto Biochimico Italiano — Arch Ist Biochim Ital
Archivio Italiano delle Malattie dell'Apparato Digerente — AIMAA
Archivio Italiano delle Malattie dell'Apparato Digerente [*Italy*] — Arch Ital Mal Appar Dig
Archivio Italiano di Anatomia e di Embriologia — AIAEA2
Archivio Italiano di Anatomia e di Embriologia — Arch Ital Anat Embriol
Archivio Italiano di Anatomia e Istologia Patologica — AIAIAE
Archivio Italiano di Chirurgia — AICIA
Archivio Italiano di Chirurgia — AICIAO
Archivio Italiano di Chirurgia — Arch Ital Chir
Archivio Italiano di Clinica Medica — Arch Ital Clin Med
Archivio Italiano di Dermatologia, Sifilografia, e Venereologia — Arch Ital Dermatol Sifilogr Venereol
Archivio Italiano di Dermatologia, Venereologia, e Sessuologia — Arch Ital Dermatol Venereol Sessuol
Archivio Italiano di Istologia Patologica — Arch Ital Anat Istol Patol
Archivio Italiano di Medicina Sperimentale — Arch Ital Med Sper
Archivio Italiano di Otologia, Rinologia, e Laringologia — AIORA
Archivio Italiano di Otologia, Rinologia, e Laringologia — Arch Ital Otol Rinol Laringol
Archivio Italiano di Otologia, Rinologia-Laringologia, e Patologia Cervico-Facciale — Arch Ital Otol Rinol-Laringol Patol Cervico-Facciale
Archivio Italiano di Patologia e Clinica dei Tumori — AIPUA
Archivio Italiano di Patologia e Clinica dei Tumori — AIPUAN
Archivio Italiano di Patologia e Clinica dei Tumori — Arch Ital Patol Clin Tumori
Archivio Italiano di Pediatria e Puericoltura — Arch Ital Pediatr Pueri
Archivio Italiano di Scienze Coloniati e di Parassitologia — Arch Ital Sci Colon Parassitol
Archivio Italiano di Scienze Farmacologiche — AISFAR
Archivio Italiano di Scienze Farmacologiche — Arch Ital Sci Farmacol
Archivio Italiano di Scienze Mediche Coloniali — Arch Ital Sc Med Colon
Archivio Italiano di Scienze Mediche Tropicali e di Parassitologia — AISMAE
Archivio Italiano di Scienze Mediche Tropicali e di Parassitologia — Arch Ital Sci Med Trop Parassitol
Archivio Italiano di Urologia — Arch Ital Urol
Archivio Italiano di Urologia, Andrologia — Arch Ital Urol Androl
Archivio Italiano di Urologia e Nefrologia — AIUNAR
Archivio Italiano di Urologia e Nefrologia — Arch Ital Urol Nefrol
Archivio Italiano per le Malattie Nervose — Arch Ital Malatt Nerv
Archivio Italiano per le Malattie Nervose e Mentali — Arch Ital Mal Nerv Ment
Archivio Libri Italiani su Calcolatore Electronico [*Database*] — ALICE
Archivio Monaldi — Arch Monaldi
Archivio Monaldi per la Tisiologia e le Malattie dell'Apparato Respiratorio — AMTIC
Archivio Monaldi per la Tisiologia e le Malattie dell'Apparato Respiratorio — Arch Monaldi Tisiol Mal Appar Respir
Archivio Muratoriano — AM
Archivio Muratoriano — AMur
Archivio. Ospedale al Mare — AOSMAM
Archivio. Ospedale al Mare — Arch Osp Mare
Archivio per la Zoologia, l'Anatomia, e la Fisiologia [*Genova*] — Archivio Zool Anat
Archivio per l'Alto Adige — ARAA
Archivio per l'Alto Adige — Arch A Ad
Archivio per l'Antropologia e la Etnologia — AANEBC
Archivio per l'Antropologia e la Etnologia — Arch Antrop e Etnol
Archivio per l'Antropologia e la Etnologia — Arch Antropol Etnol
Archivio per l'Antropologia e la Etnologia — Archiv Antropol Etnol
Archivio per l'Antropologia e l'Etnologia — AAE
Archivio per l'Antropologia e l'Etnologia — Arch Antr Etn
Archivio per l'Antropologia e l'Etnologia — Arch per l Ante l Etn
Archivio per l'Antropologia e l'Etnologia — Archivio Antropol Etnol
Archivio per l'Antropologia e l'Etnologia — Archivio Per L Antropol E L Etnol
Archivio per le Scienze Mediche [*Torino*] — Arch Sci Med
Archivio per le Scienze Mediche — ASMEA
Archivio per le Scienze Mediche — ASMEAU
Archivio per le Scienze Mediche (Torino) — Arch Sc Med (Torino)
Archivio per lo Studio della Fisiopatologia e Clinica del Ricambio — Arch Stud Fisiopatol Clin Ricamb
Archivio per lo Studio delle Tradizioni Populari — ATP
Archivio Putti di Chirurgia degli Organi di Movimento — APCOB
Archivio Putti di Chirurgia degli Organi di Movimento — Arch Putti Chir Organi Mov
Archivio. Reale Deputazione Romana di Storia Patria — ADRS
Archivio. Reale Deputazione Romana di Storia Patria — ADRSP
Archivio. Reale Deputazione Romana di Storia Patria — Arch Deputazione Romana Stor Patria
Archivio. Reale Deputazione Romana di Storia Patria — ARDRSP
Archivio. Societa Romana di Storia Patria — Arch Stor Patria
Archivio. Societa Romana di Storia Patria — ASRS
Archivio. Societa Romana di Storia Patria — ASRSP
Archivio Stomatologico — ACSMA6
Archivio Stomatologico — Arch Stomatol
Archivio Stomatologico — ARCSB
Archivio Storico — Archiv Stor
Archivio Storico del Risorgimento Umbrio — ASRU
Archivio Storico della Calabria — Arch Stor Cal
Archivio Storico di Belluno, Feltre, e Cadore — ABFC
Archivio Storico di Corsica — ASC
Archivio Storico di Terra di Lavoro — ASTL
Archivio Storico Italiano — A St It
Archivio Storico Italiano — Arch Stor
Archivio Storico Italiano — Arch Stor I
Archivio Storico Italiano — Arch Stor Ital
Archivio Storico Italiano — ASI
Archivio Storico Lodigiano — ASLod
Archivio Storico Lombardo — A St Lomb
Archivio Storico Lombardo — Arch Stor Lomb
Archivio Storico Lombardo — Archivio Stor Lomb
Archivio Storico Lombardo — ASL
Archivio Storico Messinese — ASM
Archivio Storico per Belluno, Feltre, e Cadore — ASBFC
Archivio Storico per la Calabria e la Lucania — Arch Stor Cal Luc
Archivio Storico per la Calabria e la Lucania — Arch Stor Calabria
Archivio Storico per la Calabria e la Lucania — Arch Stor Cla
Archivio Storico per la Calabria e la Lucania — ASCL
Archivio Storico per la Dalmazia — A St Dal
Archivio Storico per la Dalmazia — Arch Stor Dalmazia
Archivio Storico per la Dalmazia — ASD
Archivio Storico per la Provincie Napoletane — Arch Stor Prov Nap
Archivio Storico per la Provincie Napoletane — Arch Storico per Prov Nap
Archivio Storico per la Provincie Napoletane — AS Parm
Archivio Storico per la Provincie Napoletane — ASN
Archivio Storico per la Provincie Napoletane — Ast Nap
Archivio Storico per la Sicilia Orientale — A St Sic Or
Archivio Storico per la Sicilia Orientale — Arch Stor Sic
Archivio Storico per la Sicilia Orientale — Arch Stor Sic Or
Archivio Storico per la Sicilia Orientale — Arch Stor Sicilia
Archivio Storico per la Sicilia Orientale — Arch Stor Sicilia Orient
Archivio Storico per la Sicilia Orientale — AS Sic O
Archivio Storico per la Sicilia Orientale — ASSO
Archivio Storico per le Provincie Napolitane — ASPN
Archivio Storico per le Provincie Parmensi — Arch Stor Prov Parmensi
Archivio Storico per le Provincie Parmensi — ASPP
Archivio Storico Pratese — A S Prat
Archivio Storico Pratese — ASP
Archivio Storico Pugliese — A St Pugl
Archivio Storico Pugliese — Arch Stor Publiese
Archivio Storico Pugliese — Arch Stor Pugl
Archivio Storico Pugliese — ASP
Archivio Storico Sardo — Arch S Sardo
Archivio Storico Sardo — Arch Stor Sardo
Archivio Storico Sardo — AS Sard
Archivio Storico Sardo — AS Sardo
Archivio Storico Sardo — ASSar
Archivio Storico Siciliano — Arch S Sic
Archivio Storico Siciliano — Archivo St Siciliano
Archivio Storico Siciliano — ArchSS
Archivio Storico Siciliano — AS Sic
Archivio Storico Siciliano — ASS
Archivio Storico Siciliano. Serie 3 — Arch Stor Sicil Ser 3
Archivio Storico Siracusano — AS Sir
Archivio Storico Ticinese — ASTic

Archivio Svizzero di Neurologia e Psichiatria — Arch Svizz Neurol Psichiatr
Archivio Svizzero di Neurologia, Neurochirurgia, e Psichiatria — Arch Svizz Neurol Neurochir Psichiatr
Archivio Trentino — ATren
Archivio Triennale. Laboratorio di Botanica Crittogamica — Arch Triennale Lab Bot Crittog
Archivio Unione Comunita Israelitiche Italiane — AUCII
Archivio Veneto — Ar Ven
Archivio Veneto — Arch Veneto
Archivio Veneto — AV
Archivio Veneto — AVen
Archivio Veneto — NA Ven
Archivio Veneto. Serie 5 — Arch Veneto Ser 5
Archivio Veneto-Tridentino — AVT
Archivio Veterinario Italiano — Arch Vet Ital
Archivio Veterinario Italiano — Archo Vet Ital
Archivio Veterinario Italiano — AVEIA
Archivio Veterinario Italiano — AVEIAN
Archivio Zoologico Italiano — Arch Zool Ital
Archivio Zoologico Italiano — Archo Zool Ital
Archivio Zoologico Italiano — AZOIAX
Archivist. Public Archives of Canada — ARCH
Archivium Hibernicum — AH
Archivium Hibernicum — Arch Hib
Archivni Casopis — Arch Cas
Archivo Agustiniano — AAg
Archivo Agustiniano. Revista do Investigacion Historica de los P.P. Agustinos Espanoles — Arch Agustin
Archivo de Biologia Vegetal Teorica y Aplicada — Arch Biol Veg Teor Aplicada
Archivo de Derecho Publico — ADP
Archivo de Derecho Publico. Universidad de Granada — Arch Derecho Publico
Archivo de Filologia Aragonesa — AFA
Archivo de Filologia Aragonesa — ArchFAr
Archivo de Filologia Aragonesa. Institucion Fernando el Catolico de la Excma. Diputacion Provincial — Arch Filol Aragonesa
Archivo de Genealogia y Heraldica — Arch Geneal Herald
Archivo de Medicina Legal — Arch Med Leg
Archivo de Prehistoria Levantina — AP Lev
Archivo de Prehistoria Levantina — APHL
Archivo de Prehistoria Levantina — APL
Archivo de Prehistoria Levantina — Arch Hist Lev
Archivo de Prehistoria Levantina — Arch Pr Hist Lev
Archivo de Prehistoria Levantina — Arch Pr Lev
Archivo de Prehistoria Levantina — Archivo Prehist Levantina
Archivo de Prehistoria Levantina. CSIC (Consejo Superior de Investigaciones Cientificas) — Arch Prehist Levantina
Archivo Diocesano de Cuenca — ADC
Archivo Espanol de Arqueologia — A Esp A
Archivo Espanol de Arqueologia — A Esp Arqu
Archivo Espanol de Arqueologia — AEA
Archivo Espanol de Arqueologia — AEAr
Archivo Espanol de Arqueologia — AEArq
Archivo Espanol de Arqueologia — AEsp
Archivo Espanol de Arqueologia — Arch Esp A
Archivo Espanol de Arqueologia — Arch Esp Arch
Archivo Espanol de Arqueologia — Arch Esp Arq
Archivo Espanol de Arqueologia — Archiv Espan Arq
Archivo Espanol de Arqueologia — Archivo Esp Arq
Archivo Espanol de Arqueologia — Archivo Espanol Arqu
Archivo Espanol de Arqueologia [*Madrid*] — ArEspArq
Archivo Espanol de Arqueologia. CSIC (Consejo Superior de Investigaciones Cientificas) — Arch Espan Arqueol
Archivo Espanol de Arte — A Es A
Archivo Espanol de Arte — A Esp A
Archivo Espanol de Arte — AEA
Archivo Espanol de Arte — Arch Esp A
Archivo Espanol de Arte — Arch Esp Ar
Archivo Espanol de Arte — Arch Esp Art
Archivo Espanol de Arte — Archiv Espan Arte
Archivo Espanol de Arte — Archivo Esp Arte
Archivo Espanol de Arte. CSIC (Consejo Superior de Investigaciones Cientificas) — Arch Espan Arte
Archivo Espanol de Arte y Arqueologia — A Esp
Archivo Espanol de Arte y Arqueologia — AEAA
Archivo Espanol de Arte y Arqueologia — Arch Esp
Archivo Espanol de Morfologia — Arch Esp Morfol
Archivo Giuridico — AG
Archivo Hispalense — AH
Archivo Hispalense — Arch Hisp
Archivo Hispalense — ArH
Archivo Hispalense. Revista Historica, Litteraria, y Artistica — Ar Hisp
Archivo Ibero-Americano [*Madrid*] — AIA
Archivo Ibero-Americano [*Madrid*] — ArchIA
Archivo Ibero-Americano — Archiv Ibero
Archivo Ibero-Americano [*Madrid*] — ArI
Archivo Iberoamericano de Historia de la Medicina y de Antropologia Medica — Arch Ib Am Hist Med
Archivo Ibero-Americano (Madrid) — Arch Ibero Am Madrid
Archivo Jose Marti [*Cuba*] — AJM
Archivo Jose Marti (Habana) — Arch J Marti Hav
Archivo per la Storia Ecclesiastica dell'Umbria — ASEU
Archivo. Revista de Ciencias Historicas — Arch Revista Ci Hist
Archivo Storico Lodigiano — Arch Stor Lodigiano
Archivo Teologico Granadino [*Granada*] — ArTGran
Archivo Teologico Granadino — ATG
Archivos. Academia Ecuatoriana de Medicina — Arch Acad Ecuat Med
Archivos Argentinos de Dermatologia — Arch Argent Dermatol
Archivos Argentinos de Neurologia — Arch Argent Neurol
Archivos Argentinos de Pediatria — AHAPAS
Archivos Argentinos de Pediatria — Arch Argent Pediatr
Archivos Argentinos de Reumatologia — AHARAY
Archivos Argentinos de Reumatologia — Arch Argent Reumatol
Archivos Argentinos de Tisiologia y Neumonologia — AATNAY
Archivos Argentinos de Tisiologia y Neumonologia — Arch Argent Tisiol Neumonol
Archivos. Asociacion Peruana para el Progreso de la Ciencia — Arch Asoc Peruana Progr Ci
Archivos Brasileiros de Medicina — Arch Brasil Med
Archivos. Clinica e Instituto de Endocrinologia (Montevideo) — Arch Clin Inst Endocrinol (Montevideo)
Archivos. Colegio Medico de El Salvador — Arch Col Med El Salv
Archivos. Colegio Medico de El Salvador — Arch Col Med El Salvador
Archivos. Conferencia de Medicos del Hospital Ramos-Mejia — Arch Conf Med Hosp Ramos Mejia
Archivos Cubanos de Cancerologia — Arch Cubanos Cancerol
Archivos de Biologia Andina — Arch Biol Andina
Archivos de Biologia y Medicina Experimentales [*Chile*] — ABMXA
Archivos de Biologia y Medicina Experimentales — ABMXA2
Archivos de Biologia y Medicina Experimentales — Arch Biol M
Archivos de Biologia y Medicina Experimentales — Arch Biol Med Exp
Archivos de Biologia y Medicina Experimentales. Suplemento — Arch Biol Med Exp Supl
Archivos de Bioquimica, Quimica, y Farmacia — Arch Bioquim Quim Farm
Archivos de Bioquimica, Quimica, y Farmacia (Tucuman) — Arch Bioquim Quim Farm (Tucuman)
Archivos de Bioquimica, Quimica, y Farmacia (Tucuman) — Archos Bioquim Quim Farmac (Tucuman)
Archivos de Bioquimica, Quimica, y Farmacia. Universidad Nacional de Tucuman — Arch Bioquim
Archivos de Bromatologia — Archos Bromat
Archivos de Bronconeumologia — Arch Bronconeumol
Archivos de Cardiologia y Hematologia — Arch Cardio y Hematol
Archivos de Criminologia, Neuropsiquiatria, y Disciplinas Conexas — ACNP
Archivos de Criminologia Neuro-Psiquiatria y Disciplinas Conexas — Arch Criminol Neuro Psiquiatr Discip Conexas
Archivos de Dermatologia e Syphiligraphia de Sao Paulo — Arch Dermatol Syphiligr Sao Paulo
Archivos de Estudios Medicos Aragoneses — Arch Estud Med Aragon
Archivos de Farmacia y Bioquimica del Tucuman — AFBTAV
Archivos de Farmacia y Bioquimica del Tucuman — Arch Farm Bioquim Tucuman
Archivos de Farmacologia y Toxicologia — AFTOD7
Archivos de Farmacologia y Toxicologia — Arch Farmacol Toxicol
Archivos de Histologia Normal y Patologica — Arch Histol Norm Patol
Archivos de Historia de la Medicina Argentina — Arch Hist Med Argent
Archivos de Historia Medica de Venezuela — Arch Hist Med Venezuela
Archivos de Hospitales Universitarios — AHUNA
Archivos de Hospitales Universitarios (Havana) — Arch Hosp Univ (Havana)
Archivos de Investigacion Medica — AIVMB
Archivos de Investigacion Medica — AIVMBU
Archivos de Investigacion Medica — Arch Inv M
Archivos de Investigacion Medica — Arch Invest Med
Archivos de Medicina Experimental — Arch Med Exp
Archivos de Medicina (Lisbon) — Arch Med (Lisbon)
Archivos de Medicina Veterinaria — Arch Med Vet
Archivos de Medicina Veterinaria (Valdivia) — Arch Med Vet (Valdivia)
Archivos de Neurobiologia [*Madrid*] — Arch Neurobiol
Archivos de Neurobiologia — ARNBBK
Archivos de Neurobiologica — ARNBB
Archivos de Odontoestomatologia — Arch Odontoestomatol
Archivos de Oftalmologia de Buenos Aires — AOBAA3
Archivos de Oftalmologia de Buenos Aires — Arch Oftalmol B Aires
Archivos de Oftalmologia Hispano-Americanos — Arch Oftal Hispano-Am
Archivos de Oftalmologia Hispano-Americanos — Arch Oftalmol Hisp-Am
Archivos de Pediatria del Uruguay — APURAK
Archivos de Pediatria del Uruguay — Arch Pediatr Urug
Archivos de Psiquiatria y Criminologia. Medicina Legal — Archivos Psiquiat Y Criminol
Archivos de Zootecnia — Arch Zootec
Archivos de Zootecnia — Archos Zootecnia
Archivos de Zootecnia — AZOTAW
Archivos del Folklore Chileno — AC
Archivos del Folklore Chileno (Santiago) — Arch Folk Chil Santiago
Archivos del Folklore Chileno. Universidad de Chile — AFCU
Archivos del Folklore Cubano — AFC
Archivos do Instituto Biologico (Sao Paulo) — Arch Inst Biol Sao Paulo
Archivos Espanoles de Farmacologia Experimental — Arch Esp Farmacol Exp
Archivos Espanoles de Urologia — Arch Esp Urol
Archivos. Facultad de Medicina de Madrid — AFMMBW
Archivos. Facultad de Medicina de Madrid — Arch Fac Med Madr
Archivos. Facultad de Medicina de Madrid — Arch Fac Med Madrid
Archivos. Facultad de Medicina de Zaragoza — Arch Fac Med Zaragoza
Archivos. Facultad de Medicina de Zaragoza. Suplemento — Arch Fac Med Zaragoza Supl
Archivos Farmaceuticos (Bago) — Arch Farm (Bago)
Archivos. Fundacion Roux-Ocefa — Arch Fund Roux-Ocefa
Archivos. Fundacion Roux-Ocefa — FRXAAJ
Archivos. Fundacion Roux-Ocefa — FRXZZ
Archivos. Hospital de la Cruz Roja de Barcelona — Arch Hosp Cruz Roja
Archivos. Hospital Rosales — Arch Hosp Rosales

Archivos. Hospital Universitario General Calixto Garcia — Arch Hosp Univ Gen Calixto Garcia
Archivos. Hospital Vargas — Arch Hosp Vargas
Archivos. Hospital Vargas (Caracas) — Arch Hosp Vargas (Caracas)
Archivos Iberoamericanos de Historia de la Medicina — AIHM
Archivos Iberoamericanos de Historia de la Medicina. CSIC (Consejo Superior de Investigaciones Cientificas) — Arch Ibero Am Hist Medicina
Archivos Iberoamericanos de Historia de la Medicina y Antropologia Medica [*A publication*] — Arch Iberoamer Hist Med
Archivos. Instituto Antropologia (Natal) — Archos Inst Antrop (Natal)
Archivos. Instituto Biologico — Arch Inst Biol
Archivos. Instituto Biologico (Sao Paulo) — Archos Inst Biol (S Paulo)
Archivos. Instituto de Aclimatacion (Almeria, Espana) — Arch Inst Aclim (Almeria Esp)
Archivos. Instituto de Aclimatacion (Almeria, Espana) — Archos Inst Aclim (Almeria)
Archivos. Instituto de Aclimatacion. Consejo Superior de Investigaciones Cientificas — Arch Inst Aclim Cons Super Invest Ci
Archivos. Instituto de Biologia Andina (Lima) — Arch Inst Biol Andina (Lima)
Archivos. Instituto de Cardiologia de Mexico — Arch I Card
Archivos. Instituto de Cardiologia de Mexico — Arch Inst Cardiol Mex
Archivos. Instituto de Estudios Africanos — AIEA
Archivos. Instituto de Estudios Africanos — Arch IE Afr
Archivos. Instituto de Estudios Africanos — Arch Inst Est Afr
Archivos. Instituto de Estudios Africanos [*Madrid*] — Arch Inst Estud Afr
Archivos. Instituto de Estudios Africanos. CSIC (Consejo Superior de Investigaciones Cientificas) — Arch Inst Est Africanos
Archivos. Instituto de Farmacologia Experimental [*Madrid*] — AIFEA
Archivos. Instituto de Farmacologia Experimental — Arch Inst Farm Exp
Archivos. Instituto de Farmacologia Experimental (Madrid) — Arch Inst Farmacol Exp (Madrid)
Archivos. Instituto de Farmacologia Experimental (Medicina) — Arch Inst Farmacol Exp (Med)
Archivos Internacionales de la Hidatidosis — Arch Int Hidatidosis
Archivos Latinoamericanos de Nutricion — ALANBH
Archivos Latinoamericanos de Nutricion — ALN
Archivos Latinoamericanos de Nutricion — Arch Latinoam Nutr
Archivos Latinoamericanos de Nutricion — Arch Latinoamer Nutr
Archivos Latinoamericanos de Nutricion. Organo Oficial. Sociedad Latinoamericano de Nutricion — SLN/ALN
Archivos Leoneses — AL
Archivos Leoneses — Ar Leon
Archivos Leoneses. CSIC (Consejo Superior de Investigaciones Cientificas) — Arch Leoneses
Archivos Medicos de Cuba — Arch Med Cuba
Archivos Medicos Mexicanos [*Mexico*] — Arch Med Mex
Archivos Medicos (Mexico City) — Arch Med (Mexico City)
Archivos Medicos Panamenos — Arch Med Panameno
Archivos Mexicanos de Anatomia — Arch Mex Anat
Archivos Mexicanos de Neurologia y Psiquiatria — Arch Mex Neurol Psiquiatr
Archivos Mexicanos de Venereologia y Dermatologia — Arch Mex Venereol Dermatol
Archivos Mexicanos de Venereo-Sifilis y Dermatologia — Arch Mex Venereo Sifilis Dermatol
Archivos Mineiros de Dermato-Syphiligraphia — Arch Mineir Dermato Syphiligr
Archivos. Museu Paranaie — Archos Mus Paranaie
Archivos Peruanos de Patologia y Clinica — Arch Peru Patol Clin
Archivos Peruanos de Patologia y Clinica (Lima) — Arch Peru Patol Clin (Lima)
Archivos. Real Instituto Bacteriologico Camara Pestana — Arch R Inst Bacteriol Camara Pestana
Archivos. Sociedad Americana de Oftalmologia y Optometria — Arch S A Of
Archivos. Sociedad Americana de Oftalmologia y Optometria — Arch Soc Am Oftalmol Optom
Archivos. Sociedad Americana de Oftalmologia y Optometria — SAOABX
Archivos. Sociedad Canaria de Oftalmologia — Arch Soc Canaria Oftalmol
Archivos. Sociedad Canaria de Oftalmologia — ASOFDC
Archivos. Sociedad de Biologia de Montevideo — Arch Soc Biol Montev
Archivos. Sociedad de Biologia de Montevideo — Archos Soc Biol Montev
Archivos. Sociedad de Biologia de Montevideo — ASBLAU
Archivos. Sociedad de Biologia de Montevideo. Suplemento — Arch Soc Biol Montevideo Supl
Archivos. Sociedad de Estudios Clinicos de la Habana — Arch Soc Estud Clin Habana
Archivos. Sociedad Espanola de Oftalmologia — Arch Soc Esp Oftalmol
Archivos. Sociedad Espanola de Oftalmologia — ASEOAK
Archivos. Sociedad Oftalmologica Hispano-Americana — Arch Soc Oftalmol Hisp-Am
Archivos. Sociedad Oftalmologica Hispano-Americana — ASOHAF
Archivos Uruguayos de Medicina, Cirugia y Especialidades — Arch Uruguayos Med
Archivos Uruguayos de Medicina, Cirujia, y Especialidades — Arch Urug Med Cir Espec
Archivos Uruguayos de Medicina, Cirujia, y Especialidades — AUMCA4
Archivos Venezolanas de Puericultura y Pediatria. Sociedad Venezolana de Puericultura y Pediatria — SVPP/A
Archivos Venezolanos de Folklore — AVF
Archivos Venezolanos de Folklore (Caracas) — Arch Venez Folk Caracas
Archivos Venezolanos de Medicina Tropical y Parasitologia Medica — Arch Venez Med Trop Parasitol Med
Archivos Venezolanos de Medicina Tropical y Parasitologia Medica — AVMPAG
Archivos Venezolanos de Nutricion — Arch Venez Nutr
Archivos Venezolanos de Nutricion — Archos Venez Nutr
Archivos Venezolanos de Nutricion — AVNUA2
Archivos Venezolanos de Patologia Tropical y Parasitologia Medica — Arch Venez Patol Trop Parasitol Med
Archivos Venezolanos de Patologia Tropical y Parasitologia Medica — AVPTA9
Archivos Venezolanos de Puericultura y Pediatria — Arch Venez Pueric Pediatr
Archivos Venezolanos de Puericultura y Pediatria — AVPPAV
Archivum [*Oviedo*] — Arch
Archivum Balatonicum — Arch Balaton
Archivum Balatonicum — Arch Balatonicum
Archivum Chirurgicum Neerlandicum — ACNRA
Archivum Chirurgicum Neerlandicum — Arch Chir Neerl
Archivum Combustionis — ACOME
Archivum Combustionis — Arch Combust
Archivum de Dermatologia Experimentale et Functionale — Arch Dermatol Exp Funct
Archivum Eurasiae Medii Aevi — A Euras
Archivum Europae Centro-Orientalis — AECO
Archivum Europae Centro-Orientalis — Arch Eur Centro Orient
Archivum Europae Centro-Orientalis — ArchEurCO
Archivum Franciscanum Historicum [*Firenze*] — AFH
Archivum Franciscanum Historicum — Arch Franciscanum Hist
Archivum Fratrum Praedicatorum [*Roma*] — AFP
Archivum Fratrum Praedicatorum — Arch Fratrum Praedicatorum
Archivum Heraldicum — Arch Herald
Archivum Histologicum Japonicum — AHJPB6
Archivum Histologicum Japonicum — AHTJA
Archivum Histologicum Japonicum — Arch Hist J
Archivum Histologicum Japonicum — Arch Hist Jap
Archivum Histologicum Japonicum — Arch Histol Jpn
Archivum Historiae Pontificiae — AHP
Archivum Historiae Pontificiae [*Rome*] — ArHPont
Archivum Historicum Carmelitanum — Arch Hist Carm
Archivum Historicum Societatis Iesu — AHSI
Archivum Historicum Societatis Iesu — Arch Hist Soc Iesu
Archivum Historicum Societatis Iesu — Archivum Hist Soc Iesu
Archivum Historicum Societatis Jesu — Arch Hist Soc Jesu
Archivum Historii, Filozofii, i Mysli Spolecznej — AHF
Archivum Hydrobiologii i Rybactwa — Arch Hydrobiol Rybactwa
Archivum Immunologiae et Therapiae Experimentalis — AITEA
Archivum Immunologiae et Therapiae Experimentalis — Arch Immunol Ther Exp
Archivum Immunologiae et Therapiae Experimentalis (English Translation) — Arch Immunol Ther Exp Engl Transl
Archivum Immunologiae et Therapiae Experimentalis (Warszawa) — Arch Immunol Ther Exp (Warsz)
Archivum Latinitatis Medii Aevi — ALMA
Archivum Linguisticum — ALing
Archivum Linguisticum — Arch Ling
Archivum Linguisticum — Arch Linguist
Archivum Linguisticum — Arch Linguisticum
Archivum Linguisticum — Archiv Ling
Archivum Linguisticum — ArchL
Archivum Linguisticum — ArL
Archivum Mathematicum (Brno) — Arch Math (Brno)
Archivum Melitense. Malta Historical and Scientific Society/Societa Storico-Scientifica Matenese — Arch Melit
Archivum Orientale Pragense — AOP
Archivum Ottomanicum — ArOtt
Archivum Romanicum — AR
Archivum Romanicum — Arch Rom
Archivum Romanicum — Arch Roman
Archivum Romanicum — Archiv Rom
Archivum Romanicum — ARom
Archivum Societatis Zoologicae-Botanicae Fennicae "Vanamo" — Arch Soc Zool-Bot Fenn "Vanamo"
Archivum Societatis Zoologicae-Botanicae Fennicae "Vanamo" — ASZBAI
Archivum Veterinarium Polonicum — Arch Vet Pol
Archivum Veterinarium Polonicum — PARWAC
Archiwa, Biblioteki, i Muzea Koscielne — ABMK
Archiwum Akustyki — Arch Akust
Archiwum Automatyki i Telemechaniki — AATMA
Archiwum Automatyki i Telemechaniki — Arch Autom Telemech
Archiwum Automatyki i Telemechaniki — Arch Automat i Telemech
Archiwum Automatyki i Telemechaniki — Arch Automat Telemech
Archiwum Budowy Maszyn — Arch Budowy Masz
Archiwum Budowy Maszyn — Arch Budowy Maszyn
Archiwum Budowy Maszyn — AWBMA
Archiwum Chemji i Farmacji — Arch Chem Farm
Archiwum Elektrotechniki [*Warsaw*] — Arch Elektrotech
Archiwum Elektrotechniki — ARELA
Archiwum Energetyki — Arch Energ
Archiwum Energetyki — AREGB
Archiwum Glownej Komisji Badania Zbrodni Hitlerowskich — AGKBZH
Archiwum Gornictwa — AGORA
Archiwum Gornictwa — Arch Gorn
Archiwum Gornictwa — Archwm Gorn
Archiwum Gornictwa i Hutnictwa — Arch Gorn Hutn
Archiwum Historii Medycyny — Arch Hist Med
Archiwum Historii Medycyny — ARHMB
Archiwum Historii Medycyny — ARHMBN
Archiwum Historii Medycyny (Warszawa) — Arch Hist Med (Warsz)
Archiwum Hutnictwa — AHUTA
Archiwum Hutnictwa — Arch Hutn
Archiwum Hutnictwa — Archwm Hutn
Archiwum Hydrotechniki — AHDRA
Archiwum Hydrotechniki — Arch Hydrotech
Archiwum Immunologii i Terapii Doswiadczalnej — Arch Immunol Ter Dosw

Archiwum Inzynierii Ladowej — AIZLA
Archiwum Inzynierii Ladowej — Arch Inz Ladowej
Archiwum Mechaniki Stosowanej [*Archives of Mechanics*] — AMESA
Archiwum Mechaniki Stosowanej [*Archives of Mechanics*] — Arch Mech Stosow
Archiwum Mechaniki Stosowanej [*Archives of Mechanics*] — Arch Mech Stosowanej
Archiwum Medycyny Sadowej i Kryminologii — Arch Med Sadowej Kryminol
Archiwum Mineralogiczne — Arch Mineral
Archiwum Mineralogiczne — ARWMA
Archiwum Nauki o Materialach — ANAMD
Archiwum Nauki o Materialach [*Poland*] — Arch Nauki Mater
Archiwum Ochrony Srodowiska — AOSRD6
Archiwum Ochrony Srodowiska — Arch Ochr Srodowiska
Archiwum Procesow Spalania [*Poland*] — Arch Procesow Spalania
Archiwum Termodynamiki — Arch Termodyn
Archiwum Termodynamiki — ATERD
Archiwum Termodynamiki i Spalania — Arch Termodyn Spal
Archiwum Towarzystwa Naukowego we Lwowie. Dzial 3. Matematyczno-Przyrodniczy — Arch Towarz Nauk We Lwowie Dzial 3 Mat Przyr
Archiwum Zydowskiego Instytutu Historycznego — AZIH
Arcispedale S. Anna di Ferrara — AAFRA
Arcispedale S. Anna di Ferrara [*Italy*] — Arcisp S Anna di Ferrara
Arco — AO
Arco di Ulisso. Collana di Testi e Documonti nelle Lingue Originali — Arco di Ulisso
Arctic — ARCT
Arctic Aeromedical Laboratory. Technical Note — AALTN
Arctic Aeromedical Laboratory. Technical Report — AALTR
Arctic Aeromedical Laboratory (United States). Technical Documentary Report — Arct Aeromed Lab (US) Tech Doc Rep
Arctic Aeromedical Laboratory (United States). Technical Note — Arct Aeromed Lab (US) Tech Note
Arctic Aeromedical Laboratory (United States). Technical Report — Arct Aeromed Lab (US) Tech Rep
Arctic and Alpine Research — ARAR
Arctic and Alpine Research — Arct Alp Res
Arctic and Alpine Research — Arctic Alp Res
Arctic and Alpine Research — ATLPA
Arctic and Alpine Research — ATLPAV
Arctic and Alpine Research (Boulder, Colorado) — Arct Alp Res (Boulder Colo)
Arctic and Northern Development Digest — ARND
Arctic Anthropology — AANT
Arctic Anthropology — ARANBP
Arctic Anthropology — Arct Anthropol
Arctic Anthropology — Arctic Anthropol
Arctic Anthropology — Artic Anth
Arctic Bibliography — Arct Bibl
Arctic Bibliography — Arct Bibliogr
Arctic Bibliography. US Department of Defense — Arctic Bibliogr
Arctic Bulletin — ARBU
Arctic Bulletin — ARBUD
Arctic Bulletin — ARBUDJ
Arctic Bulletin — Arct Bull
Arctic Bulletin — Arctic Bul
Arctic Circle — ARCC
Arctic Circular — ARCI
Arctic Coastal Zone Management. Newsletter — ACZMN
Arctic Explorer. Travel Arctic. Northwest Territories [*Canada*] — AREX
Arctic Gas Profile — AGP
Arctic in Colour — ARIC
Arctic Institute of North America. Annual Report — AIANAT
Arctic Institute of North America. Annual Report — Arct Inst N Am Annu Rep
Arctic Institute of North America. Annual Report — Arct Inst North Am Annu Rep
Arctic Institute of North America. Research Paper — AINARP
Arctic Institute of North America. Research Paper — Arctic Inst North America Research Paper
Arctic Institute of North America. Special Publication — AIASAA
Arctic Institute of North America. Special Publication — Arct Inst N Am Spec Publ
Arctic Institute of North America. Special Publication — Arctic Inst North America Special Pub
Arctic Institute of North America. Technical Paper — AIATAD
Arctic Institute of North America. Technical Paper — Arct Inst N Am Tech Pap
Arctic Institute of North America. Technical Paper — Arct Inst North America Tech Pap
Arctic Institute of North America. Technical Paper — Arctic Inst North America Tech Paper
Arctic International Wildlife Range Society. Newsletter — AIWR
Arctic Land Use Research Program Report. ALUR (Canada) — Arct Land Use Res Program Rep ALUR (Can)
Arctic Land Use Research Report — ALUR Rep
Arctic Medical Research — Arctic Med Res
Arctic Medical Research Report. Nordic Council — AMR
Arctic Medical Research Report. Nordic Council — AMRR
Arctic News — ARNE
Arctic Offshore. Publication of the Alaska Oil and Gas Association — AROF
Arctic Petroleum Review — APOA
Arctic Policy Review — ARPR
Arctic Research in the United States — ARUS
Arctic Science and Technology Information System [*Database*] — ASTIS
Arctic Seas Bulletin. Canadian Arctic Resources Committee — ARSB
Arctos. Acta Philologica Fennica — AAPF
Arctos. Acta Philologica Fennica — Arc
Arcturus. Department of Education. Northwest Territories [*Canada*] — ARCU
Ardenne et Famenne. Art-Archeologie-Histoire-Folklore — A&F
Arden's Sydney Magazine — Arden's Sydney Mag
Area and Culture Studies [*Tokyo*] — A & CS
Area Development — ADEVD
Area Development — Area Dev
Area Resource File [*Database*] — ARF
Areco's Quarterly Index to Periodical Literature on Aging — Arecos Quart Ind Per Lit Aging
Areito — AR
Areito (New York) — ANY
Arena — Ar
Arena Review — Arena Rev
Arena Tekstil — Arena Teks
Arerugi — ARERAM
Arethusa — Areth
AREUEA [*American Real Estate and Urban Economics Association*] **Journal** — REU
AREUEA Journal. American Real Estate and Urban Economics Association — AREUEA Jrnl Amer Real Estate and Urban Economics Assn
Argensola — Arg
Argenteuil Symposia Series [*Elsevier Book Series*] — ASS
Argenteuil Symposium — Argenteuil Symp
Argentina Austral (Buenos Aires) — Arg Austral BA
Argentina. Comision Nacional de Energia Atomica. CNEA NT — Argent Com Nac Energ At CNEA NT
Argentina. Comision Nacional de Energia Atomica. Department of Radiobiology. Progress Report — Argent Com Nac Energ At Dep Radiobiol Prog Rep
Argentina. Comision Nacional de Energia Atomica. Informe — Argent Com Nac Energ At Inf
Argentina. Comision Nacional de Energia Atomica. Publicaciones. Serie Informe — Argent Com Nac Energ At Publ Ser Inf
Argentina. Direccion de Minas, Geologia, e Hidrologia. Boletin — Argent Dir Minas Geol Hidrol Bol
Argentina. Direccion de Minas y Geologia. Anales — Argent Dir Minas Geol An
Argentina. Direccion de Minas y Geologia. Boletin — Argent Dir Minas Geol Bol
Argentina. Direccion de Minas y Geologia. Publicacion — Argent Dir Minas Geol Publ
Argentina. Direccion General de Industria Minera. Anales — Argent Dir Gen Ind Min An
Argentina. Direccion General de Industria Minera. Boletin — Argent Dir Gen Ind Minera Bol
Argentina. Direccion General de Industria Minera. Publicacion — Argent Dir Gen Ind Min Publ
Argentina. Direccion General de Minas y Geologia. Boletin — Argent Dir Gen Minas Geol Bol
Argentina. Direccion General de Minas y Geologia. Publicacion — Argent Dir Gen Minas Geol Publ
Argentina. Direccion Nacional de Geologia y Mineria. Anales — Argent Dir Nac Geol Min An
Argentina. Direccion Nacional de Geologia y Mineria. Boletin — AMMBAD
Argentina. Direccion Nacional de Geologia y Mineria. Boletin — Argent Dir Nac Geol Min Bol
Argentina. Direccion Nacional de Geologia y Mineria. Informe Tecnico — Argent Dir Nac Geol Min Inf Tec
Argentina. Direccion Nacional de Geologia y Mineria. Publicacion — Argent Dir Nac Geol Min Publ
Argentina. Direccion Nacional de Mineria. Boletin — Argent Dir Nac Min Bol
Argentina. Direccion Nacional de Quimica. Boletin Informativo — Argent Dir Nac Quim Bol Inf
Argentina Electroenergetica — Argent Electroenerg
Argentina. Instituto Nacional de Geologia y Mineria. Anales — Argent Inst Nac Geol Min An
Argentina. Instituto Nacional de Geologia y Mineria. Boletin — Argent Inst Nac Geol Min Bol
Argentina. Instituto Nacional de Tecnologia Agropecuaria. Manual Agropecuario [*A publication*] — Argent Inst Nac Tecnol Agropecu Man Agropecu
Argentina. Instituto Nacional de Tecnologia Industrial. Boletin Tecnico — Argent Inst Nac Tecnol Ind Bol Tec
Argentina. Republica. Comision Nacional de Energia Atomica. Publicaciones. Serie Quimica — Argent Repub Com Nac Energ At Publ Ser Quim
Argentina. Republica. Comision Nacional de Energia Atomica. Report CNEA — Argent Repub Com Nac Energ At CNEA
Argentina. Republica. Direccion Nacional de Geologia y Mineria. Anales — Argent Repub Dir Nac Geol Min An
Argentina. Republica. Direccion Nacional de Geologia y Mineria. Boletin — Argent Repub Dir Nac Geol Min Bol
Argentina. Republica. Direccion Nacional de Geologia y Mineria. Informe Tecnico — Argent Repub Dir Nac Geol Min Inf Tec
Argentina. Republica. Direccion Nacional de Geologia y Mineria. Publicacion — Argent Repub Dir Nac Geol Min Publ
Argentina. Republica. Estudios de Geologia y Mineria Economica. Serie Argentina — Argent Repub Estud Geol Min Econ
Argentina. Republica. Instituto Nacional de Geologia y Mineria. Boletin — Argent Repub Inst Nac Geol Min Bol
Argentina. Republica. Instituto Nacional de Geologia y Mineria. Revista — Argent Repub Inst Nac Geol Min Rev
Argentina. Republica. Ministerio de Agricultura. Direccion de Informaciones. Publicacion Miscelanea — Argent Repub Minist Agric Dir Inf Publ Misc
Argentina. Republica. Ministerio de Economia de la Nacion. Direccion Nacional de Geologia y Mineria. Anales — Argent Repub Minist Econ Nac Dir Nac Geol Min An

Argentina. Republica. Ministerio de Economia de la Nacion. Direccion Nacional de Geologia y Mineria. Publicacion — Argent Repub Minist Econ Nac Dir Nac Geol Min Publ
Argentina. Republica. Ministerio de Industria y Comercio de la Nacion. Direccion Nacional de Mineria. Anales — Argent Repub Minist Ind Comer Nac Dir Nac Min An
Argentina Republica. Ministerio de Industria y Comercio de la Nacion. Direccion Nacional de Mineria. Boletin — Argent Repub Minist Ind Comer Nac Dir Nac Min Bol
Argentina. Republica. Ministerio de Industria y Comercio de la Nacion. Direccion Nacional de Mineria. Publicacion — Argent Repub Minist Ind Comer Nac Dir Nac Min Publ
Argentina. Republica. Secretaria de Agricultura Ganaderia. Direccion de Informaciones. Publicacion Miscelanea — Argent Repub Secr Agric Ganad Dir Inf Publ Misc
Argentina. Republica. Subsecretaria de Mineria. Estudios de Geologia y Mineria Economica. Serie Argentina — Argent Repub Subsecr Min Estud Geol Min Econ Ser Argent
Argentina. Secretaria de Industria y Comercio. Boletin — Argent Secr Ind Comer Bol
Argentina Servicio de Hidrografia Naval. Boletin — Argent Serv Hidrogr Naval Bol
Argentina. Servicio Geologico Nacional. Boletin — Argent Serv Geol Nac Bol
Argentina. Servicio Nacional Minero Geologica. Revista — Argent Serv Nac Min Geol Rev
Argentina. Servicio Nacional Minero Geologico. Boletin — AMGBCJ
Argentina. Servicio Nacional Minero Geologico. Boletin — Argent Serv Nac Min Geol Bol
Argentina Textil — Argent Text
Argive Heraeum — AH
Argomenti de Farmacoterapia — Argomenti Farmacoter
Argonne National Laboratory. Energy and Environmental Systems Division. Report ANL/CNSV — ANLSD
Argonne National Laboratory. Energy and Environmental Systems Division. Technical Report — Argonne Natl Lab Energy Envirn Syst Div Tech Rep
Argonne National Laboratory. Fusion Power Program. ANL/FPP Technical Memorandum — Argonne Natl Lab Fusion Power Program ANL/FPP Tech Mem
Argonne National Laboratory. High Energy Physics Division. Report — Argonne Natl Lab High Energy Phys Div Rep
Argonne National Laboratory. News Bulletin — Argonne Natl Lab News Bull
Argonne National Laboratory. Office of Electrochemical Project Management. Report ANL/OEPM — Argonne Natl Lab Off Electrochem Proj Manage Rep ANL/OEPM
Argonne National Laboratory. Physics Division. Report — ANL/PHY Rep
Argonne National Laboratory. Physics Division. Report — Argonne Natl Lab Phys Div Rep
Argonne National Laboratory. Report — Argonne Natl Lab Rep
Argonne National Laboratory. Report ANL — Argonne Natl Lab Rep ANL
Argonne National Laboratory. Report ANL/OTEC — Argonne Natl Lab Rep ANL/OTEC
Argonne National Laboratory. Report ANL-CT — Argonne Natl Lab Rep ANL-CT
Argonne National Laboratory. Reviews [*United States*] — ANRVA
Argonne National Laboratory. Reviews — Argonne Natl Lab Rev
Argonne National Laboratory. Technical Report ANL/CNSV-TM — Argonne Natl Lab Tech Rep ANL/CNSV-TM
Argonne National Laboratory. Technical Report ANL/EES-TM — Argonne Natl Lab Tech Rep ANL/EES-TM
Argonne National Laboratory. Water Resources Research Program (Report) ANL/WR [*A publication*] — Argonne Natl Lab Water Resour Res Program (Rep) ANL/WR
Argonne Reviews — Argonne Rev
Argonne Reviews — ARRWB
Argosy — ARGOA
Argument — RGUMD
Argumentation and Advocacy — IAAA
Argumente — ARUMD
Argus Journal — Argus J
Argus Law Reports — ALR
Argus Law Reports — Arg LR
Argus Law Reports — Arg Rep
Argus Law Reports — Argus L Rep
Argus Law Reports — Argus LR
Argus Law Reports (Current Notes) — ALR (CN)
Argus Law Reports (Current Notes) — Argus LR (CN)
Argus of Arab Business — Argus Arab Bus
Argus Reports — Ar Rep
Argus Reports (Newspaper) (Victoria) — Argus (Newspr) (VIC)
Arheologia Moldovei — A Mold
Arheologia Moldovei — AM
Arheologia Moldovei — Arh Mol
Arheologia Moldovei — Arh Mold
Arheologia Moldovei — Arh Moldovei
Arheologija un Etnografija — AE
Arheologija un Etnografija — Arhun Etn
Arheologija un Etnografija — AuE
Arheoloski Pregled — AP
Arheoloski Pregled — Ar Preg
Arheoloski Pregled — Arh Pr
Arheoloski Pregled — Arh Preg
Arheoloski Pregled — Arh Pregl
Arheoloski Pregled — Arh Pregled
Arheoloski Pregled Arheolosko Drustvo Jugoslavije — A Pregl
Arheoloski Radovi i Rasprave — A Rad Raspr
Arheoloski Radovi i Rasprave — ARR
Arheoloski Vestnik [*Ljubljana*] — A Ves
Arheoloski Vestnik [*Ljubljana*] — Arch Vestnik
Arheoloski Vestnik — Arh Vest
Arheoloski Vestnik — Arh Vestnik
Arheoloski Vestnik — ArhV
Arheoloski Vestnik — AV
Arheoloski Vestnik (Ljubljana) — A Ves L
Arheoloski Vestnik (Ljubljana) — Arheoloski Vest (L)
Arhitektura SSSR — Arhitekt SSSR
Arhiv Biologiceskih Nauk/Archives des Sciences Biologiques — Arh Biol Nauk
Arhiv Bioloskih Nauka — Arh Biol Nauka
Arhiv Bioloskih Nauka — AVBNA
Arhiv Bioloskih Nauka — AVBNAN
Arhiv Ministarstva Poljoprivrede (Yugoslavia) — Arh Minist Poljopr (Yugoslavia)
Arhiv Russkogo Protistologiceskogo Obscestva/Archives. Societe Russe de Protistologie — Arh Russk Protistol Obsc
Arhiv za Farmaciju — ARFMA
Arhiv za Farmaciju [*Belgrade*] — ARFMAC
Arhiv za Farmaciju — Arh Farm
Arhiv za Farmaciju (Belgrade) — Arh Farm (Belgr)
Arhiv za Hemiju i Farmaciju — Arh Hem Farm
Arhiv za Higijenu Rada — Arh Hig Rada
Arhiv za Higijenu Rada i Toksikologiju — AHRTA
Arhiv za Higijenu Rada i Toksikologiju — AHRTAN
Arhiv za Higijenu Rada i Toksikologiju — Arh Hig Rad Toksikol
Arhiv za Higijenu Rada i Toksikologiju — Arh Hig Rada Toksikol
Arhiv za Kemiju — Arh Kem
Arhiv za Kemiju i Tehnologiju — Arh Kem Tehnol
Arhiv za Poljoprivredne Nauke — APNAA
Arhiv za Poljoprivredne Nauke — APNAA2
Arhiv za Poljoprivredne Nauke — Arh Poljopr Nauke
Arhiv za Poljoprivredne Nauke — Arh Poljopriv Nauke
Arhiv za Poljoprivredne Nauke i Tehniku — APNTAP
Arhiv za Poljoprivredne Nauke i Tehniku — Arh Poljopr Nauke Teh
Arhiv za Rudarstvo i Tehnologiju — Arh Rud Tehnol
Arhiv za Tehnologiju — Arh Tehnol
Arhivele Olteniei — AO
Arhivele Olteniei — Arh Olt
Ariadne — ARI
Arid Lands Newsletter — Arid Lands Newsl
Arid Lands Resource Information Paper — ALRIAI
Arid Lands Resource Information Paper — Arid Lands Resour Inf Pap
Arid Soils. Their Genesis, Geochemistry, Utilization — Arid Soils Their Genesis Geochem Util
Arid Zone Newsletter. Division of Land Research. Commonwealth Scientific and Industrial Research Organisation — Arid Zone Newsl Div Land Res CSIRO
Arid Zone Research — Arid Zone Res
Arid Zone Research. United Nations Educational, Scientific, and Cultural Organization — Arid Zone Res UNESCO
Aridnye Pochvy Ikh Genezis Geokhimiya Ispol'zovanie — Aridnye Pochvy Ikh Genezis Geokhim Ispol
Ariel: a Review of International English Literature — Ariel E
Ariel, A Review of International English Literature — PARI
Arion's Dolphin — Ari D
Aris and Phillips Central Asian Studies — Aris Phil C
Aristoteleion Panepistemion Thessalonikis Epetiris tis Geoponikis kai Dasologikis Skolis — Aristot Panepist Thessalonikis Epet Geopon Dasolog Skol
Aristoteleion Panepistemion Thessalonikis Epistimoniki Epetiris Geoponikis kai Dasologikis Skolis — ATESD8
Aristotelian Society. Supplementary Volume — Aris Soc
Arithmetic Teacher — Arith Teach
Arithmetic Teacher — IATE
Arizona Academy of Science. Journal — Ariz Acad Sci J
Arizona Academy of Science. Journal — Arizona Acad Sci Jour
Arizona Administrative Digest — Ariz Admin Dig
Arizona. Agricultural Experiment Station. Bulletin — Ariz Agric Exp Stn Bull
Arizona Agricultural Experiment Station. Bulletin — Arizona Agric Exp Sta Bull
Arizona. Agricultural Experiment Station. Mimeographed Report — Ariz Agric Exp Stn Mimeogr Rep
Arizona. Agricultural Experiment Station. Publications — Ariz Ag Exp
Arizona. Agricultural Experiment Station. Report — Ariz Agric Exp Stn Rep
Arizona. Agricultural Experiment Station. Research Report — Ariz Agric Exp Stn Res Rep
Arizona. Agricultural Experiment Station. Research Report — AZARAO
Arizona. Agricultural Experiment Station. Technical Bulletin — Ariz Agric Exp Stn Tech Bull
Arizona. Agricultural Experiment Station. Technical Bulletin — AZATAU
Arizona and the West — AriW
Arizona and the West — Ariz and West
Arizona and the West — Ariz West
Arizona and the West — ArizW
Arizona Appeals Reports — Ariz App
Arizona Bar Briefs — Ariz Bar Briefs
Arizona Bar Journal — Ariz BJ
Arizona. Bureau of Mines. Bulletin — Ariz Bur Mines Bull
Arizona. Bureau of Mines. Bulletin — Arizona Bur Mines Bull
Arizona. Bureau of Mines. Bulletin. Geological Series — Ariz Bur Mines Bull Geol Ser
Arizona. Bureau of Mines. Bulletin. Mineral Technology Series — Ariz Bur Mines Bull Mineral Technology Ser
Arizona. Bureau of Mines. Circular — Ariz Bur Mines Circ
Arizona. Bureau of Mines. Field Notes — Ariz Bur Mines Field Notes
Arizona. Bureau of Mines. Field Notes — FNAMA

Arizona Business — ABB
Arizona Business — Ariz Bus
Arizona Business — ARZ
Arizona Business Gazette — Ariz Bsn G
Arizona. Commission of Agriculture and Horticulture. Annual Report — AAHRAK
Arizona. Commission of Agriculture and Horticulture. Annual Report — Ariz Comm Agric Hortic Annu Rep
Arizona Dairy Newsletter. University of Arizona. Cooperative Extension Service — Ariz Dairy Newsl Univ Ariz Coop Ext Serv
Arizona Dental Journal — ADEJB
Arizona Dental Journal — Ariz Dent J
Arizona. Department of Mineral Resources. Annual Report — Ariz Dept Mineral Res Ann Rept
Arizona Farmer-Stockman — Ariz Farmer Stockman
Arizona Foreign Language Teachers Forum — AFLT Forum
Arizona Forestry Notes — AFONA
Arizona Forestry Notes — AFONAA
Arizona Forestry Notes — Ariz For Notes
Arizona Forestry Notes. School of Forestry. Northern Arizona University — Ariz For Note Sch For Nth Ariz Univ
Arizona. Game and Fish Department. Wildlife Bulletin — Ariz Game Fish Dep Wildl Bull
Arizona. Game and Fish Department. Wildlife Bulletin — AZWBAI
Arizona Geological Society Digest — Ariz Geol Soc Dig
Arizona Geological Society. Digest. Annual — Ariz Geol Soc Digest Ann
Arizona Geological Society. Southern Arizona Guidebook — Ariz Geol Soc South Ariz Guideb
Arizona Highways — Ariz H
Arizona Highways — AZHIA
Arizona Historical Review — Ariz His R
Arizona Historical Review — Ariz Hist Rev
Arizona Land and People — ALAPDP
Arizona Land and People — Ariz Land & People
Arizona Law Review — ALRED
Arizona Law Review — Ariz L Rev
Arizona Law Review — Ariz Law R
Arizona Law Review — Ariz LR
Arizona Law Review — AZ L
Arizona Law Review — AZ LR
Arizona Legislative Service — Ariz Legis Serv
Arizona Legislative Service (West) — Ariz Legis Serv (West)
Arizona Librarian — Ariz Libn
Arizona Librarian — Ariz Librn
Arizona Medicine — Ariz Med
Arizona Medicine — Arizona Med
Arizona Medicine — ARMEA
Arizona Medicine — ARMEAN
Arizona Mining Journal — Ariz Min J
Arizona Monthly — Ariz M
Arizona Music News — AMN
Arizona Nurse — Ariz Nurse
Arizona Official Compilation of Administrative Rules and Regulations — Ariz Comp Admin R & Regs
Arizona Quarterly — AQ
Arizona Quarterly — Ariz Q
Arizona Quarterly — Arizona Q
Arizona Quarterly — ArQ
Arizona Quarterly — AzQ
Arizona Quarterly (Tucson) — Ariz Quart Tucson
Arizona Real Estate Press — Ariz REP
Arizona Reports — Ariz
Arizona Reports — AZ
Arizona Republic — Ariz Repub
Arizona Review — AR
Arizona Review — Ariz R
Arizona Review — Arizona R
Arizona Review. AR — Ariz Rev AR
Arizona Revised Statutes Annotated — Ariz Rev Stat Ann
Arizona State Bureau of Mines. Bulletin — Ariz St Bur Mines B
Arizona State Land Department. Water Resources Report — Ariz State Land Dep Water Resour Rep
Arizona State Land Department. Water Resources Report — Ariz State Land Dept Water Res Rept
Arizona State Law Forum — Ariz St LF
Arizona State Law Journal — Ariz St L J
Arizona State Law Journal — Ariz State Law J
Arizona State Law Journal — Arizona State LJ
Arizona State Law Journal — ASLJD
Arizona State University. Anthropological Research Papers — Ariz SU Ant
Arizona State University. Business Teacher — ASU Bus Tchr
Arizona Supreme Court Reports — Ariz
Arizona Teacher — Ariz Teach
Arizona University. Agricultural Experiment Station. Bulletin — Ariz Univ Agr Expt Bull
Arizona University. Agricultural Experiment Station. Bulletin. Physical Science Bulletin — Ariz Univ Agr Expt Bull Phys Sci Bull
Arizona University. Agricultural Experiment Station. Technical Bulletin — Ariz Univ Agric Exp Stn Tech Bull
Arizona. University. Agricultural Experment Station. Report — Ariz Univ Agric Exp Stn Rep
Arizona University. Laboratory of Tree-Ring Research. Papers — Ariz Univ Lab Tree-Ring Res Pap
Arizona University. Lunar and Planetary Laboratory. Communications — Ariz Univ Lunar Planet Lab Commun
Arizona. Water Commission. Bulletin — Ariz Water Comm Bull
Arizona-Nevada Academy of Science. Journal — Ariz Nev Acad Sci J
Arizoniana (Journal of Arizona History) — A (Jr A)
Arjungnagimmat. Inuit Cultural Institute — ARJU
Ark River Review — Ark Riv
Arkansas Academy of Science. Proceedings — AKASAO
Arkansas Academy of Science. Proceedings — Ark Acad Sci Proc
Arkansas Academy of Science. Proceedings — Arkansas Acad Sci Proc
Arkansas. Agricultural Experiment Station. Bulletin — AKABA7
Arkansas. Agricultural Experiment Station. Bulletin — Arkansas Agric Exp Stn Bull
Arkansas. Agricultural Experiment Station. Mimeograph Series — AKAMA6
Arkansas. Agricultural Experiment Station. Mimeograph Series — Arkansas Agric Exp Stn Mimeogr Ser
Arkansas. Agricultural Experiment Station. Publications — Ark Ag Exp
Arkansas. Agricultural Experiment Station. Report Series — AKARAL
Arkansas. Agricultural Experiment Station. Report Series — Arkansas Agric Exp Stn Rep Ser
Arkansas. Agricultural Experiment Station. Research Series — Arkansas Agric Exp Stn Res Ser
Arkansas. Agricultural Experiment Station. Research Series — RSUSEV
Arkansas. Agricultural Experiment Station. Special Report — Arkansas Agric Exp Stn Spec Rep
Arkansas. Agricultural Experiment Station. Special Report — AUARAN
Arkansas Animal Morbidity Report — Arkansas Anim Morb Rep
Arkansas Business — Arkansas B
Arkansas Business and Economic Review — ARK
Arkansas Business and Economic Review — Ark Bus and Econ R
Arkansas Cattle Business — Arkansas Cattle Bus
Arkansas Dental Journal — AKDJA
Arkansas Dental Journal — Arkansas Dent J
Arkansas. Division of Geology. Bulletin — Arkansas Div Geol Bull
Arkansas. Engineering Experiment Station. Bulletin — Arkansas Eng Exp Stn Bull
Arkansas Farm Research — Ark Farm Res
Arkansas Farm Research — Arkans Fm Res
Arkansas Farm Research — Arkansas Farm Res
Arkansas Farm Research. Arkansas Agricultural Experiment Station — Arkansas Farm Res Arkansas Agric Exp Stn
Arkansas Farm Research. Report Series. University of Arkansas Agricultural Experiment Station — Arkansas Farm Res Rep Ser
Arkansas Gazette — Ark Gazet
Arkansas. Geological and Conservation Commission. Bulletin — Arkansas Geol Conserv Comm Bull
Arkansas. Geological and Conservation Commission. Information Circular — Arkansas Geol Comm Inform Circ
Arkansas. Geological and Conservation Commission. Information Circular — Arkansas Geol Conserv Comm Inf Circ
Arkansas. Geological and Conservation Commission. Water Resources Circular — Arkansas Geol Conserv Comm Water Resour Circ
Arkansas. Geological and Conservation Commission. Water Resources Summary — Arkansas Geol Conserv Comm Water Resour Summ
Arkansas. Geological Commission. Bulletin — Arkansas Geol Comm Bull
Arkansas. Geological Commission. Water Resources Circular — Arkansas Geol Comm Water Resour Circ
Arkansas. Geological Commission. Water Resources Summary — Arkansas Geol Comm Water Resour Summ
Arkansas. Geological Survey — Ark G S
Arkansas. Geological Survey. Bulletin — Arkansas Geol Surv Bull
Arkansas Historical Association. Report — Ark Hist Assn Rpt
Arkansas Historical Association. Publications — Ark His As
Arkansas Historical Association. Publications — Ark Hist Assoc Publ
Arkansas Historical Quarterly — AHQ
Arkansas Historical Quarterly — ArHQ
Arkansas Historical Quarterly — Ark Hist Q
Arkansas Historical Quarterly — Ark Hist Quar
Arkansas Historical Quarterly — Arkansas Hist Q
Arkansas Historical Quarterly — ArkH
Arkansas Historical Quarterly — ArkHQ
Arkansas Industrial University. Agricultural Experiment Station. Bulletin — Arkansas Industr Univ Agric Exp Sta Bull
Arkansas Law Review — Ark L Rev
Arkansas Law Review — Ark Law R
Arkansas Law Review — Ark LR
Arkansas Law Review — Arkansas L Rev
Arkansas Lawyer — Ark Law
Arkansas Libraries — Ark Lib
Arkansas Libraries — Arkansas Lib
Arkansas Medical Society. Journal — Ark Med Soc J
Arkansas Medical Society. Journal — Arkansas Med Soc J
Arkansas Nurse — Ark Nurse
Arkansas Nutrition Conference. Proceedings — Arkansas Nutr Conf Proc
Arkansas Register — Ark Reg
Arkansas Reports — Ark
Arkansas. Resources and Development Commission. Division of Geology. Bulletin — Arkansas Resour Dev Comm Div Geol Bull
Arkansas. Resources and Development Commission. Division of Geology. Bulletin. Information Circular — Ark Res Devel Comm Div Geology Bull Inf Circ
Arkansas State Nurses' Association. Newsletter — Ark State Nurses Assoc Newsl
Arkansas Statutes Annotated — Ark Stat Ann
Arkansas University. Engineering Experiment Station. Research Report — Arkansas Univ Eng Exp Sta Res Rep

Arkansas University. Engineering Experiment Station. Research Report Series — Arkansas Univ Eng Exp Stn Res Rep Ser
Arkansas University (Fayetteville). Agricultural Experiment Station. Bulletin — Arkansas Univ (Fayetteville) Agric Exp Stn Bull
Arkansas. University. Fayetteville. Agricultural Experiment Station. Mimeograph Series — Arkansas Univ Fayetteville Agric Exp Stn Mimeogr Ser
Arkansas University (Fayetteville). Agricultural Experiment Station. Report Series — Arkansas Univ (Fayetteville) Agric Exp Stn Rep Ser
Arkansas. University. Fayetteville. Agricultural Experiment Station. Special Report — Arkansas Univ Fayetteville Agric Exp Stn Spec Rep
Arkansas University. Institute of Science and Technology. Research Series — Ark Univ Inst Sci and Technology Research Ser
Arkansas University. Seismological Bulletin — Arkansas Univ Seismol Bull
Arkansas Water and Sewage Conference and Short Course. Proceedings — Arkansas Water Sewage Conf Short Course Proc
Arkansas Water Works and Pollution Control Conference and Short School. Proceedings — Arkansas Water Works Pollut Control Conf Short Sch Proc
Arkeoloj Muezeleri Yayinlari — Ark Muez Yayim
Arkhangel'skii Lesotekhnicheskii Institut. Trudy — Arkhang Lesotekh Inst Tr
Arkheograficheskii Ezhegodnik — AE
Arkheograficheskii Ezhogodnik — Arkh Ez
Arkheologicheskie Issledovaniia na Ukraine — Arkh Issl
Arkheologicheskie Issledovaniia v Gruzii — Ark Issl Gruz
Arkheologicheskie Izviestiia i Zametki. Moskovskoe Arkheologicheskoe Obshchestvo — AIZ
Arkheologicheskie Otkrytiia — Ark Otkr
Arkheologicheskie Raskopi v Armenii — Arkh Rask
Arkheologicheskii Sbornik — A Sbor
Arkheologicheskii Sbornik — Arh Sb
Arkheologicheskii Sbornik — Arkh Sbor
Arkheologicheskii Sbornik — Arkh Sbornik
Arkheologichi Pamiatniki URSR — Ark Pam URSR
Arkheologichni Pamiatky Ursr — AP
Arkheologichni Pamiatky URSR — Arch Pamjatki URSR
Arkheologichni Pamiatky URSR — Arh Pam URSR
Arkheologichni Pamiatky Ursr — Arkh Pam
Arkheologiia — AK
Arkheologiia [*Kiev*] — Arkh
Arkheologiia/Archeologie (Kiev) — AK
Arkheologiia i Etnografiia Bashkirii — AEB
Arkheologiia i Etnografiia Bashkirii — Arkhi Etn
Arkheologiia i Istoriia Bospora. Sbornik Statei — AIB
Arkheologiia (Kiev) — Ark (Kiev)
Arkheologiia Organ na Arkheologicheskiia Institut i Muzei pri B'lgarskata Akademiia na Naukite — Arkheologiia
Arkheologija. Publies par l'Academie des Sciences d'Ukraine — ArkUkr
Arkheologiya (Kiev) — Ar (Kiev)
Arkheologiya (Kiev) — ARKLAY
Arkhimedes — AKMDA
Arkhitektura i Stroitelstvo Leningrada — Arkhit Stroit Leningrada
Arkhiv Anatomii, Gistologii, i Embriologii — AAGEA
Arkhiv Anatomii, Gistologii, i Embriologii — AAGEAA
Arkhiv Anatomii, Gistologii, i Embriologii — Arkh Anat Gistol Embriol
Arkhiv Biologicheskikh Nauk — Arkh Biol Nauk
Arkhiv Klinicheskoi i Eksperimental'noi Meditsiny (Moskva) — Arkh Klin i Eksper Med (Moskva)
Arkhiv Meditsinskikh Nauk — Arkh Med Nauk
Arkhiv Patologii — Arkh Patol
Arkhiv Patologii — ARPTA
Arkhiv Patologii — ARPTAF
Arkhiv Russkogo Protistologicheskogo Obshchestva — Arkh Russk Protist Obsh
Arkhiv Samizdata. Sobranie Documentov Samizdata — AS
Arkhivi Ukraini. Naukovo Informatsiinii Biuleten' Arkhivnogo Upravliniia pri Radi Ministriv URSR — Arkhivi Ukr
Arkif foer Landtmaen och Traegards-Odlare — Ark Landtm Traeg Odlare
Arkitekten — Ark
Arkiv foer Astronomi — AASYA
Arkiv foer Astronomi — Ark Astron
Arkiv foer Botanik — AKVBAA
Arkiv foer Botanik — Ark Bot
Arkiv foer det Fysiske Seminar i Trondheim — Ark Fys Semin Trondheim
Arkiv foer Fysik — Ark Fys
Arkiv foer Geofysik — AGFYA
Arkiv foer Geofysik — Ark Geofys
Arkiv foer Inre Medicine — Ark Inre Med
Arkiv foer Kemi — Ark Kemi
Arkiv foer Kemi — ARKEAD
Arkiv foer Kemi, Mineralogi, och Geologi — Ark Kemi Miner Geol
Arkiv foer Kemi, Mineralogi, och Geologi [*Sweden*] — Ark Kemi Mineral Geol
Arkiv foer Matematik — AKMTA
Arkiv foer Matematik — Ark Mat
Arkiv foer Matematik — Ark Matemat
Arkiv foer Matematik, Astronomi, och Fysik [*Sweden*] — Ark Mat Astron Fys
Arkiv foer Mineralogi och Geologi — AMNGA
Arkiv foer Mineralogi och Geologi — AMNGAX
Arkiv foer Mineralogi och Geologi — Ark Mineral Geol
Arkiv foer Nordisk Filologi — ANF
Arkiv foer Nordisk Filologi — Arkiv
Arkiv foer Nordisk Filologi — Arkiv f Nord Filologi
Arkiv foer Nordisk Filologi [*Christiania*] — Arkiv Nord Filol
Arkiv foer Zoologi — Ark Zool
Arkiv foer Zoologi — ARZOA
Arkiv foer Zoologi — ARZOAG
Arkiv foer Zoologi (Stockholm) — Ark Zool (Stockholm)
Arkkitehti — ARKK-A
Ark-Light Newsletter — Ark Light Newsl
Arkticheskii i Antarkticheskii Nauchno-Issledovatel'skii Institut. Trudy — Ark Antarkt Nauchno Issled Inst Tr
ARL Mechanical Engineering Report. Australia Aeronautical Research Laboratories — ARL Mech Eng Rep Aust Aeronaut Res Lab
Arlington Quarterly — ArlQ
ARLIS [*Art Libraries Society/North America*] **Newsletter** — ARLIS Newsl
Armada International — Arma Int
Armas y Letras — ALet
[*The*] **Armchair Detective** — Arm D
[*The*] **Armchair Detective** — Armchair Det
[*The*] **Armchair Detective** — TAD
Armed Forces — Arm Frc
Armed Forces and Society — AFS
Armed Forces and Society — Armed Forces Soc
Armed Forces and Society — GARM
Armed Forces Chemical Journal — Armed Forces Chem J
Armed Forces Comptroller — AFC
Armed Forces Journal — AFJ
Armed Forces Journal International — Arm FJ Int
Armed Forces Medical Journal [*Arab Republic of Egypt*] — AFMADW
Armed Forces Medical Journal [*India*] — AFMIBK
Armed Forces Medical Journal [*US*] — Armed Forces Med J
Armed Forces Medical Journal (Arab Republic of Egypt) — Armed Forces Med J (Arab Repub Egypt)
Armed Forces Medical Journal (India) — Armed Forces Med J (India)
Armed Forces Special Weapons Project [*later, DASA*]. Technical Publications — AFSWP-TP
Armees d'Aujourd'hui — Armees Aujourd
Armeezeitung [*Wien*] — Armeeztg
Armeezeitung [*Wien*] — AZ
Armement — ARMED
Armement. Bulletin d'Information et de Liaison — Armement Bull Inf Liaison
Armenian Numismatic Journal — Armenian N J
Armenian Review — Arm Rev
Armenian Review — Armen Rev
Armidale and District Historical Society. Journal — ADHS
Armidale and District Historical Society. Journal — Armidale Dist Hist Soc J
Armidale and District Historical Society. Journal — Armidale Hist Soc J
Armidale and District Historical Society. Journal and Proceedings — Armdale & Dist Hist Soc J & Proc
Armidale Teachers' College. Bulletin — Armid Teach Coll Bul
Armidale Teachers' College. Bulletin — Armidale Teach Coll Bull
Armidale. University of New England. Exploration Society. Report — Armidale New Engl Univ Explor Soc Rep
Armjanskii Gosudarstvennyi Pedagogiceskii Institut Imeni H. Abovjana. Sbornik Naucnyh Trudov. Serija Fiziko-Matematiceskaja — Armjan Gos Ped Inst Sb Naucn Trud Ser Fiz-Mat
Armored Cavalry Journal — Armored Cavalry J
Armotsementnye Konstruktsii — Armotsem Konstr
Armour Research Foundation. Report — Armour Res Found Rep
Arms and Explosives — Arms Explos
Arms Control and Disarmament — ArmC
Arms Control Today — Arms Con T
Armstrong Aerospace Medical Research Laboratory. Technical Report AAMRL-TR (US) — Armstrong Aerosp Med Res Lab Tech Rep AAMRL TR (US)
Army Administrator — Army Adm
Army Aviation Digest — AAD
Army Communicator [*United States*] — Army Comm
Army Digest — AD
Army Lawyer — Army Law
Army Lawyer — Army Lawy
Army Logistician — ALOG
Army Logistician [*United States*] — Army Log
Army Logistician — Army Logis
Army Materials and Mechanics Research Center. Report AMMRC MS (US) — Army Mater Mech Res Cent Rep AMMRC MS (US)
Army Materials Technology Conference Series — Army Mater Technol Conf Ser
Army Medical Bulletin — Army Med Bull
Army Medical Department. Reports (London) — Army Med Dept Rep (London)
Army Medical Research and Development Command. Biomedical Laboratory Technical Report (US) — Army Med Res Dev Command Biomed Lab Tech Rep (US)
Army Quarterly — ArQ
Army Quarterly and Defence Journal — Army Q Def J
Army Quarterly and Defence Journal — Army Quart Defence J
Army R D and A [*Research, Development, and Acquisition*] [*R, D & A United States*] [*Later,*] — ARDAD
Army Research and Development [*R, D & A*] [*United States*] [*Later,*] — ARDVA
Army Research and Development [*Later, R, D & A*] — Army Res & Devel
Army Reserve Magazine — Army Reserv
Army Review (London) — ARL
Army Scientific and Technical Intelligence Bulletin — ASTIB
Armyanskii Khimicheskii Zhurnal — Arm Khim Zh
Armyanskii Khimicheskii Zhurnal — Armyanskii Khim Zh
Armyanskii Nauchno-Issledovatel'skii Institut Stroitel'nykh Materialov i Sooruzhenii Nauchnye Soobshcheniya — Arm Nauchno-Issled Inst Stroit Mater Sooruzh Nauchn Soobshch
Armyanskii Nauchno-Issledovatel'skii Institut Vinogradarstva, Vinodeliya, i Plodovodstva. Trudy — Arm Nauchno Issled Inst Vinograd Vinodel Plodovod Tr
Armyanskii Nauchno-Issledovatel'skii Institut Zhivotnovodstva i Veterinarii. Nauchnye Trudy — Arm Nauchno Issled Inst Zhivotnovod Vet Nauchn Tr

Armyanskii Sel'skokhozyaistvennyi Institut. Sbornik Nauchnykh Trudov — Arm Skh Inst Sb Nauchn Tr
Army-Navy-Air Force Journal — ANAFJ
ARN [*Association of Rehabilitation Nurses*] **Journal** — ARN J
Arnold Arboretum. Harvard University. Journal — Arnold Arbor Harv Univ J
Arnold Arboretum. Journal — Arnold Arboretum J
Arnold Bax Society. Bulletin — Bax S
Arnold Bennett Newsletter — ABN
Arnold O. Beckman Conference in Clinical Chemistry. Proceedings — Arnold O Beckman Conf Clin Chem Proc
Arnold Schoenberg Institute. Journal — Schoenberg Inst
Arnoldia [*Boston*] — ARNOAO
Arnoldia Rhodesia — ARNPBS
Arnoldia (Zimbabwe) — Arnold (Zim)
Arnoldia Zimbabwe — AZIMDI
Arnoldian — Ardn
ARO (US Army Research Office) Report — ARO Rep
Aroma Research. Proceedings of the International Symposium on Aroma Research. Central Institute for Nutrition and Food Research — Aroma Res Proc Int Symp A
Aromatic Amino Acids in the Brain. Symposium — Aromat Amino Acids Brain Symp
Aromatic and Heteroaromatic Chemistry — Aromat Heteroaromat Chem
Arqueologia Boliviana — Arqu Bol
Arqueologia e Historia — Arque Hist
Arqueologia e Historia [*Lisbon*] — Arqueol Hist
Arqueologo Portugues — AP
Arqueologo Portugues — Arch Portugues
Arqueologo Portugues — Arq Port
Arqueologo Portugues — Arq Portugues
Arqueologo Portugues — Arqu Port
Arquitectura — ARQT
Arquitectura (Habana) — Arquitec Hav
Arquitecturas Bis — Arquitec Bis
Arquitetura (Rio de Janeiro) — Arquitet Rio
Arquivo Brasileiro de Medicina Veterinaria e Zootecnia — ABMZDB
Arquivo Brasileiro de Medicina Veterinaria e Zootecnia — Arq Bras Med Vet Zootec
Arquivo de Anatomia e Antropologia — AAA
Arquivo de Anatomia e Antropologia — AAANA7
Arquivo de Anatomia e Antropologia — Arq Anat Antrop
Arquivo de Anatomia e Antropologia — Arq Anat Antropol
Arquivo de Beja — A Beja
Arquivo de Beja — Arq Beja
Arquivo de Beja. Boletim da Camara Municipal — ABBCM
Arquivo de Bibliografia Portuguesa — ABP
Arquivo de Medicina Legal — Arq Med Leg
Arquivo de Medicina Popular — AMP
Arquivo de Patologia — APALA4
Arquivo de Patologia — Arq Patol
Arquivo de Viana do Castelo — AVC
Arquivo do Alto Minho — AAM
Arquivo do Distrito de Aveiro — ADA
Arquivo Historico da Madeira — AHM
Arquivo. Instituto Gulbenkian de Ciencia. A. Estudos Matematicos e Fisico-Matematicos — Arquivo Inst Gulbenkian Ci A Estud Mat Fis-Mat
Arquivo Transtagano — AT
Arquivos Brasileiros de Cardiologia — ABCAA
Arquivos Brasileiros de Cardiologia — ABCAAJ
Arquivos Brasileiros de Cardiologia — Arq Bras Cardiol
Arquivos Brasileiros de Cardiologia — Arq Brasil Cardiol
Arquivos Brasileiros de Endocrinologia — Arq Bras Endocrinol
Arquivos Brasileiros de Endocrinologia e Metabologia — ABENA
Arquivos Brasileiros de Endocrinologia e Metabologia — ABENAY
Arquivos Brasileiros de Endocrinologia e Metabologia — Arq Bras Endocrinol Metabol
Arquivos Brasileiros de Medicina — ABMEAD
Arquivos Brasileiros de Medicina — Arq Bras Med
Arquivos Brasileiros de Medicina Naval — Arq Bras Med Nav
Arquivos Brasileiros de Nutricao — ABNUAW
Arquivos Brasileiros de Nutricao — Arq Bras Nutr
Arquivos Brasileiros de Oftalmologia — AQBOAP
Arquivos Brasileiros de Oftalmologia — Arq Bras Oftal
Arquivos Brasileiros de Oftalmologia — Arq Bras Oftalmol
Arquivos Brasileiros de Psicologia Aplicada — Arq Bras Ps
Arquivos Brasileiros de Psicologia Aplicada — Arquivos Brasil Psicol Ap
Arquivos Brasileiros de Psicotecnica — AQBPA
Arquivos Brasileiros de Psicotecnica (Rio de Janeiro) — Arquiv Bras Psicotec Rio
Arquivos Brasileiros de Tuberculose e Doencas do Torax — Arq Bras Tuberc Doencas Torax
Arquivos Catarinenses de Medicina — Arq Catarinenses Med
Arquivos. Centro Cultural Portugues — ACCP
Arquivos. Centro Cultural Portugues [*Paris*] — ArCCP
Arquivos. Centro Cultural Portugues — Arq Centro Cult Port
Arquivos. Centro de Estudos da Faculdade de Odontologia. Universidade de Minas Gerais (Belo Horizonte) — Arq Cent Estud Fac Odontol Univ Minas Gerais (Belo Horiz)
Arquivos. Centro de Estudos da Faculdade de Odontologia. Universidade Federal de Minas Gerais — Arq Cent Estud Fac Odontol Univ Fed Minas Gerais
Arquivos. Centro de Estudos do Curso de Odontologia. Universidade Federal de Minas Gerais — Arq Cent Estud Curso Odontol Univ Fed Minas Gerais
Arquivos. Congresso Internacional de Microbiologia — Arq Congr Int Microbiol
Arquivos da Universidade da Bahia (Salvador, Brazil) — Arquiv Univ Bahia Salvador
Arquivos de Biologia [*Sao Paulo*] — ARBLAN
Arquivos de Biologia e Tecnologia [*Curitiba*] — ABTTAP
Arquivos de Biologia e Tecnologia — Arq Biol Tecnol
Arquivos de Biologia e Tecnologia (Curitiba) — Arq Biol Tecnol (Curitiba)
Arquivos de Biologia (Sao Paulo) — Arq Biol (Sao Paulo)
Arquivos de Botanica do Estado de Sao Paulo — ABOPAM
Arquivos de Botanica do Estado de Sao Paulo — Arq Bot Estado Sao Paulo
Arquivos do Bromatologia — Arq Bromatol
Arquivos de Ciencias do Mar — Arq Cienc Mar
Arquivos de Cirurgia Clinica e Experimental (Sao Paulo) — Arq Cir Clin Exp (Sao Paulo)
Arquivos de Dermatologia e Sifiligrafia de Sao Paulo — Arq Dermatol Sifiligr Sao Paulo
Arquivos de Entomologia. Serie A — Arq Entomol Ser A
Arquivos de Entomologia. Serie B — Arq Entomol Ser B
Arquivos de Gastroenterologia — Arq Gastroenterol
Arquivos de Geologia — Arq Geol
Arquivos de Geologia. Universidade do Recife. Curso de Geologia — Arq Geol Univ Recife Curso Geol
Arquivos de Geologia. Universidade do Recife. Escola de Geologia de Pernambuco — Arq Geol Univ Recife Esc Geol Pernambuco
Arquivos de Higiene e Saude Publica — Arq Hyg Saude Publica
Arquivos de Higiene e Saude Publica (Sao Paulo) — Arq Hig Saude Publica (Sao Paulo)
Arquivos de Higiene (Rio De Janeiro) — Arq Hig (Rio De J)
Arquivos de Historia de Cultura Portuguesa — AHCP
Arquivos de Neuro-Psiquiatria — ANPIA
Arquivos de Neuro-Psiquiatria — Arq Neuro-Psiquiatr
Arquivos de Oncologia — Arq Oncol
Arquivos de Oncologia — ARQOA5
Arquivos de Oncologia (Salvador, Brazil) — Arq Oncol (Salvador Braz)
Arquivos de Patologia [*Lisbon*] — AQPTA
Arquivos de Patologia Geral e Anatomia Patologica — Arq Patol Geral Anat Patol
Arquivos de Patologia Geral e Anatomia Patologica. Universidade de Coimbra [*A publication*] — APGAAZ
Arquivos de Patologia Geral e Anatomia Patologica. Universidade de Coimbra — Arq Patol Geral Anat Patol Univ Coimbra
Arquivos de Patologia (Lisbon) — Arq Patol (Lisbon)
Arquivos de Pediatria — Arq Pediat
Arquivos de Tisiologia — AQTSA
Arquivos de Tisiologia — Arq Tisiol
Arquivos de Zoologia — Arq Zool
Arquivos de Zoologia [*Sao Paulo*] — ARQZA4
Arquivos de Zoologia do Estado de Sao Paulo — Arq Zool Estado Sao Paulo
Arquivos de Zoologia do Estado de Sao Paulo — AZSPA6
Arquivos de Zoologia (Sao Paulo) — Arq Zool (Sao Paulo)
Arquivos. Departamento de Assistencia a Psicopates. Estado de Sao Paulo — Arq Dep Assist Psicop S Paulo
Arquivos do Instituto de Antropologia. Universidad do Rio Grande do Norte (Natal, Brazil) — Arquiv Inst Antrop Univ R Grande Norte Natal
Arquivos do Instituto de Direito Social (Sao Paulo) — Arquiv Inst Direit Soc S Paulo
Arquivos do Servico Florestal — Arq Serv Florest
Arquivos Economicos (Brasilia) — Arquiv Econ Brasilia
Arquivos. Escola de Veterinaria. Universidade Federal de Minas Gerais — Arq Esc Vet Univ Fed Minas Gerais
Arquivos. Escola de Veterinaria. Universidade Federal de Minas Gerais — Arq Esc Vet Univ Minas Gerais
Arquivos. Escola Superior de Veterinaria. Universidade do Estado de Minas Gerais — Arq Esc Super Vet Univ Estado Minas Gerais
Arquivos. Escola Superior de Veterinaria. Universidade Rural. Estado de Minas Gerais — Arq Esc Super Vet Univ Rur Estado Minas Gerais
Arquivos. Estacao de Biologia Marinha da Universidade Federal do Ceara — Arq Estac Biol Mar Univ Ceara
Arquivos. Estacao de Biologia Marinha da Universidade Federal do Ceara — Arq Estac Biol Mar Univ Fed Ceara
Arquivos. Faculdade de Higiene e Saude Publica. Universidade de Sao Paulo — Arq Fac Hig S Paul
Arquivos. Faculdade de Higiene e Saude Publica. Universidade de Sao Paulo — Arq Fac Hig Saude Publica Univ Sao Paulo
Arquivos. Faculdade Nacional de Medicina — Arq Fac Nac Med
Arquivos. Faculdade Nacional de Medicina (Rio De Janeiro) — Arq Fac Nac Med (Rio De Janeiro)
Arquivos. IBIT [*Instituto Brasileiro para Investigacao da Tuberculose*] — Arq IBIT
Arquivos. Instituto Bacteriologico. Camara Pestana — Arq Inst Bacteriol Cam Pestana
Arquivos. Instituto Bacteriologico. Camara Pestana — Arq Inst Bacteriol Camara Pestana
Arquivos. Instituto Bacteriologico Camara Pestana (Lisbon) — Arq Inst Bacteriol Camara Pestana (Lisbon)
Arquivos. Instituto Biologico [*Sao Paulo*] — AIBOA3
Arquivos. Instituto Biologico — Arq Inst Biol
Arquivos. Instituto Biologico (Sao Paulo) — Arq Inst Biol (Sao Paulo)
Arquivos. Instituto Biologico (Sao Paulo). Suplemento — Arq Inst Biol (Sao Paulo) Supl
Arquivos. Instituto de Anatomia. Universidade do Rio Grande Do Sul — Arq Inst Anat Univ Rio Grande Do Sul
Arquivos. Instituto de Anatomia. Universidade Federal do Rio Grande Do Sul — Arq Inst Anat Univ Fed Rio Grande Sul
Arquivos. Instituto de Biologia Animal (Rio De Janeiro) — Arq Inst Biol Anim (Rio De J)
Arquivos. Instituto de Biologia do Exercito — Arq Inst Biol Exerc

Arquivos. Instituto de Biologia do Exercito (Rio De Janeiro) — Arq Inst Biol Exerc (Rio De Janeiro)
Arquivos. Instituto de Biologia Vegetal [*Rio De Janeiro*] — AIBVAO
Arquivos. Instituto de Biologia Vegetal — Arq Inst Biol Veg
Arquivos. Instituto de Biologia Vegetal (Rio De Janeiro) — Arq Inst Biol Veg (Rio De J)
Arquivos. Instituto de Pesquisas Agronomicas — APQAAH
Arquivos. Instituto de Pesquisas Agronomicas — Arq Inst Pesqui Agron
Arquivos. Instituto de Pesquisas Agronomicas (Recife) — Arq Inst Pesqui Agron (Recife)
Arquivos. Instituto de Pesquisas Veterinarias "Desiderio Finamor" — AIPVAQ
Arquivos. Instituto de Pesquisas Veterinarias "Desiderio Finamor" — Arq Inst Pesqui Vet Desiderio Finamor
Arquivos. Instituto Militar de Biologia (Rio De Janeiro) — Arq Inst Mil Biol (Rio De Janeiro)
Arquivos Interamericanos de Reumatologia — Arq Interam Reumatol
Arquivos. Jardim Botanico do Rio De Janeiro — AJBJAT
Arquivos. Jardim Botanico do Rio De Janeiro — Arq Jard Bot Rio De J
Arquivos. Jardim Botanico do Rio De Janeiro — Arq Jard Bot Rio De Janeiro
Arquivos Mineiros de Leprologia — AMLPAG
Arquivos Mineiros de Leprologia — Arq Min Leprol
Arquivos. Museu Bocage — Arq Mus Bocage
Arquivos. Museu Bocage — MNLAB9
Arquivos. Museu Bocage. Notas e Suplementos — Arq Mus Boc Nota Sup
Arquivos. Museu Bocage. Serie A — AMBAER
Arquivos. Museu Bocage. Serie A — Arq Mus Bocage Ser A
Arquivos. Museu Bocage. Serie B. Notas — AMBNDV
Arquivos. Museu Bocage. Serie B. Notas — Arq Mus Bocage Ser B Notas
Arquivos. Museu Bocage. Serie C. Suplementos — AMBSDC
Arquivos. Museu Bocage. Serie C. Suplementos — Arq Mus Bocage Ser C Supl
Arquivos. Museu de Historia Natural. Universidade Federal de Minas Gerais — AMHGD6
Arquivos. Museu de Historia Natural. Universidade Federal de Minas Gerais — Arq Mus Hist Nat Univ Fed Minas Gerais
Arquivos. Museu Nacional do Rio De Janeiro — AMNJA8
Arquivos. Museu Nacional do Rio De Janeiro — Arq Mus Nac Rio De J
Arquivos. Museu Nacional do Rio de Janeiro — Arq Mus Nac Rio De Janeiro
Arquivos. Museu Nacional do Rio De Janeiro — Arqu Mus Nac
Arquivos. Museu Paranaense — AQMPAF
Arquivos. Museu Paranaense — Arq Mus Parana
Arquivos Portugueses de Bioquimica — Arq Port Bioquim
Arquivos. Revista Bimestral. Ministerio da Educacao e Saude (Rio de Janeiro) — Arquiv Rio
Arquivos Rio-Grandenses de Medicina. Sociedade de Medicina de Porto Alegre — Arq Rio Grandenses Med
Arquivos. Seminario de Estudos Galegos — Arq Semin Estud Galegos
Arquivos. Seminario d'Estudos Galegos — ASEG
Arquivos. Servico Florestal [*Rio De Janeiro*] — ASFJAA
Arquivos. Servico Florestal (Rio De Janeiro) — Arq Serv Florestal (Rio De J)
Arquivos. Universidade de Bahia. Faculdade de Filosofia — AUBFF
Arquivos. Universidade de Bahia. Faculdade de Medicina — Arq Univ Bahia Fac Med
Arquivos. Universidade do Recife. Instituto da Terra. Divisao de Ciencias Geograficas — Arq Univ Recife Inst Terra Div Ci Geogr
Arquivos. Universidade Federal Rural do Rio De Janeiro — Arq Univ Fed Rural Rio De Janeiro
ARR Report. Australian Road Research Board — ARR Rep Aust Road Res Board
Arran Naturalist — Arran Nat
Arret de la Cour de Cassation de Belgique — Cass
Arrets et Avis du Conseil d'Etat — Arr et Av Cons Etat
Arrow — AW
Ars Aequi; Juridisch Studentenblad — AA
Ars Asiatica — Ars As
Ars Combinatoria — ACOMD
Ars Combinatoria [*Canada*] — Ars Comb
Ars Combinatoria — Ars Combin
Ars Curandi em Odontologia — Ars Curandi Odontol
Ars Hispaniae — Ars Hisp
Ars Hungarica — Ars H
Ars Islamica — AI
Ars Islamica — Ars Isl
Ars Islamica — Ars Islam
Ars Journal — Ars J
ARS [*American Rocket Society*] **Journal** — ARS Jnl
Ars Medici [*Edition Francaise*] — ARSMBA
Ars Medici Drug Series — Ars Med Drug Ser
Ars Medici (Edition Francaise) — Ars Med (Ed Fr)
Ars Musica Denver — Ars Mus Den
ARS NE. United States Agricultural Research Service. Northeastern Region — ARS NE US Agric Res Serv Northeast Reg
Ars Orientalis — Ars Orient
Ars Orientalis — ArsOr
Ars Pharmaceutica — APHRA
Ars Pharmaceutica — Ars Pharm
Ars Pharmaceutica. Revista. Facultad de Farmacia. Universite de Granada — Ars Pharm
Ars Poetica — AP
ARS S. United States Agricultural Research Service. Southern Region — ARS S US Agric Res Serv South Reg
Ars Semiotica — Ars S
Ars Semiotica — Ars Semiot
ARS. US Department of Agriculture. Agricultural Research Service — ARS US Dep Agric Agric Res Serv
Ars Veterinaria — Ars Vet
Arsberaettelse. Kungliga Humanistiska Vetenskapssamfundet i Lund — AKHVL
Arsberaettelse. Kungliga Humanistiska Vetenskapssamfundet i Lund — Arsberaettelse Lund
Arsberaettelse. Sverings Geologiska Undersoekning — Arsber Sver Geol Unders
Arsberetning fra Danmarks Fiskeri og Havundersogelser — Arsber Danm Fisk Havund
Arsberetning Norges Fiskerier — Arsberet Nor Fisk
Arsberetning. Statens Forsoegsmejeri — Arsberet Statens Forsoegsmejeri
Arsberetning Vedkommende Norges Fiskerier — Arsberet Vedkomm Nor Fisk
Arsbok. Finska Vetenskaps Societeten — Arsb Finska Vetensk Soc
Arsbok. Foreningen Skogstradsforadling — Arsb Foren Skogstradsfor
Arsbok. Sodermanlands Lans Hushallningssallskaps — Arsb Sodermanlands Lans Hushallningssallsk
Arsbok. Sveriges Meteorologisk och Hydrologiska Institut — Arsb Sver Met Hydrol Inst
Arsbok Utgiven av Seminarierna i Slaviska Sprak, Jamforande Sprakforskning, Finsk-Ugriska Sprak och Ostasiatiska Sprak Vid Lunds Universitet — ASLund
Arsbok. Vetenskaps-Societetn i Lund — Arsb Vet Soc Lund
Arsenical Pesticides. Symposium — Arsenical Pestic Symp
Arsmelding Statens Smabrukslaerarskole — Arsmelding St Smabrlaerarsk
Arson Analysis Newsletter — Arson Anal Newsl
Arsskrift. Bohuslaens Hembygdsfoerbund — A Bohuslaens Hembygds
Arsskrift den Kongelige Veterinaer og Landbohoejskole — Arsskr K Vet Landbohoejsk
Arsskrift foer Modersmalslararnas Forening — Arsskr f Modersmalslararnas Foren
Arsskrift foer Norske Skogplanteskoler — Arsskr Nor Skogplanteskoler
Arsskrift fran Alnarps Lantbruks-, Mejeri, och Traedgardsinstitut — Arsskr Alnarps Lantbruks Mejeri Traedgardsinstitut
Arsskrift Universitet — Arsskr Univ
Arstryck. Etnografiska Museum — EM/A
Art and Archaeology — A & A
Art and Archaeology — AA
Art and Archaeology — Art & Arch
Art and Archaeology. Research Papers — AARP
Art and Archaeology. Research Papers — Art Archaeol Res Papers
Art and Archaeology. Technical Abstracts [*Information service or system*] — AATA
Art and Archaeology. Technical Abstracts — Art Archaeol Tech Abstr
Art and Archaeology. Technical Abstracts — ArtArch
Art and Archaeology Technical Abstracts — IIC Abstracts
Art and Architecture — AA
Art and Architecture — ARAC
Art and Australia — Art and Aust
Art and Decoration — Art & Dec
Art and Industry — Art & Ind
Art and Letters — AL
Art and the Law — Art & L
Art Bibliographies Modern — ABM
Art Bulletin — AB
Art Bulletin — ABul
Art Bulletin — ABull
Art Bulletin — Art Bul
Art Bulletin — Art Bull
Art Bulletin — ArtB
Art Bulletin — GABU
Art Criticism — Art Crit
Art, Design, Photo — Art Des Photo
Art Digest — AD
Art Direction — Art Dir
Art Direction — Art Direct
Art Direction — ARTDA
Art Education — Art Educ
Art et Architecture — Art & Archre
Art/Film/Criticism — Art
Art for Humanity — AH
Art Galleries and Museums Association of Australia and New Zealand. News Bulletin — AGMA News Bul
Art Gallery of New South Wales. Quarterly — Art Gall NSW Q
Art History — Art Hist
Art History — PARH
Art in America — AIA
Art in America — ArAm
Art in America — Art Am
Art in America — Art in Am
Art in America — Art in Amer
Art in America — GARA
Art Index — AInd
Art Index — Art Ind
Art Index — ArtI
Art Institute of Chicago. Bulletin — Art Inst of Chicago Bull
Art International — AI
Art International — Art Int
Art Journal — AJ
Art Journal — Art J
Art Journal — Art Jnl
Art Journal — Art Jour
Art Journal — GABJ
Art Journal. Paris Edition — Art J P E
Art Libraries Journal — Art Lib J
Art Libraries Journal — Art Libraries Jnl
Art Monthly — Art Mthly
Art New Zealand — Art NZ

Art News — AN
Art News — ArNe
Art News — Art N
Art News — ARTNB
Art Psychotherapy — Art Psychot
Art Quarterly — AQ
Art Quarterly [*Detroit*] — Art Quart
Art Quarterly — ArtQ
Art Quarterly — At Quart
Art Scholar — AS
Art Stamps — Art St
Art Studies. Medieval, Renaissance, and Modern — Art S
Art Teacher — Art Teach
Art Teachers Association of Victoria. Journal — ATAVJ
Art Teachers Association of Victoria. News Sheet — ATAV News
Art Teachers Association of Victoria. News Sheet — ATAV News Sheet
Art, Technology, Health, Physical Education, and Science of Human Living Seri es — Art Technol Health Phys Educ Sci Hum Living Ser
Arta si Arheologia — A & A
Arta si Arheologia Revista [*Iasi*] — A Arh
ARTbibliographies. Current Titles — ARTbibliogr Curr Titles
Artbibliographies Modern — Ab
ARTbibliographies Modern — ARTbibliogr Mod
Arte Antica e Moderna — AAM
Arte Cristiana — ACr
Arte do Dancar — Arte Dan
Arte e Poesia — ArteP
Arte e Storia — A e St
Arte e Storia — Arte e Stor
Arte Espanol — A Esp
Arte Espanol. Revista. Sociedad Espanola de Amigos del Arte — Art Espanol
Arte Etrusca — AE
Arte Figurativa — AF
Arte Informa — Arte Info
Arte Lombarda — Art Lomb
Arte Lombarda — Arte Lomb
Arte (Milan) — ArM
Arte Musical — Arte Mus
Arte Popular em Portugal — APP
Arte Stampa — ArtSt
Arte Veneta — Art Ven
Arte Veneta — Arte Ven
Arte y Variedades — Arte y Var
Artech House Communication and Electronic Defense Library — Artech House Commun Electron Def Lib
Artech House Telecom Library — Artech House Telecom Lib
Arterioscleros Thrombos — Arterioscler Thromb
Arteriosclerosis and Thrombosis — Arter Throm
Arteriosclerosis (Dallas) — ARTRD
Arteriosclerosis, Thrombosis, and Vascular Biology — Arterioscler Thromb Vasc Biol
Artes Graficas (Buenos Aires) — Artes Graf BA
Artes Plasticas (Habana) — Art Plast Hav
Artesania y Folklore de Venezuela — AFV
Artforum — Artf
Artforum — IAFO
Artha Vijnana — Artha Vij
Artha Vijnana — AV
Artha Vijnana — AXB
Artha Vijnana. Journal of the Gokhale Institute of Politics and Economics [*A publication*] — Artha Vijnana J Gokhale Inst Polit Econ
Artha Vikas — Artha Vik
Arthaniti — Arth
Arthritis and Musculoskeletal and Skin Diseases Database — AMS
Arthritis and Rheumatism — ARHEA
Arthritis and Rheumatism — Arth Rheum
Arthritis and Rheumatism — Arthritis Rheum
Arthropods of Florida and Neighboring Land Areas — Arthropods Fla Neighboring Land Areas
Arthur Andersen Chronicle — A A Chron
Arthurian Literature — Arthurian Lit
Arthuriana — A
Arti Figurative. Rivista d'Arte Antica e Moderna — AFig
Arti Figurative. Rivista d'Arte Antica e Moderna — Arti Fig
Arti Musices — Arti M
Arti Musices — Arti Mus
Arti. Societa Pontaniana (Napoli) — Atti Pont
Artibus Asiae — AA
Artibus Asiae — AAS
Artibus Asiae — Art As
Artibus Asiae — Art Asiae
Artibus Asiae — Artibus A
Artibus Asiae — Artibus As
Artificial Cells, Blood Substitutes, and Immobilization Biotechnology — Artif Cells Blood Substit Immobil Biotechnol
Artificial Earth Satellites (USSR) — Artif Earth Satell (USSR)
Artificial Fiber — Artif Fiber
Artificial Intelligence [*Elsevier Book Series*] — AI
Artificial Intelligence — Artif Intel
Artificial Intelligence — Artif Intell
Artificial Intelligence Abstracts — Artif Intell Abstr
Artificial Intelligence in Medicine — Artif Intell Med
Artificial Life — Artif Life
Artificial Lungs for Acute Respiratory Failure. Theory and Practice. Papers Presented at the International Conference on Membrane Lung Technology and Prolonged Extracorporeal Perfusion — Artif Lungs Acute Respir Failure Pap Int Conf
Artificial Organs — Artif Organs
Artificial Organs Today — Artif Organs Today
Artificial Rainfall Newsletter — Artif Rainf Newsl
Artificial Satellites [*Poland*] — Artif Satell
Artificial Silk and Staple Fibre Journal of Japan — Artif Silk Staple Fibre J Jpn
Artificial Silk World — Artif Silk World
Artigas-Washington (Montevideo) — Artig Wash Monte
Artikkel-Indeks Tidsskrifter [*Database*] — AITI
Artisan et les Arts Liturgiques — AALi
Artium Scriptores. Oesterreichische Akademie der Wissenschaften. Philosophisch-Historische Klasse. Sitzungsberichte — Art Script
ARTnews — GARN
Arts Action — Arts Act
Arts and Architecture — A & A
Arts and Architecture — Arts & Arch
Arts and Architecture — Arts & Archre
Arts and Culture of the North — AACN
Arts and Decoration — Arts & D
Arts and Decoration — Arts and Dec
Arts and Humanities Citation Index — AHCI
Arts and Humanities Citation Index — Arts & Hum Cit Ind
Arts and Humanities Citation Index — Arts Humanit Citation Index
Arts and Letters. India and Pakistan — IAL
Arts and Sciences — A & S
Arts Asiatiques — Ar As
Arts Asiatiques — ArA
Arts Asiatiques — Arts Asiat
Arts d'Afrique Noire — Arts Afr Noire
Arts d'Afrique Noire — Arts d Afr Noire
Arts Documentation Monthly — Arts Doc Mthly
Arts Documentation Service [*Database*] — ARTSDOC
Arts et Lettres du Quebec — Arts Let Quebec
Arts et Manufactures — ARMUB
Arts et Manufactures — Arts Manuf
Arts et Metiers — Arts Metiers
Arts et Traditions Populaires — ATP
Arts in Alaska. Newsletter. Alaska State Council on the Arts — ASIN
Arts in Ireland — Arts Ir
Arts in Psychotherapy — Arts Psychother
Arts in Society — ARSOB
Arts in Society — ART
Arts in Society — Arts in Soc
Arts in Society — ArtsS
Arts in Society — AS
Arts in Society — ASoc
Arts International — Arts Int
Arts, Letters, Printers and Publishers, and Systems — ALPS
Arts Magazine — Art Mag
Arts Magazine — Arts
Arts Magazine — Arts Mag
Arts Magazine — PARM
Arts Manitoba — Arts Man
Arts of Asia — Art Asia
Arts of Asia — Arts As
Arts Report. Tennessee Arts Commission — Art Rep Tenn Art Com
Arts Reporting Service — Arts Reptg Ser
Arts Review — Arts Rev
Arts Review Yearbook and Directory — Arts Rev Yearb Dir
Arts Victoria — Art Vict
Artscanada — Artscan
Artworkers News — Artwork N
Arup Journal — Arup J
Arup Journal — Arup Jnl
Arviap Nipinga. Eskimo Point — AVNP
Arxius de la Seccio de Ciences — Arx Sec Cien
Arxivs. Seccio de Ciencies. Institut d'Estudis Catalans — Arxivs Secc Ci Inst Estud Catalans
Aryan Path — AP
Aryan Path — ArP
Arzneibuch der Deutschen Demokratischen Republik. Kommentare — Arzneib DDR Komment
Arzneibuch Kommentare. Deutsche Demokratische Republik — Arzneib Komment DDR
Arzneimittelallergie. Kongress der Deutschen Gesellschaft fuer Allergie- und Immunitaetsforschung — Arzneimittelallerg Kongr Dtsch Ges Allerg Immunitaetsforsch
Arzneimittel-Forschung [*Drug Research*] — ARZNA
Arzneimittel-Forschung [*Drug Research*] — Arznei-For
Arzneimittel-Forschung [*Drug Research*] — Arzneim-Forsch
Arzneimittel-Forschung [*Drug Research*] — Arzneimittel-Forsch
Arzneimittel-Forschung. Beiheft — Arzneim Forsch Beih
Arzneimittel-Forschung. Beiheft — AZBAZ
Arzneimittel-Forschung/Drug Research — Arzneim Forsch Drug Res
Arzneykundige Annalen — Arzneyk Ann
Arzt, Apotheker, Krankenhaus — Arzt Apoth Krankenhaus
Arzt im Krankenhaus — Arzt Krankenh
AS. Cooperative Extension Service. Purdue University — AS Coop Ext Serv Purdue Univ
ASA [*Australian Society of Accountants*] **Bulletin** — ASA Bull

Asa Gray Bulletin. A Botanical Quarterly Published in the Interests of the Gray Memorial Botanical Association. The Botanical Gardeners Association. University of Michigan Botanical Club — Asa Gray Bull
ASA [*American Society of Agronomy*] **Newsletter** — ASA Newsl
ASA [*American Society of Agronomy*] **Publication** — ASA Publ
ASA [*American Society of Agronomy*] **Special Publication** — ASA Spec Publ
ASA Special Publication. American Society of Agronomy — ASA Spec Publ Am Soc Agron
ASA [*Australian Society of Accountants*] **Technical Bulletin** — ASA Tech Bul
ASAE [*American Society of Agricultural Engineers*] **Publication** — ASAE Publ
ASAE [*American Society of Agricultural Engineers*] **Publication** — ASPUD
ASAE [*American Society of Agricultural Engineers*] **Technical Paper** — ASAE Tech Pap
ASAIHL (Association of Southeast Asian Institutions of Higher Learning) Bulletin — ASAIHL Bul
ASAIO [*American Society for Artificial Internal Organs*] **Journal** — ASAIO J
Asamblea Latinoamericana de Fitoparasitologia — Asamblea Latinoam Fitoparasitol
ASB [*Association of Southeastern Biologists*] **Bulletin** — ASB Bull
Asbury Seminarian — AS
Asbury Seminarian [*Wilmore, KY*] — AsbSem
ASC [*American Society for Cybernetics*] **Communications** — ASC Commun
ASC University of Kentucky. Cooperative Extension Service — ASC Univ Ky Coop Ext Serv
ASCAP [*American Society of Composers, Authors, and Publishers*] **Copyright Law Symposium** — ASCAP Copyright L Sym
ASCAP [*American Society of Composers, Authors, and Publishers*] **in Action** — ASCAP
ASCAP [*American Society of Composers, Authors, and Publishers*] **in Action** — AT
ASCAP [*American Society of Composers, Authors, and Publishers*] **Today** — ASCAP
ASCE [*American Society of Civil Engineers*] **Annual Combined Index** — ASCE Annu Comb Index
ASCE [*American Society of Civil Engineers*] **Combined Sewer Separation Project. Technical Memorandum** — ASCE Combined Sewer Separation Proj Tech Memo
ASCE [*American Society of Civil Engineers*] **Engineering Issues** — ASCE Eng Issues
ASCE [*American Society of Civil Engineers*] **Engineering Issues. Journal of Professional Activities** — ASCE Eng Issues J Prof Activ
ASCE [*American Society of Civil Engineers*] **Journal of Professional Activities** — ASCE J Prof Activ
ASCE [*American Society of Civil Engineers*] **Journal of the Construction Division** — ASCE J Constr Div
ASCE [*American Society of Civil Engineers*] **Journal of the Engineering Mechanics Division** — ASCE J Eng Mech Div
ASCE [*American Society of Civil Engineers*] **Journal of the Environmental Engineering Division** — ASCE J Environ Eng Div
ASCE [*American Society of Civil Engineers*] **Journal of the Geotechnical Engineering Division** — ASCE J Geotech Eng Div
ASCE [*American Society of Civil Engineers*] **Journal of the Hydraulics Division** [*A publication*] — ASCE J Hydraul Div
ASCE [*American Society of Civil Engineers*] **Journal of the Irrigation and Drainage Division** — ASCE J Irrig Drain Div
ASCE [*American Society of Civil Engineers*] **Journal of the Power Division** — ASCE J Power Div
ASCE [*American Society of Civil Engineers*] **Journal of the Sanitary Engineering Division** — ASCE J Sanit Eng Div
ASCE [*American Society of Civil Engineers*] **Journal of the Soil Mechanics and Foundations Division** — ASCE J Soil Mech Found Div
ASCE [*American Society of Civil Engineers*] **Journal of the Structural Division** — ASCE J Struct Div
ASCE [*American Society of Civil Engineers*] **Journal of the Surveying and Mapping Division** — ASCE J Surv Mapp Div
ASCE [*American Society of Civil Engineers*] **Journal of the Urban Planning and Development Division** — ASCE J Urban Plann Dev Div
ASCE [*American Society of Civil Engineers*] **Journal of the Waterways, Harbors, and Coastal Engineering Division** — ASCE J Waterw Harbors Coastal Eng Div
ASCE [*American Society of Civil Engineers*] **Manuals and Reports on Engineering Practice** — ASCE Man Rep Eng Pract
ASCE [*American Society of Civil Engineers*] **Publications Abstracts** — ASCE Publ Abstr
ASCE [*American Society of Civil Engineers*] **Publications Information** — ASCE Publ Inf
ASCE [*American Society of Civil Engineers*] **Transportation Engineering Journal** [*A publication*] — ASCE Transp Eng J
ASCE [*American Society of Civil Engineers*] **Urban Water Resources Research Program. Technical Memorandum** — ASCE Urban Water Resour Res Program Tech Mem
ASCE [*American Society of Civil Engineers*] **Urban Water Resources Research Program. Technical Memorandum** — AUWTB
ASCE [*American Society of Civil Engineers*] **Urban Water Resources Research Program. Technical Memorandum IHP** [*International Hydrological Programme*] — ASCE Urban Water Resour Res Program Tech Memo IHP
ASCE [*American Society of Civil Engineers*] **Urban Water Resources Research Program. Technical Memorandum IHP** [*International Hydrological Programme*] — AUWMD
Aschaffenburgs Monatsschrift fuer Kriminalpsychologie — Mschr Kriminalpsych
Aschener Blaetter fuer Aufbereiten Verkoken Brikettieren — Aschener Bl Aufbereit Verkoken Briket
ASCI (Administrative Staff College of India) Journal of Management — ASCI (Admin Staff Col India) J Mgt
ASCI [*Administrative Staff College of India*] **Journal of Management** — ASC
ASDC [**American Society of Dentistry for Children]Journal of Dentistryfor Children** — ASDC J Dent Child
ASEA [*Allmaenna Svenska Elektriska Aktiebolaget*] **Journal** — ASEA J
ASEA [*Allmaenna Svenska Elektriska Aktiebolaget*] **Research** — ASEA Res
ASEA [*Allmaenna Svenska Elektriska Aktiebolaget*] **Tidning** — ASEA Tidn
ASEA [*Allmaenna Svenska Elektriska Aktiebolaget*] **Zeitschrift** — ASEA Z
ASEAN (Association of South East Asian Nations) Business Quarterly — ASEAN (Assn South East Asian Nations) Bus Q
ASEAN [*Association of South East Asian Nations*] **Business Quarterly** — ASEAN Bus
ASEAN [*Association of South East Asian Nations*] **Food Journal** — ASEAN Food J
ASEAN Food Journal — ASEAN Food Jnl
ASEAN [*Association of South East Asian Nations*] **Journal of Clinical Sciences** — ASEAN J Clin Sci
ASEE [*American Society for Engineering Education*] **Annual Conference Proceedings** — ACOPD
Asepelt Series — Asepelt S
Asfar. Publikaties van het Documentatiebureau Islam-Christendom van de Rijksuniversiteit te Leiden — Asfar Publ Documentatiebureau Islam-Chris Rijksuniv Leiden
ASHA. Journal of the American Speech and Hearing Association — ASHA
ASHA. Journal of the American Speech and Hearing Association — ASHA J Am Speech Hear Assoc
ASHA [*American Speech and Hearing Association*] **Monographs** — ASHA Monogr
ASHA [*American Speech and Hearing Association*] **Reports** — ASHA Rep
ASHA [American Speech and hearing Association] Supplement — ASHA Suppl
Asher's Guide to Botanical Periodicals — Ash G Bot Per
Asher's Guide to Botanical Periodicals — Ashers Guide Bot Period
Ashikaga Institute of Technology. Research Reports — Ashikaga Inst Technol Res Rep
Ashmolean Museum — Ash M
ASHRAE [*American Society of Heating, Refrigerating, and Air-Conditioning Engineers*] **Handbook and Product Directory** — ASHRAE Handb Prod Dir
Asia — A
Asia [*New York*] — As
Asia and Africa Review — Asia Afr R
Asia and Africa Review — Asia Afr Rev
Asia and Oceania Congress of Endocrinology — Asia & Oceania Cong Endocrinol
Asia and Pacific — Asia Pac
Asia and the Americas — AAm
Asia and the Americas — Asia
Asia Electronics Union. Journal — AEU
Asia Foundation News — Asia Found News
Asia Letter. An Authoritative Analysis of Asian Affairs — ASB
Asia Major — AM
Asia Major — As Ma
Asia Major — AsM
Asia Mining [*Manila*] — Asia Min
Asia Monitor — Asia Mon
Asia Oceania Congress of Perinatology — Asia Oceania Congr Perinatol
Asia Oceania Journal of Obstetrics and Gynaecology — Asia Oceania J Obstet Gynaecol
Asia Pacific Business — ASIA
Asia Pacific Communications in Biochemistry — Asia Pac Commun Biochem
Asia Pacific Community — Asia Pac Com
Asia Pacific International Journal of Management Development — Asia Pac Int Jnl Manage Dev
Asia Pacific Journal of Pharmacology — Asia Pac J Pharmacol
Asia Pacific Shipping — Asia Ship
Asia Pacific Top Management Digest — Asia Pac Top Manage Dig
Asia Quarterly — As Q
Asia Quarterly — Asia Q
Asia Quarterly — Asia Quart
Asia Research Bulletin — ANC
Asia Research Bulletin — Asia Res Bul
Asian Affairs — AA
Asian Affairs — Asian Aff
Asian Affairs — PASF
Asian Affairs. An Americaan Review — PAAA
Asian Affairs. Journal of the Royal Central Asian Society (London) — Asian Aff (London)
Asian Affairs (London) — As Aff (L)
Asian Affairs (New York) — As Aff (NY)
Asian Affairs (New York) — Asian Aff (New York)
Asian and African Studies — AAS
Asian and African Studies. Bratislava — AASB
Asian and African Studies (Bratislava) — As Afr Stud (B)
Asian and African Studies (Bratislava) — Asian & African Stud (Bratislava)
Asian and African Studies (Jerusalem) — AASJ
Asian and African Studies. Journal. Israeli Oriental Society — Asian Afr Stud
Asian and Pacific Census Forum — Asian Pac Cens Forum
Asian and Pacific Council. Food and Fertilizer Technology Center. Book Series — Asian Pac Counc Food Fert Technol Cent Book Ser
Asian and Pacific Council. Food and Fertilizer Technology Center. Extension Bulletin — Asian Pac Counc Food Fert Technol Cent Ext Bull
Asian and Pacific Council. Food and Fertilizer Technology Center. Newsletter — Asian Pac Counc Food Fert Technol Cent Newsl
Asian and Pacific Council. Food and Fertilizer Technology Center. Technical Bulletin — Asian Pac Counc Food Fert Technol Cent Tech Bull
Asian and Pacific Population Programme News — Asian Pac Popul Programme News
Asian Archives of Anaesthesiology and Resuscitation — Asian Arch Anaesthesiol Resusc
Asian Book Trade Directory — As Bk Tr Dir

Asian Building and Construction — Asian Bldg & Construction
Asian Business [*Hong Kong*] — ABN
Asian Business and Industry [*Later, Asian Business*] — Asian Bus
Asian Business and Industry [*Later, Asian Business*] — Asian Bus and Industry
Asian Cancer Conference — Asian Cancer Conf
Asian Computer Yearbook — Asia Comp Yearbk
Asian Congress of Obstetrics and Gynaecology. Proceedings — Asian Congr Obstet Gynaecol Proc
Asian Cultural Studies — ACS
Asian Culture Quarterly — As Cult Q
Asian Defence Journal — As Def J
Asian Defense Journal — ADJ
Asian Development. Quarterly Newsletter — Asian Dev
Asian Economic Review — AEV
Asian Economic Review — Asian Econ R
Asian Economic Review. Journal. Indian Institute of Economics — Asian Econ Rev
Asian Economics — Asian Econ
Asian Economies — As Econ
Asian Environment — Asian Environ
Asian Executive Report — Asian Exec Rep
Asian Finance — AFN
Asian Finance — Asian Fin
Asian Folklore Studies — AFS
Asian Folklore Studies — As Folk Stud
Asian Folklore Studies — Asia Folkl Stud
Asian Folklore Studies — Asian Folk
Asian Folklore Studies — Asian Folkl Stud
Asian Folklore Studies — PAFS
Asian Geotechnology Engineering Database — AGE
Asian Institute of Technology. Newsletter — Asian Inst Tech Newsl
Asian Institute of Technology. Review — Asian Inst Tech Rev
Asian Journal of Chemistry — Asian J Chem
Asian Journal of Dairy Research — Asian J Dairy Res
Asian Journal of Economics — Asia J Econ
Asian Journal of Infectious Diseases — Asian J Infect Dis
Asian Journal of Medicine — AFMDBX
Asian Journal of Medicine — Asian J Med
Asian Journal of Modern Medicine — AJMMAP
Asian Journal of Modern Medicine — Asian J Mod Med
Asian Journal of Pharmaceutical Sciences — Asian J Pharm Sci
Asian Journal of Pharmacy — Asian J Pharm
Asian Journal of Physics — Asian J Phys
Asian Journal of Plant Science — Asian J Plant Sci
Asian Labour — As Lab
Asian Marketing Monitor — AMM
Asian Medical Journal [*Tokyo*] — Asian Med J
Asian Medical Journal — Asian Med Jnl
Asian Messenger — Asia Mes
Asian Music — AMus
Asian Music — As Music
Asian Music — Asian M
Asian Music — Asian Mus
Asian Music — ASM
Asian Outlook — As Outlook
Asian Outlook — AsO
Asian Pacific Journal of Allergy and Immunology — Asian Pac J Allergy Immunol
Asian Pacific Quarterly of Cultural and Social Affairs — APQ
Asian Pacific Quarterly of Cultural and Social Affairs — Asian Pacif Quart Cult Soc Aff
Asian Pacific Review — Asian Pac Rev
Asian Perspectives — AP
Asian Perspectives — Asian Persp
Asian Perspectives — Asian Perspect
Asian Perspectives (Honolulu) — As Perspect (H)
Asian Perspectives (Seoul) — As Perspect (S)
Asian Philosophical Studies — A Ph S
Asian Profile — As Profile
Asian Profile — AsP
Asian Quarterly — AQ
Asian Review — AR
Asian Review — Asian R
Asian Review — Asian Rev
Asian Social Science Bibliography with Annotations and Abstracts — Asian Soc Sci Bibliogr Annot Abstr
Asian Student — AsSt
Asian Studies — Asian Stud
Asian Studies — ASt
Asian Studies. Professional Review — Asian Stud Prof R
Asian Survey — AS
Asian Survey — As Surv
Asian Survey — Asian S
Asian Survey — Asian Surv
Asian Survey — AsS
Asian Survey — FES
Asian Survey — IASS
Asian Symposium on Medicinal Plants and Spices — Asian Symp Med Plants Spices
Asian Thought and Society — As Thought Soc
Asian Wall Street Journal — Asian Wall St J
Asian Wall Street Journal — Asian WSJ
Asian Wall Street Journal — AWSJ
Asian-Australasian Journal of Animal Sciences — Asian Australas J Anim Sci
Asian-Australasian Journal of Animal Sciences — Asian Australasian J Anim Sci
Asian-Pacific Congress of Cardiology. Proceedings — Asian Pac Congr Cardiol Proc
Asian-Pacific Congress of Clinical Biochemistry — Asian Pac Congr Clin Biochem
Asian-Pacific Corrosion Control Conference — Asian Pac Corros Control Conf
Asian-Pacific Weed Science Society Conference — Asian Pac Weed Sci Soc Conf
Asia-Pacific Chemicals — Asia Pac Chem
Asia-Pacific Journal of Operational Research — Asia Pacific J Oper Res
Asia-Pacific Journal of Public Health — Asia Pac J Public Health
Asia-Pacific Petroleum Directory — Asia Pac Pet Dir
Asia-Philippines Leader — Le
Asiatic Annual Register — AAR
Asiatic Quarterly — AQ
Asiatic Quarterly Review — AQR
Asiatic Research Bulletin — ARB
Asiatic Researches — AsR
Asiatic Review — AR
Asiatic Review — Asia R
Asiatic Review — Asiat Rev
Asiatic Review — Asiatic R
Asiatic Review. New Series — Asiatic R ns
Asiatic Society Journal — Asiat Soc J
Asiatic Society Monographs — ASM
Asiatic Society of Bengal. Journal — ASB
Asiatic Society of Bengal. Proceedings — ASBP
Asiatic Society of Japan. Transactions — Asiatic Soc Japan Trans
Asiatic Society of Pakistan. Journal — ASP
Asiatic Society of Pakistan. Journal — ASPJ
Asiatic Society of Pakistan. Publication — ASPP
Asiatische Forschungen — AF
Asiatische Forschungen — As For
Asiatische Studien — AS
Asiatische Studien — As St
Asiatische Studien — Asiat Stud
Asiatische Studien — Asiatische Stud
Asiatische Studien — AsS
Asiatische Studien — ASt
Asiatische Studien/Etudes Asiatiques — ASEA
Asiatische Studien/Etudes Asiatiques — Asi St/Et As
Asiatisches Jahrbuch — AJ
ASIDIC [*Association of Information and Dissemination Centers*] **Newsletter** — ASIDIC News
Asie du Sud-est et Monde Insulinden — ASEMI
Asie du Sud-Est et Monde Insulindien — As SE Monde Insul
Asie du Sud-Est et Monde Insulindien — Asie Sud-Est Monde Insulind
Asie et l'Afrique — As A
Asie Nouvelle — Asie Nouv
Asien, Afrika, Lateinamerika — AAL
Asien, Afrika, Lateinamerika — Asien Afr Lateinam
Asien (Berlin) — AsB
ASILS [*Association of Student International Law Societies*] **International Law Journal** — ASILS Intl LJ
ASIS [*American Society for Information Science*] **News** — ASNED
ASIS [*American Society for Information Science*] **Newsletter** — AISNC
ASIS [*American Society for Information Science*] **Newsletter** — ASIS Newsl
ASL [*American Scientific Laboratories*] **Research Report** — ASL Res Rep
ASL [*American Scientific Laboratories*] **Research Report** — ASRRAQ
ASLE (American Society of Lubrication Engineers) Annual Meeting. Preprints — ASLE (Am Soc Lubr Eng) Annu Meet Prepr
ASLE [*American Society of Lubrication Engineers*] **Annual Meeting. Preprints** — ASLE Annu Meet Prepr
ASLE [*American Society of Lubrication Engineers*] **Papers** — ASLE Pap
ASLE [*American Society of Lubrication Engineers*] **Preprints** — ASLE Prepr
ASLE [*American Society of Lubrication Engineers*] **Proceedings. International Conference on Solid Lubrication** — ASLE Proc Int Conf Solid Lubr
ASLE [*American Society of Lubrication Engineers*] **Special Publication** — ASLE Spec Publ
ASLE [*American Society of Lubrication Engineers*] **Transactions** — ASLE Trans
Aslib Information — AI
Aslib Information — Aslib Inf
Aslib Information — Aslib Info
Aslib Information — ASY
Aslib Occassional Publications — Aslib Occas Publ
Aslib Proceedings — APD
Aslib Proceedings — Aslib Proc
Aslib. Proceedings — AslP
ASM [*American Society for Metals*] **Transactions Quarterly** — ASM Trans Q
ASM [*American Society for Metals*] **Transactions Quarterly** — ASM Trans Quart
ASM [*American Society for Metals*] **Transactions Quarterly** — ASMTQ
Asmat Sketch Book — Asmat Sketch Bk
ASME [*American Society of Mechanical Engineers*] **Air Pollution Control Division. National Symposium** — ASME Air Pollut Control Div Nat Symp
ASME [*American Society of Mechanical Engineers*] **Air Pollution Control Division. Regional Meeting** — ASME Air Pollut Control Div Reg Meet
- ASME Appled Mechanics Western Conference [*Japan Society of Mechanical Engineers*] [*American Society of Mechanical Engineers*] — JSME Pap Jt JSME ASME Appl Mech West Conf
ASME [*American Society of Mechanical Engineers*] **National Waste Processing Conference. Proceedings** — ASME Nat Waste Process Conf Proc
ASME-ANS [*American Society of Mechanical Engineers Advanced Nuclear Systems*] **International Conference on Advanced Nuclear Energy Systems. Papers** — ASME ANS Int Conf Adv Nucl Energy Syst Pap
ASNA [*Alabama State Nurses' Association*] **Reporter** — ASNA Reporter

Asociacion Argentina de Farmacia y Bioquimica Industrial — Asoc Argent Farm Bioquim Ind
Asociacion Argentina de Microbiologia. Revista — Asoc Argent Microbiol Rev
Asociacion Argentina de Mineralogia, Petrologia, y Sedimentologia. Revista — Asoc Argent Mineral Petrol Sediment Rev
Asociacion Colombiana de Bibliotecarios. Boletin — Asoc Colombiana Bibl Bol
Asociacion Cubana de Bibliotecarios. Boletin — Asoc Cuba Bibl Bol
Asociacion de Ingenieros Agronomos. Revista [*Uruguay*] — Asoc Ing Agron Rev
Asociacion de Ingenieros Agronomos. Revista — RAIAA
Asociacion de Ingenieros del Uruguay. Revista de Ingenieria — Asoc Ing Uruguay Rev Ingenieria
Asociacion de Investigacion Tecnica de la Industria Papelera Espanola. Jornadas Tecnicas Papeleras — Asoc Invest Tec Ind Papelera Esp Jorn Tec Papeleras
Asociacion de Tecnicos Azucareros de Cuba. ATAC — Asoc Tec Azucar Cuba ATAC
Asociacion de Tecnicos Azucareros de Cuba. Boletin Oficial — Asoc Tec Azucar Cuba Bol Of
Asociacion Dental Mexicana. Revista — Asoc Dent Mex Rev
Asociacion Espanola de Farmaceuticos de Hospitales. Revista — Asoc Esp Farm Hosp Rev
Asociacion Espanola para el Progreso de las Ciencias. Anales — Asoc Esp Prog Cienc An
Asociacion Farmaceutica Mexicana. Revista — Asoc Farm Mex Rev
Asociacion Folklorica Argentina. Anales — AFA
Asociacion Geologica Argentina. Monografia — Asoc Geol Argent Monogr
Asociacion Geologica Argentina. Revista — Asoc Geol Argent Rev
Asociacion Latinoamericana de Entomologia. Publicacion — ALEPB9
Asociacion Latinoamericana de Entomologia. Publicacion — Asoc Latinoam Entomol Publ
Asociacion Latinoamericana de Produccion Animal. Memoria — ALPMBL
Asociacion Latinoamericana de Produccion Animal. Memoria — Asoc Latinoam Prod Anim Mem
Asociacion Matematica Espanola — Asoc Mat Espanola
Asociacion Medica Argentina. Revista — Asoc Med Argent Rev
Asociacion Medica de los Ferrocarriles Nacionales de Mexico. Revista Medica — Asoc Med Ferrocarriles Nac Mex Rev Med
Asociacion Medica de Puerto Rico — Asoc Med PR
Asociacion Mexicana de Geofisicos de Exploracion. Boletin — Asoc Mexicana Geofisicos Explor Bol
Asociacion Mexicana de Geologos Petroleros. Boletin — Asoc Mex Geol Pet Bol
Asociacion Mexicana de Tecnicos de las Industrias de la Celulosa y del Papel. Boletin — Asoc Mex Tec Ind Celul Pap Bol
Asociacion Nacional de Bibliotecarios, Arquiveros, y Arqueologos [*Madrid*] — ANABA
Asociacion Nacional de Ingenieros Agronomos. Boletin — Asoc Nac Ing Agron Bol
Asociacion Odontologica Argentina. Revista — Asoc Odontol Argent Rev
Asociacion para la Historia de la Ciencia Espanola — AHCE
Asociacion Quimica Espanola de la Industria del Cuero. Boletin Tecnico — Asoc Quim Esp Ind Cuero Bol Tec
Asociacion Venezolana de Geologia Mineria y Petroleo. Boletin — Asoc Venez Geol Min Pet Bol
Asoma (Puerto Rico) — APR
Asomante — As
Asomante — Aso
ASP Counterattack — ASP Ctrattack
ASPAC Quarterly of Cultural and Social Affairs — ASPAC Q Cul & Soc Aff
Aspects Actuels des Mycoses. Journees Internationales de Biologie — Aspects Actuels Mycoses Journ Int Biol
Aspects de la France et du Monde — AFM
Aspects de la France et du Monde — Asp Fr
Aspects of Adhesion — Aspects Adhes
Aspects of Allergy and Applied Immunology — AAAIBR
Aspects of Allergy and Applied Immunology — Aspects Allergy Appl Immunol
Aspects of Applied Biology — Aspects Appl Biol
Aspects of Education — Aspects Ed
Aspects of Education — Aspects of Ed
Aspects of Educational Technology — Asp Educ Technol
Aspects of Energy Conversion. Proceedings of a Summer School — Aspects Energy Convers Proc Summer Sch
Aspects of Fish Parasitology. Symposium of the British Society for Parasitology — Aspects Fish Parasitol Symp Br Soc Parasitol
Aspects of Greek and Roman Life — AGRL
Aspects of Homogeneous Catalysis — AHCADU
Aspects of Homogeneous Catalysis — Aspects Homogeneous Catal
Aspects of Mathematics — Aspects of Math
Aspects of Mathematics. E — Aspects of Math E
Aspects of Microbiology — ASMIEC
Aspects of Microbiology — Aspects Microbiol
Aspects of Nuclear Structure and Function — Aspects Nucl Struct Funct
Aspects of Plant Sciences — APLSDF
Aspects of Plant Sciences — Aspects Pl Sci
Aspects of Plant Sciences — Aspects Plant Sci
Aspects Statistiques de la Region Parisienne — Aspects Statist Region Paris
Aspekte Komplexer Systeme — Asp Komplexer Systeme
Aspekten van Internationale Samenwerking — IWX
Aspen Anthology — Aspen
Aspen Anthology — Aspen A
Aspen Journal for the Arts — Aspen J Art
Aspen Journal of the Arts — Aspen J
Aspetti Letterari — ALet
Asphalt Institute. Construction Series — Asphalt Inst Constr Ser
Asphalt Institute. Information Series — Asphalt Inst Inf Ser
Asphalt Institute. Quarterly — Asphalt Inst Q
Asphalt Institute. Research Series — Asphalt Inst Res Ser
Asphalt Paving Technology — Asphalt Paving Technol
Asphalt Teerindustrie. Zeitung — Asphalt Teerind Ztg
Asphalt und Teer. Strassenbautechnik [*Germany*] — Asphalt Teer Strassenbautech
Aspirantskie Raboty Nauchno Issledovatel'skii Institut po Udobrenii i Insektofungitsidam (Moscow) — Aspir Rab Nauchno Issled Inst Udobr Insektofungits (Moscow)
Aspirin and Related Drugs. Their Actions and Uses. Proceedings of the Symposium — Aspirin Relat Drugs Their Actions Uses Proc Symp
ASR [*Automatizovane Systemy Rizeni*] **Bulletin INORGA** — ASR Bull INORGA
ASRE [*American Society of Refrigerating Engineers*] **Journal** — ASRE J
Assam Agricultural University. Journal of Research — Assam Agric Univ J Res
Assam Department of Agriculture. Fruit Series — Assam Dept Agric Fruit Ser
Assam Review and Tea News — Assam Rev Tea News
Assam Science Society. Journal — Assam Sci Soc J
Assaults on Federal Officers — Assaults Fed Off
ASSE Journal — ASSE J
Assemblee Generale. Commission Internationale Technique de Sucrerie — Assem Gen Comm Int Tech Sucr
Assemblees du Seigneur [*Bruges*] — AssSeign
Assembly and Fastener Engineering — Assem Fastener Eng
Assembly Automation — Assem Autom
Assembly Engineering — Assem Eng
Assembly Engineering — Assembly Eng
Assembly. European Federation of Chemical Engineering — Assem Eur Fed Chem Eng
Assessment and Evaluation in Higher Education — Assess & Eval in Higher Educ
Assessment in Higher Education — Assessment in Higher Ed
Assessment of Environmental Pollution. Proceedings. National Symposium — Assess Environ Pollut Proc Natl Symp
Assessment of Pharmacodynamic Effects in Human Pharmacology. Symposium — Assess Pharmacodyn Eff Hum Pharmacol Symp
Assessment of Radioactive Contamination in Man. Proceedings. Symposium on Assessment of Radioactive Organ and Body Burdens — Assess Radioact Contam Man Proc Symp
Assessment of the Arctic Marine Environment. Selected Topics. Based on a Symposium Held in Conjunction with Third International Conference on Port and Ocean Engineering under Arctic Conditions — Assess Arct Mar Environ Sel Top Symp
Assessors Journal — Assess J
Assessors Journal — Assessors J
ASSET. Abstracts of Selected Solar Energy Technology — AASTD
Assignment Children — ASCHDQ
Assignment Children — Assignment Chil
Assignment Children — Assignment Child
Assises Annuelles. Association Quebecoise des Techniques de l'Eau — Assises Annu Assoc Que Tech Eau
Assises Francaises de Gynecologie. Rapports — Assises Fr Gynecol Rapp
Assistance Informations [*France*] — Assist Inf
Assistant Librarian — Assist Libn
Assistant Librarian — Assistant Librn
Assistant Librarian — Asst Libn
Assistenz [*Germany*] — ASZ
Assistenza Sociale — Assist Soc
Assistenza Sociale — Assistenza Soc
Assiut Journal of Agricultural Sciences — Assiut J Agric Sci
Assiut University. Faculty of Engineering. Bulletin — Assiut Univ Fac Eng Bull
Assiut University. Faculty of Science. Bulletin — Assiut Univ Fac Sci Bull
Assocation of Geography Teachers of Ireland. Journal — Assoc Geog Teach Ir J
Associacao Brasileira das Industrias da Alimentacao. Revista — Assoc Bras Ind Aliment Rev
Associacao Brasileira das Industrias da Alimentacao. Setor de Alimentos Calorico Proteicos. Revista — Assoc Bras Ind Aliment Setor Aliment Calorico Proteicos Rev
Associacao Brasileira de Metais. Boletim — Assoc Bras Met Bol
Associacao Brasileira de Metais. Congresso Anual — Assoc Bras Met Congr Anu
Associacao Brasileira de Metais. Noticiario — Assoc Bras Met Not
Associacao Brasileira de Pesquisas sobre Plantas Aromaticas e Oleos Essenciais. Boletim — Assoc Bras Pesqui Plant Aromat Oleos Essen Bol
Associacao Brasileira de Quimica. Seccao Regional de Sao Paulo. Simposio de Fermentacao — Assoc Bras Quim Secc Reg Sao Paulo Simp Ferment
Associacao Industrial de Angola. Boletim — Assoc Ind Angola Bol
Associacao Medica Brasileira. Revista — Assoc Med Bras Rev
Associacao Medica de Minas Gerais. Revista da AMMG — Assoc Med Minas Gerais Rev AMMG
Associacao Paulista de Cirurgioes Dentistas. Revista — Assoc Paul Cir Dent Rev
Associacao Portuguesa para o Progresso das Ciencias — APPC
Associacao Tecnica Brasileira de Celulose e Papel. Boletim — Assoc Tec Bras Celul Pap Bol
Associacion Latinoamericana de Entomologia. Publicacion — Assoc Latinoam Entomol Publ
Associate Committee on Instructional Technology. Newsletter/Bulletin. Comite Associe de Technologie Pedagogique — ACIT News/Bu CATP
Associate News — Assoc News
Associated Electrical Industries Engineering — Assoc Electr Ind Eng
Associated Electrical Industries Engineering Review — Assoc Electr Ind Eng Rev
Associated Industries of New York State. Bulletin — Assoc Ind NY Bull
Associated Scientific and Technical Societies of South Africa. Annual Proceedings — Assoc Sci Tech Soc S Afr Annu Proc

Associated Scientific and Technical Societies of South Africa. Annual Proceedings — ATSAAL
Associated Technical Services, Inc. List of Translations — ATS List Transl
Association and Society Manager — ASM
Association and Society Manager — Assoc Soc Manager
Association and Society Manager — ASY
Association Belge de Photographie et de Cinematographie. Bulletin — Assoc Belge Photogr Cinematogr Bull
Association Belge de Radioprotection. Annales — Assoc Belge Radioprot Ann
Association Belge des Technologues de Laboratoire. Revue — Assoc Belge Technol Lab Rev
Association Belge pour le Developpement Pacifique de l'Energie Atomique. Bulletin d'Information — Assoc Belge Dev Pac Energ At Bull Inf
Association Belgo-Neerlandaise pour l'Etude des Cereales. Comptes Rendus — Assoc Belgo Neerl Etude Cereales CR
Association Bulletin. International Association of Milk Dealers — Assoc Bull Int Assoc Milk Dealers
Association Canadienne des Bibliothecaires de Langue Francaise. Bulletin — ACBLF Bul
Association Canadienne des Bibliothecaires de Langue Francaise. Bulletin — Assn Canadienne Bibl Langue Francaise Bul
Association Canadienne des Bibliothecaires de Langue Francaise. Bulletin — Assoc Can Bibl Lang Fr Bull
Association Canadienne des Dietetistes. Journal — Assoc Can Diet J
Association Canadienne-Francaise pour l'Avancement des Sciences. Annales — Assoc Can Fr Av Sci Ann
Association Canadienne-Francaise pour l'Avancement des Sciences. Annales — Assoc Canadienne-Francaise Av Sci Annales
Association. Commissioners of Agriculture of Southern States. Proceedings — Assoc Comm Agric South States Proc
Association de Cadres Dirigeants de l'Industrie pour le Progres Social et Economique. Bulletin — Assoc Cadres Dir Industr B
Association de Geographes Francais. Bulletin — AGFB
Association de Geographes Francais. Bulletin — Assoc Geogr Fr Bull
Association de Geographes Francais. Bulletin — Assoc Geographes Francais Bull
Association de Recherche sur les Techniques de Forage et de Production. Comptes Rendus du Colloque — Assoc Rech Tech Forage Prod CR Colloq
Association de Recherche sur les Techniques d'Exploitation du Petrole. Comptes Rendus du Colloque de l'ARTEP — Assoc Rech Tech Exploit Pet CR Colloque ARTEP
Association des Bibliothecaires Francais. Annuaire — Assoc Bibl Fr Ann
Association des Bibliothecaires Francais. Bulletin d'Informations — Ass Bibliot Fr Bull Inf
Association des Bibliothecaires Francais. Bulletin d'Informations — Assn Bibl Francais Bull Inf
Association des Bibliothecaires Francais. Bulletin d'Informations — Assoc Bibl Francais Bul
Association des Biochimistes des Hopitaux du Quebec. Bulletin — Assoc Biochim Hop Que Bull
Association des Geologues du Bassin de Paris. Bulletin — Assoc Geol Bassin Paris Bull
Association des Geologues du Bassin de Paris. Bulletin d'Information — Assoc Geol Bassin Paris Bull Inf
Association des Ingenieurs Electriciens Sortis de l'Institut Electrotechnique Montefiore. Bulletin [*Belgium*] — Assoc Ing Electr Sortis Inst Electrotech Montefiore Bull
Association des Ingenieurs Electriciens Sortis de l'Institut Electrotechnique Montefiore. Bulletin — BEEMA
Association des Ingenieurs Sortis de l'Universite Libre de Bruxelles. Bulletin Technique — Assoc Ing Sortis Univ Libre Bruxelles Bull Tech
Association des Licencies de l'Universite de Liege. Bulletin — Assn D Licen Univ Liege Bul
Association des Naturalistes de l'Enseignement Agricole Public. Bulletin Trimestriel — Assoc Nat Enseign Agric Public Bull Trimest
Association Executives Buyers' Guide and Meeting Planner — Assoc Exec Buy Gui Meet Plan
Association for African Studies. Nagoya University. Preliminary Report of African Studies — Assoc Afr Stud Nagoya Univ Prelim Rep Afr Stud
Association for Asian Studies. Newsletter — Assn Asian Stud Newsletter
Association for Computing Machinery. Communications — Assoc Comput Mach Commun
Association for Computing Machinery Computing Surveys — ACM Comput Surveys
Association for Computing Machinery. Journal — Assn Comp Mach J
Association for Computing Machinery. Proceedings. Annual Conference — Assoc Comput Mach Proc Annu Conf
Association for Computing Machinery. Proceedings of National Conference — ACM Proc Nat Conf
Association for Education by Radio. Journal — Assn Ed Radio J
Association for Hospital Medical Education. Journal — AHME J
Association for International Cancer Research. Symposia — AIRSEV
Association for International Cancer Research. Symposia — Assoc Int Cancer Res Symp
Association for Jewish Studies. Newsletter — AJSN
Association for Jewish Studies Newsletter — Assoc Jewish Stud Newsl
Association for Recorded Sound Collections. Journal — ARSC
Association for Recorded Sound Collections. Journal — ARSCJ
Association for Recorded Sound Collections. Journal — Assoc Recor
Association for Recorded Sound Collections. Newsletter — ARSC
Association for Religious Education Aspects of Education. Bulletin — AREA
Association for Research in Nervous and Mental Disease. Proceedings — A Res Nerv Ment Dis Proc
Association for Research in Nervous and Mental Disease. Research Publications [*A publication*] — Assoc Res Nerv Ment Dis Res Publ
Association for Research in Nervous and Mental Disease. Series of Research Publications — Assoc Res Nerv Ment Dis Ser Res Publ
Association for Student Teaching. Yearbook — Assn Stud Teach Yrbk
Association for Supervision and Curriculum Development. Yearbook — Assn for Sup & Curric Develop Yearbook
Association for Supervision and Curriculum Development. Yearbook — Assn Sup & Curric Devel Yrbk
Association for the Advancement of Agricultural Sciences in Africa. Journal — Assoc Adv Agric Sci Afr J
Association for the Advancement of Medical Instrumentation Technology Analysis and Review — Assoc Adv Med Instrum Technol Anal Rev
Association for the Advancement of Medical Instrumentation Technology. Assessment Report — Assoc Adv Med Instrum Technol Assess Rep
Association for the Advancement of Polish Studies. Bulletin — Assoc Adv Pol Stud Bul
Association for the Welfare of Children in Hospital. New South Wales. Newsletter — AWCH NSW Newsletter
Association for Tropical Biology Bulletin — Assoc Trop Biol Bull
Association Foret-Cellulose — AFOCEL
Association Francaise de Gemmologie. Bulletin — Assoc Fr Gemmol Bull
Association Francaise des Chimistes des Industries du Cuir. Conference — Assoc Fr Chim Ind Cuir Conf
Association Francaise des Techniciens du Petrole. Revue — Assoc Fr Tech Pet Rev
Association Francaise pour la Cybernetique Economique et Technique. Annuaire — Assoc Fr Cybern Econ Tech Annu
Association Francaise pour l'Avancement des Sciences. Comptes-Rendus — As Franc C R
Association Francaise pour l'Avancement des Sciences. Comptes-Rendus — Ass Franc Avance Sc C R
Association Francaise pour l'Avancement des Sciences. Conferences Faites En — Assoc Franc Avancem Sci Conf
Association Francaise pour l'Etude du Quaternaire. Bulletin — Assoc Fr Etude Quat Bull
Association Francaise pour l'Etude du Sol. Bulletin — Assoc Fr Etude Sol Bull
Association Guillaume Bude. Bulletin — AGB
Association Internationale de Geologie de l'Ingenieur. Bulletin — Assoc Int Geol Ing Bull
Association Internationale de Limnologie Theoretique et Appliquee. Communications — Assoc Int Limnol Theor Appl Commun
Association Internationale de Limnologie Theoretique et Appliquee. Travaux — Assoc Int Limnol Theor Appl Trav
Association Internationale des Distributions d'Eau. Congres — Assoc Int Distrib Eau Congr
Association Internationale des Documentalistes et Techniciens de l'Information. Bulletin — Assoc Int Doc Tech Inf Bull
Association Internationale des Sciences Hydrologiques. Publication — Assoc Int Sci Hydrol Publ
Association Internationale d'Etudes du Sud-Est Europeen. Bulletin [*Bucharest*] — AESEE
Association Internationale d'Odonto Stomatologie Infantile. Journal — Assoc Int Odonto Stomatol Infant J
Association Internationale pour l'Etude de la Mosaique Antique. Bulletin d'Information — AIEMA
Association Internationale pour l'Etude des Argiles — Assoc Int Etude Argiles
Association Management — AMG
Association Management — ASM
Association Management — Assn Mgt
Association Management — Assoc Manage
Association Men (Rural Manhood) — Assn Men
Association Nationale des Services d'Eau (Belgium). Bulletin d'Information — Assoc Natl Serv Eau (Belg) Bull Inf
Association Nationale pour la Protection contre l'Incendie. Dossier Technique — Assoc Natl Prot Incendie Dossier Tech
Association Nucleaire Canadienne. Congres International Annuel — Assoc Nucl Can Congr Int Ann
Association of American Agricultural Colleges and Experiment Stations. Proceedings — Assn Am Ag Coll & Exp Pro
Association of American Anatomists. Proceedings — Assn Am Anat Proc
Association of American Colleges. Bulletin — Assn Am Col Bul
Association of American Fertilizer Control Officials. Official Publication — Assoc Am Fert Control Off Off Publ
Association of American Geographers. Annals — AAAGA
Association of American Geographers. Annals — As Am Geog
Association of American Geographers. Annals — Assn Am Geog Ann
Association of American Geographers. Annals — Assoc Am Geographers Annals
Association of American Geographers. Commission on College Geography. Publication — Assoc Am Geogr Comm Coll Geogr Publ
Association of American Geographers. Commission on College Geography. Resource Paper — Assoc Am Geographers Comm Coll Geography Resource Paper
Association of American Geologists and Naturalists. Reports — As Am G Rp
Association of American Law Schools. Proceedings — AALS Proc
Association of American Library Schools. Newsletter — AALS News
Association of American Physicians and Surgeons. Newsletter — AAPS Newsletter
Association of American Physicians. Transactions — Assoc Am Physicians Trans
Association of American Plant Food Control Official. Official Publication — Assoc Am Plant Food Control Off Off Publ
Association of American Railroads. Yearbook of Railroad Facts — AAR Facts
Association of Asphalt Paving Technologists. Conference — Assoc Asphalt Paving Technol

Association of Asphalt Paving Technologists. Proceedings. Technical Sessions — Assoc Asphalt Paving Technol Proc Tech Sess
Association of British Columbia Drama Educators. Newsletter — ABCDE News
Association of British Orientalists. Bulletin — BABO
Association of British Orientalists. Bulletin of Near Eastern and Indian Studies — BABO
Association of British Orientalists. Bulletin of Oriental Studies — BABO
Association of Canadian Educators of the Hearing Impaired. Journal/Association Canadienne des Educateurs des Deficients-Auditifs. Revue — ACEHI J/REV ACEDA
Association of Canadian Universities for Northern Studies. Occasional Publications — ACUNSOP
Association of Clinical Pathologists Symposia — Assoc Clin Pathol Symp
Association of College and Research Libraries. Monographs — ACRL Monogr
Association of Consulting Engineers Directory — Assoc Cons Eng Dir
Association of Departments of English. Bulletin — ADEB
Association of Departments of Foreign Languages. Bulletin — ADFLB
Association of Economic Biologists. Coimbatore. Proceedings — Assoc Econ Biol Coimbatore Proc
Association of Education by Radio-Television. Journal — AERTJ
Association of Educational Psychologists. Journal — AEPJ
Association of Educators of Gifted, Talented, and Creative Children in British Columbia. Journal — AEGTCC J
Association of Engineering Geologists. Annual Meeting. Guide to Field Trips [*A publication*] — Assoc Eng Geol Annu Mtg Guide Field Trips
Association of Engineering Geologists. Annual Meeting. Guidebook — Assoc Eng Geol Annu Mtg Guideb
Association of Engineering Geologists. Annual Meeting. Program and Abstracts — Assoc Eng Geol Ann Meet Program Abstr
Association of Engineering Geologists. Bulletin — Assoc Eng Geol Bull
Association of Engineering Societies. Journal — As Eng Soc J
Association of Food and Drug Officials of the United States. Quarterly Bulletin — Assoc Food Drug Off US Q Bull
Association of Food and Drug Officials. Quarterly Bulletin — Assoc Food and Drug Off Q Bull
Association of Governing Boards of State Universities and Allied Institutions. Proceedings — Assn of Gov Bds of State Univ & Allied Insts Proc
Association of Green Crop Driers. Yearbook — Assoc Green Crop Driers Yearb
Association of Home Appliance Manufacturers. Trends and Forecasts — AHAM
Association of Hospital and Institution Libraries. Quarterly — AHIL Q
Association of Industrial Medical Officers. Transactions — Assoc Ind Med Off Trans
Association of Iron and Steel Electrical Engineers. Proceedings — Assoc Iron Steel Electr Eng Proc
Association of Japanese Portland Cement Engineers. Review of General Meeting — Assoc Jpn Portland Cem Eng Rev Gen Meet
Association of Kineticists of India. Bulletin — Assoc Kinet India Bull
Association of Mental Health Chaplains. Forum — AMHC Forum
Association of Metal Sprayers. Papers. Symposium on Engineering Applications of Metal Spraying — Assoc Met Sprayers Pap Symp Eng Appl Met Spraying
Association of Mine Managers of South Africa. Circulars — Assoc Mine Mangr S Afr Circ
Association of Mine Managers of South Africa. Papers and Discussions — Assoc Mine Mangr S Afr Pap Discuss
Association of Official Agricultural Chemists. Journal — Assn Offic Ag Chem J
Association of Official Agricultural Chemists. Journal — Assoc Official Agr Chemists Jour
Association of Official Analytical Chemists. Journal — Assoc Off Anal Chem J
Association of Official Analytical Chemists. Journal — Assoc Off Analyt Chemists J
Association of Official Seed Analysts. Proceedings — Assoc Off Seed Anal Proc
Association of Operating Room Nurses. Journal — AORN J
Association of Pacific Coast Geographers. Yearbook — Assoc Pacific Coast Geographers Yearbook
Association of Public Analysts. Journal — Assoc Public Analysts J
Association of Research Libraries. Minutes — ARL Mins
Association of School Business Officials of the United States and Canada. Proceedings — Assn Sch Bsns Officials US & Canada Proc
Association of Short-Circuit Testing Authorities. Publication — ASS Short-Circuit Test Auth Publ
Association of South East Asian Nations. Food Journal — Assoc South East Asian Nations Food J
Association of Southern Agricultural Workers. Proceedings — Assoc South Agric Work Proc
Association of Special Libraries of the Philippines. Bulletin — ASLP Bul
Association of Special Libraries of the Philippines. Bulletin — ASLP Bull
Association of State Library Agencies. President's Newsletter — ASLA Pres Newsl
Association of Teachers of Russian. Journal — ATRJ
Association of the Bar of the City of New York. Record — Assn Bar City NY Rec
Association of Trial Lawyers of America. Law Journal — A Trial Law Am LJ
Association of University Programs in Health Administration. Program Notes — Assoc Univ Programs Health Admin Program Notes
Association of Veterinary Anaesthetists of Great Britain and Ireland. Journal — Assoc Vet Anaesth GB Irel J
Association Quebecoise des Techniques de l'Eau. Assises Annuelles — Assoc Que Tech Eau Assises Annu
Association Quebecoise des Techniques de l'Eau. Congres AQTE — Assoc Que Tech Eau Congr AQTE
Association Regionale pour l'Etude et la Recherche Scientifiques. Bulletin — Assoc Reg Etude Rech Sci Bull
Association Regionale pour l'Etude et la Recherche Scientifiques. Bulletin — Assoc Reg Etude Sci Bull
Association Royale des Anciens Etudiants en Brasserie. Universite de Louvain. Bulletin — Assoc R Anc Etud Brass Univ Louvain Bull
Association Scientifique Internationale du Cafe. Colloque — Assoc Sci Int Cafe Colloq
Association Senegalaise pour l'Etude du Quaternaire de l'Ouest Africain. Bulletin de Liaison — ASQBA7
Association Senegalaise pour l'Etude du Quaternaire de l'Ouest Africain. Bulletin de Liaison — Assoc Senegal Etud Quat Ouest Afr Bull Liaison
Association Senegalaise pour l'Etude du Quaternaire de l'Ouest Africain. Bulletin de Liaison — Assoc Senegal Etude Quat Afr Bull Liaison
Association Suisse des Chimistes et Techniciens de l'Industrie des Vernis et Couleurs. Bulletin — Assoc Suisse Chim Tech Ind Vernis Couleurs Bull
Association Technique de l'Industrie du Gaz en France. Proceedings — Assoc Tech Ind Gaz
Association Technique de l'Industrie Papetiere. Bulletin — Assoc Tech Ind Papet Bull
Association Technique pour l'Energie Nucleaire. Bulletin d'Information — Assoc Tech Energ Nucl Bull Inf
Associations' Publications in Print [*Database*] — APIP
Associazione Elettrotecnica ed Elettronica Italiana. Rendiconti della Riunione Annuale — Assoc Elettrotec Elettron Ital Rend Riun Annu
Associazione Elettrotecnica Italiana. Rendiconti della Riunione Annuale — Assoc Elettrotec Ital Rend Riun Annu
Associazione Geofisica Italiana. Atti del Convegno Annuale — AGIAA
Associazione Geofisica Italiana. Atti del Convegno Annuale [*Italy*] — Assoc Geofis Ital Atti Conv Annu
Associazione Industriali Metallurgici Meccanici Affini. Notiziario Tecnico AMMA — Assoc Ind Metall Mecc Affini Not Tec AMMA
Associazione Italiana Biblioteche. Bollettino d'Informazioni — AIB Boll
Associazione Italiana Biblioteche. Bollettino d'Informazioni — Assn Italiana Bibl Boll Inf
Associazione Italiana Biblioteche. Quaderni del Bollettino d'Informazioni — Assoc Ital Bibl Quad Bol Inf
Associazione Italiana di Fisica Sanitaria e di Protezione contro le Radiazioni. Atti del Congresso Nazionale — Assoc Ital Fis Sanit Prot Radiaz Atti Congr Naz
Associazione Italiana di Metallurgia. Atti Notizie — Assoc Ital Metall Atti Not
Associazione Italiana Industriali Prodotti Alimentari. Bollettino — Assoc Ital Ind Prod Aliment Bol
Associazione Italiana Tecnici Industrie Vernici Affini. Bollettino — Assoc Ital Tec Ind Vernici Affini Boll
Associazione Metallurgici Meccanici Affini. Notiziario Tecnico AMMA — Assoc Metall Mecc Affini Not Tec AMMA
Associazione Nazionale degli Ingegneri ed Architetti Italiani. Quaderni — Ass Naz Ing Architetti Ital Quad
Associazione Scientifica di Produzione Animale. Congresso Nazionale — Assoc Sci Prod Anim Congr Naz
Assortiment des Oeuvres Specialises et Scientifiques. Ecole Polytechniques a Brno. A — Assortiment Oeuvres Spec Sci Ec Polytech Brno A
Assortiment des Oeuvres Specialises et Scientifiques. Ecole Polytechniques a Brno. B — Assortiment Oeuvres Spec Sci Ec Polytech Brno B
Assuntos Europeus — Assuntos Eur
Assurandoren — Assd
Assuring Radiation Protection. Annual National Conference on Radiation Control — Assuring Radiat Prot Annu Natl Conf Radiat Control
Assyrian and English Glossary [*Johns Hopkins University*] — Assyr Engl Glossary
Assyrian Dictionary — AD
Assyriological Miscellanies — Assy Misc
Assyriological Studies — Assyr S
Assyriological Studies — Assyriol Studies
Assyriological Studies — AssyrSt
Assyriological Studies. Oriental Institute. University of Chicago — AS
Assyriologische Bibliothek — A Bib
Assyriologische Bibliothek — AB
Assyriologische Studien — Assyr S
Assyriologische Studien — Assyriol Stud
Assyrische Rechtsurkunden — ARU
Astarte — ASTTB9
Astarte. Journal of Arctic Biology — ASTT
Asthetische Medizin (Berlin) — Asthet Med (Berl)
Asthma and Bronchial Hyperreactivity. Congress. European Society of Pneumology — Asthma Bronchial Hyperreact Congr Eur Soc Pneumol
Astin Bulletin [*Leiden*] — Astin Bull
ASTM (American Society for Testing and Materials) Data Series — ASTM (Am Soc Test Mater) Data Ser
ASTM [*American Society for Testing and Materials*] **Cement, Concrete, and Aggregates** — ASTM Cem Concr Aggregates
ASTM [*American Society for Testing and Materials*] **Data Series** — ASTM Data Ser
ASTM [*American Society for Testing and Materials*] **Data Series** — ATDSAY
ASTM [*American Society for Testing and Materials*] **Geotechnical Testing Journal** — ASTM Geotech Test J
ASTM [*American Society for Testing and Materials*] **Journal of Testing and Evaluation** — ASTM J Testing Evaln
ASTM [*American Society for Testing and Materials*] **Proceedings** — ASTM Proc
ASTM [*American Society for Testing and Materials*] **Special Technical Publication** — ASTM SP
ASTM [*American Society for Testing and Materials*] **Special Technical Publication** — ASTM Spec Tech Publ
ASTM [*American Society for Testing and Materials*] **Special Technical Publication** — ASTTA8
ASTM [*American Society for Testing and Materials*] **Standardization News** — ASTM Stand N
ASTM [*American Society for Testing and Materials*] **Standardization News** — ASTM Stand News

ASTM [*American Society for Testing and Materials*] **Standardization News** — ASTM Stdn News
ASTM [*American Society for Testing and Materials*] **Standardization News** — STDNA
ASTM [*American Society for Testing and Materials*] **Standards** — ASTM Stand
ASTM [*American Society for Testing and Materials*] **Standards** — ASTM Std
ASTM [*American Society for Testing and Materials*] **Tentative Standards** — ASTM Tentative Stand
Astonishing Stories — Ash
Astonishing Stories — AST
Astounding Science Fiction — ASF
Astounding Stories Yearbook — ASY
Astrofizicheskie Issledovaniya — Astrofiz Issled
Astrofizicheskie Issledovaniya. Izvestiya Spetsial'noi Astrofizicheskoi Observatorii — Astrofiz Issled Izv Spets Astrofiz Obs
Astrofizicheskie Issledovaniya (Leningrad) — Astrofiz Issled (Leningrad)
Astrofizicheskie Issledovaniya (Sofia) — Astrofiz Issled (Sofia)
Astrofizika — Astrofiz
Astrology '77 — Astrol 77
Astrology '78 — Astrol 78
Astrology Now — Astrol Now
Astrometriya i Astrofizika — Astrom Astrofiz
Astrometriya i Astrofizika — Astrometriya & Astrofiz
Astrometriya i Astrofizika — SAAFA
Astronautica Acta — Astronaut Acta
Astronautical Sciences Review — Astronaut Sci Rev
Astronautics and Aeronautics — A & A
Astronautics and Aeronautics — Astro Aeron
Astronautics and Aeronautics — Astronaut Aeronaut
Astronautics and Aerospace Engineering — Astronaut Aerosp Eng
Astronautics and Aerospace Engineering — Astronautics Aerospace Eng
Astronautische Forschungsberichte. Deutsche Rakete Gesellschaft eV — Astronaut Forschungsber Dtsch Raketen Ges eV
Astronautische Forschungsberichte. Hermann Oberth Gesellschaft — Astronaut Forschungsber Hermann Oberth Ges
Astronomia-Optika Institucio. Universitato de Turku. Informo — Astron-Opt Inst Univ Turku Inf
Astronomical and Astrophysical Transactions — Astron Astrophys Trans
Astronomical Circulars. Academia Sinica — Astron Circ Acad Sin
Astronomical Ephemeris — Astro Ephem
Astronomical Herald — Astron Her
Astronomical Journal — Astron J
Astronomical Journal — Astronom J
Astronomical Society of Australia. Proceedings — Astron Soc Aust Proc
Astronomical Society of Australia. Publications — Astron Soc Aust Publ
Astronomical Society of India. Bulletin — Astron Soc India Bull
Astronomical Society of Japan. Publications — Astron Soc Jpn Publ
Astronomical Society of the Pacific Conference Series — Astron Soc Pac Conf Ser
Astronomical Society of the Pacific. Leaflet — Astron Soc Pac Leafl
Astronomical Society of the Pacific. Publications — Astron Soc Pacific Pubs
Astronomicheskii Kalendar (Moscow) — Astron Kal (Moscow)
Astronomicheskii Tsirkulyar [*Former USSR*] — Astron Tsirk
Astronomicheskii Vestnik — Astron Vestn
Astronomicheskii Zhurnal — Astron Zh
Astronomicheskii Zhurnal — Astronom Zh
Astronomie (Paris) — Astron (Paris)
Astronomie (Paris). Supplement — Astron (Paris) Suppl
Astronomie und Raumfahrt — Astron Raumfahrt
Astronomische Abhandlungen als Ergaenzungshefte zu den Astronomischen Nachrichten — Astron Abhandl Ergaenzungshefte Astron Nachr
Astronomische Nachrichten — Astron Nach
Astronomische Nachrichten — Astron Nachr
Astronomische Nachrichten — Astronom Nachr
Astronomische Zeitschrift — Astron Zs
Astronomischer Jahresbericht — Astron Jahresber
Astronomisk Tidsskrift — Astron Tidsskr
Astronomiska Saellskapet — Astron Saellsk
Astronomiya Itogi Nauki i Tekhniki — Astronomiya Itogi Nauki Tekh
Astronomy — GAST
Astronomy and Astrophysics — Astron
Astronomy and Astrophysics — Astron Astr
Astronomy and Astrophysics — Astron Astrophys
Astronomy and Astrophysics — Astronom and Astrophys
Astronomy and Astrophysics. Abstracts — AAABC
Astronomy and Astrophysics. Abstracts — Ast & AstroAb
Astronomy and Astrophysics. Abstracts — Astron Astrophys Abstr
Astronomy and Astrophysics Library — Astronom Astrophys Lib
Astronomy and Astrophysics Supplement Series — Astr Ast SS
Astronomy and Astrophysics. Supplement Series — Astron Astrophys Suppl Ser
Astronomy and Astrophysics. Supplement Series — Astronom Astrophys Ser
Astronomy and Space — Astron & Space
Astronomy Express — Astron Ex
Astronomy (Milwaukee) — Astron (Milwaukee)
Astronomy Quarterly — Astron Q
Astrophysica Norvegica — ASNOA
Astrophysica Norvegica [*Norway*] — Astrophys Norv
Astrophysical Journal — Astrophys J
Astrophysical Journal. Letters to the Editor — Astrophys J Lett Ed
Astrophysical Journal. Supplement — Astrophys J Suppl
Astrophysical Journal. Supplement Series — APJSA
Astrophysical Journal. Supplement Series — Astroph J S
Astrophysical Journal. Supplement Series — Astrophys J Suppl Ser
Astrophysical Letters — Astrophys L
Astrophysical Letters — Astrophys Lett
Astrophysics — Astrophys
Astrophysics and Gravitation. Proceedings of the Solvay Conference on Physics [*A publication*] — Astrophys Gravitation Proc Solvay Conf Phys
Astrophysics and Space Physics Reviews — Astrophys Space Phys Rev
Astrophysics and Space Science — Astro Sp Sc
Astrophysics and Space Science — Astrophys Space Sci
Astrophysics and Space Science Library — ASSLAD
Astrophysics and Space Science Library [*Reidel, Dordrecht*] — Astrophys Space Sci Lib
Astrophysics and Space Science Library — Astrophys Space Sci Libr
Astrophysics (English Translation) — Astrophysics (Engl Transl)
Asufaruto — ASUHA
Asuntos Agrarios — Asuntos Agr
Asutustoiminnan Aikakauskirja — Asutustoiminnan Aikak
Asymmetric Organic Synthesis. Proceedings. Nobel Symposium — Asymmetric Org Synth Proc Nobel Symp
Asymptotic Analysis — Asymptotic Anal
AT Times — ATTID
ATA [*Alberta Teachers Association*] **Magazine** — ATA Mag
Ata Reumatologica Brasileira — ASPND7
Ata Reumatologica Brasileira — Ata Reumatol Bras
ATAC (Asociacion de Tecnicos Azucareros de Cuba) — ATAC (Asoc Tec Azucar Cuba)
ATAC (Asociacion de Tecnicos Azucareros de Cuba) — ATACC7
ATAC. Revista Bimestral. Asociacion de Tecnicos Azucareros de Cuba — ATAC Rev Bimest Asoc Tec Azucar Cuba
ATACC [*Alberta Teachers' Association, Computer Council*] **Journal** — ATACC J
Atalanta — ATLNDS
Atalanta Norvegica — Atalanta Norv
Atalanta Norvegica — ATLABL
AT&T Technical Journal — AT&T Tech J
Atas. Instituto de Micologia da Universidade Federal de Pernambuco — Atas Inst Micol Univ Fed Pernambuco
Atas. Instituto de Micologia da Universidade Federal de Pernambuco — PUIAA7
Atas. Simposio Regional de Geologia — Atas Simp Reg Geol
Atas. Simposio Sobre a Biota Amazonica — ASBA
Atas. Sociedade de Biologia do Rio De Janeiro — Atas Soc Biol Rio De J
Atas. Sociedade de Biologia do Rio De Janeiro — Atas Soc Biol Rio De Janeiro
Ataturk Universitesi Fen Bilimleri Dergisi — Ataturk Univ Fen Bilimleri Derg
Ataturk Universitesi Fen Fakultesi Dergisi — Ataturk Univ Fen Fak Derg
Ataturk University Journal of Sciences — Ataturk Univ J Sci
ATB [*Acta Technica Belgica*] **Metallurgie** — ATB Metall
ATCP [*Asociacion Mexicana de Tecnicos de las Industrias de la Celulosa y del Papel*] — ATCP
Atelier des Photographen — Atelier
Atelier des Photographen und Allgemeine Photographenzeitung — Atelier Photogr Allg Photographztg
Atelier des Photographen und Deutsche Photographische Kunst — Atelier Photogr Dtsch Photogr Kunst
Atemwegs- und Lungenkrankheiten — Atemwegs- Lungenkr
Atemwegs- und Lungenkrankheiten — Atemwegs Lungenkrankh
Atencion Medica — Aten Med
Atencion Primaria — Aten Primaria
Atene e Roma — AeR
Atene e Roma — AR
Atene e Roma — At R
Atene e Roma — At Roma
Atene e Roma — Ate R
Atene e Roma — Atene Rom
Atenea — At
Atenea — Ate
Atenea [*Chile*] — ATEN
Atenea. Facultad de Artes y Ciencias (Puerto Rico) — ATENEA PR
Ateneo Cientifico. Memoria Leida en la Junta General — Ateneo Ci
Ateneo Parmense — At Parm
Ateneo Parmense. Acta Bio-Medica — Ateneo Parmense Acta Bio-Med
Ateneo Parmense. Acta Naturalia — Ateneo Parmense Acta Nat
Ateneo Parmense. Collana di Monografie — At Par Col Monogr
Ateneo Parmense. Sezione 1. Acta Bio-Medica — Ateneo Parmense Sez 1
Ateneo Parmense. Sezione 2. Acta Naturalia [*Italy*] — Ateneo Parmense Sez 2
Ateneo Puertorriqueno — AtP
Ateneo Veneto — AtV
Ateneo Veneto — AV
Ateneo Veneto. Rivista di Scienze, Lettere, ed Arti — At Ven
Ateneum Kaplanskie — AK
Ateneum Kaplanskie [*Wloclawek, Poland*] — AtKap
ATES [*Aquifer Thermal Energy Storage*] **Newsletter** — ATES Newsl
ATES [*Aquifer Thermal Energy Storage*] **Newsletter** — ATNED
ATF Colada — ATFCC
ATHA [*Association for Traditional Hooking Artists*] **Newsletter** — ATHHA Newsl
Athena. Syngramma Periodikon tes en Athenais Epistemonikes Hetaireias — Athen
Athenaeum — Ath
Athenaeum fuer Wissenschaft, Kunst, und Leben — Athenaeum Wiss
Athenaeum. Studi Periodici di Letteratura e Storia dell'Antichita. Universita di Pavia — Athenae
Athenaeum. Studi Periodici di Letteratura e Storia dell'Antichita. Universita di Pavia — Athenaeum Pavia
Athenaion Literaturwissenschaft — ALit
Athene. The American Magazine of Hellenic Thought — Ath
Athenian Agora — Ag
Athenian Tribute Lists — ATL
Athenische Mitteilungen — AM
Athenische Mitteilungen. Beiheft — Ath Mitt-BH

Athens Annals of Archaeology — AAA
Atherogenesis. Proceedings of the International Symposium — Atherogenesis Proc Int Symp
Atherosclerosis — Atheroscler
Atherosclerosis and Coronary Heart Disease. Hahnemann Symposium — Atheroscler Coron Heart Dis Hahnemann Symp
Atherosclerosis Drug Discovery — Atheroscler Drug Discovery
Atherosclerosis. Proceedings. International Symposium on Atherosclerosis — Atheroscler Proc Int Symp
Atherosclerosis Reviews — Atheroscler Rev
Athletic Administration — Ath Adm
Athletic Administration — Athl Adm
Athletic Business — Ath Bus
Athletic Educator's Report — Athl Educ Rep
Athletic Journal — Ath J
Athletic Journal — Athl J
Athletic Journal — Athletic J
Athletic Management — Ath Management
Athletic Purchasing and Facilities — Ath Pur and Fac
Athletic Training — Ath Train
Athletic Training — Athl Train
Athletics Coach — Ath Coach
Athletics Coach — Athl Coach
Athlone French Poets — AFrP
Athro Arfon — AA
ATIRA [*Ahmedabad Textile Industry's Research Association*] **Technical Digest** — ATIRA Tech Dig
Atkinson's Saturday Evening Post — Atkinsons Saturday Eve Post
ATLA. Alternatives to Laboratory Animals — ATLA Alt Lab Anim
ATLA-Alternatives to Laboratory Animals — ATLA-Alt L
Atlanta Business Chronicle [*United States*] — Atlan Bs C
Atlanta Constitution [*United States*] — Atlan Cons
Atlanta Economic Review — Atl Econ R
Atlanta Economic Review — Atlanta Econ R
Atlanta Economic Review — Atlanta ER
Atlanta Historical Journal — Atlanta Hist J
Atlanta Journal/Atlanta Constitution Weekend — Atlanta Jou
Atlanta Magazine — Atlanta M
Atlanta Medicine — Atlanta Med
Atlanta Professional — Atl Prof
Atlantic — GTAT
Atlantic Advocate — Atl Adv
Atlantic Advocate — Atlan Adv
Atlantic Business — ATIC
Atlantic Canada Teacher — ACT
Atlantic Communication Arts Directory — Atlan Com Dir
Atlantic Community Quarterly — Atl Com Q
Atlantic Community Quarterly — Atl Community Quar
Atlantic Community Quarterly — Atlan Com Q
Atlantic Community Quarterly — Atlantic Community Q
Atlantic Community Quarterly — PACQ
Atlantic Economic Journal — AEJ
Atlantic Economic Journal — Atlantic Econ J
Atlantic Fisherman — Atl Fisherman
Atlantic Insight — Atlan Insight
Atlantic Medical Journal — Atl Med J
Atlantic Monthly — AM
Atlantic Monthly — AMo
Atlantic Monthly — AMon
Atlantic Monthly — Atl
Atlantic Monthly — Atl M
Atlantic Monthly — Atl Mo
Atlantic Monthly — Atlan
Atlantic Monthly — Atlan Mo
Atlantic Monthly — Atlan Mon
Atlantic Monthly — Atlantic
Atlantic Monthly — AtM
Atlantic Monthly — AtMo
Atlantic Naturalist — Atl Nat
Atlantic Papers — Atlantic Pap
Atlantic Province Reports [*Information service or system*] — APR
Atlantic Provinces Book Review — Atl Pro Bk R
Atlantic Provinces Library Association. Bulletin — APLA Bull
Atlantic Provinces Reports [*Canada*] — APR
Atlantic Quarterly — AQ
Atlantic Report (Ottawa) — Atl Rep (Ottawa)
Atlantic Salmon Journal — Atl Salmon J
Atlantic Salmon References — Atl Salmon Ref
Atlantic Truck Transport Review — Atlan Tr Tran Rev
Atlantic Workshop — Atl Workshop
Atlantic Workshop. Proceedings — Atl Workshop Proc
Atlantica and Iceland Review — ATIR
Atlantica and Iceland Review — IGC
Atlantico — Atl
Atlantida — At
Atlantida — Atl
Atlantida. Mensario Artistico, Literario, e Social para Portugal e Brasil — A
Atlantida. Orgao do Instituto Acoriano de Cultura — AOIAC
Atlantide Report — Atl Rep
Atlantis — AT
Atlantis — Atla
Atlantisch Perspektief — ATL
Atlas Archeologique de l'Algerie — AAA
Atlas de Radiologie Clinique [*France*] — Atlas Radiol Clin
Atlas de Radiologie Clinique — ATRCA
Atlas de Radiologie Clinique. Presse Medicale — Atlas Radiol Clin Presse Med
Atlas. Division of Fisheries and Oceanography. Commonwealth Scientific and Industrial Organisation — Atlas Div Fish Oceanogr CSIRO
Atlas Fizicheskikh Svoistv Mineralov i Porod Khibinskikh Mestorozhdenii — Atlas Fiz Svoistv Miner Porod Khibinskikh Mestorozhd
Atlas Newsletter — Atlas Newsl
Atlas of Australian Resources — Atlas of Aust Resources
Atlas of Binary Alloys. A Periodic Index — Atlas Bin Alloy Period Index
Atlas of Japanese Fossils — Atlas Jap Fossils
Atlas of Protein Sequence and Structure — Atlas Protein Sequence Struct
Atlas. Pennsylvania. Bureau of Topographic and Geologic Survey — Atlas Pa Bur Topogr Geol Surv
Atlas World Press Review — ASC
Atlas World Press Review — Atlas W P Rev
Atlin Claim — ATCL
Atlin News Miner — AT
ATM. Archiv fuer Technisches Messen und Industrielle Messtechnik — ATM Arch Tech Mess Ind Messtech
ATM. Archiv fuer Technisches Messen und Messtechnische Praxis — ATM Arch Tech Mess Messtech Prax
ATM. Archiv fuer Technisches Messen und Messtechnische Praxis — ATM Mess Pr
ATM. Archiv fuer Technisches Messen und Messtechnische Praxis — ATM Messtech Prax
Atmosfernoe Elektrichestvo Trudy Vsesoyuznogo Simpoziuma po Atmosfernomu Elektrichestvu — Atmos Elektr Tr Vses Simp
Atmosfernyi Ozon — Atmos Ozon
Atmosfernyi Ozon. Materialy Mezhduvedomstvennogo Soveshchaniya po Atmosfernomu Ozonu — Atmos Ozon Mater Mezhduved Soveshch
Atmosferos Apsauga nuo Uztersimu — Atmos Apsauga Uztersimu
Atmosferos Fizika — Atmos Fiz
Atmosphere — ATMO
Atmosphere Pollution Bulletin — Atm Poll Bull
Atmosphere-Ocean [*Canada*] — Atmos-Ocean
Atmospheric and Oceanic Physics — Atmos Oceanic Phys
Atmospheric and Oceanic Physics (English Edition) — Atmos Oceanic Phys (Engl Ed)
Atmospheric Chemistry and Air Pollution. Seminar — Atmos Chem Air Pollut Semin
Atmospheric Chemistry Problems and Scope — Atmos Chem Probl Scope
Atmospheric Corrosion — Atmos Corros
Atmospheric Environment — ATEN
Atmospheric Environment — Atmos Env
Atmospheric Environment — Atmos Envir
Atmospheric Environment — Atmos Environ
Atmospheric Ozone Optics of Atmosphere Solar Radiation (Belsk) — Atmos Ozone Opt Atmos Sol Radiat (Belsk)
Atmospheric Physics — Atmos Phys
Atmospheric Pollution. Proceedings of the International Colloquium — Atmos Pollut Proc Int Colloq
Atmospheric Propagation and Remote Sensing — Atmos Propag Remote Sens
Atmospheric Quality Improvement. Technical Bulletin — Atmos Qual Improv Tech Bull
Atmospheric Research — Atmos Res
Atmospheric Sciences Report. Alberta Research Council — Atmos Sci Rep Alberta Res Counc
Atmospheric Technology — Atmos Technol
Atoll Research Bulletin — At Res B
Atoll Research Bulletin — Atoll Res Bull
Atom Enerjisi Komisyonu. Genel Sekreterligi. Seri B (Turkey) — At Enerj Kom Gen Sekr Seri B (Turk)
Atom Enerjisi Komisyonu (Turkey) Bilimsel Yayinlar Seri — At Enerj Kom (Turkey) Bilimsel Yayin Seri
Atom Enerjisi Komisyonu (Turkey). Report K — At Enerj Kom (Turk) K
Atom Indonesia — At Indones
Atom Indonesia — Atom Indones
Atom Industry — At Ind
Atom und Strom — At Strom
Atom und Strom — At und Strom
Atom und Strom — Atom U Strom
Atomedia Philippines — Atomedia Philipp
Atomes et Radiations — At Radiat
Atomic Absorption Newsletter — At Absorpt Newsl
Atomic Absorption Newsletter — Atom Absorpt Newsl
Atomic and Molecular Physics — At Mol Phy
Atomic and Molecular Physics. Proceedings. National Workshop — At Mol Phys Proc Natl Workshop
Atomic and Molecular Physics. US/Mexico Symposium — At Mol Phys US Mex Symp
Atomic Data [*Later, Atomic Data and Nuclear Data Tables*] — At Data
Atomic Data and Nuclear Data Tables — ADNDA
Atomic Data and Nuclear Data Tables — At Data Nucl Data Tables
Atomic Data and Nuclear Data Tables — Atomic Data
Atomic Data Workshop — At Data Workshop
Atomic Diffusion in Semiconductors — At Diffus Semicond
Atomic Energy Board. Report PEL (South Africa) — At Energy Board Rep PEL (S Afr)
Atomic Energy Board. Report PER [*South Africa*] — At Energy Board Rep PER
Atomic Energy Board (Republic of South Africa). Report — At Energy Board (Repub S Afr) Rep
Atomic Energy Bulletin [*Japan*] — At Energy Bull
Atomic Energy Centre. Dacca. AECD Report — At Energy Cent Dacca AECD Rep
Atomic Energy Centre. Report PAECL [*Atomic Energy Centre, Lahore, Pakistan*] — At Energy Cent Rep PAECL Pak

Atomic Energy Control Board. Research Report — At Energy Control Board Res Rep
Atomic Energy Establishment (Trombay, India). Reports — At Energy Establ (Trombay India) Rep
Atomic Energy Establishment Winfrith. Memorandum — At Energy Establ Winfrith Memo
Atomic Energy Establishment Winfrith. Report — At Energy Establ Winfrith Rep
Atomic Energy in Australia — At Energy Aust
Atomic Energy in Australia — At Eng
Atomic Energy in Australia — Atom Ener A
Atomic Energy in Australia — Atomic Energy in Aust
Atomic Energy Law Journal — At Energy Law J
Atomic Energy Law Journal — Atomic Energy L J
Atomic Energy Law Journal — Atomic Energy Law J
Atomic Energy Law Journal — Atomic Eng LJ
Atomic Energy Law Reports — At Energy Law Rep
Atomic Energy Law Reports — CAELB
Atomic Energy Levels and Grotrian Diagrams [*Elsevier Book Series*] — AEL
Atomic Energy Minerals Centre (Pakistan). Report — At Energy Miner Cent (Pak) Rep
Atomic Energy Minerals Centre. Report AEMC (Pakistan) — At Energy Miner Cent Rep AEMC (Pak)
Atomic Energy Newsletter — At En Newsl
Atomic Energy of Canada Limited. AECL (Report) — At Energy Can Ltd AECL (Rep)
Atomic Energy of Canada Limited. Materials Research in AECL — At Energy Can Ltd Mat Res AECL
Atomic Energy Organization of Iran. Scientific Bulletin — At Energy Organ Iran Sci Bull
Atomic Energy Organization of Iran. Technical Bulletin — At Energy Organ Iran Tech Bull
Atomic Energy (Peking) — At Energy (Peking)
Atomic Energy Research Establishment, Great Britain. Analytical Method — At Energy Res Establ GB Anal Method
Atomic Energy Research Establishment (Great Britain). Bibliography — At Energy Res Establ (GB) Bibliogr
Atomic Energy Research Establishment, Great Britain. Lectures — At Energy Res Establ GB Lect
Atomic Energy Research Establishment (Great Britain). Memorandum — At Energy Res Establ (GB) Mem
Atomic Energy Research Establishment (Great Britain). Memorandum — At Energy Res Establ (GB) Memo
Atomic Energy Research Establishment (Great Britain). Report — At Energy Res Establ (GB) Rep
Atomic Energy Research Establishment (Great Britain). Translation — At Energy Res Establ (GB) Transl
Atomic Energy Research Establishment [*Great Britain*]. Registered Publications Section — AERE/RPS
Atomic Energy Research Establishment. Report AERE-G (United Kindgom) — At Energy Res Establ Rep AERE G (UK)
Atomic Energy Research. Quarterly Report [*Japan*] — At Energy Res Q Rep
Atomic Energy Review — AER
Atomic Energy Review — At En Rev
Atomic Energy Review — At Energy Rev
Atomic Energy Review — Atom Ener R
Atomic Energy Review. Special Issue — At Energy Rev Spec Issue
Atomic Energy Science and Technology — At Energy Sci Technol
Atomic Energy (Sydney) [*Australia*] — At Energy (Sydney)
Atomic Energy Yearbook — At En Yb
Atomic Engineering Technology — At Eng Technol
Atomic Inner-Shell Processes — At Inn Shell Processes
Atomic Masses and Fundamental Constants — At Masses Fundam Constants
Atomic Masses and Fundamental Constants. Proceedings of the International Conference on Atomic Masses and Fundamental Constants — At Masses Fundam Constants Proc Int Conf M
Atomic Physics — At Phys
Atomic Power — At Power
Atomic Power Review — At Pow R
Atomic Processes and Applications — At Processes Appl
Atomic Scientists Journal — At Sci J
Atomic Scientists News — At Sci News
Atomic Spectra and Oscillator Strengths for Astrophysics and Fusion Research — At Spectra Oscillator Strengths Astrophys Fusion Res
Atomic Spectroscopy — At Spectrosc
Atomic Structure and Mechanical Properties of Metals — At Struct Mech Prop Met
Atomic Weapons Research Establishment (United Kingdom). Report. Series O — At Weapons Res Establ (UK) Rep O
Atomic World — At World
Atomics — Atom
Atomics and Atomic Engineering — At At Eng
Atomics and Atomic Technology — At At Technol
Atomics and Nuclear Energy — ANE
Atomics and Nuclear Energy — At Nucl En
Atomics and Nuclear Energy [*England*] — At Nucl Energy
Atomics. Engineering and Technology — At Eng Tech
Atom-Informationen — At-Inf
Atomisation and Spray Technology — Atomisation Spray Technol
Atomkernenergie — Atomkernene
Atomkernenergie Kerntechnik — Atomkernenerg Kerntech
ATOMKI [*Atommag Kutato Intezet*] **Koezlemenyek** — ATOMKI Kozl
ATOMKI [*Atommag Kutato Intezet*] **Koezlemenyek. Supplement** — AKZMA
Atomnaya Energetika Itogi Nauki i Tekhniki — At Energ Itogi Nauki Tekh
Atomnaya Energiya — At En
Atomnaya Energiya [*Former USSR*] — At Energ
Atomnaya Energiya [*Former USSR*] — Atomn Energ
Atomnaya Energiya [*Former USSR*] — Atomnaya En
Atomnaya Energiya Prilozhenie — At Energ Prilozh
Atomnaya Energiya (USSR) — At Energiya (USSR)
Atomnaya Spektroskopiya i Spektral'nyi Analiz. Materialy Respublikanskogo Soveshchaniya — At Spektrosk Spekr Anal Mater Resp Soveshch
Atomnaya Tekhnika za Rubezhom — At Tekh Rubezhom
Atomno-Vodorodnaya Energetika i Tekhnologiya — At-Vodorodnaya Energ Tekhnol
Atomno-Vodorodnaya Energetika i Tekhnologiya — AVETD
Atomnye Elektricheskie Stantsii — AESTD
Atomnye Elektricheskie Stantsii [*Former USSR*] — At Elektr Stn
Atomnye Stolknoveniya — At Stolknoveniya
Atomo, Petrol, Elettricita [*Italy*] — Atomo Petrol Elet
Atompraxis — Atomprax
Atoms and Nuclei — At Nucl
Atoms in Japan — At Jpn
Atoms in Japan. Supplement — ATJSA
Atoms in Strong Fields — At Strong Fields
Atoms in Unusual Situations — At Unusual Situat
Atomtechnikai Tajekoztato — Atomtech Tajek
Atomwirtschaft Atomtechnik — ATI
Atomwirtschaft Atomtechnik — Atomwirtsch
Atomwirtschaft Atomtechnik — Atomwirtsch Atomtech
Atoomenergie en Haar Toepassingen — Atoomenerg Haar Toepass
Atoomenergie en Haar Toepassingen — Atoomenerg Toepass
Atos. Academia de Medicina de Sao Paulo — At Acad Med S Paulo
ATQ. The American Transcendental Quarterly — PATQ
ATR: Australian Telecommunication Research — ATR Aust Telecommun Res
Atrazine Information Sheet. Geigy Agricultural Chemicals. Atrazine Herbicides [*A publication*] — Atrazine Inform Sheet Geigy Agr Chem Atrazine Herbic
Attempt at Sedimentological Characterization of Carbonate Deposits — Attempt Sedimentol Charact Carbonate Deposits
Atti. Accademia Anatomico-Chirurgica (Perugia) — Atti Accad Anat Chir (Perugia)
Atti. Accademia Cosentina — AA Cos
Atti. Accademia Cosentina — Atti Ac Cos
Atti. Accademia Cosentina — Atti C Cos
Atti. Accademia de' Geogrofili — Atti Accad Geogrof
Atti. Accademia degli Arcadi — AAAr
Atti. Accademia dei Fisiocritici in Siena — Atti Accad Fisiocrit Siena
Atti. Accademia dei Fisiocritici in Siena. Sezione Agraria — Atti Accad Fisiocrit Siena Sez Agrar
Atti. Accademia dei Fisiocritici in Siena. Sezione Medico-Fisica — AAMFA
Atti. Accademia dei Fisiocritici in Siena. Sezione Medico-Fisica — AAMFA9
Atti. Accademia dei Fisiocritici in Siena. Sezione Medico-Fisica — Atti Accad Fisiocrit Siena Sez Med-Fis
Atti. Accademia dei Lincei — AAL
Atti. Accademia dei Lincei. Rendiconti. Classe di Scienze Morali, Storiche, e Filologiche — AALR
Atti. Accademia dei Lincei. Transunti — AALT
Atti. Accademia delle Scienza di Torino. Classe di Scienze Morali, Storiche, e Filologiche — Atti Accad Sci Torino Cl Sci Mor Stor Filol
Atti. Accademia delle Scienze di Ferrara — AASRA7
Atti. Accademia delle Scienze di Ferrara — Atti Accad Sci Ferrara
Atti. Accademia delle Scienze di Siena. Detta de Fisiocritici — AFISAT
Atti. Accademia delle Scienze di Siena detta de' Fisiocritici — Atti Accad Sci Siena
Atti. Accademia delle Scienze di Siena. Detta de Fisiocritici — Atti Accad Sci Siena Fisiocrit
Atti. Accademia delle Scienze di Torino — A Tor
Atti. Accademia delle Scienze di Torino — AAT
Atti. Accademia delle Scienze di Torino — Atti Ac Torino
Atti. Accademia delle Scienze di Torino — Atti Acc Sci Torino
Atti. Accademia delle Scienze di Torino — Atti Acc Scienze Torino
Atti. Accademia delle Scienze di Torino — Atti Accad Sci Torino
Atti. Accademia delle Scienze di Torino — Atti Accad Scienze di Torino
Atti. Accademia delle Scienze di Torino — Atti Torino
Atti. Accademia delle Scienze di Torino. Classe di Scienze Fisiche, Matematiche, e Naturali — Atti Accad Sci Torino Cl Sci Fis Mat Nat
Atti. Accademia delle Scienze di Torino. Classe di Scienze Fisiche, Matematiche, e Naturali — Atti Accad Sci Torino Cl Sci Fis Mat Natur
Atti. Accademia delle Scienze di Torino. Classe di Scienze Morali, Storiche, e Filologiche — AASTM
Atti. Accademia delle Scienze di Torino. I — Atti Accad Sci Torino I
Atti. Accademia delle Scienze di Torino. I. Classe di Scienze Fisiche, Matematiche, e Naturali — AATFAA
Atti. Accademia delle Scienze di Torino. I. Classe di Scienze Fisiche, Matematiche, e Naturali — Atti Accad Sci Torino I Cl Sci Fis Mat Nat
Atti. Accademia delle Scienze Fisiche e Matematiche — Atti Accad Sci Fis
Atti. Accademia delle Scienze Fisiche e Matematiche di Napoli — Atti Accad Sci Fis Mat Napoli
Atti. Accademia delle Scienze. Istituto di Bologna — AASB
Atti. Accademia delle Scienze. Istituto di Bologna. Classe di Scienze Fisiche. Memorie — Atti Accad Sci Ist Bologna Cl Sci Fis Mem
Atti. Accademia delle Scienze. Istituto di Bologna. Classe di Scienze Fisiche. Memorie. Serie IV — Atti Accad Sci Ist Bologna Cl Sci Fis Mem Ser IV
Atti. Accademia delle Scienze. Istituto di Bologna. Classe di Scienze Fisiche. Rendiconti — Atti Accad Sci Ist Bologna Cl Sci Fis Rend
Atti. Accademia delle Scienze. Istituto di Bologna. Classe di Scienze Fisiche. Rendiconti. Serie XIII — Atti Accad Sci Ist Bologna Cl Sci Fis Rend Ser XIII
Atti. Accademia delle Scienze. Istituto di Bologna. Classe di Scienze Fisiche. Rendiconti. Serie XIII — Atti Accad Sci Istit Bologna Cl Sci Fis Rend XIII
Atti. Accademia delle Scienze. Istituto di Bologna. Memorie — Mem Bologna

Atti. Accademia delle Scienze. Istituto di Bologna. Rendiconti — Atti Accad Sci Ist Bologna Ren
Atti. Accademia delle Scienze. Istituto di Bologna. Rendiconti — Rend Bologna
Atti. Accademia di Agricoltura, Scienze, e Lettere di Verona — AAV
Atti. Accademia di Medicina de Torino — Atti Accad Med Torino
Atti. Accademia di Palermo — AAP
Atti. Accademia di Scienze, Lettere, e Arti di Palermo — AASP
Atti. Accademia di Scienze, Lettere, e Arti di Palermo — At Acc Sc Pa
Atti. Accademia di Scienze, Lettere, e Arti di Palermo — Atti Accad Palermo
Atti. Accademia di Scienze, Lettere, e Arti di Palermo — Atti Pal
Atti. Accademia di Scienze, Lettere, ed Arti. Agiati in Rovereto — Atti Accad Sci Lett Arti Agiati Rovereto
Atti. Accademia di Scienze, Lettere, ed Arti di Palermo — AAPal
Atti. Accademia di Scienze, Lettere, ed Arti di Palermo — AASLA
Atti. Accademia di Scienze, Lettere, ed Arti di Palermo — Atti Accad Sci Lett Arti Palermo
Atti. Accademia di Scienze, Lettere, ed Arti di Palermo — Atti Palermo
Atti. Accademia di Scienze, Lettere, ed Arti di Palermo. Parte Prima. Scienze — AASLAN
Atti. Accademia di Scienze, Lettere, ed Arti di Palermo. Parte Prima. Scienze — Atti Accad Sci Lett Arti di Palermo Parte I
Atti. Accademia di Scienze, Lettere, ed Arti di Palermo. Parte Prima. Scienze — Atti Accad Sci Lett Arti Palermo Parte I
Atti. Accademia di Scienze, Lettere, ed Arti di Palermo. Parte Prima. Scienze — Atti Accad Sci Lett Arti Palermo Parte Prima Sci
Atti. Accademia di Scienze, Lettere, ed Arti di Palermo. Parte Prima. Scienze. Serie Quarta — Atti Accad Sci Lett Arti Palermo Parte I 4
Atti. Accademia di Scienze, Lettere, ed Arti di Palermo. Serie Quarta. Scienze — Atti Accad Sci Lett Arti Palermo Ser Quarta Sci
Atti. Accademia di Scienze, Lettere, ed Arti di Udine — AAU
Atti. Accademia di Scienze, Lettere, ed Arti di Udine — Atti Ac Udine
Atti. Accademia di Scienze Morali e Politiche della Societa Nazionale di Scienze, Lettere, ed Arti di Napoli — AAN
Atti. Accademia di Scienze Morali e Politiche di Napoli — AASN
Atti. Accademia Fiorentina — AAF
Atti. Accademia Fisio-Medico-Statistica di Milano — Atti Accad Fis-Med-Statist Milano
Atti. Accademia Gioenia di Scienze Naturali in Catania — AAGCA4
Atti. Accademia Gioenia di Scienze Naturali in Catania — Atti Accad Gioenia Sci Nat Catania
Atti. Accademia Italiana della Vite e del Vino (Siena) — Atti Accad Ital Vite Vino (Siena)
Atti. Accademia Ligure di Scienze e Lettere — AALGA7
Atti. Accademia Ligure di Scienze e Lettere — Atti Acc Lig
Atti. Accademia Ligure di Scienze e Lettere — Atti Accad Ligure Sci Lett
Atti. Accademia Ligure di Scienze e Lettere di Genova — AA Lig
Atti. Accademia Ligure di Scienze e Lettere di Genova — AAL
Atti. Accademia Ligure di Scienze e Lettere di Genova — Atti Acad Lig Sci Lettere Genova
Atti. Accademia Ligure di Scienze e Lettere di Genova — Atti Genoa
Atti. Accademia Ligure di Scienze e Lettere (Genoa) — Atti Accad Ligure Sci Lett (Genoa)
Atti. Accademia Mariana Salesiana — AAMS
Atti. Accademia Medica Lombarda — AAMLAR
Atti. Accademia Medica Lombarda — Atti Acc Med Lomb
Atti. Accademia Medica Lombarda — Atti Accad Med Lomb
Atti. Accademia Medica Lombarda — Atti Accad Med Lombarda
Atti. Accademia Nazionale dei Lincei — AANL
Atti. Accademia Nazionale dei Lincei — Ac Naz Linc A
Atti. Accademia Nazionale dei Lincei — Atti Acc Naz Linc
Atti. Accademia Nazionale dei Lincei — Atti Accad Naz Lincei
Atti. Accademia Nazionale dei Lincei — Atti Linc
Atti. Accademia Nazionale dei Lincei. Classe di Scienze Fisiche, Matematiche, e Naturali. Rendiconti — Atti Accad Naz Lincei Cl Sci Fis Mat Nat Rend
Atti. Accademia Nazionale dei Lincei. Memorie. Classe de Scienze Morali, Storiche, e Filologiche — AANLM
Atti. Accademia Nazionale dei Lincei. Memorie. Classe di Scienze Fisiche, Matematiche, e Naturali — Atti Accad Naz Lincei Mem Cl Sci Fis Mat Nat
Atti. Accademia Nazionale dei Lincei. Memorie. Classe di Scienze Fisiche, Matematiche, e Naturali. Sezione 1a. Matematica, Meccanica, Astronomia, Geodesia, e Geofisica — Atti Accad Naz Lincei Mem Cl Sci Fis Mat Nat Sez 1a
Atti. Accademia Nazionale dei Lincei. Memorie. Classe di Scienze Fisiche, Matematiche, e Naturali. Sezione 1a. Matematica, Meccanica, Astronomia, Geodesia, e Geofisica — Atti Accad Naz Lincei Mem Cl Sci Fis Mat Natur Sez 1a
Atti. Accademia Nazionale dei Lincei. Memorie. Classe di Scienze Fisiche, Matematiche, e Naturali. Sezione 2a. Fisica, Chimica, Geologia, Paleontologia, e Mineralogia — Atti Accad Naz Lincei Mem Cl Sci Fis Mat Nat Sez 2a
Atti. Accademia Nazionale dei Lincei. Memorie. Classe di Scienze Fisiche, Matematiche, e Naturali. Sezione 3a — AALBAQ
Atti. Accademia Nazionale dei Lincei. Memorie. Classe di Scienze Fisiche, Matematiche, e Naturali. Sezione 3a. Botanica, Zoologia, Fisiologia, Patologia — Atti Accad Naz Lincei Mem Cl Sci Fis Mat Nat Sez 3a
Atti. Accademia Nazionale dei Lincei. Memorie Classe di Scienze Morale, Storiche, e Filologiche — Atti Accad Naz Lincei Mem Cl Sci Mor Stor Filol
Atti. Accademia Nazionale dei Lincei. Memorie. Classe di Scienze Morali, Storiche, e Filologiche — MAL
Atti. Accademia Nazionale dei Lincei. Memorie. Classe di Scienze Morali, Storiche, e Filologiche — MALinc
Atti. Accademia Nazionale dei Lincei. Memorie. Classe di Scienze Morali, Storiche, e Filologiche — MALincei
Atti. Accademia Nazionale dei Lincei. Notizie degle Scavi di Antichita Communicate — AANLN
Atti. Accademia Nazionale dei Lincei. Rendiconti. Classe di Scienze Fisiche, Matematiche, e Naturali — AANLAW
Atti. Accademia Nazionale dei Lincei. Rendiconti. Classe di Scienze Fisiche, Matematiche, e Naturali — Accad Naz Lincei Atti Cl Sci Fis Mat e Nat Rend
Atti. Accademia Nazionale dei Lincei. Rendiconti. Classe di Scienze Fisiche, Matematiche, e Naturali — Att ANL R F
Atti. Accademia Nazionale dei Lincei. Rendiconti. Classe di Scienze Fisiche, Matematiche, e Naturali — Atti Accad Naz Lincei Rend Cl Sci Fis Mat & Nat
Atti. Accademia Nazionale dei Lincei. Rendiconti. Classe di Scienze Fisiche, Matematiche, e Naturali — Atti Accad Naz Lincei Rend Cl Sci Fis Mat Natur
Atti. Accademia Nazionale dei Lincei. Rendiconti. Classe di Scienze Fisiche, Matematiche, e Naturali (Serie 8) — Atti Accad Naz Lincei Rend Cl Sci Fis Mat Natur (8)
Atti. Accademia Nazionale dei Lincei. Rendiconti. Classe di Scienze Morali, Storiche, e Filologiche — AANLR
Atti. Accademia Nazionale dei Lincei (Serie Ottava) — Atti Accad Naz Lincei (Serie Ottava)
Atti. Accademia Nazionale di Scienze Morali e Politiche (Napoli) — AANMP
Atti. Accademia Nazionale di Scienze Morali e Politiche. Napoli — At Acc Nap
Atti. Accademia Nazionale di Scienze Morali e Politiche (Napoli) — Atti Acc (Nap)
Atti. Accademia Nazionale di Scienze Morali e Politiche (Napoli) — Atti Nap
Atti. Accademia Nazionale Italiana di Entomologia. Rendiconti [*Italy*] — Atti Accad Naz Ital Entomol Rend
Atti. Accademia Olimpica — Atti Acc Olimp
Atti. Accademia Peloritana — Atti Acc Pel
Atti. Accademia Peloritana. Classe di Scienze Medico-Biologiche — Atti Accad Peloritana Cl Sci Med Biol
Atti. Accademia Peloritana dei Pericolanti. Classe di Scienze Fisiche, Matematiche, e Naturali — Atti Accad Peloritana Pericolanti Cl Sci Fis Mat Nat
Atti. Accademia Peloritana dei Pericolanti. Classe di Scienze Fisiche, Matematiche, e Naturali — Atti Accad Peloritana Pericolanti Cl Sci Fis Mat Natur
Atti. Accademia Peloritana dei Pericolanti. Classe di Scienze Medico-Biologiche — Atti Accad Peloritana Pericolanti Cl Sci Med Biol
Atti. Accademia Pontaniana — AAN
Atti. Accademia Pontaniana [*Naples*] — AAP
Atti. Accademia Pontaniana [*Naples*] — AAPont
Atti. Accademia Pontaniana — Atti Ac Pont
Atti. Accademia Pontaniana — Atti Accad Pontan
Atti. Accademia Pontaniana — Atti Accad Pontaniana
Atti. Accademia Pontaniana (Naples) — AAPN
Atti. Accademia Pontaniana (Napoli) — At Acc Napoli
Atti. Accademia Pontificia dei Nuovi Lincei — AAPNL
Atti. Accademia Roveretana degli Agiati — A A Rov
Atti. Accademia Roveretana degli Agiati — AARA
Atti. Accademia Roveretana degli Agiati — Atti Accad Roveretana Agiati
Atti. Accademia Roveretana degli Agiati — Atti Roveretana
Atti. Accademia Scientifica Veneto-Trentino-Istriana — Atti Accad Sci Veneto-Trentino-Istriana
Atti. Associazione Genetica Italiana — AAGNA
Atti. Associazione Genetica Italiana — AAGNA3
Atti. Associazione Genetica Italiana — Att Ass Gen
Atti. Associazione Genetica Italiana — Atti Ass Genet Ital
Atti. Associazione Genetica Italiana — Atti Assoc Genet Ital
Atti. Associazione Italiana di Aerotecnica — Atti Ass Ital Aerotec
Atti. Centro Nazionale Meccanico Agricolo — Atti Cent Naz Mecc Agr
Atti. Centro Ricerche e Documentazione sull'Antichita Classica — Atti C Ant Cl
Atti. Centro Richerche Documentazione sull'Antichita Classica — Atti Ce SDIR
Atti. Centro Richerche Documentazione sull'Antichita Classica — CRDACA
Atti. Centro Studi e Documentazione sull'Italia Romana — Atti C It Rom
Atti. Civici Musei di Storia ed Arte di Trieste — ACMT
Atti. Civici Musei di Storia ed Arte di Trieste — Atti Mus Trieste
Atti. Clinica Odontoiatrica e Societa Napolitana di Stomatologia — Atti Clin Odont
Atti. Clinica Odontoiatrica e Societa Napolitana di Stomatologia — Atti Clin Odontoi Soc Napolitana Stomatol
Atti. Clinica Oto-Rino-Laringoiatrica. Universita di Palermo — Atti Clin Oto-Rino-Laringoiatr Univ Palermo
Atti. Clinica Otorinolaringologica. Reale Universita di Napoli — Atti Clin Otorinolaringol Reale Univ Napoli
Atti. Collegio degli Ingegneri di Milano — Atti Coll Ing Milano
Atti. Colloquio Slavistico di Uppsala — ACSU
Atti. Commissione Conservatrice dei Monumenti e Belle Arti. Provincia di Terra di Lavoro — Atti Com Cons Mon Prov Ter Lavoro
Atti Conferenza Avicola Europea — Atti Conf Avic Eur
Atti. Congresso del Naturalis i Italiani — Atti Cong Nat Ital
Atti. Congresso della Lega Internazionale Contro il Reumatismo — Atti Congr Lega Int Reum
Atti. Congresso dell'Unione Matematica Italiana — Atti Congr Unione Mat Ital
Atti. Congresso Geografico Italiano — Atti Congr Geogr Ital
Atti. Congresso Internazionale degli Americanisti — Atti Congr Int Amer
Atti. Congresso Internazionale dei Matematici — Atti Congr Int Mat
Atti. Congresso Internazionale dei Studi Bizantini — Atti Congr Int Stud Bizantini
Atti. Congresso Internazionale del Vetro — Atti Congr Int Vetro
Atti. Congresso Internazionale della Ceramica — Atti Congr Int Ceram
Atti. Congresso Internazionale delle Materie Plastiche — Atti Congr Int Mater Plast
Atti. Congresso Internazionale delle Materie Plastiche ed Elastomeriche — Atti Congr Int Mater Plast Elastomeriche
Atti. Congresso Internazionale di Estetica — Atti
Atti. Congresso Internazionale di Filosofia — Atti Congr Int Fil
Atti. Congresso Internazionale di Microbiologia — Atti Congr Int Microbiol
Atti. Congresso Internazionale di Panificazione — Atti Congr Int Panif

Atti. Congresso Internazionale di Standardizzazione Immunomicrobiologica — Atti Congr Int Stand Immunomicrobiol
Atti. Congresso Internazionale di Storia della Medicina — Atti Congr Int Stor Med
Atti. Congresso Internazionale di Studi Romanzi — ACISR
Atti. Congresso Internazionale per l'Elettronica — Atti Congr Int Elettron
Atti. Congresso Nazionale. Associazione Scientifica di Produzione Animale — Atti Congr Naz Assoc Sci Prod Anim
Atti. Congresso Nazionale della Sezione Apicultori Italiani — Atti Congr Naz Apic Ital
Atti. Congresso Nazionale della Societa Italiana di Biologia Marina Riassunti — Atti Congr Naz Soc Ital Biol Mar Riass
Atti. Congresso Nazionale di Archeologia Cristiana — ACNAC
Atti. Congresso Nazionale di Chimica Industriale — Atti Congr Naz Chim Ind
Atti. Congresso Nazionale di Chimica Pura ed Applicata — Atti Congr Naz Chim Pura Appl
Atti. Congresso Nazionale di Studi Romani — Atti C N St R
Atti. Congresso Nazionale di Studi Romani — Atti C St R
Atti. Congresso Nazionale d'Igiene — Atti Congr Naz Ig
Atti. Congresso Nazionale Italiano di Entomologia — Atti Congr Naz Ital Entomol
Atti. Congresso Scientifico. Rassegna Internazionale Elettronica e Nucleare — Atti Congr Sci Rass Int Elettron Nucl
Atti. Convegni Lincei [*Rome*] — Atti Convegi Lincei
Atti. Convegno di Studi Filosofici Cristiani — ACSFC
Atti. Convegno di Studi su Umanesimo e Cristianesimo — ACSUC
Atti. Convegno "Fiscalizzazione Oneri Sociala e Riforma della Previdenza Sociale" — Atti Conv Prev Soc
Atti. Convegno Internazionale dei Lipidi Alimentari e del Simposio sulla Genuinita degli Oli per l'Alimentazione — Atti Conv Int Lipidi Aliment Simp Genuinita Oli Aliment
Atti. Convegno Internazionale del Grano Duro — Atti Conv Int Grano Duro
Atti. Convegno Internazionale di Studie Etiopici — ACISE
Atti. Convegno Internazionale per la Pace e la Civita Cristiana — ACIC
Atti. Convegno Nazionale della Apicultori — Atti Conv Naz Apic
Atti. Convegno Nazionale della Qualita — Atti Conv Naz Qual
Atti. Convegno Nazionale di Tecnica Navale — Atti Conv Naz Tec Nav
Atti. Convegno Nazionale sugli Olii Essenziali e Sui Derivati Agrumari — Atti Conv Naz Olii Essenz Sui Deriv Agrum
Atti. Convegno Regionale dell'Alimentazione — Atti Conv Reg Aliment
Atti. Convegno sul Diabete Secondario — Atti Conv Diabete Second
Atti. Convegno sulla Eutrofizzazione in Italia — Atti Conv Eutrofizziazione Ital
Atti. Convegno sulla Qualita — Atti Conv Qual
Atti. Convegno-Scuola su Sintesi di Polimeri — Atti Conv Sc Sint Polim
Atti dei Georgofili — Atti Georgofili
Atti del Congresso di Storia del Risorgimento Italiano — Atti Congr Stor Risorg Ital
Atti del Congresso Internazionale di Scienze Storiche — Atti del Congr Intern di Sc Storiche
Atti del Congresso. Societa Italiana di Ortodonzia — Atti Congr Soc Ital Ortod
Atti del IV Congresso Internazionale delle Scienze Preistoriche e Protoistoriche — Atti VI Congr Internaz Sci Preistor Protoistor
Atti della Accademia delle Scienze dell'Istituto di Bologna. Classe di Scienze Fisiche. Rendiconti. Serie XIV — Atti Accad Sci Istit Bologna Cl Sci Fis Rend 14
Atti della Accademia di Scienze Lettere e Arti di Palermo. Serie V — Atti Accad Sci Lett Arti Palermo Ser 5
Atti della Accademia Pontaniana. Nuova Serie — Atti Accad Pontaniana NS
Atti della Giornate Fitopatologiche — Atti Giornate Fitopatol
Atti della Societa Peloritana di Scienze. Nuova Serie — Atti Soc Peloritana Sci NS
Atti dello VIII Congresso Internazionale di Studi Bizantini — Atti VIII Congr Internaz Studi Bizant
Atti. Deputazione di Storia Patria per la Liguria — ADSPL
Atti. Deputazione di Storia Patria per la Liguria — AS Lig
Atti. Deputazione di Storia Patria per la Liguria. Sezione di Savana — ADSPLS
Atti di Conferenze. Societa Italiana di Fisica — Atti Conf Soc Ital Fis
Atti di Ortopedia e Traumatologia — Atti Ortop Traum
Atti e Memoire. Istituto Veneto — AMIV
Atti e Memoire. Istituto Veneto — Atti Mem Ist Veneto
Atti e Memorie. Accademia di Agricoltura, Commercio, ed Arti di Verona — Atti Mem Accad Agric Commer Arti Verona
Atti e Memorie. Accademia di Agricoltura, Scienze, e Lettere. Verona — AMAAV
Atti e Memorie. Accademia di Agricoltura, Scienze, e Lettere (Verona) — Atti Mem Accad Agric Sci Lett (Verona)
Atti e Memorie. Accademia di Agricoltura, Scienze, e Lettere (Verona) — Atti Memo Acad Agric Sci Lett (Verona)
Atti e Memorie. Accademia di Padova — AAPad
Atti e Memorie. Accademia di Scienze, Lettere, ed Arti di Modena — AAM
Atti e Memorie. Accademia di Scienze, Lettere, ed Arti di Modena — AAMod
Atti e Memorie. Accademia di Scienze, Lettere, ed Arti di Modena — AMAM
Atti e Memorie. Accademia di Scienze, Lettere, ed Arti in Modena — AMA Mod
Atti e Memorie. Accademia di Scienze, Lettere, ed Arti in Modena — Atti Mem Accad Mod
Atti e Memorie. Accademia di Storia dell'Arte Sanitaria — AMAAA
Atti e Memorie. Accademia di Storia dell'Arte Sanitaria — Atti Acc Stor Arte San
Atti e Memorie. Accademia di Storia dell'Arte Sanitaria — Atti Mem Accad Stor Arte Sanit
Atti e Memorie. Accademia Nazionale di Scienze, Lettere, ed Arti (Modena) — Atti Mem Accad Naz Sci Lett Arti (Modena)
Atti e Memorie. Accademia Patavina — AAPat
Atti e Memorie. Accademia Patavina di Scienze, Lettere, ed Arti — AMAP
Atti e Memorie. Accademia Patavina di Scienze, Lettere, ed Arti — Atti Mem Accad Patav Sci Lett Arti
Atti e Memorie. Accademia Patavina di Scienze, Lettere, ed Arti — Atti Mem Accad Patavina Sci Lett Arti
Atti e Memorie. Accademia Patavina di Scienze, Lettere ed Arti. Classe di Scienze Morali, Lettere, ed Arti — Atti Mem Accad Patavina Sci Lett Arti Cl Sci Mor Lett Arti
Atti e Memorie. Accademia Petrarca — AMAPe
Atti e Memorie. Accademia Toscana di Scienze e Lettere La Colombaria [*Florence*] — Atti Acc Tosc
Atti e Memorie. Accademia Toscana la Colombaria — AATC
Atti e Memorie. Accademia Toscana la Colombaria — AMAT
Atti e Memorie. Accademia Vergiliana di Scienze, Lettere, ed Arte di Mantova — AMVM
Atti e Memorie. Accademia Virgiliana di Mantova — Atti Mem Accad Virgiliana Mantova
Atti e Memorie del Congresso Nazionale del Risorgimento — Atti Congr Naz Risorg
Atti e Memorie della Regia Deputazione di Storia Patria per le Province Modenesi — Atti Mem Stor Patria Prov Modenesi
Atti e Memorie dell'Accademia Patavina di Scienze, Lettere ed Arti. Classe di Scienze Morali — Atti Mem Accad Patavina
Atti e Memorie dell'Accademia Toscana di Scienze e Lettere La Colombaria — Atti Mem Accad Tosc Sci Lettere La Colombaria
Atti e Memorie dell'Arcadia — AMA
Atti e Memorie. Deputanzione di Storia Patria per le Provincie dell'Emilia — ADSPE
Atti e Memorie. Deputanzione di Storia Patria per l'Emilia e la Romagna — ADSPER
Atti e Memorie. Deputanzione di Storia Patria per la Provincie delle Marche — Am Marche
Atti e Memorie. Deputazione di Storia Patria per le Antiche Provincie Modenensi — AMD Mod
Atti e Memorie. Deputazione di Storia Patria per le Antiche Provincie Modenesi — ADSPM
Atti e Memorie. Deputazione di Storia Patria per le Antiche Provincie Modenesi — AMDM
Atti e Memorie. Deputazione di Storia Patria per le Antiche Provincie Modenesi — AMDSPAM
Atti e Memorie. Deputazione di Storia Patria per le Antiche Provincie Modenesi — AMSAPM
Atti e Memorie. Deputazione di Storia Patria per le Antiche Provincie Modenesi — Atti Mem Deputazione Stor Antiche Prov Modenesi
Atti e Memorie. Deputazione di Storia Patria per le Antiche Provincie Modenesi — Atti Mem Deputazione Stor Patria Antiche Prov Modenesi
Atti e Memorie. Deputazione di Storia Patria per le Antiche Provincie Modenesi — Atti Mem Modena
Atti e Memorie. Deputazione di Storia Patria per le Marche — ADSPMa
Atti e Memorie. Deputazione di Storia Patria per le Provincie delle Marche — AMDSPPM
Atti e Memorie. Deputazione di Storia Patria per le Provincie di Romagna — ADSPR
Atti e Memorie. Deputazione di Storia Patria per le Provincie di Romagna — AMSPR
Atti e Memorie. Deputazione di Storia Patria. Provincie di Romagna — AM Rom
Atti e Memorie. Deputazione di Storia Patria. Provincie di Romagna — Atti Mem Romagna
Atti e Memorie. Istituto Italiano di Numismatica — AII Num
Atti e Memorie. Istituto Italiano di Numismatica — AIIN
Atti e Memorie. Istituto Italiano di Numismatica — AIN
Atti e Memorie. Istituto Italiano di Numismatica — AMIIN
Atti e Memorie. Istituto Italiano di Numismatica — Atti e Mem Ist Ital Num
Atti e Memorie. Istituto Italiano di Numismatica — Atti e Mem Ital Num
Atti e Memorie. Reale Accademia di Mantova — Atti e Mem Mantova
Atti e Memorie. Reale Accademia di Mantova — Atti Mem M
Atti e Memorie. Reale Accademia di Scienze, Lettere, ed Arti de Modena — Atti Mem Accad Sci Lett Arti Modena
Atti e Memorie. Reale Accademia di Scienze, Lettere, ed Arti de Modena — Atti Mod
Atti e Memorie. Reale Accademia di Scienze, Lettere, ed Arti in Modena — Atti Mem R Accad Sci Lett Arti Modena
Atti e Memorie. Reale Accademia di Scienze, Lettere, ed Arti in Padova — AAP
Atti e Memorie. Reale Accademia di Scienze, Lettere, ed Arti in Padova — Atti Mem Accad Sci Lett Arti Padova
Atti e Memorie. Reale Accademia Petrarca di Lettere, Arti, e Scienze — Atti Mem Accad Petrarca Lett Arti Sci
Atti e Memorie. Reale Accademia Virgiliana — Atti Mem Acc Virg
Atti e Memorie. Reale Accademia Virgiliana — Atti Mem R Accad Virgiliana
Atti e Memorie. Reale Accademia Virgiliana di Scienze, Lettere, ed Arti di Montova — AAM
Atti e Memorie. Reale Deputazione di Storia Patria per le Marche — AMSM
Atti e Memorie. Reale Deputazione di Storia Patria per le Provincie di Romagna — Atti Mem Deputazione Stor Romagna
Atti e Memorie. Reale Deputazione di Storia Patria per le Provincie Modenesi — Atti Mem Deputazione Stor Modenesi
Atti e Memorie. Reale Deputazione di Storia Patria per le Provincie Modenesi e Parmensi — Atti Mem Deputazione Stor Modenesi Parmensi
Atti e Memorie. Reale Deputazione di Storia Patria per l'Emilia e la Romagna — Atti Mem Deputazione Stor Emilia Romagna
Atti e Memorie. Reale Deputazione di Storia Patria per l'Emilia et la Romagna — AMSER
Atti e Memorie. Regia Accademia di Scienze, Lettere, ed Arti in Padova — Atti Mem Regia Accad Sci Lett Arti Padova
Atti e Memorie. Societa Dalmata di Storia — AMSDSP
Atti e Memorie. Societa Istriana di Archeologia e Storia Patria — AMSI
Atti e Memorie. Societa Istriana di Archeologia e Storia Patria — AMSIA
Atti e Memorie. Societa Istriana di Archeologia e Storia Patria — AMSIstriana

Atti e Memorie. Societa Istriana di Archeologia e Storia Patria — ASIA
Atti e Memorie. Societa Istriana di Archeologia e Storia Patria — Atti Istr
Atti e Memorie. Societa Istriana di Archeologia e Storia Patria — Atti Mem Istriana
Atti e Memorie. Societa Istriana di Archeologia e Storia Patria — Atti Mem Soc Istriana
Atti e Memorie. Societa Istriana di Archeologia e Storia Patria — Atti Soc Istr
Atti e Memorie. Societa Magna Grecia — ASMG
Atti e Memorie. Societa Magna Grecia — Att Mem Soc Magna Grecia
Atti e Memorie. Societa Magna Grecia — Atti M Gr
Atti e Memorie. Societa Magna Grecia — Atti M Grecia
Atti e Memorie. Societa Magna Grecia — Atti Mem Soc Mag Gr
Atti e Memorie. Societa Magna Grecia — Atti Mem Soc Magna Grecia
Atti e Memorie. Societa Magna Grecia — Atti S M Graecia
Atti e Memorie. Societa Magna Grecia — Atti SMG
Atti e Memorie. Societa Tiburtina di Storia e d'Arte — AST
Atti e Memorie. Societa Tiburtina di Storia e d'Arte — Atti Mem Soc Tiburtina
Atti e Memorie. Societa Tiburtina di Storia e d'Arte — Atti Soc Tib
Atti e Memorie. Societa Tiburtina di Storia e d'Arte — Atti Soc Tiburtina
Atti e Memorie. Societa Tiburtina di Storia e d'Arte. Tivoli — AMST
Atti e Rassegna Tecnica. Societa degli Ingegneri e degli Architetti in Torino — Atti Rass Tec Soc Ing Archit Torino
Atti e Relazioni. Accademia Pugliese delle Scienze. Parte 2. Classe di Scienze Fisiche, Mediche, e Naturali — Atti Relaz Accad Pugliese Sci Parte 2
Atti. Facolta d'Ingegneria. Universita di Bologna — Atti Fac Ing Univ Bologna
Atti. Fondazion Giorgio Ronchi e Contributi. Istituto Nazionale de Ottica — Atti Fond Ronchi
Atti. Fondazione Giorgio Ronchi — Atti Fond Giorgio Ronchi
Atti. Fondazione Giorgio Ronchi — Atti Fond Ronchi
Atti. Fondazione Giorgio Ronchi e Contributi dell'Istituto Nazionale di Ottica — Atti Fond Giorgio Ronchi & Contrib Ist Naz Ottica
Atti. Giornate dell'Energia Nucleare — Atti Giornate Energ Nucl
Atti. Imperiale Accademia Pistojese di Scienze e Lettere — Atti Imp Accad Pistojese Sci
Atti. Imperiale Regia Accademia di Scienze, Lettere, ed Arti Degli Agiati di Rovereto — Atti Imp Regia Accad Rovereto
Atti. IR Accademia di Scienze. Lettere ed Arti degli Agiati in Rovereto — Atti IR Accad Sci Lett Arti Agiati Rovereto
Atti. Istituto Botanico e Laboratorio Crittogamico. Universita di Pavia — Atti Ist Bot Lab Crittogam Univ Pavia
Atti. Istituto Botanico e Laboratorio Crittogamico. Universita di Pavia — Atti Ist Bot Labor Crittog Univ Pavia
Atti. Istituto Botanico e Laboratorio Crittogamico. Universita di Pavia — IBCPAG
Atti. Istituto Botanico Giovanni Briosi e Laboratorio Crittogamica Italiano. Reale Universita di Pavia — Atti Ist Bot Giovanni Briosi
Atti. Istituto Botanico. Universita di Pavia — Atti Ist Bot Univ Pavia
Atti. Istituto Botanico. Universita. Laboratorio Crittogamico. Pavia — Atti Ist Bot Univ Lab Crittogam Pavia
Atti. Istituto di Geologia. Universita di Genova — Atti Ist Geol Univ Genova
Atti. Istituto Geologico. Universita di Pavia — AIGPAV
Atti. Istituto Geologico. Universita di Pavia — Atti Ist Geol Univ Pavia
Atti. Istituto Veneto di Scienze, Lettere, ed Arti — Atti Ist Veneto
Atti. Istituto Veneto di Scienze, Lettere, ed Arti — Atti Ist Veneto Sci Lett Arti
Atti. Istituto Veneto di Scienze, Lettere, ed Arti — Atti R Ist Ven
Atti. Istituto Veneto di Scienze, Lettere, ed Arti — Atti Ven
Atti. Istituto Veneto di Scienze, Lettere, ed Arti — Atti Venezia
Atti. Istituto Veneto di Scienze, Lettere, ed Arti. Classe di Scienze Fisiche, Matematiche, e Naturali — AIVNDZ
Atti. Istituto Veneto di Scienze, Lettere, ed Arti. Classe di Scienze Matematiche e Naturali — AIVLAQ
Atti. Istituto Veneto di Scienze, Lettere, ed Arti. Classe di Scienze Matematiche e Naturali — Atti Ist Veneto Sci Lett Arti Cl Sci Mat Nat
Atti. Istituto Veneto di Scienze, Lettere, ed Arti (Venezia). Classe di Scienze Fisiche, Matematiche, e Naturali — Atti Ist Veneto Sci Lett Arti (Venezia) Cl Sci Fis Mat Nat
Atti. Museo Civico di Storia Naturale di Trieste — Atti Mus Civico Storia Nat Trieste
Atti. Museo Civico di Storia Naturale di Triesti — ACVNAO
Atti. Museo Civico di Storia Naturale di Triesti — Atti Mus Civ Stor Nat Triesti
Atti Notizie. Associazione Italiana di Metallurgia — Atti Not Assoc Ital Metall
Atti. Pontificia Accademia delle Scienze — Atti Pontif Accad Sci
Atti. Pontificia Accademia delle Scienze. Nuovi Lincei — Atti Pontif Accad Sci Nuovi Lincei
Atti. Pontificia Accademia Romana dei Nuovi Lincei — Atti Pontif Accad Romana Nuovi Lincei
Atti. Pontificia Accademia Romana di Archeologia — APAA
Atti. Pontificia Accademia Romana di Archeologia — APARA
Atti. Pontificia Accademia Romana di Archeologia — Atti Acc Pont
Atti. Pontificia Accademia Romana di Archeologia — Atti PARA
Atti. Pontificia Accademia Romana di Archeologia — Atti Pont Acc
Atti. Pontificia Accademia Romana di Archeologia — Rend Pontif Accad
Atti. Pontificia Accademia Romana di Archeologia — Rendic Acc Pont
Atti. Pontificia Accademia Romana di Archeologia — Rendiconti Pont Acc Arch
Atti. Pontificia Accademia Romana di Archeologia. Memorie — Mem Pont Acc
Atti. Pontificia Accademia Romana di Archeologia. Rendiconti — APARAR
Atti. Real Accademia di Archeologia, Lettere, e Belle Arti (Napoli) — AAAN
Atti. Real Accademia d'Italia — AAI
Atti. Real Accademia d'Italia. Memorie. Classe di Scienze Morali, Storiche, e Filologiche — AAIM
Atti. Real Accademia d'Italia. Notizie degli Scavi di Antichita — AAIN
Atti. Real Accademia d'Italia. Rendiconti. Classe di Scienze Morali e Storiche — AAIR
Atti. Real Istituto d'Incoraggiamento alle Scienze Naturali di Napoli — Atti Real Ist Incoragg Sci Nat Napoli
Atti. Reale Accademia dei Geogrofili — Atti R Accad Geogrofili
Atti. Reale Accademia dei Geogrofili di Firenze — Atti Accad Geogrofili
Atti. Reale Accademia dei Geogrofili di Firenze — Atti Reale Accad Geogrof Firenze
Atti. Reale Accademia dei Lincei — Atti Acc Linc
Atti. Reale Accademia dei Lincei — Atti R Accad Lincei
Atti. Reale Accademia dei Lincei — Atti Reale Accad Lincei
Atti. Reale Accademia dei Lincei. Memorie. Classe di Scienze Fisiche, Matematiche, e Naturali — Atti Accad Lincei Mem Cl Sci Fis Mat Natur
Atti. Reale Accademia dei Lincei. Memorie. Classe di Scienze Fisiche, Matematiche, e Naturali — Atti R Accad Lincei Mem Cl Sc Fis Mat e Nat
Atti. Reale Accademia dei Lincei. Memorie. Classe di Scienze Morali, Storiche, e Filologiche [*Rome*] — AALM
Atti. Reale Accademia dei Lincei. Memorie. Classe di Scienze Morali, Storiche, e Filologiche — Atti Accad Lincei Mem Cl Sci Morali Stor Filol
Atti. Reale Accademia dei Lincei. Notizie degli Scavi [*Rome*] — ARALNS
Atti. Reale Accademia dei Lincei. Notizie degli Scavi — ARANS
Atti. Reale Accademia dei Lincei. Notizie degli Scavi di Antichita. Classe di Scienze Morali, Storiche, e Filologiche [*Rome*] — AALN
Atti. Reale Accademia dei Lincei. Rendiconti. Classe di Scienze Fisiche, Matematiche, e Naturale — Atti Reale Accad Lincei Rendiconti Cl Sci Fis
Atti. Reale Accademia dei Lincei. Rendiconti. Classe di Scienze Fisiche, Matematiche, e Naturali — Atti Accad Lincei Rendic Cl Sci Fis Mat Natur
Atti. Reale Accademia dei Lincei. Rendiconti. Classe di Scienze Fisiche, Matematiche, e Naturali — Atti R Accad Lincei Rendic Cl Sc Fis Mat e Nat
Atti. Reale Accademia dei Lincei. Rendiconti. Classe di Scienze Morali, Storiche, e Filologiche — Atti Accad Lincei Rendic Cl Sci Morali Stor Filol
Atti. Reale Accademia dei Lincei. Rendiconti delle Sedute Solenni — Atti Accad Lincei Rendic Sedute Solenni
Atti. Reale Accademia dei Lincei (Roma). Memorie. Classe di Scienze Fisiche, Matematiche, e Naturali — Atti R Accad Lincei (Roma) Mem Cl Sc Fis Mat e Nat
Atti. Reale Accademia dei Lincei (Roma). Rendiconti. Classe di Scienze Fisiche, Matematiche, e Naturali — Atti R Accad Lincei (Roma) Rendic Cl Sc Fis Mat e Nat
Atti. Reale Accademia della Crusca — Atti Accad Crusca
Atti. Reale Accademia della Scienze di Torino — Atti Tor
Atti. Reale Accademia delle Scienze di Torino — ARAST
Atti. Reale Accademia delle Scienze di Torino. Classe di Scienze Fisiche, Matematiche, e Naturali — Atti R Accad Sci Torino Cl Sci Fis Mat Nat
Atti. Reale Accademia delle Scienze di Torino. Classe di Scienze Morali, Storiche, e Filologiche — AAST
Atti. Reale Accademia delle Scienze di Torino. Classe di Scienze Morali, Storiche, e Filologiche — Atti Accad Sci Torino Cl Sci Morali Stor Filol
Atti. Reale Accademia delle Scienze e Belle-Lettere di Napoli — Atti Reale Accad Sci Napoli
Atti. Reale Accademia delle Scienze Medico-Chirurgiche (Napoli) — Atti Accad Sci Med Chir (Napoli)
Atti. Reale Accademia di Archeologia, Lettere, e Belle Arti di Napoli — AAN
Atti. Reale Accademia di Archeologia, Lettere, e Belle Arti di Napoli — Atti Acc Arch N
Atti. Reale Accademia di Archeologia, Lettere, e Belle Arti di Napoli — Atti Acc Arch Napoli
Atti. Reale Accademia di Scienze, Lettere, e Arti di Palermo — Atti R Accad Sci Lett Arti Palermo
Atti. Reale Accademia d'Italia. Memorie. Classe di Scienze Fisiche, Matematiche, e Naturali — Atti Accad Ital Mem Cl Sci Fis Mat Natur
Atti. Reale Accademia d'Italia. Memorie. Classe di Scienze Morali, Storiche, e Filologiche — Atti Accad Ital Mem Cl Sci Morali Stor Filol
Atti. Reale Accademia d'Italia. Rendiconti. Classe di Scienze Fisiche, Matematiche, e Naturali — Atti Accad Ital Rendic Cl Sci Fis Mat Natur
Atti. Reale Accademia d'Italia. Rendiconti. Classe di Scienze Fisiche, Matematiche, e Naturali — Atti R Accad Ital Rend Cl Sci Fis Mat Nat
Atti. Reale Accademia d'Italia. Rendiconti. Classe di Scienze Morali — Rend Acc It
Atti. Reale Accademia d'Italia. Rendiconti. Classe di Scienze Morali, Storiche, e Filologiche — Atti Accad Ital Rendic Cl Sci Morali Stor Filol
Atti. Reale Accademia d'Italia (Roma). Memorie. Classe di Scienze Morali e Storiche — AAR
Atti. Reale Accademia Economico-Agraria dei Geogrofili di Firenze — Atti Accad Econ Agrar Geogrofili Firenze
Atti. Reale Accademia Economico-Agraria dei Geogrofili di Firenze — Atti Reale Accad Econ Agrar Geogrof Firenze
Atti. Reale Accademia Lucchese di Scienze, Lettere, ed Arti — Atti Reale Accad Lucchese Sci
Atti. Reale Accademia Medico-Chirurgica (Napoli) — Atti Accad Med Chir (Napoli)
Atti. Reale Accademia Nazionale dei Lincei — Atti Accad Lincei
Atti. Reale Accademia Nazionale dei Lincei. Classe di Scienze Morali, Storiche, e Filologiche [*Rome*] — ANL
Atti. Reale Accademia Nazionale dei Lincei. Classe di Scienze Morali, Storiche, e Filologiche [*Rome*] — ANLA
Atti. Reale Accademia Nazionale dei Lincei. Memorie. Classe di Scienze Fisiche, Matematiche, e Naturale — Atti Reale Accad Naz Lincei Mem Cl Sci Fis
Atti. Reale Accademia Nazionale dei Lincei. Memorie. Classe di Scienze Fisiche, Matematiche, e Naturali — Atti Accad Naz Lincei Mem Cl Sci Fis Mat Natur
Atti. Reale Accademia Nazionale dei Lincei. Memorie. Classe di Scienze Fisiche, Matematiche, e Naturali — Atti R Accad Naz Lincei Mem Cl Sci Fis Mat Nat
Atti. Reale Accademia Nazionale dei Lincei. Rendiconti. Classe di Scienze Fisiche, Matematiche, e Naturali — Atti Accad Naz Lincei Rendic Cl Sci Fis Mat Natur

Atti. Reale Accademia Nazionale dei Lincei. Rendiconti. Classe di Scienze Fisiche, Matematiche, e Naturali — Atti R Accad Naz Lincei Rend Cl Sci Fis Mat Nat
Atti. Reale Accademia Nazionale dei Lincei. Rendiconti. Classe di Scienze Fisiche, Matematische, e Naturale — Atti Reale Accad Naz Lincei Rendiconti Cl Sci Fis
Atti. Reale Accademia Nazionale dei Lincei. Rendiconti. Classe di Scienze Morali, Storiche, e Filologiche — Atti Accad Naz Lincei Rendic Cl Sci Morali Stor Filol
Atti. Reale Accademia Nazionale dei Lincei. Rendiconti delle Sedute Solenni [*A publication*] — Atti Accad Naz Lincei Rendic Sedute Solenni
Atti. Reale Accademia Nazionale dei Lincei (Roma) — Atti R Accad Naz Lincei (Roma)
Atti. Reale Accademia Peloritana [*Messina*] — A A Pel
Atti. Reale Accademia Peloritana — Atti Accad Peloritana
Atti. Reale Accademia Peloritana — Atti R Accad Peloritana
Atti. Reale Accademia Peloritana. Classe di Scienze Fisiche, Matematiche, e Biologiche — Atti R Accad Peloritana Cl Sci Fis Mat Biol
Atti. Reale Accademia Peloritana. Classe di Scienze Fisiche, Matematiche, e Biologiche PB — Atti Accad Peloritana Cl Sci Fis Mat Biol
Atti. Reale Istituto d'Incoraggiamento di Napoli — Atti R Ist Incoraggiamento Napoli
Atti. Reale Istituto Veneto di Scienze, Lettere, ed Arti. Classe di Scienze Morali e Lettere — AIV
Atti. Reale Istituto Veneto di Scienze, Lettere, ed Arti. Classe di Scienze Morali e Lettere — AIVSML
Atti. Reale Scuola Normale Superiore di Pisa — ARSNSP
Atti. Reale Universita di Genova — Atti R Univ Genova
Atti. Regia Accademia dei Fisiocritici in Siena — Atti R Accad Fisiocrit Siena
Atti. Regia Accademia dei Fisiocritici in Siena — Atti Regia Accad Fisiocrit Siena
Atti. Regia Accademia dei Fisiocritici in Siena. Sezione Medico-Fisica — Atti Regia Accad Fisiocrit Siena Sez Med Fis
Atti. Rendiconti. Accademia Nazionale dei Lincei. Classe di Scienze Fisiche, Matematiche, e Naturali — Atti Rend Accad Naz Lincei Cl Sci Fis Mat Natur
Atti. Riuione degli Scienziati Italiani — Atti Riunione Sci Ital
Atti Scientifici. Societa Elvetica di Scienze Naturali — Atti Sci Soc Elv Sci Nat
Atti. Seminario Matematico e Fisico. Universita di Modena — ASMMA
Atti. Seminario Matematico e Fisico. Universita di Modena — Atti Sem Mat Fis Univ Modena
Atti. Seminario Matematico e Fisico. Universita di Modena — Atti Semin Mat & Fis Univ Modena
Atti. Simposio Conferme e Prospettive nell'Uso della Calcitonina — Atti Simp Conferme Prospettive Uso Calcitonina
Atti. Simposio Internazionale di Agrochimica — Atti Simp Int Agrochim
Atti. Simposio Internazionale di Zootecnia — ASTZA5
Atti. Simposio Internazionale di Zootecnia — Atti Simp Int Zootec
Atti. Simposio Nazionale sul C3 — Atti Simp Naz C3
Atti. Sindacati Ingegneri di Lombardia — Atti Sind Ing Lombardia
Atti. Societa Astronomica Italiana — Atti Soc Astron Ital
Atti. Societa dei Naturalisti di Modena — Atti Soc Naturalisti Modena
Atti. Societa dei Naturalisti e Matematici di Modena — ASNMAP
Atti. Societa dei Naturalisti e Matematici di Modena — Atti Soc Nat Mat Modena
Atti. Societa dei Naturalisti e Matematici di Modena — Atti Soc Naturalisti Mat Modena
Atti. Societa di Scienze Naturali Toscana Residente in Pisa. Memorie — Atti Soc Sci Nat Toscana Pisa Mem
Atti. Societa Elvetica delle Scienze Naturali — Atti Soc Elvet Sci Nat
Atti. Societa Elvetica di Scienze Naturali — Atti Soc Elv Sci Nat
Atti. Societa Elvetica di Scienze Naturali. Parte Scientifica — Atti Soc Elv Sci Nat Parte Sci
Atti. Societa fra i Cultori delle Scienze Mediche e Naturali in Cagliari — Atti Soc Cultori Sc Med e Nat Cagliari
Atti. Societa Italiana delle Scienze Veterinarie — ASISAI
Atti. Societa Italiana delle Scienze Veterinarie — Atti Soc Ital Sci Vet
Atti. Societa Italiana di Anatomia — Atti Soc Ital Anat
Atti. Societa Italiana di Buiatria — Atti Soc Ital Buiatria
Atti. Societa Italiana di Cancerologia. Congresso Nazionale — Atti Soc Ital Cancerol Congr Naz
Atti. Societa Italiana di Cardiologia — ASOCAY
Atti. Societa Italiana di Cardiologia — Atti Soc Ital Cardiol
Atti. Societa Italiana di Scienze Naturali (Milano) — Atti Soc Ital Sc Nat (Milano)
Atti. Societa Italiana di Scienze Naturali. Museo Civico di Storia Naturale di Milano — ASIMAY
Atti. Societa Italiana di Scienze Naturali. Museo Civico di Storia Naturale di Milano — Atti Soc Ital Sci Nat Mus Civ Stor Nat Milano
Atti. Societa Italiana di Scienze Naturali. Museo Civile di Storia Naturale [*A publication*] — Atti Soc Ital Sci Nat
Atti. Societa Italiana di Statistica — ASIS
Atti. Societa Italiana di Storia Critica delle Scienze Mediche e Naturali — Atti Soc Ital Stor Crit Sci Med Natur
Atti. Societa Italiana per il Progresso delle Scienze — ASPS
Atti. Societa Italiana per il Progresso delle Scienze — Atti Soc Ital Prog Sci
Atti. Societa Italiana per il Progresso delle Scienze — Atti Soc Ital Progr Sci
Atti. Societa Ligure di Storia Patria — ASLig
Atti. Societa Ligure di Storia Patria — ASLSP
Atti. Societa Ligure di Storia Patria — Atti Soc Lig Stor Patria
Atti. Societa Ligustica di Scienze Naturali e Geografiche — Atti Soc Ligust Sc Nat e Geogr
Atti. Societa Linguistica di Scienze e Lettere di Genova — ASLG
Atti. Societa Lombarda di Scienze Mediche e Biologiche — Atti Soc Lomb Sci Med Biol
Atti. Societa Medico-Chirurgica di Padova e Facolta di Medicina e Chirurgia della Universita di Padova — Atti Soc Med-Chir Padova Fac Med Chir Univ Padova
Atti. Societa Oftalmologica Lombarda — Atti Soc Oftalmol Lomb
Atti. Societa Peloritana di Scienze Fisiche, Matematiche, e Naturali — ASPSA
Atti. Societa Peloritana di Scienze Fisiche, Matematiche, e Naturali — ASPSAJ
Atti. Societa Peloritana di Scienze Fisiche, Matematiche, e Naturali — Atti Soc Peloritan Sci Fis Mat e Nat
Atti. Societa Peloritana di Scienze Fisiche, Matematiche, e Naturali — Atti Soc Peloritana Sci Fis Mat e Nat
Atti. Societa Peloritana di Scienze Fisiche, Matematiche, e Naturali — Atti Soc Peloritana Sci Fis Mat Nat
Atti. Societa Peloritana di Scienze Fisiche, Matematiche, e Naturali — Atti Soc Peloritana Sci Fis Mat Natur
Atti. Societa per la Preistoria e Protostoria della Regione Friuli-Venezia Giulia — Atti Soc Friuli
Atti. Societa Piemontese di Archeologia e Belle Arti — ASPA
Atti. Societa Piemontese di Archeologia e Belle Arti — ASPABA
Atti. Societa Pontaniana. Napoli — Atti Napoli
Atti. Societa Salernitana di Medicina e Chirurgia — Atti Soc Salernitana Med Chir
Atti. Societa Toscana di Scienze Naturali di Pisa. Memorie — Atti Soc Tosc Sci Nat Pisa Mem
Atti. Societa Toscana di Scienze Naturali. Processi Verbali e Memorie. Serie B — ATNBAX
Atti. Societa Toscana di Scienze Naturali. Processi Verbali e Memorie. Serie B — Atti Soc Toscana Sci Nat P V Mem Ser B
Atti. Societa Toscana di Scienze Naturali Residente in Pisa — Atti Soc Toscana Sci Nat Pisa
Atti. Societa Toscana di Scienze Naturali Residente in Pisa. Memorie — Atti Soc Toscana Sci Nat Pisa Mem
Atti. Societa Toscana di Scienze Naturali Residente in Pisa. Memorie. Serie A — ATMAAP
Atti. Societa Toscana di Scienze Naturali Residente in Pisa. Memorie. Serie A — Atti Soc Toscana Sci Nat Pisa Mem Ser A
Atti. Societa Toscana di Scienze Naturali Residente in Pisa. Memorie. Serie A — Atti Soc Toscana Sci Nat Resid Pisa Mem Ser A
Atti. Societa Toscana di Scienze Naturali Residente in Pisa. Memorie. Serie B — Atti Soc Toscana Sci Nat Pisa Mem Ser B
Atti. Societa Toscana di Scienze Naturali Residente in Pisa. Processi Verbali — Atti Soc Toscana Sci Nat Pisa P V
Atti. Societa Toscana di Scienze Naturali Residente in Pisa. Processi Verbali e Memorie. Serie A — Atti Soc Toscana Sci Nat Pisa P V Mem Ser A
Atti. Sodalizio Glottologico Milanese — ASGLM
Atti. Sodalizio Glottologico Milanese — ASGM
Atti. Solenne Distribuzione di Premi d'Agricoltura e d'Industria — Atti Solenne Distrib Premi Agric Industr
Atti. Symposium Internazionale sull'Estere di Cori e sui Glucidi Fosforilati — Atti Symp Int Estere Cori Glucidi Fosforilati
Atti. V Simposio Internazionale di Agrochimica su "Lo Zolfo in Agricoltura" — Atti V Simp Int Agrochim "Zolfo in Agricoltura"
Atti. VI Convegno della Salute — Atti Conv Salute
Atti. X Congresso Internazionale di Geografia [*Rome*] — ACIG
Attic Black Figured Lekythoi — ABL
Attic Black Figured Vase-Painters — ABF
Attic Black-Figure Vase Painters — ABV
Attic Red-Figure Vase Painters — ARFVP
Attic Red-Figure Vase Painters — ARV
Attic Red-Figure Vase Painters — ARVP
Attorney General's Information Service — AGIS
Attualita Dentale — Attual Dent
Attualita di Chemioterapia — Attual Chemioter
Attualita di Laboratorio — Attual Lab
Attualita di Ostetricia e Ginecologia — AOSGA4
Attualita di Ostetricia e Ginecologia — Attual Ostet Ginecol
Attualita Medica — Attual Med
Attualita Zoologiche — Attual Zool
Attualita Zoologiche — ATZOAU
Atualidades Agronomicas [*Sao Paulo*] — ATAGDK
Atualidades Agronomicas — Atual Agron
Atualidades Agronomicas (Sao Paulo) — Atual Agron (Sao Paulo)
Atualidades Agropecuarias — Atual Agropecu
Atualidades Agroveterinarias — Atual Agrovet
Atualidades de Fisico-Quimica Organica — Atual Fis Quim Org
Atualidades Medicas — ATMED6
Atualidades Medicas — Atual Med
Atualidades Medico Sanitarias — ATMSAB
Atualidades Medico Sanitarias — Atual Med Sanit
Atualidades Veterinarias — Atual Vet
Atualidades Veterinarias — ATVED
Atualidades Veterinarias [*Sao Paulo*] — ATVEDH
Atualidades Veterinarias (Sao Paulo) — Atual Vet (Sao Paulo)
Atuaqunik. Newsletter of Northern Quebec — ATQK
ATW. Atomwirtschaft, Atomtechnik — ATW Atomwirtsch Atomtech
Atypical Mycobacteria. Proceedings. Symposium — Atyp Mycobacteria Proc Symp
ATZ. Automobiltechnische Zeitschrift — ATZ Automobiltech Z
Au Courant — AUC
AUA [*Association of University Architects*] **Newsletter** — AUA Newsl
AUAA [*American Urological Association Allied*] **Journal** — AUAA J
Auburn University. Agricultural Experiment Station. Circular — Auburn Univ Agric Exp Stn Circ
Auburn University. Agricultural Experiment Station. Leaflet — Auburn Univ Agric Exp Stn Leafl
Auburn University. Agricultural Experiment Station. Progress Report Series — Auburn Univ Agric Exp Stn Prog Rep Ser
Auburn University. Engineering Experiment Station. Bulletin — Auburn Univ Eng Exp Stn Bull
Auburn University. Water Resources Research Institute. WRRI Bulletin — Auburn Univ Water Resour Res Inst WRRI Bull

Auckland Metro [*New Zealand*] — AK Metro
Auckland Star — Ak St
Auckland University. Law Review — Auck UL Rev
Auckland University. Law Review — Auck ULR
Auckland University. Law Review — Auckland U L Rev
Auckland University. Law Review — Auckland Univ L Rev
Auckland-Waikato Historical Journal — Ak Waik Hist J
Auctarium Bibliothecae Hagiographicae Graecae — Auctar
Auctores Britannici Medii Aevi — ABMA
Audience — Aud
Audience — Audn
Audio — Au
Audio — AUDUA
Audio — IAUD
Audio Engineering — Audio Engg
Audio Engineering Society. Journal — Audio Eng Soc J
Audio Engineering Society. Preprint — Audio Eng Soc Prepr
Audio Marketnews — Aud Mark
Audio Scene Canada — Audio Scene Can
Audio Video Canada — Audio Video Can
Audio Visual — AV
Audio Visual Guide — Audio Visual G
Audio Visual Librarian — Audio Visual Lib
Audio Visual Review Digest — AVRD
Audiologische Akustik — Audiol Akust
Audiology — Audiol
Audiology [*Japan*] — AUDJDK
Audiology — AUDLA
Audiology [*Basel*] — AUDLAK
Audiology and Neuro-Otology — Audiol Neuro Otol
Audiology (Japan) — Audiol (Jap)
Audio-Visual Bulletin (Malaysia) — AV Bul Malay
Audiovisual Communications — Audiov Commun
Audio-Visual Communications — GAVC
Audio-Visual Education — AV Ed
Audio-Visual Index — A-V Ind
Audiovisual Instruction — Audiov Instr
Audiovisual Instruction — Audiovis Instr
Audiovisual Instruction — Av I
Audiovisual Instruction — AV Inst
Audiovisual Instruction — Av Instr
Audio-Visual Language Journal — Audio-Visual Language J
Audio-Visual Language Journal — A-V L J
Audiovisual Librarian — Audiov Libr
Audiovisual Librarian — AV Libn
Audiovisual Market Place — AMP
Audiovisual Market Place — AV Mark Pl
Audio-Visual Media — A-V Media
Audio-Visual News — AV News
Auditory Biochemistry — Aud Biochem
Auditory Neuroscience — Aud Neurosci
Auditory System — Aud Syst
Audubon — Aud
Audubon — AUDUAD
Audubon — GAUD
Audubon Field Notes — AUFNA2
Audubon Magazine — Audubon Mag
Audubon Magazine — AUMGAG
Audubon Society of Rhode Island. Bulletin — Audubon Soc RI Bull
Auerbach Data Base Management — Auerbach Data Base Manage
Auerbach Data Base Management — DBMAD
Auerbach Reporter — Auerbach Rep
Aufbau — A
Aufbau — AUFB-A
Aufbereiten von PVC — Aufbereit PVC
Aufbereitungs-Technik — AT
Aufbereitungs-Technik — Aufbereit
Aufbereitungs-Technik — Aufbereit-Tech
Aufbereitungs-Technik — Aufbereitungs-Tech
Aufbereitungstechnik in Huettenwerken. Vortraege beim Metallurgischen Seminar — Aufbereitungstech Huettenwerken Vortr Metall Semin
Aufsaetze und Vortraege zur Theologie und Religionswissenschaft [*Berlin*] — AVThRw
Aufsaetze zur Portugiesischen Kulturgeschichte — APK
Aufschluss Sonderheft — Aufschluss Sonderh
Aufsteig und Niedergang der Roemischen Welt — ANRW
Aufstieg und Niedergang der Roemischen Welt — Au N
Auftakt — A
Augsburger Mathematisch-Naturwissenschaftliche Schriften — Augsbg Math Naturwiss Schrift
August — Ag
Augustana Bulletin — AB
Augustana Institute Bulletin — AIB
Augustana Library Publications — Augustana Libr Pub
Augustinian Studies — Aug Stud
Augustinian Studies — Augustin Stud
Augustiniana — Au
Augustiniana — Aug
Augustiniana (Louvain) — AugLv
Augustinianum (Rome) — AugRom
Augustinus (Madrid) — AugMad
Aujourd'hui: Art et Architecture — Aujourd'hui
Aula Pratica de Quimica Organica 1. Pratica Basica da Quimica Organica. Preparacoes. 27 Experiencias — Aula Prat Quim Org 1 Prat Basica Quim Org Prep 27 Exper
Aurea Parma — AP
Aurea Parma — APar
Auris Nasus Larynx — ANLADF
Aurora — Aur
Aus Aachens Vorzeit — AAV
Aus Aachens Vorzeit — AV
Aus dem Walde — Aus Walde
Aus dem Walde. Mitteilungen aus der Niedersaechsischen Landesforstverwaltung — Aus Walde Mitt Niedersaechs Landesforstverwalt
Aus der Arbeit des Evangelischen Bundes — AAEB
Aus der Heimat. Blaetter des Vereins fuer Gothaische Geschichte — Aus d Heimat
Aus der Natur — Aus Nat
Aus der Papyrussammlung der Universitaetsbibliothek in Lund — APUL
Aus Natur und Museum — Aus Natur Mus
Aus Politik und Zeitgeschichte — Aus Polit U Zeitgesch
Aus Politik und Zeitgeschichte. Beilage zur Wochenzeitung das Parlament — Politik u Zeitgesch
Aus Unterricht und Forschung. Korrespondenzblatt der Hoeheren Schulen Wuertembergs. Neue Folge — Aus Unterricht Forsch
Ausbildung und Fortbildung in Gesundheitsoekonomie — Ausbild Fortbild Gesundheitsoekon
Ausbreitungsrechnung und Messverfahren zur Luftueberwachung — Ausbreitungsrechn Messverfahren Luftueberwach
Auserlesene Bibliothek der Neuesten Deutschen Literatur — Auserlesene Biblioth Neuesten Deutsch Lit
Auserlesene Griechische Vasenbilder — AV
Ausfuehrliche Grammatik der Griechischen Sprache — AGGS
Ausfuehrliches Lexikon der Griechischen und Roemischen Mythologie — Lex Myth
Ausfuehrliches Lexikon der Griechischen und Roemischen Mythologie — RML
Ausgaben und Abhandlungen aus dem Gebiete der Romanischen Philologie — Ausg u Abhand
Ausgewaehlte Physikalische Methoden der Organischen Chemie — Ausgewaehlte Phys Methoden Org Chem
Ausgrabungen der Deutschen Forschungsgemeinschaft in Uruk-Warka — ADFGUW
Ausgrabungen in Berlin — Ausgr Berlin
Ausgrabungen und Funde — Au Fu
Ausgrabungen und Funde — Ausgrab Fun
Ausgrabungen und Funde. Nachrichtenblatt fuer Vor- und Fruehgeschichte — AF
Ausgrabungen und Funde. Nachrichtenblatt fuer Vor- und Fruehgeschichte — Ausgr Fu
Ausgrabungen und Funde. Nachrichtenblatt fuer Vor- und Fruehgeschichte — Ausgr Funde
Ausgrabungen zu Olympia — Ol Ausgr
AusIMM (Australasian Institute of Mining and Metallurgy) Bulletin and Proceedings — AusIMM Bull Proc
Auskunftsblatt [*Bern*] — AWM
Ausland — Au
Auslanddeutschtum und Evangelische Kirche — ADEK
Auslandmerkte/Marches Etrangers [*Lausanne*] — WMT
Auslandsanfragen. Waren Vertretungen Kooperationen — AFG
Auslandsdeutschtum und Evangelische Kirche — Auslandsdeutschtum Evang Kirche
Auslegeschrift (Switzerland) — Auslegeschrift (Switz)
AUSLOAN: Australian Inter-Library Loans Manual — AUSLOAN
Ausonia — Au
Ausonia — Aus
Auspicium — ASPCD8
Ausschuss fuer Wirtschaftliche Fertigung Mitteilungen — Ausschuss Wirtsch Fertigung Mitt
Aussenhandels-Dienst — AH Dienst
Aussenhandels-Dienst der Industriekammern und Handelskammern und Wirtschaftsverbande [*Frankfurt Am Main*] — AIH
Aussenpolitik — Aussenpol
Aussenpolitik — Aussenpoli
Aussenwirtschaft — Aussenwirt
Aussenwirtschaft. Zeitschrift fuer Internationale Wirtschaftsbeziehungen — AUW
Austauschbarkeit von Gasen. Vortraege zum Seminar — Austauschbarkeit Gasen Vortr Semin
Austin American-Statesman — Austn Amer
Austin Business Journal — Austin BJ
Austin Seminary Bulletin. Faculty Edition — Austin Sem Bul
Austral News — Aust News
Austral News (Johannesburg) — Aust News (Johannesburg)
Austral News (Montreal) — Aust News (Montreal)
Austral News (Singapore) — Aust News (Singapore)
Austral News (Wellington) — Aust News (Wellington)
Australain Database Development Asssociation [*Database*] — ADDABASE
Australasian Annals of Medicine — AAMEA6
Australasian Annals of Medicine — Aust Ann Med
Australasian Annals of Medicine — Aust Ann of Med
Australasian Annals of Medicine — Australas Ann Med
Australasian Annals of Medicine — Australasian Ann Med
Australasian Antique Collector — Ant Coll
Australasian Association for the Advancement of Science. Reports — Australasian As Rp
Australasian Baker and Millers' Journal — A'sian Baker
Australasian Baker and Millers' Journal — Australas Baker
Australasian Baker and Millers' Journal — Australas Baker Millers J
Australasian Beekeeper — Austr Beek
Australasian Beekeeper — Australas Beekpr

Australasian Biotechnology — Australas Biotechnol
Australasian Boating — A'sian Boating
Australasian Book News and Library Journal — Australasian Bk News
Australasian Bulletin of Medical Physics and Biophysics — Australas Bull Med Phys Biophy
Australasian Bulletin of Medical Physics and Biophysics — Australas Bull Med Phys Biophys
Australasian Business Conditions Bulletin — A'sian Bus Cond Bul
Australasian Catholic Record — ACR
Australasian Catholic Record — A'sian Catholic R
Australasian Catholic Record — A'sian Catholic Rec
Australasian Catholic Record [*Manly, NSW*] — AuCaRec
Australasian Catholic Record — Aus C Rec
Australasian Catholic Record — Austsn Cath Rec
Australasian Chemical Engineering Conference — Australas Chem Eng Conf
Australasian Chemist and Metallurgist — Austr Chem Met
Australasian Chemist and Metallurgist — Australas Chem Metall
Australasian Confectioner and Restaurant Journal — A'sian Confectioner
Australasian Conference on Grassland Invertebrate Ecology — Australas Conf Grassl Invertebr Ecol
Australasian Conference on Heat and Mass Transfer. Proceedings — Australas Conf Heat Mass Transfer Proc
Australasian Corrosion Association. Conference — Australas Corros Assoc Conf
Australasian Corrosion Association. Preprinted Papers of the Annual Conference — Australas Corros Assoc Prepr Pap Annu Conf
Australasian Corrosion Association. Preprinted Papers of the Annual Conference — Prepr Pap Annu Conf Australas Corros Assoc
Australasian Corrosion Association. Technical Paper of the Annual Conference — Australas Corros Assoc Tech Pap Annual Conf
Australasian Corrosion Engineering — Australas Corros
Australasian Corrosion Engineering — Australas Corros Eng
Australasian Corrosion Engineering — Australas Corros Engng
Australasian Dirt Bike — Aust Dirt Bike
Australasian Engineer — A'sian Engineer
Australasian Engineer — Aust Engineer
Australasian Engineer — Aust Engr
Australasian Engineer — Austr Eng
Australasian Engineer — Australas Eng
Australasian Engineer — Australas Engr
Australasian Engineering — A'sian Eng
Australasian Engineering and Machinery — Australas Engng Mach
Australasian Environment — Australas Environ
Australasian Exhibitor — A'sian Exhibitor
Australasian Grocer — A'sian Grocer
Australasian Hardware and Machinery — Australas Hardware Machinery
Australasian Herbarium News — Austr Herb News
Australasian Herbarium News — Australas Herb News
Australasian Home Reader — AHR
Australasian Institute of Metals. Annual Conference — Australas Inst Met Annu Conf
Australasian Institute of Metals. Annual Conference. Proceedings — Australas Inst Met Annu Conf Proc
Australasian Institute of Metals. Journal — Australas Inst Met J
Australasian Institute of Metals. Journal — J Australas Inst Metals
Australasian Institute of Metals. Metals Congress — Australas Inst Met Met Congr
Australasian Institute of Mining and Metallurgy. Bulletin — Australas Inst Min Metall Bull
Australasian Institute of Mining and Metallurgy. Conference — Australas IMM Conf
Australasian Institute of Mining and Metallurgy. Conference — Australas Inst Min Metall Conf
Australasian Institute of Mining and Metallurgy. Conference Series — Australas Inst Min Metall Conf Ser
Australasian Institute of Mining and Metallurgy. Monograph Series — Australas Inst Min Metall Monogr Ser
Australasian Institute of Mining and Metallurgy. Proceedings — A'sian Inst Min & Metallurgy Proc
Australasian Institute of Mining and Metallurgy. Proceedings — Australas Inst Min Metall Proc
Australasian Institute of Mining and Metallurgy. Proceedings — Australas Inst Mining Met Proc
Australasian Institute of Mining and Metallurgy. Proceedings — Proc Aust Inst Min and Metall
Australasian Institute of Mining and Metallurgy. Proceedings — Proc Australas Inst Min and Metall
Australasian Institute of Mining and Metallurgy Publication Series — Australas Inst Min Metall Publ Ser
Australasian Institute of Mining and Metallurgy. Symposia Series — Australas Inst Min Metall Symp Ser
Australasian Insurance and Banking Record — A'sian Insurance & Banking Rec
Australasian Insurance Journal — A'sian Insurance J
Australasian Irrigator — A'sian Irrigator
Australasian Irrigator and Pasture Improver — A/asian Irrigator
Australasian Irrigator and Pasture Improver — Aust Irrig
Australasian Irrigator and Pasture Improver — Aust Irrig Past Improver
Australasian Irrigator and Pasture Improver — Australas Irrig
Australasian Journal of Combinatorics — Australas J Combin
Australasian Journal of Dermatology — AJDEBP
Australasian Journal of Dermatology — Aust J Derm
Australasian Journal of Dermatology — Aust J Dermatol
Australasian Journal of Dermatology — Australas J Dermatol
Australasian Journal of Ecotoxicology — Australas J Ecotoxicol
Australasian Journal of Medical Technology — Australas J Med Technol
Australasian Journal of Pharmacy — A'sian J Pharmacy
Australasian Journal of Pharmacy — AUPHAY
Australasian Journal of Pharmacy — Australas J Phar
Australasian Journal of Pharmacy — Australas J Pharm
Australasian Journal of Pharmacy — Austsn J Pharm
Australasian Journal of Pharmacy. Science Supplement — AJPXA
Australasian Journal of Pharmacy. Science Supplement — AJPXA5
Australasian Journal of Pharmacy. Science Supplement — Australas J Pharm Sci Suppl
Australasian Journal of Philosophy — A/asian J Philos
Australasian Journal of Philosophy — A'sian J Phil
Australasian Journal of Philosophy — Aust J Phil
Australasian Journal of Philosophy — Austl J Phil
Australasian Journal of Philosophy — Australas J Phil
Australasian Journal of Philosophy — Austsn J Philos
Australasian Journal of Psychology and Philosophy — Aust J Ps Phil
Australasian Leather and Footwear Review — A'sian Leather and Footwear R
Australasian Leather and Footwear Review — Aust Leath Footwear Rev
Australasian Leather and Footwear Review — Australas Leath Footwear Rev
Australasian Leather Trades Review — A'sian Leather Trades R
Australasian Leather Trades Review — Australas Leath Trades Rev
Australasian Manufacturer — A'sian Manuf
Australasian Manufacturer — A'sian Manufacturer
Australasian Manufacturer — Aust Manuf
Australasian Manufacturer — Australas Manuf
Australasian Manufacturer — Australas Mfr
Australasian Manufacturer. Industrial Annual — A'sian Manuf Ind Ann
Australasian Manufacturer. Plastics Review — Australas Mfr Plast Rev
Australasian Manufacturing Engineer — Australas Manuf Eng
Australasian Medical Congress. Transactions — Australas Med Congr
Australasian Medical Gazette — Austr Med Gaz
Australasian Medical Gazette — Australas Med Gaz
Australasian Methodist Historical Society. Journal and Proceedings — AMHSJ
Australasian Methodist Historical Society. Journal and Proceedings — A'sian Meth Hist Soc J & Proc
Australasian Methodist Historical Society. Journal and Proceedings — Aust Methodist Hist Soc J Proc
Australasian Methodist Historical Society. Journal and Proceedings — Austsn Meth Hist Soc J
Australasian Methodist Historical Society. Journal and Proceedings — J & Proc A'sian Methodist Historical Soc
Australasian Methodist Historical Society. Journal and Proceedings — J & Proc Aust Methodist Hist Soc
Australasian Methodist Historical Society. Journal and Proceedings — J Proc Australas Meth Hist Soc
Australasian Model Railroad Magazine — AMRM
Australasian Nurses Journal — Australas Nurses J
Australasian Nursing Journal (Port Adelaide) — Australas Nurs J (Port Adelaide)
Australasian Oil and Gas Journal — AOGJAL
Australasian Oil and Gas Journal — A'sian Oil & Gas J
Australasian Oil and Gas Journal — Aust Oil Gas J
Australasian Oil and Gas Journal — Australas Oil Gas J
Australasian Oil and Gas Review — AOGRDE
Australasian Oil and Gas Review — Australas Oil Gas Rev
Australasian Pastoralists' Review — Austr Past Rev
Australasian Pastoralists' Review — Australas Past Rev
Australasian Performing Right Association. Journal — APRAJ
Australasian Pharmaceutical Notes and News — Australas Pharm Notes News
Australasian Photo Review — APR
Australasian Photo Review — Australas Photo Rev
Australasian Photo Review — Australas Photo Review
Australasian Photographic Review — Australas Photogr Rev
Australasian Physical and Engineering Sciences in Medicine — AUPMDI
Australasian Physical and Engineering Sciences in Medicine — Australas Phys and Eng Sci Med
Australasian Physical and Engineering Sciences in Medicine — Australas Phys Eng Sci Med
Australasian Physical Sciences in Medicine [*Later, Australasian Physical and Engineering Sciences in Medicine*] — Australas Phys Sci Med
Australasian Plant Pathology — AAPPDN
Australasian Plating and Finishing — Australas Plat Finish
Australasian Post — A'sian Post
Australasian Printer — A'sian Pr
Australasian Printer — A'sian Printer
Australasian Printer — Aust Printer
Australasian Printer — Australas Print
Australasian Printer — Australas Printer
Australasian Printer — Austsn Pr
Australasian Radiology — AURDAW
Australasian Radiology — Aust Radio
Australasian Radiology — Aust Radiol
Australasian Radiology — Australas Radiol
Australasian Railway and Locomotive Historical Society. Bulletin — A'sian R'way & Locomotive Hist Soc Bul
Australasian Small Press Review — ASPR
Australasian Software Report — ASR
Australasian Symposium on the Microcirculation — Australas Symp Microcir
Australasian Tax Decisions — ATD
Australasian Tax Decisions — Aust Tax D
Australasian Tax Reports — ATR
Australasian Tax Review — Aust Tax Rev
Australasian Tertiary Handbook Collection on Microfiche — ATHCOM
Australasian Textiles — Australas Text
Australasian Trade Review and Manufacturers Journal — Australas Trade Rev
Australasian Typographical Journal — Australas Typogr J
Australasian Universities Modern Language Association. Journal — AUMLA

Australasian Universities Modern Language Association. Proceedings of Congress — A'sian Univ Mod Lang Assoc Congress Proc
Australasian Water Well Journal — Aust Water Well J
Australia 1888 Bulletin — A 1888 B
Australia 1938-1988 Bicentennial History Project. Bulletin — A 1938-1988 B
Australia. Aeronautical Research Laboratories. Aerodynamics Report — Aust Aeronaut Res Lab Aerodyn Rep
Australia. Aeronautical Research Laboratories. Guided Weapons Note — Aust Aeronaut Res Lab Guided Weapons Note
Australia. Aeronautical Research Laboratories. Materials Note — Aust Aeronaut Res Lab Mater Note
Australia. Aeronautical Research Laboratories. Materials Note — Mater Note Aust Aeronaut Res Lab
Australia. Aeronautical Research Laboratories. Materials Report — Aust Aeronaut Res Lab Mater Rep
Australia. Aeronautical Research Laboratories. Materials Report — Mater Rep Aust Aeronaut Res Lab
Australia. Aeronautical Research Laboratories. Mechanical Engineering Note — Aust Aeronaut Res Lab Mech Eng Note
Australia. Aeronautical Research Laboratories. Mechanical Engineering Report — Aust Aeronaut Res Lab Mech Eng Rep
Australia. Aeronautical Research Laboratories. Metallurgy Note — Aust Aeronaut Res Lab Metall Note
Australia. Aeronautical Research Laboratories. Metallurgy Note — Met Note Aust Aeronaut Res Lab
Australia. Aeronautical Research Laboratories. Metallurgy Report — Aust Aeronaut Res Lab Metall Rep
Australia. Aeronautical Research Laboratories. Metallurgy Report — Metall Rep Aeronaut Res Lab Aust
Australia. Aeronautical Research Laboratories. Metallurgy Technical Memorandum — Aust Aeronaut Res Lab Metall Tech Mem
Australia. Aeronautical Research Laboratories. Metallurgy Technical Memorandum — Aust Aronaut Res Lab Metall Tech Memo
Australia. Aeronautical Research Laboratories. Metallurgy Technical Memorandum — Metall Tech Memo Aust Aeronaut Res Lab
Australia. Aeronautical Research Laboratories. Report MET (Metallurgy) — Aust Aeronaut Res Lab Rep MET
Australia. Aeronautical Research Laboratories. Structures and Materials Note [*A publication*] — Aust Aeronaut Res Lab Struct
Australia. Aeronautical Research Laboratories. Structures and Materials Note [*A publication*] — Aust Aeronaut Res Lab Struct Mater Note
Australia. Aeronautical Research Laboratories. Structures and Materials Report — Aust Aeronaut Res Lab Struct Mater Rep
Australia. Aeronautical Research Laboratories. Structures and Materials Report — Aust Aronaut Lab Struct Mater Rep
Australia. Aeronautical Research Laboratories. Structures and Materials Report — Struct Mater Rep Aust Aeronaut Res Lab
Australia. Aeronautical Research Laboratories. Structures Note — Aust Aeronaut Res Lab Struct Note
Australia. Aeronautical Research Laboratories. Structures Note — Struct Note Aust Aeronaut Res Lab
Australia. Aeronautical Research Laboratories. Structures Report — Aust Aeronaut Res Lab Struct Rep
Australia. Aeronautical Research Laboratories. Structures Report — Struct Rep Aust Aeronaut Res Lab
Australia and New Zealand Bank. Business Indicators — ANZ Ind
Australia and New Zealand Bank. Quarterly Survey — A & NZ Bank Quarterly Surv
Australia and New Zealand Bank. Quarterly Survey — ANZ Bank
Australia and New Zealand Weekly — Aust & NZ W
Australia. Australian Radiation Laboratory. Technical Report Series ARL/TR — Tech Rep Ser ARL/TR Aust Radiat Lab
Australia Building Forum — Aust Bldg Forum
Australia. Bureau of Mineral Resources. Geology and Geophysics. BMR Journal of Australian Geology and Geophysics — Aust Bur Miner Resour Geol Geophys BMR J Aust Geol Geophys
Australia. Bureau of Mineral Resources. Geology and Geophysics. Bulletin — Aust Bur Miner Resour Geol Geophys Bull
Australia. Bureau of Mineral Resources. Geology and Geophysics. Bulletin — Bull Bur Miner Resour Geol Geophys
Australia. Bureau of Mineral Resources. Geology and Geophysics. Pamphlet — Aust Bur Miner Resour Geol Geophys Pam
Australia. Bureau of Mineral Resources. Geology and Geophysics. Report — Aust Bur Miner Resour Geol Geophys Rep
Australia. Bureau of Statistics. Adoptions — Aust Bur Stat Adopt
Australia. Bureau of Statistics. Banking Australia — Aust Bur Stat Bank Aust
Australia. Bureau of Statistics. Finance Companies, Australia — Aust Bur Stat Fin Co Aust
Australia. Bureau of Statistics. Rural Industries Bulletin — Aust Bur Stat Rural Ind Bul
Australia. Bureau of Statisticss. Technical Papers — Aust Bur Stat Tech Pap
Australia. Commonwealth Advisory Council of Science and Industry. Bulletin — Aust Commonw Advis Counc Sci Ind Bull
Australia. Commonwealth Advisory Council of Science and Industry. Pamphlet — Aust Commonw Advis Counc Sci Ind Pam
Australia. Commonwealth Bureau of Census and Statistics. Monthly Bulletin of Production Statistics — Aust Prod
Australia. Commonwealth Bureau of Census and Statistics. Queensland Office. Bulletin — Q Census & Statistics Bul
Australia. Commonwealth Bureau of Census and Statistics. South Australian Office. Bulletin — SA Census & Statistics Bul
Australia. Commonwealth Council for Scientific and Industrial Research. Bulletin — Aust Commonw Counc Sci Ind Res Bull
Australia. Commonwealth Council for Scientific and Industrial Research. Pamphlet — Aust Commonw Counc Sci Ind Res Pam
Australia. Commonwealth. Council for Scientific and Industrial Research. Pamphlet — Aust Commonw CSIR Pam
Australia. Commonwealth Department of Supply. Aeronautical Research Committee. Report — Aust Commonw Dept Supply Aeronaut Res Comm Rep
Australia. Commonwealth Department of Supply. Aeronautical Research Committee. Report ACA — Aust Commonw Dep Supply Aeronaut Res Comm Rep ACA
Australia. Commonwealth Department of Supply. Aeronautical Research Consultative Committee. Report ACA — Aust Commonw Dep Supply Aeronaut Res Consult Comm Rep ACA
Australia. Commonwealth Department of Supply. Aeronautical Research Laboratories. Guided Weapons Note — Aust Commonw Dep Supply Aeronaut Res Guided Weapons Note
Australia. Commonwealth. Department of Supply. Aeronautical Research Laboratories. Guided Weapons Note — Aust Commonw Dep Supply Aeronaut Res Lab Guided Weapons Note
Australia. Commonwealth Department of Supply. Aeronautical Research Laboratories. Metallurgy Note — Aust Commonw Dep Supply Aeronaut Res Lab Metall Note
Australia. Commonwealth Department of Supply. Aeronautical Research Laboratories. Metallurgy Technical Memorandum — Aust Commonw Dep Supply Aeronaut Res Lab Metall Tech Memo
Australia. Commonwealth Department of Supply. Aeronautical Research Laboratories. Report MET (Metallurgy) — Aust Commonw Dep Supply Aeronaut Res Lab Rep MET
Australia. Commonwealth Department of Supply. Aeronautical Research Laboratories. Report SM [*Structures and Materials*] — Aust Commonw Dep Supply Aeronaut Res Lab Rep SM
Australia. Commonwealth Department of Supply. Defence Research Laboratories. Report — Aust Commonw Dep Supply Def Res Lab Rep
Australia. Commonwealth Department of Supply. Defence Research Laboratories. Report — Aust Commonw Dep Supply Def Res Lab Report
Australia. Commonwealth Department of Supply. Defence Research Laboratories. Technical Note — Aust Commonw Dep Supply Def Res Lab Tech Note
Australia. Commonwealth Department of Supply. Defence Research Laboratories. Technical Note — Aust Commonw Dep Supply Res Lab Tech Note
Australia. Commonwealth Department of Supply. Defence Standards Laboratories. Report — Aust Commonw Dep Supply Def Stand Lab Rep
Australia. Commonwealth Department of Supply. Defence Standards Laboratories. Technical Note — Aust Commonw Dep Supply Def Stand Lab Tech Note
Australia. Commonwealth Experimental Building Station. Bulletin — Commonw Exp Build Stat Bull
Australia. Commonwealth Experimental Building Station. CEBS Researchers and Facilities — Commonw Exp Build Stat RF
Australia. Commonwealth Experimental Building Station. Notes on the Science of Building — Common Exp Build Stn NSB
Australia. Commonwealth Experimental Building Station. Special Report — Commonw Exp Build Stat SR
Australia. Commonwealth Experimental Building Station. Technical Study — Commonw Exp Build Stat TS
Australia. Commonwealth Forestry and Timber Bureau. Forestry Research Notes — For Bur Aust For Res Notes
Australia. Commonwealth Forestry and Timber Bureau. Leaflet — For Bur Aust Leaf
Australia. Commonwealth Forestry and Timber Bureau. Timber Supply Review — For Bur Aust Timber Supp Rev
Australia. Commonwealth Institute of Science and Industry. Bulletin — Aust Commonw Inst Sci Ind Bull
Australia. Commonwealth Institute of Science and Industry. Pamphlet — Aust Commonw Inst Sci Ind Pam
Australia. Commonwealth Scientific and Industrial Research Organisation. Abstracts of Published Papers and List of Translations — Aust CSIRO Abstr Publ Pap List Transl
Australia. Commonwealth Scientific and Industrial Research Organisation. Animal Research Laboratories. Technical Paper — AOAPA9
Australia. Commonwealth Scientific and Industrial Research Organisation. Animal Research Laboratories. Technical Paper — Aust CSIRO Anim Res Lab Tech Pap
Australia. Commonwealth Scientific and Industrial Research Organisation. Annual Report — ASIRAF
Australia. Commonwealth Scientific and Industrial Research Organisation. Annual Report — Aust CSIRO Annu Rep
Australia. Commonwealth Scientific and Industrial Research Organisation. Bulletin — ACIBAP
Australia. Commonwealth Scientific and Industrial Research Organisation. Bulletin —Aust CSIRO Bull
Australia. Commonwealth Scientific and Industrial Research Organisation. Bulletin — Bull CSIRO
Australia. Commonwealth Scientific and Industrial Research Organisation. Chemical Research Laboratories. Technical Paper — Aust CSIRO Chem Res Lab Tech Pap
Australia. Commonwealth Scientific and Industrial Research Organisation. Coal Research Division. Location Report — Aust CSIRO Coal Res Div Locat Rep
Australia. Commonwealth Scientific and Industrial Research Organisation. Coal Research Division. Miscellaneous Report — Aust CSIRO Coal Res Div Misc Rep
Australia. Commonwealth Scientific and Industrial Research Organisation. Coal Research Division. Technical Communication — Aust CSIRO Coal Res Div Tech Commun
Australia. Commonwealth Scientific and Industrial Research Organisation. CSIRO Wildlife Research — Aust CSIRO CSIRO Wildl Res

Australia. Commonwealth Scientific and Industrial Research Organisation. Division of Animal Genetics. Research Report — Aust CSIRO Div Anim Genet Res Rep

Australia. Commonwealth Scientific and Industrial Research Organisation. Division of Animal Genetics. Research Report — RRCGDX

Australia. Commonwealth Scientific and Industrial Research Organisation. Division of Animal Health and Production. Technical Paper — AAHPAE

Australia. Commonwealth Scientific and Industrial Research Organisation. Division of Animal Health and Production. Technical Paper — Aust CSIRO Div Anim Health Prod Tech Pap

Australia. Commonwealth Scientific and Industrial Research Organisation. Division of Animal Health. Annual Report — AAHAA3

Australia. Commonwealth Scientific and Industrial Research Organisation. Division of Animal Health. Annual Report — Aust CSIRO Div Anim Health Annu Rep

Australia. Commonwealth Scientific and Industrial Research Organisation. Division of Animal Physiology. Annual Report — AUARBO

Australia. Commonwealth Scientific and Industrial Research Organisation. Division of Animal Physiology. Annual Report — Aust CSIRO Div Anim Physiol Annu Rep

Australia. Commonwealth Scientific and Industrial Research Organisation. Division of Applied Chemistry. Annual Report — ACDACX

Australia. Commonwealth Scientific and Industrial Research Organisation. Division of Applied Chemistry. Annual Report — Aust CSIRO Div Appl Chem Annu Rep

Australia. Commonwealth Scientific and Industrial Research Organisation. Division of Applied Chemistry. Technical Paper — Aust CSIRO Div Appl Chem Tech Pap

Australia. Commonwealth Scientific and Industrial Research Organisation. Division of Applied Chemistry. Technical Paper — Div Appl Chem Tech Pap CSIRO Aust

Australia. Commonwealth Scientific and Industrial Research Organisation. Division of Applied Geomechanics. Technical Memorandum — Aust CSIRO Div Appl Geomech Tech Memo

Australia. Commonwealth Scientific and Industrial Research Organisation. Division of Applied Geomechanics. Technical Paper — AAGTCN

Australia. Commonwealth Scientific and Industrial Research Organisation. Division of Applied Geomechanics. Technical Paper — Aust CSIRO Div Appl Geomech Tech Pap

Australia. Commonwealth Scientific and Industrial Research Organisation. Division of Applied Geomechanics. Technical Report — AAGRCH

Australia. Commonwealth Scientific and Industrial Research Organisation. Division of Applied Geomechanics. Technical Report — Aust CSIRO Div Appl Geomech Tech Rep

Australia. Commonwealth Scientific and Industrial Research Organisation. Division of Applied Organic Chemistry. Research Report — Aust CSIRO Div Appl Org Chem Res Rep

Australia. Commonwealth Scientific and Industrial Research Organisation. Division of Applied Organic Chemistry. Research Report — RPACDV

Australia. Commonwealth Scientific and Industrial Research Organisation. Division of Applied Organic Chemistry. Technical Paper — Aust CSIRO Div Appl Org Chem Tech Pap

Australia. Commonwealth Scientific and Industrial Research Organisation. Division of Applied Organic Chemistry. Technical Paper — Div Appl Org Chem Tech Pap CSIRO Aust

Australia. Commonwealth Scientific and Industrial Research Organisation. Division of Atmospheric Physics. Technical Paper — AAPTCY

Australia. Commonwealth Scientific and Industrial Research Organisation. Division of Atmospheric Physics. Technical Paper — Aust CSIRO Div Atmos Phys Tech Pap

Australia. Commonwealth Scientific and Industrial Research Organisation. Division of Atmospheric Physics. Technical Paper — Div Atmos Phys Tech Pap Aust CSIRO

Australia. Commonwealth Scientific and Industrial Research Organisation. Division of Building Research. Annual Report — ADBRDE

Australia. Commonwealth Scientific and Industrial Research Organisation. Division of Building Research. Annual Report — Aust CSIRO Div Build Res Annu Rep

Australia. Commonwealth Scientific and Industrial Research Organisation. Division of Building Research. Technical Paper — AUDBAO

Australia. Commonwealth Scientific and Industrial Research Organisation. Division of Building Research. Technical Paper — Aust CSIRO Div Build Res Tech Pap

Australia. Commonwealth Scientific and Industrial Research Organisation. Division of Chemical Engineering. Report — Aust CSIRO Div Chem Eng Rep

Australia. Commonwealth Scientific and Industrial Research Organisation. Division of Chemical Physics. Annual Report — Aust CSIRO Div Chem Phys Annu Rep

Australia. Commonwealth Scientific and Industrial Research Organisation. Division of Chemical Physics. Annual Report — CSCPC3

Australia. Commonwealth Scientific and Industrial Research Organisation. Division of Chemical Technology. Research Review — Aust CSIRO Div Chem Technol Res Rev

Australia. Commonwealth Scientific and Industrial Research Organisation. Division of Chemical Technology. Research Review — RDCTD8

Australia. Commonwealth Scientific and Industrial Research Organisation. Division of Chemical Technology. Research Review — Res Rev CSIRO Div Chem Technol

Australia. Commonwealth Scientific and Industrial Research Organisation. Division of Chemical Technology. Technical Paper — Aust CSIRO Div Chem Technol Tech Pap

Australia. Commonwealth Scientific and Industrial Research Organisation. Division of Chemical Technology. Technical Paper — Div Chem Technol Tech Pap CSIRO Aust

Australia. Commonwealth Scientific and Industrial Research Organisation. Division of Coal Research. Location Report — Aust CSIRO Div Coal Res Locat Rep

Australia. Commonwealth Scientific and Industrial Research Organisation. Division of Coal Research. Miscellaneous Report — Aust CSIRO Div Coal Res Misc Rep

Australia. Commonwealth Scientific and Industrial Research Organisation. Division of Coal Research. Reference LR [*Location Report*] — Aust CSIRO Div Coal Res Ref LR

Australia. Commonwealth Scientific and Industrial Research Organisation. Division of Coal Research. Technical Communication — Aust CSIRO Div Coal Res Tech Commun

Australia. Commonwealth Scientific and Industrial Research Organisation. Division of Dairy Research. Annual Report — ADRRCP

Australia. Commonwealth Scientific and Industrial Research Organisation. Division of Dairy Research. Annual Report — Aust CSIRO Div Dairy Res Annu Rep

Australia. Commonwealth Scientific and Industrial Research Organisation. Division of Entomology. Annual Report — ADETBX

Australia. Commonwealth Scientific and Industrial Research Organisation. Division of Entomology. Annual Report — Aust CSIRO Div Entomol Annu Rep

Australia. Commonwealth Scientific and Industrial Research Organisation. Division of Entomology. Technical Paper — ASEPAN

Australia. Commonwealth Scientific and Industrial Research Organisation. Division of Entomology. Technical Paper — Aust CSIRO Div Entomol Tech Pap

Australia. Commonwealth Scientific and Industrial Research Organisation. Division of Fisheries and Oceanography. Annual Report — AFOAB6

Australia. Commonwealth Scientific and Industrial Research Organisation. Division of Fisheries and Oceanography. Annual Report — Aust CSIRO Div Fish Oceanogr Annu Rep

Australia. Commonwealth Scientific and Industrial Research Organisation. Division of Fisheries and Oceanography. Circular — ACFCBE

Australia. Commonwealth Scientific and Industrial Research Organisation. Division of Fisheries and Oceanography. Circular — Aust CSIRO Div Fish Oceanogr Circ

Australia. Commonwealth Scientific and Industrial Research Organisation. Division of Fisheries and Oceanography. Fisheries Synopsis — AOFSA9

Australia. Commonwealth Scientific and Industrial Research Organisation. Division of Fisheries and Oceanography. Report — ADFOAM

Australia. Commonwealth Scientific and Industrial Research Organisation. Division of Fisheries and Oceanography. Report — Aust CSIRO Div Fish Oceanogr Rep

Australia. Commonwealth Scientific and Industrial Research Organisation. Division of Fisheries and Oceanography. Report — Rep CSIRO Div Fish Oceanogr

Australia. Commonwealth Scientific and Industrial Research Organisation. Division of Fisheries and Oceanography. Technical Paper — AFOPAG

Australia. Commonwealth Scientific and Industrial Research Organisation. Division of Fisheries and Oceanography. Technical Paper — Aust CSIRO Div Fish Oceanogr Tech Pap

Australia. Commonwealth Scientific and Industrial Research Organisation. Division of Fisheries. Technical Paper — Aust CSIRO Div Fish Tech Pap

Australia. Commonwealth Scientific and Industrial Research Organisation. Division of Food Preservation and Transport. Technical Paper — ASFPAS

Australia. Commonwealth Scientific and Industrial Research Organisation. Division of Food Preservation and Transport. Technical Paper — Aust CSIRO Div Food Preserv Transp Tech Pap

Australia. Commonwealth Scientific and Industrial Research Organisation. Division of Food Preservation. Report of Research — ADFPBQ

Australia. Commonwealth Scientific and Industrial Research Organisation. Division of Food Preservation. Report of Research — Aust CSIRO Div Food Preserv Rep Res

Australia. Commonwealth Scientific and Industrial Research Organisation. Division of Food Preservation. Technical Paper — AOFPAY

Australia. Commonwealth Scientific and Industrial Research Organisation. Division of Food Preservation. Technical Paper — Aust CSIRO Div Food Preserv Tech Pap

Australia. Commonwealth Scientific and Industrial Research Organisation. Division of Food Research. Report of Research — ACFRBP

Australia. Commonwealth Scientific and Industrial Research Organisation. Division of Food Research. Report of Research — Aust CSIRO Div Food Res Rep Res

Australia. Commonwealth Scientific and Industrial Research Organisation. Division of Food Research. Technical Paper — ACTPCM

Australia. Commonwealth Scientific and Industrial Research Organisation. Division of Food Research. Technical Paper — Aust CSIRO Div Food Res Tech Pap

Australia. Commonwealth Scientific and Industrial Research Organisation. Division of Forest Products. Forest Products Newsletter — Aust CSIRO Div For Prod For Prod Newsl

Australia. Commonwealth Scientific and Industrial Research Organisation. Division of Forest Products. Technological Paper — AFPPAL

Australia. Commonwealth Scientific and Industrial Research Organisation. Division of Forest Products. Technological Paper — Aust CSIRO Div For Prod Technol Pap

Australia. Commonwealth Scientific and Industrial Research Organisation. Division of Forest Research. Annual Report — ARCRDF

Australia. Commonwealth Scientific and Industrial Research Organisation. Division of Forest Research. Annual Report — Aust CSIRO Div For Res Annu Rep

Australia. Commonwealth Scientific and Industrial Research Organisation. Division of Horticulture. Research Report — AHRRBI

Australia. Commonwealth Scientific and Industrial Research Organisation. Division of Horticulture. Research Report — Aust CSIRO Div Hortic Res Rep

Australia. Commonwealth Scientific and Industrial Research Organisation. Division of Industrial Chemistry. Technical Paper — Aust CSIRO Div Ind Chem Tech Pap

Australia. Commonwealth Scientific and Industrial Research Organisation. Division of Irrigation Research. Annual Report — ADIRBD

Australia. Commonwealth Scientific and Industrial Research Organisation. Division of Irrigation Research. Annual Report — Aust CSIRO Div Irrig Res Annu Rep

Australia. Commonwealth Scientific and Industrial Research Organisation. Division of Irrigation Research. Report — ABIRBD

Australia. Commonwealth Scientific and Industrial Research Organisation. Division of Irrigation. Research Report — Aust CSIRO Div Irrig Res Rep

Australia. Commonwealth Scientific and Industrial Research Organisation. Division of Land Research and Regional Survey. Technical Paper — AOLPAU

Australia. Commonwealth Scientific and Industrial Research Organisation. Division of Land Research and Regional Survey. Technical Paper — Aust CSIRO Div Land Res Reg Surv Tech Pap

Australia. Commonwealth Scientific and Industrial Research Organisation. Division of Land Research. Technical Paper — Aust CSIRO Div Land Res Tech Pap

Australia. Commonwealth Scientific and Industrial Research Organisation. Division of Land Research. Technical Paper — Div Land Res Tech Pap CSIRO Aust

Australia. Commonwealth Scientific and Industrial Research Organisation. Division of Land Resources Management. Technical Paper — Aust CSIRO Div Land Resour Manage Tech Pap

Australia. Commonwealth Scientific and Industrial Research Organisation. Division of Land Resources Management. Technical Paper — Div Land Resour Manage Tech Pap CSIRO Aust

Australia. Commonwealth Scientific and Industrial Research Organisation. Division of Land Use Research. Technical Paper — ACDLAU

Australia. Commonwealth Scientific and Industrial Research Organisation. Division of Land Use Research. Technical Paper — Aust CSIRO Div Land Use Res Tech Pap

Australia. Commonwealth Scientific and Industrial Research Organisation. Division of Land Use Research. Technical Paper — Div Land Use Res Tech Pap CSIRO Aust

Australia. Commonwealth Scientific and Industrial Research Organisation. Division of Mathematical Statistics. Technical Paper — ADMPAQ

Australia. Commonwealth Scientific and Industrial Research Organisation. Division of Mathematical Statistics. Technical Paper — Aust CSIRO Div Math Stat Tech Pap

Australia. Commonwealth Scientific and Industrial Research Organisation. Division of Mechanical Engineering. Annual Report — AMEAB5

Australia. Commonwealth Scientific and Industrial Research Organisation. Division of Mechanical Engineering. Annual Report — Aust CSIRO Div Mech Eng Annu Rep

Australia. Commonwealth Scientific and Industrial Research Organisation. Division of Meteorological Physics. Technical Paper — AOMPAZ

Australia. Commonwealth Scientific and Industrial Research Organisation. Division of Meteorological Physics. Technical Paper — Aust CSIRO Div Meteorol Phys Tech Pap

Australia. Commonwealth Scientific and Industrial Research Organisation. Division of Metrology. Technical Paper — Aust Commonw Sci Ind Res Organ Div Metrol Tech Pap

Australia. Commonwealth Scientific and Industrial Research Organisation. Division of Metrology. Technical Paper — Aust CSIRO Div Metrol Tech Pap

Australia. Commonwealth Scientific and Industrial Research Organisation. Division of Mineral Chemistry. Investigation Report — Aust CSIRO Div Miner Chem Invest Rep

Australia. Commonwealth Scientific and Industrial Research Organisation. Division of Mineral Chemistry. Location Report — Aust CSIRO Div Miner Chem Locat Rep

Australia. Commonwealth Scientific and Industrial Research Organisation. Division of Mineral Chemistry. Technical Communication — Aust CSIRO Div Miner Chem Tech Commun

Australia. Commonwealth Scientific and Industrial Research Organisation. Division of Mineral Chemistry. Technical Communication — Tech Commun CSIRO Div Miner Chem

Australia. Commonwealth Scientific and Industrial Research Organisation. Division of Mineralogy. Technical Communication — Aust CSIRO Div Mineral Tech Commun

Australia. Commonwealth Scientific and Industrial Research Organisation. Division of Mineralogy. Technical Communication — Tech Commun CSIRO Div Mineral

Australia. Commonwealth Scientific and Industrial Research Organisation. Division of Nutritional Biochemistry. Research Report — Aust CSIRO Div Nutr Biochem Res Rep

Australia. Commonwealth Scientific and Industrial Research Organisation. Division of Plant Industry. Annual Report — AOPRAM

Australia. Commonwealth Scientific and Industrial Research Organisation. Division of Plant Industry. Annual Report — Aust CSIRO Div Plant Ind Annu Rep

Australia. Commonwealth Scientific and Industrial Research Organisation. Division of Plant Industry. Field Station Record — AOIRAL

Australia. Commonwealth Scientific and Industrial Research Organisation. Division of Plant Industry. Field Station Record — Aust CSIRO Div Plant Ind Field Stn Rec

Australia. Commonwealth Scientific and Industrial Research Organisation. Division of Plant Industry. Field Station Record — CSIRO Div Plant Ind Field Stn Rec Aust

Australia. Commonwealth Scientific and Industrial Research Organisation. Division of Plant Industry. Field Station Record — Field Stn Rec Aust CSIRO Div Plant Ind

Australia. Commonwealth Scientific and Industrial Research Organisation. Division of Plant Industry. Technical Paper — APIPAM

Australia. Commonwealth Scientific and Industrial Research Organisation. Division of Plant Industry. Technical Paper — Aust CSIRO Div Plant Ind Tech Pap

Australia. Commonwealth Scientific and Industrial Research Organisation. Division of Protein Chemistry. Annual Report — ARCCD4

Australia. Commonwealth Scientific and Industrial Research Organisation. Division of Soil Mechanics. Technical Paper — ASOTBI

Australia. Commonwealth Scientific and Industrial Research Organisation. Division of Soil Mechanics. Technical Paper — Aust CSIRO Div Soil Mech Tech Pap

Australia. Commonwealth Scientific and Industrial Research Organisation. Division of Soil Research. Technical Paper — ASTPCW

Australia. Commonwealth Scientific and Industrial Research Organisation. Division of Soil Research. Technical Paper — Aust CSIRO Div Soil Res Tech Pap

Australia. Commonwealth Scientific and Industrial Research Organisation. Division of Soils. Divisional Report — Aust CSIRO Div Soils Div Rep

Australia. Commonwealth Scientific and Industrial Research Organisation. Division of Soils. Divisional Report — Div Soils Div Rep CSIRO Aust

Australia. Commonwealth Scientific and Industrial Research Organisation. Division of Soils. Notes on Soil Techniques — Aust CSIRO Div Soils Notes Soil Tech

Australia. Commonwealth Scientific and Industrial Research Organisation. Division of Soils. Report on Progress — ASRPCM

Australia. Commonwealth Scientific and Industrial Research Organisation. Division of Soils. Report on Progress — Aust CSIRO Div Soils Rep Prog

Australia. Commonwealth Scientific and Industrial Research Organisation. Division of Soils. Soils and Land Use Series — Aust CSIRO Div Soils Soils Land Use Ser

Australia. Commonwealth Scientific and Industrial Research Organisation. Division of Soils. Technical Paper — Aust CSIRO Div Soils Tech Pap

Australia. Commonwealth Scientific and Industrial Research Organisation. Division of Soils. Technical Paper — Div Soils Tech Pap CSIRO Aust

Australia. Commonwealth Scientific and Industrial Research Organisation. Division of Textile Industry. Report — Aust CSIRO Div Text Ind Rep

Australia. Commonwealth Scientific and Industrial Research Organisation. Division of Textile Industry. Report — Rep Aust CSIRO Div Text Ind

Australia. Commonwealth Scientific and Industrial Research Organisation. Division of Textile Industry. Report — Rep CSIRO Div Text Ind Aust

Australia. Commonwealth Scientific and Industrial Research Organisation. Division of Tropical Agronomy. Annual Report — Aust CSIRO Div Trop Agron Annu Rep

Australia. Commonwealth Scientific and Industrial Research Organisation. Division of Tropical Agronomy. Technical Paper — Aust CSIRO Div Trop Agron Tech Pap

Australia. Commonwealth Scientific and Industrial Research Organisation. Division of Tropical Crops and Pastures. Technical Paper — Aust CSIRO Div Trop Crops Pastures Tech Pap

Australia. Commonwealth Scientific and Industrial Research Organisation. Division of Tropical Crops and Pastures. Tropical Agronomy. Technical Memorandum — Aust CSIRO Div Trop Crops Pastures Trop Agron Tech Memo

Australia. Commonwealth Scientific and Industrial Research Organisation. Division of Tropical Crops and Pastures. Tropical Agronomy. Technical Memorandum — Trop Agron Tech Memo Aust CSIRO Div Trop Crops Pastures

Australia. Commonwealth Scientific and Industrial Research Organisation. Division of Tropical Pastures. Annual Report — Aust CSIRO Div Trop Pastures Annu Rep

Australia. Commonwealth Scientific and Industrial Research Organisation. Division of Tropical Pastures. Technical Paper — Aust CSIRO Div Trop Pastures Tech Pap

Australia. Commonwealth Scientific and Industrial Research Organisation. Division of Tropical Pastures. Technical Paper — Div Trop Pastures Tech Pap CSIRO Aust

Australia. Commonwealth Scientific and Industrial Research Organisation. Division of Water and Land Resources. Divisional Report — Aust CSIRO Div Water Land Resour Div Rep

Australia. Commonwealth Scientific and Industrial Research Organisation. Division of Water and Land Resources. Natural Resources Series — Aust CSIRO Div Water Land Resour Nat Resour Ser

Australia. Commonwealth Scientific and Industrial Research Organisation. Division of Water Resources. Divisional Report — Aust CSIRO Div Water Resour Div Rep

Australia. Commonwealth Scientific and Industrial Research Organisation. Division of Wildlife and Rangelands Research. Technical Paper — Aust CSIRO Div Wildl Rangelands Res Tech Pap

Australia. Commonwealth Scientific and Industrial Research Organisation. Division of Wildlife Research. Report — Aust CSIRO Div Wildl Res Rep

Australia. Commonwealth Scientific and Industrial Research Organisation. Division of Wildlife Research. Technical Paper — Aust CSIRO Div Wildl Res Tech Pap

Australia. Commonwealth Scientific and Industrial Research Organisation. Food Preservation Quarterly — Aust CSIRO Food Preserv Q

Australia. Commonwealth Scientific and Industrial Research Organisation. Food Preservation Quarterly — CFPQAC

Australia. Commonwealth Scientific and Industrial Research Organisation. Food Research Quarterly — Aust CSIRO Food Res Q

Australia. Commonwealth Scientific and Industrial Research Organisation. Food Research Quarterly — CFRQAM

Australia. Commonwealth Scientific and Industrial Research Organisation. Forest Products Laboratory. Division of Applied Chemistry. Technological Paper — ACSPCH
Australia. Commonwealth Scientific and Industrial Research Organisation. Forest Products Laboratory. Division of Applied Chemistry. Technological Paper — Aust CSIRO For Prod Lab Div Appl Chem Technol Pap
Australia. Commonwealth Scientific and Industrial Research Organisation. Forest Products Laboratory. Division of Building Research. Technological Paper — Aust CSIRO For Prod Lab Div Build Res Technol Pap
Australia. Commonwealth Scientific and Industrial Research Organisation. Forest Products Laboratory. Technological Paper — AFBTBW
Australia. Commonwealth Scientific and Industrial Research Organisation. Forest Products Laboratory. Technological Paper — Aust CSIRO For Prod Lab Technol Pap
Australia. Commonwealth Scientific and Industrial Research Organisation. Groundwater Research. Technical Paper — GRTPEP
Australia. Commonwealth Scientific and Industrial Research Organisation. Institute of Biological Resources. Division of Water and Land Resources. Technical Memorandum — Aust CSIRO Inst Biol Resour Div Water Land Resour Tech Memo
Australia. Commonwealth Scientific and Industrial Research Organisation. Institute of Natural Resources and Environment. Division of Water Resources. Technical Memorandum — Aust CSIRO Inst Nat Resour Environ Div Water Resour Tech Mem
Australia. Commonwealth Scientific and Industrial Research Organisation. Irrigation Research Stations. Technical Paper — AUIRAT
Australia. Commonwealth Scientific and Industrial Research Organisation. Irrigation Research Stations. Technical Paper — Aust CSIRO Irrig Res Stn Tech Pap
Australia. Commonwealth Scientific and Industrial Research Organisation. Irrigation Research Stations. Technical Paper — Aust CSIRO Irrig Res Stn Techn Pap
Australia. Commonwealth Scientific and Industrial Research Organisation. Land Research Series — ASLRAU
Australia. Commonwealth Scientific and Industrial Research Organisation. Land Research Series — Aust CSIRO Land Res Ser
Australia. Commonwealth Scientific and Industrial Research Organisation. Land Resources Laboratories. Division of Soils. Biennial Report — Aust CSIRO Land Resour Lab Div Soils Bienn Rep
Australia. Commonwealth Scientific and Industrial Research Organisation. Land Resources Laboratories. Division of Soils. Biennial Report — BRCSDT
Australia. Commonwealth Scientific and Industrial Research Organisation. Land Resources Management Technical Paper — Aust CSIRO Land Resour Manage Tech Pap
Australia. Commonwealth Scientific and Industrial Research Organisation. Land Resources Management. Technical Paper — LRMPDA
Australia. Commonwealth Scientific and Industrial Research Organisation. Marine Biochemistry Unit. Annual Report — Aust CSIRO Mar Biochem Unit Annu Rep
Australia. Commonwealth Scientific and Industrial Research Organisation. Marine Biochemistry Unit. Annual Report — CMBUC5
Australia. Commonwealth Scientific and Industrial Research Organisation. Marine Laboratories Report — Aust CSIRO Mar Lab Rep
Australia. Commonwealth Scientific and Industrial Research Organisation. Marine Laboratories. Report — RCMLDR
Australia. Commonwealth Scientific and Industrial Research Organisation. Mineragraphic Investigations. Technical Paper — Aust CSIRO Mineragraphic Invest Tech Pap
Australia. Commonwealth Scientific and Industrial Research Organisation. Minerals Research Laboratories. Annual Report — Aust CSIRO Miner Res Lab Annu Rep
Australia. Commonwealth Scientific and Industrial Research Organisation. Minerals Research Laboratories. Annual Report — CSMRCP
Australia. Commonwealth Scientific and Industrial Research Organisation. Minerals Research Laboratories. Investigation Report — Aust CSIRO Miner Res Lab Invest Rep
Australia. Commonwealth Scientific and Industrial Research Organisation. Mining Department. University of Melbourne. Ore Dressing Investigations. Report — Aust CSIRO Min Dep Univ Melbourne Ore Dressing Invest Rep
Australia. Commonwealth Scientific and Industrial Research Organisation. National Measurement Laboratory. Biennial Report — Aust CSIRO Natl Meas Lab Bienn Rep
Australia. Commonwealth Scientific and Industrial Research Organisation. National Measurement Laboratory. Biennial Report — BRNLDT
Australia. Commonwealth Scientific and Industrial Research Organisation. National Measurement Laboratory. Technical Paper — Aust CSIRO Natl Meas Lab Tech Pap
Australia. Commonwealth Scientific and Industrial Research Organisation. National Measurement Laboratory. Technical Paper — Natl Meas Lab Tech Pap CSIRO Aust
Australia. Commonwealth Scientific and Industrial Research Organisation. National Standards Laboratory. Biennial Report — Aust CSIRO Natl Stand Lab Bienn Rep
Australia. Commonwealth Scientific and Industrial Research Organisation. National Standards Laboratory. Biennial Report — CSNSAV
Australia. Commonwealth Scientific and Industrial Research Organisation. National Standards Laboratory. Technical Paper — ANSPAO
Australia. Commonwealth Scientific and Industrial Research Organisation. National Standards Laboratory. Technical Paper — Aust CSIRO Nat Stand Lab Tech Pap
Australia. Commonwealth Scientific and Industrial Research Organisation. National Standards Laboratory. Technical Paper — Aust CSIRO Natl Stand Lab Tech Pap
Australia. Commonwealth Scientific and Industrial Research Organisation. National Standards Laboratory. Technical Paper — Natl Stand Lab Tech Pap CSIRO Aust
Australia. Commonwealth Scientific and Industrial Research Organisation. Soil Mechanics Section. Technical Memorandum — ACSTBS
Australia. Commonwealth Scientific and Industrial Research Organisation. Soil Mechanics Section. Technical Memorandum — Aust CSIRO Soil Mech Sect Tech Memo
Australia. Commonwealth Scientific and Industrial Research Organisation. Soil Mechanics Section. Technical Paper — AUSMBV
Australia. Commonwealth Scientific and Industrial Research Organisation. Soil Mechanics Section. Technical Paper — Aust CSIRO Soil Mech Sect Tech Pap
Australia. Commonwealth Scientific and Industrial Research Organisation. Soil Publication — ASSPAP
Australia. Commonwealth Scientific and Industrial Research Organisation. Soil Publication — Aust CSIRO Soil Publ
Australia. Commonwealth Scientific and Industrial Research Organisation. Soils and Land Use Series — AOSLAJ
Australia. Commonwealth Scientific and Industrial Research Organisation. Soils and Land Use Series — Aust CSIRO Soils Land Use Ser
Australia Commonwealth Scientific and Industrial Research Organisation. Tropical Crops and Pastures. Annual Report — ARCPEA
Australia. Commonwealth Scientific and Industrial Research Organisation. Tropical Crops and Pastures. Annual Report — Aust CSIRO Trop Crops Pastures Ann Rep
Australia. Commonwealth Scientific and Industrial Research Organisation. Tropical Crops and Pastures. Divisional Report — Aust CSIRO Trop Crops & Pastures Div Rep
Australia Commonwealth Scientific and Industrial Research Organisation. Tropical Crops and Pastures. Divisional Report — CTCRDH
Australia. Commonwealth Scientific and Industrial Research Organisation. Wheat Research Unit. Annual Report — Aust CSIRO Wheat Res Unit Annu Rep
Australia Commonwealth Scientific and Industrial Research Organisation. Wheat Research Unit. Annual Report — CWRUAH
Australia. Commonwealth Scientific and Industrial Research Organisation. Wildlife Research — Aust CSIRO Wildl Res
Australia. Commonwealth Scientific and Industrial Research Organisation. Wildlife Survey Section. Technical Paper — Aust CSIRO Wildl Surv Sect Tech Pap
Australia. Commonwealth Scientific and Industrial Research Organization and the School of Mines of Western Australia. Kalgoorlie. Ore Dressing Investigations — Aust CSIRO Sch Mines West Aust Kalgoorlie Ore Dressing Inves
Australia. Commonwealth Scientific and Industrial Research Organization. Coal Research Laboratory Location Report — Aust CSIRO Coal Res Lab Locat Rep
Australia. Defence Research Laboratories. Paint Notes — Aust Def Res Lab Paint Notes
Australia. Defence Research Laboratories. Plating Notes — Aust Def Res Lab Plat Notes
Australia. Defence Standards Laboratories. DSL Report — Def Stand Lab DSL Rep
Australia. Defence Standards Laboratories. Report — Aust Def Stand Lab Rep
Australia. Defence Standards Laboratories. Report — Def Stand Lab Rep
Australia. Defence Standards Laboratories. Report — Rep Def Stand Lab Aust
Australia. Defence Standards Laboratories. Technical Memorandum — Aust Def Stand Lab Tech Mem
Australia. Defence Standards Laboratories. Technical Memorandum — Aust Def Stand Lab Tech Memo
Australia. Defence Standards Laboratories. Technical Memorandum — Def Stand Lab Tech Memo
Australia. Defence Standards Laboratories. Technical Note — Aust Def Stand Lab Tech Note
Australia. Defence Standards Laboratories. Technical Note — Def Stand Lab Tech Note
Australia. Defence Standards Laboratories. Technical Note — Tech Note Def Stand Lab Aust
Australia. Department of Agriculture. Biology Branch. Technical Paper — Aust Dep Agric Biol Branch Tech Pap
Australia. Department of Defence. Materials Research Laboratories. Report — Aust Dep Def Mater Res Lab Rep
Australia. Department of Defence. Materials Research Laboratories. Technical Note — Aust Dep Def Mater Res Lab Tech Note
Australia. Department of Defence. Weapons Research Establishment. Technical Report — Aust Dep Def Weapons Res Establ Tech Rep
Australia. Department of Foreign Affairs. International Treaties and Conventions — Aust DFA Treaty Series
Australia. Department of Health. Australian Radiation Laboratory. Technical Report Series ARL/TR — Aust Dep Health Aust Radiat Lab Tech Rep ARL/TR
Australia. Department of Health. Australian Radiation Laboratory. Technical Report Series ARL/TR — Aust Dep Health Aust Radiat Lab Tech Rep Ser ARL/TR
Australia. Department of Munitions. Paint Notes — Aust Dep Munitions Paint Notes
Australia. Department of Primary Industry. Fisheries Paper — Fish Pap Dep Prim Ind
Australia. Department of Primary Industry. Fisheries Report — Fish Rep Dep Prim Ind
Australia. Department of Supply. Aeronautical Research Laboratories. Mechanical Engineering Note — Aust Dep Supply Aeronaut Res Lab Mech Eng Note

Australia. Department of Supply. Aeronautical Research Laboratories. Structures and Materials Note — Aust Dep Supply Aeronaut Res Lab Struct Mater Note
Australia. Department of Supply. Aeronautical Research Laboratories. Structures and Materials Note — Struct Mater Note Aust Aeronaut Res Lab
Australia. Department of Supply. Defence Research Laboratories. Paint Notes — Aust Dep Supply Def Res Lab Paint Notes
Australia. Department of Supply. Defence Research Laboratories. Plating Notes — Aust Dep Supply Def Res Lab Plat Notes
Australia. Education Research and Development Committee. Annual Report — Aust Educ Res Dev Com Ann Rep
Australia. Fisheries Department. Fisheries Information Publication — Aust Fish Dept Fish Inf Publ
Australia. Government Public Relations Office. Ministerial Press Statements — Aust Press Statement
Australia. House of Representatives. Parliamentary Debates — Aust Parl Deb House Rep
Australia. Industries Assistance Commission. Annual Report — Aust Ind Assist Com Ann Rep
Australia. Materials Research Laboratories. Report — Aust Mater Res Lab Rep
Australia. Materials Research Laboratories. Report — Rep Mater Res Lab Aust
Australia. Materials Research Laboratories. Technical Note — Aust Mater Res Lab Tech Note
Australia. Materials Research Laboratories. Technical Note — Tech Note Mater Res Lab Aust
Australia. National Measurement Laboratory. Technical Paper — Aust Natl Meas Lab Tech Pap
Australia. New Zealand Conference on Pain — Aust NZ Conf Pain
Australia Newsletter — ADQ
Australia Now — Aust Now
Australia Now — Austral N
Australia. Parliament. House of Representatives. Parliamentary Debates — Aust Parl H of R Parl Deb
Australia. Parliament. Senate. Parliamentary Debates — Aust Parl Deb Senate
Australia. Parliament. Senate. Parliamentary Debates — Aust Parl Sen Parl Deb
Australia. Patent Office. Australian Official Journal of Patents — Aust Pat Off Aust Off J Pat
Australia. Patent Office. Australian Official Journal of Patents, Trade Marks, and Designs — Aust Pat Off Aust Off J Pat Trade Marks Des
Australia. Patent Specification (Petty) — Aust Pat Specif (Petty)
Australia Today — Aust Today
Australia. Weapons Research Establishment. Technical Report — Aust Weapons Res Establ Tech Rep
Australia (Western). Department of Mines. Annual Report — Aust (West) Dep Mines Annu Rep
Australia (Western). Department of Mines. Mineral Resources of Western Australia. Bulletin — Aust West Dep Mines Miner Resour West Aust Bull
Australia (Western). Department of Mines. Report of the Mineralogist, Analyst, and Chemist — Aust (West) Dep Mines Rep Mineral Anal Chem
Australia (Western). Geological Survey. Mineral Resources Bulletin — Aust (West) Geol Surv Miner Resour Bull
Australia (Western). Report of the Director of Government Chemical Laboratories — Aust (West) Rep Dir Gov Chem Lab
[*The*] **Australian** — A
[*The*] **Australian** — Aus
[*The*] **Australian** — Aust
Australian Aborigines Annual Bibliography — Aust Aborig
Australian Acacias — Aust Acacias
Australian Academic and Research Libraries — AARL
Australian Academic and Research Libraries — Aust Acad and Res Lib
Australian Academic and Research Libraries — Aust Acad Res Libr
Australian Academic and Research Libraries — Australian Acad and Res Lib
Australian Academy of Science. Reports — Aust Acad Sci Rep
Australian Academy of Science. Science and Industry Forum. Forum Report — Aust Acad Sci Sci Ind Forum Forum Rep
Australian Academy of Science. Science and Industry Forum. Forum Report — Forum Rep Sci Ind Forum Aust Acad Sci
Australian Academy of Science. Silver Jubilee Symposium — Aust Acad Sci Silver Jubilee Symp
Australian Academy of the Humanities. Proceedings — Aust Acad H
Australian Accountancy Progress — Aust Accountancy Progress
Australian Accountancy Student — Aust Accountancy Student
Australian Accountancy Student — Aust Acct Stud
Australian Accountant — Aust Acc
Australian Accountant — Aust Accnt
Australian Accountant — Aust Accountant
Australian Accountant — Aust Acct
Australian Accountant — Aust Acctnt
Australian Advances in Veterinary Science — Aust Adv Vet Sci
Australian Advertising Rate and Data Service — AARDS
Australian Aeronautical Research Committee. Report — Aust Aeronaut Res Comm Rep
Australian Aeronautical Research Committee. Report ACA — Aust Aeronaut Comm Rep ACA
Australian Aeronautical Research Committee. Report ACA — Aust Aeronaut Res Comm Rep ACA
Australian Agricultural Newsletter — Aust Agric News
Australian Amateur Mineralogist — Aust Amat Miner
Australian Amateur Mineralogist — Aust Amateur Mineral
Australian Amateur Mineralogist — Aust Amateur Mineralogist
Australian and New Zealand Association for the Advancement of Science. Congress — ANZAAS Congress
Australian and New Zealand Association for the Advancement of Science. Congress. Papers — Aust NZ Assoc Adv Sci Congr Pap
Australian and New Zealand Association for the Advancement of Science. Congress. Papers — Pap Congr Aust NZ Assoc Adv Sci
Australian and New Zealand Association for the Advancement of Science. Papers — ANZAAS Papers
Australian and New Zealand Association for the Advancement of Science. Report — Australian and New Zealand Assoc Adv Sci Rept
Australian and New Zealand Association of Inspectors of Schools. Journal — ANZ Insp Sch J
Australian and New Zealand Conveyancing Report — ACR
Australian and New Zealand Conveyancing Report — ACV
Australian and New Zealand Conveyancing Report — ANZ Conv R
Australian and New Zealand Environmental Report — ANV
Australian and New Zealand Environmental Report — Aust & NZ Environ Rep
Australian and New Zealand Environmental Report — Aust New Zeal Environ Rep
Australian and New Zealand General Practitioner — Aust & NZ General Practitioner
Australian and New Zealand General Practitioner — Aust NZ Gen Practnr
Australian and New Zealand General Practitioner — Austr NZ Gen Pract
Australian and New Zealand Income Tax Reports — AITR
Australian and New Zealand Insurance Cases — ANZ Insurance Cases
Australian and New Zealand Insurance Reporter — AIN
Australian and New Zealand Journal of Criminology — ANZJ Crim
Australian and New Zealand Journal of Criminology — ANZJC
Australian and New Zealand Journal of Criminology — Aust & NZ J Criminol
Australian and New Zealand Journal of Criminology — Aust NZ J C
Australian and New Zealand Journal of Criminology — Austl and NZJ Criminology
Australian and New Zealand Journal of Developmental Disabilities — ANZDDQ
Australian and New Zealand Journal of Developmental Disabilities — Aust NZ J Dev Disabil
Australian and New Zealand Journal of Medicine — Aust NZ J M
Australian and New Zealand Journal of Medicine — Aust NZ J Med
Australian and New Zealand Journal of Medicine. Supplement — Aust NZ J Med Suppl
Australian and New Zealand Journal of Obstetrics and Gynaecology — Aust NZ J O
Australian and New Zealand Journal of Obstetrics and Gynaecology — Aust NZ J Obstet Gynaec
Australian and New Zealand Journal of Obstetrics and Gynaecology — Aust NZ J Obstet Gynaecol
Australian and New Zealand Journal of Obstetrics and Gynaecology — Austr NZ J Obst Gynaec
Australian and New Zealand Journal of Obstetrics and Gynaecology — Australian New Zeal J Obstet Gynaecol
Australian and New Zealand Journal of Obstetrics and Gynaecology — AZOGB
Australian and New Zealand Journal of Obstetrics and Gynaecology (Supplement) — Aust NZ J Obstet Gynaecol (Suppl)
Australian and New Zealand Journal of Ophthalmology — ANZOEQ
Australian and New Zealand Journal of Ophthalmology — Aust NZ J Ophthalmol
Australian and New Zealand Journal of Psychiatry — Aust NZ J P
Australian and New Zealand Journal of Psychiatry — Aust NZ J Psychiat
Australian and New Zealand Journal of Psychiatry — Aust NZ J Psychiatry
Australian and New Zealand Journal of Sociology — ANZJOS
Australian and New Zealand Journal of Sociology — ANZJS
Australian and New Zealand Journal of Sociology — Aust NZ J Soc
Australian and New Zealand Journal of Sociology — Aust NZ J Sociol
Australian and New Zealand Journal of Sociology — Aust NZ Soc
Australian and New Zealand Journal of Sociology — Austral N Zealand J Sociol
Australian and New Zealand Journal of Sociology — Australian and NZ J Sociol
Australian and New Zealand Journal of Surgery — Aust & NZ J Surgery
Australian and New Zealand Journal of Surgery — Aust NZ J S
Australian and New Zealand Journal of Surgery — Aust NZ J Surg
Australian and New Zealand Journal of Surgery — Austr NZ J Surg
Australian and New Zealand Journal of Surgery — Australian New Zeal J Surg
Australian and New Zealand Rose Annual — Aust NZ Rose A
Australian and New Zealand Symposium on the Microcirculation — Aust NZ Symp Microcirc
Australian and New Zealand Weekly — Aust NZ W
Australian and Pacific Book Prices Current — Aust & Pac Book Prices Curr
Australian Anthropological Journal — AAJ
Australian Arabian Horse News — Aust Arab Horse News
Australian Argus Law Reports — AALR
Australian Argus Law Reports — ALR
Australian Argus Law Reports — Aust Argus L Rep
Australian Argus Law Reports — Austl Argus LR
Australian Army — Army
Australian Army Journal — Aust Army J
Australian Art Index [*Database*] — AARTI
Australian Association of Neurologists. Proceedings — Aust Assoc Neurol Proc
Australian Atomic Energy Commission. AAEC/E. Report — Aust AEC AAEC/E Rep
Australian Atomic Energy Commission. AAEC/TM. Report — Aust AEC AAEC/TM Rep
Australian Atomic Energy Commission. Information Paper — Aust AEC Inf Pap
Australian Atomic Energy Commission Research Establishment. AAEC/E — Aust AEC Res Establ AAEC/E
Australian Atomic Energy Commission. Research Establishment. Report — Aust AEC Res Establ Rep
Australian Atomic Energy Commission. Research Establishment. Report AAEC/S — Aust AEC Res Establ Rep AAEC/S
Australian Atomic Energy Commission. TRG Report — Aust AEC TRG Rep
Australian Atomic Energy Symposium. Proceedings of a Symposium on the Peaceful Uses of Atomic Energy. University of Sydney, June 2-6, 1958 — Aust At Energy Symp Proc

Australian Audio-Visual News — AAVN
Australian Author — Aust Auth
Australian Automobile Trade Journal — Aust Automobile Trade J
Australian Automotive Engineering and Equipment — Aust Automot Eng & Equip
Australian Aviation Newsletter — Aust Aviat Newsl
Australian Aviation Newsletter — Aust Aviation Newsletter
Australian Aviation Yearbook — Aust Aviat Yb
Australian Aviculture — Aust Avicult
Australian Baker and Millers' Journal — Auct Baker
Australian Banker — Aust Bank
Australian Bankruptcy Bulletin — ABB
Australian Bankruptcy Cases — ABC
Australian Bankruptcy Cases — Aust Bankr Cas
Australian Bankruptcy Cases — Austl Bankr Cas
Australian Bankruptcy Cases — Austr BC
Australian Baptist — Aust Baptist
Australian Bar Gazette — Aust Bar Gaz
Australian Bar Review — Aust Bar Rev
Australian Bee Journal — Aust Bee J
Australian Beekeeper — Austral Beekeeper
Australian Biblical Review — ABR
Australian Biblical Review [*Melbourne*] — AuBiR
Australian Biblical Review — Aus BR
Australian Biblical Review [*Melbourne*] — AusBiR
Australian Biblical Review — Aust Bib R
Australian Bibliography of Agriculture [*Database*] — ABOA
Australian Biochemical Society. Proceedings — Aust Biochem Soc Proc
Australian Bird Bander — Aust Bird Bander
Australian Birdwatcher — ABWADK
Australian Birdwatcher — Aust Birdwatcher
Australian Boating — Aust Boating
Australian Boating Industry — Aust Boat Ind
Australian Book Auction Records — Aust Book Auction Rec
Australian Book Review — ABR
Australian Book Review — Aust Book R
Australian Book Review — Aust Book Rev
Australian Book Review. Children's Books and Educational Supplement — Aust Book Rev Children's Book & Ed Suppl
Australian Books in Print [*Information service or system*] — ABIP
Australian Bookseller and Publisher — AB & P
Australian Brewing and Wine Journal — Aust Brewing Wine J
Australian Brewing and Wine Journal — Austr Brew Wi J
Australian British Business Directory — Aust Brit Bus Dir
Australian Builder — Aust Bldr
Australian Builder — Aust Builder
Australian Building Forum — Aust Build Forum
Australian Building Research Congress. Proceedings — Proc Aust Bldg Res Congr
Australian Building Research Congress. Proceedings — Proc Aust Build Res Congr
Australian Building Science and Technology — Aust Build Sci Technol
Australian Building Specification — ABS
Australian Building Technology — Aust Build Technol
Australian Bulletin of Labour — Aust Bull Labour
Australian Bush Nursing Journal — Aust Bush Nursing J
Australian Business — AB
Australian Business [*Database*] — AUSB
Australian Business — Aust Bus
Australian Business Brief and Hansard Service [*Database*] — BBHS
Australian Business Computer — ABC
Australian Business Index — ABI
Australian Business Index [*Information service or system*] — ABIX
Australian Business Law Review — A Bus L Rev
Australian Business Law Review — ABLR
Australian Business Law Review — ABU
Australian Business Law Review — Aust Bus L Rev
Australian Business Law Review — Aust Bus Law R
Australian Business Law Review — Aust Business L Rev
Australian Business Law Review — Austl Bus L Rev
Australian Business Law Review — Austr Bus LR
Australian Camera and Cine — Aust Camera
Australian Canegrower — Aust Canegrow
Australian Canning Convention. Proceedings — Aust Canning Convention
Australian Canning Convention. Proceedings — Aust Canning Convention Procs
Australian Capital Territory. Reports — ACTR
Australian Catholic Digest — Aust Catholic D
Australian Catholic Historical Society. Journal — ACHSJ
Australian Catholic Historical Society. Journal — Aust Cath Hist Soc J
Australian Catholic Historical Society. Journal — JACHS
Australian Catholic Record [*Sydney*] — AusCR
Australian Catholic Record [*Sydney*] — AusCRec
Australian Catholic Truth Society. Record — Aust Catholic Truth Soc Rec
Australian Ceramic Conference. Proceedings — Aust Ceram Conf Proc
Australian Ceramic Conference. Proceedings — Proc Aust Ceram Conf
Australian Ceramic Conference. Proceedings — Proc Aust Ceramic Conf
Australian Chemical Abstracts — Aust Chem Abstr
Australian Chemical Abstracts — Austr Chem Abstr
Australian Chemical Engineering — Aust Chem Eng
Australian Chemical Engineering — Aust Chem Engineering
Australian Chemical Engineering — Aust Chem Engng
Australian Chemical Engineering. Conference — Aust Chem Eng Conf
Australian Chemical Institute. Journal and Proceedings — Aust Chem Inst J Proc
Australian Chemical Institute. Journal and Proceedings — Austr Chem Inst J Pr
Australian Chemical Institute Journal and Proceedings. Supplement — Aust Chem Inst J Proc Suppl
Australian Chemical Processing — Aust Chem Proc
Australian Chemical Processing — Aust Chem Process
Australian Chemical Processing — Aust Chem Processing
Australian Chemical Processing and Engineering — ACPE
Australian Chemical Processing and Engineering — Aust Chem Process Eng
Australian Chemical Processing and Engineering — Aust Chem Process Engng
Australian Chess Lore — ACL
Australian Child and Family Welfare — ACFW
Australian Child and Family Welfare — Aust Child Fam Welfare
Australian Children Limited — Auct Child Limited
Australian Children Limited — Aust Child Ltd
Australian Children Limited — Aust Children Ltd
Australian Christian — Aust Christian
Australian Church Quarterly — Aust Church Q
Australian Church Record — Aust Church Rec
Australian Citizen Limited — Aust Citizen Ltd
Australian Citrus News — Aust Citrus News
Australian Civil Engineering — Aust Civ Eng
Australian Civil Engineering — Aust Civ Engng
Australian Civil Engineering and Construction — Aust Civ Engng Constr
Australian Civil Engineering and Construction — Aust Civil Eng Construc
Australian Civil Engineering and Construction — Austr Civ Eng Constr
Australian Clay Minerals Conference. Proceedings — Proc Aust Clay Miner Conf
Australian Climatological Summary — Aust Climatol Summ
Australian Clinical Review — Aust Clin Rev
Australian Coal Association (Research) Limited. Report — Aust Coal Ass (Res) Rep
Australian Coal Industry Research Laboratories. Published Report. PR — Aust Coal Ind Res Lab Publ Rep PR
Australian Coal Preparation Conference — Aust Coal Prep Conf
Australian Coal Report — AUS
Australian Coal, Shipping, Steel, and the Harbour — Aust Coal & Harbour
Australian Coal, Shipping, Steel, and the Harbour — Harbour
Australian Coalmining and Mine Mechanisation — Aust Coalmining
Australian Coin Review — ACR
Australian Coin Review — Aust Coin
Australian College Libraries — ACL
Australian College Libraries Activities Network [*Database*] — CLANN
Australian College of Education. Victorian Chapter. Newsletter — Aust Coll Educ Vic Chapter Newsl
Australian College of Speech Therapists. Journal — Aust Coll Speech Ther J
[*The*] **Australian Comic Collector** — TACC
Australian Commercial Journal — ACJ
Australian Commercial Journal — Austl Com J
Australian Company Law and Practice — ACP
Australian Company Law Cases — ACC
Australian Company Law Cases — ACLC
Australian Company Law Cases — Aust Comp Law Cases
Australian Company Law Reports — ACLR
Australian Computer Bulletin — ACB
Australian Computer Bulletin — Aus Comp Bul
Australian Computer Bulletin — Aust Comput Bull
Australian Computer Journal — Aus Comp J
Australian Computer Journal — Aust Comput J
Australian Computer Journal — Austral Comput J
Australian Computer Science Communications — Aust Comput Sci Commun
Australian Computer Science Communications — Austral Comput Sci Comm
Australian Conference on Chemical Engineering — Aust Conf Chem Eng
Australian Conference on Nuclear Techniques of Analysis. Proceedings — Aust Conf Nucl Tech Anal Proc
Australian Conference on Nuclear Techniques of Analysis. Proceedings — Proc Aust Conf Nucl Tech Anal
Australian Conference on Nuclear Techniques of Analysis. Summary of Proceedings — Aust Conf Nucl Tech Anal Summ Proc
Australian Conference on Nuclear Techniques of Analysis. Summary of Proceedings — Summ Proc Aust Conf Nucl Tech Anal
Australian Conservation Foundation. Newsletter — Aust Conserv Found Newsl
Australian Conservation Foundation. Newsletter — Newsl Aust Conserv Fdn
Australian Conservation Foundation. Newsletter — Newsl Aust Conserv Found
Australian Construction Law Reporter — ACLR
Australian Consumer Sales and Credit Law Reporter — ASC
Australian Conveyancer and Solicitors' Journal — AC & SJ
Australian Conveyancer and Solicitors' Journal — Aust Conv
Australian Conveyancer and Solicitors' Journal — Aust Conv Sol J
Australian Conveyancer and Solicitors' Journal — Aust Conveyancer
Australian Copyright Council. Bulletin — ACCB
Australian Cordial Maker, Brewer, and Bottler's Gazette — Aust Cordial Maker
Australian Corporate Affairs Reporter — ACA
Australian Corrosion Engineering — Aust Corr Eng
Australian Corrosion Engineering — Aust Corros Eng
Australian Corrosion Engineering — Aust Corros Engng
Australian Corrosion Engineering — Aust Corrosion Eng
Australian Cotton Grower — Aust Cott Grow
Australian Cotton Grower — Austr Cott Grow
Australian Cotton Grower, Farmer, and Dairyman — Aust Cott Grow Fmr Dairym
Australian Cotton Grower, Farmer, and Dairyman — Austr Cott Grow Farm Dairym
Australian Council for Aeronautics. Report ACA — Aust Counc Aeronaut Rep ACA
Australian Council for Educational Administration. Bulletin — Aust Counc Educ Admin
Australian Council for Educational Research. Bulletin — ACER Bull
Australian Council for Educational Research. Test News — ACER Test News

Australian Country Magazine — Aust Country
Australian Country Magazine — Aust Country Mag
Australian Country Magazine — Aust Ctry Mag
Australian Criminal Reports — A Crim R
Australian Criminal Reports — ACR
Australian Culturist — Aust Culturist
Australian Current Law — ACL
Australian Current Law Bulletin — ACL Bull
Australian Current Law Digest — ACLD
Australian Current Law Review — ACL Rev
Australian Current Law Review — ACLR
Australian Current Law Review — Aust CL Rev
Australian Current Law Review — Aust Curr L Rev
Australian Current Law Review — Aust Curr Law Rev
Australian Dairy Review — Aust Dairy R
Australian Dairy Review — Aust Dairy Rev
Australian Defence Scientific Service. Aeronautical Research Laboratories. Report — Aust Def Sc Serv ARL Report
Australian Defence Scientific Service. Materials Research Laboratory. Technical Note — Aust Def Sci Serv Mater Res Lab Tech Note
Australian Defence Scientific Service. Weapons Research Establishment. Technical Note — Aust Def Sci Serv Weapons Res Est Tech Note
Australian Demographic Review — Aust Demographic R
Australian Dental Journal — Aust Dent J
Australian Dental Journal — Aust Dental J
Australian Dental Journal — Austr Dent J
Australian Dental Mirror — Aust Dent Mirr
Australian Dental Mirror — Austr Dent Mirr
Australian Dental Summary — Aust Dent Summ
Australian Dictionary of Biography — ADB
Australian Digest — AD
Australian Digest — Aust Digest
Australian Digest Bulletin — ADB
Australian Director — Aust Dir
Australian Director — Aust Director
Australian Directory of Music Organisations — ADMO
Australian Directory of Music Research — ADMR
Australian Doctor Weekly — Aust Dr Wkly
Australian Draftsmen — Aust Draftsmen
Australian Dried Fruit News — Aust Dried Fruit News
Australian Drug and Medical Information Group. Bulletin — ADMIG Bulletin
Australian Early Childhood Resource Booklets — Aust Early Child Resource Booklets
Australian Earth Sciences Information System [*Database*] — AESIS
Australian Earth Sciences Information System. Quarterly — AESIS Quarterly
Australian Economic History Review — AEHR
Australian Economic History Review — Aust Econ H
Australian Economic History Review — Aust Econ Hist R
Australian Economic History Review — Aust Econ Hist Rev
Australian Economic History Review — Austral Econ Hist R
Australian Economic History Review — Australian Econ Hist R
Australian Economic History Review — Australian Econ Hist Rev
Australian Economic News Digest — Aust Econ News Dig
Australian Economic Papers — AEP
Australian Economic Papers — Aust Econ
Australian Economic Papers — Aust Econ Pap
Australian Economic Papers — Austral Econ Pap
Australian Economic Papers — Australian Econ Pas
Australian Economic Review — AER
Australian Economic Review — Aust Econ Rev
Australian Economic Review — Australian Econ R
Australian Education Index [*Australian Council for Educational Research*] [*Information service or system*] — AEI
Australian Education Index — Aus Educ Ind
Australian Education Index — Aust Educ Index
Australian Education Researcher — Aust Educ Res
Australian Education Review — Aust Educ R
Australian Education Review — Aust Educ Rev
Australian Electrical World — Aust Elec World
Australian Electrical World — Aust Elect Wld
Australian Electrical World — Aust Electr World
Australian Electrochemistry Conference — Aust Electrochem Conf
Australian Electronics Bulletin — Aust Electron Bull
Australian Electronics Engineering — Aust Electron Eng
Australian Electronics Engineering — Aust Electron Engng
Australian Electronics Monthly — Aust Electron M
Australian Encyclopaedia — AE
Australian Encyclopaedia — Aust Encycl
Australian Endeavourer — Aust Endeavourer
Australian Engineering Database — ENGINE
Australian Entomological Magazine — Aust Ent Mag
Australian Entomological Magazine — Aust Entomol Mag
Australian Entomological Society. Journal — Aust Entomol Soc J
Australian Entomological Society. Miscellaneous Publication — Aust Entomol Soc Misc Publ
Australian Estate and Gift Duty Reporter — AEG
Australian Estate and Gift Duty Reporter — AEGR
Australian Evaluation Newsletter — Aust Eval Newsl
Australian Exporter — Aust Exporter
Australian External Territories — Aust Ext Terr
Australian External Territories — Aust External Terr
Australian Factory — Aust Fact
Australian Factory — Aust Factory
Australian Family Law and Practice — AFL
Australian Family Law Cases — FLC
Australian Family Physician — Aust Fam Physician
Australian Family Physician — Austral Fam Physician
Australian Family Safety — Aust Fam Safe
Australian Farm Management Journal — Aust Fm Mgmt J
Australian Fashion News — Aust Fashion News
Australian Federal Tax Reporter — AFT
Australian Federal Tax Reporter — FTR
Australian Federation of University Women. Bulletin — AFUW Bul
Australian Financial Review — AFR
Australian Financial Review [*Database*] — AFRE
Australian Financial Review — Aust Fin Rev
Australian Financial Review — Aust Financ Rev
Australian Financial Review — Aust Financial R
Australian Financial Review — Aust Financial Rev
Australian Financial Review — Austrl Fin
Australian Financial Review — FR
Australian Financial Times — Aust Financial Times
Australian Finishing — Aust Finish
Australian Finishing Review — Aust Finish Rev
Australian Fisheries — Aust Fish
Australian Fisheries Education Leaflet — Aust Fish Educ Leafl
Australian Fisheries Newsletter — Aust Fish Newsl
Australian Fisheries Paper — Aust Fish Pap
Australian Food Manufacturer and Distributor — Aust Fd Manuf
Australian Food Manufacturer and Distributor — Aust Fd Mf
Australian Food Manufacturer and Distributor — Aust Fd Mfr
Australian Food Manufacturer and Distributor — Aust Food Manuf
Australian Food Manufacturer and Distributor — Aust Food Manuf Distrib
Australian Food Manufacturer and Distributor — Aust Food Mfr Distrib
Australian Foreign Affairs and Trade — Aust Foreign Aff Trade
Australian Foreign Affairs Record — AFAR
Australian Foreign Affairs Record — Aust For Aff R
Australian Foreign Affairs Record — Aust Foreign Aff Rec
Australian Foreign Affairs Record — Austral For Aff Rec
Australian Foreign Affairs Record — Australian For Affairs Rec
Australian Forest Grower — Aust For Grow
Australian Forest Industries Journal — Aust For Ind J
Australian Forest Industries Journal — Aust Forest Inds J
Australian Forest Industries Journal and Australian Logger — Aust For Ind J Aust Log
Australian Forest Journal — Aust For J
Australian Forest Research — Aust For Res
Australian Forest Research — Aust Forest
Australian Forest Research — Aust Forest Res
Australian Forest Research. Forest Research Institute — Austral Forest Res
Australian Forest Resources — Aust For Resour
Australian Forest Tree Nutrition Conference. Contributed Papers — Aust For Tree Nutr Conf Contrib Pap
Australian Forester — Aust Forester
Australian Forestry — Aust For
Australian Forestry — Aust Forestry
Australian Forestry — Austr For
Australian Forestry Journal — Austr For J
Australian Forestry Journal — Australian For J
Australian Forestry (Perth) — Aust For (Perth)
Australian Foundry Trade Journal — Aust Found Trade J
Australian Foundry Trade Journal — Aust Foundry Trade J
Australian Fracture Group Conference. Proceedings — Aust Fract Group Conf Proc
Australian Fracture Group Conference. Proceedings — Conf Aust Fract Group Proc
Australian Fruitgrower, Fertiliser, and Poultry Farmer — Austral Fruitgrower
Australian Furnishing Trade Journal — Aust Furn Trade J
Australian Garden and Field — Austral Gard Field
Australian Garden History Society. Journal — Australian Garden History Soc Jnl
Australian Gas Bulletin — Aust Gas Bull
Australian Gas Journal — Aust Gas J
Australian Gem and Treasure Hunter — Aust Gem
Australian Gemmologist — Aust Gemmol
Australian Gemmologist — Aust Gemmologist
Australian Gems and Crafts — Aust Gems
Australian Genealogist — Aust Geneal
Australian Genealogist — Aust Genealogist
Australian Geographer — AG
Australian Geographer — Aust Geog
Australian Geographer — Aust Geogr
Australian Geographer — Aust Geographer
Australian Geographer — Austr Geogr
Australian Geographical Record — Aust Geog Rec
Australian Geographical Record — Aust Geog Record
Australian Geographical Record — Aust Geogr Rec
Australian Geographical Society. Report — Austr Geogr Soc Rep
Australian Geographical Studies — Aust Geog S
Australian Geographical Studies — Aust Geog Stud
Australian Geographical Studies — Aust Geog Studies
Australian Geographical Studies — Aust Geogr Stud
Australian Geographical Studies — Aust Geogr Studies
Australian Geologist — Aust Geol
Australian Geomechanics Journal — Aust Geomech J
Australian Geomechanics Journal — Aust Geomechanics J
Australian Gliding — Aust Gliding
Australian Goat World — Aust Goat World
Australian Gourmet — Aust Gourmet
Australian Government Analytical Laboratories. Report of Investigations — Aust Gov Anal Lab Rep Invest

Australian Government Analytical Laboratories. Report of Investigations — Rep Invest Aust Gov Anal Lab
Australian Government Digest — AGD
Australian Government Publications [*Information service or system*] — AGP
Australian Government Publications — Aust Gov Publ
Australian Government Weekly Digest — AGWD
Australian Grade Teacher — AGT
Australian Grade Teacher — Aust Grade Teach
Australian Grapegrower [*Later, Australian Grapegrower and Winemaker*] — Aust Grapegr
Australian Grapegrower and Winemaker — Aust Grapegrow
Australian Hand Weaver and Spinner — Aust Hand Weaver
Australian Hardware Journal — Aust Hardware J
Australian Health Education Advisory Digest — AHEAD
Australian Hereford Annual — Aust Hereford A
Australian Hereford Annual — Aust Hereford Ann
Australian Hereford Annual — Aust Hereford Annu
Australian Hereford Journal — Aust Hereford J
Australian Hi-Fi — Aust Hi-Fi
Australian High Court and Federal Court Practice — AHF
Australian Highway — Aust Highway
Australian Highway — Aust Hwy
Australian Historical Association. Bulletin — AHAB
Australian Historical Bibliography — Australian Hist Bibliogr
Australian Historical Society. Journal and Proceedings — J Proc Aust Hist Soc
Australian History Teacher — Aust Hist Teach
Australian Home Beautiful — Aust Home Beaut
Australian Home Journal — Aust Home J
Australian Homemaker — Aust Homemaker
Australian Horticultural Magazine and Garden Guide — Austral Hort Mag Gard Guide
Australian Hospital — Aust Hosp
Australian Hospital — Aust Hospital
Australian House and Garden — Aust House and Garden
Australian House and Garden — Aust House Gard
Australian Housing — Aust Housing
Australian Humanities Research Council. Annual Report — Aust Human Res Cncl A Rept
[*The*] **Australian Hymn Book** — AHB
Australian Immigration: Consolidated Statistics — Aust Immigr Consol Stat
Australian in Facts and Figures — Facts & Figures
Australian Income Tax Guide — ATG
Australian Income Tax Guide — ITG
Australian Income Tax Law and Practice — AITL & P
Australian Income Tax Reports — AITR
Australian Industrial and Mining Standard — Aust Ind Min Stand
Australian Industrial Law Review — AIL
Australian Industrial Law Review — AILR
Australian Industrial Law Review — Aust Ind LR
Australian Industrial Relations Database — IREL
Australian Industrial Research Directory — AIRD
Australian Industrial Safety, Health, and Welfare — ASH
Australian Industries Development Association. Bulletin — AID
Australian Industries Development Association. Director Reports — Aust Ind Dev Assoc Dir Repts
Australian Industries Development Association. Director Reports — Aust Ind Development Assn Director Report
Australian Institute of Aboriginal Studies. Newsletter — AIAS News
Australian Institute of Aboriginal Studies. Newsletter — Austr Inst Aborig Stud Newsletter
Australian Institute of Energy National Conference. Papers — Aust Inst Energy Natl Conf Pap
Australian Institute of Energy News Journal — Aust Inst Energy News J
Australian Institute of Family Studies. Working Paper — Aust Inst Fam Stud Work Pap
Australian Institute of International Affairs. New South Wales Branch — Aust Inst Internat Aff NSW Br
Australian Institute of Librarians. Proceedings — Australian Inst Libn Proc
Australian Institute of Marine Science. Monograph Series — Aust Inst Mar Sci Monogr Ser
Australian Institute of Petroleum. South Australian Branch. Annual Seminar — Aust Inst Pet South Aust Branch Annu Semin
Australian Insurance and Banking Record — AIBR
Australian Intercollegian — Aust Intercollegian
Australian Jazz Quarterly — AJQ
Australian Jewish Herald — Aust Jewish Herald
Australian Jewish Historical Society. Journal — AJHS J
Australian Jewish Historical Society. Journal and Proceedings — Aust Jewish Hist Soc J Proc
Australian Jewish Historical Society. Journal and Proceedings — J Proc Aust Jewish Hist Soc
Australian Jewish News — AJN
Australian Jewish News — Aust Jewish News
Australian Jewish Outlook — Aust Jewish Outlook
Australian Joint Copying Project — AJCP
Australian Journal — AJ
Australian Journal — Aust J
Australian Journal for Health, Physical Education, and Recreation — AUHJ
Australian Journal for Health, Physical Education, and Recreation — AUS J HPER
Australian Journal for Health, Physical Education, and Recreation — Aust J Health Phys Edu Recreation
Australian Journal for Health, Physical Education, and Recreation — Aust J Health Phys Educ Recreation
Australian Journal. Institute of Transport — Aust J Inst Trans
Australian Journal of Adult Education — Aust J Adult Ed
Australian Journal of Adult Education — Aust J Adult Educ
Australian Journal of Advanced Nursing — Aust J Adv Nurs
Australian Journal of Agricultural Economics — Aust J Ag E
Australian Journal of Agricultural Economics — Aust J Ag Econ
Australian Journal of Agricultural Economics — Aust J Agr Econ
Australian Journal of Agricultural Economics — Aust J Agric Econ
Australian Journal of Agricultural Economics — Austral J Agr Econ
Australian Journal of Agricultural Economics — Austral J Agric Econ
Australian Journal of Agricultural Research — Aust J Ag R
Australian Journal of Agricultural Research — Aust J Ag Res
Australian Journal of Agricultural Research — Aust J Agr
Australian Journal of Agricultural Research — Aust J Agr Res
Australian Journal of Agricultural Research — Aust J Agric Res
Australian Journal of Agricultural Research — Austr J Agric Res
Australian Journal of Agricultural Research — Austral J Agric Res
Australian Journal of Alcoholism and Drug Dependence — AJADD
Australian Journal of Alcoholism and Drug Dependence — Aust J Alcohol & Drug Depend
Australian Journal of Applied Science — AJAS
Australian Journal of Applied Science — Aust J Appl Sci
Australian Journal of Applied Science — Austr J Appl Sci
Australian Journal of Applied Science — Austral J Appl Sci
Australian Journal of Architecture and Arts — Aust J Arch & Arts
Australian Journal of Biblical Archaeology — AJBA
Australian Journal of Biblical Archaeology — Au JBA
Australian Journal of Biblical Archaeology [*Sydney*] — AusJBibArch
Australian Journal of Biblical Archaeology — Aust J Biblical Archaeol
Australian Journal of Biological Sciences — Aust J Biol
Australian Journal of Biological Sciences — Aust J Biol Sci
Australian Journal of Biological Sciences — Austr J Biol Sci
Australian Journal of Biological Sciences — Austral J Biol Sci
Australian Journal of Biotechnology — Aust J Biotechnol
Australian Journal of Botany — AJB
Australian Journal of Botany — AJBTA
Australian Journal of Botany — Aust J Bot
Australian Journal of Botany — Aust J Botany
Australian Journal of Botany — Austr J Bot
Australian Journal of Botany — Austral J Bot
Australian Journal of Botany. Supplementary Series — Aust J Bot Suppl Ser
Australian Journal of Botany. Supplementary Series. Supplement — Aust J Bot Suppl Ser Suppl
Australian Journal of Botany. Supplementary Series. Supplement — Aust J Bot Supplry Ser Suppl
Australian Journal of Chemical Engineers — Aust J Chem Eng
Australian Journal of Chemistry — AJCHAS
Australian Journal of Chemistry — Aust J Chem
Australian Journal of Chemistry — Austr J Chem
Australian Journal of Chemistry — Austral J Chem
Australian Journal of Clinical and Experimental Hypnosis — AJCHDV
Australian Journal of Clinical and Experimental Hypnosis — Aust J Clin Exp Hypn
Australian Journal of Coal Mining Technology and Research — Aust J Coal Min Technol Res
Australian Journal of Cultural Studies — AJCS
Australian Journal of Dairy Technology — AJDTAZ
Australian Journal of Dairy Technology — Aust J Dair
Australian Journal of Dairy Technology — Aust J Dairy Tech
Australian Journal of Dairy Technology — Aust J Dairy Technol
Australian Journal of Dairy Technology — Aust J Dairy Technology
Australian Journal of Dairy Technology. Supplement — Aust J Dairy Technol Suppl
Australian Journal of Dentistry — Aust J Dent
Australian Journal of Dentistry — Aust J Dentistry
Australian Journal of Dentistry — Austr J Dent
Australian [*later, Australasian*] **Journal of Dermatology** — Aust J Derm
Australian [*later, Australasian*] **Journal of Dermatology** — Aust J Dermatol
Australian [*later, Australasian*] **Journal of Dermatology** — Austr J Derm
Australian Journal of Developmental Disabilities — AUJDDT
Australian Journal of Developmental Disabilities — Aust J Dev Disabil
Australian Journal of Developmental Disabilities — Aust J Dev Disabilities
Australian Journal of Early Childhood — Aust J Early Child
Australian Journal of Earth Sciences — Aust J Earth Sci
Australian Journal of Ecology — AJECDQ
Australian Journal of Ecology — Aust J Ecol
Australian Journal of Education — AJE
Australian Journal of Education — Aust J Ed
Australian Journal of Education — Aust J Educ
Australian Journal of Experimental Agriculture — AJEAEL
Australian Journal of Experimental Agriculture — Aust J Exp Agric
Australian Journal of Experimental Agriculture — Aust J Exper Agric
Australian Journal of Experimental Agriculture and Animal Husbandry — AAAHAN
Australian Journal of Experimental Agriculture and Animal Husbandry — Aust J Ex A
Australian Journal of Experimental Agriculture and Animal Husbandry — Aust J Exp Agr Anim Husb
Australian Journal of Experimental Agriculture and Animal Husbandry — Aust J Exp Agric An Husb
Australian Journal of Experimental Agriculture and Animal Husbandry — Aust J Exp Agric Anim Husb
Australian Journal of Experimental Agriculture and Animal Husbandry — Aust J Exper Agric
Australian Journal of Experimental Agriculture and Animal Husbandry — Austral J Exp Agric Anim Husb

Australian Journal of Experimental Biology and Medical Science — AJEBAK
Australian Journal of Experimental Biology and Medical Science — Aust J Ex B
Australian Journal of Experimental Biology and Medical Science — Aust J Exp B
Australian Journal of Experimental Biology and Medical Science — Aust J Exp Biol
Australian Journal of Experimental Biology and Medical Science — Aust J Exp Biol Med Sci
Australian Journal of Experimental Biology and Medical Science — Aust J Expl Biol Med Sci
Australian Journal of Experimental Biology and Medical Science — Austr J Exp Biol Med Sci
Australian Journal of Family Law — AJFL
Australian Journal of Family Therapy — Aust J Fam Ther
Australian Journal of Forensic Sciences — AJFS
Australian Journal of Forensic Sciences — Aust J For Sci
Australian Journal of Forensic Sciences — Aust J Forensic Sci
Australian Journal of Forensic Sciences — Aust Jnl of Forensic Sciences
Australian Journal of Forensic Sciences — Austl J For Sci
Australian Journal of French Studies — AJFS
Australian Journal of French Studies — Aust J Fr S
Australian Journal of French Studies — Aust J Fr Stud
Australian Journal of French Studies — Aust J French Stud
Australian Journal of French Studies — Australian J French Stud
Australian Journal of Geodesy, Photogrammetry, and Surveying — Aust J Geod Photogramm and Surv
Australian Journal of Grape and Wine Research — Aust J Grape Wine Res
Australian Journal of Higher Education — AJHE
Australian Journal of Higher Education — Aust J Higher Ed
Australian Journal of Higher Education — Aust J Higher Educ
Australian Journal of Higher Education — Austral J High Educ
Australian Journal of Hospital Pharmacy — AUHPAI
Australian Journal of Hospital Pharmacy — Aust J Hosp Pharm
Australian Journal of Human Communication Disorders — Austral J Hum Commun Dis
Australian Journal of Instrument Technology — Aust J Instrum Tech
Australian Journal of Instrument Technology — Aust J Instrum Technol
Australian Journal of Instrument Technology — Aust J Instrument Tech
Australian Journal of Instrument Technology — Aust J Instrument Technology
Australian Journal of Instrument Technology — Austr J Instr Techn
Australian Journal of Instrumentation and Control — Aust J Inst
Australian Journal of Instrumentation and Control — Aust J Instrum Control
Australian Journal of Law and Society — AJLS
Australian Journal of Law and Society — Aust JL & Soc
Australian Journal of Management — AJM
Australian Journal of Management — Aust J Manage
Australian Journal of Management — Australian J Mgt
Australian Journal of Marine and Freshwater Research — AJMFA
Australian Journal of Marine and Freshwater Research — AJMFA4
Australian Journal of Marine and Freshwater Research — Aust J Mar
Australian Journal of Marine and Freshwater Research — Aust J Mar Freshw Res
Australian Journal of Marine and Freshwater Research — Aust J Mar Freshwat Res
Australian Journal of Marine and Freshwater Research — Aust J Mar Freshwater Res
Australian Journal of Marine and Freshwater Research — Austr J Mar Freshwat Res
Australian Journal of Marine and Freshwater Research — Austral J Mar Freshwater Res
Australian Journal of Medical Laboratory Science — Aust J Med Lab Sci
Australian Journal of Medical Technology — Aust J Med Technol
Australian Journal of Mental Retardation — AJMNA
Australian Journal of Mental Retardation — Aust J Ment Retard
Australian Journal of Music Education — AJME
Australian Journal of Music Education — AJMEA
Australian Journal of Music Education — Aust J Music Ed
Australian Journal of Music Education — Aust J Music Educ
Australian Journal of Music Education — Australian J Mus Ed
Australian Journal of Ophthalmology — AJOHBL
Australian Journal of Ophthalmology — Aust J Ophthalmol
Australian Journal of Optometry — Aust J Optom
Australian Journal of Optometry — Aust J Optometry
Australian Journal of Pharmaceutical Sciences — AJPSBP
Australian Journal of Pharmaceutical Sciences — Aust J Pharm Sci
Australian Journal of Pharmacy — Aust J Pharm
Australian Journal of Pharmacy — Aust J Pharmacy
Australian Journal of Pharmacy — Austr J Pharm
Australian Journal of Pharmacy. Supplement — Aust J Pharm Suppl
Australian Journal of Physical Education — Aust J Phys Ed
Australian Journal of Physical Education — Aust J Phys Educ
Australian Journal of Physical Education — Aust J Physical Educ
Australian Journal of Physics — Aust J Phys
Australian Journal of Physics — Austr J Phys
Australian Journal of Physics — Austral J Phys
Australian Journal of Physics. Astrophysical Supplement — Aust J Phys Astrophys Suppl
Australian Journal of Physiotherapy — Aust J Physiother
Australian Journal of Physiotherapy — Aust J Physiotherapy
Australian Journal of Plant Physiology — AJPPCH
Australian Journal of Plant Physiology — Aust J Pl Physiol
Australian Journal of Plant Physiology — Aust J Plan
Australian Journal of Plant Physiology — Aust J Plant Physiol
Australian Journal of Politics and History — AJ Pol & Hist
Australian Journal of Politics and History — AJPH
Australian Journal of Politics and History — AusJP
Australian Journal of Politics and History — Aust J Pol and Hist
Australian Journal of Politics and History — Aust J Pol Hist
Australian Journal of Politics and History — Aust J Poli
Australian Journal of Politics and History — Aust J Poli & Hist
Australian Journal of Politics and History — Aust J Polit Hist
Australian Journal of Politics and History — Aust J Politics & History
Australian Journal of Politics and History — Aust J Politics Hist
Australian Journal of Politics and History — Austral J Polit Hist
Australian Journal of Psychological Research — Aust J Psych Res
Australian Journal of Psychological Research — Aust J Psychological Research
Australian Journal of Psychology — AJP
Australian Journal of Psychology — ASJPA
Australian Journal of Psychology — ASJPAE
Australian Journal of Psychology — Aust J Psyc
Australian Journal of Psychology — Aust J Psych
Australian Journal of Psychology — Aust J Psychol
Australian Journal of Psychology — Aust J Psychology
Australian Journal of Psychology — Austr J Psychol
Australian Journal of Psychology — Australian J Psychol
Australian Journal of Public Administration — AJPA
Australian Journal of Public Administration — Aust J Pub Admin
Australian Journal of Public Administration — Aust J Publ
Australian Journal of Public Health — Aust J Public Health
Australian Journal of Reading — AJR
Australian Journal of Reading — Aust J Reading
Australian Journal of Remedial Education — Aust J Rem Educ
Australian Journal of Science — AJSIA9
Australian Journal of Science — Aust J Sci
Australian Journal of Science — Aust J Science
Australian Journal of Science — Austr J Sci
Australian Journal of Science & Medicine in Sport — AUS J Sci & Med
Australian Journal of Science and Medicine in Sport — Aust J Sci Med Sport
Australian Journal of Scientific Research — AJSR
Australian Journal of Scientific Research — Aust J Scient Res
Australian Journal of Scientific Research — Aust J Scientific Research
Australian Journal of Scientific Research. Series A. Physical Sciences — Aust J Sci Res Ser A
Australian Journal of Scientific Research. Series B. Biological Sciences — Aust J Sci Res B
Australian Journal of Scientific Research. Series B. Biological Sciences — Aust J Sci Res Ser B
Australian Journal of Scientific Research. Series B. Biological Sciences — Austral J Sci Res Ser B Biol Sci
Australian Journal of Screen Theory — Aus J Screen Theory
Australian Journal of Screen Theory — Aust J of Screen Th
Australian Journal of Social Issues — AJ Soc Iss
Australian Journal of Social Issues — AJSI
Australian Journal of Social Issues — Aust J Soc
Australian Journal of Social Issues — Aust J Soc Issues
Australian Journal of Social Issues — Aust J Social Iss
Australian Journal of Social Issues — Aust J Social Issues
Australian Journal of Social Issues — Aust Jnl of Social Issues
Australian Journal of Social Issues — Austral J Soc Issues
Australian Journal of Social Work — AJSW
Australian Journal of Social Work — Aust J Soc Work
Australian Journal of Social Work — Aust J Social Work
Australian Journal of Soil and Water Conservation — Aust J Soil Water Conserv
Australian Journal of Soil Research — ASORA
Australian Journal of Soil Research — ASORAB
Australian Journal of Soil Research — Aust J Soil
Australian Journal of Soil Research — Aust J Soil Res
Australian Journal of Sport Sciences — Aus J Sport Sci
Australian Journal of Sports Medicine — Aus J Sports Med
Australian Journal of Sports Medicine and Exercise Sciences — Aust J Sp Med Ex Sci
Australian Journal of Statistics — AUJSA
Australian Journal of Statistics — Aust J Stat
Australian Journal of Statistics — Aust J Statist
Australian Journal of Statistics — Aust J Stats
Australian Journal of Statistics — Austr J St
Australian Journal of Statistics — Austral J Statist
Australian Journal of Statistics — Australian J Statis
Australian Journal of Teacher Education — Aust J Teach Educ
Australian Journal of Teaching Practice — Aust J Teach Pract
Australian Journal of Zoology — AJZOA
Australian Journal of Zoology — AJZOAS
Australian Journal of Zoology — Aust J Zool
Australian Journal of Zoology — Austr J Zool
Australian Journal of Zoology. Supplementary Series — AJZSA6
Australian Journal of Zoology. Supplementary Series — Aust J Zool Suppl Ser
Australian Journal of Zoology. Supplementary Series — Aust J Zool Supplry Ser
Australian Journal of Zoology. Supplementary Series. Supplement — Aust J Zool Supplry Ser Suppl
Australian Junior Farmer — Aust Junior Farmer
Australian Jurist — Aust Jr
Australian Jurist — Aust Jur
Australian Jurist — Austr Jur
Australian Jurist Reports — A Jur Rep
Australian Jurist Reports — AJR
Australian Jurist Reports — Aust Jr R
Australian Jurist Reports — Aust Jur
Australian Jurist Reports — Aust Jur Rep
Australian Jurist Reports — Austl Jur R
Australian Jurist Reports (Notes of Cases) — AJR (NC)

Australian Labour Law Reporter — ALL
Australian Labour Law Reporter — ALLR
Australian Lapidary Magazine — Aust Lapidary
Australian Law Journal — ALJ
Australian Law Journal — ALJOD
Australian Law Journal — Aust L J
Australian Law Journal — Aust Law J
Australian Law Journal — Austl LJ
Australian Law Journal — Austr LJ
Australian Law Journal. Reports — ALJR
Australian Law Journal. Reports — Aust LJ Rep
Australian Law Journal. Reports — Austl LJ Rep
Australian Law Librarians' Group. Newsletter — ALLG Newsletter
Australian Law News — ALN
Australian Law News — Aust Law News
Australian Law News — Aust LN
Australian Law Reform Agencies Conference — ALRAC
Australian Law Reform Commission. Discussion Paper — ALRC DP
Australian Law Reports — ALR
Australian Law Reports — Aust L Rep
Australian Law Review — Aust Law Rev
Australian Law Times — ALT
Australian Law Times — Aust LT
Australian Law Times — Austr LT
Australian Lawyer — Aust Law
Australian Lawyer — Aust Lawyer
Australian Leather Journal — Austr Leath J
Australian Leather Journal. Boot and Shoe Recorder — Aust Leath J
Australian Leather Journal. Boot and Shoe Recorder — Aust Leather J
Australian Leather Trades Review — Aust Leath Tr Rev
Australian Left Review — ALR
Australian Legal Monthly Digest — ALMD
Australian Legal Monthly Digest — Aus Leg Mon Dig
Australian Legal Monthly Digest — Aust Leg Mon Dig
Australian Legal Monthly Digest — LMD
Australian Legal Profession Digest — ALPD
Australian Legal Workers Group. Newsletter — ALWG Newsletter
Australian Leisure Index [*Database*] — ALI
Australian Letters — AusL
Australian Letters — Aust Lett
Australian Liberal — Aust Liberal
Australian Library and Information Research — ALIR
Australian Library Annual Reports on Microfiche — ALARM
Australian Library Journal — ALJ
Australian Library Journal — AULJA
Australian Library Journal — Aust Lib J
Australian Library Journal — Aust Libr J
Australian Library Journal — Australian Lib J
Australian Library Journal. Supplement — Aust Libr J Suppl
Australian Library News — ALN
Australian Lilium Society Bulletin — Austral Lilium Soc Bull
Australian Lilum Society Quarterly — Austral Lilum Soc Quart
Australian Literary Letter — Aust Literary Letter
Australian Literary Studies — ALS
Australian Literary Studies — Aust Lit S
Australian Literary Studies — Aust Lit St
Australian Literary Studies — Aust Lit Stud
Australian Machinery and Production Engineering — AMPDA
Australian Machinery and Production Engineering — Aust Mach Prod Eng
Australian Machinery and Production Engineering — Aust Mach Prod Engng
Australian Machinery and Production Engineering — Aust Machinery & Prod Eng
Australian Machinery and Production Engineering — Austr Mach Prod Eng
Australian Magazine — AM
Australian Magazine — Aust Mag
Australian Mammalogy — AUMACY
Australian Mammalogy — Aust Mammal
Australian Management Review — Aust Manag R
Australian Manager — Aust Man
Australian Manager — Aust Manager
Australian Manager — Aust Mgr
Australian Marine Science Bulletin — Aust Mar Sci Bull
Australian Marine Sciences Newsletter — Aust Mar Sci Newsl
Australian Marketing Researcher — AMR
Australian Marxist Review — Aust Marxist Rev
Australian Master Tax Guide Updater — MTGU
Australian Mathematical Society. Bulletin — Aust Math Soc Bul
Australian Mathematical Society. Bulletin — Aust Math Soc Bull
Australian Mathematical Society. Gazette — Austral Math Soc Gaz
Australian Mathematical Society. Journal — Aust Math Soc J
Australian Mathematical Society. Journal. Series A — Aust Math Soc J Ser A
Australian Mathematical Society Lecture Series — Austral Math Soc Lect Ser
Australian Mathematics Teacher — Aust Math Teach
Australian Mathematics Teacher — Aust Maths Teach
Australian Mathematics Teacher — Australian Math Teacher
Australian Mechanical Engineering — Aust Mech Eng
Australian Mechanical Engineering — Aust Mech Engng
Australian Mechanical Engineering — Aust Mech Engr
Australian Mechanical Engineering — Austr Mech Eng
Australian Medical Association. Gazette — AMA Gazette
Australian Medical Journal — Aust Med J
Australian Medical Journal — Austr Med J
Australian Medical Journal — Austral Med J
Australian Medical Journal — Australian M J
Australian Merino Wool Campaign — Aust Merino Wool Campaign
Australian Meteorological Magazine — Aust Met Mag
Australian Meteorological Magazine — Aust Meteorol Mag
Australian Methods Engineer — Aust Methods Eng
Australian Milk and Dairy Products Journal — Aust Milk Dairy Prod J
Australian Miner — AUMID
Australian Mineral Development Laboratories [*AMDEL*]. Bulletin — Aust Min Dev Lab Bull
Australian Mineral Development Laboratories [*AMDEL*]. Bulletin — Aust Min Dev Labs Bull
Australian Mineral Development Laboratories [*AMDEL*]. Bulletin — Aust Miner Dev Lab Bull
Australian Mineral Development Laboratories [*AMDEL*]. Report — Aust Miner Dev Lab Rep
Australian Mineral Industry — AUMIA
Australian Mineral Industry — Aust Min Ind
Australian Mineral Industry — Aust Miner Ind
Australian Mineral Industry. Annual Review — Aust Miner Ind Annu Rev
Australian Mineral Industry. Quarterly — Aust Miner Ind Q
Australian Mineral Industry. Quarterly — Australian Mineral Industry Q
Australian Mineral Industry. Review — Aust Miner Ind Rev
Australian Mineral Industry. Review — Austr Min Ind Rev
Australian Mineral Industry. Statistics — Aust Min Ind Stat
Australian Mineral Industry. Statistics — Aust Miner Ind Stat
Australian Mineral Industry. Statistics — Austr Min Ind Stat
Australian Mineralogist — Aust Mineral
Australian Mining — AUMNA
Australian Mining — Aust Min
Australian Mining — Aust Mining
Australian Mining — Austral M
Australian Mining and Engineering Review — Aust Min Eng Rev
Australian Mining and Engineering Review — Aust Min Engng Rev
Australian Mining and Petroleum Law Journal — AMPLJ
Australian Mining and Petroleum Law Journal — Aust Min Pet Law J
Australian Mining Council. Newsletter — Aust Min Counc Newsl
Australian Mining, Minerals, and Oil — AMMO
Australian Mining Standard — Aust Min Stand
Australian Mining Year Book — Aust Min Year Book
Australian Model Railway Magazine — Aust Mod Rail
Australian Monthly — AM
Australian Monthly Motor Manual — Aus Mo Motor Manual
Australian Monthly Weather Report — Austr Mth Weath Rep
Australian Monthly Weather Report and Meteorological Abstract — Aust Mon Weath Rep
Australian Motor Cycle News — Aust Mot Cycle News
Australian Motor Sports — Aust Motor Sports
Australian Motorist — Aust Motorist
Australian Municipal Information [*Database*] — AMIS
Australian Municipal Journal — Aust Munic J
Australian Museum. Magazine — AUMMAY
Australian Museum. Magazine — Aust Mus Mag
Australian Museum. Magazine — Aust Museum Mag
Australian Museum. Magazine — Austr Mus Mag
Australian Museum Magazine — Austral Mus Mag
Australian Museum [*Sydney*]. Memoirs — AUNMA5
Australian Museum. Records — Aust Mus Rec
Australian Museum (Sydney). Memoirs — Aust Mus (Syd) Mem
Australian Museum (Sydney). Memoirs — Aust Mus (Sydney) Mem
Australian Music Directory — Aust Mus Dir
Australian Musical News and Musical Digest — Aust Musical News & D
Australian National Advisory Committee for UNESCO [*United Nations Educational, Scientific, and Cultural Organization*]. Information Circular — UNESCO Inf Circ
Australian National Bibliography [*Information service or system*] — ANB
Australian National Bibliography [*Information service or system*] — Aust Nat Bibliogr
Australian National Clay — ANCLAY
Australian National Clay — Aust Nat Clay
Australian National Clay — Aust Natn Clay
Australian National Drug Information Service [*Database*] — NDIS
Australian National University. Department of Engineering Physics. Energy Conversion Technical Report — Energy Convers Tech Rep Aust Natl Univ Dep Eng Phys
Australian National University. Historical Journal — ANUHJ
Australian National University. News — ANU News
Australian National University. News — Aust Nat Univ News
Australian National University. Research School of Pacific Studies. Department of Geography. Publication — Aust Nat Univ Res Sch Pacif Stud Geog Pub
Australian National University. Research School of Physical Sciences. Department of Engineering Physics. Publication — Aust Natl Univ Res Sch Phys Sci Dep Eng Phys Publ
Australian National University. Research School of Physical Sciences. Department of Engineering Physics. Publication — Publ Aust Natl Univ Res Sch Phys Sci Dep Eng Phys
Australian National University. Social Science Monograph — ANUSSM
Australian Natural History — AUNHA
Australian Natural History — Aust Nat H
Australian Natural History — Aust Nat Hist
Australian Natural History — Aust Natur His
Australian Natural History — Aust Natur Hist
Australian Natural History — Aust Natural History
Australian Naturalist — Aust Nat
Australian Naturalist — Austr Nat
Australian Naturalist. Journal and Magazine. New South Wales Naturalists' Club — Austral Naturalist

Australian News Digest — AND
Australian News Review — Aust News R
Australian Nuclear Science and Technology Organisation. Report — Aust Nucl Sci Technol Organ Rep
Australian Nuclear Science and Technology Organisation. Report. ANSTO/E — Aust Nucl Sci Technol Organ Rep ANSTO E
Australian Numerical Meteorology Research Centre (Melbourne). Annual Report — Aust Num Meteor Res Centr (Melb) Ann Rep
Australian Numismatic Journal — ANJ
Australian Numismatic Journal — Aust Num J
Australian Numismatic Journal — Aust Numismatic J
Australian Numismatic Society. Report — Aust Num Soc Rept
Australian Numismatic Society. Report — Aust Numismatic Soc Rep
Australian Nurses' Journal — Aust Nurses J
Australian Nurses' Journal (Melbourne) — Aust Nurses J (Melbourne)
Australian OCCA [*Oil and Colour Chemists Association*] **Proceedings and News** [*A publication*] — Aust OCCA Proc News
Australian Occupational Therapy Journal — Aust Occup Ther J
Australian Occupational Therapy Journal — Aust Occupational Ther J
Australian Official Journal of Patents — Aust Off J Pat
Australian Official Journal of Patents — Austral Off J Pat
Australian Official Journal of Patents, Trade Marks, and Designs — AOJP
Australian Official Journal of Patents, Trade Marks, and Designs — AOJPTMD
Australian Official Journal of Patents, Trade Marks, and Designs — Aust Off J Pat
Australian Official Journal of Patents, Trade Marks, and Designs — Austr Off J Pat
Australian Official Journal of Patents, Trade Marks, and Designs. Patent Abridgments Supplement — Aust Off J Pat Trade Marks Des Pat Abr Suppl
Australian Official Journal of Patents, Trade Marks, and Designs. Patent Abridgments Supplement — Australian Offic J Pat Pat Abridgments Suppl
Australian Oil and Colour Chemists Association. Proceedings and News — Aust Oil Colour Chem Assoc Proc News
Australian Oil Seed Grower — Aust Oil Seed Gr
Australian Orchid Review — Aust Orchid Rev
Australian Orchid Review — Austral Orchid Rev
Australian Orthodontic Journal — Aust Orthod J
Australian Outdoors — Aust Outdoors
Australian Outlook — AO
Australian Outlook — AuO
Australian Outlook — Aust Out
Australian Outlook — Aust Outl
Australian Outlook — Aust Outloo
Australian Outlook — Aust Outlook
Australian Outlook — Austral O
Australian Outlook — Austral Outlook
Australian Packaging — Aust Packaging
Australian Packaging — Austral Pkg
Australian Packaging [*Sydney*] — AUZ
Australian Paediatric Journal — AUPJB
Australian Paediatric Journal — Aust Paedia
Australian Paediatric Journal — Aust Paediat J
Australian Paediatric Journal — Aust Paediatr J
Australian Paediatric Journal — Aust Paediatric J
Australian Paint Journal — Aust Paint J
Australian Paint Journal — Austral Paint J
Australian Paint Journal. Incorporating the Australian Finishing Review — Aust Paint J Aust Finish Rev
Australian Paint Journal. Supplement — Aust Paint J Suppl
Australian Parks [*Later, Australian Parks and Recreation*] — Aust Parks
Australian Parks and Recreation — Aust Parks
Australian Parks and Recreation — Aust Parks Recreat
Australian Pastoralist — Aust Past
Australian Pastoralist — Austr Past
Australian (Patent Document) — Aust Pat Doc
Australian Pay-Roll Tax Manual — APY
Australian Periodicals Index — API
Australian Personal Computer — APC
Australian Personnel Management — APM
Australian Petroleum Exploration Association. Journal — Aust Pet Explor Assoc J
Australian Photographic Journal — Aust Photogr J
Australian Photographic Journal — Austr Photogr J
Australian Photography — Aust Phot
Australian Physicist — AUPHB
Australian Physicist — Aust Phys
Australian Physicist — Aust Physicist
Australian Physiological and Pharmacological Society. Proceedings — Aust Physiol Pharmacol Soc Proc
Australian Planning Appeal Decisions — APA
Australian Planning Appeal Decisions — APAD
Australian Planning Institute. Journal — API Journal
Australian Planning Institute. Journal — Aust Plan Inst J
Australian Planning Institute. Journal — Aust Plann Inst J
Australian Planning Institute. Journal — Austral Plan Inst J
Australian Plant Disease Recorder — Aust Pl Dis Rec
Australian Plant Disease Recorder — Aust Plant Dis Rec
Australian Plant Disease Recorder — Austr Pl Dis Rec
Australian Plant Disease Recorder — Austral Pl Dis Rec
Australian Plant Introduction Review — Aust Plant Introd Rev
Australian Plant Pathology Society. Newsletter — Aust Plant Pathol Soc Newsl
Australian Plants — Aust Pl
Australian Plants — Aust Plants
Australian Plastics — Aust Plast
Australian Plastics — Austr Plast
Australian Plastics and Allied Trades Review — Aust Plast All Trades Rev
Australian Plastics and Allied Trades Review — Austr Plast All Trade Rev
Australian Plastics and Rubber — Aust Plast Rubb
Australian Plastics and Rubber — Aust Plast Rubber
Australian Plastics and Rubber Buyers Guide — Aust Plast & Rubber Buy Guide
Australian Plastics and Rubber Journal — Aust Plas Rubb J
Australian Plastics and Rubber Journal — Aust Plast Rubber J
Australian Plastics and Rubber Journal — Aust Plastics & Rubber J
Australian Plastics and Rubber Journal — Austr Plast Rubb J
Australian Plastics Journal — Aust Plast J
Australian Plastics Journal — Aust Plastics J
Australian Plastics Year Book — Aust Plast Yb
Australian Plastics Year Book — Aust Plastics Yrbk
Australian Pocket Oxford Dictionary — APOD
Australian Police Journal — Aust Police J
Australian Political Register [*Database*] — APOL
Australian Popular Photography — Aust Pop Phot
Australian Post Office Research Laboratories. Report — Aust Post Office Res Lab Rep
Australian Power Engineering — Aust Power Eng
Australian Power Engineering — Aust Pwr Engng
Australian Prayer Book [*An*] — AAPB
Australian Pre-School Association. Biennial Conference — Aust Pre-School Assn Biennial Conf
Australian Pre-School Association. Victorian Branch. Newsletter — APA VIC News
Australian Pre-School Quarterly — Aust Pre-Sch Quart
Australian Pre-School Quarterly — Aust Pre-School Q
Australian Pre-School Quarterly — Aust Pre-School Quart
Australian Printer — Aust Pr
Australian Process Engineering — Aust Process Eng
Australian Process Engineering — Aust Processs Engng
Australian Psychologist — Aust Psych
Australian Psychologist — Aust Psychl
Australian Psychologist — Aust Psychol
Australian Public Affairs Information Service [*Information service or system*] — APAIS
Australian Public Affairs Information Service [*Information service or system*] — Aus PAIS
Australian Public Affairs Information Service — Aust Public Aff Inf Serv
Australian Public Affairs Information Service [*Information service or system*] — Austral Publ Aff Inform Serv
Australian Pulp and Paper Industry Technical Association. Proceedings — APPITA Proc
Australian Pulp and Paper Industry Technical Association. Proceedings — Aust Pulp Pap Ind Tech Assoc Proc
Australian Pump Journal — Aust Pump J
Australian Quarterly — A Quart
Australian Quarterly — AQ
Australian Quarterly — AuQ
Australian Quarterly — Aus Quart
Australian Quarterly — AusQ
Australian Quarterly — AUSQA
Australian Quarterly — Aust Q
Australian Quarterly — Aust Qly
Australian Quarterly — Aust Quart
Australian Quarterly — Austr Q
Australian Quarterly — Austral Quart
Australian Radiation Laboratory. Technical Report — ARL/TR
Australian Radiation Laboratory. Technical Report ARL/TR — Aust Radiat Lab Tech Rep ARL/TR
Australian Radiation Laboratory. Technical Report Series ARL/TR — Aust Radiat Lab Tech Rep Ser ARL/TR
Australian Radiation Records — Aust Radiat Rec
Australian Radiation Records — Austr Rad Rec
Australian Railway Historical Society. Bulletin — ARHS Bull
Australian Railway Historical Society. Bulletin — Aust Railway Hist Soc Bul
Australian Ranger Bulletin — ARB
Australian Red Cross Quarterly — Aust Red Cross Q
Australian Refrigeration, Air Conditioning, and Heating — ARFHA
Australian Refrigeration, Air Conditioning, and Heating — Aust Refrig Air Con Heat
Australian Refrigeration, Air Conditioning, and Heating — Aust Refrig Air Cond Heat
Australian Refrigeration, Air Conditioning, and Heating — Aust Refrig Air Condit
Australian Refrigeration, Air Conditioning, and Heating — Aust Refrig Air Condit Heat
Australian Refrigeration Review — Aust Refrig Rev
Australian Renewable Energy Resources Index — ARERI
Australian Reporter — Aust Rep
Australian Representative Basins Program Report. Series Report — Aust Represent Basins Program Rep Ser Rep
Australian Reptile Park. Records — Aust Reptile Park Rec
Australian Rhodes Review — Aust Rhodes R
Australian Road Haulage Journal — Aust Road Haulage J
Australian Road Index — Aust Rd Index
Australian Road Research — ARDRA
Australian Road Research — Aust Rd Res
Australian Road Research — Aust Road Res
Australian Road Research — Aust Road Research
Australian Road Research Board. ARR Reports — Aust Road Res Board ARR Rep
Australian Road Research Board. Bulletin — Aust Road Res Bd Bull
Australian Road Research Board. Bulletin — Aust Road Res Board Bull
Australian Road Research Board. Conference — Aust Road Res Board Conf

Australian Road Research Board. Proceedings — Proc Aust Road Res Bd
Australian Road Research Board. Proceedings — Proc Aust Road Research Board
Australian Road Research Board. Proceedings of the Conference — Aust Road Res Board Proc Conf
Australian Road Research Board. Special Report — Aust Road Res Bp Spec Rep
Australian Road Research in Progress — ARRIP
Australian Road Research in Progress — Aust Rd Res Progress
Australian Road Research. Reports — Aust Rd Res Rep
Australian Rose Annual — Aust Rose A
Australian Rose Annual — Aust Rose Annu
Australian Rubber — Aust Rubber
Australian Safety News — Aust Saf News
Australian Sales Tax Guide — ATX
Australian Sales Tax Guide — AXT
Australian School Librarian — Aust Sch L
Australian School Librarian — Aust Sch Lib
Australian School Librarian — Aust Sch Libr
Australian School Librarian — Aust Sch Librn
Australian School Librarian — Aust School Libr
Australian Science Abstracts — Aust Sci Abstr
Australian Science Abstracts — Austr Sci Abstr
Australian Science Fiction Review — ASFR
Australian Science Index [*Information service or system*] — ASI
Australian Science Index [*Information service or system*] — Aus Sci Ind
Australian Science Index [*Information service or system*] — Aust Sci Index
Australian Science Index [*Information service or system*] — Austr Sci Ind
Australian Science Index [*Information service or system*] — Austral Sci Index
Australian Science Newsletter — Aust Sci Newsl
Australian Science Teachers' Journal — Aust Sci Teach J
Australian Science Teachers' Journal — Aust Science Teachers J
Australian Scientific and Technological Reports — AUSTRE
Australian Scientific and Technological Reports on COM — AUSTRE on COM
Australian Scientific Liaison Office (London). Report — ASLO (London) Rep
Australian Scientist — Aust Sci
Australian Scientist — Aust Scient
Australian Scientist — Aust Scientist
Australian Seacraft Magazine — Aust Seacraft
Australian Seacraft Magazine — Aust Seacraft Mag
Australian Seacraft, Power, and Sail — Aust Seacraft
Australian Securities Law Cases — ASLC
Australian Securities Law Reporter — ASLR
Australian Securities Law Reporter — ASR
Australian Seed Producers Review — Aust Seed Prod Rev
Australian Serials in Print — ASIP
Australian Shell News — Aust Shell News
Australian Shipping and Shipbuilding — Aust Ship Shipbuild
Australian Shorthorn — Aust Shorthorn
Australian Ski Year Book — Aust Ski
Australian Ski Year Book — Aust Ski YB
Australian Social Welfare — ASW
Australian Social Welfare — Aust Soc Welfare
Australian Society for Education through the Arts. Bulletin — ASEA Bul
Australian Society for Education through the Arts. Bulletin — ASEA Bull
Australian Society for the Study of Labour History. Bulletin — Aust Soc Study Lab Hist Bull
Australian Society of Accountants. South Australian Division. Convention Reports — Aust Soc Accountants SA Convention
Australian Society of Animal Production. New South Wales Branch. Bulletin — Aust Soc Anim Prod NSW Branch Bull
Australian Society of Animal Production. Victorian Branch. Federal Council. Bulletin — Aust Soc Anim Prod Victorian Branch Fed Counc Bull
Australian Society of Dairy Technology. Technical Publication — Aust Soc Dairy Tech Tech Pub
Australian Society of Dairy Technology. Technical Publication — Aust Soc Dairy Techn Tech Publ
Australian Society of Dairy Technology. Technical Publication — Aust Soc Dairy Technol Tech Pub
Australian Society of Dairy Technology. Technical Publication — Aust Soc Dairy Technol Tech Publ
Australian Society of Dairy Technology. Technical Publication — Tech Publ Aust Soc Dairy Technol
Australian Society of Educational Technology. Yearbook — ASET Yearb
Australian Society of Exploration Geophysicists. Bulletin — ASEGB
Australian Society of Exploration Geophysicists. Bulletin — Aust Soc Explor Geophys Bull
Australian Society of Exploration Geophysicists. Bulletin — Australian Soc Explor Geophys Bull
Australian Society of Legal Philosophy. Bulletin — ASLP Bulletin
Australian Society of Legal Philosophy. Proceedings — ASLP Proceedings
Australian Society of Soil Science. Soils News — Aust Soc Soil Sci Soils News
Australian Society of Sugar Cane Technologists. Proceedings of the Conference — Aust Soc Sugar Cane Technol Proc Conf
Australian Society of Sugar Cane Technologists. Proceedings of the Conference — Proc Conf Aust Soc Sugar Cane Technol
Australian Software Locator [*Database*] — SOFT
Australian Special Libraries News — ASLN
Australian Special Libraries News — Aust Spec Libr News
Australian Speleo Abstracts — Aus Speleo Abstr
Australian Stamp Bulletin — Aust Stamp Bull
Australian Stamp Monthly — Aust Stamp M
Australian Stamp Monthly — Aust Stamp Mo
Australian Standard [*Sydney*] — Aust Stand
Australian Standard Specifications — Aust Stand Specif
Australian Standard Specifications. Standards Association of Australia — Aust Stand Specif Stand Ass Aust
Australian Standards Quarterly — Aust Stand Q
Australian Standards Quarterly — Austr Stand Q
Australian Statesman and Mining Standard — Aust Statesm Min Stand
Australian Statesman and Mining Standard — Austr Statesm Min Stand
Australian Stock Exchange Journal — Aust Stock Exch J
Australian Stock Exchange Journal — Aust Stock Exchange J
Australian Stock Exchange Journal — SEJ
Australian Stud and Farm Monthly — Aust Stud & Farm M
Australian Stud Book — ASB
Australian Student — Aust Stud
Australian Studies in Legal Philosophy — Aust Stud Legal Philos
Australian Studies Newsletter — Aust Stud Newsl
Australian Sugar Journal — Aust Sug J
Australian Sugar Journal — Aust Sugar J
Australian Sugar Journal — Austr Sug J
Australian Sugar Journal — Austral Sugar J
Australian Sugar Year Book — Aust Sugar Yr Bk
Australian Sugar Year Book — Austral Sugar Year Book
Australian Sugar Yearbook — Aust Sug Yb
Australian Superannuation and Employee Benefits Guide — ASP
Australian Superannuation Practice — ASP
Australian Surveyor — Aust Surv
Australian Surveyor — Aust Survey
Australian Surveyor — Aust Surveyor
Australian Surveyor — Austr Surv
Australian Systematic Botany — Aust Syst Bot
Australian TAFE [*Department of Technical and Further Education*] **Teacher** — Aust TAFE Teach
Australian Tax Cases — ATC
Australian Tax Decisions — ATD
Australian Tax Decisions — Austl Tax
Australian Tax Decisions — Austr Tax D
Australian Tax Review — AT Rev
Australian Tax Review — Aust Tax Rev
Australian Tax Review — Austl Tax Rev
Australian Tax Review — Austr Tax R
Australian Teacher — Aust Teach
Australian Teacher of the Deaf — ATD
Australian Teacher of the Deaf — Aust T Deaf
Australian Teacher of the Deaf — Aust Teach Deaf
Australian Teacher of the Deaf — Aust Teacher of the Deaf
Australian Teacher of the Deaf — Austral Teacher Deaf
Australian Teachers' Federation. Report — ATF Rep
Australian Teachers' Federation. Report — Aust Teach Fed Rep
Australian Technical Journal — Aust Teach J
Australian Technology Magazine — Aust Technol Mag
Australian Technology Review — Aust Technol Rev
Australian Telecommunication Research — ATR
Australian Telecommunication Research — Aust Telecomm Res
Australian Telecommunication Research — Aust Telecomm Research
Australian Telecommunication Research — Aust Telecommun Res
Australian Telecommunications Development Association. Annual Report — Aust Telecommun Dev Assoc
Australian Territories — Aust Terr
Australian Territories — Aust Territ
Australian Territories — Aust Territories
Australian Territories — Austr Terr
Australian Theatre Yearbook — Aust Theatre Yrbk
Australian Thermodynamics Conference — Aust Thermodyn Conf
Australian Timber Journal — Aust Timb J
Australian Timber Journal — Aust Timber J
Australian Timber Journal — Austr Timb J
Australian Timber Journal and Building Products Merchandiser — Aust Timb J
Australian Tobacco Grower's Bulletin — Aust Tob Grow Bull
Australian Tobacco Grower's Bulletin — Austral Tobacco Growers Bull
Australian Tobacco Journal — Aust Tob J
Australian Tobacco Journal — Aust Tobacco J
Australian Tobacco Journal — Austr Tob J
Australian Torts Reporter — ATOR
Australian Tractor Test — Aust Tract Test
Australian Tractor Testing Committee. Australian Tractor Test — Aust Tract Test Comm Aust Tract Test
Australian Trade Chronicle — Aust Trade Chronicle
Australian Trade Practices Report — ATP
Australian Trade Practices Reporter — ATPR
Australian Transport — Aust Transp
Australian Transport — Aust Transport
Australian Transport — AUTRB
Australian Transport Index — ATI
Australian Transport Information Directory [*Database*] — ATID
Australian Transport Information Directory — Aust Transport Inf Dir
Australian Transport Literature Information System [*Database*] — ATLIS
Australian Transport Research in Progress [*Database*] — ATRIP
Australian Travel Goods and Handbags and Accessories — Aust Travel Goods
Australian Traveller — Aust Traveller
Australian Treaty Series — ATS
Australian University — Aust Univ
Australian Uranium News — AUNED
Australian Uranium News — Aust Uranium News
Australian Urban Studies — Aust Urban Stud
Australian Veterinary Association. Victorian Division. Annual General Meeting. Proceedings — Vict Vet Proc

Australian Veterinary Association. Victorian Division. Victorian Veterinary Proceedings — Vict Vet Proc
Australian Veterinary Journal — Aust Vet J
Australian Veterinary Journal — Austr Vet J
Australian Veterinary Journal — AUVJA
Australian Veterinary Practitioner — Aust Vet Pr
Australian Veterinary Practitioner — Aust Vet Pract
Australian Video and Cinema — Aust Vid Cin
Australian Video and Communications — Aust Vid Comm
Australian Video Review — AVR
Australian Waste Conference — Aust Waste Conf
Australian Waste Disposal Conference — Aust Waste Disposal Conf
Australian Waste Management and Control Conference. Papers — Aust Waste Manage Control Conf Pap
Australian Water and Wastewater Association. Federal Convention — Aust Water Wastewater Assoc Fed Conv
Australian Water and Wastewater Association. International Convention — Aust Water Wastewater Assoc Int Conv
Australian Water and Wastewater Association. Summer School — Aust Water Wastewater Assoc Summer Sch
Australian Water Resources Council. Conference Series — Aust Water Resour Counc Conf Ser
Australian Water Resources Council. Hydrological Series — Aust Wat Resour Coun Hydrol Ser
Australian Water Resources Council. Hydrological Series — Aust Water Resour Counc Hydrol Ser
Australian Water Resources Council. Hydrological Series — AWRHA
Australian Water Resources Council. Stream Gauging Information — Aust Water Resour Counc Stream Gauging Inf
Australian Water Resources Council. Technical Paper — Aust Water Resour Coun Tech Pap
Australian Water Resources Council. Technical Paper — Aust Water Resour Counc Tech Pap
Australian Water Resources Council. Technical Paper — AWRTAQ
Australian Weed Control Handbook — Aust Weed Control Handb
Australian Weeds — Aust Weed
Australian Weeds — Aust Weeds
Australian Weeds — AUWEDT
Australian Weeds Conference. Proceedings — Aust Weeds Conf Proc
Australian Week-End Review of Current Books, the Arts, and Entertainments — Week-End R
Australian Welder — Aust Weld
Australian Welding Engineer — Aust Weld Engr
Australian Welding Engineer — Austr Weld Eng
Australian Welding Journal — Aust Weld J
Australian Welding Journal — Aust Welding J
Australian Welding Journal — AUWJA
Australian Welding Research — Aust Weld Res
Australian Welding Research Association. Bulletin — Aust Weld Res Ass Bull
Australian Wild Life — Austr Wild Life
Australian Wild Life — Austral Wild Life
Australian Wildlife Research — Aust Wild R
Australian Wildlife Research — Aust Wildl Res
Australian Wildlife Research — AWLRAO
Australian Wine, Brewing, and Spirit Review — Aust Wine Brew Spirit Rev
Australian Wine, Brewing, and Spirit Review — Aust Wine Brewing and Spir Rev
Australian Wine, Brewing, and Spirit Review — Aust Wine Brewing Spir Rev
Australian Women's Weekly — Aust Womens W
Australian Women's Weekly — AWW
Australian Women's Weekly — WW
Australian Wool Board. Report — Aust Wool Bd Rep
Australian Wool Bureau. Wool Statistical Service — Aust Wool Bur Wool Stat Service
Australian Wool Bureau. Wool Statistical Service. Australian Wool. Statistical Analysis — Aust Wool Bur Wool Stat Service Aust Wool Stat Analysis
Australian Wool. Statistical Analysis — Aust Wool Stat Analysis
Australian Wool Testing Authority. Textile Testing Bulletin — Aust Wool Test Auth Text Test Bull
Australian Worker's Compensation Guide — AWK
Australian Workshop on Advanced Protein Electrophoretic Techniques — Aust Workshop Adv Protein Electroph Tech
Australian Workshop on Coal Hydrogenation — Aust Workshop Coal Hydrogenation
Australian Workshop on Coal Hydrogenation. Abstract and Papers — Abstr Pap Aust Workshop Coal Hydrogenation
Australian Writer's Workshop — AWW
Australian Yearbook of International Law — Aust YB Intl L
Australian Yearbook of International Law — Aust Yearbook Int L
Australian Yearbook of International Law — Aust Yr Bk IL
Australian Yearbook of International Law — Aust Yr Book Int Law
Australian Yearbook of International Law — Austl YB Int'l L
Australian Yearbook of International Law — AYBIL
Australian Zoologist — Aust Zoo
Australian Zoologist — Aust Zool
Australian Zoologist — Aust Zoologist
Australian Zoologist — AUZOA3
Australian-American Association in Canberra. News Bulletin — Aust-American Assn Canb News Bul
Australian-American Association. Monthly Journal [*Sydney*] — Mo J Australian-American Assoc
Australian-American Journal — Aust-American J
Australian-New Zealand Conference on Geomechanics. Proceedings — Aust NZ Conf Geomech Proc
Australia's Heritage — Aust's Heritage
Australia's Mining Monthly — Aust Min Mon
Australia's Neighbours — AN
Australia's Neighbours — Aust Neigh
Australia's Neighbours — Aust Neighb
Australia's Neighbours — Aust Neighbours
Australia's Neighbours — Austr Neighb
Australisch-Neuseelaendische Studien zur Deutschen Sprache und Literatur — ANSDL
Australisch-Neuseelaendische Studien zur Deutschen Sprache und Literatur — ANSDSL
Austria. Geologische Bundesanstalt. Jahrbuch — Austria Geol Bunesanst Jahrb
Austria. Geologische Bundesanstalt. Verhandlungen — Austria Geol Bundesanst Verh
Austria. Machinery and Steel — Austria Mach Steel
Austria. Patent Document — Austria Pat Doc
Austria, Patentamt, Oesterreichisches Patentblatt — Austria Patentamt Oesterr Patentbl
Austria Tabakwerke. Fachliche Mitteilungen — Austria Tabakwerke Fachliche Mitt
Austria. Zentralanstalt fuer Meteorologie und Geodynamik. Arbeiten — Austria Zentralanst Meteorol Geodynamik Arb
Austrian Journal of Oncology — Austrian J Oncol
Austrian Journal of Oncology — OZOKAN
Austrian Trade News — Aus Trade
Austrian-Italian-Yugoslav Chemical Engineering Conference. Proceedings — Austrian Ital Yugosl Chem Eng Conf Proc
Austrobaileya — AUSTDK
Auswaertige Politik — Auswaert Politik
Auswahl der Besten Auslaendischen Geographischen und Statistischen Nachrichten zur Aufklaerung der Voelker- und Landeskunde — Auswahl Besten Ausl Geogr Statist Nachr Voelker Landesk
Auswahl der Kleinen Schriften, Welche in der Arzneiwissenschaft, Chemie, Chirurgie, und Botanik Herausgekommen — Auswahl Kleinen Schriften Arzneiwiss
Auswahl der Medicinischen Aufsaetze und Beobachtungen aus den Nuernbergischen Gelehrten Unterhandlungen — Auswahl Med Aufsaetze Beob Nuernberg Gel Unterhandl
Auswahl Oekonomischer Abhandlungen. Welche die Freye Oekonomische Gesellschaft zu St. Petersburg in Teutscher Sprache Erhalten Hat — Auswahl Oekon Abh Freya Oekon Ges St Petersburg
Auszuege aus den Europaeischen Patentschriften — Auszuege Europ Patentschr
Auszuege aus den Protokollen der Gesellschaft fuer Natur- und Heilkunde in Dresden — Auszuege Protok Ges Natur Heilk Dresden
Auszuege Auslegeschriften Patentschriften — Auszuege Auslegeschr Patentschr
Auszug aus den Protocollen ueber die Versammlungen der Ersten Classe. Leipziger Oekonomische Societaet — Auszug Protoc Versamml Ersten Cl
Aut Aut — AA
Auteursrecht — AUC
AutEx Trading Information System [*Database*] — TIS
Authentic Science Fiction — Aut
Author Biographies Master Index — ABMI
Author/Publisher News and Views — Auth Pub N V
Autisme Infantile — Autisme Infant
Auto Chemicals (Tokyo) — Auto Chem (Tokyo)
Auto Collector News — Auto Col N
Auto Merchandising News — Auto Merch
Auto + Motortechniek — AUT
Auto Movilismo y Turismo (Lima) — Auto Turismo Lima
Auto Sport Canada — Auto Sp Can
Auto Technik — Auto Tech
Auto-Cite [*Database*] — AC
Autogene Industrie — Autogene Ind
Autogene Metallbearbeitung — Autogene Metallbearb
Autogenous Industry — Autogenous Ind
Autogestion et Socialisme — Autogestion et Social
Autograph Collectors Journal — Autograph Collect J
Autoimmunity and Endocrine Disease — Autoimmun Endocr Dis
Automated Analysis of Drugs and Other Substances of Pharmaceutical Interest — Autom Anal Drugs Other Subst Pharm Interest
Automated Library Information System [*Database*] — ALIS
Automated Manufacturing Report — Autom Manuf Rep
Automated Reasoning Series — Automat Reason Ser
Automatenmarkt — AME
Automatic and Remote Control. Proceedings. International Congress. International Federation of Automatic Control — Autom Remote Control Proc Int Congr Int Fed Autom Control
Automatic Control [*Japan*] — Autom Control
Automatic Control and Computer Sciences — Autom Control and Comput Sci
Automatic Control and Computer Sciences — Autom Control Comput Sci
Automatic Control and Computer Sciences — Automat Control and Computer Sci
Automatic Control and Computer Sciences — Automat Control Comput Sci
Automatic Control and Computer Sciences (English Translation) — Autom Control Comput Sci (Engl Transl)
Automatic Control Theory and Applications — Autom Control Theory & Appl
Automatic Control Theory and Applications — Automat Control Theory Appl
Automatic Control Theory and Applications — Automatic Control Theory Appl
Automatic Data Processing Information Bulletin — Autom Data Process Inf Bull
Automatic Data Processing Information Bulletin — Automat Data Process Inform B
Automatic Documentation and Mathematical Linguistics — ADML
Automatic Documentation and Mathematical Linguistics — Autom Doc Math Linguist
Automatic Documentation and Mathematical Linguistics — Automat Document and Math Linguistics
Automatic Electric Technical Journal — AETJA
Automatic Electric Technical Journal — Autom Elec Tech J

Automatic Electric Technical Journal — Automat Elec Tech J
Automatic Machining — Autom Mach
Automatic Monitoring and Measuring — Autom Monit and Meas
Automatic Monitoring and Measuring — Automat Monit Mea
Automatic Monitoring and Measuring (English Translation) — Autom Monit Meas (Engl Transl)
Automatic New Structure Alert — ANSA
Automatic Programming — Automat Programming
Automatic Subject Citation Alert — ASCA
Automatic Subject Citation Alert — Autom Subj Citation Alert
Automatic Welding [*Former USSR*] — Autom Weld
Automatic Welding (English Translation) — Autom Weld (Engl Transl)
Automatic Welding (English Translation) — AUWEA
Automatic Welding (USSR) — Aut Weld R
Automatic Welding (USSR) — Automat Weld (USSR)
Automatica [*United States*] — ATCAA
Automatica si Electronica — AUELA
Automatica si Electronica — Autom si Electron
Automatica: The Journal of IFAC [*International Federation of Automatic Control*] — Automatica-J IFAC
Automatie, Maandblad voor Meettechniek en Regeltechniek, Mechanisering, en Automatisering [*Baarn*] — ATY
Automation — ATMNA
Automation and Control — Auto and Con
Automation and Control — Autom and Control
Automation and Instrumentation. Proceedings. International Convention on Automation and Instrumentation — Autom Instrum Proc Int Conv
Automation and Remote Control — AURCA
Automation and Remote Control [*Former USSR*] — Autom Remote Control
Automation and Remote Control [*Former USSR*] — Automat Remote Contr
Automation and Remote Control — Automat Remote Control
Automation and Remote Control (USSR) — Aut Remot (R)
Automation (Cleveland) — Automation (Cleve)
Automation Computers Applied Mathematics — Automat Comput Appl Math
Automation in Housing and Systems Building News — Auto Housg
Automation in Microbiology and Immunology. Papers. Symposium on Rapid Methods and Automation in Microbiology — Autom Microbiol Immunol Pap Symp
Automatique et Informatique Industrielles — Autom et Inf Ind
Automatique et Informatique Industrielles — Autom Inform Ind
Automatisation Documentaire. Recherches et Reflexions — Autom Doc Rech Reflexions
Automatisches Schweissen — Autom Schweissen
Automatisering Gids — AUR
Automatisierungspraxis fuer Grundlagen Geratebau und Betriebserfahrungen — Automatisierungspraxis
Automatisme — AUMTA
Automatisme et Telecommande. Comptes-Rendus. Congres International — Autom Telecommande C R Congr Int
Automatizace — AUTMA
Automatizovane Systemy Rizeni - Bulletin INORGA — Autom Syst Rizeni
Automazione e Strumentazione — ATSZA
Automazione e Strumentazione — Autom Strum
Automedica — AUMDC
Automobile Abstracts — Automobile Abs
Automobile Credit — Auto Cred
Automobile Engineer [*England*] — AUENA
Automobile Engineer — Auto Eng
Automobile Law Reports. Commerce Clearing House — Auto L Rep CCH
Automobile Quarterly — Automob Q
Automobile Technology [*Japan*] — Automob Technol
Automobil-Industrie [*Germany*] — ATOIA
Automobiltechnische Zeitschrift — Automobiltech Z
Automotive Abstracts — Automot Abstr
Automotive Age — Auto Age
Automotive and Aviation Industries — Automot Aviat Ind
Automotive and Aviation Industries — Automotive & Aviation Ind
Automotive Chain Store — Auto Chn S
Automotive Competitive Assessment Data Bank — COMPASS
Automotive Design and Development — Automot Des Dev
Automotive Design Engineering — ADEGB
Automotive Design Engineering — Automot Des Eng
Automotive Electronics. International Conference — Automot Electron Int Conf
Automotive Engineer — AE
Automotive Engineer — Automot Engr
Automotive Engineer (London) — Automot Eng (Lond)
Automotive Engineering — Aut Eng
Automotive Engineering — Automot Eng
Automotive Engineering — Automot Engng
Automotive Engineering — IAUE
Automotive Engineering (Pittsburgh) — Automot Eng (Pittsb)
Automotive Industries — AUINA
Automotive Industries — Auto Ind
Automotive Industries — Automot Ind
Automotive Industries. Truck and Off Highway — Auto Highwy
Automotive Industry — Automotive Ind
Automotive News — Auto News
Automotive News — Automot N
Automotive News — Automot News
Automotive News — IAUN
Automotive Rebuilder — Auto Rbldr
Automotive Service News [*Japan*] — Automot Serv News
Automotive Topics — Automot Top
Autores e Livros. Suplemento Literario de A Manha (Rio de Janeiro) — Autor Livr Rio
Autotech Magazine — Autotech Mag
AUTOTESTCON [*Automatic Testing Conference*] **Proceedings** — AUPRD
Autotransaction Industry Report — Auto Ind Rep
Autour de la Bible [*Paris*] — AuB
Autoxidation and Antioxidants — Autoxid Antioxid
Autumn — AT
Aux Frontieres de la Spectroscopie Laser. Ecole d'Ete de Physique Theorique — Aux Front Spectrosc Laser Ec Ete Phys Theor
Auxilia ad Codicem Juris Canonici — ACJC
AV Communication Review — AV
AV Communication Review — AV Comm R
AV Communication Review — AV Commun Rev
AV Communication Review — AVCR
Avances en Alimentacion y Mejora Animal — AATAAT
Avances en Alimentacion y Mejora Animal — Av Aliment Mejora Anim
Avances en Alimentacion y Mejora Animal — Avances Aliment Mejora Anim
Avances en Alimentacion y Mejora Animal. Suplemento — Av Aliment Mejora Anim Supl
Avances en Produccion Animal — APANDD
Avances en Produccion Animal — Av Prod Anim
Avances en Terapeutica — Av Ter
Avances Tecnicos Cenicafe — Av Tec Cenicafe
Avant Scene Theatre — Avant Sc Th
Avant-Scene Cinema — Avant Sc C
Avant-Scene Cinema — Avant Scene
AVC Delivery and Development [*Formerly, Audio-Visual Communications*] — GAVC
Avco Corporation. Research Reports — Avco Corp Res Rep
Avenir Agriculture — Avenir Agr
Avenir Medical — Avenir Med
Avenir Militaire [*Paris*] — Avenir Milit
Avenue Magazine — Ave Mag
Average Monthly Weather Outlook — AWO
Avery Index to Architectural Periodicals — Avery
Avery Index to Architectural Periodicals — Avery Index Archit Period
Avery Index to Architectural Periodicals of Columbia University — Avery Ind Archit Per
Avery Index to Architectural Periodicals. Second Edition. Revised and Enlarged. Supplement — Avery Index Archit Period Second Ed Revis Enlarged Suppl
Avesta Stainless Bulletin — Avesta Stainless Bull
Avhandlinger. Utgitt av Det Norske Videnskaps-Akademi — Avh Norske Vid Akad
Avhandlinger Utgitt av det Norske Videnskaps-Akademi i Oslo. Serie I. Matematisk-Naturvidenskapelig Klasse — Avh Norske Vidensk Akad Oslo Ser 1 Mat Naturvidensk Kl
Avhandlinger Utgitt av Norsk Videnskaps-Akademi I Oslo — ANVA
Avhandlinger Utgitt av Norsk Videnskaps-Akademi I Oslo. I. Matematisk-Naturvidenskapelig Klasse — Avh Nor Vidensk-Akad Oslo I
Avhandlinger Utgitt av Norsk Videnskaps-Akademi I Oslo. I. Matematisk-Naturvidenskapelig Klasse. Ny Serie — Avh Norsk Vid-Akad Oslo I NS
Avhandlinger Utgitt av Norsk Videnskaps-Akademi I Oslo. II — ANVAO
Avhandlinger Utgitt av Norsk Videnskaps-Akademi I Oslo. Matematisk-Naturvidenskapelig Klasse — AUNVAW
Avhandlinger Utgitt av Norsk Videnskaps-Akademi I Oslo. Matematisk-Naturvidenskapelig Klasse — Avh Utgitt Nor Vidensk-Akad Oslo Mat-Naturvidensk Kl
Aviacija i Kosmonavtika — AIK
Aviakosmicheskaia i Ekologicheskaia Meditsina — Aviakosm Ekolog Med
Avian and Mammalian Wildlife Toxicology. Conference — Avian Mamm Wildl Toxicol Conf
Avian Biology — AVBIDB
Avian Biology — Avian Biol
Avian Diseases — AVDIA
Avian Diseases — Avian Dis
Avian Endocrinology. Proceedings. International Symposium on Avian Endocrinology — Avian Endocrinol Proc Int Symp
Avian Pathology — Avian Pathol
Avian Pathology — AVPADN
Avian Pathology. Journal. WVPA (World Veterinary Poultry Association) — Avian Pathol J WVPA
Avian Physiology [*Monograph*] — Avian Physiol
Avian Research — Avian Res
Aviation Age — AVIAA
Aviation Age — Aviat Age
Aviation Cases. Commerce Clearing House — Av Cas CCH
Aviation Daily — Aviation Da
Aviation Historical Society of Australia. Journal — Av Hist Soc Aust J
Aviation Historical Society of Australia. Journal — J Aviat Hist Soc Aust
Aviation Law Reports. Commerce Clearing House — Av L Rep CCH
Aviation Medicine — Aviat Med
Aviation Medicine — AVMED
Aviation News — Aviation N
Aviation News — AVN
Aviation Research Monographs — Aviat Res Monogr
Aviation Review — Aviat Rev
Aviation Safety Digest — ASD
Aviation/Space — Aviat Sp
Aviation, Space, and Environmental Medicine — ASEMC
Aviation, Space, and Environmental Medicine — ASEMCG
Aviation, Space, and Environmental Medicine — Aviat Sp En
Aviation, Space, and Environmental Medicine — Aviat Spac Environ Med
Aviation, Space, and Environmental Medicine — Aviat Space Environ Med
Aviation Trader — Aviat Tr
Aviation Week — Aviation W

Aviation Week — AW
Aviation Week and Space Technology — Avia Week
Aviation Week and Space Technology — Aviat Week Space Technol
Aviation Week and Space Technology — AWS
Aviation Week and Space Technology — AWSTA
Aviatsionnaya Promyshlennost — Aviats Promst
Aviatsionnaya Tekhnika — Aviats Tekh
Aviatsiya i Khimiya — Aviats Khim
Aviatsiya i Kosmonavtika [*Former USSR*] — Aviat Kosmonavt
Aviatsiya i Kosmonavtika — AVKOA
Avicultura Tecnica — Avicult Tec
Avicultural Magazine — Avic Mag
Avicultural Magazine — Avicult Mag
Avicultural Magazine — AVMGAN
Avishkar — AVISD
Avocado Grower — Avoc Grow
Avocado Grower — Avocado Grow
Avon Fantasy Reader — AFR
Avon Science Fiction Reader — ASFR
Avon Science Fiction Reader — ASR
Avtodorozhnik Ukrainy — Avtodorozhnik Ukr
Avtogennoe Delo — Avtog Delo
Avtoklavnye Betony i Izdeliya na Ikh Osnove — Avtoklavn Betony Izdeliya Ikh Osn
Avtomaticeskoe Upravlenie i Vycislitel'naja Tehnika — Avtomat Upravl i Vycisl Tehnika
Avtomaticheskaya Svarka — AVSVA
Avtomaticheskaya Svarka — Avtom Svarka
Avtomaticheskii Kontrol i Upravlenie pri Obogashchenii i Gidrometallurgii Tsvetnykh Metallov — Avtom Kontrol Upr Obogashch Gidrometall Tsvetn Met
Avtomaticheskoe Upravlenie i Vychislitel'naya Tekhnika — Avtomat Upravlenie i Vychisl Tekhn
Avtomatika i Izchislitelna Tekhnika — Avtomat Izchisl Tekhn
Avtomatika i Priborostroenie. Informasionnyi Nauchno-Tekhnicheskii — Avtom Priborostr Inf Nauchno Tekh
Avtomatika i Telemekhanika — AVTEA
Avtomatika i Telemekhanika — Avtom Telemekh
Avtomatika i Vychislitel'naya Tekhnika — Avtom & Vychisl Tekh
Avtomatika i Vychislitel'naya Tekhnika (1961-66) — AVVTA
Avtomatika i Vychislitel'naya Tekhnika. Akademiya Nauk Latviiskoi SSR — Avtomat i Vychisl Tekhn
Avtomatika i Vychislitel'naya Tekhnika. Minskii Radiotekhnicheskii Institut — Avtomat i Vychisl Tekhn
Avtomatika i Vycislitel'naja Tehnika (Minsk) [*Minskii Radiotekhnicheskii Institut*] — Avtomat i Vycisl Tehnika (Minsk)
Avtomatika i Vycislitel'naja Tehnika (Riga) [*Akademija Nauk Latviiskoi SSR*] — Avtomat i Vycisl Tehn (Riga)
Avtomatika, Telemekhanika, i Svyaz — ATSVA
Avtomatika, Telemekhanika, i Svyaz — Avtom Telemekh Svyaz
Avtomatizatsiya i Kompleksnaya Mekhanizatsiya Khimiko Tekhnologicheskikh Protsessov — Avtom Kompleksn Mekh Khim Tekhnol Protsessov
Avtomatizatsiya i Kontrol'no-Izmeritel'nye Pribory v Neftepererabatyvayushchei i Neftekhimicheskoi Promyshlennosti — AKPOD
Avtomatizatsiya i Mekhanizatsiya Protsessov Lit'ya — Avtom Mekh Protsessov Litya
Avtomatizatsiya i Priborostroenie — Avtom Priborostr
Avtomatizatsiya Khimicheskikh Proizvodstv (Kiev) — Avtom Khim Proizvod (Kiev)
Avtomatizatsiya Khimicheskikh Proizvodstv (Moscow) — Avtom Khim Proizvod (Moscow)
Avtomatizatsiya Khimicheskoi Promyshlennosti — Avtom Khim Promsti
Avtomatizatsiya, Mekhanizatsiya i Oborudovanie Protsessov Tsellyulozno-Bumazhnogo Proizvodstva — Avtom Mekh Oborud Protsessov Tsellyul Bum Proizvod
Avtomatizatsiya Mikrobiologicheskikh i Elektrofiziologicheskikh Issledovanii — Avtom Mikrobiol Elektrofiziol Issled
Avtomatizatsiya Nauchnykh Issledovanii. Materialy Vsesoyuznoi Shkoli po Avtomatizatsii Nauchnykh Issledovanii — Avtom Nauchn Issled Mater Vses Shk
Avtomatizatsiya Nauchnykh Issledovanii v Khimii — Avtom Nauchn Issled Khim
Avtomatizatsiya Nauchnykh Issledovanii v Khimii i Khimicheskoi Tekhnologii. Materialy Vsesoyuznoi Shkoly — Avtom Nauchn Issled Khim Khim Tekhnol Mater Vses Shk
Avtomatizatsiya Proektirovaniya v Elektronike — Avtom Proekt Elektron
Avtomatizatsiya Proizvodstvennykh Protsessov — Avtom Proizvod Protsessov
Avtomatizatsiya Proizvodstvennykh Protsessov Tsvetnoi Metallurgii — Avtom Proizvod Protsessov Tsvetn Metall
Avtomatizatsiya Proizvodstvennykh Protsessov v Mashinostroenii i Priborostroenii (Lvov) — Avtom Proizvod Protsessov Mashinostr Priborostr (Lvov)
Avtomatizatsiya Staleplavil'nogo Proizvodstva — ASPZA
Avtomatizatsiya Staleplavil'nogo Proizvodstva [*Former USSR*] — Avtom Staleplavil'n Proizvod
Avtomatizatsiya Tekhnologicheskikh Protsessov Khimicheskikh Proizvodstv — Avtom Tekhnol Protsessov Khim Proizvod
Avtomatizatsiya Tsitologicheskoi Diagnostiki Opukholei — Avtom Tsitol Diagn Opukholei
Avtomatizirovannye Sistemy Upravlenija i Pribory Avtomatiki — Avtom Sist Upr Prib Avtom
Avtomatizirovannye Sistemy Upravlenija i Pribory Avtomatiki — Avtomat Sistemy Upravlenija i Pribory Avtomat
Avtometriia — AVMEBI
Avtometrija Akademija Nauk SSSR — Avtometrija
Avtomobil ni Dorogi i Dorozhne Budivnitstvo — Avtomob Dorogi Dorozhne Budiv
Avtomobile- i Traktorostroenie — Avtomob Traktorostr
Avtomobil'naya i Traktornaya Promyshlennost — Avtomob Trakt Promst
Avtomobil'naya Promyshlennost — AVPRA
Avtomobil'naya Promyshlennost [*Former USSR*] — Avtomob Prom-St
Avtomobil'nye Dorogi — AVNDA
Avtomobil'nye Dorogi — Avtomob Dorogi
Avtomobil'nyi — Avto
Avtomobil'nyi Transport — AVTRA
Avtomobil'nyi Transport i Dorogi — Avtomob Transp Dorogi
Avtomobil'nyi Transport Kazakhstana [*Kazakh SSR*] — Avtomon Transp Kaz
Avtomobil'nyi Transport (Kiev) — Avtomob Transp (Kiev)
Avtomobil'nyi Transport (Moscow) — Avtomob Transp (Moscow)
Avtotraktornoe Delo — Avtotrakt Delo
Avulso. Divisao de Fomento da Producao Mineral (Brazil) — Avulso Div Fom Prod Miner (Braz)
Avulso. Laboratorio da Producao Mineral (Brazil) — Avulso Lab Prod Miner (Braz)
Avvenire Agricolo — AVAGA
Avvenire Agricolo — Avven Agr
Avvenire Agricolo — Avvenire Agric
AWA [*Alberta Wilderness Association*] **Newsletter** — AWAN
AWA [*Amalgamated Wireless Australasia*] **Technical Review** — AWA Tech Rev
Awamia. Revue de la Recherche Agronomique Marocaine — Awamia Rev Rech Agron Maroc
Awamia. Revue de la Recherche Agronomique Marocaine — AWMIA2
Awards in Nuclear Medicine and Radiopharmacology — Awards Nucl Med Radiopharmacol
Awasis — Awas
AWF [*Ausschuss fuer Wirtschaftliche Fertigung*] **Mitteilungen** — AWF Mitt
AWRA Monograph Series — AWRA Monogr Ser
AWRE (Atomic Weapons Research Establishment) Report O — AWRE Rep O
AWRE (Atomic Weapons Research Establishment) Report. Series R. United Kingdom Atomic Energy Authority — AWRE Rep Ser R UK At Energ Auth
AWWA (American Water Works Association) Seminar on Control of Inorganic Contaminants — AWWA Semin Control Inorg Contam
AWWA (American Water Works Association) Seminar on Minimizing and Recycling Water Plant Sludge — AWWA Semin Minimizing Recycl Water Plant Sludge
AWWA (American Water Works Association) Seminar on Water Treatment Waste Disposal. Proceedings — AWWA Semin Water Treat Waste Disposal Proc
AWWA (American Water Works Association) Seminar Proceedings. Controlling Corrosion within Water Systems — AWWA Semin Proc Controlling Corros Water Syst
AWWA [*American Water Works Association*] **Annual Conference. Proceedings** — AWWA Annu Conf Proc
AWWA [*American Water Works Association*] **Disinfection Seminar. Proceedings** — AWWA Disinfect Semin Proc
AWWA [*American Water Works Association*] **Seminar on Controlling Corrosion within Water Systems. Proceedings** — AWWA Semin Controlling Corros Water Syst Proc
AWWA [*American Water Works Association*] **Seminar on Ozonation. Recent Advances and Research Needs** — AWWA Semin Ozonation
AWWA [*American Water Works Association*] **Seminar on Water Chlorination Principles and Practices** — AWWA Semin Water Chlorination Princ Pract
AWWA [*American Water Works Association*] **Water Quality Technology Conference. Proceedings** — AWWA Water Qual Technol Conf Proc
Axel Heiberg Island Research Reports. Geology. McGill University — Axel Heiberg Isl Res Rep Geol McGill Univ
Axis — AX
AY. Purdue University Cooperative Extension Service — AY Purdue Univ Coop Ext Serv
Ayasofya Muezesi Yilligi — Ayasofia Muez Yil
Aylesford Review — AYLR
Ayrshire Archaeological and Natural History Collections. Series 2 — Ayrshire Archaeol Natur Hist Collect 2 Ser
Az Alfoeldi Tudomanyos Gyuejtemeny. Az Alfoeldi Tudomanyos Intezet Evkoenyve. Annales de l'Institut Scientifique de l'Alfoeld — Alfoeldi Tud Gyuejt
Az Egri Muzeum Evkoenyve — Egri Muz Ev
Az Erdelyi Muzeum-Egyesulet Evkoenyve — Erdelyi Muz Egyes Evk
Az Erdeszeti es Faipari Egyetem Tudomanyos Koezlemenyei. Wissenschaftliche Mitteilungen der Universitaet fuer Forst- und Holzwirtschaf — Erdesz Faip Egyet Tud Koezlem
Az Erdoe (Temesvar) — Erdoe Temesvar
Az Iparmuveszeti Muzeum Evkoenyvei — AIME
Az Orszagos Erdeszeti-Egyesuelet Evkoenyve — Orsz Erdesz Egyes Evk
Azabu Daigaku Juigakubu Kenkyu Hokoku — ADJHDO
Azabu Juika Daigaku Kenkyu Hokoku [*Bulletin. Azabu Veterinary College*] — AJDKA8
Azabu Juika Daigaku Kenkyu Hokoku/Bulletin. Azabu Veterinary College — Azabu Juika Daigaku Kenkyu Hokoku Bull
Azerbaidzanskii Gosudarstvennyi Universitet Imeni M. Kirova. Ucenye Zapiski — Azerbaidzan Gos Univ Ucen Zap
Azerbaidzanskii Gosudarstvennyi Universitet Imeni S. M. Kirova. Ucenye Zapiski. Serija Fiziko-Matematiceskih Nauk — Azerbaidzan Gos Univ Ucen Zap Ser Fiz-Mat Nauk
Azerbaidzhanskii Gosudarstvennyi Meditsinskii Institut Materialy Nauchnoi Konferentsii — Azerb Gos Med Inst Mater Nauchn Konf
Azerbaidzhanskii Gosudarstvennyi Meditsinskii Institut. Uchenye Zapiski — Azerb Gos Med Inst Uch Zap
Azerbaidzhanskii Gosudarstvennyi Nauchno-Issledovatel'skii i Proektnyi Institut Neftyanoi Promyshlennosti. Trudy — Azerb Gos Nauchno Issled Proektn Inst Neft Promsti Tr
Azerbaidzhanskii Institut Nefti i Khimii. Trudy — Azerb Inst Nefti Khim Tr

Azerbaidzhanskii Khimicheskii Zhurnal — Azerb Khim Zh
Azerbaidzhanskii Khimicheskii Zhurnal — AZKZA
Azerbaidzhanskii Meditsinskii Zhurnal — Azerb Med Zh
Azerbaidzhanskii Meditsinskii Zhurnal — Azerbaidzhan Med Zhurnal
Azerbaidzhanskii Meditsinskii Zhurnal — AZMZA
Azerbaidzhanskii Nauchno-Issledovatel'skii Institut Gematologii i Perelivaniya Krovi. Sbornik Nauchnykh Trudov — Azerb Nauchno Issled Inst Gematol Pereliv Krovi Sb Nauchn Tr
Azerbaidzhanskii Nauchno-Issledovatel'skii Institut Oftal'mologii. Sbornik Trudov — Azerb Nauchno-Issled Inst Oftalmol Sb Tr
Azerbaidzhanskii Nauchno-Issledovatel'skii Institut Sadovodstva, Vinogradarstva i Subtropicheskikh Kul'tur. Trudy — Azerb Nauchno Issled Inst Sadovod Vinograd Subtyrop Kult Tr
Azerbaidzhanskii Nauchno-Issledovatel'skii Institut Shelkovodstva. Trudy — Azerb Nauchno Issled Inst Shelkovod Tr
Azerbaidzhanskii Sel'skokhozyaistvennyi Institut imeni S. Agamaliogly. Trudy — Azerb Skh Inst S Agamaliogly Tr
Azerbajdzan SSR Elmler Akademijasynyn Herberleri. Izvestija Akademii Nauk Azerbajdzanskoj SSR — Azerb Ak Heberleri
Azerbajdzanskij Filial Akademii Nauk SSSR. SSCI Elmler Aqademijasb Azerbajcan Filialb — Azerbajdzansk Fil Akad Nauk SSSR
Azerbajdzhanskoe Neftyanoe Khozyajstvo — Azerb Neft Khoz
Azia i Afrika Segodnia — AAS
Aziia i Afrika Segodnia — AzAS
Azija i Afrika Segodnja — Azija i Afr Segodnja
Azotul in Agricultura — Azotul Agric
Aztlan — PAZT

B

B + U. Bouw en Uitvoering van Gemeentewerken; Maandblad voor Functionarissen van de Diensten van Publieke en Openbare Werken — BUL
BA [*Bansilal Amritlal*] **College of Agriculture Magazine** [*India*] — BA Coll Agric Mag
Babel. International Journal of Translation [*Budapest*] — Ba
Babel. Journal of the Australian Federation of Modern Language Teachers Association [*Darlinghurst, New South Wales*] — Bab J A
Babesch. Bulletin Antieke Beschaving — B An B
Babesch. Bulletin Antieke Beschaving — B Ant Beschav
Babesch. Bulletin Antieke Beschaving — BBAB
Babesch. Bulletin Antieke Beschaving — Bull Ant B
Babesch. Bulletin Antieke Beschaving — Bull Ant Besch
Baby John — Baby J
Babyloniaca. Etudes de Philologie Assyro-Babylonienne [*Paris*] — Bab
Babyloniaca. Etudes de Philologie Assyro-Babylonienne — Babyl
Babylonian and Oriental Record — BOR
[*The*] **Babylonian Expedition of the University of Pennsylvania. Series A: Cuneiform Texts** — BE
[*The*] **Babylonian Expedition of the University of Pennsylvania. Series A: Cuniform Texts** — BEUP
Babylonian Expedition. University of Pennsylvania — BE
Babylonian Inscriptions in the Collection of James B. Nies. Yale University — BIN
Babylonian Inscriptions in the Collection of James B. Nies. Yale University — NBC
Babylonian Magic and Sorcery — BMS
Bach — BA
Bach, Johann Sebastian. Neue Ausgabe Saemtlicher Werke — NBA
Bachelor of Arts — Bach of Arts
Bach-Jahrbuch — B JB
Bach-Jahrbuch — BachJb
BACIE [*British Association for Commercial and Industrial Education*] **Journal** — BACIE J
Background Notes — Backgr Notes
Background Notes on the Countries of the World. US Department of State — Back Notes
Background Papers for a Workshop on the Tropospheric Transport of Pollutants to the Ocean — Background Pap Workshop Tropospheric Transp Pollut Ocean
Background to Collecting — Backgr Collect
Background to Migraine. Migraine Symposium — Background Migraine Migraine Symp
Background to Migraine. Migraine Symposium — BGMGAV
Backgrounder — BCKGD
Backpacker — GBAC
Backpacking Journal — Backpacking J
Baconiana — Ba
Bacteria, Bacteriophages, and Fungi — Bact Bacteriophages Fungi
Bacterial Immunoglobulin-Binding Proteins — Bact Immunoglobulin Binding Proteins
Bacterial Infections of Respiratory and Gastrointestinal Mucosae — Bact Infect Respir Gastrointest Mucosae
Bacterial Transport — Bact Transp
Bacteriologia, Virusologia, Parazitologia, Epidemiologia — Bacteriol Virusol Parazitol Epidemiol
Bacteriologia, Virusologia, Parazitologia, Epidemiologia (Bucharest) — Bacteriol Virusol Parazitol Epidemiol (Buchar)
Bacteriological News — Bacteriol News
Bacteriological Proceedings — Bact Proc
Bacteriological Proceedings — Bacteriol Proc
Bacteriological Reviews — Bact R
Bacteriological Reviews — Bact Rev
Bacteriological Reviews — Bact Rs
Bacteriological Reviews — Bacteriol Rev
Bacteriological Reviews — BAREA
Bad Hersfelder Jahresheft — Bad Hersfelder Jh
Badania Fizjograficzne nad Polska Zachodnia. B. Biologia — Badan Fizjogr Pol Zachod
Badener Neujahrsblaetter — Bad N
Badger Pharmacist. Wisconsin Pharmaceutical Association — Badger Pharm
Badische Fundberichte — Bad FB
Badische Fundberichte — Bad Fber
Badische Fundberichte — Bad Fu Ber
Badische Fundberichte — BF
Badische Geologische Abhandlungen — Bad Geol Abh
Badische Historische Kommission. Neujahrsblaetter — Badische Hist Komm Neujahrsbl
Badische Notarszeitschrift — Bad Not Z
Badische Rechtspraxis — Bad Rechtsprax
Badischer Obst- und Gartenbau — Bad Obst Gartenbau
Badminton Magazine — Bad M
Badminton Review — Badminton Rev
Baecker und Konditor — Baecker Konditor
Baender, Bleche, Rohre — BBROA
Baer von Berlin — Baer Berl
Baessler-Archiv [*Berlin*] — Baessler-Arch
Baessler-Archiv. Beitraege zur Voelkerkunde — BABV
Baessler-Archiv. Beitraege zur Voelkerkunde — Baessler-Arch
Baessler-Archiv. Beitraege zur Volkskunde — Baessler Arch
Baessler-Archiv. Museen fuer Voelkerkunde — MV/BA
Baetica; Estudios de Arte, Geografia, e Historia — Baetica
Baghdad Chamber of Commerce. Commercial Bulletin. Bi-Weekly — CHS
Baghdad University. College of Science. Bulletin — Baghdad Univ Coll Sci Bull
Baghdader Mitteilungen [*Berlin*] — BaM
Baghdader Mitteilungen — BM
Baghdader Mitteilungen des Deutschen Archaeologischen Instituts. Abteilung Baghdad [*Berlin*] — BaghMitt
Baghdader Mitteilungen. Deutsches Archaeologisches Institut. Abteilung Baghdad — Ba Mitt
Baghdader Mitteilungen. Deutsches Archaeologisches Institut. Abteilung Baghdad — Baghdader Mitt
Baghdader Mitteilungen. Deutsches Archaeologisches Institut. Abteilung Baghdad — MDAI Bag Abt
Bahia. Annuario Energetico — Bahia Ener
Bahia. Balanco Energetico Consolidado — Bahia Bal E
Bahia, Brazil. Centro de Estatistica e Informacoes. Anuario Estatistico — Bahia Braz Cent Estat Inf An Estat
Bahia. Centro de Pesquisas e Desenvolvimento. Boletim Tecnico — Bahia Cent Pesqui Desenvolvimento Bol Tec
Bahnarzt — BahnA
Bailey's Industrial Oil and Fat Products [*Monograph*] — Baileys Ind Oil Fat Prod
Baillieres Clinical Endocrinology and Metabolism — Baillieres Clin Endocrinol Metab
Baillieres Clinical Gastroenterology — Baillieres Clin Gastroenterol
Baillieres Clinical Haematology — Baillieres Clin Haematol
Baillieres Clinical Neurology — Baillieres Clin Neurol
Baillieres Clinical Obstetrics and Gynaecology — Baillieres Clin Obstet Gynaecol
Baillieres Clinical Rheumatology — Baillieres Clin Rheumatol
Bajan and South Caribbean — Bajan S Carib
Bakasha LePatent — Bakasha LePat
Bakelite Review — Bakelite Rev
Baker and Millers' Journal — Baker Millers J
Baker and Millers' Journal — Baker Millr J
Baker, J. T., Chemical Company. Product Bulletin — Baker J T Chem Co Prod Bull
Baker Street Journal — BakerSJ
Baker Street Journal — BSJ
Baker's Digest — Baker's
Baker's Digest — Baker's Dig
Baker's Review — Baker's Rev
Baker's Technical Digest — Baker's Tech Dig
Bakersfield Californian — Baker Calif
Bakery Industry — Bakery Ind
Bakery Production and Marketing — Baker Prod
Bakery Production and Marketing — BKQ
Baking Industry — Baking Ind
Baking Technology — Baking Technol
Bakish Materials Corporation. Publication — Bakish Mater Corp Publ
Bakker. Actueel Vakblad voor de Broodbakkerij. Banketbakkerij [*Nijmegen*] — BAK
Bakkerij Wetenschap — Bakkerij Wet
Bakkerswereld — BKW
Baksteen. Tweemaandelijks Tijdschrift Gewijd aan de Technische en Esthetische Eigenschappen van Gebakken Kleiproducten — BKH
Balai Penelitian Industri. Bulletin Penelitian — Balai Penelitian Ind Bull Penelitian
Balance of Payments Statistics [*Information service or system*] — BOPS
Balance Sheet — Bal Sheet
Balasovkii Gosudarstvennyi Pedagogiceskii Institut. Ucenye Zapiski — Balasov Gos Ped Inst Ucen Zap
Balaton Symposium on Particle Physics — Balaton Symp Part Phys

Baldwin's Official Edition. Kentucky Revised Statutes, Annotated — KY Rev Stat Ann (Baldwin)
Baldwin's Ohio Legislative Service — Ohio Legis Serv (Baldwin)
Balgarska Dialektologija — BDial
Balgarska Muzyka — Balgarska M
Balgarski Ezik — BE
Balgarski Ezik i Literatura — BEL
Balgarsko Ovostarstvo i Gradinarstvo — Balg Ovostarstvo Gradinarstvo
Balkan Archiv — BA
Balkan Studies — B St
Balkan Studies — Bal St
Balkan Studies — Balk St
Balkan Studies — Balk Stud
Balkan Studies — Balkan St
Balkan Studies — Balkan Stud
Balkan Studies — BASU
Balkan-Kutatasainak Tudomanyos Eredmenyei — Balkan Kutat Tud Eredm
Balkansko Ezikoznanie — Balk Ez
Balkansko Ezikoznanie — Balk Ezik
Balkansko Ezikoznanije — B Ez
Balkansko Ezikoznanije — BalkE
Ball and Roller Bearing Engineering — Ball & Roller Bear Engng
Ball and Roller Bearing Engineering — Ball Roller Bear Eng
Ball Bearing Journal — Ball Bear J
Ball State Business Review — Ball St Bus Rev
Ball State Business Review — BSB
Ball State Commerce Journal — BSCJ
Ball State Journal for Business Educators — Ball State J
Ball State Monographs — Ball St Monogr
Ball State Teachers College Forum [*Later, Ball State University Forum*] — BSTCF
Ball State University Forum — Ball St Uni
Ball State University Forum — BSUF
Ballade Tidsskrift for Ny Musikk — Ballade
Ballet News — Ballet N
Ballet Review — Ballet Rev
Ballistic Materials and Penetration Mechanics — Ballist Mater Penetration Mech
Balloon Research and Technology Symposium — Balloon Res Technol Symp
Balneologia Bohemica — Balneol Bohem
Balneologia Bohemica — BLBHAE
Balneologia Polska — Balneol Pol
Balneological Society of Japan. Journal — Balneol Soc Japan Jour
Balston Conference on Nuclear Physics — Balston Conf Nucl Phys
Baltic Review — Bal R
Baltic Review — Balt Rev
Baltic Review [*New York*] — BR
Baltic Sea Environment. Proceedings — Baltic Sea Environ Proc
Baltic Sea Environment. Proceedings — BSEPE4
Baltimore Bulletin of Education — Baltimore B of Ed
Baltimore Business Journal — Baltimr BJ
Baltimore Journal of Medicine — Baltimore Journ Med
Baltimore Manufacturers' Record — Baltimore Manuf Rec
Baltimore Medical and Physical Recorder — Baltimore Med Phys Rec
Baltimore Municipal Journal — Baltimore Munic J
Baltimore Museum of Art. News — Baltimore Mus Art N
Baltimore Museum of Art. News — Baltimore Mus N
Baltische Hefte — B He
Baltische Hefte — Balt H
Baltische Monatschefte — Balt Mh
Baltische Monatsschrift — BM
Baltische Studien — Bal St
Baltische Studien — Balt Stud
Baltische Studien — Baltische Stud
Baltische Wochenschrift fuer Landwirtschaft, Gewerbefleiss, und Handel — BaltW
Baltisches Recht — Balt Recht
Baltisk Revy — Balt Revy
Balwant Vidyapeeth Journal of Agricultural and Scientific Research — Balwant Vidyapeeth J Agr Sci Res
Balwant Vidyapeeth Journal of Agricultural and Scientific Research — Balwant Vidyapeeth J Agric Sci Res
BAM Amts- und Mitteilungsblatt — BAM Amts Mitteilungsbl
BAM Berlin Amtsblatt und Mitteilungsblatt der Bundesanstalt fuer Materialpruefung — BAM Amtsbl Mitteilungsbl
BAM, Bundesanstalt fuer Materialpruefung. Forschungsbericht — BAM Bundesanst Materialpruef Forschungsber
Bamberger Abhandlungen und Forschungen — BAF
BAM-Berichte. Forschung und Entwicklung in der Bundesanstalt fuer Materialpruefung — BAM-Ber
Bamboo Journal — Bamboo J
Bambou. Periodique Illustre (Paris) — Bambou Paris
Bamidgeh — BMGHA
Bamidgeh. Bulletin of Fish Culture in Israel — Bamidgeh Bull Fish Cult Isr
Banach Center. Publications [*Warsaw*] — Banach Center Publ
Banaras Metallurgist — Banaras Metall
Banasthali Patrika — BP
Banater Zeitschrift fuer Landwirthschaft, Handel, Kuenste, und Gewerbe — Banater Z Landw
Banber Erevani Hamalsarani-Vestnik Erevanskogo Universiteta — Banb Erev Hamal
Banber Matenadarani — BM
Banbury Report — Banbury Rep
Banca d'Italia. Bollettino — Banca d'Italia Bol
Banca Nazionale del Lavoro. Quarterly Review — Banca Naz Lav Quart R
Banca Nazionale del Lavoro. Quarterly Review — Banca Nazionale del Lavoro Q R
Banca Nazionale del Lavoro. Quarterly Review — BLN
Banca Nazionale del Lavoro. Quarterly Review — BNL
Bancaria — BAS
Banco Central. Boletin Informativo [*Madrid*] — BAW
Banco Central de Bolivia. Boletin Estadistico — Banco Central Bolivia Bol Estadistico
Banco Central de Reserra de El Salvador. Revista Mensual — El Salv M
Banco de Angola. Boletim Trimestral — Banco Angola Bol Trim
Banco de Espana — Bnc Espana
Banco de Guatemala. Informe Economico — BOO
Banco de la Republica. Revista — BRC
Banco de Vizcaya. Revista Financiera — Banco Vizcaya
Banco do Brasil. Boletim Trimestral — Banco Brasil Bol Trim
Banco Nacional da Habitacao. Orcamento Plurianual — Banc Nacl Habit Orca Plurian
Banco Nacional da Habitacao. Relatorio de Atividades — Banc Nacl Habit Relator Ativid
Banco Nacional de Comercio Exterior. Comercio de Exterior — CXT
Banco Nacional de Comercio Exterior, SA, Mexico. Annual Report — Banco Nacl
Banco Nacional de Panama — Banco Nacl Panama Cuad
Banco Roma. Review of the Economic Conditions in Italy — Banco Roma
Bandaoti Xuebao — PTTPD
Banff Conference on Reproductive Immunology — Banff Conf Reprod Immunol
Bangabasi College Magazine [*Calcutta*] — Bangabasi College Mag
Bangabasi Morning College Magazine [*Calcutta*] — Bangabasi Morning College Mag
Bangalore Theological Forum — Bangalore Th F
Bangason Bango Hakhoe Chi — BBHCD
Bangkok Bank. Monthly Review — BAD
Bangkok Bank. Monthly Review — Bangkok Bank Mo R
Bangladesh Academy of Sciences. Journal — Bangladesh Acad Sci J
Bangladesh Agricultural Sciences Abstracts — Bangladesh Agr Sci Abstr
Bangladesh Agricultural Sciences Abstracts — Bangladesh Agric Sci Abstr
Bangladesh Bank. Bulletin — BQU
Bangladesh Council of Scientific and Industrial Research Laboratories. Chittagong. Research Bulletin — Bangladesh CSIRL Chittagong Res Bull
Bangladesh Development Studies — Bangla Dev Stud
Bangladesh Development Studies — Bangladesh Dev Stud
Bangladesh Development Studies — Bangladesh Devel Stud
Bangladesh Development Studies — BGLE
Bangladesh Development Studies — PCJ
Bangladesh Geological Survey. Records — Bangladesh Geol Surv Rec
Bangladesh Historical Studies — Bangla Hist Stud
Bangladesh Horticulture — BAHODP
Bangladesh Horticulture — Bangladesh Hortic
Bangladesh Journal of Agricultural Sciences — Bangladesh J Agric Sci
Bangladesh Journal of Agriculture — Bangladesh J Agric
Bangladesh Journal of Agriculture — BJOADD
Bangladesh Journal of Animal Sciences — Bangladesh J Anim Sci
Bangladesh Journal of Biological and Agricultural Sciences [*Later, Bangladesh Journal of Biological Sciences*] — Bangladesh J Biol Agric Sci
Bangladesh Journal of Biological Sciences — Bangladesh J Biol Sci
Bangladesh Journal of Botany — Bangladesh J Bot
Bangladesh Journal of Botany — BJBTB
Bangladesh Journal of Jute and Fibre Research — Bangladesh J Jute Fibre Res
Bangladesh Journal of Scientific and Industrial Research — Bangladesh J Sci Ind Res
Bangladesh Journal of Scientific and Industrial Research — BJSIB
Bangladesh Journal of Scientific and Industrial Research — BJSIBL
Bangladesh Journal of Scientific Research — Bangladesh J Sci Res
Bangladesh Journal of Scientific Research — BJSRDG
Bangladesh Journal of Soil Science — Bangladesh J Soil Sci
Bangladesh Journal of Zoology — Bangladesh J Zool
Bangladesh Medical Research Council. Bulletin — Bangladesh Med Res Counc Bull
Bangladesh Pharmaceutical Journal — Bangladesh Pharm J
Bangladesh Veterinary Journal — Bangladesh Vet J
Bangor Daily News — Bangor Dail
Banjo Newsletter — Banjo N
Bank Advertising News — Bank Ad News
Bank Analysis System [*Database*] — BANKANAL
Bank Compliance — Bank Comp
Bank Directory of Canada — Bank Dir Can
Bank Executive's Report — Bank Exec Rep
Bank fuer Gemeinwirtschaft. Aussenhandelsdienst — BCD
Bank Installment Lending Newsletter — Bank Install Lend Newsl
Bank Letter den Danske Landsmandsbank — Danske Bnk
Bank Leumi Le-Israel. Economic Review — BXK
Bank Markazi Iran. Bulletin — BQL
Bank Marketing — Bank Mark
Bank Marketing — BMR
Bank Marketing — BNM
Bank Marketing Magazine — Bank Mktg M
Bank Marketing Report — Bank Mark Rep
Bank Marketing Report — Bank Mktg R
Bank Negara Malaysia. Bulletin — BNMB
Bank Negara Malaysia. Quarterly Economic Bulletin — BKN
Bank Note Reporter — BNR
Bank of Canada. Review — Bank Can R
Bank of Canada Weekly Financial Statistics [*Database*] — WBANK
Bank of China. Economic Review — BCER
Bank of England. Quarterly Bulletin — Bank Eng Q Bull
Bank of England. Quarterly Bulletin — Bank Eng QB
Bank of England. Quarterly Bulletin — Bank England Q Bul

Bank of England. Quarterly Bulletin — BEF
Bank of England. Quarterly Bulletin — BEQB
Bank of Finland. Monthly Bulletin — Bank Finland Mo Bul
Bank of Finland. Monthly Bulletin — Bank Finland Mthly B
Bank of Finland. Monthly Bulletin — BFMB
Bank of Finland. Monthly Bulletin — BOF
Bank of Ghana Quarterly Economic Bulletin — Bank of Ghana Q Econ Bull
Bank of Hawaii. Monthly Review — Bk Hawaii
Bank of Israel. Bulletin [*Jerusalem*] — BIB
Bank of Israel. Current Banking Statistics — Bank Isr Cur Bank Stat
Bank of Israel. Economic Review — BKB
Bank of Jamaica. Bulletin — BAE
Bank of Japan. Monthly Economic Review — BJG
Bank of Korea. Quarterly Economic Review — BKO
Bank of London and South America. Review — Bank London and South Am R
Bank of London and South America. Review — Bank London South Amer R
Bank of London and South America. Review — BLF
Bank of London and South America. Review — BOLSA
Bank of Montreal. Business Review — Bank Montreal Bus R
Bank of New South Wales. Review — Bank NSW R
Bank of New South Wales. Review — Bank NSW Re
Bank of New South Wales. Review — Bank NSW Rev
Bank of New South Wales. Review — Bank of NSW R
Bank of New South Wales. Review — BSW
Bank of Nova Scotia. Monthly Review — Bank Nova Scotia Mo R
Bank of Nova Scotia. Monthly Review — BNSMR
Bank of Papua New Guinea. Quarterly Economic Bulletin — BBP
Bank of Sierra Leone Economic Review — Bank of Sierra Leone Econ Rev
Bank of Sierra Leone. Economic Review — Bank Sierra Leone Econ R
Bank of Sudan. Economic and Financial Bulletin — Bank Sudan Ec Fin Bull
Bank of Tanzania. Economic Bulletin — BZX
Bank of Thailand. Monthly Bulletin — Bank Thailand Mo Bul
Bank of Thailand. Monthly Bulletin — BTD
Bank of Thailand. Quarterly Bulletin — Bank Thailand Q Bul
Bank Reports — BNK
Bank Systems and Equipment — Bank Sys
Bank Systems and Equipment — Bank Syst and Equip
Bank Systems and Equipment — BSE
Bank Systems and Equipment — BSY
Bank van de Nederlandse Antillen. Quarterly Bulletin — BNI
Bankbedrijf en Effectenbedrijf — BBY
Bank-Betrieb — Bank-Betr
Banker — B
Banker — BKR
Banker — BNKRB
Banker-Farmer — Banker-F
Banker's Business — Bankers Bus
Bankers' Institute of Australasia. Journal — J Bankers Inst Australas
Bankers' Journal — Bankers J
Bankers' Magazine — Bank
Bankers' Magazine — Bank Mag
Bankers' Magazine — Bankers' M
Bankers' Magazine — Bankers' Mag
Bankers' Magazine — BM
Bankers' Magazine — BZE
Bankers' Magazine (London) — Bank M (L)
Bankers' Magazine (London) — Bank M (Lond)
Bankers' Magazine (New York) — Bank M (NY)
Bankers Magazine of Australasia — Bank Mag A/sia
Bankers Magazine of Australasia — Bankers M Australasia
Bankers Magazine of Australasia — Bankers Mag
Bankers Magazine of Australasia — Bankers Mag A'sia
Bankers Magazine of Australasia — Bankers Mag Aust
Bankers Magazine of Australasia — Bankers Mag Australas
Bankers' Monthly — Bankers M
Bankers' Monthly — Bankers' Mo
Bankers' Monthly — Bankers' Mon
Bankers' Monthly — BKM
Bankhistorisches Archiv — Bankhist Archiv
Banking. American Bankers Association — Banking Am Bankers Assn
Banking Law Journal — BAN
Banking Law Journal — Ban LJ
Banking Law Journal — Bank Law J
Banking Law Journal — Bank LJ
Banking Law Journal — Banking Law J
Banking Law Journal — Banking LJ
Banking Law Journal — Bk LJ
Banking Law Journal Digest. Federal Supplement — Bank Law J Dig Fed Sup
Banknote Quarterly — BQ
Banko Janakari. A Journal of Forestry Information for Nepal — Banko Janakari J For Inf Nepal
Bankruptcy Court Decisions — BCD
Bankruptcy Law Reports [*Commerce Clearing House*] — Bankr L Rep
Bankwirtschaft — B Wi
Bankwissenschaft — B Wi
Bankwissenschaft — BW
Bano Biggyan Patrika — BBPAD
Banque Centrale de Madagascar. Bulletin Mensuel de Statistiques — Banque Centrale Madagascar Bul Mensuel Statis
Banque Centrale des Etats de l'Afrique de l'Ouest. Notes d'Information et Statistiques — Banque Centrale Etats Afr Ouest Notes Info et Statis
Banque Centrale des Etats de l'Afrique de l'Ouest. Notes d'Information et Statistiques — BCM
Banque de Donnees Internationales de Biometrie Humaine et d'Ergonomie [*Database*] — ERGODATA
Banque de Donnees Locales [*Database*] — BDL
Banque de Donnees Macroeconomique [*Database*] — BDM
Banque de Donnees Socio-economiques des Pays Mediterraneens [*Database*] — MEDISTAT
Banque de Donnees Urbaines de Paris et de la Region d'Ile de France [*Database*] — BDU
Banque de France. Bulletin Trimestriel — Banque Fr Bul Trim
Banque de France. Bulletin Trimestriel — BBB
Banque de la Republique du Burundi. Bulletin Mensuel — Banque Repub Burundi Bul Mensuel
Banque de la Republique du Burundi. Bulletin Trimestriel — Banque Repub Burundi Bul Trim
Banque de Terminologie du Quebec [*Database*] — BTQ
Banque des Etats de l'Afrique Centrale. Etudes et Statistiques — Banque Etats Afr Centrale Etud et Statis
Banque d'Information Industrielle [*Database*] — BII
Banque d'Informations Automatisees sur les Medicaments [*Database*] — BIAM
Banque d'Informations sur les Recherches [*Database*] — BIR
Banque du Zaire. Bulletin Trimestriel — Banque Zaire Bul Trim
Banque Francaise et Italienne pour l'Amerique du Sud. Etudes Economiques — Banque Franc Ital Amer Sud Et Econ
Banque Marocaine du Commerce Exterieur. Monthly Information Review — Banque Marocaine du Commerce Exterieur Mo Info R
Banque Nationale de Belgique. Bulletin — Banque Nat Belgique Bul
Banque Nationale de Belgique. Bulletin — Banque Nationale de Belgique Bul
Banque Nationale de Paris. Revue Economique — Banque Nat Paris R Econ
Banque Nationale Suisse. Bulletin Mensuel — BNS
Bansilal Amritlal Agricultural College. Magazine — Bansilal Amritlal Agric Coll Mag
Bansky Obzor — Bansk Obz
Banta's Greek Exchange — Banta's Greek Exch
Bantu Studies — Bantu Stud
Bantu Studies — BS
Banyaszat — BANYB
Banyaszati es Kohaszati Lapok — Banyasz Kohasz Lapok
Banyaszati es Kohaszati Lapok. Banyaszat — Banyasz Kohasz Lap Banyasz
Banyaszati es Kohaszati Lapok. Banyaszat — Banyasz Kohasz Lapok Banyasz
Banyaszati es Kohaszati Lapok. Banyaszat Kulonszam — Banyasz Kohasz Lapok Banyasz Kulonszam
Banyaszati es Kohaszati Lapok. Koeolaj es Foeldgaz — Banyasz Kohasz Lapok Koeolaj Foeldgaz
Banyaszati es Kohaszati Lapok. Kohaszat — Banyasz Kohasz Lapok Kohasz
Banyaszati es Kohaszati Lapok. Kohaszat — BKLKB
Banyaszati es Kohaszati Lapok. Melleklet. Aluminum — Banyasz Kohasz Lapok Mellek Alum
Banyaszati es Kohaszati Lapok. Ontode — Banyasz Kohasz Lapok Ontode
Banyaszati Kutato Intezet Kozlemenyei — Banyasz Kut Intez Kozl
Banyaszati Kutato Intezet Kozlemenyei [*Hungary*] — Banyasz Kut Intez Kozlem
Banyaszati Kutato Intezet Kozlemenyei. Kulonszam — Banyasz Kut Intez Kozl Kulonszam
Banyaszati Lapok — Banyasz Lapok
BANZ [*British-Australian-New Zealand*] **Antarctic Research Expedition. Report. Series B** — BANZ Antarct Exped Rep Ser B
Baptist Bulletin — Bapt B
Baptist History and Heritage — Bapt H Heri
Baptist History and Heritage — Bapt Hist and Heritage
Baptist History and Heritage — BHH
Baptist Information Retrieval System [*Database*] — BIRS
Baptist Quarterly — BapQ
Baptist Quarterly [*London*] — Bapt Q
Baptist Quarterly — BQ
Baptist Quarterly Review [*London*] — Bapt Q
Baptist Reformation Review — Bapt Ref R
Bar Bulletin of the Boston Bar Association — Bar Bull Boston
Bar Code News — BCN
Bar Examiner — B Exam
Bar Examiner — Bar Exam
Bar Gazette — Bar Gaz
Barat Review — Barat R
Barbados. Annual Report. Department of Science and Agriculture — Barbados Annu Rep Dep Sci Agric
Barbados Museum and Historical Society. Journal — Bar Mus Hist Soc J
Barbados Nursing Journal — Barbados Nurs J
Barbour's Supreme Court Reports [*New York*] — Barb
BARC (Bangladesh Agricultural Research Council) Soils and Irrigation Publication — BARC Soils Irrig Publ
Barcelona — B
Barcelona. Instituto de Investigaciones Geologicas. Publicaciones — Barc Inst Invest Geol Publ
Barcelona. Instituto Provincial de Paleontologia. Actividades — Barc Inst Prov Paleontol Actividades
Barcelona. Instituto Provincial de Paleontologia. Boletin Informativo [*Sabadell*] — Barc Inst Prov Paleontol Bol Inf
Barcelona. Instituto Provincial de Paleontologia. Paleontologia y Evolucion [*A publication*] — Barc Inst Prov Paleontol Paleontol Evol
Barcelona Universidad. Facultad de Ciencias. Miscellanea Alcobe — Barc Univ Fac Cienc Misc Alcobe
Barcelona Universidad. Instituto Geologia. Memorias y Communicaciones — Barc Univ Inst Geol Mem Commun
Barclays Review — BAC
Barclays Review — BAQ
Barclays Review — Barclays R
Barclays Review — Barclays Rev
Bardsey Observatory Report — Bardsey Obs Rep
Bardsey Observatory Report — RBOBDY

Baretti — Bar
Bargaining Report — Bargaining Rep
Bari International Conference — Bari Int Conf
Barid Hollanda — BHE
Barley Genetics Newsletter — Barley Genet Newsl
Barley Genetics. Proceedings. International Barley Genetics Symposium — Barley Genet Proc Int Barley Genet Symp
Barnaul'skii Gosudarstvennyi Pedagogiceskii Institut. Ucenye Zapiski — Barnaul Gos Ped Inst Ucen Zap
Barnes and Noble Critical Study Series — Barn Nob Cr
Baroda Journal of Nutrition — Baroda J Nutr
Baroda Museum and Picture Gallery. Bulletin — BBMPG
Baroid News Bulletin — Baroid News Bull
Baroid News Bulletin — BNBUD
Barossa Historical Bulletin — Barossa Hist Bull
Barrasiha-Ye Tarikhi — ByT
Barre du Jour — BdJ
Barrister — Bar
Barron's — BAR
Barron's Financial Weekly — BRR
Barron's Index — Barrons Ind
Barrow (W. J.) Research Laboratory. Publication — Barrow (W J) Res Lab Publ
Bartlett Tree Research Laboratory. Bulletin — Bartlett Tree Res Lab Bull
Bartonia. Proceedings. Philadelphia Botanical Club — Bartonia Proc Phila Bot Club
Baruka Rebyu — BAREDB
Baryon Resonances. Conference — Baryon Reson Conf
Base and User — BUSED
Base Bleed. International Symmposium on Special Topics in Chemical Propulsion — Base Bleed Int Symp Spec Top Chem Propul
Base d'Information Robert Debre [*Database*] — BIRD
Baseball Canada — Baseb Can
Baseball (Ottawa) — Baseb (Ott)
Basel Institute for Immunology. Annual Report — ARBIDH
Basel Institute for Immunology. Annual Report — Basel Inst Immunol Annu Rep
Baselbieter Heimatblaetter — BHb
Baselbieter Heimatbuch — BHB
BASF (Badische Anilin- und Soda-Fabrik) Mitteilungen fuer den Landbau — BASF Mitt Landbau
BASF (Badische Anilin- und Soda-Fabrik) Review (English Edition) — BASF Rev (Engl Ed)
BASF [*Badische Anilin- und Sodafabrik*] **Information** — BASF Inf
BASF [*Badische Anilin- und Sodafabrik*] **Review** — BASF Rev
BASF [*Badische Anilin- und Soda-Fabrik*] **Symposium** — BASF Symp
Bashkirskaya Neft. Tekhnicheskii Byulleten — Bashk Neft
Bashkirskii Gosudarstvennyi Meditsinskii Institut. Sbornik Nauchnykh Trudov — Bashk Gos Med Inst Sb Nauchn Tr
Bashkirskii Khimicheskii Zhurnal — Bashk Khim Zh
Bashkirskii Nauchno-Issledovatel'skii Institut po Stroitel'stvu. Trudy — Bashk Nauchno Issled Inst Stroit Tr
Basic and Applied Histochemistry — BAHID
Basic and Applied Histochemistry — Basic Appl Histochem
Basic and Clinical Aspects of Neuroscience — Basic Clin Aspects Neurosci
Basic and Clinical Cardiology — Basic Clin Cardiol
Basic and Clinical Endocrinology — Basic Clin Endocrinol
Basic and Clinical Endocrinology — BCLEDT
Basic and Clinical Immunology — Basic and Clin Immunol
Basic and Clinical Nutrition — Basic Clin Nutr
Basic and Clinical Nutrition — BCNUDJ
Basic Biology in Color Series — Basic Biol Color Ser
Basic Data Report. Maryland. Geological Survey — Basic Data Rep Md Geol Surv
Basic Data Report. West Virginia. Geological and Economic Survey — Basic Data Rep WV Geol Econ Surv
Basic Data Series. Ground-Water Release. Kansas Geological Survey — Basic Data Ser Ground Water Release Kans Geol Surv
Basic Documentation/World Fertility Survey — Basic Doc World Fertil Surv
Basic Education — BE
Basic Environmental Problems of Man in Space. Proceedings. International Symposium — Basic Environ Probl Man Space Proc Int Symp
B.A.S.I.C. Key to the World's Biological Research. Biological Abstracts Subject Index. Biological Abstracts, Inc. — BASIC
Basic Life Sciences — Basic Life Sci
Basic Life Sciences — BLFSB
Basic Neurochemistry. 2nd Edition — Basic Neurochem 2nd Ed
Basic Pharmacology Therapeutics [*Japan*] — Basic Pharmacol Ther
Basic Plasma Processes on the Sun. Proceedings. Symposium. International Astronomical Union — Basic Plasma Processes Sun Proc Symp Int Astron Union
Basic Record Report. United States Department of Interior. Geological Survey [*A publication*] — Basic Rec Rep US Dep Inter Geol Surv
Basic Records Report. Louisiana Department of Public Works — Basic Rec Rep LA Dep Public Works
Basic Research in Cardiology — Bas R Card
Basic Research in Cardiology — Basic Res Cardiol
Basic Science in Toxicology. Proceedings. International Congress of Toxicology — Basic Sci Toxicol Proc Int Congr Toxicol
Basic Science Principles of Nuclear Medicine — Basic Sci Princ Nucl Med
Basic Sleep Mechanisms — Basic Sleep Mech
Basin Planning Report. Allegheny Basin Regional Water Resources Planning Board — Basin Plann Rep Allegheny Basin Reg Water Resour Plann Board
Basin Planning Report ARB (Allegheny River Basin). New York State Department of Environmental Conservation — Basin Plann Rep ARB NY State Dep Environ Conserv
Basin Planning Report BRB [*Black River Basin*]. New York State Department of Environmental Conservation — Basin Plann Rep BRB NY State Dep Environ Conserv
Basin Planning Report. New York State Department of Environmental Conservation. Series ARB — Basin Plann Rep NY State Dept Environ Conserv ARB
Basin Planning Report. New York State Department of Environmental Conservation. Series ORB — Basin Plann Rep NY State Dep Environ Conserv ORB
Basin Planning Report. New York State Water Resources Commission. Series ENB — Basin Plann Rep NY State Water Resour Comm ENB
Basin Planning Report. New York State Water Resources Commission. Series ENB — NWRBBE
Basis and Practice of Neuroanaesthesia [*Monograph*] — Basis Pract Neuroanaesth
Basis of an Individual Physiology — Basis Individ Physiol
Baskerville Chemical Journal — BASKAV
Baskerville Chemical Journal — Baskerville Chem J
Baskirskii Gosudarstvennyi Universitet. Ucenye Zapiski — Baskir Gos Univ Ucen Zap
Basler Beitraege zur Chirurgie — Basler Beitr Chir
Basler Beitraege zur Deutschen Literatur- und Geistesgeschichte — BBLG
Basler Beitraege zur Ethnologie — Basler Beitr Ethnol
Basler Beitraege zur Geographie — Basler Beitr Geogr
Basler Beitraege zur Geschichtswissenschaft — Basler Beitr Gesch Wiss
Basler Beitraege zur Geschichtswissenschaft — BBG
Basler Jahrbuch — Basler Jb
Basler Jahrbuch fuer Historische Musikpraxis — Basler
Basler Juristische Mitteilungen [*Switzerland*] — BJM
Basler Stadtbuch — BS
Basler Studien zur Deutschen Sprache und Literatur — BSDSL
Basler Veroeffentlichungen zur Geschichte der Medizin und der Biologie — Basler Veroeffentl Gesch Med Biol
Basler Zeitschrift fuer Geschichte und Altertumskunde — Basler Z Gesch Altertumskde
Basler Zeitschrift fuer Geschichte und Altertumskunde — Basler Z Gesch Altertumskunde
Basler Zeitschrift fuer Geschichte und Altertumskunde — Basler Z Gesch & Altertumsk
Basler Zeitschrift fuer Geschichte und Altertumskunde — BaZ
Basler Zeitschrift fuer Geschichte und Altertumskunde — BZG
Basler Zeitschrift fuer Geschichte und Altertumskunde — BZGA
Basler Zeitschrift fuer Geschichte und Altertumskunde — BZGAK
Basrah Natural History Museum. Publication — Basrah Nat Hist Mus Publ
Basrah Natural History Museum. Publication — BNHPDH
Bass Sound Post — Bass Sound
Bastan Chenassi va Honar-Eiran — B Chl
Bat Research News — Bat Res News
Bataille — BAT
Bateman Eichler and Hill Richards. News Release — Bateman E
Bateman Eichler and Hill Richards. Research Report — Bateman E
Baths and Bath Engineering — Baths Bath Eng
Baths Service and Recreation Management — Baths Serv Rec Mgmt
Bati Edebiyatlari Arastirma Dergisi (Ankara, Turkey) — BEAD (Ankara Turkey)
Batiment International [*France*] — Batim Int
Batiment International/Building Research and Practice — Batim Int Build Res Pract
Battelle Information (Frankfurt) — Battelle Inf (Frankfurt)
Battelle Memorial Institute. Battelle Institute Materials Science Colloquia — Battelle Mem Inst Battelle Inst Mater Sci Colloq
Battelle Memorial Institute. Defense Ceramic Information Center. DCIC Report — Battelle Mem Inst DCIC Rep
Battelle Memorial Institute. Defense Metals Information Center. DMIC Memorandum — Battelle Mem Inst DMIC Memo
Battelle Memorial Institute. Defense Metals Information Center. DMIC Report — Battelle Mem Inst DMIC Rep
Battelle Memorial Institute. Defense Metals Information Center. DMIC Report — Battelle Meml Inst Def Met Inf Cent DMIC Rep
Battelle Memorial Institute. Materials Science Colloquia — Battelle Inst Mater Sci Colloq
Battelle Memorial Institute. Probable Levels of R and D Expenditures — Battel R & D
Battelle Monographs — Battelle Mg
Battelle Pacific Northwest Laboratories. Report BNWL — Battelle Pac Northwest Lab Rep BNWL
Battelle Pacific Northwest Laboratory. Technical Report PNL — Battelle Pac Northwest Lab Tech Rep PNL
Battelle Pacific Northwest Laboratory. Technical Report PNL-SA — Battelle Pac Northwest Lab Tech Rep PNL SA
Battelle Research Outlook — Battelle Res Outlook
Battelle Technical Review — BATRA
Battelle Technical Review — Battelle Tech R
Battelle Today — Battelle T
Battelle-Institut. Bericht (Frankfurt/Main) — Battelle Inst Ber Frankfurt Main
Batteries [*New York*] — BATTDW
Battery Bimonthly — Battery Bimon
Battery Council International Convention — Battery Counc Int Conv
Battery Council. International Convention. Proceedings — Battery Counc Int Conv Proc
Battery Council International Meeting — Battery Counc Int Meet
Battery Man — BAMAB
Battery Man — Battery Mn
Battery Research and Development Conference. Proceedings — Battery Res Dev Conf Proc
Bau und Betrieb — Bau Betr

Bauelemente der Elektrotechnik — Bauelem Elektrotech
Bauen fuer die Landwirtschaft — Bauen Landwirtsch
Bauen und Wirtschaft — Bauen Wirtsch
Bauen und Wohnen — BAWOA
Bauforschungsprojekte [*Database*] — BAUFO
Baugeschichte - Bauplanung — Baugesch Bauplan
Bauginia. Zeitschrift. Basler Botanische Gesellschaft — Bauginia Z Basler Botan Ges
Bauinformation. Wissenschaft und Technik [*Germany*] — Bauinf Wiss Tech
Bauingenieur — BANGA
Bauingenieur Praxis — Bauing Prax
Baukunst und Werkform — Bau & Werk
Baum Bugle — Baum B
Baum Bugle: A Journal of Oz — BaumB
Baumarkt. Zeitschrift fuer Wirtschaftliche Unternehmensfuehrung — DBA
Baumaschine und Bautechnik — Baumasch Bautech
Baumaschine und Bautechnik — BMBTA
Baumaschine und Bautechnik — BMBTAN
Baumaschinendienst — BDBAD
Baumeister — BAUMA
Baumwoll-Industrie — Baumwoll Ind
Bauobjektdokumentation [*Database*] — BODO
Bauplanung-Bautechnik — BABAB
Bauplanung-Bautechnik — Bauplanung Bautech
Baupraxis — BAPXB
Bausteine zum Deutschen Nationaltheater — BDN
Bausteine zur Geschichte der Literatur bei den Slaven — BGLS
Bausteine zur Volkskunde und Religionswissenschaft — BVR
Baustoffindustrie. Ausgabe A. Primaerbaustoffe [*German Democratic Republic*] — Baustoffind Ausg A
Baustoffindustrie. Ausgabe B. Bauelemente — Baustoffind Ausg B
Bautechnik. Ausgabe A — Bautechnik Ausg A
Bautechnik, Beilage. Zeitschriftenschau fuer das Gesamte Bauingenieurwesen — Bautechnik Beil Zeitschriftenschau Gesamte Bauingenieurwes
Bautechnik-Archiv — Bautech-Arch
Bauteile Report — Bauteile Rep
Bauverwaltung — BAUVA
Bauwelt — BAWTA
Bauwirtschaft — BWTSA
Bauxite Symposium — Bauxite Symp
Bauzeitung — BAZTA
Bay Area Worker — Bay Workr
Bay Cities Garden Monthly — Bay Cities Gard Monthy
Bay State Librarian — Bay St Librn
Bay State Librarian — Bay State Libn
Bay State Monthly — Bay State Mo
Bayer Colorist — Bayer Color
Bayer Farben Revue. Special Edition (USA) — Bayer Farben Rev Spec Ed (USA)
Bayer Mitteilungen fuer die Gummi Industrie (English Translation) — Bayer Mitt Gummi Ind (Engl Transl)
Bayerische Akademie der Wissenschaften. Jahrbuch — Bayer Akad Wiss Jahrb
Bayerische Akademie der Wissenschaften. Jahrbuch — Bayerische Akad Wiss Jahrbuch
Bayerische Akademie der Wissenschaften. Mathematisch-Naturwissenschaftliche Abteilung. Abhandlungen — Bayer Akad Wiss Math-Naturw Abt Abh
Bayerische Akademie der Wissenschaften. Mathematisch-Naturwissenschaftliche Klasse. Abhandlungen — Bayer Akad Wiss Math-Natur Kl Abh
Bayerische Akademie der Wissenschaften. Mathematisch-Naturwissenschaftliche Klasse. Abhandlungen — Bayer Akad Wiss Math-Naturwiss Kl Abh
Bayerische Akademie der Wissenschaften. Mathematisch-Naturwissenschaftliche Klasse. Abhandlungen. Neue Folge [*Munich*] — Bayer Akad Wiss Math-Natur Kl Abh NF
Bayerische Akademie der Wissenschaften. Mathematisch-Naturwissenschaftliche Klasse. Sitzungsberichte — Bayer Akad Wiss Math-Natur Kl S-B
Bayerische Akademie der Wissenschaften. Mathematisch-Naturwissenschaftliche Klasse. Sitzungsberichte — Bayer Akad Wiss Math-Natur Kl Sitzungsber
Bayerische Akademie der Wissenschaften. Mathematisch-Naturwissenschaftliche Klasse. Sitzungsberichte — Bayer Akad Wiss Math-Naturwiss Kl Sitzungsber
Bayerische Akademie der Wissenschaften. Philosophisch-Historische Abteilung. Abhandlungen — Bayer Akad Wiss Philos-Hist Abt Abh
Bayerische Akademie der Wissenschaften. Philosophisch-Historische Klasse. Sintzungsbericht — Bayer Akad Wiss Philos Hist Kl Sitzungsber
Bayerische Akademie der Wissenschaften. Philosophisch-Historische Klasse. Sitzungsberichte — BADWS
Bayerische Akademie der Wissenschaften. Philosophisch-Historische Klasse. Sitzungsberichte — BAW PHK
Bayerische Akademie der Wissenschaften. Philosophisch-Historische Klasse. Sitzungsberichte — BAWS
Bayerische Akademie der Wissenschaften. Philosophisch-Philologische und Historiche Klasse. Abhandlungen — Bayer Akad d Wiss Philos-Philol u Hist Kl Abhandl
Bayerische Akademie der Wissenschaften. Sitzungsberichte — Bayer Sitzb
Bayerische Berufsschule — Bayer Berufsschule
Bayerische Bienen-Zeitung — Bayer Bienenztg
Bayerische Gemeinde- und Verwaltungszeitung — Bayer Gemeinde u Verwztg
Bayerische Staatssammlung fuer Palaeontologie und Historische Geologie. Mitteilungen — Bayer Staatssamml Palaeontol Hist Geol Mitt
Bayerische Staatszeitung und Bayerischer Staatsanzeiger — Bayer Staatsztg Bayer Staatsanz
Bayerische Verwaltungsblaetter — BAVED
Bayerische Verwaltungsblaetter — Bayer Verwaltungsbl
Bayerische Volksmusik — Bayerische Volksm
Bayerische Vorgeschichtsblaetter — Bay Vg Bl
Bayerische Vorgeschichtsblaetter — Bayer Vorgeschbl
Bayerische Vorgeschichtsblaetter — BVBl
Bayerische Vorgeschichtsblaetter — Vgbl
Bayerische Zeitschrift fuer Vermessungswesen — Bayer Z Vermessungswesen
Bayerischer Landwirtschaftsrat Vierteljahresschrift — Bayer Landwirtschaftsrat Vierteljahresschr
Bayerischer Literaerischer und Markantilischer Anzeiger fuer Literatur-und Kunstfreunde. Im In- und Auslande — Bayer Lit Merkantil Anz Literatur Kunstfr
Bayerisches Aerzteblatt — Bayer Aerztebl
Bayerisches Aerztliches Korrespondenzblatt — Korr Bl Bayr
Bayerisches Bildungswesen — Bayer Bildungswesen
Bayerisches Landesstraf- und Verordnungsgesetz — L St VG
Bayerisches Landwirtschaftliches Jahrbuch — Bayer Landw Jb
Bayerisches Landwirtschaftliches Jahrbuch — Bayer Landwirt Jahrb
Bayerisches Landwirtschaftliches Jahrbuch — Bayer Landwirtsch Jahrb
Bayerisches Landwirtschaftliches Jahrbuch — Bayer Landwirtsch Jb
Bayerisches Landwirtschaftliches Jahrbuch — BYLJA
Bayerisches Landwirtschaftliches Jahrbuch. Sonderheft — Bayer Landwirtsch Jahrb Sonderh
Bayerisches Zahnaerzteblatt — B Zb
Bayerisches Zahnaerzteblatt — BZ Bl
Bayerland — BAYED
Bayer-Mitteilungen fuer die Gummi-Industrie — Bayer Mitt Gummi Ind
Bayer-Symposium — Bayer-Symp
Bayer-Symposium — BAYSAH
Baylor Business Review — BBR
Baylor Business Studies — Baylor Bus Stud
Baylor Business Studies — Baylor Bus Studies
Baylor Business Studies — BBZ
Baylor Dental Journal — Baylor Dent J
Baylor Dental Journal — BYDAA
Baylor Geological Studies. Bulletin — Baylor Geol Stud Bull
Baylor Law Review — Bay LR
Baylor Law Review — Baylor L Rev
Baylor Law Review — Baylor Law
Baylor Law Review — Baylor Law R
Baylor Law Review — BLR
Baylor Law Review — By LR
Baylor Nursing Educator — Baylor Nurs Educ
Bayreuther Blaetter — BB
Bayreuther Mathematische Schriften — Bayreuth Math Schr
Bazele Fizico-Chimice ale Intaririi Liantilor Anorganici — Bazele Fiz Chim Intaririi Liantilor Anorg
Bazele Matematice ale Cercetarii Operationale — Bazele Mat Cercetarii Oper
BB [*B'nai Brith in Australia*] **Bulletin** — BB Bul
BBA [*Biochimica et Biophysica Acta*] **Library** — BBA Libr
BBA [*Biochimica et Biophysica Acta*] **Library** — BBALAJ
BBC [*British Broadcasting Corporation*] **Engineering** — BBC Eng
BBC [*British Broadcasting Corporation*] **Engineering Division. Monograph** — BBC Eng Div Monogr
BBC [*Brown, Boveri & Cie.*] **Nachrichten** — BBC Nachr
BBC [*Brown, Boveri & Cie.*] **Nachrichten** — BBCNA
BBR. Brunnenbau, Bau von Wasserwerken, Rohrleitungsbau — BBBRD
BBR. Brunnenbau, Bau von Wasserwerken, Rohrleitungsbau — BBR Brunnenbau Bau Wasserwerken
BBR. Brunnenbau, Bau von Wasserwerken, Rohrleitungsbau. Impressum — BBR Impressum
BC [*British Columbia*] **Building Tradesman** — BC Build Trade
BC [*British Columbia*] **Business** — BCB
BC [*British Columbia*] **Business Magazine** — BC Bus Mag
BC [*British Columbia*] **Economic Development** — BC Econ Dev
BC [*British Columbia*] **Farmways** — BC Farmw
BC [*British Columbia*] **Market News** — BC Mark N
BC [*British Columbia*] **Musher** [*Canada*] — BCMU
BC [*British Columbia*] **Outdoors** [*Canada*] — BCOD
BC [*British Columbia*] **Perspectives** — BC Persp
BC [*British Columbia*] **Research** — BC Res
BC [*British Columbia*] **Runner** — BC Run
BC [*British Columbia*] **School Librarians Association. Reviews** — BCSLA Reviews
BC [*British Columbia*] **Science Teacher** — BC Sci Teach
BC [*British Columbia*] **Sea Angling Guide** — BC Sea Ang G
BC [*British Columbia*] **Shellfish Mariculture Newsletter** — BC Shellf Maricult Newsl
BC [*British Columbia*] **Studies** [*Canada*] — BCST
BC [*British Columbia*] **Track Monthly** — BC Track M
BCA [*Business Committee for the Arts*] **News** — BCA News
BCIRA [*British Cast Iron Research Association*] **Abstracts of Foundry Literature** — BCIRA Abstr Foundry Lit
BCIRA [*British Cast Iron Research Association*] **Abstracts of International Foundry Literature** — BCIRA Abstr Int Foundry Lit
BCIRA [*British Cast Iron Research Association*] **Abstracts of International Literature on Metal Castings Production** — BCIRA Abstr Int Lit Metal Cast Prod
BCIRA [*British Cast Iron Research Association*] **Journal** — BCIRA J
BCLA [*British Columbia Library Association*] **Reporter** — BCLA Rept
BCPC (British Crop Protection Council) Monograph — BCPC Monogr

BCPC (British Crop Protection Council) Symposium Proceedings — BCPC Symp Proc
BCRA [*British Carbonization Research Association*] **Review** — BCRA Rev
BCRA [*British Carbonization Research Association*] **Review** — BCRAD
BCSIR [*Banglaesh Council of Scientific and Industrial Research*] **Laboratories. Chittagong. Research Bulletin** — BCSIR Lab Chittagong Res Bull
BCSLA [*British Columbia School Librarians' Association*] **Reviews** — BCSLA R
BCURA [*British Coal Utilization Research Association*] **Gazette** — BCURA Gaz
BCURA [*British Coal Utilisation Research Association*] **Quarterly Gazette** — BCURA Q Gaz
BC-X. Canadian Forestry Service. Pacific Forest Research Centre — BC-X Can For Serv Pac For Res Cent
Bead Journal — Bead J
Bealoideas — Be
Beam Foil Spectroscopy — Beam Foil Spectros
Beam Foil Spectroscopy. Proceedings of the International Conference on Beam Foil Spectroscopy — Beam Foil Spectros Proc Int Conf
BEAMA [*British Electrical and Allied Manufacturers Association*] **Journal** — BEAJA
BEAMA [*British Electrical and Allied Manufacturers Association*] **Journal** — BEAMA J
Bear Hills Native Voice [*Hobbema, Alberta*] — BH
Bearing Steels; The Rating of Nonmetallic Inclusion. Symposium — Bear Steels Rating Nonmet Inclusion Symp
Bears Bluff Laboratories. Progress Report — Bears Bluff Lab Prog Rep
Beaufort Bulletin. Dome Petroleum Ltd. — BEFT
Beaufort Bulletin. Dome Petroleum Ltd. — BFBU
Beaufort Outlook. Newsletter from the Northern Office of the Beaufort Sea Alliance — BFOL
Beaufort Sea Project. Technical Report — BSPTR
Beaufortia Series of Miscellaneous Publications. Zoological Museum. University of Amsterdam — Beaufortia Ser Misc Publ Zool Mus Univ Amsterdam
Beaux Arts. Chronique des Arts et de la Curiosite — CA
Beaux-Arts — BxA
Beaux-Arts Institute of Design. Bulletin — Beaux-Arts Inst Des Bul
Beaver — Bea
Beaver [*Canada*] — BEAV
Beaver County Legal Journal [*Pennsylvania*] — B Co Leg J'nal
Beaver County Legal Journal [*Pennsylvania*] — Beaver
Beaver County Legal Journal [*Pennsylvania*] — Beaver County LJ
Beaver County Legal Journal (Pennsylvania) — Beaver County LJ (PA)
Beaver. Exploring Canada's History — IBEA
BECAN [*Bioengineering Current Awareness Notification*] **Biomechnics and Orthopaedics** — BECAN Biomechan Orthopaed
BECAN [*Bioengineering Current Awareness Notification*] **Electrodes for Medicine and Biology** — BECAN Electrod Med Biol
BECAN [*Bioengineering Current Awareness Notification*] **Equipment for the Disabled Population** — BECAN Equip Disabled Pop
BECAN [*Bioengineering Current Awareness Notification*] **Instrumentation and Techniques in Cardiology** — BECAN Instr Tech Cardiol
Bechtel Briefs — BEBR
Bechuanaland Protectorate. Geological Survey Department. Mineral Resources Report — Bechuanaland Prot Geol Surv Dep Miner Resour Rep
Beck Isoliertechnik — Beck Isoliertech
Beckacite Nachrichten — Beckacite Nachr
Beckett Circle — BeckettC
Beckman Bulletin — Beckman Bull
Beckman Instruments, Incorporated. Technical Report — Beckman Instrum Inc Tech Rep
Beckman Report — Beckman Rep
Beckman Report — BECRB
Bedford Institute of Oceanography. Collected Contributions — BIOCC
Bedford Institute of Oceanography. Report Series — BIORS
Bedfordshire Archaeological Journal — Bedford Arch J
Bedfordshire Archaeological Journal — Bedfordshire Archaeol J
Bedi Kartlisa — Bedi Kart
Bedi Kartlisa — BK
Bedrijf en Techniek [*Amsterdam*] — BET
Bedrijfsdocumentaire; Magazine op het Gebied van Praktisch Management — BDR
Bedrijfseconoom — BE
Bedrijfshuishouding. Magazine voor Interne en Civiele Diensten — MOC
Bedrijfskunde Tijdschrift voor Management — MHP
Bedrijfsontwikkeling. Editie Akkerbouw. Maandblad voor Agrarische Produktie. Verwerking en Afzet — Bedrijfsontwikkeling Ed Akkerbouw
Bedrijfsontwikkeling. Editie Tuinbouw — Bedrijfsontwikkeling Ed Tuinbouw
Bedrijfsontwikkeling. Editie Veehouderij — Bedrijfsontwikkeling Ed Veehouderij
Bedrijfsontwikkeling; Maandblad voor Agrarische Produktie, Verwerking, en Afzet — MLV
Bedrijfsvoering; Tijdschrift voor Organisatiekunde en Arbeidskunde, Produktie, Onderhoud, Inkoop, en Logistiek — ATE
Bee Genetics Information Bulletin — Bee Genet Inf Bull
Bee Kingdom Leaflet — Bee Kingdom Leafl
Bee World — Bee Wld
Beecham Colloquium — Beecham Colloq
Beecham Colloquium on Aspects of Infection — Beecham Colloq Aspects Infect
Beecham Colloquium on Infections — Beecham Colloq Infect
Beef Cattle Science Handbook — Beef Cattle Sci Handb
Beef Research Report — Beef Res Rep
Beef Research Report (Bureau of Agricultural Economics) — Beef Res Rep (Bur Agric Econ)
Beekeepers Bulletin — Beekprs Bull
Bee-Keepers Magazine — Beekprs Mag
Bee-Keepers News — Beekprs News
Bee-Keepers Record — Beekprs Rec
Bee-Keeping Annual — Beekeep A
Beekeeping Division Leaflet. Forest Department (Tanganyika) — Beekeep Div Leafl (Tanganyika)
Beekeeping Information. Cooperative Extension Service (Ohio) — Beekeep Inf Coop Ext Serv (Ohio)
Beekeeping (Queensland) — Beekeep (QD)
Beethoven Journal — Beethoven J
Beethoven-Jahrbuch — Be Jb
Beethoven-Jahrbuch — BeethovenJb
Beet-Sugar Technology [*Monograph*] — Beet Sugar Technol
Begg Journal of Orthodontic Theory and Treatment — Begg J Orthod Theory Treat
Begg Journal of Orthodontic Theory and Treatment — BJOTA
Behandlung und Verwertung Kommunaler Abwasserschlaemme — Behandl Verwert Kommunaler Abwasserschlaemme
Behandlung von Industrieabwaessern — Behandl Industrieabwaessern
Behandlungen der Rheumatoiden Arthritis mit D-Penicillamin. Symposion — Behandl Rheumatoiden Arthritis D-Penicillamin Symp
Behavior and Pathology of Aging in Rhesus Monkeys — Behav Pathol Aging Rhesus Monkeys
Behavior Genetics — Behav Genet
Behavior Genetics — BHGNA
Behavior Modification — Behav Modif
Behavior Research and Therapy — BRT
Behavior Research and Therapy — BRTHA
Behavior Research Methods — BRMCEW
Behavior Research Methods and Instrumentation — Behav Res M
Behavior Research Methods and Instrumentation — Behav Res Methods Instrum
Behavior Research Methods and Instrumentation — BRMIA
Behavior Research Methods, Instruments, and Computers — Behav Res Methods Instrum & Comput
Behavior Research of Severe Developmental Disabilities — Behav Res Severe Dev Disabil
Behavior Science Notes — Behav Sci N
Behavior Science Notes — Behavior Sci Notes
Behavior Science Research — Behav Sci R
Behavior Science Research. Journal of Comparative Studies. Human Relations Area Files — HRAF/BSR
Behavior Therapy — Behav Ther
Behavior Therapy — Behavior Ther
Behavior Today — Behav Today
Behavioral and Brain Sciences — BBSCDH
Behavioral and Brain Sciences — Behav Brain Sci
Behavioral and Neural Biology — Behav Neural Biol
Behavioral and Neural Biology — BNBID
Behavioral and Social Sciences Librarian — Behav and Soc Sci Libr
Behavioral and Social Sciences Librarian — Behav Soc Sci Libr
Behavioral and Social Sciences Librarian — Behavioral & Social Sci Libn
Behavioral Assessment — Behav Assess
Behavioral Assessment — BEHSDV
Behavioral Biology — Behav Biol
Behavioral Biology — Behavioral Bio
Behavioral Biology — BHBLA
Behavioral Counseling Quarterly — Behav Couns Quart
Behavioral Ecology and Sociobiology — Behav Ecol Sociobiol
Behavioral Engineering — BEJUA
Behavioral Group Therapy — Behav Gr Ther
Behavioral Medicine — Behav Med
Behavioral Medicine Abstracts — Behav Med Abstr
Behavioral Medicine and Stress Management News — Behav Med Stress Man N
Behavioral Medicine Update — Behav Med Upd
Behavioral Models and the Analysis of Drug Action. Proceedings. OHOLO Conference — Behav Models Anal Drug Action Proc OHOLO Conf
Behavioral Neurochemistry — Behav Neurochem
Behavioral Neuropsychiatry — Behav Neuropsychiatry
Behavioral Neuropsychiatry — BNEPB
Behavioral Neuroscience — Behav Neurosci
Behavioral Neuroscience — BENEDJ
Behavioral Neuroscience — IBNE
Behavioral Pharmacology — Behav Pharmacol
Behavioral Pharmacology. The Current Status — Behav Pharmacol Curr Status
Behavioral Science — Behav Sc
Behavioral Science — Behav Sci
Behavioral Science — Behavioral Sci
Behavioral Science — BEHSA
Behavioral Science — BSci
Behavioral Science — PBSC
Behavioral Sciences and the Law — Behav Sci Law
Behavioral Toxicology — Behav Toxicol
Behaviour — Behav
Behaviour and Chemical State of Irradiated Ceramic Fuels. Proceedings. Panel — Behav Chem State Irradiat Ceram Fuels Proc Panel
Behaviour and Information Technology — Behav and Inf Technol
Behaviour and Information Technology — Behaviour Inf Tech
Behaviour Research and Therapy — Behav Res T
Behaviour Research and Therapy — Behav Res Ther
Behaviour Research and Therapy — Behaviour Res & Ther
Behaviour Research and Therapy — PBRT
Behaviour Science Research — Behaviour Sci Res
Behavioural Abstracts — Behav Abstr
Behavioural and Political Animal Studies — Behav Polit Anim Stud
Behavioural Brain Research — Behav Brain Res
Behavioural Pharmacology — Behav Pharm
Behavioural Processes — Behav Processes
Behavioural Psychotherapy — Behav Psychother

Behavioural Sciences and Community Development — BECD
Behavioural Sciences and Community Development — Behav Sci Com Dev
Behavioural Sciences and Community Development — Behav Sci Community Develop
Behring Institute Mitteilungen [*Germany*] — Behring Inst Mitt
Behring Institute. Research Communications — Behring Inst Res Commun
Behringwerk Mitteilungen — Behringwerk Mitt
Beiaard — B
Beiblaetter zu den Annalen der Physik — Beibl Ann Phys
Beiblatt zur Anglia — Bei
Beiblatt zur Anglia — Beibl
Beiblatt zur Anglia — Beiblatt
Beiheft. Archiv fuer Orientforschung [*Graz*] — BAfO
Beiheft. Internationale Zeitschrift fuer Vitamin- und Ernaehrungsforschung — Beih Int Z Vitam-Ernaehrungsforsch
Beiheft. Zeitschriften des Schweizerischen Forstvereins — Beih Z Schweiz Forstver
Beiheft zur Internationalen Zeitschrift fuer Vitaminforschung — Beih Int Z Vitaminforsch
Beihefte. Archiv fuer Schiffs und Tropen-Hygiene — Beihefte Arch Schiffs- u Tropen-Hyg
Beihefte. Berichten der Naturhistorischen Gesellschaft zu Hannover — Beih Ber Naturhist Ges Hannover
Beihefte der Pharmazie — Beih Pharmazie
Beihefte. Schweizerische Bienenzietung — Beih Schweiz Bienenztg
Beihefte. Sydowia Annales. Mycologici. Serie II — Beih Sydowia Ann Mycol Ser II
Beihefte. Tuebinger Atlas des Vorderen Orients. Reihe A. Naturwissenschaften [*A publication*] — Beih Tueb Atlas Vorderen Orients Reihe A Naturwiss
Beihefte. Zeitschrift Elemente der Mathematik — Beihefte Elem Math
Beihefte. Zeitschrift fuer die Alttestamentliche Wissenschaft [*Giessen/Berlin*] — BZAW
Beihefte. Zeitschrift fuer die Neutestamentliche Wissenschaft und die Kunde der Alteren Kirche [*Giessen/Berlin*] — BZNW
Beihefte. Zeitschrift fuer Religions und Geistesgeschichte — BZR Gg
Beihefte. Zeitschrift fuer Romanische Philologie — Z Beih
Beihefte. Zeitschrift Wirkendes Wort — BZWW
Beihefte. Zentralblatt fuer Gewerbehygiene und Unfallverhuetung — Beih Zentralbl Gewerbehyg Unfallverhuet
Beihefte zu den Veroeffentlichungen fuer Naturschutz und Landschaftspflege in Baden-Wuerttemberg — Beih Veroeff Naturschutz Landschaftspflege Baden Wurttumb
Beihefte zu Material und Organismen — Beih Mater Org
Beihefte zum Botanischen Centralblatt — Beih Bot Centralbl
Beihefte zum Ja — BzJA
Beihefte zum Jahrbuch der Albertus-Universitaet zu Koenigsberg — Jb Albertus Univ Koenigsberg Beih
Beihefte zur Geologie — Beih Geol
Beihefte zur Nova Hedwigia — Beih Nov Hedwigia
Beihefte zur Philosophia Naturalis — Beih Philo Nat
Beihefte zur Vierteljahrsschrift fuer Sozial- und Wirtschaftsgeschichte — Beih Vierteljarh Soz Wirtsch
Beihefte zur Wissenschaft des Alten Testaments — Beihh Wiss AT
Beihefte zur Zeitschrift fuer Romanische Philologie — Beihefte zur Zischr f Roman Philol
Beijing International Symposium on Hydrogen Systems — Beijing Int Symp Hydrogen Syst
Beijing International Symposium on Pyrotechnics and Explosives — Beijing Int Symp Pyrotech Explos
Beijing Review — Beijing R
Beijing Review — IBEI
Beijing Review — PKC
Beilage der Zeitschrift fuer Medizinische Laboratoriumsdiagnostik — Beil Z Med Laboratoriumsdiagn
Beilage zur Allgemeine Zeitung (Muenchen) — BAZM
Beilage zur Anhalter Kurier — BAK
Beira Alta. Arquivo Provincial — BAAP
Beispiele Angewandter Forschung. Fraunhofer Gesellschaft zur Foerderung der Angewandten Forschung — Beispiele Angew Forsch Fraunhofer Ges Foerd Angew Forsch
Beitraege aus der Plasmaphysik — Beitr Pl Physik
Beitraege aus der Plasmaphysik — Beitr Plasmaphys
Beitraege aus der Plasmaphysik — BPPHA
Beitraege Datenverarbeitung und Unternehmensforschung — Beitr Datenverarb Unternehmensforsch
Beitraege der Wetterauischen Gesellschaft fuer die Gesammte Naturkunde. Zur Botanik — Beitr Wetterauischen Ges Gesammte Naturk Bot
Beitraege des Bezirks-Naturkundemuseums Stralsund — Beitr Bez Naturkundemus Stralsund
Beitraege fuer die Forstwirtschaft [*Germany*] — Beitr Forstwirtsch
Beitraege fuer Saechsische Kirchengeschichte — BSaechsKG
Beitraege Geobotanischen Landesaufnahme der Schweiz — Beitr Geobot Landesaufn Schweiz
Beitraege zu der Naturgeschichte des Schweizerlandes — Beitr Naturgesch Schweizerl
Beitraege zu Verschiedenen Wissenschaften von Einigen Oesterreichischen Gelehrten — Beitr Verschiedenen Wiss
Beitraege zum Assyrischen Woerterbuch — BA Wb
Beitraege zum Internationalen Kongress fuer Geschichte der Wissenschaft — Beitr Int Kongr Gesch Wiss
Beitraege zum Mathematisch-Naturwissenschaftlichen Unterricht — Beitr Math-Naturwiss Unterr
Beitraege zum Sonderschulwesen und zur Rehabilitationspaedagogik — Beit Sonderschulwesen Rehabilitationspaedagog
Beitraege zum Studium Fundamentale — Beitr Stud Fund
Beitraege zur Aegyptischen Bauforschung und Altertumskunde — BABA
Beitraege zur Aegyptischen Bauforschung und Altertumskunde [*Cairo*] — Beitrage Bf
Beitraege zur Agrarwissenschaft — Beitr Agrarwiss
Beitraege zur Alexander-von-Humboldt-Forschung — Beitr Alexander von Humboldt Forsch
Beitraege zur Algebra und Geometrie — Beitraege Algebra Geom
Beitraege zur Allgemeinen Botanik — Beitr Allg Bot
Beitraege zur Allgemeinen und Vergleichenden Archaeologie — BAVA
Beitraege zur Allgemeinen und Vergleichenden Archaeologie — Beitr Allg A
Beitraege zur Alten Geschichte — BAG
Beitraege zur Analysis — Beitraege Anal
Beitraege zur Anthropologie und Urgeschichte Bayerns — BAUB
Beitraege zur Anthropologie und Urgeschichte Bayerns — Bayr Beitr
Beitraege zur Anthropologie und Urgeschichte Bayerns — Beitr Anthr u Urgesch Bayern
Beitraege zur Anthropologie und Urgeschichte Bayerns — Btr Anthropol Bayern
Beitraege zur Assyriologie und Semitischen Sprachwissenschaft — BA
Beitraege zur Assyriologie und Semitischen Sprachwissenschaft — BAS
Beitraege zur Assyriologie und Semitischen Sprachwissenschaft — BASS
Beitraege zur Bayerischen Kirchengeschichte — BBKG
Beitraege zur Bayerischen Kirchengeschichte — Btr Bayer Kirchgesch
Beitraege zur Biblischen Landes- und Altertumskunde — BBLA
Beitraege zur Biblischen Landes- und Altertumskunde — BBLAK
Beitraege zur Biologie der Pflanzen — Beitr Biol Pfl
Beitraege zur Biologie der Pflanzen — Beitr Biol Pflanz
Beitraege zur Biologie der Pflanzen — BEPFA
Beitraege zur Chemischen Physiologie und Pathologie — BCPAA
Beitraege zur Chemischen Physiologie und Pathologie [*Germany*] — Beitr Chem Physiol Pathol
Beitraege zur Deutschen Klassik — BDK
Beitraege zur Deutschen Klassik. Abhandlungen — BDKA
Beitraege zur Deutschen Philologie — BDP
Beitraege zur Deutschen Volks- und Altertumskunde — BDVA
Beitraege zur Deutschen Volks- und Altertumskunde — Beitr Deut Volks Alter
Beitraege zur Deutschen Volks- und Altertumskunde — Beitr Deutsch Volks Altertumskunde
Beitraege zur Englischen Philologie — BEP
Beitraege zur Englischen Philologie — BEPh
Beitraege zur Entomologie — Beitr Ent
Beitraege zur Entomologie — Beitr Entomol
Beitraege zur Entwicklungsmechanischen Anatomie der Pflanzen — Beitr Entwicklungsmech Anat Pflanz
Beitraege zur Erforschung der Deutschen Sprache — BEDS
Beitraege zur Erforschung der Sprache und Kultur Englands und Nordamerikas — Beitr Engl u Nordamerikas
Beitraege zur Erforschung Mecklenburgischer Naturschutzgebiete — Beitr Erforsch Mecklenburg Naturschutzgeb
Beitraege zur Evangelischen Theologie [*Munich*] — BEvTh
Beitraege zur Foerderung Christlicher Theologie [*Guetersloh*] — BFChTh
Beitraege zur Foerderung Christlicher Theologie [*Guetersloh*] — BFTh
Beitraege zur Forschungstechnologie [*Berlin*] — Beitr Forschungstech
Beitraege zur Forschungstechnologie — Beitr Forschungstechnol
Beitraege zur Geographie, Geschichte, und Staatenkunde — Beitr Geogr
Beitraege zur Geologie der Schweiz. Geotechnische Serie — Beitr Geol Schweiz Geotech Ser
Beitraege zur Geologie der Schweiz. Kleinere Mitteilungen — Beitr Geol Schweiz Kleinere Mitt
Beitraege zur Geologie und Palaeontologie von Sumatra — BGPSum
Beitraege zur Geologie von Thueringen — Beitr Geol Thueringen
Beitraege zur Geologischen Erforschung der Deutschen Schutzgebiete — Btr Geol Erforsch Dt Schutzgeb
Beitraege zur Geologischen Karte der Schweiz — Beitr Geol Karte Schweiz
Beitraege zur Geophysik — Beitr Geoph
Beitraege zur Geophysik — Beitr Geophysik
Beitraege zur Gerichtlichen Medizin — BEGMA
Beitraege zur Gerichtlichen Medizin — Beitr Gerichtl Med
Beitraege zur Geschichte der Abtei Werden — BGAW
Beitraege zur Geschichte der Abtei Werden — Btr Gesch Abtei Werden
Beitraege zur Geschichte der Deutschen Arbeiterbewegung — BeG
Beitraege zur Geschichte der Deutschen Arbeiterbewegung — BZG
Beitraege zur Geschichte der Deutschen Sprache und Literatur [*Halle*] — Beitr
Beitraege zur Geschichte der Deutschen Sprache und Literatur — Beitr Gesch Dtsch Sprache
Beitraege zur Geschichte der Deutschen Sprache und Literatur [*Halle*] — BGDSL
Beitraege zur Geschichte der Deutschen Sprache und Literatur — Btr Gesch Dt Spr
Beitraege zur Geschichte der Deutschen Sprache und Literatur (Halle) — BGDSLH
Beitraege zur Geschichte der Deutschen Sprache und Literatur (Halle) — (Halle) Beitr
Beitraege zur Geschichte der Deutschen Sprache und Literatur (Hermann Paul und Wilhelm Braune, Editors) — PBSB
Beitraege zur Geschichte der Deutschen Sprache und Literatur (Tuebingen) — BGDSLT
Beitraege zur Geschichte der Landwirtschaftswissenschaften — Beitr Gesch Landwirtschaftswiss
Beitraege zur Geschichte der Pharmazie — Beitr Gesch Pharm
Beitraege zur Geschichte der Pharmazie und Ihrer Nachbargebiete — Beitr Gesch Pharm Ihrer Nachbargeb
Beitraege zur Geschichte der Philosophie und Theologie des Mittelalters — Beitr Gesch Phil Mittelalters
Beitraege zur Geschichte der Philosophie und Theologie des Mittelalters — BGPTM

Beitraege zur Geschichte der Stadt Rostock — Btr Gesch Rostock
Beitraege zur Geschichte der Technik und Industrie. Jahrbuch des Vereines Deutscher Ingenieure — Beitr Gesch Tech Ind
Beitraege zur Geschichte der Universitaet Erfurt — Beitr Gesch Univ Erfurt
Beitraege zur Geschichte der Universitaet Erfurt — BeGUE
Beitraege zur Geschichte der Universitaet Halle-Wittenberg — Beitr Gesch Univ Halle-Wittenberg
Beitraege zur Geschichte des Alten Moenchtums und des Benediktinerordens [*A publication*] — Beitr Gesch Moenchtums Benediktinerordens
Beitraege zur Geschichte des Bergbaus und Huettonwesens — Beitr Gesch Bergaus Huettenwes
Beitraege zur Geschichte des Buchwesens — Beitraege Gesch Buchw
Beitraege zur Geschichte des Niederrheins — BGNrh
Beitraege zur Geschichte Dortmunds und der Grafschaft Mark — BGDM
Beitraege zur Geschichte, Statistik, Naturkunde und Kunst von Tyrol und Vorarlberg — Beitr Gesch Tyrol Vorarlberg
Beitraege zur Geschichte und Lehre der Reformierten Kirche [*Neukirchen*] — BGLRK
Beitraege zur Geschichte von Stadt und Stift Essen — BGSSE
Beitraege zur Historischen Theologie [*Tuebingen*] — BeitrHistTh
Beitraege zur Historischen Theologie [*Tuebingen*] — BHTh
Beitraege zur Hygiene und Epidemiologie — Beitr Hyg Epidemiol
Beitraege zur Infusionstherapie und Klinische Ernaehrung — Beitr Infusionsther Klin Ernaehr
Beitraege zur Infusionstherapie und Klinische Ernaehrung. Forschung und Praxis — Beitr Infusionsther Klin Ernaehr Forsch Prax
Beitraege zur Infusionstherapie und Transfusionsmedizin — Beitr Infusionsther Transfusionsmed
Beitraege zur Inkunabelkunde. Gesellschaft fuer Typenkunde des 15 Jahrhunderts-Wiegendruck-Gesellschaft — Beitr Inkunabelk
Beitraege zur Intensiv und Notfallmedizin — Beitr Intensiv Notfallmed
Beitraege zur Kenntnis der Babylonischen Religion — BBR
Beitraege zur Kenntnis der Babylonischen Religion — BKBR
Beitraege zur Kenntnis des Orients — BKO
Beitraege zur Kinder- und Jugendliteratur — BKJ
Beitraege zur Klinik der Infektionskrankheiten — BKlIKr
Beitraege zur Klinik der Tuberkulose — Btr Klin Tuberk
Beitraege zur Klinik der Tuberkulose und Spezifischen Tuberkulose-Forschung — Beitr Klin Tuberk Spezif Tuber-Forsch
Beitraege zur Klinik der Tuberkulose und Spezifischen Tuberkulose-Forschung — Beitr Klin Tuberk Spezif Tuberk Forsch
Beitraege zur Klinik der Tuberkulose und Spezifischen Tuberkulose-Forschung — Beitr Klin Tuberkulose Spezif Tuberkulose Forsch
Beitraege zur Klinik und Erforschung der Tuberkulose und der Lungenkrankheiten — Beitr Klin Erforsch Tuberk Lungenkr
Beitraege zur Klinischen Chirurgie — Beitr Klin Chir
Beitraege zur Klinischen Neurologie und Psychiatrie — Beitr Klin Neurol Psychiatr
Beitraege zur Kolonialforschung. Ergaenzungsband — Beitr Kolonialf Ergaenzungsband
Beitraege zur Konfliktforschung — Beitr Konfl
Beitraege zur Konfliktforschung — Beitr Konfliktforsch
Beitraege zur Krebsforschung — Beitr Krebsforsch
Beitraege zur Kryptogamenflora der Schweiz — Beitr Kryptogamenfl Schweiz
Beitraege zur Kryptogamenflora der Schweiz — Beitr Kryptogamenflora Schweiz
Beitraege zur Krystallographie und Mineralogie — Beitr Krystallogr Mineral
Beitraege zur Kulturgeschichte des Mittelalters und der Renaissance — BKMR
Beitraege zur Kunde der Indogermanischen Sprachen — BKIDGRS
Beitraege zur Kunde der Indogermanischen Sprachen — BKIS
Beitraege zur Kunde der Indogermanischen Sprachen (A. Bezzenberger, Editor) — Bezzenb Beitr
Beitraege zur Kunde Est-, Liv-, und Kurlands — BKEst
Beitraege zur Kunde Preussens — Beitr Kunde Preussens
Beitraege zur Landes und Volkeskunde von Elsass-Lothringen — Beitr z Land u Volk v Elsass-Loth
Beitraege zur Linguistik und Informationsverarbeitung — BLI
Beitraege zur Mathematik, Informatik, und Nachrichtentechnik — Beitr Math Informatik Nachrichtentech
Beitraege zur Meereskunde — Beitr Meer
Beitraege zur Mineralogie und Petrographie — Beitr Miner Petrogr
Beitraege zur Mineralogie und Petrographie — Beitr Mineralogie u Petrographie
Beitraege zur Mittelstandsforschung — Beitr Mittelstandforsch
Beitraege zur Morphologie und Physiologie der Pflanzenzelle — Beitr Morphol Physiol Pflanzenzelle
Beitraege zur Musikwissenschaft — B Mw
Beitraege zur Musikwissenschaft — Beitr Musik
Beitraege zur Musikwissenschaft [*DDR*] — BeitrMw
Beitraege zur Musikwissenschaft — BzMW
Beitraege zur Namenforschung — B z Nf
Beitraege zur Namenforschung — Beitr Nam F
Beitraege zur Namenforschung — Beitr Namenforsch
Beitraege zur Namenforschung — Beitraege Namen
Beitraege zur Namenforschung — BN
Beitraege zur Namenforschung — BNF
Beitraege zur Namenforschung [*Heidelberg*] — BZN
Beitraege zur Natur- und Heilkunde (Heilbronn) — Beitr Natur Heilk Heilbronn
Beitraege zur Naturdenkmalpflege — BNDpfl
Beitraege zur Naturdenkmalpflege — Btr Natdenkmalpfl
Beitraege zur Naturgeschichte — Beitr Naturgesch
Beitraege zur Naturkunde — Beitr Naturk
Beitraege zur Naturkunde der Wetterau — Beitr Naturkd Wetterau
Beitraege zur Naturkunde Niedersachsens — Beitr Naturk Niedersachsens
Beitraege zur Naturkunde Niedersachsens — Beitr Naturkd Niedersachsens
Beitraege zur Naturkunde Preussens. Herausgegeben von der Koeniglichen Physikalisch-Oekonomischen Gesellschaft zu Koenigsberg — Beitr Naturk Preussens
Beitraege zur Naturkundlichen Forschung im Oberrheingebiet — Beitr Naturk Forsch Oberrheingeb
Beitraege zur Naturkundlichen Forschung in Suedwestdeutschland — Beitr Naturk Forsch Suedwdtl
Beitraege zur Naturkundlichen Forschung in Suedwestdeutschland — Beitr Naturk Forsch Suedwestdeut
Beitraege zur Naturkundlichen Forschung in Suedwestdeutschland — Beitr Naturkd Forsch Suedwestdtsch
Beitraege zur Naturkundlichen Forschung in Suedwestdeutschland — Beitr Naturkd Forsch Suedwestdtschl
Beitraege zur Naturkundlichen Forschung in Suedwestdeutschland. Beihefte — Beitr Naturkd Forsch Suedwestdtsch Beih
Beitraege zur Naturkundlichen Forschung in Suedwestdeutschland. Beihefte — Beitr Naturkd Forsch Suedwestdtschl Beih
Beitraege zur Neotropischen Fauna — Beitr Neotrop Fauna
Beitraege zur Neueren Literaturgeschichte — BNL
Beitraege zur Neuren Literaturgeschichte — Beitraege z Neur Literaturgesch
Beitraege zur Neurochirurgie — Beitr Neurochir
Beitraege zur Numerischen Mathematik — Beitr Numer Math
Beitraege zur Numerischen Mathematik — Beitraege Numer Math
Beitraege zur Oberpfalzforschung — BOP
Beitraege zur Onkologie — Beitr Onkol
Beitraege zur Orthopaedie und Traumatologie — Beitr Orthop Traumatol
Beitraege zur Orthopaedie und Traumatologie — BOTRA
Beitraege zur Palaeontologie von Oesterreich — Beitr Palaeontol Oesterr
Beitraege zur Pathologie — Beitr Path
Beitraege zur Pathologie — Beitr Pathol
Beitraege zur Pathologie — BTPGA
Beitraege zur Pathologischen Anatomie und zur Allgemeinen Pathologie — Beitr Path Anat u Allg Path
Beitraege zur Pathologischen Anatomie und zur Allgemeinen Pathologie — Beitr Pathol Anat Allg Pathol
Beitraege zur Pathologischen Anatomie und zur Allgemeinen Pathologie — BPAAA
Beitraege zur Pathologischen Anatomie und zur Allgemeinen Pathologie — BpAaP
Beitraege zur Petrefacten-Kunde — Beitr Petrefacten Kunde
Beitraege zur Pflanzenzucht — B Pfl Z
Beitraege zur Pflanzenzucht — Beitr Pflanzenzucht
Beitraege zur Pflanzenzucht — Btr Pflanzenzucht
Beitraege zur Philosophie — BP
Beitraege zur Philosophie des Deutschen Idealismus — B Ph DI
Beitraege zur Philosophie und Psychologie — BPP
Beitraege zur Physik der Atmosphaere — Beitr Phys Atmos
Beitraege zur Physik der Freien Atmosphaere — B Ph Fr A
Beitraege zur Physiologie — B Phl
Beitraege zur Praktischen Theologie — BP Th
Beitraege zur Radioastronomie — Beitr Radioastron
Beitraege zur Radioastronomie — BRDAA
Beitraege zur Rechtsgeschichte Tirols — BRgT
Beitraege zur Rechtsgeschichte Tirols — Btr Rechtsgesch Tirols
Beitraege zur Religionsgeschichte des Altertums [*Halle/S.*] — BRA
Beitraege zur Rheinischen Naturgeschichte. Herausgegeben von der Gesellschaft fuer Befoerderung der Naturwissenschaften zu Freiburg im Breisgau — Beitr Rhein Naturgesch
Beitraege zur Rheumatologie — Beitr Rheumatol
Beitraege zur Romanischen Philologie — BRP
Beitraege zur Romanischen Philologie — BRPh
Beitraege zur Saarlaendischen Archaeologie und Kunstgeschichte — BSAK
Beitraege zur Saarlaendischen Archlichen Archaeologie des Mittelmeer-Kulturraumes — BAM
Beitraege zur Saechsischen Kirchengeschichte — BSKG
Beitraege zur Schweizerdeutschen Mundartforschungen — BSM
Beitraege zur Sexualforschung — Beitr Sexualforsch
Beitraege zur Silikose-Forschung — Beitr Silikose-Forsch
Beitraege zur Silikose-Forschung (Pneumokoniose) — Beitr Silikose-Forsch (Pneumokoniose)
Beitraege zur Silikose-Forschung. Sonderband — Beitr Silikose-Forsch Sonderb
Beitraege zur Sittenlehre, Oekonomie, Arzneywissenschaft, Naturlehre, und Geschichte in Ihrem Allgemeinen Umfange — Beitr Sittenl
Beitraege zur Statistik des Koenigreichs Bayern — BStB
Beitraege zur Tabakforschung — Beitr Tabakforsch
Beitraege zur Tabakforschung International — Beitr Tabakforsch Int
Beitraege zur Technikgeschichte Tirols — Beitr Technikgesch Tirols
Beitraege zur Tropischen Landwirtschaft und Veterinaermedizin — Beitr Trop Landwirtsch Veterinaermed
Beitraege zur Tropischen und Subtropischen Landwirtschaft und Tropenveterinaermedizin — Beitr Trop Subtrop Landwirtsch Tropenveterinaermed
Beitraege zur Turn- und Sportwissenschaft — Btr Turn u Sportwisse
Beitraege zur Urologie — Beitr Urol
Beitraege zur Vaterlandskunde fuer Inner-Oesterreichs Einwohner — Beitr Vaterlandsk Inner Oesterreichs Einwohner
Beitraege zur Vogelkunde — Beitr Vogelkd
Beitraege zur Vogelkunde — BEVOA
Beitraege zur Volks- und Voelkerkunde — Beitr Z Volks U Voelkerkunde
Beitraege zur Wirkstofforschung — Beitr Wirkstofforsch
Beitraege zur Wissenschaft vom Alten Testament — BWAT
Beitraege zur Wissenschaft vom Alten und Neuen Testament [*Leipzig/Stuttgart*] — BWANT
Beitraege zur Wissenschaft vom Alten und Neuen Testament [*Leipzig/Stuttgart*] — BWAuNT

Beitraege zur Wissenschaftlichen Botanik (Stuttgart) — Beitr Wiss Bot Stuttgart
Beitraege zur Wissenschaftsgeschichte — Beitr Wissenschaftsgesch
Beitraege zur Wuerttembergischen Apothekengeschichte — Beitr Wuerttemb Apothekengesch
Beitrage zu Wirtschafts- und Wahrungsfragen und zur Bankgeschichte — Beitr Wirtsch U Wahrungsfragen U Bankgesch
Beitrage zur Kolonial- und Ueberseegeschichte — Beit Kolon Uebersee
Beke es Szocializmus — Beke es Szocial
Bekes Megyei Muzeumok Kozlemenyei — Bekes M K
Bekes Megyei Muzeumok Kozlemenyei — BMMK
Belaruskaia Litaratura — BLL
Belaruskaia Medychnaia Dumka — Belarusk Med Dumka
Belaruskaia Mova. Mizhvuzauski Zbornik — BMM
Belaruskaja Linhvistyka — Bel L
Belastingbeschouwingen. Onafhankelijk Maandblad voor Belastingrecht en Belastingpraktijk — MBR
Belastinggids — BG
Belastingsconsulent — BC
Belastungsgrenzen von Kunststoff Bauteilen — Belastungsgrenzen Kunstst Bauteilen
Beleggers Belangen — BGH
Belehrende Herbarsbeilage — Belehrende Herbarsbeil
Beleid en Maatschappij — BDL
Beleid en Maatschappij — Beleid en Mij
Beleidsanalyse — BYA
Belfagor — Bel
Belfast Natural History and Philosophical Society. Proceedings and Reports — Belfast Nat Hist Phil Soc Proc
Belfast Naturalists' Field Club — Belfast Nat Fld Cl
Belfast Telegraph — BTE
Belgarsko Muzikoznanie — B Muz
Belgian American Trade Review — Belg Rev
Belgian Business — BQO
Belgian Journal of Food Chemistry and Biotechnology — Belg J Food Chem Biotechnol
Belgian Journal of Food Chemistry and Biotechnology — BJFBE6
Belgian Journal of Operations Research Statistics and Computer Science — Belg J Oper Res Statist Comput Sci
Belgian Plastics — Belg Plast
Belgian Review of International Law — Belgian R Internat Law
Belgicatom Bulletin [*Belgium*] — Belgicatom Bull
Belgicatom Bulletin d'Information — Belgicatom Bull Inf
Belgie/Economische en Handelsvoorlichting — BLT
Belgique Apicole — Belg Apic
Belgique Coloniale et Commerce International — Belg Col
Belgique Medicale — Belgique Med
Belgisch Archief — Belg Arch
Belgisch Institut tot Verbetering van de Beit Driemaandelijkse Publikatie — Belg Inst Verbetering Beit Driemaand Publ
Belgisch Staatsblad — BS
Belgisch Staatsblad — Staatsbl
Belgisch Tijdschrift voor Fysische Geneeskunde en Rehabilitatie — Belg Tijdschr Fys Geneeskd Rehabil
Belgisch Tijdschrift voor Geneeskunde — Belg Tijdschr Geneeskd
Belgisch Tijdschrift voor Muziek-Wetenschap/Revue Belge de Musicologie — R Belge Musicol
Belgisch Tijdschrift voor Radiologie — Belg Tijdschr Radiol
Belgisch Tijdschrift voor Reumatologie en Fysische Geneeskunde — Belg Tijdschr Reumatol Fys Geneeskd
Belgisch Tijdschrift voor Sociale Zekerheid — Belg Tijds Soc Zekerh
Belgisch Tijdschrift voor Sociale Zekerheid — BTSZ
Belgische Chemische Industrie — Belg Chem Ind
Belgische Fruit-Revue. Organ der Vlaamsche Pomologische Verenigingen — Belg Fruit Rev
Belgische Kleding — BEG
Belgisch-Nederlands Tijdschrift voor Oppervlaktetechnieken van Metalen — BNOTA
Belgisch-Nederlands Tijdschrift voor Oppervlaktetechnieken van Metalen — Belg Ned Tijdschr Oppervlatke Tech Met
Belgium. Economic and Technical Information. English Edition — Belg Econ
Belgium Economy and Technique — Belg E & T
Belgium. Service Geologique. Memoire — Belg Serv Geol Mem
Belgium. Service Geologique. Professional Paper — Belg Serv Geol Prof Pap
Belgrade — Be
Belgravia — Belgra
Belizean Studies. Belizean Institute of Social Research and Action and St. John's College — BISRA/BS
Bell Journal of Economics — BEL
Bell Journal of Economics — Bell J Econ
Bell Journal of Economics — Bell J Econom
Bell Journal of Economics — BJECD
Bell Journal of Economics — BYM
Bell Journal of Economics and Management Science [*Later, Bell Journal of Economics*] — Bell J Econ and Manage Sci
Bell Journal of Economics and Management Science [*Later, Bell Journal of Economics*] — Bell J Econ Manage Sci
Bell Journal of Economics and Management Science [*Later, Bell Journal of Economics*] — BJEMA
Bell Laboratories Record — Bell Lab Re
Bell Laboratories Record — Bell Lab Rec
Bell Laboratories Record — BELR
Bell Laboratories Record — BLRCA
Bell System Technical Journal — Bell Syst T
Bell System Technical Journal — Bell Syst Tech J
Bell System Technical Journal — Bell System Tech J
Bell System Technical Journal — BSTJ
Bell System Technical Journal — BSTJA
Bell Telephone Magazine — Bell Tel Mag
Bell Telephone Magazine — Bell Telephone Mag
Bell Telephone System. Technical Publications. Monographs — Bell Teleph Syst Tech Publ Monogr
Belle Glade AREC. Research Report EV. Florida University. Agricultural Research and Education Center — Belle Glade AREC Res Rep EV Fla Univ Agric Res Educ Cent
Belle Glade EREC Research Report EV. Florida University Agricultural Research and Education Center — Belle Glade EREC Res Rep EV Fla Univ Agric Res Educ Cent
Belle W. Baruch Library in Marine Science — Belle W Baruch Libr Mar Sci
Belleten (Ankara) — BA
Belleten. Tuerk Tarih Kurumu — Bel
Belleten. Tuerk Tarih Kurumu — BTTK
Belleten. Tuerk Tarih Kurumu — TTK
Belleten Turk Tarih Kurumu — Belleten
Belli Law Journal — Belli LJ
Belmontia. Miscellaneous Publications in Botany. I. Taxonomy — Belmontia 1 Taxon
Belmontia. Miscellaneous Publications in Botany. III. Horticulture — Belmontia 3 Hort
Beloit Poetry Journal — Bel Po J
Beloit Poetry Journal — Beloit
Beloit Poetry Journal — Beloit Poet
Beloit Poetry Journal — BPJ
Belorussian Review — Beloruss Rev
Belorussian Review [*Munich*] — BLR
Belorussian Review — BR
Belorusskaya Nauchnaya Konferentsiya Onkologov. Materialy — Beloruss Nauchn Konf Onkol Mater
Belorusskii Nauchno-Issledovatel'skii Institut Melioratsii i Vodnogo Khozyaistva. Trudy — Beloruss Nauchno Issled Inst Melior Vodn Khoz Tr
Belorusskii Nauchno-Issledovatel'skii Kozhno-Venerologicheskii Institut. Sbornik Nauchnykh Trudov — Beloruss Nauchno Issled Kozhno Venerol Inst Sb Nauchn Tr
Belorusskii Politekhnicheski Institut. Teoreticheskaya i Prikladnaya Mekhanika — Teoret i Prikl Mekh
Beltsville Symposia in Agricultural Research — Beltsville Symp Agric Res
Beltz Monographien — Beltz Monogr
Bemerkungen der Kuhrpfaelzischen Physikalisch-Oekonomischen Gesellschaft — Bemerk Kuhrpfaelz Phys Oekon Ges
Bench and Bar — B & B
Bench and Bar — B Bar
Bench and Bar — Bench & B
Bench and Bar of Minnesota — Bench and B Minn
Benchmark Papers in Acoustics — Benchmark Pap Acoust
Benchmark Papers in Analytical Chemistry — Benchmark Pap Anal Chem
Benchmark Papers in Behavior — Benchmark Pap Behav
Benchmark Papers in Biochemistry — Benchmark Pap Biochem
Benchmark Papers in Biochemistry — BPABDM
Benchmark Papers in Biological Concepts — Benchmark Pap Biol Concep
Benchmark Papers in Ecology — Benchmark Pap Ecol
Benchmark Papers in Ecology — BPECDB
Benchmark Papers in Electrical Engineering and Computer Science — Benchmark Papers Electrical Engrg Comput Sci
Benchmark Papers in Genetics — Benchmark Pap Genet
Benchmark Papers in Genetics — BPGEDR
Benchmark Papers in Geology — Benchmark Pap Geol
Benchmark Papers in Geology — BPGEES
Benchmark Papers in Human Physiology — Benchmark Pap Hum Physiol
Benchmark Papers in Human Physiology — BPHPDV
Benchmark Papers in Inorganic Chemistry — Benchmark Pap Inorg Chem
Benchmark Papers in Microbiology — Benchmark Pap Microbiol
Benchmark Papers in Microbiology — BPMIDZ
Benchmark Papers in Nuclear Physics — Benchmark Pap Nucl Phys
Benchmark Papers in Optics — Benchmark Pap Opt
Benchmark Papers in Organic Chemistry — Benchmark Pap Org Chem
Benchmark Papers in Physical Chemistry and Chemical Physics — Benchmark Pap Phys Chem Chem Phys
Benchmark Papers in Polymer Chemistry — Benchmark Pap Polym Chem
Benchmark Papers in Soil Science — Benchmark Pap Soil Sci
Benchmark Papers in Systematic and Evolutionary Biology — Benchmark Pap Syst Evol Biol
Benchmark Papers in Systematic and Evolutionary Biology — BPSBDA
Benchmark Papers on Energy — Benchmark Pap Energy
Benchmark Soils Project. Technical Report Series — Benchmark Soils Proj Tech Rep Ser
Bendix Technical Journal — Bendix Tech J
Bendix Technical Journal — BXTJA
Benedictina — Ben
Benedictine Review — BR
Benedictiner Monatsschrift — BMS
Benediktinische Monatshefte [*Beuron*] — BM
Benediktinische Monatsschrift — BndM
Benefits International — BEI
Benefits Review Board Service. Matthew Bender — Ben Rev Bd Serv MB
Benelumat Revue — BFA
Benelux — BEN
Be-ne-lux Genealogist — Benelux Geneal
Benelux Nieuws [*Belgium*] — BN
Bengal Agricultural Journal — Bengal Agric J
Bengal Past and Present — Bengal P P
Bengal Past and Present — BPP

Bengal Public Health Journal — Bengal Public Health J
Bengal Veterinarian — Bengal Vet
Beni Culturali e Ambientali (Sicilia) — BCA (Sic)
Benin Review — Benin R
Benin Review — Benin Rev
Benn Electronics Executive — Benn Electron Exec
Bennington Review — BR
Benn's Press Directory International — Benn Pr Dir Int
Bentley's Miscellany — Bentley
Bentley's Quarterly Review — Bent Q
Benzene and Its Industrial Derivatives — Benzene Its Ind Deriv
Benzene in the Work Environment — Benzene Work Environ
Benzene Magazine — Benzene Mag
Benzole Digest — Benzole Dig
Benzole Producers Limited. Information Circular — Benzole Prod Ltd Inf Circ
Benzole Producers Limited. Research Paper — Benzole Prod Ltd Res Pap
Beograd Matematicki Institut. Zbornik Radova. Nouvelle Serie — Zb Rad Math Inst Beograd NS
Beor's Queensland Law Reports — QL Beor
Beratende Ingenieure — BEIND
Beratende Ingenieure [*Germany*] — Beratende Ing
Berceo — Berc
Berdyanskii Opytnyi Neftemaslozavod. Trudy — Berdyanskii Opytn Neftemaslozavod Tr
Beretning- Faellesudvalget for Statens Mejeri- og Husdyrbrugsforsoeg (Denmark) — Beret Faellesudvalget Statens Mejeri Husdyrbrugsfors (Den)
Beretning fra Faellesudvalget foer Statens Planteavls- og Husdyrbrugsforsog — Beret Faellesudvalget Statens Planteavls-Husdyrbrugsfors
Beretning fra Forsoegslaboratoriet — Beret Forsogslab
Beretning fra Forsoegslaboratoriet Kungliga Veterinaer- og Landbohoejskoles Landoekonomiske Forsoegslaboratorium — Beret Forsoegslab K Vet Landbohoejsk Landoekon Forsoegslab
Beretning fra Forsoegslaboratoriet Udgivet af Statens Husdyrbrugsudvalg — Beret Forsoegslab Statens Husdyrbrugsudvalg
Beretning fra Statens Forogsmejeri — Beret Statens Forogsmejeri
Beretning fra Statens Husdyrbrugsforsog — Beret Statens Husdyrbrugsfors
Beretning fra Statsfrokontrollen (Denmark) — Beretn Statsfrokontr (Denmark)
Beretning til Ministeriet for Landbrug og Fiskeri fra Den Danske Biologiske Station — Beretn d Biol S
Beretninger fra Forsogslaboratoriet — Beretn Forsogsl
Berg Technik — Berg Tech
Berg- und Huettenmaennische Monatshefte — Berg Huettenmaenn Monatsh
Berg- und Huettenmaennische Monatshefte [*Austria*] — Berg Huttenmann Monatsh
Berg- und Huettenmaennische Monatshefte — BHMMA
Berg- und Huettenmaennische Monatshefte. Montanistische Hochschule in Leoben — BEHMA
Berg- und Huettenmaennische Monatshefte. Montanistische Hochschule in Leoben [*Austria*] — Berg Huettenmaenn Monatsh Montan Hochsch Leoben
Berg- und Huettenmaennische Monatshefte. Supplementum — Berg Huettenmaenn Monatsh Suppl
Berg- und Huettenmaennische Zeitung — Berg u Huettenm Ztg
Berg- und Huettenmaennisches Jahrbuch. Montanistische Hochschule in Leoben — Berg Huettenmaenn Jahrb Montan Hochsch Leoben
Bergakademie — BERGA
Bergbau — BERGD
Bergbau Rohstoffe Energie — Bergbau Rohst Energ
Bergbau Rundschau — Bergbau Rundsch
Bergbau und Energiewirtschaft — BEENA
Bergbau und Energiewirtschaft [*Germany*] — Bergbau Energiewirtsch
Bergbau und Wirtschaft — Bergbau Wirtsch
Bergbau-Archiv — BEGAA
Bergbau-Archiv [*Germany*] — Bergbau-Arch
Bergbautechnik — BETKA
Bergbauwissenschaften — Bergbauwiss
Bergbauwissenschaften und Verfahrenstechnik im Bergbau und Huettenwesen — Bergbauwiss Verfahrenstech Bergbau Huettenwes
Bergbauwissenschaften und Verfahrenstechnik im Bergbau und Huettenwesen — Bergbauwissen Verfahrenstech Bergbau Huettenwes
Bergbauwissenschaften und Verfahrenstechnik im Bergbau und Huettenwesen — BVBHAG
Bergens Museums. Aarbok — BM Aa
Bergens Museums. Aarbok — BMA
Bergens Museums. Aarbok — BMARB
Bergens Museums. Aarbok. Naturvitenskapelig Rekke — Bergens Mus Arbok Naturvitensk Rekke
Bergens Museums. Skrifter — Bergens Mus Skr
Berger-Burger Newsletter — Berger Burger Newsl
Bergische Forschungen — Bergische Forschgg
Bergmann Schaefer Lehrbuch der Experimentalphysik — Bergmann Schaefer Lehrb Experimentalphys
Bergonum — Berg
Bericht. Algemeen Proefstation der AVROS — Ber Alg Proefst AVROS
Bericht. Arbeitstagung der Arbeitsgemeinschaft der Saatzuchtleiter — Ber Arbeitstag Arbeitsgem Saatzuchtleiter
Bericht ATWD. Physikalisch-Technische Bundesanstalt — Ber ATWD Phys Tech Bundesanst
Bericht der Deutschen Orchideen-Gesellschaft — Ber Deutsch Orchideen Ges
Bericht der Deutschen Pharmazeutischen Gesellschaft — Ber Deut Pharm Ges
Bericht der Freien Vereinigung fuer Pflanzengeographie und Systematische Botanik — Ber Freien Vereinigung Pflanzengeogr
Bericht der Informatik-Forschungsgruppen — Ber Inform Forschungsgr
Bericht der Naturforschenden Gesellschaft Freiburg — Ber Natf Ges Freiburg
Bericht der Senckenbergischen Naturforschenden Gesellschaft — Ber Senckenberg Naturforsch Ges
Bericht der Senckenbergischen Naturforschenden Gesellschaft [*Frankfurt*] — Ber Senckenbg Naturf Ges
Bericht der Zuercherischen Botanischen Gesellschaft — Ber Zuercherischen Bot Ges
Bericht des Botanischen Vereines in Landshut. Bayern Anerkannter Verein — Ber Bot Vereines Landshut
Bericht des Botanischen Vereins zu Landshut — Ber Bot V Landshut
Bericht des Lehrerklubs fuer Naturkunde — Ber Lehrerklubs Naturk
Bericht des Naturwissenschaftlichen Vereines in Aussig — Ber Naturiwss Vereines Aussig
Bericht des Naturwissenschaftlichen Vereines zu Regensburg — Ber Naturwiss Vereines Regensburg
Bericht des Naturwissenschaftlichen Vereins fuer Bielefeld und Umgegend EV — Ber Naturwiss Ver Bielefeld Umgegend EV
Bericht des Naturwissenschaftlichen Vereins fuer Bielefeld und Umgegend EV [*A publication*] — BNVUDY
Bericht des Naturwissenschaftlichen Vereins fuer Schwaben — Ber Naturwiss Vereins Schwaben
Bericht des Naturwissenschaftlichen Vereins fuer Schwaben und Neuburg a.V. in Augsburg, fruerher Naturhistorischen Vereins in Augsburg — Ber Naturwiss Vereins Schwaben Augsburg
Bericht des Naturwissenschaftlich-Medizinischen Vereins Innsbruck — Ber Naturwiss Med Vereins Innsbruck
Bericht des Offenbacher Vereins fuer Naturkunde — Ber Offenbacher Vereins Naturkd
Bericht des Offenbacher Vereins fuer Naturkunde — BOVNDK
Bericht des Offenbacher Vereins fuer Naturkunde ueber seine Thaetigkeit — Ber Offenbacher Vereins Naturk Thaetigk
Bericht des Vereines fuer Naturkunde in Fulda — Ber VF Naturk Fulda
Bericht des Vereines zum Schutze und zur Pflege der Alpenflanzen — Ber Vereines Schutze Pflege Alpenpfl
Bericht des Vereins Carnuntum in Wien — BVC
Bericht des Vereins fuer Naturkunde zu Fulda — Ber Vereins Naturk Fulda
Bericht des Vereins zum Schutze der Alpenpflanzen — Ber Vereins Schutze Alpenpfl
Bericht des Vereins zur Erforschung der Heimischen Pflanzenwelt. Halle — Ber Vereins Erforsch Heimischen Pflanzenwelt Halle
Bericht des Westpreussischen Botanisch-Zoologischen Vereines — BWpBZV
Bericht. Deutsche Gesellschaft fuer Holzforschung — Ber Dtsch Ges Holzforsch
Bericht. Deutsche Ophthalmologische Gesellschaft — BDOGA
Bericht. Deutsche Ophthalmologische Gesellschaft [*Germany*] — Ber Dtsch Ophthalmol Ges
Bericht. Ernst-Mach-Institut [*Freiburg*] — Ber Ernst-Mach-Inst
Bericht. Forschungsinstitut der Cechoslavakischen Zuckerindustrie in Prag — Ber Forschungsinst Cech Zuckerind Prag
Bericht. Forschungsinstitut der Zuckerindustrie fuer Boehmen und Machren in Prag — Ber Forschungsinst Zuckerind Boehm Machren Prag
Bericht. Geobotanische Forschungsinstitut Ruebel in Zuerich — Ber Geobot Forschungsinst Ruebel Zuerich
Bericht. Gesellschaft fuer Innere Medizin der Deutschen Demokratischen Republik — Ber Ges Inn Med DDR
Bericht. Historischer Verein fuer das Fuerstbistum (Bamberg) — BHVBamberg
Bericht. Historischer Verein fuer das Fuerstbistum (Bamberg) — BHVFB
Bericht. Institut fuer Festkoerpermechanik der Fraunhofer-Gesellschaft — Ber Inst Festkoerpermech Fraunhofer-Ges
Bericht. Institut fuer Hochenergiephysik. Oesterreichische Akademie der Wissenschaften (Wien) — Ber Inst Hochenergiephys (Wien)
Bericht. Jyvaeskylae Universitaet. Mathematisches Institut — Ber Univ Jyvaeskyla Math Inst
Bericht. Kernforschungszentrum Karlsruhe — Ber Kernforschungszentr Karlsruhe
Bericht. Max-Planck-Institut fuer Kernphysik (Heidelberg) — Ber MPI Kernphys (Heidelberg)
Bericht. Max-Planck-Institut fuer Physik und Astrophysik. Institut fuer Extraterrestrische Physik — Ber MPI Phys Astrophys Inst Extraterr Phys
Bericht. Max-Planck-Institut fuer Plasmaphysik. Garching bei Muenchen — Ber MPI Plasmaphys Garching
Bericht. Max-Planck-Institut fuer Stroemungsforschung [*Germany*] — Ber Max-Planck-Inst Stroemungsforsch
Bericht. Max-Planck-Institut fuer Stroemungsforschung — Ber MPI Stroemungsforsch
Bericht. Naturhistorische Gesellschaft zu Hannover — Ber Naturhist Ges Hannover
Bericht. Oberhessische Gesellschaft fuer Natur und Heilkunde zu Giessen. Naturwissenschaftliche Abteilung — Ber Oberhess Ges Nat Heikd Giessen Naturwiss Abt
Bericht. Physikalisch-Technische Bundesanstalt, Braunschweig und Berlin — BPTBBD
Bericht. Roemisch-Germanische Kommission — Ber RGK
Bericht. Roemisch-Germanische Kommission — BRGK
Bericht. Staatliche Denkmalpflege im Saarland — Ber Saarland
Bericht. Staatliche Denkmalpflege im Saarland. Beitraege zur Archaeologie und Kunstgeschichte — Ber Staat Denkmaf Saarland
Bericht. Studiengruppe fuer Systemforschung (Heidelberg) — Ber Studiengruppe Systemforsch (Heidelberg)
Bericht ueber das Internationale Seminar Kernstrukturphysik und Automatisierung — Ber Int Semin Kernstrukturphys Autom
Bericht ueber das Museum Francisco-Carolinum — Ber Mus Francisco Carol
Bericht ueber den Annaberg-Buchholzer-Verein fuer Naturkunde — Ber Annaberg Buchholzer Verein Naturk
Bericht ueber den Botanischen Garten und das Botanische Institut der Universitaet Bern — Ber Bot Gart Bot Inst Univ Bern
Bericht ueber den Botanischen Garten und das Botanische Institut in Bern — Ber Bot Gard Bot Inst Bern

Bericht ueber den Naturwissenschaftlichen Verein zu Zerbst — Ber Naturwiss Verein Zerbst
Bericht ueber die Ausgrabungen in Olympia [*1936-*] — Ol Ber
Bericht ueber die Detmolder Studientage fuer Lehrer an Berufsbildenden Schulen — Ber Detmolder Studientage
Bericht ueber die Durum- und Teigwaren-Tagung — Ber Durum Teigwaren Tag
Bericht ueber die Durum-Teigwaren-Tagung. Vortraege — Ber Durum Teigwaren Tag Vortr
Bericht ueber die Getreidechemiker-Tagung (Detmold) [*Germany*] — Ber Getreidechem-Tag (Detmold)
Bericht ueber die Getreidetagung (Detmold) — Ber Getreidetag (Detmold)
Bericht ueber die Jahrestagung der Deutschen Gesellschaft fuer Arbeitsmedizin — Ber Jahrestag Dtsch Ges Arbeitsmed
Bericht ueber die Musikcwissenschaftlichen Arbeiten in der DDR [*Deutsche Demokratische Republik*] — Ber Musikw Arb DDR
Bericht ueber die Oesterreichische Literatur der Zoologie, Botanik, und Paleontologie — Ber Oesterr Lit Zool Bot
Bericht ueber die Physikalisch-Chemische Untersuchung des Rheinwassers — Ber Phys Chem Unters Rheinwassers
Bericht ueber die Senckenbergische Naturforschende Gesellschaft — Ber Senckenberg Naturf Ges
Bericht ueber die Sitzungen der Naturforschenden Gesellschaft zu Halle — Ber Sitzungen Naturf Ges Halle
Bericht ueber die Taetigkeit der Naturwissenschaftlichen Gesellschaft Isis. Bautzen — Ber Taetigkeit Naturwiss Ges Isis Bautzen
Bericht ueber die Taetigkeit Jahrbuch der St. Gallischen Naturwissenschaftlichen Gesellschaft — Ber Taetigk Jahrb St Gallischen Naturwiss Ges
Bericht ueber die Tagung fuer Baeckerei-Technologie — Ber Tag Baeckerei Technol
Bericht ueber die Tagung fuer Getreidechemie — Ber Tag Getreidechem
Bericht ueber die Tagung fuer Lebensmittelrheologie — Ber Tag Lebensmittelrheol
Bericht ueber die Tagung fuer Muellerei Technologie — Ber Tag Muellerei Technol
Bericht ueber die Tagung fuer Muellerei-Technologie. Vortraege Gehalten Anlaesslich der Tagung der Arbeitsgemeinschaft Getreideforschung — Ber Tag Muellerei-Technol Vortr Tag
Bericht ueber die Thaetigkeit des Naturwissenschaftlichen Vereins in Lueneburg — Ber Thaetigk Naturwiss Vereins Lueneburg
Bericht ueber die Thaetigkeit des Offenbacher Vereins fuer Naturkunde — Ber Thaetigk Offenbacher Vereins Naturk
Bericht ueber die Verhandlungen der Naturforschenden Gesellschaft in Basel — Ber Verh Naturf Ges Basel
Bericht ueber die zur Bekanntmachung Geeigneten Verhandlungen der Koeniglich Preussischen Akademie der Wissenschaften zu Berlin — Ber Bekanntm Verh Koenigl Preuss Akad Wiss Berlin
Bericht ueber die Zusammenkunft der Deutschen Ophthalmologischen Gesellschaft — Ber Zusammenkunft Dtsch Ophthalmol Ges
Bericht ueber Landwirtschaft — BERLA
Bericht ueber Rassenkeuze — Ber Rassenkeuze
Bericht und Abhandlungen des Clubs fuer Naturkunde. Section des Bruenner Lehrervereins — Ber Abh Clubs Naturk
Bericht zur Deutschen Landeskunde — Ber Dtsch Landeskd
Berichte. Abwassertechnische Vereinigung — Ber Abwassertech Ver
Berichte. Arbeitsgemeinschaft Ferromagnetismus — Ber Arbeitsgem Ferromagn
Berichte. Arbeitsgemeinschaft Saechsischer Botaniker — Ber Arbeitsgem Saechs Bot
Berichte aus dem Physiologischen Laboratorium und der Versuchsanstalt des Landwirthschaftlichen Instituts — Ber Physiol Lab Versuchsanst Landw Inst
Berichte aus den Sitzungen der Joachim Jungius-Gesellschaft der Wissenschaften — Ber Sitzungen Joachim Jungius Gesellsch Wiss
Berichte aus der Bonner Universitatsklinik und Poliklinik fuer Mund-, Zahn-, und Kieferkrankheiten — Ber Bonn Univ Poliklin Mund Zahn Kieferkr
Berichte aus der Forschungsstelle Nedri As Hveragerdi Island — Ber Forschungsstelle Nedri As Hveragerdi Isl
Berichte aus der Forschungsstelle Nedri As Hveragerdi Island — RINRBM
Berichte aus der Mathematik — Ber Math
Berichte aus der Oekologischen Forschung — Ber Oekol Forsch
Berichte aus Wasserguete- und Abfallwirtschaft. Technische Universitaet Muenchen — Ber Wasserguete Abfallwirtsch Tech Univ Muenchen
Berichte. Bayerische Botanische Gesellschaft zur Erforschung der Heimischen Flora — Ber Bayer Bot Ges Erforsch Heim Flora
Berichte Biochemie und Biologie — BBCBB
Berichte Biochemie und Biologie — Ber Biochem Biol
Berichte. Bunsengesellschaft fuer Physikalische Chemie — BBPCA
Berichte. Bunsengesellschaft fuer Physikalische Chemie — Ber Bun Ges
Berichte. Bunsengesellschaft fuer Physikalische Chemie — Ber Bunsen Ges
Berichte. Bunsengesellschaft fuer Physikalische Chemie — Ber Bunsenges Phys Chem
Berichte der Arbeitsgruppe Mathematisierung — Ber Arbeitsgruppe Math
Berichte der Deutschen Botanischen Gesellschaft — Ber Deutsch Bot Ges
Berichte der Deutschen Chemischen Gesellschaft — BDChG
Berichte der Deutschen Pharmaceutischen Gesellschaft. Bericht ueber die Pharmacognostische Literatur aller Laender — Ber Deutsch Pharm Ges Ber Pharmacogn Lit Aller Laender
Berichte der Fachausschuesse. Deutsche Glastechnische Gesellschaft — Ber Fachausschuesse Dtsch Glastech Ges
Berichte der Gesellschaft fuer Mathematik und Datenverarbeitung — Ber Gesellsch Math Datenverarb
Berichte der Kongresses der Internationalen Messtechnischen Konfoederation — Ber Kongr Int Messtech Konfoed
Berichte der Mathematisch-Statistischen Sektion in der Forschungsgesellschaft Joanneum — Ber Math Statist Sekt Forschungsgesellsch Joanneum
Berichte der Naturforschenden Gesellschaft Uri — Ber Naturf Ges Uri
Berichte der Naturforschenden Gesellschaft zu Freiburg — Ber Naturf Ges Freiburg
Berichte der Roemisch-Germanische Kommission des Deutschen Archaeologischen Instituts — Ber RGKO
Berichte der Roemisch-Germanische Kommission des Deutschen Archaeologischen Instituts — Ber Roem Germ Kom
Berichte der Roemisch-Germanische Kommission des Deutschen Archaeologischen Instituts — Bericht Rom-Germ Komm
Berichte des Hahn-Meitner-Instituts fuer Kernforschung (Berlin) — Ber Hahn-Meitner-Inst Kernforsch (Berlin)
Berichte des Naturwissenschaftlichen Vereins in Dessau — Ber Naturwiss Vereins Dessau
Berichte des Naturwissenschaftlichen Vereins zu Regensburg — Ber Naturwiss Ver Regensburg
Berichte des Vereins Natur und Heimat und des Naturhistorischen Museums zu Luebeck — Ber Ver Nat Heimat Naturhist Mus Luebeck
Berichte des Vereins Natur und Heimat und des Naturhistorischen Museums zu Luebeck — BVNLDN
Berichte. Deutsche Botanische Gesellschaft — BEDBA
Berichte. Deutsche Botanische Gesellschaft — Ber Deu Bot
Berichte. Deutsche Botanische Gesellschaft — Ber Deut Bot Ges
Berichte. Deutsche Botanische Gesellschaft — Ber Dt Bot Ges
Berichte. Deutsche Botanische Gesellschaft — Ber Dtsch Bot Ges
Berichte. Deutsche Chemische Gesellschaft — BDCGA
Berichte. Deutsche Chemische Gesellschaft — Ber
Berichte. Deutsche Chemische Gesellschaft — Ber Deut Chem Ges
Berichte. Deutsche Chemische Gesellschaft — Ber Dt Chem Ges
Berichte. Deutsche Chemische Gesellschaft [*Germany*] — Ber Dtsch Chem Ges
Berichte. Deutsche Chemische Gesellschaft — Berichte
Berichte. Deutsche Chemische Gesellschaft. Abteilung A. Vereins Nachriften — Ber Dtsch Chem Ges A
Berichte. Deutsche Chemische Gesellschaft. Abteilung B. Abhandlungen — Ber Dtsch Chem Ges B
Berichte. Deutsche Gesellschaft fuer Geologische Wissenschaften. Reihe A. Geologie und Palaeontologie — Ber Dtsch Ges Geol Wiss Reihe A
Berichte. Deutsche Gesellschaft fuer Geologische Wissenschaften. Reihe B. Mineralogie und Lagerstaettenforschung — Ber Dtsch Ges Geol Wiss Reihe B
Berichte. Deutsche Keramische Gesellschaft — BDKGA
Berichte. Deutsche Keramische Gesellschaft — Ber Deut Keram Gesell
Berichte. Deutsche Keramische Gesellschaft — Ber Dtsch Keram Ges
Berichte. Deutsche Pharmazeutische Gesellschaft — Ber Dtsch Pharm Ges
Berichte. Deutsche Physikalische Gesellschaft — Ber Dtsch Phys Ges
Berichte. Deutsche Wissenschaftliche Kommission fuer Meeresforschung — Ber D W Meer
Berichte. Deutsche Wissenschaftliche Kommission fuer Meeresforschung — Berichte Dtsch Wiss Komm Meeresforsch
Berichte. Deutscher Ausschuss fuer Stahlbau — Ber Deut Ausschusses Stahlbau
Berichte. Deutscher Wetterdienst — Ber Deut Wetterdienst
Berichte. Deutscher Wetterdienst — Ber Dtsch Wetterdienstes
Berichte. Deutscher Wissenschaftliche Kommission fuer Meeresforschung — Ber Dtsch Wiss Komm Meeresforsch
Berichte. Deutsches Industrielinstitut zur Wirtschaftspolitik — Dt Indinst Ber Wirtpol
Berichte. Eidgenoessische Anstalt fuer das Forstliche Versuchswesen — Ber Eidg Anst Forstl Versuchswes
Berichte. Forschungsinstitut fuer Osten und Orient [*Vienna*] — BFOO
Berichte. Forschungszentrum. Mathematisch-Statistische Sektion (Graz) — Ber Math-Statist Sekt Forschungszentrum (Graz)
Berichte. Gehalten im Kontaktstudium "Werkstoffkunde Eisen und Stahl" — Ber Kontaktstud Werkstoffkd Eisen Stahl
Berichte. Geobotanische Institut der Eidgenoessischen Technischen Hochschule Stiftung Ruebel Zuerich — Ber Geobot Inst Eidg Tech Hochsch Stift Ruebel Zuer
Berichte. Geologische Gesellschaft in der Deutschen Demokratischen Republik fuer das Gesamtgebiet der Geologischen Wissenschaft — Ber Geol Ges DDR Gesamtgeb Geol Wiss
Berichte. Geologische Gesellschaft in der Deutschen Demokratischen Republik fuer das Gesamtgebiet der Geologischen Wissenschaft [*Germany*] — Ber Geol Ges Dtsch Demokrat Repub Gesamtgeb Geol Wiss
Berichte. Gesellschaft fuer Kohlentechnik — BEKOA
Berichte. Gesellschaft fuer Kohlentechnik [*Germany*] — Ber Ges Kohlentech
Berichte. Institut fuer Tabakforschung (Dresden) [*Germany*] — Ber Inst Tabakforsch (Dresden)
Berichte. Institut fuer Tabakforschung. Wohlsdorf-Biendorf — Ber Inst Tabakforsch Wohlsdorf-Biendorf
Berichte. Institut fuer Textil und Faserforschung (Stuttgart) — Ber Inst Tex Faserforsch (Stuttgart)
Berichte. Internationale Gesellschaft fuer Getreidechemie — Ber Int Ges Getreidechem
Berichte. Internationale Kongress fuer Photographie — Ber Intern Kongr Phot
Berichte. Kernforschungsanlage Juelich — Ber Kernforschungsanlage Juelich
Berichte. Kernforschungsanlage Juelich — BKEJA
Berichte. Kernforschungsanlage Juelichgesellschaft mit Beschraenkter Haftung [*A publication*] — Ber Kfa Juelich
Berichte. Limnologische Flusstation Freudenthal Munden — Ber Limnol Flusst Freudenthal Munden
Berichte. Naturforschende Gesellschaft (Augsburg) — Ber Naturforsch Ges (Augsb)
Berichte. Naturforschende Gesellschaft (Bamberg) — Ber Naturforsch Ges (Bamberg)
Berichte. Naturforschende Gesellschaft (Freiburg) — Ber Naturforsch Ges (Freiburg)

Berichte. Naturforschende Gesellschaft (Freiburg Im Breisgau) — BEFBAZ
Berichte. Naturforschende Gesellschaft (Freiburg Im Breisgau) — Ber Naturforsch Ges (Freib I Br)
Berichte. Naturforschende Gesellschaft (Freiburg Im Breisgau) — Ber Naturforsch Ges (Freiburg Breisgau)
Berichte. Naturwissenschaftlich-Medizinischer Verein in Innsbruck — Ber Naturw Med Ver Innsbruck
Berichte. Naturwissenschaftlich-Medizinischer Verein in Innsbruck — Ber Naturwiss-Med Ver Innsb
Berichte. Netherlands. Plantenziektenkundige Dienst — Ber Neth Plantenziektenkundige Dienst
Berichte. Oesterreichische Studiengesellschaft fuer Atomenergie — Ber Oesterr Studienges Atomenerg
Berichte. Ohara Institut fuer Landwirtschaftliche Biologie — Ber Ohara Inst Landw Biol
Berichte. Ohara Institut fuer Landwirtschaftliche Biologie. Okayama Universitaet — Ber Ohara Inst Landwirtsch Biol Okayama Univ
Berichte. Ohara Institut fuer Landwirtschaftliche Forschungen in Kurashiki — Ber Ohara Inst Landwirtsch Forsch Kurashiki
Berichte. Ohara Institut fuer Landwirtschaftliche Forschungen. Okayama Universitaet — Ber Ohara Inst Landwirtsch Forsch Okayama Univ
Berichte. Physikalisch-Medizinische Gesellschaft zu Wuerzburg — Ber Phys-Med Ges Wuerzb
Berichte. Physikalisch-Medizinische Gesellschaft zu Wuerzburg — BPMGA
Berichte. Physikalisch-Technische Bundesanstalt, Braunschweig und Berlin — Ber Phys Tech Bundesanst Braunschweig Berlin
Berichte. Physiologisches Laboratorium und der Versuchsanstalt des Landwirtschaftlichen Instituts der Universitaet Halle — Ber Physiol Lab Versuchsanst Landwirtsch Inst Univ Halle
Berichte. Preussische Kunstsammlungen [*Berlin*] — BPK
Berichte. Preussische Kunstsammlungen — BPKS
Berichte. Schweizerische Botanische Gesellschaft — Ber Schweiz Bot Ges
Berichte. Schweizerische Botanische Gesellschaft — BSBG
Berichte. Schweizerische Botanische Gesellschaft — BSBGA
Berichte. Schweizerische Botanische Gesellschaft/Bulletin de la Societe Botanique Suisse — Ber Schweiz Bot Ges Bull Soc Bot Suisse
Berichte. Technisch Wissenschaftliche Abteilung des Verbandes Keramischer Gewerke in Deutschland — Ber Tech Wiss Abt Verb Keram Gewerke Dtschl
Berichte. Technische Akademie Wuppertal — Ber Tech Akad Wuppertal
Berichte ueber den 24 Kongress der Deutschen Gesellschaft fuer Psychologie — Ber Kongr Dt Ges Psychol
Berichte ueber die Arbeiten an der Mathematisch-Physicalischen Klasse der Koeniglich Bayerischen Akademie der Wissenschaften — Ber Arbeiten Math Phys Kl Koenigl Bayer Akad Wiss
Berichte ueber die Gesamte Biologie. Abteilung A. Berichte ueber die Wissenschaftliche Biologie — Ber Gesamte Biol Abt A Ber Wiss Biol
Berichte ueber die Gesamte Biologie. Abteilung B. Berichte ueber die Gesamte Physiologie und Experimentelle Pharmakologie — Ber Gesamte Biol Abt B Ber Gesamte Physiol
Berichte ueber die Gesamte Gynaekologie und Geburtshilfe — BgG
Berichte ueber die Gesamte Physiologie — Berr Ges Physiol
Berichte ueber die Gesamte Physiologie und Experimentelle Pharmakologie — Ber Gesamte Physiol Exp Pharmakol
Berichte ueber die Petroleum Industrie — Ber Pet Ind
Berichte ueber die Pharmakognostische Litteratur Aller Laender, Herausgegeben von der Deutschen Pharmaceutischen Gesellschaft — Ber Pharmakogn Litt Aller Laender
Berichte ueber die Tagung fuer Baeckerei-Technologie. Vortraege, gehalten Anlaesslich der Tagung der Arbeitsgemeinschaft Getreideforschung — Ber Tag Baeckerei-Technol Vortr Tag
Berichte ueber die Tagung im Nordwestdeutscher Forstverein — Ber Tag Nordwestdtsch Forstver
Berichte ueber die Verhandlungen der Sachsischen Akademie der Wissenschaften — Berr Vhdlgg Saechs Akad Wiss
Berichte ueber die Verhandlungen der Saechsischen Gesellschaft der Wissenschaft zu Leipzig — Ber Leipz
Berichte ueber die Verhandlungen der Saechsischen Gesellschaft der Wissenschaft zu Leipzig — Ber Saechs Ges Wiss
Berichte ueber die Verhandlungen der Saechsischen Gesellschaft der Wissenschaft zu Leipzig — Ber Saechs Gesell
Berichte ueber die Versammlung Deutscher Forstmaenner — Ber Versamml Deutsch Forstmaenner
Berichte ueber die Versammlung Deutscher Naturforscher und Aerzte — Ber Versamml Deutsch Naturf Aerzte
Berichte ueber die Wissenschaftliche Biologie — Ber Wiss Biol
Berichte ueber Land- und Forstwirtschaft in Deutsch-Ostafrika — Ber Land Forstw Deutsch Ostafrika
Berichte ueber Landwirtschaft — Ber Landwirtsch
Berichte ueber Landwirtschaft. Bundes Ministerium fuer Ernaehrung, Landwirtschaft, und Forsten — Ber Landwirt Bundes Min Ernaehr Landwirt Forsten
Berichte ueber Landwirtschaft. Neue Folge — Ber Landwirt N F
Berichte ueber Landwirtschaft. Sonderheft — Ber Landwirtsch Sonderh
Berichte ueber Landwirtschaft. Zeitschrift fuer Agrarpolitik und Landwirtschaft — BZA
Berichte ueber Verhandlungen der Deutschen Weinbau-Kongresse — BDWK
Berichte. Ukrainische Wissenschaftliche Forschungs Institut fuer Physikalische Chemie — Ber Ukr Wiss Forsch Inst Phys Chem
Berichte und Informationen. Europaeische Gemeinschaften — Ber Inf Europ Gem
Berichte und Informationen. Europaeische Gemeinschaften — BRIFB
Berichte und Informationen. Kommission der Europaeischen Gemeinschaften — Ber Inf KEG
Berichte und Mittheilungen des Altertumsvereins in Wien — BMAW
Berichte. Verhandlungen der Saechsischen Akademie der Wissenschaften — BSAW
Berichte. Verhandlungen der Saechsischen Akademie der Wissenschaften zu Leipzig [*Berlin*] — BAL
Berichte. Verhandlungen der [*Koeniglich*] **Saechsischen Akademie der Wissenschaften zu Leipzig** — BVSAW
Berichte. Verhandlungen der Saechsischen Akademie der Wissenschaften zu Leipzig — BVSAWL
Berichte. Verhandlungen der Saechsischen Akademie der Wissenschaften zu Leipzig — VSAL
Berichte. Verhandlungen der Saechsischen Akademie der Wissenschaften zu Leipzig. Mathematisch-Naturwissenschaftliche Klasse [*Germany*] — Ber Verh Saechs Akad Wiss Leipzig Math-Naturwiss Kl
Berichte. Verhandlungen der Saechsischen Akademie der Wissenschaften zu Leipzig. Mathematisch-Naturwissenschaftliche Klasse — Ber Verhandl Saechs Akad Wiss Leipzig Math Naturwiss Kl
Berichte. Verhandlungen der Saechsischen Akademie der Wissenschaften zu Leipzig. Mathematisch-Naturwissenschaftliche Klasse — BEVSA
Berichte. Verhandlungen der Saechsischen Akademie der Wissenschaften zu Leipzig. Mathematisch-Physische Klasse — Ber Verh Saechs Akad Wiss Leipzig Math Phys Kl
Berichte. Verhandlungen der Saechsischen Akademie der Wissenschaften zu Leipzig. Philologisch-Historische Klasse — Ber Verhandl Saechs Akad Wiss Leipzig Philol Hist Kl
Berichte. Verhandlungen der Saechsischen Gesellschaft der Wissenschaft zu Leipzig — BSAWL
Berichte. Verhandlungen der Saechsischen Gesellschaft der Wissenschaften [*Berlin*] — BSGW
Berichte. Verhandlungen der Saechsischen Gesellschaft der Wissenschaften — BVSGW
Berichte. Verhandlungen der Saechsischen Gesellschaft der Wissenschaften zu Leipzig. Philologisch-Historische Klasse — Ber Verhandl Saechs Ges Wiss Leipzig Philol Hist
Berichte vom Internationalen Kongress fuer Grenzflaechenaktive Stoffe — Ber Int Kongr Grenzflaechenaktive Stoffe
Berichte zur Deutschen Landeskunde — BDL
Berichte zur Raumforschung und Raumplanung — Ber Raumforsch und Raumplanung
Berichte zur Wissenschaftsgeschichte — Ber Wissenschaftsgesch
Berichten. Afdeling Tropische Producten van het Koninklijke Institut por de Tropen — Ber Afd Trop Prod K Inst Trop
Berichten en Mededeelingen van het Genootschap Voor Landbouw en Kruidkunde te Utrecht — Ber Meded Genootsch Landb Utrecht
Berichten over de Buitenlandse Handel — BEE
Berichten. Rijksdienst voor het Oudheidkundige Bodemonderzoek — Ber Rijksd Oudh Bod
Berichten. Rijksdienst voor het Oudheidkundige Bodemonderzoek — BROB
Berichten uit het Buitenland — KBO
Berichtigungsliste der Griechischen Papyrusurkunden aus Aegypten — BGPA
Berichtsband ueber den EAST (European Academy of Surface Technology)-Kongress — Berichtsband EAST Kongr
Berigt Nopens de Gouvernments Kina-Onderneming op Java — Ber Gouv Kina Ondern Java
Bering Sea Oceanography — Bering Sea Oceanogr
Berita Anthropologi — BA
Berita Biologi — Berita Biol
Berita Selulosa — BSELB
Berkala Ilmu Kedokteran [*Journal of the Medical Sciences*] [*Indonesia*] — Berkala Ilmu Kedokt
Berkala Ilmu Kedokteran [*Journal of the Medical Sciences*] — Berkala Ilmu Kedokt Gadjah Mada
Berkeley — Berk
Berkeley Buddhist Studies Series — Berk Bud St
Berkeley Journal of Sociology — Ber J Soc
Berkeley Journal of Sociology — Berkeley J Sociol
Berkeley Religious Studies Series — Berk Relig
Berkeley Review — BeR
Berkeley Symposia on Mathematical Statistics and Probability — Berk Symp Math Stat Prob
Berks, Bucks, and Oxon. Archaeological Journal — BBOJ
Berks County Historical Society. Papers — BeCHS
Berks County Historical Society. Papers — BerksCoHS
Berks County Law Journal — Berk Co LJ
Berks County Law Journal — Berks
Berks County Law Journal — Berks Co
Berkshire Archaeological Journal — Berks AJ
Berkshire Archaeological Journal — Berkshire A J
Berkshire Archaeological Journal — Berkshire Arch J
Berkshire Archaeological Journal — Berkshire Archaeol J
Berkshire Historical and Scientific Society — Berkshire Hist Sc Soc
Berlin Freie Universitaet. FU Pressedienst Wissenschaft — Berl Freie Univ FU Pressedienst Wiss
Berlin. Winckelmannsprogramm der Archaeologischen Gesellschaft — Berl Winck Prog
Berlin-Brandenburgische Akademie der Wissenschaften. Berichte und Abhandlungen — Berlin Brandenburgische Akad Wiss Ber Abh
Berliner Beitraege zur Archaeometrie — Berl Beitr Archaeom
Berliner Beitraege zur Namenforschung — BBN
Berliner Beitraege zur Romanischen Philologie — BBRP
Berliner Beitraege zur Vor- und Fruehgeschichte — BBV
Berliner Beitraege zur Vor- und Fruehgeschichte — BBVF
Berliner Beytraege zur Landwirthschaftswissenschaft — Berliner Beytr Landwirthschaftswiss
Berliner Blaetter fuer Muenz-, Siegel- und Wappenkunde — BBMSWK
Berliner Blaetter fuer Vor- und Fruehgeschichte — Ber Bl V Frue Gesch

Berliner Byzantinistische Arbeiten — BBA
Berliner Byzantinistische Arbeiten. Deutsche Akademie der Wissenschaften zu Berlin — BByzA
Berliner Entomologische Zeitschrift — Berl Ent Z
Berliner Geowissenschaftliche Abhandlungen. Reihe A — Berl Geowissenschaftliche Abh Reihe A
Berliner Gesellschaft fuer Anthropologie. Verhandlungen — Berl Gesell F Anthropol Verhandl
Berliner Griechische Urkunden — Berl Griech Urkdn
Berliner Illustrierte Zeitung — BIZ
Berliner Jahrbuch fuer Vor- und Fruehgeschichte — Ber Jhb
Berliner Jahrbuch fuer Vor- und Fruehgeschichte — Berl Jb f Vor-u Fruehgesch
Berliner Jahrbuch fuer Vor- und Fruehgeschichte — Berliner Jahr Vor Fruehgesch
Berliner Jahrbuch fuer Vor- und Fruehgeschichte — BJV
Berliner Jahrbuch fuer Vor- und Fruehgeschichte — BJVF
Berliner Juedische Gemeinde-Zeitung — BJGZ
Berliner Klassiker Texte — Berl Klass Text
Berliner Klassiker Texte — BKT
Berliner Klinische Wochenschrift — Berl Klin Wchnschr
Berliner Klinische Wochenschrift — Berl Klin Wschr
Berliner Leihgabe Griechischer Papyri — P Berl Leihg
Berliner Medizinische Zeitschrift — Berliner Med Z
Berliner Monatshefte fuer Internationale Aufklaerung — Berliner Mh
Berliner Morgenpost — BM
Berliner Munzblaetter — BMBL
Berliner Museen — B Mu
Berliner Museen — Berl Mus
Berliner Museen — BMus
Berliner Museen. Berichte aus den Preusssischen Kunstsammlungen — Ber Kunsts
Berliner Museen. Berichte aus den Preusssischen Kunstsammlungen — Ber Mus
Berliner Museen. Berichte aus den Preusssischen Kunstsammlungen — Berliner Mus
Berliner Numismatische Zeitschrift — Berl Num Z
Berliner Numismatische Zeitschrift — Berl Num Zeit
Berliner Numismatische Zeitschrift — Berl NZ
Berliner Numismatische Zeitschrift — Berliner Num Z
Berliner Numismatische Zeitschrift — Berliner Numism Ztschr
Berliner Numismatische Zeitschrift — BNZ
Berliner Numismatische Zeitschrift — Num Z
Berliner Philologische Wochenschrift — Berl Phil Woch
Berliner Philologische Wochenschrift — Berliner Philol Wochenschr
Berliner Philologische Wochenschrift — BPhW
Berliner Philologische Wochenschrift — BPW
Berliner Philologische Wochenschrift — BPWS
Berliner Statistik — Berl Stat
Berliner Statistik — Berliner Statis
Berliner Studien fuer Klassische Philologie und Archaeologie — BSt
Berliner Studien fuer Klassische Philologie und Archeologie — B St KPA
Berliner Studienreihe zur Mathematik — Berl Studienreihe Math
Berliner Tieraerztliche Wochenschrift — Berl Tieraerztl Wchnschr
Berliner Tieraerztliche Wochenschrift — Berliner Tieraerztl Wochenschr
Berliner und Muenchener Tieraerztliche Wochenschrift — BEMTA
Berliner und Muenchener Tieraerztliche Wochenschrift — Berl Muench Tieraerztl Wochenschr
Berliner und Muenchener Tieraerztliche Wochenschrift — Berl Muench Tieraerztl Wschr
Berliner Volks-Zeitung — BVZ
Berliner Wetterkarte. Supplement [*Germany*] — Berl Wetterkarte Suppl
Berliner Wetterkarte. Supplement — BWESA
Berliner Wirtschaft; Mitteilungen der Industriekammer und Handelskammer zu Berlin — BWX
Berliner Wirtschaftsbericht — B Wirtsch B
Berliner Wirtschaftsbericht — BWB
Berliner Zahnaerztliche Halbmonatsschrift — BZHM
Berliner Zeitung — BZ
Berliner Zeitung am Mittag — BZM
Berlingske Tidende — BT
Berlinische Blaetter — Berlin Blaett
Berlinische Sammlungen zur Befoerderung der Arzneywissenschaft, der Naturgeschichte, der Haushaltungskunst, Cameralwissenschaft und der Dahin Einschlagenden Litteratur — Berlin Samml Befoerd Arzneywiss
Berlinisches Jahrbuch fuer die Pharmacie — Berl Jahrb Pharm
Berlinisches Magazin, oder Gesammlete Schriften und Nachrichten fuer die Liebhaber der Arzneywissenschaft, Naturgeschichte und der Angenehmen Wissenschaften Ueberhaupt — Berlin Mag
Bermondsey Book — BB
Bermuda Biological Station for Research. Contributions — Bermuda Biol Sta Res Contr
Bermuda. Biological Station for Research. Special Publication — Bermuda Biol Stn Res Spec Publ
Bermuda. Historical Quarterly — Berm Hist Q
Bermuda Historical Society. Occasional Publications — Bermuda Hist Soc Occas Publ
Bermuda. Report of the Director of Agriculture and Fisheries — Bermuda Rep Dir Agric Fish
Berner Beitraege zur Geschichte der Medizin und der Naturwissenschaften — Berner Beitr Gesch Med Naturwiss
Bernice Pauahi Bishop Museum. Bulletin — Bernice Pauahi Bishop Museum Bull
Bernice Pauahi Bishop Museum. Bulletin. Special Publication — Bernice Pauahi Bishop Museum Bull Special Pub
Bernice Pauahi Bishop Museum. Occasional Papers — Bernice Pauahi Bishop Mus Oc P
Bernice Pauahi Bishop Museum. Special Publication — Bernice P Bishop Mus Spec Publ
Bernische Blaetter fuer Landwirthschaft — Bern Blaett Landw
Beroepsvervoer — BVR
Bertrand Russell Memorial Lecture in Philosophy and Science — B Russell Mem Lect Phil Sci
Berufs-Dermatosen — BERUA
Berufs-Dermatosen — Berufs-Derm
Berufsgenossenschaft — BGNSA
Berufspaedagogische Zeitschrift — BPZ
Berytus Archaeological Studies — Berytus
Besancon Universite. Annales Scientifiques. Serie 3. Geologie — Besancon Univ Ann Sci Ser 3
Beschreibende Bibliographien — BBib
Beschrijvende Rassenlijst voor Fruitgewassen — Beschr Rassenlijst Fruitgew
Beschrijvende Rassenlijst voor Groentegewassen — Beschr Rassenlijst Groentegew
Beskontaktnye Elektricheskie Mashiny — Beskontaktn Elektr Mash
Besluit van de Regent — BReg
Besluit van de Regent — BRgt
Bessarione — Bess
Best of Business — Best Bus
Best of Newspaper Design — Best News Des
Best Sellers — Best
Best Sellers — Best Sell
Best Sellers — BS
Bestimmung der Isotopenverteilung in Markierten Verbindungen — Bestimm Isotopenverteil Markierten Verbindungen
Best's Insurance News — Best's Ins N
Best's Review. Life/Health Insurance Edition — Best Life
Best's Review. Life/Health Insurance Edition — Best's Life
Best's Review. Life/Health Insurance Edition — Bests R
Best's Review. Life/Health Insurance Edition — Bests R Life Ed
Best's Review. Life/Health Insurance Edition — Best's Rev Life Health Insur Ed
Best's Review. Life/Health Insurance Edition — BLH
Best's Review. Property/Casualty Insurance Edition — Best's Rev Prop/Casualty Insur Ed
Best's Review. Property/Casualty Insurance Edition — BIP
Best's Review. Property/Liability Edition — Bests Prop
Best's Review. Property/Liability Edition — Bests R Prop Ed
Best's Review. Property/Liability Edition — Best's R Property Ed
Bestuurswetenschappen — BWT
Beszamolo a Vizgazdalkodasi Tudomanyos Kutato Intezet Munkajarol — Beszamolo Vizgazdalkodasi Tud Kut Intez Munkajarol
Beta Adrenerge Blocker und Hochdruck Internationales Symposion — Beta Adrenerge Blocker Hochdruck Int Symp
Beta Adrenergic Blockers and Hypertension — Beta Adrenergic Blockers Hypertens
Beta Blocker in der Hypertonie Behandlung — Beta Blocker Hypertonie Behandl
Beta Blockers. Present Status and Future Prospects. An International Symposium — Beta Blockers Present Status Future Prospects Int Symp
Beta Phi Research Exchange — Beta Phi Research Exch
Beta-Aluminas and Beta Batteries. Proceedings. International Workshop — Beta Aluminas Beta Batteries Proc Int Workshop
Betablocker Gegenwart und Zukunft Internationales Symposium — Betablocker Ggw Zukunft Int Symp
Beteram (Tel Aviv) — BTA
Beth Hamikra. Bulletin of the Israel Society for Biblical Research and the World Jewish Biblical Society — Beth Hamikra
Beth Israel Hospital. Seminars in Medicine — Beth Isr Hosp Semin Med
Beth Israel Hospital. Seminars in Medicine — Beth Israel Hosp Semin Med
Beth Mikra — BM
Beton, Herstellung, Verwendung — Beton Herstellung Verwend
Beton, Herstellung, Verwendung — BTONA
Beton, Herstellung, Verwendung — BZM
Beton i Zhelezobeton [*Tiflis*] — BEZHDK
Beton i Zhelezobeton — BTZBA
Beton- und Stahlbetonbau — BESTA
Betongtekniske Publikasjoner — Betongtek Publ
Betons Industriels [*France*] — Betons Ind
Betonstein Zeitung — Betonstein Ztg
Betonstein Zeitung — BEZEA
Betontechnische Berichte [*Germany*] — Betontech Ber
Beton-Teknik — Bet-Tek
Betonwerk und Fertigteil-Technik [*Germany*] — Betonwerk Fertigteil-Tech
Betrieb (Duesseldorf) — BETRD
Betriebs-Berater. Zeitschrift fuer Recht und Wirtschaft — BBM
Betriebs-Berater. Zeitschrift fuer Recht und Wirtschaft — Betr-Berat
Betriebs-Oekonom — Betr-Oekon
Betriebs-Technik — Betr-Tech
Betriebswirtschaft — Betriebswirtsch
Betriebswirtschaftliche Forschung und Praxis — Betriebswirtsch Forsch Praxis
Betriebswirtschaftliche Forschung und Praxis — BTF
Betriebswirtschaftliche Mitteilungen fuer den Wirtschaftsberater — Betriebswirt Mitt Wirtberater
Betriebswirtschaftliche Mitteilungen fuer den Wirtschaftsberater — Betriebswirtsch Mitt Wirtschaftsberat
Betriebswirtschaftliche Rundschau — Bw R
Betrifft Erziehung [*Germany*] — Betr Erz
Better Business [*New Zealand*] — Better Bus
Better Ceramics Through Chemistry. Symposium — Better Ceram Chem Symp
Better Crops with Plant Food — Bett Crops Pl Fd
Better Crops With Plant Food — Better Crops With Pl Food
Better Farming — Better F
Better Homes and Gardens — Bet Hom & Gard

Better Homes and Gardens — BHGDA
Better Homes and Gardens — GBHG
Better Roads — BEROA
Betterave et les Industries Agricoles — Betterave Ind Agr
Betuwsche Rassenlijst voor Fruit van de Nederlandsche Fruittelers Organisatie — Betuwsche Rassenlijst Fruit
Between Librarians — Bet Libns
Between Librarians — Betw Libns
Between the Species. A Journal of Ethics — Between Spec J Ethics
Between Worlds — BW
Betz Indicator — Betz Indic
Beurteilungskriterien fuer Chemotherapeutika — Beurteilungskriterien Chemother
Beverage Industry — Beverage
Beverage Industry — Beverage Ind
Beverage Industry Annual Manual — Bev Ann
Beverage World — Bev
Beverage World — Bev Wld
Beverage World 100 — Bev Wld 100
Beverage World Periscope. Late Breaking News and Analysis — Bev Wld P
Bewirtschaftung Fester Abfaelle Berichte Internationaler Kongress — Bewirtsch Fester Abfaelle Ber Int Kongr
Beyond Baroque — Bey B
Beyond Fiction — BFF
Beyond Infinity — BDI
Beytraege zur Botanik — Beytr Bot
Beytraege zur Geschichte der Erfindungen — Beytr Gesch Erfind
Beytraege zur Natuerlichen Oekonomischen und Politischen Geschichte der Ober- und Niederlausiz — Beytr Natuerl Oekon Polit Gesch Ober Niederlausiz
Beytraege zur Naturkunde des Herzogthums Zelle — Beytr Naturk Herzogth Zelle
Bezopasnost Gornykh Rabot — Bezop Gorn Rab
Bezopasnost Truda na Proizvodstve Issledovaniya i Ispytaniya Spravochnoe Posobie 2-e Izdanie — Bezop Tr Proizvod Issled Ispyt Sprav Posobie 2-e Izd
Bezopasnost Truda v Promyshlennosti — Bezop Tr Prom-St
Bezzenbergers Beitraege — BB
BF Goodrich Co. Economic and Business Facts and Forecasts — Goodrich
BfS-ISH-Berichte (Bundesamt fuer Strahlenschutz. Institut fuer Strahlenhygiene) — BfS ISH Ber
B.G. Rudolph Lectures in Judaic Studies — RLJS
BGA (Bundesgesundheitsamt) Schriften — BGA Schr
Bhagirath — BHAGA
Bhagirath. The Irrigation and Power Quarterly — Bhagirath Irrig Power Q
Bharat Ka Rajpatra — GZINB
Bharata Manisha Quarterly — Bhar Ma Q
Bharatiya Vidya — BhV
Bharatiya Vidya — BV
Bhavan's Journal — Bhavan's J
BHM. Berg- und Huttenmaennische Monatshefte — BHM Berg u Huttenm Mh
BHP [*Broken Hill Proprietary Ltd.*] **Journal** — BHP J
BHP [*Broken Hill Proprietary Ltd.*] **Journal** — BHP Jo
BHP [*Broken Hill Proprietary Ltd.*] **Review** — BHP R
BHP [*Broken Hill Proprietary Ltd.*] **Review** — BHP Rev
BHP [*Broken Hill Proprietary Ltd.*] **Technical Bulletin** — BHP Tech Bull
BHP [*Broken Hill Proprietary Ltd.*] **Technical Bulletin (Australia)** — BPHBA
BI [*Bibliographisches Institut*] **Hochschultaschenbuecher** — BI Hochschultaschenb
BI [*Business International Corp.*] **Middle East Marketing Conditions. Egypt** — BI Mid East Market Cond Egypt
Biafra Review — Biafra R
Bianco e Nero — Bian & Nero
Bi-annual Review of Allergy — Biann Rev Allergy
Bibbia e Oriente — B e O
Bibbia e Oriente — Bib Or
Bibbia e Oriente — BiO
Bibel und Kirche — B u K
Bibel und Kirche [*Stuttgart*] — BiKi
Bibel und Leben [*Duesseldorf*] — BiLeb
Bibel und Leben [*Duesseldorf*] — BL
Bibel und Liturgie [*Klosterneuburg, Austria*] — BiLit
Bible and Spade — B and S
Bible and the Ancient Near East — BANE
Bible Collector — Bib Col
Bible e Vie Chretienne — Bib VC
Bible et Terre Sainte — B&TS
Bible et Terre Sainte (Nouvelle Serie) [*Paris*] — BiTerS
Bible et Vie Chretienne [*Maredsous*] — BiViChr
Bible et Vie Chretienne [*Maredsous*] — BiVieChr
Bible et Vie Chretienne [*Paris*] — BVC
Bible Today — Bible T
Bible Today — BiTod
Bible Today — BT
Bible Translator — Bib Transl
Bible Translator — BiTr
Bible Translator — BiTrans
Bible Translator — BT
Bible Translator. Practical Papers — Bib Tr P
Bible Translator. Practical Papers. Numbers 2 and 4 — Bib Tr No 2 No 4
Bible Translator. Technical Papers — Bib Tr T
Bible Translator. Technical Papers. Numbers 1 and 3 — Bib Tr No 1 No 3
Biblebhashyam — Biblebas
Biblia y Fe [*Madrid*] — ByF
Biblica [*Rome*] — Bbl
Biblica — Bi
Biblica — Bib
Biblica [*Rome*] — Bibl
Biblica et Orientalia. Pontificum Institutum Biblicum — Bib Or Pont
Biblical and Patristic Studies — BPS
Biblical Archaeologist — BA
Biblical Archaeologist — BiA
Biblical Archaeologist — Bib Ar
Biblical Archaeologist — Bib Arch
Biblical Archaeologist — Bibl A
Biblical Archaeologist — Bibl Arch
Biblical Archaeologist — Bibl Archaeolo
Biblical Archaeologist — PBIA
Biblical Archaeology Review — BAR
Biblical Archaeology Review — Bib Arch R
Biblical Archaeology Review — Bib Arch Rev
Biblical Archeologist — Bib A
Biblical Archeologist — Bibl Archeol
Biblical Research — Bib Res
Biblical Research [*Chicago*] — BiR
Biblical Research [*Chicago*] — BiRes
Biblical Research — BR
Biblical Research. Papers of the Chicago Society of Biblical Research [*Amsterdam*] — BiblRes
Biblical Review — Bib R
Biblical Review — Biblical Rev
Biblical Review — BR
Biblical Theology Bulletin — Bib Th Bul
Biblical Theology Bulletin [*Rome*] — BibTB
Biblical Theology Bulletin — BTB
Biblical Viewpoint — BV
Biblical World — Bi W
Biblical World — Bi Wld
Biblical World — Bib World
Biblical World [*Chicago*] — BW
Bibliofilia — B
Bibliofilia — BF
Bibliofilia — Bi
Bibliofilia — Biblio
Bibliografia Argentina de Artes y Letras (Buenos Aires) — Bibliogr Arg Art Letr BA
Bibliografia Brasileira Odontologia — Bibliogr Bras Odontol
Bibliografia de Ciencias Historicas — Bibliogr Ci Hist
Bibliografia de Historia de America — Bib Hist Am
Bibliografia, Documentacion, y Terminologia — BDT
Bibliografia Economica de Mexico — Bibliogr Econ Mex
Bibliografia Ecuatoriana — BE
Bibliografia Espanola [*Database*] — BIBL
Bibliografia Extranjera Depositada en la Biblioteca Nacional [*Database*] — BNBE
Bibliografia Filologica do Centro de Estudos Filologica de Lisboa — Bibl Filol
Bibliografia Geologiczna Poliski — Bibliogr Geol Pol
Bibliografia Hispanica — BH
Bibliografia Hispanica — BHisp
Bibliografia Hispanica — BiH
Bibliografia Hispanica. Instituto Nacional del Libro Espanol — Bibliogr Hisp
Bibliografia Internazionale di Scienze ed Arti — Bibliogr Internaz Sci Art
Bibliografia Italiana — BI
Bibliografia Italiana sull'Educazione dei Sordi — Biblio Ital Educ Sordi
Bibliografia Medico-Biologica — Bibliogr Med Biol
Bibliografia (Mexico) — Bibliogr Mex
Bibliografia Missionaria — Bibliogr Mission
Bibliografia Nazionale Italiana — BNI
Bibliografia y Documentation (Caracas) — Bibliogr Doc Caracas
Bibliografias. Biblioteca Conmemorativa Orton. Instituto Interamericano de Ciencias Agricolas — Bibliogr Bibl Conmem Orton Inst Interamer Cienc Agr
Bibliografica Farmaceutica — Bibliogr Farm
Bibliografico de Turrialba. Suplemento — Turrialba Supl
Bibliografija Vostoka. Bibliography of the Orient (Moscow and Leningrad) — Bibliogr Vostoka Moscow Leningrad
Bibliographer — Bibliog
Bibliographia Asiatica — Bibl Asiatica
Bibliographia Cartographica — BC
Bibliographia Cartographica — Bibliogr Carto
Bibliographia Chimica — Bibliogr Chim
Bibliographia Forestalis. Forstliche Bibliographie der Internationalen Forstzentrale — Bibliogr Forest
Bibliographia Genetica — Bibliogr Genet
Bibliographia Neuroendocrinologica — Bib Neuroendocr
Bibliographia Phytosociologica Syntaxonomica — Bibliogr Phytosociol Syntaxon
Bibliographia Phytosociologica Syntaxonomica — BPSYDB
Bibliographia Scientiae Naturalis Helvetica [*Bern*] — Biblio Sci Nat Helv
Bibliographic Index — Bibl
Bibliographic Index — Bibl Ind
Bibliographic Index — Bibliogr Index
Bibliographic Index of Health Education Periodicals [*Information service or system*] — BIHEP
Bibliographic Index of Health Education Periodicals. BIHEP — Bibliogr Index Health Educ Period
Bibliographic Index of Library Documents [*Database*] — BILD
Bibliographic Information on Southeast Asia [*Database*] — BISA
Bibliographic Series. Institute of Paper Chemistry — Bibliogr Ser Inst Pap Chem
Bibliographic Series. Institute of Paper Chemistry — IPCBA
Bibliographica Genetica Medica — Bibliogr Genet Med
Bibliographical Bulletin of the Greek Language — BGL
Bibliographical Bulletin. United States Department of Agriculture. Library — Biblphical Bull US Dep Agric Libr
Bibliographical Contributions. United States Department of Agriculture. Library — Biblphical Contr US Dep Agric Libr

Bibliographical Register — Bibliog Reg
Bibliographical Series. International Atomic Energy Agency — Bibliogr Ser IAEA
Bibliographical Series. Oregon State University. Forest Research Laboratory — Bibliogr Ser Ore For Res Lab
Bibliographical Series. Science Library. Science Museum — Bibliogr Ser Sci Libr Sci Mus
Bibliographical Society (London) — Bibliog Soc
Bibliographical Society of America — Bibliog Soc Amer
Bibliographical Society of America. Papers — Bib Soc Am
Bibliographical Society of America. Papers — Bibl Soc Am Pa
Bibliographical Society of America. Papers — Biblio Soc Am
Bibliographical Society of America. Papers — Bibliog Soc Am Pa
Bibliographical Society of America. Papers — BSAP
Bibliographical Society of America. Papers — BSP
Bibliographical Society of Ireland. Publications — Bibliog Soc Ir
Bibliographical Society [*London*]. Publications — BSP
Bibliographical Society. University of Virginia — Bibliog Soc Univ Virginia
Bibliographie Africaine/Afrikaanse Bibliografie — Bibliogr Afr Afr Bibliogr
Bibliographie Americaniste. Linguistique Amerindienne. Societe des Americanistes — Bib Am Ling Am Soc Am
Bibliographie Analytique de l'Afrique Antique — BAAA
Bibliographie Anatomique — Biblphie Anat
Bibliographie Annuelle de Madagascar — Bibliogr Annu Madagascar
Bibliographie de Belgique — BB
Bibliographie de Belgique — Bibl Bel
Bibliographie de la Belgique — Bibliogr Belgique
Bibliographie de la France — BF
Bibliographie de la France — Biblio France
Bibliographie de la Litterature Francaise du Moyen Age a Nos Jours — Bib Lit Fr Moy Age N Jou
Bibliographie de la Philosophie — BP
Bibliographie de la Philosophie — BPh
Bibliographie der Biologie. Internationales Institut fuer Bibliographie der Medizin und der Nachbargebiete — Bibliogr Biol
Bibliographie der Deutschen Bibliographien — Bib Deut Bib
Bibliographie der Pflanzenschutzliteratur — Bibl Pflanz
Bibliographie der Pflanzenschutzliteratur — Bibliogr Pflanzenschutzlit
Bibliographie der Schweizerischen Naturwissenschaftlichen Literatur. Bibliographie Scientifique Suisse — Bibliogr Schweiz Naturwiss Lit
Bibliographie der Wirtschaftspresse — Bibl Wirtschaftspresse
Bibliographie der Wirtschaftspresse — BWO
Bibliographie Internationale des Sciences Sociales — BISS
Bibliographie Linguistique — Bibl
Bibliographie Linguistique — BL
Bibliographie Linguistischer Literatur [*Database*] — BLL
Bibliographie Moderne — BMod
Bibliographie Padagogik — Bib Padagog
Bibliographie Philosophie — Bibliogr Phil
Bibliographie Scientifique Francaise. Bureau Francais du Catalogue International de la Litterature Scientifique — Bibliogr Sci Franc
Bibliographie Selective des Publications Officielles Francaises — Bibl Selective Pubns Officielles Fr
Bibliographie von Deutschland — Bibliogr Deutsch
Bibliographie zur Bestrahlung von Lebensmitteln [*Germany*] — Bibliogr Bestrahlung Lebensm
Bibliographie zur Geschichte der Deutschen Arbeiterbewegung — Bibl Gesch Dt Arbeiterbewegung
Bibliographie zur Juedisch-Hellenistischen und Intertestamentarischen Literatur — BJHIL
Bibliographie zur Offentlichen Unternehmung und Verwaltung [*Database*] — BOWI
Bibliographie zur Umweltradioaktivitaet in Lebensmitteln [*Germany*] — Bibliogr Umweltradioakt Lebensm
Bibliographien des Deutschen Wetterdienstes — Biblphien Dt Wetterd
Bibliographien und Studien — Bibliogr Stud
Bibliographien zum Studium der Deutschen Sprache und Literatur — BSSL
Bibliographien zur Deutsche Barockliteratur — BzDB
Bibliographien zur Deutschen Literatur des Mittelalters — BDLM
Bibliographies Analytiques sur l'Afrique Centrale — Bibliogr Anal Afr Cent
Bibliographies and Literature of Agriculture. United States Department of Agriculture. Economics and Statistics Service — Bibliogr Lit Agric US Dep Agric Econ Stat Serv
Bibliographies. Entomological Society of America — Bib Ent Soc Am
Bibliographies in Paint Technology — Bibliogr Paint Technol
Bibliographies of Australian Writers [*State Library of South Australia*] — Bibs of Aust Writers
Bibliographies of New England History — Bib N Eng Hist
Bibliographies of the History of Science and Technology — Bibliograph Hist Sci Tech
Bibliographique Officiel des Imprimes Publies en Pologne. Bulletin — BOP
Bibliographische Reihe der Kernforschungsanlage Juelich — Bibliogr Reihe Kernforschungsanlage Juelich
Bibliography and Index of Geology — Bibl & Ind Geol
Bibliography and Index of Geology — BiblGeo
Bibliography and Index of Geology — Bibliogr Index Geol
Bibliography and Index of Geology Exclusive of North America — Bibliogr Index Geol Exclus North Am
Bibliography and Index of Geology Exclusive of North America — BIGENA
Bibliography and Index of Micropaleontology — Bibliogr Index Micropaleontology
Bibliography and Subject Index of South African Geology — Bibliogr Subj Index S Afr Geol
Bibliography. Bee Research Association — Biblphy Bee Research Ass
Bibliography. Commonwealth Bureau of Soils — Bibliogr Bur Soils
Bibliography, Documentation, Terminology — Bibl Docum Terminology
Bibliography, Documentation, Terminology — Bibliog Doc Terminology
Bibliography for the Control of Anxiety, Fear, and Pain in Dentistry — Bib Cont Anx Fear Pain Dent
Bibliography in Irradiation of Foods [*Germany*] — Bibliogr Irradiat Foods
Bibliography. International Bee Research Association — Biblphy Int Bee Res Ass
Bibliography of Agriculture — BibAg
Bibliography of Agriculture — Bibliogr Agric
Bibliography of Agriculture — BOA
Bibliography of Agriculture. US Department of Agriculture (Washington, DC) — Bibliogr Agric Washington
Bibliography of Agriculture (Washington) — Biblphy Agric (Wash)
Bibliography of Appraisal Literature — Bibliogr Apprais Lit
Bibliography of Books for Children — Bibliogr Books Child
Bibliography of Economic Geology — Bibliogr Econ Geol
Bibliography of English Language and Literature — Bibl Engl Lang & Lit
Bibliography of English Language and Literature — Bibliogr Engl Lit
Bibliography of Forestry and Forest Products/Bibliographie des Forets et Products Forestieres/Bibliografia de la Silvicultura y Productos Forestale — Bibliogr Forest Forest Prod
Bibliography of Geological Literature on Atomic Energy Raw Materials — Bibliogr Geol Lit At Energy Raw Mater
Bibliography of Manichaean Materials — BMM
Bibliography of North American Geology — Bibliogr North Am Geol
Bibliography of Periodical Literature on the Near and Middle East — BPLNME
Bibliography of Philosophy — BOP
Bibliography of Reproduction — Bibl Repro
Bibliography of Reproduction — Bibliogr Reprod
Bibliography of Reviews in Chemistry — Bibliogr Rev Chem
Bibliography of Scientific and Industrial Reports — Bibliogr Sci Ind Rep
Bibliography of South African Government Publications — Bibliogr S Afr Gov Publ
Bibliography of Systematic Mycology. Commonwealth Mycological Institute — Bibliogr Syst Mycol
Bibliography of Technical Reports — Bibliogr Tech Rep
Bibliography of the English-Speaking Caribbean — Bibliogr Engl Speak Carib
Bibliography of the History of Art/Bibliographic d'Histoire d l'Art — BHA
Bibliography of the History of Medicine — BHM
Bibliography of the History of Medicine — Bibliogr Hist Med
Bibliography on the High Temperature Chemistry and Physics of Gases and Plasmas — Bibliogr High Temp Chem Phys Gases Plasmas
Bibliography on the High Temperature Chemistry and Physics of Materials — Bibliogr High Temp Chem Phys Mater
Bibliography on the High Temperature Chemistry and Physics of Materials in the Condensed State — Bibliogr High Temp Chem Phys Mater Condens State
Biblionews and Australian Notes and Queries — BANQ
Biblios. Revista da Faculdade de Letras da Universidade de Coimbra — BRFLUC
Biblioteca Bio-Bibliografica della Terra Santa. Nova Serie — BBBNS
Biblioteca Clasica Gredos — Bibl Clas Gredos
Biblioteca Critica della Letteratura Italiana — Bibl Crit d Lett Ital
Biblioteca de Automatica, Informatica, Electronica, Management. Seria Practica — Bibl Automat Inform Electron Management Ser Practica
Biblioteca de Autores Cristianos — BAC
Biblioteca de Autores Espanoles — BAE
Biblioteca de la Revista Matematica Iberoamericana — Bibl Rev Mat Iberoamericana
Biblioteca Dedalo — Bibl Dedalo
Biblioteca del Leonardo — Bibl d Leonardo
Biblioteca della Liberta — Bibl Liberta
Biblioteca della Scuole Italiane — Biblioteca Scuole Ital
Biblioteca della Societa Storica Subalpina — Bibl d Soc Stor Subalpina
Biblioteca dell'Archivum Romanicum — BAR
Biblioteca dell'Archivum Romanicum. Serie II. Linguistica — Bibl Arch Roman Ser II Linguistica
Biblioteca delle Scuole Italiane — Bibl d Scuole Ital
Biblioteca delle Scuole Italiane — Bibl d Scuole Italiane
Biblioteca di Critica Storica e Letteraria — Bibl di Crit Stor e Lett
Biblioteca di Cultura — Bibl di Cult
Biblioteca di Cultura Contemporanea — BCC
Biblioteca di Cultura Moderna — BCM
Biblioteca di Cultura Moderna — Bibl di Cult Mod
Biblioteca di Nuncius. Studi e Testi — Bibl Nuncius Studi Testi
Biblioteca di Saggi e Lezioni Accademiche — Bibl di Saggi e Lez Accad
Biblioteca di Storia della Scienza — Bibl Storia Sci
Biblioteca General del Consejo Superior de Invistigaciones Cientificas. Boletin Semestral — Bibl Gen CSIC
Biblioteca Germanica di Lettere, Arti, e Scienze — Bibliot German Lett
Biblioteca Hispana — BHis
Biblioteca Jose Jeronimo Triana — Bibl Jose Jeronimo Triana
Biblioteca Jose Jeronimo Triana — BJJTEC
Biblioteca Moderna Mondadori — BMM
Biblioteca Mondadori — Bibl Mondadori
Biblioteca Nacional Jose Marti. Revista — Biblioteca Nac Jose Marti R
Biblioteca Profesorului de Matematica — Bibl Profes Mat
Biblioteca (Rio de Janeiro) — Bibl Rio
Biblioteca Storica Toscana. Sezione di Storia del Risorgimento — Bibl Stor T
Biblioteca Universitaria y Provincial Barcelona. Boletin de Noticias — Bibl Univ Prov Barc Bol Not
Bibliotechka Sel'skogo Profsoiuznogo Aktivista — Bibl Sel'sk Profsoiuznogo Akt
Bibliotecologia (Buenos Aires) — Bibliotec BA
Bibliotek for Laeger — Bibl Laeger
Bibliotek for Laeger — Bibl Lg
Biblioteka Analiz Literackich — BALit
Biblioteka Inzynierii Oprogramowania — Bib Inz Oprogram
Biblioteka Inzynierii Oprogramowania — Bibl Inz Oprogram

Biblioteka Juznoslovenskog Filologa — BJF
Biblioteka Matematyczna — Bibl Mat
Biblioteka Mechaniki Stosowanej — Bibl Mech Stos
Biblioteka Naukowa Inzyniera — Bibl Nauk Inz
Biblioteka Pisarzy Polskich i Obcych — BPP
Biblioteka Polska — B Pol
Biblioteka Problemow — Bibl Problem
Biblioteka Slovesnika — BS
Biblioteka Vracha — Bibliot Vrach
Bibliotekaren — Biblt
Bibliotekarz — B
Bibliotekininkystes ir Bibliografijos Klausimai — BBK
Biblioteksaarbog — Biblaa
Biblioteksbladet — BBL
Biblioteksbladet — Bibl
Bibliotheca Aegyptiaca — BA
Bibliotheca Africana — Bibliotheca Afr
Bibliotheca Anatomica — BIANA
Bibliotheca Anatomica — Bibl Anat
Bibliotheca Anatomica — Bibl Anatom
Bibliotheca Arnamagnaeana — B Arn
Bibliotheca Biotheoretica — Bibl Biotheor
Bibliotheca Biotheoretica — Biblioth Biotheor
Bibliotheca Cardiologica — Bibl Cardio
Bibliotheca Cardiologica — Bibl Cardiol
Bibliotheca Cardiologica (Switzerland) — BCSCA
Bibliotheca Celtica — BC
Bibliotheca Classica Orientalis — BCO
Bibliotheca Classica Orientalis — Bi Cl Or
Bibliotheca Classica Orientalis — Bibl Class Or
Bibliotheca Classica Orientalis — Bibl Class Orient
Bibliotheca Critica — Biblioth Crit
Bibliotheca Critica Nova — Biblioth Crit Nova
Bibliotheca de Farmacia, Chimica, Fisica, Medicina, Chirurgia, Terapeutica, Storia Naturale — Bibliot Farm
Bibliotheca Diatomologica — Bibl Diatomol
Bibliotheca Diatomologica — BIDIEA
Bibliotheca Gastroenterologica — BGSGB
Bibliotheca Gastroenterologica — Bibl Gastro
Bibliotheca Gastroenterologica — Bibl Gastroenterol
Bibliotheca Geographorum Arabicorum — BGA
Bibliotheca Gynaecologica — Bibl Gynaecol
Bibliotheca Haematologica — Bibl Haem
Bibliotheca Haematologica — Bibl Haemat
Bibliotheca Haematologica — Bibl Haematol
Bibliotheca Haematologica — BIHAA
Bibliotheca Hagiographica Graeca — BHG
Bibliotheca Hagiographica Latina — BHL
Bibliotheca Hagiographica Orientalis — BHO
Bibliotheca Historica Sueo-Gothica — Bibl Hist Sueo-Gothica
Bibliotheca Humanitatis Historica — BHH
Bibliotheca Humanitatis Historica — Bibl Hum Hist
Bibliotheca Indica — BI
Bibliotheca Indica — Bibliotheca Ind
Bibliotheca Islamica — BI
Bibliotheca Lichenologica — Bibl Lichenol
Bibliotheca Lichenologica — BLICD3
Bibliotheca Mathematica [*Elsevier Book Series*] — BM
Bibliotheca Medica — Bibl M
Bibliotheca Medica Canadiana — Bibl Med Can
Bibliotheca Medica Cassel — Biblioth Med Cassel
Bibliotheca (Merida, Venezuela) — Bibl Merida
Bibliotheca Mesopotamica — Bib Mes
Bibliotheca Mesopotamica — BM
Bibliotheca Microbiologica — Bibl Microbiol
Bibliotheca Microbiologica — BMPMB
Bibliotheca Mycologica — Bibl Mycol
Bibliotheca Mycologica — BIMYDY
Bibliotheca Nicotiana — Biblioth Nicotiana
Bibliotheca Normannica — Bibl Norm
Bibliotheca Nutrito et Dieta — Bibl Nutr D
Bibliotheca Nutrito et Dieta — Bibl Nutr Dieta
Bibliotheca Nutrito et Dieta (Switzerland) — BNDSA
Bibliotheca Ophthalmologica — Bibl Ophthalmol
Bibliotheca Ophthalmologica — BOPSA
Bibliotheca Orientalis — Bibl Or
Bibliotheca Orientalis — Bibl Orient
Bibliotheca Orientalis — Bibl Oriental
Bibliotheca Orientalis — Biblioth Orient
Bibliotheca Orientalis — BibO
Bibliotheca Orientalis — BiOr
Bibliotheca Orientalis — BO
Bibliotheca Oto-Rhino-Laryngologica — Bibl Oto-Rhino-Laryngol
Bibliotheca Paediatrica — Bibl Paediatr
Bibliotheca Patrum Ecclesiasticorum Selectissima — BPES
Bibliotheca Philologica Classica — BPhC
Bibliotheca Phonetica — Bibl Phonet
Bibliotheca Phonetica — Bibl Phonetica
Bibliotheca Phonetica — BIPNA
Bibliotheca Phycologica — Bibl Phycol
Bibliotheca Phycologica — BIPHDW
Bibliotheca Primatologica — Bibl Primatol
Bibliotheca Primatologica — BPRMA
Bibliotheca Psychiatrica — Bibl Psych
Bibliotheca Psychiatrica — Bibl Psychiatr
Bibliotheca Psychiatrica et Neurologica — Bibl Psychiatr Neurol
Bibliotheca Psychiatrica et Neurologica (Switzerland) — BPNSA
Bibliotheca Radiologica — Bibl Radiol
Bibliotheca Radiologica [*Switzerland*] — BRSRA
Bibliotheca Romana — BR
Bibliotheca Sacra — Bib Sac
Bibliotheca Sacra — Bib Sacra
Bibliotheca Sacra — Bibl Sac
Bibliotheca Sacra — Bibl Sacra
Bibliotheca Sacra — BS
Bibliotheca Sacra — BSa
Bibliotheca Scriptorum Graecorum et Romanorum Teubneriana — Bibl Script Gr Rom Teub
Bibliotheca Scriptorum Graecorum et Romanorum Teubneriana — Bibl Teubn
Bibliotheca Scriptorum Graecorum et Romanorum Teubneriana — T
Bibliotheca Scriptorum Graecorum et Romanorum Teubneriana — Teubner
Bibliotheca Theologica Norvegica — BTN
Bibliotheca Tuberculosea — Bibl Tuberc
Bibliotheca Tuberculosea — BICTA
Bibliotheca Tuberculosea et Medicinae Thoracalis — Bibl Tub Me T
Bibliotheca Tuberculosea et Medicinae Thoracalis — Bibl Tuberc Med Thorac
Bibliotheca "Vita Humana" — Bibl "Vita Hum"
Bibliotheca "Vita Humana" — BVHUA
Bibliotheca Zoologica — Bibliotheca Zool
Bibliotheek en Samenleving — OPI
Bibliotheekleven — BL
Bibliothek der Alten Welt — BAW
Bibliothek der Kirchenvaeter — BKV
Bibliothek der Neuesten Physisch-Chemischen, Metallurgischen, Technologischen, und Pharmaceutischen Literatur — Biblioth Neuesten Phys Chem Lit
Bibliothek des Literarischen Vereins in Stuttgart — Biblioth Lit Ver Stuttg
Bibliothek des Literarischen Vereins (Stuttgart) — BLVS
Bibliothek Klassischer Texte — Bibl Klass Texte
Bibliothek und Wissenschaft — B & W
Bibliothek und Wissenschaft — BibW
Bibliothek von Anzeigen und Auszuegen Kleiner, Meist Akademischer, Schriften — Biblioth Anz Auszuegen Kleiner Schriften
Bibliotheque Archeologique et Historique de l'Institut Francais d'Archeologie d'Istanbul — BAHIFAI
Bibliotheque Archeologique et Historique. Institut Francais d'Archeologie de Beyrouth — BAH
Bibliotheque Bonaventurienne. Series "Textes" — BBST
Bibliotheque Britannique. Sciences et Arts — Bibl Br Sci Arts
Bibliotheque de la Faculte Catholique de Theologie de Lyon — BFCTL
Bibliotheque de la Faculte de Philosophie et Lettres de l'Universite de Liege — BFPhLL
Bibliotheque de la Faculte de Philosophie et Lettres de l'Universite de Liege — BFPLUL
Bibliotheque de la Pleiade — B de P
Bibliotheque de la Pleiade — Bibl de la Pleiade
Bibliotheque de la Revue de Litterature Comparee — Bibl RLC
Bibliotheque de la Revue de Litterature Comparee — BRLC
Bibliotheque de la Revue des Cours et Conferences — Bibl de la R d C et Conf
Bibliotheque de la Revue des Cours et Conferences — Bibl de la R d Cours et Conf
Bibliotheque de la Revue des Cours et Conferences — Bibl de la Rev d C et Conf
Bibliotheque de la Revue des Cours et Conferences — Bibl de la Rev d Cours et Conf
Bibliotheque de la Revue des Cours et Conferences — Bibl de RCC
Bibliotheque de la Revue des Cours et Conferences — BRCC
Bibliotheque de la Revue d'Histoire Ecclesiastique — Biblioth de la Rev d Hist Eccles
Bibliotheque de la Societe d'Histoire Ecclesiastique de la France — Bibl de la Soc d Hist Eccl de la France
Bibliotheque de l'Ecole de Hautes Etudes — Bibl de H Et
Bibliotheque de l'Ecole de Hautes Etudes — Bibl de l Ec H Et
Bibliotheque de l'Ecole de Hautes Etudes — Bibl Ec H Et
Bibliotheque de l'Ecole des Chartes — BEC
Bibliotheque de l'Ecole des Chartes — BECh
Bibliotheque de l'Ecole des Chartes — Bibl Ec Chartes
Bibliotheque de l'Ecole des Chartes — Bibl Ecole Chartes
Bibliotheque de l'Ecole des Hautes Etudes Belfagor — BEHE
Bibliotheque de l'Institut de Droit Canonique de l'Universite de Strasbourg — BIDCUS
Bibliotheque de l'Institut Francais a l'Universite de Budapest — Bibl de l Inst Franc a l Univ de Budapest
Bibliotheque de l'Institut Francais de Florence — Bibl de l Inst Franc de Florence
Bibliotheque de Philosophie — Bibl de Philos
Bibliotheque de Philosophie Contemporaine — B Ph C
Bibliotheque de Philosophie Contemporaine — Bibl de Philos Contemp
Bibliotheque de Sociologie Contemporaine — BSC
Bibliotheque de Theologie — BT
Bibliotheque de Theologie Historique — BTH
Bibliotheque de Theologie. Serie 4. Histoire de la Theologie — Bibl Theol
Bibliotheque des Centres d'Etudes Superieures Specialisees — BCESS
Bibliotheque des Centres d'Etudes Superieures Specialisees. Travaux du Centre d'Etudes Superieures Specialisees d'Histoire de Religions de Strasbourg — BCETCEHRS
Bibliotheque des Ecoles Francaises d'Athenes et de Rome — BEAR
Bibliotheque des Ecoles Francaises d'Athenes et de Rome — BEFAR
Bibliotheque des Ecoles Francaises d'Athenes et de Rome — Bibl Ec Franc
Bibliotheque des Textes Philosophiques — Bibl Text Philos
Bibliotheque des Textes Philosophiques — BTP

Bibliotheque d'Etudes. Institute Francais d'Archeologie Orientale — Bibl IFAO
Bibliotheque d'Etudes. Institute Francais d'Archeologie Orientale — BIFAOr
Bibliotheque d'Histoire des Sciences — Bibl Hist Sci
Bibliotheque d'Histoire Litteraire et de Critique — Bibl d Hist Litt et de Critique
Bibliotheque d'Humanisme et Renaissance — BHR
Bibliotheque d'Humanisme et Renaissance — Bibl Hum R
Bibliotheque d'Humanisme et Renaissance — Bibl Hum Renaissance
Bibliotheque d'Humanisme et Renaissance — Bibl Humanisme Renaissance
Bibliotheque d'Humanisme et Renaissance — BiblH & R
Bibliotheque d'Humanisme et Renaissance — BiH
Bibliotheque d'Humanisme et Renaissance — BiHR
Bibliotheque d'Humanisme et Renaissance. Travaux et Documents — Bibl d H et Ren
Bibliotheque d'Humanisme et Renaissance. Travaux et Documents — Bibl Hum et Ren
Bibliotheque d'Humanisme et Renaissance. Travaux et Documents — Bibl Hum Renaiss
Bibliotheque du Museon (Louvain) — BML
Bibliotheque du XV Siecle — Bibl du XV S
Bibliotheque du XV Siecle — Bibl du XV Siecle
Bibliotheque. Ecole des Hautes Etudes Sciences, Philologiques, et Historiques — BEH Et
Bibliotheque Elzevirienne — Bibl Elzev
Bibliotheque Elzevirienne — Biblioth Elzev
Bibliotheque. Faculte de Philosophie et Lettres. Universite de Liege — BFLL
Bibliotheque Francaise — Bibl Franc
Bibliotheque Francaise — Biblioth Franc
Bibliotheque Francaise du Moyen Age — BFMA
Bibliotheque Francaise du Moyen Age — Bibl Franc du M A
Bibliotheque Francaise et Romane — BFR
Bibliotheque Generale Illustree — Bibl Gen Ill
Bibliotheque Historique — BH
Bibliotheque Historique des Curiosites Litteraires — Bibl Hist des Curiosites Litteraires
Bibliotheque Historique Vaudoise — Bibl Hist Vaudoise
Bibliotheque Internationale de Critique — Biblioth Intern de Critique
Bibliotheque Italienne, ou Tableau des Progres des Sciences et des Arts en Italie (Turin) — Biblioth Ital Turin
Bibliotheque Litteraire de la Renaissance — Bibl Litt de la Renaiss
Bibliotheque Litteraire de la Renaissance — Bibl Litt de la Renaissance
Bibliotheque Litteraire de la Renaissance — Bibl Litter de la Renaiss
Bibliotheque Litteraire de la Renaissance — Bibl Litter de la Renaissance
Bibliotheque Litteraire de la Renaissance — Biblioth Litt de la Renaiss
Bibliotheque Litteraire de la Renaissance — Biblioth Litt de la Renaissance
Bibliotheque Litteraire de la Renaissance — Biblioth Litteraire de la Renaiss
Bibliotheque Litteraire de la Renaissance — Biblioth Litteraire de la Renaissance
Bibliotheque Medico-Physique du Nord — Biblioth Med Phys N
Bibliotheque Meridionale — Bibl Meridionale
Bibliotheque Nationale — Bibl Nat
Bibliotheque Nationale — BN
Bibliotheque Norbertine — BN
Bibliotheque Philosophique de Louvain — Bibl Philos Louvain
Bibliotheque Scientifique Albert Blanchard — Bibl Sci Albert Blanchard
Bibliotheque Scientifique Internationale — Biblioth Sci Int
Bibliotheque. Societe pour l'Etude des Langues Africaines — Biblioth SELAF
Bibliotheque Theatrale Illustree — Bibl Theatrale Ill
Bibliotheque Universelle. Agriculture — Biblioth Universelle Agric
Bibliotheque Universelle de Geneve — Bibl Univers Geneve
Bibliotheque Universelle des Sciences, Belles Lettres, et Arts. Sciences et Arts — Bibl Univers Sci B L Arts Sci Arts
Bibliotheque Universelle et Revue de Geneve — Bibl Univers Rev Gen
Bibliotheque Universelle et Revue Suisse — Bibl Univers Rev Suisse
Bibliotheque Universelle et Revue Suisse — Bibl Universelle Rev Suisse
Bibliotheque Universelle et Revue Suisse — BURS
Bibliotheque Universelle et Revue Suisse et Etrangere. Nouvelle Periode — Bibl Univers Rev Suisse Etrang Nouv Periode
Bibliotheque Universitaire. Grenoble. Publications — Biblio Univ Grenoble Publ
Biblische Beitraege — BB
Biblische Notizen — BNo
Biblische Notizen. Beitraege zur Exegetischen Diskussion — Bib Not
Biblische Studien [*Neukirchen*] — BiblStud
Biblische Studien [*Neukirchen*] — BSt
Biblische Studien (Freiburg) — BSt(F)
Biblische Untersuchungen [*Regensburg*] — BUnt
Biblische Zeitfragen — B Zfr
Biblische Zeitfragen — B Ztfr
Biblische Zeitfragen [*Muenster*] — BZF
Biblische Zeitschrift — BbZ
Biblische Zeitschrift — Bib Z
Biblische Zeitschrift — Bib Zeit
Biblische Zeitschrift — BiblZ
Biblische Zeitschrift — BiZ
Biblische Zeitschrift — BZ
Biblischer Kommentar — BK
Biblischer Kommentar. Altes Testament — BKAT
Biblisches Reallexikon — BRL
Biblos — Bi
Biblos — Bib
BIBRA [*British Industrial Biological Research Association*] **Bulletin** — BIBRA Bull
Bickel's Coin and Medal News. Munt en Medaljenuus — Bickel C M N
Bicycle Forum — Bic Forum
Bicycles Bulletin — Bicycles Bull
Bicycling — GBIK
Bicycling News Canada — Bic N Can
BIDICS (Bond Index to the Determinations of Inorganic Crystal Structures) — BIDICS (Bond Index Determinations Inorg Cryst Struct)
Bidrag till Kaennedom af Finlands Natur och Folk — Bidr Kaennedom Finl Natur Folk
Bidrag till Kaennedom of Finlands Natur Och Folk — Bidr Kaenned Finlds Nat
Bidrag Till Kundskab Over Naturvidenskaberne — Bidrag Kundskab Naturvidensk
Biedermanns Zentralblatt — Biedermanns Zentralbl
Biedermanns Zentralblatt. Abteilung A. Allgemeiner und Referierender Teil — Biedermanns Zentralbl Abt A
Biedermanns Zentralblatt. Abteilung B. Tierernaehrung — Biedermanns Zentralbl Abt B
Biekorf — B
Bielefeld Encounters in Physics and Mathematics — Bielefeld Encount Phys Math
Bielefelder Beitraege zur Ausbildungsforschung und Studienreform — Bielefelder Beitr Ausbildungsforsch Studienreform
Bienen-Blatt fuer des Bundesgebiet — Bienenbl Bundesgebiet
Bienenwirtschaftliches Zentralblatt — Bienenw Zbl
Bienen-Zeitung — Bienen Ztg
Bien-Etre Social Canadien — Bien-Etre Soc Canadien
Biennial Anaerobe Discussion Group International Symposium — Bienn Anaerobe Discuss Group Int Symp
Biennial Conference. Carbon. Extended Abstracts and Program — Bienn Conf Carbon Ext Abstr Program
Biennial Congress. International Deep Drawing Research Group — Bienn Congr Int Deep Drawing Res Group
Biennial Congress. International Solar Energy Society — Bienn Congr Int Sol Energy Soc
Biennial International CODATA [*Committee on Data for Science and Technology*] **Conference** — Bienn Int CODATA Conf
Biennial Report. California State Board of Forestry — Bienn Rep Calif State Board Forest
Biennial Report. California Waste Management Board — Bien Rep Cal Waste Man Bd
Biennial Report. Hawaii Agricultural Experiment Station — Bien Rep Hawaii Agr Exp Sta
Biennial Report. Hawaii Institute of Geophysics — Bienn Rep Hawaii Geophys
Biennial Report. Hawaii Institute of Geophysics — Bienn Rep Hawaii Inst Geophys
Biennial Report. Iowa. Book of Agriculture. Iowa State Department of Agriculture — Bien Rep Iowa Book Agr
Biennial Report. Meat Research Institute — Bien Rep Meat Res Ins
Biennial Report. Nevada State Department of Agriculture — Bien Rep Nev State Dept Agr
Biennial Review of Anthropology — Bienn Rev Anthropol
Biennial. Studi Storia Arte Medicina — Bienn Studi Stor Arte Med
Biergrosshandel. Zeitschrift fuer den Gesamten Biergrosshandel und Getrankegrosshandel — BIK
Bifidobacteria and Microflora — Bifidobact Microflora
Big Deal — Big D
Big Farm Management — Big Farm Manage
Big Mama Rag — Big Mama
Big Sky Economics. Montana State University. Cooperative Extension Service — Big Sky Econ Mont Stat Univ Coop Ext Serv
Big Table — BT
Bigaku — B
Bihang till Kongliga Svenska Vetenskaps-Akademiens Handlingar (Stockholm) — Bihang K Svenska Vetensk-Akad Handl (Stockholm)
Bihar Academy of Agricultural Sciences. Proceedings — Bihar Acad Agr Sci Proc
Bihar and Orissa Research Society. Journal — BORS
Bihar Research Society. Journal — BRS
Bijblad bij de Industriele Eigendom — BIE
Bijblad bij de Industriele Eigendom — Bijbl I E
Bijblad bij de Industriele Eigendom — Bijbl Ind Eig
Bijblad op het Staatsblad — Bb
Bijdrage tot de Kennis der Boomsoorten van Java — Bijd Kennis Boomsoorten Java
Bijdragen — Bi
Bijdragen en Mededeelingen der Dialectencommissie van de Koninklijke Akademie van Wetenschappen te Amsterdam — Bijdragen Dialectencommissie
Bijdragen en Mededeelingen der Dialectencommissie van de Koninklijke Akademie van Wetenschappen te Amsterdam — BMD
Bijdragen en Mededeelingen der Dialectencommissie van de Koninklijke Akademie van Wetenschappen te Amsterdam — BMDial
Bijdragen en Mededeelingen Uitgegeven door de Vereeniging Geire — BMGeire
Bijdragen en Mededeelingen van het Genootschap voor de Joodsche Wetenschap in Nederland — BMGJW
Bijdragen en Mededeelingen van het Historisch Genootschap — BMHG
Bijdragen en Mededelingen Betreffende de Geschiedenis der Nederlanden — BMGN
Bijdragen. Tijdschrift voor Filosofie en Theologie [*Nijmegen/Brugge*] — Bijdr
Bijdragen tot de Dierkunde — Bijd Dierkunde
Bijdragen tot de Dierkunde — Bijdr Dierk
Bijdragen tot de Dierkunde — Bijdr Dierkd
Bijdragen tot de Dierkunde — BJDIAD
Bijdragen tot de Geschiedenis — BG
Bijdragen tot de Geschiedenis Bijzonderlijk van het Aloude Hertogdom Brabant — BGHB
Bijdragen tot de Geschiedenis der Geneeskunde. Nederlandsche Maatschappij tot Bevordering der Geneeskunst — Bijdr Gesch Geneesk
Bijdragen tot de Geschiedenis Inzonderheid van het oud Hertogdom Brabant — BGIHB

Bijdragen tot de Taal, Land- en Volkenkunde — Bijd Volk
Bijdragen tot de Taal- Land- en Volkenkunde van Nederlandsch-Indie — Bijd Volk Ned Indie
Bijdragen tot de Taal-Land- en Volkenkunde — Bijdrag Taal-Land- Volkenk
Bijdragen tot de Taal-Land- en Volkenkunde — Bijdragen
Bijdragen tot de Taal-Land- en Volkenkunde — BijdrTLV
Bijdragen tot de Taal-Land- en Volkenkunde — BTLV
Bijdragen tot de Taal-Land- en Volkenkunde van Nederlandsche-Indie — Bijdr Taal- Land-en Volkenk Nederl-Indie
Bijdragen tot de Taal-Land- en Volkenkunde van Nederlandsche-Indie — Bijdragen Nederl-Indie
Bijdragen tot de Taal-Land- en Volkenkunde van Nederlandsche-Indie — BTLVNI
Bijdragen Uitgegeven door en Philosophische en Theologische Faculteiten der Noord- en Zuid-Nederlandse Jezuieten — BFNJ
Bijdragen van de Philosophische en Theologische Faculteiten der Nederlandsche Jezuieten — BP
Bijdragen voor de Geschiedenis der Nederlanden — BGN
Bijdragen voor de Geschiedenis der Nederlanden — Bijdr Gesch Ndl
Bijdragen voor de Geschiedenis der Nederlanden — Bijdr Gesch Nederl
Bijdragen voor de Geschiedenis van de Provincie der Minderbroeders in de Nederlanden — BGPMN
Bijdragen voor de Geschiedenis van het Bisdom van Haarlem — BGBH
Bijdragen voor Vaderlandsche Geschiedenis en Oudheidskunde — BVG
Bijdragen voor Vaderlandsche Geschiedenis en Oudheidskunde — BVGO
Bijlagen bij de Handelingen van de Tweede Kamer der Staten Generaal — Bijl Hand Tw K der St Gen
Bijvoegsel tot het Staatsblad — Bijv Stb
Bijvoegsel tot het Staatsblad — BS
Bijzondere Publicaties van het Bosbouwproefstation/Pengumuman Isti Mewa Balai Penjelidiken Kehutanan — Bijzondere Publ Bosbouwproefstat
Biken Journal — Biken J
Biken Journal — BIKJA
Bilateral Seminars. International Bureau — Bilateral Semin Int Bur
Bild der Wissenschaft — Bild Wiss
Bild der Wissenschaft — BIWIA
Bild und Ton — BITOA
Bildende Kunst — BK
Bilder Griechischen Vasen — BV
Bildung und Erziehung — Bildung Erzieh
Bile Acid Meeting. Proceedings — Bile Acid Meet Proc
Bile Acid Metabolism in Health and Disease. Proceedings of the Bile Acid Meeting — Bile Acid Metab Health Dis Proc Bile Acid Meet
Bile Acids as Therapeutic Agents. From Basic Science to Clinical Practice. Proceedings. Falk Symposium — Bile Acids Ther Agents Proc Falk Symp
Bilingual Education Paper Series — Biling Ed Pap Ser
Bilingual Review — BR
Bilingual Review/Revista Bilingue — Biling Rev
Bilingual Review/Revista Bilingue — BR/RB
Bilirubin Metabolism in the Newborn. International Symposium — Bilirubin Metab Newborn Int Symp
Biljeske. Institut za Oceanografiju i Ribarstvo (Split) — Biljeske Inst Oceanogr Ribar (Split)
Bill of Rights Journal — Bill Rights J
Billboard — BB
Billboard — BILLA
Billboard — GBIL
Billboard Country Music Sourcebook — Billboard Co Mus Sour
Billboard Information Network [*Database*] — BIN
Billboard International Audio Video Tape Directory — Billboard Int Aud Vid Tape Dir
Billboard International Buyer's Guide — Billboard Int Buy G
Billboard International Recording Equipment and Studio Directory — Billboard Int Rec Equip St Dir
Billboard International Talent and Touring Directory — Billboard Int Tal Tour Dir
Billings Gazette — BIZ
Billings Geological Society. Annual Field Conference. Guidebook — Billings Geol Soc Annu Field Conf Guideb
Bilten Dokumentacije — BDGAA
Bilten Dokumentacije [*Yugoslavia*] — Bilt Dok
Bilten. Drushtvo na Matematicharite i Fizicharite od Narodna Republika Makedonija — Bilten Drushtvo Mat Fiz Nar Repub Makedonija
Bilten Poslovnog Udruzenja Proizvodaca Biljnih Ulja i Masti — Bilt Poslovnog Udruzenja Proizvodaca Biljnih Ulja Masti
Bilten Poslovnog Udruzenja Proizvodaca Biljnih Ulja i Masti — BPUPBQ
Bilten za Farmaceutskoto Drustvo za Makedonija — Bilt Farm Drus Maked
Bilten za Farmaceutskoto Drustvo za Socijalisticka Republika Makedonija — Bilt Farm Drus Soc Repub Makedonija
Bilten za Hematologiju i Transfuziju — Bilt Hematol Transfuz
Bilten za Hmelj i Sirak — Bilt Hmelj Sirak
Bilten za Hmelj Sirak i Lekovito Bilje — Bilt Hmelj Sirak Lek Bilje
Bilten za Sojuzot za Zdruzenijata za Farmacevtite i Farmacevtskite Tehnicari za SR Makedonija — Bilt Sojuzot Zdruzenijata Farm Farm Teh SR Maked
Bilychnis — Bil
Bi-Monthly Bulletin. North Dakota Agricultural Experiment Station — Bi-M Bull N Dak Agric Exp Stn
Bimonthly Business Review — Bimon Bus Rev
Bi-Monthly Law Review — Bi Mo Law R
Bimonthly Research Notes. Canada Department of Environment — BMRN
Bi-Monthly Research Notes. Canada Department of Forestry — Bi-M Res Notes Canada Dep For
BIN [*Boreal Institute for Northern Studies*] **Bibliographic Series** — BIN Bibliogr Ser
Binnenschiffahrts-Nachrichten — Binnenschiffahrts-Nachr
Binnenschiffahrts-Nachrichten — BSNRB
Bio Med — BOMDD
Bio Medical Instrumentation — Bio Med Instrum
Bio Membrane News CSIRO [*Commonwealth Scientific and Industrial Research Organisation*] **Biomembrane Committee** — CSIRO Bio Mem News
Bio Systems — Bio Syst
Bio/Technology — BT
Bio/Technology. The International Monthly for Industrial Biology — Biotechnol
Bio Times — BTMSD
Bioactive Molecules — Bioact Mol
Bioantioksidanty v Luchevom Porazhenii i Zlokachestvennom Roste — Bioantioksidant Luchevom Porazhenii Zlokach Roste
Biobehavioral Reviews — Biobehav Rev
Biocatalysis and Biotransformation — Biocatal Biotransform
Bioceramics and the Human Body. Proceedings. International Congress — Bioceram Hum Body Proc Int Congr
Biochemia Clinica Bohemoslovaca — Biochem Clin Bohemoslov
Biochemical Actions of Hormones — Biochem Actions Horm
Biochemical Analysis of Membranes — Biochem Anal Membr
Biochemical and Biophysical Perspectives in Marine Biology — Biochem Biophys Perspect Mar Biol
Biochemical and Biophysical Research Communications — BBRCA
Biochemical and Biophysical Research Communications — Bioc Biop R
Biochemical and Biophysical Research Communications — Biochem Biophys Res Commun
Biochemical and Clinical Aspects of Pteridines — Biochem Clin Aspects Pteridines
Biochemical and Molecular Medicine — Biochem Mol Med
Biochemical and Structural Dynamics of the Cell Nucleus — Biochem Struct Dyn Cell Nucl
Biochemical Archives — Biochem Arch
Biochemical Aspects of Plant Parasite Relationships. Proceedings of the Symposium — Biochem Aspects Plant Parasite Relat Proc Symp
Biochemical Bulletin (New York) — Biochem Bull (NY)
Biochemical Clinics — Biochem Clin
Biochemical Correlates of Brain Structure and Function — Biochem Correl Brain Struct Funct
Biochemical Education [*England*] — Biochem Educ
Biochemical Effects of Environmental Pollutants — Biochem Eff Environ Pollut
Biochemical Endocrinology — Biochem Endocrinol
Biochemical Engineering. Stuttgart. Proceedings. International Symposium on Biochemical Engineering — Biochem Eng Stuttgart Proc Int Symp
Biochemical Genetics — BIGEB
Biochemical Genetics — Biochem Gen
Biochemical Genetics — Biochem Genet
Biochemical Interaction between Plants and Insects — Biochem Interact Plants Insects
Biochemical Journal — BIJOA
Biochemical Journal — Biochem J
Biochemical Journal. Molecular Aspects — Biochem J Mol Asp
Biochemical Medicine — BIMDA
Biochemical Medicine — Biochem Med
Biochemical Medicine and Metabolic Biology — Biochem Med Metab Biol
Biochemical Medicine and Metabolic Biology — BMMBES
Biochemical Methods for Monitoring Risk Pregnancies — Biochem Methods Monit Risk Pregnancies
Biochemical Pharmacology — BCPCA
Biochemical Pharmacology — Bioch Pharm
Biochemical Pharmacology — Biochem Pharmac
Biochemical Pharmacology — Biochem Pharmacol
Biochemical Preparations — Biochem Prep
Biochemical Problems of Lipids. Proceedings. International Conference — Biochem Probl Lipids Proc Int Conf
Biochemical Reviews (Bangalore) — Biochem Rev (Bangalore)
Biochemical Society. Special Publications — Biochem Soc Spec Publ
Biochemical Society. Symposia — Biochem Soc Symp
Biochemical Society. Symposia — BSSYA
Biochemical Society. Transactions — BCSTB
Biochemical Society. Transactions — Bioch Soc T
Biochemical Society. Transactions — Biochem Soc Trans
Biochemical Spectroscopy — Biochem Spectros
Biochemical Systematics [*Later, Biochemical Systematics and Ecology*] — Biochem Syst
Biochemical Systematics and Ecology — Biochem Syst Ecol
Biochemie und Physiologie der Pflanzen — Bioc Phy Pf
Biochemie und Physiologie der Pflanzen — Biochem Physiol Pflanz
Biochemie und Physiologie der Pflanzen — BPP
Biochemie und Physiologie der Pflanzen. BPP — Biochem Physiol Pflanz BPP
Biochemija Tarybu Lietuvoje — Biochem Tarybu Lietuvoje
Biochemische Befunde in der Differentialdiagnose Innerer Krankheiten — Biochem Befunde Differentialdiag Inn Kr
Biochemische Zeitschrift — Biochem Z
Biochemische Zeitschrift — BIZEA
Biochemisches Centralblatt — Biochem Centralbl
Biochemistry — BICHA
Biochemistry — Biochem
Biochemistry [*English Translation*] — BIORA
Biochemistry: a Series of Monographs — Biochem Ser Monogr
Biochemistry and Cell Biology — BCBIEQ
Biochemistry and Cell Biology — Biochem Cell Biol
Biochemistry and Cytology of Plant Parasite Interaction Symposium — Biochem Cytol Plant Parasite Interact Symp
Biochemistry and Experimental Biology — BEXBB
Biochemistry and Experimental Biology — Biochem Exp Biol
Biochemistry and Molecular Biology International — Biochem Mol Biol Int
Biochemistry and Molecular Biology of Fishes — Biochem Mol Biol Fishes
Biochemistry and Neurological Disease — Biochem Neurol Dis

Biochemistry and Pathology of Connective Tissue — Biochem Pathol Connect Tissue
Biochemistry and Physiology of Substance Abuse — Biochem Physiol Subst Abuse
Biochemistry (English Translation of Biokhimiya) — Biochemistry (Engl Transl Biokhimiya)
Biochemistry International — Biochem Int
Biochemistry. Life Science Advances — Biochem Life Sci Adv
Biochemistry of Adenosylmethionine. Proceedings of an International Symposium on the Biochemistry of Adenosylmethionine — Biochem Adenosylmethionine Proc Int Symp
Biochemistry of Animal Development — Biochem Anima Dev
Biochemistry of Bacterial Growth. 2nd Edition — Biochem Bact Growth 2nd Ed
Biochemistry of Cell Differentiation — Biochem Cell Differ
Biochemistry of Cell Differentiation. Federation of European Biochemical Societies. Meeting — Biochem Cell Differ Fed Eur Biochem Soc Meet
Biochemistry of Collagen — Biochem Collagen
Biochemistry of Copper — Biochem Copper
Biochemistry of Cutaneous Epidermal Differentiation. Proceedings of the Japan-US Seminar on Biochemistry of Cutaneous Epidermal Differentiation — Biochem Cutaneous Epidermal Differ Proc Jpn US Semin
Biochemistry of Development — Biochem Dev
Biochemistry of Disease — Biochem Dis
Biochemistry of Disease (New York) — Biochem Dis (NY)
Biochemistry of Exercise. Proceedings of the International Symposium on Exercise Biochemistry — Biochem Exercise Proc Int Symp
Biochemistry of Folic Acid and Related Pteridines — Biochem Folic Acid Relat Pteridines
Biochemistry of Lipids, Lipoproteins, and Membranes — Biochem Lipids Lipoproteins Membr
Biochemistry of Membrane Transport — Biochem Membr Transp
Biochemistry of Parasites and Host Parasite Relationships. Proceedings of the International Symposium on the Biochemistry of Parasites and Host Parasite Relationships — Biochem Parasites Host Parasite Relat Proc Int Symp
Biochemistry of Peptide Antibiotics [*Monograph*] — Biochem Pept Antibiot
Biochemistry of Plants. A Comprehensive Treatise — Biochem Plants Compr Treatise
Biochemistry of Sensory Functions — Biochem Sens Funct
Biochemistry of Smooth Muscle. Proceedings of the Symposium — Biochem Smooth Muscle Proc Symp
Biochemistry of the Acute Allergic Reactions. International Symposium — Biochem Acute Allerg React Int Symp
Biochemistry of the Developing Brain — Biochem Developing Brain
Biochemistry of Women. Clinical Concepts — Biochem Women Clin Concepts
Biochemistry of Women. Methods for Clinical Investigation — Biochem Women Methods Clin Invest
Biochemistry of Wood — B o W
Biochemistry. Series One — Biochemistry Ser One
Biochemistry-USSR — Biochem SSR
Biochimica Applicata — Biochim Appl
Biochimica e Biologia Sperimentale — BBSPA
Biochimica e Biologia Sperimentale — Biochim Biol Sper
Biochimica e Terapia Sperimentale — Biochim Ter Sper
Biochimica et Biophysica Acta — BBA
Biochimica et Biophysica Acta — BBACA
Biochimica et Biophysica Acta — Bioc Biop A
Biochimica et Biophysica Acta — Biochim Biophys Acta
Biochimica et Biophysica Acta. B. Bioenergetics — Biochim Biophys Acta B
Biochimica et Biophysica Acta. B. Bioenergetics — Biochim Biophys Acta Bioenerg
Biochimica et Biophysica Acta. BR. Reviews on Bioenergetics — Biochim Biophys Acta BR
Biochimica et Biophysica Acta. Enzymology — BBEZA
Biochimica et Biophysica Acta. Enzymology — Biochim Biophys Acta Enzymol
Biochimica et Biophysica Acta. G. General Subjects — BBGSB
Biochimica et Biophysica Acta. G. General Subjects — Biochim Biophys Acta G
Biochimica et Biophysica Acta. G. General Subjects — Biochim Biophys Acta General Subjects
Biochimica et Biophysica Acta/International Journal of Biochemistry and Biophysics — Biochim Biophys Acta Int J Biochem Biophys
Biochimica et Biophysica Acta. Library — Biochim Biophys Acta Libr
Biochimica et Biophysica Acta. Lipids and Lipid Metabolism — Biochim Biophys Acta Lipids Lipid Metab
Biochimica et Biophysica Acta. M. Biomembranes — BBBMB
Biochimica et Biophysica Acta. M. Biomembranes — Biochim Biophys Acta Biomembranes
Biochimica et Biophysica Acta. M. Biomembranes — Biochim Biophys Acta M
Biochimica et Biophysica Acta. MR. Reviews on Biomembranes — Biochim Biophys Acta MR
Biochimica et Biophysica Acta. Nucleic Acids and Protein Synthesis — BBNPA
Biochimica et Biophysica Acta. Nucleic Acids and Protein Synthesis — Biochim Biophys Acta Nucl Acids Protein Synth
Biochimica et Biophysica Acta. P. Protein Structure — BBPTB
Biochimica et Biophysica Acta. P. Protein Structure — Biochim Biophys Acta P
Biochimica et Biophysica Acta. P. Protein Structure — Biochim Biophys Acta Protein Struct
Bioclimat Numero Special — Bioclimat Numero Spec
Biocomplex Investigation in Kazakhstan — Biocomplex Invest Kaz
Bioconjugate Chemistry — Bioconjug Chem
Bioconjugate Chemistry — Bioconjugate Chem
BioCycle — BCYCD
Biodeterioration Investigation Techniques — Biodeterior Invest Tech
Biodeterioration Research Titles — Biodeter Res Titles
Biodynamica — BIODA
Bioelectrochemistry and Bioenergetics — BEBEBP
Bioelectrochemistry and Bioenergetics — Bioelectr B
Bioelectrochemistry and Bioenergetics — Bioelectrochem Bioenerg
Bioelectrochemistry Principles and Practice — Bioelectrochem Prin Pract
Bio-energy Directory — Bioen Dir
Bio-Energy Re-News — BERND
Bioengineering Abstracts — Bioeng Abstr
Bioethics Quarterly — Bioethics Q
Bioethius. Texte und Abhandlungen zur Geschichte der Exakten Wissenschaften — Bioethius Texte Abh Gesch Exakt Wissensch
Biofeedback and Self-Regulation — BGGPB
Biofeedback and Self-Regulation — Biofeedback and Self-Regul
Biofeedback and Self-Regulation — Biofeedback Self-Regul
Biofizika — BIOFA
Biofizika — Biofiz
Biofizika i Biokhimiya Myshechnogo Sokrashcheniya — Biofiz Biokhim Myshechnogo Sokrashcheniya
Biofizika i Radiobiologiya — Biofiz Radiobiol
Biofizika Rastenii. Materialy Vsesoyuznogo Simpoziuma po Molekulyarnoi i Prikladnoi Biofizike Rastenii — Biofiz Rast Mater Vses Simp Mol Prikl Biofiz Rast
Biofizika Zhivoi Kletki — Biofiz Zhivoi Kletki
Biofuels Report — BFRPD
Biofuels Report — Biofuels Rep
Biogas and Alcohol Fuels Production — BAFPD
Biogas and Alcohol Fuels Production — Biogas Alcohol Fuels Prod
Biogenic Amines — Biog Amine
Biogenic Amines — Biog Amines
Biogeochemistry — Biogeochemi
Biogeochemistry of Devils Lake, North Dakota — Biogeochem Devils Lake ND
Biogeograficheskaya Nauchnaya Konferentsiya Materialy — Biogeogr Nauchn Konf Mater
Biogeokhimiya Diageneza Osadkov Okeana — Biogeokhim Diageneza Osadkov Okeana
Biografias [*Database*] — BIOG
Biographical Directory. American Political Science Association — Biograph Dir Am Pol Sci Ass
Biographical Memoirs. Fellows of the Royal Society — Biogr Mem Fellows R Soc
Biographical Memoirs. Fellows of the Royal Society — Biogr Mem Fellows Roy Soc
Biographical Memoirs. National Academy of Sciences — Biogr Mem Natl Acad Sci
Biographical Memoirs. National Academy of Sciences (United States of America) — Biogr Mem Nat Acad Sci (USA)
Biographical Memoirs. Royal Society — Biog Mem R Soc
Biographie Nationale. Academie Royale des Sciences, des Lettres, et des Beaux-Arts de Belgique — Biogr Nat Acad Roy Belg
Biographien Hervorragender Naturwissenschaftler, Techniker, und Mediziner — Biogr Hervorragender Naturwiss Tech Med
Biographien Hervorragender Naturwissenschaftler, Techniker, und Mediziner — Biograph Hervorrag Naturwiss Tech Medizin
Biographisches Jahrbuch fuer Altertumskunde — Biogr Jb Altertskde
Biographoi. Vitarum Scriptores Graeci Minores — BGM
Biographoi. Vitarum Scriptores Graeci Minores — Biogr Gr
Biography and Genealogy Master Index — BGMI
Biography Index — Biog Ind
Biography Index — Biogr Index
Biography Index — Biol
Biography News — BN
Bioinorganic Chemistry — BICHB
Bioinorganic Chemistry — Bioinorg Ch
Bioinorganic Chemistry — Bioinorg Chem
Bio-Joule Newsletter [*Canada*] — Bio-Joule Newsl
Biokhimicheskaya Genetika Ryb. Materialy Vsesoyuznogo Soveshchaniya po Biokhimicheskoi Genetike Ryb — Biokhim Genet Ryb Mater Vses Soveshch
Biokhimicheskie Aspekty Introduktsii Otdalennoi Gibridizatsii i Filogenii Rastenii — Biokhim Aspekty Introd Otdalennoi Gibrid Filogenii Rast
Biokhimicheskie i Tekhnologicheskie Protsessy v Pishchevoi Promyshlennosti — Biokhim Tekhnol Protsessy Pishch Promsti
Biokhimicheskie Issledovaniya v Protsesse Selektsii Kukuruzy — Biokhim Issled Protsesse Sel Kukuruzy
Biokhimicheskie Metody Issledovaniya v Gigiene — Biokhim Metody Issled Gig
Biokhimichna Zhurnal — Biokhim Zh
Biokhimiya [*Moscow*] — BIOHA
Biokhimiya — Biokhim
Biokhimiya Chainogo Proizvodstva — Biokhim Chain Prozvod
Biokhimiya Kul'turnykh Rastenii Moldavu — Biokhim Kul't Rast Mold
Biokhimiya Nasekomykh — Biokhim Nasekomykh
Biokhimiya Plodov i Ovoshchei — Biokhim Plodov Ovoshchei
Biokhimiya Rastenii — Biokhim Rast
Biokhimiya v Litovskoi SSR. Materialy S'ezda Biokhimikov Litovskoi SSR — Biokhim Lit SSR Mater S'ezda Biokhim Lit SSR
Biokhimiya Vinodeliya — Biokhim Vinodel
Biokhimiya Zerna i Khlebopeeheniya — Biokhim Zerna Khlebopeeh
Biokompleksnye Issledovaniya v Kazakhstane — Biokompleksnye Issled Kaz
Biokon Reports — Biokon Rep
Biologia — Biol
Biologia [*Budapest*] — BIOLD5
Biologia [*Bratislava*] — BLOAA
Biologia Acuatica — Biol Acuatica
Biologia Africana — Biol Afr
Biologia (Bratislava) — Biol (Bratislava)
Biologia. Casopis Slovenskej Akademie vied Bratislava — Biologia Bratisl
Biologia Contemporanea — BICODM

Biologia Contemporanea — Biol Contemp
Biologia Culturale — BioC
Biologia Culturale — Biol Culturale
Biologia et Industria — Biol Ind
Biologia Gabonica — Biol Gabonica
Biologia Gallo-Hellenica — Biol Gallo-Hell
Biologia Gallo-Hellenica — Biol Gallo-Hellenica
Biologia Generalis — Biol Gen
Biologia Medica (Niteroi, Brazil) — Biol Med (Niteroi Brazil)
Biologia Neonatorum [*Later, Biology of the Neonate*] — BINEA
Biologia Neonatorum [*Later, Biology of Neonate*] — BINEAA
Biologia Neonatorum [*Later, Biology of Neonate*] — Biol Neonat
Biologia Neonatorum [*Later, Biology of the Neonate*] — Biol Neonatorum
Biologia Pesquera — Biol Pesq
Biologia Plantarum — Biol Plant
Biologia Plantarum — Biologia Pl
Biologia Plantarum [*Prague*] — BPABA
Biologia Plantarum [*Prague*] — BPABAJ
Biologia Plantarum (Prague) — Biol Plant (Prague)
Biologia w Szkole — Biol Szkole
Biologia y Clinica Hematologica — Biol Clin Hematol
Biologiai Koezlemenyek — BIKOA
Biologiai Koezlemenyek — Biol Koezl
Biologiai Koezlemenyek — Biol Koezlem
Biologiai Koezlemenyek — Biol Kozl
Biologiai Koezlemenyek. Pars Biologica — Biol Koezlem Pars Biol
Biologic Effects of Light. Proceedings of a Symposium — Biol Eff Light Proc Symp
Biologica Latina — Biol Lat
Biologica Latina — Biologica Lat
Biologica. Trabajos. Instituto de Biologia "Juan Noe." Facultad de Medicina de la Universidad de Chile — Biol Trab Inst Biol "Juan Noe" Fac Med Univ Chile
Biological Abstracts — BA
Biological Abstracts — BioAb
Biological Abstracts — Biol Abs
Biological Abstracts — Biol Abstr
Biological Abstracts on Compact Disc — BA on CD
Biological Abstracts on Tape [*Database*] — BAT
Biological Abstracts/Reports, Reviews, Meetings [*Formerly, BIOI*] — BA/RRM
Biological Abstracts/RRM [*Reports, Reviews, Meetings*] — Biol Abstr RRM
Biological Actions of Dimethyl Sulfoxide — Biol Actions Dimethyl Sulfoxide
Biological Agriculture and Horticulture — BAH
Biological Agriculture and Horticulture — Biol Agric & Hortic
Biological Agriculture and Horticulture. An International Journal — Biol Agric Hort Int J
Biological Amplification Systems in Immunology — Biol Amplification Syst Immunol
Biological and Agricultural Index — BAI
Biological and Agricultural Index — BioAg
Biological and Agricultural Index — Biol Agric Index
Biological and Agricultural Index — Biol & Agr Ind
Biological and Artificial Membranes and Desalination of Water. Proceedings of the Study Week — Biol Artif Membr Desalin Water Proceed Study Week
Biological and Clinical Aspects of the Fetus — Biol Clin Aspects Fetus
Biological and Clinical Basis of Radiosensitivity. Report. Proceedings. Conference — Biol Clin Basis Radiosensitivity Rep Proc Conf
Biological and Environmental Effects of Low Level Radiation. Proceedings of a Symposium on Biological Effects of Low Level Radiation Pertinent to Protection of Man and His Environment — Biol Environ Eff Low Level Radiat Proc Symp
Biological and Pharmaceutical Bulletin — Biol Pharm Bull
Biological Applications of Electron Spin Resonance — Biol Appl Electron Spin Reson
Biological Aspects of Inorganic Chemistry. Symposium — Bil Aspects Inorg Chem Symp
Biological Asymmetry and Handedness — Biol Asymmetry Handedness
Biological Basis of Clinical Effect of Bleomycin — Biol Basis Clin Eff Bleomycin
Biological Board of Canada. Bulletin — Biol Board Can Bull
Biological Bulletin — Biol B
Biological Bulletin — Biol Bul
Biological Bulletin — Biol Bull
Biological Bulletin — PBIB
Biological Bulletin. Department of Biology. College of Science. Tunghai University — Biol Bull Dep Biol Coll Sci Tunghai Univ
Biological Bulletin. Marine Biological Laboratory (Woods Hole) [*Massachusetts*] — Biol Bull Mar Biol Lab (Woods Hole)
Biological Bulletin of India — Biol Bull India
Biological Bulletin of Poznan — Biol Bull Poznan
Biological Bulletin (Woods Hole) [*Massachusetts*] — Biol Bull (Woods Hole)
Biological Chemistry — Biol Chem
Biological Chemistry Hoppe-Seyler — Biol Chem Hoppe-Seyler
Biological Conference "Oholo." Annual Meeting — Biol Conf "Oholo" Annu Meet
Biological Conservation — BICOB
Biological Conservation — Biol Conser
Biological Conservation — Biol Conserv
Biological Council Series. Drug Action at the Molecular Level — Biol Counc Ser Drug Action Mol Level
Biological Cybernetics — BICYA
Biological Cybernetics — Biol Cybern
Biological Cybernetics — Biol Cybernet
Biological Cybernetics — Biol Cybernetics
Biological Diagnosis of Brain Disorders. Proceedings. International Conference — Biol Diag Brain Disord Proc Int Conf
Biological Effects of Asbestos. Proceedings. Working Conference — Biol Eff Asbestos Proc Work Conf
Biological Effects of Heavy Metals — Biol Eff Heavy Met
Biological Effects of Neutron Irradiation. Proceedings. Symposium. Effects of Neutron Irradiation upon Cell Function — Biol Eff Neutron Irradiat Proc Symp
Biological Effects of Nonionizing Radiation. Conference — Biol Eff Nonioniz Radiat Conf
Biological Fraternity — Biol Fraternity
Biological Handbooks — Biol Handb
Biological Identification with Computers. Proceedings of a Meeting — Biol Identif Comput Proc Meet
Biological Implications of Metals in the Environment. Proceedings of the Annual Hanford Life Sciences Symposium — Biol Implic Met Environ Proc Annu Hanford Life Sci Symp
Biological Journal — Biol J
Biological Journal. Linnean Society — Biol J Linn
Biological Journal. Linnean Society — Biol J Linn Soc
Biological Journal. Linnean Society of London — Biol J Linn Soc Lond
Biological Journal. Nara Women's University — Biol J Nara Women's Univ
Biological Journal. Okayama University — Biol J Okayama Univ
Biological Laboratory of Owens College. Manchester University. Studies — Biol Lab Owens Coll Stud
Biological Macromolecules — Biol Macromol
Biological Macromolecules and Assemblies — Biol Macromol Assem
Biological Magazine/Okinawa Seibutsu Gekhai — Biol Mag
Biological Mass Spectrometry — Biol Mass S
Biological Mass Spectrometry — Biol Mass Spectrom
Biological Membranes — Biol Membr
Biological Memoirs — Biol Mem
Biological Memoirs — BMEMDK
Biological Monitoring of Exposure to Chemicals. Metals — Biol Monit Exposure Chem Met
Biological Monitoring of Water and Effluent Quality. Symposium — Biol Monit Water Effluent Qual Symp
Biological Notes. Illinois Natural History Survey — Biol Notes
Biological Notes. Illinois Natural History Survey — Biol Notes Ill Nat Hist Surv
Biological Oceanography — Biol Oceanogr
Biological Oceanography — BOJODV
Biological Papers. University of Alaska — Biol Pap Univ Alaska
Biological Papers. University of Alaska — BPUA
Biological Papers. University of Alaska. Special Report — Biol Pap Univ Alaska Spec Rep
Biological Papers. University of Alaska. Special Report — BPUASR
Biological Properties. Mammalian Surface Membrane. Symposium — Biol Prop Mamm Surf Membr Symp
Biological Psychiatry — Biol Psychi
Biological Psychiatry — Biol Psychiatry
Biological Psychiatry — BIPCB
Biological Psychology — Biol Psychol
Biological Psychology — BLPYA
Biological Psychology Bulletin — Biol Psych Bul
Biological Psychology Bulletin [*Oklahoma City*] — BPCBAT
Biological Psychology Bulletin (Oklahoma City) — Biol Psychol Bull (Okla City)
Biological Reactive Intermediates, Formation Toxicity, and Inactivation. Proceedings of an International Conference on Active Intermediates, Formation Toxicity, and Inactivation — Biol React Intermed Proc Int Conf
Biological Regulation and Development — Biol Regul Dev
Biological Research [*Santiago*] — Biol Res
Biological Research in Pregnancy and Perinatology — Biol Res Pregnancy Perinatol
Biological Research in Pregnancy and Perinatology — BRPPDH
Biological Research Reports. University of Jyvaeskylae — Biol Res Rep Univ Jyvaeskylae
Biological Resources and Natural Conditions. Mongolian People's Republic — Biol Resour Nat Cond Mong People's Repub
Biological Review. City College of New York — Biol Rev City Coll NY
Biological Reviews — Biol R
Biological Reviews — Biol Rs
Biological Reviews. Cambridge Philosophical Society — Biol Rev
Biological Reviews. Cambridge Philosophical Society — Biol Rev Camb Philos Soc
Biological Reviews. Cambridge Philosophical Society — Biol Rev Cambridge Phil Soc
Biological Reviews. Cambridge Philosophical Society — BRCPA
Biological Reviews. Cambridge Philosophical Society — PBIR
Biological Rhythms in Neuroendocrine Activity — Biol Rhythms Neuroendocr Act
Biological Role of Porphyrins and Related Structures. Papers. Conference — Biol Role Porphyrins Relat Struct Pap Conf
Biological Roles of Sialic Acid — Biol Roles Sialic Acid
Biological Science — Biol Sci
Biological Science Bulletin. University of Arizona — Biol Sci Bull Univ Arizona
Biological Science (Tokyo) — Biol Sci (Tokyo)
Biological Sciences Curriculum Study. Bulletin — BCUBAS
Biological Sciences Curriculum Study. Bulletin — Biol Sci Curric Study Bull
Biological Sciences Curriculum Study. Bulletin — Biol Sci Curriculum Study Bull
Biological Signals — Biol Signals
Biological Signals. Proceedings of a Symposium — Biol Signals Proc Symp
Biological Society of Nevada. Memoirs — Biol Soc Nev Mem
Biological Society of Nevada. Occasional Papers — Biol Soc Nev Occas Pap
Biological Society of Pakistan. Monograph — Biol Soc Pak Monogr
Biological Society of Washington. Proceedings — Biol Soc Wash Proc
Biological Society of Washington. Proceedings — Biol Soc Washington Proc
Biological Structures and Morphogenesis — Biol Struct Morphog
Biological Studies. Catholic University of America — Biol Stud Catholic Univ Amer
Biological Symposia — Biol Symp
Biological Trace Element Research — Biol Trace Elem Res

Biological Trace Element Research — BTERD
Biological Wastes — Biol Wastes
Biologically Inspired Physics — Biol Inspired Phys
Biologicheskaya Aktivnost Nekotorykh Aminotiolov i Aminosul'fidov — Biol Akt Nek Aminotiolov Aminosul'fidov
Biologicheskaya Flora Moskovskoi Oblasti — Biol Flora Mosk Obl
Biologicheskaya Nauka. Sel'skomu i Lesnomu Khozyatsteu — Biol Nauka Sel'sk Lesn Khoz
Biologicheskaya Produktivnost Yuzhnykh Morei — Biol Prod Yuzhn Morei
Biologicheskaya Rol Mikroelementov i Ikh Primenenie v Sel'skom Khozyaistve i Meditsine — Biol Rol Mikroelem Ikh Primen Sel'sk Khoz Med
Biologicheski Aktivnye Soedineniya Rastenii Sibirskoi Flory — Biol Akt Soedin Rast Sib Flory
Biologicheski Aktivnye Veshchestva Mikroorganizmov — Biol Akt Veshchestva Mikroorg
Biologicheski Aktivnye Veshchestva Mikroorganizmov i Ikh Ispol'zovanie — Biol Akt Veshchestva Mikroorg Ikh Ispol'z
Biologicheski Aktivnye Veshchestva v Zhizni Rastenii i Zhivotnykh — Biol Akt Veshchestva Zhizni Rast Zhivotn
Biologicheskie Issledovaniya na Severo Vostoke Evropeiskoi Chasti SSSR — Biol Issled Sev Vostoke Evr Chasti SSSR
Biologicheskie Membrany — Biol Memb
Biologicheskie Membrany — Biol Membr
Biologicheskie Nauki [*Moscow*] — Biol Nauki
Biologicheskie Osnovy Bor'by s Obrastaniem — Biol Osn Bor'by Obrastaniem
Biologicheskie Osnovy Oroshaemogo Zemledeliya. Materialy Vsesoyuznogo Soveshchaniya "Biologicheskie Osnovy Oroshaemogo Zemledeliya" — Biol Osn Oroshaemogo Zemled Mater Vses Soveshch
Biologicheskie Osnovy Povysheniya Produktivnosti Sel'skokhozyaistvennykh Rastenii — Biol Osn Povysh Prod Skh Rast
Biologicheskie Povrezhdeniya Stroitel'nykh i Promyshlennykh Materialov — Biol Povrezhdeniya Stroit Prom Mater
Biologicheskie Problemy Severa Tezisy Dokladov Simpozium — Biol Probl Sev Tezisy Dokl Simp
Biologicheskie Produktsionnye Protsessy v Basseine Volgi — Biol Prod Protsessy Basseine Volgi
Biologicheskie Protsessy i Mineral'nyi Obmen v Pochvakh Kol'skogo Poluostrova [*A publication*] — Biol Protsessy Miner Obmen Pochvakh Kol'sk Poluostrova
Biologicheskie Provrezhdeniya Stroitel'nykh i Promyshlennykh Materialov — BPSPBG
Biologicheskie Resursy Bodoemov Moldavii — Biol Resur Bodoemov Mold
Biologicheskie Resursy i Prirodnye Usloviya Mongol'skoi Narodnoi Respubliki — Biol Resur Prir Usloviya Mong Nar Resp
Biologicheskie Svoistva Khimicheskikh Soedinenii — Biol Svoistva Khim Soedin
Biologicheskii Zhurnal — Biol Zh
Biologicheskii Zhurnal — Biol Zhur
Biologicheskii Zhurnal Armenii — Biol Zh Arm
Biologicheskii Zhurnal Armenii — Biol Zh Armenii
Biologicheskoe Deistvie Bystrykh Neitronov — Biol Deistvie Bystrykh Neitronov
Biologicheskoe Deistvie i Gigienicheskoe Znachenie Atmosfernykh Zagryaznenii [*A publication*] — Biol Deistvie Gig Znach Atmos Zagryaz
Biologicheskoe Deistvie Radiatsii [*Ukrainian SSR*] — Biol Deistvie Radiats
Biologicheskoe Deistvie Ul'trafioletovogo Izlucheniya. Doklady Vsesoyuznoi Soveshchanii — Biol Deistvie Ul'trafiolet Izluch Dokl Vses Soveshch
Biologichnii Zbirnik. L'vivs'kii Derzhaenii Universitet — Biol Zb L'viv Derzh Univ
Biologicke Listy — BILIA
Biologicke Listy — Biol Listy
Biologicke Prace — Biol Pr
Biologicke Prace, Slovenskej Akademie Vied — Biol Prace Slov Akad Vied
Biologicky Sbornik. Slovenskej Akademie Vied a Umeni — Biol Sborn Slov Akad Vied
Biologickych Listu — Biol Listu
Biologie Cellulaire — BICED
Biologie Cellulaire — Biol Cel
Biologie Cellulaire — Biol Cell
Biologie de Cristallin au Cours de Developpement et de la Senescence. Colloque — Biol Crist Cours Dev Senescence Colloq
Biologie de la Peau. Cours Francophone Annuel — Biol Peau Cours Francophone Annu
Biologie du Comportement — BIBEDL
Biologie du Comportement — Biol Comport
Biologie du Sol. Bulletin International d'Informations — Biol Sol
Biologie du Sol. Microbiologie — Biol Sol Microbiol
Biologie et Gastro-Enterologie — BGENA
Biologie et Gastro-Enterologie — Biol Gastro
Biologie et Gastro-Enterologie — Biol Gastro-Enterol
Biologie in Unserer Zeit — Biol Unserer Zeit
Biologie Medical Milano. Edizione per l'Italia [*Milano*] — Biol Med Milano Ed Ital
Biologie Medicale — BIMEA
Biologie Medicale (Paris) — Biol Med (Paris)
Biologie-Ecologie Mediterraneenne — Biol Ecol Med
Biologieunterricht — BIUNA
Biologiia Moria — Biol Moria
Biologike Zaklad Pol'nohospodarstvo — Biol Zakl Pol'nohospod
Biologisch Jaarboek — Biol Jaarb
Biologisch Jaarboek [*Gent*] — Biol Jb
Biologische Abhandlungen — Biol Abh
Biologische Bundesanstalt fuer Land- und Forstwirtschaft Merkblatt — Biol Bundesanst Land Forstwirtsch Merkbl
Biologische Heilkunst — Biol Heilkunst
Biologische Rundschau — Biol Rdsch
Biologische Rundschau — Biol Rundsch
Biologische Rundschau — Biol Rundschau
Biologische Rundschau — BIRUA
Biologisches Zentralblatt — Biol Zbl
Biologisches Zentralblatt — Biol Zentralbl
Biologisches Zentralblatt — BIZNA
Biologischeskii i Vsesoyuzni Institut Eksperimental'noi Veterinarii — Biol Vses Inst Eksp Vet
Biologiske Meddelelser — Biol Meddr
Biologiske Meddelelser Kongelige Danske Videnskabernes Selskab — Biol Medd K Dan Vidensk Selsk
Biologiske Meddelelser Kongelige Danske Videnskabernes Selskab — KVBMAS
Biologiske Skrifter — Biol Skr
Biologiske Skrifter. Kongelige Dansk Videnskabernes Selskab — Biol Skr K Dan Vidensk Selsk
Biologiski Aktivo Savienojumu Kimijas Tehnologija Rigas Politehniskaja Instituta — BASIDS
Biologiski Aktivo Savienojumu Kimijas Tehnologija Rigas Politehniskaja Instituta — Biol Akt Savienojumu Kim Tehnol Rigas Politeh Inst
Biologist [*Champaign, IL*] — BGSTB
Biologist [*London*] — BLGTB
Biologiya Baltiiskogo Morya — BBMODN
Biologiya Baltiiskogo Morya — Biol Balt Morya
Biologiya i Akklimatizatsiya Obez'yan. Materialy Simpoziuma — Biol Akklim Obez'yan Mater Simp
Biologiya i Khimiya — Biol Khim
Biologiya i Selektsiya Mikroorganizmov — Biol Sel Mikroorg
Biologiya Khimiya Geografiya — Biol Khim Geogr
Biologiya Laboratornykh Zhivotnykh — Biol Lab Zhivotn
Biologiya Luchistykh Gribkov — Biol Luchistykh Gribkov
Biologiya Mikroorganizmov i Ikh Ispol'zovanie v Narodnom Khozyaistve — Biol Mikroorg Ikh Ispol'z Nar Khoz
Biologiya Morya [*Kiev*] — BIMOA
Biologiya Morya — Biol Morya
Biologiya Morya (Vladivostok) — Biol Morya (Vladivost)
Biologiya Reprodakisli Kletok — Biol Reprod Kletok
Biologiya Shkole — Biol Shk
Biologiya Vnutrennykh Vod — Biol Vnutr Vod
Biologiya Vnutrennykh Vod. Informatsionnyi Byulleten — Biol Vnutr Vod Inf Byull
Biologiya Vnutrennykh Vod. Informatsionnyi Byulleten — BVIBA
Biologizace a Chemizace Zivocisne Vyroby-Veterinaria — Biol Chem Zivocisne Vyroby Vet
Biology and Chemistry of Eucaryotic Cell Surfaces. Proceedings. Miami Winter Symposia — Biol Chem Eucaryotic Cell Surf Proc Miami Winter Symp
Biology and Clinical Applications of Interleukin-2. Proceedings. Meeting — Biol Clin Appl Interleukin 2 Proc Meet
Biology and Control of Soil-Borne Plant Pathogens. International Symposium on Factors Determining the Behavior of Plant Pathogens in Soil — Biol Control Soil-Borne Plant Pathog Int Symp
Biology and Fertility of Soils — Biol Fertil Soils
Biology and Human Affairs — Biol Hum Aff
Biology and Philosophy — Biol & Philos
Biology and Philosophy — BIOPEI
Biology and Society — Biol Soc
Biology Bulletin. Academy of Sciences of the USSR — Biol Bull Acad Sci USSR
Biology Bulletin of the Russian Academy of Sciences. Translation of Izvestiya Akademii Nauk. Seriya Biologich — Biol Bull Russ Acad Sci Transl of Izvest Akad Nauk Ser Biol
Biology Digest — Biol Dig
Biology International — Biol Int
Biology International — BYILDJ
Biology of Aging and Development — Biol Aging Dev
Biology of Behaviour — Biol Behav
Biology of Brain Dysfunction — Biol Brain Dysfunct
Biology of Brain Dysfunction — Biol Brain Dysfunction
Biology of Cancer. 2nd Edition — Biol Cancer 2nd Ed
Biology of Carbohydrates — Biol Carbohydr
Biology of Cephalopods. Proceedings of a Symposium — Biol Cephalopods Proc Symp
Biology of Crustacea — BCRUD5
Biology of Crustacea — Biol Crustacea
Biology of Cytoplasmic Microtubules. Papers. Conference — Biol Cytoplasmic Microtubules Pap Conf
Biology of Diatoms — Biol Diatoms
Biology of Human Fetal Growth — Biol Hum Fetal Growth
Biology of Hystricomorph Rodents. Proceedings of a Symposium — Biol Hystricomorph Rodents Proc Symp
Biology of Nitrogen Fixation — Biol Nitrogen Fixation
Biology of Penguins — Biol Penguins
Biology of Reproduction — Biol Reprod
Biology of Reproduction — BIREB
Biology of Reproduction. Supplement — Biol Reprod Suppl
Biology of Schizophrenia. Proceedings of the International Symposium of the Tokyo Institute of Psychiatry — Biol Schizophr Proc Int Symp Tokyo Inst Psychiatry
Biology of the Actinomycetes and Related Organisms — Biol Actinomycetes Relat Org
Biology of the Baltic Sea — Biol Baltic Sea
Biology of the Cell — Biol Cell
Biology of the Laboratory Rabbit — Biol Lab Rabbit
Biology of the Neonate — Biol Neonat
Biology of the Neonate — Biol Neonate
Biology of the Neonate — BNEOB
Biology of the Nocardiae — Biol Nocardiae
Biology of the Oceanic Pacific. Proceedings. Annual Biology Colloquium — Biol Oceanic Pac Proc Annu Biol Colloq

Biology of the Seal. Proceedings of the Symposium — Biol Seal Proc Symp
Biology of the Uterus — Biol Uterus
Biology of World Resources Series — Biol World Res Ser
Bioloshki Fakultet na Univerzitetot Kiril i Metodij Skopje Godishen Zbornik — Biol Fak Univ Kiril Metod Skopje God Zb
Bioloshki Fakultet na Univerzitetot Kiril i Metodij Skopje Godishen Zbornik [*A publication*] — GZBBDG
Bioloski Glasnik — BIGLA
Bioloski Glasnik — Biol Glas
Bioloski Vestnik — Biol Vestn
Biolyuminestsentsiya v Tikhom Okeane. Materialy Simpoziuma Tikhookeanskogo Nauchnogo Kongressa — Biolyumin Tikhom Okeane Mater Simp Tikhookean Nauchn Kongr
Biomass Abstracts — BIABE
Biomass Digest — Biomass Dig
Biomass Digest — BMSSD
Biomass Energy Institute. Newsletter — BENSD
Biomass Energy Institute. Newsletter [*Canada*] — Biomass Energy Inst Newsl
Biomass for Energy, Environment, Agriculture, and Industry. Proceedings of the European Biomass Conference — Biomass Energy Environ Agric Ind Proc Eur Biomass Conf
Biomass for Energy, Industry, and Environment. E.C. Conference — Biomass Energy Ind Environ EC Conf
Biomaterials, Artificial Cells, and Artificial Organs — Biomater Artif Cells Artif Organs
Biomaterials, Artificial Cells, and Immobilization Biotechnology — Biomater Artif Cells Immobilization Biotechnol
Biomaterials, Medical Devices, and Artificial Organs — Biomat Med
Biomaterials, Medical Devices, and Artificial Organs — Biomater Med Dev Artif Organs
Biomaterials, Medical Devices, and Artificial Organs — Biomater Med Devices and Artif Organs
Biomaterials, Medical Devices, and Artificial Organs — Biomater Med Devices Artif Organs
Biomaterials, Medical Devices, and Artificial Organs — BMDOA
Bio-Mathematics — Bio-Math
Bio-Mathematics — RBIMBZ
Biomechanical Transport Processes — Biomech Transp Processes
Biomechanics Symposium Presented at the Joint Applied Mechanics Fluids Engineering and Bioengineering Conference — Biomech Symp Jt Appl Mech Fluids Eng Bioeng Conf
Biomedica Biochimica Acta — Biomed Biochim Acta
Biomedical and Clinical Aspects of Coenzyme Q — Biomed Clin Aspects Coenzyme Q
Biomedical and Clinical Aspects of Coenzyme Q. Proceedings of the International Symposium — Biomed Clin Aspects Coenzyme Q Proc Int Symp
Biomedical and Environmental Mass Spectrometry — BEMS
Biomedical and Environmental Mass Spectrometry — Biomed Environ Mass Spectrom
Biomedical and Environmental Sciences — Biomed Environ Sci
Biomedical Applications — Biomed Appl
Biomedical Applications — JCBADL
Biomedical Applications of Biotechnology — Biomed Appl Biotechnol
Biomedical Applications of Gas Chromatography — Biomed Appl Gas Chromatogr
Biomedical Applications of Immobilized Enzymes and Proteins — Biomed Appl Immobilized Enzymes Proteins
Biomedical Applications of Polymers — Biomed Appln Polym
Biomedical Bulletin — Biomed Bull
Biomedical Business International — BBI
Biomedical Chromatography — Biomed Chro
Biomedical Chromatography — Biomed Chromatogr
Biomedical Communications — Biomed Commun
Biomedical Electronics — Biomed Elect
Biomedical Engineering — BIMEB
Biomedical Engineering [*English Translation*] — BIOEA
Biomedical Engineering [*New York*] — Biomed Eng
Biomedical Engineering (Berlin) — Biomed Eng (Berl)
Biomedical Engineering Current Awareness Notification [*Database*] — BECAN
Biomedical Engineering Current Awareness Notification — Biomed Engng Curr Aware Notif
Biomedical Engineering (English Translation) — Biomed Eng (Engl Transl)
Biomedical Engineering (English Translation of Meditsinskaya Tekhnika) — Biomed Eng (Engl Transl Med Tekh)
Biomedical Engineering (London) — Biomed Eng (Lond)
Biomedical Engineering (New York) — Biomed Eng (NY)
Bio-Medical Engineering (Tokyo) — Bio Med Eng (Tokyo)
Biomedical Engineering (USSR) — Biomed Eng (USSR)
Biomedical Instrumentation and Technology — Biomed Instrum Technol
Biomedical Laboratory Technical Report. United States Army Medical Research and Development Command — Biomed Lab Tech Rep US Army Med Res Dev Command
Biomedical Letters — Biomed Lett
BIOMEDICAL LETTERS — BIOMEDICAL LETT
Biomedical Mass Spectrometry — Biomed Mass
Biomedical Mass Spectrometry — Biomed Mass Spectrom
Biomedical Mass Spectrometry — BMSYA
Bio-Medical Materials and Engineering — Bio Med Mater Eng
Bio-Medical Materials and Engineering — Biomed Mater Eng
Biomedical Materials Symposium — Biomed Mater Symp
Biomedical Peptides, Proteins, and Nucleic Acids — Biomed Pept Proteins Nucleic Acids
Bio-Medical Preview. National Society for Medical Research — Bio Med Preview
Bio-Medical Purview — Bio-Med Purv
Bio-Medical Reports of the 406 Medical Laboratory — Bio-Med Rep 406 Med Lab
Biomedical Research — Biomed Res
Biomedical Research — BRESD
Biomedical Research Applications of Scanning Electron Microscopy — Biomed Res Appl Scanning Electron Micros
Biomedical Research on Trace Elements — Biomed Res Trace Elem
Biomedical Sciences Instrumentation — Biomed Sci Instrum
Biomedical Sciences Instrumentation — BMSIA
Biomedical Sciences (Tokyo) — Biomed Sci (Tokyo)
Biomedical Technical Report. Beckman Instruments, Inc. — Biomed Tech Rep Beckman Instrum Inc
Biomedical Technology Information Service — BMT
Biomedical Thermology. Proceedings. International Symposium — Biomed Thermol Proc Int Symp
Biomedicine — BIMDB
Biomedicine and Pharmacotherapy — Biomed Pharmacother
Biomedicine and Pharmacotherapy — BIPHEX
Biomedicine and Physiology of Vitamin B12. Proceedings. International Symposium — Biomed Physiol Vitam B12 Proc Int Symp
Biomedicine and Therapeutics (Tokyo) — Biomed Ther (Tokyo)
Biomedicine Express [*Paris*] — Biomed Expr
Biomedicine Express (Paris) — Biomed Express (Paris)
Biomedizinische Technik [*Berlin*] — Biomed Tech
Biomedizinische Technik — BMZTA
Biomedizinische Technik (Berlin) — Biomed Tech (Berlin)
Biomedizinische Technik. Biomedical Engineering — Biomed Tech Biomed Eng
Biomembranes — BOMBB
Biomembranes, Lipids, Proteins, and Receptors. Proceedings of a NATO Advanced Study Institute — Biomembr Lipids Proteins Recept Proc NATO Adv Study Inst
Biometeorologia Czlowieka — Biometeorol Czlowieka
Biometeorological Research Centre (Leiden). Monograph Series — Biometeorol Res Cent (Leiden) Monogr Ser
Biometrae Bulletin — Biom Bull
Biometrical Journal — Biom J
Biometrical Journal — Biometrical J
Biometrical Journal. Journal of Mathematical Methods of Biosciences — Biom J
Biometrics — Biom
Biometrics — BIOMA
Biometrie Humaine — Biom Hum
Biometrie Humaine — Biometrie Hum
Biometrie Humaine — SBHRAL
Biometrie in der Chemisch-Pharmazeutischen Industrie — Biom Chem Pharm Ind
Biometrie-Praximetrie — Biomet-Praximet
Biometrie-Praximetrie — Biometr-Praxim
Biometrika — BIOKA
Biometrika — Biom
Biometrische Zeitschrift — Biom Z
Biometrische Zeitschrift — Biom Zeit
Biometrische Zeitschrift — Biometr Z
Biometrische Zeitschrift — BIZEB
Biometrische Zeitschrift. Zeitschrift fuer Mathematische Methoden in den Biowissenschaften — Biom Z
Bionika — BNKAB
Bionika i Matematicheskoe Modelirovanie v Biologii — Bionika Mat Model Biol
Bioorganic and Medicinal Chemistry — Bioorg Med Chem
Bioorganic and Medicinal Chemistry Letters — Bioorg Med Chem Lett
Bioorganic Chemistry — Bioorg Chem
Bioorganic Chemistry Frontiers — Bioorg Chem Front
Bioorganic Marine Chemistry — Bioorg Mar Chem
Bioorganicheskaya Khimiya — BIKHD
Bioorganicheskaya Khimiya — Bioorg Khim
Bio-oriented Technology Research Advancement Instution Techno News — Bio Oriented Technol Res Adv Inst Techno News
BIOP [*Board on International Organizations and Programs*] **Newletter** [*United States*] — BINED
BIOP [*Board of International Organizations and Programs*] **Newsletter** — BIOP Newsl
BioPharm Manufacturing — BioPharm Manuf
Biopharmaceutics and Drug Disposition — Biopharm Drug Dispos
Biophysical Chemistry — Biophys Ch
Biophysical Chemistry — Biophys Chem
Biophysical Journal — BIOJA
Biophysical Journal — Biophys J
Biophysical Journal. Supplement — Biophys J Suppl
Biophysical Journal. Supplement — BPJSA
Biophysical Society Abstracts. Annual Meetings — Biophys Soc Abstr Ann Meetings
Biophysical Society. Annual Meeting. Abstracts — Biophys Soc Annu Meet Abstr
Biophysical Society. Symposium — Biophys Soc Symp
Biophysics [*English Translation*] — BIOPA
Biophysics [*English Translation of Biofizika*] — BIOPAE
Biophysics — Biophys
Biophysics (English Translation of Biofizika) — Biophysics (Engl Transl Biofizika)
Biophysics of Membrane Transport. School Proceedings. School on Biophysics of Membrane Transport — Biophys Membr Transp
Biophysics of Structure and Mechanism — Biophys Str
Biophysics of Structure and Mechanism — Biophys Struct Mech
Biophysics of Structure and Mechanism — BSMHB
Biophysik [*Berlin*] — BPYKA
Biophysikalisches Centralblatt — Biophys Centralbl
Biopolimery i Kletka — BIKLEK

Biopolimery i Kletka — Biopolim Kletka
Biopolymers — BIPMA
Biopolymers and Cell — Biopolym Cell
Biopolymers Symposia — Biopolym Symp
Bioprocess Engineering — Bioprocess Eng
Bioprocess Technology — Bioprocess Technol
Bioprocessing Technology [*Database*] — BT
Bioquimica Clinica — Bioquim Clin
Bioquimica Clinica — Bioquim Clini
BioResearch Index [*Later, BA/RRM*] — BIOI
BioResearch Index [*Later, BA/RRM*] — BioRes Index
BioResearch Index [*Later, BA/RRM*] — BRI
Bioresearch Titles — Biores Titles
Biorheology [*England*] — BRHLA
Biorheology. Supplement — Biorheol Suppl
Bios Boissons Conditionnement — Bios Boissons Cond
Bios. Rivista di Biologia Sperimentale e Generale (Genoa) — Bios Genoa
Bios (Unadilla, New York) — Bios (Unadilla NY)
BIOS [*Baffin Island Oil Spill Project*] **Working Report** — BIOSW
BioScience — BioSci
BioScience — BISNA
Bioscience — GBSC
BioScience. American Institute of Biological Sciences — BioSci Am Inst Biol Sci
Bioscience and Industry — Bioscience & Ind
Bioscience and Industry — HAKOD4
Bioscience and Microflora — Biosci Microflora
Bioscience Report. Abo Akademi — Biosci Rep Abo Akad
Bioscience Reports — Biosci Rep
Bio-Sciences — BIOSE
Biosciences Communications — Biosci Commun
Biosensors and Bioelectronics — Biosens Bioelectron
Biosfera i Chelovek Materialy Vsesoyuznogo Simpoziuma — Biosfera Chel Mater Vses Simp
Biosintez i Sostoyanie Khlorofillov v Rastenii — Biosint Sostoyanie Khlorofillov Rast
BIOSIS/CAS Registry Number Concordance [*Database*] — BIOCAS
Biosources Digest — BIDID
Biosources Digest — Biosources Dig
Biosynthesis — Biosyn
Biosynthesis and Biodegradation of Cellulose — Biosynth Biodegrad Cellul
Biosynthesis of Antibiotics — Biosynth Antibiot
Biosynthetic Products for Cancer Chemotherapy — Biosynth Prod Cancer Chemother
Biosynthetic Products for Cancer Chemotherapy — BPCCDZ
Biotech Patent News — Biotech Pat News
BioTechForum. Advances in Molecular Genetics — BioTechForum Adv Mol Genet
Biotechnic and Histochemistry — Biotech His
Biotechnic and Histochemistry — Biotech Histochem
Biotechniek [*The Netherlands*] — BTNKA
Bio-Technology [*New York*] — BTCHDA
Biotechnology Action Programme — BAP
Biotechnology Advances — BIADDD
Biotechnology Advances — Biotechnol Adv
Biotechnology and Applied Biochemistry — BABIEC
Biotechnology and Applied Biochemistry — Biotechnol Appl Biochem
Biotechnology and Bioengineering — BIBIA
Biotechnology and Bioengineering — Biotech Bio
Biotechnology and Bioengineering — Biotech Bioeng
Biotechnology and Bioengineering — Biotechnol Bioeng
Biotechnology and Bioengineering. Symposium — Biotechnol Bioeng Symp
Biotechnology and Bioindustry — Biotechnol Bioind
Biotechnology and Biotechnological Equipment — Biotechnol Biotechnol Equip
Biotechnology and Genetic Engineering Reviews — Biotechnol Genet Eng Rev
Biotechnology and Nutrition. Proceedings. International Symposium — Biotechnol Nutr Proc Int Symp
Biotechnology and Plant Protection. Viral Pathogenesis and Disease Resistance. Proceedings of the International Symposium — Biotechnol Plant Prot
Biotechnology Annual Review — Biotechnol Annu Rev
Biotechnology Business News — Biotechnol Bus News
Biotechnology. Current Progress — Biotechnol Curr Prog
Biotechnology Education — Biotechnol Educ
Biotechnology Handbooks — Biotechnol Handb
Biotechnology in Agricultural Chemistry — Biotechnol Agric Chem
Biotechnology in Agriculture — Biotechnol Agric
Biotechnology in Agriculture and Forestry — BAFOEG
Biotechnology in Agriculture and Forestry — Biotechnol Agric For
Biotechnology International. Trends and Perspectives — Biotech
Biotechnology Law Report — Biotechnol Law Rep
Biotechnology Letters [*England*] — Biotechnol Lett
Biotechnology Monographs — Biotechnol Monogr
Biotechnology News — Biotechnol News
Biotechnology of Blood — Biotechnol Blood
Biotechnology Patent Digest — Biotechn Pat Dig
Biotechnology Progress — Biotechnol Prog
Biotechnology Series — Biotechnol Ser
Biotechnology Techniques — Biotechnol Tech
Biotechnology Therapeutics — Biotechnol Ther
Biotecnologia Aplicada — Biotecnol Apl
Biotekhnologiya i Biotekhnika — Biotekhnol Biotekh
Biotekniikan Laboratorio, Tiedonanto (Valtion Teknillinen Tutkimuskeskus) — Biotek Lab Tied (Valt Tek Tutkimuskeskus)
Biotelemetry [*Later, Biotelemetry and Patient Monitoring*] — Biotelemetr
Biotelemetry and Patient Monitoring — Biotelem Patient Monit
Biotest Bulletin — Biotest Bull
Bioticheskie Komponenty Nazemnykh Ekosistem Tyan Shanya — Bioticheskie Komponenty Nazemn Ekosistem Tyan Shanya
Biotrop Bulletin — Biotrop Bull
Biotropica — BTROA
Biotypologie. Bulletin. Societe de Typologie — Biotypologie Bul Soc Typ
Biovigyanam — BIOVD
BIR [*British Institute of Radiology*] **Bulletin** — BIR Bull
Birbal Sahni Institute of Palaeobotany. Birbal Sahni Memorial Lecture [*Luchnow*] — Birbal Sahni Inst Palaeobot Birbal Sahni Mem Lect
Birbal Sahni Institute of Palaeobotany. Special Publication — Birbal Sahni Inst Palaeobot Spec Publ
Bird Behaviour — Bird Behav
Bird Control Seminar. Proceedings — Bird Control Semin Proc
Bird Effort — Bird E
Bird Keeping in Australia — Bird Keeping
Bird Lore [*Pennsylvania*] — Bird L
Bird-Banding — Bird-Band
Birger Sjoberg Sallskapet — BSS
Birkmeyer. Enzyklopaedie der Rechtswissenschaft — Enz Rechtswiss
Birla Archaeological and Cultural Research Institute. Research Bulletin — Birla Archaeol Cult Res Inst Res Bull
Birmingham Historical Journal — Birmingham Hist J
Birmingham [*England*] **Philosophical Society. Proceedings** — Birmingham Ph Soc Pr
Birmingham Photographic Society. Journal — BPS
Birmingham Post — B'ham Post
Birmingham Post — BMP
Birmingham University. Chemical Engineer — BIRMA
Birmingham University. Chemical Engineer — Birmingham Univ Chem Eng
Birmingham University. Historical Journal — Birmingham Univ Hist
Birth and the Family Journal — Birth Fam J
Birth and the Family Journal — Birth Family J
Birth Defects Information Systems [*Database*] — BDIS
Birth Defects. Original Article Series — Birth Defects
Birth Defects. Original Article Series — Birth Defects Orig Artic Ser
Birth Defects. Original Article Series — BTHDA
BIS [*Brain Information Service*] **Conference Report** — BIS Conf Rep
Bisbabharati Patrika — BP
Biserica Orthodoxa Romana — BOR
Biserica Ortodoxa Romana — Biserica Ortod Romana
Bismuth Institute. Bulletin (Brussels) — Bismuth Inst Bull (Brussels)
BISRA [*British Iron and Steel Research Association*] **Open Report** — BISRA Open Rep
Bit Nordisk Tidskrift fuer Informationsbehandling — Bit Nord Tidskr Informationsbehandl
Bitamin — BTMNA
Bitki Koruma Bulteni — Bitki Koruma Buelt
Bitki Koruma Bulteni — Bitki Koruma Bul
Bitki Koruma Bulteni. Ek Yayin — Bitki Koruma Bul Ek Yayin
Bitki Koruma Bulteni. Plant Protection Bulletin — Bitki Koruma Bul Plant Prot Bull
Bits and Pieces — BIPID
Bitumen — BITUA
Bitumen, Teere, Asphalte, Peche — BITAA
Bitumen, Teere, Asphalte, Peche, und Verwandte Stoffe — Bitumen Teere Asphalte Peche
Bitumen, Teere, Asphalte, Peche, und Verwandte Stoffe — BTAPB
Bituminization of Low and Medium Level Radioactive Wastes. Proceedings of a Seminar — Bitum Low Medium Level Radioact Wastes Proc Semin
Bituminous Coal Research, Incorporated. Technical Report — Bitum Coal Res Inc Tech Rep
Biuletyn Centralnego Laboratorium Technologii Przetworstwa i Przechowalnictwa Zboz w Warszawie — Biul Cent Lab Technol Przetworstwa Przechow Zboz Warszawie
Biuletyn Centralnej Stacji Oceny Pasz. Instytut Zootechniki w Polsce — Biul Cent Stacji Oceny Pasz Inst Zootech Pol
Biuletyn Centralnogo Instytutu Ochrony Pracy — Biul Cent Inst Ochr Pr
Biuletyn Fonograficzny — B Fon
Biuletyn Fonograficzny — BFo
Biuletyn Geologiczny — Biul Geol
Biuletyn Glownego Instytutu Gornictwa — BGIGA
Biuletyn Glownego Instytutu Gornictwa [*Poland*] — Biul Gl Inst Gorn
Biuletyn Glownego Instytutu Wlokiennictwa — Biul Gl Inst Wlok
Biuletyn Historii Sztuki — BHS
Biuletyn Informacyjny — Biul Inform
Biuletyn Informacyjny. Barwniki i Srodki Pomocnicze — Biul Inf Barwniki Srodki Pomocnicze
Biuletyn Informacyjny. Centralnego Laboratorium Przemyslu Tytoniowego — Biul Inf Cent Lab Przem Tytoniowego
Biuletyn Informacyjny. Geologia. Geofizyka oraz Ekonomika i Technika Prac Geologicznych — Biul Inf Geol Geofiz Ekon Tech Prac Geol
Biuletyn Informacyjny. Glowny Instytut Elektrotechniki — Biul Inf Gl Inst Elektrotech
Biuletyn Informacyjny. Instytut Badawezo Projektowy Przemyslu Farb i Lakierow — Biul Inf Inst Badaw Proj Przem Farb Lakierow
Biuletyn Informacyjny. Instytut Farb i Lakierow — Biul Inf Inst Farb Lakierow
Biuletyn Informacyjny. Instytut Przemyslu Tworzyw i Farb — Biul Inf Inst Przem Tworzyw Farb
Biuletyn Informacyjny. Instytut Przemyslu Wiazacych Materialow Budowlanych (Krakow) — Biul Inf Inst Przem Wiazacych Mater Budow (Krakow)
Biuletyn Informacyjny. Instytut Techniki Budowlanej — Biul Inf Inst Tech Budow
Biuletyn Informacyjny. Instytutu Lekow — Biul Inf Inst Lekow
Biuletyn Informacyjny. Instytutu Materialow Ogniotrwalych — Biul Inf Inst Mater Ogniotrwalych

Biuletyn Informacyjny Instytutu Techniki Cieplnej — Biul Inf Inst Tech Cieplnej
Biuletyn Informacyjny. Instytutu Zbozowego w Warszawie — Biul Inf Inst Zbozowego Warszawie
Biuletyn Informacyjny. Instytutu Zbozowego w Warszawie — Biul Inform Inst Zboz Warszawie
Biuletyn Informacyjny. Komisji Krystalografii PAN [*Polska Akademia Nauk*] — Biul Inf Kom Krystalogr PAN
Biuletyn Informacyjny. Materialow Ogniotrwalych — Biul Inf Mater Ogniotrwalych
Biuletyn Informacyjny. Naukowo Technicznej. Instytut Techniki Budowlanej — Biul Inf Nauk Tech Inst Tech Budow
Biuletyn Informacyjny. Osrodek Badawczo-Rozwojowy Przemyslu Barwnikow — Biul Inf Osr Badaw Rozwoj Przem Barwnikow
Biuletyn Informacyjny. Panstwowy Instytut Elektrotechniczny — Biul Inf Panst Inst Elektrotech
Biuletyn Informacyjny Przemyslu Farb i Lakierow — Biul Inf Przem Farb Lakierow
Biuletyn Informacyjny. Zakladu Narodowego Ossolinskich Biblioteki Polskiej Akademii Nauk — B Inf Zak Narod
Biuletyn. Instytut Geologiczny (Warsaw) — Biul Inst Geol (Warsaw)
Biuletyn. Instytut Maszyn Przeplywowych Polskiej Akademii Nauk w Gdansku — Biul Inst Masz Przeplyw Pol Akad Nauk Gdansku
Biuletyn. Instytut Metali Niezelaznych — Biul Inst Met Niezelaz
Biuletyn. Instytuta Spawalnictwa. Gliwice — BISWA
Biuletyn. Instytutu Bibliograficznego — Biul IB
Biuletyn. Instytutu Energetyki — Biul Inst Energ
Biuletyn. Instytutu Energetyki (Warsaw) — Biul Inst Energ (Warsaw)
Biuletyn. Instytutu Genetyki i Hodowli Zwierzat Polskiej Akademii Nauk [*Poland*] — Biul Inst Genet Hodowli Zwierzat Pol Akad Nauk
Biuletyn. Instytutu Geologicznego — BIUGA
Biuletyn. Instytutu Gospodarstwa Spolecznego — Biul IGS
Biuletyn Instytutu Hodowii i Aklimatyzacji Roslin — Biul Inst Hodowii Rosl
Biuletyn. Instytutu Hodowli i Aklimatyzacji Roslin — Biul Inst Hodowli Aklim Rosl
Biuletyn. Instytutu Hodowli i Aklimatyzacji Roslin (Warszawa) — Biul Inst Hodowli Aklimat Ros (Warszawa)
Biuletyn. Instytutu Mechaniki Precyzyjnej — Biul Inst Mech Precyz
Biuletyn. Instytutu Medycyny Morskiej i Tropikalne w Gdyni — Biul Inst Med Morsk Trop Gdyni
Biuletyn. Instytutu Medycyny Morskiej i Tropikalnej Akademii Lekarskiej w Gdansku — Biul Inst Med Morsk Trop Akad Lek Gdansku
Biuletyn. Instytutu Medycyny Morskiej w Gdansku — Biul Inst Med Morsk Gdansk
Biuletyn. Instytutu Medycyny Morskiej w Gdansku — Biul Inst Med Morsk Gdansku
Biuletyn. Instytutu Naftowego — BIINA
Biuletyn. Instytutu Naftowego — Biul Inst Naft
Biuletyn. Instytutu Naftowego — Biul Inst Naftowego
Biuletyn. Instytutu Naukowo-Badawczego Przemyslu Weglowego Komunikat — Biul Inst Nauk Badaw Przem Weglowego Komun
Biuletyn. Instytutu Ochrony Roslin [*Poznan*] — Biul Inst Ochr Rosl
Biuletyn. Instytutu Przemyslu Cukrowniczego — Biul Inst Przem Cukrow
Biuletyn. Instytutu Roslin Leczniezych — Biul Inst Rosl Lecz
Biuletyn. Instytutu Spawalnictwa — Biul Inst Spawalnictwa
Biuletyn. Instytutu Spawalnictwa (Gliwice) — Biul Inst Spawal (Gliwice)
Biuletyn. Instytutu Spawalnictwa (Gliwice) — Biul Inst Spawalnictwa (Gliwice)
Biuletyn. Instytutu Technologii Drewna — Biul Inst Tech Drewna
Biuletyn. Instytutu Weglowego. Komunikat — Biul Inst Weglowego Komun
Biuletyn. Instytutu Weterynarny w Pulawy — Biul Inst Weter Pulawy
Biuletyn. Instytutu Wlokiennictwa — Biul Inst Wlok
Biuletyn. Instytutu Ziemniaka — Biul Inst Ziemniaka
Biuletyn. Instytutu Ziemniaka (Koszalin, Poland) — Biul Inst Ziemniaka (Koszalin Pol)
Biuletyn Koksownika — Biul Koksownika
Biuletyn. Kwarantanny i Ochrony Roslin Ministerstwo Rolnictwa (Warszawa) — Biul Kwarant Ochr Ros Min Roln (Warszawa)
Biuletyn Lubelskiego Towarzystwa Naukowego Biologia — Biul Lubel Tow Nauk Biol
Biuletyn Lubelskiego Towarzystwa Naukowego. Geografia — Biul Lubel Tow Nauk Geogr
Biuletyn Lubelskiego Towarzystwa Naukowego. Matematyka-Fizyka-Chemia — Biul Lubel Tow Nauk Mat Fiz Chem
Biuletyn Lubelskiego Towarzystwa Naukowego. Matematyka-Fizyka-Chemia — Biul Lubel Towarz Nauk Mat Fiz Chem
Biuletyn Lubelskiego Towarzystwa Naukowego. Sectio A-D. Supplement — Biul Lubel Tow Nauk Sect A-D Suppl
Biuletyn Lubelskiego Towarzystwa Naukowego. Wydzial 2. Biologia — Biul Lubel Tow Nauk Wydz 2
Biuletyn Lubelskiego Towarzystwa Naukowego. Wydzial 3. Geografia — Biul Lubel Tow Nauk Wydz 3
Biuletyn Nauczyciela Opolskiego — BNO
Biuletyn Naukowy Instytutu Nauk Ekonomicznych Universytetu Warszawskiego — B Nauk Inst Nauk Ekon Univ Warszaw
Biuletyn Numizmatyczny — B Num
Biuletyn Numizmatyczny — Biul Num
Biuletyn Numizmatyczny — BN
Biuletyn Panstwowego Instytutu Ksiazki — Biul PIK
Biuletyn. Panstwowy Instytut Geologiczny — Biul Panstw Inst Geol
Biuletyn. Panstwowy Instytut Naukowy Leczniczych Surowcow Roslinnych w Poznaniu — Biul Panst Inst Nauk Leczn Surow Ros Poznaniu
Biuletyn. Panstwowy Instytutu Medycyny Morskiej i Tropikalnej w Gdansku — Biul Panstw Inst Med Morsk Trop Gdansku
Biuletyn Peryglacjalny — Biul Peryglac
Biuletyn Polonistyczny — BP
Biuletyn Polskiego Towarzystwa Farmaceutycznego — Biul Pol Tow Farm
Biuletyn Polskiego Towarzystwa Jezykoznawczego — BPTJ
Biuletyn Prasowy Polonia — B Pol
Biuletyn Producenta Pieczarek — Biul Prod Pieczarek
Biuletyn Przemyslowego Instytutu Automatyki i Pomiarow MERA-PIAP — Biul Przem Inst Autom Pomiarow MERA PIAP
Biuletyn Sluzby Sanitarno Epidemiologiczej Wojewodztwa Katowickiego — Biul Sluzby Sanit Epidemiol Wojewodztwa Katowickiego
Biuletyn Techniczny, Elektrownie, i Elektrocieplownie [*Poland*] — Biul Tech Elektrownie Elektrocieplownie
Biuletyn Warzywniczy — Biul Warzywniczy
Biuletyn Wojskowej Akademii Medycznej — Biul Wojsk Akad Med
Biuletyn Wojskowej Akademii Technicznej Imienia Jaroslawa Dabrowskiego — Biul Wojsk Akad Tech
Biuletyn Wojskowej Akademii Technicznej Imienia Jaroslawa Dabrowskiego — BWATA
Biuletyn Zaklad Badan Naukouyeh Gornoslaskiego Okregu Przemyslowego Polskiej Akademii Nauk — Biul Zakl Badan Nauk Gornoslask Okregu Przem Pol Akad Nauk
Biuletyn Zaklad Ochrony Srodowiska Regionow Przemyslowych Polskiej Akademii Nauk — Biul Zakl Ochr Srodowiska Reg Przem Pol Akad Nauk
Biuletyn Zjednoczenia Przemyslu Chemii Gospodarczej Pollena — Biul Zjednoczenia Przem Chem Gospod Pollena
Biuletyn Zydowskiego Instytutu Historycznego — Biul Zydowskiego Inst Hist
Biuletyn Zydowskiego Instytutu Historycznego — BZIH
Biuletyn Zydowskiego Instytutu Historycznego w Polsci — Biul Zydowskiego Inst Hist Pol
Biulleten Eksperimentalnoi Biologii i Meditsiny — Biull Eksp Biol Med
Biulleten Glavnogo Botanicheskogo Sada — Biull Gl Bot Sada
Biulleten Glavnogo Botanicheskogo Sada (Leningrad) — Biul Gl Bot Sada (Leningrad)
Biulleten Gosudarstvennyi Nikitskii Botanicheskii Sad — Biul Gos Nikitsk Bot Sad
Biulleten Izobretenii [*Former USSR*] — Biull Izobret
Biulleten Nauchno-Tekhnicheskoi Informatsii po Agronomicheskoi Fizike — Biul Nauchno Tekh Inf Agron Fiz
Biulleten Nauchno-Tekhnicheskoi Informatsii po Maslichnym Kul'turam — Biul Nauchno Tekh Inf Maslichn Kult
Biulleten Nauchno-Tekhnicheskoi Informatsii Vsesoiuznyi Nauchno-Issledovatel'skii Instituta Risa — Biul Nauchno-Tekh Inf Vses Nauchno-Issled Inst Risa
Biulleten Nauchnykh Rabot. Vsesoiuznyi Nauchno-Issledovatel'skii Institut Zhivotnovodstva — Biul Nauchn Rabot Vses Nauchno Issled Inst Zhivotnovod
Biulleten Vsesoiuznogo Kardiologicheskogo Nauchnogo Tsentra AMN SSSR — Biull Vsesoiuznogo Kardiol Nauchn Tsentr AMN SSSR
Biulleten Vsesoiuznogo Nauchno-Issledovatel'skogo Instituta Kukuruzy — Biull Vses Nauchno-Issled Inst Kukuruzy
Biulleten. Vsesoiuznyi Institut Gel'mintologii — Biul Vses Inst Gel'mintol
Biulleten Vsesoiuznyi Nauchno-Issledovatel'skii Institut Zashchity Rastenii [*A publication*] — Biul Vses Nauchno Issled Inst Zashch Rast
Biweekly Cryogenics Current Awareness Service — BCCCD
Biweekly Cryogenics Current Awareness Service — Biwkly Cryog Curr Aware Serv
Biweekly Scientific and Technical Intelligence Summary — BSTIS
Biyokimya Dergisi — Biyokim Derg
Bizantion-Nea Hellas — BzNH
Bizarre Fantasy Tales — BFT
Bizarre Mystery Magazine — Biz
BJR [British Journal of Radiology] Supplement — BJR Suppl
Bjulleten Akademiji Nauk Uzbekskoj SSR — Bjull Akad Nauk Uz SSR
Bjulleten Dialektologiceskogo Sektora Instituta Russkogo Jazyka — BDSekt
Bjulleten Glavnogo Botaniceskogo Sada — Bjull Glavn Bot Sada
Bjulleten Gosudarstvennogo Nikitskogo Botaniceskogo Sada — Bjull Gos Nikit Bot Sada
Bjulleten' Habarovskogo Lesnogo Pitomnika — Bjull Habarovsk Lesn Pitomn
Bjulleten Inostrannoj Kommerceskoj Informacii Prilozenie — B Inostr Kommerc Inform Priloz
Bjulleten' Jarovizacii — Bjull Jarov
Bjulleten Moskovskogo Obscestva Ispytatelej Prirody. Otdel Biologiceskij — Bjull Mosk Obsc Ispyt Prir Otd Biol
Bjulleten' Moskovskogo Obscestva Ispytatelej Prirody. Otdel Geologiceskij/ Bulletin. Societe des Naturalistes de Moscou. Section Geologique — Bjull Moskovsk Obsc Isp Prir Otd Geol
Bjulleten' Sibirskogo Botaniceskogo Sada — Bjull Sibirsk Bot Sada
Bjulleten' Tihookeanskogo Komiteta Akademii Nauk SSSR/Bulletin. Pacific Committee. Academy of Sciences. USSR — Bjull Tihookeansk Komiteta Akad Nauk SSSR
Bjulleten' Vsesojuznogo Naucno-Issledovatel'skogo Instituta Zascity Rastenij — Bjull Vsesojuzn Naucno Issl Inst Zasc Rast
Bjulleteni Rukopisnogo Otdela Puskinskogo Doma — BROPD
Bjulletin Instituta Teoreticeskoi Astronomii. Akademija Nauk Sojuza Sovetskih Socialisticeskih Respublik — Bjull Inst Teoret Astronom
BK Technical Review — BK Tech Rev
BKSTS [*British Kinematograph Sound and Television Society*] **Journal** — BKSTS J
Black Academy Review — BA Rev
Black American Literature Forum — BALF
Black American Literature Forum — Bl Amer Lit Forum
Black American Literature Forum — Black Am L
Black American Literature Forum — PBAL
Black Americans Information Directory — BAID
Black Art [*London*] — BLA
Black Belt Magazine — Bl Belt Mag
Black Books Bulletin — Bl Bks B
Black Business News — Black Bus News
Black Church — BlackCh
Black Coal in Australia — Black Coal Aust
Black Collegian — Black Col
Black Collegian — Black Coll

Black Collegian — GBLC
Black Diamond — BLDIA
Black Elegance — BE
Black Enterprise — B Ent
Black Enterprise — BEn
Black Enterprise — Black Ent
Black Enterprise — Black Enterp
Black Enterprise — BLEND
Black Experience — BIE
Black Forum — Black F
Black Fox Magazine — Black Fox Mag
Black Hills Engineer — Black Hills Eng
Black I: A Canadian Journal of Black Expression — BlackIC
Black Images: A Critical Quarterly on Black Arts and Culture — BlackI
Black Information Index — Black Inf Index
Black Law Journal — Bl LJ
Black Law Journal — Black L J
Black Liberation — Blk Lib
Black Mountain Review — Black Mtn Rev
Black Music and Jazz Review — Black Mus Jazz Rev
Black Music Research Journal — BMR
Black Music Research Journal — BMR J
Black News Digest — Black N Dig
Black Oracle — Bl Orcl
Black Orpheus — BO
Black Panther — Blk Panth
Black Perspective in Music — BI
Black Perspective in Music — Black Per M
Black Perspective in Music — Black Perspective M
Black Perspective in Music — PBPM
Black Perspectives in Music — BPiM
Black Review — BlackR
Black Rock Forest. Bulletin — Black Rock For Bull
Black Rock Forest. Bulletin — Black Rock Forest Bull
Black Rock Forest. Papers — Black Rock For Pap
Black Sacred Music — Black Sacred Mus
Black Scholar — B Sch
Black Scholar — BKSCA
Black Scholar — Black Sch
Black Scholar — Blk Schol
Black Scholar — BlS
Black Scholar — BlSch
Black Scholar — BS
Black Scholar — GBLS
Black Sociologist — Black Soc
Black Times — BT
Black Warrior Review — BWR
Black World — BL W
Black World — Black W
Blackford — Blackf
Blackwell Newsletter — Blackwell Newsl
Blackwood's Magazine — BKMGA
Blackwood's Magazine — Black
Blackwood's Magazine — Black Mag
Blackwood's Magazine — Blackw
Blackwood's Magazine — Blackwood's Mag
Blackwood's Magazine — BlM
Blackwood's Magazine — Blwd Mag
Blackwood's Magazine — BM
Blad foer Bergshandteringens Vaenner — Bl Bergshandteringens Vaenner
Blaetter der Bergakademie Freiberg — Bl Bergakad Freiberg
Blaetter der Rilke-Gesellschaft — BRG
Blaetter der Staatsoper — Bll Staatsoper
Blaetter der Thomas Mann Gesellschaft — BTMG
Blaetter des Schwaebischen Albvereins (Tuebingen) — Tuebingen Bl Albver
Blaetter des Vereins fuer Landeskunde in Niederoesterreich — Blaett Vereins Landesk Niederoesterreich
Blaetter fuer Administrative Praxis — Bl Adm Pr
Blaetter fuer Christliche Archaeologie und Kunst — BCA
Blaetter fuer das Bayerische Gymnasialschulwesen — BBG
Blaetter fuer das Bayerische Gymnasialschulwesen — Bl Gymnasialschulwesen
Blaetter fuer das Bayerische Gymnasialschulwesen — BlBGym
Blaetter fuer das Bayerische Gymnasialschulwesen — Bll Bayer Gymnschulw
Blaetter fuer das Gymnasialschulwesen — Bll Gymnschulw
Blaetter fuer Deutsche Landesgeschichte — BDLG
Blaetter fuer Deutsche Landesgeschichte — Bl D Lg
Blaetter fuer Deutsche Landesgeschichte — Bl Deutsche Landesgesch
Blaetter fuer Deutsche Landesgeschichte — Bl Dt Landesgesch
Blaetter fuer Deutsche Philosophie — Bl D Ph
Blaetter fuer Deutsche Philosophie — Bl Deut Phil
Blaetter fuer Deutsche Philosophie — Bl Dte Philos
Blaetter fuer Deutsche Philosophie. Zeitschrift der Deutsche Philosophische Gesellschaft — BDPH
Blaetter fuer Deutsche und Internationale Politik — BDIPD
Blaetter fuer Deutsche und Internationale Politik — Bl Dt und Internat Pol
Blaetter fuer Deutsche und Internationale Politik — Bl Dtsch Int Polit
Blaetter fuer Deutsche und Internationale Politik — Blaett Dtsche u Int Polit
Blaetter fuer Geschichte der Technik. Oesterreichisches Forschungsinstitut fuer Geschichte der Technik — Bl Gesch Tech
Blaetter fuer Grundstuecks, Bau-, und Wohnungsrecht — BGBWD
Blaetter fuer Grundstuecks, Bau-, und Wohnungsrecht [*Germany*] — Bl Grundstuecks Bau-Wohnungsrecht
Blaetter fuer Heimatkunde — Bl H
Blaetter fuer Heimatkunde — Bl Heimatkd
Blaetter fuer Heimatkunde — BlfH
Blaetter fuer Heimatkunde. Historischer Verein fuer Steiermark — Bl HK
Blaetter fuer Internationales Privatrecht — BlIntPR
Blaetter fuer Juedische Geschichte und Literatur — BJGL
Blaetter fuer Kirchengeschichte Pommerns — BKGP
Blaetter fuer Klinische Hydrotherapie und Verwandte Heilmethoden [Wien und Leipzig] — Bll Klin Hydrotherap
Blaetter fuer Literarische Unterhaltung — Blaett Lit Unterhalt
Blaetter fuer Muenzfreunde — BMFR
Blaetter fuer Muenzfreunde und Muenzforschung — BfM
Blaetter fuer Muenzfreunde und Muenzforschung — Bl Muefreunde F
Blaetter fuer Muenzfreunde und Muenzforschung — Bl Muenzfreunde Muenzforsch
Blaetter fuer Muenzfreunde und Muenzforschung — BMF
Blaetter fuer Musikfreunde — BfM
Blaetter fuer Naturkunde und Naturschutz — Blaett Naturk Naturschutz
Blaetter fuer Obst-, Wein-, Gartenbau, und Kleintierzucht — Blaett Obst Wein Gartenbau Kleintierzucht
Blaetter fuer Pfaelzische Kirchengeschichte — BPKG
Blaetter fuer Pflanzenbau und Pflanzenzuechtung — Blaett Pflanzenbau Pflanzenzuecht
Blaetter fuer Rechtspflege in Thueringen und Anhalt — Bll Rechtspfl Thuering
Blaetter fuer Technikgeschichte — Blaett Technikgesch
Blaetter fuer Technikgeschichte. Forschungsinstitut fuer Technikgeschichte in Wien — Bl Technikgesch
Blaetter fuer Untersuchungs- und Forschungs-Instrumente — Bl Unters Forsch Instrum
Blaetter fuer Vergleichende Rechtswissenschaft — BlverglR
Blaetter fuer Wuerttembergische Kirchengeschichte — Bl Wuerttemb Kirchengesch
Blaetter fuer Wuerttembergische Kirchengeschichte — Bl Wuerttemberg Kirchenges
Blaetter fuer Wuerttembergische Kirchengeschichte — BWKG
Blaetter fuer Zuckerruebenbau — Bl Zuckerruebenbau
Blagoveshchenskii Gosudarstvennyi Meditsinskii Institut. Trudy — Blagoveshch Gos Med Inst Tr
Blagoveshchenskii Sel'skokhozyaistvennyi Institut. Trudy — Blagoveshch Skh Inst Tr
Blair and Ketchum's Country Journal — Blair & Ketchum's
Blake; an Illustrated Quarterly — Blake Ill Q
Blake; an Illustrated Quarterly — Blake Q
Blake Newsletter — BlakeN
Blake Studies — Blake Stud
Blake Studies — BlakeS
Blast Furnace and Steel Plant — Blast F & Steel Pl
Blast Furnace and Steel Plant — Blast Furn Steel Plant
Blast Furnace and Steel Plant — BLFSA
Blast Furnace, Coke Oven, and Raw Materials. Proceedings — Blast Furn Coke Oven Raw Mater Proc
Blatt fuer Patent-, Muster-, und Zeichenwesen — Bl Patentw
Bleacher, Finisher, and Textile Chemist — Bleacher Finish Tex Chem
Blech, Rohre, Profile — BRPFD
B'lgarska Akademija na Naukite. Teoreticna i Prilozna Mehanika — Teoret Priloz Meh
Blick durch die Wirtschaft — BW
Blick durch die Wirtschaft — FFE
Blick in die Wissenschaft — Blick Wiss
Blick ins Museum. Mitteilungen aus den Staatlichen Wissenschaftlichen Museen Dresden — Blick Mus
Blindness, Visual Impairment, Deaf-Blindness — Blind Vis Impair Deaf Blind
BLL [*British Library Lending Division*] **Review** — BLL Rev
BLM (Bonniers Litterara Magasin) — BLM (Bon Lit)
BLMRA [*British Leather Manufacturers' Research Association*] **Journal** — BLMRA J
Blodau'r Ffair — BFf
Bloembollencultuur — WBC
Bloembollenexport — BLB
Blood Bank Technology. 2nd Edition — Blood Bank Technol 2nd Ed
Blood Cells — BLCED
Blood Cells, Molecules, and Diseases — Blood Cells Mol Dis
Blood Coagulation and Fibrinolysis — Blood Coagul Fibrinolysis
Blood Pressure — Blood Press
Blood Pressure Control — Blood Pres Cont
Blood Pressure. Supplement — Blood Press Suppl
Blood Purification — Blood Purif
Blood Reviews — Blood Rev
Blood Therapy Journal — Blood Ther J
Blood Transfusion and Immunohaematology — Blood Transfus Immunohaematol
Blood Vessels — Blood Vess
Blue Book and Catalog Edition. Annual Buyers' Guide — Blue Book Cat Ed Annu Buyers Guide
Blue Book of Soap and Sanitary Chemicals — Blue Book Soap Sanit Chem
Blue Chip Economic Indicators — Blue Chip
Blue Cloud Quarterly — Blue Cloud Q
Blue Cross Association. Research Series — Blue Cross Assoc Res Ser
Blue Cross Reports — Blue Cross Rep
Blue Guitar — BG
Blue Jay — BJAY
Blue Jeans Magazine — BJ
Blue Sky Law Reports. Commerce Clearing House — Blue Sky L Rep CCH
Bluegrass — BLBIA
Bluegrass Literary Review — B L Rev
Bluegrass Literary Review — Bluegrass Lit Rev
Bluegrass Music News — BM
Bluegrass Unlimited — BGU
Bluegrass Unlimited — Bluegrass
Bluehende Kakteen. Deutsche Kakteengesellschaft — Blueh Kakteen

Blues Unlimited — Blues
Blues Unlimited — BU
Blues World — BW
Blumen-Kalender — Blumen Kalender
Blumen-Zeitung — Blumen Zeitung
Blut. Sonderbaende — Blut Sonderb
Blut. Supplement — Blut Suppl
BMA [*British Medical Association*] **Press Cuttings Database** — BMAP
BMFT [*Bundesministerium fuer Forschung und Technologie*] **Mitteilungen** — BMFT Mitt
BMI: The Many Worlds of Music — BMI
BMJ. British Medical Journal — BMJ Br Med J
BML. Bollettino di Microbiologia e Indagini di Laboratorio — BML Boll Microbiol Indag Lab
BMR [*Bureau of Mineral Resources, Geology, and Geophysics*] **Bulletin** — BMR Bull
BMR [*Australia. Bureau of Mineral Resources. Geology and Geophysics*] **Journal of Australian Geology and Geophysics** — BMR J Aust Geol Geophys
BMWI Tagesnachrichten — BTAED
BN. Bianco e Nero — BN Bian Ner
BNA [*Bureau of National Affairs*] **Administrative Practice Manual** — BNA Admin Pract Man
B'nai B'rith International Jewish Monthly — BBIJM
BNF [*British Nutrition Foundation*] **Bulletin** — BNF Bull
BNF [*British Nutrition Foundation*] **Information Bulletin** — BNF Inf Bull
BNF [*British Nutrition Foundation*] **Nutrition Bulletin** — BNF Nutr Bull
BNF Nutrition Bulletin. British Nutrition Foundation — BNF Nutr Bull Br Nutr Found
BNH [*Banco Nacional da Habitacao*] **Em Resumo** — BNH Em Res
BNH [*Banco Nacional da Habitacao*] **Relatorio de Atividades** — BNH Relat Atividad
BNIST [*Bureau National de l'Information Scientifique et Technique*] **Rapport Annuel** — BNIST Rapp Annu
Board Manufacture and Practice — Board Mfr
Board of Agriculture and Fisheries. Annual Reports of Proceedings under the Diseases of Animals Acts (London) — Bd Agric and Fish Ann Rep Proc Dis Anim Acts (London)
Board of Contract Appeals Decisions. Commerce Clearing House — BCA CCH
Board of Greenkeeping Research. British Golf Unions. Journal — Board Greenkeeping Res Brit Golf Unions J
Boardroom Reports — Boardroom
Boating — GBOT
Boating Abstracts — BoAb
Boating Business — Boat Bus
Bobbin Magazine — Bobbin Mag
BOCAAD. Bulletin of Computer-Aided Architectural Design — BOCAAD Bull Comput Aided Archit Des
Bochu Kagaku — BOCKA
Bochumer Anglistische Studien — BAS
Bochumer Arbeiten zur Sprach- und Literaturwissenschaft — BASL
Bockernas Varld — BoV
Boden Wand und Decke — BWDEB
Bodenbiologie Microbiologie — Bodenbiol Microbiol
Bodenkultur — BODEA
Bodenkunde und Pflanzenernaehrung — Bodenkd Pflanzenernaehr
Bodenkundliche Forschungen — Bodenk Forsch
Bodenkundliche und Pflanzenernaehrung — Bodenk Pflanzenernaehr
Bodleian Library Record — BLR
Bodleian Library Record — Bod Lib Rec
Bodleian Library Record — Bodl Libr Rec
Bodleian Library Record — Bodleian Lib Rec
Bodleian Library Record — Bodleian Libr Rec
Bodleian Quarterly Record — Bodleian Quart Rec
Bodleian Quarterly Record — BQR
Body Politic — Body Pol
Boei Eisei — BOEIA
Boei Ika Daigakko Zasshi — BIDZD
Boekblad — NBO
Boekenschouw voor Godsdienst, Wetenschap en Kunst — BGWK
Boekverkoper — BOK
Boergyogyaszati es Venerologiai Szemle — Boergyogy Venerol Sz
Boerhaave Series for Postgraduate Medical Education — Boerhaave Ser Postgrad Med Educ
Boersenblatt fuer den Deutschen Buchandel — BoeDB
Boersenblatt fuer den Deutschen Buchhandel — BDBHA
Boersenblatt fuer den Deutschen Buchhandel [*Germany*] — Boersenbl Dtsch Buchhandel
Boersen-Zeitung — Boersen-Ztg
Boersen-Zeitung — BOZED
Boethius. Texte und Abhandlungen zur Geschichte der Mathematik und der Naturwiss — Boethius Texte Abh Gesch Math Naturwiss
Bog og Naal — B o N
Bogazici Universitesi Dergisi. Muhendislik — Bogazici Univ Derg Muhendislik
Bogazici Universitesi Dergisi. Temel Bilimler — Bogazici Univ Derg Temel Bilimler
Bogazici Universitesi Dergisi. Temel Bilimler. Kimya — Bogazici Univ Derg Temel Bilimler Kim
Bogazici Universitesi Journal. Engineering — Bogazici Univ J Eng
Bogazici Universitesi Journal. Sciences — Bogazici Univ J Sci
Bogazici Universitesi Journal. Sciences. Chemistry — Bogazici Univ J Sci Chem
Bogens Verden — Bg V
Bogens Verden — BV
Boghazkoei-Studien — Bo St
Boghazkoei-Studien [*Vorderasiatische Aegyptische Gesellschaft*] — Boghazkoei Stud
Boghazkoei-Texte in Umschrift — BoTU
Bogormen — Bgorm
Bogoslovni Vestnik — BV
Bogoslovska Smotra — BS
Bogoslovski Glasnik — BG
Bogvennen — Bgv
Bohemia. Jahrbuch des Collegium Carolinum — Bo
Bohr- und Sprengpraxis — Bohr Sprengprax
Bohrtechniker Zeitung — Bohrtech Ztg
Boiler Engineer [*Japan*] — Boiler Eng
Boiler Maker and Plate Fabricator — Boiler Maker Plate Fabr
Bois et Forets des Tropiques — BFTRA
Bois et Forets des Tropiques — Bois For Trop
Bois et Forets des Tropiques — Bois Forets Trop
Bok og Bibliotek — Bo B
Bok og Bibliotek — Bok og Bibl
Bolero — B
Boletim ABCP [*Associacao Tecnica Brasileira de Celulose e Papel*] — Bol ABCP
Boletim. Academia Nacional de Farmacia — Bol Acad Nac Farm
Boletim. Academia Nacional de Medicina — Bol Acad Nac Med
Boletim. Academia Nacional de Medicina (Brazil) — Bol Acad Nac Med (Braz)
Boletim. Academia Nacional de Medicina (Rio De Janeiro) — Bol Acad Nac Med (Rio De J)
Boletim. Academia Portuguesa do Ex-Libris — BAPE
Boletim. Academia Portuguesa do Ex-Libris — BAPEL
Boletim Apicola — Bolm Apic
Boletim. Associacao Brasileira de Fisicos em Medicina [*Brazil*] — Bol Assoc Bras Fis Med
Boletim. Associacao Brasileira de Pesquisas sobre Plantas Aromaticas e Oleos Essenciais — Bol Assoc Bras Pesqui Plant Aromat Oleos Essen
Boletim. Associacao Brasileira de Pesquisas sobre Plantas Aromaticas e Oleos Essenciais — Bol Assoc Bras Pesqui Plant Aromat Oleos Essenc
Boletim. Associacao Brasileira de Pharmaceuticos — Bol Assoc Bras Pharm
Boletim. Associacao Brasileira de Quimica — Bol Assoc Bras Quim
Boletim. Associacao Central da Agricultura Portuguesa — BACAP
Boletim. Associacao de Filosofia Natural — BAFN
Boletim. Associacao de Filosofia Natural (Portugal) — Bol Assoc Filos Nat (Portugal)
Boletim. Associacao Quimica do Brasil — Bol Assoc Quim Brasil
Boletim. Associacao Tecnica Brasileira de Celulose e Papel — Bol Assoc Tec Bras Celul Pap
Boletim. Banco Central do Brasil — Bol Banco Cent Brasil
Boletim Bibliografico. Biblioteca Publica Municipal (Sao Paulo) — Bol Bibliogr S Paulo
Boletim Bibliografico Brasileiro — BBBr
Boletim Bibliografico Brasileiro (Rio de Janeiro) — Bol Bibliogr Bras Rio
Boletim Biologica (Sao Paulo) — Bol Biol (S Paulo)
Boletim. Casa Regional da Beira-Douro — BCRBD
Boletim Cearense de Agronomia — Bol Cear Agron
Boletim. Centro de Estudos do Hospital dos Servidores do Estado (Rio De Janeiro) — Bol Cent Estud Hosp Servidores Estado (Rio De J)
Boletim Cientifico BC. Centro de Energia Nuclear na Agricultura — Bol Cient BC Cent Energ Nucl Agric
Boletim Clinico dos Hospitals Civis de Lisboa — Bol Clin Hosp Civis Lisb
Boletim. Comissao Geografica e Geologica do Estado de Sao Paulo — Bol Com Geogr Geol Estado Sao Paulo
Boletim. Comissao Nacional de Energia Nuclear (Brazil) — Bol Com Nac Energ Nucl (Braz)
Boletim. Comissao Reguladora de Cereais do Arquipelago dos Acores — BCRCA
Boletim. Commissao Geographica e Geologica do Estado de Sao Paulo — Bol Commiss Geogr Estado Sao Paulo
Boletim. Conselho Nacional de Pesquisas (Brazil) — Bol Cons Nac Pesqui (Braz)
Boletim. Conselho Nacional de Pesquisas (Brazil) — Bol Cons Nac Pesqui (Brazil)
Boletim Cultural — BCu
Boletim Cultural. Camara Municipal do Porto — BC
Boletim Cultural. Camara Municipal do Porto — BCCMP
Boletim Cultural da Guine Portuguesa — BCGP
Boletim Cultural da Guine Portuguesa — BCGuineP
Boletim Cultural da Guine Portuguesa — Bol Cult Guine Port
Boletim Cultural da Guine Portuguesa — Bol Cult Guine Portug
Boletim da Associacao Brasileira de Normas Tecnicas (Rio de Janeiro) — Bol Assoc Bras Normas Tec Rio
Boletim da Biblioteca da Camara dos Deputados (Rio de Janeiro, Brasilia) — Bol Bibl Cam Deputados Rio Brasilia
Boletim da Biblioteca Publica Municipal de Matosinhos — BBPMM
Boletim da Comissao de Planejamento Economico (Salvador, Brazil) — Bol CPE Salvador
Boletim da Equipe de Odontologia Sanitaria — Bol Equipe Odontol Sanit
Boletim da Federacao Brasileira de Associacoes de Bibliotecarios (Sao Paulo) — Bol Fed Bras Assoc Bibl S Paulo
Boletim da Federacao Nacional dos Produtores de Trigo — BFNPT
Boletim da Junta Nacional da Cortica — BJNC
Boletim da Sociedade Brasileira de Direito Internacional (Rio de Janeiro) — Bol Soc Bras Direito Intern Rio
Boletim da Sociedade Brasileira de Geografia (Rio de Janeiro) — Bol Soc Bras Geogr Rio
Boletim da Sociedade Brasileira de Matematica. Nova Serie — Bol Soc Brasil Mat NS
Boletim da Sociedade Broteriana — Bol Soc Brot
Boletim da Superintendencia dos Servicos do Cafe (Sao Paulo) — Bol Superin Serv Cafe S Paulo
Boletim da Universidade de Sao Paulo. Botanica — Bol Univ Sao Paulo Bot

Boletim de Agricultura (Belo Horizonte, Brazil) — Bol Agric (Belo Horizonte Braz)
Boletim de Agricultura (Belo Horizonte, Brazil) — Bol Agric (Belo Horizonte Brazil)
Boletim de Agricultura. Departmento de Producao Vegetal (Minas Gerais) — Bol Agr Dept Prod Veg (Minas Gerais)
Boletim de Agricultura. Directoria de Publicidade Agricola (Sao Paulo) — Bol Agr Dir Publ Agr (Sao Paulo)
Boletim de Agricultura do Estado de Sao Paulo — Bol Agric Estado Sao Paulo
Boletim de Agricultura (Sao Paulo) — Bol Agr S Paulo
Boletim de Agricultura (Sao Paulo) — Bol Agric Sao Paulo
Boletim de Agricultura, Zootechnia, e Veterinaria. Bello Horizonte — Bol Agric Zootech e Vet Bello Horizonte
Boletim de Antropologia. Instituto de Antropologia. Universidade do Ceara (Fortaleza, Brazil) — Bol Antrop Fortaleza
Boletim de Ariel — B d A
Boletim de Assistencia Medicaos Indigenas e da Luta Contra a Moleatia do Sono (Luanda) — Bol Assist Med Indigen (Luanda)
Boletim de Bioestatistica e Epidemiologia — Bol Bioestat Epidem
Boletim de Ciencias do Mar — Bol Cienc Mar
Boletim de Ciencias Economicas — Bol Ciencias Econs
Boletim de Dentistica Operatoria — Bol Dent Oper
Boletim de Divulgacao. Instituto de Oleos (Rio De Janeiro) — Bol Divulg Inst Oleos (Rio De Janeiro)
Boletim de Electroquimica e Corrosao — Bol Electroquim Corros
Boletim de Estudos Classicos — BEC
Boletim de Estudos de Pesca — Bol Estud Pesca
Boletim de Estudos. Superintendencia do Desenvolvimento do Nordeste. Divisao de Geologia (Brazil) — Bol Estud Supt Desenvolvimento Nordeste Div Geol (Braz)
Boletim de Etnografia — BE
Boletim de Faculdade de Filosofia, Ciencias, e Letras. Universidade de Sao Paulo. Botanica — Biol Fac Filos Univ Sao Paulo Bot
Boletim de Filologia — BdF
Boletim de Fisiologia Animal (Sao Paulo) — Bol Fisiol Anim (Sao Paulo)
Boletim de Geociencias da Petrobras — Bol Geocienc Petrobras
Boletim de Geologia. Universidade Federal do Rio De Janeiro. Instituto de Geociencias — Bol Geol Univ Fed Rio De Janeiro Inst Geocienc
Boletim de Industria Animal — Bol Ind Anim
Boletim de Industria Animal — Bolm Ind Anim
Boletim de Inseminacao Artificial — Bol Insemin Artif
Boletim de Inseminacao Artificial — Bol Inseminacao Artif
Boletim de Matematica, Estatistica, e Fisica — Bol Mat Estatist Fis
Boletim de Matematica, Estatistica, e Fisica (Araraquara, Brazil) — Bol Mat Estat Fis (Araraquara Braz)
Boletim de Matematica, Estatistica, e Fisica (Araraquara, Brazil) — Bol Mat Estat Fis (Araraquara Brazil)
Boletim de Materias Dentarios — Bol Mat Dent
Boletim de Minas (Portugal Direccao-Geral de Minas e Servicos Geologicos) — Bol Minas (Port Dir-Geral Minas Serv Geol)
Boletim de Numismatica (Brasil) — Bol Num (Brasil)
Boletim de Oncologia — Bol Oncol
Boletim de Pesquisa. Centro de Tecnologia Agricola e Alimentar EMBRAPA [*Empresa Brasileira de Pesquisa Agropecuaria*] — Bol Pesqui Cent Tecnol Agric Aliment EMBRAPA
Boletim de Pesquisa. EMBRAPA [*Empresa Brasileira de Pesquisa Agropecuaria*]. Centro de Tecnologia Agricola e Alimentar — Bol Pesqui EMBRAPA Cent Tecnol Agric Alimen
Boletim de Psicologia — Bol Psicol
Boletim de Psiquiatria — Bol Psiquiatr
Boletim de Sociedade Portuguesa de Matematica — Bol Soc Port Mat
Boletim de Zoologia — Bol Zool
Boletim de Zoologia e Biologia Marinha [*Later, Boletim de Zoologia*] — Bol Zool Biol Mar
Boletim de Zoologia e Biologia Marinha (Nova Serie) [*Later, Boletim de Zoologia*] — Bol Zool Biol Mar (Nova Ser)
Boletim de Zoologia. Museu Paraense Emilio Goeldi — Bol Zool Mus Para Emilio Goeldi
Boletim de Zoologia. Universidade de Sao Paulo — Bolm Zool Univ S Paulo
Boletim de Zootecnia — Bol Zootec
Boletim Demografico (Brazil) — Bol Demografico (Brazil)
Boletim. Departamento de Engenharia Quimica. Escola Politecnica. Universidad e de Sao Paulo — Bol Dept Eng Quim Esc Politec Univ Sao Paulo
Boletim. Departamento de Engenharia Quimica. Escola Politecnica. Universidade de Sao Paulo — Bol Dep Eng Quim Esc Politec Univ Sao Paulo
Boletim. Departamento de Matematica e Estatistica (Araraquara, Brazil) — Bol Dep Mat Estat (Araraquara Braz)
Boletim. Departamento de Quimica. Escola Politecnica. Universidade de Sao Paulo — Bol Dep Quim Esc Politec Univ Sao Paulo
Boletim. Departamento Nacional da Producao Mineral (Brasil) — Bol Dep Nac Prod Miner (Brasil)
Boletim Didatico. Escola de Agronomia Eliseu Maciel (Pelotas, Brazil) — Bol Didat Esc Agron Eliseu Maciel (Pelotas Braz)
Boletim Didatico. Escola de Agronomia Eliseu Maciel (Pelotas, Brazil) — Bol Didat Esc Agron Eliseu Maciel (Pelotas Brazil)
Boletim. Divisao de Fomento da Producao Mineral (Brazil) — Bol Div Fom Prod Miner (Braz)
Boletim. Divisao Nacional de Dermatologia Sanitaria — Bol Div Nac Dermatol Sanit
Boletim. Divisao Nacional de Lepra — Bol Div Nac Lepra
Boletim do Arquivo Municipal. Camara Municipal de Braga — BAM
Boletim do Centro Latino-Americano de Pesquisas em Ciencias Sociais (Rio de Janeiro) — Bol Cent Lat Am Pesq Cien Soc Rio
Boletim do Departamento de Estradas de Rodagem (Sao Paulo) — Bol Dept Estradas Rodagem S Paulo
Boletim do Grupo Amigos de Braganca — BGAB
Boletim do INBAPO (Instituto Paranaense de Botanica) — Bol INPABO
Boletim do Instituto Joaquim Nabuco de Pesquisas Sociais (Recife, Brazil) — Bol Inst J Nabuco Pesq Soc Recife
Boletim do Jardim Botanico (Rio de Janeiro) — Bol Jard Bot Rio De Janeiro
Boletim do Leite — Bol Leite
Boletim do Leite e Seus Derivados [*Rio De Janeiro*] — Bol Leit
Boletim do Leite e Seus Derivados — Bol Leite Seus Deriv
Boletim do Ministerio da Agricultura, Industria e Commercio (Rio de Janeiro) — Bol Min Agr Indus Com Rio
Boletim do Ministerio da Agricultura (Rio de Janeiro) — Bol Min Agr Rio
Boletim do Ministerio do Trabalho, Industria e Commercio (Rio de Janeiro) — Bol Min Trab Indus Com Rio
Boletim do Museu Nacional. Geologia (Rio de Janeiro) — Bol Mus Nac Geol Rio
Boletim do Museu Nacional. Antropologia (Rio de Janeiro) — Bol Mus Nac Antrop Rio
Boletim do Museu Nacional (Rio de Janeiro) — Bol Mus Nac Rio
Boletim do Museu Nacional. Zoologia (Rio de Janeiro) — Bol Mus Nac Zool Rio
Boletim do Museu Paraense de Historia Natural e Ethnographia — Bol Mus Paraense Hist Nat
Boletim do Museu Paraense Emilio Goeldi (Belem, Brazil) — Bol Mus Paraense E Goeldi Belem
Boletim do Rotary Club de Braga — BRCB
Boletim do Sanatorio (Sao Lucas) — Bol Sanat (Sao Lucas)
Boletim do Servico Nacional de Pesquisas Agronomicas — Bol Serv Nac Pesq Agron
Boletim do Trabalho Industrial — BTI
Boletim Epidemiologico (Rio De Janeiro) — Bol Epidemiol (Rio De J)
Boletim. Escola Agricola "Luiz De Queiroz" — Bolm Esc Agric "Luiz Queiroz"
Boletim. Escola de Farmacia (Coimbra) — Bol Esc Farm (Coimbra)
Boletim. Escola de Farmacia. Universidade de Coimbra — Bol Esc Farm Univ Coimbra
Boletim. Escola de Farmacia. Universidade de Coimbra. Edicao Cientifica — Bol Esc Farm Univ Coimbra Ed Cien
Boletim. Escola de Farmacia. Universidade de Coimbra. Edicao Didactica. Noticias Farmaceuticas — Bol Esc Farm Univ Coimbra Ed Didact Not Farm
Boletim. Escola Superior de Agricultura "Luiz De Queiroz." Universidade de Sao Paulo — Bol Esc Super Agric "Luiz De Queiroz" Univ Sao Paulo
Boletim. Escola Superior de Farmacia. Universidade de Lisboa — Bol Esc Super Farm Univ Lisboa
Boletim. Estacao de Biologia Marinha. Universidade do Ceara — Bol Estac Biol Mar Univ Ceara
Boletim. Estacao de Biologia Marinha. Universidade Federal do Ceara — Bol Estac Biol Mar Univ Fed Ceara
Boletim. Faculdade de Ciencias Agrarias do Para — Bol Fac Cienc Agrar Para
Boletim. Faculdade de Direito (Coimbra) — Bol Fac Dir (Coimbra)
Boletim. Faculdade de Farmacia e Odontologia de Ribeirao Preto — Bol Fac Farm Odontol Ribeirao Preto
Boletim. Faculdade de Farmacia. Universidade de Coimbra (Coimbra) — Bol Fac Farm Coimbra (Coimbra)
Boletim. Faculdade de Farmacia. Universidade de Coimbra. Edicao Cientifica — Bol Fac Farm Univ Coimbra Ed Cient
Boletim. Faculdade de Farmacia. Universidade de Coimbra. Edicao Didactica. Noticias Farmaceuticas — Bol Fac Farm Univ Coimbra Ed Didact Not Farm
Boletim. Faculdade de Farmacia. Universidade de Lisboa — Bol Fac Farm Univ Lisboa
Boletim. Faculdade de Filosofia, Ciencias, e Letras. Universidade de Sao Paulo. Serie Botanica — Bol Fac Filos Cienc Let Univ Sao Paulo Bot
Boletim. Faculdade de Filosofia, Ciencias, e Letras. Universidade de Sao Paulo. Serie Botanica — Bol Fac Filos Cienc Let Univ Sao Paulo Ser Bot
Boletim. Faculdade de Filosofia, Ciencias, e Letras. Universidade de Sao Paulo. Serie Geologia — Bol Fac Filos Cienc Let Univ Sao Paulo Geol
Boletim. Faculdade de Filosofia, Ciencias, e Letras. Universidade de Sao Paulo. Serie Mineralogia — Bol Fac Filos Cienc Let Univ Sao Paulo Mineral
Boletim. Faculdade de Filosofia, Ciencias, e Letras. Universidade de Sao Paulo. Serie Quimica — Bol Fac Filos Cienc Let Univ Sao Paulo Quim
Boletim. Faculdade de Filosofia, Ciencias, e Letras. Universidade de Sao Paulo. Serie Zoologia — Bol Fac Filos Cienc Let Univ Sao Paulo Ser Zool
Boletim. Faculdade de Odontologia de Piracicaba — Bol Fac Odontol Piracicaba
Boletim. Faculdade de Odontologia de Piracicaba. Universidade Estadual de Campinas — Bol Fac Odontol Piracicaba Univ Estadual Campinas
Boletim Fitossanitario — Bol Fitossanit
Boletim. Fundacao Goncalo Moniz — Bol Fund Goncalo Moniz
Boletim Geografico — Bol Geog
Boletim Geografico — Bol Geogr
Boletim Geografico. Instituto Brasileiro de Geografia e Estatistica (Rio de Janeiro) — Bol Geogr Rio
Boletim Geral do Ultramar — BGU
Boletim. Hospital da Faculdade de Medicina. Universidade da Bahia — Bol Hosp Fac Med Univ Bahia
Boletim. Hospital das Clinicas. Faculdade de Medicina. Universidade da Bahia — Bol Hosp Clin Fac Med Univ Bahia
Boletim. Hospital. Hospital Geral de Santo Antonio-Porto — Bol Hosp Hosp Geral Santo Antonio Porto
Boletim. Hospital Prof. Edgard Santos. Faculdade de Medicina. Universidade da Bahia — Bol Hosp Prof Edgard Santos Fac Med Univ Bahia
Boletim IG. Universidade de Sao Paulo. Instituto de Geociencias — Bol IG Univ Sao Paulo Inst Geocien
Boletim Informativo ABIA/SAPRO [*Associacao Brasileira das Industrias da Alimentacao. Setor de Alimentos Calorico-Proteicos*] — Bol Inf ABIA/SAPRO
Boletim Informativo do Instituto Brasileiro de Bibliografia e Documentacao (Rio de Janeiro) — Bol Inform Inst Bras Bibliogr Doc Rio
Boletim Informativo. Instituto de Biologia Maritima — Bol Inf Inst Biol Marit
Boletim Informativo. Instituto de Cacau da Bahia — Bol Inform Inst Cacau Bahia
Boletim Informativo. Sociedade Brasileira de Radiologia — BISRD

Boletim Informativo. Sociedade Brasileira de Radiologia — Bol Inf Soc Bras Radiol
Boletim. INPA [*Instituto Nacional de Pesquisas da Amazonia*]. Botanica — Bol INPA Bot
Boletim. INPA [*Instituto Nacional de Pesquisas da Amazonia*]. Patologia Tropical — Bol INPA Pat Trop
Boletim. INPA [*Instituto Nacional de Pesquisas da Amazonia*]. Patologia Tropical — Bol INPA Patol Trop
Boletim. INPA [*Instituto Nacional de Pesquisas da Amazonia*]. Pesquisas Florestais — Bol INPA Pesqui Florestais
Boletim. INPA [*Instituto Nacional de Pesquisas da Amazonia*]. Tecnologia — Bol INPA Tecnol
Boletim. Instituto Agronomico Campinas — Bol Inst Agron Campinas
Boletim. Instituto Agronomico do Estado de Sao Paulo — Bol Inst Agron Estado Sao Paulo
Boletim. Instituto Agronomico (Sao Paulo) — Bol Inst Agron (Sao Paulo)
Boletim. Instituto Biologico da Bahia — Bol Inst Biol Bahia
Boletim. Instituto Brasileiro de Sciencias — Bol Inst Brasil Sci
Boletim. Instituto Central de Biociencias. Serie Botanica — Bol Inst Cent Biocienc Ser Bot
Boletim. Instituto Central de Fomento Economica da Bahia — Bol Inst Centr Fomento Econ Bahia
Boletim. Instituto de Angola [*Luanda*] — B Inst Angola
Boletim. Instituto de Angola — Bol Inst Angola
Boletim. Instituto de Angola — Bolm Inst Angola
Boletim. Instituto de Biologia e Pesquisas Tecnologicas — Bol Inst Biol Pesqui Tecnol
Boletim. Instituto de Biologia Marinha. Universidade Federal do Rio Grande Do Norte — Bol Inst Biol Mar Univ Fed Rio Grande Do Norte
Boletim. Instituto de Botanica (Sao Paulo) — Bol Inst Bot (Sao Paulo)
Boletim. Instituto de Ciencias Biologicas e de Geociencias. Communicacoes Malacologicas — Bol Inst Cienc Biol Geocienc Commun Malacol
Boletim. Instituto de Ciencias Naturais. Universidade do Rio Grande Do Sul [*A publication*] — Bol Inst Cienc Nat Univ Rio Grande Do Sul
Boletim. Instituto de Ecologia e Experimentacao Agricolas — Bol Inst Ecol Exp Agric
Boletim. Instituto de Geociencias e Astronomia. Universidade de Sao Paulo — Bol Inst Geocienc Astron Univ Sao Paulo
Boletim. Instituto de Geologia. Universidade de Recife. Mineralogia — Bol Inst Geol Univ Recife Mineral
Boletim. Instituto de Historia Natural Curitiba Botanica — Bol Inst Hist Nat Curitiba Bot
Boletim. Instituto de Investigacao Cientifica de Angola — Bol Inst Invest Cient Angola
Boletim. Instituto de Investigacao Cientifica de Angola — Bol Inst Investig Cient Angola
Boletim. Instituto de Microbiologia. Universidade Federal do Rio Grande Do Sul — Bol Inst Microbiol Univ Fed Rio Grande Do Sul
Boletim. Instituto de Oceanografia. Sao Paulo Universidade (Sao Paulo) — Bol Inst Oceanogr Sao Paulo
Boletim. Instituto de Pesquisas Cirurgicas (Rio De Janeiro) — Bol Inst Pesqui Cir (Rio De J)
Boletim. Instituto de Pesquisas Veterinarias "Desiderio Finamor" — Bol Inst Pesqui Vet "Desiderio Finamor"
Boletim. Instituto de Quimica Agricola (Rio De Janeiro) — Bol Inst Quim Agric (Rio De Janeiro)
Boletim. Instituto de Tecnologia de Alimentos [*Campinas, Brazil*] — BIALB
Boletim. Instituto de Tecnologia de Alimentos — Bol Inst Tecnol Aliment
Boletim. Instituto de Tecnologia de Alimentos (Campinas, Brazil) — Bol Inst Tecnol Aliment (Campinas Braz)
Boletim. Instituto de Tecnologia Rural. Universidade do Ceara — Bol Inst Tecnol Rural Univ Ceara
Boletim. Instituto do Azeite e Produtos Oleaginosos — Bol Inst Azeite Prod Oleaginosos
Boletim. Instituto dos Produtos Florestais - Cortica — Bol Inst Prod Florestais Cortica
Boletim. Instituto dos Produtos Florestais. Madeiras e Derivados — Bol Inst Prod Florestais Madeiras Deriv
Boletim. Instituto dos Produtos Florestais. Resinosos — Bol Inst Prod Florestais Resinosos
Boletim. Instituto Geografico e Geologico (Sao Paulo State) — Bol Inst Geogr Geol (Sao Paulo State)
Boletim. Instituto Historico da Ilha Terceira — BIHIT
Boletim. Instituto Kuribara de Ciencia Natural Brasileira — Bol Inst Kuribara Ci Nat Brasil
Boletim. Instituto Luis de Camoes — BILC
Boletim. Instituto Nacional de Investigacao Industrial. Electroquimica e Corrosao (Portugal) — Bol Inst Nac Invest Ind Electroquim Corros (Port)
Boletim. Instituto Nacional de Pesquisas da Amazonia. Pesquisas Florestais — Bol Inst Nac Pesqui Amazonia Pesqui Florestais
Boletim. Instituto Nacional de Pesquisas da Amazonia. Tecnologia — Bol Inst Nac Pesqui Amazonia Tecnol
Boletim. Instituto Nacional de Tecnologia (Rio De Janeiro) — Bol Inst Nac Tecnol (Rio De Janeiro)
Boletim. Instituto Oceanografico — Bol Inst Oceanogr
Boletim. Instituto Oceanografico. Universidade de Sao Paulo — Bol Inst Oceanogr Univ Sao Paulo
Boletim. Instituto Tecnologico (Rio Grande Do Sul) — Bol Inst Tecnol (Rio Grande Sul)
Boletim. Instituto Zimotecnico (Sao Paulo) — Bol Inst Zimotec (Sao Paulo)
Boletim Internacional de Bibliografia Luso-Brasileira [*Lisboa*] — BIBLB
Boletim. IPA [*Instituto de Pesquisas Agronomicas*]. PSM [*Programa de Sorgo e Milheto*] — Bol IPA PSM
Boletim. Junta Geral Distrito Autonomo Ponta Delgada — Bol Junta Geral Distr Auton Ponta Delgada
Boletim. Junta Nacional da Cortica — Bol Junta Nac Cortica
Boletim. Laboratorio de Producao Mineral (Brazil) — Bol Lab Prod Miner (Braz)
Boletim Mensal de Estatistica (Portugal) — Bol Mensal Estatistica (Portugal)
Boletim Mensal. Sociedade de Lingua Portuguesa — BMP
Boletim Mensal. Sociedade de Lingua Portuguesa — BMSLP
Boletim Mineiro de Geografia — Bol Min Geogr
Boletim Mineralogico — Bol Mineral
Boletim Mineralogico (Recife, Brazil) — Bol Mineral (Recifec Braz)
Boletim. Ministerio de Sanidad y Asisteneta Social (Venezuela) — Bol Minist Sanid Asist Soc (Venez)
Boletim. Museu Botanico Municipal (Curitiba) — Bol Mus Bot Munic (Curitiba)
Boletim. Museu de Historia Natural UFMG [*Universidade Federal de Minas Gerais*]. Botanica — Bol Mus Hist Nat UFMG Bot
Boletim. Museu de Historia Natural UFMG [*Universidade Federal de Minas Gerais*]. Geologia — Bol Mus Hist Nat UFMG Geol
Boletim. Museu de Historia Natural UFMG [*Universidade Federal de Minas Gerais*]. Zoologia — Bol Mus Hist Nat UFMG Zool
Boletim. Museu e Laboratorio Mineralogico e Geologicao. Faculdade de Ciencias. Universidade de Lisboa — Bol Mus Lab Mineral Geol Fac Cienc Univ Lisboa
Boletim. Museu Municipal do Funchal — Bol Mus Munic Funchal
Boletim. Museu Nacional (Rio De Janeiro) — Bol Mus Nac (Rio De Janeiro)
Boletim. Museu Nacional (Rio De Janeiro). Antropologia — Bol Mus Nac (Rio De J) Antropol
Boletim. Museu Nacional (Rio De Janeiro). Botanica — Bol Mus Nac (Rio De J) Bot
Boletim. Museu Nacional (Rio De Janeiro). Geologia — BOJAAK
Boletim. Museu Nacional (Rio De Janeiro). Geologia — Bol Mus Nac (Rio De J) Geol
Boletim. Museu Nacional (Rio De Janeiro). Geologia — Bol Mus Nac (Rio De Janeiro) Geol
Boletim. Museu Nacional (Rio De Janeiro). Nova Serie. Geologia — Bol Mus Nac (Rio De J) Nova Ser Geol
Boletim. Museu Nacional (Rio De Janeiro). Zoologia — Bol Mus Nac (Rio De J) Zool
Boletim. Museu Paraense Emilio Goeldi — BMPEAE
Boletim. Museu Paraense Emilio Goeldi — Bol Mus Para Emilio Goeldi
Boletim. Museu Paraense Emilio Goeldi — Bol Mus Paraense Emilio Goeldi
Boletim. Museu Paraense Emilio Goeldi. Geologia — Bol Mus Para Emilio Goeldi Geol
Boletim. Museu Paraense Emilio Goeldi. Nova Serie. Antropologia — Bol Mus Para Emilio Goeldi Nova Ser Antropol
Boletim. Museu Paraense Emilio Goeldi. Nova Serie. Antropologia — Bol Mus Paraense Emilio Goeldi Nova Ser Antropol
Boletim. Museu Paraense Emilio Goeldi. Nova Serie. Antropologia — BPGAAC
Boletim. Museu Paraense Emilio Goeldi. Nova Serie. Antropologia (Belem) — Bol Mus Paraense E Goeldi NS Antrop Belem
Boletim. Museu Paraense Emilio Goeldi. Nova Serie. Botanica — Bol Mus Para Emilio Goeldi Nova Ser Bot
Boletim. Museu Paraense Emilio Goeldi. Nova Serie. Botanica — Bol Mus Paraense Emilio Goeldi Nova Ser Bot
Boletim. Museu Paraense Emilio Goeldi. Nova Serie. Botanica — Bolm Mus Para Emilio Goeldi Bot
Boletim. Museu Paraense Emilio Goeldi. Nova Serie. Geologia — Bol Mus Para Emilio Goeldi Nova Ser Geol
Boletim. Museu Paraense Emilio Goeldi. Nova Serie. Geologia — Bol Mus Paraense Emilio Goeldi Nova Ser Geol
Boletim. Museu Paraense Emilio Goeldi. Nova Serie. Zoologia — Bol Mus Para Emilio Goeldi Nova Ser Zool
Boletim. Museu Paraense Emilio Goeldi. Serie Antropologia — BMPAE6
Boletim. Museu Paraense Emilio Goeldi. Serie Antropologia — Bol Mus Para Emilio Goeldi Ser Antropol
Boletim. Museu Paraense Emilio Goeldi. Serie Botanica — BMPBE9
Boletim. Museu Paraense Emilio Goeldi. Serie Botanica — Bol Mus Para Emilio Goeldi Ser Bot
Boletim. Museu Paraense Emilio Goeldi. Serie Zoologia — BMPZED
Boletim. Museu Paraense Emilio Goeldi. Serie Zoologia — Bol Mus Para Emilio Goeldi Ser Zool
Boletim Odontologico Paulista — Bol Odont Paul
Boletim. Ordem dos Medicos — Bol Ord Med
Boletim Paranaense de Geociencias — Bol Parana Geocienc
Boletim Paranaense de Geografia — Bol Par Geogr
Boletim Paranaense de Geografia — Bol Parana Geogr
Boletim Paranense de Geografia. Associacao dos Geografas Brasileiros. Seccao Regional do Parana — Bol Paran Geogr
Boletim Paulista de Geografia — Bol Paul Geogr
Boletim Paulista de Geografia. Associacao dos Geografos Brasileiros (Sao Paulo) — Bol Paulista Geogr S Paulo
Boletim Pecuario — Bol Pecu
Boletim Pecuario — BP
Boletim Pecuario. Direccao Geral dos Servicos Pecuarios (Portugal) — Bol Pecuar Dir Geral Serv Pecuar (Portugal)
Boletim Pecuario (Lisbon) — Bol Pecu (Lisb)
Boletim. Real Sociedad Espanola de Historia Natural. Seccion Biologica — Bolm Real Soc Esp Hist Nat Secc
Boletim. Servico de Odontologia Sanitaria. Secretaria da Saude. Rio Grande do Sul (Porto Alegre) — Bol Serv Odontol Sanit (Porto Alegre)
Boletim. Servicos de Geologia e Minas de Angola — Bol Serv Geol Minas Angola
Boletim. Servicos de Geologia e Minas (Mocambique) — Bol Serv Geol Minas (Mocambique)
Boletim. Sociedade Brasileira de Agronomia — Bol Soc Bras Agron
Boletim. Sociedade Brasileira de Entomologia — Bol Soc Bras Ent
Boletim. Sociedade Brasileira de Entomologia — Bolm Soc Bras Ent
Boletim. Sociedade Brasileira de Geologia — Bol Soc Bras Geol

Boletim. Sociedade Brasileira de Matematica — Bol Soc Brasil Mat
Boletim. Sociedade Brasileira de Medicina Veterinaria — Bol Soc Bras Med Vet
Boletim. Sociedade Brasileira de Tuberculose — Bol Soc Bras Tuberc
Boletim. Sociedade Broteriana — Bol Soc Broteriana
Boletim. Sociedade Broteriana — Bolm Soc Broteriana
Boletim. Sociedade Cearense de Agronomia — Bol Soc Cear Agron
Boletim. Sociedade Cearense de Agronomia — Bol Soc Cearense Agron
Boletim. Sociedade Cearense de Agronomia — Bolm Soc Cearense Agron
Boletim. Sociedade de Chimica de Sao Paulo — Bol Soc Chim Sao Paulo
Boletim. Sociedade de Engenharia do Rio Grande Do Sul — Bol Soc Eng Rio Grande Do Sul
Boletim. Sociedade de Estudios Filologicos — BSEF
Boletim. Sociedade de Estudos de Macambique — BSEM
Boletim. Sociedade de Estudos de Mocambique — Bol Soc Estud Mocambique
Boletim. Sociedade de Geografia de Lisboa — Bol Soc Geogr Lisboa
Boletim. Sociedade de Geografia de Lisboa — BSGL
Boletim. Sociedade de Medicina e Cirugia de Sao Paulo — Bol Soc Med e Cirug S Paulo
Boletim. Sociedade Geologica de Portugal — Bol Soc Geol Port
Boletim. Sociedade Geologica de Portugal — BSGP
Boletim. Sociedade Paranaense de Matematica. 2 Serie [*Panama*] — Bol Soc Paran Mat 2
Boletim. Sociedade Paulista de Medicina Veterinaria — Bol Soc Paul Med Vet
Boletim. Sociedade Portuguesa de Cardiologia — Bol Soc Port Cardiol
Boletim. Sociedade Portuguesa de Ciencias Naturais — Bol Soc Port Cienc Nat
Boletim. Sociedade Portuguesa de Entomologia — Bol Soc Port Entomol
Boletim. Sociedade Portuguesa de Entomologia — BSPEEQ
Boletim. Sociedade Portuguesa de Quimica — Bol Soc Port Quim
Boletim. Superintendencia dos Servicos do Cafe (Sao Paulo) — Bol Supt Serv Cafe (Sao Paulo)
Boletim Tecnico. Brazil Departamento Nacional de Obras Contra as Secas — Bol Tec Braz Dep Nac Obras Contra Secas
Boletim Tecnico BT. Centro de Energia Nuclear na Agricultura — Bol Tec BT Cent Energ Nucl Agric
Boletim Tecnico. Centro de Pesquisa Agropecuaria do Tropico Umido — Bol Tec Cent Pesqui Agropecu Trop Umido
Boletim Tecnico. Centro de Pesquisa do Cacau (Itabuna, Brazil) — Bol Tec Cent Pesqui Cacau (Itabuna Braz)
Boletim Tecnico. Centro de Pesquisas e Desenvolvimento (Estado da Bahia) — Bol Tec Cent Pesqui Desenvolvimento (Estado Bahia)
Boletim Tecnico. Centro de Tecnologia Agricola e Alimentar — Bol Tec Cent Tecnol Agric Aliment
Boletim Tecnico. Centro de Tecnologia Agricola e Alimentar (Brazil) — BTCAB
Boletim Tecnico. Centro de Tecnologia Agricola e Alimentar (Rio De Janeiro) [*A publication*] — Bol Tec Cent Tecnol Agric Aliment (Rio De Janeiro)
Boletim Tecnico Cientifico. Universidade de Sao Paulo. Escola Superior Agricultura "Luiz de Queiroz" — Bol Tec Cient Univ Sao Paulo Esc Super Agri Luiz de Queiroz
Boletim Tecnico COPERSUCAR [*Cooperativa Central dos Produtores de Acucar e Alcool do Estado de Sao Paulo*] — Bol Tec COPERSUCAR
Boletim Tecnico. Departamento de Producao Vegetal Secretaria de Agricultura do Parana — Bol Tec Dep Prod Veg Secr Agric Parana
Boletim Tecnico. Departamento Nacional de Obras Contra as Secas — Bol Tec Dep Nac Obras Contra Secas
Boletim Tecnico. Departamento Nacional de Obras Contra as Secas (Brazil) — Bol Tec Dep Nac Obras Contra Secas (Braz)
Boletim Tecnico. Divisao de Pedologia e Fertilidade do Solo (Brazil) — Bol Tec Div Pedol Fertil Solo (Braz)
Boletim Tecnico. Divisao de Pesquisa Pedologica (Brazil) — Bol Tec Div Pesqui Pedol (Braz)
Boletim Tecnico. Divisao de Tecnologia Agricola e Alimentar (Brazil) — Bol Tec Div Tecnol Agric Aliment (Braz)
Boletim Tecnico. Divisao de Tecnologia Agricola e Alimentar (Brazil) — Bol Tec Div Tecnol Agric Aliment (Brazil)
Boletim Tecnico. Equipe de Pedologia e Fertilidade do Solo (Brazil) — Bol Tec Equipe Pedol Fertil Solo (Braz)
Boletim Tecnico. Equipe de Pedologia e Fertilidade do Solo (Brazil) — Bol Tec Equipe Pedol Fertil Solo (Brazil)
Boletim Tecnico. Fundacao Instituto Agronomico do Parana — Bol Tec Fund Inst Agron Parana
Boletim Tecnico IAPAR [*Instituto Agronomico do Parana*] — Bol Tec IAPAR
Boletim Tecnico. Instituto Agronomico — Bol Tec Inst Agron
Boletim Tecnico. Instituto Agronomico do Estado de Sao Paulo — Bol Tecn Inst Agron Estado Sao Paulo
Boletim Tecnico. Instituto Agronomico do Leste (Cruz Das Almas) — Bol Tec Inst Agron Leste (Cruz Das Almas)
Boletim Tecnico. Instituto Agronomico do Nordeste — Bol Tec Inst Agron Nordeste
Boletim Tecnico. Instituto Agronomico do Norte — Bol Tec Inst Agron Norte
Boletim Tecnico. Instituto Agronomico do Norte — Bolm Tec Inst Agron N
Boletim Tecnico. Instituto Agronomico do Norte (Belem) — Bol Tec Inst Agron Norte (Belem)
Boletim Tecnico. Instituto Agronomico do Sul — Bol Tec Inst Agron Sul
Boletim Tecnico. Instituto Agronomico do Sul (Brazil) — Bol Tec Inst Agron Sul (Braz)
Boletim Tecnico. Instituto Agronomico do Sul (Pelotas) — Bol Tec Inst Agron Sul (Pelotas)
Boletim Tecnico. Instituto Agronomico do Sul (Pelotas, Brazil) — Bol Tec Inst Agron Sul (Pelotas Brazil)
Boletim Tecnico. Instituto de Pesquisa Agropecuaria do Norte — Bol Tec Inst Pesqui Agropecu Norte
Boletim Tecnico. Instituto de Pesquisas e Experimentacao Agropecuarias do Norte — Bol Tec Inst Pesqui Exp Agropecu Norte
Boletim Tecnico. Instituto de Pesquisas e Experimentacao Agropecuarias do Norte — Bol Tec IPEAN
Boletim Tecnico. Instituto de Pesquisas e Experimentacao Agropecuarias do Norte — Bolm Tec Inst Pesq Exp Agropecuar N
Boletim Tecnico. Instituto de Pesquisas e Experimentacao Agropecuarias do Sul (Brazil) — Bol Tec Inst Pesqui Exp Agropecu Sul (Braz)
Boletim Tecnico. Instituto Florestal — Bol Tec Inst Florest
Boletim Tecnico. Instituto Florestal — IFBTBI
Boletim Tecnico. PETROBRAS [*Petroleo Brasileiro SA*] [*Centro de Pesquisas e Desenvolvimento*] — Bol Tec PETROBRAS
Boletim Tecnico. Servico Nacional de Levantamento e Conservacao de Solos — Bol Tec Serv Nac Levantamento Conserv Solos
Boletim Tecnico. Servico Nacional de Levantamento e Conservacao de Solos — BSNSDN
Boletim Tecnico. Universidade Federal Rural do Rio De Janeiro. Instituto de Agronomia. Departamento de Solos — Bol Tec Univ Fed Rural Rio De Janeiro Inst Agron Dep Solos
Boletim Trimestral Subcomissao Catarinense de Folclore da Comissao Nacional Brasileira de Folclore do Instituto Brasileiro de Educacao, Ciencia, e Cultura — BCF
Boletim. Universidade de Sao Paulo. Instituto de Geociencias — Bol Univ Sao Paulo Inst Geocienc
Boletim. Universidade de Sao Paulo. Instituto de Geociencias e Astronomia — Bol Univ Sao Paulo Inst Geocien Astron
Boletim. Universidade do Parana. Botanica — Bol Univ Parana Bot
Boletim. Universidade do Parana. Conselho de Pesquisas. Departamento de Medicina Preventiva. Monografia — Bol Univ Parana Cons Pesqui Dep Med Pre Monogr
Boletim. Universidade do Parana. Farmacognosia — Bol Univ Parana Farm
Boletim. Universidade do Parana. Farmacognosia — Bol Univ Parana Farmacogn
Boletim. Universidade do Parana. Farmacognosia — BPFRAO
Boletim. Universidade do Parana. Geologia — Bol Univ Parana Geol
Boletim. Universidade do Parana. Instituto de Geologia. Serie Geologia — Bol Univ Parana Inst Geol Geol
Boletim. Universidade do Parana. Zoologia — Bol Univ Parana Zool
Boletim. Universidade do Rio Grande Do Sul. Escola de Geologia — Bol Univ Rio Grande Sul Esc Geol
Boletim. Universidade Federal do Parana. Botanica — Bol Univ Fed Parana Bot
Boletim. Universidade Federal do Parana. Fisica Teorica [*Brazil*] — Bol Univ Fed Parana Fis Teor
Boletim. Universidade Federal do Parana. Fisica Teorica (Brazil) — BUFFB
Boletim. Universidade Federal do Parana. Instituto de Geologia. Serie Geologia — Bol Univ Fed Parana Inst Geol Geol
Boletim. Universidade Federal do Parana. Zoologia — Bol Univ Fed Parana Zool
Boletim. Universidade Federal do Parana. Zoologia — Bolm Univ Parana Zool
Boletin. Academia Aragonesa de Nobles y Bellas Artes de San Luis de Zaragoza — BANAZ
Boletin. Academia Argentina de Buenas Letras — BAABL
Boletin. Academia Argentina de Letras — BAAL
Boletin. Academia Argentina de Letras (Buenos Aires) — Bol Acad Arg Letr BA
Boletin. Academia Chilena de Historia (Santiago) — Bol Acad Chil Hist Santiago
Boletin. Academia Chilena de la Historia — Bola
Boletin. Academia Chilena (Santiago) — Bol Acad Chil Santiago
Boletin. Academia Colombiana — BAC
Boletin. Academia Colombiana — BACol
Boletin. Academia Colombiana (Bogota) — Bol Acad Col Bogota
Boletin. Academia Cubana de la Lengua — BACL
Boletin. Academia Cubana de la Lengua (Habana) — Bol Acad Cubana Leng Hav
Boletin. Academia de Artes y Ciencias — BAAC
Boletin. Academia de Bellas Artes de Cordoba — BABC
Boletin. Academia de Bellas Artes de Valladolid — BABA
Boletin. Academia de Bellas Artes y Ciencias Historicas de Toledo — BABAT
Boletin. Academia de Ciencias, Bellas Letras, y Nobles Artes de Cordoba — BACBLNAC
Boletin. Academia de Ciencias del Instituto de Chile — Bol Acad Cien Inst Chile
Boletin. Academia de Ciencias en Cordoba — Bol Acad Cienc Cordoba
Boletin. Academia de Ciencias Exactas, Fisicas, y Naturales — Bol Acad Cienc Exactas Fis Nat
Boletin. Academia de Ciencias Exactas, Fisicas, y Naturales de Madrid — Bol Acad Ci Exact Madrid
Boletin. Academia de Ciencias Fisicas, Matematicas, y Naturales [*Caracas, Venezuela*] — Bol Acad Cienc Fis Mat Natur
Boletin. Academia de Ciencias Fisicas, Matematicas, y Naturales (Caracas) — Bol Acad Cien Fis Mat Nat Caracas
Boletin. Academia de Ciencias Fisicas, Matematicas, y Naturales (Caracas, Venezuela) — BOCVA
Boletin. Academia de Ciencias Fisicas, Matematicas, y Naturales (Caracas, Venezuela) — Bol Acad Cienc Fis Mat Nat (Caracas)
Boletin. Academia de Ciencias Fisicas (Republica Argentina) — Bol Acad Cienc (Repub Argent)
Boletin. Academia de Ciencias Naturales y Artes de Barcelona — Bol Acad Ci Nat Barcelona
Boletin. Academia de Ciencias Politicas y Sociales — ACPS/B
Boletin. Academia de Ciencias Politicas y Sociales — BACPS
Boletin. Academia de Historia del Valle del Cauca (Cali, Colombia) — Bol Acad Hist Valle Cauca Cali
Boletin. Academia de la Historia — BAH
Boletin. Academia Galega — BAG
Boletin. Academia Galega de Ciencias — Bol Acad Galega Cienc
Boletin. Academia Hondurena de la Lengua — BAHL
Boletin. Academia Nacional de Ciencias (Argentina) — Bol Acad Nac Cienc (Argent)
Boletin. Academia Nacional de Ciencias (Cordoba) — Bol Acad Nac Cienc (Cordoba)
Boletin. Academia Nacional de Historia — B Acad Nac Hist

Boletin. Academia Nacional de Historia (Quito) — Bol Acad Nac Hist Quito
Boletin. Academia Nacional de la Historia — ANH/B
Boletin. Academia Nacional de la Historia — BANH
Boletin. Academia Nacional de la Historia [*Venezuela*] — BolA
Boletin. Academia Nacional de la Historia (Caracas) — Bol Acad Nac Hist Caracas
Boletin. Academia Nacional de la Historia (Quito) — BANHQ
Boletin. Academia Nacional de Medicina (Buenos Aires) — Bol Acad Nac Med (B Aires)
Boletin. Academia Norteamericana de la Lengua Espanola — BANLE
Boletin. Academia Panamena de la Historia (Panama) — Bol Acad Panamena Hist Panama
Boletin. Academia Puertorriquena de la Historia — BAPH
Boletin. Academia Venezolana — BAV
Boletin. Academia Venezolana Correspondiente a la Espanola — BAVC
Boletin. Academia Venezolana. Correspondiente de la Espanola (Caracas) — Bol Acad Venez Corr Espanola Caracas
Boletin. Administracion Nacional del Agua (Argentina) — Bol Adm Nac Agua (Argent)
Boletin Administrativo. Secretaria de Salud Publica de la Nacion — Bol Secr Sal Publ
Boletin Aereo. Instituto Panamericano de Geografia e Historia — Bol Aer Inst Panam Geo Hist
Boletin. Agencia Geral das Colonias — Bol Agencia Geral Colon
Boletin Agricola. Asociacion de Agricultores del Rio Culiacan — Bol Agric Asoc Agric Rio Culiacan
Boletin Agricola (Limburgerhof, Germany) — Bol Agric (Limburgerhof Ger)
Boletin Agricola (Mendoza, Argentina) — Bol Agric (Mendoza Argent)
Boletin Agricola. Sociedad Antioquena de Agricultores — Bol Agric
Boletin Agro-Pecuario — Bol Agro-Pec
Boletin Agropecuario. Compania Colombiana de Alimentos Lacteos — Bol Agropecu Com Colomb Aliment Lacteos
Boletin Americanista (Barcelona) — Bol Am Barcelona
Boletin Antropologico. Publicacion. Museo de Arqueologia, Etnografia, y Folklore (Sucre) — Bol Antrop Sucre
Boletin. Anuario Bibliografico Cubano (Habana) — Bol Anuar Bibliogr Cubano Hav
Boletin. Archivo General de la Nacion — BAGN
Boletin. Archivo General de la Nacion (Caracas) — Bol Arch Gen Nac Caracas
Boletin. Archivo General de la Nacion (Ciudad Trujillo, Santo Domingo) — Bol Arch Gen Nac C Trujillo S Domingo
Boletin. Archivo General de la Nacion (Mexico) — Bol Arch Gen Nac Mex
Boletin. Archivo General del Gobierno (Guatemala) — Bol Arch Gen Gob Guat
Boletin. Archivo Nacional — BAN
Boletin. Archivo Nacional de Historia (Quito) — Bol Arch Nac Hist Quito
Boletin. Archivo Nacional (Habana) — Bol Arch Nac Hav
Boletin (Argentina). Servicio Geologico Nacional — Bol (Argent) Serv Geol Nac
Boletin (Argentina). Servicio Nacional Minero Geologico — Bol (Argent) Serv Nac Min Geol
Boletin Argentino Forestal — Bol Argent For
Boletin Arqueologico — BA
Boletin Arqueologico — Bol Arqu
Boletin Arqueologico de Tarragona — BAT
Boletin Arqueologico de Tarragona — Bol Arq
Boletin Arqueologico. Real Sociedad Arqueologica Tarraconense de la Comision Provincial de Monumentos y del Museo Arqueologico Provincial — B Arqueol
Boletin. Asociacion Argentina de Electrotecnicos — Bol Asoc Argent Electrotec
Boletin. Asociacion Argentina de Odontologia para Ninos — Bol Asoc Argent Odontol Ninos
Boletin. Asociacion Chilena de Proteccion de la Familia — Bol Asoc Chil Prot Fam
Boletin. Asociacion Colombiana de Bibliotecarios (Bogota) — Bol Asoc Col Bibl Bogota
Boletin. Asociacion Costarricense de Bibliotecarios (San Jose) — Bol Asoc Costa Bibl S Jose
Boletin. Asociacion Cubana de Bibliotecarios (La Habana) — Bol Asoc Cubana Bibl Hav
Boletin. Asociacion de Peritos Forestales — Bol Asoc Peritos Forest
Boletin. Asociacion Espanola de Amigos de la Arqueologia — B Esp A
Boletin. Asociacion Espanola de Entomologia — Bol Asoc Esp Entomol
Boletin. Asociacion Espanola de Orientalistas — B Esp Or
Boletin. Asociacion Espanola de Orientalistas — BAEO
Boletin. Asociacion Europea de Profesores de Espanol — BAEPE
Boletin. Asociacion Filatelica (Bahia Blanca, Argentina) — Bol Asoc Filat Bahia Blanca
Boletin. Asociacion Folklorica (Argentina) — BAFA
Boletin. Asociacion General de Agricultures (Guatemala) — Bol Asoc Gen Agric Guatemala
Boletin. Asociacion Medica de Puerto Rico — Bol Asoc Med PR
Boletin. Asociacion Medica de Puerto Rico — Bol Asoc Med Puerto Rico
Boletin. Asociacion Mexicana de Bibliotecarios (Mexico) — Bol Asoc Mex Bibl Mex
Boletin. Asociacion Mexicana de Geofisicos de Exploracion — Bol Asoc Mex Geofis Explor
Boletin. Asociacion Mexicana de Geologos Petroleros — Bol Asoc Mex Geol Pet
Boletin. Asociacion Mexicana de Geologos Petroleros — Bol Asoc Mex Geol Petrol
Boletin. Asociacion Mexicana de Geologos Petroleros — BOMXA
Boletin. Asociacion Nacional de Ingenieros Agronomos — Bol Asoc Nac Ing Agron
Boletin. Asociacion Nacional de Ingenieros Agronomos — Bol Asoc Nac Ingen Agron
Boletin. Asociacion Peruana de Bibliotecarios (Lima) — Bol Asoc Peruana Bibl Lima
Boletin. Asociacion Tucumana de Folklore — BATF
Boletin. Asociacion Uruguaya para el Progreso de la Ciencia — Bol Asoc Urug Prog Cienc
Boletin. Asociacion Venezolana de Enfermeras Profesionales — Bol Asoc Venez Enferm Prof
Boletin. Asociacion Venezolana de Geologia, Mineria, y Petroleo — Bol Asoc Venez Geol Min Pet
Boletin Auriense — B Aur
Boletin. AVGMP [*Asociacion Venezolana de Geologia, Mineria, y Petroleo*] — Bol AVGMP
Boletin Azucarero Mexicano — Bol Azucar Mex
Boletin. Banco Central de Venezuela (Caracas) — Bol Banco Cent Venez Caracas
Boletin Bibliografico — BBib
Boletin Bibliografico Agricola. Ministerio de Agricultura — B Bibliogr Agricola
Boletin Bibliografico Agricola (Turrialba, Costa Rica) — Bol Bibliogr Agric Turrialba
Boletin Bibliografico Agropecuario. Universidad de Narino (Pasto, Colombia) — Bol Bibliogr Agrop Pasto
Boletin Bibliografico (Bahia Blanca, Argentina) — Bol Bibliogr Bahia Blanca
Boletin Bibliografico. Biblioteca. Camara de Diputados (Lima) — Bol Bibliogr Bibl Cam Diputados Lima
Boletin Bibliografico. Biblioteca Central. Ministerio de Trabajo y Asuntos Indigenas (Lima) — Bol Bibliogr Bibl Cent Min Trab Asunt Indig Lima
Boletin Bibliografico. Biblioteca. Universidad Mayor de San Marcos (Lima) — Bol Bibliogr Bibl Univ S Marcos Lima
Boletin Bibliografico Cerlal — Bol Bib Cer
Boletin Bibliografico de Antropologia Americana — B Bibliogr Antropol Americana
Boletin Bibliografico de Antropologia Americana — BBAA
Boletin Bibliografico de Antropologia Americana — Bol Bibl Antropol Amer
Boletin Bibliografico de Antropologia Americana (Mexico) — Bol Bibliogr Antrop Am Mex
Boletin Bibliografico de Geofisica y Oceanografia Americanas — Bol Bibliog Geofisica y Oceanografia Am
Boletin Bibliografico de Geofisica y Oceanografia Americanas (Mexico) — Bol Bibliogr Geofis Oceano Am Mex
Boletin Bibliografico. Departamento de Bibliotecas. Ministerio de Agricultura (Buenos Aires) — Bol Bibliogr Dept Bibl Min Agr BA
Boletin Bibliografico Dominicano (Ciudad Trujillo) — Bol Bibliogr Dom C Trujillo
Boletin Bibliografico. Facultad de Agronomia. Universidad Central de Venezuela — Bol Bibliogr Fac Agron Univ Cent Venez
Boletin Bibliografico. Facultad de Ciencias Juridicas y Sociales. Universidad Nacional de La Plata (La Plata, Argentina) — Bol Bibliogr Bibl Fac Cien Jur Soc La Plata
Boletin Bibliografico Forestal [*Chile*] — Bol Bibl
Boletin Bibliografico. Instituto Forestal Latinoamericano de Investigacion y Capacitacion — Bol Bibliogr Inst Forest Latinoamer Invest
Boletin Bibliografico Mexicano — BBM
Boletin Bibliografico Mexicano. Instituto Panamericano de Bibliografia y Documentacion (Mexico) — Bol Bibliogr Mex Mex
Boletin Bibliografico Mexicano Porrua — BBMP
Boletin Bibliografico (Mexico) — BBM
Boletin Bibliografico (Peru) — Bol Biblio (Peru)
Boletin Bibliografico. Secretaria de Hacienda y Credito Publico (Mexico) — Bol Bibliogr Sec Hac Cred Publ Mex
Boletin Bibliografico Semestral. Publicacion. Banco de Guatemala — Bol Bibliogr Semes Guat
Boletin. Biblioteca Americana y de Bellas Artes — BBIBA
Boletin. Biblioteca Central y de las Bibliotecas Departamentales. Universidad Catolica de Chile (Santiago) — Bol Bibl Cent Univ Cato Santiago
Boletin. Biblioteca de los Tribunales del Distrito Federal (Caracas) — Bol Bibl Trib D F Caracas
Boletin. Biblioteca de Menendez Pelayo — BBMP
Boletin. Biblioteca de Menendez Pelayo — Bol Bibl Menendez Pelayo
Boletin. Biblioteca del Colegio de Abogados (Lima) — Bol Bibl Col Abogad Lima
Boletin. Biblioteca General. Universidad del Zulia (Maracaibo, Venezuela) — Bol Bibl Gen Maracaibo
Boletin. Biblioteca Ibero Americana de Bellas Artes (Mexico) — Bol Bibl Ibero Am Bellas Art Mex
Boletin. Biblioteca Menendez Pelayo — B Bibl M Pelayo
Boletin. Biblioteca Museo Balaguer — B Bibl Mus Balaguer
Boletin. Biblioteca Nacional (Caracas) — Bol Bibl Nac Caracas
Boletin. Biblioteca Nacional (Guatemala) — Bol Bibl Nac Guat
Boletin. Biblioteca Nacional (Lima) — Bol Bibl Nac Lima
Boletin. Biblioteca Nacional (Mexico) — Bol Bibl Nac Mex
Boletin. Biblioteca Nacional (Quito) — Bol Bibl Nac Quito
Boletin. Biblioteca Nacional (San Salvador) — Bol Bibl Nac S Salvador
Boletin. Biblioteca Nacional (Santiago) — Bol Bibl Nac Santiago
Boletin. Biblioteca National (Lima) — BBNL
Boletin. Biblioteca National (Mexico) — BBNM
Boletin. Biblioteca-Museo-Balaguer — BBMB
Boletin Biologico — Bol Biol
Boletin. Camara de Comercio (Caracas) — Bol Cam Com (Caracas)
Boletin. Catedra de Fitopatologia. Universidad Nacional La Plata — Bol Catedra Fitopatol Univ Nac La Plata
Boletin. Centro de Cooperacion Cientifica (Montevideo) — Bol Cent Coop Cientif Monte
Boletin. Centro de Estudiantes de Derecho (Sucre) — Bol Cent Estudiant Der Sucre
Boletin. Centro de Estudios del Siglo XVIII, Oviedo — BOCES XVIII
Boletin. Centro de Historia Larense (Barquisimeto, Venezuela) — Bol Cent Hist Larense Barquisimeto
Boletin. Centro de Investigaciones Antropologicas de Mexico — Bol Centro Invest Antropol Mexico

Boletin. Centro de Investigaciones Antropologicas de Mexico (Mexico) — Bol Cent Invest Antrop Mex
Boletin. Centro de Investigaciones Biologicas. Universidad del Zulia — Bol Cent Invest Biol Univ Zulia
Boletin. Centro de Investigaciones Historicas (Guayaquil) — Bol Cent Invest Hist Guayaquil
Boletin. Centro Excursionista de Els Blaus — B Centro Excursionista Els Blaus
Boletin. Centro Nacional de Alimentacion y Nutricion (Spain) — Bol Cent Nac Aliment Nutr (Spain)
Boletin. Centro Naval — Bol Cent Nav
Boletin. Centro Panamericano de Fiebre Aftosa — Bol Cent Panam Fiebre Aftosa
Boletin Chileno de Parasitologia — Bol Chil Parasitol
Boletin Cientifico. Centro de Investigaciones Oceanograficas e Hidrograficas (Cartegena, Colombia) — Bol Cient Cent Invest Oceanogr Hidrogr (Cartagena Colomb)
Boletin Cientifico. Compania Administradora del Guano (Lima) — Bol Cientif Lima
Boletin Cientifico. Sociedad Sanchez Oropeza — Bol Ci Soc Sanchez Oropeza
Boletin Clacso — Bol Clac
Boletin. Clinica de Endocrinologia y Metabolismo — Bol Clin Endocrinol Metab
Boletin. Colegio de Profesionales de la Enfermeria de Puerto Rico — Bol Col Prof Enferm PR
Boletin. Colegio de Quimicos de Puerto Rico — Bol Col Quim PR
Boletin. Comision de Fomento Minero (Mexico) — Bol Com Fom Min (Mex)
Boletin. Comision de Monumentos de Burgos — BCMB
Boletin. Comision de Monumentos de Lugo — BCML
Boletin. Comision de Monumentos de Valladolid — BCMV
Boletin. Comision Nacional de Panama (UNESCO) (Panama) — Bol Comis Nac Panama UNESCO Panama
Boletin. Comision Permanente de la Asociacion de Academias de la Lengua Espanola — Bol Com Perm Asoc Acad Lengua Espan
Boletin. Comision Provincial de Monumentos de Navarra — BCPN
Boletin. Comision Provincial de Monumentos de Orense — BCPO
Boletin. Comision Provincial de Monumentos de Orense — BCPOrense
Boletin. Comision Provincial de Monumentos Historicos y Artisticos de la Ciudad de Lugo — B Com Monum Hist Art Lugo
Boletin. Comision Provincial de Monumentos Historicos y Artisticos de Lugo [*A publication*] — B Lugo
Boletin. Comision Provincial de Monumentos Historicos y Artisticos de Lugo — BCM Lugo
Boletin. Comision Provincial de Monumentos Historicos y Artisticos de Lugo — BCML
Boletin. Comision Provincial de Monumentos Historicos y Artisticos de Lugo — BCPM Lugo
Boletin. Comision Provincial de Monumentos Historicos y Artisticos de Orense — BCM Or
Boletin. Comision Provincial de Monumentos Historicos y Artisticos de Orense — BCMO
Boletin. Comision Provincial de Monumentos Historicos y Artisticos de Orense — BCPM Orense
Boletin. Comision Provincial de Monumentos Historicos y Artisticos de Orense — BCPMHAO
Boletin. Comision Provincial de Monumentos Historicos y Artisticos de Orense — BO
Boletin. Comision Provincial de Monumentos Historicos y Artisticos Orense — B Com Prov Monum Hist Art Orense
Boletin. Comision Provincial de Monumentos y de la Institucion Fernan Gonzalez de la Ciudad de Burgos — B Com Prov Monum Inst F Gonzalez Burgos
Boletin. Comite de Archivos (La Habana) — Bol Com Arch Hav
Boletin. Compania Administradora del Guano — Bol Cia Adm Guano
Boletin. Compania Administradora del Guano — Bol Comp Admin Guano
Boletin. Corporacion Venezolana de Fomento — Bol Corp Venez Fomento
Boletin. Cuerpo de Ingenieros de Minas del Peru — Bol Cuerpo Ing Minas Peru
Boletin Cultural y Bibliografico [*Bogota*] — BCB
Boletin Cultural y Bibliografico (Bogota) — Bol Cult Bibliogr Bogota
Boletin de Agricultura. Diputacion Provincial de Baleares — B Agricultura
Boletin de Agricultura, Mineria, e Industrias — Bol Agr
Boletin de Agricultura Tropical — Bol Agric Trop
Boletin de Arqueologia (Bogota) — Bol Arqueol Bogota
Boletin de Bellas Artes [*Seville*] — B Bel Art
Boletin de Bibliografia Antioquena (Medellin, Colombia) — Bol Bibliogr Antioq Medellin
Boletin de Bibliografia Botanica — Bol Bibliogr Bot
Boletin de Bibliografia Yucateca — Bol Bibliogr Yucat Merida
Boletin de Biblioteca — Bol Biblioteca
Boletin de Bibliotecas y Bibliografia — BBB
Boletin de Bosques, Pesca i Caza — Bol Bosques
Boletin de Ciencia y Tecnologia. Departamento de Asuntos Culturales. Union Panamericana — Bol Cienc Tecnol Dep Asuntos Cult Union Panam
Boletin de Ciencias Medicas (Guadalajara, Mexico) — Bol Ci Med Guadalajara
Boletin de Ciencias Politicas y Sociales — Bol Ciencias Pol y Socs
Boletin de Combustibles y Petroquimica — Bol Combust Petroquim
Boletin de Comunicaciones (La Habana) — Bol Comunic Hav
Boletin de Dialectologia Espanola — BDE
Boletin de Divulgacion. Estacion Experimental Agropecuaria. Instituto Nacional de Tecnologia Agropecuaria (Pergamino, Argentina) — Bol Divul Estac Exp Agropec INTA (Pergamino)
Boletin de Divulgacion Ganaderia — Boln Divulg Ganad
Boletin de Divulgacion (Pergamino) — Boln Divulg (Pergamino)
Boletin de Divulgacion Tecnica. Instituto de Patologia Vegetal (Buenos Aires) — Bol Divulg Tec Inst Patol Veg (B Aires)
Boletin de Documentacion. Fondo para la Investigacion Economica y Social — Bol Docum Fondo Invest Econ Soc
Boletin de Edificacion — Bol Ed
Boletin de Educacion Paraguaya (Asuncion) — Bol Educ Paraguay Asuncion
Boletin de Entomologia Venezolana — Bol Entomol Venez
Boletin de Estadistica — Bol Estadistica
Boletin de Estudios Asturianos — BEA
Boletin de Estudios de Economia. Universidad Comercial de Deusto — B Est Econ
Boletin de Estudios de Teatro (Buenos Aires) — Bol Estud Teatro BA
Boletin de Estudios Economicos — Bol Estud Econ
Boletin de Estudios Geograficos (Mendoza, Argentina) — Bol Estud Geogr Mendoza
Boletin de Estudios Geograficos. Universidad Nacional de Cuyo — Bol Estud Geogr Univ Nac Cuyo
Boletin de Estudios Germanicos — BEG
Boletin de Estudios Historicos (Pasto, Colombia) — Bol Estud Hist Pasto
Boletin de Estudios Historicos sobre San Sebastiano — BoE
Boletin de Estudios Latinoamericanos. Centro de Estudios y Documentacion Latinoamericanos [*Amsterdam*] — CEDLA/B
Boletin de Estudios Latinoamericanos y del Caribe — BEL
Boletin de Estudios Latinoamericanos y del Caribe — BLH
Boletin de Estudios Latinoamericanos y del Caribe — Bol Estud Latinoam y Caribe
Boletin de Estudios Latinoamericanos y del Caribe — Bol Estud Latinoamer
Boletin de Estudios Medicos y Biologicos — BEMBA
Boletin de Estudios Medicos y Biologicos — Bol Estud Med Biol
Boletin de Estudios Medicos y Biologicos. Universidad Nacional Autonoma de Mexico — Bol Estud Med Biol Univ Nac Auton Mex
Boletin de Estudios Oaxaquenos (Oaxaca, Mexico) — Bol Estud Oaxaquenos Oaxaca
Boletin de Estudios Politicos (Mendoza, Argentina) — Bol Estud Pol Mendoza
Boletin de Estudios y Documentacion del Serem — Bol Est Doc Serem
Boletin de Farmacia Militar — Bol Farm Mil
Boletin de Filologia — B Fil
Boletin de Filologia — BF
Boletin de Filologia Espanola — BFE
Boletin de Filologia. Instituto de Estudios Superiores del Uruguay — BFU
Boletin de Filologia. Instituto de Filologia. Universidade de Chile — BFUCH
Boletin de Filologia (Montevideo) — BFM
Boletin de Filologia (Montevideo) — Bol Filol Monte
Boletin de Filologia (Rio De Janeiro) — BFR
Boletin de Filologia (Santiago) — Bol Filol Santiago
Boletin de Fomento. Secretaria de Fomento y Agricultura (San Jose, Costa Rica) — Bol Fomento San Jose
Boletin de Geologia (Caracas) — Bol Geol (Caracas)
Boletin de Geologia (Caracas). Publicacion Especial — Bol Geol (Caracas) Publ Espec
Boletin de Geologia. Direccion de Geologia (Venezuela) — Bol Geo Dir Geol (Venez)
Boletin de Geologia. Direccion de Geologia (Venezuela) — Bol Geol Dir Geol (Venez)
Boletin de Geologia. Publicacion Especial — Bol Geol Publ Espec
Boletin de Geologia. Publicacion Especial. Direccion de Geologia (Venezuela) — Bol Geol Publ Espec Dir Geol (Venez)
Boletin de Geologia. Universidad Industrial de Santander — Bol Geol Univ Ind Santander
Boletin de Geologia (Venezuela). Direccion de Geologia — Bol Geol (Venez) Dir Geol
Boletin de Higiene y Epidemiologia — Bol Hig Epidemiol
Boletin de Historia Antigua. Academia Colombiana de Historia — B Hist Antig
Boletin de Historia Natural — Bol Historia Nat
Boletin de Historia Natural. Sociedad "Felipe Poey" — Bol Hist Nat Soc "Felipe Poey"
Boletin de Historia Natural. Sociedad Felipe Poey (La Habana) — Bol Hist Nat Soc F Poey Hav
Boletin de Historia Natural. Sociedad Felipe Poey. Universidad de la Habana — Bol Hist Nat Soc Felipe Poey Univ Habana
Boletin de Historia y Antiguedades — BHA
Boletin de Historia y Antiguedades — BoH
Boletin de Historia y Antiguedades (Bogota) — Bol Hist Antig Bogota
Boletin de Informacion Bromatologica — Bol Inf Bromatol
Boletin de Informacion. Consejo General de Colegios Veterinarios de Espana — B Inf Consejo Gener Col Veterinarios Esp
Boletin de Informacion Dental. Ilustre Consejo General de Colegios de Odontologos y Estomatologos de Espana — Bol Inf Dent Ilustre Cons Gen Col Odontol Estomatol Esp
Boletin de Informacion Dental (Madrid) — Bol Inf Dent (Madr)
Boletin de Informacion Documental — B Inf Doc
Boletin de Informacion Judicial [*Mexico*] — Bol Info Jud
Boletin de Informacion. Ministerio de Agricultura (Madrid) — Bol Inform Minist Agric (Madrid)
Boletin de Informacion. Secretariado Iberoamericano de Municipios — Bol Info Secretar Iberoam Mun
Boletin de Informacion Tecnica. Asociacion de Investigacion Tecnica de las Industrias de la Madera y Corcho — Bol Inform Tec Asoc Invest Tec Ind Madera
Boletin de Informacion Tecnica. Departamento de Metales No Ferreos. Consejo Superior de Investigaciones Cientificas (Spain) — Bol Inf Tec Dep Met No Ferreos CSIC (Spain)
Boletin de Informacion Tecnica. Departamento de Metales No Ferreos. Patronato Juan de la Cierva de Investigacion Tecnica — Bol Inf Tec Dep Met No Ferreos
Boletin de Informacion Tecnica. Negromex, SA. Departamento de Servicio Tecnico — Bol Inf Tec Negromex SA Dep Serv Tec
Boletin de Informaciones Cientificas Nacionales — Bol Inf Cient Nac
Boletin de Informaciones Cientificas Nacionales (Quito) — Bol Inform Cientif Nac Quito

Boletin de Informaciones Parasitarias Chilenas — Bol Inf Parasit Chil
Boletin de Informaciones Petroleras — Bol Inf Pet
Boletin de Informaciones Petroleras (Buenos Aires) — Bol Inform Petrol BA
Boletin de Informaciones Petroliferas, Yacimientos, e Industrias (Buenos Aires) — Bol Inform Petrol Yac Indus BA
Boletin de Ingenieros — Bol Ing
Boletin de Instruccion Publica [*Mexico*] — Bol Instr Publ
Boletin de la Sociedad Cientifica, Literaria, y Artistica — Bol Soc Ci Lit Artist
Boletin de la Sociedad de Historia, Geografia, y Estadistica de Aguascalientes — Bol Soc Hist Aguascalientes
Boletin de la Sociedad Nacional Agraria — Bol Soc Nac Agrar
Boletin de la Union Panamericana — BUP
Boletin de Literaturas Hispanicas (Santa Fe, Argentina) — Bol Lit Hisp Santa Fe
Boletin de los Hospitales — Bol Hosp
Boletin de Matematicas — Bol Mat
Boletin de Medicina — Bol Med
Boletin de Medicina, Cirugia, y Farmacia (Madrid) — Bol Med Cirug y Farm (Madrid)
Boletin de Minas — Bol Minas
Boletin de Minas, Industria, y Construcciones — Bol Minas Ind Constr
Boletin de Minas y Energia — Bol Minas y Energia
Boletin de Minas y Petroleo — Bol Minas Pet
Boletin de Minas y Petroleo — Bol Minas y Petroleo
Boletin de Mineralogia (Mexico City) — Bol Mineral (Mexico City)
Boletin de Miras y Petroleo [*Chile*] — Bol Min Petr
Boletin de Museos y Bibliotecas de Guatemala — Bol Mus Bibl Guat
Boletin de Musica y Artes Visuales — Mus y Artes
Boletin de Musica y Artes Visuales (Washington, DC) — Bol Music Art Vis Wash
Boletin de Noticias. Instituto de Fomento Algodonero (Bogota) — Bol Not Inst Fom Algodonero (Bogota)
Boletin de Obras Sanitarias de la Nacion (Argentina) — Bol Obras Sanit Nac (Argent)
Boletin de Oceanografia y Pescas — Bol Oceanogr Pesc
Boletin de Odontologia — Bol Odont
Boletin de Odontologia (Bogota) — Bol Odontol (Bogota)
Boletin de Pastoral Liturgica — BP Lit
Boletin de Patologia Medica — Bol Patol Med
Boletin de Patologia Medica (Madrid) — Bol Patol Med (Madr)
Boletin de Patologia Vegetal y Entomologia Agricola — Bol Patol Veg Entomol Agric
Boletin de Patologia Vegetal y Entomologia Agricola — Boln Patol Veg Ent Agric
Boletin de Petroleo y Minas — Bol Pet Minas
Boletin de Planificacion — Bol Planificacion
Boletin de Politica Cultural — BPC
Boletin de Prehistoria de Chile. Universidad de Chile — UC/BPC
Boletin de Produccion Animal — Bol Prod Anim
Boletin de Produccion y Fomento Agricola — Bol Prod Fom Agric
Boletin de Produccion y Fomento Agricola (Buenos Aires) — Bol Produc Fom Agri BA
Boletin de Protesis — Bol Protes
Boletin de Quimica. Clinica — Bol Quim Clin
Boletin de Radiactividad — Bol Radiact
Boletin de Resenas. Serie Agricultura — Bol Resenas Ser Agric
Boletin de Resenas. Serie Ganaderia (Havana) — Bol Resenas Ser Ganad
Boletin de Resenas. Suelos y Agroquimica — Bol Resenas Suelos Agroquim
Boletin de Resenas. Viandas, Hortalizas, y Granos — Bol Resenas Viandas Hortalizas Granos
Boletin de Salubridad e Higiene — Bol Salubr Hig
Boletin de Salud Publica — Bol Salud Publica
Boletin de Sanidad Militar — Bol Sanid Mil
Boletin del Ministerio de Fomento — Bol Minist Fomento
Boletin del Petroleo — Bol Pet
Boletin del Petroleo — Bol Petroleo
Boletin del Poeta — BolP
Boletin del Quimico Peruano — Bol Quim Peru
Boletin del Secretariado Tecnico — B Secretar
Boletin Dental Uruguayo — Bol Dent Urug
Boletin. Departamento de Biologia. Facultad de Ciencias. Universidad Nacional de Colombia — Bol Dep Biol Fac Cienc Univ Nac Colombia
Boletin. Departamento de Geologia. Universidad de Sonora — Bol Dep Geol Uni Son
Boletin. Departamento de Quimica. Instituto Tecnologico y de Estudios Superiores (Monterrey) — Bol Dep Quim Inst Tecnol Estud Super (Monterrey)
Boletin. Departamento Forestal (Montevideo, Uruguay) — Bol Dep For (Uruguay)
Boletin Dermatologico Sanitario — Bol Dermatol Sanit
Boletin. Direccion de Agricultura y Ganaderia (Peru) — Bol Dir Agric Ganad (Peru)
Boletin. Direccion de Malariologia y Saneamiento Ambiental — Bol Dir Malariol Saneamiento Ambiental
Boletin. Direccion General de Agricultura (Peru) — Bol Dir Gen Agric (Peru)
Boletin. Direccion General de Archivos y Bibliotecas — B Direc Gen Arch Bibl
Boletin. Direccion General de Archivos y Bibliotecas — BDGAB
Boletin. Direccion General de Odontologia (Santa Fe) — Bol Dir Gen Odontol (Santa Fe)
Boletin. Direccion General Forestal y de Caza (Mexico) — Bol Dir Gen Forest Caza Mex
Boletin. Direccion Nacional de Geologia y Mineria (Argentina) — Bol Dir Nac Geol Min (Argent)
Boletin. Direcion General de Archivos y Bibliotecas (Madrid) — Bol Dir Gen Arch Bibl Madrid
Boletin Divulgativo. Instituto Nacional de Investigaciones Forestales (Mexico) — Bol Divulg Inst Nac Invest For (Mex)
Boletin Divulgativo. Ministerio de Agricultura y Ganaderia — Bol Divulg Minist Agric Ganad
Boletin Eclesiastico de Filipinas — BEF
Boletin Eclesiastico de Filipinas — Bol Eclesias Fil
Boletin Epidemiologico — Bol Epidemiol
Boletin. Escuela Nacional de Agricultura (Lima) — Bol Esc Nac Agr (Lima)
Boletin. Escuela Nacional de Bibliotecarios y Archivistas (Mexico) — Bol Escuela Nac Bibl Arch Mex
Boletin. Escuela Nacional de Ciencias Biologicas — Bol Esc Nac Ci Biol
Boletin. Escuela Nacional de Ingenieros (Peru) — Bol Esc Nac Ing (Peru)
Boletin. Estacion Agricola Experimental (Chihuahua, Mexico) — Bol Estac Agric Exp Chihuahua
Boletin. Estacion Central de Ecologia — Bol Estac Cent Ecol
Boletin. Estacion Central de Ecologia (Spain) — Bol Estac Cent Ecol (Spain)
Boletin. Estacion Experimental Agricola de la Provincia de Tucuman — Bol Estac Exp Agric Tucuman
Boletin. Estacion Experimental Agricola de Tucuman — Bol Estac Exp Agric Tucuman
Boletin. Estacion Experimental Agricola "La Molina" — Bol Estac Exp Agr "La Molina"
Boletin. Estacion Experimental Agricola "La Molina" — Bol Estac Exp Agric "La Molina"
Boletin. Estacion Experimental Agricola "La Molina" (Lima) — Bol Estac Exp Agric "La Molina" (Lima)
Boletin. Estacion Experimental Agricola (Rio Piedras, Puerto Rico) — Bol Estac Exp Agric (Rio Piedras PR)
Boletin. Estacion Experimental Agricola "Tingo Maria" — Bol Estac Exp Agr "Tingo Maria"
Boletin. Estacion Experimental Agricola "Tingo Maria" — Boln Estac Exp Agric "Tingo Maria"
Boletin. Estacion Experimental Agropecuaria de Presidencia Roque Saenz Pena (Argentina) — Bol Estac Exp Agropec Pres Roque Saenz Pena (Argentina)
Boletin Estadistico Trimestral (Argentina) — Bol Estadistico Trim (Argentina)
Boletin Estadistico Trimestral (Bolivia) — Bol Estadistico Trim (Bolivia)
Boletin Experimental. Servicio Agricola Interamericano (La Paz) — Bol Exp Serv Agric Interam (La Paz)
Boletin. Facultad de Agronomia. Universidad de la Republica (Montevideo) — Bol Fac Agron Univ Repub (Montevideo)
Boletin. Facultad de Agronomia. Universidad de San Carlos — Bol Fac Agron
Boletin. Facultad de Agronomia. Universidad de San Carlos de Guatemala — Bol Fac Agron Univ San Carlos Guatemala
Boletin. Facultad de Ciencias Forestales. Universidad de Los Andes — Bol Fac Cienc For Univ Los Andes
Boletin. Facultad de Derecho y Ciencias Sociales — BFDC
Boletin. Facultad de Derecho y Ciencias Sociales (Cordoba) — Bol Fac Der Cienc Soc (Cordoba)
Boletin. Facultad de Derecho y Ciencias Sociales. Universidad Nacional de Cordoba (Cordoba, Argentina) — Bol Fac Der Cien Soc Cordoba
Boletin. Facultad de Ingenieria de Montevideo — Bol Fac Ing Montevideo
Boletin. Facultad de Ingenieria. Universidad de la Republica — Bol Fac Ing Univ Repub
Boletin. Facultad de Ingenieria y Agrimensura de Montevideo — Bol Fac Ing Agrimensura Montevideo
Boletin. Facultad de Ingenieria y Agrimensura de Montevideo — Bol Fac Ing y Agrimensura Montevideo
Boletin. Facultad de Ingenieria y Agrimensura. Universidad de la Republica — Bol Fac Ing Agrimens Univ Repub
Boletin. Facultad de Ingenieria y Ramas Anexas. Universidad de Montevideo — Bol Fac Ing Ramas Anexas Univ Montevideo
Boletin. Facultad Nacional de Agronomia — Bol Fac Nac Agron
Boletin. Facultade de Dereito — B Fac Dereito
Boletin. Federacion Medica del Ecuador — Bol Fed Med Ecuador
Boletin Forestal (Caracas) — Bol Forest Caracas
Boletin Forestal y de Industrias Forestales para America Latina. Oficina Forestal Regional de la FAO [*Food and Agriculture Organization*] — Bol For Ind For Amer Lat FAO
Boletin Genetico — Bol Genet
Boletin Genetico (English Edition) — Bol Genet (Engl Ed)
Boletin Geologico (Bogota) — Bol Geol Bogota
Boletin Geologico (Columbia). Instituto Nacional de Investigaciones Geologico-Mineras — Bol Geol (Colomb) Inst Nac Invest Geol Min
Boletin Geologico Ingeominas — Bol Geol Ingeominas
Boletin Geologico. Instituto Geografico Nacional (Guatemala) — Bol Geol Inst Geogr Nac (Guatem)
Boletin Geologico. Instituto Geologico Nacional (Bogota, Colombia) — Boln Geol (Bogota)
Boletin Geologico. Instituto Geologico Nacional (Colombia) — Bol Geol Inst Geol Nac (Colomb)
Boletin Geologico. Servicio Geologico Nacional (Colombia) — Bol Geol Serv Geol Nac (Colomb)
Boletin Geologico y Minero — BGMIA
Boletin Geologico y Minero — Bol Geol Min
Boletin Geologico y Minero — Bol Geol Miner
Boletin Geologico y Minero (Espana) — Bol Geol Min (Esp)
Boletin. GEOMINAS — Bol GEOMINAS
Boletin Historial (Cartagena, Colombia) — Bol Hist Cartagena
Boletin Historico — BHist
Boletin Historico (Caracas) — Bol Hist Caracas
Boletin Historico del Valle (Cali, Colombia) — Bol Hist Valle Cali
Boletin Historico (Montevideo) — Bol Hist Monte
Boletin. Hospital Civil de San Juan De Dios (Quito) — Bol Hosp Civ San Juan De Dios (Quito)
Boletin. Hospital de Vina del Mar — Bol Hosp Vina del Mar
Boletin. Hospital Oftalmologico de Nuestra Senora de la Luz — Bol Hosp Oftalmol Nuestra Senora de la Luz
Boletin Iberoamericano de Cultura Tecnica — Bol Iberoam Cult Tec
Boletin IIE [*Instituto de Investigaciones Electricas*] — BOIID

Boletin IIE [*Instituto de Investigaciones Electricas*] — Bol IIE
Boletin Indigenista — Boln Indig
Boletin Indigenista (Mexico) — Bol Indig Mex
Boletin Indigenista Venezolano — BIV
Boletin Indigenista Venezolano (Caracas) — Bol Indig Venez Caracas
Boletin Indigenista Venezolano. Organo de la Comision Indigenista. Ministerio de Justicia — VMJ/BIV
Boletin. INED [*Institucion Nacional de Examen y Diagnostico*] — Bol INED
Boletin Informativo — BI
Boletin Informativo (Argentina). Direccion Nacional de Quimica — Bol Inf (Argent) Dir Nac Quim
Boletin Informativo. Asociacion Venezolana de Geologia, Mineria, y Petroleo [*A publication*] — Bol Inf Asoc Venez Geol Min Pet
Boletin Informativo. Asociacion Venezolana de Geologia, Mineria, y Petroleo [*A publication*] — BVGPA
Boletin Informativo. Biblioteca. Facultad de Filosofia y Letras. Universidad Nacional de Tucuman (Tucuman, Argentina) — Bol Inform Bibl Fac Filos Letr Tucuman
Boletin Informativo. Centro Nacional de Investigaciones de Cafe — Bol Inf Cent Nac Invest Cafe
Boletin Informativo de Circular Farmaceutica — Bol Inf Cir Farm
Boletin Informativo de Circular Farmaceutica — Bol Inf Circ Farm
Boletin Informativo. DNQ [*Direccion Nacional de Quimica*] — Bol Inf DNQ
Boletin Informativo. Estacion Experimental Agricola de Tucuman — Bol Inf Estac Exp Agri Tucuman
Boletin Informativo. Instituto Cubano de Investigaciones Tecnologicas — Bol Inf Inst Cubano Invest Tecnol
Boletin Informativo. Instituto de Botanica — Bol Inf Inst Bot
Boletin Informativo. Instituto Forestal — Bol Inform Inst Forest
Boletin Informativo. Instituto Forestal (Santiago-De-Chile) — Bol Inform Inst For (Chile)
Boletin Informativo. Instituto Interamericano de Ciencias Agricolas — Bol Inform Inst Interamer Ci Agric
Boletin Informativo. Instituto Nacional de Tecnologia Agropecuaria. Instituto de Fitotecnia — Bol Inform Inst Nac Tec Agropec Inst Fitotec
Boletin Informativo. Ministerio de Relaciones Exteriores (Quito) — Bol Inform Min Rel Ext Quito
Boletin Informativo (Santiago) — Bol Inform Santiago
Boletin Informativo. Secretaria General del Movimiento — BISGM
Boletin Informativo. Seminario de Derecho Politico — BISDP
Boletin Informativo. Sociedad Colombiana de Quimicos Farmaceuticos — Bol Inf Soc Colomb Quim Farm
Boletin Informativo y Bibliografico — BIB
Boletin. Institucion Fernan Gonzalez de Burgos. CSIC (Consejo Superior de Investigacion Cientificas) — B Inst F Gonzalez
Boletin. Institucion Fernan-Gonzales — BJF
Boletin. Institucion Fernan-Gonzales — Bol Inst Fer Gonz
Boletin. Institucion Fernan-Gonzalez — BIFG
Boletin. Institucion Fernan-Gonzalez (Burgos) — B(Burgos)
Boletin. Institucion Nacional de Examen y Diagnostico — Bol Inst Nac Examen Diagn
Boletin. Institucion Sancho el Sabio — BISS
Boletin. Institucion Sancho el Sabio — Bol Sancho Sabio
Boletin. Instituto Bacteriologico de Chile — Bol Inst Bacteriol Chile
Boletin. Instituto Boliviano del Petroleo — Bol Inst Boliv Pet
Boletin. Instituto Botanica. Universidad de Quito — Bol Inst Bot Univ Quito
Boletin. Instituto Botanico. Universidad Central (Quito) — Bol Inst Bot Univ Cent (Quito)
Boletin. Instituto Caro y Cuerva — Boln Inst Caro Cuerva
Boletin. Instituto Caro y Cuervo — BICC
Boletin. Instituto Caro y Cuervo — Ca Cu
Boletin. Instituto Caro y Cuervo (Bogota) — Bol Inst Caro Cuervo Bogota
Boletin. Instituto de Agricultura Tropical. Universidad de Puerto Rico — Bol Inst Agric Trop Univ PR
Boletin. Instituto de Antropologia — BIA
Boletin. Instituto de Antropologia (Medellin, Colombia) — Bol Inst Antrop Medellin
Boletin. Instituto de Antropologia. Universidad de Antioquia, Medellin — Bol Inst Antropol Univ Antioquia Medellin
Boletin. Instituto de Biologia Marina (Mar Del Plata) — Bol Inst Biol Mar (Mar Del Plata)
Boletin. Instituto de Biologia Marina. Universidades Nacionales de Buenos Aires — Bol Inst Biol Mar
Boletin. Instituto de Ciencias Naturales. Universidad Central del Ecuador — Bol Inst Cienc Nat Univ Cent Ecuador
Boletin. Instituto de Clinica Quirurgica — Bol Inst Clin Quir
Boletin. Instituto de Derecho Comparado de Mexico (Mexico, DF) — Bol Inst Der Comp Mex
Boletin. Instituto de Derecho Comparado (Quito) — Bol Inst Der Comp Quito
Boletin. Instituto de Estudios Asturianos — B Inst Est Asturianos
Boletin. Instituto de Estudios Asturianos — BIEA
Boletin. Instituto de Estudios Asturianos — Bol Inst Est Astur
Boletin. Instituto de Estudios Economicos y Financieros (La Plata, Argentina) — Bol Inst Estud Econ Finan La Plata
Boletin. Instituto de Estudios Giennenses — BIE Gien
Boletin. Instituto de Estudios Giennenses — BIEG
Boletin. Instituto de Estudios Giennenses — Bol Inst Est Giennenses
Boletin. Instituto de Estudios Helenicos — B Inst Est Hel
Boletin. Instituto de Estudios Helenicos — BIEH
Boletin. Instituto de Estudios Helenicos. Universidad de Barcelona. Facultad de Filosofia y Letras — B Inst Est Hel
Boletin. Instituto de Estudios Medicos y Biologicos — Bol Inst Estud Med Biol
Boletin. Instituto de Estudios Medicos y Biologicos. Universidad Nacional Autonoma de Mexico — BOEMA
Boletin. Instituto de Estudios Medicos y Biologicos. Universidad Nacional de Mexico — Bol Inst Estud Med Biol Univ Nac Mex
Boletin. Instituto de Estudios Politicos — Bol Inst Estud Polit
Boletin. Instituto de Filologia. Universidad de Chile — BFC
Boletin. Instituto de Folklore — BIFV
Boletin. Instituto de Folklore — Boletin IF
Boletin. Instituto de Folklore — Inst Folk
Boletin. Instituto de Folklore (Caracas) — Bol Inst Folk Caracas
Boletin. Instituto de Fomento Algodonero — Bol Inst Fomento Algodonero
Boletin. Instituto de Genetica. Sociedad Nacional Agraria (Lima) — Bol Inst Genet Soc Nac Agrar (Lima)
Boletin. Instituto de Geografia (Lima) — Bol Inst Geogr Lima
Boletin. Instituto de Geologia — Bol Inst Geol
Boletin. Instituto de Geologia (Mexico) — Bol Inst Geol (Mex)
Boletin. Instituto de Geologia. Universidad Nacional Autonoma de Mexico — Bol Inst Geol Univ Nac Auton Mex
Boletin. Instituto de Historia Argentina Doctor Emilio Ravignani (Buenos Aires) — Bol Inst Hist Arg BA
Boletin. Instituto de Investigacion de los Recursos Marinos (Callao) — Bol Inst Invest Recur Mar (Callao)
Boletin. Instituto de Investigacion Textil y de Cooperacion Industrial. Universidad Politecnica de Barcelona — Bol Inst Invest Text Coop Ind Univ Politec Barcelona
Boletin. Instituto de Investigaciones Agronomicas (Spain) — Bol Inst Invest Agron (Spain)
Boletin. Instituto de Investigaciones Bibliograficas — BIIB
Boletin. Instituto de Investigaciones Bibliograficas — Bol Inst Invest Bibliogr
Boletin. Instituto de Investigaciones Cientificas. Universidad de Nuevo Leon — Bol Inst Invest Cient Univ Nuevo Leon
Boletin. Instituto de Investigaciones Electricas — Bol Inst Invest Electr
Boletin. Instituto de Investigaciones Folkloricas. Universidad Interamericana (Panama) — BIFP
Boletin. Instituto de Investigaciones Geologicas (Chile) — Bol Inst Invest Geol (Chile)
Boletin. Instituto de Investigaciones Historicas — BIIH
Boletin. Instituto de Investigaciones Historicas (Buenos Aires) — Bol Inst Invest Hist BA
Boletin. Instituto de Investigaciones Literarias — BIIL
Boletin. Instituto de Investigaciones Sociales y Economicas (Panama) — Bol Inst Invest Soc Econ Panama
Boletin. Instituto de Investigaciones Veterinarias (Maracay) — Bol Inst Invest Vet (Maracay)
Boletin. Instituto de Investigaciones Veterinarias (Maracay, Venezuela) — Bol Inst Invest Vet (Maracay Venez)
Boletin. Instituto de las Espanas — BIE
Boletin. Instituto de Legislacion Comparada y Derecho Internacional (Panama) — Bol Inst Legis Comp Der Intern Panama
Boletin. Instituto de Literatura Chilena (Santiago) — Bol Inst Lit Chil Santiago
Boletin. Instituto de Literatura y Linguistica — BILL
Boletin. Instituto de Matematica, Astronomia, y Fisica — Bol Inst Mat Astron Fis
Boletin. Instituto de Medicina Experimental para el Estudio y Tratamiento del Cancer (Buenos Aires) — Bol Inst Med Exp Estud Trat Cancer (Buenos Aires)
Boletin. Instituto de Numismatica e Historia de San Nicolas de los Arroyos [*Argentina*] — Bol Inst Num Hist San Nicolas
Boletin. Instituto de Patologia Medica (Madrid) — Bol Inst Patol Med (Madrid)
Boletin. Instituto de Quimica. Universidad Nacional Autonoma de Mexico — Bol Inst Quim Mexico
Boletin. Instituto de Quimica. Universidad Nacional Autonoma de Mexico — Bol Inst Quim Univ Nac Auton Mex
Boletin. Instituto de Salud Publica de Chile — Bol Inst Salud Publica Chile
Boletin. Instituto de Sociologia (Buenos Aires) — Bol Inst Sociol BA
Boletin. Instituto de Tonantzintla — Bol Inst Tonantzintla
Boletin. Instituto del Mar del Peru (Callao) — Bol Inst Mar Peru (Callao)
Boletin. Instituto Espanol de Londres — BIE
Boletin. Instituto Espanol de Oceanografia — Bol Inst Esp Oceanogr
Boletin. Instituto Forestal de Investigaciones y Experiencias (Madrid) — Bol Inst For Invest Exp (Madrid)
Boletin. Instituto Forestal de Investigaciones y Experiencias (Madrid) — Bol Inst For Invest Exper (Madrid)
Boletin. Instituto Forestal Latino Americano de Investigacion y Capacitacion (Merida, Venezuela) — Bol Inst Forest Latinoam Invest Capacit Merida
Boletin. Instituto Forestal Latino-Americano de Investigacion y Capacitacion — Bol Inst For Lat-Am Invest Capac
Boletin. Instituto Forestal Latino-Americano de Investigacion y Capacitacion — Bol Inst For Latino-Am Invest Capac
Boletin. Instituto Forestal Latinoamericano de Investigacion y Capacitacion — Bol Inst Forest Latinoamer Invest
Boletin. Instituto Frances — BIF
Boletin. Instituto Geologico y Minero de Espana — Bol Inst Geol Min Esp
Boletin. Instituto Indigenista Nacional (Guatemala) — Bol Inst Indig Nac Guat
Boletin. Instituto Inter-Americano del Nino — BIIN
Boletin. Instituto Interamericano del Nino — Bol Inst Interam Nino
Boletin. Instituto Inter-Americano del Nino (Montevideo) — Bol Inter Am Child Inst Monte
Boletin. Instituto Internacional Americano de Proteccion a la Infancia — Bol Inst Int Am Prot Infanc
Boletin. Instituto Marco Fidel Suarez (Medellin, Colombia) — Bol Inst M F Suarez Medellin
Boletin. Instituto Mexicana del Cafe — Bol Inst Mex Cafe
Boletin. Instituto Nacional de Alimentacion (Montevideo) — Bol Inst Nac Aliment (Montevideo)
Boletin. Instituto Nacional de Antropologia e Historia de Mexico — Bol Inst Nac Antropol Hist Mexico
Boletin. Instituto Nacional de Higiene (Caracas) — Bol Inst Nac Hig (Caracas)

Boletin. Instituto Nacional de Higiene de Alfonso XIII — Bol Inst Nac Hig Alfonso XIII
Boletin. Instituto Nacional de Investigacion y Fomento Mineros (Peru) — Bol Inst Nac Invest Fom Min (Peru)
Boletin. Instituto Nacional de Investigaciones Agronomicas — Bol Inst Nac Invest Agron
Boletin. Instituto Nacional de Investigaciones Agronomicas (Madrid) — Bol Inst Nac Invest Agron (Madr)
Boletin. Instituto Nacional de Investigaciones Agronomicas (Spain) — Bol Inst Nac Invest Agron (Spain)
Boletin. Instituto Nacional de Investigaciones y Experiencias Agronomicas y Forestales — Bol Inst Nac Invest Exper Agron For
Boletin. Instituto Nacional de Neumologia (Mexico) — Bol Inst Nac Neumol (Mex)
Boletin. Instituto Nacional de Prevision Social (Buenos Aires) — Bol Inst Nac Prev Soc BA
Boletin. Instituto Nacional Mejia (Quito) — Bol Inst Nac Mejia Quito
Boletin. Instituto Oceanografico (Cumana, Venezuela) — Bol Inst Oceanogr (Cumana Venez)
Boletin. Instituto Oceanografico. Universidad de Oriente — Bol Inst Oceanogr Univ Oriente
Boletin. Instituto Oceanografico. Universidad de Oriente (Cumana) — Bol Inst Oceanogr Univ Oriente (Cumana)
Boletin. Instituto Psicopedagogico Nacional (Lima) — Bol Inst Psicopedagog Nac Lima
Boletin. Instituto Psiquiatrico. Facultad de Ciencias Medicas de Rosario — Bol Inst Psiquiatr Fac Cienc Med Rosario
Boletin. Instituto Riva Agueero — BIRA
Boletin. Instituto Sudamericano del Petroleo (Montevideo) — Bol Inst Sudam Pet (Montevideo)
Boletin. Instituto Sudamericano del Petroleo (Montevideo) — Bol Inst Sudam Petrol Monte
Boletin Interamericano de Musica — BIM
Boletin Interamericano de Musica/Inter-American Music Bulletin — Bol Interamer M
Boletin Interamericano de Musica/Inter-American Music Bulletin — Intam Mus B
Boletin Interamericano de Musica (Washington, DC) — Bol Interam Music Wash
Boletin. Jardin Botanico. Mexico City — Bol Jard Bot Mexico City
Boletin. Jardin Botanico Nacional — BJBNDL
Boletin. Jardin Botanico Nacional — Bol Jard Bot Nac
Boletin. Junta Auxiliar. Sociedad Mexicana de Geografia y Estadistica (Guadalajara, Mexico) — Bol Junt Aux Soc Mex Geogr Estad Guadalajara
Boletin. Junta do Control de Energia Atomica — BJCEA
Boletin. Junta do Control de Energia Atomica [*Peru*] — Bol Junta Control Energ At
Boletin. Laboratorio de la Clinica "Luis Razetti" — Bol Lab Clin "Luis Razetti"
Boletin. Laboratorio de Paleontologia de Vertebrados — Bol Lab Paleontol Vertebr
Boletin. Laboratorio Quimico Nacional — Bol Lab Quim Nac
Boletin. Laboratorio Quimico Nacional (Colombia) — Bol Lab Quim Nac (Colomb)
Boletin. Laboratorio Quimico Nacional (Colombia) — Bol Lab Quim Nac (Colombia)
Boletin Latino-Americano de Musica — BLAM
Boletin. Liga Contra el Cancer — Bol Liga Cancer
Boletin Matematico — Bol Mat
Boletin Medico Britanico — Bol Med Brit
Boletin Medico de Chile — Bol Med Chile
Boletin Medico. Hospital Infantil — Bol Med Hosp Inf
Boletin Medico. Hospital Infantil de Mexico — Bol Med Hosp Infant Mex
Boletin Medico. Hospital Infantil de Mexico (English Edition) — Bol Med Hosp Infant Mex (Engl Ed)
Boletin Medico. Hospital Infantil de Mexico (Spanish Edition) — Bol Med Hosp Infant Mex (Span Ed)
Boletin Medico Informativo — Bol Med Inf
Boletin Medico. Instituto Mexicano del Seguro Social — Bol Med Inst Mex Seg Soc
Boletin Medico. Universidad Autonoma de Guadalajara — Bol Med Univ Auton Guadalajara
Boletin Medico. Universidad Autonoma de Guadalajara — Bol Med Univ Guad
Boletin Medico-Quirurgico — Bol Med Quir
Boletin Medico-Social. Caja de Seguro Obligatorio — Bol Med Soc
Boletin Mensual de Estadistica — Bol Mens Estadist
Boletin Mensual de Estadistica — Bol Mensual Estadistica
Boletin Mensual de Estadistica Agraria — Bol Mensual Estadistica Agraria
Boletin Mensual de Estadisticas Agricolas — Bol Mens Estad Agri
Boletin Mensual de Estadisticas Agricolas — Bol Mensual Estadisticas Agrics
Boletin Mensual. Instituto Nacional de Alimentacion (Montevideo) — Bol Mens Inst Nac Aliment (Montevideo)
Boletin Mensual. Observatorio del Ebro — Bol Mens Obs Ebro
Boletin Mensual. Observatorio del Ebro. Seria A — Bol Mens Obs Ebro Ser A
Boletin Meteorologico (Ecuador) — Bol Met (Ecuad)
Boletin Meteorologico y Seismologico — Bol Met Seism
Boletin Mexicano de Derecho Comparado — BMD
Boletin Mexicano de Derecho Comparado — Bol Mexic Der Comp
Boletin Mexicano de Reumatologia — Bol Mex Reumatol
Boletin (Mexico). Comision de Fomento Minero — Bol (Mex) Com Fom Min
Boletin (Mexico). Consejo de Recursos Naturales No Renovables — Bol (Mex) Cons Recur Nat No Renov
Boletin Minero — Bol Minero
Boletin Minero e Industrial — B Minero E Ind
Boletin Minero e Industrial — Bol Min Ind
Boletin Minero (Mexico City) — Bol Min (Mexico City)
Boletin. Ministerio de Agricultura (Buenos Aires) — Bol Minist Agric Buenos Aires
Boletin. Ministerio de Relaciones Exteriores (Montevideo) — Bol Min Rel Ext Monte
Boletin. Musei Arqueologico Provincial de Orense — B M Arq Or
Boletin. Musei Arqueologico Provincial de Orense — BMAP Orense
Boletin. Museo Arqueologico Provincial de Orense — BM Arq Or
Boletin. Museo Bolivariano (Lima) — Bol Mus Bolivar Lima
Boletin. Museo de Arte Colonial (Bogota) — Bol Mus Arte Colonial Bogota
Boletin. Museo de Ciencias Naturales — Bol Mus Cienc Nat
Boletin. Museo de Ciencias Naturales (Caracas) — Bol Mus Cien Nat Caracas
Boletin. Museo de Ciencias Naturales y Antropologicas Juan Cornelio Moyano [*A publication*] — BMCMEB
Boletin. Museo de Ciencias Naturales y Antropologicas Juan Cornelio Moyano — Bol Mus Cienc Nat Antropol Juan Cornelio Moyano
Boletin. Museo de Historia Natural Javier Prado — Bol Mus Hist Nat Javier Prado
Boletin. Museo de Historia Natural "Javier Prado" — Boln Mus Hist Nat Javier Prado
Boletin. Museo de Historia Natural Javier Prado (Lima) — Bol Mus Hist Nat J Prado Lima
Boletin. Museo de Motivos Populares Argentinos Jose Hernandez — BMJH
Boletin. Museo de Valparaiso — Bol Mus Valp
Boletin. Museo del Hombre Dominicano — MHD/B
Boletin. Museo Nacional de Historia Natural (Chile) — Boln Mus Nac Hist Nat (Chile)
Boletin. Museo Nacional de Historia Natural (Santiago) — Bol Mus Nac Hist Nat Santiago
Boletin. Museo Provincial de Bellas Artes de Zaragoza — B Mus Prov Bellas Artes Zaragoza
Boletin. Museo Social Argentino — Bol Mus Soc Argent
Boletin Nacional de Minas — Bol Nac Minas
Boletin Nicaraguense de Bibliografia y Documentacion — BNB
Boletin Nucleo — Bol Nucl
Boletin. Observatorio del Ebro. Serie A — Bol Obs Ebro Ser A
Boletin Odontologico (Buenos Aires) — Bol Odontol (B Aires)
Boletin Odontologico Mexicano — Bol Odont Mex
Boletin Odontologico Mexicano — Bol Odontol Mex
Boletin Oficial [*Argentina*] — BO
Boletin Oficial. Asociacion de Quimicos de Puerto Rico — Bol Of Asoc Quim PR
Boletin Oficial. Asociacion de Tecnicos Azucareros de Cuba — Bol Of Asoc Tec Azucar Cuba
Boletin Oficial. Asociacion Nacional de Ingenieros Agronomos — Bol Of Asoc Nac Ing Agron
Boletin Oficial. Colegio Quimicos de Puerto Rico — Bol Of Col Quim PR
Boletin Oficial del Estado [*Spain*] — Bol Of Estado
Boletin Oficial del Estado — Boln Of Estado
Boletin Oficial. Direccion de Minas e Industrias (Lima) — Bol Of Dir Min Indus Lima
Boletin Oficial. Propiedad Industrial. 2. Patentes y Modelos de Utilidad — Bol Of Prop Ind 2
Boletin. Oficina Sanitaria Panamericana — B Of San Pa
Boletin. Oficina Sanitaria Panamericana — Bol Of Sanit Panam
Boletin. Oficina Sanitaria Panamericana — Bol Ofic Sanit Panamer
Boletin. Oficina Sanitaria Panamericana — Bol Oficina Sanit Panam
Boletin. Oficina Sanitaria Panamericana. English Edition — Bol Of Sanit Panam Engl Ed
Boletin. Oficina Sanitaria Panamericana. English Edition — Bol Ofic Sanit Panam Engl Ed
Boletin. Oficina Sanitaria Panamericana. English Edition — BPAHA3
Boletin. Oficina Sanitaria Panamericana (Washington, DC) — Bol Of Sanit Panam Wash
Boletin Oftalmologico — Bol Oftal
Boletin Paleontologico de Buenos Aires — Bol Paleontol B Aires
Boletin para Bibliotecas Agricolas — Bol Bibl Agric
Boletin (Peru). Comision Carta Geologica Nacional — Bol (Peru) Com Carta Geol Nac
Boletin Popular. Direccion General de Agricultura de Guatemala. Ministerio de Agricultura (Guatemala) — Bol Popular Min Agric (Guatemala)
Boletin. Proyecto Bibliografico del Sur (Lima) — Bol Proy Bibliogr Lima
Boletin. Publicaciones del Museo y de la Sociedad Arqueologica de la Serena — Bol Mus Soc Arqueol la Serena
Boletin. Real Academia de Buenas Letras de Barcelona — B Acad Letras Barcelona
Boletin. Real Academia de Buenas Letras de Barcelona — BABL
Boletin. Real Academia de Buenas Letras de Barcelona — BABLB
Boletin. Real Academia de Buenas Letras de Barcelona — BALB
Boletin. Real Academia de Buenas Letras de Barcelona — Bol Acad Buenas Letras Barcelona
Boletin. Real Academia de Buenas Letras de Barcelona — BRABLB
Boletin. Real Academia de Ciencias, Bellas Letras, y Nobles Artes de Cordoba — Bol Acad Cordoba
Boletin. Real Academia de Ciencias, Bellas Letras, y Nobles Artes de Cordoba — BRA Cor
Boletin. Real Academia de Ciencias, Bellas Letras, y Nobles Artes de Cordoba — BRA Cord
Boletin. Real Academia de Ciencias, Bellas Letras, y Nobles Artes de Cordoba — BRACC
Boletin. Real Academia de Ciencias. Buenas Letras y Bellas Artes de la Ciudad de Cordoba — B Acad Ci Letras Artes Cordoba
Boletin. Real Academia de Cordoba — BAC
Boletin. Real Academia de Cordoba — BRAC
Boletin. Real Academia de la Historia — B Ac Hist
Boletin. Real Academia de la Historia — B Acad Hist
Boletin. Real Academia de la Historia — B Real Acad
Boletin. Real Academia de la Historia — BAHist

Boletin. Real Academia de la Historia — Bol A de la H
Boletin. Real Academia de la Historia — Bol Ac Hist
Boletin. Real Academia de la Historia [*Madrid*] — Bol Acad Hist
Boletin. Real Academia de la Historia [*Madrid*] — Bol R Ac Hist
Boletin. Real Academia de la Historia — Bol RAH
Boletin. Real Academia de la Historia — Bol Real Ac
Boletin. Real Academia de la Historia [*Madrid*] — Bol Real Acad Hist
Boletin. Real Academia de la Historia [*Madrid*] — Bolet R Acad Hist
Boletin. Real Academia de la Historia — BolR
Boletin. Real Academia de la Historia — BRAH
Boletin. Real Academia Espanola — B Acad Espan
Boletin. Real Academia Espanola — B Real Acad
Boletin. Real Academia Espanola — BAE
Boletin. Real Academia Espanola — Bol R Ac Esp
Boletin. Real Academia Espanola — BRAE
Boletin. Real Academia Gallega — B Acad Gallega
Boletin. Real Academia Gallega — BRAG
Boletin. Real Sociedad de Geografia [*Madrid*] — Bol Real Soc Geogr
Boletin. Real Sociedad de Geografia (Madrid) — Bol Soc Geogr (Madrid)
Boletin. Real Sociedad Espanola de Historia Natural — Bol R Soc Esp Hist Nat
Boletin. Real Sociedad Espanola de Historia Natural — Bol R Soc Espan Hist Nat
Boletin. Real Sociedad Espanola de Historia Natural — Boln R Soc Esp Hist Nat
Boletin. Real Sociedad Espanola de Historia Natural. Seccion Biologica — Bol R Soc Esp Hist Nat Secc Biol
Boletin. Real Sociedad Espanola de Historia Natural. Seccion Geologica — Bol R Soc Esp Hist Nat Secc Geol
Boletin. Real Sociedad Geografica — B Soc Geogr
Boletin. Real Sociedad Geografica — BRSG
Boletin. Real Sociedad Vascongada de Amigos del Pais — B Soc Vascongada
Boletin. Real Sociedad Vascongada de Amigos del Pais — BRSV
Boletin. Real Sociedad Vascongada de Amigos del Pais — BRSVAP
Boletin. Real Sociedad Vascongada de Amigos del Pais — BSVasc
Boletin. Revista Peruana de Pediatria — Bol Rev Peru Pediat
Boletin. Revista. Universidad de Madrid — Bol Rev Univ Madrid
Boletin Rural. Instituto Nacional de Tecnologia Agropecuaria — Boln Rur Inst Nac Tecnol Agropec
Boletin. Secretaria de Industria y Comercio (Argentina) — Bol Secr Ind Comer (Argent)
Boletin. Secretaria de Industria y Comercio (Buenos Aires) — Bol Sec Indus Com BA
Boletin. Seminario de Cultura Mexicano (Mexico) — Bol Semin Cult Mex Mex
Boletin. Seminario de Derecho Publico (Santiago) — Bol Semin Der Publ Santiago
Boletin. Seminario de Estudios de Arte y Arqueologia — Bol Arte Arq Valladolid
Boletin. Seminario de Estudios de Arte y Arqueologia — Bol del SEAA
Boletin. Seminario de Estudios de Arte y Arqueologia — Bol Sem Est Arte Arq
Boletin. Seminario de Estudios de Arte y Arqueologia — BSAA
Boletin. Seminario de Estudios de Arte y Arqueologia — BSEA
Boletin. Seminario de Estudios de Arte y Arqueologia — BSEAA
Boletin. Seminario de Estudios de Arte y Arqueologia de Valladolid — B Sem Est Arte Arqueol Valladolid
Boletin. Seminario de Estudios de Arte y Arqueologia. Universidad de Valladolid — B Vallad
Boletin. Seminario de Estudios de Arte y Arqueologia. Universidad de Valladolid — BSAAV
Boletin. Seminario de Estudios de Arte y Arqueologia. Universidad de Valladolid — BSAV
Boletin. Seminario de Estudios de Arte y Arqueologia (Valladolid) — B Sem EAA (Valladolid)
Boletin. Seminario (Santa Fe, Argentina) — Bol Semin Santa Fe
Boletin. Serie D. Estudios Especiales. Instituto de Geologia y Mineria. Republica del Peru [*Lima*] — Bol Ser D Estud Espec Inst Geol Miner Repub Peru
Boletin. Servicio de Defensa Contra Plagas e Inspeccion Fitopatologica (Spain) — Bol Serv Def Contra Plagas Inspeccion Fitopatol (Spain)
Boletin. Servicio de Plagas Forestales — Bol Serv Plagas For
Boletin. Servicio de Plagas Forestales — Bol Serv Plagas Forest
Boletin. Servicio de Plagas Forestales (Spain) — Bol Serv Plagas For (Spain)
Boletin. Servicio Geologico Nacional de Nicaragua — Bol Serv Geol Nac Nicaragua
Boletin. Servicio Geologico Nacional de Nicaragua (Managua) — Bol Serv Geol Nac Managua
Boletin. Servicio Geologico Nacional (Nicaragua) — Bol Serv Geol Nac (Nicar)
Boletin. Servicio Medico Nacional de Empleados (Chile) — Bol Serv Med Nac Empl (Ch)
Boletin. Servicio Nacional de Salud (Chile) — Bol Serv Nac Sal (Ch)
Boletin sobre Suelos Derivados de Cenizas Volcanicas — Bol Suelos Deriv Cenizas Volcanicas
Boletin. Sociedad Argentina de Angiologia — Bol Soc Argent Angiol
Boletin. Sociedad Argentina de Botanica — Bol Soc Arg Bot
Boletin. Sociedad Argentina de Botanica — Bol Soc Argent Bot
Boletin. Sociedad Argentina de Botanica (La Plata, Buenos Aires) — Bol Soc Arg Botan La Plata BA
Boletin. Sociedad Argentina de Estudios Geograficos Gaea — Bol Soc Arg Est Gaea
Boletin. Sociedad Argentina de Estudios Geograficos GAEA (Buenos Aires) — Bol Soc Arg Estud Geogr BA
Boletin. Sociedad Argentina de Investigacion Operativa — BSAIO
Boletin. Sociedad Arqueologica Luliana — B Soc Arqueol Luliana
Boletin. Sociedad Astronomica de Mexico — Bol Soc Astr Mex
Boletin. Sociedad Boliviana de Pediatria — Bol Soc Boliv Pediat
Boletin. Sociedad Botanica de Mexico — Bol Soc Bot Mex
Boletin. Sociedad Botanica de Mexico — Bol Soc Botan Mex
Boletin. Sociedad Botanica del Estado de Jalisco — Bol Soc Bot Estado Jalisco
Boletin. Sociedad Castellano-Astur-Leonosa de Pediatria — Bol Soc Cast Leon Pediat
Boletin. Sociedad Castellonense de Cultura — B Soc Castell Cult
Boletin. Sociedad Castellonense de Cultura — Bol Soc Castell Cult
Boletin. Sociedad Castellonense de Cultura — BSCC
Boletin. Sociedad Catalana de Pediatria — Bol Soc Catal Pediat
Boletin. Sociedad Chilena de Obstetricia y Ginecologia — Bol Soc Chil Obstet Ginec
Boletin. Sociedad Chilena de Obstetricia y Ginecologia — Bol Soc Chil Obstet Ginecol
Boletin. Sociedad Chilena Quimica — Bol Soc Chil Quim
Boletin. Sociedad Cientifica Hispano-Marroqui de Alcazarquivir — Bol Soc Cient Hispano-Marroqui
Boletin. Sociedad Colombiana de Ciencias Naturales — Bol Soc Col Cienc Nat
Boletin. Sociedad Colombiana de Quimicos Farmaceuticos — Bol Soc Colomb Quim Farm
Boletin. Sociedad Cubana de Dermatologia y Sifilografia — Bol Soc Cub Derm Sif
Boletin. Sociedad Cubana de Dermatologia y Sifilografia — Bol Soc Cubana Dermatol Sifilogr
Boletin. Sociedad de Bibliotecarios de Puerto Rico (San Juan) — Bol Soc Bibl Puerto Rico S Juan
Boletin. Sociedad de Biologia de Concepcion — Bol Soc Biol Concepcion
Boletin. Sociedad de Biologia de Santiago De Chile — Bol Soc Biol Santiago De Chile
Boletin. Sociedad de Cirugia de Chile — Bol Soc Cirug Chile
Boletin. Sociedad de Cirugia del Uruguay — Bol Soc Cir Urug
Boletin. Sociedad de Cirugia del Uruguay — Bol Soc Cirug Urug
Boletin. Sociedad de Fomento Fabril — Bol Soc Fom Fabril
Boletin. Sociedad Dental de Guatemala — Bol Soc Dent Guatem
Boletin. Sociedad Espanola de Amigos de los Castillos — B Soc Espan Amigos Castillos
Boletin. Sociedad Espanola de Ceramica — Bol Soc Esp Ceram
Boletin. Sociedad Espanola de Ceramica y Vidrio — Bol Soc Esp Ceram Vidr
Boletin. Sociedad Espanola de Ceramica y Vidrio — Bol Soc Esp Ceram Vidrio
Boletin. Sociedad Espanola de Excursiones — B Soc Espan Excurs
Boletin. Sociedad Espanola de Excursiones — BSEE
Boletin. Sociedad Espanola de Historia de la Farmacia — Bol Soc Esp Hist Farm
Boletin. Sociedad Espanola de Historia de la Medicina — Bol Soc Esp Hist Med
Boletin. Sociedad Estomatologica Argentina — Bol Soc Estomatol Argent
Boletin. Sociedad General de Autores de Espana — BSGAE
Boletin. Sociedad Geografica de Colombia (Bogota) — Bol Soc Geogr Bogota
Boletin. Sociedad Geografica de Lima — Bol Soc Geogr Lima
Boletin. Sociedad Geografica de Lima — SGL/B
Boletin. Sociedad Geografica de Sucre (Bolivia) — Bol Soc Geogr Sucre
Boletin. Sociedad Geografica e Historica (Sucre, Bolivia) — Bol Soc Geogr Hist Sucre
Boletin. Sociedad Geografica (La Paz) — Bol Soc Geogr La Paz
Boletin. Sociedad Geografica Nacional (Madrid) — BSGM
Boletin. Sociedad Geologica Boliviana — Bol Soc Geol Boliv
Boletin. Sociedad Geologica del Peru — Bol Soc Geol Peru
Boletin. Sociedad Geologica Mexicana — Bol Soc Geol Mex
Boletin. Sociedad Matematica Mexicana — Bol Soc Mat Mexicana
Boletin. Sociedad Matematica Mexicana. Segunda Serie [*Mexico City*] — Bol Soc Mat Mexicana 2
Boletin. Sociedad Medica del Centro Materno Infantil Gral Maximino Avila Camacho [*Mexico*] — Bol Soc Med Cent Materno Infant Gral Maximino Avila Camacho
Boletin. Sociedad Medico-Quirurgica del Centro de la Republica — Bol Soc Med Quir Centro Republ
Boletin. Sociedad Mexicana de Geografia y Estadistica (Mexico) — Bol Soc Mex Geogr Estad Mex
Boletin. Sociedad Mexicana de Historia y Filosofia de la Medicina — Bol Soc Mex Hist Filos Med
Boletin. Sociedad Mexicana de Micologia — Bol Soc Mex Mico
Boletin. Sociedad Mexicana de Micologia — Bol Soc Mex Micol
Boletin. Sociedad Mexicana de Micologia — BSMMDY
Boletin. Sociedad Nacional de Mineria del Peru (Lima) — Bol Soc Nac Mineria Lima
Boletin. Sociedad Nacional de Mineria (Peru) — Bol Soc Nac Min (Peru)
Boletin. Sociedad Nacional de Mineria y Petroleo — Bol Soc Nac Min Pet
Boletin. Sociedad Nacional de Mineria y Petroleo — Bol Soc Nac Mineria Petrol
Boletin. Sociedad Peruana de Botanica — Bol Soc Peruana Bot
Boletin. Sociedad Quimica del Peru — Bol Soc Quim Peru
Boletin. Sociedad Valenciana de Pediatria — Bol Soc Valencia Pediatr
Boletin. Sociedad Venezolana de Ciencias Naturales — Bol Soc Venez Cienc Nat
Boletin. Sociedad Venezolana de Ciencias Naturales — Boln Soc Venez Cienc Nat
Boletin. Sociedad Venezolana de Ciencias Naturales (Caracas) — Bol Soc Venez Cien Nat Caracas
Boletin. Sociedad Venezolana de Cirugia — Bol Soc Venez Cir
Boletin. Sociedad Venezolana de Espeleologia — Bol Soc Venez Espeleol
Boletin. Sociedad Venezolana de Geologos — Bol Soc Venez Geol
Boletin. Sociedade Brasileira de Matematica — Bol Soc Bras Mat
Boletin Tecnico Arpel — Bol Tec Arpel
Boletin Tecnico. Asociacion Interamericana de Bibliotecarios y Documentalistas Agricolas — Bol Tec Asoc Interam Bibl Doc Agric
Boletin Tecnico. Centro de Investigaciones Agricolas "Alberto Boerger" — Bol Tec Cent Invest Agric Alberto Boerger
Boletin Tecnico. Departamento de Investigacion Agricola. Ministerio de Agricultura. Direccion de Agricultura y Pesca (Chile) — Bol Tec Dept Invest Agr Min Agr Dir Agr Pesca (Chile)
Boletin Tecnico. Direccion General de Sanidad — Bol Tec Dir Gen Sanid

Boletin Tecnico. Escuela de Ingenieria Forestal. Universidad de Chile — Bol Tec Esc Ingen For Univ Chile
Boletin Tecnico. Escuela Nacional de Agricultura Chapingo — Bol Tec Esc Nac Agr Chapingo
Boletin Tecnico. Escuela Superior de Agricultura "Antonio Narro." Universidad de Coahuila (Saltillo) — Bol Tec Es Super Agric Antonio Narro Univ Coahuila Saltillo
Boletin Tecnico. Escuela Superior de Agricultura "Antonio Narro." Universidad de Coahuila (Saltillo) — Bol Tec Esc Super Agric Antonio Narro Univ Coahuila Saltillo
Boletin Tecnico. Facultad de Agronomia. Universidad de Chile — Boln Tec Fac Agron Univ Chile
Boletin Tecnico. Facultad de Ciencias Biologicas. Universidad de Nuevo Leon — Bol Tecn Fac Ci Biol Univ Nuevo Leon
Boletin Tecnico. Federacion Nacional de Cafeteros (Colombia) — Bol Tec Feder Nac Cafeteros (Colombia)
Boletin Tecnico. Federacion Nacional de Cafeteros de Colombia — Bol Tec Fed Nac Cafeteros Colomb
Boletin Tecnico. Instituto de Fitotecnia — Bol Tecn Inst Fitotecn
Boletin Tecnico. Instituto de Fomenta Algodonero (Bogota) — Bol Tec Inst Fom Algodonero (Bogota)
Boletin Tecnico. Instituto Experimental de Investigacion y Fomento Agricola-Ganadero (Sante Fe) — Bol Tec Inst Exp Invest Fom Agric Ganad (St Fe)
Boletin Tecnico. Instituto Forestal. Santiago-De-Chile — Bol Tec Inst For Chile
Boletin Tecnico. Instituto Nacional de Investigaciones Forestales (Mexico) — Bol Tec Inst Nac Invest For (Mex)
Boletin Tecnico. Instituto Nacional de Tecnologia Industrial (Argentina) — Bol Tec Inst Nac Tecnol Ind (Argent)
Boletin Tecnico. Instituto Provincial Agropecuario — Bol Tec Inst Prov Agropecu
Boletin Tecnico. Instituto Provincial Agropecuario (Mendoza) — Bol Tec Inst Prov Agropecu (Mendoza)
Boletin Tecnico. Ministerio de Agricultura (Colombia) — Bol Tec Min Agr (Colombia)
Boletin Tecnico. Ministerio de Agricultura e Industrias (San Jose, Costa Rica) — Bol Tec Minist Agric Ind (San Jose Costa Rica)
Boletin Tecnico. Ministerio de Agricultura (Guatemala) — Bol Tec Min Agr (Guatemala)
Boletin Tecnico. Ministerio de Agricultura y Cria — Bol Tecn Minist Agric
Boletin Tecnico. Ministerio de Agricultura y Ganaderia (Costa Rica) — Bol Tec Minist Agric Ganad (Costa Rica)
Boletin Tecnico. Peru. Servicio de Investigacion y Promocion Agraria — Bol Tec Peru Serv Invest Promoc Agr
Boletin Tecnico (San Jose, Costa Rica) — Bol Tec S Jose
Boletin Tecnico. Universidad Central de Venezuela. Instituto de Materiales y Modelos Estructurales — Bol Tec Univ Cent Venez Inst Mater Modelos Estruct
Boletin Tecnico. Universidad de Chile. Facultad de Ciencias Forestales — Bol Tec Univ Chile Fac Cienc For
Boletin Trimestral. Banco de Angola — Bnc Angola
Boletin Trimestral de Estadistica Municipal (Caracas) — Bol Trim Estad Munici Caracas
Boletin Trimestral de Experimentacion Agropecuaria — Bol Trimest Exp Agropecu
Boletin Trimestrial. Hospital del Vina Del Mar — Bol Trimest Hosp Vina Del Mar
Boletin. Unesco para las Bibliotecas — BUB
Boletin. Union Panamericana (Washington, DC) — Bol Un Pan Wash
Boletin. Universidad de Chile — Bol Univ Chile
Boletin. Universidad de Chile — BUC
Boletin. Universidad de Granada — B Univ Granada
Boletin. Universidad de Granada — BUG
Boletin. Universidad de la Republica. Faculdad de Agronomia (Montevideo) — Boln Univ (Montevideo) Fac Agron
Boletin. Universidad de la Republica. Facultad de Agronomia (Montevideo) — Bol Univ Repub Fac Agron (Montevideo)
Boletin. Universidad de Los Andes. Facultad de Ciencias Forestales — Bol Univ Los Andes Fac Cienc For
Boletin. Universidad de Madrid — BUM
Boletin. Universidad de Santiago de Compostela — B Univ Santiago
Boletin. Universidad de Santiago de Compostela — BU Comp
Boletin. Universidad de Santiago de Compostela — BUSC
Boletin. Universidad Nacional de Ingenieria (Lima) — Bol Univ Nac Ing Lima
Boletin. Universidad Nacional de Ingenieria (Peru) — Bol Univ Nac Ing (Peru)
Boletin Uruguayo de Sociologia — Bol Urug Sociol
Boletines. Sociedad Argentina de Angiologia — Bol Soc Arg Angiol
Boletines y Trabajos. Sociedad Argentina de Cirujanos — Bol Soc Arg Ciruj
Boletines y Trabajos. Sociedad Argentina de Cirujanos — Bol Trab Soc Argent Cir
Boletines y Trabajos. Sociedad de Cirugia de Buenos Aires — Bol Trab Soc Cir Buenos Aires
Boletines y Trabajos. Sociedad de Cirugia de Buenos Aires — Bol y Trab Soc Cirug Buenos Aires
Boletines y Trabajos. Sociedad de Cirugia de Cordoba — Bol Soc Cirug Cord
Boletinos Tecnicos. Sociedad Agronomica Mexicana — Bol Tecn Soc Agron Mex
Bolex Reporter — Bolex Rep
Bolezni Rastenij. Morbi Plantarum. Jahrbuch fuer Pflanzenkrankheiten — Bolezni Rast
Bolezni Sel'skokhozyaistvennykh Zhivotnykh. Sbornik SAO VASKhNIL — Bolezni Skh Zhivotn Sb SAO VASKhNIL
Bolezni Sel'skokhozyaistvennykh Zhivotnykh. Trudy UzNIVI — Bolezni Skh Zhivotn Tr UzNIVI
Bolgarskii Fizicheskii Zhurnal [*Bulgaria*] — Bolg Fiz Zh
Bolgarskii Tabak — Bolg Tab
Bolivar — Bo
Bolivar — Bol
Bolivia. Departamento Nacional de Geologia. Boletin — Bolivia Dep Nac Geol Bol
Bolivia. Instituto Nacional de Estadistica. Boletin Estadistico Mensual — Bolivia Inst Nac Estadist Bol Estadist Mens
Bolivia. Instituto Nacional de Estadistica. Boletin Estadistico Trimestral — Bolivia Inst Nac Estadist Bol Estadist Trimest
Bolivia. Ministerio de Minas y Petroleo. Departamento Nacional de Geologia. Boletin — Bolivia Minist Minas Pet Dep Nac Geol Bol
Bolivia. Servicio Geologico. Boletin — Bolivia Serv Geol Bol
Bolleti del Diccionari de la Llengua Catlana — BDLIC
Bolleti. Societat Arqueologica Lubliana — BSAL
Bolletini di Litteratura Moderna — BLM
Bolletino Civico. Istituto Colombiano — B Civico Ist Colombiano
Bolletino della Badia Greca di Grottaferrata — Boll Badia Greca Grottaferrata
Bolletino di Storia della Filosofia — Boll Stor Fil
Bolletino. Reale Istituto Botanico. Universita Parmense — Boll Reale Ist Bot Univ Parmense
Bolletino. Societa d'Esplorazione Commerciale — BSECA
Bolletino. Societa Geografica (Genoa) — BSGG
Bolletino. Societa Geografica Italiana — Boll Soc Geogr It
Bolletino Storico-Bibliografico Subalpino — BollS
Bollettino. Accademia Medica de Genova — Boll Accad Med Genova
Bollettino. Accademia Medica Pistoiese Filippo Pacini — Boll Accad Med Pistoiese Filippo Pacini
Bollettino. Accademia Medico-Chirurgica di Bologna — Boll Accad Med-Chir Bologna
Bollettino. Accademia Svizzera delle Scienze Mediche — Boll Accad Svizz Sci Med
Bollettino. Amicizia Ebraico-Cristiana di Firenze — BAEC
Bollettino. Amicizia Ebraico-Cristiana di Firenze — BAmicEbrCr
Bollettino Annuale. Musei Ferraresi — B Ann Mus Ferr
Bollettino Archeologico Napoletano — Boll Napol
Bollettino. Archivio Paleografico Italiano — BAPI
Bollettino. Archivio Storico del Banco di Napoli — BABN
Bollettino. Associazione Archeologica Romana — BAAR
Bollettino. Associazione degli Africanisti Italiani — BAAI
Bollettino. Associazione degli Africanisti Italiani — Boll Assoc Afr Ital
Bollettino. Associazione degli Africanisti Italiani — Boll Assoc African Ital
Bollettino. Associazione Internazionale degli Studi Mediterranei — Boll Ass Int Stud Med
Bollettino. Associazione Internazionale degli Studi Mediterranei — Boll St M
Bollettino. Associazione Internazionale degli Studi Mediterranei — BSM
Bollettino. Associazione Internazionale degli Studi Mediterranei — BStM
Bollettino. Associazione Italiana de Chimica Tessile e Coloristica — Boll Assoc Ital Chim Tess Color
Bollettino. Associazione Italiana delle Industrie delle Zucchero e dell'Alcool — Boll Assoc Ital Ind Zucchero Alcool
Bollettino. Associazione Italiana pro Piante Medicinal Aromatiche ed Altre Piante Utili — Boll Assoc Ital Piante Med Aromat Altre Piante Utili
Bollettino. Associazione Italiana Tecnici Industrie Vernici Affini — Boll Assoc Ital Tec Ind Vernici Affini
Bollettino. Associazione Mathesis. Societa Italiana di Matematica — Boll Mathesis
Bollettino. Associazione Medica Marchigiana — Boll Ass Med March
Bollettino. Associazione Medica Tridentina — Boll Ass Med Trid
Bollettino. Associazione Medica Triestina — Boll Ass Med Triest
Bollettino. Associazione Mineraria Italiana — Boll Ass Min Ital
Bollettino. Associazione Ottica Italiana — Boll Ass Ott Ital
Bollettino. Associazione per gli Studi Mediterranei — BASM
Bollettino. Associazione Romana di Entomologia — Boll Assoc Rom Entomol
Bollettino. Badia Greca di Grottaferrata — B Grottaf
Bollettino. Banca d'Italia — Bol Banca Italia
Bollettino Biblico [*Associazione Biblica Italiana*] — Boll Bibl
Bollettino Bibliografico Della Botanica Italiana — Boll Bibliogr Bot Ital
Bollettino Camera Agrumaria de Messina — Boll Camera Agrum Messina
Bollettino. Centro Camuno di Studi Preistorici — B Camuno St Pr Istor
Bollettino. Centro Camuno di Studi Preistorici — BCCSP
Bollettino. Centro Camuno di Studi Preistorici — Boll Centro Camuno
Bollettino. Centro di Studi di Poesia Italiana e Straniera [*Roma*] — BCSP
Bollettino. Centro di Studi Filologici e Linguistici Siciliani — B Fil Ling Sic
Bollettino. Centro di Studi Filologici e Linguistici Siciliani — BCSF
Bollettino. Centro di Studi Filologici e Linguistici Siciliani — BCSFLS
Bollettino. Centro di Studi Filologici e Linguistici Siciliani — BCSic
Bollettino. Centro di Studi Filologici e Linguistici Siciliani — BCSS
Bollettino. Centro di Studi Onomastici [*G. D. Serra*] — BCSO
Bollettino. Centro di Studi per la Storia dell'Architettura — BC St Stor Archit
Bollettino. Centro di Studi per la Storia dell'Architettura — BCSSA
Bollettino. Centro di Studi per la Storia dell'Architettura — Boll Centro
Bollettino. Centro di Studi per la Storia dell'Architettura — Boll Centro Architettura
Bollettino. Centro di Studi Vichiani — BCSV
Bollettino. Centro di Studi Vichiani — Boll Centro Stud Vichiani
Bollettino. Centro Internazionale A. Beltrame di Storia dello Spazio e del Tempo — Boll Centro Int Beltrame Stor Spaz Tempo
Bollettino. Centro Internazionale di Studi d'Architettura Andrea Palladio — BCSA
Bollettino. Centro Internazionale per lo Studio dei Papiri Ercolanesi [*Cronache Ercolanesi*] [*Napoli*] — BCPE
Bollettino Chimico Farmaceutico — Boll Chim Farm
Bollettino. Circolo Numismatico Napoletano — B Circ Num Nap
Bollettino. Circolo Numismatico Napoletano — Boll Circ Num Napoletano
Bollettino. Comitato Glaciologico Italiano. Serie 3 — Boll Com Glaciol Ital Ser 3
Bollettino. Comitato per la Preparazione dell'Edizione Nazionale dei Classici Greci e Latini — Boll Com

Bolletino. Comitato per la Preparazione dell'Edizione Nazionale dei Classici Greci e Latini — Boll Com Prep Ed Naz Class Greci Lat
Bolletino. Comitato per la Preparazione dell'Edizione Nazionale dei Classici Greci e Latini — BPEC
Bollettino. Commemorazione del XVI Centenario del Concilio di Nicea — BCCCN
Bollettino. Commissione Archeologica Comunale di Roma — BCAC
Bollettino. Commissione Archeologica Comunale di Roma — BCACR
Bollettino. Commissione Archeologica Comunale di Roma — BCAR
Bollettino. Commissione Archeologica Comunale di Roma — BCR
Bollettino. Commissione Archeologica Comunale di Roma — Bo Co
Bollettino. Commissione Archeologica Comunale di Roma — Boll Comm
Bollettino. Commissione Archeologica Comunale di Roma — Boll della Comm Arch Com di Roma
Bollettino. Commissione Archeologica de Governatorato di Roma — Boll Gov
Bollettino Critico di Cose Francescane — BCCF
Bollettino d'Arte — BA
Bollettino d'Arte — BDA
Bollettino d'Arte — Boll Arte
Bollettino d'Arte — Boll d A
Bollettino d'Arte. Ministero della Pubblica Istruzione — B Arte
Bollettino d'Arte. Ministero della Pubblica Istruzione — BAMPI
Bollettino d'Arte. Ministero della Pubblica Istruzione — Bol Arte
Bollettino d'Arte. Ministero della Pubblica Istruzione — Boll d'Arte
Bollettino d'Arte. Ministero della Pubblica Istruzione — Boll d'Arte MPI
Bollettino degli Olii e dei Grassi — Boll Olii Grassi
Bollettino degli Studi Inglesi in Italia — BSII
Bollettino dei Brevetti per Invenzioni, Modelli, e Marchi — Boll Brev Invenz Modelli Marchi
Bollettino dei Chimici dei Laboratori Provinciali — Boll Chim Lab Prov
Bollettino dei Chimici Igienisti. Parte Scientifica — Boll Chim Ig Parte Sci
Bollettino dei Chimici. Unione Italiana dei Laboratori Provinciali — Boll Chim Unione Ital Lab Prov
Bollettino dei Chimici. Unione Italiana dei Laboratori Provinciali. Parte Scientifica — Bol Chim Un Italiana Lb Prov Par Scien
Bollettino dei Chimici. Unione Italiana dei Laboratori Provinciali. Parte Scientifica — Boll Chim Unione Ital Lab Prov Parte Sci
Bollettino dei Chimici. Unione Italiana dei Laboratori Provinciali. Parte Scientifica — Boll Chim Unione Ital Parte Sci
Bollettino dei Classici — Boll Class
Bollettino dei Classici. Comitato per la Preparazione dell'Edizione Nazionale dei Classici Greci e Latini — B Cl Gr Lat
Bollettino dei Musei Comunali di Roma — Boll MC
Bollettino dei Musei Comunali di Roma — Boll Musei Com Roma
Bollettino del Circolo Numismatico Napolitano — BCNN
Bollettino del Domus Mazziniana — BDM
Bollettino del Medici Svizzeri — Boll Med Svizz
Bollettino della Badia Greca di Grottaferrata — BBGG
Bollettino della Capitale — BC
Bollettino della Carta dei Dialetti Italiani — BCDI
Bollettino della Cotoniera — Boll Coton
Bollettino della Laniera — Boll Laniera
Bollettino della Sezione di Novara della Regia Deputazione Subalpina di Storia Patria — BSNS
Bollettino della Societa Africana d'Italia — BSAI
Bollettino dell'Atlante Linguistico Italiano — BALI
Bollettino dell'Atlante Linguistico Mediterraneo — BALM
Bollettino delle Epizoozie — Boll Epizooz
Bollettino delle Malattie dell'Orecchio, della Gola, del Naso — BMOGA
Bollettino delle Malattie dell'Orecchio, della Gola, del Naso — Boll Mal Orecch Gola Naso
Bollettino delle Malattie dell'Orecchio, della Gola, del Naso [*Italy*] — Boll Mal Orecchio Gola Naso
Bollettino delle Pubblicazioni Italiane Ricevute per Diritto di Stampa — BPI
Bollettino delle Publicatione Italiane — BPI
Bollettino delle Reale Orto Botanico e Giardino Coloniale di Palermo — Boll Reale Orto Bot Giardino Colon Palermo
Bollettino delle Riviste — Boll Riv
Bollettino delle Scienze Mediche — Boll Sci Med
Bollettino delle Scienze Mediche — BUSCA
Bollettino delle Scienze Mediche di Bologna — Boll Sc Med Bologna
Bollettino dell'Economia Pubblica — Bol Econ Pubblica
Bollettino Demografico-Meteorico — Boll Dem Met
Bollettino. Deputazione di Storia Patria per l'Umbria — BDSPU
Bollettino. Deputazione di Storia Patria per l'Umbria — BDU
Bollettino. Deputazione di Storia Patria per l'Umbria — Boll St Patria Umbria
Bollettino di Archeologia Cristiana — BA Cr
Bollettino di Archeologia Cristiana — BAC
Bollettino di Archeologia e Storia Dalmata — BASD
Bollettino di Associazione Italiana Pro Piante Medicinali, Aromatiche, ed Altre Piante Utili — Boll Assoc Ital Piante Med
Bollettino di Bibliografia e Storia delle Scienze Matematiche — Boll Bibliogr Stor Sci Mat
Bollettino di Chimica Clinica — Boll Chim Clin
Bollettino di Filologia Classica — BFC
Bollettino di Filologia Classica — Bo Fi Cl
Bollettino di Filologia Classica — Boll F Cl
Bollettino di Filologia Classica — Boll Fil Cl
Bollettino di Filologia Classica — Boll Fil Class
Bollettino di Geodesia e Scienze Affini [*Florence*] — Boll Geod Sci Affini
Bollettino di Geodesia e Scienze Affini — Boll Geodes
Bollettino di Geofisica Teorica ed Applicata — Boll Geofis Teor Appl
Bollettino di Geofisica Teorica ed Applicata — Boll Geofis Teorica Appl
Bollettino di Geofisica Teorica ed Applicata. Osservatorio Geofisico — Boll Geof Teor Appl
Bollettino di Informazioni Italiani — Bol Inform Ital
Bollettino di Matematica — Boll Mat
Bollettino di Meteorologia e di Idrologia Agraria — Boll Meteorol Idrol Agrar
Bollettino di Microbiologia e Indagini di Laboratorio — Boll Microbiol Indag Lab
Bollettino di Oceanologia Teorica ed Applicata — Boll Oceanol Teor ed Appl
Bollettino di Oncologia — Boll Oncol
Bollettino di Pesca, Piscicoltura, e Idrobiologia — Boll Pesca Piscic Idrobiol
Bollettino di Psicologia Applicata — B Psic Appl
Bollettino di Psicologia Applicata — Boll Psicol App
Bollettino di Psicologia Applicata — Boll Psicol Appl
Bollettino di Psicologia Applicata. Inserto — Boll Psicol Appl Inserto
Bollettino di Ricerche. Centro Sperimentale Enologico F. Paulson (Marsala) — Boll Ric Cent Sper Enol F Paulson (Marsala)
Bollettino di Ricerche e Informazioni. Centro Regionale Sperimentale per l'Industria Enologia F. Paulsen (Marsala) — Boll Ric Inf Cent Reg Sper Ind Enol F Paulsen (Marsala)
Bollettino di Ricerche. Regione Siciliana. Centro Sperimentale Enologia F. Paulsen (Marsala) — Boll Ric Reg Sicil Cent Sper Enol F Paulsen (Marsala)
Bollettino di Storia della Scienze Matematiche — Boll Stor Sci Mat
Bollettino di Storia dell'Arte — Boll St A
Bollettino di Storia dell'Arte (Salerno) — Boll St Arte (Salerno)
Bollettino di Storia delle Scienze Matematiche — Boll Storia Sci Mat
Bollettino di Storia Piacentina — BSPiac
Bollettino di Studi Latini — B St Lat
Bollettino di Studi Latini — BStud Lat
Bollettino di Studi Mediterranei — BSM
Bollettino di Studi Storici ed Archeologici di Tivoli e Regione — BSSAT
Bollettino di Zoologia — Boll Zool
Bollettino di Zoologia Agraria e di Bachicoltura — Boll Zool Agr Bachic
Bollettino di Zoologia Agraria e di Bachicoltura — Boll Zool Agr Bachicolt
Bollettino di Zoologia Agraria e di Bachicoltura — Boll Zool Agrar Bachic
Bollettino di Zoologia Agraria e di Bachicoltura — Boll Zool Agrar Bachicolt
Bollettino di Zoologia Agraria e di Bachicoltura — BOZAA
Bollettino di Zoologia (Napoli) — Boll Zool (Napoli)
Bollettino d'Informazioni. Associazione Italiana di Diritto Marittimo — Boll Ass It Dir Mar
Bollettino d'Informazioni. Consociazione Nazionale Infermiere Professionali e Assistenti Sanitare Visitatrici (Rome) — Boll Inf Consoc Naz (Rome)
Bollettino d'Informazioni Costituzionali e Parlamentari — Boll Cost Parl
Bollettino d'Informazioni per l'Industria Olearia e Saponiera — Boll Inf Ind Olearia Sapon
Bollettino d'Oculistica — Boll Ocul
Bollettino d'Oculistica — BOOCA
Bollettino e Atti. Reale Accademia Medica di Roma — Boll Atti R Accad Med Roma
Bollettino e Memorie. Societa Piemontese de Chirurgia — Boll Mem Soc Piemont Chir
Bollettino e Memorie. Societa Tosco Umbro Emiliana di Medicina Interna — Boll Mem Soc Tosco Umbro Emiliana Med Interna
Bollettino Economico. Camera de Commercio. Industria, Artigianato, e Agricoltura de Ravenna — B Ec Cam Commerc Ravenna
Bollettino Economico. Consiglio Provinciale delle Corporazioni di Cagliari — Boll Cons Cagliari
Bollettino Economico della Camera di Commercio, Industria, Artigianato, e Agricoltura — BECC
Bollettino Economico della Camera di Commercio, Industria, Artigianato, e Agricoltura (Ravenne) — BECC (Ravenne)
Bollettino ed Atti. Accademia Medica di Roma — Boll Atti Accad Med Roma
Bollettino ed Atti. Societa Italiana de Endocrinologia — Boll Atti Soc Ital Endocrinol
Bollettino. Facolta Agraria. Universita di Pisa — Boll Fac Agrar Univ Pisa
Bollettino. Federazione Internazionale. Associazioni di Chimica Tessile e Coloristica — Boll Fed Int Assoc Chim Tess Color
Bollettino. Federazione Mineraria — Boll Fed Miner
Bollettino. Fondazione Sen Pascale Centro per la Diagnosi e la Cura dei Tumori — Boll Fond Sen Pascale Cent Diagn Cura Tumori
Bollettino Forense — Boll For
Bollettino Internazionale delle Opere Scientifiche Medicina — Boll Int Opere Sci Med
Bollettino Internazionale di Informazioni sul Latino — BIL
Bollettino. Istituto Agrario di Scandicci — Boll Ist Agrar Scandicci
Bollettino. Istituto Centrale del Restauro — B I Cent Rest
Bollettino. Istituto Centrale del Restauro — B Ist Rest
Bollettino. Istituto Centrale del Restauro — Boll ICR
Bollettino. Istituto Centrale del Restauro — Boll Ist Rest
Bollettino. Istituto Centrale di Restauro — BICR
Bollettino. Istituto Centrale di Restauro — Boll Ist Restauro
Bollettino. Istituto Centrale per la Patologia del Libro Alfonso Gallo — Boll Ist Cent Patol Libro Alfonso Gallo
Bollettino. Istituto de Lingue Estere [*Genoa, Italy*] — BILEUG
Bollettino. Istituto dei Entomologia. Universita degli Studi di Bologna — Boll Ist Entomol Univ Studi Bologna
Bollettino. Istituto dei Tumori di Napoli — Boll Ist Tumori Napoli
Bollettino. Istituto Dermatologico S. Gallicano — Boll Ist Dermatol S Gallicano
Bollettino. Istituto di Alimentazione e Dietologia — Boll Ist Aliment Dietol
Bollettino. Istituto di Correspondenza Archeologica — B Ist C
Bollettino. Istituto di Corrispondenza Archeologica — Bdl
Bollettino. Istituto di Corrispondenza Archeologica — BICA
Bollettino. Istituto di Diritto Romano — BIDR
Bollettino. Istituto di Entomologia — Boll Ist Entomol
Bollettino. Istituto di Entomologia Agraria e Osservatorio di Fitopatologia di Palermo — BEFPA
Bollettino. Istituto di Entomologia Agraria e Osservatorio di Fitopatologia di Palermo — Boll Ist Ent Agr Oss Fitopat Palermo

Bollettino. Istituto di Entomologia Agraria e Osservatorio di Fitopatologia di Palermo — Boll Ist Entomol Agrar Oss Fitopatol Palermo
Bollettino. Istituto di Entomologia Agraria e Osservatorio di Fitopatologia di Palermo — Boll Ist Entomol Agrar Osse Fitopatol Palermo
Bollettino. Istituto di Entomologia. Universita degli Studi di Bologna — Boll Ist Ent Univ Bologna
Bollettino. Istituto di Filologia Greca — B Fil Gr
Bollettino. Istituto di Filologia Greca. Universita di Padova — B Fil Gr Padova
Bollettino. Istituto di Filologia Greca. Universita di Padova — BIFG
Bollettino. Istituto di Lingue Estere [*Genova*] — BILE
Bollettino. Istituto di Lingue Estere (Genoa) — BILEUG
Bollettino. Istituto di Lingue Estere (Genova) — BILEG
Bollettino. Istituto di Patologia del Libro — Bol Ist Pato Lib
Bollettino. Istituto di Patologia del Libro — Boll Ist Patol Libro
Bollettino. Istituto di Patologia del Libro — Boll Ist Patologia Lib
Bollettino. Istituto di Patologia del Libro Alfonso Gallo — Boll Ist Patol Libr
Bollettino. Istituto di Patologia del Libro Alfonso Gallo — Boll Ist Patol Libro Alfonso Gallo
Bollettino. Istituto di Storia della Societa e dello Stato Veneziano — BISV
Bollettino. Istituto di Storia e di Arte del Lazio Meridionale — B Lazio Merid
Bollettino. Istituto di Storia e di Arte del Lazio Meridionale — BISLM
Bollettino. Istituto di Studi Verdiani — Bol Ist Stud Verdiani
Bollettino. Istituto Nazzionale di Archeologia e Storia dell'Arte — BIA
Bollettino. Istituto Nazzionale di Archeologia e Storia dell'Arte — BIASA
Bollettino. Istituto Nazzionale di Archeologia e Storia dell'Arte — Boll Ist Arch St Arte
Bollettino. Istituto Nazzionale di Archeologia e Storia dell'Arte — Boll Ist Naz Arche St Arte
Bollettino. Istituto Sieroterapico Milanese — B Ist Sier
Bollettino. Istituto Sieroterapico Milanese — Boll Ist Sieroter Milan
Bollettino. Istituto Storico e di Cultura dell'Arma del Genio — Boll Ist Stor Cult Arma Genio
Bollettino. Istituto Storico Italiano — BISI
Bollettino. Istituto Storico Italiano dell'Arte Sanitaria — Boll Ist Stor Ital Arte Sanit
Bollettino. Istituto Storico Italiano e Archivio Muratoriano — BISIAM
Bollettino. Istituto Storico Italiano per il Medioevo e Archivio Muratoriano — BISIMAM
Bollettino. Istituto Storico Italiano per il Medioevo e Archivio Muratoriano — Boll Ist Stor It
Bollettino Italiano di Numismatica — BIN
Bollettino Italiano di Numismatica e di Arte della Medaglia — BMCCP
Bollettino. Laboratori Chimici Provinciali — Boll Lab Chim Prov
Bollettino. Laboratori Chimici Provinciali — Boll Laboratori Chim Prov
Bollettino. Laboratorio di Entomologia Agraria — Boll Lab Entol Agr
Bollettino. Laboratorio di Entomologia Agraria "Filippo Silvestri" — Boll Lab Entomol Agrar Filippo Silvestri
Bollettino. Laboratorio di Entomologia Agraria "Filippo Silvestri" di Portici — BLESA
Bollettino. Laboratorio di Entomologia Agraria "Filippo Silvestri" di Portici — BLESAS
Bollettino. Laboratorio di Entomologia Agraria "Filippo Silvestri" di Portici [*Italy*] — Boll Lab Entomol Agrar Portici
Bollettino Linguistico per la Storia e la Cultura Regionale — BLSCR
Bollettino Malacologico — BMALDV
Bollettino Malacologico — Boll Malacol
Bollettino Malacologico. Unione Malacologica Italiana — Boll Malacol Unione Malacol Ital
Bollettino Mensile. Camera di Commercio Industria e Agricoltura (Perugia) — Boll Mens Cam Com Ind Agr (Perugia)
Bollettino Mensile di Statistica — B Stat M
Bollettino Mensile di Statistica — Bol Mensile Statis
Bollettino Mensile d'Informazioni e Notizie. Reale Stazione di Patologia Vegetale di Roma e Reale Osservatorio Fitopatologico per la Provincia di Roma e gli Abruzzi — Boll Mens Inform Notiz Sta Patol Vegetale Roma
Bollettino Mensile. Societa Svizzera per l'Industria del Gas e dell'Acqua Potabile — Boll Mens Soc Svizz Ind Gas Acqua Potabile
Bollettino Metallografico — Boll Metallogr
Bollettino. Monumenti. Musei e Gallerie Pontificie — B Mon Mus Pont
Bollettino. Musei Civici Veneziani — BMC Venezia
Bollettino. Musei e Istituti Biologici. Universita di Genova — Boll dei Mus Is Biol Univ Genova
Bollettino. Musei e Istituti Biologici. Universita di Genova — Boll Mus Ist Biol Univ Genova
Bollettino. Musei Ferraresi — BM Ferr
Bollettino. Museo Civico di Padova — B Mus Padova
Bollettino. Museo Civico di Padova — Bol Museo Civico Padova
Bollettino. Museo Civico di Padova — Boll Mus Civico Padova
Bollettino. Museo Civico di Padova — Boll Museo Civico Padova
Bollettino. Museo Civico di Storia Naturale di Venezia — Boll Mus Civ Stor Nat Ven
Bollettino. Museo Civico di Storia Naturale di Venezia — Boll Mus Civ Stor Nat Venezia
Bollettino. Museo Civico di Storia Naturale di Verona — B Mus Natur Verona
Bollettino. Museo Civico di Storia Naturale di Verona — Boll Mus Civ Stor Nat Verona
Bollettino. Museo della Civilta Romana — BMCR
Bollettino. Museo dell'Impero Romana — BM Imp R
Bollettino. Museo dell'Impero Romano — B Mus Imp
Bollettino. Museo dell'Impero Romano — BMIR
Bollettino. Museo di Zoologia. Universita di Torino — Boll Mus Zool Univ Torino
Bollettino Numismatico di Luigi Simonetti — BollN
Bollettino Paleontologico Italiano — Boll Pal
Bollettino Paleontologico Italiano — BPI
Bollettino. Reale Accademia de Scienze, Lettere, e Belle Arti di Palermo — BASP
Bollettino. Reale Accademia Medica di Roma — Boll R Accad Med Roma
Bollettino. Reale Istituto di Archeologia e Storia dell'Arte — BIA
Bollettino. Reale Istituto di Archeologia e Storia dell'Arte — BIAA
Bollettino. Reale Societa Geografica Italiana — BRSGI
Bollettino. Reale Stazione di Patologia Vegetale di Roma — Boll Sta Patol Vegetale
Bollettino. Reale Universita Italiana per Stranieri di Perugia — BRP
Bollettino. Regia Deputazione di Storia Patria per la Liguria — BRDSPL
Bollettino. Regia Deputazione di Storia Patria per l'Umbria — BRDSPU
Bollettino. Regia Deputazione di Storia Patria per l'Umbria — BSPU
Bollettino. Regia Stazione di Patologia Vegetale (Rome) — Boll Regia Stn Patol Veg (Rome)
Bollettino. Regia Stazione Sperimentale per l'Industria della Carta e lo Studio delle Fibre Tessile Vegetali — Boll Stn Sper Ind Carta Stud Fibre Tess Veg
Bollettino. Regia Stazione Sperimentale per l'Industria della Carta e lo Studio delle Fibre Tessili Vegetali — Boll Regia Stn Sper Ind Carta Stud Fibre Tess Veg
Bollettino. Regia Stazione Sperimentale per l'Industria delle Pelli e delle Materie Concianti Napoli — Boll Regia Stn Sper Ind Pelli Mater Concianti Napoli
Bollettino. Regio Istituto Superiore Agrario di Pisa — Boll Regio Is Super Agrar Pisa
Bollettino. Regio Istituto Superiore Agrario di Pisa — Boll Regio Ist Super Agrar Pisa
Bollettino Schermografico — Boll Schermogr
Bollettino Scientifico — Boll Scient
Bollettino Scientifico. Facolta di Chimica Industriale di Bologna [*Italy*] — Boll Sci Fac Chim Ind Bologna
Bollettino Scientifico. Facolta di Chimica Industriale di Bologna — BSFCA
Bollettino Scientifico. Facolta di Chimica Industriale. Universita di Bologna — Boll Sci Fac Chim Ind Univ Bologna
Bollettino. Sedute della Accademia Gioenia di Scienze Naturali in Catania — Boll Sedute Accad Gioenia Sci Nat Catania
Bollettino Senese — BS
Bollettino Senese di Storia Patria — Boll Senese Stor Patria
Bollettino Senese di Storia Patria — BSSP
Bollettino. Servizio Geologico d'Italia — Boll Serv Geol Ital
Bollettino. Servizio Geologico d'Italia — BOSGA
Bollettino. Sezione Italiana. Societa Internazionale di Microbiologia — Boll Sez Ital Soc Int Microbiol
Bollettino Sistematico di Bibliografia Romana — BSBR
Bollettino. Societa Adriatica di Scienze (Trieste) — Boll Soc Adriat Sci (Trieste)
Bollettino. Societa Adriatica di Scienze (Trieste). Supplemento — Boll Soc Adriat Sci (Trieste) Suppl
Bollettino. Societa di Biologia Sperimentale — Boll Soc Biol Sper
Bollettino. Societa di Medicina e Chirurgia del Salento — Boll Soc Med Chir Salento
Bollettino. Societa di Naturalisti di Napoli — Boll Soc Nat Napoli
Bollettino. Societa di Naturalisti di Napoli — BONNA
Bollettino. Societa di Studi Valdesi — Bol Soc St Vald
Bollettino. Societa di Studi Valdesi — BSSV
Bollettino. Societa Entomologica Italiana — Boll Soc Ent Ital
Bollettino. Societa Entomologica Italiana — Boll Soc Entomol Ital
Bollettino. Societa Eustachiana — Boll Soc Eustachiana
Bollettino. Societa Filologica Friulana — BSFF
Bollettino. Societa Filologica Romana — BSFR
Bollettino. Societa Geografica Italiana — Boll Soc Geog
Bollettino. Societa Geografica Italiana — Boll Soc Geogr Ital
Bollettino. Societa Geografica Italiana — BSGI
Bollettino. Societa Geografica Italiana — BSGIA
Bollettino. Societa Geologica Italiana — BOGIA
Bollettino. Societa Geologica Italiana — Boll Soc Geol Ital
Bollettino. Societa Internazionale di Microbiologia. Sezione Italiana — Boll Soc Int Microbiol Sez Ital
Bollettino. Societa Italiana di Biologia Sperimentale — B Ital Biol
Bollettino. Societa Italiana di Biologia Sperimentale — Boll Soc Ital Biol Sper
Bollettino. Societa Italiana di Biologia Sperimentale — Boll Soc Ital Biol Sperim
Bollettino. Societa Italiana di Biologia Sperimentale — BSIBA
Bollettino. Societa Italiana di Cardiologia — Boll Soc Ital Cardiol
Bollettino. Societa Italiana di Cardiologia — BOTLA
Bollettino. Societa Italiana di Ematologia — Boll Soc Ital Ematol
Bollettino. Societa Italiana di Farmacia Ospedaliera — Boll Soc Ital Farm Osp
Bollettino. Societa Italiana di Fisica — Bol Soc Ital Fis
Bollettino. Societa Italiana di Fisica — Boll Soc Ital Fis
Bollettino. Societa Italiana di Fisica — BOSFA
Bollettino. Societa Italiana di Patologia — Boll Soc Ital Patol
Bollettino. Societa Medica Lazzaro Spallanzani con Sede in Reggio Emilia — Boll Soc Med Lazzaro Spallanzani Reggio Emilia
Bollettino. Societa Medico-Chirurgica Bresciana — Boll Soc Med Chir Brescia
Bollettino. Societa Medico-Chirurgica (Cremona) — Boll Soc Med Chir (Cremona)
Bollettino. Societa Medico-Chirurgica della Provincia di Varese — Boll Soc Med Chir Prov Varese
Bollettino. Societa Medico-Chirurgica di Catania — Boll Soc Med Chir Catania
Bollettino. Societa Medico-Chirurgica di Modena — Boll Soc Med Chir Modena
Bollettino. Societa Medico-Chirurgica di Pavia — Boll Soc Med-Chir Pavia
Bollettino. Societa Medico-Chirurgica di Pisa — Boll Soc Med Chir Pisa
Bollettino. Societa Medico-Chirurgica di Reggio Emilia — Boll Soc Med Chir Reggio Emilia
Bollettino. Societa Medico-Chirurgica e Ospedali Provincia di Cremona — Boll Soc Med-Chir Osp Prov Cremona
Bollettino. Societa Paleontologica Italiana — Boll Soc Paleontol Ital
Bollettino. Societa Paleontologica Italiana — BSPIA

Bollettino. Societa Pavese di Storia Patria — Boll Soc Pavese Stor Patria
Bollettino. Societa Pavese di Storia Patria — BPSP
Bollettino. Societa Pavese di Storia Patria — BSPS
Bollettino. Societa Pavese di Storia Patria — BSPSP
Bollettino. Societa per gli Studi Storici, Archeologici, ed Artistici nella Provincia di Cuneo — Boll Soc Studi Stor Prov Cuneo
Bollettino. Societa Piemontese di Archeologia — BSPA
Bollettino. Societa Piemontese di Archeologia e Belle Arti — BSPABA
Bollettino. Societa Piemontese di Archeologia e di Belle Arti — Boll Soc Piemontese
Bollettino. Societa Piemontese di Archeologia e di Belle Arti — BS Piem
Bollettino. Societa Romana per gli Studi Zoologici — Boll Soc Rom Stud Zool
Bollettino. Societa Sarda di Scienze Naturali — Boll Soc Sarda Sci Nat
Bollettino. Societa Sismologica Italiana — Boll Soc Sismol Ital
Bollettino. Societa Storica Maremmana — BS Mar
Bollettino. Societa Zoologica Italiana — Boll Soc Zool Ital
Bollettino. Stazione di Patologia Vegetale di Roma — Boll Sta Patol Veg
Bollettino. Stazione di Patologia Vegetale di Roma — Boll Staz Patol Veg Roma
Bollettino. Stazione di Patologia Vegetale di Roma — Boll Stn Patol Veg Roma
Bollettino. Stazione Sperimentale per l'Industria della Pelli e delle Materie Concianti (Napoli-Torino) — Boll Stn Sper Ind Pelli Mater Concianti (Napoli Torino)
Bollettino Storico Catanese — Boll Stor Cat
Bollettino Storico Catanese — BSC
Bollettino Storico Catanese — BSCat
Bollettino Storico Cremonese — Boll St Cremonese
Bollettino Storico Cremonese — Boll Stor Crem
Bollettino Storico Cremonese — Boll Stor Cremonese
Bollettino Storico Cremonese — BS Cr
Bollettino Storico Cremonese — BSC
Bollettino Storico della Svizzera Italiana — Boll St Sv It
Bollettino Storico della Svizzera Italiana — Boll Stor Svizz Ital
Bollettino Storico della Svizzera Italiana — Boll Stor Svizzera Italiana
Bollettino Storico della Svizzera Italiana — BSI
Bollettino Storico della Svizzera Italiana — BSSI
Bollettino Storico Livornese — BSL
Bollettino Storico Mantovano — BSM
Bollettino Storico per la Provincia de Novara — BSPN
Bollettino Storico per la Provincia di Novara — Boll St Novara
Bollettino Storico per la Provincia di Novara — Boll Stor Novara
Bollettino Storico Piacentino — Boll S P
Bollettino Storico Piacentino — Boll St Piacentino
Bollettino Storico Piacentino — BSP
Bollettino Storico Pisano — Boll Stor Pisano
Bollettino Storico Pisano — BSPis
Bollettino Storico Pistoiese — BSP
Bollettino Storico Pistoiese — BSPi
Bollettino Storico-Bibliografico Subalpino — BSB Subalpino
Bollettino Storico-Bibliografico Subalpino — BSBS
Bollettino Svizzero di Mineralogia e Petrografia — Boll Svizz Mineral Petrogr
Bollettino Tecnico della Coltivazione del Tabacchi — Boll Tecn Coltiv Tabacchi
Bollettino Tecnico FINSIDER [*Societa Finanziaria Siderurgica*] [*Italy*] — Boll Tec FINSIDER
Bollettino Tecnico FINSIDER [*Societa Finanziaria Siderurgica*] — BTFIA
Bollettino Tecnico. Regio Istituto Sperimentale per la Coltivazione dei Tabacchi Leonardo Angeloni — Boll Tec Regio Ist Sper Coltiv Tab Leonardo Angeloni
Bollettino Ufficiale. Camera di Commercio, Industria, e Agricoltura di Udine — Boll Uffic Cam Com Ind Agr Udine
Bollettino Ufficiale. Regia Stazione Sperimentale per la Seta (Italy) — Boll Uffic Regia Stn Sper Seta (Italy)
Bollettino Ufficiale. Stazione Sperimentale per l'Industria delle Essenze e dei Derivati degli Agrumi in Reggio Calabria — Boll Uffic Stn Sper Ind Essenze Deriv Agrumi Reggio Calabria
Bollettino. Ufficio Geologico d'Italia — Boll Uffic Geol Ital
Bollettino. Unione Matematica Italiana — BLUMA
Bollettino. Unione Matematica Italiana — Boll Un Mat Ital
Bollettino. Unione Matematica Italiana — Boll Unione Mat Ital
Bollettino. Unione Matematica Italiana. A — Boll Un Mat Ital A
Bollettino. Unione Matematica Italiana. B — Boll Un Mat Ital B
Bollettino. Unione Matematica Italiana. C. Serie V. Analisi Funzionale e Applicazioni — Boll Un Mat Ital C 5
Bollettino. Unione Matematica Italiana. Series IV [*Italy*] — Boll Unione Mat Ital Ser IV
Bollettino. Unione Matematica Italiana. Series IV — BUIMB
Bollettino Universitario Italiano per Stranieri — Boll Stran
Bollingen Series — BS
Bologna Medica — Bologna Med
Bolsa Review — Bolsa Rev
Bolton Landing Conference. Proceedings — Bolton Landing Conf Proc
Bolyai Society Mathematical Studies — Bolyai Soc Math Stud
Bombay Asiatic Society — BAS
Bombay Geographical Magazine — BGM
Bombay Geographical Magazine — Bombay Geogr Mag
Bombay Historical Society. Journal — BHS
Bombay Hospital Journal — Bombay Hosp J
Bombay Secretariat — BS
Bombay Selections — B Sel
Bombay Technologist — Bombay Technol
Bombay University Journal — Bombay Univ J
Bombay University. Journal — BUJ
Bome in Suid-Afrika — Bome S-Afr
Bon Appetit — GBON
Bondsspaarbanken — VNS
Bone and Mineral — Bone Miner
Bone and Mineral Research — Bone Miner Res
Bone and Tooth. Proceedings. European Symposium — Bone Tooth Proc Eur Symp
Bone Metabolism [*Japan*] — Bone Metab
Bones and Joints — Bones Jt
Bonn. Pressereferat des Bundesministeriums fuer Forschung und Technologie. Mitteilungen — BMFT Mitteilungen
Bonn University. Physikalisches Institut. Technical Report BONN-HE — Bonn Univ Phys Inst Tech Rep BONN HE
Bonn University. Physikalisches Institut. Technical Report BONN-IR — Bonn Univ Phys Inst Tech Rep BONN IR
Bonner Arbeiten zur Deutschen Literatur — BADL
Bonner Arbeiten zur Deutschen Literatur — Bonner Arbeiten
Bonner Beitraege — BB
Bonner Biblische Beitraege — BBB
Bonner County Genealogical Society Quarterly — Bonner County Geneal Soc Quart
Bonner Energie-Report — Bonner Energ-Rep
Bonner Geographische Abhandlungen — Bonn Geogr Abh
Bonner Geschichtsblaetter — BG
Bonner Geschichtsblaetter — BonG
Bonner Hefte zur Vorgeschichte — BHVG
Bonner Hefte zur Vorgeschichte — Bonn Hefte Vg
Bonner Historische Forschungen — BHF
Bonner Jahrbuecher — BJ
Bonner Jahrbuecher — BJbb
Bonner Jahrbuecher — Bonn Jb
Bonner Jahrbuecher — Bonner Jb
Bonner Jahrbuecher des Rheinischen Landesmuseums in Bonn und des Vereins von Altertumsfreunden im Rheinlande — B Jb
Bonner Jahrbuecher des Rheinischen Landesmuseums in Bonn und des Vereins von Altertumsfreunden in Rheinlande — Bonn Jahrb
Bonner Jahrbuecher des Rheinischen Landesmuseums in Bonn und des Vereins von Altertumsfreunden in Rheinlande — Bonn Jhb
Bonner Jahrbuecher des Rheinischen Landesmuseums in Bonn und des Vereins von Altertumsfreunden in Rheinlande — Bonner J
Bonner Jahrbuecher des Rheinischen Landesmuseums in Bonn und des Vereins von Altertumsfreunden in Rheinlande — Bonner Jahrb
Bonner Jahrbuecher. Jahrbuecher des Vereins von Altertumsfreunden im Rheinlande — Bonn Jbb
Bonner Mathematische Schriften — Bonn Math Schr
Bonner Mathematische Schriften [*Bonn*] — Bonner Math Schriften
Bonner Orientalistische Studien — BOS
Bonner Rechtswissenschaftliche Abhandlungen — Bonner Rechtswiss Abh
Bonner Studien zur Englischen Philologie — Bo Stud
Bonner Zeitschrift fuer Theologie und Seelsorge — BZThS
Bonner Zeitschrift fuer Theologie und Seelsorge — BZTS
Bonner Zoologische Beitraege — Bonn Zool Beitr
Bonner Zoologische Monographien — Bonn Zool Monogr
Bonniers Litteraera Magasin — BLM
Bonniers Litteraera Magasin — BLMag
Bonniers Litteraera Magasin — Bonn Litt Mag
Bonniers Litteraerae Magasin — Bonniers Litt Mag
Bonniers Litterara Magasin — BLM
Bonniers Maenadstidning [*Stockholm*] — BM
Bonsai Bulletin. Bonsai Society of Greater New York — Bonsai Bull New York
Bonsai Bulletin. Quarterly. Pennsylvania Bonsai Society (Philadelphia) — Bonsai Bull Philadelphia
Bonsai Journal — Bonsai J
Bont. Maandblad voor het Bontbedrijf — BVB
Book Arts Review — BAR
Book Auction Records — Book Auct Rec
Book Buyer [*Later, Lamp*] — Bk Buyer
Book Collecting and Library Monthly — Bk Collecting & Lib Mo
Book Collector — BC
Book Collector — BCol
Book Collector — Bk Coll
Book Collector — Bk Collec
Book Collector — Bk Collector
Book Collector — Book Coll
Book Collector — Book Collec
Book Collector — Book Collect
Book Collector's Market — BCM
Book Collector's Quarterly — BCQ
Book Collector's Quarterly — Book Coll Qtr
Book Forum — B Forum
Book Forum — BF
Book Forum — Bk Forum
Book League Monthly — BLM
Book List. Society for Old Testament Studies [*Manchester*] — BL
Book List. Society for Old Testament Studies — BLOT
Book. Metals Society — Book Met Soc
Book Notes — BN
Book of Abstracts. International Conference on Atomic Spectroscopy — Book Abstr Int Conf At Spectrosc
Book of ASTM [*American Society for Testing and Materials*] **Standards** — Book ASTM Stand
Book of Awards [*New Zealand*] — BA
Book of Papers. American Association of Textile Chemists and Colorists. International Conference and Exhibition — Book Pap Am Assoc Text Chem Color Int Conf Exhib
Book of Papers. Canadian Textile Seminar International — Book Pap Can Text Semin Int

Book of Papers. International Conference and Exhibition. AATCC [*American Association of Textile Chemists and Colorists*] — Book Pap Int Conf Exhib AATCC
Book of Papers. International Technical Conference. American Association of Textile Chemists and Colorists — Book Pap Int Tech Conf Am Assoc Tex Chem Color
Book of Papers. National Technical Conference — Book Pap Nat Tech Conf
Book of Papers. National Technical Conference. AATCC [*American Association of Textile Chemists and Colorists*] — Book Pap Natl Tech Conf AATCC
Book of Papers. National Technical Conference. American Association of Textile Chemists and Colorists — Book Pap Natl Tech Conf Am Assoc Text Chem Color
Book of Papers. Technical Symposium. Nonwovens. Innovative Fabrics for the Future — Book Pap Tech Symp Nonwovens Innovative Fabr Future
Book of Proceedings. Annual Industrial Air and Water Pollution/Contamination Control Seminar — Book Proc Annu Ind Air Water Pollut Contam Control Semin
Book of Proceedings. Annual Industrial Air Pollution/Contamination Control Seminar — Book Proc Annu Ind Air Pollut Contam Contr Semin
Book of Proceedings. Annual Industrial Air Pollution Control Seminar — Book Proc Annu Ind Air Pollut Control Semin
Book of the Month Club. News — BMCN
Book of Weird Tales [*A*] — BKW
Book Production Industry — Book Prod
Book Production Industry — BPI
Book Publishers Directory — Book Pub Dir
Book Report — BR
Book Research Quarterly — BRQ
Book Review Data Base [*Kirkus*] — BRDB
Book Review Digest [*Information service or system*] — Bk Rev Dig
Book Review Digest — Book Rev Digest
Book Review Digest [*Information service or system*] — BoRv
Book Review Digest [*Information service or system*] — BRD
Book Review Editors File [*Database*] — BREF
Book Review Index — Bk Rev Ind
Book Review Index — Book Revi Index
Book Review Index to Social Science Periodicals — Book Rev Index Soc Sci Period
Book Reviews — Book R
Book Reviews of the Month — Bk Rev Mo
Book Reviews of the Month — Book Rev Mon
Book Supplement. Journal of Child Psychology and Psychiatry — Book Suppl J Child Psychol Psychiatr
Book Times — Bk T
Book Trolley — Bk Trolley
Book Trolley — BKTLA
Book Week — B Wk
Book Week — Bk Wk
Book World — Bk World
Book World — BkW
Book World [*Chicago Tribune*] — BW
Book World (Washington Post) — BW (WP)
Bookbinding and Book Production — Bkbinding & Bk Production
Bookbird — Bkbird
Booklegger — Bookleger
Booklegger Magazine — Bklegger
Booklet. Forestry Commission (London) — Bookl For Comm (Lond)
Booklet. International Colloquium on Magnetic Films and Surfaces — Bookl Int Colloq Magn Films Surf
Booklet. Timber Preservers' Association of Australia — Bookl Timb Pres Assoc Aust
Bookletter Southeast — Booklet SE
Bookline Alert. Missing Books and Manuscripts [*Database*] — BAMBAM
Booklist — Bkl
Booklist — BL
Booklist — PBKL
Booklist and Subscription Books Bulletin [*Later, Booklist*] — Bklist
Booklist and Subscription Books Bulletin [*Later, Booklist*] — Booklist
Booklist and Subscription Books Bulletin [*Later, Booklist*] — Booklist and SBB
Booklovers' Magazine — Bookl M
Booklover's Magazine — Booklover's M
Bookman [*Published in US*] — Amer Bookman
Bookman — B
Bookman — Bk
Bookman — Bm
Bookman — Bookm
Bookman (London) — BkL
Bookman (London) — Bkman (Lond)
Bookman (London) — Bookm (Lond)
Bookman's Journal — BJ
Bookmark — Bkmark
Bookmark. New York State Library — Bookmark
Bookmark. University of Idaho — Bkmark (Idaho)
Book-News — Bk-News
Books Abroad — BA
Books Abroad — Bk Abroad
Books Abroad — Bks Abroad
Books Abroad — Books
Books Abroad (Norman, Oklahoma) — Bks Abrd Norman
Books and Bookmen — BB
Books and Bookmen — Bk & Bkmen
Books and Bookmen — Bks & Bkmn
Books and Libraries at the University of Kansas — Bks & Libs
Books and Writers — BW
Books at Brown — BBr
Books at Iowa — BI
Books at Iowa — BkIA
Books from Finland — BF
Books in Canada — BIC
Books in Canada — Bks in Can
Books in French — Book Fr
Books in Library and Information Science [*New York*] — Books in Library and Information Sci
Books in Print — B Pr
Books in Print South Africa — BIPSA
Books in Scotland — Books in Scot
Books in Series — BIS
Books in the Earth Sciences and Related Topics — Books Earth Sci Relat Top
Books of the Month — B of M
Books of the Times — BOT
Books of the Times (New York) — BOT (New York)
Books Today [*Sunday Chicago Tribune*] — Bks Today
Boole Press Conference Series — Boole Press Conf Ser
Boosey & Hawkes Newsletter — BHN
Bopp und Reuther. Technische Mitteilungen — Bopp Reuther Tech Mitt
Bor es Cipotechnika — Bor Cipotech
Bor- es Cipotechnika, -Piac — Bor Cipotech Piac
Bor. Poluchenie, Struktura, i Svoistva. Materialy Mezhdunarodnogo. Simpoziuma po Boru — Bor Poluch Strukt Svoistva Mater Mezhdunar Simp Boru
Boraszati Lapok (Budapest) — Borasz Lapok Budapest
Boraszati Lapok (Pest) — Borasz Lapok Pest
Bor'ba s Gazom i Pyl'yu v Ugol'nykh Shakhtakh — Bor'ba Gazom Pyl'yu Ugol'n Shakhtakh
Bor'ba s Tuberkulezom — Bor'ba Tuberk
Bordeaux Chirurgicale [*France*] — Bordeaux Chir
Bordeaux Medical — Bord Med
Bordeaux Medical — Bordeaux Med
Borden Review of Nutrition Research — BRNR
Borden's Review of Nutrition Research — Borden's Rev Nutr Res
Borderland of Psychiatry — Borderl Psychiatry
Borderlands of Neurology — Borderl Neurol
Boreal — BORL
Boreal Institute for Northern Studies. Contribution Series — BINSCS
Boreal Institute for Northern Studies. Occasional Publication — BINSOP
Boreal Institute for Northern Studies. University of Alberta. Annual Report [*A publication*] — Boreal Inst North Stud Univ Alberta Annu Rep
Boreal Institute for Northern Studies. University of Alberta. Occasional Publication — Boreal Inst North Stud Univ Alberta Occas Publ
Boreal Northern Titles [*Database*] — BNT
Boreales. Revue du Centre de Recherches Inter-Nordiques — BOLS
Borehole Water Journal — Borehole Water J
Borgyogyaszati es Venerologiai Szemle — Borgyogy Venerol Sz
Born og Boger — Bo og Bo
Borneo Research Bulletin — Bor Res B
Bornesagens Tidende — Bo T
Bornholmske Samlinger — Bh S
Bornholmske Samlinger — Bornholm Sam
Borsen — BN
Borsen Zeitung — BZ
Borsenblatt fuer den Deutschen Buchhandel — BDB
Borsodi Szemle — Borsod Szle
Bosbou in Suid-Afrika — Bosb Suid-Afr
Bosbou in Suid-Afrika — Bosbou S-Afr
Bosbouwproefstation TNO. Korte Mededeling — Bosbouwproefstn TNO Korte Meded
Bosch Technische Berichte — Bosch Tech Ber
Boschbouwkundig Tijdschrift — Boschbouwk Tijdschr
Bosquejo Historico de Etnografia Portuguesa — BHEP
Bossche Bijdragen — BB
Boston Bar Journal — BBJ
Boston Bar Journal — Boston BJ
Boston Business Journal — Boston Bsn
Boston College. Environmental Affairs Law Review — BC Env Aff LR
Boston College. Environmental Affairs Law Review — BC Environ Aff Law R
Boston College. Environmental Affairs Law Review — BC Envtl Aff L Rev
Boston College. Environmental Affairs Law Review — Boston Col Environmental Affairs Law R
Boston College Environmental Affairs Law Review — Boston Coll Env Aff Law Rev
Boston College. Environmental Affairs Law Review — Boston Coll Environ Aff Law Rev
Boston College Environmental Affairs Law Review — PBCE
Boston College. Industrial and Commercial Law Review — BC Ind & Com L R
Boston College. Industrial and Commercial Law Review — BC Ind & Com L Rev
Boston College. Industrial and Commercial Law Review — BC Ind Com'l L Rev
Boston College. Industrial and Commercial Law Review — BC Indus & Com L Rev
Boston College. Industrial and Commercial Law Review — Bost Coll Ind L Rev
Boston College. Industrial and Commercial Law Review — Boston Col Ind and Commer Law R
Boston College. Industrial and Commercial Law Review — Boston Col Ind Com L Rev
Boston College. International and Comparative Law Journal — BC Int'l and Comp LJ
Boston College. International and Comparative Law Journal — Boston Col Int'l & Comp LJ
Boston College. International and Comparative Law Review — BC Int'l and Comp L Rev

Boston College. International and Comparative Law Review — Boston Col Int Comp L Rev
Boston College. International and Comparative Law Review — Boston Col Internat and Comparative Law R
Boston College. Law Review — BCL
Boston College. Law Review — BCL Rev
Boston College. Law Review — BCLR
Boston College. Law Review — Boston Col Law R
Boston College Press Anthropological Series — Boston Coll Press Anthrop Ser
Boston College. Studies in Philosophy — Boston Col Stud Phil
Boston Globe — BG
Boston Globe — Bostn Glbe
Boston Globe Index — Bostn Glbe Ind
Boston Herald American — Bost Her Am
Boston Journal of Natural History — Boston J N H
Boston Journal of Natural History — Boston J Nat Hist
Boston Journal of Philosophy and the Arts — Boston J Ph
Boston Magazine — Boston M
Boston Magazine — IBOS
Boston Medical and Surgical Journal — Boston Med and S J
Boston Medical and Surgical Journal — Boston Med Surg J
Boston Medical and Surgical Quarterly — BMSQ
Boston Medical Quarterly — BMQ
Boston Medical Quarterly — Boston Med Q
Boston Monthly Magazine — Bost Mo
Boston Museum. Bulletin — BMB
Boston Museum of Fine Arts. Bulletin — Boston Mus Bul
Boston Observer — Bost Obs
Boston Public Library. Quarterly — Bos Pub Lib Q
Boston Public Library. Quarterly — Boston Pub Lib Quar
Boston Public Library Quarterly — Boston Publ Libr Quart
Boston Public Library. Quarterly — BPLQ
Boston Quarterly — Bost Q
Boston Review — Bost R
Boston Review — Boston R
Boston Society of Civil Engineers. Journal — Boston Soc C E J
Boston Society of Natural History. Memoirs — Boston Soc of Nat Hist Memoirs
Boston Society of Natural History. Occasional Papers — Bost Soc Natur Hist Occ Pa
Boston Society of Natural History. Occasional Papers — Boston Soc of Nat Hist Occ Papers
Boston Society of Natural History. Proceedings — Bost Soc Natur Hist Proc
Boston Society of Natural History. Proceedings — Boston Soc of Nat Hist Proc
Boston State Hospital. Monograph Series — Boston State Hosp Monogr Ser
Boston Studies in the Philosophy of Science — Boston Stud Philos Sci
Boston Studies in the Philosophy of Science — Boston Studies Philos Sci
Boston Symphony Orchestra. Concert Bulletin — Bost Sym Concert Bul
Boston Symphony Orchestra. Program Notes — Bost Sym
Boston University. Africana Libraries. Newsletter — Bost Univ Afr Lib Newsl
Boston University. Business Review — Bost Univ Bus Rev
Boston University. Journal — Bos U J
Boston University. Journal — BUJ
Boston University. Law Review — Bos U Law Rev
Boston University. Law Review — Bost UL Rev
Boston University. Law Review — Boston U LR
Boston University. Law Review — Boston UL Rev
Boston University. Law Review — Boston Univ Law R
Boston University. Law Review — BU L Rev
Boston University. Law Review — BUL
Boston University. Law Review — BULR
Boston University. Studies in English — Bost Univ St Engl
Boston University. Studies in English — BUSE
Boston University. Studies in Philosophy and Religion — Boston U St
Bostonian — Bost
Botanic Advertiser and Rhode Island Record of Modern Medical Reform — Bot Advertiser Rhode Island Rec Med Reform
Botanic Gardens (Adelaide). Miscellaneous Bulletin — Misc Bull Botanic Gdn (Adelaide)
Botanic Gardens (Singapore). Annual Report — Bot Gard (Singapore) Annu Rep
Botanic Journal (Boston) — Bot J Boston
Botanic Ledger and Family Journal of Health — Bot Ledger Family J Health
Botanic Sentinel and Literary Gazette — Bot Sentinel Lit Gaz
Botanica Acta — Bot Acta
Botanica Gothoburgensia. Acta Universitatis Gothoburgensis — Bot Gothob
Botanica Gothoburgensia. Acta Universitatis Gothoburgensis — Bot Gothob Acta Univ Gothob
Botanica Helvetica — Bot Helv
Botanica Lithuanica — Bot Lith
Botanica Marina — Bot Mar
Botanica Marina — Botan Marin
Botanica Marina. Supplement — Bot Mar Suppl
Botanica Oeconomica — Bot Oecon
Botanica Rhedonica. Serie A — Bot Rhedonica Ser A
Botanical Abstracts — Bot Abstr
Botanical Bulletin — Bot Bull
Botanical Bulletin. Academia Sinica — Bot Bull Ac Sin
Botanical Bulletin. Academia Sinica — Bot Bull Acad Sinica
Botanical Bulletin. Academia Sinica — Botan B A S
Botanical Bulletin. Academia Sinica. Institute of Botany. New Series — Bot Bull Acad Sinica Inst Bot New Ser
Botanical Bulletin. Academia Sinica (Taipei) — Bot Bull Acad Sin (Taipei)
Botanical Exchange Club and Society. British Isles — Bot Exch Club Soc Brit Isles
Botanical Gazette — Bot Gaz
Botanical Gazette — Botan Gaz
Botanical Gazette — PBOG
Botanical Gazette (Chicago) — Bot Gaz (Chicago)
Botanical Journal — Bot J
Botanical Journal. Linnean Society [*London*] — Bot J Linn Soc
Botanical Journal. Linnean Society [*London*] — Botan J Lin
Botanical Journal. Linnean Society (London) — Bot J Linn Soc (Lond)
Botanical Leaflets. A Series of Studies in the Systematic Botany of Miscellaneous Dicotyledonous Plants — Bot Leafl
Botanical Magazine — Bot Mag
Botanical Magazine [*Tokyo*] — Botan Mag
Botanical Magazine/Shokubutsu-Gaku Zasshi. Tokyo Botanical Society — Bot Mag Tokyo
Botanical Magazine. Special Issue — Bot Mag Spec Issue
Botanical Magazine (Tokyo) — Bot Mag (Tokyo)
Botanical Miscellany — Bot Misc
Botanical Monographs (New Delhi) — Bot Monogr (New Delhi)
Botanical Monographs (Oxford) — Bot Monogr (Oxf)
Botanical Museum Leaflets. Harvard University — Bot Mus Leafl
Botanical Museum Leaflets. Harvard University — Bot Mus Leafl Harv Univ
Botanical Repository. For New and Rare Plants — Bot Repos
Botanical Review — Bot R
Botanical Review — Bot Rev
Botanical Review — Botan Rev
Botanical Review — BR
Botanical Review — PBOR
Botanical Society. British Isles Proceedings — Bot Soc Br Isl Proc
Botanical Society. British Isles. Proceedings — Bot Soc Brit Isles Proc
Botanical Society of Edinburgh. Transactions — Bot Soc Edinb Trans
Botanical Society of Edinburgh. Transactions — Bot Soc Edinburgh Trans
Botanical Survey of South Africa. Memoir — Bot Surv S Afr Mem
Botanical Transactions. Yorkshire Naturalists Union — Bot Trans Yorkshire Naturalists Union
Botaniceskie Materialy Gerbarija Glavnogo Botaniceskogo Sada SSSR/Notulae Systematicae ex Herbario Horti Botanici Petropolitanae USSR — Bot Mater Gerb Glavn Bot Sada SSSR
Botaniceskie Materialy Gerbarija Instituta Botaniki Akademii Nauk Uzbekskoj SSR — Bot Mater Gerb Inst Bot Akad Nauk Uzbeksk SSR
Botaniceskie Materialy Otdela Sporovyh Rastenij/Notulae Systematicae e Sectione Cryptogamica — Bot Mater Otd Sporov Rast
Botaniceskij Zurnal — Bot Z
Botaniceskij Zurnal SSSR/Journal Botanique de l'URSS — Bot Zurn SSSR
Botaniceskoe Obozrenie. Conspectus Literaturae Botanicae — Bot Obozr
Botanicheski Institut. Izvestiya. Bulgarska Akademiya na Naukite — Bot Inst Izv Bulg Akad Nauk
Botanicheskie Materialy Gerbariya Botanicheskogo Instituta. Akademii Nauk — Bot Mater Gerb Bot Inst Akad Nauk
Botanicheskie Materialy Gerbariya Instituta Botaniki. Akademii Nauk Kazakhskoi — Bot Mater Gerb Inst Bot Akad Nauk Kaz
Botanicheskie Materialy Gerbariya Instituta Botaniki. Akademii Nauk Kazakhskoi SSR — Bot Mater Gerb Inst Bot Akad Nauk Kaz SSR
Botanicheskii Zhurnal (Leningrad) — Bot Zh (Leningr)
Botanicheskii Zhurnal (Moscow) — Bot Zh (Moscow)
Botanicheskii Zhurnal (SSSR) — Bot Zh (SSSR)
Botanichnyi Zhurnal (Kiev) — Bot Zh (Kiev)
Botanicnyj Zurnal/Journal Botanique. Academie des Sciences de la RSS d'Ukraine (Kiev) — Bot Zurn Kiev
Botanico-Medical Recorder — Bot Med Rec
Botanico-Medical Reformer. Or a Course of Lectures Introductory to a Knowledge of True Medical Science (Mount Vernon, Ohio) — Bot Med Reformer Mount Vernon
Botanico-Periodicum-Huntianum — BPH
Botanika. Issledovaniya. Belorusskoe Otdelenie Vsesoyuznogo Botanicheskogo Obshchestva — Bot Issled Beloruss Otd Vses Bot O-Va
Botanikai Koezlemenyek — Bot Koezl
Botanikai Koezlemenyek — Bot Koezlem
Botanikai Koezlemenyek — Bot Kozl
Botanikos Klausimai — Bot Klausimai
Botanique — BTNQA
Botanique et Biologie Vegetale — Bot Biol Veg
Botanisch Jaarboek — Bot Jaarb
Botanische Abhandlungen aus dem Gebiet der Morphologie und Physiologie — Bot Abh
Botanische Blaetter zur Befoerderung des Selbststudiums der Pflanzenkunde auch Besonders fuer Frauenzimmer — Bot Blaett Befoerd Selbststud Pflanzenk
Botanische Jahrbuecher fuer Systematik Pflanzengeschichte und Pflanzengeographie — Bot Jahrb Syst Pflanzengesch Pflanzengeogr
Botanische Jahrbuecher fuer Systematik Pflanzengeschichte und Pflanzengeographie — Bot Jb
Botanische Mitteilungen — Bot Mitt
Botanische Mitteilungen aus den Tropen — Bot Mitt Tropen
Botanische Studien — Bot Stud
Botanische Studien — BS
Botanische Untersuchungen. Landwirthschaftliche Lehranstalt. Physiologisches Laboratorium (Berlin) — Bot Untersuch Berlin
Botanische Zeitung — Bot Ztg
Botanische Zeitung. 2. Abteilung — Bot Zeitung 2 Abt
Botanische Zeitung (Berlin) — Bot Zeitung Berlin
Botanischer Verein zu Hamburg EV. Berichte — Bot Ver Ham EV Ber
Botanisches Archiv — Bot Arch
Botanisches Archiv der Gartenbaugesellschaft des Oesterreichischen Kaiserstaates — Bot Arch Gartenbauges Oesterr Kaiserstaates
Botanisches Centralblatt — BotC
Botanisches Centralblatt. Beihefte. Zweite Abteilung-Systematik. Pflanzengeographie. Angewandte Botanik — Bot Centralbl Beih 2 Abt

Botanisches Centralblatt fuer Deutschland — Bot Centralbl Deutschl
Botanisches Jahrbuch fuer Jedermann — Bot Jahrb Jedermann
Botanisches Magazin. Edited by Roemer and Usteri — Bot Mag Roemer Usteri
Botanisches Zentralblatt — Bot Zblt
Botanisch-Phaenologische Beobachtungen in Boehmen — Bot Phaenol Beob Boehmen
Botanisk Haves Virksomhed Beretning — Bot Haves Virksomhed Beret
Botanisk Tidsskrift — Bot T
Botanisk Tidsskrift — Bot Tidsskr
Botanisk Tidsskrift — Botan Tids
Botaniska Notiser — Bot Not
Botaniska Notiser — Bot Notis
Botaniska Notiser — Bot Notiser
Botaniska Notiser — Botan Notis
Botaniska Notiser. Supplement — Bot Not Suppl
Botanists' Chronicle — Bot Chron
Botetourt Bibliographical Society. Publications — BBSP
Bothnian Bay Reports — BBR
Botswana. Geological Survey and Mines Department. Annual Report — Botswana Geol Surv Mines Dep Annu Rep
Botswana. Geological Survey Department. Bulletin — Botswana Geol Surv Dep Bull
Botswana. Geological Survey Department. Mineral Resources Report — Botswana Geol Sur Dep Miner Resour Rep
Botswana. Geological Survey. District Memoir — Botswana Geol Surv Dist Mem
Botswana Magazine — Botswana Mag
Botswana Notes and Records — BN & R
Botswana Notes and Records — Botswana Notes Rec
Botswana Notes and Records — Botswana Notes Recs
Bottin des Femmes Professionnelles et Commercantes — Bot Fem Prof Com
Bottin Eglise de Montreal — Bot Egl Montreal
Bottomline — BLN
Bottomline — BTL
Botucatu Cientifica. Serie A. Ciencias Agrarias — Botucatu Cient Ser A
Botucatu Cientifica. Serie B. Ciencias Biomedicas — Botucatu Cient Ser B
BOU (British Ornithologists' Union) Check-List — BOU (Br Ornithol Union) Check-List
BOU [*British Ornithologists' Union*] **Check-List** — BCLIE8
Boulainviller's Life of Mohammed [*Monograph*] — BLM
Boumajnaja Promyshlennost — Boumajnaja Promst
Boundary 2 — Bound
Boundary 2 — PBTO
Boundary Two — Bound Two
Boundary-Layer Meteorology — Boundary-Layer Meteorol
Bourgogne Medicale — Bourg Med
Bourne Society. Local History Records — Bourne Soc Local Hist Rec
Bourse aux Cuirs de Belgique — Bourse Cuirs Belg
Bouteille a la Mer — Bout
Bouw. Onafhankelijk Weekblad voor de Bouw — BWG
Bouw/Werk. De Bouw in Feiten, Cijfers, en Analyses — BWY
Bouwadviseur Opinievormend Beroepstijdschrift voor Adviseurs — RIG
Bouwbedrijf — BOP
Bouwbelangen — BWL
Bouwhandel — HFB
Bouwkroniek. Weekblad voor de Bouwvakken en Aanverwante Vakken. Aanbestedingsbulletin voor Alle Werken en Leveringen — BWR
Bouwmarkt — BFH
Bouwsteenen. Jaarboek der Vereeniging voor Nederlandsche Muziekgeschiedenis [*A publication*] — Bouwsteenen J V N M
Bouwstenen voor een Geschiedenis der Toonkunst in de Nederlanden — Bouwstenen
Bouwwereld. Universeel Veertiendaags Vaktijdschrift voor de Bouwnijverheid — VBO
Bovagblad — BAG
Bovine Practitioner — Bovine Pract
Bowdoin Scientific Review. A Fortnightly Journal — Bowdoin Sci Rev
Bowhunting World — Bowhunting Wld
Bowker Annual of Library and Book Trade Information — Bowker Ann
Bowker's International Serials Database — BISD
Bowker's Publisher Authority Database — BPAD
Bowlers Journal — Bowl J
Bowling Green Studies in Applied Philosophy — Bowl Gr St
Bowling-Fencing Guide — Bowl Fenc G
Boxboard Containers — Boxbrd Con
Boxboard Containers — BXV
Boxspring — Box
Boyce Thompson Institute. Contributions — Boyce Thompson Inst Contrib
Boyce Thompson Institute for Plant Research. Professional Papers — Boyce Thompson Inst Plant Res Prof Pap
Boyer Museum Collection — Boyer Mus Coll
Boy's Life — IBOY
Bozart and Contemporary Verse — Bozart
BP [*British Petroleum*] **Accelerator** — BP Accel
BP [*Benzin und Petroleum AG Hamburg*] **Kurier** — BP Kur
BP [*Benzin und Petroleum AG Hamburg*] **Kurier** — BPKUD
BP. Purdue University. Cooperative Extension Service — BP Purdue Univ Coop Ext Serv
BP [*British Petroleum*] **Shield International** — BP Shield Int
BPF (British Plastics Federation) Composites Congress — BPF Compos Congr
BPN [*Butane-Propane News*] — BPN
BPT [*Bereich Projekttraegerschaften*]**-Bericht** — BPT Ber
BRA [*British Rheumatic Association*] **Review** — BRA Rev
Brabant Agricole et Horticole — Brabant Agric Hortic
Bracara Augusta. Revista Cultural da Camara Municipal de Braga — B Aug
Bracara Augusta. Revista Cultural da Camara Municipal de Braga — BA
Bracara Augusta. Revista Cultural de Camara Municipal de Braga — Brac Aug
Brackish Water as a Factor in Development — Brackish Water Factor Dev
Bracton Law Journal — Brac LJ
Bracton Law Journal — Bracton LJ
Bradea. Boletim do Herbarium Bradeanum — Bradea Bol Herb Bradeanum
Bradford — Bradf
Bradford Antiquary — Bradford Ant
Bradford Antiquary — Bradford Antiq
Bradley Fighting Vehicle. US Army White Paper, 1986 — Brad Fight
Bragantia — BRGTAF
Brahms-Studien — Brahms-Stud
Brain and Behavior Research Monograph Series — AGHVA6
Brain and Behavior Research Monograph Series — Brain Behav Res Monogr Ser
Brain and Cogitation — Brain Cogit
Brain and Cognition — Brain Cogn
Brain and Development — BDEVDI
Brain and Development — Brain Dev
Brain and Development — NTHAA7
Brain and Language — B and L
Brain and Language — Brain Lang
Brain and Language — BRLGA
Brain and Nerve [*Tokyo*] — NOTOA6
Brain, Behavior, and Evolution — Brain Behav
Brain, Behavior, and Evolution — Brain Behav Evol
Brain, Behavior, and Evolution — BRBEBE
Brain, Behavior, and Immunity — Brain Behav Immun
Brain Dysfunction — Brain Dysfunct
Brain Dysfunction in Infantile Febrile Convulsions. Symposium — Brain Dysfunct Infant Febrile Convulsions Symp
Brain Edema. Proceedings. International Symposium — Brain Edema Proc Int Symp
Brain Function. Proceedings. Conference — Brain Funct Proc Conf
Brain Injury — Brain Inj
Brain. Journal of Neurology — BRAIA
Brain Metabolism and Cerebral Disorders — Brain Metab Cereb Disord
Brain/Mind Bulletin — Brain/Mind
Brain Pathology — Brain Pathol
Brain Peptides — Brain Pep
Brain Research — Brain Res
Brain Research — BRREA
Brain Research — BRREAP
Brain Research. Brain Research Reviews — Brain Res Brain Res Rev
Brain Research Bulletin — Brain Res Bull
Brain Research Bulletin — BRBUD
Brain Research Bulletin — BRBUDU
Brain Research Bulletin — BRRAB
Brain Research. Cognitive Brain Research — Brain Res Cogn Brain Res
Brain Research. Cognitive Brain Research — Brain Res Cognit Brain Res
Brain Research. Developmental Brain Research — Brain Res Dev Brain Res
Brain Research. Molecular Brain Research — Brain Res Mol Brain Res
Brain Research Reviews — Brain Res Rev
Brain Research Reviews — BRERD
Brain Research Reviews — BRERD2
Brain Stimulation Reward. Collection of Papers Prepared for the International Conference — Brain Stimul Reward Collect Pap Int Conf
Brain Topography — Brain Topogr
Brain-Endocrine Interaction — Brain Endocr Interact
Brains of Chemical Engineer — Brains Chem Eng
Brake and Front End — Brake FE
Brandfare og Brandvaern — Bf o Bv
Brandon's Shipper and Forwarder — Brand Ship Forward
Brandschutz Deutsche Feuerwehrzeitung — Brandschutz Dtsch Feuerwehrztg
Brandstoffen Visie. Vakblad voor de Mandel in Aardolieprodukten en Vaste Brandstoffen — GBL
Brandstofnavorsingsinstituut van Suid-Afrika. Bulletein — Brandstofnavorsingsinst S Afr Bull
Branntwein-Industrie (Moscow) — Branntwein Ind (Moscow)
Branntweinwirtschaft — Branntweinwirt
Branntweinwirtschaft — BWWSAP
Brasil Acucareiro — BrA
Brasil Acucareiro — BRACA2
Brasil Acucareiro — Bras Acucareiro
Brasil Acucareiro — Brasil Acucar
Brasil Acucareiro (Rio de Janeiro) — Bras Acuc Rio
Brasil Apicola — Brasil Apic
Brasil Florestal — Bras Flores
Brasil. Instituto Brasileiro de Bibliographia e Documentacao. Noticias — Noticias
Brasil Odontologico — Bras Odont
Brasil Textil — Bras Text
Brasilia — Bras
Brasilia. Instituto de Estudos Brasileiros. Faculdade de Letras de Coimbra — B
Brasil-Medico — Bras-Med
Brasil-Medico — BRMRA5
Brasov International School — Brasov Int Sch
Brass and Wind News — BW
Brass and Woodwind Quarterly — Brass & Wood Q
Brass and Woodwind Quarterly — BWQ
Brass Bulletin — Brass B
Brass Founder and Finisher — Brass Founder Finsh
Brass World and Plater's Guide — Brass W
Brasserie et Malterie — Brass Malt
Brasseur Francais — Brass Fr
Brassey's Annual and Armed Forces Yearbook — Brass Ann Arm Forc Yb

Brassey's Naval Annual — Brass Nav A
Brassey's Naval Record [*Database*] — BNR
Bratislavske Lekarske Listy — BLLIAX
Bratislavske Lekarske Listy — Bratisl Lek Listy
Bratskii Vestnik — BV
Bratskij Vestnik — Br Vest
Brau Industrie — Brau Ind
Brau- und Malzindustrie — Brau Malzind
Brauer- und Hopfen-Zeitung Gambrinus — Brau Hopfen Ztg Gambrinus
Brauer und Maelzer — Brau Maelzer
Brauerei- und Getraenke-Rundschau — Brau Getraenke Rundsch
Brauerei. Wissenschaftliche Beilage — Brauerei Wiss Beil
Brauerei-Rundschau — Brau Rundsch
Brauerei-Rundschau — BRRUD
Braunkohle — Braunk
Braunkohle Bergbautechnik — Braunkohle Bergbautech
Braunkohle, Waerme, und Energie — Braunkohle Waerme Energ
Braunschweiger Anglistische Arbeiten — BAA
Braunschweiger Jahrbuch — BrJ
Braunschweiger Naturkundliche Schriften — BNSCDX
Braunschweiger Naturkundliche Schriften — Braunschweiger Naturkd Schr
Braunschweigische Heimat — Braun H
Braunschweigische Konserven-Zeitung — Braunschw Konserv Z
Braunschweigische Konserven-Zeitung — Braunschw Konserv Ztg
Braunschweigische Wissenschaftliche Gesellschaft. Abhandlungen — Braunschweig Wiss Ges Abh
Braunschweigische Wissenschaftliche Gesellschaft, Sitzungsberichte, und Mitteilungen. Sonderheft — Braunschw Wiss Ges Sitzungsber Mitt Sonderh
Braunschweigisches Jahrbuch — Braun J
Braunschweigisches Jahrbuch — Braunschw Jb
Braunschweigisches Magazin — Braunschweig Mag
Brauwissenschaft — Brauwiss
Brazda — B
Brazil. A Monthly Publication on Trade and Industry — BRX
Brazil. Camara dos Deputados. Biblioteca. Boletim — Brazil Camara Deput Bibl Bol
Brazil. Camara dos Deputados. Documentacao e Informacao — Brazil Camara Deput Document Inform
Brazil. Comissao Nacional de Energia Nuclear. Boletim — Braz Com Nac Energ Nucl Bol
Brazil. Conselho Nacional do Petroleo. Relatorio — Brazil Cons Nac Petrol Relat
Brazil. Departamento Nacional da Producao Mineral. Anuario Mineral Brasileiro — Braz Dep Nac Prod Miner Anu Miner Bras
Brazil. Departamento Nacional da Producao Mineral. Boletim — Braz Dep Nac Prod Miner Bol
Brazil. Departamento Nacional da Producao Mineral. Divisao de Aguas. Boletim — Braz Dep Nac Prod Miner Div Aguas
Brazil. Departamento Nacional da Producao Mineral. Laboratorio da Producao Mineral. Boletim — Braz Dep Nac Prod Miner Lab Prod Miner Bol
Brazil. Departamento Nacional de Obras Contra as Secas. Servico de Piscicultura. Publicacao. Serie 1 C — Braz Dep Nac Obras Secas Serv Piscic Publ Ser 1 C
Brazil. Departmento Nacional da Producao Mineral. Laboratorio da Producao Mineral. Avulso — Brazil Dep Nac Prod Miner Lab Prod Miner Avulso
Brazil. Divisao de Fomento da Producao Mineral. Avulso — Braz Div Fom Prod Miner Avulso
Brazil. Divisao de Fomento da Producao Mineral. Boletim — Braz Div Fom Prod Miner Bol
Brazil. Divisao de Fomento da Producao Mineral. Memoria — Braz Div Fom Prod Miner Mem
Brazil. Divisao de Geologia e Mineralogia. Avulso — Braz Div Geol Mineral Avulso
Brazil. Divisao de Geologia e Mineralogia. Boletim — Braz Div Geol Mineral Bol
Brazil. Divisao de Geologia e Mineralogia. Boletim — Brazil Div Geol Mineral Bol
Brazil. Divisao de Geologia e Mineralogia. Notas Preliminares e Estudos — Braz Div Geol Mineral Notas Prelim Estud
Brazil. Divisao de Geologia e Mineralogia. Notas Preliminares e Estudos — Brazil Div Geol Mineral Notas Prelim Estud
Brazil. Divisao de Pesquisa Pedologica. Boletim Tecnico — Braz Div Pesqui Pedol Bol Tec
Brazil. Divisao de Tecnologia Agricola e Alimentar. Boletim Tecnico — Braz Div Tecnol Agric Aliment Bol Tec
Brazil. Equipe de Pedologia e Fertilidade do Solo. Boletim Tecnico — Braz Equipe Pedol Fertil Solo Bol Tec
Brazil. Escritorio de Pesquisas e Experimentacao. Equipe de Pedologia e Fertilidade da Solo. Boletim Tecnico — Braz Escritorio Pesqui Exp Equipe Pedol Fertil Solo Bol Tec
Brazil. Fundacao Servicos de Saude Publica. Revista — Braz Fund Serv Saude Publica Rev
Brazil. Instituto Agronomico da Nordeste. Boletim Tecnico — Braz Inst Agron Nordeste Bol Tec
Brazil. Instituto de Oleos. Boletim — Braz Inst Oleos Bol
Brazil. Instituto Nacional da Propriedade Industrial. Revista da Propriedade Industrial — Braz Inst Nac Propr Ind Rev Propr Ind
Brazil Journal — JBG
Brazil. Laboratorio da Producao Mineral. Avulso — Braz Lab Prod Miner Avulso
Brazil. Laboratorio da Producao Mineral. Boletim — Braz Lab Prod Miner Bol
Brazil. Ministerio da Agricultura. Centro de Tecnologia Agricola e Alimentar. Boletim Tecnico — Braz Minist Agric Cent Tecnol Agric Aliment Bol Tec
Brazil. Ministerio da Agricultura. Centro Nacional de Ensino e Pesquisas Agronomicas. Instituto Agronomico do Nordeste. Boletim Tecnico — Braz Minist Agric Inst Agron Nordeste Bol Tec
Brazil. Ministerio da Agricultura. Departamento Nacional da Producao Animal. Revista — Braz Minist Agric Dep Nac Prod Anim Rev
Brazil. Ministerio da Agricultura. Departamento Nacional da Producao Mineral. Divisao de Geologia e Mineralogia. Avulso — Braz Minist Agric Dep Nac Prod Miner Div Geol Mineral Avulso
Brazil. Ministerio da Agricultura. Departamento Nacional da Producao Mineral. Divisao de Geologia e Mineralogia. Monografia — Braz Minist Agric Dep Nac Prod Miner Div Geol Mineral Monogr
Brazil. Ministerio da Agricultura. Departamento Nacional da Producao Mineral. Divisao do Fomento da Producao Mineral. Boletim — Braz Minist Agric Dep Nac Prod Miner Div Fom Prod Miner Bol
Brazil. Ministerio da Agricultura. Departamento Nacional da Producao Mineral. Laboratorio da Producao Mineral. Avulso — Braz Minist Agric Dep Nac Prod Miner Lab Prod Miner Avulso
Brazil. Ministerio da Agricultura. Departamento Nacional da Producao Mineral. Laboratorio da Producao Mineral. Boletim — Braz Minist Agric Dep Nac Prod Miner Lab Prod Miner Bol
Brazil. Ministerio da Agricultura. Departmento Nacional da Producao Mineral. Divisao de Aguas. Boletim — Braz Minist Agric Dep Nac Prod Miner Div Aguas Bol
Brazil. Ministerio da Agricultura. Instituto de Oleos (Rio de Janiero). Boletim — Braz Minist Agric Inst Oleos Rio de Janiero Bol
Brazil. Ministerio da Agricultura. Servico de Informacao Agricola. Estudos Tecnicos — Braz Minist Agric Serv Inf Agric Estud Tec
Brazil. Ministerio das Minas e Energia. Departamento Nacional da Producao Mineral. Boletim — Braz Minist Minas Energ Dep Nac Prod Miner Bol
Brazil. Ministerio das Minas e Energia. Departamento Nacional da Producao Mineral. Boletim — Brazil Minist Minas Energ Dep Nac Prod Miner Bol
Brazil. Ministerio das Minas e Energia. Departamento Nacional da Producao Mineral. Laboratorio da Producao Mineral. Boletim — Braz Minist Minas Energ Dep Nac Prod Miner Lab Prod Miner Bo
Brazil. Patent Document — Braz Pat Doc
Brazil. Servico de Fomento da Producao Mineral. Avulso — Braz Serv Fom Prod Miner Avulso
Brazil. Servico de Fomento da Producao Mineral. Boletim — Braz Serv Fom Prod Miner Bol
Brazil. Servico de Informacao Agricola. Estudos Teemcos — Braz Serv Inf Agric Estud Tee
Brazil. Servico Especial de Saude Publica. Revista — Braz Serv Espec Saude Publica Rev
Brazil. Superintendencia do Desenvolvimento do Nordeste. Divisao de Geologia. Boletim de Estudos — Braz Supt Desenvolvimento Nordeste Div Geol Bol Estud
Brazil. Superintendencia do Desenvolvimento do Nordeste. Divisao de Geologia. Serie Especial — Braz Supt Desenvolvimento Nordeste Div Geol Ser Espec
Brazil. Superintendencia do Desenvolvimento do Nordeste. Divisao de Geologia. Serie Geologia Economica — Braz Supt Desenvolvimento Nordeste Div Geol Ser Geol Econ
Brazil. Superintendencia do Desenvolvimento do Nordeste. Divisao de Geologia. Serie Geologia Especial — Braz Supt Desenvolvimento Nordeste Div Geol Ser Geol Espec
Brazilian American Survey (Rio de Janeiro) — Braz Am Surv Rio
Brazilian Business — Brazilian Bus
Brazilian Economic Studies — Braz Econ Stud
Brazilian Economic Studies — Brazilian Econ Studies
Brazilian Economic Studies — BRR
Brazilian Economy. Trends and Perspectives — Braz Econ
Brazilian International Journal of Adapted Physical Education Research — BRAZ Int J Adapt PE Res
Brazilian Journal of Botany — Braz J Bot
Brazilian Journal of Botany — RRBODI
Brazilian Journal of Chemical Engineering — Braz J Chem Eng
Brazilian Journal of Genetics — Braz J Genet
Brazilian Journal of Genetics — RBGED3
Brazilian Journal of Medical and Biological Research — BJMRDK
Brazilian Journal of Medical and Biological Research — Braz J Med Biol Res
Brazilian Journal of Medical and Biological Research/Revista Brasileira de Pesquisas Medicas e Biologicas — Braz J Med Biol Res Rev Bras Pesqui Med Biol
Brazilian Journal of Plant Physiology — Braz J Plant Physiol
Brazilian Journal of Sports Medicine — Braz J Sports Med
Brazilian Journal of Veterinary Research — Braz J Vet Res
Brazilian Studies — Brazil S
Brazilian Symposium on Theoretical Physics. Proceedings — Braz Symp Theor Phys Proc
Brazil-Medico — Brazil-Med
BRE [*Building Research Establishment*] **Digest** — BRE Dig
Bread Manufacturer and Pastrycook of Western Australia — Bread Manuf WA
Breast Cancer. Advances in Research and Treatment — Breast Cancer Adv Res Treat
Breast Cancer Research and Treatment — BCTRD6
Breast Cancer Research and Treatment — Breast Cancer Res Treat
Breast. Diseases of the Breast — Breast Dis Breast
Breast Feeding and the Mother — Breast Feed Mother
Brecha (Montevideo) — BrechaM
Brecht Heute - Brecht Today — BrechtH
Brecht-Jahrbuch — Brecht J
Breeder's Gazette — Breeder's Gaz
Breifny Antiquarian Society Journal — Breifny Antiq Soc J
Brem- und Verdische Bibliothek, Worin zur Aufnahme der Wissenschaften. Allerley Brauchbare Abhandlungen und Anmerkungen Mitgetheilet Werden — Brem Verdische Biblioth
Bremer Archaeologische Blaetter — BAB
Bremer Archaeologische Blaetter — Br Bl
Bremer Archaeologische Blaetter — Brem A Bl
Bremer Archaeologische Blaetter — Bremer Arch Bl

Bremer Beitraege zur Naturwissenschaft — Bremer Beitr Naturwiss
Bremer Briefe zur Chemie — Bremer Briefe Chem
Bremisches Jahrbuch — Br Jb
Brenesia — BRNSBE
Brennerei Zeitung — Brennerei Ztg
Brenner-Studien — Bren-S
Brennkrafttechnische Gesellschaft. Jahrbuch — Brennkrafttech Ges Jahrb
Brennstoff- und Waermewirtschaft [*Germany*] — Brennst Waermewirtsch
Brennstoff- und Waermewirtschaft — Brennstoff u Waermewirtsch
Brennstoff- und Waermewirtschaft — BRNWA
Brennstoff-Chemie — Br Ch
Brennstoff-Chemie — Brennst-Chem
Brennstoff-Waerme-Kraft [*Fuel, Heat, Power*] — Brennst-Waerme-Kraft
Brennstoff-Waerme-Kraft [*Fuel, Heat, Power*] — Brenns-Waerme-Kraft
Brennstoff-Waerme-Kraft [*Fuel, Heat, Power*] — Brenn-Waerme
Brennstoff-Waerme-Kraft [*Fuel, Heat, Power*] — BWK
Brent Unemployment Bulletin — Brent Unempl Bull
Breslauer Zeitung — Brs Z
Brethren Life and Thought — BLT
Brethren Life and Thought — Breth Life
Brettener Jahrbuch fuer Kultur und Geschichte — BJKG
Brettener Jahrbuch fuer Kultur und Geschichte — Brett J
Brevet Canadien. Brevet de Redelivrance — Brev Can Brev Redelivrance
Brevet d'Importation (Belgium) — Brev Import Belg
Brevet d'Invention (Belgium) — Brev Invent (Belg)
Brevet d'Invention (France) — Brev Invent (Fr)
Brevet Special de Medicament (France) — Brev Spec Med Fr
Brevetto per Invenzione Industriale (Italy) — Brev Invenz Ind (Italy)
Breviora — BRVRAG
Breviora Geologica Asturica — BGAOAT
Breviora Geologica Asturica — Breviora Geol Asturica
Brewer and Maltster — Brew Maltster
Brewers Digest — BRDGAT
Brewers Digest — Brew Dig
Brewers' Guardian — Brew Guardian
Brewers' Guardian — BRGUAI
Brewers' Guild Journal — Brew Guild J
Brewers' Guild Journal — BRGIAG
Brewers Journal — Brew J
Brewers' Journal and Hop and Malt Trades' Review — Brew J Hop Malt Trades Rev
Brewers Journal (Chicago) — Brew J Chicago
Brewers' Journal (London) — Brew J (London)
Brewers' Journal (New York) — Brew J NY
Brewers Journal (Philadelphia) — Brew J (Philadelphia)
Brewer's Journal. Western Brewer — Brew J West Brew
Brewers Technical Review — Brew Tech Rev
Brewing and Distilling International — Brew Distill Int
Brewing Chemists' News Letter — Brew Chem News Lett
Brewing Review — Brew Rev
Brewing Science — Brew Sci
Brewing Trade Review — Brew Trade Rev
Brewing Trade Review. Supplement — Brew Trade Rev Suppl
BRH [*Bureau of Radiological Health*] **Bulletin** — BRH Bull
BRI [*Building Research Institute*] **Occasional Report** — BRI Occ Rep
Briarcliff Quarterly — Briar Q
Briarpatch. Saskatchewan's Independent Monthly Newsmagazine [*Canada*] — BRPT
Brick and Clay Record — B & C Rec
Brick and Clay Record — Brick Clay Rec
Brick Bulletin — Brick Bull
Brick Development Research Institute. Technical Notes on Clay Products — Brick Dev Res Inst Tech Notes Clay Prod
Brick Technical Note — Brick Tech Note
Brickbuilder — Brickb
Bridge Engineering — Bridge Eng
Brief Clinical and Laboratory Observations — Brief Clin Lab Observations
Briefing. Committee of Vice-Chancellors and Principals — Briefing CVCP
Brigantium. Museo Arqueologico e Historico — Brigant
Brigham Young University. Geology Studies — Brigham Young Univ Geol Stud
Brigham Young University. Geology Studies — BYGSA
Brigham Young University. Law Review — Brig Yo ULR
Brigham Young University. Law Review — Brigham Young U L Rev
Brigham Young University. Law Review — Brigham Young Univ L Rev
Brigham Young University. Law Review — Brigham YULR
Brigham Young University. Law Review — BYU L Rev
Brigham Young University. Law Review — BYU LR
Brigham Young University. Research Studies. Geology Series — Brigham Young Univ Res Stud Geol Ser
Brigham Young University. Science Bulletin. Biological Series — Brigham Young Univ Sci Bull Biol Ser
Brigham Young University. Science Bulletin. Biological Series — BYBBA
Brigham Young University. Science Bulletin. Biological Series — BYBBAJ
Brigham Young University. Studies — Brigham You
Brigham Young University. Studies — BYUS
Bright Lights — BRLI
Bright Lights — Brt Lgts
Brighton Crop Protection Conference. Pests and Diseases — Brighton Crop Prot Conf Pests Dis
Brimleyana — BRIMD7
Brinkman's Cumulatieve Catalogus van Boeken — Brink Boeken
Brinkman's Cumulatieve Catalogus van Boeken in Nederland en Vlaanderen Uitgegeven of Herdrukt met Aanvullingen over Voorafgaande Jaren — BCB
Brisbane Courier — BC
Brisbane Courier Reports (Newspaper) (Queensland) — BC (Newspr) (Q)
Bristol Chamber of Commerce. Journal — BSCJA
Bristol Medico-Chirurgical Journal — Bristol Med-Chir J
Bristol Naturalists' Society. Proceedings — Bristol Nat Soc Proc
Bristol University. Department of Agriculture and Horticulture. Bulletin — Bristol Univ Dep Agric Hortic Bull
Bristol University. Proceedings. Speleological Society — Bristol Univ Spel Soc Proc
Bristol University. Spelaeological Society. Proceedings — Bristol Univ Spelaeol Soc Proc
Bristol-Myers Cancer Symposia — BCSYDM
Bristol-Myers Cancer Symposia — Bristol-Myers Cancer Symp
Bristol-Myers Nutrition Symposia — Bristol-Myers Nutr Symp
Bristol-Myers Squibb Cancer Symposia — Bristol Myers Squibb Cancer Symp
Bristol-Myers Squibb/Mead Johnson Nutrition Symposia — Bristol Myers Squibb Mead Johnson Nutr Symp
Britannica Book of the Year — BBY
Britannica Book of the Year — Brit Bk Yr
Britannica Review of Foreign Language Education — Britannica R For Lang Educ
Britische und Irische Studien zur Deutschen Sprache und Literatur — BISDSL
British [*Patent Document*] — Brit
British Abstracts — Br Abstr
British Abstracts A1. General, Physical, and Inorganic Chemistry — Br Abstr A1
British Abstracts A2. Organic Chemistry — Br Abstr A2
British Abstracts A3. Physiology and Biochemistry — Br Abstr A3
British Abstracts B1. Chemical Engineering, Fuels, Metallurgy, Applied Electrochemistry, and Industrial Inorganic Chemistry — Br Abstr B1
British Abstracts B2. Industrial Organic Chemistry — Br Abstr B2
British Abstracts B3. Agriculture, Foods, Sanitation — Br Abstr B3
British Abstracts C. Analysis and Apparatus — Br Abstr C
British Abstracts of Medical Sciences — Br Abstr Med Sci
British Abstracts of Medical Sciences — Brit Abstr Med Sci
British Academy Classical and Medieval Logic Texts — British Acad Classical Medieval Logic Texts
British Academy [*London*]. Proceedings — Brit Acad Proc
British Agricultural Bulletin — Br Agric Bull
British Agricultural Bulletin — Brit Agric Bull
British Almanac Companion — Br Alma Comp
British Alternative Press Index — BAPI
British Amended [*Patent document*] — Brit Amended
British and Colonial Druggist — Br Colon Drug
British and Colonial Pharmacist — Brit Colon Pharm
British and Colonial Printer and Stationer — Brit Col Print
British and Foreign Evangelical Review — Brit & For Evang R
British and Foreign Medico-Chirurgical Review (London) — Brit Foreign Med Chir Rev London
British and Foreign Review — Brit & For R
British and Foreign Scientific Magazine and Journal of Scientific Inventions — Brit Foreign Sci Mag
British and Overseas Pharmacist's Yearbook — Brit Overs Pharm Yb
British Antarctic Survey. Bulletin — BASB
British Antarctic Survey. Bulletin — Br Antarct Surv Bull
British Antarctic Survey. Data — BASD
British Antarctic Survey. Scientific Reports — BASSR
British Antarctic Survey. Scientific Reports — Br Antarct Surv Sci Rep
British Archaeological Abstracts — BAA
British Archaeological Abstracts — Br Arch Abs
British Archaeological Abstracts — Br Archaeol Abstr
British Archaeological Abstracts — Brit AA
British Archaeological Abstracts — Brit Arch Ab
British Archaeological Association. Conference Transactions — British Archaeological Assocn Conference Trans
British Archaeological Association. Journal — BAAJ
British Archaeological Reports — BAR
British Archaeological Reports — Brit Archaeol Rep
British Association for American Studies. Bulletin — BAASB
British Association for American Studies. Bulletin — Brit Assoc Am Studies Bull
British Association for the Advancement of Science. Report — Brit As Rp
British Association for the Advancement of Science. Report — Brit Assn Adv Sci Rpt
British Astronomical Association. Circular — Br Astron Assoc Circ
British Bee Journal — Br Bee J
British Bee Journal and Beekeepers' Adviser — Brit Bee J
British Beet Grower and Empire Producer — Brit Beet Grower
British Birds — Br Birds
British Birds — Brit Birds
British Book News — BBN
British Book News — Brit Bk N
British Book News — Brit Bk News
British Book News. Children's Supplement — Brit Bk N C
British Books in Print — Br Bks Print
British Bryological Society. Transactions — Brit Bryol Soc Trans
British Bulletin of Publications — BBP
British Bulletin of Spectroscopy — Br Bull Spectrosc
British Bulletin of Spectroscopy — Brit Bull Spectrosc
British Business — BB
British Business — BBU
British Business [*England*] — Br Bus
British Business — Br Business
British Business — Brit Busin
British Business — Brit Busn
British Business — BTJ
British Cactus and Succulent Journal — Br Cactus & Succulent J
British Caribbean Supplement of New Commonwealth — Br Car Suppl

British Cast Iron Research Association. Bureau Bulletin — Br Cast Iron Res Assoc Bur Bull
British Cast Iron Research Association. Journal of Research and Development — Br Cast Iron Res Assoc J Res Dev
British Cast Iron Research Association. Journal of Research and Development [*A publication*] — Br Cast Iron Res Assoc Jrna Res Dev
British Cave Research Association. Transactions — Br Cave Res Assoc Trans
British Cave Research Association. Transactions — Brit Cave Res Ass Trans
British Ceramic Abstracts — Br Ceram Abstr
British Ceramic Abstracts — Brit Cer Abstr
British Ceramic Proceedings — Br Ceram Proc
British Ceramic Research Association. Special Publication — Br Ceram Res Assoc Spec Publ
British Ceramic Research Association. Special Publications — B Ceram RA Spec Publ
British Ceramic Research Association. Special Publications — Br Cer Res Assoc Spec Publ
British Ceramic Research Association. Technical Notes — B Ceram RA Tech Note
British Ceramic Review [*England*] — Br Ceram Rev
British Ceramic Society. Proceedings — Br Ceram Soc Proc
British Ceramic Society. Transactions — British Ceramic Soc Trans
British Ceramic Transactions and Journal — Br Ceram Trans J
British Chemical Abstracts — Brit Chem Abstr
British Chemical Abstracts. A. Pure Chemistry — Br Chem Abstr A
British Chemical Abstracts. A1 — Br Chem Abstr A1
British Chemical Abstracts. B. Applied Chemistry — Br Chem Abstr B
British Chemical Abstracts. Collective Index — Brit Chem Abstr Coll Ind
British Chemical and Physiological Abstracts — Brit Chem Phys Abstr
British Chemical and Physiological Abstracts. B — Br Chem Physiol Abstr B
British Chemical and Physiological Abstracts. B1 — Br Chem Physiol Abstr B1
British Chemical and Physiological Abstracts. B2 — Br Chem Physiol Abstr B2
British Chemical and Physiological Abstracts. B3 — Br Chem Physiol Abstr B3
British Chemical and Physiological Abstracts. C — Br Chem Physiol Abstr C
British Chemical Digest — Br Chem Dig
British Chemical Engineering — Br Chem Eng
British Chemical Engineering — Br Chem Engng
British Chemical Engineering — Brit Chem Eng
British Chemical Engineering and Process Technology — BCPTA
British Chemical Engineering and Process Technology — Br Chem Eng Process Technol
British Chemical Engineering and Process Technology — Br Chem Engng Process Technol
British Clayworker — Br Claywkr
British Clayworker — Br Clayworker
British Clayworker — Brit Clayw
British Coal Utilisation Research Association. Monthly Bulletin — BCURA
British Coal Utilisation Research Association. Monthly Bulletin — Br Coal Util Res Ass Mon Bull
British Columbia Administrator — BC Admin
British Columbia and Yukon Territory — Br Columbia Yukon Ter
British Columbia Art Teachers' Association. Journal — BC Art Teach Assn J
British Columbia Association of School Supervisors of Instruction. News — BCASSI News
British Columbia Business Educators' Association. Newsletter — BC Bus Ed Assn News
British Columbia Collective Bargaining Environment — Br Columbia Col Barg Env
British Columbia Collective Bargaining Outlook — Br Columbia Col Barg Outl
British Columbia Collective Bargaining Review — Br Columbia Col Barg Rev
British Columbia Counsellor — BC Couns
British Columbia Decisions Weekly Headnotes — Br Columbia Dec Week Headn
British Columbia. Department of Mines and Petroleum Resources. Bulletin — BC Dep Mines Pet Resour Bull
British Columbia. Department of Mines and Petroleum Resources. Bulletin — BMPBA
British Columbia. Department of Mines and Petroleum Resources. Bulletin — Brit Columbia Dep Mines Petrol Resour Bull
British Columbia Department of Mines. Annual Report — BC Dep Mines Annu Rep
British Columbia. Department of Mines. Annual Report. Bulletin — British Columbia Dept Mines Ann Rept Bull
British Columbia. Department of Mines. Bulletin — BC Dep Mines Bull
British Columbia. Department of Mines. Non Metallic Mineral Investigations Report — BC Dep Mines Non Met Miner Invest Rep
British Columbia. Department of Recreation and Conservation. Annual Report — BC Dep Recreat Conserv Annu Rep
British Columbia English Teachers' Association. Journal — BC Engl Teach J
British Columbia. Forest Service. Annual Report — BC For Serv Annu Rep
British Columbia. Forest Service. Forest Research Review — BC For Serv For Res Rev
British Columbia. Forest Service. Research Notes — BC For Serv Res Notes
British Columbia. Forest Service. Technical Publication — BC For Serv Tech Publ
British Columbia Forest Service-Canadian Forestry Service. Joint Report — BC For Serv Can For Serv Jt Rep
British Columbia Forest Service-Canadian Forestry Service. Joint Report — JRBSDA
British Columbia Gazette — BC Gaz
British Columbia Historical Quarterly — BC His Q
British Columbia Historical Quarterly — Brit Columbia Hist Quart
British Columbia Journal of Special Education — BC J Spec Ed
British Columbia Library Quarterly — BC Lib Q
British Columbia Library Quarterly — BCLQ
British Columbia Library Quarterly — Br Columb Libr Q
British Columbia Library Quarterly — Brit Columbia Lib Q
British Columbia Lumberman — BC Lumberm
British Columbia Medical Journal — Br Columbia Med J
British Columbia Medical Journal — Brit Col Med J
British Columbia. Minister of Mines and Petroleum Resources. Annual Report — BC Minist Mines Pet Resour Annu Rep
British Columbia. Ministry of Agriculture. Publications — BC Minist Agric Publ
British Columbia. Ministry of Energy, Mines, and Petroleum Resources. Bulletin — BC Minist Energy Mines Pet Resour Bull
British Columbia. Ministry of Energy, Mines, and Petroleum Resources. Paper — BC Minist Energy Mines Pet Resour Pap
British Columbia. Ministry of Forests. Forest Research Review — BC Minist For For Res Rev
British Columbia. Ministry of Forests. Forest Research Review — BFFRAM
British Columbia. Ministry of Forests. Research Note — BC Minist For Res Note
British Columbia. Ministry of Forests. Research Note — BFRNA2
British Columbia. Ministry of Mines and Petroleum Resources. Bulletin — BC Minist Mines Pet Resour Bull
British Columbia Music Educator — BC Mus Ed
British Columbia Professional Engineer — BC Prof Eng
British Columbia Professional Engineer — BCPEA
British Columbia Provincial Museum of Natural History and Anthropology. Handbook — BC Prov Mus Nat Hist Anthropol Handb
British Columbia Provincial Museum of Natural History and Anthropology. Report — BC Prov Mus Nat Hist Anthropol Rep
British Columbia Research — BC Res
British Columbia. Research Council. Annual Report — BC Res Counc Annu Rep
British Columbia. Research Council. Technical Bulletin — BC Res Counc Tech Bull
British Columbia School Counsellors' Association. Newsletter — BC Sch Couns News
British Columbia Teachers' Federation. Newsletter — BCTF News
British Columbia University. Department of Geology. Report — BC Univ Dep Geol Rep
British Columbia University. Department of Geology. Report — British Columbia Univ Dept Geology Rept
British Columbia Water and Waste Association. Proceedings of the Annual Conference — BC Water Waste Assoc Proc Annu Conf
British Columbia Water and Waste School — BC Water Waste Sch
British Columbia's Western Living — Br Columbia West Liv
British Commonwealth Occupation News — BCON
British Communications and Electronics — BCELA
British Communications and Electronics [*England*] — Br Commun Electron
British Constructional Engineer — Br Constr Eng
British Constructional Steelworks Association. Publications — Brit Constr Steelworks Ass Publ
British Corrosion Journal — Br Corros J
British Corrosion Journal — Br Corrosion J
British Corrosion Journal — Brit Corros J
British Corrosion Journal — Brit Corrosion J
British Council News — Br Council News
British Crop Protection Conference. Pests and Diseases. Proceedings — Br Crop Prot Conf Pests Dis Proc
British Crop Protection Council. Monograph — Br Crop Prot Counc Monogr
British Deaf News — Brit Deaf News
British Decorator — Br Decorator
British Defence Technology — Brit Def T
British Delphinium Society's Yearbook — Brit Delphinium Soc Yearb
British Dental Annual — Br Den Annu
British Dental Journal — BDJOA
British Dental Journal — Br Dent J
British Dental Journal — Br Dental J
British Dental Journal — Brit Dent J
British Dental Surgery Assistant — Br Dent Surg Assist
British Ecological Society. Symposium — Br Ecol Soc Symp
British Ecological Society. Symposium — Brit Ecol Soc Symp
British Education Index [*Bibliographic database*] [*British Library*] — BEI
British Education Index — Br Educ Index
British Education Index — BritEdI
British Educational Research Journal — B Ednl Research J
British Educational Research Journal — Br Educ Res J
British Electrical and Allied Manufacturers' Association Journal — Br Electr Allied Manuf Assoc J
British Engine, Boiler, and Electrical Insurance Company. Technical Report — Brit Engine Boiler Elec Ins Co Tech Rep
British Engine Technical Reports — BETRC
British Engine Technical Reports — Br Eng Tech Rep
British Engine Technical Reports — Br Engine Tech Rep
British Engineer — Brit Eng
British Engineering — Brit Eng
British European Airways Magazine — Brit Europ Airw Mag
British Expertise in Science and Technology [*Database*] — BEST
British Farmer and Stockbreeder — Br Farmer Stockbreed
British Fern Gazette — Br Fern Gaz
British Florist — Brit Florist
British Food Journal — Br Food J
British Food Journal and Hygienic Review — Br Food J Hyg Rev
British Food Journal and Hygienic Review [*Later, British Food Journal*] — Brit Food J
British Food Manufacturing Industries Research Association. Scientific and Technical Surveys — Br Food Manuf Ind Res Assoc Sci Tech Surv
British Foundryman — Br Foundryman
British Foundryman — Brit Foundrym

British Gas Corporation External Reports. Research Communications and Midlands Research Station Reports — Brit Gas Corp Ext Rep Res Commun MRS Rep
British Geological Literature. New Series — Br Geol Lit New Ser
British Geologist — Br Geol
British Granite and Whinstone Federation. Journal — Brit Granite Whinstone Fed J
British Grassland Society. Journal — Brit Grassland Soc J
British Grassland Society. Occasional Symposium — Br Grassl Soc Occas Symp
British Guiana. Department of Agriculture. Sugar Bulletin — Br Guiana Dep Agric Sugar Bull
British Guiana. Geological Survey Department. Bulletin — Br Guiana Geol Surv Dep Bull
British Guiana. Geological Survey Department. Mineral Resources Pamphlet — Br Guiana Geol Surv Dep Miner Resour Pam
British Guiana. Geological Survey Department. Report — Br Guiana Geol Surv Dep Rep
British Guiana Medical Annals — Brit Guiana Med Annals
British Guiana Medical Annual — Br Gui Med Annual
British Guiana Medical Annual and Hospital Reports — Brit Gui Med Ann
British Gynaecological Journal — Brit Gyn J
British Heart Journal — Br Heart J
British Heart Journal — Brit Heart J
British Heritage — BritH
British History Illustrated — Br Hist Illus
British Honduras. Department of Agriculture and Fisheries. Annual Report — Br Honduras Dep Agric Fish Annu Rep
British Honduras. Department of Agriculture. Annual Report — Br Honduras Dep Agric Annu Rep
British Hospital and Social Service Journal — Brit Hosp Soc Serv J
British Hotelier and Restaurateur — BHR
British Humanities Index [*Library Association Publishing Ltd.*] [*London*] — BHI
British Humanities Index — Br H I
British Humanities Index — Br Humanit Index
British Humanities Index — Brit Hum
British Industrial Finishing (Leighton Buzzard, England) — Br Ind Finish (Leighton Buzzard Engl)
British Industrial Finishing (London) — Br Ind Finish (London)
British Ink Maker — Br Ink Maker
British Ink Maker — Br Ink Mkr
British Ink Maker — Brit Ink Maker
British Ink Maker — Britsh Ink
British Institute for Organ Studies Journal — BIOS
British Institute of Radiology. Special Report — Br Inst Radiol Spec Rep
British Institute of Recorded Sound. Bulletin — BIRS
British Iron and Steel Research Association. Open Report — Br Iron Steel Res Assoc Open Rep
British Isles Bee Breeders' Association. News — Br Isles Bee Breeders' News
British Journal for Eighteenth Century Studies — Br J Eighteenth Century Stud
British Journal for Eighteenth-Century Studies — Brit J 18th Cent Stud
British Journal for the History of Science — BJHS
British Journal for the History of Science — BJHSAT
British Journal for the History of Science — Br J Hist S
British Journal for the History of Science — Br J Hist Sci
British Journal for the History of Science — Brit J Hist Sci
British Journal for the History of Science — PBJH
British Journal for the Philosophy of Science — BJPIA5
British Journal for the Philosophy of Science — Br J Phil S
British Journal for the Philosophy of Science — Br J Philos Sci
British Journal for the Philosophy of Science — Brit J Phil Sci
British Journal for the Philosophy of Science — Brit J Philos Sci
British Journal for the Philosophy of Science — British J Philos Sci
British Journal for the Philosophy of Science — PBJP
British Journal of Actinotherapy — Br J Actinother
British Journal of Actinotherapy and Physiotherapy — Br J Actinother Physiother
British Journal of Addiction — Br J Addict
British Journal of Addiction — Brit J Addict
British Journal of Administrative Law — Br J Adm L
British Journal of Administrative Management — BJA
British Journal of Aesthetics — BJA
British Journal of Aesthetics — BJEMA
British Journal of Aesthetics — Br J Aesth
British Journal of Aesthetics — Brit J Aes
British Journal of Aesthetics — Brit J Aesth
British Journal of Aesthetics — Brit J Aesthet
British Journal of Aesthetics — Brit J Aesthetics
British Journal of Aesthetics — PBJA
British Journal of Anaesthesia — BJANA
British Journal of Anaesthesia — Br J Anaest
British Journal of Anaesthesia — Br J Anaesth
British Journal of Anaesthesia — Brit J Anaesth
British Journal of Animal Behaviour — Br J Anim Behav
British Journal of Applied Physics — Br J Appl Phys
British Journal of Applied Physics — Brit J Ap Phys
British Journal of Applied Physics — Brit J Appl Phys
British Journal of Applied Physics. Supplement — Br J Appl Phys Suppl
British Journal of Audiology — BJAYAC
British Journal of Audiology — Br J Audiol
British Journal of Audiology — Br J Audiology
British Journal of Audiology — Brit J Audiol
British Journal of Audiology. Supplement — Br J Audiol Suppl
British Journal of Biomedical Science — Br J Biomed Sci
British Journal of Cancer — BJCAAI
British Journal of Cancer — Br J Canc
British Journal of Cancer — Br J Cancer
British Journal of Cancer — Brit J Cancer
British Journal of Cancer. Supplement — Br J Cancer Suppl
British Journal of Children's Diseases — Brit J Child Dis
British Journal of Clinical Equipment — Br J Clin Equip
British Journal of Clinical Pharmacology — BCPHBM
British Journal of Clinical Pharmacology — Br J Cl Ph
British Journal of Clinical Pharmacology — Br J Clin Pharmacol
British Journal of Clinical Practice — BJCP
British Journal of Clinical Practice — Br J Clin P
British Journal of Clinical Practice — Br J Clin Pract
British Journal of Clinical Practice — Br J Clin Prat
British Journal of Clinical Practice — Brit J Clin Pract
British Journal of Clinical Practice. Symposium Supplement — Br J Clin Pract Symp Suppl
British Journal of Clinical Psychology — BJCPDW
British Journal of Clinical Psychology — Br J Clin Psychol
British Journal of Criminology — B J Criminology
British Journal of Criminology — BJ Crim
British Journal of Criminology — Br J Crimin
British Journal of Criminology — Br J Criminology
British Journal of Criminology — Brit J Crim
British Journal of Criminology — Brit J Criminol
British Journal of Criminology — Brit J Criminology
British Journal of Criminology — Brit J of Crimin
British Journal of Criminology — PBJC
British Journal of Delinquency — BJ Delinq
British Journal of Delinquency — Brit J Delinq
British Journal of Dental Science and Prosthetics — Br J Dent Sci Prosthetics
British Journal of Dermatology — BJDEAZ
British Journal of Dermatology — Br J Derm
British Journal of Dermatology — Br J Dermatol
British Journal of Dermatology — Brit J Dermat
British Journal of Dermatology — Brit J Dermatol
British Journal of Dermatology and Syphilis — Br J Dermatol Syph
British Journal of Dermatology. Supplement — BJDSA9
British Journal of Dermatology. Supplement — Br J Dermatol Suppl
British Journal of Developmental Psychology — BJDPE4
British Journal of Developmental Psychology — Br J Dev Psychol
British Journal of Diseases of the Chest — BJDCA
British Journal of Diseases of the Chest — BJDCAT
British Journal of Diseases of the Chest — Br J Dis Ch
British Journal of Diseases of the Chest — Br J Dis Chest
British Journal of Diseases of the Chest — Brit J Dis Chest
British Journal of Disorders of Communication — B J Disorders of Communication
British Journal of Disorders of Communication — BJDEB
British Journal of Disorders of Communication — Br J Dis Co
British Journal of Disorders of Communication — Brit J Dis Commun
British Journal of Disorders of Communication — Brit J Disord Commun
British Journal of Educational Psychology — B J Ednl Psych
British Journal of Educational Psychology — BJEP
British Journal of Educational Psychology — BJESA
British Journal of Educational Psychology — BJESAE
British Journal of Educational Psychology — Br J Ed Psy
British Journal of Educational Psychology — Br J Educ Psychol
British Journal of Educational Psychology — Brit J Ed Psychol
British Journal of Educational Psychology — Brit J Educ Psychol
British Journal of Educational Studies — B J Ednl Studies
British Journal of Educational Studies — BJES
British Journal of Educational Studies — Br J Educ S
British Journal of Educational Studies — Br J Educ Stud
British Journal of Educational Studies — Brit J Ed Studies
British Journal of Educational Studies — Brit J Educ Stud
British Journal of Educational Technology — B J Ednl Technology
British Journal of Educational Technology — Br J Educ T
British Journal of Educational Technology — Br J Educ Tech
British Journal of Experimental Biology — BJEBA
British Journal of Experimental Biology — Br J Exp Bio
British Journal of Experimental Biology — Br J Exp Biol
British Journal of Experimental Pathology — BJEPA
British Journal of Experimental Pathology — BJEPA5
British Journal of Experimental Pathology — Br J Ex Pat
British Journal of Experimental Pathology — Br J Exp Path
British Journal of Experimental Pathology — Br J Exp Pathol
British Journal of Experimental Pathology — Brit J Exper Path
British Journal of Family Planning — BJFPDD
British Journal of Family Planning — Br J Fam Plann
British Journal of General Practice — Br J Gen Pract
British Journal of Guidance and Counselling — B J Guidance & Counseling
British Journal of Guidance and Counselling — Br J Guid Couns
British Journal of Haematology — BJHEA
British Journal of Haematology — BJHEAL
British Journal of Haematology — Br J Haem
British Journal of Haematology — Br J Haematol
British Journal of Haematology — Br J Haematology
British Journal of Haematology — Brit J Haemat
British Journal of Herpetology — Brit J Herpe
British Journal of Hospital Medicine — BJHMA
British Journal of Hospital Medicine — BJHMAB
British Journal of Hospital Medicine — Br J Hosp Med
British Journal of Hospital Medicine — Brit J Hosp Med
British Journal of Industrial Medicine — BJIMA
British Journal of Industrial Medicine — BJIMAG

British Journal of Industrial Medicine — Br J Ind Me
British Journal of Industrial Medicine — Br J Ind Med
British Journal of Industrial Medicine — Br J Ind Medicine
British Journal of Industrial Medicine — Brit J Ind Med
British Journal of Industrial Medicine — Brit J Indust Med
British Journal of Industrial Medicine — Brit J Industr Med
British Journal of Industrial Relations — BJ Ind Rel
British Journal of Industrial Relations — BJI
British Journal of Industrial Relations — BJIR
British Journal of Industrial Relations — Br J Ind Relations
British Journal of Industrial Relations [*United Kingdom*] — BRI
British Journal of Industrial Relations — Brit J Ind Rel
British Journal of Industrial Relations — Brit J Industr Relat
British Journal of Industrial Safety — Br J Ind Saf
British Journal of Inebriety — Br J Inebriety
British Journal of In-Service Education — B J In-Service Ed
British Journal of Inservice Education — Br J Inserv Educ
British Journal of International Studies — Br J Int Stud
British Journal of International Studies — Brit J Int Stud
British Journal of Law and Society — BJLS
British Journal of Law and Society — Br J Law Soc
British Journal of Law and Society — Brit J L & Soc
British Journal of Law and Society — Brit J Law & Soc
British Journal of Law and Society — Brit JL & Soc'y
British Journal of Mathematical and Statistical Psychology — B J Ma St Ps
British Journal of Mathematical and Statistical Psychology — B J Math & Stat Psych
British Journal of Mathematical and Statistical Psychology — BJMSA
British Journal of Mathematical and Statistical Psychology — Br J Math S
British Journal of Mathematical and Statistical Psychology — Br J Math Stat Psychol
British Journal of Mathematical and Statistical Psychology — Brit J Math & Stat Psychol
British Journal of Mathematical and Statistical Psychology — British J Math Statist Psych
British Journal of Mathematical and Statistical Psychology [*London*] — British J Math Statist Psychology
British Journal of Medical Education — BJMEAC
British Journal of Medical Education — Br J Med Educ
British Journal of Medical Psychology — BJMPA
British Journal of Medical Psychology — BJMPAB
British Journal of Medical Psychology — BJMPs
British Journal of Medical Psychology — Br J Med Ps
British Journal of Medical Psychology — Br J Med Psychol
British Journal of Medical Psychology — Brit J M Psychol
British Journal of Medical Psychology — Brit J Med Psychol
British Journal of Mental Subnormality — BJ Mental Subnormality
British Journal of Mental Subnormality — BJMSBL
British Journal of Mental Subnormality — Br J Ment S
British Journal of Mental Subnormality — Br J Ment Subnorm
British Journal of Mental Subnormality — Brit J Ment Subnorm
British Journal of Music Education — Brit J Mus Ed
British Journal of Music Therapy — BJMTD
British Journal of Neurosurgery — Br J Neurosurg
British Journal of Non-Destructive Testing — BJNTA
British Journal of Non-Destructive Testing — Br J Non-Destr Test
British Journal of Non-Destructive Testing — Brit J Non-Destruct Test
British Journal of Nutrition — BJNUA
British Journal of Nutrition — BJNUAV
British Journal of Nutrition — Br J Nutr
British Journal of Nutrition — Brit J Nutr
British Journal of Nutrition. Proceedings of the Nutrition Society — Brit J Nutr Proc Nutr Soc
British Journal of Obstetrics and Gynaecology — BJOGA
British Journal of Obstetrics and Gynaecology — BJOGAS
British Journal of Obstetrics and Gynaecology — Br J Obst G
British Journal of Obstetrics and Gynaecology — Br J Obstet Gynaecol
British Journal of Occupational Safety — BJOCA
British Journal of Occupational Safety — Br J Occup Saf
British Journal of Ophthalmology — BJOPA
British Journal of Ophthalmology — BJOPAL
British Journal of Ophthalmology — Br J Ophth
British Journal of Ophthalmology — Br J Ophthalmol
British Journal of Ophthalmology — Brit J Ophth
British Journal of Ophthalmology — Brit J Ophthalmol
British Journal of Oral and Maxillofacial Surgery — BJOSEY
British Journal of Oral and Maxillofacial Surgery — Br J Oral Maxillofac Surg
British Journal of Oral Surgery [*Later, British Journal of Oral and Maxillofacial Surgery*] — BJOSB
British Journal of Oral Surgery [*Later, British Journal of Oral and Maxillofacial Surgery*] — BJOSBV
British Journal of Oral Surgery [*Later, British Journal of Oral and Maxillofacial Surgery*] — Br J Oral S
British Journal of Oral Surgery [*Later, British Journal of Oral and Maxillofacial Surgery*] — Br J Oral Surg
British Journal of Orthodontics — Br J Orthod
British Journal of Pharmaceutical Practice — Br J Pharm Pract
British Journal of Pharmacology — BJPCB
British Journal of Pharmacology — BJPCBM
British Journal of Pharmacology — Br J Pharm
British Journal of Pharmacology — Br J Pharmac
British Journal of Pharmacology — Br J Pharmacol
British Journal of Pharmacology — Brit J Pharmacol
British Journal of Pharmacology and Chemotherapy [*Later, British Journal of Pharmacology*] — BJPCA
British Journal of Pharmacology and Chemotherapy [*Later, British Journal of Pharmacology*] — BJPCAL
British Journal of Pharmacology and Chemotherapy [*Later, British Journal of Pharmacology*] — Br J Pharmac Chemother
British Journal of Pharmacology and Chemotherapy [*Later, British Journal of Pharmacology*] — Br J Pharmacol Chemother
British Journal of Pharmacology and Chemotherapy — Brit J Pharmacol
British Journal of Pharmacology and Chemotherapy [*Later, British Journal of Pharmacology*] — Brit J Pharmacol Chemother
British Journal of Photography — BJP
British Journal of Photography — Br J Photogr
British Journal of Photography — Brit J Phot
British Journal of Photography — Brit J Photo
British Journal of Photography — Brit Jl Photogr
British Journal of Photography — BRJFA
British Journal of Photography. Annual — Br J Photogr Ann
British Journal of Physical Education — B J Physical Ed
British Journal of Physical Education — BJPEBS
British Journal of Physical Education — BR J PE
British Journal of Physical Education — Br J Phys Ed
British Journal of Physical Medicine — Br J Phys Med
British Journal of Physiological Optics — BJPOAN
British Journal of Physiological Optics — Br J Phys O
British Journal of Physiological Optics — Br J Physiol Opt
British Journal of Plastic Surgery — BJPSA
British Journal of Plastic Surgery — BJPSAZ
British Journal of Plastic Surgery — Br J Pl Sur
British Journal of Plastic Surgery — Br J Plast Surg
British Journal of Plastic Surgery — Brit J Plast Surg
British Journal of Political Science — Br J Poli S
British Journal of Political Science — Br J Polit Sci
British Journal of Political Science — Brit J Pol Sci
British Journal of Political Science — Brit J Polit Sci
British Journal of Political Science — British J Pol Science
British Journal of Political Science — BrJP
British Journal of Political Science — PBJS
British Journal of Preventive and Social Medicine — BJPVA
British Journal of Preventive and Social Medicine — BJPVAA
British Journal of Preventive and Social Medicine — Br J Prev S
British Journal of Preventive and Social Medicine — Br J Prev Soc Med
British Journal of Preventive and Social Medicine — Brit J Prev Soc Med
British Journal of Psychiatric Social Work — Brit J Psych Soc Work
British Journal of Psychiatry — BJ Psychiatry
British Journal of Psychiatry — BJPSB
British Journal of Psychiatry — BJPYA
British Journal of Psychiatry — BJPYAJ
British Journal of Psychiatry — Br J Psych
British Journal of Psychiatry — Br J Psychi
British Journal of Psychiatry — Br J Psychiat
British Journal of Psychiatry — Br J Psychiatry
British Journal of Psychiatry — Brit J Psychiat
British Journal of Psychiatry. Special Publication — BJPSB2
British Journal of Psychiatry. Special Publication — Br J Psychiatry Spec Publ
British Journal of Psychiatry. Supplement — Br J Psychiatry Suppl
British Journal of Psychology — B J Psych
British Journal of Psychology — BJP
British Journal of Psychology — BJPs
British Journal of Psychology — BJSGAE
British Journal of Psychology — Br J Psycho
British Journal of Psychology — Br J Psychol
British Journal of Psychology — Brit J Psychol
British Journal of Psychology — PBSY
British Journal of Psychology. General Section — BJSGA
British Journal of Psychology. Medical Section — Br J Psychol Med Sect
British Journal of Radiology — BJRAA
British Journal of Radiology — BJRAAP
British Journal of Radiology — Br J Radiol
British Journal of Radiology — Brit J Radiol
British Journal of Radiology — Brit Jour Radiol
British Journal of Radiology. Special Report — Br J Radiol Spec Rep
British Journal of Radiology. Supplement — BJRSAB
British Journal of Radiology. Supplement — Br J Radiol Suppl
British Journal of Religious Education — BJ Religious Ed
British Journal of Rheumatology — BJRHDF
British Journal of Rheumatology — Br J Rheumatol
British Journal of Sexual Medicine — BJMEDF
British Journal of Sexual Medicine — Br J Sex Med
British Journal of Social and Clinical Psychology — B J Social and Clinical Psych
British Journal of Social and Clinical Psychology — BJCPB
British Journal of Social and Clinical Psychology — BJCPBU
British Journal of Social and Clinical Psychology — BJSCP
British Journal of Social and Clinical Psychology — Br J Soc Cl
British Journal of Social and Clinical Psychology — Br J Soc Clin Psychol
British Journal of Social and Clinical Psychology — Brit J Social & Clin Psychol
British Journal of Social Medicine — BJSMAW
British Journal of Social Medicine — Br J Soc Med
British Journal of Social Psychiatry — Br J Soc Ps
British Journal of Social Psychiatry — Brit J Social Psychiat
British Journal of Social Psychology — BJSPDA
British Journal of Social Psychology — Br J Soc Psychol
British Journal of Social Work — Br J Soc W
British Journal of Social Work — Br J Soc Wk
British Journal of Social Work — Brit J Soc Work
British Journal of Sociology — B J Sociology

British Journal of Sociology — BJOSA
British Journal of Sociology — BJS
British Journal of Sociology — Br J Soc
British Journal of Sociology — Br J Sociol
British Journal of Sociology — Br J Sociology
British Journal of Sociology — Brit J Soc
British Journal of Sociology — Brit J Sociol
British Journal of Sociology — Brit Jour Sociol
British Journal of Sociology — BrJS
British Journal of Sociology — PBJO
British Journal of Sports Medicine — Br J Sports Med
British Journal of Statistical Psychology — B J Stat Psych
British Journal of Surgery — BJSUA
British Journal of Surgery — BJSUAM
British Journal of Surgery — Br J Surg
British Journal of Surgery — Brit J Surg
British Journal of Teacher Education — BJ Teach Ed
British Journal of the Sociology of Education — Br J Sociol Educ
British Journal of Tuberculosis — BJTBA4
British Journal of Tuberculosis — Br J Tuberc
British Journal of Tuberculosis — Brit J Tuberc
British Journal of Tuberculosis and Diseases of the Chest — BJTUAR
British Journal of Tuberculosis and Diseases of the Chest — Br J Tuberc Dis Chest
British Journal of Urology — BJURA
British Journal of Urology — BJURAN
British Journal of Urology — Br J Urol
British Journal of Urology — Brit J Urol
British Journal of Venereal Diseases — BJVDA
British Journal of Venereal Diseases — BJVDAK
British Journal of Venereal Diseases — Br J Ven Dis
British Journal of Venereal Diseases — Br J Vener Dis
British Journal of Venereal Diseases — Brit J Ven Dis
British Journal of Venereal Diseases — Brit J Vener Dis
British Journal on Alcohol and Alcoholism — Br J Alcohol Alcohol
British Kinematography — Brit Kinemat
British Kinematography — BRKIA
British Kinematography, Sound, and Television — Br Kinematogr
British Kinematography, Sound, and Television — Br Kinematogr Sound and Telev
British Kinematography, Sound, and Television — Brit Kinemat Sound and Telev
British Kinematography, Sound, and Television — Brit Kinematogr Sound Telev
British Knitting Industry — Br Knitting Ind
British Librarianship and Information Science — Br Lib Inf Sci
British Library Catalogue. Humanities and Social Sciences [*Database*] — HSS
British Library Journal — BLJ
British Library Journal — Brit Lib J
British Library Journal — Brit Libr J
British Library. Lending Division. Review — BLL Review
British Library News — Br Libr News
British Library Research and Development Newsletter — Brit Lib Res Dev Newsletter
British Library Research and Development Reports — Br Libr Res Dev Rep
British Lithium Congress — Br Lithium Congr
British Medical Bulletin — BMB
British Medical Bulletin — BMBUA
British Medical Bulletin — BMBUAQ
British Medical Bulletin — Br Med B
British Medical Bulletin — Br Med Bull
British Medical Bulletin — Brit M Bull
British Medical Journal — BMJOA
British Medical Journal — BMJOAE
British Medical Journal — Br Med J
British Medical Journal — Brit Med J
British Medical Journal — Brit MJ
British Medical Journal Epitome — BMJE
British Medical Journal. Practice Observed Edition — Br Med J Pract Obs
British Mining — Br Min
British Museum Catalogs. Bronzes. Catalogue of the Bronzes, Greek, Roman, and E truscan in the Department of Greek and Roman Antiquities — BMC Bronzes
British Museum Catalogs. Coins. Roman Empire. Coins of the Roman Empire — BMC Emp
British Museum Catalogs. Coins. Roman Empire. Coins of the Roman Empire — BMC Rom Emp
British Museum Catalogs. Coins. Roman Republic. Coins of the Roman Republic — BMC RR
British Museum. Catalogs. Vases. Catalogue of the Greek and Etruscan Vases — BM Vases
British Museum. General Catalogue of Printed Books — BMGC
British Museum (London) — BML
British Museum (Natural History). Bulletin. Geology — Br Mus (Nat Hist) Bull
British Museum (Natural History). Bulletin. Geology — Br Mus (Nat Hist) Bull Geol
British Museum (Natural History). Bulletin. Geology — British Mus (Nat History) Bull Geology
British Museum (Natural History). Bulletin. Zoology — Br Mus (Nat Hist) Bull Zool
British Museum (Natural History). Economic Series — BMEPAQ
British Museum (Natural History). Economic Series — Br Mus (Nat Hist) Econ Ser
British Museum (Natural History). Economic Series — Brit Mus (Nat Hist) Econom Ser
British Museum (Natural History). Fossil Mammals of Africa — BMFAAK
British Museum (Natural History). Fossil Mammals of Africa — Br Mus (Nat Hist) Fossil Mammals Afr
British Museum (Natural History). Mineralogy Leaflet — Br Mus (Nat Hist) Mineral Leafl
British Museum (Natural History). Palaeontology Leaflet — Br Mus (Nat Hist) Palaeontol Leafl
British Museum (Natural History). Publication — BMNPA3
British Museum (Natural History). Publication — Br Mus (Nat Hist) Publ
British Museum (Natural History). Report — BMNRBA
British Museum (Natural History). Report — Br Mus (Nat Hist) Rep
British Museum. Quarterly — BM
British Museum. Quarterly — BM Qu
British Museum. Quarterly — BMQ
British Museum. Quarterly — Br M Qu
British Museum Quarterly — Br Mus Q
British Museum. Quarterly — Brit Mus Q
British Museum. Quarterly — Brit Mus Quart
British Museum. Quarterly — Brit Mus Quarterly
British Museum. Quarterly — BrMQ
British Museum. Subject Index — Brit Mus Subj Index
British Museum. Yearbook — Br Mus Yearbook
British Museum. Yearbook — Brit Mus Yearb
British Mycological Society. Bulletin — BMYBA
British Mycological Society. Symposium — BMYSD2
British Mycological Society. Symposium — Br Mycol Soc Symp
British Mycological Society. Transactions — Br Mycol Soc Trans
British Mycological Society. Transactions — Brit Mycol Soc Trans
British National Bibliography — BNB
British National Bibliography — Br Nat Bibliography
British National Bibliography [*London*] — British Nat Biblio
British Non-Ferrous Metals Research Association. Annual Report — Br Non Ferrous Met Res Assoc Ann Rep
British Non-Ferrous Metals Research Association. Bulletin — Br Non Ferrous Met Res Assoc Bull
British Non-Ferrous Metals Research Association. Research Monograph — Br Non Ferrous Met Res Assoc Res Monogr
British Nuclear Energy Conference Journal — Br Nucl Energy Conf J
British Nuclear Energy Society. Symposium. Advanced Gas-Cooled Reactor. Papers — Br Nucl Energy Soc Symp Adv Gas Cooled React Pap
British Numismatic Journal — Br Numismatic J
British Numismatic Journal — Brit Numis J
British Numismatic Journal, Including the Proceedings of the British Numismatic Society — BNJ
British Nutrition Foundation. Information Bulletin — Br Nutr Found Inf Bull
British Nutrition Foundation. Nutrition Bulletin — Br Nutr Found Nutr Bull
British Orthoptic Journal — BOTJAT
British Orthoptic Journal — Br Orthopt J
British Orthoptic Journal — Brit Orth J
British Osteopathic Journal — Brit Osteop J
British Osteopathic Review — Brit Osteop Rev
British Paper and Board Makers Association. Proceedings of the Technical Section — Br Pap Board Makers Assoc Proc Tech Sect
British Paperbacks in Print — Br PIP
British Patent Abstracts. Section CH. Chemical — Brit Pat Abs Sect CH Chem
British Pest Control Conference — Br Pest Control Conf
British Petroleum Equipment — Brit Petr Equipm
British Petroleum Equipment News — Br Pet Equip News
British Petroleum Equipment News — Brit Petr Equipm Ne
British Pharmacological Society. 50th Anniversary Meeting — Br Pharmacol Soc 50th Anniv Meet
British Phycological Bulletin [*Later, British Phycological Journal*] — BPYBA3
British Phycological Bulletin [*Later, British Phycological Journal*] — Br Phycol Bull
British Phycological Bulletin — Brit Phycol Bull
British Phycological Journal — BPHJA
British Phycological Journal — BPHJAA
British Phycological Journal — Br Phycol J
British Plastics [*Later, European Plastics News*] — B Plastics
British Plastics [*Later, European Plastics News*] — Br Plast
British Plastics [*Later, European Plastics News*] — Brit Plast
British Plastics [*Later, European Plastics News*] — BRPLA
British Plastics and Moulded Products Trader — Br Plast Moulded Prod Trader
British Plastics and Moulded Products Trader. Supplement — Br Plast Moulded Prod Trader Suppl
British Plastics and Rubber — BP & R
British Plastics and Rubber — Br Plast Rubber
British Plastics and Rubber — Br Plastics Rubber
British Plastics and Rubber — Brit Plast Rubb
British Plastics and Rubber — RPA
British Plastics Federation. Reinforced Plastics Technical Conference — Br Plast Fed Reinf Plast Tech Conf
British Plastics Yearbook — Brit Plast Yb
British Political Sociology. Yearbook — Brit Polit Sociol Yb
British Polymer Journal — BPOJA
British Polymer Journal — Br Polym J
British Polymer Journal — Brit Polym J
British Portland Cement Research Association. Pamphlets — Br Portland Cem Res Assoc Pam
British Poultry Science — BPOSA
British Poultry Science — BPOSA4
British Poultry Science — Br Poult Sc
British Poultry Science — Br Poult Sci
British Poultry Science — Brit Poult Sci
British Poultry Science — Brit Poultry Sci
British Power Engineering — BPOEA
British Power Engineering [*England*] — Br Power Eng

British Printer — Br Print
British Printer — Brit Print
British Printer — Brit Printer
British Psychological Society. Bulletin — Br Psych Soc Bull
British Pteridological Society. Bulletin — BPSBA7
British Pteridological Society. Bulletin — Br Pteridol Soc Bull
British Public Opinion — BPOPD
British Public Opinion — Br Public Opin
British Quarterly Review — Brit Q
British Quarterly Review — Brit Quar Rev
British Rayon and Silk Journal — Br Rayon Silk J
British Regional Geology — Br Reg Geol
British Reports, Translations, and Theses — Br Rep Transl Theses
British Reports, Translations, and Theses — Brit Repts Transl Theses
British Reports, Translations, and Theses — British Reports Transl & Theses
British Review of Economic Issues — British R Econ Issues
British Rheumatic Association. Review — Brit Rheum Ass Rev
British Rheumatism and Arthritis Association. Review — BRAR
British Rubber Producers' Research Association. Technical Bulletin — Br Rubber Prod Res Assoc Tech Bull
British School at Athens. Annual — Brit Sch Athens Ann
British School at Athens. Annual — BSA
British School at Rome. Papers — Brit Sch at Rome Papers
British School of Archaeology at Rome. Papers — BSR
British School of Archaeology in Egypt. Publications — BSAE
British Schools Exploring Society. News — BSES News
British Science News — Br Sci News
British Science News — Brit Sci News
British Small Animal Veterinary Association. Congress. Proceedings — Br Small Anim Vet Assoc Congr Proc
British Soap Manufacturer — Br Soap Manuf
British Society for Cell Biology. Symposium — Br Soc Cell Biol Symp
British Society for Cell Biology. Symposium — BSCSD2
British Society for Developmental Biology Symposium — Br Soc Dev Biol Symp
British Society for Middle East Studies Bulletin — BRISMES Bull
British Society for Parasitology. Symposia — Br Soc Parasitol Symp
British Society of Animal Production. Proceedings — Br Soc Anim Prod Proc
British Society of Franciscan Studies — Brit Soc Fran Stud
British South Africa Company. Publication. Mazoe Citrus Experimental Station — Br S Afr Co Publ Mazoe Citrus Exp Stn
British Space Fiction Magazine — BSP
British Standard Specification — Brit Stand
British Standards Institution. British Standard — Brit Stand Inst Brit Stand
British Standards Yearbook — Br Stan Yrbk
British Steel — Br Steel
British Steel — BRSTB
British Steel — SRI
British Steel Corporation. General Steels Division. Report — Br Steel Corp Gen Steels Div Rep
British Steel Corporation. Open Report — Br Steel Corp Open Rep
British Steel Corporation. Open Report — BRSOA
British Steel Corporation. Reports — Br Steel Corp Rep
British Steelmaker — Br Steelmaker
British Steelmaker — Brit Steelmaker
British Steelmaker — BSTEA
British Studies Monitor — Br Stud Monit
British Studies Monitor — Brit Stud Mon
British Studies Monitor — BrSM
British Studies Monitor — BSM
British Sugar Beet Review — Br Sug Beet Rev
British Sugar Beet Review — Br Sugar Beet Rev
British Sugar Beet Review — Brit Sug Beet Rev
British Sugar Beet Review — BRSUAA
British Sulphur Corporation Ltd. Quarterly Bulletin — Br Sulphur Corp Q Bull
British Sulphur Corporation Ltd. Statistical Supplement — BSC Stat
British Tax Review — BR Tax R
British Tax Review — Brit Tax Rev
British Tax Review — British Tax R
British Tax Review — BTR
British Technology Index [*Later, Current Technology Index*] — Br Technol Index
British Technology Index [*Later, Current Technology Index*] — Brit Techl
British Technology Index [*Later, Current Technology Index*] — BTI
British Telecom Journal — Br Telecom J
British Telecom Journal — Brit Telec
British Telecom Journal — POT
British Telecommunications Engineering — Br Telecom Engng
British Telecommunications Engineering — Br Telecommun Eng
British Territories in Borneo. Annual Report. Geological Survey Department — Br Territ Borneo Annu Rep Geol Sur Dep
British Territories in Borneo. Geological Survey Department. Annual Report — Br Territ Borneo Geol Surv Dep Annu Rep
British Territories in Borneo. Geological Survey Department. Bulletin — Br Territ Borneo Geol Surv Dep Bull
British Territories in Borneo. Geological Survey Department. Report — Br Territ Borneo Geol Surv Dep Rep
British Thoracic and Tuberculosis Association. Review — Br Thorac Tuber Assoc Rev
British Travel News — Br Travel News
British Travel News — BTN
British UK Patent Application — Brit UK Pat Appl
British Universities Annual — B Universities Annual
British Veterinary Journal — Br Vet J
British Veterinary Journal — Brit Vet J
British Veterinary Journal — BVJ
British Veterinary Journal — BVJOA
British Veterinary Journal — BVJOA9
British Water Supply — Br Wat Supply
British Weed Control Conference. Proceedings — Br Weed Control Conf Proc
British Welding Journal — Br Weld J
British Welding Journal — Brit Weld J
British Welding Journal — BRWJA
British Wire Journal — Br Wire J
British Year Book of International Law — Brit Y Book
British Yearbook of International Law — Br Int Law
British Yearbook of International Law — Brit Yb Int Law
British Yearbook of International Law — Brit Yb Int'l L
British Yearbook of International Law — Brit Yearb Internat Law
British Yearbook of International Law — Brit Yearbook Int L
British Yearbook of International Law — BY
British Yearbook of International Law — BYB
British Yearbook of International Law — BYIL
British-American Trade News — Brit Am Tr N
Brittonia — BRTAAN
Brixia Sacra — BS
BRMA [*British Rubber Manufacturers' Association Ltd.*] **Review** — BRMA Rev
Brno Studies in English — BSE
Brno. Universita. Prirodovedecka Fakulta. Scripta Geologia — Brno Univ Prirod Fak Scr Geol
Broad Way Clinical Supplement [*England*] — Broad Way Clin Suppl
Broad Way Clinical Supplement — BWCSA
Broadcast [*United Kingdom*] — Bcast
Broadcast Advertisers Reports [*Database*] — BAR
Broadcast Banking — Broadcast Bank
Broadcast Databook — Broad Datab
Broadcast Equipment Today — Broadcast Equip Today
Broadcast Management/Engineering — BM/E
Broadcast Technology — Broadcast Technol
Broadcasters Audience Research Board [*Database*] — BARB
Broadcasters Database — BDB
Broadcasting — B
Broadcasting — B/C
Broadcasting — Brdcstng
Broadcasting — GBRD
Broadcasting Business — Broadcasting Bus
Broadcasting Magazine — Broadcast
Broadcasting Systems and Operations — Broadcast Syst and Oper
Broadsheet. Royal College of Pathologists of Australia — Broadsheet R Coll Pathol Aust
Broadside Series — Broad
Broadway — Broadw
Brock University. Department of Geological Sciences. Research Report Series — Brock Univ Dep Geol Sci Res Rep Ser
Brodil'naya Promyshlennost — Brodil'naya Prom
Broiler Growing — Broil Grow
Broken Hill Historical Society. Journal and Proceedings — J Proc Broken Hill Hist Soc
Broken Hill Proprietary Ltd. Research Division. Information Circular — BHP Res Div Inf Circ
Brolga Review — Brolga R
Bromatologia i Chemia Toksykologiczna — BCTKA
Bromatologia i Chemia Toksykologiczna — BCTKAG
Bromatologia i Chemia Toksykologiczna — Bromatol Chem Toksykol
Bromley Local History — Bromley Local Hist
Bromma Hembygds-Forenings Arsskrift — Bromma Hembygds-Foren Arsskr
Brompton Hospital Reports — Brompt Hosp Rep
Bronches — BRONA
Bronches — BRONA3
Broncho-Pneumologie — Broncho Pneumol
Broncho-Pneumologie — BRPNDB
Bronte Society. Transactions — BST
Brook Lodge Conference on Lung Cells in Disease. Proceedings — Brook Lodge Conf Lung Cells Dis Proc
Brookgreen Bulletin — Brookgreen Bul
Brookhaven National Laboratory. Lectures in Science. Vistas in Research — BNLVAI
Brookhaven National Laboratory. Lectures in Science. Vistas in Research — Brookhaven Natl Lab Lect Sci Vistas Res
Brookhaven National Laboratory. National Neutron Cross Section Center. Report. BNL-NCS — Brookhaven Natl Lab Natl Neutron Cross Sect Cent Rep BNL NCS
Brookhaven National Laboratory. National Nuclear Data Center. Report — Brookhaven Natl Lab Natl Nucl Data Cent Rep
Brookhaven National Laboratory. Report. BNL — Brookhaven Natl Lab Rep BNL
Brookhaven Symposia in Biology — Brook S Bio
Brookhaven Symposia in Biology — Brookh Symp Biol
Brookhaven Symposia in Biology — Brookhaven Symp Biol
Brookhaven Symposia in Biology — BSBIA
Brookhaven Symposia in Biology — BSBIAW
Brookings Annual Report — Brookings Ann Rep
Brookings Bulletin — BROBA
Brookings Bulletin — Brook Bul
Brookings Bulletin — Brookings Bull
Brookings Papers on Economic Activity — BIM
Brookings Papers on Economic Activity — BPE
Brookings Papers on Economic Activity — BPEA
Brookings Papers on Economic Activity — BPEAD
Brookings Papers on Economic Activity — Brook Pap Econ Act
Brookings Papers on Economic Activity — Brookings
Brookings Papers on Economic Activity — Brookings P
Brookings Papers on Economic Activity — Brookings Pa Econ Activ

Brookings Papers on Economic Activity — Brookings Pap Econ Activ
Brookings Papers on Economic Activity — Brookings Pas Econ Activity
Brookings Review — Brookings R
Brookings Review — Brookng R
Brookings Review — BRR
Brookings Review — BRV
Brooklyn Barrister — Brooklyn Bar
Brooklyn Botanic Garden. Annual Report — BKBGA4
Brooklyn Botanic Garden. Annual Report — Brooklyn Bot Gard Annu Rep
Brooklyn Botanic Garden. Memoirs — Brooklyn Bot Gard Mem
Brooklyn Botanic Garden. Record — Brookl Bot Gard Rec
Brooklyn Botanic Garden. Record — Brooklyn Bot Gard Rec
Brooklyn Botanic Garden. Record. Plants and Gardens — Brooklyn Bot Gard Rec Plants Gard
Brooklyn Botanic Garden. Record. Plants and Gardens — BRPGDO
Brooklyn Hospital. Journal — Brooklyn Hosp J
Brooklyn Institute of Arts and Sciences. Museum Bulletin — Brooklyn Mus Bul
Brooklyn Journal of International Law — Brook J Int L
Brooklyn Journal of International Law — Brookl J Int L
Brooklyn Journal of International Law — Brooklyn J Int L
Brooklyn Journal of International Law — Brooklyn J Intl L
Brooklyn Law Review — BR
Brooklyn Law Review — Br LR
Brooklyn Law Review — Brook LR
Brooklyn Law Review — Brookl L Rev
Brooklyn Law Review — Brooklyn L Re
Brooklyn Law Review — Brooklyn L Rev
Brooklyn Law Review — Brooklyn Law R
Brooklyn Medical Journal — Brookl Med J
Brooklyn Museum. Annual — Brookl Mus Ann
Brooklyn Museum. Annual — Brooklyn Mus Ann
Brooklyn Museum. Bulletin — Br MB
Brooklyn Museum Bulletin — Brookl M Bu
Brooklyn Museum. Bulletin — Brookl Mus Bull
Brooklyn Museum. Journal — Brookl Mus J
Brooklyn Museum Quarterly — Bklyn Mus Q
Brooklyn Museum. Quarterly — Br MQ
Brooklyn Museum. Quarterly — Brook Mus Q
Brooklyn Museum. Quarterly — Brookl Mus Quart
Brookville Society of Natural History. Bulletin — Brookville Soc N H B
Broom and Broom Corn News — Broom Broom Corn News
Broom Corn Review — Broom Corn Rev
Brot und Gebaeck — Brot Gebaeck
Brot und Gebaeck — BROTA
Brot und Gebaeck — BROTAL
Broteria — Brot
Broteria Genetica — Broteria Genet
Broteria. Revista Contemporanea de Cultura — BRCC
Broteria. Serie de Ciencias Naturais — Broteria Ser Cienc Nat
Broteria. Serie Trimestral. Ciencias Naturais — BRORAF
Broteria. Serie Trimestral. Ciencias Naturais — Broteria Ser Trimest Cienc Nat
Brotherhood of Maintenance of Way Employees. Journal — BMWEJ
Brown American — Brown Am
Brown Boveri Mitteilungen [*Brown Boveri Review*] — Brown Boveri Mitt
Brown Boveri Review — BRBOA
Brown Boveri Review — Brown Bov R
Brown Boveri Review — Brown Boveri Rev
Brown Boveri Symposium on Corrosion in Power Generating Equipment — Brown Boveri Symp Corros Power Gener Equip
Brown Boveri Symposium on Nonemissive Electrooptic Displays — Brown Boveri Symp Nonemissive Electroopt Disp
Brown Boveri und Cie Nachrichten — Brown Boveri Cie Nachr
Brown University. Human Development Letter — Brown Univ Hum Dev Let
Brown University. Studies — BUS
Browning Institute. Studies — BIS
Browning Institute. Studies — Browning In
Browning Institute. Studies — Browning Inst Stud
Browning Newsletter — BN
Browning Society. Notes — BSNotes
Brown's Chancery Cases — Bro CC
Brownson's Quarterly Review — Brownson
Brownson's Quarterly Review — Brownsons Q R
BRPRA [*British Rubber Producers' Research Association*] **Technical Bulletin** — BRPRA Techn Bull
BRS [*Bibliographic Retrieval Services*] **Bulletin** — BRS Bull
Bruel and Kjaer Technical Review — Bruel & Kjaer Tech Rev
Brugger Neujahrsblaetter. Kulturgesellschaft des Bezirks Brugg — BrN
Bruker Report — Bruker Rep
Brunei Museum Journal — BMJ
Brunei Museum. Journal — Brun Mus J
Brunn-Bruckmann — Br Br
Brunnenbau Bau von Wasserwerken Rohrleitungsbau — Brunnenbau Bau Rohrleitungsbau
Brunner/Mazel Psychosocial Stress Series — BMPSEQ
Brunner/Mazel Psychosocial Stress Series — Brunner/Mazel Psychosoc Stress Ser
Brunonia — BRUND2
Bruns' Beitraege zur Klinischen Chirurgie — BBKCA
Bruns' Beitraege zur Klinischen Chirurgie — BBKCA8
Bruns' Beitraege zur Klinischen Chirurgie — Bruns' Beitr Klin Chir
Bruns Beitraege zur Klinischen Chirurgie — BrunsBtr
Brush and Pencil — Brush & P
Brussels. Musees Royaux d'Art et d'Histoire. Bulletin — Brussels Mus Roy Bul
Brussels. Musees Royaux des Beaux-Arts Belgiques. Bulletin — Brus Mus Roy Beaux Arts Bull
Brussels Museum of Musical Instruments. Bulletin — Brus Museum
Brussels Museum of Musical Instruments. Bulletin — Brussels Museum M Instruments Bul
Brussels. Universite Libre. Institut de Philologie et d'Histoire. Annuaire [*A publication*] — Ann Phil Hist
Bruxelles. Cahiers du Journal des Poetes — Br Cah JdP
Bruxelles Medical — BRMEA
Bruxelles Medical — BRMEAY
Bruxelles Medical — Brux Med
Bruxelles Medical — Bruxelles Med
Brygmesteren — BRYGAW
Brygmesteren — Brygm
Bryologist — BRYOA
Bryologist — BRYOAM
Bryologist — Bryol
Bryophytorum Bibliotheca — BRBIDS
Bryophytorum Bibliotheca — Bryophytorum Bibl
BS. Betriebssicherheit [*Austria*] — BESID
BSA [*Building Societies Association*] **European Bulletin** — BSA Eur Bul
BSAP Occasional Publication. An Occasional Publication. British Society of Animal Production — BSAP Occas Publ Occas Publ Br Soc Anim Prod
BSBI [*Botanical Society of the British Isles*] **Conference Reports** — BBICAW
BSBI [*Botanical Society of the British Isles*] **Conference Reports** — BSBI Conf Rep
BSCP [*Biological Sciences Communication Project*] **Communique** — BSCP Commun
BSFA [*British Steel Founders' Association*] **Bulletin** — BSFA Bull
BSI [*British Standards Institution*] **News** — BSI News
BSI [*British Standards Institution*] **News** — BSINA
BSI [*British Standards Institution*] **Sales Bulletin** — BSI Sales Bull
BTH [*British Thomson-Houston Co.*] **Activities** — BTH Act
BTTA [*British Thoracic and Tuberculosis Association*] **Review** [*Scotland*] — BTTA Rev
Buccal and Nasal Administration as an Alternative to Parenteral Administration. Minutes. European Symposium — Buccal Nasal Adm Altern Parenter Adm Minutes Eur Symp
Buch und Bibliothek — Buch und Bibl
Bucharest. Universitatea. Analele. Geologie — Buchar- Univ- An Geol
Bucharest. Universitatea. Analele. Seria Stiintele Naturii — Buchar Univ An Ser Stiint Nat
Bucherei des Augenarztes — Buch Augenarzt
Buchreihe Atomkernenergie — Buchr Atomkernenerg
Buchreihe der Cusanus-Gesellschaft — Buchr Cusanus Ges
Bucimul Romanu — BR
Bucknell Review — BR
Bucknell Review — Bucknell Re
Bucknell Review — Bucknell Rev
Bucknell Review — BuR
Bucks County Historical Society. Papers — BuCHS
Bucks County Historical Society. Papers — BucksCoHS
Budapest Regisegei — BPR
Budapest Regisegei — BR
Budapest Regisegei — Bud Reg
Budapest Regisegei — Budapest Reg
Budapest Regisegei. Budapesti Toerteneti Muzeum — Bp Reg
Budapest Regisegei. Budapesti Toerteneti Muzeum — BudR
Budapesti Muszaki Egyetem Elemiszerkemiai Tanszekenek Kozlemenyei — Budapesti Musz Egy Elemiszerkem Tansz Kozl
Budapesti Muszaki Egyetem Mezogazdasagi Kemiai Technologiai Tanszekenek Evkonyve — Budapesti Musz Egy Mezogazd Kem Technol Tansz Evk
Budapesti Muszaki Egyetem Mezogazdasagi Kemiai Technologiai Tanszekenek Kozlemenyei — Budapesti Musz Egy Mezogazd Kem Technol Tansz Kozl
Budapesti Szemle — B Sz
Budapesti Szemle — Bp Szle
Budavox Telecommunication Review — Budavox Telecommun Rev
Buddhist Research Information — BRI
Buddhist Text Information — BTI
Budget and Program Newsletter — Budget Program Newsl
Budget and Program Newsletter [*United States*] — BUPRD
Budget of the US Government — Budget
Budget of the US Government. Special Analyses — Budget SA
Budivel'ni Materialy i Konstruktsii — Budiv Mater Konstr
Budownictwo Rolnicze — Budownictwo Roln
Buecher des Archiv fuer Bienenkunde — Buecher Arch Bienenk
Buecher fuer die Wirtschaft — Buecher Wirt
Buecherei des Augenarztes — BAUGA
Buecherei des Augenarztes — Buech Augenarzt
Buecherei des Frauenarztes — Buech Frauenarztes
Buecherei Fachlicher und Wissenschaftlicher Schriften der Technischen Hochschule in Brno — Buech Fachlicher Wiss Schr Tech Hochsch Brno
Buecherei Fachlicher und Wissenschaftlicher Schriften der Technischen Hochschule in Brno. B — Buech Fachlicher Wiss Schr Tech Hochsch Brno B
Buecherei fuer Bienenkunde — Buecherei Bienenk
Buecherei und Bildung — BuB
Buecherei und Bildungspflege — BueBpfl
Buecherei Winter — BW
Buendner Monatsblatt — Buendner Mbl
Buenos Aires — BA
Buenos Aires Literaria — BAL
Buenos Aires Musical — BAM
Buenos Aires Musical — Buenos Aires M
Buenos Aires Musical — Buenos Aires Mus
Buenos Aires (Province). Comision de Investigaciones Cientificas. Monografias — Buenos Aires (Prov) Com Invest Cient Monogr
Buerger im Staat — BUESD
Buerotechnik — Buerotech

Buerotechnik Automation und Organisation — Buerotech Autom & Organ
Buerotechnik und Organisation — Buerotech und Org
Buffalo Fine Arts Academy. Albright Art Gallery. Notes — Buffalo Gal Notes
Buffalo Historical Society. Publications — Buffalo Hist Soc Publ
Buffalo Law Review — Bu LR
Buffalo Law Review — Buff L Rev
Buffalo Law Review — Buff Law R
Buffalo Law Review — Buff LR
Buffalo Law Review — Buffalo L Rev
Buffalo News — Buffalo Nw
Buffalo Philharmonic. Program Notes — Buffalo Phil
Buffalo Society of Natural Sciences. Bulletin — Buffalo Soc N Sc B
Buffalo Society of Natural Sciences. Bulletin — Buffalo Soc Nat Sci Bull
BUFORA (British Unidentified Flying Object Research Association) Bulletin — BUFORA Bull
Buggalo Nam Newsletter — BNN
Build International (English Edition) — Build Int (Engl Ed)
Builder — Build
Builder Architect Contractor Engineer — Build Arch Contr Eng
Builder (New South Wales) — Builder (NSW)
Builder NSW [*New South Wales*] — Build NSW
Builders and Timber Merchants Journal — Builders Timber Merchants J
Builders' Journal — Build J
Building — Bldg
Building — Build
Building — BULDB
Building Age and National Builder — Bldg Age
Building and Architecture — Build & Archit
Building and Architecture — Building & Arch
Building and Construction — Build & Cons
Building and Construction and Cazaly's Contract Reporter (Melbourne, Victoria) — Build & Cons (VIC)
Building and Construction Legal Reporting Service — BCLRS
Building and Contract Journal for Ireland — Build Cont J Ir
Building and Decorating Materials — Build & Decorating Materials
Building and Decorating Materials — Build Decorating Mat
Building and Engineering — Build & Eng
Building and Engineering Review — Build Eng Rev
Building and Environment — Bldg & Environment
Building and Environment — Bldg Env
Building and Environment — Bldg Envir
Building and Environment — Bldg Environ
Building and Environment [*England*] — Build Environ
Building and Manufacturing — Build & Manuf
Building Blocks. Aboriginal Rights and Constitutional Update — BUBL
Building Briefs. Division of Building Research. Commonwealth Scientific and Industrial Research Organisation — Build Briefs Div Build Res CSIRO
Building Conservation — Bldg Conserv
Building Conservation — Bldg Conservation
Building Construction in Texas — Build Constr Tex
Building Design — Bldg Des
Building Design — Bldg Design
Building Design and Construction — BDCSB
Building Design and Construction — Bldg Desgn
Building Design and Construction — Build Des Constr
Building Design Journal — Build Des Jnl
Building Digest — Build Dig
Building Economics Letter — Build Econ Let
Building Economist — Bldg Econ
Building Economist — Bldg Economist
Building Economist — Build Econ
Building Energy Progress — BENPD
Building Energy Progress — Build Energy Prog
Building Forum — Bldg Forum
Building Forum — Build Forum
Building (Hobart) — Build (Hobart)
Building Ideas — BUIDD
Building Ideas — Build Ideas
Building Information Bulletin [*New Zealand*] — Build Inf Bull
Building, Lighting, and Engineering — Build Light Eng
Building, Lighting, and Engineering — Build Ltg Engng
Building, Lighting, and Engineering — Building Ltg and Engng
Building, Lighting, and Engineering — Building Ltg Engng
Building Machinery and Construction Methods — Build Mach Constr Methods
Building Maintenance — Build Maint
Building Management Abstracts — Bldg Mgmt Abs
Building Material News — BMN
Building Materials — Bldg Mater
Building Materials [*Sydney*] — Build Mater
Building Materials — Build Materials
Building Materials and Equipment — Bldg Mater
Building Materials and Equipment — Build Mater
Building Materials and Equipment — Build Mater & Equip
Building Materials and Equipment (Sydney) — Build Mater Equip (Syd)
Building Materials (Chicago) — Build Mater (Chicago)
Building Materials, Components, and Equipment — Build Mat
Building Materials Digest — Build Mat Dig
Building Materials List — Bldg Mats List
Building Materials Magazine [*Australia*] — Build Mater Mag
Building Materials Magazine [*Australia*] — BUMMB
Building Materials (Moscow) — Build Mater Moscow
Building Monthly — Build Mon
Building Official and Code Administrator [*United States*] — BOCDA
Building Official and Code Administrator [*United States*] — Build Off Code Adm
Building Operating Management — Bldg Opr
Building Operating Management — Build Oper Manage
Building Owner and Manager — Build Own Man
Building Products — Bldg Products
Building Products News — BPN
Building Products News — Build Prod News
Building Products Report — Build Prod Rep
Building Refurbishment — Bldg Refurb
Building Refurbishment and Maintenance — Bldg Refurbishment & Maintenance
Building Research — BRJNA
Building Research — Build Res
Building Research and Practice — Bld Res Prac
Building Research and Practice — Bldg Res Practice
Building Research and Practice — Bldg Research & Practice
Building Research and Practice — Build Res Pract
Building Research Association of New Zealand. Building Information Bulletin — Bldg Research Assocn New Zealand Bldg Information Bull
Building Research Association of New Zealand. Technical Paper P — Build Res Assoc NZ Tech Pap P
Building Research Establishment. Digest — Build Res Establ Dig
Building Research Establishment (Station). Digest — Build Res Estab (Sta) Digest
Building Research Institute Quarterly — Build Res Inst Q
Building Research News — Build Res News
Building Research News. National Research Council of Canada — BRNNRC
Building Research Note. National Research Council of Canada. Division of Building Research — Build Res Note Natl Res Counc Can Div Build Res
Building Research Station. Current Papers — BRSCB
Building Research Station. Current Papers [*England*] — Build Res Stn Curr Pap
Building Research (Washington, DC) — Bldg Res (Washington DC)
Building Science — Bldg Sci
Building Science — BS
Building Science — Build Sci
Building Science — BUSCB
Building Science Series. United States National Bureau of Standards — Build Sci Ser Natl Bur Stand
Building Science Series. United States National Bureau of Standards — Build Sci Ser Natl Bur Stand US
Building Science Series. United States National Bureau of Standards — Building Sci Ser Nat Bur Stand US
Building Seals and Sealants — Build Seals Sealants
Building Services — Bldg Serv
Building Services — Bldg Services
Building Services — Build Serv
Building Services and Environmental Engineer — Bldg Serv Environ Engr
Building Services and Environmental Engineer — Bldg Services & Environmental Engineer
Building Services and Environmental Engineer — Bldg Services Environ Engnr
Building Services and Environmental Engineer — BSEND
Building Services and Environmental Engineer (England) — Build Serv Environ (Eng)
Building Services Engineer — Bldg Serv Engr
Building Services Engineer — Bldg Services Engineer
Building Services Engineer — Build Serv Eng
Building Services Engineering Research and Technology — Bld Serv Enging Res Tech
Building Services Engineering Research and Technology — Build Serv Eng Res
Building Services Engineering Research and Technology — Build Serv Eng Res and Technol
Building Societies Gazette — Bldg Soc Gaz
Building Specification — Bldg Specif
Building Specification — Bldg Specification
Building Standards [*United States*] — Build Stand
Building Study. Division of Building Research. Commonwealth Scientific and Industrial Research Organisation — Bldg Study Div Bldg Res CSIRO
Building Supply and Home Centers — Bldg S Home
Building Supply News — Bldg SN
Building Supply News — Build Sup N
Building Systems Design — Bldg Systems Design
Building Systems Design — Bldg Systm
Building Systems Design — Build Syst Des
Building Technical File — Bldg Tech File
Building Technology and Management — Bld Technol Mgmnt
Building Technology and Management — Bldg Tech Mgmt
Building Technology and Management — Bldg Technol Mgmt
Building Technology and Management [*England*] — Build Technol Manage
Building Technology and Management — BUTMB
Building Trades Journal — Bldg Trades J
Building Trades Journal — Bldg Trades Jnl
Building with Steel — Bldg with Steel
Building with Steel — Build Steel
Building Worker — Build Worker
Building-Permit Activity [*Florida*] — Build Perm
Buildings — BLDGA
Buildings Energy Conservation — Build En Conserv
Buildings for Education — Build Ed
Buildings Journal — Build Jnl
Buildings: the Construction and Building Management Journal — Bldgs
Built Environment — BENV
Built Environment — Built Env
Built Environment — Built Envir
Built Environment — Built Environ
Bujqesia Socialiste — Bujq Soc
Bukowinaer Landwirtschaftliche Blaetter (Czernowitz) — Bukow Landw Bl Czernowitz
Bukowiner Schule — BS

Buletin Balai Penelitian Perkebunan Bedan — BBPMAT
Buletin Balai Penelitian Perkebunan Medan — Bul Balai Penelitian Perkebunan Medan
Buletin Fizik — Bul Fiz
Buletin i Institutit te Shkencave — BISchk
Buletin i Shkencave Mjekesore — Bul Shkencave Mjekesore
Buletin i Shkencave Natyrore — Bul Shkencave Nat
Buletin i Universitetit Shteteror te Tiranes. Seria Shkencat Shoqerore — BUSS
Buletin i Universitetit Shteteror te Tiranes. Seria Shkencat Shoqerore — BUST
Buletin i Universitetit te Tiranes Enver Hoxha. Seria Shkencat Mjekesore — Bul Univ Tiranes Enver Hoxha Ser Shkencat Mjekesore
Buletin Information. Laboratorul Central Coloristic — Bul Inf Lab Cent Color
Buletin Kebun Raya. Botanical Gardens of Indonesia — Bul Kebun Raya Bot Gard Indones
Buletin. Merkaz Volkani (Bet Dagan, Israel) — Bul Merkaz Volkani (Bet Dagan Isr)
Buletin peer Shkencat Biologijke — Bul Shkencat Biol
Buletin Penelitian Hutan — BPHUED
Buletin Penelitian Hutan — Bul Penelitian Hutan
Buletin Penelitian Teknologi Hasil Pertanian — Bul Penelitian Teknol Hasil Pertanian
Buletin pentru Inventii si Marci — Bul Invent Marci
Buletin per Shkencat Shoqerore — BSS
Buletin PPTM [*Pusat Pengembangan Teknologi Mineral*] — Bul PPTM
Buletin Pusat Pengembangan Teknologi Mineral — Bul Pusat Pengembangan Teknol Miner
Buletin Stiintific. Academia Republicii Populare Romane/Bulletin Scientifique. Academie de la Republique Populaire Roumaine/Naucnyj Vestnik. Akademija Rumynskoj Narodnoj Respubliki — Bul Sti Acad Republ Populare Romane
Buletin Stiintific. Academia Republicii Populare Romine — BSARPR
Buletin Stiintific. Academia Republicii Populare Romine — Bul Stiint Acad Repub Pop Rom
Buletin Stiintific. Institutul Pedagogic (Baia Mare). Seria B. Biologie, Fizico-Chimie, Matematica — Bul Stiint Inst Pedagog (Baia Mare) Ser B
Buletin Tehnico-Informativ. Central de Cercetari pentru Materiale de Protectie — Bul Teh Inf Cent Cercet Mater Prot
Buletin Tehnico-Informativ. Laboratorului Central de Cercetari pentru Lacuri si Cerneluri Bucuresti — Bul Teh Inf Lab Cent Cercet Lacuri Cerneluri Bucuresti
Buletin. Universiteti Shteteror te Tiranes. Fakulteti i Shkencave te Natyres — Bul Univ Shteteror Tiranes Shk Nat
Buletin. Universiteti Shteteror te Tiranes. Seria Shkencat Mjekesore — Bul Univ Shteteror Tiranes Ser Shkencat Mjekesore
Buletin. Universiteti Shteteror te Tiranes. Seria Shkencat Natyrore — Bul Univ Shteteror Tiranes Ser Shkencat Nat
Buletin. Universiteti Shteteror te Tiranes. Seria Shkencat Natyrore — Buletin Univ Shtet Tiranes Shkencat Nat
Buletin. Universiteti Shteteror te Tiranes. Seria Shkencat Shoqerore — BUT
Buletini i Shkencave Bujqesore — Bul Shken Bujqesore
Buletini i Shkencave Bujqesore — Bul Shkencave Bujqesore
Buletini i Shkencave Bujqesore Tirana. Institute i Larte Shteteror i Bujqesise — Bul Shken Bujqesore Tirana Inst Larte Shteteror Bujqesise
Buletinul Academiei de Stiinte a Republicii Moldova. Stiinte Biologice si Chimice — Bul Acad Stiinte Repub Mold Stiinte Biol Chim
Buletinul Akademiei. Stiince a RSS Moldovenest — Bul Akad Stiince RSS Moldoven
Buletinul Bibliotecii Romane — BBR
Buletinul Bibliotecii Romane — Bul Bibl Romane
Buletinul. Comisiunii Monumentelor Istorice — BCM
Buletinul Comisiunii Monumentelor Istorice a Romaniei — B Mon Ist
Buletinul Comisiunii Monumentelor Istorice a Romaniei — BCMI
Buletinul Comisiunii Monumentelor Istorice a Romaniei — BCMIR
Buletinul Comisiunii Monumentelor Istorice a Romaniei — Bul Com Mon Ist
Buletinul Comisiunii Monumentelor Istorice a Romaniei — Bul Mon Ist
Buletinul Culturii Tutunului — Bul Cult Tutun
Buletinul de Cercetari Piscicole — BCPCB7
Buletinul de Cercetari Piscicole — Bul Cercet Piscic
Buletinul de Informatii al Societatii Naturalistilor din Romania — Bul Inform Soc Nat Romania
Buletinul de Standardizare — Bul Stand
Buletinul de Stiinta si Tehnica al Institutului Politehnic din Timisoara — Bul Stiinta Teh Inst Politeh Timisoara
Buletinul Erbarului Institutului Botanic din Bucuresti — Bul Erb Inst Bot Bucuresti
Buletinul Facultatii de Agronomie din Cluj — Bul Fac Agron Cluj
Buletinul Facultatii de Stiinte din Cernauti — Bul Fac Sti Cernauti
Buletinul Facultatii de Stiinte din Cernauti — Bul Fac Stiinte Cernauti
Buletinul Informativ al Academiei de Stiinte Agricole si Silvice — Bul Inf Acad Stiinte Agric Silvice
Buletinul. Institutului Agronomic Cluj-Napoca — BIACDA
Buletinul. Institutului Agronomic Cluj-Napoca — Bul Inst Agron Cluj Napoca
Buletinul. Institutului Agronomic Cluj-Napoca. Institutul Agronomic "Dr. Petru Groza" — Bul Inst Agron Cluj Napoca Inst Agron Dr Petru Groza
Buletinul. Institutului Agronomic Cluj-Napoca. Seria Agricultura — BIAAD4
Buletinul. Institutului Agronomic Cluj-Napoca. Seria Agricultura — Bul Inst Agron Cluj Napoca Ser Agric
Buletinul. Institutului Agronomic Cluj-Napoca. Seria Zootehnie si Medicina Veterinara — BIAVDX
Buletinul Institutului Agronomic Cluj-Napoca. Seria Zootehnie si Medicina Veterinara — Bul Inst Agron Cluj-Napoca Ser Zooteh Med Vet
Buletinul Institutului de Cercetari Piscicole — Bul Inst Cercet Piscic
Buletinul. Institutului de Cercetari si Proiectari Piscicole — BCPPAB
Buletinul. Institutului de Cercetari si Proiectari Piscicole — Bul Inst Cercet Proiect Piscic
Buletinul. Institutului de Filologie Romaina "Alexandru Philippide" [*Iasi*] — BIFR
Buletinul. Institutului de Filologie Romaina "Alexandru Philippide" (Iasi) — BIFRI
Buletinul. Institutului de Petrol, Gaze, si Geologie — BIPGA
Buletinul. Institutului de Petrol, Gaze, si Geologie [*Romania*] — Bul Inst Pet Gaze Geol
Buletinul. Institutului de Studii si Projectari Energetice — Bul Inst Stud & Proj Energ
Buletinul. Institutului de Studii si Projectari Energetice — Bul Inst Stud si Project Energ
Buletinul. Institutului de Studii si Projectari Energetice — ISPBA
Buletinul Institutului Politehnic Buchuresti. Seria Electronica — Bul Inst Politehn Bucurestl Ser Electron
Buletinul Institutului Politehnic Buchuresti. Seria Energetica — Bul Inst Politehn Bucuresti Ser Energet
Buletinul. Institutului Politehnic Bucuresti — Bul Inst Politeh Bucur
Buletinul. Institutului Politehnic Bucuresti — Bul Inst Politeh Bucuresti
Buletinul. Institutului Politehnic Bucuresti — Bul Inst Politehn Bucuresti
Buletinul Institutului Politehnic Bucuresti. Seria Automatica-Calculatoare — Bul Inst Politehn Bucuresti Ser Automat Calc
Buletinul Institutului Politehnic Bucuresti. Seria Chimie — Bul Inst Politeh Bucuresti Ser Chim
Buletinul Institutului Politehnic Bucuresti. Seria Constructii de Masini — Bul Inst Politehn Bucuresti Ser Construc Mas
Buletinul Institutului Politehnic Bucuresti. Seria Metalurgie — Bul Inst Politeh Bucuresti Ser Metal
Buletinul Institutului Politehnic Bucuresti. Seria Transporturi-Aeronave — Bul Inst Politehn Bucuresti Ser Transport Aeronave
Buletinul. Institutului Politehnic din Brasov. Seria A. Mecanica — Bul Inst Politeh Brasov A
Buletinul. Institutului Politehnic din Brasov. Seria B. Economie Forestiera — BPEFA
Buletinul. Institutului Politehnic din Brasov. Seria B. Economie Forestiera — Bul Inst Polit Brasov Ser B Econ For
Buletinul. Institutului Politehnic din Iasi — Bul Inst Politeh Iasi
Buletinul Institutului Politehnic din Iasi. Sectia 2. Chimie — Bul Inst Politeh Iasi Sect 2 Chim
Buletinul Institutului Politehnic din Iasi. Sectia 2. Chimie si Inginerie Chimica — Bul Inst Politeh Iasi Sect 2 Chim Ing Chim
Buletinul Institutului Politehnic din Iasi. Sectia 5. Constructii Arhit ectura — Bul Inst Politeh Iasi Sect 5
Buletinul Institutului Politehnic din Iasi. Sectia 6. Imbunatatiri Funciare — Bul Inst Politeh Iasi Sect 6
Buletinul Institutului Politehnic din Iasi. Sectia 7. Textile, Pielarie — Bul Inst Politeh Iasi Sect 7
Buletinul. Institutului Politehnic din Iasi. Sectia I. Matematica, Mecanica Teoretica, Fizica — BMTFA
Buletinul. Institutului Politehnic din Iasi. Sectia I. Matematica, Mecanica Teoretica, Fizica — Bul Inst Politeh Iasi I
Buletinul. Institutului Politehnic din Iasi. Sectia I. Matematica, Mecanica Teoretica, Fizica — Bul Inst Politeh Iasi Sect I
Buletinul. Institutului Politehnic din Iasi. Sectia II. Chimie — Bul Inst Politeh Iasi Sect II
Buletinul. Institutului Politehnic din Iasi. Sectia III. Electrotehnica, Electronica Automatizari — Bul Inst Politeh Iasi III
Buletinul. Institutului Politehnic din Iasi. Sectia III. Electrotehnica, Electronica Automatizari — Bul Inst Politeh Iasi Sect III
Buletinul. Institutului Politehnic din Iasi. Sectia IV. Mecanica Tehnica — Bul Inst Politeh Iasi Sect IV
Buletinul. Institutului Politehnic din Iasi. Sectia V — Bul Inst Politeh Iasi Sect V
Buletinul. Institutului Politehnic din Iasi. Seria Noua — Bul Inst Politehn Iasi
Buletinul. Institutului Politehnic din Iasi. Seria Noua — Bul Inst Politehn Iasi NS
Buletinul. Institutului Politehnic "Gheorghe Gheorghiu-Dej" Bucuresti — BIGBA
Buletinul. Institutului Politehnic "Gheorghe Gheorghiu-Dej" Bucuresti — Bul Inst Politeh Gheorghe Gheorghiu Dej Bucur
Buletinul. Institutului Politehnic "Gheorghe Gheorghiu-Dej" Bucuresti — Bul Inst Politeh Gheorghe Gheorghiu Dej Bucuresti
Buletinul. Institutului Politehnic "Gheorghe Gheorghiu-Dej" Bucuresti. Seria Chimie — Bul Inst Politeh Gheorghe Gheorghiu Dej Bucuresti Ser Chim
Buletinul. Institutului Politehnic "Gheorghe Gheorghiu-Dej" Bucuresti. Seria Chimie-Metalurgie — Bul Inst Politeh Bucuresti Ser Chim Metal
Buletinul. Institutului Politehnic "Gheorghe Gheorghiu-Dej" Bucuresti. Seria Chimie-Metalurgie — Bul Inst Politeh Chim-Metal
Buletinul Institutului Politehnic. Gheorghe Gheorghiu-Dej. Bucuresti. Seria Chimie-Metalurgie — Bul Inst Politeh Gheorghe Gheorghiu Dej Bucuresti Ser Chim M
Buletinul. Institutului Politehnic "Gheorghe Gheorghiu-Dej" Bucuresti. Seria Chimie-Metalurgie [*Bucharest*] — Bul Inst Politehn Bucuresti Ser Chim-Metal
Buletinul Institutului Politehnic. Gheorghe Gheorghiu-Dej. Bucuresti. Seria Electrotechnica — Bul Inst Politeh Gheorghe Gheorghiu Dej Bucuresti Ser Electro
Buletinul. Institutului Politehnic "Gheorghe Gheorghiu-Dej" Bucuresti. Seria Electrotehnica — BIPED
Buletinul. Institutului Politehnic "Gheorghe Gheorghiu-Dej" Bucuresti. Seria Electrotehnica — Bul Inst Politehn Bucuresti Ser Electrotehn
Buletinul. Institutului Politehnic "Gheorghe Gheorghiu-Dej" Bucuresti. Seria Mecanica — BPGMD
Buletinul. Institutului Politehnic "Gheorghe Gheorghiu-Dej" Bucuresti. Seria Mecanica — Bul Inst Politeh Bucuresti Ser Mec
Buletinul. Institutului Politehnic "Gheorghe Gheorghiu-Dej" Bucuresti. Seria Mecanica — Bul Inst Politeh Gheorghe Gheorghiu Dej Bucuresti Ser Mec
Buletinul. Institutului Politehnic "Gheorghe Gheorghiu-Dej" Bucuresti. Seria Mecanica — Bul Inst Politeh Mec
Buletinul. Institutului Politehnic "Gheorghe Gheorghiu-Dej." Seria Chimie-Metalurgie [*Romania*] — Bul Inst Politeh Gheorghe Gheorghiu Dej Chim-Metal

Buletinul. Institutului Politehnic "Gheorghe Gheorghiu-Dej." Seria Electrotehnica [*Romania*] — Bul Inst Politeh Gheorghe Gheorghiu Dej Electroteh
Buletinul. Institutului Politehnic "Gheorghe Gheorghiu-Dej." Seria Mecanica [*Romania*] — Bul Inst Politeh Gheorghe Gheorghiu Dej Mec
Buletinul Laboratoarelor — Bul Laborat
Buletinul Monumentelor Istorica — Bul Mon Ist
Buletinul Politehnicii "Gh. Asachi" din Iasi — Bul Politeh Gh Asachi Iasi
Buletinul Sectorului Piscicol. Ministerul Industriei Alimentare. Romania — Bul Sect Piscic Minist Ind Aliment Rom
Buletinul si Memorie. Societatii de Medicina Veterinaria din Bucuresti — Bul si Mem Soc Med Vet Bucuresti
Buletinul. Societatii de Geografie al Romaniei — BSGR
Buletinul. Societatii de Stiinte din Cluj — Bul Soc Stiinte Cluj
Buletinul. Societatii de Stiinte din Cluj — Bulet Cluj
Buletinul. Societatii de Stiinte Geologice din Republica Socialista Romania [*A publication*] — BSSGC
Buletinul. Societatii de Stiinte Geologice din Republica Socialista Romania [*A publication*] — Bull Soc Stiinte Geol Repub Soc Rom
Buletinul Societatii Geografice din Republica Socialista Romania — BSGR
Buletinul Societatii Geografice din Republica Socialista Romania — BSGRSR
Buletinul Societatii Geografice Romane — BSGR
Buletinul. Societatii Geografice Romine — BSG
Buletinul Societatii Naturalistilor din Romania — BSNR
Buletinul Societatii Naturalistilor din Romania — Bul Soc Naturalistilor Romania
Buletinul. Societatii Numismatice Romane — BSN
Buletinul. Societatii Numismatice Romane — BSNR
Buletinul. Societatii Regale Romane de Geografie — Bul Soc Rom Geogr
Buletinul Statistic al Romaniei — BSR
Buletinul Stiintific al Institutului Politehnic Cluj-Napoca. Seria. Electrotehnica, Energetica, Informatica — Bul Stiint Inst Politeh Cluj Napoca Ser Electroteh Energ Inf
Buletinul Stiintific al Institutului Politehnic Cluj-Napoca. Seria Matematica Aplicada, Mecanica — Bul Stiint Inst Politehn Cluj Napoca Ser Mat Apl Mec
Buletinul Stiintific al Universitat. Universitatii Craiova [*Romania*] — Bul Stiint Univ Craiova
Buletinul Stiintific al Universitatii Craiova — BSUCA
Buletinul Stiintific. Institutul de Constructii (Bucuresti) — Bul Stiint Inst Constr (Bucuresti)
Buletinul Stiintific. Institutului Politehnic [*Cluj*] — BSIPA
Buletinul Stiintific. Institutului Politehnic (Cluj) — Bul Sti Inst Politehn (Cluj)
Buletinul Stiintific. Institutului Politehnic (Cluj) — Bul Stiint Inst Politeh (Cluj)
Buletinul Stiintific. Institutului Politehnic (Cluj). Seria Constructii — Bul Sti Inst Politehn (Cluj) Ser Construc
Buletinul Stiintific. Institutului Politehnic (Cluj). Seria Electromecanica — Bul Sti Inst Politehn (Cluj) Ser Electromec
Buletinul Stiintific. Institutului Politehnic (Cluj). Seria Electromecanica — Bul Stiint Inst Politeh (Cluj) Ser Electromec
Buletinul Stiintific. Institutului Politehnic (Cluj). Seria Electromecanica — Bul Stiint Inst Politehn (Cluj) Ser Electromec
Buletinul Stiintific. Institutului Politehnic (Cluj). Seria Mecanica — Bul Sti Inst Politehn (Cluj) Ser Mec
Buletinul Stiintific. Institutului Politehnic (Cluj). Seria Mecanica — Bul Stiint Inst Politehn (Cluj) Ser Mec
Buletinul Stiintific. Institutului Politehnic (Cluj-Napoca) — Bul Stiint Inst Politeh (Cluj-Napoca)
Buletinul Stiintific. Institutului Politehnic Cluj-Napoca. Seria Electrotehnica-Electrotechnica-Energetica-Informatica — Bul Stiint Inst Politehn Cluj Napoca Ser Electroteh Energet
Buletinul Stiintific si Tehnic al Institutului Politehnic Traian Vuia Timisoara — Bul Stiint Teh Inst Politeh Traian Vuia Timisoara
Buletinul Stiintific si Tehnic. Institutului Politehnic (Timisoara) — BSPTA
Buletinul Stiintific si Tehnic. Institutului Politehnic (Timisoara) — Bul Stiint Teh Inst Politeh (Timisoara)
Buletinul Stiintific si Tehnic. Institutului Politehnic "Traian Vuia" (Timisoara) — Bul Sti Tehn Inst Politehn "Traian Vuia" (Timisoara)
Buletinul Stiintifice. Academia Romana. Sectia de Stiinte Isotrice, Filozofice, si Economice — B St Ac
Buletinul Stiintifice. Academia Romana. Sectia de Stiinte Isotrice, Filozofice si Economice — BSA
Buletinul Tutunului — Bul Tutunului
Buletinul. Universitatea din Brasov — Bul Univ Brasov
Buletinul. Universitatea din Brasov. Seria C — Bul Univ Brasov Ser C
Buletinul. Universitatii din Brasov. Seria A. Mecanica Aplicata Constructii de Masini — Bul Univ Brasov Ser A Mec Apl
Buletinul. Universitatii din Brasov. Seria C. Matematica, Fizica, Chimie, Stiinte Naturale — Bul Univ Brasov Ser C Mat Fiz Chim Sti Natur
Buletinul Universitatii din Galati. Fascicula 2. Matematica, Fizica, Mecanica Teoretica — Bul Univ Galati Fasc 2
Buletinul Universitatii din Galati. Fascicula 4. Constructii de Masini. Frigotehnie. Constructii Navale — Bul Univ Galati Fasc 4
Buletinul Universitatii din Galati. Fascicula 6. Tehnologia si Chimia Produselor Alimentare — Bul Univ Galati Fasc 6
Buletinul Universitatii din Galati. Fascicula VI. Technologia si Chimia Produselor Alimentare — Bul Univ Galati Fasc VI Techn Chim Prod Aliment
Buletinul Universitatilor "V Babes" si "Bolyai" (Cluj). Seria Stiintele Natura — Bul Univ V Babes Bolyai (Cluj) Ser Stiint Nat
Bulgarian Academy of Sciences. Communications. Department of Chemistry — Bulg Acad Sci Commun Dep Chem
Bulgarian Films — Bulg F
Bulgarian Foreign Trade — BFT
Bulgarian Geophysical Journal — Bulg Geophys J
Bulgarian Historical Review/Revue Bulgare d'Histoire — Bulg Hist
Bulgarian Journal of Physics — Bulg J Phys
Bulgarian Journal of Physics — Bulgar J Phys
Bulgarian Journal of Plant Physiology — Bulg J Plant Physiol
Bulgarian Mathematical Monographs — Bulgar Math Monographs
Bulgarian Tobacco — Bulg Tob
Bulgarische Tabak — Bulg Tab
Bulgarska Akademiya na Naukite. Doklady — Bulg Akad Nauk Dokl
Bulgarska Akademiya na Naukite. Geologicheski Institut. Izvestiya. Seriya Inzhenerna Geologiya i Khidrogeologiya — Bulg Akad Nauk Geol Inst Izv Ser Inzh Geol Khidrogeol
Bulgarska Akademiya na Naukite. Geologicheski Institut. Izvestiya. Seriya Paleontologiya — Bulg Akad Nauk Geol Inst Izv Ser Paleontol
Bulgarska Akademiya na Naukite. Institut po Okeanografiya i Ribno Stopanstvo Izvestiya — Bulg Akad Nauk Inst Okeanogr Ribno Stop Izv
Bulgarska Akademiya na Naukite. Izvestiya na Instituta za Zhivotnovudstvo — Bulg Akad Nauk Izv Inst Zhivotnovud
Bulgarska Akademiya na Naukite. Izvestiya na Khimicheskiya Institut — Bulg Akad Nauk Izv Khim Inst
Bulgarska Akademiya na Naukite. Izvestiya na Mikrobiologicheskiya Institut — Bulg Akad Nauk Izv Mikrobiol Inst
Bulgarska Akademiya na Naukite. Izvestiya na Tekhnicheskiya Institut — Bulg Akad Nauk Izv Tekh Inst
Bulgarska Akademiya na Naukite. Otdelenie za Geologo-Geografski i Khimicheski Nauki. Izvestiya na Geologicheskiya Institut — Bulg Akad Nauk Otd Geol Geogr Khim Nauki Izv Geol Inst
Bulgarska Akademiya na Naukite. Otdeleniye za Biologichni Nauki. Zoologicheski Institut si Muzey. Izvestiya — Bulg Akad Nauk Zool Inst Muz Izv
Bulgarska Muzika — Bulgar Muz
Bulgarski Ezik — Bulg Ez
Bulgarski Tiutiun — Bulg Tiutiun
Bulgarski Tyutyun — Bulg Tyutyun
Bulgarsko Geofizichno Spisanie — BGSPD
Bulgarsko Geofizichno Spisanie [*Bulgaria*] — Bulg Geofiz Spis
Bulgarsko Geologichesko Druzhestvo. Spisanie — Bulg Geol Druzh Spis
Bulgarsko Muzikoznanie — Bulgarsko Muz
Bulgarsko Muzikoznanie. Bulgarska Akademiia na Naukite. Institut za Muzikoznanie — Bulg Muzik Bulg Akad Nauk Inst Muzik
Bulgarsko Spisanie po Fiziologiya na Rasteniyata — Bulg Spis Fiziol Rast
Bulk Solids Handling — Bulk Solids Handl
Bulk Systems International — Bulk Syst Int
Bullarium Romanum — BR
Bulleid Memorial Lectures — Bulleid Mem Lect
Bulleti. Associacio Catalana d'Antropologia — BACA
Bulleti de Dialectologia Catalana — BDC
Bulleti de la Societat Catalana de Matematiques — Bull Soc Catalana Mat
Bulleti Informatiu. Institut de Prehistoria i Arqueologia. Diputacio Provincial de Barcelona — BA Barcel
[*The*] **Bulletin** — B
[*The*] **Bulletin** — BLTND
[*The*] **Bulletin** — Bul
Bulletin A. Pennsylvania Bureau of Topographic and Geologic Survey — Bull A Pa Bur Topogr Geol Surv
Bulletin A. University of Arizona. Cooperative Extension Service — Bull A Univ Ariz Coop Ext Serv
Bulletin A. University of Arizona. Extension Service — Bull A Ariz Univ Ext Serv
Bulletin. Aberdeen and North of Scotland College of Agriculture — Bull Aberd N Scotl Coll Agric
Bulletin. Aberdeen University. African Studies Group — B Aberdeen Univ Afr Stud Group
Bulletin. Academie de Belgique. Classe des Lettres et des Sciences Morales et Politiques — Bull Academ Belg
Bulletin. Academie de Chirurgie Dentaire (Paris) — Bull Acad Chir Dent (Paris)
Bulletin. Academie de Medecine — B Acad Med
Bulletin. Academie de Medecine de Roumanie — BAMRAM
Bulletin. Academie de Medecine de Roumanie — Bull Acad Med Roum
Bulletin. Academie de Medecine (Paris) — Bull Acad Med (Paris)
Bulletin. Academie de Science de St. Petersbourg — BASP
Bulletin. Academie Delphinale — B Delph
Bulletin. Academie Delphinale — BAD
Bulletin. Academie Delphinale — Bull Acad Delph
Bulletin. Academie Dentaire (Paris) — Bull Acad Dent (Paris)
Bulletin. Academie des Inscriptions et Belles-Lettres — BAIBL
Bulletin. Academie des Sciences Agricoles et Forestieres — BAAFBT
Bulletin. Academie des Sciences Agricoles et Forestieres — Bull Acad Sci Agric For
Bulletin. Academie des Sciences Agricoles et Forestieres (Bucharest) — BAAFB
Bulletin. Academie des Sciences Agricoles et Forestieres (Bucharest) — Bull Acad Sci Agric For Bucharest
Bulletin. Academie des Sciences de l'URSS — BASURSS
Bulletin. Academie des Sciences de l'URSS — Bull Acad Sci URSS
Bulletin. Academie des Sciences de l'URSS. Classe des Sciences Chimiques — Bull Acad Sci URSS Cl Sci Chim
Bulletin. Academie des Sciences de l'URSS. Classe des Sciences Mathematiques et Naturelles — Bull Acad Sci URSS Cl Sci Math Nat
Bulletin. Academie des Sciences de l'URSS [*Union des Republiques Socialistes Sovietiques*]. Classe des Sciences Techniques — Bull Acad Sci URSS Cl Sci Tech
Bulletin. Academie des Sciences de l'URSS [*Union des Republiques Socialistes Sovietiques*]. Serie Biologique — Bull Acad Sci URSS Ser Biol
Bulletin. Academie des Sciences de l'URSS. Serie Geographique et Geophysique — Bull Acad Sci URSS Ser Geogr Geophys
Bulletin. Academie des Sciences de l'URSS. Serie Geologique — Bull Acad Sci URSS Ser Geol
Bulletin. Academie des Sciences de l'URSS. Serie Physique — Bull Acad Sci URSS Ser Phys

Bulletin. Academie des Sciences de Russie — BASR
Bulletin. Academie des Sciences de St. Petersbourg — Bull Acad Sci St Petersbourg
Bulletin. Academie des Sciences et Lettres de Montpellier — Bull Acad Sci Lett Montpellier
Bulletin. Academie des Sciences Mathematiques et Naturelles. Academie Royale Serbe. Serie A. Sciences Mathematiques et Physiques — Bull Acad Sci Math Nat Acad R Serbe A
Bulletin. Academie des Sciences Mathematiques et Naturelles. Academie Royale Serbe. Serie A. Sciences Mathematiques et Physiques (Belgrade) — Bull Acad Sci Math Natur (Belgrade) A
Bulletin. Academie des Sciences Mathematiques et Naturelles. Academie Royale Serbe. Serie B. Sciences Naturelles — Bull Acad Sci Math Nat Acad R Serbe B
Bulletin. Academie d'Hippone — BAH
Bulletin. Academie d'Hippone — BHipp
Bulletin. Academie du Var — B Var
Bulletin. Academie du Var — BAV
Bulletin. Academie Ebroicienne — Bull Acad Ebroic
Bulletin. Academie et de la Societe Lorraines des Sciences [*Nancy*] — BASLS
Bulletin. Academie et de la Societe Lorraines des Sciences (Nancy) — B Nancy
Bulletin. Academie et Societe Lorraines des Sciences — B Lorraine
Bulletin. Academie et Societe Lorraines des Sciences — BASLAY
Bulletin. Academie et Societe Lorraines des Sciences — Bull Acad Soc Lorraines Sci
Bulletin. Academie Imperiale des Sciences de Petrograd — Bull Acad Imp Sci Petrograd
Bulletin. Academie Imperiale des Sciences de St. Petersbourg — Bull Acad Imp Sc St Petersb
Bulletin. Academie Imperiale des Sciences de St. Petersbourg — Bull Acad Imp Sci St Petersbourg
Bulletin. Academie Internationale de Geographie Botanique — Bull Acad Int
Bulletin. Academie Malgache — BAMalgache
Bulletin. Academie Malgache — Bull Ac Malg
Bulletin. Academie Malgache — Bull Acad Malg
Bulletin. Academie Malgache — Bull Acad Malgache
Bulletin. Academie Malgache — BUMTAW
Bulletin. Academie Nationale de Medecine [*Paris*] — BANMAC
Bulletin. Academie Nationale de Medecine [*France*] — Bull Acad Nat Med
Bulletin. Academie Nationale de Medecine [*Paris*] — Bull Acad Natl Med
Bulletin. Academie Nationale de Medecine (Paris) — Bull Acad Natl Med (Paris)
Bulletin. Academie Polonaise de Cracovie — BAPC
Bulletin. Academie Polonaise des Sciences — Bull Ac Polon Sci
Bulletin. Academie Polonaise des Sciences — Bull Acad Pol Sci
Bulletin. Academie Polonaise des Sciences. Classe 2. Agrobiologie, Biologie, Sciences Medicales — Bull Acad Pol Sci Cl 2
Bulletin. Academie Polonaise des Sciences. Classe 3. Mathematique, Astronomie, Physique, Chimie, Geologie, et Geographie — Bull Acad Pol Sci Cl 3
Bulletin. Academie Polonaise des Sciences et des Lettres — BAPSL
Bulletin. Academie Polonaise des Sciences. Serie des Sciences Biologiques — B Pol Biol
Bulletin. Academie Polonaise des Sciences. Serie des Sciences Biologiques — BAPBAN
Bulletin. Academie Polonaise des Sciences. Serie des Sciences Biologiques — Bull Acad Pol Sci Biol
Bulletin. Academie Polonaise des Sciences. Serie des Sciences Biologiques — Bull Acad Pol Sci Ser Sci Biol
Bulletin. Academie Polonaise des Sciences. Serie des Sciences Biologiques — Bull Acad Polon Sci Ser Sci Biol
Bulletin. Academie Polonaise des Sciences. Serie des Sciences Chimiques — B Pol Chim
Bulletin. Academie Polonaise des Sciences. Serie des Sciences Chimiques — Bull Acad Pol Sci Ser Sci Chim
Bulletin. Academie Polonaise des Sciences. Serie des Sciences Chimiques, Geologiques, et Geographiques — Bull Acad Pol Sci Ser Sci Chim Geol Geogr
Bulletin. Academie Polonaise des Sciences. Serie des Sciences de la Terre [*A publication*] — B Pol Sci T
Bulletin. Academie Polonaise des Sciences. Serie des Sciences de la Terre [*A publication*] — BPSTBS
Bulletin. Academie Polonaise des Sciences. Serie des Sciences de la Terre [*A publication*] — Bull Acad Pol Sci Ser Sci Terre
Bulletin. Academie Polonaise des Sciences. Serie des Sciences Geologiques et Geographiques — BPGGA
Bulletin. Academie Polonaise des Sciences. Serie des Sciences Geologiques et Geographiques — Bull Acad Pol Sci Ser Sci Geol Geogr
Bulletin. Academie Polonaise des Sciences. Serie des Sciences Mathematiques, Astronomiques, et Physiques — B Pol Math
Bulletin. Academie Polonaise des Sciences. Serie des Sciences Mathematiques, Astronomiques, et Physiques — Bull Acad Pol Sci Ser Sci Math Astron et Phys
Bulletin. Academie Polonaise des Sciences. Serie des Sciences Mathematiques, Astronomiques, et Physiques — Bull Acad Pol Sci Ser Sci Math Astron Phys
Bulletin. Academie Polonaise des Sciences. Serie des Sciences Mathematiques, Astronomiques, et Physiques — Bull Acad Polon Sci Ser Sci Math Astronom Phys
Bulletin. Academie Polonaise des Sciences. Serie des Sciences Physiques et Astronomiques — Bull Acad Pol Sci Ser Sci Phys Astron
Bulletin. Academie Polonaise des Sciences. Serie des Sciences Physiques et Astronomiques — Bull Acad Pol Sci Ser Sci Phys et Astron
Bulletin. Academie Polonaise des Sciences. Serie des Sciences Techniques — B Pol Techn
Bulletin. Academie Polonaise des Sciences. Serie des Sciences Techniques — Bull Acad Pol Sci Ser Sci Tech
Bulletin. Academie Polonaise des Sciences. Serie des Sciences Techniques — Bull Acad Polon Sci Ser Sci Tech
Bulletin. Academie pour l'Histoire de la Culture Materielle — BACM
Bulletin. Academie Royale d'Archeologie de Belgique — BARAB
Bulletin. Academie Royale de Belgique [*Brussels*] — BARB
Bulletin. Academie Royale de Belgique. Classe des Beaux-Arts — Bull Acad Roy Belg Cl Beaux Arts
Bulletin. Academie Royale de Belgique. Classe des Lettres et des Sciences Morales et Politiques — BuA
Bulletin. Academie Royale de Belgique. Classe des Lettres et des Sciences Morales et Politiques — Bul Ac R
Bulletin. Academie Royale de Belgique. Classe des Lettres et des Sciences Morales et Politiques — Bull Acad Roy Belg Cl Lett
Bulletin. Academie Royale de Belgique. Classe des Lettres et des Sciences Morales et Politiques — Bull Acad Roy Belgique Cl Lett Sci Moral Polit
Bulletin. Academie Royale de Belgique. Classe des Sciences — Bull Acad R Belg Cl Sci
Bulletin. Academie Royale de Belgique. Classe des Sciences — Bull Acad Roy Belg Cl
Bulletin. Academie Royale de Belgique. Classe des Sciences — Bull Acad Roy Belgique Cl Sci
Bulletin. Academie Royale de Langue et de Litterature Francaises — BALF
Bulletin. Academie Royale de Langue et de Litterature Francaises — BARLLF
Bulletin. Academie Royale de Langue et de Litterature Francaises — Bull ALLF
Bulletin. Academie Royale de Medecine de Belgique — BARMAW
Bulletin. Academie Royale de Medecine de Belgique [*Mededeelingen van de Koninklijke Belgische Academie voor Geneeskunde*] — Bull Acad Med Belg
Bulletin. Academie Royale de Medecine de Belgique — Bull Acad R Med Belg
Bulletin. Academie Royale de Medecine de Belgique — Bull Acad Roy Med Belgique
Bulletin. Academie Royale de Medicine (Paris) — Bull Acad Roy Med (Paris)
Bulletin. Academie Serbe des Sciences. B. Sciences Naturelles — Bull Acad Serbe Sci B Sci Nat
Bulletin. Academie Serbe des Sciences. Classe des Sciences Mathematiques et Naturelles — Bull Acad Serbe Sci Cl Sci Math Nat
Bulletin. Academie Serbe des Sciences. Classe des Sciences Mathematiques et Naturelles. Sciences Naturelles — Bull Acad Serbe Sci Cl Sci Math Nat Sci Nat
Bulletin. Academie Serbe des Sciences et des Arts. Classe des Sciences Mathematiques et Naturelles — Bull Acad Serbe Sci Arts Cl Sci Math Nat
Bulletin. Academie Serbe des Sciences et des Arts. Classe des Sciences Mathematiques et Naturelles — Bull Acad Serbe Sci Arts Cl Sci Math Natur
Bulletin. Academie Serbe des Sciences et des Arts. Classe des Sciences Mathematiques et Naturelles. Nouvelle Serie [*Belgrade*] — Bull Acad Serbe Sci Arts Cl Sci Math Natur NS
Bulletin. Academie Serbe des Sciences et des Arts. Classe des Sciences Mathematiques et Naturelles. Sciences Mathematiques — Bull Acad Serbe Sci Arts Cl Sci Math Natur Sci Math
Bulletin. Academie Serbe des Sciences et des Arts. Classe des Sciences Mathematiques et Naturelles. Sciences Naturelles — Bull Acad Serbe Sci Arts Cl Sci Math Nat Sci Nat
Bulletin. Academie Serbe des Sciences et des Arts. Classe des Sciences Medicales [*Belgrade*] — Bull Acad Serbe Sci Arts Cl Sci Med
Bulletin. Academie Serbe des Sciences et des Arts. Classe des Sciences Techniques [*Belgrade*] — Bull Acad Serbe Sci Arts Classe Sci Tech
Bulletin. Academie Serbe des Sciences et des Arts. Classe des Sciences Techniques — Bull Acad Serbe Sci et Arts Cl Sci Tech
Bulletin. Academie Suisse des Sciences Medicales — BSAMA5
Bulletin. Academie Suisse des Sciences Medicales — Bull Acad Sui Sci Med
Bulletin. Academie Suisse des Sciences Medicales — Bull Acad Suisse Sci Med
Bulletin. Academie Tchecoslovaque d'Agriculture — Bull Acad Tchec Agric
Bulletin. Academie Veterinaire de France — BAVFAV
Bulletin. Academie Veterinaire de France — Bull Acad Vet Fr
Bulletin. Academie Veterinaire de France — Bull Acad Vet France
Bulletin. Academy of Dentistry for the Handicapped — Bull Acad Dent Handicap
Bulletin. Academy of General Dentistry — Bull Acad Gen Dent
Bulletin. Academy of Medical Sciences. USSR — Bull Acad Med Sci USSR
Bulletin. Academy of Medicine of Toledo — Bull Acad Med Tol
Bulletin. Academy of Medicine of Toledo and Lucas County [*Ohio*] — Bull Acad Med Toledo
Bulletin. Academy of Medicine of Toronto — Bull Acad Med Tor
Bulletin. Academy of Medicine of Toronto — Bull Acad Med Toronto
Bulletin. Academy of Sciences. Armenian SSR. Natural Sciences — Bull Acad Sci Arm SSR Nat Sci
Bulletin. Academy of Sciences. Azerbaidjan SSR [*Soviet Socialist Republic*] — Bull Acad Sci Azerb SSR
Bulletin. Academy of Sciences. DPR [*Democratic People's Republic*] **Korea** — Bull Acad Sci DPR Korea
Bulletin. Academy of Sciences. Georgian SSR — Bull Acad Sci Georgian SSR
Bulletin. Academy of Sciences of Georgia — Bull Acad Sci Georgia
Bulletin. Academy of Sciences of St. Louis — Bull Acad Sci St Louis
Bulletin. Academy of Sciences of the Georgian SSR — Bull Acad Sci Ga SSR
Bulletin. Academy of Sciences of the United Provinces of Agra and Oudh, India — Bull Acad Sci United Prov Agra Oudh India
Bulletin. Academy of Sciences of the USSR. Division of Chemical Science — B Acad Sci
Bulletin. Academy of Sciences of the USSR. Division of Chemical Science — Bull Acad Sci USSR Div Chem Sci
Bulletin. Academy of Sciences of the USSR. Geologic Series — Bull Acad Sci USSR Geol Ser
Bulletin. Academy of Sciences of the USSR. Physical Sciences — Bull Acad Sci USSR Phys Sci

Bulletin. Academy of Sciences of the USSR. Physical Series — Bull Acad Sci USSR Phys Ser
Bulletin. Academy of Sciences of the USSR. Physical Series (Columbia Technical Translations) — Bull Acad Sci USSR Phys Ser (Columbia Tech Transl)
Bulletin. Academy of Sciences of the USSR. Physical Series (English Translation) — Bull Acad Sci USSR Phys Ser (Engl Transl)
Bulletin. Academy of Sciences. USSR. Geophysics Series — Bull Acad Sci USSR Geophys Ser
Bulletin. Activity of the Institute for Geology and Subsurface Research [*Athens*] — Bull Act Inst Geol Subsurf Res
Bulletin. Adler Museum of the History of Medicine — Bull Adler Mus Hist Med
Bulletin. Administration Penitentiaire — Bul Admin Penitentiaire
Bulletin. Advisory Council for Scientific and Industrial Research (Canada) — Bull Advis C Sci I R (Can)
Bulletin. Advisory Council for Scientific and Industrial Research (Canada) — Bull Advis Counc Sci Ind Res (Can)
Bulletin. Aeronautical Research Institute. University of Tokyo — Bull Aeronaut Res Inst Univ Tokyo
Bulletin. Afghan Geological and Mineral Survey — Bull Afghan Geol Miner Surv
Bulletin. Africa Institute of South Africa — Bull Afr Inst S Afr
Bulletin. African Studies Association of the United Kingdom — Bull Afr Stud Assoc
Bulletin. Agence Economique des Colonies Autonomes et des Territoires Africains sous Mandat — B Ag Econ Colon Auto Ter Afr
Bulletin. Agence Economique des Colonies Autonomes et des Territoires Africains sous Mandat (France) — Bull Agence Econ Colon Auton Territ Afr Mandat (Fr)
Bulletin. Agence Generale des Colonies — B Ag Gen Colon
Bulletin. Agence Generale des Colonies (France) — Bull Agence Gen Colon (Fr)
Bulletin. Agence Internationale de l'Energie Atomique — B Agenc Int Energie Atom
Bulletin. Agence Internationale de l'Energie Atomique — Bull AIEA
Bulletin. Agency of Industrial Science and Technology (Japan) — Bull Agency Ind Sci Technol Jpn
Bulletin Agricole — Bull Agric
Bulletin Agricole de la Societe d'Agriculture et des Quatre Comices du Bas-Rhin/Neue Ackerbau-Zeitung der Ackerbau-Gesellschaft und der Vier Comitien des Niederrheins — Bull Agric Soc Agric Bas Phin
Bulletin Agricole du Congo — Bull Agr Congo
Bulletin Agricole du Congo — Bull Agric Congo
Bulletin Agricole du Congo Belge — Bul Agric Congo Belge
Bulletin Agricole du Congo Belge — Bull Agr CB
Bulletin Agricole du Congo Belge — Bull Agric Cong Belg
Bulletin Agricole du Congo Belge — Bull Agric Congo Belg
Bulletin Agricole du Rwanda — Bull Agric Rwanda
Bulletin Agricole. Institut Scientifique de l'Indochine — Bull Agric Inst Sci Indochine
Bulletin Agricole. Societe d'Agriculture et des Quatre Comices du Departement du Bas-Rhin — Bull Agric Soc Agric Dep Bas Rhin
Bulletin. Agricultural and Forestry College. Suwon — Bull Agric Coll Suwon
Bulletin. Agricultural and Mechanical College of Texas — Bull Agric Mech Coll Texas
Bulletin. Agricultural and Mechanical College of Texas. Texas Engineering Experiment Station. Bulletin — Bull Agric Mech Coll Tex Tex Eng Exp Stn Bull
Bulletin. Agricultural Chemical Society of Japan — BACOAV
Bulletin. Agricultural Chemical Society of Japan — Bl Agric Chem Soc Jap
Bulletin. Agricultural Chemical Society of Japan — Bull Agr Chem Soc Jap
Bulletin. Agricultural Chemical Society of Japan — Bull Agric Chem Soc Jpn
Bulletin. Agricultural Chemicals Inspection Station — Bull Agric Chem Insp Stn
Bulletin. Agricultural Chemicals Inspection Station [*Tokyo*] — NKHOAK
Bulletin. Agricultural Chemicals Inspection Station (Tokyo) — Bull Agric Chem Insp Stn (Tokyo)
Bulletin. Agricultural Department (Assam) — Bull Agric Dep (Assam)
Bulletin. Agricultural Department (Tasmania) — Bull Agric Dep (Tasm)
Bulletin. Agricultural Engineering Research Station. Nogyo Doboku Shikenjo Hokou [*Japan*] — Bull Agri Eng Res Stn
Bulletin. Agricultural Experiment Station. Alabama Polytechnic Institute — Bull Agric Exp Stn Ala Polytech Inst
Bulletin. Agricultural Experiment Station. Kungchuling/Manchukuo Kung Chu Ling Noji Shikenjo Hokoku — Bull Agric Exp Sta Kungchuling
Bulletin. Agricultural Experiment Station. North Carolina — Bull Agric Exp Stn NC
Bulletin. Agricultural Experiment Station. North Carolina State University — Bull Argic Exp Stn N Carol St Univ
Bulletin. Agricultural Experiment Station. North Dakota State University — Bull Agric Exp Stn ND State Univ
Bulletin. Agricultural Experiment Station (Rehovoth) — Bull Agric Exp Stn (Rehovoth)
Bulletin. Agricultural Experiment Station. Rio Piedras, Puerto Rico — Bull Agric Exp Stn Rio Piedras PR
Bulletin. Agricultural Experiment Station. South Dakota State University — Bull Agric Exp Stn SD State Univ
Bulletin. Agricultural Experiment Station (Tahreer Province) — Bull Agric Exp Stn (Tahreer Prov)
Bulletin. Agricultural Experiment Stations. Florida — Bull Agric Exp Stn Fla
Bulletin. Agricultural Experiment Stations. Georgia — Bull Agric Exp Stn Ga
Bulletin. Agricultural Intelligence and Plant Diseases. Monthly — Bull Agric Intell Plant Dis Mon
Bulletin. Agricultural Research Institute. Iregszemcse, Hungary — Bull Agric Res Inst Iregszemcse Hung
Bulletin. Agricultural Research Institute of Kanagawa Prefecture — Bull Agric Res Inst Kanagawa Prefect
Bulletin. Agricultural Research Institute (Pusa) — Bull Agr Res Inst (Pusa)
Bulletin. Agricultural Research Station (Rehovat) — Bull Agr Res Sta (Rehovat)
Bulletin. Agricultural Science (Hungary) — Bull Agric Sci (Hung)
Bulletin. Agricultural Society. Cairo. Technical Section — Bull Agric Soc Cairo Tech Sect
Bulletin Agronomique. Institut de Recherches Agronomiques Tropicales et des Cultures Vivrieres — Bull Agron Inst Rech Agron Trop Cult Vivrieres
Bulletin. Aichi Agricultural Experiment Station — Bull Aichi Agr Exp Sta
Bulletin. Aichi Environmental Research Center — Bull Aichi Environ Res Cent
Bulletin. Aichi Gakugei University — Bull Aichi Gakugei Univ
Bulletin. Aichi Institute of Technology — Bull Aichi Inst Technol
Bulletin. Aichi Institute of Technology. Part B — Bull Aichi Inst Technol Part B
Bulletin. Aichi Prefecture Agricultural Experiment Station/Aichi-Ken Nogyo Shikenjo Iho — Bull Aichi Prefect Agric Exp Sta
Bulletin. Aichi University of Education. Natural Science [*Kariya*] — Bull Aichi Univ Ed Natur Sci
Bulletin. Aichi-Ken Agricultural Experiment Station — Bull Aichi Ken Agric Exp Stn
Bulletin. Aichi-ken Agricultural Research Center. Series A. Food Crop — Bull Aichi ken Agric Res Cent Ser A
Bulletin. Aichi-ken Agricultural Research Center. Series B. Horticulture — Bull Aichi ken Agric Res Cent Ser B
Bulletin. Aichi-ken Agricultural Research Center. Series D. Sericulture — Bull Aichi ken Agric Res Cent Ser D
Bulletin. Akademie Serbe des Sciences. Classe des Sciences Medicales — Bull Akad Serbe Sci Cl Sci Med
Bulletin. Akita Agricultural Experiment Station — Bull Akita Agric Exp Stn
Bulletin. Akita Fruit-Tree Experiment Station — Bull Akita Fruit Tree Exp Stn
Bulletin. Akita Prefectural College of Agriculture — Bull Akita Prefect Coll Agric
Bulletin. Akron Dental Society [*Ohio*] — AKDDA
Bulletin. Akron Dental Society [*Ohio*] — Bull Akron Dent Soc
Bulletin. Alabama Agricultural Experiment Station. Auburn University — Bull Ala Agr Exp Sta
Bulletin. Alabama Agricultural Experiment Station. Auburn University — Bull Ala Agric Exp Sta
Bulletin. Alabama Agricultural Experiment Station. Auburn University — Bull Ala Agric Exp Stn
Bulletin. Alabama. Geological Survey — Bull Ala Geol Surv
Bulletin. Alameda County Dental Society — Bull Alameda Cty Dent Soc
Bulletin. Alameda-Contra Costa Medical Association [*California*] — Bull Alameda-Contra Costa Med Assoc
Bulletin. Alaska Agricultural Experiment Station — Bull Alaska Agr Exp Sta
Bulletin. Alaska Agricultural Experiment Station — Bull Alaska Agric Exp Stn
Bulletin. Alberta Research Council — Bull Alberta Res Counc
Bulletin. Alexandria Faculty of Medicine — Bull Alexandria Fac Med
Bulletin Algerien de Carcinologie — Bull Alger Carcinol
Bulletin. Allegheny County Medical Society [*Pennsylvania*] — Bull Allegheny County Med Soc
Bulletin. Alliance Israelite Universelle — BAIU
Bulletin. All-Union Institute of Agricultural Microbiology — Bull All Union Inst Agric Microbiol
Bulletin. All-Union Scientific Research Cotton Institute — Bull All Union Sci Res Cotton Inst
Bulletin. All-Union Scientific Research Institute of Fertilizers and Agro-Soil Science. Leningrad Department — Bull All Union Sci Res Inst Fert Agro Soil Sci Leningrad Dep
Bulletin. Allyn Museum — Bull Allyn Mus
Bulletin. Alumni Association. Utsunomiya Agricultural College — Bull Alumni Assoc Utsunomiya Agric Coll
Bulletin. American Academy of Arts and Sciences — Bull Amer Acad Arts Sci
Bulletin. American Academy of Dermatology — Bull Am Acad Dermatol
Bulletin. American Academy of Medicine — Bull Acad M
Bulletin. American Academy of Orthopaedic Surgeons — Bull Am Acad Orthopaedic Surg
Bulletin. American Academy of Psychiatry and the Law — Bul Am Acad Psy and L
Bulletin. American Academy of Psychiatry and the Law — Bull Am Acad Psychiatr Law
Bulletin. American Academy of Psychiatry and the Law — Bull Am Acad Psychiatry Law
Bulletin. American Academy of Religion — Bull Am Acad Rel
Bulletin. American Anthropological Association — B Am Anth A
Bulletin. American Anthropological Association — Bull Am Anthr Ass
Bulletin. American Association of Botanical Gardens and Arboreta — Bull Am Assoc Bot Gard Arboreta
Bulletin. American Association of Dental Editors — Bull Am Assoc Dent Ed
Bulletin. American Association of Hospital Dentists — Bull Am Assoc Hosp Dent
Bulletin. American Association of Nurse Anesthetists — Bull Am Assoc Nurse Anesth
Bulletin. American Association of Petroleum Geologists — B Am Ass Petrol Geol
Bulletin. American Association of Petroleum Geologists — BAAPA
Bulletin. American Association of Petroleum Geologists — Bull Am Ass Petrol Geol
Bulletin. American Association of Petroleum Geologists — Bull Am Assoc Pet Geol
Bulletin. American Association of Petroleum Geologists — Bull Amer Assoc Petrol Geol
Bulletin. American Association of Public Health Dentists — Bull Am Ass Publ Hlth Dent
Bulletin. American Association of Public Health Physicians — Bull Am Ass Publ Hlth Phys
Bulletin. American Association of University Professors — Bull Am Ass Univ Prof
Bulletin. American Association of Variable Star Observers — Bull Am Assoc Variable Star Obs
Bulletin. American Astronomical Society — Bull Am Astron Soc

Bulletin. American Astronomical Society — Bull Amer Astron Soc
Bulletin. American Cancer Society — Bull Am Cancer Soc
Bulletin. American Ceramic Society — Bull Am Cer Soc
Bulletin. American Ceramic Society — Bull Am Ceram Soc
Bulletin. American College of Physicians — Bull Am Coll Physicians
Bulletin. American College of Surgeons — Bull Am Coll Surg
Bulletin. American Congress on Surveying and Mapping — Bul Am Cong Surv Map
Bulletin. American Council of Learned Societies — Bull ACLS
Bulletin. American Council of Learned Societies — Bull Amer Counc Learned Soc
Bulletin. American Dahlia Society — Bull Am Dahlia Soc
Bulletin. American Dahlia Society — Bull Amer Dahlia Soc
Bulletin. American Dental Association — Bull Am Dent Ass
Bulletin. American Foundrymen's Association — Bull Am Foundrymen's Assoc
Bulletin American Fuchsia Society — Bull Amer Fuchsia Soc
Bulletin. American Game Protective Association — Bull Am Game Protect Ass
Bulletin. American Geographical Society — B Am Geogr Soc
Bulletin. American Geographical Society — BAGS
Bulletin. American Group. International Institute for Conservation of Historic and Artistic Works — Bull Am Group IIC
Bulletin. American Historical Collection — B Am Hist Col
Bulletin. American Historical Collection — BAHC
Bulletin. American Horticultural Society — Bull Amer Hort Soc
Bulletin. American Hosta Society — Bull Am Hosta Soc
Bulletin. American Institute of Chemical Engineers — Bull Am Inst Chem Eng
Bulletin. American Institute of Mining and Metallurgical Engineers — Bull Am Inst Min Metall Eng
Bulletin. American Institute of Mining Engineers — Bull Amer Inst Min Eng
Bulletin. American Institute of Swedish Arts, Literature, and Science — BAI
Bulletin. American Library Association — BALA
Bulletin. American Malacological Union, Incorporated — Bull Am Malacol Union Inc
Bulletin. American Mathematical Society — B Am Math S
Bulletin. American Mathematical Society — BAMOA
Bulletin. American Mathematical Society — BAMS
Bulletin. American Mathematical Society — Bull Am Math Soc
Bulletin. American Mathematical Society — Bull Amer Math Soc
Bulletin. American Mathematical Society. New Series — Bull Amer Math Soc NS
Bulletin. American Meteorological Society — B Am Meteor
Bulletin. American Meteorological Society — BAMIA
Bulletin. American Meteorological Society — Bull Am Meteorol Soc
Bulletin. American Meteorological Society — Bull Amer Meteorol Soc
Bulletin. American Museum of Natural History — Bull Am Mus Nat Hist
Bulletin. American Musicological Society — BAMS
Bulletin. American Orchid Society — Bull Am Orchid Soc
Bulletin. American Pharmaceutical Association — Bull Am Pharm Assoc
Bulletin. American Physical Society — B Am Phys S
Bulletin. American Physical Society — BAPSA
Bulletin. American Physical Society — Bl Am Phys Soc
Bulletin. American Physical Society — Bull A Phys Soc
Bulletin. American Physical Society — Bull Am Phys Soc
Bulletin. American Poinsettia Society — Bull Amer Poinsettia Soc
Bulletin. American Pomological Society — Bull Amer Pomol Soc
Bulletin. American Protestant Hospital Association — Bull Am Prot Hosp Assoc
Bulletin. American Railway Engineering Association — Bull Amer Railw Eng Assoc
Bulletin. American School of Prehistoric Research — B Am Pr Hist Res
Bulletin. American School of Prehistoric Research — BASPR
Bulletin. American School of Prehistoric Research — Bull Am Sch Prehist Res
Bulletin. American School of Prehistoric Research — Bull Am Sch Prehist Research
Bulletin. American Schools of Oriental Research — B Amer School Orient
Bulletin. American Schools of Oriental Research — BASOR
Bulletin. American Schools of Oriental Research — Bull Amer Orient
Bulletin. American Schools of Oriental Research — Bull Amer Sch Orient Res
Bulletin. American Schools of Oriental Research in Jerusalem and Bagdad — BASO
Bulletin. American Schools of Oriental Research. Supplementary Series — BASORSS
Bulletin. American Society for Information Science — Am Soc Info Science Bul
Bulletin. American Society for Information Science — BASIC
Bulletin. American Society for Information Science — BASIS
Bulletin. American Society for Information Science — Bull Am Soc Inf Sci
Bulletin. American Society for Information Science — Bull Am Soc Inform Sci
Bulletin. American Society of Bakery Engineers — Bull Amer Soc Bakery Eng
Bulletin. American Society of Hospital Pharmacists — Bull Am Soc Hosp Pharm
Bulletin. American Society of Papyrologists — B Am S Pap
Bulletin. American Society of Papyrologists — B Am Soc P
Bulletin. American Society of Papyrologists — BASP
Bulletin. American Society of Papyrologists — Bull Am Soc Pap
Bulletin. American Society of Veterinary Clinical Pathologists — Bull Am Soc Vet Clin Pathol
Bulletin. American Swedish Institute — BASI
Bulletin. American Zinc Institute — Bull Am Zinc Inst
Bulletin. Americana College of Nurse-Midwifery — Bull Am Coll Nurse Midwifery
Bulletin. Amis des Arts et des Sciences de Tournus — B Art Tournus
Bulletin. Amnesty International. Canadian Section — Bul Amnesty Int Can Sect
Bulletin. Analysis and Testing — BAT
Bulletin Analytique de Bibliographie Hellenique — BBH
Bulletin Analytique de Documentation Politique, Economique, et Sociale Contemporaine — Bul Analytique Docum
Bulletin Analytique d'Entomologie Medical et Veterinaire — Bull Anal Ent Med Vet
Bulletin Analytique d'Entomologie Medicale et Veterinaire — Bull Anal Entomol Med Vet
Bulletin Analytique d'Histoire Romaine — B Anal Hist Rom
Bulletin Analytique d'Histoire Romaine — B Analyt Hist Rom
Bulletin Analytique d'Histoire Romaine [*Strasbourg*] — Bull Anal d Hist Rom
Bulletin. Anciens Eleves de l'Ecole Francaise de Meunerie — Bull Anc Eleves Ec Fr Meun
Bulletin. Anciens Eleves de l'Ecole Francaise de Meunerie — Bull Anciens Eleves Ecole Franc Meun
Bulletin. Ancient Orient Museum [*Tokyo*] — B Anc Or Mus
Bulletin and Foundry Abstracts. British Cast Iron Research Association — Bull Foundry Abstr Br Cast Iron Res Assoc
Bulletin Annuel. Federation Internationale de Laiterie — Bull Annu Fed Int Lait
Bulletin Annuel. Musee d'Ethnographie de la Ville de Geneve — B Annu Mus Ethnogr Geneve
Bulletin Annuel. Musee d'Ethnographie de la Ville de Geneve — BAMEG
Bulletin Annuel. Societe Ariegeoise des Sciences, Lettres, et Arts — Bull Ariegeois
Bulletin Annuel. Societe d'Archeologie et d'Histoire du Tonnerrois — BSAHT
Bulletin Annuel. Societe Suisse de Chronometrie et Laboratoire Suisse de Recherches Horlogeres — BSCLA
Bulletin Annuel. Societe Suisse de Chronometrie et Laboratoire Suisse de Recherches Horlogeres — Bull Ann Soc Suisse Chronom et Lab Suisse Rech Horlogeres
Bulletin Annuel. Societe Suisse de Chronometrie et Laboratoire Suisse de Recherches Horlogeres — Bull Annu Soc Suisse Chronom Lab Suisse Rech Horlog
Bulletin. Anthropological Institute [*Nagoya*] — B Anthropol Inst
Bulletin. Anthropological Survey of India — Bul Anthro Surv India
Bulletin. Antivenin Institute of America — Bull Antivenin Inst Am
Bulletin. Aomori Agricultural Experiment Station — Bull Aomori Agr Exp Sta
Bulletin. Aomori Agricultural Experiment Station — Bull Aomori Agric Exp Stn
Bulletin. Aomori Apple Experiment Station — Bull Aomori Apple Exp Stn
Bulletin. Aomori Apple Experiment Station/Aomori-Ken Ringo Shikenjo Hokoku — Bull Aomori Apple Exp Sta
Bulletin Apicole — Bull Apic
Bulletin Apicole de Documentation Scientifique et Technique et d'Information — Bull Apic Doc Sci Tech Inf
Bulletin. APM [*Australian Paper Manufacturers*] **Forests Proprietary Ltd.** — Bull APM Forests
Bulletin. Applied Botany and Plant Breeding — Bull Appl Bot Plant Breed
Bulletin. Applied Botany. Genetics and Plant Breeding — Bull Appl Bot Genet Plant Breed
Bulletin. Applied Botany. Genetics and Plant Breeding. Series C. Supplement — Bull Appl Bot Genet Plant Breed Ser C
Bulletin Archeologique. Comite des Travaux Historiques — BCTH
Bulletin Archeologique. Comite des Travaux Historiques et Archeologiques [*A publication*] — BAC
Bulletin Archeologique. Comite des Travaux Historiques et Scientifiques — BACT
Bulletin Archeologique. Comite des Travaux Historiques et Scientifiques [*Paris*] — BACTH
Bulletin Archeologique. Comite des Travaux Historiques et Scientifiques [*Paris*] — BACTHS
Bulletin Archeologique. Comite des Travaux Historiques et Scientifiques — Bull Arch Comite
Bulletin Archeologique. Comite des Travaux Historiques et Scientifiques [*Paris*] — BullArch
Bulletin Archeologique. Comite des Travaux Historiques et Scientifiques (Paris) — BA (Paris)
Bulletin Archeologique de Provence — BA Prov
Bulletin Archeologique du Comite des Travaux Historiques et Scientifiques. Ministere d'Education Nationale — B Archeol
Bulletin Archeologique du Vexin Francais — BA Vexin
Bulletin Archeologique du Vexin Francais — BAVF
Bulletin Archeologique du Vexin Francais — Bull Vexin
Bulletin Archeologique, Historique, et Artistique. Societe Archeologique de Tarn-et-Garonne — B Tarn-et-Garone
Bulletin Archeologique, Historique, et Artistique. Societe Archeologique de Tarn-et-Garonne — BAHASA
Bulletin Archeologique, Historique, et Artistique. Societe Archeologique de Tarn-et-Garonne — Bull Arch Hist
Bulletin Archeologique, Historique, et Artistique. Societe Archeologique de Tarn-et-Garonne — Bull Archeol
Bulletin Archeologique, Historique, et Artistique. Societe Archeologique de Tarn-et-Garonne — Bull Archeol Tarn
Bulletin Archeologique, Historique, et Folklorique. Musee du Rethelois et du Porcien — B Rethel
Bulletin. ARERS [*Association Regionale des Amis de l'Universite et de l'Enseignement Superieur pour la Promotion de l'Etude et la Recherche Scientifiques*] — AREBA8
Bulletin. Arizona Agricultural Experiment Station — Bull Ariz Agr Exp Sta
Bulletin. Arizona Agricultural Experiment Station — Bull Ariz Agric Exp Stn
Bulletin. Arizona Agricultural Experiment Station. Cooperating Extension Service — Bull Ariz Agr Exp Sta Coop Ext Serv
Bulletin. Arizona Water Commission — Bull Ariz Water Comm
Bulletin. Arkansas Agricultural Experiment Station — Bull Ark Agr Exp Sta
Bulletin. Arkansas Agricultural Experiment Station — Bull Ark Agric Exp Stn
Bulletin. Arkansas Agricultural Experiment Station — Bull Arkansas Agric Exp Stn
Bulletin. Armenian Branch. Academy of Sciences. USSR — Bull Arm Branch Acad Sci USSR
Bulletin. Art Institute of Chicago — Bul Art Inst Chic
Bulletin. Arts and Science Division. University of the Ryukyus. Mathematics and Natural Sciences — Bull Arts Sci Div Univ Ryukyus Math Natur Sci

Bulletin. ASIS [*American Society for Information Science*] — BAS
Bulletin. Associated State Engineering Societies — Bull Assoc State Eng Soc
Bulletin. Associated State Engineering Societies. Yearbook — Bull Assoc State Eng Soc Yearb
Bulletin. Association Amicale des Anciens Eleves de la Faculte des Lettres de Paris — BAAFLP
Bulletin. Association Canadienne des Bibliothecaires de Langue Francaise — Bull Ass Can Bibliot Lang Fr
Bulletin. Association de Cadres Dirigeants de l'Industrie pour le Progres Social et Economique — B Assoc Cadres Dir Industr Progres Soc Econ
Bulletin. Association de Demographes du Quebec — Assoc Demographes Quebec Bul
Bulletin. Association de Geographes Francais — B Ass Geogr Fr
Bulletin. Association des Amis de Flaubert — BAF
Bulletin. Association des Amis de l'Art Copte — BAAAC
Bulletin. Association des Amis de l'Universite de Liege — AUL
Bulletin. Association des Amis de l'Universite de Liege — Bul Un L
Bulletin. Association des Amis de l'Universite de Liege — Bull Univ Lg
Bulletin. Association des Amis de Rabelais et de la Deviniere — BAARD
Bulletin. Association des Amis de Rabelais et de la Deviniere — BAR
Bulletin. Association des Amis de Rabelais et de la Deviniere — BARD
Bulletin. Association des Amis des Eglises et de l'Art Coptes — BAEC
Bulletin. Association des Anatomistes — Bull Assoc Anat
Bulletin. Association des Anatomistes (Nancy) — Bull Assoc Anat (Nancy)
Bulletin. Association des Anatomistes (Paris) — Bull Ass Anat (Paris)
Bulletin. Association des Anciens Eleves de l'Ecole Francaise de Meunerie [*A publication*] — AEMBB
Bulletin. Association des Anciens Eleves de l'Ecole Francaise de Meunerie [*France*] — Bull Assoc Anciens Eleves Ecole Fr Meun
Bulletin. Association des Anciens Eleves de l'Institut des Industries de Fermentation de Bruxelles [*Belgium*] — Bull Assoc Anc Eleves Inst Ind Ferment Bruxelles
Bulletin. Association des Anciens Eleves de l'Institut Superieur des Fermentations de Gand — Bull Assoc Anc Eleves Super Ferment Gand
Bulletin. Association des Anciens Etudiants de l'Ecole Superieure de Brasserie de l'Universite de Louvain — Bull Assoc Anc Etud Brass Univ Louv
Bulletin. Association des Anciens Etudiants de l'Ecole Superieure de Brasserie de l'Universite de Louvain — Bull Assoc Anc Etud Ec Super Brass Univ Louv
Bulletin. Association des Anciens Etudiants de l'Ecole Superieure de Brasserie de l'Universite de Louvain — Bull Assoc Anc Etud Ec Super Brass Univ Louvain
Bulletin. Association des Anciens Etudiants en Brasserie de l'Universite de Louvain — Bull Assoc Anc Etud Brass Univ Louvain
Bulletin. Association des Biochimistes des Hopitaux du Quebec — Bull Assoc Biochim Hop Que
Bulletin. Association des Chimistes — Bl Assoc Chim
Bulletin. Association des Chimistes — Bull Assoc Chim
Bulletin. Association des Chimistes de Sucrerie, de Distillerie, et des Industries Agricoles de France et des Colonies — Bull Assoc Chim Sucr Distill Ind Agric Fr Colon
Bulletin. Association des Chimistes de Sucrerie et de Distillerie de France et des Colonies — Bull Assoc Chim Sucr Distill Fr Colon
Bulletin. Association des Diplomes de Microbiologie. Faculte de Pharmacie de Nancy — Bull Ass Dipl Microbiol Nancy
Bulletin. Association des Diplomes de Microbiologie. Faculte de Pharmacie de Nancy — Bull Ass Diplomes Microbiol Fac Pharm Nancy
Bulletin. Association des Diplomes de Microbiologie. Faculte de Pharmacie de Nancy — Bull Assoc Diplomes Microbiol Fac Pharm Nancy
Bulletin. Association des Enseignants de Mathematiques. Serie B [*Rabat*] — Bull Assoc Enseign Math Ser B
Bulletin. Association des Geographes Francais — AGF/B
Bulletin. Association des Geographes Francais — B Ass Geogr Franc
Bulletin. Association des Geographes Francais — B Assoc Geogr Franc
Bulletin. Association des Geographes Francais — Bull Ass Geogr Fr
Bulletin. Association des Gynecologues et Obstetriciens de Langue Francaise — Bull Assoc Gynecol Obstet Lang Fr
Bulletin. Association des Juristes Europeens — Bull Ass Jur Eur
Bulletin. Association des Medecins de Langue Francaise — Bull Ass Med Lang Fr
Bulletin. Association des Mines d'Amiante du Quebec — Bul Assoc Mine Am Quebec
Bulletin. Association d'Oceanographie Physique — Bull Ass Oceanogr Phys
Bulletin. Association for Literary and Linguistic Computing — Bul Assoc Lit Ling Comp
Bulletin. Association for Science and Mathematics Education Penang — Bull Assoc Sci Math Educ Penang
Bulletin. Association for Tropical Biology — Bull Assoc Trop Biol
Bulletin. Association Francaise de Gemmologie — Bull AFG
Bulletin. Association Francaise des Ingenieurs, Chimistes, et Techniciens des Industries du Cuir et Documents et Informations du Centre Technique du Cuir — Bull Assoc Fr Ing Chim Tech Ind Cuir Doc Inf Cent Tech Cuir
Bulletin. Association Francaise des Ingenieurs et Techniciens du Cinema — Bull Assoc Fr Ing Tech Cinema
Bulletin. Association Francaise des Techniciens du Petrole [*France*] — Bull Assoc Fr Tech Pet
Bulletin. Association Francaise d'Etudes Chinoises — Bul Assoc Franc Etud Chin
Bulletin. Association Francaise pour l'Avancement des Sciences — B Ass Av Sci
Bulletin. Association Francaise pour l'Avancement des Sciences — Bull Ass Franc Avance Sci
Bulletin. Association Francaise pour l'Etude du Cancer — Bull Ass Franc Canc
Bulletin. Association Francaise pour l'Etude du Cancer — Bull Assoc Fr Etude Cancer
Bulletin. Association Francaise pour l'Etude du Sol — BUFSA
Bulletin. Association Francaise pour l'Etude du Sol — Bull Ass Fr Etude Sol
Bulletin. Association Francaise pour l'Etude du Sol — Bull Assoc Fr Etud Sol
Bulletin. Association Francaise pour l'Etude du Sol — Bull Assoc Fr Etude Sol
Bulletin. Association Guillaume Bude — B Bude Suppl
Bulletin. Association Guillaume Bude — BAGB
Bulletin. Association Guillaume Bude [*Paris*] — BAssBude
Bulletin. Association Guillaume Bude [*Paris*] — BBude
Bulletin. Association Guillaume Bude — BGB
Bulletin. Association Guillaume Bude — Bul Ass Guil Bude
Bulletin. Association Guillaume Bude — Bul Bude
Bulletin. Association Guillaume Bude — Bull Ass Bude
Bulletin. Association Guillaume Bude — Bull Ass Guillaume Bude
Bulletin. Association Guillaume Bude — Bull Assoc Guillaume Bude
Bulletin. Association Guillaume Bude — Bull Bude
Bulletin. Association Guillaume Bude — Bull G Bude
Bulletin. Association Guillaume Bude. Supplement Critique — BAGB SC
Bulletin. Association Internationale de Geologie de l'Ingenieur — Bull Assoc Int Geol Ing
Bulletin. Association Internationale de la Securite Sociale — B As Int S Soc
Bulletin. Association Internationale de la Securite Sociale — Bull Ass Int Sec Soc
Bulletin. Association Internationale des Documentalistes — Bull Assoc Int Doc
Bulletin. Association Internationale des Documentalistes et Techniciens de l'Information — Bull Assoc Int Doc Tech Inf
Bulletin. Association Internationale d'Etudes du Sud-Est Europeen — Bull AI Et SE Eur
Bulletin. Association Internationale d'Hydrologie Scientifique — Bull Ass Int Hydrol Scient
Bulletin. Association Internationale du Froid. Monthly — Bull Assoc Int Froid Mon
Bulletin. Association Internationale pour la Protection de l'Enfance — Bul Enf
Bulletin. Association Internationale pour l'Histoire du Verre — BAHV
Bulletin. Association Lyonnaise de Recherches Archeologiques — BALA
Bulletin. Association Mathematique du Quebec — Bul/AMQ
Bulletin. Association Medicale Corporative — Bull Ass Med Corp
Bulletin. Association Medicale Haitienne — Bull Ass Med Hait
Bulletin. Association of British Theological and Philosophical Libraries — Bull ABTPL
Bulletin. Association of Engineering Geologists — Bull Assoc Eng Geol
Bulletin. Association of Engineering Geologists — Bull Assoc Engng Geol
Bulletin. Association of Kineticists of India — Bull Assoc Kinet India
Bulletin. Association of Minnesota Entomologists — Bull Assoc Minn Entomol
Bulletin. Association of Operative Millers — Bull Ass Oper Millers
Bulletin. Association of the Technic for Animal Hygiene — Bull Assoc Tech Anim Hyg
Bulletin. Association Permanente des Congres Belges de la Route — Bull Assoc Perm Congr Belg Route
Bulletin. Association Philomathique d'Alsace et de Lorraine — Bull Ass Philomath Alsace et Lorraine
Bulletin. Association Philomatique d'Alsace et de Lorraine — Bull Assoc Philom Alsace Lorraine
Bulletin. Association Pro Aventico — B Ass Pro Aventico
Bulletin. Association pro Aventico — BAA
Bulletin. Association Quebecoise pour l'Etude du Quaternaire — Bulletin-AQQUA
Bulletin. Association Regionale pour l'Etude et la Recherche Scientifiques — Bull ARERS
Bulletin. Association Regionale pour l'Etude et la Recherche Scientifiques — Bull Assoc Reg Etude Rech Sci
Bulletin. Association Royal des Anciens Etudiants en Brasserie de l'Universite de Louvain — Bull Assoc R Anc Etud Brass Univ Louv
Bulletin. Association Royale des Anciens Etudiants en Brasserie de l'Universite de Louvain — Bull Assoc R Anc Etud Brass Univ Louvain
Bulletin. Association Scientifique Algerienne — Bull Assoc Sci Alger
Bulletin. Association Suisse des Electriciens — Bull Ass Suisse El
Bulletin. Association Suisse des Electriciens — Bull Ass Suisse Elec
Bulletin. Association Suisse des Electriciens — Bull Assoc Suisse Electr
Bulletin. Association Technique de Fonderie — Bull Ass Tech Fo
Bulletin. Association Technique de Fonderie — Bull Assoc Tech Fonderie
Bulletin. Association Technique de l'Industrie Papetiere — Bull Ass Tech Ind Pap
Bulletin. Association Technique de l'Industrie Papetiere — Bull Assoc Tech Ind Papet
Bulletin. Association Technique Maritime et Aeronautique — BATMA
Bulletin. Association Technique Maritime et Aeronautique [*France*] — Bull Assoc Tech Mar Aeronaut
Bulletin. Association Technique Maritime et Aeronautique — Bull Assoc Tech Marit Aeronaut
Bulletin. Astronomical Institutes of Czechoslovakia — B Astr I Cz
Bulletin. Astronomical Institutes of Czechoslovakia — Bull Astron Inst Czech
Bulletin. Astronomical Institutes of Czechoslovakia — Bull Astronom Inst of Czechoslovakia
Bulletin. Astronomical Institutes of the Netherlands — Bull Astr Inst Neth
Bulletin. Astronomical Institutes of the Netherlands — Bull Astron Inst Neth
Bulletin. Astronomical Institutes of the Netherlands. Supplement Series — BAINB
Bulletin. Astronomical Institutes of the Netherlands. Supplement Series — Bull Astron Inst Neth Suppl Ser
Bulletin. Astronomical Society of India — Bull Astron Soc India
Bulletin Astronomique — Bull Astr
Bulletin Astronomique [*France*] — Bull Astron
Bulletin Astronomique. Observatoire Royale de Belgique — Bull Astron Observ Belg

Bulletin. Atomic Energy Research Institute of Korea — Bull At Energy Res Inst Korea
Bulletin. Auckland Institute and Museum — B Auckland Inst Mus
Bulletin. Auckland Institute and Museum — Bull Auckl Inst Mus
Bulletin. Australasian Institute of Mining and Metallurgy — Bull Australas Inst Min Metall
Bulletin. Australian Association of Occupational Therapists — Bul Aust Assn Occupational Therapists
Bulletin. Australian Mathematical Society — ANLBA
Bulletin. Australian Mathematical Society — Bull Aust Math Soc
Bulletin. Australian Mathematical Society — Bull Austral Math Soc
Bulletin. Australian Mineral Development Laboratories — Bull Aust Miner Dev Lab
Bulletin. Australian Road Research Board — Bull Aust Road Res Bd
Bulletin. Australian Society for the Study of Labour History — Bul Aust Soc Stud Lab Hist
Bulletin. Australian Society for the Study of Labour History — Bull Aust Soc Stud Lab Hist
Bulletin. Australian Society of Exploration Geophysicists — Bull Aust Soc Explor Geophys
Bulletin. Australian Welding Research Association — Bull Aust Weld Res Assoc
Bulletin. Australian-Asian Association of Victoria — Bul Aust Asian Assn of Vic
Bulletin aux Producteurs — Bul Prod
Bulletin. Ayer Clinical Laboratory of the Pennsylvania Hospital — Bull Ayer Clin Lab PA Hosp
Bulletin. Azabu University of Veterinary Medicine — Bull Azabu Univ Vet Med
Bulletin. Azabu Veterinary College — Bull Azabu Vet Coll
Bulletin B. Oklahoma Agricultural Experiment Station — Bull B Okla Agric Exp Stn
Bulletin B. Wyoming Agricultural Experiment Station — Bull B Wyo Agric Exp Stn
Bulletin Balai Penelitian Perkebunan Medan — Bull Balai Penelitian Perkebunan Medan
Bulletin. Banque Nationale — Bull BN
Bulletin. Banque Nationale de Belgique — B Banque Nat Belgique
Bulletin. Banque Nationale de Belgique — Bul Belg
Bulletin. Basic Science Research Institute. Inha University — Bull Basic Sci Res Inst Inha Univ
Bulletin. Basrah Natural History Museum — Bull Basrah Nat Hist Mus
Bulletin Baudelairien — B Baud
Bulletin Belge de Metrologie [*Service de la Metrologie*] — Bull Belg Metrol
Bulletin. Belgian Physical Society — Bull Belg Phys Soc
Bulletin Belgicatom — BUBEA
Bulletin Belgicatom — Bull Belgicatom
Bulletin. Bell Museum of Pathobiology — Bull Bell Mus Pathobiol
Bulletin. Benelux — Bull Benelux
Bulletin. Benelux — Bull BNL
Bulletin. Bergen County Dental Society — Bull Bergen Cty Dent Soc
Bulletin. Bernice P. Bishop Museum — Bull Bernice P Bishop Mus
Bulletin Bibliographique — Bul Bibl
Bulletin Bibliographique de CREDIF [*Centre de Recherche et d'Etude pour la Diffusion du Francais*] **Service de Documentation** — CREDIF
Bulletin Bibliographique de Pedologie. Office de la Recherche Scientifique et Technique d'Outre-Mer — Bull Biblphique Pedol ORSTOM
Bulletin Bibliographique et Pedagogique du Musee Belge — Bull Bibliogr Pedag Musee Belge
Bulletin Bibliographique et Pedagogique du Musee Belge — Bullet Mus Belge
Bulletin Bibliographique et Pedagogique. Musee Belge — Bull Mus Belge
Bulletin Bibliographique. Musee Belge — BBMB
Bulletin Bibliographique. Musee Belge — BBPMB
Bulletin Bibliographique. Musee Belge — BMB
Bulletin Bibliographique. Musee Belge — MBBull
Bulletin Bibliographique. Societe Internationale Arthurienne — BBSIA
Bulletin Bibliographique. Societe Rencesvals — Bull Bibl Soc Rencesvals
Bulletin. Bibliotheque Nationale — Bull Bibl Natl
Bulletin Bimensual. Societe Linneenne de Lyon — Bull Bimens Soc Linn Lyon
Bulletin Bimestriel — Bull Bime
Bulletin Bimestriel. INACOL [*Institut National pour l'Amelioration des Conserves de Legumes*] — Bull Bimest INACOL
Bulletin Bimestriel. Institut National pour l'Amelioration des Conserves de Legumes (Belgium) — Bull Bimest Inst Natl Amelior Conserves Legumes (Belg)
Bulletin Bimestriel. Societe de Comptabilite de France — B Bimestr Soc Comptabil France
Bulletin. Bingham Oceanographic Collection — Bull Bingham Oceanogr Collect
Bulletin. Bingham Oceanographic Collection. Yale University — Bull Bingham Oceanogr Collect Yale Univ
Bulletin. Biochemical Research Laboratory. Bulgarian Academy of Sciences — Bull Biochem Res Lab Bulg Acad Sci
Bulletin. Biogeographical Society of Japan — Bull Biogeogr Soc Japan
Bulletin. Biogeographical Society of Japan — Bull Biogeogr Soc Jpn
Bulletin. Biological Association. University of Amoy/Hsia-Ta Shengwu-Hsueeh-Hui Ch'i K'an — Bull Biol Assoc Univ Amoy
Bulletin. Biological Board of Canada — Bull Biol Board Can
Bulletin. Biological Research Centre (Baghdad) — Bull Biol Res Cent (Baghdad)
Bulletin. Biological Research Centre. Publication (Baghdad) — Bull Biol Res Cent Publ (Baghdad)
Bulletin. Biological Society of Hiroshima University — Bull Biol Soc Hiroshima Univ
Bulletin. Biological Society of Washington — Bull Biol Soc Wash
Bulletin Biologique de la France et de la Belgique — BUBFA
Bulletin Biologique de la France et de la Belgique — Bull Biol Fr Belg
Bulletin Biologique de la France et de la Belgique — Bull Biol France et Belgique
Bulletin. Biology (Beijing) — Bull Biol (Beijing)
Bulletin. Bismuth Institute — Bull Bismuth Inst
Bulletin. Bismuth Institute (Brussels) — Bull Bismuth Inst Brussels
Bulletin. Board of Celtic Studies — B Celt St
Bulletin. Board of Celtic Studies — BBCS
Bulletin. Board of Celtic Studies — Bull BCS
Bulletin. Board of Celtic Studies [*Cardiff*] — Bull Bd Celtic Studies
Bulletin. Board of Celtic Studies — Bull Board Celtic Stud
Bulletin. Board of Celtic Studies/Bwletin y Bwrdd Gwybodau Celtaidd — B Bd Celt S
Bulletin. Board of Science and Art (New Zealand) — Bull Board Sci Art (NZ)
Bulletin. Boris Kidric Institute of Nuclear Sciences — Bull Boris Kidric Inst Nucl Sci
Bulletin. Boris Kidric Institute of Nuclear Sciences. Biology — Bull Boris Kidric Inst Nucl Sci Biol
Bulletin. Boris Kidric Institute of Nuclear Sciences. Ceramics and Metallurgy — Bull Boris Kidric Inst Nucl Sci Ceram Metall
Bulletin. Boris Kidric Institute of Nuclear Sciences. Chemistry — BKBCB
Bulletin. Boris Kidric Institute of Nuclear Sciences. Chemistry — Bull Boris Kidric Inst Nucl Sci Chem
Bulletin. Boris Kidric Institute of Nuclear Sciences. Electronics — Bull Boris Kidric Inst Nucl Sci Electron
Bulletin. Boris Kidric Institute of Nuclear Sciences. Nuclear Engineering — Bull Boris Kidric Inst Nucl Sci Nucl Eng
Bulletin. Boris Kidric Institute of Nuclear Sciences. Physics — Bull Boris Kidric Inst Nucl Sci Phys
Bulletin. Boris Kidric Institute of Nuclear Sciences. Supplement — BKISA
Bulletin. Boris Kidric Institute of Nuclear Sciences. Supplement — Bull Boris Kidric Inst Nucl Sci Suppl
Bulletin. Boston Society of Natural History — Bull Boston Soc Nat Hist
Bulletin. Botanic Gardens of Buitenzorg — Bull Bot Gard Buitenzorg
Bulletin. Botanical Society. College of Science (Nagpur) — Bull Bot Soc Coll Sci (Nagpur)
Bulletin. Botanical Society. Government Science College (Jabalpur (MP) India) [*A publication*] — Bull Bot Soc Gov Sci Coll (Jabalpur (MP) India)
Bulletin. Botanical Society of Bengal — Bull Bot Soc Bengal
Bulletin. Botanical Society. University of Saugar — Bull Bot Soc Univ Saugar
Bulletin. Botanical Survey of India — Bull Bot Surv India
Bulletin. Brackishwater Aquaculture Development Centre — Bull Brackishwater Aquacult Dev Cent
Bulletin. British Antarctic Survey [*Cambridge*] — Bull Br Antarct Surv
Bulletin. British Arachnological Society — Bull Br Arachnol Soc
Bulletin. British Bee-Keepers Association. Research Committee — Bull Br Beekprs Ass Res Comm
Bulletin. British Carnation Society — Bull Brit Carnation Soc
Bulletin. British Cast Iron Research Association — Bull Br Cast Iron Res Assoc
Bulletin. British Columbia Department of Mines and Petroleum Resources — Bull BC Dep Mines Pet Resour
Bulletin. British Columbia. Ministry of Energy, Mines, and Petroleum Resources — Bull BC Minist Energy Mines Pet Resour
Bulletin. British Columbia. Ministry of Mines and Petroleum Resources — Bull BC Minist Mines Pet Resour
Bulletin. British Columbia Police Commission — Bul Br Columbia Police Com
Bulletin. British Hydromechanics Research Association — Bull Br Hydromech Res Ass
Bulletin. British Interplanetary Society — Bull Br Interplanet Soc
Bulletin. British Museum — B Br Mus
Bulletin. British Museum (Natural History) — Bull Brit Mus Natur Hist
Bulletin. British Museum (Natural History). Botany — Bull Br Mus (Nat Hist) Bot
Bulletin. British Museum. Natural History. Botany Series — Bull Brit Mus Natur Hist Bot Ser
Bulletin. British Museum (Natural History). Entomology — Bull Br Mus (Nat Hist) Entomol
Bulletin. British Museum (Natural History). Entomology. Supplement — Bull Br Mus (Nat Hist) Entomol Suppl
Bulletin. British Museum (Natural History). Geology — Bull Br Mus (Nat Hist) Geol
Bulletin. British Museum (Natural History). Geology — Bull Brit Mus Natur Hist Geol
Bulletin. British Museum (Natural History). Geology. Supplement — Bull Br Mus (Nat Hist) Geol Suppl
Bulletin. British Museum (Natural History). Historical Series — Bull Br Mus (Nat Hist) Hist Ser
Bulletin. British Museum (Natural History). Mineralogy — Bull Br Mus Nat Hist Mineral
Bulletin. British Museum. Natural History. Zoology — Brit Museum Nat Hist Bull Zool
Bulletin. British Museum (Natural History). Zoology — Bull Br Mus (Nat Hist) Zool
Bulletin. British Museum (Natural History). Zoology. Supplement — Bull Br Mus (Nat Hist) Zool Suppl
Bulletin. British Mycological Society — Bull Br Mycol Soc
Bulletin. British Non-Ferrous Metals Research Association — Bull Br Non Ferrous Met Res Assoc
Bulletin. British Ornithologists' Club — BBOC
Bulletin. British Ornithologists' Club — Bull Br Ornithol Club
Bulletin. British Psychological Society — B Br Psycho
Bulletin. British Psychological Society — Brit Psychol Soc Bull
Bulletin. British Psychological Society — Bull B Psych Soc
Bulletin. British Psychological Society — Bull Brit Psychol Soc
Bulletin. British School of Archaeology, Jerusalem [*1922-25, after 1927 included in PEFOS*] — BBSAJ
Bulletin. British Society for the History of Science — Bull Brit Soc Hist Sci
Bulletin. British Society of Rheology — Bull Br Soc Rheol
Bulletin. Bromeliad Society — Bull Bromeliad Soc
Bulletin. Bronx County Dental Society — Bull Bronx Cty Dent Soc
Bulletin. Brooklyn Entomological Society — Bull Brooklyn Ent Soc

Bulletin. Brooklyn Entomological Society — Bull Brooklyn Entomol Soc
Bulletin. Brooklyn Museum — BBM
Bulletin. Buddhist Cultural Institute. Ryukoku University — B Buddhist Cult Inst Ryukoku Univ
Bulletin. Buffalo General Hospital — Bull Buffalo Gen Hosp
Bulletin. Buffalo Naturalists' Field Club — Bull Buffalo Naturalists Field Club
Bulletin. Buffalo Society of Natural Sciences — Bull Buffalo Soc Nat Sci
Bulletin. Builders Association of India — Bul Build Assoc India
Bulletin. Bureau de Recherches Geologiques et Minieres — Bull Bur Rech Geol Min
Bulletin. Bureau de Recherches Geologiques et Minieres [*France*] — Bull Bur Rech Geol Minieres
Bulletin. Bureau de Recherches Geologiques et Minieres. Deuxieme Serie. Section 2. Geologie des Gites Mineraux — Bull Bur Rech Geol Minieres Deuxieme Ser Sect 2
Bulletin. Bureau de Recherches Geologiques et Minieres. Deuxieme Serie. Section 3. Hydrogeologie - Geologie de l'Ingenieur — Bull Bur Rech Geol Minieres Deuxieme Ser Sect 3
Bulletin. Bureau de Recherches Geologiques et Minieres (France) — Bull Bur Rech Geol Min Fr
Bulletin. Bureau de Recherches Geologiques et Minieres (France). Section 1. Geologie de la France — Bull Bur Rech Geol Minieres (Fr) Sect 1
Bulletin. Bureau de Recherches Geologiques et Minieres (France). Section 2. Geologie Appliquee — Bull Bur Rech Geol Minieres (Fr) Sect 2
Bulletin. Bureau de Recherches Geologiques et Minieres (France). Section 2. Geologie Appliquee — Bull Bur Rech Geol Minieres Sec 2 Geol Appl
Bulletin. Bureau de Recherches Geologiques et Minieres (France). Section 3. Hydrogeologie - Geologie de l'Ingenieur — Bull Bur Rech Geol Minieres (Fr) Sect 3
Bulletin. Bureau de Recherches Geologiques et Minieres (France). Section 4. Geologie Generale — Bull Bur Rech Geol Minieres (Fr) Sect 4
Bulletin. Bureau de Recherches Geologiques et Minieres. Section 1. Geologie de la France — Bull Bur Rech Geol Min Sect 1 Fr
Bulletin. Bureau de Recherches Geologiques et Minieres. Section 2. Geologie Appliquee. Chronique des Mines (France) — Bull Bur Rech Geol Min Sect 2 Geol Appl Chron Mines (Fr)
Bulletin. Bureau de Recherches Geologiques et Minieres. Section 2. Geologie Appliquee (France) — Bull Bur Rech Geol Min Sect 2 Geol Appl (Fr)
Bulletin. Bureau de Recherches Geologiques et Minieres. Section 2. Geologie des Gites Mineraux (France) — Bull Bur Rech Geol Min Sect 2 Geol Gites Miner (Fr)
Bulletin. Bureau de Recherches Geologiques et Minieres. Section 3. Hydrogeologie - Geologie de l'Ingenieur (France) — Bull Bur Rech Geol Min Sect 3 (Fr)
Bulletin. Bureau de Recherches Geologiques et Minieres. Section II. Geologie Appliquee — Bull Bur Rech Geol Min Sect II Geol Appl
Bulletin. Bureau de Recherches Geologiques et Minieres. Serie 2. Section 1 — Bull Bur Rech Geol Minieres Ser 2 Sect 1
Bulletin. Bureau de Recherches Geologiques et Minieres. Serie 2. Section 2 [*France*] — Bull Bur Rech Geol Minieres Ser 2 Sect 2
Bulletin. Bureau de Recherches Geologiques et Minieres. Serie 2. Section 3 — Bull Bur Rech Geol Minieres Ser 2 Sect 3
Bulletin. Bureau de Recherches Geologiques et Minieres. Serie 2. Section 4 — Bull Bur Rech Geol Minieres Ser 2 Sect 4
Bulletin. Bureau d'Ethnologie (Port-au-Prince) — Bull Bur Ethnol Port Au Prince
Bulletin. Bureau of Agricultural Intelligence and Plant Diseases — Bull Bur Agric Intell Plant Des
Bulletin. Bureau of American Ethnology — B Bur Am Ethnol
Bulletin. Bureau of American Ethnology — BBAE
Bulletin. Bureau of Animal Industry. United States Department of Agriculture — Bull Bureau Animal Indust US Dept Agric
Bulletin. Bureau of Bio Technology — Bull Bur Bio Technol
Bulletin. Bureau of Chemistry. United States Department of Agriculture — Bull Bur Chem US Dep Agric
Bulletin. Bureau of Entomology. United States Department of Agriculture — Bull Bur Ent US Dep Agric
Bulletin. Bureau of Geology and Topography (New Jersey) — Bull Bur Geol Topogr (NJ)
Bulletin. Bureau of Mineral Resources. Geology and Geophysics (Australia) — Bull Bur Miner Resour Geol Geophys (Aust)
Bulletin. Bureau of Mines and Geology (State of Montana) — Bull Bur Mines Geol (State Montana)
Bulletin. Bureau of Standards (US) — Bull Bur Stand US
Bulletin. Business Historical Society — Bull Bus Hist Soc
Bulletin. Bussey Institution — Bull Bussey Inst
Bulletin. Byzantine Institute — BByzI
Bulletin. Byzantine Institute of America — B Byz
Bulletin. Byzantine Institute of America — BBI
Bulletin. Calcutta Mathematical Society — BCMSB
Bulletin. Calcutta Mathematical Society — Bull Calcutta Math Soc
Bulletin. Calcutta School of Tropical Medicine — BCSTA
Bulletin. Calcutta School of Tropical Medicine — Bull Calcutta Sch Trop Med
Bulletin. California Academy of Sciences — Bul Calif Acad Sci
Bulletin. California Agricultural Experiment Station — Bull Calif Agr Exp Sta
Bulletin. California Agricultural Experiment Station — Bull Calif Agric Exp Stn
Bulletin. California Department of Agriculture — Bull Calif Dep Agric
Bulletin. California Department of Agriculture — Bull Calif Dept Agr
Bulletin. California. Division of Mines and Geology — Bull Calif Div Mines Geol
Bulletin. California State Mining Bureau — Bull Calif State Min Bur
Bulletin. Canada Corporations — Bul Can Corp
Bulletin. Canada Corporations. Bankruptcy and Insolvency — Bul Can Corp Bankrupt Insolv
Bulletin. Canadian Biochemical Society — Bull Can Biochem Soc
Bulletin. Canadian Celtic Arts Association — Bul Can Celt Art Assoc
Bulletin. Canadian Folk Music Society — Bul Can Folk Mus Soc
Bulletin. Canadian Institute of Mining and Metallurgy — Bull Can Inst Min Metall
Bulletin. Canadian Mining Institute — Bull Can Min Inst
Bulletin. Canadian Petroleum Geology — Bull Canad Petrol Geol
Bulletin. Canadian Wheat Board — Bull Can Wheat Board
Bulletin. Cancer Institute. Okayama University Medical School — Bull Cancer Inst Okayama Univ Med Sch
Bulletin. Canton Christian College — Bull Canton Christian Coll
Bulletin. Caoutchoucs de l'Institut Francais d'Outre-Mer — Bull Caoutch Inst Fr Outre Mer
Bulletin. Cardiovascular Research Center — Bul Card Res Cent
Bulletin. Cardiovascular Research Center (Houston) — Bull Cardiovas Res Cent (Houston)
Bulletin. Carnegie Institute of Technology. Mining and Metallurgical Investigations — Bull Carnegie Inst Technol Min Metall Invest
Bulletin. Carnegie Museum of Natural History — Bull Carnegie Mus Nat Hist
Bulletin. Center for Children's Books — Bul Child Bks
Bulletin. Center for Children's Books — Bull CCB
Bulletin. Central Asia Scientific Research Cotton Institute — Bull Cent Asia Sci Res Cotton Inst
Bulletin. Central Bank of Ceylon — Bul Cent Bank Ceylon
Bulletin. Central Building Research Institute (Roorkee, India) — Bull Cent Build Res Inst (Roorkee India)
Bulletin. Central Food Technological Research Institute (Mysore) — Bull Cent Food Technol Res Inst (Mysore)
Bulletin. Central Glass and Ceramic Research Institute (Calcutta) — Bull Cent Glass Ceram Res Inst (Calcutta)
Bulletin. Central Helminthological Laboratory. Bulgarian Academy of Sciences — Bull Cent Helminthol Lab Bulg Acad Sci
Bulletin. Central Inspection Institute of Weights and Measures (Tokyo) — Bull Cent Insp Inst Weights Meas (Tokyo)
Bulletin. Central Leather Research Institute (Madras) — Bull Cent Leather Res Inst (Madras)
Bulletin. Central Marine Fisheries Research Institute — Bull Cent Mar Fish Res Inst
Bulletin. Central Mississippi Valley American Studies Association — BCMVASA
Bulletin. Central Research Institute. University of Kerala (India). Series C. Natural Science — Bull Cent Res Inst Univ Kerala (India) Ser C Nat Sci
Bulletin. Central Research Institute. University of Kerala (Trivandrum). Series C. Natural Science — Bull Cent Res Inst Univ Kerala (Trivandrum) Ser C
Bulletin. Central Research Institute. University of Travancore — Bull Cent Res Inst Univ Trav
Bulletin. Central Research Laboratory. Osaka Institute of Technology — Bull Central Res Lab OIT
Bulletin. Centre Belge d'Etude et de Documentation des Eaux — Bull Cent Belge Etude Doc Eaux
Bulletin. Centre de Compilation de Donnees Neutroniques — BDCNB
Bulletin. Centre de Compilation de Donnees Neutroniques [*France*] — Bull Cent Compilation Donnees Neutroniques
Bulletin. Centre de Documentation d'Etudes Juridiques, Economiques, et Sociales — B Centre Docum Et Jur Econ Soc
Bulletin. Centre de Physique Nucleaire. Universite Libre de Bruxelles [*A publication*] — Bull Cent Phys Nucl Univ Lib Bruxelles
Bulletin. Centre de Physique Nucleaire. Universite Libre de Bruxelles — Bull Cent Phys Nucl Univ Libre Bruxelles
Bulletin. Centre de Recherches Agronomiques de Bingerville — Bull Centr Rech Agron Bingerville
Bulletin. Centre de Recherches de Pau — Bull Cent Rech Pau
Bulletin. Centre de Recherches et d'Enseignement de l'Antiquite (Angers) [*A publication*] — B (Angers)
Bulletin. Centre de Recherches et d'Essais de Chatou — BCREA
Bulletin. Centre de Recherches et d'Essais de Chatou [*France*] — Bull Cent Rech Essais Chatou
Bulletin. Centre d'Etudes et de Discussion de Litterature Francaise. Universite de Bordeaux — BCEDLFB
Bulletin. Centre d'Etudes et de Recherches Scientifiques (Biarritz) — Bull Cent Etud Rech Sci (Biarritz)
Bulletin. Centre d'Information du Material et des Articles de Bureau — Bull CIMAB
Bulletin. Centre d'Information et d'Etude du Credit — B Centre Inform Et Credit
Bulletin. Centre Europeen de la Culture — B Centre Europ Cult
Bulletin. Centre International des Engrais Chimiques — Bull Cent Int Engrais Chim
Bulletin. Centre Marin des Blanchons — Bul Cent Mar Blanch
Bulletin. Centre of Excellence in Geology. University of Peshawar — Bull Cent Excellence Geol Univ Peshawar
Bulletin. Centre of Leisure Studies. Acadia University — Bul Cent Leisure Stud Acadia Univ
Bulletin. Centre Polonais de Recherches Scientifiques de Paris — Bull Centre Pol Rech Sci Paris
Bulletin. Centre Protestant d'Etudes — BCPE
Bulletin. Centre Textile de Controle et de Recherche Scientifique — Bull Cent Text Controle Rech Sci
Bulletin. Centres de Recherches Exploration-Production ELF [*Essences et Lubrifiants de France*] **- Aquitaine** — BCRED
Bulletin. Centres de Recherches Exploration-Production ELF [*Essences et Lubrifiants de France*] **- Aquitaine** — Bull Cent Rech Explor ELF Aquitaine
Bulletin. Centres de Recherches Exploration-Production ELF [*Essences et Lubrifiants de France*] **- Aquitaine** — Bull Cent Rech Explor Prod ELF Aquitaine
Bulletin. Centres de Recherches Exploration-Production ELF [*Essences et Lubrifiants de France*] **- Aquitaine** — Bull Centres Rech Explor-Prod ELF-Aquitaine
Bulletin. Centres d'Etudes Techniques Agricoles — Bull CETA
Bulletin. Cercle Archeologique Hesbaye-Condroz — B Hesbaye-Condroz
Bulletin. Cercle Archeologique Hesbaye-Condroz — Bull Cerc Arch Hesbaye-Condroz

Bulletin. Cercle Archeologique, Litteraire, et Artistique de Malines — BCAM
Bulletin. Cercle Belge de Linguistique — BCBL
Bulletin. Cercle Benelux d'Histoire de la Pharmacie — Bull Cerc Benel Hist Pharm
Bulletin. Cercle Benelux d'Histoire de la Pharmacie — Bull Cercle Benelux Hist Pharm
Bulletin. Cercle d'Etudes des Metaux — Bull Cercle Etud Met
Bulletin. Cercle d'Etudes des Metaux — Bull Cercle Etud Metaux
Bulletin. Cercle d'Etudes Numismatiques — B Cercle Num
Bulletin. Cercle d'Etudes Numismatiques — BCEN
Bulletin. Cercle Ernest Renan [*Paris*] — BullCER
Bulletin. Cercle Francois Laurent — Bull CFL
Bulletin. Cercle Gabriel-Marcel — Bul Cerc Gabriel Marcel
Bulletin. Cercle General d'Horticulture — Bull Cercle Gen Hort
Bulletin. Cercle Historique et Archeologique de Courtrai — BCHAC
Bulletin. Cercle Juif — Bul Cerc Juif
Bulletin. Cercle Linguistique de Copenhague — BCLC
Bulletin. Cercle Zoologique Congolais — Bull Cercle Zool Congolais
Bulletin CETIOM. Centre Technique Interprofessionnel des Oleagineux Metropolitains — Bull CETIOM Cent Tech Interprof Ol Metrop
Bulletin. Ceylon Fisheries. Ceylon Department of Fisheries — Bull Ceyl Fish
Bulletin. Chambre de Commerce d'Agriculture, d'Industrie, et des Mines du Gabon — Chambre Commer Gabon Bul
Bulletin. Chambre de Commerce Francaise et Organe Officiel du Tourisme Francaise en Australie — Bul Chambre Com Francaise
Bulletin. Charleston Museum — Bull Charleston Mus
Bulletin. Chemical Research Institute of Non-Aqueous Solutions. Tohoku University [*Japan*] — Bull Chem Res Inst Non-Aqueous Solutions Tohoku Univ
Bulletin. Chemical Society of Japan — B Chem S J
Bulletin. Chemical Society of Japan — BCSJA
Bulletin. Chemical Society of Japan — Bl Chem Soc Jap
Bulletin. Chemical Society of Japan — Bull Chem Soc Jap
Bulletin. Chemical Society of Japan — Bull Chem Soc Japan
Bulletin. Chemists and Technologists of Macedonia — Bull Chem Technol Macedonia
Bulletin. Chest Disease Research Institute. Kyoto University — Bull Chest Dis Res Inst Kyoto Univ
Bulletin. Chiba College of Agriculture — Bull Chiba Agric
Bulletin. Chiba College of Horticulture/Chiba Koto Engeigakko Gakujutsu Hokoku — Bull Chiba Coll Hort
Bulletin. Chiba Prefectural Research Institute for Environmental Pollution — Bull Chiba Prefect Res Inst Environ Pollut
Bulletin. Chiba Prefecture Agricultural Experiment Station [*Japan*] — Bull Chiba Prefect Agri Exp Stn
Bulletin. Chiba Sericultural Experiment Station — Bull Chiba Seric Exp Stn
Bulletin. Chiba-ken Agricultural Experiment Station — Bull Chiba-Ken Agr Exp Sta
Bulletin. Chicago Academy of Sciences — Bull Chic Acad Sci
Bulletin. Chicago Herpetological Society — Bull Chic Herpetol Soc
Bulletin. Chichibu Museum of Natural History — Bull Chichibu Mus Nat Hist
Bulletin. Chinese Association for the Advancement of Science — Bull Chin Assoc Adv Sci
Bulletin. Chinese Association for the Advancement of Science — Bull Chin Assoc Advancem Sci
Bulletin. Chinese Botanical Society — Bull Chin Bot Soc
Bulletin Chirurgical des Accidents du Travail — Bull Chir Accid Trav
Bulletin. Christian Association for Psychological Studies — Bul Christ Assoc Psych Stud
Bulletin. Christian Institutes of Islamic Studies — BCIIS
Bulletin. Christian Institutes of Islamic Studies — Bul Chr Inst Islamic St
Bulletin. Chubu Institute of Technology — Bull Chubu Inst Technol
Bulletin. Chugoku Agricultural Experiment Station. Series A, D, and E — Bull Chugoku Agr Exp Sta Ser A Ser D Ser E
Bulletin. Chugoku National Agricultural Experiment Station — Bull Chugoku Agr Exp Sta
Bulletin. Chugoku National Agricultural Experiment Station. Series A (Crop Division) — Bull Chugoku Natl Agric Exp Stn Ser A
Bulletin. Chugoku National Agricultural Experiment Station. Series A (Crop Division) — Bull Chugoku Natl Agric Exp Stn Ser A (Crop Div)
Bulletin. Chugoku National Agricultural Experiment Station. Series B (Livestock Division) — Bull Chugoku Natl Agric Exp Stn Ser B
Bulletin. Chugoku National Agricultural Experiment Station. Series B (Livestock Division) — Bull Chugoku Natl Agric Exp Stn Ser B (Livest Div)
Bulletin. Chugoku National Agricultural Experiment Station. Series E (Environment Division) — Bull Chugoku Natl Agric Exp Stn Ser E
Bulletin. Chugoku National Agricultural Experiment Station. Series E (Environment Division) — Bull Chugoku Natl Agric Exp Stn Ser E (Environ Div)
Bulletin. Chukyo Women's College — Bull Chukyo Women's Coll
Bulletin. Chukyo Women's University — Bull Chukyo Women's Univ
Bulletin. Chungking Institute of Industrial Research — Bull Chungking Inst Ind Res
Bulletin. Cincinnati Dental Society — Bull Cinci Dent Soc
Bulletin. Cincinnati Dental Society — CNDBA
Bulletin. Cincinnati Historical Society — BCHS
Bulletin. City Hospital of Akron [*United States*] — Bull City Hosp Akr
Bulletin. Claremont Pomological Club — Bull Claremont Pomol Club
Bulletin. Classe des Lettres et des Sciences Morales et Politiques. Academie Royale de Belgique — B Acad Roy Belg
Bulletin. Classe des Sciences. Academie Royale de Belgique — B CSAR Belg
Bulletin. Classe des Sciences. Academie Royale de Belgique — Bull Cl Sci Acad R Belg
Bulletin. Classe des Sciences. Academie Royale de Belgique — Bull Cl Sci Acad Royale Belg
Bulletin. Classe des Sciences. Academie Royale de Belgique — Bull Classe Sci Acad Roy Belg
Bulletin. Classe des Sciences. Academie Royale de Belgique. 5e Serie — Bull Cl Sci Acad R Belg 5e Ser
Bulletin. Classe Physico-Mathematique. Academie Imperiale des Sciences de St. Petersbourg — Bull Cl Phys Math Acad Imp Sci St Petersbourg
Bulletin. Classification Society — Bull Classific Soc
Bulletin. Clemson Agricultural Experiment Station — Bull Clemson Agr Exp Sta
Bulletin. Clemson University. Cooperative Extension Service — Bull Clemson Univ Coop Ext Serv
Bulletin. Cleveland Dental Society — Bull Cleve Dent Soc
Bulletin. Cleveland Medical Library — Bull Cleveland Med Libr
Bulletin. Cleveland Medical Library Association — Bull Cleve Med Libr Assoc
Bulletin. Cleveland Museum of Art — B Clev Mus
Bulletin. Cleveland Museum of Art — B Cleveland Mus Art
Bulletin. Cleveland Museum of Art — BCMA
Bulletin. Cleveland Museum of Art — Bull Cleveland Museum
Bulletin. Cleveland Scientific and Technical Institution — Bull Cleveland Sci Tech Inst
Bulletin. Coconut Research Institute (Ceylon) — Bull Cocon Res Inst (Cey)
Bulletin. Coconut Research Institute (Ceylon) — Bull Cocon Res Inst (Ceylon)
Bulletin. College Art Association of America — Bull Coll Art Ass
Bulletin. College of Agricultural Sciences (Mosonmagyarovar, Hungary) — Bull Coll Agric Sci (Mosonmagyarovar Hung)
Bulletin. College of Agriculture and Forestry. University of Nanking — Bull Coll Agr Forest Univ Nanking
Bulletin. College of Agriculture and Veterinary Medicine. Nihon University — Bull Coll Agric Vet Med Nihon Univ
Bulletin. College of Agriculture. Research Center. Washington State University — Bull Coll Agric Res Cent Wash St Univ
Bulletin. College of Agriculture. Research Center. Washington State University — Bull Coll Agric Res Cent Wash State Univ
Bulletin. College of Agriculture. Tokyo Imperial University — Bull Coll Agric Tokyo Imp Univ
Bulletin. College of Agriculture. University of Teheran — Bull Coll Agric Univ Teheran
Bulletin. College of Agriculture. Utsunomiya University — Bull Coll Agr Utsunomiya Univ
Bulletin. College of Agriculture. Utsunomiya University — Bull Coll Agric Utsunomiya Univ
Bulletin. College of Arts and Sciences. Baghdad — Bull Coll Arts Baghdad
Bulletin. College of Engineering. Hosei University — Bull Coll Eng Hosei Univ
Bulletin. College of Engineering. National Taiwan University — Bull Coll Eng Natl Taiwan Univ
Bulletin. College of Foreign Studies (Yokohama). Natural Science — Bull Coll Foreign Stud (Yokohama) Nat Sci
Bulletin. College of General Education. Nagoya City University. Natural Science Section — Bull Coll Gen Educ Nagoya City Univ Nat Sci Sect
Bulletin. College of Science (Baghdad) — Bull College Sci (Baghdad)
Bulletin. College of Science. Part 1 [*Baghdad*] — Bull Coll Sci 1
Bulletin. College of Science. University of Baghdad — Bull Coll Sci Univ Baghdad
Bulletin. College of Science. University of the Ryukyus — Bull Coll Sci Univ Ryukyus
Bulletin. Colonial Institute of Amsterdam — B Colon Inst Amst
Bulletin Colorado Agricultural College. Colorado Experiment Station — Bull Colorado Agric Coll Colorado Exp Sta
Bulletin. Colorado Agricultural Experiment Station — Bull Colo Agr Exp Sta
Bulletin. Colorado Agricultural Experiment Station — Bull Colo Agric Exp Stn
Bulletin. Colorado Department of Agriculture — Bull Colo Dept Agr
Bulletin. Colorado State University. Agricultural Experiment Station — Bull Colo St Univ Agric Exp Stn
Bulletin. Colorado State University. Agricultural Experiment Station — Bull Colo State Univ Agr Exp Sta
Bulletin. Colorado State University. Experiment Station — Bull Colo State Univ Exp Stn
Bulletin. Colorado State University Experiment Station — Bull Colorado State Univ Exp Sta
Bulletin. Colorado Veterinary Medical Association — Bull Colo Vet Med Ass
Bulletin. Colorado Veterinary Medical Association — Bull Colo Vet Med Assoc
Bulletin. Comite Archeologique de Lezoux — B Lezoux
Bulletin. Comite Archeologique de Lezoux — BCA Lezoux
Bulletin. Comite Central Industriel — CCI
Bulletin. Comite Central Industriel de Belgique — Bull Comite Centr Ind
Bulletin. Comite de l'Asie Francaise — BCAF
Bulletin. Comite des Forets — Bull Com For
Bulletin. Comite des Travaux Historiques et Scientifiques — BCTH
Bulletin. Comite des Travaux Historiques et Scientifiques. Section d'Archeologie — BCTA
Bulletin. Comite d'Etudes [*Paris*] — BullComEt
Bulletin. Comite d'Etudes. Compagnie de S. Sulpice [*Paris*] — BComEtSulp
Bulletin. Comite d'Etudes Historiques et Scientifiques de l'Afrique Occidentale Francaise — Bull Comite Etud Hist Sci Afr Occident Franc
Bulletin. Comite Flamand de France — BCFF
Bulletin. Commission Archeologique de Narbonne — BA Narb
Bulletin. Commission Archeologique de Narbonne — BCAN
Bulletin. Commission Archeologique de Narbonne — Bull Comm Arch Narbonne
Bulletin. Commission Belge de Bibliographie — Bull Comm Belge Bibl
Bulletin. Commission Departementale de Monuments Historiques du Pas-De-Calais — B Pas De Calais
Bulletin. Commission des Antiquites de Seine-Maritime — BCASM
Bulletin. Commission Geologique de Finlande — Bull Comm Geol Finl
Bulletin. Commission Historique et Archeologique de la Mayenne — B Mayenne
Bulletin. Commission Historique et Archeologique de la Mayenne — BCHAM

Bulletin. Commission Historique et Archeologique de la Mayenne — Bull Comm Hist Archeol Mayenne
Bulletin. Commission Internationale pour l'Exploration Scientifique de la Mer Mediterranee — Bull Commiss Int Explor Sci Mer Medit
Bulletin. Commission Nationale de la Republique Populaire Roumaine pour l'UNESCO — BR UNESCO
Bulletin. Commission Royale de Toponymie et de Dialectologie — BCRTD
Bulletin. Commission Royale de Toponymie et de Dialectologie — BCTD
Bulletin. Commission Royale de Toponymie et de Dialectologie — BTD
Bulletin. Commission Royale des Anciennes Lois et Ordonnances de Belgique — Bul ALO
Bulletin. Commission Royale des Anciennes Lois et Ordonnances de Belgique — Bull Anc Lois et Ord Belg
Bulletin. Commission Royale des Monuments et des Sites — BCMS
Bulletin. Commission Royale d'Histoire — BC Hist
Bulletin. Commission Royale d'Histoire — BCH
Bulletin. Commission Royale d'Histoire — BCRH
Bulletin. Commissions Royales d'Art et d'Archeologie — BCRAA
Bulletin. Committee on Archives. United Church of Canada — Bul Com Arch Un Ch Can
Bulletin. Commonwealth Bureau of Pastures and Field Crops — Bull Commonw Bur Past Fld Crops
Bulletin. Commonwealth Bureau of Pastures and Field Crops — Bull Commonw Bur Pastures Field Crops
Bulletin. Commonwealth Scientific and Industrial Research Organisation — Bull Commonw Sci Ind Res Org
Bulletin. Commonwealth Scientific and Industrial Research Organisation — Bull Commonw Scient Ind Res Org
Bulletin. Commonwealth Scientific and Industrial Research Organisation (Australia) — Bull Commonw Sci Industr Res Organ (Aust)
Bulletin. Commonwealth Scientific and Industrial Research Organisation (Australia) — Bull IRO (Aust)
Bulletin. Communaute Economique Europeenne — BCEE
Bulletin. Communaute Europeenne du Charbon et de l'Acier — B CECA
Bulletin. Compressed Gas Manufacturers Association [*United States*] — Bull Compr Gas Man Ass
Bulletin. Confederation Generale de la Publicite — Bul Confed Gen Pub
Bulletin. Confederation Generale de la Publicite. English Edition — Bul Confed Gen Pub Eng Ed
Bulletin. Connecticut Agricultural Experiment Station — Bull Conn Agr Exp Sta
Bulletin. Connecticut Agricultural Experiment Station — Bull Conn Agric Exp Sta
Bulletin. Connecticut Agricultural Experiment Station. New Haven — Bull Conn Agric Exp Stn New Haven
Bulletin. Connecticut Agriculture Experiment Station — Bull Connecticut Agr Exp Sta
Bulletin. Connecticut Arboretum — Bull Connecticut Arbor
Bulletin. Connecticut Historical Society — Bull Conn Hist Soc
Bulletin. Connecticut State Geological and Natural History Survey — Bull Conn St Geol Nat Hist Surv
Bulletin. Co-Operative Extension Service. College of Agriculture. University of Idaho — Bull Co-Op Ext Serv Coll Agric Univ Idaho
Bulletin. Cooperative Extension Service. Colorado State University — Bull Coop Ext Serv Colo State Univ
Bulletin. Cooperative Extension Service. Montana State University — Bull Coop Ext Serv Mont State Univ
Bulletin. Cooperative Extension Service. Ohio State University — Bull Coop Ext Serv Ohio St Univ
Bulletin. Cooperative Extension Service. University of Connecticut — Bull Coop Ext Serv Univ Conn
Bulletin. Cooperative Extension Service. University of Georgia. College of Agriculture — Bull Coop Ext Serv Univ GA Coll Agric
Bulletin. Copper and Brass Research Association — Bull Copper Brass Res Assoc
Bulletin. Copyright Society of the USA — B Copyrgt S
Bulletin. Copyright Society of the USA — Bull Cop Soc
Bulletin. Copyright Society of the USA — Bull Copyright Soc'y
Bulletin. Copyright Society of the USA — Bull Copyright Soc'y USA
Bulletin. Copyright Society of the USA — Bull Cr Soc
Bulletin. Copyright Society of the USA — Bull C'right Soc'y
Bulletin. Copyright Society of the USA — Copy Soc Bull
Bulletin. Cornell University. Agricultural Experiment Station — Bull Cornell Univ Agric Exp Stn
Bulletin. Cornell University. Engineering Experiment Station — Bull Cornell Univ Eng Exp St
Bulletin. Council for Research in Music Education — B C Res Mus
Bulletin. Council for Research in Music Education — BRM
Bulletin. Council for Research in Music Education — Bull Council Res Mus Educ
Bulletin. Council of University Classical Departments — CUCD Bulletin
Bulletin. Council on the Study of Religion — Bul Council Stud Rel
Bulletin. Crimean Astrophysical Observatory — Bull Crimean Astrophys Obs
Bulletin Critique — BC
Bulletin Critique — Bull Crit
Bulletin Critique du Livre Francais — BCLF
Bulletin Critique du Livre Francais — BCr
Bulletin. Czechoslovak Medical Association in Great Britain — Bull Czech Med Ass Great Brit
Bulletin. Dahlia Society of Michigan — Bull Dahlia Soc Michigan
Bulletin. Daito Bunka University [*Japan*] — Bull Daito Bunka Univ
Bulletin d'Ancienne Litterature Chretienne Latine [*Maredosous*] — BALC
Bulletin d'Ancienne Litterature et d'Archeologie Chretienne — B Anc Lit
Bulletin d'Ancienne Litterature et d'Archeologie Chretienne — BALAC
Bulletin d'Ancienne Litterature et d'Archeologie Chretiennes — BLAC
Bulletin d'Arabe Chretien — Bul Arab Chret
Bulletin d'Archeologie Algerienne [*Paris*] — B Arch Alg
Bulletin d'Archeologie Algerienne — BA Alg
Bulletin d'Archeologie Algerienne — BA Alger
Bulletin d'Archeologie Algerienne — BAA
Bulletin d'Archeologie Algerienne [*Paris*] — BM Jewell
Bulletin d'Archeologie Algerienne — Bull Arch Alg
Bulletin d'Archeologie et d'Histoire Dalmate — BAHD
Bulletin d'Archeologie Luxembourgeoise — BA Lux
Bulletin d'Archeologie Marocaine — BA Maroc
Bulletin d'Archeologie Marocaine — BAM
Bulletin d'Archeologie Marocaine — Bul Arch Maroc
Bulletin d'Archeologie Marocaine — Bull Arch Maroc
Bulletin d'Archeologie Sud-Est Europeenne — BA Sud Est Eur
Bulletin d'Archeologie Sud-Est Europeenne — BASE Eur
Bulletin d'Archeologie Sud-Est Europeenne — Bul ASE
Bulletin d'Audiophonologie — Bull Audiophonol
Bulletin de Atlas Linguistique du Cameroun — Bull de ALCAM
Bulletin de Biologie et de Medecine Experimentale de l'URSS — Bull Biol Med Exp URSS
Bulletin de Carignan — Bul Carignan
Bulletin de Chimie Clinique — Bull Chim Clin
Bulletin de Colonisation Comparee — B Colon Comp
Bulletin de Colonisation Comparee — Bul Col Comp
Bulletin de Conjoncture Regionale — B Conjonct Region
Bulletin de Conjoncture Regionale. Supplement — B Conjoncture Suppl
Bulletin de Correspondance Hellenique — BCH
Bulletin de Correspondance Hellenique — Bul Corresp Hellenique
Bulletin de Correspondance Hellenique — Bul Hel
Bulletin de Correspondance Hellenique — Bull Corr Hell
Bulletin de Correspondance Hellenique — Bull Corr Hellenique
Bulletin de Correspondance Hellenique — Bull Corresp Hellen
Bulletin de Correspondance Hellenique. Supplement — BCH Supp
Bulletin de Cultures Ethniques et de Civilisations Comparees — BCECC
Bulletin de Documentation — B Doc
Bulletin de Documentation — Bul Docum
Bulletin de Documentation. Association Internationale des Fabricants de Superphosphates — Bull Docum Ass Int Fabr Superphos
Bulletin de Documentation Bibliographique — Bul Doc Bibliog
Bulletin de Documentation Bibliographique — Bull Doc Bibliog
Bulletin de Documentation. Centre d'Information du Chrome Dur — BDCDA
Bulletin de Documentation. Centre d'Information du Chrome Dur [*France*] — Bull Doc Cent Inf Chrome Dur
Bulletin de Documentation Economique — Bul Docum Econ
Bulletin de Documentation Pratique de Securite Sociale et de Legislation du Travail — B Docum Prat Secur Soc Legisl Trav
Bulletin de Documentation Rhenane — BXD
Bulletin de Droit Nucleaire — Bull de Droit Nucl
Bulletin de Droit Nucleaire — Bull Droit Nucl
Bulletin de Droit Tchecoslovaque — B Dr Tchecosl
Bulletin de Droit Tchecoslovaque — Bull de Droit Tchecoslovaque
Bulletin de Geographie Historique et Descriptive — BGHD
Bulletin de Geographie Historique et Descriptive — Bull Geogr Hist
Bulletin de Geographie Historique et Descriptive (Paris) — BGHDP
Bulletin de Geophysique — Bull Geophys
Bulletin de Guerre des Biologistes Pharmaciens — Bull Guerre Biol Pharm
Bulletin de la Carte et de la Vegetation de la Provence et des Alpes du Sud — Bull Carte Veg Provence Alpes Sud
Bulletin de la Jurisprudence Immobiliere et de la Construction — Bull Jur Immob
Bulletin de la Murithienne — Bull Murithienne
Bulletin de la Protection des Vegetaux — Bull Prot Veg
Bulletin de la Protection des Vegetaux — Bull Protect Veg
Bulletin de la Sante Publique — B Sante P
Bulletin de la Societe Belge d'Etudes Coloniales — Bull Soc Belge Etudes Colon
Bulletin de la Societe Centrale Forestiere de Belgique — Bull Soc Centr Forest Belgique
Bulletin de la Societe d'Agriculture du Department de l'Ardeche — Bull Soc Agric Dep Ardeche
Bulletin de la Societe de l'Histoire de Paris et de l'Ile-de-France — Bull de la Soc de l Hist de Paris et de l Ile de France
Bulletin de la Societe des Naturalistes Dinantais — Bull Soc Naturalistes Dinantais
Bulletin de la Societe des Sciences et des Lettres de Lodz. Serie. Recherches sur les Deformations — Bull Soc Sci Lett Lodz Ser Rech Deform
Bulletin de la Societe des Sciences Naturelles et Historiques de l'Ardeche — Bull Soc Sci Nat Ardeche
Bulletin de la Societe des Sciences Physiques and Naturelles de Toulouse — Bull Soc Sci Phys Nat Toulouse
Bulletin de la Societe d'Etudes Scientifiques d'Angers — Bull Soc Etudes Sci Angers
Bulletin de la Societe d'Histoire Naturelle de Colmar — Bull Soc Hist Nat Colmar
Bulletin de la Societe d'Horticulture de la Sarthe — Bull Soc Hort Sarthe
Bulletin de la Societe Linneenne du Nord de la France — Bull Soc Linn N France
Bulletin de la Societe Royal Belge de Geographie — BSBG
Bulletin de la Vie Musicale Belge — BVmB
Bulletin de l'Academie de Medecine de Paris — Bul Acad De Med Paris
Bulletin de l'Academie Royale de Belgique — Bull de l Acad Roy de Belgique
Bulletin de l'Academie Veterinaire de France — Bull Acad Veterin France
Bulletin de l'Administration des Prisons — BAP
Bulletin de l'Administration des Prisons — Bull Adm Pr
Bulletin de l'Afrique Noire — Bul Afr Noire
Bulletin de l'Agriculture et de l'Horticulture — Bull Agric Hort
Bulletin de l'Alde a l'Implantation Monastique — Bull AIM
Bulletin de l'Arco — Bul Arco

Bulletin de l'Association Francaise des Chimistes des Industries du Cuir et Documents Scientifiques et Techniques des Industries du Cuir — Bull Assoc Fr Chim Ind Cuir Doc Sci Tech Ind Cuir
Bulletin de l'Association Pyreneenne pour l'Echange des Plantes — Bull Assoc Pyren Echange Pl
Bulletin de l'Etude en Commun de la Mediterranee — Bull Etud Commun Mediter
Bulletin de l'Herbier Boissier — Bull Herb Boissier
Bulletin de l'Hygiene Professionnelle — Bull Hyg Prof
Bulletin de Liaison. Centre d'Etudes des Peintures Murales Romaines — Bulletin de Liaison
Bulletin de Liaison. Centre International d'Etude des Textiles Anciens — B Textil Anc
Bulletin de Liaison. Centre International d'Etude des Textiles Anciens — BCETA
Bulletin de Liaison. Centre International d'Etude des Textiles Anciens — Bull Text Anc
Bulletin de Liaison de la Recherche en Informatique et Automatique [*Rocquencourt*] — Bull Liaison Rech Inform Automat
Bulletin de Liaison des Laboratoires des Ponts et Chaussees — Bull Liaison Lab Ponts Chaussees
Bulletin de Liaison du Centre Universitaire de Recherches de Developpement. Universite d'Abidjan — Bull de Liaison Cent Univ Rech Dev Abidjan
Bulletin de Liaison du Laboratoire. Laboratoire de la Profession des Peintures Bitry Thiais (France) — Bull Liaison Lab Lab Prof Pein Bitry Thiais (Fr)
Bulletin de Liaison et d'Information — Bul Liaison et Info
Bulletin de Liaison et d'Information. Administration Centrale de l'Economie et des Finances — B Liaison Inform Adm Centr Econ Finances
Bulletin de Liaison. Groupe Polyphenols — Bull Liaison Groupe Polyphenols
Bulletin de l'Institut Francaise d'Afrique Noire — Bull Inst Franc Afrique Noire
Bulletin de l'Institut Royal des Sciences Naturelles de Belgique/Koninklijk Belgisch Instituut voor Natuurwetenschappen. Mededelingen — Bull Inst Roy Sci Nat Belgique
Bulletin de Litterature Chretienne — BLC
Bulletin de Litterature Ecclesiastique — B Lit E
Bulletin de Litterature Ecclesiastique — BLE
Bulletin de Litterature Ecclesiastique — Bull de Litt Eccles
Bulletin de Litterature Ecclesiastique — Bull Ecc
Bulletin de l'Office International de la Vigne et du Vin — Bull Off Int Vin
Bulletin de l'OIV [*Office International de la Vigne et du Vin*] — Bull OIV
Bulletin de l'Universite de Brasov. Serie C — Bull Univ Brasov Ser C
Bulletin de l'Universite de l'Asie Centrale — Bull Univ Asie Cent
Bulletin de Madagascar — B Mad
Bulletin de Madagascar — BMadagascar
Bulletin de Madagascar — Bull de Madagascar
Bulletin de Medecine Legale et de Toxicologie Medicale — Bull Med Leg Toxicol Med
Bulletin de Metrologie — Bull Metrol
Bulletin de Microscopie Appliquee — Bull Micr Appl
Bulletin de Microscopie Appliquee — Bull Microscopie Appl
Bulletin de Mineralogie [*France*] — Bull Mineral
Bulletin de Nos Communautes — BC
Bulletin de Numismatique — B Num
Bulletin de Pharmacie du Sud-Est — Bull Pharm Sud Est
Bulletin de Philosophie Medievale — Bull Phil Mediev
Bulletin de Photogrammetrie — Bull Photogramm
Bulletin de Physiopathologie Respiratoire — B Physiopa
Bulletin de Physiopathologie Respiratoire — BPPRA
Bulletin de Physio-Pathologie Respiratoire — Bull Physio Pathol Respir
Bulletin de Physiopathologie Respiratoire (Nancy) — Bull Physiopathol Respir (Nancy)
Bulletin de Psychologie — B Psychol
Bulletin de Renseignements Agricoles — B Rens Agr
Bulletin de Science et Technique. Institut Polytechnique de Timisoara — Bull Sci Tech Inst Polytech Timisoara
Bulletin de Statistique (Belgium) — Bul Statis (Belgium)
Bulletin de Statistique (Bruxelles) — B Statist (Bruxelles)
Bulletin de Statistique et de Documentation — Bul Statis et Docum
Bulletin de Statistique (Rwanda) — Bul Statis (Rwanda)
Bulletin de Statistique Suisse — BSS
Bulletin de Taxes et Tarifs — Bul Tax Tarif
Bulletin de Theologie Africaine — Bul Th Africa
Bulletin de Theologie Ancienne et Medievale — BTAM
Bulletin de Theologie Ancienne et Medievale — BTh
Bulletin de Theologie Biblique [*Rome*] — BTBib
Bulletin de Vanier — Bul Van
Bulletin. Debating Association of Pennsylvania Colleges — BDAPC
Bulletin. Deccan College Research Institute — B Deccan Coll Res Inst
Bulletin. Deccan College Research Institute — BDC
Bulletin. Deccan College Research Institute — Bull Deccan Coll Res Inst
Bulletin d'Ecologie — BUECD
Bulletin d'Ecologie — Bull Ecol
Bulletin. Delaware Agricultural Experiment Station — Bull Del Agric Exp Stn
Bulletin. Delaware County Medical Society [*Pennsylvania*] — Bull Delaware County Med Soc
Bulletin. Delaware. Geological Survey — Bull Del Geol Surv
Bulletin. Deli Proefstation Medan — Bull Deli Proefstat Medan
Bulletin Dentaire — Bull Dent
Bulletin. Dental Guidance Council for Cerebral Palsy — Bull Dent Guid Counc Cereb Palsy
Bulletin. Department of Agricultural Economics. University of Manchester — Bull Dept Agr Econ Univ Manchester
Bulletin. Department of Agricultural Research. Royal Tropical Institute (Amsterdam) — Bull Dep Agric Res R Trop Inst (Amsterdam)
Bulletin. Department of Agricultural Research. Royal Tropical Institute (Amsterdam) — Bull Dep Agric Res Trop Inst (Amst)
Bulletin. Department of Agricultural Technical Services (Republic of South Africa) — Bull Dept Agr Tech Serv (Repub S Afr)
Bulletin. Department of Agricultural Technical Services (South Africa) — Bull Dep Agric Tech Serv (S Afr)
Bulletin. Department of Agricultural Technical Services (Transvaal) — Bull Dep Agric Tech Serv (Transv)
Bulletin. Department of Agriculture and Forestry (Union of South Africa) — Bull Dep Agric For (Un S Afr)
Bulletin. Department of Agriculture and Industries (Western Australia) — Bull Dept Agric and Indust (West Australia)
Bulletin. Department of Agriculture (British Columbia) — Bull Dep Agric (Br Columb)
Bulletin. Department of Agriculture (Ceylon) — Bull Dep Agric (Ceyl)
Bulletin. Department of Agriculture (Cyprus) — Bull Dep Agric (Cyp)
Bulletin. Department of Agriculture (Dominion of Canada) — Bull Dep Agric (Dom Can)
Bulletin. Department of Agriculture. Government Research Institute. Formosa/Taiwan Sotokufu Chuo Kenkyu Jo, Nogyo-Bu Iho — Bull Dept Agric Gov Res Inst Formosa
Bulletin. Department of Agriculture (Kingston) — Bull Dept Agric Kingston
Bulletin. Department of Agriculture (Madras) — Bull Dep Agric (Madras)
Bulletin. Department of Agriculture (Mysore State). Entomology Series — Bull Dept Agr (Mysore) Entomol Ser
Bulletin. Department of Agriculture (New Zealand) — Bull Dep Agric (NZ)
Bulletin. Department of Agriculture. North-West Territories — Bull Dep Agric NW Terr
Bulletin. Department of Agriculture (Quebec) — Bull Dep Agric (Queb)
Bulletin. Department of Agriculture (Tanganyika) — Bull Dept Agr (Tanganyika)
Bulletin. Department of Agriculture (Tasmania) — Bull Dep Agric (Tas)
Bulletin. Department of Agriculture (Tasmania) — Bull Dep Agric (Tasm)
Bulletin. Department of Agriculture (Tasmania) — Tas Dep Agric Bull
Bulletin. Department of Agriculture (Trinidad and Tobago) — B Dept Ag (Trinidad)
Bulletin. Department of Agriculture (Western Australia) — Bull Dep Agric (West Aust)
Bulletin. Department of Agronomy. Mosonmagyarovar College of Agricultural Sciences — Bull Dept Agron Mosonmagyarovar Coll Agr Sci
Bulletin. Department of Antiquities of the State of Israel — BDASI
Bulletin. Department of Archaeology and Anthropology [*Taipei*] — B Dept Archaeol Anthropol
Bulletin. Department of Biology. Yenching University/Yen Ta Sheng Wu Pu Ts'ung K'an — Bull Dept Biol Yenching Univ
Bulletin. Department of Civil Engineering. University of Queensland — Bull Dep Civ Eng Queensl Univ
Bulletin. Department of Civil Engineering. University of Queensland — Bull Dep Civ Engng QD Univ
Bulletin. Department of English (Calcutta) — BDEC
Bulletin. Department of Entomology. Kansas State University — Bull Dep Ent Kans St Univ
Bulletin. Department of Forestry (Pretoria, South Africa) — Bull Dep For (S Afr)
Bulletin. Department of Forestry. University of Ibadan — Bull Dep For Univ Ibadan
Bulletin. Department of General Education. College of Science and Technology. Nihon University — Bull Dept Gen Ed College Sci Tech Nihon Univ
Bulletin. Department of General Education. Nagoya City University. Natural Science Section — Bull Dept Gen Educ Nagoya City Univ Nat Sci Sect
Bulletin. Department of General Education. Tokyo Medical and Dental University — Bull Dep Gen Educ Tokyo Med Dent Univ
Bulletin. Department of Geology. Hebrew University (Jerusalem) — Bull Dep Geol Heb Univ (Jerusalem)
Bulletin. Department of Home Economics. Kyoritsu Women's Junior College — Bull Dep Home Econ Kyoritsu Womens Jr Coll
Bulletin. Department of Labor — Bul Dept Labor
Bulletin. Department of Land Records and Agriculture (Madras) — Bull Dept Land Rec Madras
Bulletin. Department of Mines (British Columbia) — Bull Dep Mines (Br Columbia)
Bulletin. Department of Scientific and Industrial Research (New Zealand) — Bull Dep Sci Ind Res (NZ)
Bulletin. Department of Sociology (Okinawa) — B Dept Sociol (Okinawa)
Bulletin. Department of Zoology. University of the Panjab. New Series — Bull Dep Zool Univ Panjab New Ser
Bulletin. Department of Zoology. University of the Panjab. New Series — PUZBAR
Bulletin der Schweizerischen Gesellschaft fuer Anthropologie und Ethnologie — BSAE
Bulletin des Amis d'Orange — BA Orange
Bulletin des Anciens Eleves de l'Ecole de Meunerie ENSMIC [*Ecole Nationale Superieure de Meunerie et des Industries Cerealieres*] — Bull Anc Eleves Ec Meun ENSMIC
Bulletin des Antiquites Luxembourgeoises — B Ant Lux
Bulletin des Antiquites Luxembourgeoises — BAL
Bulletin des Archives d'Anvers — BAA
Bulletin des Arrets de la Cour de Cassation. Chambre Criminelle [*France*] — Bull Crim
Bulletin des Arrets de la Cour de Cassation. Chambres Civiles. Deuxieme Section Civile — Bull Civ II
Bulletin des Arrets de la Cour de Cassation. Chambres Civiles. Premiere Section Civile [*France*] — Bull Civ I
Bulletin des Arrets de la Cour de Cassation. Chambres Civiles. Troisieme Section Civile [*France*] — Bull Civ III
Bulletin des Assurances — Bul Ass
Bulletin des Assurances — Bull Ass
Bulletin des Bibliophiles Liegeois — BBL

Bulletin des Bibliotheques de France — BBF
Bulletin des Bibliotheques de France — Bul Bibl de France
Bulletin des Bibliotheques de France — Bull Bibl de France
Bulletin des Bibliotheques de France — Bull Bibl Fr
Bulletin des Bibliotheques de France — Bull Bibl France
Bulletin des Bibliotheques de France — Bull Biblioth Fr
Bulletin des Bibliotheques et des Archives — BBA
Bulletin des Biologistes Pharmaciens — Bull Biol Pharm
Bulletin des Brevets (Budapest) — Bull Brev Budapest
Bulletin des Brevets et Bulletin Central des Marques — Bull Brev Bull Cent Marques
Bulletin des Cereales et des Plantes a Fecule — Bull des Cereales Plant Fecule
Bulletin des Communautes Europeennes — B Commun Europ
Bulletin des Contributions — BC
Bulletin des Contributions — Bull Contr
Bulletin des Contributions Directes — BCD
Bulletin des Contributions Directes — Bull Contrib Dir
Bulletin des Engrais — Bull Engrais
Bulletin des Etudes Arabes — BEA
Bulletin des Etudes Francaises — BEF
Bulletin des Etudes Parnassiennes — BEP
Bulletin des Etudes Portugaises — B E Port
Bulletin des Etudes Portugaises. Institut Francais au Portugal — BEP
Bulletin des Etudes Portugaises. Institut Francais au Portugal — BEPIF
Bulletin des GTV (Groupements Techniques Veterinaires). Dossiers Techniques Veterinaires — Bull GTV (Group Tech Vet) Dossiers Tech Vet
Bulletin des Jeunes Romanistes — BJR
Bulletin des Juridictions Indigenes — BJI
Bulletin des Juridictions Indigenes — Bull Jurid Indig
Bulletin des Juridictions Indigenes du Droit Coutumier — Bul Jur I
Bulletin des Laboratoires des Ponts et Chaussees — Bull Lab Ponts Chaussees
Bulletin des Lettres — BL
Bulletin des Matieres Grasses. Institut Colonial de Marseille — Bull Matieres Grasses Inst Colon Marseille
Bulletin des Medecins Suisses — Bull Med Suisses
Bulletin des Musees et Monuments Lyonnais — B Mus Mon Lyon
Bulletin des Musees et Monuments Lyonnais — BM Lyon
Bulletin des Musees et Monuments Lyonnais — Bull Mus Mon Lyonn
Bulletin des Musees Royaux des Arts Decoratifs et Industriels a Bruxelles — BMB
Bulletin des Naturalistes de Mons et du Borinage — Bull Nat Mons
Bulletin des Neuesten und Wissenswuerdigsten aus der Naturwissenschaft, so wie den Kuensten, Manufakturen, Technischen Gewerben, der Landwirthschaft der Buergerlichen Haushaltung — Bull Neuesten Wissenswuerd Naturwiss
Bulletin des Parlers du Calvados — BP Calv
Bulletin des Questions et Reponses Parlementaires — BQRP
Bulletin des Questions et Reponses Parlementaires — Bull Quest Rep Parlem
Bulletin des Recherches Agronomiques de Gembloux — Bull Rech Agron Gembloux
Bulletin des Recherches Historiques — Bul D Rech Hist
Bulletin des Sante et Production Animales en Afrique — Bull Sante Prod Anim Afr
Bulletin des Sciences Geographiques, Economie Publique, Voyages — Bull Sci Geogr
Bulletin des Sciences Geologiques [*Strasbourg*] — Bull Sci Geol
Bulletin des Sciences Mathematiques — B Sci Math
Bulletin des Sciences Mathematiques — BSM
Bulletin des Sciences Mathematiques — Bull Sci Math
Bulletin des Sciences Mathematiques (2e Serie) [*Paris*] — Bull Sci Math (2)
Bulletin des Sciences Naturelles et de Geologie — B Sc Nat
Bulletin des Sciences Naturelles et de Geologie — BSNG
Bulletin des Sciences Pharmacologiques — Bull Sci Pharmacol
Bulletin des Sciences Physiques et Naturelles en Neerlande — Bull Sci Phys Nat Neerl
Bulletin des Sciences Politiques — BSP
Bulletin des Sciences Politiques — Bul Pol
Bulletin des Sciences. Societe Philomathique de Paris — Bull Sc Soc Philomat Paris
Bulletin des Seances. Academie de Nimes — B Ac N
Bulletin des Seances. Academie de Nimes — B Ac Nimes
Bulletin des Seances. Academie de Nimes — Bull Nimes
Bulletin des Seances. Academie Royale des Sciences d'Outre-Mer [*Bruxelles*] — B Acad Roy Sci O Mer
Bulletin des Seances. Academie Royale des Sciences d'Outre-Mer — B Seances Acad Roy Sci O-Mer
Bulletin des Seances. Academie Royale des Sciences d'Outre-Mer — Bull Sean Acad Roy Sci Outre-Mer
Bulletin des Seances. Academie Royale des Sciences d'Outre-Mer — Bull Seances Acad Roy Sci Outre Mer
Bulletin des Seances. Academie Royale des Sciences d'Outre-Mer (Brussels) [*A publication*] — Bull Seances Acad R Sci Outre-Mer (Brussels)
Bulletin des Seances. Cercle Archeologique de Mons — BSCAM
Bulletin des Seances. Institut Royal Colonial Belge — Bull IRCB
Bulletin des Seances. Institut Royal Colonial Belge — Bull Seances IRCB
Bulletin des Seances. Institut Royal Colonial Belge/Bulletin der Zittingen. Koninklijk Belgisch Koloniaalinstitut — Bull Seances Inst Roy Colon Belge
Bulletin des Seances. Societe des Sciences de Nancy et Reunion Biologique de Nancy — Bull Seanc Soc Sci Nancy
Bulletin des Soies Kinugasa — Bull Soies Kinugasa
Bulletin des Stations d'Experimentation Agricole Hongroises. B. Elevage — Bull Stn Exp Agric Hong B
Bulletin des Statistiques Agricoles — Bul Stat Agr
Bulletin des Stupefiants — B Stupefiants
Bulletin des Transports Internationaux par Chemins de Fer — B Tr Int Ch Fer
Bulletin des Travaux de l'Institut Pharmaceutique d'Etat (Warsaw) — Bull Trav Inst Pharm Etat (Warsaw)
Bulletin des Travaux. Societe de Pharmacie de Bordeaux — Bull Trav Soc Pharm Bordeaux
Bulletin des Travaux. Societe de Pharmacie de Lyon — Bull Tra Soc Pharm Lyon
Bulletin des Travaux. Societe de Pharmacie de Lyon — Bull Trav Soc Pharm Lyon
Bulletin des Tribunaux de Police Congolais — BTPC
Bulletin des Tribunaux de Police Congolais — Bull Trib Pol Cong
Bulletin d'Etudes et de Recherches Techniques — Bull Etud Rech Tech
Bulletin d'Etudes Orientales — B Et Or
Bulletin d'Etudes Orientales — B Et Orient
Bulletin d'Etudes Orientales — BEO
Bulletin d'Etudes Orientales — Bull Et Orient
Bulletin d'Etudes Orientales — Bull Etud Orient
Bulletin d'Etudes Orientales — Bull Etudes Orient
Bulletin d'Etudes Orientales (Damascus) — BEOD
Bulletin d'Etudes Orientales. Institut Francais de Damas — BEOR
Bulletin d'Etudes Orientales. Institut Francais de Damas — Bull Etud Or
Bulletin d'Histoire du Theatre Portugais — BHTP
Bulletin d'Histoire et Exegese de l'Ancien Testament [*Louvain*] — BHEAT
Bulletin d'Histoire et Exegese de l'Ancien Testament [*Louvain*] — BHET
Bulletin d'Histologie Appliquee — Bull Histol Appl
Bulletin d'Information. ANSEAU — Bull Inf ANSEAU
Bulletin d'Information. Association Belge pour le Developpement Pacifique de l'Energie Atomique — BBDAA
Bulletin d'Information. Association Belge pour le Developpement Pacifique de l'Energie Atomique [*Belgium*] — Bull Inf Assoc Belge Dev Pac Energ At
Bulletin d'Information. Association Internationale pour l'Etude de la Mosaique Antique — B Ass Mos Ant
Bulletin d'Information. Association Internationale pour l'Etude de la Mosaique Antique — BAIEMA
Bulletin d'Information. Association Internationale pour l'Etude de la Mosaique Antique — BAMA
Bulletin d'Information. Association Internationale pour l'Etude de la Mosaique Antique — Bull AIEMA
Bulletin d'Information. Association Nationale des Services d'Eau (Belgium) [*A publication*] — Bull Inf Assoc Nat Serv Eau (Belg)
Bulletin d'Information. Association Technique pour la Production et l'Utilisation de l'Energie Nucleaire — Bull Inf Ass Tech Prod Util Energ Nucl
Bulletin d'Information. Association Technique pour l'Energie Nucleaire — Bull Inf Assoc Tech Energ Nucl
Bulletin d'Information. ATEN [*Association Technique pour l'Energie Nucleaire*] [*France*] — Bull Inf ATEN
Bulletin d'Information. ATEN [*Association Technique pour l'Energie Nucleaire*]. Supplement [*France*] — Bull Inf ATEN Suppl
Bulletin d'Information. Bureau National de Metrologie — Bull Inf Bur Natl Metrol
Bulletin d'Information. Centre de Documentation pour l'Education en Europe — B Inform Centre Docum Educ Europe
Bulletin d'Information. Centre de Donnees Stellaires — Bull Inf Centre Donnees Stellaires
Bulletin d'Information. Centre National de la Cinematographie — B Inform C N C
Bulletin d'Information. Centre National pour l'Exploitation des Oceans [*France*] — Bull Inf Cent Natl Exploit Oceans
Bulletin d'Information. CETAMA — BCETB
Bulletin d'Information. CNEEMA (Centre National d'Etudes et d'Experimentation de Machinisme Agricole) — Bull Inf CNEEMA (Cent Natl Etud Exp Mach Agric)
Bulletin d'Information CORESTA. Centre de Co-operation pour les Recherches Scientifiques Relatives au Tabac — Bull Inform CORESTA
Bulletin d'Information. Corporation Professionnelle des Conseillers d'Orientation du Quebec — Bul Info Corp Prof Cons Orient Quebec
Bulletin d'Information de la Region Parisienne — B Inform Region Paris
Bulletin d'Information de la Region Parisienne — Bul Info Region Parisienne
Bulletin d'Information de l'Institut pour l'Etude Agronomique du Congo — Bull Inform Inst Etude Agron Congo
Bulletin d'Information. Departement d'Economie et de Sociologie Rurales [*A publication*] — B Inform Dept Econ Sociol Rur
Bulletin d'Information. Departement d'Economie et de Sociologie Rurales [*Paris*] — Bul Info
Bulletin d'Information des Centrales Electriques — BICEB
Bulletin d'Information des Centrales Electriques [*France*] — Bull Inf Cent Electr
Bulletin d'Information des Riziculteurs de France — Bull Inf Rizic Fr
Bulletin d'Information Economique de la Caisse Nationale des Marches de l'Etat — B Inform Econ Caisse Nat Marches Etat
Bulletin d'Information en Anthropologie Medicale et en Psychiatrie Transculturelle — Bul Info Anthro Med Psych Transcult
Bulletin d'Information et de Bibliographie — Bull Inf Bibliogr
Bulletin d'Information et de Coordination. Association Internationale des Etudes Byzantines — BICByz
Bulletin d'Information et de Documentation. Banque Nationale — B Inf Doc BN
Bulletin d'Information et de Documentation. Banque Nationale — BBN
Bulletin d'Information et de Documentation. Banque Nationale — Bul BN
Bulletin d'Information et de Liaison. Association Internationale des Etudes Patristiques — BILPatr
Bulletin d'Information. FNAMI — B Inf FNAMI
Bulletin d'Information. Haut Comite d'Etude et d'Information sur l'Alcoolisme — B Inform Haut Comite Et Inform Alcool
Bulletin d'Information. Institut de Reboisement de Tunis — Bull Inform Inst Rebois Tunis
Bulletin d'Information. Institut de Recherche et d'Histoire des Textes — BIIRHT
Bulletin d'Information. Institut de Recherche et d'Histoire des Textes — BIRT

Bulletin d'Information. Institut d'Etude Economique et Sociale des Classes Moyennes — B Inf
Bulletin d'Information. Institut National pour l'Etude Agronomique du Congo Belge — Bull Inf INEAC
Bulletin d'Information. Institut National pour l'Etude Agronomique du Congo Belge (INEAC) — Bull Inform Inst Nat Etud Agron Congo (INEAC)
Bulletin d'Information. Institut Textile de France Nord — Bull Inf Inst Text Fr Nord
Bulletin d'Information. ITF [*Institut Textile de France*] **Nord** — Bull Inf ITF Nord
Bulletin d'Information. Laboratoire Cooperatif — Bull Info Lab Coop
Bulletin d'Information. Laboratoire d'Analyse Lexicologique — BILAL
Bulletin d'Information. Ministere de l'Agriculture — Bull Inf Minist Agric
Bulletin d'Information. Office de Commercialisation — BDN
Bulletin d'Information Officiel. Association des Pharmaciens des Etablissements de Sante du Quebec — Bul Info Off Assoc Pharm Etablis Sante Quebec
Bulletin d'Information Regionale Champagne-Ardenne — B Inform Region Champagne-Ardenne
Bulletin d'Information. Societe d'Archeologie et d'Histoire de Waremme et Environs — B Waremme
Bulletin d'Information. Societe d'Archeologie et d'Histoire de Waremme et Environs — BSAHW
Bulletin d'Information. Station Experimentale d'Aviculture de Ploufragan — Bull Inf Stn Exp Avic Ploufragan
Bulletin d'Information sur la Chine — Bul Inf Chine
Bulletin d'Information sur les Applications Industrielles des Radioelements — Bull Inf Appl Ind Radioelem
Bulletin d'Information sur les Generateurs Isotopiques — Bull Inf Generateurs Isot
Bulletin d'Information. UGGI [*Union Geodesique et Geophysique Internationale*] — Bull Inf UGGI
Bulletin d'Informations Economiques — B Inform Econ
Bulletin d'Informations Scientifiques et Techniques — Bull Inf Sci Tech
Bulletin d'Informations Scientifiques et Techniques. Commissariat a l'Energie Atomique — B In Sci T
Bulletin d'Informations Scientifiques et Techniques. Commissariat a l'Energie Atomique [*France*] — BUIAA
Bulletin d'Informations Scientifiques et Techniques. Commissariat a l'Energie Atomique [*France*] — Bull Inf Sci Tech Commis Energ At
Bulletin d'Informations Scientifiques et Techniques (Paris) — Bull Inf Sci & Tech (Paris)
Bulletin d'Informations Techniques. Centre Technique du Bois — Bull Inform Tech Centre Tech Bois
Bulletin d'Informations Techniques. Charbonages de France — Bull Inf Tech Charbon Fr
Bulletin d'Instrumentation Nucleaire — BINUA
Bulletin d'Instrumentation Nucleaire — Bull Instrum Nucl
Bulletin. Direction des Etudes et Recherches. Electricite de France. Serie A. Nucleaire, Hydraulique, Thermique — Bull Dir Etud Rech Electr Fr Ser A
Bulletin. Direction des Etudes et Recherches. Electricite de France. Serie B. Reseaux Electriques Materiels Electriques — Bull Dir Etud Rech Electr Fr
Bulletin. Direction des Etudes et Recherches. Electricite de France. Serie C. Matematiques, Informatiques — Bull Dir Etud Rech Electr Fr
Bulletin. Direction des Etudes et Recherches. Serie A — Bull Dir Etud & Rech A
Bulletin. Direction des Etudes et Recherches. Serie A — Bull Dir Etud & Rech Ser A
Bulletin. Direction des Etudes et Recherches. Serie A (France) — EFDNA
Bulletin. Direction des Etudes et Recherches. Serie A. Supplement (France) — EFBSA
Bulletin. Direction des Etudes et Recherches. Serie B — Bull Dir Etud & Rech B
Bulletin. Direction des Etudes et Recherches. Serie B — Bull Dir Etud & Rech Ser B
Bulletin. Direction des Etudes et Recherches. Serie B (France) — EFDBA
Bulletin. Direction des Etudes et Recherches. Serie C — Bull Dir Etud & Rech C
Bulletin. Direction des Etudes et Recherches. Serie C — Bull Dir Etud & Rech Ser C
Bulletin. Direction des Etudes et Recherches. Serie C. Mathematiques. Informatique — Bull Direction Etudes Recherches Ser C Math Informat
Bulletin. Direction des Mines et de la Geologie (Afrique Equatoriale) — Bull Dir Mines Geol (Afr Equa)
Bulletin. Directorate General of Mineral Resources (Saudia Arabia) — Bull Dir Gen Miner Resour Saudi Arabia
Bulletin. Division of Human Relations — B Divis Hum Relat
Bulletin. Division of Mineral Resources (Virginia) — Bull Div Miner Resour (VA)
Bulletin. Division of Plant Industry. New South Wales Department of Agriculture — Bull Div Plant Ind NSW Dept Agr
Bulletin. Division of Plant Pathology. Agricultural Experiment Station. Formosa/Taiwan Nosakubutsu Byogai Mokuroku — Bull Div Pl Pathol Agric Exp Sta Formosa
Bulletin. Division of Silviculture. Department of Forests of Papua and New Guinea — Bull Div Silv Dep For Papua & N Guinea
Bulletin. Division of Vegetable Physiology and Pathology. United States Department of Agriculture — Bull Div Veg Physiol Path US Dep Agric
Bulletin. Dolmetsch Foundation — Dolmetsch B
Bulletin. Dominion of Canada. Department of Agriculture — Bull Canada Dept Agric
Bulletin du Bibliophile — BBibl
Bulletin du Bibliophile et du Bibliothecaire — B Bibl
Bulletin du Bibliophile et du Bibliothecaire — BB
Bulletin du Bibliophile et du Bibliothecaire — BBB
Bulletin du Bibliophile et du Bibliothecaire — Bull du Bibl
Bulletin du Bibliophile et du Bibliothecaire — Bull du Biblioph
Bulletin du Bureau de Recherches Geologiques et Minieres. Section 4. Geologie Generale (France) — Bull Bur Rech Geol Min Sect 4 Fr
Bulletin du Cancer [*Paris*] — B Cancer
Bulletin du Cancer — BUCAB
Bulletin du Cancer [*Paris*] — Bull Cancer
Bulletin du Cancer (Paris) — Bull Cancer (Paris)
Bulletin du Cancer. Radiotherapie — Bull Cancer Radiother
Bulletin du Cange — BD
Bulletin du Cange. Archivum Latinitatis Medii Aevi — Arch LMA
Bulletin du Cange. Archivum Latinitatis Medii Aevi — BCALMA
Bulletin du Cercle d'Etudes Numismatiques — B Cercl Num
Bulletin du Cercle d'Etudes Numismatiques — CEN
Bulletin du Cercle Vaudois de Botanique — Bull Cercle Vaud Bot
Bulletin du Citoyen — Bul Citoyen
Bulletin du Comite des Travaux Historiques et Scientifiques. Section de Histoire — Bull Comite Trav Hist Sect Hist
Bulletin du Comite d'Etudes Historiques et Scientifiques de l'Afrique Occidentale Francaise — Bul Comite D Etudes Hist Et Sci De L Afrique Occid Fr
Bulletin du Credit National — B Cred Nat
Bulletin du Dictionnaire Wallon — BDW
Bulletin du Jardin Botanique de l'Etat / Bulletin van den Rijksplantentuin — Bull Jard Bot Etat
Bulletin du Laboratoire Professionnel — Bull Lab Prof
Bulletin du Musee d'Anthropologie Prehistorique [*Monaco*] — BMAP
Bulletin du Museum d'Histoire Naturelle (Paris) — Bull Mus Hist Nat Paris
Bulletin du Protestantisme Francais — BPF
Bulletin du Service de Biogeographie. Universite de Montreal — Bull Serv Biogeogr Univ Montreal
Bulletin du Service de la Carte Geologique d'Alsace et de Lorraine — Bull Serv Carte Geol Alsace Lorraine
Bulletin du Statec — B Statec
Bulletin du Static — Bul Static
Bulletin. Duke University School of Forestry — Bull Duke Univ Sch For
Bulletin. Earth and Mineral Sciences Experiment Station. Pennsylvania State University — Bull Earth Miner Sci Exp Sta PA State Univ
Bulletin. Earth and Mineral Sciences Experiment Station. Pennsylvania State University — Bull Earth Miner Sci Exp Stn PA State Univ
Bulletin. Earth Science Faculty. Ege University (Izmir) — Bull Earth Sci Fac Ege Univ (Izmir)
Bulletin. Earthquake Research Institute. University of Tokyo — Bull Earthquake Res Inst Univ Tokyo
Bulletin. East of Scotland College of Agriculture — Bull East Scotl Coll Agric
Bulletin. Ecole de la Meunerie Belge — Bull Ec Meun Belge
Bulletin. Ecole Francaise d'Extreme-Orient — B Ecole Fr Ex Or
Bulletin. Ecole Francaise d'Extreme-Orient — BEEO
Bulletin. Ecole Francaise d'Extreme-Orient — BEFEO
Bulletin. Ecole Francaise d'Extreme-Orient [*Hanoi*] — Bull Ecole Franc Extreme-Orient
Bulletin. Ecole Nationale Superieure Agronomique de Nancy — Bull Ec Natl Super Agron Nancy
Bulletin. Ecole Nationale Superieure Agronomique de Nancy — Bull Ec Natn Sup Agron Nancy
Bulletin. Ecole Nationale Superieure Agronomique de Nancy — Bull Ecole Nat Super Agron Nancy
Bulletin. Ecole Nationale Superieure d'Agronomie et des Industries Alimentaires — Bull Ec Nat Super Agron Ind Aliment
Bulletin. Ecole Nationale Superieure d'Agronomie et des Industries Alimentaires — Bull Ec Natl Super Agron Ind Aliment
Bulletin. Ecole Superieure d'Agriculture de Tunis — Bull Ecole Super Agr Tunis
Bulletin. Ecological Society of America — Bull Ecol Soc Amer
Bulletin Economique et Financier — Bul Econ et Fin
Bulletin Economique et Social du Maroc — B Econ Soc Maroc
Bulletin Economique et Social du Maroc — BEM
Bulletin Economique et Social du Maroc — Bul Econ et Soc Maroc
Bulletin Economique et Social du Maroc — Bull Econ et Soc Maroc
Bulletin Economique Mensuelle — Bull Econom
Bulletin Economique pour l'Afrique — B Econ Afr
Bulletin Economique pour l'Europe — B Econ Europe
Bulletin. Edinburgh School of Agriculture — Bull Edinburgh Sch Agr
Bulletin. Educational Research Institute. Faculty of Education. University of Kagoshima — Bull Educ Res Inst Fac Educ Univ Kagoshima
Bulletin EGU — BEGUB
Bulletin. Ehime Agricultural Experiment Station — Bull Ehime Agr Exp Sta
Bulletin. Ehime Prefectural Agricultural Experiment Station — Bull Ehime Prefect Agric Exp Stn
Bulletin. Ehime University Forest — Bull Ehime Univ For
Bulletin. Eidgenoessisches Gesundheitsamt. Beilage B — BEGBA
Bulletin. Eidgenoessisches Gesundheitsamt. Beilage B [*Switzerland*] — Bull Eidgenoess Gesundh Beil B
Bulletin. Eighth District Dental Society [*Kenmore, New York*] — Bull Eighth Dist Dent Soc
Bulletin. Electron Microscope Society of India — BEMID
Bulletin. Electron Microscope Society of India — Bull Electron Microsc Soc India
Bulletin. Electrotechnical Laboratory [*Japan*] — Bull Electrotech Lab
Bulletin. Electrotechnical Laboratory (Tokyo) — Bull Electrotech Lab (Tokyo)
Bulletin. Eleventh District Dental Society [*Jamaica, New York*] — Bull Eleventh Dist Dent Soc NY
Bulletin. Engineering Experiment Station. Oregon State College — Bull Eng Exp Stn Oreg State Coll
Bulletin. Engineering Research Institute of Kyoto University [*Japan*] — Bull Eng Res Inst Kyoto Univ
Bulletin. Enseignement Public du Gouvernement Cherifien — Bull Enseign Public Gouvernement Cherifien
Bulletin. Entomological Society of America — Bull Ent Soc Am
Bulletin. Entomological Society of America — Bull Entomol Soc Am
Bulletin. Entomological Society of America — Bull Entomol Soc Amer
Bulletin. Entomological Society of Egypt — BSEEAZ

Bulletin. Entomological Society of Egypt — Bull Entomol Soc Egypt
Bulletin. Entomological Society of Egypt. Economic Series — Bull Ent Soc Egypt Econ Ser
Bulletin. Entomological Society of Egypt. Economic Series — Bull Entomol Soc Egypt Econ Ser
Bulletin. Entomological Society of Nigeria — Bull Entomol Soc Nigeria
Bulletin. Environmental Pollution Control and Research Center. Shizuoka Prefecture — Bull Environ Pollut Control Res Cent Shizuoka Prefect
Bulletin Epigraphique — B Ep
Bulletin Epigraphique — BE
Bulletin Epigraphique — Bull Ep
Bulletin Epigraphique — Bull Epigr
Bulletin Epigraphique [*Paris*] — Bull Epigraph
Bulletin Epigraphique de la Gaule — Bull Epigr Gaule
Bulletin Epigraphique (Paris) — B Ep P
Bulletin. Equine Research Institute — BEQIDC
Bulletin. Equine Research Institute — Bull Equine Res Inst
Bulletin Escher Wyss — Bull Escher Wyss
Bulletin. Essex County [*New Jersey*] **Dental Society** — Bull Essex Cty Dent Soc
Bulletin et Annales. Societe Entomologique de Belgique — Bull Ann Soc Entomol Belg
Bulletin et Annales. Societe Royale Belge d'Entomologie — Bull Ann Soc R Belge Entomol
Bulletin et Annales. Societe Royale d'Entomologie de Belgique — Bull Ann Soc R Entomol Belg
Bulletin et Annales. Societe Royale d'Entomologie de Belgique — Bull Ann Soc Roy Entomol Belg
Bulletin et Annales. Societe Royale Entomologique de Belgique — Bull Annls Soc R Ent Belg
Bulletin et Memoires. Academie Royale de Medecine de Belgique — Bull Mem Acad R Med Belg
Bulletin et Memoires. Faculte Nationale de Medecine et de Pharmacie de Dakar — Bull Mem Fac Natl Med Pharm Dakar
Bulletin et Memoires. Institut des Fouilles de Prehistoire et d'Archeologie des Alpes-Maritimes — BMIPA
Bulletin et Memoires. Institut des Fouilles de Provence et des Prealpes — BIFP
Bulletin et Memoires. Societe Archeologique de Bordeaux — B Mem Soc Arch Bordeaux
Bulletin et Memoires. Societe Archeologique de Bordeaux — BMSAB
Bulletin et Memoires. Societe Archeologique de Bordeaux — Bull Mem Bordeaux
Bulletin et Memoires. Societe Archeologique de Bordeaux — Bull Mem Soc Arch Bordeaux
Bulletin et Memoires. Societe Archeologique et Historique de la Charente — Bull Mem Soc Archeol Hist Charente
Bulletin et Memoires. Societe Archeologique et Historique de l'Arrondisement de Fougeres — B Fougeres
Bulletin et Memoires. Societe Archeologique et Historique de l'Arrondisement de Fougeres — BMSF
Bulletin et Memoires. Societe d'Anthropologie de Paris — Bull Soc Anthr Paris
Bulletin et Memoires. Societe d'Anthropologie de Paris — Bull Soc Anthrop Paris
Bulletin et Memoires. Societe de Medecine de Paris — Bull Mem Soc Med Paris
Bulletin et Memoires. Societe de Medecine de Paris — Bull Soc Med Par
Bulletin et Memoires. Societe d'Emulation de Montbeliard — B Montbeliard
Bulletin et Memoires. Societe d'Emulation de Montbeliard — SEM
Bulletin et Memoires. Societe des Antiquaires de l'Ouest — BMSAO
Bulletin et Memoires. Societe des Chirurgiens de Paris — Bull Mem Soc Chir Paris
Bulletin et Memoires. Societe des Chirurgiens de Paris — SCHPB
Bulletin. European Association for Theoretical Computer Science — Bull Eur Assoc Theor Comput Sci
Bulletin. European Chiropractors' Union — Bull Eur Chiro Union
Bulletin. European Communities [*Luxembourg*] — Bull Eur Communities
Bulletin. European Communities. Supplement — BECSB
Bulletin. European Communities. Supplement [*Luxembourg*] — Bull Eur Communities Suppl
Bulletin. European Society of Human Genetics — B Eur S Hum
Bulletin. European Southern Observatory [*Germany*] — Bull Eur South Obs
Bulletin Europeen de Physiopathologie Respiratoire — BEPRD
Bulletin Europeen de Physiopathologie Respiratoire — Bull Eur Physiopathol Respir
Bulletin. Europese Gemeenschappen. Europese Gemeenschap voor Kolen en Staal, Europese Economische Gemeenschap, Europese Gemeenschap voor Atoomenergie — BYH
Bulletin. Evangelical Theological Society [*Later, Journal. Evangelical Theological Society*] — BETS
Bulletin. Evangelical Theological Society [*Later, Journal. Evangelical Theological Society*] — BEvTSoc
Bulletin. Evangelical Theological Society [*Later, Journal. Evangelica l Theological Society*] — BullETHS
Bulletin. Experiment Station. Tuskegee Normal and Industrial Institute. Tuskegee Institute, Alabama — Bull Exp Sta Tuskegee Normal Industr Inst
Bulletin. Experimental Building Station — EBS Bulletin
Bulletin. Experimental Farm College of Agriculture. Ehime University — Bull Exp Farm Coll Agr Ehime Univ
Bulletin. Experimental Farms Branch. Department of Agriculture (Canada) — Bull Exp Fms Brch Dep Agric (Can)
Bulletin. Experimental Forest of National Taiwan University — Bull Exp For Natl Taiwan Univ
Bulletin. Experimental Station for Horse Breeding (Slatinany) — Bull Exp Stn Horse Breed (Slatinany)
Bulletin Exterieur — Bull Ext
Bulletin. Faculte de Medecine d'Istanbul — Bull Fac Med Istanbul
Bulletin. Faculte des Lettres de Lille — BFL
Bulletin. Faculte des Lettres de Strasbourg — BFLS
Bulletin. Faculte des Lettres de Strasbourg — BFS
Bulletin. Faculte des Lettres de Strasbourg — Bull Strasb
Bulletin. Faculte des Sciences. Universite Franco-Chinoise de Peiping — Bull Fac Sci Univ Fr Chin Peiping
Bulletin. Facultes Catholiques de Lyon — BFCL
Bulletin. Faculty of Agricultural Sciences (Mosonmagyarovar, Hungary) — Bull Fac Agric Sci (Mosonmagyarovar Hung)
Bulletin. Faculty of Agriculture. Cairo University — Bull Fac Agric Cairo Univ
Bulletin. Faculty of Agriculture. Hirosaki University — Bull Fac Agric Hirosaki Univ
Bulletin. Faculty of Agriculture. Kagoshima University — Bull Fac Agr Kagoshima Univ
Bulletin. Faculty of Agriculture. Kagoshima University — Bull Fac Agric Kagoshima Univ
Bulletin. Faculty of Agriculture. Meiji University — Bull Fac Agr Meiji Univ
Bulletin. Faculty of Agriculture. Meiji University — Bull Fac Agric Meiji Univ
Bulletin. Faculty of Agriculture. Mie University — Bull Fac Agric Mie Univ
Bulletin. Faculty of Agriculture. Miyazaki University — Bull Fac Agric Miyazaki Univ
Bulletin. Faculty of Agriculture. Niigata University — Bull Fac Agr Niigata Univ
Bulletin. Faculty of Agriculture. Niigata University — Bull Fac Agric Niigata Univ
Bulletin. Faculty of Agriculture. Saga University — Bull Fac Agric Saga Univ
Bulletin. Faculty of Agriculture. Saga University — SDNID7
Bulletin. Faculty of Agriculture. Shimane University — Bull Fac Agr Shimane Univ
Bulletin. Faculty of Agriculture. Shimane University — Bull Fac Agric Shimane Univ
Bulletin. Faculty of Agriculture. Shinshu University/Shinshu Daigaku Nogakubu Gakujitsu Hokoku — Bull Fac Agric Shinshu Univ
Bulletin. Faculty of Agriculture. Shizuoka University — Bull Fac Agr Shizuoka Univ
Bulletin. Faculty of Agriculture. Shizuoka University — Bull Fac Agric Shizuoka Univ
Bulletin. Faculty of Agriculture. Tamagawa University — Bull Fac Agric Tamagawa Univ
Bulletin. Faculty of Agriculture. Tokyo University of Agriculture and Technology — Bull Fac Agric Tokyo Univ Agric Technol
Bulletin. Faculty of Agriculture. Tottori University — Bull Fac Agric Tottori Univ
Bulletin. Faculty of Agriculture. University of Miyazaki — Bull Fac Agr Univ Miyazaki
Bulletin. Faculty of Agriculture. University of Miyazaki — Bull Fac Agric Univ Miyazaki
Bulletin. Faculty of Agriculture. Yamaguchi University — Bull Fac Agr Yamaguchi Univ
Bulletin. Faculty of Agriculture. Yamaguchi University — YDNGAU
Bulletin. Faculty of Agriculture. Yamaguti University — Bull Fac Agric Yamaguti Univ
Bulletin. Faculty of Arts. Alexandria University [*Majallat Kulliyat al-Adab. Jami'at al-Iskandaruyah*] — Bull Alexandria Univ Fac Arts
Bulletin. Faculty of Arts. Egyptian University — Bull Egypt Univ Fac Arts
Bulletin. Faculty of Arts. Fuad University. Arabic Section [*Cairo*] — BFA
Bulletin. Faculty of Arts. University of Egypt [*Cairo*] — BFA
Bulletin. Faculty of Arts. University of Egypt [*Cairo*] — BUE
Bulletin. Faculty of Arts. University of Egypt (Cairo) — BFAC
Bulletin. Faculty of Bioresources. Mie University — Bull Fac Bioresour Mie Univ
Bulletin. Faculty of Education. Chiba University — Bull Fac Educ Chiba Univ
Bulletin. Faculty of Education. Hirosaki University — Bull Fac Educ Hirosaki Univ
Bulletin. Faculty of Education. Hiroshima University — Bull Fac Educ Hiroshima Univ
Bulletin. Faculty of Education. Hiroshima University. Part 3 (Science and Technology) — Bull Fac Educ Hiroshima Univ Part 3 (Sci Tech)
Bulletin. Faculty of Education. Kagoshima University. Natural Science — Bull Fac Ed Kagoshima Univ Natur Sci
Bulletin. Faculty of Education. Kanazawa University. Natural Science — Bull Fac Educ Kanazawa Univ Nat Sci
Bulletin. Faculty of Education. Kobe University — Bull Fac Educ Kobe Univ
Bulletin. Faculty of Education. Kochi University. Series 3 — Bull Fac Educ Kochi Univ Ser 3
Bulletin. Faculty of Education. University of Kagoshima — Bull Fac Ed Univ Kagoshima
Bulletin. Faculty of Education. University of Kagoshima. Natural Science — Bull Fac Educ Univ Kagoshima Nat Sci
Bulletin. Faculty of Education. Utsunomiya University — UFEBB
Bulletin. Faculty of Education. Utsunomiya University. Section 2 — Bull Fac Ed Utsunomiya Univ Sect 2
Bulletin. Faculty of Education. Utsunomiya University. Section 2 — Bull Fac Educ Utsunomiya Univ Sect 2
Bulletin. Faculty of Education. Wakayama University. Natural Science — Bull Fac Educ Wakayama Univ Nat Sci
Bulletin. Faculty of Education. Yamaguchi University — Bull Fac Educ Yamaguchi Univ
Bulletin. Faculty of Engineering. Alexandria University [*Egypt*] — Bull Fac Eng Alexandria Univ
Bulletin. Faculty of Engineering. Cairo University — Bull Fac Eng Cairo Univ
Bulletin. Faculty of Engineering. Hiroshima University — Bull Fac Eng Hiroshima Univ
Bulletin. Faculty of Engineering. Hiroshima University — Bull Fac Engrg Hiroshima Univ
Bulletin. Faculty of Engineering. Hokkaido University — Bull Fac Eng Hokkaido Univ
Bulletin. Faculty of Engineering. Ibaraki University — Bull Fac Eng Ibaraki Univ
Bulletin. Faculty of Engineering. Kyushu Sangyo University — Bull Fac Eng Kyushu Sangyo Univ

Bulletin. Faculty of Engineering. Miyazaki University — Bull Fac Eng Miyazaki Univ
Bulletin. Faculty of Engineering. Miyazaki University — Bull Fac Engrg Miyazaki Univ
Bulletin. Faculty of Engineering. Tokushima University — Bull Fac Eng Tokushima Univ
Bulletin. Faculty of Engineering. Toyama University [*Japan*] — Bull Fac Eng Toyama Univ
Bulletin. Faculty of Engineering. University of Alexandria. Chemical Engineering [*Egypt*] — Bull Fac Eng Univ Alexandria Chem Eng
Bulletin. Faculty of Engineering. Yokohama National University — Bull Fac Eng Yokohama Natl Univ
Bulletin. Faculty of Engineering. Yokohama University — Bull Fac Eng Yokohama Univ
Bulletin. Faculty of Fisheries. Hokkaido University — Bull Fac Fish Hokkaido Univ
Bulletin. Faculty of Fisheries. Mie University — Bull Fac Fish Mie Univ
Bulletin. Faculty of Fisheries. Nagasaki University [*Japan*] — Bull Fac Fish Nagasaki Univ
Bulletin. Faculty of Forestry. University of British Columbia — Bull Fac For Univ BC
Bulletin. Faculty of General Education. Utsunomiya University. Section 2 — Bull Fac Gen Educ Utsunomiya Univ Sect 2
Bulletin. Faculty of Home Life Science. Fukuoka Women's University — Bull Fac Home Life Sci Fukuoka Women's Univ
Bulletin. Faculty of Home Life Science. Fukuoka Women's University — FJDKDW
Bulletin. Faculty of Horticulture and Viticulture. University of Agriculture [*Budapest*] — Bull Fac Hort Univ Sci Agric
Bulletin. Faculty of Liberal Arts and Education. Shiga University. Part 2. Natural Science/Shiga Daigaku Gakugeibu Kenkyu Ranshu — Bull Fac Liberal Arts Shiga Univ Pt 2 Nat Sci
Bulletin. Faculty of Liberal Arts. Ibaraki University (Natural Science) — Bull Fac Lib Arts Ibaraki Univ (Nat Sci)
Bulletin. Faculty of Pharmacy. Cairo University — Bull Fac Pharm Cairo Univ
Bulletin. Faculty of Pharmacy. Kinki University — Bull Fac Pharm Kinki Univ
Bulletin. Faculty of School Education. Hiroshima University. Part I — Bull Fac Sch Educ Hiroshima Univ Part I
Bulletin. Faculty of School Education. Hiroshima University. Part I — HDGKDR
Bulletin. Faculty of School Education. Hiroshima University. Part II — Bull Fac Sch Educ Hiroshima Univ Part II
Bulletin. Faculty of School Education. Hiroshima University. Part II — Bull Fac School Ed Hiroshima Univ Part II
Bulletin. Faculty of School Education. Hiroshima University. Part II — HDGDD6
Bulletin. Faculty of Science. Alexandria University — Bull Fac Sci Alexandria Univ
Bulletin. Faculty of Science and Engineering. Chuo University — Bull Fac Sci Eng Chuo Univ
Bulletin. Faculty of Science and Engineering. Chuo University — Bull Fac Sci Engrg Chuo Univ
Bulletin. Faculty of Science. Assiut University — Bull Fac Sci Assiut Univ
Bulletin. Faculty of Science (Cairo) — Bull Fac Sci (Cairo)
Bulletin. Faculty of Science. Cairo University — Bull Fac Sci Cairo Univ
Bulletin. Faculty of Science. Ibaraki University. Series A. Mathematics — Bull Fac Sci Ibaraki Univ Ser A
Bulletin. Faculty of Science. Ibaraki University. Series A. Mathematics — Bull Fac Sci Ibaraki Univ Series A
Bulletin. Faculty of Science. King Abdul Aziz University — Bull Fac Sci King Abdul Aziz Univ
Bulletin. Faculty of Science. Riyad University. Series II — Bull Fac Sci Riyad Univ
Bulletin. Faculty of Textile Fibers. Kyoto University of Industrial Arts and Textile Fibers — Bull Fac Textile Fibers Kyoto Univ Ind Arts Textile Fibers
Bulletin. Far Seas Fisheries Research Laboratory (Shimizu) — Bull Far Seas Fish Res Lab (Shimizu)
Bulletin. Farm Management and Land Utilization. Series H — Bull Farm Manage Land Util Ser H
Bulletin. Farouk I University. Faculty of Arts [*Cairo*] — Bull Farouk I Univ Fac Arts
Bulletin. Federal Ministry of Agriculture (Salisbury) — Bull Fed Min Agr (Salisbury)
Bulletin. Federation Belge des Societes de Sciences Mathematiques, Physiques, Chimiques, Naturelles, Medicales, et Appliquees — Bull Fed Belg Soc Sci
Bulletin. Federation des Avoues — Bull Av
Bulletin. Federation des Avoues — Bull des Avoues
Bulletin. Federation des Avoues de Belgique — BFA
Bulletin. Federation des Femmes du Quebec — Bul Fed Femmes Quebec
Bulletin. Federation des Industries Belges — Bull FIB
Bulletin. Federation des Industries Belges — FIB
Bulletin. Federation des Industries Chimiques de Belgique — Bull Fed Ind Chim Bel
Bulletin. Federation des Societes de Gynecologie et d'Obstetrique de Langue Francaise — BFSGA
Bulletin. Federation des Societes de Gynecologie et d'Obstetrique de Langue Francaise — Bull Fed Soc Gynecol Obstet Lang Fr
Bulletin. Federation des Societes d'Histoire Naturelle de Franche-Comte — Bull Fed Soc Hist Nat Franche-Comte
Bulletin. Federation des Societes d'Horticulture de Belgique — Bull Fed Soc Hort Belgique
Bulletin. Federation Internationale de Laiterie — Bull Fed Int Lait
Bulletin. Federation Internationale des Associations des Chimistes du Textile et de la Couleur — Bull Fed Int Assoc Chim Text Couleur
Bulletin. Field Geology Club of South Australia — Bull Field Geol Club South Aust
Bulletin. Fifth District Dental Society (Fresno) [*California*] — Bull Fifth Dist Dent Soc (Fresno)
Bulletin. Fifth District Dental Society of the State of New York [*Syracuse, NY*] — Bull Fifth Dist Dent Soc State NY
Bulletin. Filiales de la Societe de Biologie de Paris — Bull Fil Soc Biol Paris
Bulletin. First Agronomy Division. Tokai-Kinki National Agricultural Experiment Station — Bull First Agron Div Tokai-Kinki Nat Agr Exp Sta
Bulletin. First Agronomy Division. Tokai-Kinki National Agricultural Experiment Station — Bull First Agron Div Tokai-Kinki Natl Agric Exp Stn
Bulletin. Fisheries Research Board of Canada — Bull Fish Res Board Can
Bulletin. Fisheries Research Station (Ceylon) — Bull Fish Res Stn (Ceylon)
Bulletin. Fishery Experiment Station. Government General of Chosen. Series B — Bull Fish Exp Stn Gov Gen Chosen Ser B
Bulletin. Florida Agricultural Experiment Station — Bull Fla Agr Exp Sta
Bulletin. Florida Agricultural Experiment Station — Bull Fla Agric Exp Stn
Bulletin. Florida Agricultural Extension Service — Bull Fla Agric Ext Serv
Bulletin. Florida Cooperative Extension Service. University of Florida — Bull Fla Coop Ext Serv Univ Fla
Bulletin. Florida Department of Agriculture — Bull Fla Dep Agric
Bulletin. Florida Department of Agriculture. Division of Plant Industry — Bull Fla Dept Agr Div Plant Ind
Bulletin. Florida Nurserymen and Growers Association — Bull Florida Nurserymen Growers Assoc
Bulletin. Florida State Museum. Biological Sciences — Bull Fla State Mus Biol Sci
Bulletin. Florida State University. Tallahassee — Bul Florida St Univ Tallahassee
Bulletin. Florida University. Agricultural Experiment Station — Bull Fla Univ Agr Exp Sta
Bulletin. Fogg Art Museum — BFAM
Bulletin. Fogg Art Museum — Bull Fogg Art Mus
Bulletin Folklorique d'Ile-De-France — BFIF
Bulletin. Fonds de Recherches Forestieres. Universite Laval — Bull Fonds Rech For Univ Laval
Bulletin. Food Industrial Experiment Station. Hiroshima Prefecture — Bull Food Ind Exp Stn Hiroshima Prefect
Bulletin for Australian Industry — Bul Aust Ind
Bulletin for Australian Industry — Bul Aust Industry
Bulletin for Industrial Psychology and Personnel Practice — Bul Ind Psychol
Bulletin for International Fiscal Documentation — B Int Fis D
Bulletin for International Fiscal Documentation — B Int Fisc Docum
Bulletin for International Fiscal Documentation — BFD
Bulletin for International Fiscal Documentation — BIFD
Bulletin for International Fiscal Documentation — Bul Int Fiscal Doc
Bulletin for International Fiscal Documentation — Bul Internat Fiscal Docum
Bulletin for International Fiscal Documentation — Bul Internat Fiscal Documentation
Bulletin for International Fiscal Documentation — Bull for Internat Fiscal Docum
Bulletin for International Fiscal Documentation — Bull for Int'l Fisc Doc
Bulletin for International Fiscal Documentation — Bull Int Fisc Doc
Bulletin for Medical Research. National Society for Medical Research — Bull Med Res Natl Soc Med Res
Bulletin for Psychologists — Bul for Psych
Bulletin for the History of Chemistry — Bull Hist Chem
Bulletin. Ford Forestry Center — Bull Ford For Cent
Bulletin. Foreign Language Association of Virginia — BFLAV
Bulletin. Forest Department. Kampala (Uganda) — Bull For Dep (Uganda)
Bulletin. Forest Products Research. Ministry of Technology (London) — Bull For Prod Res (Lond)
Bulletin. Forestry and Forest Products Research Institute — Bull For For Prod Res Inst
Bulletin. Forestry and Forest Products Research Institute — RSHKA6
Bulletin. Forestry and Timber Bureau — Bull For Timb Bur
Bulletin. Forestry and Timber Bureau (Canberra, Australia) — Bull For Timb Bur (Aust)
Bulletin. Forestry Commission (London) — Bull For Comm (Lond)
Bulletin. Forestry Commission of Tasmania — Bull For Comm Tasm
Bulletin. Forestry Society of Korea/Chosen Sanrin-Kaiho — Bull Forest Soc Korea
Bulletin. Forests Commission of Tasmania — Bull Forests Comm Tasm
Bulletin. Forests Commission of Victoria — Bull For Comm Vict
Bulletin. Forests Commission of Victoria — Bull Forest Comm Vict
Bulletin. Forests Department of Western Australia — Bull For Dep W Aust
Bulletin. Forests Department of Western Australia — Bull For Dep West Aust
Bulletin. Forests Department of Western Australia — Bull Forest Dep WA
Bulletin. Forests Department of Western Australia — Bull Forests Dep West Aust
Bulletin. Fort Wayne Medical Society [*Indiana*] — Bull Ft Wayne Med Soc
Bulletin. Fouad I University. Faculty of Arts [*Giza*] — Bull Fouad I Univ Fac Arts
Bulletin Francais de la Peche et de la Pisciculture — BFPPE2
Bulletin Francais de la Peche et de la Pisciculture — Bull Fr Peche Piscic
Bulletin Francais de Pisciculture — Bul Franc Piscicul
Bulletin Francais de Pisciculture — Bull Fr Piscic
Bulletin Francais de Pisciculture — Bull Franc Piscicult
Bulletin. Freshwater Fisheries Research Laboratory [*Tokyo*] — TSKHAY
Bulletin. Freshwater Fisheries Research Laboratory (Tokyo) — Bull Freshw Fish Res Lab (Tokyo)
Bulletin. Freshwater Fisheries Research Laboratory (Tokyo) — Bull Freshwater Fish Res Lab (Tokyo)
Bulletin. Friends' Historical Association — B Friends Hist Ass
Bulletin. Friends Historical Association — BFHA
Bulletin. Friends Historical Association — Bull Friends Hist Ass
Bulletin. Friends Historical Association [*Philadelphia*] — Bull Frnds Hist Assn
Bulletin. Fruit Tree Research Station. Ministry of Agriculture and Forestry. Series E (Akitsu) — Bull Fruit Tree Res Stn Minist Agric For Ser E (Akitsu)
Bulletin. Fruit Tree Research Station. Series A [*Yatabe*] — KSHAB2

Bulletin. Fruit Tree Research Station. Series A (Hiratsuka) — Bull Fruit Tree Res Stn Ser A (Hiratsuka)
Bulletin. Fruit Tree Research Station. Series A (Yatabe) — Bull Fruit Tree Res Stn Ser A (Yatabe)
Bulletin. Fruit Tree Research Station. Series B (Okitsu) — Bull Fruit Tree Res Stn Ser B (Okitsu)
Bulletin. Fruit Tree Research Station. Series C (Morioka) — Bull Fruit Tree Res Stn Ser C (Morioka)
Bulletin. Fruit Tree Research Station. Series D [*Kuchinotsu*] — KJHKD5
Bulletin. Fruit Tree Research Station. Series D (Kuchinotsu) — Bull Fruit Tree Res Stn Ser D (Kuchinotsu)
Bulletin. Fruit Tree Research Station. Series E [*Akitsu*] — BFTADA
Bulletin. Fruit Tree Research Station. Series E (Akitsu) — Bull Fruit Tree Res Stn Ser E (Akitsu)
Bulletin. Fuel Research Institute of South Africa — Bull Fuel Res Inst S Afr
Bulletin. Fuji Women's College — Bull Fuji Women's Coll
Bulletin. Fukui Prefectural Textile Engineering Research Institute — Bull Fukui Prefect Text Eng Res Inst
Bulletin. Fukuoka Agricultural Experiment Station — Bull Fukuoka Agr Exp Stn
Bulletin. Fukuoka Prefectural Agricultural Experiment Station — Bull Fukuoka Pref Agr Exp Sta
Bulletin. Fukuoka. Ringyo Shikenjo — Bull Fukuoka Ringyo Shikenjo
Bulletin. Fukuoka University of Education. Part 3. Mathematics, Natural Sciences, and Technology — Bull Fukuoka Univ Educ Part 3 Math Nat Sci Technol
Bulletin. Fukuoka University of Education. Part 3. Mathematics, Natural Sciences, and Technology — FDKNEF
Bulletin. Fukuoka University of Education. Part 3. Mathematics, Natural Sciences, and Technology — FKDNEF
Bulletin. Fukuoka University of Education. Part 3. Natural Sciences — Bull Fukuoka Univ Ed 3
Bulletin. Fukuoka University of Education. Part 3. Natural Sciences — Bull Fukuoka Univ Educ Part 3 Nat Sci
Bulletin. Fukuoka University of Education. Part 3. Natural Sciences — FKDRAN
Bulletin. Fukuokaken Forest Experiment Station — Bull Fukuokaken For Exp Sta
Bulletin. Fukushima Prefectural Fisheries Experimental Station — Bull Fukushima Prefect Fish Exp Stn
Bulletin Galenica — Bull Galenica
Bulletin. Garden Club of America — Bull Gard Club Amer
Bulletin. Geisinger Medical Center — Bull Geisinger Med Cent
Bulletin General Congregatio Santi-Spiritus — BGCSS
Bulletin General de Therapeutique Medicale, Chirurgicale, et Obstetricale (Paris) — Bull Gen Therap (Paris)
Bulletin General et Universel des Annonces et des Nouvelles Scientifiques — Bull Gen Universel Annonces Nouv Sci
Bulletin. Genessee County Medical Society [*Michigan*] — Bull Genessee County Med Soc
Bulletin. Geochemical Society of India — Bull Geochem Soc India
Bulletin Geodesique — Bull Geod
Bulletin Geodesique — Bull Geodesique
Bulletin. Geographical Society of Philadelphia — B Geogr Soc Phila
Bulletin. Geographical Society of Philadelphia — Bull Geogr Soc Phila
Bulletin. Geographical Survey Institute — Bull Geogr Surv Inst
Bulletin. Geological and Mineral Resources Department (Sudan) — Bull Geol Miner Resour Dep (Sudan)
Bulletin. Geological and Natural History Survey — Bull Geol Nat Hist Surv
Bulletin. Geological Institute. Bulgarian Academy of Sciences. Series Geotectonics — Bull Geol Inst Bulg Acad Sci Ser Geotecton
Bulletin. Geological Institutions of the University of Uppsala — Bull Geol Inst Univ Upps
Bulletin. Geological, Mining, and Metallurgical Society of India — Bull Geol Min Metall Soc India
Bulletin. Geological, Mining, and Metallurgical Society of Liberia — Bull Geol Min Metall Soc Liberia
Bulletin. Geological Society of America — B Geol Soc Am
Bulletin. Geological Society of America — BGSA
Bulletin. Geological Society of America — Bull Geol Soc Am
Bulletin. Geological Society of America — Bull Geol Soc Amer
Bulletin. Geological Society of America. Part 1 — Bull Geol Soc Am Part 1
Bulletin. Geological Society of China — Bull Geol Soc China
Bulletin. Geological Society of Denmark — Bull Geol Soc Den
Bulletin. Geological Society of Denmark — Bull Geol Soc Denmark
Bulletin. Geological Society of Denmark — MDGFA
Bulletin. Geological Society of Finland — Bull Geol Soc Finl
Bulletin. Geological Society of Greece — Bull Geol Soc Greece
Bulletin. Geological Society of Malaysia — Bull Geol Soc Malays
Bulletin. Geological Society of Turkey — Bull Geol Soc Turk
Bulletin. Geological Survey Department (Malawi) — Bull Geol Surv Dep (Malawi)
Bulletin. Geological Survey Department (Republic of Botswana) — Bull Geol Surv Dep (Botswana)
Bulletin. Geological Survey Division (Jamaica) — Bull Geol Surv Div (Jamaica)
Bulletin. Geological Survey Division (Solomon Islands) — Bull Geol Surv Div (Solomon Isl)
Bulletin. Geological Survey of Canada — Bull Geol Surv Can
Bulletin. Geological Survey of Georgia — Bull Geol Surv G
Bulletin. Geological Survey of Georgia [*United States*] — Bull Geol Surv Georgia
Bulletin. Geological Survey of Great Britain — BUGGA
Bulletin. Geological Survey of Great Britain — Bull Geol Surv GB
Bulletin. Geological Survey of Great Britain — Bull Geol Surv Gr Brit
Bulletin. Geological Survey of Greenland — Bull Geol Surv Greenland
Bulletin. Geological Survey of Guyana — Bull Geol Surv Guyana
Bulletin. Geological Survey of India. Series A. Economic Geology — Bull Geol Surv India A
Bulletin. Geological Survey of Indonesia — Bull Geol Surv Indones
Bulletin. Geological Survey of Ireland — Bull Geol Surv Irel
Bulletin. Geological Survey of Israel — Bull Geol Surv Israel
Bulletin. Geological Survey of Japan — Bull Geol Surv Jap
Bulletin. Geological Survey of Japan — Bull Geol Surv Jpn
Bulletin. Geological Survey of New South Wales — Bull Geol Surv NSW
Bulletin. Geological Survey of Prague — Bull Geol Surv Prague
Bulletin. Geological Survey of Rhodesia — Bull Geol Surv Rhod
Bulletin. Geological Survey of South Africa — Bull Geol Surv S Afr
Bulletin. Geological Survey of South Australia — Bull Geol Surv S Aust
Bulletin. Geological Survey of Taiwan — Bull Geol Surv Taiwan
Bulletin. Geological Survey of Tanzania — Bull Geol Surv Tanz
Bulletin. Geological Survey of Western Australia — Bull Geol Surv West Aust
Bulletin. Geologinen Tutkimuslaitos (Finland) — Bul Geol Tutkimuslaitos (Fin)
Bulletin. Geologiska Institut. Universitet Upsala — Bull Geol Inst Univ Ups
Bulletin. Geophysical Observatory. Haile Sellassie I University [*Ethiopia*] — Bull Geophys Obs Haile Sellassie I Univ
Bulletin. Georgetown University Medical Center — Bull Georgetown Univ Med Cent
Bulletin. Georgia Academy of Science — BUCDA
Bulletin. Georgia Academy of Science — Bull GA Acad Sci
Bulletin. Georgia Agricultural Experiment Station — Bull GA Agr Exp Sta
Bulletin. Georgia Agricultural Experiment Station — Bull GA Agric Exp Stn
Bulletin- Geoteknisk Institut (Copenhagen) — Bull Geotek Inst (Copenhagen)
Bulletin. Geothermal Resources Council (Davis, California) — Bull Geotherm Resour Counc (Davis Calif)
Bulletin. Ghana Geological Survey — Bull Ghana Geol Surv
Bulletin. Gifu College of Education — Bull Gifu College E
Bulletin. Gifu College of Education — Bull Gifu College Ed
Bulletin. Government Forest Experiment Station — Bull Gov Forest Exp Sta
Bulletin. Government Forest Experiment Station [*Tokyo*] — Bull Govt Forest Expt Sta
Bulletin. Government Forest Experiment Station (Meguro) — Bull For Exp Sta (Meguro)
Bulletin. Government Forest Experiment Station (Tokyo) — Bull Gov For Exp Stn (Tokyo)
Bulletin. Government Industrial Research Institute (Osaka) — Bull Gov Ind Res Inst (Osaka)
Bulletin. Government Museum. New Series. Natural History Section — Bull Gov Mus New Ser Nat Hist Sect
Bulletin. Great Britain Forest Products Research — Bull GB For Prod Res
Bulletin. Great Britain Forestry Commission — Bul GB For Com
Bulletin. Greene County Medical Society [*Missouri*] — Bull Greene County Med Soc
Bulletin. Greenville County Medical Society [*South Carolina*] — Bull Greenville County Med Soc
Bulletin. Groenlands Geologiske Undersoegelse — BGGUA
Bulletin. Groenlands Geologiske Undersoegelse [*Denmark*] — Bull Groenl Geol Unders
Bulletin. Groenlands Geologiske Undersoegelse — Bull Gronl Geol Unders
Bulletin. Groupe Archeologique du Nogentais — B GA Nogent
Bulletin. Groupe Belge des Auditeurs. Academie de Droit International de La Haye — BGB
Bulletin. Groupe Belge des Auditeurs et Anciens Auditeurs. Academie de Droit International de La Haye — Bul Ac Int
Bulletin. Groupe de Travail pour l'Etude de l'Equilibre Foret-Gibier — Bull Groupe Trav Etud Equilib Foret-Gibier
Bulletin. Groupe de Travail pour l'Etude de l'Equilibre Foret-Gibier — Bull Groupe Trav Etud Equilibre Foret-Gibier
Bulletin. Groupe d'Etude des Rythmes Biologiques — Pull Groupe Etud Rythmes Biol
Bulletin. Groupe Francais des Argiles — Bull Groupe Fr Argiles
Bulletin. Groupe Francais des Argiles — Bull Grpe Fr Argiles
Bulletin. Groupe Francais d'Humidimetrie Neutronique — BGFND
Bulletin. Groupe Francais d'Humidimetrie Neutronique — Bull Groupe Fr Humidimetrie Neutron
Bulletin. Groupe Francais d'Humidimetrie Neutronique [*France*] — Bull Groupe Fr Humidimetrie Neutronique
Bulletin. Groupement Archeologique de Seine-et-Marn — BGASM
Bulletin. Groupement Archeologique de Seine-Et-Marne — B Group Seine Marne
Bulletin. Groupement Archeologique du Maconnais — BGA Mac
Bulletin. Groupement Europeen pour la Recherche Scientifique en Stomatologie et Odontologie — Bull Group Eur Rech Sci Stomatol Odontol
Bulletin. Groupement International pour la Recherche Scientifique en Stomatologie — BGRSA
Bulletin. Groupement International pour la Recherche Scientifique en Stomatologie — Bull Group Int Rech Sci Stomatol
Bulletin. Groupement International pour la Recherche Scientifique en Stomatologie et Odontologie — Bull Group Int Rech Sci Stomatol Odontol
Bulletin. Groupes de Recherches Archeologiques du Departement de la Loire — BGRL
Bulletin. Haffkine Institute — BHFIA
Bulletin. Haffkine Institute — Bull Haffkine Inst
Bulletin. Hakodate Marine Observatory — Bull Hakodate Mar Observ
Bulletin Halte — Bul Halte
Bulletin. Hardy Plant Society — Bull Hardy Pl Soc
Bulletin. Harvard Forestry Club — Bull Harvard Forest Club
Bulletin. Harvard Medical Alumni Association — Bull Harvard Med Alumni Ass
Bulletin. Hatano Tobacco Experiment Station — Bull Hatano Tob Exp Stn
Bulletin. Heart Institute (Japan) — BHIJA
Bulletin. Heart Institute (Japan) — Bull Hear Inst (Jpn)
Bulletin. Heart Institute (Japan) — Bull Heart Inst (Jpn)
Bulletin Hebdomadaire Fabrimetal — BHFabrimetal
Bulletin. Hellenic Veterinary Medical Society — Bull Hell Vet Med Soc
Bulletin. Hemlock Arboretum at Far Country — Bull Hemlock Arbor
Bulletin. Hennepin County Medical Society [*Minnesota*] — Bull Hennepin County Med Soc

Bulletin. Highway Research Board — Bull Highw Res Bd
Bulletin. Hiroshima Agricultural College — Bull Hiroshima Agric Coll
Bulletin. Hiroshima Food Research Institute — Bull Hiroshima Food Res Inst
Bulletin. Hiroshima Jogakuin College — Bull Hiroshima Jogakuin Coll
Bulletin. Hiroshima Prefectural Agricultural Experiment Station — Bull Hiroshima Prefect Agric Exp Stn
Bulletin. Hiroshima Prefectural Food Technological Research Center — Bull Hiroshima Prefect Food Technol Res Cent
Bulletin. Hiroshima Prefectural Institute of Public Health — Bull Hiroshima Prefect Inst Public Health
Bulletin Hispanique — B Hispan
Bulletin Hispanique — BH
Bulletin Hispanique — BHi
Bulletin Hispanique — BHisp
Bulletin Hispanique — BIH
Bulletin Hispanique — Bull Hisp
Bulletin Hispanique — Bull Hispanique
Bulletin. Histoire Naturelle. Societe Linneenne de Bordeaux — Bull Hist Nat Soc Linn Bordeaux
Bulletin. Historical and Philosophical Society of Ohio — BHPSO
Bulletin. Historical Metallurgy Group — Bull Hist Metal Group
Bulletin. Historical Society of Montgomery County — BHSM
Bulletin. Historical Society of Montgomery County — BHSMCo
Bulletin Historique. Diocese de Lyon — BHDL
Bulletin Historique et Litteraire. Societe de l'Histoire du Protestantisme Francais — BHPF
Bulletin Historique et Philologique. Comite des Travaux Historiques et Scientifiques — BHPCTHS
Bulletin Historique et Philologique du Comite des Travaux Scientifiques — PHPh
Bulletin Historique et Scientifique de l'Auvergne — B Auvergne
Bulletin Historique et Scientifique de l'Auvergne — BHSA
Bulletin Historique, Scientifique, Litteraire, Artistique et Agricole. Societe Academique du Puy et de la Haute-Loire — Bull Hist Haute-Loire
Bulletin Historique. Societe des Antiquitaires de la Morinie — BHSAM
Bulletin. History of Medicine — BuH
Bulletin. Hoblitzelle Agricultural Laboratory. Texas Research Foundation — Bull Hoblitzelle Agr Lab Tex Res Found
Bulletin. Hoblitzelle Agricultural Laboratory. Texas Research Foundation — Bull Hoblitzelle Agric Lab Tex Res Found
Bulletin. Hokkaido Agricultural Experiment Station/Hokkaido Noji Shikenjo Iho — Bull Hokkaido Agric Exp Sta
Bulletin. Hokkaido Forest Experiment Station — Bull Hokkaido For Exp Stn
Bulletin. Hokkaido Prefectural Agricultural Experiment Station — Bull Hokkaido Pref Agr Exp Sta
Bulletin. Hokkaido Prefectural Agricultural Experiment Station — Bull Hokkaido Prefect Agric Exp Stn
Bulletin. Hokkaido Regional Fisheries Research Laboratories — Bull Hokkaido Reg Fish Res Lab
Bulletin. Hokuriku National Agricultural Experiment Station — Bull Hokuriku Natl Agric Exp Stn
Bulletin. Holly Society of America — Bull Holly Soc Amer
Bulletin Horticole (Liege) — Bull Hortic (Liege)
Bulletin. Horticultural Research Station (Ministry of Agriculture and Forestry). Series A (Hiratsuka) — Bull Hortic Res Stn (Minist Agric For) Ser A (Hiratsuka)
Bulletin. Horticultural Research Station (Ministry of Agriculture and Forestry). Series B (Okitsu) — Bull Hortic Res Stn (Minist Agric For) Ser B (Okitsu)
Bulletin. Horticultural Research Station (Ministry of Agriculture and Forestry). Series C (Morioka) — Bull Hortic Res Stn (Minist Agric For) Ser C (Morioka)
Bulletin. Horticultural Research Station (Ministry of Agriculture and Forestry). Series D (Kurume) — Bull Hortic Res Stn (Minist Agric For) Ser D (Kurume)
Bulletin. Horticultural Research Station. Series A. Hiratsuka/Engei Shikenjo Hokoku. A. Hiratsuka — Bull Hort Res Sta Ser A Hiratsuka
Bulletin. Horticultural Research Station. Series D. Kurume/Engei Shikenjo Hokoku. D. Kurume — Bull Hort Res Sta Ser D Kurume
Bulletin. Hospital for Joint Diseases — Bull Hosp Joint Dis
Bulletin. Hospital for Joint Diseases — Bull Hosp Jt Dis
Bulletin. Hospital for Joint Diseases. Orthopaedic Institute — Bull Hosp Jt Dis Orthop Inst
Bulletin. Hot Spring Research Institute. Kanagawa Prefecture — Bull Hot Spring Res Inst Kanagawa Prefect
Bulletin. Hudson County Dental Society — Bull Hudson Cty Dent Soc
Bulletin. Hunan Medical College — Bull Hunan Med Coll
Bulletin. Hygienic Laboratory. United States Marine Hospital Service — Bull Hyg Lab US Mar Hosp Serv
Bulletin. Hygienic Laboratory. United States Public Health and Marine Hospital Service — Bull Hyg Lab US Pub Health and Mar Hosp Serv
Bulletin. Hygienic Laboratory. United States Public Health Service — Bull Hyg Lab US Pub Health Serv
Bulletin. Hyogo Prefectural Agricultural Center for Experiment, Extension, and Education — Bull Hyogo Prefect Agric Cent Exp Ext Educ
Bulletin. Hyogo Prefectural Agricultural Experiment Station — Bull Hyogo Pref Agr Exp Sta
Bulletin. Hyogo Prefectural Agricultural Experiment Station/Hyogo-Kenritsu Nogyo Shikenjo Kenkyu Hokoku — Bull Hyogo Prefect Agric Exp Sta
Bulletin. Hyogo Prefectural Agricultural Institute — Bull Hyogo Prefect Agric Inst
Bulletin. Hyogo Prefectural Forest Experiment Station — Bull Hyogo Prefect For Exp Stn
Bulletin. Ibaraki Prefectural Forest Experiment Station — Bull Ibaraki Prefect For Exp Stn
Bulletin. Idaho Agricultural Experiment Station — Bull Idaho Agr Exp Sta
Bulletin. Idaho Agricultural Experiment Station — Bull Idaho Agric Exp Stn
Bulletin. Idaho Bureau of Mines and Geology — Bull Idaho Bur Mines Geol
Bulletin. Idaho Forest, Wildlife, and Range Experiment Station — Bull Idaho For Wildl Range Exp Stn
Bulletin. Idaho, Oregon, and Washington Agricultural Experiment Stations and US Department of Agriculture — Bull Idaho Oreg Wash Agr Exp Sta US Dept Agr
Bulletin. Illinois Agricultural Experiment Station — Bull Ill Agr Exp Sta
Bulletin. Illinois Cooperative Crop Reporting Service — Bull Ill Coop Crop Rep Serv
Bulletin. Illinois Foreign Language Teachers Association — BIFLTA
Bulletin. Illinois Natural History Survey — Bull Ill Nat Hist Surv
Bulletin. Illinois Natural History Survey — Bull Illinois Nat Hist Surv
Bulletin. Illinois Natural History Survey — INHBA
Bulletin. Illinois State Geological Survey — Bull Ill St Geol Surv
Bulletin. Illinois State Geological Survey — Bull Ill State Geol Surv
Bulletin. Illinois State Laboratory of Natural History — Bull Ill St Lab Nat Hist
Bulletin Illustre de la Wallonie — B Ill Wall
Bulletin. Imperial Bureau of Pastures and Forage Crops — Bull Imp Bur Pastures Forage Crops
Bulletin. Imperial Forest Experiment Station/Ringyo Shiken Hokoku — Bull Imp Forest Exp Sta
Bulletin. Imperial Institute — B Imp Inst
Bulletin. Imperial Institute [*London*] — Bull Imp Inst
Bulletin. Imperial Institute (London) — Bull Imp Inst (London)
Bulletin. Imperial Institute of Great Britain — Bull Imp Inst Gr Brit
Bulletin. Imperial Sericultural Station (Tokyo) — Bull Imp Seric Stn (Tokyo)
Bulletin in Applied Statistics — BIAS
Bulletin. Independent Biological Laboratories (Kefar-Malal) — Bull Indep Biol Lab (Kefar-Malal)
Bulletin. India Section. Electrochemical Society — Bull India Sect Electrochem Soc
Bulletin. Indian Council of Agricultural Research — Bull Indian Coun Agric Res
Bulletin. Indian Geologists' Association — Bull Indian Geol Ass
Bulletin. Indian Institute of the History of Medicine — Bull Indian Inst Hist Med
Bulletin. Indian National Science Academy — Bull Indian Natl Sci Acad
Bulletin. Indian Phytopathological Society — Bull Indian Phytopathol Soc
Bulletin. Indian Society for Malaria and Other Communicable Diseases — Bull Indian Soc Malar Commun Dis
Bulletin. Indian Society of Earthquake Technology — Bull Indian Soc Earthqu Technol
Bulletin. Indian Society of Soil Science — Bull Indian Soc Soil Sci
Bulletin. Industrial Developers Association of Canada — Bul Ind Dev Assoc Can
Bulletin. Industrial Research Center of Ehime Prefecture — Bull Ind Res Cent Ehime Prefect
Bulletin. Industrial Research Institute of Ehime Prefecture — Bull Ind Res Inst Ehime Prefect
Bulletin. Industrial Research Institute of Kanagawa Prefecture [*Japan*] — Bull Ind Res Inst Kanagawa Prefect
Bulletin. Infirmieres Catholiques du Canada — Bull Infirm Cathol Can
Bulletin. Institut Agronomique et Stations de Recherches de Gembloux [*Belgium*] — Bull Inst Agron Gembloux
Bulletin. Institut Agronomique et Stations de Recherches de Gembloux — Bull Inst Agron Sta Rech Gembloux
Bulletin. Institut Agronomique et Stations de Recherches de Gembloux — Bull Inst Agron Stn Rech Gembloux
Bulletin. Institut Agronomique et Stations de Recherches de Gembloux — Bull Inst Agron Stns Rech Gembloux
Bulletin. Institut Agronomique et Stations de Recherches de Gembloux. Hors Serie — Bull Inst Agron Stn Rech Gembloux Hors Ser
Bulletin. Institut Archeologique Bulgare — Bl Bulg
Bulletin. Institut Archeologique Bulgare — BIA Bulg
Bulletin. Institut Archeologique Bulgare — BIAB
Bulletin. Institut Archeologique Liegeois — B A Liege
Bulletin. Institut Archeologique Liegeois — BIAL
Bulletin. Institut Archeologique Liegeois — Bull Inst Arch Liegeois
Bulletin. Institut Archeologique Liegeois — Bull Inst Archeol Liegeois
Bulletin. Institut Belge de Droit Compare — Bul D Cpr
Bulletin. Institut de Geologie du Bassin d'Aquitaine — Bull Inst Geol Bassin Aquitaine
Bulletin. Institut de Geologie. Universite Louis Pasteur de Strasbourg — Bull Inst Geol Univ Louis Pasteur Strasbourg
Bulletin. Institut de l'Email Vitrifie — Bull Inst Email Vitrifie
Bulletin. Institut de Medecine Experimentale — Bull Inst Med Exp
Bulletin. Institut de Phonetique de Grenoble — BIPG
Bulletin. Institut de Physique. Universite Libre de Bruxelles [*Belgium*] — Bull Inst Phys Univ Libre Bruxelles
Bulletin. Institut de Recherches Economiques — B Inst Rech Econ
Bulletin. Institut de Recherches Economiques et Sociales — Bull Inst Econ Soc
Bulletin. Institut de Recherches Economiques et Sociales. Universite de Louvain — BIRESUL
Bulletin. Institut de Recherches Scientifiques au Congo — BIRSC
Bulletin. Institut de Sociologie Solvay — Bull Inst Sociol Solvay
Bulletin. Institut de Zoologie et Musee. Academie Bulgare des Sciences — Bull Inst Zool Mus Acad Bulg Sci
Bulletin. Institut d'Egypte — BIE
Bulletin. Institut d'Egypte — Bull Inst Eg
Bulletin. Institut d'Egypte — Bull Inst Egypt
Bulletin. Institut d'Egypte — Bull Inst Egypte
Bulletin. Institut des Peches Maritimes du Maroc — Bull Inst Peches Marit Maroc
Bulletin. Institut des Sciences Economiques — Bul Ec
Bulletin. Institut d'Etudes Centrafricaines — Bul IEC
Bulletin. Institut d'Etudes Centrafricaines — Bull Inst Etudes Centrafr
Bulletin. Institut du Desert d'Egypte — Bull Inst Desert Egypte
Bulletin. Institut du Pin — Bull Inst Pin
Bulletin. Institut du Verre — Bull Inst Verre
Bulletin. Institut Economique de Paris — B Inst Econ Paris
Bulletin. Institut Egyptien — Bull Inst Egypt

Bulletin. Institut et Observatoire Physique du Globe du Puy De Dome — Bull Inst Obs Phys Globe Puy De Dome
Bulletin. Institut Fondamental d'Afrique Noire — B Inst Fondam Afr Noire
Bulletin. Institut Fondamental d'Afrique Noire — Bull Inst Fondam Afr Noire
Bulletin. Institut Fondamental d'Afrique Noire. Serie A. Sciences Naturelles — Bull Inst Fondam Afr Noire Ser A Sci Nat
Bulletin. Institut Francais d'Afrique Noire — B Inst Fr Afr Noire
Bulletin. Institut Francais d'Afrique Noire — Bull IFAN
Bulletin. Institut Francais d'Afrique Noire — Bull Inst Fr Afr Noire
Bulletin. Institut Francais d'Afrique Noire. Serie A — Bull Inst Fr Afr Noire Ser A
Bulletin. Institut Francais d'Afrique Noire. Serie A. Sciences Naturelles — Bull Inst Fr Afr Noire Ser A Sci Nat
Bulletin. Institut Francais d'Amerique Latine — Bull IFAL
Bulletin. Institut Francais d'Archeologie Orientale — BIAO
Bulletin. Institut Francais d'Archeologie Orientale — BIFAO
Bulletin. Institut Francais d'Archeologie Orientale [*Cairo*] — BJFAO
Bulletin. Institut Francais d'Archeologie Orientale — Bull IFAO
Bulletin. Institut Francais d'Archeologie Orientale [*Cairo*] — Bull IFAOC
Bulletin. Institut Francais d'Archeologie Orientale — Bull Inst Fr Archeol Orient
Bulletin. Institut Francais d'Archeologie Orientale [*Cairo*] — Bull Inst Franc
Bulletin. Institut Francais d'Archeologie Orientale [*Cairo*] — Bull Inst Franc Archeol Orient
Bulletin. Institut Francais d'Archeologie Orientale (Cairo) — Bull Cairo
Bulletin. Institut Francais d'Etudes Andines — B Inst Franc Et Andines
Bulletin. Institut Francais d'Etudes Andines — IFEA/B
Bulletin. Institut Francais du Cafe et du Cacao — Bull Inst Fr Cafe Cacao
Bulletin. Institut Francais en Espagne — B Inst Franc Espagne
Bulletin. Institut General Psychologique — Bull Inst Gen Psychol
Bulletin. Institut Historique Belge de Rome — B Inst Hist Belg Rom
Bulletin. Institut Historique Belge de Rome — BIBR
Bulletin. Institut Historique Belge de Rome — BIHBR
Bulletin. Institut Historique Belge de Rome — Bull Inst Hist Belg Rome
Bulletin. Institut Historique Belge de Rome — Bull Inst Hist Belge
Bulletin. Institut International d'Administration Publique — B Inst Int Adm Publ
Bulletin. Institut International d'Administration Publique — Bull Inst Int Adm Publique
Bulletin. Institut International d'Administration Publique — Inst Internat Admin Publique Bul
Bulletin. Institut International de Bibliographie — BIB
Bulletin. Institut International de Bibliographie — Bull Inst Int Bibliogr
Bulletin. Institut International de Statistique — Bull Inst Int Stat
Bulletin. Institut International de Statistique — Bull Inst Internat Statist
Bulletin. Institut International du Froid — Bull Inst Int Froid
Bulletin. Institut International du Froid. Annexe [*France*] — Bull Inst Int Froid Annexe
Bulletin. Institut International du Froid. Annexe — IRBAA
Bulletin. Institut National de la Sante et de la Recherche Medicale — BSRMA
Bulletin. Institut National de la Sante et de la Recherche Medicale (Paris) — Bull Inst Natl Sante Rech Med (Paris)
Bulletin. Institut National d'Hygiene (Paris) — Bull Inst Natl Hyg (Paris)
Bulletin. Institut National Genevois — Bull Inst Nat Genevois
Bulletin. Institut National Scientifique et Technique d'Oceanographie et de Peche — Bull Inst Natl Sci Rech Oceanogr Peche
Bulletin. Institut National Scientifique et Technique d'Oceanographie et de Peche de Salammbo — Bull Inst Natl Sci Tech Oceanogr Peche Salammbo
Bulletin. Institut Oceanographique (Monaco) — Bull Inst Oceanogr (Monaco)
Bulletin. Institut Oinoue de Recherches Agronomiques et Biologiques/Oinoue Rinogaku Kenkyusho. Kenkyu Hokoku — Bull Inst Oinoue Rech Agron
Bulletin. Institut Pasteur [*Paris*] — B I Pasteur
Bulletin. Institut Pasteur [*Paris*] — BIPAA
Bulletin. Institut Pasteur [*Paris*] — Bull Inst Pasteur
Bulletin. Institut Pasteur (Paris) — Bull Inst Pasteur (Paris)
Bulletin. Institut Polytechnique a Ivanovo-Vosniesensk — Bull Inst Polytech Ivanovo Vosniesensk
Bulletin. Institut pour l'Etude de l'Europe Sud-Orientale — BISO
Bulletin. Institut Provincial de Cooperation Agricole — Bull Inst Prov Coop Agr
Bulletin. Institut Royal des Sciences Naturelles de Belgique — Bull Inst R Sci Nat Belg
Bulletin. Institut Royal des Sciences Naturelles de Belgique — Bull Inst Sci Natur Belg
Bulletin. Institut Royal des Sciences Naturelles de Belgique. Biologie — Bull Inst R Sci Nat Belg Biol
Bulletin. Institut Royal des Sciences Naturelles de Belgique. Entomologie — Bull Inst R Sci Nat Belg Entomol
Bulletin. Institut Royal des Sciences Naturelles de Belgique. Sciences de la Terre — Bull Inst R Sci Nat Belg Sci Terre
Bulletin. Institut Royal du Patrimoine Artistique [*Brussels*] — BIPA
Bulletin. Institut Royal du Patrimoine Artistique — BIRPA
Bulletin. Institut Scientifique (Rabat) — Bull Inst Sci (Rabat)
Bulletin. Institut Technique du Porc — Bull Inst Tech Porc
Bulletin. Institut Textile de France — Bull Inst Text Fr
Bulletin. Institute for Agricultural Research on Rolling Land (Tokyo) — Bull Inst Agric Res Rolling Land (Tokyo)
Bulletin. Institute for Agricultural Research. Tohoku University — Bull Inst Agr Res Tohoku Univ
Bulletin. Institute for Agricultural Research. Tohoku University — Bull Inst Agric Res Tohoku Univ
Bulletin. Institute for Basic Science. Inha University — Bull Inst Basic Sci Inha Univ
Bulletin. Institute for Chemical Preparations in Agriculture. Academy of Agricultural Sciences. Bulgaria — Bull Inst Chem Prep Agric Acad Agric Sci Bulg
Bulletin. Institute for Chemical Reaction Science. Tohoku University — Bull Inst Chem React Sci Tohoku Univ
Bulletin. Institute for Chemical Research. Kyoto University — BICRA
Bulletin. Institute for Chemical Research. Kyoto University — Bull Inst Chem Res Kyoto Univ
Bulletin. Institute for Geological and Geophysical Research (Belgrade). Series A. Geology — Bull Inst Geol Geophys Res (Belgrade) Ser A
Bulletin. Institute for Geological and Geophysical Research (Belgrade). Series B. Engineering Geology and Hydrogeology — Bull Inst Geol Geophys Res (Belgrade) Ser B
Bulletin. Institute for Geological and Geophysical Research (Belgrade). Series C. Applied Geophysics — Bull Inst Geol Geophys Res (Belgrade) Ser C
Bulletin. Institute for Geological and Geophysical Research. Series A. Geology (English Translation) — Bull Inst Geol Geophys Res Ser A (Engl Transl)
Bulletin. Institute for Geological and Geophysical Research. Series B. Engineering Geology and Hydrogeology (English Translation) — Bull Inst Geol Geophys Res Ser B (Engl Trans)
Bulletin. Institute for Geological and Geophysical Research. Series C. Applied Geophysics (English Translation) — Bull Inst Geol Geophys Res Ser C (Eng Trans)
Bulletin. Institute for Industrial and Social Development [*South Korea*] — BIIDD
Bulletin. Institute for Industrial and Social Development [*South Korea*] — Bull Inst Ind Soc Dev
Bulletin. Institute for Material Science and Engineering. Faculty of Engineering. Fukui University — Bull Inst Mater Sci Eng Fac Eng Fukui Univ
Bulletin. Institute for Medical Research. Federated Malay States — Bull Inst Med Research FMS
Bulletin. Institute for Medical Research. Federation of Malaya — Bull Inst Med Res Fed Malaya
Bulletin. Institute for Medical Research (Kuala Lumpur) — Bull Inst Med Res (Kuala Lumpur)
Bulletin. Institute for Medical Research of Malaya — Bull Inst Med Res Malaya
Bulletin. Institute for Medical Research. University of Madrid — Bull Inst Med Res Univ Madr
Bulletin. Institute for the Study of the USSR — BIS
Bulletin. Institute for the Study of the USSR — BSUSSR
Bulletin. Institute for the Study of the USSR — Bull Inst Study USSR
Bulletin. Institute of Applied Geology. King Abdulaziz University [*Jeddah*] — Bull Inst Appl Geol King Abdulaziz Univ
Bulletin. Institute of Arab-American Affairs — BIA
Bulletin. Institute of Archaeology — BIA
Bulletin. Institute of Archaeology [*London*] — BInstArch
Bulletin. Institute of Archaeology — Bull Inst Arch
Bulletin. Institute of Archaeology (London) — B Inst A (London)
Bulletin. Institute of Archaeology. University of London — B Inst Archaeol
Bulletin. Institute of Archaeology. University of London — BIA London
Bulletin. Institute of Archaeology. University of London — BIAL
Bulletin. Institute of Archaeology. University of London — Bull Inst Archaeol Univ London
Bulletin. Institute of Atomic Energy. Kyoto University [*Japan*] — Bull Inst At Energ Kyoto Univ
Bulletin. Institute of Atomic Energy. Kyoto University — Bull Inst At Energy Kyoto Univ
Bulletin. Institute of Balneotherapeutics [*Japan*] — Bull Inst Balneother
Bulletin. Institute of Chemistry. Academia Sinica [*Taiwan*] — BICMA
Bulletin. Institute of Chemistry. Academia Sinica [*Taiwan*] — Bull Inst Chem Acad Sin
Bulletin. Institute of Classical Studies — Bull Inst Class Studies
Bulletin. Institute of Classical Studies. University of London — BICS
Bulletin. Institute of Classical Studies. University of London — BICSL
Bulletin. Institute of Classical Studies. University of London — Bul Cl Lo
Bulletin. Institute of Classical Studies. University of London — Bull Inst Cl St
Bulletin. Institute of Classical Studies. University of London — Bull Inst Classic Stud
Bulletin. Institute of Communication Research — B Inst Communication Res
Bulletin. Institute of Constitutional Medicine. Kumamoto University — Bull Inst Const Med Kumamoto Univ
Bulletin. Institute of Corrosion Science and Technology — Bull Inst Corros Sci Technol
Bulletin. Institute of Development Studies — B Inst Develop Stud
Bulletin. Institute of Ethnology. Academia Sinica — B Inst Ethnol Acad Sinica
Bulletin. Institute of Filipino Geologists — Bull Inst Filip Geol
Bulletin. Institute of Gas Technology — Bull Inst Gas Technol
Bulletin. Institute of General and Comparative Pathology. Bulgarian Academy of Sciences — Bull Inst Gen Comp Pathol Bulg Acad Sci
Bulletin. Institute of Geological Sciences — Bull Inst Geol Sci
Bulletin. Institute of Geophysics. National Central University [*Taiwan*] — Bull Inst Geophys Natl Cent Univ
Bulletin. Institute of Historical Research — B I Hist R
Bulletin. Institute of Historical Research — BIHR
Bulletin. Institute of Historical Research — Bull Inst Hist Res
Bulletin. Institute of Historical Research (London University) — Bull Inst Hist Res LU
Bulletin. Institute of History and Philology. Academia Sinica — B Inst Philol Acad Sinica
Bulletin. Institute of History and Philology. Academia Sinica — BIHP
Bulletin. Institute of History of Medicine — Bull Inst Hist Med
Bulletin. Institute of History of Medicine (Hyderabad) — B Inst Hist Med (Hyderabad)
Bulletin. Institute of History of Medicine. Johns Hopkins University — Bull Inst Hist Med Johns Hopk Univ
Bulletin. Institute of Immunological Science. Hokkaido University — Bull Inst Immunol Sci Hokkaido Univ
Bulletin. Institute of Jamaica. Science Series — B Inst Jam Sci
Bulletin. Institute of Jamaica. Science Series — Bull Inst Jam Sci Ser
Bulletin. Institute of Jewish Studies — BIJS
Bulletin. Institute of Jewish Studies — Bull Inst Jew St
Bulletin. Institute of Marine Medicine in Gdansk — Bull Inst Mar Med Gdansk

Bulletin. Institute of Maritime and Tropical Medicine in Gdynia — Bull Inst Mar Trop Med Gdynia
Bulletin. Institute of Maritime and Tropical Medicine in Gdynia — Bull Inst Marit Trop Med Gdynia
Bulletin. Institute of Mathematics. Academia Sinica — Bull Inst Math Acad Sinica
Bulletin. Institute of Mathematics and Its Applications — Bull Inst Math Appl
Bulletin. Institute of Metal Finishing — Bull Inst Met Finish
Bulletin. Institute of Metals — Bull Inst Met
Bulletin. Institute of Mineral Deposits. Chinese Academy of Geological Sciences [*Beijing*] — Bull Inst Miner Deposits Chin Acad Geol Sci
Bulletin. Institute of Modern History. Academia Sinica — B Inst Mod Hist Acad Sinica
Bulletin. Institute of Modern History. Academica Sinica — Bul
Bulletin. Institute of Natural Education in Shiga Heights — Bull Inst Nat Educ Shiga Heights
Bulletin. Institute of Nutrition. Bulgarian Academy of Sciences — Bull Inst Nutr Bulg Acad Sci
Bulletin. Institute of Oceanography and Fisheries — Bull Inst Oceanogr Fish
Bulletin. Institute of Paper Chemistry — Bull Inst Pap Chem
Bulletin. Institute of Physical and Chemical Research — Bull Inst Phys Chem Res
Bulletin. Institute of Physics (London) — Bull Inst Phys (Lond)
Bulletin. Institute of Physics (Malaysia) — Bull Inst Phys (Malays)
Bulletin. Institute of Post Graduate Medical Education and Research — Bull Inst Post Grad Med Educ Res
Bulletin. Institute of Public Health (Tokyo) — Bull Inst Public Health (Tokyo)
Bulletin. Institute of Radiation Breeding [*Japan*] — Bull Inst Radiat Breed
Bulletin. Institute of Space and Aeronautical Science. University of Tokyo [*A publication*] — Bull Inst Space Aeronaut Sci Univ Tokyo
Bulletin. Institute of Space and Aeronautical Science. University of Tokyo. A — Bull Inst Space & Aeronaut Sci Univ Tokyo A
Bulletin. Institute of Space and Aeronautical Science. University of Tokyo. B — Bull Inst Space & Aeronaut Sci Univ Tokyo B
Bulletin. Institute of Traditional Cultures — B Inst Trad Cult
Bulletin. Institute of Traditional Cultures — BITC
Bulletin. Institute of Vitreous Enamellers — Bull Inst Vitreous Enamellers
Bulletin. Institute of Zoology. Academia Sinica [*Taipei*] — B I Zool AS
Bulletin. Institute of Zoology. Academia Sinica (Taipei) — Bull Inst Zool Acad Sin (Taipei)
Bulletin. Institution of Engineers — Bull Inst Eng
Bulletin. Institution of Engineers (India) — BEGIA
Bulletin. Institution of Engineers (India) — Bull Inst Eng (India)
Bulletin. Institution of Mining and Metallurgy — Bull Inst Min Metall
Bulletin. Institution of Sanitary Engineers — Bull Inst Sanit Eng
Bulletin. Instituts de Medecine — Bull Inst Med
Bulletin. Instituut voor de Tropen Afdeling Agrarisch Onderzoek — Bull Inst Tropen Afd Agrar Onderz
Bulletin Interieur des Cadres — BIC
Bulletin Interministeriel pour la Rationalisation des Choix Budgetaires — B Interminist Rational Choix Budget
Bulletin International. Academie Croate des Sciences et des Beaux-Arts. Classe des Sciences Mathematiques et Naturelles — Bull Int Acad Croate Sci Cl Sci Math
Bulletin International. Academie des Sciences du Cracovie — Bull Int Acad Sci Cracovie
Bulletin International. Academie des Sciences du Cracovie. Classe des Sciences Mathematiques et Naturelles — Bull Int Acad Sci Cracovie Cl Sci Math Natur
Bulletin International. Academie des Sciences du Cracovie. Classe des Sciences Mathematiques et Naturelles. Serie A. Sciences Mathematiques — Bull Int Acad Sci Cracovie Cl Sci Math Natur Ser A
Bulletin International. Academie des Sciences et des Lettres du Cracovie — Bull Int Acad Sci Lett Cracovie
Bulletin International. Academie des Sciences et des Lettres du Cracovie. Serie A — Bull Int Acad Sci Lett Cracovie Ser A
Bulletin International. Academie Polonaise des Sciences et des Lettres — B Ac Pol
Bulletin International. Academie Polonaise des Sciences et des Lettres — BIAP
Bulletin International. Academie Polonaise des Sciences et des Lettres — BIAPSL
Bulletin International. Academie Polonaise des Sciences et des Lettres. Classe des Sciences Mathematiques et Naturelles. Serie A. Sciences Mathematiques — BIAMA
Bulletin International. Academie Polonaise des Sciences et des Lettres. Classe des Sciences Mathematiques et Naturelles. Serie A. Sciences Mathematiques [*Poland*] — Bull Int Acad Pol Sci Lett Cl Sci Math Nat Ser A
Bulletin International. Academie Polonaise des Sciences et des Lettres. Classe des Sciences Mathematiques et Naturelles. Serie B. Sciences Naturelles — Bull Int Acad Pol Sci Lett Cl Sci Math Nat Ser B
Bulletin International. Academie Polonaise des Sciences et des Lettres. Classe des Sciences Mathematiques et Naturelles. Serie B-1. Botanique — Bull Int Acad Pol Sci Lett Cl Sci Math Nat Ser B 1
Bulletin International. Academie Polonaise des Sciences et des Lettres. Classe des Sciences Mathematiques et Naturelles. Serie B-2. Zoologie — Bull Int Acad Pol Sci Lett Cl Sci Math Nat Ser B-2
Bulletin International. Academie Yougoslave des Sciences et des Beaux-Arts. Classe des Sciences Mathematiques et Naturelles — Bull Int Acad Yougoslave Cl Sci Math Natur
Bulletin International. Academie Yougoslave des Sciences et des Beaux-Arts. Classe des Sciences Mathematiques et Naturelles [*Yugoslavia*] — Bull Int Acad Yougoslave Sci Beaux-Arts Cl Sci Math Nat
Bulletin International. Academie Yougoslave des Sciences et des Beaux-Arts. Classe des Sciences Mathematiques et Naturelles — Bull Int Acad Yougoslave Sci Cl Sci Math
Bulletin International. Academie Yougoslave des Sciences et des Beaux-Arts. Classe des Sciences Mathematiques et Naturelles — BUSLA
Bulletin International. Academie Yougoslave (Zagreb) — Bull (Zagreb)
Bulletin International. Academie Yugoslave des Sciences et des Beaux-Arts et Belles-Lettres (Zagreb) — B Ac (Zagr)
Bulletin. International Association for Educational and Vocational Guidance [*A publication*] — B Int Assoc Educ Vocat Guidance
Bulletin. International Association for Shell and Spatial Structures — Bull Int Assoc Shell Spat Struct
Bulletin. International Association for Shell Structures — Bull Int Ass Shell Struct
Bulletin. International Association of Engineering Geology — BIEGB
Bulletin. International Association of Engineering Geology — Bull Int Assoc Eng Geol
Bulletin. International Association of Medical Museums — Bull Int Ass Med Mus
Bulletin. International Association of Medical Museums — Bull Int Assoc Med Mus
Bulletin. International Association of Paper Historians — Bull Intern Assocn Paper Hist
Bulletin. International Association of Scientific Hydrology — BIAHA
Bulletin. International Association of Scientific Hydrology — Bull Int Ass Sci Hydrol
Bulletin. International Association of Scientific Hydrology — Bull Int Assoc Sci Hydrol
Bulletin. International Association of Wood Anatomists — Bull Int Ass Wood Anatomists
Bulletin. International Bureau of the American Republics — Bul Am Repub
Bulletin. International Centre for Heat and Mass Transfers — Bull Int Cent Heat Mass Transf
Bulletin. International Commission on Irrigation and Drainage — Bull ICID
Bulletin. International Committee of Historical Sciences — BICH
Bulletin. International Committee of Historical Sciences — BICHS
Bulletin. International Committee of Historical Sciences — Bull Int Comm Hist Sci
Bulletin. International Committee of Historical Sciences — Bull Internat Comm Hist Sci
Bulletin. International Committee on Urgent Anthropological and Ethnological Research — B Int Committee on Urg Anthropol Ethnol Res
Bulletin. International Committee on Urgent Anthropological and Ethnological Research — B Int Committee Urgent Anthro Ethno Res
Bulletin. International Committee on Urgent Anthropological and Ethnological Research — BICAER
Bulletin. International Committee on Urgent Anthropological and Ethnological Research — Bull Int Comm on Urgent Anthrop Ethnol Res
Bulletin. International Committee on Urgent Anthropological and Ethnological Research — ICUAER/B
Bulletin. International Committee on Urgent Anthropological Research (Vienna) — Bull Intern Com Anthrop Ethnol Res Vienna
Bulletin. International Dairy Federation — BIDFD
Bulletin International des Douanes — BID
Bulletin. International Institute for Social History — Bull Internat Inst Soc Hist
Bulletin. International Institute of Refrigeration — Bull Int Inst Refrig
Bulletin. International Office of Epizootics — Bull Int Off Epizoot
Bulletin. International Organization for Septuagint and Cognate Studies — Bul Septuagint St
Bulletin. International Pacific Salmon Fisheries Commission — Bul Int Pac Salmon Fish Com
Bulletin. International Peat Society — Bull Int Peat Soc
Bulletin. International Potash Institute — Bull Int Potash Inst
Bulletin. International Railway Congress Association — Bull Int Ry Congr Ass
Bulletin International. Services de Sante des Armees de Terre, de Mer, et de l'Air — Bull Int Ser Sante Armees Terre Mer Air
Bulletin. International Social Security Association — Bull ISSA
Bulletin. International Society for Tropical Ecology — Bull Int Soc Trop Ecol
Bulletin. International Tin Research and Development Council — Bull Int Tin Res
Bulletin. International Union Against Cancer — BCANA
Bulletin. International Union Against Cancer [*Switzerland*] — Bull Int Union Cancer
Bulletin. International Union Against Tuberculosis — Bull Int Un Tub
Bulletin. International Union Against Tuberculosis — Bull Int Union Tuberc
Bulletin. International Union Against Tuberculosis — UTTBA
Bulletin Interparlementaire — B Interparl
Bulletin. Iowa Agricultural Experiment Station — Bull Io Agric Exp St
Bulletin. Iowa Agricultural Experiment Station — Bull Iowa Agr Exp Sta
Bulletin. Iowa Nurses Association — Bull Iowa Nurses Assoc
Bulletin. Iowa State University of Science and Technology. Engineering Experiment Station — Bull Iowa State Univ Sci Technol Eng Exp Stn
Bulletin. Iranian Institute — B Iran Inst
Bulletin. Iranian Institute of America — BII
Bulletin. Iranian Institute of America [*New York*] — BIIA
Bulletin. Iranian League — BIL
Bulletin. Iranian Mathematical Society — Bull Iranian Math Soc
Bulletin. Iranian Petroleum Institute — Bull Iran Pet Inst
Bulletin. Iranian Petroleum Institute — Bull Iranian Petrol Inst
Bulletin. Iraq Natural History Museum (University of Baghdad) — Bull Iraq Nat Hist Mus (Univ Baghdad)
Bulletin. Iron and Steel Institute — Bull Iron Steel Inst
Bulletin. Isaac Ray Medical Library — Bull Isaac Ray Med Libr
Bulletin. Ishikawa Prefecture College of Agriculture — Bull Ishikawa Prefect Coll Agric
Bulletin. Ishikawa-Ken Agricultural Experiment Station — Bull Ishikawa-Ken Agric Exp Stn
Bulletin. Israel Chemical Society — Bull Isr Chem Soc
Bulletin. Israel Exploration Society [*BJPES*] [*Jerusalem*] [*Formerly,*] — BIES

Bulletin. Israel Physical Society — Bull Isr Phys Soc
Bulletin. Israel Society of Special Libraries and Information Centres — Bull Isr Soc Spec Libr & Inf Cent
Bulletin. Istanbul Technical University — Bull Istanbul Tech Univ
Bulletin Italien — BI
Bulletin Italien — BItal
Bulletin Italien — Bull It
Bulletin Italien — Bull Ital
Bulletin. Iwate University Forests — Bull Iwate Univ For
Bulletin. Iwate-Ken Agricultural Experiment Station — Bull Iwate-Ken Agr Exp Sta
Bulletin. Jackson Memorial Hospital and the School of Medicine of the University of Florida — Bull Jacks Mem Hosp
Bulletin. Jamaica Geological Survey — Bull Jam Geol Surv
Bulletin. Japan Electronic Materials Society — Bull Jpn Electron Mater Soc
Bulletin. Japan Entomological Academy — Bull Jpn Entomol Acad
Bulletin. Japan Institute of Metals — Bull Jpn Inst Met
Bulletin. Japan Mining Industry Association — Bull Jpn Min Ind Assoc
Bulletin. Japan Petroleum Institute — BUJPA
Bulletin. Japan Petroleum Institute — Bull Jap Pet Inst
Bulletin. Japan Petroleum Institute — Bull Japan Pet Inst
Bulletin. Japan Petroleum Institute — Bull Jpn Pet Inst
Bulletin. Japan Sea Regional Fisheries Research Laboratories — Bull Jpn Sea Reg Fish Res Lab
Bulletin. Japan Society of Grinding Engineers — Bull Jap Soc Grinding Eng
Bulletin. Japan Society of Mechanical Engineers — Bull Jpn Soc Mech Eng
Bulletin. Japan Society of Precision Engineering — Bull Jap Soc Precis Eng
Bulletin. Japan Society of Precision Engineering — Bull Japan Soc Precis Engng
Bulletin. Japan Society of Precision Engineering — Bull Jpn Soc Precis Eng
Bulletin. Japanese Society of Mechanical Engineers — Bull Japan Soc Mech Engrs
Bulletin. Japanese Society of Phycology — Bull Jpn Soc Phycol
Bulletin. Japanese Society of Scientific Fisheries — B Jap S S F
Bulletin. Japanese Society of Scientific Fisheries — Bull Jap Soc Sci Fish
Bulletin. Japanese Society of Scientific Fisheries — Bull Jpn Soc Sci Fish
Bulletin. Japanese Society of Tuberculosis — Bull Jpn Soc Tuberc
Bulletin. Jardin Botanique de Buitenzorg — Bull Jard Bot Buitenzorg
Bulletin. Jardin Botanique de l'Etat a Bruxelles — Bull Jard Bot Etat Brux
Bulletin. Jardin Botanique National de Belgique — Bull Jard Bot Natl Belg
Bulletin. Jardin Botanique National de Belgique — Bull Jard Bot Natn Belg
Bulletin. Jealott's Hill Research Station — Bull Jealott's Hill Res St
Bulletin. Jersey Society — Bull Jersey Soc
Bulletin. Jeunesse Prehistorique et Geologique de France — B Jeun Fr
Bulletin. Jewish Hospital [*United States*] — Bull Jew Hosp
Bulletin. Jewish Palestine Exploration Society — B Jew Pal Soc
Bulletin. Jewish Palestine Exploration Society — BJewPES
Bulletin. Jewish Palestine Exploration Society — BJPES
Bulletin. Jewish Palestine Exploration Society — Bull Jew Pal Expl Soc
Bulletin. John Rylands Library — Bull J Ryl Libr
Bulletin. John Rylands Library — Bull John Rylands Libr
Bulletin. John Rylands Library — Bull Rylands Libr
Bulletin. John Rylands Library. University of Manchester — B John Ryl
Bulletin. John Rylands Library. University of Manchester — BJR
Bulletin. John Rylands Library. University of Manchester — BJRL
Bulletin. John Rylands Library. University of Manchester — BJRLM
Bulletin. John Rylands Library. University of Manchester — BRL
Bulletin. John Rylands Library. University of Manchester — Bul J Rylands
Bulletin. John Rylands University Library. Manchester — Bull John Rylands Univ Libr Manchester
Bulletin. Johns Hopkins Hospital — Bull Johns Hopk Hosp
Bulletin. Johns Hopkins Hospital — Bull Johns Hopkins Hosp
Bulletin. Johns Rylands Library Manchester — Bull J Rylands Libr
Bulletin. Josai Dental University — Bull Josai Dent Univ
Bulletin. Josselyn Botanical Society of Maine — Bull Josselyn Bot Soc Maine
Bulletin. JSAE [*Japan Society of Automotive Engineers*] — Bull JSAE
Bulletin. JSME [*Japan Society of Mechanical Engineers*] — B JSME
Bulletin. JSME [*Japan Society of Mechanical Engineers*] — Bull JSME
Bulletin. Kagawa Agricultural Experiment Station — Bull Kagawa Agr Exp Sta
Bulletin. Kagawa Agricultural Experiment Station — Bull Kagawa Agric Exp Stn
Bulletin. Kagawa Prefecture Agricultural Experiment Station — Bull Kagawa Prefect Agric Exp Stn
Bulletin. Kagoshima Imperial College of Agriculture and Forestry — Bull Kagoshima Imp Coll Agric
Bulletin. Kagoshima Prefectural Junior College. Natural Sciences — Bull Kagoshima Prefect Jr Coll Nat Sci
Bulletin. Kagoshima University Forest — Bull Kagoshima Univ For
Bulletin. Kanagawa Agricultural Experiment Station — Bull Kanagawa Agric Exp Stn
Bulletin. Kanagawa Horticultural Experiment Station — Bull Kanagawa Hort Exp Stn
Bulletin. Kanagawa Horticultural Experiment Station — Bull Kanagawa Hortic Exp Stn
Bulletin. Kanagawa Prefectural Environmental Center — Bull Kanagawa Prefect Environ Cent
Bulletin. Kanagawa Prefectural Museum of Natural Science — Bull Kanagawa Prefect Mus Nat Sci
Bulletin. Kanagawa-Ken Agricultural Experiment Station/Kanagawa Ken Noji Shiken Seiseki — Bull Kanagawa Ken Agric Exp Sta
Bulletin. Kansas Agricultural Experiment Station — Bull Kans Agr Exp Sta
Bulletin. Kansas Agricultural Experiment Station — Bull Kans Agric Exp Stn
Bulletin. Kansas City Veterinary College. Quarterly — Bull Kansas City Vet Coll Quart
Bulletin. Kansas Engineering Experiment Station — Bull Kans Eng Exp Stn
Bulletin. Kansas State Agricultural College — Bull Kans St Agric Coll
Bulletin. Kansas State Geological Survey — Bull Kans State Geol Surv
Bulletin. Karachi Geographical Society — Bull Karachi Geogr Soc
Bulletin. Kent County Medical Society [*California*] — Bull Kent County Med Soc
Bulletin. Kentucky Agricultural Experiment Station — Bull Kent Agr Exp St
Bulletin. Kentucky Agricultural Experiment Station — Bull Kent Agric Exp St
Bulletin. Kentucky Agricultural Experiment Station — Bull KY Agr Exp Sta
Bulletin. Kentucky Agricultural Experiment Station — Bull KY Agric Exp Stn
Bulletin. Kentucky Geological Survey — Bull Kent Geol Surv
Bulletin. Kentucky Geological Survey — Bull Kentucky Geol Surv
Bulletin. Kern County Medical Society [*California*] — Bull Kern County Med Soc
Bulletin. Kesennuma Miyagi Prefectural Fisheries Experiment Station — Bull Kesennuma Miyagi Prefect Fish Exp Stn
Bulletin. King County Medical Society [*Washington*] — Bull King County Med Soc
Bulletin. Kisarazu Technical College — Bull Kisarazu Tech Coll
Bulletin. Kobayasi Institute of Physical Research — Bull Kobayasi Inst Phys Res
Bulletin. Kobe Medical College — Bull Kobe Med Coll
Bulletin. Kobe Women's College — Bull Kobe Women's Coll
Bulletin. Kobe Women's College. Domestic Science Department — Bull Kobe Women's Coll Domest Sci Dep
Bulletin. Kobe Women's University. Faculty of Home Economics — Bull Kobe Women's Univ Fac Home Econ
Bulletin. Kochi Technical College — Bull Kochi Tech Coll
Bulletin. Konan Women's College — B Konan Women Coll
Bulletin. Koninklijke Belgische Botanische Vereniging — Bull K Belg Bot Ver
Bulletin. Koninklijke Nederlandse Oudheidkundige Bond — BKNOB
Bulletin. Koninklijke Nederlandse Oudheidkundige Bond — Bull KNOB
Bulletin. Koninklijke Nederlandse Oudheidkundige Bond — KNOB
Bulletin. Koninklijke Nederlandse Oudheidkundige Bond — NKNOB
Bulletin. Korea Ocean Research and Development Institute — Bull Korea Ocean Res & Dev Inst
Bulletin. Korea Ocean Research and Development Institute — HKYSDK
Bulletin. Korean Academy of Science — Bull Korean Acad Sci
Bulletin. Korean Chemical Society [*South Korea*] — BKCSD
Bulletin. Korean Chemical Society [*South Korea*] — Bull Korean Chem Soc
Bulletin. Korean Fisheries Society — Bull Korean Fish Soc
Bulletin. Korean Fisheries Society [*South Korea*] — HSHKA
Bulletin. Korean Fisheries Technological Society [*South Korea*] — BKFSD
Bulletin. Korean Fisheries Technological Society — Bull Korean Fish Technol Soc
Bulletin. Korean Institute of Metals and Materials — Bull Korean Inst Met Mater
Bulletin. Korean Mathematical Society — Bull Korean Math Soc
Bulletin. Korean Research Center — BKRC
Bulletin. Kwasan Observatory — Bull Kwasan Observ
Bulletin. Kyoto Daigaku Institute for Chemical Research — Bull Kyoto Daigaku Inst Chem Res
Bulletin. Kyoto Educational University. Series B. Mathematics and Natural Science — KBSEA
Bulletin. Kyoto Gakugei University. Series B. Mathematics and Natural Science — Bull Kyoto Gakugei Univ Ser B Math Nat Sci
Bulletin. Kyoto Prefectural University Forests — Bull Kyoto Prefect Univ For
Bulletin. Kyoto University Forests — Bull Kyoto Univ For
Bulletin. Kyoto University Observatory — Bull Kyo Univ Obs
Bulletin. Kyoto University of Education. Series B. Mathematics and Natural Science — Bull Kyoto Univ Ed Ser B
Bulletin. Kyoto University of Education. Series B. Mathematics and Natural Science — Bull Kyoto Univ Educ Ser B Math Nat Sci
Bulletin. Kyushu Agricultural Experiment Station — Bull Kyushu Agr Exp Sta
Bulletin. Kyushu Agricultural Experiment Station — Bull Kyushu Agric Exp Stn
Bulletin. Kyushu Agricultural Experiment Station/Kyushu Nogyo Shikenjo Iho — Bull Kyushu Agric Exp Sta
Bulletin. Kyushu Institute of Technology — Bull Kyus Inst Technol
Bulletin. Kyushu Institute of Technology — Bull Kyushu Inst Technol
Bulletin. Kyushu Institute of Technology — KKDKA
Bulletin. Kyushu Institute of Technology. Mathematics and Natural Science — Bull Kyushu Inst Tech Math Natur Sci
Bulletin. Kyushu Institute of Technology. Mathematics and Natural Science — Bull Kyushu Inst Technol Math Nat Sci
Bulletin. Kyushu Institute of Technology. Science and Technology — Bull Kyushu Inst Technol Sci & Technol
Bulletin. Kyushu University Forests — Bull Kyushu Univ For
Bulletin. Kyushu University Forests/Kyushu Daigaku Nogaku-Bu Enshurin Hokoku — Bull Kyushu Univ Forests
Bulletin. Laboratoire Central d'Energie. Academie Bulgare des Sciences — Bull Lab Cent Energ Acad Bulg Sci
Bulletin. Laboratoire de Biologie Appliquee (Paris) — Bull Lab Biol Appl (Paris)
Bulletin. Laboratoire de Geologie. Faculte des Sciences de Caen — Bull Lab Geol Fac Sci Caen
Bulletin. Laboratoire d'Etudes Politiques et Administratives — Bul Lab Etud Polit Admin
Bulletin. Laboratoire du Musee de Louvre — B Labor Mus Louvre
Bulletin. Laboratoire du Musee du Louvre — Bull Lab Louvre
Bulletin. Laboratoire Maritime de Dinard — Bull Lab Marit Dinard
Bulletin. Laboratoires de Geologie, Mineralogie, Geophysique, et Musee Geologique. Universite de Lausanne — Bull Lab Geol Mineral Geophys Mus Geol Univ Laus
Bulletin. Laboratoires de Geologie, Mineralogie, Geophysique, et Musee Geologique. Universite de Lausanne — Bull Lab Geol Mineral Geophys Mus Geol Univ Lausanne
Bulletin. Laboratories of Natural History. Iowa State University — Bull Lab Nat Hist Iowa State Univ
Bulletin. Landbouwproefstation in Suriname — Bull Landbproefstn Suriname
Bulletin Legislatif Belge — BLB
Bulletin Legislatif Dalloz [*France*] — BLD
Bulletin Legislatif Dalloz — Bul Leg Dalloz
Bulletin Lembaga Penelitian Peternakan — BLPPD9
Bulletin Lembaga Penelitian Peternakan — Bull Lembaga Penelitian Peternakan

Bulletin. Leo Baeck Institute — BLBI
Bulletin. Liberia Geological Survey — Bull Liberia Geol Surv
Bulletin. Librairie Ancienne et Moderne — BLAM
Bulletin Linguistique et Ethnologique — BLE
Bulletin Linguistique et Ethnologique. Institut Granducal (Luxembourg) — BLux
Bulletin Linguistique. Faculte des Lettres de Bucarest — BL
Bulletin Linguistique. Faculte des Lettres de Bucarest — BLB
Bulletin. Lloyd Library of Botany, Pharmacy, and Materia Medica — Bull Lloyd Libr Bot Pharm Mater Med
Bulletin. London Mathematical Society — Bull London Math Soc
Bulletin. Long Island Horticultural Society — Bull Long Island Hort Soc
Bulletin. Los Angeles County Medical Association — Bull Los Angeles County Med Ass
Bulletin. Los Angeles County Museum of Natural History. Contributions in Science — Bull Los Ang Cty Mus Nat Hist Sci
Bulletin. Los Angeles Dental Society — Bull Los Angeles Dent Soc
Bulletin. Los Angeles Neurological Societies — Bull LA Neurol Soc
Bulletin. Los Angeles Neurological Societies — Bull Los Ang Neurol Soc
Bulletin. Los Angeles Neurological Societies — Bull Los Angeles Neurol Soc
Bulletin. Louisiana Agricultural Experiment Station — Bull LA Agr Exp Sta
Bulletin. Louisiana Agricultural Experiment Station — Bull LA Agric Exp Stn
Bulletin. Louisiana Cooperative Extension Service — Bull LA Coop Ext Serv
Bulletin. Louisiana Library Association (New Orleans) — Bull La Libr Assoc New Orleans
Bulletin. Lucknow National Botanic Gardens — Bull Lucknow Natl Bot Gard
Bulletin. Lutheran Theological Seminary [*Gettysburg*] — BLTSG
Bulletin. Madhya Pradesh Agriculture Department — Bull Madhya Pradesh Agric Dep
Bulletin. Madras Development Seminar Series — B Madras Dev Sem Ser
Bulletin. Madras Government Museum. Natural History Section — Bull Madras Gov Mus Nat Hist Sect
Bulletin. Maine Agricultural Experiment Station — Bull ME Agric Exp Stn
Bulletin. Maine Forestry Department — Bull ME For Dep
Bulletin. Maine Geological Survey — Bull Maine Geol Surv
Bulletin. Maine Life Sciences and Agriculture Experiment Station — Bull Maine Life Sci Agric Exp Stn
Bulletin. Maine University Agricultural Experiment Station — Bull ME Agric Exp Sta
Bulletin. Maison Franco-Japonais — BMFJ
Bulletin. Maison Franco-Japonaise — Bull Maison Franco Jap
Bulletin. Malaysia Kementerian Pertanian — Bull Malays Kementerian Pertanian
Bulletin. Malaysia Ministry of Agriculture and Rural Development — Bull Malays Minist Agric Rural Dev
Bulletin. Malaysian Mathematical Society — Bull Malaysian Math Soc
Bulletin. Malaysian Mathematical Society. Second Series [*Kuala Lumpur*] — Bull Malaysian Math Soc (2)
Bulletin. Malaysian Ministry of Agriculture and Rural Development — Bull Malaysian Min Agric Rural Dev
Bulletin. Management Consulting Institute — Bul Man Consult Inst
Bulletin. Manila Medical Society — Bull Manila Med Soc
Bulletin. Margaret Hague Maternity Hospital — Bull Margaret Hague Maternity Hospital
Bulletin. Marine Biological Station of Asamushi — Bull Mar Biol Stn Asamushi
Bulletin. Maryland Agricultural Experiment Station — Bull MD Agr Exp Sta
Bulletin. Maryland Agricultural Experiment Station — Bull MD Agric Exp Stn
Bulletin. Maryland Herpetological Society — Bull MD Herpetol Soc
Bulletin. Maryland Office of Animal Health and Consumer Services — Bull Md Off Anim Health Consum Serv
Bulletin. Mason Clinic — Bull Mason Clinic
Bulletin. Massachusetts Agricultural Experiment Station — Bull Mass Agr Exp Sta
Bulletin. Massachusetts Agricultural Experiment Station — Bull Mass Agric Exp Sta
Bulletin. Massachusetts Audubon Society — Bull Mass Audubon Soc
Bulletin. Massachusetts Nurses Association — Bull Mass Nurses Assoc
Bulletin. Mathematical Association of India — Bull Math Assoc India
Bulletin Mathematique [*Romania*] — BMSSB
Bulletin Mathematique [*Romania*] — Bull Math
Bulletin Mathematique. Societe des Sciences Mathematiques de la Republique Socialiste de Roumanie — Bull Math Soc Sci Math RS Roumanie
Bulletin Mathematique. Societe des Sciences Mathematiques de la Republique Socialiste de Roumanie. Nouvelle Serie — Bull Math Soc Sci Math RS Roumanie NS
Bulletin. Mechanical Engineering Laboratory — Bull Mech Eng Lab
Bulletin. Mechanical Engineering Laboratory of Japan — BMEGA
Bulletin Medecine Legale, Toxicologie, Urgence Medicale. Centre Anti-Poisons — Bull Med Leg Toxicol Urgence Med Cent Anti Poisons
Bulletin. Medelhausmuseet — Bull Medel
Bulletin. Medelhausmuseet — Medelh Bull
Bulletin Medical — Bull Med
Bulletin. Medical College of Virginia — Bull Med Coll V
Bulletin. Medical College of Virginia — Bull Med Coll VA
Bulletin Medical du Katanga — Bull Med Katanga
Bulletin Medical du Nord — Bull Med Nord
Bulletin. Medical Library Association — B Med Lib A
Bulletin. Medical Library Association — BMLA
Bulletin. Medical Library Association — Bull Med Libr Ass
Bulletin. Medical Library Association — Bull Med Libr Assoc
Bulletin Medical (Paris) — Bull Med (Paris)
Bulletin. Medical Staff of Methodist Hospitals of Dallas — Bull Med Staff Methodist Hosp Dallas
Bulletin. Meiji College of Pharmacy [*Japan*] — Bull Meiji Coll Pharm
Bulletin. Menninger Clinic — B Menninger
Bulletin. Menninger Clinic — Bull Menninger Clin
Bulletin Mensuel. Academie Delphinale — BMAD
Bulletin Mensuel. Alliance Israelite Universelle — BMAIU
Bulletin Mensuel. Banque Royale du Canada — Bul Mens Banque Roy Can
Bulletin Mensuel. Bureau des Relations Publiques de l'Industrie Sucriere — Bul Mens Bur Relat Pub Ind Sucriere
Bulletin Mensuel de la Societe des Sciences de Nancy — Bull Mens Soc Sci Nancy
Bulletin Mensuel de Statistique d'Outre-Mer — B Mens Stat O-Mer
Bulletin Mensuel de Statistique (France) — Bul Mensuel Statis (France)
Bulletin Mensuel de Statistique (France) — Fr Bul Stat
Bulletin Mensuel de Statistique (Gabon) — Bul Mensuel Statis (Gabon)
Bulletin Mensuel de Statistique Industrielle (France) — Fr Ind M
Bulletin Mensuel de Statistique (Ivory Coast) — Bul Mensuel Statis (Ivory Coast)
Bulletin Mensuel de Statistique (Tunisia) — Bul Mensuel Statis (Tunisia)
Bulletin Mensuel de Statistiques Industrielles — Bul Mens Stat Indust
Bulletin Mensuel des Naturalistes Belges — Bull Mens Nat Belg
Bulletin Mensuel des Publications Francaises — BMPFr
Bulletin Mensuel des Statistiques (Cameroon) — Bul Mensuel Statis (Cameroon)
Bulletin Mensuel des Statistiques (Congo People's Republic) — Bul Mensuel Statis (Congo People's Republic)
Bulletin Mensuel des Statistiques du Travail — Bul Mensuel Statis Trav
Bulletin Mensuel des Statistiques du Travail. Supplement — B Mens Statist Trav Suppl
Bulletin Mensuel d'Informations [*Paris*] — Bull Mens Inf
Bulletin Mensuel du Commerce Exterieur. Union Economique Belgo-Luxembourgeoise — Bul Mens Com Exter Un Econ Belg Lux
Bulletin Mensuel. Ecole Superieure d'Agriculture et de Viticulture d'Angers — Bull Mens Ecole Super Agr Viticult Angers
Bulletin Mensuel. Office International d'Hygiene Publique — Bull Mens Off Int Hyg Publique
Bulletin Mensuel. Office International d'Hygiene Publique — Bull Off Int Hyg Publ
Bulletin Mensuel. Societe de Medecine Militaire Francaise — Bull Mens Soc Med Mil Fr
Bulletin Mensuel. Societe des Naturalistes Luxembourgeois — Bull Mens Soc Natur Luxembourgeois
Bulletin Mensuel. Societe des Sciences de Semur — BSSS
Bulletin Mensuel. Societe Linneenne de Lyon — Bull Mens Soc Linn Lyon
Bulletin Mensuel. Societe Linneenne et des Societes Botanique de Lyon, d'Anthropologie, et de Biologie de Lyon Reunies — Bull Mens Soc Linn Soc Bot Lyon
Bulletin Mensuel. Societe Nationale d'Horticulture de France — Bull Mens Soc Natl Hortic Fr
Bulletin Mensuel. Societe Polymathique du Morbihan — BMSPM
Bulletin Mensuel. Societe Polymathique du Morbihan — Bull Soc Polymath Morbihan
Bulletin Mensuel. Societe Polymatique de Morbihan — B Morbihan
Bulletin Mensuel. Societe Veterinaire Pratique de France — Bull Mens Soc Vet Prat France
Bulletin. Metals Museum [*Japan*] — Bull Met Mus
Bulletin. Metropolitan Museum of Art — B Metr Mus
Bulletin. Metropolitan Museum of Art [*New York*] — B Metr Mus A
Bulletin. Metropolitan Museum of Art — BMM
Bulletin. Metropolitan Museum of Art — BMMA
Bulletin. Metropolitan Museum of Art — Bull Metr Mus
Bulletin. Metropolitan Museum of Art [*New York*] — Bull Metr Mus Art
Bulletin. Metropolitan Museum of Art — Bull MMA
Bulletin. Metropolitan Museum of Art (New York) — BMMANY
Bulletin Meunerie Francaise — Bull Meun Fr
Bulletin. Michigan Agricultural College — Bull Mich Agric Coll
Bulletin. Michigan Agricultural College. Experiment Station — Bull Mich Agric Coll Exp Stn
Bulletin. Michigan Dental Hygienists Association — Bull Mich Dent Hyg Assoc
Bulletin. Michigan State Dental Society — Bull Mich State Dent Soc
Bulletin. Michigan State University — Bull Mich St Univ
Bulletin. Microscopical Society of Canada — Bull Microsc Soc Can
Bulletin. Midwest Modern Language Association — B Midwest M
Bulletin. Midwest Modern Language Association — BMMLA
Bulletin. Midwest Modern Language Association — Bul Midw MLA
Bulletin. Mie Agricultural Technical Center — Bull Mie Agric Tech Cent
Bulletin. Millard Fillmore Hospital — Bull Millard Fillmore Hosp
Bulletin. Mineral Industries Experiment Station. Pennsylvania State University — Bull Miner Ind Exp Stn PA State Univ
Bulletin. Mineral Research and Exploration Institute (Turkey) — Bull Miner Res Explor Inst (Turk)
Bulletin. Mineral Research and Exploration Institute (Turkey). Foreign Edition — Bull Miner Res Explor Inst (Turk) Foreign Ed
Bulletin. Mineral Research and Exploration Institute (Turkey). Foreign Edition — Bull Mineral Res Explor Inst (Turkey)
Bulletin. Mining and Metallurgical Society of America — Bull Min Met Soc Am
Bulletin. Ministere de l'Interieur — B Min Inter
Bulletin. Ministere de l'Interieur — Bul Int
Bulletin. Ministry of Agriculture and Fisheries (New Zealand) — Bull Minist Agric Fish (NZ)
Bulletin. Ministry of Agriculture and Lands (Jamaica) — Bull Min Agr Land (Jamaica)
Bulletin. Ministry of Agriculture and Rural Development (Malaysia) — Bull Minist Agric Rural Dev (Malays)
Bulletin. Ministry of Agriculture (Egypt) — Bull Min Agr (Egypt)
Bulletin. Ministry of Agriculture (Egypt) Technical and Scientific Service [*A publication*] — Bull Minist Agric (Egypt) Tech Scient Serv
Bulletin. Ministry of Agriculture, Fisheries, and Food — Bull Minist Agric Fish Fd
Bulletin. Ministry of Agriculture, Fisheries, and Food (Great Britain) — Bull Minist Agric Fish Food (GB)

Bulletin. Ministry of Agriculture, Fisheries, and Food (London) — Bull Minist Agric Fish Fd (Lond)
Bulletin. Ministry of Agriculture (Quebec) — Bull Minist Agric (Queb)
Bulletin. Ministry of Education/Chiao-Yue Kung Pao — Bull Minist Educ
Bulletin. Minnesota Geological Survey — Bull Minn Geol Surv
Bulletin. Misaki Marine Biological Institute. Kyoto University — Bull Misaki Mar Biol Inst
Bulletin. Misaki Marine Biological Institute. Kyoto University — Bull Misaki Mar Biol Inst Kyoto Univ
Bulletin. Mississippi Agricultural and Forestry Experiment Station — Bull Miss Agric For Exp Stn
Bulletin. Mississippi Agricultural and Mechanical College — Bull Miss Agric Mech Coll
Bulletin. Mississippi Agricultural Experiment Station — Bull Miss Agric Exp Stn
Bulletin. Mississippi Geological, Economic, and Topographical Survey — Bull Mississippi Geol Econ Topogr Surv
Bulletin. Mississippi State University. Agricultural Experiment Station — Bull Miss Agric Exp Sta
Bulletin. Mississippi State University. Agricultural Experiment Station — Bull Miss State Univ Agr Exp Sta
Bulletin. Missouri Academy of Science. Supplement — Bull MO Acad Sci Suppl
Bulletin. Missouri Botanical Garden — Bull MO Bot Gdn
Bulletin. Missouri Historical Society — B Miss Hist Soc
Bulletin. Missouri Historical Society — BMHS
Bulletin. Missouri Historical Society — Bull MO Hist Soc
Bulletin. Missouri Historical Society — BuMH
Bulletin. Missouri School of Mines. Technical Series — Bull Miss Sch Min Tech Ser
Bulletin. Miyagi Agricultural College — Bull Miyagi Agr Coll
Bulletin. Miyagi Agricultural College — Bull Miyagi Agric Coll
Bulletin. Miyazaki Agricultural Experiment Station — Bull Miyazaki Agr Exp Sta
Bulletin. Mizunami Fossil Museum — Bull Mizunami Fossil Mus
Bulletin. Monmouth County [*New Jersey*] **Dental Society** — Bull Monmouth Cty Dent Soc
Bulletin. Monroe County Medical Society [*New York*] — Bull Monroe County Med Soc
Bulletin. Montana Agricultural Experiment Station — Bull Mont Agr Exp Sta
Bulletin. Montana Agricultural Experiment Station — Bull Montana Agric Exp Stn
Bulletin. Montana State College. Agricultural Experiment Station — Bull Mont State Coll Agric Exp Stn
Bulletin. Montana State College. Cooperative Extension Service — Bull Mont State Coll Coop Ext Serv
Bulletin. Montana State University. Biological Series — Bull Montana State Univ Biol Ser
Bulletin. Montgomery-Bucks Dental Society — Bull Montg-Bucks Dent Soc
Bulletin. Montreal Botanical Gardens — Bull Montreal Bot Gard
Bulletin Monumental — B Mon
Bulletin Monumental — B Monument
Bulletin Monumental — BM
Bulletin Monumental — Bull Mon
Bulletin Monumental. Societe Francaise d'Archeologie — BM
Bulletin. Moravian Music Foundation — Bul Mor Mus Found
Bulletin. Morioka Tobacco Experiment Station — Bull Morioka Tob Exp Stn
Bulletin. Mount Desert Island Biological Laboratory — BMDIA
Bulletin. Mount Desert Island Biological Laboratory — Bull Mt Desert Isl Biol Lab
Bulletin. Mukogawa Women's University. Food Science — Bull Mukogawa Womens Univ Food Sci
Bulletin. Mukogawa Women's University. Natural Science [*Japan*] — Bull Mukogawa Women's Univ Nat Sci
Bulletin. Musashino Academia Musicae — Bul Musashino Academia M
Bulletin. Musee Basque — BMB
Bulletin. Musee d'Anthropologie Prehistorique — B Mus Anthropol Prehist
Bulletin. Musee d'Anthropologie Prehistorique de Monaco — Bull du Mus d Anthrop Prehistorique de Monaco
Bulletin. Musee d'Anthropologie Prehistorique (Monaco) — B Mus (Monaco)
Bulletin. Musee d'Anthropologie Prehistorique (Monaco) — BM (Monaco)
Bulletin. Musee d'Anthropologie Prehistorique (Monaco) — Bull Mus Anthr Prehist (Monaco)
Bulletin. Musee d'Art et d'Histoire de Geneve — Bull Mus Art Hist Geneve
Bulletin. Musee de Beyrouth — BM Beyr
Bulletin. Musee de Beyrouth — BM Beyrouth
Bulletin. Musee de Beyrouth — BMB
Bulletin. Musee de Beyrouth — BMusBeyr
Bulletin. Musee de Beyrouth — Bull Mus Beyrouth
Bulletin. Musee d'Histoire Naturelle de Marseille — Bull Mus Hist Nat Marseille
Bulletin. Musee Historique de Mulhouse — B Mus Mulhouse
Bulletin. Musee Historique de Mulhouse — BMHM
Bulletin. Musee Historique de Mulhouse — Bull Mus Hist Mulhouse
Bulletin. Musee Hongrois des Beaux Arts — BMHBA
Bulletin. Musee Hongrois des Beaux Arts — BMusHongr
Bulletin. Musee Hongrois des Beaux-Arts — Bull Mus Hong
Bulletin. Musee National de Burgas — BMNB
Bulletin. Musee National de Varsovie — B Mus Vars
Bulletin. Musee National de Varsovie — BMNV
Bulletin. Musee National de Varsovie — Bull M Nat Varsovie
Bulletin. Musee National Hongrois des Beaux-Arts — BMHB
Bulletin. Musee National Hongrois des Beaux-Arts — Bull BA
Bulletin. Musee Royal d'Histoire Naturelle de la Belgique — Bull Mus Hist Nat Belg
Bulletin. Musee Royal d'Histoire Naturelle de la Belgique — Bull Mus Hist Natur Belg
Bulletin. Musee Royal d'Histoire Naturelle de la Belgique — Bull Mus R Hist Nat Belg
Bulletin. Musees de France — BMF
Bulletin. Musees de France — BMusFr
Bulletin. Musees de la Ville d'Angers — BM Angers
Bulletin. Musees et Monuments Lyonnais — Bull Mus Lyon
Bulletin. Musees Royaux d'Art et d'Histoire [*Bruxelles*] — B Mus Art
Bulletin. Musees Royaux d'Art et d'Histoire — BMAH
Bulletin. Musees Royaux d'Art et d'Histoire — BMRAH
Bulletin. Musees Royaux d'Art et d'Histoire [*Brussels*] — Bull Mus Roy Art et Hist
Bulletin. Musees Royaux d'Art et d'Histoire — Bull Musees Royaux
Bulletin. Musees Royaux d'Art et d'Histoire (Brussels) — Bull Mus Roy Bruxelles
Bulletin. Musees Royaux des Beaux-Arts — BMRBA
Bulletin. Musees Royaux des Beaux-Arts de Belgique — BMBA
Bulletin. Musees Royaux des Beaux-Arts de Belgique — BMBAB
Bulletin. Musees Royaux des Beaux-Arts de Belgique — Bull Mus Roy Beaux Arts Belg
Bulletin Museum Boymans van Beuningen — BMBB
Bulletin. Museum d'Histoire Naturelle — B Mus Hist Nat
Bulletin. Museum d'Histoire Naturelle de Marseille — Bull Mus Hist Nat Mars
Bulletin. Museum d'Histoire Naturelle du Pays Serbe — Bull Mus Hist Nat Pays Serbe
Bulletin. Museum Haaretz [*Tel Aviv*] — BMH
Bulletin. Museum National d'Histoire Naturelle [*Paris*] — Bull Mus Natl Hist Nat
Bulletin. Museum National d'Histoire Naturelle. Botanique [*Paris*] — Bull Mus Natl Hist Nat Bot
Bulletin. Museum National d'Histoire Naturelle. Ecologie Generale [*Paris*] [*A publication*] — Bull Mus Natl Hist Nat Ecol Gen
Bulletin. Museum National d'Histoire Naturelle (Paris) — Bull Mus Nat Hist Nat (Paris)
Bulletin. Museum National d'Histoire Naturelle. Section A. Zoologie, Biologie, et Ecologie Animales — BMNADT
Bulletin. Museum National d'Histoire Naturelle. Section A. Zoologie, Biologie, et Ecologie Animales — Bull Mus Natl Hist Nat Sect A Zool Biol Ecol Anim
Bulletin. Museum National d'Histoire Naturelle. Section B. Adansonia Botanique. Phytochimie — BMNBDW
Bulletin. Museum National d'Histoire Naturelle. Section B. Andansonia Botanique. Phytochimie — Bull Mus Natl Hist Nat Sect B Andansonia Bot Phytochim
Bulletin. Museum National d'Histoire Naturelle. Section B. Botanique, Biologie, et Ecologie Vegetales. Phytochimie — BMNPD6
Bulletin. Museum National d'Histoire Naturelle. Section B. Botanique, Biologie, et Ecologie Vegetales. Phytochimie — Bull Mus Natl Hist Nat Sect B Bot Biol Ecol Veg Phytochim
Bulletin. Museum National d'Histoire Naturelle. Section C. Sciences de la Terre. Paleontologie, Geologie, Mineralogie — BMNMDV
Bulletin. Museum National d'Histoire Naturelle. Serie 3. Sciences de la Terre [*Paris*] — Bull Mus Natl Hist Nat Sci Terre
Bulletin. Museum National d'Histoire Naturelle. Serie 3. Sciences de la Terre [*Paris*] — Bull Mus Natl Hist Nat Ser 3 Sci Terre
Bulletin. Museum National d'Histoire Naturelle. Zoologie [*Paris*] — Bull Mus Natl Hist Nat Zool
Bulletin. Museum of Comparative Zoology — Bull Mus Comp Zool
Bulletin. Museum of Comparative Zoology at Harvard University — Bull Mus Comp Zool Harv
Bulletin. Museum of Comparative Zoology at Harvard University — Bull Mus Comp Zool Harv Univ
Bulletin. Museum of Far Eastern Antiquities — B Mus Far East Antiq
Bulletin. Museum of Far Eastern Antiquities [*Stockholm*] — BMFEA
Bulletin. Museum of Far Eastern Antiquities [*Stockholm*] — Bull Far Eastern Antiquities
Bulletin. Museum of Far Eastern Antiquities — Bull Mus Far East Antiquities
Bulletin. Museum of Fine Arts [*Boston*] — B Mus F A
Bulletin. Museum of Fine Arts [*Boston*] — BMFA
Bulletin. Museum of Fine Arts [*Boston*] — Bull MFA
Bulletin. Museum of Fine Arts [*Boston*] — MFA B
Bulletin. Museum of Fine Arts. Boston — BMFAB
Bulletin. Museum of Fine Arts (Boston) — BMusB
Bulletin. Museum of Fine Arts. Boston — Bull Bus FA
Bulletin. Museum of Fine Arts (Boston) — Bull Mus Fine Arts (Boston)
Bulletin. Museum of Fine Arts (Boston) — Bull Museum (Boston)
Bulletin. Museum of Jewish Antiquities — BMJA
Bulletin. Museum of Mediterranean and Near Eastern Antiquities — BMNE
Bulletin. Museum of Natural History. University of Oregon — Bull Mus Nat Hist Univ Oregon
Bulletin. Mysore Geologists Association — Bull Mysore Geol Assoc
Bulletin. Nagano Agricultural Experiment Station — Bull Nagano Agr Exp Sta
Bulletin. Nagaoka Municipal Science Museum — Bull Nagaoka Munic Sci Mus
Bulletin. Nagoya City University. Department of General Education. Natural Science Section — Bull Nagoya City Univ Dep Gen Educ Nat Sci Sect
Bulletin. Nagoya Institute of Technology — Bull Nagoya Inst Tech
Bulletin. Nagoya Institute of Technology — Bull Nagoya Inst Technol
Bulletin. Naikai Regional Fisheries Research Laboratory [*Japan*] — Bull Naikai Reg Fish Res Lab
Bulletin. Naniwa University. Series A. Engineering and Natural Sciences — Bull Naniwa Univ Ser A
Bulletin. Naniwa University. Series B. Agricultural and Natural Science — Bull Naniwa Univ Ser B
Bulletin. Nanjing Institute of Geology and Mineral Resources — Bull Nanjing Inst Geol Miner Resour
Bulletin. Nansei Regional Fisheries Research Laboratories — Bull Nansei Reg Fish Res Lab
Bulletin. Nara Agricultural Experiment Station — Bull Nara Agric Exp Stn
Bulletin. Nara University of Education. Natural Science — Bull Nara Univ Ed Natur Sci
Bulletin. Nara University of Education. Natural Science — Bull Nara Univ Educ Nat Sci
Bulletin. National Association for Music Therapy — BNAMC
Bulletin. National Association of Secondary-School Principals — BNAP

Bulletin. National Association of Watch and Clock Collectors — Bull Nat Ass Watch Clock Collect
Bulletin. National Association of Wool Manufacturers — Bull Nat Assoc Wool Manuf
Bulletin. National Botanic Garden [*Lucknow*] — BNBGAP
Bulletin. National Botanic Garden [*Lucknow, India*] — Bull Natl Bot Gard
Bulletin. National Botanic Garden (Lucknow) — Bull Natl Bot Gard (Lucknow)
Bulletin. National Chrysanthemum Society — Bull Natl Chrysanthemum Soc
Bulletin. National Clearinghouse for Poison Control Centers — Bul Nat Clearh Poison Cont Cent
Bulletin. National District Heating Association — Bull Nat Dist Heat Assoc
Bulletin. National Formulary Committee — Bull Nat Formul Comm
Bulletin. National Gallery of South Australia — Bul Nat Gallery of SA
Bulletin. National Geographical Society of India — B Nat Geogr Soc India
Bulletin. National Geophysical Research Institute (India) — Bull Nat Geophys Res Inst (India)
Bulletin. National Geophysical Research Institute (India) — Bull Natl Geophys Res Inst (India)
Bulletin. National Grassland Research Institute [*Japan*] — Bull Natl Grassl Res Inst
Bulletin. National Hygienic Laboratory (Tokyo) — Bull Natl Hyg Lab (Tokyo)
Bulletin. National Institute of Agricultural Sciences. Series A (Physics and Statistics) — Bull Natl Inst Agric Sci Ser A
Bulletin. National Institute of Agricultural Sciences. Series A (Physics and Statistics) (Japan) — Bull Natl Inst Agric Sci Ser A (Phys Stat)
Bulletin. National Institute of Agricultural Sciences. Series B (Soils and Fertilizers) (Japan) — Bull Natl Inst Agric Sci Ser B (Soils Fert) (Japan)
Bulletin. National Institute of Agricultural Sciences. Series C [*Japan*] — Bull Natl Inst Agri Sci Ser C
Bulletin. National Institute of Agricultural Sciences. Series C (Plant Pathology and Entomology) — Bull Natl Inst Agric Sci Ser C (Plant Pathol Entomol)
Bulletin. National Institute of Agricultural Sciences. Series D (Physiology and Genetics) (Japan) — Bull Natl Inst Agric Sci Ser D (Physiol Genet) (Japan)
Bulletin. National Institute of Agricultural Sciences. Series D (Plant Physiology, Genetics, and Crops in General) — Bull Natl Inst Agric Sci Ser D Plant Physiol Genet Crops Gen
Bulletin. National Institute of Agricultural Sciences. Series E. Horticulture/ Nogyo Gijutsu Kenkyusho Hokoku. E. Engei — Bull Natl Inst Agric Sci Ser E Hort
Bulletin. National Institute of Agricultural Sciences. Series G (Animal Husbandry) (Japan) — Bull Natl Inst Agric Sci Ser G (Anim Husb)
Bulletin. National Institute of Agricultural Sciences (Tokyo) — Bull Natn Inst Agric Sci (Tokyo)
Bulletin. National Institute of Agrobiological Resources — Bull Natl Inst Agrobiol Resour
Bulletin. National Institute of Agro-Environmental Sciences (Japan) — Bull Natl Inst Agro Environ Sci Jpn
Bulletin. National Institute of Animal Health (Japan) — Bull Natl Inst Anim Health (Jpn)
Bulletin. National Institute of Animal Industry — Bull Nat Inst Anim Ind
Bulletin. National Institute of Animal Industry (Chiba) — Bull Natl Inst Anim Ind (Chiba)
Bulletin. National Institute of Animal Industry (Ibaraki) — Bull Natl Inst Anim Ind (Ibaraki)
Bulletin. National Institute of Geology and Mining (Bandung, Indonesia) — Bull Nat Inst Geol Min (Bandung Indonesia)
Bulletin. National Institute of Hygienic Sciences — Bull Nat Inst Hyg Sci
Bulletin. National Institute of Hygienic Sciences (Tokyo) — Bull Natl Inst Hyg Sci (Tokyo)
Bulletin. National Institute of Hygienic Sciences (Tokyo) [*Japan*] — Bull Natn Inst Hyg Sci (Tokyo)
Bulletin. National Institute of Oceanography (India) — Bull Natl Inst Oceanogr (India)
Bulletin. National Institute of Sciences of India — Bull Nat Inst Sci India
Bulletin. National Institute of Sciences of India — Bull Natl Inst Sci India
Bulletin. National Institute of Sciences of India — Bull Natn Inst Sci India
Bulletin. National Medical and Dental Association and National Advocates Society [*Chicago*] — Bull Natl Med Dent Assoc Natl Advocates Soc
Bulletin. National Museum of Ethnology — Bull Natn Mus Ethnol
Bulletin. National Museum (Singapore) — Bull Natl Mus (Singapore)
Bulletin. National Pearl Research Laboratory [*Japan*] — Bull Natl Pearl Res Lab
Bulletin. National Pearl Research Laboratory (Japan) — Bull Nat Pearl Res Lab (Jpn)
Bulletin. National Research Council of the Philippines — Bull Natl Res Counc Philipp
Bulletin. National Research Council. Philippines — Bull Natl Res Council Philipp
Bulletin. National Research Council (US) — Bull Nat Res Counc (US)
Bulletin. National Research Development Corporation [*England*] — Bull NRDC
Bulletin. National Research Institute for Pollution and Resources [*Japan*] — Bull Natl Inst Pollut Resour
Bulletin. National Research Institute for Pollution and Resources (Japan) — Bull Natl Res Inst Pollut Resour Jpn
Bulletin. National Research Institute of Aquaculture — Bull Natl Res Inst Aquacult
Bulletin. National Research Institute of Fisheries Engineering — Bull Natl Res Inst Fish Eng
Bulletin. National Research Institute of History and Philology. Academia Sinica — BHPAS
Bulletin. National Research Institute of Tea [*Japan*] — Bull Natl Res Inst Tea
Bulletin. National Research Institute of Vegetables, Ornamental Plants, and Tea. Series B. Tea — Bull Natl Res Inst Veg Ornamental Plants Tea Ser B Tea
Bulletin. National Research Laboratory of Metrology [*Japan*] — Bull Nat Res Lab Metrology
Bulletin. National Research Laboratory of Metrology [*Japan*] — Bull Natl Res Lab Metrol
Bulletin. National Research Laboratory of Metrology [*Japan*] — Bull Natl Res Lab Metrology
Bulletin. National Science Board, Philippine Islands — Bull Nat Sci Brd
Bulletin. National Science Foundation — Bull Natl Sci Found
Bulletin. National Science Museum. Series A (Zoology) (Japan) — Bull Natl Sci Mus Ser A (Zool)
Bulletin. National Science Museum. Series B (Botany) (Japan) — Bull Natl Sci Mus Ser B (Bot)
Bulletin. National Science Museum. Series C (Geology and Paleontology) [*Japan*] — Bull Natl Sci Mus Ser C (Geol Paleontol)
Bulletin. National Science Museum. Series C (Geology) [*Later, Bulletin. National Science Museum. Series C. (Geology and Paleontology)*] **(Japan)** — Bull Natl Sci Mus Ser C (Geol)
Bulletin. National Science Museum. Series D (Anthropology) [*Japan*] — Bull Natl Sci Mus Ser D (Anthropol)
Bulletin. National Science Museum. Series E. Physical Sciences and Engineering (Tokyo) — Bull Natl Sci Mus Ser E Tokyo
Bulletin. National Science Museum (Tokyo) — Bull Natl Sci Mus (Tokyo)
Bulletin. National Science Museum (Tokyo) — Bull Natn Sci Mus (Tokyo)
Bulletin. National Society of India for Malaria and Other Mosquito Borne Disease — Bull Nat Soc Ind Malar
Bulletin. National Speleological Society [*United States*] — Bull Nat Spel Soc
Bulletin. National Speleological Society [*United States*] — Bull Natl Speleol Soc
Bulletin. National Tuberculosis Association [*United States*] — Bull Nat Tub Ass
Bulletin. National Tuberculosis Association [*US*] — Bull Natl Tuberc Assoc
Bulletin. National Tuberculosis Respiratory Disease Association [*US*] — Bull Natl Tuberc Respir Dis Assoc
Bulletin. Nationale Plantentuin van Belgie — Bull Natl Plant Belg
Bulletin. Natural History Museum, Balboa Park [*United States*] — Bull Nat Hist Mus
Bulletin. Natural History Museum in Belgrade — BNHMB6
Bulletin. Natural History Museum in Belgrade — Bull Nat Hist Mus Belgr
Bulletin. Natural History Museum in Belgrade. Series A. Mineralogy, Geology, Paleontology — Bull Nat His Mus Belgr Ser A Mineral Geol Paleontol
Bulletin. Natural History Museum in Belgrade. Series B. Biological Sciences — Bull Nat Hist Mus Belgr Ser B Biol Sci
Bulletin. Natural History Museum in Belgrade. Series B. Biological Sciences — Bull Nat Hist Mus Belgrade B
Bulletin. Natural History Research Center. University of Baghdad — Bull Nat Hist Res Cent Univ Baghdad
Bulletin. Natural History Society of British Columbia — Bull Nat Hist Soc British Columbia
Bulletin. Natural History Society of New Brunswick — Bull Nat Hist Soc New Br
Bulletin. Natural History Survey. Chicago Academy of Sciences — Bull Nat Hist Surv Chicago Acad Sci
Bulletin. Nebraska Agricultural Experiment Station — Bull Nebr Agric Exp St
Bulletin. Nederlandse Oudheidkundige Bond — BNOB
Bulletin. Neurological Institute of New York — Bull Neurol Inst NY
Bulletin. Nevada Agricultural Experiment Station — Bull Nev Agr Exp St
Bulletin. Nevada Bureau of Mines and Geology — Bull Nev Bur Mines Geol
Bulletin. New England Medical Center — Bull New Engl Med Cent
Bulletin. New England Rose Society — Bul NE Rose Soc
Bulletin. New Hampshire Agricultural Experiment Station — Bull N Hampshire Agric Exper Station
Bulletin. New Hampshire Agricultural Experiment Station — Bull New Hamps Agric Exp Stn
Bulletin. New Hampshire Agricultural Experiment Station — Bull NH Agric Exp Stn
Bulletin. New Hampshire Public Libraries — Bul NHPL
Bulletin. New Jersey Academy of Science — B NJ Acad S
Bulletin. New Jersey Academy of Science — Bull NJ Acad Sci
Bulletin. New Jersey Agricultural Experiment Station — Bull New Jers Agric Exp St
Bulletin. New Jersey Agricultural Experiment Station — Bull New Jers Agric Exp Stn
Bulletin. New Jersey Agricultural Experiment Station — Bull NJ Agr Exp Sta
Bulletin. New Jersey Association of Osteopathic Physicians and Surgeons — Bul NJ Assoc Osteopath Phys Surg
Bulletin. New Jersey Bureau of Geology and Topography — Bull NJ Bur Geol Topogr
Bulletin. New Jersey Society of Dentistry for Children — Bull NJ Soc Dent Child
Bulletin. New Jersey State Soil Conservation Committee — Bull New Jers St Soil Conserv Comm
Bulletin. New Mexico Agricultural Experiment Station — Bull N Mex Agr Exp Sta
Bulletin. New Mexico Agricultural Experiment Station — Bull New Mex Agric Exp Stn
Bulletin. New Series. Report. Agricultural Experiment Station. Agricultural and Mechanical College — Bull New Ser Rep Agric Exp Sta Agric Coll
Bulletin. New York Academy of Medicine — B NY Ac Med
Bulletin. New York Academy of Medicine — Bull New York Acad Med
Bulletin. New York Academy of Medicine — Bull NY Acad Med
Bulletin. New York Agricultural Experiment Station — Bull NY Agr Exp Sta
Bulletin. New York. Agricultural Experiment Station (Ithaca) — Bull NY Agric Exp Stn Ithaca
Bulletin. New York Botanical Garden — Bull New York Bot Gard
Bulletin. New York C. S. Lewis Society — BNYLS
Bulletin. New York County Dental Society — Bull NY Cty Dent Soc
Bulletin. New York Medical College. Flower and Fifth Avenue — Bull NY Med Coll Flower Fifth Ave
Bulletin. New York Public Library — BNPL
Bulletin. New York Public Library — BNYPL
Bulletin. New York Public Library — Bul NYPL
Bulletin. New York Public Library — Bull NY Pub Lib
Bulletin. New York Public Library — Bull NY Publ Libr
Bulletin. New York Public Library — Bull NY Public Libr

Bulletin. New York Public Library — Bull NYPL
Bulletin. New York Public Library — New York Pub Lib Bull
Bulletin. New York Public Library (New York) — Bull Publ Libr NY
Bulletin. New York State Agricultural Experiment Station — Bull NY St Agric Exp St
Bulletin. New York State Agricultural Experiment Station — Bull NY St Agric Exp Stn
Bulletin. New York State Conservation Department — Bull NY St Conserv Dep
Bulletin. New York State Department of Agriculture — Bull NY St Dep Agric
Bulletin. New York State Flower Industries — Bull NY State Flower Ind
Bulletin. New York State Museum — Bull NY St Mus
Bulletin. New York State Museum — Bull NY State Mus
Bulletin. New York State Museum and Science Service — Bull NY St Mus Sci Serv
Bulletin. New York State Museum and Science Service — Bull NY State Mus Sci Serv
Bulletin. New York State Society of Anesthesiologists — Bull NY State Soc Anesthesiol
Bulletin. New York State Society of Dentistry for Children — BNSDA
Bulletin. New York Zoological Society — Bull NY Zool Soc
Bulletin. New Zealand Astronomical Society. Variable Star Section — Bull NZ Astr Soc
Bulletin. New Zealand Department of Scientific and Industrial Research — Bull NZ Dep Scient Ind Res
Bulletin. New Zealand Department of Scientific and Industrial Research — Bull NZ Dept Sci Ind Res
Bulletin. New Zealand Department of Scientific and Industrial Research — NEZSA
Bulletin. New Zealand Geological Survey — Bull NZ Geol Surv
Bulletin. New Zealand Geological Survey. New Series — Bull NZ Geol Surv New Ser
Bulletin. New Zealand National Society for Earthquake Engineering — BNZED
Bulletin. New Zealand National Society for Earthquake Engineering — Bull NZ Natl Soc Earthq Eng
Bulletin. New Zealand Society for Earthquake Engineering — Bull NZ Soc Earthquake Eng
Bulletin. New Zealand Society of Periodontology — Bull NZ Soc Periodontol
Bulletin. Newark [*New Jersey*] **Dental Club** — Bull Newark Dent Club
Bulletin. Nigerian Forestry Departments — Bull Niger For Dep
Bulletin. Nigerian Forestry Departments — Bull Nigerian For Dep
Bulletin. Niigata University Forests — Bull Niigata Univ For
Bulletin. Ninth District Dental Society [*White Plains, New York*] — Bull Ninth Dist Dent Soc
Bulletin. Nippon Agricultural Research Institute/Nihon Nogyo Kenkyusho Hokoku — Bull Nippon Agric Res Inst
Bulletin. Nippon Dental College. General Education — Bull Nippon Dent Coll Gen Educ
Bulletin. Nippon Dental University. General Education — Bull Nippon Dent Univ Gen Educ
Bulletin. Nippon Veterinary and Zootechnical College — Bull Nippon Vet Zootech Coll
Bulletin. Norges Geologiske Undersokelse — Bull Norg Geol Unders
Bulletin. North American Gladiolus Council — Bull N Am Gladiolus Counc
Bulletin. North Carolina Board of Health — Bull North Carolina Bd Health
Bulletin. North Carolina Department of Conservation and Development — Bull N Carol Dep Conserv Dev
Bulletin. North Carolina Division of Mineral Resources — Bull NC Div Miner Resour
Bulletin. North Carolina Division of Resource Planning and Evaluation. Mineral Resources Section — Bull NC Div Resour Plann Eval Miner Resour Sect
Bulletin. North Carolina State University. Agricultural Experiment Station — Bull N Carol St Univ Agric Exp Stn
Bulletin. North Dakota Agricultural Experiment Station — Bull N Dak Agr Exp Sta
Bulletin. North Dakota Agricultural Experiment Station — Bull N Dak Agric Exp Stn
Bulletin. North Dakota Agricultural Experimental Station — Bull N Dak Agric Exp St
Bulletin. North of Scotland College of Agriculture — Bull N Scot Coll Agr
Bulletin. North of Scotland College of Agriculture — Bull N Scotl Coll Agric
Bulletin. North of Scotland College of Agriculture — Bull North Scotl Coll Agric
Bulletin. North of Scotland College of Agriculture. Beekeeping Department — Bull N Scotl Coll Agric Beekeep Dep
Bulletin. Northern District Dental Society [*Atlanta, Georgia*] — Bull North Dist Dent Soc
Bulletin. Northern Rhodesia Department of Agriculture — Bull N Rhodesia Dept Agr
Bulletin. NRLM [*National Research Laboratory of Metrology*] — Bull NRLM
Bulletin. Nutrition Institute of the United Arab Republic — Bull Nutr Inst UAR
Bulletin. Observatoire du Puy De Dome — Bull Obs Puy De Dome
Bulletin. Ocean Research Institute. University of Tokyo — Bull Ocean Res Inst Univ Tokyo
Bulletin. Oceanographical Institute of Taiwan — Bull Oceanogr Inst
Bulletin OEPP [*Organisation Europeenne et Mediterraneenne pour la Protection des Plantes*] — Bull OEPP
Bulletin Oerlikon [*Switzerland*] — Bull Oerlikon
Bulletin of African Studies in Canada — Bull Afr Stud Canada
Bulletin of Alloy Phase Diagrams — Bull Alloy Phase Diagrams
Bulletin of Analysis and Testing — Bull Anal Test
Bulletin of Animal Behavior — Bull Anim Behav
Bulletin of Animal Health and Production in Africa — BAHAD
Bulletin of Animal Health and Production in Africa — Bull Anim Health Prod Afr
Bulletin of Animal Health and Production in Africa/Bulletin de la Sante et de la Production Animales en Afrique — Bull Anim Health Prod Afr Bull Sante Prod Anim Afr
Bulletin of Aquatic Biology — Bull Aquat Biol
Bulletin of Aquatic Biology — Bull Aquatic Biol
Bulletin of Arts and Science Division. Ryukyu University/Ryukyu Daigaku Bunrui Gakubu Kiyo — Bull Arts Sci Div Ryukyu Univ
Bulletin of Atmospheric Radioactivity [*Japan*] — Bull Atmos Radioactiv
Bulletin of Baltic Studies — BBS
Bulletin of Basic Science Research — Bull Bas Sci Res
Bulletin of Basic Science Research — Bull Basic Sci Res
Bulletin of Bibliography — BB
Bulletin of Bibliography — Bul B
Bulletin of Bibliography — Bul Bibliog
Bulletin of Bibliography — Bull Bibl
Bulletin of Bibliography — Bull Bibliog
Bulletin of Bibliography and Dramatic Index — BBDI
Bulletin of Bibliography and Dramatic Index — Bul of Bibliography
Bulletin of Bibliography and Magazine Notes — Bull Bibliogr Mag Notes
Bulletin of Bibliography (Boston) — Bull Bibliogr Boston
Bulletin of Black Theatre — BBT
Bulletin of Black Theatre — Bul Black Theatre
Bulletin of Brewing Science — Bull Brew Sci
Bulletin of Business Research — Bul Bus Res
Bulletin of Business Research. Ohio State University — Bul Bus Research Ohio State Univ
Bulletin of Canadian Petroleum Geology — BCPG
Bulletin of Canadian Petroleum Geology — BCPGA
Bulletin of Canadian Petroleum Geology — Bull Can Pet Geol
Bulletin of Canadian Petroleum Geology — Bull Can Petrol Geol
Bulletin of Canadian Studies — Bul Can Stud
Bulletin of Canadian Welfare Law — BCWL
Bulletin of Canadian Welfare Law — Bull Can Welfare L
Bulletin of Central Research Institute Fukuoka University — Bul Central Res Inst Fukuoka Univ
Bulletin of Centre for Informatics — Bull Centre Inform
Bulletin of Chemical Thermodynamics — Bull Chem Thermodyn
Bulletin of Cheng Kung University. Science and Engineering — Bull Cheng Kung Univ Sci Eng
Bulletin of Chinese Materia Medica — Bull Chin Mater Med
Bulletin of Chinese Studies — BCS
Bulletin of Chinese Studies/Chung Kuo Wen Hua Yen Chin Hui Kán — Bull Chin Stud
Bulletin of Clinical Neurosciences — Bull Clin Neurosci
Bulletin of Computer Aided Architectural Design — Bull of Computer Aided Archtl Design
Bulletin of Concerned Asian Scholars — Asian Sch
Bulletin of Concerned Asian Scholars — B Asian Schol
Bulletin of Concerned Asian Scholars — B Con As Sc
Bulletin of Concerned Asian Scholars — B Concern As Schol
Bulletin of Concerned Asian Scholars — B Concerned Asian Scholars
Bulletin of Current Documentation — Bull Curr Doc
Bulletin of Documentation. International Superphosphate Manufacturers Association. Agricultural Committee — Bull Doc Int Superphosphate Mfr Ass Agr Comm
Bulletin of Economic Research — B Econ Res
Bulletin of Economic Research — BER
Bulletin of Economic Research [*British*] — BOE
Bulletin of Economic Research — YOR
Bulletin of Economic Research (England) — Bul Econ Research (England)
Bulletin of Education and Research — Bul Ed & Res
Bulletin of Educational Development and Research — Bull Educ Dev & Res
Bulletin of Endemic Diseases — Bull Endem Dis
Bulletin of Endemic Diseases — Bull Endemic Diseases
Bulletin of Endemic Diseases (Baghdad) — Bull Endem Dis (Baghdad)
Bulletin of Engineering Geology and Hydrogeology [*English Translation*] [*Yugoslavia*] — BEGHA
Bulletin of Engineering Geology and Hydrogeology (English Translation) [*Yugoslavia*] — Bull Eng Geol Hydrogeol (Engl Transl)
Bulletin of Entomological Research — B Ent Res
Bulletin of Entomological Research — BER
Bulletin of Entomological Research — BEREA
Bulletin of Entomological Research — Bull Ent Res
Bulletin of Entomological Research — Bull Entomol Res
Bulletin of Entomology — Bull Entomol
Bulletin of Environmental Contamination and Toxicology — B Envir Con
Bulletin of Environmental Contamination and Toxicology — BECTA
Bulletin of Environmental Contamination and Toxicology — Bull Envir Contam Toxic
Bulletin of Environmental Contamination and Toxicology — Bull Environ Contam
Bulletin of Environmental Contamination and Toxicology — Bull Environ Contam Toxicol
Bulletin of Environmental Education — BEE
Bulletin of Environmental Sciences [*South Korea*] — Bull Environ Sci
Bulletin of Environmental Sciences [*South Korea*] — HKROD
Bulletin of Environmental Sciences. Hanyang University [*Republic of Korea*] — Bull Environ Sci
Bulletin of Epizootic Diseases of Africa — Bull Epizoot Dis Afr
Bulletin of Experimental Biology and Medicine — B Exp B Med
Bulletin of Experimental Biology and Medicine [*English Translation*] — BEXBA
Bulletin of Experimental Biology and Medicine — Bull Exp Biol Med
Bulletin of Experimental Biology and Medicine (English Translation of Byulleten' Eksperimental'noi Biologii i Meditsiny) — Bull Exp Biol Med (Eng Transl Byull Eksp Biol Med)
Bulletin of Fisheries Research and Development — Bull Fish Res Dev
Bulletin of Fisheries Research and Development — RIDPE3

Bulletin of Forest Experiment Station. Government of Taiwan/Taiwan Ringyo Shikenjo Hokoku — Bull Forest Exp Sta Gov Taiwan
Bulletin of Forest Research Institute — Bull Forest Res Inst
Bulletin of General Education. Dokkyo University. School of Medicine — Bull Gen Ed Dokkyo Univ School Medicine
Bulletin of Genetics [*China*] — Bull Genet
Bulletin of Geology (Warsaw) — Bull Geol Warsaw
Bulletin of Geophysics. National Central University (Taiwan) — Bull Geophys Natl Cent Univ Taiwan
Bulletin of Grain Technology [*India*] — BUGTA
Bulletin of Grain Technology — Bull Grain Technol
Bulletin of High Points — B H Points
Bulletin of Hispanic Studies — B Hispan S
Bulletin of Hispanic Studies — BHS
Bulletin of Historical Research in Music Education — B Historical Res
Bulletin of Hokkaido Underground Resource Investigation [*Japan*] — Bull Hokkaido Underground Resour Invest
Bulletin of Human Body Measurement — Bull Hum Body Meas
Bulletin of Hydrobiological Research — Bull Hydrobiol Res
Bulletin of Hygiene — Bull Hyg
Bulletin of Indonesian Economic Studies — B Indo Econ Stud
Bulletin of Indonesian Economic Studies — B Indones Econ Stud
Bulletin of Indonesian Economic Studies — BIS
Bulletin of Indonesian Economic Studies — Bul Indonesian Econ Studies
Bulletin of Indonesian Economic Studies [*Canberra*] — IESB
Bulletin of Industrial Technology — Bull Ind Techn
Bulletin of Informatics and Cybernetics — Bull Inform Cybernet
Bulletin of International Folk Music Council — BIFMC
Bulletin of International News — BIN
Bulletin of Ishinomaki Senshu University — Bull Ishinomaki Senshui Univ
Bulletin of Islamic Studies — Bull Islam Stud
Bulletin of Kochi Women's College/Kochi Joshi Daigaku Kiyo — Bull Kochi Womens Coll
Bulletin of Koshien University. B — Bull Koshien Univ B
Bulletin of Laboratory of Food Technology. Hachinohe Institute of Technology — Bull Lab Food Technol Hachinohe Inst Technol
Bulletin of Latin American Research — BLAR
Bulletin of Law, Science, and Technology — Bull L Sci and Tech
Bulletin of Marine Science — B Marin Sci
Bulletin of Marine Science — BMRSA
Bulletin of Marine Science — Bull Mar Sci
Bulletin of Marine Science — Bull Marine Sci
Bulletin of Marine Science of the Gulf and Caribbean [*Later, Bulletin of Marine Science*] — Bull Mar Sci Gulf Caribb
Bulletin of Marine Science of the Gulf and Caribbean [*Later, Bulletin of Marine Science*] — Bull Marine Sci Gulf and Caribbean
Bulletin of Marine Science of the Gulf and Caribbean. University of Miami Marine Laboratory — Bull Mar Sci Gulf Caribbean
Bulletin of Massachusetts Natural History — Bull Mass Nat Hist
Bulletin of Materials Science [*India*] — Bull Mat Sci
Bulletin of Materials Science [*India*] — Bull Mater Sci
Bulletin of Materials Science — BUMSD
Bulletin of Materials Science (India) — Bull Mater Sci (India)
Bulletin of Mathematical Biology — B Math Biol
Bulletin of Mathematical Biology — BMTBA
Bulletin of Mathematical Biology — Bull Math Biol
Bulletin of Mathematical Biology — Bull Math Biology
Bulletin of Mathematical Biophysics — BMBIA
Bulletin of Mathematical Biophysics — Bull Mat Biophys
Bulletin of Mathematical Biophysics — Bull Math Biophys
Bulletin of Mathematical Statistics — B Math Stat
Bulletin of Mathematical Statistics — Bull Math Statist
Bulletin of Mathematics [*London*] — Bull Math
Bulletin of Mechanical Engineering Education — BMEEB
Bulletin of Mechanical Engineering Education — Bull Mech Eng Educ
Bulletin of Mechanical Engineering Education — Bull Mech Engng Educ
Bulletin of Medical Science (Philadelphia) — Bull Med Science Philad
Bulletin of Medieval Canon Law — BMCL
Bulletin of Meditteranean Archaeology — BMA
Bulletin of Microbiology — Bull Microbiol
Bulletin of Microbiology — MIBUBI
Bulletin of Miscellaneous Information. Department of Agriculture. Imperial College of Agriculture — Bull Misc Inform Dept Agric Imp Coll Agric
Bulletin of Miscellaneous Information. Royal Botanic Gardens — Bull Misc Inf R Bot Gard
Bulletin of Miscellaneous Information. Royal Botanic Gardens (Kew) — Bull Misc Inf (Kew)
Bulletin of Miscellaneous Information. Royal Botanic Gardens (Kew) — Bull Misc Inform Roy Bot Gard (Kew)
Bulletin of Molecular Biology and Medicine — Bull Mol Biol Med
Bulletin of Mukogawa Women's University — Bull Mukogawa Women's Univ
Bulletin of Mukogawa Women's University. Pharmaceutical Sciences — Bull Mukogawa Women's Univ Pharm Sci
Bulletin of Mycology — Bull Mycol
Bulletin of Mycology — BUMYDG
Bulletin of National Fisheries. University of Pusan. Natural Sciences — Bull Natl Fish Univ Pusan Nat Sci
Bulletin of National Fisheries. University of Pusan. Natural Sciences — PSCKAR
Bulletin of Natural Sciences (Wellington) — Bull Nat Sci (Wellington)
Bulletin of Number Theory and Related Topics — Bull Number Theory Related Topics
Bulletin of Osaka Kun'ei Women's Junior College — Bull Osaka Kun'ei Women's Jr Coll
Bulletin of Osaka Prefectural College of Technology — Bull Osaka Prefect College Tech
Bulletin of Pathology (Chicago, Illinois) — BPAIA
Bulletin of Pathology (Chicago, Illinois) — Bull Pathol (Chicago)
Bulletin of Peace Proposals — B Peace Propos
Bulletin of Peace Proposals — BPPRD
Bulletin of Peace Proposals — Bull Peace Propos
Bulletin of Peony News. American Peony Society — Bull Peony News
Bulletin of Pharmacology (Beijing) — Bull Pharmacol (Beijing)
Bulletin of Pharmacy — Bull Pharm
Bulletin of Pharmacy (Istanbul) — Bull Pharm (Istanbul)
Bulletin of Polish Medical Science and History — Bull Pol Med Sci Hist
Bulletin of Popular Information. Arnold Arboretum Harvard University — Bull Popular Inform Arnold Arbor
Bulletin of Prosthetics Research — BPR
Bulletin of Prosthetics Research — BPRRB
Bulletin of Prosthetics Research — Bull Prosthet Res
Bulletin of Pure and Applied Sciences — Bull Pure Appl Sci
Bulletin of Pure and Applied Sciences. Section B. Plant Sciences — Bull Pure Appl Sci Sec B
Bulletin of Pure and Applied Sciences. Section E. Mathematics — Bull Pure Appl Sci Sec E Math
Bulletin of Radiation Protection — BRPRD
Bulletin of Radiation Protection [*India*] — Bull Radiat Prot
Bulletin of Reprints — Bul Repr
Bulletin of Research. College of Agriculture and Veterinary Medicine. Nihon University — Bull Res Coll Agr Vet Med Nihon Univ
Bulletin of Research. College of Agriculture and Veterinary Science. Nihon University — Bull Res Coll Agric Vet Sci Nihon Univ
Bulletin of Research in Music Education — Bull Res Music Ed
Bulletin of Research in the Humanities — B Res Hum
Bulletin of Research in the Humanities — BRH
Bulletin of Research in the Humanities — Bull Res Hum
Bulletin of Research in the Humanities — Bull Res Humanit
Bulletin of Research Institute of Natural Sciences. Okayama University of Scienc — Bull Res Inst Nat Sci Okayama Univ Sci
Bulletin of Rural Economics and Sociology — Bull Rur Econ Sociology
Bulletin of Sanyo Gakuen College — Bull Sanyo Gakuen Coll
Bulletin of Sanyo Gakuen Junior College — Bull Sanyo Gakuen Jr Coll
Bulletin of Science, Technology, and Society — Bull Sci Technol Soc
Bulletin of Shizuoka Prefecture Agricultural Experiment Station/Shizuoka-Ken Nogyo Shikenjo Kenkyu Hokoku — Bull Shizuoka Prefect Agric Exp Sta
Bulletin of Small Scale Industry in Africa — Bull Small Scale Ind in Afr
Bulletin of Spanish Studies — BSS
Bulletin of Statistics. Office of Planning and Statistics. Office of the High Commissioner — Bul Stat Off Plan Stat Off High Com
Bulletin of Stomatology. Kyoto University — Bull Stomatol Kyoto Univ
Bulletin of Sugar Beet Research — Bull Sugar Beet Res
Bulletin of Sugar Beet Research. Supplement — Bull Sugar Beet Res Suppl
Bulletin of Suicidology — Bul Suicidol
Bulletin of Suicidology — Bull Suicidol
Bulletin of Symbolic Logic — Bull Symbolic Logic
Bulletin of Taiwan Forestry Research Institute in Co-Operation with Taiwan Forest Bureau — Bull Taiwan For Res Inst Co Op Taiwan For Bur
Bulletin of Teikoku-Gakuen — Bull Teikoku Gakuen
Bulletin of the Allahabad Mathematical Society — Bull Allahabad Math Soc
Bulletin of the Atomic Scientists — Atomic Sci
Bulletin of the Atomic Scientists — B Atom Sci
Bulletin of the Atomic Scientists — BAS
Bulletin of the Atomic Scientists — Bul Atomic Sci
Bulletin of the Atomic Scientists — Bull At Sci
Bulletin of the Atomic Scientists — Bull Atom Sci
Bulletin of the Atomic Scientists — Bull Atom Scient
Bulletin of the Atomic Scientists — GTBA
Bulletin of the Belgian Mathematical Society. Simon Stevin — Bull Belg Math Soc Simon Stevin
Bulletin of the California Insect Survey — Bull Calif Insect Surv
Bulletin of the Chinese Academy of Geological Sciences — Bull Chin Acad Geol Sci
Bulletin of the College of Liberal Arts Kyushu Sangyo University — Bull College Liberal Arts Kyushu Sangyo Univ
Bulletin of the Comediantes — B Com
Bulletin of the Comediantes — B Comediant
Bulletin of the Comediantes — BC
Bulletin of the European Communities — BEC
Bulletin of the Experiment Forest. Tokyo University of Agriculture and Technology — Bull Exp For Tokyo Univ Agric Technol
Bulletin of the Experimental Animals — Bull Exp Anim
Bulletin of the Faculty of Home Economics. Hiroshima Women's University — Bull Fac Home Econ Hiroshima Womens Univ
Bulletin of the Faculty of Home Economics. Kobe Women's University — Bull Fac Home Econ Kobe Women's Univ
Bulletin of the Faculty of Human Environmental Science. Fukuoka Women's University — Bull Fac Hum Environ Sci Fukuoka Womens Univ
Bulletin of the Faculty of Human Life and Environmental Science. Hiroshima Women's University — Bull Fac Hum Life Environ Sci Hiroshima Womens Univ
Bulletin of the Faculty of Science and Engineering Chuo University. Seres I. Mathematics — Bull Fac Sci Engrg Chuo Univ Ser I Math
Bulletin of the Faculty of Science. Assiut University. C. Mathematics — Bull Fac Sci Assiut Univ C
Bulletin of the Faculty of the Liberal Arts Chukyo University — Bull Fac Liberal Arts Chukyo Univ
Bulletin of the Georgian Academy of Science — Bull Georg Acad Sci
Bulletin of the Graduate School of Social and Cultural Studies. Kyushu University — Bull Grad Sch Soc Cult Stud Kyushu Univ

Bulletin of the Greek Mathematical Society — Bull Greek Math Soc
Bulletin of the Hiruzen Research Institute. Okayama University of Science — Bull Hiruzen Res Inst Okayama Univ Sci
Bulletin of the History of Dentistry — BHDEA
Bulletin of the History of Dentistry — Bull Hist Dent
Bulletin of the History of Medicine — B Hist Med
Bulletin of the History of Medicine — BHM
Bulletin of the History of Medicine — Bull Hist Med
Bulletin of the Institute of Combinatorics and its Applications — Bull Inst Combin Appl
Bulletin of the Interest Group in Pure and Applied Logics — Bull IGPL
Bulletin of the Northern Territory of Australia — Bull Nth Terr Austr
Bulletin of the Polish Academy of Sciences. Mathematics — Bull Polish Acad Sci Math
Bulletin of the Polish Academy of Sciences. Technical Sciences — Bull Polish Acad Sci Tech Sci
Bulletin of the Shiga Prefectural Livestock Research and Improvement Institute — Bull Shiga Prefect Livest Res Improv Inst
Bulletin of the Transilvania University of Brasov. Series B. Mathematics, Economic Sciences, Philology, Medicine, Physics, Chemistry, Sports — Bull Transilvania Univ Brasov Ser B
Bulletin of the Transylvania University of Brasov. Seria C. Mathematics. Physics. Chemistry — Bull Transylv Univ Brasov Ser C
Bulletin of the University of Electro-Communications — Bull Univ Electro Comm
Bulletin of the Zambia Language Group — B Zambia Lang Group
Bulletin of Thermodynamics and Thermochemistry — Bull Thermodyn & Thermochem
Bulletin of Tibetology — B Tibetol
Bulletin of Tibetology — BT
Bulletin of Toyama Food Research Institute — Bull Toyama Food Res Inst
Bulletin of Vegetable Crops Research Work — BIWAA9
Bulletin of Vegetable Crops Research Work — Bull Veg Crops Res Work
Bulletin of Volcanic Eruptions (Tokyo) — Bull Volcanic Eruptions (Tokyo)
Bulletin of War Medicine — Bull War Med
Bulletin of Zoological Nomenclature — Bull Zool Nom
Bulletin of Zoological Nomenclature — Bull Zool Nomencl
Bulletin of Zoology — Bull Zool
Bulletin. Office de la Protection de l'Enfance — Bul OPE
Bulletin. Office International de la Viticulture — B Off Int Vitic
Bulletin. Office International des Epizooties — Bull Off Int Epizoot
Bulletin. Office International des Instituts d'Archeologie et d'Histoire de l'Art — B Off Int
Bulletin. Office International des Instituts d'Archeologie et d'Histoire de l'Art — BOIA
Bulletin. Office International d'Hygiene Publique — B Off Int Hyg Publ
Bulletin. Office Internationale. Instituts d'Archeologie et d'Histoire de l'Art [*Paris*] — B Off Inst
Bulletin. Office National de Coordination des Allocations Familiales — Bull ONAF
Bulletin. Office National Meteorologique [*France*] — BONM
Bulletin. Office of Experiment Stations. United States Department of Agriculture — Bull Office Exper Stations US Dept Agric
Bulletin Officiel. Association des Medecins Dentistes de France — Bull Off Ass Med Dent Fr
Bulletin Officiel. Chambre de Commerce (Bruxelles) — B Offic Ch Com (Bruxelles)
Bulletin Officiel de la Propriete Industrielle [*Berne*] — Bull Offic
Bulletin Officiel de la Propriete Industrielle. Abreges — Bull Off Propr Ind Abr
Bulletin Officiel de la Propriete Industrielle. Brevets d'Invention, Abreges, et Listes — Bull Off Propr Ind Brev Invent Abr Listes
Bulletin Officiel de la Propriete Industrielle (France) — Bull Offic Propriete Ind (Fr)
Bulletin Officiel de Ruanda-Urundi — BORU
Bulletin Officiel des Chemins de Fer — BOC
Bulletin Officiel. Direction des Recherches Scientifiques et Industrielles et des Inventions (France) — Bull Off Dir Rech Sci Ind Inv (Fr)
Bulletin Officiel du Congo Belge — BO
Bulletin Officiel. Office International du Cacao et du Chocolat — Bull Off Off Int Cacao Choc
Bulletin Officiel. Societe Internationale de Psychoprophylaxie Obstetricale — Bull Off Soc Int Psycho Proph Obstet
Bulletin. Ogata Institute for Medical and Chemical Research — Bull Ogata Inst Med Chem Res
Bulletin. Ohio Agricultural Experiment Station — Bull Ohio Agr Exp Sta
Bulletin. Ohio Agricultural Experiment Station — Bull Ohio Agric Exp St
Bulletin. Ohio Agricultural Experiment Station — Bull Ohio Agric Exp Stn
Bulletin. Ohio Biological Survey — Bull Ohio Biol Surv
Bulletin. Ohio Engineering Experiment Station — Bull Ohio Eng Exp St
Bulletin. Ohio State University. Co-Operative Extension Service — Bull Ohio St Univ Co-Op Ext Serv
Bulletin. Ohio State University. Cooperative Extension Service — Bull Ohio State Univ Coop Ext Serv
Bulletin. Oil and Natural Gas Commission [*India*] — Bull Oil Nat Gas Comm
Bulletin. Oil and Natural Gas Commission (India) — Bull Oil Natur Gas Comm (India)
Bulletin. Oita Institute of Technology — Bull Oita Inst Technol
Bulletin. Oji Institute for Forest Tree Improvement — Bull Oji Inst For Tree Impr
Bulletin. Oji Institute for Forest Tree Improvement — Bull Oji Inst Forest Tree Improv
Bulletin. Okayama College of Science — Bull Okayama Coll Sci
Bulletin. Okayama Tobacco Experiment Station — Bull Okayama Tob Exp Stn
Bulletin. Okayama University of Science — Bull Okayama Univ Sci
Bulletin. Okayama University of Science. A. Natural Science — Bull Okayama Univ Sci A Nat Sci
Bulletin. Okayama University of Science. B. Human Sciences — Bull Okayama Univ Sci B Hum Sci
Bulletin. Okinawa Prefectural Agricultural Experiment Station/Okinawa Kenritsu Noji Shikenjo — Bull Okinawa Prefect Agric Exp Sta
Bulletin. Oklahoma Agricultural Experiment Station — Bull Okla Agric Exp St
Bulletin. Oklahoma Agricultural Experiment Station — Bull Okla Agric Exp Stn
Bulletin. Oklahoma Anthropological Society — Bull Okla Anthrop Soc
Bulletin. Oklahoma Geological Survey — Bull Okla Geol Surv
Bulletin. Oklahoma Geological Survey — Bull Oklahoma Geol Surv
Bulletin. Oklahoma Ornithological Society — Bull Okla Ornithol Soc
Bulletin. Oklahoma State Dental Association — Bull Okla Dent Ass
Bulletin. Oklahoma State University. Agricultural Experiment Station — Bull Okla State Univ Agr Exp Sta
Bulletin on Inventions — BULIB
Bulletin on Inventions [*United States*] — Bull Invent
Bulletin on Narcotics — B Narcotics
Bulletin on Narcotics [*Switzerland*] — BNUNA
Bulletin on Narcotics — Bull Narc
Bulletin on Narcotics — Bull Narcotics
Bulletin on Narcotics (United Nations) — Bul Narcotics (UN)
Bulletin on Rheumatic Diseases — BRDIA
Bulletin on Rheumatic Diseases — Bull Rheum Dis
Bulletin on Training — Bull Train
Bulletin. Ontario Agricultural College — Bull Ont Agric Coll
Bulletin. Ontario College of Pharmacy — Bull Ont Coll Pharm
Bulletin. Ontario Department of Agriculture — Bull Ont Dep Agric
Bulletin. Ontario Medical Association — Bull Ont Med Ass
Bulletin. Operations Research Society of America — Bull Op Res Soc Am
Bulletin. Operations Research Society of America — Bull Oper Res Soc Am
Bulletin. Operations Research Society of America — Bull ORSA
Bulletin. Ophthalmological Society of Egypt — BOSYA
Bulletin. Ophthalmological Society of Egypt — Bull Ophth Soc Eg
Bulletin. Ophthalmological Society of Egypt — Bull Ophthalmol Soc Egypt
Bulletin. Orange County Medical Association [*California*] — Bull Orange County Med Assoc
Bulletin. Ordre des Pharmaciens (Brussels) — Bull Ordre Pharm (Brussels)
Bulletin. Ordre National des Pharmaciens — Bull Ordre Natl Pharm
Bulletin. Oregon Agricultural College — Bull Ore Agric Coll
Bulletin. Oregon Agricultural Experiment Station — Bull Ore Agric Exp Stn
Bulletin. Oregon Agricultural Experiment Station — Bull Oreg Agr Exp Sta
Bulletin. Oregon Agricultural Experiment Station — Bull Oreg Agric Exp St
Bulletin. Oregon Entomological Society — Bull Ore Ent Soc
Bulletin. Oregon State University. Forest Research Laboratory — Bull Ore For Res Lab
Bulletin. Organisatie voor Natuurwetenschappelijk Onderzoek in Indonesiee/ Bulletin. Organization for Scientific Research in Indonesia — Bull Organ Natuurw Onderz Indonesiee
Bulletin. Organisation Internationale de Metrologie Legale — Bull Organ Int Metrol Leg
Bulletin. Organisation Mondiale de la Sante — Bull Org Mond Sante
Bulletin. Ornithological Society of New Zealand — Bull Orn Soc NZ
Bulletin. Orton Society — Bull Orton Soc
Bulletin. Osaka Agricultural Research Center — Bull Osaka Agric Res Cent
Bulletin. Osaka Industrial Research Institute — Bull Osaka Ind Res Inst
Bulletin. Osaka Medical School — Bull Os Med Sch
Bulletin. Osaka Medical School — Bull Osaka Med Sch
Bulletin. Osaka Medical School. Supplement — Bull Osaka Med Sch Suppl
Bulletin. Osaka Municipal Technical Research Institute [*Japan*] — Bull Osaka Munic Tech Res Inst
Bulletin. Osaka Museum of Natural History — Bull Osaka Mus Nat Hist
Bulletin. Osaka Prefectural Technical College — Bull Osaka Prefect Tech College
Bulletin. Otago Catchment Board — Bull Otago Catchm Bd
Bulletin. Oxford University. Institute of Statistics — B Oxf Univ Inst Statist
Bulletin. Oxford University. Institute of Statistics — BOUIS
Bulletin. Oxford University. Institute of Statistics — Bull Oxf Univ Inst Stat
Bulletin P. New South Wales Department of Agriculture. Division of Plant Industry — Bull P NSW Dep Agric Div Plant Ind
Bulletin. Pacific Coast Society of Orthodontists [*US*] — Bull Pac Coast Soc Orthod
Bulletin. Pacific Orchid Society of Hawaii — Bull Pac Orchid Soc Hawaii
Bulletin. Pacific Orchid Society of Hawaii — Bull Pacif Orchid Soc Haw
Bulletin. Pacific Tropical Botanical Garden — Bull Pac Trop Bot Gard
Bulletin. Palestine Exploration Society — BPES
Bulletin. Palestine Museum — BPM
Bulletin. Palestine Museum [*Jerusalem*] — PMB
Bulletin. Pan American Health Organization — BPAH
Bulletin. Pan American Health Organization — Bull Pan Am Health Organ
Bulletin. Pan American Health Organization — PAHO/B
Bulletin. Pan American Union — B Pan Am Un
Bulletin. Pan American Union — BPAU
Bulletin. Pan American Union — Bul Pan Am Union
Bulletin. Pan American Union (Washington, DC) — Bull Pan Am Un Wash
Bulletin. Parenteral Drug Association — Bull Parenter Drug Assoc
Bulletin. Parenteral Drug Association — BUYRA
Bulletin. Passaic County Dental Society — Bull Passaic Cty Dent Soc
Bulletin. Patent and Trademark Institute of Canada — Bul Pat Tradem Inst Can
Bulletin. Patna Science College Philosophical Society — Bull Patna Sci Coll Philos Soc
Bulletin. Peabody Museum of Natural History — Bull Peab Mus Nat Hist
Bulletin. Peak District Mines Historical Society [*Matlock Bath*] — Bull Peak Dist Mines Hist Soc
Bulletin Pedagogique — B Pedag
Bulletin. Peking Society of Natural History — Bull Peking Soc Nat Hist
Bulletin. Pennsylvania Agricultural Experiment Station — Bull PA Agr Exp Sta
Bulletin. Pennsylvania Agricultural Experiment Station — Bull PA Agric Exp Stn

Bulletin. Pennsylvania Agricultural Experiment Station — Bull Penns Agric Exp St
Bulletin. Pennsylvania Flower Growers — Bull Pa Flower Grow
Bulletin. Pennsylvania State Dental Society — Bull Penns St Dent Soc
Bulletin. Pennsylvania State Modern Language Association — BPSMLA
Bulletin. Pennsylvania State University. Agricultural Experiment Station — Bull PA State Univ Agr Exp Sta
Bulletin. Permanent International Association of Navigation Congresses — B Perm Int Ass Nav Congr
Bulletin. Permanent International Association of Navigation Congresses — Bull Perm Int Assoc Navig Congr
Bulletin. Permanent International Association of Navigation Congresses — Bull Perma Int Ass Navig Congr
Bulletin. Permanent International Association of Navigation Congresses — Bull Permanent Int Assoc Navigation Congresses
Bulletin. Pharmaceutical Research Institute (Osaka) — Bull Pharm Res Inst (Osaka)
Bulletin. Philadelphia Astronautical Society — Bull Philadelphia Astronaut Soc
Bulletin. Philadelphia County Dental Society — Bull Phila Cty Dent Soc
Bulletin. Philadelphia Herpetological Society — Bull Phila Herpetol Soc
Bulletin. Philadelphia Museum of Art — B Phila Mus
Bulletin. Philippine Biochemical Society — Bull Philipp Biochem Soc
Bulletin. Philological Society of Calcutta — BPhSC
Bulletin. Philological Society of Calcutta — BPSC
Bulletin Philologique et Historique — BPH
Bulletin Philologique et Historique — BPHist
Bulletin Philologique et Historique — Bull Philol Hist
Bulletin Philologique et Historique. Comite des Travaux Historiques et Scientifiques [*Paris*] — BPCTH
Bulletin Philologique et Historique. Comite des Travaux Historiques et Scientifiques [*Paris*] — BPHCTHS
Bulletin Philologique et Historique. Comite des Travaux Historiques et Scientifiques — Bull Philol Hist
Bulletin Philologique et Historique. Comite des Travaux Historiques et Scientifiques (Paris) — BPHP
Bulletin. Philosophical Society of Washington [*District of Columbia*] — Bull Phil Soc Wash
Bulletin. Phonetic Society of Japan — BPhSJ
Bulletin. Physical Fitness Research Institute — Bull Phys Fitness Res Inst
Bulletin. Pittsburgh University — Bull Pittsb Univ
Bulletin. Plankton Society of Japan — Bull Plankton Soc Jpn
Bulletin. Plant Board of Florida — Bull Plant Bd Fla
Bulletin. Plant Physiology (Beijing) — Bull Plant Physiol (Beijing)
Bulletin. Polish Academy of Sciences. Biological Sciences — Bull Pol Acad Sci Biol Sci
Bulletin. Polish Academy of Sciences. Biology — Bull Pol Acad Sci Biol
Bulletin. Polish Academy of Sciences. Chemistry — Bull Pol Acad Sci Chem
Bulletin. Polish Academy of Sciences. Earth Sciences — Bull Pol Acad Sci Earth Sci
Bulletin. Polish Institute of Arts and Sciences in America — BPIAS
Bulletin. Polish Institute of Arts and Sciences in America — Bull Pol Inst Arts Sci Am
Bulletin. Polish Institute of Arts and Sciences in America — Bull Pol Inst Arts Sci Amer
Bulletin. Polish Institute of Arts and Sciences in America — Bull Pol Inst Arts Sci America
Bulletin Polytec. Ecole Polytechnique de Montreal — Bul Polytec Ecole Polytech Montreal
Bulletin. Post-Graduate Committee in Medicine. University of Sydney — BPCMUS
Bulletin. Post-Graduate Committee in Medicine. University of Sydney — Bul Post-Graduate Ctee in Medicine Univ of Syd
Bulletin. Postgraduate Institute of Medical Education and Research (Chandigarh) — Bull Postgrad Inst Med Educ Res (Chandigarh)
Bulletin pour la Conservation des Monuments Historiques d'Alsace — BMHA
Bulletin. Poznanskie Towarzystwo Przyjaciol Nauk. Serie D — Bull Poznan Tow Przyjaciol Nauk Ser D
Bulletin. Presbyterian Historical Society of Ireland — Bull Pres Hist Soc Ir
Bulletin. Press Exchange and Documentation Centre of Apimondia — Bull Press Exchange Documn Cent Apimondia
Bulletin. Presse- und Informationsamt der Bundesregierung — Bull Presse-Informationsamt Bundesregier
Bulletin. Primary Tungsten Association — Bull Primary Tungsten Assoc
Bulletin. Prince of Wales Museum of Western India — B Prince of Wales Mus West India
Bulletin. Proceedings. National Institution for the Promotion of Science — Nat Inst Bull
Bulletin Professionel et Technique des Pecheurs Maritimes — BPTPM
Bulletin. Psychonomic Society — B Psychon S
Bulletin. Psychonomic Society — BPNSB
Bulletin. Psychonomic Society — BPS
Bulletin. Psychonomic Society — Bull Psychon Soc
Bulletin. Public Health Institute of Hyogo Prefecture — Bull Public Health Inst Hyogo Prefect
Bulletin. Puerto Rico Agricultural Experiment Station. Insular Station (Rio Piedras) — Bull Puerto Rico Agric Exp Stn Insular Stn (Rio Piedras)
Bulletin. Punjab Agricultural University — Bull Punjab Agric Univ
Bulletin. Pusan Fisheries College (Natural Sciences) — Bull Pusan Fish Coll (Nat Sci)
Bulletin. Quebec Asbestos Mining Association — Bul Quebec Asbest Min Assoc
Bulletin. Quezon Institute (Manila) — Bull Quezon Inst (Manila)
Bulletin. Rabinowitz Fund for the Exploration of Ancient Synagogues — BRF
Bulletin. Radio and Electrical Engineering Division. National Research Council of Canada — Bull Radio Electr Eng Div Nat Res Counc Can
Bulletin. Radio and Electrical Engineering Division. National Research Council of Canada — Bull Radio Electr Eng Div Natl Res Counc Can
Bulletin. Radio and Electrical Engineering Division. National Research Council of Canada — NRRBA
Bulletin. Radioisotope Research Institute. Tokyo University of Agriculture — Bull Radioisot Res Inst Tokyo Univ Agric
Bulletin. Raffles Museum — Bull Raffles Mus
Bulletin. Ramakrishna Mission Institute of Culture — B Rama Miss Inst Cult
Bulletin. Ramakrishna Mission Institute of Culture — B Ramakr Miss Inst
Bulletin Regional. Amis de Montlucon — BA Montl
Bulletin. Regional Research Laboratory (Jammu) — Bull Reg Res Lab (Jammu)
Bulletin. Republic Institution for the Protection of Nature and the Museum of Natural History in Titograd — Bull Repub Inst Prot Nat Mus Nat Hist Titograd
Bulletin. Research Council (Israel) — Bull (Israel) Res Counc
Bulletin. Research Council of Israel — B Res Council Isr
Bulletin. Research Council of Israel — BRCI
Bulletin. Research Council of Israel [*Jerusalem*] — BResClsr
Bulletin. Research Council of Israel — Bull Res Coun Israel
Bulletin. Research Council of Israel — Bull Res Counc Isr
Bulletin. Research Council of Israel — Bull Res Council Israel
Bulletin. Research Council of Israel. Section A. Chemistry — Bull Res Counc Isr Sect A Chem
Bulletin. Research Council of Israel. Section A. Mathematics, Physics, and Chemistry — Bull Res Counc Isr Sect A Math Phys Chem
Bulletin. Research Council of Israel. Section B. Biology and Geology — Bull Res Counc Isr Sect B Biol Geol
Bulletin. Research Council of Israel. Section B. Zoology — Bull Res Counc Isr Sect B Zool
Bulletin. Research Council of Israel. Section C. Technology — BRICA
Bulletin. Research Council of Israel. Section C. Technology — Bull Res Counc Isr Sect C Technol
Bulletin. Research Council of Israel. Section D. Botany — Bull Res Counc Isr Sect D Bot
Bulletin. Research Council of Israel. Section D. Botany — Bull Res Council Israel Sect D Bot
Bulletin. Research Council of Israel. Section E. Experimental Medicine — Bull Res Counc Isr Sect E Exp Med
Bulletin. Research Council of Israel. Section F. Mathematics and Physics — Bull Res Counc Isr Sect F
Bulletin. Research Council of Israel. Section G. Geo-Sciences — Bull Res Counc Isr Sect G
Bulletin. Research Council of Israel. Section G. Geo-Sciences — Bull Res Counc Isr Sect G Geo-Sci
Bulletin. Research Institute for Applied Mechanics. Kyushu University [*Japan*] — Bull Res Inst Appl Mech Kyushu Univ
Bulletin. Research Institute for Diathetic Medicine. Kumamoto University — Bull Res Inst Diathetic Med Kumamoto Univ
Bulletin. Research Institute for Food Science. Kyoto University — Bull Res Inst Food Sci Kyoto Univ
Bulletin. Research Institute for Material Science and Engineering. Faculty of Engineering. Fukui University — Bull Res Inst Mater Sci Eng Fac Eng Fukui Univ
Bulletin. Research Institute for Polymers and Textiles — Bull Res Inst Polymers Textiles
Bulletin. Research Institute for Scientific Measurements. Tohoku University — Bull Res Inst Sci Meas Tohoku Univ
Bulletin. Research Institute of Applied Electricity — Bull Res Inst Appl Electr
Bulletin. Research Institute of Electronics. Shizuoka University — Bull Res Inst Electron Shizuoka Univ
Bulletin. Research Institute of Fermentation. Yamanashi University [*Japan*] — Bull Res Inst Ferment Yamanashi Univ
Bulletin. Research Institute of Mineral Dressing and Metallurgy [*Japan*] — Bull Res Inst Min Dressing Metall
Bulletin. Research Institute of Mineral Dressing and Metallurgy. Tohoku University [*Japan*] — Bull Res Inst Miner Dressing Metall Tohoku Univ
Bulletin. Research Institute. Sumatra Plantations Association — Bull Res Inst Sumatra Plant Assoc
Bulletin. Research Institute. University of Kerala (Trivandrum). Series A. Physical Sciences — Bull Res Inst Univ Kerala (Trivandrum) Ser A
Bulletin. Research Laboratory for Nuclear Reactors. Tokyo Institute of Technology — BRLTD
Bulletin. Research Laboratory for Nuclear Reactors. Tokyo Institute of Technology — Bull Res Lab Nucl React Tokyo Inst Technol
Bulletin. Research Laboratory of Precision Machinery and Electronics — Bull Res Lab Precis Mach and Electron
Bulletin. Research Laboratory of Precision Machinery and Electronics — Bull Res Lab Precis Mach Electron
Bulletin. Research Laboratory of Precision Machinery and Electronics. Tokyo Institute of Technology — Bull Res Lab Precis Mach Electron Tokyo Inst Technol
Bulletin. Reserve Bank of India — BRBI
Bulletin. Reserve Bank of New Zealand — Bull Reserve Bank
Bulletin. Rhode Island Agricultural Experiment Station — Bull Rhode Isl Agric Exp Stn
Bulletin. Rhode Island Agricultural Experiment Station — Bull RI Agric Exp Stn
Bulletin. Rhode Island School of Design. Museum Notes — BRISD
Bulletin. Rhode Island School of Design. Museum Notes — BRISDMN
Bulletin. Rhode Island School of Design. Museum Notes — Rhode Island
Bulletin. Rhode Island School of Design. Museum Notes (Providence) — B (Providence)
Bulletin. Rhodesia Geological Survey — Bull Rhod Geol Surv
Bulletin. Richmond County Medical Society [*Georgia*] — Bull Richmond County Med Soc
Bulletin. Rijksmuseum — Bull Rijksmus

Bulletin. Riverside County Medical Association [*California*] — Bull Riverside County Med Assoc
Bulletin. Rocky Mountain Modern Language Association — BRMMLA
Bulletin. Royal College of Psychiatrists — Bull R Col Psychiatr
Bulletin. Royal Ontario Museum. Art and Archaeology Division — BROM
Bulletin. Royal Ontario Museum. Art and Archaeology Division — BROMA
Bulletin. Royal Ontario Museum. Art and Archaeology Division — Bull ROM
Bulletin. Royal Society of New Zealand — Bull Roy Soc New Zealand
Bulletin. Royal Society of New Zealand — Bull Soc NZ
Bulletin. Rubber Growers Association — Bull Rubber Grow Assoc
Bulletin. Rubber Research Institute of Malaya — Bull Rubber Res Inst Malaya
Bulletin. Saga Agricultural Experiment Station — Bull Saga Agr Exp Sta
Bulletin. Saga Agricultural Experiment Station/Saga-Ken Nogyo Shikenjo Kenkyu Hokoku — Bull Saga Agric Exp Sta
Bulletin. Saginaw County Medical Society [*Michigan*] — Bull Saginaw County Med Soc
Bulletin. Saitama Horticultural Experiment Station — Bull Saitama Hortic Exp Stn
Bulletin. Salesian Polytechnic — Bull Salesian Polytech
Bulletin. San Diego County Dental Society — Bull San Diego Cty Dent Soc
Bulletin. San Mateo [*California*] **County Dental Society** — Bull San Mateo Cty Dent Soc
Bulletin. San Mateo County Medical Society [*California*] — Bull San Mateo County Med Soc
Bulletin. Santa Clara County Medical Society — Bull Santa Clara County Med Soc
Bulletin. Sapporo Branch. Forestry Experiment Station/Hokkaido Ringyo Shiken Hokoku — Bull Sapporo Branch Forest Exp Sta
Bulletin. School of Engineering and Architecture of Sakarya — BSESD
Bulletin. School of Engineering and Architecture of Sakarya — Bull School Eng Archit Sakarya
Bulletin. School of Forestry. Montana State University — Bull Sch For Mont St Univ
Bulletin. School of Forestry. Stephen F. Austin State College — Bull Sch For S F Austin St Coll
Bulletin. School of Medicine. University of Maryland — Bull Sch Med Univ MD
Bulletin. School of Oriental and African Studies — B Sch Or Afr Stud
Bulletin. School of Oriental and African Studies — B Sch Orien
Bulletin. School of Oriental and African Studies — B Sch Orient Afr Stud
Bulletin. School of Oriental and African Studies — BOAS
Bulletin. School of Oriental and African Studies — BSOA
Bulletin. School of Oriental and African Studies — BSOAS
Bulletin. School of Oriental and African Studies — Bull Sch Orient Afr Stud
Bulletin. School of Oriental and African Studies — Bull Sch Oriental Afr Stud
Bulletin. School of Oriental and African Studies — Bull School Orient African Stud
Bulletin. School of Oriental and African Studies — Bull SOAS
Bulletin. School of Oriental and African Studies. University of London — BSOSt
Bulletin. School of Oriental Studies — BSOS
Bulletin. School of Oriental Studies — Bull Sch Orient Stud
Bulletin. Schweizerische Akademie der Medizinischen Wissenschaften — B Sc Ak Med
Bulletin. Schweizerische Akademie der Medizinischen Wissenschaften — BSAMA
Bulletin. Schweizerische Akademie der Medizinischen Wissenschaften — Bull Schweiz Akad Med Wiss
Bulletin. Schweizerische Gesellschaft fuer Anthropologie und Ethnologie — Bull Schweiz Ges Anthropol Ethnol
Bulletin. Schweizerischer Elektrotechnischer Verein [*Switzerland*] — Bull Schweiz Electrotech Ver
Bulletin. Schweizerischer Elektrotechnischer Verein — Bull SEV
Bulletin. Schweizerischer Elektrotechnischer Verein — BUSKA
Bulletin. Science and Engineering Research Laboratory. Waseda University — Bull Sci Eng Res Lab Waseda Univ
Bulletin. Science and Technology Agency [*Japan*] — Bull Sci Technol Agency
Bulletin. Sciences de la Terre. Universite de Poitiers — Bull Sci Terre Univ Poitiers
Bulletin. Scientific and Technical Documentation Centre (Egypt) — Bull Sci Tech Doc Cent (Egypt)
Bulletin. Scientific Laboratories of Denison University — Bull Sci Lab Denison Univ
Bulletin. Scientific Researches. Alumni Association. Morioka College of Agriculture and Forestry/Morioka Kono Dosokai Gakujutsu Iho — Bull Sci Res Alumni Assoc Morioka Coll Agric
Bulletin Scientifique. Academie Imperiale des Sciences de Saint Petersbourg [*A publication*] — Bull Sci Acad Imp Sci Saint Petersbourg
Bulletin Scientifique. Association des Ingenieurs Electriciens Sortis de l'Institut Electrotechnique (Montefiore) — Bul Sci AIM
Bulletin Scientifique. Association des Ingenieurs Electriciens Sortis de l'Institut Electrotechnique (Montefiore) — Bull Sci Assoc Ing Electr Inst Electrotech (Montefiore)
Bulletin Scientifique. Conseil des Academies de la RSF de Yougoslavie — Bull Sci Cons Acad RSF Yougosl
Bulletin Scientifique. Conseil des Academies de la RSF de Yougoslavie. Section A [*Zagreb*] — Bull Sci Conseil Acad RSF Yougoslav Sect A
Bulletin Scientifique. Conseil des Academies de la RSF de Yougoslavie. Section A. Sciences Naturelles, Techniques, et Medicales — Bull Sci Cons Acad RSF Yougosl Sect A Sci Nat Tech Med
Bulletin Scientifique. Conseil des Academies des Sciences et des Arts de la RSF de Yougoslavie. Section A. Sciences Naturelles, Techniques, et Medicales — BSYSA
Bulletin Scientifique. Conseil des Academies des Sciences et des Arts de la RSF de Yougoslavie. Section A. Sciences Naturelles, Techniques, et Medicales — Bull Sci Cons Acad Sci Arts RSF Yougosl Sect A
Bulletin Scientifique de Bourgogne — Bull Sci Bourgogne
Bulletin Scientifique de la France et de la Belgique — Bull Scient Fr Belg
Bulletin Scientifique de la France et de la Belgique — Bull Scient France et Belgique
Bulletin Scientifique. Ecole Polytechnique de Timisoará — BSEPT
Bulletin Scientifique. Ecole Polytechnique de Timisoara. Comptes Rendus des Seances. Societe Scientifique de Timisoara — Bull Sci Ecole Polytech Timisoara
Bulletin Scientifique et Economique. Bureau de Recherches Minieres de l'Algerie — Bull Sci Econ Bur Rech Minieres Alger
Bulletin Scientifique et Historique de l'Auvergne — Bull Sci Hist Auvergne
Bulletin Scientifique et Industriel de la Maison Roure Bertrand Fils — Bull Sci Ind Maison Roure Bertrand Fils
Bulletin Scientifique, Historique, et Litteraire du Department du Nord et des Pays Voisins — Bull Sci Dep Nord Pays Voisins
Bulletin Scientifique. Institut Textile de France — Bull Sci Inst Text Fr
Bulletin Scientifique. Institut Textile de France — Bull Sci ITF
Bulletin Scientifique Roumain — Bull Sci Roumain
Bulletin Scientifique. Section A. Sciences Naturelles, Techniques, et Medicales — Bull Sci Sect A
Bulletin. Scottish Association of Geography Teachers — Bull Scott Assoc Geogr Teach
Bulletin. Scottish Georgian Society — Bull Scott Georgian Soc
Bulletin. Scripps Institution of Oceanography of the University of California — Bull Scripps Inst Oceanogr Univ Calif
Bulletin. Sea View Hospital — Bull Sea View Hosp
Bulletin. Second Agronomy Division. Tokai-Kinki National Agricultural Experiment Station — Bull Sec Agron Div Tokai-Kinki Natl Agric Exp Stn
Bulletin. Second Agronomy Division. Tokai-Kinki National Agricultural Experiment Station — Bull Second Agron Div Tokai-Kinki Nat Agr Exp Sta
Bulletin. Second District Dental Society [*Brooklyn, New York*] — Bull Second Dist Dent Soc
Bulletin. Section de Geographie. Actes du 96e Congres National des Societes Savantes — B Sect Geogr Soc Sav
Bulletin. Section de Geographie. Comite des Travaux Historiques et Scientifiques — BGCTH
Bulletin. Section de Geographie. Comite des Travaux Historiques et Scientifiques. Ministere de l'Instruction Publique et des Beaux Arts. Ministere de l'Education Nationale — Bull Sect Geogr Comite Trav Hist Sci
Bulletin. Section de Geographie de Paris. Congres des Societies Savantes. Congres de Strasbourg — B Sec GP
Bulletin. Section d'Histoire Moderne et Contemporaine — BSHMC
Bulletin. Section d'Histoire Moderne et Contemporaine. Comite des Travaux Historiques et Scientifiques — Bull Sect Hist Mod Contemp
Bulletin. Section Historique. Academie Roumaine — BH Ac Roum
Bulletin. Section Historique. Academie Roumaine — BHAR
Bulletin. Section Historique. Academie Roumaine — BSH
Bulletin. Section Historique. Academie Roumaine — BSHAR
Bulletin. Section Historique. Academie Roumaine — Bull Sect Hist Acad Roumaine
Bulletin. Section of Logic — Bull Sect Log
Bulletin. Section Scientifique. Academie Roumaine — Bull Sect Sc Ac Roum
Bulletin. Section Scientifique. Academie Roumaine — Bull Sect Sci Acad Roum
Bulletin SEDEIS [*Societe d'Etudes et de Documentation Economiques, Industrielles, et Sociales*] — BSEDEIS
Bulletin. Seikai Regional Fisheries Research Laboratory — Bull Seikai Reg Fish Res Lab
Bulletin. Seishin Igaku Institute — Bull Seishin Igaku Inst
Bulletin. Seishin Igaku Institute (Seishin Igaku Kenkyusho Gyosekishu) — Bull Seishin Igaku Inst (Seishin Igaku Kenkyusho Gyosekishu)
Bulletin. Seismological Society of America — B Seis S Am
Bulletin. Seismological Society of America — Bull Seism Soc Am
Bulletin. Seismological Society of America — Bull Seismol Soc Am
Bulletin. Seismological Society of America — Bull Seismol Soc Amer
Bulletin Seismologique (Warsaw) — Bull Seismol (Warsaw)
Bulletin Semestriel. Association des Classiques de l'Universite de Liege — BACILg
Bulletin. Seoul National University Forests — Bull Seoul Natl Univ For
Bulletin. Seoul National University Forests/Seoul Taehakkyo Yonsuplim Pogo — Bull Seoul Natl Univ For Seoul Taehakkyo Yonsuplim Pogo
Bulletin. Sericultural Experiment Station. Government General of Chosen — Bull Ser Exp Stn Gov Gen Chosen
Bulletin. Sericultural Experiment Station. Government-General of Chosen — Bull Seric Exp Stn Gov Gen Chosen
Bulletin. Sericultural Experiment Station (Tokyo) — Bull Seric Exp Stn (Tokyo)
Bulletin. Sericultural Experimental Station of Miyagi Prefecture — Bull Seric Exp Stn Miyagi Prefect
Bulletin. Sericulture and Silk Industry — Bull Seric Silk Ind
Bulletin. Serie C. Societe Geologique et Mineralogique de Bretagne — Bull Ser C Soc Geol Mineral Bretagne
Bulletin. Service Botanique et Agronomique de Tunisie — Bull Serv Bot Agron Tunis
Bulletin. Service de Culture et d'Etudes du Peuplier et du Saule — Bull Serv Cult Etud Peuplier et Saule
Bulletin. Service de la Carte Geologique. Algerie. Serie 1. Paleontologie — Bull Serv Carte Geol Alger Ser 1
Bulletin. Service de la Carte Geologique. Algerie. Serie 4. Geophysique — Bull Serv Carte Geol Alger Ser 4
Bulletin. Service de la Carte Geologique d'Alsace et de Lorraine — Bull Serv Carte Geol Als Lorr
Bulletin. Service de la Carte Geologique de la France — B Serv Carte Geol
Bulletin. Service de la Carte Geologique de la France — Bull Serv Carte Geol Fr
Bulletin. Service de la Carte Geologique de l'Algerie — B Serv Carte Geol Alg
Bulletin. Service de la Carte Geologique de l'Algerie — Bull Serv Carte Geol Alger

Bulletin. Service de la Carte Geologique de l'Algerie. Serie 2. Stratigraphie — Bull Serv Carte Geol Alger Ser 2
Bulletin. Service de la Carte Geologique de l'Algerie. Serie 3. Geologie Appliquee — Bull Serv Carte Geol Alger Ser 3
Bulletin. Service de la Carte Geologique de l'Algerie. Serie 5. Petrographie — Bull Serv Carte Geol Alger Ser 5
Bulletin. Service de la Carte Geologique de l'Algerie. Serie 6. Metallogenie — Bull Serv Carte Geol Alger Ser 6
Bulletin. Service de la Carte Phytogeographique — B Serv Carte Phytogeogr
Bulletin. Service des Etudes et de la Documentation Economiques. Office de la Statistique Generale — Bull Serv Et
Bulletin. Service des Instruments de Mesure — Bull Serv Instrum Mes
Bulletin. Service Geologique de la Republique Rwandaise — Bull Serv Geol Rwandaise
Bulletin Service Geologique de Pologne — Bull Serv Geol Pol
Bulletin. Service Geologique du Luxembourg — Bull Serv Geol Luxemb
Bulletin. Service Geologique et Geophysique. RP de Serbie — Bull Serv Geol Geophys RP Serbie
Bulletin. Service Geologique (Rwanda) — Bull Serv Geol (Rwanda)
Bulletin. Service Medical du Travail — Bull Serv Med Trav
Bulletin. Service Social des Caisses d'Assurance Maladie — B Serv Soc Caisses Assur Malad
Bulletin. Service Tunisien des Statistiques — B Serv Tunis Statist
Bulletin. Shanghai Science Institute — Bull Shanghai Sci Inst
Bulletin. Shanghai Science Institute — Bull SSI
Bulletin. Shemane Agricultural Experiment Station — Bull Shemane Agric Exp Stn
Bulletin. Shenyang Institute of Geology and Mineral Resources — Bull Shenyang Inst Geol Miner Resour
Bulletin. Shiga Prefectural Agricultural Experiment Station — Bull Shiga Pref Agr Exp Sta
Bulletin. Shiga Prefecture Agricultural Experiment Station — Bull Shiga Prefect Agric Exp Stn
Bulletin. Shih Yen Pao Kao. Taiwan Forest Research Institute — Bull Shih Yen Pao Kao Taiwan For Res Inst
Bulletin. Shikoku Agricultural Experiment Station — Bull Shikoku Agr Exp Sta
Bulletin. Shikoku Agricultural Experiment Station — Bull Shikoku Agric Exp Stn
Bulletin. Shikoku National Agricultural Experiment Station — Bull Shikoku Natl Agric Exp Stn
Bulletin. Shikoku National Agricultural Experiment Station. Extra Issue — Bull Shikoku Natl Agric Exp Stn Extra Issue
Bulletin. Shimane Agricultural College — Bull Shimane Agr Coll
Bulletin. Shimane Agricultural College — Bull Shimane Agric Coll
Bulletin. Shimane Agricultural Experiment Station — Bull Shimane Agr Exp Sta
Bulletin. Shimane Agricultural Experiment Station — Bull Shimane Agric Exp Stn
Bulletin. Shimane Prefecture Forestry Experiment Station — Bull Shimane Prefect For Exp Stn
Bulletin. Shimane University. Natural Science [*Japan*] — Bull Shimane Univ Nat Sci
Bulletin. Shinshu University Forest/Shinshu Daigaku Nogaku-Bu Enshurin Hokoku — Bull Shinshu Univ Forest
Bulletin. Shinshu University Forests — Bull Shinshu Univ For
Bulletin. Shizuoka Agricultural Experiment Station — Bull Shizuoka Agr Exp Sta
Bulletin. Shizuoka Daigaku Nogaku-Bu — Bull Shizuoka Daigaku Nogaku-Bu
Bulletin. Shizuoka Prefectural Agricultural Experiment Station — Bull Shizuoka Pref Agr Exp Sta
Bulletin. Shizuoka Prefectural Fisheries Experiment Station — Bull Shizuoka Prefect Fish Exp Stn
Bulletin. Shizuoka Prefecture Forestry Experiment Station — Bull Shizuoka Prefect For Exp Stn
Bulletin. Shizuoka Prefecture Institute of Public Health — Bull Shizuoka Prefect Inst Public Health
Bulletin. Shrimp Culture Research Center — Bull Shrimp Cult Res Cent
Bulletin Signaletique — B Sign
Bulletin Signaletique — BS
Bulletin Signaletique — Bull Signal
Bulletin Signaletique 101. Sciences de l'Information. Documentation — BS 101
Bulletin Signaletique 221. Gitologie Economie Miniere — Bull Signal 221
Bulletin Signaletique. Art et Archeologie — BSAA
Bulletin Signaletique. Entomologie Medicale et Veterinaire — Bull Signal Ent Med Vet
Bulletin Signaletique. Histoire des Sciences et des Techniques — BSHST
Bulletin Signaletique. Histoire et Science de la Litterature — BSHSL
Bulletin Signaletique. Polymeres, Peintures, Bois, Cuirs — Bull Sign Polym Peint Bois Cuirs
Bulletin Signaletique. Sciences de l'Education — BS Sci Ed
Bulletin Signaletique. Sciences du Langage — BS Sci L
Bulletin Signaletique. Sciences Humaines, Etc. [*Paris*] — BSignHum
Bulletin Signaletique. Sciences Religieuses — BS Sci R
Bulletin Signaletique. Section 17. Biologie et Physiologie Vegetales — Bull Signal 17 Biol Physiol Veg
Bulletin Signaletique. Sociologie-Ethnologie — BS Soc Ethn
Bulletin. Sinai Hospital of Detroit — Bull Sinai Hosp Detroit
Bulletin. Singapore National Institute of Chemistry — Bull Singapore Natl Inst Chem
Bulletin. Singapore National Institute of Chemistry — Bulletin Singapore Natl Inst Chem
Bulletin Skloprojektu — Bull Skloprojektu
Bulletin. Sloane Hospital for Women in the Columbia-Presbyterian Medical Center — Bull Sloane Hosp Women Columbia-Presbyt Med Cent
Bulletin. Slovenskej Pol'nohospodarskej Akademie. Vyskumneho Ustavu Potravinarskeho — BSVPB
Bulletin. Slovenskej Pol'nohospodarskej Akademie. Vyskumneho Ustavu Potravinarskeho — Bull Slov Pol'nohospod Akad Vysk Ustavu Potravin
Bulletin Social des Industriels — BSI
Bulletin Social des Industriels — Bul Soc Ind
Bulletin Social des Industriels. Association des Patrons et Ingenieurs Catholiques de Belgique — Bull Soc Ind
Bulletin. Societe Academique d'Agriculture des Sciences, Arts, et Belles-Lettres du Departement de l'Aube — BSA Aube
Bulletin. Societe Academique d'Agriculture des Sciences, Arts, et Belles-Lettres du Departement de l'Aube — Bull Acad Agric Aube
Bulletin. Societe Alsacienne de Construction Mecanique — Bull Soc Alsac Constr Mec
Bulletin. Societe Anatomique de Paris — Bull Soc Anat Paris
Bulletin. Societe Archeologique Alexandrine — Bull Soc Archeol Alexandr
Bulletin. Societe Archeologique Bulgare — B Soc Bulg
Bulletin. Societe Archeologique Bulgare — BSAB
Bulletin. Societe Archeologique d'Alexandrie — BArchAlex
Bulletin. Societe Archeologique d'Alexandrie — BSAA
Bulletin. Societe Archeologique d'Alexandrie — Bull Alex
Bulletin. Societe Archeologique de Bordeaux — BSAB
Bulletin. Societe Archeologique de la Correze — BSACorreze
Bulletin. Societe Archeologique de Sens — BSAS
Bulletin. Societe Archeologique de Sens — Bull Arch Sens
Bulletin. Societe Archeologique de Touraine — BSAT
Bulletin. Societe Archeologique d'Eure-et-Loir — BSAEL
Bulletin. Societe Archeologique du Finistere — BSA Finistere
Bulletin. Societe Archeologique du Finistere — Bull Soc Archeol Finistere
Bulletin. Societe Archeologique du Finstere — BSA Fin
Bulletin. Societe Archeologique du Limousin — BSAL
Bulletin. Societe Archeologique du Midi de la France — BSAM
Bulletin. Societe Archeologique du Midi de la France — BSAMF
Bulletin. Societe Archeologique du Midi de la France — Bull Soc Arch du Midi de la France
Bulletin. Societe Archeologique et Historique de Beauvais — B Beauvais
Bulletin. Societe Archeologique et Historique de Beauvis — BSAHB
Bulletin. Societe Archeologique et Historique de l'Orleannais — B Orleans
Bulletin. Societe Archeologique et Historique de l'Orleannais — BSAHO
Bulletin. Societe Archeologique et Historique de Nantes et de Loire-Atlantique — BSAHNantes
Bulletin. Societe Archeologique et Historique des Hauts Cantons de l'Herault — B Soc Arch HCH
Bulletin. Societe Archeologique et Historique du Chatillonnais — Bull Soc Arch Hist Chatillonnais
Bulletin. Societe Archeologique et Historique du Limousin — B Limousin
Bulletin. Societe Archeologique et Historique du Limousin — B Soc Archeol Hist Limousin
Bulletin. Societe Archeologique et Historique du Limousin — BSAHL
Bulletin. Societe Archeologique et Historique du Limousin — BSAHLimousin
Bulletin. Societe Archeologique et Scientifique de Noyon — BSAH Noy
Bulletin. Societe Archeologique et Statistique de la Drome — BSASD
Bulletin. Societe Archeologique, Historique, et Artistique de Vieux Papier — Bull Soc Archeol Hist Artist Vieux Pap
Bulletin. Societe Archeologique, Historique, Litteraire, et Scientifique du Gers — BSAG
Bulletin. Societe Archeologique, Historique, Litteraire, et Scientifique du Gers — BSAHG
Bulletin. Societe Archeologique, Historique, Litteraire, et Scientifique du Gers — Bull Gers
Bulletin. Societe Archeologique, Scientifique, e Litteraire du Vendomois — Bull Soc Archeol Sci Litt Vendomois
Bulletin. Societe Archeologique, Scientifique, et Litteraire de Beziers — Bull Beziers
Bulletin. Societe Archeologique, Scientifique, et Litteraire de Beziers — Bull Soc Arch Sci Lettr de Beziers
Bulletin. Societe Archeologique, Scientifique, et Litteraire du Vendomois — B Vendome
Bulletin. Societe Archeologique, Scientifique, et Litteraire du Vendomois — BSAV
Bulletin. Societe Belfortaine d'Emulation — B Belfort
Bulletin. Societe Belfortaine d'Emulation — BSBE
Bulletin. Societe Belfortaine d'Emulation — Bull Belfort
Bulletin. Societe Belge de Geologie — BSBGD
Bulletin. Societe Belge de Geologie [*Belgium*] — Bull Soc Belge Geol
Bulletin. Societe Belge de Geologie, de Paleontologie, et d'Hydrologie [*Later, Bulletin. Societe Belge de Geologie*] — B Soc Belge Geol Paleont Hydrol
Bulletin. Societe Belge de Geologie, de Paleontologie, et d'Hydrologie [*Later, Bulletin. Societe Belge de Geologie*] — BSBPA
Bulletin. Societe Belge de Geologie, de Paleontologie, et d'Hydrologie [*Later, Bulletin. Societe Belge de Geologie*] — Bull Soc Belg Geol Paleontol Hydrol
Bulletin. Societe Belge de Geologie, de Paleontologie, et d'Hydrologie — Bull Soc Belge Geol Paleontol Hydrol
Bulletin. Societe Belge de Physique — Bull Soc Belge Phys
Bulletin. Societe Belge des Ingenieurs et des Industriels — Bull Soc Belge Ing Ind
Bulletin. Societe Belge d'Etudes et d'Expansion — B Soc Belge Et Exp
Bulletin. Societe Belge d'Etudes et d'Expansion — SBelEx
Bulletin. Societe Belge d'Etudes Geographiques — B Soc Belge Et Geogr
Bulletin. Societe Belge d'Etudes Napoleoniennes — Bull Soc Belge Etud Napoleon
Bulletin. Societe Belge d'Ophtalmologie — Bull Soc Belge Ophtalmol
Bulletin. Societe Bibliographique des Publications Populaires — BSBPP
Bulletin. Societe Botanique de France — BSBFA
Bulletin. Societe Botanique de France — Bull Soc Bot Fr
Bulletin. Societe Botanique de France — Bull Soc Bot France
Bulletin. Societe Botanique de France. Actualites Botaniques — Bull Soc Bot Fr Actual Bot
Bulletin. Societe Botanique de France. Lettres Botaniques — Bull Soc Bot Fr Lett Bot

Bulletin. Societe Botanique de France. Memoires — Bull Soc Bot Fr Mem
Bulletin. Societe Botanique de France. Premiere Partie — B S Bot Fr I
Bulletin. Societe Botanique de Geneve — Bull Soc Bot Geneve
Bulletin. Societe Botanique Suisse — Bull Soc Bot Suisse
Bulletin Societe Bretonne de Geographie — BSBG
Bulletin. Societe Canadienne de Biochimie — Bull Soc Can Biochim
Bulletin. Societe Canadienne des Relations Publiques — Bul Soc Can Rel Publ
Bulletin. Societe Centrale d'Agriculture du Departement de l'Herault — Bull Soc Centr Agric Dep Herault
Bulletin. Societe Centrale de Medecine Veterinaire — Bull Soc Centr Med Vet
Bulletin. Societe Centrale Forestiere de Belgique — Bull Soc Cent For Belg
Bulletin. Societe Chateaubriand — BSC
Bulletin. Societe Chimique (Beograd) — Bull Soc Chim (Beogr)
Bulletin. Societe Chimique (Beograd) — Bull Soc Chim (Beograd)
Bulletin. Societe Chimique de Belgique — Bl Soc Chim Belg
Bulletin. Societe Chimique de France — BSCFA
Bulletin. Societe Chimique de France — Bull Soc Chim
Bulletin. Societe Chimique de France — Bull Soc Chim de France
Bulletin. Societe Chimique de France — Bull Soc Chim Fr
Bulletin. Societe Chimique de France — Bull Soc Chim France
Bulletin. Societe Chimique de France. Deuxieme Partie — B S Ch Fr II
Bulletin. Societe Chimique de France. Deuxieme Partie — Bull Soc Chim Fr 2
Bulletin. Societe Chimique de France. Deuxieme Partie. Chimie Organique, Biochimie — Bull Soc Chim Fr Part 2
Bulletin. Societe Chimique de France. Documentation — Bull Soc Chim Fr Doc
Bulletin. Societe Chimique de France. Memoires — Bull Soc Chim Fr Mem
Bulletin. Societe Chimique de France. Premiere Partie — B S Ch Fr I
Bulletin. Societe Chimique de France. Premiere Partie. Chimie Analytique, Chimie Minerale, Chimie Physique — Bull Soc Chim Fr 1
Bulletin. Societe Chimique de France. Premiere Partie. Chimie Analytique, Chimie Minerale, Chimie Physique — Bull Soc Chim Fr Part 1
Bulletin. Societe d'Acupuncture — Bull Soc Acup
Bulletin. Societe d'Agriculture d'Alger — Bull Soc Agric Alg
Bulletin. Societe d'Agriculture, Sciences, et Arts de la Sarthe — BSA Sarthe
Bulletin. Societe d'Agriculture, Sciences, et Arts de la Sarthe — Bull Soc Agr Sci Arts Sarthe
Bulletin. Societe d'Agriculture, Sciences, et Arts de la Sarthe — Bull Soc Agric Sarthe
Bulletin. Societe d'Anatomie Pathologique — Bull Soc Anat Pathol
Bulletin. Societe d'Anthropologie — B Soc Anthrop
Bulletin. Societe d'Anthropologie (Brussels) — BSAB
Bulletin. Societe d'Anthropologie de Paris — Bull Anthrop
Bulletin. Societe d'Anthropologie de Paris — Bull Soc Anthropol Paris
Bulletin. Societe d'Anthropologie (Lyon) — BSAL
Bulletin. Societe d'Apiculture des Alpes-Maritimes — Bull Soc Apic Alpes-Marit
Bulletin. Societe d'Archeologie Copte — BA Copt
Bulletin. Societe d'Archeologie Copte — BSA Copt
Bulletin. Societe d'Archeologie Copte — BSAC
Bulletin. Societe d'Archeologie Copte — Bull Copte
Bulletin. Societe d'Archeologie Copte — Bull Soc Arch Copte
Bulletin. Societe d'Archeologie d'Alexandrie — B Soc Arch Al
Bulletin. Societe d'Archeologie d'Alexandrie — BSA Al
Bulletin. Societe d'Archeologie d'Alexandrie — BSA Alex
Bulletin. Societe d'Archeologie d'Alexandrie — Bull Soc Alex
Bulletin. Societe d'Archeologie d'Alexandrie — SAA
Bulletin. Societe d'Archeologie et de Statistique de la Drome — B Drome
Bulletin. Societe d'Archeologique Champenoise — B Soc A Champ
Bulletin. Societe d'Archeologique Champenoise — BSAC
Bulletin. Societe d'Archeologique Champenoise — Bull Soc Arch Champenoise
Bulletin. Societe d'Art et d'Histoire du Diocese de Liege — BSAH Liege
Bulletin. Societe d'Art et d'Histoire du Diocese de Liege — BSAHDL
Bulletin. Societe de Borda — BS Borda
Bulletin. Societe de Borda — Bull Borda
Bulletin. Societe de Borda — Bull Soc Borda
Bulletin. Societe de Botanique du Nord de la France — Bull Soc Bot N Fr
Bulletin. Societe de Botanique du Nord de la France — Bull Soc Bot Nord Fr
Bulletin. Societe de Chimie Biologique — BSCIA
Bulletin. Societe de Chimie Biologique *[France]* — Bull Soc Chim Biol
Bulletin. Societe de Chimie Industrielle — Bl Soc Chim Ind
Bulletin. Societe de Chimie Industrielle — BSCNA
Bulletin. Societe de Chimie Industrielle *[France]* — Bull Soc Chim Ind
Bulletin. Societe de Chimistes. Republique Populaire de Bosnie et Herzeqovine — Bull Soc Chim Repub Pop Bosnie Herzeqovine
Bulletin. Societe de Chirurgie de Paris — Bull Soc Chir Paris
Bulletin. Societe de Geographie — BSG
Bulletin. Societe de Geographie — Bull Soc Geographie
Bulletin. Societe de Geographie Commerciale de Paris — B Soc Geogr Comml Paris
Bulletin. Societe de Geographie Commerciale de Paris — BSGCP
Bulletin. Societe de Geographie Commerciale du Havre — BSGCH
Bulletin. Societe de Geographie d'Anvers — BSGA
Bulletin. Societe de Geographie de Lille — B Soc Geogr
Bulletin. Societe de Geographie de Lille — BSGLi
Bulletin. Societe de Geographie de Lyon — BSGL
Bulletin. Societe de Geographie de Marseille — B Soc Geogr Mars
Bulletin. Societe de Geographie de Paris — B Soc Geogr Paris
Bulletin. Societe de Geographie de Paris — BSGP
Bulletin. Societe de Geographie de Quebec — BSGQ
Bulletin. Societe de Geographie de Rochefort — BSGR
Bulletin. Societe de Geographie de Toulouse — B Soc Geogr Toul
Bulletin. Societe de Geographie d'Egypte — B Soc Geogr Eg
Bulletin. Societe de Geographie d'Egypte — BSGE
Bulletin. Societe de Geographie et d'Archeologie d'Oran — BSGAO
Bulletin. Societe de Geographie et d'Etudes Coloniales de Marseille — B Soc Geogr Etud Colon Mars
Bulletin. Societe de Geographie Hellenique — B Soc Geogr Hellen
Bulletin. Societe de Langue et Litterature Wallonnes — BSLLW
Bulletin. Societe de Lettres de Lund — B Lund
Bulletin. Societe de l'Histoire de l'Art Francais — BSHAF
Bulletin. Societe de l'Histoire de l'Ile Maurice — Bull Soc Hist Ile Maurice
Bulletin. Societe de l'Histoire du Protestantisme Francais — BSHP
Bulletin. Societe de l'Histoire du Protestantisme Francais — BSHPF
Bulletin. Societe de l'Histoire du Protestantisme Francais — BudS
Bulletin. Societe de l'Histoire du Protestantisme Francais — Bull SHPF
Bulletin. Societe de l'Industrie Minerale de St. Etienne — Bull Soc Ind Miner St Etienne
Bulletin. Societe de Linguistique de Paris — B Soc Ling P
Bulletin. Societe de Linguistique de Paris — B Soc Linguist Paris
Bulletin. Societe de Linguistique de Paris — BSL
Bulletin. Societe de Linguistique de Paris — BSLP
Bulletin. Societe de Linguistique de Paris — Bull SL
Bulletin. Societe de Linguistique de Paris — Bull Soc Linguistique Paris
Bulletin. Societe de Microscopie du Canada — Bull Soc Microsc Can
Bulletin. Societe de Mythologie de France — B Soc Myth Franc
Bulletin. Societe de Pathologie Exotique — B Soc Path Exot
Bulletin. Societe de Pathologie Exotique — Bull Soc Path Exot
Bulletin. Societe de Pathologie Exotique — Bull Soc Pathol Exot
Bulletin. Societe de Pathologie Exotique — Bull Soc Pathol Exotique
Bulletin. Societe de Pathologie Exotique et de ses Filiales — B Soc Path Exot Fil
Bulletin. Societe de Pathologie Exotique et de Ses Filiales — BSPEA
Bulletin. Societe de Pathologie Exotique et de Ses Filiales — Bull Soc Path Exot
Bulletin. Societe de Pathologie Exotique et de Ses Filiales — Bull Soc Pathol Exot Filiales
Bulletin. Societe de Pediatrie de Paris — Bull Soc Pediat Paris
Bulletin. Societe de Pharmacie de Bordeaux — BSPBA
Bulletin. Societe de Pharmacie de Bordeaux — Bull Soc Pharm Bord
Bulletin. Societe de Pharmacie de Bordeaux — Bull Soc Pharm Bordeaux
Bulletin. Societe de Pharmacie de Bruxelles — Bull Soc Pharm Bruxelles
Bulletin. Societe de Pharmacie de Lille — Bull Soc Pharm Lille
Bulletin. Societe de Pharmacie de Marseille — Bull Soc Pharm Mars
Bulletin. Societe de Pharmacie de Marseille — Bull Soc Pharm Marseille
Bulletin. Societe de Pharmacie de Nancy — Bull Soc Pharm Nancy
Bulletin. Societe de Pharmacie de Strasbourg — Bull Soc Pharm Strasb
Bulletin. Societe de Pharmacie de Strasbourg — Bull Soc Pharm Strasbourg
Bulletin. Societe de Prehistoire du Maroc — BSPM
Bulletin. Societe de Thanatologie — B Soc Thanatologie
Bulletin. Societe de Vieux Papier — Bull Soc Vieux Papier
Bulletin. Societe d'Emulation du Bourbonnais — BSE Bour
Bulletin. Societe d'Emulation du Bourbonnais — BSE Bourbonn
Bulletin. Societe d'Emulation du Bourbonnais — BSEBourbonnais
Bulletin. Societe d'Emulation Historique et Litteraire d'Abbeville — B Abbeville
Bulletin. Societe d'Emulation Historique et Litteraire d'Abbeville — BSE Abb
Bulletin. Societe d'Encouragement pour l'Industrie Nationale — Bull Soc Encour Ind Natl
Bulletin. Societe d'Encouragement pour l'Industrie Nationale — Bull Soc Encour Industr Natl
Bulletin. Societe des Agriculteurs de France — Bull Soc Agric Fr
Bulletin. Societe des Agriculteurs de France — Bull Soc Agricrs Fr
Bulletin. Societe des Amis d'Andre-Marie Ampere — Bull Soc Amis Andre-Marie Ampere
Bulletin. Societe des Amis de Marcel Proust et de Combray — BSAP
Bulletin. Societe des Amis de Montaigne — BSAM
Bulletin. Societe des Amis de Port-Royal — BSAPR
Bulletin. Societe des Amis de Vienne — BSA
Bulletin. Societe des Amis de Vienne — BSA Vienne
Bulletin. Societe des Amis des Sciences de Poznan. Serie B. Sciences Mathematiques et Naturelles — Bull Soc Amis Sci Poznan Ser B
Bulletin. Societe des Amis des Sciences et des Lettres de Poznan — Bull Soc Amis Sci Lett Poz
Bulletin. Societe des Amis des Sciences et des Lettres de Poznan. Serie B. Sciences Mathematiques et Naturelles — BPZBA
Bulletin. Societe des Amis des Sciences et des Lettres de Poznan. Serie B. Sciences Mathematiques et Naturelles — Bull Soc Amis Sci Lett Poznan Ser B
Bulletin. Societe des Amis des Sciences et des Lettres de Poznan. Serie C. Medecine — Bull Soc Amis Sci Lett Poznan Ser C
Bulletin. Societe des Amis des Sciences et des Lettres de Poznan. Serie D. Sciences Biologiques — Bull Soc Amis Sci Lett Poznan Ser D
Bulletin. Societe des Amis des Sciences et des Lettres de Poznan. Serie D. Sciences Biologiques — Bull Soc Amis Sci Lett Poznan Ser D Sci Biol
Bulletin. Societe des Amis du Musee d'Arras — BM Arras
Bulletin. Societe des Amis du Musee de Dijon — BM Dijon
Bulletin. Societe des Amis du Musee de Dijon — BMD
Bulletin. Societe des Antiquaires de l'Ouest — Bull Soc Antiquaires Ouest
Bulletin. Societe des Antiquaires de l'Ouest et des Musees de Poitiers — BSAO
Bulletin. Societe des Antiquaires de l'Ouest et des Musees de Poitiers — BSAOuest
Bulletin. Societe des Antiquaires de l'Ouest et des Musees de Poitiers — Bull Soc Ant Ouest
Bulletin. Societe des Antiquaires de Normandie — BSAN
Bulletin. Societe des Antiquaires de Normandie — BSANormandie
Bulletin. Societe des Antiquaires de Picardie — Bull Soc Antiq Picardie
Bulletin. Societe des Auteurs, Compositeurs, et Editeurs — SABAM
Bulletin. Societe des Bibliolatres de France — BSBF
Bulletin. Societe des Bibliophiles Belges Seant a Mons — BSBB
Bulletin. Societe des Bibliophiles Belges Seant a Mons — BSBBM
Bulletin. Societe des Bibliophiles Liegeois — BSBL
Bulletin. Societe des Etudes de Lettres (Lausanne) — BELL

Bulletin. Societe des Etudes du Lot — Bull Soc Et Lot
Bulletin. Societe des Etudes Indochinoises — B Soc Et Indoch
Bulletin. Societe des Etudes Indochinoises — B Soc Et Indochinoises
Bulletin. Societe des Etudes Indochinoises [*Saigon*] — BSEI
Bulletin. Societe des Etudes Indochinoises — BSEIC
Bulletin. Societe des Etudes Indochinoises — BSI
Bulletin. Societe des Etudes Indochinoises — BSIC
Bulletin. Societe des Etudes Litteraires, Scientifiques, et Artistiques du Lot — BSELot
Bulletin. Societe des Etudes Litteraires, Scientifiques et Artistiques du Lot — Bull Lot
Bulletin. Societe des Ingenieurs Civils de France — Bull Soc Ing Civ Fr
Bulletin. Societe des Lepidopteristes Francais — Bull Soc Lepid Fr
Bulletin. Societe des Mathematiciens et des Physiciens de la Republique Populaire de Macedoine — Bull Soc Math Phys Macedoine
Bulletin. Societe des Naturalistes de Moscou. Section Geologique — Bull Soc Nat Moscou Sect Geol
Bulletin. Societe des Naturalistes de Voroneje — Bull Soc Nat Voroneje
Bulletin. Societe des Naturalistes et des Archeologiques de l'Ain — B Ain
Bulletin. Societe des Naturalistes et des Archeologiques de l'Ain — BSN Ain
Bulletin. Societe des Naturalistes et des Archeologues de l'Ain — Bull Soc Nat Archeol Ain
Bulletin. Societe des Naturalistes Luxembourgeois — Bull Soc Nat Lux
Bulletin. Societe des Parlers de France — B Parl
Bulletin. Societe des Professeurs d'Histoire et de Geographie — Bull Soc Prof Hist Geogr
Bulletin. Societe des Professeurs Francais en Amerique — SPFA
Bulletin. Societe des Sciences, Agriculture, et Arts du Departement du Bas-Rhin — Bull Soc Sci Dep Bas Rhin
Bulletin. Societe des Sciences Anciennes — Bull Soc Sci Anc
Bulletin. Societe des Sciences de Cluj. Roumanie — Bull Soc Sci Cluj Roum
Bulletin. Societe des Sciences de Nancy — Bull Soc Sci Nancy
Bulletin. Societe des Sciences et des Lettres de Lodz — BSSL
Bulletin. Societe des Sciences et des Lettres de Lodz — Bull Soc Sci Lett Lodz
Bulletin. Societe des Sciences et des Lettres de Lodz — Bull Soc Sci Lettres Lodz
Bulletin. Societe des Sciences et des Lettres de Lodz. Classe 3. Sciences Mathematiques et Naturelles — Bull Soc Sci Lett Lodz Cl 3
Bulletin. Societe des Sciences et des Lettres de Lodz. Classe 4. Sciences Medicales — Bull Soc Sci Lett Lodz Cl 4
Bulletin. Societe des Sciences Geologiques. Republique Socialiste de Roumanie — Bull Soc Sci Geol Repub Soc Roum
Bulletin. Societe des Sciences Historiques de l'Yonne — BSHY
Bulletin. Societe des Sciences Historiques de l'Yonne — BSSY
Bulletin. Societe des Sciences Historiques et Naturelles de la Corse — B Corse
Bulletin. Societe des Sciences Historiques et Naturelles de la Corse — BSSHC
Bulletin. Societe des Sciences Historiques et Naturelles de la Corse — BSSHN
Bulletin. Societe des Sciences Historiques et Naturelles de l'Yonne — B Yonne
Bulletin. Societe des Sciences Historiques et Naturelles de l'Yonne — BSSHNY
Bulletin. Societe des Sciences Historiques et Naturelles de Semur-en-Auxois — BSS
Bulletin. Societe des Sciences Historiques et Naturelles de Semur-en-Auxois — BSSHS
Bulletin. Societe des Sciences Historiques et Naturelles de Semur-en-Auxois — Bull Soc Semur
Bulletin. Societe des Sciences, Lettres, et Arts de Bayonne — B Bayonne
Bulletin. Societe des Sciences Medicales du Grand-Duche de Luxembourg — B S Sci Med
Bulletin. Societe des Sciences Medicales du Grand-Duche de Luxembourg — BMGLA
Bulletin. Societe des Sciences Medicales du Grand-Duche de Luxembourg — Bull Soc Sci Med Grand-Duche Luxemb
Bulletin. Societe des Sciences Medicales du Grand-Duche de Luxembourg — Bull Soc Sci Med Gr-Duche Luxemb
Bulletin. Societe des Sciences Naturelles — Bull Soc Sci Nat
Bulletin. Societe des Sciences Naturelles de l'Ouest de la France [*A publication*] — Bull Soc Sci Nat Ouest Fr
Bulletin. Societe des Sciences Naturelles de l'Ouest de la France — Bull Soc Sci Nat Ouest France
Bulletin. Societe des Sciences Naturelles de Neuchatel — Bull Soc Sci Nat Neuchatel
Bulletin. Societe des Sciences Naturelles de Tunisie — B Soc Sci Nat Tunisie
Bulletin. Societe des Sciences Naturelles de Tunisie — Bull Soc Sci Nat Tun
Bulletin. Societe des Sciences Naturelles de Tunisie — Bull Soc Sci Nat Tunis
Bulletin. Societe des Sciences Naturelles du Maroc — Bull Soc Sci Nat Mar
Bulletin. Societe des Sciences Naturelles du Maroc — Bull Soc Sci Nat Maroc
Bulletin. Societe des Sciences Naturelles et Physiques du Maroc — Bull Soc Sci Nat Phys Mar
Bulletin. Societe des Sciences Naturelles et Physiques du Maroc — Bull Soc Sci Nat Phys Maroc
Bulletin. Societe des Sciences Physiques, Naturelles, et Climatologiques de l'Algerie — Bull Soc Sci Phys Algerie
Bulletin. Societe des Sciences Veterinaires de Lyon — Bull Soc Sc Vet Lyon
Bulletin. Societe des Sciences Veterinaires de Lyon — Bull Soc Sci Vet Lyon
Bulletin. Societe des Sciences Veterinaires et de Medecine Comparee de Lyon — Bull Soc Sci Vet Med Comp Lyon
Bulletin. Societe d'Ethnographie du Limousin et de la Marche — B Soc Ethnogr Limousin Marche
Bulletin. Societe d'Ethnozootechnie — Bull Soc Ethnozootech
Bulletin. Societe d'Etude des Sciences Naturelles de Nimes — B Nimes
Bulletin. Societe d'Etude des Sciences Naturelles de Nimes — BSESNN
Bulletin. Societe d'Etude des Sciences Naturelles de Nimes — BSSNN
Bulletin. Societe d'Etudes Camerounaises — BSEC
Bulletin. Societe d'Etudes Dantesques. Centre Universitaire Mediterraneen — BSED
Bulletin. Societe d'Etudes d'Avallon — B Avalon
Bulletin. Societe d'Etudes d'Avallon — BSE Av
Bulletin. Societe d'Etudes de la Province de Cambrai — BSEPC
Bulletin. Societe d'Etudes Historiques, Scientifiques, et Litteraires des Hautes-Alpes — B Hautes-Alpes
Bulletin. Societe d'Etudes Oceaniennes — B Soc Et Ocean
Bulletin. Societe d'Etudes Oceaniennes — BSEO
Bulletin. Societe d'Etudes Oceaniennes — Bull Soc Etud Oceaniennes
Bulletin. Societe d'Etudes Scientifiques de l'Aude — B Soc Et Sci Aude
Bulletin. Societe d'Etudes Scientifiques de l'Aude — BSE Aude
Bulletin. Societe d'Etudes Scientifiques de Lyon — Bull Soc Etudes Sci Lyon
Bulletin. Societe d'Etudes Scientifiques de Sete et de la Region — B Sete
Bulletin. Societe d'Etudes Scientifiques de Sete et de la Region — Bull Sete
Bulletin. Societe d'Etudes Scientifiques et Archeologiques de Draguignan — B Draguignan
Bulletin. Societe d'Histoire de la Medecine — BSHM
Bulletin. Societe d'Histoire du Maroc — B Maroc
Bulletin. Societe d'Histoire du Maroc — BSH Maroc
Bulletin. Societe d'Histoire du Maroc — Bull Soc Hist Maroc
Bulletin. Societe d'Histoire et d'Archeologie de Beaucaire — BSHAB
Bulletin. Societe d'Histoire et d'Archeologie de Bretagne — B Bretagne
Bulletin. Societe d'Histoire et d'Archeologie de Bretagne — BSHA Br
Bulletin. Societe d'Histoire et d'Archeologie de Gand — BHAG
Bulletin. Societe d'Histoire et d'Archeologie de Geneve — B Geneve
Bulletin. Societe d'Histoire et d'Archeologie de Geneve — BSHA Geneve
Bulletin. Societe d'Histoire et d'Archeologie de la Maurienne — B Maurienne
Bulletin. Societe d'Histoire et d'Archeologie de la Maurienne — BSHA Maur
Bulletin. Societe d'Histoire et d'Archeologie de l'Arrondissement de Provins — B Provins
Bulletin. Societe d'Histoire et d'Archeologie de l'Arrondissement de Provins — BHS Prov
Bulletin. Societe d'Histoire et d'Archeologie de l'Arrondissement de Provins — Provins
Bulletin. Societe d'Histoire et d'Archeologie de Saverne et des Environs — B Saverne
Bulletin. Societe d'Histoire et d'Archeologie de Vichy et des Environs — B Vichy
Bulletin. Societe d'Histoire et d'Archeologie de Vichy et des Environs — BSHAV
Bulletin. Societe d'Histoire et de Geographie de la Region de Setif — BSHS
Bulletin. Societe d'Histoire Moderne — BSHM
Bulletin. Societe d'Histoire Moderne — Bull Soc Hist Mod
Bulletin. Societe d'Histoire Naturelle d'Autun — Bull Soc Hist Nat Autun
Bulletin. Societe d'Histoire Naturelle de l'Afrique du Nord — Bull Soc Hist Nat Afr Nord
Bulletin. Societe d'Histoire Naturelle de l'Afrique du Nord — Bull Soc Hist Natur Afr Nord
Bulletin. Societe d'Histoire Naturelle de Metz — Bull Soc Hist Nat Metz
Bulletin. Societe d'Histoire Naturelle de Toulouse — Bull Soc Hist Nat Toulouse
Bulletin. Societe d'Histoire Naturelle du Doubs — Bull Soc Hist Nat Doubs
Bulletin. Societe d'Horticulture et d'Acclimation du Maroc — Bull Soc Hort Maroc
Bulletin. Societe d'Obstetrique et de Gynecologie de Paris — Bull Soc Obst Gynec
Bulletin. Societe d'Oceanographie de France — B Soc Oceanogr Fr
Bulletin. Societe d'Ophtalmologie de Paris — Bull Soc Ophtalmol Paris
Bulletin. Societe d'Ophtalmologie d'Egypte — Bull Soc Ophtal Egy
Bulletin. Societe Entomologique de France — Bull Soc Ent Fr
Bulletin. Societe Entomologique de France — Bull Soc Entomol Fr
Bulletin. Societe Entomologique de Mulhouse — Bull Soc Ent Mulhouse
Bulletin. Societe Entomologique d'Egypte — Bull Soc Ent Egypte
Bulletin. Societe Entomologique d'Egypte — Bull Soc Entomol Egypte
Bulletin. Societe Entomologique Suisse — Bull Soc Entomol Suisse
Bulletin. Societe Ernest Renan — BSER
Bulletin. Societe Forestiere de Franche-Comte et Belfort — Bull Soc For Franche-Comte
Bulletin. Societe Fouad I d'Entomologie — Bull Soc Fouad I Entomol
Bulletin. Societe Francaise d'Archeologie Classique — BSF
Bulletin. Societe Francaise d'Archeologie Classique — BSFAC
Bulletin. Societe Francaise de Ceramique — B S Fr Cer
Bulletin. Societe Francaise de Ceramique — Bull Soc Fr Ceram
Bulletin. Societe Francaise de Dermatologie et de Syphiligraphie — B S Fr D Sy
Bulletin. Societe Francaise de Dermatologie et de Syphiligraphie — Bull Soc Fr Dermatol Syphiligr
Bulletin. Societe Francaise de Microscopie — Bull Soc Fr Micros
Bulletin. Societe Francaise de Mineralogie — Bull Soc Fr Mineral
Bulletin. Societe Francaise de Mineralogie et de Cristallographie — B S Fr Min
Bulletin. Societe Francaise de Mineralogie et de Cristallographie — B Soc Fr Min Crist
Bulletin. Societe Francaise de Mineralogie et de Cristallographie — Bull Soc Fr Miner Cristallogr
Bulletin. Societe Francaise de Mineralogie et de Cristallographie — Bull Soc Fr Mineral Cristallogr
Bulletin. Societe Francaise de Mineralogie et de Cristallographie — Bull Soc Fr Mineral et Cristallogr
Bulletin. Societe Francaise de Mycologie Medicale — Bull Soc Fr Mycol Med
Bulletin. Societe Francaise de Numismatique — BSF
Bulletin. Societe Francaise de Numismatique — BSFN
Bulletin. Societe Francaise de Numismatique — Bull SFN
Bulletin. Societe Francaise de Numismatique (Paris) — B Num (Paris)
Bulletin. Societe Francaise de Numismatique (Paris) — Bull Soc Fr Num Paris
Bulletin. Societe Francaise de Philosophie — B S Ph
Bulletin. Societe Francaise de Philosophie — BSFP
Bulletin. Societe Francaise de Philosophie — Bull Soc Fr Phil

Bulletin. Societe Francaise de Photogrammetrie [*Later, Bulletin. Societe Francaise de Photogrammetrie et de Teledetection*] — Bull Soc Fr Photogramm
Bulletin. Societe Francaise de Photogrammetrie et de Teledetection — Bull Soc Fr Photogramm et Teledetect
Bulletin. Societe Francaise de Photographie — Bull Soc Franc Phot
Bulletin. Societe Francaise de Physiologie Vegetale — Bull Soc Fr Physiol Veg
Bulletin. Societe Francaise de Physiologie Vegetale — Bull Soc Franc Physiol Veg
Bulletin. Societe Francaise de Sociologie — B Soc Franc Sociol
Bulletin. Societe Francaise d'Egyptologie — BSF
Bulletin. Societe Francaise d'Egyptologie [*Paris*] — BSFE
Bulletin. Societe Francaise d'Egyptologie [*Paris*] — BSocFrEg
Bulletin. Societe Francaise des Electriciens — BSFEA
Bulletin. Societe Francaise des Electriciens [*France*] — Bull Soc Fr Electr
Bulletin. Societe Francaise d'Etudes Mariales — BSFEM
Bulletin. Societe Francaise d'Histoire de la Medecine — BHM
Bulletin. Societe Francaise d'Histoire des Hopitaux — Bull Soc Fr Hist Hop
Bulletin. Societe Francaise d'Histoire Naturelle des Antilles — B Soc Fr Hist Nat Ant
Bulletin. Societe Francaise d'Hygiene — Bull Soc Franc Hyg
Bulletin. Societe Franco-Japonaise de Paris — Bull Soc Franco Jap Paris
Bulletin. Societe Franco-Japonaise des Sciences Pures et Appliquees — Bull Soc Fr Jpn Sci Pures Appl
Bulletin. Societe Fribourgeoise des Sciences Naturelles — Bull Soc Frib Sci Nat
Bulletin. Societe Geographie de l'Egypte — BSGRE
Bulletin. Societe Geographie de l'Est (Nancy) — BSGEN
Bulletin. Societe Geologique de Belgique — B Soc Geol Belg
Bulletin. Societe Geologique de Belgique — Bull Soc Geol Belg
Bulletin. Societe Geologique de France — B Soc Geol Fr
Bulletin. Societe Geologique de France — BSGF
Bulletin. Societe Geologique de France — Bull Soc Geol Fr
Bulletin. Societe Geologique de France — Bull Soc Geol France
Bulletin. Societe Geologique de France. Notes et Memoires — B Soc Geol Fr Notes Mem
Bulletin. Societe Geologique de France. Supplement. Compte Rendu Sommaire des Seances — Bull Soc Geol Fr Suppl
Bulletin. Societe Geologique de Normandie — Bull Soc Geol Normandie
Bulletin. Societe Geologique et Mineralogique de Bretagne — Bull Soc Geol Mineral Bretagne
Bulletin. Societe Geologique et Mineralogique de Bretagne. Serie C — Bull Soc Geol Mineral Bretagne Ser C
Bulletin. Societe Historique, Archeologique, et Artistique du Giennois — BSH Gien
Bulletin. Societe Historique de Paris et de l'Ile de France — BSHPIF
Bulletin. Societe Historique et Archeologique de Corbeil, d'Etampes et du Hurepoix — BSH Corbeil
Bulletin. Societe Historique et Archeologique de Langres — B Langres
Bulletin. Societe Historique et Archeologique de l'Orne — BSHA Or
Bulletin. Societe Historique et Archeologique de Nogent-sur-Marne et du Canton de Nogent — B Nogent
Bulletin. Societe Historique et Archeologique de Nogent-sur-Marne et du Canton de Nogent — BSHAN
Bulletin. Societe Historique et Archeologique du Perigord — B Perigord
Bulletin. Societe Historique et Archeologique du Perigord — BSHAP
Bulletin. Societe Historique et Archeologique du Perigord — BSHAPerigord
Bulletin. Societe Historique et Archeologique du Perigord — Bull Soc Hist Archeol Perigord
Bulletin. Societe Historique et Archeologique. Les Amis des Antiquites de Parthenay — B Parthenay
Bulletin. Societe Historique et Archeologique. Les Amis des Antiquites de Parthenay — BSHA Par
Bulletin. Societe Historique et Scientifique des Deaux-Sevres — BSHDS
Bulletin. Societe Imperiale des Naturalistes de Moscou — Bull Soc Imp Nat Moscou
Bulletin. Societe Industrielle d'Amiens — Bull Soc Ind Amiens
Bulletin. Societe Industrielle de Mulhouse — Bull Soc Ind Mulhouse
Bulletin. Societe Industrielle de Mulhouse — Bull Societe Ind Mulhouse
Bulletin. Societe Industrielle de Rouen — Bull Soc Ind Rouen
Bulletin. Societe Internationale de Chirurgie — Bull Soc Int Chir
Bulletin. Societe Internationale des Electriciens — Bull Soc Int Electr
Bulletin. Societe Internationale pour l'Etude de la Philosophie Medievale — BPhM
Bulletin. Societe Internationale pour l'Etude de la Philosophie Medievale — Bull Soc Int Et Phil Med
Bulletin. Societe J. K. Huysmans — Bull JKH
Bulletin. Societe Khedivale de Geographie — BSKG
Bulletin. Societe Khediviale de Geographie — Bull Soc Khediv Geogr
Bulletin. Societe Languedocienne de Geographie — B Soc Langued Gegr
Bulletin. Societe Languedocienne de Geographie — Bul Soc Lang Geog
Bulletin. Societe les Naturalistes Parisiens — Bull Soc Naturalistes Parisiens
Bulletin. Societe Liegeoise de Musicologie — Bul Soc Liegeoise Musicol
Bulletin. Societe Linneenne — B Soc Linn
Bulletin. Societe Linneenne de Bordeaux — Bull Soc Linn Bord
Bulletin. Societe Linneenne de Bordeaux — Bull Soc Linn Bordeaux
Bulletin. Societe Linneenne de Lyon — Bull Soc Linn Lyon
Bulletin. Societe Linneenne de Normandie — Bull Soc Linn Normandie
Bulletin. Societe Linneenne de Provence — Bull Soc Linn Provence
Bulletin. Societe Litteraire et Historique de la Brie — B Soc Litt Hist Brie
Bulletin. Societe Litteraires et Historiques de la Brie — Bull Brie
Bulletin. Societe Lorraine des Etudes Locales dans l'Enseignement Public — BSLELEP
Bulletin. Societe Lorraine des Sciences — Bull Soc Lorraine Sci
Bulletin. Societe Lorraine des Sciences. Memoires — Bull Soc Lorraine Sci Mem
Bulletin. Societe Mathematique de Belgique — Bull Soc Math Belg
Bulletin. Societe Mathematique de Belgique. Serie A — Bull Soc Math Belg Ser A
Bulletin. Societe Mathematique de Belgique. Serie B — Bull Soc Math Belg Ser B
Bulletin. Societe Mathematique de France — B S Math Fr
Bulletin. Societe Mathematique de France — Bull Soc Math Fr
Bulletin. Societe Mathematique de France — Bull Soc Math France
Bulletin. Societe Mathematique de France. Memoire — Bull Soc Math Fr Mem
Bulletin. Societe Mathematique de Grece — Bull Soc Math Grece
Bulletin. Societe Mathematique de Grece. Nouvelle Serie — Bull Soc Math Grece NS
Bulletin. Societe Medicale d'Afrique Noire de Langue Francaise — Bull Soc Med Afr Noire
Bulletin. Societe Medicale d'Afrique Noire de Langue Francaise — Bull Soc Med Afr Noire de Langue Fr
Bulletin. Societe Medicale d'Afrique Noire de Langue Francaise — Bull Soc Med Afr Noire Lang Fr
Bulletin. Societe Medicale des Hopitaux de Lyon — Bull Soc Med Hop Lyon
Bulletin. Societe Medicale des Hopitaux Universitaires de Quebec — Bull Soc Med Hop Univ Quebec
Bulletin. Societe Medico-Chirurgicale de l'Indo-Chine — Bull Soc Med-Chir Indo-Chine
Bulletin. Societe Mycologique de France — Bull Soc Mycol Fr
Bulletin. Societe Mycologique de Geneve — Bull Soc Mycol
Bulletin. Societe Nationale des Antiquaires de France — B Ant Fr
Bulletin. Societe Nationale des Antiquaires de France — BAF
Bulletin. Societe Nationale des Antiquaires de France — BMSAF
Bulletin. Societe Nationale des Antiquaires de France — BSAF
Bulletin. Societe Nationale des Antiquaires de France — BSAFrance
Bulletin. Societe Nationale des Antiquaires de France — BSNA
Bulletin. Societe Nationale des Antiquaires de France — BSNAF
Bulletin. Societe Nationale des Antiquaires de France — Bull Ant Fr
Bulletin. Societe Nationale des Antiquaires de France — Bull Soc Ant
Bulletin. Societe Nationale des Antiquaires de France — Bull Soc Ant France
Bulletin. Societe Nationale des Antiquaires de France — Bull Soc Nat Antiq Fr
Bulletin. Societe Nationale des Antiquaires de France — Bull Soc Nat Antiqu France
Bulletin. Societe Nationale des Antiquaires de France — Bull Soc Nat Fr
Bulletin. Societe Nationale des Antiquaires de France — Bullet Soc Nat Fr
Bulletin. Societe Neuchatelloise de Geographie — B Soc Neuch Geogr
Bulletin. Societe Neuchatelloise des Sciences Naturelles — Bull Soc Neuchatel Sci Nat
Bulletin. Societe Nivernaise des Lettres, Sciences, et Arts — Bull Soc Nivernaise
Bulletin. Societe Normande d'Archeologie Prehistorique et Historique — BSNAP
Bulletin. Societe Normande d'Archeologie Prehistorique et Historique — Bull Soc Norm Arch Prehist Hist
Bulletin. Societe Philomathique de Paris — Bull Soc Philomath Paris
Bulletin. Societe Philomatique de Paris — Bull Soc Philomat Paris
Bulletin. Societe Philomatique de Perpignan — Bull Soc Philom Perpignan
Bulletin. Societe Philomatique Vosgienne — B Soc Vosg
Bulletin. Societe Philomatique Vosgienne — Bull Soc Philom Vosg
Bulletin. Societe Phycologique de France — Bull Soc Phycol Fr
Bulletin. Societe Polonaise de Linguistique — BSPL
Bulletin. Societe Portugaise des Sciences Naturelles — Bull Soc Port Sci Nat
Bulletin. Societe Portugaise des Sciences Naturelles — Bull Soc Portugaise Sc Nat
Bulletin. Societe pour la Conservation des Monuments Historiques d'Alsace — Bull Soc Cons Mon Hist Alsace
Bulletin. Societe pour la Conservation des Monuments Historiques d'Alsace — Bull Soc Conserv Monum Hist Als
Bulletin. Societe pour l'Histoire des Eglises Wallonnes — BHEW
Bulletin. Societe pour l'Histoire des Eglises Wallonnes — BSHEW
Bulletin. Societe Prehistorique de France — Bull Preh
Bulletin. Societe Prehistorique de l'Ariege — B Ariege
Bulletin. Societe Prehistorique de l'Ariege — Bull Soc Prehist Ariege
Bulletin. Societe Prehistorique Francaise — B Soc Prehist Fr
Bulletin. Societe Prehistorique Francaise — B Soc Prehist Franc
Bulletin. Societe Prehistorique Francaise — BSPF
Bulletin. Societe Prehistorique Francaise — Bull Soc Prehist Fr
Bulletin. Societe Prehistorique Francaise — Bull Soc Prehist France
Bulletin. Societe Prehistorique Francaise — Bull SPF
Bulletin. Societe Prehistorique Francaise. Comptes Rendus Mensuels — B Soc Prehist Franc C R Mens
Bulletin. Societe Prehistorique Francaise. Etudes et Travaux — B Pr Hist Fr
Bulletin. Societe Romande d'Apiculture — Bull Soc Romande Apic
Bulletin. Societe Roumaine de Neurologie, Psychiatrie, Psychologie, et Endocrinologie — Bull Soc Roum Neurol Psychiatr Psychol Endocrinol
Bulletin. Societe Royale Belge d'Anthropologie — B Soc Roy Belge Anthropol
Bulletin. Societe Royale Belge d'Anthropologie et de Prehistoire — B Belg Anthrop
Bulletin. Societe Royale Belge d'Anthropologie et de Prehistoire — B Soc Roy Belge Anthropol Prehis
Bulletin. Societe Royale Belge d'Anthropologie et de Prehistoire — BSBAP
Bulletin. Societe Royale Belge d'Anthropologie et de Prehistoire — BSRBAP
Bulletin. Societe Royale Belge d'Anthropologie et de Prehistoire — Bull Soc R Belge Anthrop et Prehist
Bulletin. Societe Royale Belge d'Anthropologie et de Prehistoire — Bull Soc Roy Belg Anthr Prehist
Bulletin. Societe Royale Belge de Gynecologie et d'Obstetrique — Bull Soc R Belge Gynecol Obstet
Bulletin. Societe Royale Belge des Electriciens — Bull Soc R Belge Electr
Bulletin. Societe Royale Belge des Electriciens — Bull Soc Roy Belg Elec

Bulletin. Societe Royale d'Agriculture, Sciences, et Arts du Mans — Bull Soc Roy Agric Mans
Bulletin. Societe Royale d'Archeologie d'Alexandrie — BSRAA
Bulletin. Societe Royale de Botanique de Belgique — Bull Soc Bot Belg
Bulletin. Societe Royale de Botanique de Belgique — Bull Soc R Bot Belg
Bulletin. Societe Royale de Geographie d'Anvers — BSRGA
Bulletin. Societe Royale de Geographie d'Egypte — BSGE
Bulletin. Societe Royale de Geographie d'Egypte — BSRGE
Bulletin. Societe Royale de Pharmacie de Bruxelles — Bull Soc R Pharm Bruxelles
Bulletin. Societe Royale de Pharmacie de Bruxelles — Bull Soc Roy Pharm Bruxelles
Bulletin. Societe Royale de Vieux-Liege — BSRV-L
Bulletin. Societe Royale des Sciences de Liege — Bull Soc R Sci Liege
Bulletin. Societe Royale des Sciences de Liege — Bull Soc Roy Sci Liege
Bulletin. Societe Royale Entomologique d'Egypte — Bull Soc R Entomol Egypte
Bulletin. Societe Royale Forestiere Belge — B Soc Roy For Belge
Bulletin. Societe Royale Forestiere de Belgique — Bull Soc For Belg
Bulletin. Societe Royale Forestiere de Belgique — Bull Soc R For Belg
Bulletin. Societe Royale Forestiere de Belgique/Tijdschrift van de Koninklijke Belgische Bosbouwmaatschappij — Bull Soc R For Belg Tijdschr K Belg Bosbouwmaatsch
Bulletin. Societe Scientifique de Bretagne — Bull Soc Sci Bretagne
Bulletin. Societe Scientifique de Bretagne — Bull Soc Scient Bretagne
Bulletin. Societe Scientifique d'Hygiene Alimentaire et d'Alimentation Rationnelle — Bull Soc Sci Hyg Aliment Aliment Ration
Bulletin. Societe Scientifique d'Hygiene Alimentaire et d'Alimentation Rationnelle de l'Homme — Bull Soc Hyg Aliment
Bulletin. Societe Scientifique d'Hygiene Alimentaire et d'Alimentation Rationnelle de l'Homme — Bull Soc Sci Hyg Aliment Aliment Ration Homme
Bulletin. Societe Scientifique et Litteraire du Limbourg — BSL
Bulletin. Societe Scientifique et Litteraire du Limbourg — BSSLL
Bulletin. Societe Scientifique et Medicale de l'Ouest — Bull Soc Scient Med Ouest
Bulletin. Societe Scientifique, Historique, et Archeologique de la Correze — BSH Correze
Bulletin. Societe Suisse des Americanistes — B Soc Suisse Am
Bulletin. Societe Suisse des Americanistes — B Soc Suisse American
Bulletin. Societe Suisse des Americanistes — SSA/B
Bulletin. Societe Suisse des Americanistes (Geneva) — Bull Soc Suisse Am Geneva
Bulletin. Societe Suisse des Amis de l'Extreme-Orient — BSSAEO
Bulletin. Societe Sultanieh de Geographie — BSSG
Bulletin. Societe Theophile Gautier — BSTG
Bulletin. Societe Toulousaine d'Etudes Classiques — BSTEC
Bulletin. Societe Tournaisienne de Paleontologie et de Prehistoire — B Tournal
Bulletin. Societe Tournaisienne de Paleontologie et de Prehistoire — BSTPP
Bulletin. Societe Vaudoise des Sciences Naturelles — Bull Soc Vaud Sci Nat
Bulletin. Societe Vaudoise des Sciences Naturelles — Bull Soc Vaudoise Sci Nat
Bulletin. Societe Vervietoise d'Archeologie et d'Histoire — BSVAH
Bulletin. Societe Veterinaire Hellenique — Bull Soc Vet Hell
Bulletin. Societe Zoologique de France — B S Zool Fr
Bulletin. Societe Zoologique de France — Bull Soc Zool Fr
Bulletin. Societe Zoologique de France — Bull Soc Zool France
Bulletin. Societe Zoologique de France. Supplement — Bull Soc Zool Fr Suppl
Bulletin. Societes Archeologiques d'Eure-Et-Loir — B Soc Arch Eure-Et-Loir
Bulletin. Societes Chimiques Belges — B S Chim Be
Bulletin. Societes Chimiques Belges — BSBQA
Bulletin. Societes Chimiques Belges — Bull Soc Chim Belg
Bulletin. Societes d'Histoire et d'Archeologie de la Meuse — BSHAM
Bulletin. Societes d'Ophtalmologie de France — Bull Soc Ophtal Fr
Bulletin. Societes d'Ophtalmologie de France — Bull Soc Ophtalmol Fr
Bulletin. Society for African Church History — Bull Soc Afr Church Hist
Bulletin. Society for African Church History — BuSA
Bulletin. Society for Analytical Chemistry — Bull Soc Analyt Chem
Bulletin. Society for Italian Studies — BSIS
Bulletin. Society for Latin American Studies — Bull Soc Lat Am Stud
Bulletin. Society for the Promotion of Engineering Education — Bull Soc Promot Eng Educ
Bulletin. Society of Arts. Massachusetts Institute of Technology — Bull Soc Arts Mass Inst Technol
Bulletin. Society of Naval Architects and Marine Engineers — Bull Soc Nav Archit Mar Eng
Bulletin. Society of Pharmacological and Environmental Pathologists — Bull Soc Pharmacol Environ Pathol
Bulletin. Society of Photographic Science and Technology of Japan — Bull Soc Photogr Sci Technol Jpn
Bulletin. Society of Plant Ecology/Shokubutsu Seitai-Gaku Kaiho — Bull Soc Pl Ecol
Bulletin. Society of Salt Science. Japan — Bull Soc Salt Sci Jpn
Bulletin. Society of Scientific Photography of Japan — Bull Soc Sci Photogr Jpn
Bulletin. Society of Sea Water Science (Japan) — Bull Soc Sea Water Sci (Jpn)
Bulletin. Society of Vector Ecologists — Bull Soc Vector Ecol
Bulletin. Soil Bureau Department of Scientific and Industrial Research (New Zealand) — Bull Soil Bur (NZ)
Bulletin. Soil Survey of Great Britain — Bull Soil Surv Gt Br
Bulletin Solidarnosc — Bul Solidar
Bulletin. Sommaires des Periodiques Francais et Etrangers — BS
Bulletin. Sonoma County Medical Association [*California*] — Bull Sonoma County Med Assoc
Bulletin. South African Cultural History Museum — Bull S Afr Cult Hist Mus
Bulletin. South African Institute of Assayers and Analysts — BSIAD
Bulletin. South African Institute of Assayers and Analysts — Bull S Afr Inst Assayers Anal
Bulletin. South Carolina Academy of Science — Bull SC Acad Sci
Bulletin. South Carolina Agricultural Experiment Station — Bull SC Agric Exp Stn
Bulletin. South Carolina. State Development Board — Bull SC State Dev Board
Bulletin. South Dakota Agricultural Experiment Station — Bull S Dak Agr Exp Sta
Bulletin. South Dakota Agricultural Experiment Station — Bull S Dak Agric Exp St
Bulletin. South Dakota Geological Survey — Bull SD Geol Surv
Bulletin. South Texas Geological Society — BSTGA
Bulletin. South Texas Geological Society — Bull S Tex Geol Soc
Bulletin. South Texas Geological Society — Bull South Tex Geol Soc
Bulletin. Southern California Academy of Sciences — Bull S Cal Acad Sci
Bulletin. Southern California Academy of Sciences — Bull South Calif Acad Sci
Bulletin. Southern California Academy of Sciences — Bull Sth Calif Acad Sci
Bulletin. Southern Pacific General Hospital — Bull South Pac Gen Hosp
Bulletin. Southern Research Institute — Bul S Res Inst
Bulletin. Southern Research Institute — Bull South Res Inst
Bulletin. Southwestern Association of Petroleum Geologists — Bull SW Ass Petrol Geol
Bulletin. Soviet Section. International Pedologists Association — Bull Sov Sect Int Pedol Assoc
Bulletin. Special Astrophysical Observatory (North Caucasus) — Bull Spec Astrophys Obs (North Caucasus)
Bulletin. Special Libraries Council of Philadelphia and Vicinity — Bull Spec Libr Coun Phila
Bulletin. Speleological Society of the District of Columbia — Bull Speleol Soc DC
Bulletin. Spokane County Medical Society [*Washington*] — Bull Spokane County Med Soc
Bulletin. Sport Fishing Institute — BSFIA
Bulletin. Sport Fishing Institute — Bull Sport Fish Inst
Bulletin. St. Francis Hospital and Sanatorium (Roslyn, New York) — Bull St Francis Hosp Sanat (Roslyn NY)
Bulletin. St. Marianna University. School of Medicine. General Education — Bull St Marianna Univ Sch Med Gen Educ
Bulletin. Standard Oil Company of California — BSTCA
Bulletin. Standard Oil Company of California — Bull Stand Oil Co Calif
Bulletin. State Agricultural Experiment Station (Auburn, Alabama) — Bull State Agric Exp Sta Alabama
Bulletin. State Biological Survey of Kansas — Bull State Biol Surv Kans
Bulletin. State Board of Agriculture. Dover, Delaware — Bull State Board Agric Dover Del
Bulletin. State Fruit Experiment Station. Southwest Missouri State University (Mountain Grove) — Bull State Fruit Exp Stn Southwest MO State Univ (Mt Grove)
Bulletin. State Geological Survey of Kansas — Bull State Geol Surv Kansas
Bulletin. State Geologist (Wyoming) — Bull State Geol (Wyo)
Bulletin. State Institute of Agricultural Microbiology (Leningrad) — Bull State Inst Agric Microbiol Leningrad
Bulletin. State Institute of Marine and Tropical Medicine in Gdansk — Bull State Inst Mar Trop Med Gdansk
Bulletin. State Nikita Botanical Gardens — Bull State Nikita Bot Gard
Bulletin. State Plant Board of Florida — Bull State Plant Board Fla
Bulletin. State University of Iowa — Bull State Univ Iowa
Bulletin. Stations d'Experimentation Agricole Hongroises. A. Production Vegetale — Bull Stn Exp Agric Hong A
Bulletin. Stations d'Experimentation Agricole Hongroises. C. Horticulture — Bull Stn Exp Agric Hong C
Bulletin. Statistical Society of New South Wales — Bull Statist Soc NSW
Bulletin Statistique Agricole — Bul Statis Agric
Bulletin Statistique et Economique — Bul Statis et Econ
Bulletin Statistique Mensuel [*Beirut*] — BSM
Bulletin Statistique Mensuel. Comite des Forges de France — Bull St Mens Com Forg Fr
Bulletin Statistique Mensuel (Lebanon) — Bul Statis Mensuel (Lebanon)
Bulletin. Storrs Agricultural Experiment Station. University of Connecticut — Bull Storrs Agric Exp Stn Univ Conn
Bulletin. Storrs Agricultural Station — Bull Storrs Agric Stn
Bulletin. Studiorum Novi Testamenti Societas — BulSNTS
Bulletin. Sugadaira Biological Laboratory — Bull Sugadaira Biol Lab
Bulletin Suisse de Mycologie — Bull Suisse Mycol
Bulletin sur les Politiques Liberales — Bul Polit Liberal
Bulletin. Suzugamine Women's College. Natural Science — Bull Suzugamine Women's Coll Nat Sci
Bulletin. Swaziland Department of Agriculture — Bull Swazild Dep Agric
Bulletin. Swedish Corrosion Institute — Bull Swed Corros Inst
Bulletin. Taichung District Agricultural Improvement Station — Bull Taichung Dist Agric Improv Stn
Bulletin. Taichung District Agricultural Improvement Station — TCNPEX
Bulletin. Taipei Medical College — Bull Taipei Med Coll
Bulletin. Taiwan Agricultural Research Institute — Bull Taiwan Agric Res Inst
Bulletin. Taiwan Forestry Research Institute — Bull Taiwan For Res Inst
Bulletin. Taiwan Forestry Research Institute — Bull Taiwan Forestry Res Inst
Bulletin. Tall Timbers Research Station — Bull Tall Timbers Res Stn
Bulletin. Tamagawa-Gakuen Women's Junior College — Bull Tamagawa-Gakuen Women's Jr Coll
Bulletin. Tea Division. Tokai Kinki Agricultural Station — Bull Tea Div Tokai Kinki Agric Stn
Bulletin. Tea Research Station (Kanaya, Japan) — Bull Tea Res Stn (Kanaya Jpn)
Bulletin. Tea Research Station. Ministry of Agriculture and Forestry [*Japan*] — Bull Tea Res Stn Minist Agric For
Bulletin. Tea Research Station. Ministry of Agriculture and Forestry/Chagyo Shikenjo Kenkyu Hokoku — Bull Tea Res Sta Minist Agric

Bulletin (Technical). Agricultural Experiment Stations (Florida) — Bull Tech Agric Exp Stn Fla
Bulletin. Technical Association of Graphic Arts of Japan — Bull Tech Assoc Graphic Arts Jpn
Bulletin. Technical Forest Academy — Bull Tech For Acad
Bulletin. Technical University of Istanbul — Bull Tech Univ Istanbul
Bulletin Technique AIBr [*Association des Ingenieurs Sortis de l'Universite Libre de Bruxelles*] — Bull Tech AIBr
Bulletin Technique Apicole — Bull Tech Api
Bulletin Technique. Bureau Veritas [*France*] — BTBVA
Bulletin Technique. Bureau Veritas — Bull Tech Bur Veri
Bulletin Technique. Centre de Recherches Zootechniques et Veterinaires de Theix — Bull Tech Cent Rech Zootech Vet Theix
Bulletin Technique. Chambre Syndicale des Mines de Fer de France — Bull Tech Chambre Synd Mines Fer Fr
Bulletin Technique de la Suisse Romande — BTQSA
Bulletin Technique de la Suisse Romande — Bull Tech Suisse Romande
Bulletin Technique de la Suisse Romande — Bull Techn Suisse Rom
Bulletin Technique de l'Houille et Derives. Institut National de l'Industrie Charbonniere — Bull Tech Houille Deriv Inst Natl Ind Charbon
Bulletin Technique de l'Institut de l'Email Vitrifie — Bull Tech Inst Email Vitrifie
Bulletin Technique de Securite et Salubrite. Institut National des Industries Extractives — BTSCB
Bulletin Technique de Securite et Salubrite. Institut National des Industries Extractives — Bull Tech Secur Salubr Inst Natl Ind Extr
Bulletin Technique. Departement de Genetique Animale [*France*] — Bull Tech Dep Genet Anim
Bulletin Technique des Mines de Fer de France — BTFFA
Bulletin Technique des Mines de Fer de France — Bull Tech Mines Fer Fr
Bulletin Technique d'Information — Bull Tech Inf
Bulletin Technique d'Information des Ingenieurs des Services Agricoles — BTIIA6
Bulletin Technique d'Information des Ingenieurs des Services Agricoles — Bull Tech Inf Ing Serv Agric
Bulletin Technique d'Information des Ingenieurs des Services Agricoles — Bull Tech Inf Ingrs Servs Agric
Bulletin Technique d'Information. Ministere de l'Agriculture (France) — Bull Tech Inf Min Agric (France)
Bulletin Technique d'Information. Ministere de l'Agriculture (France) — Bull Tech Inform Min Agr (France)
Bulletin Technique. Division des Sols. Province de Quebec - Ministere de l'Agriculture — Bull Tech Div Sols Queb Minist Agric
Bulletin Technique du Genie Rural [*France*] — Bull Tech Genie Rural
Bulletin Technique. Edite par l'Union Suisse des Lithographes et la Societe Suisse des Patrons Lithographes — Bull Tech Union Suisse Lithogr Soc Suisse Patrons Lithogr
Bulletin Technique/Gattefosse Report — Bull Tech Gattefosse Rep
Bulletin Technique PTT [*Schweizerische Post-, Telephon- und Telegraphenbetrieben*] — Bull Tech PTT
Bulletin Technique. Societe Francaise des Constructions Babcock et Wilcox — BTFCA
Bulletin Technique. Societe Francaise des Constructions Babcock et Wilcox [*France*] — Bull Tech Soc Fr Constr Babcock et Wilcox
Bulletin Technique. Societe Francaise des Constructions Babcock et Wilcox — Bull Tech Soc Fr Constr Babcock Wilcox
Bulletin Technique. Societe Royale Belge des Ingenieurs et des Industriels — Bull Tech Soc R Belge Ing Ind
Bulletin Technique. Societe Standard Francaise des Petroles — Bull Techn Soc Stand Petroles
Bulletin Technique. Valorisation et Utilisation des Combustibles. Institut National des Industries Extractives — Bull Tech Valorisation Util Combust Inst Natl Ind Extr
Bulletin Technique Vevey — BTVVA
Bulletin Technique Vevey — Bull Tech Vevey
Bulletin. Technological Institute of Plant Products. Athens — Bull Technol Inst Plant Prod Athens
Bulletin. Tennessee Agricultural Experiment Station — Bull Tenn Agric Exp Stn
Bulletin. Tennessee. Division of Geology — Bull Tenn Div Geol
Bulletin. Tennessee Nurses Association — Bull Tenn Nurses Assoc
Bulletin. Tenth District Dental Society (Rockville Centre) [*New York*] — Bull Tenth Dist Dent Soc (Rockville Centre)
Bulletin. Texas Agricultural Experiment Station — B Tex Agric Exp Stn
Bulletin. Texas Agricultural Experiment Station — Bull Tex Agr Exp Sta
Bulletin. Texas Agricultural Experiment Station — Bull Tex Agric Exp St
Bulletin. Texas Agricultural Experiment Station — Bull Tex Agric Exp Stn
Bulletin. Texas Archaeological Society — BTAS
Bulletin. Texas Memorial Museum — Bull Tex Mem Mus
Bulletin. Texas Nurses Association — Bull Tex Nurses Assoc
Bulletin. Texas Ornithological Society — Bull Tex Ornithol Soc
Bulletin. Textile Institute. Faculty of Engineering. Yamagata University — Bull Text Inst Fac Eng Yamagata Univ
Bulletin. Textile Research Institute (Japan) — Bull Text Res Inst (Jpn)
Bulletin. Thailand National Commission for UNESCO — Bull Thailand Nat Com UNESCO
Bulletin. The National Anti-Vivisection Society — Bull Natl Anti Vivisection Soc
Bulletin Thomiste — BThom
Bulletin. Tobacco Research Institute — Bull Tob Res Inst
Bulletin. Tobacco Research Institute. Taiwan Tobacco and Wine Monopoly Bureau — Bull Tob Res Inst Taiwan Tob Wine Monop Bur
Bulletin. Tochigi Agricultural Experiment Station — Bull Tochigi Agr Exp Sta
Bulletin. Tochigi Prefectural Dairy Experimental Institute — Bull Tochigi Prefect Dairy Exp Inst
Bulletin. Tohoku Institute of Technology. Section B. Sciences — Bull Tohoku Inst Technol Sect B
Bulletin. Tohoku National Agricultural Experiment Station — Bull Tohoku Nat Agr Exp Sta
Bulletin. Tohoku National Agricultural Experiment Station — Bull Tohoku Natl Agric Exp Stn
Bulletin. Tohoku National Agricultural Experiment Station — Bull Tohoku Natn Agric Exp Stn
Bulletin. Tohoku National Agricultural Experiment Station (Morioka) — Bull Tohoku Natol Agr Exp Stn (Morioka)
Bulletin. Tohoku National Agricultural Experiment Station/Tohoku Nogyo Shikenjo Kenkyu Hokoku — Bull Tohoku Natl Agric Exp Sta
Bulletin. Tohoku Regional Fisheries Research Laboratory — Bull Tohoku Reg Fish Res Lab
Bulletin. Tokai Regional Fisheries Research Laboratory — Bull Tokai Reg Fish Res Lab
Bulletin. Tokai-Kinki National Agricultural Experiment Station — Bull Tokai-Kinki Agr Exp Sta
Bulletin. Tokai-Kinki National Agricultural Experiment Station — Bull Tokai-Kinki Nat Agr Exp Sta
Bulletin. Tokai-Kinki National Agricultural Experiment Station — Bull Tokai-Kinki Natl Agric Exp Stn
Bulletin. Tokyo College of Domestic Science — Bull Tokyo Coll Domest Sci
Bulletin. Tokyo College of Photography — Bull Tokyo Coll Photogr
Bulletin. Tokyo Dental College — Bull Tokyo Dent Coll
Bulletin. Tokyo Gakugei University — Bull Tokyo Gakugei Univ
Bulletin. Tokyo Gakugei University — TGUBA
Bulletin. Tokyo Gakugei University. Series 4 — Bull Tokyo Gakugei Univ Ser 4
Bulletin. Tokyo Imperial University Forests/Nogaku-Bu Enshurin Hokoku — Bull Tokyo Imp Univ Forests
Bulletin. Tokyo Institute of Technology — BTITA
Bulletin. Tokyo Institute of Technology — Bull Tokyo Inst Technol
Bulletin. Tokyo Institute of Technology. Series A — Bull Tokyo Inst Technol Ser A
Bulletin. Tokyo Kasei Daigaku — Bull Tokyo Kasei Daigaku
Bulletin. Tokyo Medical and Dental University — BTMDA
Bulletin. Tokyo Medical and Dental University — Bull Tokyo Med Dent Univ
Bulletin. Tokyo Metropolitan Isotope Research Center — Bull Tokyo Metrop Isot Res Cent
Bulletin. Tokyo Metropolitan Rehabilitation Center of the Physically and Mentally Handicapped — Bull Tokyo Metro Rehab Cent Phys Ment Handcp
Bulletin. Tokyo Science Museum — Bull Tokyo Sci Mus
Bulletin. Tokyo University Forests — Bull Tokyo Univ For
Bulletin. Toledo [*Ohio*] **Dental Society** — Bull Toledo Dent Soc
Bulletin. Toronto East Medical Association — Bull Toronto East Med Assoc
Bulletin. Torrey Botanical Club — B Tor Bot C
Bulletin. Torrey Botanical Club — BTBCA
Bulletin. Torrey Botanical Club — Bull Torr Bot Club
Bulletin. Torrey Botanical Club — Bull Torrey Bot Club
Bulletin. Tottori Agricultural Experiment Station — Bull Tottori Agr Exp Sta
Bulletin. Tottori Fruit Tree Experiment Station/Tottori-Ken Kaju Shikenjo Kenkyu Hokoku — Bull Tottori Fruit Tree Exp Sta
Bulletin. Tottori Tree Fruit Experiment Station — Bull Tottori Tree Fruit Exp Stn
Bulletin. Tottori University Forests — Bull Tottori Univ For
Bulletin. Tottori University Forests/Tottori Daigaku Nogaku-Bu Fusoku Enshurin Hokoku — Bull Tottori Univ Forests
Bulletin. Tottori Vegetable and Ornamental Crops Experiment Station — Bull Tottori Veg Ornamental Crops Exp Stn
Bulletin. Toyama Agricultural Experiment Station — Bull Toyama Agric Exp Stn
Bulletin. Toyama Prefectural Livestock Experiment Station — Bull Toyama Prefect Livest Exp Stn
Bulletin. Tri-County Dental Society [*Morristown, New Jersey*] — Bull Tri Cty Dent Soc
Bulletin Trimestriel. Association Centrale des Veterinaires — Bull Trim Ass Cent Vet
Bulletin Trimestriel. Banque Centrale du Mali — Bul Trimest Ban Cent Mali
Bulletin Trimestriel. Banque de France — B Trim Banque France
Bulletin Trimestriel. Centre Textile de Controle et de Recherche Scientifique — Bull Trimest Cent Text Controle Rech Sci
Bulletin Trimestriel de la Societe Forestiere Francaise des Amis des Arbres — Bull Trimest Soc Forest Franc Amis Arbres
Bulletin Trimestriel de l'Association des Anciens Eleves de l'Ecole Superieure de Brasserie de l'Universite de Louvain — Bull Trimest Assoc Anc Eleves Ec Super Brass Univ Louvain
Bulletin Trimestriel des Antiquites Africaines Recueillies par les Soins de la Societe de Geographie et d'Archeologie de la Province d'Oran — BOran
Bulletin Trimestriel d'Information du Carbure de Calcium et de l'Acetylene — Bull Trimest Inf Carbure Calcium Acetylene
Bulletin Trimestriel du CEBEDEAU [*Centre Belge d'Etude et de Documentation de l'Eau*] — Bull Trimest CEBEDEAU
Bulletin Trimestriel. Ecole Nationale de la Sante Publique — B Trim Ecole Nat Sante Publ
Bulletin Trimestriel INACOL [*Institut National pour l'Amelioration des Conserves de Legumes*] — Bull Trimest INACOL
Bulletin Trimestriel. Institut Archeologique du Luxembourg — BIA Lux
Bulletin Trimestriel. Institut Archeologique du Luxembourg — BTIAL
Bulletin Trimestriel. Institut Archeologique du Luxembourg — BTIALux
Bulletin Trimestriel. Institut Archeologique du Luxembourg — Bull Trim Inst Arch Luxembourg
Bulletin Trimestriel. Institut National pour l'Amelioration des Conserves de Legumes (Belgium) — Bull Trimest Inst Natl Amelior Conserves Legumes (Belg)
Bulletin Trimestriel. Les Amis du Musee Oceanographique de Monaco — Bull Trimestriel Amis Mus Oceanogr Monaco
Bulletin Trimestriel. Societe Academique des Antiquaires de la Morinie — BSAM

Bulletin Trimestriel. Societe Academique des Antiquaires de la Morinie — BSAMorinie
Bulletin Trimestriel. Societe Academique des Antiquaires de la Morinie — BTSAAM
Bulletin Trimestriel. Societe Archeologique de Touraine — B Tours
Bulletin Trimestriel. Societe Archeologique de Touraine — BSA Touraine
Bulletin Trimestriel. Societe de Geographie et d'Archeologie de la Province d'Oran — Bull Oran
Bulletin Trimestriel. Societe de Geographie et d'Archeologie de la Province d'Oran — Soc Geo A Oran
Bulletin Trimestriel. Societe des Antiquaires de Picardie — BSAP
Bulletin Trimestriel. Societe des Antiquaires de Picardie — BSAPicardie
Bulletin Trimestriel. Societe des Antiquaires de Picardie — BTSAP
Bulletin Trimestriel. Societe d'Histoire Naturelle des Amis de la Museum d'Autun — Bull Trimest Soc Hist Nat Amis Mus Autun
Bulletin Trimestriel. Societe Forestiere de Franche-Comte et des Provinces de l'Est [*Salins-Les-Bains*] — Bull Soc For Franche-Comte
Bulletin Trimestriel. Societe Mycologique de France — Bull Trim Soc Mycol Fr
Bulletin Trimestriel. Societe Mycologique de France — Bull Trimest Soc Mycol Fr
Bulletin Trimestriel. Societe Royale Belge des Electriciens — Bull Trimest Soc R Belge Electr
Bulletin. Tufts New England Medical Center — Bull Tufts N Engl Med Cent
Bulletin. Tufts New England Medical Center — Bull Tufts New Engl Med Cent
Bulletin. Tulane Medical Faculty — Bull Tulane Med Fac
Bulletin. Tulane University Medical Faculty — Bull Tulane Univ Med Fac
Bulletin. Turkish Medical Society — Bull Turk Med Soc
Bulletin. Tuskegee Normal and Industrial Institute Experiment Station — Bull Tuskegee Normal Industr Inst Exp Sta
Bulletin. Uganda Society — Bull Uganda Soc
Bulletin UICN (Union Internationale pour la Conservation de la Nature et de ses Resources) — Bull UICN
Bulletin. Ukrainian Scientific Research Institute of Grain Culture — Bull Ukr Sci Res Inst Grain Cult
Bulletin. UNESCO [*United Nations Educational, Scientific, and Cultural Organization*] **Regional Office for Education in Asia** — B UNESCO Reg Off Educ
Bulletin. UNESCO Regional Office for Education in Asia — Bul UNESCO Reg Off Ed Asia
Bulletin. UNESCO Regional Office for Science and Technology for the Arab States (UNESCO SC/ROSTAS) — Bull UNESCO Reg Off Sci Technol Arab States UNESCO SC/ROSTAS
Bulletin. Union [*New Jersey*] **County Dental Society** — Bull Union Cty Dent Soc
Bulletin. Union des Agriculteurs d'Egypte — Bull Union Agric Egypte
Bulletin. Union des Oceanographes de France — Bull Union Oceanogr Fr
Bulletin. Union des Physiciens — BTUPA
Bulletin. Union des Physiciens — Bull Union Physiciens
Bulletin. Union Internationale Contre la Tuberculose — Bull Un Int Tub
Bulletin. Union Medicale Balkanique — Bull Union Med Balk
Bulletin. Union Syndicale des Agriculteurs d'Egypte — Bull Union Synd Agric Egypte
Bulletin. Union Syndicale des Apiculteurs — Bull Synd Apic
Bulletin. Union Syndicale des Apiculteurs Picards — Bull Union Synd Apic Picards
Bulletin Uniprojektu — Bull Uniprojektu
Bulletin. United Bible Societies — Bull United Bible Soc
Bulletin. United Planters' Association of Southern India. Scientific Department — Bull United Plant Assoc South Ind Sci Dep
Bulletin. United States Army Medical Department — Bull US Army Med Dep
Bulletin. United States Bureau of Fisheries — Bull US Bur Fish
Bulletin. United States Bureau of Mines — Bull US Bur Min
Bulletin. United States Bureau of Mines — Bull US Bur Mines
Bulletin. United States Coast and Geodetic Survey — Bull US Cst Geod Surv
Bulletin. United States Department of Agriculture — Bull US Dept Agric
Bulletin. United States Geological Survey — Bull US Geol Surv
Bulletin. United States Golf Association. Green Committee — Bull US Golf Assoc Green Comm
Bulletin. United States National Museum — Bull US Nat Mus
Bulletin. United States National Museum — Bull US Natl Mus
Bulletin. United States National Museum — Bull US Natn Mus
Bulletin. Universite de Lyon — BUL
Bulletin. Universite de Lyon — Bull Univ Lyon
Bulletin. Universite de Strasbourg — BUS
Bulletin. Universite de Toulouse — BUT
Bulletin. Universite d'Etat de l'Asie Centrale — Bull Univ Etat Asie Cent
Bulletin. Universite l'Aurore — BUA
Bulletin. University College of Medicine (Calcutta) — Bull Univ Coll Med (Calcutta)
Bulletin. University College of Medicine. Calcutta University — Bull Univ Coll Med Calcutta Univ
Bulletin. University Forest. Kyushu Imperial University — Bull Univ Forest Kyushu Imp Univ
Bulletin. University of Agricultural Sciences. Godollo, Hungary — Bull Univ Agric Sci Godollo Hung
Bulletin. University of Alberta — Bull Univ Alberta
Bulletin. University of California. Division of Agricultural Sciences — Bull Univ Calif Div Agric Sci
Bulletin. University of Cape Town. Chamber of Mines Precambrian Research Unit — Bull Univ Cape Town Chamber Mines Precambrian Res Unit
Bulletin. University of Florida. Agricultural Extension Service — Bull Univ Fla Agric Ext Serv
Bulletin. University of Florida. Cooperative Extension Service — Bull Univ Fla Coop Ext Serv
Bulletin. University of Florida, Gainesville. Institute of Food and Agricultural Experiment Stations — Bull Univ Fla Gainesville Inst Food Agric Sci Agric Exp Stn
Bulletin. University of Georgia. College of Agriculture. Cooperative Extension Service — Bull Univ GA Coll Agr Coop Ext Serv
Bulletin. University of Idaho. College of Agriculture. Extension Service — Bull Univ Idaho Coll Agr Ext Serv
Bulletin. University of Illinois. Agricultural Experiment Station — Bull Ill Agric Exp Sta
Bulletin. University of Illinois. Engineering Experiment Station — Bull Univ Ill Eng Exp Stat
Bulletin. University of Iowa. Institute of Agricultural Medicine — Bull Univ Iowa Inst Agr Med
Bulletin. University of Iowa. Museum of Art — Bul Univ Iowa Mus Art
Bulletin. University of Kentucky. Office of Research and Engineering Services — Bull Univ KY Off Res Eng Serv
Bulletin. University of Maryland. Cooperative Extension Service — Bull Univ MD Coop Ext Serv
Bulletin. University of Maryland. School of Medicine — Bull Univ MD Sch Med
Bulletin. University of Miami School of Medicine and Jackson Memorial Hospital — Bull Univ Miami Sch Med
Bulletin. University of Miami School of Medicine and Jackson Memorial Hospital — Bull Univ Miami Sch Med Jackson Mem Hosp
Bulletin. University of Minnesota. Institute of Technology. Engineering Experiment Station — Bull Univ Minn Eng Exp Stat
Bulletin. University of Missouri at Rolla. Technical Series — Bull Univ MO Rolla Tech Ser
Bulletin. University of Missouri. College of Agriculture. Experiment Station — Bull Univ MO Coll Agr Exp Sta
Bulletin. University of Missouri. Engineering Experiment Station Series — Bull Univ Mo Eng Exp Stn Ser
Bulletin. University of Missouri School of Mines and Metallurgy — Bull Univ Mo Sch Mines Metall
Bulletin. University of Nebraska State Museum — Bull Univ Neb St Mus
Bulletin. University of Nebraska State Museum — Bull Univ Nebr State Mus
Bulletin. University of Osaka Prefecture. Series A. Engineering and Natural Sciences — Bull Univ Osaka Prefecture Ser A
Bulletin. University of Osaka Prefecture. Series A. Sakai — Bull Univ Osaka Prefect Ser A
Bulletin. University of Osaka Prefecture. Series B — Bull Univ Osaka Pref Ser B
Bulletin. University of Osaka Prefecture. Series B. Agriculture and Biology — Bull Univ Osaka Prefect Ser B
Bulletin. University of Osaka Prefecture. Series B. Agriculture and Biology [*A publication*] — Bull Univ Osaka Prefect Ser B Agric Biol
Bulletin. University of Pittsburgh — BUP
Bulletin. University of Puerto Rico. Agricultural Experiment Station. Rio Piedras — Bull Univ PR Agric Exp Stn Rio Piedras
Bulletin. University of Rhode Island. Agricultural Experiment Station — Bull Univ RI Agric Exp Stn
Bulletin. University of Rhode Island. Cooperative Extension Service — Bull Univ RI Coop Ext Serv
Bulletin. University of Tennessee. Agricultural Experiment Station — Bll Univ Tenn Agr Exp Sta
Bulletin. University of Tennessee. Agricultural Experiment Station — Bull Univ Tenn Agric Exp Stn
Bulletin. University of the Ryukyus. Science and Engineering Division. Mathematics and Natural Sciences — Bull Sci Engrg Div Univ Ryukyus Math Natur Sci
Bulletin. University of Washington. Engineering Experiment Station — Bull Univ Wash Eng Exp Stat
Bulletin. University of Wisconsin. Engineering Series — Wis U Bul Eng S
Bulletin. University of Wisconsin. Science Series — Bull Univ Wisconsin Sci Ser
Bulletin. University of Wisconsin. Studies in Science — Bull Univ Wisconsin Stud Sci
Bulletin. USSR Institute of Agricultural Microbiology — Bull USSR Inst Agric Microbiol
Bulletin Ustavu Russkeho Jazyka a Literatury — BURJL
Bulletin Usuel des Lois et Arretes — B Us L Ar
Bulletin Usuel des Lois et Arretes — Bull Us
Bulletin. Utah Agricultural Experiment Station — Bull Utah Agr Exp Sta
Bulletin. Utah Agricultural Experiment Station — Bull Utah Agric Exp Stn
Bulletin. Utah Engineering Experiment Station — Bull Utah Eng Exp Stn
Bulletin. Utah Engineering Experiment Station — UEEBA
Bulletin. Utah Geological and Mineral Survey — Bull Utah Geol Miner Surv
Bulletin. Utsunomiya Agricultural College. Series A. Agricultural Sciences, Forestry, Veterinary Science, Agricultural Engineering, Agricultura Chemistry — Bull Utsunomiya Agric Coll Ser A
Bulletin. Utsunomiya Agricultural College. Series B. Agricultural and Forest Economics — Bull Utsunomiya Agric Coll Ser B
Bulletin. Utsunomiya Tobacco Experiment Station — Bull Utsunomiya Tob Exp Stn
Bulletin. Utsunomiya University Forests — Bull Utsunomiya Univ For
Bulletin. Utsunomiya University. Section 2 — Bull Utsunomiya Univ Sect 2
Bulletin. UV Spectrometry Group — Bull UV Spectrom Group
Bulletin V. Luna General Hospital Medical Society — Bull V Luna Gen Hosp Med Soc
Bulletin. Valley Dental Society [*Encino, California*] — Bull Val Dent Soc
Bulletin van de Belgische Vereniging voor Geologie. Paleontologie en Hydrologie — Bull Belg Ver Geol Paleontol Hydrol
Bulletin van de Directe Belastingen — BDB
Bulletin van de Directe Belastingen — Bull Dir Bel
Bulletin van de Generale Bankmaatschappij — BYL
Bulletin van de Vereeniging tot Bevordering der Kennis van de Antike Beschaving — B A Besch

Bulletin van de Vereeniging tot Bevordering der Kennis van de Antike Beschaving — BVAB
Bulletin van het Algemeen Proefstation voor de Landbouw — Bull Alg Proefstat Landb
Bulletin van het Koninklijke Belgische Instituut voor Natuurwetenschappen. Aardwetenschappen — Bull K Belg Inst Natuurwet Aardwet
Bulletin van het Koninklijke Belgische Instituut voor Natuurwetenschappen. Biologie — Bull K Belg Inst Natuurwet Biol
Bulletin van het Koninklijke Belgische Instituut voor Natuurwetenschappen. Entomologie — Bull K Belg Inst Natuurwet Entomol
Bulletin van het Proefstation voor Cacao te Salatiga — Bull Proefstat Cacao Salatiga
Bulletin van Volksgezondheid — B Vgzh
Bulletin. Vancouver Medical Association — Bull Vanc Med Ass
Bulletin. Vancouver Medical Association — Bull Vancouver Med Assoc
Bulletin. Vegetable and Ornamental Crops Research Station. Series A — Bull Veg Ornamental Crops Res Stn Ser A
Bulletin. Vegetable and Ornamental Crops Research Station. Series B [*Morioka*] — YSHBDP
Bulletin. Vegetable and Ornamental Crops Research Station. Series B (Morioka) [*A publication*] — Bull Veg Ornamental Crops Res Stn Ser B (Morioka)
Bulletin. Vegetable and Ornamental Crops Research Station. Series C — Bull Veg Ornamental Crops Res Stn Ser C
Bulletin. Vegetable and Ornamental Crops Research Station. Series C (Kurume) [*A publication*] — Bull Veg Ornamental Crops Res Stn Ser C (Kurume)
Bulletin. Vegetable Crops Research Institute (Kecskemet, Hungary) — Bull Veg Crops Res Inst Kecskemet Hung
Bulletin. Vereinigung der Schweizerischen Petroleum-Geologen und -Ingenieure — Bull Ver Schweiz Pet-Geol Ing
Bulletin. Vereinigung der Schweizerischen Petroleum-Geologen und -Ingenieure — Bull Ver Schweiz Petrol Geol-Ing
Bulletin. Vereinigung der Schweizerischen Petroleum-Geologen und -Ingenieure — BUVSA
Bulletin. Vermont Agricultural Experiment Station — Bull Verm Agric Exp St
Bulletin. Vermont Agricultural Experiment Station — Bull VT Agric Exp Stn
Bulletin. Vermont. Geological Survey — Bull Vt Geol Surv
Bulletin Veterinaire (Lisbon) — Bull Vet (Lisb)
Bulletin. Veterinary Institute in Pulawy — Bull Vet Inst Pulawy
Bulletin. Veterinary Institute of Infectious and Parasitic Diseases. Academy of Agricultural Sciences. Bulgaria — Bull Vet Inst Infect Parasit Dis Acad Agric Sci Bulg
Bulletin. Veterinary Research Laboratory (Anyang, South Korea) — Bull Vet Res Lab Anyang South Korea
Bulletin. Veterinary Virus Research Institute. Academy of Agricultural Sciences. Bulgaria — Bull Vet Virus Res Inst Acad Agric Sci Bulg
Bulletin. Victoria Memorial Museum of the Geological Survey of Canada — B Victoria Mem
Bulletin. Victoria Memorial Museum of the Geological Survey of Canada — Bull Vict Mem Mus
Bulletin. Victorian Institute of Educational Research — Bul VIER
Bulletin. Victorian Institute of Educational Research — Bull Vict Inst Educ Res
Bulletin. Vie Musicale Belge [*Bulletin van het Belgisch Muziekleven*] — Bul Vie M Belge
Bulletin vir Dosente — Bull Dosente
Bulletin. Virginia Agricultural Experiment Station — Bull VA Agr Exp Sta
Bulletin. Virginia Agricultural Experiment Station — Bull VA Agric Exp Stn
Bulletin. Virginia Agricultural Experiment Station — Bull Virg Agric Exp St
Bulletin. Virginia Agricultural Extension Service — Bull VA Agric Ext Serv
Bulletin. Virginia Division of Mineral Resources — Bull Va Div Miner Resour
Bulletin. Virginia Geological Survey — Bull VA Geol Surv
Bulletin. Virginia Polytechnic Institute. Agricultural Extension Service — Bull VA Polytech Inst Agr Ext Serv
Bulletin. Virginia Polytechnic Institute and State University. Virginia Water Resources Research Center — Bull VA Polytech Inst State Univ VA Water Resources Cent
Bulletin. Virginia Polytechnic Institute. Engineering Experiment Station Series — Bull Va Polytech Inst Eng Exp Stn Ser
Bulletin. Virginia Sections of the American Chemical Society — Bull VA Sect Amer Chem Soc
Bulletin. Virginia State Dental Association — Bull Virg Dent Ass
Bulletin. Virginia Water Resources Research Center — Bull VA Water Resour Res Cent
Bulletin. Volcanological Society of Japan — Bull Volcanol Soc Jpn
Bulletin Volcanologique — Bull Volcan
Bulletin Volcanologique — Bull Volcanol
Bulletin Volcanologique — BUVOA
Bulletin Volcanologique (Rome) — Bull Volcanol Rome
Bulletin. Vyskumneho Ustavu Papieru a Celulozy — Bull Vysk Ustavu Pap Celul
Bulletin. Vyskumneho Ustavu Potravinarskeho — Bull Vysk Ustavu Potravin
Bulletin. Vyskumneho Ustavu Potravinarskeho — BVUPD
Bulletin. Vyskumneho Ustavu Priemyslu Celulozy — Bull Vysk Ustavu Priem Celul
Bulletin Vysoke Skoly Russkeho Jazyka a Literatury — BVSRJL
Bulletin. Wagner Free Institute of Science — Bull Wagner Free Inst Sci
Bulletin. Wakayama Fruit Tree Experiment Station — Bull Wakayama Fruit Tree Exp Stn
Bulletin. Waseda Applied Chemical Society — Bull Waseda Appl Chem Soc
Bulletin. Washington Agricultural Experiment Station — Bull Wash Agr Exp Sta
Bulletin. Washington Agricultural Experiment Station — Bull Wash Agric Exp St
Bulletin. Washington Agricultural Experiment Station — Bull Wash Agric Exp Stn
Bulletin. Washington Agricultural Experiment Station — Bull Washington Agric Exp Stn
Bulletin. Washington. Division of Geology and Earth Resources — Bull Wash Div Geol Earth Resour
Bulletin. Washington Geological Survey — Bull Wash Geol Surv
Bulletin. Washington State College Extension Service — Bull Wash St Coll Ext Serv
Bulletin. Washington State Institute of Technology — Bull Wash State Inst Technol
Bulletin. Washington State University. Agricultural Research Center — Bull Wash State Univ Agric Res Cent
Bulletin. Washington State University. College of Agriculture Research Center — Bull Wash State Univ Coll Agric Res Cent
Bulletin. Water Research Foundation of Australia — Bull Wat Res Fdn Aust
Bulletin. Water Resources Research Center (Blacksburg, Virginia) — Bull Water Resour Res Cent Blacksburg Va
Bulletin. Welding Research Council — Bull Weld Res Counc
Bulletin. Welsh Plant Breeding Station. University College of Wales — Bull Welsh Pl Breed Stn
Bulletin. West of Scotland Agricultural College — Bull W Scotl Agric Coll
Bulletin. West Virginia Association of College English Teachers — BWVACET
Bulletin. West Virginia University. Agricultural Experiment Station — Bull W Va Agric Exp Sta
Bulletin. West Virginia University. Agricultural Experiment Station — Bull W Va Univ Agr Exp Sta
Bulletin. Western Society of Engineers — Bull West Soc Eng
Bulletin. Wheat and Sunflower Research Institute. Tolbouhin. Academy of Agricultural Sciences. Bulgaria — Bull Wheat Sunflower Res Inst Tolbouhin Acad Agric Sci Bulg
Bulletin. Wildlife Disease Association — Bull Wildl Dis
Bulletin. Wildlife Disease Association — Bull Wildl Dis Assoc
Bulletin. Wisconsin Agricultural Experiment Station — Bull Wis Agr Exp Sta
Bulletin. Wisconsin Agricultural Experiment Station — Bull Wis Agric Exp Stn
Bulletin. Wisconsin Agricultural Experiment Station — Bull Wisc Agric Exp St
Bulletin. Wisconsin Natural History Society — Bull Wisconsin Nat Hist Soc
Bulletin. Woman's Auxiliary to American Medical Association — Bull Wom Aux Amer Med Ass
Bulletin. Wood Research Laboratory. Virginia Polytechnic Institute — Bull Wood Res Lab VA Polyt Inst
Bulletin. Woods and Forests Department of South Australia — Bull Wds For Dep S Aust
Bulletin. Woods and Forests Department of South Australia — Bull Woods Forests Dep S Aust
Bulletin. World Health Organization — B WHO
Bulletin. World Health Organization — Bull WHO
Bulletin. World Health Organization — Bull Wld Hlth Org
Bulletin. World Health Organization — Bull World Health Organ
Bulletin. Wyoming Agricultural Experiment Station — B Wyo Agric Exp Stn
Bulletin. Wyoming Agricultural Experiment Station — Bull Wyo Agr Exp Sta
Bulletin. Wyoming Agricultural Experiment Station — Bull Wyo Agric Exp Stn
Bulletin. Wyoming Agricultural Extension Service — Bull Wyo Agric Ext Serv
Bulletin. Wyoming Department of Agriculture. Division of Statistics and Information — Bull Wyo Dept Agr Div Statist Inform
Bulletin. Wyoming Experiment Station — Bull Wyo Exp Stn
Bulletin. Wyoming University. Cooperative Extension Service — Bull Wyo Univ Coop Ext Serv
Bulletin Y. National Fertilizer Development Center (United States) — Bull Y Natl Fert Dev Cent (US)
Bulletin. Yale University Art Gallery — B Yale
Bulletin. Yale University Art Gallery — B Yale U
Bulletin. Yale University School of Forestry — Bull Yale Sch For
Bulletin. Yale University. School of Forestry — Bull Yale Univ Sch For
Bulletin. Yamagata Agricultural College/Yamagata Kenritsu Norin Senmon Gakko Kenkyu Hokoku — Bull Yamagata Agric Coll
Bulletin. Yamagata University. Agricultural Science — Bull Yamagata Univ Agric Sci
Bulletin. Yamagata University. Engineering — Bull Yamagata Univ Eng
Bulletin. Yamagata University. Medical Science — Bull Yamagata Univ Med Sci
Bulletin. Yamagata University. Medical Science — YMJODW
Bulletin. Yamagata University. Natural Science — Bull Yamagata Univ Nat Sci
Bulletin. Yamagata University. Natural Science — Bull Yamagata Univ Natur Sci
Bulletin. Yamaguchi Agricultural Experiment Station — Bull Yamaguchi Agric Exp Stn
Bulletin. Yamaguchi Medical School — Bull Yamaguchi Med Sch
Bulletin. Yamaguchi Prefectural Poultry Breeding Station — Bull Yamaguchi Prefect Poult Breed Stn
Bulletin. Yamanashi Agricultural Experiment Station — Bull Yamanashi Agric Exp Stn
Bulletin. Yamanashi Agricultural Research Center — Bull Yamanashi Agric Res Cent
Bulletin. Yamanashi Fruit Tree Experiment Station — Bull Yamanashi Fruit Tree Exp Stn
Bulletin. Yamanashi Prefectural Agricultural Experiment Station — Bull Yamanashi Pref Agr Exp Sta
Bulletin. Yamanashi Prefectural Agricultural Experiment Station/Yamanashi-Ken Nogyo Shikenjo Hokoku — Bull Yamanashi Prefect Agric Exp Sta
Bulletin. Yamanashi Prefectural Forest Experiment Station — Bull Yamanashi For Exp Sta
Bulletin. Yichang Institute of Geology and Mineral Resources — Bull Yichang Inst Geol Miner Resour
Bulletin. Yichang Institute of Geology and Mineral Resources. Chinese Academy of Geological Sciences — Bull Yichang Inst Geol Miner Resour Chin Acad Geol Sci
Bulletin. Yokohama City University — B Yokohama City Univ
Bulletin. Zambia Language Group — Bull Zambia Language Grp
Bulletin. Zimbabwe Geological Survey — Bull Zimbabwe Geol Surv

Bulletin. Zoological Society College of Science (Nagpur) — Bull Zool Soc Coll Sci (Nagpur)
Bulletin. Zoological Society of Egypt — Bull Zool Soc Egypt
Bulletin. Zoological Survey of India — Bull Zool Surv India
Bulletin. Zoologisch Museum Universitet van Amsterdam — Bull Zool Mus Univ Amsterdam
Bulletino del Laboratorio ed Orto Botanico della Reale Universita di Siena — Bull Lab Orto Bot Reale Univ Siena
Bulletino di Archeologia e Storia Dalmata — BAD
Bulletino. Istituto di Diritto Romano — Bullett Istit Dir Rom
Bulletino Nautico e Geografico di Roma — Bull Naut Geogr Roma
Bulletins. Academie Royalc de Belgique — B Ac Belg
Bulletins. Academie Royale de Belgique — Belg Ac Bull
Bulletins. Academie Royale de Belgique — Bull Ac Belgique
Bulletins. Academie Royale de Belgique — Bull Acad Roy Belg
Bulletins. Academie Royale de Belgique. Classe des Lettres, des Sciences Morales et Politiques — Bull de l'Ac Roy de Belg Cl Let
Bulletins. Academie Royale des Sciences, des Lettres, et des Beaux Arts de Belgique — Bull Acad Roy Sci Belgique
Bulletins de l'Academie Royale des Sciences, des Lettres, et des Beaux Arts de Belgique. Classe des Sciences — Bull Acad Roy Sci Belgique Cl Sci
Bulletins. Ecological Research Committee-NFR (Statens Naturvetenskapliga Forskningsrad) — Bull Ecol Res Comm-NFR (Statens Naturvetensk Forskningsrad)
Bulletins et Memoires. Ecole Nationale de Medecine et de Pharmacie de Dakar — Bull Mem Ec Natl Med Pharm Dakar
Bulletins et Memoires. Ecole Preparatoire de Medecine et de Pharmacie de Dakar — Bull Mem Ec Prep Med Pharm Dakar
Bulletins et Memoires. Faculte de Medecine et de Pharmacie de Dakar — Bull Mem Fac Med Pharm Dakar
Bulletins et Memoires. Societe Anatomique de Paris — Bull et Mem Soc Anat Paris
Bulletins et Memoires. Societe Centrale de Medecine Veterinaire — Bull et Mem Soc Centr Med Vet
Bulletins et Memoires. Societe d'Anthropologie — B Mem Soc Anthrop
Bulletins et Memoires. Societe d'Anthropologie — BMSA
Bulletins et Memoires. Societe d'Anthropologie de Paris — B M S Anthr
Bulletins et Memoires. Societe d'Anthropologie de Paris — B Mem Soc Anthr
Bulletins et Memoires. Societe d'Anthropologie de Paris — B Soc Anthropol Paris
Bulletins et Memoires. Societe d'Anthropologie de Paris — Bull Mem Soc Anthropol Paris
Bulletins et Memoires. Societe d'Anthropologie de Paris — Bull Soc Anthropol
Bulletins et Memoires. Societe d'Anthropologie de Paris — Bulls et Mem Soc Anthrop Paris
Bulletins et Memoires. Societe de Chirurgie de Paris — Bull et Mem Soc Chir Paris
Bulletins et Memoires. Societe de Therapeutique — Bull et Mem Soc Therap
Bulletins et Memoires. Societe d'Emulation des Cotes-du-Nord — SECN
Bulletins et Memoires. Societe Francaise d'Ophtalmologie — Bull Mem Soc Fr Ophtalmol
Bulletins et Memoires. Societe Medicale des Hopitaux de Bucarest — Bull et Mem Soc Med Hop Bucarest
Bulletins et Memoires. Societe Medicale des Hopitaux de Paris — BMSMA
Bulletins et Memoires. Societe Medicale des Hopitaux de Paris — BSMHA
Bulletins et Memoires. Societe Medicale des Hopitaux de Paris — Bull et Mem Soc Med Hop Paris
Bulletins et Memoires. Societe Medicale des Hopitaux de Paris — Bull Soc Med Hop Pa
Bulletins et Memoires. Societe Medicale des Hopitaux de Paris — Bull Soc Med Hop Paris
Bulletins et Memoires. Societe Nationale de Chirurgie — Bull Mem Soc Natl Chir
Bulletins et Memoires. Societe Nationale de Chirurgie (Paris) — Bull et Mem Soc Nat Chir (Paris)
Bulletins. Geological Survey of India. Series B. Engineering Geology and Ground Water — Bull Geol Surv India Ser B
Bulletins. Indian Industrial Research — Bull Indian Ind Res
Bulletins of American Paleontology — B Am Pal
Bulletins of American Paleontology — Bull Am Paleontol
Bulletins of American Paleontology — Bull Am Paleontology
Bulletins of American Paleontology — Bulls Am Paleontology
Bulletins of Marine Ecology — Bull Mar Ecol
Bulletins. Office of the Surgeon General. United States War Department — Bull Office Surg Gen US War Dept
Bulletins on Soviet Economic Development — Bull Soviet Econ Dev
Bulletin's Science Series — Bull Sci Ser
Bulletins. Societe de Zoologie d'Anvers — Bull Soc Zool Anvers
Bulletins. Societe des Antiquaires de Picardie — B Picardie
Bulletins. Societe des Antiquaires de Picardie — Picardie
Bullettino Archeologico Napoletano — BAN
Bullettino Archeologico Napoletano — Bull Arch Nap
Bullettino Archeologico Napoletano — Bull Nap
Bullettino Archeologico Napoletano — Bull Napol
Bullettino. Commissione Archeologica Comunale di Roma — Bull Com Roma
Bullettino. Commissione Archeologica Comunale di Roma — Bull Comunale
Bullettino. Commissione di Antichita e Belle Arte in Sicilia — B Comm Sicilia
Bullettino. Commissione di Antichita e Belle Arte in Sicilia — Bull Comm Ant Sic
Bullettino dei Musei Civici Veneziani — BMCV
Bullettino della Societa Filologica Romana — Bull d Soc Filol Rom
Bullettino. Deputazione Abruzzesi di Storia Patria — BDA
Bullettino. Deputazione Abruzzesi di Storia Patria — BDASP
Bullettino di Archeologia Cristiana — B A Crist
Bullettino di Archeologia Cristiana — Bullettino Archeol Crist
Bullettino di Associazione Napolitana di Medici e Naturalisti — Bull Assoc Napol Med
Bullettino di Paleontologia Italiana — Bull d Paleont
Bullettino di Paleontologia Italiana — Bull Paleot Ital
Bullettino di Paletnologia Italiana — BPIt
Bullettino di Paletnologia Italiana — Bull di Paletn Ital
Bullettino di Paletnologia Italiana — Bull Pal
Bullettino. Instituto di Correspondenza Archeologica — B Inst
Bullettino. Instituto di Correspondenza Archeologica — Bull Cor Arch
Bullettino. Instituto di Correspondenza Archeologica — Bull d Inst Corr Arch
Bullettino. Instituto di Correspondenza Archeologica — Bullet dell Inst Arch
Bullettino. Istituto di Diritto Romano "Vittorio Scialoja" — Bd I Dir Rom
Bullettino. Istituto di Diritto Romano. Vittorio Scialoja — Bdl
Bullettino. Istituto di Diritto Romano Vittorio Scialoja — Bull IDR
Bullettino. Istituto di Diritto Romano Vittorio Scialoja — Bull Ist Dir Rom
Bullettino. Istituto Storico Italiano per il Medio Evo e Archivio Muratorino — BIME
Bullettino. Museo dell'Impero Romana — Bull Imp
Bullettino. Museo dell'Impero Romana — Bull Impero
Bullettino. Museo dell'Impero Romana — Bull Mus
Bullettino. Museo dell'Impero Romana — Bull Mus Imp
Bullettino. Museo dell'Impero Romana — Bull Mus Imp Rom
Bullettino Sienese di Storia Patria — B Siena
Bull's-Eye News — BEN
Bumagodelatel'noe Mashinostroenie — Bumagodel Mashinostr
Bumazhnaya i Derevoobrabatyvayushchaya Promyshlennost — Bum Derevoobrab Promst
Bumazhnaya Promyshlennost — Bum Promst
Bumazhnaya Promyshlennost — Bumaz Prom
Bumazhnaya Promyshlennost — Bumazh Prom
Bumazhnaya Promyshlennost — BUMPA
Bund [*Bern*] — B
Bunda College of Agriculture. Research Bulletin — Bunda Coll Agric Res Bull
Bunder Jahrbuch — BundJb
Bundesamt fuer Strahlenschutz. Institut fuer Strahlenhygiene Berichte — Bundesamt Strahlenschutz Inst Strahlenhyg Ber
Bundesanstalt fuer Arbeitsschutz. Schriftenreihe. Gefaehrliche Arbeitsstoffe — Bundesanst Arbeitsschutz Schriftenr Gefaehrliche Arbeitsst
Bundesanstalt fuer Forst- und Holzwirtschaft. Merkblaetter — Bundesanst Forst Holzwirtsch Merkbl
Bundesanstalt fuer Materialpruefung. Forschungsbericht — Bundesanst Materialpruef Forschungsber
Bundesanstalt fuer Materialpruefung. Jahresbericht — Bundesanst Materialpruef Jahresber
Bundesanstalt fuer Materialpruefung-Berichte — Bundesanst Materialpruef Ber
Bundesanstalt fuer Pflanzenschutz Flugblatt — Bundesanst Pflanzenschutz Flugbl
Bundesanstalt fuer Wasserbau. Mitteilungsblatt (Federal Republic of Germany) — Bundesanst Wasserbau Mitteilungsbl Fed Repub Ger
Bundesanzeiger. Beilage — Bundesanzeiger Beil
Bundesapothekerkammer zur Wissenschaftlichen Fortbildung. Schriftenreihe. Gelbe Reihe — Bundesapothekerkammer Wiss Fortbild Schriftenr Gelbe Reihe
Bundesapothekerkammer zur Wissenschaftlichen Fortbildung. Schriftenreihe. Gruene Reihe — Bundesapothekerkammer Wiss Fortbild Schriftenr Gruene Reihe
Bundesarbeitsblatt — BNDSD
Bundesarbeitsblatt — Bundesarbeitsbl
Bundesbaublatt — BUBBA
Bundesblatt [*Switzerland*] — BB
Bundesforschungsanstalt fuer Ernaehrung. Berichte — Bundesforschungsanst Ernaehr Ber
Bundesforschungsanstalt fuer Fischerei. Institut fuer Kuesten- und Binnenfischerei. Veroeffentlichungen — Bundesforschungsanst Fisch Inst Kuesten Binnenfisch Veroeff
Bundesgesetzblatt fuer die Republik Oesterreich — BGROD
Bundesgesetzblatt fuer die Republik Oesterreich — Bundesgesetzbl Repub Oesterr
Bundesgesundheitsamt. Berichte — Bundesgesundheitsamt Ber
Bundesgesundheitsamt. BGA Schriften — Bundesgesundheitsamt BGA Schr
Bundesgesundheitsblatt — BDGHA
Bundesgesundheitsblatt [*Germany*] — Bundesges
Bundesministerium der Verteidigung. Forschungsbericht aus der Wehrmedizin — Bundesminister Verteidigung Forschungsber Wehrmed
Bundesministerium der Verteidigung. Forschungsbericht aus der Wehrtechnik — Bundesminister Verteidigung Forschungsber Wehrtech
Bundesministerium fuer Bildung und Wissenschaft. Forschungsbericht — Bundesminist Bild Wiss Forschungsber
Bundesministerium fuer Bildung und Wissenschaft. Forschungsbericht. Kernforschung — Bundesminist Bild Wiss Forschungsber Kernforsch
Bundesministerium fuer Forschung und Technologie. Forschungsbericht DV. Datenverarbeitung — Bundesminist Forsch Technol Forschungsber DV
Bundesministerium fuer Forschung und Technologie. Forschungsbericht. Humanisierung des Arbeitslebens — Bundesminist Forsch Technol Forschungsber Hum Arbeitslebens
Bundesministerium fuer Forschung und Technologie. Forschungsbericht K. Kernforschung — Bundesminist Forsch Technol Forschungsber K
Bundesministerium fuer Forschung und Technologie. Forschungsbericht M. Meeresforschung — Bundesminist Forsch Technol Forschungsber M
Bundesministerium fuer Forschung und Technologie. Forschungsbericht. Meeresforschung — Bundesminist Forsch Technol Forschungsber Meeresforsch
Bundesministerium fuer Forschung und Technologie. Forschungsbericht T. Technologische Forschung und Entwicklung — Bundesminist Forsch Technol Forschungsber T

Bundesministerium fuer Forschung und Technologie. Forschungsbericht W. Weltraumforschung — Bundesminist Forsch Technol Forschungsber W
Bundesministerium fuer Forschung und Technologie. Forschungsbericht W. Weltraumforschung — Bundesminist Forsch Technol Forschungsber Weltraumforsch
Bundesministerium fuer Forschung und Technologie. Mitteilungen — BFTMB
Bundesministerium fuer Wissenschaftliche Forschung. Forschungsbericht K 69-03. Kernforschung — Bundesminist Wiss Forsch Forschungsber K 69 03 Kernforsch
Bundesrat - Drucksache — BUNDD
Bundessteuerblatt — BS Bl
Bundesverfassung [*Switzerland*] — BV
Bundesversuchsinstitut fuer Kulturtechnik und Technische Bodenkunde — Bundes Vers Inst Kulturtech Tech Bodenk
Bundeszollblatt — BZ Bl
Bundner Monatsblatt. Zeitschrift fuer Bundnerische Geschichte, Heimat-und Volkskunde — B Mb
Bundnerisches Monatsblatt — BUNDMB
Bungaku — BG
Bungaku Ronshu [*Studies on Literature*] — BGRS
Bunko Kenkyu — BUKKA
Bunseki Kagaku — BNSKA
Bunseki Kagaku — Bunseki Kag
Bunsen-Gesellschaft fuer Physikalische Chemie. Berichte — Bunsen Ges Phys Chem Ber
Bunting and Lyon's Guide to Private Schools — Bunting Lyon
Burda-Marketing Info System [*Database*] — MADIS
Burdekin-Townsville Region, Queensland. Resource Series — Burdekin-Townsville Reg QD Resour Ser
Bureau de Recherches Geologiques et Minieres. Bulletin. Section 2. Geologie des Gites Mineraux (France) — Bur Rech Geol Min Bull Sect 2 Geol Gites Miner (Fr)
Bureau de Recherches Geologiques et Minieres. Documents (France) — Bur Rech Geol Min Doc (Fr)
Bureau de Recherches Geologiques et Minieres. Memoire (France) — Bur Rech Geol Min Mem Fr
Bureau et Informatique — Bur Inform
Bureau Farmer — Bur Farmer
Bureau for Inspecting and Testing Commercial Commodities (China). Bulletin — Bur Insp Test Commer Commod (China) Bull
Bureau of American Ethnology. Annual Report — Bur Am Ethnol Annual Report
Bureau of American Ethnology. Bulletin — Bur Am Ethn
Bureau of Corporate Affairs. Bulletin — Corp Bulletin
Bureau of Economic Geology. University of Texas at Austin. Mineral Resource Circular — Bur Econ Geol Univ Tex Austin Miner Resour Circ
Bureau of Land Management. Alaska. News Release — BLMNR
Bureau of Meteorology. Bulletin [*Australia*] — Met Bur Bull
Bureau of Meteorology. Meteorological Study [*Australia*] — Met Bur Met Study
Bureau of Meteorology. Meteorological Study [*Australia*] — Met Study Bur Met
Bureau of Meteorology. Meteorological Study [*Australia*] — Meteorol Stud Meteorol Bur
Bureau of Meteorology. Meteorological Summary [*Australia*] — Met Bur Met Summ
Bureau of Meteorology. Meteorological Summary [*Australia*] — Met Summary Met Bur
Bureau of Meteorology. Project Report [*Australia*] — Met Bur Proj Rep
Bureau of Meteorology. Working Paper [*Australia*] — Met Bur Working Paper
Bureau of Mineral Resources. 1:250,000 Geological Series [*Australia*] — Min Res Bur 1:250000 Geol Ser
Bureau of Mineral Resources. 1 Mile Geological Series [*Australia*] — Min Res Bur 1 Mile Geol Ser
Bureau of Mineral Resources. Bulletin [*Australia*] — Min Res Bur Bull
Bureau of Mineral Resources. Geological Map [*Australia*] — Min Res Bur Geol Map
Bureau of Mineral Resources, Geology, and Geophysics. Bulletin [*Canberra*] — AGGBA9
Bureau of Mineral Resources. Geology and Geophysics. Bulletin (Australia) — Bur Miner Resour Geol Geophys Bull (Aust)
Bureau of Mineral Resources, Geology, and Geophysics. Bulletin (Canberra) — Bur Miner Resour Geol Geophys Bull (Canberra)
Bureau of Mineral Resources, Geology, and Geophysics. Report [*Canberra*] — AGGRAN
Bureau of Mineral Resources. Geology and Geophysics. Report (Australia) — Bur Miner Resour Geol Geophys Rep (Aust)
Bureau of Mineral Resources, Geology, and Geophysics. Report (Canberra) — Bur Miner Resour Geol Geophys Rep (Canberra)
Bureau of Mineral Resources. Geophysical Observatory Report [*Australia*] — Min Res Bur Geophys Obs Rep
Bureau of Mineral Resources Journal of Australian Geology and Geophysics — Bur Miner Resour J Aust Geol Geophys
Bureau of Mineral Resources. Pamphlet [*Australia*] — Min Res Bur Pamph
Bureau of Mineral Resources. Petroleum Search Subsidy Acts. Publication [*Australia*] — Min Res Bur Petrol Search Pub
Bureau of Mineral Resources. Petroleum Search Subsidy Acts. Publication [*Australia*] [*A publication*] — Min Res Bur Petrol Search Publ
Bureau of Mineral Resources. Petroleum Search Subsidy Acts. Publication [*Australia*] — Min Res Bur Petrol Search Public
Bureau of Mineral Resources. Report [*Australia*] — Min Res Bur Rep
Bureau of Mineral Resources. Summary Report [*Australia*] — Min Res Bur Sum Rep
Bureau of Mines. Information Circular [*United States*] — Bur Mines Inf Circ
Bureau of Mines. Open File Report [*United States*] — XMOFA
Bureau of Mines Open File Report (United States) — Bur Mines Open File Rep US
Bureau of Mines. Report of Investigations [*United States*] — Bur Mines Rep Invest
Bureau of Mines. Research [*United States*] — BMRED
Bureau of Mines. Research [*Washington, DC*] — Bur Mines Res
Bureau of Mines. Technology News [*United States*] — Bur Mines Technol News
Bureau of Mines. Technology News [*United States*] — TNBMD
Bureau of Plant Industry Library. Current Author Entries — Bur Pl Industr Libr Curr Author Entries
Bureau of Standards (United States). Circular — Bur Stand (US) Cir
Bureau of Standards (United States). Miscellaneous Publication — Bur Stand US Misc Publ
Bureau of Standards (US). Bulletin — Bur Stand (US) Bull
Bureau of Standards (US). Scientific Papers — Bur Stand US Sci Pap
Bureau of Steel Manufacturers of Australia. Paper Presented at the Annual Meeting — Bureau of Steel Manuf
Bureau of Sugar Experiment Stations (Brisbane). Annual Report — Bur Sugar Exp Stn (Brisbane) Annu Rep
Bureau of Sugar Experiment Stations (Brisbane). Technical Communications — Bur Sugar Exp Stn (Brisbane) Tech Commun
Bureau of Sugar Experiment Stations. Queensland Technical Communications — Bur Sugar Exp St Queensl Tech Commun
Bureau of Veterinary Medicine. Technical Report FDA/BVM (US Food and Drug Administration) — Bur Vet Med Tech Rep FDA BVM US Food Drug Adm
Bureaucrat — BUR
Burenie i Ispytanie Neftyanykh i Gazovykh Skvazhin v Oslozhennykh Usloviyakh Uzbekistana — Buren Ispyt Neft Gazov Skvazhin Oslozhennykh Usloviyakh Uzb
Burg Monographs in Science [*Basel*] — Burg Monographs in Sci
Burgenlaendische Bienenzucht — Burgenlaend Bienenzucht
Burgenlaendische Heimatblaetter — BGLD Hb
Burgenlaendische Heimatblaetter — BHb
Burgenlaendische Heimatblaetter — Burg Hbl
Burgenlaendische Heimatblaetter — Burgenl Heim Bl
Burgenlaendische Heimatblaetter — Burgenl Heimatbl
Burgenlaendische Heimatblaetter — BurgHb
Burger's Medicinal Chemistry — Burgers Med Chem
Buridava Studii si Materiale — Buridava
Burke's Newsletter — BN
Burlington Magazine — BM
Burlington Magazine — Burl M
Burlington Magazine — Burl Mag
Burlington Magazine — Burlington Mag
Burma Forest Bulletin — Burma For Bull
Burma Medical Journal — BMDJA
Burma Medical Journal — Burma Med J
Burma Weekly Bulletin — BWB
Burning River News — Bur River
Burns Chronicle — Burns Chron
Burns, Including Thermal Injury — Burns Incl Therm Inj
Burns' Indiana Statutes, Annotated Code Edition — Ind Code Ann (Burns)
Buro und EDV. Zeitschrift fuer Buroorganisation und Datentechnik — RBU
Burrelle's Hispanic Media Directory — Burrell
Burroughs Clearing House — Burroughs Clear House
Burschenschaftliche Blaetter — Burschensch Bll
Bursians Jahresbericht ueber die Fortschritte der Klassischen Altertumswissenschaft — Bursian
Bursians Jahresbericht ueber die Fortschritte der Klassischen Altertumswissenschaft — Jahresb Fortschr Altertswiss
Bursians Jahresbericht ueber die Fortschritte der Klassischen Altertumswissenschaft — JB
Bursians Jahresbericht ueber die Fortschritte der Klassischen Altertumswissenschaft — JFAW
Bus and Track Transport — Bus Track Trans
Bus Transportation — Bus Transp
Busan Women's University. Journal [*South Korea*] — Busan Women's Univ J
Busan Women's University. Journal — BWUJD
Business [*Formerly, Atlanta Economic Review*] — AEC
Business Abroad — Bsns Abroad
Business Administration — BA
Business Administration — Bus Adm
Business Administration [*England*] — BUSAB
Business Administration (Great Britain) — Bus Admin (Great Britain)
Business America — BAM
Business America — BUAMD
Business America — Bus Am
Business America — COR
Business America — GBAM
Business and Economic Dimensions [*Florida*] — Bus and Econ Dim
Business and Economic Dimensions — Bus and Econ Dimensions
Business and Economic Perspectives — Bus and Econ Perspectives
Business and Economic Review — BER
Business and Economic Review (University of South Carolina) — Bus and Econ R (Univ SC)
Business and Finance — BNC
Business and Finance (Ireland) — Bus and Fin (Ireland)
Business and Finance (Ireland) — Irish Bus
Business and Health — Bus Health
Business and Industry Taiwan — Bus Taiwan
Business and Law Review [*Database*] — BLR
Business and Professional Ethics Journal — Bus Prof Ethics J
Business and Professional Ethics Journal — IBPE
Business and Public Affairs — Bus and Public Affairs
Business and Society — BAS
Business and Society — BSS
Business and Society — Bus & Scty

Business and Society — Bus and Society
Business and Society — Bus Soc
Business and Society Review — BUS
Business and Society Review — Bus & Scty R
Business and Society Review — Bus & Soc
Business and Society Review — Bus & Soc R
Business and Society Review — Bus and Society R
Business and Society Review — Bus and Socy Rev
Business and Society Review — Bus Soc Rev
Business and Society Review — Busin Soc R
Business and Technology Sources — Bsns & Tech Sources
Business and Tcchnology Videolog — Bus Tech Video
Business and the Media — Bus Media
Business and Trade — Bus Trade
Business Archives and History — BAH
Business Archives and History — Bus Arch & Hist
Business Archives and History — Bus Archs Hist
Business Archives Council of Australia. Bulletin — Bull Bus Archs Coun Aust
Business Archives Council of Australia. Bulletin — Bus Archives Council Aust Bul
Business Archives Council of Australia. New South Wales Branch. Bulletin — Bus Arch Cncl Aust Bull
Business Archives Council of Australia. Publications — Bus Archives Council Aust Pub
Business Asia — Bus Asia
Business Asia. Weekly Report to Managers of Asia/Pacific Operations — BNV
Business Atlanta — Bsn Atlant
Business Automation — B Automatn
Business Automation — Bsns Automation
Business Automation — Business Automn
Business Barometer of Central Florida — Bus Barometer
Business Briefing — Bus Brief
Business China — BCF
Business China — Bus China
Business Communications Review — BCR
Business Communications Review — Bus Comm
Business Computer Systems — BCS
Business Computer Systems — Bus Comp Sys
Business Computing and Communications — Bus Comput Commun
Business Conditions Digest — BCD
Business Conditions Digest — BFM
Business Conditions Digest — Bus Cond Dig
Business Conditions Digest — Bus Conditions Dig
Business Eastern Europe — BDO
Business Eastern Europe — Bus E Eur
Business Economics — BEC
Business Economics — Bus Econ
Business Economics — Busin Econ
Business Economics and Finance Series — Bus Econ Fin Ser
Business Economist — BE
Business Economist — Bus Economist
Business Economist — Busin Economist
Business Education Association of Metropolitan New York. Journal — BEA J
Business Education Council. Newsletter — Bus Ed News
Business Education Forum — Bsns Ed Forum
Business Education Forum — Bus Ed Forum
Business Education Forum — Bus Educ Forum
Business Education Index — Bus Educ Ind
Business Education Index — Bus Educ Index
Business Education Journal — BEJ
Business Education Journal — Bus Ed J
Business Education World — Bsns Ed World
Business Education World — Bus Ed World
Business Equipment Digest — Business Equip Dig
Business Europe — Bus Europe
Business Europe. A Weekly Report to Managers. Europe, Middle-East, and Africa — BDZ
Business Exchange — Bus Exch
Business Finance Review — Bus Fin Rev
Business Forms Reporter — Bus Form Rep
Business Forum — BFO
Business Forum — Bus Forum
Business Franchise Guide. Commerce Clearing House — Bus Franchise Guide CCH
Business Graduate — Bus Grad
Business History — BH
Business History — BHI
Business History — Bus Hist
Business History — Bus History
Business History — Business Hist
Business History Review — BHR
Business History Review — BHV
Business History Review — Bsns Hist R
Business History Review — Bus Hist R
Business History Review — Bus Hist Rev
Business History Review — Business Hist Rev
Business History Society. Bulletin — Bus Hist Soc Bull
Business Horizons — B Hor
Business Horizons — BHO
Business Horizons — BHZ
Business Horizons — Bus Horiz
Business Horizons — Bus Horizn
Business Horizons — Bus Horizons
Business in Brief — Bus in Brief
Business in Thailand — BHC
Business Index — BI
Business India — BUIND
Business India — Bus India
Business Information — Bus Inf
Business Information Desk Reference — BIRD
Business Information Technology — Bus Inf Technol
Business Insurance — BI
Business Insurance — Binsurance
Business Insurance — BIS
Business Insurance — Bus Insur
Business Insurance — Business Insur
Business International — Bus Intnl
Business International — BUT
Business International Index — BII
Business International Index — Bus Int Ind
Business International. Money Report — Bus Int Mo
Business Japan — BJP
Business Japan — BUJ
Business Japan — Bus Ja
Business Japan — Bus Jap
Business Japan — Bus Japan
Business Japan — Bus Jpn
Business Journal (Manila) — Bus J (Manila)
Business Journal of New Jersey — Bus Jrl NJ
Business Journal (Philadelphia) — (Phil) Busn
Business Journal (Philippines) — Phil Jrl
Business Journal (San Jose, California) — Bus J (San Jose)
Business Latin America — BLA
Business Latin America — Bus Latin A
Business Law Cases for Australia [*Commerce Clearing House*] — ABL
Business Law Memo — Bus Law Memo
Business Law Reports — BLR
Business Law Review — BLR
Business Law Review — Bus L Rev
Business Law Review — Bus Law R
Business Law Review — Bus LR
Business Law Review — Business LR
Business Law Review (Butterworths) — Bus L Rev (Butterworths)
Business Laws of Oman — Bus Laws Oman
Business Lawyer — BL
Business Lawyer — BLW
Business Lawyer — Bus L
Business Lawyer — Bus Law
Business Lawyer — Bus Lawyer
Business Lawyer. Special Issue — BLS
Business Librarian — BULID
Business Life [*Canada*] — BUSL
Business Literature — Bsns Lit
Business Literature — Bus Lit
Business Location File — Bus Loc File
Business Magazine — Bus Mag
Business Management — Bsns Mgt
Business Management (London) — Bsns Mgt (London)
Business Marketing — Bus Mark
Business Marketing — Bus Mktg
Business Matters — Bus Matters
Business Memo from Belgium — Belg Memo
Business Mexico — Bus Mexico
Business Monitor. Monthly Statistics — BM
Business Monitor. Rubber — Busin Monitor Rubb
Business Monitor. Synthetic Resins and Plastics Materials — Busin Monitor Synth
Business Month — BM
Business News. Facts, Analysis, Information — BNJ
Business North [*Canada*] — BUSN
Business North Carolina — Busines NC
Business Organizations and Agencies Directory — Business Org Agen Dir
Business Overseas — Bus Overseas
Business Owner — BOR
Business Owner — BSO
Business Periodicals Index — BPI
Business Periodicals Index — Bus Period Index
Business Periodicals Index — BusI
Business Periodicals Ondisc [*Database*] — BPO
Business Press of Orange County — Orange Cty
Business Printer — Bus Print
Business Publications Index and Abstracts — Bus Pub Ind Abst
Business Publisher — Bus Publ
Business Quarterly — BQU
Business Quarterly [*Canada*] — BSQ
Business Quarterly — Bus Q
Business Quarterly — Business Q
Business Radio Buyers' Guide — Bus Radio Buy G
Business Record — Bsn Record
Business Review — BR
Business Review [*Australia*] — BRW
Business Review — Bsns Revw
Business Review — Bus Rev
Business Review — Busin R
Business Review — Business R
Business Review — Business Rev
Business Review (Bangkok) — BBK
Business Review (Bangkok) — Bus R (Bangkok)
Business Review. Federal Reserve Bank of Philadelphia — FRB
Business Review. Kobe University — Bus Rev Kobe Univ

Business Review (Montreal) — B (Montreal)
Business Review (Thailand) — (Thai) Bus R
Business Review. University of Washington — BRVWA
Business Review. Washington University — Bus Rev Wash Univ
Business Review Weekly — BR
Business Review Weekly — BRW
Business Review Weekly [*Financial Review Information Service*] [*Information service or system*] — BRWE
Business Review. Wells Fargo Bank — BWF
Business SA [*South Africa*] — BSSAD
Business Science Experts [*Database*] — WEX
Business Scotland — Bus Scotland
Business Screen — Bus Scr
Business Service Checklist — BSCL
Business Software Database — BSD
Business Software Review — Bus Software Rev
Business Statistics. US Department of Commerce — Bus Stat
Business Systems — Bus Syst
Business Systems and Equipment — BS
Business Systems and Equipment — BSEQA
Business Systems and Equipment — Bus Syst & Equip
Business Systems Update — Bus Syst Update
Business Teachers Association of New York State. Journal — BTA J
Business. The Magazine of Managerial Thought and Action — ATX
Business Times — Busn Times
Business Times. An Economic and Business Review — BTS
Business Today — Bus Today
Business Traveler — Bus Trav
Business Traveler International — BTI
Business Traveler's Report — Bus Trav Rep
Business Trends. A Concise and Systematic Weekly Report to Management on the Argentine Economy — BTR
Business Trends Survey — Bus Tr Surv
Business Unix Journal — Bus Unix Jnl
Business Update — Bus Update
Business Venezuela — Bus Venezuela
Business Venezuela — BWA
Business Venture Profiles [*Database*] — BVP
Business View of Southwest Florida — Bsn SW Fla
Business Week — Bsns W
Business Week — Bus W
Business Week — Bus Week
Business Week — BUW
Business Week — BUWEA
Business Week — BW
Business Week — BWE
Business Week. Industrial/Technology Edition — Bus Week Ind Technol Ed
Business Worcester — Bs Worcstr
Business World — Bsns W
Businessman's Law — Bus Law
Bussei — BUSIB
Bussei Kenkyu — BUSKB
Busseiron Kenkyu — BUKEA
Busushchee Nauki — BDNKA
Butane Propane — BUTPA
Butler University Botanical Studies — Butler Univ Bot Stud
Butler's Money Fund Report — Butler
Butlleti. Associacio Catalana d'Antropologia, Etnologia, i Prehistoria — BACAEP
Butlleti de la Seccio de Matematiques — Butl Sec Mat
Butlleti de la Societat Catalana de Matematiques — Butl Soc Catalana Mat
Butlleti. Institucio Catalana d'Historia Natural — Butl Inst Catalana Hist Nat
Butlleti. Seccio de Matematiques. Societat Catalana de Ciencies Fisiques, Quimiques, i Matematiques — Butl Sec Mat Soc Catalana Cienc Fis Quim Mat
Butlleti. Societat Catalana de Ciencies Fisiques, Quimiques, i Matematiques. Segona Epoca — Butl Soc Catalana Cienc Fis Quim Mat 2
Butsuri. Physical Society of Japan — Butsuri Phys Soc Jap
Butter and Cheese Journal — Butter & Cheese J
Butter, Cheese, and Milk Products Journal — Butter Cheese Milk Prod J
Butterworth-Heinemann International Medical Reviews. Neurology — Butterworth Heinemann Int Med Rev Neurol
Butterworth-Heinemann Series in Chemical Engineering — Butterworth Heinemann Ser Chem Engrg
Butterworths International Medical Reviews. Cardiology — BMRCDL
Butterworths International Medical Reviews. Cardiology — Butterworths Int Med Rev Cardiol
Butterworths International Medical Reviews. Clinical Endocrinology — Butterworths Int Med Rev Clin Endocrinol
Butterworths International Medical Reviews. Clinical Endocrinology — CLEYDQ
Butterworths International Medical Reviews. Clinical Pharmacology and Therapeutics — Butterworths Int Med Rev Clin Pharmacol Ther
Butterworths International Medical Reviews. Clinical Pharmacology and Therapeutics — CPTHDA
Butterworths International Medical Reviews. Gastroenterology — Butterworths Int Med Rev Gastroenterol
Butterworths International Medical Reviews. Gastroenterology — GASTDE
Butterworths International Medical Reviews. Hematology — BIMHEI
Butterworths International Medical Reviews. Hematology — Butterworths Int Med Rev Hematol
Butterworths International Medical Reviews. Neurology — BMRNDK
Butterworths International Medical Reviews. Neurology — Butterworths Int Med Rev Neurol
Butterworths International Medical Reviews. Obstetrics and Gynecology — BMRODN
Butterworths International Medical Reviews. Obstetrics and Gynecology — Butterworths Int Med Rev Obstet Gynecol
Butterworths International Medical Reviews. Ophthalmology — BMOPDB
Butterworths International Medical Reviews. Ophthalmology — Butterworths Int Med Rev Ophthalmol
Butterworths International Medical Reviews. Orthopaedics — BMORDH
Butterworths International Medical Reviews. Orthopaedics — Butterworths Int Med Rev Orthop
Butterworths International Medical Reviews. Otolaryngology — BIRODT
Butterworths International Medical Reviews. Otolaryngology — Butterworths Int Med Rev Otolaryngol
Butterworths International Medical Reviews. Pediatrics — Butterworths Int Med Rev Pediatr
Butterworths International Medical Reviews. Rheumatology — Butterworths Int Med Rev Rheumatol
Butterworths International Medical Reviews. Surgery — Butterworths Int Med Rev Surg
Butterworths International Medical Reviews. Urology — Butterworths Int Med Rev Urol
Butterworth's Property Reports — BPR
Buvoha Mededelingen — BVM
Buying for the Farm — Buy Farm
Buzzworm. The Environmental Journal — PBUZ
Bwletin Cymdeithas Emynau Cymru — BCEC
BWPA [*British Wood Preserving Association*] **News Sheet** — BWPA News Sheet
By og Bygd. Norsk Folkemuseums Arbok — BOB
Bydgoskie Towarzystwo Naukowe. Prace Wydzialu Nauk Technicznych. Seria A — Bydgoskie Tow Nauk Pr Wydz Nauk Tech Ser A
Bydgoskie Towarzystwo Naukowe. Wydzial Nauk Przyrodniczych. Prace. Seria A — Bydgoskie Tow Nauk Wydz Nauk Przyr Pr Ser A
Bydgoskie Towarzystwo Naukowe. Wydzial Nauk Przyrodniczych. Prace. Seria B — Bydgoskie Tow Nauk Wydz Nauk Przyr Pr Ser B
Bydgoskie Towarzystwo Naukowe Wydzial Nauk Technicznych. Prace. Seria B — Bydgoskie Tow Nauk Wydz Nauk Tech Pr Ser B
Bydgoszcz. Whzsza Szkola Pedagogiczna. Zeszyty Naukowe. Problemy Matematyczne — Problemy Mat
Bygge Forum — Byg F
Byggmestern — BYGEA
Byggvaruregistret [*Database*] — BVR
Bygmesteren — Bygm
Bygningsstatiske Meddelelser — Bygnin Medd
Bygningsstatiske Meddelelser — BYMEA
Bylgarski Plodove Zelenchutsi i Konservi — Bylg Plodove Zelenchutsi Konserv
Byrd Polar Research Center — BPRCCS
Byron Journal — Byron J
Byte — BYT
BYTE Information Exchange [*Database*] — BIX
BYTE. The Small Systems Journal. Special IBM Issue — BYTE Spcl
BYU [*Brigham Young University*] **Law Review** — BYU
Byuleten Brashovskogo Universiteta. Seriya C — Byul Brashovskogo Univ Ser C
Byuletin. Institut po Stuklo i Fina Keramika — Byul Inst Stuklo Fina Keram
Byulleten' Abastumanskaya Astrofizicheskaya Observatoriya Akademiya Nauk Gruzinskoi SSR [*Georgian SSR*] — Byull Abastumanskaya Astrofiz Obs Akad Nauk Gruz SSR
Byulleten' Akademii Nauk Uzbekskoi SSR — Byull Akad Nauk Uzb SSR
Byulleten' Akademiya Nauk Gruzinskoi SSR Abastumanskaya Astrofizicheskaya Observatoriya [*Georgian SSR*] — Byull Akad Nauk Gruz SSR Abastumanskaya Astrofiz Obs
Byulleten' Astronomicheskikh Institutov Chekhoslovakii — Byull Astron Inst Chekh
Byulleten' Azerbaidzhanskogo Nauchno Issledovatel'skogo Instituta Khlopkovodstva — Byull Azerb Nauchno Issled Inst Khlopkovod
Byulleten' Belogo Morya — Byull Belogo Morya
Byulleten' Botanicheskogo Sada Akademii Nauk Armyanskoi SSR — Byull Bot Sada Akad Nauk Arm SSR
Byulleten' Botanicheskogo Sada Erevan — Byull Bot Sada Erevan
Byulleten' Eksperimental'noi Biologii i Meditsiny — BEBMA
Byulleten' Eksperimental'noi Biologii i Meditsiny — Byull Eksp Biol Med
Byulleten Gipromeza — Byull Gipromeza
Byulleten'. Glavno Upravlenie na Stroitelnite Voiski (Sofia) — Byul Gl Upr Stroit Voiski (Sofia)
Byulleten' Glavnogo Botanicheskogo Sada [*Leningrad*] — Byull Gl Bot Sada
Byulleten Glavnogo Botanicheskogo Sada — Byull Glav Bot Sada
Byulleten' Glavnogo Botanicheskogo Sada (Leningrad) — Byull Glavn Bot Sada (Leningr)
Byulleten Gosplana — Byull Gosplana
Byulleten' Gosudarstvennogo Nikitskogo Botanicheskogo Sada — Byull Gos Nikitsk Bot Sada
Byulleten. Gosudarstvennyi Makeevskii Nauchno-Issledovatel'skii Institut po Bezopasnosti Rabot v Gornoi Promyshlennosti — Byull Gos Makeev Nauchno Issled Inst Bezop Rab Gorn Promsti
Byulleten' Informatsii Tsentralnoi Geneticheskoi Laboratorii Imeni I. V. Michurina — Byull Inf Tsentr Genet Lab Im I V Michurina
Byulleten' Informatsionnogo Tsentral'nogo po Yadernym Dannym — BITYA
Byulleten' Informatsionnogo Tsentral'nogo po Yadernym Dannym — Byull Inf Tsentra Yad Dannym
Byulleten' Instituta Astrofiziki Akademiya Nauk Tadzhikskoi SSR — Byull Inst Astrofiz Akad Nauk Tadzh
Byulleten' Instituta Astrofiziki Akademiya Nauk Tadzhikskoi SSR — Byull Inst Astrofiz Akad Nauk Tadzh SSR
Byulleten Instituta Biologii Akademiya Nauk Belorusskoi SSR — Byull Inst Biol Akad Nauk Beloruss SSR
Byulleten Instituta Biologii Vodokhranilishch. Akademiya Nauk SSSR — Byull Inst Biol Vodokhran Akad Nauk SSSR
Byulleten' Instituta Biologii Vodokhranilishcha — Byull Inst Biol Vodokhran

Byulleten' Instituta Biologiya Akademii Nauk Belorusskoi SSR — Byull Inst Biol Akad Nauk B SSR
Byulleten' Instituta Metallokeramiki i Spetsial'nykh Splavov Akademiya Nauk Ukrainskoi SSR — Byull Inst Metallokeram Spets Splavov Akad Nauk Ukr SSR
Byulleten Instituta Morskoi i Tropicheskoi Meditsiny v Gdyne — Byull Inst Morsk Trop Med Gdyne
Byulleten' Instituta Teoreticheskoi Astronomii [*Former USSR*] — Byull Inst Teor Astron
Byulleten' Instituta Teoreticheskoi Astronomii Akademiya Nauk SSSR — Byull Inst Teor Astron Akad Nauk SSSR
Byulleten Izobretenii — Byull Izobret
Byulleten' Izobretenii — BYZOA
Byulleten Izobretenii i Tovarnykh Znakov — Byull Izobret Tovarnykh Znakov
Byulleten' Kavkazskogo Instituta Mineral'nogo Syr'ya — Byull Kavk Inst Miner Syrya
Byulleten' Kirgizskogo Nauchno-Issledovatel'skogo Instituta Zemledeliya — Byull Kirg Nauchno Issled Inst Zemled
Byulleten' Kirgizskogo Nauchno-Issledovatel'skogo Instituta Zemledeliya — Byull Kirgiz Nauch Issled Inst Zemled
Byulleten' Kirgizskogo Nauchno-Issledovatel'skogo Instituta Zemledeliya — Byull Kirgiz Nauchno-Issled Inst Zeml
Byulleten' Komissii po Izucheniyu Chetvertichnogo Perioda Akademiya Nauk SSSR — Byull Kom Izuch Chetvertichn Perioda Akad Nauk SSSR
Byulleten' Komissii po Kometam i Meteoram Astronomicheskogo Sovieta Akademii Nauk SSSR — Byull Kom Kometam Meteoram Astron Sov Akad Nauk SSSR
Byulleten' Komissii po Opredeleniyu Absolyutnogo Vozrasta Geologicheskikh Formatsii — BKOAA
Byulleten' Komissii po Opredeleniyu Absolyutnogo Vozrasta Geologicheskikh Formatsii [*Former USSR*] — Byull Kom Opred Absol Geol Form
Byulleten' Komissii po Opredeleniyu Absolyutnogo Vozrasta Geologicheskikh Formatsii Akademiya Nauk SSSR — Byull Kom Opred Absol Vozrasta Geol Form Akad Nauk SSSR
Byulleten. Kraevoi Dermato-Venerologicheskii Institut Kazakhstana — Byull Kraev Derm Venerol Inst Kaz
Byulleten' Leningradskii Institut Organizatsii i Okhrany Truda — Byull Leningr Inst Organ Okhr Tr
Byulleten' Leningradskogo Otdeleniya Institut Udobrenii i Agropochvovedeniya — Byull Leningr Otd Inst Udobr Agropochvoved
Byulleten' Mezhdunarodnogo Obshchestva po Torfu — Byull Mezhdunar O-Va Torfu
Byulleten' Mezhdunarodnykh Agenstv Atomnoi Energii — BMAAA
Byulleten' Moskovskogo Obshchestva Ispytatelei Prirody Kalininskii Otdel — Byull Mosk Ova Ispyt Prir Kalinin Otd
Byulleten' Moskovskogo Obshchestva Ispytatelei Prirody Otdel Biologicheskii — BYMOA
Byulleten' Moskovskogo Obshchestva Ispytatelei Prirody Otdel Biologicheskii — Byull Mosk Obshch Ispyt Prir
Byulleten' Moskovskogo Obshchestva Ispytatelei Prirody Otdel Biologicheskii — Byull Mosk Ova Ispyt Prir Otd Biol
Byulleten' Moskovskogo Obshchestva Ispytatelei Prirody Otdel Geologicheskii — BMPGA
Byulleten' Moskovskogo Obshchestva Ispytatelei Prirody Otdel Geologicheskii — Byull Mosk Ova Ispyt Prir Otd Geol
Byulleten Moskovskoho Obshchestva Ispytatelei Prirody. Otdel Biologicheskii — Byull Mosk Obshch Isp Prir Otd Biol
Byulleten' Nauchno Issledovatel'skogo Instituta Malyarii i Meditsinskoi Parazitologii — Byull Nauchno Issled Inst Malyarii Med Parazitol
Byulleten' Nauchno Issledovatel'skogo Khimiko Farmatsevticheskogo Instituta — Byull Nauchno Issled Khim Farm Inst
Byulleten Nauchnogo Avtomotornogo Instituta — Byull Nauchn Avtomot Inst
Byulleten' Nauchnogo Studencheskogo Obshchestva Kazakhskii Gosudarstvennyi Universitet — Byull Nauchn Stud Ova Kaz Gos Univ
Byulleten Nauchno-Issledovatel'skogo Instituta Chainoi Promyshlennosti — Byull Nauchno Issled Inst Chain Promsti
Byulleten' Nauchno-Issledovatel'skogo Instituta Malyarii i Meditsinskoi Parazitologii — Byull Nauch-Issled Inst Malyarii Med Parazitol
Byulleten Nauchno-Issledovatel'skogo Instituta po Khlopkovodstvu — Byull Nauchno Issled Inst Khlopkovod
Byulleten' Nauchno-Tekhnicheskogo Soveta po Metallurgii Legkikh Metallov — Byull Nauchno Tekh Sov Metall Legk Met
Byulleten' Nauchno-Tekhnicheskogo Soveta po Metallurgii Tyazhilykh Tsvetnykh Metallov [*Poland*] — Byull Nauchno-Tekh Sov Metall Tyazh Tsvetn Met
Byulleten' Nauchno-Tekhnicheskogo Soveta po Obogashcheniyu Rud Tsvetnykh Metallov [*Romania*] — Byull Nauchno-Tekh Sov Obogashch Rud Tsvetn Met
Byulleten' Nauchno-Tekhnicheskogo Soveta po Obrabotke Tsvetnykh Metallov i Vtorichnoi Metallurgii [*Czechoslovakia*] — Byull Nauchno-Tekh Sov Obrab Tsvetn Met Vtorichnoi Metall
Byulleten' Nauchno-Tekhnicheskoi Informatsii — Byull Nauchno-Tekh Inf
Byulleten' Nauchno-Tekhnicheskoi Informatsii Armyanskogo Nauchno-Issledovatel'skogo Instituta Zemledeliya — Byull Nauchno Tekh Inf Arm Nauchno Issled Inst Zemled
Byulleten' Nauchno-Tekhnicheskoi Informatsii Belorusskogo Nauchno-Issledovatel'skogo Instituta Zemledeliya — Byull Nauchno Tekh Inf Beloruss Nauchno Issled Inst Zemled
Byulleten' Nauchno-Tekhnicheskoi Informatsii Gosudarstvennyi Geologicheskii Komitet SSSR — Byull Nauchno Tekh Inf Gos Geol Kom SSSR
Byulleten' Nauchno-Tekhnicheskoi Informatsii Litovskogo Nauchno-Issledovatel'skogo Instituta Zhivotnovodstva — Byull Nauchno Tekh Inf Litov Nauchno Issled Inst Zhivotnovod
Byulleten' Nauchno-Tekhnicheskoi Informatsii Ministerstvo Geologii i Okhrany Nedr SSSR — Byull Nauchno Tekh Inf Minist Geol Okhr Nedr SSSR
Byulleten' Nauchno-Tekhnicheskoi Informatsii Ministerstvo Geologii SSSR — Byull Nauchno Tekh Inf Minist Geol SSSR
Byulleten' Nauchno-Tekhnicheskoi Informatsii Nauchno-Issledovatel'skogo Instituta Pchelovodstva — Byull Nauchno Tekh Inf Inst
Byulleten Nauchno-Tekhnicheskoi Informatsii ONTI VIEMS — Byull Nauchno Tekh Inf ONTI VIEMS
Byulleten' Nauchno-Tekhnicheskoi Informatsii po Agronomicheskoi Fizike — Byull Nauchno-Tekh Inf Agron Fiz
Byulleten' Nauchno-Tekhnicheskoi Informatsii po Maslichnym Kulturam — Byull Nauchno Tekh Inf Maslichn Kult
Byulleten' Nauchno-Tekhnicheskoi Informatsii po Sel'skokhozyaistvennoi Mikrobiologii — Byull Nauchno-Tekh Inf S-Kh Mikrobiol
Byulleten Nauchno-Tekhnicheskoi Informatsii Sibirskogo Nauchno-Issledovatel'skogo Instituta Zhivotnovodstva — Byull Nauchno Tekh Inf Sib Nauchno Issled Inst Zhivotnovod
Byulleten' Nauchno-Tekhnicheskoi Informatsii (Sumskaya Gosudarstvennaya Sel'skokhozyaistvennaya Opytnaya Stantsiya) — Byull Nauchno-Tekh Inf (Sumskaya Gos Skh Opytn Stn)
Byulleten' Nauchno-Tekhnicheskoi Informatsii Tadzhikskogo Nauchno-Issledovatel'skogo Instituta Sel'skogo Khozyaistva — Byull Nauchno Tekh Inf Tadzh Nauchno Issled Inst Sel'sk Khoz
Byulleten' Nauchno-Tekhnicheskoi Informatsii Tsentralnoi Torfobolotnoi Opytnoi Stantsii — Byull Nauchno Tekh Inf Tsentr Torfobolotnoi Opytn Stant
Byulleten' Nauchno-Tekhnicheskoi Informatsii Turkmenskogo Nauchno-Issledovatel'skogo Instituta Zemledeliya — Byull Nauchno Tekh Inf Turkm Nauchno Issled Inst Zemled
Byulleten' Nauchno-Tekhnicheskoi Informatsii Ukrainskii Nauchno-Issledovatel'skii Institut Metallov — Byull Nauchno Tekh Inf Ukr Nauchno Issled Inst Met
Byulleten Nauchno-Tekhnicheskoi Informatsii. Ukrainskii Nauchno-Issledovatel'skii Trubnyi Institut — Byull Nauchno Tekh Inf Ukr Nauchno Issled Trubn Inst
Byulleten' Nauchno-Tekhnicheskoi Informatsii Ukrainskii Nauchno-Issledovatel'skii Uglekhimicheskii Institut — Byull Nauchno Tekh Inf Ukr Nauchno Issled Uglekhim Inst
Byulleten' Nauchno-Tekhnicheskoi Informatsii Ukrainskogo Nauchno-Issledovatel'skogo Instituta Ogneuporov — Byull Nauchno Tekh Inf Ukr Nauchno Issled Inst Ogneuporov
Byulleten' Nauchno-Tekhnicheskoi Informatsii Ural'skogo Nauchno-Issledovatel'skogo Instituta Chernykh Metallov — Byull Nauchno Tekh Inf Ural Nauchno Issled Inst Chern Met
Byulleten Nauchno-Tekhnicheskoi Informatsii Vsesoyuznogo Instituta Gel'mintologi — Byull Nauchno Tekh Inf Vses Inst Gelmintol
Byulleten' Nauchno-Tekhnicheskoi Informatsii Vsesoyuznogo Nauchno-Issledovatel'skogo Instituta Ogneuporov — Byull Nauchno Tekh Inf Vses Nauchno Issled Inst Ogneuporov
Byulleten Nauchno-Tekhnicheskoi Informatsii Vsesoyuznyi Nauchno-Issledovatel'sk ii Trubnyi Institut — Byull Nauchno Tekh Inf Vses Nauchno Issled Trub Inst
Byulleten' Naukovoi Informatsii po Zemlerobstvu — Byul Nauk Inf Zemlerob
Byulleten NIKhFI — Byull NIKhFI
Byulleten' Obmena Opytom Lakokrasochnoi Promyshlennosti — Byull Obmena Opytom Lakokras Promsti
Byulleten' Obshchestva Estestvoispytatelei pri Voronezhskom Gosudarstvennom Universitete — Byull Ova Estestvoispyt Voronezh Gos Univ
Byulleten' po Fiziologii Rastenii — Byull Fiziol Rast
Byulleten' po Ovoshchevodstvu — Byull Ovoshchevod
Byulleten Pochvennogo Instituta imeni V.V. Dokuchaeva — Byull Poch Inst im V V Dokuchaeva
Byulleten' Pochvoveda — Byull Pochvoveda
Byulleten' Sakharotresta — Byull Sakharotresta
Byulleten' Sovet po Seismologii — BSSIA
Byulleten' Sovet po Seismologii [*Former USSR*] — Byull Sov Seismol
Byulleten' Sovetskoi Antarkticheskoi Ekspeditsii — BUSEB
Byulleten' Sovetskoi Antarkticheskoi Ekspeditsii [*Former USSR*] — Byull Sov Antarkt Eksped
Byulleten' Sredneaziatskogo Gosudarstvennogo Universiteta — Byull Sredneaziat Gos Univ
Byulleten Sredneaziatskogo Nauchno-Issledovatel'skogo Instituta po Khlopkovodstvu — Byull Sredneaziat Nauchno Issled Inst Khlopkovod
Byulleten' Stantsii Opticheskogo Nablyudeniya Iskusstvennykh Sputnikov Zemli — BSONA
Byulleten' Stantsii Opticheskogo Nablyudeniya Iskusstvennykh Sputnikov Zemli [*Former USSR*] — Byull Stn Opt Nablyudeniya Iskusstvennykh Sputnikov Zemli
Byulleten' Stroitel'noi Tekhniki — BYSTA
Byulleten' Stroitel'noi Tekhniki [*Former USSR*] — Byull Stroit Tekh
Byulleten' Studencheskogo Nauchnogo Obshchestva Kazakhskii Gosudarstvennyi Universitet — Byull Stud Nauchn Ova Kaz Gos Univ
Byulleten' Studencheskogo Nauchnogo Obshchestva Leningradskii Gosudarstvennyi Universitet — Byull Stud Nauchn Ova Leningr Gos Univ
Byulleten' Tekhnicheskoi Informatsii po Stroitel'stvu — Byull Tekh Inf Stroit
Byulleten' Tekhnicheskoi Informatsii Sovet Narodnogo Khozyaistva Kurskogo Ekonomicheskogo Administrativnogo Raiona — Byull Tekh Inf Sov Nar Khoz Kursk Ekon Adm Raiona
Byulleten' Tekhniko-Ehkonomicheskoj Informatsii. Gosudarstvennyj Nauchno-Issledovatel'skij Institut Nauchnoj i Tekhnicheskoj Informatsii — Byull Tekh-Ehkon Inf Gos Nauchno-Issled Inst Nauchn Tekh Inf
Byulleten' Tekhniko-Ekonomicheskoi Informatsii — BTEKA
Byulleten' Tekhniko-Ekonomicheskoi Informatsii — Byull Tekh Ekon Inf
Byulleten' Tekhniko-Ekonomicheskoi Informatsii Gosudarstvennyi Nauchno-Issledovatel'skii Institut Nauchnoi i Tekhnicheskoi Informatsii [*Former USSR*] — Byull Tekh-Ekon Inf Gos Nauchno-Issled Inst Nauchn Tekh Inf
Byulleten Tekhniko-Ekonomicheskoi Informatsii. Ministerstvo Morskogo Flota — Byull Tekh Ekon Inf Minist Morsk Flota

Byulleten' Tekhniko-Ekonomicheskoi Informatsii Morskogo Flota — Byull Tekh Ekon Inf Mork Flota
Byulleten Tekhniko-Ekonomicheskoi Informatsii Morskogo Flota — Byull Tekh Ekon Inf Morsk Flota
Byulleten' Tekhniko-Ekonomicheskoi Informatsii Sovet Narodnogo Khozyaistva Belorusskoi SSR — Byull Tekh Ekon Inf Sov Nar Khoz B SSR
Byulleten Tekhniko-Ekonomicheskoi Informatsii. Sovet Narodnogo Khozyaistva Bryanskogo Ekonomicheskogo Administrativnogo Raiona — Byull Tekh Ekon Inf Sov Nar Khoz Bryansk Ekon Adm Raiona
Byulleten Tekhniko-Ekonomicheskoi Informatsii. Sovet Narodnogo Khozyaistva Khar'kovskogo Ekonomicheskogo Administrativnogo Raiona — Byull Tekh Ekon Inf Sov Nar Khoz Khark Ekon Adm Raiona
Byulleten Tekhniko-Ekonomicheskoi Informatsii. Sovet Narodnogo Khozyaistva Rostovskogo Ekonomicheskogo Administrativnogo Raiona — Byull Tekh Ekon Inf Sov Nar Khoz Rostov Ekon Adm Raiona
Byulleten Tekhniko-Ekonomicheskoi Informatsii. Sovet Narodnogo Khozyaistva Stalingradskogo Ekonomicheskogo Administrativnogo Raiona — Byull Tekh Ekon Inf Sov Nar Khoz Stalingr Ekon Adm Raiona
Byulleten' Tekhniko-Ekonomicheskoi Informatsii Sovet Narodnogo Khozyaistva Stalinskogo Ekonomicheskogo Administrativnogo Raiona — Byull Tekh Ekon Inf Sov Nar Khoz Stalinskogo Ekon Adm Raiona
Byulleten' Tsentra po Yadernym Dannym — BTIDA
Byulleten' Tsentra po Yadernym Dannym [*Former USSR*] — Byull Tsentra Yad Dannym
Byulleten. Tsentral'nyi Institut Informatsii Chernoi Metallurgii — Byull Tsentr Inst Inf Chern Metall
Byulleten. Tsentral'nyi Nauchno-Issledovatel'skii Institut Tekhnologii i Mashinostroeniya — Byull Tsentr Nauchno Issled Inst Tekhnol Mashinostr
Byulleten' Tsvetnoi Metallurgii — Byull Tsvetn' Metall
Byulleten' Ural'skogo Otdeleniya Moskovskogo Obshchestva Ispytatelei Prirody — Byull Ural Otd Mosk Ova Ispyt Prir
Byulleten' Vil'nyusskoi Astronomicheskoi Observatorii — BVAOD
Byulleten' Vil'nyusskoi Astronomicheskoi Observatorii [*Lithuanian SSR*] — Byull Vil'nyus Astron Obs
Byulleten' Vostochno Sibirskoi Fenologicheskoi Komissii — Byull Vost Sib Fenol Kom
Byulleten' Vsesoyuznogo Astronomo-Geodezicheskogo Obshchestva — Byull Vses Astron Geod Ova
Byulleten Vsesoyuznogo Instituta Eksperimental'noi Meditsiny — Byull Vses Inst Eksp Med
Byulleten' Vsesoyuznogo Instituta Eksperimental'noi Veterinarii — Byull Vses Inst Eksp Vet
Byulleten' Vsesoyuznogo Instituta Gel'mintologii — Byull Vses Inst Gel'mintol
Byulleten' Vsesoyuznogo Instituta Rastenievodstva — Byull Vses Inst Rastenievod
Byulleten' Vsesoyuznogo Kardiologicheskogo Nauchnogo Tsentra AMN SSSR — Byull Vses Kardiol Nauchn Tsentra AMN SSSR
Byulleten' Vsesoyuznogo Nauchno-Issledovatel'skogo Geologicheskogo Instituta — Byull Vses Nauchno Issled Geol Inst
Byulleten' Vsesoyuznogo Nauchno-Issledovatel'skogo Instituta Agrolesomelioratsii — Byull Vses Nauchno-Issled Inst Agrolesomelior
Byulleten' Vsesoyuznogo Nauchno-Issledovatel'skogo Instituta Chainoi Promyshlennosti — Byull Vses Nauchno Issled Inst Chain Promsti
Byulleten Vsesoyuznogo Nauchno-Issledovatel'skogo Instituta Chainoi Promyshlennosti i Subtropicheskikh Kul'tur — Byull Vses Nauchno Issled Inst Chain Promsti Subtrop Kult
Byulleten' Vsesoyuznogo Nauchno-Issledovatel'skogo Instituta Chaya i Subtropicheskikh Kul'tur — Byull Vses Nauchno-Issled Inst Chaya Subtrop Kul't
Byulleten' Vsesoyuznogo Nauchno-Issledovatel'skogo Instituta Eksperimental'noi Veterinarii Imeni Ya. R. Kovalenko — Byull Vses Nauchno Issled Inst Eksp Vet Im Ya R Kovalenko
Byulleten. Vsesoyuznogo Nauchno-Issledovatel'skogo Instituta Fiziologii i Biokhimii i Pitaniya Sel'skokhozyaistvennyk Zhivotnykh — Byull Vses Nauchno-Issled Inst Fiziol Biokhim Skh Zhivotn
Byulleten' Vsesoyuznogo Nauchno-Issledovatel'skogo Instituta Kukuruzy — Byull Vses Nauchno-Issled Inst Kukuruzy
Byulleten Vsesoyuznogo Nauchno-Issledovatel'skogo Instituta po Khlopkovodstvu — Byull Vses Nauchno Issled Inst Khlopkovod
Byulleten' Vsesoyuznogo Nauchno-Issledovatel'skogo Instituta Rastenievodstva Imeni N. I. Vavilova — BVIRA
Byulleten' Vsesoyuznogo Nauchno-Issledovatel'skogo Instituta Rastenievodstva Imeni N. I. Vavilova [*Former USSR*] — Byull Vses Nauchno-Issled Inst Rastenievod Im N I Vavilova
Byulleten' Vsesoyuznogo Nauchno-Issledovatel'skogo Instituta Tsementov — Byull Vses Nauchno Issled Inst Tsem
Byulleten' Vsesoyuznogo Nauchno-Issledovatel'skogo Instituta Udobrenii i Agropochvovedeniya — Byull Vses Nauchno Issled Inst Udobr Agropochvoved
Byulleten' Vsesoyuznogo Nauchno-Issledovatel'skogo Instituta Zashchity Rastenii — Byull Vses Nauchno-Issled Inst Zashch Rast
Byulleten' Vsesoyuznogo Ordena Lenina Instituta Eksperimental'noi Veterinarii [*A publication*] — Byull Vses Ordena Lenina Inst Eksp Vet
Byulleten' Vsesoyuznoi Koordinatsionnoi Komissee po Mikroelementam — Byull Vses Koord Kom Mikroelem
Byulleten Vsesoyuznoi Koordinatsionnoi Komissii po Mikroelementam. Akademiya Nauk Latviiskoi SSR — Byull Vses Koord Kom Mikroelem Akad Nauk Latv SSR
Byulleten' Vulkanologicheskikh Stantsii Akademiya Nauk SSSR — Byull Vulkanol Stn Akad Nauk SSSR
Byulleten' Vulkanologicheskikh Stantsii na Kamchatke Akademiya Nauk SSSR — Byull Vulkanol Stn Kamchatke Akad Nauk SSSR
Byulleteni Otdela Zemledeliya. Gosudarstvennyi Institut Opytnoi Agronomii — Byull Otd Zemled Gos Inst Opytn Agron
Byzantina — Byz
Byzantina kai Metabyzantina — BKM
Byzantina kai Metabyzantina — Byzantinak
Byzantina Neerlandica — BN
Byzantina Neerlandica — Byz Neer
Byzantina Neerlandica — Byz Neerl
Byzantina Neerlandica — Byz Neerland
Byzantina Vindobonensia — BV
Byzantina-Metabyzantina — Byz-Met
Byzantina-Metabyzantina — ByzMetabyz
Byzantine and Modern Greek Studies — BMGS
Byzantine and Modern Greek Studies — Byzantine M
Byzantine Studies — Byzantine S
Byzantinische Forschungen — Byz F
Byzantinische Forschungen — Byz Forsch
Byzantinische Papyri in der Koenigliche Hof- und Staatsbibliothek zu Muenchen — P Monac
Byzantinische Zeitschrift — ByZ
Byzantinische Zeitschrift — Byz Zeitschr
Byzantinische Zeitschrift — Byz Zeitschrift
Byzantinische Zeitschrift — Byz Zs
Byzantinische Zeitschrift — Byzant Z
Byzantinische Zeitschrift — Byzantin Z
Byzantinische Zeitschrift — Byzantin Ztschr
Byzantinische Zeitschrift — Byzantinische Z
Byzantinische Zeitschrift — ByzZ
Byzantinische Zeitschrift — BZ
Byzantinisches Archiv — Byz Arch
Byzantinisch-Neugriechische Jahrbuecher — B Ng Jb
Byzantinisch-Neugriechische Jahrbuecher — BN Jbb
Byzantinisch-Neugriechische Jahrbuecher — BNCJ
Byzantinisch-Neugriechische Jahrbuecher — BNGrJb
Byzantinisch-Neugriechische Jahrbuecher — BNJ
Byzantinisch-Neugriechische Jahrbuecher — BNJb
Byzantinisch-Neugriechische Jahrbuecher — ByJ
Byzantinisch-Neugriechische Jahrbuecher — Byz J
Byzantinisch-Neugriechische Jahrbuecher — Byz Jb
Byzantinisch-Neugriechische Jahrbuecher — Byz-Neugr Jahrb
Byzantinisch-Neugriechische Jahrbuecher — BYZNGJB
Byzantino-Bulgarica — Byz Bul
Byzantino-Bulgarica — Byz-Bulg
Byzantino-Slavica — BS
Byzantino-Slavica — BSL
Byzantino-Slavica — Bysl
Byzantino-Slavica — Byzantinosl
Byzantino-Slavica — ByzS
Byzantino-Slavica — ByzSl
Byzantino-Slavica. Sbornik pro Studium Byzantskoslovanskych Vztahu — Byz Slav
Byzantion — Byz
Byzantion; Revue Internationale des Etudes Byzantines — Byzant

C

C & CA [*Cement and Concrete Association*] **Technical Report** — C & CA Tech Rep
C. C. Furnas Memorial Conference — C C Furnas Meml Conf
C. Kansas State University. Cooperative Extension Service — C Kans State Univ Coop Ext Serv
C. Missouri University. Cooperative Extension Service — C Mo Univ Coop Ext Serv
C. S. Lewis Society. Bulletin [*New York*] — CSLBull
C. University of Nevada. Cooperative Extension Service. Max C. Fleischmann College of Agriculture — C Univ Nev Coop Ext Serv Max C Fleischmann Coll Agric
C_1 Molecule Chemistry — C_1 Mol Chem
CA. A Bulletin of Cancer Progress — CA
CA. A Bulletin of Cancer Progress — CA Bull
CA. A Bulletin of Cancer Progress — CA Bull Cancer Prog
CA. A Cancer Journal for Clinicians — CA
CA. A Cancer Journal for Clinicians — CA Cancer J Clin
CA. A Cancer Journal for Clinicians — CAMCA
CA [*Chartered Accountant*] **Magazine** [*Canadian Institute of Chartered Accountants*] — CA Mag
CA [*Chemical Abstracts*] **Magazine** — CA Magazin
CA [*Chartered Accountant*] **Magazine** — CAM
CA Magazine. Journal of Commercial Art — CA Mag J Commer Art
CA Magazine. Journal of Commercial Art — CAMZA
CA Quarterly. Facts and Figures on Austria's Economy — CA Qtrly
CA [*Committee Assignment*] **Report. Technical Association of the Pulp and Paper Industry** — CA Rep Tech Assoc Pulp Pap Ind
Cabinet Maker and Retail Furnisher — CAO
Cabinet of Natural History and American Rural Sports — Cab Nat Hist Amer Rural Sports
Cable Libraries — Cable Lib
Cable Marketing — Cable Mktg
Cable On-line Data Exchange [*Database*] — CODE
Cable Report — Cable Rpt
Cable Television Business — Cable TV B
Cable Television Business Directory. CATV Suppliers Phone Book — Cable TVBD
Cable Television Engineering — Cable Telev Eng
Cable TV Advertising — Cable TV Adv
Cable TV Finance — Cable TV Fin
Cable TV Programming — Cable TV Pro
Cable TV Regulation — Cable TV Reg
Cable TV Security — Cable TV Sec
Cablecasting, Cable TV Engineering — Cablecast Cable TV Eng
Cables et Transmission — Cabl Transm
Cables et Transmission — Cables & Transm
Cables et Transmission — Cables Transm
Cabo Verde — CaboV
Cacao Chocolade en Suikerwerken — Cacao Choc Suikerwerken
Cacao en Colombia — Cacao Colomb
Cacau Atualidades — Cacau Atual
Cacciatore Italiano — Cacciat Ital
Cacciatore Trentino — Cacciat Trent
CACS (Chemical Analysis Center. Saitama University) Forum — CACS Forum
Cactaceas y Suculentas Mexicanas — Cact Suc Mex
Cactaceas y Suculentas Mexicanas — Cact Suculentas Mex
Cactus and Succulent Journal — Cact Succ J
Cactus and Succulent Journal [*United States*] — Cactus Succ J
Cactus and Succulent Journal — Cactus Succulent J
Cactus and Succulent Journal. Cactus and Succulent Society of New South Wales (Woollahra, Australia) — Cact Succ J Woollahra
Cactus and Succulent Journal of Great Britain — Cact Succ J Gr Br
Cactus and Succulent Journal of Great Britain — Cact Succ J Gr Brit
Cactus and Succulent Journal of Great Britain — Cactus Succ J Gt Br
Cactus and Succulent Journal of Great Britain — Cactus Succulent J GB
Cactus. Bulletin Bimestriel (Mont St. Amaud, France) — Cactus Mont St Amaud
Cactus Digest. Henry Shaw Cactus Society — Cact Digest
Cactus Journal — Cact J
Cactus Journal (Croydon, England) — Cact J Croydon
CAD/CAM [*Computer-Aided Design/Computer-Aided Manufacturing*] **Technology** — CAD/CAM Tech
Cadastro Oleicola. Registo Portugues — Cadastro Oleic Registo Port
Cadence — Cad
Cadence Magazine — Cadence
Caderno Omega — Cad Omega
Caderno Omega. Universidade Federal Rural de Pernambuco — Cad Omega Univ Fed Rural Pernambuco
Cadernos Brasileiros — CadB
Cadernos Brasileiros — CBr
Cadernos Brasileiros (Rio de Janeiro) — Cad Bras Rio
Cadernos Cientificos. Instituto Pasteur de Lisboa — Cad Cient
Cadernos da Amazonia — Cad Amazonia
Cadernos de Biblioteconomia — Cad Bibliotecon
Cadernos de Debate — Cad Deb
Cadernos de Historia e Filosofia da Ciencia — Cad Hist Filos Cienc
Cadernos Mensais de Estatistica e Informacao. Editados pelo Instituto da Vinho da Porto — Cad Mens Estat Inf Inst Vinho Porto
Cadiz Medico — Cad Med
Cadmium Abstracts — Cadmium Abstr
Cadres et Professions — Cadres et Profes
Caducee — Cad
Caduceo. Revista Grafica Espanola Economico Financiera — Cad
Caduceus — Cad
CAED Report. Iowa State University of Science and Technology. Center for Agricultural and Economic Development — CAED Rep Iowa State Univ Sci Tech Center Agr Econ Develop
Caesaraugusta. Seminario de Arqueologia y Numismatica Aragonesas — Caesaraug
Cafe, Cacao, The — CACAA
Cafe de El Salvador. Revista. Asociacion Cafetalera de El Salvador (San Salvador) — Cafe Salvador S Salvador
Cafe Solo — Cafe
Caffer. Comitato Italiano Caffe e del Bureau Europeen du Cafe — Caffer Com It Caffe
Cahier Canadien Claudel — CCanC
Cahier. Centre de Recherches en Developpement Economique — Cah Cent Rech Dev Econ
Cahier. Centre Technique du Bois — Cah Centre Tech Bois
Cahier d'Archeologie du Nordest — CANE
Cahier de la Societe de Chimie Organique et Biologique — Cah Soc Chim Org Biol
Cahier des Annales de Normandie — Cah Ann Norm
Cahier d'Etudes Medievales — Cah Etud Mediev
Cahier d'Information. Departement d'Oceanographie. Universite du Quebec a Rimouski — Cah Inf Dep Oceanogr Univ Que Rimouski
Cahier d'Information du Bureau Eurisotop — Cah Inf Bur Eurisotop
Cahier d'Information. Universite du Quebec a Rimouski. Department d'Oceanographie — Cah Inf Univ Que Rimouski Dep Oceanogr
Cahier du Corps des Maitres de Stage des Hopitaux. Universite Libre de Bruxelles — Cah Corps Maitres Stage Hop Univ Libre Bruxelles
Cahier Special des Charges — CSCh
Cahier. Supplement aux Annales du Service des Antiquites de l'Egypte [*Cairo*] — CASAE
Cahiers. Academie Luxembourgeoise — C A L
Cahiers Africains d'Administration Publique — C Afr Adm Publ
Cahiers Africains de la Securite Sociale — C Afr Secur Soc
Cahiers Albert Le Grand — Cah Albert Le Grand
Cahiers Albert Roussel — Cah Albert Roussel
Cahiers Algeriens de la Sante — Cah Alg San
Cahiers Algeriens de Litterature Comparee — CALC
Cahiers. Alliance Israelite Universelle — CAIU
Cahiers. Alliance Israelite Universelle [*Mahberet*] — CAIUM
Cahiers Alsaciens d'Archeologie, d'Art, e d'Histoire — Cah Alsac Archeol Art Hist
Cahiers Alsaciens d'Archeologie, d'Art, et d'Histoire — CAAH
Cahiers Alsaciens d'Archeologie, d'Art, et d'Histoire — Cah Als
Cahiers Alsaciens d'Archeologie, d'Art, et d'Histoire — Cah Als Arch
Cahiers Alsaciens d'Archeologie d'Art et d'Histoire — Cah Als Arch Art Hist
Cahiers Alsaciens d'Archeologie d'Art et d'Histoire — Cah Alsaciens
Cahiers Alsaciens d'Archeologie d'Art et d'Histoire — Cah Arch et Hist Alsace
Cahiers Alsaciens d'Archeologie d'Art et d'Histoire — CAHA
Cahiers Alsaciens d'Archeologie d'Art et d'Histoire — Cahiers Alsaciens
Cahiers Alsaciens d'Archeologie d'Art et d'Histoire — Cahiers Arch et Hist Alsace
Cahiers Apicoles — Cah Apic
Cahiers Archeologiques — Ca Ar
Cahiers Archeologiques — Cah A
Cahiers Archeologiques — Cah Arch
Cahiers Archeologiques — Cah Archeol
Cahiers Archeologiques — CArch
Cahiers Archeologiques. Fin de l'Antiquite et Moyen-age — CA

Cahiers Archeologiques. Fin de l'Antiquite et Moyen-age — Cahiers Arch
Cahiers Archeologiques. Fin de l'Antiquite et Moyen-age — Cahiers Archeol
Cahiers. Association des Universites Parliellement ou Entierement de Langue Francaise — Cah AUPELF
Cahiers. Association Internationale des Etudes Francaises — CAEF
Cahiers. Association Internationale des Etudes Francaises — Cah Ass Int Et Fr
Cahiers. Association Internationale des Etudes Francaises — CAIEF
Cahiers. Association Interuniversitaire de l'Est — Cah Assoc Interuniv Est
Cahiers Benjamin Constant — CBC
Cahiers Bleus Veterinaires — Cah Bleus Vet
Cahiers Bruxellois — Cah Brux
Cahiers Bruxellois — CB
Cahiers Canadiens de Musique [*Canada Music Book*] — Cah Canadiens M
Cahiers CEDAF (Centre d'Etudes et de Documentation Africaines) — CaC
Cahiers. Centre d'Etudes de Recherche Operationnelle — Cah Cent Etud Rech Oper
Cahiers. Centre d'Etudes de Recherche Operationnelle [*Brussels*] — Cahiers Centre Etudes Rech Oper
Cahiers. Centre d'Etudes de Recherche Operationnelle — Cahiers Centre Etudes Recherche Oper
Cahiers. Centre d'Etudes de Recherche Operationnelle — CCERO
Cahiers. Centre d'Etudes des Coutumes — C Centre Et Coutumes
Cahiers. Centre d'Etudes Irlandaises — CCEI
Cahiers. Centre Scientifique et Technique du Batiment — Cahiers CSTB
Cahiers. Centre Scientifique et Technique du Batiment — CSTB
Cahiers. Centre Universitaire d'Histoire Contemporaine de Louvain — CCUHCL
Cahiers. CERBOM [*Centre d'Etudes et de Recherche de Biologie et d'Oceanographie Medicale*] — Cah CERBOM
Cahiers. Cercle Ernest Renan [*Paris*] — CahCerclERenan
Cahiers. Cercle Ernest Renan pour Libres Recherches d'Histoire du Christianisme [*Paris*] — CCER
Cahiers Cesairiens — Cahiers C
Cahiers Charles De Foucauld — Cah Ch Foucauld
Cahiers. College de Medecine des Hopitaux de Paris — Cah Coll Med Hop Paris
Cahiers. College de Medecine des Hopitaux de Paris — CCMDA
Cahiers. Comites de Prevention du Batiment et des Travaux Publics [*France*] — Cah Com Prev Batim Trav Publics
Cahiers. Comites de Prevention du Batiment et des Travaux Publics — CCPBA
Cahiers d'Acoustique — Cah Acoust
Cahiers d'Aerodynamique — Cah Aerod
Cahiers d'Analyse Textuelle — Cah Anal Text
Cahiers d'Analyse Textuelle. Les Belles Lettres [*Liege*] — CAT
Cahiers d'Anesthesiologie — CAANB
Cahiers d'Anesthesiologie — Cah Anesth
Cahiers d'Anesthesiologie — Cah Anesthesiol
Cahiers d'Animation Spirituelle — Cah Anim Spirit
Cahiers d'Anthropologie et Biometrie Humaine — Cah Anthropol Biom Hum
Cahiers d'Anthropologie et d'Ecologie Humaines — C Anthropol Ecol Hum
Cahiers d'Archeologie Biblique — CAB
Cahiers d'Archeologie du Nord-Est — Cah Nord Est
Cahiers d'Archeologie et d'Histoire d'Alsace — CAHA
Cahiers d'Archeologie et d'Histoire du Berry — Cah Arch Hist Berry
Cahiers d'Archeologie et d'Histoire du Berry — Cah Archeol Hist Berry
Cahiers d'Archeologie et d'Histoire du Berry — Cah Berry
Cahiers d'Archeologie et d'Histoire du Berry — CAHB
Cahiers d'Archeologie et d'Histoire du Berry — CBerry
Cahiers d'Archeologie Regionale — CAR
Cahiers d'Archeologie Subaquatique — C A Subaqu
Cahiers d'Archeologie Subaquatique — Cah A Subaqu
Cahiers d'Archeologie Subaquatique — Cah Arch Subaqu
Cahiers d'Art — Cah Art
Cahiers de Biologie Marine — Cah Bio Mar
Cahiers de Biologie Marine — Cah Biol Mar
Cahiers de Biologie Marine — CBIMA
Cahiers de Bruges — Cah Bruges
Cahiers de Bruges — CB
Cahiers de Byrsa — Byrsa
Cahiers de Byrsa — Cah Byrsa
Cahiers de Byrsa — CB
Cahiers de Byrsa. Tunis. Musee Lavigerie — C d Byrsa
Cahiers de Byrsa. Tunis. Musee Lavigerie — Cah Byr
Cahiers de Centreau — Cah Cent
Cahiers de Chimie Organique — Cah Chim Org
Cahiers de Chirurgie — Cah Chir
Cahiers de Civilisation Medievale — Cah Civ Med
Cahiers de Civilisation Medievale — Cah Civ Mediev
Cahiers de Civilisation Medievale — Cah Civilisation Medievale
Cahiers de Civilisation Medievale — CCM
Cahiers de Civilisation Medievale — CCMe
Cahiers de Civilisation Medievale Xe-XIIe Siecles — Cah CM
Cahiers de Documentation de la Chambre de Commerce et d'Industrie de Marseille — C Docum Ch Com Marseille
Cahiers de Droit — C de D
Cahiers de Droit — Cahiers
Cahiers de Droit de l'Entreprise — C Dr Entreprise
Cahiers de Droit Europeen — C Dr Europ
Cahiers de Droit Europeen — Cah de Droit Eur
Cahiers de Droit Europeen — Cah Dr Eur
Cahiers de Droit Europeen — CDE
Cahiers de Droit (Quebec) [*Canada (already exists in GUS II database)*] — Cah de Droit (Quebec)
Cahiers de Geographie de Quebec — CAGQ
Cahiers de Geographie de Quebec — Cahiers Geog Quebec
Cahiers de Geographie de Quebec. Universite Laval. Institut de Geographie — ULIG/C
Cahiers de Geographie Physique — Cah Geogr Phys
Cahiers de Josephologie [*Montreal, PQ*] — CarJos
Cahiers de Kinesitherapie — Cah Kinesither
Cahiers de la Biloque — Cah Biloque
Cahiers de la Ceramique, du Verre, et des Arts du Feu — C Cer
Cahiers de la Cinematheque — Cahiers Cinematheque
Cahiers de la Compagnie Madeleine Renaud-Jean Louis Barrault — CCRB
Cahiers de la Compagnie Madeleine Renaud-Jean Louis Barrault — CRB
Cahiers de la Delegation Archeologique Francaise. Iran — CDAFI
Cahiers de la Documentation — Cah Docum
Cahiers de la Haute-Loire — CHL
Cahiers de la Maboke — Cah Maboke
Cahiers de la Nouvelle Journee — Cah Nouv Journee
Cahiers de la Nouvelle Revue Thologique — Cah Nouv Rev Theol
Cahiers de la Pleiade — Cah Pleiade
Cahiers de la Pleiade — CaPL
Cahiers de la Presse Francaise — Cah Presse Fr
Cahiers de la Recherche Agronomique — Cah Rech Agron
Cahiers de la Recherche Agronomique. Institut National de la Recherche Agronomique (Morocco) — Cah Rech Agron Inst Rech Agron (Morocco)
Cahiers de la Revue Biblique [*Paris*] — CRB
Cahiers de la Revue d'Histoire et de Philosophie Religieuses — CRHPR
Cahiers de la Revue d'Histoire et de Philosophie Religieuses Publies par la Faculte de Theologie Protestanto de l'Universite de Strasbourg — Cahiers de la Rev d Hist et de Philos Religieuses
Cahiers de la Thermique — Cah Therm
Cahiers de l'Actualite Religieuse — Cah A R
Cahiers de l'Amitie Charles Peguy — CACP
Cahiers de l'Amitie Charles Peguy — Cah Am Ch P
Cahiers de l'Analyse des Donnees — CADOD
Cahiers de l'Art Sacre — Cah Art Sacre
Cahiers de l'Asie du Sud-Est — Cah As Se
Cahiers de l'Enfance — Cah Enf
Cahiers de l'ENSBANA — Cah ENSBANA
Cahiers de Lexicologie — Cah Lex
Cahiers de Lexicologie — CdL
Cahiers de Lexicologie — CLe
Cahiers de Lexicologie — CLex
Cahiers de l'Expansion Regionale — Cah Expansion Reg
Cahiers de l'Herne — Cahiers Herne
Cahiers de Linguistique Asie Orientale — Cah Ling As Or
Cahiers de Linguistique Theorique et Appliquee — Cah Ling
Cahiers de Linguistique Theorique et Appliquee — CLTA
Cahiers de Linguistique. Universite du Quebec — CLUQ
Cahiers de l'Institut d'Etudes Polonaises en Belgique — Cah Inst Et Pol Belg
Cahiers de l'Iroise — Cah Iroise
Cahiers de Litterature et de Linguistique Appliquee — CLLA
Cahiers de l'ONAREST (Office National de la Recherche Scientifique et Technique du Cameroun) — Cah ONAREST
Cahiers de l'Oronte [*Beirut*] — Cah Or
Cahiers de l'Oronte [*Beirut*] — CO
Cahiers de l'Ouest — CO
Cahiers de Mariemont — Cah Mariemont
Cahiers de Mariemont — CM
Cahiers de Medecine — Cah Med
Cahiers de Medecine [*Paris*] — CAHMB
Cahiers de Medecine. Assises de Medecine — Cah Med Assises Med
Cahiers de Medecine du Travail — Cah Med Trav
Cahiers de Medecine. Europa Medica — Cah Med Eur Med
Cahiers de Medecine Interprofessionnelle [*France*] — Cah Med Interprof
Cahiers de Medecine Interprofessionnelle — CMIPB
Cahiers de Medecine (Paris) — Cah Med Paris
Cahiers de Medecine Veterinaire — Cah Med Vet
Cahiers de Micropaleontologie — Cah Micropaleontol
Cahiers de Notes Documentaires — Cah Notes Doc
Cahiers de Notes Documentaires — CNDIB
Cahiers de Notes Documentaires. Securite et Hygiene du Travail — Cah Notes Doc
Cahiers de Notes Documentaires. Securite et Hygiene du Travail — Cah Notes Doc Secur Hyg Trav
Cahiers de Nutrition et de Dietetique — Cah Nutr Diet
Cahiers de Pedologie. Office de la Recherche Scientifique et Technique d'Outre-Mer — Cah Pedol ORSTOM
Cahiers de Physique [*France*] — Cah Phys
Cahiers de Physique. Theorie, Syntheses, et Mises au Point — Cah Phys
Cahiers de Prothese — Cah Prothese
Cahiers de Psychiatrie — Cah Psych
Cahiers de Quentovic — Cah Quentovic
Cahiers de Readaptation — Cah Readapt
Cahiers de Recherches. Institut de Papyrologie et d'Egyptologie de Lille — CRIPEL
Cahiers de Saint-Michel de Cuxa — CA St Michel de Cuxa
Cahiers de Saint-Michel de Cuxa — Cah St Michel
Cahiers de Sante Communautaire — Cah San Commun
Cahiers de Science Appliquee — Cah Sci Appl
Cahiers de Sexologie Clinique — Cah Sexol Clin
Cahiers de Sociologie Economique — C Soc Econ
Cahiers de Sociologie Economique — Cah Soc Ec
Cahiers de Sociologie Economique — Cah Sociol Econ
Cahiers de Sociologie et de Demographie Medicales — C Soc Dem Med
Cahiers de Sociologie et de Demographie Medicales — C Sociol Demogr Medic
Cahiers de Sociologie et de Demographie Medicales — Cah Sociol Demogr Med
Cahiers de Synthese Organique — Cah Synth Org
Cahiers de Topologie et Geometrie Differentielle — Cahiers Topologie Geom Differentielle

Cahiers de Topologie et Geometrie Differentielle Categoriques — Cahiers Topologie Geom Differentielle Categ
Cahiers de Toxicologie Clinique et Experimentale — Cah Toxicol Clin Exp
Cahiers de Tunisie — C Tunisie
Cahiers de Tunisie — Cah de Tunisie
Cahiers de Tunisie — Cah Tun
Cahiers de Tunisie — Cah Tunisie
Cahiers de Tunisie — CAHT
Cahiers de Tunisie — CT
Cahiers Debussy — Cah Debussy
Cahiers d'Education Civique — Cah Educ Civ
Cahiers. Delegation Archeologique Francaise en Iran — DAFI
Cahiers. Delegation Francaise en Iran — Cah Del Fr Iran
Cahiers des Ameriques Latines — C Amer Lat
Cahiers des Ameriques Latines — Cah Am Lat
Cahiers des Ameriques Latines — CAL
Cahiers des Ameriques Latines — CDAL
Cahiers des Ameriques Latines. Serie Sciences de l'Homme — C Amer Lat Ser Sci Homme
Cahiers des Ameriques Latines. Serie Sciences de l'Homme — Cah Am Latines Ser Sciences Homme
Cahiers des Annales — Cah Ann
Cahiers des Dix — CaD
Cahiers des Etudes Anciennes — Cah Etud Anc
Cahiers des Etudes Anciennes — CEA
Cahiers des Ingenieurs Agronomes — C Ingen Agron
Cahiers des Ingenieurs Agronomes — Cah Ing Agron
Cahiers des Ingenieurs Agronomes — Cah Ingnrs Agron
Cahiers des Naturalistes — Cah Nat
Cahiers des Naturalistes — Cah Naturalistes
Cahiers des Naturalistes — CNat
Cahiers des Religions Africaines — Cah Relig Afr
Cahiers des Religions Africaines — Cah Religions Afr
Cahiers d'Etudes Africaines — C Et Afr
Cahiers d'Etudes Africaines — CaE
Cahiers d'Etudes Africaines — Cah Et Afr
Cahiers d'Etudes Africaines — Cah Etud Af
Cahiers d'Etudes Africaines — Cah Etud Afr
Cahiers d'Etudes Africaines — CEAfr
Cahiers d'Etudes Africaines. Revue Trimestrielle — Cah d'Et Afr
Cahiers d'Etudes Biologiques — Cah Etud Biol
Cahiers d'Etudes Cathares — Cah Et Cath
Cahiers d'Etudes Cathares — CEC
Cahiers d'Etudes de Radio-Television — CER-T
Cahiers d'Etudes Medievales — CEM
Cahiers d'Etudes Romanes — CER
Cahiers d'Hermes — Cah Herm
Cahiers d'Histoire — Ca H
Cahiers d'Histoire — Ca Hist
Cahiers d'Histoire — Cah Hist
Cahiers d'Histoire — CH
Cahiers d'Histoire de la Revolution Francaise — CHRF
Cahiers d'Histoire Egyptienne — Cah Hist Eg
Cahiers d'Histoire Egyptienne [*Cairo*] — CHE
Cahiers d'Histoire et d'Archeologie — C Hist Arch
Cahiers d'Histoire et d'Archeologie — Cah Hist Arch
Cahiers d'Histoire et d'Archeologie — CHA
Cahiers d'Histoire et de Folklore — CHF
Cahiers d'Histoire et de Philosophie des Sciences. Nouvelle Serie — Cahiers Hist Philos Sci Nouv Ser
Cahiers d'Histoire et de Philosophie des Sciences. Nouvelle Serie — Cahiers Hist Philos Sci Nouvelle Ser
Cahiers d'Histoire. Institut Maurice Thorez — C Hist Inst Maurice Thorez
Cahiers d'Histoire. Institut Maurice Thorez — Inst Maurice Thorez Cah Hist
Cahiers d'Histoire Mondiale — Cah Hist Mondiale
Cahiers d'Histoire Mondiale — Cahiers d'Hist Mond
Cahiers d'Histoire Mondiale — CaHM
Cahiers d'Histoire Mondiale/Journal of World History — Cah Hist M
Cahiers d'Histoire Mondiale/Journal of World History — Cah Hist Mond
Cahiers d'Histoire Mondiale/Journal of World History — CHM
Cahiers d'Histoire Mondiale/Journal of World History [*Paris*] — CHMond
Cahiers d'Histoire Mondiale/Journal of World History — J Wld Hist
Cahiers d'Histoire Mondiale/Journal of World History/Cuadernos de Historia Mundial — Cah Hist Mond J Wld Hist
Cahiers d'Histoire Mondiale (Paris) — Cahiers Hist Mond Paris
Cahiers d'Histoire Publies par les Universites de Clermont-Lyon-Grenoble — CHCLG
Cahiers d'Histoire. Societe Historique de Quebec — Cah Hist Soc Hist Que
Cahiers d'Information du Chef de Personnel — C Inform Chef Personnel
Cahiers d'Information Station de Biologie Marine de Grande-Riviere — Cah Inf Stn Biol Mar Grande-Riviere
Cahiers d'Informations Techniques/Revue de Metallurgie — Cah Inf Tech Rev Metall
Cahiers d'Informations Techniques/Revue de Metallurgie — CITMD
Cahiers d'Odonto-Stomatologie — Cah Odonto-Stomatol
Cahiers d'ORL [*Oto-Rhino-Laryngologie*] — Cah ORL
Cahiers d'Outre-Mer — C O-Mer
Cahiers d'Outre-Mer — Cah d Outre Mer
Cahiers d'Outre-Mer — Cah OM
Cahiers d'Outre-Mer — Cah O-Mer
Cahiers d'Outre-Mer — Cah Outre-Mer
Cahiers d'Outre-Mer — CaOM
Cahiers du Bazadais — C Ba
Cahiers du Centre de Logique — Cahiers Centre Logique
Cahiers du Centre d'Etudes et de Recherches de Biologie et d'Oceanographie Medicale — Cah Centr Etudes Rech Biol
Cahiers du Centre d'Etudes et de Recherches Ethnologiques — Cah Cent Etud et Rech Ethnol
Cahiers du Centre d'Etudes Regionales (Antilles-Guyane) — Cah Cent Etud Reg Ant Guy
Cahiers du Cinema — C Cinema
Cahiers du Cinema — Cah Cinema
Cahiers du Cinema — Cah du Cinema
Cahiers du Cinema — Cahiers
Cahiers du Cinema — CC
Cahiers du Cinema in English — Cahiers in Eng
Cahiers du Communisme — C Communisme
Cahiers du Communisme — CaCo
Cahiers du Communisme — Cah Communisme
Cahiers du Monde Hispanique et Luso-Bresilien — C Monde Hisp Luso-Bresil
Cahiers du Monde Hispanique et Luso-Bresilien — Cah Monde Hisp Luso-Bresil
Cahiers du Monde Hispanique et Luso-Bresilien — CMHLB
Cahiers du Monde Nouveau — Cah M Nouv
Cahiers du Monde Russe et Sovietique — C Monde Russe Sov
Cahiers du Monde Russe et Sovietique — Cah Mon Rus
Cahiers du Monde Russe et Sovietique — Cah Monde Russ Soviet
Cahiers du Monde Russe et Sovietique — CaM
Cahiers du Monde Russe et Sovietique — CMRS
Cahiers du Nursing [*Montreal*] — Cah Nurs
Cahiers du Pacifique — Cah Pac
Cahiers du Seminaire Ch. Gide — CSP
Cahiers du Seminaire d'Econometrie — Cah Sem Econ
Cahiers du Seminaire d'Histoire des Mathematiques. Serie 2 — Cahiers Sem Hist Math Ser 2
Cahiers du Sud — Cah Sud
Cahiers du Sud — CS
Cahiers du Vingtieme Siecle — CaVS
Cahiers Economiques de Bretagne — C Econ Bretagne
Cahiers Economiques de Bruxelles — C Econ Bruxelles
Cahiers Economiques de Bruxelles — Cah Econ Br
Cahiers Economiques de Bruxelles — Cah Econ Brux
Cahiers Economiques de Bruxelles — Cah Econs Bruxelles
Cahiers Economiques de Bruxelles — CEK
Cahiers Economiques et Monetaires — Cah Econs et Monetaires
Cahiers Economiques et Monetaires — CCF
Cahiers Economiques et Sociaux [*Kinshasa*] — C Econ Soc
Cahiers Economiques et Sociaux — Cah Econ Soc
Cahiers Economiques et Sociaux — Cah Econs et Soc
Cahiers Economiques Monetaires — C Econ Monet
Cahiers Elisabethains — Cah Elis
Cahiers Elisabethains — CahiersE
Cahiers Europeens — C Europ
Cahiers Evangiles — CE
Cahiers. Faculte des Sciences. Universite Mohammed 5. Serie Biologie Animale — Cah Fac Sci Univ Mohammed Ser Bio Anim
Cahiers Ferdinand de Saussure — CFS
Cahiers Francais — C Franc
Cahiers Francais — Cah Fr
Cahiers Francais; Revue Periodique de l'Actualite Politique, Economique, Sociale, et Culturelle de la France — CAN
Cahiers Francophones — CahiersF
Cahiers Geologiques — Cah Geol
Cahiers Geologiques — Cahiers Geol
Cahiers Geologiques de Thoiry — Cah Geol Thoiry
Cahiers Gerard De Nerval — CGN
Cahiers. Groupe de Recherches. Armee Romaine et les Provinces — CGRAR
Cahiers. Groupe de Recherches sur l'Armee Romaine et les Provinces — Cah Armee Rom
Cahiers. Groupe Francais de Rheologie — Cah Groupe Fr Rheol
Cahiers. Groupe Francois-Thureau-Dangin — CGFTD
Cahiers. Groupe Francois-Thureau-Dangin [*Paris*] — CTD
Cahiers. Groupe Francois-Thureau-Dangin. I [*Paris, 1960*] — CahTD
Cahiers Haut-Marnais — C Ht M
Cahiers Haut-Marnais — Cah Haut Marnais
Cahiers. Institut d'Amenagement et d'Urbanisation de la Region Parisienne — C Inst Amenag Urb Region Paris
Cahiers. Institut d'Amenagement et d'Urbanisme de la Region d'Ile-De-France — CHIA
Cahiers. Institut de Linguistique de Louvain — CdIL
Cahiers. Institut de Linguistique. Universite Louvain — CILUL
Cahiers. Institut du Moyen Age Grec et Latin — CIMAGL
Cahiers. Institut du Moyen-Age Grec et Latin — CIMGL
Cahiers. Institut du Moyen-Age Grec et Latin. Universitaire Copenhagen — CIMA
Cahiers. Institut Francais d'Amerique Latine — Cah I F A L
Cahiers Internationaux — Cah Int
Cahiers Internationaux de la Resistance — Cah Internat Resistance
Cahiers Internationaux de Sociologie — C Int Sociol
Cahiers Internationaux de Sociologie — Cah Int Soc
Cahiers Internationaux de Sociologie — Cah Int Sociol
Cahiers Internationaux de Sociologie — Cah Int Sociologie
Cahiers Internationaux de Sociologie — Cah Internat Sociol
Cahiers Internationaux de Sociologie — CI Soc
Cahiers Internationaux de Sociologie — CIS
Cahiers Internationaux. Revue Internationale du Monde du Travail — Cah Internat
Cahiers Irlandais — Cahiers I
Cahiers Ivoiriens de Recherche Economique et Sociale — Cah Ivoiriens de Rech Econ et Sociale

Cahiers Ivoiriens de Recherche Economique et Sociale — Cah Ivoiriens Rech Econ et Soc
Cahiers J. K. Huysmans — Cah JKH
Cahiers Jean Cocteau — CJC
Cahiers Jean Giraudoux — CJG
Cahiers Juridiques de l'Electricite et du Gaz — Cah Juridiques Electr Gaz
Cahiers. Laboratoire d'Hydrobiologie de Montereau [*France*] — Cah Lab Hydrobiol Montereau
Cahiers. Laboratoire d'Hydrobiologie de Montereau — CLHMD
Cahiers Leopold Delisle — Cah Leopold Delisle
Cahiers Leoppold Delisle. Societe Parisienne d'Histoire et d'Archeologi e Norman des — CLD
Cahiers. Ligue Catholique de l'Evangile — CLE
Cahiers Ligures de Prehistoire et d'Archeologie — C Ligures Prehist Archeol
Cahiers Ligures de Prehistoire et d'Archeologie — Cah Lig
Cahiers Ligures de Prehistoire et d'Archeologie — Cahiers Lig Prehist Arch
Cahiers Ligures de Prehistoire et d'Archeologie — CLPA
Cahiers Linguistiques d'Ottawa — CLO
Cahiers Lorrains — Cah Lor
Cahiers Lorrains — CL
Cahiers Mathematiques — Cahiers Math
Cahiers Mathematiques de l'Ecole Polytechnique Federale de Lausanne — Cahiers Math Ecole Polytech Fed Lausanne
Cahiers Mathematiques Montpellier. Universite des Sciences et Techniques du Languedoc — Cahiers Math Montpellier
Cahiers Maynard — CM
Cahiers Medicaux — Cah Med
Cahiers Medicaux Lyonnais — Cah Med Lyon
Cahiers Meduliens — C Med
Cahiers Meduliens — Cah Med
Cahiers Meduliens — Cah Medul
Cahiers. Musee Forezien — Cah Mus Forezien
Cahiers Numismatiques — Cah Num
Cahiers Numismatiques — Cahiers Num
Cahiers Numismatiques — CahN
Cahiers Numismatiques — CN
Cahiers Oceanographiques — Cah Oceanogr
Cahiers Oceanographiques (France) — COOFA
Cahiers Oceanographiques. Supplement — Cah Oceanogr Suppl
Cahiers Odontostomatologiques (Touraine) — Cah Odontostomatol (Touraine)
Cahiers. Office de la Recherche Scientifique et Technique d'Outre-Mer — Cah ORSTOM
Cahiers. Office de la Recherche Scientifique et Technique d'Outre-Mer. Serie Pedologie — Cah Off Rech Sci Tech Outre-Mer Ser Pedol
Cahiers. Office de la Recherche Scientifique et Technique pour l'Outre-Mer. Serie Sciences Humaines — Cah ORSTOM Sci Hum
Cahiers. ORSTOM [*Office de la Recherche Scientifique et Technique d'Outre-Mer*]. Hydrobiologie — Cah ORST Hy
Cahiers. ORSTOM [*Office de la Recherche Scientifique et Technique d'Outre-Mer*]. Hydrologie — COSHB
Cahiers. ORSTOM [*Office de la Recherche Scientifique et Technique d'Outre-Mer*]. Oceanographie — Cah ORST Oc
Cahiers. ORSTOM [*Office de la Recherche Scientifique et Technique d'Outre-Mer*]. Physiologie des Plantes Tropicales Cultivees — Cah ORSTOM Physiol Plant Trop Cult
Cahiers ORSTOM. Physiologie des Plantes Tropicales Cultivees. Office de la Recherche Scientifique et Technique d'Outre-Mer — Cah ORSTOM Physiol Pl Trop Cult
Cahiers. ORSTOM [*Office de la Recherche Scientifique et Technique d'Outre-Mer*]. Serie Biologie — Cah ORSTOM Ser Biol
Cahiers. ORSTOM [*Office de la Recherche Scientifique et Technique d'Outre-Mer*]. Serie Entomologie Medicale — Cah ORSTOM Ser Entomol Med
Cahiers. ORSTOM [*Office de la Recherche Scientifique et Technique d'Outre-Mer*]. Serie Entomologie Medicale et Parasitologie — Cah ORSTOM Ser Entomol Med Parasitol
Cahiers. ORSTOM [*Office de la Recherche Scientifique et Technique d'Outre-Mer*]. Serie Hydrobiologie — Cah ORSTOM Ser Hydrobiol
Cahiers. ORSTOM [*Office de la Recherche Scientifique et Technique d'Outre-Mer*]. Serie Hydrologie — Cah ORSTOM Ser Hydrol
Cahiers. ORSTOM [*Office de la Recherche Scientifique et Technique d'Outre-Mer*]. Serie Oceanographie — Cah ORSTOM Ser Oceanogr
Cahiers. ORSTOM [*Office de la Recherche Scientifique et Technique d'Outre-Mer*]. Serie Pedologie — Cah ORSTOM Ser Pedol
Cahiers. ORSTOM [*Office de la Recherche Scientifique et Technique d'Outre-Mer*]. Serie Pedologie — Cahiers ORSTOM Pedologie
Cahiers ORSTOM. [*Office de la Recherche Scientifique et Technique d'Outre-Mer. France*] **Serie Physiologie des Plantes Tropicales Cultivees** — Cah ORSTOM Ser Physiol Plant Trop Cultiv
Cahiers. ORSTOM [*Office de la Recherche Scientifique et Technique d'Outre-Mer*]. Serie Sciences Humaines — C ORSTOM Ser Sci Hum
Cahiers. ORSTOM [*Office de la Recherche Scientifique et Technique d'Outre-Mer*]. Serie Sciences Humaines — Cah ORSTOM Ser Sci Hum
Cahiers Pedagogiques — C Pedag
Cahiers Pedagogiques. Institut d'Etudes Occitanes — C Pedag Inst Et Occitanes
Cahiers Pedopsychiatriques — Cah Pedopsych
Cahiers Philosophiques Africains — Cah Phil Afr
Cahiers Pierre Loti — Cah P L
Cahiers Points et Contrepoints — Cah P et CP
Cahiers Pologne-Allemagne — Cah Pologne Allemagne
Cahiers pour l'Analyse — Cah Anal
Cahiers Protestants — Cah Prot
Cahiers Quebecois de Demographie — Cah Quebecois Demographie
Cahiers Raciniens — Cah Rac
Cahiers Raciniens — CRa
Cahiers Renaniens — Cahiers R
Cahiers Rene de Lucinge — Cah Rene de Lucinge
Cahiers Roumains d'Etudes Litteraires — CREL
Cahiers Saint-John Perse — CSJP
Cahiers Sarregueminois — Cah Sar
Cahiers Scientifiques — Cahiers Sci
Cahiers Scientifiques (Supplement to Bois et Forets des Tropiques) — Cahiers Sci (Suppl Bois Forets Trop)
Cahiers. Seminar d'Histoire des Mathematiques — Cah Seminar Hist Math
Cahiers Sextil Puscariu — CSP
Cahiers Simone Weil — CSW
Cahiers Sioniens [*Paris*] — CahSion
Cahiers Sioniens [*Paris*] — CS
Cahiers Sioniens [*Paris*] — CSion
Cahiers Socialistes — Cah Soc
Cahiers. Societe Asiatique — CSA
Cahiers Staeliens — Cah Staeeliens
Cahiers Staeliens — Cahiers S
Cahiers Techniques. Centre National de Coordination des Etudes et Recherches sur la Nutrition et l'Alimentation — Cah Tech Cent Nat Coord Etud Rech Nutr Aliment
Cahiers Techniques de l'Art — Cah Tech
Cahiers Techniques de l'Art — Cahiers Techniques
Cahiers - Theatre Louvain — CTL
Cahiers Thomistes — CT
Cahiers Universitaires Catholiques — CUC
Cahiers van de Stichting Bio-Wetenschappen en Maatschappij — Cah Sticht Bio-Wet Maatsch
Cahiers Victoriens et Edouardiens — Cah Vict Ed
Cahiers Victoriens et Edouardiens — Cah Victoriens Edouardiens
Cahiers Victoriens et Edouardiens — CVE
Cahiers Vilfredo Pareto — Cah V Paret
Cahiers Vilfredo Pareto. Revue Europeenne des Sciences Sociales — Cah Vilfredo Pareto
Cahiers voor Bedrijfsgeneeskunde — Cah Bedrijfsgeneeskd
Cahiers Zairois de la Recherche et du Developpement — C Zair Rech Develop
Cahiers Zairois de la Recherche et du Developpement — Cah Zairois Rech et Dev
Cahiers Zairois d'Etudes Politiques et Sociales — C Zair Et Polit Soc
Cahiers Zairois d'Etudes Politiques et Sociales — Cah Zair Et Polit Soc
Cahiers Zairois d'Etudes Politiques et Sociales — Cah Zairois Etud Pol et Soc
Cahiers Zairois d'Etudes Politiques et Sociales — Cah Zairois Etud Polit et Soc
CAHPER [*Canadian Association for Health, Physical Education, and Recreation*] **Journal** — CAHJ
CAHPER [*Canadian Association for Health, Physical Education, and Recreation*] **Journal** — CAHPER J
CAHS [*Canadian Aviation Historical Society*] **Journal** — CAHS
CAIC [*Computer Assisted Instruction Center*] **Technical Memo. Florida State University** — CAI
Caiman Barbudo — CB
Cairn. Archives of the Canadian Rockies Newsletter — CARN
Cairo Document — CD
Cairo Papyri — P Cair
Cairo Studies in English — Cairo St Engl
Cairo Studies in English — CaiSE
Cairo University. Faculty of Agriculture. Bulletin — Cairo Univ Fac Agric Bull
Cairo University. Faculty of Pharmacy. Bulletin — Cairo Univ Fac Pharm Bull
Cairo University. Faculty of Science. Bulletin — Cairo Univ Fac Sci Bull
Cairo University. Herbarium. Publications — Cairo Univ Herb Publ
Cairo University. Medical Journal — Cairo Univ Med J
Caisse Israelite de Demarrage Economique — CIDE
Cakavska Ric — CaR
Calabria Nobilissima — CalN
Calabria Nobilissima — CaN
Calabria Nobilissma. Periodico di Arte, Storia, e Letteratura Calabrese — Cal Nob
Calcified Tissue International — Calcif Tissue Int
Calcified Tissue Research [*Later, Calcified Tissue International*] — Calc Tiss Res
Calcified Tissue Research [*Later, Calcified Tissue International*] — Calcif Tiss
Calcified Tissue Research [*Later, Calcified Tissue International*] — Calcif Tissue Res
Calcified Tissue Research [*Later, Calcified Tissue International*] — CATRB
Calcified Tissues. Proceedings of the European Symposium — Calcif Tissues Proc Eur Symp
Calcitonin Proceedings. International Symposium — Calcitonin Proc Int Symp
Calcium and Cell Function — Calcium Cell Funct
Calcoin News — CN
Calculi. Department of Classics. Dartmouth — Calc
Calculus of Variations and Partial Differential Equations — Calc Var Partial Differential Equations
Calcutta Historical Journal — Calcutta Hist J
Calcutta Journal of Medicine — Calc J M
Calcutta Journal of Natural History and Miscellany of the Arts and Sciences in India — Calcutta J Nat Hist
Calcutta Medical Journal — Calcutta Med J
Calcutta Medical Review — Calc Med Rev
Calcutta Review — Calc Rev
Calcutta Review — Calcutta R
Calcutta Review — CalR
Calcutta Review — CR
Calcutta Sanskrit College Research Series — CSCRS
Calcutta Statistical Association. Bulletin — Calcut St
Calcutta Statistical Association. Bulletin — Calcutta Statist Assoc Bull
Calcutta Statistical Association. Bulletin — CSA
Caldas Medico — Cald Med
Caledonian Medical Journal — Caled Med J

Calendario Forestale Italiano — Cal For Ital
CALF News. Concerning America's Livestock Feeders — CALF News Concern Am Livest Feeders
Calgary Archaeologist. University of Calgary [*Canada*] — CAAR
Caliban — Cal
Caliche — Cal
CALICO [*Computer-Assisted Language Learning and Instruction Consortium*] **Journal** — CALICO J
Calicut University Research Journal — Calicut Univ Res J
California — ICAL
California Academy of Sciences — Cal Ac Sc
California Academy of Sciences. Memoirs — Cal Ac Sc Mem
California Academy of Sciences. Memoirs — Calif Acad Sci Mem
California Academy of Sciences. Occasional Papers — Cal Ac Sc Oc P
California Academy of Sciences. Occasional Papers and Proceedings — Calif Acad Sci Occasional Paper Proc
California Academy of Sciences. Proceedings — Cal Ac Sc Pr
California Academy of Sciences. Proceedings — California Acad Sci Proc
California Administrative Code — Cal Admin Code
California Administrative Notice Register — Cal Admin Notice Reg
California Advance Legislative Service (Deering) — Cal Adv Leg Serv (Deering)
California. Agricultural Experiment Station. Bulletin — Calif Agric Exp Stn Bull
California. Agricultural Extension Service. Circular — Calif Agric Ext Serv Circ
California Agriculture — CAGRA
California Agriculture — Cal Agr
California Agriculture — Calif Agr
California Agriculture — Calif Agric
California Agriculture. California Agricultural Experiment Station — Calif Agric Calif Agric Exp Stn
California Air Environment — Calif Air Environ
California Air Quality Data — Calif Air Qual Data
California Air Quality Data — CAQDA
California and Western Medicine — Calif West Med
California and Western Medicine — California West Med
California and Western States Grape Grower — Calif West States Grape Grow
California Anthropologist — Calif Anthropol
California Appellate Reports — Cal App
California Art and Nature — Calif Art Nat
California Association of Nurse Anesthetists — CANA
California Avocado Society Yearbook — Calif Avocado Soc Yearb
California Bee Times — Calif Bee Times
California Birds — Calif Birds
California Business — Calif Bus
California Business Education Journal — Calif Bus Ed J
California Cattleman — Calif Cattleman
California Citation News — Calif Cit News
California Citrograph — Cal Citrograph
California Citrograph — Calif Citrogr
California Connections [*Database*] — CALCON
California Cooperative Oceanic Fisheries Investigations. Atlas — Calif Coop Oceanic Fish Invest Atlas
California Cooperative Oceanic Fisheries Investigations. Reports — Calif Coop Oceanic Fish Invest Rep
California Countryman — Cal Countryman
California Cultivator — Cal Cultivator
California Culturist. A Journal of Agriculture, Horticulture, Mechanism, and Mining — Calif Cult
California Dairyman — Cal Dairym
California Dental Association. Journal — CDA J
California. Department of Agriculture. Biennial Report — Calif Dep Agric Bienn Rep
California. Department of Agriculture. Bulletin — Calif Ag Bul
California. Department of Agriculture. Bulletin — Calif Dep Agric Bull
California. Department of Agriculture. Bureau of Entomology. Occasional Papers — Calif Dep Agric Bur Entomol Occas Pap
California. Department of Agriculture. Bureau of Entomology. Occasional Papers — Calif Dept Agric Bur Entomol Occas Pap
California. Department of Agriculture. Monthly Bulletin — Calif Dep Agric Mon Bull
California. Department of Conservation. Division of Mines and Geology. Special Report — Calif Dep Conserv Div Mines Geol Spec Rep
California. Department of Fish and Game. Fish Bulletin — Calif Dep Fish Game Fish Bull
California. Department of Fish and Game. Game Bulletin — Calif Dep Fish Game Game Bull
California. Department of Food and Agriculture. Laboratory Services-Entomology. Occasional Papers — Calif Dep Food Agric Lab Serv-Entomol Occas Pap
California. Department of Natural Resources. Division of Mines. Bulletin — Calif Dep Nat Resour Div Mines Bull
California. Department of Natural Resources. Division of Mines. Bulletin — Calif Dept Nat Res Div Mines Bull
California. Department of Natural Resources. Division of Mines. Economic Mineral Map — Calif Dept Nat Res Div Mines Econ Mineral Map
California. Department of Natural Resources. Division of Mines. Mineral Information Service — Calif Dept Nat Res Div Mines Mineral Inf Service
California. Department of Natural Resources. Division of Mines. Report of State Mineralogist — Calif Dept Nat Res Div Mines Rept State Mineralogist
California. Department of Natural Resources. Division of Mines. Special Report — Calif Dep Nat Resour Div Mines Spec Rep
California. Department of Natural Resources. Division of Mines. Special Report — Calif Dept Nat Res Div Mines Special Rept
California. Department of Natural Resources. Division of Soil Conservation. Bulletin — Calif Dep Nat Resour Div Soil Conserv Bull
California. Department of Public Works. Division of Water Resources. Bulletin — Calif Dept Public Works Div Water Res Bull
California. Department of Public Works. Division of Water Resources. Water Quality Investigations Report — Calif Dept Public Works Div Water Res Water Quality Inv Rept
California. Department of Water Resources. Bulletin — Calif Dept Water Res Bull
California. Department of Water Resources. Bulletin — California Dept Water Resources Bull
California. Department of Water Resources. Division of Resources. Planning Bulletin — Calif Dept Water Res Div Res Plan Bull
California. Department of Water Resources. Report — Calif Dept Water Res Rept
California. Division of Forestry. Fire Control Experiments — Calif Div For Fire Control Exp
California. Division of Forestry. Fire Control Notes — Calif Div For Fire Control Notes
California. Division of Mines and Geology. Bulletin — Calif Div Mines Geol Bull
California. Division of Mines and Geology. Bulletin — California Div Mines and Geology Bull
California. Division of Mines and Geology. Bulletin — CDMBA
California. Division of Mines and Geology. County Report — Calif Div Mines Geol Cty Rep
California. Division of Mines and Geology. County Report — Calif Div Mines Geol Rep
California. Division of Mines and Geology. Geologic Data Map — Calif Div Mines Geol Geol Data Map
California. Division of Mines and Geology. Map Sheet — California Div Mines and Geology Map Sheet
California. Division of Mines and Geology. Map Sheet Series — Calif Div Mines Geol Map Sheet Ser
California. Division of Mines and Geology. Mineral Information Service — California Div Mines and Geology Mineral Inf Service
California. Division of Mines and Geology. Report of the State Geologist — Calif Div Mines Geol Rep State Geol
California. Division of Mines and Geology. Special Publication — Calif Div Mines Geol Spec Publ
California. Division of Mines and Geology. Special Report — Calif Div Mines Geol Spec Rep
California. Division of Mines and Geology. Special Report — California Div Mines and Geology Spec Rept
California. Division of Oil and Gas. Annual Report — Calif Div Oil Gas Annu Rep
California Education — Calif Ed
California Elementary School Administrators Association. Monographs — Calif El Sch Adm Assn Mon
California Elementary School Administrators Association. Yearbook — Calif El Sch Adm Assn Yearbook
California English Journal — Cal Engl J
California English Journal — CEJ
California Farmer — Calif Farmer
California Farmer. Central Edition — Calif Farmer Cent Ed
California Feeders' Day — Calif Feeders Day
California Fire Control Notes. California Division of Forestry — Calif Fire Control Note Calif Div For
California Fire Prevention Notes. California Division of Forestry — Calif Fire Prev Note Calif Div For
California Fish and Game — CAFGA
California Fish and Game — Cal Fl Ga
California Fish and Game — Calif Fish
California Fish and Game — Calif Fish Game
California Florist — Calif Florist
California Folklore Quarterly — Cal Folkl Q
California Folklore Quarterly — Calif Folklore Qu
California Folklore Quarterly — CFQ
California Forestry — Calif Forest
California Forestry and Forest Products — Cal For For Prod
California Forestry and Forest Products — Calif For For Prod
California Forestry and Forest Products. University of California. Forest Products Laboratory — Calif For & For Prod Calif For Prod Lab
California Forestry Note — Calif For Note
California Geographer — Calif Geogr
California Geography — Cal Geogr
California Geology — Calif Geol
California Geology — California Geol
California Grower — Calif Grower
California Grower and Rancher. Sacramento Valley Edition — Calif Grow Rancher Sacramento Val Ed
California Highways and Public Works — Calif Highw Public Works
California Historical Courier — Calif Hist Courier
California Historical Quarterly — CaHQ
California Historical Quarterly — Calif Hist Q
California Historical Quarterly [*San Francisco*] — CHQ
California Historical Society. Quarterly — C H Soc Q
California Historical Society. Quarterly [*San Francisco*] — Calif Hist Soc Q
California Historical Society. Quarterly [*San Francisco*] — Calif Hist Soc Quar
California Historical Society. Quarterly [*San Francisco*] — CHSQ
California History — Calif Hist
California History Nugget — Cali His Nugget
California Horticultural Journal — Calif Hortic J
California Horticulturist and Floral Magazine — Calif Hort Fl Mag
California Hospitals — Calif Hosp
California Housing Outlook — Calif Hous
California Institute of Technology. Division of Geological Sciences. Contributions — Calif Inst Technology Div Geol Sci Contr

California Institute of Technology. Earthquake Engineering Research Laboratory (Report) EERL — Calif Inst Technol Earthquake Eng Res Lab (Rep) EERL
California Institute of Technology. Jet Propulsion Laboratory. Special Publication JPL SP — Calif Inst Technol Jet Propul Lab Spec Publ JPL SP
California Institute of Technology. Jet Propulsion Laboratory. Technical Memorandum — Calif Inst Technol Jet Propul Lab Tech Memo
California Institute of Technology. Jet Propulsion Laboratory. Technical Report — Calif Inst Technol Jet Propul Lab Tech Rep
California Journal — Cal J
California Journal of Development — Cal J Dev
California Journal of Educational Research — Cal J Educ Res
California Journal of Educational Research — Calif J Ed Res
California Journal of Educational Research — Calif J Edu
California Journal of Elementary Education — Calif J El Ed
California Journal of Mines and Geology — Cal J Min
California Journal of Mines and Geology — Calif J Mines Geol
California Journal of Mines and Geology — Calif Jour Mines and Geology
California Journal of Mines and Geology — CJMGA
California Journal of Secondary Education — Calif J Sec Ed
California Journal of Teacher Education — Calif Jnl Teach Educ
California Journal of Technology — Cal J Tech
California Journal of Technology — Cal J Techn
California Landscape Management — Calif Landscape Manage
California Law Review — CA LR
California Law Review — CAL
California Law Review — Cal L Rev
California Law Review — Cal Law R
California Law Review — Cal LR
California Law Review — Calif L Rev
California Law Review — CL Rev
California Law Review — ICLR
California Lawyer — Cal Law
California Legislative Service (West) — Cal Legis Serv (West)
California Librarian — Cal Libr
California Librarian — Calif Libn
California Librarian — Calif Librn
California Library Directory — CLD
California Library Statistics — CLS
California Library Statistics and Directory — Calif Lib Stat Dir
California Magazine — Calif Mag
California Management Review — Cal Man Rev
California Management Review — Cal Mgmt Rev
California Management Review — Cal Mgt R
California Management Review — Calif Manag
California Management Review — Calif Manag R
California Management Review — Calif Manage Rev
California Management Review — Calif Management Rev
California Management Review — Calif Mgt R
California Management Review — CMD
California Management Review — CMR
California Manufacturers Register [*Database*] — CMR
California Medical and Surgical Reporter — Cal Med Surg Rep
California Medical Bulletin — Cal Med Bull
California Medical Journal — Cal Med J
California Medicine — Cal Med
California Medicine — Calif Med
California Medicine — California Med
California Medicine — CAMEA
California Mental Health News — Cal Ment Hlth Ne
California Miners' Association — Cal M As
California Mining Journal — Calif Min J
California Mining Journal — CLMJA
California Minority Business Enterprises Directory — Calif Min Bus Ent Dir
California Mosquito and Vector Control Association. Proceedings and Papers of the Annual Conference — Calif Mosq Vector Control Assoc Proc Pap Annu Conf
California Mosquito Control Association. Proceedings and Papers of the Annual Conference — Calif Mosq Control Assoc Proc Pap Annu Conf
California Natural History Guides — Calif Nat Hist Guides
California Nurse — Calif Nurs
California Nurse — Calif Nurse
California Nurses Association. Bulletin — CNA Bull
California Oil Fields — Calif Oil Fields
California Oil World — Calif Oil World
California Oil World and Petroleum Industry — Calif Oil World Pet Ind
California Oil World and Petroleum Industry — COWPA
California Olive Industry News — Calif Olive Industr News
California Palace of the Legion of Honor. Museum Bulletin — Calif Pal Leg Hon Bul
California Physical Geography Club. Bulletin — Cal Phys Geog Club B
California Polytechnic Journal — Cal Polyt J
California Poultry Journal — Cal Poult J
California Poultry Letter. University of California Cooperative Extension — Calif Poult Lett Univ Calif Coop Ext
California Poultry Tribune — Cal Poult Trib
California Public Employee Relations — Cal Public Employee Relations
California Public Library Salary Survey — Calif Pub Lib Sal Surv
California Publications in Classical Archaeology — Cal Publ Class Arch
California Quarterly — Cal Q
California Quarterly — Calif Q
California Quarterly — CaQ
California Quarterly of Secondary Education — Cal Q Sec Ed
California Reporter — Cal R
California Reports — Cal
California Safety News — Cal Saf Ne
California Savings and Loan Journal — Cal Savings and Loan J
California School Libraries — Calif Sch Lib
California School Libraries — Calif Sch Libr
California Schools — Calif Sch
California Sewage Works Journal — Cal Sew WJ
California Sewage Works Journal — Calif Sewage Works J
California Slavic Studies — Cal Sl St
California Slavic Studies — Cal SS
California Slavic Studies — Calif Slavic Stud
California Slavic Studies — California Slav Stud
California Slavic Studies — CSS
California Socialist — Calif Social
California State Bar Journal — Cal St BJ
California State Bar Journal — Calif St Bar Jnl
California State Commission of Horticulture. Monthly Bulletin — Cal State Comm Hort B
California State Department of Education. Bulletin — Calif State Dept Education Bull
California. State Department of Public Health. Monthly Bulletin — Calif State Dep Public Health Mon Bull
California. State Department of Public Health. Quarterly Bulletin — Calif State Dep Public Health Q Bull
California. State Department of Public Health. Weekly Bulletin — Calif State Dep Public Health Wkly Bull
California State Journal of Medicine — Cal St J Med
California State Journal of Medicine — Calif State J Med
California State Library Newsletter — CSLN
California State Mining Bureau — Cal St M Bur
California State Mining Bureau. Annual Report. Bulletin — Cal St M Bur An Rp B
California State Publications — CSP
California State University (Chico). Regional Programs Monograph — Calif State Univ (Chico) Reg Programs Monogr
California State Water Pollution Control Board. Publication — Calif State Water Pollut Control Board Publ
California State Water Pollution Control Board. Publication — Calif State Water Pollution Control Board Pub
California State Water Resources Board. Bulletin — Calif State Water Res Board Bull
California State Water Resources Control Board. Publication — Calif State Water Resour Control Board Publ
California Studies in Classical Antiquity — Cal St Class Ant
California Studies in Classical Antiquity — Calif St Cl Ant
California Studies in Classical Antiquity — CSCA
California Studies in the History of Science — California Stud Hist Sci
California Turfgrass Culture. California University. Berkeley Cooperative Extension Service — Calif Turfgrass Cult Calif Univ Berkeley Coop Ext Serv
California Union List of Periodicals [*Database*] — CULP
California. University. Agricultural Experiment Station. Bulletin — Calif Univ Agric Exp Stn Bull
California. University. Agricultural Experiment Station. Circular — Calif Univ Agric Exp Stn Circ
California University. Agricultural Experiment Station. Ground Water Studies — Calif Univ Agr Expt Sta Ground Water Studies
California University (Berkeley). Water Resources Center. Desalination Report — Calif Univ (Berkeley) Water Resour Cent Desalin Rep
California University. Chronicle — Calif Univ Chron
California University. Institute of Transportation and Traffic Engineering. Information Circular — Calif Univ Inst Transp and Traffic Eng Inf Circ
California University. Memoirs — Calif Univ Mem
California University. Publications. Department of Geology. Bulletin — Cal Univ Dp G B
California University [*Berkeley*]. Publications in Agricultural Science — Cal Univ Pub
California University. Publications in Astronomy — Calif Univ Pubs Astronomy
California University. Publications in Geography — Cal Univ Pub Geog
California University. Publications in Geography — Calif Univ Pubs Geography
California University. Publications in Geological Sciences — Calif Univ Publ Geol Sci
California University. Publications in Geological Sciences — Calif Univ Pubs Geol Sci
California University. Publications in Geological Sciences — California Univ Pubs Geol Sci
California University. Publications in Zoology — Calif Univ Pubs Zoology
California University. Publications. Seismography Stations. Bulletin — Cal Univ Seism Sta B
California University (Riverside). Campus Museum. Contributions — Calif Univ (Riverside) Campus Mus Contrib
California University. Scripps Institution of Oceanography. Annual Report — Calif Univ Scripps Inst Oceanogr Annu Rep
California University. Scripps Institution of Oceanography. Bulletin — Calif Univ Scripps Inst Oceanogr Bull
California University. Scripps Institution of Oceanography. Contributions — Calif Univ Scripps Inst Oceanogr Contrib
California University. Scripps Institution of Oceanography. Reference Series — Calif Univ Scripps Inst
California University. Scripps Institution of Oceanography. Reference Series — Calif Univ Scripps Inst Oceanogr Ref Ser
California University. Scripps Institution of Oceanography. SIO Reference — Calif Univ Scripps Inst Oceanography SIO Reference
California University. Scripps Institution of Oceanography. Submarine Geology Report — Calif Univ Scripps Inst Oceanography Submarine Geology Rept

California University. Water Resources Center Archives. Archives Series Report. Contributions — Calif Univ Water Res Center Archives Archives Ser Rept Contr
California. University. Water Resources Center. Contribution — Calif Univ Water Resour Cent Contrib
California University. Water Resources Center. Report — Calif Univ Water Resour Cent Rep
California University. Water Resources Center. Report — California Univ Water Resources Center Rept
California Unreported Cases — Cal Unrep
California Vector Views — Calif Vector Views
California Veterinarian — Calif Vet
California Water Pollution Control Association. Bulletin — Calif Water Pollut Control Assoc Bull
California Water Pollution Control Association. Bulletin — CWPBA
California Water Resources Center Report — Calif Water Resour Cent Rep
California Weed Conference. Proceedings — Calif Weed Conf Proc
California Western International Law Journal — CA WILJ
California Western International Law Journal — Cal W Int LJ
California Western International Law Journal — Cal W Int'l LJ
California Western International Law Journal — Calif W Int Law J
California Western International Law Journal — Calif W Int'l LJ
California Western International Law Journal — Calif West Int'l LJ
California Western International Law Journal — Calif Western Int L J
California Western Law Review — CA WLR
California Western Law Review — Cal W LR
California Western Law Review — Cal Western Law R
California Western Law Review — Cal WL Rev
California Western Law Review — Calif West L Rev
California Western Law Review — Calif Western L Rev
California Western Law Review — Calif WL Rev
California Western Law Review — California West L Rev
California Western Law Review — CWLR
Californian Illustrated Magazine — Calif M
Californian Law Review — Californian Law Rev
California's Health — Cal Hlth
California's Health — Calif Health
Californium-252 Progress — Californium 252 Prog
Californium-252 Progress — CFTPB
Calitatea Productiei si Metrologie — Calitatea Prod & Metrol
Callaloo — GCAL
Cal-Neva Token Ledger — Cal Neva TL
Calore — CALOA
Calore e Tecnologia — Calore Tecnol
Calorie — CALOD
Calorimetry and Thermal Analysis — Calorim Therm Anal
CALPHAD. Computer Coupling of Phase Diagrams and Thermochemistry — CALPHAD Comput Coupling Phase Diagrams and Thermochem
Calvin Theological Journal — Cal Th J
Calvin Theological Journal — Calv Theol J
Calvin Theological Journal [*Grand Rapids, MI*] — CalvTJ
Calvin Theological Journal — CTJ
Calwer Hefte zur Foerderung Biblischen Glaubens und Christlichen Lebens — CalwerH
Camara de Comercio de Bogota. Revista — Camara Comer Bogota R
Camara de Comercio de Bogota. Revista — CCZ
Camara de Industria y Comercio Argentino-Alemana — CAA
Camara Textil de Mexico. Revista Tecnica — Camara Text Mex Rev Tec
Cambio Internacional (Ecuador) — CIE
Cambio (Mexico) — COM
Camborne School of Mines Magazine — Camborne Sch Mines Mag
Cambrian Archaeological Association. Monographs and Collections — Cambrian Archaeol Ass Monogr Collect
Cambrian Law Review — Cambrian L Rev
Cambrian Law Review — Cambrian Law R
Cambrian Law Review — Cambrian LR
Cambridge Abstracts — Cam Abs
Cambridge Ancient History — C Anc H
Cambridge Ancient History — CAH
Cambridge Ancient History — Cambr Anc Hist
Cambridge Anthropology — Cambridge Anthrop
Cambridge Anthropology — Cambridge Anthropol
Cambridge Antiquarian Society. Proceedings — Camb ASP
Cambridge Bibliographical Society — Camb Bibliog Soc
Cambridge Bibliographical Society. Transactions — Cambr Bibl Soc Trans
Cambridge Biological Studies — Cambr Biol Stud
Cambridge Classical Studies — CCS
Cambridge Classical Texts and Commentaries — CCTC
Cambridge Computer Science Texts — Cambridge Comput Sci Texts
Cambridge Economic Policy Review — Cambridge Econ Pol R
Cambridge Economic Policy Review — Cambridge Econ Policy Rev
Cambridge Economic Policy Review — CEPR
Cambridge Edition of the Works of Immanuel Kant — Cambridge Ed Works Immanuel Kant
Cambridge Environmental Chemistry Series — Cambridge Environ Chem Ser
Cambridge Greek and Latin Classics — CGLC
Cambridge Greek Testament for Schools and Colleges — CGT
Cambridge Historical Journal — Camb Hist J
Cambridge Historical Journal — Cambridge Hist J
Cambridge Historical Journal — CHJ
Cambridge History of Science Series — Cambridge Hist Sci Ser
Cambridge Institute of Education. Bulletin — Cambridge Inst Ed Bulletin
Cambridge International Series on Parallel Computation — Cambridge Internat Ser Parallel Comput
Cambridge Journal — Camb J
Cambridge Journal — Cambridge J
Cambridge Journal — CamJ
Cambridge Journal — CJ
Cambridge Journal of Economics — Cambridge J Econ
Cambridge Journal of Economics — Cambridge J Economics
Cambridge Journal of Economics — ICJE
Cambridge Journal of Education — Cam J Educ
Cambridge Journal of Education — Cambridge J Ed
Cambridge Journal of Education — Cambridge J Educ
Cambridge Law Journal — Camb L J
Cambridge Law Journal — Cambr LJ
Cambridge Law Journal — Cambridge LJ
Cambridge Law Journal — CLJ
Cambridge Lecture Note in Physics — Cambridge Lecture Notes Phys
Cambridge Left — CL
Cambridge Mathematical Library — Cambridge Math Lib
Cambridge Mathematical Textbooks — Cambridge Math Textbooks
Cambridge Mediaeval History — CMH
Cambridge Medieval Celtic Studies — Cambridge Medieval Celtic Stud
Cambridge Medieval Celtic Studies — CMCS
Cambridge Medieval History — C Med H
Cambridge Modern History — Camb Mod Hist
Cambridge Monographs in Experimental Biology — Camb Monogr Exp Biol
Cambridge Monographs on Applied and Computational Mathematics — Cambridge Monogr Appl Comput Math
Cambridge Monographs on Mathematical Physics — Cambridge Mongraphs Math Phys
Cambridge Monographs on Mechanics — Cambridge Monogr Mech
Cambridge Monographs on Mechanics and Applied Mathematics — Cambridge Monogr Mech Appl Math
Cambridge Monographs on Mechanics and Applied Mathematics — Cambridge Monographs Mech Appl Math
Cambridge Monographs on Physics — Cambridge Monographs Phys
Cambridge Nonlinear Science Series — Cambridge Nonlinear Sci Ser
Cambridge Opera Journal — Camb Opera J
Cambridge Oriental Series — Cambr Or Ser
Cambridge Philosophical Society. Biological Reviews — Cambridge Philos Soc Biol Rev
Cambridge Philosophical Society. Mathematical Proceedings — Cambridge Philos Soc Math Proc
Cambridge Philosophical Society. Proceedings — Cambridge Ph Soc Pr
Cambridge Philosophical Society. Transactions — Camb Philos Soc Trans
Cambridge Quarterly — Camb Q
Cambridge Quarterly — Cambridge Q
Cambridge Quarterly — CamQ
Cambridge Quarterly — CQ
Cambridge Quarterly of Healthcare Ethics — Camb Q Healthc Ethics
Cambridge Review — CamR
Cambridge Science Classics — Cambridge Sci Classics
Cambridge Studies in Advanced Mathematics — Cambridge Stud Adv Math
Cambridge Studies in Biological Anthropology — Camb Stud Biol Anthropol
Cambridge Studies in Biotechnology — Camb Stud Biotechnol
Cambridge Studies in Biotechnology — CSBIED
Cambridge Studies in French — CSF
Cambridge Studies in Linguistics — CSL
Cambridge Studies in Mathematical Biology — Cambridge Stud Math Biol
Cambridge Studies in Mathematical Biology — CSMBDC
Cambridge Studies in Medieval Life and Thought — CSMLT
Cambridge Studies in Modern Biology — Camb Stud Mod Biol
Cambridge Studies in Modern Biology — CAMBDM
Cambridge Studies in Modern Optics — Cambridge Stud Mod Opt
Cambridge Studies in Philosophy — Cambridge Stud Philos
Cambridge Studies in Probability, Induction, and Decision Theory — Cambridge Stud Probab Induc Decis Theory
Cambridge Studies in Russian Literature — CSRL
Cambridge Studies in Social Anthropology — Cambridge Stud Soc Anthropology
Cambridge Texts in Applied Mathematics — Cambridge Texts Appl Math
Cambridge Texts in the Physiological Sciences — Camb Texts Physiol Sci
Cambridge Texts in the Physiological Sciences — CESSDT
Cambridge Tracts in Mathematics — Cambridge Tracts in Math
Cambridge Tracts in Mathematics and Mathematical Physics [*Later, Cambridge Tracts in Mathematics*] — Cambr Tr Math
Cambridge Tracts in Theoretical Computer Science — Cambridge Tracts Theoret Comput Sci
Cambridge University Agricultural Society. Magazine — Cambr Univ Agr Soc Mag
Cambridge University Engineering and Aeronautical Societies. Journal — Cambr Univ Eng Aeronaut
Cambridge University. Engineering Department. Report CUED/A-Turbo — Cambridge Univ Eng Dep Rep CUED A Turbo
Cambridge University. Engineering Department. Report CUED/C/MATS — Cambridge Univ Eng Dep Rep CUED C MATS
Cambridge University Engineering Society. Journal — Cambr Univ Eng Soc J
Cambridge University Library Bulletin — Camb Univ Lib Bull
Cambridge University Medical Society. Magazine — Cambr Univ Med Soc Mag
Cambridge University Medical Society. Magazine — Cambridge Univ Med Soc Mag
Cambridge Urban and Architectural Studies — Cambridge Urban Architect Stud
Cambridgeshire and Huntingdonshire Archaeological Society — CHAS
CAMCORE Bulletin on Tropical Forestry — CAMCORE Bull Trop For
Camden Society. Publications — CS
Camellia Journal — Camellia J
Camellia Review. Publication. Southern California Camellia Society — Camellia Rev
Camellian. South Carolina Camellia Society — Camellian S Carolina

Camera — CMRAD
Camera and Cine — Camera
Camera Club — Cam Club
Camera (English Edition) — Camera (Engl Ed)
Camera Notes — Cam Not
Camera Obscura — Cam Obs
Camera Obscura — Camera Obsc
Cameron and Carroll — C & C
Cameron Synthetic Fuels Report — Cameron Synth Fuels Rep
Cameron Synthetic Fuels Report — CSFRD
Cameroon. Bulletin. Direction des Mines et de la Geologie — Cameroon Bull Dir Mines Geol
Cameroon. National Office for Scientific and Technical Research of Cameroon. Onarest Scientific Papers — Cameroon Natl Off Sci Tech Res Cameroon Onarest Sci Pap
Cameroons. French. Bulletin. Direction des Mines et de la Geologie — Cameroons Fr Bull Dir Mines Geol
Cameroun Agricole, Pastoral, et Forestier — Cameroun Agric Pastor For
Cameroun. Direction des Mines et de la Geologie. Activites Minieres au Cameroun — Cameroun Dir Mines Geol Act Minieres Cameroun
Cameroun Territoire. Bulletin de la Direction des Mines et de la Geologie — Cameroun Territ Bull Dir Mines Geol
Camp de l'Arpa — CdA
CAMP [*Cable Advertising, Merchandising, and Programming*] **Report** — CAMP Rpt
Campaign — C
Campaign — CMPN
Campaigner — Campaign
Campbell Law Review — Campbell L Rev
Campbell Soup Company. Department of Agricultural Research. Bulletin — Campbell Soup Dep Agric Res Bull
Campbell Soup Company. Department of Agricultural Research. Research Monograph — Campbell Soup Co Dep Agric Res Res Monogr
Campbell Soup Company. Department of Agricultural Research. Research Monograph — Campbell Soup Dep Agric Res Res Monogr
Camping Magazine — Camp Mag
Camping Magazine — Camping
Camping Magazine — ICAM
Campo. Banco Agricola de Bolivia (La Paz) — Campo La Paz
Campo. Diarios e Emissoras Associadas do Rio Grande do Sul (Porto Alegre) — Campo Porto Alegre
Campo y Suelo Argentino — Campo Suelo Argent
Campus Life — CaL
Canada Agriculture — CAAGB
Canada Agriculture — Can Agric
Canada. Agrometeorology Research and Service. Chemistry and Biology Research Institute. Research Branch Technical Bulletin — CARSCT
Canada. An Historical Magazine — Can Hist Mag
Canada and the World — Can & World
Canada and the World — GCTW
Canada. Arctic Land Use Research Program Report — Can Arct Land Use Res Prog Rep
Canada. Arctic Land Use Research Program. Report ALUR — Can Arct Land Use Res Program Rep ALUR
Canada. Board of Grain Commissioners. Grain Research Laboratory. Annual Report — Can Board Grain Comm Grain Res Lab Annu Rep
Canada. Centre de Recherches Forestieres des Laurentides. Rapport d'Information LAU-X (Edition Francaise) — Can Cent Rech For Laurentides Rapp Inf LAUX Ed Fr
Canada. Centre de Terminologie. Bulletin de Terminologie — Can Cent Terminol Bull Terminol
Canada. Centre for Inland Waters. Data Report Series — CCIWD
Canada. Centre for Inland Waters. Field Report Series — CCIWF
Canada. Centre for Inland Waters. Manuscript Report Series — CCIWM
Canada. Centre for Inland Waters. Technical Note Series — CCIWT
Canada Centre for Mineral and Energy Technology. CANMET Report — Can Cent Miner Energy Technol CANMET Rep
Canada. Centre for Mineral and Energy Technology. Publications — Can Cent Miner Energy Technol Publ
Canada. Centre for Mineral and Energy Technology. Scientific Bulletin — Can Cent Miner Energy Technol Sci Bull
Canada Centre for Mineral and Energy Technology. Special Publication — Can Cent Miner Energy Technol Spec Publ
Canada. Climatological Studies — CACS
Canada Commerce — Can Commer
Canada Commerce — Can Commerce
Canada Commerce — CIJ
Canada Communicable Disease Report — Can Commun Dis Rep
Canada Crafts — Can Crafts
Canada Defence Research Board. Handbook — Canada Defence Research Board Handb
Canada. Defence Research Establishment. Ottawa. Reports — CDREOR
Canada. Department of Agriculture. Annual Report — Can Dep Agric Annu Rep
Canada. Department of Agriculture. Bulletin — Can Dep Agric Bull
Canada. Department of Agriculture. Circular — Can Dep Agric Circ
Canada. Department of Agriculture. Extension Circular — Can Dep Agric Ext Circ
Canada. Department of Agriculture. Farmers' Bulletin — Can Dep Agric Farmers Bull
Canada. Department of Agriculture. Plant Research Institute. Agrometeorology Section. Technical Bulletin — Can Dep Agric Plant Res Inst Agro-Meteorol Sect Tech Bull
Canada. Department of Agriculture. Plant Research Institute. Agrometeorology Section. Technical Bulletin — CPATBH
Canada. Department of Agriculture. Publication — Can Dep Agric Publ
Canada. Department of Agriculture. Publication — Canada Ag
Canada. Department of Agriculture. Research Branch Monograph — Can Dep Agric Res Branch Monogr
Canada. Department of Agriculture. Research Branch Report — Can Dep Agric Res Branch Rep
Canada. Department of Agriculture. Technical Bulletin — Can Dep Agric Tech Bull
Canada. Department of Energy, Mines, and Resources. Earth Physics Branch. Memoir — Can Dep Energy Mines Resources Earth Phys Br Mem
Canada. Department of Energy, Mines, and Resources. Earth Physics Branch. Mineral Report — Can Dep Energy Mines Resources Earth Phys Br Mineral Rep
Canada. Department of Energy, Mines, and Resources. Earth Science Branch. Information Circular — Can Dep Energy Mines Resources Earth Sci Br Inform Circ
Canada. Department of Energy, Mines, and Resources. Geological Survey of Canada. Bulletin — Can Dep Energy Mines Resour Geol Surv Can Bull
Canada. Department of Energy, Mines, and Resources. Geological Survey of Canada. Geological Survey Paper — Can Dep Energy Mines Resour Geol Surv Can Geol Surv Pap
Canada. Department of Energy, Mines, and Resources. Inland Waters Branch. Technical Bulletin — EMRIWTB
Canada. Department of Energy, Mines, and Resources. Mineral Resources Division. Mineral Information Bulletin — Can Dep Energy Mines Resour Miner Resour Div Miner Inf Bull
Canada. Department of Energy, Mines, and Resources. Mines Branch. Investigation Report — Can Dep Energy Mines Resour Mines Branch Invest Rep
Canada. Department of Energy, Mines, and Resources. Mines Branch. Monograph — Can Dep Energy Mines Resour Mines Branch Monogr
Canada. Department of Energy, Mines, and Resources. Mines Branch. Technical Bulletin — Can Dep Energy Mines Resour Mines Branch Tech Bull
Canada. Department of Energy, Mines, and Resources. Report — Can Dep Energy Mines Resources Rep
Canada. Department of Environment. Forestry Service Information Report CC-X — Can Dep Environ For Serv Inf Rep CCX
Canada. Department of Fisheries and Forestry. Annual Report — Can Dep Fish For Annu Rep
Canada. Department of Fisheries and Forestry. Annual Report of the Forest Insect and Disease Survey — Can Dept Forestry Disease Surv
Canada. Department of Fisheries and Forestry. Bimonthly Research Notes — Can Dep Fish For Bimon Res Notes
Canada. Department of Fisheries and Forestry. Bimonthly Research Notes — Can Dept Forestry Bimo Res Note
Canada. Department of Fisheries and Forestry. Canadian Forestry Service. Information Report — Can Dep Fish For Can For Ser Inf Rep
Canada. Department of Fisheries and Forestry. Canadian Forestry Service. Information Report FF-X — Can Dep Fish For Can For Serv Inf Rep FF-X
Canada. Department of Fisheries and Forestry. Canadian Forestry Service. Publication — Can Dep Fish For Can For Serv Publ
Canada. Department of Fisheries and Forestry. Departmental Publications — Can Dept Forestry Publ
Canada. Department of Fisheries and Forestry. Forestry Branch Departmental Publication — Can Dep Fish For For Branch Dep Publ
Canada. Department of Fisheries and Forestry. Forestry Branch Publication — Can Dep Fish For For Branch Publ
Canada. Department of Fisheries and Forestry. Research News — Can Dept Forestry Res News
Canada. Department of Fisheries and Oceans. Canadian Special Publication of Fisheries and Aquatic Sciences — Can Dep Fish Oceans Can Spec Publ Fish Aquat Sci
Canada. Department of Fisheries and Oceans. Ocean Dumping Report — Can Dep Fish Oceans Ocean Dumping Rep
Canada. Department of Fisheries. Annual Report — Can Dep Fish Annu Rep
Canada. Department of Fisheries. Trade News — Can Dep Fish Trade News
Canada. Department of Forestry and Rural Development. Annual Report — Can Dep For Rural Dev Annu Rep
Canada. Department of Forestry and Rural Development. Annual Report. Forest Insect and Disease Survey — Can Dep For Rural Dev Annu Rep For Insect Dis Surv
Canada. Department of Forestry and Rural Development. Bi-Monthly Research Notes — Can Dep For Rural Dev Bi-Mon Res Notes
Canada. Department of Forestry and Rural Development. Forestry Branch. Department Publication — Can Dep For Rural Dev For Branch Dep Publ
Canada. Department of Forestry and Rural Development. Forestry Branch. Information Report FF-X — Can Dep For Rural Dev For Branch Inf Rep FF-X
Canada. Department of Forestry and Rural Development. Publication — Can Dep For Rural Dev Publ
Canada. Department of Forestry. Forest Entomology and Pathology Branch. Annual Report. Forest Insect and Disease Survey — CFPIAM
Canada. Department of Forestry. Forest Entomology and Pathology Branch. Bi-Monthly Progress Report — Can Dep For For Entomol Pathol Branch Bi-Mon Prog Rep
Canada. Department of Indian Affairs and Northern Development. Environmental Studies — Can Dep Indian Aff North Dev Environ Stud
Canada. Department of Indian and Northern Affairs. Arctic Land Use Research Program. Report ALUR — Can Dep Indian North Aff Arct Land Use Res Program Rep ALUR
Canada. Department of Mines and Resources. Geological Survey of Canada. Paper — Can Dep Mines Resour Geol Surv Can Pap
Canada. Department of Mines and Resources. Mines and Geology Branch. Bureau of Geology and Topography. Economic Geology Series — Can Dep Mines Resour Bur Geol Topogr Econ Geol Ser
Canada. Department of Mines and Technical Surveys. Geographical Branch. Bibliographical Series — Canada Dept Mines and Tech Surveys Geog Br Bibl Ser

Canada. Department of Mines and Technical Surveys. Geographical Bulletin — Canada Dept Mines and Tech Surveys Geog Bull
Canada. Department of Mines and Technical Surveys. Geographical Paper — Canada Dept Mines and Tech Surveys Geog Paper
Canada. Department of Mines and Technical Surveys. Geological Survey of Canada. Bulletin — Can Dep Mines Tech Surv Geol Surv Can Bull
Canada. Department of Mines and Technical Surveys. Geological Survey of Canada. Economic Geology Report — Can Dep Mines Tech Surv Geol Surv Can Econ Geol Rep
Canada. Department of Mines and Technical Surveys. Geological Survey of Canada. Paper — Can Dep Mines Tech Surv Geol Surv Can Pap
Canada. Department of Mines and Technical Surveys. Memoir — Canada Dept Mines and Tech Surveys Mem
Canada. Department of Mines and Technical Surveys. Mineral Information Bulletin — Can Dep Mines Tech Surv Miner Inf Bull
Canada. Department of Mines and Technical Surveys. Mineral Resources Division. Mineral Information Bulletin — Can Dep Mines Tech Surv Miner Resour Div Miner Inf Bull
Canada. Department of Mines and Technical Surveys. Mineral Resources Division. Mineral Report — Can Dep Mines Tech Surv Miner Resour Div Miner Rep
Canada. Department of Mines and Technical Surveys. Mines Branch. Memorandum Series — Can Dep Mines Tech Surv Mines Branch Memo Ser
Canada. Department of Mines and Technical Surveys. Mines Branch. Monograph — Can Dep Mines Tech Surv Mines Branch Monogr
Canada. Department of Mines and Technical Surveys. Mines Branch. Radioactivity Division. Topical Report — Can Dep Mines Tech Surv Mines Branch Radioact Div Top Rep
Canada. Department of Mines and Technical Surveys. Mines Branch. Report — Can Dep Mines Tech Surv Mines Branch Rep
Canada. Department of Mines and Technical Surveys. Mines Branch. Technical Bulletin — Can Dep Mines Tech Surv Mines Branch Tech Bull
Canada. Department of Mines and Technical Surveys. Mines Branch. Technical Paper — Can Dep Mines Tech Surv Mines Branch Tech Pap
Canada. Department of Mines and Technical Surveys. Miscellaneous Paper Series — Canada Dept Mines and Tech Surveys Misc Paper Ser
Canada Department of Mines. Mines Branch. Memorandum Series — Can Dep Mines Mines Branch Memo Ser
Canada Department of Mines. Mines Branch. Report — Can Dep Mines Mines Branch Rep
Canada. Department of Mines. Mines Branch. Summary Report — Can Mines Br Sum Rp
Canada. Department of Resources and Development. Forestry Branch. Forest Products Laboratory Division. Technical Note — Can Dep Resour Dev For Branch For Prod Lab Div Tech Note
Canada. Department of Resources and Development. National Parks Branch. National Museum of Canada. Bulletin — Can Dep Resour Dev Natl Parks Branch Natl Mus Can Bull
Canada. Department of the Environment. Canadian Forestry Service. Northern Forest Research Centre. Information Report — Can Dep Environ Can For Ser North For Res Cent Inf Rep
Canada. Department of the Environment. Canadian Forestry Service. Northern Forest Research Centre. Information Report NOR-X — Can Dep Environ Can For Serv North For Res Cent Inf Rep NORX
Canada. Department of the Environment. Fisheries and Marine Service. Data Report Series — CEN
Canada. Department of the Environment. Fisheries and Marine Service. Miscellaneous Special Publication — CFMSMSP
Canada. Department of the Environment. Fisheries and Marine Service. Technical Report — CFMSTR
Canada. Department of the Environment. Fisheries and Marine Service. Technical Report Series — C
Canada. Department of the Environment. Inland Waters Branch. Report Series — Can Dep Environ Inland Waters Branch Rep Ser
Canada. Department of the Environment. Inland Waters Directorate. Sediment Data for Canadian Rivers — Can Dep Environ Inland Waters Dir Sediment Data Can Rivers
Canada. Department of the Environment. Marine Sciences Directorate. Manuscript Report Series — Can Dep Environ Mar Sci Dir Manuscr Rep Ser
Canada. Department of the Interior. Report of the Chief Astronomer — Can Dp Interior Rp Chief Astronomer
Canada. Department of the Interior. Superintendent of Mines. Report — Can Dp Interior Sup Mines Rp
Canada. Department of Trade and Commerce. Board of Grain Commissioners. Grain Research Laboratory. Annual Report — Can Dep Trade Commer Board Grain Comm Grain Res Lab Annu Rep
Canada. Dominion Grain Research Laboratory. Annual Report — Can Dom Grain Res Lab Annu Rep
Canada Dominion Observatory Contributions. Publications — Canada Dominion Observatory Contr Pub
Canada. Earth Physics Branch. Publications — Can Earth Phys Branch Publ
Canada. Environmental Conservation Directorate. Solid Waste Management Branch. Report EPS [*Environmental Protection Service*] — Can Environ Conserv Dir Solid Waste Manage Branch Rep EPS
Canada. Environmental Protection Service. Economic and Technical Review Report — Can Environ Prot Serv Econ Tech Rev Rep
Canada. Environmental Protection Service. Economic and Technical Review Report EPS 3 — Can Environ Prot Serv Econ Tech Rev Rep EPS 3
Canada. Environmental Protection Service. Solid Waste Management Branch. Report EPS — Can Environ Prot Serv Solid Waste Manage Branch Rep EPS
Canada. Environmental Protection Service. Surveillance Report EP — Can Environ Prot Serv Surveill Rep EP
Canada. Environmental Protection Service. Technology Development Report — Can Environ Prot Serv Technol Dev Rep
Canada. Fisheries and Environment Canada. Occasional Paper — Can Fish Environ Can Occas Pap
Canada. Fisheries and Marine Service. Data Report. Series Cen-D — Can Fish Mar Serv Data Rep Ser Cen-D
Canada. Fisheries and Marine Service. Industry Report — Can Fish Mar Serv Ind Rep
Canada. Fisheries and Marine Service. Industry Report — FMSCD2
Canada. Fisheries and Marine Service. Manuscript Report — Can Fish Mar Serv Manuscr Rep
Canada. Fisheries and Marine Service. Manuscript Report — FMSRDD
Canada. Fisheries and Marine Service. Miscellaneous Special Publication — Can Fish Mar Serv Misc Spec Publ
Canada. Fisheries and Marine Service. Northern Operations Branch. Pacific Region. Data Report Series — PAC
Canada. Fisheries and Marine Service. Pacific Marine Science Report — CPMSR
Canada. Fisheries and Marine Service Resource Branch. Maritimes Region. Information Publication MAR-N — Can Fish Mar Serv Resour Branch Marit Reg Inf Publ MAR-N
Canada. Fisheries and Marine Service Resource Development Branch. Halifax Progress Report — Can Fish Mar Serv Resour Dev Branch Halifax Prog Rep
Canada. Fisheries and Marine Service Resource Development Branch. Maritimes Region. Report — Can Fish Mar Serv Resour Dev Branch Marit Reg Rep
Canada. Fisheries and Marine Service. Resource Development Branch. Maritimes Region Technical Report. Series Mar-T — TSMRD9
Canada. Fisheries and Marine Service. Technical Report — Can Fish Mar Serv Tech Rep
Canada. Fisheries and Marine Service. Technical Report. Series Cen-T — Can Fish Mar Serv Tech Rep Ser Cen-T
Canada. Fisheries and Oceans. Canadian Contractor Report of Hydrography and Ocean Sciences — CFOCCRH
Canada. Fisheries and Oceans. Ocean Science and Surveys. Technical Note Series — CFOTNS
Canada. Fisheries Research Board. Biological Station. St. Andrews, NB General Series Circular — Can Fish Res Board Biol Stn St Andrews NB Gen Ser Circ
Canada. Fisheries Research Board. Journal — Can Fish Res Board J
Canada. Fisheries Service. Resource Development Branch. Halifax Progress Report — Can Fish Serv Resour Dev Branch Halifax Prog Rep
Canada Folk Bulletin — Can Folk B
Canada. Forest Entomology and Pathology Branch. Annual Report — Can For Entomol Pathol Branch Annu Rep
Canada. Forest Products Research Branch. Annual Report — Can For Prod Res Branch Annu Rep
Canada. Forest Products Research Branch. Technical Note — Can For Prod Res Branch Tech Note
Canada. Forest Research Branch. Annual Report — Can For Res Branch Annu Rep
Canada. Forestry Branch. Departmental Publication — Can For Branch Dep Publ
Canada. Forestry Branch Publication — Can For Branch Publ
Canada. Forestry Service. Bi-Monthly Research Notes — Can For Serv Bi-Mon Res Notes
Canada. Forestry Service. Chemical Control Research Institute. Information Report CC-X — Can For Serv Chem Control Res Inst Inf Rep CCX
Canada. Forestry Service. Department of the Environment. Internal Report CC-16 — Can For Serv Dep Environ Intern Rep CC 16
Canada. Forestry Service. Forest Fire Research Institute. Information Report — Can For Ser For Fire Res Inst Info Rep
Canada Francais — Can Franc
Canada Francais — CF
Canada Gazette. Part I — Can Gaz Part I
Canada Gazette. Part II — Can Gaz Part II
Canada. Geological Survey — Can G S
Canada. Geological Survey. Annual Report — Can G S An Rp
Canada. Geological Survey. Bulletin — Can Geol Surv Bull
Canada. Geological Survey. Bulletin — Canada Geol Survey Bull
Canada. Geological Survey. Economic Geology Report — Can Geol Surv Econ Geol Rep
Canada. Geological Survey. Economic Geology Report — Canada Geol Survey Econ Geology Rept
Canada. Geological Survey. Geophysics Paper — Canada Geol Survey Geophysics Paper
Canada. Geological Survey. Map — Can Geol Surv Map
Canada. Geological Survey. Map — Canada Geol Survey Map
Canada. Geological Survey. Map — CGOMA
Canada. Geological Survey. Memoir — Can G S Mem
Canada. Geological Survey. Memoir — Can Geol Surv Mem
Canada. Geological Survey. Memoir — Canada Geol Survey Mem
Canada. Geological Survey. Miscellaneous Report — Can Geol Surv Misc Rep
Canada. Geological Survey. Museum Bulletin — Can G S Mus B
Canada. Geological Survey. Paper — Can Geol Surv Pap
Canada. Geological Survey. Paper — Canada Geol Survey Paper
Canada. Geological Survey. Preliminary Series. Map — Canada Geol Survey Prelim Ser Map
Canada. Geological Survey. Summary Report — Can G S Sum Rp
Canada. Honorary Advisory Council for Scientific and Industrial Research. Bulletin — Can Honorary Advis CSIR Bull
Canada. Honorary Advisory Council Scientific and Industrial Research. Report — Can Honorary Advis Counc Sci Ind Res Rep
Canada. Indian and Northern Affairs. Environmental Studies — Can Indian North Aff Environ Stud
Canada. Industrial Meteorology Studies. Environment Canada. Atmospheric Environment — CIMS

Canada. Inland Waters Branch. Report Series — Can Inland Waters Branch Rep Ser
Canada. Inland Waters Branch. Scientific Series — Can Inland Waters Branch Sci Ser
Canada. Inland Waters Directorate. Report Series — Can Inland Waters Dir Rep Ser
Canada. Inland Waters Directorate. Scientific Series — Can Inland Waters Dir Sci Ser
Canada. Inland Waters Directorate. Scientific Series — CIWDSS
Canada. Inland Waters Directorate. Sediment Data for Canadian Rivers — Can Inland Waters Dir Sediment Data Can Rivers
Canada. Inland Waters Directorate. Social Science Series — CIWDSSS
Canada. Inland Waters Directorate. Technical Bulletin — CIWDTB
Canada. Inland Waters Directorate. Water Quality Interpretive Report — Can Inland Waters Dir Water Qual Interpret Rep
Canada. Inland Waters Directorate. Water Quality Interpretive Reports — CIWQIR
Canada Institute of Particle Physics Summer School. Proceedings — Can Inst Part Phys Summer Sch Proc
Canada Lancet and Practitioner — Can Lanc
Canada. Marine Environmental Data Service. Technical Report — CMEDSTR
Canada. Marine Sciences Directorate. Department of Fisheries and Oceans. Manuscript Report — CMSDMR
Canada Medical and Surgical Journal — Canada Med Surg J
Canada Medical Journal and Monthly Record of Medical and Surgical Science — Canada Med J
Canada. Meteorological Translations — CAMT
Canada. Mineral Resources Branch. Mineral Bulletin — Can Miner Resour Branch Miner Bull
Canada. Mineral Resources Branch. Mineral Bulletin — CNMBB
Canada. Mineral Resources Branch. Mineral Information Bulletin — Can Miner Resour Branch Miner Inf Bull
Canada. Mineral Resources Branch. Mineral Report — Can Miner Resour Branch Miner Rep
Canada. Mineral Resources Division. Mineral Bulletin — Can Miner Resour Div Miner Bull
Canada. Mineral Resources Division. Operators List — Can Miner Resour Div Oper List
Canada. Mines Branch. Information Circular — Can Mines Branch Inf Circ
Canada. Mines Branch. Information Circular — CMICA
Canada. Mines Branch. Investigation Report — Can Mines Branch Invest Rep
Canada. Mines Branch. Memorandum Series — Can Mines Branch Memo Ser
Canada. Mines Branch. Monograph — Can Mines Branch Monogr
Canada. Mines Branch. Radioactivity Division. Topical Report — Can Mines Branch Radioact Div Top Rep
Canada. Mines Branch. Rapports. Division des Mines — Can Mines Branch Rapp Div Mines
Canada. Mines Branch. Report — Can Mines Branch Rep
Canada. Mines Branch. Research Report — Can Mines Branch Res Rep
Canada. Mines Branch. Technical Bulletin — Can Mines Branch Tech Bull
Canada. Mines Branch. Technical Bulletin — CMTBB
Canada. Mines Branch. Technical Paper — Can Mines Branch Tech Pap
Canada Music Book — Can Mus Bk
Canada. National Aeronautical Establishment. Mechanical Engineering Report — Can Natl Aeronaut Establ Mech Eng Rep
Canada. National Aeronautical Establishment. Mechanical Engineering Report MS — Can Natl Aeronaut Establ Mech Eng Rep MS
Canada. National Museum Bulletin. Natural History Paper. Special Contributions — Canada Natl Mus Bull Nat History Paper Special Contr
Canada. National Research Council. Division of Mechanical Engineering. Laboratory Technical Report — Can Natl Res Counc Div Mech Eng Lab Tech Rep
Canada News-Wire [*Database*] — CNW
Canada - North of 60 — CANS
Canada - North of 60. Newsletter — CANSN
Canada. Northern Forest Research Centre. Information Report NOR-X — Can North For Res Cent Inf Rep NOR-X
Canada. Northern Forest Research Centre. Information Reports — CNOR
Canada. Northern Science Research Group. Reports — CNSRG
Canada. Northern Science Research Group. Social Science Notes — CNSRGSSN
Canada Now Social Studies Magazine for Schools — CANW
Canada Nucleaire — Can Nucl
Canada. Ocean and Aquatic Sciences Central Region. Technical Notes — COAST
Canada. Pacific Forest Research Centre. Report. BC X — Can Pac For Res Cent Rep BC X
Canada. Patent Document — Can Pat Doc
Canada. Patent Office. Patent Office Record — Can Pat Off Pat Off Rec
Canada. Resource Development Branch. Fisheries Service. Halifax Progress Report — Can Resour Dev Branch Fish Ser Halifax Prog Rep
Canada. Statistics Canada. Biscuits and Confectionery — Can Stat Can Biscuits Confect
Canada. Statistics Canada. Coarse Grains Review — Can Stat Can Coarse Grains Rev
Canada. Statistics Canada. Coastwise Shipping Statistics — Can Stat Can Coastwise Shipping Stat
Canada. Statistics Canada. Consumer Credit — Can Stat Can Consumer Credit
Canada. Statistics Canada. Consumption, Production and Inventories of Rubber — Can Stat Can Consumption Rubber
Canada. Statistics Canada. Honey Production and Value. Production Forecast — Can Stat Can Honey
Canada. Statistics Canada. Index of Farm Production — Can Stat Can Index Farm Prod
Canada. Statistics Canada. New Manufacturing Establishments in Canada — Can Stat Can New Manuf
Canada. Statistics Canada. Shorn Wool Production — Can Stat Can Shorn Wool
Canada. Statistics Canada. Tuberculosis Statistics — Can Stat Can Tuberc Stat
Canada. Supreme Court Reports — SCR
Canada. Task Force on Northern Oil Development. Report — CTNOR
Canada. Victoria Memorial Museum. Bulletin — Can Victoria Mem Mus B
Canada. Water Resources Branch. Water Resources Paper — Can Water Resour Branch Water Resour Pap
Canada. Water Resources Branch. Water Resources Paper S. Sediment — Can Water Resour Branch Water Resour Pap S
Canada Weekly — Can W
Canada West — CAWE
Canada. Western Forest Products Laboratory. Information Report VP-X — Can West For Prod Lab Inf Rep VP X
Canada-Mongolia Review — Can-Mong R
Canada's Business Climate — CBU
Canada's Domestic Consumption of Forest Products, 1960-2000 — Cda Forest
Canada's Foundry Journal — Can Foundry J
Canada's Mental Health — Can Ment He
Canada's Mental Health — Can Ment Health
Canada's Mental Health — Can Ment Hlth
Canada's Mental Health — Can Mental Health
Canada's Mental Health — Can's Mental Health
Canada-United States Law Journal — Can-US Law J
Canada-United States Law Journal — Can-US LJ
Canada-West Indies Magazine — Can WI Mag
Canadian Acoustics/Acoustique Canadienne — Can Acoust Acoust Can
Canadian Administrator — Can Admin
Canadian Advertising Rates and Data — CNA
Canadian Aeronautic and Space Institute. Transactions — CAETB
Canadian Aeronautic and Space Institute. Transactions — Can Aeronaut Space Inst Trans
Canadian Aeronautical Journal — Can Aeron J
Canadian Aeronautical Journal — Can Aeronaut J
Canadian Aeronautics and Space Journal — Can Aer Spa
Canadian Aeronautics and Space Journal — Can Aeronaut and Space J
Canadian Aeronautics and Space Journal — Can Aeronaut Space J
Canadian Aeronautics and Space Journal — CSPJA
Canadian Agricultural Engineering — Can Agr Eng
Canadian Agricultural Engineering — Can Agric Eng
Canadian Agricultural Insect Pest Review — Can Agric Insect Pest Rev
Canadian Agriculture — Can Agr
Canadian Aircraft Industries — Can Aircr Ind
Canadian Alpine Journal — CALJ
Canadian Alpine Journal — Can Al J
Canadian Alpine Journal — Canadian Alpine Jour
[*The*] **Canadian Amateur** — TCA
Canadian Anaesthetists' Society. Journal — Can Anae S J
Canadian Anaesthetists' Society. Journal — Can Anaesth Soc J
Canadian Anaesthetists' Society. Journal — Canad Anaesth Soc J
Canadian Anaesthetists' Society. Journal — CANJA
Canadian and International Education — Can Int Educ
Canadian and International Education/Education Canadienne et Internationale [*A publication*] — Can Inter Ed/Ed Can
Canadian Annual Review — CAR
Canadian Antiquarian and Numismatic Journal — Canad Antiq Numis J
Canadian Antiques and Art Dealers Yearbook — Can Ant Art Deal Ybk
Canadian Antiques Collector — Can Ant Coll
Canadian Applied Mathematics Quarterly — Canad Appl Math Quart
Canadian Archaeological Association. Bulletin — CAAB
Canadian Architect — CAARA
Canadian Architect — Can Arch
Canadian Architect — Canadian Archt
Canadian Architect Yearbook — Can Arch Ybk
Canadian Arctic Resources Committee. Monograph. Yukon Series — CARCMYS
Canadian Art — Can Art
Canadian Association for American Studies. Bulletin — CAAS Bull
Canadian Association of College and University Libraries. Newsletter — CACUL Newsl
Canadian Association of Geographers. Education Committee. Bulletin — Canadian Assoc Geographers Education Comm Bull
Canadian Association of Native Peoples. Bulletin — CANP
Canadian Association of Radiologists Journal — Can Assoc Radiol J
Canadian Association of University Teachers/Association Canadienne des Professeurs d'Universite. Bulletin — CAUT ACPU Bul
Canadian Audubon — Can Aud
Canadian Audubon — Can Audubon
Canadian Author and Bookman — Can Auth & Book
Canadian Automotive Trade — Can Automot Trade
Canadian Automotive Trade — CAUTA
Canadian Aviation — Can Av
Canadian Aviation — Cdn Aviat
Canadian Banker [*Formerly, Canadian Banker and ICB Review*] — Can Bank
Canadian Banker [*Formerly, Canadian Banker and ICB Review*] — Can Banker
Canadian Banker [*Formerly, Canadian Banker and ICB Review*] — CBI
Canadian Banker and ICB [*Institute of Canadian Bankers*] **Review** [*Canadian Banker*] [*Later,*] — Can Banker & ICB R
Canadian Banker and ICB [*Institute of Canadian Bankers*] **Review** [*Canadian Banker*] [*Later,*] — Can Banker ICB Rev
Canadian Banker and ICB [*Institute of Canadian Bankers*] **Review** [*Canadian Banker*] [*Later,*] — Cdn Bnk Rv
Canadian Bankruptcy Reports — Can Bank R
Canadian Bankruptcy Reports — Can Bankr

Canadian Bankruptcy Reports — Can Bankr Rep
Canadian Bar Association. Continuing Education Seminars — Can Bar Assoc Cont Educ Sem
Canadian Bar Association. Year Book — Can B Year Book
Canadian Bar Journal — Can B J
Canadian Bar Journal — Can Bar J
Canadian Bar Journal. New Series — Can Bar J (NS)
Canadian Bar Review — Can B Rev
Canadian Bar Review — Can Bar R
Canadian Bar Review — Can Bar Rev
Canadian Bar Review — Can BR
Canadian Bar Review — Canad Bar Rev
Canadian Bar Review — CBR
Canadian Bee Journal — Can Bee J
Canadian Bee Journal — Canad Bee J
Canadian Beekeeping — Can Beekeep
Canadian Biochemical Society. Bulletin — Can Biochem Soc Bull
Canadian Book Review Annual — CBRA
Canadian Bookman — Can Bkman
Canadian Bookman — Canad Bookm
Canadian Books in Print — CBIP
Canadian Building Digest — CABD
Canadian Building Digest — Can Build Dig
Canadian Building Digest — Canadian Bldg Digest
Canadian Building News — Can Build News
Canadian Bulletin of Fisheries and Aquatic Sciences — Can Bull Fish Aquat Sci
Canadian Bulletin of Fisheries and Aquatic Sciences — CBFAS
Canadian Bulletin of Fisheries and Aquatic Sciences — CBFSDB
Canadian Bulletin on Nutrition — Can Bull Nutr
Canadian Business — CABUA
Canadian Business — Can Bus
Canadian Business — CB
Canadian Business and Current Affairs [*Database*] — CBCA
Canadian Business Economics — Can Bus Econ
Canadian Business Index — Can Bus Index
Canadian Business Index [*Micromedia Ltd.*] [*Database Toronto, ON*] — CBI
Canadian Business Law Journal — Can Bus LJ
Canadian Business Law Journal — CBJ
Canadian Business Law Journal — CBL
Canadian Business Magazine — Can Bus Mag
Canadian Business Magazine — Canada Bus
Canadian Business Magazine — CBS
Canadian Business Periodicals Index [*Later, Canadian Business Index*] — Can BPI
Canadian Business Periodicals Index [*Later, Canadian Business Index*] — Can Bus Period Index
Canadian Business Periodicals Index [*Later, Canadian Business Index*] — CBPI
Canadian Business Review — Can Bus R
Canadian Business Review — Can Bus Rev
Canadian Business Review — CAS
Canadian Business Review — CB Review
Canadian Business Review — CBU
Canadian Business Trends. Monthly Indicators — Can Bus Tr M Ind
Canadian Business Trends. Quarterly Indicators — Can Bus Tr Q Ind
Canadian Camping — Can Camp
Canadian Cancer Conference — Can Cancer Conf
Canadian Cancer Conference — CNCCA
Canadian Cancer Conference. Proceedings — Can Cancer Conf Proc
Canadian Capital Markets — Can Cap Mark
Canadian Cartographer — Can Cartogr
Canadian Cases on the Law of Torts — Can Cases L Torts
Canadian Cases on the Law of Torts — CCLT
Canadian Catholic Historial Association Report — Canad Cath Hist Assoc Rep
Canadian Cattlemen — Can Cattlemen
Canadian Cement and Concrete Review — Can Cem Concr Rev
Canadian Centenary Series — Can Cent Ser
Canadian Centre for Folk Culture Studies Papers. National Museum of Man Mercury Series — CCFCSP
Canadian Ceramic Society. Journal — Can Ceram Soc J
Canadian Ceramic Society. Journal — Canadian Ceramic Soc Jour
Canadian Chartered Accountant [*Later, CA Magazine*] — Can Chart Acc
Canadian Chartered Accountant [*Later, CA Magazine*] — Can Chart Account
Canadian Chartered Accountant [*Later, CA Magazine*] — Can Chart Acct
Canadian Chemical Education — Can Chem Educ
Canadian Chemical Journal — Can Chem J
Canadian Chemical News — Can Chem News
Canadian Chemical News — CCHNEE
Canadian Chemical News — Cdn Chem N
Canadian Chemical Processing — Can Chem Proc
Canadian Chemical Processing — Can Chem Process
Canadian Chemical Processing — Canad Chem Process
Canadian Chemical Processing — CCPRA
Canadian Chemical Processing — Cdn Chem P
Canadian Chemical Register — Can Chem Reg
Canadian Chemistry and Metallurgy — Can Chem & Met
Canadian Chemistry and Metallurgy — Can Chem Met
Canadian Chemistry and Metallurgy — Can Chem Metall
Canadian Chemistry and Process Industries — Can Chem & Process Ind
Canadian Chemistry and Process Industry — Can Chem Process
Canadian Chemistry and Process Industry — Can Chem Process Ind
Canadian Children's Literature — Can Child Lit
Canadian Children's Literature — CCL
Canadian Churchman — CACH
Canadian Civil Aircraft Register — Can Civ Aircr Reg
Canadian Clay and Ceramics Quarterly — Can Clay Ceram Q
Canadian Collector — Can Collector
Canadian College of Teachers. Occasional Papers — CCT Occ Pap
Canadian Colleges Sport Scene — Can Coll Sp Sc
Canadian Colorist and Textile Processor — Can Color Text Process
Canadian Committee on Ecological Land Classification. Newsletter — CCELCN
Canadian Communications and Power Conference. Proceedings — Can Commun Power Conf Proc
Canadian Communications and Power Conference. Proceedings — CCPPD
Canadian Communications Network Letter [*Telecommunications service*] — NL
Canadian Community Law Journal — Can Community LJ
Canadian Competition Policy Record — Can Competition Pol
Canadian Composer — Can Comp
Canadian Composer — Can Composer
Canadian Composer — ICMP
Canadian Conservationist — CACO
Canadian Consulting Engineer — Can Consult Eng
Canadian Consumer — CACOD
Canadian Consumer — Can Consum
Canadian Consumer — Can Consumer
Canadian Consumer — ICNS
Canadian Contractor Report of Hydrography and Ocean Sciences — Can Contract Rep Hydrogr Ocean Sci
Canadian Contractor Report of Hydrography and Ocean Sciences — CCRHOS
Canadian Contractor Report of Hydrography and Ocean Sciences — CCRSEB
Canadian Controls and Instrumentation — Can Controls & Instrum
Canadian Controls and Instrumentation — Can Controls Instrum
Canadian Controls and Instrumentation — CCISA
Canadian Controls and Instrumentation — Cdn Contrl
Canadian Controls and Instruments — Can Controls Instruments
Canadian Copper — Can Copper
Canadian Corporate Names [*Database*] — CNAM
Canadian Corporations [*Database*] — CanCorp
Canadian Counsellor — Can Coun
Canadian Counsellor/Conseiller Canadien — Can Couns/Cons Can
Canadian Criminal Cases — Can CC
Canadian Criminal Cases [*Database*] — CCC
Canadian Critical Care Nursing Journal — Can Crit Care Nurs J
Canadian Current Law — Can CL
Canadian Cyclist — Can Cyc
Canadian Dairy and Ice Cream Journal — Can Dairy Ice Cream J
Canadian Dairy and Ice Cream Journal — Canad Dairy Ice Cream J
Canadian Data Report of Fisheries and Aquatic Sciences — Can Data Rep Fish Aquat Sci
Canadian Data Report of Hydrography and Ocean Sciences — Can Data Rep Hydrogr Ocean Sci
Canadian Data Report of Hydrography and Ocean Sciences — CDHSDZ
Canadian Datasystems — Can Data
Canadian Datasystems — Can Datasyst
Canadian Datasystems — Cdn Data
Canadian Defence Quarterly — Can DQ
Canadian Dental Hygienist — Can Dent Hyg
Canadian Dimension — Can Dimen
Canadian Dimension — Dimension
Canadian Dimension — ICDI
Canadian Directory of Completed Master's Theses in Nursing [*Database*] — CAMN
Canadian Distributor and Retailer — Can Dist Ret
Canadian Doctor — Can Doct
Canadian Doctor — Canad Doctor
Canadian Druggist — Can Drug
Canadian Dun's Market Identifiers [*Database*] — CDMI
Canadian Dyer and Color User — Can Dyer Color User
Canadian Education and Research Digest — Can Ed Res Digest
Canadian Education and Research Digest — Can Educ Res Dig
Canadian Education Association. Newsletter — CEA News
Canadian Education Index [*Repertoire Canadien sur l'Education*] — Can Educ Index
Canadian Education Index [*Repertoire Canadien sur l'Education*] — CanEdI
Canadian Education Index [*Repertoire Canadien sur l'Education*] — CEI
Canadian Electrical Association. Transactions of the Engineering and Operating Division — Can Electr Assoc Trans Eng Oper Div
Canadian Electrical Association. Transactions of the Engineering and Operating Division — CEAEA
Canadian Electrical Engineering Journal — Can Electr Eng J
Canadian Electronics Engineering — CAEEA
Canadian Electronics Engineering — Can Electron Eng
Canadian Electronics Engineering — Cdn Elec E
Canadian Energy News — CAEN
Canadian Energy News — Can Energy News
Canadian Engineer — Can Eng
Canadian Engineer — CE
Canadian Entomologist — CAE
Canadian Entomologist — CAENA
Canadian Entomologist — Can Ent
Canadian Entomologist — Can Entm
Canadian Entomologist — Can Entom
Canadian Entomologist — Can Entomol
Canadian Entomologist — Canad Ent
Canadian Entomologist — Canad Entom
Canadian Environment — Can Environ
Canadian Environmental Control Newsletter — CECN
Canadian Environmental Law News — Can Environ Law News
Canadian Essay and Literature Index — Can Essay Lit Index
Canadian Ethnic Studies — CAES
Canadian Ethnic Studies — Can Ethnic Stud

Canadian Ethnic Studies — Can Ethnic Studies
Canadian Ethnic Studies/Etudes Ethniques au Canada — CE Studies
Canadian Family Physician — Can Fam Physician
Canadian Family Physician — Canad Fam Physician
Canadian Farm Economics — Can Farm Ec
Canadian Farm Economics — Can Farm Econ
Canadian Federal Corporations and Directors [*Database*] — CFCD
Canadian Federation of Biological Societies. Proceedings — Can Fed Biol Soc Proc
Canadian Federation of Biological Societies. Proceedings — PCBSA2
Canadian Feed and Grain Journal — Can Feed Grain J
Canadian Fiction Magazine — Can Fic Mag
Canadian Fiction Magazine — CFM
Canadian Field-Naturalist — CAFN
Canadian Field-Naturalist — CAFNA
Canadian Field-Naturalist — Can Fie Nat
Canadian Field-Naturalist — Can Field-Nat
Canadian Field-Naturalist — Can Field-Natur
Canadian Field-Naturalist — Can Fld Nat
Canadian Field-Naturalist — Canad Fld-Nat
Canadian Financial Database — CFD
Canadian Fish Culturist — Can Fi Cu
Canadian Fish Culturist — Can Fish Cult
Canadian Fisheries. Exports — Can Fish Exp
Canadian Fisheries. Imports — Can Fish Imp
Canadian Fisheries Reports — Can Fish Rep
Canadian Fisherman — Can Fisherm
Canadian Fisherman — Can Fisherman
Canadian Folk Music Bulletin — Can Folk Mus Bulletin
Canadian Folk Music Journal — Can Folk Mus
Canadian Folk Music Journal — CFMJ
Canadian Food Bulletin — Can Food Bull
Canadian Food Industries — Can Food Ind
Canadian Food Journal — Can Fd J
Canadian Food Packer — Can Food Pack
Canadian Food Packer — Can Food Packer
Canadian Forces Dental Services Quarterly — Can Forces Dent Serv Q
Canadian Forest Industries — Can For Ind
Canadian Forest Industries — Canad For Ind
Canadian Forest Industries — Cdn Forest
Canadian Forest Industries — CFOI
Canadian Forestry Journal — Can For J
Canadian Forestry Magazine — Can For M
Canadian Forestry Service. Annual Report of the Forest Insect and Disease Survey — Can For Serv Annu Rep For Insect Dis Surv
Canadian Forestry Service. Chemical Control Research Institute. File Report — Can For Serv Chem Control Res Inst File Rep
Canadian Forestry Service. Chemical Control Research Institute. Report CC-X — Can For Serv Chem Control Res Inst Rep CC-X
Canadian Forestry Service. Forest Fire Research Institute. Information Report FF-X — Can For Serv For Fire Res Inst Inf Rep FF-X
Canadian Forestry Service. Forest Fire Research Institute. Miscellaneous Report FF-X — Can For Serv For Fire Res Inst Misc Rep FF-X
Canadian Forestry Service. Forest Management Institute. Information Report FMR-X — Can For Serv For Manage Inst Inf Rep FMR-X
Canadian Forestry Service. Forest Pest Management Institute. Information Report FPM-X — Can For Serv For Pest Manage Inst Inf Rep FPM-X
Canadian Forestry Service. Forest Pest Management Institute. Information Report. FPM-X — RFFID4
Canadian Forestry Service. Forest Pest Management Institute. Report FPM-X — Can For Serv For Pest Manage Inst Rep FPM-X
Canadian Forestry Service. Forestry Publication — CFSFP
Canadian Forestry Service. Forestry Technical Report — Can For Serv For Tech Rep
Canadian Forestry Service. Forestry Technical Report — CFSFTR
Canadian Forestry Service. Great Lakes Forestry Centre. Information Report O-X — Can For Serv Gt Lakes For Cent Inf Rep O-X
Canadian Forestry Service. Northern Forest Research Centre. Forestry Report — Can For Serv North For Res Cent For Rep
Canadian Forestry Service. Northern Forest Research Centre. Forestry Report — CFRTBW
Canadian Forestry Service. Northern Forest Research Centre. Information Report NOR-X — Can For Serv North For Res Cent Inf Rep NOR-X
Canadian Forestry Service. Northern Forest Research Centre. Information Report NOR-X — CNRXAV
Canadian Forestry Service. Pacific Forest Research Centre BC-P — Can For Serv Pac For Res Cent BC-P
Canadian Forestry Service. Pacific Forest Research Centre. Forest Pest Leaflet — Can For Serv Pac For Res Cent For Pest Leafl
Canadian Forestry Service. Pacific Forest Research Centre. Forest Pest Leaflet — FLCFDQ
Canadian Forestry Service. Pacific Forest Research Centre. Information Report BC-X — Can For Serv Pac For Res Cent Inf Rep BC-X
Canadian Forestry Service. Pacific Forest Research Centre. Information Report BC-X — CPFIA8
Canadian Forestry Service. Pacific Forest Research Centre. Report BC-P — CFPFDG
Canadian Forestry Service. Pacific Forest Research Centre. Report BC-R — Can For Serv Pac For Res Cent Rep BC-R
Canadian Forestry Service. Pacific Forest Research Centre. Report BC-X — Can For Serv Pac For Res Cent Rep BC-X
Canadian Forestry Service. Pacific Forest Research Centre. Report BC-X — RBCPDG
Canadian Forestry Service. Petawawa National Forestry Institute. Information Report PI-X — Can For Serv Petawawa Natl For Inst Inf Rep PI-X
Canadian Forestry Service. Publication — Can For Serv Publ
Canadian Forestry Service. Publication — CFOPB5
Canadian Forestry Service. Research News — CFSR
Canadian Forum — CAFO
Canadian Forum — Can F
Canadian Forum — Can Forum
Canadian Forum — Canad Forum
Canadian Forum — CF
Canadian Forum — GCAF
Canadian Foundryman — Can Foundryman
Canadian Foundryman and Electroplater — Can Foundryman Electroplat
Canadian Fruitgrower — Can Fruitgrower
Canadian Fruitgrower — Canad Fruitgrower
Canadian Gas Journal — Can Gas J
Canadian Genealogist — Can Geneal
Canadian Geographer — Can Geog
Canadian Geographer — Can Geogr
Canadian Geographer — Can Geographer
Canadian Geographer — CNGGA
Canadian Geographer — CNGGAR
Canadian Geographer — PCGE
Canadian Geographer/Le Geographe Canadien. Canadian Association of Geographers — CAG/CG
Canadian Geographic — Can Geogr
Canadian Geographic — Can Geographic
Canadian Geographic — CG
Canadian Geographic — CGJ
Canadian Geographic — PCGO
Canadian Geographical Journal [*Later, Canadian Geographic*] — Can Geog J
Canadian Geographical Journal [*Later, Canadian Geographic*] — Can Geogr J
Canadian Geographical Journal [*Later, Canadian Geographic*] — Canad Geog J
Canadian Geographical Journal — Canad Geogr J
Canadian Geographical Journal — CanGJ
Canadian Geographical Journal [*Later, Canadian Geographic*] — CGEJ
Canadian Geographical Journal — CGJ
Canadian Geography — Can Geogr
Canadian Geophysical Bulletin — Can Geoph Bull
Canadian Geophysical Bulletin — Can Geophys Bull
Canadian Geophysical Bulletin — CGBUA
Canadian Geotechnical Journal — Can Geotech J
Canadian Geotechnical Journal — Canadian Geotech Jour
Canadian Geotechnical Journal — CGJO
Canadian Geotechnical Journal — CGJOA
Canadian Gladiolus Society Quarterly — Canad Gladiolus Soc Quart
Canadian Government Publications Quarterly — Can Gov Publ Q
Canadian Government Publications Quarterly — CGPQA
Canadian Government Series — Can Gov Ser
Canadian Grain Research Laboratory. Annual Report — Can Grain Res Lab Annu Rep
Canadian Grain Research Laboratory. Report — Can Grain Res Lab Rep
Canadian Heritage — CAHE
Canadian Heritage — Can Heritage
Canadian Historic Sites. Occasional Papers in Archaeology and History — CHSOP
Canadian Historical Association. Annual Report — Can Hist Ass Ann Rep
Canadian Historical Association. Annual Report — Can Hist Assoc Ann Rep
Canadian Historical Association. Historical Papers — Can Hist Assn
Canadian Historical Association. Report — Can Hist Assn Rep
Canadian Historical Association. Report — Canad Hist Assn Rep
Canadian Historical Review — CAHR
Canadian Historical Review — Can His R
Canadian Historical Review — Can Hist R
Canadian Historical Review — Can Hist Rev
Canadian Historical Review — Canad Hist Rev
Canadian Historical Review — Canadian Hist Rev
Canadian Historical Review — CanHR
Canadian Historical Review — CHR
Canadian Historical Review — PCHR
Canadian Home Economics Journal — Can Home Ec J
Canadian Home Economics Journal — CHEJ
Canadian Home Economics Journal/Revue Canadienne d'Economie Familiale — Can Home Econ J Rev Can Econ Familiale
Canadian Horticultural Magazine — Canad Hort Mag
Canadian Horticulture and Home Magazine — Can Hort
Canadian Horticulturist and Beekeeper — Can Hort Beek
Canadian Hospital — CAHOA
Canadian Hospital — CAHOAX
Canadian Hospital — Can Hosp
Canadian Hospital — Canad Hosp
Canadian Hotel and Restaurant — CHR
Canadian Hydrological Operational Multipurpose Subprogramme [*Database*] — CHOMS
Canadian Import Tribunal [*Database*] — CIT
Canadian Index to Geoscience Data — Can Ind Geosci Data
Canadian Indian Artcrafts. National Indian Arts and Crafts Advisory Committee — CIAC
Canadian Industry Report of Fisheries and Aquatic Sciences — Can Ind Rep Fish Aquat Sci
Canadian Industry Report of Fisheries and Aquatic Sciences — CIRFAS
Canadian Insect Pest Review — Can Insect Pest Rev
Canadian Insect Pest Review — CIPRA2
Canadian Institute of Food Science and Technology. Journal — Can I Food
Canadian Institute of Food Science and Technology. Journal — Can Inst Food Sci Technol J
Canadian Institute of Food Science and Technology. Journal — CFSTB3

Canadian Institute of Food Science and Technology Journal/Journal de l'Institute Canadien de Science et Technologie Alimentaire — Can Inst Food Sci Technol J J Inst Can Sci Technol Aliment
Canadian Institute of Food Technology. Journal — Can Inst Food Technol J
Canadian Institute of Food Technology. Journal — CIFJAU
Canadian Institute of International Affairs — Can Inst Int Aff
Canadian Institute of Mining and Metallurgy and the Mining Society of Nova Scotia. Transactions — Can Inst Min Metall Min Soc NS Trans
Canadian Institute of Mining and Metallurgy. Bulletin — Can Inst Min Metall Bull
Canadian Institute of Mining and Metallurgy. Bulletin — Canadian Inst Mining Met Bulletin
Canadian Institute of Mining and Metallurgy. Bulletin [*Montreal*] — CIM Bulletin
Canadian Institute of Mining and Metallurgy. Petroleum Society. Annual Technical Meeting — Can Inst Min Metall Pet Soc Annu Tech Meet
Canadian Institute of Mining and Metallurgy. Special Volume — Can Inst Min Met Spec Vol
Canadian Institute of Mining and Metallurgy. Transactions — Canadian Inst Mining and Metallurgy Trans
Canadian Institute Proceedings — Can Inst Pr
Canadian Insurance — CI
Canadian Insurance — CIN
Canadian Interiors — CI
Canadian Inventory of Historic Building [*Database*] — CIHB
Canadian Jewish Historical Society. Journal — CJHSJ
Canadian Jewish News — CJN
Canadian Journal [*Toronto*] — Can J
Canadian Journal for Exceptional Children — Can Jnl Except Child
Canadian Journal of African Studies — Can J Afr S
Canadian Journal of African Studies — Can J Afr Stud
Canadian Journal of African Studies — Can J Afr Studies
Canadian Journal of African Studies — Canad J Afr Stud
Canadian Journal of African Studies — CanJA
Canadian Journal of African Studies — CJAS
Canadian Journal of Agricultural Economics — Can J Ag Ec
Canadian Journal of Agricultural Economics — Can J Agr Econ
Canadian Journal of Agricultural Economics — Can J Agric Econ
Canadian Journal of Agricultural Economics — Canad J Agric Econ
Canadian Journal of Agricultural Economics/Revue Canadienne d'Economie Rurale — Can J Agric Econ Rev Can Econ Rurale
Canadian Journal of Agricultural Science — Can J Ag Sci
Canadian Journal of Agricultural Science — Can J Agr Sci
Canadian Journal of Agricultural Science — Can J Agric Sci
Canadian Journal of Anaesthesia — Can J Anaesth
Canadian Journal of Animal Science — Can J Anim
Canadian Journal of Animal Science — Can J Anim Sci
Canadian Journal of Animal Science — CNJNA
Canadian Journal of Animal Science — CNJNAT
Canadian Journal of Anthropology — Can J Anthropol
Canadian Journal of Anthropology — CJN
Canadian Journal of Applied Physiology — Can J Appl Physiol
Canadian Journal of Applied Sport Sciences — Can J Appl Sport Sci
Canadian Journal of Applied Sport Sciences — Can J Appl Sport Sciences
Canadian Journal of Applied Sport Sciences — CJSCDG
Canadian Journal of Archaeology — CJA
Canadian Journal of Behavioural Science — Can J Beh S
Canadian Journal of Behavioural Science — Can J Behav Sci
Canadian Journal of Behavioural Science — CJBSAA
Canadian Journal of Behavioural Science/Revue Canadienne des Sciences du Comportement — Can J Beh Sc/R Can Sc Comport
Canadian Journal of Biochemistry — Can J Bioch
Canadian Journal of Biochemistry — Can J Biochem
Canadian Journal of Biochemistry — CJBIA
Canadian Journal of Biochemistry — CJBIAE
Canadian Journal of Biochemistry and Cell Biology — Can J Biochem Cell Biol
Canadian Journal of Biochemistry and Cell Biology — Can Jnl Biochem Cell Biol
Canadian Journal of Biochemistry and Cell Biology — CJBBDU
Canadian Journal of Biochemistry and Physiology — Can J Biochem Physiol
Canadian Journal of Biochemistry and Physiology — Canad J Biochem
Canadian Journal of Biochemistry and Physiology — CJBPAZ
Canadian Journal of Botany — Can J Bot
Canadian Journal of Botany — Canad J Bot
Canadian Journal of Botany — CJBO
Canadian Journal of Botany — CJBOA
Canadian Journal of Botany — CJBOAW
Canadian Journal of Botany/Journal Canadien de Botanique — Can J Bot J Can Bot
Canadian Journal of Cardiology — Can J Cardiol
Canadian Journal of Chemical Engineering — Can J Ch En
Canadian Journal of Chemical Engineering — Can J Chem Eng
Canadian Journal of Chemical Engineering — Can J Chem Engng
Canadian Journal of Chemical Engineering — Canad J Chem Engng
Canadian Journal of Chemical Engineering — CJCEA
Canadian Journal of Chemistry — Can J Chem
Canadian Journal of Chemistry — Canad J Chem
Canadian Journal of Chemistry — CJCHA
Canadian Journal of Chemistry — CJCHAG
Canadian Journal of Civil Engineering — Can J Civ Eng
Canadian Journal of Civil Engineering — Can J Civ Engng
Canadian Journal of Civil Engineering — CJCE
Canadian Journal of Civil Engineering/Revue Canadienne de Genie Civil — Can J Civ Eng/Rev Can Genie Civ
Canadian Journal of Comparative Medicine — Can J Com M
Canadian Journal of Comparative Medicine — Can J Comp Med
Canadian Journal of Comparative Medicine — CJCMA
Canadian Journal of Comparative Medicine — CJCMAV
Canadian Journal of Comparative Medicine and Veterinary Science [*Later, Canadian Journal of Comparative Medicine*] — Can J Comp Med Vet Sci
Canadian Journal of Comparative Medicine and Veterinary Science [*Later, Canadian Journal of Comparative Medicine*] — CNJMAQ
Canadian Journal of Corrections [*Later, Canadian Journal of Criminology*] — Can J Corr
Canadian Journal of Corrections [*Later, Canadian Journal of Criminology*] — Can J Correction
Canadian Journal of Criminology — Can J Criminology
Canadian Journal of Criminology — PCJC
Canadian Journal of Criminology and Corrections [*Later, Canadian Journal of Criminology*] — Can J Crim
Canadian Journal of Criminology and Corrections [*Later, Canadian Journal of Criminology*] — Can J Crim & Correct
Canadian Journal of Criminology and Corrections [*Later, Canadian Journal of Criminology*] — Can J Criminology & Corr
Canadian Journal of Development Studies — Can J Development Studies
Canadian Journal of Development Studies (Ottawa) — Can J Development Studies (Ottawa)
Canadian Journal of Early Childhood Education — Cdn J ECE
Canadian Journal of Earth Sciences — Can J Earth
Canadian Journal of Earth Sciences — Can J Earth Sci
Canadian Journal of Earth Sciences — CJES
Canadian Journal of Earth Sciences — CJESA
Canadian Journal of Earth Sciences — CJESAP
Canadian Journal of Economics — Can J Ec
Canadian Journal of Economics — Can J Econ
Canadian Journal of Economics — Canad J Econ
Canadian Journal of Economics — CJ
Canadian Journal of Economics — CJD
Canadian Journal of Economics — CJE
Canadian Journal of Economics — CJECB
Canadian Journal of Economics and Political Science [*Later, Canadian Journal of Economics*] — Can J Econ & Pol Sci
Canadian Journal of Economics and Political Science [*Later, Canadian Journal of Economics*] — Can J Econ Pol Sci
Canadian Journal of Economics and Political Science [*Later, Canadian Journal of Economics*] — Can J Econ Polit Sci
Canadian Journal of Economics and Political Science — Canad J Econ Polit Sci
Canadian Journal of Economics and Political Science — CEPS
Canadian Journal of Economics and Political Science [*Later, Canadian Journal of Economics*] — CJE
Canadian Journal of Economics and Political Science [*Later, Canadian Journal of Economics*] — CJEPS
Canadian Journal of Economics/Revue Canadienne d'Economique. University of Toronto Press. Canadian Economics Association — Can J Econ Rev Can Econ Univ Toronto Press Can Econ Assoc
Canadian Journal of Education — Can J Ed
Canadian Journal of Educational Communication — Can J Ed Comm
Canadian Journal of English Language Arts — Can Jnl Engl Lang Arts
Canadian Journal of Experimental Psychology — Can J Exp Psychol
Canadian Journal of Fabrics — Can J Fabr
Canadian Journal of Family Law — Can J Fam L
Canadian Journal of Family Law — Can J Family Law
Canadian Journal of Fisheries and Aquatic Sciences — Can J Fish Aquat Sci
Canadian Journal of Fisheries and Aquatic Sciences — Can J Fish Aquatic Sci
Canadian Journal of Fisheries and Aquatic Sciences — CJFA
Canadian Journal of Fisheries and Aquatic Sciences — CJFSDX
Canadian Journal of Fisheries and Aquatic Sciences. Journal Canadien des Sciences Halieutiques et Aquatiques — Can J Fish Aquat Sci J Can Sci Halieutiques Aquat
Canadian Journal of Forest Research — Can J For Res
Canadian Journal of Forest Research — Can J Forest Res
Canadian Journal of Forest Research — CJFR
Canadian Journal of Forest Research — CJFRAR
Canadian Journal of Forest Research/Journal Canadien de Recherche Forestiere — Can J For Res J Can Rech For
Canadian Journal of Gastroenterology — Can J Gastroenterol
Canadian Journal of Genetics and Cytology — Can J Gen Cyt
Canadian Journal of Genetics and Cytology — Can J Genet
Canadian Journal of Genetics and Cytology — Can J Genet Cytol
Canadian Journal of Genetics and Cytology — CNJGA
Canadian Journal of Genetics and Cytology — CNJGA8
Canadian Journal of Higher Education — Can J Higher Ed
Canadian Journal of History — Can J His
Canadian Journal of History — Can J Hist
Canadian Journal of History — Can Jour Hist
Canadian Journal of History — CanJH
Canadian Journal of History — CJH
Canadian Journal of History — CJHi
Canadian Journal of History — PCJH
Canadian Journal of History of Sport — Can J Hist Sport
Canadian Journal of History of Sport and Physical Education [*Later, Canadian Journal of History of Sport*] — Can J Hist Sport Phys Educ
Canadian Journal of Hospital Pharmacy — Can J Hosp Pharm
Canadian Journal of Hospital Pharmacy — CJHPAV
Canadian Journal of Industry — Canad J
Canadian Journal of Industry, Science, and Art — Canad J Industr
Canadian Journal of Information Science — Can J Info Science
Canadian Journal of Irish Studies — CJIS
Canadian Journal of Italian Studies — C J It S
Canadian Journal of Italian Studies — Can J Ital
Canadian Journal of Latin American and Caribbean Studies — CJLACS
Canadian Journal of Linguistics — Can J L
Canadian Journal of Linguistics — Can J Ling

Canadian Journal of Linguistics — Can J Lingu
Canadian Journal of Linguistics — Canad Jour
Canadian Journal of Linguistics — Canad Jour L
Canadian Journal of Linguistics — CJL
Canadian Journal of Mathematics — Can J Math
Canadian Journal of Mathematics [*Ottawa, Ontario*] — Canad J Math
Canadian Journal of Mathematics — CDJM
Canadian Journal of Mathematics — CJMAA
Canadian Journal of Medical Science — Can J Med Sci
Canadian Journal of Medical Science — Canad J Med Sc
Canadian Journal of Medical Science — CJMSAV
Canadian Journal of Medical Technology — Can J Med T
Canadian Journal of Medical Technology — Can J Med Techn
Canadian Journal of Medical Technology — Can J Med Technol
Canadian Journal of Medical Technology — Canad J Med Tech
Canadian Journal of Medical Technology — Canad J Med Technol
Canadian Journal of Medical Technology — CJMTA
Canadian Journal of Medical Technology — CJMTAY
Canadian Journal of Medicine and Surgery — Can J Med Surg
Canadian Journal of Microbiology — Can J Micro
Canadian Journal of Microbiology — Can J Microb
Canadian Journal of Microbiology — Can J Microbiol
Canadian Journal of Microbiology — Canad J Microbiol
Canadian Journal of Microbiology — CJMIA
Canadian Journal of Microbiology — CJMIAZ
Canadian Journal of Native Education — Can J Nat Ed
Canadian Journal of Native Education — CJNE
Canadian Journal of Native Studies — Can Jnl Nat Stud
Canadian Journal of Native Studies — CJNS
Canadian Journal of Neurological Sciences — Can J Neurol Sci
Canadian Journal of Neurological Sciences — CJNSA2
Canadian Journal of Occupational Therapy — Can J Occup Ther
Canadian Journal of Oncology — Can J Oncol
Canadian Journal of Ophthalmology — CAJOB
Canadian Journal of Ophthalmology — CAJOBA
Canadian Journal of Ophthalmology — Can J Ophth
Canadian Journal of Ophthalmology — Can J Ophthalm
Canadian Journal of Ophthalmology — Can J Ophthalmol
Canadian Journal of Optometry — Can J Optom
Canadian Journal of Otolaryngology — Can J Otolaryngol
Canadian Journal of Otolaryngology — CJOLAK
Canadian Journal of Pharmaceutical Sciences — Can J Ph Sc
Canadian Journal of Pharmaceutical Sciences — Can J Pharm Sci
Canadian Journal of Pharmaceutical Sciences — CNJPA
Canadian Journal of Pharmaceutical Sciences — CNJPAZ
Canadian Journal of Philosophy — Can J Phil
Canadian Journal of Philosophy — CJPhil
Canadian Journal of Philosophy — PCJP
Canadian Journal of Physics — Can J Phys
Canadian Journal of Physics — Canad J Phys
Canadian Journal of Physics — CJPHA
Canadian Journal of Physics — CJPHAD
Canadian Journal of Physiology and Pharmacology — Can J Physiol Pharm
Canadian Journal of Physiology and Pharmacology — Can J Physiol Pharmacol
Canadian Journal of Physiology and Pharmacology — Can J Physl
Canadian Journal of Physiology and Pharmacology — Canad J Physiol Pharmacol
Canadian Journal of Physiology and Pharmacology — CJPPA
Canadian Journal of Physiology and Pharmacology — CJPPA3
Canadian Journal of Plant Pathology — Can J Plant Pathol
Canadian Journal of Plant Pathology/Revue Canadienne de Phytopathologie — Can J Plant Pathol Rev Can Phytopathol
Canadian Journal of Plant Science — Can J Pl Sci
Canadian Journal of Plant Science — Can J Plant
Canadian Journal of Plant Science — Can J Plant Sci
Canadian Journal of Plant Science — Canad J Pl Sci
Canadian Journal of Plant Science — CPLSA
Canadian Journal of Plant Science — CPLSAY
Canadian Journal of Plant Science/Revue Canadienne de Phytotechnie — Can J Plant Sci Rev Can Phytotech
Canadian Journal of Political and Social Theory — Can J Pol and Soc Theory
Canadian Journal of Political and Social Theory — Canad J Polit Soc Theory
Canadian Journal of Political and Social Theory — Cn Jour
Canadian Journal of Political Science — Can J Pol Sc
Canadian Journal of Political Science — Can J Pol Sci
Canadian Journal of Political Science — Can J Pol Science
Canadian Journal of Political Science — Can J Poli
Canadian Journal of Political Science — Canad J Polit Sci
Canadian Journal of Political Science — CJPS
Canadian Journal of Political Science — PCPS
Canadian Journal of Political Science (Ontario) — Can J Pol Science (Ont)
Canadian Journal of Psychiatric Nursing — Can J Psychiatr Nurs
Canadian Journal of Psychiatric Nursing — Canad J Psychiatr Nurs
Canadian Journal of Psychiatry — Can J Psychiatry
Canadian Journal of Psychiatry — Canad J Psychiatr
Canadian Journal of Psychology — Can J Psych
Canadian Journal of Psychology — Can J Psychol
Canadian Journal of Psychology — Canad J Psychol
Canadian Journal of Psychology — CJP
Canadian Journal of Psychology — CJPs
Canadian Journal of Psychology — CJPSA
Canadian Journal of Psychology — CJPSAC
Canadian Journal of Psychology — PCSY
Canadian Journal of Public Health — Can J Publ
Canadian Journal of Public Health — Can J Publ Hlth
Canadian Journal of Public Health — Can J Public Health
Canadian Journal of Public Health — Canad J Public Health
Canadian Journal of Public Health — CJPEA
Canadian Journal of Public Health — CJPEA4
Canadian Journal of Public Health — CJPH
Canadian Journal of Radiography, Radiotherapy, Nuclear Medicine — Can J Radiogr Radiother Nucl Med
Canadian Journal of Radiography, Radiotherapy, Nuclear Medicine — Canad J Radiogr Radiother Nucl Med
Canadian Journal of Radiography, Radiotherapy, Nuclear Medicine [*English Edition*] — CJRMD7
Canadian Journal of Radiography, Radiotherapy, Nuclear Medicine (English Edition) — Can J Radiogr Radiother Nucl Med (Engl Ed)
Canadian Journal of Religious Thought — Can J Rel Thought
Canadian Journal of Remote Sensing — Can J Remote Sens
Canadian Journal of Remote Sensing — Can J Remote Sensing
Canadian Journal of Research — Can J Res
Canadian Journal of Research in Semiotics — Can Jnl Res Semiot
Canadian Journal of Research in Semiotics — CJRS
Canadian Journal of Research. Section A. Physical Sciences — Can J Res Sect A
Canadian Journal of Research. Section B. Chemical Sciences — Can J Res Sect B
Canadian Journal of Research. Section C. Botanical Sciences — Can J Res Sect C
Canadian Journal of Research. Section C. Botanical Sciences — Can J Res Sect C Bot Sci
Canadian Journal of Research. Section C. Botanical Sciences — CNRCA2
Canadian Journal of Research. Section D. Zoological Sciences — Can J Res Sect D
Canadian Journal of Research. Section D. Zoological Sciences — Can J Res Sect D Zool Sci
Canadian Journal of Research. Section D. Zoological Sciences — CNRDA5
Canadian Journal of Research. Section E. Medical Sciences — Can J Res Sect E
Canadian Journal of Research. Section E. Medical Sciences — Can J Res Sect E Med Sci
Canadian Journal of Research. Section E. Medical Sciences — CNRMAW
Canadian Journal of Research. Section F. Technology — Can J Res Sect F
Canadian Journal of Science, Literature, and History — Can J Sci
Canadian Journal of Soil Science — Can J Soil
Canadian Journal of Soil Science — Can J Soil Sci
Canadian Journal of Soil Science — Canad J Soil Sci
Canadian Journal of Soil Science — CJSSA
Canadian Journal of Soil Science — CJSSAR
Canadian Journal of Spectroscopy — Can J Spect
Canadian Journal of Spectroscopy — Can J Spectrosc
Canadian Journal of Spectroscopy — Can J Spectry
Canadian Journal of Spectroscopy — CJSPAI
Canadian Journal of Sport Sciences — Can J Sport Sci
Canadian Journal of Statistics — Can J Statis
Canadian Journal of Statistics — Canad J Statist
Canadian Journal of Statistics — Cand J St
Canadian Journal of Surgery — Can J Surg
Canadian Journal of Surgery — Canad J Surg
Canadian Journal of Surgery — CJSUA
Canadian Journal of Surgery — CJSUAX
Canadian Journal of Technology — Can J Technol
Canadian Journal of Theology — Can J Th
Canadian Journal of Theology — Can JT
Canadian Journal of Theology [*Toronto*] — CanadianJTH
Canadian Journal of Theology [*Toronto*] — CanadJT
Canadian Journal of Theology — CJT
Canadian Journal of University Continuing Education — Can J Univ Cont Ed
Canadian Journal of Veterinary Research — Can J Vet Res
Canadian Journal of Veterinary Research/Revue Canadienne de Recherche Veterinaire — Can J Vet Res Rev Can Rech Vet
Canadian Journal of Zoology — Can J Zool
Canadian Journal of Zoology — Canad J Zool
Canadian Journal of Zoology — Canad J Zoology
Canadian Journal of Zoology — CJZ
Canadian Journal of Zoology — CJZOA
Canadian Journal of Zoology — CJZOAG
Canadian Journal on Aging — CJOA
Canadian Journal on Mental Retardation — Can Jnl Ment Ret
Canadian Journalism Database — CJD
Canadian Labour — Can Lab
Canadian Labour — Can Labour
Canadian Labour — Can Lbr
Canadian Labour — CDL
Canadian Labour Arbitration Summaries [*Database*] — CLAS
Canadian Law Times and Review — Canad Law Times R
Canadian Lawyer — Can Law
Canadian Lawyer — Can Lawyer
Canadian Legal Aid Bulletin — Can Legal Aid Bul
Canadian Library — Can Lib
Canadian Library — Canad Lib
Canadian Library Association. Bulletin — Can Lib Assn Bul
Canadian Library Association. Bulletin — Canad Lib Assn Bul
Canadian Library Association. Bulletin — Canadian Lib Assn Bul
Canadian Library Association. Feliciter — Canad Lib Assn Feliciter
Canadian Library Bulletin — Can Lib Bull
Canadian Library Handbook — CLH
Canadian Library Journal — Can Lib J
Canadian Library Journal — Can Libr J

Canadian Library Journal — Canad Lib J
Canadian Library Journal — CLJ
Canadian Literary Magazine — Can Lit Mag
Canadian Literature — Can L
Canadian Literature — Can Lit
Canadian Literature — PCLI
Canadian Machine-Readable Cataloging [*Database*] — CAN/MARC
Canadian Machinery and Manufacturing News — Can Mach Manu News
Canadian Machinery and Metalworking — Can Mach Metalwork
Canadian Machinery and Metalworking — Cdn Machin
Canadian Machinery and Metalworking — CMCHA
Canadian Machinery and Metalworking Directory and Buying Guide — Cdn Mach D
Canadian Magazine — Can M
Canadian Magazine — Can Mag
Canadian Magazine — Canad M
Canadian Magazine Index [*Database*] — CMI
Canadian Magazine of Politics, Science, Art, and Literature — Can Mag Polit Sci Art Lit
Canadian Manager — CMA
Canadian Manager — CNM
Canadian Manuscript Report of Fisheries and Aquatic Sciences — Can Manuscr Rep Fish Aquat Sci
Canadian Manuscript Report of Fisheries and Aquatic Sciences — CMRFAS
Canadian Market Data Index — Can Mark Data Ind
Canadian Materials — CM
Canadian Mathematical Bulletin — Can Math B
Canadian Mathematical Bulletin — Can Math Bull
Canadian Mathematical Bulletin — CMBUA
Canadian Mathematical Society Series of Monographs and Advanced Texts — Canad Math Soc Ser Monographs Adv Texts
Canadian Mathematics Teacher — Can Math Teach
Canadian Medical Association. Journal — Can MAJ
Canadian Medical Association. Journal — Can Med A J
Canadian Medical Association. Journal — Can Med Ass J
Canadian Medical Association. Journal — Can Med Assn J
Canadian Medical Association. Journal — Can Med Assoc J
Canadian Medical Association. Journal — Canad MAJ
Canadian Medical Association. Journal — Canad Med Assn J
Canadian Medical Association. Journal — Canad Med Assoc J
Canadian Medical Association. Journal — CMAJ
Canadian Medical Association. Journal — CMAJA
Canadian Medical Association. Journal — CMAJAX
Canadian Metallurgical Quarterly — CAMQA
Canadian Metallurgical Quarterly — Can Met Quart
Canadian Metallurgical Quarterly — Can Metal Q
Canadian Metallurgical Quarterly — Can Metall Q
Canadian Metals — Can Met
Canadian Metals and Metallurgical Industries — Can Met Metall Ind
Canadian Metalworking — Can Metalwork
Canadian Metalworking/Machine Production — Can Metalwork/Mach Prod
Canadian Metalworking Production — Can Metalwork Prod
Canadian Military Journal — Can Ml J
Canadian Milling and Feed Journal — Can Milling Feed
Canadian Milling and Feed Journal — Can Milling Feed J
Canadian Milling and Grain Journal — Can Milling Grain J
Canadian Mineral Industry. Review — Can Miner Ind Rev
Canadian Mineral Processors. Annual Meeting — Can Miner Process Annu Meet
Canadian Mineralogist — CAMI
Canadian Mineralogist — CAMIA
Canadian Mineralogist — Can Mineral
Canadian Minerals Yearbook — Can Miner Yearb
Canadian Minerals Yearbook — CMYBA
Canadian Mines Handbook — Cdn Mine H
Canadian Mining and Metallurgical Bulletin — Can Min & Met Bul
Canadian Mining and Metallurgical Bulletin — Can Min & Metallurg Bull
Canadian Mining and Metallurgical Bulletin — Can Min Met
Canadian Mining and Metallurgical Bulletin — Can Min Metall Bull
Canadian Mining and Metallurgical Bulletin — Can Mining Met Bul
Canadian Mining and Metallurgical Bulletin — CMMBA
Canadian Mining Institute. Bulletins — Can Min Inst Bull
Canadian Mining Journal — CAMJ
Canadian Mining Journal — CAMJA
Canadian Mining Journal — Can Min J
Canadian Mining Journal — Can Mining J
Canadian Mining Journal — CM
Canadian Mining Journal — CMJ
Canadian Mining Review — Can M Rv
Canadian Modern Language Review — CMLR
Canadian Monthly — Canad Mo
Canadian Municipal Utilities — Can Munic Util
Canadian Music Educator — Can Mus Ed
Canadian Music Journal — Can Mus J
Canadian Musician — Can Mus
Canadian National Power Alcohol Conference — Can Natl Power Alcohol Conf
Canadian Native Law Bulletin. Native Law Centre. University of Saskatchewan — CNLB
Canadian Native Law Reporter. Native Law Centre. University of Saskatchewan — CNLR
Canadian Native News Service — CNNS
Canadian Natural Science News — Canad Nat Sci News
Canadian Naturalist and Geologist — Canad Naturalist Geol
Canadian Naturalist and Geologist and Proceedings of the Natural History Society of Montreal — Can Nat
Canadian Network Papers. National Library of Canada — CANWP
Canadian News Index — Can News Index
Canadian News Index [*Database*] — CNI
Canadian Nuclear Association. Annual International Conference — Can Nucl Assoc Annu Int Conf
Canadian Nuclear Association. Annual International Conference (Proceedings) — Can Nucl Assoc Annu Int Conf (Pro)
Canadian Nuclear Association. Report — Can Nucl Assoc Report
Canadian Nuclear Association. Report CNA [*Canadian Nuclear Association*] — Can Nucl Assoc Rep CNA
Canadian Nuclear Society. Annual Conference. Proceedings — Can Nucl Soc Annu Conf Proc
Canadian Nuclear Society. Annual Conference. Transactions — Can Nucl Soc Annu Conf Trans
Canadian Nuclear Society. Transactions — Can Nucl Soc Trans
Canadian Nuclear Technology — Can Nucl Technol
Canadian Nuclear Technology — CNUTA
Canadian Numismatic Journal — CNJ
Canadian Nurse — Can Nurse
Canadian Nurse — Canad Nurse
Canadian Nurse — CANNB
Canadian Nurse — CANU
Canadian Nurse — CANUA
Canadian Oil and Gas Handbook — Canada O & G
Canadian Oil and Gas Industries — Can Oil Gas Ind
Canadian Operating Room Nursing Journal — Can Oper Room Nurs J
Canadian Operating Statistics [*Database*] — COPS
Canadian Operational Research Society. Journal — Can Oper Res Soc J
Canadian Optician — Can Opt
Canadian Oral History Association. Journal/Societe Canadienne d'Histoire Orale. Journal — COHAJ
Canadian Packaging — Can Packag
Canadian Packaging — Can Pkg
Canadian Packaging — Cdn Pkg
Canadian Packaging — CPC
Canadian Paint and Finishing — Can Paint Finish
Canadian Paint and Varnish — Can Paint Varn
Canadian Paper Money Journal — CPMJ
Canadian Papers in Rural History — Can Pap Rural Hist
Canadian Patent — Can Pat
Canadian. Patent Document — Can
Canadian Patent Office. Record — Can Pat Office Rec
Canadian Patent Office. Record — Can Pat Office Recd
Canadian Patent. Reissue — Can Pat Reissue
Canadian Patent Reporter [*Information service or system*] — Can P R
Canadian Patent Reporter [*Information service or system*] — Can Pat Rep
Canadian Patent Reporter [*Information service or system*] — CPR
Canadian Peat Society. Bulletin — Can Peat Soc B
Canadian Periodical Index — Can Ind
Canadian Periodical Index — Can Period Index
Canadian Periodical Index — CanI
Canadian Periodicals Index [*Database*] — CPI
Canadian Personnel and Industrial Relations Journal (Including the Canadian Training Digest) — Can Pers
Canadian Personnel and Industrial Relations Journal (Including the Canadian Training Digest) — Can Psl & Ind Rel J
Canadian Personnel and Industrial Relations Journal (Including the Canadian Training Digest) — Canad Person Industr Relat J
Canadian Perspective — Can Persp
Canadian Pest Management Society. Proceedings of the Annual Meeting — Can Pest Manage Soc Proc Annu Meet
Canadian Petro Engineering — Can Pet Eng
Canadian Petro Engineering — Can Petro Eng
Canadian Petro Engineering — CPEGA
Canadian Petroleum — Can Pet
Canadian Petroleum — Can Petrol
Canadian Petroleum — CAPE
Canadian Petroleum — CPETA
Canadian Petroleum Association Statistics [*Database*] — CPASTATS
Canadian Pharmaceutical Journal — Can Pharm J
Canadian Pharmaceutical Journal — CPJ
Canadian Pharmaceutical Journal — CPJOAC
Canadian Philosophical Reviews — Can Phil Rev
Canadian Plains Proceedings — Can Plains Proc
Canadian Plant Disease Survey — Can Plant Dis Surv
Canadian Plant Disease Survey — CPDSAS
Canadian Plastics — Can Plast
Canadian Plastics — Can Plastics
Canadian Plastics — Canad Plast
Canadian Plastics — Cdn Plast
Canadian Plastics — CPG
Canadian Plastics Directory and Buyer's Guide — Cdn Plast D
Canadian Podiatrist — Can Pod
Canadian Poetry — Can Po
Canadian Poetry — Can Poetry
Canadian Poultry Review — Can Poult Rev
Canadian Poultry Review — Can Poultry Rev
Canadian Poultry Review — CNPRA3
Canadian Power Engineer — CPOEA
Canadian Power Engineering — Can Power Eng
Canadian Power Engineering and Plant Maintenance — Can Power Eng Plant Maint
Canadian Power Engineering and Plant Maintenance — CPOEB
Canadian Practitioner — Canad Pract
Canadian Practitioner and Review — Canad Pract and Rev
Canadian Press Network [*Database*] — CPN

Canadian Printer and Publisher — Can Printer Publ
Canadian Psychiatric Association. Journal — Can Psychi
Canadian Psychiatric Association. Journal — Can Psychiatr Assoc J
Canadian Psychiatric Association. Journal — Canad Psychiat AJ
Canadian Psychiatric Association. Journal — Canad Psychiat Ass J
Canadian Psychiatric Association. Journal — CPAJA
Canadian Psychological Review — Can Psych R
Canadian Psychological Review — Can Psychol Rev
Canadian Psychological Review — CPREDP
Canadian Psychologist — Can Psychol
Canadian Psychologist — CAPSAH
Canadian Psychology — Can Psychology
Canadian Psychology — CPSGD2
Canadian Psychology/Psychologie Canadienne — Can Psych Psych Can
Canadian Public Administration — Can Public Admin
Canadian Public Administration — CPC
Canadian Public Administration/Administration Publique du Canada — Can Pub Admin
Canadian Public Administration/Administration Publique du Canada — Can Publ Ad
Canadian Public Administration/Administration Publique du Canada — Canad Publ Adm
Canadian Public Health Journal — Can Public Health J
Canadian Public Policy — Can Pub Pol
Canadian Public Policy — Can Pub Policy
Canadian Public Policy — Can Public Policy
Canadian Public Policy — Canad Publ Pol
Canadian Public Policy (Guelph) — Can Public Policy (Guelph)
Canadian Pulp and Paper Association. Technical Section. Annual Meeting. Preprints of Papers — Can Pulp Pap Assoc Tech Sect Annu Meet Prepr Pap
Canadian Pulp and Paper Association. Technical Section. Preprints of Papers. Annual Meeting — Can Pulp Pap Assoc Tech Sect Prepr Pap Annu Meet
Canadian Pulp and Paper Association. Technical Section. Transactions — Can Pulp Pap Assoc Tech Sect Trans
Canadian Pulp and Paper Industry — Can Pulp Paper Ind
Canadian Pulp and Paper Industry — Cdn P & P
Canadian Pulp and Paper Industry — CNPIA
Canadian Quill — Can Quill
Canadian Record of Natural History and Geology — Can Rec N H
Canadian Record of Natural History and Geology. With Proceedings. Natural History Society of Montreal — Canad Rec Nat Hist Geol
Canadian Record of Science — Can Rec Sc
Canadian Regulatory Reporter [*Database*] — CRR
Canadian Renewable Energy News — Can Renewable Energy News
Canadian Research — Can Res
Canadian Research and Development [*Later, Canadian Research*] — Can Res Dev
Canadian Research and Development [*Later, Canadian Research*] — CRDVA
Canadian Research Institute of Launderers and Cleaners. Technical Report — Can Res Inst Launderers Clean
Canadian Research Institute of Launderers and Cleaners. Technical Report — Can Res Inst Launders Clean Tech
Canadian Review — Can Rev
Canadian Review of American Studies — C Rev AS
Canadian Review of American Studies — Can R Am St
Canadian Review of American Studies — Can Rev Am Stud
Canadian Review of American Studies — Can Rev Amer Stud
Canadian Review of American Studies — CRAS
Canadian Review of Comparative Literature/Revue Canadienne de Litterature Comparee — Can R Com L
Canadian Review of Comparative Literature/Revue Canadienne de Litterature Comparee — Can Rev Comp Lt
Canadian Review of Comparative Literature/Revue Canadienne de Litterature Comparee — CRCL
Canadian Review of Sociology and Anthropology — Can R Soc
Canadian Review of Sociology and Anthropology — Can R Soc A
Canadian Review of Sociology and Anthropology — Can R Soc Anthr
Canadian Review of Sociology and Anthropology — Can R Sociol & Anthrop
Canadian Review of Sociology and Anthropology — Can R Sociol Anth
Canadian Review of Sociology and Anthropology — Can Rev Sociol Anthropol
Canadian Review of Sociology and Anthropology — Canad R Sociol Anthropol
Canadian Review of Sociology and Anthropology — CRSA
Canadian Review of Sociology and Anthropology — PCRS
Canadian Review of Studies in Nationalism — Can R Stud Nat
Canadian Review of Studies in Nationalism — Can R Studies Nationalism
Canadian Review of Studies in Nationalism — Can Rev Stud Natl
Canadian Risk Management and Business Insurance — RMBI
Canadian Rose Annual — Canad Rose Annual
Canadian Runner — Can Run
Canadian Sales Tax Reports. Commerce Clearing House — Can Sales Tax Rep CCH
Canadian School Executive — Can Sch Exec
Canadian Science Monthly — Can Sc Mo
Canadian Scientist — Can Sci
Canadian Semiconductor Technology Conference — Can Semicond Technol Conf
Canadian Services Medical Journal — Can Serv Med J
Canadian Services Medical Journal — CSMDA
Canadian Services Medical Journal — CSMDAF
Canadian Shipping and Marine Engineering — Canadian Shipp & Mar Engng
Canadian Slavic Studies — CanS
Canadian Slavic Studies — CSS
Canadian Slavonic Papers — Can Sl P
Canadian Slavonic Papers — Can Slav P
Canadian Slavonic Papers — Can Slavonic Pa
Canadian Slavonic Papers — Can Slavonic Pap
Canadian Slavonic Papers — Canad Slavonic Pap
Canadian Slavonic Papers — CanSP
Canadian Slavonic Papers — CSLP
Canadian Slavonic Papers — CSP
Canadian Society of Environmental Biologists. Newsletter/Bulletin — CSEB
Canadian Society of Forensic Science. Journal — Can Soc Forensic Sci J
Canadian Society of Laboratory Technologists. Bulletin — Canad Soc Lab Technol Bull
Canadian Society of Petroleum Geologists. Memoir — Can Soc Pet Geol Mem
Canadian Society of Petroleum Geologists. Reservoir — CSPG Reservoir
Canadian Soil Information System [*Database*] — CanSIS
Canadian Special Publication of Fisheries and Aquatic Sciences — Can Spec Publ Fish Aquat Sci
Canadian Special Publication of Fisheries and Aquatic Sciences — CSPSD
Canadian Special Publication of Fisheries and Aquatic Sciences — CSPSDA
Canadian Spectroscopy — Can Spectrosc
Canadian Spectroscopy — Can Spectry
Canadian Spectroscopy — CASPA
Canadian Standards [*Database*] — CANSTAN
Canadian Standards Association. CSA Standard — Can Stand Ass CSA Stand
Canadian Statistical Review — Can Stat Rev
Canadian Statistical Review — Can Statis R
Canadian Statistical Review. Weekly Supplement — Can Statis Rev WS
Canadian Stock Options [*Database*] — CDNOPT
Canadian Structural Engineering Conference — Can Struct Eng Conf
Canadian Student — Can Stud
Canadian Studies Bulletin — Can Stud Bul
Canadian Studies in Economics — Can St Ec
Canadian Studies in German Language and Literature — CSGLL
Canadian Studies in Population — Can Studies Population
Canadian Sulfur Symposium — Can Sulfur Symp
Canadian Surveyor — Can Surv
Canadian Surveyor — Can Surveyor
Canadian Surveyor — CASU
Canadian Surveyor — CASUA
Canadian Symposium of Remote Sensing. Proceedings — Can Symp Remote Sensing Proc
Canadian Symposium on Catalysis. Preprints — Can Symp Catal Prepr
Canadian Symposium on Nonwovens and Disposables — Can Symp Nonwovens Disposables
Canadian Symposium on Water Pollution Research — Can Symp Water Pollut Res
Canadian Tax Journal — Can Tax J
Canadian Tax Journal — CTJ
Canadian Tax News — Can Tax News
Canadian Tax Reports. Commerce Clearing House — Can Tax Rep CCH
Canadian Taxation — Can Taxation
Canadian Taxation. A Journal of Tax Policy — Can Tax J Tax Policy
Canadian Technical Asphalt Association. Proceedings of the Annual Conference — Can Tech Asphalt Assoc Proc Annu Conf
Canadian Technical Report of Fisheries and Aquatic Sciences — Can Tech Rep Fish Aquat Sci
Canadian Technical Report of Fisheries and Aquatic Sciences — CTRFAS
Canadian Technical Report of Hydrography and Ocean Sciences — Can Tech Rep Hydrogr Ocean Sci
Canadian Technical Report of Hydrography and Ocean Sciences — CTRHOS
Canadian Textile Journal — Can Text J
Canadian Textile Journal — CTJ
Canadian Textile Journal — CTJOA
Canadian Textile Seminar. International Book of Papers — Can Text Semin Int Book Pap
Canadian Theatre Review — Can Theat R
Canadian Theatre Review — Can Theatre R
Canadian Theatre Review — CTR
Canadian Theses — Can Theses
Canadian Tobacco Grower — Can Tob Grower
Canadian Token — CT
Canadian Trade Index [*Database*] — CTIX
Canadian Trade Marks [*Database*] — TMRK
Canadian Transportation [*Later, Canadian Transportation and Distribution Management*] — Can Transp
Canadian Transportation and Distribution Management — CTD
Canadian Transportation Documentation System [*Database*] — CTDS
Canadian Underwriter — CU
Canadian Union Catalogue of Books [*Database*] — UCB
Canadian Union Catalogue of Library Materials for the Handicapped [*Database*] — CANUC:H
Canadian Union Catalogue of Serials [*Database*] — UCS
Canadian University Music Review — Can U Mus R
Canadian University. Music Review — CUMR
Canadian Vending — Can Vending
Canadian Veterinary Journal — Can Vet J
Canadian Veterinary Journal — CNVJA9
Canadian Veterinary Record — Can Vet Record
Canadian Veterinary Record — Canad Vet Rec
Canadian Vocational Journal — Can Voc J
Canadian Water Resources Journal — Can Water Resour J
Canadian Water Resources Journal — CWRJ
Canadian Weather Review — Can W Rev
Canadian Weekly Bulletin — CWB
Canadian Welder and Fabricator — Can Welder Fabr
Canadian Welfare — Can Wel
Canadian Welfare — Can Welfare
Canadian Welfare — CW

Canadian Wildlife and Fisheries Newsletter — CWFN
Canadian Wildlife Service — Can Wildl Serv
Canadian Wildlife Service — CWLSBG
Canadian Wildlife Service. Occasional Papers — Can Wildl Serv Occas Pap
Canadian Wildlife Service. Occasional Papers — CWOPAL
Canadian Wildlife Service. Occasional Papers — CWSOP
Canadian Wildlife Service. Progress Notes — Can Wildl Serv Prog Notes
Canadian Wildlife Service. Progress Notes — CWPNBL
Canadian Wildlife Service. Progress Notes — CWSPN
Canadian Wildlife Service. Report Series — Can Wildl Serv Rep Ser
Canadian Wildlife Service. Report Series — CWRSBC
Canadian Wildlife Service. Report Series — CWSRS
Canadian Women of Note [*Database*] — CWON
Canadian Woodlands Review — Can Woodl Rev
Canadian Yearbook of International Law — Can YB Int'l L
Canadian Yearbook of International Law — Can Yb of Internat
Canadian Yearbook of International Law — Can YBIL
Canadian Yearbook of International Law — Can Yearb Int Law
Canadian Yearbook of International Law — Can Yearbook Int L
Canadian Yearbook of International Law — Canad Yb Int Law
Canadiana — Can
Canadian-American Review of Hungarian Studies — Can Am Rev Hung Stud
Canadian-American Review of Hungarian Studies — CARHS
Canadian-American Slavic Studies — Can Am Sl Stud
Canadian-American Slavic Studies — Can Amer Slav Stud
Canadian-American Slavic Studies — Can Slav Stud
Canadian-American Slavic Studies — Can-Am Slav
Canadian-American Slavic Studies — CanSS
Canadian-American Slavic Studies — CASS
Canberra and District Historical Society. Addresses — Canb Hist Soc Add
Canberra and District Historical Society. Newsletter — Canb Hist Soc News
Canberra Anthropology — Canberra Anthrop
Canberra Anthropology — Canberra Anthropol
Canberra Comments — Canb Comments
Canberra Historical Journal — CDHS
Canberra Letter — Canb Letter
Canberra Survey — Canb Survey
Canberra Survey — Canberra Surv
Canberra Times — CT
Canberra University College. Gazette — Canb Univ Col Gaz
Canberra University College. Gazette — Canb Univ Coll Gaz
Canberra University College. Gazette — CUC Gaz
Canberra Viewpoint — Canb Viewpoint
Canberra Weekly — Canb Weekly
CANCAM Proceedings. Canadian Congress of Applied Mechanics — CANCAM Proc Can Congr Appl Mech
CANCAS. Collegiate Academy of the North Carolina Academy of Sciences — CANCAS Coll Acad NC Acad Sci
Cancer and Metastasis Reviews — Cancer Metastasis Rev
Cancer Biochemistry - Biophysics — CABCD
Cancer Biochemistry - Biophysics — CABCD4
Cancer Biochemistry - Biophysics — Canc Bioc B
Cancer Biochemistry - Biophysics — Cancer Biochem Biophys
Cancer Biology and Biosynthesis [*Monograph*] — Cancer Biol Biosynth
Cancer Biology Reviews — Cancer Biol Rev
Cancer Biotherapy — Cancer Biother
Cancer Biotherapy and Radiopharmaceuticals — Cancer Biother Radiopharm
Cancer Bulletin — Canc Bull
Cancer Bulletin — Cancer Bull
Cancer Causes and Control [*Oxford*] — Cancer Causes Control
Cancer Cells [*Cold Spring Harbor*] — CACEEG
Cancer Cells — Cancer Cel
Cancer Chemical Journal — Can Chem J
Cancer Chemotherapy Abstracts — Canc Chemoth Abstr
Cancer Chemotherapy Abstracts — CCA
Cancer Chemotherapy and Biological Response Modifiers — Cancer Chemother Biol Response Modif
Cancer Chemotherapy and Pharmacology — Cancer Chemother Pharmacol
Cancer Chemotherapy and Pharmacology — CCPHDZ
Cancer Chemotherapy Annual [*Elsevier Book Series*] — CCA
Cancer Chemotherapy Reports — Canc Chemother Rep
Cancer Chemotherapy Reports — Cancer Chem Rep
Cancer Chemotherapy Reports — Cancer Chemother Rep
Cancer Chemotherapy Reports — CNCRA6
Cancer Chemotherapy Reports. Part 1 — Canc Ch P 1
Cancer Chemotherapy Reports. Part 1 — Cancer Chemother Rep Part 1
Cancer Chemotherapy Reports. Part 1 — CCROBU
Cancer Chemotherapy Reports. Part 2 — Canc Ch P 2
Cancer Chemotherapy Reports. Part 2 — Cancer Chemother Rep Part 2
Cancer Chemotherapy Reports. Part 2 — CCSUBJ
Cancer Chemotherapy Reports. Part 3 — Canc Ch P 3
Cancer Chemotherapy Reports. Part 3 — Cancer Chemother Rep Part 3
Cancer Chemotherapy Reports. Part 3 — CCYPBY
Cancer Chemotherapy Reports. Supplement — Canc Chemother Rep Suppl
Cancer Chemotherapy Screening Data — Cancer Chemother Screening Data
Cancer Chemotherapy Screening Data — CCRCAR
Cancer Clinical Trials — Cancer Clin Trials
Cancer Clinical Trials — CCTRDH
Cancer Communications — Cancer Commun
Cancer Current Literature Index — Canc Curr Lit Ind
Cancer Cytology — CACYA4
Cancer Cytology — Cancer Cytol
Cancer Detection and Prevention — Cancer Detect Prev
Cancer Detection and Prevention — CDPRD
Cancer Detection and Prevention — CDPRD4
Cancer Drug Delivery — Canc Drug D
Cancer Drug Delivery — Canc Drug Del
Cancer Drug Delivery — Cancer Drug Deliv
Cancer Drug Delivery — CDDED7
Cancer Epidemiology, Biomarkers, and Prevention — Cancer Epidemiol Biomarkers Prev
Cancer Focus — CAFOER
Cancer Forum — CAFODQ
Cancer Gene Therapy — Cancer Gene Ther
Cancer Genetics and Cytogenetics — Cancer Genet Cytogenet
Cancer Genetics and Cytogenetics — CGCYD
Cancer Genetics and Cytogenetics — CGCYDF
Cancer Immunology and Immunotherapy — Cancer Immunol Immunother
Cancer Immunology and Immunotherapy — CIIMDN
Cancer Investigation — CAIN
Cancer Investigation — Cancer Invest
Cancer Investigation — CI
Cancer Investigation — CINVD7
Cancer Journal — Canc J
Cancer Journal for Clinicians — Can J Clin
Cancer Journal from Scientific American — Cancer J Sci Am
Cancer Letters — CALEDQ
Cancer Letters — Cancer Lett
Cancer Letters (Shannon, Ireland) — Cancer Lett Shannon Irel
Cancer Literature [*Database*] — CANCERLIT
Cancer Metastasis Reviews — Canc Met Rev
Cancer News — CANW
Cancer News Journal — Canc NJ
Cancer Nursing — Ca Nurs
Cancer Nursing — Cancer Nurs
Cancer Nursing Letter — Cancer Nurs Let
Cancer Progress — Cancer Progr
Cancer Rehabilitation — Cancer Rehabil
Cancer Research — Canc Res
Cancer Research — Cancer Res
Cancer Research — CNREA8
Cancer Research and Clinical Oncology — Cancer Res Clin Oncol
Cancer Research and Clinical Oncology — ZKKOBW
Cancer Research Campaign. Annual Report — Canc Res Campaign Annu Rep
Cancer Research Campaign. Annual Report — Cancer Res Campaign Annu Rep
Cancer Research Institute. Slovak Academy of Sciences. Annual Report — Canc Res Inst Slovak Acad Annu Rep
Cancer Research Institute. Slovak Academy of Sciences. Annual Report — Cancer Res Inst Slovak Acad Sci Annu Rep
Cancer Research Institute. Slovak Academy of Sciences. Annual Report — CSARCX
Cancer Research Projects [*Database*] — CANCERPROJ
Cancer Research. Supplement — Cancer Res Suppl
Cancer Review — Canc Rev
Cancer Reviews — Cancer Rev
Cancer Seminar — Cancer Semin
Cancer Seminar — CASEA
Cancer Supplement — Cancer Suppl
Cancer Surveys — Cancer Surv
Cancer Surveys — CASUD7
Cancer Therapy Abstracts — Canc Ther Abst
Cancer Treatment and Research — Cancer Treat Res
Cancer Treatment Reports — Cancer Treat Rep
Cancer Treatment Reports — CTRRD
Cancer Treatment Reports — CTRRDO
Cancer Treatment Reviews — Cancer T R
Cancer Treatment Reviews — Cancer Treat Rev
Cancer Treatment Reviews — CTRED
Cancer Treatment Reviews — CTREDJ
Cancer Treatment Symposia — Canc Treat Symp
Cancer Treatment Symposia — Cancer Treat Symp
Cancer Treatment Symposia — CTSYEH
Candela — C
Candid Quarterly Review of Public Affairs — Candid
Candle — CD
Candollea — CNDLAR
Candy and Snack Industry — Candy Ind
Candy and Snack Industry — Candy Snack Ind
Candy Industry and Confectioners Journal — Candy Ind Confect J
Cane Growers Quarterly Bulletin — Can Grow Q Bull
Cane Growers Quarterly Bulletin — Cane Gr Quart Bull
Cane Growers Quarterly Bulletin — Cane Grow Q Bull
Cane Growers Quarterly Bulletin — Cane Growers Q Bul
Cane Growers Quarterly Bulletin — CNQBAS
Canebrake Agricultural Experiment Station Bulletin — Canebrake Agric Exp Sta Bull
Canine Practice — Canine Pract
Canine Practice — CPCEAF
CANMET [*Canada Centre for Mineral and Energy Technology*] **Report** [*Ottawa*] — CANMET Rep
CANMET [*Canada Centre for Mineral and Energy Technology*] **Special Publication** — CANMET Spec Publ
Canner Packer World — Can/Pack
Canners Journal (Tokyo) — Canners J (Tokyo)
Canning and Packing — Cann Pack
Canning House Library Bulletin (London) — Canning H Libr Bull London
Canning Industry — Cann Ind
Canning Trade — Cann Trade
Canning Trade — CATRAY
Canoe & Kayak — Canoe

Canoe Magazine — Canoe
Canoma. Canada Department of Energy, Mines, and Resources — CANO
Canon Law Abstracts — Canon Law
Canon Law Abstracts — Canon Law Abstr
Canon Law Society of America. Proceedings — CLSAP
Canoniste — Can
Canoniste Contemporain — Can C
CanPlast. Proceedings. Conference. Society of the Plastics Industry of Canada — CanPlast Proc Conf Soc Plast Ind Can
Canstatt's Jahresbericht ueber die Fortschritte in der Pharmacie und Verwandten Wissenschaften — Canstatts Jahresber Fortschr Pharm Verwandten Wiss
Cansteiner Kolloquium — Cansteiner Kolloq
Canteras y Explotaciones — Canteras Explot
Canterbury Chamber of Commerce. Agricultural Bulletin — Canterbury Chamber Commer Agric Bull
Canterbury Chamber of Commerce. Agricultural Bulletin — CCCBAH
Canterbury Chamber of Commerce. Bulletin [*New Zealand*] — CCC Bul
Canterbury Engineering Journal — Canterbury Eng J
Canterbury Engineering Journal — CEGJB
Canterbury Law Review — Canterbury L Rev
Canterbury Mountaineer [*New Zealand*] — Cant Mount
Canterbury Music Bulletin — Cant Mus Bull
Canticle — CAN
Canto Gregoriano — Canto Greg
Canto Libre — Canto Lib
Cantrill's Filmnotes — Cantrill's F
Cantrill's Filmnotes — Cantrill's Fmnts
Canyon Cinema News — Cany C News
Caoutchouc et la Gutta Percha — Caoutch Gutta Percha
Caoutchouc Moderne — Caoutch Mod
Caoutchoucs et Latex Artificiels — Caoutch Latex Artif
Caoutchoucs et Plastiques — Caoutch Plast
Cape Librarian — Cap Libn
Cape Librarian — Cape Librn
Cape Monthly Magazine — CMM
Cape Of Good Hope. Department of Nature Conservation. Investigational Report [*A publication*] — Cape Of Good Hope Dep Nat Conserv Invest Rep
Cape Of Good Hope. Department of Nature Conservation. Investigational Report — CGIRAL
Cape Of Good Hope. Department of Nature Conservation. Report — Cape Good Hope Dep Nat Conserv Rep
Cape Of Good Hope. Department of Nature Conservation. Report — Cape Of Good Hope Dep Nat Conserv Rep
Cape Of Good Hope. Department of Nature Conservation. Report — CGHRBH
Cape Town. University. Department of Geology. Precambrian Research Unit. Annual Report — Cape Town Univ Dep Geol Precambrian Res Unit Annu Rep
Capilla Alfonsina. Boletin — BCA
Capilla Alfonsina Boletin — Capil Alfonsina Bol
Capillarity Today. Proceedings. Advanced Workshop on Capillarity — Capillarity Today Proc Adv Workshop Capillarity
Capita Zoologica — Capita Zool
Capital and Class — Capital
Capital and Class — PCNC
Capital Chemist — Cap Chem
Capital. Das Deutsche Wirtschaftsmagazin — CTZ
Capital District Business Review — Cap Dist Bs
Capital Goods Review — Capital Goods R
Capital Markets Report [*Database*] — CMR
Capital Nursing — Cap Nurs
Capital University. Law Review — Cap U LR
Capital University. Law Review — Cap UL Rev
Capital University. Law Review — Capital U L Rev
Capital University. Law Review — Capital ULR
Capital University. Law Review — Capital Univ L Rev
Capitol Studies — Cap Stud
Capitol Studies — Capitol Stud
Capitoli — Cap
Capitolium — Cap
Capitolium — Capit
Capsule Information Series. Montana Agricultural Experiment Station — Capsule Inf Ser Mont Agric Exp Stn
Captain Future — CAF
Captain Future — CF
Captive Insurance Concept — Captv Insur
Capuchin Annual — Cap Ann
Car and Driver — C/D
Car and Driver — Car & Dr
Car and Driver — GCAR
Caravan Kampeersport. Maandblad voor Caravan/Kampeerliefhebbers — CAR
Caravel — CV
Caravelle — Car
Carbide and Tool Journal — Carbide Tool J
Carbide Engineering — Car Eng
Carbide Engineering — Carbide Eng
Carbide Journal — Carbide J
Carbide Journal — CBJNA
Carbohydrate Chemistry — Carbohydr Chem
Carbohydrate Chemistry of Substances of Biological Interest. Proceedings. International Congress of Biochemistry — Carbohydr Chem Subst Biol Interest Proc Int Congr Biochem
Carbohydrate. Comprehensive Biochemistry — Carbohydr Compr Biochem
Carbohydrate Letters — Carbohydr Lett
Carbohydrate Metabolism. Comprehensive Biochemistry — Carbohydr Metab Compr Biochem
Carbohydrate Metabolism in Pregnancy and the Newborn. International Colloquium — Carbohydr Metab Pregnancy Newborn Int Colloq
Carbohydrate Metabolism. Quantitative Physiology and Mathematical Modeling — Carbohydr Metab Quant Physiol Math Model
Carbohydrate Polymers — Carbohydr Polym
Carbohydrate Research — Carbohy Res
Carbohydrate Research — Carbohyd Res
Carbohydrate Research — Carbohydr Res
Carbohydrate Research — CRBRAT
Carbon Dioxide and Climate. A Second Assessment — Carbon Dio
Carbon Dioxide Review — Carbon Dioxide Rev
Carbon News — Carb Ne
Carbon Review — Carbon Rev
Carbonization Research Report — Carbonization Res Rep
Carbonization Research Report — CRRED
Carcinogenesis [*London*] — CRNGDP
Carcinogenesis: A Comprehensive Survey — Carcinog Compr Surv
Carcinogenesis: A Comprehensive Survey — CCSUDL
Carcinogenesis Abstracts — Carcinog Abst
Carcinogenesis Technical Report Series. United States National Cancer Institute — Carcinog Tech Rep Ser US Natl Cancer Inst
CARD [*Center for Agricultural and Rural Development*] **Report** — CARD Rep
Cardiac News Letter. Chest and Heart Association — Card Ne Lett
Cardiac Practice — Card Pract
Cardiff Naturalist's Society. Transactions — CNST
Cardiganshire Natural History Bulletin — Card Nat Hist Bull
Cardiologia — Card
Cardiologia — CARDAG
Cardiologia [*Rome*] — CARDDJ
Cardiologia Hungarica — Cardil Hung
Cardiologia Pratica — Card Prat
Cardiologia Pratica — Cardiol Prat
Cardiologisches Bulletin — Cardiol Bull
Cardiologisches Bulletin — CLBCBB
Cardiology — CAGYAO
Cardiology. An International Perspective. Proceedings. World Congress of Cardiology — Cardiol Int Perspect Proc World Congr
Cardiology Clinics — Cardiol Clin
Cardiology. Proceedings of the World Congress of Cardiology — Cardiol Proc World Congr
Cardiovascular and Interventional Radiology — CAIRDG
Cardiovascular and Interventional Radiology — Cardiovasc Intervent Radiol
Cardiovascular and Interventional Radiology — Cardiovasc Interventional Radiol
Cardiovascular and Pulmonary Technology. Journal — CVP
Cardiovascular Clinics — Cardiovasc Clin
Cardiovascular Clinics — CCLIB
Cardiovascular Diseases Bulletin. Texas Heart Institute — CADIDW
Cardiovascular Diseases Bulletin. Texas Heart Institute — Cardiovasc Dis Bull Tex Heart Inst
Cardiovascular Diseases (Houston) — Cardiovas Dis (Houston)
Cardiovascular Diuretic Review — Cardiovasc Diuretic Rev
Cardiovascular Drug Reviews — Cardio Dr R
Cardiovascular Drug Therapy. The Hahnemann Symposium — Cardiovasc Drug Ther Hahnemann Symp
Cardiovascular Drugs — CADRDP
Cardiovascular Drugs — Cardiovasc Drugs
Cardiovascular Drugs and Therapy — Cardiovasc Drugs Ther
Cardiovascular Flow Dynamics and Measurements (North Atlantic Treaty Organization. Advanced Study Institute on Cardiovascular Flow Dynamics) — Cardiovasc Flow Dyn Meas (NATO Adv Study Inst)
Cardiovascular Medicine — CAMEEW
Cardiovascular Medicine — Cardiovasc Med
Cardiovascular Medicine — CMEDD4
Cardiovascular Medicine [*New York*] — CMRPD3
Cardiovascular Medicine (New York) — Cardiovasc Med (NY)
Cardiovascular Nursing — Cardiovasc Nurs
Cardiovascular Physiology — Cardiovasc Physiol
Cardiovascular Radiology — Cardiovasc Radiol
Cardiovascular Research — Cardio Res
Cardiovascular Research — Cardiovas Res
Cardiovascular Research — Cardiovasc Res
Cardiovascular Research — CVREAU
Cardiovascular Research Center. Bulletin [*Houston*] — Cardiovasc Res Cent Bull
Cardiovascular Research Center. Bulletin [*Houston*] — CRCBAK
Cardiovascular Research Center. Bulletin (Houston) — Cardiovasc Res Cent Bull (Houston)
Cardiovascular Research. Supplement — Cardiovas Res Suppl
Cardiovascular Review — Cardiovas Rev
Cardiovascular Surgery — Cardiovasc Surg
Cardiovascular System — Cardiovasc Syst
Cardiovascular Therapy — Cardiovasc Ther
Cardozo Arts and Entertainment Journal — Car A and E J
Cardozo Law Review — Cardozo L Rev
Career Development Bulletin — Career Dev Bul
Career Development Quarterly — GCDQ
Career Information System [*Database*] — CIS
Careers and Guidance Teacher — Careers Guid Teach
Careers Bulletin — Careers Bull
Careers Journal — Careers J
Carey's American Museum — Carey's Mus
Cargese Lectures in Physics — Cargese Lect Phys
Cargill Crop Bulletin — Cargill Crop Bull
Cargo Systems International — Cargo Syst Int
Cargo Systems International — CSYIB
Caribbean Agriculture — Caribb Agr

Caribbean Agriculture — Caribb Agric
Caribbean Agriculture — Caribbean Agric
Caribbean Agriculture — CRAGAP
Caribbean Basin Economic Survey — Carib Basin Econ Surv
Caribbean Basin Economic Survey — CBESD
Caribbean Business — Caribb Bus
Caribbean Commission. Monthly Information Bulletin — Car Commn Mon Inf B
Caribbean Economic Review — Car Econ Rev
Caribbean Educational Bulletin — CEB
Caribbean Forester — Car For
Caribbean Forester — CARIAV
Caribbean Forester — Caribb For
Caribbean Forester — Caribbean Forest
Caribbean Forester (Rio Piedras, Puerto Rico) — Carib Forest Rio Piedras
Caribbean Geography (Jamaica) — CGJ
Caribbean Geological Conference. Transactions — Caribb Geol Conf Trans
Caribbean Historical Review — Car Hist Rev
Caribbean Insight (London) — CIL
Caribbean Islands Water Resources Congress — Caribb Isl Water Resour Congr
Caribbean Journal of African Studies — CJAfS
Caribbean Journal of Mathematical and Computing Sciences — Caribbean J Math Comput Sci
Caribbean Journal of Mathematics — Caribbean J Math
Caribbean Journal of Religious Studies — Carib J Rel St
Caribbean Journal of Science — Car J Sci
Caribbean Journal of Science — Caribb J Sci
Caribbean Journal of Science — Caribbean Jour Sci
Caribbean Journal of Science — CRJSA4
Caribbean Journal of Science and Mathematics — Caribb J Sci Math
Caribbean Journal of Science and Mathematics — Caribbean J Sci Math
Caribbean Journal of Sciences (Mayaguez, Puerto Rico) — Carib Jour Sc Mayaguez
Caribbean Medical Journal — Car Med J
Caribbean Medical Journal — Carib Med J
Caribbean Medical Journal — Caribb Med J
Caribbean Medical Journal — CMJUA9
Caribbean Monthly Bulletin — Carib Bul
Caribbean Monthly Bulletin — CMB
Caribbean Quarterly — Car Quart
Caribbean Quarterly — Carib Q
Caribbean Quarterly — Caribb Q
Caribbean Quarterly — CarQ
Caribbean Quarterly — CQ
Caribbean Quarterly (Kingston, Jamaica, Port of Spain, Trinidad) — Carib Quart Kingston Port of Spain
Caribbean Quarterly. University of the West Indies — UWI/CQ
Caribbean Review — Caribbean R
Caribbean Review — CarR
Caribbean Review — CRI
Caribbean Review. Florida International University. Office of Academic Affairs — FIU/CR
Caribbean Studies — Car Stud
Caribbean Studies — Carib Stud
Caribbean Studies — Caribb Stud
Caribbean Studies — Caribbean S
Caribbean Studies — Caribbean Stud
Caribbean Studies — CarS
Caribbean Studies — CS
Caribbean Studies Newsletter — CSN
Caribbean Studies. University of Puerto Rico. Institute of Caribbean Studies — UPR/CS
Caribbean Technological Abstracts — Caribb Technol Abstr
Caribbean Today — CTY
Caribbean Update — Carib Updat
Caribbean Yearbook of International Relations — Caribb Yb Int Relat
Caribe Contemporaneo — CCO
Caribe Universidad de Hawaii — CUH
Caribou News [*Canada*] — CABN
Caridad Ciencia y Arte — Caridad Cienc Arte
Caries Research — CAREBK
Caries Research — Caries Res
Carindex Social Sciences — Carindex Soc Sci
Caring for the Older Veteran — Old Vetern
Carinthia 2 — CATHA4
Carinthia 2. Sonderheft — Carinthia 2 Sonderh
Carinthia. Mitteilungen des Geschichtsverein fuer Kaernten — Carinthia
Carinthia. Zeitschrift fuer Vaterlanskunde, Belehrung, und Unterhaltung — Car
Caritas. Zeitschrift des Schweizerischen Caritasverbandes — CV
Carl Neuberg Society for International Scientific Relations. Transactions of the Symposium — Trans Symp Carl Neuberg Soc
Carle Clinic and Carle Foundation. Selected Papers — Carle Clin Carle Found Sel Pap
Carle Hospital Clinic and Carle Foundation. Selected Papers — Carle Hosp Clin Carle Found Sel Pap
Carle Selected Papers — Carle Sel Pap
Carleton Germanic Papers — CGP
Carleton Miscellany — Carl Mis
Carleton Miscellany — Carleton Misc
Carleton Miscellany — CM
Carleton Newsletter — CarlN
Carleton University. Department of Geology. Geological Paper — Carleton Univ Dep Geol Geol Pap
Carleton University. Department of Geology. Geological Paper — Carleton Univ Dept Geology Geol Paper
Carleton-Ottawa Mathematical Lecture Note Series — Carleton Ottawa Math Lecture Note Ser
Carlsberg Research Communications — Carlsberg Res Commun
Carlsberg Research Communications — CRCODS
Carlyle Newsletter — CNew
Carmarthenshire Antiquary — C Antiq
Carmarthenshire Antiquary — Carmarthenshire Antiq
Carmarthenshire Historian — CH
Carmelus — Car
Carmina — CA
Carmina Latina Epigraphica — C Epigr
Carmina Latina Epigraphica — Carm Lat Epigr
Carmina Latina Epigraphica — CE
Carmina Latina Epigraphica — CL Ep
Carmina Latina Epigraphica — CLE
Carnation Craft. American Carnation Society — Carnation Craft ACS
Carnation Nutrition Education Series — Carnation Nutr Educ Ser
Carnegie College of Physical Education (Leeds). Research Papers in Physical Education — Carnegie Coll Physical Ed Research Papers
Carnegie Institute of Technology. Bulletin. Coal Mining Investigations — Carnegie Inst Technol Bull Coal Min Invest
Carnegie Institute of Technology. Coal Research Laboratory. Contribution — Carnegie Inst Technol Coal Res Lab Contri
Carnegie Institute of Technology. Coal Research Laboratory. Contributions — Carnegie Inst Technol Coal Res Lab Contrib
Carnegie Institute of Technology. Cooperative Bulletin. Mining and Metallurgical Investigations — Carnegie Inst Technol Coop Bull Min Metall Invest
Carnegie Institution of Washington. Papers from the Geophysical Laboratory [*A publication*] — Carnegie Inst Wash Pap Geophys Lab
Carnegie Institution of Washington. Papers from the Geophysical Laboratory [*A publication*] — Carnegie Inst Washington Pap Geophys Lab
Carnegie Institution of Washington. Publication — Carnegie Inst Wash Publ
Carnegie Institution of Washington. Publication — CIWPAV
Carnegie Institution of Washington. Year Book — Carnegie Inst Wash Year Book
Carnegie Institution of Washington. Year Book — CIWYAO
Carnegie Magazine — Carn Mag
Carnegie Magazine — Carnegie Mag
Carnegie Magazine — CarnM
Carnegie Museum Botany Pamphlet — Carnegie Mus Bot Pam
Carnegie Museum of Natural History. Annals — Carnegie Mus Annals
Carnegie Museum of Natural History. Annals. Memoirs — Carnegie Mus An Mem
Carnegie Museum of Natural History. Annual Report — Carnegie Mus Nat Hist Annu Rep
Carnegie Museum of Natural History. Annual Report — CNHABF
Carnegie Museum of Natural History. Special Publication — Carnegie Mus Nat Hist Spec Publ
Carnegie Museum of Natural History. Special Publication — SPCHDX
Carnegie Research Papers — Carnegie Res Papers
Carnegie Scholarship Memoirs — Carnegie Scholarship Mem
Carnegie Series in American Education — Carn Ser Am Educ
Carnegie Series in English — Carn SE
Carnegie Series in English — CaSE
Carnegie Series in English — CSE
Carnegie-Mellon University, Pittsburgh. Transportation Research Institute. TRI Research Report — Carnegie-Mellon Univ TRI Res Rep
Carnegie-Rochester Conference Series on Public Policy [*Elsevier Book Series*] [*A publication*] — CR
Carnes y Mercados — Carnes Merc
Carnet Musical — Carnet Mus
Carnets de l'Enfance/Assignment Children — CARN
Carnets de l'Enfance/Assignment Children — Carn Enfance
Carnets de l'Enfance/Assignment Children — Carnets Enfance
Carnets de l'Enfance/Assignment Children — Carnets Enfance Assignment Child
Carnets de l'Enfance/Assignment Children — CENCBM
Carnets de Zoologie — Carnets Zool
Carnets de Zoologie — CZOOA5
Carnivore [*Seattle*] — CRNVD2
Carnivore. Carnivore Research Institute [*Petersburg, IL*] — CARV
Carnivore Genetics Newsletter — Carniv Genet Newsl
Carnivore Genetics Newsletter — Carnivore Genet Newsl
Carnivore Genetics Newsletter — CGN
Carnivore Genetics Newsletter — CGNWAR
Carnuntum Jahrbuch — Carn Jb
Carnuntum-Jahrbuch — Carnuntum Jb
Carolimetrie et Analyse Thermique — Carolim Anal Therm
Carolina Biology Readers — Carol Biol Readers
Carolina Camellias — Carol Camellias
Carolina Journal of Pharmacy — Car J Pharm
Carolina Journal of Pharmacy — Carol J Pharm
Carolina Lecture Series — Carolina Lecture Ser
Carolina Planning — CAPLD
Carolina Planning — Carol Plann
Carolina Playbook — CarP
Carolina Quarterly — CAR Q
Carolina Quarterly — Carol Q
Carolina Quarterly — Carolina Q
Carolina Quarterly — CQ
Carolina Tips — Carol Tips
Carolina Tips — CTIPB5
Carolinea — CAROEJ
Carotenoid Chemistry and Biochemistry. Proceedings of the International Symposium on Carotenoids — Carotenoid Chem Biochem Proc Int Symp Carotenoids

Carotenoids in Photosynthesis — Carotenoids Photosynth
Carousel Quarterly — Carousel Q
Carovana — Car
Carre Bleu — CRBL-A
Carrefour — Car
Carrobbio; Rivista di Studi Bolognesi — Carrobbio
Carroll Business Bulletin — Carroll Bus Bul
Carrosserie — ENH
Carswell's Practice Cases — Carswell's Prac
Carswell's Practice Cases — Carswell's Prac Cases
Carswell's Practice Cases — CPC
Carta (Chile). Instituto de Investigaciones Geologicas — Carta (Chile) Inst Invest Geol
Carta Geologica de Chile — Carta Geol Chile
Carta Geologica de Chile. Instituto de Investigaciones Geologicas — Carta Geol Chile Inst Invest Geol
Carta Informativa (Costa Rica) — CICR
Carta Mensal (Rio de Janeiro) — Carta Mens Rio
Carta Semanal (Mexico, DF) — Carta Sem Mex
Carte Archeologique de la Gaule Romaine — CAGR
Carte Segrete — Carte
Carte Segrete — CSeg
Cartel; Review of Monopoly Development and Consumer Protections — Cart
Cartographic Journal — Cart J
Cartographic Journal — Cartogr J
Cartography — Cartogr
Cartonnages et Emballages Modernes — AXL
Carus Mathematical Monographs — Carus Math Monogr
Carus Mathematical Monographs — Carus Math Monographs
Carvao, Informacao, e Pesquisa — Carvao Inf Pesqui
Carvao, Informacao, e Pesquisa [*Brazil*] — CIPED
Caryologia — CARYAB
Casa de la Cultura Ecuatoriana (Quito) — Casa Cult Equat Quito
Casa de las Americas — CA
Casa de las Americas — CAm
Casa de las Americas — CasaA
Casa de las Americas — CDLA
Casa de las Americas (La Habana) — Casa Am Hav
Casabella — CSBL-A
Cascadian Regional Library — CAREL
Case and Comment — C & C
Case and Comment — Case & Com
Case Studies in Atomic Physics — Case Stud At Phys
Case Studies in Atomic Physics — CSAPC
Case Studies in Dental Emergencies — Case Stud Dent Emerg
Case Studies in Health Administration — Case Stud Health Adm
Case Western Reserve. Journal of International Law — Case W Res
Case Western Reserve. Journal of International Law — Case W Res J Int L
Case Western Reserve. Journal of International Law — Case West J Int Law
Case Western Reserve. Journal of International Law — Case West Res J Int'l L
Case Western Reserve Journal of International Law — Case West Reserve J Int Law
Case Western Reserve. Journal of International Law — CWR J Int L
Case Western Reserve. Law Review — Cas W Res L Rev
Case Western Reserve. Law Review — Case W Res L Rev
Case Western Reserve. Law Review — Case W Reserve L Rev
Case Western Reserve. Law Review — Case W Reserve Law R
Case Western Reserve. Law Review — Case West Res L Rev
Case Western Reserve. Law Review — Case West Reserve L Rev
Case Western Reserve. Law Review — CWL
Case Western Reserve. Law Review — CWR LR
Case Western Reserve University. Department of Mechanical and Aerospace Engineering. Technical Report FTAS/TR — Case West Reserve Univ Dep Mech Aerosp Eng Tech Rep
Case Western Reserve University. Studies in Anthropology — Case West Reserve
Casella-Reidel Archiv. Wissenschaftliche Reihe. Cerebrum I — Casella Reidel Arch Wiss Reihe Cerebrum
Cashflow — CFL
Cashflow Classics — Casflow C
Cashflow Magazine — Cashflow
Cashflow Magazine — Cashflow M
Cashflow Magazine — CWM
CASI [*Canadian Aeronautics and Space Institute*] **Transactions** — CASI Trans
CASL [*Centro Academico Sarmento Leite*] **Revista Cientifica** — CASL Rev Cient
Casopis Ceske Spolecnosti Entomologicke — Cas Ceske Spol Ent
Casopis Ceskeho Museum — Cas Ceskeho Mus
Casopis Ceskenho Lekarstnitva — Cas Cesk Lek
Casopis Ceskenho Musea — CCM
Casopis Ceskoslovenske. Spolecnosti Entomologicke — Cas Cesk Spol Entomol
Casopis Ceskoslovenske. Spolecnosti Entomologicke — Cas Cesk Spolecnosti Entomol
Casopis Ceskoslovenske. Spolecnosti Entomologicke — CSOPAR
Casopis Ceskoslovenskeho Lekarnictva — Cas Ceskoslov Lekarn
Casopis Katolickeko Duckovenstva a Prilohou — CKD
Casopis Lekaru Ceskych — Cas Lek Cesk
Casopis Lekaru Ceskych — CLCEA
Casopis Lekaru Ceskych — CLCEAL
Casopis Matice Moravske — Cas Matice Morav
Casopis Matice Moravske — CMM
Casopis Moravskeho Musea (Brne) — Cas Morav Mus (Brne)
Casopis. Moravskeho Musea v Brne — CMMB
Casopis Moravskeho Musea. Vedy Prirodni — Cas Morav Mus Vedy Prir
Casopis Moravskeho Musea. Vedy Spolcenske — Casopis Moravskeho Musea
Casopis Moravskeho Musea Zemskeho. Acta Musei Moraviensis — Cas Morav Mus Zemsk
Casopis Musealnej Slovenskej Splocnosti — CMSS
Casopis Narodniho Muzea [*Prague*] — CANMAN
Casopis Narodniho Muzea [*Prague*] — CNM
Casopis Narodniho Muzea. Historicke Muzeum Rocnik [*Prague*] — Cas Narod Muz
Casopis Narodniho Muzea. Oddil Prirodovedny [*Prague*] — Cas Nar Muz Oddil Priroddoved
Casopis Narodniho Muzea (Prague) — Cas Nar Muz (Prague)
Casopis Narodniho Muzea v Praze. Rada Prirodovedna — Cas Nar Muz Praze Rada Prirodoved
Casopis Narodniho Muzea v Praze. Rada Prirodovedna — CMOPAJ
Casopis Ovocnickeho Spolku Pro Kralovstvi Ceske — Cas Ovocn Spolku Kral Ceske
Casopis Pracovniho Lekarstvi — Cas Prac Lek
Casopis pro Mineralogii a Geologii — Cas Mineral Geol
Casopis pro Moderni Filologii — CMF
Casopis pro Moderni Filologii — CpMF
Casopis pro Moderni Filologii a Literatury — CMFL
Casopis pro Prumysl Chemicky — Cas Prum Chem
Casopis pro Slovanske Jazyky, Literaturu, a Dejiny SSSR — CSJ
Casopis pro Slovanske Jazyky, Literaturu, a Dejiny SSSR — CSLJa
Casopis Rodopisne Spolecnosti Ceskoslovenske — CRodSpol
Casopis Slezskeho Musea. Serie A. Historia Naturalis. Acta Musei Silesiae — Cas Slez Mus Ser A Hist Nat
Casopis Slezskeho Muzea — Cas Sl Muz
Casopis Slezskeho Muzea — Cas Slezske Muz
Casopis Slezskeho Muzea — CSM
Casopis Slezskeho Muzea. Serie A. Scientiae Naturales — Cas Slezskeho Muz Ser A Sci Nat
Casopis Slezskeho Muzea. Serie A. Vedy Prirodni — Cas Slezskeho Muz Ser A Vedy Prir
Casopis Slezskeho Muzea. Serie A. Vedy Prirodni — CASNAH
Casopis Slezskeho Muzea. Vedy Prirodni (Acta Musei Silesiae. Series A. Scientiae Naturales) — Cas Slezskeho Muz Vedy Prir Acta Mus Silesiae Ser A Sci Nat
Casopis Vlasteneckeho Spolku Musejniho v Olomouci — CVSMO
Casopis Vlasteneckeho Spolku Muzejniho v Olomouci — Casopis Vlast Spolku Olomouci
Casopis za Zgodovino in Narodopisje — CasZ
Casopis za Zgodovino in Narodopisje — CZN
Casopis Zemskeho Spolku Steparskeho Pro Kralovstvi Ceske. Zeitschrift des Landes-Obstbaumzucht-Vereines fuer das Koenigreich Boehmen — Cas Zemsk Spolku Step Kral Ceske
Cassava Program Annual Report — Cassava Prog Ann Rep
Cassella Riedel Archiv Cerebrum 1 — Cassella Riedel Arch Cerebrum 1
Cassier's Magazine — Cass M
Cassier's Magazine — Cassier
Cassier's Magazine — Cassiers M
Cassier's Magazine — Cassiers Mag
Cassinia — CASSAW
Cassinia. A Journal of Ornithology of Eastern Pennsylvania, Southern New Jersey, and Delaware — Cassinia J Ornithol East Penn South NJ Del
Cassoe Newsletter — Cassoe Nesl
Cast Metals — Cast Met
Cast Metals Institute. Electric Ironmelting Conference — Cast Met Inst Electr Ironmelting Conf
Cast Metals Research Journal — Cast Met Res J
Castanea — CSTNAC
Casting and Forging [*Japan*] — Cast Forg
Casting and Forging of Steel [*Japan*] — Cast Forg Steel
Casting and Forging (Osaka) — Cast Forg (Osaka)
Casting Engineering — Cast Eng
Casting Engineering/Foundry World — Cast Eng/Foundry World
Casting, Forging, and Heat Treatment (Osaka) — Cast Forg Heat Treat (Osaka)
Castrum Peregrini — C
Castrum Peregrini — Ca Per
Castrum Peregrini — CP
Castrum Peregrini — CPe
Catalog of Books represented by Library of Congress Printed Cards — LOC
Catalog of New Publications. Noyes Data Corp. — Noyes
Catalog Showroom Merchandiser — Cat Show Merch
Cataloging and Classification Quarterly — Cat and Classif Q
Cataloging and Classification Quarterly — CCQUD
Cataloging Service Bulletin — CSB
Catalogo Colectivo de Publicaciones Periodicas [*Database*] — CPUP
Catalogo Italiano Riviste su Calcolatore Elettronico [*Database*] — CIRCE
Catalogue and Index. Library Association Cataloguing and Indexing Group — Cat Index
Catalogue des Invertebres de la Suisse. Museum d'Histoire Naturelle de Geneve — Cat Invertebres Suisse Mus Hist Nat Geneve
Catalogue des Manuscrits Alchimiques Grecs — CMA
Catalogue des Manuscrits Alchimiques Grecs — CMAG
Catalogue des Manuscrits Alchimiques Latins — CMA Lat
Catalogue des Manuscrits Alchimiques Latins — CMAL
Catalogue des Monnaies de l'Empire Romain. Bibliotheque Nationale — CMERBN
Catalogue des Textes Hittites — CTH
Catalogue of American Amphibians and Reptiles — CAPBAY
Catalogue of American Amphibians and Reptiles — Cat Am Amphib Reptiles
Catalogue of British Official Publications — Cat Br Off Publications
Catalogue of Byzantine Coins in the Dumbarton Oaks Collection and in the Whittemore Collection — CBCDO

Catalogue of Byzantine Coins in the Dumbarton Oaks Collection and Whittemore Collection — DOC
Catalogue of Calcareous Nannofossils. Edizioni Tecnoscienza [*Rome*] — Cat Calcareous Nannofossils
Catalogue of Egyptian Scarabs, Scaraboids, Seals, and Amulets in the Palestine Archeological Museum — CESSA
Catalogue of Egyptian Scarabs, Scaraboids, Seals, and Amulets in the Palestine Archeological Museum — CSPM
Catalogue of Greek and Latin Papyri and Ostraca in the Possession of the University of Aberdeen — P Aberd
Catalogue of the Epstean Collection — Epst Cat
Catalogue of Type Invertebrate Fossils. Geological Survey of Canada — Cat Type Invertebr Fossils Geol Surv Can
Catalogue of Type Invertebrate Fossils. Geological Survey of Canada — CTICD2
Catalogus Codicum Astrologorum Graecorum — Cat Cod Astr Gr
Catalogus Codicum Astrologorum Graecorum — CCAG
Catalogus Codicum Hagiograhicorum Latinorum Bibliothecarum Romanorum Praeter quam Vaticanae — Catal Cod Hag Lat
Catalogus Codicum Hagiograhicorum Latinorum Bibliothecarum Romanorum Praeter quam Vaticanae — Catal Lat Rom
Catalogus Codicum Hagiographicorum Bibliothecae Regiae Bruxellensis — Catal Lat Brux
Catalogus Codicum Hagiographicorum Graecorum Bibliothecae Nationalis Parisiensis — Catal Cod Hag Gr B
Catalogus Codicum Hagiographicorum Graecorum Bibliothecae Nationalis Parisiensis — Catal Gr Paris
Catalogus Codicum Hagiographicorum Graecorum Bibliothecae Vaticanae — Catal Graec Vatic
Catalogus Codicum Hagiographicorum Graecorum Germaniae, Gelgii, Angliae — Catal Cod Hag Gr Ger
Catalogus Codicum Hagiographicorum Graecorum Germaniae, Gelgii, Angliae — Catal Graec Germ
Catalogus Codicum Hagiographicorum Latinorum Antiquiorum Saeculo XVI qui Asservantur in Bibliotheca Nationalis Parisiensis — Catal Cod Hag La Ant
Catalogus Faunae Austriae — Cat Faunae Austriae
Catalogus Faunae Poloniae — Cat Faunae Pol
Catalogus Faunae Poloniae — KAFPAC
Catalogus Fossilium Austriae — Cat Fossilium Austriae
Catalogus Translationum et Commentariorium/Medieval and Renaissance Latin Translations and Commentaries — Cat Trans C
Catalogus Translationum et Commentariorum. Medieval and Renaissance Latin Translations and Commentaries. Annotated Lists and Guides — CTC
Catalysis by Metal Complexes — Catal Met Complexes
Catalysis in Organic Syntheses — Catal Org Synth
Catalysis Letters — Catal Lett
Catalysis Letters. Supplement — Catal Lett Suppl
Catalysis of Organic Reactions — Catal Org React
Catalysis. Proceedings of the International Congress on Catalysis — Catal Proc Int Congr
Catalysis Reviews — Catal Rev
Catalysis Reviews. Science and Engineering — Catal Rev Sci Eng
Catalysis Today — Catal Today
Catalyst — Cat
Catalyst — Cata
Catalyst for Environmental Quality — Catal Environ Qual
Catalyst for Environmental Quality — Catalyst Envir Qual
Catalyst Resource on the Work Force and Women [*Database*] — CRFW
Catalysts in Chemistry — Catal Chem
Catechistes [*Paris*] — Cat
Catequesis Latinoamericana — Cateques Latinoamer
Catequesis Latinoamericana (Mexico) — CLM
Caterer and Hotelkeeper — CHK
Catering — Cater
Catering Industry Employee — CIE
Catering Times — CT
Catgut Acoustical Society Journal — CASJ
Cathedral Service Book — CSB
Catheterization and Cardiovascular Diagnosis — Cathet Cardiovasc Diagn
Catheterization and Cardiovascular Diagnosis — Catheterization Cardiovasc Diagn
Catheterization and Cardiovascular Diagnosis — CCDIDC
Catholic Biblical Quarterly — Ca Bi Q
Catholic Biblical Quarterly — Cath Bib Q
Catholic Biblical Quarterly — Cath Bibl Q
Catholic Biblical Quarterly — CBQ
Catholic Biblical Quarterly — PCBQ
Catholic Charismatic — Cath Charis
Catholic Choirmaster — Cath Choirmaster
Catholic Digest — C Dgst
Catholic Documentation — Cath Doc
Catholic Documentation — Catholic Doc
Catholic Educational Association. Bulletin — Cath Educ Assn Bul
Catholic Educational Review — Cath Ed R
Catholic Educational Review — CER
Catholic Encyclopedia — Cath Ency
Catholic Encyclopedia — CE
Catholic Health Association of Canada. Review — CHAC Rev
Catholic Historical Review — C Hist
Catholic Historical Review — CatH
Catholic Historical Review — Cath His R
Catholic Historical Review — Cath Hist R
Catholic Historical Review — Cath Hist Rev
Catholic Historical Review — CathHR
Catholic Historical Review — Cathol Hist Rev
Catholic Historical Review — CHR
Catholic Historical Review — PCRE
Catholic Hospital — Cath Hosp
Catholic Hospital — Cathol Hosp
Catholic Lawyer — C Lawyer
Catholic Lawyer — Cath Law
Catholic Lawyer — Cath Lawyer
Catholic Lawyer — Catholic Law
Catholic Library World — Cath Lib W
Catholic Library World — Cath Lib World
Catholic Library World — Cath Libr Wld
Catholic Library World — CLW
Catholic Library World (Glen Ellyn, Ill) — Cathol Libr World Glen Ellyn
Catholic Life in Poland — Cat Life Pol
Catholic Mind — C Mind
Catholic Mind — Cath M
Catholic Mind — Cath Mind
Catholic Nurse (Wallsend) — Cathol Nurse (Wallsend)
Catholic Periodical and Literature Index — Cathl
Catholic Periodical and Literature Index — Cathol Period Lit Index
Catholic Periodical and Literature Index — CPLI
Catholic Periodical Index — Cathol Period Index
Catholic Record Society. Publications — Cath Rec Soc Pub
Catholic School Journal — Cath Sch J
Catholic School Paper — CSP
Catholic Telegraph — Cat Tel
Catholic Theological Society of America. Proceedings — CTSAP
Catholic Trustee — Catholic Trust
Catholic University. Bulletin — Cath Univ Bull
Catholic University. Bulletin — CUB
Catholic University. Law Review — Cath UL Rev
Catholic University. Law Review — Cath ULR
Catholic University. Law Review — Catholic U L Rev
Catholic University. Law Review — Catholic ULR
Catholic University. Law Review — Catholic Univ L Rev
Catholic University. Law Review — CULR
Catholic University of America. Biological Series — Catholic Univ Amer Biol Ser
Catholic University of America. Biological Studies — CABSAF
Catholic University of America. Biological Studies — Cath Univ Am Biol Stud
Catholic University of America. Biological Studies — Cathol Univ Am Biol Stud
Catholic University of America. Bulletin — Cath Univ Bull
Catholic University of America. Bulletin — CUAB
Catholic University of America. Law Review — Cath U Law
Catholic University of America. Law Review — Cath UALR
Catholic University of America. Law Review — Cath Univ Law Rev
Catholic University of America. Law Review — Catholic UALR
Catholic University of America. Law Review — CUALR
Catholic University of America. Patristic Studies — CUAPS
Catholic University of America. Studies in Romance Languages and Literatures — CUASRL
Catholic University of America. Studies in Romance Languages and Literatures — CUASRLL
Catholic Weekly — Catholic W
Catholic Worker — Cath Work
Catholic World — Cath World
Catholic World — CathW
Catholic World — CaW
Catholic World — CW
Catholic World — Cwd
Catholic World — ICWO
Catholica — Cath
Catholicisme. Hier, Aujourd'hui, Demain [*Paris*] — Cath
Catholic-Presbyterian — Cath-Presb
Cations of Biological Significance — Cations Biol Significance
Cato Journal — CAJOD
Cato Journal — Cato J
Cato Journal — CTJ
Cats Magazine — GCAT
Cattleman — CTLMAA
Cattlemen. The Beef Magazine — Cattlemen Beef Mag
Caucasian Review — Caucas Rev
Cava-Cristallas Svizzer — Cava Crist Svizz
Cavalry Journal — Cavalry J
Cave Geology — Cave Geol
Cave Research Group of Great Britain. Newsletter — Cave Res Group News
Cave Research Group of Great Britain. Transactions — Cave Res Group GB Trans
Cave Research Group of Great Britain. Transactions — Cave Res Group Great Britain Trans
Cave Science — Cave Sci
Caveat Emptor — Caveat
Cawthron Institute (Nelson, New Zealand). Report — Cawthron Inst (Nelson NZ) Rep
Cawthron Institute. Publications — Cawthron Inst Publs
Cawthron Institute [*Nelson, New Zealand*]. **Report** — CIARAT
Caxton Magazine — Cax
Cayey — CY
CB Review (Philippines) — CBP
CBA [*Council for British Archaeology*] **Research Report** — CBA Res Rep
CBC (Citizens Budget Commission) Quarterly — CBC (Citizens Budget Comm) Q
CBC [*Canadian Broadcasting Corporation*] **Northern Service Press Releases** — CBCNS

CBI (Confederation of British Industry) Review — CBI (Confederation British Industry) R
CBI [*Cement- och Betonginstitutet*] **Forskning** — CBI Forsk
CBI [*Confederation of British Industry*] **Industrial Trends** — CBI Ind Trends
CBI [*Confederation of British Industry*] **Industrial Trends Survey** — CBI Ind Trends Surv
CBI Newsbulletin — CFI
CBI [*Cement- och Betonginstitutet*] **Rapporter** — CBI Rapp
CBI [*Cement- och Betonginstitutet*] **Reports** — CBI Rep
CBI [*Cement- och Betonginstitutet*] **Research** — CBI Res
CCAM [*Chambre de Commerce et d'Industrie de Marseille*] **Information** — CCAM Info
CCAR [*Central Conference of American Rabbis*] **Yearbook** — CCARY
CCB. Review for Chocolate Confectionery and Bakery — CCB Rev Choc Confect Bakery
CCH [*Commerce Clearing House*] **Dominion Report Service** [*Database*] — DRS
CCH [*Commerce Clearing House*] **Dominion Tax Cases** [*Database*] — DTC
CCLA [*Correspondence Chess League of Australia*] **Record** — CCLA Record
CCLP. Contents of Current Legal Periodicals — CCLP Contents Curr Leg Period
CCMS [*North Atlantic Treaty Organization. Committee on the Challenges of Modern Society*] **Report** — CCMS Rep
C-CORE [*Centre for Cold Ocean Resources Engineering*] **Publications** — C-CORE
CCQ. Critical Care Quarterly — CCCQDV
CCQ: Critical Care Quarterly — CCQ Crit Care Q
CCS: Centro de Ciencias da Saude — CCS Cent Cienc Saude
CCS. Ciencia, Cultura, Saude — CCS Cienc Cult Saude
CD Data Report [*Database*] — CDDR
CD. North Carolina Agricultural Extension Service — CD NC Agric Ext Serv
CDHA [*California Dental Hygienists Association*] **Journal** — CDHA Jnl
CD-ROM [*Compact Disc Read Only Memory*] **Review** — CD-ROM Rev
Ce Fastu — CeF
Ce Fastu — CF
CEA [*College English Association*] **Chap Book** — CEAC
CEA (Chemical Engineering in Australia) — CEA (Chem Eng Aust)
CEA [*College English Association*] **Critic** — CEA
CEA [*College English Association*] **Critic** — CEACrit
CEA [*College English Association*] **Forum** — CEAF
CEA [*Cahiers d'Etudes Anciennes*] **Notes d'Information** [*France*] — CEA Notes Inf
Cebecoskoop — MCL
CEC [*Consolidated Electrodynamics Corporation*] **Recordings** [*United States*] — CECRA
Ceceno-Ingusskii Gosudarstvennyi Pedagogiceskii Institut. Ucenye Zapiski — Ceceno-Ingus Gos Ped Inst Ucen Zap
Cechoslovakisches Archiv fuer Dermatologie und Syphilis — Cech Arch Dermatol Syph
Cecidologia Indica — CECIAI
Cecidologia Indica — Cecidol Indica
Cecidologia Internationale — Cecidol Int
Cecidologia Internationale — CEINEX
CED [*Committee for Economic Development*] **Newsletter** — CED Newsl
CEER (Chemical Economy and Engineering Review) — CEER (Chem Econ Eng Rev)
CEGB [*Central Electricity Generating Board*] **Abstracts** — CEGB Abs
CEGB (Central Electricity Generating Board) Research — CEGB Cent Electr Generating Board
CEGB [*Central Electricity Generating Board*] **Digest** [*England*] — CEGB Dig
CEGB [*Central Electricity Generating Board*] **Research** — CEGB Res
CEGB [*Central Electricity Generating Board*] **Research** [*England*] — CERED
CEGB [*Central Electricity Generating Board*] **Technical Disclosure Bulletin** [*England*] — CEGB Tech Disclosure Bull
CEGB [*Central Electricity Generating Board*] **Technical Disclosure Bulletin** [*England*] — CETDA
CEGS [*Council on Education in the Geological Sciences*] **Programs Publication** — CEGPAP
CEGS [*Council on Education in the Geological Sciences*] **Programs Publication** — CEGS Programs Publ
Cela Zimes — CZ
Celestial Mechanics — Celest Mech
Celestial Mechanics — Celestial Mech
Celestial Mechanics and Dynamical Astronomy — Celestial Mech Dynam Astronom
Celjabinskii Gosudarstvennyi Pedagogiceskii Institut. Trudy — Celjabinsk Gos Ped Inst Trudy
Cell Adhesion and Communication — Cell Adhes Commun
Cell and Chromosome Newsletter — CCHNDD
Cell and Chromosome Newsletter — Cell Chromosome Newsl
Cell and Chromosome Research — CCREE3
Cell and Chromosome Research — Cell Chromosome Res
Cell and Muscle Motility — Cell Muscle Motil
Cell and Muscle Motility — CMUMD9
Cell and Tissue Kinetics — Cell Tiss K
Cell and Tissue Kinetics — Cell Tissue Kinet
Cell and Tissue Kinetics — CTKIAR
Cell and Tissue Research — Cell Tis Re
Cell and Tissue Research — Cell Tissue Res
Cell and Tissue Research — CTSRC
Cell and Tissue Research — CTSRCS
Cell Biochemistry and Function — CBF
Cell Biochemistry and Function — CBFUDH
Cell Biochemistry and Function — Cell Biochem Funct
Cell Biology: a Series of Monographs — Cell Biol Ser Monogr
Cell Biology and Toxicology — Cell Biol T
Cell Biology and Toxicology — Cell Biol Toxicol
Cell Biology Communications — Cell Biol Commun
Cell Biology International — Cell Biol Int
Cell Biology International Reports — CBRPDS
Cell Biology International Reports — Cell Biol Int Rep
Cell Biology Monographs — CBMODY
Cell Biology Monographs — CEBIEH
Cell Biology Monographs — Cell Biol Monogr
Cell Biophysics — CBIOD
Cell Biophysics — Cell Biophys
Cell Culture and Its Application. International Cell Culture Congress — Cell Cult Its Appl Int Cell Cult Congr
Cell Culture Methods for Molecular and Cell Biology — Cell Cult Methods Mol Cell Biol
Cell Culture Methods for Molecular and Cell Biology — CMMBE5
Cell Differentiation — Cell Differ
Cell Differentiation — CLDFAT
Cell Differentiation and Development — Cell Differ Dev
Cell Growth and Differentiation — Cell Growth & Differ
Cell Interactions. Proceedings. Lepetit Colloquium — Cell Interact Proc Lepetit Colloq
Cell Membranes (New York). Methods and Reviews — Cell Membr (NY)
Cell Messengers at Fertilization. Proceedings. Symposium. British Society for Developmental Biology and the Society for the Study of Fertility — Cell Messengers Fert Proc Symp Br Soc Dev Biol Soc Study Fert
Cell Monograph Series — Cell Monogr Ser
Cell Motility — Cell Motil
Cell Motility — CMOTDY
Cell Motility and the Cytoskeleton — Cell Motil Cytoskeleton
Cell Motility and the Cytoskeleton — CMCYEO
Cell Proliferation — Cell Prolif
Cell Regulation — Cell Regul
Cell Structure and Function — Cell Struct Funct
Cell Structure and Function — CSFUDY
Cell Surface Reviews — Cell Surf Rev
Cell Surface Reviews [*Elsevier Book Series*] — CSR
Cell Surface Reviews — CSREDC
Cell Technology (Tokyo) — Cell Technol (Tokyo)
Cell Transplantation — Cell Transplant
Cells and Materials — Cells Mater
Cellular and Molecular Aspects of Endotoxin Reactions. Proceedings. Congress. International Endotoxin Society — Cell Mol Aspects Endotoxin React Proc Congr Int Endotoxin Soc
Cellular and Molecular Biology — Cell Mol Biol
Cellular and Molecular Biology — CMBID4
Cellular and Molecular Biology Letters — Cell Mol Biol Lett
Cellular and Molecular Biology Research — Cell Mol Biol Res
Cellular and Molecular Mechanisms of Inflammation — Cell Mol Mech Inflammation
Cellular and Molecular Neurobiology — Cell Mol Neurobiol
Cellular and Molecular Neurobiology — CMN
Cellular and Molecular Neurobiology — CMNEDI
Cellular and Molecular Physiology of Cell Volume Regulation [*monograph*] — Cell Mol Physiol Cell Vol Regul
Cellular Biology of the Uterus — Cell Biol Uterus
Cellular Business — CLB
Cellular Communication during Ocular Development. Papers. Symposium — Cell Commun Ocul Dev Pap Symp
Cellular Engineering — Cell Eng
Cellular Immunology — Cell Immun
Cellular Immunology — Cell Immunol
Cellular Immunology — CLIMB8
Cellular Interactions — Cell Interact
Cellular Physiology and Biochemistry — Cell Physiol Biochem
Cellular Polymers — Cell Polym
Cellular Sales and Marketing [*Database*] — CS & M
Cellular Senescence and Somatic Cell Genetics — Cell Senescence Somatic Cell Genet
Cellular Signalling — Cell Signal
Cellular Signalling — Cell Signalling
Cellule — CELLA4
Cellules Solaires — Cell Sol
Celluloid Industrie — Celluloid Ind
Celluloid und Plastische Massen — Celluloid Plast Massen
Cellulosa e Carta — Cellul Carta
Cellulosa e Carta — CLCAA9
Cellulose Chemistry and Technology — CECTA
Cellulose Chemistry and Technology — Cell Chem T
Cellulose Chemistry and Technology — Cellul Chem Technol
Cellulose Chemistry and Technology — Cellulose Chem Technol
Cellulose Communications — Cellul Commun
Cellulose Industry — Cellul Ind
Cellulose-Chemie — Cellul Chem
Celoslovenska Geologicka Konferencia. Materialy — Celosloven Geol Konf Mater
Celostatna Konferencia o Termickej Analyze — Celostatna Konf Term Anal
Celostatna Konferencia o Termickej Analyze. Zbornik — Celostatna Konf Term Anal Zb
Celostatne Dni Tepelneho Spracovania. Konferencia so Zahranicnou Ucastou — Celostatne Dni Tepelneho Spracovania Konf Zahr Ucastou
Celostatni Konference "Makrotest". Sbornik Prednasek — Celostatni Konf Makrotest Sb Prednasek
Celovek i Obscestvo — Celovek i Obsc
Celtiberia — Celt
Celtic Magazine — Celt Mag
Celtic Review — Celtic R
Celtica — Ce
Celtica. Caderno de Estudos Galaico-Portugueses — CCEGP

Celuloza, Papir, Grafika — Celul Pap Grafika
Celuloza si Hartie — Celul Hartie
Celuloza si Hirtie — Celul Hirtie
Celuloza si Hirtie — Celuloza Hirt
Celuloza si Hirtie — CsH
Cement Age — Cem Age
Cement and Cement Manufacture — Cem Cem Manuf
Cement and Concrete — CECOB
Cement and Concrete Association. Research Report — Cem Concrete Ass Res Rep
Cement and Concrete Association. Technical Report — Cem Concr Assoc Tech Rep
Cement and Concrete (Delhi) — Cem Concr (Delhi)
Cement and Concrete Research — Cem Concr Res
Cement and Concrete Research — Cement Concrete Res
Cement and Concrete (Tokyo) — Cem Concr (Tokyo)
Cement and Lime Manufacture — Cem Lime Manuf
Cement and Lime Manufacture — Cem Lime Mf
Cement Association of Japan. Review of General Meeting. Technical Session — Cem Assoc Jpn Rev Gen Meet Tech Sess
Cement Composites — Cem Compos
Cement, Concrete, and Aggregates — Cem Concr Aggregates
Cement (English Translation of Tsement) — Cement (Engl Transl)
Cement Era — Cem Era
Cement Industry (Tokyo) — Cem Ind (Tokyo)
Cement, Lime, and Gravel — Cem Lime Grav
Cement, Lime, and Gravel — Cem Lime Gravel
Cement Mill and Quarry — Cem Mill Quarry
Cement och Betong — Cem Betong
Cement- och Betonginstitutet. Forskning — Cem Betonginst Forsk
Cement Record — Cem Rec
Cement Research Institute of India. Abstracts — CRI Abstr
Cement Research Institute of India. Monograph MS — Cem Res Inst India Monogr MS
Cement Research Institute of India. Research Bulletin — Cem Res Inst India RB
Cement Technology — Cem Technol
Cement. Vapno, Azbestocement, Sadra — Cem Vapno Azbestocem Sadra
Cement Wapno Gips — Cem Wapno Gips
Cemento Armato — Cem Armato
Cemento-Hormigon — Cem Hormigon
Cements Research Progress — Cem Res Prog
Cement-Wapno-Beton — Cem Wapno Beton
CEN. Construction Equipment News — CEN Constr Equip News
Cenicafe — CENIA5
Cenicafe. Avances Tecnicos — Cenicafe Av Tec
Cenni Storici del Museo Civico di Storia Naturale di Trieste — Cenni Stor Mus Civ Stor Nat Trieste
Cenni Storici. Museo Civico di Storia Naturale di Trieste — Cenni Storici Mus Civico Storia Nat Trieste
Cenobio — C
Censo de Archivos [*Database*] — CARC
Censo de Bibliotecas [*Database*] — CBIB
Censo de Museos de Espana [*Database*] — CMUS
Census Access System [*Database*] — CENSAC
Centaurus — Cent
Centennial Magazine — Centennial Mag
Centennial Review — Centen Rev
Centennial Review — Centennial Rev
Centennial Review — CentR
Centennial Review — CeR
Centennial Review — CR
Centennial Review of Arts and Sciences [*Later, Centennial Review*] — CRAS
Center for Children's Books. Bulletin — CCB
Center for Children's Books. Bulletin — CCB-B
Center for Children's Books. Bulletin — Center Child Bk Bull
Center for Cuban Studies Newsletter — CCSN
Center for Editions of American Authors. Newsletter — CEAAN
Center for Great Lakes Studies. University of Wisconsin-Milwaukee. Special Report — Cent Great Lakes Stud Univ Wis Milwaukee Spec Rep
Center for High-Energy Forming. Proceedings. International Conference — Cent High Energy Form Proc Int Conf
Center for High-Energy Forming. Proceedings. International Conference — Cent High-Energy Form Pro
Center for Highway Research. Research Report. University of Texas at Austin — Cent High Res Res Rep Tex Austin
Center for Highway Research. Research Report. University of Texas at Austin — Cent Highw Res Res Rep Univ Tex Austin
Center for History of Chemistry News — Cent Hist Chem News
Center for North Atlantic Studies. Newsletter — CNS
Center for Northern Studies and Research. McGill University. News Notes — CNSRNN
Center for Northern Studies (Wolcott, Vermont). Contributions — CNSVC
Center for Oceans Law and Policy. University of Virginia. Oceans Policy Studies — COLPS
Center for Settlement Studies. University of Manitoba. Research Reports — Cent SS RR
Center for Settlement Studies. University of Manitoba. Series 2. Research Reports — CSSRR
Center for Settlement Studies. University of Manitoba. Series 5. Occasional Papers — CSSOP
Center Journal — Center J
Center Magazine — C Mag
Center Magazine — Cent Mag
Center Magazine — Center
Center Magazine — Center M
Center Magazine — Center Mag
Center Magazine — Cn
Center News — CENN
Centers for Disease Control. Publications — CDC
CENTO [*Central Treaty Organization*] **Conference on Land Classification for Non-Irrigated Lands** — CENTO Conf Ld Classif Non-Irrig Lds
CENTO [*Central Treaty Organization*] **Scientific Programme. Report** — CENTO Sci Programme Rep
Centraal Bureau voor de Statistiek. Bibliotheek en Documentatiedienst. Lijst van Aanwinsten — LCB
Centraal Economisch Plan — Centr Econ Plan
Centraal Instituut voor Materiaal Onderzoek. Afdeling Corrosie. Circulaire — Cent Inst Mater Onderz Afd Corros Circ
Centraal Instituut voor Materiaal Onderzoek. Afdeling Corrosie. Circulaire — Cent Inst Mater Onderz Afde Corros Circ
Centraal Instituut voor Materiaal Onderzoek. Afdeling Corrosie. Mededeling — Cent Inst Mater Onderz Afd Corr Mededе
Centraal Instituut voor Materiaal Onderzoek. Afdeling Corrosie. Mededeling — Cent Inst Mater Onderz Afd Corros Meded
Centraal Instituut voor Materiaal Onderzoek. Afdeling Hout. Circulaire — Cent Inst Mater Onderz Afd Hout Circ
Centraal Instituut voor Materiaal Onderzoek. Afdeling Verf. Circulaire — Cent Inst Mater Onderz Afd Verf Circ
Centraal Planbureau. Bibliotheek. Aanwinsten [*'S-Gravenhage*] — ABP
Centraal Rubberstation. Mededeeling — Cent Rubberstn Meded
Centraal Technisch Instituut TNO. Afdeling Warmtetechniek. Verslag — Cent Tech Inst TNO Afd Warmtetech Versl
Centraal Technisch Instituut TNO. Verslag — Cent Tech Inst TNO Versl
Central African Journal of Medicine — CAJMA3
Central African Journal of Medicine — Cent Afr J Med
Central African Journal of Medicine — Central African J Med
Central Arecanut Research Station. Technical Bulletin — Cent Arecanut Res St Tech Bull
Central Asian Review — CAR
Central Asian Review — CAsR
Central Asian Review — Centr Asian Rev
Central Asiatic Journal — CAJ
Central Asiatic Journal — CAsJ
Central Asiatic Journal — Cent Asia J
Central Asiatic Journal — Centr Asiat J
Central Asiatic Studies — CAS
Central Bank of Barbados. Quarterly Report — Central Bank Barbados Q Rept
Central Bank of Barbados. Quarterly Report — CEQ
Central Bank of Cyprus. Bulletin — CKP
Central Bank of Egypt. Annual Report — Bk Egypt A
Central Bank of Ireland. Annual Report — Centr Bank Ireland Annu Rep
Central Bank of Ireland. Quarterly Bulletin — Centr Bank Ireland Quart B
Central Bank of Ireland. Quarterly Bulletin — Central Bank Ireland Q Bul
Central Bank of Ireland. Quarterly Bulletin — CKI
Central Bank of Libya. Economic Bulletin — Central Bank Libya Econ Bul
Central Bank of Libya. Economic Bulletin — NBB
Central Bank of Malta. Quarterly Review — Central Bank Malta QR
Central Bank of Malta. Quarterly Review — CLD
Central Bank of Nigeria. Annual Report and Statement of Accounts — Bk Nigeria
Central Bank of Nigeria. Economic and Financial Review — Central Bank Nigeria Econ and Fin R
Central Bank of Nigeria. Economic and Financial Review (Lagos) — CNL
Central Bank of the Bahamas. Quarterly Review — CFA
Central Bank of Trinidad and Tobago. Quarterly Economic Bulletin — Central Bank Trinidad and Tobago Q Econ Bul
Central Bank of Trinidad and Tobago. Quarterly Economic Report — CSA
Central Electricity Generating Board. CEGB [*Central Electricity Generating Board. London*] **Research** — Cent Electr Gener Board CEGB Res
Central European Federalist — Cent Eur Fed
Central European Federalist — CEUFA
Central European History — CEH
Central European History — Cen Eur Hist
Central European History — CenE
Central European History — Cent Eur H
Central European History — Cent Eur Hist
Central European Journal for Operations Research and Economics — Central European J Oper Res Econom
Central European Journal of Public Health — Cent Eur J Public Health
Central Gaulish Potters — CGP
Central Glass and Ceramic Research Institute. Bulletin — Cent Glass Ceram Res Inst Bull
Central Inland Fisheries Research Institute (Barrackpore). Annual Report — Cent Inland Fish Res Inst (Barrackpore) Annu Rep
Central Inland Fisheries Research Institute (Barrackpore). Annual Report — CIFRBL
Central Inland Fisheries Research Institute (Barrackpore). Bulletin — Cent Inland Fish Res Inst (Barrackpore) Bull
Central Inland Fisheries Research Institute (Barrackpore). Bulletin — CIFBA6
Central Inland Fisheries Research Institute (Barrackpore, India). Survey Report — Cent Inland Fish Res Inst (Barrackpore India) Surv Rep
Central Inland Fisheries Research Institute (Barrackpore). Miscellaneous Contribution — Cent Inland Fish Res Inst (Barrackpore) Misc Contri
Central Inland Fisheries Research Institute (Barrackpore). Miscellaneous Contribution — Cent Inland Fish Res Inst (Barrackpore) Misc Contrib
Central Inland Fisheries Research Institute (Barrackpore). Miscellaneous Contribution — CFMCBO
Central Inland Fisheries Research Institute (Barrackpore). Survey Report — Cent Inland Fish Res Inst (Barrackpore) Surv Rep

Central Inland Fisheries Research Institute (Barrackpore). Survey Report — CIFSBO
Central Institute of Physics. Institute for Physics and Nuclear Engineering. Report (Romania) — Cent Inst Phys Inst Phys Nucl Eng Rep (Romania)
Central Institute of Physics. Report (Bucharest) — Cent Inst Phys Rep (Bucharest)
Central Institute of Physics Topics in Theoretical Physics — Cent Inst Phys Top Theor Phys
Central Japan Journal of Orthopaedic and Traumatic Surgery — Cent Jpn J Orthop Traumatic Surg
Central Laboratory for Radiological Protection. Warsaw. Report — Cent Lab Radiol Prot Warsaw Rep
Central Laboratory for Radiological Protection. Warsaw. Technical Report Cent Lab Radiol Prot Warsaw Tech Rep
Central Law Journal — Central Law J
Central Luzon State University Science Journal — CLSU Sci Jnl
Central Luzon State University. Scientific Journal — Cent Luzon State Univ Sci J
Central Marine Fisheries Research Institute. Bulletin — Cent Mar Fish Res Inst Bull
Central Marine Fisheries Research Institute. CMFRI Bulletin — Cent Mar Fish Res Inst CMFRI Bull
Central Medical Journal. Seminar Reports (Moscow) — Cent Med J Semin Rep (Moscow)
Central Nervous System and Behavior. Transactions. Conference on the Central Nervous System and Behavior — Cent Nerv Syst Behav Trans Conf
Central Nervous System Pharmacology Series — Cent Nerv Syst Pharmacol Ser
Central Nervous System. Pharmacology Series — CNSSEP
Central Nervous System Trauma — Cent Nerv Syst Trauma
Central New York Business Review — C NY Bs Rv
Central Ohio Scientific Association of Urbana, Ohio. Proceedings — Central Ohio Sc As Pr
Central Opera Service. Bulletin — CE
Central Opera Service. Bulletin — Central Opera
Central Opera Services Bulletin — COSB
Central Pharmaceutical Journal — Cent Phar J
Central Plantation Crops Research Institute [*Kasaragod*]. Annual Report — CPIAAX
Central Plantation Crops Research Institute (Kasaragod). Annual Report — Cent Plant Crops Res Inst (Kasaragod) Annu Rep
Central Queensland Herald — Central Q Herald
Central Research Institute for Agriculture. Contributions (Bogor, Indonesia) — Cent Res Inst Agric Contrib (Bogor Indones)
Central Research Institute for Physics. Report KFKI — Cent Res Inst Phys Rep KFKI
Central Research Institute of Electric Power Industry. Report (Tokyo) — Cent Res Inst Electr Power Ind Rep Tokyo
Central Research Institute of Electric Power Industry. Technical Report (Tokyo) — Cent Res Inst Electr Power Ind Tech Rep (Tokyo)
Central Soil Salinity Research Institute. Bulletin — Cent Soil Salinity Res Inst Bull
Central States Speech Journal — Cent St Spe
Central States Speech Journal — CSSJ
Central Treaty Organization Scientific Programme. Report — Cent Treaty Organ Sci Programme Rep
Central Unit on Environmental Pollution. Pollution Paper (Great Britain) — Cent Unit Environ Pollut Pollut Pap G B
Centralblatt der Bauverwaltung — CdBv
Centralblatt fuer Agrikulturchemie und Rationellen Wirtschaftsbetrieb — Centralbl Agrikulturchem Ration Wirtschaftsbetr
Centralblatt fuer Allgemeine Pathologie und Pathologische Anatomie — CAPPA
Centralblatt fuer Allgemeine Pathologie und Pathologische Anatomie — Centralbl Allg Path u Path Anat
Centralblatt fuer Bakteriologie, Parasitenkunde, und Infektionskrankheiten. Erste Abteilung. Medizinisch-Hygienische Bakteriologie Virusforschung, und Tierische Parasitologie. Originale — Centralbl Bakteriol 1 Abt Originale
Centralblatt fuer Bakteriologie, Parasitenkunde, und Infektionskrankheiten. Erste Abteilung. Medizinisch-Hygienische Bakteriologie, Virusforschung, und Tierische Parasitologie. Referate — Centralbl Bakteriol 1 Abt Ref
Centralblatt fuer Bakteriologie und Parasitenkunde — Centralbl Bakteriol
Centralblatt fuer Bakteriologie und Parasitenkunde. Zweite Abteilung — Centralbl Bakteriol Parasitenk 2 Abt
Centralblatt fuer Bibliothekwesen — CBW
Centralblatt fuer Bibliothekwesen — Zbl Bibliothw
Centralblatt fuer Chirurgie — Centralbl Chir
Centralblatt fuer Chirurgie — CfCh
Centralblatt fuer das Gesamte Forstwesen — Cbl Ges Forstw
Centralblatt fuer das Gesamte Forstwesen [*Austria*] — CEGFA
Centralblatt fuer das Gesamte Forstwesen — Centbl Ges Forstw
Centralblatt fuer das Gesamte Forstwesen — Centralbl Gesamte Forstwes
Centralblatt fuer das Gesamte Forstwesen — Zbl Ges Forstw
Centralblatt fuer die Gesammte Landescultur des In- und Auslandes — Centralbl Gesammte Landescult In Ausl
Centralblatt fuer die Krankheiten der Harn- und Sexualorgane — CHKSex
Centralblatt fuer die Krankheiten der Harn- und Sexualorgane — Zbl Krkht Harnorg
Centralblatt fuer die Maehrischen Landwirthe — Centralbl Maehr Landwirthe
Centralblatt fuer Innere Medicin — Centralbl Innere Med
Centralblatt fuer Mineralogie, Geologie, und Palaeontologie — Centralbl Miner
Centralblatt fuer Mineralogie, Geologie, und Palaeontologie — CMGPA
Centralblatt fuer Pathologie — Cf Pa
Centralblatt fuer Physiologie — Zbl Physiol
Centralblatt fuer Praktische Augenheilkunde — CprAh
Centralblatt fuer Rechtswissenschaft — CBl Rw
Central-European Journal of Immunology — Cent Eur J Immunol
Centralized Title Service — CTS
Centralne Laboratorium Ochrony Radiologicznej. Raport — Cent Lab Ochr Radiol Rap
Centralne Laboratorium Ochrony Radiologicznej. Raport — Cent Lab Ochron Radiol Rap
Centralne Laboratorium Ochrony Radiologicznej. Raport Techniczny — Cent Lab Ochr Radiol Rap Tech
Centralne Laboratorium Przemyslu Tytoniowego. Biuletyn Informacyjny — Cent Lab Przem Tytoniowego Biul Inf
Centre Belge d'Etude de la Corrosion. Rapport Technique — Cent Belge Etude Corros Rapp Tech
Centre Belge d'Etude et de Documentation des Eaux. Bulletin Mensuel — CEBEA
Centre Belge d'Etude et de Documentation des Eaux. Bulletin Mensuel [*Belgium*] — Cent Belge Etude Doc Eaux Bull Mens
Centre Belge d'Etude et de Documentation des Eaux. Journal Mensuel — Cent Belge Etude Doc Eaux J Mens
Centre (Canada) — CRC
Centre d'Actualisation Scientifique et Technique de l'INSA [*Institut National des Sciences Appliques. France*] **Monographies** — Cent Actual Sci Tech INSA Monogr
Centre de Documentation de Musique Internationale. Bulletin — CDMI Bul
Centre de Documentation Siderurgique. Circulaire d'Informations Techniques — Cent Doc Sider Cir Inf Tech
Centre de Documentation Siderurgique. Circulaire d'Informations Techniques — Cent Doc Sider Circ Inf Tech
Centre de Documentation Universitaire — CDU
Centre de Formation Technique et de Perfectionnement. Union des Fabricants de Biscuits, Biscottes, Aliments Dietetiques, et Divers. Bulletin — Cent Form Tech Perfect Bull
Centre de Geomorphologie de Caen. Bulletin — Cent Geomorphol Caen Bull
Centre de Mathematique Sociale. Ecole Pratique des Hautes Etudes. Mathematiques et Sciences Humaines — Math Sci Humaines
Centre de Recherches Agronomiques de l'Etat. Gembloux. Note Technique — Cent Rech Agron Etat Gembloux Note Tech
Centre de Recherches Archeologiques Cahier — Cent Rech Archeol Cah
Centre de Recherches de Pau. Bulletin — Centre Recherches Pau Bull
Centre de Recherches du Fer-Blanc. Bulletin (Thionville, France) — Cent Rech Fer Blanc Bull (Thionville Fr)
Centre de Recherches Ecologiques et Phytosociologiques de Gembloux. Communication — Cent Rech Ecol Phytosociol Gembloux Commun
Centre de Recherches Ecologiques et Phytosociologiques de Gembloux. Communication — CEPCAV
Centre de Recherches Forestieres des Laurentides. Rapport d'Information LAU-X (Edition Francaise) — Cent Rech For Laurentides Rapp Inf LAU X Ed Fr
Centre de Recherches. Institut d'Etudes Hispaniques — CRIEH
Centre de Recherches Metallurgiques. Metallurgical Reports — Cent Rech Metall Metall Rep
Centre de Recherches Oceanographiques (Abidjan). Document Scientifique Provisoire — Cent Rech Oceanogr (Abidjan) Doc Sci Provisoire
Centre de Recherches Oceanographiques (Abidjan). Documents Scientifiques — Cent Rech Oceanogr (Abidjan) Doc Sci
Centre de Recherches Oceanographiques [*Abidjan*]. Document Scientifique Provisoire — CODSBM
Centre de Recherches Oceanographiques [*Abidjan*]. Documents Scientifiques — CRODAI
Centre de Recherches Routieres. Comptes Rendus CR (Brussels) — Cent Rech Routieres CR CR (Brussels)
Centre de Recherches Scientifiques et Techniques de l'Industrie des Fabrications Metalliques. Section. Fonderie. Report FD — Cent Rech Sci Tech Ind Fab Met Sect Fonderie Rep FD
Centre de Recherches Scientifiques et Techniques de l'Industrie des Fabrications Metalliques. Section Plastiques. Report PL — Cent Rech Sci Tech Ind Fabr Met Sect Plast Rep PL
Centre de Recherches Industrielles en Afrique Centrale. Sciences. Techniques. Informations CRIAC — Cent Rech Ind Afr Cent Sci Tech Inf CRIAC
Centre d'Etude de l'Azote — Cent Etude Azote
Centre d'Etude de l'Energie Nucleaire. Rapport. BLG — Cent Etude Energ Nucl BLG
Centre d'Etude, de Recherches, et d'Essais Scientifiques du Genie Civil. Universite de Liege. Memoires — Cent Etude Rech Essais Sci Genie Univ Liege Mem
Centre d'Etudes de l'Emploi. Cahiers — Centre Etud Emploi Cah
Centre d'Etudes, de Recherches, et d'Essais Scientifiques du Genie Civil. Universite de Liege. Memoires — Cent Etud Rech Essais Sci Genie Civ Univ Liege Mem
Centre d'Etudes et de Documentation Sociales. Bulletin Mensuel — Centre Etud et Docum Socs Bul
Centre d'Etudes et de Documentation Sociales (Liege) — Centre Et Docum Soc (Liege)
Centre d'Etudes et de Recherches Scientifiques (Biarritz). Bulletin — Cent Etud Rech Sci (Biarritz) Bull
Centre d'Etudes Nordiques. Collection Nordicana. University of Laval — CENCN
Centre d'Etudes Nucleaires de Saclay. Serie Bibliographies — Cent Etud Nucl Saclay Ser Bibliogr
Centre d'Etudes Superieures de la Siderurgie Francaise. Rapport — Cent Etud Super Sider Fr Rapp
Centre d'Information du Chrome Dur. Bulletin de Documentation — Cent Inf Chrome Dur Bull Doc
Centre d'Information du Chrome Dur. Bulletin de Documentation — Centre Inform Chrome Dur Bull Doc

Centre d'Information du Nickel pour Toutes Applications Techniques et Industrielles. Serie A. Alliages — Cent Inf Nickel Toutes Appl Tech Ind Ser A
Centre d'Information du Nickel pour Toutes Applications Techniques et Industrielles. Serie C. Fontes au Nickel — Cent Inf Nickel Toutes Appl Tech Ind Ser C
Centre d'Information du Nickel pour Toutes Applications Techniques et Industrielles. Serie D. Nickelage — Cent Inf Nickel Toutes Appl Tech Ind Ser D
Centre d'Information du Nickel pour Toutes Applications Techniques et Industrielles. Serie X. Applications du Nickel — Cent Inf Nickel Toutes Appl Tech Ind Ser X
Centre d'Information et d'Etudes du Credit. Bulletin — Centre Info et Etud Credit Bul
Centre for Agricultural Publications and Documentation [*Wageningen*]. Annual Report — PCAABC
Centre for Agricultural Publications and Documentation (Wageningen). Annual Report — Cent Agric Publ Doc (Wageningen) Annu Rep
Centre for Environmental Studies. Conference Papers — CES Conf Paps
Centre for Environmental Studies. Information Papers — CES Inf Paps
Centre for Environmental Studies. Occasional Papers — CES Occ Paps
Centre for Environmental Studies. Policy Series — CES Policy Series
Centre for Environmental Studies. Research Papers — CES Res Paps
Centre for Environmental Studies. Research Series — CES Res Series
Centre for Environmental Studies. Review — CES Rev
Centre for Environmental Studies. University Working Papers — CES Univ Wkng Paps
Centre for Environmental Studies. Working Papers — CES Wkng Paps
Centre for International Relations. Queen's University. Northern Studies Series — CIRQNS
Centre for International Relations. Queen's University. Northern Studies Series — CIRQNSS
Centre for Overseas Pest Research. Miscellaneous Report — Cent Overseas Pest Res Misc Rep
Centre for Overseas Pest Research. Miscellaneous Report — CPRMBD
Centre for Overseas Pest Research. Report — Cent Overseas Pest Res Rep
Centre for Overseas Pest Research. Report — COVPAY
Centre for Pure and Applied Differential Geometry (PADGE) — Centre Pure Appl Differential Geom PADGE
Centre International des Engrais Chimiques. Assemblee Generale. Rapports — Cent Int Engrais Chim Assem Gen Rapp
Centre International des Engrais Chimiques. Symposium — Cent Int Engrais Chim Symp
Centre Meridional de Recherche sur le Dix-Septieme Siecle — CMR 17
Centre National de Coordination des Etudes et Recherches sur la Nutrition et l'Alimentation. Cahiers Techniques [*France*] — Cent Natl Coord Etud Rech Nutr Aliment Cah Tech
Centre National de Documentation Scientifique et Technique. Rapport d'Activite — Cent Natl Doc Sci Tech Rap Act
Centre National de la Recherche Scientifique [*Translation of Courrier du CNRS*] — Cent Nat Rech Sci
Centre National de la Recherche Scientifique. Groupe Francais des Argiles. Bulletin — CNRS Groupe Fr Argiles Bull
Centre National de la Recherche Scientifique. Groupe Francais des Argiles. Compte Rendu des Reunions d'Etudes — Cent Nat Rech Sci Groupe Fr Argiles R Reun Etude
Centre National de la Recherche Scientifique. Groupe Francais des Argiles. Compte Rendu des Reunions d'Etudes — CNRS Groupe Fr Argiles CR Reun Etud
Centre National de Recherches Metallurgiques. Memoires [*Belgium*] — Cent Natl Rech Metall Mem
Centre National de Recherches Metallurgiques. Metallurgical Reports [*Belgium*] — Cent Natl Rech Metall Metall Rep
Centre National de Recherches Scientifiques et Techniques pour l'Industrie Cimentiere. Rapport de Recherche — Cent Natl Rech Sci Tech Ind Cimentiere Rapp Rech
Centre National de Recherches Scientifiques et Techniques pour l'Industrie Cimentiere. Rapport de Recherche — Centre Nat Rech Sci Tech Ind Cimentiere Rapp Rech
Centre National pour l'Exploitation des Oceans. Publications. Serie Actes de Colloques (France) — Cent Natl Exploit Oceans Publ Ser Actes Colloq (Fr)
Centre National pour l'Exploitation des Oceans. Publications. Serie Rapports Scientifiques et Techniques (France) — Cent Nat Exploit Oceans Publ Ser Rapp Sci Tech (Fr)
Centre National pour l'Exploitation des Oceans. Publications. Serie Rapports Scientifiques et Techniques (France) — Cent Natl Exploit Oceans Publ Ser Rapp Sci Tech (Fr)
Centre National pour l'Exploitation des Oceans. Rapport Annuel — Cent Natl Exploit Oceans Rapp Annu
Centre National pour l'Exploitation des Oceans. Rapport Annuel — CEOABL
Centre Nucleaire TRICO [*Training, Research, Isotope Production Reactor. Congo*]. Rapport de Recherche — Cent Nucl TRICO Rapp Rech
Centre of Advanced Study in Geology. Publication (Chandigarh, India) — Cent Adv Study Geol Publ (Chandigarh India)
Centre Regional d'Etudes Nucleaires de Kinshasa. Rapport de Recherche — Cent Reg Etud Nucl Kinshasa Rapp Rech
Centre Scientifique et Technique de la Construction. Note d'Information Technique — Centre Sci & Tech Constr Note Inf Tech
Centre Technique de l'Union. Bulletin — Cent Tech Union Bull
Centre Technique des Industries Mecaniques. Memoires Techniques — Cent Tech Ind Mec Mem Tech
Centre Technique Forestier Tropical (Nogent Sur Marne, France). Note Technique — Cent Tech For Trop (Nogent Sur Marne Fr) Note Tech
Centre Technique Forestier Tropical (Nogent Sur Marne, France). Publication — Cent Tech For Trop (Nogent Sur Marne Fr) Publ
Centre Technique Interprofessionnel des Oleagineux Metropolitains. Bulletin CETIOM — Cent Tech Interprof Ol Metrop Bull CETIOM
Centre Textile de Controle et de Recherche Scientifique. Bulletin — Cent Text Controle Rech Sci Bull
Centres de Recherches Exploration-Production Elf-Aquitaine. Bulletin — Cent Rech Explor Prod Elf Aquitaine Bull
Centro Agricola — CEAGD5
Centro Agricola — Cent Agric
Centro Azucar — CEAZD
Centro Azucar [*Cuba*] — Cent Azucar
Centro (Buenos Aires) — Cent BA
Centro Cientifico Tropical. Estudio Ocasional — Cent Cient Trop Estud Ocas
Centro Cientifico Tropical. Estudio Ocasional (San Jose, Costa Rica) — Cent Cient Trop Estud Ocas (San Jose, Costa Rica)
Centro de Ciencias Biomedicas. Revista. Universidade Federal de Santa Maria — Cent Cienc Biomed Rev Univ Fed St Maria
Centro de Ciencias da Educacao. Boletim — Cent Cienc Educ Bol
Centro de Ciencias Rurais. Revista. Universidade Federal de Santa Maria — Cent Cienc Rurais Rev Univ Fed St Maria
Centro de Ciencias Saude. Revista. Universidade Federal de Santa Maria — Cent Cienc Saude Rev Univ Fed St Maria
Centro de Cultura Scientifica. Revista (Pelotas, Brazil) — Cent Cult Sci Rev (Pelotas, Brazil)
Centro de Cultura Valenciana — CCV
Centro de Edafologia y Biologia Aplicada de Salamanca. Anuario — Cent Edafol Biol Apl Salamanca Anu
Centro de Energia Nuclear na Agricultura. Boletim Cientifico BC — Cent Energ Nucl Agric Bol Cient BC
Centro de Energia Nuclear na Agricultura. Boletim Tecnico BT — Cent Energ Nucl Agric Bol Tec BT
Centro de Estudios de Recursos Odontologicos para el Nino — Cent Estud Recur Odontol Nino
Centro de Estudios Mayas-Cuadernos — CEMC
Centro de Estudos Demograficos. Revista — Centro Estud Demograficos R
Centro de Estudos Rurais e Urbanos. Cadernos — Centro Estud Rurais e Urbanos Cad
Centro de Estudos Zoologicos. Universidade do Brasil. Avulso — ACZBA8
Centro de Estudos Zoologicos. Universidade do Brasil. Avulso — Cent Estud Zool Univ Brasil Avulso
Centro de Investigacion de Biologia Marina. Contribucion Tecnica — Cent Invest Biol Mar Contrib Tec
Centro de Investigacion de Biologia Marina. Contribucion Tecnica — CIBMAJ
Centro de Investigacion y Accion Social. Revista — Centro Investigacion y Accion Soc R
Centro de Investigacion y Desarrollo en Tecnologia de Pinturas. Anales — Cent Invest Desarrollo Tecnol Pint An
Centro de Investigaciones Agricolas Alberto Boerger. Boletin Tecnico — Cent Invest Agric Alberto Boerger Bol Tec
Centro de Investigaciones Agricolas del Noreste. Informe de Investigacion Agricola — CAIIAK
Centro de Investigaciones Agricolas del Noreste. Informe de Investigacion Agricola — Cent Invest Agric Noreste Inf Invest Agric
Centro de Investigaciones Agronomicas Maracay. Monografia — Cent Invest Agron Maracay Monogr
Centro de Investigaciones Agronomicas Maracay. Monografia — CIAMAE
Centro de Investigaciones Agropecuarias de la Region Centro Occidental. Boletin Tecnico — Cent Invest Agropecu Reg Cent Occident Bol Tec
Centro de Investigaciones Oceanograficas e Hidrograficas. Boletin Cientifico (Cartagena, Colombia) — Cent Invest Oceanogr Hidrogr Bol Cient (Cartagena, Colomb)
Centro de Investigaciones Tecnologicas. Informe de Investigacion (Pando, Uruguay) — Cent Invest Tecnol Inf Invest (Pando Urug)
Centro de Investigaciones Tecnologicas. Publicacion (Pando, Uruguay) — Cent Invest Tecnol Publ (Pando, Urug)
Centro de Pesquisa Agropecuaria do Tropico Umido. Boletim Technico — Cent Pesqis Agropecu Trop Umido Bol Tec
Centro de Pesquisa Agropecuaria do Tropico Umido EMBRAPA [*Empresa Brasileira de Pesquisa Agropecuaria*] — Cent Pesqui Agropecu Trop Umido
Centro de Pesquisas do Cacau. Boletim Tecnico (Itabuna, Brazil) — Cent Pesqui Cacau Bol Tec Itabuna Braz
Centro de Pesquisas e Desenvolvimento. Boletim Tecnico (Estado da Bahia) — Cent Pesqui Desenvolvimento Bol Tec (Estado Bahia)
Centro de Quimicos Industriales. Buenos Aires. Publicacion — Cent Quim Ind Buenos Aires Publ
Centro de Quimicos Industriales. Buenos Aires. Revista — Cent Quim Ind Buenos Aires Rev
Centro di Reumatologia. Bollettino. Ospedali Riuniti di Roma — Cent Reumatol Boll Osp Riuniti Roma
Centro di Studi per la Lotta Antitermitica. Pubblicazione — Cent Studi Lotta Antitermitica Pubbl
Centro di Studi per l'Ingegneria Agraria. Memorie ed Atti — CEIAA
Centro di Studi per l'Ingegneria Agraria. Memorie ed Atti [*Italy*] — Cent Stud Ing Agrar Mem Atti
Centro di Studio per la Citogenetica Vegetale. Consiglio Nazionale delle Richerche. Pubblicazioni — Cent Stud Citogenet Veg Pubbl
Centro Editor de America Latina — CEAL
Centro Intercultural de Documentacion. Sondeos — CIDS
Centro Interdisciplinario de Ciencias Marinas. Investigaciones Marinas — Cent Interdiscip Cienc Mar Invest Mar
Centro Internacional de Agricultura Tropical [*CIAT*]. Annual Report — Cent Int Agric Trop Annu Rep
Centro Internacional de Agricultura Tropical [*CIAT*]. Annual Report — CIATB2
Centro Internacional de Agricultura Tropical (CIAT). Series CE — Cent Int Agric Trop (CIAT) Ser CE

Centro Internacional de Agricultura Tropical (CIAT). Series EE — Cent Int Agric Trop (CIAT) Ser EE
Centro Internacional de Agricultura Tropical (CIAT). Series FE — Cent Int Agric Trop (CIAT) Ser FE
Centro Internacional de Agricultura Tropical (CIAT). Series GE — Cent Int Agric Trop (CIAT) Ser GE
Centro Internacional de Agricultura Tropical (CIAT). Series JE — Cent Int Agric Trop (CIAT) Ser JE
Centro Internacional de Agricultura Tropical [*CIAT*]. Series CE — Cent Int Agric Trop Ser CE
Centro Internacional de Agricultura Tropical [*CIAT*]. Series CE — CIACDL
Centro Internacional de Agricultura Tropical [*CIAT*]. Series EE — Cent Int Agric Trop Ser EE
Centro Internacional de Agricultura Tropical [*CIAT*]. Series EE — SECTDQ
Centro Internacional de Agricultura Tropical [*CIAT*]. Series FE — Cent Int Agric Trop Ser FE
Centro Internacional de Agricultura Tropical [*CIAT*]. Series FE — SFCTDX
Centro Internacional de Agricultura Tropical [*CIAT*]. Series GE — CATGD4
Centro Internacional de Agricultura Tropical [*CIAT*]. Series GE — Cent Int Agric Trop Ser GE
Centro Internacional de Agricultura Tropical [*CIAT*]. Series JE — CIJED4
Centro Internacional de Agricultura Tropical [*CIAT*]. Series Seminars — Cent Int Agric Trop Ser Semin
Centro Internacional de Agricultura Tropical [*CIAT*]. Series Seminars — SCIADJ
Centro Internacional de Agricultura Tropical [*CIAT*]. Technical Bulletin — Cent Int Agric Trop Tech Bull
Centro Internacional de Agricultura Tropical [*CIAT*]. Technical Bulletin — CIATC3
Centro Internacional de Mejoramiento de Maiz y Trigo. News — CIMMYT News
Centro Italiano Smalti Porcellanati. Notiziario — Cent Ital Smalti Porcellanati Not
Centro Italiano Smalti Porcellanati. Notiziario Informativo — Cent Ital Smalti Porcellanati Not Inf
Centro Linceo Interdisciplinare di Scienze Matematiche e Loro Applicazioni. Contributi — Cent Linceo Interdiscip Sci Mat Loro Appl Contrib
Centro Nacional de Agricultura (Costa Rica). Boletin Tecnica — Cent Nac Agric (Costa Rica) Bol Tec
Centro Nacional de Alimentacion y Nutricion (Spain). Boletin — Cent Nac Aliment Nutr (Spain) Bol
Centro Nacional de Investigaciones Cientificas. Revista CENIC. Ciencias Biologicas — Cent Nac Invest Cient Rev CENIC Cienc Biol
Centro Nacional de Investigaciones Cientificas. Revista CENIC. Ciencias Fisicas [*Cuba*] — Cent Nac Invest Cient Rev CENIC Cienc Fis
Centro Nacional de Investigaciones Cientificas. Revista CENIC. Ciencias Quimicas [*Cuba*] — Cent Nac Invest Cient Rev CENIC Cienc Quim
Centro Nacional de Investigaciones de Cafe. Avances Tecnicos [*Colombia*] — Cent Nac Invest Cafe Av Tec
Centro Nacional de Investigaciones de Cafe. Boletin Tecnico [*Chinchina*] — BTCCDT
Centro Nacional de Investigaciones de Cafe. Boletin Tecnico (Chinchina) — Cent Nac Invest Cafe Bol Tec (Chinchina)
Centro pro Unione. Bulletin — Centro pro Un Bul
Centro (San Luis Potosi, Mexico) — Cent S L Potosi
CENTRO. Serie. Azucar. Revista Cientifica. Universidad Central de Las Villas [*Cuba*] — CENTRO Ser Azucar
CENTRO. Serie. Quimica y Tecnologia Quimica. Revista Cientifica. Universidad Central de las Villas [*Cuba*] — CENTRO. Ser Quim Tecnol Quim
Centro Studi e Documentazione sull'Italia Romana — CSDIR
Centros de Investigacion de Baja California and Scripps Institution of Oceanography. Transactions — Cent Invest Baja Calif Scripps Inst Oceanogr Trans
Centrul de Cercetare pentru Materiale de Protectie. Buletin Tehnico-Informativ — Cent Cercet Mater Prot Bul Teh Inf
Centrum voor Landbouwdocumentatie. Literatuuroverzicht — Cent Landbouwdoc Literatuuroverz
Centrum voor Landbouwpublikaties en Landbouwdocumentatie Literatuuroverzicht — Cent Landbouwpubl Landbouwdoc Literatuuroverz
Centrum voor Wiskunde en Informatica. Newsletter — CWI Newslett
Century — C
Century Dictionary — Cent D
Century Magazine — Cent
Century Magazine — Cent Mag
Century Magazine — CM
Ceol. Journal of Irish Music — Ceol
CEP [*Council on Economic Priorities*] **Newsletter** — CEP Newsl
CEP [*Council on Economic Priorities*] **Newsletter** — CEPND
CEPAL (Comision Economica para America Latina) Review — CEPAL
CEPAL [*Comision Economica para America Latina*] **Review** — CEPAL Rev
CEPEC [*Centro de Pesquisas do Cacau*] **Informe Tecnico** — CEPEC Inf Tec
CEPEC [*Centro de Pesquisas do Cacau*] **Informe Tecnico** — CPCIAR
Cephalalgia — CEPHDF
CEPLAC [*Comissao Executiva do Plano da Lavoura Cacaueira*] **Boletim Tecnico** — CEPLAC Bol Tec
CEPLAC [*Comissao Executiva do Plano da Lavoura Cacaueira*] **Boletim Tecnico** — CEPLAO
CEPLAC [*Comissao Executiva do Plano da Lavoura Cacaueira*] **Comunicacao Tecnica** [*A publication*] — CECTBI
CEPLAC [*Comissao Executiva do Plano da Lavoura Cacaueira*] **Comunicacao Tecnica** — CEPLAC Comun Tec
Ceramic Abstracts — Ceram Abstr
Ceramic Abstracts — Ceramic Abstr
Ceramic Age — Ceram Age
Ceramic- and Carbon-Matrix Composites — Ceram Carbon Matrix Compos
Ceramic Awareness Bulletin [*Defense Ceramic Information Center*] — Ceram Awareness Bull
Ceramic Bulletin — Ceram Bull
Ceramic Chemists' Conference on Silicate Analysis — Ceram Chem Conf Sil Anal
Ceramic Engineering and Science Proceedings — Ceram Eng Sci Proc
Ceramic Films and Coatings — Ceram Films Coat
Ceramic Forum International [*Germany*] — Ceram Forum Int
Ceramic Industries Journal — CRIJA
Ceramic Industry — Cer Ind
Ceramic Industry — Ceram Ind
Ceramic Industry — CRI
Ceramic Industry (Chicago) — Ceram Ind Chicago
Ceramic Monographs — Ceram Monogr
Ceramic Powder Processing Science. Proceedings. International Conference — Ceram Powder Process Sci Proc Int Conf
Ceramic Powder Science — Ceram Powder Sci
Ceramic Processing Science and Technology — Ceram Process Sci Technol
Ceramic Research Institute. Tokoname. Aichi Prefecture. News — Ceram Res Inst Tokoname Aichi Prefect News
Ceramic Review — Ceramic R
Ceramic Superconductors. Research Update — Ceram Supercond Res Update
Ceramic Transactions — Ceram Trns
Ceramica y Cristal — Ceram Crist
Ceramica y Vidrio — Ceram Vidrio
Ceramichte e Laterizi — Ceram Laterizi
Ceramics and Glass. Science and Technology — Ceram Glass Sci Technol
Ceramics in Severe Environments. Proceedings. University Conference on Ceramic Science — Ceram Severe Environ Proc Univ Conf Ceram Sci
Ceramics Industries Journal — Ceram Ind J
Ceramics International — Ceram Int
Ceramics International [*United Kingdom*] — Ceramics Int
Ceramics International — CINND
Ceramics International News [*Italy*] — Ceram Int News
Ceramics Japan — Ceram Jap
Ceramics Japan — Ceram Jpn
Ceramics Monthly — Ceram Mo
Ceramics Monthly — Ceramics Mo
Ceramics Monthly — ICMO
Ceramika Budowlana — CEBUD
Ceramika Budowlana — Ceram Budow
Ceramika Prace Komisji Ceramicnyj Polska Akademie Nauk Oddzial w Krakowie — Ceram Pr Kom Ceram Pol Akad Nauk Oddzial Krak
Ceramique et Verrerie — Ceram Verrerie
Ceramique, Verrerie, Emaillerie — Ceram Verrerie Emaill
Ceramiques Industrielles (Sevres, France) — Ceram Ind (Sevres Fr)
Ceramurgia International — CEIND
Ceramurgia International — Ceramurg Int
Ceramurgia International — Ceramurgia Int
Ceramurgia, Tecnologia Ceramica — Ceramurgia Tec Ceram
Ceramurgia, Tecnologia Ceramica — CRGIA
Cerberus Elektronik — Cerberus Elektron
Cerberus Report — Cerberus R
CERBOM [*Centre d'Etudes et de Recherches de Biologie et d'Oceanographie Medicale*] **Rapport d'Activite** [*France*] — CERBOM Rapp Act
Cercetari Agronomice in Moldova — Cercet Agron Moldova
Cercetari Arheologice — CA
Cercetari Arheologice in Bucuresti — CAB
Cercetari Arheologice in Bucuresti — Cercet Arh Buc
Cercetari de Linguistica — C Ling
Cercetari de Linguistica — CLin
Cercetari de Muzicologie — C Mz
Cercetari de Muzicologie — Cercetari Muzicol
Cercetari in Domeniul Constructiilor Hidrotehnice — Cercet Domeniul Constr Hidroteh
Cercetari Istorice [*Bucharest*] — C Ist
Cercetari Istorice [*Iasi*] — Cerc Ist
Cercetari Istorice — Cercet Ist
Cercetari Istorice (Bucharest) — Cerc Ist (Buch)
Cercetari Istorice (Iasi) — Cercet Ist (Iasi)
Cercetari Metalurgice — Cercet Met
Cercetari Metalurgice — Cercet Metal
Cercetari Metalurgice — CERMB
Cercetari Metalurgice. Institutul de Cercetari Metalurgice (Bucharest) — Cercet Metal Inst Cercet Metal (Bucharest)
Cercetari Miniere. Institutul de Cercetari Miniere — Cercet Miniere Inst Cercet Miniere
Cercetari Numismatice — Cercet Num
Cercetari Numismatice. Muzeul de Istorie — Cerc Num
Cercle Archeologique de Malines. Bulletin — CAMBull
Cercle Archeologique de Mons. Annales — CAMAn
Cercle Archeologique d'Enghien. Annales — CAE
Cercle Archeologique d'Enghien. Annales — CAEAn
Cercle Archeologique du Pays de Waes. Annales — CAPWAn
Cercle d'Etudes Numismatiques. Bulletin — CENB
Cercle Historique et Archeologique de Courtrai. Bulletin — CHAC
Cercle Historique et Archeologique de Courtrai. Bulletin — CHACBull
Cereal Chemistry — CECHAF
Cereal Chemistry — Cereal Chem
Cereal Chemists Bulletin — Cereal Chem Bull
Cereal Crop Series. Indian Council of Agricultural Research — Cereal Crop Ser Indian Counc Agr Res
Cereal Foods World — Cereal F W
Cereal Foods World — Cereal Foods World
Cereal Foods World — CFW
Cereal Foods World — CFWODA
Cereal Research Communications — Cereal Res Commun
Cereal Research Communications — CRCMCL

Cereal Rusts Bulletin — Cereal Rusts Bull
Cereal Science Today — Cereal Sci Today
Cerebral Circulation and Metabolism — Cereb Circ Metab
Cerebral Circulation and Metabolism. Papers. International Symposium on Cerebral Blood Flow — Cereb Cir Metab Pap Int Symp Cereb Blood Flow
Cerebral Cortex — Cereb Cortex
Cerebral Palsy Bulletin — CEPBA
Cerebral Palsy Journal — Cereb Palsy J
Cerebral Palsy Review — CBPRA
Cerebral Palsy Review — Cereb Palsy Rev
Cerebral Vascular Diseases — Cereb Vas Dis
Cerebral Vascular Diseases. International Conference — Cereb Vas Dis Int Conf
Cerebral Vascular Diseases. Transactions of the Conference — Cere Vasc Dis Trans Conf
Cerebrovascular and Brain Metabolism Reviews — Cerebrovasc Brain Metab Rev
Cerebrovascular Diseases — Cereb Dis
Cerebrovascular Diseases — Cerebrovasc Dis
Cerebrovascular Diseases. Princeton Stroke Conference — Cerebrovasc Dis Princeton Stroke Conf
Cerevisia and Biotechnology — Cerevisia Biotechnol
Cerf-Volant — CV
CERI (Central Research Institute) Journal of Education — CERI J Ed
Cermica — CERMA
CERN [*Conseil Europeen pour la Recherche Nucleaire*] **Accelerator School. General Accelerator Physics Course** — CERN Accel Sch Gen Accel Phys Course
CERN (Conseil Europeen pour la Recherche Nucleaire) Accelerator School. Applied Geodesy for Particle Accelerators — CERN Accel Sch Appl Geod Part Accel
CERN (Conseil Europeen pour la Recherche Nucleaire) School of Physics. Proceedings — CERN Sch Phys Proc
CERN (Conseil Europeen pour la Recherche Nucleaire) Symposium on High Energy Accellerators and Pion Physics. Proceedings — CERN Symp High Energy Pion Phys Proc
CERN [*Conseil Europeen pour la Recherche Nucleaire*] **High Energy Reaction Analysis Group Report** — CERN High Energy React Anal Group Rep
CERN [*Conseil Europeen pour la Recherche Nucleaire*] **Report** — CERN Rep
CERN-JINR [*Conseil Europeen pour la Recherche Nucleaire. Joint Institute of Nuclear Research*] **School of Physics** — CERN JINR Sch Phys
Cerpadla Potrubi Armatury — CPARD
Cerrahpasa Tip Fakultesi Dergisi — Cerrahpasa Tip Fak Derg
CERT. Civil Engineering and Road Transport [*New Zealand*] — CERT
Certificado de Adicion (Spain) — Certif Adicion (Spain)
Certificat d'Addition a un Brevet Special Medicament (France) — Certif Addit Brev Spec Med Fr
Certificat d'Addition au Certificat d'Utilite (France) — Certif Addit Certif Util Fr
Certificat d'Utilite (France) — Certif Util Fr
Certificated Engineer — Certif Eng
Certificated Engineer — Certifd Engr
Certified Dental Technician — Certif Dent Tec
Certified Engineer — Certif Eng
CES (Centre Environmental Studies) Review — CES (Centre Environmental Studies) R
CES. Computer Enhanced Spectroscopy — CES Comput Enhanced Spectrosc
Cesare Barbieri Courier — CBC
Ceska a Slovenska Farmacie — Ceska Slov Farm
Ceska a Slovenska Psychiatrie — Ceska Slov Psychiatr
Ceska Dermatologie — Ceska Dermatol
Ceska Gynekologie — Ceska Gynekol
Ceska Literatura — Cesk Lit
Ceska Literatura — CL
Ceska Literatura — CLit
Ceska Mykologie — Ceska Mykol
Ceske Lesnicke Rozhledy — Ceske Lesn Rozhl
Ceske Museum Filologicke — Ceske Museum Filol
Ceske Museum Filologicke — CMF
Ceske Vysoke Uceni Technicke v Praze. Prace. I. Stavebni — Ceske Vys Uceni Tech Praze Pr I
Ceske Vysoke Uceni Technicke v Praze. Prace. Rada 4. Technicko-Teoreticka — Ceske Vys Uceni Tech Praze Pr Rada 4
Ceskoslovenska Akademie Ved — CSAV
Ceskoslovenska Akademie Ved. Casopis pro Pestovani Matematiky — Casopis Pest Mat
Ceskoslovenska Akademie Ved. Ekonomicko-Matematicky Obzor — Ekonom-Mat Obzor
Ceskoslovenska Akademie Ved. Geograficky Ustav (Brno). Studia Geographica — Ceskoslovensk Akad Ved Geog Ustav (Brno) Studia Geog
Ceskoslovenska Akademie Ved. Geograficky Ustav Zpravy [*Brno*] — Cesk Akad Ved Geogr Ustav Zpr
Ceskoslovenska Akademie Ved. Laborator Radiologicke Dozimetrie. Report LRD — Cesk Akad Ved Lab Radiol Dozim Rep LRD
Ceskoslovenska Akademie Ved. Publikace — Cesk Akad Ved Publ
Ceskoslovenska Akademie Ved. Studia Geophysica et Geodaetica — Cesk Akad Ved Stud Geophys Geod
Ceskoslovenska Akademie Ved. Ustav Fyziky Plazmatu. Research Report IPP CZ — Cesk Akad Ved Ustav Fyz Plazmatu Res Rep IPPCZ
Ceskoslovenska Akademie Ved. Ustav Jaderne Fyziky. Report. — Cesk Akad Ved Ustav Jad Fyz Rep
Ceskoslovenska Akademie Ved. Vedecke Informace CSAV — Cesk Akad Ved Ved Inf CSAV
Ceskoslovenska Akademie Zemedelska. Ustav Vedeckotechnickych Informaci pro Zemedelstvi. Sbornik. Potravinarske Vedy — Cesk Akad Zemed Ustav Vedeckotech Inf Zemed Sb Potravin Vedy
Ceskoslovenska Biologie — Cesk Biol
Ceskoslovenska Dermatologie — Cesk Dermatol
Ceskoslovenska Dermatologie — Cslka Derm
Ceskoslovenska Epidemiologie, Mikrobiologie, Immunologie — Cesk Epidemiol Mikrobiol Immunol
Ceskoslovenska Epidemiologie, Mikrobiologie, Immunologie — Cs Epidem
Ceskoslovenska Farmaceuticka Spolecnost. Sbornik Prednasek Sjezdu — Cesk Farm Spol Sb Prednasek Sjezdu
Ceskoslovenska Farmacie — Cesk Farm
Ceskoslovenska Farmacie — Cs Farm
Ceskoslovenska Farmacie — Cslka Farm
Ceskoslovenska Fysiologie — Cesk Fysiol
Ceskoslovenska Fysiologie — Cs Fysiol
Ceskoslovenska Fysiologie — Cslka Fysiol
Ceskoslovenska Gastroenterologie a Vyziva — Cesk Gastroenterol Vyz
Ceskoslovenska Gastroenterologie a Vyziva — Cs Gastrent Vyz
Ceskoslovenska Gynekologie — CEGYA
Ceskoslovenska Gynekologie — Cesk Gynekol
Ceskoslovenska Gynekologie — Cs Gynek
Ceskoslovenska Hygiena — Cesk Hyg
Ceskoslovenska Hygiena Epidemiologie, Mikrobiologie, Imunologie — Cesk Hyg Epidemiol Mikrobiol Imunol
Ceskoslovenska Informatika. Teorie a Praxe — Cesk Inf
Ceskoslovenska Informatika. Teorie a Praxe — Cesk Inf Teor a Praxe
Ceskoslovenska Kozarstvi — Cesk Kozarstvi
Ceskoslovenska Mikrobiologie — Cesk Mikrobiol
Ceskoslovenska Mikrobiologie — Ceskoslov Mikrobiol
Ceskoslovenska Morfologie — Cesk Morfol
Ceskoslovenska Neurologie [*Later, Ceskoslovenska Neurologie a Neurochirurgie*] — Cesk Neurol
Ceskoslovenska Neurologie [*Later, Ceskoslovenska Neurologie a Neurochirurgie*] — Cs Neur
Ceskoslovenska Neurologie [*Later, Ceskoslovenska Neurologie a Neurochirurgie*] — CSKNA
Ceskoslovenska Neurologie a Neurochirurgie — Cesk Neurol Neurochir
Ceskoslovenska Oftalmologie — CEOFA
Ceskoslovenska Oftalmologie — Cesk Oftalmol
Ceskoslovenska Oftalmologie — Cs Oft
Ceskoslovenska Onkologie — Cesk Onkol
Ceskoslovenska Onkologie — Cs Onkol
Ceskoslovenska Otolaryngologie — CEOTA
Ceskoslovenska Otolaryngologie — Cesk Otolaryngol
Ceskoslovenska Parasitologie — Cesk Parasitol
Ceskoslovenska Parasitologie — Cs Parasit
Ceskoslovenska Patologie — Cesk Patol
Ceskoslovenska Patologie. Priloha. — Cesk Patol Priloha
Ceskoslovenska Pediatrie — CEPEA
Ceskoslovenska Pediatrie — Cesk Pediatr
Ceskoslovenska Pediatrie — Cs Pediat
Ceskoslovenska Psychiatrie — CEPYA
Ceskoslovenska Psychiatrie — Cesk Psychiatr
Ceskoslovenska Psychiatrie — Cs Psych
Ceskoslovenska Psychologie — CEPSB
Ceskoslovenska Psychologie — Cesk Psycho
Ceskoslovenska Psychologie — Cesk Psychol
Ceskoslovenska Psychologie — Cs Psych
Ceskoslovenska Radiologie — CERAB
Ceskoslovenska Radiologie — Cesk Radiol
Ceskoslovenska Rentgenologie — Cesk Rentgenol
Ceskoslovenska Rentgenologie — Cs Rentgen
Ceskoslovenska Rusistika — CRu
Ceskoslovenska Rusistika — CRus
Ceskoslovenska Rusistika — CsR
Ceskoslovenska Standardizace — Cesk Stand
Ceskoslovenska Standardizace — CESTD
Ceskoslovenska Stomatologie — Ce Sta
Ceskoslovenska Stomatologie — CES A
Ceskoslovenska Stomatologie — Cesk Stomatol
Ceskoslovenska Stomatologie — Cslka Stomat
Ceskoslovenske Botanicke Listy — Ceskoslov Bot Listy
Ceskoslovenske Zdravotnictvi — Cesk Zdrav
Ceskoslovenske Zdravotnictvi — Cs Zdrav
Ceskoslovensky Casopis Historicky — CesC
Ceskoslovensky Casopis Historicky — Cesk Cas Hist
Ceskoslovensky Casopis Historicky — CSCH
Ceskoslovensky Casopis pro Fysiku — CKCFA
Ceskoslovensky Casopis pro Fysiku. Sekce A — Cesk C Fys
Ceskoslovensky Casopis pro Fysiku. Sekce A [*Prague*] — Cesk Cas Fys
Ceskoslovensky Casopis pro Fysiku. Sekce A — Cesk Cas Fys A
Ceskoslovensky Casopis pro Fysiku. Sekce A — Cesk Cas Fys Sekce A
Ceskoslovensky Spisovatel — CSp
Ceskoslovensky Terminologicky Casopis — CSTC
Ceskoslovensky Terminologicky Casopis — CTC
Cesky Casopis Filologicky — CCF
Cesky Jazyk a Literatura — CJL
Cesky Jazyk a Literatura — CJLit
Cesky Lid — CLid
Cesky Vcelar — Cesky Vcel
CESRL Report. University of Texas at Austin. Department of Civil Engineering. Structures Research Laboratory — CESRL Rep Univ Tex Austin Dep Civ Eng Struct Res Lab
CESSID. Centre d'Etudes Superieures de la Siderurgie Francaise. Rapport — CESSID Cent Etud Super Sider Fr Rapp
CETIM Informations. Centre Technique des Industries Mechaniques — CETIM Informations

Ceylon Association for the Advancement of Science. Proceedings of the Annual Session — Ceylon Assoc Adv Sci Proc Annu Sess
Ceylon Coconut Journal — Ceylon Coconut J
Ceylon Coconut Planters' Review — Ceylon Coconut Plant Rev
Ceylon Coconut Quarterly — Ceylon Coconut Q
Ceylon Dental Journal — Ceylon Dent J
Ceylon. Department of Fisheries. Bulletin — Ceylon Dep Fish Bull
Ceylon. Department of Mineralogy. Geological Survey of Ceylon. Memoir. — Ceylon Dep Mineral Geol Surv Ceylon Mem
Ceylon Economist — CE
Ceylon. Fisheries Research Station. Progress Reports. Biological and Technological — Ceylon Fish Res St Prog Rep Biol Technol
Ceylon Forester — Ceylon For
Ceylon Forester — Ceylon Forest
Ceylon. Geological Survey. Memoir — Ceylon Geol Surv Mem
Ceylon Institute of Scientific and Industrial Research. Natural Products Section. Natural Products Technical Notes Series — Ceylon Inst Sci Ind Res Nat Prod Sect Nat Prod Tech Notes Ser
Ceylon Journal of Historical and Social Studies — Cey J Hist Soc Stud
Ceylon Journal of Historical and Social Studies — CJHSS
Ceylon Journal of Medical Science — Ceylon J Med Sci
Ceylon Journal of Science. Anthropology — Ceylon J Sci Anthropol
Ceylon Journal of Science. Biological Sciences — Ceylon J Sci Biol Sci
Ceylon Journal of Science. Medical Science — Ceylon J Sci Med Sci
Ceylon Journal of Science. Section A. Botany — Ceylon J Sci Sect A Bot
Ceylon Journal of Science. Section B. Zoology — Ceylon J Sci Sect B
Ceylon Journal of Science. Section B. Zoology — Ceylon J Sci Sect B Zool
Ceylon Journal of Science. Section C. Fisheries — Ceylon J Sci Sect C
Ceylon Journal of Science. Section C. Fisheries — Ceylon J Sci Sect C Fish
Ceylon Journal of Science. Section D. Medical Science — Ceylon J Sci Sect D
Ceylon Journal of Science. Section D. Medical Science — Ceylon J Sci Sect D Med Sci
Ceylon Medical Journal — Ceylon Med J
Ceylon. National Museums Administration. Report of the Director. Part IV. Education, Science, and Art — Ceylon Nat Mus Adm Rep Dir Part IV Educ Sci Art
Ceylon. National Museums Administration. Report of the Director. Part IV. Education, Science, and Art (E) — Ceylon Natl Mus Adm Rep Dir Part IV Educ Sci Art (E)
Ceylon National Museums. Ethnographic Series — Ceylon Natl Mus Ethnogr Ser
Ceylon Rubber Research Scheme. Quarterly Circular — Ceylon Rubber Res Scheme Q Circ
Ceylon Today — C Td
Ceylon Veterinary Journal — Ceylon Vet J
Ceylon Veterinary Journal — CVTJA
CFEM [*Comision Forestal del Estado de Michoacan*] **Serie Tecnica** — CFEM Ser Tec
CFI [*Ceramic Forum International*] **Berichte der Deutschen Keramischen Gesellsch aft** — CCFDD
CFI Ceramic Forum International. Beihefte — CFI Ceram Forum Int Beih
CFI. Ceramic Forum International. Berichte der Deutschen Keramischen Gesellschaft — CFI Ceram Forum Int
CFI (Ceramic Forum International). Berichte der Deutschen Keramischen Gesellschaft — CFI (Ceram Forum Int) Ber Dtsch Keram Ges
CFI (Ceramic Forum International). Berichte der Deutschen Keramischen Gesellschaft — CFI(Ceram Forus Int) Ber DKG
CFI (Commonwealth Forest Institute) Occasional Papers — CFI (Commonw For Inst) Occas Pap
CFO [*Colorado Field Ornithologists*] **Journal** — CFO J
CFS. Courier Forschungsinstitut Senckenberg — CFS Cour Forschungsinst Senckenberg
Chacaras e Quintais — Chacaras Quint
Chagyo Shikenjo Kenkyu Hokoku. Bulletin. National Research Institute of Tea — Chagyo Shikenjo Kenkyu Hokoku Bull Natl Res Inst Tea
Chain Drug Review. Reporter for the Chain Drug Store Industry — Chain Drug R
Chain Marketing and Management — Chn Mktg
Chain Merchandiser — Chn Merch
Chain Reaction — Chain React
Chain Store Age — Chn Store
Chain Store Age — CQG
Chain Store Age. Administration Edition — Chain Store Age Adm Ed
Chain Store Age. Drug Store Edition. Annual Report of the Chain Drug Industry — Chn Stor D
Chain Store Age. Executive Edition — Chain Store Age Exec
Chain Store Age. Executive Edition — CHS
Chain Store Age. General Merchandise Edition [*Later, Chain Store Age. General Merchandise Trends*] — Chain Store Age Gen Merch Ed
Chain Store Age. General Merchandise Trends Edition — Chn Str GM
Chain Store Age Supermarkets — Chain Store Age Supermark
Chaleur et Climats — Chal Clim
Chaleur et Climats — Chal Climats
Chaleur et Industrie — Cha Ind
Chaleur et Industrie [*France*] — Chal Ind
Challenge — CHL
Challenge — CHLGB
Challenge for Change. Access. National Film Board of Canada — CFCA
Challenge in Educational Administration — Challenge in Ed Admin
Challenge. Magazine of Economic Affairs — CHA
Challenges to Montana Agriculture — Challenges Mont Agr
Chalmers Tekniska Hoegskola. Doktorsavhandlingar — Chalmers Tek Hogsk Doktorsavh
Chalmers Tekniska Hoegskola. Handlingar — Chalmers Tek Hoegsk Handl
Chalmers Tekniska Hoegskola. Institutionen foer Vattenfoersoerjnings-och Avloppsteknik. Publikation — Chalmers Tek Hoegsk Inst Vattenfoersoerjnings Avloppstek Pub
Chalmers Tekniska Hoegskola. Publikation B — Chalmers Tek Hoegsk Publ B
Chamber Music — Chamber Mus
Chamber Music — ChM
Chamber of Agriculture of Victoria. Yearbook — Chamber of Ag Vic Yrbk
Chamber of Mines. Journal — Chamber Mines J
Chamber of Mines. Journal — CHMJB
Chamber of Mines. Newsletter — Chamb Mines Newsl
Chamber of Mines. Newsletter [*Johannesburg*] — Chamber Mines Newsl
Chamber of Mines. Newsletter [*South Africa*] — CMNLD
Chamber Tombs at Mycenae — Ch T
Chamber Tombs at Mycenae — CT
Chamber's Edinburgh Journal — Chamb J
Chamber's Journal — CJ
Chambre de Commerce, d'Agriculture, et d'Industrie de la Republique Togolaise. Bulletin Mensuel — CXA
Chambre de Commerce, d'Agriculture, et d'Industrie du Niger. Bulletin — CKN
Chambre de Commerce de Tunis. Bulletin — CCD
Chambre de Commerce et d'Industrie d'Anvers. Bulletin — CAV
Chambre de Commerce et d'Industrie de Nouvelle Caledonie. Bulletin — CPJ
Chambre de Commerce et d'Industrie. Republique Populaire du Benin. Bulletin Hebdomadaire d'Information et de Documentation — CKD
Chambre de Commerce Francaise au Canada. Revue — Chambre Commer Fr Can R
Chambre de Commerce Francaise en Australie. Bulletin — Chambre de Commerce Francaise Bul
Chambre de Commerce France-Amerique Latine — CML
Chambre de Commerce. Republique de Cote D'Ivoire. Bulletin Mensuel — Chambre Commer Repub Cote D'Ivoire Bul Mensuel
Chambres d'Agriculture — Ch Agric
Champignon. Algemene Nederlandse Champignon-Kwekers Vereniging (Netherlands) — Champignon Netherlands
Changchun Dizhi Xueyuan Xuebao — CTCPD
Change — CML
Change — CNG
Change — GCHA
Change (Paris) — Change (Par)
Change to Metric Information Service — CMIS
Changes Socialist Monthly — Changes
Changing Education — Chang Ed
Changing Face of Breadstuffs (Milling and Baking News. Special Edition) — Milling S
Changing Japanese Attitudes Toward Modernization [*Monograph*] — CJA
Changing Scene — Chang Scene
Changing Scene — CHSCD
Changing the Structure of Medicare Benefits. Issues and Options. Congressional Budget Office — CBO Med Ben
Changing Times — Cha Ti
Changing Times — Chang Times
Changing Times — Changing T
Changing Times — CNGTA
Changing Times — GCHT
Changsha Communications University. Journal — J Changsha Comm Univ
Channel Isles Annual Anthology — Channel Isles Annu Anthol
Channels — GCHS
Channels of Communications — Ch
Chanoyu Quarterly — Chanoyu Q
Chantiers de France — CFRMB
Chantiers de France — Chantiers Fr
Chantiers Magazine [*France*] — Chantiers Mag
Chantiers Magazine — CHMNA
Chapingo. Sociedad de Alumnos. Escuela Nacional de Agricultura — Chapingo Soc Alum Esc Nac Agric
Chapman and Hall Computing — Chapman and Hall Comput
Chapman and Hall Mathematics Series — Chapman and Hall Math Ser
Charge and Field Effects in Biosystems-3. International Symposium on Charge and Field Effects in Biosystems — Charge Field Eff Biosyst 3 Int Symp
Charged and Reactive Polymers — Charged React Polym
Charged Particle Tracks in Solids and Liquids. Proceedings. L. H. Gray Conference — Charged Part Tracks Solids Liq Proc L H Gray Conf
Charisma — Char
Charite-Annalen — Charite Ann
Charities — Char
Charities Review — Char R
Charles Babbage Institute Newsletter — Charles Babbage Inst Newslett
Charles Babbage Institute Reprint Series for the History of Computing — Charles Babbage Inst Reprint Ser Hist Comput
Charles Lamb Bulletin — Ch L B
Charles Lamb Society. Bulletin — CLS
Charles Lamb Society. Bulletin — CLSB
Charles Rennie Mackintosh Society. Newsletter (Glasgow) — Charles Rennie Mackintosh Soc Newsletter (Glasgow)
Charleston Gazette — Charlstn G
Charleston Medical Journal and Review — Charleston Med J R
Charlotte Medical Journal — Charlotte Med J
Charlotte News — Charlotte N
Charlotte Observer — Charlot Obs
Chartae Latinae Antiquiores — Ch L
Chartae Latinae Antiquiores — ChLA
Chartae Latinae Antiquiores — CLA
Chartered Accountant in Australia — Char Acctnt Aust
Chartered Accountant in Australia — Chart Acc in Aust
Chartered Accountant in Australia — Chart Accnt in Aust

Chartered Accountant in Australia — Chart Accountant in Aust
Chartered Accountant in Australia — Chart Acct
Chartered Accountant in Australia — Chartered Accountant Aust
Chartered Builder — Chart Build
Chartered Builder — Chart Builder
Chartered Engineer — Chart Eng
Chartered Institute of Transport. Journal [*England*] — Chart Inst Transp J
Chartered Institute of Transport. Journal — Chartered Inst Transport J
Chartered Institute of Transport. Journal — CITJD
Chartered Land Surveyor/Chartered Minerals Surveyor — Chart Land Surv Chart Miner Surv
Chartered Mechanical Engineer — Chart Mech E
Chartered Mechanical Engineer — Chart Mech Eng
Chartered Mechanical Engineer — Chart Mech Engr
Chartered Mechanical Engineer — CHMGA
Chartered Mechanical Engineer — CME
Chartered Municipal Engineer — Chart Munic Eng
Chartered Quantity Surveyor — Chart Quant Surv
Chartered Secretary — Chart Sec
Chartered Surveyor [*Later, Chartered Surveyor Weekly*] — Chart Surv
Chartered Surveyor [*Later, Chartered Surveyor Weekly*] — CHSUA
Chartered Surveyor. Building and Quantity Surveying Quarterly — Chartered Surveyor Bldg & Quantity Surveying Qly
Chartered Surveyor. Land Hydrographic and Minerals Quarterly [*England*] — Chart Surv Land Hydrogr Miner Q
Chartered Surveyor. Land Hydrographic and Minerals Quarterly — CSLHA
Chartered Surveyor. Rural Quarterly [*England*] — Chart Surv Rural Q
Chartered Surveyor. Rural Quarterly — CSRQA
Chartered Surveyor. Urban Quarterly — Chartered Surveyor Urban Qly
Chartered Surveyor Weekly — Chart Surv Wkly
Chartered Surveyor Weekly — CSW
Chase Economic Bulletin — Chase Econ Bul
Chase Economic Observer — Chase Econ Observer
Chase Economic Observer — Chase Obsv
Chase Manhattan Bank. International Finance — Chase Fin
Chasqui — CHA
Chatelaine — ICHA
Chaucer Review — Chaucer R
Chaucer Review — Chaucer Rev
Chaucer Review — ChauR
Chaucer Review — PCHA
Chaucer Society — Chaucer Soc
Chaud-Froid-Plomberie — CFPOB
Chauffage, Ventilation, Conditionnement [*France*] — Chauf Vent Cond
Chauffage, Ventilation, Conditionnement — Chauff Vent Con
Chauffage, Ventilation, Conditionnement — CHVCA
Chautauquan — Chaut
Chayanica Geologica — Chayanica Geol
Chayon Kwahak Taehak Nomunjip — CKTND
ChEC Series on Chemical Engineering Computing — ChEC Ser Chem Eng Comput
Checkout. Management im Modernen Handel — CCP
ChED. Chemie. Experiment + Didaktik — ChED Chem Exp Didakt
Chefmagazin fuer Kleinbetriebe und Mittelbetriebe — GEB
Cheiron. The Tamil Nadu Journal of Veterinary Science and Animal Husbandry [*A publication*] — Cheiron Tamil Nadu J Vet Sci Anim Husb
Cheju University. Journal — Cheju Univ J
Cheju University. Journal. Natural Sciences — Cheju Univ J Nat Sci
Cheju University. Journal (South Korea) — CUJSD
Chekhoslovatskaya Biologiya — Chekh Biol
Chekhoslovatskaya Biologiya — Chekhoslov Biol
Chekhoslovatskaya Fiziologiya — Chekh Fiziol
Chekhoslovatskii Fizicheskii Zhurnal — Chek Fiz Zh
Chekhoslovatskii Zhurnal Gigieny Truda i Professional'nykh Zabolevanii — Chek Zh Gig Tr Prof Zabol
Chekhoslovatskoe Meditsinskoe Obozrenie — Chekh Med Obozr
Chelates in Analytical Chemistry — Chelates Anal Chem
Chelovek i Biosfera — Chel Biosfera
Chelsea — Chel
Chelsea Journal — CJ
Cheltenham Magazine — Cheltenham Mag
Chelyabinskii Meditsinskii Institut. Sbornik Nauchnykh Trudov — Chelyab Med Inst Sb Nauchn Tr
Chelyabinskii Politekhnicheskii Institut. Trudy — Chelyab Politekh Inst Tr
Chem Show Guide. Special Advertising Supplement from Chemical Engineering — Chem Eng S
Chemia Analityczna [*Warszawa*] — Chemia Analit
Chemia Analityczna (Warszawa) — CANWA
Chemia Analityczna (Warszawa) — Chem Anal (Warszawa)
Chemia i Inzynieria Chemiczna — Chem Inz Chem
Chemia i Inzynieria Ekologiczna — Chem Inz Ekol
Chemia i Technologia Chemiczna — Chem Technol Chem
Chemia (Politechnika Szczecinska) — Chemia Politech Szczecin
Chemia Stosowana — Chem Stosow
Chemia Stosowana — CSTWA
Chemia Stosowana. Seria A — Chem Stosow Ser A
Chemia Stosowana. Seria A. Kwartalnik Poswiecony Zagadnieniom Technologii Chemicznej — CSAKA
Chemia Stosowana. Seria B — Chem Stosow Ser B
Chemia Stosowana. Seria B. Kwartalnik Poswiecony Zagadnieniom Inzynierii i Aparatury Chemicznej — CSBKA
Chemia Szkole — Chem Szk
Chemica Scripta — Chem Scr
Chemica Scripta — Chem Scripta
Chemica Scripta — Chemica Scr
Chemica Scripta — CSRPB
Chemical Abstracts [*Chemical Abstracts Service*] [*Database*] — CA
Chemical Abstracts — Chem Abstr
Chemical Abstracts — ChemAb
Chemical Abstracts. Annual Subject Index — Chem Abstr Subj Ind
Chemical Abstracts. Decennial Cumulative Subject Index — Chem Abstr Cum Subj Index
Chemical Abstracts. Macromolecular Sections — Chem Abs Macromol
Chemical Abstracts of Japan — Chem Abstr Jpn
Chemical Abstracts. Physical and Analytical Chemistry Section — Chem Abst Phy Anal Chem Sect
Chemical Abstracts Service. Report — CAS
Chemical Abstracts Service Source Index [*Database*] — CASSI
Chemical Abstracts Service. Source Index — Chem Abstr Serv Source Index
Chemical Abstracts Service. Source Index Quarterly — C A Source Index
Chemical Activity Status Report [*Database*] — CASR
Chemical Age — C A
Chemical Age — CHAGA
Chemical Age — Chem Age
Chemical Age International — CAGIB
Chemical Age International — Chem Age Int
Chemical Age (London) — Chem Age (Lond)
Chemical Age (New York) — Chem Age (NY)
Chemical Age of India — CHAIA
Chemical Age of India — Chem Age India
Chemical Age Project File [*Database*] — CAPF
Chemical Age Survey — Chem Ag Sv
Chemical Analysis. A Series of Monographs on Analytical Chemistry and Its Applications — Chem Anal Ser Monogr Anal Chem Appl
Chemical Analysis. A Series of Monographs on Analytical Chemistry and Its Applications (New York) — Chem Anal (New York)
Chemical Analysis and Biological Fate. Polynuclear Aromatic Hydrocarbons. International Symposium — Chem Anal and Biol Fate Polynucl Aromat Hydrocarbons Int Sym
Chemical Analysis (New York). A Series of Monographs — Chem Anal NY
Chemical and Biochemical Engineering Quarterly — Chem Biochem Eng Q
Chemical and Dynamical Evolution of Our Galaxy. Proceedings. IAU [*International Astronomical Union*] **Colloquium** — Chem Dyn Evol Our Galaxy Proc IAU Colloq
Chemical and Engineering Data Series — Chem Eng Data Ser
Chemical and Engineering News — C & E News
Chemical and Engineering News — C & EN
Chemical and Engineering News — CENEA
Chemical and Engineering News — Chem & Eng N
Chemical and Engineering News — Chem and Engin News
Chemical and Engineering News — Chem & Engng News
Chemical and Engineering News — Chem Eng News
Chemical and Engineering News — Chem Engn News
Chemical and Engineering News — CLN
Chemical and Engineering News — GCEN
Chemical and Environmental Science — Chem Environ Sci
Chemical and Metallurgical Engineering — Chem & Met Eng
Chemical and Metallurgical Engineering — Chem Met Eng
Chemical and Metallurgical Engineering — Chem Metall Eng
Chemical and Metallurgical Engineering — CMENA
Chemical and Petroleum Engineering — Chem & Pet Engng
Chemical and Petroleum Engineering — Chem Pet Eng
Chemical and Petroleum Engineering [*English Translation*] — CPTEA
Chemical and Petroleum Engineering (English Translation) — Chem Pet Eng (Engl Transl)
Chemical and Pharmaceutical Bulletin — Chem Pharm
Chemical and Pharmaceutical Bulletin — Chem Pharm Bull
Chemical and Pharmaceutical Bulletin (Tokyo) — Chem Pharm Bull (Tokyo)
Chemical and Pharmaceutical Bulletin (Tokyo) — CPBTA
Chemical and Physical Processes in Combustion — Chem Phys Processes Combust
Chemical and Process Engineering — Chem and Process Eng
Chemical and Process Engineering [*Later, Process Engineering*] — Chem & Process Engng
Chemical and Process Engineering — Chem Process Eng
Chemical and Process Engineering [*London*] — CPENA
Chemical and Process Engineering and Atomic World — Chem Process Eng At World
Chemical and Process Engineering (London) — Chem Process Eng London
Chemical Applications of Nonlinear Raman Spectroscopy [*monograph*] — Chem Appl Nonlinear Raman Spectrosc
Chemical Bank. Economic Forecast Summary — Chem Bk Frct
Chemical Bank. Weekly Economic Package — Chem Bk Econ
Chemical, Biomedical, and Environmental Instrumentation — Chem Biomed and Environ Instrum
Chemical, Biomedical, and Environmental Instrumentation — Chem Biomed Environ Inst
Chemical, Biomedical, and Environmental Instrumentation — Chem Biomed Environ Instrum
Chemical Bulletin — Chem Bull
Chemical Bulletin (Beijing) — Chem Bull (Beijing)
Chemical Business — Chem Bus
Chemical Business NewsBase [*Database*] — CBNB
Chemical Business (Supplement to Chemical Marketing Reporter) — CMR Chem Bus
Chemical Carcinogenesis Research Information System [*Database*] — CCRIS
Chemical Carcinogens [*Monograph*] — Chem Carcinog
Chemical Changes in Food during Processing. Proceedings. Basic Symposium — Chem Changes Food Process Proc Basic Symp

Chemical Coaters Association. Annual National Technical Seminar — Chem Coaters Assoc Annu Natl Tech Semin
Chemical Coatings Conference. Powder Coatings Session. Technical Papers — Chem Coat Conf Powder Coat Sess Tech Pap
Chemical Coatings Conference. Technical Papers — Chem Coat Conf Tech Pap
Chemical, Color, and Oil Daily — Chem Color Oil Daily
Chemical, Color, and Oil Record — Chem Color Oil Rec
Chemical Communications — CCOMA
Chemical Communications [*Journal of the Chemical Society. Section D*] — Chem Commun
Chemical Communications — Chem Communs
Chemical Communications (Cambridge) — Chem Commun Cambridge
Chemical Communications. Journal of the Chemical Society — Chem Commun J Chem Soc
Chemical Communications. University of Stockholm — Chem Commun Univ Stockholm
Chemical Concepts — CHCOD
Chemical Concepts — Chem Concepts
Chemical Congress of the North American Continent — Chem Congr North Am Cont
Chemical Control Research Institute (Ottawa). Information Report — Chem Control Res Inst (Ottawa) Inf Rep
Chemical Control Research Institute. Ottawa. Internal Report CC-16 — Chem Control Res Inst Ottawa Int Rep CC 16
Chemical Corps Journal — Chem Corps J
Chemical Correspondence — Chem Corr
Chemical Dependencies — Chem Depend
Chemical Division Transactions. American Society for Quality Control — Chem Div Trans Am Soc Qual Control
Chemical Economy and Engineering Review — CECEB
Chemical Economy and Engineering Review — CEER
Chemical Economy and Engineering Review — Chem Econ
Chemical Economy and Engineering Review — Chem Econ Eng Rev
Chemical Education [*Japan*] — Chem Educ
Chemical Education (Seoul) — Chem Ed (Seoul)
Chemical Educator [*Electronic Publication*] — Chem Educ
Chemical Engineer — Chem Eng
Chemical Engineer — Chem Engr
Chemical Engineer — Chemical Engnr
Chemical Engineer. Birmingham University — Chem Eng Birmingham Univ
Chemical Engineer Diary and Process Industries News — Chem Engr Diary & Process Ind News
Chemical Engineer (London) — Chem Engr (Lond)
Chemical Engineer (Rugby) — Chem Eng (Rugby)
Chemical Engineering [*New York*] — CHEEA
Chemical Engineering — Chem Eng
Chemical Engineering — Chem Engng
Chemical Engineering Abstracts [*Database*] — CEA
Chemical Engineering and Machinery (Lanzhou, People's Republic of China) — Chem Eng Mach Lanzhou Peoples Repub China
Chemical Engineering and Mining Review — Chem Eng & Min R
Chemical Engineering and Mining Review — Chem Eng and Min Rev
Chemical Engineering and Mining Review — Chem Engng Min Rev
Chemical Engineering and Processing — Chem Eng Process
Chemical Engineering and Technology — Chem Eng Technol
Chemical Engineering and the Works Chemist — Chem Eng Works Chem
Chemical Engineering at Supercritical Fluid Conditions [*Monograph*] — Chem Eng Supercrit Fluid Cond
Chemical Engineering (Australia) — Chem Eng (Aust)
Chemical Engineering (Australia) — Chem Engng (Aust)
Chemical Engineering. Chemical Technology for Profit Minded Engineers — CMM
Chemical Engineering (China) — Chem Eng China
Chemical Engineering Communications — Chem Eng Comm
Chemical Engineering Communications — Chem Eng Commun
Chemical Engineering Communications — Chem Engng Commun
Chemical Engineering Communications — Chem Engng Communications
Chemical Engineering Costs Quarterly — Chem Eng Costs Q
Chemical Engineering Education — CHEDA
Chemical Engineering Education — Chem Eng Educ
Chemical Engineering Fundamentals — Chem Eng Fundam
Chemical Engineering Group. Society of Chemical Industry. London. Proceedings — Chem Eng Group Soc Chem Ind London Proc
Chemical Engineering in a Changing World. Proceedings. Plenary Sessions. World Congress on Chemical Engineering — Chem Eng Changing World Proc Plenary Sess World Congr Chem E
Chemical Engineering in Australia — Chem Eng Aust
Chemical Engineering Index — CEI
Chemical Engineering (International Edition) — CEIED
Chemical Engineering (International Edition) — Chem Eng (Int Ed)
Chemical Engineering (Japan) — Chem Eng (Jpn)
Chemical Engineering Journal — Chem Eng J
Chemical Engineering Journal — Chem Engng J
Chemical Engineering Journal — Chem Engng Journal
Chemical Engineering Journal — Chem Engrg J
Chemical Engineering Monographs [*Elsevier Book Series*] — CEM
Chemical Engineering Monographs — CENMD
Chemical Engineering Monographs [*Netherlands*] — Chem Eng Monogr
Chemical Engineering (New York) — Chem Eng (NY)
Chemical Engineering Progress — CEP
Chemical Engineering Progress — CEPRA
Chemical Engineering Progress — Chem Eng P
Chemical Engineering Progress — Chem Eng Pr
Chemical Engineering Progress — Chem Eng Prog
Chemical Engineering Progress — Chem Eng Progr
Chemical Engineering Progress — Chem Engng Prog
Chemical Engineering Progress — Chem Engng Progress
Chemical Engineering Progress. Monograph Series — Chem Eng Prog Monogr Ser
Chemical Engineering Progress. Symposium Series — CEPSA
Chemical Engineering Progress. Symposium Series — Chem Eng Prog Symp Ser
Chemical Engineering Progress. Symposium Series — Chem Eng Progr Symp Ser
Chemical Engineering Research and Design — Chem Eng Res and Des
Chemical Engineering Research and Design — Chem Engng Res Des
Chemical Engineering Research Bulletin (Dacca) — CERBD
Chemical Engineering Research Bulletin (Dhaka) — Chem Eng Res Bull Dhaka
Chemical Engineering Science — CESCA
Chemical Engineering Science — Chem Eng Sc
Chemical Engineering Science — Chem Eng Sci
Chemical Engineering Science — Chem Engng Sci
Chemical Engineering Science — Chem Engng Science
Chemical Engineering (Tokyo) — Chem Eng (Tokyo)
Chemical Engineering World — CEWOA
Chemical Engineering World — Chem Eng World
Chemical Engineering World — Chem Engng World
Chemical Engineer's Digest (Tokyo) — Chem Eng Dig (Tokyo)
Chemical Equipment News — Chem Equip News
Chemical Equipment Preview — Chem Equip Preview
Chemical Era [*India*] — Chem Era
Chemical Era — CHERD
Chemical Evaluation Search and Retrieval System [*Database*] — CESARS
Chemical Evolution of the Early Precambrian. College Park Colloquium on Chemical Evolution — Chem Evol Early Precambrian College Park Colloq
Chemical Factory (Tokyo) — Chem Fact (Tokyo)
Chemical Farming — Chem Farming
Chemical Fertilizers. Proceedings. International Congress — Chem Fert Proc Int Congr
Chemical Geology — Chem Geol
Chemical Geology — Chem Geology
Chemical Geology — CHGEA
Chemical Guide to Europe — Chem G Eur
Chemical Hazards in Industry [*Database*] — CHI
Chemical Hazards Response Information System [*Database*] — CHRIS
Chemical Health and Safety — Chem Health Saf
Chemical Immunology — Chem Immunol
Chemical Industries — Chem Ind
Chemical Industries (New York) — Chem Ind (NY)
Chemical Industries Week — Chem Ind Week
Chemical Industry and Engineering — Chem Ind
Chemical Industry and Engineering — Chem Ind and Engng
Chemical Industry and Engineering — Chem Ind Eng
Chemical Industry and Engineering (Beijing) — Chem Ind Eng (Beijing)
Chemical Industry and Engineering Progress (Beijing) — Chem Ind Eng Prog Beijing
Chemical Industry and Engineering (Tianjin) — Chem Ind Eng Tianjin
Chemical Industry Developments — Chem Ind Dev
Chemical Industry (Japan) — Chem Ind (Jpn)
Chemical Industry (Japan). Supplement — Chem Ind (Jpn) Suppl
Chemical Industry Notes [*Chemical Abstracts Service*] [*Bibliographic database*] [*A publication*] — CIN
Chemical Industry (Peking) — Chem Ind Peking
Chemical Industry Scheme for Assistance in Freight Emergencies — CHEMSAFE
Chemical Industry (Shanghai) — Chem Ind Shanghai
Chemical Industry (Tenali, India) — Chem Ind (Tenali India)
Chemical Information and Computer Sciences. Journal — Chem Info
Chemical Information. Information in Chemistry, Pharmacology, and Patents — Chem Inf
Chemical Information Systems [*Monograph*] — Chem Inf Sys
Chemical Insight — Chem Insgt
Chemical Institute of Canada. Joint Conference with the American Chemical Society. Abstracts of Papers — Chem Inst Can J Conf Am Chem Soc Abstr Pap
Chemical Instrumentation — Chem Instr
Chemical Instrumentation — Chem Instrum
Chemical Instrumentation [*New York*] — CHINB
Chemical Journal. Association of Official Analytical Chemists [*Database*] — CJAOAC
Chemical Journal of Chinese Universities — Chem J Chin Univ
Chemical Journal of John Wiley and Sons [*Database*] — CJWILEY
Chemical Journals. American Chemical Society [*Database*] — CJACS
Chemical Journals. Royal Society of Chemistry [*Database*] — CJRSC
Chemical Journals. VCH Verlagsgesellschaft [*Database*] — CJVCH
Chemical Laboratory Report. Department of Mines (New South Wales) — Chem Lab Rep Dep Mines (NSW)
Chemical Laboratory Report (Hiroshima) — Chem Lab Rep Hiroshima
Chemical Laboratory Report. New South Wales. Department of Mines — Chem Lab Rep NSW Dep Mines
Chemical Machinery — Chem Mach
Chemical Marketing and Economics Reprints — CME Reprnt
Chemical Marketing Newspaper — Chem Mark Newspaper
Chemical Marketing Reporter — Chem Mark Rep
Chemical Marketing Reporter — Chem Market Reptr
Chemical Marketing Reporter — Chem Mkt R
Chemical Marketing Reporter — Chem Mkt Rept
Chemical Marketing Reporter — Chem Mktg Rep
Chemical Marketing Reporter — CMKRA
Chemical Marketing Reporter — OPD

Chemical Markets — Chem Mark
Chemical Monthly — Chem Mon
Chemical Mutagens — Chem Mutagens
Chemical News — Chem N
Chemical News — Chem News
Chemical News — CNEWA
Chemical News and Journal of Industrial Science — Chem News
Chemical News and Journal of Industrial Science — Chem News J Ind Sci
Chemical News and Journal of Physical Science — Chem News J Phys Sci
Chemical Papers — Chem Pap
Chemical Physics — Chem Phys
Chemical Physics Letters — Chem P Lett
Chemical Physics Letters — Chem Phys Lett
Chemical Physics Letters — CHPLB
Chemical Physics of Solids and Their Surfaces — Chem Phys Solids Their Surf
Chemical Plant (Tokyo) — Chem Plant (Tokyo)
Chemical Pretreatment of Nuclear Waste for Disposal. Proceedings of an American Chemical Society Symposium — Chem Pretreat Nucl Waste Disposal Proc Am Chem Soc Symp
Chemical Preview — Chem Preview
Chemical Problems Connected with the Stability of Explosives — Chem Probl Connected Stab Explos
Chemical Process Control. Proceedings. Engineering Foundation Conference — Chem Process Control Proc Eng Found Conf
Chemical Process Hazards with Special Reference to Plant Design. International Symposium — Chem Process Hazards Spec Ref Plant Des Int Symp
Chemical Processing — Chem Process
Chemical Processing — Chem Processing
Chemical Processing [*London*] — CPROA
Chemical Processing and Engineering — CPENB
Chemical Processing and Engineering. Annual (Bombay) — Chem Process Eng Annu (Bombay)
Chemical Processing and Engineering (Bombay) — Chem Process Eng (Bombay)
Chemical Processing (Chicago) — Chem Process Chicago
Chemical Processing (Chicago) — CHPCA
Chemical Processing (London) — Chem Process (London)
Chemical Processing of Advanced Materials — Chem Process Adv Mater
Chemical Processing Review — Chem Process Rev
Chemical Processing (Sydney) [*Australia*] — Chem Proc (Sydney)
Chemical Processing (Sydney) — Chem Process (Sydney)
Chemical Products and Aerosol News — Chem Prod Aerosol News
Chemical Products and the Chemical News [*England*] — Chem Prod Chem News
Chemical Progress — Chem Progr
Chemical Propulsion Abstracts [*Database*] — CPA
Chemical Purchasing — Chem Purch
Chemical Reaction Engineering and Technology — Chem React Eng Technol
Chemical Reaction Engineering. Houston. International Symposium on Chemical Reaction Engineering — Chem React Eng Houston Int Symp
Chemical Reaction Engineering. International Symposium on Chemical Reaction Engineering — Chem React Eng Int Symp
Chemical Reaction Engineering. Plenary Lectures. Based on the International Symposium on Chemical Reaction Engineering — Chem React Eng Plenary Lect Int Symp
Chemical Reaction Engineering. Proceedings. European Symposium — Chem React Eng Proc Eur Symp
Chemical Reaction Engineering Reviews. Houston. International Symposium on Chemical Reaction Engineering — Chem React Eng Rev Houston Int Symp Chem React Eng
Chemical Reactions Documentation Service [*Database*] — CRDS
Chemical Reactivity in Liquids. Fundamental Aspects. Proceedings. International Meeting. Societe Francaise de Chimie. Division de Chimie Physique — Chem React Liq Proc Int Meet Soc Fr Chim Div Chim Phys
Chemical Record-Age — Chem Rec-Age
Chemical Regulation in Plants/Shokubutsu no Kagaku Chosetsu/The Society of Chemical Regulation of Plants — Chem Regulat Pl
Chemical Regulation Reporter — Chem Regul Rep
Chemical Regulation Reporter. Bureau of National Affairs — Chem Reg Rep BNA
Chemical Regulations and Guidelines System [*Database*] — CRGS
Chemical Research and Application — Chem Res Appl
Chemical Research in Chinese Universities — Chem Res Chin Univ
Chemical Research in Toxicology — Chem Res Toxicol
Chemical Review (Japan) — Chem Rev (Jpn)
Chemical Reviews — Chem R
Chemical Reviews — Chem Rev
Chemical Reviews — CHREA
Chemical Rubber Company. Critical Reviews in Environmental Control — CRC Critical Reviews in Environmental Control
Chemical Safety Data Sheet — Chem Saf Data Sheet
Chemical Senses — Chem Sens
Chemical Senses — Chem Senses
Chemical Senses and Flavor — Chem Senses
Chemical Sensor Technology — Chem Sens Technol
Chemical Sensors — Chem Sens
Chemical Separations. Developed from Selected Papers Presented at the International Conference on Separations Science and Technology — Chem Sep Dev Sel Pap Int Conf Sep Sci Technol
Chemical Society. Faraday Discussions — Chem Soc Faraday Discuss
Chemical Society. Faraday Symposia — Chem Soc Faraday Symp
Chemical Society. Faraday Transactions 1 — CS Faraday Transactions 1
Chemical Society. Journal [*London*] — Chem Soc J
Chemical Society of Ethiopia. Bulletin — Chem Soc Ethiop Bull
Chemical Society. Reviews [*London*] — Chem Soc Re
Chemical Society. Reviews [*London*] — Chem Soc Rev
Chemical Society. Reviews — CSRVB
Chemical Society. Special Publication [*London*] — Chem Soc Spec Publ
Chemical Specialities Manufacturers Association. Proceedings. Annual Meeting — Chem Spec Manuf Assoc Proc Annu Meet
Chemical Specialties Manufacturers Association. Proceedings of the Mid-Year Meeting — Chem Spec Manuf Assoc Proc Mid-Year Meet
Chemical Speciation and Bioavailability — Chem Speciation Bioavailability
Chemical Take-Off — Chem Take-Off
Chemical Technology — Chem Tech
Chemical Technology — Chem Technol
Chemical Technology — CHMTB
Chemical Technology, a Series of Monographs [*New York*] — Chem Technol
Chemical Technology Review — Chem Tech Rev
Chemical Thermodynamics — Chem Thermodyn
Chemical Times and Trends — Chem Times Trends
Chemical Times (Athens). Section B — Chem Times (Athens) B
Chemical Titles [*Information service or system*] — Chem Titles
Chemical Titles [*Information service or system*] — CT
Chemical Titles. Chicago Psychoanalytic Literature Index — Chem Titles Chicago Psychoanal Lit Index
Chemical Trade Journal and Chemical Engineer — Chem Trade J Chem Eng
Chemical Trade Magazine — Chem Trade Mag
Chemical Vapor Deposition — Chem Vapor Deposition
Chemical Vapor Deposition. International Conference — Chem Vap Deposition Int Conf
Chemical Warfare Bulletin — Chem Warf Bull
Chemical Week — Chem W
Chemical Week — Chem Week
Chemical Week — CHWKA
Chemical Week — CMI
Chemical Week — CWE
Chemical Weekly — Chem Wkly
Chemical Worker — Chem Wkr
Chemical World — Chem World
Chemical World (Shanghai) — Chem World (Shanghai)
Chemical Zoology — Chem Zool
Chemical-Biological Activities [*Database*] — CBAC
Chemically Modified Surfaces — Chem Modif Surf
Chemically Modified Surfaces. Proceedings. Symposium on Chemically Modified Surfaces — Chem Modif Surf Proc Symp
Chemicals and Petro-Chemicals Journal — Chem Jrl
Chemicals and Petro-Chemicals Journal — Chem Petro-Chem J
Chemicals and Petro-Chemicals Journal — CPCJD
Chemicals and Polymers Production Statistics — CAPPS
Chemicals for the Automotive Industry — Chem Automot Ind
Chemicals in Agriculture — Chem Agric
Chemicals in Progress Bulletin — Chem Prog Bull
Chemicals in the Oil Industry. Proceedings. International Symposium — Chem Oil Ind Proc Int Symp
Chemicals, Polymers, Rubber, and Plastics Industry News — Chem Polym Rubber Plast Ind News
Chemicke Listy — Chem Listy
Chemicke Listy — CHLSA
Chemicke Listy pro Vedu a Prumysl — Chem Listy Vedu Prum
Chemicke Obzor — Chem Obz
Chemicke Strojirenstvi. Stavitelstvi a Pristrojova Technika — Chem Strojir Stavitelstvi Pristrojova Tech
Chemicke Vlakna — Chem Vlakna
Chemicke Zvesti — Chem Zvesti
Chemicky Prumysl — Chem Prum
Chemicky Prumysl — CHPUA
Chemicky Prumysl. Priloha — Chem Prum Priloha
Chemico-Biological Interactions — CBINA
Chemico-Biological Interactions — Chem-Bio In
Chemico-Biological Interactions — Chem-Biol Interact
Chemico-Biological Interactions — Chem-Biol Interactions
Chemico-Biological Interactions — Chemico-Biol Interactions
Chemie a Lide — Chem Lide
Chemie and Techniek Revue. Bijlage — Chem Tech Rev Bijl
Chemie Arbeit in Werk und Labor — Chem Arb Werk Labor
Chemie der Erde — CERDA
Chemie der Erde — Chem Erde
Chemie der Nuklearen Entsorgung — Chem Nukl Entsorgung
Chemie der Zelle und Gewebe — Chem Zelle Gewebe
Chemie en Techniek (Amsterdam) — Chem Tech (Amsterdam)
Chemie. Experiment und Didaktik — CHEDC
Chemie. Experiment und Didaktik — Chem Exp Didakt
Chemie. Experiment und Technologie — Chem Exp + Technol
Chemie. Experiment und Technologie — Chem Exp Technol
Chemie fuer Labor und Betrieb — Chem Lab Betr
Chemie fuer Labor und Betrieb — CHLBA
Chemie im Kraftwerk — Chem Kraftwerk
Chemie in der Schule — Chem Sch
Chemie in Nichtwaessarigen Ionisierenden Loesungsmitteln — Chem Nichtwaessrigen Ionis Loesungsm
Chemie in Unserer Zeit — Chem Unserer Zeit
Chemie in Unserer Zeit — CUNZA
Chemie Kunststoffe Aktuell — Chem Kunst Aktuell
Chemie Magazine [*Belgium*] — Chem Mag
Chemie Magazine — CHMAD
Chemie, Mikrobiologie, Technologie der Lebensmittel — Chem Mikrobiol Technol Lebensm
Chemie, Physik, und Technologie der Kunststoffe in Einzeldarstellungen — Chem Phys Technol Kunst Einzeldarst

Chemie und Instrument (Leiden) — Chem Instrum Leiden
Chemie und Technik in der Landwirtschaft — Chem Tech Landwirt
Chemie und Technik in der Landwirtschaft — Chemie Tech Landw
Chemie und Technik Revue — Chem Tech Rev
Chemie und Verteidigung — Chem Verteidigung
Chemie-Anlagen und Verfahren — CHAVB
Chemie-Anlagen und Verfahren — Chem-Anlagen Verfahren
Chemiefasern/Textil-Industrie — CFTXA
Chemiefasern/Textil-Industrie — Chemfasern
Chemiefasern/Textilindustrie — Chemiefasern/Textilind
Chemiefasern/Textil-Industrie — Chemiefasern/Text-Ind
Chemiefasern/Textil-Industrie. Zeitschrift fuer die Gesamte Textil Industrie — RZE
Chemiefasern und Textil-Anwendungstechnik [*Later, Chemiefasern/Textil-Industrie*] — Chemiefasern Text-Anwendungstech
Chemiefasern und Textil-Anwendungstechnik/Textil-Industrie — CFTTA
Chemiefasern und Textil-Anwendungstechnik/Textil-Industrie — Chemiefasern + Text-Anwendungstech Text Ind
Chemie-Ingenieur-Technik — Chemie-Ingr-Tech
Chemie-Ingenieur-Technik — Chem-Ing-T
Chemie-Ingenieur-Technik — Chem-Ing-Tech
Chemie-Ingenieur-Technik — CITEA
Chemieunterricht — CMUTB
Chemija ir Chemine Technologija. Kauno-Politechnikos Instituto Jubiliejines Mokslines-Technines Konferencijos. Darbai — Chem Chem Technol Kauno Politech Inst Jubiliejines Mokslines
Chemik — CHGLA
Chemika Chronika — Chem Chron
Chemika Chronika. Epistemonike Ekdosis [*Greece*] — Chem Chron Epistem Ekdosis
Chemika Chronika. Genike Ekdosis — Chem Chron Genike Ekdosis
Chemika Chronika. Section A — Chem Chron A
Chemika Chronika. Section B — Chem Chron B
Chemiker- und Techniker-Zeitung. Allgemeine-Oesterreichische — Chem Tech Ztg
Chemiker Zeitung — Chem Zeitung
Chemiker-Zeitung — Chem Zeit
Chemiker-Zeitung — Chem-Zeitun
Chemiker Zeitung — Chom-Ztg
Chemiker-Zeitung — CMKZA
Chemiker-Zeitung. Chemie, Technische Chemie, Chemiewirtschaft; mit Chemie-Borse und Bezugsquellen fuer die Chemische Industrie — CZI
Chemiker-Zeitung. Chemische Apparatur — Chem-Ztg Chem Appar
Chemiker-Zeitung. Chemische Apparatur — CZCAA
Chemiker-Zeitung. Chemische Apparatur. Verfahrenstechnik — Chem Ztg Chem Appar Verfahrenstech
Chemins du Monde — Chem
Chemiosmotic Proton Circuits in Biological Membranes [*Monograph*] — Chemiosmotic Proton Circuits Biol Membr
Chemioterapia Oncologica — Chemioter Oncol
Chemisation of Socialistic Agriculture — Chem Soc Agric
Chemisch Magazine — CHM
Chemisch Magazine — CMAGD
Chemisch Metallurgische Zeitschrift — Chem Metall Z
Chemisch Technische Fabrikant — Chem Tech Fabr
Chemisch Technische Rundschau und Anzeiger der Chemischen Industrie — Chem Tech Rundsch Anz Chem Ind
Chemisch Technische Uebersicht — Chem Tech Uebers
Chemisch Weekblad [*Later, Chemisch Weekblad/Chemische Courant*] — Chem Weekbl
Chemisch Weekblad [*Later, Chemisch Weekblad/Chemische Courant*] — CHWEA
Chemisch Weekblad/Chemische Courant — CHW
Chemisch Weekblad Magazine [*Later, Chemisch Magazine*] — Chem Weekb Mag
Chemische Ackersmann — Chem Ackersmann
Chemische Analyse — Chem Analyse
Chemische Annalen fuer die Freunde der Naturlehre, Arzneygelahrtheit, Haushaltungskunst, Manufacturen — Chem Ann Freunde Naturl
Chemische Apparatur — Chem Appar
Chemische Apparatur. Supplement — Chem Appar Suppl
Chemische Berichte — CHBEA
Chemische Berichte — Chem Ber
Chemische en Pharmaceutische Technik (Dordrecht, Netherlands) — Chem Pharm Tech (Dordrecht Neth)
Chemische Fabrik — Chem Fab
Chemische Fabrik [*Germany*] — Chem Fabr
Chemische Industrie — Chemische
Chemische Industrie [*Duesseldorf*] — CHIUA
Chemische Industrie (Berlin) — Chem Ind (Berlin)
Chemische Industrie (Berlin). Gemeinschaftsausgabe — Chem Ind (Berlin) Gemeinschaftsausg
Chemische Industrie (Berlin). Nachrichtenausgabe — Chem Ind (Berlin) Nachrichtenausg
Chemische Industrie (Duesseldorf) — Chem Ind (Duesseldorf)
Chemische Industrie (Duesseldorf). Supplementum — Chem Ind Duesseldorf Suppl
Chemische Industrie. English Edition — Chem Ind Engl Ed
Chemische Industrie International — Chem Ind Int
Chemische Industrie International [*English Translation*] — CHIIA
Chemische Industrie International (English Translation) [*Germany*] — Chem Ind Int (Engl Transl)
Chemische Industrie. Jahrbuch — Chem Ind Jahrb
Chemische Industrie. Zeitschrift fuer die Deutsche Chemiewirtschaft — CEN
Chemische Nachrichten — Chem Nachr
Chemische Novitaeten — Chem Novit
Chemische Praxis — Chem Prax
Chemische Produktion — Chem Prod
Chemische Produktion — CHPRD
Chemische Reihe — Chem Reihe
Chemische Revue ueber die Fett und Harz Industrie — Chem Rev Fett Harz Ind
Chemische Rundschau — Chem Rund
Chemische Rundschau — Chem Rundschau
Chemische Rundschau [*Solothurn, Switzerland*] — CHRUA
Chemische Rundschau. Europaeische Wochenzeitung fuer Chemie, Pharmazeutik, und die Lebensmittelindustrie — CHX
Chemische Rundschau. Farbbeilage — Chem Rundsch Farbbeilage
Chemische Rundschau fuer Mitteleuropa und der Balkan — Chem Rdsch Mitteleur
Chemische Rundschau Magazine — Chem Rundsch Mag
Chemische Rundschau (Solothurn) [*Switzerland*] — Chem Rundsch (Solothurn)
Chemische Technik — Chem Tech
Chemische Technik (Berlin) — Chem Tech Berlin
Chemische Technik (Heidelberg) — Chem Tech (Heidelberg)
Chemische Technik (Leipzig) — Chem Tech Leipzig
Chemische Umschau auf dem Gebiete der Fette, Oele, Wachse, und Harze — Chem Umsch Geb Fette Oele Wachse Harze
Chemischer Apparatebau — Chem Apparatebau
Chemischer Informationsdienst — Chem Inf Dienst
Chemischer Informationsdienst — Chem Infd
Chemischer Informationsdienst — Chem Informationsdienst
Chemischer Informationsdienst — ChemInform
Chemischer Informationsdienst — CMIDB
Chemischer Informationsdienst. Anorganische und Physikalische Chemie — Chem Informationsdienst Anorg Phys Chem
Chemischer Informationsdienst. Organische Chemie — Chem Informationsdienst Org Chem
Chemisches Journal fuer die Freunde der Naturlehre — Chem J Freunde Natur
Chemisches Zentralblatt — C
Chemisches Zentralblatt — Chem Zent Bl
Chemisches Zentralblatt — Chem Zentr
Chemisches Zentralblatt — Chem Zentralbl
Chemisch-Pharmaceutisches Centralblatt — Chem Pharm Centralbl
Chemisch-Technische Industrie — Chem Tech Ind
Chemisch-Technische Rundschau (Berlin) — Chem Tech Rundsch (Berlin)
Chemisch-Technische Umschau — Chem Tech Umsch
Chemist and Druggist — Chem Drug
Chemist and Druggist Export Review — Chem Drug Export Rev
Chemist-Analyst — CHANA
Chemistry — CHRYA
Chemistry. A European Journal — Chem Eur J
Chemistry and Biochemistry of Amino Acids, Peptides, and Proteins — Chem Biochem Amino Acids Pept Proteins
Chemistry and Biochemistry of Plant Pigments [*Monograph*] — Chem Biochem Plant Pig
Chemistry and Biochemistry of Walnut Trees — Chem Biochem Walnut Trees
Chemistry and Biology [*London*] — Chem Biol
Chemistry and Biology of Beta-Lactam Antibiotics [*Monograph*] — Chem Biol Beta Lactam Antibiot
Chemistry and Biology of Hydroxamic Acids. Proceedings. International Symposium on Chemistry and Biology of Hydroxamic Acids — Chem Biol Hydroxamic Acids Proc Int Symp
Chemistry and Biology of Peptides. Proceedings. American Peptide Symposium — Chem Biol Pept Proc Am Pept Symp
Chemistry and Biology (Tokyo) — Chem Biol (Tokyo)
Chemistry and Chemical Engineering — Chem Chem Eng
Chemistry and Chemical Industry [*North Korea*] — Chem Chem Ind
Chemistry and Ecology — Chem Ecol
Chemistry and Industry — Chem & Ind
Chemistry and Industry — Chem Ind
Chemistry and Industry — Chem Indus
Chemistry and Industry — Chemy Ind
Chemistry and Industry in New Zealand — Chem Ind NZ
Chemistry and Industry (London) — Chem Ind (Lond)
Chemistry and Industry (London) — Chem Ind London
Chemistry and Industry of Forest Products — Chem Ind For Prod
Chemistry and Industry Review — Chem Ind Rev
Chemistry and Life — Chem Life
Chemistry and Life — Chemy Life
Chemistry and Pharmacology of Drugs — Chem Pharmacol Drugs
Chemistry and Physics of Carbon — Chem Phys Carbon
Chemistry and Physics of Carbon — CPHCA
Chemistry and Physics of Fracture — Chem Phy Fract
Chemistry and Physics of Lipids — Chem Phys L
Chemistry and Physics of Lipids — Chem Phys Lipids
Chemistry and Physics of Solid Surfaces — Chem Phy Solid Surf
Chemistry and Software — Chem Software
Chemistry and Technology of Fuels and Oils — Chem Tech Fuels Oils
Chemistry and Technology of Fuels and Oils — Chem Technol Fuels Oils
Chemistry and Technology of Fuels and Oils (English Translation) — Chem Technol Fuels Oils Engl Transl
Chemistry and Technology of Pectin — Chem Technol Pectin
Chemistry and Use of Organophosphorus Compounds. Transactions. Conference — Chem Use Organophosphorus Compd Trans Conf
Chemistry and Uses of Molybdenum. Proceedings. International Conference — Chem Uses Molybdenum Proc Int Conf
Chemistry Express. Journal. Kinki Chemical Society — Chem Express
Chemistry for Protection of the Environment. Proceedings. International Conference — Chem Prot Environ Proc Int Conf
Chemistry for the Future. Proceedings. IUPAC Congress — Chem Future Proc IUPAC Congr
Chemistry in Agriculture. International Congress — Chem Agric Int Congr

Chemistry in Australia — Chem Aust
Chemistry in Britain — Chem Br
Chemistry in Britain — Chem Brit
Chemistry in Britain — Chem in Br
Chemistry in Britain — Chem in Britain
Chemistry in Britain — Chems Brtn
Chemistry in Canada — Chem Can
Chemistry in Canada — Chem Cda
Chemistry in Ecology — CE
Chemistry in New Zealand — Chem NZ
Chemistry in Sierra Leone — Chem Sierra Leone
Chemistry in Sri Lanka — Chem Sri Lanka
Chemistry International — Chem Int
Chemistry International — CI
Chemistry (Kyoto). Supplement [*Japan*] — Chemistry (Kyoto) Suppl
Chemistry Leaflet — Chem Leafl
Chemistry Letters — Chem Lett
Chemistry of Amidines and Imidates [*Monograph*] — Chem Amidines Imidates
Chemistry of Foods and Beverages. Recent Developments [*Monograph*] — Chem Foods Beverages Recent Def
Chemistry of Heterocyclic Compounds — Chem Heterocycl Comp
Chemistry of Heterocyclic Compounds (English Translation) — Chem Heterocycl Compd (Engl Transl)
Chemistry of Heterocyclic Compounds. Proceedings. Symposium on Chemistry of Hetercyclic Compounds — Chem Heterocycl Compd Proc Symp
Chemistry of Heterocyclic Compounds (USSR) — Chem Heterocycl Comp (USSR)
Chemistry of High Polymers [*Japan*] — Chem High Polym
Chemistry of Inorganic Ring Systems — Chem Inorg Ring Syst
Chemistry of Interfaces. Proceeding. European Conference — Chem Interfaces Proc Eur Conf
Chemistry of Lignans [*Monograph*] — Chem Lignans
Chemistry of Marine Sediments [*Monograph*] — Chem Mar Sediments
Chemistry of Materials — Chem Mater
Chemistry of Mercury [*monograph*] — Chem Mercury
Chemistry of Metal CVD (Chemical Vapor Deposition) [*monograph*] — Chem Met CVD
Chemistry of Natural Compounds — Chem Nat Compd
Chemistry of Natural Compounds — Chem Nat Compounds
Chemistry of Natural Compounds (English Translation) — Chem Nat Compd Engl Transl
Chemistry of Non-Aqueous Solvents [*Monograph*] — Chem Non Aqueous Solvents
Chemistry of Organic Selenium and Tellurium Compounds [*Monograph*] — Chem Org Selenium Tellurium Compd
Chemistry of Organic Sulfur Compounds — Chem Org Sulfur Compd
Chemistry of Peptides and Proteins — Chem Pept Proteins
Chemistry of Peroxides [*monograph*] — Chem Peroxides
Chemistry of Plant Protection — Chem Plant Prot
Chemistry of Sulphinic Acids, Esters, and Their Derivatives — Chem Sulphinic Acids Esters Their Deriv
Chemistry of the Carbon-Carbon Triple Bond [*Monograph*] — Chem Carbon Carbon Triple Bond
Chemistry of the Hydrazo, Azo, and Azoxy Groups [*Monograph*] — Chem Hydrazo Azo Azoxy Groups
Chemistry, Oil, and Gas in Romania — Chem Oil Gas Rom
Chemistry, Oil, and Gas in Romania — COGCA
Chemistry, Physical Chemistry, and Applications of Surface Active Substances. Proceedings. International Congress on Surface Active Substances — Chem Phys Chem Appl Surf Act Subst Proc Int Congr
Chemistry, Physics, and Application of Surface Active Substances. Proceedings. International Congress on Surface Active Substances — Chem Phys Appl Surf Act Subst Proc Int Congr
Chemistry Review (Deddington, United Kingdom) — Chem Rev Deddington UK
Chemistry Seminar for Honours Students. University of Singapore — Chem Semin Honours Stud Univ Singapore
Chemists Quarterly — Chem Q
Chemoautomatyka — CMAUA
Chemometrics and Intelligent Laboratory Systems — Chemom Intell Lab Syst
Chemometrics and Species Identification — Chemom Species Identif
Chemoreception in Marine Organisms [*Monograph*] — Chemorecept Mar Org
Chemoreception in the Carotid Body. International Workshop — Chemorecept Carotid Body Int Workshop
Chemotherapie Journal — Chemother J
Chemotherapy — Chemothera
Chemotherapy and Immunity — Chemother Immun
Chemotherapy Fact Sheet — Chemother Fact Sheet
Chemotherapy of Infectious Disease [*monograph*] — Chemother Infect Dis
Chemotherapy. Proceedings. International Congresss of Chemotherapy — Chemother Proc Int Congr Chemother
Chemotherapy. Proceedings of the International Congress of Chemotherapy — Chemother Pro Int Congr Chemother
Chemsa — CHEMD
Chemtech — CHTED
CHEMTECH — ICTK
Chemtech (United States) [*Formerly, Chemical Technology*] — Chemtech (US)
Chemtracts. Analytical, Physical, and Inorganic Chemistry — Chemtracts Anal Phys Inorg Chem
Chemtracts. Inorganic Chemistry — Chemtracts Inorg Chem
Chemtracts. Organic Chemistry — Chemtracts Org Chem
Chemurgic Digest — Chem Digest
Chemurgic Digest — Chemurg Dig
Chemurgic Digest — Chemurgic Dig
Chemurgic Papers — Chemurg Pap
Chercheurs de la Wallonie — Ch W
Chernaya Metallurgiya — Chern Metall
Chesapeake Bay Institute. Johns Hopkins University. Technical Report — Chesapeake Bay Inst Johns Hopkins Univ Tech Rep
Chesapeake Science — Chesapeake Sci
Chest, Heart, and Stroke Journal — Chest Heart Stroke J
Chest Surgery Clinics of North America — Chest Surg Clin N Am
Chester and North Wales Architectural, Archaeological, and Historical Society. Journal — CASJ
Chesterton Review — C Rev
Chesterton Review — Chesterton Rev
ChET. Chemie. Experiment und Technologie [*Germany*] — ChET Chem Exp Technol
Chetham Society — Chet Soc
Chetvertichnyi Period — Chetvertichn Period
Cheval de Troie — Chev Troie
Chevron World — CHWOD
Chi Kuang — CHIKD
Chi Lin Ta Hsueh Hsueh Pao. Tzu Jan K'o Hsueh Pan — CLTPD
Chiake Epitheoresis — ChE
Chiang Mai Medical Bulletin — Chiang Mai Med Bull
Chiangmai University. Science Faculty. Journal — Chiangmai Univ Sci Fac J
Chiba Daigaku Engeigakubu Gakujutsu Hokoko — CDEGA
Chiba Daigaku Kogakubu Kenkyu Hokoku — CDKKA
Chiba Foundation. Colloquia on Ageing — Chiba Found Colloq Ageing
Chiba Medical Journal — Chiba Med J
Chiba-Ken Nogyo Shikenjo Kenkyu Hokoku — CKNSA
Chicago — ICHI
Chicago Academy of Sciences. Bulletin. Natural History Miscellanea — Chicago Acad Sci Bull Nat History Misc
Chicago Architectural Journal — Chicago Archtl Jnl
Chicago Art Institute. Bulletin — Chicago Art Inst Bul
Chicago Art Institute. Calendar — Chicago Art Inst Cal
Chicago Art Institute. Quarterly — Chicago Art Inst Q
Chicago Bar Record — Chi B Rec
Chicago Bar Record — Chicago B Rec
Chicago Bar Record — Chicago Bar Rec
Chicago Board Options Exchange Guide. Commerce Clearing House — Chicago Bd Options Ex Guide CCH
Chicago Chemical Bulletin — Chicag Chem Bull
Chicago Daily News — CDN
Chicago Daily News. Panorama — CDNP
Chicago Dairy Produce — Chicago Dairy Prod
Chicago Dental Society. Review — CDS Rev
Chicago Field Museum of Natural History — Chicago Fld Mus Nat Hist
Chicago Herpetological Society. Newsletter — Chicago Herpetol Soc Newsl
Chicago Historical Society. Proceedings — Chic Hist Soc Proc
Chicago History of Science and Medicine — Chicago His
Chicago History of Science and Medicine — Chicago Hist Sci Med
Chicago Jewish Forum — CJF
Chicago Journal of Theoretical Computer Science — Chicago J Theoret Comput Sci
Chicago Journalism Review — Chi Jrl R
Chicago Journalism Review — CJR
Chicago Lectures in Mathematics — Chicago Lectures in Math
Chicago Lectures in Physics — Chicago Lectures Phys
Chicago Legal News — Chic Leg News
Chicago Library System Communicator — Chi Lib Sys Com
Chicago Medical Examiner — Chicago Med Exam
Chicago Medical Record — Chicago Med Rec
Chicago Medical Recorder — Chicago Med Recorder
Chicago Medical School Quarterly — Chic Med Sch Q
Chicago Medicine — Chicago Med
Chicago Natural History Museum. Annual Report — Chic Nat Hist Mus Annu Rep
Chicago Naturalist — Chicago Nat
Chicago Psychoanalytic Literature Index — Chicago Psychoanal Lit Ind
Chicago Psychoanalytic Literature Index — Chicago Psychoanal Lit Index
Chicago Review — Chic R
Chicago Review — Chicago R
Chicago Review — Chicago Rev
Chicago Review — ChiR
Chicago Review — PCHI
Chicago Schools Journal — Chicago Sch J
Chicago Studies — Chicago Stds
Chicago Studies — Chicago Studs
Chicago Studies [*Mundelein, IL*] — ChicSt
Chicago Sun Book Week — CSBW
Chicago Sunday Tribune — CST
Chicago Symphony Orchestra. Program Notes — Chi Sym
Chicago Theological Seminary. Register — ChicTSemReg
Chicago Theological Seminary. Register — CTS Reg
Chicago Tribune — Chicago Trib
Chicago Tribune — Chicg Trib
Chicago Tribune — CHTRD
Chicago Tribune — CT
Chicago Tribune Magazine — Chi T M
Chicago. University. Department of Geography. Research Paper — Chic Univ Dep Geogr Res Pap
Chicago. University. Department of Geography. Research Paper — Chicago Univ Dept Geography Research Paper
Chicago-Kent Law Review — Chicago-Kent L Rev
Chicago-Kent Law Review — Chi-Kent L Rev
Chicago-Kent Law Review — Chi-Kent LR
Chicago-Kent Law Review — Chi-Kent Rev
Chicago-Kent Law Review — CK

Chicago-Kent Law Review — CKLR
Chicano Law Review — Chicano L Rev
Chicorel Abstracts to Reading and Learning Disabilities — CARLD
Chicorel Abstracts to Reading and Learning Disabilities — Chicorel Abst Read Learn Disab
Chicorel Abstracts to Reading and Learning Disabilities — Chicorel Abstr Read Learn Disabil
Chief Counsel. Annual Report. United States Internal Revenue Service — Chief Coun
Chief Executive — CE
Chief Executive — CEX
Chief Executive — CHE
Chief Executive Monthly — Chief Executive Mon
Chieh P'ou Hsueh Pao — CPHPA
Chih Wu Hsueh Pao — CHWHA
Chih Wu Hsueh Pao. Acta Botanica Sinica — Chih Wu Hsueh Pao Acta Bot Sin
Chi'i Hsiang Hsueh Pao — CHIHA
Chiiki Kaihatsu — CHKAD
Chijil Kwa Chiri — CHKWA
Chijil Kwangmul Chosa Yongu Pokoso — RGMNA
Chikusan Shikenjo Kenkyu — CSKKA
Chikyukagaku (Geochemistry) Nagoya — Chikyukagaku (Geochem)
Chikyukagaku (Nippon Chikyu Kagakkai) — CKNKD
Child Abuse and Neglect — Child Abuse Negl
Child and Youth Care Quarterly — Child Youth Care Q
Child and Youth Services — Child & Youth Serv
Child and Youth Services — Child Youth Serv
Child Behaviour Therapy — Child Behav Ther
Child Care Health and Development — Child Care Health Dev
Child Care Information Exchange — Child Care Inf Exch
Child Care Quarterly — Child Care
Child Care Quarterly — Child Care Q
Child Development — CD
Child Development — CHDEA
Child Development — Child Dev
Child Development — Child Devel
Child Development — GCHD
Child Development Abstracts — ChildDevAb
Child Development Abstracts and Bibliography — CDAB
Child Development Abstracts and Bibliography — Child Dev Abstr Bibliogr
Child Development Abstracts and Bibliography — Child Developm Absts Biblio
Child Health and Development — Child Health Dev
Child Health Magazine — Child Health M
Child Nephrology and Urology — Child Nephr
Child Protective Services in New York State. Annual Report — Child Prot Serv NY St Ann Rep
Child Psychiatry and Human Development — Child Psych
Child Psychiatry and Human Development — Child Psych & Human Devel
Child Psychiatry and Human Development — Child Psychiatry Hum Dev
Child Psychiatry Quarterly — Child Psy Q
Child Study Journal — Child St J
Child Study Journal — Child Stud J
Child Study Journal — CHSTA
Child Welfare — Child Wel
Child Welfare — GCHW
Childhood Education — C Ed
Childhood Education — CE
Childhood Education — Child Ed
Childhood Education — Childh Educ
Childhood Education — GCED
Childhood Environment and Adult Disease — Child Environ Adult Dis
Childhood Obesity — Child Obes
Children and Exercise — Child Exercise
Children and Exercise. Proceedings. International Symposium — Child Exercise Proc Int Symp
Children in Contemporary Society — Child Contemp Soc
Children in the Tropics (English Edition) — Child Trop (Engl Ed)
Children. The Parents' Magazine — Child Par M
Children Today — Child Today
Children Today — CT
Children Today — GCTY
Children's Book Review Index — CBRI
Children's Book Review Service — CBRS
Children's Business — Childs Bsn
Children's Digest — Child D
Children's Health Care — Child Health Care
Children's Health Care. Journal of the Association for the Care of Children's Health — CHC J
Children's Legal Rights Journal — Child Legal Rights J
Children's Libraries Newsletter — Ch Lib Newsl
Children's Libraries Newsletter — Child Lib News
Children's Libraries Newsletter — Childrens Lib News
Children's Libraries Newsletter — CLN
Children's Literature — Child Lit
Children's Literature — ChildL
Children's Literature — Childr Lit
Children's Literature Abstracts — Child Lit Abstr
Children's Literature Abstracts — CLA
Children's Literature. An International Journal — PCLT
Children's Literature Association. Quarterly — CLAQ
Children's Literature in Education — Child Lit Educ
Children's Literature Review — CLR
Children's Magazine Guide — Child Mag Guide
Children's Playmate Magazine — Playmate
Children's Theatre Review — Child Theat Rev
Children's Understanding of Reading Language — CURL
Child's Nervous System — Childs Nerv Syst
Chile Economic News — Chile Econ N
Chile Economic Report — CHC
Chile Economic Report — Chile Econ
Chile. Universidad. Departamento de Astronomia. Publicaciones — CUDPB
Chile. Universidad. Facultad de Ciencias Fisica y Matematicas. Instituto de Geologia. Publicacion — Chile Univ Fac Cienc Fis Mat Inst Geol Publ
Chile-America (Roma) — CAR
Chilean Nitrate Agricultural Service. Information — Chil Nitrate Agric Serv Inf
Chillan, Chile. Estacion Experimental. Boletin Tecnico — Chillan Chile Estac Exp Bol Tec
Chilton Market Forecast — Chilton MF
Chilton's Food Engineering — Chiltons Food Eng
Chilton's Food Engineering — Food Engin
Chilton's Food Engineering International — Chiltons Food Eng Int
Chimica — Chim
Chimica Acta Turcica — CATUA
Chimica Acta Turcica — Chim Acta Turc
Chimica delle Pitture-Vernici e Smalti — Chim Pitture Vernici Smalti
Chimica Didactica — CHDID
Chimica Didactica — Chim Didact
Chimica e l'Industria — Chim Ind
Chimica e l'Industria — Chimica e Ind
Chimica e l'Industria (Milan) — Chim Ind Milan
Chimica e l'Industria (Milan). Supplemento — Chim Ind Milan Suppl
Chimica e l'Industria (Milan). Supplemento. Quaderni dell'Ingegnere Chimico Italiano — Chim Ind Milan Suppl Quad Ing Chim Ital
Chimica e l'Industria (Milano) — Chimica Ind (Milano)
Chimica nel Mondo — Chim Mondo
Chimica nell Industria, nell Agricultura, nella Biologia e nelle Realizzazioni Corporative — Chim Ind Agric Biol Realizz Corp
Chimica nella Scuola — Chim Sc
Chimica Therapeutica — Chim Ther
Chimie Actualites [*France*] — Chim Actual
Chimie Actualites — Chimie Act
Chimie Analitica (Bucharest) [*Romania*] — Chim Anal (Bucharest)
Chimie Analytique — Chim Analyt
Chimie Analytique (Paris) — Chim Anal (Paris)
Chimie, Chimie Physique, et Applications des Agents de Surface. Compte-Rendu. Congres International de la Detergence — Chim Chim Phys Appl Agents Surf CR Congr Int Deterg
Chimie des Hautes Temperatures. Colloque National — Chim Hautes Temp Colloq Natl
Chimie des Peintures — Chim Peint
Chimie des Peintures, des Encres, des Plastiques, des Adhesifs, et de Leurs Composants — Chim Pein Encres Plast Adhes Leurs Composants
Chimie des Peintures et Vernis — Chim Peint Vernis
Chimie des Substances Naturelles — Chim Subst Nat
Chimie et Industrie — Chimie & Ind
Chimie et Industrie - Genie Chimique — Chim Ind - Genie Chim
Chimie et Industrie (Paris) — Chim Ind (Paris)
Chimie et Industrie (Paris). Supplement Mensuel — Chim Ind (Paris) Suppl Mens
Chimie et Technique — Chim Tech
Chimie Macromoleculaire — Chim Macromol
Chimie Magazine — Chimie Mag
Chimie, Microbiologie, Technologie Alimentaire — Chim Microbiol Technol Aliment
Chimie Moderne [*France*] — Chim Mod
Chimie Moderne — CIMOA
Chimie Nouvelle — Chim Nouv
Chimie, Physique, et Applications Pratiques des Agents de Surface. Compte-Rendu. Congres International de la Detergence — Chim Phys Appl Prat Agents Surf CR Congr Int Deterg
Chimie Pure et Appliquee — Chim Pure Appl
Chimie Therapeutique — Chim Ther
Chimika Chronika — Chim Chron
Chimika Chronika (Athens) — Chim Chron (Athens)
Chimika Chronika. General Edition — Chim Chron Gen Ed
Chimika Chronika. Section A — Chim Chron A
Chimika Chronika. Section B — Chim Chron B
Chimizarea Agriculturii — Chim Agric
China Agriculture to the Year 2000 — China Agri
China Aktuell — CAW
China Brewing — China Brew
China Business and Trade — China Bus Trade
China Business Report — CBR
China Business Review — China Bus R
China Business Review — CHR
China Business Review — UCH
China Chemical Reporter — China Chem Rep
China Chemical Week — China Chem Week
China Clay Trade Review — China Clay Trade Rev
China Cotton Journal/Shang Ch'ang Ho Chi Hua Sha Lien Hui K'an — China Cotton J
China Daily — China Dly
China Daily (North American Edition) — China Dly North Am Ed
China Economic Model and Projections — China Econ
China Economic Report — China Econ Rept
China Environmental Science — China Environ Sci
China Fisheries Monthly — China Fish Mon
China Geographer [*Los Angeles*] — China Geog
China Informatie — CXE
China International Business — China Internat Bus
China Journal — China J

China. Journal of Chinese Materia Medica — China J Chin Mater Med
China Journal of Science and Arts — China J Sci Arts
China Law Reporter — China L Rep
China Long-Term Development Issues and Options — China Long
China Market — EAR
China Medical Journal — China Med J
China Medical Missionary Journal — China Med Miss J
China News Analysis [*Hong Kong*] — China News Anal
China News Analysis — CNA
China Newsletter — CHI
China Phone Book and Business Directory — CPB
China Pictorial — CP
China Pulp and Paper — China Pulp Pap
China Quarterly [*London*] — China Q
China Quarterly — China Quart
China Quarterly — ChiQ
China Quarterly — CQ
China Quarterly — CQO
China Quarterly — GCHQ
China Reconstructs — China Recon
China Reconstructs — China Reconstr
China Reconstructs — CR
China Report — China Rep
China Report — CRB
China Report — CRep
China Report. Science and Technology — China Rep Sci Technol
China Review — China Rev
China Review (Hong Kong) — CRHK
China Science and Technology Abstracts — CTASD
China Science and Technology Abstracts. Series I. Mathematics, Astronomy, Physics — China Sci Tech Abstracts Ser I Math Astronom Phys
China Science and Technology Abstracts. Series II. Chemistry, Earth Science, Energy Sources — China Sci Technol Abstr Ser II
China Science and Technology Abstracts. Series III. Industry Technology — China Sci & Technol Abstr Ser III
China Surfactant Detergent and Cosmetics — China Surfactant Deterg Cosmet
China To-Day — CT
China Trade and Economic Newsletter [*London*] — CEL
China Trade Report — China Trade Rep
China Trade Report — CTN
China Weekly — CW
China Weekly Review — China W R
China Weekly Review — China Wkly Rev
China Yearbook — China Ybk
China-Japan-United States Trilateral Seminar on Organometallic Chemistry — China Jpn US Trilateral Semin Organomet Chem
China's Foreign Trade — CFT
China's Foreign Trade [*Peking*] — China For Tr
China's Medicine — China Med
China's Medicine — China's Med
China's Medicine — CHMEB
China's Medicine [*Peking*] — CHMEBA
China's Medicine (Peking) — China's Med (Peking)
China's Screen — China's
Chinchilla. Anales Historicos de la Medicina en General y Biografico-Bibliograficos de la Espanola en Particular — Chinchilla Anal Hist Med Gen Bio Bib
Chinese Agricultural Science [*People's Republic of China*] — Chin Agric Sci
Chinese and Japanese Repository of Facts and Events in Science, History, and Art Relating to Eastern Asia — Chin Jap Repos Facts Events Sci
Chinese Animal Husbandry and Veterinary Medicine [*People's Republic of China*] — Chin Anim Husb Vet Med
Chinese Animal Husbandry Journal — Chin Anim Husb J
Chinese Annals of Mathematics [*Shanghai*] — Chinese Ann Math
Chinese Annals of Mathematics. Series A. Shuxue Niankan — Chinese Ann Math Ser A
Chinese Annals of Mathematics. Series B. Shuxue Niankan — Chinese Ann Math Ser B
Chinese Art Society of America. Archives — ACAS
Chinese Art Society of America. Archives — ACASA
Chinese Astronomy [*Later, Chinese Astronomy and Astrophysics*] — Chin Astron
Chinese Astronomy [*Later, Chinese Astronomy and Astrophysics*] — Chinese Astronom
Chinese Astronomy and Astrophysics — CAA
Chinese Astronomy and Astrophysics — Chinese Astronom Astrophys
Chinese Atomic Energy Council. Bulletin — Chin At Energy Counc Bull
Chinese Bee Journal [*Taiwan*] — Chin Bee J
Chinese Biochemical Society. Journal — Chin Biochem Soc J
Chinese Bioscience — Chin Biosci
Chinese Chemical Industry and Engineering — Chin Chem Ind Eng
Chinese Cooperative Catalog [*Library of Congress*] — CCC
Chinese Culture — C Cul
Chinese Culture — ChC
Chinese Culture — Chin Cult
Chinese Culture — Chinese Cult
Chinese Economic Journal — Chin Econ J
Chinese Economic Monthly — Chin Econ Monthly
Chinese Economic Studies — CES
Chinese Economic Studies — Chin Econ S
Chinese Economic Studies [*New York*] — Chin Econ Stud
Chinese Economic Studies — Chinese Econ Studies
Chinese Education — Chin Educ
Chinese Forestry Science — Chin For Sci
Chinese International Summer School of Physics — Chin Int Summer Sch Phys
Chinese Journal of Administration — CJA
Chinese Journal of Anesthesiology — Chin J Anesthesiol
Chinese Journal of Animal Husbandry — Chin J Anim Husb
Chinese Journal of Animal Science — Chin J Anim Sci
Chinese Journal of Antibiotics — Chin J Antibiot
Chinese Journal of Applied Chemistry — Chin J Appl Chem
Chinese Journal of Applied Ecology — Chin J Appl Ecol
Chinese Journal of Applied Mechanics — Chinese J Appl Mech
Chinese Journal of Applied Probability and Statistics — Chinese J Appl Probab Statist
Chinese Journal of Archaeology — Chin J Archaeol
Chinese Journal of Atomic and Molecular Physics — Chin J At Mol Phys
Chinese Journal of Biotechnology — Chin J Biotechnol
Chinese Journal of Cardiology — Chin J Cardiol
Chinese Journal of Cardiology (Beijing) — Chin J Cardiol (Beijing)
Chinese Journal of Cell Biology — Chin J Cell Biol
Chinese Journal of Chromatography — Chin J Chromatogr
Chinese Journal of Clinical Pharmacology — Chin J Clin Pharmacol
Chinese Journal of Computers — Chin J Comput
Chinese Journal of Contemporary Mathematics — Chinese J Contemp Math
Chinese Journal of Dermatology [*People's Republic of China*] — Chin J Dermatol
Chinese Journal of Disinfection — Chin J Disinfect
Chinese Journal of Endocrinology and Metabolism — Chin J Endocrinol Metab
Chinese Journal of Epidemiology — Chin J Epidemiol
Chinese Journal of Experimental and Clinical Virology — Chin J Exp Clin Virol
Chinese Journal of Geochemistry — Chin J Geochem
Chinese Journal of Gynecology and Obstetrics [*People's Republic of China*] — Chin J Gynecol Obstet
Chinese Journal of Hematology — Chin J Hematol
Chinese Journal of High Pressure Physics — Chin J High Pressure Phys
Chinese Journal of Immunology — Chin J Immunol
Chinese Journal of Industrial Hygiene and Occupational Diseases — Chin J Ind Hyg Occup Dis
Chinese Journal of Infrared Research — Chin J Infrared Res
Chinese Journal of Infrared Research. A — Chin J Infrared Res A
Chinese Journal of Internal Medicine — CHHNAB
Chinese Journal of Internal Medicine [*People's Republic of China*] — Chin J Intern Med
Chinese Journal of Lasers — Chin J Lasers
Chinese Journal of Low Temperature Physics — Chin J Low Temp Phys
Chinese Journal of Magnetic Resonance — Chin J Magn Reson
Chinese Journal of Marine Drugs — Chin J Mar Drugs
Chinese Journal of Materials Science — Chin J Mater Sci
Chinese Journal of Mathematics — Chinese J Math
Chinese Journal of Mechanical Engineering — Chin J Mech Eng
Chinese Journal of Mechanics [*People's Republic of China*] — Chin J Mech
Chinese Journal of Medicinal Chemistry — Chin J Med Chem
Chinese Journal of Metal Science and Technology — Chin J Met Sci Technol
Chinese Journal of Microbiology [*Later, Chinese Journal of Microbiology and Immunology*] — Chin J Microbiol
Chinese Journal of Microbiology [*Later, Chinese Journal of Microbiology and Immunology*] — CJMBAE
Chinese Journal of Microbiology and Immunology [*Taipei*] — CKWCD9
Chinese Journal of Microbiology and Immunology [*Beijing*] — ZWMZDP
Chinese Journal of Microbiology and Immunology (Beijing) — Chin J Microbiol Immunol (Beijing)
Chinese Journal of Microbiology and Immunology (Taipei) — Chin J Microbiol Immunol (Taipei)
Chinese Journal of Neurology and Psychiatry — Chin J Neurol Psychiatry
Chinese Journal of Nonferrous Metals — Chin J Nonferrous Met
Chinese Journal of Nuclear Physics — Chin J Nucl Phys
Chinese Journal of Numerical Mathematics and Applications — Chinese J Numer Math Appl
Chinese Journal of Nutrition — Chin J Nutr
Chinese Journal of Obstetrics and Gynecology — Chin J Obstet Gynecol
Chinese Journal of Oceanology and Limnology — Chin J Oceanol Limnol
Chinese Journal of Oceanology and Limnology — CJOL
Chinese Journal of Oncology — CCLCDY
Chinese Journal of Oncology — Chin J Oncol
Chinese Journal of Operations Research — Chinese J Oper Res
Chinese Journal of Ophthalmology — Chin J Ophthalmol
Chinese Journal of Ophthalmology [*People's Republic of China*] — Chin J Ophthalmology
Chinese Journal of Organic Chemistry — Chin J Org Chem
Chinese Journal of Orthopedics — Chin J Orthop
Chinese Journal of Orthopedics — ZGZAE6
Chinese Journal of Otorhinolaryngology [*People's Republic of China*] — Chin J Otorhinolaryngol
Chinese Journal of Parasitic and Infectious Diseases — Chin J Parasit Infect Dis
Chinese Journal of Pathology — Chin J Pathol
Chinese Journal of Pediatrics [*People's Republic of China*] — Chin J Pediatr
Chinese Journal of People's Health — Chin J Peoples Health
Chinese Journal of Pharmaceuticals — Chin J Pharm
Chinese Journal of Pharmacology and Toxicology — Chin J Pharmacol Toxicol
Chinese Journal of Physics — Chin J Phys
Chinese Journal of Physics [*Peking*] [*English translation*] — CHJPB
Chinese Journal of Physics [*Taipei*] — CJOPA
Chinese Journal of Physics (New York) — Chin J Phys (New York)
Chinese Journal of Physics (Peking) — Chin J Phys (Peking)
Chinese Journal of Physics (Peking) — Chinese J Phys (Peking)
Chinese Journal of Physics (Taipei) — Chin J Phys (Taipei)
Chinese Journal of Physiology — Chin J Physiol
Chinese Journal of Physiology — CJPYA
Chinese Journal of Physiology (Beijing) — Chin J Physiol Beijing
Chinese Journal of Physiology. Metabolism Series — Chin J Physiol Metab Ser
Chinese Journal of Physiology. Report Series — Chin J Physiol Rep Ser

Chinese Journal of Physiology (Taipei) — Chin J Physiol (Taipei)
Chinese Journal of Polymer Science — Chin J Polym Sci
Chinese Journal of Power Sources — Chin J Power Sources
Chinese Journal of Preventive Medicine — Chin J Prev Med
Chinese Journal of Preventive Medicine — CHYCDW
Chinese Journal of Public Health — Chin J Public Health
Chinese Journal of Radiological Medicine and Protection — Chin J Radiol Med Prot
Chinese Journal of Radiology — Chin J Radiol
Chinese Journal of Semiconductors — Chin J Semicond
Chinese Journal of Space Science — Chin J Space Sci
Chinese Journal of Spectroscopy Laboratory — Chin J Spectrosc Lab
Chinese Journal of Stomatology — Chin J Stomatol
Chinese Journal of Surgery [*People's Republic of China*] — Chin J Surg
Chinese Journal of Surgery — CHWCAJ
Chinese Journal of the Science of Agriculture — Chin J Sci Agr
Chinese Journal of Traumatology — Chin J Traumatol
Chinese Journal of Tuberculosis — Chin J Tuber
Chinese Journal of Tuberculosis and Respiratory Diseases — Chin J Tuberc Respir Dis
Chinese Journal of Veterinary Medicine — Chin J Vet Med
Chinese Journal of Virology — Chin J Virol
Chinese Journal of Zoology — Chin J Zool
Chinese Law and Government — Chin L and Gov
Chinese Law and Government — Chin Law G
Chinese Law and Government [*New York*] — Chin Law Govt
Chinese Law and Government — Chinese L & Govt
Chinese Law and Government — Chinese Law Gvt
Chinese Literature [*Peking*] — Chin Lit
Chinese Literature — ChinL
Chinese Literature — ChLit
Chinese Literature — CL
Chinese Literature. Essays, Articles, Reviews — Chin Lit Es
Chinese Literature. Essays, Articles, Reviews — CLEAR
Chinese Literature Monthly — CLM
Chinese Medical Journal — Chin Med J
Chinese Medical Journal — Chinese MJ
Chinese Medical Journal [*English Edition*] — CMJODS
Chinese Medical Journal (English Edition) — Chin Med J (Engl Ed)
Chinese Medical Journal (Peking) — Chin Med J (Peking)
Chinese Medical Sciences Journal — Chin Med Sci J
Chinese Music — Chinese M
Chinese Music — Chinese Mus
Chinese Pen [*Taipei*] — Chin Pen
Chinese Pharmaceutical Bulletin — Chin Pharm Bull
Chinese Pharmaceutical Journal (Beijing) — Chin Pharm J (Beijing)
Chinese Pharmaceutical Journal (Taipei) — Chin Pharm J Taipei
Chinese Physics [*United States*] — Chin Phys
Chinese Physics — Chinese Phys
Chinese Physics — CHPHD
Chinese Physics Letters — Chin Phys L
Chinese Physics Letters — Chinese Phys Lett
Chinese Quarterly Journal of Mathematics — Chinese Quart J Math
Chinese Recorder and Missionary Journal — ChRMJ
Chinese Republic Studies. Newsletter — Chin Repub Stud
Chinese Science — Chin Sci
Chinese Science and Technology — Chin Sci Tech
Chinese Science Bulletin — Chinese Sci Bull
Chinese Social and Political Science Review — Chin Social & Pol Sci R
Chinese Social and Political Science Review [*Peking*] — CSPSR
Chinese Sociology and Anthropology — Chin Soc A
Chinese Sociology and Anthropology [*New York*] — Chin Sociol Anthro
Chinese Sociology and Anthropology — CSA
Chinese Students' Monthly. Chinese Students Alliance of Eastern States, USA — Chin Stud Monthly
Chinese Studies in History — Chin Stud
Chinese Studies in History [*New York*] — Chin Stud Hist
Chinese Studies in History — Chinese Stud Hist
Chinese Studies in History — CSH
Chinese Studies in Literature — Chin St Lit
Chinese Studies in Philosophy — Chin St Ph
Chinese Studies in Philosophy — Chin Stud Phil
Chinese Studies in Philosophy [*New York*] — Chin Stud Philo
Chinese Studies in Philosophy — CSP
Chinese Traditional and Herbal Drugs — Chin Tradit Herb Drugs
Chinese Veterinary Journal — Chin Vet J
Chinese-American Joint Commission on Rural Reconstruction. Plant Industry Series — Chin Am J Comm Rural Reconstr Plant Ind Ser
Chinese-American Joint Commission on Rural Reconstruction (Taiwan). Special Bulletin — Chin Am J Comm Rural Reconstr (Taiwan) Spec Bull
Chinese-American Joint Commission on Rural Reconstruction (Taiwan) Special Bulletin — Chin Am Jt Comm Rural Reconstr (Taiwan) Spec Bull
Chinetsu Gijutsu — CGIJD
Ching Chi Pu Kuo Li Taiwan Ta Hsueh Ho Pan Yu Yeh Sheng Wu Shih Yen So Yen Chiu Pao Kao — RIFBAZ
Ching Feng — CFeng
Ch'ing Hua Ta Hsueh Hsueh Pao — CHHPA
Chipper Snacker — Chip Snack
Chiral Dynamics. Theory and Experiment. Proceedings of the Workshop — Chiral Dyn Theory Exp Proc Workshop
Chironomus — CRNSBP
Chiropractic History — Chiro Hist
Chiropractic Sports Medicine — Chiropractic Sports Med
Chirurgia [*Bucharest*] — CRGAA3
Chirurgia degli Organi di Movimento — Chir Org Movimento
Chirurgia degli Organi di Movimento — Chir Organi Mov
Chirurgia degli Organi di Movimento — CHOMA9
Chirurgia e Patologia Sperimentale — Chir Patol Sper
Chirurgia e Patologia Sperimentale — CHPAAC
Chirurgia Gastroenterologica [*English Edition*] — CHRGA6
Chirurgia Gastroenterologica (English Edition) — Chir Gastroenterol (Engl Ed)
Chirurgia Generale — Chir Gen
Chirurgia Italiana — Chir Ital
Chirurgia Italiana — CHITAY
Chirurgia Maxillofacialis et Plastica — Chir Maxillofac Plast
Chirurgia Maxillofacialis et Plastica — CMXPAU
Chirurgia Narzadow Ruchu i Ortopedia Polska — Chir Narzadow Ruchu Ortop Pol
Chirurgia Narzadow Ruchu i Ortopedia Polska — CNROA4
Chirurgia Plastica — Chir Plast
Chirurgia Plastica et Reconstructiva — Chir Plast Reconstr
Chirurgia Plastica et Reconstructiva — CPLRBW
Chirurgia Toracica — Chir Torac
Chirurgia Veterinaria Referate. Abstracts — Chir Vet Ref Abstr
Chirurgie Aktuell — Chir Aktuell
Chirurgie Pediatrique — Chir Pediatr
Chirurgie Pediatrique — CPEDDP
Chirurgien-Dentiste de France — Chir-Dent Fr
Chirurgische Praxis — Chir Prax
Chirurgische Praxis — CHPXBE
Chirurgische Therapie des Mammakarzinoms, Oesterreichische Chirurgentagung — Chir Ther Mammakarzinoms Oesterr Chirurgentag
Chirurgisches Forum fuer Experimentelle und Klinische Forschung — CFEKA7
Chirurgisches Forum fuer Experimentelle und Klinische Forschung — Chir Forum Exp Klin Forsch
Chisa. Main Lectures. International Congress on Chemical Engineering, Equipment Design, and Automation — Chisa Main Lect Int Congr Chem Eng Equip Des Autom
Chishitsu Chosajo Geppo — CHCGA
Chishitsu Chosajo Geppo — CHCGAX
Chishitsu Chosajo Hokoku [*Geological Survey of Japan. Report*] — CCHHAQ
Chishitsu Chosasho Nenpo — CCNED
Chishitsu Nyusu — CHNYB
Chishitsugaku Zasshi — CHTZA
Chishitsugaku Zasshi — CHTZA5
Chisholm Gazette — Chisholm Gaz
Chislennye Metody Mekhaniki Sploshnoi Sredy [*Former USSR*] — Chislennye Metody Mekh Sploshnoi Sredy
Chislennye Metody Mekhaniki Sploshnoi Sredy — CMMSC
Chislennye Metody v Dinamike Razrezhennykh Gazov — Chislennye Metody Din Razrezh Gazov
CHISS [*Centre Haitien d'Investigation en Science Sociales*] **Cahiers** — CHISS Cah
Chitaniumu Jirukoniumu — CHJIA
Chittagong University. Studies. Part II. Science — Chittagong Univ Stud Part II Sci
Chittagong University. Studies. Part II. Science — CUSCDP
Chitty's Law Journal — Chitty LJ
Chitty's Law Journal — Chitty's L J
Chlorine in Coal. Proceedings. International Conference — Chlorine Coal Proc Int Conf
Chmelarske Listy — Chmel Listy
Chocolaterie. Confiserie de France — Choc Confiserie Fr
Choice — CE
Choice — Ch
Choice — CHO
Choice — PCHO
Choices. The Magazine of Food, Farm, and Resource Issues — Choices Mag Food Farm Resour Issues
Choir and Organ — CaO
Cho-Koon Kenkyu — CKKKA
Cholinergic Neurotransmission. Functional and Clinical Aspects. Proceedings. Nobel Symposium — Cholinergic Neurotransm Funct Clin Aspects Proc Nobel Symp
Chongi Hakhoe Chi — CGHCA
Chongqing Daxue Xuebao — CPAOD
Chonnam Medical Journal — Chonnam Med J
Chonnam Medical Journal — CVCHD
Choral and Organ Guide — Choral G
Choral Journal — ChJ
Choral Journal — Choral J
Choral Journal — CJ
Choristers Guild. Letters — CGL
Chosen Bulletin/Chosen Iho — Chosen Bull
Chosen Gakuno — CSGH
Chowder Review — Chowder
CHRA [*Canadian Health Record Association*] **Recorder** — CHRA Rec
Christ to the World — Chr World
Christ und Welt — CW
Christelijk Arbeidssecretariaat — CAS
Christelijk Historisch Tijdschrift — CHT
Christelijk Oosten en Hereniging — COH
Christelijk-Historische Unie — CHU
Christentum und Wissenschaft — C & W
Christentum und Wissenschaft [*Leipzig*] — CuW
Christian Art [*Boston*] — Chris Art
Christian Brothers Studies — Christ Brothers Stud
Christian Century — C Cent
Christian Century — CC
Christian Century — ChC
Christian Century — ChCen

Christian Century — Chr C
Christian Century — Chr Cent
Christian Century — Christ Cen
Christian Century [*Chicago*] — ChristCent
Christian Century — Christian Cent
Christian Century — GTCC
Christian College News — CCN
Christian College News Service — CCNS
Christian Disciple — Chr Disc
Christian Doctrine — Ch D
Christian East — CE
Christian Educators Journal — CEJ
Christian Examiner — Chr Exam
Christian Examiner — Christian Exam
Christian Herald — C Her
Christian Herald — CH
Christian Herald — ICHH
Christian Home — C Home
Christian Inquirer. Canadian Edition — Christ Inq Can Ed
Christian Jewish Relations — CJR
Christian Leadership Letter — Christ Lead Let
Christian Liberty — ChL
Christian Librarian — Christ Libr
Christian Librarian — CLi
Christian Life — C Life
Christian Life — CL
Christian Literature — Chr Lit
Christian Literature — Christian Lit
Christian Management Review — Christ Man Rev
Christian Medical Society. Journal — CMJ
Christian Ministry — C Min
Christian Ministry — Chr Ministry
Christian Monthly Spectator — Chr Mo Spec
Christian News from Israel — Ch NI
Christian News from Israel [*Jerusalem*] — ChrNIsrael
Christian News from Israel — CNFI
Christian News from Israel — CNI
Christian Nurse — Christ Nurse
Christian Observer — Chr Obs
Christian Periodical Index — CHPI
Christian Periodical Index — Chr Per Ind
Christian Periodical Index — Christ Period Index
Christian Perspectives — ChrPer
Christian Quarterly — Chr Q
Christian Quarterly — Christian Q
Christian Quarterly Review — Chris Q
Christian Quarterly Spectator — Chr Q Spec
Christian Quarterly Spectator — Christian Q Spec
Christian Reader — C Read
Christian Remembrance — Chr Rem
Christian Review — Chr R
Christian Scholar — ChS
Christian Scholar — CS
Christian Scholar's Review — Ch S R
Christian Scholar's Review — Chr Sch R
Christian Scholar's Review — Christ Sch Rev
Christian Scholar's Review — ChSRev
Christian Scholar's Review — CSR
Christian Science Journal — CSJ
Christian Science Monitor — Chr Sci Mon
Christian Science Monitor — Chr Sci Monitor
Christian Science Monitor — Chris Sc Mon
Christian Science Monitor — Christ Sci Mon
Christian Science Monitor — Christian Sci Mon
Christian Science Monitor — Christian Sci Monitor
Christian Science Monitor — CSM
Christian Science Monitor Magazine — Chr Sci Monit Mag
Christian Science Monitor. Magazine Section — C S Mon Mag
Christian Science Monitor. Magazine Section — Christian Sci Mon Mag
Christian Science Monitor. Magazine Section — CSMMS
Christian Science Quarterly — CSQ
Christian Standard — C Stand
Christian Union — Chr Un
Christian Union [*New York*] — CHRU
Christian Union — ChU
Christiana Albertina. Kieler Universitaets Zeitschrift — Christiana Albertina Kiel Univ Z
Christianity and Crisis — C & C
Christianity and Crisis — Chr & Cr
Christianity and Crisis — Chr & Crisis
Christianity and Crisis — Chr Cris
Christianity and Crisis — ICCC
Christianity and Literature — C and L
Christianity and Literature — Christ Lit
Christianity Today — C Today
Christianity Today — Chr T
Christianity Today — Chr Today
Christianity Today [*Washington, DC*] — ChristTod
Christianity Today — CT
Christianity Today — GCTO
Christliche Kunstblaetter — Ch K
Christliche Orient in Vergangenheit und Gegenwart — Christl Orient
Christliche Schule — Chr Sch
Christliche Welt — CW
Christlich-Juedisches Arbeitsgemeinschaft — CJA
Christlich-Juedisches Forum — ChrJF
Christlich-Paedagogische Blaetter — Christl Paedag Bll
Christmas Tree Growers Journal — Christmas Tree Grow J
Christopher Street — CS
Christopher Street — ICST
Chromatin and Chromosomal Protein Research — Chromatin Chromosomal Protein Res
Chromatographia — CHRGB7
Chromatographia — Chromatogr
Chromatographic Methods — Chromatogr Methods
Chromatographic Reviews — Chromat Rev
Chromatographic Reviews — Chromatogr Rev
Chromatographic Reviews — CRRVAJ
Chromatographic Science — Chromatogr Sci
Chromatographic Science Series — CHGSAL
Chromatographic Science Series — Chromatogr Sci Ser
Chromatographic Society International Symposium on Chiral Separations — Chromatogr Soc Int Symp Chiral Sep
Chromatographie, Electrophorese. Symposium International — Chromatogr Electrophor Symp Int
Chromatographie sur Colonne. Reunion Internationale sur les Methodes de Separation — Chromatogr Colonne Reun Int Methodes Sep
Chromatography Bulletin — Chromatog Bull
Chromatography Communications — Chromatogr Commun
Chromatography Newsletter — Chromatogr Newsl
Chromatography Newsletter — Chromatography Newsl
Chromatography of Environmental Hazards [*Elsevier Book Series*] — CEH
Chromatography Symposia Series — Chromatogr Symp Ser
Chromosoma [*Berlin*] — CHROAU
Chromosoma — Chromos
Chromosome Information Service — Chromo Inf Serv
Chromosome Information Service (Tokyo) — Chromos Inform Serv (Tokyo)
Chromosome Information Service (Tokyo) — Chromosome Inf Serv (Tokyo)
Chromosome Research — Chromosome Res
Chromosome Variations in Human Evolution — Chromosome Var Hum Evol
Chromosomes Today — CHRTB
Chromosomes Today — CHRTBC
Chronache di Chimica [*Italy*] — Chron Chim
Chronache di Chimica — CROCB
Chronica Botanica — CHRBAP
Chronica Botanica — Chron Bot
Chronica Dermatologica — Chron Dermatol
Chronica Dermatologica — CRDMBP
Chronica Horticulturae — CHHOAE
Chronica Horticulturae — Chron Hortic
Chronica Naturae — Chron Nat
Chronica Nicotiana — Chron Nicotiana
Chronicle of Australian Education — Chron Aust Ed
Chronicle of Higher Education — C H Ed
Chronicle of Higher Education — CHE
Chronicle of Higher Education — Chron Higher Educ
Chronicle of Higher Education — GCHE
Chronicle of International Communication — Chron Int Com
Chronicle (Toowoomba) — TC
Chronicle. West India Committee — Chron WI Comm
Chronicle. West Indian Committee — CWIC
Chronicle. World Health Organization — Chron WHO
Chronicles of Culture — Chron Cult
Chronicles of Oklahoma — ChrO
Chronicles of Oklahoma — Chronicles Okla
Chronicles of Oklahoma — ChronOkla
Chronicles of Oklahoma — CO
Chronicles of Oklahoma — COO
Chronicles of Oklahoma — Okla Chronicles
Chronik. Wiener Goetheverein — CWGV
Chronique Aluminum — Chron Alum
Chronique Archeologique. Association Culturelle du Groupe Total — Chron A Ass Cul
Chronique Archeologique du Pays de Liege — CAPL
Chronique Archeologique du Pays de Liege — Ch Arch Liege
Chronique Archeologique du Pays de Liege — Chronique Arch Liege
Chronique de la Recherche Miniere [*Paris*] — Chron Rech Min
Chronique de la Recherche Miniere [*France*] — Chron Rech Miniere
Chronique de Politique Etrangere — Chr Pol Et
Chronique de Politique Etrangere — Chron Pol Etrang
Chronique de Politique Etrangere — Chron Pol Etrangere
Chronique de Politique Etrangere — Chron Polit Etr
Chronique de Politique Etrangere — Chron Politique Etrangere
Chronique de Politique Etrangere — CPE
Chronique d'Egypte — C d Eg
Chronique d'Egypte — C Eg
Chronique d'Egypte — CdE
Chronique d'Egypte — CE
Chronique d'Egypte — Chr Eg
Chronique d'Egypte — ChrE
Chronique d'Egypte — Chro E
Chronique d'Egypte — Chron d'Eg
Chronique d'Egypte — Chron Eg
Chronique d'Egypte — Chron Egypte
Chronique des Lettres Francaises — CLF
Chronique des Mines Coloniales — Chron Mines Colon
Chronique des Mines d'Outre-Mer et de la Recherche Miniere — Chron Mines Outre Mer Rech Min
Chronique des Mines et de la Recherche Miniere — Chron Mines Rech Min
Chronique d'Hydrogeologie — Chron Hydrogeol

Chronique 'Egypte — Chrd'Eg
Chronique Medicale — Chron Med
Chronique Miniere Coloniale — Chron Min Colon
Chronique. Organisation Mondiale de la Sante — Chron OMS
Chronique Sociale de France — Chron Soc Fr
Chronique Sociale de France — Chron Soc France
Chronique Sociale de France — Chron Social Fr
Chronique. Societe Vervietoise d'Archeologie et d'Histoire — CSVAH
Chroniques d'Actualite — Chron Actual
Chroniques d'Actualite — Chrons Actualite
Chroniques d'Orient — C Or
Chroniques d'Orient — Chron Or
Chronmy Przyrode Ojczysta — Chron Przyr Ojczysta
Chronmy Przyrode Ojczysta — Chronmy Przyr Ojczysta
Chronmy Przyrode Ojczysta — CPZOAO
Chronobiologia — CBLGA2
Chronobiologia. Organ of the International Society for Chronobiology — Chronobiologia Organ Int Soc Chronobiology
Chronobiology International — CHBIE4
Chronobiology International — Chronobiol Int
Chronolog — CHROD
Chronology of Mycenaean Pottery — Chron
Chronology of Mycenaean Pottery — Chron MP
Chronos. Vakblad voor de Uurwerkbranche — CHH
CHS Faculty Review — CHS Fac Rev
Chteniia v Imperatorskom Obshchestve Istorii i Drevnostei Rossisskikh — ChOIDR
Chteniia v Moskovskom Obshchestve Liubiteli Dukhovnogo Prosveshcheniia — ChOLDP
Ch'uan-Kuo Ti-I-Chieh Yeh-Chin Kuo-Ch Eng Wu-Li Hua-Hsueh Hsueh-Shu Pao-Kao-Hui Lun-Wen Chi — CTYKA
Chuban Kenkyu [*Studies on Chinese Language and Literature*] — CBKK
Chugoku Agricultural Research — Chugoku Agr Res
Chugoku Agricultural Research/Chugoku Nogyo Kenkyu — Chugoku Agric Res
Chugoku and Shikoku Districts Journal. Japan Society of Obstetrics and Gynecology — Chugoku Shikoku Dist J Jpn Soc Obstet Gynecol
Chugoku Bungaku Ho — C Bun H
Chugoku Gogaku — CG
Chugoku No Bunka To Shakai [*Chinese Culture and Society*] — CBS
Chugoku Nogyo Shikenjo Hokoku. A. Sakumotsu-Bu — CNASAX
Chugoku Nogyo Shikenjo Hokoku. B. Chikusan-Bu — CNSBB5
Chugoku Nogyo Shikenjo Hokoku. E. Kankyo-Bu — CNEKAT
Chuko To Tanko — CHTTA
Chung Chi Hsueh-Pao — CCHP
Chung Chi Journal — CCJ
Chung Yang Yen Chiu Yuan Chih Wu Hsueh Hui K'an — BBASA6
Chung Yang Yen Chiu Yuan T'ung Wu Yen Chiu So Chi K'an — BIZYAS
Chung Yuan Journal — Chung Yuan J
Chung-Ang Journal of Medicine [*South Korea*] — Chung-Ang J Med
Chung-Ang Journal of Medicine — CJMED
Chung-Ang Journal of Medicine — CJMEDQ
Chung-Ang Uihak — CHUIAR
Chungara. Universidad del Norte. Departamento de Antropologia — UN/C
Chung-Hua Chieh Heh Heh Hu Hsi Hsi Chi Ping Tsa Chih [*Chinese Journal of Tuberculosis and Respiratory Diseases*] — CCHCDE
Chung-Hua Erh K'o Tsa Chih [*Chinese Journal of Pediatrics*] — CHETA
Chung-Hua Erh K'o Tsa Chih [*Chinese Journal of Pediatrics*] — CHETAE
Chung-Hua Erh Pi Yen Hou K'o Tsa Chih — CHEYAT
Chung-Hua Fang She Hsueh Tsa Chih — CHFSAG
Chung-Hua Fu Ch'an K'o Tsa Chih [*Chinese Journal of Obstetrics and Gynecology*] — CHFCA
Chung-Hua Fu Ch'an K'o Tsa Chih [*Chinese Journal of Obstetrics and Gynecology*] — CHFCA2
Chung-Hua Hsin Hsuch Kuan Ping Tsa Chih — CHHCDF
Chung-Hua I Hsueh Tsa Chih [*Chinese Medical Journal*] — CHHTAT
Chung-Hua Lin Hsueh Chi K'an. Quarterly Journal of Chinese Forestry — Chung Hua Lin Hsueh Chi K'an Q J Chin For
Chung-Hua Min Kuo Hsiao Erh K'o I Hsueh Hui Tsa Chi — CHEKAL
Chung-Hua Nei K'o Tsa Chih — CHHNA
Chung-Hua Nung Hsueh Hui Pao — CHNHA
Chung-Hua Nung Yeh Yen Chiu/Journal of Agriculture Research of China — Chung-Hua Nung Yeh Yen Chiu J Agric Res China
Chung-Hua Wai K'o Tsa Chih — CHWCA
Chung-Kuo Hsu Mu Shou I — CKHMA
Chung-Kuo K'o-Hsueh-Yuan Lan-Chou Hua-Hsueh Wu-Li Yen-Chiu-So Yen-Chiu Pao-Kao Chi-K'an — CLPCA
Chung-Kuo Kung Ch'eng Hsueh K'an — CKCKD
Chung-Kuo Lin Yeh K'o Hsueh/Chinese Forestry Science — Chung-Kuo Lin Yeh K'o Hsueh Chin For Sci
Chung-Kuo Nung Yeh Hua Hsueh Hui Chih [*Journal of the Chinese Agriculture Chemical Society*] — CKNHA
Chung-Kuo Nung Yeh Hua Hsueh Hui Chih/Journal of the Chinese Agriculture Chemical Society — Chung-Kuo Nung Yeh Hua Hsueh Hui Chih J Chin Agric Chem Soc
Chung-Kuo Nung Yeh K'o Hsueh [*Scientia Agricultura Sinica*] — CKNYA
Chung-Kuo Nung Yeh K'o Hsueh/Scientia Agricultura Sinica — Chung-Kuo Nung Yeh K'o Hsueh Sci Agric Sin
Chung-Kuo Shui Sheng Wu Hui Pao — CSWPA
Chung-Kuo Yu-Wen — CKYW
Chungnam Journal of Sciences [*South Korea*] — Chungnam J Sci
Chungnam Journal of Sciences — CJOSD
Chungnam Medical Journal — Chungnam Med J
Chungnam National University. Research Institute of Chemical Spectroscopy. Reports — Chungnam Natl Univ Res Inst Chem Spectrosc Rep
Chung-Shan Ta Hsueh Hsueh Pao. Tzu Jan K'o Hsueh — CHTHA
Chung-Shan University Journal. Natural Sciences Edition [*People's Republic of China*] — Chung-Shan Univ J Nat Sci Ed
Chung-Wai Literary Monthly — CWLM
Chung-yang Yen-chiu Yuean Chin-tai Shih Yen-chiu So Chi-k'an — ChunY
Chuo Daigaku Rikogakubu Kiyo — CDSEA
Church Administration — CA
Church and Home — Ch & H
Church and Society — Ch Soc
Church and Synagogue Libraries — C & SLib
Church Herald — Ch Her
Church History — CH
Church History — Ch Hist
Church History — ChH
Church History — CHist
Church History — Church Hist
Church History — ChurH
Church History — PCHH
Church History. American Society of Church History. University of Chicago — ASCH/CH
Church History (Chicago) — CHC
Church Missionary Intelligencer — Ch Mis I
Church Missionary Intelligencer — CMI
Church Missionary Review — Church Mis R
Church Missionary Review — CMR
Church Music — Ch Music
Church Music — Chu
Church Music (London) — Church Mus (London)
Church Music (St. Louis) — Church Mus (St L)
Church Musician — CM
Church of England Historical Society. Journal — C of E Hist Soc J
Church of England Historical Society. Journal — CEHSJ
Church of England Historical Society. Journal — Church Eng Hist Soc J
Church of Scotland Committee on Publications — CSCP
Church Quarterly — Ch Q
Church Quarterly Review — Ch Q
Church Quarterly Review — Ch Q R
Church Quarterly Review — Church Q
Church Quarterly Review — Church Q R
Church Quarterly Review — Church Qtr Rev
Church Quarterly Review — Church Quart Rev
Church Quarterly Review — Church Quartl Revw
Church Quarterly Review — CQR
Church Review — Church R
Church Teachers — ChT
Churchman — Chm
Churchman — Chmn
Chuvashskii Sel'skokhozyaistvennyi Institut. Sbornik Nauchnykh Rabot Molodykh Uchenykh — Chuv Skh Inst Sb Nauchn Rab Molodykh Uch
Chymia et Industria — Chymia Ind
CIAT [*Centro Internacional de Agricultura Tropical*] **Annual Report** — CIAT Annu Rep
CIAT [*Centro Internacional de Agricultura Tropical*] **Series Seminars** — CIAT Ser Semin
CIB [*Conseil International du Batiment pour la Recherche, l'Etude, et la Documentation*] **Congress** — CIB Congr
Ciba Clinical Symposia — Ciba Clin Symp
Ciba Collection of Medical Illustrations — Ciba Collect Med Illus
Ciba Foundation. Colloquia on Endocrinology — Ciba Found Colloq Endocrinol
Ciba Foundation. Study Group — Ciba Found Study Group
Ciba Foundation. Symposium — Ciba Fdn Symp
Ciba Foundation. Symposium — Ciba Found Symp
Ciba Foundation. Symposium — CIBSB
Ciba Journal — Ciba J
Ciba Lectures in Microbial Biochemistry — CBLBA
Ciba Lectures in Microbial Biochemistry — Ciba Lect Microb Biochem
Ciba Review — Ciba R
Ciba Review — Ciba Rev
Ciba Rundschau — Ciba Rundsch
Ciba Symposia — CBASA
Ciba Symposia — Ciba
Ciba Symposia — Ciba Symp
Ciba-Geigy Journal — Ciba Geigy J
Ciba-Geigy Review — Ciba Geig Rev
Ciba-Geigy Technical Notes — Ciba-Geigy Tech Notes
CIBCASIO (Centros de Investigacion de Baja California and Scripps Institution of Oceanography) Transactions — CIBCASIO Trans
CIC Informations. Bulletin d'Informations Generales — CIC Inform B Inform Gen
CICIAMS [*Comite International Catholique des Infirmieres et Assistantes Medico-Sociales*] **Nouvelles** — CICIAMS Nouv
Ciclo Combustible U-Th. Simposio. Congresso Nucleare — Ciclo Combust U Th Congr Nucl
Cidade de Evora. Boletim da Comissao Municipal de Turismo — CEBCMT
CIDI (Centro de Iniziativa Democratica degli Insegnanti) Quaderni — CIDI Quad
CIEA [*Central Institute for Experimental Animals*] **Preclinical Reports** — CIEA Preclin Rep
Ciel et Terre. Societe Belge d'Astronomie — Ciel Terre
Ciencia — Cienc
Ciencia Agronomica — Cienc Agron
Ciencia Biologica — CBBMC
Ciencia Biologica — Cienc Biol
Ciencia Biologica. B. Ecologia e Sistematica — Cienc Biol B
Ciencia Biologica. Biologia Molecular e Cellular — Cienc Biol Biol Mol Cel
Ciencia Biologica (Coimbra) [*Portugal*] — Cienc Biol (Coimbra)
Ciencia Biologica, Ecologia, e Sistematica — Cienc Biol Ecol Sist
Ciencia Biologica. Molecular and Cellular Biology — Cienc Biol Mol Cell Biol

Ciencia Biologica. Serie C. Biologia Molecular e Celular — Cien Biol Ser C Biol Mol Cel
Ciencia (Botucatu, Brazil). Revista do Centro Academico Piraja da Silva — Ciencia Botucatu Braz
Ciencia, Cultura, Saude — Cienc Cult Saude
Ciencia da Informacao — Ciencia Info
Ciencia e Cultura (Sao Paulo) — Cienc Cult (S Paulo)
Ciencia e Cultura (Sao Paulo) — Cienc Cult (Sao Paulo)
Ciencia e Cultura (Sao Paulo). Suplemento — Cienc Cult (Sao Paulo) Supl
Ciencia e Cultura (Sao Paulo). Suplemento — RRACD
Ciencia e Cultura. Sociedade Brasileira para o Progresso da Ciencia — Cienc Cult Soc Bras Progr Cienc
Ciencia e Industria Farmaceutica — Cienc Ind Farm
Ciencia e Investigacion — Cienc Invest
Ciencia e Investigacion Agraria — Cienc Invest Agrar
Ciencia e Investigacion (Buenos Aires) — Cien Invest BA
Ciencia e Investigacion (Buenos Aires) — Cienc Invest (B Aires)
Ciencia e Natura (Santa Maria, Brazil) — Cienc Nat (S Maria Braz)
Ciencia e Pratica — Cienc Prat
Ciencia e Tecnica Fiscal — Ciencia e Tec Fiscal
Ciencia e Tecnica Vitivinicola — Cienc Tec Vitivini
Ciencia e Tecnologia de Alimentos — Cienc Tecnol Aliment
Ciencia Forestal — Cienc For
Ciencia Interamericana — CI
Ciencia Interamericana — Cienc Interam
Ciencia Interamericana. Departamento de Asuntos Cientificos. Union Panamericana — Ci Interamer
Ciencia (Mexico) — Cien Mex
Ciencia Revista Hispanoamericana de Ciencias Puras y Aplicadas (Mexico) — CM
Ciencia Tomista — C Tom
Ciencia Tomista — Cien Tom
Ciencia Tomista — Cien Tomista
Ciencia Tomista — CiT
Ciencia Tomista — CT
Ciencia Tomista. Publicacion Trimestral de los P.P. Dominicos Espanoles — Ci Tomista
Ciencia y Cultura (Maracaibo) — Cienc Cult (Maracaibo)
Ciencia y Cultura (Maracaibo, Venezuela) — Cien Cult Maracaibo
Ciencia y Desarrollo — Cienc Desarrollo
Ciencia y Fe — CiFe
Ciencia y Fe (San Miguel, Argentina) — Cien Fe S Miguel
Ciencia y Naturaleza — Cienc Nat
Ciencia y Naturaleza (Quito) — Cien Natur Quito
Ciencia y Naturaleza (Quito) — Cienc Nat (Quito)
Ciencia y Sociedad — Ciencia y Soc
Ciencia y Tecnica — Cienc & Tec
Ciencia y Tecnica (Buenos Aires) — Cienc Tec (Buenos Aires)
Ciencia y Tecnica de la Soldadura (Madrid) — Cienc Tec Soldadura (Madrid)
Ciencia y Tecnica en el Mundo — Cienc Tec Mundo
Ciencia y Tecnica en la Agricultura. Ganado Porcino — Cienc Tec Agric Ganado Porcino
Ciencia y Tecnica en la Agricultura. Proteccion de Plantas — Cienc Tec Agric Prot Plant
Ciencia y Tecnica en la Agricultura. Veterinaria — Cienc Tec Agric Vet
Ciencia y Tecnologia — Cienc Tecn
Ciencia y Tecnologia — Ciencia Tecnol
Ciencia y Tecnologia de Alimentos Internacional — Cienc Tecnol Aliment Int
Ciencia y Tecnologia del Mar. Comite Oceanografico Nacional [*Valparaiso, Chile*] — Cienc Tec Mar
Ciencia y Tecnologia Nuclear — Cienc Tecnol Nucl
Ciencia y Tecnologia (San Jose, Costa Rica) — Cienc Tecnol (San Jose Costa Rica)
Ciencia y Tecnologia (Washington, DC) — Cienc Tecnol Washington DC
Ciencias Administrativas — Cienc Adm
Ciencias Administrativas (Argentina) — CAA
Ciencias Administrativas (La Plata, Argentina) — Cien Admin La Plata
Ciencias. Asociacion Espanola por el Progreso de las Ciencias (Madrid) — Ciencias Madrid
Ciencias Biologicas. Academia de Ciencias de Cuba — Cienc Biol Acad Cienc Cuba
Ciencias Biologicas (Luanda) — Cienc Biol (Luanda)
Ciencias da Terra — Cienc Terra
Ciencias da Terra — CIETD
Ciencias de la Agricultura — Cienc Agric
Ciencias de la Tierra y del Espacio — Cienc Tierra Espacio
Ciencias e Investigacion — Ci Invest
Ciencias Economicas. Facultad de Ciencias Economicas. Universidad de Antioquia (Medellin, Colombia) — Cien Econ Medellin
Ciencias Economicas Sociais — Cien Econ Soc
Ciencias Forestales — CSFSD
Ciencias Marinas — Cienc Mar
Ciencias Matematicas [*Havana*] — Cienc Mat
Ciencias Naturales. Boletin. Real Sociedad Vascongada de Amigos del Pais. Supplemento — Cienc Nat Bol R Soc Vascongada Amigos Pais Suppl
Ciencias Neurologicas — Cienc Neurol
Ciencias Politicas y Sociales (Mexico) — Cien Pol Soc Mex
Ciencias. Serie 1. Matematica [*Havana*] — Ciencias Ser 1 Mat
Ciencias. Serie 3. [*Quimica*] — Ciencias Ser 3
Ciencias. Serie 4. Ciencias Biologicas (Havana) — Cienc Ser 4 Cienc Biol (Havana)
Ciencias. Serie 5. Bioquimica Farmaceutica — Ciencias Ser 5
Ciencias. Serie 8. Investigaciones Marinas (Havana) — Cienc Ser 8 Invest Mar (Havana)
Ciencias. Serie 10. Botanica (Havana) — Cienc Ser 10 Bot (Havana)
Ciencias Sociales. Colombia (Medillin) — CSMC
Ciencias Sociales (Cumana, Venezuela) — Cien Soc Cumana
Ciencias Sociales (Washington, DC) — Cien Soc Wash
Ciencias Tecnicas Fisicas y Matematicas — Cienc Tec Fis Mat
Ciencias Tecnicas Fisicas y Matematicas — CTFMD
Ciencias Veterinarias — Cienc Vet
Ciencias Veterinarias (Maracay, Venezuela) — Cienc Vet Maracay Venez
Ciencias Veterinarias y Alimentas y Nutricion Animal — Cienc Vet Aliment Nutr Anim
Cieplownictwo, Ogrzewnictwo, Wentylacja — Ciep Ogrz Went
Cieplownictwo, Ogrzewnictwo, Wentylacja — Cieplownictwo Ogrzewnictwo Went
CIFA (Committee for Inland Fisheries of Africa) Technical Paper — CIFA (Comm Inland Fish Afr) Tech Pap
CIFRI (Central Inland Fisheries Research Institute) Seminar — CIFRI (Cent Inland Fish Res Inst) Semin
CIG. Cryogenics and Industrial Gases — CIG Cryog Indus Gases
CIIG [*Construction Industry Information Group*] **Bulletin** — CIIG Bull
CILA [*Centre Internationale de Linguistique Appliquee*] **Bulletin** — CILA B
CIM [*Canadian Institute of Mining and Metallurgy*] **Bulletin** — CIM Bull
CIM [*Canadian Institute of Mining and Metallurgy*] **Bulletin** — CIMB
CIM [*Computer Integrated Manufacturing*] **Magazine** — CIM Mag
Cimarron Review — CimR
Cimbebasia. Memoir — Cimbebasia Mem
Cimbebasia. Series A — Cimbebasia Ser A
Ciment si Beton — Cim Beton
Cimento Bulteni — Cimento Bul
Cimento Mustahsilleri Bulteni — Cimento Mustahsilleri Bul
Ciments, Betons, Platres, Chaux — CBPCD
Ciments, Betons, Platres, Chaux [*France*] — Cim Betons Platres Chaux
Cincinnati Art Museum Bulletin — CAMB
Cincinnati Art Museum. Bulletin — Cin Art B
Cincinnati Art Museum. Bulletin — Cincinnati Mus Bull
Cincinnati Art Museum. Bulletin. New Series — Cincinnati Mus Bul NS
Cincinnati Art Museum. News — Cincinnati Mus N
Cincinnati Bar Association. Journal — Cin BAJ
Cincinnati Business Courier — Cincin Bsn
Cincinnati Business Journal — Cincin BJ
Cincinnati Classical Studies — CCS
Cincinnati Dental Society. Bulletin — Cinci Dent Soc Bull
Cincinnati Enquirer — Cincin Enq
Cincinnati Historical Society. Bulletin — CHSB
Cincinnati Historical Society Bulletin — CiH
Cincinnati Journal of Medicine — Cincinnati J Med
Cincinnati Law Review — Ci LR
Cincinnati Medicine — Cincinnati Med
Cincinnati Quarterly Journal of Science — Cincinnati Quart J Sci
Cincinnati Symphony Orchestra. Program Notes — Cin Sym
Cincinnati Symphony Orchestra. Program Notes — Cinc Sym Prog Notes
Cine Cubano — C Cubano
Cine Cubano — CC
Cine Revue — C Revue
Cine Tracts — C Tracts
Cinefantastique — C Fantas
Cineforum — C Forum
Cinegram Magazine — Cinegram
Cinema 77 — C77
Cinema 83 — C 83
Cinema Canada — C Can
Cinema Canada — Cinema Can
Cinema Canada — ICIA
Cinema Journal — Cinema J
Cinema Journal — CJ
Cinema Nuovo — C Nuovo
Cinema Papers — C Papers
Cinema Papers — Cinema P
Cinema Pratique — C Pratiq
Cinema Quebec — C Quebec
Cinema (Romania) — C (Romania)
Cinema Societa — C Societa
Cinema (United States) — C (US)
Cinema (Zurich) — C (Zurich)
Cinemagic — C Magic
Cinemanews — C News
Cinemasud — Csud
Cinemateca Revista — Cinemateca Rev
Cinematografia [*Database*] — CINE
Cinematographe — Cinematgr
CINEP/PLUS. Bulletin du Centre d'Ingenierie Nordique de l'Ecole Polytechnique — CINP
Cineradiography with Photons or Particles. European Conference — Cineradiogr Photons Part Eur Conf
Cineschedario-Letture Drammatiche — C Let Dram
Cinquante Millions de Consommateurs — CCX
CIO [*Chief Information Officer*] **Letter** — CIO Let
CIO [*Chief Information Officer*] **Monthly** — CIO Mo
CIP [*Centre International de la Pomme de Terre*] **Circular. International Potato Center** — CIP Circ Int Potato Cent
CIP [*Capital Improvement Project*] **Newsletter** — CIP Newsl
CIPAC [*Collaborative International Pesticides Analytical Council*] **Monograph** — CIPAC Monogr
CIPS [*Canadian Information Processing Society*] **Review** — CIPS Rev
Circolo Speleologico Romano. Notiziario — Circ Speleol Rom Not
Circuits and Systems — Circuits Syst
Circuits Manufacturing — Circuits Manuf
Circuits Manufacturing — Circuits Mfg

Circuits, Systems, and Signal Processing — CSSP
Circulaire d'Informations Techniques. Centre de Documentation Siderurgique — Circ Inf Tech Cent Doc Sider
Circulaire Ministerielle — Circ Min
Circulaire. Ministre de la Defense Nationale — Circ Def Nat
Circulaire. Ministre de la Justice — Circ Just
Circulaire. Ministre de l'Interieur — Circ Int
Circulaire. Ministre des Affaires Etrangeres — Circ Aff Etr
Circulaire. Ministre des Finances — Circ Fin
Circular A. North Dakota State University of Agriculture and Applied Science. Extension Service — Circ A N Dak State Univ Agr Appl Sci Ext Serv
Circular. Agricultural Experiment Station. Purdue University — Circ Agric Exp Stn Purdue Univ
Circular. Agricultural Extension Service. University of Arkansas — Circ Agric Ext Serv Univ Ark
Circular. Agricultural Extension Service. Washington State University — Circ Agric Ext Serv Wash St Univ
Circular. Alabama Agricultural Experiment Station — Circ Ala Agr Exp Sta
Circular. Alabama Geological Survey — Circ Ala Geol Surv
Circular. Alabama Polytechnic Institute. Extension Service — Circ Ala Polytech Inst Ext Serv
Circular. Alaska. Agricultural Experiment Station — Circ Alaska Agric Exp Stn
Circular. Alaska Agricultural Experiment Station. School of Agriculture and Land Resources Management — Circ Alaska Agric Exp Stn Sch Agric Land Resour Manage
Circular ANR [*Agricultural and Natural Resources*] **Alabama Cooperative Extension Service. Auburn University** — Circ ANR Ala Coop Ext Serv Auburn Univ
Circular. Arizona Agricultural Extension Service — Circ Ariz Agric Ext Serv
Circular. Arizona Bureau of Mines — Circ Ariz Bur Mines
Circular. Arkansas State Plant Board — Circ Ark St Pl Bd
Circular. Association of Mine Managers of South Africa — Circ Assoc Mine Managers S Afr
Circular. Auburn University. Agricultural Extension Service — Circ Auburn Univ Agr Ext Serv
Circular. Bureau of Entomology. United States Department of Agriculture — Circ Bur Ent US Dep Agric
Circular. California Agricultural Experiment Station — Circ Calif Agric Exp Stn
Circular. California Agricultural Extension Service — Circ Calif Agr Ext Serv
Circular. Canadian Beekeepers' Council — Circ Can Beekprs Coun
Circular. Centro de Investigaciones Agricolas de El Bajio (CIAB) — Circ Cent Invest Agr El Bajio (CIAB)
Circular. Centro de Investigaciones Agricolas del Noroeste (CIANO) — Circ Cent Invest Agr Noroeste (CIANO)
Circular. Centro de Investigaciones Agricolas del Sudeste — Circ Cent Invest Agr Sudeste
Circular. Centro de Investigaciones del Basicas (CIB) — Circ Cent Invest Basicas (CIB)
Circular. Clemson Agricultural College. Extension Service — Circ Clemson Agr Coll Ext Serv
Circular. Clemson University Cooperative Exension Service — Circ Clemson Univ Coop Ext Serv
Circular. College of Agriculture Research Center. Washington State University — Circ Coll Agric Res Cent Wash State Univ
Circular. College of Agriculture. University of Illinois — Circ Coll Agric Univ Ill
Circular. Comision de Parasitologia Agricola (Mexico) — Circular Com Parasitol Agric (Mexico)
Circular. Connecticut Agricultural Experiment Station. New Haven — Circ Conn Agric Exp Stn New Haven
Circular. Cooperative Extension Service. North Dakota State University — Circ Coop Ext Serv N Dak St Univ
Circular. Cooperative Extension Service. University of Georgia — Circ Coop Ext Serv Univ GA
Circular. Cooperative Extension Service. University of Hawaii — Circ Coop Ext Serv Univ Hawaii
Circular. Cooperative Extension Service. University of Illinois — Circ Coop Ext Serv Univ Ill
Circular. Department of Agriculture. Canada — Circ Dep Agric Can
Circular. Division of Fisheries and Oceanography. Commonwealth Scientific and Industrial Research Organisation — Circ Div Fish Oceanogr CSIRO
Circular. Division of Food Research. Commonwealth Scientific and Industrial Research Organisation — Cir Div Food Res CSIRO
Circular. Division of Food Research. Commonwealth Scientific and Industrial Research Organisation — Circ Div Fd Res CSIRO
Circular. Division of Mechanical Engineering. Commonwealth Scientific and Industrial Research Organisation — Circ Div Mech Eng CSIRO
Circular E. Oklahoma State University. Cooperative Extension Service — Circ E Okla State Univ Coop Ext Serv
Circular. Engineering Section. Commonwealth Scientific and Industrial Research Organisation — Circ Eng Sec CSIRO
Circular. Estacion Experimental Agricola de Tucuman — Circ Estac Exp Agric Tucuman
Circular. Estacion Experimental Agricola La Molina — Circ Estac Exp Agric La Molina
Circular EX. Alabama Cooperative Extension Service. Auburn University — Circ EX Ala Coop Ext Serv Auburn Univ
Circular Farmaceutica — Circ Farm
Circular Farmaceutica. Boletin Informativo — Circ Farm Bol Inf
Circular. Florida Agricultural Experiment Station — Circ Fla Agric Exp Stn
Circular. Florida Agricultural Extension Service — Circ Fla Agric Ext Serv
Circular. Florida Cooperative Extension Service — Circ Fla Coop Ext Serv
Circular. Florida University. Agricultural Extension Service — Circ Fla Univ Agr Ext Serv
Circular. Geological Survey of Alabama — Circ Geol Surv Ala
Circular. Geological Survey of Georgia — Circ Geol Surv GA
Circular. Georgia Agricultural Experiment Stations — Circ GA Agr Exp Sta
Circular HE. Alabama Cooperative Extension Service. Auburn University — Circ HE Ala Coop Ext Serv Auburn Univ
Circular. Horticulture and Biology Service. Nova Scotia Department of Agriculture and Marketing — Circ Hort Biol Serv Nova Scot Dep Agric Mktg
Circular. Illinois Agricultural Experiment Station — Circular Illinois Agric Exper Station
Circular. Illinois Department of Agriculture — Circ Ill Dep Agric
Circular. Illinois Natural History Survey — Circ Ill Nat Hist Surv
Circular. Illinois Natural History Survey — Circ Ill Natur Hist Surv
Circular. Illinois State Geological Survey — Circ Illinois State Geol Surv
Circular. Illinois State Geological Survey Division — Circ Ill State Geol Surv Div
Circular. Instituto Agronomico — Circ Inst Agron
Circular. Instituto Agronomico (Campinas, Brazil) — Circ Inst Agron (Campinas Braz)
Circular. Instituto Agronomico do Estado de Sao Paulo — Circ Inst Agron Estado Sao Paulo
Circular. Instituto Agronomico do Norte (Brazil) — Circ Inst Agron Norte Braz
Circular. Instituto Agronomico do Norte (Brazil) — Circ Inst Agron Norte (Brazil)
Circular. Instituto Agronomico do Sul (Pelotas) — Circ Inst Agron Sul (Pelotas)
Circular. Instituto Agronomico do Sul (Pelotas, Brazil) — Circ Inst Agron Sul Pelotas Braz
Circular. Instituto de Pesquisas Agronomicas de Pernambuco — Circ Inst Pesqui Agron Pernambuco
Circular. Instituto de Pesquisas Agropecuarias do Norte — Circ Inst Pesqui Agropecu Norte
Circular. Instituto de Pesquisas Agropecuarias do Sul — Circ Inst Pesqui Agropecu Sul
Circular. Instituto de Pesquisas Agropecuarias do Sul (Brazil) — Circ Inst Pesqui Agropecu Sul (Braz)
Circular. Instituto de Pesquisas e Experimentacao Agropecuarias do Norte — Circ Inst Pesq Exp Agropecuar N
Circular. Instituto de Pesquisas e Experimentacao Agropecuarias do Sul (Brazil) — Circ Inst Pesqui Exp Agropecu Sul Braz
Circular. Kansas Agricultural Experiment Station — Circ Kans Agr Exp Sta
Circular. Kansas Agricultural Experiment Station — Circ Kans Agric Exp Stn
Circular. Kansas State Entomological Commission — Circ Kans St Ent Commn
Circular. Kansas State University of Agriculture and Applied Science. Extension Service — Circ Kans State Univ Agr Appl Sci Ext Serv
Circular. Kansas University Extension Service — Circ Kans Univ Ext Serv
Circular. Kentucky Agricultural Experiment Station — Circ KY Agric Exp Stn
Circular. Kentucky University. Agricultural Extension Service — Circ KY Univ Agr Ext Serv
Circular. Line Elevators Farm Service — Circ Line Elevators Farm Serv
Circular. Louisiana Agricultural Experiment Station — Circ LA Agr Exp Sta
Circular. Missouri University. College of Agriculture. Extension Service — Circ MO Univ Coll Agr Ext Serv
Circular. Montana Agricultural Experiment Station — Circ Mont Agr Exp Sta
Circular. Montana State College. Cooperative Extension Service — Circ Mont State Coll Coop Ext Serv
Circular. Montana State University. Cooperative Extension Service — Circ Mont State Univ Coop Ext Serv
Circular. National Bureau of Standards (United States) — Circ Natl Bur Stand (US)
Circular. Nevada University. Max C. Fleischmann College of Agriculture. Cooperative Extension Service — Circ Coop Ext Serv Max C Fleischmann Coll Agric Nevada Univ
Circular. New Jersey Agricultural Experiment Station — Circ New Jers Agric Exp Stn
Circular. New Jersey Agricultural Experiment Station — Circ NJ Agr Exp Sta
Circular. New Jersey Agricultural Experiment Station — Circ NJ Agric Exp Stn
Circular. New Jersey Department of Agriculture — Circ New Jers Dep Agric
Circular. New Mexico Bureau of Mines and Mineral Resources — Circ New Mex Bur Mines Miner Resour
Circular. New Mexico State Bureau of Mines and Mineral Resources — Circ New Mex St Bur Mines Miner Resour
Circular. New Mexico State University. Agricultural Extension Service — Circ N Mex State Univ Agr Ext Serv
Circular. New Mexico State University. Cooperative Extension Service — Circ NM State Univ Coop Ext Serv
Circular. New York State Museum — Circ New York State Mus
Circular. North Carolina Agricultural Extension Service — Circ N Carol Agric Ext Serv
Circular. North Dakota Agricultural College. Agricultural Extension Service — Circ N Dak Agr Coll Agr Ext Serv
Circular of Information. Agricultural Experiment Station. Oregon State University — Circ Inf Agric Exp Stn Oreg State Univ
Circular of Information. Oregon State College. Agricultural Experiment Station — Circ Inform Oreg State Coll Agr Exp Sta
Circular. Oklahoma Agricultural Experiment Station — Circ Okla Agric Exp Stn
Circular. Oklahoma Geological Survey — Circ Okla Geol Surv
Circular. Oklahoma Geological Survey — Circ Oklahoma Geol Surv
Circular. Oklahoma State University of Agriculture and Applied Science. Agricultural Extension Service — Circ Okla State Univ Agr Appl Sci Agr Ext Serv
Circular. Ontario Agricultural College — Circ Ont Agric Coll
Circular. Ontario Department of Agriculture — Circ Ont Dep Agric
Circular. Oregon Agricultural Experiment Station — Circ Ore Agric Exp Stn
Circular. Oregon State College. Engineering Experiment Station — Circ Oreg State Coll Eng Exp
Circular. Oregon State College. Engineering Experiment Station — Circ Oreg State Coll Eng Exp Stn
Circular. Oregon State University. Engineering Experiment Station — Circ Oreg State Univ Eng Exp St
Circular. Pennsylvania Agricultural Experiment Station — Circ PA Agric Exp Stn

Circular. Pennsylvania State University. Agricultural Extension Service — Circ Pa State Univ Agric Ext Serv
Circular. Pennsylvania State University. Earth and Mineral Sciences Experiment Station — Circ PA State Univ Earth Miner Sci Exp St
Circular. Pennsylvania University Extension Service — Circ PA Univ Ext Serv
Circular. Purdue University. Agricultural Experiment Station — Circ Purdue Univ Agric Exp Stn
Circular. Rubber Research Institute of Malaya — Circ Rubber Res Inst Malaya
Circular S. Florida Agricultural Experiment Stations. Institute of Food and Agricultural Sciences. University of Florida — Circ S Fla Agric Exp Stn Inst Food Agric Sci Univ Fla
Circular S. Florida University Agricultural Experiment Station — Circ S Fla Univ Agr Exp Sta
Circular. Saskatchewan Research Council. Geology Division — Circ Sask Res Counc Geol Div
Circular. Secretaria da Agricultura. Seccao de Informacoes e Publicidade Agricola (Porto Alegre) — Circ Secr Agr Secc Inform Publ Agr (Porto Alegre)
Circular Series. Oregon State College. Engineering Experiment Station — Cir Ser Oreg State Coll Eng Exp Stn
Circular Series. Oregon State College. Engineering Experiment Station — Circ Ser Oreg State Coll Eng Exp Stn
Circular Series. West Virginia Geological and Economic Survey — Circ Ser W Va Geol Econ Sur
Circular. South Carolina Agricultural Experiment Station — Circ SC Agric Exp Stn
Circular. South Dakota Agricultural Experiment Station — Circ S Dak Agr Exp Sta
Circular. South Florida Agricultural Experiment Station — Circ S Fla Agric Exp Stn
Circular. Texas Agricultural Experiment Station — Circ Tex Agric Exp Stn
Circular. Texas Forest Service — Circ Tex For Serv
Circular to Schools — Circ to Sch
Circular. United States Department of Agriculture — Circ US Dep Agric
Circular. United States Department of Agriculture — Circ USDA
Circular. United States Geological Survey — Circ US Geol Surv
Circular. United States National Bureau of Standards — Circ US Natn Bur Stand
Circular. University of Florida. Agricultural Extension Service — Circ Univ Fla Agric Ext Serv
Circular. University of Florida. Cooperative Extension Service — Circular Univ Fla Coop Ext Serv
Circular. University of Georgia. College of Agriculture. Cooperative Extension Service — Circ Univ GA Coll Agr Coop Ext Serv
Circular. University of Illinois. College of Agriculture. Cooperative Extension Service — Circ Univ Ill Coll Agr Coop Ext Serv
Circular. University of Illinois. Cooperative Extension Service — Circ Univ Ill Coop Ext Serv
Circular. University of Kentucky Agricultural Experiment Station — Circ Univ Ky Agric Exp Stn
Circular. University of Kentucky. Agricultural Extension Service — Circ Univ KY Agr Ext Serv
Circular. University of Nebraska. College of Agriculture and Home Economics. Agricultural Experiment Station — Circ Univ Nebr Coll Agr Home Econ Agr Exp Sta
Circular. University of Nevada. Max C. Fleischmann College of Agriculture. Agricultural Extension Service — Circ Univ Nev Max C Fleischmann Coll Agr Agr Ext Serv
Circular. University of Tennessee. Agricultural Experiment Station — Circ Univ Tenn Agric Exp Stn
Circular. University of Wisconsin. College of Agriculture. Extension Service — Circ Univ Wis Coll Agr Ext Serv
Circular. Utah Agricultural Experiment Station — Circ Utah Agric Exp Stn
Circular. Utah Geological and Mineral Survey — Circ Utah Geol Miner Surv
Circular. Virginia Polytechnic Institute. Agricultural Extension Service — Circ VA Polytech Inst Agr Ext Serv
Circular. Washington Agriculture Experiment Station — Circ Wash Agr Exp Sta
Circular. Washington State University. College of Engineering — Circ Wash State Univ Coll Eng
Circular. Washington State University. Cooperative Extension Service — Circ Wash State Univ Coop Ext Serv
Circular. West Virginia. Agricultural Experiment Station — Circ WV Agric Exp Stn
Circular. West Virginia Agricultural Experiment Station — Circular West Virginia Agric Exper Station
Circular. West Virginia University Agricultural and Forestry Experiment Station — Circ W Va Univ Agric For Exp Stn
Circular. Wild Flower Preservation Society — Circ Wild Fl Preserv Soc
Circular. Wisconsin University of Agriculture. Extension Service — Circ Wis Univ Agric Ext Serv
Circular. Wyoming. Agricultural Experiment Station — Circ Wy Agric Exp Stn
Circular. Wyoming Agricultural Extension Service — Circ Wyo Agric Ext Serv
Circulars. American Paint and Varnish Manufacturers' Association. Scientific Section — Circ Am Paint Varn Manuf Assoc Sci Sect
Circulars. Electrotechnical Laboratory — Circ Electrotech Lab
Circulars. Electrotechnical Laboratory (Tokyo, Japan) — Circ Electrotech Lab (Tokyo)
Circulars. Electrotechnical Laboratory (Tokyo, Japan) — Circ Electrotech Lab (Tokyo Japan)
Circulars. National Paint, Varnish, and Lacquer Association. Scientific Section — Circ Natl Paint Varn Lacquer Assoc Sci Sect
Circulars. National Varnish Manufacturers' Association — Circ Natl Varn Manuf Assoc
Circulars. Paint Manufacturers' Association of the United States. Educational Bureau. Scientific Section — Circ Paint Manuf Assoc US Educ Bur Sci Sect
Circulating Regulatory Factors and Neuroendocrine Function — Circ Regul Factors Neuroendocr Funct
Circulation — CIRCAZ
Circulation Control — Circ Control
Circulation et Metabolisme du Cerveau — Circ Metab Cerveau
Circulation Research — Circ Res
Circulation Research — Circulation Res
Circulation Research — CIRUAL
Circulation Research. Supplement — Circ Res Suppl
Circulation. Supplement — Circ Suppl
Circulation. Supplement — Circulation Suppl
Circulatory Shock — Circ Shock
Circulatory Shock — CRSHA
Circulatory Shock — CRSHAG
Circulatory Shock (Supplement) — Circ Shock (Suppl)
Circulo Argentino de Odontologia. Boletin — Circ Argent Odontol Bol
Circumpolar Journal — CPJO
Cirkulaer. Jordbrukstekniska Institutet — Cirk Jordbrukstek Inst
CIRP [*College International pour l'Etude Scientifique des Techniques de Production Mecanique*] **Annals** — CIRAA
CIRP [*College International pour l'Etude Scientifique des Techniques de Production Mecanique*] **Annals** — CIRP Ann
CIRPHO [*Cercle International de Recherches Philosophiques par Ordinateur*] **Review** — CIRPHO
Cirugia Bucal — Cir Bucal
Cirugia del Uruguay — Cir Urug
Cirugia Espanola — Cir Esp
Cirugia Pediatrica — Cir Pediatr
Cirugia y Cirujanos — Cir Cir
Cirugia y Cirujanos [*Mexico*] — Cir Cirujanos
Cirurgia, Ginecologia, y Urologia — Cir Ginecol Urol
CIS [*Congressional Information Service*] **Abstracts on Cards** — CIS Abstr
CIS. Chromosome Information Service — CIS Chromosome Inf Serv
CIS [*Congressional Information Service*] **Index** — CIS Ind
CIS [*Congressional Information Service*] **Index** — CISI
CIS [*Congressional Information Service*] **Index to Publications of the United States Congress** — CIS/Index Publ US Congr
Cislennye Metody Mehaniki Splosnoi Stredy — Cisl Metody Meh Splosn Stredy
Cistercian Studies — Cist Stud
Cisterciensercbronik — CistC
CISTI [*Canada Institute for Scientific and Technical Information*] **Serials** [*Database*] — CISTISER
Cistota Ovzdusia — CIOVD
CITE [*Construction Information-Training Education Project*] **News** — CITE N
Citeaux — Cit
Citeaux. Commentarii Cistercienses — CCC
Citeaux. Commentarii Cistercienses — CCCist
Citeaux in de Nederlande — CitN
CITES Reports. Convention on International Trade in Endangered Species of Wild Fauna and Flora — CITE
Cithara — Cit
Citibank. Monthly Economic Letter — Citibank
Citibank. Monthly Economic Letter — Citibank Mo Econ Letter
Citibase-Weekly [*Database*] — CBW
Cities of the Eastern Roman Provinces — CERP
Citinskii Gosudarstvennyi Pedagogiceskii Institut. Ucenye Zapiski — Citin Gos Ped Inst Ucen Zap
Citizen Register — Citzn Reg
Citizens Bulletin — Cit Bul
Citrograph — CITGAN
Citrus and Subtropical Fruit Journal [*South Africa*] — Citrus Subtrop Fruit J
Citrus and Subtropical Fruit Journal — CSFJA
Citrus and Subtropical Fruit Journal — CSFJAW
Citrus and Vegetable Magazine — Citrus Veg Mag
Citrus and Vegetable Magazine — CVGMAX
Citrus Engineering Conference. Transactions — Citrus Eng Conf Trans
Citrus Grower — Citrus Grow
Citrus Grower — CTGAAH
Citrus Grower and Sub-Tropical Fruit Journal — CGSFAZ
Citrus Grower and Sub-Tropical Fruit Journal — Citrus Grow Sub-Trop Fruit J
Citrus Grower (Uitenhage, South Africa) — Citrus Grow Uitenhage S Afr
Citrus Industry — CIINAN
Citrus Industry — Citrus Ind
Citrus Industry — Citrus Industr
Citrus Industry Magazine — Citrus Ind Mag
Citrus Magazine — Citrus Mag
Citrus Magazine — CTRMA6
Citta di Vita — CV
City Club Bulletin (Chicago) — City Club Bul Chic
City College Vector — City Coll Vector
City Facts and Abstracts [*Database*] — CFA
City Invincible — CI
City of God — Cit God
City of London Law Review — London L Rev
City of Stoke-On-Trent Museum. Archaeological Society. Reports — City Stoke-On-Trent Mus Archaeol Soc Rep
Ciudad de Dios — CD
Ciudad de Dios — CdD
Civic Development — Civ Develop
Civic Development — Civic Dev
Civic Information and Techniques Exchange [*Database*] — CIVITEXT
Civil Aeronautics Administration. Journal — CAA J
Civil Aeronautics Administration. Journal — Civil Aero J
Civil and Military Law Journal — Civ and Mil LJ
Civil and Military Law Journal — Civ & Military LJ
Civil Defence Bulletin — Civ Def Bull
Civil Defence Bulletin — Civil Defence Bul

Civil Engineering — Ci Eng
Civil Engineering — Civ Eng
Civil Engineering [*London*] — Civ Engng
Civil Engineering — Civil Eng
Civil Engineering — Civil Enging
Civil Engineering — CVEGA
Civil Engineering. American Society of Civil Engineers — Civ Engng ASCE
Civil Engineering. American Society of Civil Engineers — Civil Engineering ASCE
Civil Engineering and Public Works Review — Civ Eng Pub Works Rev
Civil Engineering and Public Works Review — Civ Eng Public Works Rev
Civil Engineering and Public Works Review — Civ Engng Publ Wks Rev
Civil Engineering, Construction, and Public Works Journal [*India*] — CECJA
Civil Engineering, Construction, and Public Works Journal [*India*] — Civ Eng Constr Public Works J
Civil Engineering Contractor — Civ Eng Contract
Civil Engineering for Practicing and Design Engineers — CEPED
Civil Engineering for Practicing and Design Engineers — Civ Engng Pract & Des Engrs
Civil Engineering for Practicing and Design Engineers — Civil Enging Practicing Des Engrs
Civil Engineering (Great Britain) — Civ Engn (GB)
Civil Engineering in Japan — Civ Eng Jpn
Civil Engineering in South Africa — Civ Eng S Afr
Civil Engineering (London) — Civ Eng (London)
Civil Engineering (London) — Civ Engng (Lond)
Civil Engineering (New York) — Civ Eng (NY)
Civil Engineering (Peking) — Civ Eng (Peking)
Civil Engineering Surveyor — Civil Enging Surv
Civil Engineering Transactions. Institution of Engineers of Australia — Civ Eng Trans
Civil Engineering Transactions. Institution of Engineers of Australia — Civ Eng Trans Inst Eng Aust
Civil Engineering Transactions. Institution of Engineers of Australia — Civ Engng Trans
Civil Engineering Transactions. Institution of Engineers of Australia — Civ Engng Trans Instn Engrs Aust
Civil Engineering Transactions. Institution of Engineers of Australia — CVETB
Civil Liberties Reporter — Civ Lib Rptr
Civil Liberties Review — Civ Lib Rev
Civil Liberties Review — Civil Liberties R
Civil Liberties Review — Civil Liberties Rev
Civil Rights — Civ Rts
Civil Rights Digest — Civ Rights Digest
Civil Rights Digest — Civ Rts Dig
Civil Rights Digest — Civil Rights Dig
Civil Rights Research Review — Civil Rights Research R
Civil Service Journal — Civ Serv J
Civil Service Journal — CSJ
Civil War History — Civ War Hist
Civil War History — Civil War H
Civil War History — Civil War Hist
Civil War History — CiW
Civil War History — CWH
Civil War History — PCIV
Civil War Times Illustrated — Civ War T Illus
Civil War Times Illustrated — Civ War Times Illus
Civilian Defense — Civ Def
Civilizations. International Institute of Differing Civilizations — IIDC/C
Civilta Cattolica — CC
Civilta Cattolica — CCa
Civilta Cattolica — CCatt
Civilta Cattolica — Civ Cattol
Civilta Cattolica — Civilta Catt
Civilta Classica e Cristiana — CCC
Civilta Classica e Cristiana — Civ Cl Crist
Civilta delle Macchine — Civilta Macch
Civilta Fascista — CV
Civilta Moderna — Civ Mod
Civilta Moderna — CM
Civis Mundi — OWB
Cizi Jazyky ve Skole — CJa
Cizi Jazyky ve Skole — CJS
Cizi Jazyky ve Skole — CJVS
CL & CL. Computational Linguistics and Computer Languages [*Budapest*] — CL & CL Comput Linguist Comput Lang
CLA [*College Language Association*] **Journal** — CLAJ
CLA Journal. Official Quarterly Publication. College Language Association — CLA J
Cladistics — CLADEC
Cladistics. International Journal. Willi Hennig Society — Cladistics Int J Willi Hennig Soc
Claflin College. Review — CCR
Clan Gunn Society. Magazine — Clan Gunn Soc Mag
Clan MacLeod Magazine — Clan MacLeod Mag
Clan Munro Magazine — Clan Munro Mag
CLAO (Contact Lens Association of Ophthalmologists) Journal — CLAO (Contact Lens Assoc Ophthalmol) J
CLAO [*Contact Lens Association of Ophthalmologists*] **Journal** — CLAO J
Clara Rhodos — C Rh
Clara Rhodos — C Rhod
Clara Rhodos — ClRh
Clara Rhodos — CR
Claremont Quarterly — Clare Q
Clarendon Library of Logic and Philosophy — Clarendon Lib Logic Philos
Clarendon Medieval and Tudor Series — CMTS
Claridad (Puerto Rico) — CPR
Claridad Weekly — Claridad
Clarinet — Clar
Clarinet — CLAWA
Clarke Institute of Psychiatry. Monograph Series — ClPMAL
Clarke Institute of Psychiatry. Monograph Series — Clarke Inst Psychiatry Monogr Ser
Clark's Digest-Annotator — Clarks Dig Annot
Clartes Syndicales. Revue de Pensee et d'Action Syndicale — Clart Synd
Clasicos del Pensamiento — Clas Pensam
Class Action Reports — Cl Act Rep
Classes Preparatoires aux Grandes Ecoles Scientifiques — Class Prepartoires Ecoles Scl
Classic CD [*Formerly, Classical*] — GCLA
Classic Film Collector — Classic F Col
Classic Images — Classic
Classica et Mediaevalia — C & M
Classica et Mediaevalia — Cl Med
Classica et Mediaevalia — Cl Mediaev
Classica et Mediaevalia — Clae
Classica et Mediaevalia [*Aarhus*] — ClassMed
Classica et Mediaevalia — CM
Classica et Medievalia — Cl et Med
Classical [*Later, Classic CD*] — GCLA
Classical and Medieval Literature Criticism — CMLC
Classical and Modern Literature — Class Mod L
Classical and Modern Literature. Quarterly — CML
Classical and Quantum Gravity — Classical Quantum Gravity
Classical Antiquity — Cl Antiq
Classical Antiquity — PCLS
Classical Bulletin — CB
Classical Bulletin [*Chicago*] — Cl B
Classical Bulletin — Cl Bull
Classical Bulletin — Class B
Classical Bulletin [*St. Louis, MO*] — ClassBull
Classical Bulletin (Chicago) — Cl Bull C
Classical Folia — CF
Classical Folia — CFol
Classical Folia — ClaF
Classical Journal — CJ
Classical Journal — ClaJ
Classical Journal — Class J
Classical Journal [*Chicago*] — Class Journ
Classical Journal — Classic Jnl
Classical Journal — Classical J
Classical Journal — CLJ
Classical Journal and Scholars Review — CJSR
Classical Journal and Scholars Review — Class J
Classical Journal and Scholars Review — Class J SR
Classical Journal and Scholars Review — Class Journ
Classical Journal and Scholars Review — ClJ
Classical Journal (Chicago) — Cl Journ (C)
Classical Journal (Chicago) — Class J (C)
Classical Journal (London) — Class J (L)
Classical Journal (Malta) — CJ(Malta)
Classical Journal. Virgil Society. Malta Branch [*Valetta*] — Cl Journ
Classical Museum — C Mu
Classical Museum — Cl Mus
Classical Music Magazine — Classical Mus Mag
Classical Outlook — Cl O
Classical Outlook — Class Out
Classical Outlook — CO
Classical Outlook. Journal. American Classical League — Cl Outlook
Classical Philology — C Phil
Classical Philology — Cl Ph
Classical Philology — Cl Phil
Classical Philology — Cl Philol
Classical Philology — Cl Phy
Classical Philology — Class Phil
Classical Philology — Class Philol
Classical Philology — Classical Philol
Classical Philology [*Chicago*] — ClassPh
Classical Philology — CLP
Classical Philology — CP
Classical Philology — CPh
Classical Philology — PCLP
Classical Quarterly — C Qu
Classical Quarterly — Cl Q
Classical Quarterly — Cl Qu
Classical Quarterly — Cl Quart
Classical Quarterly — Class Q
Classical Quarterly — Class Quart
Classical Quarterly — Class Quartl
Classical Quarterly — Classical Q
Classical Quarterly — CQ
Classical Quarterly — PCLQ
Classical Quarterly Review — CQR
Classical Review — Cl R
Classical Review — Cl Rev
Classical Review — Class R
Classical Review — Class Rev
Classical Review — CR
Classical Review. New Series — Class R NS
Classical Review. New Series — Class Rev N Ser

Classical Roman Law — CRL
Classical Views — CLV
Classical Views — CV
Classical Weekly — Cl Weekly
Classical Weekly [*New York*] — ClassW
Classical Weekly — CW
Classical World — Cl W
Classical World — Cl World
Classical World — Class W
Classical World — Class World
Classical World — Classic World
Classical World — CW
Classici della Scienza — Class Sci
Classici e Neo-Latini — CeN
Classici e Neo-Latini — CN
Classicos de la Ciencias — Clas Cienc
Classics in Applied Mathematics — Classics Appl Math
Classics in Mathematics — Classics Math
Classics of Soviet Mathematics — Classics Soviet Math
Classification Society. Bulletin — Class Soc Bull
Classified Abstract Archive of the Alcohol Literature — Classified Abstr Arch Alcohol Lit
Classiques de l'Histoire de France du Moyen Age — CHFMA
Classiques du XXe Siecle — CVS
Classiques Francais du Moyen Age — CFMA
Classiques Garnier — CG
Classiques Verts — Class Verts
Classroom Computer Learning — GCCL
Classroom Resource Materials Series — Classr Res Mater Ser
Claudel Studies — Claudel St
Claudel Studies — ClaudelS
Clausthaler Geologische Abhandlungen — Clausthaler Geol Abh
Clausthaler Hefte zur Lagerstaettenkund und Geochemie der Mineralischen Rohstoffe — Clausthaler Hefte Lagerstaettenk Geochemie Miner Rohst
Clavier — Cl
Clavier — Cla
Clavier — CLAVA
Clavileno — Cl
Clavileno — Clav
Clavis Patrum Graecorum — CPG
Clay Minerals — Clay Miner
Clay Minerals. Bulletin [*Later, Clay Minerals*] — Clay Miner Bull
Clay Products Journal of Australia — Clay Prod J
Clay Products Journal of Australia — Clay Prod J Aust
Clay Products Journal of Australia — Clay Prod J Austr
Clay Products News and Ceramic Record — Clay Prod News Ceram Rec
Clay Record — Clay Rec
Clay Research — Clay Res
Clay Resources Bulletin. Louisiana Geological Survey — Clay Resour Bull La Geol Surv
Clay Science (Tokyo) — Clay Sci (Tokyo)
Claycraft and Structural Ceramics — Claycraft Struct Ceram
Clay-Industry — Clay Ind
Clays and Clay Minerals — CCM
Clays and Clay Minerals — Clay Clay M
Clays and Clay Minerals — Clays Clay Miner
Clays and Clay Minerals. Proceedings. Conference — Clays Clay Miner Proc Conf
CLB. Chemie fuer Labor und Betrieb — CLB Chem Labor Betr
CLB. Chemie fuer Labor und Betrieb. Beilage. Lernen und Leisten — CLB Chem Labor Betr Beil
Clean Air [*Parkville, Victoria*] — CLNABV
Clean Air [*Brighton, England*] — CNAIB4
Clean Air (Brighton, England) — CNAIB
Clean Air Conference. Proceedings — Clean Air Conf Proc
Clean Air Journal — Clean Air J
Clean Air. Special Edition — Clean Air Spec Ed
Clean Air. Special Edition — KSTKBO
Clean Air Year Book — CAYBAB
Clean Fuels from Biomass and Wastes. Symposium Papers — Clean Fuels Biomass Wastes Symp Pap
Clean Technology — Clean Technol
Cleaners and Dyers Advertiser — Clean Dyers Advert
Cleaning and Laundry World (Chicago) — Clean Laundry World (Chicago)
Cleaning Maintenance and Big Building Management — Cleaning Maint Big Bldg Mgmt
Clearing House — Clear H
Clearing House — Clearing H
Clearing House — ICLH
Clearing House for Local Authority Social Services Research — Clearing Hse L A Soc Serv Res
Clearing House Journal — Clearing House J
Clearinghouse Bulletin of Research in Human Organization — Clgh Bull Res Hum Organ
Clearinghouse Review — Clear R
Clearinghouse Review — Clearinghouse R
Clearinghouse Review — Clearinghouse Rev
Cleft Palate Craniofacial Journal — Clef Pal CR
Cleft Palate Journal — Clef Pal J
Cleft Palate Journal — Cleft Palate J
Cleft Palate Journal — CLPJA
Cleft Palate-Craniofacial Journal — Cleft Palate Craniofac J
Clemson Agricultural College. Agronomy Department. Mimeographed Series — Clemson Agric Coll Agron Dept Mimeogr Ser
Clemson Agricultural College of South Carolina. Agricultural Experiment Station. Annual Report — Clemson Agric Exp Sta Annual Rep
Clemson Agricultural College of South Carolina. Agricultural Experiment Station. Miscellaneous Series — Clemson Agric Exp Sta Misc Ser
Clemson University. College of Engineering. Engineeri ng Experiment Station. Bulletin — Clemson Univ Coll Eng Eng Exp Sta Bull
Clemson University. College of Forest and Recreation Resources. Department of Forestry. Forest Research Series — Clemson Univ Coll For Recreat Resour Dep For For Res Ser
Clemson University. Department of Forestry. Forest Research Series — Clemson Univ Dep For For Res Ser
Clemson University. Department of Forestry. Forest Research Series — CUFRB3
Clemson University. Department of Forestry. Forestry Bulletin — CFBUBN
Clemson University. Department of Forestry. Forestry Bulletin — Clemson Univ Dep For For Bull
Clemson University. Department of Forestry. Technical Paper — Clemson Univ Dep For Tech Pap
Clemson University. Department of Forestry. Technical Paper — CUFTA8
Clemson University. Review of Industrial Management and Textile Science — Clemson Univ Rev Ind Manage Text Sci
Clemson University Water Resources Research Institute. Technical Report — Clemson Univ Water Resour Res Inst Tech Rep
[*The*] **Clergy Monthly** [*Ranchi, Bihar, India*] — CleM
[*The*] **Clergy Monthly** [*Ranchi, Bihar, India*] — ClergyM
[*The*] **Clergy Monthly** [*Ranchi, Bihar, India*] — ClM
[*The*] **Clergy Monthly** — ClMthly
Clergy Review — Clergy Rev
[*The*] **Clergy Review** [*London*] — ClergyR
[*The*] **Clergy Review** [*London*] — ClR
Clermont. Universite. Annales Scientifiques. Geologie et Mineralogie — Clermont Univ Ann Sci Geol Mineral
Cleveland Bar Association. Journal — Clev B A J
Cleveland Bar Association. Journal — Clev B Assn J
Cleveland Bar Association. Journal — Clev Bar Ass'n J
Cleveland Clinic. Cardiovascular Consultations — Cleveland Clin Cardiovasc Consult
Cleveland Clinic. Journal of Medicine — Cleve Clin J Med
Cleveland Clinic. Quarterly — CCQUA8
Cleveland Clinic. Quarterly — Cleve Clin Q
Cleveland Clinic. Quarterly — Cleveland Clin Q
Cleveland Clinic. Quarterly — Cleveland Clin Quart
Cleveland Institution of Engineers. Proceedings — Cleveland Inst Eng Proc
Cleveland Medical Journal — Cleveland Med J
Cleveland Museum of Art. Bulletin — Cleveland Mus Bull
Cleveland Museum of Natural History. Museum News — Cleveland Mus Nat History Mus News
Cleveland Museum of Natural History. Science Publications — Cleveland Mus Nat History Sci Pubs
Cleveland Orchestra. Program Notes — Clev Orch
Cleveland State Law Review — Clev St L R
Cleveland State Law Review — Clev St L Rev
Cleveland State Law Review — CSLR
Cleveland Symposium on Macromolecules — Cleveland Symp Macromol
Cleveland-Marshall Law Review — Clev-Mar L Rev
Cleveland-Marshall Law Review — CM
Cleveland-Marshall Law Review — CMLR
Clima Commerce International — Clima Comm Internat
Climate Control [*India*] — Clim Control
Climate Monitor. Climatic Research Unit. University of East Anglia — CLMO
Climate of the Arctic. Alaska Science Conference — Clim Arc Alaska Sci Conf
Climatic Change — CLCHD
Climatic Change — CLCHDX
Climatic Change — Clim Change
Climatic Perspectives — CLPS
Climatological Data — CD
Climatological Data — Climat Data
Climatological Studies. Environment Canada. Atmospheric Environment — CSEV
Climax International Conference on the Chemistry and Uses of Molybdenum — Climax Int Conf Chem Uses Molybdenum
Cling Peach Quarterly. California Canning Peach Association — Cling Peach Quart
Clinic All-Round [*Japan*] — Clin All-Round
Clinica — CLNAAU
Clinica Chimica Acta — CCATAR
Clinica Chimica Acta — Clin Chim A
Clinica Chimica Acta — Clin Chim Acta
Clinica Chimica Acta — Clinica Chim Acta
Clinica Dietologica — CLDID7
Clinica Dietologica — Clin Dietol
Clinica e Laboratorio (Rome) — Clin Lab Rome
Clinica e Terapeutica (Sao Paulo) — Clin Ter Sao Paulo
Clinica Europa — Clin Eur
Clinica Geral [*Sao Paulo*] — CLGEB8
Clinica Geral (Sao Paulo) — Clin Geral (Sao Paulo)
Clinica Ginecologica — Clin Ginecol
Clinica Higiene e Hidrologia — Clin Hig Hidrol
Clinica Latina — Clin Latina
Clinica Medica Italiana — Clin Med Ital
Clinica Nuova — Clin Nuova
Clinica Oculistica — Clin Oculist
Clinica Odonto-Protesica — Clin Odonto Protes
Clinica Ortopedica — Clin Ortop
Clinica Ostetrica e Ginecologica — Clin Ostet Ginecol

Clinica Otorinolaringoiatrica — Clin Otorinolaringoiatr
Clinica Otorinolaringoiatrica — COURA
Clinica Otorinolaringoiatrica [*Catania*] — COURAZ
Clinica Otorinolaringoiatrica (Catania) — Clin Otorinolaringoiatr (Catania)
Clinica Pediatrica — Clin Pediat
Clinica Pediatrica — Clinica Pediat
Clinica Pediatrica (Bologna) — Clin Pediatr Bologna
Clinica Terapeutica — Clin Ter
Clinica Terapeutica — Clinica Terap
Clinica Terapeutica — CLTEA4
Clinica Terapeutica. Supplemento — Clin Ter Suppl
Clinica Veterinaria — Clin Vet
Clinica Veterinaria [*Milan*] — CLVEAE
Clinica Veterinaria (Milan) — Clin Vet (Milan)
Clinica World Medical Device News — CLN
Clinica y Laboratoria — Clin Lab
Clinica y Laboratoria — CLLAAK
Clinical Allergy [*England*] — CLAGB
Clinical Allergy — CLAGBI
Clinical Allergy — Clin Allergy
Clinical Anatomy — Clin Anat
Clinical and Biochemical Analysis — CBAND5
Clinical and Biochemical Analysis — Clin Biochem Anal
Clinical and Diagnostic Laboratory Immunology — Clin Diagn Lab Immunol
Clinical and Diagnostic Virology — Clin Diagn Virol
Clinical and Experimental Allergy — Clin Exp Al
Clinical and Experimental Allergy — Clin Exp Allergy
Clinical and Experimental Dermatology — CEDEDE
Clinical and Experimental Dermatology — Clin Exp Dermatol
Clinical and Experimental Dialysis and Apheresis — CEDAD2
Clinical and Experimental Dialysis and Apheresis — Clin Exp Dial Apheresis
Clinical and Experimental Gnotobiotics. Proceedings. International Symposium on Gnotobiology — Clin Exp Gnotobiotics Proc Int Symp
Clinical and Experimental Hypertension — CEHYDQ
Clinical and Experimental Hypertension — Clin Exp Hypertens
Clinical and Experimental Hypertension. Part A. Theory and Practice — CEHADM
Clinical and Experimental Hypertension. Part A. Theory and Practice — Clin Exp Hypertens A
Clinical and Experimental Hypertension. Part A. Theory and Practice — Clin Exp Hypertens Part A Theory Pract
Clinical and Experimental Hypertension. Part B. Hypertension in Pregnancy — Clin Exp Hypertens B
Clinical and Experimental Hypertension. Part B. Hypertension in Pregnancy — Clin Exp Hypertens Part B
Clinical and Experimental Immunology — CEXIA
Clinical and Experimental Immunology — CEXIAL
Clinical and Experimental Immunology — Clin Exp Im
Clinical and Experimental Immunology — Clin Exp Immunol
Clinical and Experimental Immunology — Clin Exper Immunol
Clinical and Experimental Immunoreproduction — CIEMDT
Clinical and Experimental Immunoreproduction — Clin Exp Immunoreprod
Clinical and Experimental Metastasis — CEM
Clinical and Experimental Metastasis — CEXMD2
Clinical and Experimental Metastasis — Clin & Exp Metastasis
Clinical and Experimental Metastasis — Clin Exp Metastasis
Clinical and Experimental Neurology — Clin Exp Neurol
Clinical and Experimental Nutrition — Clin Exp Nutr
Clinical and Experimental Obstetrics and Gynecology — CEGOAM
Clinical and Experimental Obstetrics and Gynecology — Clin Exp Obstet Gynecol
Clinical and Experimental Pharmacology and Physiology — CEXPB
Clinical and Experimental Pharmacology and Physiology — Clin Exp Ph
Clinical and Experimental Pharmacology and Physiology — Clin Exp Pharmcol Physiol
Clinical and Experimental Pharmacology and Physiology. Supplement — Clin Exp Pharmacol Physiol Suppl
Clinical and Experimental Psychiatry — Clin Exp Psychiatry
Clinical and Experimental Rheumatology — Clin Exp Rheumatol
Clinical and Experimental Studies in Gastroenterology and Hematology. Papers — Clin Exp Stud Gastroenterol Hematol Pap
Clinical and Experimental Studies in Immunotherapy. Proceedings. International Symposium — Clin Exp Stud Immunother Proc Int Symp
Clinical and Investigative Medicine — Clin Invest
Clinical and Investigative Medicine — Clin Invest Med
Clinical and Investigative Medicine — CNVMDL
Clinical and Laboratory Haematology — Clin Lab Haematol
Clinical Anesthesia — Clin Anesth
Clinical Approaches to Problems of Childhood — Clin Approaches Probl Child
Clinical Approaches to Problems of Childhood — CLPCBD
Clinical Aspects of Metabolic Bone Disease. Proceedings. International Symposium on Clinical Aspects of Metabolic Bone Disease — Clin Aspects Metab Bone Dis Proc Int Symp Clin Aspects Metab
Clinical Autonomic Research — Clin Auton Res
Clinical Bacteriology (Tokyo) — Clin Bacteriol (Tokyo)
Clinical Behavior Therapy — Clin Behav Ther
Clinical Behavior Therapy Review — Clin Behav Therapy Rev
Clinical, Biochemical, and Nutritional Aspects of Trace Elements — Clin Biochem Nutr Aspects Trace Elem
Clinical Biochemistry [*Ottawa*] — CLBIA
Clinical Biochemistry — CLBIAS
Clinical Biochemistry — Clin Bioch
Clinical Biochemistry — Clin Biochem
Clinical Biochemistry (Amsterdam) — Clin Biochem (Amsterdam)
Clinical Biochemistry of Domestic Animals [*monograph*] — Clin Biochem Domest Anim
Clinical Biochemistry of the Elderly [*Monograph*] — Clin Biochem Elderly
Clinical Biochemistry (Ottawa) — Clin Biochem Ottawa
Clinical Biochemistry Reviews (New York) — Clin Biochem Rev (NY)
Clinical Biofeedback and Health — Clin Biofeedback Health
Clinical Biomechanics — Clin Biomech
Clinical Bulletin — CLBUA
Clinical Bulletin [*Memorial Sloan-Kettering Cancer Center*] — CLBUAU
Clinical Bulletin — Clin Bull
Clinical Bulletin (Memorial Sloan-Kettering Cancer Center) — Clin Bull (Mem Sloan-Kettering Cancer Cent)
Clinical Cardiology — CLCADC
Clinical Cardiology — Clin Cardiol
Clinical Cardiovascular Physiology [*monograph*] — Clin Cardiovasc Physiol
Clinical Cellular Immunology. Molecular and Therapeutic Reviews — Clin Cell Immunol Mol Ther Rev
Clinical Chemist (New York) — Clin Chem NY
Clinical Chemistry [*Winston-Salem, North Carolina*] — CLCHA
Clinical Chemistry — CLCHAU
Clinical Chemistry — Clin Chem
Clinical Chemistry and Chemical Toxicology of Metals. Proceedings. International Symposium — Clin Chem Chem Toxicol Met Proc Int Symp
Clinical Chemistry Lookout [*Database*] — CCL
Clinical Chemistry Newsletter — Clin Chem Newsl
Clinical Chemistry of Monoamines — Clin Chem Monoamines
Clinical Chemistry (Winston-Salem, North Carolina) — Clin Chem (Winston Salem North Carolina)
Clinical Conference on Cancer — Clin Conf Cancer
Clinical Cytology: Series of Monographs — CLCYAD
Clinical Cytology: Series of Monographs — Clin Cytol Ser Monogr
Clinical Decisions in Obstetrics and Gynecology — Clin Decis Obstet Gynecol
Clinical Dialysis and Transplant Forum. Proceedings — Clin Dial Transplant Forum Proc
Clinical Disorders in Pediatric Nutrition — Clin Disord Pediatr Nutr
Clinical Disorders of Fluid and Electrolyte Metabolism — Clin Disord Fluid Electrolyte Metab
Clinical Drug Investigation — Clin Drug Invest
Clinical Drug Trials and Tribulations — Clin Drug Trials Tribulations
Clinical Dysmorphology — Clin Dysmorphol
Clinical Echocardiography — Clin Echocardiogr
Clinical Ecology — Clin Ecol
Clinical Electroencephalography — CEEGAM
Clinical Electroencephalography — Clin EEG
Clinical Electroencephalography — Clin Electr
Clinical Electroencephalography — Clin Electroencephalogr
Clinical Endocrinology — CLECA
Clinical Endocrinology — CLECAP
Clinical Endocrinology — Clin Endocr
Clinical Endocrinology — Clin Endocrinol
Clinical Endocrinology and Metabolism — Clin Endocrinol Metab
Clinical Endocrinology (New York) — Clin Endocrinol NY
Clinical Endocrinology (Oxford) — Clin Endocrinol (Oxford)
Clinical Engineer — Clin Engineer
Clinical Engineering — CLENDR
Clinical Engineering — Clin Eng
Clinical Engineering Information Service — Clin Eng Inf Serv
Clinical Engineering News — Clin Eng News
Clinical Enzymology — Clin Enzymol
Clinical Gastroenterology — Clin Gastroenterol
Clinical Genetics — CLGNA
Clinical Genetics — CLGNAY
Clinical Genetics — Clin Genet
Clinical Genetics Seminar — Clin Genet Semin
Clinical Gerontologist — CLGEDA
Clinical Gerontologist — CLGR
Clinical Gerontologist — Clin Gerontol
Clinical Gynecology and Obstetrics [*Tokyo*] — RFUSA4
Clinical Gynecology and Obstetrics (Tokyo) — Clin Gynecol Obstet (Tokyo)
Clinical Hemorheology — Clin Hemorh
Clinical Hemorheology — Clin Hemorheol
Clinical Imaging — Clin Imaging
Clinical Immunobiology — Clin Immunobiol
Clinical Immunology and Immunopathology — CLIIA
Clinical Immunology and Immunopathology — CLIIAT
Clinical Immunology and Immunopathology — Clin Immun
Clinical Immunology and Immunopathology — Clin Immunol Immunopathol
Clinical Immunology Newsletter — CIMNDC
Clinical Immunology Newsletter — Clin Immunol Newsl
Clinical Immunology. Proceedings. IUIS [*International Union of Immunological Societies*] **Conference on Clinical Immunology** — Clin Immunol Proc IUIS Conf
Clinical Immunology Reviews — CIMRDO
Clinical Immunology Reviews — Clin Immunol Rev
Clinical Infectious Diseases — Clin Infect Dis
Clinical Investigator — Clin Invest
Clinical Journal — Clin J
Clinical Journal of Pain — Clin J Pain
Clinical Journal of Sport Medicine — Clin J Sport Med
Clinical Journal of Sport Medicine — Clinical J Sport Med
Clinical Kinesiology — Clinical Kines
Clinical Lab Letter — CLL
Clinical Laboratory Assays. New Technology and Future Directions. Papers presented at the Annual Clinical Laboratory Assays Conference — Clin Lab Assays Pap Annu Clin Lab Assays Conf

Clinical Law Journal and Newsletter — Clin Law Jnl Newsl
Clinical Librarian Quarterly — Clin Libr Q
Clinical Management in Physical Therapy — Clin Manage Phys Ther
Clinical Materials — Clin Mater
Clinical Medicine — Clin Med
Clinical Medicine — CLMEA3
Clinical Medicine and Surgery — Clin Med Surg
Clinical Microbiology and Infection — Clin Microbiol Infect
Clinical Microbiology Reviews — Clin Microbiol Rev
Clinical Microbiology (Tokyo) — Clin Microbiol Tokyo
Clinical Molecular Pathology — Clin Mol Pathol
Clinical Monographs in Hematology — Clin Mon Hemat
Clinical Nephrology — Clin Nephrol
Clinical Nephrology — CLNHBI
Clinical Nephrology — CN
Clinical Neurology [*Tokyo*] — RISHBH
Clinical Neurology and Neurosurgery — Clin Neurol
Clinical Neurology and Neurosurgery — Clin Neurol Neurosurg
Clinical Neurology and Neurosurgery — CNNSBV
Clinical Neurology (Tokyo) — Clin Neurol (Tokyo)
Clinical Neuropathology — Clin Neuropathol
Clinical Neuropathology — CLNPDA
Clinical Neuropharmacology — Clin Neuropharmacol
Clinical Neuropharmacology — CLNEDB
Clinical Neuropsychology — Clin Neuropsychol
Clinical Neuropsychology — CLNYD3
Clinical Neuroscience — Clin Neurosci
Clinical Neurosurgery — Clin Neurosurg
Clinical Neurosurgery — CLNEA
Clinical Notes on Respiratory Diseases — Clin Notes Respir Dis
Clinical Notes on Respiratory Diseases — CNRCB
Clinical Notes on Respiratory Diseases — CNRD
Clinical Notes On-Line [*Database*] — CNOL
Clinical Nuclear Medicine — Clin Nucl Med
Clinical Nuclear Medicine — CNMED
Clinical Nuclear Medicine — CNMEDK
Clinical Nutrition — Clin Nutr
Clinical Nutrition — CLNUEQ
Clinical Nutrition (Philadelphia) — Clin Nutr (Phila)
Clinical Obstetrics and Gynecology — Clin Obst Gynec
Clinical Obstetrics and Gynecology — Clin Obstet Gynecol
Clinical Obstetrics and Gynecology — CO & G
Clinical Obstetrics and Gynecology — COGYA
Clinical Obstetrics and Gynecology — COGYAK
Clinical Oncology — Clin Oncol
Clinical Oncology — CLOND
Clinical Oncology — CLOND9
Clinical Oncology. Royal College of Radiologists — Clin Oncol R Coll Radiol
Clinical Oncology (Tianjin) — Clin Oncol (Tianjin)
Clinical Orthopaedic Surgery — RISEB8
Clinical Orthopaedics — Clin Orthop
Clinical Orthopaedics — CORPA
Clinical Orthopaedics and Related Research — Clin Orthop
Clinical Orthopaedics and Related Research — Clin Orthop Relat Res
Clinical Orthopaedics and Related Research — CORTB
Clinical Orthopaedics and Related Research — CORTBR
Clinical Orthopedic Surgery [*Japan*] — Clin Orthop Surg
Clinical Otolaryngology — Clin Otolaryngol
Clinical Otolaryngology and Allied Sciences — COTSD2
Clinical Otolaryngology and Allied Sciences (Oxford) — Clin Otolaryngol Allied Sci (Oxf)
Clinical Otolaryngology (Oxford) — Clin Otolaryngol (Oxf)
Clinical Pediatrics [*Philadelphia*] — Clin Pediat
Clinical Pediatrics — Clin Pediatr
Clinical Pediatrics [*Philadelphia*] — CPEDA
Clinical Pediatrics — CPEDAM
Clinical Pediatrics (New York) — Clin Pediatr NY
Clinical Pediatrics (Philadelphia) — Clin Pediatr (Phila)
Clinical Pediatrics (Philadelphia) — Clin Pediatr (Philadelphia)
Clinical Pharmacokinetics — Clin Pharmacokinet
Clinical Pharmacokinetics — CPKNDH
Clinical Pharmacology [*monograph*] — Clin Pharmacol
Clinical Pharmacology — CLPHEV
Clinical Pharmacology and Drug Epidemiology — Clin Pharmacol Drug Epidemiol
Clinical Pharmacology and Drug Epidemiology [*Elsevier Book Series*] — CPDE
Clinical Pharmacology and Therapeutics — Clin Pharm
Clinical Pharmacology and Therapeutics — Clin Pharmacol Ther
Clinical Pharmacology and Therapeutics — Clin Pharmacol Therap
Clinical Pharmacology and Therapeutics — CLPTA
Clinical Pharmacology and Therapeutics — CLPTAT
Clinical Pharmacology and Therapeutics (London) — Clin Pharmacol Ther London
Clinical Pharmacology and Therapeutics. Proceedings. Interamerican Congress of Clinical Pharmacology and Therapeutics — Clin Pharmacol Ther Proc Interam Congr
Clinical Pharmacology and Therapeutics Series — Clin Pharmacol Ther Ser
Clinical Pharmacology (New York) — Clin Pharmacol (NY)
Clinical Pharmacology of Biotechnology Products. Proceedings. Esteve Foundation Symposium — Clin Pharmacol Biotechnol Prod Proc Esteve Found Symp
Clinical Pharmacology Research — Clin Pharmacol Res
Clinical Pharmacology Research — CPHRDE
Clinical Pharmacy — CPHADV
Clinical Pharmacy Education and Patient Education. Proceedings. European Symposium on Clinical Pharmacy — Clin Pharm Educ Patient Educ Proc Eur Symp Clin Pharm
Clinical Pharmacy Symposium — Clin Pharm Symp
Clinical Physics and Physiological Measurement — Clin Phys and Physiol Meas
Clinical Physics and Physiological Measurement — CPPM
Clinical Physics and Physiological Measurement — CPPMD5
Clinical Physiology — Clin Physiol
Clinical Physiology — CLPHDU
Clinical Physiology — CP
Clinical Physiology and Biochemistry — Clin Physiol Biochem
Clinical Physiology and Biochemistry — CPB
Clinical Physiology and Biochemistry — CPBIDP
Clinical Physiology (Oxford) — Clin Physiol (Oxf)
Clinical Physiology (Tokyo) — Clin Physiol (Tokyo)
Clinical Practice Guideline. Quick Reference Guide for Clinicians — Clin Pract Guidel Quick Ref Guide Clin
Clinical Preventive Dentistry — Clin Prev Dent
Clinical Preventive Dentistry — Clin Prevent Dent
Clinical Preventive Dentistry — CPRDDM
Clinical Proceedings (Cape Town) — Clin Proc (Cape Town)
Clinical Proceedings. Children's Hospital National Medical Center — Clin Proc Child Hosp Natl Med Cent
Clinical Proceedings. Children's Hospital National Medical Center — CPNMAQ
Clinical Proceedings. Children's Hospital of the District of Columbia [*Later, Clinical Proceedings. Children's Hospital National Medical Center*] — Clin Proc Child Hosp DC
Clinical Proceedings. Children's Hospital of the District of Columbia [*Later, Clinical Proceedings. Children's Hospital National Medical Center*] — CPCHAO
Clinical Protocols [*Database*] — CLINPROT
Clinical Psychiatry [*Japan*] — Clin Psychiatr
Clinical Psychiatry (Tokyo) — Clin Psychiatry (Tokyo)
Clinical Psychology Review — Clin Psychol Rev
Clinical Radiology — Clin Radiol
Clinical Radiology — CLRAA
Clinical Radiology — CLRAAG
Clinical Rehabilitation — Clin Rehabil
Clinical Report [*Japan*] — Clin Rep
Clinical Reproduction and Fertility — Clin Reprod Fertil
Clinical Reproduction and Fertility — CRFEDD
Clinical Reproductive Neuroendocrinology. International Seminar on Reproductive Physiology and Sexual Endocrinology — Clin Reprod Neuroendocrinol Int Semin
Clinical Research — Clin Res
Clinical Research — CLREA
Clinical Research — CLREAS
Clinical Research Centre Symposium — Clin Res Cent Symp
Clinical Research Centre. Symposium (Harrow, England) — Clin Res Cent Symp (Harrow Engl)
Clinical Research Practices and Drug Regulatory Affairs — Clin Res Pract Drug Regul Aff
Clinical Research Practices and Drug Regulatory Affairs — CRPADH
Clinical Research Practices and Drug Regulatory Affairs — CRPD
Clinical Research Proceedings — Clin Res Proc
Clinical Research Reviews — Clin Res Rev
Clinical Respiratory Physiology — Clin Respir Physiol
Clinical Review and Research Notes — Clin Rev Res Notes
Clinical Reviews in Allergy — Clin Rev Allergy
Clinical Reviews in Allergy and Immunology — Clin Rev Allergy Immunol
Clinical Rheumatology — Clin Rheumatol
Clinical Science — Clin Sc
Clinical Science [*Oxford*] [*Clinical Science and Molecular Medicine*] [*Later,*] — Clin Sci
Clinical Science and Molecular Medicine — Clin Sc Mol
Clinical Science and Molecular Medicine — Clin Sci Mol Med
Clinical Science and Molecular Medicine — CSMMCA
Clinical Science and Molecular Medicine. Supplement — Clin Sci Mol Med Suppl
Clinical Science (Colchester) — Clin Sci Colch
Clinical Science (London) — Clin Sci (Lond)
Clinical Science (Oxford) [*Later, Clinical Science and Molecular Medicine*] — Clin Sci (Oxf)
Clinical Science. Supplement — Clin Sci Suppl
Clinical Social Work Journal — Clin S Work
Clinical Social Work Journal — PCSW
Clinical Sociology Review — Clin Sociol Rev
Clinical Studies — Clin Stud
Clinical Studies [*Elsevier Book Series*] — CS
Clinical Supervisor. The Journal of Supervision in Psychotherapy and Mental Health — Clin Superv
Clinical Surgery [*Japan*] — Clin Surg
Clinical Symposia — CICSA
Clinical Symposia — Clin Symp
Clinical Technical Report. Beckman Instruments, Inc. — Clin Tech Rep Beckman Instrum Inc
Clinical Therapeutics — Clin Ther
Clinical Therapeutics — CLTHDG
Clinical Toxicology — Clin Toxic
Clinical Toxicology — Clin Toxicol
Clinical Toxicology — CTOXA
Clinical Toxicology — CTOXAO
Clinical Toxicology Bulletin — Clin Toxicol Bull
Clinical Toxicology Bulletin — CTXBA3
Clinical Toxicology Consultant — Clin Toxicol Consult
Clinical Toxicology of Commercial Products [*Dartmouth Medical School; University of Rochester*] [*Database - inactive*] — CTCP

Clinical Transplantation — Clin Transplant
Clinical Transplants — Clin Transpl
Clinical Trials Journal — Clin Trials J
Clinical-Biochemical Aspects of Internal Diseases — Clin Biochem Aspects Intern Dis
Clinically Important Adverse Drug Interactions [*Elsevier Book Series*] — CIADI
Clinically Important Adverse Drug Interactions — Clin Important Adverse Drug Interact
Clinician [*Panjim-Goa, India*] — CLCNB
Clinics in Anaesthesiology — Clin Anaesthesiol
Clinics in Andrology — Clin Androl
Clinics in Chest Medicine — CCHMD
Clinics in Chest Medicine — Clin Chest Med
Clinics in Critical Care Medicine — Clin Crit Care Med
Clinics in Dermatology — Clin Dermatol
Clinics in Diagnostic Ultrasound — Clin Diagn Ultrasound
Clinics in Endocrinology and Metabolism — CEDMB2
Clinics in Endocrinology and Metabolism — Clin End Me
Clinics in Gastroenterology — CGSTA
Clinics in Gastroenterology — CGSTA9
Clinics in Gastroenterology — Clin Gastro
Clinics in Gastroenterology — Clin Gastroenterol
Clinics in Gastroenterology. Supplement — Clin Gastroenterol Suppl
Clinics in Geriatric Medicine — Clin Geriatr Med
Clinics in Haematology — CLHMB3
Clinics in Haematology — Clin Haemat
Clinics in Haematology — Clin Haematol
Clinics in Laboratory Medicine — Clin Lab Med
Clinics in Obstetrics and Gynaecology. Supplement — Clin Obstet Gynaecol Suppl
Clinics in Perinatology — Clin Perinatol
Clinics in Perinatology — CLPED
Clinics in Perinatology — CLPEDL
Clinics in Plastic Surgery — Clin Plast Surg
Clinics in Podiatric Medicine and Surgery — Clin Podiatr Med Surg
Clinics in Podiatry — Clin Pod
Clinics in Podiatry — Clin Podiatry
Clinics in Rheumatic Diseases — Clin Rheum Dis
Clinics in Rheumatic Diseases — CRHDDK
Clinics in Sports Medicine — Clin Sports Med
Clinics of Japan — Clin Jpn
Clinics of Respiratory Organs — Clin Respir Organs
Clinics of the Virginia Mason Hospital — Clin Virginia Mason Hosp
Clinique des Hopitaux des Enfants et Revue Retrospective Medico-Chirugicale et Hygienique — Clin Hop Enfants
Clinique Ophtalmologique — Clin Ophtalmol
Clinique Ophtalmologique — CLIOAD
Clinton Laboratories. Technical Paper — Clinton Lab Tech Pap
Clio — CLMDAY
Clio — PCLO
Clio Medica — Clio Med
Clio Medica — CM
CLM [*Culham Laboratory Reports*] **Report. United Kingdom Atomic Energy Authority** — CLM Rep UK At Energy Auth
Clogher Record — Clogher Rec
Clothing and Textiles Research Journal — Clothing Text Res J
Clothing Research Journal — Cloth Res Jnl
CLR [*Council on Library Resources*] **Recent Developments** — CLR Recent Devt
CLR [*Council on Library Resources*] **Recent Developments** — CLRDA
CLS [*Christian Legal Society*] **Quarterly** — CLS Q
CLSU (Central Luzon State University) Scientific Journal — CLSU Sci J
CLU [*Chartered Life Underwriters*] **Journal** — CLU
CLU [*Chartered Life Underwriters*] **Journal** — CLU J
Club du Livre Francais — CLF
Club du Meilleur Livre — CML
Club Francais de la Medaille — CFM
Club Series. University of North Carolina. State College of Agriculture and Engineering. Agricultural Extension Service — Club Ser Univ NC State Coll Agr Eng Agr Ext Serv
Clujul Medical — Cluj Med
Clujul Medical — Clujul Med
Clustering Phenomena in Nuclei [*Vieweg, Braunschweig*] — Clustering Phenom Nuclei
CM. Canadian Materials for Schools and Libraries — CM
CMFRI [*Central Marine Fisheries Research Institute*] **Bulletin** — CMFBD3
CMFRI [*Central Marine Fisheries Research Institute*] **Bulletin** — CMFRI Bull
CMI [*Commonwealth Mycological Institute*] **Descriptions of Pathogenic Fungi and Bacteria** — CMI Descr Pathog Fungi Bact
CMI [*Commonwealth Mycological Institute*] **Descriptions of Pathogenic Fungi and Bacteria** — CMIFAR
CMMI (Council of Mining and Metallurgical Institutions) Congress — CMMI Congr
CMP Newsletter — CMP
C-MRS (Chinese Materials Research Society) International Symposia Proceedings — C MRS Int Symp Proc
CMS (Clay Minerals Society) Workshop Lectures — CMS Workshop Lect
CMU [*Central Mindanao University*] **Journal of Science and Technology** — CMUJST
CN [*Consmetic News*] — CN
CNA (Canadian Nuclear Association) Report — CNA Rep
CNE. Communication/Navigation Electronics — CNE Commun Navig Electron
CNEA (Argetina. Comision Nacional de Energia Atomica) Informe — CNEA Inf
CNEN-RT/BIO (Italy. Comitato Nazionale Energia Nucleare) — CNEN RT BIO Italy Com Naz Energ Nucl
CNEN-RT/FIMA (Italy. Comitato Nazionale Energia Nucleare) — CNEN RT FIMA Italy Com Naz Energ Nucl
CNEN-RT/ING (Italy. Comitato Nazionale Energia Nucleare) — CNEN RT ING Italy Com Naz Energ Nucl
CNEP [*Comision Nacional para la Erradicacion del Paludismo*] **Boletin** — CNEP Bol
CNEP (Comision Nacional para la Erradicacion del Paludismo) Boletin — CNEP (Com Nac Errad Palud) Bol
CNET (France. Centre National d'Etudes des Telecommunications) Annales des Telecommunications — CNET Ann Telecommun
CNFRA. Comite National Francais des Recherches Antarctiques — CNFRA Com Nat Fr Rech Antarct
CNFS. Commercial News for the Foreign Service — CNFS Commer News For Serv
CNRM (Centre National de Recherches Metallurgiques). Metallurgical Reports [*Belgium*] — CNRM (Cent Natl Rech Metall) Metall Rep
CNRM (Centre National de Recherches Metallurgiques) Metallurgical Reports [*Belgium*] — CNRM Metall Rep
CNRM [*Centre National de Recherches Metallurgiques*]. Metallurgical Reports — CNRM
CNRS (Centre National de la Recherche Scientifique) Research (New York) — CNRS Res
CNS Drug Reviews — CNS Drug Rev
Coach and Athlete — Coach and Athl
Coaching Clinic — Coach Clin
Coaching Clinic — Coach Clinic
Coaching Journal and Bus Review — Coaching J Bus Rev
Coaching Review — Coach Rev
Coaching Science Update — Coach Sci Update
Coaching Women's Athletics — Coach Women's Athl
Coaching Women's Athletics — Coach Women's Athletics
Coal Abstracts [*England*] — Coal Abstr
Coal Age — CBU
Coal Age — COLAA
Coal and Base Minerals of Southern Africa — Coal Base Miner South Afr
Coal and Coke Sessions. Canadian Chemical Engineering Conference — Coal Coke Sess Can Chem Eng Conf
Coal and Energy Quarterly — Coal Energy Q
Coal and Iron (Kharkov) — Coal Iron Kharkov
Coal Canada Focus — Coal Can Foc
Coal Conference and Exposition — Coal Conference and Expo
Coal Convention. Session Papers. Set 4. Coal Preparation — Coal Conv Sess Pap Set 4 Coal Prep
Coal Conversion — Coal Convers
Coal Geology Bulletin — Coal Geol Bul
Coal Geology Bulletin. West Virginia Geological and Economic Survey — Coal Geol Bull WV Geol Econ Surv
Coal, Gold, and Base Minerals of Southern Africa — CGBMA
Coal, Gold, and Base Minerals of Southern Africa — Coal Gold Base Miner South Afr
Coal, Gold, and Base Minerals of Southern Africa — Coal Gold Base Miner Sthn Afr
Coal Industry News — Coal Ind N
Coal Liquid Mixtures. European Conference — Coal Liq Mixtures Eur Conf
Coal Management Techniques Symposia — Coal Manage Tech Symp
Coal Mine Drainage Research Symposia — Coal Mine Drain Res Symp
Coal Miner — COA
Coal Mining and Processing — CMPRB
Coal Mining and Processing — Coal M & P
Coal Mining and Processing — Coal Min Process
Coal Mining (Chicago) — Coal Min (Chicago)
Coal Mining Technology — Coal Min Technol
Coal News [*London*] — COANB
Coal Observer — Coal Obs
Coal Operator — Coal Oper
Coal Outlook — Coal Outlk
Coal Preparation — Coal Prep
Coal Preparation and Utilization Symposium — Coal Prep Util Symp
Coal Preparation (Gordon & Breach) — Coal Prep (Gordon & Breach)
Coal Preparation Symposia — Coal Prep Symp
Coal Preparation (Thunderbird Enterprises) — Coal Prep Thunderbird Enterp
Coal Preparation (Tokyo) — Coal Prep (Tokyo)
Coal Processing Technology — Coal Process Technol
Coal Quarterly — Coal Q
Coal Research in CSIRO [*Commonwealth Scientific and Industrial Research Organisation*] — Coal Res CSIRO
Coal Science and Chemistry — Coal Sci Chem
Coal Science and Technology — Coal Sci Technol
Coal Science and Technology [*Elsevier Book Series*] — CST
Coal Science Technology (Peking) — Coal Sci Technol (Peking)
Coal Situation — Coal Situat
Coal Situation (Chase Bank) — Chase Coal
Coal Slurry Fuels Preparation and Utilization. Proceedings. International Symposium — Coal Slurry Fuels Prep Util Proc Int Symp
Coal Tar (Tokyo) — Coal Tar (Tokyo)
Coal Technology — Coal Technol
Coal Technology — COTED
Coal Technology Europe — Coal Technol Eur
Coal Technology (Houston) — Coal Technol (Houston)
Coal Technology (New York) — Coal Technol NY
Coal Technology Report — Coal Technol Rep
Coal Testing Conference. Proceedings — Coal Test Conf Proc
Coal Utilization — Coal Util
Coal Utilization — COUTA
Coal Utilization Symposia — Coal Util Symp

Coal Week International — Coal Wk I
Coast Artillery Journal — Coast Artillery J
Coastal Bend Medicine [*Texas*] — Coastal Bend Med
Coastal Engineering — Coastal Eng
Coastal Engineering — Coastal Engng
Coastal Engineering in Japan — Coastal Eng Japan
Coastal Engineering in Japan — Coastal Eng Jpn
Coastal Engineering in Japan — Coastal Engng Japan
Coastal Research Notes — Coastal Res Notes
Coastal Water Research Project Biennial Report (Southern California) — Coastal Water Res Proj Bienn Rep South Calif
Coastal Zone. Informal Newsletter of the Resources of the Pacific and Western Arctic Coasts of Canada — COZE
Coastal Zone Management Journal — Coast Zone Manage J
Coastal Zone Management Journal — Coastal Zone Manage J
Coastal Zone Management Journal — Coastal Zone Mgt J
Coastal Zone Management Journal — CZMJB
Coat of Arms — CoA
Coating Conference. Proceedings — Coat Conf Proc
Coatings, Community, and Care. International Conference — Coat Community Car Int Conf
Cobalt — COBAA
Cobalt and Cobalt Abstracts — Cobalt Cobalt Abstr
Cobalt (English Edition) — Cobalt Engl Ed
Cobblestone — Cobble
Coblenzer Zeitschrift fuer Heimatkunde — CoblZH
Cobouw. Dagblad voor de Bouwwereld — COB
Coccidioidomycosis. Proceedings. International Conference on Coccidioidomycosis — Coccidioidomycosis Proc Int Conf
Cochlear-Research. Symposium — Cochlear Res Symp
Cockerill Sambre Acier [*Belgium*] — Cockerill
Cocoa Research Institute. Council for Scientific and Industrial Research. Annual Report — Cocoa Res Inst CSIR Annu Rep
Cocoa Research Institute. Council for Scientific and Industrial Research. Annual Report — WACRAX
Cocoa Research Institute. Ghana Academy of Sciences. Annual Report — Cocoa Res Inst Ghana Acad Sci Annu Rep
Cocoa Research Institute. Ghana Academy of Sciences. Annual Report — CRGAB4
Cocoa Research Institute. Tafo, Ghana. Technical Bulletin — Cocoa Res Inst Tafo Ghana Tech Bull
Cocobro-Jaarboekje — Cocobro Jaarb
Coconut Bulletin — COCBAX
Coconut Bulletin — Coconut Bull
Coconut Research Institute. Bulletin — CCIBAD
Coconut Research Institute. Bulletin — Coconut Res Inst Bull
Cocuk Sagligi ve Hastaliklari Dergisi — Cocuk Sagligi Hastaliklari Derg
CODATA [*Committee on Data for Science and Technology*] **Bulletin** — CODATA Bull
CODATA [*Committee on Data for Science and Technology*] **Newsletter** [*France*] — CODATA Newsl
CODATA [*Committee on Data for Science and Technology*] **Special Report** — CODATA Spec Rep
Code Administratif [*France*] — C Adm
Code Civil Suisse — CC
Code de Commerce — Co
Code de l'Organisation Judiciaire du Congo — C Org Jud
Code de Procedure Penale [*France*] — C Pr Pen
Code des Droits de Succession — C Succ
Code des Droits de Timbre — CT
Code des Juridictions Indigenes — C Jur Ind
Code des Obligations [*Switzerland*] — CO
Code des Taxes Assimilees aux Impots sur les Revenus — CTAIR
Code du Travail [*France*] — C Trav
Code du Travail — CTr
Code Forestier — For
Code Judiciaire — C Jud
Code of Alabama — Ala Code
Code of Civil Procedure (India) — (India) Code Civ Proc
Code of Colorado Regulations — Colo Code Regs
Code of Criminal Procedure (India) — (India) Code Crim Proc
Code of Federal Regulations — Code Fed Reg
Code of Georgia, Annotated (Harrison) — GA Code Ann (Harrison)
Code of Justinian [*Roman law*] — Code J
Code of Laws of South Carolina Annotated. Code of Regulations — SC Code Regs
Code of Laws of South Carolina Annotated (Lawyers Co-Op) — Sc Code Ann (Law Co-Op)
Code of Maryland Regulations — MD Regs Code
Code of Massachusetts Regulations — Mass Regs Code
Code of Theodosius [*Roman law*] — Code Th
Code of Virginia Annotated — Va Code Ann
Code Penal Suisse — CP
Codex Iustinianus — C Iust
Codice Civile Svizzero — CC
Codice de Procedura Civile [*Italy*] — CPC
Codice della Navigazione [*Italy*] — C Nav
Codice delle Obligazioni [*Switzerland*] — CO
Codice di Commercio [*Italy*] — C Comm
Codice Penale [*Italy*] — CP
Codice Penale Svizzero — CP
Codices Latini Antiquiores — Codd Lat Ant
Codices Manuscripti — Cod Man
Codigo Civil — CC
Codigo Civil [*Argentina*] — Cod Civ
Codigo Civil para el Distrito Federal [*Mexico*] — CCDF
Codigo Comercial [*Brazil*] — C Co
Codigo de Comercio [*Argentina*] — Cod Com
Codigo de Processo Civil [*Brazil*] — CPC
Codigo de Processo Penal [*Brazil*] — CPP
Codigo Federal de Procedimientos Civiles [*Mexico*] — CFPC
Codigo Federal de Procedimientos Penales [*Mexico*] — CFPP
Codigo Fiscal de la Federacion [*Mexico*] — CFF
Codigo Penal [*Argentina*] — Cod Pen
Codigo Penal [*Brazil*] — CP
Codigo Penal para el Distrito Federal [*Mexico*] — CPDF
Codigo Procedimiento en Materia Penal de la Nacion [*Argentina*] — Cod Proc Pen
Codigo Procesal Civil y Comercial de la Nacion [*Argentina*] — Cod Proc Civ y Com
Codigo Tributario Nacional [*Brazil*] — CTN
Codrul Cosminului — CC
Coedwigwr. The Forester. Magazine. Forestry Society. University College of North Wales — Coedwigwr Univ Col Wales
Coeur [*Paris*] — CEURBY
Coeur et Medecine Interne — Coeur Med I
Coeur et Medecine Interne — Coeur Med Interne
Coeur et Medecine Interne — CUMIA
Coeur et Medecine Interne — CUMIAA
Coeur et Toxiques. Compte-Rendu. Reunion des Centres de Poisons — Coeur Toxiques CR Reun Cent Poisons
CoEvolution Quarterly — COEQD
CoEvolution Quarterly — CoEv Q
CoEvolution Quarterly — CoEvolution Qly
CoEvolution Quarterly — CoEvolutn
Coffee and Cacao Journal — CCAJAV
Coffee and Cacao Journal — Coffee Cacao J
Coffee and Tea Industries and the Flavor Field — Coffee Tea Ind Flavor Field
Coffee Brewing Institute. Publication — Coffee Brew Inst Publ
Coffee Research Foundation [*Kenya*]. Annual Report — CRFABX
Coffee Research Foundation (Kenya). Annual Report — Coffee Res Found (Kenya) Annu Rep
Cogenic Report — Cogenic Rep
COGLAC [*Coal Gasification, Liquefaction, and Conversion to Electricity*] **Newsletter** — COGLAC Newsl
Cognition — CGSTB
Cognition — CGTNAU
Cognition [*The Hague*] — Cog
Cognitive Brain Research — Cognit Brain Res
Cognitive Psychology — Cog Psyc
Cognitive Psychology — Cog Psychol
Cognitive Psychology — Cognitive Psychol
Cognitive Psychology — CPsy
Cognitive Psychology — ICOG
Cognitive Rehabilitation — Cognit Rehabil
Cognitive Science — C Sc
Cognitive Science — Cognit Sci
Cognitive Science Series — Cognitive Sci Ser
Cognitive Therapy and Research — Cognit Ther Res
Coherent Technology in Fiber Optic Systems — Coherent Technol Fiber Opt Syst
Coil Coating Review — Coil Coat Rev
Coil Winding International — Coil Winding Int
Coimbra — C
Coimbra Medica — COIMAS
Coimbra Medica — Coimbra Med
Coimbra Medica. Revista Mensal de Medicina e Cirurgia — Coimbra Med Rev Mens Med Cir
Coimbra. Universidade. Museu e Laboratorio Mineralogico e Geologico. Memorias e Noticias. [*Coimbra, Portugal*] — Coimbra Univ Mus Lab Mineral Geol Mem Not
Coin Monthly — CMonth
COIN [*Communication and Information Technology*] **Reports** — COIN Rep
Coin Review — Coin Rev
Coin Slot Location — COl
Coin, Stamp, and Antique News — CSAN
Coin World — CW
Coinage of the Roman Republic — CRR
Coinage of the Roman Republic — RRC
Coins and Antiquities Ltd. Fixed Price List [*London*] — C Antiq FPL
Coins Annual — CMAnnual
Coins, Incorporating Coins and Medals — CM
Coins, Medals, and Currency Digest and Monthly Catalogue — CMCD
Coins, Medals, and Currency Weekly — CMC
Coins, Stamps, and Collecting — CSC
Coir Quarterly Journal — Coir Q J
Coke and Chemistry USSR [*English Translation*] — COKCA
Coke and Chemistry USSR — Coke Chem R
Coke and Chemistry USSR — Coke Chem USSR
Coke and Coal Chemicals Monthly. Energy Data Report — Coke Coal Chem Mon Energy Data Rep
Coke and Smokeless-Fuel Age — Coke Smokeless Fuel Age
Coke Research Report [*England*] — Coke Res Rep
Coke Research Report — COKRA
Colburn's New Monthly Magazine — Colburn
Colby College. Monographs — CCM
Colby College. Monographs — ColCM
Colby Library. Quarterly — CLQ
Colby Library Quarterly — Colby Lib Qtr
Colby Library. Quarterly — Colby Libr

Colchester Archaeological Group. Annual Bulletin — Colchester Archaeol Group Annu Bull
Cold Regions Research and Engineering Laboratory. Monograph — CRREL Monograph
Cold Regions Research and Engineering Laboratory. Report — CRREL Report
Cold Regions Science and Technology [*Netherlands*] — Cold Reg Sci Technol
Cold Regions Science and Technology — CRST
Cold Regions Science and Technology — CRSTD
Cold Regions Technical Digest — CRTD
Cold Spring Harbor Conference on Cell Proliferation — Cold Spring Harbor Conf Cell Proliferation
Cold Spring Harbor Conferences on Cell Proliferation — CSHCAL
Cold Spring Harbor Monograph Series — Cold Spring Harbor Monogr Ser
Cold Spring Harbor Reports in the Neurosciences — Cold Spring Harbor Rep Neurosci
Cold Spring Harbor Symposia on Quantitative Biology — Cold S Harb
Cold Spring Harbor Symposia on Quantitative Biology — Cold Spr Harb Symp
Cold Spring Harbor Symposia on Quantitative Biology — Cold Spring Harb Symp Quant Biol
Cold Spring Harbor Symposia on Quantitative Biology — Cold Spring Harbor Symp Quant Biol
Cold Spring Harbor Symposia on Quantitative Biology — Cold Spring Harbor Symp Quantit Biol
Cold Spring Harbor Symposia on Quantitative Biology — CSHSA
Cold Spring Harbor Symposia on Quantitative Biology — CSHSAZ
Cold Storage and Produce Review — Cold Storage Prod Rev
Colecao das Leis [*Brazil*] — Colecao
Colecao Documentos Brasileiros — CDB
Colecao Ensaio — CEn
Colecao General Benicio — CGB
Colecao Poetas de Hoje — CPH
Colecao Studium — CSt
Coleccion Agropecuaria. Instituto Nacional de Tecnologia Agropecuaria (Argentina) — Colec Agropec Inst Nac Tec Agropec (Argentina)
Coleccion Al-Andalus — Colec Al Andalus
Coleccion de Monografias. Organismo Internacional de Energia Atomica — Colecc Monogr Org Int Energ At
Coleccion de Monografias y Memorias de Matematicas [*Madrid*] — Col Monograf Mem Mat
Coleccion de Monografias y Memorias de Matematicas — Colec Monograf Mem Mat
Coleccion de Textos de Agronomia y Veterinaria — Colecc Textos Agron Vet
Coleccion Diario de Navarra — Colecc Diario Navarra
Coleccion Enrique Perez Arbelaez — Colec Enrique Perez Arbelaez
Coleccion Estadistica — Colec Estadist
Coleccion Estudios CIEPLAN [*Corporacion de Investigaciones Economicas para Latinoamerica*] — Coleccion Estud CIEPLAN
Coleccion Monografias — Colec Monograf
Coleccion Montano — Colec Montano
Colecciones Ciencias Fisico-Quimicas y Matematicas — Colec Cienc Fisico Quim Mat
Colegas (Antioquia, Colombia) — CSA
Colegio de Bibliotecarios Colombianos (Medellin, Colombia) — Colegio Bibl Col Medellin
Colegio de Quimicos de Puerto Rico. Revista — Col Quim PR Rev
Colegio de Quimicos e Ingenieros Quimicos de Costa Rica. Revista — Col Quim Ing Quim Costa Rica Rev
Colegio Farmaceutico — Col Farm
Colegio Interamericano de Defensa Revista — Col Interam Defensa R
Colegio Medico — Col Med
Colegio Medico Vida Medica — Col Med Vida Med
Colegio Quimico-Farmaceutico — Col Quim-Farm
Colegio Quimico-Farmaceutico — CQFMAR
Colegio Universitario de Cayey. Boletin — CUCB
Colegio Universitario de Gerona. Seccion de Ciencias. Anales — Col Univ Gerona Secc Cien An
Colemania — CLMNDX
Coleopterists' Bulletin — COBLAO
Coleopterists' Bulletin — Coleopt Bull
Coleopterists' Bulletin — Coleopts Bull
Coletanea do Instituto de Tecnologia de Alimentos (Campinas, Brazil) — Colet Inst Tecnol Aliment Campinas Braz
Coletanea. Instituto de Tecnologia de Alimentos — CITAC7
Coletanea. Instituto de Tecnologia de Alimentos — Colet Inst Tecnol Aliment
Coletanea. Instituto de Tecnologia de Alimentos — Coletanea Inst Tecnol Aliment
Coletanea. Instituto Tecnologia de Alimentos — Colet Inst Tecnol Alim
Collaborative Proceedings Series. International Institute for Applied Systems Analysis — Collab Proc Ser Int Inst Appl Syst Anal
Collage Magazine — Collage Mag
Collagen and Related Research — Coll Relat Res
Collagen and Related Research — Collagen Relat Res
Collagen and Related Research. Clinical and Experimental — Collagen Relat Res
Collana Accademica. Accademia Patavina di Scienze, Lettere, ed Arti — Collana Accad Accad Patav Sci Lett Arti
Collana Atti di Congressi — Collana Atti Congr
Collana di Aggiornamento e Cultura Matematica — Coll Aggiorn Cult Mat
Collana di Matematica — Coll Mat
Collana di Monografie. Ateneo Parmense — CMAPAH
Collana di Monografie. Ateneo Parmense — Collana Monogr Ateneo Parmense
Collana di Monografie di Rassegna Medica Sarda — Collana Monogr Rass Med Sarda
Collana di Monografie di Veterinaria Italiana — Collana Monogr Vet Ital
Collana di Monografie sugli Oli Essenziali e Sui Derivati Agrumari — Collana Monogr Oli Essenz Sui Deri Agrum
Collana di Scienze Matematiche — Coll Sci Mat
Collana di Studi — Coll Studi
Collana di Testi e Documenti per lo Studio dell'Antichita — CTD
Collana Verde. Ministero dell'Agricoltura e della Foreste (Roma) — Collana Verde Minist Agric For (Roma)
Collationes Brugenses et Gandavenses — CBG
Collationes Brugenses et Gandavenses [*Brugge*] — ColBG
Collationes Brugenses et Gandavenses [*Gent, Belgium*] — CollBrugGand
Collationes Gandavenses — ColG
Collectanea ad Omnem Rem Botanicam Spectantia (Zurich) — Collect Rem Bot Spectantia Zurich
Collectanea Alexandrina. Reliquiae Minores Poetarum Graecorum Aetatis Ptolemaicae 323-146 A.C. Epicorum, Elegiacorum, Lyricorum, Ethicorum — Coll Alex
Collectanea Biblica Latina [*Rome*] — CBL
Collectanea Botanica [*Barcelona*] — COBOAX
Collectanea Botanica (Barcelona) — Collect Bot (Barc)
Collectanea Cisterciensa [*Forges, Belgium*] — ColctCist
Collectanea Cisterciensia — CCist
Collectanea Cisterciensia — Coll Cist
Collectanea Commissionis Synodalis [*Peking*] — CCS
Collectanea Franciscana — CF
Collectanea Franciscana [*Rome*] — ColcFranc
Collectanea Franciscana [*Rome*] — ColeFranc
Collectanea Franciscana — Coll Fran
Collectanea Mathematica — Collect Math
Collectanea Mechlinensia [*Mechelen, Belgium*] — ColctMech
Collectanea Mechlinensia [*Mechelen, Belgium*] — ColetMech
Collectanea Mechlinensia [*Mechelen, Belgium*] — CollMech
Collectanea Mechlinensia [*Mechelen, Belgium*] — ColMech
Collectanea Ordinis Cisterciensium Reformatorum — COCR
Collectanea Pharmaceutica Suecica — Collect Pharm Suec
Collectanea Theologica [*Warsaw*] — ColctT
Collectanea Theologica [*Warsaw*] — ColeT
Collectanea Theologica — CT
Collectanea Theologica Universitatis Fujen [*Taipei, Taiwan*] — ColcTFujen
Collecteanea Franciscana — Collecteanea Francisc
Collected Essays by the Members of the Faculty [*Kyoritsu Women's Junior College*] — CEMF
Collected Papers. Changchun Institute of Applied Chemistry. Academia Sinica — Collect Pap Changchun Inst Appl Chem Acad Sin
Collected Papers. Faculty of Science. Osaka Imperial University. Series A. Mathematics — Collect Pap Fac Sci Osaka Imp Univ Ser A
Collected Papers. Faculty of Science. Osaka Imperial University. Series B. Physics — Collect Pap Fac Sci Osaka Imp Univ Ser B
Collected Papers. Faculty of Science. Osaka Imperial University. Series C. Chemistry — Collect Pap Fac Sci Osaka Imp Univ Ser C
Collected Papers. Faculty of Science. Osaka University. Series B. Physics — Collect Pap Fac Sci Osaka Univ Ser B
Collected Papers. Faculty of Science. Osaka University. Series C. Chemistry — Collect Pap Fac Sci Osaka Univ Ser C
Collected Papers from the Medical Research Laboratory of Parke, Davis and Company — Collect Pap Med Res Lab Parke Davis Co
Collected Papers in Medicine. Mayo Clinic and Mayo Foundation — Collect Pap Med Mayo Clin Mayo Found
Collected Papers in Medicine. Mayo Clinic and Mayo Foundation — CPMMAL
Collected Papers in Surgery. Mayo Clinic and Mayo Foundation [*A publication*] — Collect Pap Surg Mayo Clin Mayo Found
Collected Papers in Surgery. Mayo Clinic and Mayo Foundation — CPSMBI
Collected Papers. Institute of Applied Chemistry. Academia Sinica — Collect Pap Inst Appl Chem Acad Sin
Collected Papers. Institute of Applied Chemistry. Chinese Academy of Sciences — Collect Pap Inst Appl Chem Chin Acad Sci
Collected Papers. Institute of Chemistry. Academia Sinica — Collect Pap Inst Chem Acad Sin
Collected Papers. International Congress on Glass — Collect Pap Int Congr Glass
Collected Papers. Japan Society of Civil Engineers — Collect Pap Jpn Soc Civ Eng
Collected Papers. Lister Institute of Preventive Medicine — Collect Papers Lister Inst Prevent Med
Collected Papers. Macaulay Institute for Soil Research — Collect Pap Macaulay Inst Soil Res
Collected Papers. Mathematical Society. Wakayama University — Collect Papers Math Soc Wakayama Univ
Collected Papers. Mayo Clinic and Mayo Foundation — Collect Pap Mayo Clin Mayo Found
Collected Papers of International Symposium on Molecular Beam Epitaxy and Related Clean Surface Techniques — Collect Pap Int Symp Mol Beam Epitaxy Relat Clean Surf Tech
Collected Papers on Earth Sciences. Nagoya University. Department of Earth Sciences — Collect Pap Earth Sci Nagoya Univ Dep Earth Sci
Collected Papers on Medical Science. Fukuoka University — Collect Pap Med Sci Fukuoka Univ
Collected Papers on Technological Sciences. Fukuoka University — Collect Pap Technol Sci Fukuoka Univ
Collected Papers. Research Laboratory of Parke, Davis & Company — Collect Pap Res Lab Parke Davis Co
Collected Papers. School of Hygiene and Public Health. Johns Hopkins University — Collect Papers School Hyg and Pub Health Johns Hopkins Univ
Collected Reports. Natural Science Faculty. Palacky University [*Olomouc*] — AUONAD

Collected Reports. Natural Science Faculty. Palacky University (Olomouc) — Collect Rep Nat Sci Fac Palacky Univ (Olomouc)
Collected Studies Series — Collect Studies Ser
Collected Studies Series [*London*] — Collected Studies Ser
Collected Works on Cardio-Pulmonary Disease — Coll Works Cardio-Pulm Dis
Collected Works on Cardio-Pulmonary Disease — Collect Works Cardio-Pulm Dis
Collected Works on Cardio-Pulmonary Disease — CWCDA
Collected Works on Cardio-Pulmonary Disease — CWCDAR
Collecting and Breeding — Collect Breed
Collection Alea-Saclay. Monographs and Texts in Statistical Physics — Collect Alea Saclay Monogr Texts Statist Phys
Collection. Amis de l'Histoire — Coll Amis Hist
Collection and Reuse of Waste Oils. Proceedings. European Congress on Waste Oils — Collect Reuse Waste Oils Proc Eur Congr Waste Oils
Collection Blain Faye Martin — Collect Blain Faye Martin
Collection. Colloques et Seminaires. Institut Francais du Petrole — Collect Colloq Semin Inst Fr Pet
Collection. Colloques et Seminaires. Institut Francais du Petrole — IPTCB
Collection Complete, Decrets, Ordonnances, Reglements, et Avis du Conseil d'Etat (Duvergier et Bocquet) [*France*] — Duv & Boc
Collection d'Auteurs Francais — Coll d Aut Franc
Collection de Biologie Evolutive — Collect Biol Evol
Collection de Biologie Moleculaire — Collect Biol Mol
Collection de la Chaire Aisenstadt — Collect Chaire Aisenstadt
Collection de la Direction des Etudes et Recherches d'Electricite de France ESE — Coll Dir Etudes Rech Elect France ESE
Collection de la Societe de l'Histoire de France — Coll de la Soc de l Hist de France
Collection de la Societe de l'Histoire de France — Coll de la Soc de l Histoire de France
Collection de Medecine Legale et de Toxicologie Medicale — Collect Med Leg Toxicol Med
Collection de Monographies de Botanique et de Biologie Vegetale — CMBBBF
Collection de Monographies de Botanique et de Biologie Vegetale — Collect Monogr Bot Biol Veg
Collection de Tourisme Litteraire et Historique — Coll de Tourisme Litt et Histor
Collection de Travaux. Academie Internationale d'Histoire des Sciences — Coll de Trav
Collection d'Ecologie — Coll d'Ecologie
Collection d'Ecologie — Collect Ecologie
Collection des Chefs-d'Oeuvre Meconnus — CCM
Collection des Classiques Populaires — Coll des Class Populaires
Collection des Travaux. Academie Internationale d'Histoire des Sciences — Coll Travaux Acad Internat Hist Sci
Collection des Travaux. Academie Internationale d'Histoire des Sciences — Collect Trav Acad Int Hist Sci
Collection des Travaux. Academie Internationale d'Histoire des Sciences — Collect Travaux Acad Internat Hist Sci
Collection des Travaux Chimiques de Tchecoslovaquie — Collect Trav Chim Tchec
Collection des Travaux Chimiques Tcheques — Collect Trav Chim Tcheques
Collection des Travaux. Universite de Brazzaville — Collect Trav Univ Brazzaville
Collection des Travaux. Universite de Brazzaville — CTUBDP
Collection des Universites de France — Collect Univ France
Collection des Universites de France. Association Guillaume Bude — Bude
Collection des Universites de France. Association Guillaume Bude — CB
Collection des Universites de France. Association Guillaume Bude — CUF
Collection d'Etudes Publiee par le Musee de la Vie Wallonne — Colln Etud Mus Vie Wallonne
Collection d'Histoire des Sciences [*Paris*] — Coll Hist Sci
Collection Didactique — Collect Didact
Collection. Direction des Etudes et Recherches d'Electricite de France — Coll Dir Etudes Rech Elec France
Collection. Direction des Etudes et Recherches d'Electricite de France — Collect Dir Etudes Rech Elec France
Collection du Commissariat a l'Energie Atomique. Serie Scientifique — Collect Commissariat Energ Atom Ser Sci
Collection Dunod Informatique — Collect Dunod Inform
Collection. Ecole Francaise de Rome — Collect Ec Fr Rome
Collection. Ecole Normale Superieure de Jeunes Filles — Coll Ecole Norm Sup Jeunes Filles
Collection. Ecole Normale Superieure de Jeunes Filles — Collect Ecole Norm Sup Jeunes Filles
Collection Economie et Statistiques Avancees — Collect Econom Statist Av
Collection Enseignement des Sciences [*Paris*] — Collect Enseignement Sci
Collection Enseignement des Sciences — Collect Enseignement Sci
Collection Episteme — Collect Episteme
Collection for Improvement of Husbandry and Trade — Collect Improv Husb Trade
Collection Historique — Coll Histor
Collection Historique de l'Institut d'Etudes Slaves — Coll Hist Inst Et Slav
Collection Historique des Grands Philosophes — Coll Hist des Grands Philosophes
Collection Langages et Algorithmes de l'Informatique — Collect Lang Algorithmes Inform
Collection Langues et Litteratures de l'Afrique Noire — CLLAN
Collection Latomus — Coll Latomus
Collection Latomus — CollLat
Collection "Les Grands Problemes de la Biologie." Monographie — CGPBA8
Collection "Les Grands Problemes de la Biologie." Monographie — Collect Grands Probl Biol Monogr
Collection Maitrise de Mathematiques Pures — Collect Maitrise Math Pures
Collection Major — Collect Major
Collection Management — Coll Manage
Collection Mathematiques Appliquees pour la Maitrise — Collect Math Appl Maitrise
Collection Methodes — Collect Methodes
Collection Monographies. Agence Internationale de l'Energie Atomique — Collect Monogr Agence Int Energ At
Collection of Czechoslovak Chemical Communications — CCCCAK
Collection of Czechoslovak Chemical Communications — Coll Czech
Collection of Czechoslovak Chemical Communications — Coll Czech Chem Communications
Collection of Czechoslovak Chemical Communications — Collec Czechosl Chem Commun
Collection of Czechoslovak Chemical Communications — Collect Czech Chem Commun
Collection of Czechoslovak Chemical Communications — Collect Czechoslovak Chem Commun
Collection of Czechoslovak Chemical Communications — Colln Czech Chem Commun
Collection of Lectures. International Symposium of Furan Chemistry — Collect Lect Int Symp Furan Chem
Collection of Papers. International Conference on Electronic Properties of Two-Dimensional Systems — Collect Pap Int Conf Electron Prop Two Dimens Syst
Collection of Papers Presented at the Annual Symposium on Fundamental Cancer Research — Collect Pap Annu Symp Fundam Cancer Res
Collection of Papers Presented at the Annual Symposium on Fundamental Cancer Research — SFCRAO
Collection of Papers Presented. International Symposium on Animal Toxins — Collect Pap Int Symp Anim Toxins
Collection of Papers Presented. Symposium on Atomic Interactions and Space Physics — Collect Pap Symp At Interact Space Phys
Collection of Research Works from the Paper and Pulp Industry — Collect Res Works Pap Pulp Ind
Collection of Scientific Communications. Charles University. Faculty of Medicine. Hradec Kralove — Collect Sci Commun Charles Univ Fac Med Hradec Kralove
Collection of Scientific Papers Commemorating the 20th Anniversary of the Foundation of the Shizuoka College of Pharmacy — Collect Sci Pap Commem 20th Anniv Found Shizuoka Coll Pharm
Collection of Scientific Papers. Economic Agricultural University (Ceske Budejovice). Biological Part — Collect Sci Pap Econ Agric Univ (Ceske Budejovice) Biol Part
Collection of Scientific Works. Estonian Research Institute of Animal Breeding and Veterinary — Collect Sci Works Est Res Inst Anim Breed Vet Sci
Collection of Scientific Works. Faculty of Medicine. Charles University (Hadec Kralove) — Collect Sci Works Fac Med Charles Univ (Hradec Kralove)
Collection of Scientific Works. Faculty of Medicine. Charles University (Hradec Kralove) — SVLKAO
Collection of Technical Papers. AIAA/ASME/SAE Structural Dynamics and Materials Conference — Collect Tech Pap AIAA/ASME/SAE Struct Dyn Mater Conf
Collection of Technical Papers. AIAA/ASME/SAE Structures, Structural Dynamics, and Materials Conference — Collect Tech Pap AIAA ASME SAE Struct Struct Dyn Mater Conf
Collection of Technical Papers. AIAA/ASME Structures, Structural Dynamics, and Materials Conference — Collect Tech Pap AIAA ASME Struct Struct Dyn Mater Conf
Collection of Theses. Kwang Woon Institute of Technology [*Republic of Korea*] [*A publication*] — Collect Theses Kwang Woon Inst Technol
Collection of Treatises Published by the Faculty of Humanity. University of Fukuoka [*Japan*] — Collect Treatises Fac Hum Univ Fukuoka
Collection of Voyages and Travels by J. Churchill [*Monograph*] — CVT
Collection Philosophica — Coll Phil
Collection Points. Serie Sciences — Collect Points Ser Sci
Collection. Programmation Recherche Operationnelle Appliquee — Coll Programmation Rech Oper Appl
Collection Recherches Interdisciplinaires — Coll Rech Interdiscip
Collection Regards sur la Science — Collect Regards Sci
Collection Science et Technique du Petrole — Collect Sci Tech Pet
Collection Sciences dans l'Histoire — Collect Sci Hist
Collection Sciences et Philosophie Arabes — Coll Sci Philos Arabes
Collection. Societe Francaise de la Tuberculose et des Maladies Respiratoires — Collect Soc Fr Tuber Mal Respir
Collection Technique et Scientifique des Telecommunications — Collect Tech Sci Telecomm
Collection Techniques Avancees de l'Informatique — Collect Tech Av Inform
Collection UNESCO D'Oeuvres Representatives Serie Persane — Coll UNESCO Oeuvres Represent Ser Persane
Collectionneur Francais — Coll Fr
Collections. American Statistical Association — Coll Am Statis Assn
Collections de Statistique Agricole. Etudes — Coll Statist Agric Et
Collections. Institut National de la Statistique et des Etudes Economiques. Serie C. Comptes et Planification — Collns INSEE Ser C
Collections. Institut National de la Statistique et des Etudes Economiques. Serie D. Demographie et Emploi — Collns INSEE Ser D
Collections. Institut National de la Statistique et des Etudes Economiques. Serie E. Entreprises — Collns INSEE Ser E
Collections. Institut National de la Statistique et des Etudes Economiques. Serie M. Menages — Collns INSEE Ser M
Collections. Institut National de la Statistique et des Etudes Economiques. Serie R. Regions — Collns INSEE Ser R
Collections Litteratures Africaines — CLA
Collections. Massachusetts Historical Society — Coll Mass Hist Soc
Collections. Ryukyu Forestry Experiment Station/Ryukyu Ringyo Shikenjo Shuho — Collect Ryukyu Forest Exp Sta

Collective Bargaining, Negotiations, and Contracts. Bureau of National Affairs — Collective Bargaining Negot & Cont BNA
Collective Effects in Condensed Media. Winter School of Theoretical Physics — Collect Eff Condens Media Winter Sch Theor Phys
Collective Methods of Acceleration. Papers Presented. International Conference on Collective Methods of Acceleration — Collect Methods Accel Pap Int Conf
Collective Phenomena [*London*] — CLPNAB
Collective Phenomena — Collect Phenom
College and Research Libraries — C & RL
College and Research Libraries — Col & Res Lib
College and Research Libraries — Col and Research Libs
College and Research Libraries — Coll & Res Lib
College and Research Libraries — Coll Roc Li
College and Research Libraries — Coll Res Libr
College and Research Libraries — College & Research Lib
College and Research Libraries — CRL
College and Research Libraries News — Col and Research Libs News
College and Research Libraries News — Coll & Res Lib N
College and University — C & U
College and University — Col & Univ
College and University — Col Univ
College and University — Coll & Univ
College and University Business — Col & Univ Bsns
College and University Business — Coll & Univ Bus
College and University Journal — Col & Univ J
College and University Journal — Coll & Univ J
College Art Journal — CAJ
College Art Journal — Coll Art J
College Board Review — Coll Bd R
College Canada — College Can
College Composition and Communication — CCC
College Composition and Communication — Col Comp & Comm
College Composition and Communication — Coll Comp & Comm
College Composition and Communication — Coll Composition & Commun
College Courant — Coll Courant
College English — CE
College English — Co Engl
College English — ColEng
College English — Coll Eng
College English — Coll Engl
College English — CollE
College English — GCOL
College Language Association. Journal — CLA
College Language Association Journal — CLAS
College Law Digest. National Association of College and University Attorneys — College L Dig Natl Assn College & Univ Attys
College Literature — Col Lit
College Literature — Coll L
College Literature — Coll Lit
College Literature — PCOL
College Management — Col Mgt
College Management — Coll Mgt
College Mathematics Journal — College Math J
College Mathematics Journal — PCMJ
College Media Director Newsletter — Coll Media Dir Newsl
College Music Symposium — CLMBB
College Music Symposium — CMS
College Music Symposium — Coll Music
College Music Symposium — College M Symposium
College Music Symposium — College Mus
College Musician — Coll Musician
College News — Coll News
College of Agriculture (Nagpur). Magazine — Coll Agric (Nagpur) Mag
College of Agriculture (Nagpur). Magazine — NAGMA
College of Agriculture. National Taiwan University. Special Publication — Coll Agric Nat Taiwan Univ Spec Publ
College of Agriculture Research Center. Washington State University. Circular — Coll Agric Res Cent Wash State Univ Circ
College of Agriculture. University of Tehran. Bulletin — Coll Agric Univ Tehran Bull
College of American Pathologists. Aspen Conference on Diagnostic Immunology — Coll Am Pathol Aspen Conf Diagn Immunol
College of Hawaii Publications. Bulletins — Coll Hawaii Publ Bull
College of Medicine. Annals (Mosul) — Coll Med Ann (Mosul)
College of Physicians and Surgeons of Ontario. Interim Report — Coll Phys Surg Ont Int Rep
College of Physicians of Philadelphia. Transactions and Studies — Coll Physicians Philadelphia Trans Stud
College of the Bible. Quarterly [*Lexington, KY*] — ColBiQ
College of Tropical Agriculture. Miscellaneous Publication. University of Hawaii — Coll Trop Agric Misc Publ Univ Hawaii
College Park Colloquium on Chemical Evolution. Proceedings — College Park Colloq Chem Evol Proc
College Physical Education Association. Proceedings — Col Phys Ed Assn Proc
College Press Service — Col Press
College Press Service — Coll Press
College Recruitment Database — CRD
College Student Journal — Coll Stud J
College Student Personnel Abstracts — Coll Stud Pers Abstr
College Student Personnel Abstracts — ColStuAb
Collegiate News and Views — CNV
Collegiate News and Views — Coll N & V
Collegium — Coll
Collegium Antropologicum — Coll Antropol
Collegium Internationale Neuro-Psychopharmacologicum. Congress — Coll Int Neuro Psychopharmacol Congr
Collegium Internationale Neuro-Psychopharmacologicum. Proceedings. Congress — Coll Int Neuro Psychopharmacol Proc Congr
Collegium Logicum. Annals of the Kurt-Goedel Society — Coll Logicum Ann Kurt Goedel Soc
Collegium Veterinarium — Coll Vet
Colletion Academique. Composee des Memoires, Actes, ou Journaux des Plus Celebres Academies and Societes Litteraires. Partie Etrangere — Collect Acad Pt Etrangere
Collier Bankruptcy Cases. Second Series. Matthew Bender — Collier Bankr Cas 2d MB
Collier's — C
Collier's Encyclopedia Yearbook — Collier's Yrbk
Collier's Law of Bankruptcy — Collier Bankr
Collier's National Weekly — Collier's
Colliery Engineer (Scranton, Pennsylvania) — Colliery Eng (Scranton PA)
Colliery Engineering — Colliery Eng
Colliery Engineering (London) — Colliery Eng (London)
Colliery Engineering. Supplement — Colliery Eng Suppl
Colliery Guardian [*England*] — CLGUA
Colliery Guardian — Colliery Guard
Colliery Guardian and Journal. Coal and Iron Trades. Supplement — Colliery Guardian J Coal Iron Trades Suppl
Colliery Guardian and Journal of the Coal and Iron Trades — Colliery Guardian J Coal Iron Trades
Collision Spectroscopy — Collision Spectrosc
Collisions and Half-Collisions with Lasers. Tavola Rotonda — Collisions Half Collisions Lasers Tavola Rotonda
Colloid and Interface Science. Proceedings of the International Conference on Colloids and Surfaces — Colloid Interface Sci Pro Int Conf
Colloid and Polymer Science — Coll Polym Sci
Colloid and Polymer Science — Colloid P S
Colloid and Polymer Science — Colloid Polym Sci
Colloid and Polymer Science — Colloid Polymer Sci
Colloid and Polymer Science — CPMSB6
Colloid and Polymer Science. Supplement — Colloid Polym Sci Suppl
Colloid Chemistry — Colloid Chem
Colloid Journal of the USSR [*English Translation*] — COJOA
Colloid Journal of the USSR — Colloid J
Colloid Journal of the USSR — Colloid J USSR
Colloid Journal (Translation of Kolloidnyi Zhurnal) — Colloid J Transl of Kolloidn Zh
Colloid Journal. USSR. English Translation — Colloid J USSR Engl Transl
Colloid Science — Colloid Sci
Colloid Surface Science Symposium — Colloid Surf Sci Symp
Colloid Symposium Annual — Colloid Symp Annu
Colloid Symposium Monograph — Colloid Symp Monogr
Colloidal Surface-Active Agents — Colloidal Surf Act Agents
Colloides en Biologie. Clinique et Therapeutique — Colloides Biol Clin Ther
Colloids and Surfaces — Coll Surfaces
Colloids and Surfaces — Colloids and Surf
Colloids and Surfaces — Colloids Surf
Colloids and Surfaces — COSUD
Colloids and Surfaces — COSUD3
Colloque. Club "Jules Gonin" — Colloq Club Jules Gonin
Colloque de Medecine Nucleaire de Langue Francaise — Colloq Med Nucl Lang Fr
Colloque de Metallurgie — Colloq Metall
Colloque de Metallurgie — CQMTA
Colloque de Metallurgie de Saclay — Colloq Metall Saclay
Colloque. Groupement pour l'Avancement de la Biochimie Marine (GABIM) — Colloq Group Av Biochim Mar GABIM
Colloque. INSERM [*Institut National de la Sante et de la Recherche Medicale*] — CINMDE
Colloque. INSERM (Institut National de la Sante et de la Recherche Medicale) — Colloq INSERM (Inst Natl Sante Rech Med)
Colloque. Institut National de la Sante et de la Recherche Medicale [*France*] — Colloq Inst Natl Sante Rech Med
Colloque International Berthelot-Vieille-Mallard-Le Chatelier. Actes — Colloq Int Berthelot Vieille Mallard Le Chatelier Actes
Colloque International Consacre aux Essais sur Bitumes et Materiaux Bitumineux — Colloq Int Essais Bitumes Mater Bitum
Colloque International d'Astrophysique — Colloq Int Astrophys
Colloque International d'Astrophysique. Communications — Colloq Int Astrophys Commun
Colloque International de Biologie de Saclay — Colloq Int Biol Saclay
Colloque International de Physique et Chimie des Surfaces — Colloq Int Phys Chim Surf
Colloque International de Spectrochimie. Comptes Rendus — Colloq Int Spectrochim CR
Colloque International de Technologie — Colloq Int Technol
Colloque International. Soudage et Fusion par Faisceau d'Electrons — Colloq Int Soudage Fusion Faisceau Electrons
Colloque International sur la Blennorragie. Comptes Rendus — Colloq Int Blennorragie
Colloque International sur la Blennorragie. Comptes Rendus — Colloq Int Blennorragie CR
Colloque International sur la Chimie des Cafes. Comptes Rendus — Colloq Int Chim Cafes C R
Colloque International sur la Prevention et le Traitement des Toxicomanies. Conferences — Colloq Int Prev Trait Toxicomanies Conf
Colloque International sur la Pulverisation Cathodique et ses Applications — Colloq Int Pulverisation Cathod Ses Appl

Colloque International sur l'Electricite Solaire. Comptes Rendus — Colloq Int Electr Sol
Colloque International sur les Materiaux Granulaires. Comptes Rendus — Colloq Int Mater Granulaires CR
Colloque International sur les Methodes Analytiques par Rayonnements X. Comptes Rendus — Colloq Int Methodes Anal Rayonnem X CR
Colloque International sur les Plantes Aromatiques et Medicinales du Maroc — Colloq Int Plant Aromat Med Maroc
Colloque International sur les Problemes Biochimiques des Lipides — Colloq Int Probl Biochim Lipides
Colloque International sur les Refractaires — Colloq Int Refract
Colloque National d'Hygiene de l'Environnement et des Collectivites. Comptes Rendus — Colloq Natl Hyg Environ Collect CR
Colloque Procede. Conference Internationale sur les Metaux Lourds dans l'Environnement — Colloq Procede Conf Int Met Lourds Environ
Colloque Scientifique International sur le Cafe — CICRD8
Colloque Scientifique International sur le Cafe — Colloq Sci Int Cafe
Colloque. Societe Francaise de Microbiologie — Colloq Soc Fr Microbiol
Colloque. Societe Francaise de Microbiologie. Section de Microbiologie Industrielle et de Biotechnologie — Colloq Soc Fr Microbiol Sect Microbiol Ind Biotechnol
Colloque sur la Pollution et la Protection des Eaux de la Region Rhone-Alpes. Comptes Rendus — Colloq Pollut Prot Eaux Reg Rhone Alpes CR
Colloque sur l'Information en Chimie. Compte Rendu — Colloq Inf Chim CR
Colloque Weyl — Colloq Weyl
Colloques de l'INRA (Institut National de la Recherche Agronomique) — Colloq INRA
Colloques. Institut National de la Recherche Agronomique — Colloq Inst Natl Rech Agron
Colloques Internationaux. Centre National de la Recherche Scientifique — COINAV
Colloques Internationaux. Centre National de la Recherche Scientifique — Colloq Int Cent Natl Rech Sci
Colloques Internationaux. Centre National de la Recherche Scientifique — Colloq Int CNRS
Colloques Internationaux. Centre National de la Recherche Scientifique — Colloq Internat CNRS
Colloques Internationaux. Centre National de la Recherche Scientifique — Colloques Int Cent Natn Rech Scient
Colloques Internationaux. Centre National de la Recherche Scientifique — Colloques Internat CNRS
Colloques Internationaux de la Pathologie des Insectes — Colloques Int Path Insectes
Colloques Nationaux. Centre National de la Recherche Scientifique — Colloques Nat CNRS
Colloques Nationaux du Centre National de la Recherche Scientifique. Chimie des Hautes Temperatures — Colloq Nationaux CNRS Chim Hautes Temp
Colloques Phytosociologiques — Colloq Phytosociol
Colloques Phytosociologiques — CPHYDZ
Colloqui del Sodalizio — Colloqui Sod
Colloquia Germanica — ColGer
Colloquia Germanica — Coll G
Colloquia Germanica — Colloq Ger
Colloquia Mathematica. Societatis Janos Bolyai [*Elsevier Book Series*] — CM
Colloquia Mathematica. Societatis Janos Bolyai — Colloq Math Soc Janos Bolyai
Colloquia on Topical Questions in Biochemistry. Proceedings. International Congress of Biochemistry — Colloq Top Quest Biochem Proc Int Congr Biochem
Colloquia Pflanzenphysiologie. Humboldt-Universitaet zu Berlin — Colloq Pflanzenphysiol Humboldt Univ Berlin
Colloquies on Art and Archaeology in Asia — Colloq Art
Colloquis. Societat Catalana de Biologia — Colloq Soc Catalana Biol
Colloquium Atomspektrometrische Spurenanalytik — Colloq Atomspektrom Spurenanal
Colloquium der Deutschen Gesellschaft fuer Physiologische Chemie — Colloq Dtsch Ges Physiol Chem
Colloquium der Gesellschaft fuer Biologische Chemie — Colloq Ges Biol Chem
Colloquium. Freien Universitaet — Col
Colloquium. Gesellschaft fuer Biologische Chemie in Mosbach — CGBCA9
Colloquium. Gesellschaft fuer Biologische Chemie in Mosbach — Colloq Ges Biol Chem Mosbach
Colloquium. Gesellschaft fuer Physiologische Chemie — CGPCAB
Colloquium. Gesellschaft fuer Physiologische Chemie — Colloq Ges Physiol Chem
Colloquium in Biological Sciences — Colloq Biol Sci
Colloquium in Biological Sciences. Blood-Brain Transfer — Colloq Biol Sci Blood Brain Transfer
Colloquium in Biological Sciences. Cellular Signal Transduction — Colloq Biol Sci Cell Signal Transduction
Colloquium. International Potash Institute — Colloq Int Potash Inst
Colloquium. International Potash Institute. Proceedings — Colloq Int Potash Inst Proc
Colloquium Mathematicum — Coll Math
Colloquium Mathematicum [*Warsaw*] — Colloq Math
Colloquium on Amino Acid Analysis — Colloq Amino Acid Anal
Colloquium on Application and Fabrication Technology of Plastics — Colloq Appl Fabr Technol Plast
Colloquium on Conservation Problems in Antarctica. Proceedings — Colloq Conserv Probl Antarct Proc
Colloquium on Electronic Filters — Colloq Electron Filters
Colloquium on Electroplating — Colloq Electroplat
Colloquium on Forest Fertilization — Colloq For Fert
Colloquium on Material and Energy Conservation in Powder Metallurgy. Reports and Papers — Colloq Mater Energy Conserv Powder Metall Rep Pap
Colloquium on Myoglobin — Colloq Myoglobin
Colloquium on Use of Iodinated Density-Gradient Media for Biological Separations — Colloq Use Iodinated Density Gradient Media Biol Sep
Colloquium Pedobiologiae — Colloq Pedobiologiae
Colloquium Proceedings. Potassium Institute — Colloq Proc Potassium Inst
Colloquium Scientificum Facultatis Medicae Universitatis Carolinae et Congressus Morphologicus Symposia. Papers — Colloq Sci Fac Med Univ Carol Congr Morphol Symp Pap
Colloquium Spectroscopicum Internationale. Acta — Colloq Spectrosc Int Acta
Colloquium Spectroscopicum Internationale. Comptes Rendus — Colloq Spectrosc Int CR
Colloquium Spectroscopicum Internationale. Gesamtausgabe der Vortraege und Referate — Colloq Spectrosc Int Gesamtausg Vortr Ref
Colloquium Spectroscopicum Internationale. Plenary Lectures and Reports — Colloq Spectrosc Int Plenary Lect Rep
Colloquium Spectroscopicum Internationale. Proceedings — Colloq Spectro Int Pro
Colloquium St. Jans Hospital. Bruges, Belgium — Colloq St Jans Hosp Bruges Belg
Colloquiumsberichte. Instituts fuer Gerbereichemie. Technischen Hochschule (Darmstadt) — Colloquiumsber Inst Gerbereichem Tech Hochsch (Darmstadt)
Colmenero Espanol — Colmen Esp
Colombia. Armada Nacional. Centro de Investigaciones Oceanograficas e Hidrograficas. Boletin Cientifico — Colomb Armada Nac Cent Invest Oceanogr Hidrogr Bol Cient
Colombia. Instituto Geografico "Agustin Codazzi." Departamento Agrologico. Publicaciones — Colomb Inst Geogr Agustin Codazzi Dep Agrol Publ
Colombia. Instituto Geografico "Agustin Codazzi." Direccion Agrologica. Publicaciones — Colomb Inst Geogr Agustin Codazzi Dir Agrol Publ
Colombia. Instituto Geologica Nacional. Compilacion de los Estudios Geologicos Oficiales en Colombia — Colomb Inst Geol Nac Compil Estud Geol Of Colomb
Colombia. Ministerio de Agricultura. Division de Investigacion. Informacion Tecnica — Colomb Minist Agric Div Invest Inf Tec
Colombia. Ministerio de Minas y Energia. Memoria — Colomb Minist Minas Energ Mem
Colombia. Ministerio de Minas y Petroleas. Instituto Nacional de Investigaciones Geologico-Mineras. Boletin Geologico — Colomb Minist Minas Pet Inst Nac Invest Geol Min Bol Geol
Colombia. Ministerio de Minas y Petroleos. Servicio Geologico Nacional. Boletin Geologico — Colomb Minist Minas Pet Serv Geol Nac Bol Geol
Colombia Republica. Ministerio de Minas y Petroleos. Laboratorio Quimico Nacional. Boletin — Colomb Repub Minist Minas Pet Lab Quim Nac Bol
Colombia. Servicio Geologico Nacional. Compilacion de los Estudios Geologicos Oficiales en Colombia — Colomb Serv Geol Nac Compil Estud Geol Of Colomb
Colombia Today — COT
Colombo Law Review — Colombo L Rev
Colonial and Asiatic Review — C & AR
Colonial Geology and Mineral Resources — Colon Geol Miner Rsrc
Colonial Geology and Mineral Resources — Colonial Geology and Mineral Res
Colonial Geology and Mineral Resources. Supplement Series. Bulletin Supplement — Colon Geol Miner Resour Suppl Bull Suppl
Colonial Geology and Mineral Resources. Supplement Series. Bulletin Supplement — Colon Geol Miner Resour Suppl Ser Bull Suppl
Colonial Homes — ICOH
Colonial Newsletter — ColN
Colonial Plant and Animal Products — Colon Pl Anim Prod
Colonial Plant and Animal Products — Colon Plant Anim Prod
Colonial Plant and Animal Products — CPAPA4
Colonial Research Publications — Colonial Research Pub
Colonial Society of Massachusetts. Publications — Col Soc Mass Publ
Colonial Society of Massachusetts. Transactions — Col Soc Mass Trans
Colonial Waterbirds — Colon Waterbirds
Colonial Waterbirds — COWAEW
Colonic Carcinogenesis — Colonic Carcinog
Colonies Autonomes — Colon Auton
Colonies et Marine — Colon Mar
Colony and Protectorate of Kenya. Department of Agriculture. Bulletin — Colony Prot Kenya Dep Agric Bull
Coloquio Artes — ColA
Coloquio Cientifico Internacional Sobre el Cafe — Coloq Cient Int Cafe
Coloquio de Estratigrafia y Paleogeografia del Triasico y Permico de Espana — Coloq Estratigr Paleogeogr Triasico Permico Esp
Coloquio Letras — Coloquio
Coloquio (Lisbon) — Col(L)
Coloquio sobre a Quimica dos Cafes. Atas — Coloq Quim Cafes Atas
Coloquio sobre Investigaciones y Recursos del Mar Caribe y Regiones Adyacentes. Contribuciones — Coloq Invest Recur Mar Caribe Reg Adyacentes Contrib
Coloquios de Politica Ultramarina Internacionalmente Relevante — CPUIR
Coloquios sobre Metodologia das Ciencias Sociais Lisboa — CMCS
Color Centers and Crystal Luminescence. Proceedings. International Conference — Color Cent Cryst Lumin Proc Int Conf
Color Design — Color Des
Color Engineering — Color Eng
Color Materials [*Japan*] — Color Mater
Color Research and Application — Color Res and Appl
Color Research and Application — Color Res Appl
Color Trade Journal and Textile Chemist — Color Tr J
Colorado A&M News — Colo A&M News
Colorado Agricultural and Mechanical College. Colorado Agricultural Experiment Station. Annual Report — Colo Agric Mech Coll Colo Agric Exp Stn Annu Rep
Colorado. Agricultural Experiment Station. Annual Report — CLGAAT

Colorado. Agricultural Experiment Station. Annual Report — Colo Agric Exp Stn Annu Rep
Colorado. Agricultural Experiment Station. Bulletin — CAPBBZ
Colorado. Agricultural Experiment Station. Bulletin — Colo Agric Exp Stn Bull
Colorado. Agricultural Experiment Station. Popular Bulletin — Colo Agric Exp Stn Pop Bull
Colorado. Agricultural Experiment Station. Publications — Colo Ag Exp
Colorado. Agricultural Experiment Station. Technical Bulletin — Colo Agric Exp Stn Tech Bull
Colorado Anthropologist — Col Anthro
Colorado Bar Association — Colo Bar Assn
Colorado. Bureau of Mines. Annual Report — Colo Bur Mines Ann Rept
Colorado Business — Colo Bus
Colorado Business Magazine — COLO
Colorado Business Review — Col Bus Rev
Colorado Business Review — Colo Bus R
Colorado Country Life — Colo Country Life
Colorado Court of Appeals Reports — Colo App
Colorado. Department of Game, Fish, and Parks. Special Report — Colo Dep Game Fish Parks Spec Rep
Colorado. Division of Game, Fish, and Parks. Fisheries Research Review — Colo Div Game Fish Parks Fish Res Rev
Colorado Division of Game, Fish, and Parks. Game Research Review — Colo Div Game Fish Parks Game Res Rev
Colorado. Division of Game, Fish, and Parks. Game Research Review — Colo Div Game Parks Game Res Rev
Colorado. Division of Game, Fish, and Parks. Special Report — CGFPAY
Colorado. Division of Game, Fish, and Parks. Special Report — Colo Div Game Fish Parks Spec Rep
Colorado. Division of Wildlife. Division Report — Colo Div Wildl Div Rep
Colorado. Division of Wildlife. Division Report — DRCWDT
Colorado. Division of Wildlife. Special Report — Colo Div Wildl Spec Rep
Colorado. Division of Wildlife. Special Report — CWSPA7
Colorado. Division of Wildlife. Technical Publication — Colo Div Wildl Tech Publ
Colorado. Division of Wildlife. Technical Publication — TPCWDL
Colorado Energy Factbook — Colo Energy Factbook
Colorado Engineer — Colo Engineer
Colorado Experiment Station Bulletin — Colorado Exp Sta Bull
Colorado Farm and Home Research — Colo Farm & Home Res
Colorado Farm and Home Research. Colorado Agricultural Experiment Station — Colorado Farm Home Res
Colorado Field Ornithologist — CFORAA
Colorado Field Ornithologist — Colo Field Ornithol
Colorado Fisheries Research Review — CFIRBF
Colorado Fisheries Research Review — Colo Fish Res Rev
Colorado. Game, Fish, and Parks Department. Special Report — Colo Game Fish Parks Dep Spec Rep
Colorado Game Research Review — CGRRAW
Colorado Game Research Review — Colo Game Res Rev
Colorado. Geological Survey. Bulletin — CGBLB
Colorado. Geological Survey. Bulletin — Colo Geol Surv Bull
Colorado Geological Survey. Information Series — Colo Geol Surv Inf Ser
Colorado. Geological Survey. Map Series — Colo Geol Surv Map Ser
Colorado Geological Survey. Resource Series — Colo Geol Surv Resour Ser
Colorado. Geological Survey. Special Publication — Colo Geol Surv Spec Publ
Colorado Ground Water Basic Data Report — Colo Ground Water Basic Data Rep
Colorado Historical Society. Monograph Series — Col Hist Soc Mono Ser
Colorado Journal of Pharmacy — COJPA8
Colorado Journal of Pharmacy — Colo J Pharm
Colorado Journal of Research in Music Education — CO
Colorado Journal of Research in Music Education — Colo J Res Mus Ed
Colorado Lawyer — Colo Law
Colorado Library Association. Bulletin — CLA Bull
Colorado Library Association. Bulletin — Colo Lib Assn Bul
Colorado Magazine — CM
Colorado Magazine — ColM
Colorado Magazine — Colo Mag
Colorado Magazine — ColoM
Colorado Medical Journal — Colo Med J
Colorado Medicine — COLMA9
Colorado Medicine — Colo Med
Colorado Medicine — Colorado Med
Colorado Mining Association. Mining Year Book — Colo Min Assoc Min Year Book
Colorado Music Educator — COL
Colorado Nurse — Colo Nurse
Colorado Nurse Update — Colo Nurse Update
Colorado Outdoors — Colo Outdoors
Colorado Outdoors — COOUA
Colorado Quarterly — ColoQ
Colorado Quarterly — ColQ
Colorado Rancher and Farmer — Colo Rancher Farmer
Colorado Register — Colo Reg
Colorado Reports — Colo
Colorado Research in Linguistics — CRIL
Colorado Revised Statutes — Colo Rev Stat
Colorado School of Mines. Alumni Magazine — Colo Sch Mines Alumni Mag
Colorado School of Mines. Magazine — Colo Sch Mines Mag
Colorado School of Mines. Mineral and Energy Resources Bulletin — Colo Sch Mines Mineral Energy Resources Bul
Colorado School of Mines. Mineral Industries Bulletin — Colo Sch Mines Miner Ind Bull
Colorado School of Mines. Professional Contributions — Colo Sch Mines Prof Contrib
Colorado School of Mines. Professional Contributions — Colorado School Mines Prof Contr
Colorado School of Mines. Quarterly — Colo Sch Mines Q
Colorado School of Mines. Quarterly — Colo Sch Mines Quart
Colorado School of Mines. Quarterly — CSMQD
Colorado School of Mines. Quarterly Bulletin — Color Sch Mines Q Bull
Colorado Scientific Society. Proceedings — Colo Sci Soc Proc
Colorado Seed Laboratory Bulletin. Colorado Agricultural Experiment Station — Colorado Seed Lab Bull
Colorado State University. Agricultural Experiment Station. Annual Report — Colo State Univ Agric Exp Stn Annu Rep
Colorado State University. Agricultural Experiment Station. Bulletin — Colo State Univ Agric Exp Stn Bull
Colorado State University. Agricultural Experiment Station. Technical Bulletin — CASTA
Colorado State University. Agricultural Experiment Station. Technical Bulletin — Colo State Univ Agric Exp Stn Tech Bull
Colorado State University. Annual Report — CASRAT
Colorado State University. Annual Report — Colo State Univ Annu Rep
Colorado State University. Colorado Water Resources Research Institute. Information Series — Colo State Univ Colo Water Resour Res Inst Inf Ser
Colorado State University. Experiment Station. Bulletin — CEXSBI
Colorado State University. Experiment Station. Bulletin — Colo State Univ Exp Stn Bull
Colorado State University. Experiment Station. Bulletin — Colo State Univ Expt Sta Bull
Colorado State University. Experiment Station. Progress Report — Prog Rep Exp Stn Colorado State Univ
Colorado State University. Experiment Station. Technical Bulletin — CASTAZ
Colorado State University. Experiment Station. Technical Bulletin — Colo State Univ Exp Stn Tech Bull
Colorado State University (Fort Collins). Hydrology Papers — Colo State Univ (Fort Collins) Hydrol Pap
Colorado State University (Fort Collins). Project Themis Technical Reports — Colo State Univ (Fort Collins) Proj Themis Tech Rep
Colorado State University News — Colo State Univ News
Colorado State University. Range Science Department. Range Science Series — Colo State Univ Range Sci Dep Range Sci Ser
Colorado State University. Range Science Department. Range Science Series — Colo State Univ Range Sci Dep Sci Ser
Colorado State University. Range Science Department. Range Science Series — CSRSAH
Colorado State University. Water Management Technical Report — Water Manage Techn Rep Colorado State Univ
Colorado University. Engineering Experiment Station Circular. Highway Series. Studies. General Series — Colo Univ Eng Expt Sta Circ Highway Ser Studies Gen Ser
Colorado. University Studies. Series in Chemistry and Pharmacy — Colo Univ Stud Ser Chem Pharm
Colorado. Water Conservation Board. Ground Water Series. Circular — Colo Water Conserv Board Ground Water Ser Circ
Colorado Water Conservation Board. Ground-Water Series Bulletin. Circular — Colo Water Conserv Board Ground-Water Ser Bull Circ
Colorado Water Resources Circular — Colo Water Resour Circ
Colorado Water Resources Research Institute. Information Series — Colo Water Resour Res Inst Inf Ser
Colorado Water Resources Research Institute. Technical Report — Colo Water Resour Res Inst Tech Rep
Colorado-Wyoming Academy of Science. Journal — Colorado-Wyoming Acad Sci Jour
Colorado-Wyoming Academy of Science. Journal — Colo-Wyo Acad Sci Jour
Colour Society. Journal — Colour Soc J
Colourage — COLOB
Colourage Annual — Colour Annu
Colouristical Review — Colour Rev
Col-Pa. Coloquios de la Catedra de Paleontologia. Madrid, Universidad, Facultad de Ciencias — Col-Pa Madr Univ Fac Cienc
Colston Papers — Colston Pap
Colston Research Society. Proceedings of the Symposium — Colston Res Soc Proc Symp
Colston Research Society. Proceedings of the Symposium — PCRSAE
Colt Newsletter — Colt News
Coltivatore e Giornale Vinicolo Italiano — Colt G Vinic Ital
Coltivatore e Giornale Vinicolo Italiano — Coltiv G Vinic Ital
Coltivatore e Giornale Vinicolo Italiano — Coltiv Giorn Vinicolo Ital
Coltivazione — Colt
Colton's Journal of Geography and Collateral Sciences. A Record of Discovery, Exploration, and Survey — Coltons J Geogr Collat Sci
Colture Protette — Colt Prot
Colture Protette — Colt Protette
Columbia Essays on Modern Writers — CEMW
Columbia Forum — ColF
Columbia Forum — Colum Forum
Columbia Historical Society. Records — Col Hist Soc Rec
Columbia Historical Society. Records — Colum His S
Columbia Historical Society. Records — Columbia Hist Soc Rec
Columbia Human Rights Law Review — Col Hu Ri LR
Columbia Human Rights Law Review — Col Hum RL Rev
Columbia Human Rights Law Review — Colum Hum Rts L Rev
Columbia Human Rights Law Review — Colum Human Rights L Rev
Columbia Journal of Environmental Law — Col J Env L
Columbia Journal of Environmental Law — Col J Environ L
Columbia Journal of Environmental Law — Colum J Environ L
Columbia Journal of Environmental Law — Colum J Envtl L
Columbia Journal of Law and Social Problems — CJL

Columbia Journal of Law and Social Problems — Col J L and Soc Prob
Columbia Journal of Law and Social Problems — Col JL & Soc Probl
Columbia Journal of Law and Social Problems — Colum J L & Soc Prob
Columbia Journal of Law and Social Problems — Colum J Law & Soc Prob
Columbia Journal of Law and Social Problems — Columb J L
Columbia Journal of Law and Social Problems — Columbia J Law and Social Problems
Columbia Journal of Law and Social Problems — Columbia J of L and Soc Probl
Columbia Journal of Transnational Law — Col J Tr L
Columbia Journal of Transnational Law — Col J Transnat'l L
Columbia Journal of Transnational Law — Colum J Transnat L
Columbia Journal of Transnational Law — Colum J Transnat'l Law
Columbia Journal of Transnational Law — Columb J Tr
Columbia Journal of Transnational Law — Columbia J Transnat Law
Columbia Journal of Transnational Law — Columbia J Transnational Law
Columbia Journal of World Business — CJB
Columbia Journal of World Business — CJW
Columbia Journal of World Business — CJWB
Columbia Journal of World Business — Col J World Bus
Columbia Journal of World Business — Colum J World Bus
Columbia Journal of World Business — Columb J W
Columbia Journal of World Business — Columb Jrl
Columbia Journal of World Business — Columbia J Wld Busin
Columbia Journal of World Business — Columbia J World Bus
Columbia Journalism Review — C
Columbia Journalism Review — CJORD
Columbia Journalism Review — CJR
Columbia Journalism Review — Col Jour Rev
Columbia Journalism Review — ColJR
Columbia Journalism Review — Colum Journalism R
Columbia Journalism Review — Columbia J-Ism R
Columbia Journalism Review — Columbia Journalism Rev
Columbia Journalism Review — GCJR
Columbia Law Review — Cb LR
Columbia Law Review — CLR
Columbia Law Review — Col L Rev
Columbia Law Review — Col Law Review
Columbia Law Review — Col LR
Columbia Law Review — Colum L Rev
Columbia Law Review — Columb Law
Columbia Law Review — Columbia Law R
Columbia Law Review — Columbia Law Rev
Columbia Law Review — CR
Columbia Law Review — ICLV
Columbia Library. Columns — CLC
Columbia Library. Columns — Columbia Lib C
Columbia Library. Columns — Columbia Libr Col
Columbia Library. Columns — Columbia Libr Columns
Columbia Studies in the Classical Tradition — CSCT
Columbia University. Contributions to Anthropology — CUCA
Columbia University. East Asian Institute. Studies — EAIS
Columbia University. Forum — CUF
Columbia University. Germanic Studies — CUGS
Columbia University. Quarterly — Colum Univ Q
Columbia University. Quarterly — Columbia U Q
Columbia University. Quarterly — CUQ
Columbia University. Working Papers in Linguistics — CUWPL
Columbus Business Journal — Columb Bsn
Columbus [*Ohio*] **Dental Society. Bulletin** — Columbus Dent Soc Bull
Columbus Dispatch — Colum Disp
Columbus Gallery of Fine Arts. Bulletin [*Columbus, Ohio*] — Columbus Gal Bul
Columbus Medical Bulletin — Columbus Med Bul
Columbus News Index [*Database*] — CNI
Column Chromatography. International Symposium on Separation Methods — Column Chromatogr Int Symp Sep Methods
Combat Crew — Com Crew
Combinatorial Chemistry — Comb Chem
Combinatorics, Probability, and Computing — Combin Probab Comput
Combined Cumulative Index to Pediatrics — Comb Cumul Index Pediatr
Combined Health Information Database — CHID
Combined Proceedings. International Plant Propagators' Society — Comb Proc Int Plant Propagators Soc
Combustion — COMBA
Combustion and Flame — CBFMA
Combustion and Flame — CBFMAO
Combustion and Flame — Comb Flame
Combustion and Flame — Combust and Flame
Combustion and Flame — Combust Flame
Combustion and Reaction Kinetics — Combust React Kinet
Combustion Engineering — Comb Eng
Combustion Engineering Association. Document [*England*] — Combust Eng Assoc Doc
Combustion Engines. Reduction of Friction and Wear. International Conference — Combust Engines Reduct Frict Wear Int Conf
Combustion, Explosion, and Shock Waves [*Former USSR*] — Combust Explos Shock Waves
Combustion, Explosion, and Shock Waves (USSR) — Comb Expl (R)
Combustion Institute. Canadian Section. Spring Technical Meeting — Combust Inst Can Sect Spring Tech Meet
Combustion Institute. Eastern Section. Fall Technical Meeting — Combust Inst East Sect Fall Tech Meet
Combustion Science and Technology — CBSTB
Combustion Science and Technology — Comb Sci T
Combustion Science and Technology — Combust Sci Technol
Combustion Science and Technology — Combustion Sci Tech
Combustion Science and Technology. Book Series — Combust Sci Technol Book Ser
Combustion Toxicology — Combust Toxicol
Combustione e Combustibile — Combust Combust
Comenius-Blaetter fuer Volkserziehung — CBV
Comentarios Bibliograficos Americanos — CBA
Comercio e Mercados — Comer e Mercados
Comercio Exterior. Banco Nacional de Comercio Exterior — BNCE/CE
Comercio Exterior de Mexico — CEM
Comercio Exterior de Mexico — Com Ext Mexico
Comercio Exterior de Mexico — Comer Exterior Mexico
Comercio Exterior de Mexico — Comercio Exterior de Mexico
Comercio y Desarrollo — Com Des
Comercio y Produccion — Comer y Produccion
Comercio y Produccion — Comercio Prod
Comet Stories — COM
Comicorum Atticorum Fragmenta — CAF
Comicorum Graecorum Fragmenta — CGF
Comicorum Graecorum Fragmenta i Papyri Reperta — CGF Pap
Comicorum Graecorum Fragmenta i Papyri Reperta — CGFPR
Comision de Fomento Minera. Boletin (Mexico) — Com Fom Min Bol (Mex)
Comision de Investigaciones Cientificas de la Provincia de Buenos Aires. Monografias — Com Invest Cient Prov Buenos Aires Monogr
Comision de Investigaciones Cientificas de la Provincia de Buenos Aires. Publicacion — Com Invest Cient Prov Buenos Aires Publ
Comision de Investigaciones Cientificas. Provincia de Buenos Aires. Informes — Com Invest Cient Prov Buenos Aires Inf
Comision Interamericana del Atun Tropical. Boletin — Com Interam Atun Trop Bol
Comision Nacional de Energia Atomica (Argentina). Informe — Com Nac Energ At (Argent) Inf
Comision Nacional de Energia Nuclear (Mexico). Publicacion — Com Nac Energ Nucl (Mex) Publ
Comision Nacional de Valores. Boletin — Comision Nac Valores Bol
Comision Nacional para le Erradicacion del Paludismo. Boletin — Com Nac Errad Palud Bol
Comissao das Linhas Telegraficas Estrategicas Mato Grosso ao Amazonas — Comiss Linhas Telegr Estrateg Mato Grosso Amazonas
Comissao Nacional de Energia Nuclear (Brazil). Boletim — Com Nac Energ Nucl (Braz) Bol
Comissao Nacional de Energia Nuclear (Brazil). Publicacao — Com Nac Energ Nucl (Braz) Publ
Comissao Reguladora dos Cereais do Arquipelago dos Acores [*Ponta Delgada*] — CRCAA
Comitato Glaciologico Italiano. Bollettino — CGIB
Comitato Glaciologico Italiano. Bollettino. Serie Seconda — Com Glaciol Ital Boll Ser 2
Comitato Nazionale per la Ricerca e per lo Sviluppo dell'Energia Nucleare e delle Energie Alternative. Notiziario — Com Naz Ric Sviluppo Energ Nucl Energ Altern Not
Comitato Nazionale per le Ricerche Nucleari (Italy). Notiziario — Com Naz Ric Nucl (Italy) Not
Comitato Nazionale per le Ricerche Nucleari. Rapporto Tecnico (Italy) — Com Naz Ric Nucl Rapp Tec (Italy)
Comitato Nazionale per l'Energia Nucleare. Notiziario — Com Naz Energ Nucl Not
Comitato Nazionale per l'Energia Nucleare. Notiziario — Comitato Naz Energia Nucleare Notiz
Comitato Nazionale per l'Energia Nucleare. Notiziario (Italy) — Com Naz Energ Nucl Not (Italy)
Comitato Nazionale per l'Energia Nucleare. Rapporto Tecnico CNEN-RT/BIO (Italy) — Com Naz Energ Nucl Rapp Tec CNEN-RT/BIO (Italy)
Comitato Nazionale per l'Energia Nucleare. Rapporto Tecnico CNEN-RT/CHI (Italy) — Com Naz Energ Nucl Rapp Tec CNEN-RT/CHI (Italy)
Comitato Nazionale per l'Energia Nucleare. Rapporto Tecnico CNEN-RT/DISP (Italy) — Com Naz Energ Nucl Rapp Tec CNEN-RT/DISP (Italy)
Comitato Nazionale per l'Energia Nucleare. Rapporto Tecnico CNEN-RT/FARE-SDI — Com Naz Energ Nucl Rapp Tec CNEN-RT/FARE SDI
Comitato Nazionale per l'Energia Nucleare. Rapporto Tecnico CNEN-RT/FARE-SIN — Com Naz Energ Nucl Rapp Tec CNEN-RT/FARE SIN
Comitato Nazionale per l'Energia Nucleare. Rapporto Tecnico CNEN-RT/FI (Italy) — Com Naz Energ Nucl Rapp Tec CNEN-RT/FI (Italy)
Comitato Nazionale per l'Energia Nucleare. Rapporto Tecnico CNEN-RT/FIMA (Italy) — Com Naz Energ Nucl Rapp Tec CNEN-RT/FIMA (Italy)
Comitato Nazionale per l'Energia Nucleare. Rapporto Tecnico CNEN-RT/ING (Italy) — Com Naz Energ Nucl Rapp Tec CNEN-RT/ING (Italy)
Comitato Nazionale per l'Energia Nucleare. Rapporto Tecnico CNEN-RT/MET (Italy) — Com Naz Energ Nucl Rapp Tec CNEN-RT/MET (Italy)
Comitato Nazionale per l'Energia Nucleare. Rapporto Tecnico CNEN-RT/PROT (Italy) — Com Naz Energ Nucl Rapp Tec CNEN-RT/PROT (Italy)
Comitato Nazionale per l'Energia Nucleare. Rapporto Tecnico RT/AI (Italy) — Com Naz Energ Nucl Rapp Tec RT/AI (Italy)
Comitato Nazionale per l'Energia Nucleare. Rapporto Tecnico RT/BIO (Italy) — Com Naz Energ Nucl Rapp Tec RT/BIO (Italy)
Comitato Nazionale per l'Energia Nucleare. Rapporto Tecnico RT/CHI (Italy) — Com Naz Energ Nucl Rapp Tec RT/CHI (Italy)
Comitato Nazionale per l'Energia Nucleare. Rapporto Tecnico RT/DISP (Italy) — Com Naz Energ Nucl Rapp Tec RT/DISP (Italy)
Comitato Nazionale per l'Energia Nucleare. Rapporto Tecnico RT/EC (Italy) — Com Naz Energ Nucl Rapp Tec RT/EC (Italy)
Comitato Nazionale per l'Energia Nucleare. Rapporto Tecnico RT/EL (Italy) — Com Naz Energ Nucl Rapp Tec RT/EL (Italy)
Comitato Nazionale per l'Energia Nucleare. Rapporto Tecnico RT/FI (Italy) — Com Naz Energ Nucl Rapp Tec RT/FI (Italy)

Comitato Nazionale per l'Energia Nucleare. Rapporto Tecnico RT/FIMA (Italy) — Com Naz Energ Nucl Rapp Tec RT/FIMA (Italy)
Comitato Nazionale per l'Energia Nucleare. Rapporto Tecnico RT/GEN (Italy) — Com Naz Energ Nucl Rapp Tec RT/GEN (Italy)
Comitato Nazionale per l'Energia Nucleare. Rapporto Tecnico RT/GEO (Italy) — Com Naz Energ Nucl Rapp Tec RT/GEO (Italy)
Comitato Nazionale per l'Energia Nucleare. Rapporto Tecnico RT/GIU (Italy) — Com Naz Energ Nucl Rapp Tec RT/GIU (Italy)
Comitato Nazionale per l'Energia Nucleare. Rapporto Tecnico RT/ING (Italy) — Com Naz Energ Nucl Rapp Tec RT/ING (Italy)
Comitato Nazionale per l'Energia Nucleare. Rapporto Tecnico RT/MET (Italy) — Com Naz Energ Nucl Rapp Tec RT/MET (Italy)
Comitato Nazionale per l'Energia Nucleare. Rapporto Tecnico RT/PROT (Italy) — Com Naz Energ Nucl Rapp Tec RT/PROT (Italy)
Comitato Nazionale per l'Energia Nucleare. Reprints — Com Naz Energ Nucl Repr
Comite Arctique International. Newsletter — CAIN
Comite Consultatif de Photometrie. Travaux — Com Consult Photom Trav
Comite Consultatif de Thermometrie. Session — Com Consult Thermom Sess
Comite Consultatif d'Electricite. Travaux — Com Consult Electr Trav
Comite Consultatif pour la Definition du Metre. Rapport — Com Consult Definition Metre Rapp
Comite Consultatif pour la Definition du Metre. Travaux — Com Consult Definition Metre Trav
Comite Consultatif pour les Etalons de Mesure des Radiations Ionisantes. Travaux — Com Consult Etalons Mes Radiat Ionis Trav
Comite Consultatif pour les Etalons de Mesure des Rayonnements Ionisants. Section 1. Rayons X et Y. Electrons — Com Consult Etalons Mes Rayonnem Ionis Sect 1
Comite Consultatif pour les Etalons de Mesure des Rayonnements Ionisants. Section 2. Mesure des Radionucleides — Com Consult Etalons Mes Rayonnem Ionis Sect 2
Comite Consultatif pour les Etalons de Mesure des Rayonnements Ionisants. Section 3. Mesures Neutroniques — Com Consult Etalons Mes Rayonnem Ionis Sect 3
Comite Consultatif pour les Etalons de Mesure des Rayonnements Ionisants. Section 4. Etalons d'Energie Alpha — Com Consult Etalons Mes Rayonnem Ionis Sect 4
Comite des Travaux Historiques et Scientifiques. Bulletin Archeologique — CTHBAr
Comite des Travaux Historiques et Scientifiques. Bulletin Archeologique — CTHBull
Comite des Travaux Historiques et Scientifiques. Bulletin Historique et Philologique — CTHBullH
Comite Directivo para la Investigacion de los Recursos Minerales (Mexico). Boletin — Com Dir Invest Recur Miner (Mex) Bol
Comite Flamand de France. Annales — CFFAn
Comite International de Thermodynamique et de Cinetique Electrochimiques. Comptes Rendus — Com Int Thermodyn Cinet Electrochim CR
Comite International de Thermodynamique et de Cinetique Electrochimiques. Comptes Rendus de la Reunion — Com Int Thermodyn Cinet Electrochim CR Reun
Comite International des Poids et Mesures. Comite Consultatif de Photometrie. Travaux — Com Int Poids Mes Com Consult Photom Trav
Comite International des Poids et Mesures. Comite Consultatif de Thermometrie. Session — Com Int Poids Mes Com Consult Thermom Sess
Comite International des Poids et Mesures. Comite Consultatif de Thermometrie. Travaux — Com Int Poids Mes Com Consult Thermom Trav
Comite International des Poids et Mesures. Comite Consultatif d'Electricite. Travaux — Com Int Poids Mes Com Consult Electr Trav
Comite International des Poids et Mesures. Comite Consultatif pour la Definition du Metre. Travaux — Com Int Poids Mes Com Consult Def Metre Trav
Comite International des Poids et Mesures. Comite Consultatif pour la Definition du Metre. Travaux — Com Int Poids Mes Com Consult Definition Metre Trav
Comite International des Poids et Mesures. Comite Consultatif pour les Etalons de Mesure des Radiations Ionisantes. Travaux — Com Int Poids Mes Com Consult Etalons Mes Radiat Ionis Trav
Comite International des Poids et Mesures. Proces-Verbaux des Seances — Com Int Poids Mes PV Seances
Comite International des Sciences Historiques. Recueil — Recu Com Internat Sci Hist
Comite International pour l'Etude des Bauxites, de l'Alumine, et d'Aluminium. Travaux — Com Int Etude Bauxites Alumine Alum Trav
Comite International pour l'Etude des Bauxites, des Oxydes, et des Hydroxydes d'Aluminium. Travaux — Com Int Etude Bauxites Oxydes Hydroxydes Alum Trav
Comite Special du Katanga. Annales du Service des Mines et du Service Geographique et Geologique — Com Spec Katanga Ann Ser Mines Ser Geogr Geol
Comitetul de Stat pentru Energia Nucleara. Institutul de Fizica Atomica. Report (Romania) — Com Stat Energ Nucl Inst Fiz At Rep (Rom)
Comitetul Geologic (Romania). Studii Tehnice si Economice — Com Geol (Rom) Stud Teh Econ
COMLINE Business Analysis [*Database*] — CBA
COMLINE Industrial Monitor [*Database*] — CIM
Command Paper [*London*] — Cmd
Commander's Digest — CDI
Commander's Digest — Comman Dig
Comment — C
Comment on Education — Comment on Ed
Commentaire de l'Ancien Testament [*Neuchatel*] — CAT
Commentari — Com
Commentari. Accademia di Brescia — C A Brescia
Commentari dell'Ateneo di Brescia — CAB
Commentaria in Aristotelem Graeca — CAG
Commentaries in Plant Science — Comment Plant Sci
Commentaries on Research in Breast Disease — Comment Res Breast Dis
Commentaries on Research in Breast Disease — CRBDDO
Commentarii Mathematici Helvetici — Comm Math H
Commentarii Mathematici Helvetici — Comment Math Helv
Commentarii Mathematici. Universitatis Sancti Pauli — Comment Math Univ St Paul
Commentarii Societatis Regiae Scientiarum Gottingensis — Comment Soc Regiae Sci Gott
Commentario. Pontificia Academia Scientiarum — Comment Pontif Acad Sci
Commentarj. Accademia di Scienze, Lettere, Agricultura, ed Arti del Dipartimento del Mella — Comment Accad Sci Dip Mella
Commentary — COM
Commentary — Commen
Commentary — COMNB
Commentary — Comny
Commentary — Comt
Commentary — Ctary
Commentary — GCOM
Commentary. American Jewish Committee — AJC/C
Commentary (New York) — CNY
Commentary on Herodotus — CH
Commentary on Herodotus — COH
Commentationes Balticae — CB
Commentationes Balticae — CBalt
Commentationes Balticae — Comment Balt
Commentationes Biologicae — Commentat Biol
Commentationes Biologicae. Societas Scientiarum Fennica — CMBI
Commentationes Biologicae. Societas Scientiarum Fennica — COBGA
Commentationes Biologicae. Societas Scientiarum Fennica — COBGA9
Commentationes Biologicae. Societas Scientiarum Fennica — Commentat Biol Soc Sci Fenn
Commentationes Humanarum Litterarum. Societas Scientiarum Fennica — CHLSSF
Commentationes Humanarum Litterarum. Societas Scientiarum Fennica — CSF
Commentationes Mathematicae. Special Issue — Comment Math Special Issue
Commentationes Mathematicae. Universitatis Carolinae — CMUC
Commentationes Mathematicae. Universitatis Carolinae — Comment Math Univ Carolin
Commentationes Mathematicae. Universitatis Carolinae — Comment Math Univ Carolinae
Commentationes Physico-Mathematicae — Comm Phys-M
Commentationes Physico-Mathematicae — Commentat Phys-Math
Commentationes Physico-Mathematicae — CPHMA
Commentationes Physico-Mathematicae. Dissertationes — Commentat Phys Math Diss
Commentationes Physico-Mathematicae. Societas Scientiarum Fennica — Comment Phys Math Soc Sci Fenn
Commentationes Physico-Mathematicae. Supplement — Commentat Phys-Math Suppl
Commentationes Pontificiae. Academiae Scientiarum — Commentat Pontif Acad Sci
Commentationes Pontificiae. Academiae Scientiarum — CPASAD
Commentationes Societatis Physico-Medicae Apud Universitatem Literarum Caesaream Mosquensem Institutae — Commentat Soc Phys Med Univ Lit Caes Mosq
Commentationes Vindobonenses — C Vind
Commentationes Vindobonenses — CV
Comments on Agricultural and Food Chemistry — Comments Agric Food Chem
Comments on Astrophysics [*United States, England*] — Comments Astrophys
Comments on Astrophysics and Space Physics [*Later, Comments on Astrophysics*] — COASB
Comments on Astrophysics and Space Physics [*Later, Comments on Astrophysics*] — Comments Astrophys Space Phys
Comments on Astrophysics. Comments on Modern Physics. Part C — Comments Astrophys Comments Mod Phys Part C
Comments on Atomic and Molecular Physics — CAMPB
Comments on Atomic and Molecular Physics — Comments At Mol Phys
Comments on Condensed Matter Physics — Comments Condens Matter Phys
Comments on Contemporary Psychiatry — CCPYAF
Comments on Contemporary Psychiatry — Com Con Psy
Comments on Contemporary Psychiatry — Comments Contemp Psychiatry
Comments on Earth Sciences. Geophysics — CESGA
Comments on Earth Sciences. Geophysics — Comments Earth Sci Geophys
Comments on Inorganic Chemistry — Comments Inorg Chem
Comments on Modern Biology — Comments Mod Biol
Comments on Modern Chemistry — Comments Mod Chem
Comments on Modern Chemistry. Part B — Comments Mod Chem Part B
Comments on Modern Physics — Comments Mod Phys
Comments on Modern Physics. Part B — Comments Mod Phys Part B
Comments on Modern Physics. Part D — Comments Mod Phys Part D
Comments on Molecular and Cellular Biophysics — CMCB
Comments on Molecular and Cellular Biophysics — Comments Mol Cell Biophys
Comments on Molecular and Cellular Biophysics. Comments on Modern Biology. Part A — Comments Mol and Cell Biophys Comments Mod Biol Part A
Comments on Nuclear and Particle Physics — CNPPA
Comments on Nuclear and Particle Physics — Comments Nucl & Part Phys
Comments on Nuclear and Particle Physics — Comments Nucl Part Phys
Comments on Nuclear and Particle Physics. Supplement — Comments Nucl Part Phys Suppl
Comments on Plasma Physics and Controlled Fusion — C Pl Phys C Fus

Comments on Plasma Physics and Controlled Fusion — Comments Plasma Phys & Controlled Fusion
Comments on Plasma Physics and Controlled Fusion — Comments Plasma Phys Controll Fus
Comments on Plasma Physics and Controlled Fusion [*England*] — Comments Plasma Phys Controlled Fusion
Comments on Solid State Physics — C Sol St Phys
Comments on Solid State Physics — Comments Solid State Phys
Comments on Solid State Physics — COSPB
Comments on Toxicology — Comments Toxicol
Commerce [*India*] — CMCEA
Commerce — CWI
Commerce America — Com Amer
Commerce America — Commer Am
Commerce and Finance — Comm & Fin
Commerce Business Daily [*Department of Commerce*] [*Information service or system*] — CBD
Commerce Business Daily [*Department of Commerce*] — COBD
Commerce Canada — Com Canada
Commerce du Levant — Commer Levant
Commerce et Cooperation — Com Et Coop
Commerce et Cooperation — Commerce et Coop
Commerce Exterieur Albanais — CEE
Commerce Exterieur Tchecoslovaque — Com Ext Tchecosl
Commerce Franco-Suisse — CFR
Commerce in Belgium — CXG
Commerce (India) — Comm (India)
Commerce, Industrial, and Mining Review — Commer Ind & Min Rev
Commerce, Industrial, and Mining Review — Commerce Ind & Min R
Commerce International — CHA
Commerce International — CIT
Commerce International — Commerce Int
Commerce International — Comrc Intl
Commerce Moderne — Com Mod
Commerce Monthly — Comm M
Commerce Reporter — Com Rep
Commerce Reports — Comm Rep
Commerce Today — Com Today
Commerce Today — Comm Today
Commerce Today — Commer Today
Commercial and Financial Chronicle — Comm & Fin Chr
Commercial and Financial Chronicle — Comm & Fin Chron
Commercial and Financial Chronicle. Statistical Section — Com and Fin Chr
Commercial Appeal — Commercial
Commercial Applications of Precision Manufacturing at the Sub-Micron Level [*London*] — Commer Appl Precis Manuf Sub Micron Level
Commercial Bank of Australia. Economic Review — Commer Bank Australia Econ R
Commercial Bank of Greece. Economic Bulletin — CBB
Commercial Bulletin for Teachers in Secondary Schools — Comm Bul
Commercial Car Journal — Commer Car J
Commercial Courier — MAC
Commercial Education — Comm Ed
Commercial Fertilizer — Comm Fert
Commercial Fertilizer — Commer Fert
Commercial Fertilizer and Plant Food Industry — Commer Fert Plant Food Ind
Commercial Fertilizer and Plant Food Industry. Yearbook — Commer Fert Plant Food Ind Yearb
Commercial Fertilizer Yearbook — Commer Fert Yearb
Commercial Finance Journal — Commer Fin J
Commercial Fisheries Abstracts — Commer Fish Abstr
Commercial Fisheries Review [*Later, Marine Fisheries Review*] — CFKEA
Commercial Fisheries Review [*Later, Marine Fisheries Review*] — CFREAK
Commercial Fisheries Review [*Later, Marine Fisheries Review*] — CFRV
Commercial Fisheries Review [*Later, Marine Fisheries Review*] — COFR
Commercial Fisheries Review [*Later, Marine Fisheries Review*] — Commer Fish Rev
Commercial Fishing — Com Fish
Commercial Fishing Newsletter — Comm Fish Newsl
Commercial Grower — Comml Grow
Commercial Horticulture — Com Hort
Commercial Index — Commer Ind
Commercial Intelligencer — CI
Commercial Investment Journal — CIJ
Commercial Investment Journal — Com Invest Jnl
Commercial Law Association. Bulletin — CLA Bulletin
Commercial Law Association. Bulletin — CLAB
Commercial Law Association. Bulletin — Cmcl Law Assoc Bull
Commercial Law Association. Bulletin — Com L Assoc Bull
Commercial Law Association. Bulletin — Comm L Assoc Bull
Commercial Law Journal — CML
Commercial Law Journal — Com L J
Commercial Law Journal — Com Law Jnl
Commercial Letter. Canadian Imperial Bank of Commerce — Commer Letter Can Imperial Bank Commer
Commercial Motor — Comm Mot
Commercial Motor — Commer Motor
Commercial News USA — Commer News USA
Commercial Pan America (Washington, DC) — Commer Pan Am Wash
Commercial Rabbit — Commer Rabbit
Commercial Space — Cmcl Space
Commercial Standards Monthly — Commer Stand Mon
Commercial Vehicles — Comm Veh
Commercial West — Commer W
Commercium Litterarium ad Rei Medicae et Scientiae Naturali Incrementum Institutum — Commercium Lit Rei Med et Sc Nat
Commercium. Maandblad voor Economisch, Administratief, en Ondernemersonderwijs — KMI
Commerece Moderne — Comm Mod
Commissariat a l'Energie Atomique. Clefs — Commis Energ At Clefs
Commissariat a l'Energie Atomique (France). Bulletin d'Informations Scientifiques et Techniques — Commis Energ At (Fr) Bull Inf Sci Tech
Commissariat a l'Energie Atomique (France). Rapport — Commis Energ At (Fr) Rapp
Commissariat a l'Energie Atomique (France). Service de Documentation. Serie Bibliographie — Comm Energie At (Fr) Serv Doc Ser Bibliogr
Commissariat a l'Energie Atomique (France). Service de Documentation. Serie Bibliographie — Commis Energ At (Fr) Serv Doc Ser Bibliogr
Commissariat a l'Energie Atomique. Note CEA-N (France) — Commis Energ At Note CEA N (Fr)
Commissariat a l'Energie Atomique. Rapport CEA-CONF (France) — Commis Energ At Rapp CEA CONF (Fr)
Commissie voor Hydrologisch Onderzoek TNO [*Nederlandse Centrale Organisatie voor Toegepast Natuurwetenschappelijk Onderzoek*] — CHOVA2
Commissie voor Hydrologisch Onderzoek TNO [*Nederlandse Centrale Organisatie voor Toegepast Natuurwetenschappelijk Onderzoek*]. Verslag van de Technische Bijeenkomst — Comm Hydrol Onderz TNO Versl Tech Bijeenkomst
Commissie voor Hydrologisch Onderzoek TNO [*Nederlandse Centrale Organisatie voor Toegepast Natuurwetenschappelijk Onderzoek*]. Verslag van de Technische Bijeenkomst — Comm Hydrol Onderz TNO Versl Tech Bijeenkomsten
Commissie voor Hydrologisch Onderzoek TNO [*Nederlandse Centrale Organisatie voor Toegepast Natuurwetenschappelijk Onderzoek*]. Verslagen en Mededelingen — Comm Hydrol Onderz TNO Versl Meded
Commission de Toponymie et Dialectologie — CTD
Commission des Communautes Europeennes — Comm Communautes Eur
Commission des Communautes Europeennes/Commissione delle Comunita Europee/Commission of the European Communities. Eur Report — CECED9
Commission for Scientific Research in Greenland. Newsletter — CSRG
Commission for Technical Co-Operation in Africa. Publication — Comm Tech Co Op Afr Publ
Commission Geologique de Finlande. Bulletin — CGFE
Commission Internationale des Industries Agricoles et Alimentaires. Symposium International — Comm Int Ind Agric Aliment Symp Int
Commission Internationale pour l'Exploration Scientifique de la Mer Mediterranee. Rapports et Proces-Verbaux des Reunions — Comm Int Explor Sci Mer Mediterr Rapp PV Reun
Commission Internationale Technique de Sucrerie. Comptes Rendus de l'Assemblee Generale — Comm Int Tech Sucr CR Assem Gen
Commission of the European Communities. Eur Report — Comm Eur Communities Eur Rep
Commission of the European Communities. Eurisotop Office. Information Booklet — Comm Eur Communities Eurisotop Off Inf Bookl
Commission of the European Communities. Eurosotop Office. ITE-Report — Comm Eur Communities Eurosotop Off ITE Rep
Commission of the European Communities. Information on Agriculture — CEIADR
Commission of the European Communities. Information on Agriculture — Comm Eur Communities Inf Agric
Commission of the European Communities. Report EUR — Comm Eur Communities Rep EUR
Commission Royale d'Histoire. Bulletin — CRHBull
Commissione delle Comunita Europee — Comm Comunita Eur
Commissione Internazionale per la Protezione delle Acque. Italo-Svizzere Rapporti — Comm Int Prot Acque Italo-Svizz Rapp
Commissione Internazionale per la Protezione delle Acque Italo-Svizzere. Rapporti — PQCSD6
Commissione Italiana del Comitato Internazionale di Geofisica. Pubblicazioni — Comm Ital Com Int Geofis Pubbl
Commissione Italiana per la Geofisica. Pubblicazioni — Comm Ital Geofis Pubbl
Commissions Royales d'Art et d'Archeologie. Bulletin — CRAABull
Committee Assignment Report CAR. Technical Association of the Pulp and Paper Industry — Comm Assignment Rep CAR Tech Assoc Pulp Pap Ind
Committee for Co-Ordination of Joint Prospecting for Mineral Resources in Asian Off-Shore Areas. Newsletter — CCOP Newsl
Committee for High Arctic Scientific Research Liaison and Information Exchange [*CHARLIE*]. News Bulletin — CHAR
Committee for Hydrological Research TNO (Central Organization for Applied Scientific Research in the Netherlands). Proceedings and Informations — Comm Hydrol Res TNO (Cent Organ Appl Sci Res Neth) Proc Inf
Committee for Hydrological Research TNO [*Central Organization for Applied Scientific Research in the Netherlands*]. Proceedings and Information — Comm Hydrol Res TNO Proc Inf
Committee for Inland Fisheries of Africa. Technical Paper — Comm Inland Fish Afr Tech Pap
Committee of Directors of Polytechnics Press. Information — CDP Press Inf
Committee on Alkali Reactions in Concrete. Danish National Institute of Building Research and the Academy of Technical Sciences. Progress Report. Series A. Alkali Reactions in Concrete. General — Comm Alkali React Concr Prog Rep A
Committee on Alkali Reactions in Concrete. Danish National Institute of Building Research and the Academy of Technical Sciences. Progress Report. Series D. Aggregate Types of Denmark — Comm Alkali React Concr Prog Rep D

Committee on Alkali Reactions in Concrete. Danish National Institute of Building Research and the Academy of Technical Sciences. Progress Report. Series F. Alkali Contents of Concrete Components — Comm Alkali React Concr Prog Rep F
Committee on Alkali Reactions in Concrete. Danish National Institute of Building Research and the Academy of Technical Sciences. Progress Report. Series H. Methods of Evaluation of Alkali Reactions — Comm Alkali React Concr Nat Prog Rep H
Committee on Alkali Reactions in Concrete. Danish National Institute of Building Research and the Academy of Technical Sciences. Progress Report. Series I. Inhibition of Alkali Reactions by Admixtures — Comm Alkali React Concr Prog Rep I
Committee on Alkali Reactions in Concrete. Danish National Institute of Building Research and the Academy of Technical Sciences. Progress Report. Series N. Observed Symptoms of Deterioration — Comm Alkali React Concr Prog Rep N
Committee on Alkali Reactions in Concrete. Danish National Institute of Building Research and the Academy of Technical Sciences. Progress Report. SeriesH. Methods of Evaluation of Alkali Reactions — Comm Alkali React Concr Prog Rep H
Committee on Alkali Reactions in Concrete. Danish National Institute of Building Research and the Academy of Technical Sciences. Progress Report. SeriesL. Inhibition of Alkali Reactions by Admixtures — Comm Alkali React Concr Prog Rep L
Committee on Data for Science and Technology. Bulletin — Comm Data Sci Technol Bull
Committee on Data for Science and Technology. Special Report (International Council of Scientific Unions) — Comm Data Sci Technol Spec Rep (ICSU)
Committee on Problems of Drug Dependence. Proceedings of the Annual Scientific Meeting. United States National Research Council — Comm Probl Drug Depend Proc Annu Sci Meet US Nat Res Counc
Committee on the Challenges of Modern Society. Air Pollution — Com Challenges of Mod Soc Air Pollution
Committee on the Safety of Nuclear Installations. Report — Comm Saf Nucl Install Rep
Commodities Magazine — Commod Mag
Commodities Magazine — Commodities M
Commodity Bulletin. Department of Agriculture of New South Wales. Division of Marketing and Economics — Commod Bul Dep Agric NSW Div Mark Econ
Commodity Futures Law Reports. Commerce Clearing House — Comm Fut L Rep CCH
Commodity Journal — COJ
Commodity Journal — COMJD
Commodity Journal — Commod J
Commodity Journal — Commod Jrl
Commodity Prices — CP
Commodity Production Statistics [*Database*] — ICPDATA
Commodity Trading Digest — Comm Trad Dig
Commodity Year Book — CYB
Common Cause Magazine — GCCM
Common Cause Membership — Common Cause M
Common Ground — CG
Common Law Lawyer — Comm L Law
Common Market Business Reports — CNN
Common Market Business Reports (Spain) — CSB
Common Market Law Reports — CMLR
Common Market Law Reports — Comm Mkt L Rep
Common Market Law Reports — Comm Mkt LR
Common Market Law Review — Comm Mkt L Rev
Common Market Law Review — Common Market Law R
Common Market News — CMN
Common Market Reports. Commerce Clearing House — Common Mkt Rep CCH
Common Sense — Common
Common Sense. Journal of Information for Environmentally Concerned Citizens. Kootenay Environmental Institute [*Galena Bay, British Columbia*] — COSE
Commoner and Glass Worker — Commoner Glass Work
Commonweal — C
Commonweal — Comm
Commonweal — Comw
Commonweal — Cweal
Commonweal — GCOW
Commonwealth — CW
Commonwealth — Cwealth
Commonwealth — Cwl
Commonwealth Agricultural Bureaux. Annotated Bibliography [*Database*] — CAB Annot Bibliogr
Commonwealth Agriculturist — Common Agric
Commonwealth Agriculturist — Commonw Agric
Commonwealth Agriculturist — Cwealth Agriculturist
Commonwealth Arbitration Awards and Determinations — CAA
Commonwealth Arbitration Reports — CAR
Commonwealth Arbitration Reports — Comm AR
Commonwealth Arbitration Reports — Commw Arb
Commonwealth Arbitration Reports — Commw Art
Commonwealth Bureau of Animal Breeding and Genetics. Technical Communication — Commonw Bur Anim Breed Genet Tech Commun
Commonwealth Bureau of Animal Breeding and Genetics. Technical Communication — TCBAAQ
Commonwealth Bureau of Animal Health. Review Series — Commonw Bur Anim Health Rev Ser
Commonwealth Bureau of Animal Health. Review Series — CWAHAT
Commonwealth Bureau of Animal Nutrition. Technical Communication — Commonw Bur Anim Nutr Tech Commun
Commonwealth Bureau of Animal Nutrition. Technical Communication — TCANAQ
Commonwealth Bureau of Dairy Science and Technology. Technical Communication — Commonw Bur Dairy Sci Technol Tech Commun
Commonwealth Bureau of Horticulture and Plantation Crops (Great Britain). Technical Communication — Commonw Bur Hortic Plant Crops (GB) Tech Commun
Commonwealth Bureau of Horticulture and Plantation Crops. Technical Communication — CWAPAJ
Commonwealth Bureau of Nutrition. Technical Communication — Commonw Bur Nutr Tech Commun
Commonwealth Bureau of Nutrition. Technical Communication — TCCND5
Commonwealth Bureau of Pastures and Field Crops. Bulletin — Commonw Bur Pastures Field Crops Bull
Commonwealth Bureau of Pastures and Field Crops (Great Britain). Review Series — Commonw Bur Pastures Field Crops (GB) Rev Ser
Commonwealth Bureau of Pastures and Field Crops. Hurley Berkshire Bulletin — BUPFA5
Commonwealth Bureau of Pastures and Field Crops. Hurley Berkshire Bulletin — Commonw Bur Pastures Field Crops Hurley Berkshire Bull
Commonwealth Bureau of Plant Breeding and Genetics. Technical Communication [*A publication*] — Commonw Bur Plant Breed Genet Tech Commun
Commonwealth Bureau of Soil Science. Technical Communication — Commonw Bur Soil Sci Tech Commun
Commonwealth Bureau of Soils. Special Publication — Commonw Bur Soils Spec Publ
Commonwealth Bureau of Soils. Special Publication — SPCSDW
Commonwealth Bureau of Soils. Technical Communication — Commonw Bur Soils Tech Commun
Commonwealth Bureau of Soils. Technical Communication — CWBSAX
Commonwealth Club of California. Transactions — Commonwealth Club Cal Transactions
Commonwealth Council for Educational Administration. Newsletter — CCEA Newsl
Commonwealth Council for Educational Administration. Studies in Educational Administration — CCEA SEA
Commonwealth Development — Commonw Dev
Commonwealth Employees Compensation Decisions — CCD
Commonwealth Employees Compensation Notes — CCN
Commonwealth Engineer — Commonw Eng
Commonwealth Engineer — Commonw Engr
Commonwealth Engineer — Commwth Eng
Commonwealth Engineer — Cwealth Eng
Commonwealth Essays and Studies — CE and S
Commonwealth Experimental Building Station. Notes on the Science of Building — Commw Exp Build Stat NSB
Commonwealth Fertilizer — Commonw Fert
Commonwealth Forestry Bureau. Technical Communication — CFBTAJ
Commonwealth Forestry Bureau. Technical Communication — Commonw For Bur Tech Commun
Commonwealth Forestry Review — Com For Rev
Commonwealth Forestry Review — Commonw For Rev
Commonwealth Forestry Review — Commonw Forest Rev
Commonwealth Forestry Review — CWFRA
Commonwealth Forestry Review — CWFRAG
Commonwealth Geological Liaison Office. Liaison Report — Commonw Geol Liaison Off Liaison Rep
Commonwealth Geological Liaison Office. Special Liaison Report [*London*] — Commonw Geol Liaison Off Spec Liaison Rep
Commonwealth Institute of Biological Control. Miscellaneous Publication — CIBMBK
Commonwealth Institute of Biological Control. Miscellaneous Publication — Commonw Inst Biol Control Misc Publ
Commonwealth Institute of Helminthology (Saint Albans). Technical Communication — Commonw Inst Helminthol (Albans) Tech Commun
Commonwealth Jeweller and Watchmaker — Cwealth Jeweller
Commonwealth Jeweller and Watchmaker — Cwealth Jeweller and Watchmaker
Commonwealth Journal — Commonw J
Commonwealth Journal — Commonwealth J
Commonwealth Journal. Society for Growing Australian Plants — Commonw J Soc Growing Austral Pl
Commonwealth Law Bulletin — CLB
Commonwealth Law Bulletin — Comm LB
Commonwealth Law Bulletin — Commw LB
Commonwealth Law Reports — CLR
Commonwealth Law Reports — Comm LR
Commonwealth Law Reports — Commonw L Rep
Commonwealth Law Reports — Commw LR
Commonwealth Law Reports (Australia) — CLR (Aust)
Commonwealth Mining and Metallurgical Congress. Proceedings — Commonw Min Metall Congr Proc
Commonwealth Mycological Institute. Descriptions of Pathogenic Fungi and Bacteria — Commonw Mycol Inst Descr Pathog Fungi Bact
Commonwealth Mycological Institute. Mycological Papers — CMIMAE
Commonwealth Mycological Institute. Mycological Papers — Commonw Mycol Inst Mycol Pap
Commonwealth Mycological Institute. Phytopathological Papers — CMPYAH
Commonwealth Mycological Institute. Phytopathological Papers — Commonw Mycol Inst Phytopathol Pap
Commonwealth Novel in English — CNIE
Commonwealth of Puerto Rico Rules and Regulations — Pr R & Regs
Commonwealth Parliamentary Debates — CPD
Commonwealth Parliamentary Debates (House of Representatives) — CPD (HR)

Commonwealth Parliamentary Debates (House of Representatives) — CPD (R)
Commonwealth Parliamentary Debates (Senate) — CPD (S)
Commonwealth Parliamentary Papers — CPP
Commonwealth Phytopathological News — Comm Phytopathol News
Commonwealth Phytopathological News — Commonw Phytopath News
Commonwealth Phytopathological News — Commonwealth Phytopathol
Commonwealth Public Service Arbitration Reports — CPSAR
Commonwealth Public Service Arbitration Reports — CPSR
Commonwealth Public Service Board. Bulletin — Cwealth Pub Serv Board Bul
Commonwealth Quarterly — ComQ
Commonwealth Record — Comm Rec
Commonwealth Record — CR
Commonwealth Record — Cwlth Record
Commonwealth Regional Renewable Energy Resources Index — CRRERI
Commonwealth Road Transport Index — Commonwealth Road Trans Index
Commonwealth Scientific and Industrial Research Organisation. Division of Building Research. Technical Paper — CSIRO Div Build Res Tech Pap
Commonwealth Scientific and Industrial Research Organisation. Division of Chemical Technology. Research Review — CSIRO Div Chem Technol Res Rev
Commonwealth Scientific and Industrial Research Organisation. Division of Food Processing. Technical Paper — CSIRO Div Food Proc Tech Pap
Commonwealth Scientific and Industrial Research Organisation. Division of Plant Industry. Report — CSIRO Div Plant Ind Rep
Commonwealth Scientific and Industrial Research Organisation. Division of Soils. Technical Papers — CSIRO Div Soils Tech Pap
Commonwealth Scientific and Industrial Research Organisation. Division of Water Resources Research. Natural Resources Series — CSIRO Div Water Res Res Nat Res Ser
Commonwealth Scientific and Industrial Research Organisation. Marine Laboratories. Fishery Situation Report — CSIRO Mar Lab Fish Sit Rep
Commonwealth Scientific and Industrial Research Organization — Commonw Sci Ind Res Organ
Commonwealth Scientific and Industrial Research Organization. Division of Tropical Crops and Pastures Technical Paper — CSIRO Div Trop Crops Pastures Tech Pap
Commonwealth Taxation Board of Review Decisions — CTBR
Commonwealth Taxation Board of Review Decisions. New Series — CTBR NS
Commonwealth Taxation Board of Review Decisions. Old Series — CTBROS
Communaute Europeenne de l'Energie Atomique. EURATOM Rapport — Communaute Eur Energ At EURATOM Rapp
Communicable Disease Report — CDR
Communicable Disease Report — Communicable Disease Rep
Communicable Disease Report. CDR Review — Commun Dis Rep CDR Rev
Communicable Disease Report. CDR Supplement — Comun Dis Rep CDR Suppl
Communicable Disease Report. CDR Weekly — Commun Dis Rep CDR Wkly
Communicated Abstracts. International Congress. International Union of Crystallography — Commun Abstr Int Congr Int Union Crystallogr
Communicating Nursing Research — Commun Nurs Res
Communicating with Children — Commun Child
Communicatio Socialis — Comm Soc
Communication Abstracts — Commun Abstr
Communication Age — CAG
Communication Age — Commctn Age
Communication and Broadcasting — COBRD
Communication and Broadcasting — Comm Broadc
Communication and Broadcasting — Commun Broadc
Communication and Broadcasting [*England*] — Commun Broadcast
Communication and Cognition — Comm Cognition
Communication and Cognition Monographies — Comm Cognition Monograph
Communication and Control Engineering Series — Comm Control Engrg Ser
Communication and Cybernetics — Commun and Cybernet
Communication and Cybernetics — Commun Cybern
Communication and Electronics — Com & Electronics
Communication Arts — CA
Communication Arts Magazine — Commun Arts Mag
Communication. Balai Penjelidikan dan Pemakaian Karet — Commun Balai Penjelidikan Pemakaian Karet
Communication. Centre de Recherches Zootechniques. Universite de Louvain — Commun Cent Rech Zootech Univ Louv
Communication. Centre de Recherches Zootechniques. Universite de Louvain — CRZLAT
Communication. Department of Agricultural Research. Royal Tropical Institute [*Amsterdam*] — RTICBT
Communication. Department of Agricultural Research. Royal Tropical Institute (Amsterdam) — Commun Dep Agric Res R Trop Inst (Amst)
Communication. Department of Anatomy. University of Lund (Sweden) — Commun Dep Anat Univ Lund (Swed)
Communication Education — CEd
Communication Education — Comm Educ
Communication Education — ICED
Communication Engineering — Commun Eng
Communication et Langages — Communic et Lang
Communication. Forest Research Institute — Commun Forest Res Inst
Communication. Institut de Thermique Appliquee. Ecole Polytechnique Federale de Lausanne [*Switzerland*] — Commun Inst Therm Appl Ec Polytech Fed Lausanne
Communication. Institute of Forestry Research. Agricultural University (Wageningen) [*Netherlands*] — Commun Inst For Res Agric Univ (Wageningen)
Communication. Kodak Research Laboratories — Comm
Communication Monographs — Com M
Communication Monographs [*Falls Church, Virginia*] — Comm Mon
Communication Monographs — Comm Monogr
Communication Monographs — GCMM
Communication. NV [*Naamloze Vennootschap*] **Koninklijke Nederlandsche Springstoffenfabrieken** — Commun K Ned Springstoffenfabr
Communication. NV [*Naamloze Vennootschap*] **Koninklijke Nederlandsche Springstoffenfabrieken** — Commun NV K Ned Springstoffenfabr
Communication on Applied Mathematics and Computation — Comm Appl Math Comput
Communication Quarterly — Comm Q
Communication Quarterly — Commun Quart
Communication Quarterly — PCMQ
Communication Research — Comm Res
Communication Research — PCMR
Communication Research Trends — Comm Res Trends
Communication. Royal Dutch Explosive Manufactories — Commun R Dutch Explos Manuf
Communication. Rubber Research Institute of Malaysia — Commun Rubber Res Inst Malays
Communication Studies — ICOS
Communication Studies Bulletin [*United Kingdom*] — Communication Studies Bull
Communication Systems — Commun Sys
Communication Technology Impact — CTI
Communication. Wool Research Organisation of New Zealand — Commun Wool Res Organ NZ
Communication World — CMW
Communicationes. Bibliotheca Historiae Medicae Hungarica — Comm Bibl Hist Med Hungar
Communicationes de Historià Artis Medicinae — Comm Hist Art Med
Communicationes. Instituti Forestalis Cechosloveniae — Commun Inst For Cech
Communicationes. Instituti Forestalis Cechosloveniae — Commun Inst For Csl
Communicationes Instituti Forestalis Cechosloveniae — Commun Inst Forest Cechosloveniae
Communicationes. Instituti Forestalis Fenniae — Commun Inst For Fenn
Communicationes Rei Cretariae Romanae Fautores — Communic Rei Cret Rom Faut
Communicationes Sectionis Botanicae Societatis Biologicae Hungariae. B Sectio — Commun Sect Bot Soc Biol Hung B Sect
Communicationes Veterinariae — Commun Vet
Communicationes Veterinariae — CVETAA
Communications. ACM [*Association for Computing Machinery*] — CACM
Communications. ACM [*Association for Computing Machinery*] — Comm ACM
Communications. ACM [*Association for Computing Machinery*] — Commun ACM
Communications. ACM [*Association for Computing Machinery*] — GACM
Communications Africa — Communic Afr
Communications. All-Russian Institute of Metals — Commun All Russ Inst Met
Communications. American Ceramic Society — Commun Am Ceram Soc
Communications and Distributed Resources Report [*Database*] — CDR
Communications and Distributed Resources Report — Comm and Dist Res
Communications and Electronics [*England*] — Commun Electron
Communications and Electronics (London) — Communs Electron (Lond)
Communications and the Law — Com and L
Communications and the Law — Com & Law
Communications and the Law — Com Law
Communications and the Law — Commun & Law
Communications. Archives Centrales de l'Orgue/Mededelingen. Centraal Orgelarchief — Comm Archives Centrales Orgue
Communications Artistiques et Historiques. Congres International du Verre — Commun Artistiques Hist Congr Int Verre
Communications. Association Internationale de Limnologie Theoretique et Appliquee — Commun Assoc Int Limnol Theor Appl
Communications Australia — Commun Aust
Communications. Chinese Biochemical Society — Commun Chin Biochem Soc
Communications. Coal Research Institute (Prague) — Commun Coal Res Inst (Prague)
Communications. Conference International sur la Planification et la Gestion des Eaux — Commun Conf Int Planif Gestion Eaux
Communications. Czech-Polish Colloquium on Chemical Thermodynamics and Physical Organic Chemistry — Commun Czech Pol Colloq Chem Thermodyn Phys Org Chem
Communications. Department of Chemistry. Bulgarian Academy of Sciences — Commun Dep Chem Bulg Acad Sci
Communications. Dublin Institute for Advanced Studies. Series A — Comm Dublin Inst Adv Studies Ser A
Communications. Dublin Institute for Advanced Studies. Series A — Commun Dublin Inst Adv Stud A
Communications. Dublin Institute for Advanced Studies. Series A — Commun Dublin Inst Adv Stud Ser A
Communications. Dublin Institute for Advanced Studies. Series D. Geophysical Bulletin — Commun Dublin Inst Adv Stud Ser D
Communications. Dublin Institute of Advanced Studies. Geophysical Bulletin — Comm Dublin Inst Adv Stud Geophys Bull
Communications. Ecole de Medecine Veterinaire. Universite de l'Etat a Gand — Commun Ec Med Vet Univ Etat Gand
Communications en Langues Etrangeres. Institut de Recherches des Ressources Hydrauliques (Budapest) — Commun Lang Etrang Inst Rech Ressour Hydraul (Budapest)
Communications Engineering International — Commun Eng Int
Communications Equipment and Systems Design — Commun Equip & Syst Des
Communications Equipment Manufacturers — Commun Equip Manu
Communications. Faculte de Medecine Veterinaire. Universite de l'Etat Gand — Commun Fac Med Vet Univ Etat Gand
Communications. Faculte de Medecine Veterinaire. Universite de l'Etat Gand [*A publication*] — MFDGAW
Communications. Faculte des Sciences. Universite d'Ankara — CMFAAV
Communications. Faculte des Sciences. Universite d'Ankara — Commun Fac Sci Univ Ankara

Communications. Faculte des Sciences. Universite d'Ankara. Serie A. Mathematiques-Physique-Astronomie — Comm Fac Sci Univ Ankara Ser A
Communications. Faculte des Sciences. Universite d'Ankara. Serie A. Mathematiques-Physique-Astronomie — Commun Fac Sci Univ Ankara Ser A
Communications. Faculte des Sciences. Universite d'Ankara. Serie A2. Physique — Commun Fac Sci Univ Ankara Ser A2
Communications. Faculte des Sciences. Universite d'Ankara. Serie B. Chimie — Commun Fac Sci Univ Ankara Ser B
Communications. Faculte des Sciences. Universite d'Ankara. Serie C — Communs Fac Sci Univ Ankara
Communications. Faculte des Sciences. Universite d'Ankara. Serie C. Biologie — CFABEW
Communications. Faculte des Sciences. Universite d'Ankara. Serie C. Biologie [*A publication*] — Commun Fac Sci Univ Ankara Ser C Biol
Communications. Faculte des Sciences. Universite d'Ankara. Serie C. Sciences Naturelles — CAKCAC
Communications. Faculte des Sciences. Universite d'Ankara. Serie C. Sciences Naturelles — Commun Fac Sci Univ Ankara Ser C
Communications. Faculte des Sciences. Universite d'Ankara. Serie C. Sciences Naturelles — Commun Fac Sci Univ Ankara Ser C Sci Nat
Communications. Faculte des Sciences. Universite d'Ankara. Serie C1. Geologie — CFSGDY
Communications. Faculte des Sciences. Universite d'Ankara. Serie C2. Botanique — CFSBDJ
Communications. Faculte des Sciences. Universite d'Ankara. Serie C3. Zoologie — CFSZDN
Communications. Faculte des Sciences. Universite d'Ankara. Serie C-I. Geologie — Commun Fac Sci Univ Ankara Ser C I Geol
Communications. Faculte des Sciences. Universite d'Ankara. Serie C-II. Botanique — Commun Fac Sci Univ Ankara Ser C II Bot
Communications. Faculte des Sciences. Universite d'Ankara. Serie C-III. Zoologie — Commun Fac Sci Univ Ankara Ser C III Zool
Communications. Faculte des Sciences. Universite d'Ankara. Series B. Chemistry and Chemical Engineering — Commun Fac Sci Univ Ankara Ser B Chem Chem Eng
Communications. Faculty of Veterinary Medicine. State University (Ghent) — Commun Fac Vet Med State Univ (Ghent)
Communications. Fondation du Caoutchouc (Delft) — Commun Fond Caoutch (Delft)
Communications in Africa — Communications in Afr
Communications in Algebra — Comm Algeb
Communications in Algebra — Comm Algebra
Communications in Algebra — Commun Algebra
Communications in Analysis and Geometry — Comm Anal Geom
Communications in Applied Cell Biology — Commun Appl Cell Biol
Communications in Applied Numerical Methods — Comm Appl Numer Methods
Communications in Behavioral Biology. Part A. Original Articles — CBBAA2
Communications in Behavioral Biology. Part A. Original Articles — Commun Behav Biol Part A Orig Artic
Communications in Japan — Comm Jap
Communications in Mathematical Physics — CMPHA
Communications in Mathematical Physics — Comm Math P
Communications in Mathematical Physics — Comm Math Phys
Communications in Mathematical Physics — Commun Math Phys
Communications in Numerical Methods in Engineering — Comm Numer Methods Engrg
Communications in Partial Differential Equations — Comm Part D
Communications in Partial Differential Equations — Comm Partial Differential Equations
Communications in Partial Differential Equations — Commun Part Differ Equ
Communications in Physics (Hanoi) — Commun Phys Hanoi
Communications in Psychopharmacology — Commun Psychopharmacol
Communications in Psychopharmacology — CPSZDP
Communications in Soil Science and Plant Analysis — Comm Soil S
Communications in Soil Science and Plant Analysis — Commun Soil Sci Plant Anal
Communications in Soil Science and Plant Analysis — CSOSA
Communications in Soil Science and Plant Analysis — CSOSA2
Communications in Statistics — Comm Statis
Communications in Statistics — Commun Stat
Communications in Statistics. Econometric Reviews — Comm Statist Econometric Rev
Communications in Statistics. Part A. Theory and Methods — Comm St A
Communications in Statistics. Part A. Theory and Methods — Comm Statist A Theory Methods
Communications in Statistics. Part A. Theory and Methods — Comm Statist Theory Methods
Communications in Statistics. Part A. Theory and Methods — Commun Stat A
Communications in Statistics. Part A. Theory and Methods — Commun Stat Part A Theory Methods
Communications in Statistics. Part A. Theory and Methods — Commun Stat Theory and Methods
Communications in Statistics. Part B. Simulation and Computation — Comm St B
Communications in Statistics. Part B. Simulation and Computation — Comm Statist B Simulation Comput
Communications in Statistics. Part B. Simulation and Computation — Comm Statist Simulation Comput
Communications in Statistics. Part B. Simulation and Computation — Commun Stat B
Communications in Statistics. Part B. Simulation and Computation — Commun Stat Part B
Communications in Statistics. Part B. Simulation and Computation — Commun Stat Simulation and Comput
Communications in Statistics. Part B. Simulation and Computation — CSSCD
Communications in Statistics. Part C. Sequential Analysis — Comm Statist Sequential Anal
Communications in Statistics. Stochastic Models — Comm Statist Stochastic Models
Communications in Statistics. Theory and Method — Commun Statist Theory Method
Communications in the Analytic Theory of Continued Fractions — Comm Anal Theory Contin Fractions
Communications in Theoretical Physics — Comm Th Phy
Communications in Theoretical Physics — Comm Theoret Phys
Communications in Theoretical Physics — Commun Theor Phys
Communications in Theoretical Physics (Allahabad) — Comm Theoret Phys Allahabad
Communications. Indonesian Rubber Research Institute — Commun Indones Rubber Res Inst
Communications Industry Report — Comm Ind Rep
Communications. Institut des Recherches sur le Charbon (Prague) — Commun Inst Rech Charbon (Prague)
Communications. Institute of Marine Biology. Far Eastern Scientific Center. Academy of Sciences. USSR — Commun Inst Mar Biol Far East Sci Cent Acad Sci USSR
Communications. Instituti Forestalis Cechosloveniae — CIFCA9
Communications. Instituti Forestalis Fenniae — MJULAO
Communications. Institution of Gas Engineers — Commun Inst Gas Eng
Communications International — CINTD
Communications International — Comm Intnl
Communications International — Commun Int
Communications. International Association of Theoretical and Applied Limnology — Commun Int Assoc Theor Appl Limnol
Communications. International Association of Theoretical and Applied Limnology — IVTMAS
Communications. Jajasan Penjelidikan dan Pemakain Karet — Commun Jajasan Penjelidikan Pemakain Karet
Communications. Joint Institute for Nuclear Research (Dubna) — Commun J Inst Nucl Res (Dubna)
Communications. Kamerlingh Onnes Laboratory. University of Leiden — Commun Kamerlingh Onnes Lab Univ Leiden
Communications. Kamerlingh Onnes Laboratory. University of Leiden. Supplement — Commun Kamerlingh Onnes Lab Univ Leiden Suppl
Communications Law Bulletin — CLB
Communications Law Bulletin [*Australia*] — Commu LB
Communications. Lunar and Planetary Laboratory — Commun Lunar & Planet Lab
Communications. Mathematical Institute. Rijksuniversiteit Utrecht — Commun Math Inst Rijksuniv Utrecht
Communications. Musee National de l'Ermitage — ComErm
Communications. Netherlands Indies Rubber Research Institute — Commun Neth Indies Rubber Res Inst
Communications News — Comm News
Communications News — Comms N
Communications News — Commun News
Communications Officielles. Association Internationale de la Science du Sol — Commun Off Assoc Int Sci Sol
Communications on Applied Nonlinear Analysis — Comm Appl Nonlinear Anal
Communications on Physics — Commun Phys
Communications on Pure and Applied Mathematics — Com P A Math
Communications on Pure and Applied Mathematics — Comm Pure Appl Math
Communications on Pure and Applied Mathematics — Commun Pure Appl Math
Communications on Pure and Applied Mathematics — CPAMA
Communications on the Science and Practice of Brewing. Wallerstein Laboratory — Commun Sci Pract Brew Wallerstein Lab
Communications. Physical Laboratory. University of Leiden — Commun Phys Lab Univ Leiden
Communications. Plastics Department. Rubber Foundation. Delft — Commun Plast Dep Rubber Found Delft
Communications. Research Institute of the Sumatra Planters' Association. Rubber Series — CMSRAB
Communications. Research Institute of the Sumatra Planters' Association. Rubber Series — Commun Res Inst SPA Rubber Ser
Communications. Research Institute of the Sumatra Planters' Association. Rubber Series — Commun Res Inst Sumatra Plant Assoc Rubber Ser
Communications. Royal Society of Edinburgh — Commun R Soc Edinburgh
Communications. Royal Society of Edinburgh. Physical Sciences — Comm Roy Soc Edinburgh Phys Sci
Communications. Royal Society of Edinburgh. Physical Sciences — Commun R Soc Edinburgh Phys Sci
Communications. Rubber Foundation. Amsterdam — Commun Rubber Found Amsterdam
Communications. Rubber Foundation (Delft) — Commun Rubber Found (Delft)
Communications Satellite Corporation Technical Review — Commun Stell Corp Tech Rev
Communications. Section de Matieres Plastiques. Fondation du Caoutchouc (Delft) — Commun Sect Matieres Plast Fond Caoutch (Delft)
Communications. Societe Ceramique Tchecoslovaque — Commun Soc Ceram Tchec
Communications. Sugar Milling Research Institute — Commun Sugar Milling Res Inst
Communications. Swedish Sugar Corporation — Commun Swed Sugar Corp
Communications Systems and Management — Commun Syst and Manage
Communications Technology Impact — Communication Tech Impact
Communications. Veterinary College. State University of Ghent — Commun Vet Coll State Univ Ghent
Communications. World Fertilizer Congress — Commun World Fert Congr
Communicator of Scientific and Technical Information [*Later, Communicator*] — Commun Sci & Tech Inf

Communicator of Technical Information [*Later, Communicator*] — Commun Tech Inf
Communicator's Journal — CCJ
Communicator's Journal — CMJ
Communio. International Catholic Review — Commun
Communio Viatorum — Com Via
Communio Viatorum [*Prague*] — CV
Communio Viatorum. A Theological Quarterly [*Prague*] — CommViat
Communion — Commun
Communique Newsletter [*Milwaukee, Wisconsin*] — Commun Newsl
Communist China Digest — Communist China Dig
Communist Chinese Scientific Abstracts — Communist Chin Sci Abstr
Communist Review — Communist R
Communist Review — Communist Rev
Communita Internazionale — Com Internaz
Communities — Communit
Community Action — Commun Action
Community Analysis Studies — Community Anal Stud
Community and Junior College Journal — CMJPB
Community and Junior College Journal — Com & Jr Coll
Community and Junior College Journal — Com & Jr Coll J
Community and Junior College Journal — Community Jr Coll J
Community and Junior College Libraries — Community and Junior Coll Libr
Community and Local Government Information Review — CALGIR
Community Care — Commun Care
Community College Frontiers — Com Coll Front
Community College Review — Com Coll R
Community Colleges of Canada — Com Col Can
Community Contact — COCN
Community Dental Health [*London*] — Community Dent Health
Community Dentistry and Oral Epidemiology — CDOEAP
Community Dentistry and Oral Epidemiology — Comm Den Or
Community Dentistry and Oral Epidemiology — Community Dent Oral Epidemiol
Community Development Abstracts — Community Dev Abstr
Community Development and Panchayati Raj Digest — Com Dev Pancha Raj D
Community Development Bulletin — CDB
Community Development Bulletins — Community Dev B
Community Development Journal — Com Dev J
Community Development Journal — Com Develop J
Community Development Journal — Comm Dev J
Community Development Journal — Commun Dev J
Community Development Journal — Community Dev J
Community Development Journal — Community Devel J
Community Development Journal — Community Develop J
Community Development Journal — Community Development J
Community Economics. University of Wisconsin. Department of Agricultural Economics. Cooperative Extension Service — Community Econ Univ Wis Dep Agric Econ Coop Ext Serv
Community Education Newsletter — Community Educ Newsl
Community Health — CH
Community Health [*Bristol*] — COHEBY
Community Health — Comm Health
Community Health — Community Hlth
Community Health (Bristol) — COHEB
Community Health Education Monographs — CHEM
Community Health in South Africa — Communit Health S Afr
Community Health Services Bulletin — Com Hlth Serv Bul
Community Health Studies — Comm Heal S
Community Health Studies [*Australia*] — Community Health Stud
Community Medicine — Community Med
Community Mental Health Journal — CMHJAY
Community Mental Health Journal — Com Men Health J
Community Mental Health Journal — Com Ment Health J
Community Mental Health Journal — Comm Ment H
Community Mental Health Journal — Community Ment Health J
Community Mental Health Journal — Community Ment Hlth J
Community Mental Health Journal — PCMH
Community Mental Health Review [*Later, Prevention in Human Services*] — Community Ment Health Rev
Community Newspapers — Comnty
Community Nursing [*US*] — Community Nurs
Community Nutritionist — Community Nutr
Community Planning Review — Com Plan R
Community Property Journal — Comm Prop J
Community Property Journal — Community Prop J
Community Research Center. Fairbanks North Star Borough. Special Report — CRCFBSR
Community Service Newsletter — Cmmty Serv
Community Transport Quarterly — Commun Transport Q
Commutation and Transmission — Commutat and Transm
Commutation et Electronique — CELCA
Commutation et Electronique — Commutat & Electron
Commutation et Electronique — Commutation Electron
Commuter World — Commuter W
Compagnie Francaise des Petroles. Notes et Memoires — Cie Fr Pet Notes Mem
Compagnie Francaise des Petroles. Notes et Memoires — Compagn Franc Petrol Notes Mem
Compalloy. Proceedings. International Congress on Compatibilizers and Reactive Polymer Alloying — Compalloy. Proc Int Congr Compat React Polym Alloying
Companies and Securities Bulletin — CSB
Companion Animal Practice — Companion Anim Pract
Companion to Microbiology — Companion Microbiol
Companion to the Botanical Magazine — Companion Bot Mag
Company and Securities Law Journal [*Australia*] — C & SLJ
Company and Securities Law Journal — CLSJ
Company and Securities Law Journal [*Australia*] — Co & Sec Law Journal
Company Credit Reports [*Database*] — CCR
Company Director and Professional Administrator [*New Zealand*] — Co Dir
Company Director and Professional Administrator [*New Zealand*] — Co Dir Prof Adm
Company Facts and Addresses [*Database*] — COAD
Company Law Cases — CLC
Company Law Cases (Commerce Clearing House) [*Australia*] — (CCH) CLC
Company Lawyer — Comp Lawy
Company Lawyer — Company Law
Company of Master Mariners of Australia. Journal — Comp Master Marin Aust J
Company of Master Mariners of Australia. Journal — J Company Master Mar Aust
Comparative and General Pharmacology — Comp Gen Pharmacol
Comparative and General Pharmacology — CPGPAY
Comparative and International Law Journal of Southern Africa — Comp & Int LJ South Africa
Comparative and International Law Journal of Southern Africa — Comp & Int'l LJS Afr
Comparative and International Law Journal of Southern Africa — Comp Int Law J South Afr
Comparative and International Law Journal of Southern Africa — Comp Int Law J Sth Afr
Comparative Animal Nutrition — CANUDG
Comparative Animal Nutrition — Comp Anim Nutr
Comparative Biochemistry and Physiology — CBCPA
Comparative Biochemistry and Physiology — CBCPAI
Comparative Biochemistry and Physiology — Comp Biochem Physiol
Comparative Biochemistry and Physiology. A. Comparative Physiology — CBPAB5
Comparative Biochemistry and Physiology. A. Comparative Physiology — Comp Bioc A
Comparative Biochemistry and Physiology. A. Comparative Physiology — Comp Biochem Physiol A Comp Physiol
Comparative Biochemistry and Physiology. B. Comparative Biochemistry — CBPBB
Comparative Biochemistry and Physiology. B. Comparative Biochemistry — CBPBB8
Comparative Biochemistry and Physiology. B. Comparative Biochemistry — Comp Bioc B
Comparative Biochemistry and Physiology. B. Comparative Biochemistry — Comp Biochem Physiol B
Comparative Biochemistry and Physiology. B. Comparative Biochemistry — Comp Biochem Physiol B Comp Biochem
Comparative Biochemistry and Physiology. Biochemistry and Molecular Biology — Comp Biochem Physiol Biochem Mol Biol
Comparative Biochemistry and Physiology. C. Comparative Pharmacology [*Later, Comparative Biochemistry and Physiology. C. Comparative Pharmacology and Toxicology*] — CBPCBB
Comparative Biochemistry and Physiology. C. Comparative Pharmacology [*Later, Comparative Biochemistry and Physiology. C. Comparative Pharmacology and Toxicology*] — Comp Bioc C
Comparative Biochemistry and Physiology. C. Comparative Pharmacology [*Later, Comparative Biochemistry and Physiology. C. Comparative Pharmacology and Toxicology*] — Comp Biochem Physiol C
Comparative Biochemistry and Physiology. C. Comparative Pharmacology [*Later, Comparative Biochemistry and Physiology. C. Comparative Pharmacology and Toxicology*] — Comp Biochem Physiol C Comp Pharmacol
Comparative Biochemistry and Physiology. C. Comparative Pharmacology and Toxicology — CBPCEE
Comparative Biochemistry and Physiology. C. Comparative Pharmacology and Toxicology — Comp Biochem Physiol C Comp Pharmacol Toxicol
Comparative Biochemistry and Physiology of Transport. Proceedings of the Meeting. International Conference on Biological Membranes — Comp Biochem Physiol Transp Proc Meet Int Conf
Comparative Biochemistry and Physiology. Part A. Physiology — Comp Biochem Physiol A Physiol
Comparative Biochemistry and Physiology. Part B. Biochemistry and Molecular Biology — Comp Biochem Physiol B Biochem Mol Biol
Comparative Biochemistry and Physiology. Part C. Pharmacology, Toxicology, and Endocrinology — Comp Biochem Physiol C Pharmacol Toxicol Endocrinol
Comparative Biochemistry and Physiology. Pharmacology, Toxicology, and Endocrinology — Comp Biochem Physiol Pharmacol Toxicol Endocrinol
Comparative Biochemistry and Physiology. Physiology — Comp Biochem Physiol Physiol
Comparative Biochemistry. Molecular Evolution. Comprehensive Biochemistry — Comp Biochem Mol Evol Compr Biochem
Comparative Civilizations Review — C C Rev
Comparative Civilizations Review — Comp Civ R
Comparative Criticism — C Crit
Comparative Data Report — Comp Data Rep
Comparative Drama — CD
Comparative Drama — CDr
Comparative Drama — CoD
Comparative Drama — Comp Drama
Comparative Drama — CompD
Comparative Drama — CompDr
Comparative Drama — PCDR
Comparative Drama Conference. Papers — CDCP
Comparative Education — Comp Ed
Comparative Education — Comp Educ
Comparative Education — Compar Educ
Comparative Education — Comparative Ed

Comparative Education Review — CER
Comparative Education Review — Comp Ed R
Comparative Education Review — Comp Edu Re
Comparative Education Review — Comp Educ R
Comparative Education Review — Compar Educ Rev
Comparative Education Review — Comparative Educ R
Comparative Endocrinology. Proceedings. Columbia University Symposium on Comparative Endocrinology — Comp Endocrinol Proc Columbia Univ Symp
Comparative Endocrinology. Proceedings. International Symposium on Comparative Endocrinology — Comp Endocrinol Proc Int Symp
Comparative Haematology International — Comp Haematol Int
Comparative Immunology, Microbiology, and Infectious Diseases — CIMIDV
Comparative Immunology, Microbiology, and Infectious Diseases — Comp Immunol Microbiol Infect Dis
Comparative Juridical Review — Comp Jur Rev
Comparative Juridical Review — Comp Jurid Rev
Comparative Labor Law — Comp Lab Law
Comparative Law Review — Comp L Rev
Comparative Law Review. Japan Institute of Comparative Law — Comp L Rev Japan Inst
Comparative Law Series. United States Bureau of Foreign and Domestic Commerce. General Legal Bulletin — Comp L Ser
Comparative Literature — CL
Comparative Literature — CoLi
Comparative Literature — Comp L
Comparative Literature — Comp Lit
Comparative Literature — GCLT
Comparative Literature News-Letter — CLNL
Comparative Literature Studies — CLS
Comparative Literature Studies — Comp Lit St
Comparative Literature Studies — Comp Lit Stud
Comparative Literature Studies — PCOS
Comparative Medicine East and West — CMEW
Comparative Medicine East and West — CMEWDR
Comparative Medicine East and West — Comp Med East West
Comparative Pathobiology — Comp Pathobiol
Comparative Pathology Bulletin — Comp Pathol Bull
Comparative Pathology Bulletin — CPBLAV
Comparative Physiology — Comp Physiol
Comparative Physiology and Ecology — Comp Physiol Ecol
Comparative Physiology and Ecology — CPECD
Comparative Physiology and Ecology — CPECDM
Comparative Political Studies — Comp Pol Stud
Comparative Political Studies — Comp Poli S
Comparative Political Studies — Comp Polit Stud
Comparative Political Studies — Compar Pol Stud
Comparative Political Studies — Comparative Pol Studies
Comparative Political Studies — CPS
Comparative Political Studies — PCPU
Comparative Politics — ComP
Comparative Politics — Comp Pol
Comparative Politics — Comp Polit
Comparative Politics — Comp Politics
Comparative Politics — CPo
Comparative Politics — CPS
Comparative Politics — PCPO
Comparative Politics. City University of New York, Political Science Program [*A publication*] — CUNY/CP
Comparative Romance Linguistics Newsletter — CRLN
Comparative Strategy — Comp Strat
Comparative Studies in Society and History — Comp Stud S
Comparative Studies in Society and History — Comp Stud Soc & Hist
Comparative Studies in Society and History — Comp Stud Soc Hist
Comparative Studies in Society and History — Comp Studs Soc Hist
Comparative Studies in Society and History — ComS
Comparative Studies in Society and History — CSSH
Comparative Studies in Society and History — PCSS
Comparative Studies in Sociology — Comp Stud Social
Comparative Urban Research — Comp Urb Res
Compass — Comp
Compass. Sigma Gamma Epsilon — CSGEA
Compendium. Dagelijks Overzicht van de Buitenlandse Pers — CMK
Compendium de Investigaciones Clinicas Latinoamericanas — CLATDP
Compendium de Investigaciones Clinicas Latinoamericanas — Compend Invest Clin Latinoam
Compendium. Deutsche Gesellschaft fuer Mineraloelwissenschaft und Kohlechemie [*Germany*] — Compend Dtsch Ges Mineraloelwiss Kohlechem
Compendium of Continuing Education in Dentistry — Compend Contin Educ Dent
Compendium of Papers Presented. National Convention. Canadian Manufacturers of Chemical Specialties Association — Compend Pap Natl Conv Can Manuf Chem Spec Assoc
Compendium of Technical Papers. Annual Meeting. Institute of Transportation Engineers — Compend Tech Pap Annu Meet Inst Transp Eng
Compendium on Continuing Education for the Practicing Veterinarian — Compend Contin Educ Pract Vet
Compensation and Benefits Review — Compens Benefits Rev
Compensation Medicine — Compens Med
Compensation Planning Journal — CMJ
Compensation Planning Journal — Comp Plan Jnl
Compensation Review — Comp R
Compensation Review — Comp Rev
Compensation Review — Compens R
Compensation Review — Compens Rev
Compensation Review — CRE
Compilacion de los Estudios Geologicos Oficiales en Colombia. Instituto Geologico Nacional (Colombia) — Compil Estud Geol Of Colomb Inst Geol Nac (Colomb)
Compilation of Research Work Accomplished in the Welding Research Institute (Bratislava) — Compil Res Work Accomplished Weld Res Inst (Bratislava)
Compilation of Research Work Accomplished. Welding Research Institute. Bratislava — Compil Res Work Weld Res Inst Bratislava
Complement — CMPLDF
Complement and Inflammation. Laboratory and Clinical Research — Complement Inflammation
Complete Abstracts of Japanese Chemical Literature — Complete Abstr Jpn Chem Lit
Complete Chemical Abstracts of Japan — Complete Chem Abstr Jpn
Complete Specification (Australia) — Complete Specif (Aust)
Complete Specification (India) — Complete Specif (India)
Complete Texts of Lectures of Congress of Apimondia in Prague. Translations — Complete Texts Lect Congr Apimondia Prague Transl
Complex Chemical Reaction Systems. Mathematical Modelling and Simulation. Proceedings. Workshop — Complex Chem React Syst Proc Workshop
Complex Chemistry — Complex Chem
Complex Investigations of Water Reservoirs — Complex Invest Water Reservoirs
Complex Variables. Theory and Application — Complex Variables Theory Appl
Complexation Chromatography — Complexation Chromatogr
Complexity International [*Electronic Publication*] — Complexity Int
Component Technology — Component Technol
Component Technology — CPTHA
Components Report — Components Rep
Composer — Co
Composer — COM
Composers News-Record — Comp News-Rec
Composite Interfaces. Proceedings. International Conference on Composite Interfaces — Compos Interfaces Proc Int Conf
Composite Manufacturing Technology — Compos Manuf Technol
Composite Materials — Compos Mater
Composite Materials for Offshore Operations. Proceedings of the International Workshop — Compos Mater Offshore Oper Proc Int Workshop
Composite Materials. Lectures Delivered at the Institution of Metallurgists Refresher Course — Compos Mater Lect Inst Metall Refresher Course
Composite Materials Series — Compos Mater Ser
Composite Polymers — Compos Polym
Composite Structures. Proceedings. International Conference on Composite Structures — Compos Struct Proc Int Conf
Composite Structures. Proceedings. International Conference on Composite Structures — Compos Struct Proc Int Conf Compos Struct
Composite Wood — Compos Wood
Composite Wood — CW
Composites — CPSOA
Composites Engineering — Compos Eng
Composites (Guildford, United Kingdom) — Composites (Guildford UK)
Composites Manufacturing — Compos Manuf
Composites Science and Technology — Comp Sci T
Composites Science and Technology — Compos Sci Technol
Composites Technology Review — Comp Tech Rev
Composites Technology Review — Compos Technol Rev
Composites Technology Review — Composites Technol Rev
Compositio Mathematica — CMPMA
Compositio Mathematica — Comp Math
Compositio Mathematica — Compositio Math
Compost Science [*Later, Bio Cycle*] — COMPA
Compost Science [*Later, Bio Cycle*] — COMPAN
Compost Science [*Later, Bio Cycle*] — Compost Sci
Compost Science/Land Utilization [*Later, Bio Cycle*] — Compost Sci Land Util
Comprehensive Analysis of the Environment. Proceedings. Soviet-American Symposium — Compr Anal Environ Proc Sov Am Symp
Comprehensive Analytical Chemistry — Compr Anal Chem
Comprehensive Core Medical Library [*Database*] — CCML
Comprehensive Education — Comprehensive Ed
Comprehensive Endocrinology — Compr Endocrinol
Comprehensive Immunology — COIMDV
Comprehensive Immunology — Compr Immunol
Comprehensive Nursing Monthly (Tokyo) — Comprehensive Nurs Mon (Tokyo)
Comprehensive Nursing Quarterly — Compr Nurs Q
Comprehensive Pediatric Nursing — Compr Pediatr Nurs
Comprehensive Psychiatry — Comp Psychi
Comprehensive Psychiatry — Compr Psychiatry
Comprehensive Psychiatry — Comprehensive Psychiat
Comprehensive Psychiatry — COPYA
Comprehensive Psychiatry — COPYAV
Comprehensive Therapy — Compr Ther
Comprehensive Therapy — COTHD3
Comprehensive Virology — Compr Virol
Comprendre — Co
Compressed Air — Comp Air
Compressed Air — Compres Air
Compressed Air — Compress Air
Compressed Air Magazine — Comp Air Mag
Compressed Air Magazine — Compressed Air Mag
Compressed Gas Association. Annual Report — Compressed Gas Assoc Annu Rep
Compressed Gas Association. Technical Supplement to the Annual Report — Compressed Gas Assoc Tech Suppl Annu Rep
Compte Rendu. Assemblee. Commission Internationale Technique de Sucrerie — CR Assem Comm Int Tech Sucr

Compte Rendu. Association Lyonnaise de Recherches Archeologiques — CRAL
Compte Rendu. Colloque National sur l'Information en Chimie CNIC [*Centre National de l'Information Chimique*] — CR Colloq Natl Inf Chim CNIC
Compte Rendu. Colloque sur l'Information en Chimie — CR Colloq Inf Chim
Compte Rendu. Commission Imperiale Archeologique (St. Petersbourg) — CR (Petersb)
Compte Rendu. Conference du COLUMA (Comite Francais de Lutte contre les Mauvaises Herbes) — CR Conf COLUMA
Compte Rendu. Conference Internationale de Spectroscopie Raman — CR Conf Int Spectrosc Raman
Compte Rendu. Conference Internationale de Spectroscopie Raman. Processus Lineaires et Non Lineaires — CR Conf Int Spectrosc Raman
Compte Rendu. Conference Internationale sur le Pergelisol — CR Conf Int Pergelisol
Compte Rendu. Conference Mondiale de l'Energie — CR Conf Mond Energ
Compte Rendu. Congres. Confederation Internationale de la Mesure — CR Congr Confed Int Mes
Compte Rendu. Congres de l'Industrie du Gaz [*France*] — CR Congr Ind Gaz
Compte Rendu. Congres International de Biochimie — CR Congr Int Biochim
Compte Rendu. Congres International de Chemie Industrielle — Congr Industr Chem
Compte Rendu. Congres International de Microbiologie — CR Congr Int Microbiol
Compte Rendu. Congres National de Transfusion Sanguine — CR Congr Natl Transfus Sang
Compte Rendu. Cycle International de Conferences PRO AQUA — CR Cycle Int Conf PRO AQUA
Compte Rendu de la Rencontre de Moriond — CR Rencontre Moriond
Compte Rendu Definitif. Assemblee. Institut International de Recherches Betteravieres — CR Definitif Assem Inst Int Rech Better
Compte Rendu des Seances de la Chambre des Deputes du Grand-Duche de Luxembourg — CR
Compte Rendu des Seances. Societe de Biogeographie — CR Seances Soc Biogeogr
Compte Rendu des Seances. Societe de Physique et d'Histoire Naturelle de Geneve — CR Seances Soc Phys Hist Nat Geneve
Compte Rendu des Seances. Societe Serbe de Geologie — CR Seances Soc Serbe Geol
Compte Rendu des Travaux. Congres International du Verre — CR Trav Congr Int Verre
Compte Rendu des Travaux de la Societe Nationale Havraise d'Etudes Diverses — Compt Rend Trav Soc Natl Havraise Etudes Diverses
Compte Rendu des Travaux. Societe d'Agriculture, Histoire Naturelle, et Arts Utiles de Lyon — Compt Rend Trav Soc Agric Lyon
Compte Rendu Hebdomadaire des Seances. Academie des Sciences de Jekaterinoslaw — CR Hebd Seanc Acad Sci Jekaterinoslaw
Compte Rendu. Industrie du Gaz. Congress International — CR Ind Gaz Congr Int
Compte Rendu. Journees d'Etudes sur les Herbicides. Conference du COLUMA [*Comite Francais de Lutte contre les Mauvaises Herbes*] — CR Journ Etud Herb Conf COLUMA
Compte Rendu. Proces-Verbaux et Memoires. Association Bretonne — CR PV Mem Ass Breton
Compte Rendu. Rencontre Assyriologique Internationale — CRR
Compte Rendu. Rencontre Assyriologique Internationale — CRRA
Compte Rendu. Rencontre Assyriologique Internationale — CRRAI
Compte Rendu. Reunion des Centres de Poisons — CR Reun Cent Poisons
Compte Rendu. Seminaire R and D Bioenergetique — CR Semin R D Bioenerg
Compte Rendu. Seminaire sur le Controle des Effluents Radioactifs — CR Semin Controle Effluents Radioact
Compte Rendu Sommaire des Seances. Societe de Biogeographie — CR Somm Seanc Soc Biogeogr
Compte Rendu Sommaire des Seances. Societe Geologique de France — CR Somm Seances Soc Geol Fr
Compte Rendue. Colloque de l'AEN sur la Radioecologie Marine — CR Colloq AEN Radioecol Mar
Compte-Rendu. Activite. Institut de Recherches des Ressources Hydrauliques — CR Act Inst Rech Ressour Hydraul
Compte-Rendu Analytique des Travaux du Conseil Colonial. Puis Conseil de Legislation — CRA
Compte-Rendu. Conference sur la Sante et la Securite Professionnelles — CR Conf Sante Secur Prof
Compte-Rendu. Congres International de la Detergence — CR Congr Int Deterg
Compte-Rendu de l'Association Strasbourgeoise des Amis de l'Histoire Naturelle — Compt Rend Assoc Strasbourg Amis Hist Nat
Compte-Rendu du Congres. Physico-Chimie et Siderurgie — CR Congr Phys Chim Sider
Comptes Economiques [*Beirut*] — CE
Comptes Rendus. Academie Agricole Georgi Dimitrov — CR Acad Agric Georgi Dimitrov
Comptes Rendus. Academie Agricole Georgi Dimitrov (Sofia) — CR Acad Agric (Sofia)
Comptes Rendus. Academie Bulgare des Sciences — Compt Rend Acad Bulg Sci
Comptes Rendus. Academie Bulgare des Sciences — CR Acad Bulg Sci
Comptes Rendus. Academie Bulgare des Sciences — CR Acad Bulgare Sci
Comptes Rendus. Academie d'Agriculture de France — Compt Rend Acad Agr France
Comptes Rendus. Academie des Inscriptions et Belles Lettres — CAIBL
Comptes Rendus. Academie des Inscriptions et Belles Lettres — CRAcl
Comptes Rendus. Academie des Inscriptions et Belles Lettres — CRAI
Comptes Rendus. Academie des Inscriptions et Belles Lettres — CRAIBL
Comptes Rendus. Academie des Inscriptions et Belles-Lettres — Compt Rend Acad Inscript Belles Lett
Comptes Rendus. Academie des Sciences — Compt Rend Acad Sci
Comptes Rendus. Academie des Sciences — Comptes Rend
Comptes Rendus. Academie des Sciences — CR Acad Sci
Comptes Rendus. Academie des Sciences Agricoles en Bulgarie — CR Acad Sci Agric Bulg
Comptes Rendus. Academie des Sciences de l'Union des Republiques Sovietiques Socialistes — CASURSS
Comptes Rendus. Academie des Sciences de l'URSS. Serie A — CR Acad Sci URSS Ser A
Comptes Rendus. Academie des Sciences de Russie — CRASR
Comptes Rendus. Academie des Sciences de Russie. Serie A — CR Acad Sci Russ Ser A
Comptes Rendus. Academie des Sciences (Paris) — CR Acad Sci (Paris)
Comptes Rendus. Academie des Sciences. Serie 1 — CR Acad Sci Ser 1
Comptes Rendus. Academie des Sciences. Serie 2. Mecanique, Physique, Chimie, Sciences de l'Univers, Sciences de la Terre — CR Acad Sci Ser 2
Comptes Rendus. Academie des Sciences. Serie 3. Sciences de la Vie — CR Acad Sci Ser 3
Comptes Rendus. Academie des Sciences. Serie Generale. La Vie des Sciences [*A publication*] — CR Acad Sci Ser Gen Vie Sci
Comptes Rendus. Academie des Sciences. Serie III. Sciences de la Vie — CR Acad Sci III
Comptes Rendus. Academie Polonaise des Sciences et des Lettres — CRAP
Comptes Rendus. Assemblee Generale. Commission Internationale Technique de Sucrerie — CR Assem Gen Comm Int Tech Sucr
Comptes Rendus. Association Belgo-Neerlandaise pour l'Etude des Cereales — CR Assoc Belgo Neerl Etude Cereales
Comptes Rendus. Association des Anatomistes — CAANA
Comptes Rendus. Association des Anatomistes — CR Assoc Anat
Comptes Rendus. Association Internationale d'Essais de Semences — CR Assoc Int Essais Semences
Comptes Rendus. Colloque de l'ARTEP [*Association de Recherche sur les Techniques d'Exploitation du Petrole*] — CR Colloq ARTEP
Comptes Rendus. Colloque de Medecine Nucleaire de Langue Francaise — CR Colloq Med Nucl Lang Fr
Comptes Rendus. Colloque International sur l'Electronique Nucleaire — CR Colloq Int Electron Nucl
Comptes Rendus. Colloque Regional. Institut International de la Potasse — CR Colloq Reg Inst Int Potasse
Comptes Rendus. Colloques Internationaux d'Astrophysique de Liege — CR Colloq Int Astrophys Liege
Comptes Rendus. Conference Interafricaine des Sols — CR Conf Interafr Sols
Comptes Rendus. Conference Internationale sur la Metallurgie du Plutonium — CR Conf Int Metall Plutonium
Comptes Rendus. Conference Triennale. Association Europeenne pour la Recherche sur la Pomme de Terre — CR Conf Trienn Assoc Eur Rech Pomme Terre
Comptes Rendus. Congres Annuel. Societe Nucleaire Canadienne — CR Congr Annu Soc Nucl Can
Comptes Rendus. Congres. Association Scientifique des Pays de l'Ocean Indien — CR Congr Assoc Sci Pays Ocean Indien
Comptes Rendus. Congres de l'Union Phytopathologique Mediterraneenne — CR Congr Union Phytopathol Mediterr
Comptes Rendus. Congres Europeen de Biopharmacie et Pharmacocinetique — CR Congr Eur Biopharm Pharmacocinet
Comptes Rendus. Congres International d'Angeiologie — CR Congr Int Angeiol
Comptes Rendus. Congres International de Genetique — CR Congr Int Genet
Comptes Rendus. Congres International de la Science du Sol — CR Congr Int Sci Sol
Comptes Rendus. Congres International de Lutte Contre les Ennemis des Plantes — CR Congr Int Lutte Ennemis Plant
Comptes Rendus. Congres International de Mecanique des Roches — CR Congr Int Mec Roches
Comptes Rendus. Congres International de Medecine Tropicale et d'Hygiene — Compt Rend Cong Internat Med Trop et Hyg
Comptes Rendus. Congres International de Psychotherapie — CR Congr Int Psychother
Comptes Rendus Congres International du Vide — CR Congr Int Vide
Comptes Rendus. Congres International sur les Phenomenes de Contact Electrique — CR Congr Int Phenom Contact Electr
Comptes Rendus. Congres International Technique et Chimique des Industries Agricoles — CR Congr Int Tech Chim Ind Agric
Comptes Rendus. Congres Internationaux de Chimie Industrielle — CR Congr Int Chim Ind
Comptes Rendus. Congres Mondial de Psychiatrie — CR Congr Mond Psychiatr
Comptes Rendus. Congres Mondial du Traitement de Surface des Metaux — CR Congr Mond Trait Surf Met
Comptes Rendus. Congres National des Societes Savantes. Section des Sciences — Compt Rend Congr Nat Soc Savant Sect Sci
Comptes Rendus. Congres. Societe Europeenne d'Hematologie — CR Congr Soc Eur Hematol
Comptes Rendus. Congres. Union Internationales des Instituts des Recherches Forestieres — CR Congr Union Int Inst Rech For
Comptes Rendus de la Seance Publique Annuelle. Academie de la Pharmacie — CR Seance Publ Ann Acad Pharm
Comptes Rendus de la Semaine Geologique. Comite National Malgache de Geologie — CR Sem Geol Com Nat Malgache Geol
Comptes Rendus de l'Academie des Sciences. Serie IIa. Sciences de la Terre et des Planetes — CR Academie Sci Ser IIa Sci Terre Planetes
Comptes Rendus de l'Academie des Sciences. Serie IIb. Mecanique Physique, Chimie, Astronomie — CR Academie Sci Ser IIb Mec Phys Chim Astron
Comptes Rendus de Recherches et Bibliographie sur l'Immigration — CR Rech Bibl Immigr

Comptes Rendus de Recherches. Institut pour l'Encouragement de la Recherche Scientifique dans l'Industrie et l'Agriculture [*Belgium*] — CR Rech Inst Encour Rech Sci Ind Agric
Comptes Rendus de Recherches. IRSIA (Institut pour l'Encouragement de la Recherche Scientifique dans l'Industrie et l'Agriculture) — CR Rech IRSIA
Comptes Rendus de Seances. Academie des Sciences. Serie I. Mathematique — CR Seances Acad Sci Ser I
Comptes Rendus de Seances. Academie des Sciences. Serie II. Mecanique, Physique, Chimie, Sciences de la Terre, Sciences de l'Univers — CR Acad Sci Ser II Mec Phys
Comptes Rendus de Seances. Academie des Sciences. Serie III. Sciences de la Vie — CR Seances Acad Sci Ser III Sci Vie
Comptes Rendus de Therapeutique et de Pharmacologie Clinique — CR Ther Pharmacol Clin
Comptes Rendus des Journees Nationales sur les Composites — CR Journ Natl Compos
Comptes Rendus des Seances. Academie d'Agriculture de France — CR Acad Agric Fr
Comptes Rendus des Seances. Academie d'Agriculture de France — CR Seances Acad Agric Fr
Comptes Rendus des Seances. Academie des Inscriptions et Belles Lettres — CR Ac Inscr
Comptes Rendus des Seances. Academie des Inscriptions et Belles-Lettres — Compt Rend Acad
Comptes Rendus des Seances. Academie des Inscriptions et Belles-Lettres — Cpt Rend Seanc Acad Inscr
Comptes Rendus des Seances. Academie des Inscriptions et Belles-Lettres [*Paris*] — CR Acad Insc
Comptes Rendus des Seances. Academie des Inscriptions et Belles-Lettres — CRSAIBL
Comptes Rendus des Seances. Academie des Inscriptions et Belles-Lettres (Paris) — Comptes Rendus (Paris)
Comptes Rendus des Seances. Academie des Sciences de Roumanie — CR Seances Acad Sci Roum
Comptes Rendus des Seances. Academie des Sciences (Paris). Serie I. Mathematique — CR Acad Sci (Paris) Ser I Math
Comptes Rendus des Seances. Academie des Sciences (Paris). Serie II. Mecanique, Physique, Chimie, Sciences de la Terre, Sciences de l'Univers — CR Acad Sci (Paris) Ser II Mec Phys Chim Sci
Comptes Rendus des Seances. Academie des Sciences (Paris). Serie III. Sciences de la Vie — CR Acad Sci (Paris) Ser III Sci Vie
Comptes Rendus des Seances. Academie des Sciences. Serie 2. Mecanique-Physique, Chimie, Sciences de l'Univers, Sciences de la Terre — CR Seances Acad Sci Ser 2
Comptes Rendus des Seances. Academie des Sciences. Serie A. Sciences Mathematiques [*France*] — CR Seances Acad Sci Ser A
Comptes Rendus des Seances. Academie des Sciences. Serie B. Sciences Physiques [*France*] — CR Seances Acad Sci Ser B
Comptes Rendus des Seances. Academie des Sciences. Serie C. Sciences Chimiques — CHDCA
Comptes Rendus des Seances. Academie des Sciences. Serie C. Sciences Chimiques [*France*] — CR Seances Acad Sci Ser C
Comptes Rendus des Seances. Academie des Sciences. Serie D. Sciences Naturelles — CHDDA
Comptes Rendus des Seances. Academie des Sciences. Serie D. Sciences Naturelles [*France*] — CR Seances Acad Sci Ser D
Comptes Rendus des Seances. Academie des Sciences. Serie II. Mecanique, Physique, Chimie, Sciences de la Terre, Sciences de l'Univers — CR Seances Acad Sci Ser II
Comptes Rendus des Seances. Academie des Sciences. Serie III. Sciences de la Vie — CR Seances Acad Sci III
Comptes Rendus des Seances. Academie des Sciences. Serie III. Sciences de la Vie — CR Seances Acad Sci Ser III
Comptes Rendus des Seances. Academie des Sciences. Vie Academique — CR Seances Acad Sci Vie Acad
Comptes Rendus des Seances. Congres Francais d'Oto-Rhino-Laryngologie — CR Seances Congr Fr Oto Rhino Laryngol
Comptes Rendus des Seances et Memoires. Societe de Biologie et des Ses Filiales — CR Seances Mem Soc Biol Ses Fil
Comptes Rendus des Seances. Institut de Geologie Roumaine — CRSIGR
Comptes Rendus des Seances. Institut des Sciences de Roumanie. Ancienne Academie des Sciences de Roumanie — CR Seances Inst Sci Roum Anc Acad Sci Roum
Comptes Rendus des Seances. Institut Geologique de Roumanie — CR Seances Inst Geol Roum
Comptes Rendus des Seances. Institut Geologiques de Roumanie (French Edition) — CR Seances Inst Geol Roum Fr Ed
Comptes Rendus des Seances Mensuelles. Societe des Sciences Naturelles et Physiques du Maroc — CR Seanc Mens Soc Sci Nat Phys Maroc
Comptes Rendus des Seances Mensuelles. Societe des Sciences Naturelles et Physiques du Maroc — CR Seances Mens Soc Sci Nat Phys Maroc
Comptes Rendus des Seances Mensuelles. Societe des Sciences Naturelles et Physiques du Maroc — CR Soc Sci Nat Phys Maroc
Comptes Rendus des Seances Publiques. Institut Royal des Pays-Bas — Compt Rend Seances Publiques Inst Roy Pays Bas
Comptes Rendus des Seances. Republique Populaire Roumaine. Comite Geologique — CR Seances Repub Pop Roum Com Geol
Comptes Rendus des Seances. Societe de Biologie — CR Seanc Soc Biol
Comptes Rendus des Seances. Societe de Biologie et de Ses Filiales — CR Seanc Soc Biol Fil
Comptes Rendus des Seances. Societe de Biologie et de Ses Filiales — CR Seances Soc Biol Fil
Comptes Rendus des Seances. Societe de Biologie et de Ses Filiales — CR Soc Biol
Comptes Rendus des Seances. Societe de Biologie et de Ses Filiales [*A publication*] — CRSBA
Comptes Rendus des Seances. Societe de Biologie et de Ses Filiales et Associees (Paris) — Compt Rend Soc Biol (Paris)
Comptes Rendus des Seances. Societe de Biologie (Paris) — CR Seances Soc Biol (Paris)
Comptes Rendus des Seances. Societe de Biologie (Paris) — CR Soc Biol (Paris)
Comptes Rendus des Seances. Societe de Physique (Warsaw) — CR Soc Phys Warsaw
Comptes Rendus des Travaux du Congres International de Biochimie — CR Trav Congr Int Biochim
Comptes Rendus des Travaux du Laboratoire Carlsberg. Serie Chimique et Serie Physiologique — CR Carlsb L
Comptes Rendus des Travaux. Faculte des Sciences. Universite de l'Aix Marseille — CR Trav Fac Sci Univ Aix Marseille
Comptes Rendus des Travaux. Laboratoire Carlsberg — CR Tr Lab C
Comptes Rendus des Travaux. Laboratoire Carlsberg — CR Trav Carlsb
Comptes Rendus des Travaux. Laboratoire Carlsberg — CR Trav Lab Carlsberg
Comptes Rendus des Travaux. Laboratoire Carlsberg. Serie Chimique — CR Trav Lab Carlsberg Ser Chim
Comptes Rendus des Travaux. Laboratoire Carlsberg. Serie Physiologique — CR Trav Lab Carlsberg Ser Physiol
Comptes Rendus des Travaux. Societe Royale d'Economie Politique de Belgique — CR Soc Roy Econ Pol
Comptes Rendus (Doklady). Academie des Sciences de l'Union des Republiques Sovietiques Socialistes — CR (Dokl) Acad Sci URSS
Comptes Rendus du Colloque Etudiant Annuel — CR Colloq Etud Annu
Comptes Rendus du Congres International d'Arrieration Mentale — CR Congr Int Arrieration Ment
Comptes Rendus du Congres International de Mecanique des Sols et des Travaux de Fondations — CR Congr Int Mec Sols Trav Fond
Comptes Rendus du Congres International du Froid — CR Congr Int Froid
Comptes Rendus du Groupe Linguistique d'Etudes Chamito-Semitiques — CR Groupe Linguistique Etud Chamito Semitiques
Comptes Rendus et Rapports. Congres International des Matieres Plastiques — CR Rapp Congr Int Matieres Plast
Comptes Rendus. Groupe Linguistique d'Etudes Chamito-Semitiques [*Paris*] — CRdGLECS
Comptes Rendus Hebdomadaires des Seances. Academie d'Agriculture de France [*A publication*] — CR Acad Agric France
Comptes Rendus Hebdomadaires des Seances. Academie d'Agriculture de France [*A publication*] — CR Hebd Seances Acad Agric Fr
Comptes Rendus Hebdomadaires des Seances. Academie des Sciences — Comptes Rendus
Comptes Rendus Hebdomadaires des Seances. Academie des Sciences — CR Acad Sci
Comptes Rendus Hebdomadaires des Seances. Academie des Sciences — CR Hebd Seanc Acad Sci
Comptes Rendus Hebdomadaires des Seances. Academie des Sciences — CR Hebd Seances Acad Sci
Comptes Rendus Hebdomadaires des Seances. Academie des Sciences (Paris) — Compt Rend Acad Sc (Paris)
Comptes Rendus Hebdomadaires des Seances. Academie des Sciences (Paris). Serie A et B — CR Acad Sci (Paris) Ser A-B
Comptes Rendus Hebdomadaires des Seances. Academie des Sciences (Paris). Serie D. Sciences Naturelles — CR Hebd Seanc Acad Sci (Paris) D
Comptes Rendus Hebdomadaires des Seances. Academie des Sciences. Serie 2. Mecanique-Physique, Chimie, Sciences de l'Univers, Sciences de la Terre — CR Hebd Acad Sci Ser 2
Comptes Rendus Hebdomadaires des Seances. Academie des Sciences. Serie 2. Mecanique-Physique, Chimie, Sciences de l'Univers, Sciences de la Terre — CR Hebd Seances Acad Sci Ser 2
Comptes Rendus Hebdomadaires des Seances. Academie des Sciences. Serie 3. Sciences de la Vie — CR Hebd Seances Acad Sci Ser 3
Comptes Rendus Hebdomadaires des Seances. Academie des Sciences. Serie A. Sciences Mathematiques — CR Ac Sci A
Comptes Rendus Hebdomadaires des Seances. Academie des Sciences. Serie A. Sciences Mathematiques — CR Hebd Seances Acad Sci Ser A
Comptes Rendus Hebdomadaires des Seances. Academie des Sciences. Serie A. Sciences Mathematiques — CR Hebd Seances Acad Sci Ser A Sci Math
Comptes Rendus Hebdomadaires des Seances. Academie des Sciences. Serie A. Sciences Mathematiques — CRH Acad Sci Ser A Sci Math
Comptes Rendus Hebdomadaires des Seances. Academie des Sciences. Serie B. Sciences Physiques — CR Ac Sci B
Comptes Rendus Hebdomadaires des Seances. Academie des Sciences. Serie B. Sciences Physiques — CR Hebd Seances Acad Sci Ser B
Comptes Rendus Hebdomadaires des Seances. Academie des Sciences. Serie B. Sciences Physiques — CRH Acad Sci Ser B Sci Phys
Comptes Rendus Hebdomadaires des Seances. Academie des Sciences. Serie C. Sciences Chimiques — CR Ac Sci C
Comptes Rendus Hebdomadaires des Seances. Academie des Sciences. Serie C. Sciences Chimiques — CR Hebd Seances Acad Sci Ser C
Comptes Rendus Hebdomadaires des Seances. Academie des Sciences. Serie C. Sciences Chimiques — CR Hebd Seances Acad Sci Ser C Sci Chim
Comptes Rendus Hebdomadaires des Seances. Academie des Sciences. Serie C. Sciences Chimiques — CRH Acad Sci Ser C Sci Chim
Comptes Rendus Hebdomadaires des Seances. Academie des Sciences. Serie D. Sciences Naturelles — CR Ac Sci D
Comptes Rendus Hebdomadaires des Seances. Academie des Sciences. Serie D. Sciences Naturelles — CR Hebd Seances Acad Sci Ser D
Comptes Rendus Hebdomadaires des Seances. Academie des Sciences. Serie D. Sciences Naturelles — CR Hebd Seances Acad Sci Ser D Sci Nat
Comptes Rendus Hebdomadaires des Seances. Academie des Sciences. Serie D. Sciences Naturelles — CRH Acad Sci Ser D Sci Natur

Comptes Rendus Hebdomadaires des Seances. Academie des Sciences. Serie II — CR Hebd Seances Acad Sci Ser II
Comptes Rendus Hebdomadaires des Seances. Academie des Sciences. Vie Academique (Paris) [*Later, Comptes Rendus des Seances. Academie des Sciences. Vie Academique*] — CR Acad Sci (Paris) Vie Academique
Comptes Rendus Hebdomaidaires des Seances. Academie des Sciences — CRAS
Comptes Rendus. Journees Internationales d'Etude des Piles a Combustible — CR Journ Int Etud Piles Combust
Comptes Rendus Mensuels des Seances. Academie des Sciences Coloniales — CR Mens Seanc Acad Sci Colon
Comptes Rendus. Reunion Annuelle. Societe de Chimie Physique — CR Reun Annu Soc Chim Phys
Comptes Rendus. Reunion. Association des Anatomistes — CR Reun Assoc Anat
Comptes Rendus. Societe des Physiologistes Suisses — CR Soc Physiol Suisses
Comptes Rendus. Societe des Sciences et des Lettres de Lodz — CRSL
Comptes Rendus. Societe des Sciences et des Lettres de Poznan — CRSP
Comptes Rendus. Societe des Sciences et des Lettres de Varsovie — CRSVa
Comptes Rendus. Societe des Sciences et des Lettres de Wroclaw — Compt Rend Soc Sci Wroclaw
Comptes Rendus. Societe des Sciences et des Lettres de Wroclaw — CR Soc Sci Lett Wroclaw
Comptes Rendus. Societe des Sciences et des Lettres de Wroclaw — CRSW
Comptes Rendus. Societe des Sciences et des Lettres. Universite Catholique de Lublin — CRSLub
Comptes Rendus. Societe Francaise de Gynecologie — CR Soc Fr Gynecol
Comptes Rendus. Societe Francaise de Gynecologie — CR Soc Franc Gynec
Comptes Rendus. Societe Geologique de Finlande — CR Soc Geol Finl
Comptes Rendus. Societe Geologique de France — CR Soc Geol Fr
Comptes Rendus Sommaire des Seances. Societe Geologique de France — CR Soc Geol Fr
Comptes Rendus Sommaire des Seances. Societe Geologique de France — CR Som Seances Soc Geol Fr
Comptes Rendus. Symposium International sur les Jets Moleculaires — CR Symp Int Jets Mol
Comptes Rendus. Symposium sur le Traitement des Eaux Usees — CR Symp Trait Eaux Usees
Comptes Rendus Trimestriels. Academie des Sciences d'Outre-Mer — CR Trim Acad Sci O-Mer
Comptes Rendus Trimestriels des Seances. Academie des Sciences d'Outre-Mer — Compt Rend Acad Sci Outre-Mer
Comptes Rendus Trimestriels des Seances. Academie des Sciences d'Outre-Mer — CR Trim Seances Acad Sci Outre Mer
Comptes-Rendus des Seances. Academie des Inscriptions et Belles-Lettres [*Paris*] — C R Ac
Comptes-Rendus des Seances. Academie des Inscriptions et Belles-Lettres [*Paris*] — C R Acad Inscr
Comptes-Rendus des Seances. Academie des Inscriptions et Belles-Lettres [*Paris*] — Comptes Rend Bell Let
Comptes-Rendus des Seances. Communications de l'Academie des Sciences Coloniales — Compt Rend Seances Commun Acad Sci Colon
Comptes-Rendus des Travaux du Carlsberg Laboratoriet — Compt Rend Trav Carlsberg Lab
Comptes-Rendus du Symposium International sur les Decharges et l'Isolement Electrique dans le Vide — CR Symp Int Decharges Isol Electr Vide
Comptes-Rendus et Memoires. Societe d'Histoire et d'Archeologie de Senlis — SHA Senlis
Comptes-Rendus Hebdomadaires des Seances et Memoires. Societe de Biologie — Compt Rend Hebd Seances Mem Soc Biol
Comptes-Rendus. Societe de Geographie — CRSG
Computable. Automatiseringsvakblad voor de Benelux — CTQ
Computation in Education. Mathematics, Science, and Engineering — Comput Ed Math Sci Engrg
Computational and Theoretical Polymer Science — Comput Theor Polym Sci
Computational Chemistry (Singapore). Reviews of Current Trends — Comput Chem Singapore
Computational Complexity — Comput Complexity
Computational Economics — Comput Econom
Computational Geometry — Comput Geom
Computational Imaging and Vision — Comput Imaging Vision
Computational Intelligence — Comput Intelligence
Computational Linguistics — CompL
Computational Linguistics — Comput L
Computational Linguistics and Computer Languages — CLCL
Computational Linguistics and Computer Languages — Comput Linguist and Comput Lang
Computational Mathematics and Analysis Series — Comput Math Anal Ser
Computational Mathematics and Mathematical Physics — Comput Math Math Phys
Computational Mathematics and Modeling — Comput Math Model
Computational Mechanics Advances — Comput Mech Adv
Computational Mechanics. Solids, Fluids, Engineered Materials, Aging Infrastructure, Molecular Dynamics, Heat Transfer, Manufacturing Processes, Optimization, Fracture and Integrity — Comput Mech
Computational Microelectronics — Comput Microelectron
Computational Models of Cognition and Perception — Comput Models Cognition Percept
Computational Nonlinear Mechanics in Aerospace Engineering — Comput Nonlinear Mech Aerosp Eng
Computational Optimization and Applications — Comput Optim Appl
Computational Physics. Proceedings of the International Conference on Computational Physics — Comput Phys Proc Int Conf
Computational Polymer Science — Comput Polym Sci
Computational Statistics — Comput Statist
Computational Statistics and Data Analysis — Comput Stat and Data Anal
Computational Statistics Quarterly — CSQ Comput Statist Quart
Computational Techniques — Comput Tech
Compute — GCOE
Computer — Comput
Computer Abstracts — ComAb
Computer Abstracts — Comput Abstr
Computer Advertising News, Incorporated into Adweek's Computer and Electronics Marketing — Comp Ad New
Computer Age — Comput Age
Computer Aided Geometric Design — Comput Aided Geom Design
Computer Analysis of Thermochemical Data — Comput Anal Thermochem Data
Computer Analyzed Newspaper Data On-line [*Database*] — CAN DO
Computer and Control Abstracts [*Database*] — CCA
Computer and Control Abstracts [*IEE*] [*Information service or system*] — Comput & Contr Abstr
Computer and Control Abstracts [*IEE*] [*Information service or system*] — Comput Control Abstr
Computer and Control Abstracts [*IEE*] [*Information service or system*] — Comput Control Abstracts
Computer and Data Processor Technology — Comput and Data Process Technol
Computer and Information Systems — CIS
Computer and Information Systems — Comput & Info Sys
Computer and Information Systems — Comput Inf Syst
Computer and Information Systems Abstracts Journal — Comput Inf Syst Abstr J
Computer and Telecommunications Acronyms — CTA
Computer Applications — Comput Appl
Computer Applications Digest — CAD
Computer Applications in Archaeology — Comput Appl Archaeol
Computer Applications in Shipping and Shipbuilding [*Elsevier Book Series*] — CASS
Computer Applications in the Biosciences — COABER
Computer Applications in the Biosciences — Comput Appl Biosci
Computer Applications in the Laboratory — Comput Appl Lab
Computer Applications in the Natural and Social Sciences — Comput Appl Nat and Soc Sci
Computer Applications. New Series — Comput Appl New Ser
Computer Applications Service — Comput Appl Serv
Computer Architecture News — Comput Archit News
Computer Assisted Trading System [*Database*] — CATS
Computer Book Review [*Database*] — CBR
Computer Bulletin — Comp Bul
Computer Bulletin — Comput Bull
Computer Business News — Comput Bus News
Computer Business News — Comput Busn
Computer Communication Review — Comput Commun Rev
Computer Communications — COC
Computer Communications — Comp Comm
Computer Communications — Comput Commun
Computer Compacts — Comp Compacts
Computer Contributions — Comput Contrib
Computer Data — Comp Data
Computer Data — Comput Data
Computer Decisions — Comp Dec
Computer Decisions — Comp Decisions
Computer Decisions — Comput Decis
Computer Design — CD
Computer Design — Comp Des
Computer Design — Comput Des
Computer Design and Architecture Series [*Elsevier Book Series*] — CDAS
Computer Digest — Computer D
Computer Education — Comput Educ
Computer Education — Computer Educ
Computer Elements and Systems — Comput Elem Syst
Computer Engineering Series — Comput Engrg Ser
Computer Engineering Series — Computer Engrg Ser
Computer Enhanced Spectroscopy — CES
Computer Enhanced Spectroscopy — Comput Enhanc Spectrosc
Computer Enhanced Spectroscopy — Comput Enhanced Spectrosc
Computer Equipment Review — Comput Equip Rev
Computer Fraud and Security Bulletin — Comput Fraud and Secur Bull
Computer Graphics — Comp Graphics
Computer Graphics and Art — Comput Graphics and Art
Computer Graphics and Image Processing — Comput Graphics and Image Process
Computer Graphics and Image Processing — Comput Graphics Image Process
Computer Graphics Forum — CGF
Computer Graphics Forum — Comp Gra Forum
Computer Graphics Technology — Comp Graph Technol
Computer Graphics World — Comp G Wld
Computer Graphics World — Comp Graph Wrld
Computer Graphics World — Comput Graphics World
Computer Index of Neutron Data [*Database*] — CINDA
Computer Industry Report — Comp Ind Rpt
Computer Information — Comput Inf
Computer Journal — CJ
Computer Journal — Comp J
Computer Journal — Comput J
Computer Journal — Computer J
Computer Language Magazine [*Database*] — CLM
Computer Languages — CLAND
Computer Languages — Comput Lang

Computer Law and Tax Report — Comp Law
Computer/Law Journal — Comp Law J
Computer/Law Journal — Comp LJ
Computer/Law Journal — Comput/Law J
Computer Law/Journal — Computer LJ
Computer Literature Index — CLI
Computer Literature Index — Comp Lit Index
Computer Management — Comp Manage
Computer Management — Comp Mgmt
Computer Management — Comput Manage
Computer Management — Comput Mgmt
Computer Marketplace — Comput Marketplace
Computer Merchandising — Comp Merch
Computer Methods and Programs in Biomedicine — CMPBEK
Computer Methods and Programs in Biomedicine — Comput Method Program Biomed
Computer Methods and Programs in Biomedicine — Comput Methods Programs Biomed
Computer Methods for Macromolecular Sequence Analysis — Comput Methods Macromol Sequence Anal
Computer Methods in Applied Mechanics and Engineering — Comp Methods Appl Mech Eng
Computer Methods in Applied Mechanics and Engineering — Comput Methods Appl Mech & Eng
Computer Methods in Applied Mechanics and Engineering — Comput Methods Appl Mech & Engng
Computer Methods in Applied Mechanics and Engineering — Comput Methods Appl Mech Eng
Computer Methods in Applied Mechanics and Engineering — Comput Methods Appl Mech Engrg
Computer Methods in the Geosciences — Comp Methods Geosci
Computer Modeling and Simulation in Engineering — Comput Model Simul Engrg
Computer Modeling in Corrosion — Comput Model Corros
Computer Monographs — CMONDG
Computer Monographs — Comput Monogr
Computer Multiple Listing Service [*Database*] — CMLS
Computer Music Journal — CMJ
Computer Music Journal — Comput Mus
Computer Music Journal — Comput Music J
Computer Music Journal — Computer Mus J
Computer Negotiations Report — C N Report
Computer Networks — Comp Net
Computer Networks — Comput Networks
Computer News — Comput News
Computer Performance — Comp Perf
Computer Performance — Comput Performance
Computer Peripherals Review — Comput Peripherals Rev
Computer Personnel — Comp Pers
Computer Personnel — Comput Pers
Computer Personnel Research Proceedings — CPR Proc
Computer Physics Communications — Comp Phys Comm
Computer Physics Communications — Comput Phys Comm
Computer Physics Communications — Comput Phys Commun
Computer Physics Communications — Computer Ph
Computer Physics Reports — Comput Phys Rep
Computer Praxis — Comput Prax
Computer Products Directory [*Database*] — CDP
Computer Program Abstracts [*NASA*] — Comput Program Abstr
Computer Program Abstracts [*NASA*] — CPA
Computer Program Users Manual CSIRO [*Commonwealth Scientific and Industrial Research Organisation. Division of Applied Geomechanics*] — CSIRO Div Appl Geomech Prog Circ
Computer Programs for Chemistry — Comput Programs Chem
Computer Programs in Biomedicine — Comput Programs Biomed
Computer Programs in Biomedicine — Computer Pr
Computer Programs in Biomedicine — COPMBU
Computer Publishers and Publications — CP & P
Computer Ramblings. Extension Computer Services. South Dakota State University. Cooperative Extension Service — Comput Ramblings Ext Comput Serv SD State Univ Coop Ext Serv
Computer Report. Department of Architectural Science. University of Sydney — Comput Rep Dep Archit Sci Syd Univ
Computer Reseller News — Comp Resell
Computer Retail News. The Newspaper for Systems and Software Retailing — Comp Rtl
Computer Retrieval of Information on Scientific Projects [*Database*] — CRISP
Computer Science and Applied Mathematics — Comput Sci Appl Math
Computer Science and Informatics — Comput Sci and Inf
Computer Science and Scientific Computing — Comput Sci Sci Comput
Computer Science and Scientific Computing. Proceedings. ICASE [*Institute for Computer Applications in Systems Engineering*] **Conference on Scientific Computing** — Comput Sci Sci Comput Pro ICASE Conf
Computer Science Classics — Comput Sci Classics
Computer Science in Economics and Management — Comput Sci Econom Management
Computer Science Journal of Moldova — Comput Sci J Moldova
Computer Science Monographs (Tokyo) — Comput Sci Monographs (Tokyo)
Computer Science Texts — Comput Sci Texts
Computer Science Workbench — Comput Sci Workbench
Computer Security Journal — CSJ
Computer Software Engineering Series — Comput Software Engrg Ser
Computer Sports World [*Database*] — CSW
Computer Studies in the Humanities and Verbal Behavior — Comput Stud Hum & Verbal Behav
Computer Studies in the Humanities and Verbal Behavior — CSHVB
Computer Survey — Comput Surv
Computer Systems — Comput Syst
Computer Systems in Southern Africa — Comput Syst Sthn Afr
Computer Talk — Comp Talk
Computer Talk — Comput Talk
Computer Terminals Review — Comput Terminals Rev
Computer Times with Computacards — Comput Times with Computacards
Computer Using Educators of BC [*British Columbia*] **Journal** [*Canada*] — CUE J
Computer Vision. Graphics and Image Processing — Comput Vision Graphics and Image Process
Computer Week — Comput Week
Computer Weekly — Comp Wkly
Computer Weekly — Comput Wkly
Computer Weekly — Computor Wkly
Computer Weekly International — Comput Wkly Int
Computer World — Comput World
Computer-Aided Chemical Engineering — Comput Aided Chem Eng
Computer-Aided Design — Comput Aided Des
Computer-Aided Design — Computer Aided Des
Computer-Aided Design of Electronic Circuits [*Elsevier Book Series*] — CADEC
Computer-Enhanced Analytical Spectroscopy [*Monograph*] — Comput Enhanced Anal Spectrosc
Computerized Acquisitions Systems Series — Comput Acquis Syst Ser
Computerized Administration of Patent Documents Reclassified According to the IPC [*International Patent Classification*] [*Database*] — CAPRI
Computerized AIDS Information Network [*Database*] — CAIN
Computerized Cataloging Systems Series — Comput Cat Syst Ser
Computerized Circulation Systems Series — Comput Circ Syst Ser
Computerized Equipment Pricing System [*Database*] — CEPS
Computerized Medical Imaging and Graphics — Comput Med Imaging Graph
Computerized Medical Imaging and Graphics — Comput Med Imaging Graphics
Computerized Radiology — Comput Radiol
Computerized Radiology — COMRDW
Computerized Register of Voice Research [*Database*] — CRVR
Computerized Serials Systems Series — Comput Ser Syst Ser
Computerized Tomography — Comput Tomogr
Computerized Tomography — CTOMD
Computerized Tomography — CTOMDS
Computermarkt — COP
Computers and Applied Chemistry (China) — Comput Appl Chem (China)
Computers and Artificial Intelligence — Comput Artificial Intelligence
Computers and Automation [*Later, Computers and People*] — Comp & Automation
Computers and Automation [*Later, Computers and People*] — Comput Autom
Computers and Automation and People — Comput and Autom and People
Computers and Biomedical Research — CBMRB7
Computers and Biomedical Research — Comput and Biomed Res
Computers and Biomedical Research — Comput Biom
Computers and Biomedical Research — Comput Biomed Res
Computers and Chemical Engineering — Comput & Chem Eng
Computers and Chemical Engineering — Comput Chem Eng
Computers and Chemical Engineering — Computers & Chem Engng
Computers and Chemistry — Comp Chem
Computers and Chemistry — Comput Chem
Computers and Education — Comp & Educ
Computers and Education — Comput and Educ
Computers and Education — Computers and Ed
Computers and Education — Computers and Educ
Computers and Electrical Engineering — Comput & Electr Eng
Computers and Electrical Engineering — Comput Electr Eng
Computers and Electrical Engineering — Comput Electr Engrg
Computers and Electronics in Agriculture — Comput Electron Agric
Computers and Fluids — Comp Fluids
Computers and Fluids — Comput and Fluids
Computers and Fluids — CPFLBI
Computers and Geology — Comput Geol
Computers and Geosciences — Comput & Geosci
Computers and Geosciences — Comput Geosci
Computers and Geosciences — Computers Geosci
Computers and Graphics — Comput & Graphics
Computers and Graphics — Comput Graphics
Computers and Industrial Engineering — Comput and Ind Eng
Computers and Industrial Engineering — Comput Ind Eng
Computers and Law — Comp & L
Computers and Law — Computers and L
Computers and Math Series — Comput and Math Ser
Computers and Mathematics with Applications — Comp and Maths with Appls
Computers and Mathematics with Applications — Comput & Math with Appl
Computers and Mathematics with Applications — Comput Math Appl
Computers and Medicine — Comp & Med
Computers and Medicine — Comput Med
Computers and Medieval Data Processing — Comput and Medieval Data Process
Computers and Operations Research — CMO
Computers and Operations Research — CMORA
Computers and Operations Research — CMORAP
Computers and Operations Research — Comp Oper Res
Computers and Operations Research — Comput & Oper Res
Computers and Operations Research — Comput Oper Res
Computers and People — CAP
Computers and People — Comp & People
Computers and People — Comput and People
Computers and People — Computer Pe
Computers and Security — Comp and Sec
Computers and Security — Comput and Secur

Computers and Society — Comput and Soc
Computers and Standards — Comp Stan
Computers and Standards — Comp Stand
Computers and Standards — CS
Computers and Structures — Comput and Struct
Computers and Structures — Comput and Structures
Computers and Structures — Comput Struct
Computers and the Humanities [*Database*] — CHum
Computers and the Humanities [*Database*] — Comput & Human
Computers and the Humanities [*Database*] — Comput & Humanities
Computers and the Humanities [*Database*] — Comput Hum
Computers and the Humanities [*Database*] — Computer Hu
Computers and the Humanities [*Database*] — CPHCC
Computers and the Humanities — PCNH
Computers and Their Applications — Comput Appl
Computers and Translation — CaT
Computers, Control, and Information Theory — Comput Control Inf Theory
Computers, Environment, and Urban Systems [*England*] — Comput Environ Urban Syst
Computers in Biology and Medicine — CBMDAW
Computers in Biology and Medicine — Comput Biol and Med
Computers in Biology and Medicine — Comput Biol Med
Computers in Cardiology — Comput Cardiol
Computers in Chemical and Biochemical Research — CCBCAF
Computers in Chemical and Biochemical Research — Comp Chem Biochem Res
Computers in Chemical and Biochemical Research — Comput Chem Biochem Res
Computers in Chemical Education and Research. Proceedings. International Conference on Computers in Chemical Research, Education, and Technology — Comput Chem Educ Res Proc Int Conf
Computers in Chemistry — COCHDK
Computers in Chemistry and Instrumentation — Comput Chem Instrum
Computers in Education — Comp in Ed
Computers in Education — GCIE
Computers in Healthcare — CIH
Computers in Healthcare — Comput Healthc
Computers in Hospitals — Comput Hosp
Computers in Industry — CINUD
Computers in Industry — Comp Indus
Computers in Industry [*Netherlands*] — Comput Ind
Computers in Mathematical Sciences Education — Comp Math Sci Educ
Computers in Music Research — Computers Mus Res
Computers in Nursing — Comput Nurs
Computers in Psychiatry/Psychology — Comput Psychiatry/Psychol
Computers in Schools — Comput Sch
Computers in Science — Comput Sci
Computerwoche — Computrwoc
Computerworld — Computrwld
Computerworld — Computwrld
Computerworld — CW
Computerworld Buyer's Guide — Comp Wld BG
Computerworld Extra — Computrwl X
Computerworld Focus — Comp Focus
Computerworld Office Automation — Comput OA
Computerworld Office Automation — Compwrld OA
Computerworld on Communications — Comput OC
Computerworld on Communications — Compwrld on Comm
Computing — CO
Computing. Archiv fuer Elektronisches Rechnen — Comput Arch Elektron Rechn
Computing. Archiv fuer Informatik und Numerik — Comput Arch Inf Num
Computing Canada — CCD
Computing Canada — Comp Cda
Computing Canada Focus — Comp Cda F
Computing for Business — Comp Bus
Computing Journal Abstracts — Computing J Abs
Computing Machinery Field — Comput Mach Fi
Computing Machinery Field — Comput Mach Field
Computing Newsletter for Schools of Business — Comput Newsl Schools Bus
Computing Practices Special Reports — Comp Pract Sp Rep
Computing Reviews — Comp Rev
Computing Reviews — Comput Rev
Computing Reviews — ComRev
Computing Reviews — CR
Computing Reviews. Bibliography and Subject Index of Current Computing Literature — Comput Rev Bibliogr Subj Index Curr Comput Lit
Computing South Africa — Comput S Afr
Computing. Supplementum [*Vienna*] — Comput Suppl
Computing. Supplementum — Computing Suppl
Computing Surveys — Comp Surv
Computing Surveys — Comput Surv
Computing Surveys — Comput Survey
Computing Surveys — Comput Surveys
Computing Today — Comput Today
COMSAT [*Communications Satellite Corp.*] **Technical Review** — COMSAT Tech Rev
COMSAT [*Communications Satellite Corp.*] **Technical Review** — CSTRC
COMSAT [*Communications Satellite Corp.*] **Technical Review** — CTR
Comunicacao e Sociedade — Comunicacao e Soc
Comunicacao-Missao de Estudos Agronomicos do Ultramar (Lisbon) — Comun Missao Estud Agron Ultramar (Lisb)
Comunicacion — CN
Comunicacion. Instituto Forestal de Investigaciones y Experiencias (Madrid) [*A publication*] — Comun Inst For Invest Exp (Madrid)
Comunicacion Tecnica. Instituto Nacional del Carbon y Sus Derivados "Francisco Pintado Fe" — Comun Tec Inst Nac Carbon Sus Deri Francisco Pintado Fe
Comunicacion y Cultura — Comun y Cult
Comunicaciones Biologicas — COBIEJ
Comunicaciones Biologicas — Comun Biol
Comunicaciones Botanicas. Museo de Historia Natural de Montevideo — Comun Bot Mus Hist Nat Montev
Comunicaciones Botanicas. Museo de Historia Natural de Montevideo — MNCBAY
Comunicaciones de las Reuniones Cientificas de la Sociedad Espanola de Mineralogia — Comun Reun Cient Soc Esp Mineral
Comunicaciones del Instituto Nacional de Investigaciones de las Ciencias Naturales Anexo al Museo Argentino de Ciencias Naturales Bernardino Rivadavia. Serie Ciencias Botanicas — Comun Inst Nac Invest Ci Nat Ser Ci Bot
Comunicaciones. INIA (Instituto Nacional de Investigaciones Agrarias). Serie General — Comun INIA (Inst Nac Invest Agrar) Ser Gen
Comunicaciones. INIA (Instituto Nacional de Investigaciones Agrarias). Serie Produccion Animal — Comun INIA (Inst Nac Invest Agrar) Ser Prod Anim
Comunicaciones. INIA (Instituto Nacional de Investigaciones Agrarias). Serie Tecnologia — Comun INIA (Inst Nac Invest Agrar) Ser Tecnol
Comunicaciones. INIA (Instituto Nacional de Investigaciones Agrarias). Serie Tecnologia Agraria — Comun INIA (Inst Nac Invest Agrar) Ser Tecnol Agrar
Comunicaciones. INIA [*Instituto Nacional de Investigaciones Agrarias*]. Serie General — CISGDL
Comunicaciones. INIA [*Instituto Nacional de Investigaciones Agrarias*]. Serie Produccion Animal — CSPADO
Comunicaciones. INIA [*Instituto Nacional de Investigaciones Agrarias*] **Serie Produccion Animal (Spain)** — Comun INIA Ser Prod Anim (Spain)
Comunicaciones. INIA [*Instituto Nacional de Investigaciones Agrarias*]. Serie Produccion Vegetal — CIPVDH
Comunicaciones. INIA [*Instituto Nacional de Investigaciones Agrarias*]. Serie Produccion Vegetal — Comun INIA Ser Prod Veg
Comunicaciones. INIA [*Instituto Nacional de Investigaciones Agrarias*]. Serie Production Vegetal — Comun INIA Ser Prod Veg Inst Nac Invest Agrar
Comunicaciones. INIA [*Instituto Nacional de Investigaciones Agrarias*]. Serie Proteccion Vegetal — CISIDR
Comunicaciones. INIA [*Instituto Nacional de Investigaciones Agrarias*]. Serie Proteccion Vegetal — Comun INIA Prot Veg
Comunicaciones. INIA [*Instituto Nacional de Investigaciones Agrarias*]. Serie Proteccion Vegetal — Comun INIA Ser Prot Veg
Comunicaciones. INIA [*Instituto Nacional de Investigaciones Agrarias*]. Serie Proteccion Vegetal (Spain) — Comun INIA Ser Pro Veg (Spain)
Comunicaciones. INIA [*Instituto Nacional de Investigaciones Agrarias*]. Serie Recursos Naturales — CIRND3
Comunicaciones. INIA [*Instituto Nacional de Investigaciones Agrarias*]. Serie Recursos Naturales — Comun INIA Ser Recur Nat
Comunicaciones. INIA [*Instituto Nacional de Investigaciones Agrarias*]. Serie Tecnologia Agraria — CISTDQ
Comunicaciones. INIA(Instituto Nacional de Investigaciones Agrarias). Serie Higiene y Sanidad Animal (Spain) — Comun (Inst Nac Invest Agrar) Ser Hig Sanid Anim (Spain)
Comunicaciones. INIA(Instituto Nacional de Investigaciones Agrarias). Serie Produccion Animal (Spain) — Comun (Inst Nac Invest Agrar) Ser Prod Anim (Spain)
Comunicaciones. INIA(Instituto Nacional de Investigaciones Agrarias). Serie Proteccion Vegetal (Spain) — Comun (Inst Nac Invest Agrar) Ser Prot Veg (Spain)
Comunicaciones. INIA(Instituto Nacional de Investigaciones Agrarias). Serie Tecnologia Agraria (Spain) — Comun (Inst Nac Invest Agrar) Ser Tecnol Agrar (Spain)
Comunicaciones. Instituto de Ciencias Naturales y Matematicas. Universidad de El Salvador — Comun Inst Cienc Nat Mat Univ El Salvador
Comunicaciones. Instituto Nacional de Investigacion de las Ciencias Naturales. Ciencias Botanicas — CNCBAQ
Comunicaciones. Instituto Nacional de Investigacion de las Ciencias Naturales. Ciencias Botanicas — Comun Inst Nac Invest Cienc Nat Cienc Bot
Comunicaciones. Instituto Tropical de Investigaciones Cientificas — Comun Inst Trop Invest Cient
Comunicaciones. Instituto Tropical de Investigaciones Cientificas — CTUSA5
Comunicaciones. Instituto Tropical de Investigaciones Cientificas (San Salvador) — Comunic S Salvador
Comunicaciones. Instituto Tropical de Investigaciones Cientificas, Universidad de El Salvador — Comun Inst Trop Invest Ci Univ El Salvador
Comunicaciones. Museo Argentino de Ciencias Naturales "Bernardino Rivadavia" e Instituto Nacional de Investigacion de las Ciencias Naturales. Ciencias Botanicas — CBRBAH
Comunicaciones. Museo Argentino de Ciencias Naturales "Bernardino Rivadavia" e Instituto Nacional de Investigacion de las Ciencias Naturales. Zoologia — CMAZAD
Comunicaciones Paleontologicas. Museo de Historia Natural de Montevideo — Comun Paleontol Mus Hist Nat Montev
Comunicaciones Paleontologicas. Museo de Historia Natural de Montevideo — CPMHA6
Comunicaciones Presentadas a las Jornadas del Comite Espanol de la Detergencia — Comun Jorn Com Esp Deterg
Comunicaciones Presentadas al Coloquio de Investigaciones sobre el Agua — Comun Coloq Invest Agua
Comunicaciones. Sociedad Malacologica del Uruguay — Comun Soc Malacol Urug
Comunicaciones. Sociedad Malacologica del Uruguay — CSMLA5
Comunicaciones. Universidad de El Salvador. Instituto de Ciencias Naturales y Matematicas — Comun Univ El Salvador Inst Cienc Nat Mat

Comunicaciones Zoologicas. Museo de Historia Natural de Montevideo — Comun Zool Mus Hist Nat Montev
Comunicaciones Zoologicas. Museo de Historia Natural de Montevideo — CZMMAN
Comunicacoes. Museu de Ciencias. PUCRGS [*Pontificia Universidade Catolica do Rio Grande Do Sul*] — CMCPDU
Comunicacoes. Museu de Ciencias. PUCRGS (Pontificia Universidade Catolica do Rio Grande Do Sul) — Comun Mus Cienc PUCRGS (Pontif Univ Catol Rio Grande Do Sul)
Comunicacoes. Museu de Ciencias. PUCRGS [*Pontificia Universidade Catolica do Rio Grande Do Sul*]. Serie Zoologia — CMPZBL
Comunicacoes. Servicos Geologicos de Portugal — CGEPAT
Comunicacoes. Servicos Geologicos de Portugal — Comun Serv Geol Port
Comunicacoes. Servicos Geologicos de Portugal — CSGP
Comunicado. Instituto Agronomico do Sul — Com Inst Agron Sul
Comunicado Tecnico. EMBRAPA [*Empresa Brasileira de Pesquisa Agropecuaria*] **Centro de Pesquisa Agropecuaria do Tropico Umido** — Comun Tec EMBRAPA Cent Pesqui Agropecu Trop Umido
Comunicado Tecnico. Empresa de Pesquisa Agropecuaria da Bahia — Comun Tec Empresa Pesqui Agropecu Bahia
Comunicado Tecnico. Empresa de Pesquisa Agropecuaria do Estado do Rio De Janeiro — Comun Tec Empresa Pesqui Agropecu Estado Rio De J
Comunicados Tecnicos. Instituto de Ecologia e Experimentacao Agricolas — Comun Tec Inst Ecol Exp Agric
Comunicados Tecnicos. Instituto de Ecologia e Experimentacao Agricolas — CTEAA7
Comunicari de Botanica — CBTNAT
Comunicari de Botanica — Comun Bot
Comunicari de Botanica — Comunicari Bot
Comunicari de Zoologie — Comun Zool
Comunicari de Zoologie — COZOAH
Comunicari Stiintifice Prezentate la Sesiunea. Centrul de Cercetari pentru Metalurgie. Institutul Politehnic Bucuresti — Comun Stiint Ses Cent Cercet Metal Inst Politeh Bucuresti
Comunicari Stiintifice. Simpozion de Biodeteriorare si Climatizare — Comun Stiint Simp Biodeterior Clim
Comunicarile. Academiei Republicii Populare Romine — Comun Acad Rep Pop Romine
Comunicarile. Academiei Republicii Populare Romine — Comun Acad Repub Pop Rom
Comunicarile Academiei Republicii Populare Romine — Comun Acad Republ Populare Romine
Comunicazioni i Studi — C St
Comunidad — CD
Comunidad Latinoamericana de Escritores. Boletin — CLEB
Comunita Internazionale — Comun Intern
Comunita Internazionale — Comunita Int
Comunita Internazionale — Comunita Internaz
CONA [*Canadian Orthopaedic Nurses Association*] **Journal** — CONA J
Concast Technology News [*Switzerland*] — Concast Technol News
Concelho de Santo Tirso. Boletim Cultural — CSTBC
Concentrated Milk Industries — Conc Milk Ind
Concepts in Immunopathology — COIMEW
Concepts in Immunopathology — Concept Immunopathol
Concepts in Pediatric Neurosurgery — Concepts Pediatr Neurosurg
Concepts in Pediatric Neurosurgery — COPNDZ
Concepts in Toxicology — Concepts Toxicol
Concepts in Toxicology — COTOEP
Concern Bulletin — Concern Bull
Concerned Theater of Japan — CTJ
Concerning Poetry — Conc Poet
Concerning Poetry — ConcPo
Concerning Poetry — ConP
Concerning Poetry — CP
Conch Review of Books — C Rev B
Conchiglie [*Milan*] — CGLIA9
Conciliation Courts Review — Conciliation Courts R
Concilium. Internationale Zeitschrift fuer Theologie [*Einsiedeln/Zurich/Mainz*] — Conc
Concilium Tridentinum — Conc Trid
Concimi e Concimazione — Concimi Concimaz
Concise Dictionary of American Literary Biography — CDALB
Conclusions du Ministere Public — Concl
Concordia Historical Institute. Quarterly — CHIQ
Concordia Historical Institute. Quarterly — Concor H Inst Q
Concordia Historical Institute Quarterly — ConH
Concordia Journal — CJ
Concordia Journal — Concor J
Concordia Theological Monthly — Conc Theol Mthly
Concordia Theological Monthly — Concor
Concordia Theological Monthly — Concord Theol Mthl
Concordia Theological Monthly [*St. Louis, MO*] — ConcTM
Concordia Theological Monthly — ConTM
Concordia Theological Monthly — CThM
Concordia Theological Monthly — CTM
Concordia Theological Quarterly — Concor Th Q
Concours Medical — COMEAO
Concours Medical — Concours Med
Concrete Abstracts — Concr Abstr
Concrete and Constructional Engineering — Concr Constr Eng
Concrete and Constructional Engineering — Concr Constru Eng
Concrete and Constructional Engineering. Supplement — Concr Constr Eng Suppl
Concrete Cement Age — Concr Cem Age
Concrete Construction — Concr Constr
Concrete Engineering — Concr Eng
Concrete Engineering for Engineers, Architects, and Contractors — Concr Eng Eng Archit Contract
Concrete Institute of Australia. News — Concr Inst Aust News
Concrete International. Design and Construction — Concr Int Des Constr
Concrete Journal [*Japan*] — Concr J
Concrete Precasting Plant and Technology — Concr Precast Plant Technol
Concrete Products — Concrete P
Concrete Quarterly — Concr Quart
Concrete Quarterly — Concrete Q
Concrete Quarterly — Concrete Qly
Concrete Research and Technology — Concr Res Technol
Concrete Society. Technical Report — Concr Soc Tech Rep
Concrete Technology and Design — Concr Technol Des
Concrete Works — Concrete Wks
Concursos y Certamenes Culturales [*Database*] — CECU
Conde Nast Traveler — PCNT
Condensed Matter News — Condens Matter News
Condensed Matter Studies by Nuclear Methods. Proceedings. Zakopane School on Physics — Condens Matter Stud Nucl Methods Proc Zakopane Sch Phys
Condensed Matter Theories — Condens Matter Theor
Condensed Systems of Low Dimensionality — Condens Syst Low Dimens
Condiment Science and Technology — Condiment Sci Technol
Condition Monitoring and Diagnostic Technology — Cond Monit Diagn Technol
Conditional Reflex — Cond Refl
Conditional Reflex — Cond Reflex
Conditional Reflex — COREBG
Conditionnement Embouteillage. Revue Mensuelle de l'Embouteillage et des Industries du Conditionnement, Traitement, Distribution, Transport — RCS
Conditions — Condition
Condizionamneto dell'Aria — Condiz dell'Aria
Condotta Medica — Condotta Med
Confectie. Sociaal, Economisch, en Technisch Maandblad voor de Confectie Industrie in de Beneluxlanden — CFX
Confectionery Manufacture — Confect Manuf
Confectionery Production — Confect Prod
Confectionery Production — CPW
Confederacao Nacional do Comercio — Confed Nac Com
Confederation Nationale de la Mutualite de la Cooperation et du Credit Agricoles Congres — Confed Nat Mutualite Coop Cred Agric Congres
Confederation of British Industry. News — CBI News
Confederazione Generale dell'Industria Italiana Notiziario — Confederazione Gen Ind Ital Notiz
Conference — Co
Conference. Australasian Corrosion Association — Conf Australas Corros Assoc
Conference Avicole Europeenne — Conf Avic Eur
Conference Board. Announcements of Mergers and Acquisitions — CB Merger
Conference Board. Business Management Record — Conf Bd Bsns Mgt Rec
Conference Board. Business Record — Conf Bd Bsns Rec
Conference Board. Cumulative Index — CB Index
Conference Board Data Base — CBDB
Conference Board. Information Bulletin — CB Bul
Conference Board. Manufacturing Investment Statistics. Capital Appropriations [*A publication*] — CB Cap A
Conference Board. Manufacturing Investment Statistics. Capital Investment and Supply Conditions — CB Cap Inv
Conference Board. Record — Conf Bd Rec
Conference Board. Record — Conf Board Rec
Conference Board. Record — Conference Bd Rec
Conference Board. Report 814. Managing the International Company. Building a Global Perspective — CB Rpt 814
Conference Board. Report 815. Corporate Directorship Practices. Compensation — CB Rpt 815
Conference Board. Report 818. Compensating Foreign Service Personnel — CB Rpt 818
Conference Board. Report 820. Corporate Contributions Function — CB Rpt 820
Conference Board. Report 821. Who Is Top Management — CB Rpt 821
Conference Board. Report 823. Impact of Social Welfare Policies in the United States — CB Rpt 823
Conference Board. Report 824. Insurance Deregulation. Issues and Perspectives — CB Rpt 824
Conference Board. Report 825. Regional Perspectives on Energy Issues — CB Rpt 825
Conference Board. Report 826. Planning for Staff and Support Units — CB Rpt 826
Conference Board. Report 831. Flexible Employee Benefit Plans. Companies' Experiences — CB Rpt 831
Conference Board. Report 832. Corporate Voluntary Contributions in Europe — CB Rpt 832
Conference Board. Report 834. Corporate Aid Programs in Twelve Less-Developed Countries — CB Rpt 834
Conference Board. Report 835. Adapting Products for Export — CB Rpt 835
Conference Board. Report 837. Organizing and Managing for Energy Efficiency [*A publication*] — CB Rpt 837
Conference Board. Report 838. Managing Business-State Government Relations — CB Rpt 838
Conference Board. Report 839. New Patterns in Organizing for Financial Management — CB Rpt 839
Conference Board. Report 842. Research and Development. Key Issues for Management — CB Rpt 842
Conference Board. Report 844. Manufacturing. New Concepts and New Technology to Meet New Competition — CB Rpt 844
Conference Board. Report 845. Organizing Corporate Marketing — CB Rpt 845

Conference Board. Report 846. Economic Overview 1983. Medium-Term Corporate Forecasts — CB Rpt 846
Conference Board. Report 847. Developing Strategic Leadership — CB Rpt 847
Conference Board. Report 849. Innovations in Managing Human Resources — CB Rpt 849
Conference Board. Report 850. Managing National Accounts — CB Rpt 850
Conference Board. Report 851. From Owner to Professional Management. Problems in Transition — CB Rpt 851
Conference Board. Report 852. Regulating International Data Transmission. Impact on Managing International Business — CB Rpt 852
Conference Board. Report 853. International Patterns of Inflation. A Study in Contrasts — CB Rpt 853
Conference Board. Report 855. Federal Budget Deficits and the US Economy — CB Rpt 855
Conference Board. Report 859. Inflation Adjustment of the Individual Income Tax. Indexation or Legislation — CB Rpt 859
Conference Board. Report 860. Managing Older Workers. Company Policies and Attitudes — CB Rpt 860
Conference Board. Report 861. Managing International Public Affairs — CB Rpt 861
Conference Board. Report 863. Corporate R & D Strategy. Innovation and Funding Issues — CB Rpt 863
Conference Board. Report 864. US Economy to 1990 — CB Ec 1990
Conference Board. Report 865. New Look in Wage Policy and Employee Relations — CB Rpt 865
Conference Board. Report 867. Facing Strategic Issues. New Planning Guides and Practices — CB Rpt 867
Conference Board. Report 868. Corporations and Families. Changing Practices and Perspectives — CB Rpt 868
Conference Board. Report 869. Annual Survey of Corporate Contributions — CB Corp Con
Conference Board. Report 870. Trends in Corporate Education and Training — CB Rpt 870
Conference Board. Report 872. World Economy in the 1980's — CB Rpt 872
Conference Board. Report 873. Refocusing the Company's Business — CB Rpt 873
Conference Board. Report 874. Developing New Leadership in a Multinational Environment — CB Rpt 874
Conference Board. Report 876. Competitive Leverage — CB Rpt 876
Conference Board. Report 881. Meeting Human Needs. Corporate Programs and Partnerships — CB Rpt 881
Conference Board. Report 882. Annual Survey of Corporate Contributions. 1986 Edition — CB Rpt 882
Conference Board. Report 883. Corporate Strategies for Controlling Substance Abuse — CB Rpt 883
Conference Board. Report 886. Board Committees in European Companies — CB Rpt 886
Conference Board. Report 887. Screening Requests for Corporate Contributions [*A publication*] — CB Rpt 887
Conference Board. Statistical Bulletin — CB Stat
Conference Board Utility Investment Report — Conf Board Util Invest Rep
Conference Board. Worldbusiness — C B Worldbus
Conference Circompolaire sur l'Ecologie du Nord. Compte Rendu — Conf Circompolaire Ecol Nord R
Conference Digest. Institute of Physics (London) — Conf Dig Inst Phys (London)
Conference Digest. International Conference on Infrared and Millimeter Waves — Conf Dig Int Conf Infrared Millimeter Waves
Conference Digest. International Electrical, Electronics Conference Exposition — Conf Dig Int Electr Electron Conf Expo
Conference. European Society for Comparative Physiology and Biochemistry — Conf Eur Soc Comp Physiol Biochem
Conference Europeenne de l'Aviculture — Conf Eur Avic
Conference Europeenne des Plastiques et des Caoutchoucs. Comptes Rendus — Conf Eur Plast Caoutch CR
Conference Europeenne sur la Microcirculation — Conf Eur Microcirc
Conference Europeenne sur la Microcirculation/Conferenza Europea di Microcircolazione — EKMZAD
Conference Forestiere Interafricaine. Communications — Conf For Interafr Commun
Conference Geologique des Caraibes. Publication — Conf Geol Caraibes Publ
Conference. German Biochemical Society — Conf Ger Biochem Soc
Conference. Gesellschaft fuer Aerosolforschung — Conf Ges Aerosolforsch
Conference. Gesellschaft fuer Biologische Chemie — Conf Ges Biol Chem
Conference Interafricaine des Sols — Conf Interafr Sols
Conference Internationale de Metallisation — Conf Int Met
Conference Internationale de Spectroscopie Raman — Conf Int Spectrosc Raman
Conference Internationale de Thermodynamique Chimique. Compte Rendu — Conf Int Thermodyn Chim CR
Conference Internationale d'Histoire Economique. Communications — Commun Conf Internat Hist Econ
Conference Internationale sur la Metallurgie du Beryllium. Communications — Conf Int Metall Beryllium Commun
Conference Internationale sur la Meteorologie des Carpates — Conf Int Meteorol Carpates
Conference Internationale sur la Physique des Nuages. Communications — Conf Int Phys Nuages Commun
Conference Internationale sur la Physique et la Chimie des Mineraux d'Amiante. Resumes des Communications — Conf Int Phys Chim Miner Amiante Resumes Commun
Conference Internationale sur la Production Thermo-Ionique d'Energie Electrique — Conf Int Prod Thermo Ionique Energ Electr
Conference Internationale sur la Protection des Reacteurs — Conf Int Prot React
Conference Internationale sur le Pergelisol — Conf Int Pergelisol
Conference Internationale sur les Metaux Lourds dans l'Environnement. Colloque Procede — Conf Int Met Lourds Environ Colloq Procede
Conference Internationale sur les Petroles Lourds Bruts et les Sables Bitumineux — Conf Int Pet Lourds Bruts Sables Bitum
Conference Internationale sur les Phenomenes d'Ionisation dans les Gaz. Comptes Rendus — Conf Int Phenom Ionis Gaz CR
Conference Internationale sur les Recherches Cacaoyeres. Memoires — Conf Int Rech Cacaoyeres Mem
Conference Internationale sur les Sources d'Ions. Comptes Rendus — Conf Int Sources Ions CR
Conference Mondiale de l'Energie. Compte Rendu — Conf Mond Energ CR
Conference. National Association of Corrosion Engineers. Proceedings — Conf Natl Assoc Corros Eng Proc
Conference of Actuaries in Public Practice. Proceedings — CPP
Conference of College Teachers of English of Texas. Proceedings — CCTE
Conference on Adrenal Cortex. Transactions — Conf Adrenal Cortex Trans
Conference on Advanced Composites — Conf Adv Compos
Conference on Advances in Magnetic Materials and Their Applications — Conf Adv Magn Mater Their Appl
Conference on African Geology — Conf Afr Geol
Conference on Anaerobic Digestion and Solids Handling. Proceedings — Conf Anaerobic Dig Solids Handl Proc
Conference on Analytical Chemistry in Energy Technology — Conf Anal Chem Energy Technol
Conference on Application of Science and Technology for the Benefit of Less Developed Areas. United Nations — Conf Appl Sci Technol Benefit Less Devel Areas UN
Conference on Application of Small Accelerators — Conf Appl Small Accel
Conference on Applied Chemistry. Unit Operations and Processes — Conf Appl Chem Unit Oper Processes
Conference on Applied Crystallography. Proceedings — Conf Appl Crystallogr Proc
Conference on Atmospheric Radiation. Preprints — Conf Atmos Radiat Prepr
Conference on Biological Antioxidants. Transactions — Conf Biol Antioxid Trans
Conference on Biological Waste Treatment. Proceedings — Conf Biol Waste Treat Proc
Conference on Blood Clotting and Allied Problems. Transactions — Conf Blood Clotting Allied Probl Trans
Conference on Capturing the Sun through Bioconversion. Proceedings — Conf Capturing Sun Bioconver Pro
Conference on Carbon. Extended Abstracts and Program — Conf Carbon Ext Abstr Program
Conference on Catalysis in Organic Syntheses — Conf Catal Org Symth
Conference on Ceramics for Electronics — Conf Ceram Electron
Conference on Charitable Foundations. New York University. Proceedings — Conf on Char Found NYU Proc
Conference on Clay Mineralogy and Petrology. Proceedings — Conf Clay Mineral Petrol Proc
Conference on Compatibility of Propellants, Explosives, and Pyrotechnics with Plastics and Additives — Conf Compat Propellants Explos Pyrotech Plast Addit
Conference on Connective Tissues. Transactions — Conf Connect Tissues Trans
Conference on Coordination Chemistry. Proceedings — Conf Coord Chem Proc
Conference on Copper Coordination Chemistry — Conf Copper Coord Chem
Conference on Cotton Growing Problems. Report and Summary of Proceedings — Conf Cotton Grow Probl Rep Summ Proc
Conference on Culture of Marine Invertebrate Animals. Proceedings — Conf Cult Mar Invertebr Anim Proc
Conference on Cutaneous Toxicity — Conf Cutaneous Toxic
Conference on Dimensioning and Strength Calculations — Conf Dimens Strength Cal
Conference on Elastoplastics Technology. Papers — Conf Elastoplast Technol Pap
Conference on Electrical Insulation and Dielectric Phenomena. Annual Report — Conf Electr Insul Dielectr Phenom Annu Rep
Conference on Environmental Aspects of Non-Conventional Energy Resources — Conf Environ Aspects Non Conv Energy Resour
Conference on Environmental Chemicals. Human and Animal Health. Proceedings [*A publication*] — Conf Environ Chem Hum Anim Health Proc
Conference on Experimental Medicine and Surgery in Primates — Conf Exp Med Surg Primates
Conference on Extremely High Temperatures. Proceedings — Conf Extremely High Temp Proc
Conference on Factors Regulating Blood Pressure. Transactions — Conf Factors Regul Blood Pressure Trans
Conference on Fluid Machinery. Proceedings — Conf Fluid Mach Proc
Conference on Glass Problems — Conf Glass Probl
Conference on Great Lakes Research. Proceedings — Conf Great Lakes Res Proc
Conference on Halophilic Microorganisms — Conf Halophilic Microorg
Conference on Hemoglobin Switching — Conf Hemoglobin Switching
Conference on High Molecular Compounds — Conf High Mol Compd
Conference on Human Relations in Industry. Proceedings — Conf Hum Rel Ind Proc
Conference on In Situ Composites. Proceedings — Conf In Situ Compos Proc
Conference on Industrial Carbon and Graphite. Papers Read at the Conference — Conf Ind Carbon Graphite Pap
Conference on Industrial Energy Conservation Technology — Conf Ind Energy Conserv Technol
Conference on Installation Engineering — Conf Install Eng
Conference on Instrumentation for the Iron and Steel Industry — Conf Instrum Iron Steel Ind
Conference on Liver Injury. Transactions — Conf Liver Inj Trans
Conference on Macromolecular Synthesis — Conf Macromol Synth

Conference on Materials Engineering — Conf Mater Eng
Conference on Materials for Coal Conversion and Utilization. Proceedings — Conf Mater Coal Convers Util Proc
Conference on Metabolic Aspects of Convalescence. Transactions — Conf Metab Aspects Convalescence Trans
Conference on Metabolic Interrelations. Transactions — Conf Metab Interrelat Trans
Conference on Methods in Air Pollution and Industrial Hygiene Studies. Plenary Session — Conf Methods Air Pollut Ind Hyg Stud Plenary Sess
Conference on Molecular Spectroscopy. Proceedings — Conf Mol Spectrosc Proc
Conference on Mononuclear Phagocytes — Conf Mononucl Phagocytes
Conference on Nerve Impulse. Transactions — Conf Nerve Impulse Trans
Conference on Neuropharmacology. Transactions — Conf Neuropharmacol Trans
Conference on Optical Fiber Sensor-Based Smart Materials and Structures — Conf Opt Fiber Sens Based Smart Mater Struct
Conference on Personal Finance Law. Quarterly Report — Conf Pers Fin L Q Rep
Conference on Personal Finance Law. Quarterly Report — Conf Pers Fin LQR
Conference on Plasma Physics and Controlled Nuclear Fusion Research — Conf Plasma Phys Controlled Nucl Fusion Res
Conference on Polysaccharides in Biology. Transactions — Conf Polysaccharides Biol Trans
Conference on Precision Electromagnetic Measurements. CPEM Digest — Conf Precis Electromagn Meas CPEM Dig
Conference on Problems of Aging. Transactions — Conf Probl Aging Trans
Conference on Problems of Consciousness. Transactions — Conf Probl Conscious Trans
Conference on Problems of Early Infancy. Transactions — Conf Probl Early Infancy Trans
Conference on Problems of Infancy and Childhood. Transactions — Conf Probl Infancy Child Trans
Conference on Prostaglandins in Fertility Control — Conf Prostaglandins Fertil Control
Conference on Pulverized Fuel. Proceedings at the Conference — Conf Pulverized Fuel Proc Conf
Conference on Radiation Protection in Accelerator Environments. Proceedings — Conf Radiat Prot Accel Environ Proc
Conference on Radioprotectors and Anticarcinogens — Conf Radioprot Anticarcinog
Conference on Reading (University of Chicago). Proceedings — Conf Read (Univ Chicago)
Conference on Reading (University of Pittsburgh). Report — Conf on Read (Univ Pittsburgh) Rep
Conference on Recent Advances in Adaptive and Sensory Materials and Their Applications — Conf Recent Adv Adapt Sens Mater Their Appl
Conference on Refractory Concretes — Conf Refract Concr
Conference on Renal Function. Transactions — Conf Renal Funct Trans
Conference on Research on the Radiotherapy of Cancer. Proceedings — Conf Res Radiother Cancer Proc
Conference on Shock and Circulatory Homeostasis. Transactions — Conf Shock Circ Homeostasis Trans
Conference on Silicate Industry and Silicate Science — Conf Silic Ind Silic Sci
Conference on Solid State Devices and Materials — Conf Solid State Devices Mater
Conference on Solid State Devices. Proceedings — Conf Solid State Devices Proc
Conference on Spectroscopy and Its Applications. Proceedings — Conf Spectrosc Its Appl Proc
Conference on Superconductivity and Applications — Conf Supercond Appl
Conference on Superconductivity in D- and F-Band Metals — Conf Supercond D F Band Met
Conference on Superionic Conductors. Chemistry, Physics, and Applications. Proceedings — Conf Superionic Conduct Chem Phys Appl Pro
Conference on Tests of Electroweak Theories. Polarized Processes and Other Phenomena — Conf Tests Electroweak Theor Polariz Processes Other Phenom
Conference on the Analysis of Cement and Associated Silicate Materials. Proceedings — Conf Anal Cem Assoc Silic Mate Proc
Conference on the Climatic Impact Assessment Program. Proceedings — Conf Clim Impact Assess Program Proc
Conference on the Control of Gaseous Sulphur and Nitrogen Compound Emission — Conf Control Gaseous Sulphur Nitrogen Comp Emiss
Conference on the Environmental Impact of Water Chlorination — Conf Environ Impact Water Chlorination
Conference on the Marine Transportation, Handling, and Storage of Bulk Chemicals. Proceedings — Conf Mar Transp Handl Storage Bulk Chem Proc
Conference on the Mathematics of Finite Elements and Applications. Proceedings — Conf Math Finite Elem Appl Proc
Conference on the Mining and Coking of Coal — Conf Min Coking Coal
Conference on the Production, Properties, and Testing of Aggregates. Papers — Conf Prod Prop Test Aggregates Pap
Conference on the Restoration of Coastal Vegetation in Florida. Proceedings — Conf Restor Coastal Veg Fla Proc
Conference on the Safety Techniques of Chemical Processing in Agriculture. Proceedings — Conf Saf Tech Chem Process Agric Proc
Conference on the Standardization of Methodology of Water Pollution. Proceedings — Conf Stand Methodol Water Pollut Proc
Conference on Thermal Conductivity. Proceedings — Conf Therm Conduct Proc
Conference on Thermodynamics and National Energy Problems. Report — Conf Thermodyn Natl Energy Probl Rep
Conference on Trace Substances in Environmental Health — Conf Trace Subst Environ Health
Conference on Transport Theory. Proceedings — Conf Transp Theory Proc
Conference on Tribology. Lectures — Conf Tribol Lect
Conference on Uranium Mining Technology. Proceedings — Conf Uranium Min Technol Proc
Conference on Urethanes and the Environment. Preprints — Conf Urethanes Environ Prepr
Conference on Vitamin C — Conf Vitam C
Conference on Water Chlorination. Environmental Impact and Health Effects — Conf Water Chlorination Environ Impact Health Eff
Conference on Weather Modification. American Meterological Society. Preprints — Conf Weather Modif Am Meteorol Soc Prepr
Conference on Welding — Conf Weld
Conference on Wood Gluing. Proceedings — Conf Wood Gluing Proc
Conference on Zinc Coatings in All Their Aspects. Papers — Conf Zinc Coat All Their Aspects Pap
Conference Paper. International Seminar on Modern Synthetic Methods — Conf Pap Int Semin Mod Synth Methods
Conference Papers. Annual Conference on Materials for Coal Conversion and Utilization — Conf Pap Annu Conf Mater Coal Convers Util
Conference Papers. European Industrial Research Management Association — Conf Pap Eur Ind Res Manage Assoc
Conference Papers in Applied Physical Sciences — Conf Pap Appl Phys Sci
Conference Papers Index [*Cambridge Scientific Abstracts*] [*Bethesda, MD*] [*Information service or system*] — CPI
Conference Papers. Institute of Metallurgical Technicians (London) — Conf Pap Inst Metall Tech (London)
Conference Papers. International Coal Utilization Conference and Exhibition — Conf Pap Int Coal Util Conf Exhib
Conference Papers. International Cosmic Ray Conference — Conf Pap Int Cosmic Ray Conf
Conference Papers. International Pipeline Technology Convention — Conf Pap Int Pipeline Technol Conv
Conference Papers. Joint Conference on Applications of Air Pollution Meteorology — Conf Pap Jt Conf Appl Air Pollut Meteorol
Conference Proceedings. American Association for Contamination Control. Annual Technical Meeting — Conf Proc Am Assoc Contam Control Annu Tech Meet
Conference Proceedings and Lecture Notes in Algebraic Geometry — Conf Proc Lecture Notes Algebraic Geom
Conference Proceedings and Lecture Notes in Geometry and Topology — Conf Proc Lecture Notes Geom Topology
Conference Proceedings and Lecture Notes in Mathematical Physics — Conf Proc Lecture Notes Math Phys
Conference Proceedings. Annual Convention. Wire Association International — Conf Proc Annu Conv Wire Assoc Int
Conference Proceedings. Annual Symposium on Computer Architecture — Conf Proc Annu Symp Comput Archit
Conference Proceedings. European Conference on Controlled Fusion and Plasma Physics — Conf Proc Eur Conf Controlled Fusion Plasma Phys
Conference Proceedings. European Microwave Conference — Conf Proc Eur Microwave Conf
Conference Proceedings. Ferrous Divisional Meeting. Wire Association International — Conf Proc Ferrous Div Meet Wire Assoc Int
Conference Proceedings Index [*Database*] — CPI
Conference Proceedings. International Conference on Fire Safety — Conf Proc Int Conf Fire Saf
Conference Proceedings. International Conference on Nondestructive Testing — Conf Proc Int Conf Nondestr Test
Conference Proceedings. International Symposium on Plasma Chemistry — Conf Proc Int Symp Plasma Chem
Conference Proceedings. Intersociety Energy Conversion Engineering Conference [*A publication*] — Conf Proc Intersoc Energy Convers Eng Conf
Conference Proceedings. Joint Conference on Sensing of Environmental Pollutants — Conf Proc Jt Conf Sens Environ Pollut
Conference Proceedings. Ocean Energy Conference — Conf Proc Ocean Energy Conf
Conference Proceedings OFS. International Conference on Optical Fiber Sensors — Conf Proc OFS Int Conf Opt Fiber Sens
Conference Proceedings. Purdue Agricultural Computing Conference — Conf Proc Purdue Agric Comput Conf
Conference Proceedings. Recycling World Congress — Conf Proc Recycl World Congr
Conference Proceedings. UK Section. International Solar Energy Society — Conf Proc UK Sect Int Sol Energy Soc
Conference Proceedings. World Hydrogen Energy Conference — Conf Proc World Hydrogen Energy Conf
Conference Publications. Institution of Mechanical Engineers — Conf Publ Inst Mech Eng
Conference Record. Annual Pulp and Paper Industry Technical Conference — Conf Rec Annu Pulp Pap Ind Tech Conf
Conference Record. Asilomar Conference on Circuits Systems and Computers — Conf Rec Asilomar Conf Circuits Syst Comput
Conference Record. IAS [*IEEE Industry Applications Society*] **Annual Meeting** — Conf Rec IAS Annu Meet
Conference Record. IEEE [*Institute of Electrical and Electronics Engineers*] **Photovoltaic Specialists Conference** — Conf Rec IEEE Photovoltaic Spec Conf
Conference Record. International Conference on Conduction and Breakdown in Dielectric Liquids — Conf Rec Int Conf Conduct Breakdown Dielectr Liq
Conference Report. Australian Institute of Parks and Recreation — Conf Rep R Aust Inst Parks Rec
Conference Reports. Botanical Society. British Isles — Conf Rep Bot Soc Brit Isles
Conference Series. Australasian Institute of Mining and Metallurgy — Conf Ser Australas Inst Min Metall
Conference Series. Australian Water Resources Council — Conf Ser Aust Water Resour Counc

Conference Series. Institute of Physics — Conf Ser Inst Phys
Conference sur Betons Refractaires — Conf Betons Refract
Conference sur le Role du Poisson dans l'Alimentation. Documents de Travail — Conf Role Poisson Aliment Doc Trav
Conference sur les Mesures Electromagnetiques de Precision — Conf Mes Electromagn Precis
Conference. Textile Institute (Manchester, England) — Conf Text Inst Manchester Engl
Conference Trisannuelle. Association Europeenne pour la Recherche sur la Pomme de Terre — Conf Trisannuelle Assoc Eur Rech Pomme Terre
Conference. Union Internationale de Chimie. Comptes Rendus — Conf Union Int Chim CR
Conferences and Exhibitions [*Later, Conferences and Exhibitions International*] — C & E
Conferences and Exhibitions International — CEI
Conferences and Exhibitions International — Conf Exhib Int
Conferences de Reanimation et de Medecine d'Urgence de l'Hopital Raymond Poincare — Conf Reanim Med Urgence Hop Raymond Poincare
Conferences in Energy, Physics, and Mathematics [*Database*] — CONF
Conferences. Institut de Linguistique de Paris — CILP
Conferences. Institut Maurice Thorez — Inst Maurice Thorez Confs
Conferences Invitees. Table Ronde Internationale. Symposium International de Chimie des Plasmas — Conf Invitees Table Ronde Int Symp Int Chim Plasmas
Conferences Originales. Congres International de la Detergence — Conf Orig Congr Int Deterg
Conferences. Palais de la Decouverte. Serie A — Conf Palais Decouverte Ser A
Conferences Plenieres et Principales aux Sections Presentees au Congres International de Chimie Pure et Appliquee — Conf Plenieres Princ Sect Congr Int Chim Pure Appl
Conferences Presentees au Colloque International sur la Prevention et le Traitement de l'Alcoolisme — Conf Colloq Int Prev Trait Alcool
Conferences Presentees au Colloque International sur la Prevention et le Traitement des Toxicomanies — Conf Colloq Int Prev Trait Toxicomanies
Conferences Publiques. Universite de Damas — Conf Publiques Univ Damas
Conferencia — Conf
Conferencia de Fisico-Quimica Organica — Conf Fis Quim Org
Conferencia Interamericana de Agricultura [*Caracas*] — CFIAAV
Conferencia Interamericana de Agricultura (Caracas) — Conf Interam Agric (Caracas)
Conferencia Interamericana de Radioquimica — Conf Interam Radioquim
Conferencia Inter-Americana en Tecnologia de Materiales — Conf Inter Am Tecnol Mater
Conferencia Interamericana sobre la Ensenanza de la Quimica — Conf Interam Ensenanza Quim
Conferencia Internacional de Investigaciones en Cacao. Memorias — Conf Int Invest Cacao Mem
Conferencia Internacional de Pesquisas em Cacau. Memorias — Conf Int Pesqui Cacau Mem
Conferencia Internacional sobre Crudos Pesados y Arenas Bituminosas — Conf Int Crudos Pesados Arena Bitum
Conferencias de Bioquimica — Conf Bioquim
Conferencias. Instituto Nacional de Investigaciones Agronomicas. Ministerio Agricultura (Spain) — Conf Inst Nac Invest Agron Min Agr (Spain)
Conferencias. Instituto Nacional de Investigaciones Agronomicas (Spain) — Conf Inst Nac Invest Agron (Spain)
Conferentia Hungarica pro Therapia et Investigatione in Pharmacologia — Conf Hung Ther Invest Pharmacol
Conferentia Hungarica pro Therapia et Investigatione in Pharmacologia. Societas Pharmacologica Hungarica — Conf Hung Ther Invest Pharmacol Soc Pharmacol Hung
Conferenza Avicola Europea. Atti — Conf Avic Eur Atti
Conferenza Europea di Microcircolazione — Conf Eur Microcirc
Conferenze. Deselec Lefebvre — CDL
Conferenze e Studi. Accademia Polacca delle Scienze. Biblioteca e Centro di Studi a Roma — Conf e Studi Accad Polacca Sci Bibl Centro Studi Roma
Conferenze. Seminario di Matematica. Universita di Bari — Confer Sem Mat Univ Bari
Confinement de la Radioactivite dans l'Utilisation de l'Energie Nucleaire. Actes du Congres International — Confinement Radioact Util Energ Nucl Actes Congr Int
Confinia Neurologica — CONEAT
Confinia Neurologica — Confin Neurol
Confinia Neurologica — Confinia Neurol
Confinia Psychiatrica — CFPSA
Confinia Psychiatrica — Conf Psych
Confinia Psychiatrica — Confin Psychiat
Confinia Psychiatrica — Confin Psychiatr
Confinia Psychiatrica/Confins de la Psychiatrie — CFPSAI
Confins de la Psychiatrie — Confins Psychiatr
Conflict. An International Journal — Conf
Conflict Management and Peace Science — Conflict Mgt and Peace Science
Conflict Quarterly — Conflict Q
Confluence — CF
Confluence — Cfl
Confluence — Con
Confluence — Conf
Confluences. Revue des Lettres et des Arts — Confl
Confluencia (Caracas) — CNC
Conformational Analysis. Scope and Present Limitations Papers Presented at the International Symposium — Conform Anal Pap Int Symp
Conformations and Forces in Protein Folding — Conform Forces Protein Folding
Confrontation — Confr
Confrontation — Confrontat
Confrontations Pharmacologiques — Confront Pharmacol
Confrontations Radio-Anatomo-Cliniques [*France*] — Confront Radio-Anatomo-Clin
Confructá — CONFA
Confructa — CONFAW
Confructa-Studien — Confructa Stud
Cong Nazionale — Cong Nazion
Congenital Anomalies — Congenital Anom
Congenital Anomalies — SEIJAN
Congenital Diseases in Childhood. Medical and Socio-Medical Aspects. Symposium — Congenital Dis Child Med Socio Med Aspects Symp
Congenital Disorders of Erythropoiesis. Symposium — Congenital Disord Erythropoiesis Symp
Congenital Disorders of the Urea Cycle and Ammonia Detoxication — Congenital Disord Urea Cycle Ammonia Detoxication
Congiuntura Economica Laziale — Congiuntura Econ Laziale
Congiuntura Economica Lombarda — Congiunt Econ Lombarda
Congiuntura Italiana — Congiuntura Ital
Congo Belge et Ruanda-Urundi. Service Geologique. Memoire — Congo Belge Ruanda Urundi Serv Geol Mem
Congo Illustre — CIL
Congo-Afrique — CAfr
Congregational Magazine — Cong M
Congregational Quarterly — Cong Q
Congregational Review — Cong R
Congregational Review — Congreg R
Congregationalist — Cong
Congregationalist — Congre
Congregationalist Monthly Review — Cong Mo
Congres Aeronautique Europeen. Comptes Rendus — Congr Aeronaut Eur CR
Congres Annuel. Societe Nucleaire Canadienne — Congr Annu Soc Nucl Can
Congres Archeologique de France — Congr A Fr
Congres Archeologique de France — Congres Archeol
Congres Archeologique de France — Congres Archeol de France
Congres. Association des Pediatres de Langue Francaise. Rapports — Congr Assoc Pediatr Lang Fr Rapp
Congres. Association Europeenne pour l'Amelioration des Plantes — Congr Assoc Eur Amelior Plant
Congres. Association Francaise pour l'Avancement des Sciences [*Nancy*] — CAFSB2
Congres. Association Francaise pour l'Avancement des Sciences (Nancy) — Congr Assoc Fr Av Sci (Nancy)
Congres. Association Geologique Carpatho-Balkanique. Bulletin — Congr Assoc Geol Carpatho-Balkan Bull
Congres de College Francais de Pathologie Vasculaire — Congr Coll Fr Pathol Vas
Congres des Relations Industrielles. Universite Laval. Rapport — Congres des Rel Ind
Congres des Societes de Pharmacie de France. Comptes Rendus — Congr Soc Pharm Fr CR
Congres d'Expertise Chimique. Volume Special des Conferences et Communications — Congr Expert Chim Vol Spec Conf Commun
Congres du Groupement pour l'Avancement des Methodes d'Analyse Spectrographique des Produits Metallurgiques — Congr Group Av Methodes Anal Spectrogr Prod Metall
Congres et Colloques. Universite de Liege — Congr Colloq Univ Liege
Congres Europeen. Centres de Lutte Contre les Poisons. Rapports et Communications — Congr Eur Cent Lutte Poisons Rapp Commun
Congres Europeen de Biopharmacie et Pharmacocinetique — Congr Eur Biopharm Pharmacocinet
Congres Europeen de Spectroscopie des Molecules Biologiques — Congr Eur Spectrosc Mol Biol
Congres Europeen sur les Groupes Sanguins et le Polymorphisme Biochimique des Animaux — Congr Eur Groupes Sang Polymorphisme Biochem Anim
Congres. Federation Internationale de la Precontrainte. Procedes — Congr Fed Int Precontrainte Pro
Congres Francais d' Acoustique — Congr Fr Acoust
Congres Francais d'Anesthesiologie. Rapports — Congr Fr Anesthesiol Rapp
Congres Francais de Medecine. Rapports — Congr Fr Med Rapp
Congres Francais de Medecine. Rapports. l'Agregation Plaquettaire — Congr Fr Med Rapp Agregation Plaquettaire
Congres Francais de Medecine. Rapports. Les Prostaglandines — Congr Fr Med Rapp Prostaglandines
Congres Francais d'Oto-Rhino-Laryngologie. Comptes Rendus des Seances — Congr Fr Oto Rhino Laryngol CR Seances
Congres International Annuel. Association Nucleaire Canadienne — Congr Int Annu Assoc Nucl Can
Congres International. Association des Societes Nationales Europeennes et Mediterraneennes de Gastro-Enterologie — Congr Int Assoc Soc Natl Eur Mediterr Gastro Enterol
Congres International da Chauffage Industriel. Thermique et Thermodynamique Appliquees. Comptes Rendus — Congr Int Chauffage Ind Therm Thermodyn Appl CR
Congres International d'Anthropologie — CIA
Congres International d'Anthropologie et d'Archeologie Prehistorique — CIAAP
Congres International d'Astronautique. Compte Rendu — Congr Int Astronaut CR
Congres International de Biochimie. Compte Rendu — Congr Int Biochim CR
Congres International de Biochimie. Rapports des Symposiums — Congr Int Biochim Rapp Symp
Congres International de Biochimie. Resumes des Communications — Congr Int Biochim Resumes Commun
Congres International de Botanique. Rapports et Communications — Congr Int Bot Rapp Commun

Congres International de Botanique. Rapports et Communications Parvenus avant le Congres — Congr Int Bot Rapp Commun
Congres International de Chimie Pure et Appliquee — Congr Int Chim Pure Appl
Congres International de Corrosion Metallique — Congr Int Corros Met
Congres International de Cybernetique. Actes — Congr Int Cybern Actes
Congres International de Dermatologie et de Syphilis — Cong Int De Dermat Et De Syph
Congres International de Gastro-Enterologie — Congr Int Gastro Enterol
Congres International de Geographie — CIG
Congres International de Geographie (Cairo) — CIGC
Congres International de Gerontologie — Congr Int Gerontol
Congres International de la Chimie des Ciments. Procedes — Congr Int Chim Cim Proc
Congres International de la Corrosion Marine et des Salissures — Congr Int Corros Mar Salissures
Congres International de la Detergence — Congr Int Deterg
Congres International de la Preparation de Minerais. Compte Rendu — Congr Int Prep Minerais CR
Congres International de la Recherche Textile Lainiere — Congr Int Rech Text Lainiere
Congres International de la Vigne du Vin — CIVTA4
Congres International de la Vigne du Vin — Congr Int Vigne Vin
Congres International de la Vigne et du Vin. Comptes Rendus — Congr Int Vigne Vin CR
Congres International de l'Air Pur. Compte Rendu — Congr Int Air Pur CR
Congres International de Laiterie — Congr Int Lait
Congres International de Laiterie. Rapport du Congres — Congr Int Lait Rapp Congr
Congres International de l'Electrostatique. Comptes Rendus — Congr Int Electrost CR
Congres International de l'Email Vitrifie — Congr Int Email Vitrifie
Congres International de Mecanique des Roches — Congr Int Mec Roches
Congres International de Medecine — Cong Int De Med
Congres International de Medecine. Comptes Rendus — Cong Internat Med C R
Congres International de Medicine du Travail — Congr Int Med Trav
Congres International de Microbiologie. Compte Rendu — Congr Int Microbiol CR
Congres International de Microscopie Electronique. Comptes Rendus — Congr Int Microsc Electron CR
Congres International de Mineralurgie. Compte Rendu — Congr Int Mineralurgie CR
Congres International de Neurologie. Rapports et Discussions — Congr Int Neurol Rapp Discuss
Congres International de Pathologie Infectieuse. Communications — Congr Int Pathol Infect Commun
Congres International de Patologie Infectiouse. Communicari — Congr Int Patol Infect Commun
Congres International de Pharmacie. Comptes Rendus — Congr Int Pharm CR
Congres International de Reproduction Animale et Insemination Artificielle — CIRIBK
Congres International de Reproduction Animale et Insemination Artificielle — Congr Int Reprod Anim Insemin Artif
Congres International de Reproduction Animale et Insemination Artificielle — Congr Int Reprod Anim Insemination Artif
Congres International de Stereologie. Rapport — Congr Int Stereol Rapp
Congres International de Stratigraphie et de Geologie du Carbonifere. Compte Rendu — Congr Int Stratigr Geol Carbonif CR
Congres International de Stratigraphie et de Geologie du Carbonifere. Compte Rendu — Congr Int Stratigr Geol Carbonifere C R
Congres International de Stratigraphie et de Geologie du Carbonifere. Compte Rendu — CSGCAG
Congres International de Technologie Pharmaceutique. Exposes — Congr Int Technol Pharm Expo
Congres International de Therapeutique — Congr Int Ther
Congres International de Therapeutique. Compte Rendu — Congr Int Ther CR
Congres International de Therapeutique. Rapports et Communications — Congr Int Ther Rapp Commun
Congres International d'Electrothermie — Congr Int Electrothermie
Congres International des Huiles Essentielles — Congr Int Huiles Essent
Congres International des Industries Agricoles. Comptes Rendus — Congr Int Ind Agric CR
Congres International des Jus de Fruits — Congr Int Jus Fruits
Congres International des Maladies du Thorax — Congr Int Mal Thorax
Congres International des Metaux Legers — Congr Int Met Legers
Congres International des Sciences Anthropologiques et Ethnologiques — Congr Int Sci Anthropol Ethnol
Congres International des Sciences Neurologiques — Congr Int Sci Neurol
Congres International des Textiles Artificiels et Synthetiques — Congr Int Text Artif Synth
Congres International d'Histochimie et de Cytochimie — Congr Int Histochim Cytochim
Congres International du Beton Manufacture. Comptes Rendus — Congr Int Beton Manuf CR
Congres International du Pain — Congr Int Pain
Congres International du Verre. Communications Artistiques et Historiques — Congr Int Verre Commun Artistiques Hist
Congres International du Verre. Communications Scientifiques et Techniques — Congr Int Verre Commun Sci Tech
Congres International du Verre. Compte Rendu des Travaux — Congr Int Verre CR Trav
Congres International Hydrogene et Materiaux — Congr Int Hydrogene Mater
Congres International Informatique et Genie Chimique — Congr Int Inf Genie Chim
Congres International pour l'Essai des Materiaux — Congr Int Essai Mater
Congres International. Societe Francaise de Radioprotection — Congr Int Soc Fr Radioprot
Congres International sur la Maconnerie en Briques — Congr Int Maconnerie Briques
Congres International sur l'Alteration et la Conservation de la Pierre — Congr Int Alteration Conserv Pierre
Congres International sur le Carbone — Congr Int Carbone
Congres International sur le Colza — Congr Int Colza
Congres International sur le Gaz Naturel Liquefie. Memoires — Congr Int Gaz Nat Liquefie Mem
Congres International sur le Transfert de Chaleur — Congr Int Transfert Chal
Congres International sur les Maladies du Betail — Congr Int Mal Betail
Congres International sur les Phenomenes de Contact Electrique — Congr Int Phenom Contact Electr
Congres International sur l'Optique des Rayons X et la Microanalyse — Congr Int Opt Rayons X Microanal
Congres International Technique et Chimique des Industries Agricoles. Comptes Rendus — Congr Int Tech Chim Ind Agric CR
Congres Mondial d'Alimentation Animale — Congr Mond Aliment Anim
Congres Mondial de la Filtration — Congr Mond Filtr
Congres Mondial de Medecine Aeronautique — Congr Mond Med Aeronaut
Congres Mondial du Petrole. Actes et Documents — Congr Mond Pet Actes Doc
Congres Mondial du Recyclage. Textes de la Conference — Congr Mond Recyclage Textes Conf
Congres Mondial Scientifique du Tabac — Congr Mond Sci Tab
Congres Mondial Veterinaire. Rapports — Congr Mond Vet Rapp
Congres National de l'Electrolyse et des Traitements de Surface — Congr Natl Electrolyse Trait Surf
Congres National des Sciences Medicales. Communications des Invites Etrangers — Congr Natl Sci Med Commun Invites Etrang
Congres National des Societes Savantes. Comptes Rendus. Section des Sciences — Congr Natl Soc Savantes CR Sect Sci
Congres National. Societes Savantes. Section des Sciences. Comptes Rendus — Congr Natl Soc Savantes Sect Sci C R
Congres Pomologique — Congres Pomol
Congres pour l'Avancement des Etudes de Stratigraphie et de Geologie du Carbonifere. Compte Rendu — CGGFA9
Congres pour l'Avancement des Etudes de Stratigraphie et de Geologie du Carbonifere. Compte Rendu — Congr Av Etud Stratigr Geol Carbonif CR
Congres pour l'Avancement des Etudes de Stratigraphie et de Geologie du Carbonifere. Compte Rendu — Congr Av Etud Stratigr Geol Carbonifere C R
Congres Prehistorique de France. Compte Rendu — Congres Prehist France
Congres Prehistorique de France. Compte Rendu — CPF
Congres Scientifique International du Tabac. Actes — Congr Sci Int Tab Actes
Congres Scientifiques de France — Congr Sci France
Congres. Societe Francaise de Physique. Actes — Congr Soc Fr Phys Actes
Congres. Societe Geographique de Paris — CSGP
Congres Technique International de l'Industrie des Peintures et des Industries Associees. Compte Rendu — Congr Tech Int Ind Peint Ind Assoc CR
Congres. Union Therapeutique Internationale. Comptes Rendus — Congr Union Ther Int CR
Congresboek. Wereldcongres voor Oppervlaktebehandeling van Metalen — Congresb Wereldcongr Oppervlaktebehandel Met
Congreso Anual de la Region Tropical. Sociedad Americana de Ciencias Horticolas — Congr Anu Reg Trop Soc Am Cienc Hortic
Congreso Anual. Sociedad Americana de Ciencias Horticolas. Region Tropical — Congr Anu Soc Am Cienc Hortic Reg Trop
Congreso Chileno de Obstetricia y Ginecologia — Congr Chil Obstet Ginecol
Congreso Cientifico Mexicano. Memoria. Ciencias Fisicas y Matematicas — Cong Cient Mexicano Mem Cienc Fisicas y Matematicas
Congreso de Biofarmacia y Farmacocinetica — Congr Biofarm Farmacocinet
Congreso de Quimica del Continente de America del Norte — Congr Quim Cont Am Norte
Congreso Geologico Argentino. Relatorio — Congr Geol Argent Relat
Congreso Ibero Latino Americano de Dermatologia. Memorias — Congr Ibero Lat Am Dermatol Mem
Congreso Ibero-Americano de Geologia Economica — Congr Ibero-Am Geol Econ
Congreso Ibero-Americano de Geologia Economica. La Geologia en el Desarrollo de los Pueblos. Memorias — Congr Ibero Am Geol Econ Mem
Congreso ILAFA [*Instituto Latinoamericano del Fierro y el Acero*]-Colada Continua y Metalurgia en Cuchara — Congr ILAFA Colada Continua Metal Cuchara
Congreso ILAFA-Carbon (Instituto Latinoamericano del Fierro y el Acero) — Congr ILAFA Carbon
Congreso Internacional de Ciencias Fisiologicas. Simposios y Conferencias — Congr Int Cienc Fisiol Simp Conf
Congreso Internacional de Corrosion Marina e Incrustaciones — Congr Int Corros Mar Incrustaciones
Congreso Internacional de Estudios Pirenaicos. Resumen de las Comunicaciones — Congr Int Estud Pirenaicos Resumen Comun
Congreso Internacional de Geoquimica Organica. Actas — Congr Int Geoquim Org Actas
Congreso Internacional de Hematologia. Conferencias — CIHMBG
Congreso Internacional de Hematologia. Conferencias — Congr Int Hematol Conf
Congreso Internacional de Industrias Agricolas. Actas — Congr Int Ind Agric Actas
Congreso Internacional de la Leche y Sus Derivados — Congr Int Leche Sus Deriv
Congreso Internacional de Pediatria — Congr Int Pediatr
Congreso Internacional Sobre Salud Ocupacional — Congr Int Salud Ocup
Congreso Latinoamericano de Petroquimica — Congr Latinoam Petroquim
Congreso Latinoamericano de Siderurgia. Memoria Tecnica — Congr Latinoam Sider Mem Tec

Congreso Mundial de Etologia Aplicade a la Zootecnia. Sesiones Plenarias y Mesas Redondas — Congr Mund Etol Apl Zootec Ses Plenarias Mesas Redondas
Congreso Mundial de Gastroenterologia. Informe — Congr Mund Gastroenterol Inf
Congreso Mundial de la Investigacion Agronomica — Congr Mund Invest Agron
Congreso Mundial sobre Contaminacion del Aire. Actas — Congr Mund Contam Aire Actas
Congreso Nacional de Biofarmacia y Farmacocinetica. Actas — Congr Nac Biofarm Farmacocinet Actas
Congreso Nacional de Ciencia y Technologia Metalurgicas — Congr Nac Cienc Tecnol Metal
Congreso Nacional de Farmaceuticos en la Industria. Actas — Congr Nac Farm Ind Actas
Congreso Nacional de Metalurgia. Anales — Congr Nac Metal An
Congreso Nacional de Petroquimica — Congr Nac Petroquim
Congreso Nacional de Tuberculosis y Enfermedades Respiratorias — CNTEBJ
Congreso Nacional de Tuberculosis y Enfermedades Respiratorias — Congr Nac Tuberc Enferm Respir
Congreso Venezolano de Cirugia — Congr Venez Cir
Congreso Venezolano de Cirugia — CVZOAW
Congress and the Presidency — Cong and Presidency
Congress Bi-Weekly — CBW
Congress Chemistry in Agriculture — Congr Chem Agric
Congress. Collegium Internationale Neuro-Psychopharmacologicum. Proceedings — Congr Coll Int Neuro Psychopharmacol Proc
Congress. Council of Mining and Metallurgical Institutions — Congr Counc Min Metall Inst
Congress. European Association for Research on Plant Breeding — Congr Eur Assoc Res Plant Breed
Congress. European Federation of Corrosion — Congr Eur Fed Corros
Congress. European Society for Experimental Surgery. Abstracts — Congr Eur Soc Exp Surg Abst
Congress. European Society for Photobiology — Congr Eur Soc Photobiol
Congress. European Society of Parenteral and Enteral Nutrition — Congr Eur Soc Parenter Enteral Nutr
Congress. Federation Europeenne de la Corrosion. Preprints — Congr Fed Eur Corros Prepr
Congress. Federation of Asian and Oceanian Biochemists. Proceedings — Congr Fed Asian Oceanian Biochem Proc
Congress. German Society of Hematology — Congr Ger Soc Hematol
Congress. Hungarian Pharmacological Society. Proceedings — Congr Hung Pharmacol Soc Pro
Congress in Print — Congr Print
Congress. International Association of Seed Crushers — Congr Int Ass Seed Crushers
Congress. International Commission for Optics — Congr Int Comm Opt
Congress. International Council. Aeronautical Sciences — Congr Int Counc Aeronaut Sci
Congress. International Potash Institute — Congr Int Potash Inst
Congress. International Primatological Society — Congr Int Primatol Soc
Congress. International Radiation Protection Society — Congr Int Radiat Prot Soc
Congress. International Society for the Study of Hypertension in Pregnancy — Congr Int Soc Study Hypertens Pregnancy
Congress. International Society of Blood Transfusion — Congr Int Soc Blood Transfus
Congress. International Solar Energy Society — Congr Int Sol Energy Soc
Congress. International Union for Electrodeposition and Surface Finishing. Proceedings — Congr Int Union Electrodeposition Surf Finish Proc
Congress. International Union of Physiological Sciences — Congr Int Union Physiol Sci
Congress. Italian Association for the Study of the Liver — Congr Ital Assoc Study Liver
Congress. Leather Industry — Congr Leather Ind
Congress Monthly — Cong M
Congress of Bulgarian Microbiologists — Congr Bulg Microbiol
Congress of Developmental and Comparative Immunology — Congr Dev Comp Immunol
Congress of Heterocyclic Chemistry — Congr Heterocycl Chem
Congress of International Federation of Societies of Cosmetic Chemists. Preprint of Scientific Papers — Congr Int Fed Soc Cosmet Chem Prepr Sci Pap
Congress of Microbiology. Materials. Congress of Bulgarian Microbiologists — Congr Microbiol Mater Congr Bulg Microbiol
Congress of Queensland Cooperatives. Papers and Proceedings — Cong of Q Coop
Congress on Developments in Biophysical Methods — Congr Dev Biophys Methods
Congress on Material Testing — Congr Mater Test
Congress on Material Testing. Lectures — Congr Mater Test Lect
Congress on Occupational Health — Congr Occup Health
Congress Proceedings. International Congress on Animal Reproduction and Artificial Insemination — Congr Proc Int Congr Anim Reprod Artif Insemin
Congress Proceedings. Recycling World Congress — Congr Proc Recycl World Congr
Congress Series. Sudan Medical Association — Congr Ser Sudan Med Assoc
Congress. Society for Forensic Haemogenetics — Congr Soc Forensic Haemogenet
Congress Weekly — Con W
Congress Weekly (New York) — CWN
Congress. World Federation of Hemophilia — Congr World Fed Hemophilia
Congressi. Convegni e Simposi Scientifici. Consiglio Nazionale delle Richerche — Congr Conv Simp Sci CNR
Congressi Italiani di Medicina — CMDCDU
Congressi Italiani di Medicina — Congr Ital Med
Congressi, Mostra Internazionale delle Industrie per le Conserve Alimentari — Congr Mostra Int Ind Conserve Aliment
Congressional Digest — Cong Dig
Congressional Digest — Cong Digest
Congressional Digest — Congr Dig
Congressional Digest — GCON
Congressional Globe — Cong Globe
Congressional Quarterly. Weekly Report — Cong Q W Rept
Congressional Quarterly Weekly Report — GCQW
Congressional Record — Cong Rec
Congressional Record — Congr Rec
Congressional Record [*United States*] — CR
Congressional Record. Daily Edition [*US*] — Congr Rec Dly
Congressional Studies — Congress St
Congressional Yellow Book — Congr Yellow Book
Congresso Anual da ABM [*Associacao Brasileira de Metais*] — Congr Anu ABM
Congresso Brasileiro de Apicultura — Congr Bras Apic
Congresso Brasileiro de Ceramica — Congr Bras Ceram
Congresso Brasileiro de Energia — Congr Bras Energ
Congresso Brazileiro de Geografia — Cong Braz De Geog
Congresso de Historia Nacional. Annaes — Cong De Hist Nac Annaes
Congresso della Associazione Internazionale di Gerontologia — Congr Assoc Int Gerontol
Congresso di Scienze Farmaceutiche. Conferenze e Comunicazioni — Congr Sci Farm Conf Comun
Congresso do Mundo Portugues — CMP
Congresso e Exposicao Regional das Beiras — CERB
Congresso Europeo di Medicina Aeronautica e Spaziale — Congr Eur Med Aeronaut Spaz
Congresso Internacional de Filosofia. Anais (Sao Paulo) — CIF-SP
Congresso Internacional de Oleos Essenciais — Congr Int Oleos Essenc
Congresso Internacional de Quimica do Cimento. Anais — Congr Int Quim Cimento An
Congresso Internationale della Fucinatura — Congr Int Fucinatura
Congresso Internazionale di Panificazione. Atti — Congr Int Panif Atti
Congresso Internazionale di Studi sul Carciofo — Congr Int Studi Carciofo
Congresso Internazionale per le Malattie Infettive. Communicazioni — Congr Int Mal Infett Commun
Congresso Internazionale sui Fenomeni d'Ionizzazione nei Gas. Rendiconti — Congr Int Fenom Ioniz Gas Rend
Congresso Internazionale sul Latte e Derivati — Congr Int Latte Deriv
Congresso Luso-Espanhol de Farmacia — Congr Luso Esp Farm
Congresso Mondiale della Sperimentazione Agraria — Congr Mond Sper Agrar
Congresso Nazionale. Associazione Italiana di Fisica Sanitaria e di Protezione contro le Radiazioni. Atti — Congr Naz Assoc Ital Fis Sanit Prot Radiaz Atti
Congresso Nazionale dei Chimici dei Laboratori Provinciali di Igiene Profilassi — Congr Naz Chim Lab Prov Ig Profil
Congresso Nazionale di Chimica Inorganica. Atti — Congr Naz Chim Inorg Atti
Congresso Nazionale di Fisica. Communicazioni — Congr Naz Fis Commun
Congresso Nazionale di Storia dell'Arte — Congr Naz Stor Arte
Congresso Nazionale. Societa Italiana per gli Studi sulla Fertilita e la Sterilita. Atti — Congr Naz Soc Ital Studi Fertil Steril Atti
Congresso Nucleare — Congr Nucl
Congresso Nucleare. Atti Ufficiali. Congresso Internazionale per l'Energia Nucleare — Congr Nucl Atti Uffic Congr Int Energ Nucl
Congresso Nucleare di Roma. Atti — Congr Nucl Roma Atti
Congresso Ribatejano Santarem — CR
Congressus Internationalis Dermatologiae — Congr Int Dermatol
Congressus Morphologicus Symposia — Congr Morphol Symp
Congressus Numerantium — Congr Numer
Congressus Numerantium — Congress Numer
Conjonction. Institut Francais d'Haiti — IFH/C
Conjoncture Economique au Maroc — Conjoncture Econ Maroc
Conjoncture Economique Lorraine — Conjonct Econ Lorr
Conjoncture Economique Marocaine — Conjonct Econ Maroc
Conjugated Plant Hormones. Structure, Metabolism, and Function. Proceedings. International Symposium — Conjugated Plant Horm Proc Int Symp
Conjugation Reactions in Drug Biotransformation. Proceedings. Symposium — Conjugation React Drug Biotransform Proc Symp
Conjunctuur — CQK
Conjuntura Economica — CJU
Conjuntura Economica — Conjunt Econ
Conjuntura Economica — Conjuntura Econ
Connaissance de la Loire — Connaiss Loire
Connaissance de la Vigne et du Vin — Connaiss Vigne Vin
Connaissance de la Vigne et du Vin — CVVIDV
Connaissance des Arts — C Art
Connaissance des Arts — Conn Arts
Connaissance des Arts — Connais Art
Connaissance des Arts — Connaiss Arts
Connaissance des Plastiques — Connaiss Plast
Connaissance d'Israel — Conn Israel
Connaitre le Sous-Sol. Un Atout pour l'Amenagement Urbain. Colloque National — Connaitre Sous Sol Atout Amenagement Urbain Colloq Natl
Connchord — CH
Connecticut Academy of Arts and Sciences. Memoirs (New Haven) — Conn Acad Arts & Sci Mem (New Haven)
Connecticut Academy of Arts and Sciences. Transactions — Conn Acad Arts & Sci Trans
Connecticut. Agricultural Experiment Station. Bulletin [*New Haven*] — CNABAG
Connecticut. Agricultural Experiment Station. Bulletin [*New Haven*] — Conn Agr Expt Sta Bull

Connecticut. Agricultural Experiment Station. Bulletin (New Haven) — Conn Agric Exp Stn Bull (New Haven)
Connecticut. Agricultural Experiment Station. Circular [*New Haven*] — CNACAJ
Connecticut. Agricultural Experiment Station. Circular (New Haven) — Conn Agric Exp Stn (New Haven) Circ
Connecticut. Agricultural Experiment Station. Department of Entomology. Special Bulletin — CESBBA
Connecticut. Agricultural Experiment Station. Department of Entomology. Special Bulletin — Conn Agric Exp Stn Dep Entomol Spec Bull
Connecticut Agricultural Experiment Station. Forestry Publication — Connecticut Agric Exp Sta Forest Publ
Connecticut. Agricultural Experiment Station (Storrs). Miscellaneous Publication — Conn Agric Exp Stn (Storrs) Misc Publ
Connecticut. Agricultural Experiment Station (Storrs). Research Report — Conn Agric Exp Stn (Storrs) Res Rep
Connecticut Appellate Reports — Conn App
Connecticut Arboretum Bulletin — BCARDD
Connecticut Arboretum Bulletin — Conn Arbor Bull
Connecticut Bar Journal — CBJ
Connecticut Bar Journal — Con BJ
Connecticut Bar Journal — Conn B J
Connecticut Bar Journal — Conn Bar J
Connecticut Business — Conn Busn
Connecticut Circuit Court Reports — Conn Cir Ct
Connecticut General Statutes, Annotated (West) — Conn Gen Stat Ann (West)
Connecticut. Geological and Natural History Survey. Bulletin — Conn Geol Natur Hist Surv Bull
Connecticut Government — Conn Govt
Connecticut Greenhouse Newsletter. University of Connecticut. Cooperative Extension Service — Conn Greenhouse Newsl Univ Conn Coop Ext Ser
Connecticut Health Bulletin — Conn Health Bull
Connecticut Health Bulletin — Conn Hlth Bull
Connecticut Historical Society. Bulletin — CHSB
Connecticut Historical Society Bulletin — ConHS
Connecticut Historical Society. Bulletin — Conn Hist Soc Bull
Connecticut Historical Society. Bulletin — ConnHSB
Connecticut Historical Society. Collections — Conn His S
Connecticut Historical Society. Collections — Conn Hist Soc Coll
Connecticut Industry — Conn Ind
Connecticut Labor Department. Bulletin — Conn Lab Dep Bull
Connecticut Law Journal — Conn LJ
Connecticut Law Review — Con L Rev
Connecticut Law Review — Con LR
Connecticut Law Review — Conn L Rev
Connecticut Law Review — Conn LR
Connecticut Law Review — Connecticut L Rev
Connecticut Legislative Service — Conn Legis Serv
Connecticut Libraries — Conn Lib
Connecticut Library Association. Bulletin — Conn Lib Assn Bul
Connecticut Magazine [*New Haven*] — Conn M
Connecticut Medicine — CNMEAH
Connecticut Medicine — Conn Med
Connecticut Medicine — Connecticut Med
Connecticut Medicine Journal — Conn Med J
Connecticut. Mineral Folios — Conn Mineral Folio
Connecticut Nursing News — Conn Nurs News
Connecticut Occupational Therapy Bulletin — Con Occup Ther Bull
Connecticut Periodical Index — Conn Per Ind
Connecticut Public Acts — Conn Pub Acts
Connecticut Public and Special Acts (Regular and Special Sessions) — Conn Acts (Reg Spec Sess)
Connecticut Reports — Conn
Connecticut Review — Conn R
Connecticut Review — Conn Rev
Connecticut Special Acts — Conn Spec Acts
Connecticut. State Agricultural Experiment Station. Publications — Conn State Ag Exp
Connecticut. State Geological and Natural History Survey. Bulletin — Conn State Geol Nat Hist Surv Bull
Connecticut. State Geological and Natural History Survey. Miscellaneous Series — Conn State Geol Nat Hist Surv Misc Ser
Connecticut. State Geological and Natural History Survey. Quadrangle Report — Conn State Geol Nat Hist Surv Quadrangle Rep
Connecticut. State Geological and Natural History Survey. Report of Investigations — Conn State Geol Nat Hist Surv Rep Invest
Connecticut State Medical Journal — Conn State Med J
Connecticut State Medical Journal — CSMJAX
Connecticut. Storrs Agricultural Experiment Station. Bulletin — CNBUAA
Connecticut. Storrs Agricultural Experiment Station. Bulletin — Conn Storrs Agric Exp Stn Bull
Connecticut. Storrs Agricultural Experiment Station. Miscellaneous Publication — Conn Storrs Agric Exp Stn Misc Publ
Connecticut. Storrs Agricultural Experiment Station. Progress Report — CAXPAE
Connecticut. Storrs Agricultural Experiment Station. Progress Report — Conn Storrs Agric Exp Stn Prog Rep
Connecticut. Storrs Agricultural Experiment Station. Research Report — CASRBU
Connecticut. Storrs Agricultural Experiment Station. Research Report — Conn Storrs Agric Exp Stn Res Rep
Connecticut. Storrs Agricultural Station. Bulletin — Conn Storrs Agric Stn Bull
Connecticut Supplement — Conn Supp
Connecticut. University. Agricultural Experiment Station. Research Report — Conn Univ Agric Exp Stn Res Rep
Connecticut. University Engineering Experiment Station. Bulletin — Conn Univ Eng Exp Stn Bull
Connecticut Urban Research Report — Conn Urban Res Rep
Connecticut Vegetable Growers' Association. Proceedings. Annual Meeting — Conn Veg Grow Assoc Proc Annual Meet
Connecticut Water Resources Bulletin — Conn Water Resour Bull
Connecticut Water Resources Bulletin — Connecticut Water Resources Bull
Connecticut Water Resources Bulletin — CWCBAL
Connecticut Water Resources Commission. Connecticut Water Resources Bulletin — Conn Water Res Comm Conn Water Res Bull
Connecticut Woodlands — Conn Woodl
Connecticut Woodlands — Conn Woodlands
Connecticut Woodlands — CWODAJ
Connections Journal — Connections J
Connective Tissue — Connect Tissue
Connective Tissue Diseases — Connect Tissue Dis
Connective Tissue Research — Conn Tiss Res
Connective Tissue Research — Connect Tis
Connective Tissue Research — Connect Tissue Res
Connective Tissue Research — CVTRBC
Connective Tissue Research. Chemistry, Biology, and Physiology. Proceedings. European Connective Tissue Clubs Meeting — Connect Tissue Res Proc Eur Connect Tissue Clubs Meet
Connective Tissues — Conn Tiss
Connective Tissues. Biochemistry and Pathophysiology — Connect Tissues Biochem Pathophysiol
Connective Tissues. Transactions. Conference — Connect Tissues Trans Conf
Connector Symposium. Proceedings — Connector Symp Proc
Connexions — Conn
Connoisseur — Conn
Connoisseur — ICON
Connotation — Conn
Conquest — CONQAV
Conquest — Conqu
Conquest. Journal of the Research Defence Society — Conquest J Res Def Soc
Conquest of Bacterial Disease. Dr. Albert Wander-Gedenkvorlesung — Conquest Bact Dis Dr Albert Wander Gedenkvorlesung
Conradiana — Conrad
CONRIM [*Committee on Natural Resource Information Management*] **Newsletter** [*Anchorage, Alaska*] — CNRM
Consciousness and Cognition — Conscious Cogn
Consecrated Life — Con Life
Conseil de la Recherche et du Developpement Forestiers du Quebec. Etude — Cons Rech Dev For Que Etude
Conseil de la Recherche et du Developpement Forestiers du Quebec. Etude — ECRQDQ
Conseil Economique Wallon. Revue — Cons Econ Wallon R
Conseil General des Peches pour la Mediterranee, Debata et Documents Techniques — Cons Gen Peches Mediterr Debata Doc Tech
Conseil International de Chimie — Conseil Int Chim
Conseil International pour l'Exploration de la Mer. Bulletin Statistique des Peches Maritimes — Con Int Explor Mer Bull Stat Peches Marit
Conseil International pour l'Exploration de la Mer. Bulletin Statistique des Peches Maritimes — Cons Int Explor Mer Bull Stat Peches Marit
Conseil International pour l'Exploration de la Mer. Bulletin Statistique des Peches Maritimes — CSPMBO
Conseil International pour l'Exploration de la Mer. Zooplankton Sheet — CIZSAL
Conseil International pour l'Exploration de la Mer. Zooplankton Sheet — Cons Int Explor Mer Zooplankton Sheet
Conseil National de Recherches Canada. Programme de Standards de Chimie Analytique Marine. Rapport — Cons Natl Rech Can Programme Stand Chim Anal Mar Rapp
Conseil National de Recherches du Canada. Bulletin — Cons Natl Rech Can Bull
Conseil National de Recherches du Canada. Division de Genie Mecanique. Rapport Technique de Laboratoire — Cons Natl Rech Can Div Genie Mec Rapp Tech Lab
Conseil National de Recherches du Canada. Rapport Annuel — Cons Natl Rech Can Rapp Annu
Conseil Permanent International Pour l'Exploration de la Mer — Cons Perm
Conseil Permanent International pour l'Exploration de la Mer. Journal du Conseil — Journ Cons
Conseil Scientifique International de Recherche sur les Trypanosomiases et leur Controle — Cons Sci Int Rech Trypanosomiases Controle
Conseil Scientifique International de Recherches sur les Trypanosomiases — Cons Sci Int Rech Trypanosomiases
Conseil Scientifique International de Recherches sur les Trypanosomiases — ITRMB5
Conseil Scientifique International de Recherches sur les Trypanosomiases et leur Controle — PUCODM
Conseil Scientifique pour l'Afrique au Sud du Sahara. Publication — Cons Sci Afr Sud Sahara Publ
Conseiller du Commerce Exterieur [*Paris*] — CCM
Conseiller du Commerce Exterieur — Cons Com Ext
Conseiller du Commerce Exterieur — Cons Com Exter
Consejo de Recursos Minerales. Boletin de Informacion — CRM Boletin de Informacion
Consejo de Recursos Naturales No Renovables. Publicacion (Mexico) — Cons Recur Nat No Renov Publ (Mex)
Consejo Superior de Investigaciones Cientificas. Biblioteca General. Boletin [*Madrid*] — Consejo Sup Invest Cient Bibl Bol
Consejo Superior de Investigaciones Cientificas. Centro de Edafologia y Biologia Aplicada. Anuario — CSIC Cent Edafol Biol Apl Anu

Consejo Superior de Investigaciones Cientificas. Estudios Geologicos [*Madrid*] — CSIC Estud Geol
Consejo Superior de Investigaciones Cientificas. Patronato Juan De La Cierva de Investigaciones Tecnicas. Cuaderno — CSIC Patronato Juan De La Cierva Invest Tec Cuad
Conselho Estadual de Cultura — CEC
Consensus Development Conference Summaries. National Institutes of Health — Consensus Dev Conf Summ Natl Inst Health
Consensus. Informatietijdschrift over Energie Mol — CEU
Conservation and Productivity of Natural Waters. Proceedings. Symposium — Conserv Prod Nat Waters Proc Symp
Conservation and Recycling — Conserv & Recycling
Conservation and Recycling — Conserv Recycl
Conservation and Recycling [*England*] — Conserv Recycling
Conservation and Recycling — CRECD
Conservation and Recycling — CRECD2
Conservation Canada — COCA
Conservation Foundation Letter — Conserv Found Lett
Conservation Foundation Letter — Conservation Found Letter
Conservation Magazine — Conserv M
Conservation News — Conserv News
Conservation News. National Wildlife Federation — CONS
Conservation of Cotton — Conserv Cotton
Conservation of Nature [*Japan*] — Conserv Nat
Conservation of Stone. Proceedings. International Symposium — Conserv Stone Proc Int Symp
Conservation Paper — Conserv Pap
Conservation Research Report. United States Department of Agriculture — Conserv Res Rep US Dep Agric
Conservation Research Report. United States Department of Agriculture. Agricultural Research Service — Conserv Res Rep US Dep Agric Agric Res Serv
Conservation Research Report. US Agricultural Research Service — Conserv Res Rep US Agr Res Serv
Conservation Series. Department of the Capital Territory — Conser Ser Dep Cap T
Conservation Series. Department of the Capital Territory — Conserv Ser Dep Cap T
Conservation Volunteer — Conserv Volunteer
Conservationist — CNSVAU
Conservationist — Conserv
Conservationist — GTCO
Conservative Digest — GCDI
Conservative Judaism — CJ
Conservative Judaism — Cons Jud
Conservative Review — Conserv R
Conservator. Vaktijdschrift voor de lisfrica Branche — CON
Conserve e Derivati Agrumari — CDAPAM
Conserve e Derivati Agrumari — Conserve Deriv Agrum
Conserver Society Notes [*Canada*] — Conserver Soc Notes
Consfatuire de Sudura si Incercari de Metale — Consfatuire Sudura Incercari Met
Consigna — Cons
Consolidacao das Leis do Trabalho [*Brazil*] — CLT
Consolidated Freight Classification — Consol Frt Classif
Consolidated Regulations of Canada — Can Cons Regs
Consommation — ANK
Consortium Newsletter — Consort Newsl
Consortium Quarterly — Consortium Q
Conspectus of History — Conspect Hist
Constituicao, Endocrinologie, e Metabolismo — Const Endocr Metab
Constituicao Federal [*Brazil*] — CF
Constitution and Properties of Steels — Const Prop Steels
Constitution Federale [*Switzerland*] — CST
Constitutional Acts of Canada [*Database*] — CAC
Constitutional and Parliamentary Information — Constitutional and Parliamentary Info
Construccion Arquitectura Urbanismo — CAU
Constructeur. Vaktijdschrift voor het Werktuigbouwkundig Construeren naar Functie, Vorm, en Kostprijs — GIE
Constructia de Masini — Constr Mas
Constructia de Masini — Constru Masini
Constructii (Bucharest) — CNTIB
Constructing in Steel. The User and the Maker. Proceedings. Conference — Constr Steel User Maker Proc Conf
Construction — Constr
Construction and Engineering [*Philippines*] — CE
Construction and Road Transport — Constr Road Trans
Construction Contracting — Constr Contracting
Construction Engineering Research Laboratory. Technical Report — Constr Eng Res Lab Tech Rep
Construction Equipment News — CEN
Construction Glues for Plywood, Laminating, Prefabricating, Joining, and Assembly — Constr Glues Plywood Laminating Prefabricating Joining Assem
Construction in Hawaii — Cons Hawai
Construction in Southern Africa — Constr S Afr
Construction in Southern Africa — Constr South Afr
Construction in Southern Africa — Constr Sthn Afr
Construction Industry Forecast — Constr Frct
Construction Industry Manufacturers Association. Outlook — CIMA Outlk
Construction Lawyer — Construction Law
Construction Machinery [*Japan*] — Constr Mach
Construction Machinery and Equipment — Constr Mach Equip
Construction Management — CM
Construction Mechanization (Tokyo) — Constr Mech (Tokyo)
Construction Metallique — Constr Met
Construction Metallique — Constr Metal
Construction Methods — Constr Meth
Construction Methods and Equipment — Constr Methods Equip
Construction Navale en Commposites. Colloque — Constr Nav Compos Colloq
Construction News — Constr News
Construction News (London) — Constr News (London)
Construction News Magazine — CNMAD
Construction News Magazine [*England*] — Constr News Mag
Construction News Magazine — Constr News Magazine
Construction Papers — Constr Paps
Construction Plant and Equipment — Constr Plant & Equip
Construction Plant and Equipment — Constr Plant Equip
Construction References — Constr Ref
Construction Reports. C22-83-9. Housing Completions — C22-83-9
Construction Reports. C25-83-9. New One-Family Houses Sold and for Sale — C25-83-9
Construction Reports. C40-85-5. Housing Units Authorized by Building Permits and Public Contracts — C40-85-5
Construction Review — Const Rev
Construction Review — Constr R
Construction Review — Constr Rev
Construction Review — Construction R
Construction Review — CORE
Construction Review — CRE
Construction Specifier — Constr Specifier
Construction Technical Bulletin — Constr Tech Bull
Constructional Review — Constr Rev
Constructional Review — Constrl Rev
Constructional Review — Constructional R
Constructional Review. Technical Supplement — Constrl Rev Tech Suppl
Construction-Amenagement — Construct-Amenag
Constructive Approximation — Constr Approx
Constructive Quarterly — Constr Q
Construire — Constr
Consudel. Maandblad voor de Benelux, Gewijd aan de Belangen van Industrie en Handel op het Gebied van Cacao, Chocolade, Suikerwerken, Koek, Banket, Biscuit Enz — CNF
Consultant [*Philadelphia*] — CNSLAY
Consultants and Consulting Organizations Directory [*Database*] — CCOD
Consultants News — CN
Consultatio de Universali Commercio Litterario — Consultatio Universali Commercio Litt
Consultation on Genetic Predisposition to Toxic Effects of Chemicals — Consult Genet Predispos Toxic Eff Chem
Consulting Engineer — Consult En
Consulting Engineer — Consult Eng
Consulting Engineer — Consult Engr
Consulting Engineer (Barrington, Illinois) — Consult Eng (Barrington, Illinois)
Consulting Engineer (London) — Consult Eng (London)
Consulting Engineer (St. Joseph, Michigan) — Consult Eng (St Joseph Mich)
Consultor Bibliografico (Mexico) — Consultor Bibliogr Mex
Consumentengids — CMG
Consumer Affairs Newsletter — Consum Aff Newsl
Consumer Briefing Summary — Consum Brief Summ
Consumer Buying Prospects — Consumer Buying Prosp
Consumer Credit Letter [*Database*] — CCL
Consumer Credit Letter — Consum Credit Let
Consumer Drug Information [*Database*] — CDIF
Consumer Electronics — CE
Consumer Electronics Annual Review — Consmr Elc
Consumer Guide Magazine — ICGM
Consumer Health Perspectives — Consum Health Perspect
Consumer Law Today — Cons L Today
Consumer Liaison Service Leaflet CSIRO [*Commonwealth Scientific and Industrial Research Organisation*]. Division of Food Research — CSIRO Consumer Liaison Ser Leaflet
Consumer Markets Update — Consum Mark Upd
Consumer News — Cons N
Consumer News — Consumer N
Consumer Price Index [*Database*] — CPI
Consumer Reports — Cons Rep
Consumer Reports — Consmr Rpt
Consumer Reports — Consum Rep
Consumer Reports — Consumer Rep
Consumer Reports — CR
Consumer Reports — CRF
Consumer Reports — GCOR
Consumer Reports Buying Guide — Consmr BG
Consumer Reports (Consumers Union of United States, Inc.) — Consum Rep (Consum Union US)
Consumer Research Bulletin — CR
Consumer's Digest — GCOD
Consumer's Index — Consum Ind
Consumers Index to Product Evaluations and Information Sources — Consum Index Prod Eval Inf Source
Consumers' Research Magazine — Con Res Mag
Consumers' Research Magazine — Cons Res Mag
Consumers' Research Magazine — Consum Res Mag
Consumers' Research Magazine — Consumers Res Mag
Consumers' Research Magazine — CSU
Consumers' Research Magazine — GCRM
Contabilidad. Administracion — Contabilidad Admin
Contabilidad y Finanzas — CyF
Contact — CNTA
Contact — Con

Contact [*Canadian Studies Foundation*] — Cont
Contact and Intraocular Lens Medical Journal — CILJDT
Contact and Intraocular Lens Medical Journal — Contact Intraocul Lens Med J
Contact Dermatitis — CODEDG
Contact. Journal of Urban and Environmental Affairs — CJUADK
Contact. Journal of Urban and Environmental Affairs — CONT
Contact. Journal of Urban and Environmental Affairs — Contact J Urban Environ Aff
Contact Lens Medical Bulletin — CNLMA2
Contact Lens Medical Bulletin — Contact Lens Med Bull
Contact Lens Society of America. Journal — CLSOAT
Contact Lens Society of America. Journal — Contact Lens Soc Am J
Contact List of Electronic Music [*Canada (already exists in GUS II database)*] — CLEM
Contacto (Uruguay) — COU
Container News — CWA
Containerisation International — Containerisation Int
Containers and Packaging — Cont & Packag
Containment and Dispersion of Gases by Water Sprays — Containment Dispersion Gases Water Sprays
Contaminacion Ambiental — CONAEL
Contaminacion Ambiental — Contam Ambiental
Contaminacion y Prevencion — Contam Prev
Contaminacion y Prevencion — CyP
Contaminants and Sediments — Contam Sediments
Contamination Control — CNCNAS
Contamination Control — Contam Control
Contamination Control. Biomedical Environments — CCBEA
Contamination Control. Biomedical Environments — CCBEAL
Contamination Control. Biomedical Environments — Contam Control Biomed Environ
Contemplative Review — Contemp Rev
Contemporaneo — Contemp
Contemporaries and Makers — CM
Contemporary Administrator — Contemp Adm
Contemporary Administrator for Long-Term Care — Contemp Adm Long Term Care
Contemporary Agriculture — Contemp Agric
Contemporary Agriculture — SAPOAB
Contemporary Anesthesia Practice — Contemp Anesth Pract
Contemporary Asia Review — Contemp As R
Contemporary Australian Management — CAM
Contemporary Biophysics — Contemp Biophys
Contemporary China — CC
Contemporary China — Contemp China
Contemporary Concepts in Physics — Contemp Concepts Phys
Contemporary Crises — Cont Crises
Contemporary Crises — Contemp Crises
Contemporary Drug Problems — Cont Drug P
Contemporary Drug Problems — Contemp Drug
Contemporary Drug Problems — Contemp Drug Prob
Contemporary Drug Problems — Contemp Drug Problems
Contemporary Drug Problems — PCDP
Contemporary Education — Cont Ed
Contemporary Education — Cont Educ
Contemporary Education — Contemp Ed
Contemporary Education — Contemp Educ
Contemporary Education Review — Contemp Educ Rev
Contemporary Educational Psychology — Contemp Educ Psychol
Contemporary Endocrinology — Contemp Endocrinol
Contemporary Evaluation Research — Contemp Eval Res
Contemporary French Civilization — CFC
Contemporary French Civilization — Cont Fr Civ
Contemporary Hematology/Oncology — CHONDF
Contemporary Hematology/Oncology — Contemp Hematol Oncol
Contemporary Indian Literature — CIL
Contemporary Inorganic Materials. Proceedings. German-Yugoslav Meeting on Materials Science and Development — Contemp Inorg Mater Proc Ger Yugosl Meet
Contemporary Inorganic Materials. Proceedings. Yugoslav-German Meeting on Materials Science and Development — Contemp Inorg Mater Proc Yugosl Ger Meet Mater Sci Dev
Contemporary Issues in Clinical Biochemistry — Contemp Issues Clin Biochem
Contemporary Issues in Clinical Nutrition — CICNEV
Contemporary Issues in Clinical Nutrition — Contemp Issues Clin Nutr
Contemporary Issues in Infectious Diseases — Contemp Issues Infect Dis
Contemporary Issues in Nephrology — Contemp Issues Nephrol
Contemporary Issues in Small Animal Practice — Contemp Issue Small Anim Pract
Contemporary Japan — CJ
Contemporary Japan — CJap
Contemporary Japanese Agriculture/Atarashi Nihon No Nogoyo — Contemp Jap Agric
Contemporary Jewish Record [*New York*] — CJR
Contemporary Jewish Record — Cont Jew Rec
Contemporary Jewish Record — Contemp Jewish Rec
Contemporary Keyboard — Cont Keybd
Contemporary Literature — ConL
Contemporary Literature — ConLit
Contemporary Literature — Cont Lit
Contemporary Literature — Contemp Lit
Contemporary Literature — PCYL
Contemporary Longterm Care — Contemp Longterm Care
Contemporary Marxism — Cont Marx
Contemporary Marxism — Contemp M
Contemporary Mathematicians — Contemp Mathematicians
Contemporary Metabolism — Contemp Metab
Contemporary Microbial Ecology. Proceedings. International Symposium on Microbial Ecology — Contemp Microb Ecol Proc Int Symp
Contemporary Music Review — Cont Mus R
Contemporary Musicians — CM
Contemporary Nephrology — Contemp Nephrol
Contemporary Neurology Series — Contemp Neurol Ser
Contemporary Nursing Series — Contemp Nurs Ser
Contemporary Nutrition — Contemp Nutr
Contemporary Ob/Gyn — Contemp Ob Gyn
Contemporary Ophthalmology — Contemp Ophthalmol
Contemporary Orthopaedics — Contemp Orthop
Contemporary Orthopaedics — CORTDT
Contemporary Pharmacy Practice — Contemp Pharm Pract
Contemporary Philosophy — Cont Philos
Contemporary Physics — Cont Phys
Contemporary Physics — Contemp Phys
Contemporary Physics — ICPH
Contemporary Physics. Trieste Symposium. Proceedings. International Symposium on Contemporary Physics. International Centre for Theoretical Physics — Contemp Phys Trieste Symp Proc Int Symp
Contemporary Poetry — Con P
Contemporary Poetry — Cont P
Contemporary Poetry and Prose — CPP
Contemporary Poland — CNM
Contemporary Poland — Contemp Poland
Contemporary Politics — Contemp Polit
Contemporary Problems in Cardiology — Contemp Probl Cardiol
Contemporary Psychoanalysis — Cont Psycha
Contemporary Psychoanalysis — Contemp Psychoanal
Contemporary Psychoanalysis — CPPSBL
Contemporary Psychology — Cont Psycho
Contemporary Psychology — Contemp Psychol
Contemporary Psychology — CP
Contemporary Psychology — CPJ
Contemporary Radiology — Contemp Rad
Contemporary Religions in Japan — CRJ
Contemporary Research Topics in Nuclear Physics. Proceedings. Workshop — Contemp Res Top Nucl Phys Proc Workshop
Contemporary Review — ConR
Contemporary Review — Cont R
Contemporary Review — Contemp
Contemporary Review — Contemp R
Contemporary Review — Contemp Rev
Contemporary Review — CoR
Contemporary Review — CoRe
Contemporary Review — CR
Contemporary Review — ICRV
Contemporary Scripts — Contemp Scripts
Contemporary Sociology — Cont Sociol
Contemporary Sociology — Contemp Soc
Contemporary Sociology — Contemp Sociol
Contemporary Sociology — Contemp Sociology
Contemporary Sociology — CS
Contemporary Sociology — ICSY
Contemporary Sociology. Journal of Reviews — CSJR
Contemporary Soviet Mathematics — Contemp Soviet Math
Contemporary Studies in Theology [*London*] — CST
Contemporary Surgery — Contemp Surg
Contemporary Surgery — CSGYAF
Contemporary Themes in Biochemistry. Proceedings. Federation of Asian and Oceanian Biochemists Congress — Contemp Themes Biochem Proc Fed Asian Oceanian Biochem Congr
Contemporary Thought Quarterly — CTQ
Contemporary Topics in Analytical and Clinical Chemistry — Contemp Top Anal Clin Chem
Contemporary Topics in Immunobiology — Contemp Top Immunobiol
Contemporary Topics in Immunobiology — CTIBBV
Contemporary Topics in Immunochemistry — Contemp Top Immunochem
Contemporary Topics in Molecular Immunology — Contemp Top Mol Immunol
Contemporary Topics in Molecular Immunology — CTMIB4
Contemporary Topics in Polymer Science — Contemp Top Polym Sci
Contemporary Trends in Diuretic Therapy. Proceedings. Symposium — Contemp Trends Diuretic Ther Proc Symp
Contemporary Writers in Christian Perspective — CWCP
Contents of Contemporary Mathematical Journals — CCMJ
Contents of Contemporary Mathematical Journals — Contents Contemp Math J
Contents of Contemporary Mathematical Journals and New Publications — Contents Contemp Math J New Publ
Contents of Current Legal Periodicals — CCLP
Contents of Current Legal Periodicals — Contents Curr Leg Period
Contents of Recent Economics Journals — Contents Recent Econ J
Contents of Recent Economics Journals — CREJ
Contents of Recent Economics Journals — Econ Cont
Contents of Selected Periodicals — CSP
Contents of Selected Periodicals - Technical — CSP-T
Contents Pages in Management — Contents Pages Manage
Contests in Mathematics — Contests Math
Conti Elektro Berichte — CELBA
Conti Elektro Berichte [*Germany*] — Conti Elektro Ber
Continental Birdlife — COBLES
Continental Birdlife — Cont Birdlife
Continental Comment — Continentl

Continental Iron and Steel Trade Reports. Iron and Steel Trade Market Reports and Special Information — WWK
Continental Metallurgical and Chemical Engineering — Cont Metall Chem Eng
Continental Monthly — Contin Mo
Continental Paint and Resin News [*England*] — Cont Paint Resin News
Continental Shelf Research — Cont Shelf Res
Continental Shelf Research — CSR
Continentaler Stahlmarkt (Frankfurt Am Main) — CTF
Continuazione degli Atti. Reale Accademia Economico-Agraria dei Georgofili di Firenze — Contin Atti R Accad Econ Agrar Georgofili Firenze
Continuing Education for the Family Physician — Continuing Ed Fam Physician
Continuing Education for the Family Physician — Continuing Educ for the Fam Physician
Continuing Education in New Zealand — Contin Educ
Continuing Education in Nursing Focus — CE Focus
Continuing Education Lectures (Society of Nuclear Medicine. Southeastern Chapter) — Contin Edu Lect (Soc Nucl Med Southeast Chapter)
Continuing Medical Education Newsletter — Continuing Med Educ Newsletter
Continuo — Cont
Continuous Casting of Steel. Proceedings. Process Technology Conference — Contin Cast Steel Proc Process Technol Conf
Continuous Cultivation of Microorganisms. Proceedings. Symposium on Continuous Cultivation of Microorganisms — Contin Cultiv Microorg Proc Symp
Continuous Learning — Cont Learning
Continuous Plating Seminar. Proceedings — Contin Plat Semin Proc
Continuous Transcutaneous Blood Gas Monitoring. International Symposium — Contin Transcutaneous Blood Gas Monit Int Symp
Continuum Mechanics and Thermodynamics — Contin Mech Thermodyn
Continuum Models of Discrete Systems. Proceedings. International Conference on Continuum Models of Discrete Systems — Continuum Models Discrete Syst Proc Int Conf
Contour — Con
Contra Costa Dental Bulletin [*US*] — Contra Costa Dent Bull
Contraception — CCPTAY
Contraception — Contracept
Contraception-Fertilite-Sexualite — CFSXAE
Contraception-Fertilite-Sexualite — Contracept-Fertil-Sex
Contraceptive Delivery Systems — CDESDK
Contraceptive Delivery Systems — Contracept Delivery Syst
Contract Interiors — Contract Int
Contract Interiors — Contract Inter
Contract Journal [*England*] — Contract J
Contract Journal — Contract Jnl
Contract Journal — CTC
Contract Management — CTM
Contract Record and Engineering Review [*Canada*] — Contract Rec Eng Rev
Contract Report. US Army Engineer Waterways Experiment Station — Contract Rep US Army Eng Waterw Exp Stn
Contracting and Construction Engineer — Contract & Constr Eng
Contracting and Construction Equipment — Contracting
Contracting and Public Works — Contracting
Contractor — Contract
Contractor Profit News [*Also, an information service or system*] — CPN
Contractor Report. European Space Research Organization — Contract Rep Eur Space Res Organ
Contracts Cases, Federal. Commerce Clearing House — Cont Cas Fed CCH
Contrat Social — Contrat Soc
Contrat Social. Revue Historique et Critique des Faits et des Idees — Contr Soc
Contribucion al Estudio de las Ciencias Fisicas y Matematicas. Serie Matematico Fisica — Contrib Estud Cienc Fis Mat Ser Mat Fis
Contribucion al Estudio de las Ciencias Fisicas y Matematicas. Serie Tecnica — Contrib Estud Cienc Fis Mat Ser Tec
Contribuciones — CON
Contribuciones Cientificas. Facultad de Ciencias Exactas y Naturales. Universidad de Buenos Aires. Serie Botanica — Contrib Cient Fac Cienc Exactas Nat Univ B Aires Ser Bot
Contribuciones Cientificas. Facultad de Ciencias Exactas y Naturales. Universidad de Buenos Aires. Serie Botanica — CUBBA2
Contribuciones Cientificas. Facultad de Ciencias Exactas y Naturales. Universidad de Buenos Aires. Serie C. Quimica — Contrib Cient Univ Buenos Aires Fac Cienc Exactas Nat Ser C
Contribuciones Cientificas. Facultad de Ciencias Exactas y Naturales. Universidad de Buenos Aires. Serie Geologia — Contrib Cient Fac Cienc Exactas Nat Univ B Aires Ser Geol
Contribuciones Cientificas. Facultad de Ciencias Exactas y Naturales. Universidad de Buenos Aires. Serie Quimica — CBAQAB
Contribuciones Cientificas. Facultad de Ciencias Exactas y Naturales. Universidad de Buenos Aires. Serie Quimica — Contrib Cient Fac Cienc Exactas Nat Univ B Aires Ser Quim
Contribuciones Cientificas. Facultad de Ciencias Exactas y Naturales. Universidad de Buenos Aires. Serie Zoologia — CCBZAG
Contribuciones Cientificas. Facultad de Ciencias Exactas y Naturales. Universidad de Buenos Aires. Serie Zoologia — Contrib Cient Fac Cienc Exactas Nat Univ B Aires Ser Zool
Contribuciones Cientificas y Tecnologicas — Contrib Cient Tecnol
Contribuciones del Instituto Antarctico Argentino — Contr Inst Antarc Argent
Contribuciones. Instituto Antartico Argentino — Contrib Inst Antarct Argent
Contribuciones. Instituto Antartico Argentino — Contrib Inst Antart Argent
Contribuciones. Universidad Tecnica del Estado. Santiago — Contrib Univ Tec Estado Santiago
Contribuicoes Avulsas. Instituto Oceanografico Sao Paulo — CAVOAZ
Contribuicoes Avulsas. Instituto Oceanografico Sao Paulo — Contrib Avulsas Inst Oceanogr Sao Paulo
Contribuicoes para o Estudo da Antropologia Portuguesa — CEAPAT
Contribuicoes para o Estudo da Antropologia Portuguesa — Contrib Estudo Antropol Port
Contributed Papers. European Conference on Controlled Fusion and Plasma Physics — Contrib Pap Eur Conf Controlled Fusion Plasma Phys
Contributed Papers. International Conference on Phenomena in Ionized Gases — Contrib Pap Int Conf Phenom Ioniz Gases
Contributed Papers. Workshop on ECR Ion Sources — Contrib Pap Workshop ECR Ion Sources
Contributi. Centro Lindeo Interdisciplinare di Scienze Matematiche e loro Applicazioni [*Rome*] — Contrib Centro Linceo Interdisc Sci Mat Appl
Contributi del Centro Linceo Interdisciplinare di Scienze Matematiche e Loro Applicazioni — Contrib Cent Linceo Interdiscip Sci Mat Loro Appl
Contributi. Istituto di Archeologia. Universita Milan — C Ista Milano
Contributi. Istituto di Archeologia. Universita Milan — CIA
Contributi. Istituto di Filologia Moderna — CIFM
Contributi. Istituto di Ricerche Agrarie Milano — Contrib Ist Ric Agrar Milano
Contributi. Istituto di Ricerche Agrarie Milano — IAGCBP
Contributi. Istituto di Storia Antica [*Milan*] — CISA
Contributi Scientifico. Pratici per una Migliore Conoscenza ed Utilizzazione del Legno — Contr Sci Prat Migl Conosc Util Legno
Contributii Botanice — Contrib Bot
Contributii Botanice. Universitatea Babes-Bolyai din Cluj-Napoca. Gradina Botanica — Contrib Bot Univ Babes Bolyai Cluj Napoca Gradina Bot
Contribution. Alberta Research — Contrib Alberta Res
Contribution. Canada Department of Forestry. Forest Research Branch — Contr Canada Dep For Forest Res Brch
Contribution des Sciences Neurologiques a la Psychopharmacologie et le Systeme Moteur. Colloques Internationaux — Contrib Sci Neurol Psychopharmacol Syst Mot Colloq Int
Contribution. Fonds de Recherches Forestieres. Universite Laval — Contr Fonds Rech For Univ Laval
Contribution. Institute of Forest Products. University of Washington. College of Forest Resources — Contr Inst For Prod Univ Wash
Contribution on the Paleolimnology of Lake Biwa and the Japanese Pleistocene — Contrib Paleolimnol Lake Biwa Jpn Pleistocene
Contribution on the Paleolimnology of Lake Biwa and the Japanese Pleistocene — PLBPDP
Contribution Papers. American Institute of Mining and Metallurgical Engineers — Contrib Pap Am Inst Min Metall Eng
Contribution. Research Council of Alberta — Contrib Res Counc Alberta
Contribution to Music Education — Con Mus Ed
Contribution. University of California. Water Resources Center — Contrib Univ Calif Water Resour Cent
Contribution. University of Massachusetts. Department of Geology and Geography — Contrib Univ Mass Dep Geol Geogr
Contribution. Welder Wildlife Foundation — Contrib Welder Wildl Found
Contribution. Welder Wildlife Foundation — CWWFAV
Contributions. American Entomological Institute [*Ann Arbor*] — AEICA8
Contributions. American Entomological Institute (Ann Arbor) — Contrib Am Entomol Inst (Ann Arbor)
Contributions. American Institute of Mining and Metallurgical Engineers — Contrib Am Inst Min Metall Eng
Contributions. Ames Botanical Laboratory — Contr Ames Bot Lab
Contributions. Arctic Institute. Catholic University of America — CBAIAL
Contributions. Arctic Institute. Catholic University of America — Contrib Arct Inst Cathol Univ Am
Contributions. Bears Bluff Laboratories — CBLLAH
Contributions. Bears Bluff Laboratories — Contrib Bears Bluff Lab
Contributions. Biological Laboratory. Chinese Association for the Advancement of Science. Section Botany — Contr Biol Lab Chin Assoc Advancem Sci Sect Bot
Contributions. Biological Laboratory. Kyoto University — CBLKAE
Contributions. Biological Laboratory. Kyoto University — Contrib Biol Lab Kyoto Univ
Contributions. Biological Laboratory. Science Society of China. Botanical Series — Contrib Biol Lab Sci Soc China Bot Ser
Contributions. Biological Laboratory. Science Society of China. Zoological Series — Contrib Biol Lab Sci Soc China Zool Ser
Contributions. Botanical Laboratory. Johns Hopkins University — Contr Bot Lab Johns Hopkins Univ
Contributions. Boyce Thompson Institute — CBTIAE
Contributions. Boyce Thompson Institute for Plant Research — Contr Boyce Thompson Inst Pl Res
Contributions. Boyce Thompson Institute for Plant Research — Contrib Boyce Thompson Inst
Contributions. Central Research Institute for Agriculture [*Bogor*] — CIRADW
Contributions. Central Research Institute for Agriculture (Bogor) — Contrib Cent Res Inst Agric (Bogor)
Contributions. Central Research Institute for Food Crops [*Bogor*] — CCRCDU
Contributions. Central Research Institute for Food Crops — Contrib Cent Res Inst Food Crops
Contributions. Cryptogamic Laboratory. Harvard University — Contr Cryptog Lab Harvard Univ
Contributions. Cushman Foundation for Foraminiferal Research — CCFFAA
Contributions. Cushman Foundation for Foraminiferal Research — Contrib Cushman Found Foraminiferal Res
Contributions. Danish Pharmacopoeia Commission — Contrib Dan Pharmacopoeia Comm
Contributions. Departement de Biologie. Universite Laval (Quebec) — Contrib Dep Biol Univ Laval (Que)
Contributions. Department of Geology and Mineralogy. Niigata University — Contrib Dep Geol Mineral Niigata Univ
Contributions. Department of Geology and Mineralogy. Niigata University — NDRCAJ

Contributions. Department of Horticulture. University of Illinois — Contr Dep Hort Univ Ill
Contributions. Department of Limnology. Academy of Natural Sciences of Philadelphia — CLNSAG
Contributions. Department of Limnology. Academy of Natural Sciences of Philadelphia — Contrib Dep Limnol Acad Nat Sci Phila
Contributions d'Istanbul a la Science Clinique — Contrib Istanbul Sci Clin
Contributions d'Istanbul a la Science Clinique — NEILA8
Contributions du Centre de Recherches et d'Etudes Oceanographiques — Contr Centr Rech Etudes Oceanogr
Contributions. Dudley Herbarium — CDHBAF
Contributions. Dudley Herbarium — Contrib Dudley Herb
Contributions. Dudley Museum — CDMUAT
Contributions. Dudley Museum — Contrib Dudley Mus
Contributions. Faculty of Science. Haile Selassie I University. Series C. Zoology — Contrib Fac Sci Haile Selassie I Univ Ser C Zool
Contributions. Faculty of Science. University College of Addis Ababa (Ethiopia). Series C. Zoology — Contrib Fac Sci Univ Coll Addis Ababa (Ethiop) Ser C Zool
Contributions. Faculty of Science. University College of Addis Ababa (Ethiopia). Series C. Zoology — UAFZAG
Contributions from the Biological Laboratory. Chinese Association for the Advancement of Science — Contr Biol Lab Chin Assoc Advancem Sci
Contributions from the Department of Physics. Faculty of Science. University of Tokyo — Contrib Dep Phys Fac Sci Univ Tokyo
Contributions from the Institute of Geology and Paleontology. Tohoku University — Contr Inst Geol Tohoku Univ
Contributions from the Laboratory. Marine Biological Association — Contr Lab Mar Biol Assoc
Contributions from the Laboratory of Botany. National Academy of Peiping — Contr Lab Bot Natl Acad Peiping
Contributions from the United States National Herbarium. Smithsonian Institution — Contr US Natl Herb
Contributions. General Agricultural Research Station [*Bogor*] — PMBRAZ
Contributions. General Agricultural Research Station (Bogor) — Contrib Gen Agric Res Stn (Bogor)
Contributions. Geophysical Institute. Kyoto University — Contrib Geophys Inst Kyoto Univ
Contributions. Geophysical Institute. Slovak Academy of Sciences — Contrib Geophys Inst Slovak Acad Sci
Contributions. Geophysical Institute. Slovak Academy of Sciences. Series of Meteorology — Contrib Geophys Inst Slovak Acad Sci Ser Meteorol
Contributions. Geophysical Observatory. Haile Sellassie I University. Series A — Contrib Geophys Obs Haile Sellassie I Univer Ser A
Contributions. Gray Herbarium. Harvard University — CGHHAK
Contributions. Gray Herbarium. Harvard University — Contrib Gray Herb Harv Univ
Contributions. Gray Herbarium of Harvard University — Contr Gray Herb
Contributions. Henry Shaw School of Botany. Washington University — Contr Henry Shaw School Bot
Contributions. Herbarium Australiense — Contr Herb Aust
Contributions. Herbarium Australiense — Contrib Herb Aust
Contributions. Herbarium Australiense — CTHAAM
Contributions. Hong Kong Biochemical Association — Contrib Hong Kong Biochem Assoc
Contributions. Horticultural Institute. Taihoku Imperial University/Taihoku Teikoku Daigaku Rinogakubu Engeigaku Kyoshitsu Kiyo — Contr Hort Inst Taihoku Imp Univ
Contributions in Drama and Theatre Studies — Contr Drama
Contributions in Labor History — Contrib Lab Hist
Contributions in Marine Science — CMSCA
Contributions in Marine Science — CMSCAY
Contributions in Marine Science — Contr Mar S
Contributions in Marine Science — Contr Marine Sci
Contributions in Marine Science — Contrib Mar Sci
Contributions in Medical History — Contrib Med Hist
Contributions in Microbial Geochemistry — Contrib Microb Geochem
Contributions in Military History — Contrib Mil Hist
Contributions in Science — Contr Sc
Contributions in Science — Contr Sci
Contributions in Science (Los Angeles) — Contrib Sci (Los Ang)
Contributions. Institut de Botanique. Universite de Montreal — CBBMA4
Contributions. Institut de Botanique. Universite de Montreal — Contr Inst Bot Univ Montreal
Contributions. Institut de Botanique. Universite de Montreal — Contrib Inst Bot Univ Montreal
Contributions. Institut Royal de Meteorologie de Belgique — Contr Inst Met Belg
Contributions. Institute of Botany. National Academy of Peiping — Contr Inst Bot Natl Acad Peiping
Contributions. Institute of Chemistry. National Academy of Peiping — Contrib Inst Chem Nat Acad Peiping
Contributions. Institute of Geology and Paleontology. Tohoku University — Contrib Inst Geol Paleontol Tohoku Univ
Contributions. Institute of Geology and Paleontology. Tohoku University — TDRCAH
Contributions. Institute of Low Temperature Science [*Japan*] — CLTS
Contributions. Institute of Low Temperature Science. Hokkaido University — Contrib Inst Low Temp Sci Hokkaido Univ
Contributions. Institute of Low Temperature Science. Hokkaido University. Series A — Contrib Inst Low Temp Sci Hokkaido Univ Ser A
Contributions. Institute of Low Temperature Science. Hokkaido University. Series B — CILBA2
Contributions. Institute of Low Temperature Science. Hokkaido University. Series B — Contrib Inst Low Temp Sci Hokkaido Univ B
Contributions. Institute of Low Temperature Science. Hokkaido University. Series B — Contrib Inst Low Temp Sci Hokkaido Univ Ser B
Contributions. Institute of Low Temperature Science. Series A — Contrib Inst Low Temp Sci A
Contributions. Institute of Low Temperature Science. Series A — Contrib Inst Low Temp Sci Ser A
Contributions. Institute of Physics. Natural Academy of Peiping — Contrib Inst Phys Nat Acad Peiping
Contributions. Iowa Corn Research Institute — Contr Iowa Corn Res Inst
Contributions. Iowa Corn Research Institute — Contrib Iowa Corn Res Inst
Contributions. Jardin Botanique de Rio De Janeiro — Contr Jard Bot Rio J
Contributions. Jefferson Physical Laboratory of Harvard University — Contr Jeff Phys Lab Harv
Contributions. Laboratory of Vertebrate Biology. University of Michigan — Contr Lab Vertebr Biol
Contributions. Laboratory of Vertebrate Biology. University of Michigan — Contrib Lab Vertebr Biol Univ Mich
Contributions. Laboratory of Vertebrate Biology. University of Michigan — UMVBA6
Contributions. Laboratory of Vertebrate Genetics. University of Michigan — Contr Lab Vertebr Genet Univ Mich
Contributions. Life Sciences. Royal Ontario Museum — Contr Life Sci Roy Ontario Mus
Contributions. Lunar Science Institute — Contrib Lunar Sci Inst
Contributions. Macedonian Academy of Sciences and Arts. Section of Biological and Medical Sciences — Contrib Maced Acad Sci Arts Sect Biol Med Sci
Contributions. Macedonian Academy of Sciences and Arts. Section of Natural Sciences and Mathematics — Contrib Maced Acad Sci Arts Sect Nat Sci Math
Contributions. Meteoritical Society — Contrib Meteorit Soc
Contributions. Museum of Geology. University of Michigan — Contr Mus Geol
Contributions. Museum of Paleontology. University of Michigan — Contr Mus Paleont
Contributions. Museum of Paleontology. University of Michigan — Contrib Mus Paleontol Univ Mich
Contributions. Museum of Paleontology. University of Michigan — UMMPA3
Contributions. Museum of the American Indian — Contrib Mus Am Indn
Contributions. National Research Institute of Geology. Academia Sinica — Contrib Nat Res Inst Geol Acad Sin
Contributions. New South Wales National Herbarium — CNWHA8
Contributions. New South Wales National Herbarium — Contr New South Wales Natl Herb
Contributions. New South Wales National Herbarium — Contr NSW Natn Herb
Contributions. New South Wales National Herbarium — Contrib NSW Herb
Contributions. New South Wales National Herbarium — Contrib NSW Natl Herb
Contributions. New South Wales National Herbarium. Flora Series — Contrib NSW Natl Herb Flora Ser
Contributions. New South Wales National Herbarium. Flora Series — CWHFAO
Contributions. New York Botanical Garden — Contr New York Bot Gard
Contributions of HKBA (Hong Kong Biochemical Association) — Contrib HKBA
Contributions of Science to the Development of the Textile Industry. Joint Conference — Contrib Sci Dev Text Ind Jt Conf
Contributions on Plant Genetics — Contr Pl Genet
Contributions. Perkins Observatory — Contrib Perkins Obs
Contributions. Perkins Observatory. Series 1 — Contrib Perkins Obs Ser 1
Contributions. Perkins Observatory. Series 2 — Contrib Perkins Obs Ser 2
Contributions. Queensland Herbarium — Contr Qd Herb
Contributions. Queensland Herbarium — Contrib Qd Herb
Contributions. Queensland Herbarium — Contrib Queensl Herb
Contributions. Scripps Institution of Oceanography — Contrib Scripps Inst Oceanogr
Contributions. Seto Marine Biological Laboratory. Kyoto University — Contr Seto Mar Biol Lab
Contributions. Shanghai Institute of Entomology — Contrib Shanghai Inst Entomol
Contributions. Society for Research on Meteorites — Contrib Soc Res Meteorites
Contributions. Station Biologique du St. Laurent, Canada — Contrib Stn Biol St Laurent Can
Contributions. Symposium on Immunology. Gesellschaft fuer Allergie und Immunitaetsforschung — Contrib Symp Immunol Ges Allerg Immunitaetsforsch
Contributions. Tennessee University. Botanical Laboratory — Contr Tennessee Univ Bot Lab
Contributions to Applied Statistics — Cont Appl St
Contributions to Asian Studies — ContAS
Contributions to Asian Studies — Contrib As Stud
Contributions to Asian Studies — Contrib Asian St
Contributions to Atmospheric Physics — Contrib Atmos Phys
Contributions to Canadian Biology and Fisheries — Contrib Can Biol Fish
Contributions to Canadian Economics — CCE
Contributions to Canadian Mineralogy — Contrib Can Mineral
Contributions to Current Research in Geophysics — Contrib Curr Res Geophys
Contributions to Economic Analysis [*Elsevier Book Series*] — CEA
Contributions to Economic Analysis [*Amsterdam*] — Contrib Econom Anal
Contributions to Epidemiology and Biostatistics — Contrib Epidemiol Biostat
Contributions to European Fusion Theory Conference — Contrib Eur Fusion Theory Conf
Contributions to Geology — Contrib Geol
Contributions to Geology. Special Paper — CGSPBW
Contributions to Geology. Special Paper — Contrib Geol Spec Pap
Contributions to Geology. University of Wyoming — Contrib Geol Univ Wyo
Contributions to Geology. University of Wyoming — WUGGAO
Contributions to Gynecology and Obstetrics — CGOBD6
Contributions to Gynecology and Obstetrics — Contrib Gynecol Obstet
Contributions to Human Development — CHDEDZ

Contributions to Human Development — Cont Hum De
Contributions to Human Development — Contrib Hum Dev
Contributions to Indian Economic History — CIEH
Contributions to Indian Sociology — Contrib Ind Sociol
Contributions to Infusion Therapy and Clinical Nutrition — Contrib Infusion Ther Clin Nutr
Contributions to Marine Biology. University of Wales — Contr Mar Biol Univ Wales
Contributions to Medical Psychology — Contrib Med Psychol
Contributions to Microbiology and Immunology — CMIMBF
Contributions to Microbiology and Immunology — Contrib Microbiol Immunol
Contributions to Mineralogy and Petrology — Contr Min P
Contributions to Mineralogy and Petrology — Contrib Mineral & Petrol
Contributions to Mineralogy and Petrology — Contrib Mineral Petrol
Contributions to Mineralogy and Petrology — Contrib Mineral Petrology
Contributions to Mineralogy and Petrology/Beitraege zur Mineralogie und Petrologie [*Berlin-Heidelberg-New York*] — Contrib Mineral Petrol Beitr Mineral Petrol
Contributions to Music Education — CMUED
Contributions to Nepalese Studies — Contrib Nepal Stud
Contributions to Nephrology — CNEPDD
Contributions to Nephrology — Contrib Nephrol
Contributions to Oncology — Contrib Oncol
Contributions to Palaeontology — Contr Palaeont
Contributions to Physico-Chemical Petrology — Contrib Phys Chem Petrol
Contributions to Primatology — Contr Prim
Contributions to Primatology — Contrib Primatol
Contributions to Primatology — CPMYAN
Contributions to Sedimentology — Contrib Sedimentology
Contributions to Sensory Physiology — Contrib Sens Physiol
Contributions to Sensory Physiology — CSPHA
Contributions to Sensory Physiology — CSPHA8
Contributions to Statistics — Contrib Statist
Contributions to the Anthropology, Botany, Geology, and Zoology of the Papuan Region. Botany — Contr Anthropol Papuan Region Bot
Contributions to the Botany of Vermont — Contr Bot Vermont
Contributions to Vertebrate Evolution — Contrib Vertebr Evol
Contributions to Vertebrate Evolution — CVEVDJ
Contributions to Zoology — Contrib Zool
Contributions. United States National Herbarium — Contr US Nat Herb
Contributions. United States National Herbarium — Contrib US Natl Herb
Contributions. United States National Herbarium — CXNHAX
Contributions. University of California, San Diego. Scripps Institution of Oceanography — Contrib Univ Calif San Diego Scripps Inst Oceanogr
Contributions. University of Michigan Herbarium — Contrib Univ Mich Herb
Contributions. University of Michigan Herbarium — Contrib Univ Mich Herbar
Contributions. University of Michigan Herbarium — CUMHDA
Contributiuni Botanice din Cluj la Timisoara/Contributions Botaniques de Cluj a Timisoara [*Roumanie*] — Contr Bot Cluj Timisoara
Control Abstracts — Control Abstr
Control and Automation Process [*England*] — Control Automat Process
Control and Computers — Control and Comput
Control and Cybernetics — Control & Cybern
Control and Cybernetics — Control Cybern
Control and Cybernetics [*Polish Academy of Sciences. Institute of Applied Cybernetics*] — Control Cybernet
Control and Dynamic Systems. Advances in Theory and Applications — Control Dyn Syst
Control and Dynamic Systems. Advances in Theory and Applications — Control Dynam Systems Adv Theory Appl
Control and Instrumentation — Contl & I
Control and Instrumentation — Contr Instr
Control and Instrumentation — Contr Instrum
Control and Instrumentation — Control and Instrum
Control and Instrumentation — Control Instrum
Control and Instruments in Chemical Industry — Control Instrum Chem Ind
Control Cibernetica y Automatizacion — Control Cibern & Autom
Control Engineering — Contr Eng
Control Engineering — Contrl Eng
Control Engineering — Control Eng
Control Engineering — Control Engng
Control of Antibiotic-Resistant Bacteria. Beecham Colloquium — Control Antibiot Resist Bact Beecham Colloq
Control of Diarrhoea in Clinical Practice. Proceedings. International Symposium — Control Diarrhoea Clin Pract Proc Int Symp
Control of Feeding Behavior and Biology of the Brain in Protein-Calorie Malnutrition — Control Feed Behav Biol Brain Protein-Calorie Malnutr
Control of Gaseous Sulphur and Nitrogen Compound Emission. Papers presented at the International Conference — Control Gaseous Sulphur Nitrogen Compd Emiss Pap Int Conf
Control of Glycogen Metabolism. Proceedings. Meeting. Federation of European Biochemical Societies — Control Glycogen Metab Proc Meet Fed Eur Biochem Soc
Control of Hazardous Material Spills. Proceedings. National Conference on Control of Hazardous Material Spills — Control Hazard Mater Spills Proc Natl Conf
Control of Power Systems Conference and Exposition. Conference Record — Control Power Syst Conf Expo Conf Rec
Control of Sulphur and Other Gaseous Emissions. International Symposium — Control Sulphur Other Gaseous Emiss Int Symp
Control of Tissue Damage. Strangeways Research Laboratory 75th Anniversary Symposium — Control Tissue Damage Strangeways Res Lab 75th Anniv Symp
Control of Virus Diseases. Papers. International Conference on Comparative Virology — Control Virus Dis Pap Int Conf Comp Virol
Control Products Specifier. Special Issue of Control Engineering — Contl Eng S
Control Review — Control Rev
Control Series Bulletin. Massachusetts Agricultural Experiment Station — Contr Ser Bull Mass Agr Exp Sta
Control Series Bulletin. Massachusetts Agricultural Experiment Station. University of Massachusetts — Control Ser Bull Mass Agric Exp Stn Univ Mass
Control Series. Virginia Polytechnic Institute and State University Cooperative Extension Service — Control Ser VA Polytech Inst State Univ Coop Ext Serv
Control Systems — Control Sys
Control Technology Center. United States Environmental Protection Agency. Report EPA — Control Technol Cent US Environ Prot Agency Rep EPA
Control Theory and Advanced Technology — Control Theory Adv Tech
Control Theory and Applications — Control Theory Appl
Controle de l'Alimentation des Plantes Cultivees. Colloque Europeen et Mediterraneen — Controle Aliment Plant Cultiv Colloq Eur Mediterr
Controlled Clinical Trials — CCLTDH
Controlled Clinical Trials — Controlled Clin Trials
Controlled Clnical Trials — Control Clin Trials
Controls for Optical Systems — Controls Opt Syst
Contruction Week — Constr W
Convegno della Salute. Ereditarieta, Ambiente, Alimentazione — Conv Salute Ereditarieta Ambiente Aliment
Convegno di Studi sulla Magna Graeca — C M Gr
Convegno Internazionale di Geometria Differenziale — Conv Int Geom Diff
Convegno Internazionale sugli Idrocarburi — Conv Int Idrocarb
Convegno Internazionale sulle Acque Sotterranee. Atti. Ente Sviluppo Agricolo in Sicilia [*Palermo*] — Conv Int Acque Sotterranee Atti
Convegno Italiano di Scienza delle Macromolecole. Atti — Conv Ital Sci Macromol Atti
Convegno sulle Vitamine. Giornata della Scienza — Conv Vitam Giornata Sci
Convegno-Scuola su Caratterizzazione Molecolare di Polimeri. Atti — Conv Sc Caratt Mol Polim Atti
Convegno-Scuola su Fondamenti della Transformazione dei Materiali Polimerici Polymer Processing — Conv Sc Fondam Transform Mater Polim Polym Process
Convegno-Scuola su Sintesi di Polimeri — Conv Sc Sint Polim
Convenio IICA-ZN-ROCAP [*Instituto Interamericano de Ciencias Agricolas-Zona Norte-Regional Organization for Central America and Panama*] **Bibliografia** — CIICBP
Convenio IICA-ZN-ROCAP [*Instituto Interamericano de Ciencias Agricolas-Zona Norte-Regional Organization for Central America and Panama*] **Bibliografia** — Conv IICA-ZN-ROCAP Bibliogr
Convenio IICA-ZN-ROCAP [*Instituto Interamericano de Ciencias Agricolas-Zona Norte-Regional Organization for Central America and Panama*] **Publicacion Miscelanea** — Conv IICA-ZN-ROCAP Publ Misc
Convenio IICA-ZN-ROCAP [*Instituto Interamericano de Ciencias Agricolas-Zona Norte-Regional Organization for Central America and Panama*] **Publicacion Miscelanea** — PIICAV
Convention Addresses. National Shellfisheries Association — Conv Addresses Natl Shellfish Assoc
Convention. Battery Council International — Conv Battery Counc Int
Convention Proceedings. Agricultural and Veterinary Chemicals Association of Australia — Conven Proc Agric Vet Chem Assoc Aust
Convention Record. IRE — Conv Rec IRE
Conventional and Non Conventional Proteins. Capri Veterinary Workshop — Conv Non Conv Proteins Capri Vet Workshop
Convergence — CONVDF
Convergences Medicales — Convergences Med
Conversation in Biomolecular Stereodynamics — Conversation Biomol Stereodyn
Conversation in the Discipline Biomolecular Stereodynamics — Conversation Discip Biomol Stereodyn
Conversion of Refuse to Energy. International Conference and Technical Exhibition — Convers Refuse Energy Int Conf Tech Exhib
Converting Technology — Converting Technol
Conveyancer News — CVNS
Conveyancer and Property Lawyer — conv
Conveyancer and Property Lawyer — Conv and Prop Law
Conveyancer and Property Lawyer — Convey
Conveyancer and Property Lawyer. New Series — Conv (NS)
Conveyancer and Property Lawyer. New Series — Convey NS
Conveyancer and Property Lawyer. New Series — CPL
Convivium — Con
Convivium — Conv
Convivium (New Series) — Con(NS)
Convorbiri Literare — CLit
Convorbiri Literare — ConLit
Convorbiri Literare — ConvLit
Convulsive Therapy — Convuls Ther
Convulsive Therapy — Convulsive Ther
Coolia — COOLBM
Coombe Lodge Reports — Coombe Lodge Rep
Coombe Lodge Reports — Coombe Lodge Repts
Coop Grain Quarterly — Coop Grain Quart
Co-Op North — COOP
Cooper Monographs on English and American Language and Literature — CMEALL
Cooper Union Bulletin. Engineering and Science Series — Cooper Un Bull
Cooper Union Bulletin. Engineering and Science Series — Cooper Union Bull Eng Sci Ser
Cooper Union Museum Chronicle — Cooper Union Chron
Cooperador Dental (Buenos Aires) — Coop Dent (B Aires)

Cooperateur Agricole la Cooperative Federee de Quebec — Coop Agric Coop Fed Que
Cooperateur de France — Coop Fr
Cooperatie — NCR
Cooperation — Coop
Cooperation Agricole — Coop Agr
Cooperation Agricole — Coop Agric
Cooperation and Conflict — Coop and Conflict
Cooperation and Conflict — Coop Conflict
Cooperation Canada — Coop Can
Cooperation et Developpement — Coop et Dev
Cooperation et Developpement — Coop et Development
Cooperation Information — Coop Inf
Cooperation Internationale. Culturelle, Scientifique, Technique — Coop Internat
Cooperation Mediterraneenne pour l'Energie Solaire. Revue Internationale d'Heliotechnique [*France*] — Coop Mediterr Energ Sol Rev Int Heliotech
Cooperation Technique — Coop Tech
Cooperation-Distribution-Consommation — Coop-Distrib-Consom
Cooperativa (Bogota) — Coop Bogota
Co-Operative Bulletin of Taiwan Forestry Research Institute in Co-Operation with the Joint Commission on Rural Reconstruction — Co Op Bull Taiwan For Res Inst Co Op Jt Comm Rural Reconstr
Co-Operative Bulletin. Taiwan Forestry Research Institute — Co-Op Bull Taiwan For Res Inst
Co-Operative Bulletin. Taiwan Forestry Research Institute — TLYYA4
Cooperative Consumer — Coop Consum
Cooperative Documents Network Project [*Database*] — CODOC
Cooperative Economic Insect Report [*Department of Agriculture*] — Co-Op Econ Insect Rep
Co-Operative Electrical Research — Co-Op Electr Res
Cooperative Extension Service. College of Agriculture. University of Connecticut. Bulletin — Coop Ext Serv Coll Agric Univ Conn Bull
Co-Operative Information. International Labor Office — Coop Inf Int Labor Off
Cooperative Manager and Farmer — Coop Manager & F
Co-Operative News — Co-Op News
Co-Operative News Digest — Coop News
Cooperative Phenomena in Biology — Coop Phenom Biol
Cooperative Plant Pest Report — Coop Pl Rest Rep
Cooperative Research Report. International Council for the Exploration of the Sea — Coop Res Rep Int Council Explor Sea
Cooperative Research Report. International Council for the Exploration of the Sea. Series A — Coop Res Rep Int Counc Explor Sea Ser A
Cooperative Resources Report. Illinois State Water Survey and Illinois State Geological Survey — Coop Resour Rep Ill State Water Survey Ill State Geol Surv
Co-Operative Review — Coop Rev
Cooperatives Meat Trade Digest — Coop Meat Trade D
Cooperativesmo y Desarrollo — Coop y Desarrollo
Coordinated Occupational Information Network Database — COIN
Coordinated Regulation of Gene Expression. Proceedings. International Workshop on Coordinated Regulation of Gene Expression — Coord Regul Gene Expression Proc Int Workshop
Coordinating Research Council. CRC Report — Coord Res Counc CRC Rep
Coordinating Research Council, Inc. Report — Coord Res Counc Inc Rep
Coordination Chemistry — Coord Chem
Coordination Chemistry Reviews — Coord Ch Re
Coordination Chemistry Reviews — Coord Chem Rev
Coordination Guidelines for Wildlife Habitats. United States Forest Service. California Region — Coord Guidel Wildl Habitats US For Serv Calif Reg
Copeia — Cop
Copeia — COPAAR
Copenhagen School of Economics and Business Administration. Language Department Publications — CEBAL
Copenhagen University. Mineralogical and Geological Museum. Contributions to Mineralogy — Copenhagen Univ Mineralog Geol Mus Contr Mineralogy
Coping with Medical Issues [*Elsevier Book Series*] — CMI
Copper Abstracts — Copper Abstr
Copper Alloy Bulletin — Copp All Bull
Copper Development Association. Information Sheet — Copper Development Assocn Information Sheet
Copper Development Association. Technical Report — Copper Dev Assoc Tech Rep
Copper Development Association. Technical Survey — Copper Dev Assoc Tech Sur
Copper in the United States (Washington, DC) — Copper US Washington DC
Copper Industry (Washington, D.C.) — Copper Ind Washington DC
Copper Production (Washington, DC) — Copper Prod Washington (DC)
Copper. Quarterly Report — CPR
Copper Studies — Copper Stud
Copper Yugoslavia — Copper Yugosl
Coptic Church Review — Coptic Ch R
Coptic Studies — Coptic Stu
Copyright Bulletin — Copyright Bul
Copyright Law Decisions. Commerce Clearing House — Copyright L Dec CCH
Copyright Law Symposium. American Society of Composers, Authors, and Publishers — ASCAP Cop L Symp
Copyright Law Symposium. American Society of Composers, Authors, and Publishers — ASCAP Copyright L Symp
Copyright Law Symposium. American Society of Composers, Authors, and Publishers — Copyright L Sym (ASCAP)
Copyright Reporter — Copy Rep
Copyright Society of Australia. Newsletter — Copy Soc Aust News
Cor et Vasa — COVAAN
Coral Reefs — CORFDL
Corax — CORAD6
Cordoba Medica — Cord Med
Cordulia. Supplement — Cordulia Suppl
Corduroy — Cord
Core Journals in Obstetrics/Gynecology — Core J Obst/Gyn
Core Journals in Pediatrics — Core J Pediatr
Cork Historical and Archaeological Society. Journal — Cork Hist Arch Soc J
Cormosa Newsletter — Corm
Cormosea Newsletter — Cormosea Newsl
Corn Annual — Corn Ann
Corn Annual — Corn Annu
Corn Mimeograph. Texas Research Foundation — Corn Mimeogr Tex Res Found
Cornell Agricultural Waste Management Conference — Cornell Agric Waste Manage Conf
Cornell Agricultural Waste Management Conference. Proceedings — Cornell Agric Waste Manage Conf Proc
Cornell Electrical Engineering Conference. Proceedings — Cornell Electr Eng Conf Proc
Cornell Engineer — Cornell Eng
Cornell Extension Bulletin — Cornell Ext Bull
Cornell Extension Bulletin. New York State College of Agriculture. Extension Service — Cornell Ext Bull NY State Coll Agr Ext Serv
Cornell Feed Service. New York State College of Agriculture. Extension Service [*Cornell University*] — Cornell Feed Serv NY State Coll Agr Ext Serv
Cornell History of Science Series — Cornell Hist Sci Ser
Cornell Hotel and Restaurant Administration Quarterly — CHRAQ
Cornell Hotel and Restaurant Administration Quarterly — Cornell Hotel & Rest Adm Q
Cornell Hotel and Restaurant Administration Quarterly — Cornell Hotel & Restau Adm Q
Cornell Hotel and Restaurant Administration Quarterly — Cornell Hotel and Restaurant Admin Q
Cornell Hotel and Restaurant Administration Quarterly — Cornell Hotel Restaur Adm Q
Cornell Hotel and Restaurant Administration Quarterly — Cornell Hotel Restaurant Adm Q
Cornell Hotel and Restaurant Administration Quarterly — CQB
Cornell International Agricultural Development Bulletin — Cornell Int Agric Dev Bull
Cornell International Law Journal — Cor Int LJ
Cornell International Law Journal — Cornell I J
Cornell International Law Journal — Cornell Int L J
Cornell International Law Journal — Cornell Internat Law J
Cornell International Law Journal — Cornell Internat LJ
Cornell International Law Journal — Cornell Intl LJ
Cornell International Symposium and Workshop on the Hydrogen Economy — Cornell Int Symp Workshop Hydrogen Econ
Cornell Journal of Social Relations — Corn J Soc Rel
Cornell Journal of Social Relations — Cornell J S
Cornell Journal of Social Relations — Cornell J Soc Rel
Cornell Journal of Social Relations — Cornell J Soc Relat
Cornell Journal of Social Relations — Cornell Jnl Soc Rel
Cornell Law Forum — Cornell LF
Cornell Law Quarterly — CLQ
Cornell Law Quarterly — Cor LQ
Cornell Law Quarterly — Cornell L Q
Cornell Law Quarterly — Cornell Law Q
Cornell Law Quarterly — Cornell Law Quart
Cornell Law Review — Cor
Cornell Law Review — Cor LR
Cornell Law Review — Cornell L R
Cornell Law Review — Cornell L Rev
Cornell Law Review — Cornell Law R
Cornell Law Review — Cornell Law Rev
Cornell Library Journal — CLJ
Cornell Library Journal — Cornell Lib J
Cornell Linguistic Contributions — COL
Cornell Medical Journal — Cornell Med J
Cornell Miscellaneous Bulletin — Cornell Misc Bull
Cornell Nutrition Conference for Feed Manufacturers. Proceedings — Cornell Nutr Conf Feed Manuf Proc
Cornell Plantations — Cornell Plant
Cornell Plantations — Cornell Plantat
Cornell Review — Cornell R
Cornell Studies in Classical Philology — CSCP
Cornell Studies in Classical Philology — CSPh
Cornell Studies in English — CSE
Cornell University Agricultural Experiment Station. Bulletin — Cornell Univ Agric Exp Sta Bull
Cornell University Agricultural Experiment Station Circular — Cornell Univ Agric Exp Sta Circ
Cornell University. Agricultural Experiment Station. Publications — Cornell Ag Exp
Cornell University Conference on Agricultural Waste Management — Cornell Univ Conf Agric Waste Manage
Cornell University. Department of Structural Engineering. Report — Cornell Univ Dep Struc Eng Rep
Cornell University Libraries. Bulletin — Cornell Univ Lib Bull
Cornell University Memoirs — Cornell Univ Mem
Cornell Veterinarian — Cornell Vet
Cornell Veterinarian — Cornell Veterin
Cornell Veterinarian. Supplement — Cornell Vet Suppl
Cornell Working Papers in Linguistics — CWPL
Cornhill Magazine — CM
Cornhill Magazine — Cornh
Cornhill Magazine — Cornhill M

Cornhill Magazine — Cornhill Mag
Corning Research — Corning Res
Cornish Archaeology — Corn A
Cornish Archaeology — Cornish Arch
Cornish Archaeology — Cornish Archaeol
Cornish Institute of Engineers. Transactions — Corn Inst Eng Trans
Cornish Studies — CS
Cornishman — CN
Corno Emplumado — CE
Corno Emplumado — CEm
Corona — Co
Coronary Artery Disease — Coron Artery Dis
Coronary Heart Disease (Stuttgart). International Symposium — Coron Heart Dis (Stuttgart)
Corporate Accounting — CAC
Corporate Accounting — COA
Corporate and Industry Research Reports — CIRR
Corporate and Industry Research Reports Index [*Database*] — CIRR
Corporate Commentary — Corp Comment
Corporate Controller's and Treasurer's Report — CC & T Rpt
Corporate Counsel Review. Journal of the Corporate Counsel Section. State Bar of Texas — Corp Counsel Rev J Corp Counsel Section St B Tex
Corporate Design — COD
Corporate Director — CRD
Corporate Directorship — Corp Dir
Corporate Fitness and Recreation — Corp Fit and R
Corporate Integrated Information System [*Database*] — CIIS
Corporate Management Tax Conference — Corp Mgt Tax Conf
Corporate Monthly — Corp Month
Corporate Philanthropy — Corp Philanth
Corporate Practice Commentator — Corp Prac Com
Corporate Practice Commentator — Corp Prac Comm
Corporate Practice Commentator — Corp Prac Comment
Corporate Practice Commentator — Corp Pract Comment
Corporate Practice Series (Bureau of National Affairs) — Corp Prac Ser (BNA)
Corporate Report — Corporate Rept
Corporate Report Kansas City — Crp Rpt KC
Corporate Report Minnesota — Crp Rpt MN
Corporate Technology Database — CTD
Corporation Forms (Prentice-Hall, Inc.) — Corp Forms (P-H)
Corporation Guide. Prentice-Hall — Corp Guide P-H
Corporation Journal — Corp J
Corporation Law Guide [*Commerce Clearing House*] — Corp L Guide
Corporation Law Review — COR
Corporation Law Review — Corp L Rev
Corporation Law Review — Corp LR
Corps Gras Industriels — Corps Gras Ind
Corps Medical (Ettelbruck) — Corps Med (Ettelbruck)
Corpus Bruxellense Historiae Byzantinae — CBH Byz
Corpus Christi Geological Society. Bulletin — Corpus Christi Geol Soc Bull
Corpus Christianorum — C Ch
Corpus Christianorum — CC
Corpus Christianorum — CChr
Corpus Christianorum — Corp Christ
Corpus Christianorum. Series Latina [*Turnhout*] — CCLat
Corpus Cultus Cybelae Attidisque — CCCA
Corpus Cultus Deae Syriae — CCDS
Corpus delle Urne Etrusche di Eta Ellenistica — CUE
Corpus der Griechisch-Christlichen Inschriften von Hellas — Corp Gr Christl Inschr
Corpus der Minoischen und Mykenischen Siegel — CMMS
Corpus der Minoischen und Mykenischen Siegel — CMS
Corpus des Astronomes Byzantins — Corpus Astronom Byzantins
Corpus des Mosaieques de Tunisie — CAMT
Corpus Fontium Historiae Byzantinae [*Berlin*] — CFHB
Corpus Glossariorum Latinorum a G. Loewe Incohatum — C Gl Lat
Corpus Glossariorum Latinorum a G. Loewe Incohatum — Corp Gl
Corpus Inscriptionum Arabicorum — CIA
Corpus Inscriptionum Atticarum — CI Att
Corpus Inscriptionum Atticarum — CIA
Corpus Inscriptionum et Monumentorum Religionis Mithriacae — CIMRM
Corpus Inscriptionum et Monumentorum Religionis Mithriacae — CIRM
Corpus Inscriptionum Etruscarum — CIE
Corpus Inscriptionum Etruscarum — Corp Inscr Et
Corpus Inscriptionum Graecarum — CI Gr
Corpus Inscriptionum Graecarum [*A collection of Greek inscriptions*] [*Latin*] — CIG
Corpus Inscriptionum Graecarum — Corpus Inscript Graec
Corpus Inscriptionum Insularum Celticarum — CI Ins
Corpus Inscriptionum Iranicarum — CII
Corpus Inscriptionum Iudaicarum — CII
Corpus Inscriptionum Iudaicarum — CJI
Corpus Inscriptionum Latinarum — C
Corpus Inscriptionum Latinarum [*A collection of Latin inscriptions*] [*Latin*] — CIL
Corpus Inscriptionum Latinarum — Corp Inscr Lat
Corpus Inscriptionum Semiticarum — CI Sem
Corpus Inscriptionum Semiticarum — CIS
Corpus Inscriptionum Semiticarum — Corp Inscr Semit
Corpus Medicorum Graecorum — CMG
Corpus Medicorum Graecorum — Corp Med Graec
Corpus Medicorum Latinorum — CML
Corpus Medicorum Latinorum — Corp Med Lat
Corpus Monumentorum Religionis Dei Menis — CMRDM
Corpus of Dated Palestinian Pottery — CPP
Corpus Papyrorum Hermopolitanorum — C P Herm
Corpus Papyrorum Hermopolitanorum — Corp Papyr Hermopol
Corpus Papyrorum Judaicorum — CP Jud
Corpus Papyrorum Latinorum — CPL
Corpus Poetarum Latinorum — Corp Poet Lat
Corpus Scriptorum Christianorum Orientalium — Corp Script Christ Or
Corpus Scriptorum Christianorum Orientalium — CSCO
Corpus Scriptorum Ecclesiasticorum Latinorum — Corp Sc Eccl Lat
Corpus Scriptorum Ecclesiasticorum Latinorum — CSEL
Corpus Scriptorum Ecclesiasticorum Latinorum — CSL
Corpus Scriptorum Graecorum Paravianum — CSGP
Corpus Scriptorum Graecorum Paravianum — Paravia
Corpus Scriptorum Historiae Byzantinae — CSB
Corpus Scriptorum Historiae Byzantinae — CSH Byz
Corpus Scriptorum Historiae Byzantinae — CSHB
Corpus Scriptorum Latinorum Paravianum — C Par
Corpus Signorum Imperii Romani — CSIR
Corpus Vasorum Antiquorum — CVA
Corpus Vasorum Hispanorum — CVH
Corpusculum Poesis Epicae Graecae Ludibundae — CPEGL
Corrections Magazine — Correct Mag
Corrections Today — Correct Today
Corrections Today — PCOR
Corrective and Social Psychiatry — Corr Soc Ps
Correio Agricola — Correio Agric
Correio Elvense — CE
Correo de Honduras (Tegucigalpa) — Correo Hond Tegucigalpa
Correo de los Andes — CAn
Correo de los Andes (Argentina) — CDA
Correo Erudito — CE
Correo Fotografico Sudamericano — Corr Fotogr Sudam
Correo Literario — CLit
Correo Literario — CorL
Correspondance d'Orient. Etudes — Corresp Orient Et
Correspondance Municipale — Correspondance Munic
Correspondencia Militar [*Madrid*] — Corr Mil
Correspondent — C
Correspondent — Cor
Correspondentieblad. Orgaan der Centrale van Hogere Rijks- en Gemeente-Ambtenaren — CB
Correspondentieblad ten Dienste van de Floristiek en het Vegetatie-Onderzoek van Nederland — Correspondentiebl Dienste Florist Veg Onderz Ned
Correspondentieblad van de Broederschap der Notarissen in Nederland — Cbl Brsch Not Ned
Correspondentieblad van de Broederschap der Notarissen in Nederland — CBN
Correspondentieblad van de Broederschap der Notarissen in Nederland — Corr Blad
Correspondentieblad van de Centrale voor Hogere Rijksambtenaren — CCHR
Correspondentieblad van Hogere Rijksambtenaren — CHR
Correspondenz Blatt fuer Schweizer Aerzte — Corresp Bl Schweiz Aerzte
Correspondenzblatt des Entomologischen Vereins Iris zu Dresden — CB Iris
Correspondenzblatt des Naturforschenden Vereins zu Riga — Correspondenzbl Naturf Vereins Riga
Correspondenzblatt des Naturforschervereins zu Riga — CoBlNVR
Correspondenzblatt des Naturhistorischen Vereines fuer die Preussischen Rheinlande — Correspondenzbl Naturhist Vereines Preuss Rheinl
Correspondenzblatt. Naturforscher-Verein zu Riga — Cor-Bl Naturf-Ver Riga
Corrie Herring Hooks Series — Corrie Herring Hooks Ser
Corriere dei Ceramisti — Corr Ceram
Corriere del Farmacista — Corr Farm
Corriere del Farmacista — Corr Farmac
Corriere della Sera — CdS
Corriere della Sera — CS
Corriere Fotografico — Corr Fotogr
Corrosao e Proteccao de Materiais — Corros Prot Mater
Corrosie-Instituut TNO. Circulaire — Corros Inst TNO Circ
Corrosie-Instituut TNO. Mededeling — Corros Inst TNO Meded
Corrosion Abstracts — Corros Abstr
Corrosion and Coatings South Africa — Corros Coat S Afr
Corrosion and Degradation of Implant Materials. Symposium — Corros Degrad Implant Mater Symp
Corrosion and Its Prevention — Corros Its Prev
Corrosion and Maintenance [*India*] — Corros Maint
Corrosion and Material Protection — Corr Mater Prot
Corrosion and Material Protection — Corros Mater Prot
Corrosion and Materials — Corros Mater
Corrosion and Metal Finishing (South Africa) — Corr Met Finish (S Afr)
Corrosion and Metal Finishing. South Africa — Corros Met Finish S Afr
Corrosion Australasia — Corros Australas
Corrosion Bulletin — Corros Bull
Corrosion Bulletin (Karaikudi, India) — Corros Bull Karaikudi India
Corrosion Engineer — Corr Eng
Corrosion Engineering (Tokyo) — Corros Eng (Tokyo)
Corrosion et Anti-Corrosion [*France*] — Corros Anti-Corros
Corrosion Fatigue. Proceedings. USSR-UK Seminar on Corrosion Fatigue of Metals — Corros Fatigue Proc USSR UK Semin Corros Fatigue Met
Corrosion in Marine Environment — Corros Mar Environ
Corrosion in Marine Environment. International Sourcebook — Corros Mar Environ Int Sourceb
Corrosion of Electronic and Magnetic Materials — Corros Electron Magn Mater
Corrosion Prevention and Control — Corros Pre Contr
Corrosion Prevention and Control — Corros Prev Control
Corrosion Prevention and Control — Corrosion Prev Contr
Corrosion Prevention and Control — Corrosion Prev Control
Corrosion Prevention and Control — Corrosion Prevention

Corrosion Prevention in the Process Industries. Proceedings. NACE (National Association of Corrosion Engineers) International Symposium — Corros Prev Process Ind Proc NACE Int Symp
Corrosion Reviews — Corros Rev
Corrosion Science — Corros Sci
Corrosion Science — Corrosion Sci
Corrosion Technology [*England*] — Corros Technol
Corrosion Technology (New York) — Corros Technol NY
Corrosion Testing and Evaluation. Silver Anniversary Volume — Corros Test Eval Silver Anniv Vol
Corrosion, Traitements, Protection, Finition — Corros Trait Prot Finition
Corrosion Week. Manifestation. European Federation of Corrosion — Corros Week Manifestation Eur Fed Corros
Corrosion y Proteccion — Corros Prot
Corrugated Containers Conference. Preprints — Corrugated Containers Conf Prepr
Corrugated Newsletter — Corrugated Newsl
CORS [*Canadian Operational Research Society*] **Journal** — CORS J
Corse Historique — CHist
Corse Historique, Archeologique, Litteraire, Scientifique — Corse Hist Arch Lit Sci
Corse Historique. Etudes et Documents — Corse Hist
Corse Medicale — Corse Med
Corse Mediterranee Medicale — Corse Mediterr Med
Corsi di Cultura sull'Arte Ravennate e Bizantina — CCAB
Corsi e Seminari di Chimica. Consiglio Nazionale delle Ricerche e Fondazione "F. Giordani" — Corsi Semin Chim
Corsica Antica e Moderna — CAM
Corso di Cultura dell'Arte Ravennate e Bizantina — CCARB
Corso di Cultura dell'Arte Ravennate e Bizantina — Corsi Ravenna
Corso Teorico-Pratico sull'Utilizzazione delle Colture Cellulari nell'Indagine Tossicologica — Corso Teor Prat Util Colt Cell Indag Tossicol
Cortex — CRTXA
Cortisone Investigator — Cortisone Invest
Cosmetic Chemists. Journal of the Society — Cos Chem
Cosmetic Journal — Cosmet J
Cosmetic Medicine (Tokyo) — Cosmet Med (Tokyo)
Cosmetic News — Cosmet News
Cosmetic Technology — Cosmet Technol
Cosmetic, Toiletry, and Fragrance Association. Cosmetic Journal — Cosmet Toiletry Fragrance Assoc Cosmet J
Cosmetic World News — Cos Wld N
Cosmetic World News — CWN
Cosmetics and Perfumery — Cosmet Perfum
Cosmetics and Toiletries — Cos & Toil
Cosmetics and Toiletries — Cosmet & Toiletries
Cosmetics and Toiletries. Edizione Italiana — Cosmet Toiletries Ed Ital
Cosmetics International — Cos Intnl
Cosmetics International — CSE
Cosmic and Subatomic Physics Report — Cosmic Subatomic Phys Rep
Cosmic and Subatomic Physics Report LUIP. University of Lund. Department of Physics — Cosmic Subatomic Phys Rep LUIP Univ Lund Dep Phys
Cosmic Electrodynamics — Cosmic Electrodyn
Cosmic Ray Conference Papers. International Conference on Cosmic Rays — Cosmic Ray Conf Pap Int Conf Cosmic Rays
Cosmic Rays. Proceedings. International Conference — Cosmic Rays Proc Int Conf
Cosmic Research — Cosmic Res
Cosmic Research (English Translation) — Cosmic Res Engl Transl
Cosmic Science Fiction — Cosm
Cosmic Stories — Cos
Cosmopolitan — COS
Cosmopolitan — Cosmop
Cosmopolitan — Cosmopol
Cosmopolitan — GCOS
Cosmos [*Turin*] — C
Cosmos (Paris) — CP
Cosmos Science Fiction and Fantasy Magazine — Cos
COSPAR (Committee on Space Research) Space Research — COSPAR Space Res
COSPAR [*Committee on Space Research*] **Information Bulletin** [*Netherlands*] — COSPAR Inf Bull
Cost Accounting Standards Guide. Commerce Clearing House — Cost Accounting Stand Guide CCH
Cost and Management — COM
Cost and Management — Cost and Man
Cost and Management — Cost & Mgt
Cost and Management — Cost Manage
Cost and Management — CST
Cost Bulletin — Cost Bul
Cost Engineering — Cost Eng
Cost Engineering — CSE
Costa Azzurra Agricola-Floreale. Rivista Mensile di Floricoltura ed Orticoltura — Costa Azzurra Agric Fl
Costa Rica. Boletin de Fomento — Costa Rica B Fomento
Costa Rica. Centro de Estudios Sismologicos. Anales — Costa Rica Centro de Estudios Sismologicos An
Costa Rica. Instituto Geografico. Informe Semestral. Informe Trimestral — Costa Rica Inst Geog Informe Semestral Informe Trimestral
Costa Rica. Ministerio de Agricultura y Ganaderia. Boletin Miscelaneo — Costa Rica Minist Agric Ganad Bol Misc
Costa Rica. Ministerio de Agricultura y Ganaderia. Boletin Tecnico — Costa Rica Minist Agric Ganad Bol Tec
Costerus. Essays in English and American Language and Literature. New Series — Costerus Es
Costituzione Federale [*Switzerland*] — Cost Fed
Costruzioni Metalliche — Costr Met
Cote d'Azur Agricole et Horticole et la Revue Oleicole. Societe Centrale d'Agriculture, Horticulture, et d'Acclimatation de Nice et des Alpes-Maritimes — Cote d Azur Agric Hort
COTH [*Council of Teaching Hospitals*] **Report** — COTH Rep
Coton et Fibres Tropicales — Coton Fibr Trop
Coton et Fibres Tropicales — Coton Fibres Trop
Coton et Fibres Tropicales. Bulletin Analytique — Coton Fibres Trop Bull Anal
Coton et Fibres Tropicales. English Edition — Coton Fibres Trop Engl Ed
Cotton and Wool Situation. CWS. United States Department of Agriculture. Economics and Statistics Service — Cotton Wool Situat CWS US Dep Agric Econ Stat Serv
Cotton Counts Its Customers. Quantity of Cotton Consumed in Final Uses in the United States — Cotton Cts
Cotton Development — Cotton Dev
Cotton Digest — Cotton Dig
Cotton Dust Research Conference. Proceedings — Cotton Dust Res Conf Proc
Cotton Growing Review — Cotton Grow Rev
Cotton Growing Review. Journal. Cotton Research Corporation — Cotton Growing Rev
Cotton Improvement Conference — Cott Impr Conf
Cotton International — Cotton Int
Cotton International Edition — Cotton Int Ed
Cotton. Monthly Review of the World Situation — Cotton Rev
Cotton. Monthly Review of the World Situation — CTV
Cotton Research Corporation. Cotton Research Reports — Cotton Res Corp Cotton Res Rep
Cotton Research Corporation. Progress Reports from Experiment Stations — Cotton Res Corp Prog Rep Exp Stn
Cotton Research Institute. Sindos Science Bulletin. New Series — Cotton Res Inst Sindos Sci Bull New Ser
Cotton States Association of Commissioners of Agriculture. Proceedings — Cotton States Assoc Comm Agric Proc
Cotton. World Statistics — Cotton WS
Coulometric Analysis. Conference — Coulom Anal Conf
Council for Agricultural Science and Technology. Report — Counc Agric Sci Technol Rep
Council for British Archaeology. Annual Report — Counc Brit Archaeol Annu Rep
Council for British Archaeology. Research Reports — Counc Brit Archaeol Res Rep
Council for Mineral Technology. Report — Counc Miner Technol Rep
Council for Research in Music Education. Bulletin — CMUE B
Council for Research in Music Education. Bulletin — Council Research M Education Bul
Council for Research in Music Education. Bulletin — CRME
Council for Sciences of Indonesia. Publication — Counc Sci Indones Publ
Council for Scientific and Industrial Research. Air Pollution Research Group. Report APRG (South Africa) — CSIR Air Pollut Res Group Rep APRG (S Afr)
Council for Scientific and Industrial Research and Department of Mines and the Asbestos Mining Industry. Asbestosis Research Project. Annual Report — CSIR Dep Mines Asbestos Min Ind Asbestosis Res Proj Annu Rep
Council for Scientific and Industrial Research. National Building Research Institute. Report BOU (South Africa) — CSIR Natl Build Res Inst Rep BOU S Afr
Council for Scientific and Industrial Research (South Africa) — Counc Sci Ind Res S Afr
Council Notes — Counc Notes
Council of Europe Forum — Counc Eur For
Council of Europe. Information Bulletin — Council Eur Inf Bull
Council of Mining and Metallurgical Institutions Congress — Counc Min Metall Inst Congr
Council of Ontario Universities Quadrennial Review — Counc Ont Univ Quad Rev
Council on Anthropology and Education. Quarterly — Council Anthropol Educ Qu
Council on Economic Priorities. Newsletter — Counc Econ Prior Newsl
Council on Legal Education for Professional Responsibility. Newsletter — Council Legal Educ Prof Resp Newsl
Council on National Literatures. Quarterly World Report — CNLR
Council on the Study of Religion. Bulletin — C S R Bul
Counciline Newsletter. Canadian Council for Native Business — CCNB
Counseling and Values — C and V
Counseling and Values — Counsel & Values
Counseling and Values — Counsel Val
Counseling Psychologist — Couns Psych
Counseling Psychologist — PCOU
Counsellor's Forum — Couns For
Counselor Education and Supervision — Couns Ed Su
Counselor Education and Supervision — Counsel Ed & Sup
Counselor Education and Supervision — Counsel Educ & Superv
Countermedia. Alaska Journalism Review and Supplement — COMD
Counterpoint — Counterpt
Country Calendar — Country Cal
Country Dance and Song — CDS
Country Dance and Song Society. News — CDSS N
Country Demographic Profiles — Ctry Demogr Profiles
Country Economic Profiles [*Database*] — CEP
Country Gentleman — Country Gent
Country Gentleman — Ctry Gentleman
Country Gentleman (Dublin) — Country Gent Dublin
Country Gentleman (Philadelphia) — Country Gent Philadelphia
Country Hour Journal — Country Hour J
Country Journal — Ctry J

Country Journal — GCOJ
Country Kids — Country
Country Landowner — Ctry Landowner
Country Life [*London*] — CL
Country Life — Ctry Life
Country Life in America — Ctry Life Am
Country Life. Journal for All Interested in Country Life and Country Pursuits (London) — Country Life London
Country Living — GCOU
Country Magazine — Ctry Mag
Country Market Survey. Computers and Peripheral Equipment (Bahrain) — CMS Cmp (Bah)
Country Market Survey. Computers and Peripheral Equipment (Canada) — CMS Cmp (Cda)
Country Market Survey. Computers and Peripheral Equipment (France) — CMS Cmp (Fra)
Country Market Survey. Computers and Peripheral Equipment (Japan) — CMS Cmp (Jpn)
Country Market Survey. Computers and Peripheral Equipment (Kuwait) — CMS Cmp (Kuw)
Country Market Survey. Computers and Peripheral Equipment (Saudi Arabia) — CMS Cmp (Sau)
Country Market Survey. Computers and Peripheral Equipment (Singapore) — CMS Cmp (Sin)
Country Market Survey. Computers and Peripheral Equipment (Sweden) — CMS Cmp (Swe)
Country Market Survey. Computers and Peripheral Equipment (Taiwan) — CMS Cmp (Tai)
Country Market Survey. Computers and Peripheral Equipment (United Arab Emirates) — CMS Cmp (Emi)
Country Market Survey. Computers and Peripheral Equipment (United Kingdom) — CMS Cmp (UK)
Country Market Survey. Computers and Peripheral Equipment (Yugoslavia) — CMS Cmp (Yug)
Country Market Survey. Electric Power Systems (Colombia) — CMS EPS (Col)
Country Market Survey. Electric Power Systems (Egypt) — CMS EPS (Egy)
Country Market Survey. Electric Power Systems (Nigeria) — CMS EPS (Nig)
Country Market Survey. Electric Power Systems (Philippines) — CMS EPS (Phi)
Country Market Survey. Electric Power Systems (Saudi Arabia) — CMS EPS (Sau)
Country Market Survey. Electric Power Systems (Spain) — CMS EPS (Spa)
Country Market Survey. Electric Power Systems (Thailand) — CMS EPS (Tha)
Country Market Survey. Electric Power Systems (Yugoslavia) — CMS EPS (Yug)
Country Market Survey. Electronic Components (Austria) — CMS EIC (Aut)
Country Market Survey. Electronic Components (Mexico) — CMS EIC (Mex)
Country Market Survey. Electronic Components (Philippines) — CMS EIC (Phl)
Country Market Survey. Electronic Components (Switzerland) — CMS EIC (Swl)
Country Market Survey. Electronic Components (Taiwan) — CMS EIC (Tai)
Country Market Survey. Food Processing Packaging Equipment (Thailand) — CMS FPP (Tha)
Country Market Survey. Graphic Industries Equipment (Australia) — CMS GIE (Aus)
Country Market Survey. Graphic Industries Equipment (Japan) — CMS GIE (Jpn)
Country Market Survey. Graphic Industries Equipment (Mexico) — CMS GIE (Mex)
Country Market Survey. Graphic Industries Equipment (Netherlands) — CMS GIE (Net)
Country Market Survey. Graphic Industries Equipment (South Africa) — CMS GIE (Soa)
Country Market Survey. Graphic Industries Equipment (United Kingdom) — CMS GIE (UK)
Country Market Survey. Industrial Process Controls (Australia) — CMS IPC (Aus)
Country Market Survey. Industrial Process Controls (Brazil) — CMS IPC (Bra)
Country Market Survey. Industrial Process Controls (France) — CMS IPC (Fra)
Country Market Survey. Industrial Process Controls (Singapore) — CMS IPC (Sin)
Country Market Survey. Industrial Process Controls (South Korea) — CMS IPC (Sok)
Country Market Survey. Industrial Process Controls (Spain) — CMS IPC (Spa)
Country Market Survey. Industrial Process Controls (Taiwan) — CMS IPC (Tai)
Country Market Survey. Laboratory Instruments (Japan) — CMS Lab (Jpn)
Country Market Survey. Laboratory Instruments (Spain) — CMS Lab (Spa)
Country Market Survey. Machine Tools (Portugal) — CMS MTL (Por)
Country Market Survey. Medical Equipment (Argentina) — CMS MED (Arg)
Country Market Survey. Medical Equipment (Australia) — CMS MED (Aus)
Country Market Survey. Medical Equipment (Brazil) — CMS MED (Bra)
Country Market Survey. Medical Equipment (Canada) — CMS MED (Can)
Country Market Survey. Medical Equipment (Japan) — CMS MED (Jpn)
Country Market Survey. Mining Industry Equipment (Pakistan) — CMS MIE (Pak)
Country Market Survey. Mining Industry Equipment (Zaire) — CMS MIE (Zai)
Country Market Survey. Pollution Instrumentation and Equipment (Israel) — CMS PCE (Isr)
Country Market Survey. Pollution Instrumentation and Equipment (Philippines) [*A publication*] — CMS PCE (Phl)
Country Market Survey. Pollution Instrumentation and Equipment (Taiwan) — CMS PCE (Tai)
Country Market Survey. Pollution Instrumentation and Equipment (West Germany) — CMS PCE (W Ge)
Country Market Survey. Sporting and Recreational Equipment (Argentina) — CMS SGR (Arg)
Country Market Survey. Sporting and Recreational Equipment (Saudi Arabia) — CMS SGR (Sau)
Country Market Survey. Sporting and Recreational Equipment (Sweden) — CMS SGR (Swe)
Country Market Survey. Sporting and Recreational Equipment (Switzerland) — CMS SGR (Swi)
Country Market Survey. Sporting and Recreational Equipment (United Kingdom) — CMS SGR (UK)
Country Market Survey. Telecommunications Equipment (Argentina) — CMS TCE (Arg)
Country Market Survey. Telecommunications Equipment (China) — CMS TCE (Chn)
Country Market Survey. Telecommunications Equipment (France) — CMS TCE (Fra)
Country Market Survey. Telecommunications Equipment (Germany) — CMS TCE (Ger)
Country Market Survey. Telecommunications Equipment (Kuwait) — CMS TCE (Kuw)
Country Market Survey. Telecommunications Equipment (Pakistan) — CMS TCE (Pak)
Country Market Survey. Telecommunications Equipment (Philippines) — CMS TCE (Phl)
Country Market Survey. Telecommunications Equipment (Saudi Arabia) — CMS TCE (Sau)
Country Market Survey. Telecommunications Equipment (Spain) — CMS TCE (Spa)
Country Market Survey. Telecommunications Equipment (Thailand) — CMS TCE (Tha)
Country Market Survey. Telecommunications Equipment (United Arab Emirates) — CMS TCE (Emi)
Country Music — ICMU
Country Profiles — Ctry Profiles
Country Traders' Review — Country Traders R
Country Women — Cntry Wom
Country Women — Ctry Women
Countryside and Small Stock Journal — ICTY
Countryside Commission. Journal — Countryside Comm J
Countryside Magazine — Countryside M
Countryside Magazine and Suburban Life — Countryside M
County Court Reports (Victoria) — CCR (VIC)
County Court Reports (Victoria) — Vic CC
County Donegal Historical Society. Journal — Donegal Hist Soc J
County Employment Reporter — County Employ Rep
County Kildare Archaeological Society. Journal — Kildare Arch Soc J
County Louth Archaeological and Historical Journal — Co Louth Archaeol Hist J
County Louth Archaeological Journal — Louth Arch J
County Newsletter — County Newsl
County Report. California. Division of Mines and Geology — Cty Rep Calif Div Mines Geol
County Report. Idaho. Bureau of Mines and Geology — Cty Rep Idaho Bur Mines Geol
County Report. Kentucky Geological Survey — Cty Rep K Geol Surv
County Report. Mississippi Board of Water Commissioners — Cty Rep Miss Board Water Comm
County Resource Series. Geological Survey of Wyoming — Cty Resour Ser Geol Surv Wyo
Cour de Cassation. Chambres Reunies [*France*] — Cass Ch Reun
Cour de Cassation. Criminelle [*France*] — Cass Crim
Cour de Cassation. Deuxieme Section Civile [*France*] — Cass Civ 2e
Cour de Cassation. Premiere Section Civile [*France*] — Cass Civ 1re
Cour de Cassation. Requetes [*France*] — Cass Req
Cour de Cassation. Sociale [*France*] — Cass Soc
Cour Permanente de Justice Internationale — CPJI
Cour Permanente de Justice Internationale. Serie A/B. Recueil des Arrets. Avis Consultatifs et Ordonnances — CPJI-A/B
Cour Permanente de Justice Internationale. Serie A. Recueil des Arrets — CPJI-A
Cour Permanente de Justice Internationale. Serie B. Recueil des Avis Consultatifs — CPJI-B
Courier [*Formerly, UNESCO Courier*] — GCUN
Courier de la Bourse et de la Banque — CRB
Courier. European Community, Africa, Caribbean, Pacific — CNH
Courier Forschungsinstitut Senckenberg — Cour Forschungsinst Senckenb
Courier-Journal — COUR
Courier-Journal — Courier Jl
Courrier Apicole — Courr Apic
Courrier. Centre International pour l'Enfance — Courr Centre Int Enfance
Courrier de la Nature — Courr Nat
Courrier de la Normalisation — Courr Norm
Courrier de l'Extreme-Orient — CEO
Courrier de l'Extreme-Orient — Courr Extr-Orient
Courrier des Etablissements Neu — CENUA
Courrier des Etablissements Neu [*France*] — Courr Etabl Neu
Courrier des Pays de l'Est — Courr Pays Est
Courrier des Pays de l'Est — Courrier Pays Est
Courrier des Pays de l'Est. Mensuel d'Informations Economiques — COU
Courrier du Centre National de la Recherche Scientifique — Courrier du CNRS
Courrier du CNRS [*Centre National de la Recherche Scientifique*] — Cour CNRS
Courrier du CNRS [*Centre National de la Recherche Scientifique*]. **Supplement** — Cour CNRS Suppl
Courrier Graphique — CG
Courrier Graphique — Cour Graph
Courrier Hebdomadaire. Centre de Recherche et d'Information Socio-Politiques — CHCRISP

Courrier Hebdomadaire du CRISP (Centre de Recherche et d'Information Socio-Politiques) — Courr Hebd du CRISP
Courrier Musical de France — CMdF
Courrier Musical de France — CMF
Courrier Musical de France — Cour Mus France
Courrier Musical de France — Courrier M France
Courrier Phytochimique — Courrier Phytochim
Courrier Revue Medico-Sociale de l'Enfance — Courrier
Courrier. UNESCO — Courr UNESCO
Cours d'Analyse de l'Ecole Royale Polytechnique — Cours Anal Ecole Roy Polytech
Cours de Geometrie de la Faculte des Sciences — Cours Geom Fac Sci
Cours de Perfectionnement du Notariat — CP du N
Cours de Perfectionnement en Pediatrie pour le Practicien — Cours Perfect Pediatr Prat
Cours de Perfectionnement. Societe Suisse de Psychiatrie — Cours Perfect Soc Suisse Psychiatr
Cours et Documents de Biologie — Cours Doc Bil
Cours Specialises — Cours Spec
Court Management Journal — Court Man Jnl
Court Management Journal — Court Mgt J
Court of Review Decisions (Ratcliffe and McGrath) — R & McG Ct of Rev
Covenant Quarterly — Cov Q
Coventry Engineering Society. Journal — Coventry Eng Soc J
Covert Action — Covrt Act
Cow Moos. Newsletter for Maryland Dairymen. Maryland University. Cooperative Extension Service — Cow Moos Newsl Md Dairymen Md Univ Coop Ext Serv
COWA [*Council for Old World Archaeology*] **Survey. Current Work in Old World Archaeology** — COWA CW
Coyote's Journal — CJ
Coyoti Prints. Caribou Tribal Council Newsletter — CP
Coyuntura Economica — Coyunt Econ
Coyuntura Economica — Coyuntura Econ
CP. Corrosion y Proteccion — CP Corris Prot
CPA [*Certified Public Accountant*] **Computer Report** — CPA Comp Rep
CPA [*American Institute of Certified Public Accountants*] **Journal** — CPA
CPA [*American Institute of Certified Public Accountants*] **Journal** — CPAJ
CPCU [*Chartered Property and Casualty Underwriters*] **Journal** — CUJ
CPHERI (Central Public Health Engineering Research Institute. Nagpur, India) Bulletin — CPHERI Bull
CPI [*Consumer Price Index*] **Detailed Report. US and City Averages. US Bureau of Labor Statistics** — BLS CPI
CPI [*Current Physics Index*] **Management Service** — CPI Mgmt
CPJ Equipment Reporter — CPJ Equip Rep
CPPA [*Canadian Pulp and Paper Association*] **Monthly Newsprint Report** — CPPA Newsprint Rept
CPPA [*Canadian Pulp and Paper Association*] **Newsprint Data** — CPPA Newsprint Data
CPPA [*Canadian Pulp and Paper Association*] **Press Digest** — CPPA Press Dig
CPPA [*Canadian Pulp and Paper Association*] **Reference Tables** — CPPA Ref Tables
CPPA [*Canadian Pulp and Paper Association*] **Technical Section. Proceedings** — CPPA Tech Sect Proc
CPU-Estudios Sociales — CPU
CQ [*Call to Quarters*]. Radio Amateur's Journal — CQ Radio Amat J
CQ [*Call to Quarters*]. Radio Amateur's Journal — CQCQA
CQ Researcher [*Formerly, Editorial Research Reports*] — GERR
CR [*Chemische Rundschau*] **Magazin** — CR Mag
Craft Australia — Craft A
Craft Australia — Craft Aust
Craft Horizons — Cr H
Craft Horizons — Craft Hor
Craft Horizons — Craft Horiz
Crafts Report — Crafts Rep
Crafts'n Things — ICNT
Crain's Chicago Business — CCHI
Crain's Chicago Business — Chicago Bs
Crain's Cleveland Business — CCLE
Crain's Cleveland Business — Cleve Busn
Crain's Detroit Business — CDET
Crain's Detroit Business — Crain Detro
Crain's Illinois Business — CIL
Crain's Illinois Business — Crain Illin
Crain's New York Business — CNYB
Crain's New York Business — Crains NY
Crampton's Magazine — Cramp Mag
Cranbrook Institute of Science. Bulletin — Cranbrook Inst Sci Bull
Cranbrook Institute of Science. Bulletin. News Letter — Cranbrook Inst Sci Bull News Letter
Crane Review — CraneR
Crank. Sibley Journal of Engineering — Crank Sibley J Eng
Crassulacean Acid Metabolism. Proceedings. Annual Symposium in Botany — Crassulacean Acid Metab Proc Annu Symp Bot
Crawdaddy — Cy
CRC (Coordinating Research Council) Report — CRC Rep
CRC [*Chemical Rubber Company*] **Critical Reviews in Analytical Chemistry** — CCACB
CRC [*Chemical Rubber Company*] **Critical Reviews in Analytical Chemistry** — CRC Crit Rev Anal Chem
CRC [*Chemical Rubber Company*] **Critical Reviews in Biochemistry** — CRC Crit Rev Biochem
CRC Critical Reviews in Biochemistry and Molecular Biology — CRC Crit Rev Biochem Mol Biol
CRC [*Chemical Rubber Company*] **Critical Reviews in Biocompatibility** — CCRBES
CRC [*Chemical Rubber Company*] **Critical Reviews in Biocompatibility** — CRC Crit Rev Biocompat
CRC [*Chemical Rubber Company*] **Critical Reviews in Bioengineering** — CRC Crit Rev Bioeng
CRC [*Chemical Rubber Company*] **Critical Reviews in Biomedical Engineering** — CRC Crit Rev Biomed Eng
CRC [*Chemical Rubber Company*] **Critical Reviews in Biotechnology** — CRBTE5
CRC [*Chemical Rubber Company*] **Critical Reviews in Biotechnology** — CRC Crit Rev Biotechnol
CRC [*Chemical Rubber Company*] **Critical Reviews in Clinical Laboratory Sciences** — CRC Crit Rev Clin Lab Sci
CRC [*Chemical Rubber Company*] **Critical Reviews in Clinical Neurobiology** — CCRNEU
CRC [*Chemical Rubber Company*] **Critical Reviews in Clinical Neurobiology** — CRC C R NEU
CRC [*Chemical Rubber Company*] **Critical Reviews in Clinical Neurobiology** — CRC Crit Rev Clin Neurobiol
CRC [*Chemical Rubber Company*] **Critical Reviews in Clinical Radiology and Nuclear Medicine** — CRC Crit Rev Clin Radiol Nucl Med
CRC [*Chemical Rubber Company*] **Critical Reviews in Diagnostic Imaging** — CRC Crit Rev Diagn Imaging
CRC [*Chemical Rubber Company*] **Critical Reviews in Diagnostic Imaging** — CRDIDF
CRC [*Chemical Rubber Company*] **Critical Reviews in Environmental Control** — CCECA
CRC [*Chemical Rubber Company*] **Critical Reviews in Environmental Control** — CRC Crit Rev Environ Control
CRC [*Chemical Rubber Company*] **Critical Reviews in Food Science and Nutrition** — CRC Crit Rev Food Sci Nutr
CRC [*Chemical Rubber Company*] **Critical Reviews in Food Technology** — CRC Crit Rev Food Technol
CRC [*Chemical Rubber Company*] **Critical Reviews in Immunology** — CCRIDE
CRC [*Chemical Rubber Company*] **Critical Reviews in Immunology** — CRC Crit Rev Immunol
CRC [*Chemical Rubber Company*] **Critical Reviews in Microbiology** — CRC Crit R Microbiol
CRC [*Chemical Rubber Company*] **Critical Reviews in Microbiology** — CRC Crit Rev Microbiol
CRC [*Chemical Rubber Company*] **Critical Reviews in Microbiology** — CRVMAC
CRC Critical Reviews in Neurobiology — CRC Crit Rev Neurobiol
CRC [*Chemical Rubber Company*] **Critical Reviews in Oncology/Hematology** — CCRHEC
CRC [*Chemical Rubber Company*] **Critical Reviews in Oncology/Hematology** — CRC Crit Rev Oncol/Hematol
CRC [*Chemical Rubber Company*] **Critical Reviews in Plant Sciences** — CRC Crit Rev Plant Sci
CRC [*Chemical Rubber Company*] **Critical Reviews in Radiological Sciences** — CRC Crit Rev Radiol Sci
CRC [*Chemical Rubber Company*] **Critical Reviews in Radiological Sciences** — CRRDB
CRC [*Chemical Rubber Company*] **Critical Reviews in Solid State and Materials Sciences** — CRC Crit Rev Solid State Mater Sci
CRC [*Chemical Rubber Company*] **Critical Reviews in Solid State Sciences** — CRC Crit Rev Solid Sci
CRC Critical Reviews in Solid States Sciences — CRC Crit Rev Solid State Sci
CRC [*Chemical Rubber Company*] **Critical Reviews in Therapeutic Drug Carrier Systems** — CRC Crit Rev Ther Drug Carrier Syst
CRC [*Chemical Rubber Company*] **Critical Reviews in Therapeutic Drug Carrier Systems** — CRTSEO
CRC [*Chemical Rubber Company*] **Critical Reviews in Toxicology** — CRC Crit Rev Toxicol
CRC Handbook of Chromatography. Lipids — CRC Handb Chromatogr Lipids
CRC [*Chemical Rubber Company*] **Handbook of Experimental Aspects of Oral Biochemistry** — CRC Handb Exp Aspects Oral Biochem
CRC Handbook of HPLC (High Performance Liquid Chromatography) for the Separation — CRC Handb HPLC Sep Amino Acids Pept Proteins
CRC Handbook of Laser Science and Technology — CRC Handb Laser Sci Technol
CRC Handbook of Lasers with Selected Data on Optical Technology — CRC Handb Lasers Sel Data Opt Technol
CRC Handbook of Natural Pesticides. Methods — CRC Handb Nat Pestic Methods
CRC [*Chemical Rubber Company*] **Handbook of Naturally Occurring Food Toxicants** [*A publication*] — CRC Handb Nat Occurring Food Toxicants
CRC [*Chemical Rubber Company*] **Handbook of Nutritional Supplements** — CRC Handb Nutr Suppl
CRC Handbook of Pharmacologie Methodologies for the Study of the Neuroendocrine System — CRC Handb Pharmacol Methodol Study Neuroendocr Syst
CRC [*Chemical Rubber Company*] **Handbook of Stereoisomers. Drugs in Psychopharmacology** — CRC Handb Stereoisomers Drugs Psychopharmacol
CRC Handbook of Thermoelectrics — CRC Handb Thermoelectr
CRC Mathematical Modelling Series — CRC Math Model Ser
CRC Press Series on Discrete Mathematics and its Applications — CRC Press Ser Discrete Math Appl
CRC [*Chemical Rubber Company*] **Reviews in Biomedical Engineering** — CRBEDR
CRC [*Chemical Rubber Company*] **Reviews in Plant Sciences** — CRPSD3
CRC Series in Computational Mechanics and Applied Analysis — CRC Ser Comput Mech Appl Anal
CRD Newsletter. United States Department of Agriculture. Science and Education Administration. Extension, Community, and Rural Development — CRD Newsl US Dep Agric Ext Community Rural Dev

Creacion de Rerchesches Caraibes — CRE
Creamery and Milk Plant Monthly — Creamery Milk Plant Mon
Creamery Journal — Creamery J
Creation and Detection of the Excited State — Creat Detect Excited State
Creation/Evolution — C/E
Creation Research Society. Quarterly — Creat Res Soc Q
Creation Research Society. Quarterly — Creation Res Soc Q
Creation Research Society. Quarterly — CRSQ
Creative Child and Adult Quarterly — Creative Child Adult Q
Creative Computing — Creative Comput
Creative Computing — Creatv Comp
Creative Crafts — Cr Crafts
Creative Crafts — Creat Crafts
Creative Guitar International — CGI
Creative Moment — CMo
Creative Photography — Creat Photogr
Creative Photography — Creative Photogr
Creative Writing — Cr Wtg
Credit — CRE
Credit — CRI
Credit and Financial Management — C F Mgmt
Credit and Financial Management — CFM
Credit and Financial Management — Credit & Fin Mgt
Credit and Financial Management — Credit Financ Manage
Credit Communal de Belgique. Bulletin Trimestriel — Credit Communal Belgique Bul Trim
Credit Management — CRM
Credit Monthly — Credit M
Credit Suisse. Bulletin — Cred Suisse B
Credit Suisse. Bulletin — Credit Suisse Bul
Credit Suisse. Bulletin (Zurich) — Credit Suisse Bul (Zurich)
Credit Union Executive — CUE
Credit Union Magazine — Credit Union M
Credit Union Magazine — CUG
Credit Union Management — CUM
Credit World — Credit Wld
Credit World — CWD
Creditanstalt-Bankverein. Wirtschaftsberichte — Creditanst-Bankverein Wirtschaftsber
Creditanstalt-Bankverein. Wirtschaftsberichte — CRV
Credito Rural — Cred Rur
Creem Magazine — CRCMC
Creem Magazine — Creem M
Creep and Fracture of Engineering Materials and Structures. Proceedings of the International Conference — Creep Fract Eng Mater Struct Proc Int Conf
Creep in Structures. Symposium — Creep Struct Symp
Creighton Law Review — Cre LR
Creighton Law Review — Creighton L Rev
Crescendo & Jazz Music — Crescendo & Jazz Mus
Crescendo International — CRCFA
Crescendo International — Crescendo Int
Cresset — Cres
Cresterea Colectiilor. Caiet Selectiv de Informare Bibliotecii Academiei Republicii Socialiste Romania — Crest Colect
Cresterea Patrimoniului Muzeal Buletin — Crest Patr Muz Bul
Cretaceous Research — Cretaceous Res
Cretaceous Research — CRRSDD
Cretacico de la Peninsula Iberica — Cretacico Peninsula Iber
Cretan Seals — CS
CRI [*Carpet and Rug Institute*] **Newsletter** — CRI Newsl
CRIEPI (Central Research Institute of Electric Power Industry) Report — CRIEPI (Cent Res Inst Electr Power Ind) Rep
CRIEPI [*Central Research Institute of Electric Power Industry*] **Report** — CRCIDA
Crime and Delinquency — CAD
Crime and Delinquency — Crim & Delin
Crime and Delinquency — Crime & Delin
Crime and Delinquency — Crime & Delin'cy
Crime and Delinquency — Crime & Delinq
Crime and Delinquency — Crime Delin
Crime and Delinquency — GCDL
Crime and Delinquency Abstracts — Crime Delinq Abstr
Crime and Delinquency Literature — Crime Delinq Lit
Crime and Justice — Crime and Just
Crime and Social Justice — Crim Just
Crime and Social Justice — Crime & Soc Just
Crime and Social Justice [*Australia*] — CSJ
Crime in the United States — Crime
Crime Prevention News — CPN
Crime Prevention News — Crime Prev News
Crimen. Tijdschrift voor Criminologie en Criminalistiek — Cr
Criminal Defense — Crim Def
Criminal Injuries Compensation — Crim Inj Comp
Criminal Justice — Cr Just
Criminal Justice Abstracts — Crim Justice Abstr
Criminal Justice and Behavior — Crim J and Beh
Criminal Justice and Behavior — Crim Just & Behav
Criminal Justice and Behavior — Crim Just B
Criminal Justice and Behavior — GCJB
Criminal Justice Ethics — Crim Just Ethics
Criminal Justice Ethics — PCRJ
Criminal Justice Journal — Crim Just J
Criminal Justice Newsletter — Crim Just Newsl
Criminal Justice Periodical Index [*University Microfilms International*] [*Ann Arbor, MI Bibliographic database*] — CJPI
Criminal Justice Periodical Index — Crim Justice Period Index
Criminal Justice Quarterly — Criminal Justice Q
Criminal Justice Review — Criminal Justice R
Criminal Law Audio Series — CLAS
Criminal Law Bulletin — Crim L Bul
Criminal Law Bulletin — Crim L Bull
Criminal Law Bulletin — Crim Law Bul
Criminal Law Bulletin — Criminal Law Bul
Criminal Law Journal — CLJ
Criminal Law Journal — Crim LJ
Criminal Law Journal of India — CLJ
Criminal Law Journal of India — Cr LJ
Criminal Law Journal of India — Crim LJ Ind
Criminal Law Journal of India — Crim LJI
Criminal Law Journal (Sydney) [*Australia*] — Crim LJ (Sydney)
Criminal Law Quarterly — Crim L Q
Criminal Law Quarterly — Crim Law Q
Criminal Law Quarterly — Criminal LQ
Criminal Law Reporter — Cr Law Rep
Criminal Law Reporter — Cr LR
Criminal Law Reporter — Crim L Rep
Criminal Law Reporter — Crim L Rptr
Criminal Law Reporter. Bureau of National Affairs — Crim L Rep BNA
Criminal Law Review — Crim L R
Criminal Law Review — Crim L Rev
Criminal Law Review — Crim Law R
Criminal Law Review (England) — Crim L Rev (England)
Criminal Reports — CR
Criminal Reports — Cr R
Criminal Reports — Cr Rep
Criminal Reports [*Carswell Company*] — Crim Rep
Criminal Reports (Canada) — (Can) Crim
Criminal Reports (Canada) — Crim R (Can)
Criminal Reports. New Series — Crim Rep NS
Criminal Reports. New Series — CRNS
Criminal Reports. Third Series. Annotated — CR 3d
Criminalia — CMA
Criminalia. Organo. Academia Mexicana de Ciencias Penales (Mexico) — Criminal Mex
Criminology — Crim
Criminology — Crimin
Criminology — PCRY
Criminology an Interdisciplinary Journal — CIJ
Criminology and Penology Abstracts — CPA
Criminology and Penology Abstracts — Crim Penol Abstr
Crisia Culegere de Materiale si Studii — Crisia
Crisis — Cr
Criss-Cross Art Communications — Criss-Cross
Cristallier Suisse — Crist Suisse
Cristianesimo nella Storia — Cr St
Cristianesimo nella Storia — CrS
Cristianismo y Sociedad — Crist y Soc
Cristianismo y Sociedad — Cristianismo Soc
Cristianismo y Sociedad — CYS
Criterio — CR
Criterio — Crit
Criterio (Colombia) — COC
Criterio Economico — Criterio Econ
Criterion — Cr
Criterion — Cri
Criterion — Crit
Criterium. Letterkundig Maandblad — Crit
Critic — Crit
Critica — C
Critica — Crit
Critica Contemporanea (Caracas) — Crit Contem Caracas
Critica d'Arte — CA
Critica d'Arte — Cr d'A
Critica d'Arte [*Florence*] — Crit Ar
Critica d'Arte — Crit Arte
Critica d'Arte — Crit d A
Critica (Espana) — CAE
Critica Hispanica — CH
Critica Juridica — CJ
Critica Marxista — Crit Marx
Critica Penale — Crit Pen
Critica Politica — Crit Pol
Critica. Revista Hispano-Americana de Filosofia (Mexico) — CAM
Critica Sociale — Crit Soc
Critica Sociologica (Roma) — Crit Sociol (Roma)
Critica Storica — C Stor
Critica Storica — Crit Stor
Critica Storica — CrS
Critica Storica — CS
Critical Arts — Crit Arts
Critical Care Clinics — Crit Care Clin
Critical Care Medicine — CCM
Critical Care Medicine — CCMDC
Critical Care Medicine — Crit Care Med
Critical Care Nurse — Crit C Nurse
Critical Care Nurse — Crit Care Nurse
Critical Care Quarterly — CCCQDV
Critical Care Quarterly — CCQ
Critical Care Quarterly — Crit Care Q
Critical Care Quarterly — Crit CQ
Critical Care Update — Crit Care Update

Critical Current Limitations in High Temperature Superconductors. Proceedings. International Workshop — Crit Curr Limitations High Temp Supercond Proc Int Workshop
Critical Currents in Superconductors — Crit Curr Supercond
Critical Evaluation of Some Equilibrium Constants Involving Alkylammonium Extractants — Crit Eval Some Equil Constants Involv Alkylammonium Extr
Critical Inquiry — CI
Critical Inquiry — Crit I
Critical Inquiry — Crit Inq
Critical Inquiry — GCIQ
Critical Introduction to the Apocrypha [*A*] [*L. H. Brockinton*] — BCIA
Critical List — Crit List
Critical Mass Journal — Crit Mass J
Critical Perspectives — Crit Perspe
Critical Quarterly — CQ
Critical Quarterly — Crit Q
Critical Quarterly — Crit Quart
Critical Quarterly — CrQ
Critical Quarterly — PCRQ
Critical Reports on Applied Chemistry — Crit Rep Appl Chem
Critical Review — CR
Critical Review — Crit R
Critical Review — Crit Rev
Critical Review of Theological and Philosophical Literature — CRL
Critical Reviews in Analytical Chemistry — Cr R Anal C
Critical Reviews in Analytical Chemistry — Crit Rev Anal Chem
Critical Reviews in Biochemistry — Crit Rev Biochem
Critical Reviews in Biochemistry and Molecular Biology — Cr R Bioche
Critical Reviews in Biochemistry and Molecular Biology — Crit Rev Biochem Mol Biol
Critical Reviews in Biocompatibility — Crit Rev Biocompat
Critical Reviews in Bioengineering — Crit Rev Bioeng
Critical Reviews in Biomedical Engineering — Cr R Biomed
Critical Reviews in Biomedical Engineering — Crit Rev Biomed Eng
Critical Reviews in Biotechnology — Cr R Biotec
Critical Reviews in Biotechnology — Crit Rev Biotechnol
Critical Reviews in Clinical Laboratory — Cr R Cl Lab
Critical Reviews in Clinical Laboratory Sciences — Crit Rev Clin Lab Sci
Critical Reviews in Clinical Neurobiology — Crit Rev Clin Neurobiol
Critical Reviews in Clinical Radiology and Nuclear Medicine — Crit Rev Clin Radiol Nucl Med
Critical Reviews in Diagnostic Imaging — Cr R Diagn
Critical Reviews in Diagnostic Imaging — Crit Rev Diagn Imaging
Critical Reviews in Environmental Control — Cr R Env C
Critical Reviews in Environmental Control — Crit Rev Environ Control
Critical Reviews in Eukaryotic Gene Expression — Crit Rev Eukaryot Gene Expr
Critical Reviews in Food Science and Nutrition — Cr R F Sci
Critical Reviews in Food Science and Nutrition — Crit Rev Food Sci Nutr
Critical Reviews in Food Technology — Crit Rev Food Technol
Critical Reviews in Immunology — Cr R Immun
Critical Reviews in Immunology — Crit Rev Immunol
Critical Reviews in Microbiology — Cr R Microb
Critical Reviews in Microbiology — Crit Rev Microbiol
Critical Reviews in Neurobiology — Cr R Neur
Critical Reviews in Neurobiology — Crit Rev Neurobiol
Critical Reviews in Oncogenesis — Crit Rev Oncog
Critical Reviews in Oncology/Hematology — Cr R Onc H
Critical Reviews in Oncology/Hematology — Crit Rev Oncol/Hematol
Critical Reviews in Oral Biology and Medicine — Crit Rev Oral Biol Med
Critical Reviews in Plant Sciences — Cr R Plant
Critical Reviews in Plant Sciences — Crit Rev Plant Sci
Critical Reviews in Radiological Sciences — Crit Rev Radiol Sci
Critical Reviews in Solid State and Materials Sciences — Crit Rev Solid State Mater Sci
Critical Reviews in Solid State Sciences — Crit Rev Solid State Sci
Critical Reviews in Surface Chemistry — Crit Rev Surf Chem
Critical Reviews in Therapeutic Drug Carrier Systems — Cr R Ther
Critical Reviews in Therapeutic Drug Carrier Systems — Crit Rev Ther Drug Carrier Syst
Critical Reviews in Toxicology — Cr R Toxic
Critical Reviews in Toxicology — Crit Rev Toxicol
Critical Social Policy — Critical Soc Policy
Critical Survey — CritS
Criticism — Critm
Criticism — PCSM
Criticism. A Quarterly for Literature and the Arts — Crit
Critique — C
Critique — Critiq
Critique — Critq
Critique. A Review of Contemporary Art — Crit
Critique of Anthropology — Critique Anthrop
Critique of Anthropology — Critique of Anthropol
Critique Regionale — Critique Reg
Critique Socialiste (Paris) — Crit Social (Paris)
Critique. Studies in Contemporary Fiction — PCTQ
Critique: Studies in Modern Fiction — Crit
Critique: Studies in Modern Fiction — Critique S
Critiques de l'Economie Politique — Crit Econ Polit
Critiques de l'Economie Politique — Critiques Econ Pol
Critisch Bulletin — CrB
Crkoven Vestnik — CV
CRL [*Cosmic Ray Laboratory*] **Report. University of Tokyo. Cosmic Ray Laboratory** — CRL Rep Univ Tokyo Cosmic Ray Lab
CRM [*Centre de Recherches Metallurgiques*] **Metallurgical Reports** — CRM Metall Rep
Croatia Press — Croatia Pr
Croatia Sacra — CS
Croatian Geological Congress — Croat Geol Congr
Croatica Chemica Acta — CCACA
Croatica Chemica Acta — Croat Chem
Croatica Chemica Acta — Croat Chem A
Croissance de Jeunes Nations — CJN
Cronaca delle Belle Arti — CBA
Cronache Culturali — CCult
Cronache de Chimica — Cron Chim
Cronache di Archeologia e di Storia dell'Arte — CASA
Cronache di Archeologia e di Storia dell'Arte — CdA
Cronache di Archeologia e di Storia dell'Arte — Cr Arch
Cronache di Archeologia e di Storia dell'Arte — Cron A Stor Art
Cronache di Archeologia e di Storia dell'Arte — Cron Arch
Cronache di Archeologia e di Storia dell'Arte. Universita de Catania — Cron Catania
Cronache Economiche — CROEA
Cronache Economiche — Cron Econ
Cronache Economiche — Cronache Econ
Cronache Ercolanesi — Cron Erc
Cronache Ercolanesi — Cron Ercol
Cronache Farmaceutiche — Cron Farm
Cronache Pompeiane — Cron Pomp
Croner's Export Digest — Croner's
Croner's Reference Book for Employers — Croner's Ref Book Employ
Croner's Reference Book for Exporters — Croner's Ref Book Export
Cronica Agricola — Cron Agric
Cronica. Congreso Nacional de Arqueologia — CNA
Cronica. Congreso Nacional de Arqueologia — Congr Nac Arq
Cronica de Caracas (Caracas) — Cronica Caracas Caracas
Cronica de la UNESCO — CDU
Cronica de Vinos y Cereales — Cron Vin Cer
Cronica Dental — Cron Dent
Cronica Medica (Lima) — Cron Med (Lima)
Cronica Medica Mexicana — Cron Med Mex
Cronica Medica Mexicana — Cron Med Mexicana
Cronica Medico-Quirurgica — Cron Med Quir
Cronica Medico-Quirurgica de La Habana — Cron Med-Quir Habana
Cronica Numismatica si Arheologica — CNA
Cronica Numismatica si Arheologica — Cr NA
Cronos — Cron
Croom Helm Philosophers in Focus Series — Croom Helm Philos Focus Ser
Crop Bulletin. Canada Board of Grain Commissioners — Crop Bull Can Board Grain Comm
Crop Bulletin. Grain Research Laboratory (Canada) — Crop Bull Grain Res Lab (Can)
Crop Improvement — Crop Improv
Crop Improvements by Induced Mutation. Report of Symposium — Crop Improv Induced Mutat Rep Symp
Crop Production — Crop Prod
Crop Production (Budapest) — Crop Prod Budapest
Crop Production Conference Report. Crop Quality Council — Crop Prod Conf Rep Crop Qual Counc
Crop Production (Pretoria) — Crop Prod (Pretoria)
Crop Production Science — Crop Prod Sci
Crop Protection — CP
Crop Protection — Crop Prot
Crop Protection Chemicals Reference — CPCR
Crop Protection in Northern Britain — Crop Prot North Br
Crop Research — CR
Crop Research — Crop Res
Crop Research News. New Zealand Department of Scientific and Industrial Research — Crop Res News Dep Sci Ind Res (NZ)
Crop Research News. New Zealand Department of Scientific and Industrial Research — Crop Res News NZ Dep Sci Ind Res
Crop Resources. Proceedings. Annual Meeting. Society for Economic Botany — Crop Resour Proc Annu Meet Soc Econ Bot
Crop Science — Crop Sci
Crop Science — CRPSA
Crop Soils. North Carolina State University — Crop Soil NC State Univ
Crops and Soils — CRSOA
Crops and Soils Magazine — Crops Soils Mag
Crops Research ARS [*Agricultural Research Service*] — Crop Res ARS
Cross and Crown — Cross & Cr
Cross and Crucible — Cross Crucible
Cross Currents — CC
Cross Currents — Cr Cu
Cross Currents — Cross C
Cross Currents — Cross Cur
Cross Currents — Cross Curr
Cross Currents — PCUR
Cross Section Information Storage and Retrieval System [*Database*] — CSISRS
Cross Tie Bulletin — Cross Tie Bull
Crosscurrents/Modern Critiques — CMC
Crosscurrents/Modern Fiction — CMF
Cross-Reference on Human Resources Management — Crossref Hum Resour Manage
Crown Agents Quarterly Review — Crown Agents QR
Crown Agents Review — Crown Ag R
Crown Colonist — Crown Col
Crown Colonist — Crown Colon
Crown Colonist (London) — CCL
Crown Counsel's Review — Crown C Rev
Crown Lands Law Reports — CLLR

Crown Lands Law Reports — CLR
Crown Lands Law Reports (Queensland) — CL (Q)
CRREL [*Cold Regions Research and Engineering Laboratory*] **Draft Translation** [*United States*] — CRRELDT
CRREL [*Cold Regions Research and Engineering Laboratory*] **Monograph Series** [*United States*] — CRLM
CRREL [*Cold Regions Research and Engineering Laboratory*] **Report** [*United States*] — CRREL
CRREL [*Cold Regions Research and Engineering Laboratory*] **Report** — CRREL Rep
CRREL [*Cold Regions Research and Engineering Laboratory*] **Report** [*United States*] — CRRELR
CRREL [*Cold Regions Research and Engineering Laboratory*] **Research Reports** [*United States*] — CRRELRR
CRREL [*Cold Regions Research and Engineering Laboratory*] **Special Report** [*United States*] — CRRELSR
CRREL [*Cold Regions Research and Engineering Laboratory*] **Technical Reports** [*United States*] — CRRELTR
Crude Petroleum, Petroleum Products, and Natural Gas Liquids — Crude Pet Pet Prod Nat Gas Liq
Cruise Report. Fisheries Research Vessel Kapala — Fish Res Ves Kapala Cruise Rep
Cruise Report. Flinders Institute for Atmospheric and Marine Science. Flinders University of South Australia — Flinders Inst Atmos Mar Sci Cruise Rep
Cruise Report. Geological Survey of Japan — Cruise Rep Geol Surv Jap
Cruising World — ICRU
Crushing and Grinding Trades Journal — Crushing Grinding Trades J
Crushing, Grinding, Mining, and Quarrying Journal — Crush Grind Min Quarr J
Crushing, Grinding, Mining, and Quarrying Journal — Crushing Grinding Min Quarrying J
Crustaceana [*Leiden*] — CRUSA
Crustaceana. Supplement (Leiden) — Crustaceana Suppl (Leiden)
Crux — Cr
Cruz del Sur (Caracas) — Cruz Sur Caracas
Cruz y Raya — CyR
Cry California — CCALA
Cry California — Cry Calif
Cryo Letters — Cryo Lett
Cryobiology — CRYBA
Cryobiology — Crybiol
Cryogenic and Industrial Gases — CRIGB
Cryogenic and Industrial Gases — Cryog & Ind Gases
Cryogenic Engineering [*Japan*] — Cryog Eng
Cryogenic Engineering News — Cryog Eng News
Cryogenic Engineering News — CYENA
Cryogenic Optical Systems and Instruments — Cryog Opt Syst Instrum
Cryogenic Pure et Appliquee — Cryog Pure Appl
Cryogenic Technology — Cryog Technol
Cryogenic Technology — CYTEA
Cryogenics [*England*] — CRYOA
Cryogenics — Cryog
Cryogenics. Supplement — Cryog Suppl
Cryptogamic Studies — Cryptogam Stud
Cryptogamica Helvetica — Cryptogamica Helv
Cryptogamie: Algologie — Cryptogam Algol
Cryptogamie: Bryologie et Lichenologie — Cryptogam Bryol Lichenol
Cryptogamie: Mycologie — Cryptogam Mycol
Crystal Chemistry of Non-Metallic Materials — Cryst Chem Non-Met Mater
Crystal Field Effects in Metals and Alloys (Proceedings of the International Conference on Crystal Field Effects in Metals and Alloys) — Cryst Field Eff Met Alloys (Proc Int Conf)
Crystal Growth and Characterization of Polytype Structures — Cryst Growth Charact Polytype Struct
Crystal Growth and Characterization. Proceedings. International Spring School on Crystal Growth — Cryst Growth Charact Proc Int Spring Sch Cryst Growth
Crystal Growth in Space and Related Optical Diagnostics — Cryst Growth Space Relat Opt Diagn
Crystal Lattice Defects [*Later, Crystal Lattice Defects and Amorphous Materials*] [*A publication*] — CLADA
Crystal Lattice Defects [*Later, Crystal Lattice Defects and Amorphous Materials*] [*A publication*] — Crys Lattice Defects
Crystal Lattice Defects [*Later, Crystal Lattice Defects and Amorphous Materials*] [*A publication*] — Cryst Latt
Crystal Lattice Defects [*Later, Crystal Lattice Defects and Amorphous Materials*] [*A publication*] — Cryst Lattice Defects
Crystal Lattice Defects and Amorphous Materials — Cryst Lattice Defects Amorphous Mater
Crystal Lattice Defects and Amorphous Materials — Cryst Lattice Defects and Amorphous Mater
Crystal Properties and Preparation — Cryst Prop Prep
Crystal Research and Technology — CRTED
Crystal Research and Technology — Cryst Res and Technol
Crystal Research and Technology — Cryst Res Technol
Crystal Structure Communications [*Italy*] — Cryst Struct Commun
Crystal Structures of Clay Minerals and Their X-Ray Identification — Cryst Struct Clay Miner Their X Ray Identif
Crystallographic Computing. Proceedings of an International Summer School — Crystallogr Comput Proc Int Summer Sch
Crystallographic Computing Techniques. Proceedings of an International Summer School — Crystallogr Comput Tech Proc Int Summer Sch
Crystallographic Research Center. Institute for Protein Research. Osaka University. Report — Crystallogr Res Cent Inst Protein Res Osaka Univ Rep
Crystallographic Structural Database — CSD
Crystallography and Crystal Perfection. Proceedings of a Symposium — Crystallogr Cryst Perfect Proc Symp
Crystallography in Molecular Biology — Crystallogr Mol Biol
Crystallography (Soviet Physics) — Crystallogr (Sov Phys)
Crystals. Growth, Properties, and Applications — Cryst Growth Prop Appl
CSA [*Canadian Standards Association*] **Bulletin** — CSA Bull
CSA [*Cambridge Scientific Abstracts*] **Neurosciences Abstracts** — CSA Neurosci Abstr
CSA (Scientific Council for Africa South of the Sahara). Publication — CSA Publ
CSAC [*Civil Service Association of Canada*] **Journal** — CSACJ
Csatornamue Informacio — Csatornamue Inf
CSC. Bulletin Mensuel. Confederation des Syndicats Chretiens de Belgique — CSC
CSCE [*Centre Senegalais du Commerce Exterieur*] **Informations** — CSY
CSEC [*Cesareans, Support, Education and Concern*] **Newsletter** — CSEC Newsl
CSELT [*Centro Studi e Laboratori Telecomunicazioni*] **Rapporti Tecnici** — CSELT Rapp Tec
CSELT [*Centro Studi e Laboratori Telecomunicazioni*] **Rapporti Tecnici** — CSELT Rappo Tec
CSIC Workshop on SUSY [*Supersymmetry*] **and Grand Unification. From Strings to Collider Phenomenology** — CSIC Workshop SUSY Grand Unification
CSIO [*Central Scientific Instruments Organisation*] **Communications** [*India*] — CSIO Commun
CSIR (Council for Scientific and Industrial Research, South Africa) Annual Report — CSIR (Counc Sci Ind Res S Afr) Ann Rep
CSIR [*Council for Scientific and Industrial Research*] **News (India)** — CSIR News (India)
CSIR [*South African Council for Scientific and Industrial Research*] **Report BOU** — CSIR Rep BOU
CSIR [*Council for Scientific and Industrial Research*] **Research Report** — CSIR Res Rep
CSIR [*Council for Scientific and Industrial Research*] **Research Review** — CSIR Res Rev
CSIR (South African Council for Scientific and Industrial Research) Report CENG — CSIR Rep CENG
CSIR (South African Council for Scientific and Industrial Research) Research Report BOU — CSIR Res Rep BOU
CSIR (South African Council for Scientific and Industrial Research) Special Report. Series WISK — CSIR Spec Rep WISK
CSIR [*Council for Scientific and Industrial Research*] **Special Report FIS** — CSIR Spec Rep FIS
CSIR [*South African Council for Scientific and Industrial Research*] **Special Report HOUT** — CSIR Spec Rep HOUT
CSIR [*South African Council for Scientific and Industrial Research*] **Special Report. Series CENG** — CSIR Spec Rep CENG
CSIR [*Council for Scientific and Industrial Research*] **Zoological Monograph** — CSIR Zool Monogr
CSIRO [*Commonwealth Scientific and Industrial Research Organisation*] **Abstracts** — CSIRO Abstr
CSIRO [*Commonwealth Scientific and Industrial Research Organisation*] **Animal Research Laboratories. Technical Paper** — CSIRO An Res Labs TP
CSIRO [*Commonwealth Scientific and Industrial Research Organisation*] **Annual Report** — CSIRO Annu Rep
CSIRO [*Commonwealth Scientific and Industrial Research Organisation*] **Australia. Division of Tropical Crops and Pastures. Technical Paper** — CSIRO Aust Div Trop Crops Pastures Tech Pap
CSIRO [*Commonwealth Scientific and Industrial Research Organisation*] **Bulletin** [*Australia*] — CSIRO Bull
CSIRO [*Commonwealth Scientific and Industrial Research Organisation*] **Chemical Research Laboratories. Technical Paper** — CSIRO Chem Res Lab Tech Pap
CSIRO [*Commonwealth Scientific and Industrial Research Organisation*] **Chemical Research Laboratories. Technical Paper** — CSIRO Chem Res Labs TP
CSIRO [*Commonwealth Scientific and Industrial Research Organisation*] **Coal Research Laboratory. Division of Mineral Chemistry. Investigation Report** — CSIRO Coal Res Lab Invest Rep
CSIRO [*Commonwealth Scientific and Industrial Research Organisation*] **Coal Research Laboratory. Division of Mineral Chemistry. Technical Communication** — CSIRO Coal Res Lab Tech Commun
CSIRO [*Commonwealth Scientific and Industrial Research Organisation*] **Computing Research Section. Memorandum** — CSIRO Computing Res Sect Memo
CSIRO [*Commonwealth Scientific and Industrial Research Organisation*] **Digest of Current Activities** — CSIRO Dig of Curr Act
CSIRO [*Commonwealth Scientific and Industrial Research Organisation*] **Division of Animal Genetics. Annual Report** — CSIRO Div Anim Genet Ann Rep
CSIRO [*Commonwealth Scientific and Industrial Research Organisation*] **Division of Animal Health and Production. Technical Paper** — CSIRO An Health Div TP
CSIRO [*Commonwealth Scientific and Industrial Research Organisation*] **Division of Applied Organic Chemistry. Research Report** — CSIRO Div Appl Organic Chem Res Rep
CSIRO [*Commonwealth Scientific and Industrial Research Organisation*] **Division of Atmospheric Physics. Technical Paper** [*Australia*] — CSIRO Div Atmos Phys Tech Pap
CSIRO [*Commonwealth Scientific and Industrial Research Organisation*] **Division of Building Research. Building Study** — CSIRO Build Res Div Building Study
CSIRO [*Commonwealth Scientific and Industrial Research Organisation*] **Division of Building Research. Publications** — CSIRO Div Build Res Publ
CSIRO [*Commonwealth Scientific and Industrial Research Organisation*] **Division of Building Research. Report** — CSIRO Build Res Div Rep
CSIRO [*Commonwealth Scientific and Industrial Research Organisation*] **Division of Building Research. Technical Paper** — CSIRO Build Res Div Tech Pap
CSIRO [*Commonwealth Scientific and Industrial Research Organisation*] **Division of Building Research. Technical Paper** — CSIRO Build Res Div TP

CSIRO [*Commonwealth Scientific and Industrial Research Organisation*] **Division of Chemical Physics. Annual Report** — CSIRO Div Chem Phys Ann Rep

CSIRO [*Commonwealth Scientific and Industrial Research Organisation*] **Division of Chemical Physics. Annual Report** — CSIRO Div Chem Phys Annu Rep

CSIRO [*Commonwealth Scientific and Industrial Research Organisation*] **Division of Chemical Technology. Technical Paper** — CSIRO Div Chem Technol Tech Pap

CSIRO [*Commonwealth Scientific and Industrial Research Organisation*] **Division of Coal Research. Reference TC** [*Technical Communication*] — CSIRO Coal Res Div Ref TC

CSIRO [*Commonwealth Scientific and Industrial Research Organisation*] **Division of Coal Research. Technical Communication** — CSIRO Coal Res Div Tech Commun

CSIRO [*Commonwealth Scientific and Industrial Research Organisation*] **Division of Entomology. Annual Report** — CSIRO Div Entomol Annu Rep

CSIRO [*Commonwealth Scientific and Industrial Research Organisation*] **Division of Entomology. Technical Paper** — CSIRO Entomol Div Tech Pap

CSIRO [*Commonwealth Scientific and Industrial Research Organisation*] **Division of Entomology. Technical Paper** — CSIRO Entomol Div TP

CSIRO [*Commonwealth Scientific and Industrial Research Organisation*] **Division of Fisheries and Oceanography. Circular** — CSIRO Fish Div C

CSIRO [*Commonwealth Scientific and Industrial Research Organisation*] **Division of Fisheries and Oceanography. Fisheries Synopsis** — CSIRO Fish Div Fish Synopsis

CSIRO [*Commonwealth Scientific and Industrial Research Organisation*] **Division of Fisheries and Oceanography. Oceanographical Cruise Report** — CSIRO Fish Div Oceanogrl Cruise Rep

CSIRO [*Commonwealth Scientific and Industrial Research Organisation*] **Division of Fisheries and Oceanography. Oceanographical Station List** — CSIRO Fish Div Oceanogr Station List

CSIRO [*Commonwealth Scientific and Industrial Research Organisation*] **Division of Fisheries and Oceanography. Oceanographical Station List** — CSIRO Fish Div Oceanogrl Stn List

CSIRO [*Commonwealth Scientific and Industrial Research Organisation*] **Division of Fisheries and Oceanography. Report** — CSIRO Div Fish Oceanogr Rep

CSIRO [*Commonwealth Scientific and Industrial Research Organisation*] **Division of Fisheries and Oceanography. Report** — CSIRO Fish Div Rep

CSIRO [*Commonwealth Scientific and Industrial Research Organisation*] **Division of Fisheries and Oceanography. Report (Australia)** — CSIRO Div Fish Oceanogr Rep (Aust)

CSIRO [*Commonwealth Scientific and Industrial Research Organisation*] **Division of Fisheries and Oceanography. Technical Paper** — CSIRO Fish Div Tech Pap

CSIRO [*Commonwealth Scientific and Industrial Research Organisation*] **Division of Fisheries and Oceanography. Technical Paper** — CSIRO Fish Div TP

CSIRO [*Commonwealth Scientific and Industrial Research Organisation*] **Division of Food Preservation. Circular** — CSIRO Fd Pres Div Circ

CSIRO [*Commonwealth Scientific and Industrial Research Organisation*] **Division of Food Preservation. Circular** — CSIRO Food Pres Div C

CSIRO [*Commonwealth Scientific and Industrial Research Organisation*] **Division of Food Preservation. Technical Paper** — CSIRO Fd Preserv Div Tech Pap

CSIRO [*Commonwealth Scientific and Industrial Research Organisation*] **Division of Food Preservation. Technical Paper** — CSIRO Food Pres Div TP

CSIRO [*Commonwealth Scientific and Industrial Research Organisation*] **Division of Food Research. Food Research Quarterly** — CSIRO Food Res Q

CSIRO [*Commonwealth Scientific and Industrial Research Organisation*] **Division of Food Research. Food Research Quarterly. Supplementary Series** — CSIRO Food Res Q Suppl Ser

CSIRO [*Commonwealth Scientific and Industrial Research Organisation*] **Division of Food Research. Report of Research** — CSIRO Div Food Res Rep Res

CSIRO [*Commonwealth Scientific and Industrial Research Organisation*] **Division of Forest Products. CSIRO Forest Products Technical Notes** — CSIRO For Prod Tech Notes

CSIRO [*Commonwealth Scientific and Industrial Research Organisation*] **Division of Forest Products. Forest Products Newsletter** — CSIRO For Prod Newsl

CSIRO [*Commonwealth Scientific and Industrial Research Organisation*] **Division of Forest Products. Technological Paper** — CSIRO Div Forest Prod Technol Paper

CSIRO [*Commonwealth Scientific and Industrial Research Organisation*] **Division of Forest Products. Technological Paper** — CSIRO For Prod Div Technol P

CSIRO [*Commonwealth Scientific and Industrial Research Organisation*] **Division of Forest Products. Technological Paper** — CSIRO For Prod Div Technol Pap

CSIRO [*Commonwealth Scientific and Industrial Research Organisation*] **Division of Forest Research. Annual Report** — CSIRO Div For Res Ann Rep

CSIRO [*Commonwealth Scientific and Industrial Research Organisation*] **Division of Land Research and Regional Survey. Technical Paper** — CSIRO Land Res Regional Surv Div Tech Pap

CSIRO [*Commonwealth Scientific and Industrial Research Organisation*] **Division of Land Research and Regional Survey. Technical Paper** — CSIRO Land Res Regional Surv Div TP

CSIRO [*Commonwealth Scientific and Industrial Research Organisation*] **Division of Land Use Research. Publications** — CSIRO Div Land Use Res Publ

CSIRO [*Commonwealth Scientific and Industrial Research Organisation*] **Division of Mathematical Statistics. Technical Paper** — CSIRO Math Statist Div Tech Pap

CSIRO [*Commonwealth Scientific and Industrial Research Organisation*] **Division of Mathematical Statistics. Technical Paper** — CSIRO Math Statist Div TP

CSIRO [*Commonwealth Scientific and Industrial Research Organisation*] **Division of Mechanical Engineering. Circular** — CSIRO Mech Engng Div Circ

CSIRO [*Commonwealth Scientific and Industrial Research Organisation*] **Division of Mechanical Engineering. Information Service Leaflet** — CSIRO Div Mech Eng Info Serv Leafl

CSIRO [*Commonwealth Scientific and Industrial Research Organisation*] **Division of Mechanical Engineering. Report** — CSIRO Mech Engng Div Rep

CSIRO [*Commonwealth Scientific and Industrial Research Organisation*] **Division of Meteorological Physics. Technical Paper** — CSIRO Met Phys Div Tech Pap

CSIRO [*Commonwealth Scientific and Industrial Research Organisation*] **Division of Mineral Chemistry. Investigation Report** — CSIRO Div Miner Chem Invest Rep

CSIRO [*Commonwealth Scientific and Industrial Research Organisation*] **Division of Mineral Physics. Investigation Report** — CSIRO Div Miner Phys Invest Rep

CSIRO [*Commonwealth Scientific and Industrial Research Organisation*] **Division of Mineralogy. Investigation Report** — CSIRO Div Mineral Invest Rep

CSIRO [*Commonwealth Scientific and Industrial Research Organisation*] **Division of Mineralogy. Technical Communication** — CSIRO Div Mineral Tech Commun

CSIRO [*Commonwealth Scientific and Industrial Research Organisation*] **Division of Plant Industry. Field Station Record** — CSIRO Plant Ind Div Field Sta Rec

CSIRO [*Commonwealth Scientific and Industrial Research Organisation*] **Division of Plant Industry. Field Station Record** — CSIRO Plant Ind Div Field Stn Rec

CSIRO [*Commonwealth Scientific and Industrial Research Organisation*] **Division of Plant Industry. Technical Paper** — CSIRO Plant Ind Div Tech Pap

CSIRO [*Commonwealth Scientific and Industrial Research Organisation*] **Division of Plant Industry. Technical Paper** — CSIRO Plant Ind Div TP

CSIRO [*Commonwealth Scientific and Industrial Research Organisation*] **Division of Plant Industry. Technical Paper** — CSIRO Plant Ind TP

CSIRO [*Commonwealth Scientific and Industrial Research Organisation*] **Division of Radiophysics. Report** — CSIRO Radiophys Div Rept

CSIRO [*Commonwealth Scientific and Industrial Research Organisation*] **Division of Soil Mechanics. Technical Paper** — CSIRO Soil Mech Div Tech Pap

CSIRO [*Commonwealth Scientific and Industrial Research Organisation*] **Division of Soil Mechanics. Technical Report** — CSIRO Soil Mech Div Tech Rep

CSIRO [*Commonwealth Scientific and Industrial Research Organisation*] **Division of Soils. Soils and Land Use Series** — CSIRO Soils Div SLU

CSIRO [*Commonwealth Scientific and Industrial Research Organisation*] **Division of Textile Industry. Report** — CSIRO Text Ind Div Rep

CSIRO [*Commonwealth Scientific and Industrial Research Organisation*] **Division of Textile Industry. Wool Textile News** — CSIRO Wool Text News

CSIRO [*Commonwealth Scientific and Industrial Research Organisation*] **Division of Textile Physics. Annual Report** — CSIRO Div Text Phys Ann Rep

CSIRO [*Commonwealth Scientific and Industrial Research Organisation*] **Division of Textile Physics. Report** — CSIRO Text Phys Div Rep

CSIRO [*Commonwealth Scientific and Industrial Research Organisation*] **Division of Tropical Agronomy. Annual Report** — CSIRO Div Trop Agron Annu Rep

CSIRO [*Commonwealth Scientific and Industrial Research Organisation*] **Division of Tropical Crops and Pastures. Tropical Agronomy Technical Memorandum** — CSIRO Div Trop Crops Pastures Trop Agron Tech Memo

CSIRO [*Commonwealth Scientific and Industrial Research Organisation*] **Division of Tropical Pastures. Technical Paper** — CSIRO Trop Pastures Div TP

CSIRO [*Commonwealth Scientific and Industrial Research Organisation*] **Division of Wildlife Research. Technical Paper** — CSIRO Wildl Res Div Tech Pap

CSIRO [*Commonwealth Scientific and Industrial Research Organisation*] **Division of Wildlife Research. Technical Paper** — CSIRO Wildl Res Div TP

CSIRO [*Commonwealth Scientific and Industrial Research Organisation*] **Engineering Section. Circular** — CSIRO Engng Sect C

CSIRO [*Commonwealth Scientific and Industrial Research Organisation*] **Engineering Section. Internal Report** — CSIRO Engng Sect Int Rept

CSIRO [*Commonwealth Scientific and Industrial Research Organisation*] **Food Preservation Quarterly** — CSIRO Fd Preserv Q

CSIRO [*Commonwealth Scientific and Industrial Research Organisation*] **Food Preservation Quarterly** — CSIRO Food Preserv Q

CSIRO [*Commonwealth Scientific and Industrial Research Organisation*] **Food Research Quarterly** — CSIRO Fd Res Q

CSIRO [*Commonwealth Scientific and Industrial Research Organisation*] **Forest Products Newsletter** — CSIRO For Prod Newslett

CSIRO [*Commonwealth Scientific and Industrial Research Organisation*] **Forest Products Newsletter** — CSIRO For Prod Newsletter

CSIRO [*Commonwealth Scientific and Industrial Research Organisation*] **Forest Products Newsletter** — CSIRO Forest Prod Newsl

CSIRO [*Commonwealth Scientific and Industrial Research Organisation*] **Index** — CSI

CSIRO [*Commonwealth Scientific and Industrial Research Organisation*] **Industrial Research News** — CSIRO Ind Res News

CSIRO [*Commonwealth Scientific and Industrial Research Organisation*] **Institute of Earth Resources. Investigation Report** — CSIRO Inst Earth Resour Invest Rep

CSIRO [*Commonwealth Scientific and Industrial Research Organisation*] **Institute of Earth Resources. Investigation Report** — Invest Rep CSIRO Inst Earth Resour

CSIRO [*Commonwealth Scientific and Industrial Research Organisation*] **Institute of Earth Resources. Technical Communication** — CSIRO Inst Earth Resour Tech Commun

CSIRO [*Commonwealth Scientific and Industrial Research Organisation*] **Institute of Earth Resources. Technical Communication** — Tech Commun CSIRO Inst Earth Resour

CSIRO [*Commonwealth Scientific and Industrial Research Organization*] **Institute of Energy and Earth Resources. Technical Communication** — CSIRO Inst Energ Earth Resour Tech Commun

CSIRO [*Commonwealth Scientific and Industrial Research Organisation*] **Irrigation Research Stations. Technical Paper** — CSIRO Irrig Res Stat TP

CSIRO [*Commonwealth Scientific and Industrial Research Organisation*] **Land Research Series** — CSIRO Land Res Ser

CSIRO [*Commonwealth Scientific and Industrial Research Organisation*] **Leaflet Series** — CSIRO Leaflet Ser

CSIRO [*Commonwealth Scientific and Industrial Research Organisation*] **Marine Biochemistry Unit. Annual Report** — CSIRO Mar Biochem Unit Annu Rep

CSIRO [*Commonwealth Scientific and Industrial Research Organisation*] **Marine Biochemistry Unit. Annual Report** — CSIRO Marine Biochem Unit Ann Rep
CSIRO [*Commonwealth Scientific and Industrial Research Organization*] **Marine Laboratories. Report** — CSIRO Mar Lab Rep
CSIRO [*Commonwealth Scientific and Industrial Research Organisation*] **Mineragraphic Investigations. Technical Paper** — CSIRO Minerag Invest Tech Pap
CSIRO [*Commonwealth Scientific and Industrial Research Organisation*] **Mineragraphic Investigations. Technical Paper** — CSIRO Minerag Investig TP
CSIRO [*Commonwealth Scientific and Industrial Research Organisation*] **Mineral Physics Section. Investigation Report** — CSIRO Miner Phys Sect Invest Rep
CSIRO [*Commonwealth Scientific and Industrial Research Organisation*] **Minerals Research Laboratories. Annual Report** — CSIRO Miner Res Lab Ann Rep
CSIRO [*Commonwealth Scientific and Industrial Research Organisation*] **Minerals Research Laboratories. Annual Report** — CSIRO Miner Res Lab Annu Rep
CSIRO [*Commonwealth Scientific and Industrial Research Organisation*] **Minerals Research Laboratories. Division of Mineralogy. Technical Communication** — CSIRO Miner Res Lab Div Mineral Tech Commun
CSIRO [*Commonwealth Scientific and Industrial Research Organisation*] **Minerals Research Laboratories. Investigation Report** — CSIRO Miner Res Lab Invest Rep
CSIRO [*Commonwealth Scientific and Industrial Research Organisation*] **Minerals Research Laboratories. Investigation Report** — Invest Rep CSIRO Miner Res Lab
CSIRO [*Commonwealth Scientific and Industrial Research Organisation*] **Minerals Research Laboratories. Research Review** — CSIRO Miner Res Lab Res Rev
CSIRO [*Commonwealth Scientific and Industrial Research Organisation*] **Minerals Research Laboratories. Technical Communication** — CSIRO Miner Res Lab Tech Commun
CSIRO [*Commonwealth Scientific and Industrial Research Organisation*] **Minerals Research Laboratories. Technical Communication** — Tech Commun CSIRO Miner Res Lab
CSIRO [*Commonwealth Scientific and Industrial Research Organisation*] **National Measurement Laboratory. Biennial Report** — CSIRO Natl Meas Lab Bienn Rep
CSIRO [*Commonwealth Scientific and Industrial Research Organisation*] **National Measurement Laboratory. Biennial Report** — CSIRO Natl Measure Lab Biennial Rep
CSIRO [*Commonwealth Scientific and Industrial Research Organisation*] **National Measurement Laboratory. Technical Paper** — CSIRO Natl Meas Lab Tech Pap
CSIRO [*Commonwealth Scientific and Industrial Research Organisation*] **National Standards Laboratory. Biennial Report** — CSIRO Natl Stand Lab Bienn Rep
CSIRO [*Commonwealth Scientific and Industrial Research Organisation*] **National Standards Laboratory. Circular** — CSIRO Nat Stands Lab Circ
CSIRO [*Commonwealth Scientific and Industrial Research Organisation*] **National Standards Laboratory. Division of Applied Physics. Test Pamphlet** — CSIRO Nat Stand Lab Div Appl Phys Test Pamph
CSIRO [*Commonwealth Scientific and Industrial Research Organisation*] **National Standards Laboratory. Technical Paper** — CSIRO Nat Stands Lab Tech Pap
CSIRO [*Commonwealth Scientific and Industrial Research Organisation*] **National Standards Laboratory. Technical Paper** — CSIRO Nat Stands Lab TP
CSIRO [*Commonwealth Scientific and Industrial Research Organisation*] **National Standards Laboratory. Test Pamphlet** — CSIRO Nat Stands Lab Test Pamphl
CSIRO [*Commonwealth Scientific and Industrial Research Organisation*] **Physical Metallurgy Section. Technical Paper** — CSIRO Phys Met Sec Tech Pap
CSIRO [*Commonwealth Scientific and Industrial Research Organisation*] **Science Index** — CSIRO Sci Index
CSIRO [*Commonwealth Scientific and Industrial Research Organisation*] **Soil Mechanics Section. Geotechnical Report** — CSIRO Soil Mechanics Sect Geotech Rep
CSIRO [*Commonwealth Scientific and Industrial Research Organisation*] **Soil Mechanics Section. Technical Report** — CSIRO Soil Mech Sect Tech Rep
CSIRO [*Commonwealth Scientific and Industrial Research Organisation*] **Soil Mechanics Section. Technical Report** — CSIRO Soil Mechanics Sect Tech Rep
CSIRO [*Commonwealth Scientific and Industrial Research Organisation*] **Soil Publications** — CSIRO Soil Pub
CSIRO [*Commonwealth Scientific and Industrial Research Organisation*] **Wheat Research Unit. Annual Report** — CSIRO Wheat Res Unit Annu Rep
CSIRO [*Commonwealth Scientific and Industrial Research Organisation*] **Wildlife Research** — CSIRO Wildl Res
CSIRO [*Commonwealth Scientific and Industrial Research Organisation*] **Wildlife Survey Section. Technical Paper** — CSIRO Wildl Surv Sect TP
CSIRO [*Commonwealth Scientific and Industrial Research Organisation*] **Wood Research Laboratory. Textile News** — CSIRO Text News
CSIRO [*Commonwealth Scientific and Industrial Research Organisation*] **Wool Textile Research Laboratories. Report** — CSIRO Wool Text Res Labs Rep
CSIRO [*Commonwealth Scientific and Industrial Research Organisation*] **Wool Textile Research Laboratories. Technical Paper** — CSIRO Wool Text Res Labs TP
CSIRO [*Commonwealth Scientific and Industrial Research Organisation*] **Wool Textile Research Laboratories. Trade Circular** — CSIRO Wool Text Res Labs TC
CSIROOA Bulletin. Journal of the Association of Officers of the Commonwealth Scientific and Industrial Research Organisation — CSIROOA Bul
CSIS (Center for Strategic and International Studies) Energy Policy Series — CSIS (Cent Strategic Int Stud) Energy Policy Ser
CSM (Camborne School of Mines) Journal — CSM J
CSMA. Proceedings. Mid-Year Meeting — CSMA Proc Mid Year Meet
CSNI (Committee on the Safety of Nuclear Installation) Report — CSNI Rep
CSNI (Committee on the Safety of Nuclear Installation) Specialist Meeting on Transient Two-Phase Flow — CSNI Spec Meet Transient Two Phase Flow
CSNI [*Committee on the Safety of Nuclear Installation*] **Specialist Meeting on Safety Aspects of Fuel Behaviour in Off-Normal and Accident Conditions** — CSNI Spec Meet Saf Aspects Fuel Behav Off Norm Accid Cond
CSPG [*Canadian Society of Petroleum Geologists*] **Memoir** — CSPG Mem
CSR [*Colonial Sugar Refining Company Limited*] **Agricultural Circular** — CSR Agric Circ
CSSA [*Crop Science Society of America*] **Special Publication** — CSSA Spec Publ
CST. Combustion Science and Technology — CST Combust Sci Technol
CSTA [*Canadian Society of Technical Agriculturists*] **Review** — CSTA R
CSTA [*Canadian Society of Technical Agriculturists*] **Review** — CSTA Rev
CSTC [*Centre Scientifique et Technique de la Construction*] **Revue** — CSTC Rev
CT. Journal of Computed Tomography — CT J Comput Tomogr
CT. Journal of Computed Tomography — CT J Comput Tomography
CTA [*Cine Technicians' Association*] **Journal** [*India*] — CTA J
CTA [*Chicago Transit Authority*] **Quarterly** — CTA Q
CTFA [*Cosmetic, Toiletry, and Fragrance Association*] **Cosmetic Journal** — CTFA Cosmet J
CTFA (Cosmetic, Toiletry, and Fragrance Association) Scientific Monograph Series — CTFA Sci Monogr Ser
CTI. Communication Technology Impact — CTI Commun Technol Impact
Cuaderno Cultural — Cuad Cult
Cuaderno de Actualizacion Tecnica. Asociacion Argentina de Consorcios Regionales de Experimentacion Agricola — Cuad Actual Tec Asoc Argent Consorcios Reg Exp Agric
Cuaderno de Investigacion. Instituto Eduardo Torroja de la Construccion y del Cemento — Cuad Invest Inst Eduardo Torroja Constr Cem
Cuadernos Africanos y Orientales — Cuad Afr Or
Cuadernos Americanos — CA
Cuadernos Americanos — Cu A
Cuadernos Americanos — Cuad Amer
Cuadernos Americanos. La Revista del Nuevo Mundo — Cuad Am
Cuadernos Americanos (Mexico) — Cuad Am Mex
Cuadernos Bibliograficos [*Madrid*] — CB
Cuadernos Canarios de Investigacion — CuCanl
Cuadernos. Catedra Miguel de Unamuno — Cuad Catedra M Unamuno
Cuadernos. Centro de Estudiantes de Antropologia. Universidad Mayor de San Marcos (Lima) — Cuad Lima
Cuadernos. Centro de Estudios Sindicales — Cuad Sind
Cuadernos da Area de Ciencias Marinas — Cuad Area Cienc Mar
Cuadernos de Algebra — Cuadern Algebra
Cuadernos de Antropologia (Guatemala) — Cuad Antrop Guat
Cuadernos de Aragon — CA
Cuadernos de Arqueologia e Historia de la Ciudad — CAHC
Cuadernos de Arqueologia e Historia de la Ciudad (Barcelona) — Cuad A (Barcel)
Cuadernos de Arquitectura y Urbanismo — Cuad Arquit Urban
Cuadernos de Arte Colonial — CAC
Cuadernos de Arte y Poesia — CAP
Cuadernos de Arte y Poesia (Quito) — Cuad Art Poesia Quito
Cuadernos de Bellas Artes (Mexico) — Cuad Bell Art Mex
Cuadernos de Ciencias Biologicas. Universidad de Granada — Cuad Cienc Biol Univ Granada
Cuadernos de Cirugia — Cuad Cirug
Cuadernos de Cristianismo y Sociedad — Cuadernos Cristianismo Soc
Cuadernos de Cultura Espanola — CCE
Cuadernos de Cultura Teatral — CCT
Cuadernos de Economia (Barcelona) — Cuad Econ (Barcelona)
Cuadernos de Economia (Santiago) — Cuad Econ (Santiago)
Cuadernos de Estudios Africanos — Cuad Est Afr
Cuadernos de Estudios Africanos — Cuad Est Africanos
Cuadernos de Estudios Gallegos — CEG
Cuadernos de Estudios Gallegos — Cu EG
Cuadernos de Estudios Gallegos — Cuad Est Gallegos
Cuadernos de Estudios Gallegos — Cuad Gall
Cuadernos de Estudios Gallegos — Cuad Gallegos
Cuadernos de Estudios Manchegos — CEM
Cuadernos de Estudios Manchegos — Cu EM
Cuadernos de Estudios Manchegos — Cuad Est Manchegos
Cuadernos de Estudios Manchegos — Cuad Manch
Cuadernos de Estudios Yucatecos (Merida, Yucatan) — Cuad Estud Yucat Merida
Cuadernos de Etnologia y Etnografia de Navarra — CEEN
Cuadernos de Filologia — CdF
Cuadernos de Filologia — CFil
Cuadernos de Filologia Clasica — CFC
Cuadernos de Filologia Clasica — Cuad Fil Cl
Cuadernos de Filologia Clasica — Cuad Filo Clas
Cuadernos de Filologia Clasica — Cuad Filol Cl
Cuadernos de Filosofia — C Filos
Cuadernos de Filosofia — Cuad Fil
Cuadernos de Filosofia — Cuad Filosof
Cuadernos de Geografia de Colombia — Cuad Geogr Colom
Cuadernos de Geografia de Colombia (Bogota) — Cuad Geogr Col Bogota
Cuadernos de Geologia Iberica — Cuad Geol Iber
Cuadernos de Geologia. Universidad de Granada — Cuad Geol Univ Granada
Cuadernos de Historia de Espana — CHE
Cuadernos de Historia de Espana — Cuad Hist Esp
Cuadernos de Historia de Espana — Cuad Hist Espan
Cuadernos de Historia de la Economia Catuluna — Cuad Hist Econ Cataluna
Cuadernos de Historia de la Medicina Espanola — Cuad Hist Med Esp
Cuadernos de Historia de la Medicina Espanola — Cuad Hist Med Espan
Cuadernos de Historia de la Salud Publica — Cuad Hist Salud Publica
Cuadernos de Historia del Arte (Mendoza, Argentina) — Cuad Hist Art Mendoza
Cuadernos de Historia Habanera — CHH
Cuadernos de Historia. Jeronimo Zurita — CHJZ

Cuadernos de Historia Primitiva — CHP
Cuadernos de Historia Primitiva — Cuad Hist Primit
Cuadernos de Historia Primitiva — Cuadernos Hist Prim
Cuadernos de Historia Sanitaria — Cuad Hist Sanit
Cuadernos de Historia y Arqueologia (Guayaquil) — Cuad Hist Arqueol Guayaquil
Cuadernos de Informacion Economica. Corporacion Venezolana de Fomento (Caracas) — Cuad Inform Econ Caracas
Cuadernos de Informacion Economica y Sociologica — Cuad Inform Econ Sociol
Cuadernos de Investigacion. IETCC [*Instituto Eduardo Torroja de la Construccion y del Cemento*] — Cuad Invest IETCC
Cuadernos de la Catedra de Unamuno — CCU
Cuadernos de la Corporacion Venezolana de Fomento — Cuad CVF
Cuadernos de las Facultades. Universidad de Panama (Panama) — Cuad Fac Panama
Cuadernos de Literatura — CL
Cuadernos de Literatura — CLi
Cuadernos de Literatura Contemporanea — CLC
Cuadernos de Literatura. CSIC (Consejo Superior de Investigaciones Cientificas) — Cuad Literatura
Cuadernos de Marcha — Cuad Marcha
Cuadernos de Mineralogia y Geologia. Universidad de Tucuman — Cuad Min Geol Univ Tuc
Cuadernos de Numismatica — Cuad Num
Cuadernos de Orientacion — Cuad Orient
Cuadernos de Pedagogia — Cuad Ped
Cuadernos de Politica Internacional — Cuad Pol Int
Cuadernos de Prehistoria. Universidad de Granada — CPUG
Cuadernos de Prehistoria (Universidad de Granada) — Cuad (Granada)
Cuadernos de Prehistoria. Universidad de Granada — Cuadernos Preh Granada
Cuadernos de Prehistoria. Universidad de Granda — Cuadernos Preh Granada
Cuadernos de Prehistoria y Arqueologia — Cuad Pr Hist A
Cuadernos de Prehistoria y Arqueologia Castellonense — Cuad P Arq Cast
Cuadernos de Realidades Sociales — Cuad Realidades Socs
Cuadernos de Ruedo Iberico — Cuad Ruedo Iber
Cuadernos de Trabajos. Escuela Espanola de Historia y Arqueologia en Roma [*A publication*] — Cuad Rom
Cuadernos de Trabajos. Escuela Espanola de Historia y Arqueologia. Roma — CTER
Cuadernos del Congreso — CUAD
Cuadernos del Congreso por la Libertad de la Cultura — CCLC
Cuadernos del Congreso por la Libertad de la Cultura — Cuad Congr Liber Cult
Cuadernos del Guayas — CDG
Cuadernos del Hombre Libre — CHL
Cuadernos del Idioma — CDI
Cuadernos del Idioma — CI
Cuadernos del Idioma (Buenos Aires) — Cuad Idioma BA
Cuadernos Hispanoamericanos [*Madrid*] — CH
Cuadernos Hispanoamericanos [*Madrid*] — CHA
Cuadernos Hispanoamericanos — Cuad Hisp
Cuadernos Hispanoamericanos — Cuadernos H
Cuadernos Hispanoamericanos — CuaH
Cuadernos Hispanoamericanos [*Madrid*] — CuH
Cuadernos Hispanoamericanos. Instituto de Cultura Hispanica — Cuad Hisp Am
Cuadernos. Instituto de Historia (Mexico) — Cuad Inst Hist (Mex)
Cuadernos. Instituto de Historia. Seria Antropologica [*Mexico*] — Cuad Inst Hist Ser Antr
Cuadernos. Instituto de Matematica Beppo Levi — Cuadern Inst Mat Beppo Levi
Cuadernos. Instituto Nacional de Antropologia — Cuad Inst Nac Antropol
Cuadernos. Instituto Nacional de Antropologia (Buenos Aires) — Cuad Inst Nac Antrop BA
Cuadernos. Instituto Nacional de Investigaciones Folkloricas (Buenos Aires) — Cuad Inst Nac Invest Folk BA
Cuadernos Internacionales de Historia Psicosocial del Arte — Cuad Int Hist Psicosoc Arte
Cuadernos Laborales — Cuad Laborales
Cuadernos Latinoamericanos — CH
Cuadernos Latinoamericanos de Economia Humana (Montevideo) — Cuad Latinoam Econ Humana Monte
Cuadernos Medicos — Cuad Med
Cuadernos Medicos y de Divulgacion Cientifico — Cuad Med Divulg Cient
Cuadernos Oceanograficos. Universidad de Oriente (Cumana) — Cuad Oceanogr Univ Oriente (Cumana)
Cuadernos para el Dialogo — CD
Cuadernos para el Dialogo — CpD
Cuadernos para Investigacion de la Literatura Hispanica — CILH
Cuadernos (Paris) — Cuad Paris
Cuadernos Politicos [*Ediciones Era*] — CP
Cuadernos Politicos [*Ediciones Era*] — Cuad Pol
Cuadernos Prehispanicos — CPH
Cuadernos Salmantinos de Filosofia — CSF
Cuadernos. Seminario de Historia (Lima) — Cuad Seminario Hist Lima
Cuadernos Teologicos — Cuad Teol
Cuadernos Teorema — Cuadern Teorema
Cuadernos. Universidad del Aire — CUA
Cuadernos Universitarios (Guatemala) — CUG
Cuadernos Universitarios (Leon, Nicaragua) — Cuad Univ Leon
Cuadernos Universitarios (Nicaragua) — CUN
Cuba Agricola — Cuba Agric
Cuba Bibliotecologica — CBib
Cuba Bibliotecologica — Cuba Bibl
Cuba Bibliotecologica. Colegio Nacional de Bibliotecarios Universitarios — Cuba Bibliotecol
Cuba Bibliotecologica (La Habana) — Cuba Bibliotec Hav
Cuba Contemporanea — CCont
Cuba. Direccion de Montes y Minas. Boletin de Minas — Cuba Dir Montes B Minas
Cuba Economic News — CEY
Cuba en la UNESCO — CUNESCO
Cuba Intelectual — CInt
Cuba Internacional — CAI
Cuba Internacional — CubaI
Cuba Literaria — CubaL
Cuba Ministerio de la Agricultura Juridico. Boletin — Cuba Min Agric Jur Bol
Cuba Ministerio del Commerco Exterior. Revista — Cuba Min Com Ext Rev
Cuba Noticias Economicas — Cuba Not Econ
Cuba Nueva — CubaN
Cuba Profesional — CPro
Cuba Review — Cuba Revw
Cuba Review — CubaR
Cuba Si — CSi
Cuba Socialista — CSO
Cuba Socialista — CSoc
Cuba Socialista — Cuba Soc
Cuba y America — CyA
Cuba y Espana — CyE
Cuban Journal of Agricultural Science — Cuban J Agric Sci
Cuban Studies/Estudios Cubanos — CS
Cuban Studies/Estudios Cubanos — Cuban Stud
Cuban Studies/Estudios Cubanos. University of Pittsburg. University Center for International Studies. Center for Latin American Studies — UP/CSEC
Cuban Studies Newsletter — CSN
Cuban Studies (Pittsburgh) — CSP
Cubatimes — Cuba
Cue Sheet — CS
Cue Sheet — Cue
Cuget Romanesc — CRom
Cuir. Journal Trihebdomadaire d'Informations du Cuir et de la Chaussure — CUK
Cuir Technique — Cuir Tech
Cuir Technique. Supplement — Cuir Tech Suppl
Cuivre, Laitons, Alliages — CUIVA
Cukoripar — CUKOA
Cukoripar, Melleklet — Cukoripar Mellek
Cukurova Universitesi Tip Fakultesi Dergisi — Cukurova Univ Tip Fak Derg
Culegere de Articole de la Consfatuire pe Tara de Materiale Electrotehnice — Culegere Articole Consfatuire Tara Mater Electroteh
Culegere de Studii si Cercetari (Brasov) — Cul Stud Cerc (Brasov)
Culham Laboratory. United Kingdom Atomic Energy Authority. Report CLM-R — Culham Lab UK At Energy Auth Rep CLM R
Cultivador Moderno — Cult Mod
Cultivador Moderno — Cultiv Mod
Cultivador Moderno — CUMOA
Cultivator. New York State Agricultural Society — Cultivator NY Agri Soc
Cultivos Industriales (La Plata, Argentina) — Cultiv Indus La Plata
Cults of the Greek States — CGS
Cultura [*San Salvador*] — CUL
Cultura — Cult
Cultura Atesina — Cult Atesina
Cultura Biblica — CB
Cultura Biblica — Cu Bi
Cultura Biblica [*Segovia, Spain*] — CuBib
Cultura Biblica — Cult B
Cultura Biblica — Cult Biblica
Cultura Biblica [*Segovia, Spain*] — CultBib
Cultura Biblica [*Segovia, Spain*] — CultBibl
Cultura Boliviana (Oruro, Bolivia) — Cult Boliviana Oruro
Cultura de Guatemala Universidad Rafael Landivar — CGURL
Cultura e Scuola — C & S
Cultura e Scuola — CeS
Cultura e Scuola — CS
Cultura e Scuola — Cult Sc
Cultura e Scuola — Cult Scu
Cultura e Scuola — Cult Scuol
Cultura (Ecuador) — CULE
Cultura Espanola — Cult Esp
Cultura Medica — Cult Med
Cultura Medica Moderna — Cult Med Mod
Cultura Medica Moderna — Cultura Med Mod
Cultura Mexico (Mexico) — Cult Mex Mex
Cultura Neolatina — CN
Cultura Neolatina — Cu N
Cultura Neolatina — Cult Neol
Cultura Neolatina — Cult Neolat
Cultura Politica [*Rio De Janeiro*] — CP
Cultura Politica (Rio de Janeiro) — Cult Pol Rio
Cultura (San Salvador) — Cult S Salvador
Cultura Scientifica — Cult Sci
Cultura Sovietica — CSov
Cultura Stomatologica — Cult Stomat
Cultura (Tunja, Colombia) — Cult Tunja
Cultura Universitaria — CU
Cultura Universitaria — Cult Univ
Cultura Universitaria — CUn
Cultura Universitaria (Caracas) — CUC
Cultura Universitaria. Universidad Central de Venezuela — Cult Universitaria
Cultura Universitaria. Universidad Central de Venezuela — CUUCV
Cultural Correspondence — Cult Corr

Cultural Correspondence — Cultural Cor
Cultural Events in Africa — CulEA
Cultural Forum [*New Delhi*] — CForum
Cultural Hermeneutics — Cult Hermen
Cultural Resource Report. United States Forest Service. Southwestern Region — Cult Resour Rep US For Serv Southwest Reg
Cultural Studies — Cult Stud
Cultural Survival Newsletter — Cult Surv
Cultural Survival Quarterly — CUSQ
Culturas Energeticas. Biomassa — Cult Energ Biomassa
Culture — Clt
Culture — Cul
Culture — Cult
Culture and Tradition — C & T
Culture de Zaiere et d'Afrique — CulZ
Culture et Authenticite. Revue Zairoise d'Orientation Culturelle — Cult et Authenticite
Culture Francaise — Cult Fr
Culture Francaise — Cult Franc
Culture, Illness, and Healing — CIAH
Culture, Medicine, and Psychiatry — CMPSD
Culture, Medicine, and Psychiatry — Cult Med Psych
Culture, Medicine, and Psychiatry — Cult Med Psychiatry
Cultured Dairy Products Journal — Cul Dair Prod J
Cultured Dairy Products Journal — Cult Dairy Prod J
Cultures au Zaire et en Afrique — Cultures au Zaire et en Afr
Cultures et Developpement — Cult et Devel
Cultures et Developpement — Cultures et Dev
Cultuurtechnische Dienst — CTD
Cum Notis Variorum — CNV
Cumana. Universidad de Oriente. Instituto Oceanografico. Boletin — Cumana Univ Oriente Inst Oceanogr Bol
Cumberland and Westmorland Antiquarian and Archaeological Society. Transactions — C & W Trans
Cumberland and Westmorland Antiquarian and Archaeological Society. Transactions — C&W
Cumberland and Westmorland Antiquarian and Archaeological Society. Transactions — Cumb and West AAST
Cumberland County Council. Historic Buildings Committee. Minutes — CCC Hist Bldg Ctee Min
Cumberland Law Review — Cum L Rev
Cumberland Law Review — Cum LR
Cumberland Law Review — Cumb L Rev
Cumberland Law Review — Cumberland L Rev
Cumberland Poetry Review [*British*] — CPR
Cumberland Presbyterian Quarterly Review — Cumb Q
Cumberland Seminarian — Cumberland Sem
Cumberland-Samford Law Review — Cumberland-Samford
Cumberland-Samford Law Review — Cumberland-Samford L Rev
Cumberland-Samford Law Review — Cumber-Sam L Rev
Cumberland-Samford Law Review — Cum-Sam
Cumidava Culegere de Studii si Cercetari — Cumidava
Cumulated Index Medicus — Cumul Index Med
Cumulative Abstracts of Defence Readings [*Database*] — CADRE
Cumulative Book Index [*Information service or system*] — CBI
Cumulative Book Index — Cum B Ind
Cumulative Book Index — Cum Book
Cumulative Book List — CBL
Cumulative Bulletin [*United States Internal Revenue Service*] — CB
Cumulative Bulletin [*United States Internal Revenue Service*] — Cum Bull
Cumulative Computer Abstracts — Cum Comput Abstr
Cumulative Index to Nursing and Allied Health Literature — CINAHL
Cumulative Index to Nursing and Allied Health Literature — CINL
Cumulative Index to Nursing and Allied Health Literature — Cumul Index Nurs Allied Health Lit
Cumulative Index to Nursing Literature — Cumul Index Nurs Lit
Cunobelin Yearbook. British Association of Numismatic Societies — Cunobelin
Cuoio, Pelli, Materie Concianti — CPMAA
Cuore e Circolazione — Cuore Circ
Cuore e Circolazione — Cuore Circol
Cupey — CUP
Curent Topics in Clinical and Community Psychology — Curr Top Clin Comm Psych
Curierul Farmaceutic — Curierul Farm
Curioso Americano — CAmer
Currency Collector — CC
Currency Exchange Database — CEDB
Current [*New York*] — CRETB
Current — CURRD
Current — GCDC
Current Abstracts of Chemistry [*Institute for Scientific Information*] [*Database*] — CAC
Current Abstracts of Chemistry and Index Chemicus — CAC & IC
Current Abstracts of Chemistry and Index Chemicus — Curr Abstr Chem Index Chem
Current Accounts — Cur Accts
Current Accounts — Current Accts
Current Advances in Genetics — Curr Adv Genet
Current Advances in Mechanical Design and Production. Proceedings. International Conference — Curr Adv Mech Des Prod Proc Int Conf
Current Advances in Plant Science — Curr Adv Plant Sci
Current Advances in Plant Science — Current Adv Plant Sci
Current Affairs Bulletin — CAB
Current Affairs Bulletin — CRABB
Current Affairs Bulletin — Curr Aff B
Current Affairs Bulletin — Curr Aff Bull
Current Affairs Bulletin — Curr Affairs Bull
Current Affairs Bulletin — Current Affairs Bul
Current African Issues — Curr Afr Issues
Current Agricultural Research — Curr Agric Res
Current Agricultural Research Information System [*Database*] — CARIS
Current Agriculture — Curr Agric
Current American Government — Curr Am Gov
Current Antarctic Literature — CAL
Current Anthropology — CA
Current Anthropology — CAnth
Current Anthropology — CAnthr
Current Anthropology — CUAN
Current Anthropology — Cur Anthro
Current Anthropology — Cur Anthrop
Current Anthropology — Cur Anthropol
Current Anthropology — Curr Anthr
Current Anthropology — Curr Anthrop
Current Anthropology — Curr Anthropol
Current Anthropology — Current Anthr
Current Anthropology — GCAY
Current Anthropology. University of Chicago — UC/CA
Current Applications in Radiopharmacology. Proceedings. International Symposium on Radiopharmacology — Curr Appl Radiopharmacol Proc Int Symp Radiopharmacol
Current Approaches in Toxicology — Curr Approaches Toxicol
Current Archaeology — Curr Archaeol
Current Archives Bibliography Australia — CURABA
Current Aspects of the Neurosciences — Curr Aspects Neurosci
Current Australian and New Zealand Legal Literature Index — CANZLLI
Current Australian and New Zealand Legal Literature Index — Curr Aus NZ Leg Lit Ind
Current Australian and New Zealand Legal Literature Index — Curr Aust New Z Leg Lit Index
Current Australian Serials — CAS
Current Awareness Bulletin — CAB
Current Awareness Bulletin — Curr Awareness Bull
Current Awareness in Biological Sciences [*Database*] — CABS
Current Awareness in Biological Sciences. CABS — Curr Aware Biol Sci CABS
Current Awareness - Library Literature. CALL — Curr Awareness Libr Lit CALL
Current Awareness-Library Literature — CALL
Current Background — Cur Backg
Current Bibliographic Information — CBI
Current Bibliography for Aquatic Sciences and Fisheries — CBASF
Current Bibliography for Aquatic Sciences and Fisheries — Curr Bibl Aquatic Sci & Fish
Current Bibliography for Fisheries Science. Food and Agriculture Organization — Curr Bibliogr Fish Sci
Current Bibliography of Middle East Geology — Curr Bibliogr Middle East Geol
Current Bibliography on African Affairs — CB
Current Bibliography on African Affairs — CBAA
Current Bibliography on African Affairs — Cur Bibliog African Affairs
Current Bibliography on African Affairs — Curr Bibl Afr Affairs
Current Biography — CB
Current Biography — Cur Biog
Current Biography — GCBI
Current Biography Yearbook — Cur Biog Yrbk
Current Biology — Curr Biol
Current Biotechnology Abstracts [*Database*] — CBA
Current Book Review Citations — CBRC
Current Book Review Citations — Curr Book Rev Citations
Current British Foreign Policy — Cur Brit For Pol
Current Business Reports. Advanced Monthly Retail Sales — CBR Retl A
Current Business Reports. Annual Retail Trade — CBR Retail
Current Business Reports. Monthly Retail Trade Sales and Inventories — CBR Retl M
Current Business Reports. Monthly Wholesale Trade Sales and Inventories — CBR Whsl TM
Current Business Reports. Revised Monthly Retail Sales and Inventories for January, 1974 - December, 1983 — CBR Retl S
Current Business Reports. Revised Monthly Wholesale Trade Sales and Inventories for January, 1975 - December, 1984 — CBR Whsl S
Current Cardiovascular Topics — Curr Cardiovasc Top
Current Caribbean Bibliography (Port of Spain, Trinidad) — Cur Carib Bibliogr Port Of Spain
Current Central Legislation (India) — (India) Curr Cen Leg
Current Chemical Papers — Curr Chem Pap
Current Chemical Translations — Current Chem Transl
Current Chemotherapy and Immunotherapy. Proceedings. International Congress of Chemotherapy — Curr Chemother Immunother Proc Int Congr Chemother
Current Chemotherapy. Proceedings. International Congress of Chemotherapy — Curr Chemother Proc Int Congr Chemother
Current Clinical Practice Series — Curr Clin Pract Ser
Current Clinical Topics in Infectious Diseases — Curr Clin Top Infect Dis
Current Commonwealth Publications — CCP
Current Concepts in Emergency Medicine — Curr Concepts Emerg Med
Current Concepts in Hospital Pharmacy Management — Curr Concepts Hosp Pharm Manage
Current Concepts in Migraine Research — Curr Concepts Migraine Res
Current Concepts in Nutrition — CCNTB
Current Concepts in Nutrition — Curr Concepts Nutr
Current Concepts in Plant Taxonomy — Curr Concepts Plant Taxon
Current Concepts in Surfactant Research. International Symposium on Surfactant Research — Curr Concepts Surfactant Res Int Symp

Current Concepts of Cerebrovascular Disease: Stroke — Curr Concepts Cerebrovasc Dis Stroke
Current Contents — CC
Current Contents — Curr Contents
Current Contents — CurrCont
Current Contents/Agriculture, Biology, and Environmental Sciences — CC/AB & ES
Current Contents/Agriculture, Biology, and Environmental Sciences — Curr Contents Agric Biol Environ Sci
Current Contents/Arts and Humanities — CC/A & H
Current Contents/Behavioral, Social, and Educational Sciences — Curr Contents Behav Soc Educ Sci
Current Contents/Behavioral, Social, and Management Sciences — Curr Contents Behav Soc Manage Sci
Current Contents/Clinical Medicine — Curr Contents Clin Med
Current Contents Clinical Practice — CC/CP
Current Contents Clinical Practice — Cur C Clin Prac
Current Contents/Clinical Practices — Curr Contents Clin Pract
Current Contents/Education — Curr Contents Educ
Current Contents/Engineering and Technology — Curr Contents Eng Technol
Current Contents/Engineering, Technology, and Applied Sciences — Curr Contents Eng Tech Appl Sci
Current Contents/Life Sciences — Curr Contents Life Sci
Current Contents of Pharmaceutical Publications — Curr Contents Pharm Publ
Current Contents/Physical, Chemical, and Earth Sciences — Curr Contents Phys Chem Earth Sci
Current Contents/Social and Behavioral Sciences — Curr Contents Soc Behav Sci
Current Corrosion Research in Scandinavia. Lectures held at the Scandinavian Corrosion Conference — Curr Corros Res Scand Lect Scand Corros Congr
Current Developments in Biological Nitrogen Fixation — Curr Dev Biol Nitrogen Fixation
Current Developments in Optical Design and Engineering — Curr Dev Opt Des Eng
Current Developments in Optical Engineering and Diffraction Phenomena — Curr Dev Opt Eng Diffr Phenom
Current Developments in Psychopharmacology — Curr Dev Psychopharmacol
Current Developments in Yeast Research. Proceedings. International Yeast Symposium — Curr Dev Yeast Res Proc Int Yeast Symp
Current Digest of the Soviet Press — CDSP
Current Digest of the Soviet Press — Curr Dig Sov Press
Current Digest of the Soviet Press — Current Dig Soviet Pr
Current Discussions in Theology — Curr Discussions Theol
Current Documents from the German Democratic Republic — Curr Doc Ger Dem Rep
Current Economic Comment — Curr Econ Comm
Current Economics and Business Aspects of the Wine Industry. Symposium — Curr Econ Bus Aspects Wine Ind Symp
Current Endocrine Concepts — Curr Endocr Concepts
Current Endocrinology [*Elsevier Book Series*] — CE
Current Energy Patents — CUPAD
Current Energy Patents — Curr Energy Pat
Current Engineering Practice — Curr Eng Pract
Current European Directories — Curr Eur Dir
Current Events — Cur Ev
Current Events in Jewish Life [*New York*] — CEJL
Current Eye Research — Curr Eye Res
Current Farm Economics — Curr Farm Econ
Current Farm Economics. Agricultural Experiment Station. Division of Agriculture. Oklahoma State University — Curr Farm Econ Agric Exp Stn Div Agric Okla State Univ
Current Gastroenterology — Curr Gastroenterol
Current Genetics — Curr Genet
Current Geographical Publications — CGP
Current Health — Cur Health
Current Health 2 — GCUH
Current Hematology and Oncology — Curr Hemat Onco
Current Hepatology — Curr Hepatol
Current History — CH
Current History — CHY
Current History — Cu H
Current History — Cur Hist
Current History — CurH
Current History — Curr Hist
Current History — Current Hist
Current History — GCHI
Current History Magazine of the New York Times — Cur Hist M NY Times
Current Housing Reports — CHR
Current Index to Commonwealth Legal Periodicals — Curr Ind Commonw Leg Per
Current Index to Commonwealth Legal Periodicals — Curr Index Commonw Leg Period
Current Index to Journals in Education [*United States Office of Education*] — CIJE
Current Index to Journals in Education. CIJE — Curr Index J Educ
Current Index to Legal Periodicals [*Database*] — CILP
Current Index to Statistics — CIS
Current Index to Statistics — Curr Index Stat
Current Index to Statistics; Applications-Methods-Theory — Curr Index Stat Appl Methods Theory
Current Index to Statistics; Applications-Methods-Theory — Current Index Statist Appl Methods Theory
Current Indian Statutes — Curr Indian Stat
Current Induced Reactions. International Summer Institute on Theoretical Particle Physics — Curr Induced React Int Summer Inst Theor Part Phys
Current Industrial Reports [*Census Bureau*] — Current Ind Rept
Current Industrial Reports. Aluminum Ingot and Mill Products — Curr Ind Rep Alum Ingot Mill Prod
Current Industrial Reports. Clay Construction Products — Curr Ind Rep Clay Constr Prod
Current Industrial Reports. DIB-917. Copper-Base Mill and Foundry Products — CIR DIB917
Current Industrial Reports. Fats and Oils-Oilseed Crushings — Curr Ind Rep Fats Oils Oilseed Crushings
Current Industrial Reports. Fats and Oils-Production, Consumption, and Stocks — Curr Ind Rep Fats Oils Prod Consumption Stocks
Current Industrial Reports. Flat Glass — Curr Ind Rep Flat Glass
Current Industrial Reports. Inorganic Chemicals — Curr Ind Rep Inorg Chem
Current Industrial Reports. Inorganic Fertilizer Materials and Related Products — Curr Ind Rep Inorg Fert Mater Relat Prod
Current Industrial Reports. Iron and Steel Castings — Curr Ind Rep Iron Steel Cast
Current Industrial Reports. ITA-991. Titanium Mill Products, Ingots, and Castings — CIR ITA991
Current Industrial Reports. M20A. Flour Milling Products — CIR M20A
Current Industrial Reports. M20J. Fats and Oils, Oilseed Crushings — CIR M20J
Current Industrial Reports. M20K. Fats and Oils. Production, Consumption, and Warehouse Stocks — CIR M20K
Current Industrial Reports. M22A. Finished Fabrics. Production, Inventories, and Unfilled Orders — CIR M22A
Current Industrial Reports. M22D. Consumption on the Woolen and Worsted Systems — CIR M22D
Current Industrial Reports. M22P. Cotton, Manmade Fiber Staple, and Linters — CIR M22P
Current Industrial Reports. M23I. Men's, Women's, Misses', and Juniors' Selected Apparel — CIR M23I
Current Industrial Reports. M28A. Inorganic Chemicals — CIR M28A
Current Industrial Reports. M28B. Inorganic Fertilizer Materials and Related Products — CIR M28B
Current Industrial Reports. M28C. Industrial Gases — CIR M28C
Current Industrial Reports. M28F. Paint, Varnish, and Lacquer — CIR M28F
Current Industrial Reports. M30E. Plastic Bottles — CIR M30E
Current Industrial Reports. M30E. Plastic Bottles — Curr Ind Rept Plast Bottles
Current Industrial Reports. M3-1. Manufacturers' Shipments, Inventories, and Orders — CIR M3-1
Current Industrial Reports. M31A. Footwear — CIR M31A
Current Industrial Reports. M31A. Footwear — Curr Ind Rept Footwear
Current Industrial Reports. M32D. Clay Construction Products — CIR M32D
Current Industrial Reports. M32G. Glass Containers — CIR M32G
Current Industrial Reports. M33A. Iron and Steel Castings — CIR M33A
Current Industrial Reports. M33E. Nonferrous Castings — CIR M33E
Current Industrial Reports. M33K. Inventories of Brass and Copper Wire Mill Shapes — CIR M33K
Current Industrial Reports. M34H. Closures for Containers — CIR M34H
Current Industrial Reports. M35S. Tractors, except Garden Tractors — CIR M35S
Current Industrial Reports. M36D. Electric Lamps — CIR M36D
Current Industrial Reports. M37G. Complete Aircraft and Aircraft Engines — CIR M37G
Current Industrial Reports. M37L. Truck Trailers — CIR M37L
Current Industrial Reports. M33-2. Aluminum Ingot and Mill Products — CIR M332
Current Industrial Reports. M33-3. Inventories of Steel Mill Shapes — CIR M333
Current Industrial Reports. MA-20D. Confectionery, Including Chocolate Products — CIR MA20D
Current Industrial Reports. MA-20O. Manufacturers' Pollution Abatement Capital Expenditures and Operating Costs — CIR MA20O
Current Industrial Reports. MA-22F1. Textured Yarn Production — CIR MA22F1
Current Industrial Reports. MA-22F2. Spun Yarn Production — CIR MA22F2
Current Industrial Reports. MA-22G. Narrow Fabrics — CIR MA22G
Current Industrial Reports. MA-22S. Finished Broadwoven Fabric Production — CIR MA22S
Current Industrial Reports. MA-23E. Men's and Boys' Outerwear — CIR MA23E
Current Industrial Reports. MA-23F. Women's and Children's Outerwear — CIR MA23F
Current Industrial Reports. MA-23G. Underwear and Nightwear — CIR MA23G
Current Industrial Reports. MA-23J. Brassieres, Corsets, and Allied Garments [*A publication*] — CIR MA23J
Current Industrial Reports. MA-24F. Hardwood Plywood — CIR MA24F
Current Industrial Reports. MA-24H. Softwood Plywood — CIR MA24H
Current Industrial Reports. MA-25H. Manufacturers' Shipments of Office Furniture — CIR MA25H
Current Industrial Reports. MA-26A. Pulp, Paper, and Board — CIR MA26A
Current Industrial Reports. MA-26B. Selected Office Supplies and Accessories [*A publication*] — CIR MA26B
Current Industrial Reports. MA-26F. Converted Flexible Materials for Packaging and Other Uses — CIR MA26F
Current Industrial Reports. MA-28A. Inorganic Chemicals — CIR MA28A
Current Industrial Reports. MA-28B. Sulfuric Acid — CIR MA28B
Current Industrial Reports. MA-28C. Industrial Gases — CIR MA28C
Current Industrial Reports. MA-28F. Paint and Allied Products — CIR MA28F
Current Industrial Reports. MA-28G(84)-1. Pharmaceutical Preparations, except Biologicals — CIR MA28G84
Current Industrial Reports. MA-30A. Rubber Production Shipments and Stocks — CIR MA30A
Current Industrial Reports. MA-30B. Rubber and Plastics Hose and Belting — CIR MA30B

Current Industrial Reports. MA-30D. Shipments of Selected Plastic Products — CIR MA30D
Current Industrial Reports. MA-31A. Footwear Production by Manufacturers' Selling Price — CIR MA31A
Current Industrial Reports. MA-32C. Refractories — CIR MA32C
Current Industrial Reports. MA-32E. Consumer, Scientific, Technical, and Industrial Glassware — CIR MA32E
Current Industrial Reports. MA-32J. Fibrous Glass — CIR MA32J
Current Industrial Reports. MA-33B. Steel Mill Products — CIR MA33B
Current Industrial Reports. MA-33G. Magnesium Mill Products — CIR MA33G
Current Industrial Reports. MA-33L. Insulated Wire and Cable — CIR MA33L
Current Industrial Reports. MA-34N. Heating and Cooking Equipment — CIR MA34N
Current Industrial Reports. MA-34P. Aluminum Foil Converted — CIR MA34P
Current Industrial Reports. MA-35A. Farm Machines and Equipment — CIR MA35A
Current Industrial Reports. MA-35D. Construction Machinery — CIR MA35D
Current Industrial Reports. MA-35F. Mining Machinery and Mineral Processing Equipment — CIR MA35F
Current Industrial Reports. MA-35J. Selected Air Pollution Equipment — CIR MA35J
Current Industrial Reports. MA-35L. Internal Combustion Engines — CIR MA35L
Current Industrial Reports. MA-35M. Air-Conditioning and Refrigeration Equipment — CIR MA35M
Current Industrial Reports. MA-35N. Fluid Power Products Including Aerospace — CIR MA35N
Current Industrial Reports. MA-35O. Antifriction Bearings — CIR MA350
Current Industrial Reports. MA-35P. Pumps and Compressors — CIR MA35P
Current Industrial Reports. MA-35R. Office, Computing, and Accounting Machines — CIR MA35R
Current Industrial Reports. MA-35U. Vending Machines Coin Operated — CIR MA35U
Current Industrial Reports. MA-36A. Switchgear, Switchboard Apparatus, Relays, and Industrial Controls — CIR MA36A
Current Industrial Reports. MA-36E. Electric Housewares and Fans — CIR MA36E
Current Industrial Reports. MA-36F. Major Household Appliances — CIR MA36F
Current Industrial Reports. MA-36G. Transformers — CIR MA36G
Current Industrial Reports. MA-36H. Motors and Generators — CIR MA36H
Current Industrial Reports. MA-36K. Wiring Devices and Supplies — CIR MA36K
Current Industrial Reports. MA-36L. Electric Lighting Fixtures — CIR MA36L
Current Industrial Reports. MA-36M. Home-Type Radio Receivers and TV Sets, Auto Radios, Phonos, and Record Players — CIR MA36M
Current Industrial Reports. MA-36N. Selected Electronic and Associated Products — CIR MA36N
Current Industrial Reports. MA-37D. Aerospace Industry Orders, Sales, and Backlog — CIR MA37D
Current Industrial Reports. MA-37E. Aircraft Propellers — CIR MA37E
Current Industrial Reports. MA-38B. Selected Instruments and Related Products — CIR MA38B
Current Industrial Reports. MA-38Q. Selected Atomic Energy Products — CIR MA38Q
Current Industrial Reports. MA-39A. Pens, Pencils, and Marking Devices — CIR MA39A
Current Industrial Reports. MQ-22Q. Carpets and Rugs — CIR MQ22Q
Current Industrial Reports. MQ-22T. Broadwoven Fabrics — CIR MQ22T
Current Industrial Reports. MQ-23X. Sheets, Pillowcases, and Towels — CIR MQ23X
Current Industrial Reports. MQ-32A. Flat Glass — CIR MQ32A
Current Industrial Reports. MQ-32C. Refractories — CIR MQ32C
Current Industrial Reports. MQ-34E. Plumbing Fixtures — CIR MQ34E
Current Industrial Reports. MQ-34K. Steel Shipping Drums and Pails — CIR MQ34K
Current Industrial Reports. MQ-35D. Construction Machinery — CIR MQ35D
Current Industrial Reports. MQ-35W. Metalworking Machinery — CIR MQ35W
Current Industrial Reports. MQ-36B. Electric Lamps — CIR MQ36B
Current Industrial Reports. MQ-36C. Fluorescent Lamp Ballasts — CIR MQ36C
Current Industrial Reports. MQ-C1. Survey of Plant Capacity — CIR MQ-C1
Current Industrial Reports. Refractories — Curr Ind Rep Refract
Current Industrial Reports. Selected Industrial Air Pollution Control Equipment — Curr Ind Rep Sel Ind Air Pollut Control Equip
Current Industrial Reports. Series BCDF-263 — Curr Ind Rep Ser BDCF 263
Current Industrial Reports. Series. Copper-Base Mill and Foundry Products — Curr Ind Rep Ser Copper Base Mill Foundry Prod
Current Industrial Reports. Series DIB-991 — Curr Ind Rep Ser DIB 991
Current Industrial Reports. Series DIB-9008 — Curr Ind Rep Ser DIB 9008
Current Industrial Reports. Series ITA-991 — Curr Ind Rep Ser ITA 991
Current Industrial Reports. Series ITA-9008 — Curr Ind Rep Ser ITA 9008
Current Industrial Reports. Series M20J — Curr Ind Rep Ser M20J
Current Industrial Reports. Series M26A — Curr Ind Rep Ser M26A
Current Industrial Reports. Series M28A — Curr Ind Rep Ser M28A
Current Industrial Reports. Series M28C — Curr Ind Rep Ser M28C
Current Industrial Reports. Series M28F — Curr Ind Rep Ser M28F
Current Industrial Reports. Series M33A — Curr Ind Rep Ser M33A
Current Industrial Reports. Series M33E — Curr Ind Rep Ser M33E
Current Industrial Reports. Series M33-2 — Curr Ind Rep Ser M33 2
Current Industrial Reports. Series MQ-32A — Curr Ind Rep Ser MQ 32A
Current Industrial Reports. Series MQ-32C — Curr Ind Rep Ser MQ 32C
Current Industrial Reports. Series. Pulp, Paper, and Board — Curr Ind Rep Ser Pulp Pap Board
Current Information in the Construction Industry — Current Inf Constr Ind
Current Information Series. Cooperative Extension Service. University of Idaho — Curr Inf Ser Coop Ext Serv Univ Idaho
Current Information Series. University of Idaho. College of Agriculture. Agricultural Extension Service — Curr Inform Ser Univ Idaho Coll Agr Ext Serv
Current Information System (USDA)/Canadian Agricultural Research Council — CRIS-CAR
Current Innovations in Molecular Biology — Curr Innovations Mol Biol
Current Inquiry into Language and Linguistics — CILL
Current Intelligence Digest — CIDG
Current Issues and Studies. United States National Research Council — Curr Issues Stud US Nat Res Counc
Current Issues in Commerce and Finance — CICF
Current Issues in Higher Education — Cur Issues Higher Ed
Current Issues in Higher Education. Annual Series — Cur Issues Higher Educ Ann Ser
Current Issues in Psychoanalytic Practice — Curr Issues Psychoanal Pract
Current Jodine Literature — Curr Jod Lit
Current Laboratory Practice — Curr Lab Pract
Current Labour Developments — Cur Lab Dev
Current Law — Current L
Current Law and Social Problems — Curr Law Soc Probl
Current Law and Social Problems — Curr LSP
Current Law and Social Problems — Current L & Soc Probl
Current Law and Social Problems — Current Law
Current Law Case Citator — Curr Law Case Cit
Current Law Citator — Curr Law Cit
Current Law Index — Curr Law Index
Current Law Statute Citator and Index — Curr Law Statut Cit Index
Current Law Year Book — CL
Current Law Year Book — CLYB
Current Law Year Book — Curr LYB
Current Law Year Book — Current LYB
Current Leather Literature — Curr Leather Lit
Current Legal Problems — CLP
Current Legal Problems — Curr Leg Probl
Current Legal Problems — Current Legal Prob
Current Literature — Cur Lit
Current Literature in Traffic and Transportation — Current Lit Traff Transp
Current Literature of Blood — Curr Lit Blood
Current Literature on Aging — Curr Lit Aging
Current Literature on Venereal Disease — Curr Lit Vener Dis
Current Mathematical Publications — CMP
Current Mathematical Publications — Curr Math Publ
Current Mathematical Publications — Current Math Publ
Current Medical Abstracts for Practitioners — Curr Med Abstr Practit
Current Medical Digest — Curr Med Dig
Current Medical Information and Terminology — Curr Med Info Termin
Current Medical Practice — Curr Med Pract
Current Medical Practice (India) — Curr Med Pract (India)
Current Medical Research — Curr Med Res
Current Medical Research and Opinion — Curr Med Res Opin
Current Medicine — Curr Med
Current Medicine and Drugs — Curr Med Drugs
Current Medicine for Attorneys — Current Med
Current Microbiology — Curr Microbiol
Current Municipal Problems — Cur Muni Prob
Current Municipal Problems — Curr Mun Pr
Current Municipal Problems — Current Mun Prob
Current Musicology — C Mc
Current Musicology — Curr Music
Current Musicology — Current Mus
Current Musicology — Current Musicol
Current Musicology — PCMS
Current Nephrology — Curr Nephrol
Current Neurosurgical Practice — Curr Neurosurg Pract
Current Notes — CN
Current Notes on International Affairs [*Australia*] — CRNIA
Current Notes on International Affairs — Curr Notes
Current Notes on International Affairs — Curr Notes Int Aff
Current Notes on International Affairs — Curr Notes Int Affairs
Current Notes on International Affairs — Current Notes
Current Obstetric and Gynecologic Diagnosis and Treatment — Curr Obstet Gynecol Diagn Treat
Current Opiinion in Cardiology — Curr Opin Cardiol
Current Opinion — Cur Opinion
Current Opinion — Curr Opin
Current Opinion in Biotechnology — Curr Opin Biotechnol
Current Opinion in Cell Biology — Curr Opin Cell Biol
Current Opinion in Colloid and Interface Science — Curr Opin Colloid Interface Sci
Current Opinion in Gastroenterology — Curr Opin G
Current Opinion in Gastroenterology — Curr Opin Gastroenterol
Current Opinion in General Surgery — Curr Opin Gen Surg
Current Opinion in Genetics and Development — Curr Opin Genet Dev
Current Opinion in Hematology — Curr Opin Hematol
Current Opinion in Immunology — Curr Op Im
Current Opinion in Immunology — Curr Opin Immunol
Current Opinion in Lipidology — Curr Opin Lipidol
Current Opinion in Nephrology and Hypertension — Curr Opin Nephrol Hypertens
Current Opinion in Neurobiology — Curr Opin Neurobiol
Current Opinion in Neurology — Curr Opin Neurol
Current Opinion in Obstetrics and Gynecology — Curr Opin Obstet Gynecol
Current Opinion in Oncology — Curr Opin Oncol

Current Opinion in Pediatrics — Curr Opin Pediatr
Current Opinion in Pulmonary Medicine — Curr Opin Pulm Med
Current Opinion in Radiology — Curr Opin Radiol
Current Opinion in Rheumatology — Curr Opin Rheumatol
Current Opinion in Solid State and Materials Science — Curr Opin Solid State Mater Sci
Current Opinion in Structural Biology — Curr Opin Struct Biol
Current Paper. Building Research Establishment — Curr Pap Build Res Establ
Current Papers. Aeronautical Research Council (United Kingdom) — Curr Pap Aeronaut Res Counc (UK)
Current Papers in Electrical and Electronics Engineering — CPE
Current Papers in Physics — CPP
Current Papers in Physics — Curr Pap Phys
Current Papers in Physics — Curr Papers Phys
Current Papers. Kyoto University. Department of Aeronautical Engineering — Curr Pap Kyoto Univ Dep Aeronaut Eng
Current Papers on Computers and Control — CPC
Current Perspectives in Cancer Therapy — Curr Perspect Cancer Ther
Current Perspectives in Nitrogen Fixation. Proceedings. International Symposium on Nitrogen Fixation — Curr Perspect Nitrogen Fixation Proc Int Symp
Current Pharmaceutical Design — Curr Pharm Des
Current Physics Advance Abstracts — CPAA
Current Physics Index — CPI
Current Physics Index — Curr Phys Index
Current Physics Microform — CPM
Current Plant Science and Biotechnology in Agriculture — Curr Plant Sci Biotechnol Agric
Current Podiatry — Cur Pod
Current Population Reports — CPR
Current Population Reports — Curr Pop Rep
Current Population Reports. Characteristics of Households and Persons Receiving Selected Noncash Benefits. Series P-60-148 — CPR 60-148
Current Population Reports. Characteristics of the Population below the Poverty Level. Series P-60-147 — CPR 60-147
Current Population Reports. Consumer Buying Indicators. Series P-65 — CPR 65
Current Population Reports. Consumer Income. Series P-60 — CPR 60
Current Population Reports. Consumer Income. Series P-60 [*United States*] — Curr Popul Rep Consum Income
Current Population Reports. Farm Population of the US. Series P-27-57 — CPR 27-57
Current Population Reports. Farm Population. Series P-27 — CPR 27
Current Population Reports. Federal-State Cooperative Program for Population Estimates. Series P-26 — CPR 26
Current Population Reports. Household and Family Characteristics. Series P20-398 — CPR 20-398
Current Population Reports. Money Income of Households, Families, and Persons in the US. Series P-60-146 — CPR 60-146
Current Population Reports. Money, Income, Poverty Status of Families and Persons in the US. Series P-60-149 — CPR 60-149
Current Population Reports. Population Characteristics. Series P-20 — CPR 20
Current Population Reports. Population Characteristics. Series P-20 [*United States*] — Curr Popul Rep Popul Charact
Current Population Reports. Population Estimates and Projections. Households and Families, 1986-2000. Series P-25. No.986 — CPR 25-986
Current Population Reports. Population Estimates and Projections. Series P-25 — CPR 25
Current Population Reports. Population Estimates and Projections. Series P-25 [*United States*] — Curr Popul Rep Popul Estim Proj
Current Population Reports. Series P-26. Federal-State Cooperative Program for Population Estimates — Curr Popul Rep P-26
Current Population Reports. Special Censuses. Series P-28 — CPR 28
Current Population Reports. Special Censuses. Series P-28 [*United States*] — Curr Popul Rep Spec Censuses
Current Population Reports. Special Studies. Series P-23 — CPR 23
Current Population Reports. Special Studies. Series P-23 — Curr Pop Rep Special Studies
Current Population Reports. Special Studies. Series P-23 [*United States*] — Curr Popul Rep Spec Stud
Current Practice in Gerontological Nursing — Curr Pract Gerontol Nurs
Current Practice in Obstetric and Gynecologic Nursing — Curr Pract Obstet Gynecol Nurs
Current Practice in Orthopaedic Surgery — Curr Pract Orthop Surg
Current Practice in Pediatric Nursing — Curr Pract Pediatr Nurs
Current Practices in Environmental Engineering — Curr Pract Environ Eng
Current Practices in Environmental Science and Engineering — Curr Pract Environ Sci Eng
Current Problems — Curr Probl
Current Problems in Anesthesia and Critical Care Medicine — Curr Probl Anesth Crit Care Med
Current Problems in Cancer — Curr Probl Cancer
Current Problems in Cardiology — Curr P Card
Current Problems in Cardiology — Curr Probl Cardiol
Current Problems in Clinical Biochemistry — Curr Probl Clin Biochem
Current Problems in Dermatology — APDEB
Current Problems in Dermatology — Curr Prob Dermatol
Current Problems in Dermatology — Curr Probl Derm
Current Problems in Dermatology — Curr Probl Dermatol
Current Problems in Diagnostic Radiology — CPDRD
Current Problems in Diagnostic Radiology — Curr Probl Diagn Radiol
Current Problems in Electrophotography. European Colloquium — Curr Probl Electrophotogr Eur Colloq
Current Problems in Epilepsy — Curr Probl Epilepsy
Current Problems in Immunology. Bayer-Symposium — Curr Probl Immunol Bayer Symp
Current Problems in Pediatrics — Curr Probl Pediatr
Current Problems in Pediatry — Curr Probl Ped
Current Problems in Radiology — Curr Probl Rad
Current Problems in Surgery — CPSUA
Current Problems in Surgery — Curr P Surg
Current Problems in Surgery — Curr Probl Surg
Current Psychiatric Therapies — CPSTB
Current Psychiatric Therapies — Curr Psychiatr Ther
Current Psychological Research — Cur Psychol Res
Current Psychological Research — Curr Psychol Res
Current Psychological Research and Reviews — Curr Psychol Res & Rev
Current Psychological Research and Reviews — Curr Psychol Res Rev
Current Psychological Reviews — Cur Psychol Rev
Current Psychological Reviews — Curr Psychol Rev
Current Psychology — Curr Psychol
Current Pulmonology — Curr Pulmonol
Current Radiology — Curr Radiol
Current Report. West Virginia. Agricultural Experiment Station — Curr Rep W Va Agric Exp Stn
Current Report. West Virginia University. Agricultural and Forestry Experiment Station — Curr Rep W Va Univ Agric For Exp Stn
Current Report. West Virginia University. Agricultural Experiment Station — Curr Rep W Va Univ Agr Exp Sta
Current Research — Curr Res
Current Research. Geological Survey of Canada — Curr Res Geol Surv Can
Current Research. Geological Survey of Israel — Curr Res Geol Surv Isr
Current Research in Cancer Chemotherapy — Curr Res Canc Chemoth
Current Research in Nephrology in Japan — Curr Res Nephrol Jpn
Current Research in Photosynthesis. Proceedings. International Conference on Photosynthesis — Curr Res Photosynth Proc Int Conf Photosynth
Current Research in the Netherlands. Biology — Curr Res Neth Biol
Current Research Information System [*Database*] — CRIS
Current Research on Medicinal and Aromatic Plants — Curr Res Med Arom Plants
Current Research on Medicinal and Aromatic Plants — Curr Res Med Aromat Plants
Current Research Reporter — Curr Res Rep
Current Researches in Anesthesia and Analgesia — Anesth Analg
Current Researches in Anesthesia and Analgesia — Curr Res Anesth Analg
Current Review of Agricultural Conditions in Canada — Curr Rev Agr Cond Can
Current Reviews for Nurse Anesthetists — Curr Rev Nurse Anesth
Current Reviews for Recovery Room Nurses — Curr Rev Recov Room Nurses
Current Reviews in Biomedicine — Curr Rev Biomed
Current Reviews in Respiratory Therapy — Curr Rev Respir Ther
Current Scene [*Hong Kong*] — CS
Current Scene — Cur Scene
Current Science — Cur Sci
Current Science — Curr Sc
Current Science [*India*] — Curr Sci
Current Science — Current Sci
Current Science [*India*] — CUSCA
Current Separations — Curr Sep
Current Sociology — C Soc
Current Sociology — CUO
Current Sociology — Curr Sociol
Current Sociology — PCSO
Current Sociology (Sage Publications Ltd.) — Current Sociol (Sage)
Current Soviet Leaders — Cur Sov Lead
Current Studies in Hematology and Blood Transfusion — Curr Stud Hematol Blood Transfus
Current Surgery — Curr Surg
Current Sweden — Curr Swed
Current Technology Index [*Library Association Publishing Ltd.*] [*London, England*] [*Information service or system*] — CTI
Current Technology Index — Current Tech Index
Current Themes in Tropical Science — Curr Themes Trop Sci
Current Theory and Research in Motivation. Nebraska Symposium on Motivation — Curr Theory Res Motiv Nebr Symp Motiv
Current Therapeutic Research — Curr Ther Res
Current Therapeutic Research. Clinical and Experimental — CTCEA
Current Therapeutic Research. Clinical and Experimental — Curr Ther R
Current Therapeutic Research. Clinical and Experimental — Curr Ther Res Clin Exp
Current Therapy — Curr Ther
Current Therapy in Endocrinology and Metabolism — Curr Ther Endocrinol Metab
Current Therapy (Philadelphia) — Curr Ther (Phila)
Current Titles in Electrochemistry — Curr Tit Electrochem
Current Titles in Electrochemistry — Curr Titles Electrochem
Current Titles in Turkish Science — Curr Titles Turk Sci
Current Topics in Biochemistry — Curr Top Biochem
Current Topics in Bioenergetics — Curr Top Bioenerg
Current Topics in Bioenergetics — Curr Topics Bioenerget
Current Topics in Bioenergetics — CUTBA
Current Topics in Cardiology — Curr Top Cardiol
Current Topics in Cellular Regulation — CTCRA
Current Topics in Cellular Regulation — Curr Top Cell Regul
Current Topics in Chinese Science. Section D. Biology — Curr Top Chin Sci Sect D Biol
Current Topics in Chinese Science. Section G. Medical Science — Curr Top Chin Sci Sect G Med Sci
Current Topics in Clinical Chemistry — Curr Top Clin Chem
Current Topics in Comparative Pathobiology — Curr Top Comp Pathobiol

Current Topics in Coronary Research. Papers. Symposium — Curr Top Coron Res Pap Symp
Current Topics in Critical Care Medicine — Curr Top Crit Care Med
Current Topics in Developmental Biology — CTDBA
Current Topics in Developmental Biology — Curr Top Dev Biol
Current Topics in Developmental Biology — Curr Top Devel Biol
Current Topics in Developmental Biology — Curr Topics Developm Biol
Current Topics in Electronics and Systems — Curr Top Electron Syst
Current Topics in Experimental Endocrinology — CTEEA
Current Topics in Experimental Endocrinology — Curr Top Exp Endocrinol
Current Topics in Eye Research — Curr Top Eye Res
Current Topics in Hematology — Curr Top Hematol
Current Topics in Immunology Series — Curr Top Immunol Ser
Current Topics in Materials Science [*Elsevier Book Series*] — CTMS
Current Topics in Materials Science — Curr Top Mater Sci
Current Topics in Medical Mycology — CTMMEJ
Current Topics in Medical Mycology — Curr Top Med Mycol
Current Topics in Membranes — Curr Top Membr
Current Topics in Membranes and Transport — CTMTA2
Current Topics in Membranes and Transport — Curr Top Membr Transp
Current Topics in Membranes and Transport — Curr Top Membranes Transp
Current Topics in Microbiology and Immunology — CTMIA
Current Topics in Microbiology and Immunology — Curr Top Microbiol Immunol
Current Topics in Molecular Endocrinology — Curr Top Mol Endocrinol
Current Topics in Nerve and Muscle Research. Selected Papers. Symposia held at the International Congress on Neuromuscular Diseases — Curr Top Nerve Muscle Res Sel Pap Symp Int Congr Neuromuscul
Current Topics in Neurobiology — Curr Top Neurobiol
Current Topics in Neuroendocrinology — CTNEEY
Current Topics in Neuroendocrinology — Curr Top Neuroendocrinol
Current Topics in Neuropathology — Curr Top Neuropathol
Current Topics in Nutrition and Disease — Curr Top Nutr Dis
Current Topics in Pathology — Curr Top Pathol
Current Topics in Photovoltaics — Curr Top Photovoltaics
Current Topics in Plant Physiology — Curr Top Plant Physiol
Current Topics in Pulmonary Pharmacology and Toxicology — Curr Top Pulm Pharmacol Toxicol
Current Topics in Radiation Research [*Elsevier Book Series*] — CTRR
Current Topics in Radiation Research — CTRRA
Current Topics in Radiation Research — Curr Top Radiat Res
Current Topics in Radiation Research. Quarterly — CTRQA
Current Topics in Radiation Research. Quarterly — Curr Top Radiat Res Q
Current Topics in Reproductive Endocrinology — Curr Top Reprod Endocrinol
Current Topics in Research on Synapses — CTRSES
Current Topics in Research on Synapses — Curr Top Res Synapses
Current Topics in Surgical Research — Curr Top Surg Res
Current Topics in Synthesis and Structure of Polymers. Presented at IUPAC International Symposium — Curr Top Synth Struct Polym IUPAC Int Symp
Current Topics in Thyroid Research. Proceedings of the International Thyroid Conference — Curr Top Thyroid Res Proc Int Thyroid Conf
Current Topics in Tumor Cell Physiology and Positron-Emission Tomography — Curr Top Tumor Cell Physiol Positron Emiss Tomogr
Current Topics in Veterinary Medicine — CTVMDT
Current Topics in Veterinary Medicine — Curr Top Vet Med
Current Topics in Veterinary Medicine and Animal Science — Curr Top Vet Med Anim Sci
Current Trends in Histocompatibility — Curr Trends Histocompat
Current Trends in Morphological Techniques — Curr Trends Morphol Tech
Current Trends in Optics. Invited Papers from the ICO [*International Commission for Optics*] **Meeting** — Curr Trends Opt Invited Pap Meet
Current Trends in Organic Synthesis. Proceedings. International Conference — Curr Trends Org Synth Proc Int Conf
Current US Government Periodicals on Microfiche — Curr US Gov Per Mfiche
Current Veterinary Therapy. Small Animal Practice — Curr Vet Ther
Current Work in the History of Medicine — Curr Work Hist Med
Current Work in the History of Medicine — CWHM
Currents in Alcoholism — Curr Alcohol
Currents in Modern Biology [*The Netherlands*] — CUMBB
Currents in Modern Biology — Curr Mod Biol
Currents in Modern Biology. Biosystems — Curr Mod Biol Biosyst
Currents in Photosynthesis. Proceedings. Western-Europe Conference on Photosynthesis — Curr Photosynth Proc West Eur Conf
Currents in Theology and Mission — Curr T M
Currents in Theology and Mission — CuTM
Currents. The Journal of Food, Nutrition, and Health — Curr J Food Nutr Health
Curriculum and Research Bulletin — Curric & Research Bul
Curriculum and Research Bulletin — Curriculum Res Bull
Curriculum Australia — Curric Aust
Curriculum Inquiry — Curric Inq
Curriculum Inquiry — Curric Inquiry
Curriculum Journal [*Philippines*] — CJ
Curriculum News — Curric News
Curriculum Perspective — Curriculum Perspect
Curriculum Review — Cur R
Curriculum Review — Curric R
Curriculum Study and Educational Research Bulletin — Curric Stud and Ed Res B
Curriculum Theory Network — Curric Theo
Cursillos y Conferencias. Instituto Lucas Mallada — Cursillos Conf Inst Lucas Mallada
Curso. Escuela de Optica Cuantica — Curso Esc Opt Cuantica
Curso Roso de Luna. Investigacion y Economia de los Recursos Geologico-Mineros. Actas — Curso Roso de Luna Invest Econ Recur Geol Min Actas
Cursos y Conferencias — CuCo
Cursos y Conferencias — CyC
Cursos y Conferencias. Biblioteca de Universidade de Coimbra — CCBUC
Cursos y Conferencias (Buenos Aires) — Cursos Conf BA
Cursos y Congresos. Universidad de Santiago De Compostela — Cursos Congr Univ Santiago De Compostela
Curtis's Botanical Magazine. New Series — Curtis's Bot Mag New Ser
Curtius' Studien zur Griechischen und Lateinischen Grammatik — St Griech Lat Gramtk
Cushman Foundation for Foraminiferal Research. Contributions — Cushman Found Foram Research Contr
Cushman Foundation for Foraminiferal Research. Contributions. Special Publication — Cushman Found Foram Research Contr Special Pub
Cushman Foundation for Foraminiferal Research. Special Publication — Cushman Found Foraminiferal Res Spec Publ
Customs Bulletin — CB
Customs Tariff Proposals — CTP
Customs Tariff Schedule for Japan, 1986 — Custom Tar J
Cutaneous and Ocular Toxicology — Cutaneous Ocul Toxicol
Cuticle Techniques in Arthropods — Cuticle Tech Arthropods
Cutting Tool Engineering — CTEGA
Cutting Tool Engineering — Cut Tool En
Cutting Tool Engineering — Cutting Tool Eng
Cuttington Research Journal — Cuttington Res J
Cuttlefish. Unalaska City School. Unalaska — CTLF
Cuvasskii Gosudarstvennyi Pedagogiceskii Institut Imeni I. Ja. Jakovleva Ucenye Zapiski [*Cheboksary*] — Cuvas Gos Ped Inst Ucen Zap
Cuvasskii Gosudarstvennyi Universitet Imeni I. N. Ul'janova Cuvasskii Gosudarstvennyi Pedagogiceskii Institut Imeni I. Ja. Jakovleva Ucenyi Zapiski — Cuvas Gos Univ I Cuvas Gos Ped Inst Ucen Zap
Cuyo. Anuario de Historia del Pensamiento Argentino — Cuy
CVGIP (Computer Vision Graphics and Image Processing) Graphical Models and Image Processing — CVGIP Graph
CVGIP (Computer Vision Graphics and Image Processing) Image Understanding — CVGIP Imag
CVP. Journal of Cardiovascular and Pulmonary Technology — CVP J Cardiovasc Pulm Technol
CW-Canadian Welfare — CW-Can Welf
Cwiczenia Laboratoryjne z Kinetyki Procesowej — Cwiczenia Lab Kinet Procesowej
Cyanamid International. Mitteilungen — Cyanamid Int Mitt
Cyanamid International. Veterinary Bulletin — Cyanamid Int Vet Bull
Cyanamid Magazine — Cyanamid Mag
Cyanamid New Product Bulletin — Cyanam New Prod Bull
Cyanide Compounds in Biology — Cyan Compd Biol
Cybernetica — Cyb
Cybernetics — Cyb
Cybernetics [*English Translation*] — CYBNA
Cybernetics and Systems — Cybern and Syst
Cybernetics and Systems — Cybern Syst
Cybernetics and Systems — Cybernet Systems
Cybernetics and Systems — CYSYDH
Cybernetics and Systems Analysis — Cybernet Systems Anal
Cybium. Bulletin de l'Association des Amis du Laboratoire des Peches Coloniales — Cyb
Cycle — GCYC
Cycle Australia — Cycle Aust
Cycle de Perfectionnement en Genie Chimique — Cycle Perfect Genie Chim
Cycle World — ICYW
Cycles — CYCLA
Cyclic Deformation, Fracture, and Nondestructive Evaluation of Advanced Materials — Cyclic Deform Fract Nondestr Eval Adv Mater
Cycling Science — Cycling Sci
Cyclopaedia of Anatomy and Physiology — Cycl Anat and Physiol
Cylchgrawn Llyfrgell Genedlaethol Cymru — CyL
CYP. Revista de Contaminacion y Prevencion — CYP
Cypher — Cyp
Cypriote Bronzework in the Mycenaean World — CBMW
Cyprus Agricultural Journal — Cypr Agric J
Cyprus Agricultural Journal — Cyprus Agric J
Cyprus Agricultural Research Institute. Annual Report — Cyprus Agric Res Inst Annu Rep
Cyprus Agricultural Research Institute. Miscellaneous Publications — Cyprus Agric Res Inst Misc Publ
Cyprus Agricultural Research Institute. Progress Report — Cyprus Agric Res Inst Prog Rep
Cyprus Agricultural Research Institute. Technical Bulletin — Cyprus Agric Res Inst Tech Bull
Cyprus Agricultural Research Institute. Technical Paper — Cyprus Agric Res Inst Tech Pap
Cyprus Department of Agriculture. Annual Report — Cyprus Dep Agric Annu Rep
Cyprus Geological Survey Department. Bulletin — Cyprus Geol Surv Dep Bull
Cyprus Geological Survey Department. Memoir — Cyprus Geol Surv Dep Mem
Cyprus Industrial Journal — Cyprus Ind
Cyprus Journal — Cyprus J
Cyprus Medical Journal — Cypr Med J
Cyprus Ornithological Society. Bulletin — Cypr Orn Soc Bull
Cyprus Popular Bank Newsletter — CPB
Cyprus Public Health — Cypr Publ Hlth
Cyprus. Republic. Ministry of Commerce and Industry. Geological Survey Department. Bulletin — Cyprus Repub Minist Commer Ind Geol Surv Dep Bull
Cytobiologie — CYTZA
Cytobiologie de la Reproduction Sexuee des Plantes Ovulees. Collque International — Cytobiol Reprod Sex Plant Ovulees Colloq Int
Cytobiologie; Zeitschrift fuer Experimentelle Zellforschung — Cytobiologie Z Exp Zellforsch

Cytobiologische Revue — Cytobiol Rev
Cytobios — CYTBA
Cytogenetics [*Switzerland*] — CYTGA
Cytogenetics — Cytogen
Cytogenetics and Cell Genetics — Cytog C Gen
Cytogenetics and Cell Genetics — Cytogenet Cell Genet
Cytokine and Growth Factor Reviews — Cytokine Growth Factor Rev
Cytokines and Molecular Therapy — Cytokines Mol Ther
Cytologia — CYTOA
Cytologia — Cytol
Cytologia. International Journal of Cytology — Cytologia Int J Cytol
Cytological and Neurological Studies. Faculty of Medicine. University of Kanazawa — Cytol Neurol Stud Fac Med Univ Kanazawa
Cytological Studies. Faculty of Medicine. University of Kanazawa — Cytol Stud Kanaz
Cytology and Genetics [*English Translation of Tsitologiya i Genetika*] — Cytol Genet
Cytology and Genetics (English Translation) — Cytol Genet (Engl Transl)
Cytology and Genetics (English Translation of Tsitologiya i Genetika) — Cytol Genet (Engl Transl Tsitol Genet)
Cytometry Supplement — Cytometry Suppl
Cytoprotection and Cytobiology. Proceedings. Symposium on Cytoprotection — Cytoprot Cytobiol Proc Symp Cytoprot
CZ Chemie-Technik — CZ Chem-Tech
Czasopismo Geograficzne [*Geographical Journal*] — Czas Geogr
Czasopismo Prawno-Historyczne — Cz PH
Czasopismo Prawno-Historyczne — Czas Praw Hist
Czasopismo Rolnicze — Czas Roln
Czasopismo Stomatologiczne — Czas Stomat
Czasopismo Stomatologiczne — Czas Stomatol
Czasopismo Stomatologiczne — CZSTA
Czasopismo Techniczne (Krakow) — Czas Tech (Krakow)
Czasopismo Techniczne. M. Mechanika — Czas Tech M
Czasopismo Towarzystwa Aptekarskiego (Lwow) — Czas Tow Aptek (L)
Czechoslovak Academy of Sciences. Botanical Institute. Hydrobiological Laboratory. Annual Report — Czech Acad Sci Bot Inst Hydrobiol Lab Annu Rep
Czechoslovak Academy of Sciences. Institute of Landscape Ecology. Hydrobiological Laboratory. Annual Report — ARCLEW
Czechoslovak Academy of Sciences. Institute of Landscape Ecology. Hydrobiological Laboratory. Annual Report — Czech Acad Sci Inst Landscape Ecol Hydrobiol Lab Annu Rep
Czechoslovak Academy of Sciences. Institute of Landscape Ecology. Section of Hydrobiology. Annual Report — ACAHE7
Czechoslovak Academy of Sciences. Institute of Landscape Ecology. Section of Hydrobiology. Annual Report — Czech Acad Sci Inst Landscape Ecol Sect Hydrobiol Annu Rep
Czechoslovak Bibliography on Industrial Hygiene and Occupational Diseases — Czech Bibliogr Ind Hyg Occup Dis
Czechoslovak Conference on Electronics and Vacuum Physics. Proceedings — Czech Conf Electron Vac Phys Proc
Czechoslovak Conference on Electronics and Vacuum Physics. Texts. Contributed Papers — Czech Conf Electron Vac Phys Texts Contrib Pap
Czechoslovak Conference on Electronics and Vacuum Physics. Texts. Survey Papers — Czech Conf Electron Vac Phys Texts Surv Pap
Czechoslovak Congress of Gastroenterology — Czech Congr Gastroenterol
Czechoslovak Economic Digest — Czechoslovak Econ Dig
Czechoslovak Economic Papers — CEP
Czechoslovak Economic Papers — Czechosl Econ Pap
Czechoslovak Film — Czech F
Czechoslovak Foreign Trade — CZE
Czechoslovak Foreign Trade — Czech Fg T
Czechoslovak Heavy Industry — Czech Heavy Ind
Czechoslovak Heavy Industry — CZHIA
Czechoslovak Journal of Physics — Czech J Phys
Czechoslovak Journal of Physics — Czechoslovak J Phys
Czechoslovak Journal of Physics — CZYPA
Czechoslovak Journal of Physics. Section A — Czech J Phys Sect A
Czechoslovak Journal of Physics. Section B — Czec J Phys
Czechoslovak Journal of Physics. Section B — Czech J Phys Sect B
Czechoslovak Journal of Physics. Section B — Czechoslovak J Phys B
Czechoslovak Mathematical Journal — CMJ
Czechoslovak Mathematical Journal — Czec Math J
Czechoslovak Mathematical Journal — Czech Math J
Czechoslovak Mathematical Journal — Czechoslovak Math J
Czechoslovak Mathematical Journal — CZMJA
Czechoslovak Medicine — Czech Med
Czechoslovak Research Work — Czech Res W
Czechoslovak Review of Tuberculosis and Pulmonary Diseases — Czech Rev Tuberc Pulm Dis
Czechoslovak Trade Journal — Czech Tr J
Czechoslovakia. Research Institutes for Crop Production. Annual Report — Czech Res Inst Crop Prod Annu Rep
Czechoslovakia. Urad pro Patenty a Vynalezy. Vestnik — Czech Urad Pat Vynalezy Vestn
Czechoslovakia. Urad pro Vynalezy a Objevy. Vestnik — Czech Urad Vynalezy Objevy Vestn
Czechoslovakian Patent Document — Czech
Czech-Polish Colloquium on Chemical Thermodynamics and Physical Organic Chemistry. Communications — Czech Pol Colloq Chem Thermodyn Phys Org Chem Commun
Czech-Polish Colloquium on Chemical Thermodynamics and Physical Organic Chemistry. Lectures — Czech Pol Colloq Chem Thermodyn Phys Org Chem Lect
Czernowitzer Wochenblatt — CWB
Czsaopismo Prawno-Historyczne — CPH
Czytelnik — Cz

D

D and B [*Dun and Bradstreet*] **Reports** — D & B Rpts
D & T. Dialysis and Transplantation — D T Dial Transplant
D. H. Lawrence Review — D H Lawren
D. H. Lawrence Review — D H Lawrence R
D. H. Lawrence Review — DHLR
D. J. Crowther Ltd. Fixed Price List — Crowther FPL
DA. Difesa Ambientale — D A Dif Ambientale
Dacca University. Bulletin — Dacca Univ Bull
Dacca University. Journal — Dacca Univ J
Dacca University. Oriental Publications Series — Dacca Univ Or Publ Ser
Dacca University. Studies — Dacca U Stud
Dacca University. Studies — Dacca Univ St
Dacca University Studies — Dacca Univ Stud
Dacca University. Studies — DUS
Dacca University Studies. Arts and Sciences — Dacca Univ Stud Arts Sci
Dacca University. Studies. Part A — Dacca Univ Stud Part A
Dacca University. Studies. Part B — Dacca Univ Stud Part B
Dacia — Dac
Dacia. Revue d'Archeologie et d'Histoire Ancienne — Dacia
Dacoromania — D
Dacoromania — Dac
Dacoromania — Dacor
Dacotah Territory — Dac Terr
Dactylography — Dactyl
Dada/Surrealism — Dada
DAE Circular. Louisiana Agricultural Experiment Station. Department of Agricultural Economics — DAE Circ LA Agr Exp Sta Dept Agr Econ
DAE Research Report. Department of Agricultural Economics and Agribusiness. Louisiana State University — DAE Res Rep Dep Agric Econ Agribusiness LA State Univ
Daedalus — Dae
Daedalus — Daed
Daedalus — DAEDA
Daedalus — GDAD
Daedalus. Journal. American Academy of Arts and Sciences — Daedalus J Amer Acad Arts Sci
Daedalus Tekniska Museets Arsbok — Daedalus Tek Mus Arsb
Daenische Bibliothek Oder Sammlung von Alten und Neuen Gelehrten Sachen aus Daenemark — Daen Biblioth
Daffodil and Tulip Year Book — Daffod Tul Yb
Daffodil and Tulip Year Book. Royal Horticultural Society — Daffodil Tulip Year Book
Daffodil Yearbook — Daffod Yb
Dagblad Scheepvaart — SPA
Dagbladpers — MDA
Dagens Industri — DGIN
Dagens Nyheter — DN
Dagestanskii Gosudarstvennyi Universitet Imeni V. I. Lenina Ucenyi Zapiski [*Makhachkala*] — Dagestan Gos Univ Ucen Zap
Dagestanskii Nauchno-Issledovatel'skii Veterinarnyi Institut. Sbornik Nauchnykh Rabot — Dagest Nauchno Issled Vet Inst Sb Nauchn Rab
Dagestanskii Sel'skokhozyaistvennyi Institut. Trudy — Dagest Skh Inst Tr
Dahlem Workshop Reports. Life Sciences Research Report — Dahlem Workshop Rep Life Sci Res Rep
Dahlem Workshop Reports. Physical, Chemical, and Earth Sciences Research Report — Dahlem Workshop Rep Phys Chem Earth Sci Res Rep
Dahlia News. New England Dahlia Society (Boston) — Dahlia News Boston
Dahlia Year Book — Dahl Yb
Dahlmann-Waitz. Quellenkunde der Deutschen Geschichte — DW
Dail Debates [*Ireland*] — Dail Deb
[*The*] **Daily Chronicle** — DC
Daily Commercial News and Shipping List — DCN
Daily Consumer News [*Database*] — DCN
Daily Engineering Articles — DEA
Daily Express [*United Kingdom*] — DE
Daily Graphic — DG
Daily Industrial Index Analyzer [*Database*] — DIIA
Daily Mail [*United Kingdom*] — DM
Daily Missouri-Mississippi River Bulletin — DMMRB
Daily Nation [*Nairobi*] — DN
Daily News — DN
Daily News [*Tanzania*] — DNS
Daily News Record — Daily News
Daily Oil Bulletin — Daily Oil Bull
Daily Oklahoman — Daily Oklah
Daily Planet — Dl Planet
Daily Telegraph [*London*] — D Tel
Daily Telegraph [*London*] — D Telegraph
Daily Telegraph — DT
Daily Telegraph Reports (Newspaper) (Tasmania) — DT (Newspr) (Tas)
Daily Times [*Lagos*] — DT
Daily Weather and River Bulletin — DW & RB
Daily World — Daily Wld
Dainichi Nippon Densen Jiho — DNDJA
Dainichi-Nippon Cables Review [*Japan*] — Dainichi-Nippon Cables Rev
Dairy and Dairy Shopkeepers Journal — Dairy Dairy Shopkeepers J
Dairy and Ice Cream Field — Dairy and Ice Cream Fld
Dairy and the Creamery Journal — Dairy Creamery J
Dairy Council Digest — Dairy Counc Dig
Dairy Council Digest — DCDI
Dairy Cow of the Future. International Seminar — Dairy Cow Future Int Semin
Dairy Effluents. Proceedings. International Dairy Federation Seminar — Dairy Effluents Proc Int Dairy Fed Semin
Dairy Engineering — Dairy Eng
Dairy Exporter — D Exp
Dairy Farmer — Dairy F
Dairy Farmer — Dairy Farm
Dairy Farmer and Dairy Beef-Producer — Dairy Farmer Dairy Beef Prod
Dairy Farming Annual — Dairy Annu
Dairy, Food, and Environmental Sanitation — Dairy Food Environ Sanit
Dairy Goat Journal — Dairy Goat J
Dairy Guidelines. Virginia Polytechnic Institute and State University Extension Division — Dairy Guidelines Va Polytech Inst State Univ Ext Div
Dairy Herd Management — Dairy Herd Manage
Dairy Herd Management — Dairy Herd Mgt
Dairy Industries [*Later, Dairy Industries International*] — Dairy Ind
Dairy Industries [*Later, Dairy Industries International*] — Dairy Indus
Dairy Industries International — DAI
Dairy Industries International — Dairy Ind
Dairy Industries International — Dairy Ind Int
Dairy Industries International — Dairy Inds
Dairy Information Bulletin — Dairy Info Bul
Dairy Produce — Dairy Prod
Dairy Promotion Review — Dairy Prom Rev
Dairy Record — Dairy Rec
Dairy Research Report — Dairy Res Rep
Dairy Research Report. Louisiana Agricultural Experiment Station — Dairy Res Rep La Agric Exp Stn
Dairy Research Report. South Australia Department of Agriculture and Fisheries — Dairy Res Rep Dep Agric Fish
Dairy Science Abstracts — Dairy Sci Abstr
Dairy Science Handbook — Dairy Sci Handb
Dairy Society International. Bulletin — Dairy Soc Int Bull
Dairy Starter Cultures [*monograph*] — Dairy Starter Cult
Dairy Tales. California University, Berkeley. Cooperative Extension Service — Dairy Tales Calif Univ Berkeley Coop Ext Serv
Dairy Tales. University of California. Berkeley. Cooperative Extension Service — Dairy Tales Univ Calif Berkeley Coop Ext Serv
Dairy World and the British Dairy Farmer — Dairy World Br Dairy Farmer
Dairyfarming Annual — Dairyfarm Annu
Dairyfarming Digest — Dairyfarming Dig
Dairyfarming Digest — Dairyfmg Dig
Dairymen's Digest. North Central Region Edition — Dairymen's Dig North Cent Reg Ed
Dairymen's Digest. Southern Region Edition — Dairymen's Digest South Reg Ed
Daito Bunka Daigaku Kangakkaishi — DBDKK
Daito Bunka Daigaku Kiyo — DBDK
Daiwa Investment Monthly — Daiwa
Dakar Medical — Dakar Med
Dakar Medical — DAMDD5
Dakota Farmer — Dakota F
Dakota Law Review — Dak L Rev
Dakota Law Review — Dak Law Rev
Dakota Law Review — Dakota Law Rev
Dakota Reports — Dakota
Dalgetys Annual Wool Digest — Dalgetys Annual Wool D
Dalgetys Annual Wool Review — Dalgetys Annual Wool R
Dalhousie Dental Journal — Dalhousie Dent J
Dalhousie Law Journal — Dal LJ
Dalhousie Law Journal — Dalhousie L J
Dalhousie Review — Da R
Dalhousie Review — Dal R

Dalhousie Review — Dal Rev
Dalhousie Review — Dalh Rev
Dalhousie Review — Dalhous Rev
Dalhousie Review — Dalhousie R
Dalhousie Review — Dalhousie Rev
Dalhousie Review — DR
Dalhousie Review — PDAL
Dalhousie University. Institute of Public Affairs. Occasional Papers — Dalhousie Univ Inst Pub Aff Occ Pap
Dalian Institute of Technology. Journal — Dalian Inst Technol J
Dallam's Opinions [*Texas*] — Dallam
Dallas — IDAL
Dallas/Fort Worth Business Journal — Dalls FW B
Dallas Medical Journal — Dall Med J
Dallas Medical Journal — Dallas Med J
Dallas Medical Journal — DAMJA
Dallas Morning News — Dallas New
Dallas Morning News — DMN
Dallas Reports — Dall R
Dallas Symphony Orchestra. Program Notes — Dallas Sym
Dalloz Analytique. Jurisprudence [*France*] — DA Jur
Dalloz Analytique. Legislation [*France*] — DAL
Dalloz Critique. Jurisprudence [*France*] — DC Jur
Dalloz Critique. Legislation [*France*] — DCL
Dalloz. Jurisprudence [*France*] — D Jur
Dalloz. Legislation [*France*] — DL
Dalloz-Sirey. Jurisprudence [*France*] — DS Jur
Dalloz-Sirey. Legislation [*France*] — DSL
Dal'nevostochnoe Petrograficheskoe Soveshchanie — Dalnevost Petrogr Soveshch
Dal'nevostochnyi Fizicheskii Sbornik — Dal'nevost Fiz Sb
Dal'nevostochnyi Matematiceskii Sbornik — Dal'nevostocn Mat Sb
Dal'nevostochnyi Nauchno-Issledovatel'skii Institut Lesnogo Khozyaistva. Sbornik Trudov — Dalnevost Nauchno Issled Inst Lesn Khoz Sb Tr
Dal'nevostochnyi Nauchno-Issledovatel'skii Institut po Stroitel'stvu Sbornik Nauchnykh Rabot — Dal'nevost Nauchno Issled Inst Stroit Sb Nauchn Rab
Dal'nevostochnyi Nauchno-Issledovatel'skii Institut Sel'skogo Khozyaistva. Trudy — Dalnevost Nauchno Issled Inst Selsk Khoz Tr
Dal'nevostochnyi Politekhnicheskii Institut imeni V. V. Kuibysheva. Trudy — Dalnevost Politekh Inst im V V Kuibysheva Tr
Dal'nevostocnyi Gosudarstvennyi Universitet Ucenyi Zapiski Serija Fiziko-Matematiceskih Nauk — Dal Nevostocn Gos Univ Ucen Zap
Dalton Transactions — Dalton Trans
Dan Viet Nam — DVN
Dana-Report. Carlsberg Foundation — Dana-Rep
Dana-Report. Carlsberg Foundation — Dana-Rep Carlsberg Found
Dana-Report. Carlsberg Foundation — DNRPAI
Dance — D
Dance and Dancers — DD
Dance Chronicle — Dance Chron
Dance Chronicle — PDCH
Dance Data Base Project — DDBP
Dance in Canada — Dance in Can
Dance Magazine — Dance
Dance Magazine — Dance Mag
Dance Magazine — DM
Dance Magazine — GDAM
Dance News — Dance N
Dance News — DN
Dance Notation Record — Dance Notat Rec
Dance Observer — DO
Dance Perspectives — Dance Per
Dance Perspectives — DP
Dance Research Annual — Dance Res A
Dance Research Annual — Dance Res An
Dance Research Journal — Dance Res J
Dance Research Journal — PDRJ
Dance Scope — Dance Sco
Dancing Times — Dancing Tim
Dandke Folkemaal — DF
Daneshgah-e Tehran. Daneshkade-ye Darusazi. Majallah — Daneshgah e Tehran Daneshkade ye Darusazi Maj
Danfoss Journal — Danfoss J
Dania Reports. Carlsberg Foundation — Dania Rep
Danish Academy of Technical Sciences. Transactions — ATS Trans
Danish Academy of Technical Sciences. Transactions — Dan Acad Tech Sci Trans
Danish Arctic Research — Dan Arct Res
Danish Arctic Station of Disko Island, Greenland. Publications — DADG
Danish Atomic Energy Commission. Research Establishment. Risoe Report — Dan AEC Res Establ Riso Rep
Danish Atomic Energy Commission. Research Establishment Risoe. Report Risoe-M — Dan AEC Res Establ Risoe Rep Risoe M
Danish Atomic Energy Commission. Research Establishment Risoe. Risoe Report — Dan AEC Res Establ Risoe Risoe Rep
Danish Foreign Office Journal — D For O J
Danish Journal — DAJO
Danish Journal. A Magazine about Denmark — DFO
Danish Journal of Plant and Soil Science — Dan J Plant Soil Sci
Danish Medical Bulletin — Dan Med B
Danish Medical Bulletin — Dan Med Bull
Danish Medical Bulletin — Danish M Bull
Danish Medical Bulletin — DMBUA
Danish Medical Bulletin. Supplement — Dan Med Bull Suppl
Danish Meteorological Institute. Climatological Papers [*Danske Meteorologiske Institut Klimatologiske Meddelelser*] — DMICP
Danish Meteorological Institute. Weather Service Report — DMIWSR
Danish Patent Document — Dan
Danish Pest Infestation Laboratory. Annual Report — ABSLAU
Danish Pest Infestation Laboratory. Annual Report — Dan Pest Infest Lab Annu Rep
Danish Review of Game Biology — Dan Rev Game Biol
Danish Review of Game Biology — DRGBAH
Danish Scientific Investigations in Iran — DSI
Danish Yearbook of Philosophy — Dan Yrbk Phil
Danish Yearbook of Philosophy — Danish Yearb Phil
Danmarks Gamle Folkeviser — DGF
Danmarks Geologiske Undersoegelse — Danm Geol Undersoeg
Danmarks Geologiske Undersoegelse — Danmarks Geol Undersoegelse
Danmarks Geologiske Undersoegelse. Afhandlinger. Raekke 1 — Dan Geol Unders Afh Raekke 1
Danmarks Geologiske Undersoegelse. Afhandlinger. Raekke 2 — Dan Geol Unders Afh Raekke 2
Danmarks Geologiske Undersoegelse. Afhandlinger. Raekke 4 — Dan Geol Unders Afh Raekke 4
Danmarks Geologiske Undersoegelse. Afhandlinger. Raekke 5 — Dan Geol Unders Afh Raekke 5
Danmarks Geologiske Undersoegelse. Arbog — Dan Geol Unders Arbog
Danmarks Geologiske Undersoegelse. II Raekke — Dan Geol Unders II Raekke
Danmarks Geologiske Undersoegelse. III Raekke — Dan Geol Unders III Raekke
Danmarks Geologiske Undersoegelse. IV Raekke — Dan Geol Unders IV Raekke
Danmarks Geologiske Undersoegelse. Rapport — Dan Geol Unders Rapp
Danmarks Geologiske Undersoegelse. Serie A — Dan Geol Unders Ser A
Danmarks Geologiske Undersoegelse. Serie B — Dan Geol Unders Ser B
Danmarks Haandvaerk — D Haa
Danmarks Naturfredningsforenings Arsskrift — Dan Naturfredningsforen Arsskr
Danmarks Statistiks TidsseriedataBank [*Database*] — DSTB
Danmarks Veterinaer- og Jordbrugsbase [*Database*] — DVJB
Danmarksposten — Dmkp
Dannzha — DANN
Dansk Aarbog foer Musikforskning — DAM
Dansk Aarbog for Musikforskning — Dansk Aarbog Mf
Dansk Akvarieblad. Akvarie- og Terrarietidsskrift — D Akvbl
Dansk Arbejde — D Arb
Dansk Artilleri-Tidsskrift — D Art-T
Dansk Atomenergikommissionens Forsoegsanlaeg Risoe. Report — Dan Atomenergikomm Forsoegsanlaeg Risoe Rep
Dansk Audiologopaedi — Dansk Audiol
Dansk Bogfortegnelse — Dansk Bog
Dansk Botanisk Arkiv — D Bot A
Dansk Botanisk Arkiv — Dan Bot Ark
Dansk Botanisk Arkiv — Dansk Botan
Dansk Botanisk Arkiv — DBA
Dansk Bryggeritidende — Dan Brygg Tid
Dansk Dendrologisk Arsskrift — Dan Dendrol Arsskr
Dansk Dendrologisk Arsskrift — Dansk Dendrol Arsskr
Dansk Erhvervsfjerkrae — Dan Erhvervsfjerkrae
Dansk Farmaceutisk Aarbog — Dan Farm Aarb
Dansk Fiskeritidende — D Fskt
Dansk Fiskeritidende — Dan Fisk Tid
Dansk Folkemal — DFM
Dansk Forsikrings Tidende — D Fs T
Dansk Fotografisk Tidsskrift — D Fot T
Dansk Froavl — D Fro
Dansk Geologisk Forening Meddelelser — Dansk Geol Foren Medd
Dansk Geologisk Forening Meddelelser — Dansk Geol Foren Meddel
Dansk Havebrug — Dan Haveb
Dansk Havetidende — Dan Havetid
Dansk Historisk Tidskrift — HTD
Dansk Ingeniorforening Spildevandskomiteen Skrift — Dan Ingeniorforen Spildevandskom Skr
Dansk Jagttidende — D Jgt
Dansk Kemi — DAKEA
Dansk Kemi — Dan Kemi
Dansk Kirkeliv Mens Tiderne Skifter — D Krkl
Dansk Kunsthaandvaerk — D Kunsth
Dansk Landbrug — Dan Landbr
Dansk Landburg — D Ldb
Dansk Maanedsskrift for Dyrlaeger — D Dl M
Dansk Medicinhistorisk Arbog — Dan Medicinhist Arbog
Dansk Missionsblad — D Miss
Dansk Musiktidsskrift — D Mus
Dansk Musiktidsskrift — Dansk Mt
Dansk Musiktidsskrift — Dansk Mus
Dansk Musiktidsskrift — DMt
Dansk Naturfredning — D Natfr
Dansk Naturfredning — Dan Naturfr
Dansk Naturfredning — Dan Naturfredning
Dansk Naturhistorisk Forening. Videnskabelige Meddelelser — DNFV
Dansk Ornithologisk Forening. Feltornithologen — Dan Ornithol Foren Feltornithol
Dansk Ornithologisk Forening. Fuglevaern — Dan Ornithol Foren Fuglevaern
Dansk Ornithologisk Forenings Tidsskrift — D Orn FT
Dansk Ornithologisk Forenings Tidsskrift — DAFT
Dansk Ornithologisk Forenings Tidsskrift — Dan Ornithol Foren Tidsskr
Dansk Ornithologisk Forenings Tidsskrift — DOFTAB
Dansk Patenttidende — Dan Patenttid
Dansk Pelsdyravl — Dan Pelsdyravl
Dansk Pelsdyrblad — Dan Pelsdyrbl

Dansk Radio Industri — D Rad I
Dansk Radio Industri — Dansk Rad Ind
Dansk Reklame — D Rkl
Dansk Rode Kors — DRK
Dansk Sang — D Sa
Dansk Selskab foer Bygningsstatik, Bygningsstatiske Meddelelser — Dan Selsk Bygningsstatik Bygningsstatiske Medd
Dansk Seminarieblad — D Smbl
Dansk Skoleslojd — D Sksl
Dansk Skovforenings Tidsskrift — D Skf T
Dansk Skovforenings Tidsskrift — Dan Skovforen Tidsskr
Dansk Skovforenings Tidsskrift — DSFT
Dansk Skovforenings Tidsskrift — DSFTA
Dansk Skovforenings Tidsskrift — DSFTA5
Dansk Skovforenings Tidsskrift — DST
Dansk Sofartstidende — D Sof
Dansk Teknisk Tidsskrift — D Tekn T
Dansk Teknisk Tidsskrift [*Denmark*] — Dan Tek Tidsskr
Dansk Teknisk Tidsskrift — Dansk Tekn Tidsskr
Dansk Teknisk Tidsskrift — DTKTA
Dansk Teologisk Tidsskrift [*Copenhagen*] — DanTTs
Dansk Teologisk Tidsskrift — Dteol T
Dansk Teologisk Tidsskrift [*Copenhagen*] — DTT
Dansk Teologisk Tidsskrift — DTTid
Dansk Tidsskrift — Dansk Tidsskr
Dansk Tidsskrift foer Farmaci — Dan Tdsskr Farm
Dansk Tidsskrift foer Farmaci — Dan Tidsskr Farm
Dansk Tidsskrift foer Farmaci — Dansk T Farm
Dansk Tidsskrift foer Farmaci — Dansk Tidssk Farm
Dansk Tidsskrift foer Farmaci — DTFAA
Dansk Tidsskrift foer Farmaci — DTFAAN
Dansk Tidsskrift foer Farmaci. Supplementum — Dan Tidsskr Farm Supple
Dansk Tidsskrift for Farmaci — D T Farm
Dansk Tidsskrift for Farmaci. Supplementum — Dan Tidsskr Farm Suppl
Dansk Toldtidende — D To
Dansk Udsyn — D Ud
Dansk Udsyn — Dan Udsyn
Dansk Udsyn — DanU
Dansk Udsyn — DU
Dansk Ugeskrift — Dansk Ugeskr
Dansk Vejtidsskrift — D Vejt
Dansk Veterinaertidsskrift — Dan Veterinaertidsskr
Dansk Veterinaertidsskrift — DAVEDJ
Danske Dyrlaegeforening. Medlemsblad — Dan Dyrlaegeforen Medlemsb
Danske Folkemaal — D Fo
Danske Folkemaal — DanF
Danske Magazin — D Mg
Danske Magazin — Dan Mag
Danske Magazin — DM
Danske Meteorologiske Institut. Meddelelser — DMIM
Danske Sprog-og Literaturselskab — DSL
Danske Studier — DS
Danske Studier — DSt
Danske Videnskabernes Selskabs Biologiske. Skrifter — DVSB
Danske Videnskabernes Selskabs Skrifter — DVSS
Dante Studies — Dante Stud
Dante Studies — DaSt
Dante Studies with the Annual Report of the Dante Society — DSARDS
Danville Quarterly Review — Danv Q
Danzig. Uniwersytet. Wydzial Biologii i Nauk o Ziemi. Zeszyty Naukowe. Geografia — Danzig Uniw Wydz Biol Nauk Ziemi Zesz Nauk Geogr
Daphnis. Zeitschrift fuer Mittlere Deutsche Literatur — Daphn
Dapim Refuiim — Dapim Refu
Dar Es Salaam Medical Journal — Dar Es Salaam Med J
Dar Es Salaam Medical Journal — DSMJBB
Dar es Salaam University Law Journal — Dar es Salaam Univ Law J
Darbai. Lietuvos Veterinarijos Akademijos — Darbai Liet Vet Akad
Daresbury Laboratory. Preprint DL/P — Daresbury Lab Prepr DL/P
Daresbury Laboratory. Preprint DL/SRF/P — Daresbury Lab Prepr DL/SRF/P
Daresbury Laboratory. Report — Daresbury Lab Rep
Daresbury Laboratory. Report DL/R — Daresbury Lab Rep DL R
Daresbury Laboratory. Report DL/SRF/R — Daresbury Lab Rep DL SRF R
Daresbury Laboratory. Technical Memorandum — Daresbury Lab Tech Memo
Daresbury Nuclear Physics Laboratory. Report — Daresbury Nucl Phys Lab Rep
Daresbury Nuclear Physics Laboratory Report DNPL/R — Daresbury Nucl Phys Lab Rep DNPL R
Daresbury Nuclear Physics Laboratory. Technical Memorandum — Daresbury Nucl Phys Lab Tech Memo
Daresbury Synchrotron Radiation Lecture Note Series — Daresbury Synchrotron Radia Lect Note Ser
Dari de Seama ale Sedintelor. Comitetul de Stat al Geologiei (Romania) — Dari Seama Sedintelor Com Stat Geol (Rom)
Dari de Seama ale Sedintelor. Institutul de Geologie si Geofizica (Bucharest) — Dari Seama Sedintelor Inst Geol Geofiz Bucharest
Dari de Seama ale Sedintelor. Institutul Geologic (Bucharest) — Dari Seama Sedintelor Inst Geol Bucharest
Dari de Seama ale Sedintelor. Institutul Geologie (Romania) — Dari Seama Sedintelor Inst Geol (Rom)
Dari de Seama ale Sedintelor. Republica Populara Romana Comitetul Geologic — Dari Seama Sedint RPR Com Geol
Dari Seama Sedintelor. Republica Populara Romana. Comitetul Geologic — Dari Seama Sedintelor Repub Pop Rom Com Geol
Darien Institute of Technology. Journal — Darien Inst Technol J
Darken Conference. Proceedings — Darken Conf Proc
Darkenu (London) — DL
Darkroom Photography — Darkroom Photogr
Darling Downs Times — DDT
Darmstaedter Beitraege zur Neuen Musik — Darmstaedter Beitr Neuen M
Darmstaedter Beitraege zur Neuen Musik — DBNM
Darshana International — Darshana Int
Dartmouth Alumni Magazine — Dartmouth Alumni Mag
Dartmouth Bi-Monthly — Dart Bi-Mo
Dartmouth College. Bulletin — Dartm Coll Bull
Darwiniana [*Buenos Aires*] — DARWAG
Darwiniana. Revista del Instituto de Botanica Darwinion — Darwin
Das Heilige Land in Vergangenheit und Gegenwart — HLVG
Das Heilige Land. Koeln — Hl L
Das Neue Testament Deutsch — NTD
Das Riesengebirge im Wort und Bild — Riesengebirge Im Wort Bild
Das Zeichen — Zei
Dasika Hronika — Dasika Hron
Dasonomia Interamericana. Instituto Interamericano de Ciencias Agricolas — Dasonomia Interamer
Data Acquisition and Processing in Biology and Medicine — DAPBAB
Data Acquisition and Processing in Biology and Medicine — Data Acquis Process Biol Med
Data Acquisition and Processing in Biology and Medicine. Proceedings of the Rochester Conference — Data Acquis Process Biol Med Proc Rochester Conf
Data Analysis in Astronomy — Data Anal Astron
Data Archive on Adolescent Pregnancy and Pregnancy Prevention [*Database*] — DAAPPP
Data Automation Digest — DAD
Data Base Newsletter — Data Base News
Data Business — Data Bus
Data Channels — Data Chan
Data Communications — Data C
Data Communications — Data Comm
Data Communications — Data Commun
Data Communications Extra — Data C Xtra
Data Dynamics — Data Dyn
Data Education — Data Ed
Data Handling in Science and Technology — Data Hand Sci Technol
Data Handling in Science and Technology — DHSTEV
Data Management — Data Manage
Data Management — Data Mgmt
Data Management — Data Mgt
Data Management — DMG
Data of Atomic Power [*Japan*] — Data At Power
Data Papers in Papua New Guinea Languages — DPPNGL
Data Processing — Data Proc
Data Processing — Data Proces
Data Processing — Data Process
Data Processing Digest — Data Proc Dig
Data Processing Digest — Data Process
Data Processing Digest — Data Process Dig
Data Processing for Education [*North American Publishing Co.*] — Data Process Educ
Data Processing in Medicine — Data Process Med
Data Processing Magazine — Data Process Mag
Data Processing Magazine — DPMAA
Data Processing Practitioner — Data Process Pract
Data Record of Oceanographic Observations and Exploratory Fishing [*Hokkaido*] — DROFAZ
Data Record of Oceanographic Observations and Exploratory Fishing (Hokkaido) — Data Rec Oceanogr Obs Explor Fish (Hokkaido)
Data Report — Data Rep
Data Report. Virginia Institute of Marine Science — Data Rep Virginia Inst Mar Sci
Data Resources Series [*Elsevier Book Series*] — DRS
Data Series. Design Institute for Physical Property Data — Data Ser Des Inst Phys Prop Data
Data Systems — Data Sys
Data Systems — Data Syst
Data Systems Engineering — DSE
Data Systems News — Data Systems N
Data Training — Data Trng
Data Users News — Data User Ns
Database [*United States*] — DTBSD
Database — DTE
Database Journal — Database J
Database Journal — Database Jrnl
Database of Antiviral and Immunomodulatory Therapies for AIDS — DAITA
Database of Offsite Waste Management — DOWM
Datamation — DAT
Datamation — DAU
Datamation — DTMNA
Datamation News Release — Datam NR
Datapro Communications Solutions — Datapro Com Sol
Datapro Management of Small Comuter Systems — Datapro Man Sm Comp Sys
Datapro Reports on Data Communications — Datapro Rep Data Commun
Datapro Reports on Minicomputers — Datapro Rep Minicomput
Datapro Reports on Office Systems — Datapro Rep Office Syst
Datas on Ecological Morphology — Datas Ecol Morphol
Date Growers' Institute. Report — Date Grow Inst Rep
Date Palm Journal — DAPJD4
Date Palm Journal — Date Palm J
Daten und Dokumente zum Umweltschutz — Daten Dok Umweltschutz
Datenbank fuer Wassergefahrdende Stoffe [*Database*] — DABAWAS
Datenjournal — DATJBM
Datennachweis Informationssystem [*Database*] — DANIS

Datenverarbeitung im Recht — Datenverarb Recht
Datenverarbeitung in der Medizin — Datenverarb Med
Datenverarbeitung in der Medizin — DVMMB7
Datum Collection. Tokai Regional Fisheries Research Laboratory — Datum Collect Tokai Reg Fish Res Lab
Datum Collection. Tokai Regional Fisheries Research Laboratory — TRDCBC
Daughters of the American Revolution. Magazine — DAR Mag
Dauphine Medical — Dauph Med
Davar. Revista Literaria — Dav
Davenport Academy of Sciences. Proceedings — Davenport Acad Sci Proc
David — DV
Davidsonia — DVDSAD
Davos Symposium — Davos Symp
Dawe Digest — Dawe Dig
Dawson Packet — DP
Day Care and Early Education — Day Care & Early Educ
Daybooks for Knossos — DB
Daybooks for Knossos — DM
Dayton Medicine — Dayton Med
DB. The Sound Engineering Magazine — DB Sound Eng Mag
DBR Paper (National Research Council of Canada. Division of Building Research) — DBR Pap Natl Res Counc Can Div Build Res
DC Bar Journal — DCB J
DC [*District of Columbia*] **Municipal Regulations** — DC Mun Regs
DDD. Diffusion and Defect Data — DDD Diffus Defect Data
DDR-Medizin-Report — DDR-Med-Rep
DDZ. Das Deutsche Zahnaerzteblatt — DDZZA
De Antiquis Ecclesiae Ritibus — AERit
De Beers Duesseldorf-Conference. Papers — De Beers Duesseldorf Conf Pap
De Bow's Commercial Review — De Bow
De Bow's Review — De Bows R
De Brabantse Folklore — Brabantse Folkl
De Colores. Journal of Emerging Raza Philosophies — DC
DE. Domestic Engineering [*Formerly, DE Journal*] — DE Dom Eng
De Duinen. Bulletin du Centre Scientifique et Culturel de l'Abbaye des Dunes et du Westhoek — Duinen
De Duisburgse Vrachtkonvenie — DVK
De Economist — DeEc
De Gids — Gids
De Gids op Maatschappelijk Gebied — De Gids
De Grafiske Fag — Graf F
De Gruyter Expositions in Mathematics — De Gruyter Exp Math
De Gruyter Series in Nonlinear Analysis and Applications — De Gruyter Ser Nonlinear Anal Appl
De Gruyter Studies in Mathematics — De Gruyter Stud Math
De Homine — DeH
De Indische Culturen — Indische Cult
DE Journal [*Later, DE. Domestic Engineering*] — DE/J
DE. Journal of Dental Engineering — DE
DE. Journal of Dental Engineering — DE J Dent Eng
De Katholick — DKath
De Katholiek (Leiden) — KathL
De Maasgouw. Orgaan voor Limbrugsche Geschiedenis, Taal-en Letterkunde — DMG
De Militaire Spectator — DMS
De Navorscher — DNav
De Nederlandse Gemeente — DNG
De Nieuwe Taglalgids — DNT
De Paul Law Review — De Paul L Rev
De Paul Law Review — DPLR
De Philosophia — De Phil
De Probatis Sanctorum Historiis — PSH
De Proprietatibus Litterarum — DPL
De Re Metallica de la Mineria y los Metales — De Re Met Min Met
De Vierde Macht — DVM
De Vrije Fries — VF
Deaconess Hospital. Medical Bulletin — Deaconess Hosp Med Bull
Deactivation and Poisoning of Catalysts — Deact Poisoning Catal
Deafness Research and Training Center — Deafness Res & Train Cent
Dealerscope Merchandising — Dealerscop
Dearborn Independent — Dearborn Ind
Death Education — Death Educ
Death Education. Pedagogy, Counseling, Care — DEED
Death Penalty Reporter — Death Pen Rep
Death Studies — Death Stud
Death Studies — PDST
Debate — DE
Debater's Magazine — DM
Debates en Antropologia. Pontificia Universidad Catolica del Peru. Departamento de Ciencias Sociales — PUCP/DA
Debrecceni Mezogazdasagi Akademia Tudomanyos Evkonyve — Debreceni Mezogazd Akad Tud Evk
Debrecceni Szemle — Debrecceni Sz
Debreceni Deri Muzeum Evkoenyve — Debre Muz Evk
Debreceni Deri Muzeum Evkoenyve — DME
Debreceni Deri Muzeum Evkoenyve — Evk Debrecen
Debreceni Deri Muzeum Evokoenyve — Debrec Muz Evk
Debreceni Mezoegazdasagi Kiserleti Intezet Evkoenyve — Debreceni Mezoegazd Kiserl Intez Evk
Debreceni Mezogazdasagi Akademia Tudomanyos Evkonyve — Debreceni Mezogazd Akad Tud Evk
Debreceni Tisza Istvan Tudomanyos Tarsasag II. Orvos-Termeszettudomanyi Osztalyanak Munkai — Debreceni Tisza Istvan Tud Tars 2 Orv Termeszettud Oszt Munka
Decachord — DD
Decade Egyptienne — Decade Egypt
Decade of Short Stories — Dec
Decalogue Journal — Decalogue J
Deccan College. Monograph Series — DCMS
Deccan College Postgraduate and Research Institute. Bulletin — DCRI
Deccan Geographer — Decc Geogr
December — D
DECHEMA [*Deutshe Gesellschaft fuer Chemisches Apparatenesen, Chemische Technik, und Biotechnologie e V*] **Biotechnology Equipment Suppliers** [*Database*] — BIOQUIP
DECHEMA [*Deutshe Gesellschaft fuer Chemisches Apparatenesen, Chemische Technik, und Biotechnologie e V*] **Corrosion Data Base** — DECOR
DECHEMA [*Deutshe Gesellschaft fuer Chemisches Apparatenesen, Chemische Technik, und Biotechnologie e V*] **Environmental Technology Equipment Databank** — DETEQ
DECHEMA [*Deutsche Gesellschaft fuer Chemisches Apparatenesen, Chemische Technik, und Biotechnologie e V*] **Equipment Suppliers Data Base** — DEQUIP
DECHEMA [*Deutsche Gesellschaft fuer Chemisches Apparatewesen, Chemische Technik, und Biotechnologie eV*] **Monographien** — DECHEMA Monogr
DECHEMA [*Deutsche Gesellschaft fuer Chemisches Apparatewesen, Chemische Technik, und Biotechnologie eV*] **Monographien** — DMDGA
DECHEMA [*Deutshe Gesellschaft fuer Chemisches Apparatenesen, Chemische Technik, und Biotechnologie e V*] **Research Institutes Databank** — DERES
DECHEMA [*Deutshe Gesellschaft fuer Chemisches Apparatenesen, Chemische Technik, und Biotechnologie e V*] **Thermophysical Property Data Bank** — DETHERM
Decheniana — DCNNAH
Decheniana Beihefte — DEBEAC
Decheniana Beihefte — Decheniana Beih
Decheniana. Verhandlungen des Naturhistorischen Vereins der Rheinlande und Westerfalens. B. Biologische Abteilung — Decheniana B Biol Abt
Deciduous Fruit Grower — Decid Fruit Grow
Deciduous Fruit Grower — Deciduous Fruit Grow
Deciduous Fruit Grower [*South Africa*] — DEFGA
Deciduous Fruit Grower. Die Sagtevrugteboer — Decid Fruit Grow Sagtevrugteboer
Decimal Research Bulletin — Decimal Research Bul
Decision — Decs
Decision Sciences — DEC
Decision Sciences — Decis Sci
Decision Sciences — DSI
Decisiones de Puerto Rico — PR Dec
Decisions. Geographic Board of Canada — Decis Geogr Bd Can
Decisions. Income Tax Board of Review — Board of Review Decisions
Decisions. United States Geographic Board — Decis US Geogr Bd
Decontamination and Decommissioning of Nuclear Facilities. Proceedings. American Nuclear Society Topical Meeting — Decontam Decomm Nucl Facil Proc Am Nucl Soc Top Meet
Decorative Arts Society. Journal — Decorative Arts Soc Jnl
Decorator and Painter for Australia and New Zealand — Decorator
Dedalo — Ded
Dedications from the Athenian Akropolis — DAA
Deep Delta Quarterly — Deep Delta Q
Deep Sea Drilling Project. Initial Reports — Deep Sea Drill Proj Initial Rep
Deep Sea Research and Oceanographic Abstracts — Deep Sea Res & Oceanogr Abstr
Deep Sea Research and Oceanographic Abstracts — Deep Sea Res Oceanogr Abstr
Deep Sea Research and Oceanographic Abstracts — DROAAK
Deep Sea Research. Part B. Oceanographic Literature Review — Deep Sea Res Part B Oceanogr Lit Rev
Deeper Pathways in High-Energy Physics — Deeper Pathways High Energy Phys
Deep-Inelastic and Fusion Reactions with Heavy Ions. Proceedings. Symposium — Deep Inelastic Fusion React Heavy Ions Proc Symp
Deep-Sea Research [*Later, Deep-Sea Research with Oceanographic Literature Review*] — Deep Sea Re
Deep-Sea Research [*Later, Deep-Sea Research with Oceanographic Literature Review*] — Deep Sea Res
Deep-Sea Research [*Later, Deep-Sea Research with Oceanographic Literature Review*] — DESRAY
Deep-Sea Research and Oceanographic Abstracts — Deep-Sea Oceanogr Abstr
Deep-Sea Research. Part A. Oceanographic Research Papers [*Later, Deep-Sea Research with Oceanographic Literature Review*] — Deep-Sea Res Part A
Deep-Sea Research. Part A. Oceanographic Research Papers [*Later, Deep-Sea Research with Oceanographic Literature Review*] — Deep-Sea Res Part A Oceanogr Res Pap
Deep-Sea Research. Part A. Oceanographic Research Papers [*Later, Deep-Sea Research with Oceanographic Literature Review*] — Deep-Sea Res Pt A Oceanogr Res Pap
Deep-Sea Research. Part A. Oceanographic Research Papers [*Later, Deep-Sea Research with Oceanographic Literature Review*] — DRPPD5
Deep-Sea Research. Part B. Oceanographic Literature Review — Deep-Sea Res Pt B Oceanogr Lit Rev
Deer Farmer — Deer Farm
Deering's Annotated California Code — Cal Code (Deering)
Deering's California General Laws Annotated — Cal Gen Laws Ann (Deering)
DEFAZET. Deutsche Farben Zeitschrift — DEFAZET Dtsche Farben Z
Defect and Diffusion Forum — Defect Diffus Forum
Defect Complexes in Semiconductor Structures. Proceedings. International School — Defect Complexes Semicond Struct Proc Int Sch
Defect Structure, Morphology and Properties of Deposits. Proceedings of a Symposium — Defect Struct Morphol Prop Deposits Proc Symp

Defects and Radiation Effects in Semiconductors. Invited and Contributed Papers from the International Conference on Defects and Radiation Effects in Semiconductors — Defects Radiat Eff Semicond Invited Contrib Pap Int Conf
Defects in Crystalline Solids [*Defects in Solids*] [*Elsevier Book Series*] [*Later,*] [*A publication*] — DCS
Defects in Semiconductors. Proceedings. Materials Research Society Annual Meeting — Defects Semicond Proc Mater Res Soc Annu Meet
Defects in Solids [*Elsevier Book Series*] — DSOL
Defektologija — Defektol
Defektoskopiya — Defektosk
Defektoskopiya Metallov — Defektoskopiya Met
Defence Aerienne — Def Aer
Defence Attache — D Atache
Defence Journal — Def J
Defence Material — D Mtr
Defence Research Abstracts. Contractors Edition [*England*] — Def Res Abs Contractors Edn
Defence Research Board of Canada. Defence Research Establishment Ottawa. Reports — DREOR
Defence Research Board of Canada. Defence Research Establishment Ottawa. Technical Note — DRETN
Defence Research Board of Canada. Defence Research Establishment Pacific. Reports — DREPR
Defence Science and Technology Organisation. Technical Note DSTO-TN — Def Sci Technol Organ Tech Note DSTO TN
Defence Science and Technology Organisation. Technical Report DSTO-GD — Def Sci Technol Organ Tech Rep DSTO-GD
Defence Science Journal — Def Sci J
Defence Science Journal [*Delhi*] — Defence Sci J
Defence Science Journal [*New Delhi*] — DSJOA
Defence Science Journal — DSJOAA
Defenders — DEFEDZ
Defenders of Wildlife — Def Wildl
Defenders of Wildlife International — Def Wildl Int
Defenders of Wildlife International — Defenders Wildl Int
Defenders of Wildlife Magazine [*Later, Defenders*] — Defenders Wildl
Defenders of Wildlife Magazine [*Later, Defenders*] — DWLIAU
Defenders of Wildlife News — Def Wildl News
Defenders of Wildlife News — Defenders Wildl News
Defenders of Wildlife News — DWINAU
Defending All Outdoors. Alberta Fish and Game Association — DAOD
Defensa Latino Americana — Def Latin A
Defensa Medico Social — Def Med Soc
Defense Africa and the Middle East — Defense A
Defense and Armament Heracles International — Defarmhera
Defense & Armament Magazine — D & A
Defense and Foreign Affairs — De For Af
Defense and Foreign Affairs Daily — D & FA Daily
Defense and Foreign Affairs Weekly — D & FA Week
Defense Budget Intelligence — DBI
Defense Daily — Def Daily
Defense de la Langue Francaise — DLF
Defense de l'Occident — Def Occident
Defense des Plantes — Def Plant
Defense des Vegetaux — Def Veg
Defense des Vegetaux — Defense Veg
Defense des Vegetaux — DEVEAA
Defense Electronics — Def Elect
Defense Electronics — Def Electron
Defense Helicopter World — Def Heli W
Defense Industry Bulletin [*DoD*] — DIB
Defense Industry Bulletin [*DoD*] — DIBtn
Defense Law Journal — Def L J
Defense Law Journal — Def Law J
Defense Law Journal — Defense L J
Defense Management Journal — D Manage J
Defense Management Journal — Def Man J
Defense Management Journal — Defense Mgt J
Defense Management Journal — DMJ
Defense Management Journal — DMJOB
Defense Markets and Technology — Def Mark Technol
Defense Metals Information Center. Batelle Memorial Institute. DMIC Report — Def Met Inf Cent Battelle Meml Inst DMIC Rep
Defense Monitor — Def Mntr
Defense Nationale — D Natl
Defense Nationale — Def Nat
Defense Nationale — Def Natl
Defense Nationale — Defense Nat
Defense Nationale. Problemes Politiques Economiques, Scientifiques, Militaires — Def Natn
Defense News — Defense Ns
Defense Nuclear Agency. Report DNA (United States) — Def Nucl Agency Rep DNA (US)
Defense of Japan, 1984 — Defense Jpn
Defense R and D Update. Space, Aeronautics, and Electronic Systems — Defens R & D
Defense Science 2001 — Def Sci
Defense Science Journal — Defense Sci J
Defense Spending and the Economy. Congressional Budget Office Study — CBO Def S
Defense Systems Management Review — Def Syst Man Rev
Defense Systems Review and Military Communications — Def Sys Rv
Defense Technical Information Center. Digest — Def Tech Inf Cent Dig
Defense Technology International — Def Tech Int
Defense Today — Def Today
Defense Transportation Journal — D Trns J
Defense Transportation Journal — Def Transp J
Defense Transportation Journal — DETJA
Deficience Mentale — Def Ment
Defining the Laboratory Animal. Symposium — Defining Lab Anim Symp
Defixionum Tebellae Atticae — DTA
Defixionum Tebellae Atticae — Tab Defix
Deformacion Metalica — Deform Met
Deformatsiya i Razrushenie v Neravnomernykh Temperaturnykh Polyakh — Deform Razrushenie Neravnomernykh Temp Polyakh
DEG Information Series. United Kingdom Atomic Energy Authority. Development and Engineering Group — DEG Inf Ser UK At Energy Auth Dev Eng Group
Degradation and Stabilization of Materials. Papers presented at the Arab International Conference in Materials Science — Degrad Stab Mater Pap Arab Int Conf Mater Sci
Degre Second. Studies in French Literature — DSec
Dejiny Ved a Techniky — Dejiny Ved Tech
Dejiny Ved a Techniky — DVT
Dejiny Ved a Techniky. Spolecnost pro Dejiny Ved a Techniky — DVT-Dejiny Ved a Techniky
DeKalb Literary Arts Journal — DeKalb
DeKalb Literary Arts Journal — DeKalb Lit
DeKalb Literary Arts Journal — DLAJ
Dekorativnoe Iskusstvo SSSR — Dek Iskusstvo
Dekorativnoe Iskusstvo SSSR — Dekor Isk SSSR
Dela Institut za Biologijo. Slovenska Akad. Znanosti in Umietnosti. Opera. Institutum Biologicum. Academia Scientiarum et Artium Slovenica — Dela Inst Biol Slov Akad Znan
Delaware. Agricultural Experiment Station. Bulletin — Del Agric Exp Stn Bull
Delaware. Agricultural Experiment Station. Bulletin — DUABA8
Delaware. Agricultural Experiment Station. Circular — Del Agric Exp Stn Circ
Delaware. Agricultural Experiment Station. Publications — Del Ag Exp
Delaware Cases — Del Cas
Delaware Chancery Reports — Del Ch
Delaware Code. Annotated — Del Code Ann
Delaware County Farm and Home News — Del Cty Farm Home News
Delaware County Institute of Science. Proceedings — Delaware Co Inst Sc Pr
Delaware. Geological Survey. Annual Report. Bulletin. Report of Investigations — Del Geol Survey Ann Rept Bull Rept Inv
Delaware. Geological Survey. Bulletin — Del Geol Surv Bull
Delaware. Geological Survey. Report of Investigations — Del Geol Surv Rep Invest
Delaware Health News — Del Hlth News
Delaware Historical Society. Papers — Delaware Hist Soc Papers
Delaware History — DeH
Delaware History — Del Hist
Delaware History — DelH
Delaware History — DH
Delaware Journal of Corporate Law — Del J Corp L
Delaware Journal of Corporate Law — DJC
Delaware Journal of Corporate Law — DJCL
Delaware Medical Journal — Del Med J
Delaware Medical Journal — DSMJA
Delaware Notes — Del Note
Delaware Notes — Del Notes
Delaware Notes — DelN
Delaware Nurse — Del Nurs
Delaware Sea Grant Technical Report. DEL-SG — Del Sea Grant Tech Rep DEL-SG
Delaware Sea Grant Technical Report Del-SG — DSGRD7
Delaware State Bar Association — Del State Bar Assn
Delaware State Medical Journal — Del St Med J
Delaware State Medical Journal — Del State Med J
Delaware. University. Agricultural Experiment Station. Bulletin — Del Univ Agric Exp Stn Bull
Delaware University. Agricultural Experiment Station. Circular — Del Univ Agric Exp Stn Circ
Delaware University. Sea Grant Program. Annual Report — Del Univ Sea Grant Program Annu Rep
Delaware University. Water Resources Seminars. Proceedings — Del Univ Water Resour Semin Proc
Delaware Valley Business Digest — Del Val Bus D
Del-Chem Bulletin — Del-Chem Bull
Delegation en Perse. Memoires — DP
Delft Hydroscience Abstracts — Delft Hydrosci Abstr
Delft Progress Report — Delft Prog Rep
Delft Progress Report — Delft Prog Report
Delft Progress Report — DPRED
Delft Progress Report. Series A. Chemistry and Physics, Chemical and Physical Engineering — Delft Prog Rep Ser A
Delft Progress Report. Series A. Chemistry and Physics, Chemical and Physical Engineering — DPRAC
Delft Progress Report. Series A-F — DPRPB
Delft Progress Report. Series B. Electrical, Electronic, and Information Engineering — Delft Prog Rep Ser B
Delft Progress Report. Series B. Electrical, Electronic, and Information Engineering — DPRBA
Delft Progress Report. Series C. Mechanical and Aeronautical Engineering and Shipbuilding — Delft Prog Rep Ser C
Delft Progress Report. Series C. Mechanical and Aeronautical Engineering and Shipbuilding — DPRCB
Delft Progress Report. Series D. Architecture, Industrial Design, Social Sciences — Delft Prog Rep Ser D

Delft Progress Report. Series E. Geosciences — Delft Prog Rep Ser E
Delft Progress Report. Series F. Mathematical Engineering, Mathematics, and Information Engineering — Delft Prog Rep Ser F
Delft Progress Report. Series F. Mathematical Engineering, Mathematics, and Information Engineering — Delft Progress Rep Ser F
Delhi Aluminium Patrika — Delhi Alum Patrika
Delhi Law Review — Del L R
Delhi Law Review — Delhi L R
Delhi Law Review — Delhi L Rev
Delhi Law Times — Delhi L Times
Deliberations. Societe Royale du Canada — Deliberations Soc R Can
Delineator — Delin
Delius Society. Journal — Delius
Delkeletdunantuli Mezogazdasagi Kiserleti Intezet Kozlemenye — Delkeletdunantuli Mezogazd Kiserl Intez Kozl
Delphinium Society Yearbook — Delphinium Soc Yearb
Delpinoa — DLPNAM
Delpinoa. Nuova Serie del Bulletino dell'Orto Botanico. Universita di Napoli — Delpinoa NS
Delta Epsilon Sigma Bulletin — DESB
Delta Journal of Science — Delta J Sci
Delta Kappa Gamma Bulletin — Delta Kappa Gamma Bull
Delta Pi Epsilon Journal — Delta Pi Epsilon J
Delta. Revue du Centre d'Etudes et de Recherche sur les Ecrivains du Sud aux Etats-Unis — Delta ES
Deltawerken. Driemaandelijks Bericht — DRD
Deltio Ellenikes Mikrobiologikes Etaireias — Delt Ell Mikrobiol Etair
Deltion Agrotikes Trapezes — Delt Agrotikes Trapezes
Deltion Archaiologikon — Delt Arch
Deltion Biblikon Meleton — Delt Bibl Melet
Deltion Hellenikes Geografikes Hetaireias — Delt Hell Geogr Het
Deltion Hellenikes Mikrobiologikes Hetaireias — Delt Hell Mikrobiol Hetair
Deltion Hellenikes Mikrobiologikes kai Hygieinologikes Hetaireias — Delt Hell Mikr Hyg Het
Deltion Hellenikes Mikrobiologikes kai Hygieinologikes Hetaireias — Delt Hell Mikrobiol Hygieinol Hetair
Deltion Hellenikes Mikrobiologikes kai Hygieinologikes Hetaireias [*Greece*] — Delt Hellen Mikrobiol Hyg Hetair
Deltion Hidrymatos Koinonikon Asphaliseon — Delt IKA
Deltion tes Christianikes Archaiologikes Hetaireias — Delt Chr
Deltion tes Christianikes Archaiologikes Hetaireias — Deltion Christ
Deltion tes Hellenikes Geolokne Hetaireias — Delt Hell Geol Hetair
Deltion tes Hellenikes Kteniatrikes Hetaireias — Delt Hell Kteniatr Hetair
Deltion tes Hellenikes Kteniatrikes Hetaireias — DNKHAR
Deltion tes Historikes kai Ethnologikes Hetaireias tes Hellados — DHEHH
Deltion tou Institoutou Technologias Phytikon Proionton — Delt Inst Technol Phytikon Proionton
Demag Nachrichten — Demag Nachr
Demain — D
Demande de Brevet d'Invention (France) — Demande Brev Invent (Fr)
Demande de Brevet Europeen — Demande Brev Eur
Demande de Certificat d'Addition (France) — Demande Certif Addit (Fr)
Demande de Certificat d'Utilite (France) — Demande Certif Util (Fr)
Dementia Reviews — Dementia Rev
Democracy — Demo
Democrat and Chronicle — Demo & Chr
Democratic Left — Demo Left
Democratic Review — Dem R
Democratic Review — Democratic R
Democrazia e Diritto — Dem Dir
Democrazia e Diritto — Democr e Dir
Demografia — Dem
Demografia — Demogr
Demografia y Economia — Demogr y Econ
Demografia y Economia — Demografia y Econ
Demografia y Economia — DYE
Demographic Bulletin [*New Zealand*] — Demogr Bull
Demographic Online Retrieval Information System [*Database*] — DORIS
Demography — DEMO
Demography — Demogr
Demography — DMGYA
Demography — DY
Demography — PDEM
Demography and Development Digest — Demogr Dev Dig
Demokratie und Recht — Demokr Recht
Demonstratio Mathematica — Demonstratio Math
Demotic Ostraca from Medinet Habu — DOMH
Demotic Ostraca from the Collections at Oxford, Paris, Berlin, and Cairo — DO
Demotische Studien [*Leipzig*] — DemStud
Dempa Digest — Dempa Dig
Den Danske Realskole — D Rsk
Den Haag. Maandblad van de Gemeente ('S-Gravenhage) — GRG
Den Indre Missions Tidende — I Miss T
Dendritic Cells in Fundamental and Clinical Immunology — Dendritic Cells Fundam Clin Immunol
Dendroflora — DENFA7
Dene Express. Fort Good Hope — DE
Dene Nation Newsletter — DENN
Den'gi i Kredit — D i K
Den'gi i Kredit — D Kred
Den'gi i Kredit — Den'gi i Kred
Deniliquin Historical Society. Newsletter — Deniliquin Hist Soc News
Denison University. Scientific Laboratories. Bulletin — Denison Univ Sc Lab B
Denison University. Scientific Laboratories. Journal — Denison Univ Sci Lab Jour
Denki Gakkai Ronbunshi. A — DGKRA
Denki Gakkai Ronbunshi. B — DGRBB
Denki Gakkai Ronbunshi. C — DGRCA
Denki Gakkai Zasshi — DGZAA
Denki Kagaku — Denki Kag
Denki Seirigaku Kenkyu [*Electrophysiology*] — DSKSAR
Denki Tsushin Daigaku Gakuho — DTDRA
Denki Tsushin Gakkai Zasshi — DTGZA
Denkmaeler Antiker Architektur — DAA
Denkmaeler Antiker Architektur — Denkmaeler Ant
Denkmaeler aus Aegypten und Aethiopien — Denkm Aeg
Denkmaeler der Malerei des Altertums — Denkmaeler Mal
Denkmaeler der Tonkunst in Bayern — DTB
Denkmaeler des Klassischen Altertums zur Erlaeuterung des Lebens der Griechen und Roemer in Religion, Kunst, und Sitte — Denkm Klass
Denkmaeler Deutscher Tonkunst — Denkm Dt Tonkunst
Denkmaeler Griechischer und Roemischer Skulptur — Denkmaeler Skulpt
Denkmaeler Griechischer und Roemischer Skulptur — DGRS
Denkmalpflege in Baden-Wuerttemberg — DBW
Denkmalpflege in Baden-Wuerttemberg — Denkm Pfl Bad Wuert
Denkmalpflege in Baden-Wuerttemberg — Denkmal Baden Wuerttemberg
Denkmalpflege in Rheinland-Pfalz — Denk Pfl Rhein Pfalz
Denkschrift des Naturhistorischen Museums. Wien — DnatMus
Denkschriften der Akademie der Wissenschaften in Wien — DAW
Denkschriften der Akademie der Wissenschaften in Wien — DAWW
Denkschriften der Allgemeinen Schweizerischen Gesellschaft fuer die Gesammten Naturwissenschaften — Denkschr Allg Schweiz Ges Gesammten Naturwiss
Denkschriften der Bayerischen Akademie der Wissenschaften zu Muenchen — MD
Denkschriften der Kaiserlichen Akademie der Wissenschaften. Mathematisch-Naturwissenschaftliche Klasse — Denkschr Kaiserl Akad Wiss Math Naturwiss Kl
Denkschriften der Kaiserlichen Akademie der Wissenschaften. Mathematisch-Naturwissenschaftliche Klasse — DKAW
Denkschriften der Kaiserlichen Akademie der Wissenschaften (Wien) — Denkschr Ak Wiss Wien
Denkschriften der Koeniglichen Bayrischen Botanischen Gesellschaft in Regensburg — Denkschr Koenigl Bayr Bot Ges Regensburg
Denkschriften der Oesterreichischen Akademie der Wissenschaften. Philosophisch-Historische Klasse — Denkschriften Wien Ak
Denkschriften der Oesterreichischen Akademie der Wissenschaften. Philosophisch-Historische Klasse — DWA
Denkschriften der Oesterreichischen Akademie der Wissenschaften. Philosophisch-Historische Klasse — OAW PHKD
Denkschriften der Oesterreichischen Akademie der Wissenschaften. Philosophisch-Historische Klasse (Wien) — Wiener Denkschr
Denkschriften der Russischen Geographischen Gesellschaft zu St. Petersburg — Denkschr Russ Geogr Ges St Petersburg
Denkschriften der Schweizerischen Naturforschenden Gesellschaft — Denkschr Schweiz Natf Ges
Denkschriften der Schweizerischen Naturforschenden Gesellschaft — DSchNG
Denkschriften der Vaterlaendischen Gesellschaft der Aerzte und Naturforscher Schwabens — Denkschr Vaterl Ges Aerzte Schwabens
Denkschriften. Schweizerische Naturforschende Gesellschaft — Denkschr Schweiz Naturforsch Ges
Denkschriften. Schweizerische Naturforschende Gesellschaft — DSNGA6
Denmark. Groenlands Geologiske Undersoegelse Rapport — Denmark Gronlands Geol Undersogelse Rapp
Denmark. Research Establishment Risoe. Report — Den Res Establ Risoe Rep
Denmark. Research Establishment Risoe. Report Risoe-M — Den Res Establ Risoe Rep Risoe M
Denmark. Research Establishment Risoe. Risoe Report — Den Res Establ Risoe Risoe Rep
Denmark Review — DNF
Denmark. Risoe National Laboratory. Report Risoe-M — Den Risoe Natl Lab Rep Risoe M
Denmark. Statens Husholdningsraad. Tekniske Meddelelser — Den Statens Husholdningsraad Tek Medd
Denmark. Technical University. Structural Research Laboratory. Report — Den Tech Univ Struct Res Lab Rep
Denosa. Department of Northern Saskatchewan — DENS
Denpa Kenkyusho Kiho — DKKIB
Denryoku Chuo Kenkyusho Hokoku — DCKHDL
Denryoku Chuo Kenkyusho Hokoku. Sogo Hokoku — DKHHD
Denryoku Chuo Kenkyusho Noden Kenkyusho Hokoku [*Agricultural Electricity Institute. Report*] — DKNHDO
Denshi Tsushin Gakkai Gijutsu Kenkyu Hokoku — DTGHD
Denshi Tsushin Gakkai Rombunshi. Part D — DTGDA
Dental Abstracts — Dent Abstr
Dental Anaesthesia and Sedation — Dent Anaesth Sedat
Dental Angles — Dent Angles
Dental Assistant — DEASA
Dental Assistant — Dent Assist
Dental Association of South Africa. Journal — Dent Assoc S Afr J
Dental Bulletin — Dent Bull
Dental Bulletin. Osaka University — Dent Bull Osaka Univ
Dental Cadmos — DECAA
Dental Cadmos — Dent Cadm
Dental Cadmos — Dent Cadmos
Dental Clinics of North America — D Clin North America
Dental Clinics of North America — DCNAA
Dental Clinics of North America — DCNAAC
Dental Clinics of North America — Dent Clin N
Dental Clinics of North America — Dent Clin N Am

Dental Clinics of North America — Dent Clin North Am
Dental Concepts — Dent Conc
Dental Concepts — Dent Concepts
Dental Concepts — DNCPA
Dental Cosmos — Dent Cosm
Dental Cosmos — Dent Cosmos
Dental Delineator — Dent Delin
Dental Dialogue — Dent Dialogue
Dental Digest — DEDIA
Dental Digest — Dent Dig
Dental Dimensions — Dent Dimens
Dental Discourse — Dent Discourse
Dental Echo — DEECAL
Dental Echo — Dent Echo
Dental Economics — Dent Econ
Dental Fabrikant — Dent Fabr
Dental Health [*London*] — DEHEA8
Dental Health (London) — Dent Health (Lond)
Dental Hygiene — Dent Hyg
Dental Hygiene — DNHYAT
Dental Images — Dent Images
Dental Items of Interest — Dent Items Interest
Dental Journal — Dent J
Dental Journal. Nihon University — Dent J Nihon Univ
Dental Journal of Australia — Dent J Aust
Dental Journal of Australia — Dent J Austr
Dental Journal of Malaysia and Singapore — Dent J Malaysia Singapore
Dental Labor (Munich) — Dent Labor (Munch)
Dental Laboratorie Bladet — Dent Lab Bl
Dental Laboratory Review — Dent Lab Rev
Dental Literature Index — Dent Ind
Dental Magazine — Dent Mag
Dental Magazine and Oral Topics — Dent Mag
Dental Magazine and Oral Topics — Dent Mag Oral Top
Dental Management — DEMAB
Dental Management — Dent Manage
Dental Materials — DEMAEP
Dental Materials — Dent Mater
Dental Materials Journal — Dent Mater J
Dental Mirror (Atlanta) — Dent Mirror (Atlanta)
Dental Mirror (Quezon City) — Dent Mirror (Quezon City)
Dental Observer — Dent Obs
Dental Outlook [*Japan*] — Dent Outlook
Dental Practice (Cincinnati) — Dent Pract (Cincinnati)
Dental Practice Management — Dent Pract Manage
Dental Practitioner — Dent Pract
Dental Practitioner and Dental Record [*England*] — Dent Pract Dent Rec
Dental Press — Dent Press
Dental Progress — DENPA3
Dental Progress — Dent Prog
Dental Quarterly — Dent Qu
Dental Radiography and Photography — Dent Radiogr Photogr
Dental Record — Dent Rec
Dental Reflector — Dent Refl
Dental Research and Graduate Study Quarterly. Northwestern University — Dent Res Grad Study Q
Dental Revue — Dent Rev
Dental Science Journal of Australia — Dent Sci J Austr
Dental Student — Dent Stud
Dental Surgeon — Dent Surg
Dental Survey — Dent Surv
Dental Survey — DESUA9
Dental Technician — Dent Tech
Dental Therapeutics Newsletter — Dent Ther Newsl
Dental Update — Dent Update
Dental World — Dent Wld
Dentiste de France — Dent Fr
Dentistry in Japan (Tokyo) — Dent Jpn (Tokyo)
Dentists' Magazine — Dent Mag
Dento Maxillo Facial Radiology — Dento Maxillo Fac Radiol
Dentsu Japan Marketing/Advertising Yearbook — DJM
Dentsu Japan Marketing/Advertising Yearbook — Jpn Market
Denver Business — Denver Bus
Denver Journal of International Law and Policy — Den J Int L and Pol
Denver Journal of International Law and Policy — Den J Int'l L & Pol'y
Denver Journal of International Law and Policy — Den JILP
Denver Journal of International Law and Policy — Denver J Int L & Pol
Denver Journal of International Law and Policy — Denver J Int Law Policy
Denver Journal of International Law and Policy — Denver J Internat Law and Policy
Denver Law Center. Journal — Den LCJ
Denver Law Center. Journal — Denver LCJ
Denver Law Journal — Den L J
Denver Law Journal — Denver L J
Denver Law Journal — Denver Law
Denver Law Journal — DJ
Denver Law Journal — Dn LJ
Denver Medical Bulletin — Denver Med Bull
Denver Medical Times — Denv Med Tim
Denver Medical Times — Denver Med Times
Denver Museum of Natural History. Museum Pictorial Popular Series. Proceedings — Denver Mus Nat History Mus Pictorial Pop Ser Proc
Denver Post — Denvr Post
Denver Post — DPST
Denver Quarterly — Den Q
Denver Quarterly — DenverQ
Denver Quarterly — DQ
Denver Western Roundup — Denver West Roundup
Departamento Nacional de Agricultura (Costa Rica). Boletin Tecnica — Dep Nac Agric (Costa Rica) Bol Tec
Departement de Biologie. College Bourget Rigaud. Bulletin — BDBBDB
Departement de Biologie. College Bourget Rigaud. Bulletin. — Dep Biol Coll Bourget Rigaud Bull
Departement d'Economie et de Sociologie Rurales. Bulletin d'Information — Dept Econ et Sociol Rurales Bul Info
Department Bulletin. United States Department of Agriculture — Dep Bull US Dep Agric
Department Bulletin. United States Department of Agriculture — Dept Bull US Dept Agric
Department Circular. United States Department of Agriculture — Dep Circ US Dep Agric
Department of Aeronautical Engineering. Kyoto University. Current Papers — Dep Aeronaut Eng Kyoto Univ Curr Pap
Department of Agriculture. Botanical Division. Bulletin — Dept Agric Bot Div Bull
Department of Agriculture. Botany Division. Annual Report — Dept Agric Bot Div Annual Rep
Department of Agriculture (Brisbane, Queensland). Bureau of Sugar Experiment Stations. Technical Communications — Dep Agric (Brisbane Queensl) Bur Sugar Exp Stn Tech Commun
Department of Agriculture. Forestry Division. Report. Chief of the Forestry Division — Dept Agric Forest Div Rep Chief Forest Div
Department of Agriculture. Microscopy Division. Food Products — Dept Agric Microscop Div Food Prod
Department of Agriculture (New South Wales). Technical Bulletin — Dep Agric (NSW) Tech Bull
Department of Agriculture. Report on Forestry — Dept Agric Rep Forest
Department of Agriculture. Special Report — Dept Agric Special Rep
Department of Agriculture. Straits Settlements and Federated Malay States. Economic Series — Dep Agric Straits Settlements Fed Malay States Econ Ser
Department of Agriculture. Straits Settlements and Federated Malay States. General Series — Dep Agric Straits Settlements Fed Malay States Gen Ser
Department of Agriculture. Straits Settlements and Federated Malay States. Scientific Series — Dep Agric Straits Settlements Fed Malay States Sci Ser
Department of Agriculture (Victoria, Australia). Technical Bulletin — Dep Agric (Victoria Aust) Tech Bull
Department of Agriculture. Victoria Technical Report Series — Dep Agric Victoria Tech Rep Ser
Department of Antiquities in Palestine. Quarterly — QAP
Department of Applied Mathematics and Theoretical Physics. University of Cambridge. Report DAMTP — Dep Appl Math Theor Phys Univ Cambridge Rep DAMTP
Department of Defence. Aeronautical Research Laboratories. Mechanical Engineering Report (Australia) — Dep Def Aeronaut Res Lab Mech Eng Rep (Aust)
Department of Defense. News Release — DOD NR
Department of Education and Science: Reports on Education [*London*] — Dept of Ed and Science Repts
Department of Elementary School Principals. Bulletin — Dept El Sch Prin B
Department of Employment. Gazette (Great Britain) — Dept Employment Gaz (Gt Britain)
Department of Energy. Environmental Measurements Laboratory. Environmental Quarterly (US) — Dep Energy Environ Meas Lab Environ Q (US)
Department of Energy. Indirect Liquefaction Contractors' Review Meeting — Dep Energy Indirect Liquefaction Contract Rev Meet
Department of Energy. Nuclear Air Cleaning Conference. Proceedings (US) — Dep Energy Nucl Air Clean Conf Proc (US)
Department of Energy. Nuclear Airborne Waste Management and Air Cleaning Conference (US) — Dep Energy Nucl Airborne Waste Manage Air Clean Conf (US)
Department of Energy. Symposium Series (US) — Dep Energy Symp Ser
Department of Engineering. Science Report. University of Oxford — Dep Eng Sci Rep Univ Oxford
Department of Forestry (Queensland). Research Note — Dep For (Queensl) Res Note
Department of Forestry (Queensland). Research Paper — Dep For (Queensl) Res Pap
Department of Forestry Technical Paper. Clemson University — Dep For Tech Pap Clemson Univ
Department of Harbours and Marine (Queensland). Fisheries Notes — Dep Harb Mar (Queensl) Fish Notes
Department of Health, Education, and Welfare. National Institute for Occupational Safety and Health. Publication (United States) — Dep Health Educ Welfare Natl Inst Occup Saf Health Publ (US)
Department of Health, Education, and Welfare. National Institutes of Health. Publication — Dep Health Educ Welfare Natl Inst Health Publ
Department of Health, Education, and Welfare. Publication — HEW
Department of Health, Education, and Welfare. Publication (Health Services Administration) (United States) — Dep Health Educ Welfare Publ (Health Serv Adm) (US)
Department of Indian and Northern Affairs. Education Section. Northern Services Division. Newsletter — IAEN
Department of Industries (Bombay). Bulletin — Dep Ind (Bombay) Bull
Department of Industries (Province of Bombay). Bulletin — Dep Ind (Prov Bombay) Bull
Department of Primary Industries. Brisbane Fisheries Branch. Fisheries Notes [*New Series*] — APFNC3
Department of Primary Industries. Brisbane Fisheries Branch. Fisheries Notes (New Series) — Dep Primary Ind Brisbane Fish Branch Fish Notes (New Ser)

Department of Primary Industries. Fisheries Research Annual Report (Port Moresby) — Dep Primary Ind Fish Res Annu Rep (Port Moresby)
Department of Secondary School Principals. Bulletin — Dept Sec Sch Prin B
Department of State. Bulletin — DEB
Department of State. Bulletin — Dep St B
Department of State. Bulletin — Dept St Bull
Department of State. Bulletin — Dept Sta Bul
Department of State. Bulletin — Dept State Bul
Department of State. Bulletin — Dept State Bull
Department of State Bulletin — GDSB
Department of State. Newsletter — Dept Sta Nl
Department of State. Newsletter — Dept State Newsletter
Department of State US Bulletin — Dep State US Bull
Department of the Capital Territory. Conservation Series [*Canberra*] — CSATD6
Department of the Capital Territory. Conservation Series (Canberra) — Dep Cap Territ Conserv Ser (Canberra)
Department of the Environment. Fire Research Station. Fire Research Technical Paper (United Kingdom) — Dep Environ Fire Res St Fire Res Tech Pap (UK)
Department of the Navy. RAN [*Royal Australian Navy*] **Reports** — Navy Dep RAN Rep
Department Store Sales Fact File — Dept S Fct
Departmental Technical Report. Texas Agricultural Experiment Station — Dep Tech Rep Tex Agric Exp Stn
DePaul Law Review — DeP
DePaul Law Review — DeP LR
Depressive Illness Series — Depressive Illness Ser
Der Alte Orient — Alt O
Der Alte Orient. Gemeinverstaendliche Darstellungen [*Leipzig*] — AO
Der Altsprachliche Unterricht — AU
Der Anaesthesist — ANATA
Der Baierischen Akademie der Wissenschaften in Muenchen. Meteorologische Ephemeriden — Baier Akad Wiss Muenchen Meteorol Ephem
Der Betrieb [*Information service or system*] — DB
Der Chirurg — CHIRAS
Der Deutsche Beamte — DDB
Der Deutsche Oekonomist — DDO
Der Herold. Vierteljahrsschrift fuer Heraldik, Genealogie, und Verwandte Wissenschaften — Herold
Der Islam — DI
Der Islam. Zeitschrift fuer Geschichte und Kultur des Islamischen Orients — Islam
Der Israelitische Volkslehrer — IV
Der Koeniglich Norwegischen Gesellschaft der Wissenschaften Schriften — Koenigl Norweg Ges Wiss Schriften
Der Kolonialdeutsche. Wissenschaftliche Beihefte — Kolonialdeutsche Wiss Beih
Der Neue Orient — DNO
Der Neue Weg — DNW
Der Oeffentliche Dienst — D Oe D
Der Oesterreichische Betriebswirt — D Oe B
Der Physikalische und Oekonomische Patriot oder Bemerkungen und Nachrichten aus der Naturhistorie, der Algemeinen Haushaltungskunst, und der Handlungskunst — Phys Oekon Patriot
Der Preussische Sammler. Zur Kaenntnis der Naturgeschichte — Preuss Sammler Kaenntn Naturgesch
Der Roemisch Kaiserlichen Akademie der Naturforscher Auserlesene Medicinisch- Chirurgisch- Anatomisch- Chymisch- und Botanische Abhandlungen — Roem Kaiserl Akad Naturf Auserlesene Med Chir Abh
Der Zoologische Garten — Zool Gart
Derbyshire Archaeological Journal — DAJ
Derbyshire Archaeological Journal — Derbyshire Arch J
Derbyshire Archaeological Journal — Derbyshire Archaeol J
Derecho de Integracion — DDI
Derecho de la Integracion — Der Integr
Derecho y Reforma Agraria Revista — Derecho Reforma Agrar Rev
Derechos y Reforma Agraria — DRA
Derevoobrabatyvaiushchaia Promyshlennost — Derev Prom
Derevoobrabatyvaiushchaia Promyshlennost — Derevoobrab Prom-St
Derevopererabatyvayushchaya i Lesokhimicheskaya Promyshlennost — Derevopererab Lesokhim Promst
Dergisi. Review of the Faculty of Forestry. University of Istanbul. Series A — Derg Rev Fac For Univ Istanbul Ser A
Deri Muzeum Evkoenyve — Deri Muz Ev
Dermatologia — Derm
Dermatologia [*Mexico*] — DERMAE
Dermatologia Ibero Latino-Americana — Derm Ib Lat Amer
Dermatologia Internationalis — DERIA
Dermatologia Internationalis — DERIA2
Dermatologia Internationalis — Dermatol Int
Dermatologia, Syphilologia, et Urologia — Dermatol Syphilol Urol
Dermatologia Tropica et Ecologia Geographica — Dermatol Trop Ecol Geogr
Dermatologia Tropica et Ecologia Geographica — DTEGA2
Dermatologic Clinics — Dermatol Clin
Dermatologic Surgery — Dermatol Surg
Dermatologica [*Basel*] — DERAAC
Dermatologica — Dermatolog
Dermatologica Supplementum — Dermatologica Suppl
Dermatologica Tropica — Dermatol Trop
Dermatologische Monatsschrift — Dermatol Monatsschr
Dermatologische Monatsschrift — DMONBP
Dermatologische Studien — D St
Dermatologische Studien — Derm St
Dermatologische Wochenschrift — Dermat Wochnschr
Dermatologische Wochenschrift — Dermatol Wochenschr
Dermatologische Zeitschrift — Dermatol Z
Dermatologische Zeitschrift — DZ
Dermatologiya i Venerologiya — Dermatol Venerol
Dermatologiya i Venerologiya — DVENA3
Dermatologiya i Venerologiya (Sofia) — Dermatol Venerol (Sofia)
Dermatology and Venereology — Dermatol Venereol
Dermatology Online Journal — Dermatol Online J
Dermatology Update — Dermatol Update
Dermatology Update — DEUPD7
Dermatosen in Beruf und Umwelt — Derm Beruf Umwelt
Dermatoses Professionnelles — BERUAG
Dermatoses Professionnelles — Dermatoses Prof
Dermato-Venerologie — Derm Vener
Dermato-Venerologie — Derm Venerol
Dermato-Venerologie — Dermato-Vener
Dermato-Venerologie [*Bucharest*] — DERVA7
Dermosifilografo — Dermos
Derwent Archaeological Society. Research Reports — Derwent Archaeol Soc Res Rep
Desalination — Desalinatn
Desarrollo Economico — Des Econ
Desarrollo Economico — Desarr Econ
Desarrollo Economico — Desarrollo Econ
Desarrollo Economico (Argentina) — DEA
Desarrollo Economico. Instituto de Desarrollo Economico y Social — IDES/DE
Desarrollo Indoamericano — Desarr Indoamer
Desarrollo Indoamericano — Desarrollo Indoam
Desarrollo Indoamericano — DI
Desarrollo Rural en las Americas — Desarr Rur Amer
Desarrollo Rural en las Americas — Desarr Rural Am
Desarrollo Rural en las Americas — DSRAB9
Desarrollo y Sociedad — Desarrollo y Soc
Descripcion del Patrimonio Historico-Artistico Espanol [*Database*] — DPHA
Description Historique des Monnaies Frapees sous l'Empire Romain Comunement Appelees Medailles Imperiales — DHM
Descriptive and Applied Linguistics — Descrip Appl Ling
Descriptive Catalogue of the Collection of Greek Coins Formed by Sir Hermann Weber — Weber
Descriptive Catalogue of the Greek Papyri in the Collection of Wilfred Merton — P Merton
Desenvolvimento e Conjuntura (Rio de Janeiro) — Desenvol Conjun Rio
Desert Botanical Garden (Phoenix). Science Bulletin — Desert Bot Gard (Phoenix) Sci Bull
Desert Institute. Bulletin — Desert Inst Bull
Desert Institute. Bulletin ARE — Desert Inst Bull ARE
Desert Institute. Bulletin ARE — DIBLAR
Desert Locust Control Organization for Eastern Africa. Technical Report — Desert Locust Control Organ E Afr Tech Rep
Desert Locust Control Organization for Eastern Africa. Technical Report — DLTRBL
Desert Magazine — Desert Mag
Desert Plant Life — Desert Pl Life
Desertification Control Bulletin — Desertification Control Bull
Design [*London*] — DEG
Design Abstracts International — Des Abst Int
Design and Components in Engineering — Des Compon Engn
Design and Management for Resource Recovery — Des Manage Resour Recovery
Design and Management for Resource Recovery — Design & Manage Resour Recovery
Design and Management for Resource Recovery — DMRRDK
Design Electronics — Des Electron
Design Engineering — Des Eng
Design Engineering — Dsgn Eng
Design Engineering (Great Britain) — Des Engng (GB)
Design Engineering (New York) — Des Eng (NY)
Design Engineering (Toronto) — Des Eng (Toronto)
Design Engineering (United States of America) — Des Engng (USA)
Design for Arts in Education — Des Arts Educ
Design for Arts in Education — GDAE
Design for Industry — Design for Ind
Design for Industry — Design Ind
Design for Special Needs — Des Special Needs
Design in Steel — Des in Steel
Design Institute for Physical Property Data. Data Series — Des Inst Phys Prop Data Data Ser
Design Magazine — Design
Design News — Des News
Design News — IDNE
Design of Anti-AIDS Drugs — Des Anti AIDS Drugs
Design Products and Applications — Des Prod Appln
Design Quarterly — Design Q
Design Quarterly — Design Qly
Design Quarterly — DQ
Design Quarterly — DSNQ
Design Quarterly — IDEQ
Design Quarterly (Heery) — Design Qly (Heery)
Design Science Collection — Design Sci Collect
Design Studies — DSS
Designs, Codes, and Crytography — Des Codes Cryptogr
Designscape — D'scape
Desinfektion und Gesundheitswesen — Desinfekt Gesundheitswes
Desinfektion und Gesundheitswesen — DSGEAX
Desinfektion und Schaedlingsbekaempfung — Desinfekt Schaedlingsbekaempf
Desinfektion und Schaedlingsbekaempfung. Ausgabe A. Desinfektion — Desinfekt Schaedlingsbekaempf Ausg A

Desinfektion und Schaedlingsbekaempfung. Ausgabe B. Schaedlingsbekaempfung — Desinfekt Schaedlingsbekaempf Ausg B
Desktop Computing — Desk Comp
Destillateur Lehrling — Destill Lehrling
Destillateur Likoerfabrikant — Destill Likoerfabr
DESY [*Deutches Elektronen-Synchroton*] **Journal** — DESY J
Det Danske Marked — D Ma
Det Forstlige Forsogsvaesen i Danmark — Forst Fv
Det Gronlandske Selskabs Aarskrift — GSA
Det Kongelige Danske Videnskabernes Selskab. Historisk-Filologiske Meddelelser [*Copenhagen*] — DVSM
Det Kongelige Danske Videnskabernes Selskab. Matematisk-Fysiske Meddelelser — Danske Vid Selsk Mat-Fys Medd
Det Kongelige Norske Videnskabers Selskabs Forhandlinger — NoVidSF
Det Kongelige Videnskapers Selskap — DKVS
Det Norske Sprak-og Litteraturselskap — NSL
Det Norske Videnskapers Selskap — DNVS
Det Skonne Odsherred — Sk Odsh
Detailhandel Magazine — HBD
Detailman Information — Detailman Inf
Detali Mashin i Pod'emno Transportnye Mashiny — Detali Mash Podemno Transp Mash
Detali Mashin (Kiev) — Detali Mash (Kiev)
Detergent Age — Deterg Age
Detergents and Specialties — Deterg Spec
Determination of Organic Structures by Physical Methods — Determ Org Struct Phys Methods
Detroit Academy of Natural Sciences. Occasional Papers — Detroit Acad Nat Sci Occasional Paper
Detroit Art Registration Information System [*Database*] — DARIS
Detroit Chemist — Detroit Chem
Detroit College of Law. Review — Det CL Rev
Detroit College of Law. Review — Det CLR
Detroit College of Law. Review — Det Coll L Rev
Detroit College of Law. Review — Det Coll LR
Detroit Dental Bulletin — Detroit Dent Bull
Detroit in Perspective — Detroit Perspect
Detroit Institute of Arts. Bulletin — Detroit Inst Bul
Detroit Lawyer — Det Law
Detroit Lawyer — Detroit Law
Detroit Medical Journal — Detr MJ
Detroit Medical Journal — Detroit Med Journ
Detroit Medical News — Detr Med Ne
Detroit Medical News — Detroit Med News
Detroit News — Detroit Nw
Detroit News — DN
Detroit Review of Medicine and Pharmacy — Detroit Rev Med and Pharm
Detroit Symphony Orchestra. Program Notes — Detroit Sym
Detskaya Literatura — Det Lit
Detskaya Literatura — DL
Deus Loci — DL
Deutsch als Fremdsprache — DaF
Deutsch Shakespeare Gesellschaft West. Jahrbuch — Deutsch Shakespeare Ges West Jahrb
Deutsch-Dominikanisches Tropenforschungsinstitut Veroeffentlichungen — Deutsch-Dominikan Tropenforschungsinstitut Veroeff
Deutsche Aerztezeitung — Deutsche Aerzte-Ztg
Deutsche Aerzte-Zeitung — Dt Aerzteztg
Deutsche Agrartechnik — Deut Agrartech
Deutsche Agrartechnik [*Germany*] — Dtsch Agrartech
Deutsche Akademie der Landwirtschaftwissenschaften zu Berlin. Tagungsberichte — Dtsch Akad Landwirtschaftwiss Berl Tagungber
Deutsche Akademie der Landwirtschaftwissenschaften zu Berlin. Tagungsberichte — TDLBAI
Deutsche Akademie der Wissenschaften zu Berlin — DAWB
Deutsche Akademie der Wissenschaften zu Berlin. Institut fuer Deutsche Sprache und Literatur — DAWBIDSL
Deutsche Akademie der Wissenschaften zu Berlin. Institut fuer Orientforschung. Mitteilungen — MIODAWB
Deutsche Akademie der Wissenschaften zu Berlin. Institut fuer Orientforschung. Veroeffentlichungen — VIODAWB
Deutsche Akademie der Wissenschaften zu Berlin. Schriften der Sektion fuer Vor- und Fruehgeschichte — Deutsche Akad Wissen Berlin Schr
Deutsche Akademie der Wissenschaften zu Berlin. Vortraege und Schriften — Dtsch Akad Wiss Berlin Vortr Schr
Deutsche Akademie der Wissenschaften zu Berlin. Zentralinstituts Physik der Erde. Veroeffentlichungen — Dtsch Akad Wiss Berlin Zentralinst Phys Erde Veroeff
Deutsche Akademie fuer Sprache und Dichtung (Darmstadt). Jahrbuch — DASD
Deutsche Akademie fuer Sprache und Dichtung (Darmstadt). Jahrbuch — DASDJ
Deutsche Allgemeine Zeitung — DAZ
Deutsche Angler-Zeitung — DAZ
Deutsche Annalen — Dtsche A
Deutsche Anthropologische Gesellschaft. Korrespondenzblatt — D Anthropol Gesell Korrespondenzbl
Deutsche Apotheker — DAPOAG
Deutsche Apotheker — Dt Apoth
Deutsche Apotheker — Dtsch Apoth
Deutsche Apotheker Post — Dt Apoth Post
Deutsche Apotheker-Biographie — Dtsch Apoth Biogr
Deutsche Apotheker-Zeitung — D Apoth Ztg
Deutsche Apotheker-Zeitung — DAZ
Deutsche Apotheker-Zeitung — DAZEA2
Deutsche Apotheker-Zeitung — Deut Apoth Z
Deutsche Apotheker-Zeitung — Dt ApothZtg
Deutsche Apotheker-Zeitung — Dtsch Apoth-Ztg
Deutsche Apotheker-Zeitung. Beilage. Apothekerpraktikant und Pharmazeutisch-Technischer Assistent — Dtsch Apoth Ztg Beil Apothekerprakt Pharm Tech Assist
Deutsche Apotheker-Zeitung. Beilage. Neue Arzneimittel, Spezialitaeten, und Geheimmittel — Dtsch Apoth Ztg Beil Neue Arzneim Spez Geheimm
Deutsche Apotheker-Zeitung. Beilage. Neue Arzneimittel und Spezialitaeten — Dtsch Apoth Ztg Beil Neue Arzneim Spez
Deutsche Apotheker-Zeitung. Beilage. Pharmazie Heute — Dtsch Apoth Ztg Beil Pharm Heute
Deutsche Apotheker-Zeitung. Beilage. Praktikantenbriefe — Dtsch Apoth Ztg Beil Praktikantenbriefe
Deutsche Aquarien- und Terrarien-Zeitschrift — Deutsche Aquarien Terrar Z
Deutsche Arbeit. Zeitschrift des Volksbundes fuer das Deutschtum im Ausland — Dt Arbeit
Deutsche Arbeiten der Universitaet Koeln — DAUK
Deutsche Arbeiten der Universitaet Koeln — Dt Arb Univ Koeln
Deutsche Aussenpolitik — DAP
Deutsche Aussenpolitik — Dt Aussenpolitik
Deutsche Aussenpolitik [*Germany*] — Dtsch Aussenpolitik
Deutsche Aussenpolitik — Dtsche Aussenpolit
Deutsche Bauerntechnik — Dt Bauern Techn
Deutsche Baumschule — Dtsch Baumsch
Deutsche Baumschule — DUBMAC
Deutsche Bauzeitschrift. Fachblatt fuer Entwurf und Ausfuehrung — DEBZA
Deutsche Bauzeitschrift. Fachblatt fuer Entwurf und Ausfuehrung — Dtsch Bauz
Deutsche Bauzeitschrift. Fachblatt fuer Entwurf und Ausfuehrung [*Germany*] — Dtsch Bauz Fachbl Entwurf Ausfuhrung
Deutsche Bauzeitung — DBZ
Deutsche Bauzeitung — DBZT-A
Deutsche Beitraege — D Bei
Deutsche Beitraege. Eine Zweimontsschrift — Dt Beitr
Deutsche Beitraege zur Geistigen Ueberlieferung — DBGU
Deutsche Beitraege zur Geotechnik — Dtsch Beitr Geotech
Deutsche Berufsschule — DBSch
Deutsche Bibliographie — DB
Deutsche Bibliographie. Das Deutsche Buch. Auswahl Wichtiger Neuerscheinungen — DBB
Deutsche Bibliographie. Halbjahres-Verzeichnis — DBHVA
Deutsche Bibliographie. Halbjahres-Verzeichnis [*Germany*] — Dtsch Bibliogr Halbjahres Verzeichnis
Deutsche Bibliographie. Woechentliches Verzeichnis. Reihe A — DBWVA
Deutsche Bibliographie. Woechentliches Verzeichnis. Reihe A [*Germany*] — Dtsch Bibliogr Woech Verzeichnis A
Deutsche Bibliographie. Woechentliches Verzeichnis. Reihe B — DBWBD
Deutsche Bibliographie. Woechentliches Verzeichnis. Reihe B [*Germany*] — Dtsch Bibliogr Woech Verzeichnis B
Deutsche Bibliographie. Woechentliches Verzeichnis. Reihe C — DBWCD
Deutsche Bibliographie. Woechentliches Verzeichnis. Reihe C [*Germany*] — Dtsch Bibliogr Woech Verzeichnis C
Deutsche Bienenkalender — Dt Bienenkal
Deutsche Bienenwirtschaft — DTBWAZ
Deutsche Bienenwirtschaft — Dtsch Bienenwirtsch
Deutsche Bienenwirtschaft. Teil 2 — Dtsch Bienenwirtsch Teil 2
Deutsche Bienenzeitung — D Bien Zt
Deutsche Bienenzeitung — Dt Bienenztg
Deutsche Bienenzucht — Dt Bienenzucht
Deutsche Botanische Gesellschaft. Berichte — Dtsch Bot Ges Ber
Deutsche Botanische Monatsschrift — D Bot Ms
Deutsche Brauerei — Dtsch Brau
Deutsche Brauwirtschaft. Beilage — Dtsch Brauwirtschaft Beil
Deutsche Buehne — DB
Deutsche Buehne — Dt Buehne
Deutsche Bundesbank. Monatsberichte mit Statistischen Beiheften — MBB
Deutsche Bundesbank. Monthly Report — Deutsche Bundesbank Mo Rept
Deutsche Bundespost. Forschungsinstitut beim FTZ. Technischer Bericht — Dtsch Bundespost Forschungsinst FTZ Tech Ber
Deutsche Chemiker-Zeitschrift — Dtsch Chem Z
Deutsche Chirurgie — D Ch
Deutsche Chirurgie — Deutsche Chir
Deutsche Dendrologische Gesellschaft. Kurzmitteilungen — Dtsch Dendrol Ges Kurzmitt
Deutsche Dendrologische Gesellschaft. Kurzmitteilungen — KDDGAU
Deutsche Destillateur Zeitung — Dtsch Destill Ztg
Deutsche Devisen-Rundschau — D Dev Rd
Deutsche Dialektgeographie — DD
Deutsche Dialektgeographie — DDG
Deutsche Drama — D Dr
Deutsche Druckgewerbe — Dtsch Druckgewerbe
Deutsche Edelstahlwerke Technische Berichte — Dtsch Edelstahlwerke Tech Ber
Deutsche Eisenbahntechnik — Dtsch Eisenbahntech
Deutsche Elektrotechnik [*Germany*] — Dtsch Elektrotech
Deutsche Entomologische Zeitschrift — DENZAX
Deutsche Entomologische Zeitschrift — Deut Entomol Z
Deutsche Entomologische Zeitschrift — Deutsche Entomol Z
Deutsche Entomologische Zeitschrift — Dt Ent Z
Deutsche Entomologische Zeitschrift — Dtsch Entomol Z
Deutsche Entomologische Zeitschrift (Berlin) — DEZB
Deutsche Entomologische Zeitschrift "Iris" — Deutsche Entom Ztschr "Iris"
Deutsche Erde — DE
Deutsche Evangelische Kirchenzeitung — Dt Evgl Kirchztg
Deutsche Faerber-Zeitung — Dtsch Faerber Ztg

Deutsche Faerber-Zeitung. Beilage — Dtsch Faerber Ztg Beil
Deutsche Farben Zeitschrift — Dtsch Farben Z
Deutsche Faserstoffe und Spinnpflanzen — Dtsch Faserst Spinnpflanzen
Deutsche Fischerei Zeitung — DFSZAV
Deutsche Fischerei Zeitung — Dtsch Fisch Ztg
Deutsche Fischerei-Rundschau — DFIRAP
Deutsche Fischerei-Rundschau — Dtsch Fisch Rundsch
Deutsche Fischereirundschau — Dtsch Fischereirundsch
Deutsche Fischwirtschaft — Dtsch Fischwirtsch
Deutsche Flugtechnik — Dtsch Flugtech
Deutsche Flungtechnik — Dtsch Flungtec
Deutsche Forschung im Osten — Dt Forsch Osten
Deutsche Forschung in Ungarn — Dt Forsch Ungarn
Deutsche Forschungs- und Versuchsanstalt fuer Luft- und Raumfahrt. Forschungsber — Deutsche Forsch Versuchsanst Luft Raumfahrt Forschungsber
Deutsche Forschungs- und Versuchsanstalt fuer Luft- und Raumfahrt. Forschungsbericht — Dtsch Forsch Versuchsanst Luft Raumfahrt Forschungsber
Deutsche Forschungs- und Versuchsanstalt fuer Luft- und Raumfahrt. Mitteilung — Dtsch Forsch Versuchsanst Luft Raumfahrt Mitt
Deutsche Forschungs- und Versuchsanstalt fuer Luft und Raumfahrt. Nachrichten [*Germany*] — Dtsch Forsch Versuchsanst Luft Raumfahrt Nachr
Deutsche Forschungsgemeinschaft Farbstoff Kommission Mitteilung — Dtsch Forschungsgem Farbst Komm Mitt
Deutsche Forschungsgemeinschaft. Farbstoffkommission. Mitteilung — Dtsch Forschungsgem Farbstoffkomm Mitt
Deutsche Forschungsgemeinschaft Kommission fuer Geowissenschaftliche Gemeinschaftsforschung Mitteilung [*Germany*] — Dtsch Forschungsgem Komm Geowiss Gemeinschaftsforsch Mitt
Deutsche Forschungsgemeinschaft. Kommission fuer Wasserforschung. Mitteilung — Dtsch Forschungsgem Komm Wasserforsch Mitt
Deutsche Forschungsgemeinschaft. Kommission zur Erforschung der Luftverunreinigung. Mitteilung — Dtsch Forschungsgem Komm Erforsch Luftverunreinig Mitt
Deutsche Forschungsgemeinschaft Kommission zur Erforschung der Luftverunreinigung. Mitteilung [*Germany*] — Dtsch Forschungsgem Komm Erforsch Luftverunreinigung Mitt
Deutsche Forschungsgemeinschaft Kommission zur Pruefung Fremder Stoffe bei Lebensmitteln Mitteilung — Dtsch Forschungsgem Komm Pruef Fremder Stoffe Lebensm Mitt
Deutsche Forschungsgemeinschaft. Kommission zur Pruefung von Rueckstaenden in Lebensmitteln. Mitteilung — Dtsch Forschungsgem Komm Pruef Rueckstaenden Lebensm Mitt
Deutsche Forschungsgemeinschaft Mitteilungen [*Germany*] — Dtsch Forschungsgem Mitt
Deutsche Forschungsgemeinschaft. Senatskommission fuer Wasserforschung. Mitteilung — Dtsch Forschungsgem Senatskomm Wasserforsch Mitt
Deutsche Forschungsgesellschaft fuer Druck- und Reproduktionstechnik. Forschungsbericht — Dtsch Forschungsges Druck Reproduktionstech Forschungsber
Deutsche Forschungsgesellschaft fuer Druck- und Reproduktionstechnik. Mitteilungen — Dtsch Forschungsges Druck Reproduktionstech Mitt
Deutsche Forstmann — Dtsch Forstm
Deutsche Fortszeitung — DFZg
Deutsche Gaertnerboerse — Dtsch Gaertnerboerse
Deutsche Gaertner-Verbands-Zeitung — Deutsche Gaertn Verbands Zeitung
Deutsche Gartenbau — DGABAC
Deutsche Gartenbau — Dtsch Gartenbau
Deutsche Gaststatte. Deutsche Hotelzeitung — DGC
Deutsche Gefluegel-Zeitung — D Gefl Ztg
Deutsche Gemeinde-Zeitung — Dt Gemeindeztg
Deutsche Geodaetische Kommission bei der Bayerischen Akademie der Wissenschaften. Reihe B. Angewandte Geodaesie — Dtsch Geod Komm Bayer Akad Wiss Reihe B
Deutsche Geodaetische Kommission bei der Bayerischen Akademie der Wissenschaften. Reihe C. Dissertationen — Dtsch Geod Komm Bayer Akad Wiss Reihe C
Deutsche Geodaetische Kommission. Veroeffentlichungen. Reihe B. Angewandte Geodaesie — Dtsch Geod Komm Veroeff Reihe B
Deutsche Geodaetische Kommission. Veroeffentlichungen. Reihe E. Geschichte und Entwicklung der Geodaesie — Deut Geod Komm Veroeff Reihe E Gesch Entwickl Geod
Deutsche Geographische Blaetter — D Geog Bl
Deutsche Geographische Blaetter — D Geogr Bl
Deutsche Geographische Blaetter — Deut Geog Blaetter
Deutsche Geographische Blaetter — DGBl
Deutsche Geologische Gesellschaft. Nachrichten — Dtsch Geol Ges Nachr
Deutsche Geologische Gesellschaft. Zeitschrift — Deutsche Geol Gesell Zeitschr
Deutsche Geologische Gesellschaft. Zeitschrift — Dtsch Geol Ges Z
Deutsche Gerichtsvollzieher-Zeitung — GVollzZ
Deutsche Geschichtsblaetter — D Geschichtbl
Deutsche Geschichtsblaetter — DG Bl
Deutsche Gesellschaft fuer Angiologie. Jahrestagung — Dtsch Ges Angiol Jahrestag
Deutsche Gesellschaft fuer Anthropologie. Korrespondenzblatt — D Gesell F Anthropol Korrespondenzbl
Deutsche Gesellschaft fuer Arbeitsmedizin. Jahrestagung — Dtsch Ges Arbeitsmed Jahrestag
Deutsche Gesellschaft fuer Bevoelkerungswissenschaft an der Universitaet Hamburg — Dtsche Ges Bevoelkerungswiss
Deutsche Gesellschaft fuer Chemisches Apparatewesen, Chemische Technik, und Biotechnologie-Monographien — Dtsch Ges Chem Apparatewes Chem Tech Biotechnol Monogr
Deutsche Gesellschaft fuer Herz- und Kreislaufforschung. Verhandlungen — Dtsch Ges Herz Kreislaufforsch Verh
Deutsche Gesellschaft fuer Holzforschung Bericht — Dtsch Ges Holzforsch Ber
Deutsche Gesellschaft fuer Metallkunde Fachberichte [*Germany*] — Dtsch Ges Metallkd Fachber
Deutsche Gesellschaft fuer Metallkunde. Hauptversammlung — Dtsch Ges Metallkd Hauptversamml
Deutsche Gesellschaft fuer Mineraloelwissenschaft und Kohlechemie — Dtsche Ges Mineraloelwiss Kohlechem
Deutsche Gesellschaft fuer Mineraloelwissenschaft und Kohlechemie. Berichte — Dtsch Ges Mineraloelwiss Kohlechem Ber
Deutsche Gesellschaft fuer Mineraloelwissenschaft und Kohlechemie. Compendium [*Germany*] — Dtsch Ges Mineraloelwiss Kohlechem Compend
Deutsche Gesellschaft fuer Qualitaetsforschung (Pflanzliche Nahrungsmittel). Congress — Dtsch Ges Qualitaetsforsch Pflanz Nahrungsm Congr
Deutsche Gesellschaft fuer Qualitaetsforschung (Pflanzliche Nahrungsmittel). Vortragstagung — Dtsch Ges Qualitaetsforsch Pflanz Nahrungsm Vortragstag
Deutsche Gesellschaft fuer Technische Zusammenarbeit. Schriftenreihe — Dtsch Ges Tech Zusammenarb Schriftenr
Deutsche Gesellschaft fuer Wissenschaftliche und Angewandte Kosmetik. Symposium — Dtsch Ges Wiss Angew Kosmet Symp
Deutsche Gesundheitswesen — DEGEA3
Deutsche Gesundheitswesen — Dtsch Gesundheitsw
Deutsche Gesundheitswesen — Dtsch Gesundheitswes
Deutsche Gewaesserkundliche Mitteilungen — DGMTAO
Deutsche Gewaesserkundliche Mitteilungen — Dtsch Gewaesserkd Mitt
Deutsche Goldschmiede-Zeitung — Dtsch Goldschmiede Z
Deutsche Handelsschullehrer-Zeitung — Dt Handelsschullehrztg
Deutsche Handelsschulwarte — DHW
Deutsche Hebe und Foerdertechnik — Dtsch Hebe Foerdertech
Deutsche Hochschule — Dt Hochschule
Deutsche Hochschulschriften — Deutsche Hochschulschrift
Deutsche Hochschulzeitung — DHZ
Deutsche Hydrographische Zeitschrift — Deutsche Hydrogr Z
Deutsche Hydrographische Zeitschrift — DHYZA7
Deutsche Hydrographische Zeitschrift — Dtsch Hydrogr Z
Deutsche Illustrierte Bienenzeitung — Dt Ill Bienenztg
Deutsche Im Osten — Dt Im Osten
Deutsche Imkerfuehrer — Dt Imkerfuehrer
Deutsche Imkerzeitung — Dt Imkerztg
Deutsche Immobilien — D Imm
Deutsche Instrumentanbau Zeitung — DIZ
Deutsche Internierten Zeitung — DIZ
Deutsche Iris- und Liliengesellschaft Jahrbuch — Deutsche Iris Lilienges Jahrb
Deutsche Israelitische Zeitung [*Regensburg*] — DtIsrZtg
Deutsche Jaegerzeitung — Dt Jaegerztg
Deutsche Juristenzeitung — DJurZ
Deutsche Juristenzeitung — DJZ
Deutsche Juristenzeitung — JurZ
Deutsche Justiz-Statistik — DJ St
Deutsche Justiz-Statistik — Dt Justizstatist
Deutsche Kameramann — Deutsch Kam
Deutsche Kautschuk-Gesellschaft Vortragstagung. Dokumenten — Dtsch Kautsch Ges Vortragstag Dok
Deutsche Keramische Gesellschaft. Berichte — Deutsche Keramische Gesell Ber
Deutsche Keramische Gesellschaft. Berichte — Dtsch Keram Ges Ber
Deutsche Keramische Gesellschaft Fachausschussbericht — Dtsch Keram Ges Fachausschussber
Deutsche Kolonialzeitung — D Kolonialzeitung
Deutsche Kolonialzeitung — DK
Deutsche Kolonialzeitung — DKZ
Deutsche Kraftfahrtforschung Strassenverkehrstechnik — Dtsch Kraftfahrtforsch Strassenverkehrstech
Deutsche Krankenpflegezeitschrift — Dtsch Krankenpflegez
Deutsche Kultur im Leben der Voelker — Dt Kult Leben Voelker
Deutsche Kunst und Denkmalpflege — D Ku Denkm Pfl
Deutsche Kunst und Denkmalpflege — DKD
Deutsche Kunst und Denkmalpflege — DKDP
Deutsche Kunstseiden Zeitung und Spezialorgan fuer Zellwolle — Dtsch Kunstseiden Ztg Spezialorgan Zellwolle
Deutsche Landtechnische Zeitschrift — Dtsch Landtech Z
Deutsche Landwirtschaft — D Lwsch
Deutsche Landwirtschaft — Deut Landwirt
Deutsche Landwirtschaft — Dt Landwirt
Deutsche Landwirtschaft — Dtsch Landwirtsch
Deutsche Landwirtschaft (Berlin) — Dt Landwirt (Berlin)
Deutsche Landwirtschaftliche Presse — D Lw Pr
Deutsche Landwirtschaftliche Rundschau — Dtsch Landwirtsch Rundsch
Deutsche Landwirtschaftliche Tierzucht — D Landw Tz
Deutsche Landwirtschaftliche Tierzucht — Dtsch Landwirtsch Tierz
Deutsche Landwirtschafts-Gesellschaft Mitteilungen — Dtsch Landwirtsch Ges Mitt
Deutsche Lebensmittel Rundschau — Deut Lebensm Rundsch
Deutsche Lebensmittel Rundschau — DLRUAJ
Deutsche Lebensmittel Rundschau — Dt LebensmittRdsch
Deutsche Lebensmittel Rundschau — Dtsch Lebensm Rundsch
Deutsche Lehrerzeitung — DLZ
Deutsche Levante-Zeitung — DLevZ
Deutsche Licht- und Wasserfach Zeitung — Dtsch Licht Wasserfach Ztg
Deutsche Literarische Zeitung — DL Zg
Deutsche Literatur — DLit
Deutsche Literatur und Sprachstudien — DLS
Deutsche Literaturdenkmale — DLD
Deutsche Literaturdenkmale — Dt Litdenkm
Deutsche Literaturzeitung — D Lit

Deutsche Literaturzeitung — DL
Deutsche Literaturzeitung — DLtz
Deutsche Literaturzeitung — DLZ
Deutsche Literaturzeitung fuer Kritik der Internationalen Wissenschaft — D Literatur Z
Deutsche Literaturzeitung fuer Kritik der Internationalen Wissenschaft — D Lz
Deutsche Lotto-Zeitung — DLZ
Deutsche Luft- und Raumfahrt. Forschungsbericht — Deut Luft Raumfahrt Forschungsber
Deutsche Luft- und Raumfahrt. Forschungsbericht — Dtsch Luftfahrt Raumfahrt Forschungsber
Deutsche Luft- und Raumfahrt. Mitteilung — Dtsch Luft Raumfahrt Mitt
Deutsche Luft- und Raumfahrt. Mitteilung — Dtsch Luftfahrt Raumfahrt Mitt
Deutsche Mechaniker-Zeitung — Dtsch Mech Ztg
Deutsche Medizinal-Zeitung — Deutsche Med-Ztg
Deutsche Medizinische Forschung — Dtsch Med Forsch
Deutsche Medizinische Wochenschrift — D Med Wochens
Deutsche Medizinische Wochenschrift — Deut Med Wo
Deutsche Medizinische Wochenschrift — Deutsche Med Wochenschr
Deutsche Medizinische Wochenschrift — DMW
Deutsche Medizinische Wochenschrift — DMWOAX
Deutsche Medizinische Wochenschrift — Dt Med Wschr
Deutsche Medizinische Wochenschrift — Dtsch Med Wochenschr
Deutsche Medizinische Wochenschrift — Dtsch Med Wschr
Deutsche Medizinische Wochenschrift. Sonderbeilage — Dtsch Med Wochenschr Sonderbeil
Deutsche Medizinische Zeitung — DMZ
Deutsche Metallwaren Industrie — Dtsch Metallwaren Ind
Deutsche Meteorologen-Tagung — Dtsch Meteorol Tag
Deutsche Milchwirtschaft — DMIWAL
Deutsche Milchwirtschaft — Dt Milchwirt
Deutsche Milchwirtschaft — Dtsch Milchwirtsch
Deutsche Milchwirtschaft (Gelsenkirchen) [*Germany*] — Dtsch Milchwirtsch (Gelsenkirchen)
Deutsche Milchwirtschaft (Leipzig) — Dtsch Milchwirtsch (Leipzig)
Deutsche Mineralogische Gesellschaft. Fortschritte der Mineralogie — Deutsche Mineralog Gesell Fortschr Mineralogie
Deutsche Molkerei- und Fettwirtschaft — Dtsch Molk Fettwirtsch
Deutsche Molkerei-Zeitung — Dtsch Molk Ztg
Deutsche Molkerei-Zeitung — Dtsch Molkerei Ztg
Deutsche Monatschefte — Dt Mh
Deutsche Monatschefte in Polen — Dt Mh Polen
Deutsche Monatsschrift fuer das Gesamte Leben der Gegenwart — Dt Mschr Ges Leben Gegenw
Deutsche Monatsschrift fuer Kolonialpolitik und Kolonisation — DMKK
Deutsche Morgenlaendische Gesellschaft — DMG
Deutsche Morgenlaendische Gesellschaft. Zeitschrift — D Morgenl Gesell Zeits
Deutsche Motor-Zeitschaft — Dtsch Mot Z
Deutsche Mueller Zeitung — Deut Mueller Ztg
Deutsche Muellerei — Dtsch Muellerei
Deutsche Muenzblaetter — Deut Muenzbl
Deutsche Muenzblaetter — DM Bl
Deutsche Nahrungsmittel. Rundschau — Dtsch Nahrungsm Rundsch
Deutsche Nationalbibliographie. Reihe A [*Leipzig*] — Deutsch Nationalbiblio Reihe A
Deutsche Nationalbibliographie. Reihe B [*Leipzig*] — Deutsch Nationalbiblio Reihe B
Deutsche Notariats-Zeitung — Dt Notariatsztg
Deutsche Oper am Rhein — Deutsche Oper
Deutsche Ophthalmologische Gesellschaft. Bericht — DOPGAM
Deutsche Ophthalmologische Gesellschaft. Bericht — Dtsch Ophthalmol Ges Ber
Deutsche Ophthalmologische Gesellschaft in Heidelberg. Bericht ueber die Zusammenkunft — Dtsch Ophthalmol Ges Heidelberg Ber Zusammenkunft
Deutsche Optikerzeitung — Dtsch Optikerztg
Deutsche Optische Wochenschrift — Dtsch Opt Wochenschrift
Deutsche Optische Wochenschrift und Central-Zeitung fuer Optik und Mechanik — Dtsch Opt Wochenschr Cent Ztg Opt Mech
Deutsche Papierwirtschaft — Deut Papierwirtsch
Deutsche Parfuemerie-Zeitung — Dtsch Parfuem Ztg
Deutsche Patent Datenbank — PATDPA
Deutsche Pelztierzuchter — Dtsch Pelztierz
Deutsche Pflanzenschutz-Tagung — Dtsch Pflanzenschutz Tag
Deutsche Philologie — DP
Deutsche Revue — D Rv
Deutsche Revue — DeutR
Deutsche Revue — DR
Deutsche Revue — DRev
Deutsche Revue — Dt Rev
Deutsche Richterzeitung — DRZg
Deutsche Richterzeitung — Dt Richterztg
Deutsche Rundschau — D Rund
Deutsche Rundschau — D Rundschau
Deutsche Rundschau — Deut Rundschau
Deutsche Rundschau — DR
Deutsche Rundschau — DRs
Deutsche Rundschau — DRu
Deutsche Rundschau — Dt Rdsch
Deutsche Rundschau — Dt Rs
Deutsche Rundschau fuer Geographie — Deutsche Rundschau Geogr
Deutsche Rundschau fuer Geographie und Statistik — DRGS
Deutsche Rundschau fuer Geographie und Statistik — Dt Rdsch Geogr Statist
Deutsche Schlacht- und Viehhof-Zeitung — Deutsche Schlacht-u Viehhof-Ztg
Deutsche Schwarzbunte — Dtsch Schwarzbunte
Deutsche Shakespeare-Gesellschaft (West Germany) — DSGW
Deutsche Sprache — DSp
Deutsche Steuer-Rundschau — D St R
Deutsche Steuerzeitung — D St Z
Deutsche Steuerzeitung — D St Zt
Deutsche Steuerzeitung — DStZg
Deutsche Steuer-Zeitung — Dtsche Steuer Z
Deutsche Stomatologie — DESTA
Deutsche Stomatologie — DESTA6
Deutsche Stomatologie — Dtsch Stomatol
Deutsche Studien — DeuS
Deutsche Studien — DS
Deutsche Studien — DSt
Deutsche Studien — Dt Stud
Deutsche Studien — Dt Studien
Deutsche Studien. Vierteljahreshefte fuer Vergleichende Gegenwartskunde — Dtsche Stud
Deutsche Studien zur Geistesgeschichte — DSG
Deutsche Suedpolarexpedition — Dt Suedpolarexp
Deutsche Tabak Zeitung — Dtsch Tab Ztg
Deutsche Tagespost — DT
Deutsche Technik — Dtsch Tech
Deutsche Technische Warte — DTW
Deutsche Texte des Mittelalters — Dt Texte Mittelalt
Deutsche Texte des Mittelalters — DTM
Deutsche Textilgewerbe — Dtsch Textilgewerbe
Deutsche Textiltechnik — Dtsch Textiltech
Deutsche Textilwirtschaft — Dtsch Textilwirtsch
Deutsche Theologie — Dt Th
Deutsche Theologie: Monatsschrift fuer die Deutsche Evangelische Kirche — DTh
Deutsche Tiefbauzeitung — D T Zg
Deutsche Tieraerztliche Wochenschrift — Deutsche Tieraerztl Wochenschr
Deutsche Tieraerztliche Wochenschrift — Dt Tieraerztl Wschr
Deutsche Tieraerztliche Wochenschrift — Dtsch Tieraerztl Wochenschr
Deutsche Tieraerztliche Wochenschrift — DTTIAF
Deutsche Tieraerztliche Wochenschrift. Beilage. Lebensmitteltierarzt — Dtsch Tieraerztl Wochenschr Beil Lebensmitteltierarzt
Deutsche Tieraerztliche Wochenschrift Tieraerztliche Rundschau — Dtsch Tieraerztl Wochenschr Tieraerztl Rundsch
Deutsche Toepfer und Ziegler Zeitung — Dtsch Toepfer Ziegler Ztg
Deutsche Tonkuenstlerzeitung — Dt Tonkuenstlerztg
Deutsche Tonkuenstlerzeitung — DTZ
Deutsche Tropenmedizinische Zeitschrift — Dtsch Tropenmed Z
Deutsche Universitaetszeitung — Dt Univ Ztg
Deutsche Universitaetszeitung — DUZ
Deutsche Vereinigung fuer die Interessen der Osteuropaeischen Juden — DVIOJ
Deutsche Versuchsanstalt fuer Luft- und Raumfahrt. Bericht — Dtsch Versuchsanst Luft Raumfahrt Ber
Deutsche Veterinaermedizinische Gesellschaft. Tagung des Arbeitsgebietes Lebensmittelhygiene — Dtsch Veterinaermed Ges Tag Arbeitsgeb Lebensmittelhyg
Deutsche Vierteljahresschrift fuer Literaturwissenschaft und Geistesgeschichte — Dt Vjschr Lit Wiss Geistesgesch
Deutsche Vierteljahrsschrift — DV
Deutsche Vierteljahrsschrift fuer Literaturwissenschaft und Geistesgeschichte — Deu Viertel
Deutsche Vierteljahrsschrift fuer Literaturwissenschaft und Geistesgeschichte — Deut Vier L
Deutsche Vierteljahrsschrift fuer Literaturwissenschaft und Geistesgeschichte — Deut Vier Lit
Deutsche Vierteljahrsschrift fuer Literaturwissenschaft und Geistesgeschichte — Deut Vierteljahrsschr Literaturwiss Geistesgesch
Deutsche Vierteljahrsschrift fuer Literaturwissenschaft und Geistesgeschichte — Dt Vischr
Deutsche Vierteljahrsschrift fuer Literaturwissenschaft und Geistesgeschichte — DtVis
Deutsche Vierteljahrsschrift fuer Literaturwissenschaft und Geistesgeschichte — DVJS
Deutsche Vierteljahrsschrift fuer Literaturwissenschaft und Geistesgeschichte — DVLG
Deutsche Vierteljahrsschrift fuer Literaturwissenschaft und Geistesgeschichte — VJ Lit
Deutsche Vierteljahrsschrift fuer Literaturwissenschaft und Geistesgeschichte — VL
Deutsche Waldenser — Dt Waldenser
Deutsche Warande en Belfort — DWB
Deutsche Wasserwirtschaft — Dt Wass Wirt
Deutsche Weinbau — Dtsch Weinbau
Deutsche Weinbau — DTWBA9
Deutsche Weinbau — DWb
Deutsche Weinbau. Wissenschaftliche Beihefte — Dtsch Weinbau Wiss Beih
Deutsche Weinrundschau — Dt Wein Rd
Deutsche Weinzeitung — Dt Wein Zt
Deutsche Wein-Zeitung — Dtsch Wein Ztg
Deutsche Wirker Zeitung — Dtsch Wirker Ztg
Deutsche Wissenschaft, Erziehung, und Volksbildung — DWEV
Deutsche Wissenschaftliche Gesellschaft fuer Erdoel, Erdgas,und Kohle. Berichte. Tagungsbericht — Dtsch Wiss Ges Erdoel Erdgas Kohle Ber Tagungsber
Deutsche Wissenschaftliche Kommission fuer Meeresforschung. Berichte — Dtsch Wiss Komm Meeresforsch Ber
Deutsche Wissenschaftliche Zeitschrift fuer Polen — Dt Wiss Z Polen
Deutsche Wissenschaftliche Zeitschrift fuer Polen — DWZP
Deutsche Wissenschaftliche Zeitschrift im Wartheland — Dt Wiss Z Warthel

Deutsche Wissenschaftlicher Dienst — DWD
Deutsche Woche — DW
Deutsche Wollen Gewerbe — Dtsch Wollen Gewerbe
Deutsche Zahn- Mund- und Kieferheilkunde — Dtsch Zahn- Mund- Kieferheilkd
Deutsche Zahn- Mund- und Kieferheilkunde — DZMKAS
Deutsche Zahn-, Mund-, und Kieferheilkunde mit Zentralblatt fuer die Gesamte Zahn-, Mund-, und Kieferheilkunde — Dtsch Zahn Mund Kieferheilkd Zentralbl Gesamte
Deutsche Zahnaerztliche Wochenschrift — Dtsch Zahnaerztl Wochenschr
Deutsche Zahnaerztliche Zeitschrift — Dtsch Zahnaerztl Z
Deutsche Zahnaerztliche Zeitschrift — DZZEA
Deutsche Zahnaerztliche Zeitschrift — DZZEA7
Deutsche Zahnheilkunde — Dt Zahnhkd
Deutsche Zeitschrift — DZT
Deutsche Zeitschrift fuer Akupunktur — Dt Zs Akup
Deutsche Zeitschrift fuer Chirurgie — Deutsche Ztschr Chir
Deutsche Zeitschrift fuer Chirurgie — Dt Z Chir
Deutsche Zeitschrift fuer Chirurgie — Dtsch Z Chir
Deutsche Zeitschrift fuer Christliche Wissenschaft und Christliches Leben — DZCW
Deutsche Zeitschrift fuer die Gesamte Gerichtliche Medizin — Dtsch Z Gesamte Gerichtl Med
Deutsche Zeitschrift fuer die Gesamte Gerichtliche Medizin — DZGGAK
Deutsche Zeitschrift fuer Geschichtswissenschaft — Dt Zs Geschwiss
Deutsche Zeitschrift fuer Geschichtswissenschaft — DZGW
Deutsche Zeitschrift fuer Kirchenrecht — DZKR
Deutsche Zeitschrift fuer Mund-, Kiefer-, und Gesichtschirurgie — Dtsch Z Mund Kiefer Gesichtschir
Deutsche Zeitschrift fuer Nervenheilkunde — D Zs N Hk
Deutsche Zeitschrift fuer Nervenheilkunde — Deutsche Ztschr Nervenh
Deutsche Zeitschrift fuer Nervenheilkunde — Dtsch Z Nervenheilkd
Deutsche Zeitschrift fuer Nervenheilkunde — DZ Nh
Deutsche Zeitschrift fuer Nervenheilkunde — DZNEAF
Deutsche Zeitschrift fuer Philosophie — Deut Z Phil
Deutsche Zeitschrift fuer Philosophie — Dt Z f Ph
Deutsche Zeitschrift fuer Philosophie — Dt Z Philos
Deutsche Zeitschrift fuer Philosophie — Dt Zs Philos
Deutsche Zeitschrift fuer Philosophie — Dtsche Z Philos
Deutsche Zeitschrift fuer Philosophie — DZ Ph
Deutsche Zeitschrift fuer Philosophie. Beiheft — DZ Ph B
Deutsche Zeitschrift fuer Sportmedizin — Dtsch Z Sportmed
Deutsche Zeitschrift fuer Verdauungs- und Stoffwechselkrankheiten — Dtsch Z Verdau Stoffwechselkr
Deutsche Zeitschrift fuer Verdauungs- und Stoffwechselkrankheiten — Dtsch Z Verdau Stoffwechselkrankh
Deutsche Zeitung — Dt Ztg
Deutsche Zeitung — DZT
Deutsche Zollbeamte — D Zoll B
Deutsche Zoologische Gesellschaft. Verhandlungen — Deutsch Zool Ges Verh
Deutsche Zuckerindustrie — Dtsch Zuckerind
Deutsche-Englische Medizinische Rundschau — Dtsch Engl Med Rundsch
Deutschen Gesellschaft fuer Geologische Wissenschaften. Berichte — Deutsch Gesell Geol Wiss Ber
Deutscher Ausschuss fuer Stahlbeton — Deut Ausschuss Stahlbeton
Deutscher Baustellen Informationsdienst — DEC
Deutscher Bundestag. Drucksache — Dtsch Bundestag Drucks
Deutscher Faerber-Kalender — Dtsch Faerber Kal
Deutscher Forschungsdienst. Sonderbericht Kernenergie [*Germany*] — Dtsch Forschungsdienst Sonderber Kernenerg
Deutscher Garten — Deutsch Gart
Deutscher Geographentag Verhandlungen — Deutscher Geographentag Verh
Deutscher Haematologenkongress — Dtsch Haematologenkongr
Deutscher Imkerkalender — Dt Imkerkal
Deutscher Kaelte und Klimatechnischer Verein. Abhandlungen — Dtsch Kaelte Klimatech Ver Abh
Deutscher Kaelte- und Klimatechnischer Verein. DKV-Statusbericht — Dtsch Kaelte Klimatech Ver DKV Statusber
Deutscher Kaelte- und Klimatechnischer Verein-Tagungsbericht — Dtsch Kaelte Klimatech Ver Tagungsber
Deutscher Kaeltetechnischer Verein. Abhandlungen — Dtsch Kaeltetech Ver Abh
Deutscher Kongress fuer Perinatale Medizin — Dtsch Kongr Perinat Med
Deutscher Militaeraerztlicher Kalender fuer die Sanitaetsoffiziere der Armee — D Militaeraerztl Kal Hamburg
Deutscher Sportaerztekongress — Dtsch Sportaerztekongr
Deutscher und Oesterreichischer Alpen-Verein. Zeitschrift — Deut Oesterr Alpen-Ver Zs
Deutscher Verband fuer Schweisstechnik. Berichte — Dtsch Verb Schweisstech Ber
Deutscher Verband fuer Wasserwirtschaft und Kulturbau. Materialien — Dtsch Verb Wasserwirtsch Kulturbau Mater
Deutscher Verein des Gas- und Wasserfaches. Schriftenreihe. Wasser — Dtsch Ver Gas Wasserfaches Schriftenr Wasser
Deutscher Verein fuer Kunstwissenschaft. Zeitschrift — Deutsch Verein Kunstwis Z
Deutscher Verein von Gas- und Wasserfachmaennern. Schriftenreihe. Gas — Dtsch Ver Gas Wasserfachmaennern Schriften Gas
Deutsches Aerzteblatt. Aerztliche Mitteilungen — Dtsch Aerztebl
Deutsches Archaeologisches Institut. Jahrbuch — Deutch Archaeol Inst Jahrb
Deutsches Archaeologisches Institut. Mitteilungen. Roemische Abteilung — Deutsch Archaeol Inst Roem Mitt
Deutsches Architektenblatt [*Germany*] — Dtsch Archit
Deutsches Archiv — DA
Deutsches Archiv fuer Erforschung des Mittelalters — DA
Deutsches Archiv fuer Erforschung des Mittelalters — DAEM
Deutsches Archiv fuer Erforschung des Mittelalters — Dt Arch Erforsch Mittelalter
Deutsches Archiv fuer Erforschung des Mittelalters Namens Monumenta Germaniae Historica — Deut Arch Erforsch Mittelalt
Deutsches Archiv fuer Geschichte des Mittelalters — DAGM
Deutsches Archiv fuer Geschichte des Mittelalters — Dt Arch Gesch Mittelalter
Deutsches Archiv fuer Innere Medizin — DAiM
Deutsches Archiv fuer Innere Medizin — Dt Arch Inn Med
Deutsches Archiv fuer Klinische Medizin — D Arch Klin Med
Deutsches Archiv fuer Klinische Medizin — DAKMAJ
Deutsches Archiv fuer Klinische Medizin — Deutsches Arch Klin Med
Deutsches Archiv fuer Klinische Medizin — Dt Arch Klin Med
Deutsches Archiv fuer Klinische Medizin — Dtsch Arch Klin Med
Deutsches Archiv fuer Landes und Volksforschung — DALV
Deutsches Archiv fuer Landes- und Volksforschung — Dt Arch Landes U Volksforsch
Deutsches Atomforum. Schriftenreihe — Dtsch Atomforum Schriftenr
Deutsches Biographisches Jahrbuch — DBJb
Deutsches Dante-Jahrbuch — DDJ
Deutsches Dante-Jahrbuch — Deutsch Dante Jahrb
Deutsches Dante-Jahrbuch — DJ
Deutsches Elektronen-Synchrotron [*Also, an information service or system*] — DESY
Deutsches Familienarchiv — Dt Familienarch
Deutsches Handwerksblatt — DH
Deutsches Handwerksblatt — DHS
Deutsches Hydrographisches Institut. Jahresbericht — Dtsch Hydrogr Inst Jahresber
Deutsches Institut fuer Wirtschaftsforschung. Economic Bulletin — Deutsches Institut fuer Wirtschaftsforschung Econ Bul
Deutsches Institut fuer Wirtschaftsforschung. Wochenbericht — Dt Inst Wirtschaftsforsch Wochenber
Deutsches Institut fuer Wirtschaftsforschung. Wochenbericht — Dtsch Inst Wirtschaftsforsch Wochenber
Deutsches Institut fuer Wirtschaftsforschung Wochenbericht — Dtsches Inst Wirtsch Forsch Wber
Deutsches Institut fuer Wirtschaftsforschung. Wochenbericht — WIK
Deutsches Institut zur Weiterbildung Medizinisch-Technischer Assistenten. Journal — Dtsch Inst Weiterbild Med Tech Assist J
Deutsches Jahrbuch fuer Musikwissenschaft — Deutsch Jahrb Musikw
Deutsches Jahrbuch fuer Numismatik — D Jb Num
Deutsches Jahrbuch fuer Numismatik — DJbN
Deutsches Jahrbuch fuer Numismatik — Dt Jb Numismat
Deutsches Jahrbuch fuer Volkskunde — DjbVk
Deutsches Jahrbuch fuer Volkskunde — DJV
Deutsches Jahrbuch fuer Volkskunde — Dt Jb Volkskde
Deutsches Kolonialblatt — Dt Kolonialbl
Deutsches Kolonialblatt — K B
Deutsches Kunstblatt — D Kbl
Deutsches Lesewerk — DLW
Deutsches Literaturblatt — DL Bl
Deutsches Magazin — Deutsch Mag
Deutsches Magazin fuer Garten- und Blumenkunde — Deutsch Mag Garten Blumenk
Deutsches Medizinisches Journal — DMJOA2
Deutsches Medizinisches Journal — Dt Med J
Deutsches Medizinisches Journal — Dtsch Med J
Deutsches Meteorologisches Jahrbuch fuer Bayern — DMJB
Deutsches Mozartfest der Deutschen Mozart-Gesellschaft — DMG
Deutsches Museum. Abhandlungen und Berichte — Dtsch Mus Abh Ber
Deutsches Orient-Jahrbuch — DOJb
Deutsches Pfarrerblatt [*Essen, Germany*] — DPfBl
Deutsches Philologen-Blatt — DphBl
Deutsches Philologen-Blatt — Dt Philologenbl
Deutsches Recht. Vereinigt mit Juristische Wochenschrift — Dt Recht
Deutsches Roheisen — Dtsch Roheisen
Deutsches Schiffahrtsarchiv — Dtsch Schiffahrtsarch
Deutsches Schiffahrtsarchiv. Zeitschrift des Deutschen Schiffartsmuseums — Deut Schiffahrtsarch
Deutsches Statistisches Zentralblatt — Dt Statist Zbl
Deutsches Steuerrecht — D St R
Deutsches Tierarzteblatt — Dtsch Tierarztebl
Deutsches Tuberkulose-Blatt — Dt Tub Bl
Deutsches Tuberkulose-Blatt — Dtsch Tuberk Bl
Deutsches Verwaltungsblatt — Dt Verw Bl
Deutsches Verwaltungsblatt und Verwaltungsarchiv — Dtsch Verwaltungsbl Verwaltungsarch
Deutsches Volkstum. Monatsschrift fuer das Deutsche Geistesleben — DVo
Deutsches Wirtschaftsinstitut Forschungshefte — Dt Wirtinst Forschhft
Deutsches Wochenblatt — Dt Wochenbl
Deutsches Wollforschungsinstitut an der Technischen Hochschule Aachen. Schriftenreihe — Dtsch Wollforschungsinst Tech Hochsch Aachen Schriftenr
Deutsches Zahnaerzteblatt — Dt Zahnaerztebl
Deutsches Zentralblatt fuer Krankenpflege — Dtsch Zentralbl Krankenpfl
Deutsche-Slawische Forschungen zur Namenkunde und Siedlungsgeschichte — DSFNS
Deutsch-Evangelisch im Auslande — DEvA
Deutsch-Evangelische Blaetter — DEBl
Deutsch-Evangelische Blaetter — DEBll
Deutsch-Franzoesische Monatshefte — DFMhe
Deutsch-Franzoesische Rundschau — DFR
Deutsch-Hebraeische Sterbeliste [*Berlin*] — DHStL
Deutsch-Israelitische Zeitung — DIZ
Deutschkundliche Arbeiten — DkA
Deutschland Archiv — DeutA

Deutschland Archiv — Dtl Arch
Deutschlands Erneuerung — Deu E
Deutschland-Union-Dienst [*Germany*] — Dtschl-Union-Dienst
Deutsch-Oesterreich — D Oe
Deutschoesterreichische Monatsschrift fuer Naturwissenschaftliche Fortbildung — Deutschoesterr Monatsschr Naturwiss Fortbild
Deutschoesterreichische Spirituisen-Zeitung — Deutschoesterr Spirit Ztg
Deutschoesterreichische Tieraerztliche Wochenschrift — Deutschoesterr Tieraerztl Wchnschr
Deutsch-Oesterreichische Tieraerztliche Wochenschrift — DoetW
Deutsch-Poinische Hefte — Dt Pol H
Deutsch-Polnische Hefte — Dt PH
Deutsch-Schwedisches Jahrbuch — Dt Schwed Jb
Deutsch-Schwedisches Symposion ueber Photomedizin. Verhandlungsbericht — Dtsch Schwed Symp Photomed Verhandlungsber
Deutsch-Skandinavisches Symposium — Dtsch Skand Symp
Deutsch-Sowjetische Arbeitstagung zu Fragen des Strahlenschutzes — Dtsch Sow Arbeitstag Fragen Strahlenschutzes
Deutsch-Taschenbuecher — Deutsch-Taschenb
Deutschtum im Ausland — Deutschtum Ausl
Deutschtum und Ausland — DA
Deutschunterricht — DU
Deutschunterricht. Arbeitshefte zu Seiner Praktischen Gestaltung — Dt Unterr
Deutschunterricht fuer Auslaender — DUA
Deuxieme Conference Internationale d'Histoire Economique — DCI
Develop Victoria Journal — Develop VIC
Develop Victoria Journal — Develop VIC J
[*The*] **Developing Child** — TDC
Developing Economies — DE
Developing Economies — Dev Econ
Developing Economies — Develop Eco
Developing Economies — Develop Econ
Developing Economies — DVE
Developing Economies — DVEC-A
Developing Education — Dev Educ
Developing Railways — Dev Rail
Development and Change — DEC
Development and Change — Dev Change
Development and Change — Develop and Change
Development and Change — Develop Cha
Development and Change — DVA
Development and Innovation for Australian Process Industries. Papers of the Australian Chemical Engineering Conference [*Newcastle, 1972*] — Dev Innovation Aust Process Ind Pap Aust Chem Eng Conf
Development and Materials Bulletin — Dev Mat Bull
Development and Materials Bulletin — Development & Materials Bull
Development and Psychopathology — Dev Psychopathol
Development Dialogue — Dev Dialogue
Development Dialogue — Develop Dialogue
Development Digest — DD
Development Digest — Devel Dig
Development Forum — Dev Forum
Development Forum [*General Edition*] — Development
Development Forum — DVS
Development Forum. Business Edition — DVI
Development Genes and Evolution — Dev Genes Evol
Development, Growth, and Differentiation — Dev Grow Differ
Development, Growth, and Differentiation — Dev Growth Differ
Development, Growth, and Differentiation — Develop Gr
Development, Growth, and Differentiation — DGDFA5
Development, Growth, and Differentiation (Nagoya) — Dev Growth Differ (Nagoya)
Development in Food Science — Dev Food Sci
Development in Mammals — Dev Mamm
Development in Mammals — DMAMDM
Development News — DEV
Development News Digest [*Later, Development Dossier*] — DND
Development Newsletter — Dev Newsl
Development of Attic Black-Figure — DAB
Development of Science. Sources for the History of Science — Develop Sci Sources Hist Sci
Development of the James Bay Region/Societe de Developpement de la Baie James — DJBR
Development Period Medicine — Dev Period Med
Development Psychobiology — Devel Psychobiol
Development Review and Outlook — Dev Rev Outl
Development Studies — Dev Stud
Development Studies (Southern Africa) — Dev Stud (Sthn Afr)
Development. Supplement — Dev Suppl
Developmental and Cell Biology — Dev Cell Biol
Developmental and Cell Biology — DVCBAP
Developmental and Comparative Immunology — DCIMDQ
Developmental and Comparative Immunology — Dev Comp Immunol
Developmental Biology — DEBIAO
Developmental Biology — Dev Biol
Developmental Biology — Devel Biol
Developmental Biology — Develop Bio
Developmental Biology — Develop Biol
Developmental Biology — Developm Biol
Developmental Biology — Devl Biol
Developmental Biology. Supplement — DEBSAK
Developmental Biology. Supplement — Dev Biol Suppl
Developmental Brain Research — Dev Brain Res
Developmental Disabilities Abstracts — Dev Disab Abstr
Developmental Dynamics — Dev Dyn
Developmental Genetics — Dev Genet
Developmental Genetics — DGNTDW
Developmental Genetics (New York) — Dev Genet (NY)
Developmental Medicine and Child Neurology — Dev Med Child Neurol
Developmental Medicine and Child Neurology — Develop Med
Developmental Medicine and Child Neurology — Develop Med Child Neurol
Developmental Medicine and Child Neurology — Developmental Med Child Neurol
Developmental Medicine and Child Neurology — DMCNA
Developmental Medicine and Child Neurology — DMCNAW
Developmental Medicine and Child Neurology. Supplement — Dev Med Child Neurol Suppl
Developmental Medicine and Child Neurology. Supplement — DMCSAD
Developmental Neuropathology of Schizophrenia — Dev Neuropathol Schizophr
Developmental Neuroscience — DENED7
Developmental Neuroscience — Dev Neurosci
Developmental Neuroscience (Basel) — Dev Neurosci (Basel)
Developmental Pharmacology and Therapeutics — Dev Pharmacol Ther
Developmental Pharmacology and Therapeutics — DPTHDL
Developmental Psychobiology — DEPBA
Developmental Psychobiology — DEPBA5
Developmental Psychobiology — Dev Psychobiol
Developmental Psychobiology — Develop Psy
Developmental Psychology — Dev Psychol
Developmental Psychology — Devel Psych
Developmental Psychology — Develop Psychol
Developmental Psychology — DEVPA
Developmental Psychology — DEVPA9
Developmental Psychology — DP
Developmental Psychology — GDPS
Developmental Psychology. Monograph — Dev Psychol Monogr
Developmental Psychology. Monograph — DVPMAL
Developmental Review — DEREES
Developmental Review — Dev Rev
Developments in Adhesives — Dev Adhes
Developments in Agricultural and Managed-Forest Ecology [*Elsevier Book Series*] — DAME
Developments in Agricultural and Managed-Forest Ecology — Dev Agric Managed For Ecol
Developments in Agricultural Economics — Dev Agric Econ
Developments in Agricultural Engineering [*Elsevier Book Series*] — DAE
Developments in Agricultural Engineering — DAENDT
Developments in Agricultural Engineering — Dev Agric Eng
Developments in Animal and Veterinary Sciences [*Elsevier Book Series*] — DAVS
Developments in Animal and Veterinary Sciences — DAVSDR
Developments in Animal and Veterinary Sciences — Dev Anim Vet Sci
Developments in Applied Spectroscopy — DAPSAS
Developments in Applied Spectroscopy — Dev Appl Spectrosc
Developments in Aquaculture and Fisheries Science — Dev Aquacult Fish Sci
Developments in Atmosphere Science [*Elsevier Book Series*] — DAS
Developments in Atmospheric Science — Dev Atmos Sci
Developments in Biochemistry [*Elsevier Book Series*] — DB
Developments in Biochemistry — DEBIDR
Developments in Biochemistry — Dev Biochem
Developments in Biodegradation of Hydrocarbons — Dev Biodegrad Hydrocarbons
Developments in Bioenergetics and Biomembranes [*Elsevier Book Series*] — DBB
Developments in Bioenergetics and Biomembranes — Dev Bioenerg Biomembr
Developments in Biological Standardization — Dev Biol Stand
Developments in Biological Standardization — Devs Biol Standardiz
Developments in Biological Standardization — DVBSA3
Developments in Block Copolymers — Dev Block Copolym
Developments in Cancer Research [*Elsevier Book Series*] — DCR
Developments in Cardiovascular Medicine — Dev Cardiovasc Med
Developments in Cell Biology [*Elsevier Book Series*] — DCB
Developments in Cell Biology — Develop in Cell Biology
Developments in Cell Biology (Amsterdam) — Dev Cell Biol (Amsterdam)
Developments in Cell Biology (London) — Dev Cell Biol (London)
Developments in Ceramic and Metal-Matrix Composites. Proceedings. Symposium — Dev Ceram Met Matrix Compos Proc Symp
Developments in Chemical Engineering and Mineral Processing — Dev Chem Eng Miner Process
Developments in Chromatography — Dev Chromatogr
Developments in Civil and Foundation Engineering — Develop Civ Found Engrg
Developments in Civil Engineering [*Elsevier Book Series*] — DCE
Developments in Civil Engineering — Develop Civ Engrg
Developments in Clinical Biochemistry — Dev Clin Biochem
Developments in Composite Materials — Dev Compos Mater
Developments in Crop Science [*Elsevier Book Series*] — DC
Developments in Crop Science — DCSCDC
Developments in Crop Science — Dev Crop Sci
Developments in Crystalline Polymers — Dev Cryst Polym
Developments in Dairy Chemistry — Dev Dairy Chem
Developments in Diabetes Research [*Elsevier Book Series*] — DDR
Developments in Economic Geology [*Elsevier Book Series*] — DEG
Developments in Economic Geology — Dev Econ Geol
Developments in Electromagnetic Theory and Applications — Develop Electromagnet Theory Appl
Developments in Endocrinology [*Elsevier Book Series*] — DIE
Developments in Endocrinology (Amsterdam) — Dev Endocrinol (Amersterdam)
Developments in Endocrinology (The Hague) — Dev Endocrinol (The Hague)
Developments in Environmental Biology of Fishes — DEBFDI
Developments in Environmental Biology of Fishes — Dev Environ Biol Fishes

Developments in Environmental Control and Public Health — Dev Environ Control Public Health
Developments in Environmental Modelling [*Elsevier Book Series*] — DEM
Developments in Environmental Modelling — Dev Environ Modell
Developments in Food Analysis Techniques — Dev Food Anal Tech
Developments in Food Colours — Dev Food Colours
Developments in Food Engineering. Proceedings of the International Congress on Engineering and Food — Dev Food Eng Proc Int Congr Eng Food
Developments in Food Microbiology — Dev Food Microbiol
Developments in Food Packaging — Dev Food Packag
Developments in Food Preservation — Dev Food Preserv
Developments in Food Preservation — Dev Food Preservation
Developments in Food Preservatives — Dev Food Preservatives
Developments in Food Proteins — Dev Food Proteins
Developments in Food Science [*Elsevier Book Series*] — DFS
Developments in Food Science — DFSCDX
Developments in Genetics [*Elsevier Book Series*] — DIG
Developments in Genetics (Amsterdam) — Dev Genet (Amsterdam)
Developments in Geochemistry — Dev Geochem
Developments in Geochemistry [*Elsevier Book Series*] — DGC
Developments in Geomathematics [*Elsevier Book Series*] — DGM
Developments in Geotechnical Engineering — Dev Geotech Eng
Developments in Geotechnical Engineering [*Elsevier Book Series*] — DGE
Developments in Geotechnical Engineering — DGEND
Developments in Geotectonics — Dev Geotectonics
Developments in Geotectonics [*Elsevier Book Series*] — DG
Developments in Halophilic Microorganisms — Dev Halophilic Microorg
Developments in Halophilic Microorganisms — Dev Halophilic Microorganisms
Developments in Halophilic Microorganisms [*Elsevier Book Series*] — DHM
Developments in Heat Exchanger Technology — Dev Heat Exch Technol
Developments in Hematology — Dev Hematol
Developments in Hydrobiology — DEHYD3
Developments in Hydrobiology — Dev Hydrobiol
Developments in Immunology — DEIMD6
Developments in Immunology — Dev Immunol
Developments in Immunology [*Elsevier Book Series*] — DI
Developments in Industrial Microbiology — Dev Ind Microbiol
Developments in Industrial Microbiology — Devel Ind Microbiol
Developments in Industrial Microbiology — DIMCAL
Developments in Industrial Microbiology Series — Dev Ind Microbiol Ser
Developments in Injection Moulding — Dev Injection Moulding
Developments in Ionic Polymers — Dev Ionic Polym
Developments in Landscape Management and Urban Planning [*Elsevier Book Series*] — DLM
Developments in Mammals [*Elsevier Book Series*] — DM
Developments in Marine Biology — Dev Mar Biol
Developments in Marine Biology [*Elsevier Book Series*] — DMB
Developments in Meat Science — Dev Meat Sci
Developments in Mechanics — Dev Mech
Developments in Mechanics — Develop in Mech
Developments in Mineral Processing — Dev Miner Process
Developments in Mineral Processing [*Elsevier Book Series*] — DMP
Developments in Molecular and Cellular Biochemistry — Dev Mol Cell Biochem
Developments in Molecular and Cellular Biochemistry — DMCBDX
Developments in Molecular Virology — Dev Mol Virol
Developments in Nephrology — Dev Nephrol
Developments in Neurology [*Elsevier Book Series*] — DIN
Developments in Neuroscience [*Elsevier Book Series*] — DN
Developments in Neuroscience (Amsterdam) — Dev Neurosci (Amsterdam)
Developments in Nuclear Medicine — Dev Nucl Med
Developments in Nutrition and Metabolism — Dev Nutr Metab
Developments in Nutrition and Metabolism [*Elsevier Book Series*] — DINM
Developments in Obstetrics and Gynecology — Dev Obstet Gynecol
Developments in Obstetrics and Gynecology — DOGYDY
Developments in Oncology — Dev Oncol
Developments in Ophthalmology — DEOPDB
Developments in Ophthalmology — Dev Ophthalmol
Developments in Optical Component Coatings — Dev Opt Compon Coat
Developments in Oriented Polymers — Dev Oriented Polym
Developments in Palaeontology and Stratigraphy — Dev Palaeontol Stratigr
Developments in Palaeontology and Stratigraphy [*Elsevier Book Series*] — DPAS
Developments in Perinatal Medicine — Dev Perinat Med
Developments in Petroleum Geology — Dev Pet Geol
Developments in Petroleum Science — Dev Pet Sci
Developments in Petroleum Science [*Elsevier Book Series*] — DPS
Developments in Petrology — Dev Petrol
Developments in Petrology [*Elsevier Book Series*] — DP
Developments in Pharmacology — Dev Pharmacol
Developments in Plant and Soil Sciences — Dev Plant Soil Sci
Developments in Plant and Soil Sciences — DVPSD8
Developments in Plant Biology — Dev Plant Biol
Developments in Plant Biology [*Elsevier Book Series*] — DPB
Developments in Plant Genetics and Breeding — Dev Plant Genet Breed
Developments in Plastics Technology — Dev Plast Technol
Developments in Polymer Characterisation — Dev Polym Charact
Developments in Polymer Degradation — Dev Polym Degrad
Developments in Polymer Fracture — Dev Polym Fract
Developments in Polymer Photochemistry — Dev Polym Photochem
Developments in Polymer Stabilisation — Dev Polym Stab
Developments in Polymerisation — Dev Polym
Developments in Polyurethane — Dev Polyurethane
Developments in Precambrian Geology — Dev Precambrian Geol
Developments in Precambrian Geology [*Elsevier Book Series*] — DPG
Developments in Psychiatry — Dev Psychiatry
Developments in Psychiatry [*Elsevier Book Series*] — DIP
Developments in PVC Production and Processing — Dev PVC Prod Process
Developments in Reinforced Plastics — Dev Reinf Plast
Developments in Rubber and Rubber Composites — Dev Rubber Rubber Compos
Developments in Rubber Technology — Dev Rubber Technol
Developments in Sedimentology — Dev Sedimentol
Developments in Sedimentology [*Elsevier Book Series*] — DS
Developments in Soft Drinks Technology — Dev Soft Drinks Technol
Developments in Soil Science — Dev Soil Sci
Developments in Soil Science [*Elsevier Book Series*] — DSS
Developments in Soil Science — DSSCDM
Developments in Solar System and Space Science [*Elsevier Book Series*] — DSSSS
Developments in Solid Earth Geophysics [*Elsevier Book Series*] — DSEG
Developments in Statistics — Dev Stat
Developments in Statistics — Develop in Statist
Developments in Toxicology and Environmental Science — Dev Toxicol Environ Sci
Developments in Toxicology and Environmental Science [*Elsevier Book Series*] [*A publication*] — DT
Developments in Toxicology and Environmental Science — DTESD
Developments in Veterinary Virology — Dev Vet Virol
Developments in Water Science [*Elsevier Book Series*] — DWS
Developpement et Civilisation — Devel Civ
Developpement et Civilisation — Develop et Civilis
Developpement et Civilisations — Dev et Civilisations
Developpement et Progres Socio-Economique — Develop Progres Socio Econ
Developpement Industriel et Scientifique — Dev Ind Sci
Deviant Behavior — DEBEDF
Deviant Behavior — Deviant Behav
Devil's Box — DevB
Devon and Cornwall. Notes and Queries — DCNQ
Devon Historian — Devon Hist
Devonshire Association — Devonshire Assoc
Devotee — Dev
DEW [*Deutsche Edelstahlwerke*] **Technische Berichte** — DEW Tech Ber
DEW [*Deutsche Edelstahlwerke*] **Technische Berichte** — DEWTA
DFBO [*Deutsche Forschungsgesellschaft fuer Blechverarbeitung und Oberflaechenbehandlung*] **Mitteilungen** — DFBO Mitt
DFG Mitteilungen. Deutsche Forschungsgemeinschaft — DFG Mitt
DFL [*Deutsche Forschungsanstalt fuer Luftfahrt*] **Bericht** — DFL Ber
DGU (Geological Survey of Denmark) Series C — DGU (Geol Surv Den) Ser C
DGU [*Geological Survey of Denmark*] **Series C** — DSECEL
Dhaka University Studies. Part B — Dhaka Univ Stud Part B
Dhaka University Studies. Part B — DUBSDX
DHEW [*Department of Health, Education, and Welfare*] **NIOSH Publication (US)** [*National Institute of Occupational Safety and Health*] — DHEW NIOSH Publ (US)
DHEW [*Department of Health, Education, and Welfare*] **Publication ADM (US)** — DHEW Publ ADM (US)
DHEW [*Department of Health, Education, and Welfare*] **Publication. HSA (US)** [*Health Services Administration*] — DHEW Publ HSA (US)
DHEW [*Department of Health, Education, and Welfare*] **Publication. NIH (US)** [*National Institutes of Health*] — DHEW Publ NIH (US)
DHHS [*Department of Health and Human Services*] **Publication. ADM (US)** — DHHS Publ ADM (US)
DHHS [*Department of Health and Human Services*] **Publication. NIOSH (US)** [*National Institute of Occupational Health and Safety*] — DHHS NIOSH Publ (US)
DHZ Markt. Vakblad voor de Doe het Zelf Ondernemer — VEJ
DIA [*Division de Investigaciones Agropecuarias*] **Boletin de Divulgacion** — DIA Bol Divulg
DIA [*Division de Investigaciones Agropecuarias*] **Boletin Tecnico** — DIA Bol Tec
DIA [*Division de Investigaciones Agropecuarias*] **Boletin Tecnico** — DIATAC
DIA [*Division de Investigaciones Agropecuarias*] **Medico** — DIA Med
DIA [*Division de Investigaciones Agropecuarias*] **Medico** — DIMEAR
DIA [*Division de Investigaciones Agropecuarias*] **Medico Uruguayo** — DIA Med Urug
Diabete [*Later, Diabete et Metabolisme*] — DBTEAD
Diabete [*Later, Diabete et Metabolisme*] — Diab
Diabete et Metabolisme — Diabete Met
Diabete et Metabolisme — Diabete Metab
Diabete et Metabolisme — DIMEDU
Diabete et Nutrition — Diabete Nutr
Diabetes — Diabet
Diabetes — DIAEAZ
Diabetes Abstracts — Diab Abstr
Diabetes and Metabolism — Diabetes Metab
Diabetes Care — Diabetes Care
Diabetes Educator — DBED
Diabetes Educator — Diabetes Educ
Diabetes Forecast — Diabetes Forecast
Diabetes Frontier — Diabetes Front
Diabetes Journal — Diabetes J
Diabetes Literature Index — Diab Lit Ind
Diabetes Literature Index — Diabetes Lit Index
Diabetes Literature Index — DLI
Diabetes Mellitus. Diagnosis and Treatment — Diabetes Mellitus Diagn Treat
Diabetes/Metabolism Reviews — Diabetes Metab Rev
Diabetes/Metabolism Reviews — Diabetes Metab Review
Diabetes/Metabolism Reviews — DMR
Diabetes/Metabolism Reviews — DMREEG
Diabetes Research — Diabetes Res

Diabetes Research and Clinical Practice — Diabetes Res Clin Prac
Diabetes Research and Clinical Practice — Diabetes Res Clin Pract
Diabetes Research and Clinical Practice — DRCPE9
Diabetic Digest — Diabet Dig
Diabetic Journal — Diabet J
Diabetic Journal of Australia — Diabetic J of Aust
Diabetic Medicine — Diabet Med
Diabetologia — DBTGAJ
Diabetologia — Diabet
Diabetologia — Diabetolog
Diabetologia Croatica — DBCRB2
Diabetologia Croatica — Diabetol Croat
Diacritics — DS
Diadora Glasilo Arheoloskoga Muzeja u Zadru — Diadora
Diagnose und Labor — Diagn Labor
Diagnosi Laboratorio e Clinica — Diagn Lab Clin
Diagnosis and Therapy [*Japan*] — Diagn Ther
Diagnosis and Treatment [*Japan*] — Diagn Treat
Diagnostic Cytopathology — Diagn Cytopathol
Diagnostic Enzymology — Diagn Enzymol
Diagnostic Gynecology and Obstetrics — Diagn Gynecol Obstet
Diagnostic Histopathology — Diagn Histopathol
Diagnostic Histopathology — DIHIDH
Diagnostic Imaging — Diagn Imaging
Diagnostic Imaging — DIIMD
Diagnostic Imaging — DIIMDY
Diagnostic Imaging in Clinical Medicine — Diagn Imag Clin Med
Diagnostic Imaging in Clinical Medicine — Diagn Imaging Clin Med
Diagnostic Imaging in Clinical Medicine — DICMD4
Diagnostic Immunology — DI
Diagnostic Immunology — Diagn Immunol
Diagnostic Immunology — DIIMEZ
Diagnostic Medicine — Diagn Med
Diagnostic Microbiology and Infectious Disease — Diagn Microbiol Infect Dis
Diagnostic Microbiology and Infectious Disease — DMID
Diagnostic Microbiology and Infectious Disease — DMIDDZ
Diagnostic Molecular Pathology — Diagn Mol Pathol
Diagnostic Radiology Series — Diagn Radiol Ser
Diagnostic Radiology Series — DRSEDL
Diagnostica — DGNSAQ
Diagnostica — Diagn
Diagnostica e Tecnica di Laboratorio — Diagn Tec Lab
Diagnosticos APEC. Associacao Promotora de Estudos de Economia — Diagnosticos APEC
Diagnostics et Traitements — Diagn Trait
Diagnostics Intelligence. Monthly Intelligence for the Medical Diagnostics Industry — Diagn Intell
Diagnostik und Intensivmedizin — Diagn Intensivmed
Diagnostik und Intensivtherapie — Diagn Intensivther
Diagnostika Plazmy [*Former USSR*] — Diagn Plazmy
Diagnostyka Laboratoryjna — Diagn Lab
Diagnostyka Laboratoryjna — DLJNAQ
Dial — D
Dial. A Magazine for Literature, Philosophy, and Religion — Di
Dial (Chicago) — Dial (Ch)
Dialect Notes — Dial Notes
Dialect Notes — DN
Dialectes Belgo-Romans — DBR
Dialectes Belgo-Romans — Dial Belg-Rom
Dialectes de Wallonie — D d W
Dialectica — D
Dialectica — Dial
Dialectica — Dialec
Dialectical Anthropology — Dial Anthro
Dialectical Anthropology — Dialectical Anthrop
Dialectics and Humanism — Dialec Hum
Dialectics and Humanism — Dialect Hum
Dialects of Ancient Gaul — DAG
Dialektika Ob'ektivnogo i Sub'ektivnogo v Poznanie i Prakticeskoj Dejatel'nosti — Dialektika Ob'ekt Sub'ekt Poznanie Prakt Dejatel'nosti
Dialektolohicnyi Bjuleten — DB
Dialektolohicnyi Bjuleten — DialB
Dialog [*Warsaw*] — Dg
Dialog — Di
Dialog — Dia
Dialog [*Minneapolis*] — Dial
Dialog. Fairleigh Dickinson University. School of Dentistry — Dialog Fairleigh Dickinson Univ Sch Dent
Dialog: Teatertidskrift (Stockholm) — DialS
Dialog (Warsaw) — Dialog (W)
Dialoghi — Di
Dialoghi — Dia
Dialoghi — Dial
Dialoghi di Archeologia — D Arch
Dialoghi di Archeologia — DdA
Dialoghi di Archeologia — Dial A
Dialoghi di Archeologia — Dial Ar
Dialoghi di Archeologia — Dial Arch
Dialoghi di Archeologia — Dial di Arch
Dialogo Dor Haemshej — DDH
Dialogo Ecumenico — Dial Ec
Dialogo Ecumenico [*Salamanca*] — DialEcum
Dialogo (Puerto Rico) — DUPR
Dialogo Social (Panama) — DSP
Dialogos. Colegio de Mexico — CM/D
Dialogos Hispanicos de Amsterdam — DHA
Dialogos (Mexico) — DM
Dialogos. Problemi della Scuola Italiana — Dial
Dialogos Revista. Departamento de Filosofia. Universidad de Puerto Rico — DPR
Dialogue. Canadian Philosophical Review — Dialogue C
Dialogue. Canadian Philosophical Review — Dialogue (Canada)
Dialogue in Instrumental Music Education — DIME
Dialogue (Milwaukee) — Dialogue (M)
Dialogue North — DIN
Dialogue North. Combined Edition — DINC
Dialogue North. Eastern Arctic Edition — DINE
Dialogue North. Western Arctic Edition — DINW
Dialogue on Diarrhoea — DDIAEW
Dialogue (Phi Sigma Tau) — Dialogue (PST)
Dialogues. Cahiers de Litterature et de Linguistique — Dial
Dialogues d'Histoire Ancienne — DHA
Dialogues d'Histoire Ancienne — Dial Hist Anc
Dialysis and Transplantation — Dial Transplant
Dialysis and Transplantation — DLTPAE
Dialysis, Transplantation, Nephrology — Dial Transplant Nephrol
Dialysis, Transplantation, Nephrology. Proceedings. Congress of the European Dialysis and Transplant Association — Dial Transplant Nephrol Pro Congr Eur Dial Transplant Assoc
Diamant. Maandelijks Tijdschrift voor de Studie van het Diamantbedrijf — DIM
Diamond and Abrasives Engineering — Diamond Abrasives Eng
Diamond and Related Materials — Diamond Relat Mater
Diamond Films and Technology — Diamond Films Technol
Diamond News and SA [*South African*] **Jeweller** — Diamond News and SA Jeweller
Diamond Research — Diamond Res
Diapason — DI
Diapason — Dia
Diapason — Diap
Diario de Centro America — DCA
Diario de Centroamerica — DLA
Diario de Justica da Uniao [*Brazil*] — DJU
Diario de Noticias (Lisbon, Portugal) — DNAL
Diario Oficial — DO
Diario Oficial (Mexico) — Diario Of Mex
Diario Oficial. Ministerio de Marina — Diario Of Minist Mar
Diario Oficial (Rio de Janeiro) — Diario Of Rio
Diarium Terrae Sanctae [*Jerusalem*] — DTS
Diatomic Research Bulletin — Diatomic Research Bull
Dibevo — MVV
Diccionario de la Real Academia Espanola — DRAE
Diccionario Griego-Espanol — DGE
Dichtung und Erkenntnis — DuE
Dichtung und Volkstum — Dicht u Volkst
Dichtung und Volkstum — DuV
Dichtung und Volkstum — DV
Dichtung und Wirklichkeit — DuW
DICIS. Doane Information Center Indexing System. Subject Index — Doane Inf Cent Index Syst Subj Index
Dickens Quarterly — DickQ
Dickens Studies — DiS
Dickens Studies Annual — DSA
Dickens Studies Newsletter — Dicken Stud Newsl
Dickens Studies Newsletter — Dickens St
Dickens Studies Newsletter — DSN
Dickensian — D
Dickensian — Dick
Dickensian — Dickens
Dickinson Law Review — Dick L R
Dickinson Law Review — Dick L Rev
Dickinson Law Review — Dickinson L Rev
Dickinson Review — DickinsonR
Dickinson Studies — Dic S
Dickinson Studies — Dickinson S
DICP (Drug Intelligence and Clinical Pharmacy) Annals of Pharmacotherapy — DICP Ann Pharmacother
DICP (Drug Intelligence and Clinical Pharmacy) The Annals of Pharmacotherapy — DICP Ann Ph
Dictionarul Limbii Romane — Dict Limb Rom
Dictionary of American Biography — DAB
Dictionary of American English — DAE
Dictionary of American Library Biography — DALB
Dictionary of American Regional English — DARE
Dictionary of American Scholars — DAS
Dictionary of American Slang — DAS
Dictionary of Americanisms — DA
Dictionary of Bahamian English — DBE
Dictionary of Canadianisms — DCan
Dictionary of Christ and the Gospels — DCG
Dictionary of Christian Antiquities — DCA
Dictionary of Christian Biography [*London*] — DCB
Dictionary of Drugs — DOD
Dictionary of Jamaican English — DJE
Dictionary of National Biography — DNB
Dictionary of Newfoundland English — DNE
Dictionary of Organic Compounds — DOC
Dictionary of Organometallic Compounds — DOMC
Dictionary of Steroids — DOS
Dictionary of the Apostolic Church — DAC
Dictionary of the Bible — DOB

Dictionary of the Older Scottish Tongue — DOST
Dictionary of the Scottish Language — DSL
Dictionnaire Apologetique — Dict Apol
Dictionnaire Classique d'Histoire Naturelle — Dict Class Hist Nat
Dictionnaire d'Archeologie Biblique — DAB
Dictionnaire d'Archeologie Chretienne et de Liturgie — DAC
Dictionnaire d'Archeologie Chretienne et de Liturgie — DACL
Dictionnaire d'Archeologie Chretienne et de Liturgie — DAL
Dictionnaire d'Archeologie Chretienne et de Liturgie — DArChr
Dictionnaire d'Archeologie Chretienne et de Liturgie — DArChrL
Dictionnaire de Biographie Francaise — DBF
Dictionnaire de Droit Canonique — DDC
Dictionnaire de la Bible — DB
Dictionnaire de la Bible — Dict Bibl
Dictionnaire de la Langue Louvite [*Paris*] — DLL
Dictionnaire de Spiritualite [*Paris*] — DSpir
Dictionnaire de Spiritualite Ascetique et Mystique, Doctrine et Histoire — Dict Sp
Dictionnaire de Spiritualite Ascetique et Mystique, Doctrine et Histoire — DSAM
Dictionnaire de Theologie Catholique — D Th C
Dictionnaire de Theologie Catholique — Dict Theol Cath
Dictionnaire de Theologie Catholique [*Paris*] — DTC
Dictionnaire des Antiquites Grecques et Romaines — DA
Dictionnaire des Antiquites Grecques et Romaines — DAGR
Dictionnaire des Antiquites Grecques et Romaines — Dict
Dictionnaire des Antiquites Grecques et Romaines — Dict Ant
Dictionnaire des Antiquites Grecques et Romaines (Daremberg and Saglio) — Dar Sag
Dictionnaire des Inscriptions Semitiques de l'Ouest — DISO
Dictionnaire des Noms Geographiques — DNG
Dictionnaire des Noms Geographiques Contenus dans les Textes Hieroglyphiques — DG
Dictionnaire d'Histoire et de Geographie Ecclesiastique — DHGE
Dictionnaire Encyclopedique de la Bible — DEB
Dictionnaire Etymologique de la Langue Latine [*Paris*] — DEL
Dictionnaire Etymologique de la Langue Latine [*Paris*] — DELL
Dictionnaire Etymologique de la Langue Latine [*Paris*] — Dict Etym
Dictionnaire Etymologique de la Langue Latine [*Paris*] — EM
Dictionnaire Geographique de l'Ancienne Egypte — Dict Geog
Didascalia — Didasc
Didaskaleion — Di
Didaskaleion — Did
Didaskalos — Didask
Diderot Studies — Did S
Diderot Studies — Diderot Stud
Diderot Studies — DS
Die Beitraege des Staatsanzeiger fuer Wuertemburg — BBSW
Die Bibel in der Welt [*Ruhr*] — BiWelt
Die Botschaft des Alten Testaments [*Stuttgart*] — BA
Die Casting Engineer — DICEA
Die Casting Engineer — Die Cast Eng
Die Castings — Die Cast
Die Christengemeinschaft [*Stuttgart*] — ChrGem
Die Deutsche Post — DDP
Die Friedenswarte — Fr Warte
Die Griechische Christliche Schriftsteller der Ersten Drei Jahrhunderten — GCS
Die Grossen Deutschen — GD
Die Haghe. Bijdragen en Mededeelingen — HBM
Die Heilige Schrift des Alten Testaments [*Herausgegeben von Herkenne und Feldmann. Bonn*] — HSAT
Die Heilige Schrift des Neuen Testaments. Bonn — HSNT
Die Holzzucht — D Hz
Die Juedische Presse [*Berlin*] — JPr
Die Justiz — DJ
Die Kultur — DK
Die Landtechnische Zeitschrift — DLZ
Die Landwirtschaftlichen Versuchsstationen — Landw Versuchsstat
Die Literatur — DL
Die Medizinischen Versuche, Nebst Bemerkungen, Welche von Einer Gesellschaft in Edinburgh Durchgesehen und Herausgegeben Werden — Med Versuche Bemerk Ges Edinburgh
Die Neue Literatur — DNL
Die Neueren Sprachen — DNS
Die Neuesten Religionsbegebenheiten mit Unpartheyischen Anmerkungen — NRB
Die Oberhessischen Kloester — OHK
Die Oekuminischen Konzile der Christenheit — OeKC
Die Ortskrankenkasse — DOK
Die Ou Testamentiese Werkgemeenskap in Suid-Afrika [*Pretoria*] — OTWerkSuidA
Die Ou Testamentiese Werkgemeenskap in Suid-Afrika [*Pretoria*] — OTWSA
Die Ou Testamentiese Werkgemeenskap in Suid-Afrika (Pretoria) — OuTWP
Die Palmyrenischen Personennamen — PP
Die Praxis des Bundesgerichts [*Basel, Switzerland*] — Pra
Die Presse — DP
Die Schriften des Alten Testaments in Auswahl Neu Uebersetzt und fuer die Gegenwart Erklaert [*Goettingen*] — SAT
Die Schriften des Alten Testaments in Auswahl Neu Uebersetzt und fuer die Gegenwart Erklaert [*Goettingen*] — SATA
Die Sumerischen und Akkadischen Hymnen und Gebete [*Zurich/Stuttgart*] — SAHG
Die Welt — DW
Die Welt des Islam — Welt Isl
Die Welt des Islams — DWI
Die Weltliteratur — DW
Diecasting and Metal Moulding — Diecast Met Mould
Diecasting and Metal Moulding — Diecasting Met Moulding
Diehlektriki i Poluprovodniki — Diehlektr Poluprovodn
Dielectric and Optical Aspects of Intermolecular Interactions — Dielectr Opt Aspects Intermol Interact
Dielectric and Related Molecular Processes — Dielectr Relat Mol Processes
Dielectric Properties of Heterogeneous Materials — Dielectr Prop Heterog Mater
Dielektriki i Poluprovodniki — Dielektr Poluprovodn
Dielektryczne i Optyczne Aspekty Oddzialywan Miedzyczasteczkowych — Dielektr Opt Aspekty Oddzialywan Miedzyczasteczkowych
Dienstreglement Loodswezen — DL
Diergeneeskundig Memorandum — Diergeneesk Memo
Diesel and Gas Turbine Progress [*Later, Diesel Progress North American*] — DGTPA
Diesel and Gas Turbine Progress [*Later, Diesel Progress North American*] — Diesel
Diesel and Gas Turbine Progress [*Later, Diesel Progress North American*] — Diesel Gas Turbine Prog
Diesel and Gas Turbine Progress [*Later, Diesel Progress North American*] — Diesel Gas Turbine Progr
Diesel and Gas Turbine Progress Worldwide [*Later, Diesel and Gas Turbine Worldwide*] — Diesel Gas Turb Prog Worldwide
Diesel and Gas Turbine Worldwide — Diesel Gas Turbine Worldwide
Diesel Engineering [*England*] — Diesel Eng
Diesel Engineers and Users Association. Publication — Diesel Eng Users Ass Publ
Diesel Engineers and Users Association. Reports — Diesel Eng Us Ass Report
Diesel Equipment Superintendent — Diesel Equip Supt
Diesel Power — DIPOA
Diesel Power and Diesel Transportation — Diesel Power Diesel Transp
Diesel Progress — Diesel Prog
Diesel Progress North American — Diesel Prog
Diesel Progress North American — Diesel Prog N Amer
Diesel Progress North American — Diesel Prog North Am
Diesel Railway Traction — Dies Rail Tract
Dietetic and Hygienic Gazette — Diet Hyg Gaz
Dietetic Currents — Diet Curr
Dietetic Currents — Diet Currents
Dietetic Gazette — Diet Gaz
Dietetique et Collectivites — Diet Collect
Dietetique et Nutrition — Diet et Nutr
Dietetique et Nutrition — Diet Nutr
Dietetique et Sante — Diet Sante
Dietologia e Dietoterapia — Dietol Dietoter
Dietskaia Meditsina — Dietsk Med
Dieu Vivant [*Paris*] — DV
Difesa Ambientale — Dif Ambientale
Difesa Sociale — Dif Soc
Difesa Sociale — DISOAJ
Difesa Sociale — DS
Differencial'nye Uravnenija i Vycislitelnaja Matematika — Differencial'nye Uravnenija i Vycisl Mat
Differential Equations — DIEQA
Differential Equations — Differ Equations
Differentiation — DFFNAW
Differentiation — Differentia
Differentsial'nye Uravneniya — Differ Uravn
Differentsial'nye Uravneniya i Ikh Primenenie — Differ Uravn Primen
Diffusion and Defect Data [*Switzerland*] — Diffus Defect Data
Diffusion and Defect Data. Solid State Data. Part A. Defect and Diffusion Forum — Diffus Defect Data Pt A
Diffusion and Defect Data. Solid State Data. Part B. Solid State Phenomena — Diffus Defect Data Pt B
Diffusion and Defect Monograph Series — Diffus Defect Monogr Ser
Diffusion Data [*Later, Diffusion and Defect Data*] — DIFDA
Diffusion Data [*Later, Diffusion and Defect Data*] — Diffus Data
Diffuzionnaya Svarka v Vakuume Metallov. Splavov i Nemetallicheskikh Materialov [*Former USSR*] — Diffuz Svarka Vak Met Splavov Nemet Mater
Diffuzionnoe Nasyshchenie i Pokrytiya na Metallakh — Diffuz Nasyshchenie Pokrytiya Met
Diffuzionnoe Soedinenie v Vakuume Metallov. Splavov i Nemetallicheskikh Materialov — Diffuz Soedin Vak Met Splavov Nemet Mater
Diffuziya v Metallakh i Splavakh. Trudy Vsesoyuznoi Konferentsii — Diffuz Met Splavakh Tr Vses Konf
Difusion Economica — Difusion Econ
Digest des Ostens — D d O
Digest. International Conference on Medical and Biological Engineering [*Sweden*] — Dig Int Conf Med Biol Eng
Digest of Agricultural Economics — Dig Agric Econ
Digest of Chiropractic Economics — Dig Chiro Econ
Digest of Decisions of the National Labor Relations Board — DLRB
Digest of Dental Science — DDS
Digest of Environmental Impact Statements — EIS
Digest of Japanese Industry and Technology — DJT
Digest of Literature on Dielectrics — Dig Lit Dielec
Digest of Literature on Dielectrics — Dig Lit Dielect
Digest of Modern Teaching — Digest Mod Teach
Digest of Neurology and Psychiatry — Dig Neurol Psychiat
Digest of Neurology and Psychiatry — Dig Neurol Psychiatry
Digest of Ophthalmology and Otolaryngology — Dig Ophthal Otolaryng
Digest of Papers. IEEE Computer Society International Conference — Dig Pap IEEE Comput Soc Int Conf

Digest of Papers. Semiconductor Test Symposium — Dig Pap Semicond Test Symp
Digest of Public General Bills [*Library of Congress*] — DPGB
Digest of Selected Health and Insurance Plans — DSHIP
Digest of Selected Pension Plans [*Bureau of Labor Statistics*] — DSPP
Digest of Statistics. International Civil Aviation Organization — Dig Stat ICAO
Digest of Technical Papers. IEEE International Solid State Circuits Conference — Dig Tech Pap IEEE Int Solid State Circuits Conf
Digest of Technical Papers. IEEE MTTS International Microwave Symposium — Dig Tech Pap IEEE MTTS Int Microwave Symp
Digest of Technical Papers. International Quantum Electronics Conference — Dig Tech Pap Int Quantum Electron Conf
Digest of Treatment — Dig Treatm
Digest. Proceedings. Annual Conference on Automatic Control — Dig Proc Annu Conf Autom Control
Digeste Social — Digeste Soc
Digestion — DIGEB
Digestion — DIGEBW
Digestion and Absorption (Tokyo) — Dig Absorpt (Tokyo)
Digestion and Metabolism in the Ruminant. Proceedings of the International Symposium on Ruminant Physiology — Dig Metab Ruminant Proc Int Symp
Digestive Diseases — DIDIEW
Digestive Diseases — Dig Dis
Digestive Diseases and Sciences — DDSCD
Digestive Diseases and Sciences — DDSCDJ
Digestive Diseases and Sciences — Dig Dis Sci
Digestive Organ and Immunology — Dig Org Immunol
Digestive Surgery — Dig Surg
Digestive Surgery — DISUD6
Digests. Intermag Conference — Dig Intermag Conf
Digital Bypass Report — Dgt Bypass
Digital Computer Newsletter — Digit Comp Newsl
Digital Design — DDS
Digital Design — Digital Des
Digital Design — Digital Dn
Digital Design. Computer Compatible Directory and Technology Review — Digital DD
Digital Processes — Digit Process
Digital Systems for Industrial Automation — Digital Syst Ind Autom
Digitale Bilddiagnostik — Digitale Bilddiagn
Dikaiomata. Auszuege aus Alexandrinischen Gesetzen und Verordnungen in einem Papyrus des Philologischen Seminars der Universitaet Halle — P Halle
Dikaiomata. Auszuege aus Alexandrinischen Gesetzen und Verordnungen in einem Papyrus des Philologischen Seminars der Universitaet Halle — PHal
Dikorastushchie i Introdutsiruemye Poleznye Rasteniya v Bashkirii — Dikorastushchie Introd Polezn Rast Bashk
Dil ve Tarih-Cografya Fakueltesi Dergisi — DTCFD
Dil ve Tarih-Cografya Fakueltesi Dergisi — Fak Derg
Diliman Review — DilR
Diliman Review — DR
Dilthey-Jahrbuch fuer Philosophie und Geschichte der Geisteswissenschaften — Dilthey Jahrb
DIMACS Series in Discrete Mathematics and Theoretical Computer Science — DIMACS Ser Discrete Math Theoret Comput Sci
Dimension Historica de Chile — DHC
Dimensioni. Revista Abruzzese di Cultura e d'Arte — Dimens
Dimensions Economiques de la Bourgogne — Dim Econ Bourgogne
Dimensions in Health Service — Dimens Health Serv
Dimensions in Health Service — DMNHA
Dimensions in Oncology Nursing — Dimens Oncol Nurs
Dimensions. [*US*] **National Bureau of Standards** — Dimen NBS
Dimensions. [*US*] **National Bureau of Standards** — Dimensions NBS
Dimensions. [*US*] **National Bureau of Standards** — DNBSB
Dimensions of Critical Care Nursing — DCCN
Dimensions of Critical Care Nursing — Dimens Crit Care Nurs
Dimensions. Ontario Metis and Non-Status Indian Association — DIMS
DIN [*Deutsches Institut fuer Normung*] **Mitteilungen** — DIMIA
DIN [*Deutsches Institut fuer Normung*] **Mitteilungen** [*Germany*] — DIN Mitt
DIN [*Deutsches Institut fuer Normung*] **Taschenbuch** [*Germany*] — DIN Taschenb
Dinamika i Prochnost Mashin — Din Prochn Mash
Dinamika i Prochnost Mashin — Din Prochn Mashin
Dinamika Sploshnoj Sredy — Din Sploshn Sredy
Dinamika Sploshnoj Sredy. Institut Gidrodinamiki Sibirskogo Otdeleniya Akademii Nauk SSSR — Dinamika Sploshn Sredy
Dinamika Teplovykh Protsessov. Materialy Respublikanskogo Seminara — Din Tepl Protsessov Mater Resp Semin
Dine Bizaad Nanil' Iih/Navajo Language Review — NLR
Dinglers Polytechnisches Journal — Dinglers Polytech J
Diogenes [*English edition*] — PDIO
Diogenes. International Council for Philosophy and Humanistic Studies — Diog Int
Diogenes. International Council for Philosophy and Humanistic Studies — ICPHS/D
Dioniso — Dion
Dioptric and Optological Review — Diopt Optol Rev
Dioptric Review and British Journal of Physiological Optics — Diopt Rev Br J Physiol Opt
Diorama — DA
Dioskuren. Jahrbuch fuer Geisteswissenschaft — Diosk
Diplomatic History — Dipl Hist
Diplomatic History — PDIP
Diplomattirium Danicum — Dipl Dan
DIPPR (Design Institute for Physical Property Data) Data Series — DIPPR Data Ser
Diquiu Huaxue (English Edition) — Diquiu Huaxue Engl Ed
Dirasat. Journal of the College of Education. University of Riyadh — Dirasat J Coll Educ Univ Riyadh
Dirasat. Medical and Biological Sciences — Dirasat Med Biol Sci
Dirasat. Natural and Engineering Sciences — Dirasat Nat Eng Sci
Dirasat. Natural and Engineering Sciences — Dirasat Nat Engrg Sci
Dirasat/Natural Science [*Amman*] — DSNJDI
Dirasat/Natural Science (Amman) — Dirasat Nat Sci (Amman)
Dirasat/Natural Science. University of Jordan — Dirasat Nat Sci Univ Jordan
Dirasat. Series B. Pure and Applied Sciences — Dirasat Ser B Pure Appl Sci
Dirasat. University of Jordan — Dirasat Univ Jordan
Dirasat. University of Jordan. Series B. Pure and Applied Sciences — Dirasat Univ Jordan Ser B
Direccion de Geologia, Minas y Petroleo (Costa Rica). Informes Tecnicos y Notas Geologias — Dir Geol Minas Pet Costa Rica Inf Tec Notas Geol
Direccion General de Agricultura (Peru). Divulgaciones e Informaciones — Dir Gen Agric (Peru) Divulg Inf
Direccion General de Archivos y Bibliotecas. Boletin — Dir Gen Bol
Direccion General de Geologia y Minas. Revista (Ecuador) — Dir Gen Geol Minas Rev Ecuador
Direccion General del Inventario Nacional Forestal. Publicacion — Dir Gen Invent Nac For Publ
Direccion General del Inventario Nacional Forestal. Publicacion — Dir Gen Inventario Nac For Publ
Direccion General del Inventario Nacional Forestal. Publicacion — MDNPAR
Direccion Nacional de la Propiedad Industrial (Argentina) — Dir Nac Propiedad Ind (Argent)
Direccion Nacional de Quimica. Boletin Informativo (Argentina) — Dir Nac Quim Bol Inf Argent
Direct Action — DA
Direct Advertising [*Later, Printing Paper Quarterly*] — d/a
Direct Current — Direct Curr
Direct Current and Power Electronics — Direct Curr & Power Electron
Direct from Cuba — Dir fr Cu
Direct from Midrex — Direct Midrex
Direct Information. Nuklearmedizin — Direct Inf Nuklearmed
Direct Information. Strahlenschutz — Direct Inf Strahlenschutz
Direct Interactions and Nuclear Reaction Mechanisms. Proceedings. Conference — Dir Interact Nucl React Mech Proc Conf
Direct Marketing — DIM
Direct Marketing — Direct Mark
Direct Marketing — DM
Direct Observation of Imperfections in Crystals. Proceedings. Technical Conference — Direct Obs Imperfections Cryst Proc Tech Conf
Direction — Direc
Direction Commerciale Francaise — DCF
Direction des Etudes et Recherches d'Electricite de France. Collection — Dir Etud Rech Electr Fr Collect
Direction des Etudes et Recherches. Electricite de France. Bulletin. Serie B. Reseaux Electriques, Materiels Electriques — Dir Etud Rech Electr Fr Bull Ser B
Direction et Gestion — Dir Gestion
Direction et Gestion des Entreprises — Dir et Gestion
Direction et Gestion des Entreprises — Dir Gestion Entr
Direction Line — DLine
Direction of Trade Statistics [*Database*] — DOTS
Directions in Applied Nutrition — Dir Appl Nutr
Directions in Chaos — Dir Chaos
Directions in Condensed Matter Physics — Dir Condensed Matter Phys
Directions in Government — Dir Gov
Directions in Health, Physical Education, and Recreation. Monograph Series — DIRH
Director — D
Director — DIR
Director [*United Kingdom*] — DRT
Director — DRTRD
Director. Journal of Business Leadership — DRB
Directorate of Ancient Monuments and Historic Buildings. Occasional Papers [*England*] — Dir Ancient Monum Hist Bldgs Occas Pap
Directors and Boards — DBO
Directors and Boards — Dir Boards
Directors and Boards — Direct Brd
Directors and Boards — Directors and Bds
Director's Annual Report. United Dental Hospital of Sydney. Institute of Dental Research — Dir Annu Rep United Dent Hosp Sydney Inst Dent Res
Directors Law Reporter — Dir LR
Directors Law Reporter — DLR
Directory. Indiana Crop Improvement Association. Seed Certification Service — Dir Indiana Crop Impr Ass Seed Certif Serv
Directory of American Research and Technology [*Database*] — DART
Directory of Australian Academic Libraries — DAAL
Directory of Australian Manufactured Scientific Equipment and Laboratoryware — DAMSEL
Directory of Australian Tertiary Education — DATE
Directory of Automated Library and Information Systems in Australia — DALIS
Directory of Biotechnology Information Resources [*Database*] — DBIR
Directory of Education Research and Research in Australia [*Database*] — DERA
Directory of Educational Journal and Newsletters — EJN
Directory of Genealogical Periodicals — Dir Geneal Per
Directory of High Technology Corporations. Supplement — Dir High Tech Corp Suppl
Directory of Online Databases [*United States*] — Dir Online Databases
Directory of Periodicals Online — DPO
Directory of Published Proceedings [*United States*] — Dir Publ Proc

Directory of Published Proceedings [*United States*] — DPPSA
Directory of Published Proceedings. Series SEMT. Science, Engineering, Medicine, and Technology — Dir Publ Proc SEMT
Directory of Research Grants — DRG
Directory of Texas Manufacturers [*Database*] — DTM
Directory of United Nations Databases and Information Systems [*Database*] — DUNDIS
Directory of Unpublished Experimental Mental Measures — Dir Unpubl Exp Ment Meas
Directory of Unpublished Experimental Mental Measures — DUEMEV
Directory of Visual Arts Organizations [*Database*] — DVA
Direito Nuclear — Direito Nucl
Direktorat Geologi. Publikasi Teknik. Seri Geologi Ekonomi (Indonesia) — Dir Geol Publ Tek Seri Geol Ekon Indones
Diritti d'Autore — Dir Aut
Diritto Automobilistico — Dir Aut
Diritto Cinematografico — Dir Cinem
Diritto Criminale e Criminologia — Dir Crim
Diritto del Lavoro — Diritto Lav
Diritto e Giurisprudenza — Dir e Giur
Diritto e Pratica dell'Assicurazione — Dir Prat Ass
Diritto e Pratica Tributaria — Dir e Prat Trib
Diritto e Pratica Tributaria — Dir Prat Trib
Diritto Ecclesiastico — DE
Diritto Ecclesiastico — Dir Eccl
Diritto ed Economia Nucleare — Dir Ec Nucl
Diritto Internazionale. Rivista Trimestrale di Dottrina e Documentazione — Dir Int
Diritto Marittimo — Dir Maritt
Diritto Pubblico della Regione Siciliana — Dir Pubbl Reg Sicil
Diritto Sanitario Moderno — Dir San Mod
Diritto Scolastico — Dir Scol
DISA [*Danske Industri Syndikat A/S*] **Information** — DISA Inf
Disability and Rehabilitation — Disabil Rehabil
Disarmament — Disarm
Disarmament and Arms Control — Disarm & Arms Control
Disaster Management — Disaster Manage
Disaster Prevention Research Institute. Annual [*Japan*] — Disaster Prev Res Inst Annu
Disaster Prevention Research Institute. Kyoto University. Bulletin — Disaster Prev Res Inst Kyoto Univ Bull
Discharge Planning Update — Disch Plann Update
Discharges and Electrical Insulation in Vacuum. Proceedings. International Symposium on Discharges and Electrical Insulation in Vacuum — Discharges Electr Insul Vac Proc Int Symp
Discipleship Journal — DJ
Disciplinary Law and Procedure Advance Sheets — Disc L and Proc Adv Sheets
Discipline and Grievances — DIGRD
Discipline and Grievances — Discip Grievances
Discographical Forum — Disco Forum
Discoteca alta Fedalta I — Discoteca
Discount Merchandiser — Discount M
Discount Merchandiser — DMS
Discourse Processes — DIPRDG
Discourse Processes — DP
Discourse Processes — DPr
Discover — GDIS
Discover the New World of Instrumentation. Proceedings. Joint Symposium — Discover New World Instrum Proc Jt Symp
Discoveries in Pharmacology — Discoveries Pharmacol
Discoveries in the Judaean Desert — Dis Jud Des
Discoveries in the Judaean Desert — DJD
Discovery [*London*] — D
Discovery — Disc
Discovery [*England*] — DISCA
Discovery [*New Haven*] — DISCAH
Discovery [*London*] — DISCBI
Discovery — Discov
Discovery — GDIY
Discovery and Excavation (Scotland) — Disc Excav (Scot)
Discovery and Excavation (Scotland) — Discovery Excav (Scot)
Discovery Reports — Discov Rep
Discovery Reports — Discovery Rep
Discrete and Computational Geometry — Discrete Comput Geom
Discrete and Continuous Dynamical Systems — Discrete Contin Dynam Systems
Discrete Applied Mathematics — Discrete Appl Math
Discrete Geometry and Convexity — Discrete Geom Convexity
Discrete Mathematics — Discr Math
Discrete Mathematics — Discrete Math
Discrete Mathematics — DSMHA
Discrete Mathematics and Applications — Discrete Math Appl
Discrete Mathematics and Theoretical Computer Science — Discrete Math Theoret Comput Sci
Discurs. Reial Academia de Farmacia de Barcelona — Discurs Reial Acad Farm Barcelona
Discussion Held at the Annual Conference. Steel Castings Research and Trade Association. Steel Foundry Practice — Discuss Annu Conf Steel Cast Res Trade Assoc
Discussion sur l'Alphabetisation — Discuss Alphabet
Discussiones Mathematicae — Discuss Math
Discussiones Mathematicae. Algebra and Stochastic Methods — Discuss Math Algebra Stochastic Methods
Discussiones Mathematicae. Differential Inclusions — Discuss Math Differential Incl
Discussiones Mathematicae. Graph Theory — Discuss Math Graph Theory
Discussions. Faraday Society — Disc Far Soc
Discussions. Faraday Society — Discn Faraday Soc
Discussions. Faraday Society — Discuss Farad Soc
Discussions. Faraday Society — Discuss Faraday Soc
Disease Markers — Dis Marker
Disease Markers — Dis Markers
Disease-a-Month — Dis Mon
Diseases of Aquatic Organisms — DAOREO
Diseases of Aquatic Organisms — Dis Aquat Org
Diseases of the Chest — DICHA
Diseases of the Chest — DICHAK
Diseases of the Chest — Dis Chest
Diseases of the Colon and Rectum — DICRA
Diseases of the Colon and Rectum — DICRAG
Diseases of the Colon and Rectum — Dis Col Rec
Diseases of the Colon and Rectum — Dis Colon Rectum
Diseases of the Esophagus — Dis Esophagus
Diseases of the Liver [*Monograph*] — Dis Liver
Diseases of the Nervous System — Dis Ner Sys
Diseases of the Nervous System — Dis Nerv Syst
Diseases of the Nervous System — Dis Nerv System
Diseases of the Nervous System — DNSYA
Diseases of the Nervous System — DNSYAG
Dishekimligi Alemi — Dishek Alemi
Dishekimligi Dergisi — Dishekim Derg
Diskretnaya Matematika — Diskret Mat
Diskretnyi Analiz i Issledovanie Operatsii — Diskret Anal Issled Oper
Diskretnyi Analiz. Sbornik Trudov — Diskret Analiz
Diskussion Deutsch — DD
Diskussionsforum Medizinische Ethik — Diskussionsforum Med Ethik
Diskussionstagung - Forschungskreis der Ernaehrungsindustrie e. V — Diskussionstag Forschungskreis Ernaehrungsind
Dislocation Modelling of Physical Systems. Proceedings. International Conference — Dislocat Modell Phys Syst Proc Int Conf
Dislocations and Mechanical Properties of Crystals. International Conference — Dislocat Mech Prop Cryst Int Conf
Dislocations in Solids [*Elsevier Book Series*] — DIS
Dislocations in Solids. Proceedings. Yamada Conference — Dislocat Solids Proc Yamada Conf
Disodium Cromoglycate in Allergic Airways Disease. Proceedings. Symposium — Disodium Cromoglycate Allerg Airways Dis Proc Symp
Disorder and Fracture — Disord Fract
Disordered Semiconductors [*Monograph*] — Disord Semicond
Disorders of Eating and Nutrients in Treatment of Brain Diseases — Disord Eat Nutr Treat Brain Dis
Disorders of Sexual Differentiation. Etiology and Clinical Delineation [*monograph*] — Disord Sex Differ Etiol Clin Delin
Disorders of the Motor Unit. Proceedings. International Meeting — Disord Mot Unit Proc Int Meet
Disorders of the Respiratory System — Disord Respir Syst
Disorders of Thrombin Formation — Disord Thrombin Form
DISP. Dokumentations- und Informationsstelle fuer Planungsfragen — DISP
Dispergirovanie Zhidkostei v Emul'giruyushchikh Apparatakh Sel'skokhozyaistvennogo Proizvodstva — Dispergirovanie Zhidk Emulgiruyushchikh Appar Skh Proizvod
Dispergirovannye Metallicheskie Plenki — Dispergirovannye Met Plenki
Dispersnye Sistemy i Ikh Povedenie v Elektricheskikh i Magnitnykh Polyakh — Dispersnye Sist Ikh Povedenie Elektr Magn Polyakh
Dispersnye Sistemy v Burenii — Dispersnye Sist Buren
Dispersnye Sistemy v Energokhimicheskikh Protsessakh — Dispersnye Sist Energokhim Protsessakh
Display System Optics — Disp Syst Opt
Displays. Technology and Applications — Disp Technol and Appl
Disposables International and Nonwoven Fabric Review — Dispos Intern
Disposal and Decontamination of Pesticides. Symposium — Disposal Decontam Pestic Symp
Disposal of Radioactive Waste. Proceedings. Information Meeting — Disposal Radioact Waste Proc Inf Meet
Disposal of Radioactive Wastes into Seas, Oceans, and Surface Waters. Proceedings. Symposium — Disposal Radioact Wastes Seas Oceans Surf Waters Proc Symp
Disposal of Radioactive Wastes into the Ground. Proceedings. Symposium — Disposal Radioact Wastes Ground Proc Symp
Disposal of Radioactive Wastes. Proceedings. Scientific Conference — Disposal Radioact Wastes Proc Sci Conf
Dispositivo — DO
Disquisitiones Mathematicae Hungaricae — Disquis Math Hungar
Disraeli Newsletter — DN
Dissent — Dis
Dissent — GDSS
Dissertation Abstracts [*Later, Dissertation Abstracts International*] — DA
Dissertation Abstracts [*Later, Dissertation Abstracts International*] — DAb
Dissertation Abstracts [*Later, Dissertation Abstracts International*] — Dis Abst
Dissertation Abstracts [*Later, Dissertation Abstracts International*] — DisA
Dissertation Abstracts [*Later, Dissertation Abstracts International*] — Diss Abs
Dissertation Abstracts [*Later, Dissertation Abstracts International*] — Diss Abstr
Dissertation Abstracts. A. Humanities and Social Sciences — Diss Abstr A
Dissertation Abstracts. B. Sciences and Engineering — Diss Abstr B
Dissertation Abstracts. B. Sciences and Engineering — Diss Abstr B Sci Eng
Dissertation Abstracts International — DAI
Dissertation Abstracts International — Diss Abstr Int
Dissertation Abstracts International — Dissert Abs Internat
Dissertation Abstracts International — Dissert Abstr Int
Dissertation Abstracts International. C. European Abstracts — Diss Abstr Int C
Dissertation Abstracts International. Retrospective Index — DAIRI

Dissertation Abstracts International. Section A — DABAA
Dissertation Abstracts International. Section B. Sciences and Engineering — DABBB
Dissertation Abstracts International. Section B. Sciences and Engineering — DABSAQ
Dissertation Abstracts International. Section B. Sciences and Engineering — Diss Abstr Int B
Dissertation Abstracts International. Section B. Sciences and Engineering — Diss Abstr Int B Sci Eng
Dissertation Abstracts International. Section B. Sciences and Engineering — Diss Abstr Int Sec B
Dissertation Abstracts International. Section B. Sciences and Engineering — Diss Abstr Int Sect B
Dissertation Abstracts International. Section C. European Dissertations — Diss Abstr Int Sect C
Dissertation. Chalmers Tekniska Hoegskola — Diss Chalmers Tek Hoegsk
Dissertation. Hohenheim Landwirtschaftliche Hochschule — Diss Hohenheim Landwirt Hochsch
Dissertationen der Johannes Kepler. Universitaet Linz — Diss Johannes Kepler Univ Linz
Dissertationen der Technischen Universitaet Wien — Diss Techn Univ Wien
Dissertationen der Universitaet (Wien) — DissUW
Dissertationen der Wirtschaftsuniversitaet Wien — Diss Wirtschaftsuniv Wien
Dissertationes Archaeologicae — Diss Arch
Dissertationes Archaeologicae Gandenses — Diss Arch Gand
Dissertationes Botanicae — DIBOD5
Dissertationes Botanicae — Diss Bot
Dissertationes Inaugurales — DI
Dissertationes Mathematicae (Rozprawy Matematyczny) — Dissertationes Math (Rozprawy Mat)
Dissertationes Pannonicae — Diss Pan
Dissertationes Pannonicae — Diss Pannon
Dissertationes Pharmaceuticae — Diss Pharm
Dissertationes Pharmaceuticae et Pharmacologicae — Diss Pharm Pharmacol
Dissertationes Pharmaceuticae et Pharmacologicae — DPHFA
Dissertations International — DI
Dissertazioni. Pontificia Accademia Roman di Archeologia — DPAA
Dissonances. Revue Musicale Independante — D
Distance Education — Distance Educ
Distant Drummer — Dist Drum
Distillate Fuel Stability and Cleanliness. Symposium — Distill Fuel Stab Cleanliness Symp
Distillation. International Symposium — Distill Int Symp
Distillers Feed Research Council. Conference Proceedings — Distill Feed Res Counc Conf Proc
Distinguished Dissertations in Computer Science — Disting Diss Comput Sci
Distinguished Lecture Series. Society of the General Physiologists — Distinguished Lect Ser Soc Gen Physiol
Distinguished Lecture Series. Society of the General Physiologists — DLSPDC
Distributed Computing — Distrib Comput
Distributed Processing Newsletter — Dist Proc
Distributie Vandaag. Maandblad over Verkooppromotie en Moderne Handelstechniek — DBF
Distribution — Distr
Distribution — Distrbutn
Distribution — DTB
Distribution Age — Distrib Age
Distribution Management — Distr Man
Distribution Manager — Distrib Mgr
Distribution of Electricity — Distrib El
Distribution of Water. Proceedings. European Regional Conference — Distrib Water Proc Eur Reg Conf
Distribution Worldwide — Distr Worldwide
Distribution Worldwide — Distrib Worldwide
Distributive Worker — Distributive Wkr
District Council Review — Dist Council Rev
District Court Reports — DCR
District Court Reports (New South Wales) — DCR (NSW)
District Heating — DIHEA
District Heating — Dist Heat
District Heating — Distr Heat
District Heating Association. Journal — Distr Heat Ass J
District Heating for New Zealand. Proceedings. Seminar — Dist Heat NZ Proc Semin
District Heating International — Dist Heat Int
District Lawyer — District Law
District Lawyer (District of Columbia) — District Law (DC)
District Memoir. Geological Survey of Botswana — Dist Mem Geol Surv Botswana
District Memoir. Geological Survey of Malaysia — Dist Mem Geol Surv Malays
District Memoir. Geological Survey of Malaysia — Dist Mem Geol Surv Malaysia
District Nursing — Dist Nurs
District of Columbia Code. Annotated — DC Code Ann
District of Columbia Libraries — DC Lib
District of Columbia Nursing Action — DC Nurs Action
District of Columbia Register — DC Reg
District of Columbia Statutes at Large — DC Stat
Distrifood. Weekblad voor de Betaillist en Groothandel in Food en Nonfood — DIS
Distrito de Braga — DdB
Distrito de Braga — Dist Braga
Distrubuzione Moderna — Distr Mod
Disturbances in Neurogenic Control of the Circulation — Disturbances Neurog Control Circ
Disturbances of Water and Electrolyte Metabolism. Symposium on Nephrology — Disturbances Water Electrolyte Metab Symp Nephrol
Ditchley Journal — Ditchley J
Diureseforschung. Fortschritte auf dem Gebiete der Inneren Medizin. Symposion — Diureseforsch Fortschr Geb Inn Med Symp
Diuretics. Chemistry, Pharmacology, and Clinical Applications. Proceedings. International Conference on Diuretics — Diuretics Chem Pharmacol Clin Appl Proc Int Conf Diuretics
Divan — Div
Diverse. Office National d'Etudes et de Recherches Aeronautiques (France) — Diverse Off Natl Etud Rech Aeronaut Fr
Diversity of Environmental Biogeochemistry — Diversity Environ Biogeochem
Divice — DIVID
Divinitas — Div
Divisao de Pesquisa Pedologica. Boletim Tecnico (Brazil) — Div Pesqui Pedol Bol Tec (Braz)
Division for Nutrition and Food Research TNO. Report — Div Nutr Food Res TNO Rep
Division of Applied Chemistry Technical Paper (Australia. Commonwealth Scientific and Industrial Research Organization) — Div Appl Chem Tech Pap Aust CSIRO
Division of Applied Organic Chemistry Technical Paper (Australia. Commonwealth Scientific and Industrial Research Organization) — Div Appl Org Chem Tech Pap Aust CSIRO
Division of Building Research Technical Paper (Australia. Commonwealth Scientific and Industrial Research Organization) — Div Build Res Tech Pap Aust CSIRO
Division of Building Research Technological Paper. Forest Products Laboratory. Commonwealth Scientific and Industrial Research Organization. Australia — Div Build Res Technol Pap For Prod Lab CSIRO Aust
Division of Chemical Technology Technical Paper (Australia. Commonwealth Scientific and Industrial Research Organization) — Div Chem Technol Tech Pap (Aust CSIRO)
Division of Electronic Products *[Series]* — DEP
Division of Entomology Technical Paper (Australia. Commonwealth Scientific and Industrial Research Organization) — Div Entomol Tech Pap Aust CSIRO
Division of Fisheries and Oceanography. Technical Paper. Australia Commonwealth Scientific and Industrial Research Organisation — Div Fish Oceanogr Tech Pap Aust CSIRO
Division of Food Preservation Technical Paper (Australia. Commonwealth Scientific and Industrial Research Organization) — Div Food Preserv Tech Pap Aust CSIRO
Division of Food Research Technical Paper (Australia. Commonwealth Scientific and Industrial Research Organization) — Div Food Res Tech Pap (Aust CSIRO)
Division of Forest Products Technological Paper (Australia. Commonwealth Scientific and Industrial Research Organization) — Div For Prod Technol Pap Aust CSIRO
Division of Land Research and Regional Survey Technical Paper (Australia. Commonwealth Scientific and Industrial Research Organization) — Div Land Res Reg Surv Tech Pap Aust CSIRO
Division of Land Resources Management Technical Paper (Australia. Commonwealth Scientific and Industrial Research Organization) — Div Land Resour Manage Tech Pap (Aust CSIRO)
Division of Land Use Research. Technical Paper. Australia Commonwealth Scientific and Industrial Research Organisation — Div Land Use Res Tech Pap Aust CSIRO
Division of Meteorological Physics Technical Paper (Australia. Commonwealth Scientific and Industrial Research Organization) — Div Meteorol Phys Tech Pap Aust CSIRO
Division of Plant Industry Technical Paper (Australia. Commonwealth Scientific and Industrial Research Organization) — Div Plant Ind Tech Pap Aust CSIRO
Division of Soil Research Technical Paper (Australia. Commonwealth Scientific and Industrial Organization) — Div Soil Res Tech Pap Aust CSIRO
Division of Soils Divisional Report (Australia. Commonwealth Scientific and Industrial Research Organization) — Div Soils Div Rep (Aust CSIRO)
Division of Tropical Agronomy. Technical Paper. Commonwealth Scientific and Industrial Research Organisation (Australia) — Div Trop Agron Tech Pap CSIRO (Aust)
Division of Tropical Crops and Pastures. Technical Paper. Commonwealth Scientific and Industrial Research Organisation (Australia) — Div Trop Crops Pastures Tech Pap CSIRO (Aust)
Divisional Report. Division of Soils. Commonwealth Scientific and Industrial Research Organisation — Div Rep Div Soils CSIRO
Divisional Reports. Department of Agriculture. British Guiana — Divl Rep Dep Agric Br Guiana
Divisional Technical Conference. Society of Plastics Engineers. Technical Papers — Div Tech Conf Soc Plast Eng Tech Pap
Divisions — DIV
Divorce. Actes du Congres International — Divorce Actes Congr Int
DIVTEC. Technical Papers (Society of Plastics Engineers. Engineering Properties and Structures Division) — DIVTEC Tech Pap Soc Plast Eng Eng Prop Struct Div
Divulgacion Cultural Odontologica — Divulg Cult Odontol
Divulgacion Historica (Mexico) — Divul Hist Mex
Divulgacion Pesquera *[Bogota]* — DPCPDS
Divulgacion Pesquera (Bogota) — Divulg Pesq (Bogota)
Divulgacion Pesquera. Direccion General de Pesca (Bogota) — Divulg Pesq Dir Gen Pesca (Bogota)
Divulgaciones Agricolas (Lima) — Divul Agri Lima
Divulgaciones Etnologicas (Barranquilla, Colombia) — Divul Etnol Barranquilla
Divulgaciones Matematicas — Divulg Mat
Divus Thomas — DT

Divus Thomas — DTh
Dix-Huitieme Siecle — DHS
Dix-Huitieme Siecle — Dix-Huit Siecle
Dixie Business — Dixie Bus
Dix-Septieme Siecle — Dix-Sept S
Dizionario Epigrafico di Antichita Romane — DEAR
Dizionario Epigrafico di Antichita Romane — Diz Epigr
Dizionario Etimologico Italiano — DEI
Dizionario Veterinario — Dizion Vet
Djela Jugoslavenske Akademije Znanosti i Umjetnosti. Opera Academiae Scientiarum et Artium Slavorum Meridionalium — Djela Jugoslav Akad Znan
DK Mitteilungen — DK Mitt
DKV [*Deutscher Kaelte- und Klimatechnischer Verein*] **Tagungsbericht** — DKV Tagungsber
DL [*Dominion Laboratory*] **Report** — DL Rep
DLG. Mitteilungen. Deutsch Landwirtschafts Gesellschaft — DLG Mit Dtsch Landwirtsch Ges
DLR-Mitteilungen — DLR Mitt
DLZ. Deutsche Landtechnische Zeitschrift — DLZ Deut Landtech Z
DLZ. Die Landtechnische Zeitschrift — DLTZA
DLZ. Die Landtechnische Zeitschrift — DLZ Die Landtech Z
DM/Disease-a-Month — DIMOA
DM/Disease-a-Month — DM
DM/Disease-a-Month — DM Dis Mon
DMB. Danish Medical Bulletin — DMB Dan Med Bull
DMB. Danish Medical Bulletin. Supplement — DMB Dan Med Bull Suppl
DMG-DRS [*Design Methods Group - Design Research*] **Journal** — DMG-DRS J
DMP. Durvoobrabotvashta i Mebelna Promishlenost — DMP Durvoobrab Mebelna Promst
DMW. Deutsche Medizinische Wochenschrift — DMW Dtsch Med Wochenschr
DMZ. Deutsche Molkerei-Zeitung — DMZ Dtsch Molk Ztg
DMZ (Deutsche Molkerei-Zeitung) Lebensmittelindustrie und Milchwirtschaft — DMZ Lebensmittelind Milchwirtsch
DNA [*Deoxyribonucleic Acid*] **and Cell Biology** — DNA Cell Biol
DNA Repair and Its Inhibition — DNA Repair Its Inhib
DNA Research — DNA Res
DNA Sequence — DNA Seq
DNA Synthesis in Vitro. Proceedings. Annual Harry Steenbock Symposium — DNA Synth in Vitro Proc Annu Harry Steenbock Symp
DnC Monthly Survey of Norwegian Trade, Industry, and Finance — DCO
Dnevnik Vserossijskogo S'ezda Russkih Botanikov — Dnevn Vserossijsk Sezda Russk Bot
DNR [*Department of Natural Resources*] **Notes. Washington (State) Department of Natural Resources** — DNR Notes Wash State Dep Nat Resour
Doane's Agricultural Report — Doanes Agr Rep
Doane's Business Magazine for American Agriculture — Doanes Bus Mag Amer Agr
Doboku Gakkai Ronbun Hokokushu — DGRHA
Dobutsugaku Zasshi [*Toyko*] — Dobuts Zasshi
Dobycha i Obogashchenie Rud Tsvetnykh Metallov — Dobycha Obogashch Rud Tsvetn Met
Dobycha i Pererabotka Goryuchikh Slantsev [*Former USSR*] — Dobycha Pererab Goryuch Slantsev
Dobycha i Pererabotka Nerudnykh Stroitel'nykh Materialov — Dobycha Pererab Nerudn Stroit Mater
Dock and Harbour Authority — DHBAA
Dock and Harbour Authority [*London*] — Dock & Harbour
Dock and Harbour Authority — Dock Harb Auth
Dock and Harbour Authority [*London*] — DOH
Dock of the Bay — Dk of Bay
Doctor Communis [*Rome*] — Doct Comm
Doctor Communis [*Rome*] — DoctCom
Doctoral Dissertations Accepted by American Universities — Doct Diss Amer Univ
Doctorate Records File [*Database*] — DRF
Doctrine and Life — DL
Doctrine and Life [*Dublin*] — DoctrLife
Document. Centre National de Recherches Forestieres — Docum Centre Nat Rech For
Document. Combustion Engineering Association [*England*] — Doc Combust Eng Assoc
Document de Seance. Rapport Parlementaire au Parlement Europeen — Doc Seance
Document de Travail [*Besancon*] — Doc Travail
Document. Illinois Department of Energy and Natural Resources — Doc Ill Dep Energy Nat Resour
Document. Illinois Institute for Environmental Quality — Doc Ill Inst Environ Qual
Document. Institute of Natural Resources (Illinois) — Doc Inst Nat Resour (Ill)
Document Management — Doc Man
Document PB. National Technical Information Service — PB
Document. Swedish Council for Building Research — Doc Swed Counc Build Res
Document Technique de la SCPA (Societe Commerciale des Potasses et de l'Azote) — Doc Tech SCPA (Soc Commer Potasses Azote)
Documenta Albana — Doc Alb
Documenta Chemica Yugoslavica — Doc Chem Yugosl
Documenta de Medicina Geographica et Tropica — Doc Med Geogr Trop
Documenta de Medicina Geographica et Tropica — Docum Med Geogr Trop
Documenta et Monumenta Orientis Antiqui — DMOA
Documenta Haematologica (Bucharest) — Doc Haematol (Bucharest)
Documenta Mathematica — Doc Math
Documenta Neerlandica et Indonesica de Morbis Tropicis — Doc Neerl Indones Morb Trop
Documenta Neerlandica et Indonesica de Morbis Tropicis — Docum Ned Indo Morbis Trop
Documenta Ophthalmologica — Doc Ophthal
Documenta Ophthalmologica — Doc Ophthalmol
Documenta Ophthalmologica — Docum Ophthal
Documenta Ophthalmologica — DOOPA
Documenta Ophthalmologica. Proceedings Series — Doc Ophthalmol Proc Ser
Documenta Physiographica Poloniae — Doc Physiogr Pol
Documenta Rheumatologica — Doc Rheum
Documenta Veterinaria — Doc Vet
Documenta Veterinaria (Brno) — Doc Vet Brno
Documenta Veterinaria (Brno) — DOVEB
Documentacion Administrativa — Docum Adm
Documentacion Administrativa — Docum Admin
Documentacion Bibliotecologica — Doc Bibl
Documentacion Critica Iberoamericana (Sevilla) — Doc Crit Iberoam Sevilla
Documentacion Economica [*Madrid*] — Docum Econ
Documentacion Economica Colombiana — Docum Econ Colombiana
Documentacion Juridica — Docum Jur
Documentary Relations of the South West [*Database*] — DRSW
Documentatie en Informatie over Toerisme — DIB
Documentatieblad. Nieuwe Reeks — DTD
Documentatieblad van het Centraal Orgaan van de Landelijke Opleidingsorganen van het Bedrijfsleven — CTI
Documentatieblad voor Onderwijs en Wetenschappen — VBV
Documentatieblad Werkgroep 18E-eeuw — Documentatiebl Werkgr 18E-eeuw
Documentatiecentrum voor Overheidspersoneel. Literatuuroverzicht — LDO
Documentatio Geographica — Doc Geogr
Documentation Abstracts — DA
Documentation Abstracts — Doc Abstr
Documentation Abstracts and Information Science Abstracts — Doc Abstr Inf Sci Abstr
Documentation Bulletin. National Research Centre (Egypt) — Doc Bull Natl Res Cent (Egypt)
Documentation Bulletin. National Research Centre (United Arab Republic) — Doc Bull Nat Res Cent (UAR)
Documentation Catholique — DC
Documentation Catholique — Doc Cath
Documentation Catholique [*Paris*] — DocC
Documentation Catholique — Docum Cath
Documentation du Biologiste Practicien — Doc Biol Pract
Documentation du Bureau Geologique (Malagasy) — Doc Bur Geol Malagasy
Documentation Economique — Doc Econ
Documentation Economique (Paris) — Docum Econ (Paris)
Documentation et Bibliotheques — Doc et Bibl
Documentation et Bibliotheques — Docum et Biblio
Documentation et Information Pedagogiques — Docum Inform Pedag
Documentation Etc. — Documen
Documentation. Europaeisches Abwasser- und Abfallsymposium — Doc Eur Abwasser Abfallsymp
Documentation. Europaeisches Abwasser- und Abfall-Symposium EAS — Doc Eur Abwasser Abfall Symp EAS
Documentation. European Sewage and Refuse Symposium EAS — Doc Eur Sewage Refuse Symp EAS
Documentation Europeenne — Docum Europ
Documentation Europeenne. Serie Syndicale et Ouvriere — Docum Eur Ser Syndicale et Ouvriere
Documentation Francaise Illustree — Docum Franc Illustr
Documentation in Public Administration — Doc Public Adm
Documentation Legislative Africaine — Docum Legis Afr
Documentation Medicale. Comite International de la Croix-Rouge — Doc Med
Documentation sur l'Europe Centrale — Docum Europe Centr
Documentation sur l'Europe Centrale — DOG
Documentazione sui Paesi de l'Est — Docum Paesi Est
Documente Privind Isotria Romaniei — DIR
Documente Privind Isotria Romaniei — Doc Rom
Documenti Antichi dell'Africa Italiana — DAI
Documenti Antichi dell'Africa Italiana — Doc Ant dell Afr Ital
Documenti Cooperativi — Doc Coop
Documenti di Vita Italiana — Doc Vita It
Documenti Diplomatici Italiani — DDI
Documentos de Investigacion Hidrologica — Doc Invest Hidrol
Documentos Politicos — Doc Polit
Documentos Tecnicos de Hidrologia — Doc Tec Hidrol
Documents. American Catholic Historical Association — ACHAD
Documents Artistiques du XV Siecle — Doc Art du XV S
Documents. Centre de Recherche d'Anthropologie. Musee de l'Homme — Docums Cent Rech Anthrop Mus Homme
Documents. Centre d'Etude des Revenus et des Couts — Doc Centre Et Revenus Couts
Documents. Centre d'Etudes Geologiques et Minieres — Documents CEGM
Documents CEPESS [*Centre d'Etudes Politiques, Economiques, et Sociales*] — Doc CEPESS
Documents. CEPESS [*Centre d'Etudes Politiques, Economiques, et Sociales*] — Docs CEPESS
Documents d'Archeologie Meridionale — Doc A Merid
Documents de Cartographie Ecologique — Doc Cartogr Ecol
Documents de Fouilles. Institut Francais d'Archeologie Orientale du Caire [*Cairo*] — DFIFAO
Documents des Laboratoires de Geologie de la Faculte des Sciences de Lyon — Doc Lab Geol Fac Sci Lyon
Documents d'Etudes. Droit Constitutionnel et Institutions Politiques — Doc d'Et Droit Const
Documents d'Etudes. Droit International Public — Doc d'Et Droit Internat Publ
Documents d'Histoire — DH

Documents d'Information et de Gestion — Doc Inform Gestion
Documents du BRGM [*Bureau de Recherches Geologiques et Minieres*] [*France*] — Doc BRGM
Documents et Rapports. Societe Paleontologique et Archeologique de l'Arrondissement Judiciaire de Charleroi — Doc Charleroi
Documents et Rapports. Societe Paleontologique et Archeologique de l'Arrondissement Judiciaire de Charleroi — DR Charl
Documents et Rapports. Societe Paleontologique et Archeologique de l'Arrondissement Judiciaire de Charleroi — DRSPAAJC
Documents Illustrating the Reigns of Augustus and Tiberius — DIRAT
Documents Illustrating the Reigns of Augustus and Tiberius — Docs Aug Tib
Documents in Mycenaean Greek — DMG
Documents in the History of Canadian Art — Doc Hist Can Art
Documents. Institut Scientifique [*Rabat*] — DISMDG
Documents. Institut Scientifique (Rabat) — Doc Inst Sci (Rabat)
Documents of Ukrainian Samvydav — Doc Ukr Sam
Documents on American Foreign Relations — DAFR
Documents on Biology — Doc Biol
Documents on International Affairs [*London*] — DIA
Documents Pedozoologiques — Doc Pedozool
Documents Phytosociologiques — Doc Phytosociol
Documents Phytosociologiques — DOPHDS
Documents Relatifs a l'Histoire des Croisades — DHC
Documents Scientifiques du XVe Siecle [*Geneva*] — Doc Sci XVe Siecle
Documents Techniques. Charbonnages de France — Doc Tech Charbon Fr
Documents Techniques. Charbonnages de France — DTCFA
Documents Techniques. Institut National de la Recherche Agronomique de Tunisie — Doc Tech Inst Natl Rech Agron Tunis
Documents Techniques. Institut National de la Recherche Agronomique de Tunisie — Docums Tech INRAT
Documents to the People — DTTP
Documents. United Nations Conference on International Organization — UNCIO
Dodekanesiakon Archeion — D Arch
Dodge/Sweet's Construction Outlook — Dodge
DOE [*US Department of Energy*] **and Transport Library Bulletin** — DOE Transp Lib Bull
DOE [*Department of Energy*] **Chemical/Hydrogen Energy Contractor Review Systems. Proceedings** — DOE Chem Hydrogen Energy Contract Rev Syst Proc
DOE [*Department of Energy*] **Energy Data Base** — EDB
DOE Nuclear Airborne Waste Management and Air Cleaning Conference — DOE Nucl Airborne Waste Manage Air Clean Conf
DOE [*US Department of Energy*] **Patents Available for Licensing** [*United States*] — DOE Pat Available Licens
DOE [*US Department of Energy*] **Patents Available for Licensing** — DPALD
DOE/TIC (United States. Department of Energy. Technical Information Center) — DOE TIC US Dep Energy Tech Inf Cent
DOE (US Department of Energy) Nuclear Air Cleaning Conference. Proceedings — DOE Nucl Air Clean Conf Proc
DOE (US Department of Energy) Symposium Series — DOE (US Dep Energy) Symp Ser
Dog World — GDOG
Doga Bilim Dergisi. Seri A — Doga Bilim Derg Seri A
Doga Bilim Dergisi. Seri A1 — Doga Bilim Derg Seri A1
Doga Bilim Dergisi. Seri A2 — Doga Bilim Derg Seri A2
Doga Bilim Dergisi. Seri D. Veterinerlik Hayvancilik ve Tarim Ormancilik — Doga Bilim Derg Seri D
Doga Bilim Dergisi. Seri D. Veterinerlik Hayvancilik ve Tarim Ormancilik — Doga Bilim Derg Seri D Vet Hayvancilik Tarim Ormancilik
Doga Bilim Dergisi. Seri D1 — Doga Bilim Derg Seri D1
Doga Bilim Dergisi. Seri D2 — Doga Bilim Derg Seri D2
Doga Biyoloji Serisi — Doga Biyol Serisi
Doga Fizik Astrofizik Serisi — Doga Fiz Astrofiz Serisi
Doga Kimya Serisi — Doga Kim Serisi
Doga Matematik Serisi — Doga Mat Serisi
Doga. Muhendislik ve Cevre Bilimleri — Doga Muhendislik Cevre Bilimleri
Doga. Serie A. Mathematical, Physical, and Biological Sciences — Doga Ser A Math Phys Biol Sci
Doga. Serie B. Engineering — Doga Ser B Eng
Doga. Serie C. Medical Sciences — Doga Ser C Med Sci
Doga. Serie D. Agriculture and Animal Husbandry — Doga Ser D Agric Anim Husb
Doga. Tarim ve Ormancilik Serisi — Doga Tarim Ormancilik Ser
Doga. Turk Biyoloji Dergisi — Doga Turk Biyol Derg
Doga. Turk Botanik Dergisi — Doga Turk Bot Derg
Doga. Turk Fizik ve Astrofizik Dergisi — Doga Turk Fiz Astrofiz Derg
Doga. Turk Kimya Dergisi — Doga Turk Kim Derg
Doga. Turk Matematik Dergisi — Doga Mat
Doga. Turk Tarim ve Ormancilik Dergisi — Doga Turk Tarim Ormancilik Derg
Doga. Turk Tip ve Eczacilik Dergisi — Doga Turk Tip Eczacilik Derg
Doga. Turk Zooloji Dergisi — Doga Turk Zool Derg
Doga. Turkish Journal of Physics — Doga Turk J Phys
Doga. Veterinerlik ve Hayvancilik Serisi — Doga Vet Hayvancilik Ser
Dohanykutato Intezet Kozlemenyei — Dohanykut Intez Kozl
Dois Distritos da Beira Litoral. Factos e Coisas do Nosso Tempo — BL
Doitsu Bungaku — DB
Doitsu Bungaku — Doi B
Doitsu Bungaku Ronko — Doit Bung Ronko
Doitsugo — Doits
Do-It-Yourselfer — D-I-Y
Dokembrii. Doklady Sovetskikh Geologov. Mezhdunarodnyi Geologicheskii Kongress — Dokembr Dokl Sov Geol Mezhdunar Geol Kongr
Dokkyo Journal of Medical Sciences — Dokkyo J Med Sci
Dokladi na Bulgarskata Akademiya na Naukite/Reports. Bulgarian Academy of Sciences — Dokl Bulg Akad Nauk
Dokladi na Yubileinata Nauchna Sesiya po Sluchai 25 Godishninata na Instituta. Vissh Mashino-Elektrotekhnicheski Institut — Dokl Yubileinata Nauchna Ses Vissh Mash Elektrotekh Inst
Dokladi. Natsionalna Nauchno-Tekhnicheska Konferentsiya po Zavaryavane v Stroitelstvoto i Montazha — Dokl Nats Nauchno Tekh Konf Zavaryavane Stroit Montazha
Doklady. Academy of Sciences. BSSR — Dokl Acad Sci BSSR
Doklady. Academy of Sciences of Belarus — Dokl Acad Sci Belarus
Doklady Academy of Sciences of the USSR. Earth Science Sections — Acad Sci USSR Dokl Earth Sci Sec
Doklady Academy of Sciences of the USSR. Earth Science Sections — Dokl Acad Sci USSR Earth Sci Sect
Doklady. Academy of Sciences. USSR. Oceanology Sections — Dokl Acad Sci USSR Oceanol Sect
Doklady Akademii Nauk — Dokl Akad Nauk
Doklady Akademii Nauk Armyanskoi SSR — Dokl Ak N Arm SSR
Doklady Akademii Nauk Armyanskoi SSR — Dokl Akad Nauk Arm SSR
Doklady Akademii Nauk Azerbajdzanskoj SSR — Dokl Ak N Az SSR
Doklady Akademii Nauk Azerbajdzanskoj SSR — Dokl Akad Nauk Az SSR
Doklady Akademii Nauk Azerbajdzanskoj SSR — Dokl Akad Nauk Azerb SSR
Doklady Akademii Nauk Belarusi — Dokl Akad Nauk Belarusi
Doklady Akademii Nauk Belorusskoi SSR — Dokl Ak N Bel SSR
Doklady Akademii Nauk Belorusskoi SSR — Dokl Akad Nauk B SSR
Doklady Akademii Nauk Belorusskoi SSR — Dokl Akad Nauk Beloruss SSR
Doklady Akademii Nauk BSSR — DBLRA
Doklady Akademii Nauk SSR — DANKA
Doklady Akademii Nauk SSSR — DAN
Doklady Akademii Nauk SSSR — DAN SSSR
Doklady Akademii Nauk SSSR — Dokl Ak SSSR
Doklady Akademii Nauk SSSR — Dokl Akad Nauk SSSR
Doklady Akademii Nauk SSSR. Biochemistry Section (English Translation) — Dokl Akad Nauk SSR Biochem Sect (Engl Transl)
Doklady Akademii Nauk SSSR. Biochemistry Section (English Translation) — Dokl Akad Nauk SSSR Biochem Sect (Engl Transl)
Doklady Akademii Nauk SSSR. Biological Sciences Section (English Translation) [*A publication*] — Dokl Akad Nauk SSSR Biol Sci Sect (Engl Transl)
Doklady Akademii Nauk SSSR. Botanical Sciences Section (English Translation) — Dokl Akad Nauk SSR Bot Sci Sect (Engl Transl)
Doklady Akademii Nauk SSSR. Botanical Sciences Section (English Translation) — Dokl Akad Nauk SSSR Bot Sci Sect (Engl Transl)
Doklady Akademii Nauk SSSR. English Translation. Biophysics Section — Dokl Akad Nauk SSSR Engl Transl Biophys Sect
Doklady Akademii Nauk SSSR. English Translation. Botanical Sciences Sections — Dokl Akad Nauk SSSR Engl Transl Bot Sci Sect
Doklady Akademii Nauk SSSR. English Translation. Chemistry Section — Dokl Akad Nauk SSSR Engl Transl Chem Sect
Doklady Akademii Nauk SSSR. English Translation. Earth Sciences Sections — Dokl Akad Nauk SSSR Engl Transl Earth Sci Sect
Doklady Akademii Nauk SSSR. English Translation. Physical Chemistry Section — Dokl Akad Nauk SSSR Engl Transl Phys Chem Sect
Doklady Akademii Nauk SSSR. English Translation. Pure Mathematics Section — Dokl Akad Nauk SSSR Engl Transl Pure Math Sect
Doklady Akademii Nauk SSSR. English Translation. Soil Science Section — Dokl Akad Nauk SSSR Engl Transl Soil Sci Sect
Doklady Akademii Nauk SSSR. Seriya A — Dokl Akad Nauk SSSR Ser A
Doklady Akademii Nauk SSSR. Seriya Biologiya — Dokl Akad Nauk SSSR Ser Biol
Doklady Akademii Nauk SSSR. Seriya Fizicheskoj Khimii — Dokl Akad Nauk SSSR Ser Fiz Khim
Doklady Akademii Nauk SSSR. Seriya Geologiya [*Former USSR*] — Dokl Akad Nauk SSSR Ser Geol
Doklady Akademii Nauk SSSR. Seriya Khimiya — Dokl Akad Nauk SSSR Ser Khim
Doklady Akademii Nauk SSSR. Seriya Matematika Fizika — Dokl Akad Nauk SSSR Ser Mat Fiz
Doklady Akademii Nauk Tadzhikskoi SSR — Dokl Akad Nauk Tadzh SSR
Doklady Akademii Nauk Ukrainskoi SSR [*Ukrainian SSR*] — Dokl Akad Nauk Ukr SSR
Doklady Akademii Nauk Ukrainskoi SSR. Seriya B. Geologicheskie, Khimicheskie, i Biologicheski Nauki — Dokl Akad Nauk Ukr SSR Ser B
Doklady Akademii Nauk Ukrainskoi SSR. Seriya B. Geologicheskie, Khimicheskie, i Biologicheski Nauki — Dokl Akad Nauk Ukr SSR Ser B Geol Khim Biol Nauki
Doklady Akademii Nauk Ukrainy — Dokl Akad Nauk Ukr
Doklady Akademii Nauk Uzbekskoi SSR — Dokl Akad Nauk Uzb SSR
Doklady Akademii Nauk Uzbekskoi SSR — Dokl Akad Nauk Uzbek SSR
Doklady Akademii Nauk Uzbekskoi SSR — Dokl Akad Nauk UzSSR
Doklady Akademii Pedagogicheskikh Nauk RSFSR — DAPNA
Doklady Akademii Pedagogicheskikh Nauk RSFSR — Dokl Akad Pedagog Nauk RSFSR
Doklady Akademii Sel'skokhozyaistvennykh Nauk v Bolgarii — Dokl Akad Skh Nauk Bolg
Doklady. Akademiya Nauk Azerbaidzhana — Dokl Akad Nauk Azerb
Doklady Akademiya Nauk Azerbaidzhana — Dokl Akad Nauk Azerbaidzhana
Doklady Akademiya Nauk Respubliki Tadzhikistan — Dokl Akad Nauk Respub Tadzhikistan
Doklady Azerbajdzanskogo Filiala. Akademii Nauk SSSR — DAAN
Doklady Biochemistry [*English Translation*] — DBIOA
Doklady Biochemistry — Dokl Biochem
Doklady. Biochemistry. Akademiia Nauk SSSR — Dokl Biochem Akad Nauk SSSR

Doklady Biochemistry (English Translation of Doklady Akademii Nauk SSSR. Seriya Biokhimiya) — Dokl Biochem (Engl Transl Dokl Akad Nauk SSSR Ser Biokhim)
Doklady Biological Sciences [*English Translation*] — DKBSA
Doklady Biological Sciences — Dokl Biol Sci
Doklady. Biological Sciences. Akademiia Nauk SSSR — Dokl Biol Sci Akad Nauk SSSR
Doklady Biological Sciences (English Translation of Doklady Akademii Nauk SSSR) — Dokl Biol Sci (Engl Transl Dokl Akad Nauk SSSR)
Doklady Biological Sciences (English Translation of Doklady Akademii Nauk SSSR. Seriya Biologiya) — Dokl Biol Sci (Engl Transl Dokl Akad Nauk SSSR Ser Biol)
Doklady Biophysics [*English Translation*] — DOKBA
Doklady Biophysics — Dokl Biophys
Doklady. Biophysics. Akademiia Nauk SSSR — Dokl Biophys Akad Nauk SSSR
Doklady Biophysics (English Translation of Doklady Akademii Nauk SSSR) — Dokl Biophys (Engl Transl Dokl Akad Nauk SSSR)
Doklady Biophysics (English Translation of Doklady Akademii Nauk SSSR. Seriya Biofizika) — Dokl Biophys (Engl Transl Dokl Akad Nauk SSSR Ser Biofiz)
Doklady Bolgarskoi Akademii Nauk — DAN Bolg
Doklady Bolgarskoi Akademii Nauk — Dokl Bolg Akad Nauk
Doklady Botanical Sciences [*English Translation of Doklady Akademii Nauk SSSR*] — DKBSB
Doklady Botanical Sciences — Dokl Bot Sci
Doklady. Botanical Sciences. Akademiia Nauk SSSR — Dokl Bot Sci Akad Nauk SSSR
Doklady Botanical Sciences (English Translation of Doklady Akademii Nauk SSSR) — Dokl Bot Sci (Engl Transl Dokl Akad Nauk SSSR)
Doklady Botanical Sciences (English Translation of Doklady Akademii Nauk SSSR. Seriya Botanika) — Dokl Bot Sci (Engl Transl Dokl Akad Nauk SSSR Ser Bot)
Doklady Chekhoslovatskogo Liteinogo Nauchnogo Issledovaniya — Dokl Chekh Liteinogo Nauchn Issled
Doklady Chemical Technology [*English Translation*] — DCHTA
Doklady Chemical Technology. Academy of Sciences of the USSR. Chemical Technology Section — Dokl Chem Technol
Doklady Chemistry [*English Translation*] — DKCHA
Doklady Chemistry — Dokl Chem
Doklady Chemistry (English Translation) — Dokl Chem Engl Transl
Doklady. Earth Sciences Sections — DKESA
Doklady Geograficheskogo Obshchestva SSSR — Dokl Geogr Ova SSSR
Doklady i Nauchnye Soobshcheniya. L'vovskii Politekhnicheskii Institut — Dokl Nauchn Soobshch Lvov Politekh Inst
Doklady i Soobscenija Filologoceskogo Fakul'teta Moskovskogo Universiteta — DoklMU
Doklady i Soobscenija Instituta Jazykozanija Akademiji Nauk SSSR — DSIJa
Doklady i Soobscenija Instituta Russkogo Jazyka — DoklIRuJa
Doklady i Soobscenija Uzgorodskogo Universiteta — DSUzU
Doklady i Soobshcheniya. Mezhdunarodnaya Konferentsiya po Merzlotovedeniyu — Dokl Soobshch Mezhdunar Konf Merzlotoved
Doklady i Soobshcheniya. Mezhdunarodnyi Kongress po Vinogradarstvu i Vinodeliyu. Sektsiya Vinodelie — Dokl Soobshch Mezhdunar Kongr Vinograd Vinodel Sekts Vinodel
Doklady i Soobshcheniya. Mezhdunarodnyi Kongress po Zashchite Rastenii — Dokl Soobshch Mezhdunar Kongr Zashch Rast
Doklady i Soobshcheniya po Kormoproizvodstvu — Dokl Soobshch Kormoproizvod
Doklady i Soobshcheniya Uzhgorodskogo Gosudarstvennogo Universiteta. Seriya Biologicheskaya — Dokl Soobshch Uzhgorod Gos Univ Ser Biol
Doklady i Soobshcheniya Uzhgorodskogo Gosudarstvennogo Universiteta. Seriya Fiziko. Matematicheskaya i Khimicheskaya — Dokl Soobshch Uzhgorod Gos Univ Ser Fiz Mat Khim
Doklady i Soobshcheniya Uzhgorodskogo Gosudarstvennogo Universiteta. Seriya Fiziko. Matematicheskikh Nauk — Dokl Soobshch Uzhgorod Gos Univ Ser Fiz Mat Nauk
Doklady i Soobshcheniya Uzhgorodskogo Gosudarstvennogo Universiteta. Seriya Khimicheskaya — Dokl Sooshch Uzhgorod Gos Univ Ser Khim
Doklady i Soobshcheniya Vsesoyuznoi Lateksnoi Konferentsii — Dokl Soobshch Vses Lateksnoi Konf
Doklady i Soobshcheniya. Vsesoyuznyi Nauchno-Issledovatel'skii Institut Ekonomiki Sel'skogo Khozyaistva — Dokl Soobshch Vses Nauch Issled Inst Ekon Selskokhoz
Doklady Instituta Geografii Sibiri i Dal'nego Vostoka — Dokl Inst Geogr Sib Dal'n Vost
Doklady Instituta Geografii Sibiri i Dal'nego Vostoka — Dokl Inst Geogr Sib Dal'nego Vostoka
Doklady Irkutskogo Protivochumnogo Instituta — Dokl Irkutsk Protivochumn Inst
Doklady k Konferentsii po Vysokomolekulyarnym Soedineniyam — Dokl Konf Vysokomol Soedin
Doklady k Mezhdunarodnomu Kongressu Pochvovedov — Dokl Mezhdunar Kongr Pochvovedov
Doklady Komissii Aeros'emki i Fotogrametrii Geograficheskogo Obshchestva SSR [*A publication*] — Dokl Kom Aeros'emki Fotogr Geogr O-Va SSR
Doklady Komissii Aeros'emki i Fotogrametrii Geograficheskogo Obshchestva SSR — Dokl Kom Aerosemki Fotogrametrii Geogr Obs SSR
Doklady Konferentsii po Fizike Plazmy i Probleme Upravlyaemogo Termoyadernogo Sinteza — Dokl Konf Fiz Plazmy Probl Upr Termoyad Sint
Doklady Konferentsii po Fizike Plazmy i Probleme Upravlyaemykh Termoyadernykh Reaktsii — Dokl Konf Fiz Plazmy Probl Upr Termoyad Reakts
Doklady Konferentsii po Vysokoprochnym Nemagnitnym Stalyam — Dokl Konf Vysokoprochn Nemagn Stalyam
Doklady Konferentsiya po Voprosam Tsito- i Gistokhimii — Dokl Konf Vopr Tsito Gistokhim
Doklady L'vovskogo Politekhnicheskogo Instituta — Dokl L'vov Politekh Inst
Doklady L'vovskogo Politekhnicheskogo Instituta Khimiya i Khimicheskaya Tekhnologiya — Dokl L'vov Politekh Inst Khim Khim Tekhnol
Doklady Mezhdunarodnoi Konferentsii po Limnologicheskomu Izucheniyu Dunaya — Dokl Mezhdunar Konf Limnol Izuch Dunaya
Doklady. Mezhdunarodnyi Geologicheskii Kongress — Dokl Mezhdunar Geol Kongr
Doklady Mezhvuzovskoi Konferentsii po Fizicheskomu i Matematicheskomu Modelirovaniya — Dokl Mezhvuz Konf Fiz Mat Model
Doklady Mezhvuzovskoi Konferentsii po Khimii Organicheskikh Kompleksnykh Soedinenii — Dokl Mezhvuz Konf Khim Org Kompleksn Soedin
Doklady Moskovskaya Ordena Lenina Sel'skokhozyaistvennaya Akademiya Imeni K. A. Timiryazeva — Dokl Mosk Ord Lenina Selskokhoz Akad Im Timiryazeva
Doklady Moskovskaya Sel'skokhozyaistvennaya Akademiya Imeni K. A. Timiryazeva [*A publication*] — Dokl Mosk Skh Akad
Doklady Moskovskogo Instituta Inzhenerov Sel'skokhozyaistvennogo Proizvodstva [*A publication*] — Dokl Mosk Inst Inzh Skh Proizvod
Doklady Moskovskogo Obshchestva Ispytatelei Prirody Obshchaya Biologiya — Dokl Mosk Ova Ispyt Prir Obshch Biol
Doklady Moskovskoi Sel'skokhozyaistvennoi Akademii Imeni K. A. Timiryazeva — Dokl Mosk Sel'Khoz Akad K A Timiryazeva
Doklady Moskovskoi Sel'skokhozyaistvennoi Akademii Imeni K. A. Timiryazeva — Dokl Mosk S-Kh Akad Im K A Timiryazeva
Doklady na Mezhdunarodnom Kongresse Teoreticheskoi i Prikladnoi Khimii — Dokl Mezhdunar Kongr Teor Prikl Khim
Doklady na Mezhdunarodnom Neftyanom Kongresse — Dokl Mezhdunar Neft Kongr
Doklady na Nauchnoi Konferentsii. Leningradskii Inzhenerno-Stroitel'nyi Institut — Dokl Nauchn Konf Leningr Inzh Stroit Inst
Doklady na Nauchnoi Sessii po Problemam Zharoprochnykh Metallov i Splavov — Dokl Nauchn Sess Probl Zharoprochn Met Splavov
Doklady na Nauchnykh Konferentsiyakh Yaroslavskii Gosudarstvennyi Pedagogicheskii Institut — Dokl Nauchn Konf Yarosl Gos Pedagog Inst
Doklady na Nauchnykh Konferentsiyakh Yaroslavskii Gosudarstvennyi Pedagogicheskii Institut — Dokl Nauchn Konf Yarosl Gosud Pedagog Inst
Doklady na Naucnych Konferencijach — DNK
Doklady na Sessii po Probleme Zharoprochnosti — Dokl Sess Probl Zharoprochn
Doklady na Vsesoyuznoi Konferentsii po Neirokhimii — Dokl Vses Konf Neirokhim
Doklady na Vyezdnoi Sessii Otdeleniya Nauk o Zemle Akademii Nauk SSSR — Dokl Vyezdnoi Sess Otd Nauk Zemle Akad Nauk SSSR
Doklady Nauchnoi Konferentsii Novokuznetskogo Gosudarstvennogo Pedagogicheskogo Instituta po Biologicheskim Naukam — Dokl Nauchn Konf Novokuz Gos Pedagog Inst Biol Naukam
Doklady Nauchno-Technicheskoi Konferentsii. Tomskii Politekhnicheskii Institut — Dokl Nauchno Tekh Konf Tomsk Politekh Inst
Doklady Ostravskogo Gorno-Metallurgicheskogo Instituta. Seriya Gorno-Geologicheskaya — Dokl Ostrav Gorno Metall Inst Ser Gorno Geol
Doklady Ostravskogo Gorno-Metallurgicheskogo Instituta. Seriya Mashinostroitel'naya — Dokl Ostrav Gorno Metall Inst Ser Mashinostroit
Doklady Ostravskogo Gorno-Metallurgicheskogo Instituta. Seriya Metallurgicheskaya — Dokl Ostrav Gorno Metall Inst Ser Metall
Doklady Otdelov i Komissii Geograficheskogo Obshchestva SSSR — Dokl Otd Kom Geogr O-Va SSSR
Doklady Physical Chemistry [*English Translation*] — DKPCA
Doklady Physical Chemistry (English Translation) — Dokl Phys Chem (Engl Transl)
Doklady Plenarnogo Zasedaniya. Konferentsiya po Svarke v Stroitel'stve — Dokl Plenarnogo Zased Konf Svarke Stroit
Doklady. Prochitannye na Soveshchanii po Teoreticheskoi i Prikladnoi Magnitnoi Gidrodinamike — Dokl Soveshch Teor Prikl Magn Gidrodin
Doklady Respublikanskoi Nauchno-Tekhnicheskoi Konferentsii po Neftekhimii — Dokl Resp Nauchno Tekh Konf Neftekhim
Doklady Rossiiskoi Akademii Nauk. Seriya A. Doklady Fiziko-Matematicheskogo i Estestvenno-Istoricheskogo Kharaktera — Dokl Ross Akad Nauk Ser A
Doklady Rossiiskoi Akademii Sel'skokhozyaistvennykh Nauk — Dokl Ross Akad Skh Nauk
Doklady Rossiiskoi Sel'skokhozyaistvennoi Akademii Imeni K. A. Timiryazeva — Dokl Ross S-Kh Akad Im K A Timiryazeva
Doklady Sel'skokhozyaistvennoi Akademii imeni Georgiya Dimitrova (Sofia) — Dokl Skh Akad Sofia
Doklady Sel'skokhozyaistvennoj Akademii Imeni Geogiya Dimitrova — Dokl Skh Akad Im Geogiya Dimitrova
Doklady Simpoziumov. Mezhdunarodnyi Biofizicheskii Kongress — Dokl Simp Mezhdunar Biofiz Kongr
Doklady Sochinskogo Otdela Geograficheskogo Obshchestva SSSR — Dokl Sochinskogo Otd Geogr Ova SSSR
Doklady Soil Science (English Translation) — Dokl Soil Sci (Engl Transl)
Doklady Soveshchaniya po Biologicheskoi Produktivnosti Vodoemov Sibiri — Dokl Soveshch Biol Prod Vodoemov Sib
Doklady Sovetskikh Geologov Mezhdunarodnyi Geologicheskii Kongress — Dokl Sov Geol Mezhdunar Geol Kongr
Doklady Sovetskikh Geologov na Sessii Mezhdunarodnogo Geologicheskogo Kongressa. Geologicheskaya Informatsiya i Matematicheskaya Geologiya — Dokl Sov Geol Sess Mezhdunar Geol Kongr Geol Inf Mat Geol
Doklady Sovetskikh Geologov na Sessii Mezhdunarodnogo Geologicheskogo Kongressa. Paleontologiya, Morskaya Geologiya — Dokl Sov Geol Sess Mezhdunar Geol Kongr Paleontol Morsk Geol
Doklady Sovetskikh Geologov na Sessii Mezhdunarodnogo Geologicheskogo Kongressa. Problema 1 — Dokl Sov Geol Sess Mezhdunar Geol Kongr Probl 1
Doklady Sovetskikh Geologov na Sessii Mezhdunarodnogo Geologicheskogo Kongressa. Problema 2 — Dokl Sov Geol Sess Mezhdunar Geol Kongr Probl 2

Doklady Sovetskikh Geologov na Sessii Mezhdunarodnogo Geologicheskogo Kongressa. Problema 3 — Dokl Sov Geol Sess Mezhdunar Geol Kongr Probl 3
Doklady Sovetskikh Geologov na Sessii Mezhdunarodnogo Geologicheskogo Kongressa. Problema 4 — Dokl Sov Geol Sess Mezhdunar Geol Kongr Probl 4
Doklady Sovetskikh Geologov na Sessii Mezhdunarodnogo Geologicheskogo Kongressa. Problema 5 — Dokl Sov Geol Sess Mezhdunar Geol Kongr Probl 5
Doklady Sovetskikh Geologov na Sessii Mezhdunarodnogo Geologicheskogo Kongressa. Problema 8 — Dokl Sov Geol Sess Mezhdunar Geol Kongr Probl 8
Doklady Sovetskikh Geologov na Sessii Mezhdunarodnogo Geologicheskogo Kongressa. Problema 11 — Dokl Sov Geol Sess Mezhdunar Geol Kongr Probl 11
Doklady Sovetskikh Geologov na Sessii Mezhdunarodnogo Geologicheskogo Kongressa. Problema 12 — Dokl Sov Geol Sess Mezhdunar Geol Kongr Probl 12
Doklady Sovetskikh Geologov na Sessii Mezhdunarodnogo Geologicheskogo Kongressa. Problema 13b — Dokl Sov Geol Sess Mezhdunar Geol Kongr Probl 13b
Doklady Sovetskikh Geologov na Sessii Mezhdunarodnogo Geologicheskogo Kongressa. Simpozium 1 — Dokl Sov Geol Sess Mezhdunar Geol Kongr Simp 1
Doklady Sovetskikh Pochvovedov k Mezhdunarodnomu Kongressu v SShA — Dokl Sov Pochvovedov Mezhdunar Kongr SShA
Doklady Sovetskikh Uchastnikov Kongressa. Mezhdunarodnyi Kongress po Mineral'nym Udobreniyam — Dokl Sov Uchastnikov Kongr Mezhdunar Kongr Miner Udobr
Doklady Tbilisskogo Nauchnogo Obshchestva Anatomii, Gistologii, i Embriologii — Dokl Tbilis Nauchn O-Va Anat Gistol Embriol
Doklady Timiryazevskaya Sel'skokhozyaistvennaya Akademiya — Dokl Timiryazevsk S-Kh Akad
Doklady Timiryazevskaya Sel'skokhozyaistvennaya Akademiya — Dokl TSKHA
Doklady TSKhA. Timiriazevskaia Sel'skokhoziaistvennaia Akademiia — Dokl TSKhA Timiriazevsk S-Kh Akad
Doklady Vsesojuznoj Ordena Lenina Akademii Sel'skohozjajstvennyh Nauk Imeni V. I. Lenina — Dokl Vsesojuzn Ordena Lenina Akad Selskohoz Nauk Lenina
Doklady. Vsesoyuznaya Akusticheskaya Konferentsiya — Dokl Vses Akust Konf
Doklady Vsesoyuznogo Geologicheskogo Ugol'nogo Soveshchaniya — Dokl Vses Geol Ugoln Soveshch
Doklady Vsesoyuznogo Seminara po Organicheskomu Veshchestvu Sovremennykh I Iskopaemykh Osadkov — Dokl Vses Semin Org Veshchestvu Sovrem Iskop Osadkov
Doklady Vsesoyuznogo Seminara po Prikladnoi Elektrokhimii — Dokl Vses Semin Prikl Elektrokhim
Doklady Vsesoyuznogo Simpoziuma po Impul'snym Davleniyam — Dokl Vses Simp Impulsnym Davleniyam
Doklady Vsesoyuznogo Simpoziuma po Vychislitel'nym Metodam v Teorii Perenosa Izlucheniya — Dokl Vses Simp Vychisl Metodam Teor Perenosa Izluch
Doklady Vsesoyuznogo Soveshchaniya po Mikroelementam — Dokl Vses Soveshch Mikroelem
Doklady Vsesoyuznogo Soveshchaniya po Teplo- i Massoperenosu — Dokl Vses Soveshch Teplo Massoperenosu
Doklady Vsesoyuznoi Akademii Sel'skokhozyaistvennykh Nauk — Dokl Vses Akad Skh Nauk
Doklady Vsesoyuznoi Akademii Sel'skokhozyaistvennykh Nauk Imeni V. I. Lenina — Dokl Vses Akad Sel'khoz Nauk
Doklady Vsesoyuznoi Akademii Sel'skokhozyaistvennykh Nauk Imeni V. I. Lenina — Dokl Vses Akad Selskokhoz Nauk V I Lenina
Doklady Vsesoyuznoi Akademii Sel'skokhozyaistvennykh Nauk Imeni V. I. Lenina [*Former USSR*] — Dokl Vses Akad S-Kh Nauk Im V I Lenina
Doklady Vsesoyuznoi Akademii Sel'skokhozyaistvennykh Nauk Imeni V. I. Lenina — DVASA
Doklady Vsesoyuznoi Konferentsii "Fizika Khrupkogo Razrusheniya" — Dokl Vses Konf "Fiz Khrupkogo Razrusheniya"
Doklady Vsesoyuznoi Konferentsii Liteishchikov — Dokl Vses Konf Liteishchikov
Doklady Vsesoyuznoi Konferentsii po Khimii Atsetilena — Dokl Vses Konf Khim Atsetilena
Doklady Vsesoyuznoi Konferentsii po Teplofizicheskim Svoistvam Veshchestv — Dokl Vses Konf Teplofiz Svoistvam Veshchestv
Doklady Vsesoyuznoi Mezhvuzovskoi Konferentsii po Khimii Organicheskikh Kompleksnykh Soedinenii — Dokl Vses Mezhvuz Konf Khim Org Kompleksn Soedin
Doklady Vsesoyuznoi Nauchno-Tekhnicheskoi Konferentsii po Vozobnovlyaemym Istochnikam Energii — Dokl Vses Nauchn Tekh Konf Vozobnovlyaemym Istochnikam Energ
Doklady Vsesoyuznoi Ordena Lenina Akademii Sel'skokhozyaistvennykh Nauk Imeni V. I. Lenina — Dokl Vses Ordena Lenina Akad S-Kh Nauk Im V I Lenina
Doklady Vtoroi Mezhvuzovskoi Konferentsii po Khimii Organicheskikh Kompleksnykh Soedinenii — Dokl Vtoroi Mezhvuz Konf Khim Org Kompleksn Soedin
Doklady Zarubezhnykh Uchastnikov. Mezhdunarodnyi Kongress po Mineral'nym Udobreniyam — Dokl Zarub Uchastnikov Mezhdunar Kongr Miner Udobr
Doklady Zasedaniya Issledovatel'skogo Komiteta Mezhdunarodnoi Federatsii po Dokumentatsii Teoreticheskie Osnovy Nauchnoi Informatsii — Dokl Zased Issled Kom Mezhdunar Fed Dok Teor Osn Nauchn Inf
Doktorsavhandlingar vid Chalmers Tekniska Hoegskola [*Sweden*] — Doktorsavh Chalmers Tek Hoegsk
Dokumentace Zemedelska a Lesnicka — Dok Zemed Lesn
Dokumentace Zemedelska a Lesnicka. Zahranicni Literatura — Dok Zemed Lesn Zahr Lit
Dokumentation — Dok
Dokumentation Arbeitsmedizin — Dok Arbeitsmed
Dokumentation der Zeit — DDZ
Dokumentation der Zeit — Dokumentat d Zeit
Dokumentation Fachbibliothek Werkbuecherei — Dok Fachbibl Werkbuech
Dokumentation Fachbibliothek Werksbuecherei — DFW
Dokumentation/Information — Dok/Inf
Dokumentation Kraftfahrwesen [*Database*] — DKF
Dokumentation Maschinenbau [*Database*] — DOMA
Dokumentation Ostmitteleuropa (Neue Folge) — Dokum Ostmitteleur (NF)
Dokumentation Schweisstechnik [*Database*] — DS
Dokumentation Strasse — Dok Str
Dokumentation und Schriftenreihe aus Wissenschaft und Praxis (Abwassertechnische Vereinigung) — Dok Schriftenr Wiss Prax Abwassertech Ver
Dokumentation Wasser [*Germany*] — Dok Wasser
Dokumentation Wasser — DOKWA
Dokumentation Zerstorungsfreie Pruefung [*Database*] — ZfP
Dokumentation zur Raumentwicklung — Dok Raum
Dokumentation zur Raumentwicklung — Dok Raumentwickl
Dokumentation zur Raumentwicklung — Dokum Raumentwicklung
Dokumentations und Informationssystem fuer Parlamentsmaterial [*Database*] — DIP
Dokumentationsdienst Asien Mitteilungen — Dokum As Mitt
Dokumente der Wissenschaftsgeschichte — Dok Wissenschaftsgesch
Dokumente zur Geschichte der Mathematik — Dokumente Gesch Math
Dokumenteshon Kenkyu — DOKEA
Doland's Medical Directory. New York Metropolitan Area Edition — Dolands Med Dir
[*The*] **Dolciani Mathematical Expositions** — Dolciani Math Exp
Dolgozatok a Magyar Kiralyi Horthy Miklos Tudomany-Egyetem Regisegtudomanyi Intezeteboel — DMKHMT ERI
Dolgozatok az Erdelyi Nemzeti Muzeum Erem-Es Regisegtarabol — Dolg Erd Nem Muz Erem Reg
Dollars and Sense — Doll & Sen
Dollars and Sense — Dollars
Domeny Cylindryczne. Szkola Zimowa Nowe Materialy Magnetyczne — Domeny Cylindryczne Szk Zimowa Nowe Mater Magn
Domestic Air Transport Policy Review — DATPR
Domestic Animal Endocrinology — Domest Anim Endocrinol
Domestic Commerce — Dom Comm
Domestic Engineering — Dom Eng
Domestic Engineering. Heat and Ventilation [*England*] — Domest Eng Heat Vent
Domestic Heating and Air Conditioning News — Domestic Heat Air Cond News
Domestic Heating News — DOHNA
Domestic Heating News [*England*] — Domest Heat News
Dominican Studies — Dom St
Dominican Studies — DS
Dominicana — Dom
Dominion Engineer — Dom Engr
Dominion Foundryman — Dom Foundrym
Dominion Law Reports [*Database*] — DLR
Dominion Law Reports — Dom LR
Dominion Law Reports (Canada) — DLR (Can)
Dominion Law Reports. Second Series — DLR 2d
Dominion Law Reports. Second Series (Canada) — DLR 2d (Can)
Dominion Law Reports. Third Series — DLR 3d
Dominion Medical Journal — Dom Med J
Dominion Museum Bulletin [*Wellington*] — Dom Mus Bull
Dominion Museum Monographs [*New Zealand*] — Dom Mus Monogr
Dominion Museum Records in Entomology (Wellington) — Dom Mus Rec Entomol (Wellington)
Dominion Museum Records in Ethnology [*New Zealand*] — Dom Mus Rec Ethnol
Dominion Museum Records in Zoology (Wellington) — Dom Mus Rec Zool (Wellington)
Dominion Observatory (Ottawa). Contributions — Dominion Observatory (Ottawa) Contr
Dominion Observatory Pamphlet [*Canada*] — Dom Obs Pamph
Dominion Observatory. Seismological Series — Dominion Observatory Seismol Ser
Dominion Report Service [*Information service or system*] — DRS
Dominion Tax Cases. Commerce Clearing House — Dominion Tax Cas CCH
Domus Medici — Dom Med
Domus Medici — Domus Med
Donauland — Donld
Donegal Annual — Donegal Ann
Donetskii Nauchno-Issledovatel'skii Institut Chernoi Metallurgii. Sbornik Trudov — Donetsk Nauchno Issled Inst Chern Metall Sb Tr
Dong-A Ronchong. Dong-A University — Dong-A Ronchong Dong-A Univ
Dongguk Journal — Dongguk J
Donnees Statistiques du Limousin — Donnees Statist Limousin
Donnees sur les Sediments. Rivieres Canadiennes — Donnees Sediments Rivieres Can
Doors to Latin America (Gainesville, Florida) — Doors Lat Am Gainesville
Dope — DE
Dopovidi Akademii Nauk Ukraini — Dopov Akad Nauk Ukr
Dopovidi Akademii Nauk Ukrains'koi RSR — Dop Akad Nauk Ukr RSR
Dopovidi Akademii Nauk Ukrains'koi RSR — Dopov Akad Nauk Ukr RSR
Dopovidi Akademii Nauk Ukrains'koi RSR — DUKRA
Dopovidi Akademii Nauk Ukrains'koi RSR. Seriya A. Fiziko-Tekhnichni ta Matematichni Nauki — DNUND
Dopovidi Akademii Nauk Ukrains'koi RSR. Seriya A. Fiziko-Tekhnichni ta Matematichni Nauki — Dop Akad Nauk Ukr RSR Ser Fiz-Tekh Mat
Dopovidi Akademii Nauk Ukrains'koi RSR. Seriya A. Fiziko-Tekhnichni ta Matematichni Nauki — Dopov Akad Nauk Uk RSR Ser A
Dopovidi Akademii Nauk Ukrains'koi RSR. Seriya A. Fiziko-Tekhnichni ta Matematichni Nauki — Dopov Akad Nauk Ukr RSR Ser A Fiz Tekh Mat Nauki
Dopovidi Akademii Nauk Ukrains'koi RSR. Seriya A. Fiziko-Tekhnichni ta Matematichni Nauki — Dopovidi Akad Nauk Ukrain RSR Ser A

Dopovidi Akademii Nauk Ukrains'koi RSR. Seriya A. Fiziko-Tekhnichni ta Matematichni Nauki — DUKAB
Dopovidi Akademii Nauk Ukrains'koi RSR. Seriya A. Tekhnichni Matematichni Nauki — Dop Ukr A
Dopovidi Akademii Nauk Ukrains'koi RSR. Seriya B. Geologichni, Khimichni, ta Biologichni Nauki — Dopov Akad Nauk Ukr RSR Ser B Geol Khim Biol Nauki
Dopovidi Akademii Nauk Ukrains'koi RSR. Seriya B. Geologiya, Geofizika, Khimiya, ta Biologiya — DBGGA
Dopovidi Akademii Nauk Ukrains'koi RSR. Seriya B. Geologiya, Geofizika, Khimiya, ta Biologiya — Dop Ukr B
Dopovidi Akademii Nauk Ukrains'koi RSR. Seriya B. Geologiya, Geofizika, Khimiya, ta Biologiya — Dopov Akad Nauk Ukr RSR B
Dopovidi Akademii Nauk Ukrains'koi RSR. Seriya B. Geologiya, Geofizika, Khimiya, ta Biologiya — Dopov Akad Nauk Ukr RSR Ser B Geol Geofiz Khim Biol
Dopovidi Akademii Nauk Ukrains'koi RSR. Seriya B. Geologiya, Geofizika, Khimiya, ta Biologiya — Dopovidi Akad Nauk Ukrain RSR Ser B
Dopovidi Akademii Nauk Ukrainskoj RSR. Seriya A. Fiziko-Tekhnichni i Matematichni Nauki — Dopov Akad Nauk Ukr RSR Ser A Fiz
Dopovidi Akademii Nauk Ukrainskoj RSR. Seriya B. Geologiya, Geofizika, Khimiya na Biologiya — Dopov Akad Nauk Ukr RSR Ser B Geol
Dopovidi Akademiji Nauk Ukrajins'koji RSR/Reports. Academy of Sciences. Ukrainian SSR/Doklady Akademii Nauk Ukrainskoj SSR — Dopov Akad Nauk Ukrajinsk RSR
Dopovidi Akademiyi Nauk Ukrayins'koyi RSR. Seriya B. Heolohichni, Khimichni, ta Biolohichni Nauky — Dopov Akad Nauk Ukr RSR Ser B Heol Khim Biol Nauky
Dopovidi Akademiyi Nauk Ukrayins'koyi RSR. Seriya B. Heolohiya, Heofizyka, Khimiya, ta Biolohiya — Dopov Akad Nauk Ukr RSR Ser B Heol Heofiz Khim Biol
Dopovidi Natsional'noi Akademii Nauk Ukraini — Dopov Nats Akad Nauk Ukr
Dopovidi ta Povidomlenniya L'vivs'koho Derzhavnoho Universytetu — Dopov Povidom Lvivsk Derzh Univ
Dopovidi ta Povidomlenniya L'vivs'koho Derzhavnoho Universytetu — Dopov Povidomlenniya L'viv Derzh Univ
Dopovidi ta Povidomlennja. Materialy Konferencij Drohobyc'koho Derzavnoho Pedahohicnoho Instytutu Imeni I. Ja. Franka. Serija Filolohicnych Nauk. Drohobyc — DPDroh
Dopovidi ta Povidomlennya L'vivs'kii Derzhvnii Institut. Sektsiya Biologii Khimii — Dopov Povidomlennya L'viv Derzh Pedagog Inst Sekts Biol Khim
Dopovidi Ukrains'koi Akademii Sil's'kogospodars'kikh Nauk — Dopov Ukr Akad Sil's'kogospod Nauk
Doris Lessing Newsletter — DLN
Dornier-Post [*English Edition*] — DOPOA
Dorogi i Mosty. Doklady Nauchnoi Konferentsii Leningradskii Inzhenerno-Stroitel'nyi Institut — Dorogi Mosty Dokl Nauchn Konf Leningr Inzh Stroit Inst
Dorpater Zeitschrift fuer Rechtswissenschaft — DZRw
Dorpater Zeitschrift fuer Theologie und Kirche — DZTK
Dorset Natural History and Archaeological Society. Proceedings — Proc Dorset Soc
Dortmund Data Bank — DDB
Dortmunder Beitraege zur Wasserforschung — Dortm Beitr Wasserforsch
Dortmundisches Magazin — Dortmund Mag
Doshida Joshidaigaku Gakujutsu Kenkyu Nenpo — DJGKN
Doshisha Daigaku Rikogaku Kenkyu Hokoku — DDRKA
Doshisha Engineering Review — Doshisha Eng Rev
Doshisha Literature — Doshisha L
Dosieren in der Kunststofftechnik — Dosieren Kunststofftech
Dosimetria ed Effetti Biologici dei Campi Elettromagnetici a Radiofrequenza — Dosim Eff Biol Campi Elettromagn Radiofreq
Doslidzennja i Materijaly z Ukrjins'koji Movy — DMUkrM
Doslidzennja z Literaturoznavstava ta Movoznavstva — DLMov
Doslidzennja z Movoznavstva Zbirnyk Statej Aspirantiv i Dysertantiv — DMov
Doslidzhennya v Tvarinnitstvi — Dosl Tvarinnitstvi
Doslidzhennya Zootekhniki L'vivskoho Zootekhnicheskoho Veterinars'koho Instituta — Dosl Zootekh L'vivskoho Zootekh Vet Inst
Dossier Mundo — Doss Mundo
Dossiers Archeologiques — Dossiers Archeol
Dossiers Bis Jeune Afrique et Economia — Doss Bis Jeune Afr Econ
Dossiers. Centre Regional Archeologique d'Alet — Doss Alet
Dossiers de la Politique Agricole Commune — Doss Polit Agric Commune
Dossiers de l'Archeologie — Doss Archeol
Dossiers de l'Archeologie (Paris) — Doss A (Paris)
Dossiers de l'Economie Lorraine — Doss Econ Lorraine
Dostizheniya Biologicheskoi Nauki — Dostizh Biol Nauki
Dostizheniya Biologii v Sel'skokhozyaistvennoe Proizvodstvo. Materialy Nauchnoi Konferentsii — Dostizh Biol Skh Proizvod Mater Nauchn Konf
Dostizheniya Metallurgii v SSSR i Zagranitsei — Dostizh Metall SSSR Zagr
Dostizheniya Nauki i Peredovogo Opyta v Sel'skom Khozyaistve — Dostizh Nauki Peredovogo Opyta Selsk Khoz
Dostizheniya Nauki i Peredovoi Opyt po Sveklovodstvu — Dostizh Nauki Peredovoi Opyt Sveklovod
Dostizheniya Nauki i Tekhniki i Peredovoi Opyt v Promyshlennosti i Stroitel'stve — Dostizh Nauki Tekh Peredovoi Opyt Promsti Stroit
Dostizheniya Nauki v Zhivotnovodstve — Dostizh Nauki Zhivotnovod
Dostizheniya Nefrologii — Dostizh Nefrol
Dostizheniya Sovetskoi Mikrobiologii — Dostizh Sov Mikrobiol
Dostizheniya Sovremennoi Farmakologii — Dostizh Sovrem Farmakol
Dostizheniya Sovremennoi Neirofarmakologii — Dostizh Sovrem Neirofarmakol
Dostizheniya Spektroskopii. S'ezd po Spektroskopii — Dostizh Spektrosk Sezd Spektrosk
Dostizheniya v Efirnomaslichnom Proizvodstve NR (Narodnaya Respublika) Bolgarii i Moldavskoi SSR — Dostizh Efirnomaslichn Proizvod NR Bolg Mold SSR
Dostizheniya v Oblasti Sozdaniya i Primeneniya Kleev v Promyshlennosti. Materialy Seminara — Dostizh Obl Sozdaniya Primen Kleev Promsti Mater Semin
Dostizheniya Veterinarnoi Gel'mintologii v Praktiku — Dostizh Vet Gelmintol Prakt
Dostizheniya Veterinarnoi Nauki i Peredovogo Opyta. Zhivotnovodstvu — Dostizh Vet Nauki Peredovogo Opyta Zhivotnovod
Dostoevsky Studies. Journal of the International Dostoevsky Society — D Studies
Dottrina Guiridica [*Database*] — DOGI
Double Dealer — Dble Dealer
Double Liaison. Chimie des Peintures — Chimie Peint
Double Liaison. Physique and Chimie des Peintures and Adhesifs — Double Liaison Phys Chim Peint Adhes
Double Liaison Physique, Chimie et Economie des Peintures et Adhesifs — Double Liason Phys Chim Econ Peint Adhes
Double Reed — DR
Douro Litoral — DL
Douro Litoral (Portugal) — DLP
Dover Books on Advanced Mathematics — Dover Books Adv Math
Dow Jones News [*Database*] — DJN
Dow Jones News Retrieval Service — DJNR
Dow Jones News Wire — DJNEWS
Down and Connor Historical Society. Journal — Down Con Hist Soc J
Down Beat — Down Bt
Down Beat — GDOB
Down to Earth — Down Earth
Down to Earth — DTE
Downbeat — Db
Downbeat — Dbt
Downs Syndrome Research and Practice — Downs Syndr Res Pract
Downside Review — DoR
Downside Review — DownR
Downside Review [*Downside Abbey, Bath, England*] — DowR
Downside Review — DR
Doxa. Rassegna Critica di Antichita Classica — DRCAC
Doxographi Graeci — D
Doxographi Graeci — DG
Doxographi Graeci — Dox Gr
Doxographi Graeci — Dox Graec
DOZ. Deutsche Optikerzeitung — DOZ Dtsch Optikerztg
Dozimetriya i Radiatsionnye Protsessy v Dozimetricheskikh Sistemakh — Dozim Radiats Protsessy Dozim Sist
DP. Dental Practice (Ewell) [*England*] — Dent Pract (Ewell)
DPW. Deutsche Papierwirtschaft — DPW Dtsch Papierwirtsch
Dr. Dobb's Journal [*Database*] — DDJ
Dr. Dobb's Journal — Dr Dobb's J
Dr. Dobb's Journal of Computer Calisthenics and Orthodontia [*Later, Dr. Dobb's Journal of Software Tools*] — Dr Dobb's J Comput Calisthenics and Orthod
Draeger Review [*Germany*] — Draeger Rev
Draegerheft — DRAEA
Draegerheft. Mitteilungen der Draegerwerk AG [*Luebeck*] — Draegerh
Drag Reduction in Polymer Solutions. Papers. Symposium — Drag Reduct Polym Solutions Pap Symp
Drag Reduction. Papers presented at the International Conference — Drag Reduct Pap Int Conf
Dragoco Berichte. English Edition — Dragoco Ber Engl Edn
Dragoco Report. English Edition — Dragoco Rep Engl Ed
Dragoco Report. Flavoring Information Service — Dragoco Rep Flavor Inf Serv
Dragoco Report. German Edition — Dragoco Rep Ger Ed
Dragonfly — Drag
Dragotsennye i Tsvetnye Kamni kak Poleznoe Iskopaemoe — Dragotsennye Tsvetn Kamni Polezn Iskop
Draht-Welt — DRWEA
Drake Law Review — DR
Drake Law Review — Dr LR
Drake Law Review — Drake L Rev
Drake Law Review — Drake Law R
Drake Law Review — Drake LR
Drama and Theatre — D & T
Drama Critique — DramC
Drama Review — Drama R
Drama Review — Drama Rev
Drama Review — DrR
Drama Review [*Formerly, Tulane Drama Review*] — TDR
Drama Survey — Drama Surv
Drama Survey — DramS
Drama Survey — DS
Drama: The Quarterly Theatre Review — DR
Drama. The Quarterly Theatre Review — IDQT
Drammatic Festivals of Athens — DFA
Drammaturgia — D
Drammaturgia — Dram
Draper Fund Report — Draper Fund Rep
Draper Fund Report — Draper Fund Rept
Draper of Australasia — Draper
Draper World Population Fund Report — Draper World Population Fund Rept
Dream World — DWD
Dredged Material Research — Dredged Mater Res
Dredging and Port Construction — DPC
Dredging and Port Construction — Dredging & Port Constr
Dreijahrestagung der Europaeischen Gesellschaft fuer Kartoffelforschung — Dreijahrestagung Eur Ges Kartoffelforsch
Dreikland [*Mainz*] — Dr

Dreiser Newsletter — DN
Dreiser Newsletter — DreiN
Dresdner Bank Wirtschaftsbericht — DBW
Dresdner Geschichts-Blaetter — DrGBL
Dresdner Journal — Dresdner Journ
Dresdner Kunstblaetter. Monatsschrift. Staatliche Kunstsammlungen Dresden — Dresdner Kunstbl
Dresdner Reihe zur Forschung — Dresdner Reihe Forsch
Dresdnisches Magazin, Oder Ausarbeitungen und Nachrichten zum Behuf der Naturlehre, der Arzneykunst, der Sitten, und der Schoenen Wissenschaften — Dresdnisches Mag
Drevarsky Vyskum — Drev Vysk
Drevarsky Vyskum — Drev Vyskum
Drevarsky Vyskum — DRVYA
Drew Gateway — DrG
Drexel Library Quarterly — DLQ
Drexel Library Quarterly — Drex Lib Q
Drexel Library Quarterly — Drexel Lib Q
Drexel Library Quarterly — Drexel Libr Q
Drexel Technical Journal — Drexel Tech J
DRI Commodities [*Database*] — DRICOM
DRI Current Economic Indicators [*Database*] — DRI-CEI
DRI Financial and Credit Statistics [*Database*] — DRIFACS
Driemaandelijkse Bladen — DmB
Driftproblem vid Avloppsreningsverk. Nordiska Symposiet om Vattenforskning — Driftprobl Avloppsreningsverk Nord Symp Vattenforsk
Drill Bit — DRBIA
Drilling — DRILA
Drilling and Production Practice — Drill Prod Pract
Drilling Contractor — Drilling Contract
Drilling - DCW [*Drilling Completion, Well Servicing*] — DRDCD
Drilling Information Services [*Database*] — DIS
Drilling News — Drill News
Drill's Pharmacology in Medicine [*monograph*] — Drills Pharmacol Med
Drip/Trickle Irrigation — Drip Trickle Irrig
Dritte Welt Magazin — Dritte Welt Mag
Driver and Traffic Safety Education Research Digest — DTSERD
Driver Education Bulletin — Driver Ed Bul
Drives and Controls International — Drives and Controls Int
Drogist. Vakblad voor Schoonheid, Gezondheid, en Hygiene — DRO
Drogistenweekblad. Onafhankelijk Vakblad voor de Drogisterijbranche — DGB
Drogownictwo — DROGA
Droguerie Francaise. La Couleur — DFA
Droit d'Auteur — D d A
Droit et Liberte, Contre le Racisme, l'Antisemitisme, pour la Paix [*Paris*] — DL
Droit et Pratique du Commerce International — Dr Pratique Com Int
Droit et Pratique du Commerce International — Droit et Pratique Commer Internat
Droit Maritime — Dr Marit
Droit Maritime Francais — Dr Marit Franc
Droit Ouvrier — Dr Ouvr
Droit Sanitaire et Social — Dr Sanit Soc
Droit Social — Dr Soc
Droperidol und Fentanyl beim Schock. Bericht ueber das Bremer Neuroleptanalgesie-Symposion — Droperidol Fentanyl Schock Ber Bremer Neuroleptanalg Symp
Drought. Lectures Presented at the Session. WMO [*World Meteorlogical Organization*] **Executive Committee** — Drought Lect Sess WMO Exec Comm
Drozhzhevaya Promyshlennost. Nauchno-Tekhnicheskii Referativnyi Sbornik — Drozhzhevaya Promst Nauchno Tekh Ref Sb
Druck Print — DRPRB
Druckspiegel — DRSPA
Drudea. Mitteilungen des Geobotanischen Arbeitskreises Sachsen-Thueringen — Drudea Mitt Geobot Sachsen-Th
Drug Absorption and Disposition. Statistical Considerations. Based on a Symposium — Drug Absorpt Dispos Stat Consid Symp
Drug Abuse and Alcoholism Review — Drug Abuse & Alcohol Rev
Drug Abuse and Social Issues. International Symposium on Drug Abuse — Drug Abuse Soc Issues Int Symp
Drug Abuse Council. Monograph Series — Drug Abu MS
Drug Abuse Council. Public Policy Series — Drug Abu PPS
Drug Abuse Current Awareness System — DACAS
Drug Abuse in Pregnancy and Neonatal Effects — Drug Abuse Pregnancy Neonat Eff
Drug Abuse Prevention Report — Drug Abuse Prev Rep
Drug Action and Drug Resistance in Bacteria — Drug Action Drug Resist Bact
Drug Action at the Molecular Level. Report. Symposium — Drug Action Mol Level Rep Symp
Drug and Alcohol Abuse Reviews — Drug Alcohol Abuse Rev
Drug and Alcohol Dependence — Drug Alcohol Depend
Drug and Allied Industries — Drug Allied Ind
Drug and Anesthetic Effects on Membrane Structure and Function — Drug Anesth Eff Membr Struct Funct
Drug and Chemical Exports — Drug Chem Exports
Drug and Chemical Toxicology — Drug Chem Toxicol
Drug and Cosmetic Industry — D & C Ind
Drug and Cosmetic Industry — DCINA
Drug and Cosmetic Industry — Drug and Cosmetic Ind
Drug and Cosmetic Industry — Drug Cosmet
Drug and Cosmetic Industry — Drug Cosmet Ind
Drug and Enzyme Targeting. Part B — Drug Enzyme Targeting Part B
Drug and Therapeutics Bulletin — DRTBB
Drug and Therapeutics Bulletin — Drug Ther Bull
Drug Bulletin — Drug Bull
Drug Delivery System — Drug Delivery Syst
Drug Delivery System Development. International Conference — Drug Delivery Syst Dev Int Conf
Drug Delivery Systems. Proceedings. International Conference — Drug Delivery Syst Proc Int Conf
Drug Dependence — Drug Depend
Drug Design and Delivery — Drug Des Delivery
Drug Design and Discovery — Drug Des Discov
Drug Development and Evaluation — Drug Dev Eval
Drug Development and Industrial Pharmacy — Drug Dev Ind Pharm
Drug Development Communications — Drug Dev C
Drug Development Communications — Drug Dev Commun
Drug Development Research — DDREDK
Drug Development Research — Drug Dev Res
Drug Digests — Drug Dig
Drug Discovery Technologies [*Monograph*] — Drug Discovery Technol
Drug Enforcement — Drug Enf
Drug Enforcement — Drug Enforce
Drug Fate and Metabolism — Drug Fate Metab
Drug Forum. Journal of Human Issues — Drug Forum J Human Issues
Drug Induced Clinical Toxicity — Drug Induced Clin Toxic
Drug Induced Diseases [*Elsevier Book Series*] — DID
Drug Induced Diseases — Drug Induced Dis
Drug Information Bulletin — Drug Inf Bull
Drug Information for the Health Professions — Drug Inf Health Prof
Drug Information Fulltext [*Database*] — DIF
Drug Information Journal — Drug Inf J
Drug Information News (Hiroshima) — Drug Inf News (Hiroshima)
Drug Intelligence [*Later, Drug Intelligence and Clinical Pharmacy*] — Drug Intell
Drug Intelligence [*Later, Drug Intelligence and Clinical Pharmacy*] — DRUIA
Drug Intelligence and Clinical Pharmacy — DICPB
Drug Intelligence and Clinical Pharmacy — Drug Intel
Drug Intelligence and Clinical Pharmacy — Drug Intel Clin Pharm
Drug Intelligence and Clinical Pharmacy — Drug Intell Clin Pharm
Drug Interactions Newsletter — DINEE2
Drug Interactions Newsletter — Drug Interact Newsl
Drug Interactions. Symposium — Drug Interact Symp
Drug Investigation — Drug Invest
Drug Measurement and Drug Effects in Laboratory Health Science. International Colloquium on Prospective Biology — Drug Meas Drug Eff Lab Health Sci Int Colloq Prospect Biol
Drug Merchandising — Drug Merch
Drug Metabolism and Disposition — DMDSAI
Drug Metabolism and Disposition — Drug Meta D
Drug Metabolism and Disposition — Drug Metab Dispos
Drug Metabolism and Disposition — Drug Metab Disposition
Drug Metabolism and Disposition. The Biological Fate of Chemicals — Drug Metab Dispos Biol Fate Chem
Drug Metabolism and Drug Interactions — Drug Metab Drug Interact
Drug Metabolism. From Microbe to Man. Symposium — Drug Metab Microbe Man Symp
Drug Metabolism. Molecular Approaches and Pharmacological Implications. Proceedings. European Workshop on Drug Metabolism — Drug Metab Proc Eur Workshop
Drug Metabolism Reviews — DMTRA
Drug Metabolism Reviews — DMTRAR
Drug Metabolism Reviews — Drug Metab
Drug Metabolism Reviews — Drug Metab Rev
Drug Metabolite Isolation and Determination — Drug Metab Isol Determ
Drug Products Information File [*Database*] — DPIF
Drug Receptor Interactions in Antimicrobial Chemotherapy. Symposium — Drug Recept Interact Antimicrob Chemother Symp
Drug Receptors and Dynamic Processes in Cells. Proceedings. Alfred Benzon Symposium — Drug Recept Dyn Processes Cells Proc Alfred Benzon Symp
Drug Research — ARZNAD
Drug Research — Drug Res
Drug Research Reports: The Blue Sheet — DRR
Drug Resistance. Mechanisms and Reversal. International Annual Pezcoller Symposium — Drug Resist Mech Reversal Int Annu Pezcoller Symp
Drug Safety — Drug Saf
Drug Stability — Drug Stab
Drug Standards — Drug Stand
Drug Store News — Drug Stor N
Drug Survival News — DRSN
Drug Therapy — Drug Ther
Drug Therapy (Biomedical Information Corporation) — Drug Ther Biomed Inf Corp
Drug Therapy for the Elderly — Drug Ther Elderly
Drug Therapy. Hospital Edition — Drug Ther Hosp Ed
Drug Therapy. Prescribing Practices and Problems — Drug Ther Prescr Pract Probl
Drug Therapy Reviews — Drug Ther Rev
Drug Therapy Reviews [*Elsevier Book Series*] — DTR
Drug Therapy Reviews — DTREDU
Drug, Vitamin, and Allied Industries — Drug Vitam Allied Ind
Druggists Circular — Drug Circ
Drug-Induced Disorders — Drug Induced Disord
Drug-Induced Liver Injury — Drug Induced Liver Inj
Drug-Induced Pathology — Drug Induced Pathol
Drug-Nutrient Interactions — DNIND4
Drug-Nutrient Interactions — Drug-Nutr
Drug-Nutrient Interactions — Drug-Nutr Interact
Drug-Nutrient Interactions — Drug-Nutrient Interact
Drug-Plastic Interactions in Parenteral Drug Administration. Proceedings. Workshop — Drug Plast Interact Parenter Drug Adm Proc Workshop

Drug-Related Damage to the Respiratory Tract — Drug Relat Damage Respir Tract
Drugs Affecting the Central Nervous System — Drugs Affecting Cent Nerv Syst
Drugs and Cerebral Function. Symposium — Drugs Cereb Funct Symp
Drugs and Diseases — Drugs Dis
Drugs and Drug Abuse Education — DADE
Drugs and Hematologic Reactions. Hahnemann Symposium — Drugs Hematol React Hahnemann Symp
Drugs and the Elderly. Perspectives in Geriatric Clinical Pharmacology. Proceedings. Symposium — Drugs Elderly Proc Symp
Drugs and the Pharmaceutical Sciences — DPHSDS
Drugs and the Pharmaceutical Sciences — Drugs Pharm Sci
Drugs, Development, and Cerebral Function. Annual Cerebral Function Symposium — Drugs Dev Cereb Funct Annu Cereb Funct Symp
Drugs in Cardiology — Drugs Cardiol
Drugs in Cerebral Palsy. Symposium — Drugs Cereb Palsy Symp
Drugs in Health Care — Drugs Health Care
Drugs in Neurology — Drugs Neuro
Drugs in Respiratory Diseases — Drugs Resp Dis
Drugs Made in Germany — DRMGAS
Drugs Made in Germany — Drugs Made Ger
Drugs of Abuse. Chemistry, Pharmacology, Immunology, and AIDS — Drugs Abuse Chem Pharmacol Immunol AIDS
Drugs of the Future — DRFUD4
Drugs of Today — DRTOBK
Drugs of Today (Barcelona) — Drugs Today (Barcelona)
Drugs under Experimental and Clinical Research — DECRDP
Drugs under Experimental and Clinical Research — Drugs Exp Clin Res
Druk en Werk — GFW
Drum. Inuvik — DR
Drumworld — DR
Drury College. Bradley Geological Field Station. Bulletin — Drury Coll Bradley G Field Sta B
Druzba Narodov — DN
Druzba Narodov — DrN
Druzhba Narodov. Ezhemesiachnyi Literaturno-Khudozhestvennyi i Obshchestvenno-Politicheskii Zhurnal — Druzh N
Drvna Industrija — DI
Drvna Industrija — DRINA
Drvna Industrija — Drvna Ind
Dry Valley Drilling Project. Bulletin. Northern Illinois University. Department of Geology — Dry Valley Drill Proj Bull
Drying Technology — Drying Technol
Dryland Agriculture — Dryland Agric
DSH [*Deafness, Speech, and Hearing*] **Abstracts** — DSH
DSH [*Deafness, Speech, and Hearing*] **Abstracts** — DSH Abstr
DSH [*Deafness, Speech, and Hearing*] **Abstracts** — DSHA
DSI [*Dairy Society International*] **Bulletin** — DSI Bull
DSIR [*Department of Scientific and Industrial Research*] **Bulletin (New Zealand)** — DSIR Bull NZ
DSIR [*Department of Scientific and Industrial Research*] **Information Series** [*New Zealand*] — DSIR Inf Ser
DTIC [*Defense Technical Information Center*] **Research and Technology Work Unit Information System** [*Database*] — R & T WUIS
DTIC [*Defense Technical Information Center*] **Technical Awareness Circular** [*Database*] — TRAC
DTS [*Digital Termination Systems*] **Directory** — DTS Direct
DTW. Deutsche Tierarztliche Wochenschrift — DTW
DTW. Deutsche Tierarztliche Wochenschrift — DTW Dtsch Tierarztl Wochenschr
Du Kunstzeitschrift — Du Kunstz
Du Pont Magazine — Du Pont Mag
Du Pont Magazine — DUPMA
Du Pont Magazine. European Edition — Du Pont Mag Eur Edn
Du Pont Modern Metal Finishing — Du Pont Mod Met Finish
Dublin Gazette — DG
Dublin Historical Record — Dublin Hist Rec
Dublin Journal of Medical Science — Dubl J Med Sci
Dublin Journal of Medical Science — Dublin J Med Sci
Dublin Magazine — DM
Dublin Magazine — Dub Mag
Dublin Magazine — Dubl Mag
Dublin Magazine — Dublin Mag
Dublin Medical Press — Dublin Med Press
Dublin Penny Journal — Dublin Pen J
Dublin Philosophical Journal and Scientific Review — Dublin Philos J Sci Rev
Dublin Quarterly Journal of Medical Science — Dublin Q J Med Sc
Dublin Quarterly Journal of Medical Science — Dublin Qtr J Med Sci
Dublin Quarterly Journal of Medical Science — Dublin Quart J Med Sci
Dublin Quarterly Journal of Science — Dublin Q J Sc
Dublin Review — DR
Dublin Review — Dub Rev
Dublin Review — Dubl Re
Dublin Review — Dublin R
Dublin Review — DublinRev
Dublin Review — DubR
Dublin University. Botanical School of Trinity College. Notes — Dublin Univ Bot Sch Trinity Coll Notes
Dublin University. Law Journal — Dublin ULJ
Dublin University. Law Review — Dublin UL Rev
Dublin University Law Review — Dublin Univ Law Rev
Dublin University. Law Review — DULR
Dublin University Magazine — Dub Univ
Dublin University Magazine — Dubl Univ Mag
DuD Fachbeitraege — DuD Fachbeitr
Dudley Educational Journal — Dudley Ednl J
Dudley Observatory Reports — Dudley Obs Rep
Duelmener Heimatblaetter — Duelmener Hb
Duerener Geschichtsblaetter — DG
Duerener Geschichtsblaetter — Duer Gesch Bl
Duesseldorfer Jahrbuch — Duesseldorfer Jahrb
Duesseldorfer Jahrbuch — DuessJ
Duessseldorfer Jahrbuch. Beitraege zur Geschichte des Niederrheins — D Jb
Duffy and Bently Report — Duf Bently Rep
Duisberger Forschungen. Schriftenreihe fuer Geschichte und Heimatkunde Duisburges — DF
Duke Bar Journal — DBJ
Duke Bar Journal — Duke B J
Duke Bar Journal — Duke Bar J
Duke Divinity School. Bulletin [*Later, Duke Divinity School. Review*] — DDSB
Duke Divinity School. Review — Duke Div R
Duke Law Journal — Du LJ
Duke Law Journal — Duke L J
Duke Law Journal — Duke Law J
Duke Mathematical Journal — Duke Math J
Duke Mathematical Journal — DUMJA
Duke University Library Newsletter — Duke Univ Lib Newsl
Duke University Library Notes — DULN
Duke University. Marine Station Bulletin — BDUMAY
Duke University. Marine Station Bulletin — Duke Univ Mar Stn Bull
Duke University Mathematics Series — Duke Univ Math Ser
Dukes' Physiology of Domestic Animals [*Monograph*] — Dukes Physiol Domest Anim
Dukovna Kultura — DK
Dulcimer Players News — Dulcimer
Dumbarton Oaks Papers — DOP
Dumbarton Oaks Papers — DOPapers
Dumbarton Oaks Papers — Dumb Pap
Dumbarton Oaks Papers — Dumbarton Oaks Pap
Dumbarton Oaks Papers — Dumbarton OP
Dumbarton Oaks Papers [*Cambridge, MA*] — DumbOaksP
Dumbarton Oaks Studies — DOS
Dumbarton Oaks Texts — DOT
Dumfriesshire and Galloway Natural History and Antiquarian Society. Transactions — DG
Dumfriesshire and Galloway Natural History Antiquarian Society. Transactions [*A publication*] — Dumfriesshire Galloway Nat Hist Antiq Soc Trans
Dun and Bradstreet Dunserve II [*Database*] — DB II
Dun and Bradstreet Reports — DAB
Dun and Bradstreet United States [*Database*] — DBUS
Dunai Vasmu Muszaki-Gazdasagi Kozlemenyei — Dunai Vasmu Musz Gazdasagi Kozl
Dunantuli Szemle — DSz
Dunantuli Szemle — Du Sz
Dun's Business Month — DBM
Dun's Business Month — DUN
Dun's Business Month — Duns
Dun's Business Month — Duns Bus M
Dun's Business Month — Dun's Bus Mon
Dun's Electronic Yellow Pages [*Database*] — EYP
Dun's Financial Profiles Report [*Database*] — DFP
Dun's Financial Records Plus [*Database*] — DFR Plus
Dun's International Review — Dun's Int R
Dun's Market Identifiers [*Database*] — DMI
Dun's Marketing Online [*Database*] — DMO
Dun's Million Dollar Directory [*Database*] — MDD
Dun's Review — DR
Dun's Review — Dun's
Dun's Review — Dun's R
Dun's Review — Duns Rev
Dun's Statistical Review — Dun's Stat R
[*The*] **Dunwoodie Review** — DunR
Duodecim — DUODA
Duodecim — DUODAG
Duodecim. Supplementum — Duodecim Suppl
DuPage Woodfield Business News — DuPage Busi
DuPont Magazine — DuPont
Duquesne Hispanic Review — DHR
Duquesne Law Review — DLRED
Duquesne Law Review — Duq
Duquesne Law Review — Duq L Rev
Duquesne Law Review — Duq LR
Duquesne Law Review — Duquesne L Rev
Duquesne Review — DR
Duquesne Review — Duq R
Duquesne Science Counselor — DSCOA9
Duquesne Science Counselor — Duquesne Sci Couns
Duquesne Studies in Language and Literature — DSLL
Duquesne Studies. Philological Series — DSPS
Duquesne Studies. Theological Series — DSTS
Duquesne University. Law Review — DULR
Duquesne University. Law Review — Duquesne U L Rev
Durabilite des Betons. Rapport — Durabilite Betons Rapp
Durability and Aging of Geosynthetics. Papers — Durability Aging Geosynth Pap
Durability of Adhesive Bonded Structures — Durability Adhes Bonded Struct
Durability of Building Materials — Durability Build Mater
Durability of Concrete. International Conference — Durability Concr Int Conf
Durability of Concrete. International Symposium. Preliminary Report — Durability Concr Int Symp Prelim Rep
Durability of Concrete. Proceedings. Symposium — Durability Concr Proc Symp
Durban Museum and Art Gallery. Annual Report — DMAGAZ

Durban Museum and Art Gallery. Annual Report — Durban Mus Art Gallery Annu Rep
Durban Museum Novitates — DMNOAM
Durban Museum Novitates — Durban Mus Novit
Durferrit Hausmitteilungen — Durferrit Hausmitt
Durham and Newcastle Research Review — Dur Newc Res Rev
Durham Research Review — DuR
Durham Research Review — Durham Res
Durham University Biological Society. Journal — Durham Univ Biol Soc J
Durham University. Department of Geography. Occasional Publications. New Series — Durham Univ Dep Geogr Occas Publ New Ser
Durham University. Journal — DUJ
Durham University. Journal — Durham Univ
Durham University. Journal — Durham Univ J
Durham University Journal — DurU
Durham University. Journal — DurUJ
Durham University Journal — DuU
Durvoobrabotvashta i Mebelna Promishlenost — Durvoobrab Mebelna Promst
Durzhaven Institut za Kontrol na Lekarstveni Sredstva. Izvestiya — Durzh Inst Kontrol Lek Sredstva Izv
Durzhaven Vestnik [*Bulgaria*] — Durzh Vestn
Dusanbinskii Gosudarstvennyi Pedagogiceskii Institut Imeni T. G. Sevcenko Ucenyi Zapiski — Dusanbin Gos Ped Inst Ucen Zap
Duscepoleznie Tchtenie — DT
Dusenia — DUSEA5
Dushanbinskii Gosudarstvennyi Pedagogicheskii Institut imeni T. G. Shevchenko. Uchenye Zapiski — Dushanb Gos Pedagog Inst im T G Shevchenko Uch Zap
Dust Topics — Dust Top
Duszpasterz Polski Zagranica [*Rome*] — DuszpPZ
Dutch Art and Architecture Today — Dutch Art & Archre Today
Dutch Birding — DUBID3
Dutch Boy Quarterly — Dutch Boy Q
Dutch Nitrogenous Fertilizer Review — Dutch Nitrogenous Fert Rev
Dutch Quarterly Review of Anglo-American Letters — DQR
Dutch Quarterly Review of Anglo-American Letters — Dutch Q Rev
Dutch Studies — DutchS
Dutch Studies (The Hague, Netherlands) — Dutch S (The Hague Netherlands)
Duxbury Series in Statistics and Decision Sciences — Duxbury Ser Statist Decis Sci
Dvar Hashavua (Tel Aviv) — DHT
DVGW [*Deutscher Verein Gas- und Wasserfachmaenner*] **-Schriftenreihe. Gas** — DVGW Schriftenr Gas
Dvigateli Vnutrennego Sgoraniya (Kharkov) [*Ukrainian SSR*] — Dvigateli Vnutr Sgoraniya (Kharkov)
Dvigateli Vnutrennego Sgoraniya (Omsk) — Dvigateli Vnutr Sgoraniya Omsk
Dvizhenie Geterogennykh Sred v Sil'nykh Magnitnykh Polyakh — Dvizhenie Geterog Sred Silnykh Magn Polyakh
Dvoinoi Sloi i Adsorbtsiya na Tverdykh Elektrodakh — Dvoinoi Sloi Adsorbts Tverd Elektrodakh
DVS [*Deutscher Verband fuer Schweisstechnik*] **Berichte** [*Germany*] — DVS Ber
DVWK (Deutscher Verband fuer Wasserwirtschaft und Kulturbau) Materialien — DVWK Mater
DVZ Deutsche Verkehrs-Zeitung [*Germany*] — DVZ Dtsch Verkehrs-Ztg
Dwight's Journal of Music — Dwights J Mus
Dyason House Papers — Dyason H P
Dyason House Papers — Dyason House Pap
Dyeing and Finishing. Nippon Senshoku Kako Kenkyukai — Dyeing Finish Nippon Senshoku Kako Kenkyukai
Dyeing Industry [*Japan*] — Dye Ind
Dyeing Industry — Dyeing Ind
Dyeing Research (Kyoto) — Dyeing Res (Kyoto)
Dyer, Textile Printer, Bleacher, and Finisher — Dyer Text Printer Bleacher Finish
Dyes and Chemicals Technical Bulletin. Paper Industry Issue — Dyes Chem Tech Bull
Dyes and Chemicals Technical Bulletin. Paper Industry Issue — Dyes Chem Tech Bull Pap Ind Issue
Dyes and Pigments — Dyes Pigm
Dyestuffs and Chemicals — Dyest Chem
Dynamic Business — DYB
Dynamic Economics [*Elsevier Book Series*] — DE
Dynamic Economics. Theory and Applications — Dynamic Econom Theory and Appl
Dynamic Mass Spectrometry — Dyn Mass Spectrom
Dynamic Psychiatry — Dyn Psychiatry
Dynamic Psychiatry — DYPSAQ
Dynamic Science Fiction — DSF
Dynamic Science Stories — DSS
Dynamic Stories — DS
Dynamic Supervision — Dyn Supervision
Dynamic Supervision — DYSUD
Dynamic Systems and Applications — Dynam Systems Appl
Dynamical Processes and Ordering on Solid Surfaces. Proceedings. Taniguchi Symposium — Dyn Processes Ordering Solid Surf Proc Taniguchi Symp
Dynamical Processes in Solid State Optics. Tokyo Summer Institute of Theoretical Physics — Dyn Processes Solid State Opt Tokyo Summer Inst Theor Phys
Dynamical Properties of Solids — Dyn Prop Solids
Dynamics and Control — Dynam Control
Dynamics of Atmospheres and Oceans — Dyn Atmos & Oceans
Dynamics of Brain Edema. Proceedings of the International Workshop on Dynamic Aspects of Cerebral Edema — Dyn Brain Edema Pro Int Workshop
Dynamics of Continuous, Discrete, and Impulsive Systems — Dynam Contin Discrete Impuls Systems
Dynamics of Heavy-Ion Collisions. Proceedings. Adriatic Europhysics Study Conference — Dyn Heavy Ion Collisions Proc Adriat Europhys Study Conf
Dynamics of Membrane Assembly — Dyn Membr Assem
Dynamics of Molecular Crystals. Proceedings. International Meeting. Societe Francaise de Chemie. Division de Chimie Physique — Dyn Mol Cryst Proc Int Meet Soc Fr Chem Div Chim Phys
Dynamics of Ovarian Function. Biennial Ovary Workshop — Dyn Ovarian Funct Bienn Ovary Workshop
Dynamics of Solids and Liquids by Neutron Scattering (1977) — Dyn Solids Liq Neutron Scattering (1977)
Dynamics of Star Clusters. Proceedings. Symposium. International Astronomical Union — Dyn Star Clusters Proc Symp Int Astron Union
Dynamics Reported. Expositions in Dynamical Systems (New Series) — Dynam Report Expositions Dynam Systems NS
Dynamik im Handel — SEU
Dynamische Psychiatrie — Dyn Psychiatr
Dynamische Psychiatrie — Dynam Psych
Dynamische Psychiatrie — DYPSAQ
Dynamite — Dyn
Dynatech Report — Dynatech Rep
Dyrevennen — Dyv
Dysmorphology and Clinical Genetics — Dysmorphol Clin Gen
Dysmorphology. Annual Review of Birth Defects — Dysmorphol Annu Rev Birth Defects
DYWIDAG [*Dyckerhoff und Widmann AG*] **Berichte** [*Germany*] — DYWIDAG Ber
Dzejas Diena — DzD
Dziennik Literacki — Dz Lit
Dziennik Polski — Dz P
Dziennik Rolniczy — Dziennik Roln
Dziennik Ustaw — Dz Ust
Dziennik Zachodni — Dz Z
Dzis i Jutro — DiJ
Dzis i Jutro — DJ
Dzveli Kartuli Enis K'atedris Stomebi — DzKarSt

E

E and MJ (Engineering and Mining Journal) Metal and Mineral Markets — E MJ Met Miner Mark
E & MS [*Earth and Mineral Sciences Experiment Station*] **Experiment Station Circular. Pennsylvania State University** — E & MS Exp Stn Circ Pa State Univ
E/E Systems Engineering Today — E/E Syst Eng Today
E Merck's Jahresberichte — E Mercks Jahresber
E. Purdue University. Cooperative Extension Service — E Purdue Univ Coop Ext Serv
EAAP [*European Association for Animal Production*] **Publication** — EAAP Publ
EAAS [*European Association for American Studies*] **Newsletter** — EAASN
EANHS [*East Africa Natural History Society*] **Bulletin** — EANHAU
EANHS [*East Africa Natural History Society*] **Bulletin** — EANHS Bull
EAP [*Employee Assistance Program*] **Digest** — EAPD
EAPR [*European Association for Potato Research*] **Abstracts of Conference Papers** — EAPR Abstr Conf Pap
EAPR Proceedings — EAPR Proc
Ear and Hearing — Ear Hear
Ear Clinics International — Ear Clin Int
Ear Clinics International — ECINE7
EAR. Edinburgh Architectural Research — EAR
Ear Magazine — Ear
Ear, Nose, and Throat Journal — Ear Nose Throat J
Ear, Nose, and Throat Journal — ENT J
Ear, Nose, and Throat Journal — ENTJDO
Ear Research (Japan) — Ear Res (Jpn)
Earlham College. Science Bulletin — Earlham Coll Sci Bull
Early American Life — IEAL
Early American Literature — EAL
Early American Literature — EAmL
Early American Literature — Early Am L
Early American Literature — Early Am Lit
Early American Literature — PEAL
Early American Literature. Newsletter — EALN
Early Child Development and Care — Early Child Dev Care
Early Child Development and Care — ECDC
Early Child Development and Care — ECDCAD
Early Childhood Bulletin — Early Child Bull
Early Childhood Education — Early Child Ed
Early Diabetes in Early Life. Proceedings. International Symposium — Early Diabetes Early Life Proc Int Symp
Early Diabetes. International Symposium on Early Diabetes — Early Diabetes Int Symp
Early Effects of Radiation on DNA — Early Eff Radiat DNA
Early English Manuscripts in facsimile — EEMF
Early English Text Society — Early Engl Text Soc
Early English Text Society — EETS
Early English Text Society. Extra Series — EETSES
Early Greek Armour and Weapons — EGA
Early Human Development — Early Hum Dev
Early Human Development — EHDEDN
Early Keyboard Journal — Early Key J
Early Music — Early Mus
Early Music — EarlyM
Early Music — EM
Early Music — PEMU
Early Music America — Early Mus America
Early Music Gazette — Early Mus G
Early Music Gazette — Early Mus Gaz
Early Music News — EMN
Early Music Today — Early Mus Today
Early Pregnancy: Biology and Medicine — Early Pregnancy Biol Med
Early Proceedings. American Philosophical Society — EPAPS
Early Scottish Text Society — ESTS
Early Years — Early Yrs
Earth and Extraterrestrial Sciences. Conference Reports and Professional Activities — Earth Extraterr Sci
Earth and Life Science Editing — Earth Life Sci Ed
Earth and Mineral Sciences — Earth Miner Sci
Earth and Mineral Sciences Experiment Station Circular. Pennsylvania State University — Earth Miner Sci Exp Stn Circ Pa State Univ
Earth and Planetary Science Letters — Earth and Planet Sci Lett
Earth and Planetary Science Letters — Earth Plan
Earth and Planetary Science Letters — Earth Planet Sci Lett
Earth and Planetary Science Letters — Earth Planetary Sci Lett
Earth and Planetary Science Letters — EPSLA
Earth Evolution Sciences — Earth Evol Sci
Earth Garden — Earth Gar
Earth Law Journal — Earth L J
Earth Law Journal [*Netherlands*] — Earth Law J
Earth Physics Branch (Canada). Publications — Earth Phys Branch (Can) Publ
Earth Research — Earth Res
Earth Research (Moscow) — Earth Res (Moscow)
Earth Resources Observation and Information Analysis System Conference. Technical Papers — Earth Resour Obs Inf Anal Syst Conf Tech Pap
Earth Science — Earth S
Earth Science — Earth Sci
Earth Science — GESC
Earth Science and Related Information. Selected Annotated Titles — Earth Sci Relat Inf Sel Annot Titles
Earth Science Bulletin — Earth Sci Bull
Earth Science Bulletin — ESCBA
Earth Science Digest — Earth Sci Dig
Earth Science Digest — Earth Sci Digest
Earth Science Institute. Special Publication — Earth Sci Inst Special Pub
Earth Science Journal — Earth Sci J
Earth Science Journal — Earth Sci Jour
Earth Science Report. College of Liberal Arts. Kyoto University — Earth Sci Rep Coll Lib Arts Kyoto Univ
Earth Science Reviews — Earth Sci R
Earth Science Reviews — Earth Sci Rev
Earth Science Reviews — ESREA
Earth Science Series (Houston) — Earth Sci Ser Houston
Earth Science (Tokyo) — Earth Sci (Tokyo)
Earth Science (Wuhan, People's Republic of China) — Earth Sci (Wuhan Peoples Repub China)
Earth Sciences — EASCD
Earth Sciences History. Journal. History of the Earth Sciences Society — Earth Sci Hist
Earth Sciences Report. Alberta Research Council — Earth Sci Rep Alberta Res Counc
Earth Shelter Digest and Energy Report — Earth Shelter Dig Energy Rep
Earth Surface Processes — Earth Surf Process
Earth Surface Processes — Earth Surf Processes
Earth Surface Processes and Landforms — Earth Surf Processes and Landforms
Earthmover and Civil Contractor — Earthmover & Civ Contrac
Earth-Oriented Applications of Space Technology [*Formerly, Advances in Earth-Oriented Applications of Space Technology*] — EOATD
Earthquake Engineering and Structural Dynamics — Earthq Engng Struct Dynam
Earthquake Engineering and Structural Dynamics — Earthquake Eng Struct Dyn
Earthquake Engineering and Structural Dynamics — Earthquake Engng & Struct Dyn
Earthquake Information Bulletin — Earth Inf Bul
Earthquake Information Bulletin — Earthqu Inf Bull
Earthquake Information Bulletin — Earthquake Inf Bull
Earthquake Information Bulletin — EIB
Earthquake Information Bulletin. US Department of the Interior. Geological Survey — Earthquake Inform Bull
Earthquake Notes — EAQNA
Earthquake Notes — Earthqu Notes
Earthquake Notes — Earthquake Not
Earthquake Prediction Research — EPR
Earthquakes in the United States — Earthquake US
Earthscan Bulletin — Earthscan Bull
Earth-Science Reviews — ESREAV
Earth-Science Reviews — PESR
East Africa Journal — E Afr J
East Africa Journal — EAJ
East Africa Law Journal — East Afr Law Jnl
East Africa Law Review — East Afr Law Rev
East African Agricultural and Forestry Journal — E Afr Agr Forest J
East African Agricultural and Forestry Journal — E Afr Agric For J
East African Agricultural and Forestry Journal — E Afric Agric & For J
East African Agricultural and Forestry Journal — E African Agric Forest J
East African Agricultural and Forestry Journal — EAFJAU
East African Agricultural and Forestry Journal — East Afr Agric For J
East African Agricultural and Forestry Research Organization. Annual Report — East Afr Agric For Res Organ Annu Rep
East African Agricultural Journal — E Afr Agric J
East African Agricultural Journal — EAAJA5
East African Agricultural Journal — East Afr Agric J

East African Agricultural Journal of Kenya, Tanganyika, Uganda, and Zanzibar — EAJKAJ
East African Agricultural Journal of Kenya, Tanganyika, Uganda, and Zanzibar — East Afr Agric J Kenya Tanganyika Uganda Zanzibar
East African Agricultural Research Institute. Amani. Annual Report — East Afr Agric Res Inst Amani Annu Rep
East African Agricultural Research Station (Amani). Annual Report — East Afr Agric Res Stn (Amani) Annu Rep
East African Agriculture and Forestry Research Organization. Forestry Technical Note — EAFNA8
East African Agriculture and Forestry Research Organization. Forestry Technical Note — East Afr Agric For Res Organ For Tech Note
East African Agriculture and Forestry Research Organization. Record of Research. Annual Report — East Afr Agric For Res Organ Rec Res Annu Rep
East African Annual — E Afr Annu
East African Common Services Organization. East African Agricultural and Forestry Research Organization. Record of Research — EAORAV
East African Common Services Organization. East African Institute for Medical Research. Annual Report — EAMRAL
East African Common Services Organization. East African Institute for Medical Research. Annual Report — East Afr Common Serv Organ East Afr Inst Med Res Annu Rep
East African Common Services Organization. East African Marine Fisheries Research Organization. Annual Report — EAFOAB
East African Economic Review — E Afr Ec Rev
East African Farmer and Planter — E Afr Farmer Plant
East African Freshwater Fisheries Research Organization. Annual Report — EAFOBC
East African Freshwater Fisheries Research Organization. Annual Report — East Afr Freshw Fish Res Org Annu Rep
East African Geographical Review — East Afr Geogr R
East African Institute for Medical Research. Annual Report — EAIABJ
East African Institute for Medical Research. Annual Report — East Afr Inst Med Res Annu Rep
East African Institute of Malaria and Vector-Borne Diseases. Annual Report — East Afr Inst Malaria Vector-Borne Dis Annu Rep
East African Institute of Social Research Conference Papers — EAISR
East African Journal of Medical Research — East Afr J Med Res
East African Journal of Rural Development — E Afr J Rur Dev
East African Law Journal — E Afr Law J
East African Library Association Bulletin — E Afr Libr Ass Bull
East African Management Journal — E Afr Mgmt J
East African Medical Journal — E Afr Med J
East African Medical Journal — EAMJA
East African Medical Journal — EAMJAV
East African Medical Journal — East Afr Med J
East African Natural Resources Research Council. Annual Report — East Afr Nat Resour Res Counc Annu Rep
East African Report on Trade and Industry — East Afr Rep Trade Ind
East African Studies — E Afr Stud
East African Trypanosomiasis Research Organization. Annual Report — East Afr Trypanosomiasis Res Organ Annu Rep
East African Trypanosomiasis Research Organization. Annual Report — EATRAM
East African Trypanosomiasis Research Organization. Report — East Afr Trypanosomiasis Res Organ Rep
East African Tuberculosis Investigation Centre. Annual Report — East Afr Tuberc Invest Cent Annu Rep
East African Tuberculosis Investigation Centre. Annual Report — EATBA8
East African Veterinary Research Organization. Annual Report — East Afr Vet Res Organ Annu Rep
East African Veterinary Research Organization. Annual Report — EAVRBX
East African Virus Research Institute. Report — East Afr Virus Res Inst Rep
East African Wildlife Journal — E Afr Wildl J
East African Wildlife Journal — E Afr Wildlife J
East African Wildlife Journal — East Afr Wildl J
East African Wildlife Journal — EAWJAD
East and West — E & W
East and West — EaW
East and West — EW
East and West — EWe
East Anglia Daily Times — EADT
East Anglian Archaeology — E Anglian Archaeol
East Arfican Weed Control Conference. Proceedings — East Afr Weed Control Conf Proc
East Asia Journal of Theology — EASJ Th
East Asian Cultural Studies — EACS
East Asian Cultural Studies — East As Cult Stud
East Asian Cultural Studies Series — EACSS
East Asian Executive Reports — E Asian Executive Rep
East Asian Pastoral Review — EAPR
East Asian Review — East As R
East Asian Review — East Asian R
East Bay Voice — East Bay
East Central Europe — E Cent Eur
East Central Europe — East Cent Eur
East China Journal of Agricultural Science — East China J Agric Sci
East End Environment — East End Environ
East End Environment — EEEVAL
East End News — E End News
East Europe — E Eur
East Europe — EE
East Europe — Eu
East European Markets — E Eur Mkts
East European Markets — EEU
East European Quarterly — E Eur Q
East European Quarterly — E Europe Q
East European Quarterly — EaE
East European Quarterly — East Eur Q
East European Quarterly — East Eur Quart
East European Quarterly — East Europ Quart
East European Quarterly — PEEQ
East Germany. Amt fuer Erfindungs- und Patentwesen. Bekanntmachungen — East Ger Amt Erfindungs Patentwes Bekanntm
East Journal of Approximations — East J Approx
East Malaysia Geological Survey. Report — East Malays Geol Surv Rep
East Malling Research Station. Annual Report — East Malling Res Stn Annu Rep
East Malling Research Station. Annual Report — EMRSAV
East Malling Research Station. Kent. Annual Report — East Malling Res Stn Kent Annu Rep
East Malling Research Station (Maidstone, England). Report — East Malling Res Stn (Maidstone England) Rep
East Midland Geographer — E Midl Geogr
East Midland Geographer — East Midl Geogr
East Pakistan Education Extension Centre Bulletin — East Pakistan Ed Ex Cen Bul
East Riding Archaeologist — E Riding Archaeol
East Siberian State University Studies — East Sib State Univ Stud
East Tennessee Historical Society — EaT
East Tennessee Historical Society. Publications — E Tenn Hist Soc Pub
East Tennessee Historical Society. Publications — East Tenn Hist Soc Publ
East Timor Report — ETR
East Turkic Review — East Turkic Rev
East/West Business and Trade — East West Bus Trade
East West Journal — East West
East West Perspectives — East West Perspect
East/West Technology Digest — East West Technol Dig
East Yorkshire Local History Series — EY Loc Hist Ser
Easter School in Agricultural Science. University of Nottingham. Proceedings — Easter Sch Agric Sci Univ Nottingham Proc
Eastern Africa Economic Review — E Afr Econ
Eastern Africa Economic Review — EAER
Eastern Africa Economic Review — East Afr Econ Rev
Eastern Africa Economic Review — Eastern Africa Econ R
Eastern Africa Journal of Rural Development — East Afr J Rur Develop
Eastern Africa Journal of Rural Development — Eastern Africa J Rural Development
Eastern Africa Law Review — EAL Rev
Eastern Africa Law Review — East Afr L Rev
Eastern Africa Law Review — East Afr LR
Eastern Analytical Symposium. Advances in Graphite Furnace Atomic Absorption Spectrometry — East Anal Symp Adv Graphite Furn At Absorpt Spectrom
Eastern Analytical Symposium. Resonance Raman Spectroscopy as an Analytical Tool — East Anal Symp Reson Raman Spectrosc Anal Tool
Eastern Analytical Symposium. Thermal Methods in Polymer Analysis — East Anal Symp Therm Methods Polym Anal
Eastern Anthropologist — E Anth
Eastern Anthropologist — E Anthropol
Eastern Anthropologist — EA
Eastern Anthropologist — EAANAH
Eastern Anthropologist — East Anthro
Eastern Anthropologist — East Anthrop
Eastern Anthropologist — East Anthropol
Eastern Anthropologist — Eastern Anthropol
Eastern Archives of Ophthalmology — East Arch Opthalmol
Eastern Buddhist — E Bud
Eastern Buddhist — E Buddhist
Eastern Buddhist — East Buddhist
Eastern Buddhist — EB
Eastern Churches Quarterly — E Ch Q
Eastern Churches Quarterly — Ea Ch Qu
Eastern Churches Quarterly — East Churches Quart
Eastern Churches Quarterly [*Ramsgate, London*] — EastChQ
Eastern Churches Quarterly — ECQ
Eastern Churches Review — East Ch R
Eastern Churches Review — ECR
Eastern Coal — East Coal
Eastern Economic Journal — EEJ
Eastern Economist — EAECA
Eastern Economist — East Econ
Eastern Economist — East Economist
Eastern Economist — EE
Eastern Economist — EED
Eastern European Business Directory — EEBD
Eastern European Economics — E Eur Econ
Eastern European Economics — Eastern Eur Econ
Eastern European Economics — EEE
Eastern Forest Products Laboratory (Canada). Report — East For Prod Lab (Can) Rep
Eastern Forest Products Laboratory. Technical Report. Forintek Canada Corporation — East For Prod Lab Tech Rep Forintek Can Corp
Eastern Fruit Grower — East Fruit Grow
Eastern Fruit Grower — EFGRAQ
Eastern Grape Grower and Winery News — East Grape Grow Winery News
Eastern Horizon — East Horiz
Eastern Horizon [*Hong Kong*] — EH
Eastern Laboratory Technical Report. Forintek Canada Corporation — East Lab Tech Rep Forintek Can Corp
Eastern Librarian — East Librn

Eastern Metals Review — East Met Rev
Eastern Metals Review — EMTRA
Eastern Offshore News. Eastcoast Petroleum Operators' Association — EONE
Eastern Pharmacist — East Pharm
Eastern Pharmacist — East Pharmst
Eastern Quarterly — East Quart
Eastern Review — East Rev
Eastern Snow Conference Annual Meetings. Proceedings — ESC
Eastern Underwriter — East Underw
Eastern Worker — East Wkr
Eastern World — E World
Eastern World — EaW
Eastern World — EW
Eastman Organic Chemical Bulletin — Eastman Org Chem Bull
East-West Center Review — EWCR
East-West Journal of Numerical Mathematics — East West J Numer Math
East-West Outlook — EW Outl
East-West Perspectives — EW Perspect
East-West Review — EWR
Eau du Quebec — EAQUDJ
Eau du Quebec — Eau Que
Eau et Air dans les Plans d'Amenagement. Compte Rendu du Cycle International de Conferences PRO AQUA — Eau Air Plans Amenagement CR Cycle Int Conf PRO AQUA
Eau et Amenagement de la Region Provencale — Eau Amenag Reg Provencale
Eau et l'Industrie — Eau Ind
Eau et l'Industrie — EINSD
Eau, l'Industrie, les Nuisances — Eau Ind Nuisances
Ebanewsletter. Daily Economic and Political News Indicators from Turkey — TIN
Ebara Engineering Review — Ebara Eng Rev
Ebara Infiruko Jiho — EIJID
Ebara-Infilco Engineering Review — Ebara Infilco Eng Rev
Ebareport. Weekly Special Survey of Turkish Business, Industrial Investment, and Contracts Markets — WSC
Ebony — GEBO
Ebsco Bulletin of Serials Changes — Ebsco Bull Ser Changes
EBTA [*Eastern Business Teachers Association*] **Journal** — EBTA J
EBTA [*Eastern Business Teachers Association*] **Yearbook** — EBTA Y
EBU [*European Broadcasting Union*] **Review** — EBU Rev
EBU [*European Broadcasting Union*] **Review. Part A** — EBU Rev A
EBU [*European Broadcasting Union*] **Review. Part A. Technical** [*Switzerland*] — EBU Rev Part A
EBU [*European Broadcasting Union*] **Review. Part A. Technical** — EBU Rev Tech
EC. Cooperative Extension Service. University of Nebraska — EC Coop Ext Serv Univ Nebr
EC. Cooperative Extension Service. University of Nebraska — EC Nebr Univ Coop Ext Serv
EC Energy Monthly — EC Energy Mon
EC [*European Communities*] **Photovoltaic Solar Energy Conference. Proceedings. International Conference** — EC Photovoltaic Sol Energy Conf Proc Int Conf
EC. Purdue University. Cooperative Extension Service — EC Purdue Univ Coop Ext Serv
EC. University of Arkansas. Cooperative Extension Service — EC Univ Arkansas Coop Ext Serv
EC. University of South Dakota. Cooperative Extension Service — EC Univ SD Coop Ext Serv
ECA [*Estudios Centroamericanos*]. Universidade Centroamericana Jose Simeon Canas [*San Salvador*] — UJSC/EA
Ecarbica Journal. Official Journal. East and Central Africa Regional Branch. International Council on Archives — Ecarbica J
Ecclesia. Encyclopedie Populaire des Connaissances Religieuses — Eccl
Ecclesiae Occidentalis Monumenta Juris Antiquissima — EOMJA
Ecclesiastica Xaveriana — Ec Xaver
Ecclesiastica Xaveriana — EX
Ecclesiastica Xaveriana [*Bogota*] — EXav
Ecclesiastical Review — Eccl Rev
Ecclesiastical Review — ER
Ecclesiasticos Pharos — EPh
ECETOC (European Centre for Ecotoxicology and Toxicology of Chemicals) Special Report — ECETOC Spec Rep
Echanges Internationaux et Developpement — Echanges Int Develop
Echangiste Universel. Revue Mensuelle des Collectionneurs de Timbres et des Numismates — Echang Univ
Echinoderm Studies — Echinoderm Stud
Echinoderm Studies — ECSTD6
Echo d'Auxerre — E Aux
Echo de la Bourse — ECB
Echo de la Brasserie — Echo Brass
Echo de l'Industrie. Revue Luxembourgeoise de la Vie Economique et Sociale — EIL
Echo des Mines et de la Metallurgie — Echo Min Met
Echo des Mines et de la Metallurgie [*France*] — Echo Mines Metall
Echo des Recherches — Echo Rech
Echo des Recherches — ECRCA
Echo Magazine — Echo
Echo Medical du Nord — Echo Med Nord
Echo Teatrolne i Muzyczne — ETiM
Echo Veterinaire — Echo Vet
Echos de la Medecine — Echos Med
Echos d'Orient — E Or
Echos d'Orient — EchO
Echos d'Orient — EO
Echos du Commonwealth — E Com
Echos. Le Quotidien de l'Economie — ECX
Eckart [*Berlin*] — Eck
Eckart Jahrbuch — Eck J
Eckart Jahrbuch [*Witten*] — Eckart J
Eclaireur Agricole et Horticule. Revue Pratique des Cultures Meriodionales et de l'Afrique du Nord et des Industries Annexes — Eclaireur Agric Hort
Eclectic Engineering Magazine [*Van Nostrand's*] — Ecl Engin
Eclectic Journal of Science — Ecl J Sci
Eclectic Magazine — Ecl M
Eclectic Museum — Ecl Mus
Eclectic Review — Ecl R
Ecletica Quimica — Eclet Quim
Ecletica Quimica — Ecletica Quim
Ecletica Quimica — ECQUDX
Eclogae Geologicae Helvetiae — Ecl Geol Helv
Eclogae Geologicae Helvetiae — Eclogae Geol Helv
Eclogae Geologicae Helvetiae — EGHVA
Eclogae Geologicae Helvetiae — EGHVAG
ECN [*Stichting Energieonderzoek Centrum Nederland*] **Report** — ECN Rep
Eco 3. Energies, Environnement, Matieres Premieres — NRE
Eco Cientifico — Eco Cient
Eco Farmaceutico — Eco Farm
Eco Industry — Eco Ind
Eco/Log Week — EW
Eco. Notiziario dell'Ecologia — Eco Not Ecol
Ecole Antique de Nimes. Bulletin Annuel — EA Nimes
Ecole Antique de Nimes. Bulletin Annuel — Ec Ant Nimes
Ecole d'Ete de Physique des Particules — Ec Ete Phys Part
Ecole d'Ete de Physique des Particules. Compte Rendu — Ec Ete Phys Part CR
Ecole d'Ete de Physique Theorique — Ec Ete Phys Theor
Ecole d'Ete de Physique Theorique. Les Houches — Ec Ete Phys Theor Les Houches
Ecole d'Ete de Roscoff — Ec Ete Roscoff
Ecole Franco-Maghrebine de Printemps de Biologie Moleculaire. Compte Rendu — Ec Fr Maghrebine Printemps Biol Mol CR
Ecole Nationale Superieure d'Agronomie et des Industries Alimentaires. Bulletin — Ecole Nat Sup Agron Ind Aliment Bull
Ecole Nationale Superieure de Biologie Appliquee a la Nutrition et a l'Alimentation. Cahiers — Ec Natl Super Biol Appl Nutr Aliment Cah
Ecole Polytechnique de Montreal. Comptes Rendus du Colloque Etudiant Annuel — Ec Polytech Montreal CR Colloq Etud Annu
Ecole Polytechnique Federale de Lausanne. Journees d'Electronique — Ec Polytech Fed Lausanne Journ Electron
Ecole Pratique des Hautes Etudes — EPHE
Ecole Pratique des Hautes Etudes. Institut de Montpellier. Memoires et Travaux — Ec Prat Hautes Etud Inst Montp Mem Trav
Ecole Pratique des Hautes Etudes. IVe Section. Sciences Historiques et Philologiques. Annuaire — EPHESHPhA
Ecole Pratique des Hautes Etudes. Ve Section. Sciences Religieuses. Annuaire [*A publication*] — EPHESRA
Ecole Superieure d'Agriculture de la Suede. Annales — Ec Super Agric Suede Ann
Ecole Superieure d'Agriculture de la Suede. Annales — LAANAQ
Ecologia [*Buenos Aires*] — ECOGDF
Ecologia Agraria. Instituto de Ecologia Agraria. Universita di Perugia — Ecol Agrar
Ecologia Mediterranea — Ecol Mediterr
Ecologia Mediterranea — EMEDDQ
Ecological Abstracts — Ecol Abstr
Ecological Approaches of Environmental Chemicals. Proceedings. International Symposium — Ecol Approaches Environ Chem Proc Int Symp
Ecological Bulletins [*Sweden*] — Ecol Bull
Ecological Bulletins - NFR [*Statens Naturvetenskapliga Forskningsrad*] — ECBUDQ
Ecological Bulletins - NFR (Statens Naturvetenskapliga Forskningsrad) — Ecol Bull - NFR (Statens Naturvetensk Forskningsrad)
Ecological Chemistry — Ecol Chem
Ecological Chemistry (Russian Edition) — Ecol Chem Russ Ed
Ecological Consequences of Global Climate Change — Ecol Consequences Global Clim Change
Ecological Entomology — Ecol Ent
Ecological Entomology — Ecol Entom
Ecological Entomology — Ecol Entomol
Ecological Entomology — EENTDT
Ecological Modelling — ECMODT
Ecological Modelling — Ecol Model
Ecological Monographs — ECMOA
Ecological Monographs — ECMOAQ
Ecological Monographs — Ecol Monogr
Ecological Monographs — EM
Ecological Monographs — PEMO
Ecological Physical Chemistry. Proceedings. International Workshop — Ecol Phys Chem Proc Int Workshop
Ecological Research — Ecol Res
Ecological Research Committee. Bulletin — Ecol Res Comm Bull
Ecological Research Committee. Bulletin — ERCBA8
Ecological Research Series — Ecol Res Ser
Ecological Review [*Deutsche Schwarzbunte*] — Ecol Rev
Ecological Review — SKENAN
Ecological Review (Sendai) — Ecol Rev (Sendai)
Ecological Society of America. Special Publication — Ecol Soc Am Spec Publ
Ecological Society of Australia. Memoirs — EAUMAC
Ecological Society of Australia. Memoirs — Ecol Soc Aust Mem
Ecological Society of Australia. Proceedings — Ecol Soc Aust Proc
Ecological Studies — Ecol Stud

Ecological Studies, Analysis, and Synthesis — Ecol Stud Anal Synth
Ecological Studies, Analysis, and Synthesis — ESASAM
Ecologie et Conservation — ECCVBW
Ecologist — ECGT
Ecologist — ECOGA
Ecologist — ECOGAC
Ecologist — EWI
Ecologist — PEGS
Ecologist Quarterly [*Ecologist*] [*England*] [*Later,*] — Ecol Q
Ecologist Quarterly — Ecologist Quart
Ecologo-Physiological Methods of Cotton Fusarium Wilt Control — Ecol Physiol Methods Cotton Fusarium Wilt Control
Ecology — EC
Ecology [*English Translation*] — ECGYA
Ecology — ECOL
Ecology [*United States*] — ECOLA
Ecology — ECOLAR
Ecology — GECO
Ecology Action Newsletter — Ecol Action Newsl
Ecology and Conservation — ECCVBW
Ecology and Conservation — Ecol Conserv
Ecology (English Translation of Ekologiya) — Ecology (Engl Transl Ekologiya)
Ecology, Environment, and Conservation — Ecol Environ Conserv
Ecology Law Quarterly — Ecol L Quart
Ecology Law Quarterly — Ecol Law Q
Ecology Law Quarterly — Ecol LQ
Ecology Law Quarterly — Ecology L Q
Ecology of Disease — Ecol Dis
Ecology of Disease — EYDIDI
Ecology of Food and Nutrition — ECFNBN
Ecology of Food and Nutrition — Ecol Food Nutr
Ecology of Food and Nutrition — Ecologn Fd Nutr
Ecology of Resource Degradation and Renewal. Symposium. British Ecological Society — Ecol Resour Degrad Renewal Symp Br Ecol Soc
Ecology. Publication. Ecological Society of America — Ecol Publ Ecol Soc Am
Ecology Review — Ecol Rev
ECOMINAS [*Empresa Colombiana de Minas*] **Boletin Mensual** [*Bogota*] — ECOMINAS Bol Mens
Econometric Data Bank — EDB
Econometric Reviews — Econometric Rev
Econometric Society Monographs — Econom Soc Monogr
Econometric Society Monographs in Pure Theory — Econom Soc Monographs Pure Theory
Econometric Society Monographs in Quantitative Economics — Econom Soc Monographs Quantitative Econom
Econometrica — ECM
Econometrica — ECMTA
Econometrica — Econ
Econometrica — EM
Econometrica — EMT
Econometrica — MET
Econometrics and Operations Research — Econom Oper Res
Econometrics and Operations Research — Econometrics Oper Res
Econometrics and Operations Research — OEUNAH
Economia — Econ
Economia Brasileira (Rio de Janeiro) — Econ Bras Rio
Economia Colombiana (Bogota) — Econ Col Bogota
Economia Colombiana. Cuarta Epoca — Econ Colombiana 4a Epoca
Economia del Lavoro — Econ Del Lav
Economia e Credito — Ec Cred
Economia e Credito — Econ e Credito
Economia e Gestao — Econ e Gestao
Economia e Lavoro — Econ e Lav
Economia e Socialismo — Econ e Socialismo
Economia e Sociologia — Econ e Sociol
Economia e Storia — Econ e Storia
Economia e Storia — ES
Economia e Storia; Rivista Italiana di Storia Economica e Sociale — Ec Stor
Economia e Storia. Rivista Italiana di Storia Economica e Sociale — Econ Stor
Economia e Storia (Seconda Serie) — Econ e Storia (2a Ser)
Economia EC — Econ EC
Economia Grancolombiana (Bogota) — Econ Grancol Bogota
Economia Industrial — Econ Ind
Economia Industrial — EIE
Economia Instituto de Investigaciones Economicas y Financieras — EE
Economia Internazionale — Econ Internaz
Economia Internazionale — ECU
Economia Internazionale — EI
Economia Internazionale delle Fonti di Energia — Econ Int Fonti Energia
Economia Internazionale delle Fonti di Energia — Econ Internaz Fonti Energia
Economia Internazionale delle Fonti di Energia — EIFEB
Economia Internazionale (Genova) — Econ Int (Genova)
Economia Internazionale. Revista. Istituto di Economia Internazionale — Econ Int
Economia Internazionale. Rivista dell'Istituto di Economia Internazionale — IEI/EI
Economia. Istruzione e Formazione Professionale — Econ Istruzione e Formazione Professionale
Economia (Lisbon) — Econ (Lisbon)
Economia Marche — Econ Marche
Economia Mundial. Revista de Economia y Finanzas — Econ Mundial
Economia Politica. Segunda Epoca — Econ Pol 2a Epoca
Economia Pubblica — Econ Pubbl
Economia Pubblica — Econ Pubblica
Economia (Quito) — Econ Quito
Economia Salvadorena — Econ Salvad
Economia Salvadorena (San Salvador) — Econ Sal S Salvador
Economia (Santiago, Chile) — Econ Santiago
Economia Trentina [*Italy*] — Econ Trentina
Economia Trentina — ECTTA
Economia y Administracion — Econ Y Adm
Economia y Ciencias Sociales — Econ Cienc Soc
Economia y Ciencias Sociales — ECS
Economia y Ciencias Sociales (Caracas) — Econ Cien Soc Caracas
Economia y Desarrollo — Econ y Desarrollo
Economia y Desarrollo — EyD
Economia y Desarrollo. Universidad de La Habana — UH/ED
Economia y Estadistica (Bogota) — Econ Estad Bogota
Economia y Finanzas Espanolas — Econ y Fin Esp
Economia y Tecnica Agricola — Econ Tecn Agric
Economic Abstracts — Econ Abstr
Economic Abstracts — EconAb
Economic Activity in Western Australia — Econ Act West Aust
Economic Activity in Western Australia — Econ Activity
Economic Activity in Western Australia — Econ Activity in WA
Economic Activity in Western Australia — Econ Activity WA
Economic Activity in Western Australia — Economic Activity in WA
Economic Affairs — Econ Aff
Economic Analysis — Ec An
Economic Analysis — Econ Analys
Economic Analysis and Policy — Econ Anal & Policy
Economic Analysis and Policy (New Series) — Econ Analysis and Policy (NS)
Economic Analysis and Workers' Management (Belgrade) — EBB
Economic Analysis and Workers' Management (Belgrade) — Econ Analysis (Belgrade)
Economic and Business Review — Econ Bus R
Economic and Commercial News — ECK
Economic and Financial Review. Central Bank of Nigeria — Econ Financ R Central Bank Nigeria
Economic and Financial Survey of Australia — Econ & Financial Survey Aust
Economic and Financial Survey of Australia — Econ Finan Surv Aust
Economic and Financial Survey of Australia — Econ Financial Surv Aust
Economic and Industrial Democracy — Econ & Ind Democ
Economic and Industrial Democracy — EID
Economic and Marketing Information for Missouri Agriculture. University of Missouri. Cooperative Extension Service — Econ Mark Inf Mo Agric Univ Mo Coop Ext Serv
Economic and Medicinal Plant Research — Econ Med Plant Res
Economic and Political Weekly — Econ Pol W
Economic and Political Weekly — Econ Polit Wkly
Economic and Political Weekly — EPW
Economic and Research Institute. Quarterly Economic Commentary — Econ and Social Research Inst Q Econ Commentary
Economic and Social History — Econ Soc Hist
Economic and Social Issues. University of California, Berkeley. Cooperative Extension Service — Econ Soc Issues Calif Univ Berkeley Coop Ext Serv
Economic and Social Issues. University of California. Berkeley. Cooperative Extension Service — Econ Soc Issues Univ Calif Berkeley Coop Ext Serv
Economic and Social Review — Econ Soc R
Economic and Social Review — Econ Soc Rev
Economic and Social Review — ESR
Economic and Social Review (Dublin) — Econ and Social R (Dublin)
Economic and Statistical Review (East Africa) — Econ and Statis R (East Africa)
Economic and Technical Review. Report EPS [*Environmental Protection Service*] **(Canada)** — Econ Tech Rev Rep EPS (Can)
Economic Annalist — Econ Ann
Economic Botany — ECBOA
Economic Botany — ECBOA5
Economic Botany — Econ Bot
Economic Botany — Econ Botan
Economic Botany. New York Botanical Garden for the Society for Economic Botany — SEB/EB
Economic Bulletin [*Sydney, Australia*] — Econ Bull
Economic Bulletin — Econ Bull
Economic Bulletin. Bank of Norway — ECBU
Economic Bulletin Board [*Database*] — EBB
Economic Bulletin. Commercial Bank of Greece — Grc Bk Eco
Economic Bulletin. Commercial Bank of Greece (Athens) — Econ B (Athens)
Economic Bulletin for Africa — Econ Afr
Economic Bulletin for Africa — Econ B Afr
Economic Bulletin for Africa — Econ Bull Afr
Economic Bulletin for Asia and the Far East [*Later, Economic Bulletin for Asia and the Pacific*] — EBAFE
Economic Bulletin for Asia and the Far East [*Later, Economic Bulletin for Asia and the Pacific*] — Econ B Asia Far East
Economic Bulletin for Asia and the Far East [*Later, Economic Bulletin for Asia and the Pacific*] — Econ Bul Asia and Far East
Economic Bulletin for Asia and the Pacific — EAE
Economic Bulletin for Asia and the Pacific — Econ B Asia Pacific
Economic Bulletin for Asia and the Pacific — Econ Bul A
Economic Bulletin for Asia and the Pacific — Econ Bul Asia and Pacific
Economic Bulletin for Europe — EBE
Economic Bulletin for Europe — EBEUA
Economic Bulletin for Europe — EBU
Economic Bulletin for Europe — Ec Bul Eur
Economic Bulletin for Europe — Econ B Europe
Economic Bulletin for Europe — Econ Bul Europe
Economic Bulletin for Europe — Econ Bull Eur
Economic Bulletin for Europe — Econ Bull for Europe
Economic Bulletin for Latin America — Econ B Latin Amer

Economic Bulletin for Latin America — Econ Bull Lat Am
Economic Bulletin. Geological Survey of West Malaysia — Econ Bull Geol Surv West Malays
Economic Bulletin (Germany) — Ger Ec Bul
Economic Bulletin. National Bank of Egypt — BNBE
Economic Bulletin. National Bank of Egypt (Cairo) — Econ B (Cairo)
Economic Bulletin of Ghana — Econ Bull Ghana
Economic Bulletin (Oslo) — Econ B (Oslo)
Economic Bulletin. Sri Lanka Geological Survey Department — Econ Bull Sri Lanka Geol Surv Dep
Economic Bulletin/Warta Cafi — EBC
Economic Commentary. Federal Reserve Bank of Cleveland — ECC
Economic Computation and Economic Cybernetics Studies and Research — Econ Comp and Econ Cyb Stud and Res
Economic Computation and Economic Cybernetics Studies and Research — Econ Comput and Econ Cybern Stud and Res
Economic Computation and Economic Cybernetics Studies and Research — Econ Comput Econ Cybern Stud Res
Economic Computation and Economic Cybernetics Studies and Research [*Bucharest*] — Econom Comp Econom Cybernet Stud Res
Economic Computation and Economic Cybernetics Studies and Research [*Bucharest*] — Econom Comput Econom Cybernet Stud Res
Economic Council of Canada. Discussion Papers — Econ Counc Can Disc Pap
Economic Crime Project. Annual Report — Econ Cr Proj A Rep
Economic Development and Cultural Change — Ec Dev Cult Change
Economic Development and Cultural Change — EcD
Economic Development and Cultural Change — Econ Dev & Cul Change
Economic Development and Cultural Change — Econ Dev Cu
Economic Development and Cultural Change — Econ Dev Cult Change
Economic Development and Cultural Change — Econ Dev Cult Chg
Economic Development and Cultural Change — Econ Devel and Cult Change
Economic Development and Cultural Change — Econ Devel Cult Ch
Economic Development and Cultural Change — Econ Devel Cult Change
Economic Development and Cultural Change — Econ Develop Cult Change
Economic Development and Cultural Change — Econ Development and Cultural Change
Economic Development and Cultural Change — EDA
Economic Development and Cultural Change — EDC
Economic Development and Cultural Change — EDC Ch
Economic Development and Cultural Change — EDCC
Economic Development and Cultural Change — EDCCA
Economic Development and Cultural Change. University of Chicago — UC/EDCC
Economic Development Programme for the Republic of South Africa — Econ Dev Prog Rep S Afr
Economic Development Review — EDR
Economic Development Review — EDV
Economic Digest — EDS
Economic Education Bulletin — Econ Educ Bul
Economic Eye — Econ Eye
Economic Forecasts. A Worldwide Survey — Eco Forcst
Economic Forum — Econ Forum
Economic Generale [*Database*] — ECODOC
Economic Geography — ECG
Economic Geography — ECGEA
Economic Geography — Econ Geog
Economic Geography — Econ Geogr
Economic Geography — Econ Geography
Economic Geography — EG
Economic Geography — EGP
Economic Geography — EGY
Economic Geography — PECG
Economic Geography (Worcester) — Econ Geogr Worcester
Economic Geology — Econ Geol
Economic Geology and the Bulletin of the Society of Economic Geologists — ECGLA
Economic Geology and the Bulletin of the Society of Economic Geologists — Econ Geol
Economic Geology and the Bulletin of the Society of Economic Geologists — Econ Geol Bull Soc Econ Geol
Economic Geology Bulletin. Thailand Department of Mineral Resources. Economic Geology Division — Econ Geol Bull Thailand Dep Miner Resour Econ Geol Div
Economic Geology Monograph — Econ Geol Monogr
Economic Geology Monograph — Econ Geology Mon
Economic Geology Report. Alberta Research Council — Econ Geol Rep Alberta Res Counc
Economic Geology Report. Geological Survey of Canada — Econ Geol Rep Geol Surv Can
Economic Geology Report. Jamaica Geological Survey Department — Econ Geol Rep Jam Geol Surv Dep
Economic Geology Report. Jamaica. Mines and Geology Division — Econ Geol Rep Jam Mines Geol Div
Economic Geology Report. Mineral Resources Division (Manitoba) — Econ Geol Rep Miner Resour Div (Manitoba)
Economic Geology Report. Research Council of Alberta — Econ Geol Rep Res Counc Alberta
Economic Geology USSR (English Translation) — Econ Geol USSR (Engl Transl)
Economic Geology. Vermont Geological Survey — Econ Geol VT Geol Surv
Economic Handbook of the World — Econ Handb Wld
Economic History — Econ Hist
Economic History — EH
Economic History of Rome — Ec Hist R
Economic History Review — Ec HR
Economic History Review — EcH
Economic History Review — Econ Hist R
Economic History Review — Econ Hist Rev
Economic History Review — EconHR
Economic History Review — EHR
Economic History Review — PECH
Economic History Review. Second Series — Econ Hist Rev Second Ser
Economic Impact. A Quarterly Review of World Economics — EOT
Economic Indicators — ECIN
Economic Indicators — Econ Indic
Economic Indicators — Econ Indicators
Economic Indicators — IECI
Economic Information on Argentina — ECA
Economic Information on Argentina — Eco Argent
Economic Information on Argentina — Econ Inf Argentina
Economic Information on Argentina — Econ Info Argentina
Economic Information Report. University of Florida. Food and Resource Economics Department. Agricultural Experiment Stations — Econ Inf Rep Food Resour Econ Dep Univ Fla Agric Exp Stns
Economic Information Report. University of Florida. Food and Resource Economics Department. Agricultural Experiment Stations — Econ Inf Rep Univ Fla Food Resour Econ Dep Agric Exp Stn
Economic Inquiry — EAT
Economic Inquiry — ECIND
Economic Inquiry — Econ Inq
Economic Inquiry — Econ Inquiry
Economic Inquiry — EIY
Economic Inquiry — WEF
Economic Investigation. Fiji. Geological Survey Department — Econ Invest Fiji Geol Surv Dep
Economic Investigation. Fiji Mineral Resources Department — Econ Invest Fiji Miner Resour Dep
Economic Issues. Department of Agricultural Economics. College of Agricultural and Life Sciences. University of Wisconsin — Econ Issues Dep Agric Econ Coll Agric Life Sci Univ Wis
Economic Journal [*United Kingdom*] — ECJ
Economic Journal — ECJOA
Economic Journal — Econ J
Economic Journal — EJ
Economic Leaflets [*Florida*] — Econ Leaf
Economic Leaflets — Econ Leaflets
Economic Letters — Econ Letters
Economic Literature Index [*Database*] — ELI
Economic Microbiology — Econ Microbiol
Economic Monograph (Melbourne, Victoria) — Econ Monograph (Vic)
Economic Monographs [*Sydney*] — Econ Monographs
Economic News — Econ News
Economic News — EN
Economic News — ENW
Economic News from Italy — Econ Italy
Economic News of Bulgaria — Ec N Bulg
Economic News of Bulgaria — EGD
Economic Outlook — EBE
Economic Outlook — Econ Outlk
Economic Outlook (California) — Econ Out (CA)
Economic Outlook (London) — Econ Outlook (London)
Economic Outlook (United Kingdom) — Eco Out (UK)
Economic Outlook USA — Econ Out US
Economic Outlook USA — Econ Outlook
Economic Outlook USA — Econ Outlook USA
Economic Outlook USA — EOUSD
Economic Outlook USA — EUS
Economic Outlook World — Econ Out W
Economic Panorama (Bancomer) — Econ Panorama (Bancomer)
Economic Paper. North Carolina Department of Conservation and Development — Econ Pap NC Dep Conserv Dev
Economic Papers — Econ Pap
Economic Papers — Econ Papers
Economic Papers — EP
Economic Papers (Australia and New Zealand) — Econ Pas (Australia and NZ)
Economic Papers (Warsaw) — Econ Pas (Warsaw)
Economic Perspectives — Econ Perspectives
Economic Perspectives [*Federal Reserve Bank of Chicago*] — ECP
Economic Planning (Helsinki) — Econ Planning (Helsinki)
Economic Planning. Journal for Agriculture and Related Industries — Econ Plann J Agric Relat Ind
Economic Policy and Developments in Norway — Norwy Econ
Economic Policy Issues — Econ Policy Issues
Economic Priorities Report — Econ Priorities Rep
Economic Proceedings. Royal Dublin Society — Econ Proc R Dublin Soc
Economic Proceedings. Royal Dublin Society — EPRDA7
Economic Progress Report — DPR
Economic Progress Report — Econ Progress Rep
Economic Progress Report (United Kingdom) — UK Report
Economic Projections to 1990. BLS Bulletin 2121. US Bureau of Labor Statistics — BLS 2121
Economic Record — Econ Rec
Economic Record — ECR
Economic Record — ER
Economic Record (Australia) — ECRDA
Economic Record (Australia) — ERA
Economic Report. Banco de Bilbao — Econ Rep Banco Bilbao
Economic Report. Department of Agricultural and Applied Economics. University of Minnesota — Econ Rep Dep Agric Appl Econ Univ Minn

Economic Report. Edinburgh School of Agriculture — Econ Rep Edinburgh Sch Agr
Economic Report. Fiji. Geological Survey Department — Econ Rep Fiji Geol Surv Dep
Economic Report. Geological Survey Department (Zambia) — Econ Rep Geol Surv Dep (Zambia)
Economic Report of the President [*Council of Economic Advisors*] [*United States*] — Econ Pres
Economic Report. Summary (Argentina) — Argent Eco
Economic Report. Zambia Geological Survey Department — Econ Rep Zambia Geol Surv Dep
Economic Reporter — Econ Reporter
Economic Research [*Nagoya, Japan*] — Econ Res
Economic Research Journal — ERJ
Economic Research Service. Reports — ERS
Economic Review — Econ R
Economic Review — Econ Rev
Economic Review — ERW
Economic Review. Bank Leumi [*Tel Aviv*] — Econ Rev Bank Leumi
Economic Review. Bank of Israel — Econ R Bank Israel
Economic Review (Colombo) — Econ R (Colombo)
Economic Review. Federal Reserve Bank of Atlanta — EAT
Economic Review. Federal Reserve Bank of Atlanta — Econ Rev Fed Reserve Bank Atlanta
Economic Review. Federal Reserve Bank of Atlanta — ECR
Economic Review. Federal Reserve Bank of Cleveland — ECV
Economic Review. Federal Reserve Bank of Cleveland — ERC
Economic Review. Federal Reserve Bank of Dallas — ERD
Economic Review. Federal Reserve Bank of Kansas City — EKC
Economic Review. Federal Reserve Bank of Richmond — ERR
Economic Review. Kansallis (Osake-Pankki) — Econ R Kansallis (Osake-Pankki)
Economic Review (Karachi) — Econ R (Karachi)
Economic Road Maps — CFE
Economic Road Maps — Road Maps
Economic Situation in the Community. European Economic Community — Ec Sit EEC
Economic Situation Report — Econ Situation Rep
Economic Society of Australia and New Zealand. New South Wales Branch. Economic Monograph — Econ Soc Aust NZ NSW Br Econ Monog
Economic Studies — Econ Stud
Economic Survey of Ancient Rome — ESAR
Economic Survey of Europe — Ec Svy Eur
Economic Survey of Finland — Ec Svy Fin
Economic Survey of Japan — Ec Svy Jpn
Economic Survey of Japan — Econ Surv Jpn
Economic Survey of Latin America — Eco Sur LA
Economic Survey of Latin America — Econ Surv Lat Am
Economic Theory — Econom Theory
Economic Theory, Econometrics, and Mathematical Economics — Econom Theory Econometrics Math Econom
Economic Titles/Abstracts — EKD
Economic Trends — Econ Trends
Economic Trends (United Kingdom) — UK Trends
Economic Week — EW
Economic Weekly — Ec W
Economic Weekly — EW
Economic World — Ec World
Economic World — Econ W
Economic World — Econ World
Economica — EA
Economica — EC
Economica — Eca
Economica — ECO
Economica — ECOM
Economica (Buenos Aires) — Econ (BA)
Economica (La Plata, Argentina) — Econ La Plata
Economica (London) — Econ (London)
Economica. Universidad Nacional de La Plata. Facultad de Ciencias Economicas. Instituto de Investigaciones Economicas — UNLP/E
Economics and Business Letter — Econ Bus Let
Economics Business Review — Econ Bus Rev
Economics for Idaho Agriculture. University of Idaho. Cooperative Extension Service — Econ Idaho Agric Univ Idaho Coop Ext Serv
Economics in Canadian Schools — Econ Can Sch
Economics Letters — ECLED
Economics Letters [*Netherlands*] — Econ Lett
Economics Letters [*Netherlands*] — Econom Lett
Economics Newsletter. South Dakota State University. Cooperative Extension Service. Economics Department — Econ Newsl SD State Univ Coop Ext Serv Econ Dep
Economics of Fruit Farming — Econ Fruit Farm
Economics of Planning — Econ Planning
Economics of Planning — EOP
Economics Pamphlet. South Dakota Agricultural Experiment Station — Econ Pam SD Agric Exp Stn
Economics Report. University of Florida. Agricultural Experiment Stations — Econ Rep Univ Fla Agric Exp Stns
Economics Report. University of Florida. Agricultural Experiment Stations. Food and Resource Economics Department — Econ Rep Univ Fla Agric Exp Stn Food Resour Econ Dep
Economie — ENM
Economie Agricole (Paris) — Econ Agr (Paris)
Economie Appliquee — EA
Economie Appliquee — EAP
Economie Appliquee — Ec Appl
Economie Appliquee — Econ Appl
Economie Appliquee — Econ Appliq
Economie Appliquee — Econ Appliquee
Economie des Pays Arabes — Econ Pays Arabes
Economie des Pays d'Afrique Noire — Econ Pays Afr N
Economie du Centre-Est — Econ Centre-Est
Economie Electrique — Econ El
Economie et Finances Agricoles — Econ et Fins Agrics
Economie et Finances Agricoles — Econ Finances Agric
Economie et Humanisme — Econ et Human
Economie et Humanisme — Econ et Humanisme
Economie et Humanisme — EHU
Economie et Medecine Animales [*France*] — ECMAA
Economie et Medecine Animales — ECMAAI
Economie et Medecine Animales — Econ Med Anim
Economie et Politique — Econ et Pol
Economie et Politique — Econ et Polit
Economie et Prevision — Econ et Prevision
Economie et Sante — Econ et Sante
Economie et Statistique — Econ et Statist
Economie et Statistique — ETU
Economie et Technique Internationale des Mines — Econ Tech Int Mines
Economie Europeenne — Econ Europ
Economie Meridionale — Econ Meridionale
Economie Rurale — Econ Rur
Economie Rurale — Econ Rurale
Economie-Geographie — Econ-Geogr
Economies et Societes — CBK
Economies et Societes — Econs et Socs
Economisch Bulletin Nederlandse Antillen — EBNA
Economisch Dagblad. Dagblad voor het Management — NTC
Economisch en Sociaal Instituut voor de Middenstand. Informatieblad — EEK
Economisch en Sociaal Tijdschrift — Econ Soc Tijds
Economisch en Sociaal Tijdschrift — Econom Soc Tijdsch
Economisch en Sociaal Tijdschrift — EST
Economisch en Sociaal Tijdschrift — ESY
Economische Politierrechter — EPR
Economische Voorlichting — EV
Economische Voorlichting Suriname — EVS
Economischen Sociaal-Historisch Jaarboek — Econ Sociaal Hist Jaarb
Economisch-Historisch Jaarboek — EHJ
Economisch-Statistische Berichten — Econ-Sta Ber
Economisch-Statistische Berichten — Econ-Statist Ber
Economisch-Statistische Berichten — ECSBA
Economisch-Statistische Berichten — ES
Economisch-Statistische Berichten — ESB
Economist — E
Economist — EC
Economist — ECI
Economist — ECN
Economist — Econ
Economist [*London*] — ECSTA
Economist — ECT
Economist — ET
Economist Financial Report — Econ Fin Rep
Economist Journal — EJM
Economista Mexicano — Econ Mex
Economiste Agricole — Econ Agric
Economiste Arabe. L'Economie et les Finances des Pays Arabes — EFP
Economiste du Tiers-Monde — Econ Tiers-Monde
Economists of the Twentieth Century — Econom Twent Century
Economy and History — E & H
Economy and History — Econ Hist
Economy and Society — Econ and Soc
Economy and Society — Econ Soc
Economy and Society — Econ Societ
Economy and Society — Economy Soc
Econotities — ENO
Ecopress Italia — ECT
Ecos de Valvanera — EV
Ecosphere [*Berkeley*] — ECSHAZ
Ecosystem Structure and Function. Proceedings. Annual Biology Colloquium — Ecosyst Struct Funct Proc Annu Biol Colloq
Ecosystems of the World — Ecosyst World
Ecosystems of the World — Ecosystems World
Ecosystems of the World [*Elsevier Book Series*] — ECWODB
Ecosystems of the World [*Elsevier Book Series*] — EW
Ecotoxicologie Marine — Ecotoxicol Mar
Ecotoxicology and Environmental Quality — Ecotoxicol Environ Qual
Ecotoxicology and Environmental Safety — Ecotoxicol Environ Saf
Ecotoxicology and Environmental Safety — Ecotoxicol Environ Safety
Ecotoxicology and Environmental Safety — EESADV
Ecotoxicology Monitoring — Ecotoxicol Monit
Ecotoxicology. Proceedings. Oikos Conference — Ecotoxicol Proc Oikos Conf
ECP [*Energy Conservation Project*] **Report** [*United States*] — ECP Rep
Ecran 79 [*France*] — Ecran
Ecrits des Saints — EdS
Ecuador. Direccion General de Geologia y Minas. Publication — Ecuador Dir Gen Geol Minas Publ
Ecuador. Direccion General Geologia y Minas. Revista — Ecuador Dir Gen Geol Minas Rev
Ecumenical Review — Ec R
Ecumenical Review — Ec Rev
Ecumenical Review — Ecum R
Ecumenical Review — Ecumen Rev

Ecumenical Review — Ecumenical R
Ecumenical Review — Ecumenical Rev
Ecumenical Review [*Geneva*] — EcuR
Ecumenical Review — ER
Ecumenical Review — PECU
Ecumenical Studies in History — Ecum St Hist
Ecumenical Studies in History — ESH
Eczacilik Bulteni — ECBUAN
Eczacilik Bulteni — Eczac Bul
Eczacilik Bulteni — Eczacilik Bul
Eczacilik Dergisi. Marmara Universitesi — Eczacilik Derg Marmara Univ
Eczacilik Fakultesi Dergisi. Hacettepe Universitesi — Eczacilik Fak Derg Hacettepe Univ
EDA [*British Electrical Development Association*] **Bulletin** — EDA Bull
Edda — Ed
Edda. Revue de Litterature — Ed
Edelmetaal, Uurwerken, Edelstenen. Maandblad voor de Edelmetaalbranche, Uurwerkenbranche, Edelstenenbranche, en Diamantbranche — MGZ
Edgar Allen News — Edg All News
Edgerton, Germeshausen, and Grier Report — Edgerton Germeshausen & Grier Rept
Edicia Matematicko-Fyzikalnej Literatury — Ed Mat Fyz Lit
Ediciones Bibliograficas (Buenos Aires) — Edic Bibliogr BA
Ediciones Catedra — Ed Cat
Ediciones Espanolas Sociedad Anonima — EDESA
Ediciones y Publicaciones Espanolas Sociedad Anonima — EPESA
Edilizia Moderna — Ed Mod
Edilizia Moderna — Edil Mod
Edinburgh Bibliographical Society. Publications — Edinburgh Bibliog Soc Pub
Edinburgh Bibliographical Society. Transactions — EBST
Edinburgh Bibliographical Society. Transactions — Edinburgh Bibliogr Soc Trans
Edinburgh Dental Hospital. Gazette — Edinb Dent Hosp Gaz
Edinburgh Geological Society. Transactions — Edinb G Soc Tr
Edinburgh Geological Society. Transactions — Edinburgh Geol Soc Trans
Edinburgh Geologist — Edinburgh Geol
Edinburgh Journal of Science — Edinburgh J Sci
Edinburgh Journal of Science, Technology, and Photographic Art — Ed J Sci
Edinburgh Journal of Science, Technology, and Photographic Art — Edinb J Sci Technol Photogr Art
Edinburgh Mathematical Notes — Edinb Math Notes
Edinburgh Medical and Surgical Journal — Edinb Med and S J
Edinburgh Medical Journal — ED MJ
Edinburgh Medical Journal — Edinb Med J
Edinburgh Medical Journal — Edinburgh Med J
Edinburgh Medical Missionary Society's Quarterly Paper — EMMSQP
Edinburgh Monthly Review — Ed Mo
Edinburgh New Philosophical Journal — Ed New Philos J
Edinburgh New Philosophical Journal — Edinburgh New Philos J
Edinburgh Philosophical Journal — Ed Philos J
Edinburgh Philosophical Journal — Edinburgh Philos J
Edinburgh Review — Ed R
Edinburgh Review — Edin R
Edinburgh Review — Edin Rev
Edinburgh Review — ER
Edinburgh School of Agriculture. Annual Report — Edinb Sch Agric Annu Rep
Edinburgh School of Agriculture. Annual Report — ESARCL
Edinburgh School of Agriculture. Experimental Work — EAEWAU
Edinburgh School of Agriculture. Experimental Work — Edinb Sch Agric Exp Work
Edinburgh University. Department of Linguistics. Work in Progress — EWIP
Edinburgh University Publications — EUP
Edinburgh University Publications. Geography and Sociology — EUP G
Edinburgh University Publications. History, Philosophy, and Economics — EUP H
Edinburgh University Publications. Language and Literature — EUP L
Edinburgh University Publications. Theology — EUP T
Edirne Tip Fakultesi Dergisi. Istanbul Universitesi — Edirne Tip Fak Derg Istanbul Univ
EDIS. Environmental Data and Information Service — EDISD
Edison Electric Institute. Bulletin — BEEIA
Edison Electric Institute. Bulletin — Edison Electr Inst Bull
Edison Electric Institute. Bulletin — EEI
Edison Electric Institute. Bulletin — EEI Bul
Edison Electric Institute. Electric Perspectives — EEI Elec P
Edison Electric Institute. Statistical Yearbook. Electric Utility Industry — Edison Electr Inst Stat Yearb Electr Util Ind
Edited Proceedings. International Cadmium Conference — Ed Proc Int Cadmium Conf
Edited Proceedings. International Conference on Hot Dip Galvanizing — Ed Proc Int Conf Hot Dip Galvanizing
Edited Proceedings. International Galvanizing Conference — Ed Proc Int Galvanizing Conf
Editeurs Francais Reunis — EFR
Edition Hebdomadaire du Journal de Debats — Edn Hebd J Deb
Editiones Arnamagnaenae — Ed Arn
Editiones Heidelbergenses — Ed Hd
Editiones Heidelbergenses — Ed Heidelb
Editiones Heidelbergenses — EH
Editions Bellarmin — Ed Bell
Editions Extraordinaires. Institut de Pharmacologie et de Toxicologie (Zagreb) — Ed Extraordinaires Inst Pharmacol Toxicol (Zagreb)
Editor and Publisher — E & P
Editor and Publisher — Ed & Pub
Editor and Publisher — Edit Publ
Editor and Publisher — EP
Editor and Publisher — GEDP
Editor and Publisher (New York) — EPNY
Editor and Publisher - the Fourth Estate — Ed Publ Fourth Estate
Editorial Cuadernos para el Dialogo — EDICUDA
Editorial Research Reports — Editorial Research Repts
Editorial Research Reports — EDRRA
Editorial Research Reports — ERR
Editorial Research Reports — GERR
Editorial Research Reports (Washington, DC) — Ed Res Rep (Wash DC)
Editorial Sudamericana, BA — SUDAM
Editorial Universitaria de Buenos Aires — EUDEBA
Editors' Notes — EdN
Edizioni Scientifiche Italiane — ESI
Edmonton Geological Society. Quarterly — Edmonton Geol Soc Q
Edmonton Geological Society. Quarterly — Edmonton Geol Soc Quart
Edmonton Journal — Edmontn Jl
Edmonton Journal — Edmonton J
Edmonton Public Library. News Notes — Edmonton P L News Notes
Edmonton Report — Edmonton Rep
Edmonton Spring Symposium — Edmonton Spring Symp
Edoth (Jerusalem) — EJ
EDP [*Electronic Data Processing*] **Analyzer** — EDP Anal
EDP [*Electronic Data Processing*] **Analyzer** — EDPAA
EDP [*Electronic Data Processing*] **Audit, Control, and Security Newsletter** — EDP A C S
EDP [*Electronic Data Processing*] **Auditor** — EDP Aud
EDP [*Electronic Data Processing*] **Europa Report** — EDP Europa
EDP [*Electronic Data Processing*] **In-Depth Reports** — EDP In-Depth Rep
EDP [*Electronic Data Processing*] **Industry Report** — EDP
EDP [*Electronic Data Processing*] **Industry Report** — EDP Indus Rep
EDP [*Electronic Data Processing*] **Japan Report** — EDP Japan
EDP [*Electronic Data Processing*] **Performance Review** — EDP Perf Rev
EDP [*Electronic Data Processing*] **Performance Review** — EDP Performance Rev
EDP [*Electronic Data Processing*] **Weekly** — EDP Weekly
EDRO [*Executive Director of Regional Operations*] **SARAP Research Technical Reports** [*Science Advisor Research Associate Program*] — EDRO SARAP Res Tech Rep
Educacao e Ciencias Sociais. Boletim do Centro Brasileiro de Pesquisas Educacionais (Rio de Janeiro) — Educ Cien Soc Rio
Educacion — ED
Educacion (Caracas) — Educ Caracas
Educacion de Adultos — EDA
Educacion Dental (Ica, Peru) — Educ Dent (Ica)
Educacion (Havanna) — EducacionH
Educacion Hoy (Colombia) — EHC
Educacion (Lima) — Educ Lima
Educacion (Managua) — EducacionM
Educacion Medica y Salud — EDMSAB
Educacion Medica y Salud — Educ Med Salud
Educacion (Mexico) — Educ Mex
Educacion Rural. Organizacion de los Estados Americanos (Rubio, Tachira, Venezuela) — Educ Rural Rubio
Educacion (San Jose, Costa Rica) — Educ S Jose
Educacion Superior — ESU
Educacion Superior y Desarrollo — Educ Sup Des
Educacion y Ciencias Humanas (Lima) — Educ Cien Humanas Lima
Educadores — ES
Education — Ed
Education — Educ
Education — Educa
Education — IDEU
Education Abstracts — EdAb
Education and Culture — EC
Education and Culture — Educ Cult
Education and Industrial Television — E & ITV
Education and Medicine — Educ and Medicine
Education and Psychology Review — Ed & Psychol Rev
Education and Safe Handling in Pesticide Application. Proceedings. International Workshop — Educ Safe Handl Pestic Appl Proc Int Workshop
Education and Social Science — Ed & Social Science
Education and Training — Ed & Training
Education and Training — Educ and Train
Education and Training — Educ & Training
Education and Training in Mental Retardation — ETMR
Education and Training of Engineering Designers. International Conference — Educ Train Eng Des Int Conf
Education and Training of the Mentally Retarded — Ed & Train Men Retard
Education and Training of the Mentally Retarded — Educ & Train Men Retard
Education and Training of the Mentally Retarded — Educ & Train Mentally Retard
Education and Training of the Mentally Retarded — ETMR
Education and Urban Society — Educ & Urban Soc
Education and Urban Society — Educ and Urban Society
Education and Urban Society — Educ Urb Soc
Education and Urban Society — Educ Urban
Education Around the World — Ed World
Education Bulletin — Educ Bull
Education Canada — Ed Can
Education Canada — Educ Can
Education Capital — Educ Cap
Education Circular. Education Department of Western Australia — Ed Circ WA
Education Circular. Education Department of Western Australia — WA Ed Circ
Education Digest — Ed Digest
Education Digest — Educ Dig

Education Digest — Educ Digest
Education Digest — GTED
Education et Culture — Educ et Cult
Education et Developpement — Educ et Develop
Education for Development — Ed for Dev
Education for Development — EFD
Education for Teaching — Ed for Teaching
Education for Victory — Educ Vict
Education Gazette — Educ Gaz
Education Gazette [*Sydney*] — Educ Gazette
Education Gazette and Teachers Aid (Victoria) — Ed Gaz & Teach Aid (Vic)
Education Gazette and Teachers Aid (Victoria) — Vic Ed Gaz
Education Gazette (New South Wales) — NSW Ed Gaz
Education Gazette. New South Wales Department of Education — Ed Gaz NSW
Education Gazette. South Australia Department of Education — Ed Gaz SA
Education Gazette. South Australia Department of Education — Educ Gaz SA
Education Gazette. South Australia Department of Education — SA Ed Gaz
Education Guardian — Educ Guard
Education in Chemistry — Ed in Chem
Education in Chemistry — EDCHA
Education in Chemistry — Educ Chem
Education in Eastern Africa — Educ East Afr
Education in Japan — Ed in Japan
Education in Large Cities — Educ Lg Cit
Education in Science — Ed in Science
Education in Science — Educ Sci
Education in the North — Ed in the North
Education Index — EdI
Education Index — Educ Ind
Education Index — Educ Index
Education Index — EI
Education Journal — Educ J
Education Law Reporter (West) — Educ L Rep (West)
Education Libraries Bulletin — Ed Lib Bulletin
Education Libraries Bulletin — Educ Libr Bull
Education Libraries Bulletin — Education Librs Bull
Education Library Service Bulletin — Educ Libr Serv Bull
Education Manitoba — Ed Man
Education Media — EdM
Education Music Magazine — Ed Mus Mag
Education Musicale — Education M
Education Nationale — Educ Nat
Education Nationale — EN
Education. New South Wales Teachers Federation — Ed NSW
Education. New South Wales Teachers Federation — Educ NSW
Education News — Ed News
Education News — Educ N
Education News — Educ News
Education Nova Scotia — Ed NS
Education of the Visually Handicapped — Ed Vis Hand
Education of the Visually Handicapped — Educ Visual
Education Office Gazette. Queensland Department of Education — Ed Off Gaz Qld
Education Office Gazette. Queensland Department of Education — Q Ed Off Gaz
Education Ontario — Ed Ont
Education Ontario — Educ Ont
Education Permanente — Educ Perm
Education (Perth, Western Australia) — Educ (WA)
Education Policy Bulletin — Educ Policy Bull
Education Quarterly — Educ Q
Education Quarterly [*New Delhi*] — EQ
Education Quarterly (India) — Ed Q India
Education Quarterly. Katmandu, Nepal College of Education — Educ Q Nepal
Education Quebec — Ed Que
Education Research — ERes
Education Research and Perspectives — Educ Res Perspect
Education Review — Educ Rev
Education Sanitaire — Ed San
Education through Technology — Educ Through Technol
Education Today — Ed Today.
Education USA — Ed USA
Education Week — GEDW
Education (Western Australia) — Ed (WA)
Educational Administration — Educ Adm
Educational Administration Abstracts — EAA
Educational Administration Abstracts — EdAd
Educational Administration Abstracts — Educ Adm Abstr
Educational Administration Abstracts — Educ Admin Abstr
Educational Administration Abstracts — EEA
Educational Administration and Supervision — Ed Adm & Sup
Educational Administration and Supervision — Educ Adm & Sup
Educational Administration and Supervision — Educ Admin Supervision
Educational Administration Bulletin — Ednl Administration Bull
Educational Administration Quarterly — Ed Adm Q
Educational Administration Quarterly — Educ Adm Q
Educational Administration Quarterly — Educ Admin
Educational Administrator — Educ Adm
Educational and Industrial Television — Educ Ind Telev
Educational and Industrial Television — Educ TV
Educational and Industrial Television — ET
Educational and Psychological Measurement — Ed & Psychol M
Educational and Psychological Measurement — Educ & Psychol M
Educational and Psychological Measurement — Educ & Psychol Meas
Educational and Psychological Measurement — Educ Psyc M
Educational and Psychological Measurement — Educ Psychol Measmt
Educational and Psychological Measurement — Educ Psychol Measure
Educational and Psychological Measurement — EPM
Educational and Psychological Measurement — EPMEA
Educational and Psychological Measurement — EPsM
Educational and Psychological Measurement — IEDP
Educational Bi-Monthly — Ed Bi-Mo
Educational Books and Equipment — Ed Books and Equip
Educational Broadcasting — EB
Educational Broadcasting — Educ Brdcstng
Educational Broadcasting International — EBI
Educational Broadcasting International [*United Kingdom*] — Ed B Int
Educational Broadcasting International — Ednl Broadcasting International
Educational Broadcasting International — Educ Broad Int
Educational Broadcasting International — Educ Broadcast Int
Educational Broadcasting Review — EBR
Educational Building Digest — Educational Bldg Digest
Educational Change and Development — Ednl Change and Dev
Educational Change and Development — Educ Change Dev
Educational Communication and Technology Journal — Educ Comm & Tech J
Educational Computing — Educ Comput
Educational Computing Organization of Ontario. Newsletter — ECOO N
Educational Development — Ednl Dev
Educational Development Centre Review — Ednl Dev Centre R
Educational Development in Korea — Educ Dev Korea
Educational Development International — Ednl Dev International
Educational Digest — Edu D
Educational Directions for Dental Auxiliaries — Educ Dir Dent Aux
Educational Directions in Dental Hygiene — Educ Dir Dent Hyg
Educational Documentation and Information — EDI
Educational Documentation and Information — Ednl Documentation and Information
Educational Documentation and Information — Educ Doc & Inf
Educational Documentation and Information Bulletin [*UNESCO*] — DI
Educational Exchange Features — Ed Ex Feat
Educational Executive's Overview — Ed Exec Overview
Educational Executives' Overview — Educ Exec Overview
Educational Experiments and Research — Ed Exp Res
Educational Film Guide — Educ Film Guide
Educational Focus — Educ Foc
Educational Focus — Educ Focus
Educational Forum — Ed F
Educational Forum — Ed Forum
Educational Forum — Educ For
Educational Forum — Educ Forum
Educational Forum — EducF
Educational Foundation. American Society of Plastic and Reconstructive Surgeons. Proceedings of the Symposium — Educ Found Am Soc Plast Reconstr Surg Proc Symp
Educational Gerontology — EDGEDA
Educational Gerontology — Educ Gerontol
Educational Horizons — Ed Horiz
Educational Horizons — EdH
Educational Horizons — Educ Horiz
Educational Innovations — Educ Innovations
Educational/Instructional Broadcasting — EIB
Educational Journal — Ed J
Educational Leadership — Ed Lead
Educational Leadership — EdL
Educational Leadership — Educ Lead
Educational Leadership — Educ Leadersh
Educational Leadership — EL
Educational Leadership — GEDL
Educational Magazine — Ed Mag
Educational Magazine — Educ Mag
Educational Management and Administration — Educ Manage Admin
Educational Media — Educ Media
Educational Media International — Educ Media Int
Educational Method — Ed Meth
Educational Microcomputing Annual — Educ Microcomp Ann
Educational Music Magazine — Educ Mus Mag
Educational Outlook — Ed Outl
Educational Outlook — Educ Outl
Educational Philosophy and Theory — Educ Phil Theor
Educational Philosophy and Theory — Educ Philos Theory
Educational Planning — Educ Plan
Educational Product Report — Ed Prod Rep
Educational Product Report — Educ Prod Rept
Educational Psychologist — Educ Psychol
Educational Quarterly (Nepal) — Ed Q Nepal
Educational Quarterly (Philippines) — Ed Q Phil
Educational Quest — Educ Quest
Educational Record — EdR
Educational Record — Educ Rec
Educational Record — Educ Recd
Educational Record — Educ Record
Educational Record — Educational Rec
Educational Record — GEDR
Educational Record. Tasmania Education Department — Ed Rec
Educational Record. Tasmania Education Department — Tas Ed Rec
Educational Records Bureau. Bulletins [*Greenwich, Connecticut*] — Ed Rec Bur Bul
Educational Records Bureau. Bulletins [*Greenwich, Connecticut*] — Educ Rec Bur Bull
Educational Research [*Oxford*] — Ed Res

Educational Research — Ednl Research
Educational Research — Educ Res
Educational Research Bulletin — Ed Res B
Educational Research Bulletin — Educ Res Bul
Educational Research Bulletin — ERB
Educational Research News — Educ Res News
Educational Research Quarterly — Educ Res Q
Educational Research Quarterly — Educ Res Quart
Educational Research Record — Ed Res Record
Educational Researcher — Educ Res
Educational Researcher — Educ Researcher
Educational Resources Information Center Clearinghouse — Educ Resour Inf Cent Clgh
Educational Review [*United Kingdom*] — Ed R
Educational Review — Ednl R
Educational Review — Educ R
Educational Review — Educa R
Educational Review — ER
Educational Review (China) — Ed R (China)
Educational Sciences — Ed Sci
Educational Sciences — Ednl Sciences
Educational Screen — Ed Screen
Educational Screen — Educ Screen
Educational Screen and Audiovisual Guide [*Later, AV Guide: The Learning Media Magazine*] — AVG
Educational Screen and Audiovisual Guide [*Later, AV Guide: The Learning Media Magazine*] — Ed Screen AV G
Educational Series. Florida Department of Natural Resources. Marine Research Laboratory — Ed Ser Fla Dep Nat Resour Mar Res Lab
Educational Series. Florida. Department of Natural Resources. Marine Research Laboratory — Educ Ser Fl Dep Nat Resour Mar Res Lab
Educational Series. Mineral Resources Division (Manitoba) — Educ Ser Miner Resour Div (Manitoba)
Educational Series. North Carolina Mineral Resources Section — Educ Ser NC Miner Resour Sect
Educational Software Report — Educ Software Rep
Educational Studies — Ed Studies
Educational Studies — Ednl Studies
Educational Studies — Educ Stud
Educational Studies — ES
Educational Studies (Ames, Iowa) — ESA
Educational Studies in Mathematics [*Dordrecht*] — Ed Stud Math
Educational Studies in Mathematics — Ednl Studies in Maths
Educational Studies in Mathematics — Educ Stud Math
Educational Supplement. Yorkshire Beekeepers Association — Educ Suppl Yorks Beekprs Ass
Educational Survey — Ed Survey
Educational Technology — Ed Tech
Educational Technology — EdT
Educational Technology — Educ Tech
Educational Technology — Educ Techn
Educational Technology — Educ Technol
Educational Television — ET
Educational Television International — Ed TV Int
Educational Theatre Journal — Ed Theatre J
Educational Theatre Journal — Educ Theatre J
Educational Theatre Journal — ETJ
Educational Theory — Ed Theory
Educational Theory — Educ Theor
Educational Theory — Educ Theory
Educational Times — ED T
Educator — EDENA
Educator's Desk Reference — EDR
Educator's Legal Service Briefs — Educ Leg Serv Br
Educazione dei Sordomuti — Educ Sordomuti
Educazione Musicale — Ed Mus
Educazione Musicale — Educazione M
Educazione Sanitaria — Educ Sanit
EDUCOM [*Educational Communications*] **Bulletin** — EDUCOM
EDUCOM [*Educational Communications*] **Bulletin** — EDUCOM Bull
EDV [*Elektronische Datenverarbeitung*] **in Medizin und Biologie** — EDV Med Biol
EDV [*Elektronische Datenverarbeitung*] **in Medizin und Biologie** — EDVBD8
Edward Cadbury Lectures — ECL
Edward Sapir Monograph Series in Language, Culture, and Cognition — ESMSLCC
EE/Systems Engineering Today — EE/Systems Eng
EEC Dangerous Chemicals Online [*Database*] — EECDNG
EEG/EMG; Zeitschrift fuer Elektroenzephalographie, Elektromyographie, und Verwandte Gebiete [*Germany*] — EEGEA
EEI [*Edison Electric Institute*] **Bulletin** — EEIBA
EEO [*Equal Employment Opportunity*] **Spotlight** — EEO Spotl
EEOC [*Equal Employment Opportunity Commission*] **Compliance Manual. Bureau of National Affairs** — EEOC Compl Man BNA
EEOC [*Equal Employment Opportunity Commission*] **Compliance Manual. Commerce Clearing House** — EEOC Compl Man CCH
EES [*Engineering Experiment Station*] **Report. University of Wisconsin-Madison. Engineering Experiment Station** — EES Rep Univ Wis Madison Eng Exp Stn
Eesti Loodus — EELOAZ
Eesti Loodusteaduse Arhiiv. 1 Ser. Geologica, Chemica, et Physica — Eesti Loodustead Arh 1 Ser
Eesti Loodusteaduse Arhiiv. 2 Seeria. Acta ad res Naturae Estonicae Perscrutandas Edita a Societate Rebus Naturae Investigandis in Universitate Tartuensi Constituta. Serie 2 — Eesti Loodustead Arh Seer 2
Eesti Loodusteaduse Arhiiv. 2 Ser. Biologica — Eesti Loodustead Arh 2 Ser
Eesti Loomakasvatuse ja Veterinaaria Teadusliku Uurimise Instituut. Teaduslike Toode Kogumik — Eesti Loomakasvatuse Vet Tead Uurim Inst Tead Toode Kogumik
Eesti NSV Teaduste Akadeemia. Fuusika Instituudi Uurimused — Eesti NSV Tead Akad Fuus Inst Uurim
Eesti NSV Teaduste Akadeemia. Fuusika ja Astronoomia Instituudi Uurimused — Eesti NSV Tead Akad Fuus Astronoom Inst Uurim
Eesti NSV Teaduste Akadeemia. Geoloogia Instituudi Uurimused — Eesti NSV Tead Akad Geol Inst Uurim
Eesti NSV Teaduste Akadeemia. Tartu Astronoomia Observatooriumi Publikatsioonik — Eesti NSV Tead Akad Tartu Astronoom Observ Publ
Eesti NSV Teaduste Akadeemia. Toimetised [*Former USSR*] — Eesti NSV Tead Akad
Eesti NSV Teaduste Akadeemia. Toimetised — Eesti NSV Tead Akad Toim
Eesti NSV Teaduste Akadeemia. Toimetised. Bioloogia — Eesti NSV Tead Akad Toim Biol
Eesti NSV Teaduste Akadeemia. Toimetised. Bioloogia — ETATA
Eesti NSV Teaduste Akadeemia. Toimetised. Bioloogia — ETATAW
Eesti NSV Teaduste Akadeemia. Toimetised. Bioloogiline Seeria [*Estonian SSR*] — Eesti NSV Tead Akad Toim Biol Ser
Eesti NSV Teaduste Akadeemia. Toimetised. Fuusika. Matemaatika — Eesti NSV Tead Akad Toim Fuus Mat
Eesti NSV Teaduste Akadeemia. Toimetised. Fuusika. Matemaatika ja Tehnikateaduste Seeria — Eesti NSV Tead Akad Toim Fuus Mat Tehnikatead Seer
Eesti NSV Teaduste Akadeemia. Toimetised. Geoloog Izvestiia Akademii Nauk Estonskoi SSR Geologiia — Eesti NSV Tead Akad Toim Geol Izv Akad Nauk Est SSR Geol
Eesti NSV Teaduste Akadeemia. Toimetised. Geoloogia — Eesti NSV Tead Akad Toim Geol
Eesti NSV Teaduste Akadeemia. Toimetised. Izvestiya. Seria Geoloogia [*Estonian SSR*] — Eesti NSV Tead Akad Toim Izv Ser Geol
Eesti NSV Teaduste Akadeemia. Toimetised. Izvestiya. Seria Keemia [*Estonian SSR*] — Eesti NSV Tead Akad Toim Izv Ser Keem
Eesti NSV Teaduste Akadeemia. Toimetised. Keemia — Eesti NSV Tead Akad Toim Keem
Eesti NSV Teaduste Akadeemia. Toimetised. Keemia. Geoloogia — Eesti NSV Tead Akad Toim Keem Geol
Eesti NSV Teaduste Akadeemia. Toimetised. Keemia. Izvestiia Akademii Nauk Estonskoi SSR Khimiia — Eesti NSV Tead Akad Toim Keem Izv Akad Nauk Est SSR Khim
Eesti NSV Teaduste Akadeemia. Toimetised. Tehniliste ja Fuusikalis-Matemaatiliste Teaduste Seeria — Eesti NSV Tead Akad Toim Teh Fuus Mat Tead Seer
Eesti NSV Teaduste Akadeemia Toimetised. Uhiskonnateaduste Seeria — ETAT
Eesti Pollumajanduse Akadeemia Teaduslike Toode Kogumik — Eesti Pollumajanduse Akad Tead Toode Kogumik
Eesti Teaduste Akadeemia Toimetised. Bioloogia — Eesti Tead Akad Toim Biol
Eesti Teaduste Akadeemia Toimetised. Keemia — Eesti Tead Akad Toim Keemia
Eesti Vabariigi Tartu Ulikooli Toimetised A. Mathematica, Physica, Medica — Eesti Vabariigi Tartu Ulik Toim A
Eesti Vabariigi Tartu Ulikooli Toimetised C. Annales — Eesti Vabariigi Tartu Ulik Toim C
Effect of the Ocean Environment on Microbial Activities. Proceedings. United States-Japan Conference on Marine Microbiology — Eff Ocean Environ Microb Act Proc US Jpn Conf
Effective Health Care — Eff Health Care
Effectivnost Udobrenii — Eff Udobr
Effects of Aging on Regulation of Cerebral Blood Flow and Metabolism. Abstracts. Satellite Symposium — Eff Aging Regul Cereb Blood Flow Metab Abstr Satell Symp
Effects of Chemical Environment on Fracture Processes. Tewksbury Symposium on Fracture — Eff Chem Environ Fract Processes Tewksbury Symp
Effects of Environment on Cells and Tissues. Proceedings. World Congress of Anatomic and Clinical Pathology — Eff Environ Cells Tissues Proc World Congr Anat Clin Pathol
Effects of Radiation on Materials. International Symposium — Eff Radiat Mater Int Symp
Effektivnost Zashchity Introdutsirovannykh Rastenii ot Vrednykh Organizmov. Materialy Koordinatsionnogo Soveshchaniya — Eff Zashch Introd Rast Vrednykh Org Mater Koord Soveshch
Effets des Rayonnements sur les Semiconducteurs. Congres International de Physique des Semiconducteurs — Eff Rayonnem Semicond Congr Int Phys Semicond
Efficience Textile — Effi Text
Efficience Textile — Effic Text
Effluent and Water Treatment Journal — Eff Wat Tre
Effluent and Water Treatment Journal — Effluent Water Treat J
Effluent and Water Treatment Journal — EWTJA
Effluent and Water Treatment Journal — EWTJAG
EFOC [*European Fiber Optics and Communications*] **Fiber Optics and Communications. Proceedings** — EFOC Fiber Opt Commun Proc
EFOC [*European Fiber Optics and Communications Exposition*] **Proceedings** — EFOC Proc
Efrydiau Athronyddol — EA
EFT Report. The Newsletter of Electronic Funds Transfer — EFT Report
EFTA [*European Free Trade Association*] **Bulletin** — EFB
EFTA [*European Free Trade Association*] **Bulletin** — EFE
EFTA [*European Free Trade Association*] **Bulletin** — EFTA Bull
EGE [*Eau-Gaz-Electricite et Applications*] **Actualites** — EGE Actual
Ege Universitesi Fen Fakultesi Dergisi. Seri B — Ege Univ Fen Fak Derg Seri B
Ege Universitesi Fen Fakultesi Ilmi Raporlar Serisi — Ege Univ Fen Fak Ilmi Rap Ser

Ege Universitesi Fen Fakultesi Ilmi Raporlar Serisi — EUFSAR
Ege Universitesi Ziraat. Fakultesi Dergisi — Ege Univ Ziraat Fak Derg
Ege Universitesi Ziraat. Fakultesi Dergisi. Seri A — Ege Univ Ziraat Fak Derg Seri A
Ege Universitesi Ziraat. Fakultesi Yayinlari — Ege Univ Ziraat Fak Yayin
Egerton College. Agricultural Bulletin — Egerton Coll Agric Bull
Egeszsegtudomany — EGESA
Egeszsegtudomany — Egesz
EGF/ESIS (European Group on Fracture/European Structural Integrity Society) Publication — EGF ESIS Publ
EGF (European Group on Fracture) Publication — EGF Publ
Egg Producer — Egg Prod
Egitto e Vicino Oriente — Eg Vic Or
Eglise aus Cent Visages — ECV
Eglise Canadienne — Egl Can
Eglise et l'Etat au Moyen Age — EEMA
Eglise et Societe — EeS
Eglise et Theologie — E & Th
Eglise et Theologie — Ee T
Eglise et Theologie — Egl Th
Eglise et Theologie — Eglise Th
Eglise Vivante — Egl Viv
Egmondiana — Egm
Egretta — EGREAF
Egri Muzeum Evkoenyve — Egri ME
Egri Muzeum Evkoenyve — Egri Muz E
Egri Muzeum Evkoenyve — EME
Egri Tanarkepzoe Foeiskola Tudomanyos Koezlemenyei. Acta Academiae Paedagogicae Agriensis — Egri Tanarkepzoe Foeisk Tud Koezlem
Egyetemes Philologiai Koezloeny — Egy Phil Koez
Egyetemes Philologiai Koezloeny — EPhK
Egyetemes Philologiai Koezloeny — EPK
Egypt Exploration Fund — EEF
Egypt Exploration Fund Memoirs — EEFM
Egypt Exploration Fund Memoirs — Egypt Explor Fund Mem
Egypt Exploration Society. Graeco-Roman Memoirs — EESGRM
Egypt Exploration Society Memoirs [*London*] — EESM
Egypt Exploration Society. Report — EESR
Egypt Geological Survey. Annals — Egypt Geol Surv Ann
Egypt Geological Survey. Paper — Egypt Geol Surv Pap
Egypt. Ministry of Agriculture. Technical Bulletin — Egypt Minist Agric Tech Bull
Egypt Research Account — ERA
Egypt Travel Magazine — Egyt Trav Mag
Egypte Contemporaine — EC
Egypte Contemporaine — Eg Cont
Egypte Contemporaine — EgC
Egypte Contemporaine — Egypte Contemp
Egypte Contemporaine. Societe Khediviale d'Economie Politique, de Statistique et de Legislation — Egypte Contemp Soc Khed
Egyptian Agricultural Organization. Bahtim Experiment Station. Technical Bulletin — Egypt Agric Organ Bahtim Exp Stn Tech Bull
Egyptian Agricultural Review — Egypt Agric Rev
Egyptian Computer Journal — Egypt Comput J
Egyptian Cotton Gazette [*Alexandria*] — ECG
Egyptian Cotton Gazette — Egypt Cott Gaz
Egyptian Cotton Gazette — Egypt Cotton Gaz
Egyptian Dental Journal — EGDJAS
Egyptian Dental Journal — Egypt Dent J
Egyptian Gazette — EGG
Egyptian Gazette (Cairo) — EGC
Egyptian Geological Survey and Mining Authority. Paper — Egypt Geol Surv Min Auth Pap
Egyptian Government School of Medicine. Records — Eg Gov School Med Rec
Egyptian Journal of Agronomy — Egypt J Agron
Egyptian Journal of Agronomy — EJAGDS
Egyptian Journal of Animal Production — EGAPBW
Egyptian Journal of Animal Production — Egypt J Anim Prod
Egyptian Journal of Bilharziasis — Egypt J Bilharz
Egyptian Journal of Bilharziasis — Egypt J Bilharziasis
Egyptian Journal of Bilharziasis — EJBLAB
Egyptian Journal of Biochemistry — Egypt J Biochem
Egyptian Journal of Biomedical Engineering — Egypt J Biomed Eng
Egyptian Journal of Botany — EGJBAY
Egyptian Journal of Botany — Egypt J Bot
Egyptian Journal of Chemistry — EGJCA3
Egyptian Journal of Chemistry — Egypt J Ch
Egyptian Journal of Chemistry — Egypt J Chem
Egyptian Journal of Chest Diseases and Tuberculosis — Egypt J Chest Dis Tuberc
Egyptian Journal of Chest Diseases and Tuberculosis — EJCDAQ
Egyptian Journal of Dairy Science — Egypt J Dairy Sci
Egyptian Journal of Food Science — Egypt J Food Sci
Egyptian Journal of Food Science — EJFSAI
Egyptian Journal of Genetics and Cytology — Egypt J Genet Cytol
Egyptian Journal of Genetics and Cytology — EJGCA9
Egyptian Journal of Geology — EGJGAF
Egyptian Journal of Geology — Egypt J Geol
Egyptian Journal of Horticulture — Egypt J Hortic
Egyptian Journal of Horticulture — EJHCAE
Egyptian Journal of Immunology — Egypt J Immunol
Egyptian Journal of Microbiology — Egypt J Microbiol
Egyptian Journal of Microbiology — EJMBA2
Egyptian Journal of Neurology, Psychiatry, and Neurosurgery — Egypt J Neurol Psychiat Neurosurg
Egyptian Journal of Occupational Medicine — Egypt J Occup Med
Egyptian Journal of Pharmaceutical Sciences — Egypt J Pharm Sci
Egyptian Journal of Pharmaceutical Sciences — EJPSBZ
Egyptian Journal of Physics — Egypt J Phys
Egyptian Journal of Physiological Science — EJPLAD
Egyptian Journal of Physiological Sciences — Egypt J Physiol Sci
Egyptian Journal of Phytopathology — Egypt J Phyopathol
Egyptian Journal of Phytopathology — Egypt J Phytopathol
Egyptian Journal of Psychiatry — Egypt J Psychiatry
Egyptian Journal of Psychology — Egypt J Psychol
Egyptian Journal of Social Medicine — Egypt J Soc Med
Egyptian Journal of Soil Science — Egypt J Soil Sci
Egyptian Journal of Soil Science — EJSSAF
Egyptian Journal of Veterinary Science — Egypt J Vet Sci
Egyptian Journal of Veterinary Science — Egypt Jnl Vet Sci
Egyptian Journal of Veterinary Science — EJVSAU
Egyptian Mail — EGM
Egyptian National Cancer Institute. Journal — Egypt Natl Cancer Inst J
Egyptian Orthopaedic Journal — Egypt Orthop J
Egyptian Pharmaceutical Bulletin — EGPBAU
Egyptian Pharmaceutical Bulletin — Egypt Pharm Bull
Egyptian Pharmaceutical Journal — EGPJBL
Egyptian Pharmaceutical Journal — Egypt Pharm J
Egyptian Pharmaceutical Reports. Pharmaceutical Society of Egypt and the Syndicate of Pharmacists — Egypt Pharm Rep
Egyptian Population and Family Planning Review — Egypt Popul Fam Plann Rev
Egyptian Religion — EgR
Egyptian Religious Texts and Representations — ERTR
Egyptian Reviews of Science — Egypt Revs Sci
Egyptian Society of Obstetrics and Gynecology. Journal — Egypt Soc Obstet Gynecol J
Egyptian Statistical Journal — Egyptian Statist J
Egyptian Sugar and Distillation Company. Sugar Cane Department. Research Bulletin — Egypt Sugar Distill Co Sugar Cane Dep Res Bull
Egyptian Sugar and Distillation Company. Sugar Cane Department. Technical Bulletin — Egypt Sugar Distill Co Sugar Cane Dep Tech Bull
Egyptian Veterinary Medical Association. Journal — Egypt Vet Med Assoc J
Egyptian Veterinary Medical Journal — Egypt Vet Med J
Ehara Jiho — EHJIA
EHD. Canada Environmental Health Directorate — EHD Can Environ Health Dir
Ehe und Familie im Privaten und Oeffentlichen Recht — E u F
Ehegesundheitsgesetz — Ehe Ges G
Ehime Daigaku Kiyo Shizenkagaku. B. Shirizu Seibutsugaku — MEUBAR
Ehime Daigaku Nogakubu Enshurin Hokoku — ENHBA5
Ehime Daigaku Nogakubu Kiyo. Memoirs of the College of Agriculture. Ehime University — Ehime Daigaku Nogaku Kiyo Mem Coll Agric Ehime Univ
Ehkonomika Neftyanoj Promyshlennosti — Ehkon Neft Prom-St
Ehksperimental'naya Khirurgiya i Anesteziologiya — Ehksp Khir Anesteziol
Ehksperimental'naya Onkologiya — Ehksp Onkol
Ehkspress-Informatsiya. Laboratornye Tekhnologicheskie Issledovaniya i Obogashchenie Mineral'nogo Syr'ya — Ehkspress-Inf Lab Tekhnol Issled Obogashch Miner Syr'ya
Ehkspress-Informatsiya. Montazh Oborudovaniya na Teplovykh Ehlektrostantsiyakh — Ehkspress-Inf Montazh Oborudovaniya Tepl Ehlektrostn
Ehkspress-Informatsiya. Neftegazovaya Geologiya i Geofizika — Ehkspress-Inf Neftegazov Geol Geofiz
Ehkspress-Informatsiya. Seriya. Regional'naya. Razvedochnaya i Promyslovaya Geofizika — Ehkspress-Inf Ser Reg Razved Promysl Geofiz
Ehkspress-Informatsiya. Stroitel'stvo Teplovykh Ehlektrostantsij — Ehkspress-Inf Stroit Tepl Ehlektrostn
Ehkspress-Informatsiya. Svarochnye Raboty — Ehkspress-Inf Svar Rab
Ehlektricheskie Stantsii — Ehlektr Stn
Ehlektrofizicheskaya Apparatura — Ehlektrofiz Appar
Ehlektrokhimiya. Akademiya Nauk SSSR. Ezhemesyachnyj Zhurnal — Ehlektrokhim
Ehlektronnaya Obrabotka Materialov — Ehlektron Obrab Mater
Ehlektronnye i Ionnye Protessy v Tverdykh Telakh — Ehlektron Ionnye Protessy Tverd Telakh
Ehlektrosvyaz' i Radiotekhnika — Ehlektrosvyaz' Radiotekh
Ehnergeticheskoe Stroitel'stvo — Ehnerg Stroit
Ehnergeticheskoe Stroitel'stvo za Rubezhom — Ehnerg Stroit Rubezhom
Ehnergetika i Ehlektrifikatsiya — Ehnerg Ehlektrif
Ehntomologicheskoe Obozrenie — Ehntomol Obozr
EHP (Environmental Health Perspectives) — EHP (Environ Health Perspect)
Ehrverskonomiske Meddelelser — EM
Ehuzu [*Benin*] — EZ
El Digest. Industrial and Hazardous Waste Management — El Dig
EIA [*Electronics Industries Association*] **Publications. New Releases** [*United States*] — EIA Publ New Releases
Eibei Bungaku [*British and American Literature: The Rikkyo Review of Arts and Letters*] — EBB
Eibungaku Shicho [*Current Thoughts in English Literature*] — EBSC
EIC [*Engineering Institute of Canada*] **News** — EIC Ne
EIC [*Engineering Institute of Canada*] **Transactions** — EIC Trans
Eichendorff-Kalender — Eichendorff Kal
Eichordnung — Eich O
Eichsfelder Heimathefte — Eichsfelder Heimath
Eichstaedter Bienenzeitung — Eichstaedter Bienenztg
Eichstaetter Pastoralblatt — Eih Pbl
Eichstaetter Studien — E St
Eickhogg-Mitteilungen [*Germany*] — Eickhogg-Mitt
Eidgenoessische Abschiede — EA
Eidgenoessische Anstalt fuer das Forstliche Versuchswesen. Mitteilungen — Eidg Anst Forstl Versuchswes Mitt

Eidgenoessische Anstalt fuer das Forstliche Versuchswesen. Mitteilungen — MEAVDO
Eidgenoessische Materialpruefungs- und Versuchsanstalt — Eidg Materialpruef Versuchsanst
Eidgenoessische Materialpruefungsanstalt an der ETH (Zurich). Bericht — Eidg Materialpruefungsanst ETH (Zurich) Ber
Eidgenoessische Technische Hochschule. Institut fuer Reaktortechnik. Bericht AF-NST — Eidg Tech Hochsch Inst Reaktortech Ber AF NST
Eidgenoessische Technische Hochschule. Versuchsanstalt fuer Wasserbau und Erdbau. Mitteilungen [*Zurich*] — Eidg Tech Hochsch Versuchsanst Wasserbau Erdbau Mitt
Eidgenoessische Technische Hochschule. Versuchsanstalt fuer Wasserbau und Erdbau. Mitteilungen Zurich — Eidge Tech Hochsch Versuchsans Wasserbau Erdbau Mitt Zurich
Eidgenoessisches Institut fuer Reaktorforschung. Bericht — EIR-Ber
Eidgenoessisches Institut fuer Reaktorforschung. EIR Bericht — Eidg Inst Reaktorforsch EIR Ber
Eidikai Meletai Edi tes Geologias tes Ellados — Eidikai Meletai Geol Ellados
Eidos. A Journal of Painting, Sculpture, and Design — Eid
EIFAC [*European Inland Fisheries Advisory Commission*] **Occasional Paper** — EIFAC Occas Pap
EIFAC [*European Inland Fisheries Advisory Commission*] **Occasional Paper** — EIOPAD
EIFAC [*European Inland Fisheries Advisory Commission*] **Technical Paper** — EIFAC Tech Pap
EIFAC [*European Inland Fisheries Advisory Commission*] **Technical Paper** — EIFPA2
Eigen Huis en Interieur — EIB
Eigen Schoon en de Brabander — ESB
Eigen Schoon en de Brabander — ESBr
Eigen Vervoer. Magazine voor Eigen Vervoerders en Verladers — INX
Eighteenth Century — E Cent
Eighteenth Century — Eighteenth Cent
Eighteenth Century: a Current Bibliography — Eight Century Curr Bibliogr
Eighteenth Century Theory and Interpretation — Eight Ct
Eighteenth Century Theory and Interpretation — Eighteenth Cent Theory Interpr
Eighteenth-Century Life — E-C Life
Eighteenth-Century Life — Eight-Ct L
Eighteenth-Century Life — Eighteenth Cent Life
Eighteenth-Century Short Title Catalogue [*Database*] — ESTCC
Eighteenth-Century Studies — ECS
Eighteenth-Century Studies — Eight-Ct St
Eighteenth-Century Studies — Eighteenth-Cent Stud
Eighteenth-Century Studies — PEIG
Eigo Seinen — Eigo S
Eigse — Eig
Eildon Tree — ET
Einbecker Jahrbuch — EJ
Einblicke in die Wissenschaft — Einblicke Wiss
Eine Heilige Kirche — E H K
Einfuehrung in die Evangelische Theologie — EETh
Einfuehrungen zur Molekularbiologie — EFMBB9
Einfuehrungen zur Molekularbiologie — Einfuehr Molekularbiol
Einfuehrungen zur Molekularbiologie — Einfuehrung Molekularbiol
Einfuehrungen zur Molekularbiologie — Einfuehrungen Molekularbiol
Einfuehrungsgesetz zum Gerichtsverfassungsgesetz — EGGVG
Einfuehrungsgesetz zur Konkursordnung — EGKO
Einheit — E
Einheit der Gesellschaftswissenschaften — Einheit Gesellschaftswiss
Einheit in Christus — Ei C
Einheit. Theoretische Zeitschrift des Wissenschaftlichen Sozialismus — Einh
Einige Wiener Papyri (Boswinkel) — P (Boswinkel)
Einige Wiener Papyri (Sijpesteijn) — P (Sijp)
Einleitung in die Altertumswissenschaft — EAW
Einsicht — Eins
Einst und Jetzt — E u J
Einst und Jetzt — EiJ
Einstein Quarterly Journal of Biology and Medicine — Einstein QJ Biol Med
Einstein Studies — Einstein Stud
Einzelarbeiten aus der Kirchengeschichte Bayerns — EKGB
Einzeldarstellungen aus Theorie und Klinik der Medizin — Einzeldarst Theor Klin Med
Einzelhandelsberater — EHA
Einzelveroeffentlichungen des Seewetteramtes — Einzelv
EIR-[*Eidgenoessisches Institut fuer Reaktorforschung*] **Bericht (Wuerenlingen)** [*A publication*] — EIR-Ber (Wuerenlingen)
Eire. Department of Agriculture. Journal — Eire Dep Agric J
Eire-Ireland — Eire Ir
Eirene. Studia Graeca et Latina — Eir
EIS. Environmental Impact Statements — EEISD
Eis- und Kaelte-Industrie — Eis Kaelte Ind
Eisei Dobutsu [*Japanese Journal of Sanitary Zoology*] — ESDBAK
Eisei Dobutsu/Japanese Journal of Sanitary Zoology — Eisei Dobutsu/Jap J Sanit Zool
Eisei Kagaku — ESKGA
Eisei Kagaku — ESKGA2
Eisei Shikenjo Hokoku [*Bulletin. National Institute of Hygienic Sciences*] — Eis Shik Hok
Eisei Shikenjo Hokoku [*Bulletin. National Institute of Hygienic Sciences*] — ESKHA
Eisei Shikenjo Hokoku [*Bulletin. National Institute of Hygienic Sciences*] — ESKHA5
Eisei Shikenjo Hokoku/Bulletin. National Institute of Hygienic Sciences — Eisei Shikenjo Hokoku/Bull Nat Inst Hyg Sci
Eisenbahn-Ingenieur — Eisenbahn-Ing
Eisenbahn-Ingenieur — ESBGA
Eisenbahnrechtliche Entscheidungen und Abhandlungen — Eisenbahnrechtl Entsch Abh
Eisenbahntechnische Rundschau — Eisenbahntech Rundsch
Eisenbahntechnische Rundschau — ER
Eisenbahntechnische Rundschau — ETRUA
Eisenhower Consortium. Bulletin — ECOBDY
Eisenhower Consortium. Bulletin — Eisenhower Consortium Bull
Eisenhower Consortium. Bulletin. United States Rocky Mountain Forest and Range Experiment Station — Eisenhower Consortium Bull Rocky Mt For Range Exp
Eisen-Zeitung — Eisen Ztg
Eisen-Zeitung. Beilage — Eisen Ztg Beil
Eiszeit — Eisz
Eiszeitalter und Gegenwart — E u G
Eiszeitalter und Gegenwart — Eisz Geg
Eiszeitalter und Gegenwart — Eiszeitalter Gegenw
Eiszeitalter und Gegenwart. Jahrbuch der Deutschen Quartaervereinigung — E & G
Eiweiss-Forschung — Eiweiss Forsch
Eiyo Syokuryo Gakkai — Eiyo Syok Gak
Eiyo To Shokuryo — EISOAU
Eiyogaku Zasshi [*Japanese Journal of Nutrition*] — EYGZAD
Eiyogaku Zasshi/Japanese Journal of Nutrition — Eiyogaku Zasshi Jap J Nutr
Eizo Joho. Medikaru — EJMED
Ekistic Index — EKI
Ekistic Index — Ekist Ind
Ekistics — EKISA
Ekistics — Ekist
Ekistics — PEKI
Ekistics; the Problems and Science of Human Settlements — Ekistics Probl Sci Hum Settl
Ekklesiastike Aletheia — EA
Ekklesiatike Aletheia — Ekkl Al
Ekologia i Technika — Ekol Tech
Ekologia Polska — Ekol Pol
Ekologia Polska — Ekol Polska
Ekologia Polska — ELPLBS
Ekologia Polska/Polish Journal of Ecology — Ekol Pol Pol J Ecol
Ekologia Polska. Seria A — Ekol Pol Ser A
Ekologia Polska. Seria A — EKPOAT
Ekologia Polska. Seria B — Ekol Pol Ser B
Ekologia Polska. Seria B — EPRDB8
Ekologia-CSSR [*Ecology-CSSR*] — EKBRD5
Ekologicheskaya Khimiya — Ekol Khim
Ekologicheskie i Fiziologicheskie Osobennosti Rastenii Yuzhnogo Urala i Ikh Resursy — Ekol Fiziol Osob Rast Yuzhn Urala Ikh Resur
Ekologiya — EKIAAK
Ekologiya [*Sofia*] — EKOLDI
Ekologiya i Fiziologiya Korennogo Rosta. Mezhdunarodnyi Simpozion — Ekol Fiziol Korennogo Rosta Mezhdunar Simp
Ekologiya i Zashchita Lesa — Ekol Zashch Lesa
Ekologiya Morya — Ekol Morya
Ekologo-Fiziologicheskie Metody v Bor'be s Fuzarioznym Viltom Khlopchatnika — Ekol Fiziol Metody Borbe Fuzarioznym Viltom Khlop
Ekonomi dan Keuangan Indonesia — EKI
Ekonomi dan Keuangan Indonesia — Ekon Keuangan
Ekonomi. Forskningsstiftelsen Skogsarbeten — Ekon Forsknstift Skogsarb
Ekonomiceskie Nauki — Ekon Nauki
Ekonomiceskie Problemy Effektivnosti Proizvodstva — Ekon Probl Effekt
Ekonomicheskaya Gazeta — Ekon Gaz
Ekonomicheskoe Sotrudnichestvo Stran-Chlenov SEV — ESSSD
Ekonomicko-Matematicky Obzor — Ekon-Mat Obz
Ekonomicko-Matematicky Obzor — Ekon-Mate O
Ekonomicky Casopis — Ekon Cas
Ekonomika i Matematiceskie Metody — Ekon Matem Metody
Ekonomika i Matematiceskie Metody — Ekon Matemat Met
Ekonomika i Matematiceskie Metody — Ekonom i Mat Metody
Ekonomika i Organizatsiya Promyshlennogo Proizvodstva — EOPPA
Ekonomika i Organiztsiya Promyslennogo Proizvodstva — Ekon Org Promysl Proizvodstva
Ekonomika Neftianoi Promyshlennosti — EKNPA
Ekonomika Neftianoi Promyshlennosti [*Former USSR*] — Ekon Neft Prom-Sti
Ekonomika, Organizatsiya,i Upravlenie v Neftepererabatyvayushchei i Neftekhimicheskoi Promyshlennosti — EOUPD
Ekonomika Poljoprivrede — Ekon Poljopr
Ekonomika Poljoprivrede — Ekon Poljopriv
Ekonomika Sel'skogo Chozjajstva — Ekon Sel'sk Choz
Ekonomika Sel'skogo Hozjajstva — Ekon Selsk Hoz
Ekonomika Sel'skogo Khozyaistva — Ekon Sel' Khoz
Ekonomika Sel'skogo Khozyaistva — Ekon Sel'sk Khoz
Ekonomika Sovetskoi Ukrainy — Ekon Sov Ukr
Ekonomika Sovetskoi Ukrainy — ESOUA
Ekonomika Stavebnictva [*Czechoslovakia*] — Ekon Stavebnictva
Ekonomika Stavebnictva — EKOSB
Ekonomika Stroitel'stva — Ekon Stroit
Ekonomika Zemedelstvi — Ekon Zemed
Ekonomisk Revy — Ekon Revy
Ekonomisk Revy (Stockholm) — Ekon R (Stockholm)
Ekonomisk Tidskrift — ET
Ekonomiska Samfundets Tidskrift — Ekon Samf T
Ekonomiska Samfundets Tidskrift — Ekon Samfund Ts
Ekonomiska Samfundets Tidskrift — EKSTB
Ekonomiya Topliva. Za — Ekon Topl Za
Ekonomiyu Materialov. Za — Ekon Mater Za
Ekonomska Revija (Ljubljana) — Ekon R (Ljubljana)

Ekotekhnologii i Resursosberezhenie — Ekotekhnol Resursosberezhenie
Ekran — Ekr
Eksperiment v Fizike Reaktorov. Materialy Vsesoyuznogo Seminara po Problemam Fiziki Raktorov — Eksp Fiz Reakt Mater Vses Semin Probl Fiz Reakt
Eksperiment v Tekhnicheskoi Mineralogii i Petrografii, po Materialam Soveshchaniya po Eksperimental'noi i Tekhnicheskoi Mineralogii i Petrografi — Eksp Tekh Mineral Petrogr Mater Soveshch
Eksperimentaalne ja Kliiniline Onkologia — Eksp Kliin Onkol
Eksperimentalna Meditsina — Eksp Med
Eksperimentalna Meditsina i Morfologiya — EKMMA8
Eksperimentalna Meditsina i Morfologiya — Eksp Med Morfol
Eksperimentalna Meditsina (Kharkov) — Eksp Med (Kharkov)
Eksperimentalnaia i Klinicheskaia Farmakologiia — Eksp Klin Farmakol
Eksperimentalnaia Klinicheskaia Stomatologiia — Eksp Klin Stomatol
Eksperimental'naja Botanika — Eksp Bot
Eksperimental'naja Chirurgija — Eksp Chir
Eksperimental'naja Chirurgija i Anesteziologija — Eksp Chir Anest
Eksperimental'naya Biologiya (Vilnius) — Eksp Biol Vilnius
Eksperimental'naya i Klinicheskaya a Radiologiya [*Ukrainian SSR*] — Eksp Klin Radiol
Eksperimental'naya i Klinicheskaya Farmakoterapiya — Eksp Klin Farmakoter
Eksperimental'naya i Klinicheskaya Meditsina — Eksp Klin Med
Eksperimental'naya i Klinicheskaya Onkologiya — Eksp Klin Onkol
Eksperimental'naya i Vozrastnaya Kardiologiya. Materialy Mezhvuzovskoi Konferentsii — Eksp Vozrastn Kardiol Mater Mezhvuz Konf
Eksperimental'naya i Vozrastnaya Kardiologiya. Trudy Nauchnoi Konferentsii — Eksp Vozrastn Kardiol Tr Nauchn Konf
Eksperimental'naya Khirurgiya — Eksp Khir
Eksperimental'naya Khirurgiya i Anesteziologiya — EKHAA
Eksperimental'naya Khirurgiya i Anesteziologiya — EKHAAF
Eksperimental'naya Khirurgiya i Anesteziologiya — Eksp Khir Anesteziol
Eksperimental'naya Meditsina (Riga) — Eksp Med (Riga)
Eksperimental'naya Onkologiya — EKSODD
Eksperimental'naya Onkologiya — Eksp Onkol
Eksperimental'naya Tekhnika i Metody Vysokotemperaturnykh Izmerenii. Sbornik Trudov Soveshchaniya — Eksp Tekh Metody Vysokotemp Izmer Sb Tr Soveshch
Eksperimental'naya Vodnaya Toksikologiya — Eksp Vodn Toksikol
Eksperimental'naya Vodnaya Toksikologiya. Materialy Vsesoyuznogo Simpoziuma po Eksperimental'noi Vodnoi Toksikologii — Eksp Vodn Toksikol Mater Vses Simp
Eksperimental'nye i Klinicheskie Issledovaniya po Antibiotikam — Eksp Klin Issled Antibiot
Eksperimental'nye Issledovaniya po Fiziologii, Biofizike, i Farmakologii — Eksp Issled Fiziol Biofiz Farmakol
Eksperimental'nye Metody i Apparatura dlya Issledovaniya Turbulentnosti. Trudy Vsesoyuznogo Soveshchaniya — Eksp Metody Appar Issled Turbul Tr Vses Soveshch
Eksperimental'nyi Infarkt Miokarda v Usloviyakh Gipotermii — Eksp Infarkt Miokarda Usloviyakh Gipotermii
Eksperimental'nyi Mutagenez Rastenii — Eksp Mutagen Rast
Eksperimental'nyi Nauchno-Issledovatel'skii Institut Kuznechno-Pressovogo Mashinostroeniya. Sbornik — Eksp Nauchno Issled Inst Kuznechno Pressovogo Mashinostr Sb
Eksperimental'nyi Nauchno-Issledovatel'skii Institut Metallorezhushchikh Stankov. Trudy — Eksp Nauchno Issled Inst Metallorezhushchikh Stankov Tr
Ekspluatatsionno Tekhnicheskie Svoistva i Primenenie Avtomobil'nykh Topliv. Smazochnykh Materialov i Sperszhidkostei — Eksp Tekh Svoistva Primen Avtomob Top Smaz Mater Sperszhidk
Ekspluatatsiya, Modernizatsiya i Remont Oborudovaniya v Neftepererabatyvayushchei i Neftekhimicheskoi Promyshlennosti — EMROD
Ekspress-Informatsiya Laboratornye Tekhnologicheskie Issledovaniya i Obogashchenie Mineral'nogo Syr'ya [*Former USSR*] — Ekspress-Inf Lab Tekhnol Issled Obogashch Miner Syr'ya
Ekspress-Informatsiya Laboratornye Tekhnologicheskie Issledovaniya i Obogashchenie Mineral'nogo Syr'ya — LTIED
Ekspress-Informatsiya. Montazh Oborudovaniya na Teplovykh Elektrostantsiyakh [*A publication*] — EIMOB
Ekspress-Informatsiya. Montazh Oborudovaniya na Teplovykh Elektrostantsiyakh [*Former USSR*] — Ekspress-Inf Montazh Oborudovaniya Teplovykh Elektrosn
Ekspress-Informatsiya. Morskoi Gidrofizicheskii Institut Akademiya Nauk Ukrainskoi SSR — Ekspress Inf Morsk Gidrofiz Inst Akad Nauk Ukr SSR
Ekspress-Informatsiya Nauchno-Issledovatel'skii Institut Sel'skogo Khozyaistva Severnogo Zaural'ya — Ekspress-Inf Nauchno-Issled Inst Sel Khoz Severn Zaural'ya
Ekspress-Informatsiya. Neftegazovaya Geologiya i Geofizika [*Former USSR*] — Ekspress-Inf Neftegazov Geol Geofiz
Ekspress-Informatsiya. Neftegazovaya Geologiya i Geofizika — ENGGD
Ekspress-Informatsiya. Seriya: Regional'naya, Razvedochnaya, i Promyslovaya Geofizika — EIPGA
Ekspress-Informatsiya. Seriya: Regional'naya, Razvedochnaya, i Promyslovaya Geofizika [*Former USSR*] — Ekspress-Inf Ser Reg Razved Prom Geofiz
Ekspress-Informatsiya. Stroitel'stvo Teplovykh Elektrostantsii — EITEA
Ekspress-Informatsiya. Stroitel'stvo Teplovykh Elektrostantsii [*Former USSR*] — Ekspress-Inf Stroit Tepl Elektrostn
Ekspress-Informatsiya. Svarochnye Raboty — EISRA
Ekspress-Informatsiya. Svarochnye Raboty [*Former USSR*] — Ekspress-Inf Svar Rab
EKT. Elektroizolacna a Kablova Technika — EKT Electroizolacna Kablova Tech
El Agricultor Lagunero — Agric Lagunero
El and Energi Elektroteknikeren — El and Energi Elektrotek
(El) Caribe — ECE
(El) Ciervo — ELC
(El) Comercio (Peru) — ECP
El Derecho [*Argentina*] — ED
El Derecho. Legislacion Argentina — EDLA
(El) Espectador. Magazin Dominical (Colombia) — ERC
El Faro a Colon (Ciudad Trujillo) — Faro Colon C Trujillo
El Libro y el Pueblo (Mexico) — Libro Pueblo Mex
El Maestro Rural (Mexico) — Maes Rural Mex
El Monitor de la Educacion Comun (Buenos Aires) — Monit Educ Comun BA
El Monte Carmelo — EMC
(El) Mundo — EM
El Museo Canario — EMC
(El) Nacional (Venezuela) — ENV
(El) Nuevo Dia — END
El Pais [*Spain*] — EP
El Palacio — El Pal
El Paso Economic Review — El Paso Econ R
El Paso Geological Society. Annual Field Trip (Guidebook) — El Paso Geol Soc Annu Field Trip (Guideb)
El Predicador Evangelico [*Buenos Aires*] — PredicadorEv
El Salvador. Direccion General de Investigaciones Agronomicas. Seccion de Agronomia. Boletin Tecnico — El Salv Dir Gen Invest Agron Secc Agron Bol Tec
El Salvador. Direccion General de Investigaciones Agronomicas. Seccion de Entomologia. Boletin Tecnico — BTSEAA
El Salvador. Direccion General de Investigaciones Agronomicas. Seccion de Entomologia. Boletin Tecnico — El Salv Dir Gen Invest Agron Secc Entomol Bol Tec
El Salvador. Servicio Geologico Nacional. Anales. Boletin. Boletin Sismologico — El Salvador Servicio Geol Nac Anales Bol Bol Sismol
El Salvador. Universidad. Instituto Tropical de Investigaciones Cientificas. Anuario Comunicaciones — El Salvador Univ Inst Tropical Inv Cient Anuario Comun
(El) Sol — ESL
(El) Tiempo — ETO
El Trimestre Economico (Mexico) — Trim Econ Mex
El Trimestre Estadistico del Ecuador (Quito) — Trim Estadis Quito
(El) Universal (Mexico) — EUM
(El) Universal (Venezuela) — EUV
EL. University of Arkansas. Cooperative Extension Service — EL Univ Arkansas Coop Ext Serv
El Urogallo (Madrid) — ELM
(El) Visitante — EV
Elabuzskii Gosudarstvennyi Pedagogiceskii Institut. Ucenye Zapiski — Elabuz Gos Ped Inst Ucen Zap
El-Amarna Tafeln. Vorderasiatische Bibliothek — AMT
El-Amarna Tafeln. Vorderasiatische Bibliothek — EA
El-Armarna-Tafeln — EAT
Elastic-Plastic Fracture. Symposium — Elastic Plast Fract Symp
Elastomerics — Elast
Elastomerics Extra — Elast Xtra
Elbinger Jahrbuch — Elbing Jb
ELCON [*Electricity Consumers Resource Council*] **Report** — ELRPD
ELDATA. International Electronic Journal of Physico-Chemical Data — ELDATA Int Electron J Phys Chem Data
Elders Weekly — Elders W
ELDO/ESRO [*European Launcher Development Organization/European Space Research Organization*] **Bulletin** [*France*] — ELDO/ESRO Bull
ELDO/ESRO [*European Launcher Development Organization/European Space Research Organization*] **Scientific and Technical Review** [*France*] — ELDO/ESRO Sci Tech Rev
Electra [*Rijswijk*] — ECTAA
Electra — ELT
Electra. Organ for Elektroinstallatorforeningen for Kobenhavn og Elektroinstallatorforeningen for Provinsen — Elec
Electric Club Journal — Electr Club J
Electric Comfort Conditioning Journal — Electr Comf Cond J
Electric Comfort Conditioning News — ECCND
Electric Comfort Conditioning News — Elec Comft
Electric Comfort Conditioning News — Electr Comf Cond News
Electric Company Magazine — Electric Comp
Electric Equipment — ELEQB
Electric Farm Power [*United States*] — EFPOD
Electric Farm Power — Electr Farm Power
Electric Forum — Electr Forum
Electric Forum [*United States*] — ELFOD
Electric Furnace Conference Proceedings — EFCPA
Electric Furnace Conference Proceedings — Electr Furn Conf Proc
Electric Furnace Conference Proceedings. Metallurgical Society of AIME. Iron and Steel Division — Elec Furnace Conf Proc AIME
Electric Furnace Conference Proceedings. Metallurgical Society of AIME. Iron and Steel Division — Electr Furn Proc Metall Soc AIME
Electric Furnace Steel — Electr Furn Steel
Electric Furnace. Steel Proceedings — Electr Furn Steel Proc
Electric Heating Journal — Electr Heat J
Electric Ironmelting Conference. Proceedings — Electr Ironmelt Conf Proc
Electric Journal — Elect J
Electric Journal — Electr J
Electric Light and Power — Electr Light & Power
Electric Light and Power — ELLPA
Electric Light and Power (Boston) — Electr Light Power (Boston)
Electric Light and Power. Energy/Generation — Electr Light Power Energy/Gener
Electric Light and Power. Energy/Generation — ELEGC

Electric Light and Power. Transmission/Distribution — Electr Light Power Transm/Distrib
Electric Light and Power. Transmission/Distribution — EPTDA
Electric Machines and Electromechanics — Electr Mach and Electromech
Electric Machines and Electromechanics — Electr Mach Electromech
Electric Machines and Electromechanics — EMELD
Electric Machines and Power Systems — Electr Mach and Power Syst
Electric Perspectives — Electr Perspect
Electric Power Annual — Elec Powr A
Electric Power Applications. IEE Journal — IJEAD
Electric Power Communicator [*Canada*] — Electr Power Commun
Electric Power Database — EPD
Electric Power Industry Abstracts [*Database*] — EPIA
Electric Power Monthly — Elec Powr M
Electric Power Monthly [*Japan*] — Electr Power Mon
Electric Power Research Institute (Report) EPRI AF — Electr Power Res Inst (Rep) EPRI AF
Electric Power Research Institute (Report) EPRI AP — ERIAD
Electric Power Research Institute. Report EPRI AP (Palo Alto, California) — Electr Power Res Inst Rep EPRI AP Palo Alto Calif
Electric Power Research Institute (Report) EPRI CS — EPRCD
Electric Power Research Institute. Report EPRI CS (Palo Alto, California) — Electr Power Res Inst Rep EPRI CS (Palo Alto Calif)
Electric Power Research Institute (Report) EPRI EA — Electr Power Res Inst (Rep) EPRI EA
Electric Power Research Institute (Report) EPRI EL — Electr Power Res Inst (Rep) EPRI EL
Electric Power Research Institute (Report) EPRI EM — Electr Power Res Inst (Rep) EPRI EM
Electric Power Research Institute (Report) EPRI ER — Electr Power Res Inst (Rep) EPRI ER
Electric Power Research Institute (Report) EPRI ER (Palo Alto, California) — Electr Power Res Inst (Rep) EPRI ER (Palo Alto Calif)
Electric Power Research Institute (Report) EPRI FP — Electr Power Res Inst (Rep) EPRI FP
Electric Power Research Institute (Report) EPRI FP (Palo Alto, California) — Electr Power Res Inst (Rep) EPRI FP (Palo Alto Calif)
Electric Power Research Institute (Report) EPRI NP — Electr Power Res Inst (Rep) EPRI NP
Electric Power Research Institute (Report) EPRI SR (Palo Alto, California) — Electr Power Res Inst (Rep) EPRI SR (Palo Alto Calif)
Electric Power Statistics — EPST
Electric Power Systems Research — Electr Power Syst Res
Electric Power Systems Research — EPSRD
Electric Railway Journal — Elec Ry J
Electric Ratemaking — ELRMD
Electric Technology [*USSR*] [*English Translation*] — ELTGA
Electric Technology (USSR) — El Technol (USSR)
Electric Technology (USSR) — Elec Technol (USSR)
Electric Technology (USSR) — Electr Technol (USSR)
Electric Times — Elec Times
Electric Traction — Elec Traction
Electric Traction — Elect Tract
Electric Vehicle Developments [*England*] — Electr Veh Dev
Electric Vehicle News — Elec Veh
Electric Vehicle News — Electr Veh News
Electric Vehicle News — EVNSA
Electric Vehicles — Electr Veh
Electric Vehicles and Batteries [*England*] — Electr Veh Batteries
Electric Vehicles and Batteries — EVBAA
Electric Welding — Electr Weld
Electrical and Electronic Abstracts — Elec & Electron Abstr
Electrical and Electronic Insulation — Electr Electron Insul
Electrical and Electronic Insulation and Related Non-Metallics — Electr Electron Insul Relat Non Met
Electrical and Electronic Trader — Elect Electron Trader
Electrical and Electronics Abstracts [*United Kingdom*] [*Information service or system*] — EEA
Electrical and Electronics Abstracts — Electr Electron Abstr
Electrical and Electronics Manufacturer — Elect Electron Mfr
Electrical and Electronics Technician Engineer — Electr and Electron
Electrical and Mechanical Engineering Transactions. Institution of Engineers of Australia — Electr Mech Eng Trans Inst Eng Aust
Electrical and Mechanical Executive Engineer — Electr and Mech Executive Eng
Electrical and Mechanical Executive Engineer [*England*] — EMEED
Electrical and Nuclear Technology — Electr Nucl Technol
Electrical Apparatus — Electr App
Electrical Business — ELBUA
Electrical Business — Electric Bus
Electrical Calculation [*Japan*] — Electr Calculation
Electrical Communication — El Commun
Electrical Communication — ELCMA
Electrical Communication — Elec Com
Electrical Communication — Elec Comm
Electrical Communication — Elec Commun
Electrical Communication — Electr Commun
Electrical Communication Laboratories. Technical Journal — Electr Commun Lab Tech J
Electrical Communication Laboratory Reports — El Commun Lab Rep
Electrical Construction and Maintenance — ECOMA
Electrical Construction and Maintenance — El Constr
Electrical Construction and Maintenance — Elec Constr Maint
Electrical Construction and Maintenance — Electr Constr and Maint
Electrical Consultant — ECNSB
Electrical Consultant — Electr Consult
Electrical Contacts — Elec Contacts
Electrical Contacts — Electr Contacts
Electrical Contracting [*United States*] — ECONB
Electrical Contracting — El Contract
Electrical Contracting — Electr Contract
Electrical Contractor — Elec Contractor
Electrical Contractor — Elect Contractor
Electrical Contractor — Electr Contract
Electrical Digest [*Canada*] — Electr Dig
Electrical Distribution — El Distrib
Electrical Distribution [*England*] — Electr Distrib
Electrical/Electronics Insulation Conference. Proceedings — Electr Electron Insul Conf Proc
Electrical Energy — El Energ
Electrical Engineer — El Eng
Electrical Engineer — Elec Eng
Electrical Engineer — Elec Engr
Electrical Engineer — Electl Engr
Electrical Engineer — Electr Eng
Electrical Engineer — ELEND
Electrical Engineer and Merchandiser — EENMA
Electrical Engineer and Merchandiser — Elec Eng & Merchandiser
Electrical Engineer and Merchandiser [*Australia*] — Electr Eng Merch
Electrical Engineer (Johannesburg) — Electr Eng (Johannesburg)
Electrical Engineer (Melbourne) — Elec Eng (Melbourne)
Electrical Engineer (Melbourne) — Elect Engr (Melb)
Electrical Engineer (Melbourne) — Electr Eng (Melb)
Electrical Engineer (Melbourne) — ELEMA
Electrical Engineer of Australia and New Zealand — Electr Eng Aust NZ
Electrical Engineering — Elec Eng
Electrical Engineering Abstracts — EEA
Electrical Engineering Abstracts — Elec Eng Abstr
Electrical Engineering Abstracts — Electr Eng Abstr
Electrical Engineering. American Institute of Electrical Engineers — El Eng
Electrical Engineering. American Institute of Electrical Engineers — Electr Eng Am Inst Electr Eng
Electrical Engineering. American Institute of Electrical Engineers — ELENA
Electrical Engineering and Electronics — Elec Engrg and Electronics
Electrical Engineering and Electronics — Elec Engrg Electron
Electrical Engineering, Communications, and Signal Processing Series — Electr Engrg Commun Signal Process Ser
Electrical Engineering in Japan — Elec En Jap
Electrical Engineering in Japan — Elec Eng Japan
Electrical Engineering in Japan — Electr Eng Jap
Electrical Engineering in Japan — Electr Eng Jpn
Electrical Engineering Review — Elec Eng Rev
Electrical Engineering Review — Electr Eng Rev
Electrical Engineering Transactions [*Australia*] — Electr Eng Trans
Electrical Engineering Transactions — ELETB
Electrical Engineering Transactions. Institution of Engineers of Australia — Elect Engng Trans Instn Engrs Aust
Electrical Engineering Transactions. Institution of Engineers of Australia — Electr Eng Trans Inst Eng Aust
Electrical Equipment — Elect Equip
Electrical Equipment — Electr Equip
Electrical India — EIDAA
Electrical India — Electr India
Electrical Industry — El Ind
Electrical Information [*Japan*] — Electr Inf
Electrical Insulation Conference. Materials and Applications — Electr Insul Conf Mater Appl
Electrical Journal — Elec J
Electrical Journal — Electr J
Electrical Journal (London) — Electr J (London)
Electrical Machines. Design and Applications. International Conference — Electr Mach Des Appl Int Conf
Electrical Magazine Ohm [*Japan*] — Electr Mag Ohm
Electrical Manufacturing — Elec Manuf
Electrical Manufacturing — Electr Manuf
Electrical Manufacturing — ELMAA
Electrical Merchandising — Elec Merch
Electrical Merchandising Week — Elec Merch W
Electrical News and Engineering — Elec News Eng
Electrical News and Engineering — Electr News Eng
Electrical News and Engineering — ENAEA
Electrical Power and Energy Systems [*England*] — Electr Power Energy Syst
Electrical Power Engineer — Elect Pwr
Electrical Power Engineer — Elect Pwr Engr
Electrical Processes in Atmospheres. Proceedings. International Conference on Atmospheric Electricity — Electr Processes Atmos Proc Int Conf Atmos Electr
Electrical Research Association. ERA Report — Elec Res Ass ERA Rep
Electrical Review — Elec R
Electrical Review — Elec Rev
Electrical Review — Elec Revw
Electrical Review — Elect Rev
Electrical Review — Electr Rev
Electrical Review [*London*] — ELREA
Electrical Review — ERV
Electrical Review International — Electr Rev Int
Electrical Review International — ERIND
Electrical Review International (London) — Electr Rev Int London
Electrical Review (London) — Electr Rev London
Electrical Supervisor — Elect Supervis
Electrical Supervisor — Electr Superv

Electrical Supervisor — ELSUA
Electrical Times — Elect Times
Electrical Times — Electr Times
Electrical Times — ELTIA
Electrical Trader — Elec Trade
Electrical Utilization and Energy Abstracts — Electr Util & Energy Abs
Electrical Week — Electr Week
Electrical Weekly — Elec W
Electrical West — Elec West
Electrical West — Electr West
Electrical West [*United States*] — ELEWA
Electrical World — Elec World
Electrical World — Elect World
Electrical World — Electr World
Electrical World — ELWOA
Electrical World — IELW
Electricheskie Stantsii — EKSTA
Electricheskii — Electrich
[*The*] **Electrician** — Elec
Electrician and Electrical Engineer — Electric
Electricidade — ELDDA
Electricidade, Energia, Electronica — Electr Energ Electron
Electricien Industriel — Electr Ind
Electricien Industriel — ELIND
Electricite — ELTCA
Electricite Automobile — Electr Automob
Electricite (Bruessel) — El (Bruessel)
Electricite de France. Bulletin de la Direction des Etudes et Recherches. Serie A. Nucleaire, Hydraulique, Thermique — Elec Fr Bull Dir Etud Rech Ser A Nucl Hydraul Therm
Electricite de France. Bulletin de la Direction des Etudes et Recherches. Serie A. Nucleaire, Hydraulique, Thermique — Electr Fr Bull Dir Etud et Rech Ser A Nucl Hydraul Therm
Electricite de France. Bulletin de la Direction des Etudes et Recherches. Serie A. Nucleaire, Hydraulique, Thermique — Electr Fr Bull Dir Etud Rech Ser A Nucl Hydraul Therm
Electricite de France. Bulletin de la Direction des Etudes et Recherches. Serie B. Reseaux Electriques, Materiels Electriques — Elec Fr Bull Dir Etud Rech Ser B Reseaux Elec Mater Elec
Electricite de France. Bulletin de la Direction des Etudes et Recherches. Serie C. Mathematiques-Informatique [*Grenoble*] — Bull Direction Etudes Rech Ser C Math Inform
Electricite de France. Bulletin de la Direction des Etudes et Recherches. Serie C. Mathematiques-Informatique — EDBCA
Electricite de France. Direction des Etudes et Recherches. Bulletin. Serie A. Nucleaire, Hydraulique, Thermique — Electr Fr Dir Etud Rech Bull Ser A
Electricite de France. Direction des Etudes et Recherches. Bulletin. Serie B. Reseaux Electriques, Materiels Electriques — Electr Fr Dir Etud Rech Bull Ser B
Electricite Solaire — Electr Sol
Electricite-Electronique Moderne — EELMA
Electricite-Electronique Moderne — Electr-Electron Mod
Electricity Canada — Elec Can
Electricity Conservation Quarterly [*India*] — ECOQD
Electricity Conservation Quarterly [*India*] — Electr Conserv Q
Electricity in Building — Elec Bldg
Electricity on the Farm Magazine — Elec Farm Mag
Electrified Industry — EINDA
Electrified Industry — Electrified Ind
Electrified Interfaces in Physics, Chemistry, and Biology — Electrified Interfaces Phys Chem Biol
Electro- and Magnetobiology — Electro Magnetobiol
Electro Conference Record — ELCRD
Electro-Acoustic Music — EAM
Electroactive Polymer Electrochemistry — Electroact Polym Electrochem
Electroanalysis — Electroanal
Electroanalytical Abstracts — ELABB
Electroanalytical Abstracts — Electroanal Abstr
Electroanalytical Chemistry — Electroanal Chem
Electrochemical and Metallurgical Industry — Electrochem Metall Ind
Electrochemical and Optical Techniques for the Study and Monitoring of Metallic Corrosion — Electrochem Opt Tech Study Monit Met Corros
Electrochemical Engineering and Energy. Proceedings of the European Symposis on Electrical Engineering — Electrochem Eng Energy Proc Eur Symp Electr Eng
Electrochemical Methods in Corrosion Research. Proceedings. International Symposium — Electrochem Methods Corros Res Proc Int Symp
Electrochemical Science and Technology of Polymers — Electrochem Sci Technol Polym
Electrochemical Society. Journal — Electrochem Soc J
Electrochemical Society. Proceedings — Electrochem Soc Proc
Electrochemical Society Symposium on Metallized Plastics — Electrochem Soc Symp Met Plast
Electrochemical Technology — Electrochem Tech
Electrochemical Technology — Electrochem Technol
Electrochemistry — ECHMB
Electrochemistry — Electrochem
Electrochemistry and Industrial Physical Chemistry [*Japan*] — Electrochem Ind Phys Chem
Electrochemistry in Industrial Processing and Biology — Electrochem Ind Process and Biol
Electrochemistry in Industrial Processing and Biology (English Translation) [*A publication*] — Electrochem Ind Process Biol (Engl Transl)
Electrochemistry of Molten and Solid Electrolytes — Electrochem Molten and Solid Electrolytes
Electrochimica Acta — El Chim Acta
Electrochimica Acta — ELCAA
Electrochimica Acta — Electr Act
Electrochimica Acta — Electrochim Acta
Electrochimica Metallorum — Electrochim Met
Electrochimica Metallorum — Electrochim Metal
Electrocomponent Science and Technology — ECSTC
Electrocomponent Science and Technology — Electrocompon Sci and Technol
Electrocomponent Science and Technology — Electrocompon Sci Technol
Electrocomponent Science and Technology — Electrocomponent Sci Technol
Electrodeposition and Surface Treatment — Electrodeposition and Surf Treat
Electroencephalography and Clinical Neurophysiology — ECNEA
Electroencephalography and Clinical Neurophysiology — ECNEAZ
Electroencephalography and Clinical Neurophysiology — EEG Cl Neur
Electroencephalography and Clinical Neurophysiology — El Enc Clin Neurophys
Electroencephalography and Clinical Neurophysiology — Electroenceph Clin Neurophysiol
Electroencephalography and Clinical Neurophysiology — Electroencephalogr and Clin Neurophysiol
Electroencephalography and Clinical Neurophysiology — Electroencephalogr Clin Neurophysiol
Electroencephalography and Clinical Neurophysiology. Supplement — EECSB3
Electroencephalography and Clinical Neurophysiology. Supplement — Electroencephalogr Clin Neurophysiol Suppl
Electrofizicheskaya Apparatura Sbornik Statei [*Former USSR*] — Elektrofiz App Sb Statei
Electrolytic Condenser Review — Electrolytic Condens Rev
Electromagnetic Compatibility. International Conference — Electromagn Compat Int Conf
Electromagnetic Waves — Electromagn Waves
Electromagnetics — ETRMD
Electromechanical Components and Systems Design — ECSDA
Electromechanical Components and Systems Design — Electromech Compon Syst Des
Electromechanical Design — Electromech Des
Electromedica — Electromed
Electromedica [*English Edition*] — ELMCBK
Electromet Metals and Alloys Review — Electromet Met Alloys Rev
Electromet Review — Electromet Rev
Electromyography [*Later, Electromyography and Clinical Neurophysiology*] — ELMYA
Electromyography [*Later, Electromyography and Clinical Neurophysiology*] — ELMYAH
Electromyography and Clinical Neurophysiology — Electromyogr Clin Neurophysiol
Electromyography and Clinical Neurophysiology — Electromyography and Clin Neurophysiol
Electromyography and Clinical Neurophysiology — EMCNA9
Electron [*Brussels*] — ELCNC4
Electron and Ion Beam Science and Technology — Electron Ion Beam Sci Technol
Electron and Ion Beam Science and Technology. International Conference — Electron Ion Beam Sci Technol Int Conf
Electron Device Letters — Electron Device Lett
Electron Holography. Proceedings of the International Workshop — Electron Hologr Proc Int Workshop
Electron Microscopy and Analysis. Proceedings. Anniversary Meeting — Electron Microsc Anal Proc Anniv Meet
Electron Microscopy and Cytochemistry. Proceedings. International Symposium — Electron Microsc Cytochem Proc Int Symp
Electron Microscopy in Biology — Electron Microsc Biol
Electron Microscopy. Proceedings. European Congress on Electron Microscopy — Electron Microsc Proc Eur Congr
Electron Microscopy. Proceedings. European Regional Conference — Electron Microsc Proc Eur Reg Conf
Electron Microscopy. Proceedings of the International Congress for Electron Microscopy — Electron Microsc Proc Int Cong
Electron Microscopy. Proceedings. Stockholm Conference — Electron Microsc Proc Stockholm Conf
Electron Microscopy Reviews — Electron Mi
Electron Microscopy Society of America. Annual Meeting. Proceedings — Electron Microsc Soc Am Annu Meet Proc
Electron Microscopy Society of America. Proceedings — Electron Microsc Soc Am Proc
Electron Microscopy Society of Southern Africa. Proceedings — Electron Micros Soc Southern Afr Proc
Electron Microscopy Society of Southern Africa. Proceedings — Electron Microsc Soc South Afr Proc
Electron Spectroscopy Theory, Techniques, and Applications — Electron Spectrosc Theory Tech Appl
Electron Spin Resonance — Electron Spin Reson
Electron Technology — Electron Technol
Electron Technology. Quarterly — Electron Technol Q
Electronic and Electrical Engineering Research Studies. Applied and Engineering — Electron Electric Engrg Res Stud Appl Engrg Math Ser
Electronic and Electrical Engineering Research Studies. Electronic Materials Series — Electron Electr Eng Res Stud Electron Mater Ser
Electronic and Radio Engineer — Electronic & Radio Eng
Electronic and Radio Technician — Electron and Radio Tech
Electronic Applications — Electron Appl
Electronic Applications Bulletin — EABUB
Electronic Applications Bulletin — El App Bull
Electronic Applications Bulletin — Electron Appl Bull

Electronic Applications. Components and Materials [*Netherlands*] — Electron Appl Components Mater
Electronic Australia — Elec Austr
Electronic Business — EBI
Electronic Business — EBU
Electronic Business — Elec Busns
Electronic Business — Electron Bus
Electronic Ceramic Materials — Electron Ceram Mater
Electronic Ceramics — Electron Ceram
Electronic Communications in Probability — Electron Comm Probab
Electronic Communicator — Electron Commun
Electronic Components — El Comp
Electronic Components — ELCCA
Electronic Components — Electron Compon
Electronic Components — Electron Components
Electronic Components and Applications — Electron Components and Appl
Electronic Components and Applications [*Netherlands*] — Electron Components Appl
Electronic Components Conference. Proceedings — Electron Compon Conf Proc
Electronic Connector Study Group. Annual Connector Symposium Proceedings — Electron Connector Stud Group Annu Connector Symp Proc
Electronic Design — Elec Des
Electronic Design — Elec Desgn
Electronic Design — Electron Des
Electronic Design — ELODA
Electronic Editions [*Database*] — EE
Electronic Education — Elec Ed
Electronic, Electro-Optic, and Infrared Countermeasures — Countrmsrs
Electronic, Electro-Optic, and Infrared Countermeasures — Electron Electro-Opt Infrared Countermeas
Electronic, Electro-Optic, and Infrared Countermeasures — Electron Electro-Optic Infrared Countermeas
Electronic Engineering — Elec Eng
Electronic Engineering [*London*] — Electr Eng
Electronic Engineering — Electron Eng
Electronic Engineering — ELEGA
Electronic Engineering (London) — Electron Eng (Lond)
Electronic Engineering Manager — Electron Eng Man
Electronic Engineering (Philadelphia) — Electron Eng (Phila)
Electronic Engineering Times — Elec Eng T
Electronic Engineering (Tokyo) — Electron Eng (Tokyo)
Electronic Equipment Engineering — EEQEA
Electronic Equipment Engineering — Electron Equip Eng
Electronic Equipment News — EEQNA
Electronic Equipment News — Electron Equip News
Electronic Industries — Electron Ind
Electronic Industries — ELIDA
Electronic Industries and Electronic Instrumentation — Electron Ind Electron Instrum
Electronic Industries and Tele-Tech — Electronic Ind & Tele-Tech
Electronic Instrument Digest — EID
Electronic Journal of Combinatorics — Electron J Combin
Electronic Journal of Differential Equations — Electron J Differential Equations
Electronic Journal of Linear Algebra — Electron J Linear Algebra
Electronic Journal of Probability — Electron J Probab
Electronic Journal of Theoretical Chemistry — Electron J Theor Chem
Electronic Learning — Electron Learn
Electronic Learning — GELL
Electronic Legislative Search System [*Database*] — ELSS
Electronic Library — Electron Libr
Electronic Library — Electron Library
Electronic Library — Electronic Libr
Electronic Mail and Message Systems — Elec M & M Sys
Electronic Market Data Book — Elec Mkt
Electronic Market Trends — Elec Mkt T
Electronic Materials and Processing Congress — Electron Mater Process Congr
Electronic Materials Information Service [*Database*] — EMIS
Electronic Materials Series — Electron Mater Ser
Electronic Measuring — Electron Meas
Electronic Music Review — Elec Mus R
Electronic News — Elec News
Electronic News — Electron News
Electronic News — Electronic N
Electronic News — EN
Electronic News Financial Fact Book and Directory — Elec Fact
Electronic Packaging and Production — Electron Packag and Prod
Electronic Packaging and Production — Electron Packag Prod
Electronic Packaging and Production — ELPPA
Electronic Product Design — Electron Prod Des
Electronic Production Methods and Equipment — Electron Prod Methods & Equip
Electronic Products — Elec Prod
Electronic Products — ELPOA
Electronic Products & Technology [*Canada (already exists in GUS II database)*] — EP & T
Electronic Products Magazine — Electr Prod
Electronic Products Magazine — Electron Prod
Electronic Progress — Elec Prog
Electronic Progress — Electron Prog
Electronic Progress — ELTPA
Electronic Properties and Mechanisms of High Tc Superconductors. Proceedings. International Workshop — Electron Prop Mech High Tc Supercond Proc Int Workshop
Electronic Publishing Abstracts — Electron Publ Abstr
Electronic Publishing Abstracts [*Database*] — EPUBS
Electronic Publishing and Bookselling — EPB
Electronic Publishing Review — Elec Pub Rv
Electronic Publishing Review — Elec Publ Rev
Electronic Publishing Review — Electron Publ Rev
Electronic Publishing Review — Electron Publishing Rev
Electronic Publishing Review — EPR
Electronic Research Announcements of the American Mathematical Society — Electron Res Announc Amer Math Soc
Electronic Rig Stats [*Database*] — ERS
Electronic Selective Archives [*Database*] — ELSA
Electronic Sound and RTE — Electron Sound and RTE
Electronic Structure and Magnetism of Inorganic Compounds — Electron Struct Magnet Inorg Comp
Electronic Structure and Properties of Semiconductors — Electron Struct Prop Semicond
Electronic Survey Computing — Electron Surv Comput
Electronic Survey Computing — Electron Surv Computing
Electronic Technology Reports [*South Korea*] — Electron Technol Rep
Electronic Technology Reports — ETRSD
Electronic Times — Electron Times
Electronic Transactions on Numerical Analysis — Electron Trans Numer Anal
Electronic Warfare Defense Electronics — Electron Warf Def Electron
Electronic Warfare Digest — Elec War D
Electronica y Fisica Aplicada — EFAPA
Electronica y Fisica Aplicada — Electron Fis Apl
Electronics — El
Electronics — ELECA
Electronics — ELECAD
Electronics — Electron
Electronics — Electronic
Electronics — GELS
Electronics Abstracts Journal — Electron Abstr J
Electronics and Biotechnology Advanced ELBA Forum Series — Electron Biotechnol Adv ELBA Forum Ser
Electronics and Communications Abstracts Journal — Electron & Communic Abstr J
Electronics and Communications Abstracts Journal — Electron Commun Abstr J
Electronics and Communications in Japan — Electr Co J
Electronics and Communications in Japan — Electron and Commun Jpn
Electronics and Communications in Japan — Electron Comm Japan
Electronics and Communications in Japan — Electron Commun Japan
Electronics and Communications in Japan — Electron Commun Jpn
Electronics and Computing Monthly — Electron and Comput Mon
Electronics and Instrumentation — ELCIA
Electronics and Instrumentation — Electron Instrum
Electronics & Music Maker Magazine [*British*] — E & MM
Electronics and Power — Electr Pow
Electronics and Power — Electron & Power
Electronics and Power — Electron Power
Electronics and Power — Electron Pwr
Electronics and Power — ELPWA
Electronics and Power. Journal of the Institution of Electrical Engineers [*A publication*] — Electron and Power
Electronics Australia — Elec Aust
Electronics Australia — Electron Aust
Electronics Australia — Electronics Aust
Electronics Digest — Electron Dig
Electronics Industry — Electron Ind
Electronics Industry, Incorporating Electronic Components — Elec Ind
Electronics Information and Planning — Electron Inf and Plann
Electronics Information and Planning — Electron Inf Plann
Electronics Information and Planning — ELPLD
Electronics Letters — Electr Lett
Electronics Letters — Electron Lett
Electronics Letters — ELLEA
Electronics Magazine — Electron Mag
Electronics Manufacturer — Electron Mfr
Electronics Product News. Supplement to Canadian Electronics Engineering — Cdn Elec P
Electronics Reliability and Microminiaturization [*England*] — Electron Reliab Microminiaturization
Electronics Report — Electron Rep
Electronics Retailing — Elec Retail
Electronics Review (Tokyo) — Electron Rev (Tokyo)
Electronics Test — Electron Test
Electronics Today — Electron Today
Electronics Today International — Elec T Intnl
Electronics Today International — Elec Tod
Electronics Today International — Electron Today Int
Electronics Today International — Electronics Today
Electronics Today International — ETI
Electronics Week [*Later, Electronics*] — Electrnc Wk
Electronics Weekly — Elec Week
Electronics Weekly — Electron Wkly
Electronics Weekly — ELWYA
Electronics World — ELCWA
Electronics World — Electron World
Electronique et Applications Industrielles — EAIND
Electronique et Applications Industrielles [*France*] — Electron Appl Ind
Electronique et Microelectronique Industrielles — Electron et Microelectron Ind
Electronique et Microelectronique Industrielles — Electron Microelectron Ind
Electronique Industrielle — Electron Ind
Electronique Industrielle — ETINA
Electronique Medicale — Electron Med
Electronique Nouvelle — Electron Nouv

Electronisch Meten — Electron Meten
Electron-Microscopy — Electron Microsc
Electro-Optical Systems Design — Electro-Opt Syst Des
Electro-Optical Systems Design — Electro-Opt Systems
Electro-Optics — Electro-Opt
Electro-Optics Report — Elec Opt Rep
Electro-optics Report — Electrooptics Rep
Electro-Optics Series — Electro Opt Ser
Electrophoresis — ELCTDN
Electrophoresis (Weinheim, Federal Republic of Germany) — Electrophoresis (Weinheim Fed Repub Ger)
Electrophotography — Electrophotogr
Electrophotography. International Conference — Electrophotogr Int Conf
Electroplating and Metal Finishing — Electroplat and Met Finish
Electroplating and Metal Finishing — Electroplat Met Finish
Electroplating and Metal Finishing — EMFIA
Electroplating and Metal Spraying — Electroplat Met Spraying
Electroplating Engineering Handbook — Electroplat Eng Handb
Electroquimica e Corrasao — Electroquim Corrasao
Electroquimica e Corrosao — Electroquim Corros
Electroresponsive Molecular and Polymeric Systems — Electroresponsive Mol Polym Syst
Electro-Revue — Electro-Rev
Electrostatics. Invited and Contributed Papers. International Conference — Electrost Invited Contrib Pap Int Conf
Electrotechnical Journal — Electrotech J
Electrotechnical Journal of Japan — Electrotech J Jpn
Electrotechnical Laboratory. Summaries of Reports [*Japan*] — ELSRB
Electrotechnics — El
Electro-Techniek — Electro-Tech
Electro-Technology — Electro-Tech
Electro-Technology — Electro-Technol
Electro-Technology [*New York*] — ELOWA
Electro-Technology [*Bangalore, India*] — ELTEA
Electro-Technology (Bangalore, India) — Electro-Technol (Bangalore India)
Electro-Technology (Beverly Shores, Indiana) — Electro Techn (Beverly Shores, Indiana)
Electro-Technology (New York) — Electro-Technol (NY)
Electrotehnica — ELTTA
Electrotehnica, Electronica, si Automatica. Seria Automatica si Electronica [*A publication*] — EAAED
Electrotehnica, Electronica, si Automatica. Serie Electrotehnica [*Romania*] — Electroteh Electron Autom Electroteh
Electrothermie International. Edition A. l'Electrothermie dans l'Equipement Technique — Electrothermie Int Ed A
Electrothermie International. Edition B. Applications Industrielles de l'Electrothermie — Electrothermie Int Ed B
Elektricestvo — El
Elektricheskaya i Teplovoznaya Tyaga — Elektr & Teplovoznaya Tyaga
Elektricheskaya i Teplovoznaya Tyaga — Elektr Teplovoz Tyaga
Elektricheskie Kontakty. Trudy Soveshchaniya po Elektricheskim Kontaktam i Kontaktnym Materialam — Elektr Kontakty Tr Soveshch
Elektricheskie Seti i Sistemy — ELSPA
Elektricheskie Stantsii — Elektr Stantsii
Elektricheskie Stantsii — Elektr Stn
Elektrichestvo — ELEKA
Elektrie — EKTRA
Elektrik Muhendisligi — Elektr Muhendisligi
Elektrische Ausruestung — Elektr Ausruestung
Elektrische Bahnen — ELBAA
Elektrische Bahnen — Elek Bahnen
Elektrische Bahnen — Elektr Bahnen
Elektrische Energie-Technik — EETED
Elektrische Energie-Technik — Elektr Energ-Tech
Elektrische Maschinen — Elektr Masch
Elektrische Nachrichten Technik — Elektr Nachr Tech
Elektrische Stahlherstellung — Elektr Stahlherstell
Elektrisches Nachrichtenwesen — Elektr Nachrichtenwes
Elektriska Svetsningsaktiebolaget. Revue. Deutsche Ausgabe — Elektr Svetsningsaktiebolaget Rev Dtsch Ausg
Elektriska Svetsningsaktiebolaget. Revue. Edition Francaise — Elektr Svetsningsaktiebolaget Rev Ed Fr
Elektrizitaetsverwertung — EKZVA
Elektrizitaetsverwertung — El Verw
Elektrizitaetswirtschaft — EKZWA
Elektrizitaetswirtschaft — El Wi
Elektro — EEROA
Elektro Medizin, Biomedizin, und Technik — Elektro Med Biomed und Tech
Elektro Promishlenost i Priborostroene — Elektro Prom-St i Priborostroene
Elektro Radio Handel — ERHAD
Elektro-Anzeiger — EKANA
Elektro-Anzeiger — El Anz
Elektro-Anzeiger — Elektro-Anz
Elektrochemische Zeitschrift — Elektrochem Z
Elektrochemische Zeitschrift — Elektrochem Zs
Elektrochimija — El Chim
Elektrodienst — ELDNB
Elektrodinamika i Fizika SVCh (Sverkhvysokaya Chastota) — Elektrodin Fiz SVCh
Elektroenergetika i Avtomatika — EEAVA
Elektroenergetika i Avtomatika — Elektroenerget i Avtomat
Elektrofizicheskaya Apparatura — Elektrofiz Appar
Elektro-Handel — E Handel
Elektro-Handel — ELKHA
Elektroiskrovaya Obrabotka Metallov — Elektroiskrovaya Obrab Met
Elektroizolacna a Kablova Technika — Elektroizol Kablova Tech
Elektroizolacna a Kablova Technika [*Czechoslovakia*] — Elektroizolacna Kablova Tech
Elektro-Jahrbuch [*Switzerland*] — Elektro-Jahrb
Elektro-Jahrbuch — ELJAA
Elektrokhimiya Margantsa — Elektrokhim Margantsa
Elektromagnitnaya Strukturo- i Defektoskopiya — Elektromagn Strukt Defekoskopiya
Elektro-Medizin — Elektro Med
Elektromeister und Deutsches Elektrohandwerk — Elektromeister & Dtsch Elektrohandwerk
Elektron in Wissenschaft und Technik — El Wiss Techn
Elektron in Wissenschaft und Technik — Elektron Wiss Tech
Elektron International — Elektron Int
Elektronaya Tekhnika. Seriya 12. Upravlenie Kachestvom i Standartizatsiya — Elektron Tekh Ser 12 Upr Kach Stand
Elektroniikka Radio Televisio [*Finland*] — Elektron Radio Telev
Elektroniikka Radio Televisio — ERT
Elektroniikka Radio Televisio — ERTLA
Elektronik — EKRKA
Elektronik — ELKOA
Elektronik Applikation — Elek App
Elektronik Applikation — Elektron Appl
Elektronik Entwicklung — Elektron Entwickl
Elektronik Heute — Elektron Heute
Elektronik Industrie — Elekt Ind
Elektronik Industrie — Elektron Ind
Elektronik Informationen — Elektron Inf
Elektronik Journal — Elektron J
Elektronik (Muenchen) — Elektron (Muenchen)
Elektronik Praxis — Elektron Prax
Elektronik - Technologie - Anwendungen - Marketing — Elektronik
Elektronika — EKNTB
Elektronika Bol'shikh Moshchnostei — EBMOA
Elektronika Bol'shikh Moshchnostei [*Former USSR*] — Elektron Bol'shikh Moshch
Elektronika i Khimiya v Kardiologii — Elektron Khim Kardiol
Elektronik-Anzeiger — Elektron Anz
Elektronik-Centralen. Report. ECR — ELKRD
Elektronikk — ELKTD
Elektronikschau — ELTRD
Elektronik-Zeitung — Elektronik
Elektronik-Zeitung [*Germany*] — Elektron-Ztg
Elektronik-Zeitung fuer Industrie, Wirtschaft, Wissenschaft, und Verwaltung [*A publication*] — EZ
Elektronische Datenverarbeitung — Elektron Datenverarb
Elektronische Informationsverarbeitung und Kybernetik — EIK
Elektronische Informationsverarbeitung und Kybernetik — Elektron Informationsverarb Kybern
Elektronische Informationsverarbeitung und Kybernetik [*Berlin*] — Elektron Informationsverarb Kybernet
Elektronische Informationsverarbeitung und Kybernetik — Elektron Informationsverarbeit Kybernetik
Elektronische Informatsionsverarbeitung und Kybernetik — EIVKA
Elektronische Rechenanlagen — Elektron Rechenanlagen
Elektronische Rechenanlagen — ELRAA
Elektronische Rechenanlagen — ER
Elektronische Rechenanlagen mit Computer Praxis — Elektron Rechenanlagen Comput Prax
Elektronisches Rechnen und Regeln — Elektron Rech Regeln
Elektronisches Rechnen und Regeln — Elektron Rechnen und Regeln
Elektronisches Rechnen und Regeln. Sonderband — Elektron Rechnen Regeln Sonderband
Elektronisches Rechnen und Regeln. Sonderband — Elektron Rechnen und Regeln Sonderband
Elektronmikroskopievereniging van Suidelike Afrika. Verrigtings [*Electron Microscopy Society of Southern Africa. Proceedings*] — Elektronmikroskopiever Suidelike Afr Verrig
Elektronmikroskopievereniging van Suidelike Afrika. Verrigtings [*Electron Microscopy Society of Southern Africa. Proceedings*] — Elektronmikroskopiever Suidelike Afr Verrigt
Elektronmikroskopievereniging van Suidelike Afrika. Verrigtings [*Electron Microscopy Society of Southern Africa. Proceedings*] — VESADE
Elektronnaya Obrabotka Materialov — Elektron Obrab Mater
Elektronnaya Obrabotka Materialov — Elektronnaya Obrab Mater
Elektronnaya Obrabotka Materialov — EOBMA
Elektronnaya Obrabotka Materialov — EOBMAF
Elektronnaya Tekhnika. Seriya 1. Elektronika [*Former USSR*] — Elektron Tekh Ser 1 Elektron
Elektronnaya Tekhnika. Seriya 1. Elektronika — ETSSD
Elektronnaya Tekhnika. Seriya 12 — Elektron Tekh Ser 12
Elektronnoe Modelirovanie [*Ukrainian SSR*] — Elektron Model
Elektronnoe Modelirovanie — ELMOD
Elektronnye i Ionnye Protsessy u Ionnykh Kristallakh — Elektron Ionnye Protsessy Ionnykh Krist
Elektronnye i Ionnye Protsessy v Tverdykh Telakh — Elektron Ionnye Protsessy Tverd Telakh
Elektrontehniski Vestnik — ELVEA
Elektro-Praktiker [*Germany*] — Elektro-Prakt
Elektro-Praktiker — EPRAD
Elektroprivreda — ELPVA
Elektropromishlenost i Priborostroene [*Bulgaria*] — Elektroprom-St Priborostr
Elektropromishlenost i Priborostroene — ELPBA
Elektrotechnicky Casopis — El Techn Cas
Elektrotechnicky Casopis — ELKCA

Elektrotechnicky Obzor — Elektrotech Obz
Elektrotechniek — Elek Tech
Elektro-Techniek — Elektro Tech
Elektrotechniek — ELTKA
Elektrotechniek Elektronica — Elektrotec
Elektrotechniek (Meppel, Netherlands) — Elektrotechniek Meppel Neth
Elektrotechniek; Technisch-Economisch Tijdschrift — ETN
Elektrotechnik — EKTCB
Elektrotechnik — EKTKA
Elektrotechnik — EKTRB
Elektrotechnik und Maschinenbau — E u M
Elektrotechnik und Maschinenbau — E und M
Elektrotechnik und Maschinenbau — Elektrotech Maschinenbau
Elektrotechnik und Maschinenbau — Elektrotech und Maschinenbau
Elektrotechnik und Maschinenbau — EM
Elektrotechnika — El Techn
Elektrotechniker — ETTCA
Elektrotechniky Casopis — Elektrotech Cas
Elektrotechnische Zeitschrift — El Techn Zs
Elektrotechnische Zeitschrift — El Z
Elektrotechnische Zeitschrift — Elek Zeit
Elektrotechnische Zeitschrift — Elektrotech Zeit
Elektrotechnische Zeitschrift — Elt Z
Elektrotechnische Zeitschrift — ETZ
Elektrotechnische Zeitschrift. Ausgabe A — Elektrotech Z A
Elektrotechnische Zeitschrift. Ausgabe A — Elektrotech Z Ausg A
Elektrotechnische Zeitschrift. Ausgabe B — Elektr Z B
Elektrotechnische Zeitschrift. Ausgabe B — Elektrotech Z Ausg B
Elektrotechnische Zeitschrift. Ausgabe B — Elektrotech Z B
Elektrotechnische Zeitschrift. ETZ — Elektrotech Z ETZ
Elektrotechnische Zeitschrift. ETZ A — Elektrotech Z ETZ A
Elektrotechnische Zeitschrift. ETZ B — Elektrotech Z ETZ B
Elektrotechnische Zeitschrift und Elektrotechnik und Maschinenbau — Elektrotech Z Elektrotech Maschinenbau
Elektro-Tehniek — LKTRD
Elektrotehnika — ELTHB
Elektrotehnika u Industriji Pogonu — Elektroteh Ind Pogonu
Elektrotehniski Vestnik — Elektroteh Vestn
Elektrotekhnicheskaya Promyshlennost. Elektrotekhnicheskie Materialy — Elektrotekh Promst Elektrotekh Mater
Elektrotekhnicheskaya Promyshlennost. Khimicheskie i Fizicheskie Istochniki Toka — Elektrotekh Promst Khim Fiz Istochniki Toka
Elektrotekhnicheskaya Promyshlennost. Seriya. Elektrotekhnicheskie Materialy — EPSMD
Elektrotekhnicheskaya Promyshlennost. Seriya. Khimicheskie i Fizicheskie Istochniki Toka — ESKTD
Elektrotekhnicheskie Materialy. Elektricheskie Kondensatory. Provoda i Kabeli — Elektrotekh Mater Elektr Kondens Provoda Kabeli
Elektrotekhnika — ELKTA
Elektroteknikeren — EKTMA
Elektroteknikeren. Elektroteknisk Todsskrift for Lys og Kraft, Telefoni og Telegrafi — Elkt
Elektroteknisk Tidsskrift — Elektrok Tidsskr
Elektroteknisk Tidsskrift — Elektrotek Tidsskr
Elektrowaerme im Technischen-Ausbau — Elektrowaerme A
Elektrowaerme im Technischen-Ausbau — Elektrowrm Tech-Ausbau
Elektrowaerme International — Elektrowaerme Int
Elektrowaerme International. Edition A. Elektrowaerme im Technischen Ausbau — EIEAD
Elektrowaerme International. Edition A. Elektrowaerme im Technischen Ausbau — Elektrowaerme Int A
Elektrowaerme International. Edition A. Elektrowaerme im Technischen Ausbau — Elektrowaerme Int A Elektrowaerme Tech Ausbau
Elektrowaerme International. Edition A. Elektrowaerme im Technischen Ausbau — Elektrowaerme Int Ed A
Elektrowaerme International. Edition B. Industrielle Electrowaerme — Elektrowaerme Int B
Elektrowaerme International. Edition B. Industrielle Elektrowaerme — EIEBD
Elektrowaerme International. Edition B. Industrielle Elektrowaerme — Elektrowaerme Int B Elektrowaerme
Elektrowaerme International. Edition B. Industrielle Elektrowaerme — Elektrowaerme Int Ed B
Elektrowelt — ELWLA
Elektrowirtschaft — ELKWA
Elelmezesi Ipar — Elelm Ipar
Elelmezesi Ipar — Elelmez Ipar
Elelmezesi Ipar — EMIPA
Elelmiszertudomany — ELMZA
Elelmiszervizgalati Kozlemenyek — Elelmiszerv Kozl
Elelmiszervizgalati Kozlemenyek — Elelmiszerviz Kozl
Elelmiszervizgalati Kozlemenyek — Elelmiszervizgalati Kozl
Elelmiszervizgalati Kozlemenyek — Elelmiszervizgalati Kozlem
Elementa ad Fontium Editiones — Elem Fontium Ed
Elementarnye Chastitsy — Elem Chastitsy
Elementarnye Chastitsy i Kosmicheskie Luchi — Elem Chastitsy Kosm Luchi
Elementary English — EE
Elementary English — El Engl
Elementary English — Elem Engl
Elementary English — ElemE
Elementary English Review — El Engl R
Elementary Particle Theory. Relativistic Groups and Analyticity. Proceedings. Nobel Symposium — Elem Part Theory Proc Nobel Symp
Elementary School Guidance and Counseling — El Sch Guid & Counsel
Elementary School Journal — El Sch J
Elementary School Journal — Elem Sch J
Elementary School Journal — Elem School J
Elementary School Journal — IESJ
Elementary School Teacher — El School T
Elemente der Mathematik — Elem Math
Elemente der Mathematik — ELMMA
Elemente der Mathematik. Supplement — Elem Math Suppl
Elementi di Lingua Etrusca — ELE
Elementos Meteorologicos e Climatologicos — Elem Met Clim
Elements — LMNTD
Elements de Doctrine Spirituelle — EDS
Elements of Mathematics — Elem Math
Elementy Teorii i Tekhniki Avtomaticheskogo Upravleniya — Elem Teor Tekh Avtom Upr
Elenchus Bibliographicus Biblicus — Elenchus Bibliogr Biblicus
Elenchus Bibliographicus Biblicus of Biblica — Elenchus Bibliogr Biblicus Biblica
Elephantine Papyri — P Eleph
Elet es Irodalom — El
Elet es Tudomany — Elet Tud
Elettrificazione — ELTZA
Elettronica e Telecomunicazioni — Elettron & Telecomun
Elettronica e Telecomunicazioni — ETTCB
Elettronica Oggi — Elettron Oggi
Elettrotecnica — Elettrotecn
Elettrotecnica — ETRTA
Elettrotecnica. Supplemento [*Italy*] — Elettrotecnica Suppl
Elettrotecnica. Supplemento — ELTSA
Elevage et Alimentation — Elev Aliment
Elevage Insemination — Elev Insemination
Elevage Porcin — Elev Porcin
Elevtheros Kosmos — Elev Kosmos
Eley Game Advisory Service. Annual Report — Eley Game Advis Serv Annu Rep
Eley Game Advisory Service. Booklet — EGASA6
Eley Game Advisory Service. Booklet — Eley Game Advis Serv Bookl
Eley Game Advisory Station. Annual Report — Eley Game Advis Stn Annu Rep
Eley Game Advisory Station. Annual Review — EGAABL
Elga Progress — Elga Prog
Elgar Society Journal — ESJ
Elgin Papers — Elgin Pap
Elgin State Hospital. Collected and Contributed Papers — Elgin State Hosp Collect Contrib Pap
ELH. English Literary History — ELH Engl L
Elias John Wilkinson Gibb Memorial Series — EJW Gibb Mem Ser
Elias John Wilkinson Gibb Memorial Series — GMS
Elin- Zeitschrift — Elin-Z
Elisha Mitchell Scientific Society. Journal — Elisha Mitchell Sci Soc J
Elizabethan Studies — ElizS
Elizabethan Theatre — E Th
Elktrosvyaz — EKZVA
Ellen Glasgow Newsletter — EGN
Ellenike Anaisthesiologia — Anaisthesiol
Ellery Queen's Mystery Magazine — EQMM
Elliott Society of Natural History of Charleston. Proceedings — Elliott Soc N H Charleston Pr
Ellipse — Elli
Ellis and Blackburn Queen's Bench Cases — El a Bl
Ellis Horwood Series. Computers and Their Applications — Ellis Horwood Ser Comput Appl
Ellis Horwood Series in Analytical Chemistry — Ellis Horwood Ser Anal Chem
Ellis Horwood Series in Artificial Intelligence — Ellis Horwood Ser Artificial Intelligence
Ellis Horwood Series in Artificial Intelligence Foundations and Concepts — Ellis Horwood Ser Artificial Intelligence Found Concepts
Ellis Horwood Series in Civil Engineering — Ellis Horwood Ser Civ Engrg
Ellis Horwood Series in Engineering Science — Ellis Horwood Ser Engrg Sci
Ellis Horwood Series in Mathematics and its Applications. Statistics and Operational Research — Ellis Horwood Ser Math Appl Statist Oper Res
Ellis Horwood Series in Mathematics and its Applications. Statistics, Operational Research, and Computational Mathematics — Ellis Horwood Ser Math Appl Statist Oper Res Comput Math
Ellis Horwood Series in Mechanical Engineering — Ellis Horwood Ser Mech Engrg
Ellis Horwood Series in Pure and Applied Physics — Ellis Horwood Ser Pure Appl Phys
Ellis Horwood Series. Mathematics and Its Applications — Ellis Horwood Ser Math Appl
Ellwanger Jahrbuch. Ein Volksbuch fuer Heimatpflege in Virngau und Ries — Ell Jb
Ellwanger Jahrbuch: Ein Volksbuch fuer Heimatpflege in Virngau und Ries — Ellwanger Jb
Elma Dill Russell Spencer Foundation Series — EDRSA2
Elma Dill Russell Spencer Foundation Series — Elma Dill Russell Spencer Found Ser
Elmore Harris Series — EHSer
Els Marges [*Barcelona*] — ELSM
Els Nostres Classics — ENC
Elsass-Lothringisches Jahrbuch — ELJ
Elsevier Business Intelligence Series — Elsevier Bus Intel Ser
Elsevier Lexica [*Elsevier Book Series*] — EL
Elsevier Oceanography Series [*Elsevier Book Series*] — ELOSA9
Elsevier Oceanography Series [*Elsevier Book Series*] — Elsevier Oceanogr Ser
Elsevier Oceanography Series [*Elsevier Book Series*] — EOS
Elsevier Oceanography Series (Amsterdam) [*Elsevier Book Series*] — Elsevier Oceanogr Ser (Amsterdam)
Elsevier Series in Forensic and Police Science [*Elsevier Book Series*] — EFPS
Elseviers Magazine — EWM

Elseviers Weekblad — EWD
Elsinore — Els
Elteknik — ETKKA
Elteknik med Aktuell Elektronik — Eltek Aktuell Elektron
Elteknik med Aktuell Elektronik — Elteknik med Aktuel Elektron
Elteknik med Aktuell Elektronik. Edition A — Eltek Aktuell Elektron A
Elucidario Regionalista de Ponte do Lima — ERPL
EM and D [*Engineering Materials and Design*] **Journal of Engineering Materials, Components, and Design** — EM & D J Eng Mater Compon Des
EM and D [*Engineering Materials and Design*] **Journal of Engineering Materials, Components, and Design** — EM D J Mater Components Des
EM and D [*Engineering Materials and Design*] **Product Data** — EM & D Prod Data
EM. Economia de Mocambique — EM Econ Mocambique
EM. Washington State University. Cooperative Extension Service — EM Wash State Univ Coop Ext Serv
EMA (Early Music Association) Bulletin — EMAB
Emailletechnische Monats Blaetter — Emailletech Mon Bl
Emailwaren-Industrie — Emailwaren Ind
Emajl - Keramika - Staklo — Emajl Keram Staklo
Emakeele Seltsi Aastaraamat — EmSA
Emakeele Seltsi Aastaraamat — ESA
Emanu-El Men's Bulletin — EEMB
Emballage Digest — Emballage Dig
Emballages Magazine — EMB
Emberiza — EMBZA6
Emberiza Vogelschutz und Vogelkunde in Rheinland Pfalz — Emberiza Vogelschutz Vogelkd Rheinl Pfalz
EMBO (European Molecular Biology Organization) Journal — EMBO (Eur Mol Biol Organ) J
EMBO [*European Molecular Biology Organization*] **Journal** — EMBO J
EMBO [*European Molecular Biology Organization*] **Journal** — EMJODG
Embouteillage Conditionnement — Embouteillage Cond
EMBRAPA. Empresa Brasileira de Pesquisa Agropecuaria — EMBRAPA Empresa Bras Pesqui Agropecu
Embryologia — EBYLA2
Embryologia — Embr
EMC. South Dakota State University. Cooperative Extension Service — EMC SD State Univ Coop Ext Serv
Emder Jahrbuch — Emder Jb
Emergency Department News — Emerg Dep News
Emergency Health Services Quarterly — EHSQ
Emergency Health Services Quarterly — Emerg Health Serv Q
Emergency Health Services Review — EHSRE2
Emergency Health Services Review — Emerg Health Serv Rev
Emergency Librarian — EL
Emergency Librarian — Emer Libr
Emergency Librarian — Emerg Lib
Emergency Librarian — Emergency Lib
Emergency Librarian — Emergency Libn
Emergency Medical Care Digest — Emerg Med Care Dig
Emergency Medical Services — Emerg Med Serv
Emergency Medical Technician Legal Bulletin — Emerg Med Tech Legal Bull
Emergency Medical Technician Legal Bulletin — EMT Legal Bull
Emergency Medicine — Emerg Med
Emergency Medicine Annual — Emerg Med Annu
Emergency Medicine Clinics of North America — Emerg Med Clin North Am
Emergency Nurse Legal Bulletin — Emerg Nurse Legal Bull
Emergency Nurse Legal Bulletin — ENLB
Emergency Planning Digest — Emerg Plann Dig
Emergency Services News — Emerg Serv News
Emerging Infectious Diseases — Emerg Infect Dis
Emerging Pharmaceuticals — Emerging Pharm
Emerita — Em
Emerita — Emer
Emerson Society. Quarterly — ESQ
Emilia Preromana — Emilia Pr Rom
Emily Dickinson Bulletin — EDB
EMIS (Electronic Materials Information Service) Datareviews Series — EMIS Datarev Ser
Emlekbeszedek a Magyar Tudomanyos Akademia Tagjai Felett — Emlekbeszedek Magyar Tud Akad Tagjai Felett
Emlekbeszedek a Magyar Tudomanyos Akademia Tagjairol — Emlekbeszedek Magyar Tud Akad Tagjairol
EMO [*Emergency Measures Organization*] **Digest** [*Canada*] — EMODA
EMO (Emergency Measures Organization) Digest (Canada) — EMO (Emerg Meas Organ) Dig
Emory Law Journal — Em LJ
Emory Law Journal — Emory L J
Emory Sources and Reprints — ESR
Emory University Journal of Medicine — Emory Univ J Med
Emory University Quarterly — Em Univ Q
Emory University Quarterly — Emory Univ Quart
Emory University Quarterly — EUQ
Emotion and Reproduction. International Congress of Psychosomatic Obstetrics and Gynecology — Emotion Reprod Int Cong Psychosom Obstet Gynecol
Empedocle — Emp
Emphasis. Nursing — Emphasis Nurs
Empire Club of Canada — Emp Club Canada
Empire Cotton Growing Corporation. Conference on Cotton Growing Problems. Report and Summary of Proceedings — Emp Cotton Grow Corp Conf Cotton Grow Probl Rep Summ Proc
Empire Cotton Growing Corporation. Progress Reports from Experiment Stations [*A publication*] — ECPRAG
Empire Cotton Growing Corporation. Progress Reports from Experiment Stations [*A publication*] — Emp Cotton Grow Corp Prog Rep Exp Stn
Empire Cotton Growing Corporation. Review — ECGWAK
Empire Cotton Growing Corporation. Review — Emp Cott Grow Corp R
Empire Cotton Growing Corporation. Review — Emp Cott Grow Rev
Empire Cotton Growing Corporation. Review — Empr Cotton Grow Rev
Empire Cotton Growing Review — Emp Cotton Growing R
Empire Digest — Emp Dig
Empire Forestry. Empire Forestry Association — Empire Forest
Empire Forestry Handbook — Emp For Handb
Empire Forestry Journal — Emp For J
Empire Forestry Journal — Empire For J
Empire Forestry Review — EFR
Empire Forestry Review — EMFRA2
Empire Forestry Review — Emp For Rev
Empire Journal of Experimental Agriculture — EJEAAR
Empire Journal of Experimental Agriculture — Emp J Exp Ag
Empire Journal of Experimental Agriculture — Emp J Exp Agric
Empire Journal of Experimental Agriculture — Emp J Expl Agric
Empire Journal of Experimental Agriculture — Empire J Exp Agr
Empire Journal of Experimental Agriculture — Empire J Exp Agric
Empire Mining and Metallurgical Congress. Proceedings — Emp Min Metall Congr Proc
Empire Producer — Emp Prod
Empire Producer — Empire Prod
Empire Production and Export — Emp Prod Exp
Empire Review — Emp R
Empire Review — Emp Rev
Empire State Report — Emp St Rep
Empire State Report — Empire State Rept
Empire State Report Weekly — Emp St Rep W
Empire Survey Review — Emp Surv Rev
Empire Survey Review — Empire Sur Rev
Empirical Economics — Empirical Econ
Empirical Research in Theatre — Empir Res T
Empirical Research in Theatre Annual — Empir Res T Ann
Empirical Studies of Psychoanalytic Theories — Empir Stud Psychoanal Theor
Empirical Studies of the Arts — EM
Employee Benefit Plan Review — EBPR
Employee Benefit Plan Review — Em Benefit
Employee Benefit Plan Review — Empl Benefit Plan Rev
Employee Benefit Plan Review — Employ Benefit Plan Rev
Employee Benefit Plan Review — EPB
Employee Benefit Research Institute. Policy Forum — ERI
Employee Benefit Research Institute. Research Report — EBR
Employee Benefits Cases. Bureau of National Affairs — Employee Benefits Cas BNA
Employee Benefits Infosource [*Database*] — EBIS
Employee Benefits Journal — EBJ
Employee Benefits Journal — Empl B Jrl
Employee Benefits Journal — Empl Benefits J
Employee Benefits Journal — Employ Benefits J
Employee Health and Fitness — EHAF
Employee Health and Fitness Newsletter — Employee Health Fitness Newsl
Employee Relations — BLS
Employee Relations — Emp Rel
Employee Relations — Employee Rel
Employee Relations — EMR
Employee Relations Law Journal — Emp Rel LJ
Employee Relations Law Journal — Empl Rel LJ
Employee Relations Law Journal — Empl Relat Law J
Employee Relations Law Journal — Employ Relat Law J
Employee Relations Law Journal — ERL
Employee Services Management — EMSM
Employer — Emp
Employers' Review — Employers R
Employment and Earnings — EMEA
Employment and Earnings — Employment
Employment and Earnings. Supplement — Emplymnt S
Employment and Training Reporter. Bureau of National Affairs — Empl & Training Rep BNA
Employment Coordinator. Research Institute of America — Empl Coordinator Research Inst Am
Employment Earnings and Hours — Employ Earn Hours
Employment Gazette — EG
Employment Gazette — Empl Gaz
Employment Gazette — Employ Gaz
Employment Issues — Employ Iss
Employment News — Empl News
Employment Practices Decisions. Commerce Clearing House — Empl Prac Dec CCH
Employment Practices Guide. Commerce Clearing House — Empl Prac Guide CCH
Employment Projections for 1995. BLS Bulletin 2197. US Bureau of Labor Statistics — BLS 2197
Employment Projections for 1995; Data and Methods. BLS Bulletin 2253. US Bureau of Labor Statistics — BLS 2253
Employment Relations Abstracts — EmAb
Employment Relations Abstracts — Empl RA
Employment Relations Abstracts — Employ Rel Abstr
Employment Relations Abstracts — Employ Relat Abstr
Employment Report — Empl Rep
Employment Report — Employ Rep
Employment Review — ETR

Employment Safety and Health Guide. Commerce Clearing House — Empl Safety & Health Guide CCH
Employment Security Review — Empl Secur Rev
Employment Service Review — Empl Serv R
Emporia State Research Studies — Emporia St Res Stud
Emporia State Research Studies — ESRS
Emporia State University. Business Review — ESU Bus Rev
Empreintes — Empr
Empresa Brasiliera de Pesquisa Agropecuaria. Centro de Tecnologia Agricola e Alimentar — Empresa Bras Pesqui Agropecu Cent Tecnol Agri
EMS [*Environmental Mutagen Society*] **Newsletter** — EMS Newsl
EMT [*Emergency Medical Technician*] **Journal** — EMT J
Emuna — Em
En Passant — En Pas
En Route Supplement — ERS
En Terre d'Islam — ETI
Enamelist Bulletin — Enamelist Bull
Encephale — ENCEA
Encephale — ENCEAN
Encephale — Enceph
Enchiridion Biblicum — Ench B
Enchiridion Biblicum. Editionis Napoli/Roma — EBn
Enchiridion Fontium Valdensium — EFV
Enchiridion Symbolorum — Ench Symb
Enchoria. Zeitschrift fuer Demotistik und Koptologie — EZDK
Enciclopedia Biografica e Bibliografica Italiana — EBBI
Enciclopedia Cattolica — E Catt
Enciclopedia Cattolica — EC
Enciclopedia Cattolica — Enc Catt
Enciclopedia de Educacion (Montevideo) — Encic Educ Monte
Enciclopedia de la Biblia — Enc Biblia
Enciclopedia de la Religion Catolica — ERC
Enciclopedia del Diritto — E d D
Enciclopedia dell'Arte Antica, Classica, e Orientale — EAA
Enciclopedia dello Spettacolo — Enc Spett
Enciclopedia di Autori Classici — EAC
Enciclopedia Ecclesiastica. Venezia — Enc Ec V
Enciclopedia Filosofica — EF
Enciclopedia Italiana — EI
Enciclopedia Italiana di Scienze, Lettere, ed Arti [*Rome*] — EI
Enciclopedia Italiana di Scienze, Lettere, ed Arti [*Rome*] — Enc It
Enciclopedia Italiana di Scienze, Lettere, ed Arti — Enc Ital
Enciclopedia Linguistica Hispanica — ELH
Enciclopedia SEI [*Societa Editrice Internazionale*] — Enc SEI
Enciclopedia Universal Ilustrada Europeo-Americana — EEAm
Enciclopedia Universal Ilustrada Europeo-Americana. Suplement Anual — EEAm S
Enciclopedia Universale dell'Arte — EUA
Enciklopedija Likovnik Umjetnosti — Enc Lik Umj
Encontro com o Folclore — EnF
Encontro Nacional de Fisica de Reatores e Termoidraulica — Encontro Nac Fis Reatores Termoidraulica
Encontros com a Civilizacao Brasileira — Encont Civ Bras
Encontros com a Civilizacao Brasileira Editora Civilizacao Brasileira — ECB
Encore American and Worldwide News — Encore
Encore Australia — Encore Aust
Encounter — E
Encounter — Ectr
Encounter — En
Encounter — ENC
Encounter — Encount
Encounter — IENC
Encounter (Christian Theological Seminary) — Encounter (Chr Theol Sem)
Encounter (Indianapolis) — Encl
Encounter (London) — EncL
Encounter Pamphlet Series — Enc Pamphl Ser
Encuentro (Nicaragua) — EN
Encyclia — ENCYDI
Encyclopaedia Americana — EA
Encyclopaedia Americana — Ency Amer
Encyclopaedia Biblica — EBIB
Encyclopaedia Britannica — E Brit
Encyclopaedia Britannica — EB
Encyclopaedia Britannica — EBr
Encyclopaedia Britannica — Enc Brit
Encyclopaedia Britannica — Ency Brit
Encyclopaedia Iranica — EIr
Encyclopaedia Judaica [*Berlin*] — EJ
Encyclopaedia Judaica. Berlin — EJB
Encyclopaedia Judaica Year Book — EnJuYB
Encyclopaedia of Archaeological Excavations in the Holy Land [*Jerusalem*] — EAEHL
Encyclopaedia of Buddhism — Enc Bud
Encyclopaedia of Buddhism — Enc Buddh
Encyclopaedia of Islam — EI
Encyclopaedia of Islam [Leiden, 1913-1942] — EI1
Encyclopaedia of Islam [2nd Ed. Leiden, 1954] — EI2
Encyclopaedia of Islam — Enc Is
Encyclopaedia of Mathematical Sciences — Encyclopaedia Math Sci
Encyclopaedia of Religion and Ethics — Encycl Rel Ethics
Encyclopaedia of Religion and Ethics — ERE
Encyclopaedia of the Social Sciences — ESS
Encyclopaedia of Veterinary Medicine, Surgery, and Obstetrics — Encycl Vet Med Surg and Obst
Encyclopaedisches Journal — Encycl J
Encyclopedia Americana — Enc Am
Encyclopedia Buying Guide — Encyc Buy G
Encyclopedia Judaica Castellana — EJC
Encyclopedia of American Business History and Biography — EABH & B
Encyclopedia of American Religions — EAR
Encyclopedia of Associations — Enc Ass
Encyclopedia of Chemical Technology — Encycl Chem Technol
Encyclopedia of Earth Sciences Series — Encycl Earth Sci Ser
Encyclopedia of Mathematics and Its Applications — Encyclopedia Math Appl
Encyclopedia of Missions — Enc Mis
Encyclopedia of Plant Anatomy — Encycl Plant Anat
Encyclopedia of Plant Physiology. New Series — Encycl Plant Physiol New Ser
Encyclopedia of Psychology — Enc Psych
Encyclopedia of Religion — Enc Rel
Encyclopedia of Southern Baptists — ESB
Encyclopedia of the Lutheran Church — ELC
Encyclopedia of Unified Science — Enc Unif Sci
Encyclopedia of Urology — Encycl Urol
Encyclopedia of Urology — HAURBR
Encyclopedia of Zionism and Israel — EZI
Encyclopedie Biologique [*Paris*] — EYBIA5
Encyclopedie Biologique (Paris) — Encycl Biol (Paris)
Encyclopedie de la Musique — Enc Mus
Encyclopedie de l'Islam — E Isl
Encyclopedie de l'Islam — EI
Encyclopedie de l'Islam — Enc I
Encyclopedie des Musiques Sacrees — EMS
Encyclopedie des Sciences Ecclesiastiques — ESE
Encyclopedie Entomologique — Encycl Entomol
Encyclopedie Entomologique — EYENAZ
Encyclopedie Francaise — Enc Fr
Encyclopedie Medico-Chirurgicale — ECMCC
Encyclopedie Medico-Chirurgicale — Encycl Med-Chir
Encyclopedie Mensuelle d'Outre-Mer — Enc Mens O Mer
Encyclopedie Mensuelle d'Outre-Mer — Ency Mens OM
Encyclopedie Mycologique — Encycl Mycol
Encyclopedie Mycologique — EYMYA6
Encyclopedie Ornithologique [*Paris*] — ENORAK
Encyclopedie Ornithologique (Paris) — Encycl Ornithol (Paris)
Encyclopedie ou Dictionnaire Raisonne des Sciences, des Arts, et des Metiers — Enc
Encyclopedie Periodique des Sciences Medico-Biologiques. Section. Biologie and Pathologie — Encycl Period Sci Med Biol Sect Biol Pathol
Encyclopedie Periodique des Sciences Medico-Biologiques. Section. Microbiologie et Applications a la Biologie — Encycl Period Sci Med Biol Sect Microbiol Appl Biol
Encyclopedie Photographique de l'Art [*Paris*] — Enc Phot
Encyclopedie Theologique — Enc Th
Encyklopaedisches Handbuch der Paedagogik — EHP
End Uses of Sulfur and Sulfuric Acid in 1982. Mineral Industry Survey — MIS Sulf U
Endangered Species Technical Bulletin — Endangered Species Tech Bull
Endeavour — ENDE
Endeavour — ENDEA
Endeavour [*Oxford*] — ENDEAS
Endeavour — PEND
Endeavour. New Series — Endeavour New Ser
Endemic Diseases Bulletin. Nagasaki University — Endem Dis Bull Nagasaki Univ
Endemic Diseases Bulletin. Nagasaki University — NDFKAH
Endocrine Bioassay Data — EBADAS
Endocrine Bioassay Data. United States Department of Health, Education, and Welfare — Endocr Bioassay Data
Endocrine Genetics and Genetics of Growth. Proceedings. International Clinical Genetics Seminar — Endocr Genet Genet Growth Proc Int Clin Genet Semin
Endocrine Journal — Endocr J
Endocrine Pathology — Endocr Pathol
Endocrine Regulations — Endocr Regul
Endocrine Research — Endocr Res
Endocrine Research — ENRSE8
Endocrine Research Communications — EDRCAM
Endocrine Research Communications — Endocr Res
Endocrine Research Communications — Endocr Res Commun
Endocrine Reviews — Endocr Rev
Endocrine Reviews Monographs — Endocr Rev Monogr
Endocrine Society of Australia. Proceedings — Endocr Soc Aust Proc
Endocrine Society of Australia. Proceedings — ESAUAS
Endocrine-Related Cancer — Endocr Relat Cancer
Endocrinologia e Scienza della Costituzione — Endocrinol Sci Cost
Endocrinologia e Scienze della Costituzione — ESDCA
Endocrinologia Experimentalis — Endocr Exp
Endocrinologia Experimentalis — Endocrinol Exp
Endocrinologia Experimentalis — ENEXA
Endocrinologia Experimentalis — ENEXAM
Endocrinologia Japonica — ECJPA
Endocrinologia Japonica — ECJPAE
Endocrinologia Japonica — Endocr Jap
Endocrinologia Japonica — Endocrinol Jpn
Endocrinologia Japonica. Supplement — Endocrinol Jpn Suppl
Endocrinology — ENDOA
Endocrinology — ENDOAO
Endocrinology — Endocrinol
Endocrinology and Metabolism — EM
Endocrinology and Metabolism — Endocrinol Metab

Endocrinology and Metabolism Clinics of North America — Endocrinol Metab Clin N Am
Endocrinology and Metabolism Clinics of North America — Endocrinol Metab Clin North Am
Endocrinology and Metabolism Series — Endocrinol Metab Ser
Endocrinology Index — EDI
Endocrinology Index — Endocrinol Ind
Endocrinology, Neuroendocrinology, Neuropeptides — Endocrinol Neuroendocrinol Neuropept
Endocrinology of Calcium Metabolism. Proceedings. Parathyroid Conference — Endocrinol Calcium Metab Proc Parathyroid Conf
Endocrinology. Proceedings. International Congress of Endocrinology — Endocrinol Proc Int Cong
Endodontics and Dental Traumatology — EDTRED
Endodontics and Dental Traumatology — Endod & Dent Traumatol
Endodontics and Dental Traumatology — Endod Dent Traumatol
Endokrinnaya Sistema Organizma i Toksicheskie Faktory Vneshnei Sredy. Materialy Konferentsii — Endokr Sist Org Toksicheskie Fakroty Vneshn Sredy Mater Konf
Endokrinnye Mekhanizmy Regulyatsii Prisposobleniya Organizma k Myshechnoi Deyatel'nosti — Endok Mekh Regul Prisposobleniya Org Myshechnoi Deyat
Endokrinologie — ENDKA
Endokrinologie — ENDKAC
Endokrinologie — Endokr
Endokrinologie — Endokrinol
Endokrynologia Polska — EDPKA2
Endokrynologia Polska — Endokr Pol
Endokrynologia Polska — Endokrynol Pol
Endoscopic Surgery and Allied Technologies — Endosc Surg Allied Technol
Endoscopy — ENDCA
Endoscopy — ENDCAM
Energetekhnologicheskow Ispol'zovanie Toplova [*Former USSR*] — Energeteknol Ispol'z Topl
Energetekhnologicheskow Ispol'zovanie Toplova — ETITA
Energetic Materials — Energ Mater
Energetica si Hidrotehnica — Energ Hidroteh
Energeticheskii Byulleten — Energ Byull
Energeticheskii Institut Imeni G. M. Krzhizhanovskogo. Sbornik Trudov — Energ Inst Im G M Krzhizhanovskogo Sb Tr
Energeticheskoe Mashinostroenie — Energ Mashinostr
Energeticheskoe Stroitel'stvo [*Former USSR*] — Energ Stroit
Energeticheskoe Stroitel'stvo za Rubezhom [*Former USSR*] — Energ Stroit Rubezhom
Energeticheskoe Stroitel'stvo za Rubezhom — ESRBB
Energetics in Metallurgical Phenomena — Energ Metall Phenom
Energetik — EGTKA
Energetika — EGKAA
Energetika (Alma-Ata) — ENAAD
Energetika i Avtomatika — Energ Avtom
Energetika i Elektrifikatsiya — Energ Elektrif
Energetika i Elektrifikatsiya (Kiev) — Energ Elektrif (Kiev)
Energetika i Elektrotekhnicheskaya Promyshlennost — Energ Elektrotekh Prom
Energetika i Elektrotekhnicheskaya Promyshlennost — Energ Elektrotekh Promst
Energetika i Transport — Energ Trans
Energetika i Transport [*Former USSR*] — Energ Transp
Energetika (Sofia, Bulgaria) — ENGTB
Energetische Nutzung von Abfallstoffen. Muelltechnisches Seminar — Energ Nutz Abfallst Muelltech Semin
Energetyka — EGYAA
Energia — NRGID
Energia del Fuego al Atomo — EFATD
Energia del Fuego al Atomo — Energ Fuego At
Energia e Industria — Energ Ind
Energia Elettrica — ENELA
Energia Elettrica — Energ El
Energia Elettrica — Energ Elet
Energia Elettrica — Energ Elettr
Energia Elettrica. A — Energ Elettr A
Energia Elettrica. B — Energ Elettr B
Energia es Atomtechnika — ENATA
Energia es Atomtechnika — Energ Atomtech
Energia es Atomtechnika — Energ es Atomtech
Energia es Atomtechnika — Energa Atom
Energia. Fontes Alternativas — Energ Fontes Altern
Energia Nuclear — Energ Nucl
Energia Nuclear — ENNCA
Energia Nuclear — ENNLAV
Energia Nuclear. Boletim Informativo do Forum Atomico Portugues (Lisbon) — Energ Nucl (Lisbon)
Energia Nuclear e Agricultura — ENAGDM
Energia Nuclear e Agricultura — Energ Nucl Agric
Energia Nuclear (Madrid) — Energ Nucl (Madrid)
Energia Nucleare [*Milan*] — Energa Nu
Energia Nucleare [*Milan*] — Energa Nucl
Energia Nucleare — ENNLA
Energia Nucleare in Agricoltura. Simposio. Congresso Nucleare — Energ Nucl Agric Cong Nucl
Energia Nucleare (Milan) — Energ Nucl (Milan)
Energia Termica — Energ Term
Energiaipari Szakirodalmi Tajekoztato — Energ Szakirod Tajek
Energie — ENERA
Energie Alternative — EHTED
Energie Alternative [*Italy*] — Energ Alternative
Energie Fluide — Energ Fluide
Energie Fluide — ENFLA
Energie Fluide et Lubrification et Hydraulique Pneumatique Asservissements [*A publication*] — Energ Fluide et Lubr Hydraul Pneum Asservissements
Energie Fluide, l'Air Industriel — EFAID
Energie Magazine — Energie Mag
Energie Nucleaire — En Nucl
Energie Nucleaire — ENNUA
Energie Nucleaire Magazine [*Later, Energie Magazine*] — Energ Nucl Mag
Energie Nucleaire (Paris) — Energ Nucl (Paris)
Energie Studie Centrum. Rapport ESC (Petten, Netherlands) — Energ Stud Cent Rapp ESC (Petten Neth)
Energie- und Kerntechnik — Energ Kerntech
Energie und Technik — Energ Tech
Energie und Technik — Energ Technik
Energie und Technik — ENTEA
Energieanwendung — EANWA
Energieanwendung, Energie- und Umwelttechnik — Energieanwend Energ Umwelttech
Energiebesparing in Bedrijf en Instelling — ENB
Energie-Brief — Energ-Brief
Energieonderzoek Centrum Nederland Report — Energieonder Cent Ned Rep
Energies — ENEGA
Energies — ENRGD
Energiespectrum — NRGSD
Energiespectrum — RCN
Energietechnik — En Techn
Energietechnik — Energ Techn
Energietechnik — Energietech
Energietechnik — ETNKA
Energietechnische Gesellschaft. Fachberichte — Energietech Ges Fachber
Energiewesen — ERGWD
Energiewirtschaftliche Tagesfragen — Energiewirtsch Tagesfr
Energiewirtschaftliche Tagesfragen — Energiewirtsch Tagesfragen
Energiewirtschaftliche Tagesfragen — EWTFA
Energinfo — EGIND
Energoexport — NRGXD
Energokhozyaistvo za Rubezhom — Energokhoz Rubezhom
Energomashinostroenie — EGSMA
Energotekhnologicheskoe Ispol'zovante Topliva — Energotekhnol Ispol'z Topl
Energy — ENERD
Energy — ENRYD
Energy — ENY
Energy — ERGYA
Energy [*South Korea*] — OINOD
Energy Abstracts for Policy Analysis [*National Science Foundation*] — Energy Abstr Policy Anal
Energy Advisory Bulletin for Texas Manufacturers — EABMD
Energy Advisory Bulletin for Texas Manufacturers — Energy Advis Bull Tex Manuf
Energy, Agriculture and Waste Management. Proceedings. Cornell Agricultural Waste Management Conference — Energy Agri Waste Manage Proc Cornell Agri Waste Manage Conf
Energy and Alternatives Magazine — ENALD
Energy and Alternatives Magazine — Energy Alternatives Mag
Energy and Buildings — Energy and Build
Energy and Buildings — Energy Bldgs
Energy and Buildings — Energy Build
Energy and Ceramics. Proceedings. International Meeting on Modern Ceramics Technologies — Energy Ceram Proc Int Meet Mod Ceram Technol
Energy and Community Planning on the Prairies. Proceedings. Symposium — Energy Community Plann Prairies Proc Symp
Energy and Development Digest — EDDID
Energy and Development Journal — Energy Dev
Energy and Ecological Modelling. Proceedings. Symposium — Energy Ecol Modell Proc Symp
Energy and Economics Data Bank — ENEC
Energy and Education — ENEDD
Energy and Education — Energy Educ
Energy and Environment [*South Africa*] — Energy Environ
Energy and Environment (Dordrecht, Netherlands) — Energy Environ Dordrecht Neth
Energy and Materials. National State-of-the-Art Symposium — Energy Mater Natl State of the Art Symp
Energy and Mineral Resources [*Database*] — E & MR
Energy and Minerals Resources — Energy Miner Resour
Energy and Physics. Proceedings. General Conference. European Physical Society — Energy Phys Proc Gen Conf Eur Phys Soc
Energy and Pollution Control [*Japan*] — Energy Pollut Control
Energy and Resources (Osaka) — Energy Resour (Osaka)
Energy and Resources Research — Energy Resour Res
Energy and the Environment — EREND
Energy and the Environment. Annual Technical Meeting — Energy Environ Annu Tech Meet
Energy and the Environment: Interactions — EEIND
Energy and the Environment. Interactions — Energy Environ Interact
Energy and the Environment (New York) — Energy Environ (NY)
Energy and the Environment (Oak Ridge, Tennessee) — Energy Environ (Oak Ridge Tenn)
Energy and the Environment. Proceedings. National Conference [*US*] — Energy Environ
Energy and the Environment. Proceedings of the National Conference — Energy Environ Proc Nat Conf
Energy at Booz-Allen — EBALD
Energy Bibliography and Index [*Database*] — EBI

Energy Business — Engy Bsns
Energy Business. The Future of Coal, 1981 and Beyond — Energy Bus
Energy Clearinghouse — ENCLD
Energy Clearinghouse — Energy Clgh
Energy, Combustion and the Environment — Energy Combust Environ
Energy Communications — Energ Commun
Energy Communications — Energy Comm
Energy Communications — Energy Commun
Energy Conservation and Environment. Federal Energy Administration. Conservation Paper (United States) — Energy Conserv Environ Fed Energy Adm Conserv Pap (US)
Energy Conservation Digest — Energy Conserv Dig
Energy Conservation News — En Conserv
Energy Conservation Report [*Canada*] — Energy Conserv Rep
Energy Conservation (Tokyo) — Energy Conserv (Tokyo)
Energy Conservation Update — Energy Conserv Update
Energy Consumer — ECOND
Energy Consumer — Energy Consum
Energy Conversion — ENERB
Energy Conversion — Energy Conv
Energy Conversion — Energy Convers
Energy Conversion. An International Journal — Energy Convers Intl J
Energy Conversion and Management — Energy Cnvers & Manage
Energy Conversion and Management — Energy Convers and Manage
Energy Conversion and Management — Energy Convers Manage
Energy Coupling in Photosynthesis. Proceedings. Harry Steenbock Symposium — Energy Coupling Photosynth Proc Harry Steenbock Symp
Energy Daily — Energy Dly
Energy Data Report. Asphalt Sales — Energy Data Rep Asphalt Sales
Energy Data Report. Coke and Coal Chemicals Monthly — Energy Data Rep Coke Coal Chem Mon
Energy Data Report. Natural and Synthetic Gas — Energy Data Rep Nat Synth Gas
Energy Data Report. Natural Gas Monthly Report — Energy Data Rep Nat Gas Mon Rep
Energy Data Report. Petroleum Refineries in the United States and US Territori es — Energy Data Rep Pet Refin US US Territ
Energy Data Report. Sales of Asphalt — Energy Data Rep Sales Asphalt
Energy Data Report. Weekly Coal Report — Energy Data Rep Wkly Coal Rep
Energy Data Report. World Crude Oil Production — Energy Data Rep World Crude Oil Prod
Energy Data Reports. Bituminous Coal and Lignite Distribution — EDR B Coal
Energy Data Reports. Carbon Black — Energy Data Rep Carbon Black
Energy Data Reports. Coal, Bituminous and Lignite — EDR Coal B & L
Energy Data Reports. Crude Petroleum, Petroleum Products, and Natural Gas Liquids — Energy Data Rep Crude Pet Pet Prod Nat Gas Liq
Energy Data Reports. Distribution of Pennsylvania Anthracite — EDR Anthrc
Energy Data Reports. Fuel Oils by Sulfur Content — Energy Data Rep Fuel Oils Sulfur Content
Energy Data Reports. Fuel Oils by Sulphur Content — EDR F Oils
Energy Data Reports. Liquefied Petroleum Sales — EDR LPS
Energy Data Reports. Natural Gas — EDR N Gas
Energy Data Reports. Natural Gas — Energy Data Rep Nat Gas
Energy Data Reports. Natural Gas Liquids — Energy Data Rep Nat Gas Liq
Energy Data Reports. Petroleum Statement — EDR Pet St
Energy Data Reports. Petroleum Statement — Energy Data Rep Pet Statement
Energy Data Reports. Sales of Fuel Oil and Kerosene — EDR Ker
Energy Data Reports. United States Imports and Exports of Natural Gas — Energy Data Rep US Imports Exports Nat Gas
Energy Detente — EDETD
Energy Detente International Price/Tax Series [*Database*] — EDPRICE
Energy Development — ENDED
Energy Development (New York). IEEE Power Engineering Society Papers — Energy Dev (New York)
Energy Developments — Energy Dev
Energy Developments in Japan — Energy Dev Jpn
Energy Dialog — ENDID
Energy Digest [*Colorado Springs, CO*] — EDIGD
Energy Digest [*Washington, DC*] — EGYDA
Energy Digest [*Bombay*] — ENDGD
Energy Digest — Energy Dig
Energy Digest (Colorado Springs, Colorado) — Energy Dig (Colo Spring Colo)
Energy Digest (London) — Energy Dig (London)
Energy Digest (Washington, DC) — Energy Dig (Wash DC)
Energy Directory — ENDRD
Energy Dollars and Sense of Conservation — ENCMD
Energy Dollars and Sense of Conservation — Energy Dollars Sense Conserv
Energy Economics — ENE
Energy Economics — Energy Econ
Energy Economics, Policy, and Management — EEPMD
Energy Economics, Policy, and Management — Energy Econ Policy Manage
Energy Economist — EYETD
Energy Educator Newsletter — EEDND
Energy Educator Newsletter — Energy Educ Newsl
Energy Engineering — Energy Eng
Energy Engineering — Energy Enging
Energy, Environment. Engineering — Energy Environ Eng
Energy Executive Directory — EEDID
Energy Executive Directory — Energy Exec Dir
Energy Exploration and Exploitation — Energy Explor Exploit
Energy File [*Vancouver, British Columbia*] — ENFL
Energy for Chemicals. Outlook and Practical Solutions. Symposium — Energy Chem Outlook Pract Solutions Symp
Energy for Industry and Commerce. Quarterly Bulletin — Energy Ind Commerce Q Bull
Energy Forum in New England — EFNED
Energy Forum in New England — Energy Forum N Engl
Energy from Biomass 1. Proceedings. Contractors' Meeting — Energy Biomass 1 Proc Contract Meet
Energy from Biomass and Wastes. Symposium Papers — Energy Biomass Wastes
Energy Highlights — ENHID
Energy in Agriculture — ENEAD
Energy in Agriculture — Energy Agri
Energy in Agriculture — Energy Agric
Energy in Buildings — Energy Bldgs
Energy in Buildings — Energy in Bldgs
Energy in Profile — En Profile
Energy in World Agriculture — Energy World Agric
Energy Index — Energy Ind
Energy Information Abstracts — Energy Inf Abstr
Energy Information Administration. Monthly Petroleum Statement (US) — Energy Inf Adm Mon Pet Statement US
Energy Information Administration. Weekly Coal Production (United States) — Energy Inf Adm Wkly Coal Prod (US)
Energy Information Resources Inventory [*Database*] — EIRI
Energy Insider — Engy Insidr
Energy Intake and Activity — Energy Intake Act
Energy International — ENEIB
Energy International — Energy Int
Energy Journal — En Jnl
Energy Journal [*New Zealand*] — Energy J
Energy Journal — ENJOD
Energy Laboratory Series — Energy Lab Ser
Energy Law Journal — Energy Law J
Energy Law Journal — Energy LJ
Energy Law Journal — Eng LJ
Energy Magazine — Energy M
Energy Management — En Manag
Energy Management — Energ Manage
Energy Management — Energy Manage
Energy Management — ENMGD
Energy Management Canada — Energ Manage Can
Energy Management (Cleveland, Ohio) — Energy Manage (Cleveland Ohio)
Energy Management (India) — Energy Manage (India)
Energy Management News — EMNED
Energy Management News — Energy Manage News
Energy Manager — Energy Mgr
Energy Meetings — EMETD
Energy Meetings [*United States*] — Energy Meet
Energy Metabolism and the Regulation of Metabolic Processes in Mitochondria. Proceedings. Symposium — Energy Metab Regul Metab Processes Mitochondria Proc Symp
Energy Metabolism of Farm Animals. Proceedings of the Symposium — Energy Metab Farm Anim Proc Symp
Energy Monitor — Energ Mon
Energy News [*Pakistan*] — ENNSD
Energy News [*United States*] — ENNWD
Energy News [*United States*] — ENTAD
Energy News Notes. CERI [*Colorado Energy Research Institute*] — ENNOD
Energy Newsletter [*United States*] — Energy Newsl
Energy Newsletter — ENWSD
Energy Nova Scotia [*Database*] — ENS
Energy (Ottawa) — EERGD
Energy People — EPEOD
Energy Perspectives — Energy Perspect
Energy Perspectives — ENPED
Energy Pipelines and Systems — Energy Pipelines Syst
Energy Pipelines and Systems — EYPSB
Energy Planning Network [*United States*] — Energy Plann Network
Energy Planning Network — EPNED
Energy Policy — EEL
Energy Policy — EGP
Energy Policy — Energ Polic
Energy Policy — Energy Pol
Energy Policy and Conservation Report — Energ Pol Con Rep
Energy Problem. Impacts on Military Research and Development. AGARD [*Advisory Group for Aerospace Research and Development*] **Annual Meeting** — Energy Probl Impacts Mil Res Dev AGARD Annu Meet
Energy Processing (Canada) — Energy Process (Can)
Energy Progress — Energy Prog
Energy Progress — ENPGD
Energy Purchasing Report — Energy Purch Rep
Energy Quarterly [*Taiwan*] — Energy Q
Energy Regulation Digest — Energ Reg Dig
Energy Report (Alton, England) — EGRTA
Energy Report (Alton, England) — Energy Rep (Alton Engl)
Energy Report. Community Information Center. Fairbanks North Star Borough — ENRE
Energy Report (Denver, Colorado) — ENRPD
Energy Report from Chase — ERCHD
Energy Report to the States — Energy Rep States
Energy Report to the States — ERSTD
Energy Research [*England*] — Energy Res
Energy Research — ENRSD
Energy Research [*Elsevier Book Series*] — ER
Energy Research Abstracts — Energy Res Abstr
Energy Research Abstracts [*Database*] — ERA
Energy Research and Development Administration. Research Abstracts — Energy Res Dev Adm Res Abstr

Energy Research and Development Administration. Symposium Series — Energy Res Dev Adm Symp Ser
Energy Research Bureau — Energy Res Bur
Energy Research Digest — Energy Res Dig
Energy Research Reports — Energy Res Rep
Energy Resources and Technology — Energy Resourc Technol
Energy Review — Energy Rev
Energy Review — ER
Energy Science and Technology — Energy Sci Technol
Energy Sources [*New York*] — EGYSA
Energy Sources — EGYSAO
Energy Sources — Energy Sources
Energy Sources — ENSOD
Energy Supply to the Year 2000 — Engy Supply
Energy Systems and Policy — Energy Syst and Policy
Energy Systems and Policy — Energy Syst Policy
Energy Systems and Policy — Energy Systems Pol
Energy Systems and Policy — ESD
Energy Systems and Policy — ESP
Energy Technology — Energy Technol
Energy Technology Conference. Proceedings — Energy Technol Conf Proc
Energy Technology. Proceedings. Energy Technology Conference — Energy Technol
Energy Technology Review — Energy Technol Rev
Energy Technology Review — ETERD
Energy Technology (Washington, DC) — Energy Technol (Wash DC)
Energy. The International Journal — Energy Int J
Energy Times [*India*] — ENTSD
Energy Topics — Energy Top
Energy Topics — ETOPD
Energy Trends — En Trends
Energy User News — Energy
Energy User News — EUSND
Energy Viewpoint — EVPTD
Energy Watch — En Watch
Energy World — Energy Wld
Energylab Newsletter — Energyl Newsl
Energyline — ERGYD
Enfant en Milieu Tropical — CHTCB5
Enfant en Milieu Tropical — Enfant Milieu Trop
Enfermedades del Torax — Enferm Torax
Enfermedades del Torax — ENFTAF
Enfermedades del Torax y Tuberculosis — Enferm Torax Tuberc
Enfermedades Infecciosas y Microbiologia Clinica — Enferm Infecc Microbiol Clin
Enfoques Educacionales (Chile) — EEC
Engage/Social Action — Engage/Soc Act
Engei Gakkai Zasshi — EGKZA
Engei Gakkai Zasshi — EGKZA9
Engei Gakkai Zasshi/Journal of the Japanese Society for Horticultural Science — Engei Gakkai Zasshi J Jap Soc Hortic Sci
Engei Shikenjo Hokoku. A. Hiratsuka — Engei Shikenjo Hokoku A
Engei Shikenjo Hokoku. A. Hiratsuka — ESHAA3
Engei Shikenjo Hokoku. B. Okitsu — ESHBA6
Engei Shikenjo Hokoku. C. Morioka — ENSHBB
Engei Shikenjo Hokoku. D. Kurume — ESHDAC
Engelhard Industries. Technical Bulletin — EITBA
Engelhard Industries. Technical Bulletin — Engelhard Ind Tech Bull
Engenharia Agricola — Eng Agric
Engenharia Civil (Sao Paulo) — Eng Civ (Sao Paulo)
Engenharia e Quimica — Eng Quim
Engenharia e Quimica — Engenh Quim
Engenharia, Mineracao, e Metalurgia (Rio de Janeiro) — Engen Miner Metal Rio
Engenharia, Mineracao, Metalurgia — Eng Min Metal
Engenharia, Mineracao, Metalurgia — Eng Mineracao Met
Engenharia, Mineracao, Metalurgia — Engenh Min Met
Engenharia na Industria — Eng Ind
Engenharia Quimica (Sao Paulo) — Eng Quim (Sao Paulo)
[*The*] **Engineer** — Eng
[*The*] **Engineer** — ENGIA
[*The*] **Engineer** — Engr
Engineer and Builder — Eng Build
Engineer and Foundryman — Eng Foundryman
Engineer Apprentice — Eng Apprent
Engineer Buyers Guide — Eng Buy Guide
Engineer (New York) — Eng (NY)
Engineered Materials Abstracts [*Database*] — EMA
Engineering — Eng
Engineering — ENGNA
Engineering — Engng
Engineering and Boiler House Review — Eng Boil H Rev
Engineering and Boilerhouse Review — Eng Boilerhouse Rev
Engineering and Building Record [*USA*] — Eng & Bu Rec
Engineering and Cement World — Eng Cem World
Engineering and Chemical Digest — Eng Chem Dig
Engineering and Contract Record — Eng Contract Rec
Engineering and Contracting — Eng Contract
Engineering and Finance — Eng Finance
Engineering and Food. Proceedings. International Congress on Engineering and Food — Eng Food Proc Int Congr
Engineering and Industrial Software Directory [*Database*] — EISD
Engineering and Instrumentation — Eng & Instrumentation
Engineering and Mining Journal — E & M Jour
Engineering and Mining Journal — EMJ
Engineering and Mining Journal — Eng & Min J
Engineering and Mining Journal — Eng Min J
Engineering and Mining Journal — Eng Mining J
Engineering and Mining Journal — Engng Min J
Engineering and Mining Journal — ENMJA
Engineering and Mining Journal Press — Eng Min J Press
Engineering and Mining Journal. Statistical Supplement — Eng Min J Stat Suppl
Engineering and Mining World — Eng Min World
Engineering and Process Economics — Eng Process Econ
Engineering and Science — Eng and Sci
Engineering and Science — Eng Sci
Engineering and Science Monthly — Eng Sci Mon
Engineering and Services Laboratory. Technical Report. ESL-TR. United States Air Force Engineering and Services Center — Eng Serv Lab Tech Rep ESL TR US Air Force Eng Serv Cent
Engineering and Technology — Eng and Technol
Engineering and Technology (Osaka) [*Japan*] — Eng Technol (Osaka)
Engineering Application of Fracture Mechanics — Eng Appl Fract Mech
Engineering Applications of Fracture Analysis. Proceedings. National Conference on Fracture — Eng Appl Fract Anal Proc Natl Conf Fract
Engineering Aspects of Magnetohydrodynamics — EASMD
Engineering Aspects of Magnetohydrodynamics — Eng Aspects Magnetohydrodyn
Engineering Aspects of Thermal Pollution. Proceedings. National Symposium on Thermal Pollution — Eng Aspects Therm Pollut Proc Natl Symp Thermal Pollut
Engineering Association of the South. Transactions — Eng As South Tr
Engineering Bulletin — Eng Bull
Engineering Bulletin. Purdue University — Eng Bull Purdue Univ
Engineering Bulletin. Purdue University. Engineering Extension Series — Eng Bull Purdue Univ Eng Ext Ser
Engineering Computations. International Journal for Computer-aided Engineering and Software — Engrg Comput
Engineering Computers — Eng Comput
Engineering Conference — Eng Conf
Engineering Conference. Proceedings [*United States*] — ECOPD
Engineering Conference. Proceedings — Eng Conf Proc
Engineering Construction World — Eng Constr World
Engineering. Cornell Quarterly — ECQUA
Engineering. Cornell Quarterly — Eng Cornell Q
Engineering Costs and Production Economics — ECP
Engineering Costs and Production Economics — ECPED
Engineering Costs and Production Economics [*Netherlands*] — Eng Costs Prod Econ
Engineering Cybernetics [*English Translation*] — ENCYA
Engineering Cybernetics — Eng Cybern
Engineering Cybernetics — Engrg Cybernetics
Engineering Design Guides — Eng Des Guides
Engineering Design International — Engng Des Int
Engineering Designer — Engng Des
Engineering Digest — EDIGA
Engineering Digest (New York) — Eng Dig (NY)
Engineering Digest (Toronto) — Eng Dig (Toronto)
Engineering Dynamics Series — Engrg Dynamics Ser
Engineering Economist — EEC
Engineering Economist — ENECA
Engineering Economist — Eng Econ
Engineering Economist — Eng Economist
Engineering Education — Eng Educ
Engineering Education — Engng Educ
Engineering Education (Lancaster, Pennsylvania) — Eng Educ (Lancaster PA)
Engineering Experiment Station Bulletin. West Virginia University — Eng Exp Stn Bull WVU
Engineering Experiment Station News — Eng Exp Stat News
Engineering Experiment Station. Oregon State College. Bulletin — Eng Exp Stn Oreg State Coll Bull
Engineering Experiment Station Publication. West Virginia University — Eng Exp Stn Publ WVU
Engineering Extension Series. Purdue University — Eng Ext Ser Purdue Univ
Engineering Field Notes. US Department of Agriculture. Forest Service. Engineering Staff — Eng Field Notes US Dep Agric For Serv Eng Staff
Engineering for Health in Hot Countries. Proceedings. WEDC (Water and Waste Engineering for Developing Countries) Conference — Eng Health Hot Countries Proc WEDC Conf
Engineering Foundation — Eng Found
Engineering Foundation Conference — Eng Found Conf
Engineering Foundation Conference on Cement Production and Use — Eng Found Conf Cem Prod Use
Engineering Foundation Conference on Enzyme Engineering — Eng Found Conf Enzyme Eng
Engineering Foundation Conference on Fluidization — Eng Found Conf Fluid
Engineering Foundation Conference. Waste Heat Utilization — Eng Found Conf Waste Heat Util
Engineering Foundation International Conference/Workshop on Small Fatigue Cracks — Eng Found Int Conf Workshop Small Fatigue Cracks
Engineering Foundation's International Conference on Separation Technology — Eng Found Int Conf Sep Technol
Engineering Fracture Mechanics — EFMEA
Engineering Fracture Mechanics — Eng Fract Mech
Engineering Geology — Eng Geol
Engineering Geology — Engng Geol
Engineering Geology (Amsterdam) — EGGOA
Engineering Geology (Amsterdam) — Eng Geol (Amsterdam)
Engineering Geology and Soils Engineering Symposium. Proceedings — Eng Geol Soils Eng Symp Proc
Engineering Geology Case Histories — Eng Geol Case Hist

Engineering Geology (Sacramento) — Eng Geol (Sacramento)
Engineering Geology Symposium. Proceedings — Eng Geol Symp Proc
Engineering Graphics — Eng Graphics
Engineering in Medicine — Eng Med
Engineering in Medicine — Engin Medic
Engineering in Medicine — Engng Med
Engineering in Medicine (Berlin) — Eng Med (Berlin)
Engineering Index — Ei
Engineering Index — Eng Ind
Engineering Index — Eng Index
Engineering Index — Engl
Engineering Index — ENI
Engineering Index Annual — Eng Index Annu
Engineering Index. Bioengineering Abstracts — Eng Index Bioeng Abstr
Engineering Index. Energy Abstracts — Eng Index Energy Abstr
Engineering Index Monthlies — Engng Index Mthlys
Engineering Index Monthly — Eng Index Mon
Engineering Index Monthly and Author Index — Eng Index Mon Author Index
Engineering Index Monthly and Author Index — Eng Index Monthly Author Index
Engineering Index of India — Eng Ind India
Engineering Industries (Iraq) — Eng Ind (Iraq)
Engineering Industries of Japan — EJB
Engineering Inspection — Eng Insp
Engineering Institute of Canada — Eng Inst Can
Engineering Institute of Canada. Transactions — Eng Inst Canada Trans
Engineering Issues — Eng Issues
Engineering Journal [*New York*] — EJASA
Engineering Journal — Eng J
Engineering Journal — Engng J
Engineering Journal [*Montreal*] — ENJOA
Engineering Journal. American Institute of Steel Construction — Eng J Am Inst Steel Constr
Engineering Journal (Canada) — Engng J (Can)
Engineering Journal (Montreal) — Eng J (Montreal)
Engineering Journal (New York) — Eng J (NY)
Engineering Journal of Singapore — Eng J Singapore
Engineering Magazine — Eng M
Engineering Magazine — Eng Mag
Engineering Magazine — Engin M
Engineering Management and Equipment Digest — Eng Man
Engineering Management International — EMI
Engineering Manpower Bulletin [*Engineers' Joint Council*] — EMB
Engineering Materials — Eng Mat
Engineering Materials [*Japan*] — Eng Mater
Engineering Materials and Design — EMTDA
Engineering Materials and Design — Eng Design
Engineering Materials and Design — Eng Mat Des
Engineering Materials and Design — Eng Mater & Des
Engineering Materials and Design — Eng Mater Des
Engineering Materials and Design — Engng Mat Des
Engineering Materials and Design — Engng Mater Des
Engineering Materials and Processing Methods — Eng Mater Process Methods
Engineering Materials (Tokyo) — Eng Mater (Tokyo)
Engineering News — Eng News
Engineering News (London) — Eng News London
Engineering News (New York) — Eng News (NY)
Engineering News (Tokyo) — Eng News (Tokyo)
Engineering News-Record — Eng N
Engineering News-Record — Eng New-Rc
Engineering News-Record — Eng News-Rec
Engineering News-Record — Engin N
Engineering News-Record — ENR
Engineering News-Record — ENREA
Engineering Opportunities — E/O
Engineering Optimization — EGOPA
Engineering Optimization — Eng Optim
Engineering Optimization — Eng Optimization
Engineering Outlook — Engng Outlook
Engineering Outlook. University of Illinois — Eng Outlook Univ Ill
Engineering Production — Eng Prod
Engineering Production — Engng Prod
Engineering Progress at the University of Florida. Leaflet Series — Eng Prog Univ Fla Leafl Ser
Engineering Progress at the University of Florida. Technical Paper Series — Eng Prog Univ Fla Tech Pap Ser
Engineering Progress. University of Florida. Bulletin — Eng Progr Univ Fla Bull
Engineering Progress. University of Florida. Technical Progress Report — Eng Progr Univ Fla Tech Progr Rep
Engineering Publication. University of New Hampshire. Engineering Experiment Station — Eng Publ Univ NH Eng Exp Stn
Engineering Report. Iowa Engineering Experiment Station. Iowa State University — Eng Rep Iowa Eng Exp Stn Iowa State Univ
Engineering Report. Iowa State College. Iowa Engineering Experiment Station — Eng Rep Iowa State Coll Iowa Eng Exp Stn
Engineering Report. Seoul National University — Eng Rep Seoul Natl Univ
Engineering Reprint. Division of Engineering Research and Development. University of Rhode Island — Eng Repr Div Eng Res Dev Univ RI
Engineering Reprint. Engineering Experiment Station. University of Rhode Island — Eng Repr Eng Exp Stn Univ RI
Engineering Research Bulletin — Eng Res Bull
Engineering Research Bulletin. Division of Engineering Research. Louisiana State University — Eng Res Bull Div Eng Res La State Univ
Engineering Research Bulletin. Louisiana State University. Division of Engineering Research — Eng Res Bull La State Univ Div Eng Res
Engineering Research Bulletin. Pennsylvania State University. College of Engineering — Eng Res Bull Pa State Univ Coll Eng
Engineering Research Bulletin. Rutgers University. College of Engineering — Eng Res Bull Rutgers Univ Coll Eng
Engineering Research News — Eng Res N
Engineering Research News — Eng Res News
Engineering Sciences Data Item — Eng Sci Data Item
Engineering Sciences Data Unit. Data Items — ESDU Data Items
Engineering Sciences Reports. Kyushu University — Eng Sci Rep Kyushu Univ
Engineering Series Bulletin. University of Missouri. Engineering Experiment Station — Eng Ser Bull Univ Mo Eng Exp Stn
Engineering Societies Library. ESL Bibliography — Eng Soc Libr ESL Bibliogr
Engineering Society of York. Proceedings — Eng Soc York Pr
Engineering Station Document. Purdue University — Eng Stn Doc Purdue Univ
Engineering Structures — Eng Struct
Engineering Structures — Engng Struct
Engineering Thermophysics in China — Engng Thermophys China
Engineering Times — Eng T
Engineering Times — Eng Times
Engineering Times — ERGTB
Engineering Times (Calcutta) — Eng Times (Calcutta)
Engineering Today — Eng Today
Engineering Today — Engng Today
Engineering Transactions. Polish Academy of Sciences. Institute of Fundamental Technological Research — Engrg Trans
Engineering Week — Eng Week
Engineering World — Eng World
Engineering-Science News — Eng-Sci News
Engineers and Engineering — Eng Eng
Engineers' and Technicians' Review — Eng Tech Rev
Engineers Australia — Eng Aust
Engineers' Bulletin — Engineers' Bull
Engineers' Club of Philadelphia. Proceedings — Eng Club Phila Pr
Engineers' Digest — ENDGA
Engineers' Digest — Eng Dig
Engineers' Digest — Engrs Dig
Engineers' Digest [*London*] — Engrs' Digest
Engineers' Digest (London) — Eng Dig (London)
Engineers' Gazette — Engineers Gaz
Engineers' Society of Western Pennsylvania. Proceedings — Eng Soc W Pa
England-Amerika-Institut — EAI
Englers Botanische Jahrbuecher fuer Systematik, Pflanzengeschichte, und Pflanzengeographie — Bot Jbb
Englische Blaetter — Engl Blaett
Englische Rundschau — ER
Englische Studien — Engl Stud
Englische Studien — ES
Englische Studien — ESn
Englische Studien — ESt
Englische Studien — EStn
Englisches Seminar — ES
English — E
English — Eng
English Abstracts of Selected Articles from Soviet Bloc and Mainland China Technical Journals. Series 1. Physics and Mathematics — Engl Abstr Sel Art Sov Bloc Mainland China Tech J Ser 1
English Abstracts of Selected Articles from Soviet Bloc and Mainland China Technical Journals. Series 2. Chemistry — Engl Abstr Sel Art Sov Bloc Mainland China Tech J Ser 2
English Abstracts of Selected Articles from Soviet Bloc and Mainland China Technical Journals. Series 3. Metals — Engl Abstr Sel Art Sov Bloc Mainland China Tech J Ser 3
English Abstracts of Selected Articles from Soviet Bloc and Mainland China Technical Journals. Series 5. Electronics and Electrical Engineering — Engl Abstr Sel Art Sov Bloc Mainland China Tech J Ser 5
English Abstracts of Selected Articles from Soviet Bloc and Mainland China Technical Journals. Series 6. Bio-Sciences — Engl Abstr Sel Art Sov Bloc Mainland China Tech J Ser 6
English Alive — Engl Alive
English and Germanic Studies — E and G Stud
English and Germanic Studies — E & Ger St
English and Germanic Studies — EG
English and Germanic Studies — EGS
English Association Pamphlets — EAP
English Bulletin — Engl Bul
English Catalogue of Books — ECB
English Catalogue of Books. Annual Issue — ECBA
English Catalogue of Books. Cumulative Issue — ECBC
English Church Music — English Church M
English Cyclopaedia — Eng Cyc
English Dance and Song — EDS
English Dance and Song — Eng Dance
English Dance and Song — EngDS
English Dialect Dictionary — EDD
English Dialect Grammar — EDG
English Education — Eng Educ
English Electric Journal — Engl El J
English Electric Journal — Engl Elec J
English Fiction in Transition, 1880-1920 [*Later, English Literature in Transition, 1880-1920*] — EFT
English Folk Dance and Song Society. Journal — Eng FD & S Soc Jl
English Heritage Monitor — Engl Heritage Monit
English Historical Documents — EHD
English Historical Review — EHR
English Historical Review — Eng His R

English Historical Review — Eng Hist R
English Historical Review — Eng Hist Rev
English Historical Review — Engl Hist R
English Historical Review — Engl Hist Rev
English Historical Review — Engl Hist Revw
English Historical Review — English His
English Historical Review — English Hist Rev
English Historical Review — EnH
English Historical Review — PEHR
English Historical Review. Supplement — EHRS
English History Bulletin for Teachers in Secondary Schools — Eng Hist Bul
English History Bulletin for Teachers in Secondary Schools — English History Bul
English History Review — Engl Hist Rev
English Illustrated Magazine — EI
English Illustrated Magazine — Eng Illust
English in Africa — E in A
English in Africa — EinA
English in Africa — Engl Afr
English in Australia — Eng in Aust
English in Australia — Engl Aust
English in Education — Engl Educ
English in Education — English in Ed
English in New Zealand — Engl NZ
English Institute. Annual — Engl Inst Ann
English Institute. Essays — EIE
English Institute. New Series — Engl Inst N
English Institute of the University of Uppsala. Essays and Studies on English Language and Literature — EIUES
English Journal — EJ
English Journal — Eng J
English Journal — Engl J
English Journal — English J
English Journal — GENJ
English Journal (College Edition) — Engl J (Col Ed)
English Journal (High School Edition) — Engl J (HS Ed)
English Language and Literature — ELL
English Language and Literature — Engl Lang Lit
English Language Education Council. Bulletin — ELEC
English Language Notes — ELN
English Language Notes — Eng Lang Notes
English Language Notes — Engl Lang N
English Language Notes — Engl Lang Not
English Language Notes — Engl Lang Notes
English Language Notes — PELN
English Language Teaching [*Later, English Language Teaching Journal*] — E Lang T
English Language Teaching [*Later, English Language Teaching Journal*] — ELT
English Language Teaching [*Later, English Language Teaching Journal*] — Eng L T
English Language Teaching — Engl Lang Tch
English Language Teaching [*Later, English Language Teaching Journal*] — Engl Lang Teach
English Language Teaching Journal — ELTJ
English Language Teaching Journal — Eng Lang Teach J
English Language Teaching Journal — English Language Teaching J
English Linguistics, 1500-1800: A Collection of Facsimile Reprints — ELCFR
English Literary Renaissance — ELR
English Literary Renaissance — ELRen
English Literary Renaissance — Engl Lit Re
English Literary Renaissance — Engl Lit Renaiss
English Literary Renaissance — Engl Lit Renaissance
English Literary Studies — ELS
English Literature and Language [*Tokyo, Japan*] — ELLS
English Literature and Language — Engl Lit Lang
English Literature in Transition, 1880-1920 — ELiT
English Literature in Transition, 1880-1920 — ELT
English Literature in Transition, 1880-1920 — Eng Lit in Trans
English Literature in Transition, 1880-1920 — Engl Lit Tr
English Literature in Transition, 1880-1920 — Engl Lit Transition
English Miscellany — EM
English Miscellany. A Symposium of History — Engl Misc
English Miscellany. St. Stephen's College (Delhi) — EMD
English Miscellany. St. Stephen's College (Delhi) — EMSCD
English Music Journal — English MJ
English Philological Studies — EPS
English Place-Name Society. Annual Volume — Engl Place-Name Soc
English Quarterly — Engl Q
English Record — Engl Rec
English Record — EngR
English Record — ERec
English Recusant Literature — ERL
English Reprint Series — ERS
English Review — Engl R
English Review — Engl Rev
English Review — English R
English Review — EngR
English Review [*London*] — EnR
English Review — ER
English Review. Salem State College — Eng Rev
English Studies — E Studies
English Studies — Eng St
English Studies — Eng Stud
English Studies — Engl Stud
English Studies [*Amsterdam*] — EngS
English Studies — ES
English Studies — ESs
English Studies — ESt
English Studies — EStud
English Studies — IENG
English Studies. A Journal of English Letters and Philology — Engl St
English Studies in Africa — Engl St Afr
English Studies in Africa — Engl Stud Afr
English Studies in Africa — English Stud Afr
English Studies in Africa — ESA
English Studies in Africa — ESAfr
English Studies in Canada — Engl St Can
English Studies in Canada — ESC
English Symposium Papers — ESP
English Teacher — Eng Teach
English Teachers Association of New South Wales. Newsletter — Eng Teach Assn NSW News
English Teachers Association of New South Wales. Newsletter — Eng Teach Assoc NSW Newsl
English Teachers Association of New South Wales. Newsletter — Engl Teach Assoc NSW Newsl
English Teachers Association of New South Wales. Newsletter — ETANSW News
English Teaching Abstracts — ETAb
English Teaching Forum — Engl Teach For
English Usage in Southern Africa — Engl Usage Sthn Afr
English-Hittite Glossary — EHGl
Englishwoman's Domestic Magazine — Eng Dom M
Englishwomen's Review — Eng WR
Enhanced Consumer Spending Patterns [*Database*] — ECSP
Enhanced Oil-Recovery Field Reports — Enhanced Oil-Recovery Field Rep
Enka Biniiru To Porima — EBIPA
Enka en Breda Rayon Revue — Enka Breda Rayon Rev
Enkabe Contact — ONN
Enkomi-Alasia. Publications. Mission Archeologique Francaise et de la Mission du Gouvernement de Chypre a Enkomi — EA
Enlace (Mexico) — EAM
Enlightenment and Dissent — Enlightenment Diss
Enlightenment Essays — EE
Enlightenment Essays — Enl E
Enoch Pond Lectures on Applied Christianity — EPLAC
Enquete Mensuelle de Conjoncture — Enquete Mens Conjonct
Enquetes du Musee de la Vie Wallonne — EMVW
Enquetes et Documents d'Histoire Africaine — Enquetes et Docum Hist Afr
Enquetes. Musee de la Vie Wallonne — EMW
Enquetes. Musee de la Vie Wallonne — Enqu Musee Vie Wall
Enquetes. Musee de la Vie Wallonne — Enquetes Mus Vie Wallonne
Enquiry — En
Enrico Fermi International Summer School of Physics [*Elsevier Book Series*] — EFI
Ensaios Ethnographicos — EE
Ensaios FEE. Fundacao de Economia e Estatistica — Ensaios FEE
Ensayos e Investigacion — Ensayos Invest
Ensayos Economicos — Ensayos Econs
Ensayos Economicos. Banco Central de la Republica Argentina — BCRA/EE
Ensayos sobre Politica Economica — Ensayos Pol Econ
Ensayos y Estudios — EE
Ensayos y Estudios — Ensay Estud
Enseignement Chretien — ECh
Enseignement Chretien — EChr
Enseignement Chretien — Ens Chr
Enseignement de la Physique. Mathematiques pour la Physique — Enseign Phys Math Phys
Enseignement des Sciences — Enseign Sci
Enseignement Mathematique — ENMAA
Enseignement Mathematique — Enseign Math
Enseignement Mathematique — Enseignement Math
Enseignement Mathematique. Revue Internationale. 2e Serie — Enseign Math 2
Enseignement Public — EPubl
Enseignement Scientifique — Enseign Sci
Enseignement Technique — Enseign Techn
Ensenanza e Investigacion en Psicologia — Ensenanza Invest Psicol
Enshurin Shuho/Reports. Kyushu University Forests — Enshurin Shuho/Rep Kyushu Univ Forests
ENT. University of Kentucky. College of Agriculture. Cooperative Extension Service — ENT Univ Ky Coll Agric Coop Ext Serv
Entente Africaine — Entente Afr
Enterprise Western Australia — Enterp Western Aust
Entertainment Law Reporter — Entertain Law Report
Entomography — ENTMEY
Entomologia Experimentalis et Applicata — Ent Exp App
Entomologia Experimentalis et Applicata — Ent Exper Appl
Entomologia Experimentalis et Applicata — Entomol Exp Appl
Entomologia Experimentalis et Applicata — Entomologia Exp Appl
Entomologia Experimentalis et Applicata — ETEAA
Entomologia Experimentalis et Applicata — ETEAAT
Entomologia Generalis — ENGND5
Entomologia Generalis — Entomol Gen
Entomologia Generalis — Entomologia Gen
Entomologia Hellenica — Entomol Hell
Entomologia Sinica — Entomol Sin
Entomologica Americana — ENAMA3
Entomologica Americana — Entomol Am
Entomologica Germanica — EGERDQ
Entomologica Germanica — Ent Germ

Entomologica Germanica — Entomol Ger
Entomologica Scandinavica — Ent Scand
Entomologica Scandinavica — Entomol Scand
Entomologica Scandinavica. Supplementum — Entomol Scand Suppl
Entomological Circular. Department of Agriculture (British Columbia) — Ent Circ Dep Agric (Br Columb)
Entomological Magazine. Entomological Society of Japan (Kyoto) — Entomol Mag Kyoto
Entomological News — Ent News
Entomological News — Entom N
Entomological News — Entom News
Entomological News — Entomol News
Entomological News — ETMNA
Entomological Review [*English Translation*] — ENREB
Entomological Review — Entomol Rev
Entomological Review (English Translation of Entomologicheskoye Obozreniye) — Entomol Rev (Engl Transl Entomol Obozr)
Entomological Series — Entomol Ser
Entomological Society of America. Annals — Entom Soc Am Ann
Entomological Society of America. North Central State Branch. Proceedings — Entomol Soc Amer N Cent State Br Proc
Entomological Society of America. Special Publication — Entomol Soc Am Spec Publ
Entomological Society of Egypt. Bulletin. Economic Series — Entomol Soc Egypt Bull Econ Ser
Entomological Society of New Zealand. Bulletin — Entomol Soc NZ Bull
Entomological Society of Nigeria. Bulletin — Entomol Soc Nig Bull
Entomological Society of Nigeria. Occasional Publication — Entomol Soc Nigeria Occas Publ
Entomological Society of Ontario. Annual Report — Entomol Soc Ont Annu Rep
Entomological Society of Ontario. Proceedings — Entomol Soc Ont Proc
Entomological Society of Quebec. Annals — Entomol Soc Que Ann
Entomological Society of Southern Africa. Journal — Entomol Soc South Afr J
Entomological World. Organ. Insect Lovers Association — Entomol World
Entomologicheskoe Obozrenie — Ent Obozr
Entomologicheskoe Obozrenie — Entomol Obozr
Entomologicke Listy — ENLIBD
Entomologicke Listy — Ent Listy
Entomologicke Listy — Entomol Listy
Entomologicke Problemy — Ent Problemy
Entomologicke Problemy — Entomol Probl
Entomologie et Phytopathologie Appliquees — Entomol Phytopathol Appl
Entomologie et Phytopathologie Appliquees — Entomologie Phytopath Appl
Entomologische Abhandlungen [*Dresden*] — SMTEBI
Entomologische Abhandlungen (Dresden) — Entomol Abh (Dres)
Entomologische Arbeiten. Museum G. Frey (Tutzing-bei Muenchen) — ETARAQ
Entomologische Arbeiten. Museum Georg Frey — Ent Arb Mus GF
Entomologische Arbeiten. Museum Georg Frey (Tutzing-bei Muenchen) — Entomol Arb Mus G Frey (Tutzing Muenchen)
Entomologische Arbeiten. Museum Georg Frey (Tutzing-bei Muenchen) — Entomol Arb Mus G Frey (Tutzing-bei Muench)
Entomologische Berichten — Ent Ber
Entomologische Berichten [*Berlin*] — ENTBAV
Entomologische Berichten [*Amsterdam*] — ETBKAV
Entomologische Berichten (Amsterdam) — Ent Ber (Amst)
Entomologische Berichten (Amsterdam) — Entomol Ber (Amst)
Entomologische Berichten (Berlin) — Ent Ber (Berlin)
Entomologische Berichten (Berlin) — Entomol Ber (Berl)
Entomologische Blaetter — Entomol Bl
Entomologische Blaetter fuer Biologie und Systematik der Kaefer — EBBSAA
Entomologische Blaetter fuer Biologie und Systematik der Kaefer — Entomol Bl Biol Syst Kaefer
Entomologische Hefte — Entomol Hefte
Entomologische Mededeelingen van Nederlandsch-Indiee — Ent Meded Ned Indiee
Entomologische Mitteilungen — Ent Mitt
Entomologische Mitteilungen. Zoologischen Museum [*Hamburg*] — EMZMAJ
Entomologische Mitteilungen. Zoologischen Museum (Hamburg) — Ent Mitt Zool Mus (Hamburg)
Entomologische Mitteilungen. Zoologischen Museum (Hamburg) — Entomol Mitt Zool Mus (Hamb)
Entomologische Mitteilungen. Zoologischen Staatsinstitut und Zoologischen Museum [*Hamburg*] — EMZSA3
Entomologische Mitteilungen. Zoologischen Staatsinstitut und Zoologischen Museum — Ent Mitt Zool St Inst
Entomologische Mitteilungen. Zoologischen Staatsinstitut und Zoologischen Museum (Hamburg) — Entomol Mitt Zool Staatsinst Zool Mus (Hamb)
Entomologische Nachrichten — Ent Nachr
Entomologische Nachrichten — Entomol Nachr
Entomologische Nachrichten und Berichte — Entomol Nachr Ber
Entomologische Zeitschrift — Ent Z
Entomologische Zeitschrift — Entomol Z
Entomologische Zeitschrift — Entomol Zs
Entomologische Zeitschrift (Frankfurt Am Main) — Ent Z (Frankf A M)
Entomologische Zeitung (Stettin) — Entom Ztg Stettin
Entomologischer Jahresbericht — Ent Jber
Entomologisches Jahrbuch — EntJ
Entomologisk Tidskrift — Ent Tidskr
Entomologisk Tidskrift — Entomol Tidskr
Entomologiske Meddelelser — Ent M
Entomologiske Meddelelser — Ent Medd
Entomologiske Meddelelser — Ent Meddr
Entomologiske Meddelelser — Entomol Medd
Entomologiske Meddelelser — ETMDAA
Entomologist — Ent
Entomologist — Entomol
Entomologiste — Ent
Entomologist's Gazette — Ent Gaz
Entomologist's Gazette — Entomol Gaz
Entomologist's Gazette — Entomologist's Gaz
Entomologist's Gazette — ETGAA5
Entomologist's Monthly Magazine — Ent Mon Mag
Entomologist's Monthly Magazine — Entom Month Mag
Entomologist's Monthly Magazine — Entomol Mon Mag
Entomologist's Monthly Magazine — Entomologist's Mon Mag
Entomologists' Newsletter — Entomol Newsl
Entomologists' Newsletter — Entomologists Newsl
Entomologist's Record — Entomol Rec
Entomologist's Record and Journal of Variation — Entomol Rec J Var
Entomologist's Report. Department of Agriculture. Tanganyika — Entomologist's Rep Dep Agric Tanganyika
Entomology Abstracts — Entomol Abstr
Entomology and Phytopathology/K'un Ch'ung Yue Chih Ping — Entomol Phytopathol
Entomology Bulletin. British Museum (Natural History) — Entomol Bull Brit Mus (Natur Hist)
Entomology Circular. Division of Plant Industry. Florida Department of Agriculture and Consumer Services — Ent Circ Div Pl Ind Fla Dep Agric Consumer Serv
Entomology Fact Sheet. University of Minnesota — Ent Fact Sheet Univ Minn
Entomology Leaflet. University of Maryland — Ent Leafl Univ MD
Entomology Memoir. South Africa. Department of Agriculture — Entomol Mem S Afr Dep Agric
Entomology Mimeo Series. Utah State University. Agricultural Extension Service — Entomol Mimeo Ser Utah State Univ Agr Ext Serv
Entomophaga — Entomoph
Entomophaga. Memoire Hors Serie — Entomophaga Mem Hors Ser
Entregas de la Licorne — ELic
Entrepreneur — Entrep
Entrepreneur Magazine — Entrepteneur
Entretiens de Bichat Chirurgie Specialites — Entret Bichat Chir Spec
Entretiens de Bichat Chirurgie Specialites — Entretiens Bichat Chir Spec
Entretiens de Bichat Medecine et Biologie — Entret Bichat Med Biol
Entretiens de Bichat Medecine et Biologie — Entretiens Bichat Med Biol
Entretiens de Bichat Stomatologie [*France*] — Entretiens Bichat Stomatol
Entretiens de Bichat Therapeutique — Entret Bichat Ther
Entretiens de Bichat Therapeutique — Entretiens Bichat Ther
Entretiens de Chize. Serie Ecologie et Ethologie — Entretiens Chize Ser Ecol Ethol
Entretiens de Chize. Serie Physiologie — Entretiens Chize Ser Physiol
Entretiens Psychiatriques — Entr Psych
Entretiens sur l'Antiquite Classique — EAC
Entretiens sur l'Antiquite Classique — Entretiens Ant Cl
Entropie — ENTPA
Entscheidungen der Gerichte und Verwaltungsbehoerden — Entsch Gerichte Verwbehoerden
Entscheidungen der Oberverwaltungsgerichte fuer das Land Nordrhein-Westfalen in Muenster — OVGE
Entscheidungen des Obersten Bayerischen Landesgerichts in Strafsachen — Ob LGS
Entscheidungen des Obersten Bayerischen Landesgerichts in Zivilsachen — Ob LGZ
Entscheidungen des Obersten Gerichts in Strafsachen [*German Democratic Republic*] — OGSt
Entscheidungen des Obersten Gerichts in Zivilsachen [*German Democratic Republic*] — OGZ
Entscheidungen des Reichsgerichts in Strafsachen — Entsch Reichsger Strafs
Entscheidungen des Reichsgerichts in Strafsachen — ERGStrafs
Entscheidungen des Reichsoberhandelsgerichtes — Entsch Reichsoberhdlsger
Entsiklopedicheskii Slovar — ES
Entsiklopedicheskii Slovar' Ruskogo Bibliograficheskogo Instituta Granat — Granat
Entsiklopediya Izmerenii. Kontrolya i Avtomatizatsii — Entsikl Izmer Kontrolya Avtom
Entwicklungsberichte der Siemens — Entw Ber Siemens
Entwicklungsberichte der Siemens und Halske Aktiengesellschaft — Entwicklungsber Siemens und Halske
Entwicklungsgeschichte und Systematik der Pflanzen — Entwicklungsgesch Syst Pflanz
Entwicklungsgeschichte und Systematik der Pflanzen. Supplementum — Entwicklungsgesch Syst Pflanz Suppl
Environment — EEN
Environment — Env
Environment — Envir
Environment — ENVTA
Environment [*Washington, DC*] — ENVTAR
Environment — GENV
Environment Action Bulletin — Env Action
Environment and Behavior — EB
Environment and Behavior — EBEH
Environment and Behavior — Envir Behav
Environment and Behavior — Environ & Behavior
Environment and Behavior — Environ Behav
Environment and Behavior — EVBHA
Environment and Behavior — PENB
Environment and Change — Environ Change
Environment and Chemistry (Dordrecht, Netherlands) — Environ Chem Dordrecht Neth
Environment and Ecology — Environ Ecol
Environment and Man — Environ Man

Environment and Planning — Env Plann
Environment and Planning — Envir Plann
Environment and Planning — Environ and Planning
Environment and Planning — IEVP
Environment and Planning. A — ENVG
Environment and Planning. A — Environ Plann A
Environment and Pollution [*Republic of Korea*] — Environ Pollut
Environment and Resource Management. Canadian Chemical Engineering Conference — Environ Resour Manage Can Chem Eng Conf
Environment Canada. Annual Report — Environ Can Annu Rep
Environment Canada. Forest Pest Management Institute. Report FPM-X — Environ Can For Pest Manage Inst Rep FPM-X
Environment Canada. Inland Waters Directorate. Scientific Series — ECIWDSS
Environment Canada. Pacific Marine Science Reports — EPMSR
Environment Centre Outlook — ECO
Environment Control in Biology [*Japan*] — Environ Control Biol
Environment/Ecology — Env
Environment in Africa. Environment and Regional Planning Research Bulletin — Environment Afr
Environment Index — Envl
Environment Index — Environ Index
Environment India — Environ India
Environment Information Abstracts — EIA
Environment Information Access — Env
Environment International — Environ Int
Environment Law Review — Environ L Rev
Environment Law Review — Environ Law Rev
Environment Libraries Automated System [*Database*] — ELIAS
Environment Midwest — EMIDD
Environment Midwest — Environ Midwest
Environment News — Environ News
Environment News. Alberta Department of the Environment — ENNE
Environment Protection Board. Gas Pipeline Newsletter — EPBGPN
Environment Protection Engineering — Environ Prot Eng
Environment Protection Service. Air Pollution Report — EPS3AP
Environment Protection Service. Environmental Impact Control Directorate. Surveillance Report — EPSnEC
Environment Protection Service. Northwest Region. Department of the Environment. Reports — EPSnNW
Environment Protection Service. Northwest Region. Technology Development Report — EPS4NW
Environment Protection Service. Water Pollution Report — EPS3WP
Environment Regulation Handbook. Environment Information Center — Envt Reg Handbook Envt Information Center
Environment Report — ENVRB
Environment Reporter Cases. Bureau of National Affairs — Envt Rep Cas BNA
Environment Southwest — Environ Southwest
Environment This Month — Environ This Mon
Environment Update. Environment Canada — ENUP
Environment Views — Environ Views
Environment Views. Alberta Department of the Environment — ENVS
Environmental Abstracts — EA
Environmental Abstracts — Environ Abstr
Environmental Action — ENACD
Environmental Action — Envir Action
Environmental Action — Environ Action
Environmental Action — Environmt
Environmental Affairs — Env Aff
Environmental Affairs — ENVA
Environmental Affairs — Environ Aff
Environmental and Ecological Biochemistry — Environ Ecol Biochem
Environmental and Experimental Botany — Env Exp Bot
Environmental and Experimental Botany — Envir & Exper Bot
Environmental and Experimental Botany — Environ and Exp Bot
Environmental and Experimental Botany — Environ & Exper Bot
Environmental and Experimental Botany — Environ Exp Bot
Environmental and Molecular Mutagenesis — Environ Mol Mutagen
Environmental and Process Monitoring Technologies — Environ Process Monit Technol
Environmental and Sanitary Engineering Research — Environ Sanit Eng Res
Environmental Awareness — Environ Awareness
Environmental Biogeochemistry and Geomicrobiology. Proceedings. International Symposium on Environmental Biogeochemistry — Environ Biogeochem Geomicrobiol Proc Int Symp
Environmental Biology — Environ Biol
Environmental Biology and Medicine — Environ Biol Med
Environmental Biology and Medicine — EVBMA
Environmental Biology of Fishes — Env Biol F
Environmental Biology of Fishes — Environ Biol Fish
Environmental Biology of Fishes — Environ Biol Fishes
Environmental Carcinogenesis and Ecotoxicology Reviews. Part C. Journal of Environmental Science and Health — Environ Carcinog Ecotoxicol Rev
Environmental Carcinogenesis Review. Part C. Journal of Environmental Science and Health — Environ Carcinog Rev Part C J Environ Sci Health
Environmental Carcinogenesis Reviews — ENCR
Environmental Carcinogenesis Reviews. Part C. Journal of Environmental Science and Health — Environ Carcinog Rev
Environmental Carcinogens Selected Methods of Analysis — Environ Carcinog Sel Methods Anal
Environmental Change in the Maritimes. Symposium — Environ Change Marit Symp
Environmental Chemicals Data and Information Network [*Database*] — ECDIN
Environmental Chemicals. Human and Animal Health. Proceedings of Annual Conference — Environ Chem Hum Anim Health
Environmental Chemistry — Environ Chem
Environmental Chemistry (Beijing) — Environ Chem Beijing
Environmental Comment — Environ Comment
Environmental Conference. Proceedings — Environ Conf Proc
Environmental Conservation — ENCO
Environmental Conservation — Envir Conserv
Environmental Conservation — Environ Conser
Environmental Conservation — Environ Conserv
Environmental Conservation Engineering [*Japan*] — Environ Conserv Eng
Environmental Contamination and Hygiene — Environ Contam Hyg
Environmental Control and Safety Management — ECSMB
Environmental Control and Safety Management — Environ Contr Safety Manage
Environmental Control Management — Environ Contr Manage
Environmental Control Management — Environ Control Manage
Environmental Control. Proceedings. Symposium — Environ Control Proc Symp
Environmental Control Symposium — Environ Control Symp
Environmental Controls for Coal Mining. Proceedings. National Seminar — Environ Controls Coal Min Proc Natl Sem
Environmental Creation — Environ Creat
Environmental Creation [*Japan*] — Environ Creation
Environmental Data Service — Env Data Serv
Environmental Data Service — Environ Data Serv
Environmental Data Services Report — Environ Data Serv Rep
Environmental Degradation of Engineering Materials in Aggressive Environments. Proceedings. International Conference on Environmental Degradation of Engineering Materials — Environ Degrad Eng Mater Aggressive Environ Proc Int Conf
Environmental Degradation of Engineering Materials in Hydrogen. Proceedings. International Conference on Environmental Degradation of Engineering Materials — Environ Degrad Eng Mater Hydrogen Proc Int Conf
Environmental Design Series — Environ Des Ser
Environmental Education — Environ Educ
Environmental Effects on Advanced Materials — Environ Eff Adv Mater
Environmental Engineering — Environ Eng
Environmental Engineering — Environ Engrg
Environmental Engineering and Pollution Control — Environ Eng Pollut Control
Environmental Engineering and Science Conference. Proceedings — Environ Eng Sci Conf Proc
Environmental Engineering (Beijing) — Environ Eng Beijing
Environmental Engineering World — Environ Eng World
Environmental Entomology — Env Entomol
Environmental Entomology — Envir Ent
Environmental Entomology — Environ Entomol
Environmental Entomology — EVETB
Environmental Ethics — ENETD
Environmental Ethics — Environ Ethics
Environmental Ethics — PEET
Environmental Ethics and Science Policy Series — Environ Ethics Sci Policy Ser
Environmental Fate [*Database*] — ENVIROFATE
Environmental Fluid Mechanics — Environ Fluid Mech
Environmental Forum — Environ Forum
Environmental Geochemistry and Health — Environ Geochem Health
Environmental Geology — Envir Geol
Environmental Geology — Environ Geol
Environmental Geology and Water Science — Environ Geol Wat Sci
Environmental Geology and Water Sciences — Environ Geol Water Sci
Environmental Geology Bulletin — Environ Geol Bul
Environmental Geology Bulletin. West Virginia Geological and Economic Survey — Environ Geol Bull WV Geol Econ Surv
Environmental Geology. Colorado Geological Survey — Environ Geol Colorado Geol Surv
Environmental Geology Notes. Illinois State Geological Survey — Environ Geol Notes Ill State Geol Surv
Environmental Geology Notes. Illinois State Geological Survey — IEGNA
Environmental Health — EH
Environmental Health [*Nagpur*] — ENHEA
Environmental Health [*London*] — ENVHA
Environmental Health [*London*] — Environ Health
Environmental Health — Environ Hlth
Environmental Health and Preventive Medicine — Environ Health Prev Med
Environmental Health Criteria — Environ Health Criter
Environmental Health Directorate. Report. EHD (Canada) — Environ Health Dir Rep EHD (Can)
Environmental Health (London) — Environ Health (Lond)
Environmental Health (Nagpur) — Environ Health (Nagpur)
Environmental Health News [*Database*] — EHN
Environmental Health Perspectives — Env Health Persp
Environmental Health Perspectives — Envir Hlth Persp
Environmental Health Perspectives — Environ Health Perspect
Environmental Health Perspectives — Environ Hlth Perspectives
Environmental Health Series. Radiological Health — Environ Health Ser Radiol Health
Environmental History Newsletter — Environ Hist Newslett
Environmental Impact Assessment Review — Environ Impact Assess Rev
Environmental Impact News — Environ Impact News
Environmental Information and Documentation Centres [*Database*] — ENDOC
Environmental Information Digest — Environ Inf Dig
Environmental Information Science — Environ Inf Sci
Environmental Issues — Environ Issues
Environmental Law — Env L
Environmental Law — Environ L
Environmental Law — Environ Law
Environmental Law — Environm L
Environmental Law — Envtl L
Environmental Law — EVLWA
Environmental Law — IEVL

Environmental Law Bulletin — ELB
Environmental Law Newsletter — ELN
Environmental Law Quarterly Newsletter — Envtl LQ Newsl
Environmental Law Reporter [*Environmental Law Institute*] — ELR
Environmental Law Reporter — ELRPA
Environmental Law Reporter — Env L Rptr
Environmental Law Reporter — Envir L Rep
Environmental Law Reporter — Environ Law Rep
Environmental Law Reporter — Envtl L Rep
Environmental Law Reporter. Environmental Law Institute — Envtl L Rep Envtl L Inst
Environmental Law Reporter of New South Wales — ELR
Environmental Law Review — Env L Rev
Environmental Letters — Envir Lett
Environmental Letters — Environ Lett
Environmental Letters — EVLTA
Environmental Management — EMNGD
Environmental Management — Environ Manage
Environmental Management Review — ENMR
Environmental Measurements Laboratory Environmental Quarterly. US Department of Energy — Environ Meas Lab Environ Q US Dep Energy
Environmental Measurements Laboratory. Environmental Report. United States Department of Energy — Environ Meas Lab Environ Rep US Dep of Energy
Environmental Measurements Laboratory. Report EML. US Department of Energy — Environ Meas Lab Rep EML US Dep Energy
Environmental Medicine. Annual Report of the Research Institute of Environmental Medicine. Nagoya University — Environ Med
Environmental Medicine (Nagoya) — Environ Med (Nagoya)
Environmental Microbiology — Environ Microbiol
Environmental Monitoring and Assessment — EMA
Environmental Monitoring and Assessment — EMASD
Environmental Monitoring and Assessment [*Netherlands*] — Environ Monit Assess
Environmental Mutagen Research Communications — Environ Mutagen Res Commun
Environmental Mutagenesis — Environ Mutagen
Environmental Mutagenesis — Environ Mutagenesis
Environmental Mutagens and Carcinogens — EMCAE8
Environmental Mutagens and Carcinogens — Environ Mutagen Carcinog
Environmental News (Karachi) — Environ News Karachi
Environmental Newsletter — Environ Newsl
Environmental Nutrition — Environ Nutr
Environmental Nutrition Newsletter — Environ Nutr Newsl
Environmental Perception Research. Working Paper — Environ Percep Res Work Pap
Environmental Periodicals Bibliography — Environ Per Bibl
Environmental Periodicals Bibliography — Environ Period Bibliogr
Environmental Physiology — Environ Physiol
Environmental Physiology — EVPHB
Environmental Physiology and Biochemistry — ENPBB
Environmental Physiology and Biochemistry — Env Phys Bi
Environmental Physiology and Biochemistry — Environ Physiol Biochem
Environmental Policy and Law — EAW
Environmental Policy and Law — Environ Pol Law
Environmental Policy and Law — Environ Policy Law
Environmental Policy and Law — Environm Policy & L
Environmental Pollution — Envir Pollu
Environmental Pollution — Environ Pollut
Environmental Pollution — ENVPA
Environmental Pollution and Health Hazards — Environ Pollut Health Hazards
Environmental Pollution (Barking) — Environ Pollut (Barking)
Environmental Pollution by Pesticides — Environ Pollut Pest
Environmental Pollution Control — Envir Poll Control
Environmental Pollution Management — Environ Pollut Manage
Environmental Pollution Management — Environ Pollut Mgmt
Environmental Pollution Management — EPM
Environmental Pollution. Proceedings. Symposium — Environ Pollut Proc Symp
Environmental Pollution. Series A. Ecological and Biological — Environ Pollut Ser A
Environmental Pollution. Series A. Ecological and Biological — Environ Pollut Ser A Ecol Biol
Environmental Pollution. Series A. Ecological and Biological — EPEBD7
Environmental Pollution. Series B. Chemical and Physical — Environ Pollut Ser B
Environmental Pollution. Series B. Chemical and Physical — Environ Pollut Ser B Chem Phys
Environmental Pollution. Series B. Chemical and Physical — EPSPDH
Environmental Professional — Environ Prof
Environmental Progress — Environ Prog
Environmental Progress — ENVPD
Environmental Protection Agency. AP (United States) — Environ Prot Agency AP US
Environmental Protection Agency. APTD [*Air Pollution Technical Data*] **(United States)** — Environ Prot Agency APTD US
Environmental Protection Agency. Office of Pesticide and Toxic Substances. Report EPA (United States) — Environ Prot Agency. Off Pestic Toxic Subst Rep EPA US
Environmental Protection Agency. Office of Pesticide Programs. Report EPA (United States) — Environ Prot Agency Off Pestic Programs Rep EPA (US)
Environmental Protection Agency. Office of Radiation Programs. Technical Report EPA (United States) — Environ Prot Agency Off Radiat Programs Tech Rep EPA (US)
Environmental Protection Agency. Office of Solid Waste Management Programs. Technical Report SW (US) — Environ Prot Agency Off Solid Waste Manage Programs Tech Rep
Environmental Protection Agency. Region 10. Report EPA (United States) — Environ Prot Agency Reg 10 Rep EPA (US)
Environmental Protection Agency (US). Publication. AP [*Air Pollution*] **Series** — Environ Prot Agency (US) Publ AP Ser
Environmental Protection Agency (US). Publication. APTD [*Air Pollution Technical Data*] **Series** — Environ Prot Agency (US) Publ APTD Ser
Environmental Protection (Beijing) — Environ Prot Beijing
Environmental Protection Bulletin — Environ Prot Bull
Environmental Protection Conference — Environ Prot Conf
Environmental Protection Service. Environmental Strategies Directorate. Economic and Technical Review — EPSnES
Environmental Protection Service. Report Series. Northern Regions — EPS NR
Environmental Protection Survey [*England*] — Environ Prot Surv
Environmental Protection (Taipei) — Environ Prot (Taipei)
Environmental Protection Technology Series — Environ Prot Technol Ser
Environmental Protection Technology Series — EPTSB
Environmental Protection Technology Series. EPA [*Environmental Protection Agency*] — Environ Prot Technol Ser EPA
Environmental Psychology [*Database*] — ENVPSYCH
Environmental Psychology and Nonverbal Behavior — Environ Psychol Nonverbal Behav
Environmental Quality — Environ Qual
Environmental Quality — EVQMA
Environmental Quality Abstracts — Environ Qual Abstr
Environmental Quality Abstracts — EQA
Environmental Quality and Safety — Environ Qual Saf
Environmental Quality and Safety. Supplement — Environ Qual Saf Suppl
Environmental Quality. Annual Report of the Council of Environmental Quality — Envir Qual
Environmental Quality Magazine — EQM
Environmental Quality Research and Development Unit. Technical Paper (New York) — Environ Qual Res Dev Unit Tech Pap (NY)
Environmental Quality Research Unit. Technical Paper (New York) — Environ Qual Res Unit Tech Pap NY
Environmental Quarterly — Environ Q
Environmental Quarterly — Environ Quart
Environmental Quarterly — ENVQA
Environmental Quarterly. United States Department of Energy. Environmental Measurements Laboratory — Environ Q US Dep Energy Environ Meas Lab
Environmental Radiation Bulletin — Environ Radiat Bull
Environmental Radiation Surveillance in Washington State. Annual Report — Environ Radiat Surveill Wash State
Environmental Radioactivity — Environ Radioact
Environmental Report. Environmental Measurements Laboratory. United States Department of Energy — Environ Rep Environ Meas Lab US Dep Energy
Environmental Research — Envir Res
Environmental Research — Environ Res
Environmental Research — ENVRA
Environmental Research Center of Saga Prefecture — Environ Res Cent Saga Prefect
Environmental Research Institute of Michigan. Annual Report — Environ Res Inst Mich Annu Rep
Environmental Research Projects [*Database*] — ENREP
Environmental Resource — Environ Resour
Environmental Review — Environ Rev
Environmental Risk Analysis for Chemicals [*Monograph*] — Environ Risk Anal Chem
Environmental Sanitation Abstract — Environ Sanit Abstr
Environmental Sanitation Review — Environ Sanit Rev
Environmental Science and Engineering — Environ Sci Eng
Environmental Science and Technology — ENT
Environmental Science and Technology — Env Sci Tec
Environmental Science and Technology — Envir Sc Technol
Environmental Science and Technology — Envir Sci & Tech
Environmental Science and Technology — Envir Sci Techn
Environmental Science and Technology — Envirn Sci
Environmental Science and Technology — Environ Sc Tech
Environmental Science and Technology — Environ Sci & Tech
Environmental Science and Technology — Environ Sci and Technol
Environmental Science and Technology — Environ Sci Technol
Environmental Science and Technology — ES & T
Environmental Science and Technology — ESTHA
Environmental Science and Technology (Dordrecht, Netherlands) — Environ Sci Technol Dordrecht Neth
Environmental Science Research — Environ Sci Res
Environmental Science Series [*Elsevier Book Series*] — ESS
Environmental Sciences — Environ Sci
Environmental Sciences and Applications — Environ Sci Appl
Environmental Sciences and Applications — ESAPDG
Environmental Sciences and Engineering Notes — Environ Sci Eng Notes
Environmental Sciences (Tokyo) — Environ Sci Tokyo
Environmental Series — Environ Ser
Environmental Space Sciences — Environ Space Sci
Environmental Space Sciences [*English translation of Kosmicheskaya Biologiya i Meditsina*] — EVSSAV
Environmental Space Sciences (English Translation of Kosmicheskaya Biologiya i Meditsina) — Environ Space Sci (Engl Transl Kosm Biol Med)
Environmental Studies. Canada. Department of Indian Affairs and Northern Development — Environ Stud Can Dep Indian Aff North Dev
Environmental Studies. Canada. Indian and Northern Affairs — Environ Stud Can Indian North Aff

Environmental Studies Revolving Funds Report — ESRFR
Environmental Systems Planning, Design, and Control. Proceedings. IFAC [*International Federation of Automatic Control*] **Symposium** — Environ Syst Plann Des Control Proc IFAC Symp
Environmental Technical Information System [*Database*] — ETIS
Environmental Technology and Economics — Environ Technol Econ
Environmental Technology Letters — Environ Technol Lett
Environmental Technology. Proceedings. European Conference on Environmental Technology — Environ Technol Proc Eur Conf
Environmental Toxicology and Chemistry — Environ Toxicol Chem
Environmental Toxicology and Chemistry — ETC
Environmental Toxicology and Chemistry — ETOCDK
Environmental Toxicology and Pharmacology — Environ Toxicol Pharmacol
Environmental Toxicology and Water Quality — Environ Toxicol Water Qual
Environmental Toxin Series — Environ Toxin Ser
Environments. Journal of Interdisciplinary Studies — ENMS
Environnement — Environ
Environnement Canada. Rapport Annuel — Environ Can Rapp Annu
Environnement et Pollution — Environ Pollut
Enzyklopaedie der Geisteswissenschaftlichen Arbeitsmethoden — EGWA
Enzyklopaedie der Psychologie in Einzeldarstellungen — EPE
Enzyklopaedie des Islam — EID
Enzymatic Release of Vasoactive Peptides. Workshop Conference Hoechst — Enzym Release Vasoact Pept Workshop Conf Hoechst
Enzyme and Microbial Technology — EMTED2
Enzyme and Microbial Technology — Enzyme Microb Technol
Enzyme Engineering — Enzyme Eng
Enzyme Engineering. Papers. Engineering Foundation Conference on Enzyme Engineering — Enzyme Eng Pap Eng Found Conf
Enzyme Physiology and Pathology — Enzyme Physiol Pathol
Enzyme Technology. Rotenburg Fermentation Symposium — Enzyme Technol Rotenburg Ferment Symp
Enzymes in Medicine — Enzymes Med
Enzymes of Biological Membranes (2nd Edition) [*Monograph*] — Enzymes Biol Membr (2nd Ed)
Enzymes-General Considerations. Comprehensive Biochemistry — Enzymes Gen Consid Compr Biochem
Enzymologia — ENZYA
Enzymologia Acta Biocatalytica — Enzymologia
Enzymologia Biologica et Clinica — Enzym Biol Clin
Enzymologia Biologica et Clinica — Enzymol Biol Clin
Enzymologia Kliniczna, Wydanie [*Monograph*] — Enzymol Klin Wyd
Enzymology and Molecular Biology of Carbonyl Metabolism — Enzymol Mol Biol Carbonyl Metab
Enzymology and Molecular Biology of Carbonyl Metabolism 2. Aldehyde Dehydrogenase, Alcohol Dehydrogenase, and Aldo-Keto Reductase. Proceedings. International Workshop — Enzymol Mol Biol Carbonyl Metab 2 Proc Int Workshop
Enzymology of Post-Translational Modification of Proteins — Enzymol Post Transl Modif Proteins
EOC [*Equal Opportunities Commission*] **Journal** — EOC Jnl
EOC [*Equal Opportunities Commission*] **Research Bulletin** — EOC Res Bul
Eolus. A Review for New Music — E
EORTC [*European Organization for Research on Treatment of Cancer*] **Cancer Chemotherapy Annual** — ECCAD5
EORTC [*European Organization for Research on Treatment of Cancer*] **Cancer Chemotherapy Annual** — EORTC Cancer Chemother Annu
Eos. Commentarii Societatis Philologae Polonorum — E
EOS. Journal of Immunology and Immunopharmacology — EOS J Immunol Immunopharmacol
EOS. Revista Espanola de Entomologia — EOS Rev Esp Entomol
EOS. Rivista di Immunologia ed Immunofarmacologia — EOS Riv Immunol Immunofarmacol
Eos. Transactions of the American Geophysical Union — Eos Trans Am Geophys Union
Eotvoes Lorand Tudomanyegyetem Evkoenyve — Eotvoes Lorand Tudomanyegyet Evk
EP. Elektropromishlenost i Priborostroene — EP Elektropromst Priborostr
EPA [*Environmental Protection Agency*] **Citizens' Bulletin** — EPA Cit Bul
EPA (Environmental Protection Agency) Environmental Protection Technology Series — EPA (Environ Prot Agency) Environ Prot Technol Ser
EPA [*Environmental Protection Agency*] **Environmental Protection Technology Series** — XPARD6
EPA (European Photochemistry Association) Newsletter — EPA Newsl
EPA [*Environmental Protection Agency*] **Journal** — EPA J
EPA [*Environmental Protection Agency*] **Journal** — GEPA
Epegrafika Vostika — EV
Epeiroetike Hestia — E Hest
Epeiroetike Hestia — EH
Epeirotike Hestia — EpH
Epeteris Epistemonikon Ereunon. Panepistemion Athenon — EEE
Epeteris Hetaireias Byzantinon Spoudon — Ep HB Sp
Epeteris Hetaireias Byzantinon Spudon — EEBS
Epeteris Hetaireias Kykladikon Meleton — EHKM
Epeteris Hetaireias Stereoelladikon Meleton — EHSM
Epeteris Mesaionikou Archeiou Akademias Athenon — EMAAA
Epeteris tes Hetaireias Byzantinon Spoudon — EHBS
Epeteris tes Hetaireias Byzantinon Spoudon — Epet
Epeteris tes Hetaireias Kretikon Spoudon — EHKS
Epeteris tou Kalabryton — EtK
Epeteris tou Kentrou Epistemonikon Ereunon Kyprou — EKEEK
Epeteris tou Kentrou Ereunes tes Hellenikes Laographias — EKEHL
Epeteris tou Kentrou Ereunes tes Historias tou Hellenikou Dikaiou — EHHD
Epeteris tou Kentrou Ereunes tes Historias tou Hellenikou Dikaiou — EKEHHD
Epeteris tou Laographikov Arkheiov — ETLA
Epeteris tou Mesaionikou Archeiou — EMA
Epeteris tou Messaionikou Archeiou — Ep Mes Arch
Epeteris tu Mesajoniku Archeiu. Paratema — EMA P
Ephemerides Carmeliticae — ECarm
Ephemerides Carmeliticae — EphC
Ephemerides Carmeliticae. Cura Pontificiae Facultatis Theologicae S. Teresiae a Jesu et Ionnis a Cruce [*Rome*] — EphCarm
Ephemerides Iuris Canonici — EIC
Ephemerides Juris Canonici — EJC
Ephemerides Liturgicae — EL
Ephemerides Liturgicae — Eph Lit
Ephemerides Liturgicae — EphL
Ephemerides Liturgicae [*Rome*] — EphLitg
Ephemerides Liturgicae. Analecta Historico-Ascetica — El A
Ephemerides Liturgicae. Jus et Praxis Liturgica — El J
Ephemerides Mariologicae [*Madrid*] — EphMar
Ephemerides Theologicae Lovanienses — Eph Th L
Ephemerides Theologicae Lovanienses — Ephem Theol Lovanienses
Ephemerides Theologicae Lovanienses — Ephemer Theologicae Lovanienses
Ephemerides Theologicae Lovanienses — EThL
Ephemerides Theologicae Lovanienses — ETL
Ephemerides Theologicae Lovanienses. Bibliotheca — E Th L B
Ephemeris Archaiologike — EA
Ephemeris Archaiologike — Eph Arch
Ephemeris Dacoromana — ED
Ephemeris Dacoromana — Eph Dac
Ephemeris Dacoromana. Annuario. Scuola Romena di Roma — Eph DR
Ephemeris Epigraphica — E Epigr
Ephemeris Epigraphica — EE
Ephemeris Epigraphica — Eph Ep
Ephemeris Epigraphica. Corpus Inscriptionum Latinarum Supplementum — EECILS
Ephemeris Epigraphica. Corpus Inscriptionum Latinarum Supplementum — Eph Epgr
Epicorum Graecorum Fragmenta — EGF
Epicorum Graecorum Fragmenta — Ep Gr Frag
Epicorum Graecorum Fragmenta — Ep Graec Frag
Epidemiologia e Prevenzione — Epidemiol Prev
Epidemiologia e Psichiatria Sociale — Epidemiol Psichiatr Soc
Epidemiologic Reviews — Epidemiol Rev
Epidemiological Bulletin — Epidemiol Bull
Epidemiological, Experimental, and Clinical Studies on Gastric Cancer. Proceedings. International Conference on Gastric Cancer — Epidemiol Exp Clin Stud Gastric Cancer Proc Int Conf
Epidemiological Review (English Translation of Przeglad Epidemiologiczny) — Epidemiol Rev (Engl Transl Przegl Epidemiol)
Epidemiologie, Mikrobiologie, Immunologie — Epidemiol Mikrobiol Immunol
Epidemiologiya Mikrobiologiya i Infektsiozni Bolesti — Epidem Mikrobiol
Epidemiologiya Mikrobiologiya i Infektsiozni Bolesti — Epidemiol Mikrobiol Infekts Boles
Epidemiology and Community Health — Epidemiol Community Health
Epidemiology and Infection — Epidemiol Infect
Epidemiology Information System [*Database*] — EIS
Epigrafia Ebraica Antica — EEA
Epigrafia Etrusca — Ep Etr
Epigrafia Greca — EG
Epigrafia Greca — Ep Gr
Epigrafia Juridica de la Espana Romana — EJER
Epigrafia Romana de Asturias — Epigr Ast
Epigrafia Romana de Asturias — ERA
Epigrafia Romana de Lerida — ERL
Epigrafika Vostoka. Sbornik Statei — Epigr Vostok
Epigrammata Graeca ex Lapidibus Conlecta — EGK
Epigrammata Graeca ex Lapidibus Conlecta — Epigr Gr
Epigrammatum Anthologia Palatina cum Planudeis — App Anth
Epigraphai Anekdotoi Anakalyphtheisai kai Ekdotheisai Hypo tou Archaiologikou Syllogou — Epig Anek
Epigraphia Indica — EI
Epigraphia Indica — Epig Indica
Epigraphia Indica. Arabic and Persian Supplement — Epi Ind A
Epigraphia Indo-Moslemica — EIM
Epigraphia Zeylanica — EZ
Epigraphica — Epig
Epigraphie. Documents du Proche-Orient Ancien — DPOA
Epigraphische Studien — Epig Stud
Epigraphische Studien — Epigr Stud
Epigraphische Studies — Epigraph Stud
Epilepsia — EPILA
Epilepsia. Revue Internationale a l'Etude de l'Epilepsie — Epileps
Epilepsy. International Symposium — Epilepsy Int Symp
Epilepsy, Pregnancy, and the Child. Proceedings. Conference — Epilepsy Pregnancy Child Proc Conf
Epilepsy Research — Epilepsy Res
Epilepsy Research. Supplement — Epilepsy Res Suppl
Epilogoe — EP
Epimethee. Essais Philosophiques — Epimethee Essais Philos
Episcopal Recorder — ER
Epistemata. Wuerzburger Wissenschaftliche Schriften, Reihe Philosophie — Epistemata Wuerzburg Wissensch Schrift Reihe Philos
Epistemologia, Historia, y Didactica de la Matematica — Epistem Hist Didact Mat
Epistemonike Epeteris. Ethnikon kai Kapodistriakon Panepistemion — Epist
Epistemonike Epeteris Kteniatrikes Scholes — Epistemon Epeteris Kteniatr Sch
Epistemonike Epeteris tes Philosophikes Scholes tou Aristoteleiou Panepistemiou — EEPSAP

Epistemonike Epeteris tes Philosophikes Scholes tou Aristoteleiou Panepistemiou Thessalonikes — EEPSAPT
Epistemonike Epeteris tes Philosophikes Scholes tou Panepistemiou Athenon — EE Ath
Epistemonike Epeteris tes Philosophikes Scholes tou Panepistemiou Athenon — EEPSPA
Epistemonike Epeteris tes Philosophikes Scholes tou Panepistemiou Athenon — Epist
Epistemonike Epeteris tes Philosophikes Scholes tou Panepistemiou Thesalonikes — EEPSTh
Epistemonike Epeteris tes Theologikes Scholes tou Panepistemiou Thessalonikes — EEThS
Epistolographi Graeci — Epist Gr
Epistolographi Graeci — Epist Graec
Epithelial Cell Biology — Epithelial Cell Biol
Epithelial-Mesenchymal Interactions. Hahnemann Symposium — Epithelial Mesenchymal Interact Hahnemann Symp
Epitheorese Klinikes Farmakologias kai Farmakokinetikes — Epitheor Klin Farmakol Farmakokinet
Epitheorese Logou Kai Technes — ELkT
Epitheorese Technes — ET
Epitheoresis Koinonikon Ereunon — EPKE
Epizootologiya i Profilaktika Prirodnoochagovykh Infektsii — Epizootol Profil Prirodnoochagovykh Infekts
Epochen der Franzoesische Literatur — Epochen d Franz Liter
Epoxy Resins and Composites — Epoxy Resins Compos
Epoxy Resins. Chemistry and Technology [*Monograph*] — Epoxy Resins Chem Technol
EPPO [*European and Mediterranean Plant Protection Organization*] **Bulletin** — EPPO Bull
EPPO (European and Mediterranean Plant Protection Organization) Publications. Series C — EPPO (Eur Mediterr Plant Prot Organ) Publ Ser C
EPPO [*European and Mediterranean Plant Protection Organization*] **Plant Health Newsletter Publications. Series B** — EPPO Plant Health Newsl Publ Ser B
EPPO [*European and Mediterranean Plant Protection Organization*] **Publications. Series C** — EPOBAK
EPPO [*European and Mediterranean Plant Protection Organization*] **Publications. Series C** — EPPO Publ Ser C
EPRI [*Electric Power Research Institute*] **Database for Environmentally Assisted Cracking** — EDEAC
EPRI [*Electric Power Research Institute*] **Journal** — EAC
EPRI [*Electric Power Research Institute*] **Journal** — EPRI J
EPRI [*Electric Power Research Institute*] **Journal** — EPRJD
EPRI [*Electric Power Research Institute*] **Report. NP** [*United States*] — EPRI Rep NP
EPRI [*Electric Power Research Institute*] **Workshop Proceedings** — EPRI Workshop Proc
EPS General Conference. Energy and Physics — EPS Gen Conf Energy Phys
Epsilon Letter — Epsilon Let
Epsilon Marketing Letter — Epsilon Market Let
Epstein-Barr Virus and Associated Diseases. Proceedings. International Symposium — Epstein Barr Virus Assoc Dis Proc Int Symp
EQL Memorandum. California Institute of Technology. Environmental Quality Laboratory — EQL Memo Calif Inst Technol Environ Qual Lab
EQS. Environmental Quality and Safety. Supplement — EQS Environ Qual Saf Suppl
Equal Employment Compliance Manual — Eq Empl Compl Man
Equal Opportunities International — Equal Opportunities Int
Equality Now — Equal Now
Equilibrium Research — Equilib Res
Equine Pharmacology Symposium. Proceedings — Equine Pharmacol Symp Proc
Equine Practice — EQPRDF
Equine Practice — Equine Pract
Equine Reproduction. Proceedings. International Symposium on Equine Reproduction — Equine Reprod Proc Int Symp
Equine Veterinary Journal — Equine Vet J
Equinox — EQNX
Equip Tips. United States Department of Agriculture. Forest Service Equipment Development Center — Equip Tips US Dep Agric For Serv Equip Dev Cent
Equipe de Pedologia e Fertilidade do Solo. Boletim Tecnico — Equipe Pedol Fertil Solo Bol Tec
Equipement Industriel. Achats et Entretien — EIAEA
Equipement Industriel. Achats et Entretien — Equip Ind Achats & Entretien
Equipement - Logement - Transports — Equipement
Equipement Mecanique [*France*] — Equip Mec
Equipment Development and Test Report. United States Forest Service. Equipment Center (San Dimas, California) — Equip Dev Test Rep US For Serv Equip Dev Ctr San Dimas Calif
Equipment Preview of Chemical Process Industries — Equip Preview Chem Process Ind
Equitable Distribution Reporter — Equit Distr Rep
ERA [*British Electrical and Allied Industries Research Association*] **Abstracts** [*A publication*] — ERA Abstr
ERA. Education Research Abstracts — ERA
ERA. Foerening foer Elektricitetens Rationella Anvaendning — ERA Foeren Elektr Ration Anvaendning
Era Magazine — Era M
Era Nova. Revista do Movimento Contemporaneo — ENRMC
Era of Arnold Bennett — EAB
Era Socialista — Era Social
Eranos — Er
Eranos Jahrbuch — Er J
Eranos Jahrbuch — Er Jb
Eranos Jahrbuch — Eranos Jhb
Eranos-Jahrbuch — EJ
Eranos-Jahrbuch [*Zurich*] — EJb
Eranos-Jahrbuch — EranJb
Eranos-Jahrbuch — Eranos
Eranos-Jahrbuch — Eranos Jahrb
Eranos-Jahrbuch — Eranos-Jb
Erasme — Er
Erasmi Opera Omnia [*Elsevier Book Series*] — EOO
Erasmus — E
Erasmus — Er
Erasmus Bibliothek — Eras B
Erasmus in English — EE
Erasmus in English — Erasmus E
Erasmus Review — Erasmus Rev
Erasmus Review — ErasmusR
Erasmus Review — ErasR
Erasmus Speculum Scientiarum — ESS
Erasmus. Speculum Scientiarum. Basel — Eras
Erasmusuniversiteit Rotterdam. Universiteitsbibliotheek. Aanwinstenlijst — ABQ
Erbe der Vergangenheit — Erbe der V
Erbe Deutscher Musik — EDM
Erbe und Auftrag — EA
Erbe und Auftrag [*Beuron*] — ErbAuf
Erbe und Auftrag — Erbe U Auftrag
Erbe und Auftrag — Eu A
Erbe und Auftrag der Reformation in den Boehmischen Laendern — EARBL
Erbschaftssteuergesetz — Erb St G
ERCE [*European Federation of Chemical Engineers*] **Publication Series** — EFCE Publ Ser
ERDA (Energy Research and Development Administration) Energy Research Abstracts — ERDA Energy Res Abstr
ERDA (Energy Research and Development Administration) Symposium Series — ERDA (Energy Res Dev Adm) Symp Ser
ERDA [*Energy Research and Development Administration*] **Symposium Series** — ERDA Symp Ser
ERDA [*Energy Research and Development Administration*] **Symposium Series** — ERDSDX
Erdelyi Muzeum — Erd M
Erdelyi Muzeum — Erd Muz
Erdelyi Muzeum — Erdelyi Muzeum
Erdelyi Muzeum-Egylet Evkoenyvei — Erd Muz
Erdelyi Muzeum-Egylet Evkoenyvei — Erd Muz Evk
Erdeszeti Ertesitoe — Erdesz Ertes
Erdeszeti es Faipari Egyetem Kiadvanyai — Erdesz Faipari Egyetem Kiad
Erdeszeti es Faipari Egyetem Tudomanyos Kozlemenyei — Erdesz Faipari Egyetem Tud Kozl
Erdeszeti es Faipari Egyetem Tudomanyos Kozlemenyei — Erdeszeti Faipari Egy Tud Kozl
Erdeszeti es Faipari Tudomanyos Kozlemenyek — Erdeszeti Faipari Tud Kozl
Erdeszeti Kiserletek — Erdeszeti Kiserl
Erdeszeti Kutatasok — Erdesz Kut
Erdeszeti Kutatasok — Erdesz Kutat
Erdeszeti Kutatasok — Erdesz Kutatas
Erdeszeti Kutatasok — Erdeszeti Kut
Erdeszeti Kutatasok — ERKUA3
Erdeszeti Ujsag — Erdesz Ujs
Erdeszettudomanyi Kozlemenyek — Erdeszettud Kozl
Erdkunde — Erdk
Erdmagnetische Berichte — Erdmagn Ber
Erdoel und Chemie (Sofia) — Erdoel Chem (Sofia)
Erdoel und Erdgas (Budapest) — Erdoel Erdgas Budapest
Erdoel und Kohle — Erd Kh
Erdoel und Kohle, Erdgas, Petrochemie — ERD
Erdoel und Kohle, Erdgas, Petrochemie — Erdoel Kohle
Erdoel und Kohle, Erdgas, Petrochemie [*Germany*] — Erdoel Kohle Erdgas Petrochem
Erdoel und Kohle, Erdgas, Petrochemie — Erdol & Kohl
Erdoel und Kohle, Erdgas, Petrochemie Vereinigt mit Brennstoff-Chemie — Erd Koh EPB
Erdoel und Kohle, Erdgas, Petrochemie Vereinigt mit Brennstoff-Chemie — Erdoel Kohle Erdgas Petrochem Brennst-Chem
Erdoel und Kohle, Erdgas, Petrochemie Vereinigt mit Brennstoff-Chemie — Erdoel Kohle Erdgas Petrochem Ver Brennst Chem
Erdoel-Erdgas Zeitschrift — Erdoel-Erdgas Z
Erdoel-Erdgas Zeitschrift. International Edition — Erdoel Erdgas Z Int Ed
Erdoel-Zeitschrift — Erdoel-Z
Erdoel-Zeitschrift fuer Bohr- und Foerdertechnik — Erdoel Z Bohr Foerdertech
Erdoemernoeki Foeiskola Evkoenyve — Erdoemern Foeisk Evk
Ere Nouvelle — EN
Eretz - Israel — EI
Eretz - Israel — Er Is
Eretz Israel. Archaeological, Historical, and Geographical Studies — Er Isr
Eretz Israel. Archaeological, Historical, and Geographical Studies — Eretz Is
Erevanskii Fizicheskii Institut. Nauchnoe Soobshchenie — Erevan Fiz Inst Nauchn Soobshch
Erevanskii Gosudarstvennyi Universitet. Ucenye Zapiski. Estestvennye Nauki — Erevan Gos Univ Ucen Zap Estesv Nauki
Erevanskii Meditsinskii Institut. Trudy — Erevan Med Inst Tr
Erevanskij Armjanskij Gosudarstvennyk Pedagogiceskij Institut Imeni Chacatur Abovjana. Sbornik Naucnych Trudov. Serija Russkogo Jazyka — EArmS
Erevna — Er
Erfahrung und Denken — Erfahr Denk

Erfahrungsheilkunde — Erf Hlkd
Erfahrungswissenschaftliche Blaetter — Erfahrungswiss Bl
Erfelijkheid in Praktijk. Orgaan van de Nederlandsche Genetische Vereeniging — Erfelijkheid Prakt
Erfurter Theologische Schriften — E Th S
Erfurtische Gelehrte Zeitungen — Erfurt Gel Zeitungen
Ergaenzungsbaende zur Zeitschrift fuer Veterinaerkunde — Ergnzngsbde Ztschr Veterinaerk
Ergaenzungsblaetter zur Allgemeinen Zeitung — Erg Bl AZ
Ergebnisse der Agrikulturchemie — Ergeb Agrikulturchem
Ergebnisse der Allgemeinen Pathologie und Pathologischen Anatomie [*West Germany*] — Erg Allg Path
Ergebnisse der Allgemeinen Pathologie und Pathologischen Anatomie — Ergeb Allg Pathol Pathol Anat
Ergebnisse der Allgemeinen Pathologie und Pathologischen Anatomie [*West Germany*] — Ergeb Allgem Pathol Pathol Anat
Ergebnisse der Allgemeinen Pathologie und Pathologischen Anatomie des Menschen und der Tiere — Ergebn Allg Path u Path Anat
Ergebnisse der Aminosaeuren-Saeulenchromatographie — Ergeb Aminosaeuren Saeulenchromatogr
Ergebnisse der Anatomie und Entwicklungsgeschichte — EAEG
Ergebnisse der Anatomie und Entwicklungsgeschichte — Ergeb Anat Entwicklungsgesch
Ergebnisse der Angewandten Mathematik — Erg Ang Math
Ergebnisse der Angewandten Physikalischen Chemie — Ergeb Angew Phys Chem
Ergebnisse der Angiologie — Ergeb Angiol
Ergebnisse der Biologie — Ergeb Biol
Ergebnisse der Biologie — Ergebn Biol
Ergebnisse der Bluttransfusionsforschung — Erg Blut Transf Forsch
Ergebnisse der Bluttransfusionsforschung — Ergeb Bluttransfusionsforsch
Ergebnisse der Chirurgie und Orthopaedie — E Ch O
Ergebnisse der Chirurgie und Orthopaedie — Erg Chir Orthop
Ergebnisse der Exakten Naturwissenschaft — Ergebn Exakt Natwiss
Ergebnisse der Exakten Naturwissenschaften — Erg Exakt Naturw
Ergebnisse der Exakten Naturwissenschaften [*Germany*] — Ergeb Exakten Naturwiss
Ergebnisse der Experimentellen Medizin — Ergeb Exp Med
Ergebnisse der Gesamten Zahnheilkunde — Ergeb Gesamten Zahnheilkd
Ergebnisse der Hochvakuumtechnik und der Physik Duenner Schichten — Ergeb Hochvakuumtech Phys Duenner Schichten
Ergebnisse der Hygiene, Bakterien-, Immunitaetsforschung, und Experimentellen Therapie — Ergebn Hyg
Ergebnisse der Hygiene, Bakteriologie, Immunitaetsforschung und Experimentellen Therapie — Ergeb Hyg Bakteriol Immunitaetsforsch Exp Ther
Ergebnisse der Immunitaetsforschung, Experimentellen Therapie, Bakteriologie und Hygiene — Ergeb Immunitaetsforsch Exp Ther Bakteriol Hyg
Ergebnisse der Inneren Medizin und Kinderheilkunde — EIMKH
Ergebnisse der Inneren Medizin und Kinderheilkunde — Erg D Inn Med u Kinderh
Ergebnisse der Inneren Medizin und Kinderheilkunde — Ergeb Inn Med Kinderheilkd
Ergebnisse der Klinischen Nuklearmedizin, Diagnostik, Therapie, Forschung, Gesellschaft fuer Nuklearmedizin. Jahrestagung — Ergeb Klin Nuklearmed Ges Nuklearmed Jahrestag
Ergebnisse der Kosmischen Physik — Ergeb Kosm Phys
Ergebnisse der Limnologie — Ergeb Limnol
Ergebnisse der Limnologie — ERLIA6
Ergebnisse der Mathematik und Ihrer Grenzgebiete — Ergeb Math Grenzgeb
Ergebnisse der Mikrobiologie, Immunitaetsforschung, und Experimentellen Therapie — Ergeb Mikrobiol Immunitatsforsch Exp Ther
Ergebnisse der Mikrobiologie und Immunitaetsforschung — CTMIA3
Ergebnisse der Mikrobiologie und Immunitaetsforschung — Ergeb Mikrobiol Immunitaetsforsch
Ergebnisse der Pathologie — CTPHBG
Ergebnisse der Pathologie — Ergeb Pathol
Ergebnisse der Pflanzengeographischen Durchforschung von Wuerttemberg, Baden, und Hohenzollern — Ergebn Pflanzengeogr Durchforsch Wuerttemberg
Ergebnisse der Physiologie, Biologischen Chemie, und Experimentellen Pharmakologie — EPBCA
Ergebnisse der Physiologie, Biologischen Chemie, und Experimentellen Pharmakologie — EPBCAQ
Ergebnisse der Physiologie, Biologischen Chemie, und Experimentellen Pharmakologie — Ergeb Physiol Biol Chem Exp Pharmakol
Ergebnisse der Physiologie, Biologischen Chemie, und Experimentellen Pharmakologie — Ergebn Physiol
Ergebnisse der Plasmaphysik und der Gaselektronik — Ergeb Plasmaphys Gaselektron
Ergebnisse der Plasmaphysik und der Gaselektronik — Ergeb Plasmaphysik Gaselektronik
Ergebnisse der Technischen Roentgenkunde — Ergeb Tech Roentgenkd
Ergebnisse der Vitamin und Hormonforschung — Ergeb Vitam Hormonforsch
Ergebnisse der Wissenschaftlichen Untersuchung des Schweizerischen Nationalparkes/Resultats des Recherches Scientifiques Entreprises au Parc National Suisse — Ergebn Wiss Untersuch Schweiz Nationalparkes
Ergebnisse Landwirtschaftlicher Forschung an der Justus Liebig-Universitaet — Ergeb Landwirtsch Forsch Justus Liebig Univ
Ergebnisse und Fortschritte der Zoologie — EFZo
Ergon tes Archaiologikes Hetaireias — EAH
Ergon tes Archaiologikes Hetaireias — Ergon
Ergonomics — ERGOA
Ergonomics — ERGOAX
Ergonomics Abstracts — Ergon Abstr
Ergonomics Abstracts — Ergonomics Abstr
Erhvervshistorisk Aarbog — E Aa
Erhvervshistorisk Arbog — Erhvervsh A
Erhvervsliv — Erhvsl
ERIC [*Educational Resources Information Center*] **Abstracts** — ERIC Abstr
ERIC [*Educational Resources Information Center*] **Current Index to Journals in Education** — ERIC Curr Index J Educ
ERIC Identifier Authority List — IAL
Ericsson Review — Ericsson Rev
Ericsson Technics — Ericsson Te
Ericsson Technics — Ericsson Tech
Eriu — Er
Erjedesipari Kutato Intezet Koslemenyei — Erjedesipari Kut Intez Kozl
Erkenntnis und Glaube — Eu G
Erkrankungen der Zootiere. Verhandlungsbericht des Internationalen Symposium ueber die Erkrankungen des Zootiere — Erkr Zootiere Verhandlungsber Int Symp
Erkunde. Archiv fuer Wissenschaftliche Geographie. Universitaet Bonn. Geographisches Institut — UBGI/E
Erlanger Arbeiten zur Deutschen Literatur — EADL
Erlanger Bausteine zur Fraenkischen Heimatforschung — Erlanger Baust Fraenk Heimatforsch
Erlanger Beitraege zur Sprach- und Kunstwissenschaft — EBSK
Erlanger Forschungen — EF
Erlanger Forschungen — Er F
Erlanger Forschungen. Reihe B. Naturwissenschaften — Erlanger Forsch Reihe B
Erlanger Geologische Abhandlungen — Erlanger Geol Abh
Erlanger Jahrbuch fuer Bienenkunde — Erlanger Jb Bienenk
Erlanger Studien — ESt
Erlanger Universitaetsreden — EUR
Erlanger Zeitschriften-Verzeichnis — EZV
Erlangische Gelehrte Anmerkungen und Nachrichten — Erlangische Gel Anmerk Nachr
Ermlaendischer Hauskalender — EHK
Ernaehrung der Pflanze — Ernaehr Pflanze
Ernaehrung in der Medizin — Ernaehr Med
Ernaehrungsforschung — ERNFA7
Ernaehrungsforschung. Institut fuer Ernaehrung (Potsdam) — Ernaehrungsforsch Inst Ernaehr (Potsdam)
Ernaehrungsforschung Wissenschaft und Praxis — Ernahrungsforsch Wiss Prax
Ernaehrungslehre und Ernaehrungspraxis — Ernaehrungsl Ernaehrungsprax
Ernaehrungslehre und- Praxis — Ernaehrungsl Prax
Ernaehrungsprobleme und Arbeitsschutz — Ernaehrungsprobl Arbeitsschutz
Ernaehrungs-Umschau — Ernaehr Umsch
Ernaehrungs-Umschau — ERUMAT
Ernaehrungswirtschaft — EWB
Ernaehrungswirtschaft. Lebensmitteltechnik (Hamburg) — Ernaehrungswirtsch Lebensmitteltech (Hamburg)
Ernaehrungswissenschaft — SALIA7
Ernst Rodenwaldt Archiv — E Rodenwaldt Arch
Ernstia — ERNSDF
Ernst-Moritz-Arndt-Universitaet Greifswald. Wissenschaftliche Zeitschrift. Mathematisch-Naturwissenschaftliche Reihe — Ernst Moritz Arndt Univ Greifsw Wiss Z Math Naturwiss Reihe
Ernst-Rodenwaldt-Archiv — Ernst Rodenwaldt Arch
Eroeterv Koezlemenyek — Eroeterv Koezl
Erosion of Ceramic Materials — Erosion Ceram Mater
ERRC Publication. United States. Agricultural Research Service. Eastern Regional Research Center — ERRC Publ US Agric Res Serv East Reg Res Cent
ERRL Publication. United States. Agricultural Research Service. Eastern Regional Research Laboratory — ERRL Publ US Agric Res Serv East Reg Res Lab
ERS Staff Report. United States Department of Agriculture. Economic Research Service — ERS Staff Rep US Dep Agric Econ Res Serv
Erste Verhandlungen der Freyen Landwirthschafts-Gesellschaft des Niederrheinischen Departements zu Strasburg — Erste Verh Freyen Landw Ges Niederrhein Dept Strasburg
ERT (Energy Resources and Technology) [*Formerly, Energy Resources Report*] — ERT (Energy Resour Technol)
Eruptive Solar Flares. Proceedings. Colloquium No. 133. International Astronomical Union — Eruptive Sol Flares Proc Colloq No 133 Int Astron Union
Erwerbungen. Stiftung zur Foerderung der Hamburgischen Kunstsammlungen — Stift Hamburg Ku Samml
Erwin von Steinbach-Stift Studien — ErS
Erythrocyte Mechanics and Blood Flow — Erythrocyte Mech Blood Flow
Erythrocyte Structure and Function. Proceedings. International Conference on Red Cell Metabolism and Function — Erythrocyte Struct Funct Proc Int Conf Red Cell Metab Funct
Erythropoiesis. Proceedings. International Conference on Erythropoiesis — Erythropoiesis Proc Int Conf
Erzeugung von Krankheitszustaenden durch das Experiment — Erzeug Krankheitszustaenden Exp
ES [*Etude Speciale*]. Ministere des Richesses Naturelles du Quebec — ES Etude Spec Minist Richesses Nat Que
ESA [*European Space Agency*] **Bulletin** [*France*] — ESA Bull
ESA. Engage/Social Action — E/SA
ESA [*European Space Agency*] **Journal** — ESA J
ESA [*European Space Agency*] **Journal** — ESAJD
ESA [*European Space Agency*] **Scientific and Technical Review** — ESA Sci and Tech Rev
ESAB [*Elektriska Svetsningsaktiebolaget*] **Revue. Deutsche Ausgabe** — ESAB Rev Dtsch Ausg
ESAB [*Elektriska Svetsningsaktiebolaget*] **Svetsaren** — ESAB Svetsaren

ESAB [*Elektriska Svetsningsaktiebolaget*] **Tidning Svetsaren** — ESAB Tidn Svetsaren
Esakia Occasional Papers of the Hikosan Biological Laboratory in Entomology — Esakia Occas Pap Hikosan Biol Lab Entomol
ESC [*Energy Studie Centrum*]. Rapport — ESC Energ Stud Cent Rapp
ESCAP [*United Nations Economic and Social Commission for Asia and the Pacific*] **Bibliographic Information System** [*Database*] — EBIS
Escola de Agronomia da Amazonia. Boletim — EAGAB9
Escola de Agronomia da Amazonia. Boletim — Esc Agron Amazonia Bol
Escola de Agronomia e Veterinaria. Anais. Universidade Federal de Goias — Esc Agron Vet An Univ Fed Goias
Escola de Agronomia e Veterinaria. Universidade Federal do Parana. Revista — Esc Agron Vet Univ Fed Parana Rev
Escola de Engenharia. Universidade de Minas Gerais. Instituto de Pesquisas Radioativas. Publicacao — Esc Eng Univ Minas Gerais Inst Pesqui Radioat Publ
Escola de Minas. Revista (Ouro Preto, Brazil) — Esc Minas Rev (Ouro Preto Braz)
Escola Secundaria (Rio de Janeiro) — Escola Secund Rio
Escola Superior de Agricultura "Luiz De Queiroz" (Sao Paulo). Boletin — Esc Super Agric Luiz De Queiroz (Sao Paulo) Bol
Escorial — E
Escorial — Es
Escorial — Esc
Escritos (Medillin) — ESM
Escuela de Agricultura. Revista Mensual — Esc Agric
Escuela de Farmacia — Esc Farm
Escuela de Farmacia Guatemala — EFGUAZ
Escuela de Farmacia Guatemala — Esc Farm Guatem
Escuela de Verano sobre Espectroscopia — Esc Veran Espectrosc
Escuela Nacional de Agricultura (Chapingo). Avances en la Ensenanza y la Investigacion — Av Ensenanza Invest Esc Nac Agric (Chapingo)
Escuela Nacional de Agricultura (Chapingo). Monografias — Esc Nac Agric (Chapingo) Monogr
Escuela Nacional de Agricultura (Chapingo). Revista — Esc Nac Agric (Chapingo) Rev
Escuela Nacional de Agricultura (Chapingo). Serie de Apuntes — Esc Nac Agric (Chapingo) Ser Apuntes
Escuela Nacional de Agricultura (Chapingo). Serie de Investigaciones — Esc Nac Agric (Chapingo) Ser Invest
Escuela Nacional de Agricultura [*Chapingo*]. Monografias — MCPAAJ
Escuela Nacional de Agricultura [*Chapingo*]. Revista — RVEAAG
Escuela Nacional de Agricultura [*Chapingo*]. Serie de Apuntes — SAPAA3
Escuela Nacional de Agricultura [*Chapingo*]. Serie de Investigaciones — SIPAAP
Escuela Nacional de Ingenieros. Boletin (Lima) — Esc Nac Ing Bol Lima
Esic-Market, Estudios de Gestion Comercial y Empresa — Esic-Market Estud Gestion Com Empr
ESIS [*European Shielding Information Service*] **Newsletter** — ESIS Newsl
ESIS Newsletter — ESISD
Esitelmat ja Poytakirjat. Suomalainen Tiedeakatemia — Esitelmat Poytak Suom Tiedeakat
Eskimo — ESKI
ESNA Working Group on Waste Irradiation. Proceedings. International Conference — ESNA Work Group Waste Irradiat Proc Int Conf
ESO/SRC/CERN Conference on Research Programmes for the New Large Telescopes — ESO SRC CERN Conf Res Programmes New Large Telesc
Espace Geographique — Espace Geogr
Espaces et Societes — Espaces et Soc
Espana Ganadera — Esp Ganad
Espana Misionera — EM
Espana Moderna — Espana Mod
Espana Nueva — EspN
Espana Sagrada — ES
Espana Sagrada — Esp Sag
Espanol Actual — EspA
Especialidades Consumidas por la Seguridad Social [*Database*] — ECOM
Especialidades Farmaceuticas en Tramite de Registro [*Database*] — TRAMIT
Especialidades Farmaceuticas Espanolas [*Database*] — ESPES
Esperienza e Ricerche. Istituto di Agronomia Generale e Coltivazioni Erbacee. Universita di Pisa — Esper Ricer Ist Agr Gen Colt Erbacee Univ Pisa
Esperienza Poetica — EPo
Esperienze Letterarie. Rivista Trimestrale di Critica e Cultura — ELet
Espionage Magazine — Espionage Mag
Espiral Letras y Arte — ELA
Esploratore — E
Esprit — E
Esprit — Es
Esprit — Espr
Esprit Createur — ECr
Esprit Createur — EsC
Esprit Createur — Esprit Cr
Esprit et Vie. Langres — EeV
Espuela de Plata — EsP
Esquire — Esq
Esquire — GESQ
Esquisses Mathematiques — Esquisses Math
ESR Applications to Polymer Research. Proceedings. Nobel Symposium — ESR Appl Polym Res Proc Nobel Symp
ESRO/ELDO [*European Space Research Organization/European Launcher Development Organization*] **Bulletin** — ESRO/ELDO Bull
Essais Catholiques — Ess C
Essais Critiques, Artistiques, Philosophiques, et Litteraires — Essais Critiques
Essay and General Literature Index — EGLI
Essay and General Literature Index — Essay Gen Lit Index
Essay-Proof Journal — EPJ
Essays and Papers. Soong Jun University [*Korea*] — Essays Pap
Essays and Papers. Soong Jun University — Essays Pap Soong Jun Univ
Essays and Studies [*London*] — E & S
Essays and Studies [*London*] — ES
Essays and Studies — Essays Stud
Essays and Studies by the Faculty of Hiroshima Jogakuin College — Essays Stud Fac Hiroshima Jogakuin Coll
Essays and Studies. Faculty of Hiroshima Jogakuin College — HJDRB5
Essays and Studies in English Language and Literature — ESELL
Essays by Divers Hands — EDH
Essays in Applied Microbiology [*monograph*] — Essays Appl Microbiol
Essays in Arts and Sciences — EAS
Essays in Arts and Sciences — Essays Arts Sci
Essays in Biochemistry — ESBIAV
Essays in Biochemistry — Essays Biochem
Essays in Chemistry — Essays Chem
Essays in Criticism — EC
Essays in Criticism — ECr
Essays in Criticism — EIC
Essays in Criticism — Ess Crit
Essays in Criticism — Essays Crit
Essays in Criticism — PEIC
Essays in Foreign Languages and Literature — EFLL
Essays in French Literature [*University of Western Australia*] — EFL
Essays in French Literature — Essays Fr L
Essays in Fundamental Immunology — Essays Fundam Immunol
Essays in Greek History — EGH
Essays in Literature — EIL
Essays in Literature — Essays Lit
Essays in Literature — PEIL
Essays in Literature. Western Illinois University — ELWIU
Essays in Medical Biochemistry — Essays Med Biochem
Essays in Neurochemistry and Neuropharmacology — ENNEDD
Essays in Neurochemistry and Neuropharmacology — Essays Neurochem Neuropharmacol
Essays in Physics — Essay Phys
Essays in Physics — Essays Phys
Essays in Poetics — Essays Poet
Essays in Public Works History — Essays Publ Works Hist
Essays in Toxicology — Essay Toxico
Essays in Toxicology — Essays Toxicol
Essays in Toxicology — ETOXAC
Essays. Institute of Liturgical Studies — EILS
Essays on Canadian Writing — ECW
Essays on Canadian Writing — Essays Can Wri
Essays on Canadian Writing — PEOC
Essays on Geology of the Azerbaijan — Essays Geol Azerb
Essays on Modern Music — Essays Mod Mus
Essence — Ess
Essence — GESS
Essential Student Algebra — Essent Student Algebra
Essentials of Islam Series — EIS
Essentials of Pharmacology [*Monograph*] — Essent Pharmacol
Essenze e Derivati Agrumari — Essenze Deriv Agrum
Essex Archaeology and History — EAH
Essex Archaeology and History — Essex Arch Hist
Essex Archaeology and History — Essex Archaeol Hist
Essex Archaeology and History. The Transactions of the Essex Archaeological Society — Transact Essex
Essex Archaeology and History. Transactions. Essex Archaeological Society — Trans Essex Arch Soc
Essex County Natural History Society. Journal — Essex Co N H Soc J
Essex Hall Lectures — EHL
Essex Institute. Annual Report — Essex Inst Annual Rep
Essex Institute. Bulletin — Essex Inst B
Essex Institute. Historical Collections — EIHC
Essex Institute. Historical Collections — EIHCA7
Essex Institute Historical Collections — EsI
Essex Institute. Historical Collections — Essex I His
Essex Institute. Historical Collections — Essex Inst Coll
Essex Institute. Historical Collections — Essex Inst Hist Coll
Essex Institute. Historical Collections — Essex Inst Hist Collect
Essex Institute. Proceedings — Essex Inst Pr
Essex Journal — Essex J
Essex Naturalist [*London*] — ESNAAX
Essex Naturalist — Essex Natur
Essex Naturalist (London) — Essex Nat (Lond)
Essex Review — Ess R
Esslinger Studien — ES
Esso Agricola — Esso Agr
Esso in the Antilles — Esso Ant
ESSO Magazine — ES
ESSO Magazine — ESSO Mag
ESSO North — ESSN
ESSO [*Standard Oil*] **Oilways International** — ESSO Oilways Int
ESSO [*Standard Oil*] **Resources News** — ESRN
Essobron — EBN
Essor Frigorifique Francais — Essor Frigorif Fr
Est et Ouest — EO
Est et Ouest. Bulletin de l'Association d'Etudes et d'Informations Politiques Internationales — Est-Ouest
Est Europeen — Est Europ
Estacion Central de Ecologia. Boletin (Spain) — Estac Cent Ecol Bol (Spain)
Estacion Experimental Agricola de La Molina. Boletin — Estac Exp Agric La Molina Bol

Estacion Experimental Agricola de Tucuman. Boletin — BIATBP
Estacion Experimental Agricola de Tucuman. Boletin — Estac Exp Agric Tucuman Bol
Estacion Experimental Agricola de Tucuman. Circular — EATCAB
Estacion Experimental Agricola de Tucuman. Circular — Estac Exp Agric Tucuman Circ
Estacion Experimental Agricola de Tucuman. Publicacion — Estac Exp Agric Tucuman Publ
Estacion Experimental Agricola de Tucuman. Publicacion Miscelanea — EATMA7
Estacion Experimental Agricola de Tucuman. Publicacion Miscelanea — Estac Exp Agric Tucuman Publ Misc
Estacion Experimental Agropecuaria Pergamino. Boletin de Divulgacion — BDEAAK
Estacion Experimental Agropecuaria Pergamino. Boletin de Divulgacion — Estac Exp Agropecu Pergamino Bol Divulg
Estacion Experimental Agropecuaria Pergamino. Publicacion Tecnico — Estac Exp Agropecu Pergamino Publ Tec
Estacion Experimental Agropecuaria Pergamino. Publicacion Tecnico — ITXPA9
Estacion Experimental de Aula dei Zaragoza. Boletin — Estac Exp Aula dei Zaragoza Bol
Estacion Experimental de Aula dei Zaragoza. Departamento de Mejora Ensayos [*A publication*] — Estac Exp Aula dei Zaragoza Dep Mejora Ens
Estacion Experimental Regional Agropecuaria Parana. Serie Notas Tecnicas — Estac Exp Reg Agropecu Parana Ser Notas Tec
Estadistica Espanola — Estadist Espanola
Estadistica Espanola — Estadistica Esp
Estadistica. Journal. Inter-American Statistical Institute (Mexico, DF; Washington, DC) — Estad Mex Wash
Estadistica Peruana (Lima) — Estad Peru Lima
Estadistica (Washington, D. C.) — EAW
Estadisticas Financieras Internacionales — EFI
Estafeta Literaria — ELit
Estafeta Literaria — EstLit
Estate Planning — EP
Estate Planning — ESP
Estate Planning — Est Plan
Estate Planning (Prentice-Hall, Inc.) — P-H Est Plan
Estates and Trusts Quarterly — Est and Tr Q
Estates and Trusts Quarterly — Estates Q
Estates and Trusts Quarterly — ETQ
Estates and Trusts Reports — Est and Tr Rep
Estates and Trusts Reports — ETR
Estates Gazette — Est Gaz
Estates Gazette — Estates Gaz
Estates Gazette Digest of Land and Property Cases — Est Gaz Dig
Estates, Gifts, and Trusts Journal — EGT
Estates Times Review — Estates Times Rev
Estel-Berichte aus Forschung und Entwicklung Unserer Werke — Estel-Ber Forsch Entwickl Unserer Werke
Estestvennye Proizvoditel'nye Sily Rossii — Estestv Proizv Sily Rossii
Esti Loodus. Tartu Ulikooli Juures Oleva Loodusuurijate Seltsi Teataja. Esti Loodus Estonian Nature/Periodical. Society of Nature Investigators. University of Tartu — Esti Loodus Tartu
Estilo. Revista de Cultura (San Luis Potosi, Mexico) — Estilo S Luis Potosi
Estomatologia e Cultura — ESCLBC
Estomatologia e Cultura — Estomatol Cult
Estonian Contributions to the International Biological Programme. Progress Report — Est Contrib Int Biol Programme Prog Rep
Estonian Papers in Phonetics — EPP
Estonskii Nauchno-Issledovatel'skii Institut Zemledeliya i Melioratsii. Sbornik Nauchnykh Trudov — Est Nauchn Issled Inst Zemled Melior Sb Nauchn Tr
Estremadura. Boletim da Junta de Provincia — EBJP
Estuaries — ESTUDO
Estuaries of the Pacific Northwest. Proceedings. Technical Conference — Estuaries Pac Northwest Proc Tech Conf
Estuarine and Coastal Marine Science — ECMSC6
Estuarine and Coastal Marine Science — Est Coas M
Estuarine and Coastal Marine Science — Estuarine Coastal Mar Sci
Estuarine Bulletin — ESBUAX
Estuarine Bulletin — Estuarine Bull
Estuarine, Coastal, and Shelf Science — ECSSD
Estuarine, Coastal, and Shelf Science — ECSSD3
Estuarine Coastal and Shelf Science — Estuar Coast Shelf Sci
Estuarine, Coastal, and Shelf Science [*England*] — Estuarine Coastal Shelf Sci
Estuarine Research — ESREDY
Estuarine Research — Estuarine Res
Estudio Agustiniano — Est Ag
Estudio (Bucaramanga, Colombia) — Estud Bucaramanga
Estudios — Est
Estudios Abulenses — E Abul
Estudios Abulenses — Est Abulenses
Estudios. Academia Literaria del Plata (Buenos Aires) — Estud BA
Estudios Afrocubanos — EA
Estudios Afrocubanos — EAf
Estudios Agrarios. Centro de Investigaciones Agrarias — Estud Agrar
Estudios Americanos — EA
Estudios Americanos [*Sevilla*] — EAm
Estudios Americanos. Revista. Escuela de Estudios Hispano Americanos de Sevilla — Est Am
Estudios Americanos (Sevilla) — Estud Am Sevilla
Estudios Andinos — Estud Andin
Estudios Andinos (Peru) — EAP
Estudios Andinos. University of Pittsburgh. Latin American Studies Center — UP/EA
Estudios Arqueologicos. Publicacion Cientifica. Universidad de Chile (Antofagasta, Chile) — Estud Arqueol Antofagasta
Estudios Biblicos — E Bibl
Estudios Biblicos — EB
Estudios Biblicos — EBl
Estudios Biblicos — EBib
Estudios Biblicos [*Madrid*] — EstB
Estudios Biblicos [*Madrid*] — EstBib
Estudios Biblicos. Organo de la Asociacion para el Fomento de Estudios Biblicos en Espana. CSIC (Consejo Superior de Investigaciones Cientificas) — Est Biblicos
Estudios (Callao, Argentina) — E (Callao)
Estudios Centroamericanos — ECA
Estudios Centroamericanos. Universidade Centroamericana Jose Simeon Canas [*San Salvador*] — UJSC/ECA
Estudios Clasicos — E Cl
Estudios Clasicos — EC
Estudios Clasicos — EClas
Estudios Clasicos — EsCl
Estudios Clasicos — Est Cl
Estudios Clasicos — Est Clas
Estudios Clasicos — Estud Cl
Estudios Clasicos — Estud Clas
Estudios Clasicos. Anejo de Bordon. Sociedad Espanola de Pedagogia — Est Clasicos
Estudios Clasicos. Suplement Serie de Textos — E Cl T
Estudios Clasicos. Suplement Serie de Traducciones — E Cl Tr
Estudios Cooperativos — Estud Coop
Estudios de Arqueologia Alavesa — EAA
Estudios de Arqueologia Alavesa — Est A Alava
Estudios de Arqueologia Alavesa — Est de Arq Alavesa
Estudios de Asia y Africa — Estud As Afr
Estudios de Cultura Maya — ECM
Estudios de Cultura Maya — Est Cult Maya
Estudios de Cultura Nahuatl — ECN
Estudios de Cultura Nahuatl — Estud Cult Nahuatl
Estudios de Derecho — EDD
Estudios de Derecho. Facultad de Derecho y Ciencias Politicas. Universidad de Antioquia (Medellin, Colombia) — Estud Der Medellin
Estudios de Derecho. Segunda Epoca — Estud Derecho 2a Epoca
Estudios de Deusto — E Deusto
Estudios de Deusto. Revista Dirigida. Profesores de las Facultades de Derecho y Economia. Universidad de Deusto — Est Deusto
Estudios de Economia — Estud Econ
Estudios de Edad Media de la Corona de Aragon — EEMCA
Estudios de Edad Media de la Corona de Aragon CSIC (Consejo Superior de Investigaciones Cientificas) — Est Edad Media Corona Aragon
Estudios de Filosofia y Religion Orientales [*Buenos Aires*] — EstFilRelOr
Estudios de Hispanofila — EstdH
Estudios de Historia Moderna — EstHM
Estudios de Historia Moderna. Centro de Estudios Historicos Internacionales. Universidad de Barcelona — Est Hist Mod
Estudios de Historia Social de Espana — EHSE
Estudios de Historia Social de Espana. CSIC (Consejo Superior de Investigaciones Cientificas) — Est Hist Social Esp
Estudios de Linguistica Aplicada — EDLA
Estudios de Poblacion — EDP
Estudios de Poblacion — Estud Poblac
Estudios Demograficos — Est Demograficos
Estudios. Duquesne University — EstD
Estudios Eclesiasticos — E Ecl
Estudios Eclesiasticos — EE
Estudios Eclesiasticos [*Madrid*] — EstE
Estudios Eclesiasticos [*Madrid*] — EstEcl
Estudios Eclesiasticos (Madrid) — EEM
Estudios Eclesiasticos. Revista Trimestral de Investigacion e Informacion Teologica. Publicada. Facultad de Teologia de la Compania de Jesus en Espana — Est Ecles
Estudios Empresariales — Estud Empresar
Estudios Empresariales — Estud Empresariales
Estudios Eruditos en Memoriam de Bonilla y San Martin — EE
Estudios Eruditos en Memoriam de Bonilla y San Martin — EEMB
Estudios Escenicos — EstE
Estudios Escenicos. Cuadernos del Instituto del Teatro — EECIT
Estudios Especiales. Servicio de Geologia y Mineria (Peru) — Estud Espec Serv Geol Min (Peru)
Estudios Extremenos; Revista Historica, Literaria, y Artistica — Estud Extremenos
Estudios Filologicos — EFil
Estudios Filologicos (Valdivia, Chile) — Estud Filol Valdivia
Estudios Filosoficos — E Fs
Estudios Filosoficos — EF
Estudios Filosoficos — Est Fil
Estudios Filosoficos — Estud Filosof
Estudios Franciscanos — EstF
Estudios Franciscanos [*Barcelona*] — EstFr
Estudios Franciscanos [*Barcelona*] — EstFranc
Estudios Franciscanos. Revista Cuatrimestral de Ciencias Eclesiasticas Publicada por los P.P. Capuchinos de Espana y America — Est Francisc
Estudios Geograficos — EG
Estudios Geograficos — Estud Geogr
Estudios Geograficos. CSIC (Consejo Superior de Investigaciones Cientificas) — Est Geogr

Estudios Geograficos (Espana) — EGE
Estudios Geograficos. Instituto "Juan Sebastian Elcano" — Estud Geogr Inst Juan Sebastian Elcano
Estudios Geologicos [*Madrid*] — EGLMA9
Estudios Geologicos — Estudios Geol
Estudios Geologicos. CSIC (Consejo Superior de Investigaciones Cientificas) — Est Geologicos
Estudios Geologicos. Instituto de Investigaciones Geologicas "Lucas Mallada" — Estud Geol Inst Invest Geol "Lucas Mallada"
Estudios Geologicos. Instituto de Investigaciones Geologicos Lucas Mallada (Madrid) — Estud Geol Inst Invest Geol Lucas Mallada (Madrid)
Estudios Geologicos (Madrid) — Estud Geol (Madr)
Estudios Historicos (Guadalajara, Mexico) — Estud Hist Guadalajara
Estudios Ibericos — EI
Estudios. Instituto Nacional de Panama (Panama) — Estud Panama
Estudios Internacionales — Estud Int
Estudios Internacionales — Estud Internac
Estudios Internacionales de Chile — EIC
Estudios Italianos — EI
Estudios Josefinos — E Jos
Estudios Josefinos — EJ
Estudios Josefinos — Est Jos
Estudios Josefinos (Valladolid) — EJV
Estudios Latinoamericanos. Polska Akademia Nauk — PAN/ES
Estudios Lulianos — ELu
Estudios Lulianos — ELul
Estudios Lulioanos — Est Lul
Estudios Marianos — E Maria
Estudios Marianos [*Madrid*] — EstMar
Estudios Medievales — Est Medievales
Estudios Missionarios — Est Miss
Estudios, Notas, y Trabelhos de Servico de Fomento Mineiro — ESFM
Estudios Onienses — Est On
Estudios Orientales — EstOr
Estudios Orientales (Mexico City) — EOMC
Estudios Paraguayos — Estud Parag
Estudios Paraguayos (Asuncion) — EPA
Estudios Pedagogicos. Instituto San Jose de Calasanz de la Excma. Diputacion de Zaragoza — Est Pedag
Estudios Politicos — Est Polit
Estudios. Revista. Padres de la Orden de la Merced — EPOM
Estudios Rurales Latinoamericanos. Consejo Latinoamericano de Ciencias Sociales. Secretaria Ejecutiva y la Comision de Estudios Rurales — CLACSO/ERL
Estudios Sefardies — E Sef
Estudios Segovianos — E Seg
Estudios Segovianos — ES
Estudios Segovianos — Est Seg
Estudios Segovianos — Estud Segov
Estudios Segovianos. Revista Historica del Centro de Estudios Segovianos — Est Segovianos
Estudios. Seminario de Prehistoria, Arqueologia, e Historia Antigua. Facultad de Filosofia y Letras de Zaragoza — Est Zaragoza
Estudios. Seminario de Prehistoria Arqueologia et Historia Antigua. Facultad de Filosofia y Letras de Zaragoza — ESPAHA
Estudios Sindicales — Estud Sindic
Estudios Sindicales — Estud Sindicales
Estudios Sindicales y Cooperativos — Estud Sindicales y Coops
Estudios Sobre el Comunismo (Santiago) — Estud Comunismo Santiago
Estudios sobre Esterilidad — Estud Esteril
Estudios sobre la Economia (Argentina) — Estud Econ (Argentina)
Estudios Sociales — ESD
Estudios Sociales Centroamericanos — ESC
Estudios Sociales Centroamericanos — Estud Soc C
Estudios Sociales Centroamericanos — Estud Soc Centroam
Estudios Sociales Centroamericanos — Estud Soc Centroamer
Estudios Sociales Centroamericanos. Consejo Superior de Universidades Centroamericanas, Confederacion Universitaria Centroamericana, Programa Centroamericano de Ciencias Sociales — CSUCA/ESC
Estudios Sociales. Revista de Ciencias Sociales — Estud Soc
Estudios Socio-Religiosos Latino-Americanos — ESRLA
Estudios Teologicos (Guatemala) — Estudios Teol (Guatemala)
Estudios Teologicos y Filosoficos — ETF
Estudios-Padres de la Orden de la Merced — EOM
Estudis d'Historia Agraria — Estud Hist Agrar
Estudis Escenics. Quaderns de l'Institut del Teatre de la Diputacio de Barcelona — EEsc
Estudis Franciscans — EF
Estudis Romanics — ER
Estudis Romanics — Est Rom
Estudis Romanics — Est Romanics
Estudis Universitaris Catalans — EUC
Estudos Agronomicos — Estud Agron
Estudos Agronomicos — Estudos Agron
Estudos Agronomicos. Missao de Estudos Agronomicos do Ultramar — Estud Agron Missao Estud Agron Ultramar
Estudos Anglo-Americanos — EAA
Estudos Brasileiros — EBra
Estudos Brasileiros. Instituto de Estudos Brasileiros (Rio de Janeiro) — Estud Bras Rio
Estudos Brasileiros. Universidad Federal do Parana. Setor de Ciencias Humanas. Centro de Estudos Brasileiros — UFP/EB
Estudos de Castelo Branco — ECB
Estudos de Quimica. Instituto Nacional de Investigacao Industrial (Portugal) — Estud Quim Inst Nac Invest Ind (Port)
Estudos do Alto Minho — EAM
Estudos e Ensaios Folcloricos em Homenagem a Renato Almeida — EEFHRA
Estudos e Informacao. Servicos Florestais e Aquicolas (Portugal) — Estud Inform Serv Flor Aquic (Portugal)
Estudos Economicos — Estud Econs
Estudos Economicos. Universidad de Sao Paulo. Instituto de Pesquisas Economicas — IPE/EE
Estudos, Ensaios, e Documentos. Junta de Investigacoes Cientificas do Ultramar (Portugal) — Estud Ensaios Doc Junta Invest Cient Ultramar (Port)
Estudos Historicos (Marilia, Brazil) — Estud Hist Marilia
Estudos Ibero-Americanos — EIA
Estudos Ibero-Americanos — Estud Ib-Am
Estudos Italianos em Portugal — EIP
Estudos Legislativos — Estud Legis
Estudos Leopoldenses — Estud Leopold
Estudos Matematica e Informatica — Estudos Mat Inform
Estudos. Notas e Trabalhos do Servico de Fomento Mineiro (Portugal) — Estud Notas Trab Serv Fom Min (Port)
Estudos, Notas, e Trabathos. Servico de Fomento Mineiro e Laboratorio da DGGM [*Direccao-Geral de Geologia e Minas*] **(Portugal)** — Estud Notas Trab Serv Fom Min Lab DGGM Portugal
Estudos sobre a Fauna Portuguesa — EFPRA3
Estudos sobre a Fauna Portuguesa — Estud Fauna Port
Estudos Sociais (Rio de Janeiro) — Estud Soc Rio
Estudos Tecnicos. Servico de Informacao Agricola (Brazil) — Estud Tec Serv Inf Agric Braz
Estudos Tecnologicos. Acta Geologica Leopoldensia — Estud Tecnol
Estudos Teologicos (Brazil) — Estudos Teol (Brazil)
Estudos Ultramarinos — EU
Estudos Universitarios [*Recife*] — EU
Estudos Universitarios: Revista de Cultura da Universidade de Pernambuco — EURCUP
Et Cetera — PETC
ET [*Enterostomal Therapy*] **Journal** — ET J
ETA. Elektrowaerme im Technischen Ausbau — EETAD
ETA. Elektrowaerme im Technischen Ausbau. Edition A — ETA Elektrowaerme Tech Ausbau Ed A
Eta Sigma Gamma — ESGM
Eta Sigma Gamma. Monograph Series — ESMS
Etat Sanitaire des Animaux de la Belgique — Etat San Animaux Belgique
Etat Solide, Rapports et Discussions. Conseil de Physique. Institut International de Physique. Solvay — Etat Solide Rapp Discuss Cons Phys Inst Int Phys Solvay
ETB - TUG. Equipement Technique du Batiment - Technische Uitrusting van het Gebouw — ETB TUG
ETC: A Review of General Semantics — ERGS
ETC: A Review of General Semantics — ETC Rev Gen
Eternelle Revue — ER
Eternity — Etr
Eternity — Ety
Eternity Magazine — Eter
ETG [*Energietechnische Gesellschaft Im Vde*] **Fachberichte** — ETG Fachber
Ethical and Religious Classics of East and West — ERCEW
Ethical Record — Eth Rec
Ethics — Et
Ethics — PETH
Ethics. An International Journal of Social, Political, and Legal Philosophy — Eth
Ethics and Animals — Ethics Animals
Ethics in Science and Medicine — ESMED9
Ethics in Science and Medicine — Ethics Sci Med
Ethiopia Geological Survey. Annual Report — Ethiop Geol Surv Annu Rep
Ethiopia Geological Survey. Bulletin — Ethiop Geol Surv Bull
Ethiopia Observer — Ethiopia Obs
Ethiopian Geographical Journal — Ethiop Geogr J
Ethiopian Herald — EH
Ethiopian Institute of Agricultural Research. Report — Ethiop Inst Agric Res Rep
Ethiopian Journal of Development Research — Ethiopian J Dev Res
Ethiopian Library Association Bulletin — Ethiopian Libr Ass Bull
Ethiopian Medical Journal — EMDJA2
Ethiopian Medical Journal — Ethiop Med J
Ethnic and Racial Studies — ERS
Ethnic and Racial Studies — Ethn Racial Stud
Ethnic and Racial Studies — Ethnic & Racial Stud
Ethnic and Racial Studies — PENR
Ethnic Groups — PEGR
Ethnic Studies — Ethn Stud
Ethnic Studies — Ethnic Stud
Ethnic Studies Bibliography — Ethnic Stud Bibliogr
[*The*] **Ethnic Studies Report** — ESR
Ethnicity and Disease — Ethn Dis
Ethnikon Mouseion — EM
Ethno History — EH
Ethnographia — Ethn
Ethnographia (Budapest) — Ethn Bud
Ethnographic Museum. University of Oslo. Yearbook — Ethnogr Mus Univ Oslo Yb
Ethnographie. Paris — Ethnog
Ethnographisch-Archaeologische Forschungen — EAF
Ethnographisch-Archaeologische Forschungen — Ethnogr Archaeol Forsch
Ethnographisch-Archaeologische Zeitschrift — EA Zeits
Ethnographisch-Archaeologische Zeitschrift — EAZ
Ethnographisch-Archaeologische Zeitschrift — Ethn Arch Z
Ethnographisch-Archaeologische Zeitschrift — Ethn Arch Zeitschr
Ethnographisch-Archaeologische Zeitschrift — Ethnogr Archaeol Z

Ethnographisch-Archaeologische Zeitschrift — Ethnogr Archaeologische Z
Ethnographisch-Archaeologische Zeitschrift — Ethnogr AZ
Ethnographisches Archiv — Ethnogr Arch
Ethnohistory — Ethn
Ethnohistory — Ethno
Ethnohistory — Ethnohist
Ethnohistory — PERY
Ethnohistory. Journal of the American Society for Ethnohistory — ASE/E
Ethnologia Americana — Ethnol Amer
Ethnologia Europaea — EthnoE
Ethnologia Europaea — Ethnol Europ
Ethnologia Fennica [*Finnish Studies in Ethnology*] — EthF
Ethnologia Fennica [*Finnish Studies in Ethnology*] — Ethnol Fennica
Ethnologia Scandinavica — Eth Sc
Ethnologia Scandinavica — Ethnol Scand
Ethnologia Slavica — Eth S
Ethnologica. Koeln — Ethnol
Ethnological Society of London. Transactions — Ethnol Soc Lond Trans
Ethnologie Francaise — EthnoF
Ethnologie Francaise — Ethnol Fr
Ethnologie Francaise — Ethnol Franc
Ethnologisch Zeitschrift [*Zuerich*] — Ethno Z
Ethnologische Zeitschrift — Ethnol Z
Ethnologische Zeitschrift — EZ
Ethnologische Zeitschrift Zuerich — Ethnol Z Zuerich
Ethnologische Zeitschrift (Zurich) — EZZ
Ethnologischer Anzeiger — Ethnol Anz
Ethnologisches Notizblatt — ENB
Ethnology — ETNLB6
Ethnology — PEGY
Ethnology. University of Pittsburgh — UP/E
Ethnomedizin. Ethnomedicine Zeitschrift fuer Interdisziplinare Forschung — Ethnomedizin
Ethno-Musicologica — Eth Mus
Ethnomusicology — Em
Ethnomusicology — ET
Ethnomusicology — Eth
Ethnomusicology — Ethmus
Ethnomusicology — Ethnomusic
Ethnomusicology — Ethnomusicol
Ethnomusicology — ETMSB
Ethnomusicology — PETU
Ethnomusicology. Selected Reports — Ethmus Sel Repts
Ethno-Psychologie — Ethno-Psych
Ethno-Psychologie — Ethno-Psychol
Ethnos — E
Ethnos — Eth
Ethnos. Statens Etnografiska Museum — SEM/E
Ethology, Ecology, and Evolution — Ethol Ecol Evol
Etimologiceskie Issledovanija po Russkomu Jazyku — EIRJa
Etizenia — ETOPBN
Etnografia Polska — Etnogr Polska
Etnografia Polska — EtPol
Etnografia Portuguesa — EP
Etnografija — E
Etnografija. Moskva — Etn
Etnologia Antropologia Culturale — Etnol Antropol Cult
Etnologia y Folklore — EyF
Etnologiska Studier — Etn St
Etnologiska Studier — Etnol Stud
Etnologiska Studier — ETNSAQ
Etnoloski Pregled — EtP
ETO (Exponential-Type Atomic Orbitals) Multicenter Molecular Integrals. Proceedings. International Conference — ETO Multicent Mol Integr Proc Int Conf
Etoiles — Et
ETR [*Eisenbahntechnische Rundschau*] — ETR
Etruscan Red-Figured Vase Painting at Caere — ERVC
Etruscan Vase-Painting — EVP
Etrusco Museo Chiusino — M Chius
Etrusco Museo Chiusino — Mus Chius
Etrusco Museo Chiusino — Museo Chius
Etruskische Spiegel — ES
Ettore Majorana International Science Series. Life Sciences — Ettore Majorana Int Sci Ser Life Sci
Ettore Majorana International Science Series. Physical Sciences — Ettore Majorana Int Sci Ser Phys Sci
Ettore Majorana International Science Series. Physical Sciences — Ettore Majorana Internat Sci Ser Phys Sci
Etude. Centre National d'Etudes et d'Experimentation de Machinisme Agricole — Etude Cent Nat Etude Experim Machin Agr
Etude de la Langue Francaise — ELF
Etude du Travail — Etude Trav
Etude Experimentale des Anti-Inflammatoires, Confrontations Pharmacologiques — Etude Exp Anti Inflammatoires Confront Pharmacol
Etude Speciale. Ministere des Richesses Naturelles du Quebec — Etude Spec Minist Richesses Nat Que
Etudes — Et
Etudes — Etu
Etudes Administratives — ETA
Etudes Africaines du CRISP (Centre de Recherche et d'Information Socio-Politique) — Etud Afr CRISP
Etudes Anglaises — EA
Etudes Anglaises — EAn
Etudes Anglaises — Et Ang
Etudes Anglaises — Et Angl
Etudes Anglaises — EtA
Etudes Anglaises — Etud Ang
Etudes Anglaises — Etud Angl
Etudes Anglaises — Etud Anglaises
Etudes Arabes — Et Ar
Etudes Archeologiques — EArch
Etudes Asiatiques — EA
Etudes Balkaniques — EB
Etudes Balkaniques — Et Balkan
Etudes Balkaniques — EtBalk
Etudes Balkaniques — EtuB
Etudes Balkaniques — Etud Balk
Etudes Balkaniques Tchecoslovaques — E B Tch
Etudes Balkaniques Tchecoslovaques — EBT
Etudes Balzaciennes — EB
Etudes Bibliques [*Paris*] — EB
Etudes Bibliques — Et B
Etudes Byzantines — EByz
Etudes Byzantines — EtByz
Etudes Camerounaises — Et Camer
Etudes Carmelitaines — Et Carm
Etudes Carmelitaines Historiques et Critiques — ECHC
Etudes Carmelitaines Mystiques et Missionnaires — ECMM
Etudes CEE [*Communaute Economique Europeenne*]. **Serie Agriculture** — Etude CEE Ser Agr
Etudes Celtiques — EC
Etudes Celtiques — ECelt
Etudes Celtiques — Et Celt
Etudes Celtiques — Et Celtiques
Etudes Celtiques — Etudes Celt
Etudes Chypriotes — Et Chypr
Etudes Cinematographiques — Etud Cinema
Etudes Cinematographiques — Etudes Cin
Etudes Classiques — E Cl
Etudes Classiques — ECLA
Etudes Classiques — Et Class
Etudes Classiques — EtCl
Etudes Classiques — EtuC
Etudes Classiques — Etud Cl
Etudes Classiques — Etud Class
Etudes Classiques — Etud Classiq
Etudes Classiques. Faculte des Lettres et Sciences Humaines d'Aix — Et Cl Aix
Etudes Congolaises — Et Cong
Etudes Congolaises — Et Congol
Etudes Corses — ECo
Etudes Creoles — EtCr
Etudes Cretoises — EC
Etudes Cretoises — Et Cret
Etudes Cretoises — Etudes Cret
Etudes Dahomeennes — ED
Etudes Dahomeennes — Et Dahom
Etudes d'Archeologie Classique — EAC
Etudes d'Archeologie Classique — ETAC
Etudes d'Archeologie Orientale [*Clermont-Ganneau*] — EAO
Etudes de la Region Parisienne — Et Region Paris
Etudes de la Region Parisienne — Etud Reg Paris
Etudes de Langue et de Litterature Francaises — ELLF
Etudes de Lettres [*Universite de Lausanne*] — EdL
Etudes de Lettres — EL
Etudes de Lettres — ELet
Etudes de Lettres — EtL
Etudes de Linguistique Appliquee — ELA
Etudes de Litterature Etrangere et Comparee — ELEC
Etudes de Metaphysique et de Morale — EMM
Etudes de Papyrologie — EP
Etudes de Papyrologie — EPap
Etudes de Papyrologie — Et P
Etudes de Papyrologie — Et Pap
Etudes de Papyrologie [*Cairo*] — EtPapyr
Etudes de Philologie, d'Archeologie et d'Histoire Anciennes — E Ph AHA
Etudes de Philologie, d'Archeologie, et d'Histoire Anciennes — EPAHA
Etudes de Philosophie Medievale — E Ph M
Etudes de Philosophie Medievale — EPM
Etudes de Philosophie Medievale — Et de Philos Mediev
Etudes de Philosophie Medievale — Etudes Philos Medievale
Etudes de Planning Familial — Et Planning Familial
Etudes de Presse — EPr
Etudes de Science Religieuse — ESR
Etudes de Theologie, de Philosophie, et d'Histoire — ETPH
Etudes de Theologie et d'Histoire de la Spiritualite — Et Th HS
Etudes de Theologie et d'Histoire de la Spiritualite — ETH
Etudes de Theologie et d'Histoire de la Spiritualite — ETHS
Etudes de Theologie Historique — Et ThH
Etudes d'Economie Rurale — Et Ec Rur
Etudes des Lettres — Et Lettres
Etudes d'Histoire Africaine — Etud Hist Afr
Etudes d'Histoire et de Philosophie Religieuses — EHPh R
Etudes d'Histoire et de Philosophie Religieuses — EHPR
Etudes d'Histoire et de Philosophie Religieuses. Universite de Strausbourg — EHPRUS
Etudes d'Histoire Litteraire et Doctrinale — EHLD
Etudes d'Histoire Moderne et Contemporaine — Et Hist Mod
Etudes d'Histoire Moderne et Contemporaine — Et Hist Mod Contemp

Etudes d'Outre-Mer — Etud OM
Etudes du Conseil Oecumenique — ECOe
Etudes Eburneennes — Et Eburn
Etudes Ecologiques — Etud Ecol
Etudes Economiques — Et Ec
Etudes Economiques et Financieres — Etud Econs et Fins
Etudes Economiques (Mons, Belgium) — Et Econ (Mons)
Etudes Economiques (Mons, Belgium) — Etud Econs (Mons)
Etudes Economiques (Paris) — Etud Econs (Paris)
Etudes Entomologiques — Etudes Entomol
Etudes Epigraphiques et Philologiques — Et Epigr et Philol
Etudes et Commentaires — EeC
Etudes et Conjoncture — Et Conj
Etudes et Conjoncture — Et et Conj
Etudes et Documents. Conseil d'Etat — Et Doc Cons d'Etat
Etudes et Documents (Education Nationale) — Et et Doc (Educ Nat)
Etudes et Documents. Societe d'Histoire et d'Art du Diocese de Meaux — ESHDM
Etudes et Documents Tchadiens — E D Tch
Etudes et Expansion — Et Et Expans
Etudes et Expansion — Etud et Expansion
Etudes et Expansion — SBP
Etudes et Notes d'Information. Direction du Batiment et des Travaux Publics et de la Conjoncture — Et Notes Inform Batiment
Etudes et Recherches. College Dominicain d'Ottawa — ERCDO
Etudes et Recherches en Informatique — Etudes Rech Inform
Etudes et Recherches. Institut de Meteorologie. Part 2. Hydrologie — Etud Rech Inst Meteorol Part 2
Etudes et Statistiques. Banque des Etats de l'Afrique Centrale. Bulletin Mensuel — Et Statist Banque Etats Afr Centr
Etudes et Travaux d'Archeologie Marocaine — ETAM
Etudes et Travaux. Ecole Marocaine d'Agriculture. Publication — Etud Trav Ec Maroc Agric Publ
Etudes et Travaux. Travaux du Centre d'Archeologie Mediterraneenne de l'Academie Polonaise de Sciences [*Warsaw*] — ET
Etudes et Travaux [*Studia i Prace*]. Travaux du Centre d'Archeologie Mediterraneenne de l'Academie Polonaise de Sciences — Et Trav
Etudes Foreziennes — EF
Etudes Francais — Etud Fr
Etudes Francaises — Et Fr
Etudes Francaises — Et Franc
Etudes Francaises — Etud Fran
Etudes Francaises — Etud Franc
Etudes Francaises — Etudes Franc
Etudes Franciscaines — EF
Etudes Franciscaines — EFran
Etudes Franciscaines — EtF
Etudes Franciscaines [*Blois*] — EtFranc
Etudes Franciscaines. Revue Mensuelle — Et Francisc
Etudes Freudiennes — Etud Freud
Etudes Gaulliennes — Et Gaul
Etudes Generales. Societe d'Histoire de l'Eglise d'Alsace — EGSHEA
Etudes Germaniques — EG
Etudes Germaniques — EGerm
Etudes Germaniques — Et Germ
Etudes Germaniques — Etud Ger
Etudes Germaniques — Etud Germaniques
Etudes Gregoriennes — Et Gr
Etudes Gregoriennes — Et Greg
Etudes Guineennes — Et Guin
Etudes Haguenoviennes — EH
Etudes Historiques — Et Hist
Etudes Historiques de Droit Canonique — Etud Hist Droit Canon
Etudes Historiques. Nouvelle Serie — Et Hist
Etudes Hongroises — Et Hong
Etudes Indo-Europeennes — EtIE
Etudes Internationales — Et Int
Etudes Internationales — Etud Int
Etudes Internationales — Etud Internat
Etudes/Inuit/Studies — EINS
Etudes Irlandaises — EI
Etudes Irlandaises — Etud Irland
Etudes Italiennes — EI
Etudes Italiennes — Et It
Etudes Italiennes — Et Ital
Etudes Italiennes — Etud Ital
Etudes Juives — Et J
Etudes Limousines — Etud Limousines
Etudes Linguistiques — ELing
Etudes Litteraires — ELit
Etudes Litteraires — Etud Lit
Etudes Maliennes — Et Mal
Etudes Maliennes — Etud Maliennes
Etudes Mariales [*Paris*] — EtMar
Etudes Mariales — Etud Mar
Etudes Mensuelles sur l'Economie et les Finances de la Syrie et des Pays Arabes [*Damascus*] — EMPA
Etudes Mongoles — E Mong
Etudes Musulmanes — Et Mu
Etudes Normandes — Et Normandes
Etudes Numismatiques — EN
Etudes Orientales — Et Or
Etudes Orientales. Institut Francaise d'Archeologie de Stamboul — Et O
Etudes Papyrologiques — EP
Etudes Peloponnesiennes — EP
Etudes Peloponnesiennes — Et Pelop
Etudes Philosophiques — EP
Etudes Philosophiques — EPh
Etudes Philosophiques — Etud Phil
Etudes Philosophiques — Etud Philos
Etudes Philosophiques et Litteraires — EPL
Etudes Polemologiques — Et Polemol
Etudes Prehistoriques — Et Pr Hist
Etudes Prehistoriques et Protohistoriques des Pays de la Loire — Et Loire
Etudes Preliminaires aux Religions Orientales dans l'Empire Romain — EPRO
Etudes Preliminaires aux Religions Orientales dans l'Empire Romain — EPRODER
Etudes Preliminaires aux Religions Orientales dans l'Empire Romain — EPROER
Etudes Psychotherapiques — EPTQAM
Etudes Psychotherapiques — Etud Psychother
Etudes Rabelaisiennes — ER
Etudes Rabelaisiennes — ERab
Etudes Religiouses, Philosophiques, Historiques, et Litteraire — ERPH
Etudes Rhodaniennes — ER
Etudes Romaines — Et Rom
Etudes Romanes de Brno — ERB
Etudes Romanes de Brno — ERBr
Etudes Romanes de Lund — ERL
Etudes Roussillonnaises — Et Rou
Etudes Rurales — Et Rur
Etudes Rurales — Etud Rur
Etudes Rurales — Etud Rurales
Etudes Salesiennes — Et Sal
Etudes Scientifiques — Etud Sci
Etudes Senegalaises — Et Seneg
Etudes Slaves and Est-Europeenes. Slavic and East European Studies — ESEE
Etudes Slaves et Est-Europeennes — ESI
Etudes Slaves et Est-Europeennes — Etud Slav E
Etudes Slaves et Est-Europeennes/Slavic and East-European Studies — Et Slav Est Eur
Etudes Slaves et Roumaines — ESLR
Etudes Slaves et Roumaines — ESR
Etudes Sociales — Etud Socs
Etudes Sociales (Paris) — Et Soc (Paris)
Etudes Sovietiques — ESov
Etudes Statistiques (Brussels) — Etud Statis (Brussels)
Etudes Statistiques. Institut National de la Statistique et des Etudes Economiques — Etude Stat Inst Nat Stat
Etudes Sud-Arabiques — ESA
Etudes Suisses d'Histoire Generale — ESHG
Etudes Suisses d'Histoire Generale — Et Suisses Hist Gen
Etudes sur le XVIIIe Siecle — Etud XVIIIe Siecle
Etudes sur les Soins et le Service Infirmier — Etud Soins Serv Infirm
Etudes sur l'Histoire des Religions — EH Rel
Etudes sur Pezenas et l'Herault — Et Pezenas
Etudes Techniques et Economiques. Seria E. Hydrogeologie (Institut de Geologie et Geophysique) — Etud Tech Econ Ser E (Inst Geol Geophys)
Etudes Thasiennes — Et Thas
Etudes Theologiques et Religieuses — E T Rel
Etudes Theologiques et Religieuses — EThR
Etudes Theologiques et Religieuses — ETR
Etudes Theologiques et Religieuses — Etud Theol
Etudes Traditionnelles — ET
Etudes Traditionnelles — Etud Trad
Etudes Tsiganes — Et Tsi
Etudes Tsiganes — ETs
Etudes Voltaiques — Et Volt
Etudes Zairoises — Et Zair
Etudes Zairoises — Etud Zairoises
Etymologicum Magnum — EM
Etymologicum Magnum — Etym Mag
Etyudy po Biogeokhimii i Agrokhimii Elementov-Biofilov — Etyudy Biogeokhim Agrokhim Elem Biofilov
ETZ. Elektrotechnische Zeitschrift — ETZ Elektrotech Z
ETZ. Elektrotechnische Zeitschrift. Archiv — ETZ Arch
ETZ. Elektrotechnische Zeitschrift. Ausgabe A [*Germany*] — ETZ Elektrotech Z Ausg A
ETZ-A. Elektrotechnische Zeitschrift. Zeitschrift fuer Elektrische Energietechnik — ETZ A Elektrotech Z
ETZ-B. Elektrotechnische Zeitschrift — ETZ B Elektrotech Z
EUCARPIA [*European Association for Research on Plant Breeding*] **Congres. Association Europeenne pour l'Amelioration des Plantes** — EUCARPIA Congr Assoc Eur Amelior Plant
EUCARPIA [*European Association for Research on Plant Breeding*] **Congres. Association Europeenne pour l'Amelioration des Plantes** — EUCRA9
Eucharistisch Tijdschrift — Euch Tijd
Euclides — Eu
Eudora Welty Newsletter — Eu W N
Eugene O'Neill Newsletter — EON
Eugenical News — Eugen News
Eugenics Laboratory. Lecture Series — Eugen Lab Lect Ser
Eugenics Laboratory. Memoirs — Eugen Lab Mem
Eugenics Laboratory. Memoirs — ULGLAM
Eugenics Quarterly — Eug Q
Eugenics Quarterly — Eugen Q
Eugenics Quarterly — EUGQAQ
Eugenics Review — Eug R
Eugenics Review — Eugen Rev
Eugenics Review — Eugenics R

Eugenics Review — EUREA
Eugenics Review — EUREAB
Eugenics Society Symposia — Eugen Soc Symp
Eugenics Society Symposia — EUSSBP
Euhemer — Euh
Euhemer. Zeszyty Filozoficzne — Euh F
Euhemer. Zeszyty Historyczne — Euh H
Eukleides. Ekdose tes Ellenikes Mathemates Etairias. A. Agymnasio. Nea Seira [*A publication*] — Eukleides A Agymnasio NS
Eul Ji Medical Journal — Eul Ji Med J
Eulenburgs Encyklopaedische Jahrbuecher der Gesamten Heilkunde — Eulenburg Enz Jbb Heilkde
Eulenspiegel-Jahrbuch — Eul J
EULEP [*European Late Effects Project Group*] **Newsletter** — EULEP Newsl
Eunomia. Ephemeridis Listy Filologicke. Supplementum — EELFS
Euntes Docete — ED
Euntes Docete [*Rome*] — EuntDoc
Euphoria et Cacophoria [*International Edition*] — EUCADT
Euphoria et Cacophoria (International Edition) — Euphoria Cacophoria (Int Ed)
Euphorion — Eu
Euphorion — Eup
Euphorion — Euph
Euphytica — EUPHAA
Euphytica. Netherlands Journal of Plant Breeding — Euphyt
Eurafrica et Tribune de Tiers-Monde — Eurafr Trib Tiers-Monde
Eurasia Septentrionalis Antiqua — ESA
EURATOM [*European Atomic Energy Community*] **Bulletin** [*Belgium*] — EURATOM Bull
EURATOM. Bulletin of the European Atomic Energy Community — EURATOM Bull Eur At Energy Community
Euratom Review — Euratom Rev
EURATOM Review. European Atomic Energy Community [*Belgium*] — EURATOM Rev Eur At Energy Community
Euriam Bulteni — Euriam Bul
Eurisotop Office Information Booklet — Euristop Off Inf Bookl
Euro Abstracts [*Database*] — EABS
Euro Abstracts. Section 2. Coal and Steel [*Luxembourg*] — Euro Abstr Sect 2
Euro Cooperation — Euro Coop
Euro Courses. Advanced Scientific Techniques — Euro Courses Adv Sci Tech
Euro Courses. Reliability and Risk Analysis — Euro Courses Reliab Risk Anal
Euro Reports and Studies — Euro Rep Stud
Euro-Asia Business Review — EuroAsia Bus Rev
Euroclay — EUCLB
Eurodoc — EQA
Euromarket Surveys. Australian/New Zealand Series — Eurom Surveys Aust NZ Series
Euromarkt Nieuws — EFI
Euromarkt Nieuws — EN
Euromath Bulletin — Euromath Bull
Euromech-Colloquium — Euromech Colloq
Euromicro Journal [*Netherlands*] — Euromicro J
Euromicro Newsletters — Euromicro Newsl
Euromoney — EME
Euromoney — ERM
Euromoney — EU
Euromoney — EUR
Euromoney Trade Finance Report — EUF
EuroMonitor Review — Euro Mon
Euronet News — ERH
Europa — E
Europa Chemie — Europ Chem
Europa Chemie — EXW
Europa Domani — Eur Domani
Europa Ethnica — Eur Ethn
Europa Ethnica — Eur Ethnica
Europa Informatie, Buitenlandse Betrekkingen — EIN
Europa Letteraria — EL
Europa Letteraria — ELet
Europa Medica (French Edition) — Eur Med (Fr Ed)
Europa Medica (Italian Edition) — Eur Med (Ital Ed)
Europa Medica (Spanish Edition) — Eur Med (Span Ed)
Europa Nucleare — Eur Nucl
Europa Orientale — Eur Orient
Europa van Morgen — EUL
Europa-Archiv — Eur A
Europa-Archiv — Eur Arch
Europa-Archiv — EUV
Europa-Archiv. Europaeischer Austauschdienst — EA
Europaeische Chirurgische Forschung — Eur Chir Forsch
Europaeische Chirurgische Forschung — EUSRBM
Europaeische Gefluegelkonferenz. Vortraege — Eur Gefluegelkonf Vortr
Europaeische Gesprache — EG
Europaeische Grundrechte — Eur Grundrechte
Europaeische Hochschulschriften — EH
Europaeische Hochschulschriften — EurH
Europaeische Hochschulschriften. Reihe 8. Chemie. Abteilung A. Pharmazie — Eur Hochschulschr Reihe 8 Chem Abt A
Europaeische Hochschulschriften. Reihe 8. Chemie. Abteilung B. Biochemie — Eur Hochschulschr Reihe 8 Chem Abt B
Europaeische Konferenz ueber Mikrozirkulation — Eur Konf Mikrozirk
Europaeische Literatur — EL
Europaeische Osten — EO
Europaeische Osten — Eur Osten
Europaeische Patentanmeldung — Eur Patentanmeld
Europaeische Revue — Eur Rev
Europaeische Revue — Europ Rev
Europaeische Rundschau — Eur Rdsch
Europaeische Rundschau — Europ Rdsch
Europaeische Sicherheit — Eur Sicherh
Europaeische Textilindustrie — Eur Textilind
Europaeische Wehrkunde — Eur Wehrkunde
Europaeische Wehrkunde — Europ Wehrkunde
Europaeische Zeitschrift der Krankenhauspharmazie — Eur Z Krankenhauspharm
Europaeische Zeitschrift fuer Cancerologie — Eur Z Cancerol
Europaeische Zeitschrift fuer Forstpathologie — Eur Z Forstpathologie
Europaeische Zeitschrift fuer Kartoffelforschung — Eur Z Kartoffelforsch
Europaeischer Wissenschaftsdienst — EWD
Europaeisches Abwasser- und Abfallsymposium — Eur Abwasser Abfallsymp
Europaeisches Abwasser- und Abfall-Symposium EAS — Eur Abwasser Abfall Symp EAS
Europaeisches Gespraech — Eu G
Europaeisches Symposium fuer Pulvermetallurgie. Vorabdrucke — Eur Symp Pulvermetall Vorabdrucke
Europe — Eu
Europe — EUP
Europe — Eur
Europe and Oil — EO
Europe and Oil [*Germany*] — Eur Oil
Europe Archiv. Zeitschrift fuer Internationale Politik — Europa Arch
Europe Daily Bulletin — Europe Daily Bull
Europe de l'Est — Eur Est
Europe de l'Est et Union Sovietique — Eur Est Union Soviet
Europe du Medicament. Realities et Ambitions. Colloque DPHM-INSERM — Eur Med Colloq DPHM INSERM
Europe en Formation — Eur en Formation
Europe France Outremer — Eur Fr Outremer
Europe France Outremer — Eur France OM
Europe in the Middle Ages. Selected Studies [*Elsevier Book Series*] — EMA
Europe Letteraria — Eu L
Europe Nouvelle — EN
Europe Nouvelle — Eur Nouv
Europe Orientale — EO
Europe Outremer — Eur Outremer
Europe Outremer — Europe O Mer
Europe Outremer. Revue Internationale — BHI
Europe Review — Eur Rev
Europe. Revue Litteraire Mensuelle — Eur Rev Lit
Europe Sud-Est. Cinquieme Serie — Eur Sud-Est 5e Ser
European Academy of Surface Technology Kongress — Eur Acad Surf Technol Kongr
European Amyloidosis Research Symposium — Eur Amyloidosis Res Symp
European and Mediterranean Plant Protection Organization. Publications. Series A — Eur Mediterr Plant Prot Organ Publ Ser A
European and Mediterranean Plant Protection Organization. Publications. Series D — Eur Mediterr Plant Prot Organ Publ Ser D
European Antiproton Symposium — Eur Antiproton Symp
European Applied Research Reports — Eur Appl Res Rep
European Applied Research Reports. Environment and Natural Resources Section — Eur Appl Res Rep Environ Nat Resour Sect
European Applied Research Reports. Nuclear Science and Technology Section — EARRD
European Applied Research Reports. Nuclear Science and Technology Section — Eur Appl Res Rep-Nucl Sci Technol Sect
European Archives of Oto-Rhino-Laryngology [*Heidelberg*] — Eur Arch Otorhinolaryngol
European Archives of Oto-Rhino-Laryngology. Supplement [*Berlin*] — Eur Arch Otorhinolaryngol Suppl
European Archives of Psychiatry and Clinical Neuroscience — Eur Arch Psychiatry Clin Neurosci
European Archives of Psychiatry and Neurological Sciences — Eur Arch Psychiatry Neurol Sci
European Association for Animal Production. Publication — EAAPAN
European Association for Animal Production. Publication — Eur Assoc Anim Prod Publ
European Association for Architectural Education. Newsheet — European Assocn for Archtl Education Newsheet
European Association for Cancer Research. Proceedings. Meeting — Eur Assoc Cancer Res Proc Meet
European Association for Research on Plant Breeding. Proceedings. Congress — Eur Assoc Res Plant Breed Proc Congr
European Association of Poison Control Centres. International Congress — Eur Assoc Poison Control Cent Int Congr
European Astronomical Meeting — Eur Astron Meet
European Atomic Energy Community. EURATOM Report — Eur At Energy Community EURATOM Rep
European Aviation and Space Medicine Congress — Eur Aviat Space Med Congr
European Bioenergetics Conference — Eur Bioenerg Conf
European Biomass Conference — Eur Biomass Conf
European Biophysics Congress. Proceedings — Eur Biophys Congr Proc
European Biophysics Journal — Eur Biophys J
European Biotechnology Information Project Bibliographic Database — EBIP
European Brewery Convention. Monograph — Eur Brew Conv Monogr
European Brewery Convention. Proceedings of the Congress — Eur Brew Conv Proc Congr
European Business — Europ Busin
European Ceramic Society. Journal — Eur Ceram Soc J
European Chemical Industry Ecology and Toxicology Centre. Technical Report — Eur Chem Ind Ecol Toxicol Cent Tech Rep

European Chemical News [*Database*] — ECN
European Chemical News — Eur Chem N
European Chemical News — Eur Chem Ne
European Chemical News [*England*] — Eur Chem News
European Chemical News — EUZ
European Chemical News. Supplement — ECN Sup
European Child and Adolescent Psychiaty — Eur Child Adolesc Psychiatry
European Clinical Section. International Association of Gerontology. Congress. Proceedings — Eur Clin Sect Int Assoc Gerontol Congr Proc
European Coal Data Bank — COALDATA
European Coal Utilisation Conference. Proceedings — Eur Coal Util Conf Proc
European Coating Symposium — Eur Coat Symp
European Colloquium on Current Trends in Quantum Chemistry. Final Report — Eur Colloq Curr Trends Quantum Chem Final Rep
European Colloquium on Echinoderms — Eur Colloq Echinoderms
European Communities Bulletin — Eur Commun Bull
European Communities Commission — Europe Communities Comm
European Communities Economic and Social Committee. Bulletin — Eur Commun Econ Soc Comm Bull
European Communities Index — EC Index
European Community — Eur Community
European Community — Europe Com
European Community (English Edition) — Eur Community (Engl Ed)
European Company for the Chemical Processing of Irradiated Fuels. Eurochemic Technical Report ETR — Eur Co Chem Process Irradiat Fuels Eurochemic Tech Rep ETR
European Conference on Advanced Materials and Processes — Eur Conf Adv Mater Processes
European Conference on Analytical Chemistry — Eur Conf Anal Chem
European Conference on Animal Blood Groups and Biochemical Polymorphism — Eur Conf Anim Blood Groups Biochem Polymorph
European Conference on Animal Blood Groups and Biochemical Polymorphism — Eur Conf Anim Blood Groups Biochem Polymorphism
European Conference on Astronomy — Eur Conf Astron
European Conference on Chemical Vapour Deposition — Eur Conf Chem Vap Deposition
European Conference on Chemistry and the Environment — Eur Conf Chem Environ
European Conference on Coal Liquid Mixtures — Eur Conf Coal Liq Mixtures
European Conference on Composite Materials — Eur Conf Compos Mater
European Conference on Controlled Fusion and Plasma Physics. Contributions — Eur Conf Controlled Fusion Plasma Phys Contrib
European Conference on Controlled Fusion and Plasma Physics. Proceedings — Eur Conf Controlled Fusion Plasma Phys Proc
European Conference on Electronic Design Automation — Eur Conf Electron Des Autom
European Conference on Flammability and Fire Retardants — Eur Conf Flammability Fire Retard
European Conference on Integrated Optics — Eur Conf Integr Opt
European Conference on Internal Friction and Ultrasonic Attenuation in Solids. Proceedings — Eur Conf Intern Frict Ultrason Attenuation Solids Proc
European Conference on Microcirculation — EKMZAD
European Conference on Microcirculation — Eur Conf Microcirc
European Conference on Mixing. Proceedings — Eur Conf Mixing Proc
European Conference on Optical Communication — Eur Conf Opt Commun
European Conference on Optical Fibre Communication — Eur Conf Opt Fibre Commun
European Conference on Optics, Optical Systems, and Applications — Eur Conf Opt Opt Syst Appl
European Conference on Organized Organic Thin Films — Eur Conf Organ Org Thin Films
European Conference on Particle Physics. Proceedings — Eur Conf Part Phys Proc
European Conference on Prenatal Diagnosis of Genetic Disorders. Proceedings — Eur Conf Prenatal Diagn Genet Disord Proc
European Conference on Spectroscopy of Biological Molecules — Eur Conf Spectrosc Biol Mol
European Congress of Allergology and Clinical Immunology. Proceedings — Eur Congr Allergol Clin Immunol
European Congress of Biopharmaceutics and Pharmacokinetics — Eur Congr Biopharm Pharmacokinet
European Congress of Biotechnology — Eur Congr Biotechnol
European Congress of Biotechnology. Preprints — Eur Congr Biotechnol Prepr
European Congress of Electron Microscopy — Eur Congr Electron Microsc
European Congress of Perinatal Medicine — Eur Congr Perinat Med
European Congress on Magnesium — Eur Congr Magnesium
European Congress on Sleep Research — Eur Congr Sleep Res
European Consortium for Mathematics in Industry — European Consort Math Indust
European Cosmetic Markets — Eur Cos Mkt
European Cotton Industry Statistics — Eur Cot Ind Stat
European Cytokine Network — Eur Cytokine Netw
European Demographic Information Bulletin — Eur Demographic Info Bul
European Demographic Information Bulletin — Europ Demogr Inform B
European Demographic Information Bulletin (The Hague) — Eur Demographic Info Bul (Hague)
European Dialysis and Transplant Association - European Renal Association. Proceedings — Eur Dial Transplant Assoc Eur Renal Assoc Proc
European Dialysis and Transplant Association. Proceedings — Eur Dial Transplant Assoc Proc
European Dialysis and Transplant Association. Proceedings of the Congress — Eur Dial Transplant Assoc Proc Congr
European Digest — Eur Dig
European Drag Reduction Meeting — Eur Drag Reduct Meet
European Drosophila Research Conference — Eur Drosophila Res Conf
European Drug Metabolism Workshop — Eur Drug Metab Workshop
European Economic and Political Survey — EEPS
European Economic and Political Survey — Europ Econ and Pol Survey
European Economic Community. Bulletin of the European Communities — EEC Bull
European Economic Community. Bulletin of the European Communities. Supplement — EEC Bull S
European Economic Review — ECR
European Economic Review — EEH
European Economic Review — EER
European Economic Review — Eur Econ R
European Economic Review — Europ Econ R
European Economy — Eur Economy
European Electric Propulsion Conference — Eur Electr Propul Conf
European Electronics — ELE
European Electro-Optics Conference — Eur Electro Opt Conf
European Electro-Optics Markets and Technology Conference — Eur Electro Opt Mark Technol Conf
European Electro-Optics Markets and Technology Conference. Proceedings — Eur Electro Opt Mark Technol Conf Proc
European Energy Prospects to 1990 — Eur Energy
European Energy Report — EFD
European Federation of Chemical Engineering. Publication Series — Eur Fed Chem Eng Publ Ser
European File — EUFID
European File [*Luxembourg*] — Eur File
European Food Symposium — Eur Food Symp
European Free Trade Association. Bulletin — EFTA
European Geophysical Society. Meeting. Abstracts — Eur Geophys Soc Meet Abstr
European Great Projects. International Seminar. Proceedings — Eur Great Proj Int Semin Proc
European Group on Fracture Publication — Eur Group Fract Publ
European Heart Journal — EHJODF
European Heart Journal — Eur Heart J
European History Quarterly — PEHQ
European Human Rights Reports — EHRR
European Industrial Relations Review — EIR
European Industrial Relations Review — EIRR
European Industrial Relations Review — EUG
European Industrial Relations Review — Eur Ind Rel R
European Industrial Relations Review — European Ind Relations Rev
European Industrial Research Management Association. EIRMA Conference Papers — Eur Ind Res Manage Assoc EIRMA Conf Pap
European Information Service — European Inf Serv
European Inland Fisheries Advisory Commission. Technical Paper — Eur Inland Fish Advis Comm Tech Pap
European Intellectual Property Review — Eur Int Pr R
European Intellectual Property Review — Eur Intell Prop R
European Intellectual Property Review — Eur Intellectual Property Rev
European Intellectual Property Review — Europ Intell Prop Rev
European Journal of Anaesthesiology — Eur J Anaesthesiol
European Journal of Anaesthesiology. Supplement — Eur J Anaesthesiol Suppl
European Journal of Applied Mathematics — European J Appl Math
European Journal of Applied Microbiology — EJAMA
European Journal of Applied Microbiology — Eur J App M
European Journal of Applied Microbiology — Eur J Appl Microbiol
European Journal of Applied Microbiology and Biotechnology — Eur J Appl Microbiol Biotechnol
European Journal of Applied Physiology and Occupational Physiology — EJAPC
European Journal of Applied Physiology and Occupational Physiology — EJAPCK
European Journal of Applied Physiology and Occupational Physiology — Eur J A Phy
European Journal of Applied Physiology and Occupational Physiology — Eur J Appl Physiol
European Journal of Applied Physiology and Occupational Physiology — Eur J Appl Physiol Occup Physiol
European Journal of Biochemistry — EJBCAI
European Journal of Biochemistry — Eur J Bioch
European Journal of Biochemistry — Eur J Biochem
European Journal of Cancer — EJCAAH
European Journal of Cancer — Eur J Canc
European Journal of Cancer — Eur J Cancer
European Journal of Cancer and Clinical Oncology — EJCOD
European Journal of Cancer and Clinical Oncology — EJCODS
European Journal of Cancer and Clinical Oncology — Eur J Cancer Clin Oncol
European Journal of Cancer. Part A — Eur J Cancer Part A
European Journal of Cancer. Part B. Oral Oncology — Eur J Cancer B Oral Oncol
European Journal of Cancer. Part B. Oral Oncology — Eur J Cancer Part B
European Journal of Cancer Prevention — Eur J Cancer Prev
European Journal of Cardiology — EJCDBR
European Journal of Cardiology — Eur J Cardiol
European Journal of Cardio-Thoracic Surgery — Eur J Cardiothorac Surg
European Journal of Cell Biology — EJCBDN
European Journal of Cell Biology — Eur J Cell Biol
European Journal of Cell Biology. Supplement — Eur J Cell Biol Suppl
European Journal of Cellular Plastics — Eur J Cell Plast
European Journal of Chiropractic — Eur J Chiro
European Journal of Clinical and Biological Research [*France*] — Eur J Clin Biol Res
European Journal of Clinical Chemistry and Clinical Biochemistry — Eur J Clin Chem Clin Biochem

European Journal of Clinical Investigation — EJCIB8
European Journal of Clinical Investigation — Eur J Cl In
European Journal of Clinical Investigation — Eur J Clin Invest
European Journal of Clinical Microbiology — Eur J Clin Microbiol
European Journal of Clinical Microbiology and Infectious Diseases — Eur J Clin Microbiol Infect Dis
European Journal of Clinical Nutrition — Eur J Clin Nutr
European Journal of Clinical Pharmacology — EJCPA
European Journal of Clinical Pharmacology — EJCPAS
European Journal of Clinical Pharmacology — Eur J Cl Ph
European Journal of Clinical Pharmacology — Eur J Clin Pharmacol
European Journal of Combinatorics — Eur J Comb
European Journal of Combinatorics — European J Combin
European Journal of Disorders of Communication — Eur J Disord Commun
European Journal of Drug Metabolism and Pharmacokinetics — EJDPD
European Journal of Drug Metabolism and Pharmacokinetics — EJDPD2
European Journal of Drug Metabolism and Pharmacokinetics — Eur J Drug Metab Pharmacokinet
European Journal of Education — Eur J Educ
European Journal of Education — European J Ed
European Journal of Emergency Medicine — Eur J Emerg Med
European Journal of Endocrinology — Eur J Endocrinol
European Journal of Engineering Education — Eur J Eng Educ
European Journal of Engineering Education — European J Engineering Ed
European Journal of Epidemiology — Eur J Epidemiol
European Journal of Experimental Musculoskeletal Research — Eur J Exp Musculoskeletal Res
European Journal of Fertility and Sterility — Eur J Fertil Steril
European Journal of Forest Pathology — EJFPA
European Journal of Forest Pathology — EJFPA9
European Journal of Forest Pathology — Eur J For Pathol
European Journal of Gastroenterology and Hepatology — Eur J Gastroenterol Hepatol
European Journal of Gynaecological Oncology — Eur J Gynaecol Oncol
European Journal of Haematology — Eur J Haematol
European Journal of Haematology. Supplementum — Eur J Haematol Suppl
European Journal of Histochemistry — Eur J Histochem
European Journal of Hospital Pharmacy — Eur J Hosp Pharm
European Journal of Human Genetics — Eur J Hum Genet
European Journal of Immunogenetics — Eur J Imm
European Journal of Immunogenetics — Eur J Immunogenet
European Journal of Immunology — EJIMAF
European Journal of Immunology — Eur J Immun
European Journal of Immunology — Eur J Immunol
European Journal of Intensive Care Medicine — Eur J I Car
European Journal of Intensive Care Medicine — Eur J Intensive Care Med
European Journal of Marketing — EJM
European Journal of Marketing — Eur J Mktg
European Journal of Mass Spectrometry in Biochemistry, Medicine, and Environmental Research — Eur J Mass Spectrom Biochem Med Environ Res
European Journal of Mechanics. A. Solids — European J Mech A Solids
European Journal of Mechanics. B. Fluids — European J Mech B Fluids
European Journal of Medical Research — Eur J Med Res
European Journal of Medicinal Chemistry — Eur J Med Chem
European Journal of Medicinal Chemistry. Chimica Therapeutica — Eur J Med Chem Chim Ther
European Journal of Medicinal Chemistry. Chimie Therapeutique — EJMCA5
European Journal of Mineralogy — Eur J Mineral
European Journal of Morphology — Eur J Morphol
European Journal of Neuroscience — Eur J Neurosci
European Journal of Nuclear Medicine — EJNMD9
European Journal of Nuclear Medicine — Eur J Nucl Med
European Journal of Obstetrics and Gynecology [*Later, European Journal of Obstetrics, Gynecology, and Reproductive Biology*] — Eur J Obstet Gynecol
European Journal of Obstetrics, Gynecology, and Reproductive Biology — EOGRAL
European Journal of Obstetrics, Gynecology, and Reproductive Biology — Eur J Obstet Gynecol Reprod Biol
European Journal of Operational Research — EJOR
European Journal of Operational Research — Eur J Oper Res
European Journal of Operational Research — European J Oper Res
European Journal of Ophthalmology — Eur J Ophthalmol
European Journal of Oral Sciences — Eur J Oral Sci
European Journal of Orthodontics — EJOODK
European Journal of Orthodontics — Eur J Orthod
European Journal of Parapsychology — EJP
European Journal of Pediatric Surgery — Eur J Ped S
European Journal of Pediatric Surgery — Eur J Pediatr Surg
European Journal of Pediatrics — EJPEDT
European Journal of Pediatrics — Eur J Ped
European Journal of Pediatrics — Eur J Pediatr
European Journal of Pharmaceutics and Biopharmaceutics — Eur J Pharm Biopharm
European Journal of Pharmacology — EJPHAZ
European Journal of Pharmacology — Eur J Pharm
European Journal of Pharmacology — Eur J Pharmacol
European Journal of Pharmacology. Environmental Toxicology and Pharmacology Section — Eur J Pharmacol Environ Toxicol Pharmacol Sect
European Journal of Pharmacology. Molecular Pharmacology Section — Eur J Pharmacol Mol Pharmacol Sect
European Journal of Pharmacology. Molecular Pharmacology Section — Eur J Ph-Mo
European Journal of Physics — Eur J Phys
European Journal of Physics — European J Phys
European Journal of Physiology — Eur J Physiol
European Journal of Political Research — Europ J Polit Res
European Journal of Population — Eur J Popul
European Journal of Radiology — Eur J Radiol
European Journal of Respiratory Diseases — EJRDD2
European Journal of Respiratory Diseases — Eur J Respir Dis
European Journal of Respiratory Diseases. Supplement — EJRSDD
European Journal of Respiratory Diseases. Supplement — Eur J Respir Dis Suppl
European Journal of Rheumatology and Inflammation — Eur J Rheumatol Inflamm
European Journal of Rheumatology and Inflammation — Eur J Rheumatol Inflammation
European Journal of Science Education — EJSEDA
European Journal of Science Education — Eur J Sci Educ
European Journal of Science Education — European J of Science Ed
European Journal of Social Psychology — Eur J Soc P
European Journal of Social Psychology — Europ J Soc Psychol
European Journal of Sociology — Eur J Sociol
European Journal of Solid State and Inorganic Chemistry — Eur J Solid State Inorg Chem
European Journal of Steroids — Eur J Steroids
European Journal of Steroids — JEPSBL
European Journal of Surgery — Eur J Surg
European Journal of Surgery. Supplement — Eur J Surg Suppl
European Journal of Surgical Oncology — Eur J Surg Oncol
European Journal of Toxicology — Eur J Toxicol
European Journal of Toxicology — JETOAS
European Journal of Toxicology and Environmental Hygiene — Eur J Toxicol Environ Hyg
European Journal of Vascular and Endovascular Surgery — Eur J Vasc Endovasc Surg
European Judaism — EJ
European Law Review — EL Rev
European Law Review — ELR
European Law Review — Europ Law R
European Law Review — European L Rev
European Linguistics. A Collection of Facsimile Reprints — Eur L Facs
European Marine Biology Symposium. Proceedings — Eur Mar Biol Symp Proc
European Materials Research Society Meeting. Symposium — Eur Mater Res Soc Meet Symp
European Materials Research Society Monographs — Eur Mater Res Soc Monogr
European Meeting on Wildfowl Conservation. Proceedings — Eur Meet Wildfowl Conserv Proc
European Monographs in Health Education Research — Eur Monogr Hlth Educ Res
European Neurology — Eur Neurol
European Neuropsychopharmacology — Eur Neuropsychopharmacol
European Numismatics — EN
European Oil and Gas Magazine [*Germany*] — Eur Oil Gas Mag
European Organization for Nuclear Research. High-Energy Reaction Analysis Group. Report — Eur Organ Nucl Res High Energy React Anal Group Rep
European Organization for Nuclear Research. Report — Eur Organ Nucl Res Rep
European Organization for Nuclear Research. Symposium on High-Energy Accelerators and Pion Physics. Proceedings — Eur Organ Nucl Res Symp High Energy Accel Pion Phys Proc
European Organization for Research on Fluorine and Dental Caries Prevention. Proceedings of the Congress — Eur Organ Res Fluorine Dent Caries Prev Proc Congr
European Organization for Research on the Treatment of Cancer. Monograph Series — Eur Organ Res Treat Cancer Monog Ser
European Organization for Research on the Treatment of Cancer. Monograph Series — Eur Organ Treat Cancer Monogr Ser
European Organization for Research on Treatment of Cancer (EORTC). Monograph Series — Eur Organ Res Treat Cancer (EORTC) Monogr Ser
European Paediatric Haematology and Oncology — Eur Paed H
European Paediatric Haematology and Oncology — Eur Paediatr Haematol Oncol
European Patent Application — Eur Pat Appl
European Patent Office. European Patent Application — Eur Pat Off Eur Pat Appl
European Peptide Symposium. Proceedings — Eur Pept Symp Proc
European Photochemistry Association. Newsletter — Eur Photochem Assoc Newsl
European Photography — European Photogr
European Photovoltaic Solar Energy Conference — Eur Photovoltaic Sol Energy Conf
European Plastics News — EPN
European Plastics News — EUN
European Plastics News — EUPNB
European Plastics News — Eur Plas N
European Plastics News — Eur Plast News
European Political Data Newsletter — Eur Pol Data Newsl
European Polymer Journal — EUPJA
European Polymer Journal — Eur Polym J
European Polymers Paint Colour Journal — Eur Polym Paint Colour J
European Potato Journal — Eur Pot J
European Potato Journal — Eur Potato J
European Poultry Science — Eur Poult Sci
European Powder Metallurgy Symposium — Eur Powder Metall Symp
European Quarterly — EQ
European Radiology — Eur Radiol
European Regional Technical Conference. Plastics and Processing — Eur Reg Tech Conf Plast Process

European Report — ER
European Research — ERS
European Research — Eur Res
European Research — Eur Research
European Research — Euro Res
European Research. Marketing, Opinion, Advertising — ERW
European Respiratory Journal — Eur Respir J
European Respiratory Journal. Supplement — Eur Respir J Suppl
European Review for Medical and Pharmacological Sciences — Eur Rev Med Pharmacol Sci
European Review of Agricultural Economics — Eur Rev Agric Econ
European Review of Agricultural Economics — Europ R Agric Econ
European Review of Agricultural Economics — EVA
European Review of Endocrinology — Eur Rev Endocrinol
European Review of Endocrinology. Supplement — Eur Rev Endocrinol Suppl
European Rubber Journal — Eur Rub Jl
European Rubber Journal — Eur Rubb J
European Rubber Journal — Eur Rubber J
European Rubber Journal — EURJA
European Rubber Journal — European Rubber J
European Rubber Journal — IRJ
European Semiconductor Production — Eur Semicond Prod
European Seminar for Sanitary Engineers. Report of the Seminar — Eur Semin Sanit Eng Rep
European Series in Applied and Industrial Mathematics. Controle, Optimisation, et Calcul des Variations — ESAIM Controle Optim Calc Var
European Shielding Information Service Newsletter — Eur Shielding Inf Serv Newsl
European Shipbuilding — Eur Shipbldg
European Shipbuilding — Eur Shipbuild
European Small Business Journal — European Sm Bus J
European Society of Toxicology. Proceedings — Eur Soc Toxicol Proc
European Solid State Device. Research Conference — Eur Solid State Device Res Conf
European Southern Observatory. Bulletin [*Germany*] — Eur South Obs Bull
European Space Agency. Bulletin — Eur Space Agency Bull
European Space Agency. Scientific and Technical Review — Eur Space Agency Sci Tech Rev
European Space Agency. Special Publication ESA SP — Eur Space Agency Spec Publ ESA SP
European Space Agency (Special Publication). ESA SP [*France*] — Euro Space Agency (Spec Publ) ESA SP
European Space Research Organization. Contractor Report — Eur Space Res Organ Contract Rep
European Space Research Organization. Technical Memorandum — Eur Space Res Organ Tech Memo
European Spectroscopy News — Eur Spectrosc News
European Spine Journal — Eur Spine J
European Structural Integrity Society Publication — Eur Struct Integr Soc Publ
European Studies in Law [*Elsevier Book Series*] — ESL
European Studies Newsletter — Europ Stud Newsl
European Studies Review — ESR
European Studies Review — Eur Stud R
European Studies Review — Eur Stud Rev
European Studies Review — Europ Stud R
European Surgical Research — Eur Surg Re
European Surgical Research — Eur Surg Res
European Symposium for Powder Metallurgy. Preprints — Eur Symp Powder Metall Prepr
European Symposium on Basic Research in Gerontology. Lectures — Eur Symp Basic Res Gerontol Lect
European Symposium on Calcified Tissues. Proceedings — Eur Symp Calcif Tissues Proc
European Symposium on Chemical Reaction Engineering — Eur Symp Chem React Eng
European Symposium on Engineering Ceramics. Proceedings — Eur Symp Eng Ceram Proc
European Symposium on Enhanced Oil Recovery — Eur Symp Enhanced Oil Recovery
European Symposium on Hormones and Cell Regulation — Eur Symp Horm Cell Regul
European Symposium on Lindane — Eur Symp Lindane
European Symposium on Marine Biology. Proceedings — Eur Symp Mar Biol Proc
European Symposium on Medical Enzymology. Proceedings — Eur Symp Med Enzymol Proc
European Symposium on Organic Micropollutants in the Aquatic Environment — Eur Symp Org Micropollut Aquat Environ
European Symposium on Polymer Spectroscopy — Eur Symp Polym Spectrosc
European Taxation — EFF
European Taxation — ET
European Taxation — Eur Tax
European Taxation — Eur Taxation
European Teacher — Eur Teach
European Technical Digests — Eur Tech Dig
European Technical Symposium on Polyimides and High-Temperature Polymers — Eur Tech Symp Polyimides High Temp Polym
European Textile Engineering Review — Eur Text Eng Rev
European Translations Centre. Quarterly Index — ETC Quart Index
European Trends — EEB
European Trends — ET
European Trends — ETR
European Tribology Congress. Proceedings — Eur Tribol Congr Proc
European University Papers. Series 8. Chemistry. Division A. Pharmacy — Eur Univ Pap Ser 8 Chem Div A
European Urology — Eur Urol
European Yearbook — Europ YB
European Yearbook — EY
Europeen, Europaer. Magazine de l'Economie et de la Culture — EUE
Europees Parlement. EP Nieuws — MBA
Europe's Largest Companies [*Database*] — ELC
Europese Documentatie — EHR
Europese Investeringsbank. Mededelingen — MFB
Europhysics Conference Abstracts [*Switzerland*] — Europhys Conf Abstr
Europhysics Conference on Macromolecular Physics. Proceedings — Europhys Conf Macromol Phys Proc
Europhysics Industrial Workshop — Europhys Ind Workshop
Europhysics Letters — Europhys Lett
Europhysics News — EUPNA
Europhysics News — Europhys News
Europlastics Monthly [*England*] — Europlas Mon
Europlastics Monthly — Europlast Mon
Euro-Spectra — Euro Spectr
Eurostat Review — Euro Rev
Eurotest Technical Bulletin — Eurotest Tech Bull
Eusko-Jakintza. Revista de Estudios Vascos — EJEV
Eusko-Jakintza. Revue des Etudes Basques — EJ
Evaluated Nuclear Data File [*Database*] — ENDF
Evaluated Nuclear Structure Data File [*Database*] — ENSDF
Evaluated Nuclear Structure Data File - MEDLIST [*Database*] — ENSDF-MEDLIST
Evaluation: A Forum for Human Services Decision-Makers — Evaluatn
Evaluation and Experiment. Some Critical Issues in Assessing Social Programs — Eval & Exper
Evaluation and Program Planning — Eval Program Plann
Evaluation and the Health Professions — Eval Health Prof
Evaluation and the Health Professions — Evaluation Health Professions
Evaluation Engineering — Eval Eng
Evaluation in Education — Eval Educ
Evaluation in Education — Evaluation in Ed
Evaluation Newsletter — Eval Newsletter
Evaluation Quarterly — Eval Q
Evaluation Quarterly — Evaluation Q
Evaluation Review — Eval Rev
Evaluation Review — Evaluation R
Evaluation Studies Review Annual — Eval Stud Rev Ann
Evaluation Studies. Review Annual — Evalu Stu
Evangelical Magazine of Wales — EMW
Evangelical Missions Quarterly — EMQ
Evangelical Missions Quarterly — Ev MQ
Evangelical Quarterly — EQ
Evangelical Quarterly — Ev Q
Evangelical Quarterly — Evang
Evangelical Quarterly — Evang Q
Evangelical Review — Evang R
Evangelical Review of Theology — ERT
Evangelie en Maatschappij — EVM
Evangelische Blaetter aus Bethlehem — EBB
Evangelische Deutschland. Beilage — Ev Dt B
Evangelische Diaspora — Evang Diaspora
Evangelische Enzyklopaedie — Ev Enz
Evangelische Jahresbriefe — Ev J
Evangelische Kirchenchor — Evan Kirchor
Evangelische Kirchenzeitung [*Berlin*] — EK
Evangelische Kirchenzeitung [*Berlin*] — EKZ
Evangelische Kommentare — EK
Evangelische Kommentare [*Germany*] — Evang Komment
Evangelische Kommentare [*Stuttgart*] — EvK
Evangelische Kommentare — EVKOD
Evangelische Kommentare [*Stuttgart*] — EvKom
Evangelische Missionszeitschrift — EMZ
Evangelische Musikzeitung [*Luzern*] — EMZ
Evangelische Musikzeitung [*Luzern*] — Evgl Musikztg
Evangelische Theologie — ET
Evangelische Theologie — Ev Th
Evangelische Theologie — Evang Th
Evangelische Theologie [*Munich*] — EvT
Evangelische Theologie (Beiheft) — EvThB
Evangelische Welt — Ev W
Evangelische Welt. Bethel bei Bielefeld [*Germany*] — EvWelt
Evangelische-Katholischer Kommentar zum Neuen Testament — EKK
Evangelischer Literaturbeobachter — ELB
Evangelisches Gemeindeblatt fuer Galizien — EG
Evangelisches Kirchenlexikon. Kirchlichtheologisches Handwoerterbuch — EKL
Evangelisches Missions-Magazin — Evang Mis Mag
Evangelisches Soziallexikon — ESL
Evangelisch-Katholischer Kommentar zum Neuen Testament. Vorarbeiten — EKKV
Evangelisch-Lutherische Kirchenzeitung [*Berlin*] — ELKZ
Evangelisch-Reformierte Kirchenzeitung — ERKZ
Evangelisch-Sozial. Beilage. Soziale Korrespondenz — Ev Soz B
Evangelizing Today's Child — EvTC
Evanglisches Forum — Ev Fo
Evans Electronic News Service [*Database*] — ENS
Evelyn Waugh Newsletter — EWN
Everglades Natural History — Everglades Nat History
Everglades Natural History. A Magazine of Natural History of South Florida — Everglades Nat Hist
Evergreen Review — ER

Evergreen Review — EV
Evergreen Review — EvR
Every Saturday — Ev Sat
Everybody's Magazine — EB
Everybody's Magazine — Everybodys M
Everyday Science — Everday Sci
Everyman's Science — Everyman's Sci
Everyman's Science — EVSCB
Evidences — Evid
Evolution — Evol
Evolution — PEVO
Evolution des Concepts et des Methodes d'Evaluation des Pollutions dans les Masses d'Eau et les Sediments — Evol Concepts Methodes Eval Pollut Masses Eau Sediments
Evolution Medicale — Evol Med
Evolution Psychiatrique — Evol Psychiatr
Evolution Psychiatrique — EVPSA
Evolutionary Biology — Evol Biol
Evolutionary Computation — Evol Comput
Evolutionary Genetics Research Reports — Evol Genet Res Rep
Evolutionary Theory — Evol Theory
Evreiskaia Entsiklopediia — EE
EWHA Medical Journal. College of Medicine. EWHA Womans University [*Korea*] — EWHA Med J Coll Med EWHA Womans
EWRSI [*East-West Resource Systems Institute*] **Newsletter** — EWRSI Newsl
EX Magazine — EX Mag
Exaktn — EXKTA
Examen de la Situacion Economica de Mexico — Exam Sit Econ Mexico
Examiner [*Quezon City*] — Ex
Examples of Mathematical Structures — Examples Math Structures
Excavaciones Arqueologicas en Espana — EAE
Excavaciones Arqueologicas en Espana — Exc Arq en Espana
Excavation at Nuzi — Ex Nuzi
Excavation Memoirs [*London*] — EM
Excavations at Dura Europos — DE
Excavations in Palestine during the years 1898-1900 — EIP
Excellence in Communication — Excel Com
Exceptional Child — Except Child
Exceptional Child Education Abstracts [*Later, ECER*] — ECEA
Exceptional Child Education Abstracts [*Later, ECER*] — Except Child Educ Abstr
Exceptional Child Education Abstracts [*Later, ECER*] — ExChAb
Exceptional Child Education Resources [*Database*] — ECER
Exceptional Child Education Resources — Except Child Educ Resour
Exceptional Children — EXCCA
Exceptional Children — Excep Child
Exceptional Children — Except Chil
Exceptional Children — GEXC
Exceptional Infant — Except Infant
Exceptional Parent — Except Parent
Exceptional Parent — GTEP
Excerpta Botanica — Excerp Bot
Excerpta Botanica. Sectio A. Taxonomica et Chorologica — Excerpta Bot Sect A Taxon Chorol
Excerpta Botanica. Sectio B. Sociologica — Excerpta Bot Sect B Sociol
Excerpta Criminologica — Excerp Criminol
Excerpta Criminologica — Excerpta Criminol
Excerpta Indonesica — EI
Excerpta Indonesica — EXY
Excerpta Medica [*Amsterdam*] — EM
Excerpta Medica — Excerpta Med
Excerpta Medica (Amsterdam) — Excerpta Med (Amst)
Excerpta Medica. International Congress Series [*Amsterdam*] — Excerpta Med Int Congr Ser
Excerpta Medica Physicians Information Retrieval and Education Service [*Database*] — EMPIRES
Excerpta Medica. Physiology — Excerpta Med Physiol
Excerpta Medica. Section 1. Anatomy, Anthropology, Embryology, and Histology [*A publication*] — Excerpta Med Sect 1
Excerpta Medica. Section 2. Physiology — Excerpta Med Sect 2
Excerpta Medica. Section 2. Physiology, Biochemistry, and Pharmacology — Excerpta Med Sect 2 Physiol Biochem Pharmacol
Excerpta Medica. Section 2A. Physiology — Excerpta Med Sect 2A
Excerpta Medica. Section 2B. Biochemistry — Excerpta Med Biochem
Excerpta Medica. Section 2B. Biochemistry — Excerpta Med Sect 2B
Excerpta Medica. Section 2C. Pharmacology and Toxicology — Excerpta Med Pharmacol Toxicol
Excerpta Medica. Section 2C. Pharmacology and Toxicology — Excerpta Med Sect 2C
Excerpta Medica. Section 3. Endocrinology — Excerpta Med Sect 3
Excerpta Medica. Section 4. Medical Microbiology and Hygiene — Excerpta Med Sect 4
Excerpta Medica. Section 4. Medical Microbiology, Immunology, and Serology — Excerpta Med Sect 4 Med Microbiol Immunol Serol
Excerpta Medica. Section 5. General Pathology and Pathological Anatomy — Excerpta Med Sect 5
Excerpta Medica. Section 6. Internal Medicine — Excerpta Med Sect 6
Excerpta Medica. Section 7. Pediatrics — Excerpta Med Sect 7
Excerpta Medica. Section 8. Neurology and Psychiatry — Excerpta Med Sect 8
Excerpta Medica. Section 9. Surgery — Excerpta Med Sect 9
Excerpta Medica. Section 10. Obstetrics and Gynecology — Excerpta Med Sect 10
Excerpta Medica. Section 11. Oto-Rhino-Laryngology — Excerpta Med Sect 11
Excerpta Medica. Section 12. Ophthalmology — Excerpta Med Sect 12
Excerpta Medica. Section 13. Dermatology and Venereology — Excerpta Med Sect 13
Excerpta Medica. Section 14. Radiology — Excerpta Med Sect 14
Excerpta Medica. Section 15. Chest Diseases, Thoracic Surgery, and Tuberculosis — Excerpta Med Sect 15
Excerpta Medica. Section 16. Cancer — Excerpta Med Sect 16
Excerpta Medica. Section 17. Public Health, Social Medicine, and Hygiene — Excerpta Med Sect 17
Excerpta Medica. Section 23. Nuclear Medicine — Excerpta Med Sect 23
Excerpta Medica. Section 29. Clinical Biochemistry — Excerpta Med Sect 29
Excerpta Medica. Section 30. Pharmacology and Toxicology — Excerpta Med Sect 30
Excerpta Medica Vocabulary [*Database*] — EVOC
Exchange for the Flower, Nursery, and Garden Center Trade — Exch Flower Nursery Gard Cent Trade
Exchequer Court Reports [*Database*] — ECR
Exchequer Court Reports [*Canada*] — Ex C R
Excise Duty Bulletin [*Database*] — EDB
Excise Tariff Proposals — ETP
Excise Tax Memoranda [*Database*] — ETM
Excursions in Recreational Mathematics Series — Excursions Rec Math Ser
Executive — EXE
Executive — Exec
Executive Administrator — Exec Admin
Executive Agreement. US State Department Series — EA
Executive Communications — Exec Com
Executive Disclosure Guide. Commerce Clearing House — Exec Disclosure Guide CCH
Executive Engineer — Executive Eng
Executive Female — Exec Female
Executive Female — EXF
Executive Fitness Newsletter — Exec Fit Newsl
Executive Health — EXHE
Executive Housekeeper — Exec Housekeeper
Executive Housekeeping Today — Exec Housekeeping Today
Executive News — Exec News
Executive Productivity — Exec Prod
Executive Reading — Exec Reading
Executive Report — Exec Reprt
Executive Sciences Institute — Exec Sci Inst
Executive Skills — Exec Skills
Executive Skills — EXS
Executive's Memory Jogger — Exec Mem Jogger
Exegesis — EXS
Exegetica. Delft — Ex
Exegetisches Handbuch zum Alten Testament — EHAT
Exempla Scripturarum — Exp Scr
Exempt Organizations Reports. Commerce Clearing House — Exempt Org Rep CCH
Exercices de la Patience — Exer Pat
Exercise and Sport Sciences Reviews — Exerc Sport Sci Rev
Exercise and Sport Sciences Reviews — Exercise Sport Sci Rev
Exercise Immunology Review — Ex Immunology Rev
Exercise Immunology Review — Exerc Immunol Rev
Exeter Hall Lectures — Ex H Lec
Exeter Papers on Economic History — Exeter Papers Econ Hist
Exhaust Gas and Air Pollution Abstracts — Exhaust Gas Air Pollut Abs
Exhibition Bulletin — EXG
Exhibition Bulletin — Exhibition Bull
Exhibitions and Conferences Gazette — Exhib & Conf Gaz
Existential Psychiatry — Exist Psychiat
Expansion — EPN
Expansion Regionale — Expans Region
Expansion Regionale — Expansion Reg
Expansion Regionale (Paris) — Expans Region (Paris)
Expatriate Review — Exp R
Expedition — Exped
Expedition — GEXP
Expedition Bulletin. University Museum. University of Pennsylvania — Expedition
Experienced Librarians and Informational Personnel in the Developing Countries of Asia and Oceania [*Database*] — ELIPA
Experiences. Bulletin. Section Belgoluxembourgeoise du Centre International de Recherches et d'Information sur l'Economie Collective — Experien
Experientia — Exp
Experientia — EXPEA
Experientia — Exper
Experientia. Supplementum — Exper Suppl
Experientia. Supplementum — Experientia Suppl
Experientia. Supplementum (Basel) — Exper Suppl (Basel)
Experientiae. Universidade Rural do Estado de Minas Gerais (Vicosa) — Experientiae Vicosa
Experiment — EX
Experiment — Exp
Experiment and Therapy (Osaka) — Exp Ther (Osaka)
Experiment Christentum — Ex Chr
Experiment Report. Ministry of Agriculture and Natural Resources (Nigeria). Midwest Region — Exp Rep Min Agr Natur Resour (Nigeria) Midwest Reg
Experiment Station Record [*Washington, DC*] — Exp St Rec
Experiment Station Record — Exp Sta Record
Experiment Station Record. Office of Experiment Station. US Department of Agriculture — Exp Sta Rec
Experiment Station Record. United States Department of Agriculture — Exp Stn Rec
Experimental Aging Research — EAGRD
Experimental Aging Research — Exp Aging Res
Experimental Agriculture — Exp Ag

Experimental Agriculture — Exp Agric
Experimental Agriculture — Exper Agric
Experimental Agriculture — Expl Agric
Experimental and Applied Acarology — Exp & Appl Acarol
Experimental and Clinical Endocrinology — Exp Clin Endocrinol
Experimental and Clinical Endocrinology and Diabetes — Exp Clin Endocrinol Diabetes
Experimental and Clinical Gastroenterology — Exp Clin Gastroenterol
Experimental and Clinical Immunogenetics — ECIME4
Experimental and Clinical Immunogenetics — Exp Clin Im
Experimental and Clinical Immunogenetics — Exp Clin Immunogenet
Experimental and Clinical Medicine (Yerevan) — Exp Clin Med Yerevan
Experimental and Clinical Oncology (Tallinn) — Exp Clin Oncol (Tallinn)
Experimental and Clinical Pharmacology — Exp Clin Pharmacol
Experimental and Clinical Psychiatry — Exp Clin Psychiatry
Experimental and Molecular Medicine — Exp Mol Med
Experimental and Molecular Pathology — EMP
Experimental and Molecular Pathology — Exp Mol Pat
Experimental and Molecular Pathology — Exp Mol Pathol
Experimental and Molecular Pathology — Exp Molec Path
Experimental and Molecular Pathology — Exp Molec Pathol
Experimental and Molecular Pathology — Exp Molecul Pathol
Experimental and Molecular Pathology. Supplement — EMPSA
Experimental and Molecular Pathology. Supplement — Exp Mol Pathol Suppl
Experimental and Toxicologic Pathology — Exp Toxicol Pathol
Experimental Animals — Exp An
Experimental Animals (Jikken Dobutsu) (Tokyo) — Exp Anim (Tokyo)
Experimental Biology — Exp Biol
Experimental Biology and Medicine — Exp Biol Med
Experimental Biology (Berlin) — Exp Biol (Berl)
Experimental Biology Online [*Electronic Publication*] — Exp Biol Online
Experimental Botany — Exp Bot
Experimental Botany: An International Series of Monographs — Exp Bot Int Ser Monogr
Experimental Brain Research — EXBRA
Experimental Brain Research — Exp Brain R
Experimental Brain Research — Exp Brain Res
Experimental Brain Research — Expl Brain Res
Experimental Brain Research. Supplementum — EBRSDP
Experimental Brain Research. Supplementum — Exp Brain Res Suppl
Experimental Cell Biology — Exp Cell Biol
Experimental Cell Research — Exp Cell Re
Experimental Cell Research — Exp Cell Res
Experimental Cell Research — Exp CR
Experimental Cell Research — Expl Cell Res
Experimental Cell Research. Supplement — Exp Cell Res Suppl
Experimental Chaos Conference — Exp Chaos Conf
Experimental Chemical Thermodynamics — Exp Chem Thermodyn
Experimental Dermatology — Exp Dermatol
Experimental Embryology and Teratology — Exp Embryol Teratol
Experimental Eye Research — Exp Eye Res
Experimental Gerontology — EXGEA
Experimental Gerontology — Exp Geront
Experimental Gerontology — Exp Gerontol
Experimental Gerontology — Expl Gerontol
Experimental Heat Transfer — Exp Heat Transfer
Experimental Hematology — EXHEB
Experimental Hematology — Exp Hemat
Experimental Hematology [*Lawrence, Kansas*] — Exp Hematol
Experimental Hematology [*Charlottesville, Virginia*] — Exp Hematol
Experimental Hematology (Copenhagen) — Exp Hematol (Copenh)
Experimental Hematology (New York) — Exp Hematol (NY)
Experimental Hematology (Oak Ridge, Tennessee) — Exp Hematol (Oak Ridge Tenn)
Experimental Hematology Today. Annual Meeting of the International Society for Experimental Hematology — Exp Hematol Today
Experimental Horticulture — Exp Hort
Experimental Horticulture — Exp Hortic
Experimental Horticulture — Expl Hort
Experimental Husbandry — Exp Husb
Experimental Husbandry — Expl Husb
Experimental Immunotoxicology [*monograph*] — Exp Immunotoxicol
Experimental Lung Research — Exp Lung Res
Experimental Magnetism — Exp Magn
Experimental Mathematics — Experiment Math
Experimental Mechanics — Exp Mech
Experimental Mechanics — Exper Mech
Experimental Medicine — Exp Med
Experimental Medicine and Microbiology — Exp Med Microbiol
Experimental Medicine and Microbiology (English Translation of Medycyna Doswiadczalna i Mikrobiologia) — Exp Med Microbiol (Engl Transl)
Experimental Medicine and Microbiology (English Translation of Medycyna Doswiadczalna i Mikrobiologia) — Exp Med Microbiol (Engl Transl Med Dosw Mikrobiol)
Experimental Medicine and Surgery — Exp Med Surg
Experimental Medicine and Surgery — Exper Med Surg
Experimental Methods in the Physical Sciences — Exp Methods Phys Sci
Experimental Mycology — Exp Mycol
Experimental Nephrology — Exp Nephrol
Experimental Neurology — EN
Experimental Neurology — EXNEA
Experimental Neurology — Exp Neurol
Experimental Neurology — Exper Neurol
Experimental Neurology. Supplement — ENUSA
Experimental Neurology. Supplement — Exp Neurol Suppl
Experimental Nuclear Physics — Exp Nucl Phys
Experimental Parasitology — Ex Paras
Experimental Parasitology — Exp Parasit
Experimental Parasitology — Exp Parasitol
Experimental Parasitology — Exper Parasitol
Experimental Parasitology — Expl Parasit
Experimental Pathology — Expl Path
Experimental Pathology (Jena) — Exp Pathol (Jena)
Experimental Pathology. Supplement — Exp Pathol Suppl
Experimental Physiology — Exp Physiol
Experimental Record. Department of Agriculture. South Australia — Exp Rec Dep Agric S Aust
Experimental Record. Department of Agriculture. South Australia — Expl Rec Dep Agric S Aust
Experimental Record. Grassland Husbandry Department. West of Scotland Agricultural College — Exp Rec Grassland Husb Dept
Experimental Reports of Equine Health Laboratory — Exp Rep Equine Health Lab
Experimental Results for Phase Equilibria and Pure Component Properties — Exp Results Phase Equilib Pure Compon Prop
Experimental Stress Analysis. Proceedings — Exp Stress Anal Proc
Experimental Technique of Physics (Lemgo, Germany) — Exp Tech Phys Lemgo Ger
Experimental Techniques — Exp Tech
Experimental Thermal and Fluid Science — Exp Therm Fluid Sci
Experimental Thermodynamics — Exp Thermodyn
Experimental Vehicle Newsletter — Veh News Ltr
Experimental Water Toxicology — Exp Water Toxicol
Experimental Work. Institute of Pomology. Skierniewice. Poland — Exp Work Inst Pomol Skierniewice Pol
Experimentation Animale — Exp Anim
Experimentation Cerebrale — Exp Cereb
Experimentelle Hirnforschung — Exp Hirnforsch
Experimentelle Medizin, Pathologie, und Klinik — Exp Med Pathol Klin
Experimentelle Pathologie — Exp Path
Experimentelle Pathologie — Exp Pathol
Experimentelle Technik der Physik [*Germany*] — Exp Tech Phys
Experimentelle Technik der Physik — Experiment Tech Phys
Experimentelle Technik der Physik (Berlin) — Exp Tech Phys Berlin
Experimentelle Veterinaermedizin — Exp Veterinaermed
Experiments in Fluids — EF
Experiments in Fluids — Exp Fluids
Experiments in Physiology and Biochemistry — Exp Physiol Biochem
Experiments in Progress. Grassland Research Institute (Hurley) — Exp Progr Grassland Res Inst (Hurley)
Expert Comptable — Ex C
Explanatory Leaflet. Intervention Board for Agricultural Produce — Explan Leafl Intervention Bd Agric Prod
Explicacion de Textos Literarios — ETL
Explicacion de Textos Literarios — Expl Text L
Explicacion de Textos Literarios — ExTL
Explicator — Ex
Explicator — Exp
Explicator — Expl
Explicator — GEXR
Exploration and Economics of the Petroleum Industry — Explor Econ Pet Ind
Exploration and Economics of the Petroleum Industry — Explor Econ Petrol Ind
Exploration and Scientific Research. Pan-American Society of Tropical Research — Explor Sci Res
Exploration du Parc National Albert — Explor Parc Nat A
Exploration Geophysics — Explor Geophys
Exploration Geophysics (Sydney) — Explor Geophys (Sydney)
Exploration Geophysics (USSR) — Explor Geophys (USSR)
Exploration in Renaissance Culture — EIRC
Exploration Review — Explor Rev
Explorations — Explor
Explorations Archeologiques de Delos — Delos
Explorations Archeologiques de Delos — EA Delos
Explorations Archeologiques de Delos — EAD
Explorations Archeologiques de Delos — ED
Explorations Archeologiques de Delos — Expl Delos
Explorations in Economic History — EEH
Explorations in Economic History — Expl Ec His
Explorations in Economic History — Explo Econ Hist
Explorations in Economic History — Explor Econ Hist
Explorations in Economic History — Explorations Econ Hist
Explorations in Economic History — IXEH
Explorations in Economic Research — Explor Econ Res
Explorations in Economic Research — Explorations Econ Research
Explorations in Entrepreneurial History — ExE
Explorations in Entrepreneurial History — Explor Entrep Hist
Explorations in Entrepreneurial History — Explorat Entrepreneurial Hist
Explorations (London) — Expl
Explore. Alberta's Outdoor Magazine — EXPL
Explorers Journal — EXJO
Explorers Journal — Explor J
Explorers Journal (New York) — Explor Jour NY
Explosion and Explosives — Explos Explos
Explosive Materials — Explos Mater
Explosives Engineer — Explos Eng
Explosives Engineer — Explosives Eng
Explosives Research and Development Establishment (Great Britain). Technical Note — Explos Res Dev Establ (GB) Tech Note
Explosivstoffe — Explosivst
Expo Data — EXX

Export — AEX
Export [*New York*] — EX
Export — EXP
Export Direction — EPE
Export Direction — Export Dir
Export Market Digest — EMD
Export Markt — EXM
Export Network [*Database*] — EN
Export (New York) — Exp (NY)
Export News — Export Nws
Export News (New Zealand) — ENN
Export Review of the British Drug and Chemical Industries — Export Rev Br Drug Chem Ind
Export Shipping Guide — Exp Ship Guide
Export Statistical Schedule (Japan) — Jpn Export
Export Turkey Magazine — ETM
Exporter. Malta's Monthly Export Journal — TEM
Exportmededelingen — EVD
Exports of Australia — Exports of Aust
Exports of Australia and New Zealand — Exports of Aust & NZ
Exposes Annuels de Biochimie Medicale — Expo Annu Biochim Med
Exposes Annuels de Biochimie Medicale — Expos Ann Biochim Med
Exposes Annuels de Biochimie Medicale — Expos Annu Biochim Med
Exposes. Congres International de Technologie Pharmaceutique — Expo Congr Int Technol Pharm
Expositiones Mathematicae. International Journal for Pure and Applied Mathematics — Exposition Math
Expositor — Exp
Expositor — Expos
Expositor and Current Anecdotes — ECA
Expositor and Homiletic Review — Exp H R
Expositor (Cleveland, Ohio, USA) — Exp USA
Expository Times — ET
Expository Times — Ex T
Expository Times — Expos T
Expository Times — Exposit Tim
Expository Times — Exposit Times
Expository Times — ExpT
Expository Times [*Edinburgh*] — ExpTim
Expovisie. Beurzen, Tentoonstellingen, Congressen, Hotellerie — BKK
Express — Exp
Express. Daily Financial Newspaper [*Athens*] — HIE
Express Ilustrowany — Ex Il
Express Translation Service List — Express Transl Serv List
Express Wieczorny — Ex W
Expression. Journal of the English Society — EESB
Expression Systems and Processes for rDNA Products — Expression Syst Processes rDNA Prod
Express-News — Express-Ne
Extel Handbook of Market Leaders — Extel Handbook Mark Leaders
Extended Abstracts and Program. Biennial Conference on Carbon — Ext Abstr Program Bienn Conf Carbon
Extended Abstracts and Program. Biennial Conference on Carbon — Extended Abstr Program Bienn Conf Carbon
Extended Abstracts. Conference on Solid State Devices and Materials — Ext Abstr Conf Solid State Devices Mater
Extended Abstracts. Meeting. International Society of Electrochemistry — Ext Abstr Meet Int Soc Electrochem
Extension — Extensn
Extension Bulletin. Agricultural Extension Service. Purdue University — Ext Bull Agric Ext Serv Purdue Univ
Extension Bulletin. Agriculture Extension Service. University of Minnesota — Ext Bull Agric Ext Serv Univ Minn
Extension Bulletin. ASPAC [*Asian and Pacific Council*]**. Food and Fertilizer Technology Center** — Ext Bull ASPAC Food Fert Technol Cent
Extension Bulletin. Cooperative Extension Service. University of Maryland — Ext Bull Coop Ext Serv Univ Md
Extension Bulletin. Cornell Agricultural Experiment Station — Ext Bull Cornell Agric Exp Stn
Extension Bulletin. Delaware University. Agricultural Extension Service — Ext Bull Del Univ Agr Ext Serv
Extension Bulletin. Department of Agriculture and Fisheries. South Australia — Ext Bull Dept Agric South Aust
Extension Bulletin. Department of Agriculture. South Australia — Ext Bull Dep Agric S Aust
Extension Bulletin E. Cooperative Extension Service. Michigan State University — Ext Bull E Coop Ext Serv Mich State Univ
Extension Bulletin E. Rutgers. The State University of New Jersey. Cooperative Extension Service — Ext Bull E Rutgers State Univ NJ Coop Ext Serv
Extension Bulletin. Florida Agricultural Experiment Station — Ext Bull Flor Agric Exp St
Extension Bulletin. Indiana Agricultural Experiment Station — Ext Bull Ind Agric Exp Stn
Extension Bulletin. Iowa State University — Ext Bull Iowa State Univ
Extension Bulletin. Maryland University. Cooperative Extension Service — Ext Bull MD Univ Coop Ext Serv
Extension Bulletin. Michigan State College — Ext Bull Mich St Coll
Extension Bulletin. Michigan State University. Cooperative Extension Service — Ext Bull Mich State Univ Coop Ext Serv
Extension Bulletin. North Dakota State University of Agriculture and Applied Science. Cooperative Extension Service — Ext Bull ND State Univ Agric Appl Sci Coop Ext Serv
Extension Bulletin. Ohio State University — Ext Bull Ohio St Univ
Extension Bulletin. Ohio State University. College of Agriculture. Cooperative Extension Service — Ext Bull Ohio State Univ Coll Agr Coop Ext Serv
Extension Bulletin. Oregon State University. Cooperative Extension Service — Ext Bull Oreg State Univ Coop Ext Serv
Extension Bulletin. Purdue University. Agricultural Extension Service — Ext Bull Purdue Univ Agric Ext Serv
Extension Bulletin. Purdue University. Department of Agricultural Extension — Ext Bull Purdue Univ Dep Agric Ext
Extension Bulletin. United States Department of Agriculture — Ext Bull US Dep Agric
Extension Bulletin. University of Delaware. Cooperative Extension Service — Ext Bull Univ Del Coop Ext Serv
Extension Bulletin. University of Maryland. Cooperative Extension Service — Ext Bull Univ MD Coop Ext Serv
Extension Bulletin. University of Minnesota. Agricultural Extension Service — Ext Bull Univ Minn Agr Ext Serv
Extension Bulletin. University of Minnesota. Agricultural Extension Service — Ext Bull Univ Minn Agric Ext Serv
Extension Bulletin. Washington State College — Ext Bull Wash St Coll
Extension Bulletin. Washington State University. College of Agriculture. Extension Service — Ext Bull Wash State Univ Coll Agr Ext Serv
Extension Bulletin. Washington State University. Cooperative Extension Service — Ext Bull Wash State Univ Coop Ext Serv
Extension Circular. Arkansas College of Agriculture — Ext Circ Ark Coll Agric
Extension Circular EC. Cooperative Extension Service. Utah State University — Ext Circ EC Coop Ext Serv Utah State Univ
Extension Circular. Illinois University — Ext Circ Ill Univ
Extension Circular. North Carolina Agricultural Experiment Station — Ext Circ N Carol Agric Exp Stn
Extension Circular. North Carolina State College of Agriculture and Engineering. Agricultural Extension Service — Ext Circ NC State Coll Agric Eng Agric Ext Serv
Extension Circular. North Carolina State University. Agricultural Extension Service — Ext Circ NC State Univ Agr Ext Serv
Extension Circular. Oregon State University. Extension Service — Ext Circ Oreg State Univ Ext Serv
Extension Circular P. Auburn University. Agricultural Extension Service — Ext Circ P Auburn Univ Agr Ext Serv
Extension Circular. Pennsylvania State College. School of Agriculture — Ext Circ PA St Coll Agric
Extension Circular. Pennsylvania State University. Agricultural Extension Service — Ext Circ Pa State Univ Agric Ext Serv
Extension Circular. Purdue University. Cooperative Extension Service — Ext Circ Purdue Univ Coop Ext Serv
Extension Circular. Purdue University. Department of Agricultural Extension — Ext Circ Purdue Univ Dept Agr Ext
Extension Circular. South Dakota College of Agriculture — Ext Circ S Dak Coll Agric
Extension Circular. South Dakota State University. Cooperative Extension Service — Ext Circ S Dak State Univ Coop Ext Serv
Extension Circular. Utah Agricultural College — Ext Circ Utah Agric Coll
Extension Circular. Washington State University. College of Agriculture. Extension Service — Ext Circ Wash State Univ Coll Agr Ext Serv
Extension Circular. Washington State University. Cooperative Extension Service — Ext Circ Wash State Univ Coop Ext Serv
Extension Course Lectures. Auckland Primary Principals Association — Ext Course Lect Ak Prim Assoc
Extension Development Unit Report — Ext Dev Unit Rep
Extension en las Americas — Ext Amer
Extension Extra ExEx. South Dakota Cooperative Extension Service — Ext Extra ExEx SD Coop Ext Serv
Extension Folder. Agricultural Extension Service. University of Minnesota — Ext Folder Agric Ext Serv Univ Minn
Extension Folder. Michigan State University — Ext Folder Mich St Univ
Extension Folder. Michigan State University of Agriculture and Applied Science. Cooperative Extension Service — Ext Folder Mich State Univ Agr Appl Sci Coop Ext Serv
Extension Folder. North Carolina Agricultural Extension Service — Ext Folder NC Agric Ext Serv
Extension Folder. North Carolina State University. Agricultural Extension Service — Ext Folder NC State Univ Agr Ext Serv
Extension Folder. University of Minnesota. Agricultural Extension Service — Ext Folder Univ Minn Agr Ext Serv
Extension Folder. University of Minnesota. Agricultural Extension Service — Ext Folder Univ Minn Agric Ext Serv
Extension Folder. University of New Hampshire. College of Agriculture. Extension Service — Ext Folder Univ NH Coll Agr Ext Serv
Extension Home Economics. Family Economics Resource Management. EHE. University of Arkansas Cooperative Extension Service — Ext Home Econ Fam Econ Resour Manage EHE Univ Arkansas Coop
Extension Leaflet. Agricultural Extension Service. Purdue University — Ext Leafl Agric Ext Serv Purdue Univ
Extension Leaflet. Ohio State University. College of Agriculture. Cooperative Extension Service — Ext Leafl Ohio State Univ Coll Agr Coop Ext Serv
Extension Leaflet. Purdue University. Agricultural Extension Service — Ext Leafl Purdue Univ Agric Ext Serv
Extension Leaflet. University of Maryland. Cooperative Extension Service — Ext Leafl Univ Md Coop Ext Serv
Extension Leaflet. Utah State University — Ext Leafl Utah St Univ
Extension Leaflet. Utah State University. Agricultural Extension Service — Ext Leafl Utah State Univ Agr Ext Serv
Extension Leaflet. Utah State University. Cooperative Extension Service — Ext Leafl Utah State Univ Coop Ext Serv
Extension Mimeo. Washington State University. College of Agriculture. Extension Service — Ext Mimeo Wash State Univ Coll Agr Ext Serv

Extension Mimeographed Circular. South Dakota State University. Cooperative Extension Service — Ext Mimeogr Circ S Dak State Univ Coop Ext Serv
Extension Miscellaneous Publication. Agricultural Extension Service. University of Minnesota — Ext Misc Publ Agric Ext Serv Univ Minn
Extension Publication. Cooperative Extension Service. University of New Hampshire — Ext Publ Coop Ext Serv Univ NH
Extension Publication. Illinois University. North Central Region — Ext Publ Ill Univ N Cent Reg
Extension Publication. Louisiana State University. Agricultural Extension Service — Ext Publ LA State Univ Agr Ext Serv
Extension Publication. Washington State College — Ext Publ Wash St Coll
Extension Review. US Department of Agriculture — Ext Rev US Dep Agric
Extension Service Bulletin. Iowa State College of Agriculture — Ext Serv Bull IA St Coll Agric
Extension Service Leaflet. College of Agriculture. Rutgers University — Ext Serv Leafl Coll Agric Rutgers Univ
Extension Service Review — ESR
Extension Service Review — Ext Serv R
Extension Service Review — Ext Serv Rev
Extension Service Review — Ext Service R
Extension Studies. Pennsylvania State University. Extension Service — Ext Stud PA State Univ Ext Serv
Extension [*O Intercambio*] **Universitaria de la Plata** — EUP
Exterminators' Log — Exterm Log
External Affairs — Ext Affairs
External Studies Gazette — External Stud Gaz
External Studies Gazette — External Studies Gaz
Externer Bericht. Kernforschungszentrum Karlsruhe — Externer Ber Kernforschungszent Karlsruhe
Externer Bericht. Kernforschungszentrum Karlsruhe — Externer Ber Kernforschungszentr Karlsruhe
Externer Bericht. Kernforschungszentrum Karlsruhe — Externer Ber Kernforschungszentrum Karlsruhe
Extracta Gynaecologica — Extr Gynaecol
Extracta Mathematicae — Extracta Math
Extracts from China Mainland Magazines [*US Consulate*] [*Hongkong*] — ECMM
Extracts from the Soviet Press on the Soviet North and Antarctic — EXSP
(Extrait de) La Revue Francaise — Ext Rev Fr
Extraits des Proces-Verbaux des Seances. Academie des Sciences et Lettres de Montpellier — Extr Proces Verbaux Seances Acad Sci Montpellier
Extra-Mural Reporter — Extra Mural Reptr
Extrapolation — Ext
Extrapolation — Extrap
Extrapolation — Extrapolat
Extrapolation — IXTP
Extreme-Orient Medical — Extr Or Med
Exuviae Sacrae Constantinopolitanae — ESC
Exxon Monograph Series — Exxon Monogr Ser
Exxon USA — EXON
Eye — EY
Eye, Ear, Nose, and Throat Journal — EENTA
Eye, Ear, Nose, and Throat Monthly — Eye Ear Nos
Eye, Ear, Nose, and Throat Monthly — Eye Ear Nose Throat Mon
Eye, Ear, Nose, and Throat Monthly — Eye Ear Nose Throat Month
Eyewitness — Eyewit
Ezegodnik Bolsoj Sovetskoj Enciklopedii — EBSE
Ezegodnik Imperatorskago Russkago Geograficeskago Obscestva — Ezeg Imp Russk Geogr Obsc
Ezegodnik Muzeja Architektury — EMA
Ezhegodnik Gosudarstvennogo Issledovatel'skogo Instituta Myasnoi Promyshlennosti — Ezheg Gos Issled Inst Myasn Promsti
Ezhegodnik Gosudarstvennogo Istoricheskogo Muzeia — EGIM
Ezhegodnik Gosudarstvennyi Istoricheskii Muzei — Ezhegodnik GIM
Ezhegodnik Imperatorskikh Teatrov — EIT
Ezhegodnik. Institut Geologii i Geokhimii. Akademiya Nauk SSSR Ural'skii Filial — Ezheg Inst Geol Geokhim Akad Nauk SSSR Ural Fil
Ezhegodnik. Institut Geologii i Geokhimii. Akademiya Nauk SSSR Ural'skii Nauchnyi Tsentr — Ezheg Inst Geol Geokhim Akad Nauk SSSR Ural Nauchn Tsentr
Ezhegodnik. Institut Tsvetnoi Metallurgii (Plovdiv) — Ezheg Inst Tsvetn Metall (Plovdiv)
Ezhegodnik Instituta Eksperimental'noi Meditsiny Akademii Meditsinskikh Nauk SSSR — Ezheg Inst Eksp Med Akad Med Nauk SSSR
Ezhegodnik Instituta Eksperimental'noi Meditsiny Akademii Meditsinskikh Nauk SSSR — TMAMAP
Ezhegodnik Instituta Geokhimii Sibirskogo Otdeleniya Akademii Nauk SSSR — Ezhe Inst Geokhim Sib Otd Akad Nauk SSSR
Ezhegodnik Instituta Geokhimii Sibirskogo Otdeleniya Akademii Nauk SSSR — Ezheg Inst Geokhim Sib Otd Akad Nauk SSSR
Ezhegodnik Instituta Geologii Komi Filiala Akademii Nauk SSSR — Ezheg Inst Geol Komi Fil Akad Nauk SSSR
Ezhegodnik Muzei Istorii Religii i Ateizma — EMIRA
Ezhegodnik Muzeja Istorii Religii i Ateizma Akademii Nauk SSSR — Ezeg Muz Ist Rel At Ak N SSSR
Ezhegodnik Nauchno-Issledovatel'skogo Instituta Metallurgii i Obogashcheniya — Ezheg Nauchno Issled Inst Metall Obogashch
Ezhegodnik Nauchno-Issledovatel'skogo Instituta Tsvetnoi Metallurgii (Plovdiv) — Ezheg Nauchno Issled Inst Tsvetn Metall (Plovdiv)
Ezhegodnik Nauchnykh Rabot Alma-Atinskii Institut Usovershenstvovaniya Vrachei — Ezheg Nauchn Rab Alma-At Inst Usovershi Vrachei
Ezhegodnik Nauchnykh Rabot Instituta Usovershenstvovaniya Vrachei Kazakhskoi SSR — Ezheg Nauchn Rab Inst Usovershi Vrachei Kaz SSR
Ezhegodnik Nauchnykh Trudov. Meditsinskaya Akademiya (Varna) — Ezheg Nauchn Tr Medska Akad (Varna)
Ezhegodnik Obshchestva Estestvoispytatelei — Ezheg Ova Estestvoispyt
Ezhegodnik Obshchestva Estestvoispytatelei Akademiya Nauk. Estonskoi SSR — Ezheg O-Va Estestvoispyt Akad Nauk Est SSR
Ezhegodnik po Geologii i Mineralogii Rossii — Ezheg Geol Mineral Ross
Ezhegodnik Pochvovedeniya — Ezheg Pochvoved
Ezhegodnik Pol'skogo Geologicheskogo Obshchestva — Ezheg Pol Geol Ova
Ezhegodnik Sibirskogo Instituta Geokhimii — Ezheg Sib Inst Geokhim
Ezhegodnik Zoologicheskogo Muzeia Akademii Nauk Sofuza Sovetskikh Sotsialisticheskikh Respublik — Ezhegodnik Zool Muz Akad Nauk SSSR
Ezhegodnik Zoologicheskogo Muzeia Rossiiskoi Akademii Nauk — Ezhegodnik Zool Muz Ross Akad Nauk
Ezik i Literatura — EiL
Ezik i Literatura — EL
Ezik i Literatura — Ez Lit
Ezik i Stil na Balgarskite Pitsateli — ESBP

F

F F Communications — F F Commun
F + I Bau — FIBBD
F und G [*Felten und Guilleaume*] **Rundschau** — F & G Rundsch
F und M, Feinwerktechnik und Messtechnik — F & M Feinwerktech Messtech
F und M, Feinwerktechnik und Messtechnik — F M-Feinw M
FAA [*Federal Aviation Administration*] **Aviation News** — FAA Aviat Ne
FAA [*Federal Aviation Administration*] **General Aviation News** — FAA Gen Av N
FABAD [*Farmasotik Bilimler Ankara Dernegi*] **Farmasotik Bilimler Dergisi** — FABAD Farm Bilimler Derg
Faberg-Mitteilungen — Faberg Mitt
Fabian Tract — Fab Tr
FABIS Newsletter. Faba Bean Information Service — FABIS Newsl Faba Bean Inf Serv
Fabrication Progress — Fabr Prog
Fabrimetal — FBB
FABS Electronic Bible [*Database*] — FEB
FABS Reference Bible [*Database*] — FRB
Fabula — Fa
Fabula — Fab
Fabula — FB
Faces — FS
Facet Books. Biblical Series — FBB
Facet Books. Historical Series — FBH
Facet Books. Social Ethics Series — FBS
Fachausschussbericht der Deutschen Glastechnischen. Gesellschaft — Fachausschussber Dtsch Glastech Ges
Fachberichte fuer Metallbearbeitung — Fachber Metallbearb
Fachberichte fuer Oberflaechentechnik — Fachber Oberflaechentech
Fachberichte Huettenpraxis Metallweiterverarbeitung — Fachber Huettenprax Metallweiterverarb
Fachberichte Huettenpraxis Metallweiterverarbeitung — Fachber Huettenpraxis Metallweiterverarb
Fachberichte Metallurgie and Werkstofftechnik. Umwelt-Verfahrenstechnik — Fachber Metall Werkstofftech Umwelt Verfahrenstech
Fachbuchreihe Schweisstechnik — Fachbuchr Schweisstech
Fachbuchreihe Schweisstechnik [*Germany*] — Fachbuchreihe Schweisstech
Fachhefte fuer Chemigraphie, Lithographie, und Tiefdruck — Fachh Chemigr
Fachhefte fuer Chemigraphie, Lithographie, und Tiefdruck — Fachh Chemigr Lithogr Tiefdruck
Fach-Informationen. Energie-Versorgung Schwaben AG — Fach Inf Energ-Versorg Schwaben AG
Fachliche Mitteilungen der Austria Tabakwerke — Fachliche Mitt Austria Tabakwerke
Fachliche Mitteilungen der Oesterreichischen Tabakregie — Fachliche Mitt Oesterr Tabakregie
Fachverband fuer Strahlenschutz. Bericht FS — Fachverb Strahlenschutz Ber FS
Facial Orthopedics and Temporomandibular Arthrology — Facial Orthop Temporomandibular Arthrol
Facial Plastic Surgery — Facial Plast Surg
Facial Plastic Surgery — FPSUEA
Facility for the Analysis of Chemical Thermodynamics [*Database*] — FACT
Fackel — Fack
Facsimile Reprint. Society for the Study of Amphibians and Reptiles — Facsim Repr Soc Study Amphibians Reptiles
Facsimile Reprint. Society for the Study of Amphibians and Reptiles — Facsimile Repr Soc Study Amphibians Reptiles
Facsimile Reprint. Society for the Study of Amphibians and Reptiles — FSARAU
Facsimile Reprints in Herpetology — Facsim Repr Herpetol
Facsimile Reprints in Herpetology — Facsimile Repr Herpetol
Facsimile Reprints in Herpetology — FRHEAJ
Facsimiles of Egyptian Hieratic Papyri in the British Museum — FEHP
FACT (Fuels and Combustion Technologies Division. ASME) American Society of Mechanical Engineers — FACT Am Soc Mech Eng
Fact Magazine — Fact Mag
Fact Sheet. College of Agriculture. University of Nevada-Reno. Nevada Cooperative Extension — Fact Sheet Coll Agric Univ Nev-Reno Nev Coop Ext
Fact Sheet. Cooperative Extension Service. University of Maryland — Fact Sheet Coop Ext Serv Univ MD
Fact Sheet. Oregon State University. Cooperative Extension Service — Fact Sheet Oreg State Univ Coop Ext Serv
Fact Sheet. South Dakota State University. Cooperative Extension Service — Fact Sheet S Dak State Univ Coop Ext Serv
Fact Sheet. United States Department of Agriculture — Fact Sheet USDA
Fact Sheet. University of Arkansas. Cooperative Extension Service — Fact Sheet Univ Arkansas Coop Ext Serv
Fact Sheet. University of Maryland. Cooperative Extension Service — Fact Sheet Univ MD Coop Ext Serv
Fact Sheet. University of Wisconsin - Extension — Fact Sh Univ Wis Ext
Fact Sheets on Sweden — Fact Sheets Swed
Fact. The Money Management Magazine — FMM
Facta Universitatis. Series. Mathematics and Informatics — Facta Univ Ser Math Inform
Facta Universitatis. Series. Mechanics, Automatic Control, and Robotics — Facta Univ Ser Mech Automat Control Robot
Facteurs Biologiques et Chimiques dans l'Alimentation des Animaux — Facteurs Biol Chim Aliment Anim
Factores Biologicos y Quimicos de la Nutricion Animal — Factores Biol Quim Nutr Anim
Factors Regulating Blood Pressure. Transactions of the Conference — Factors Regul Blood Pressure Trans Conf
Factory — FCTYA
Factory and Industrial Management — Fact Ind Manage
Factory and Industrial Management — Factory and Ind Management
Factory and Plant — Fact Pl
Factory and Plant — Fact Plant
Factory Equipment and Materials [*South Africa*] — Fact Equip Mater
Factory Laboratory — Fact Lab
Factory Management and Maintenance — Fact Man Maint
Factory Management and Maintenance — Fact Manage Maint
Factory Management and Maintenance — Factory Mgt
Factory Management and Maintenance — FMAMA
Factory Management (New York) — Fact Manage (NY)
Factory Mutual Bulletin of Loss Prevention — Fact Mut Bull Loss Prev
Facts about Film (Finland) — Facts (Finl)
Facts and Figures — Facts Fig
Facts and Figures (Germany) — German Fct
Facts and Methods for Scientific Research — Facts Methods Sci Res
Facts from Flooring. Resilient Flooring Production Estimates — Floor Fact
Facts on File — F on F
Faculdade de Ciencias Agrarias do Para. Boletim — Fac Cienc Agrar Para Bol
Faculdade de Farmacia de Coimbra. Boletim — Fac Farm Coimbra Bol
Faculdade de Farmacia e Odontologia de Araraquara. Revista — Fac Farm Odontol Araraquara Rev
Facultad de Agronomia de Montevideo. Publicacion Miscelanea — Fac Agron Montevideo Publ Misc
Facultad de Ciencias Agrarias. Universidad Austral de Chile. Boletin — Fac Cienc Agrar Univ Austral Chile Bol
Facultad de Derecho. Revista. Universidad de Zulia — Fac Derecho R Univ Zulia
Facultad de Humanidades y Ciencias. Revista (Montevideo) — Fac Humanid Cienc Rev (Montevideo)
Facultad de Ingenieria y Agrimensura (Montevideo). Publicaciones Didacticas del Instituto de Matematica y Estadistica — Fac Ingen Agrimens (Montevideo) Publ Didact Inst Mat Estadis
Facultad de Medicina de Madrid. Archivos — Fac Med Madrid Arch
Facultad de Medicina de Montevideo. Anales — Fac Med Montevideo An
Facultad de Odontologia — FO
Facultad de Odontologia de Aracatuba. Revista — Fac Odontol Aracatuba Rev
Facultad de Odontologia de Ribeirao Preto. Revista — Fac Odontol Ribeirao Preto Rev
Facultad de Quimica y Farmacia. Universidad Central del Ecuador. Revista — Fac Quim Farm Univ Cent Ecuador Rev
Facultad de Veterinaria de Leon. Anales — Fac Vet Leon An
Faculte des Lettres et Sciences Humaines. Universite de Clermont-Ferrand. Nouvelle Serie — Fac Lett Sc NS
Faculte des Sciences Agronomiques. Laboratoire de Biochimie de la Nutrition. Publication — Fac Sci Agron Lab Biochim Nutr Publ
Faculte des Sciences Agronomiques. Laboratoire de Biochimie de la Nutrition. Publication — PLBNDJ
Faculte des Sciences Agronomiques. Laboratoire de Biochimie de la Nutrition. Publication. Universite Catholique de Louvain — Fac Sci Agron Lab Biochim Nutr Publ Univ Cathol Louvain
Faculte des Sciences de Tunis. Revue — Fac Sci Tunis Rev
Faculty of Law Review — Fac L Rev
Faculty of Law Review. University of Toronto — Fac of LR
Faculty of Law Review. University of Toronto — UT Faculty LR
Faculty Research Papers [*South Korea*] — Fac Res Pap
Faculty Research Papers. Hanyang Women's Junior College — Fac Res Pap Hanyang Women's Jr Coll
Faellesudvalget foer Statens Mejeri-og Husdyrbrugsforsog Beretning — Faellesudvalget Statens Mejeri-Husdyrbrugsfors Beret
Faerberei-Zeitung — Faerbereiztg

Faerber-Zeitung — Faerber Ztg
Faerg och Lack Scandinavia — Faerg Lack Scand
Faerie Queene — FQ
Fagskrift for Bankvaaesen — Ft f B
FAH [*Federation of American Hospitals*] **Review** — FAH Rev
Fahrzeugtestdatenbank [*Database*] — TDKF
Failure Modes in Composites. Proceedings of the Symposium — Failure Modes Compos
Faim-Developpement — Faim-Develop
Faipar — FAIPA
Faipari Kutatasok — Faip Kutatas
Fair Employment Practice Cases. Bureau of National Affairs — Fair Empl Prac Cas BNA
Fairbanks North Star Borough. Community Information Center. Quarterly — FCIQ
Fairbanks North Star Borough. Community Information Center. Special Report — FBCICSR
Fairbanks North Star Borough. Impact Information Center. Report — FBIICR
Fairbanks North Star Borough. Impact Information Center. Special Reports — FBIICSR
Fairchild Tropical Garden Bulletin — Fairchild Trop Gard Bull
Fairfax Monthly — Fairfax Mon
Fairly Serious Monthly Magazine — FSM
Fairplay International Shipping Weekly — FAI
Faisneis Raithiuil Quarterly Bulletin — Faisneis
Faith and Form — FF
Faith and Freedom — Fa F
Faith and Reason — F and R
Faith and Thought. Journal of the Victoria Institute [*Croydon, Surrey*] — FThought
Faith for the Family — FFF
Fako de l'Funkcialaj Ekvacioj Japana Matematika Societo — Funkcial Ekvac
Faktory Vneshnykh Sredy i Ikh Znachenie dlya Zdorov'ya Naseleniya Respublikanskii Mezhvedomstvennyi i Sbornik — Fakt Vneshn Sred Znach Zdor Nasel Resp Mezhved Sb
Faktory Vneshykh Sredy i Ikh Znachenie dlya Zdorov'ya Naseleniya — Faktory Vneshn Sredy Ikh Znach Zdorov'ya Naseleniya
Falk Symposium [*England*] — Falk Symp
Falke Monatsschrift fuer Ornithologie und Vivarienkunde — Falke Monatsschr Ornithol
Falke Monatsschrift fuer Ornithologie und Vivarienkunde. Ausgabe A — Falke Monatsschr Ornithol Vivarienkd Ausg A
Falkland Islands Dependencies Survey. Scientific Reports — Falkl Isl Depend Surv Sci Rep
Fall — FL
Fall Joint Computer Conference Proceedings — Fall Jt Comp Conf Proc
Fall Meeting. Minerals, Metals, and Materials Society. Extractive and Processing Division — Fall Meet Miner Met Mater Soc Extr Process Div
Fall Technical Meeting. Combustion Institute. Eastern Section — Fall Tech Meet Combust Inst East Sect
Fallos de la Corte Suprema de Justicia de la Nacion [*Argentina*] — Fallos
FAMA Survey Report. Republic of Malaysia Federal Agricultural Marketing Authority — FAMA Surv Rep Malays Fed Agric Mark Auth
Familiengeschichtliche Bibliographie — Fam Bibl
Familiengeschichtliche Blaetter — FgBl
Families in Society. The Journal of Contemporary Human Services — GSCW
Famille et Developpement — Fam Dev
Familles et Pedagogues — Fam Ped
Family Advocate — Fam Adv
Family Advocate — Fam Advocate
Family and Community Health — FACH
Family and Community Health — Fam Com Hlth
Family and Community Health — Fam Community Health
Family and Home-Office Computing — GFHC
Family Archive from Tebtunis — Fam Tebt
Family Circle — FC
Family Circle — GFAC
Family Coordinator — FADOA
Family Coordinator — Fam Coord
Family Economics Review — Fam Ec Rev
Family Economics Review — Family Econ R
Family Economics Review. US Department of Agriculture. Agricultural Research Service — Fam Econ Rev US Dep Agric Agric Res Serv
Family Handyman — FAHAA
Family Handyman — Fam Handy
Family Handyman — GTFH
Family Handyman — Handyman
Family Health — Fam Health
Family Health — Family Hlth
Family Health Bulletin — FHLBA
Family Law — Fam L
Family Law — Fam Law
Family Law Finance Report — Fam Law Fin Rep
Family Law Newsletter — Fam L Newsl
Family Law Notes — Fam LN
Family Law Quarterly — Fam Law Q
Family Law Quarterly — Fam LQ
Family Law Quarterly — Family LQ
Family Law Reporter — Fam L Rep
Family Law Reporter. Bureau of National Affairs — Fam L Rep BNA
Family Law Reports — Fam LR
Family Law Review — Fam L Rev
Family Law Review — Fam LR
Family Law Tax Guide. Commerce Clearing House — Fam L Tax Guide CCH
Family Life Coordinator — Fam L Coord
Family Life Educator — Fam Life Educ
Family Life Educator — FLED
Family Life Today — FLT
Family Living Topics T. Oklahoma State University. Cooperative Extension Service — Fam Living Top T Okla State Univ Coop Ext Serv
Family Medicine — Fam Med
Family Medicine Literature Index — FAMLI
Family Physician — Fam Physician
Family Planning Digest — Family Plann Digest
Family Planning Information Service — Fam Plann Inf Serv
Family Planning (London) — Fam Plann (Lond)
Family Planning News — Fam Plan N
Family Planning Perspectives — Fam Plan Pe
Family Planning Perspectives — Fam Plann Perspect
Family Planning Perspectives — FPGPAX
Family Planning Perspectives — GFPP
Family Planning/Population Report [*US*] — Fam Plann Popul Rep
Family Planning Resume — Fam Plann Resume
Family Planning Today — Fam Plann Today
Family Practice — Fam Pract
Family Practice — Family Pract
Family Practice News — Fam Pract News
Family Practice Research Journal — Fam Pract Res J
Family Practice Survey — Fam Prac Surv
Family Process — Fam Proc
Family Process — Fam Process
Family Relations — Fam Relat
Family Relations — FAMR
Family Relations — GFAM
Family Strengths — Fam Strengths
FAMLI. Family Medicine Literature Index — FAMLI Fam Med Lit Index
Famous Fantastic Mysteries — FFM
Famous Science Fiction — FMF
Fanciful Tales of Time and Space — FTT
Fanfare — Fan
Fanfare — FF
Fanfulla della Domenica — FD
Fantasiae — FANA
Fantastic Adventures — FA
Fantastic Adventures [*1939-1953*] — FAD
Fantastic Adventures Yearbook — FAY
Fantastic Novels — FN
Fantastic Novels Magazine — FNM
Fantastic Science Fiction — FASF
Fantastic Stories — FAS
Fantastic Story Magazine — FSM
Fantastic Story Quarterly — FSQ
Fantastic Universe Science Fiction — FAU
Fantasy — Fant
Fantasy and Science Fiction — Fant & Sci Fict
Fantasy Book — FB
Fantasy Book — FBK
Fantasy Fiction — FAN
Fantasy Fiction — FanF
Fantasy Newsletter — FNL
Fantasy Stories — FanS
Fantasy Stories — FFN
Fantasy: The Magazine of Science Fiction — Fans
FAO [*Food and Agriculture Organization of the United Nations*] **Agricultural Development Papers** — FAO Agric Dev Pap
FAO [*Food and Agriculture Organization of the United Nations*] **Agricultural Development Papers** — FOADAS
FAO [*Food and Agriculture Organization of the United Nations*] **Agricultural Services Bulletin** — FAO Agric Serv Bull
FAO [*Food and Agriculture Organization of the United Nations*] **Agricultural Services Bulletin** — FASBDH
FAO [*Food and Agriculture Organization of the United Nations*] **Agricultural Studies** — FAO Agric Stud
FAO [*Food and Agriculture Organization of the United Nations*] **Agricultural Studies** — FOASA5
FAO [*Food and Agriculture Organization of the United Nations*] **Atomic Energy Series** — FAO At Energy Ser
FAO [*Food and Agriculture Organization of the United Nations*] **Atomic Energy Series** — FAO Atom En Ser
FAO [*Food and Agriculture Organization of the United Nations*] **Development Program** — FAO Dev Program
FAO [*Food and Agriculture Organization of the United Nations*] **Development Program** — FDPRBZ
FAO [*Food and Agriculture Organization of the United Nations*] **Documentation** — FAO Doc
FAO [*Food and Agriculture Organization of the United Nations*] **Economic and Social Development Series** — FAO Econ Soc Dev Ser
FAO [*Food and Agriculture Organization of the United Nations*] **Fisheries Biology Synopsis** — FABSAE
FAO [*Food and Agriculture Organization of the United Nations*] **Fisheries Biology Synopsis** — FAO Fish Biol Synop
FAO [*Food and Agriculture Organization of the United Nations*] **Fisheries Biology Technical Paper** — FAFBAH
FAO [*Food and Agriculture Organization of the United Nations*] **Fisheries Biology Technical Paper** — FAO Fish Biol Tech Pap
FAO [*Food and Agriculture Organization of the United Nations*] **Fisheries Bulletin** — FAO Fish Bull
FAO [*Food and Agriculture Organization of the United Nations*] **Fisheries Circular** — FAFCAK

FAO [*Food and Agriculture Organization of the United Nations*] **Fisheries Circular** — FAO Fish Circ
FAO [*Food and Agriculture Organization of the United Nations*] **Fisheries Reports** — FAO Fish Rep
FAO [*Food and Agriculture Organization of the United Nations*] **Fisheries Reports** — FOFRAR
FAO [*Food and Agriculture Organization of the United Nations*] **Fisheries Series** — FAO Fish Ser
FAO [*Food and Agriculture Organization of the United Nations*] **Fisheries Series** — FFSEDR
FAO [*Food and Agriculture Organization of the United Nations*] **Fisheries Synopsis** — FAFSBZ
FAO [*Food and Agriculture Organization of the United Nations*] **Fisheries Synopsis** — FAO Fish Synop
FAO [*Food and Agriculture Organization of the United Nations*] **Fisheries Technical Paper** — FAO Fish Tech Pap
FAO [*Food and Agriculture Organization of the United Nations*] **Fisheries Technical Paper** — FFTPBT
FAO (Food and Agriculture Organization) Aquaculture Bulletin — FAO Aquacult Bull
FAO [*Food and Agriculture Organization of the United Nations*] **Food and Nutrition Paper** — FAO Food Nutr Pap
FAO [*Food and Agriculture Organization of the United Nations*] **Food and Nutrition Paper** — FFNPE2
FAO [*Food and Agriculture Organization of the United Nations*] **Food and Nutrition Series** — FAO Food Nutr Ser
FAO [*Food and Agriculture Organization of the United Nations*] **Forestry and Forest Products Studies** — FAO For & For Prod Stud
FAO [*Food and Agriculture Organization of the United Nations*] **Forestry Development Paper** — FAO For Dev Pap
FAO [*Food and Agriculture Organization of the United Nations*] **Forestry Development Papers** — FAO For Developm Pap
FAO [*Food and Agriculture Organization of the United Nations*] **General Fisheries Council for the Mediterranean. Circular** — FAO Gen Fish Counc Mediterr Circ
FAO [*Food and Agriculture Organization of the United Nations*] **General Fisheries Council for the Mediterranean. Circular** — GFCCAH
FAO [*Food and Agriculture Organization of the United Nations*] **General Fisheries Council for the Mediterranean. Studies and Reviews** — FAO Gen Fish Counc Mediterr Stud Rev
FAO [*Food and Agriculture Organization of the United Nations*] **General Fisheries Council for the Mediterranean. Studies and Reviews** — FUMRA2
FAO [*Food and Agriculture Organization of the United Nations*] **Indo-Pacific Fishery Commission. Proceedings** — FAO Indo-Pac Fish Comm Proc
FAO [*Food and Agriculture Organization of the United Nations*] **Indo-Pacific Fishery Commission. Proceedings** — IFCND7
FAO [*Food and Agriculture Organization of the United Nations*] **Information Service Bulletin** — FAO Inf Serv Bull
FAO [*Food and Agriculture Organization of the United Nations*] **Informes de Pesca** — FAO Inf Pesca
FAO [*Food and Agriculture Organization of the United Nations*] **Informes de Pesca** — FIPEDX
FAO [*Food and Agriculture Organization of the United Nations*] **Manuals in Fisheries Science** — FAO Man Fish Sci
FAO [*Food and Agriculture Organization of the United Nations*] **Monthly Bulletin of Agricultural Economics and Statistics** [*FAO Monthly Bulletin of Statistics*] [*Later,*] — FAO Mo Bul Ag Econ & Stat
FAO [*Food and Agriculture Organization of the United Nations*] **Monthly Bulletin of Statistics** — MBU
FAO [*Food and Agriculture Organization of the United Nations*] **Nutrition Meetings. Report Series** — FAO Nutr Meet Rep Ser
FAO [*Food and Agriculture Organization of the United Nations*] **Nutritional Studies** — FAO Nutr Stud
FAO [*Food and Agriculture Organization of the United Nations*] **Nutritional Studies** — WHOMAP
FAO [*Food and Agriculture Organization of the United Nations*] **Pasture and Fodder Crop Studies** — FAO Pasture Fodder Crop Stud
FAO [*Food and Agriculture Organization of the United Nations*] **Pasture and Fodder Crop Studies** — FAPFAB
FAO [*Food and Agriculture Organization of the United Nations*] **Paturages et Cultures Fourrageres** — FAO Paturages Cult Fourrageres
FAO [*Food and Agriculture Organization of the United Nations*] **Plant Production and Protection Series** — FAO Plant Prod Prot Ser
FAO [*Food and Agriculture Organization of the United Nations*] **Plant Protection Bulletin** — FAO Pl Prot Bull
FAO [*Food and Agriculture Organization of the United Nations*] **Plant Protection Bulletin** — FAO Plant
FAO [*Food and Agriculture Organization of the United Nations*] **Plant Protection Bulletin** — FAO Plant Prot Bull
FAO [*Food and Agriculture Organization of the United Nations*] **Plant Protection Bulletin** — FAOPA2
FAO [*Food and Agriculture Organization of the United Nations*] **Production Yearbook** — FAO Prod Yb
FAO [*Food and Agriculture Organization of the United Nations*] **Report** — FAO Rep
FAO [*Food and Agriculture Organization of the United Nations*] **Soils Bulletin** — FAO Soils Bull
FAO [*Food and Agriculture Organization of the United Nations*] **Soils Bulletin** — FSBUDD
Far East — FE
Far East Journal — FEJ
Far East Journal of Anesthesia — Far East J Anesth
Far East Journal of Mathematical Sciences — Far East J Math Sci
Far East Medical Journal — Far East Med J
Far East Shipping — F East Ship
Far Eastern Association of Tropical Medicine — Far East Ass Trop Med
Far Eastern Ceramic Bulletin — Far East Ceram Bull
Far Eastern Ceramic Bulletin — FECB
Far Eastern Economic Review — Far E Econ R
Far Eastern Economic Review — Far East Econ R
Far Eastern Economic Review — Far Eastern Econ Rev
Far Eastern Economic Review — FEC
Far Eastern Economic Review — FEE
Far Eastern Economic Review — FEER
Far Eastern Economic Review — FER
Far Eastern Law Review — Far East LR
Far Eastern Law Review — FELR
Far Eastern Medical Journal/Tung Fong Hsueeh Tsa Chih — Far E Med J
Far Eastern Quarterly — Far East Q
Far Eastern Quarterly — Far East Quart
Far Eastern Quarterly — FEQ
Far Eastern Review — Far East R
Far Eastern Review — Far East Rev
Far Eastern Review. Engineering, Commerce, Finance — Far E Rev
Far Eastern Series — FAS
Far Eastern Survey — Far East S
Far Eastern Survey — Far East Surv
Far Eastern Survey — FES
Far Eastern University. Faculty Journal — Far East Univ Fac J
Far Eastern University. Faculty Journal — FEUFJ
Far Eastern University. Journal — JFEU
Far Point — FPt
Far Seas Fisheries Research Laboratory. S Series — Far Seas Fish Res Lab S Ser
Far Seas Fisheries Research Laboratory. S Series — FSFRAL
Far Western Forum — FWF
Faraday Discussions of the Chemical Society — Faraday Dis
Faraday Discussions of the Chemical Society — Faraday Discuss
Faraday Discussions of the Chemical Society — Faraday Discuss Chem Soc
Faraday Discussions of the Chemical Society — FDCSB7
Faraday Society. Symposia — Faraday Soc Symp
Faraday Society. Transactions — Faraday Soc Trans
Faraday Society. Transactions — TFSOA4
Faraday Special Discussions of the Chemical Society — Faraday Spec Discuss Chem Soc
Faraday Symposia of the Chemical Society — Faraday Symp Chem Soc
Faraday Symposia of the Chemical Society — FSYCA3
Faraday Symposia of the Royal Society of Chemistry — Faraday Symp R Soc Chem
Farbe und Lack — F u L
Farbe und Lack — FALAA
Farbe und Lack — Farbe & Lack
Farbe und Lack. Zentralblatt der Farbenindustrie und Lackindustrie und des Handels — FBL
Farben, Lacke, Anstrichstoffe — Farben Lacke Anstrichst
Farben Revue. Special Edition (USA) — Farben Rev Spec Ed (USA)
Farben Zeitung — Farben Ztg
Farben-Chemiker — Farben Chem
Farben-Chemiker. Beilage — Farben Chem Beil
Far-From-Equilibrium Dynamics of Chemical Systems. Proceedings. International Symposium — Far From Equilib Dyn Chem Syst Proc Int Symp
Farhang-E Iran-Zamin [*Revue Trimestrielle des Etudes Iranologiques*] — FIZ
Farm and Food Research — Farm Food Res
Farm and Food Research — FFRED
Farm and Forest (Nigeria) — Fm Forest (Nigeria)
Farm and Garden Index — Farm & Garden Ind
Farm and Garden Index — Farm Gard Index
Farm and Home Research — Farm Home Res
Farm and Home Science — Farm & Home Sci
Farm and Home Science — Farm Home Sci
Farm and Home Science — FHSCAW
Farm and Home Science — Fm Home Sci
Farm and Home Science. Utah Resources Series. Utah State University. College of Agriculture. Agricultural Experiment Station — Farm Home Sci Utah Resources Ser
Farm and Power Equipment — Farm Power Equip
Farm Audience Readership Measurement Service [*Database*] — FARMS
Farm Building Progress — Farm Bldg Progress
Farm Building R and D Studies — Farm Bldg R & D Studies
Farm Buildings Digest — Farm Bldgs Digest
Farm Buildings Topics — Farm Bldgs Topics
Farm Bulletin. Indian Council of Agricultural Research — Fm Bull Indian Coun Agric Res
Farm Business — Farm Bus
Farm Business Summary for East Central Iowa. Iowa State University. Cooperative Extension Service — Farm Bus Summ East Cent Iowa Iowa State Univ Coop Ext Serv
Farm Business Summary for Southwest Iowa. Iowa State University. Cooperative Extension Service — Farm Bus Summ Southwest Iowa Iowa State Univ Coop Ext Serv
Farm Chemicals — FARCA
Farm Chemicals — FARCAC
Farm Chemicals — Farm Chem
Farm Chemicals — Fm Chem
Farm Chemicals and Croplife — Farm Chem Croplife
Farm Economics — Fa Econ
Farm Economics — Farm Econ
Farm Economics. Facts and Opinions. Illinois University. Cooperative Extension Service — Farm Econ Facts Opin Ill Univ Coop Ext Serv
Farm Economics Facts and Opinions. University of Illinois. Department of Agricultural Economics. Cooperative Extension Service — Farm Econ Facts Opin Univ Ill Dep Agric Econ Coop Ext Serv

Farm Economics. Pennsylvania State University. Cooperative Extension Service — Farm Econ PA State Univ Coop Ext Serv
Farm Economist — Fa Econ
Farm Economist — Farm Econ
Farm Economist — Fm Economist
Farm Engineering — Farm Eng
Farm Equipment Dealer — Farm Equip Dealer
Farm Equipment News — Farm Eq
Farm Forestry — Farm For
Farm Index — Farm In
Farm Index — FI
Farm Journal — Farm J
Farm Journal [*Midwest edition*] — GFAR
Farm Journal (Calcutta) — Farm J (Calcutta)
Farm Journal (Eastern Edition) — Farm J (E Ed)
Farm Journal of British Guiana — Farm J Brit Guiana
Farm Machinery — Farm Mach
Farm Management — Fa Man
Farm Management — Farm Manage
Farm Management — Fm Mgmt
Farm Management Newsletter. Missouri Cooperative Extension Service. University of Missouri and Lincoln University — Farm Manage Newsl Mo Coop Ext Serv Univ Mo Lincoln Univ
Farm Management Notes — Farm Manage Notes
Farm Management Report. United States Department of Agriculture. Cooperative Extension Service — Farm Manage Rep USDA Coop Ext Serv
Farm Management Report. University of Hawaii. Cooperative Extension Service — Farm Manage Rep Univ Hawaii Coop Ext Serv
Farm Management Review — Farm Manage Rev
Farm Mechanization — Fa Mechan
Farm Mechanization — Farm Mech
Farm Mechanization Studies — Farm Mech Stud
Farm Policy — Farm Pol
Farm Policy — Fm Policy
Farm Policy Review Conference — Farm Policy Rev Conf
Farm Quarterly — Farm Q
Farm Quarterly — Farm Quart
Farm, Ranch, and Home Quarterly — Farm Ranch Home Q
Farm, Ranch, and Home Quarterly. Nebraska Agricultural Experiment Station — Farm Ranch Home Q Nebr Agric Exp Stn
Farm Research — Farm Res
Farm Research [*Switzerland*] — FARRA
Farm Research — FARRAN
Farm Research News — Farm Res News
Farm Research News — Fm Res News
Farm Safety Review — Farm Safety Rev
Farm Surveys Report — Farm Surveys Rep
Farm Technology — Farm Technol
Farm Technology — Fm Technol
Farmaceuta Polski (1902-1914) — Farm Pol (1902-1914)
Farmaceutici Italiani Derivati Industriali ed Affi Research Series — Farm Ital Deriv Ind Affi Res Ser
Farmaceuticky Obzor — FAOBA
Farmaceuticky Obzor — FAOBAS
Farmaceuticky Obzor — Farm Obz
Farmaceutico Brasileiro — Farm Bras
Farmaceutisch Tijdschrift voor Belgie — Farm Tijdschr Belg
Farmaceutisk Revy — FAREAI
Farmaceutisk Tidende — Farm T
Farmaceutisk Tidende — Farm Tid
Farmaceutisk Tidende (Copenhagen) — Farm Tid Copenhagen
Farmaceutisk Tidskrift — Farm Tidskr
Farmaceutiskt Notisblad — Farm Notisbl
Farmaceutski Glasnik — FAGLAI
Farmaceutski Glasnik — Farm Glas
Farmaceutski Glasnik — Farm Glasn
Farmacevtisk Revy — Farm R
Farmacevtisk Revy — Farm Revy
Farmacevtski Vestnik — Farm Vestn
Farmacevtski Vestnik — FMVTAV
Farmaci. Scientific Edition — Farm Sci Ed
Farmacia — Farm
Farmacia (Bucharest) — FRMBA
Farmacia Clinica — Farm Clin
Farmacia Moderna in Rapporto al Progresso delle Scienze Mediche Napoli — Farm Mod
Farmacia Nueva — Farm Nueva
Farmacia Nuova — Farm Nuova
Farmacia Nuova — FMNUAS
Farmacia y Quimica — Farm Q
Farmacia y Quimica — Farm y Quim
Farmacihistoriska Saellskapets Arsskrift — Farmacihist Ars
Farmacija — Farm
Farmacista Italiano — Farm Ital
Farmacja Polska — FAPOA
Farmacja Polska — Farm Pol
Farmacja Wspolczesna — Farm Wspolczesna
Farmaco — Farm
Farmaco. Edizione Pratica — Farm Ed Prat
Farmaco. Edizione Pratica — Farmaco Ed Prat
Farmaco. Edizione Pratica — Farmaco Pra
Farmaco. Edizione Pratica — FRPPAO
Farmaco. Edizione Scientifica — Farm Ed Sci
Farmaco. Edizione Scientifica [*Italy*] — Farmaco Ed Sci
Farmaco. Edizione Scientifica — Farmaco Ed Scient
Farmaco. Edizione Scientifica — Farmaco Sci
Farmaco. Edizione Scientifica — FRPSAX
Farmaco Scienza e Tecnica — Farm Sci e Tec
Farmacognosia — Farmac
Farmacognosia. Anales del Instituto Jose Celestino Mutis [*Madrid*] — Farmacog
Farmakevtikon Dheltion. Edition Scientifique — Farm Delt Ed Sci
Farmakevtikon Dheltion. Edition Scientifique — PHDLAQ
Farmakevtikon Dheltion. Epistimoniki Ekdosis — Farm Dhelt Epistim Ekdosis
Farmakologija i Toksikologija — Farm i Toksik
Farmakologija i Toksikologija — Farm Toks
Farmakologiya Alkaloidov — Farmakol Alkaloidov
Farmakologiya i Toksikologiya — Farmak Toks
Farmakologiya i Toksikologiya — Farmakol T
Farmakologiya i Toksikologiya — Farmakol Toksikol
Farmakologiya i Toksikologiya [*Moscow*] — FATOA
Farmakologiya i Toksikologiya [*Moscow*] — FATOAO
Farmakologiya i Toksikologiya (Kiev) [*Ukrainian SSR*] — Farmakol Toksikol (Kiev)
Farmakologiya i Toksikologiya (Moscow) — Farmakol Toksikol (Mosc)
Farmakologiya i Toksikologiya (Moscow) — Farmakol Toksikol (Moscow)
Farmakologiya i Toksikologiya Respublikanskii Mezhvedomstvennyi Sbornik — Farmakol Toksikol Resp Mezhved Sb
Farmakologiya i Toksikologiya Respublikanskii Mezhvedomstvennyi Sbornik — FATOBP
Farmakologiya. Khimioterapeuticheski Sredstva — Farmakol Khimioter Sredstva
Farmakologiya. Khimioterapeuticheski Sredstva. Toksikologiya. Problemy Farmakologii — Farmakol Khimioter Sredstva Toksikol Probl Farmakol
Farmakologiya. Khimioterapeuticheski Sredstva. Toksikologiya. Problemy Toksikologii — Farmakol Khimioter Sredstva Toksikol Probl Toksikol
Farmakoterapeuticke Zpravy — Farm Zpr
Farmakoterapeuticke Zpravy — Farmkoter Zpr
Farmakoterapeuticke Zpravy. Supplementum — Farmkoter Zpr Suppl
Farmalecta — Farm
Farmaseuttinen Aikakauslehti — Farm Aikak
Farmasotik Bilimler Dergisi — Farm Bilimler Derg
Farmatsevticheskii Zhurnal (St. Petersburg) — Farm Zh St Petersburg
Farmatsevtychnyi Zhurnal — Farm Z
Farmatsevtychnyi Zhurnal — Farm Zh
Farmatsevtychnyi Zhurnal [*Kiev*] — FRZKAP
Farmatsevtychnyi Zhurnal (Kharkov) — Farm Zh (Kharkov)
Farmatsevtychnyi Zhurnal (Kiev) — Farm Zh (Kiev)
Farmatsevtychnyi Zhurnal (Kiev) — Farmatsevt Zh (Kiev)
Farmatsevtychnyi Zhurnal (Leningrad) — Farm Zh (Leningrad)
Farmatsiya i Farmakologiya — Farm Farmakol
Farmer and Forester — Fmr Forester
Farmer and Stock Breeder — Fmr Stk Breed
Farmer and Stockbreeder — Farmer Stockbr
Farmer Cooperatives — Farm Coop
Farmer Cooperatives. United States Department of Agriculture. Economics Statistics and Cooperatives Service — Farmer Coop US Dep Agric Econ Stat Coop Serv
Farmer Cooperatives. US Department of Agriculture. Agricultural Cooperative Service — Farmer Coop US Dep Agric Agric Coop Serv
Farmer's Advocate and Canadian Countryman — Farmer's Advocate Can Countryman
Farmers' and Scientists' Joint Conference — Farmers' Sci Joint Conf
Farmers' Bulletin — Farmers' B
Farmers' Bulletin — Farmers Bull
Farmer's Bulletin. Department of Agriculture (Canada) — Fmrs Bull Dep Agric (Can)
Farmer's Bulletin (Rhodesia) — Fmr's Bull (Rhodesia)
Farmers' Bulletin. United States Department of Agriculture — Farm Bull US Dep Agric
Farmers' Bulletin. United States Department of Agriculture — Farmers Bull USDA
Farmers' Bulletin. United States Department of Agriculture — Fmrs Bull US Dep Agric
Farmers Leaflet. National Institute of Agricultural Botany — Farmers Leafl Natl Inst Agric Bot
Farmer's Magazine and Useful Family Companion — Farmers Mag Useful Family Companion
Farmers' Magazine (London) — Farmers Mag London
Farmers' Newsletter — Farmers Newsl
Farmers' Newsletter — Fmrs Newsl
Farmers' Report. Leeds University. Department of Agriculture. Economics Section — Farmers Rep Leeds Univ Dept Agr Econ Sect
Farmers Weekly — Farm Week
Farmers Weekly [*South Africa*] — Farmers Wkly
Farmers Weekly [*London*] — FAWEA
Farmers Weekly (Bloemfontein, South Africa) — Farmers Wkly (Bloemfontein S Afr)
Farmers Weekly (Bloemfontein, South Africa) — FAWEB
Farming Business — Farming Bus
Farming Digest — Farming Dig
Farming Forum — Fmg Forum
Farming in SA and Woman and Her Home — Farming SA
Farming in South Africa — Farm S Afr
Farming in South Africa — Farming S Afr
Farming in South Africa — Fmg S Afr
Farming in South Africa — FSAFA
Farming in South Africa. South Africa Department of Agriculture — Farming South Africa
Farming in Zambia — Fmg Zambia
Farming Mechanization — Farming Mech
Farming News and North British Agriculturist — Farm Ne

Farming Progress — Farming Progr
Farming Review — Farming Rev
Farming Review — Fmg Rev
Farming Today — Farm Today
Farmline. United States Department of Agriculture. Economic Research Service — Farmline US Dep Agric Econ Res Serv
Farmline. United States Department of Agriculture. Economics Statistics and Cooperatives Service — Farmline US Dep Agric Econ Stat Coop Serv
Farmnote. Western Australian Department of Agriculture — Farmnote West Aust Dep Agric
Farmos Medical News — Farmos Med News
Farrago — F
Farumashia — FARUA
Fascicule de la Demande (Switzerland) — Fasc Demande (Switz)
Fascicule du Brevet (Switzerland) — Fasc Brev Switz
Fasciculi Mathematici — Fasc Math
FASEB (Federation of American Societies for Experimental Biology) Journal — FASEB J
FASEB Journal. Official Publication. Federation of American Societies for Experimental Biology — FASEB J Off Publ Fed Am Soc Exp Biol
FASEB [*Federation of American Societies for Experimental Biology*] **Monographs** — FASEB Monogr
FASEB [*Federation of American Societies for Experimental Biology*] **Monographs** — FASMDG
Faserforschung und Textiltechnik — Faserf T
Faserforschung und Textiltechnik — Faserforsch Textiltech
Faserforschung und Textiltechnik — FSTXA
Faserforschung und Textiltechnik — FT
Faserstoffe und Spinnpflanzen — Faserst Spinnpflanzen
Fast Access Information Retrieval. Newsletter — FAIR Newsl
Fast Food — FF
Fast Food Management — FFM
Fast Foodservice — FFS
FAST Journal — FAST J
Fast Protein, Polypeptide, and Polynucleotide Liquid Chromatography-Symposium — Fast Protein Polypept Polynucleotide Liq Chromatogr Symp
Fast Reactor Power Stations. Proceedings. International Conference — Fast React Power Stn Proc Int Conf
Fasti Archaeologici — F Ar
Fasti Archaeologici — FA
Fasti Archaeologici — Fasti A
Fasti Capitolini — F Cap
Fasti Capitolini — Fast Cap
Fasti Consolari dell'Impero Romano — F Imp
Fasti Consolari dell'Impero Romano — Fast Cons Imp
Fasti Consolari dell'Impero Romano — FC
Fasti Hispanienses — FH
Fasti Romani — FR
Fat and Oil Chemistry, Composition, Oxidation, Processing. Scandinavian Symposium on Fats and Oils — Fat Oil Chem Scand Symp
FAT [*Forschungsvereinigung Automobiltechnik*] **Schriftenreihe** — FAT Schriftenr
Fat Science Technology — Fat Sci Technol
Fataburen — Fatab
Fataburen. Nordiska Museets och Skansens Arsbok — Fataburen
Fathers of the Church — Fa Ch
Fathers of the Church — FC
Fatigue and Fracture of Engineering Materials and Structures — Fatigue Fract Eng Mater Struct
Fatigue Design — Fatigue Des
Fatigue of Engineering Materials and Structures — Fatigue Eng Mat Struct
Fatigue of Engineering Materials and Structures — Fatigue Eng Mater and Struct
Fatigue of Engineering Materials and Structures — Fatigue Eng Mater Struct
Fatigue Strength of Metals. Papers Presented at the Conference on the Fatigue of Metals — Fatigue Strength Met Pap Conf
FATIPEC (Federation d'Associations de Techniciens des Industries des Peiintures, Vernis, Emaux et Encre d'Imprimerie de l'Europe Continentale) Congress — FATIPEC Congr
FATIS [*Food and Agriculture Technical Information Service*] **Publications** — FATIS
Fatis Review — Fat Rev
FATIS [*Food and Agriculture Technical Information Service*] **Review** — FATIS Rev
Fats and Oils-Oilseed Crushings (Current Industrial Reports) — Fats Oils Oilseed Crushings Curr Ind Rep
Fats and Oils-Production, Consumption, and Stocks (Current Industrial Reports) — Fats Oils Prod Consumption Stocks Curr Ind Rep
Faulkner Studies — Fa St
Faulkner Studies — Faulkner St
Fauna [*Oslo*] — FUNAAO
Fauna and Flora [*Transvaal*] — FAFLBE
Fauna and Flora (Transvaal) — Fauna Flora (Transvaal)
Fauna d'Italia — Fauna Ital
Fauna d'Italia — FIITA6
Fauna Entomologica Scandinavica — Fauna Entomol Scand
Fauna et Flora Laurentianae — Fauna Fl Laurent
Fauna Fennica — FAFN
Fauna Fennica — Fauna Fenn
Fauna Fennica — SFFAAM
Fauna Hungariae — Fauna Hung
Fauna Norrlandica. Department of Ecological Zoology. Umea University — FANO
Fauna Norvegica. Series A — Fauna Norv Ser A
Fauna Norvegica. Series B — Fauna Norv Ser B
Fauna Norvegica. Series C — Fauna Norv Ser C
Fauna och Flora — FOFL
Fauna och Flora [*Stockholm*] — FUOFAA
Fauna och Flora. Populaer Tidskrift foer Biologi — Fauna Fl
Fauna och Flora (Stockholm) — Fauna Flora (Stockh)
Fauna of New Zealand — Fauna NZ
Fauna Polski — Fauna Pol
Fauna Polski — FNPLAI
Faune de France — FAFRAV
Faune de France — Faune Fr
Faune du Quebec — Faune Que
Faune du Quebec — FNQBAR
Faune du Quebec. Rapport Special — Faune Que Rapp Spec
Faune du Quebec. Rapport Special — FQRSD5
Faunistic Records. University of Queensland Papers — Faun Rec Univ Qu
Faunistilisi Maerkmeid — Faun Maerkm
Faunistische Abhandlungen — Faunistische Abh
Faunistische Abhandlungen [*Dresden*] — SMTFBL
Faunistische Abhandlungen (Dresden) — Faun Abh (Dres)
Faunistische Abhandlungen. Staatliches Museum fuer Tierkunde in Dresden — Faun Abh Staatl Mus Tierk Dresden
Faunistisch-Oekologische Mitteilungen — Faun-Oekol Mitt
Faunistisch-Oekologische Mitteilungen — FOEMA7
Faunistisch-Oekologische Mitteilungen. Supplement — Faun Oekol Mitt Suppl
Faust Blaetter — Faust B
Fayum Towns and their Papyri — P Fay
Fazovye Ravnovesiya v Metallicheskikh Splavakh — Fazovye Ravnovesiya Met Splavakh
Fazovyi Khimicheskii Analiz Rud i Mineralov — Fazovyi Khim Anal Rud Mineral
FBI [*Federal Bureau of Investigation*] **Law Enforcement Bulletin** — FBI Law Enf Bul
FBI [*Federal Bureau of Investigation*] **Law Enforcement Bulletin** — FBILEB
FBI Law Enforcement Bulletin — PFBI
FBM Fertigungs-Technologie. Werkzeuge, Maschinen, Systeme — FBM Fertigungs Technol
FC [*Series*]. Society of Manufacturing Engineers — FC Soc Manuf Eng
FCAP (Faculdade de Ciencias Agrarias do Para) Informe Tecnico — FCAP (Fac Cienc Agrar Para) Inf Tec
FCS (Fish Culture Section) American Fisheries Society Publication — FCS Publ
FDA [*Food and Drug Administration*] **Clinical Experience Abstracts** — FDA Clin Exp Abstr
FDA [*Food and Drug Administration*] **Consumer** — FDA Consum
FDA [*Food and Drug Administration*] **Consumer** — FDACB
FDA [*Food and Drug Administration*] **Consumer** — GFDA
FDA [*Food and Drug Administration*] **Drug Bulletin** — FDA Drug Bull
FDA [*Food and Drug Administration*] **Drug Bulletin** — FDADA
FDA (Food and Drug Administration) Consumer — FDA Consum Food Drug Adm
FDA [*Food and Drug Administration*] **Papers** — FDA Pap
FDC [*Food, Drug, and Cosmetics*] **Control Newsletter** — FDC Cont Newsl
FDDL-F Report (Texas Agricultural Extension Service. Fish Disease Diagnostic Laboratory) — FDDL F Rep (Tex Agric Ext Serv Fish Dis Diagn Lab)
FDDL-S (Texas Agricultural Extension Service. Fish Disease Diagnostic Laboratory) — FDDL S Tex Agric Ext Serv Fish Dis Diagn Lab
FE. The Magazine for Financial Executives — FE Magazin
Fear — FER
February — F
FEBS (Federation of European Biochemical Scoieties) Congress — FEBS Congr
FEBS (Federation of European Biochemical Societies) Meeting — FEBS Fed Eur Biochem Soc Meet
FEBS [*Federation of European Biochemical Societies*] **Letters** — FEBLAL
FEBS [*Federation of European Biochemical Societies*] **Letters** — FEBS Lett
FEBS [*Federation of European Biochemical Societies*] **Proceedings of the Meeting** — FEBPBY
FEBS [*Federation of European Biochemical Societies*] **Proceedings of the Meeting** — FEBS Proc Meet
FEBS [*Federation of European Biochemical Societies*] **Symposium** — FEBS Symp
FECS (Federation of European Chemical Societies) International Conference on Chemistry and Biotechnology of Biologically Active Natural Products. Proceedings — FECS Int Conf Chem Biotechnol Biol Act Nat Prod Proc
FED Publication. American Society of Mechanical Engineers. Fluids Engineering Division — FED Publ Am Soc Mech Eng Fluids Eng Div
Feddes Repertorium — Feddes Repert
Feddes Repertorium — FRZBAW
Feddes Repertorium. Specierum Novarum Regni Vegetabilis — Feddes Repert Specierum Nov Regni Veg
Feddes Repertorium. Specierum Novarum Regni Vegetabilis — RNRVAK
Feddes Repertorium. Specierum Novarum Regni Vegetabilis. Beihefte — BRSNAN
Feddes Repertorium. Specierum Novarum Regni Vegetabilis. Beihefte — Feddes Repert Specierum Nov Regni Veg Beih
Feddes Repertorium. Zeitschrift fuer Botanische Taxonomie und Geobotanik — Feddes Repert Z Bot Taxon Geobot
Feddes Repertorium. Zeitschrift fuer Botanische Taxonomie und Geobotanik — Feddes Reprium Z Bot Taxon Geobot
Fede e Arte — Fe A
Federacion Latinoamericana de Bancos. Revista — Federacion Latinoam Bancos R
Federado Escolar — FedE
Federal Accountant — Fed Accountant
Federal and State Business Assistance Database — FSBA
Federal Applied Technology Database — FATD
Federal Assistance Program Retrieval System [*Database*] — FAPRS
Federal Audit Guide. Commerce Clearing House — Fed Audit Guide CCH
Federal Aviation Administration. Office of Environment and Energy. Technical Report FAA-EE (United States) — Fed Aviat Adm Off Environ Energy Tech Rep FAA EE (US)

Federal Bar Association. Journal — Fed BA Jo
Federal Bar Association. Journal — Fed BAJ
Federal Bar Journal [*Later, Federal Bar News and Journal*] — FEBJA
Federal Bar Journal [*Later, Federal Bar News and Journal*] — Fed B J
Federal Bar News [*Later, Federal Bar News and Journal*] — Fed BN
Federal Bar News and Journal — Fed Bar J
Federal Career Opportunities — FCO
Federal Carriers Cases. Commerce Clearing House — Fed Carr Cas CCH
Federal Carriers Reports. Commerce Clearing House — Fed Carr Rep CCH
Federal Cases — F Cas
Federal Communications Bar Journal [*Later, Federal Communications Law Journal*] — Fed Com B J
Federal Communications Bar Journal [*Later, Federal Communications Law Journal*] — Fed Comm BJ
Federal Communications Law Journal — FCL
Federal Communications Law Journal — Fed Com LJ
Federal Convention. Australian Water and Wastewater Association — Fed Conv Aust Water Wastewater Assoc
Federal Council Bulletin — FCB
Federal Court Judgments [*Database*] — FCJ
Federal Court Reporter — FCR
Federal Court Reports — FC
Federal Court Reports [*Database*] — FCR
Federal Development in Indian Education — Fed Dev Ind Educ
Federal Drug Administration. Publications — FDA
Federal Economic Review — FER
Federal Employee/Retiree Newsletter [*Information service or system*] — FERN
Federal Employment Relations Manual — Fed Employ Relat Man
Federal Energy Administration. Conservation Paper (United States) — Fed Energy Adm Conserv Pap (US)
Federal Energy Data Index [*Database*] — FEDEX
Federal Energy Regulatory Commission Reports. Commerce Clearing House — Fed Energy Reg Commn Rep CCH
Federal Environmental Assessment Review Office. Technical Report — FEARTR
Federal Estate and Gift Tax Reports [*Commerce Clearing House*] — Fed Est & Gift Tax Rep
Federal Estate and Gift Tax Reports. Commerce Clearing House — Fed Est & Gift Tax Rep CCH
Federal Excise Tax Reports. Commerce Clearing House — Fed Ex Tax Rep CCH
Federal Home Loan Bank Board. Journal — Fed Home Loan Bank Bd J
Federal Home Loan Bank Board. Journal — Fed Home Loan Bank Board J
Federal Home Loan Bank Board. Journal — Fed Home Loan Bk Bd J
Federal Home Loan Bank Board. Journal — Federal Home Loan Bank Bd J
Federal Home Loan Bank Board. Journal — FHL
Federal Home Loan Bank Board. Journal — FHLBB Jrl
Federal Home Loan Bank Board. Journal — JFHLA
Federal Income Gift and Estate Taxation. Matthew Bender — Fed Inc Gift & Est Taxn MB
Federal Institute of Industrial Research. Nigeria. Research Report — Fed Inst Ind Res Niger Res Rep
Federal Institute of Industrial Research. Technical Memorandum (Nigeria) — Fed Inst Ind Res Tech Memo (Niger)
Federal Inter-Agency Sedimentation Conference. Proceedings — Fed Inter-Agency Sediment Conf Proc
Federal Labor-Management Consultant — FLMC
Federal Law Reports — Fed L Rep
Federal Law Reports — Fed LR
Federal Law Reports — FLR
Federal Law Review — F L Rev
Federal Law Review — Fed L Rev
Federal Law Review — Fed LR
Federal Law Review — Federal L Rev
Federal Law Review — Federal Law Rev
Federal Law Review — FLR
Federal Malay States — FMS
Federal Motor Vehicle Fleet Report [*United States*] — FMVF Rpt
Federal Power Service. Matthew Bender — Fed Power Serv MB
Federal Probation — Fed Prob
Federal Probation — Fed Probat
Federal Probation — Fed Probation
Federal Probation — PFPR
Federal Public Service Journal — Fed Pub Serv J
Federal Register — Fed Reg
Federal Register — Fed Regist
Federal Register — Fedl Register
Federal Register Search System [*Database*] — FRSS
Federal Register (Washington, DC) — Fed Regist (Wash DC)
Federal Regulation of Employment Service — Fed Reg Empl Serv
Federal Reporter — F
Federal Reporter — Feder Rep
Federal Republic of Germany. Patent Document. Auslegeschrift — Fed Repub Ger Pat Doc Auslegeschr
Federal Republic of Germany. Patent Document. Offenlegungsschrift — Fed Repub Ger Pat Doc Offenlegungsschr
Federal Republic of Germany. Patent Document. Patentschrift — Fed Repub Ger Pat Doc Patentschr
Federal Research in Progress [*Database*] — FEDRIP
Federal Research Report [*Database*] — FRR
Federal Reserve Bank of Atlanta. Economic Review — Fed Atlant
Federal Reserve Bank of Dallas. Farm and Ranch Bulletin — Fed Dallas
Federal Reserve Bank of Kansas City. Monthly Review — Fed KC
Federal Reserve Bank of Minneapolis. Quarterly Review — FMN
Federal Reserve Bank of Minneapolis. Quarterly Review — FMQ
Federal Reserve Bank of New York — Fed Reserve Bank New York
Federal Reserve Bank of New York. Quarterly Review — Fed Res Bank NY
Federal Reserve Bank of New York. Quarterly Review — Fed Reserve Bank NYQ Rev
Federal Reserve Bank of New York. Quarterly Review — FNY
Federal Reserve Bank of Philadelphia. Business Review — Fed Phila
Federal Reserve Bank of Richmond. Monthly Review — Fed Richmd
Federal Reserve Bank of San Francisco. Business and Financial Letter — Fed SF BFL
Federal Reserve Bank of San Francisco. Economic Review — FSE
Federal Reserve Bank of St Louis — Fed Reserve Bank St Louis
Federal Reserve Bank of St. Louis. Monthly Review [*Later, Federal Reserve Bank of St. Louis. Review*] — Fed St L
Federal Reserve Bank of St. Louis. Review — Fed Reserve Bank St Louis Rev
Federal Reserve Bank of St. Louis. Review — FRBRD
Federal Reserve Bank of St. Louis. Review — FSL
Federal Reserve Bulletin — FED
Federal Reserve Bulletin — Fed Res Bull
Federal Reserve Bulletin — Fed Reserve B
Federal Reserve Bulletin — Fed Reserve Bull
Federal Reserve Bulletin — FRB
Federal Reserve Bulletin — FRS
Federal Reserve Monthly Chart Book — Federal Reserve Mo Chart Bk
Federal Reserve Statistical Release. Industrial Production — Fed Stat
Federal Reserve Statistical Release. Industrial Production — Fed Stat R
Federal Rules Decisions — Fed R D
Federal Rules Decisions — Fed Rules Dec
Federal Rules Decisions — FRD
Federal Science Progress — Fed Sci Prog
Federal Supplement — F Supp
Federal Support to Universities, Colleges, and Nonprofit Institutions. Fiscal Year 1982. National Science Foundation. Report No. 84-315 [*United States*] — NSF Univ
Federal Tax Articles — Fed Tax Artic
Federal Tax Coordinator Second. Research Institute of America — Fed Tax Coordinator 2d Res Inst Am
Federal Tax Guide Reports. Commerce Clearing House — Fed Tax Guide Rep CCH
Federal Times [*United States*] — Fed Times
Federal Times — FETID
Federal Trial Reports [*Database*] — FTR
Federal Yellow Book [*United States*] — Fed Yellow Book
Federated Canadian Mining Institute. Journal — Fed Can M Inst J
Federated Institution of Mining Engineers. Transactions — Fed Inst M Eng Tr
Federation Bulletin — Fed Bull
Federation Francaise des Societes de Sciences Naturelles. Bulletin Trimestriel — Fed Fr Soc Sci Nat Bull Trimest
Federation Internationale de Documentation. News Bulletin — FID News Bull
Federation Internationale de Documentation. Publication — FID Publ
Federation Internationale de Documentation. Revue de la Documentation — FID R Doc
Federation Internationale de la Precontrainte. Proceedings. Congress — Fed Int Precontrainte Proc Congr
Federation Internationale de Laiterie. Bulletin Annuel — Fed Int Lait Bull Annu
Federation Internationale des Producteurs de Jus de Fruits. Commission Scientific et Technique. Rapports — Fed Int Prod Jus Fruits Comm Sci Tech Rapp
Federation Internationale des Societes d'Ingenieurs des Techniques de l'Automobile. Congres International. Rapport — Fed Int Soc Ing Tech Automob Congr Int Rapp
Federation Museums Journal — FMJ
Federation Nationale des Infirmieres Belges — FNIB
Federation of American Hospitals. Review — Fed Am Hosp Rev
Federation of American Societies for Experimental Biology. Federation Proceedings — Fed Amer Soc Exp Biol Fed Proc
Federation of American Societies for Experimental Biology Monographs — Fed Amer Soc Exp Biol Monogr
Federation of Asian and Oceanian Biochemists Symposium — Fed Asian Oceanian Biochem Symp
Federation of Australian Music Teachers' Associations. Quarterly Magazine — Fed Aust Music Teach Assoc Q Mag
Federation of British Columbia Naturalists. Newsletter — FBCN
Federation of European Biochemical Societies Congress — Fed Eur Biochem Soc Congr
Federation of European Biochemical Societies Lecture Course — Fed Eur Biochem Soc Lect Course
Federation of European Biochemical Societies. Letters — Fed Eur Biochem Soc Lett
Federation of European Biochemical Societies. Meeting Proceedings [*England*] — Fed Eur Biochem Soc Meet Proc
Federation of European Biochemical Societies Symposium — Fed Eur Biochem Soc Symp
Federation of European Biochemical Societies. Symposium (Berlin) — Fed Eur Biochem Soc Symp (Berl)
Federation of European Microbiological Societies. FEMS Symposium — Fed Eur Microbiol Soc FEMS Symp
Federation of European Microbiological Societies Microbiology Letters — Fed Eur Microbiol Soc Microbiology Lett
Federation of Insurance Counsel. Quarterly — Federation Ins Couns Q
Federation of Insurance Counsel. Quarterly — Fed'n Ins Counsel Q
Federation of Insurance Counsel. Quarterly — FICQ
Federation of Malaya. Department of Agriculture. Bulletin — Fed Malaya Dep Agric Bull
Federation of Malaya. Department of Agriculture. Economic Series — Fed Malaya Dep Agric Econ Ser

Federation of Malaya. Department of Agriculture. General Series — Fed Malaya Dep Agric Gen Ser
Federation of Malaya. Department of Agriculture. Scientific Series — Fed Malaya Dep Agric Sci Ser
Federation of Ontario Naturalists. Newsletter — FONN
Federation Proceedings — Fed P
Federation Proceedings — Fed Proc
Federation Proceedings — Federation Proc
Federation Proceedings — FEPRA
Federation Proceedings — FEPRA7
Federation Proceedings. Federation of American Societies for Experimental Biology — Fed Proc Fed Am Soc Exp Biol
Federation Proceedings. Federation of American Societies for Experimental Biology — Fedn Proc Fedn Am Socs Exp Biol
Federation Proceedings. Translation Supplement [*United States*] — Fed Proc Transl Suppl
Federation Series on Coating Technology — Fed Ser Coat Technol
Feed Additive Compendium — Feed Addit Compend
Feed and Feeding Digest — Feed Feed Dig
Feed Bag Magazine — Feed Bag Mag
Feed Industry — Feed Ind
Feed Industry Review — Feed Ind Rev
Feed Management — Feed Manage
Feed Management — FEMAA
Feed Management. Eastern Edition — Feed Manage E Ed
Feed Situation. US Department of Agriculture. Economic Research Service — Feed Situation USDA Econ Res Serv
Feeding and Nutrition of Nonhuman Primates. Proceedings of a Symposium — Feed Nutr Nonhum Primates Proc Symp
Feedlot Management — Feedlot Manage
Feeds Illustrated — Feed Illus
Feedstuffs — FDSTA
Feedstuffs Feed Additive Compendium — Feedst Feed Addit Compend
Feingeraete Technik — Feingeraete Tech
Feingeraete Technik — FGRTA
Feinmechanik und Praezision — Feinmech Praezis
Feinwerktechnik und Messtechnik — Feinwerktech Messtech
Feinwerktechnik und Messtechnik — Feinwerktech und Messtech
Feinwerktechnik und Messtechnik — FEMED
Feinwerktechnik und Micronic — Feinwerktech & Micronic
Feira da Ladra — FL
Feiten en Cijfers. Economisch, Financieel, Sociaal, Fiscaal, Juridisch — FCA
Feld, Wald, Wasser. Schweizerische Jagdzeitung — Feld Wald Wasser Schweiz Jagdztg
Fel'dsher i Akusherka — FEAKA
Fel'dsher i Akusherka — FEAKAD
Fel'dsher i Akusherka — Fel'dsher Akush
Feldspars. Proceedings of a NATO Advanced Study Institute — Feldspars Proc NATO Adv Study Inst
Feldwirtschaft — FWSFAA
Feline Leukemia — Feline Leuk
Feline Practice — Feline Pract
Feline Practice — FELPBG
Felix Ravenna — Fel Rav
Felix Ravenna — FR
Felix Ravenna. Supplement — FRS
Fellowship — Fell
Felsmechanik und Ingenieurgeologie [*Austria*] — Felsmech Ingenieurgeol
FEM (Factory Equipment and Materials) [*South Africa*] — FEM (Fact Equip Mater)
Feminist Issues — Fem Issues
Feminist Review — Fem R
Feminist Review — Fem Rview
Feminist Review — Feminist Rev
Feminist Review — PFEM
Feminist Studies — Fem Stud
Feminist Studies — Feminist
Feminist Studies — Feminist Stud
Feminist Studies — FS
Feminist Studies — FSt
Feminist Studies — GFEM
Feministische Studies — Feministische Stud
Femipari Kutato Intezet Kozlemenyei — Femip Kut Intez Kozl
Femipari Kutato Intezet Kozlemenyei [*Hungary*] — Femip Kut Intez Kozlem
FEMS (Federation of European Microbiological Societies) Microbiology-Ecology — FEMS (Fed Eur Microbiol Soc) Microbiol Ecol
FEMS (Federation of European Microbiological Societies) Symposium — FEMS (Fed Eur Microbiol Soc) Symp
FEMS [Federation of European Microbiological Societies] Immunology and Medical Microbiological Societies — FEMS Immunol Med Microbiol
FEMS [*Federation of European Microbiological Societies*] **Microbiology Letters** — FEMS Microbiol Lett
FEMS [*Federation of European Microbiological Societies*] **Microbiology Letters** — FMLED7
FEMS Microbiology Letters. Federation of European Microbiological Societies — FEMS Microbiol Lett Fed Eur Microbiol Soc
FEMS [*Federation of European Microbiological Societies*] **Microbiology Reviews** — FEMS (Fed Eur Microbiol Soc) Microbiol Rev
FEMS [*Federation of European Microbiological Societies*] **Microbiology Reviews** — FEMS Microbiol Rev
FEMS [*Federation of European Microbiological Societies*] **Microbiology-Ecology** — FEMS Mic Ec
FEMS Symposium. Federation of European Microbiological Societies — FEMS Symp Fed Eur Microbiol Soc
Fen Bilimleri Dergisi (Marmara Universitesi) — Fen Bilimleri Derg Marmara Univ
Fen Bilimleri Dergisi (Marmara Universitesi Ataturk Egitim Fakultesi) — Fen Bilimleri Derg Marmara Univ Ataturk Egitim Fak
FEN. Factory Equipment News — FEN
Fen Fakultesi Dergisi (Ataturk Universitesi) — Fen Fak Derg (Ataturk Univ)
Fen Fakultesi Dergisi. Seri A (Ege Universitesi) — Fen Fak Derg Seri A Ege Univ
FEN. Finite Element News [*England*] — FEN Finite Elem News
Fenarete-Letture d'Italia — Fenarete
Fenedexpress — FCB
Fennia — F
Fennia — FENN
Fennia — FENNAJ
Fenno-Chemica — Fenno Chem
Fenno-Chemica och Finska Kemistsamfundets Meddelanden — Fenno Chem Fin Kemistsamf Medd
Fenway Court — Fenway C
FERIC (Forest Engineering Research Institute of Canada) Technical Report — FERIC (For Eng Res Inst Can) Tech Rep
Fermentatio — FERMA2
Fermentation and Industry — Ferment Ind
Fermentation Industry (Moscow) — Ferment Ind Moscow
Fermentation Process Development of Industrial Organisms — Ferment Process Dev Ind Org
Fermentation Technology Today. Proceedings. International Fermentation Symposium — Ferment Technol Today Proc Int Ferment Symp
Fermentnaya i Spirtovaya Promyshlennost' — Fermentn Spirt Promst
Fermentnaya i Spirtovaya Promyshlennost' — FSPMAM
Fermenty Gribov i Ikh Primenenie v Narodnom Khozyaistve — Fermenty Gribov Ikh Primen Nar Khoz
Fermenty v Evolyutsii Zhivotnykh — Fermenty Evol Zhivotn
Fermenty v Laboratornoi Diagnostike. Materialy Vsesoyuznogo S'ezda Vrachei-Laborantov — Fermenty Lab Diagn Mater Vses Sezda Vrachei Laborantov
Fermenty v Meditsine. Pishchevoi Promyshlennosti i Sel'skom Khozyaistve — Fermenty Med Pishch Promsti Selsk Khoz
Fermenty v Narodnom Khozyaistve i Meditsine — Fermenty Nar Khoz Med
Fermes Modernes — Fermes Mod
Fermi Surface. Proceedings. International Conference — Fermi Surf Proc Int Conf
Fern Bulletin. A Quarterly Devoted to Ferns — Fern Bull
Fern Gazette — FEGADG
Fern Gazette — Fern Gaz
Fernmelde-Ingenieur — Fernmelde-Ing
Fernmelde-Ingenieur — FINGA
Fernmelde-Praxis — FEPXA
Fernmelde-Praxis — Fernmelde-Prax
Fernmeldetechnische Zeitschrift [*Germany*] — Fernmeldetech Z
Fernmeldetechnische Zeitschrift — FTZ
Fernmeldetechnisches Zentralamt. Forschungsinstitut. Technischer Bericht (Germany) — Fernmeldetech Zentralamt Forschungsinst Tech Ber Ger
Fernseh- und Kino- Technik — Fernseh- & Kino- Tech
Fernseh- und Kino- Technik — FKT
Fernsehen und Bildung — Fernsehen & B
Fernwaerme International — Fern Internat
Fernwaerme International — Fernwaerme Int
Fernwaerme International — FRWMA
Fernwaerme International (Frankfurt/Main) — Fernwaerme Int (Frankfurt Main)
Ferodo International Technical News — Ferodo Int Tech News
Ferrara. Universita. Annali. Sezione 9. Scienze Geologiche e Paleontologiche [*A publication*] — Ferrara Univ Ann Sez 9
Ferroelectricity and Related Phenomena — Ferroelectr Relat Phenom
Ferroelectricity. Proceedings. International Meeting — Ferroelectr Proc Int Meet
Ferroelectrics — FEROA
Ferroelectrics — Ferroelectr
Ferroelectrics and Related Materials — Ferroelectr Relat Mater
Ferroelectrics Letters [*United Kingdom*] — Ferroelectr Lett
Ferroelectrics Letters Section — Ferroelectr Lett Sect
Ferroelectrics Physics. Proceedings. School of Ferroelectrics Physics — Ferroelectr Phys Proc Sch
Ferskvandsfiskeribladet — Fvfb
Fertigungstechnik und Betrieb — Fertigungstech Betr
Fertigungstechnik und Betrieb — FTGBA
Fertigungs-Technologie — Fertigungs Technol
Fertile Fields. Cooperative State Research Service. State Agricultural Experiment Station System — Fertile Fields Coop State Res Serv State Agric Exp Stn Syst
Fertiliser Association of India. Proceedings — Fert Assoc India Proc
Fertiliser Association of India. Proceedings No. R and D — Fert Assoc India Proc No R D
Fertiliser Association of India. Proceedings No. Tech — Fert Assoc India Proc No Tech
Fertiliser, Farming, and Food — Fert Farming Food
Fertiliser, Feedings Stuffs, and Farm Supplies Journal — Fert Feed Stuff Farm Supplies J
Fertiliser Institute (Delhi). Proceedings — Fert Inst (Delhi) Proc
Fertiliser News — FENEA
Fertiliser News — Fertil News
Fertiliser Society. Proceedings — Fert Soc Proc
Fertilite Orthogenie — FEORA2
Fertilite Orthogenie — Fertil Orthogenie
Fertility and Contraception — Fert Contracept
Fertility and Contraception — Fertil Contracept
Fertility and Sterility — Fert Ster
Fertility and Sterility — Fert Steril
Fertility and Sterility — Fertil Steril
Fertility and Sterility — FESTA

Fertility and Sterility — FESTAS
Fertility and Sterility. Proceedings. World Congress on Fertility and Sterility — Fertil Steril Proc World Congr
Fertility Regulation during Human Lactation. Proceedings. IPPF [*International Planned Parenthood Federation*] **Biomedical Workshop** — Fertil Regul Hum Lactation Proc IPPF Biomed Workshop
Fertilization and Embryogenesis in Ovulated Plants. Proceedings. International Cytoembryological Symposium — Fert Embryog Ovulated Plants Proc Int Cytoembryol Symp
Fertilizer Abstracts — Fert Abstr
Fertilizer and Feeding Stuffs Journal — Fert Feed Stuffs J
Fertilizer and Feeding Stuffs Journal — Fertil Feed Stuffs J
Fertilizer and Feeding Stuffs Journal — FFSJA5
Fertilizer Focus — Fert Focus
Fertilizer Green Book — Fert Green Bk
Fertilizer Green Book — Fert Green Book
Fertilizer Industry Round Table. Proceedings. Annual Meeting — Fert Ind Round Table Proc Annu Meet
Fertilizer Institute. Environmental Symposium — Fert Inst Environ Symp
Fertilizer International — Fert Int
Fertilizer International — Fert Intnl
Fertilizer International — FFB
Fertilizer Marketing News — Fert Mark News
Fertilizer News — Fert News
Fertilizer Progress — Fert Prog
Fertilizer Research — Fert Res
Fertilizer Research. An International Journal on Fertilizer Use and Technology — Fert Res Int J Fert Use Technol
Fertilizer Review — Fert R
Fertilizer Science and Technology Series — Fert Sci Technol Ser
Fertilizer Science (Tokyo) — Fert Soc (Tokyo)
Fertilizer Society of South Africa. Journal — Fert Soc S Afr J
Fertilizer Society of South Africa Publication — Fert Soc S Afr Publ
Fertilizer Solutions — Fert Solutions
Fertilizer Summary Data — Fert Data
Fertilizer Technology — Fert Technol
Fertilizer Technology — Fertil Technol
Fertilizer Technology — FETEDP
Fertilizers and Agriculture — Fert Agric
Fertilizers and Crops — Fert Crops
Festigkeit und Verformung bei Hoher Temperatur [*Monograph*] — Festigkeit Verform Hoher Temp
Festkoerperanalytik. Tagung — Festkoerperanal Tag
Festkoerperanalytik, Tagung, Plenar- und Hauptvortraege — Festkoerperanal Tag Plenar Hauptvortr
Festkoerperprobleme — Festkoerperprobl
Festschrift der Geographischen Gesellschaft in Muenchen — FGGM
Festschrift fuer Alfred Bertholet [*Tuebingen*] — FAB
Festschrift zu Kongress und Ausstellung Wasser — Festschr Kongr Ausstellung Wasser
Fetal and Postnatal Cellular Growth [*monograph*] — Fetal Postnatal Cell Growth
Fetal Diagnosis and Therapy — Fetal Diagn Ther
Fetal Dosimetry Workshop — Fetal Dosim Workshop
Fett in der Parenteralen Ernaehrung. Symposium in Rottach-Egern — Fett Parenter Ernaehr
Fett Wissenschaft Technologie — Fett Wiss Technol
Fettchemische Umschau — Fettchem Umsch
Fette - Seifen - Anstrichmittel — Fette Seife
Fette - Seifen - Anstrichmittel — Fette Seifen Anstrichm
Fette - Seifen - Anstrichmittel — Fette Seifen Anstrmittel
Fette - Seifen - Anstrichmittel — FSASA
Fette - Seifen - Anstrichmittel — FSASAX
Fette - Seifen - Anstrichmittel. Verbunden mit der Zeitschrift die Ernaehrungs Industrie — Fet Sei Ans
Feuerfeste Werkstoffe fuer Konverter zur Stahlerzeugung. Internationales Feuerfest-Kolloquim — Feuerfeste Werkst Konverter Stahlerzeug Int Feuerfest Kolloq
Feuille du Canton de Vaud, ou Journal d'Agriculture Pratique, des Sciences Naturelles et d'Economie Publique — Feuille Canton Vaud
Feuille Federale [*Switzerland*] — FF
Feuille Suisse des Brevets, Dessins, et Marques — Feuille Suisse Brev Dessins Marques
Feuilles d'Agriculture et d'Economie Generale. Publiees par la Societe d'Agriculture et d'Economie du Canton de Vaud — Feuilles Agric Econ Gen
Feuilles d'Histoire — FH
Feuillets de Biologie — FBIOAA
Feuillets de Biologie — Feuill Biol
Feuillets de Radiologie — Feuill Radiol
Feuillets du Praticien — FEPRB8
Feuillets du Praticien — Feuill Prat
Feuillets Mensuels d'Information de l'Amitie Charles Peguy — FA Peguy
Few-Body Problems — Few Body Probl
Few-Body Systems — Few Body Syst
Few-Body Systems. Supplementum — Few Body Syst Suppl
FFCLUSP (Faculdade de Filosofia, Ciencias, e Letras. Universidade de Sao Paulo) Boletim Quimica — FFCLUSP Bol Quim
FFHC [*Freedom from Hunger Campaign*] **Basic Studies** — FFHC Basic Stud
FFI (Forsvarets Forskningsinstitutt) Mikroskopet [*Norway*] — FFI (Forsvarets Forskningsints) Mikrosk
FFI [*Forsvarets Forskningsinstitutt*] **Mikroskopet** [*Norway*] — FFI Mikrosk
FFTC (Food and Fertilizer Technology Center) Book Series — FFTC Book Ser
FhG [*Fraunhofer-Gesellschaft*] **Berichte** — FhG Ber
FI (Forum Italicum) — FI (For Ital)
Fiamme quali Reazioni in Flusso. Simposio Internazionale di Dinamica delle Reazioni Chimiche — Fiamme Reaz Flusso Simp Int Din Reaz Chim
Fiber and Integrated Optics — Fiber and Integrated Opt
Fiber and Integrated Optics — Fiber Integr Opt
Fiber in Human Nutrition — Fiber Hum Nutr
Fiber Laser News — Fiber Laser
Fiber Optic and Laser Sensors — Fiber Opt Laser Sens
Fiber Optic Chemical Sensors and Biosensors — Fiber Opt Chem Sens Biosens
Fiber Optic Communication Technology — Fiber Opt Commun Technol
Fiber Optic Components and Reliability — Fiber Opt Compon Reliab
Fiber Optic Couplers, Connectors, and Splice Technology — Fiber Opt Couplers Connectors Splice Technol
Fiber Optic Gyros. Anniversary Conference — Fiber Opt Gyros Anniv Conf
Fiber Optic Medical and Fluorescent Sensors and Applications — Fiber Opt Med Fluoresc Sens Appl
Fiber Optic Networks and Coherent Technology in Fiber Optic Systems — Fiber Opt Networks Coherent Technol Fiber Opt Syst
Fiber Optic Sensors — Fiber Opt Sens
Fiber Optic Smart Structures and Skins — Fiber Opt Smart Struct Skins
Fiber Optic Systems for Mobile Platforms — Fiber Opt Syst Mobile Platforms
Fiber Optics and Communications — Fiber Opt Commun
Fiber Optics and Communications [*Database*] — FOC
Fiber Optics in Local Area Networks — Fiber Opt Local Area Networks
Fiber Optics News — Fiber Opt
Fiber Optics Reliability. Benign and Adverse Environments — Fiber Opt Reliab Benign Adverse Environ
Fiber Producer — Fiber Prod
Fiber Producer — FIPRD
Fiber Science and Industry — Fiber Sci Ind
Fiber Science Series — Fiber Sci Ser
Fiberoptics Report — Fiberoptcs
Fibonacci Quarterly — Fibonacci Q
Fibonacci Quarterly — Fibonacci Quart
Fibonacci Quarterly — FIBQA
Fibre and Fabric — Fibre Fabr
Fibre Chemistry — Fibre Chem
Fibre Chemistry (English Translation) — Fibre Chem (Engl Transl)
Fibre Containers and Paperboard Mills — Fibre Containers
Fibre Science and Technology — Fibre Sci Technol
Fibre Science and Technology — FSTEB
Fibre Structure — Fibre Struct
Fibres and Fabrics Journal — Fibres Fabr J
Fibres and Plastics — Fibres Plast
Fibres and Polymers — Fibres & Polym
Fibres and Textile Industries — Fibr Text Ind
Fibres and Textiles in Eastern Europe — Fibres Text East Eur
Fibres, Engineering, and Chemistry — Fibres Eng Chem
Fibres, Fabrics, and Cordage — FFC
Fibres, Fabrics, and Cordage — Fibres Fabr Cordage
Fibres Fabrics Monthly — Fibres Fabr Mon
Fibres International — Fibres Int
Fibrin Sealing in Surgical and Nonsurgical Fields — Fibrin Sealing Surg Nonsurg Fields
Fibrinolysis — Fibrinolys
Fichas de Bibliografia Potosina. Biblioteca, Universidad Autonoma de San Luis Potosi (San Luis Potosi) — Fichas Bibliogr Potos S Louis Potosi
Fichero Bibliografico Hispano-Americano — FBH
Fichero Bibliografico Hispanoamericano — Fichero Bibliogr Hispanoamer
Fichero Medico Terapeutico Purissimus — Fichero Med Ter Purissimus
Fiches de Phytopathologie Tropicale — Fiches Phytopathol Trop
Fiches d'Identification du Zooplancton — Fiches Identif Zooplancton
Fichier MARC Quebecois [*Database*] — FMQ
Fichier Micropaleontologique General — Fichier Micropaleontol Gen
Fiction International — Fic Int
Fiction International — FInt
FID (Federation Internationale de Documentation) Communications — FID Commun
FID [*Federation Internationale de Documentation*] **News Bulletin** — FIX
Fides et Historia — F et H
Fides et Historia — FH
Fides et Historia — FHist
Fides et Historia — Fides H
Fidia Research Foundation Symposium Series — Fidia Res Found Symp Ser
FIDIA [*Farmaceutici Italiani Derivati Industriali ed Affi*] **Research Series** — FIDIA Res Ser
Field Analytical Chemistry and Technology — Field Anal Chem Technol
Field and Laboratory — Field & Lab
Field and Laboratory — Field Lab
Field and Laboratory. Contributions from the Science Departments — F a L
Field and Stream — Field & S
Field and Stream — FISTB
Field and Stream [*South edition*] — GFNS
Field Artillery Journal — F Artil J
Field Columbian Museum Publications — Fld Col Mus
Field Columbian Museum. Publications. Geological Series — Field Columbian Mus Publ Geol Ser
Field Columbian Museum. Publications. Geological Series. Zoological Series — Field Col Mus Pub G S Zool S
Field Conference Guidebook. New Mexico Geological Society — Field Conf Guideb NM Geol Soc
Field Conference Guidebook. New Mexico Geological Society — NMGGA
Field Crop Abstracts — Fie Cr Abstr
Field Crop Abstracts — Field Crop Abstr
Field Crop Abstracts — Fld Crop Abstr
Field Crops Research — Field Crops Res
Field Development Newsletter — Field Dev N
Field Drainage — Field Drain

Field Facts. Soils, Insects, Diseases, Weeds, Crops. South Dakota State University. Cooperative Extension Service. Plant Science Department — Field Facts Soils Insects Dis Weeds Crops SD State Univ Coop
Field Illustrated — Field Il
Field Measurement of Dinitrogen Fixation and Denitrification. Proceedings of a Symposium — Field Meas Dinitrogen Fixation Denitrif Proc Symp
Field Museum News [*Chicago*] — FMN
Field Museum of Natural History — Fld Mus Nat Hist
Field Museum of Natural History. Anthropological Series — FMAS
Field Museum of Natural History. Anthropological Series — FMNHAS
Field Museum of Natural History. Fieldiana. Botany — Field Mus Nat Hist Fieldiana Bot
Field Museum of Natural History. Fieldiana. Technique — Field Mus Nat Hist Fieldiana Tech
Field Museum of Natural History. Fieldiana. Zoology — Field Mus Nat Hist Fieldiana Zool
Field Museum of Natural History Publications. Botanical Series — Field Mus Nat Hist Publ Bot Ser
Field Museum of Natural History Publications. Geological Series — Field Mus Nat Hist Publ Geol Ser
Field Museum of Natural History Publications. Zoological Series — Field Mus Nat Hist Publ Zool Ser
Field Naturalist — Field Nat
Field Naturalists' Quarterly — Field Naturalists Quart
Field Notes. United States Forest Service — Field Notes US For Serv
Field Reporter — Field Rep
Field Research Projects. Man and Nature Series — Field Res Proj Man Nat Ser
Field Research Projects. Natural Area Studies — Field Res Proj Nat Area Stud
Field Seed Certification Guide. Illinois Crop Improvement Association — Field Seed Certif Guide Ill Crop Impr Ass
Field Station Record. Division of Plant Industry. Commonwealth Scientific and Industrial Research Organisation — Field Stat Rec Div Plant Ind CSIRO
Field Station Record. Division of Plant Industry. Commonwealth Scientific and Industrial Research Organisation — Field Stn Rec
Field Station Record. Division of Plant Industry. Commonwealth Scientific and Industrial Research Organisation — Field Stn Rec Div Plant Ind CSIRO
Field Station Record. Division of Plant Industry. Commonwealth Scientific and Industrial Research Organisation — Fld Stn Rec Div Pl Ind CSIRO
Field Station Record. Division of Plant Industry. Commonwealth Scientific and Industrial Research Organisation — Fld Stn Rec Div Plant Ind CSIRO
Field Studies — Field Stud
Field Studies — Fld Stud
Field Testing and Instrumentation of Rock. Symposium — Field Test Instrum Rock Symp
Field Theory and the Many-Body Problem. Lectures — Field Theory Many Body Probl Lect
Fieldiana — Field
Fieldiana. Anthropological Series. Natural History Museum — Fieldiana Anthropol Ser
Fieldiana Anthropology — Fieldiana Anthropol
Fieldiana Botany — Fieldiana Bot
Fieldiana Geology — Fieldiana Geol
Fieldiana Geology. Memoirs — Fieldiana Geol Mem
Fieldiana Geology. Memoirs — Fieldiana Geology Mem
Fieldiana Technique — Fieldiana Tech
Fieldiana Zoology — Fieldiana Zool
Fieldiana Zoology. Memoirs — Fieldiana Zool Mem
Fieldiana Zoology. Memoirs — Fieldiana Zoology Mem
Fieldnotes. Arizona Bureau of Geology and Mineral Technology — Fieldnotes Arizona Bur Geol Miner Technol
Fields and Quanta — FDQTA
Fields Institute Communications — Fields Inst Commun
Fields Institute Monographs — Fields Inst Monogr
Fields within Fields within Fields — Field w Fie
FIEP [*Federation Internationale d'Education Physique*] **Bulletin** — FIEP Bull
Fiera Letteraria — FLe
Fiera Letteraria — FLett
Fifteenth-Century Studies — FCS
Fifth Estate — Fifth Est
Figaro — FIG
Figaro Litteraire — Fig Lit
Figaro Litteraire — Fig Litt
Figaro Litteraire — FigL
Figaro Litteraire — FL
Fight Against Disease — Fi Dis
Figlina. Societe Francaise d'Etude de la Ceramique Antique en Gaule — SFECAG
Figures Canadiennes — Fig Can
Figyelo — FGLOA
Fiji Agricultural Journal — Fiji Agric J
Fiji Architect — Fiji Archt
Fiji. Department of Agriculture. Bulletin — Fiji Dep Agric Bull
Fiji. Geological Survey Department. Bulletin — Fiji Geol Surv Dep Bull
Fiji. Geological Survey Department. Economic Investigation — Fiji Geol Surv Dep Econ Invest
Fiji. Geological Survey Department. Economic Report — Fiji Geol Surv Dep Econ Rep
Fiji. Geological Survey Department. Memoir — Fiji Geol Surv Dep Mem
Fiji. Mineral Resources Division. Bulletin — Fiji Miner Resour Div Bull
Fiji. Mineral Resources Division. Economic Investigation — Fiji Miner Resour Div Econ Invest
Fiji. Ministry of Lands and Mineral Resources. Mineral Resources Division. Economic Investigation — Fiji Minist Lands Miner Resour Miner Resour Div Econ Invest
Fiji Timbers and Their Uses — Fiji Timb
Filamentous Fungi — Filam Fungi
File de Istorie. Culegere de Studii, Articole si Comunicari — Fil Ist
File di Istorie. Muzeul de Istoria — FI
FIL-IDF (Federation Internationale de Laiterie - International Dairy Federation) Bulletin — FIL-IDF (Fed Int Lait Int Dairy Fed) Bull
FIL-IDF (Federation Internationale de Laiterie - International Dairy Federation) Standards — FIL-IDF (Fed Int Lait Int Dairy Fed) Stand
Filipino Forester — Filip For
Filipino Forester. Society of Filipino Foresters — Filip Forester
Filipino Teacher — Fil Teach
Filipino Teacher — FT
Film [*Amsterdam*] — OBI
Film a Divadio — F a D
Film a Doba — F & Doba
Film a Doba — F Doba
Film and Kino — F & K
Film and Kino — F & Kino
Film and Television Technician — F & TV Tech
Film Appreciation Newsletter — Film Appreciation News
Film Bulletin — F Bul
Film Comment — F Com
Film Comment — F Comment
Film Comment — FC
Film Comment — Film Comm
Film Comment — GFCO
Film Criticism — F Criticism
Film Criticism — Film C
Film Criticism — Film Crit
Film Culture — F CUL
Film Culture — F Culture
Film Culture — Film Cult
Film Culture — IFCU
Film de Recherche — Film Rech
Film Directions — F Directions
Film Dope — F Dope
Film et Televisie — F & Televisie
Film et Televisie — F & TV
Film Fan Monthly — FFM
Film Form — F Form
Film Forum Review — FFR
Film Heritage — F Her
Film Journal — F Journal
Film Journal — Film J
Film Journal — FJ
Film Kultura — F Kultura
Film Library Quarterly [*New York*] — F Lib Q
Film Library Quarterly — F Lib Quarterly
Film Library Quarterly — Film Lib Q
Film Library Quarterly — Film Libr Q
Film Library Quarterly — FLQ
Film Literature Index — Film Lit Ind
Film Literature Index — Film Lit Index
Film Literature Index — FLI
Film Making — F M
Film Music — Film Mus
Film Music Notebook — F Music Ntbk
Film Music Notes — Film Mus Notes
Film News — F News
Film News — FN
Film Psychology Review — Film Psych
Film Quarterly — F Quarterly
Film Quarterly — Film Q
Film Quarterly — FQ
Film Quarterly — GFIQ
Film Reader — F Reader
Film Review — Film Rev
Film Society Review — F Soc Rev
Film und Fernsehen — F & Fernsehen
Film und Recht — F u R
Film und Ton — F & Ton
Film und Ton Magazin — Film u Ton Mag
Film und TV Kameramann — F & TV Kam
Film/Video Producers and Distributors [*Database*] — FVPD
Filmcritica — FCR
Filme Cultura — F Cultura
Filmfacts — FF
Filmfacts — Filmf
Filmihullu — FIHUL
Filmkritik — Fkr
Filmkunst — F Kunst
Film-Lyd-Bilde — F-Lyd-Bild
Filmmakers' Monthly — Filmmakers M
Filmmakers' Monthly — FMM
Filmmakers' Newsletter — FMN
Filmograph — FGR
Filmrutan — F Rutan
Films and Filming — F & F
Films and Filming — FF
Films and Filming — Films & F
Films Illustrated — F Il
Films in Review — Films in R
Films in Review — FIR
Filmwissenschaftliche Beitraege — F Wiss Beit
Filo Metallico — Filo Met
Filoil Pipeline [*Manila*] — FP

Filologia — Fi
Filologia — Fil
Filologia (Buenos Aires) — Fil (BA)
Filologia e Letteratura — FeL
Filologia e Letteratura — Fil Let
Filologia e Letteratura — FL
Filologia. Facultad de Filosofia y Letras. Universidad Nacional de Buenos Aires (Buenos Aires) — Filol BA
Filologia. Instituto de Filologia Romancia Facultad de Filosofia y Letras. Universidad de Buenos Aires — FUBA
Filologia Moderna — Fil Mod
Filologia Moderna — FiM
Filologia Moderna — FM
Filologia Moderna — FMod
Filologia Romanza — Fil Ro
Filologia Romanza — Fil Rom
Filologia Romanza — FiR
Filologia Romanza — FRom
Filologiai Koezloeny — Fil Koezl
Filologiai Koezloeny — FK
Filologiai Kozlony/Philological Review — FK
Filologica — Filo
Filologiceskie Nauki — FN
Filologiceskie Vesti — Filol Vesti
Filologiceskij Sbornik [*Stat'i Aspirantov i Soiskatelej*]. Alma-Ata — FilSbAlm
Filologiceskoje Obozrenije — FO
Filologicke Studie — FILS
Filologija — Fil
Filologija (Zagreb) — FilZ
Filologiskt Arkiv — FA
Filoloski Pregled — Fil Pregl
Filoloski Pregled [*Belgrade*] — FP
Filomata — Fil
Filosofia — Fil
Filosofia — Filos
Filosofia — FO
Filosofia e Vita — Fil Vit
Filosofia, Letras, y Ciencias de la Educacion. Facultad de Filosofia, Letras y Ciencias de la Educacion. Universidad Central del Educador (Quito) — Filos Letr Cien Educ Quito
Filosofia y Letras — FyL
Filosofia y Letras. Facultad de Filosofia y Letras. Universidad Nacional Autonoma de Mexico (Mexico) — Filos Letr Mex
Filosofichnii Problemy Suchasnoho Przyrodoznavstva Mizhvidomchyi Naukovyi Zbirnyk — Filos Probl Suchasnoho Przyr Mizhvid Nauk Zb
Filosoficky Casopis — FC
Filosoficky Casopis CSAV [*Ceskoslovesnska Akademie Ved*] — Filosof Cas CSAV
Filosofija i Naucnyj Kommunizm — Filos Nauc Kommunizm
Filosofska Dumka — FD
Filosofska Misul — FM
Filosofskaia Entsiklopediia — FE
Filosofski Problemy Suchasnoho Pryrodoznavstva — Filos Probl Suchasnoho Pryrodozn
Filosofskie Nauki — Filos Nauki
Filosofskie Nauki — FN
Filosofskie Problemy Obscestvennogo Soznanija — Filos Probl Obsc Soznanija
Filosofskie Voprosy Fiziki — Filos Vopr Fiz
Filosofskie Voprosy Fiziki i Khimii — Filos Vopr Fiz Khim
Filosofskie Voprosy Mediciny i Biologii — Filos Vopr Medicin Biol
Filozofiai Figyelo — Filoz Figy
Filozoficky Casopis — Filoz Cas
Filson Club History Quarterly — FCHQ
Filson Club History Quarterly — FiC
Filson Club History Quarterly — Filson Club Hist Q
Filson Club History Quarterly — Filson Club Hist Quart
Filson Club Quarterly — Filson C Q
Filtration and Separation — Filtr Sep
Filtration and Separation — Filtration
Filtration and Separation — FSEPA
Filtration and Separation in Oil and Gas Drilling and Production Operations — Filtr Sep Oil Gas Drill Prod Oper
Filtration Engineering — Filtr Eng
Filtration et Techniques Separatives [*France*] — Filtr Tech Sep
Filtration et Techniques Separatives — Filtr Tech Separatives
Filtration et Techniques Separatives — FTSED
Filtration Society's Conference on Liquid-Solid Separation. The Multi-Industry Technology — Filtr Soc Conf Liq Solid Sep Multi Ind Technol
Final Control Elements — Final Control Elem
Final Report. Electric Power Research Institute EPRI EL (Palo Alto, California) — Final Rep Electr Power Res Inst EPRI EL Palo Alto Calif
Final Report. Meeting. Inter-American Nuclear Energy Commission — Fin Rep IANEC
Finance and Development — F and D
Finance and Development — FID
Finance and Development — Fin & Devel
Finance and Development — Fin and Development
Finance and Development — Fin Dev
Finance and Development — Finance & Dev
Finance and Development — Finance Dev
Finance and Development — FNDV-A
Finance and Development — FUB
Finance and Trade Review — Financ Trade Rev
Finance and Trade Review — Finance Trade R
Finance and Trade Review — UFT
Finance and Trade Review (South Africa) — Fin and Trade R (South Africa)
Finance Week — Financ Week
Finances et Developpement — Finances et Develop
Financial Analysts Journal — F Anal Jrl
Financial Analysts Journal — FAJ
Financial Analysts Journal — FIA
Financial Analysts Journal — Fin Anal J
Financial Analysts Journal — Fin Analyst
Financial Analysts Journal — Fin Analysts J
Financial Analysts Journal — Financ Anal J
Financial Analysts Journal — Financ Analysts J
[*The*] **Financial Australian** — FA
Financial Computing — FNC
Financial Executive — CNU
Financial Executive — FEX
Financial Executive — Fin Exec
Financial Executive — Financ Exec
Financial Executive — Financ Executive
Financial Executive — Financial E
Financial Gazette [*South Africa*] — FG
Financial Gazette — Fin Gaz
Financial Industry — Fin Ind
Financial Institutions Data File [*Database*] — FIDF
Financial Listing Service [*Database*] — FLS
Financial Mail — Financ Mail
Financial Mail — Fincl Mail
Financial Mail [*Johannesburg*] — FM
Financial Mail [*South Africa*] — FMAID
Financial Mail — FNL
Financial Mail (South Africa) — Fin Mail (South Africa)
Financial Management — Fin Mgt
Financial Management — Finan Manag
Financial Management — Financ Manage
Financial Management — Financial M
Financial Management — FM
Financial Management — FMA
Financial Management — FMG
Financial Market Trends [*Paris*] — FIM
Financial Planner — Fin Planner
Financial Planning — FPL
Financial Planning — FPN
Financial Planning Strategist — Fin Plan Strat
Financial Planning Today — Fin Plan Today
Financial Planning Today — Fin Planning Today
Financial Post — Fin Post
Financial Post [*Toronto*] — FPO
Financial Post Magazine — Fin Post M
Financial Post Magazine — Fin Post Mag
Financial Post Magazine — FP
Financial Practice and Education — FPE
Financial Review — Fin R
Financial Review — FR
Financial Review — FRV
Financial Services Review — FSR
Financial Strategies and Concepts — Fin Strat Con
Financial Times — Fin Times
Financial Times [*London*] — Financ Times
Financial Times — FT
Financial Times — FTS
Financial Times. European Energy Report — Financ Times Europ Energy Rep
Financial Times (Frankfurt) — FTF
Financial Times (Frankfurt Edition) — FT (Fft)
Financial Times (London Edition) — FT (London)
Financial Times (North American Edition) — Financ Times North Am Ed
Financial Times. Supplements — FTS
Financial Weekly — Fin Wkly
Financial Weekly — Financial W
Financial World — Fin World
Financial World — Finan World
Financial World — Financ World
Financial World — FIWOA
Financial World — FW
Financial World — TWO
Financieel Dagblad — FD
Financieel Dagblad — Financ Dag
Financieel Dagblad voor Handel, Industrie, Scheepvaart, en Cultures — FIN
Financieel Economisch Magazine (Amsterdam) — FEA
Financieel Ekonomische Tijd — FET
Financieel Ekonomische Tijd — VEB
Financieel Overheidsbeheer — FIO
Financiele Koerier — FIK
Financiele Koerier — FK
Financing Agriculture — Fin Agr
Financing Agriculture — Financ Agric
Finanse — Fin
Finansije — Fin
Finanstidende — Finanstid
Finanstidende — Fnst
Finansy SSSR — Fin SSSR
Finanz Rundschau — Finanz Rdsch
Finanzarchiv — FA
Finanzarchiv — Finanzarch
Finanzarchiv — FNA
Finanzas y Desarollo — FyD
Finanzas y Desarrollo — FD
Finanzierung, Leasing, Factoring — TZA

Finanzierung und Entwicklung — F und E
Finanzjournal — Finanzj
Fine Arts Journal — Fine Arts J
Fine Arts Quarterly — F Arts Q
Fine Chemical Technical Bulletin. American Cyanamid Co. — Fine Chem Tech Bull Am Cyanamid Co
Fine Chemicals — Fine Chem
Fine Chemicals Directory Data Base — FCD
Fine Homebuilding — FHB
Fine Particle Filtration and Separation — Fine Part Filtr Sep
Fine Print — Fine Pt
Fine Woodworking — Fine Wood
Finis Terrae — Fin Ter
Finis Terrae. Universidad Catolica de Chile (Santiago) — Finis Terr Santiago
Finish [*Amsterdam*] — MGN
Finishing Industries — Finish Ind
Finishing Industries — Finishing Ind
Finishing Industries — Finshng Ind
Finite Element News — Finite Elem News
Finite Elements in Analysis and Design — Finite Elem Anal Des
Finite Fields and their Applications — Finite Fields Appl
Finland Geodeettinen Laitos. Julkaisuja — Finl Geodeettinen Laitos Julk
Finland Geologinen Tutkimuslaitos. Bulletin — Finl Geol Tutkimuslaitos Bull
Finland Geologinen Tutkimuslaitos. Opas — Finl Geol Tutkimuslaitos Opas
Finland. Patent Document — Finl Pat Doc
Finland Vesitutkimuslaitos. Julkaisuja — Finl Vesitutkimuslaitos Julk
Finlande. Commission Geologique. Bulletin — Finlande Comm Geol Bull
Finlands Fiskerier — Fin Fisk
Finlands Fiskerier — Finl Fisk
Finlay — Fin
Finlay Revista Medico-Historica Cubana — Finlay Rev Med-Hist Cubana
Finnisch-Ugrische Forschungen — FUF
Finnish Academy of Science and Letters. Sodankyla Geophysical Observatory. Report — Finn Acad Sci Lett Sodankyla Geophys Obs Rep
Finnish Centre for Radiation and Nuclear Safety. Report STUK-A — Finn Cent Radiat Nucl Saf Rep STUK A
Finnish Chemical Letters — Finn Chem L
Finnish Chemical Letters — Finn Chem Lett
Finnish Dental Society. Proceedings — Finn Dent Soc Proc
Finnish Fisheries Research — Finn Fish Res
Finnish Foundation for Alcohol Studies — Finn Found Alcohol Stud
Finnish Game Research — Finn Game Res
Finnish Journal of Dairy Science — Finn J Dairy Sci
Finnish Marine Research — FIMR
Finnish Marine Research — Finn Mar Res
Finnish Music Quarterly — Finn Mus Q
Finnish Paper and Timber Journal — Fin Paper
Finnish Paper and Timber Journal — Finn Pap Timb
Finnish Paper and Timber Journal — Finn Pap Timber
Finnish Paper and Timber Journal — Finnish Pap Timber
Finnish Paper and Timber Journal — FNPTA
Finnish Periodicals Index in Economics and Business [*Database*] — FINP
Finnish Psychiatry — Finn Psychiatry
Finnish Trade Review — Fin Trade
Finnish Trade Review — Finnish Trade R
Finnish Trade Review [*Helsinki*] — FTR
Finnish-French Symposium on Water Supply and Sewerage — Finn Fr Symp Water Supply Sewerage
Finnish-German Seminar on Nuclear Waste Management — Finn Ger Semin Nucl Waste Manage
Finommechanika-Mikrotechnika — Finommech-Mikrotech
Finommechanika-Mikrotechnika — FNMKA
Finsk Militaer Tidskrift [*Helsingfors*] — Finsk Mil Tidskr
Finsk Militaer Tidskrift Helsingfors — FMT
Finsk Teologisk Tidskrift — FTT
Finsk Tidskrift — Fin Tid
Finsk Tidskrift — FiTs
Finsk Tidskrift — FT
Finsk Veterinaertidskrift — Fi Vet Tidskr
Finsk Veterinaertidskrift — Fin Veterinaertidskr
Finsk Veterinaertidskrift — Finsk Vet Tidskr
Finsk Veterinaertidskrift — Finsk Veterinaerts
Finsk Veterinaertidskrift — Finsk Veterinartidskr
Finska Kemistsamfundet. Meddelanden — Fin Kemistsamf Medd
Finska Kemistsamfundet Meddelanden — Fins Kem Med
Finska Kemistsamfundet. Meddelanden — FKAMA
Finska Kyrkohisotriska Samfundets Arsskrift — FKHSA
Finska Laekaresaellsk Handlinger — Finska Laekaresaellsk Handl
Finska Lakaresallskapets Handlingar — Fin Lakaresallsk Handl
Finska Lakaresallskapets Handlingar — FLHAA
Finska Mosskulturforeningens Arsbok — Fin Mosskulturforen Arsb
Finskt Museum — Finskt Mus
Finskt Tidskrift — Finskt T
Fiord Studies. Caswell and Nancy Sounds. New Zealand — Fiord Stud Caswell Nancy Sounds NZ
FIP (Federation Internationale de la Precontrainte) Congress. Proceedings — FIP Congr Proc
FIPA [*Federation Internationale des Producteurs Agricoles*] **Nouvelles** — FIPA Nouv
FIRA [*Furniture Industry Research Association*] **Bulletin** — FIRA Bull
FIRA (Furniture Industry Research Association) Bulletin — FIRA Bull (Furn Ind Res Ass)
FIRA (Furniture Industry Research Association) Technical Report — FIRA Tech Rep (Furn Ind Res Ass)
FIRA (Furniture Industry Research Association) Transaction — FIRA Trans (Furn Ind Res Ass)
Firat Universitesi Veteriner Fakultesi Dergisi — Firat Univ Vet Fak Derg
Fire and Casualty Cases. Commerce Clearing House — Fire & Casualty Cas CCH
Fire and Materials — Fire Mater
Fire and Water Engineering — Fire Water Eng
Fire Control Experiments. California Division of Forestry — Fire Control Exp Calif Div For
Fire Dynamics and Heat Transfer. National Heat Transfer Conference — Fire Dyn Heat Transfer Natl Heat Transfer Conf
Fire Engineering — FIENA
Fire Engineering — Fire Eng
Fire Engineers Journal — Fire Eng J
Fire Engineers Journal — Fire Engnrs J
Fire Journal — Fire J
Fire Journal (Boston) — Fire J (Boston)
Fire Management Notes. United States Department of Agriculture. Forest Service — Fire Manage Notes USDA For Serv
Fire Management Notes. US Department of Agriculture. Forest Service — Fire Manage Notes US Dep Agric For Serv
Fire Prevention [*England*] — Fire Prev
Fire Prevention News — Fire Prev N
Fire Prevention Science and Technology — Fire Prev Sci Tech
Fire Prevention Science and Technology — Fire Prev Sci Technol
Fire Prevention Science and Technology — FPSTB
Fire Prevention. Supplement — Fire Prev Suppl
Fire Protection — Fire Prot
Fire Protection — Fire Protect
Fire Protection Yearbook — Fire Prot Yearb
Fire Research Abstracts and Reviews — Fire Res Abstr & Rev
Fire Research Abstracts and Reviews — FRAR
Fire Research Abstracts and Reviews — FRARA
Fire Research (Lausanne) — Fire Res (Lausanne)
Fire Retardant Chemicals Association. Semi-Annual Meeting — Fire Retard Chem Assoc Semi Annu Meet
Fire Retardant Chemistry — Fire Retard Chem
Fire Retardants. Proceedings of International Symposium on Flammability and Fire — Fire Retard Proc Int Symp Flammability Fire Retard
Fire Safety Journal [*Switzerland*] — Fire Saf J
Fire Safety Journal — FSJOD
Fire Science Abstracts — Fie Sci Abs
Fire Science Abstracts — Fire Sci Abs
Fire Science and Technology (New York) — Fire Sci Technol NY
Fire Science and Technology (Tokyo) — Fire Sci Technol (Tokyo)
Fire Study. National Research Council of Canada. Division of Building Research — Fire Study Natl Res Counc Can Div Build Res
Fire Surveyor — Fire Surv
Fire Technology — Fire Tech
Fire Technology — Fire Technol
Fire Technology — FITCA
Fire Technology Abstracts — Fire Technol Abs
Fireweed Country. Magazine of the Yukon — FICO
Firmeninformationen-Text [*Database*] — FINF-Text
First Break — FB
First Chicago Report — First Chi
First International Conference of Economic History — First Internat Econ Hist
First National City Bank [*Later, Citibank*] **of New York. Monthly Economic Letter** [*A publication*] — First Nat City Bank
Fiscal Studies [*United Kingdom*] — FCS
Fiscale en Administratieve Praktijkvragen — FAP
Fiscale Encyclopedie de Vakstudie — Vakstudie
Fiscalite du Marche Commun — FMC
Fiscalite Europeenne — Fisc Europ
Fiscalite Europeenne — Fiscal Europ
Fiscalite Europeenne — Fiscalite Eur
Fischer Athenaeum Taschenbuecher — FAT
Fischer Taschenbuecher — Fischer Taschenb
Fischerei-Forschung — Fisch-Forsch
Fischereiforschung. Informationen fuer der Praxis — Fischereiforsch Inf Prax
Fischers Zeitschrift fuer Praxis und Gesetzgebung der Verwaltung, Zunaechst fuer das Koenigreich Sachsen — FischersZ
Fischwaren und Feinkost Industrie — Fischwaren Feinkost Ind
Fischwirtschaft mit die Fischindustrie und Fischereiwelt — Fischwirtsch Fischind Fischereiwelt
Fish and Wildlife Service (United States). Research Report — Fish Wildl Serv (US) Res Rep
Fish Culture Section Publication (American Fisheries Society) — Fish Cult Sect Publ Am Fish Soc
Fish Disease Diagnostic Laboratory. Report FDDL-F. Texas Agricultural Extension Service — Fish Dis Diagn Lab Rep FDDL F Tex Agric Ext Serv
Fish Disease Diagnostic Laboratory. Texas Agricultural Extension Service. Report FDDL-S — Fish Dis Diagn Lab Tex Agric Ext Serv Rep FDDL-S
Fish Farming International — Fish Farm Int
Fish Farming International — Fish Farming Int
Fish Health News — Fish Hlth N
Fish Industry Board. Bulletin [*New Zealand*] — FIB
Fish Meal and Oil Industry — Fish Meal Oil Ind
Fish Nutrition — Fish Nutr
Fish Nutrition and Diet Development. International Seminar — Fish Nutr Diet Dev Int Semin
Fish Oil and Blood-Vessel Wall Interactions. Proceedings. International Symposium — Fish Oil Blood Vessel Wall Interact Proc Int Symp
Fish Pathology — Fish Pathol
Fish Physiology — Fish Physiol

Fish Utilization. Contributions from Research. International Symposium — Fish Util Contrib Res Int Symp
Fisheries — FISHD
Fisheries and Marine Service (Canada). Miscellaneous Special Publication — Fish Mar Serv (Can) Misc Spec Publ
Fisheries and Marine Service (Canada). Technical Report — Fish Mar Serv (Can) Tech Rep
Fisheries and Marine Service. Fisheries Operations Directorate. Central Region. Technical Report Series (Canada) — Fish Mar Serv Fish Oper Dir Cent Reg Tech Rep Ser Can
Fisheries and Wildlife Paper (Victoria) — Fish Wildl Pap (Victoria)
Fisheries Bulletin (Dublin) — Fish Bull (Dublin)
Fisheries Bulletin. Food and Agriculture Organization — Fish Bull FAO
Fisheries Bulletin. South Africa — Fish Bull S Afr
Fisheries Management — Fish Manage
Fisheries Newsletter — Fish News
Fisheries Newsletter — Fish Newsl
Fisheries Newsletter — Fisheries Nletter
Fisheries Notes. Department of Primary Industries. Queensland — Fish Notes Dep Prim Ind Qd
Fisheries Notes. Department of Primary Industries. Queensland — Fish Notes Dep Prim Ind Queensl
Fisheries of Canada — FISC
Fisheries of the US — Fisheries
Fisheries Radiobiological Laboratory Technical Report FRL (United Kingdom) — Fish Radiobiol Lab Tech Rep FRL (UK)
Fisheries Report. Department of Agriculture — Fish Rep Dep Agric
Fisheries Research (Amsterdam) — Fish Res (Amst)
Fisheries Research Board of Canada. Annual Report — Fish Res Board Can Annu Rep
Fisheries Research Board of Canada. ARO [*Atlantic Regional Office*] **Circular** — Fish Res Board Can ARO Circ
Fisheries Research Board of Canada. Biological Station. St. Andrews, New Brunswick. General Serie Circular — Fish Res Board Can Biol Stn St Andrews NB Gen Ser Circ
Fisheries Research Board of Canada. Bulletin — Fish Res Board Can Bull
Fisheries Research Board of Canada. Bulletin — FRBCB
Fisheries Research Board of Canada. General Series Circular — Fish Res Board Can Gen Ser Circ
Fisheries Research Board of Canada. Manuscript Report Series — FRBMRS
Fisheries Research Board of Canada. Miscellaneous Special Publication — Fish Res Board Can Misc Spec Publ
Fisheries Research Board of Canada. Progress Reports of the Atlantic Coast Stations — Fish Res Board Can Prog Rep Atl Coast Stn
Fisheries Research Board of Canada. Progress Reports of the Pacific Coast Station — Fish Res Board Can Prog Rep Pac Coast Stn
Fisheries Research Board of Canada. Review — Fish Res Board Can Rev
Fisheries Research Board of Canada. Technical Paper — Fish Res Board Can Tech Pap
Fisheries Research Board of Canada. Technical Report — Fish Res Board Can Tech Rep
Fisheries Research Board of Canada. Technical Report — FRBCTR
Fisheries Research Bulletin — Fish Res Bull
Fisheries Research Bulletin. New York Conservation Department — Fish Res Bull NY Conserv Dep
Fisheries Research Bulletin (Western Australia Marine Research Laboratories) — Fish Res Bull (West Aust Mar Res Lab)
Fisheries Research Division. Occasional Publication (New Zealand) — Fish Res Div Occas Publ (NZ)
Fisheries Research Journal of the Philippines — Fish Res J Phil
Fisheries Research Technical Report (United Kingdom. Directorate of Fisheries Research) — Fish Res Tech Rep (UK Dir Fish Res)
Fisheries Statistics of British Columbia — Fish Stat BC
Fisheries Synopsis. Division of Fisheries and Oceanography. Commonwealth Scientific and Industrial Research Organisation — Fish Synopsis Div Fish Oceanogr CSIRO
Fishermen's News — FSMNA
Fishery Board of Sweden. Institute of Freshwater Research (Drottningholm). Report — Fish Board Swed Inst Freshwater Res (Drottningholm) Rep
Fishery Board of Sweden. Institute of Marine Research. Report — Fish Board Swed Inst Mar Res Rep
Fishery Board of Sweden. Series Hydrography. Report — Fish Board Swed Ser Hydrogr Rep
Fishery Bulletin — Fish B
Fishery Bulletin — Fish Bull
Fishery Industrial Research [*United States*] — FINRA
Fishery Industrial Research — Fish Ind Res
Fishery Industrial Research — Fishery Ind Res
Fishery Investigations. Ministry of Agriculture, Fisheries, and Food (Great Britain). Series II. Salmon and Freshwater Fisheries — Fish Invest Minist Agric Fish Food (GB) Ser
Fishery Investigations. Ministry of Agriculture, Fisheries, and Food (Great Britain). Series IV — Fish Invest Minist Agric Fish Food (GB) Ser IV
Fishery Investigations. Series II. Marine Fisheries. Great Britain Ministry of Agriculture, Fisheries, and Food — Fish Invest Ser II Mar Fish GB Minist Agric Fish Food
Fishery Market News — Fish Mark News
Fishery Statistics Data Base — FISHSTATS
Fishery Technology — Fish Technol
Fishery Technology [*India*] — FITEA
Fishing Boats of the World — Fish Boat Wld
Fishing Gazette — Fish Gaz
Fishing Industry News Science — FINS
Fishing News International — Fish N Intnl
Fishing News International — Fish News Int
Fishing News International — Fishg News Int
Fisica e Tecnologia — Fis e Tecnol
Fisica e Tecnologia (Bologna) — Fis Tecnol (Bologna)
Fisiologia e Medicina — Fis Med
Fisiologia e Medicina — Fisiol e Med
Fisiologia e Medicina (Rome) — Fisiol Med (Rome)
Fisk University News — Fisk Univ News
Fiskeridirektoratets Skrifter — Fisk Dir Skr
Fiskeridirektoratets Skrifter. Serie Ernaering — Fiskeridir Skr Ser Ernaer
Fiskeridirektoratets Skrifter. Serie Fiskeri — Fiskeridir Skr Ser Fisk
Fiskeridirektoratets Skrifter. Serie Havundersokelser — FISK
Fiskeridirektoratets Skrifter. Serie Havundersokelser — Fiskeridir Skr Ser Havunders
Fiskeridirektoratets Skrifter. Serie Teknologiske Undersokelser — Fiskeridir Skr Ser Teknol Unders
Fiskets Gang — Fisk Gang
Fitness & Sports Review International — Fit & Sports Rev Int
Fitness Institute. Bulletin — Fitness Inst Bull
Fitontsidy. Ikh Rol v Prirode, Izbrannye Doklady Soveshchaniya po Probleme Fitontsidov — Fitontsidy Ikh Rol Prir Izbr Dokl Soveshch Probl Fitontsidov
Fitontsidy. Rol v Biogeotsenozakh, Znachenie dlya Meditsiny, Materialy Soveshchaniya — Fitontsidy Rol Biogeotsenozakh Znach Med Mater Soveshch
Fitontsidy v Meditsine — Fitontsidy Med
Fitontsidy v Meditsine. Sel'skom Khozyaistve i Pishchevoi Promyshlennosti — Fitontsidy Med Selsk Khoz Pishch Promsti
Fitopatogennye Bakterii. Materialy Vsesoyuznoi Konferentsii po Bakterial'nym Boleznyam Rastenii — Fitopatog Bakt Mater Vses Konf Bakt Bolezn Rast
Fitopatologia — Fitopatol
Fitopatologia Brasileira — Fitopat Bras
Fitopatologia Brasileira — Fitopatol Bras
Fitopatologia Colombiana — Fitopatol Colomb
Fitopatologia Mexicana — Fitopatol Mex
Fitotecnia Latinoamericana — Fitotec Latinoam
Fitotecnia Latinoamericana — Fitotecnia Latinoam
Fitzgerald Newsletter — FitzN
Fitzgerald Newsletter — FNL
Fitzgerald-Hemingway Annual — FHA
Five-Year Economic Forecast (Japan) — Jpn Forcst
Five-Year Philippine Development Plan, 1983-1987 — Phil Pln 87
Five-Year Plan for Economic and Social Development, 1981-85 (Jordan) — Jordan Pln
FIW [*Forschungsinstitut fuer Wirtschaftsverfassung und Wettbewerb*] **Dokumentation** — FIW Dok
FIW [*Forschungsinstitut fuer Wirtschaftsverfassung und Wettbewerb*] **Schriftenreihe** — FIW Schr
Fiziceskaja Kul'tura v Skole — Fizic Kult
Fiziceskij Zurnal — Fiz Z
Fiziceskij Zurnal — Fizic Z
Fizicheskaya Elektronika (Moscow) — Fiz Elektron (Moscow)
Fizicheskaya Gazodinamika i Svoistva Gazov pri Vysokikh Temperaturakh — Fiz Gazodin Svoistva Gazov Vys Temp
Fizicheskaya Gazodinamika i Teploobmen — Fiz Gazodin Teploobmen
Fizicheskaya Gazodinamika Ionizirovannykh i Khimicheski Reagiruyushchikh Gazov — Fiz Gazodin Ioniz Khim Reagiruyushchikh Gazov
Fizicheskaya Gazodinamika, Teploobmen, i Termodinamika Gazov Vysokikh Temperatur — Fiz Gazodin Teploobmen Termodin Gazov Vys Temp
Fizicheskaya Geografiya — Fiz Geogr
Fizicheskaya Gidrodinamika i Kinetika Zhidkosti — Fiz Gidrodin Kinet Zhidk
Fizicheskaya Khimiya [*Former USSR*] — Fiz Khim
Fizicheskaya Khimiya i Tekhnologiya Silikatnykh i Neorganicheskikh Materialov — Fiz Khim Tekhnol Silik Neorg Mater
Fizicheskaya Khimiya (Krasnoyarsk) — Fiz Khim Krasnoyarsk
Fizicheskaya Khimiya (Moscow) — Fiz Khim (Moscow)
Fizicheskaya Mekhanika [*Former USSR*] — Fiz Mekh
Fizicheskie Aspekty Zagryazneniya Atmosfery. Tezisy Dokladov. Mezhdunarodnaya Konferentsiya — Fiz Aspekty Zagryaz Atmos Tezisy Dokl Mezhdunar Konf
Fizicheskie i Fiziko-Khimicheskie Metody v Eksperimente i Klinike — Fiz Fiz Khim Metody Eksp Klin
Fizicheskie i Fiziko-Khimicheskie Protsessy v Dinamicheskikh Rudoobrazuyushchikh Sistemakh — Fiz Fiz Khim Protsessy Din Rudoobraz Sist
Fizicheskie i Fiziko-Khimicheskie Svoistva Ferritov — Fiz Fiz Khim Svoistva Ferritov
Fizicheskie i Kurortnye Faktory i Ikh Lechebnow Primenenie — Fiz Kurortnye Faktory Ikh Lech Primen
Fizicheskie i Matematicheskie Metody v Koordinatsionnoi Khimii. Tezisy Dokladov. Vsesoyuznoe Soveshchanie — Fiz Mat Metody Koord Khim Tezisy Dokl Vses Soveshch
Fizicheskie Issledovaniya — Fiz Issled
Fizicheskie Metody Issledovaniya Tverdogo Tela — Fiz Metody Issled Tverd Tela
Fizicheskie Problemy Spektroskopii. Materialy Soveshchaniya — Fiz Probl Spektrosk Mater Soveshch
Fizicheskie Protsessy Gornogo Proizvodstva — Fiz Protsessy Gorn Proizvod
Fizicheskii Sbornik — Fiz Sb
Fizicheskii Sbornik. L'vovskii Gosudarstvennyi Universitet [*Ukrainian SSR*] — Fiz Sb L'vov Gos Univ
Fizicheskii Zhurnal — Fiz Zh
Fizicheskii Zhurnal. Seriya B — Fiz Zh Ser B
Fizicheskii Zhurnal. Seriya D — Fiz Zh Ser D
Fizichna Elektronika (Lvov) — Fiz Elektron (Lvov)
Fizichna Geografiya ta Geomorfologiya — Fiz Geogr Geomorfol
Fizichni i Kurortni Faktori ta Ikh Likuval'ne Zastosuvannya — Fiz Kurortni Faktori Ikh Likuvalne Zastosuvannya
Fizichni Zapiski — Fiz Zap

Fizichnii Zbirnik. L'vivs'kii Derzhavnii Universitet — Fiz Zb Lviv Derzh Univ
Fizika [*Zagreb*] — FZKAA
Fizika Aerodispersnykh Sistem — Fiz Aerodispersnykh Sist
Fizika Atmosfery — Fiz Atmos
Fizika Atmosfery i Okeana — Fiz Atmos Okeana
Fizika Atomnogo Yadra i Kosmicheskikh Luchei — Fiz At Yadra Kosm Luchei
Fizika Atomnogo Yadra. Materialy Zimnei Shkoly LIYaF (Leningradskii Institut Yadernoi Fiziki) — Fiz At Yadra
Fizika Chastits Vysokikh Energii — Fiz Chastits Vys Energ
Fizika Chastits Vysokikh Energii. Akademiya Nauk Gruzinskoi SSR. Institut Fiziki [*Georgian SSR*] — Fiz Chastits Vys Energ Akad Nauk Gruz SSR Inst Fiz
Fizika Deformatsionnogo Uprochneniya Monokristallov. Doklady Soveshchaniya po Fizike Deformatsionnogo Uprochneniya Monokristallov. Khark — Fiz Deform Uprochn Monokrist Dokl Soveshch
Fizika Deformatsionnogo Uprochneniya Splavov i Stalei. Doklady prochitannye na Seminare po Problem Fizika Deformatsionnogo Uprochneniya Splavov i Stalei — Fiz Deform Uprochn Splavov Stalei Dokl Semin
Fizika Deleniya Atomnykh Yader — Fiz Deleniya At Yader
Fizika Dielektrikov. Trudy Vsesoyuznoi Konferentsii — Fiz Dielektr Tr Vses Konf
Fizika. Doklady na Nauchnoi Konferentsii. Leningradskii Inzhenerno-Stroitel'nyi Institut. — Fiz Dokl Nauchn Konf Leningr Inzh Stroit Inst
Fizika Elementarnyh Castic i Atomnogo Jadra — Fiz Elementar Castic i Atom Jadra
Fizika Elementarnykh Chastits i Atomnogo Yadra — Fiz Ehlem Chastits At Yad
Fizika Elementarnykh Chastits i Atomnogo Yadra — Fiz Elem Chastits At Yadra
Fizika Elementarnykh Chastits i Atomnogo Yadra. Obedinennyi Institut Yadernykh Issledovanii Dubna — Fiz Elementar Chastits i Atom Yadra
Fizika Elementarnykh Chastits. Materialy Zimnei Shkoly LIYaF (Leningradskii Institut Yadernoi Fiziki) — Fiz Elem Chastits
Fizika Gazorazryadnoi Plazmy — Fiz Gazorazryadnoi Plazmy
Fizika Goreniya i Metody. Ed. Issledovaniya [*Former USSR*] — Fiz Goreniya Metody Ed Issled
Fizika Goreniya i Vzryva — Fiz Gor Vzryva
Fizika Goreniya i Vzryva — Fiz Goreniya & Vzryva
Fizika Gornykh Porod i Protsessov — Fiz Gorn Porod Protsessov
Fizika i Elektronika Tverdogo Tela — Fiz Elektron Tverd Tela
Fizika i Fiziko-Khimiya Rudoobrazuyushchikh Protsessov — Fiz Fiz Khim Rudoobraz Protsessov
Fizika i Fiziko-Khimiya Zhidkostei — Fiz Fiz-Khim Zhidk
Fizika i Khimiya. Doklady na Nauchnoi Konferentsii Leningradskogo Inzhenerno-Stroitel'nogo Instituta — Fiz Khim Dok Nauchn Konf Leningr Inzh Stroit Inst
Fizika i Khimiya Obrabotki Materialov — Fiz i Khim Obrab Mater
Fizika i Khimiya Obrabotki Materialov — Fiz Khim Obrab Mater
Fizika i Khimiya Obrabotki Materialov — FKOMA
Fizika i Khimiya Prirodnykh i Sinteticheskikh Polimerov — Fiz Khim Prir Sint Polim
Fizika i Khimiya Stekla — Fiz i Khim Stekla
Fizika i Khimiya Stekla — Fiz Khim Stekla
Fizika i Khimiya Tverdogo Tela — Fiz Khim Tverd Tela
Fizika i Mekhanika Gornykh Porod — Fiz Mekh Gorn Porod
Fizika i Melioratsiya Pochv Moldavii — Fiz Melior Pochv Mold
Fizika i Tekhnika Moshchnogo Ul'trazvuka — Fiz Tekh Moshchn Ultrazvuka
Fizika i Tekhnika Poluprovodnikov — Fiz i Tekh Poluprovodn
Fizika i Tekhnika Poluprovodnikov — Fiz Tekh Poluprovo
Fizika i Tekhnika Poluprovodnikov — Fiz Tekhn Poluprov
Fizika i Tekhnika Poluprovodnikov [*Leningrad*] — FTPPA
Fizika i Tekhnika Poluprovodnikov (Leningrad) — Fiz Tekh Poluprovodn (Leningrad)
Fizika i Tekhnika Uskoritelei Zaryazhennykh Chastits. Materialy Shkoly LIYaF [*Leningradskii Institut Yadernoi Fiziki*] — Fiz Tekh Uskorit Zaryazhennykh Chastits Mater Shk LIYaF
Fizika i Tekhnika Vysokikh Davlenii — Fiz Tekh Vys Davlenii
Fizika i Teplotekhnika Reaktorov. Atomnaya Energiya. Prilozhenie — Fiz Teplotekh Reakt At Energ Prilozh
Fizika Khrupkogo Razrusheniya. Doklady Vsesoyuznoi Konferentsii Fizik a Khrupkogo Razrusheniya — Fiz Khrupkogo Razrusheniya Dokl Vses Konf
Fizika Kondensirovannogo Sostoyaniya — Fiz Kondens Sostoyaniya
Fizika Magnitnykh Plenok — Fiz Magn Plenok
Fizika, Matematika, Mekhanika. Trudy Moskovskoi Konferentsii Molodykh Uchenykh — Fiz Mat Mekh Tr Mosk Konf Molodykh Uch
Fizika Metallov i Ikh Soedinenii — Fiz Met Ikh Soedin
Fizika Metallov i Metallovedenie — Fiz Met
Fizika Metallov i Metallovedenie — Fiz Met i Metalloved
Fizika Metallov i Metallovedenie — Fiz Metal M
Fizika Metallov i Metallovedenie — Fiz Metallov Metalloved
Fizika Metallov i Metallovedenie — FMM
Fizika Metallov i Metallovedenie — FMMEA
Fizika Metallov i Metallovedenie — FMMTA
Fizika Metallov i Metallovedenie Akademiia Nauk SSSR Ural'skii Filial [*Former USSR*] — Fiz Met Metalloved Akad Nauk SSSR Ural Fil
Fizika Mezhfaznykh Yavlenii — Fiz Mezhfaznykh Yavlenii
Fizika Mineralov — Fiz Miner
Fizika Mnogochastichnykh Sistem — Fiz Mnogochastichnykh Sist
Fizika Molekul — Fiz Mol
Fizika Nizkikh Temperatur — Fiz Nizk Temp
Fizika Nizkikh Temperatur (Kharkov) — Fiz Nizk Temp (Kharkov)
Fizika Nizkikh Temperatur (Kiev) [*Ukrainian SSR*] — Fiz Nizk Temp (Kiev)
Fizika Nizkikh Temperatur (Tbilisi) — Fiz Nizk Temp (Tbilisi)
Fizika Otkazov. Materialy Vsesoyuznogo Soveshchaniya — Fiz Otkazov Mater Vses Soveshch
Fizika Plazmy i Problemy Upravlyaemogo Termoyadernogo Sinteza [*Ukrainian SSR*] — Fiz Plazmy Probl Upr Termoyad Sin
Fizika Plazmy i Problemy Upravlyaemogo Termoyadernogo Sinteza. Doklady Konferentsii po Fizike Plazmy i Probleme Upravlyaemykh Termoyadernykh Reakt — Fiz Plazmy Probl Upr Termoyad Sint Dokl Konf
Fizika Plazmy (Moskva) — Fiz Plazmy (Moskva)
Fizika Plazmy (Tbilisi) — Fiz Plazmy (Tbilisi)
Fizika Poluprovodnikov i Poluprovodnikovaya Elektronika — Fiz Poluprovodn Poluprovodn Elektron
Fizika Prochnosti Plastichnosti Metallov i Elektrodinamicheskie Yavleniya v Veshchestve — Fiz Prochn Plast Met Elektrodin Yavleniya Veshchestve
Fizika Prochnosti. Plastichnosti Metallov i Elektrodinamicheskikh Yavlenii v Ferritakh — Fiz Prochn Plast Met Elektrodin Yavlenii Ferritakh
Fizika Rezaniya Metallov — Fiz Rezaniya Met
Fizika [*Zagreb*]. Supplement — FZKSA
Fizika Tverdogo Tela — Fiz Tverd T
Fizika Tverdogo Tela — Fiz Tverd Tel
Fizika Tverdogo Tela — Fiz Tverd Tela
Fizika Tverdogo Tela — FTT
Fizika Tverdogo Tela (Kharkov) — Fiz Tverd Tela (Kharkov)
Fizika v Shkole — Fiz Shk
Fizika v Skole — Fiz Sk
Fizika Vibratsionnogo Goreniya i Metody Ee Issledovaniya — Fiz Vib Goreniya Metody Ee Issled
Fizika Yadernykh Reaktorov — Fiz Yad Reakt
Fizika (Zagreb). Supplement [*Yugoslavia*] — Fizika (Zagreb) Suppl
Fizika Zemli — Fiz Zemli
Fizika Zemli. Itogi Nauki i Tekhniki — Fiz Zemli Itogi Nauki Tekh
Fizika Zhidkogo Sostoyaniya — Fiz Zhidk Sostoyaniya
Fizikai Szemle — FISZA
Fizikai Szemle — Fiz Sz
Fizikai Szemle — Fiz Szemle
Fizikas Instituta Raksti — Fiz Inst Rak
Fizikas un Matematikas Instituta Raksti — Fiz Mat Inst Rak
Fiziko Khimicheskie Svoistva Individual'nykh Uglevodorodov — Fiz Khim Svoistva Individ Uglevodorodov
Fiziko-Chimiceskaja Mechanika Materialov — Fiz Chim Mech Mat
Fiziko-Energeticheskii Institut. Raport FEI [*Fiziko-Energeticheskii Institut*] [*A publication*] — Fiz Energ Inst Rap FEI
Fiziko-Gazodinamicheskie Ballisticheskie Issledovaniya — Fiz Gazodin Ballist Issled
Fiziko-Geologicheskie Faktory pri Razrabotke Neftyanykh i Neftegazokondensatnykh Mestorozhdenii — Fiz Geol Faktory Razrab Neft Neftegazokondens Mestorozhd
Fiziko-Khimicheska Mekhanika — Fiz Khim Mekh
Fiziko-Khimicheskaya Mekhanika i Liofil'nost Dispersnykh Sistem — Fiz-Khim Mekh Liofil' Dispers Sist
Fiziko-Khimicheskaya Mekhanika Materialov [*Ukrainian SSR*] — Fiz-Khim Mekh Mater
Fiziko-Khimicheskie i Mediko-Biologicheskie Svoistva Prirodnykh Tseolitov — Fiz Khim Med Biol Svoistva Prir Tseolitov
Fiziko-Khimicheskie Issledovaniya i Struktura Prirodnykh Sorbentov — Fiz Khim Issled Strukt Prir Sorbentov
Fiziko-Khimicheskie Issledovaniya Massoobmennykh Protsessov — Fiz Khim Issled Massoobmennykh Protsessov
Fiziko-Khimicheskie Issledovaniya Metallurgicheskikh Protsessov — Fiz Khim Issled Metall Protsessov
Fiziko-Khimicheskie Metody Analiza — Fiz Khim Metody Anal
Fiziko-Khimicheskie Metody Analiza i Kontrolya Proizvodstva — Fiz Khim Metody Anal Kontrolya Proizvod
Fiziko-Khimicheskie Osnovy i Tekhnologiya Pererabotki Khimicheskogo Syr'ya — Fiz Khim Osn Tekhnol Pererab Khim Syrya
Fiziko-Khimicheskie Osnovy Metallurgii Margantsa. Materialy. Predstavlennye na Vsesoyuznom Soveshchanii po Metallurgii Margantsa — Fiz Khim Osn Metall Margantsa Mater Vses Soveshch
Fiziko-Khimicheskie Osnovy Proizvodstva Stali. Materialy. Dolozhennye n a Konferentsii — Fiz Khim Osn Proizvod Stali Mater
Fiziko-Khimicheskie Osnovy Proizvodstva Stali. Trudy Konferentsii po Fiziko-Khimicheskim Osonovam Proizodstva Stali — Fiz Khim Osn Proizvod Stali Tr Konf
Fiziko-Khimicheskie Osnovy Sinteza i Pererabotki Polimerov — Fiz Khim Osn Sint Pererab Polim
Fiziko-Khimicheskie Problemy Kristallizatsii [*Kazakh SSR*] — Fiz Khim Probl Krist
Fiziko-Khimicheskoe Issledovanie Prirodnykh Sorbentov i Ryada Analiticheskikh Sistem — Fiz Khim Issled Prir Sorbentov Ryada Anal Sist
Fizikokhimiya i Metallurgiya Margantsa [*Monograph*] — Fizikokhim Metall Maragantsa
Fizikokhimiya Model'nykh Kletochnykh Membran [*Monograph*] — Fizikokhim Modelnykh Kletochnykh Membr
Fiziko-Matematichesko Spisanie [*Bulgaria*] — Fiz-Mat Spis
Fiziko-Matematichesko Spisanie (Bulgaria) — FMBMA
Fiziko-Mekhanicheskie i Ekspluatatsionnye Svoistva Instrumental'nykh i Konstruktsionnykh Materialov — Fiz Mekh Ekspl Svoistva Instrum Konstr Mater
Fiziko-Tekhnicheskie Problemy Razrabotki Poleznykh Iskopaemykh — Fiz-Tekh Probl Razrab Polez Iskop
Fiziko-Tekhnicheskie Problemy Razrabotki Poleznykh Iskopaemykh — FTRIA
Fiziko-Tekhnologicheskie Voprosy Kibernetiki — Fiz Tekhnol Vopr Kibern
Fiziko-Tekhnologicheskie Voprosy Kibernetiki. Seminar [*Ukrainian SSR*] — Fiz Tekhnol Vopr Kibern Semin
Fizine Elektronika — Fiz Elektron
Fiziologia Normala si Patologica — FZNPA
Fiziologicheski Aktivnye Veshchestva [*Ukrainian SSR*] — FAVUA
Fiziologicheski Aktivnye Veshchestva — Fiziol Akt Veshchestva
Fiziologicheski Aktivnye Veshchestva [*Ukrainian SSR*] — Fiziol Aktiv Veshchestva

Fiziologicheski i Opticheski Aktivnye Polimernye Veshchestva. Trudy Vsesoyuznogo Simpoziuma po Khimii i Fiziko-Khimii Fiziologicheski i Opticheski Aktivnykh Polimernykh Veshchestv — Fiziol Opt Akt Polim Veshchestva Tr Vses Simp
Fiziologicheskie i Fiziko-Khimicheskie Mekhanizmy Regulyatsii Obmennykh Protsessov Organizma [*Former USSR*] — Fiziol Fiz-Khim Mekh Regul Obmennykh Protsessov Org
Fiziologicheskii Zhurnal [*Kiev*] — FIZHD
Fiziologicheskii Zhurnal — Fiziol Z
Fiziologicheskii Zhurnal Imeni I. M. Sechenova — Fiziol Zh Im I M Sechenova
Fiziologicheskii Zhurnal SSSR Imeni I. M. Sechenova — Fiziol Zh SSSR
Fiziologicheskii Zhurnal SSSR Imeni I. M. Sechenova — Fiziol Zh SSSR Im I M Sechenova
Fiziologicheskii Zhurnal SSSR Imeni I. M. Sechenova — FZLZA
Fiziologichnii Zhurnal (Kiev) — FZUKA
Fiziologichnij Zhurnal. Akademiya Nauk Ukrainskoj RSR — Fiziol Zh Akad Nauk Ukr RSR
Fiziologichnyi Zhurnal — Fiziol Zh
Fiziologiia Cheloveka — Fiziol Cheloveka
Fiziologiya, Biokhimiya, i Patologiya Endokrinnoi Sistemy — Fiziol Biokhim Patol Endokr Sist
Fiziologiya Cheloveka — Fiziol Chel
Fiziologiya Cheloveka i Zhivotnykh — Fiziol Chel Zhivotn
Fiziologiya Drevesnykh Rastenii — Fiziol Drev Rast
Fiziologiya i Biokhimiya Kul'turnykh Rastenii — FBKRA
Fiziologiya i Biokhimiya Kul'turnykh Rastenii — Fiziol Biokhim Kul't Rast
Fiziologiya i Biokhimiya Sil's'kogospodars'kikh Tvarin — Fiziol Biokhim Sil's'kogospod Tvarin
Fiziologiya i Patologiya Gisto-Gematicheskikh Bar'erov. Materialy Soveshchaniya po Probleme Gisto-Gematicheskikh Bar'erov — Fiziol Patol Gisto Gematicheskikh Barerov Mater Soveshch
Fiziologiya i Patologiya Vysshei Nervnoi Deyatel'nosti — Fiziol Patol Vyssh Nervn Deyat
Fiziologiya na Rasteniyata [*Sofia*] — FZRSA
Fiziologiya na Rasteniyata (Sofia) — Fiziol Rast (Sofia)
Fiziologiya Normala si Patologica — Fiziol Norm Patol
Fiziologiya Rastenii [*Moscow*] — FIRAD
Fiziologiya Rastenii — Fiziol Rast
Fiziologiya Rastenii — Fiziologiya Rast
Fiziologiya Rastenii (English Translation of Plant Physiology) [*Moscow*] — Fiziol Rast (Engl Transl Plant Physiol)
Fiziologiya Rastenii. Itogi Nauki i Tekhniki — Fiziol Rast Itogi Nauki Tekh
Fiziologiya Rastenii (Moscow) — Fiziol Rast (Mosc)
Fiziologiya Rastenii (Moscow) — Fiziol Rast (Moscow)
Fiziologiya Vodoobmena i Ustoichivosti Rastenii — Fiziol Vodoobmena Ustoich Rast
Fiziologo-Biokhimicheskie Osnovy Pitaniya Rastenii — Fiziol Biokhim Osn Pitan Rast
Fiziologo-Biokhimicheskie Osnovy Vzaimodeistviya Rastenii e Fitotsenozakh — Fiziol Biokhim Osn Vzaimodeistviya Rast Fitotsenozakh
Fiziolohichnyi Zhurnal (Kiev) — Fiziol Zh (Kiev)
Fiziolohicnyj Zurnal — Fiziol Z
Fizycheskaya Heohrafiya ta Heomorfolohiya Mizhvidomchyi Naukovyi Zbirnykh — Fiz Heohr Heomorfol Mizhvid Nauk Zb
Fizyka Dielektrykow i Radiospektroskopia — Fiz Dielektr Radiospektrosk
Fizyka i Chemia Metali (Katowice) — Fiz Chem Met (Katowice)
Fizyka w Szkole [*Poland*] — Fiz Szk
Fizyka. Wyzsza Szkola Pedagogiczna imeni Powstancow Slaskich w Opolu — Fizyka Wyzsza Szk Pedagog im Powstancow Slask Opolu
Fizykochemiczne Problemy Mineralurgii — Fizykochem Probl Mineralurgii
Flachs-, Hanf-, Juteindustrie — Flachs Hanf Juteind
Flachs und Hanf — Flachs Hanf
Flambeau — Flamb
Flame Retardancy of Polymeric Materials — Flame Retard Polym Mater
Flame Retardancy of Polymeric Materials — Flame Retardancy Polym Mater
Flame-Retardant Polymeric Materials — Flame Retard Polym Mater
Flamme et Thermique [*France*] — Flamme Therm
Flandre Judiciaire — Fl J
Flandre Judiciaire — Fl Jud
Flannery O'Connor Bulletin — FOB
Flannery O'Connor Bulletin — FOBu
Flash-Informations — Flash Inf
Flat Glass. Current Industrial Reports — Flat Glass Curr Ind Rep
Flavins and Flavoproteins. Proceedings. Conference on Flavins and Flavoproteins — Flavins Flavoproteins Proc Conf
Flavins and Flavoproteins. Proceedings. International Symposium — Flavins Flavoproteins Proc Int Symp
Flavor and Acceptability of Monosodium Glutamate. Proceedings. Symposium — Flavor Acceptability Monosodium Glutamate Proc Symp
Flavour and Fragrance Journal — Flavour Fragrance J
Flavour Industry — Flavour Ind
Flavour Science and Technology. Weurman Symposium — Flavour Sci Technol Weurman Symp
Flavours, Fruit Juices, and Spices Review — Flavours Fruit Juices Spices Rev
Fleet, Cars, Vans, and Utilities — Fleet
Fleet Street Letter — FSL
Fleischwirtschaft — Fleischw
Flemish Veterinary Journal — Flemish Vet J
Flemish Veterinary Journal — VDTIAX
Fletcher Forum — Fl Forum
Fletcher Forum — Fletcher F
Fletorja Mjeksore Shqiptare — Flet Mjeks Shquip
Fliegende Blatter aus dem Rauhen Hause zu Horn bei Hamburg — FBRH
Flight and Aircraft Engineer — Flight Aircr Eng
Flight International — Flight Int
Flight International — Flt Intnl
Flight International (London) — Flight Int (London)
Flinders Journal of History and Politics — Flinders J Hist Polit
Flinders Petrie Papyri — PPetr
Flinders University of South Australia. Institute for Atomic Studies. Technical Report FIAS-R — Flinders Univ South Aust Inst At Stud Tech Rep FIAS R
Flinders University of South Australia. Institute for Energy Studies. Report FIES — Flinders Univ South Aust Inst Energy Stud Rep FIES
Flintshire Historical Sooicty. Publications — Flintshire Hist Soc Publ
FLIP [*Future Literature in Progress*] **Magazine** — FLIP Mag
Flora and Fauna Handbook — FFHAET
Flora and Fauna Handbook — Flora & Fauna Handb
Flora and Sylva. A Monthly Review for Lovers of Garden, Woodland, Tree, or Flower. New and Rare Plants, Trees, Shrubs, and Fruits. The Garden Beautif Home Woods, and Home Landscape — Fl Sylva
Flora. Casopis Vedecko-Zahradnicky (Prague) — Flora Prague
Flora do Parana. Instituto Paranaense de Botanica Curitiba — FLAPA9
Flora do Parana. Instituto Paranaense de Botanica Curitiba — Flora Parana Inst Parana Bot Curitiba
Flora en Pomona. Bijblad Behoorende Bij De Plantenbeurs (Arnhem) — Fl Pomona Arnhem
Flora et Vegetatio Mundi — Flora Veg Mundi
Flora et Vegetatio Mundi — FVMUDL
Flora Fennica — FLFE
Flora Fennica — FLFNAS
Flora Fennica — Flora Fenn
Flora (Jena). Abteilung A. Physiologie und Biochemie [*Germany*] — Flora (Jena) Abt A
Flora (Jena). Abteilung B. Morphologie und Geobotanik [*Germany*] — Flora (Jena) Abt B
Flora. Koeniglich Saechsische Gesellschaft fuer Botanik und Gartenbau zu Dresden. Sitzungsberichte und Abhandlungen — Flora Koenigl Saechs Ges Bot Dresden Sitzungsber Abh
Flora Malesiana Bulletin — Fl Males Bull
Flora Malesiana. Bulletin — Flora Males Bull
Flora Malesiana. Series I. Spermatophyta — Flora Malesiana Ser I Spermatophyta
Flora Malesiana. Series I. Spermatophyta — FMSPA4
Flora Malesiana. Series II. Pteridophyta — FLMPB2
Flora Malesiana. Series II. Pteridophyta — Flora Malesiana Ser II Pteridophyta
Flora Neerlandica — Flora Neerl
Flora Neotropica Monograph — FLNMAV
Flora Neotropica Monograph — Flora Neotrop Monogr
Flora oder Allgemeine Botanische Zeitung — F
Flora oder Allgemeine Botanische Zeitung [*Jena*] — FABZAZ
Flora oder Allgemeine Botanische Zeitung. Abteilung A. Physiologie und Biochemie (Jena) — Flora Allg Bot Ztg Abt A Physiol Biochem (Jena)
Flora oder Allgemeine Botanische Zeitung. Abteilung B. Morphologie und Geobotanik (Jena) — Flora Allg Bot Ztg Abt B Morphol Geobot (Jena)
Flora oder Allgemeine Botanische Zeitung (Jena) — Flora Allg Bot Ztg (Jena)
Flora oder Allgemeine Botanische Zeitung (Jena) — Flora (Jena)
Flora of Ecuador — FLECDR
Flora of New South Wales — Flora NSW
Flora of New South Wales — Flora of NSW
Flora of Pakistan — Flora Pak
Flora of Texas — Flora Tex
Flora of Texas — FLTXAQ
Flora og Fauna — Fl o F
Flora og Fauna — FLFAAN
Flora og Fauna. Aarbog for Naturvenner og Naturhistoriske Samlere (Esbjerg) — Fl Fauna Esbjerg
Flora Polska: Rosliny Naczyniowe Polski i Ziem Osciennych — Flora Pol Rosl Naczyniowe Pol Ziem Osciennych
Flora Polska; Rosliny Naczyniowe Polski i Ziem Osciennych — FLPOAD
Flora. Revista al Servicio de las Ciencias Naturales y Biologicas. Instituto Ecuatoriano de Ciencias Naturales — Flora Inst Ecuat
Flora Slodkowodna Polski — Flora Slodkowodna Pol
Flora Slodkowodna Polski — FSLPAB
Flora Timarit um Islenzka Grasafraedi — Flora Timarit Isl Grasafraedi
Flora Timarit um Islenzka Grasafraedi — FLTGA9
Flora van Nederland — Flora Ned
Flora van Nederland/Flora Neerlandica — FNEEAA
Floral Cabinet and Magazine of Exotic Botany — Fl Cab
Floral Magazine. Comprising Figures and Descriptions of Popular Garden Flowers (London) — Fl Mag London
Flore de France — FLFRB7
Flore de France — Flore Fr
Flore des Serres et Jardins de l'Angleterre — Fl Serres Jard Angleterre
Flore Iconographique des Champignons du Congo — FIGCAD
Flore Iconographique des Champignons du Congo — Flore Iconogr Champignons Congo
Flore Illustree des Champignons d'Afrique Centrale — FICAAL
Flore Illustree des Champignons d'Afrique Centrale — Flore Illus Champignons Afr Cent
Florica Engineering Society. Journal — Fla Eng Soc J
Floricultural Magazine and Miscellany of Gardening — Floric Mag Misc Gard
Floriculture Indiana. Purdue University. Horticulture Department. Cooperative Extension Service — Floric Indiana Purdue Univ Hortic Dep Coop Ext Serv
Florida Academy of Sciences. Quarterly Journal — Fla Acad Sci Q J
Florida Administrative Code, Annotated — Fla Admin Code Ann
Florida Administrative Weekly — Fla Admin Weekly
Florida. Agricultural Experiment Station. Department of Soils. Mimeo Report — Fla Agric Exp Stn Dep Soils Mimeo Rep
Florida. Agricultural Experiment Stations. Annual Report — Fla Agric Exp Stn Annu Rep

Florida. Agricultural Experiment Stations. Bulletin — Fla Agric Exp Stn Bull
Florida. Agricultural Experiment Stations. Circular — Fla Agric Exp Stn Circ
Florida. Agricultural Experiment Stations. Monograph Series — Fla Agric Exp Stn Monogr Ser
Florida. Agricultural Experiment Stations. Publications — Fla Ag Exp
Florida. Agricultural Experiment Stations. Research Report — Fla Agric Exp Stn Res Rep
Florida. Agricultural Extension Service. Bulletin — Fla Agric Ext Serv Bull
Florida Agricultural Research. University of Florida. Agricultural Experiment Stations — Fla Agric Res Univ Fla Agric Exp Stn
Florida Anthropologist — Fla Anthropol
Florida Anthropologist — Flor Anthr
Florida Anthropologist — Florida Anthropol
Florida Anthropologist. Florida Anthropological Society — FAS/FA
Florida Architect — Fla Archit
Florida Association of Science Teachers. Journal — Fla Assoc Sci Teach J
Florida Banker — FL Bank
Florida Bar Journal — Fla B J
Florida Bar Journal — Florida BJ
Florida Beef Cattle Research Report. Florida Cooperative Extension Service. University of Florida — Fla Beef Cattle Res Rep Fla Coop Ext Serv Univ Fla
Florida Board of Conservation. Marine Research Laboratory. Leaflet Series — Fla Board Conserv Mar Res Lab Leafl Ser
Florida Board of Conservation. Marine Research Laboratory. Professional Papers Series — Fla Board Conserv Mar Lab Prof Pap Ser
Florida Board of Conservation. Marine Research Laboratory. Special Scientific Report — Fla Board Conserv Mar Res Lab Spec Sci Rep
Florida Board of Conservation. Marine Research Laboratory. Technical Series — Fla Board Conserv Mar Res Lab Tech Ser
Florida Builder — FL Build
Florida. Bureau of Geology. Bulletin — Fla Bur Geol Bull
Florida Bureau of Geology. Geological Bulletin — Fla Bur Geol Geol Bull
Florida Bureau of Geology. Information Circular — Fla Bur Geol Inf Circ
Florida Bureau of Geology. Report of Investigation — Fla Bur Geol Rep Invest
Florida. Bureau of Geology. Special Publication — Fla Bur Geol Spec Publ
Florida Cattleman and Livestock Journal — Fla Cattlem Livest J
Florida Citrus Nurserymens Association News — Florida Citrus Nurserymens Assoc News
Florida Conservation News — Fla Conserv News
Florida Construction Industry — FL Constr Ind
Florida Contractor and Builder — FL Cont and Build
Florida Dental Journal — Fla Dent J
Florida. Department of Agriculture and Consumer Services. Division of Plant Industry. Biennial Report — Fla Dep Agric Consum Serv Div Plant Ind Bienn Rep
Florida. Department of Agriculture and Consumer Services. Division of Plant Industry. Bulletin — Fla Dep Agric Consum Serv Div Plant Ind Bull
Florida. Department of Agriculture and Consumer Services. Division of Plant Industry. Entomology Circular — Fla Dep Agric Consum Serv Div Plant Ind Entomol Circ
Florida. Department of Agriculture and Consumer Services. Division of Plant Industry. Nematology Circular — Fla Dep Agric Consum Serv Div Plant Ind Nematol Circ
Florida. Department of Agriculture and Consumer Services. Division of Plant Industry. Plant Pathology Circular — Fla Dep Agric Consum Serv Div Plant Ind Plant Pathol Circ
Florida. Department of Agriculture. Quarterly Bulletin — Fla Ag Dept Quar B
Florida. Department of Natural Resources. Biennial Report — Fla Dep Nat Resour Bienn Rep
Florida. Department of Natural Resources. Bureau of Geology. Bulletin — Fla Dep Nat Resour Bur Geol Bull
Florida. Department of Natural Resources. Bureau of Geology. Geological Bulletin — Florida Bur Geology Geol Bull
Florida. Department of Natural Resources. Bureau of Geology. Information Circular — Fla Dep Nat Resour Bur Geol Inf Cir
Florida. Department of Natural Resources. Bureau of Geology. Information Circular — Florida Bur Geology Inf Circ
Florida. Department of Natural Resources. Bureau of Geology. Report of Investigations — Fla Dep Nat Resour Bur Geol Rep Invest
Florida. Department of Natural Resources. Bureau of Geology. Special Publication — Fla Dep Nat Resour Bur Geol Spec Publ
Florida. Department of Natural Resources. Educational Series — Fla Dep Nat Resour Educ Ser
Florida. Department of Natural Resources. Marine Research Laboratory. Educational Series — Fla Dep Nat Resour Mar Res Lab Educ Ser
Florida. Department of Natural Resources. Marine Research Laboratory. Leaflet Series — Fla Dep Nat Resour Mar Res Lab Leafl Ser
Florida. Department of Natural Resources. Marine Research Laboratory. Professional Papers Series — Fla Dep Nat Resour Mar Res Lab Prof Pap Ser
Florida. Department of Natural Resources. Marine Research Laboratory. Special Scientific Report — Fla Dept Nat Resour Mar Res Lab Spec Sci Rep
Florida. Department of Natural Resources. Marine Research Laboratory. Technical Series — Fla Dep Nat Resour Mar Res Lab Tech Ser
Florida Designers Quarterly — FDQ
Florida. Division of Geology. Information Circular — Fla Div Geol Inf Circ
Florida. Division of Geology. Report of Investigation — Fla Div Geol Rep Invest
Florida Economic Indicators — FL Econ Ind
Florida Entomologist — Fla Ent
Florida Entomologist — Fla Entomol
Florida Environmental and Urban Issues — FL Env Urb Iss
Florida Environmental and Urban Issues — Fla Environmental and Urban Issues
Florida Experiment Station Press Bulletin — Florida Exp Sta Press Bull
Florida Field Naturalist — Fla Field Nat
Florida Food and Resource Economics. Cooperative Extension Service. University of Florida — Fla Food Resour Econ Coop Ext Serv Univ Fla
Florida Foreign Language Reporter — FFLR
Florida Fruits and Flowers — Florida Fruits Fl
Florida. Geological Survey. Annual Report — Fla G S An Rp
Florida. Geological Survey. Bulletin — Fla Geol Surv Bull
Florida. Geological Survey. Bulletin — Florida Geol Surv Bull
Florida. Geological Survey. Geological Bulletin — Fla Geol Surv Geol Bull
Florida. Geological Survey. Information Circular — Fla Geol Surv Inf Circ
Florida. Geological Survey. Information Circular — Fla Geol Surv Inform Circ
Florida. Geological Survey. Information Circular — Florida Geol Surv Inform Circ
Florida. Geological Survey. Report of Investigations — Fla Geol Surv Rep Invest
Florida. Geological Survey. Report of Investigations — Florida Geol Surv Rep Invest
Florida. Geological Survey. Special Publication — Fla Geol Surv Spec Publ
Florida Grower — Fla Grow
Florida Grower and Rancher — Fla Grower Rancher
Florida Historical Quarterly — FHQ
Florida Historical Quarterly — Fla Hist Q
Florida Historical Quarterly — Fla Hist Quar
Florida Historical Quarterly — FlH
Florida Historical Society. Quarterly — Fla His S
Florida Homemaker and Gardener — Florida Homemaker Gard
Florida Libraries — Fla Lib
Florida Libraries — Fla Libr
Florida Marine Research Publications — Fla Mar Res Publ
Florida Medical Association. Journal — Fla Med Assn J
Florida Monthly — FL Monthly
Florida Music Director — DIR
Florida Naturalist — Fla Nat
Florida Naturalist — Flor Nat
Florida Nurse — Fla Nurse
Florida Quarterly — FloQ
Florida Quarterly — FlorQ
Florida Quarterly — FQ
Florida Reports — Fla
Florida Scientist — Fla Sci
Florida Sea Grant College. Report — Fla Sea Grant Coll Rep
Florida Sea Grant Marine Research Education Advisory Services. Technical Paper — Fla Sea Grant Mar Res Educ Advis Serv Tech Pap
Florida Session Law Service (West) — Fla Sess Law Serv (West)
Florida State Bar Association. Proceedings — Fla State Bar Assn Proc
Florida. State Board of Conservation. Biennial Report — Fla State Board Conserv Bien Rep
Florida. State Board of Conservation. Division of Water Survey and Research. Paper — Fla State Board Conserv Div Water Survey and Research Paper
Florida State Board of Conservation. Florida Geological Survey. Information Circular — Fla State Board Conserv Fla Geol Surv Inf Circ
Florida State Board of Conservation. Florida Geological Survey. Report of Investigations — Fla State Board Conserv Fla Geol Surv Rep Invest
Florida State Board of Conservation. Florida Geological Survey. Special Publication — Fla State Board Conserv Fla Geol Surv Spec Publ
Florida. State Board of Health. Monograph Series — Fla State Board Health Monogr Ser
Florida. State Horticultural Society. Proceedings — Proc Florida State Hortic Soc
Florida. State Horticultural Society. Quarterly — Fla St Hort Soc Q
Florida State Museum. Biological Sciences Bulletin — Fla State Mus Biol Sci Bull
Florida State Museum. Bulletin. Biological Sciences — Florida State Mus Bull Biol Sci
Florida State Plant Board. Publications — Fla State Plant Bd
Florida State University. Department of Geology. Sedimentological Research Laboratory. Contribution — Fla State Univ Dep Geol Sedimentol Res Lab Contrib
Florida State University. Department of Geology. Sedimentological Research Laboratory. Contribution — Florida State Univ Sedimentol Research Lab Contr
Florida State University. Law Review — Fla St U L Rev
Florida State University. Law Review — Fla St U LR
Florida State University. Law Review — Fla State L Rev
Florida State University. Slavic Papers — Fla St Univ Slavic Papers
Florida State University. Slavic Papers — FSUSP
Florida State University. Studies — Fla State Univ Studies
Florida State University. Studies — FSUS
Florida Statutes — Fla Stat
Florida Statutes. Annotated (West) — Fla Stat Ann (West)
Florida Supplement — Fla Supp
Florida Supplement. Second Series — Fla Supp 2d
Florida Times Union — Florida Ti U
Florida Times Union and Jacksonville Journal — Flor Ti Jack
Florida Trend — FL Trend
Florida Trend — Fla Trend
Florida. University. Agricultural Experiment Station. Circular — Fla Univ Agric Exp Stn Cir
Florida. University. Agricultural Extension Service. Bulletin — Fla Univ Agric Ext Serv Bull
Florida. University. Agricultural Extension Service. Circular — Fla Univ Agric Ext Serv Circ
Florida. University. Cooperative Extension Service. Bulletin — Fla Univ Coop Ext Serv Bull
Florida. University. Engineering and Industrial Experiment Station. Bulletin [*A publication*] — Fla Univ Eng Exp Sta Bull
Florida. University. Engineering and Industrial Experiment Station. Bulletin Series — EPFBA
Florida. University. Engineering and Industrial Experiment Station. Bulletin Series — Fla Univ Eng Ind Exp Stn Bull Ser
Florida. University. Engineering and Industrial Experiment Station. Leaflet Series — Fla Univ Eng Ind Exp Stn Leafl Ser

Florida. University. Engineering and Industrial Experiment Station. Technical Paper Series — Fla Univ Eng Ind Exp Stn Tech Pap Ser
Florida. University. Engineering and Industrial Experiment Station. Technical Progress Report — Fla Univ Eng Ind Exp Stn Tech Prog Rep
Florida. University. Engineering Progress Bulletin — Florida Univ Eng Progr Bull
Florida. University. Engineering Progress Leaflet — Florida Univ Eng Progr Leafl
Florida. University. Engineering Progress Technical Paper — Florida Univ Eng Progr Tech Pap
Florida. University. Engineering Progress Technical Progress Report — Florida Univ Eng Progr Tech Progr Rep
Florida. University. Institute of Food and Agricultural Sciences. Publication — Fla Univ Inst Food Agric Sci Publ
Florilegium Patristicum — Flor Patr
Florist and Nursery Exchange — Florist Nursery Exch
Floristilized Mjarkmed — Florist Mjarkmed
Florists' Exchange — FEHTA7
Florists' Exchange — Flor Exc
Florists' Exchange — Flor Exch
Florists' Exchange and Horticultural Trade World — Florists Exch Hortic Trade World
Florist's Journal — Florists J
Florists' Review — Flor Rev
Florists' Review — Florists Rev
Flour and Feed — FLFEAZ
Flour and Feed — Flour Feed
Flour Problems — Flour Probl
Flow. Its Measurement and Control in Science and Industry — Flow Its Meas Control Sci Ind
Flow Measurement and Instrumentation — Flow Meas Instrum
Flow Measurement and Instrumentation — Flow Measur Instrum
Flower and Garden — GFNG
Flower and Garden. Northern Edition — Flower and Gard
Flower and Garden. Southern Edition — Flower Gard South Ed
Flower and Nursery Report for Commercial Growers. California University. Berkeley. Agricultural Extension Service — Flower Nursery Rep Commer Grow Calif Univ Berkeley Agric Ext
Flower and Nursery Report for Commercial Growers. California University. Cooperative Extension — Flower Nursery Rep Commer Grow Calif Univ Coop Ext
Flower Garden — Fl Gard
Flower Grower — FLGRAB
Flower Grower — Flower Grow
Flowering Plants of Africa — Flowering Plants Afr
Flowering Plants of Africa — FPLAAD
Flowers and Gardens — Fl Gard
Fluechtlingssiedlungsgesetz — Flue SG
Flue-Cured Tobacco Farmer — FCTF
Flue-Cured Tobacco Farmer — Flue Cured Tob Farmer
Fluessiges Obst — Fluess Obst
Flugblaetter der Bekennenden Kirche — FBK
Flug-Revue — Flug-Rev
Flug-Revue International [*Germany*] — Flug-Rev Int
Flugschriften aus den Ersten Jahren der Reformation — FEJR
Flugschriften aus der Reformationszeit in Facsimile Drucken — FRZ
Flugschriften des Evangelischen Bundes — FEB
Fluid Apparecchiature Idrauliche e Pneumatiche — Fluid Apparecch Idraul & Pneum
Fluid Apparecchiature Idrauliche e Pneumatiche — Fluid Apparecchiature Idraul & Pneum
Fluid Controls Institute. FCI Standards — Fluid Contr Inst FCI Stand
Fluid Dynamics — Fluid Dyn
Fluid Dynamics — Fluid Dynam
Fluid Dynamics Research. Japan Society of Fluid Mechanics — Fluid Dynam Res
Fluid Dynamics. Transactions — Fluid Dyn Trans
Fluid Engineering [*Japan*] — Fluid Eng
Fluid Handling — Flui Handl
Fluid Handling — Fluid Handl
Fluid Mechanics and its Applications — Fluid Mech Appl
Fluid Mechanics and Its Applications — Fluid Mech Its Appl
Fluid Mechanics. Soviet Research — Fluid Mech Sov Res
Fluid Mechanics. Soviet Research — Fluid Mech Soviet Res
Fluid Mechanics. Soviet Research — FMSVA
Fluid/Particle Separation Journal — Fluid Part Sep J
Fluid Phase Equilibria — Fluid Phase Equilib
Fluid Phase Equilibria [*Netherlands*] — Fluid Phase Equilibria
Fluid Power International — Fluid Power Int
Fluid Power International — Fluid Pwr Int
Fluidex Database — Flu Data
Fluidics Quarterly — Fluid Q
Fluidics Quarterly — Fluidics Q
Fluidization. Proceedings. Engineering Foundation Conference on Fluidization — Fluid Proc Eng Found Conf Fluid
Fluidization. Proceedings of the Engineering Foundation Conference — Fluid Proc Eng Found Conf
Fluidization. Science and Technology. Conference Papers. China-Japan Symposium — Fluid Sci Technol Conf Pap China Jpn Symp
Fluidization Technology. Proceedings. International Fluidization Conference — Fluid Technol Proc Int Fluid Conf
Fluidos Hidraulica Neumatica Lubricacion — Fluidos Hidraul Neumatica Lubr
Fluids Engineering in Advanced Energy Systems. Winter Annual Meeting. American Society of Mechanical Engineers — Fluids Eng Adv Energy Syst Winter Ann Meet Am Soc Mech Eng
Fluids Handling — Fluids Handl
Fluid-Solid Surface Interactions. Proceedings. Symposium — Fluid Solid Surf Interact Proc Symp
Fluorescence and Phosphorescence Analysis [*Symposium*] — Fluoresc Phosphorescence Anal
Fluorescence News — Fluoresc News
Fluorescent Mineral Society. Journal — Fluoresc Miner Soc J
Fluoride — FLUOA4
Fluoride Abstracts — Fluoride Abstr
Fluoride Quarterly Reports — FLQRAR
Fluoride Quarterly Reports — Fluoride Q Rep
Fluoride Research — Fluoride Res
Fluorine Chemistry Reviews — Fluorine Chem Rev
Fluorocarbon and Related Chemistry — Fluorocarbon Relat Chem
Flurbereinigungsgesetz — Flur BG
Flute Journal — FJ
Flute Talk — FluT
Flutist Quarterly — Flutist Q
Flutists Quarterly — FluQ
Flygtekniska Forsoksanstalten. Meddelande — Flygtek Forsoksanst Medd
Flying — Fly
Flying — GFLY
Flying (Chicago) — FC
Flying Dutchman — FDU
Flying Saucer Review [*British*] — FSR
Flying Saucers from Other Worlds — FSO
FMDA [*Forschungen und Materialien zur Deutschen Aufklarung*] **Abteilung II. Monographien** — FMDA Abt II Monographien
FMF [*Food Manufacturer's Federation*] **Review** — FMF Rev
FMI [*Federation of Malta Industries*] **Review** — FMI Rev
FNP Journal of Food Processing and Preservation — FNP J Food Process Preserv
FNP [*Food & Nutrition Press, Inc.*] **Newsletter. Food, Nutrition, and Health** — FNP Newsl Food Nutr Health
FNR. Purdue University Cooperative Extension Service — FNR Purdue Univ Coop Ext Serv
FNS. US Department of Agriculture. Food and Nutrition Service — FNS US Dep Agric Food Nutr Serv
FOA [*Foersvarets Forskningsanstalt*] **Reports** — FOA Rep
FOC. Fiber Optics and Communications Proceedings — FOC Fiber Opt Commun Proc
Focal Points — FOPO
Focale Magazine — Focale Mag
Focus — Foc
Focus — FOX
Focus — GFOC
Focus (Amersfoort, Netherlands) — Focus Amersfoort Neth
Focus Japan — Focus Jpn
Focus Japan [*Tokyo*] — TJA
Focus/Midwest — Foc
Focus/Midwest — Focus
Focus on American Association of Critical Care Nurses [*Later, Focus on Critical Care*] — Focus AACN
Focus on Critical Care — FCCADG
Focus on Critical Care — Focus Crit Care
Focus on Exceptional Children — Foc Exc Chi
Focus on Exceptional Children — Focus Excep Child
Focus on Film — Foc F
Focus on Film — Focus on F
Focus on Floriculture. Purdue University. Cooperative Extension Service — Focus Floric Purdue Univ Coop Ext Serv
Focus on Holland — FOH
Focus on Indiana Libraries — Focus
Focus on Indiana Libraries — Focus Indiana Libr
Focus on Indonesia — Focus Indo
Focus on International and Comparative Librarianship — Focus Int Comp Librarianship
Focus on Mental Health [*Quezon City*] — FMH
Focus on Renewable Natural Resources — FNRRDF
Focus on Renewable Natural Resources — Focus Renewable Nat Resour
Focus on Renewable Natural Resources. University of Idaho. Forest, Wildlife, and Range Experiment Station — Focus Renew Nat Resour Univ Idaho For Wildl Range Exp Stn
Focus on Robert Graves — FRG
Focus Project. Folklore Computerized Studies Technical Report — Foc Proj F
Foederation Europaeischer Gewaesserschutz. Informationsblatt — Foed Eur Gewaesserschutz Informationsbl
Foeld es Ember — Foeld Ember
Foeldmuevelesuegyi Miniszterium. Allami Gazdasagok Foeigazgatosaga (Budapest) [*A publication*] — Foeldmuevel Min Allami Gazd Foeigazgatosaga (Budapest)
Foeldrajzi Ertesitoe — Foeldr Ert
Foeldrajzi Koezlemenyek — FK
Foeldrajzi Koezlemenyek — Fr K
Foeldrajzi Koezlemenyek. Mitteilungen der Ungarischen Geographischen Gesellschaft. Bulletin de la Societe Hongroise de Geographie — Foeldr Koezlem
Foeldtani Szemle — Foeldt Szemle
Foeredrag vid Pyroteknikdagen — Foeredr Pyroteknikdagen
Foerhandlingar. Geologiska Foereningen i Stockholm — Foerh Geol Foeren Stockholm
Foerhandlingar. Kungliga Fysiografiska Saellskapet — Foerh Kungl Fysiogr Saellsk
Fogg Art Museum. Acquisitions — Fogg Art Mus Acqu
Fogg Art Museum. Bulletin [*Harvard University*] — Fogg Mus Bul
Fogg Art Museum Notes — FAMN

Foglio Federale Svizzero — FF
Fogorvosi Szemle — Fogorv Sz
Fogorvosi Szemle — FOSZAE
FOGRA (Deutsche Forschungsgesellschaft fuer Druck und Reproduktionstechnik) Mitteilungen — FOGRA (Dtsche Forshungsges Druck Reproduktionstech) Mitt
FOGRA (Deutsche Forschungsgesellschaft Fuer Druckund Reproduktionstechnik) Forschungsbericht — FOGRA Forschungsber
Foi Catholique — Foi Cath
Foi et Vie — FV
Foilseachain Naisiunta Tta — FNT
Folclor Leterar — FolcL
Folder. Montana State College. Cooperative Extension Service — Folder Mont State Coll Coop Ext
Folder. Montana State University. Cooperative Extension Service — Folder Mont State Univ Coop Ext Serv
Folder. University of Arizona. Agricultural Experiment Station — Folder Univ Ariz Agric Exp Stn
Folder. University of Missouri. College of Agriculture. Extension Service — Folder Univ MO Coll Agr Ext Serv
Folding and Design — Folding Des
Foldrajzi Ertesito — Foldrajzi Ert
Foldrajzi Ertesito — Foldrajzi Ertes
Foldrajzi Koezlemenyek — Foldrajzi Koezl
Foldtani Koezlony — Foldt Koezl
Foldtani Kozlony — FOKOA9
Foldtani Kozlony — Foldt Kozl
Foldtani Kutatas — Foldt Kut
Folger Documents of Tudor and Stuart Civilization — FDTSC
Folha Medica — Fol Med
Folha Medica — Folha Med
Folha Medica — FOMEAN
Folha Medica (Rio De Janeiro) — Folha Med (Rio De Janeiro)
Folhetas de Divulgacao. Servicos Florestais e Aquicolas (Portugal) — Folh Divulg Serv Flor Aquic (Portugal)
Folia Allergologica [*Later, Folia Allergologica et Immunologica Clinica*] — FOALAI
Folia Allergologica [*Later, Folia Allergologica et Immunologica Clinica*] — Folia Allergol
Folia Allergologica et Immunologica Clinica — FAICAZ
Folia Allergologica et Immunologica Clinica — Folia Allergol Immunol Clin
Folia Ambrosiana — Fol Amb
Folia Anatomica Japonica — FAJAAY
Folia Anatomica Japonica — Folia Anat Jpn
Folia Anatomica Universitatis Conimbrigensis [*Coimbra*] — FAUCAR
Folia Anatomica Universitatis Conimbrigensis (Coimbra) — Folia Anat Univ Conimbrigensis (Coimbra)
Folia Angiologica (Pisa) — Folia Angiol (Pisa)
Folia Archaeologica — FA
Folia Archaeologica — Fol Arch
Folia Archaeologica [*Budapest*] — Folia Archaeol
Folia Archaeologica. A Magyar Nemzeti Muzeum. Toerteneti Muzeum Evkoenyve — Fol A
Folia Archaeologica (Budapest) — FA (Bud)
Folia Archeologica [*Lodz*] — Folia Arch
Folia Balcanica — Folia Balc
Folia Biochimica et Biologica Graeca — FBBGAJ
Folia Biochimica et Biologica Graeca — Folia Biochim Biol Graeca
Folia Biologica [*Cracow*] — FOBGA8
Folia Biologica [*Prague*] — FOBLAN
Folia Biologica — Fol Biol
Folia Biologica — Folia Biol
Folia Biologica (Buenos Aires) — Folia Biol Buenos Aires
Folia Biologica (Cracow) — Folia Biol (Cracow)
Folia Biologica (Krakow) — Folia Biol (Krakow)
Folia Biologica (Prague) — Folia Biol (Prague)
Folia Biologica (Praha) — Folia Biol (Praha)
Folia Botanica Miscellanea — FBMIDF
Folia Botanica Miscellanea — Folia Bot Misc
Folia Cardiologia. Supplemento — Folia Cardiol Suppl
Folia Cardiologica — FOCAAT
Folia Cardiologica — Folia Cardiol
Folia Chimica Sinica — Folia Chim Sin
Folia Chimica Theoretica Latina — Folia Chim Theor Lat
Folia Civitatis — Fol Civ
Folia Clinica. Chimica et Microscopica — Folia Clin Chim Microsc
Folia Clinica et Biologica — FCLBAR
Folia Clinica et Biologica — Folia Clin Biol
Folia Clinica et Biologica. Nova Serie — Folia Clin Biol Nova Ser
Folia Clinica Internacional — FOCIA
Folia Clinica Internacional — Folia Clin Int
Folia Clinica Internacional (Barcelona) — Folia Clin Int (Barc)
Folia Cryptogamica — Folia Cryptog
Folia Dendrologica — FODEDF
Folia Dendrologica — Folia Dendrol
Folia Dendrologica. Supplementum — FDSUDR
Folia Dendrologica. Supplementum — Folia Dendrol Suppl
Folia Dermatologica (Pisa) — Folia Dermatol Pisa
Folia Endocrinologica — FOENAA
Folia Endocrinologica — Fol Endocr
Folia Endocrinologica — Folia Endocrinol
Folia Endocrinologica Japonica — Fol Endocr Jap
Folia Endocrinologica Japonica — Folia Endocrinol Jpn
Folia Endocrinologica Japonica — NNGZAZ
Folia Endocrinologica (Pisa) — Folia Endocrinol (Pisa)
Folia Endocrinologica (Rome) — Folia Endocrinol (Rome)
Folia Entomologica Hungarica — Fol Ent Hung
Folia Entomologica Hungarica — Folia Ent Hung
Folia Entomologica Hungarica — Folia Entomol Hung
Folia Entomologica Hungarica — ROKOA5
Folia Entomologica Hungarica. Rovartani Kozlemenyek — Folia Entomol Hung Rovartani Kozl
Folia Entomologica Mexicana — FEMXAA
Folia Entomologica Mexicana — Fol Ent Mex
Folia Entomologica Mexicana — Folia Ent Mex
Folia Entomologica Mexicana — Folia Entomol Mex
Folia Facultatis Medicae — Folia Fac Med
Folia Facultatis Medicae Universitatis Comenianae Bratislaviensis — FFMDAP
Folia Facultatis Medicae Universitatis Comenianae Bratislaviensis — Folia Fac Med Univ Comenianae Bratisl
Folia Facultatis Scientiarum Naturalium Universitatis Masarykiana Brunensis. Mathematica — Folia Fac Sci Natur Univ Masaryk Brun Math
Folia Facultatis Scientiarum Naturalium Universitatis Purkynianae Brunensis: Biologia — FFUBAP
Folia Facultatis Scientiarum Naturalium Universitatis Purkynianae Brunensis: Biologia — Folia Fac Sci Nat Univ Purkynianae Brun Biol
Folia Facultatis Scientiarum Naturalium Universitatis Purkynianae Brunensis: Chemia — FFSCDL
Folia Facultatis Scientiarum Naturalium Universitatis Purkynianae Brunensis: Chemia — Folia Fac Sci Nat Univ Purkynianae Brun Chem
Folia Facultatis Scientiarum Naturalium Universitatis Purkynianae Brunensis: Physica — Folia Fac Sci Nat Univ Purkynianae Brunensis Phys
Folia Forestalia [*Helsinki*] — FLFSA9
Folia Forestalia — Fol For
Folia Forestalia — Folia For
Folia Forestalia — Folia Forest
Folia Forestalia (Helsinki) — Folia For (Helsinki)
Folia Forestalia Instituti Forestalis Fenniae — Folia For Inst For Fenn
Folia Forestalia Polonica. Seria A (Lesnictwo) — FFPOA5
Folia Forestalia Polonica. Seria A (Lesnictwo) — Folia For Pol Ser A (Lesn)
Folia Forestalia Polonica. Seria A (Lesnictwo) — Folia For Polon (Lesn)
Folia Forestalia Polonica. Seria B (Drzewnictwo) — FFPBAY
Folia Forestalia Polonica. Seria B. Drzewnictwo — Folia For Pol Ser B
Folia Forestalia Polonica. Seria B (Drzewnictwo) — Folia For Pol Ser B (Drzewnictwo)
Folia Forestalia Polonica. Seria B (Drzewnictwo) — Folia For Polon (Drzewn)
Folia Geobotanica et Phytotaxonomica — FGPBA7
Folia Geobotanica et Phytotaxonomica — Fol Geobot Phytotax
Folia Geobotanica et Phytotaxonomica — Folia Geobot Phytotaxon
Folia Geographica — Fol Geogr
Folia Geographica Danica — Fol Ggr Dan
Folia Geographica. Series Geographica-Physica — Folia Geogr Ser Geogr Phys
Folia Gynaecologica (Pavia) — Folia Gynaec (Pavia)
Folia Haematologica [*Leipzig*] — FOHEAW
Folia Haematologica — Fol Haemat
Folia Haematologica. Abteilung 2. Zentral-Organ — Folia Haematol Abt 2
Folia Haematologica (Frankfurt Am Main) — Folia Haematol (Frankfurt Am Main)
Folia Haematologica (Leipzig) — Folia Haematol (Leipz)
Folia Haematologica (Leipzig). Archiv — Folia Haematol (Leipzig) Arch
Folia Haematologica (Leipzig). Zentralorgan — Folia Haematol (Leipzig) Zentralorgan
Folia Hereditaria et Pathologica — FOHPAV
Folia Hereditaria et Pathologica — Fol Hered Path
Folia Hereditaria et Pathologica — Folia Hered Pathol
Folia Histochemica et Cytobiologica — FHCYEM
Folia Histochemica et Cytobiologica — Folia Histochem Cytobiol
Folia Histochemica et Cytochemica [*Later, Folia Histochemica et Cytobiologica*] — FHCYAI
Folia Histochemica et Cytochemica [*Later, Folia Histochemica et Cytobiologica*] — Fol Hist Cy
Folia Histochemica et Cytochemica [*Later, Folia Histochemica et Cytobiologica*] — Fol Hist Cytochem
Folia Histochemica et Cytochemica [*Later, Folia Histochemica et Cytobiologica*] — Folia Histochem Cytochem
Folia Histochemica et Cytochemica (Krakow) [*Later, Folia Histochemica et Cytobiologica*] — Folia Histochem Cytochem (Krakow)
Folia Histochemica et Cytochemica. Supplement — Folia Histochem Cytochem Suppl
Folia Historiae Artium — Fol Hist Art
Folia Horticulturea Sinica — Folia Hortic Sin
Folia Humanistica — FH
Folia Humanistica — Fol Humanis
Folia Humanistica. Ciencias, Artes, Letras — Fol Hum
Folia Humanistica. Ciencias, Artes, Letras — Folia Hum
Folia Limnologica Scandinavica — FLISAO
Folia Limnologica Scandinavica — FLSC
Folia Limnologica Scandinavica — Fol Limnol Scand
Folia Limnologica Scandinavica — Folia Limnol Scand
Folia Linguistica — FL
Folia Linguistica — FLin
Folia Linguistica — Fo Li
Folia Linguistica — Fol Ling
Folia Linguistica. Acta Societatis Linguisticae Europaeae — F Ling
Folia Linguistica. Acta Societatis Linguisticae Europaeae — FOL
Folia Lovaniensia — Fol Lov
Folia Medica — Fol Med
Folia Medica [*Plovdiv*] — FOLMA8
Folia Medica — FOMDA
Folia Medica [*Naples*] — FOMDAK
Folia Medica Bialostocensia — FMBCAG
Folia Medica Bialostocensia — Folia Med Bialostoc

Folia Medica Bialostocensia — Folia Med Bialostocensia
Folia Medica Cracoviensia — FMCRAW
Folia Medica Cracoviensia — Fol Med Cracov
Folia Medica Cracoviensia — Folia Med Cracov
Folia Medica Facultatis. Medicinae Universitatis Saraeviensis — Folia Med Fac Med Univ Saraev
Folia Medica Lodziensia — Fol Med Lodz
Folia Medica Lodziensia — Folia Med Lodz
Folia Medica (Naples) — Folia Med (Naples)
Folia Medica (Napoli) — Fol Med (Napoli)
Folia Medica Neerlandica — Fol Med Neerl
Folia Medica Neerlandica — Folia Med Neerl
Folia Medica Neerlandica — FOMNAG
Folia Medica Orientalia. Sectio 1. Folia Medicinae Internae Orientalia — Folia Med Orient Sect 1
Folia Medica (Plovdiv) — Folia Med (Plovdiv)
Folia Medico — Folia Med
Folia Mendeliana — FMDLAJ
Folia Mendeliana — Fol Mend
Folia Mendeliana Musei Moravia — Folia Mendel
Folia Microbiologica — Fol Microb
Folia Microbiologica — Fol Microbiol
Folia Microbiologica — Folia Microbiol
Folia Microbiologica — FOMIAZ
Folia Microbiologica (Prague) — Folia Microbiol (Prague)
Folia Morphologica [*Prague*] — FMORAO
Folia Morphologica — Fol Morph
Folia Morphologica — Folia Morph
Folia Morphologica [*Warsaw*] — FOMOAJ
Folia Morphologica (Prague) — Folia Morphol (Prague)
Folia Morphologica (Praha) — Folia Morphol (Praha)
Folia Morphologica (Warsaw) — Folia Morphol (Warsaw)
Folia Morphologica (Warsaw) (English translation) — Folia Morphol (Warsaw) (Engl Transl)
Folia Morphologiica (Warszawa) — Folia Morphol Warsz
Folia Musei Rerum Naturalium Bohemiae Occidentalis. Geologica — Folia Mus Rerum Nat Bohemiae Occident Geol
Folia Neuropathologica — Folia Neuropathol
Folia Neuropsiquiatrica del Sur y Este de Espana — FNPQAX
Folia Neuropsiquiatrica del Sur y Este de Espana — Folia Neuropsiquiatr Sur Este Esp
Folia Odontologica Practica — Folia Odontol Pract
Folia Oeconomica Cracoviensia — Fol Oecon Cracov
Folia Ophthalmologica — Folia Ophthalmol
Folia Ophthalmologica [*Leipzig*] — FOOPDZ
Folia Ophthalmologica Japonica — Folia Ophthalmol Jpn
Folia Ophthalmologica Japonica — NGKYA3
Folia Ophthalmologica (Leipzig) — Folia Ophthalmol (Leipz)
Folia Orientalia — FO
Folia Orientalia — Fol Or
Folia Orientalia — Folia O
Folia Orientalia — Folia Orient
Folia Parasitologica — Folia Parasit
Folia Parasitologica [*Prague*] — FPARA9
Folia Parasitologica (Prague) — Folia Parasitol (Prague)
Folia Pharmaceutica — Folia Pharm
Folia Pharmaceutica [*Istanbul*] — FOPMAS
Folia Pharmaceutica (Istanbul) — Folia Pharm (Istanbul)
Folia Pharmaceutica (Prague) — Folia Pharm Prague
Folia Pharmacologica Japonica — Fol Pharm J
Folia Pharmacologica Japonica — Folia Pharmacol Jpn
Folia Pharmacologica Japonica — NYKZAU
Folia Phoniatrica — F Phon
Folia Phoniatrica — Fol Phoniat
Folia Phoniatrica — Folia Phoniatr
Folia Phoniatrica — FOPHA
Folia Phoniatrica — FOPHAD
Folia Phoniatrica (Basel) — Folia Phoniatr (Basel)
Folia Phoniatrica et Logopedica — Folia Phoniatr Logop
Folia Primatologica — Fol Primat
Folia Primatologica — Folia Primat
Folia Primatologica — Folia Primatol
Folia Primatologica — FPRMAB
Folia Psychiatrica et Neurologica Japonica — Folia Psychiatr Neurol Jpn
Folia Psychiatrica et Neurologica Japonica — FPNJAG
Folia Quaternaria — Folia Quat
Folia Quaternaria — FOQUAN
Folia Scientifica Africae Centralis [*Congo*] — Folia Sci Afr Cent
Folia Scientifica Africae Centralis — FSAC
Folia Serologica — Fol Serol
Folia Serologica — Folia Serol
Folia Slavica — FSl
Folia Societatis Scientiarum Lublinensis — Folia Soc Sci Lublinensis
Folia Societatis Scientiarum Lublinensis. Biologia — BLTBAI
Folia Societatis Scientiarum Lublinensis. Biologia — Folia Soc Sci Lublinensis Biol
Folia Societatis Scientiarum Lublinensis. Matematyka-Fizyka-Chemia — Folia Soc Sci Lublinensis Mat Fiz Chem
Folia Societatis Scientiarum Lublinensis. Sectio A-D. Supplementum — Folia Soc Sci Lublinensis Sect A D Suppl
Folia Universitaria — Folia Univ
Folia Universitaria Cochabamba — Folia Univ Cochabamba
Folia Universitaria Cochabamba — FOUVAC
Folia Venatoria — POZBDM
Folia Veterinaria — Folia Vet
Folia Veterinaria Latina — Folia Vet Lat
Folia Veterinaria Latina — FVTLAQ
Folia Veterinaria (Prague) — Folia Vet (Prague)
Folia Zoologica — Folia Zool
Folia Zoologica — FOZODJ
Foliage Digest — Foliage Dig
Folio — F
Folio. Guide to Magazine Suppliers — Folio Supp
Folk Dance Guide — FDG
Folk. Dansk Ethnografisk Tidsskrift — FOLK
Folk Harp Journal — Folk Harp J
Folk Life — FL
Folk Life [*Cardiff*] — FoL
Folk Music Journal — FMJ
Folk Music Journal — Folk Mus J
Folk Music Journal — Folk Music
Folk og Kultur — F o K
Folk og Kultur. Arbog for Dansk Etnologi og Folkemindevidenskab — FoK
Folk og Vaern — F o V
Folkeskolen. Udgivet af Danmarks Laererforening — Flksk
Folkkultur — Folkkult
Folk-Liv — FLiv
Folklore — F
Folklore — FF
Folklore — FL
Folklore — Fo
Folklore — Folk
Folklore [*London*] — Folkl
Folklore — IFKL
Folklore Americano — FA
Folklore Americano — FAm
Folklore Americano — Folkl Am
Folklore Americano — Folklore Am
Folklore Americano. Comite Interamericano de Folklore. Instituto Panamericano de Geografia e Historia (Lima) — Folk Am Lima
Folklore Americano; Organo del Comite Interamericano de Folklore — FACI
Folklore Americas — FAm
Folklore Americas (Coral Gables, Florida) — Folk Am Coral Gables
Folklore and Folk Music Archivist — FFMA
Folklore and Folk Music Archivist — Folk Mus Arch
Folklore Archives — Folkl Arch
Folklore. Boletin del Departmento de Folklore del Instituto de Cooperacion Universitaria — FICU
Folklore Brabancon — F Brab
Folklore Brabancon — FB
Folklore Brabancon — Folkl Brabancon
Folklore (Calcutta) — FLC
Folklore (Calcutta) — Folkl (Calcutta)
Folklore (Calcutta) — Folklore C
Folklore de Champagne — Folkl Champagne
Folklore Fellows Communications — FFC
Folklore Forum — FF
Folklore Forum — FForum
Folklore Forum. Bibliographic and Special Series — FForumB
Folklore Institute. Journal — Folk Inst
Folklore Institute. Monograph Series — FIMS
Folklore Italiano — Fl
Folklore Journal — Fl J
Folk-Lore Journal — Folk-Lore J
Folklore Record — Fl R
Folk-lore Record — Folk Lore Rec
Folklore. Rivista di Tradizioni Popolari (Naples) — FN
Folklore Society Publications — Folklore Soc Pub
Folklore Studies — FLS
Folklore Studies — Folkl Stud
Folklore Studies — FolkS
Folklore Studies — FS
Folklore Studies (Peking) — Folkl St (P)
Folklore Suisse — Folkl Suisse
Folklore. Tribuna del Pensamiento Peruano — FTPP
Folkmalsstudier — FMSt
Folkminner och Folktankar — Folkm
Folks-Sztyme — FSz
Folktales of the World — FW
Folleto de Divulgacion. Instituto Forestal (Santiago De Chile) — Foll Divulg Inst For (Chile)
Folleto Tecnico. Secretaria de Agricultura y Ganaderia. Instituto Nacional de Investigaciones Agricolas (Mexico) — Fol Tec Secr Agr Ganad Inst Nac Invest Agr (Mexico)
Folleto Tecnico. Universidad Autonoma de San Luis Potosi Instituto de Geologia y Metalurgia — Foll Tec Univ Auton San Luis Potosi Inst Geol Metal
Folletos de Divulgacion Cientifica del Instituto de Biologia — Folletos Divulg Ci Inst Biol
Folletos Tecnicos Forestales — Foll Tec For
Folletos Tecnicos Forestales. Administracion Nacional de Bosques (Argentina) [*A publication*] — Foll Tec For Adm Nac Bosques (Argent)
Folya Farmasotika — Folya Farm
Fomento Agricola. Ministerio de Agricultura. Servico de Divulgacao Agricola — Fomento Agric
Fomento de Puerto Rico — Fom PR
Fonaments Prehistoria i Mon Antic als Paisos Catalans — Fonaments
Fonatana Books — FB
Fondation Universitaire Luxembourgeoise. Notes de Recherche — Fond Univ Luxemb Notes Rech

Fondation Universitaire Luxembourgeoise. Serie Notes de Recherche — Fond Univ Luxemb Ser Notes Rech
Fondation Universitaire Luxembourgeoise. Serie Notes de Recherche — NFULDA
Fondazione Giorgio Ronchi. Atti — Fond Giorgio Ronchi Att
Fondazione Iniziative Zooprofilattiche e Zootecniche. Collana — Fond Iniziative Zooprofil Zootec Collana
Fondazione Politecnica per il Mezzogiorno d'Italia. Quaderno — Fond Politec Mezzogiorno Ital Quad
Fonderia Italiana — Fonderia Ital
Fonderie Moderne — Fonderie Mod
Fonderie. Supplement — Fonderie Suppl
Fondeur d'Aujourd'hui — Fondeur
Fondo de Cultura Economica [*Mexico*] — FCE
Fondren Science Series — Fondren Sci Ser
Fonds de Recherches Forestieres. Universite Laval. Bulletin — Fonds Rech For Univ Laval Bull
Fonds de Recherches Forestieres. Universite Laval. Bulletin — LUFBBK
Fonds de Recherches Forestieres. Universite Laval. Contribution — Fonds Rech For Univ Laval Contrib
Fonds de Recherches Forestieres. Universite Laval. Contribution — QLFCAE
Fonds de Recherches Forestieres. Universite Laval. Note Technique — Fonds Rech For Univ Laval Note Tech
Fonds de Recherches Forestieres. Universite Laval. Note Technique — NTFLDX
Fonetica si Dialectologie — F & D
Fonetica si Dialectologie — FD
Fonetica si Dialectologie — FsD
FonoForum — FF
Fontaine — F
Fontaine — Font
Fontana Library — FL
Fontana Library of Theology and Philosophy — FLTP
Fontana Religious Series — FRS
Fontane Blaetter — FB
Fontane Blaetter — Fontane Bl
Fonte Nucleare nel Futuro Energetico. Atti Delle Giornate dell'Energia Nucleare — Fonte Nucl Futuro Energ Atti Giornate Energ Nucl
Fontes ad Topographiam Veteris Urbis Romae Pertinentes — Font Top Vet Urb Pert
Fontes ad Topographiam Veteris Urbis Romae Pertinentes — FTVURP
Fontes Ambrosiani — Font Amb
Fontes Archaeologici Hungariae — Fontes A H
Fontes Archaeologici Hungariae — Fontes Arch
Fontes Archaeologici Hungariae — Fontes Arch Hung
Fontes Archaeologici Posnanienses — FAP
Fontes Archaeologici Posnanienses — Font A Pos
Fontes Archaeologici Posnanienses — Fontes Arch Posnan
Fontes Archaeologici Pragenses — FAP
Fontes Archaeologici Pragenses — Fontes Arch Prag
Fontes Artis Musicae — FAM
Fontes Artis Musicae — Fon
Fontes Artis Musicae — Fon Art Mus
Fontes Artis Musicae — Fontes
Fontes Artis Musicae — FontesArtisM
Fontes Hispaniae Antiquae — FHA
Fontes Historiae Dacoromanae — FHDR
Fontes Historiae Religionum — FHR
Fontes Historiae Ukraino-Russicae — FHUR
Fontes Historicae Congregationis Passionis — FHCP
Fontes Historici Societatis Mariae — FHSM
Fontes Iuris Romani Antejustiniani — FIRA
Fontes Iuris Romani Antejustiniani — Fon Iur Rom Ant
Fontes Iuris Romani Antejustiniani — Font
Fontes Iuris Romani Antejustiniani — Font Iur Rom
Fontes Iuris Romani Antejustiniani — Font Iur Rom Antej
Fontes Iuris Romani Antiqui — FIR
Fontes Iuris Romani Antiqui — FIRA
Fontes Minores Medii Aevi — FMMA
Fontes Rerum Austriacarum — FRA
Fontes Rerum Austriacarum. Diplomataria et Acta — FRAD
Fontes Rerum Austriacarum. Fontes Juris — FRAF
Fontes Rerum Austriacarum. Scriptores — FRAS
Fontes Rerum Transylvanicarum — FRT
Fonti e Studi di Storia Ecclesiastica — FSSE
Fonti e Studi per la Storia dell'Universita di Pavia — Fonti Studi Storia Univ Pavia
Fonti per la Storia d'Italia — F St I
Fonti. Sacra Congregazione per la Chiesa Orientale. Codificazione Canonica Orientale — FCCO
Food Additive Control Series. Food and Agriculture Organization of the United Nations — F Addit Contr Ser FAO
Food Additives and Contaminants — FACOEB
Food Additives and Contaminants — Food Addit Contam
Food Additives and Contaminants. Analysis, Surveillance, Evaluation, Control — Food Addit Contam Anal Surveillance Eval Control
Food Analysis — MYG
Food and Agricultural Immunology — Food Agric Immunol
Food and Agricultural Legislation — Food Agric Leg
Food and Agriculture — F Agric
Food and Agriculture Organization of the United Nations. Committee for Inland Fisheries of Africa. CIFA Technical Paper — FAO Comm Inland Fish Afr CIFA Tech Pap
Food and Agriculture Organization of the United Nations. Irrigation and Drainage Paper — FAO Irrig Drain Pap
Food and Agriculture Organization of the United Nations. Monthly Bulletin of Agriculture — FAO Ag Bul
Food and Agriculture Organization of the United Nations. Technical Report TF-RAS — FAO Tech Rep TF-RAS
Food and Agriculture Organization of the United Nations. Timber Bulletin for Europe — FAO Timber
Food and Agriculture Technical Information Service. Review — Food Agric Tech Inf Serv Rev
Food and Beverage Marketing — Food & Bev
Food and Chemical Toxicology — FCTOD7
Food and Chemical Toxicology — Fd Chem Toxic
Food and Chemical Toxicology — Food Chem Toxicol
Food and Chemical Toxicology. An International Journal Published for the British Industrial Biological Research Organization — Food Chem Toxicol Int J Publ Br Ind Biol Res Organ
Food and Cookery Review — FCR
Food and Cosmetics Toxicology — FCTXAV
Food and Cosmetics Toxicology — Fd Cosmet Toxicol
Food and Cosmetics Toxicology — Food Cosmet
Food and Cosmetics Toxicology — Food Cosmet Toxicol
Food and Cosmetics Toxicology — Food Cosmetics Toxicol
Food and Drug Administration. Bureau of Veterinary Medicine. Technical Report FDA/BVM (United States) — Food Drug Adm Bur Vet Med Tech Rep FDA BVM (US)
Food and Drug Administration. Publication FDA — Food Drug Adm Publ FDA
Food and Drug Packaging — F & D Pkg
Food and Drugs Industry Bulletin — Food Drugs Ind Bull
Food and Fermentation Industries — Food Ferment Ind
Food and Fiber Economics. Texas Agricultural Extension Service. The Texas A & M University System — Food Fiber Econ Tex Agric Ext Serv Tex A & M Univ Syst
Food and Flowers. Hong Kong Agricultural Department — Food Fl
Food and Nonfood. Fachzeitschrift fuer Unternehmer und Fuhrungskrafte Moderner Grossformen in Lebensmittelhandel — LGE
Food and Nutrition — F Nutr
Food and Nutrition — Fd Nutr
Food and Nutrition — FN
Food and Nutrition — Food & Nutr
Food and Nutrition — Food Nutr
Food and Nutrition — HRISAK
Food and Nutrition — IFNN
Food and Nutrition Bulletin — F Nutr Bull
Food and Nutrition Bulletin — Food Nutr Bull
Food and Nutrition in Africa — Food Nutrition Afr
Food and Nutrition in History and Anthropology — Food Nutr Hist Anthropol
Food and Nutrition Information Center Catalog [*Database*] — FNIC Catalog
Food and Nutrition News — Food Nutr News
Food and Nutrition. Notes and Reviews — Fd Nutr Notes Rev
Food and Nutrition. Notes and Reviews — Fd Nutr Notes Revs
Food and Nutrition. Notes and Reviews — Food and Nutr Notes and Rev
Food and Nutrition. Notes and Reviews — Food & Nutr Notes Revs
Food and Nutrition. Notes and Reviews — Food Nutr Notes Rev
Food and Nutrition (Rome) — Food Nutr (Rome)
Food Australia — Food Aust
Food Biotechnology — Food Biotechnol
Food Biotechnology (New York) — Food Biotechnol NY
Food Business — Food Bus
Food Chemical News Guide — Fd Chem News Guide
Food Chemistry — FOCHDJ
Food Chemistry — Food Chem
Food Chemistry, Microbiology, Technology — CMTLBX
Food Chemistry, Microbiology, Technology — Food Chem Microbiol Technol
Food Development — FDEVDS
Food Development — Food Dev
Food Development — Food Devel
Food, Drug, Cosmetic Law Journal — FDLJAO
Food, Drug, Cosmetic Law Journal — Food Drug C
Food, Drug, Cosmetic Law Journal — Food Drug Cosm LJ
Food, Drug, Cosmetic Law Journal — Food Drug Cosmet Law J
Food, Drug, Cosmetic Law Quarterly — Food Drug Cosm LQ
Food, Drug, Cosmetic Law Quarterly — Food Drug Cosmet Law Q
Food, Drug, Cosmetic Law Reports. Commerce Clearing House — Food Drug Cosm L Rep CCH
Food Engineering — FDI
Food Engineering [*New York*] — FOEGAN
Food Engineering — Food Eng
Food Engineering International — Food Eng Int
Food Engineering (New York) — Food Eng (NY)
Food Engineering (Philadelphia) — Food Eng (Philadelphia)
Food Engineering Systems — Food Eng Syst
Food Equipment and Additives Suppliers and Traders [*Database*] — FEAST
Food Extrusion Science and Technology — Food Extrusion Sci Technol
Food Facts for Dietitians — Food Facts Diet
Food Farming and Agriculture. Journal for the Development of Food and Agriculture [*India*] — Food Farming Agric
Food Fish Market Review and Outlook — Food Fish Mark Rev & Outl
Food: Flavouring Ingredients Processing and Packaging — Fd Flavs Ingredients Process Packag
Food: Flavouring Ingredients Processing and Packaging — Food Flavour Ingredients Processing and Packaging
Food from Poland — Food Pol
Food Hygiene Study [*Japan*] — Food Hyg Stud
Food in Canada — Fd Can
Food in Canada — FOCNAY
Food in Canada — Food Can

Food in Canada — Food Canad
Food Industries — F Ind
Food Industries — Fd Inds
Food Industries Journal — FOIJA
Food Industries Journal — Food Ind J
Food Industries Manual — F Ind Man
Food Industries of South Africa — F Ind SA
Food Industries of South Africa — Food Ind S Afr
Food Industries Weekly — Food Ind Wkly
Food Industry — Food Ind
Food Industry (Budapest) — Food Ind (Budapest)
Food Industry (Moscow) — Food Ind (Moscow)
Food Industry of the USSR — Food Ind USSR
Food Industry Science — Food Ind Sci
Food Industry (Tokyo) — Food Ind (Tokyo)
Food Irradiation — FOIRA
Food Irradiation [*France*] — Food Irradiat
Food Irradiation [*Japan*] — SNNSB3
Food Irradiation Information — FDIIA6
Food Irradiation Information — Food Irradiat Inf
Food Irradiation (Japan) — Food Irradiat (Jpn)
Food Launch Awareness in the Retail Sector [*Database*] — FLAIRS
Food Magazine — KRN
Food Management — Food Manage
Food Manufacture — Fd Mf
Food Manufacture — FMA
Food Manufacture — FOMAAB
Food Manufacture — Food Manuf
Food Manufacture — Food Mfr
Food Manufacture Weekly — Food Manuf Wkly
Food Market Awareness Databank — FOMAD
Food Materials and Equipment — Food Mater Equip
Food Microbiology [*London*] — FOMIE5
Food Microbiology (London) — Food Microbiol (Lond)
Food Microstructure — FMICDK
Food Microstructure — Food Microstruct
Food Monitor — Food Mon
Food Monitor — FoodMonit
Food News for Consumers — Food News Consum
Food News Scanning Database — FOSCAN
Food Packer — FOPAAQ
Food Packer and Canning Age — Food Packer Cann Age
Food Policy — FNY
Food Policy — Food Pol
Food Policy — FOPOD3
Food Preservation Quarterly — Food Preserv Q
Food Preservation Quarterly — Food Preservation Q
Food Process Engineering. Proceedings. International Congress on Engineering and Food and the Eighth European Food Symposium — Food Process Eng Proc Int Congr
Food Processing — Fd Process
Food Processing — FOO
Food Processing — Food Process
Food Processing [*Chicago*] — FOPRA9
Food Processing and Marketing [*Chicago*] — Fd Process Market
Food Processing and Marketing [*Chicago*] — Food Processing Mktg
Food Processing and Marketing [*Chicago*] — FOPMBT
Food Processing and Marketing (Chicago) — Food Process Mark (Chic)
Food Processing and Marketing (London) — Food Process Mark (London)
Food Processing and Packaging — Fd Process Packag
Food Processing and Packaging — Food Process Packag
Food Processing (Chicago) — Food Process (Chic)
Food Processing (Chicago) — Food Process Chicago
Food Processing Industry — Fd Process Ind
Food Processing Industry — Food Proc
Food Processing Industry — Food Process Ind
Food Processing News — Food Proc
Food Product Development — Fd Prod Dev
Food Product Development — Food Prod
Food Product Development — Food Prod Dev
Food Product Development — Food Prod Devel
Food Product Development — FPRDAI
Food Production/Management — Food PM
Food Production/Management — Food Prod/Manage
Food RA [*Research Association*] **Online Scientific and Technical Information** [*Database*] — FROSTI
Food Regulation Enquiries [*Database*] — FOREGE
Food Research — F Res
Food Research — Fd Res
Food Research — Food Res
Food Research — FOREAE
Food Research (Chicago) — Food Res (Chicago)
Food Research Institute. Studies — Food Res Inst Stud
Food Research Institute. Studies — Food Research Inst Studies
Food Research Institute. Studies [*Stanford*] — SFRSAY
Food Research Institute. Studies in Agricultural Economics, Trade, and Development [*Stanford*] — FRSABT
Food Research Institute. Studies in Agricultural Economics, Trade, and Development (Stanford) — Food Res Inst Stud Agric Econ Trade Dev (Stanford)
Food Research Institute. Studies (Stanford) — Food Res Inst Stud (Stanford)
Food Research International — Food Res Int
Food Research Report. Division of Food Research. Commonwealth Scientific and Industrial Research Organisation — Food Res Dep Div Food Res CSIRO
Food Review — Food Rev
Food Reviews International — Food Rev Int
Food Reviews International — FRINEL
Food Safety Assessment — Food Saf Assess
Food Science — Food Sci
Food Science [*New York*] — FOSCDG
Food Science Abstracts — F Sci Abstr
Food Science Abstracts — Food Sci Abstr
Food Science and Human Nutrition — Food Sci Hum Nutr
Food Science and Technology — Food Sci Technol
Food Science and Technology [*Zurich*] — LBWTAP
Food Science and Technology. A Series of Monographs — Food Sci Technol Ser Monogr
Food Science and Technology Abstracts [*International Food Information Service*] [*Bibliographic database*] — Food Sci & Tech Abstr
Food Science and Technology Abstracts [*International Food Information Service*] [*Bibliographic database*] — Food Sci Technol Abstr
Food Science and Technology Abstracts [*International Food Information Service*] [*Bibliographic database*] — FSTA
Food Science and Technology International — Food Sci Technol Int
Food Science and Technology International (London) — Food Sci Technol Int London
Food Science and Technology International (New York) — Food Sci Technol Int NY
Food Science and Technology, International (Tsukuba, Japan) — Food Sci Technol Int Tsukuba Jpn
Food Science and Technology (London) — Food Sci Technol London
Food Science and Technology. Present Status and Future Direction. Proceedings of the International Congress of Food Science and Technology — Food Sci Technol Proc Int Congr
Food Science and Technology (Zurich) — Food Sci & Technol (Zur)
Food Science (Beijing) — Food Sci (Beijing)
Food Science (New York) — Food Sci (NY)
Food Science (Osaka) — Food Sci Osaka
Food Science (Taipei) — Food Sci (Taipei)
Food Sciences and Nutrition — Food Sci Nutr
Food Sciences and Nutrition — PFSN
Food Sciences and Technologies (Bucharest) — Food Sci Technol Bucharest
Food Service Forum — Food Serv For
Food Service Marketing — Food S Mkt
Food Service Marketing — Food Serv Mark
Food Service Marketing — Food Serv Mkt
Food Surveillance Paper — Food Surveill Pap
Food Technologist (Dunedin, New Zealand) — Food Technol Dunedin NZ
Food Technology — F Techn
Food Technology — Fd Technol
Food Technology — Food Tech
Food Technology — Food Technol
Food Technology — FOTEAO
Food Technology — IFTK
Food Technology (Chicago) — Food Technol Chicago
Food Technology in Australia — Fd Technol Aust
Food Technology in Australia — Food Tech Aust
Food Technology in Australia — Food Tech in Aust
Food Technology in Australia — Food Technol Aust
Food Technology in Australia — Food Technology in Aust
Food Technology in Australia — FTA
Food Technology in Australia — FTAUAC
Food Technology in New Zealand — Food Tech NZ
Food Technology in New Zealand — Food Technol NZ
Food Technology (Milan) — Food Technol (Milan)
Food Technology Review — Food Technol Rev
Food Trade Review — Fd Trade Rev
Food Trade Review — Food Trade R
Food Trade Review — Food Trade Rev
Food Trade Review — FTA
Food World News — Food Wld N
Foodpress, Economisch, en Technisch Weekblad voor de Voedingsmiddelenindustrie en Genotmiddelenindustrie en Groothandel in de Benelux — FDP
Foods, Nutrition, and Dental Health — Foods Nutr Dent Health
Foodservice and Hospitality — FH
Fookien Times Yearbook [*Manila*] — FTY
Foot and Ankle International — Foot Ankle Int
Foot and Mouth Disease Bulletin — Foot Mouth Dis Bull
Foote Prints on Chemicals, Metals, Alloys, and Ores — Foote Prints Chem Met Alloys Ores
Foothills Dempster Newsletter — FODN
Foothills Pipe Lines (Yukon) Limited. News Releases — FPLY
Foothills Wilderness Journal — FOWJ
Foothills Yukon Bulletin — FOYB
Footwear News — Ftwr News
Footwear News — FWN
For Fish Farmers. Mississippi State University. Cooperative Extension Service — Fish Farmers Miss State Univ Coop Ext Serv
FOR. Kentucky University Cooperative Extension Service — FOR KY Univ Coop Ext Serv
For Socialist Agricultural Science — For Social Agric Sci
For the Defense — For Def
For the Riverina Teacher — For the Riverina Teach
Forage Research — Forage Res
Forages — FORGA
Forbes — FBR
Force Ouvriere — FO
Forces. Hydro Quebec — FORC
Forces Sous-Marines — Forc Sous M

Ford Forestry Center. Michigan Technological University. Bulletin — Ford For Cent Mich Technol Univ Bull
Ford Forestry Center. Michigan Technological University. Research Notes — Ford For Cent Mich Technol Univ Res Notes
Fordham International Law Forum — Fordham Intl LF
Fordham International Law Journal — For Int LJ
Fordham International Law Journal — Fordham Int'l LJ
Fordham Law Review — Fo LR
Fordham Law Review — For LR
Fordham Law Review — Ford L Rev
Fordham Law Review — Fordham L Rev
Fordham Law Review — Fordham Law Rev
Fordham Law Review — FR
Fordham Urban Law Journal — For Urb LJ
Fordham Urban Law Journal — Ford Urban LJ
Fordham Urban Law Journal — Fordham Urb LJ
Fordham Urban Law Journal — Fordham Urban L J
Fords and Bridges — FB
Forecast. First Interstate Bank. Annual Report — Interstate
Forecast for Home Economics — Forecast Home Econ
Forecast for the Home Economist — Forecast Home Econ
Forecasts of Energy Demand and Supply (Australia). 1982-83 to 1991-92 — Engy (Austl)
Foreign Acquisitions Newsletter — FAN
Foreign Affairs — F Affairs
Foreign Affairs — FA
Foreign Affairs — FAF
Foreign Affairs — FOA
Foreign Affairs — FOR
Foreign Affairs — For Aff
Foreign Affairs — For Affairs
Foreign Affairs — Foreign Aff
Foreign Affairs Bulletin [*Thailand*] — FAB
Foreign Affairs. Council on Foreign Relations — CFR/FA
Foreign Affairs (New York) — FAN
Foreign Affairs Reports — FAR
Foreign Affairs Reports — For Aff Rep
Foreign Affairs Reports — Foreign Aff Rep
Foreign Agricultural Circular. United States Department of Agriculture. Foreign Agricultural Services. Spices. FTEA — Foreign Agric Circ US Dep Agric Serv Spices FTEA
Foreign Agricultural Economic Report. US Department of Agriculture. Economic Research Service — Foreign Agric Econ Rep US Dep Agric Econ Res Serv
Foreign Agriculture — FAG
Foreign Agriculture — FOAGB4
Foreign Agriculture — For Agric
Foreign Agriculture — Foreign Agric
Foreign Agriculture — Forgn Agr
Foreign Agriculture Circular. Canned Fruits. FCAN. United States Foreign Agricultural Service — Foreign Agric Canned Fruits FCAN US Foreign Agric Serv
Foreign Agriculture Circular. Cocoa — FAC Cocoa
Foreign Agriculture Circular. Coffee — FAC Coffee
Foreign Agriculture Circular. Cotton — FAC Cotton
Foreign Agriculture Circular. Dairy Products — FAC Dairy
Foreign Agriculture Circular. Dried Fruits. FDF. United States Department of Agriculture. Foreign Agricultural Service — Foreign Agric Circ Dried Fruit FDF USDA Foreign Agric Serv
Foreign Agriculture Circular. Grains. FG. United States Department of Agriculture. Foreign Agricultural Service — Foreign Agric Circ Grains FG US Dep Agric Foreign Agric Serv
Foreign Agriculture Circular. Horticultural Products — FAC Hort
Foreign Agriculture Circular. Livestock and Poultry Export Trade — FAC DLP
Foreign Agriculture Circular. Oilseeds and Products — FAC Oil
Foreign Agriculture Circular. Sugar, Molasses, and Honey — FAC Sugar
Foreign Agriculture Circular. Tea and Spices — FAC Tea
Foreign Agriculture Circular. Tobacco — FAC Tobac
Foreign Agriculture Circular. United States Department of Agriculture — Foreign Agric Circ US Dep Agric
Foreign Agriculture Circular. World Crop Production — FAC WCP
Foreign Agriculture Circular. World Grain Situation — FAC GrainS
Foreign Agriculture. Including Foreign Crops and Markets. US Foreign Agricultural Service — Foreign Agr Incl Foreign Crops Markets
Foreign Agriculture Trade of the United States — Foreign Agr Trade US
Foreign Agriculture. United States Department of Agriculture — FA
Foreign Agriculture. US Department of Agriculture. Foreign Agricultural Service — Foreign Agric US Dep Agric Foreign Agric Serv
Foreign Agriculture. US Foreign Agricultural Service — Foreign Agr
Foreign Agriculture (Washington, DC) — For Agr Wash
Foreign Animal Disease Report — FADR
Foreign Animal Disease Report — For Anim Dis Rep
Foreign Area Research Horizons — FAR Horiz
Foreign Broadcast Information Service — FBIS
Foreign Commerce Weekly — For Com Wkly
Foreign Commerce Weekly — For Comm
Foreign Commerce Weekly. US Bureau of Foreign and Domestic Commerce — FCW
Foreign Compound Metabolism in Mammals — Foreign Compd Metab Mamm
Foreign Economic Trends — FET
Foreign Economic Trends and Their Implications for the United States — ET
Foreign Economic Trends and Their Implications for the United States — ETI
Foreign Economic Trends and Their Implications for the United States — For Econ Trd
Foreign Economic Trends and Their Implications for the United States — Foreign Econ Trends Their Implic US
Foreign Exchange [*Database*] — FX
Foreign Exchange Rate Service [*Database*] — FX
Foreign Investment Review — FEI
Foreign Investment Review — For Investment R
Foreign Language Annals — FLA
Foreign Language Annals — Foreign Lan
Foreign Language Index — FLI
Foreign Language Index — Foreign Lang Index
Foreign Languages (Nebraska) — FL (Neb)
Foreign Legal Periodicals Index — Foreign Leg Per
Foreign Monthly Review and Continental Literary Journal — Foreign Monthly Rev Continental Lit J
Foreign Office Annual [*London*] — FOA
Foreign Office Consular Report [*London*] — FOCR
Foreign Office Treaty Series [*London*] — FOTS
Foreign Petroleum Technology — Foreign Pet Technol
Foreign Policy — For Pol
Foreign Policy — For Policy
Foreign Policy — Foreign Pol
Foreign Policy — GFOR
Foreign Policy (Ankara) — For Pol Ankara
Foreign Policy Bulletin — For Policy Bul
Foreign Policy (New York) — For Pol New York
Foreign Policy Report [*New York*] — FPR
Foreign Policy Reports — For Policy Rep
Foreign Projects Newsletter — FPR
Foreign Quarterly Review — For Q
Foreign Relations of the United States — FRUS
Foreign Report — FRP
Foreign Review — For R
Foreign Scientific Publication. National Center for Scientific, Technical, and Economic Information (Warsaw) [*Poland*] — Foreign Sci Publ Natn Cent Sci Tech Econ Inf (Warsaw)
Foreign Trade — Foreign Tr
Foreign Trade — WNT
Foreign Trade Report — FT Rep
Foreign Trade Review — FTW
Foreign Traders Index [*Database*] — FTI
Foreningen Dansk Samvirke de Dansk Atlanterhavsoer — Foren Dansk Samv Dansk Atlha
Forensic Science [*Later, Forensic Science International*] — FNSCA6
Forensic Science [*Later, Forensic Science International*] — Forensic Sci
Forensic Science Database — FORS
Forensic Science Gazette — Forensic Sci Gaz
Forensic Science International — For Sci Intl
Forensic Science International — Foren Sci I
Forensic Science International — Forensic Sci Int
Forensic Science International — FSIND
Forensic Science International — FSINDR
Forensic Science Society Journal — Forensic Sci Soc J
Forest and Bird [*New Zealand*] — For and Bird
Forest and Outdoors — For & Outdoors
Forest and Timber — For and Timb
Forest and Timber — For Timb
Forest and Timber — For Timber
Forest and Timber — Forest Timb
Forest and Timber — FOTIB3
Forest Department Bulletin. Forest Department (Zambia) — For Dep Bull For Dep (Zambia)
Forest Division Technical Note. Forest Division. (Dar Es Salaam, Tanzania) — For Div Tech Note For Div (Tanz)
Forest Ecology and Management — FECMDW
Forest Ecology and Management — For Ecol & Mgt
Forest Ecology and Management — For Ecol Manage
Forest Environmental Protection. United States Forest Service. Northern Region — FEPNDW
Forest Environmental Protection. United States Forest Service. Northern Region — For Environ Prot US For Serv North Reg
Forest Farmer — For Farmer
Forest Fire Control Abstracts — FFC Abstr
Forest Fire Control Abstracts — For Fire Control Abstr
Forest Fire Losses in Canada — Forest Fire Losses Can
Forest Fire News. Forest Fire and Atmospheric Sciences Research. Forest Service. US Department of Agriculture — For Fire News For Fire Atmos Sci Res For Serv USDA
Forest Focus — For Focus
Forest History — Forest Hist
Forest Industries — For Ind
Forest Industries — Forest Ind
Forest Industries Equipment Review — For Ind Rev
Forest Industries Review [*Later, Forest Industries*] — For Ind R
Forest Industries Review [*Later, Forest Industries*] — For Indus Rev
Forest Industry Lecture Series. University of Alberta Forestry Program — FILSUA
Forest Industry Science and Technology — For Ind Sci Technol
Forest Insect and Disease Conditions in the United States — For Insect Dis Cond US
Forest Insect and Disease Leaflet. United States Department of Agriculture. Forest Service — For Insect Dis Leafl USDA For Serv
Forest Leaves — For Leaves
Forest Management Bulletin. US Department of Agriculture. Forest Service — For Manage Bull US Dep Agric For Serv

Forest Management Note. British Columbia Forest Service — For Mgmt Note BC For Serv
Forest Notes. New Hampshire's Conservation Magazine — FONOBP
Forest Notes. New Hampshire's Conservation Magazine — For Notes
Forest Pest Leaflet — For Pest Leafl
Forest Pest Leaflet. United States Forest Service — For Pest Leafl US For Serv
Forest Pest Management Institute. Report FPM-X (Canada) — For Pest Manage Inst Rep FPMX Can
Forest Planning — For Plan
Forest Products Journal — For Prod J
Forest Products Journal — Forest Prod J
Forest Products Journal — FPJOAB
Forest Products Laboratory. General Technical Report FPL — For Prod Lab Gen Tech Rep FPL
Forest Products Laboratory. Information Circular — For Prod Lab Inf Cir
Forest Products Laboratory. Research Leaflet — For Prod Lab Res Leafl
Forest Products Market Trends — Forest PMT
Forest Products News Letter — For Prod Ne Lett
Forest Products Newsletter. Commonwealth Scientific and Industrial Research Organisation. Division of Forest Products — For Prod Newsl
Forest Products Research — For Prod Res
Forest Products Research and Development Institute. Journal — For Prod Res Dev Inst J
Forest Products Research and Industries Development Digest — For Prod Res Ind Dev Dig
Forest Products Research Bulletin (Great Britain) — For Prod Res Bull (GB)
Forest Products Research Center. Bulletin (Oregon) — For Prod Res Cent Bull (Oreg)
Forest Products Research Center. Information Circular (Oregon) — For Prod Res Cent Inf Circ (Oreg)
Forest Products Research Institute. Report (Bogor, Indonesia) — For Prod Res Inst Rep (Bogor Indones)
Forest Products Research Notes. Forest Research Institute [*New Zealand*] — For Prod Res No
Forest Products Research Record. Division of Forest Products (Zambia) — For Prod Res Rec Div For Prod (Zambia)
Forest Products Research Reports. Department of Forest Research (Nigeria) — For Prod Res Rep Dep For Res (Nigeria)
Forest Products Residuals. Papers. National Meeting. AIChE — For Prod Residuals Pap Natl Meet AIChE
Forest Products Review — Forest Products R
Forest Products Utilization Technical Report. United States Forest Service. Cooperative Forestry Division — For Prod Util Tech Rep US For Serv Coop For Div
Forest Quarterly — For Quar
Forest Record [*London*] — FORRAJ
Forest Record. Forestry Commission (London) — For Rec For Comm (Lond)
Forest Record (London) — For Rec (Lond)
Forest Recreation Research — For Recreat Res
Forest Recreation Research — FRERDC
Forest Research Bulletin. Forest Department (Zambia) — For Res Bull For Dep (Zambia)
Forest Research in India — For Res India
Forest Research in India — FORIAQ
Forest Research in the Southeast. United States Southeastern Forest Experiment Station — For Res Southeast US Southern For Exp Stn
Forest Research Information Paper. Ministry of Natural Resources (Ontario) — For Res Inf Pap Minist Natl Res (Ont)
Forest Research Institute (Bogor). Communication — For Res Inst (Bogor) Commun
Forest Research Institute [*Bogor*]. Communication — PNGUA8
Forest Research News for the Midsouth — Forest Res News Midsouth
Forest Research Note. Ontario Forest Research Centre — For Res Note Ont For Res Cent
Forest Research Pamphlet. Division of Forest Research (Zambia) — For Res Pamphl Div For Res (Zambia)
Forest Research Report. Ontario Ministry of Natural Resources — For Res Rep Ont Minist Nat Resour
Forest Research Review. British Columbia Forest Service — For Res Rev
Forest Research Series. South Carolina Agricultural Experiment Station — For Res Ser SC Agric Exp Stn
Forest Resource Report. United States Forest Service — For Res Rep
Forest Resource Report. United States Forest Service — For Resour Rep US For Serv
Forest Resources and Environment — For Resour Environ
Forest Resources Newsletter — For Resour Newslett
Forest Science — For Sci
Forest Science — Forest Sci
Forest Science — FOSCAD
Forest Science — FS
Forest Science [*Sofia*] — GONAAR
Forest Science Monographs — For Sci Monogr
Forest Science Monographs — Forest Sci Monogr
Forest Science Monographs — FOSMA9
Forest Science (Sofia) — For Sci (Sofia)
Forest Science. Supplement — For Sci Suppl
Forest Service Research Note NE. Northeastern Forest Experiment Station. Forest Service. Department of Agriculture — For Serv Res Note NE Northeast For Exp Stn US Dep Agric
Forest Service Research Paper NE (United States) — For Serv Res Pap NE (US)
Forest Soils and Forest Land Management. Proceedings. North American Forest Soils Conference — For Soils For Land Manage Proc North Am For Soils Conf
Forest Soils and Land Use. Proceedings. North American Forest Soils Conference — For Soils Land Use Proc North Am For Soils Conf
Forest Soils of Japan — For Soils Jpn
Forest Survey Notes. British Columbia Forest Service — For Surv Note BC For Serv
Forest Tree Improvement — For Tree Improv
Forest Tree Improvement — FTIPA3
Forest Tree Series. Division of Forest Research. Commonwealth Scientific and Industrial Research Organisation — For Tree Ser Div For Res CSIRO
Forest Tree Series. Forestry and Timber Bureau — Forest Tre Ser For Timb Bur
Forest Trees and Timbers of the British Empire — Forest Trees Timbers Brit Empire
Forester. Ministry of Agriculture of Northern Ireland — Forester N Ire
Forestry — Fo
Forestry [*Oxford*] — FRSTAH
Forestry Abstracts — F Ab
Forestry Abstracts — For Abstr
Forestry Abstracts — Forest Abstr
Forestry Abstracts — Forestry Abstr
Forestry Bulletin. Department of Forestry. Clemson University — For Bull Dep For Clemson Univ
Forestry Bulletin. Lin Yeh Chon K'an. Forestry Experiment Station. College of Agriculture. National Taiwan University (Taipei) — Forest Bull Taipei
Forestry Bulletin R8-FB/U. US Department of Agriculture. Forest Service. Southern Region — For Bull R8 FB U US Dep Agric For Serv South Reg
Forestry Canada. Great Lakes Forestry Centre. Information Report O-X — For Can Gt Lakes For Cent Inf Rep O-X
Forestry Chronicle — For Chron
Forestry Chronicle — Forest Chro
Forestry Chronicle — Forestry Chron
Forestry Chronicle — FRCRAX
Forestry Chronicle. Canadian Society of Forest Engineers — Forest Chron
Forestry Commission of New South Wales. Research Note — For Comm NSW Res Note
Forestry Digest (Philippines) — For Dig (Philippines)
Forestry Economics. New York State University. College of Forestry at Syracuse University — For Econ NY St Coll For
Forestry Equipment Notes. FAO [*Food and Agriculture Organization of the United Nations*] — For Equipm Note FAO
Forestry/Hsueeh Lin (Shanghai) — Forestry Shanghai
Forestry in South Africa — BOSUAN
Forestry in South Africa — For S Afr
Forestry in South Africa — Forest South Africa
Forestry Industry Monthly/Lin Ch'an Yueeh K'an — Forest Industr Monthly
Forestry. Institute of Foresters of Great Britain — For Inst For GB
Forestry Investigation. Lin-Hsun. China. Department of Agriculture and Forestry. Central Forestry Bureau — Forest Invest
Forestry. Journal. Institute of Chartered Foresters — For J Inst Chart For
Forestry. Journal. Society of Foresters of Great Britain (Oxford) — Forestry Oxford
Forestry Log — For Log
Forestry Note. Illinois. Agricultural Experiment Station. Department of Forestry — For Note Ill Agric Exp Stn Dep For
Forestry Note. University of Illinois. Agricultural Experiment Station — For Note Ill Agric Exp Sta
Forestry Occasional Paper. FAO [*Food and Agriculture Organization of the United Nations*] — For Occ Pap FAO
Forestry Quarterly [*New York*] — FOR Q
Forestry Quarterly — Forest Quart
Forestry Report. Northern Forest Research Centre. Canadian Forestry Service [*Edmonton*] — FORP
Forestry Report R8-FR. US Department of Agriculture. Forest Service. Southern Region — For Rep R8-FR US Dep Agric For Serv South Reg
Forestry Research Newsletter — Forestry Res Newsl
Forestry Research Notes — For Res Notes
Forestry Research Notes. University of Wisconsin. College of Agriculture — For Res Note Wis Coll Agric
Forestry Research Notes. Weyerhaeuser Timber Company — For Res Notes Weyerhaeuser Timber Co
Forestry Research Report. Agricultural Experiment Station. University of Illinois — For Res Rep Agric Exp Stn Univ Ill
Forestry Research Report. Agricultural Experiment Station. University of Illinois — Forestry Res Rept Agr Expt Sta Univ Ill
Forestry Research West. United States Forest Service — For Res West US For Serv
Forestry Research West. US Department of Agriculture. Forest Service — For Res West US Dep Agric For Serv
Forestry Research. What's New in the West — For Res What's New West
Forestry Science (Beijing) — For Sci Beijing
Forestry Sciences — For Sci
Forestry Sciences (Dordrecht, Netherlands) — For Sci Dordrecht Neth
Forestry Technical Notes. University of New Hampshire. Agricultural Experiment Station — For Tech Note NH Agric Exp Sta
Forestry Technical Papers — For Tech Pap
Forestry Technical Papers — Forestry Tech Paper
Forestry Technical Papers. Forests Commission of Victoria — For Tech Pap For Comm Vict
Forestry Technical Publication (Canadian Forestry Service) — For Tech Publ Can For Serv
Forestry Technical Report (Canadian Forestry Service) — For Tech Rep (Can For Serv)
Forests and People — For People
Forests Commission Victoria. Bulletin — For Comm Victoria Bull
Forests Commission Victoria. Bulletin — VFCBA9
Forests Commission Victoria. Forestry Technical Papers — FFTPAS
Forests Commission Victoria. Forestry Technical Papers — For Comm Victoria For Tech Pap

Forests Department of Western Australia. Research Paper — For Dep West Aust Res Pap
Forests Department of Western Australia. Research Paper — RPFADG
Forest-Soil Relationships in North America. Papers Presented at the North American Forest Soils Conference — For Soil Relat North Am Pap North Am For Soils Conf
Foret Privee — FOPRB
Foret-Conservation — Foret-Conserv
Forging and Heat Treating — Forg Heat Treat
Forging Industry Association's News Release — Forg Ind NR
Forging, Stamping, Heat Treating — Forg Stamping Heat Treat
Forging Topics — Forg Top
Forgotten Fantasy — FF
Forgotten People — FOPE
Forhandlingar. Teologiska Foereningen — FTF
Forhandlinger det Kongelige Norske Videnskabers Selskab — Forh K Nor Vidensk Selsk
Forintek Canada Corporation. Eastern Forest Products Laboratory. Technical Report — Forintek Can Corp East For Prod Lab Tech Rep
Forintek Canada Corporation. Eastern Laboratory. Special Publication — Forintek Can Corp East Lab Spec Publ
Forintek Canada Corporation. Laboratoire des Produits Forestiers de l'Est. Review Report — Forintek Can Corp Lab Prod For Est Rev Rep
Form und Geist — F u G
Form und Geist — FG
Form und Technik — Form Tech
Forma et Function — Forma Functio
Forma Urbis Romae — FUR
Formae Orbis Antiqui — FOA
Formage et Traitements des Metaux — Formage Trait Metaux
Formage et Traitements des Metaux — FTMEA
Formage et Traitements des Metaux. Parachevement. Assemblage — Formage Trait Met Parachevement Assem
Formaldehyde. Toxicology, Epidemiology, Mechanisms. Papers of a Meeting — Formaldehyde Toxicol Epidemiol Mech Pap Meet
Formation and Properties of Gas Bubbles Conference — Form Prop Gas Bubbles Conf
Formation and Structure of Paper. Transactions. Symposium — Form Struct Pap Trans Symp
Formation Continue — Format Continue
Formation pour l'Agriculture et le Developpement Rural — Formation Agric Develop Rur
Formazione Domani — Formazione Dom
Formazione e Aggiornamento in Matematica degli Insegnanti — Form Aggiorn Mat Insegn
Formirovanie Celovska Kommunisticeskogo Obscestva — Formirov Celov Kom Obsc
Formirovanie i Knotrol Kachestva Poverkhnostnykh Vod — Form Kontrol Kach Poverkhn Vod
Formosan Agricultural Review — Formosan Agr Rev
Formosan Science — Formosan Sci
Forno Elettrico — Forno Elettr
Fornvaennen — Fo
Fornvaennen — Forn
Fornvaennen — Fornv
Foro — FUI
Foro Amministrativo — Foro Amm
Foro Internacional — FI
Foro Internacional — Foro Int
Foro Internacional — Foro Internac
Foro Internacional. El Colegio de Mexico — CM/FI
Foro Internacional (Mexico) — Foro Intern Mex
Foro Italiano — Foro It
Foro Literario — FL
Foro Padano — Foro Pad
Foro Penale — Foro Pen
FORPRIDE [*Forest Products Research and Industries Development*] **Digest** — FORPRIDE Dig
Forschen, Planen, Bauen — Forsch Planen Bauen
Forschung auf dem Gebiete des Ingenieurwesens — Forsch Geb Ingenieurwes
Forschung auf dem Gebiete des Ingenieurwesens — Forsch Ing
Forschung auf dem Gebiete des Ingenieurwesens. Ausgabe B. Beilage — Forsch Geb Ingenieurwes Ausg B Beil
Forschung im Ingenieurwesen — FIGWA
Forschung im Ingenieurwesen — Forsch Ing Wes
Forschung im Ingenieurwesen — Forsch Ingenieurw
Forschung im Ingenieurwesen — Forsch Ingenieurwes
Forschung in der Klinik und im Labor — Forsch Klin Lab
Forschung und Beratung. Forstwirtschaft — Forsch Berat Forstw
Forschung und Beratung. Forstwirtschaft — Forsch u Berat
Forschung und Beratung. Reihe C. Wissenschaftliche Berichte und Diskussionsbeitraege — Forsch Berat Reihe C
Forschung und Information — Forsch Inf
Forschung zur Bibel [*Wuerzburg*] — FzB
Forschung zur Bremischen Kirchengeschichte — FBKG
Forschung zur Deutschen Landes und Volkskunde — FDLVK
Forschungen auf dem Gebiet der Pflanzenkrankheiten/Shokubutsu Byogai Kenkyu — Forsch Pflanzenkrankh
Forschungen auf dem Gebiet der Pflanzenkrankheiten und der Immunitaet im Pflanzenreich — Forsch Pflanzenkrankh Immunitaet Pflanzenr
Forschungen der Landes- und Volkskunde — FLVk
Forschungen der Landes- und Volkskunde — Forschgg Lds u Volkskde
Forschungen. Geographische Gesellschaft in Luebeck — Forsch Geogr Ges
Forschungen in Ephesos — FE
Forschungen in Ephesos — Fi E
Forschungen in Ephesos — Forschin Ephesos
Forschungen in Lauriacum — Fi L
Forschungen in Lauriacum — Forsch Lauriacum
Forschungen und Berichte [*Graz*] — FB
Forschungen und Berichte. Evangelische Studiengemeinschaft — Forsch Ber Evangel Studiengemeinsch
Forschungen und Berichte. Staatliche Museen — FBSM
Forschungen und Berichte. Staatliche Museen zu Berlin — Forsch Ber Staatl Mus Berlin
Forschungen und Berichte. Staatliche Museen zu Berlin — Fu B
Forschungen und Berichte zur Vor- und Fruehgeschichte in Baden-Wuerttemberg — F Ber Bad Wuert
Forschungen und Fortschritte — F & F
Forschungen und Fortschritte — FF
Forschungen und Fortschritte — Fors u Fort
Forschungen und Fortschritte — Forsch F
Forschungen und Fortschritte — Forsch Fortschr
Forschungen und Fortschritte — Forsch Fortschritte
Forschungen und Fortschritte — Forsch u Fortschr
Forschungen und Fortschritte — Forschn Fortschr
Forschungen und Fortschritte — FuF
Forschungen und Fortschritte. Korrenspondenzblatt der Deutschen Wissenschaft und Technik [*Berlin*] — For For
Forschungen und Fortschritte. Korrenspondenzblatt der Deutschen Wissenschaft und Technik — Forschu Fortschr
Forschungen und Fortschritte. Nachrichtenblatt der Deutschen Wissenschaft und Technik — Forsch Fortschr Dtsch Wiss
Forschungen und Fortschritte. Sonderheft — Fu FS
Forschungen und Materialien zur Deutschen Aufklaerung. Abteilung III. Indices — Forsch Mater Deutsch Aufklaer Abt III Indices
Forschungen und Quellen zur Kirchen- und Kulturgeschichte Ostdeutschlands — FQKGO
Forschungen und Vorarbeiten zur Austria Sacra — FVAS
Forschungen zur Brandenburgischen und Preussischen Geschichte — Forsch Brandenburg Preuss Gesch
Forschungen zur Brandenburgisch-Preussischen Geschichte — FBPG
Forschungen zur Christlichen Literatur- und Dogmengeschichte — FChrLDG
Forschungen zur Deutschen Geodaesie — Forschgg Dt Geod
Forschungen zur Deutschen Geschichte — FDG
Forschungen zur Deutschen Landes- und Volkskunde — FL Vk
Forschungen zur Deutschen Landes- und Volkskunde — Forsch D Ld u Volksk
Forschungen zur Deutschen Landes- und Volkskunde — Forsch Dt Landeskde
Forschungen zur Deutschen Sprache und Dichtung — FDSD
Forschungen zur Deutschen Weltanschauungskunde und Glaubensgeschichte — FDWG
Forschungen zur Entstehung des Urchristentums, des Neuen Testaments, und der Kirche — FEUC
Forschungen zur Geschichte der Aelteren Deutschen Literatur — FGADL
Forschungen zur Geschichte der Optik — Forsch Gesch Opt
Forschungen zur Geschichte der Philosophie und der Paedagogik — FGPP
Forschungen zur Geschichte des Innerkirchlichen Lebens — FGIL
Forschungen zur Geschichte des Neutestamentlichen Kanons und der Altchristlichen Literature — FGNK
Forschungen zur Geschichte des Paepstlichen Staatssekretariats — FGPS
Forschungen zur Geschichte Oberoesterreichs — FGO
Forschungen zur Geschichte und Lehre des Protestantismus [*Munich*] — FGLP
Forschungen zur Judenfrage — FJF
Forschungen zur Kirchen- und Dogmengeschichte — FKD
Forschungen zur Kirchen- und Dogmengeschichte (Goettingen) — FKDG
Forschungen zur Kirchen- und Geistesgeschichte — FKGG
Forschungen zur Kirchen- und Geistesgeschichte (Neue Folge) — FKG(NF)
Forschungen zur Kirchlichen Rechtsgeschichte und zum Kirchenrecht — FKRG
Forschungen zur Kunstgeschichte und Christlichen Archaeologie — FKGCA
Forschungen zur Kunstgeschichte und Christlichen Archaeologie — Forsch KA
Forschungen zur Mittelalterlichen Geschichte — F Ma G
Forschungen zur Mittelalterlichen Geschichte — Forsch Mittelalterl Gesch
Forschungen zur Mittelalterlichen und Neueren Geschichte — FMANG
Forschungen zur Neueren Literaturgeschichte — FNLG
Forschungen zur Neueren Philosophie und Ihrer Geschichte — FNPG
Forschungen zur Neueren Philosophie und Ihrer Geschichte — Fsch PG
Forschungen zur Oberrheinischen Landesgeschichte — FORLG
Forschungen zur Ost Europaeischen Geschichte — FOEG
Forschungen zur Ost Europaeischen Geschichte — FOG
Forschungen zur Ost Europaeischen Geschichte — Forsch Ost Eur G
Forschungen zur Osteuropaeischen Geschichte — Forsch Osteur Gesch
Forschungen zur Reformationsgeschichte — FRG
Forschungen zur Religion und Literatur des Alten und Neuen Testaments — FRL
Forschungen zur Religion und Literatur des Alten und Neuen Testaments — FRLANT
Forschungen zur Romanischen Philologie — FR Ph
Forschungen zur Systematischen Theologie und Religionsphilosophie — FS Th R
Forschungen zur Systematischen und Oekumenischen Theologie — FS Oe Th
Forschungen zur Volks- und Landeskunde — Forsch Volks Land
Forschungen zur Volks- und Landeskunde — FVL
Forschungen zur Volks- und Landeskunde — FVLK
Forschungen zur Volks- und Landeskunde (Bucuresti) — F (Buc)
Forschungen zur Volkskunde — FVK
Forschungen zur Vor- und Fruehgeschichte — Forsch Vor und Fruehgesch
Forschungsarbeiten aus dem Papier und Zellstoffach — Forschungsarb Pap Zellstoffach
Forschungsarbeiten des Vereins Deutscher Ingenieure — Forscharb Ver Dt Ingen

Forschungsarbeiten. Institut fuer Pflanzenoele, Proteine, und Waschmittel. Sofia — Forschungsarb Inst Pflanzenoele Proteine Waschmittel Sofia
Forschungsbericht aus dem Fachbereich Bauwesen — Forschungsber Fachbereich Bauwesen
Forschungsbericht aus der Wehrmedizin. Bundesministerium der Verteidigung — Forschungsber Wehrmed Bundesminist Verteidigung
Forschungsbericht aus der Wehrtechnik. Bundesministerium der Verteidigung — Forschungsber Wehrtech Bundesminist Verteidigung
Forschungsbericht. Bundesanstalt fuer Arbeitsschutz und Unfallforschung. Dortmund — Forschungsber Bundesanst Arbeitsschutz Unfallforsch Dortmund
Forschungsbericht. Bundesanstalt fuer Materialpruefung — Forschungsber Bundesanst Materialpruef
Forschungsbericht. Bundesministerium fuer Bildung und Wissenschaft. Kernforschung — Forschungsber Bundesminist Bild Wiss Kernforsch
Forschungsbericht. Bundesministerium fuer Bildung und Wissenschaft. Weltraumforschung — Forschungsber Bundesminist Bild Wiss Weltraumforsch
Forschungsbericht. Bundesministerium fuer Forschung und Technologie. Information und Dokumentation — Forschungsber Bundesminist Forsch Technol Inf Dok
Forschungsbericht. Bundesministerium fuer Forschung und Technologie. Kernforschung — Forschungsber Bundesminist Forsch Technol Kernforsch
Forschungsbericht. Bundesministerium fuer Forschung und Technologie. Meeresforschung — Forschungsber Bundesminist Forsch Technol Meeresforsch
Forschungsbericht. Bundesministerium fuer Forschung und Technologie. Weltraumforschung/Weltraumtechnologie — Forschungsber Bundesminist Forsch Technol Weltraumforsch Wel
Forschungsbericht. Deutsche Forschungs- und Versuchsanstalt fuer Luft- und Raumfahrt [*Germany*] — Forschungsber Dtsch Forsch Versuchsant Luft-Raumfahrt
Forschungsbericht. Deutsche Gesellschaft fuer Mineraloelwissenschaft und Kohlechemie — Forschungsber Dtsch Ges Mineraloelwiss Kohlechem
Forschungsbericht. Deutsche Luft und Raumfahrt — FBDLR
Forschungsbericht. Institut fuer Zuckerindustrie Berlin — Forschungsber Inst Zuckerind Berlin
Forschungsberichte des Landes Nordrhein-Westfalen — Forschungsber Landes Nordrhein-Westfalen
Forschungsberichte des Wirtschafts- und Verkehrsministeriums Nordrhein-Westfalen — Forschungsber Wirtsch Verkehrministr Nordrhein-Westfalen
Forschungsberichte des Wirtschafts- und Verkehrsministeriums Nordrhein-Westfalen [*Germany*] — Forschungsber Wirtsch Verkehrsminist Nordrhein-Westfalen
Forschungsberichte. Forstliche Forschungsanstalt Muenchen — Forschungsber Forstl Forschungsanst Muenchen
Forschungsberichte ueber Lebensmittel — FbLm
Forschungsberichte zur Germanistik [*Osaka-Kobe*] — FzG
Forschungsheft des Deutschen Forschungs-Instituts fuer Textilindustrie in Dresden — Forschungsh Dtsch Forsch Inst Textilind Dresden
Forschungshefte aus dem Gebiete des Stahlbaues — Forsch H Stahlbau
Forschungshefte aus dem Gebiete des Stahlbaues — Forschungsh Geb Stahlbaues
Forschungshefte fuer Schiffstechnik, Schiffbau, und Schiffsmaschinenbau — Forsch H Schiffst
Forschungshefte. Studiengesellschaft fuer Hoechstspannungsanlagen — Forschungsh Studienges Hoechstspannungsanlagen
Forschungsinstitut beim FTZ. Technischer Bericht (Germany) — Forschungsinst FTZ Tech Ber Ger
Forschungsinstitut fuer Edelmetalle an der Staatlichen Hoeheren Fachschule Schwaebisch Gmuend. Mitteilungen — Forschungsinst Edelmet Staatl Hoeheren Fachsch Schwaeb Gmuen
Forschungsinstitut fuer Wirtschaftsverfassung und Wettbewerb — FIW
Forschungskolloquium des Deutschen Ausschusses fuer Stahlbeton. Berichte — Forschungskolloq Dtsch Ausschusses Stahlbeton Ber
Forschungsreaktor Muenchen. Bericht — FRM Bericht
Forschungsvereinigung Automobiltechnik Schriftenreihe — Forschungsver Automobiltech Schriftenr
Forschungszentrum Juelich. Spezielle Berichte — Forschungszent Juelich Spez Ber
Forschungszentrum Karlsruhe. Nachrichten — Forschungszent Karlsruhe Nachr
Forschungszentrum Karlsruhe. Wissenschaftliche Berichte — Forschungszent Karlsruhe Wiss Ber
Forskning i Groenland [*Denmark*] — Forsk Groenl
Forskning och Framsteg — Forsk Framsteg
Forskning och Framsteg — FSFMA
Forskning och Teknik (Helskini) — Forsk Tek Helsinki
Forskning og Forsok i Landbruket — Forsk Fors Landbr
Forskning og Forsok i Landbruket — Forsk Fors Landbruket
Forskning Udvikling Uddannelse — Forsk Udvikling Uddannelse
Forskningsnytt — FONYA
Forskningsrapporter. Statens Tekniska Forskningscentral — Forskningsrapp Statens Tek Forskningscent
Forsoksmelding. Landbruksteknisk Institutt — Forsokmeld Landbrukstek Inst
Forst und Holz — Forst Holz
Forst- und Holzwirt — FOHWA
Forst- und Holzwirt — Forst- u Holzw
Forst und Jagd — FJ
Forst und Jagd — Forst Jagd
Forstarchiv — FA
Forstarchiv — FRTAA
Forst-Archiv zur Erweiterung der Forst- und Jagd-Wissenschaft und der Forst- und Jagd-Literatur — Forst Arch Erweit Forst Jagd Wiss
Forst-Journal — Forst J
Forstliche Bundesversuchsanstalt — Forstl Bundesversuchsanst
Forstliche Bundesversuchsanstalt Wein. Mitteilungen — Forstl Bundesversuchsanst Wein Mitt
Forstliche Bundesversuchsanstalt (Wien). Jahresbericht — Forstl Bundesversuchsanst (Wien) Jahresber
Forstliche Forschungsanstalt Muenchen. Forschungsberichte — Forstl Forschungsanst Muenchen Forschungsber
Forstliche Forschungsberichte Muenchen — Forstl Forschungsber Muenchen
Forstliche Mitteilungen — Forstl Mitt
Forstliche Umschau — FU
Forstlich-Naturwissenschaftliche Zeitschrift — Forstl Naturwiss Z
Forstlige Forsogsvaesen i Danmark — FFODAZ
Forstlige Forsogsvaesen i Danmark — Forst Forsogvaes Dan
Forstlige Forsogsvaesen i Danmark — Forstl Forsogsv Danm
Forstlige Forsogsvaesen i Danmark — Forstl Forsogsvaes Dan
Forstschutz-Merkblaetter — FMERDB
Forstschutz-Merkblaetter — Forstschutz-Merkbl
Forsttechnische Informationen — FI
Forsttechnische Informationen — Forsttech Inf
Forsttechnische Informationen — Forsttech Inform
Forstwirtschaft Holzwirtschaft — Forstwirtsch Holzwirtsch
Forstwirtschaftliches Centralblatt — Forstw Centbl
Forstwissenschaftliche Forschungen — Forstwiss Forsch
Forstwissenschaftliche Forschungen. Beihefte zum Forstwissenschaftlichen Centralblatt — Forstwiss Forsch Beih Forstwiss Centralbl
Forstwissenschaftliche Mitteilungen — Forstwiss Mitt
Forstwissenschaftliches Centralblatt — Forstwiss Cbl
Forstwissenschaftliches Centralblatt — Forstwiss Zbl
Forstwissenschaftliches Centralblatt — FWSCA
Forstwissenschaftliches Centralblatt (Hamburg) — Forstwiss Centralbl (Hamb)
Forstwissenschaftliches Zentralblatt — Forstwiss Zentbl
Forstwissenschaftliches Zentralblatt — Forstwiss Zentralbl
Fort Collins International Hydrology Symposium. Proceedings — Fort Collins Int Hydrol Symp Proc
Fort Dodge Bio-Chemic Review — Fort Dodge Bio-Chem Rev
Fort Hare Papers — FHP
Fort Hare Papers — FHPAD
Fort Hare Papers — Fort Hare Pap
Fort Hays Studies. New Series. Science Series — Fort Hays Stud New Ser Sci Ser
Fort Lauderdale News — Ft Laud Nw
Fort McMurray News — Ft McMurray News
Fort McMurray Today — FT
Fort McMurray Today. Oil Sands Business Report — FTBR
Fort Pierce ARC Research Report FTP. University of Florida. Agricultural Research Center — Fort Pierce ARC Res Rep FTP Univ Fla Agric Res Cent
Fort Pierce ARC Research Report R1. University of Florida. Agricultural Research Center — Fort Pierce ARC Res Rep R1 Univ Fla Agric Res Cent
Fort Simpson Journal — FS
Fort Smith Journal — FJ
Fort Smith News — FN
Fort Worth Star-Telegram — Worth Star T
Fortbildungskurse fuer Rheumatologie — Fortbildungskurse Rheumatol
Fortbildungskurse. Schweizerische Gesellschaft fuer Psychiatrie — Fortbildungskurse Schweiz Ges Psychiatr
Fortgesetzte Nachrichten von dem Zustande der Wissenschaften und Kuenste in den Koeniglich Daenischen Reichen und Laendern — Fortgesetzte Nachr Wiss Kuenste Koenigl Daen Reichen Laendern
Fortgesetzte Sammlung von Alten und Neuen Theologischen Sachen — FSATS
Forth Naturalist and Historian — Forth Nat Hist
Forthcoming International Scientific and Technical Conference — Forthcoming Int Sci & Tech Conf
Fortid og Nutid — FN
Fortid og Nutid — FoN
Fortids Veje — For V
Fortnightly — F
Fortnightly — Fn
Fortnightly Review — Fo R
Fortnightly Review — Fort Rev
Fortnightly Review — Fortn
Fortnightly Review — FortnR
Fortnightly Review — FR
Fortnightly Review of the Chicago Dental Society — Fortn Rev Chic Dent Soc
Fortpflanzung Besamung und Aufzucht der Haustiere — Fortpflanz Besamung Aufzucht Haustiere
Fortpflanzung, Zuchthygiene, und Haustierbesamung — Fortpflanz Zuchthyg Haustierbesamung
Fortschritt-Berichte der VDI Zeitschriften. Reihe 5. Grund- und Werkstoffe — Fortschr Ber VDI Z Reihe 5
Fortschritt-Berichte. VDI [*Verein Deutscher Ingenieure*] **Zeitschriften** — Fortschr Ber VDI Z
Fortschritt-Berichte. VDI [*Verein Deutscher Ingenieure*] **Zeitschriften. Reihe** [*Germany*] — Fortsch-Ber VDI Z Reihe
Fortschritt-Berichte. VDI [*Verein Deutscher Ingenieure*] **Zeitschriften. Reihe 2** — Fortschr Ber VDI Zeitschr Reihe 2
Fortschritt-Berichte. VDI [*Verein Deutscher Ingenieure*] **Zeitschriften. Reihe 4. Bauingenieurwesen** — FBVBA
Fortschritt-Berichte. VDI [*Verein Deutscher Ingenieure*] **Zeitschriften. Reihe 4. Bauingenieurwesen** [*Germany*] — Fortschr-Ber VDI Z Reihe 4
Fortschritt-Berichte. VDI [*Verein Deutscher Ingenieure*] **Zeitschriften. Reihe 8** — Fortschritt Ber VDI Zeitschr Reihe 8
Fortschritt-Berichte. VDI [*Verein Deutscher Ingenieure*] **Zeitschriften. Reihe 11** — Fortschritt Ber VDI Zeitschr Reihe 11
Fortschritte auf dem Gebiet der Roentgenstrahlen — Fortschr Roentgenstrahlen
Fortschritte auf dem Gebiete der Roentgenstrahlen — Fortschr Geb Roentgenstr

Fortschritte auf dem Gebiete der Roentgenstrahlen — Fortschr Geb Roentgenstrahlen
Fortschritte auf dem Gebiete der Roentgenstrahlen und der Nuklearmedizin [*A publication*] — F Roent Nuk
Fortschritte auf dem Gebiete der Roentgenstrahlen und der Nuklearmedizin [*A publication*] — FGRNA
Fortschritte auf dem Gebiete der Roentgenstrahlen und der Nuklearmedizin [*A publication*] — Fortschr Geb Roentgenstr Nuklearmed
Fortschritte auf dem Gebiete der Roentgenstrahlen Vereinigt mit Roentgenpraxis — Fortschr Geb Roentgenstr Ver Roentgenprax
Fortschritte auf dem Gebiete der Rontgenstrahlen und der Neuen Bildgebenden Verfahren — F Ront Neue
Fortschritte bei der Anwendung von Flockungsverfahren in der Abwassertechnologie. Verfahrenstechnisches Seminar — Fortschr Anwend Flockungsverfahren Abwassertechnol Verfahren
Fortschritte Chromatografischer Methoden und Ihre Anwendung in der Klinischen Biochemie Symposion Chromatografie in der Klinischen Biochemie — Fortschr Chromatogr Methoden Ihre Anwend Klin Biochem
Fortschritte der Allergielehre — Fortschr Allergiel
Fortschritte der Andrologie — Fortschr Androl
Fortschritte der Antimikrobiellen und Antineoplastischen Chemotherapie — Fortschr Antimikrob Antineoplast Chemother
Fortschritte der Arzneimittelforschung — Fortschr Arzneimittelforsch
Fortschritte der Augenheilkunde — Fortschr Augenheilkd
Fortschritte der Botanik — Fortschr Bot
Fortschritte der Chemie Organischer Naturstoffe — Fortschr Chem Org Natr
Fortschritte der Chemie Organischer Naturstoffe — Fortschr Chem Org Natstoffe
Fortschritte der Chemie Organischer Naturstoffe — Fortschr Chem Org Naturst
Fortschritte der Chemie Organischer Naturstoffe (Progress in the Chemistry of Organic Natural Products) — Fortschr Chem Org Naturst Prog Chem Org Nat Prod
Fortschritte der Chemie, Physik, und Physikalischen Chemie — FChPhphCh
Fortschritte der Chemie, Physik, und Physikalischen Chemie — Fortschr Chem Phys Phys Chem
Fortschritte der Chemischen Forschung — Fortschr Chem Forsch
Fortschritte der Diabetesforschung. Symposion — Fortschr Diabetesforsch Symp
Fortschritte der Evolutionsforschung — Fortschr Evolutionsforsch
Fortschritte der Experimentellen Tumorforschung — Fortschr Exp Tumorforsch
Fortschritte der Experimentellen und Theoretischen Biophysik — Fortschr Exp Theor Biophys
Fortschritte der Geburtshilfe und Gynaekologie — FGGYA
Fortschritte der Geburtshilfe und Gynaekologie — Fortschr Geburtshilfe Gynaekol
Fortschritte der Haematologie — Fortschr Haematol
Fortschritte der Hals- Nasen- Ohrenheilkunde — Fortschr Hals- Nasen Ohrenheilkd
Fortschritte der Hochpolymeren-Forschung — Fortschr Hochpolym-Forsch
Fortschritte der Immunitaetsforschung — Fortschr Immunitaetsforsch
Fortschritte der Kardiologie — Fortschr Kardiol
Fortschritte der Kiefer und Geschichts Chirurgie — Fortschr Kiefer Gesichtschir
Fortschritte der Kieferorthopaedie — Fortschr Kieferorthop
Fortschritte der Klinischen Pharmakologie — Fortsch Klin Pharmakol
Fortschritte der Klinischen Pharmakologie — Fortschr Klin Pharmakol
Fortschritte der Krebsforschung — Fortschr Krebsforsch
Fortschritte der Landwirtschaft — Fortschr Landwirtsch
Fortschritte der Medizin — F Med
Fortschritte der Medizin — FMDZA
Fortschritte der Medizin — Fortschr Med
Fortschritte der Medizin. Monographie [*Muenchen*] — Fortschr Med Monogr
Fortschritte der Medizin. Supplement [*Gauting*] — Fortschr Med Suppl
Fortschritte der Medizinischen Mikrobiologie — Fortschr Med Mikrobiol
Fortschritte der Medizinischen Virusforschung — Fortschr Med Virusforsch
Fortschritte der Mineralogie — F Min
Fortschritte der Mineralogie — FMRLA
Fortschritte der Mineralogie — Fortsch Min
Fortschritte der Mineralogie — Fortschr Mineral
Fortschritte der Mineralogie. Beiheft — Fortschr Miner Beih
Fortschritte der Mineralogie. Beiheft — Fortschr Mineral Beihe
Fortschritte der Mineralogie, Kristallographie, und Petrographie — Fortschr Mineral Kristallogr Petrogr
Fortschritte der Neurologie, Psychiatrie, und Ihrer Grenzgebiete — F Neur Psyc
Fortschritte der Neurologie, Psychiatrie, und Ihrer Grenzgebiete — FNPGA
Fortschritte der Neurologie, Psychiatrie, und Ihrer Grenzgebiete — Fortschr Neurol Psychiatr
Fortschritte der Neurologie, Psychiatrie, und Ihrer Grenzgebiete — Fortschr Neurol Psychiatr Grenzgeb
Fortschritte der Neurologie, Psychiatrie, und Ihrer Grenzgebiete — Fortschr Neurol Psychiatr Ihrer Grenzgeb
Fortschritte der Neurologie-Psychiatrie — Fortschr Neurol Psychiatr
Fortschritte der Ophthalmologie — FORODD
Fortschritte der Ophthalmologie — Fortsch Ophthalmol
Fortschritte der Ophthalmologie — Fortschr Ophthalmol
Fortschritte der Pflanzenzuechtung — Fortschr Pflanzenzuecht
Fortschritte der Physik — Fortschr Ph
Fortschritte der Physik — Fortschr Phys
Fortschritte der Physik — Fortschr Physik
Fortschritte der Physik — FPYKA
Fortschritte der Physik. Deutsche Physikalische Gesellschaft — Fortschr Phys Dtsche Phys Ges
Fortschritte der Physikalischen Chemie — Fortschr Phys Chem
Fortschritte der Physikalischen Wissenschaften (Moscow) — Fortschr Phys Wiss Moscow
Fortschritte der Psychosomatischen Medizin — Fortschr Psychosom Med
Fortschritte der Psychosomatischen Medizin — FPMMA
Fortschritte der Rheumatologie. Kongressband der Tagung der Deutschen Gesellschaft fuer Rheumatologie Gemeinsam mit der Schweizerischen Gesellschaft fuer Rheumatologie — Fortschr Rheumatol Kongressband Tag Dtsch Ges Rheumatol
Fortschritte der Teerfarbenfabrikation und Verwandter Industriezweige — Fortschr Teerfarbenfabr Verw Industriezweige
Fortschritte der Therapie — Fortschr Ther
Fortschritte der Tuberkuloseforschung — Fortschr Tuberkuloseforsch
Fortschritte der Verfahrenstechnik — Fortschr Verfahrenstech
Fortschritte der Verfahrenstechnik — FVFSA
Fortschritte der Verfahrenstechnik Abteilung A. Grundlagen der Verfahrenstechnik — Fortschr Verfahrenstech Abt A
Fortschritte der Verfahrenstechnik Abteilung B. Mechanische Verfahrenstechnik — Fortschr Verfahrenstech Abt B
Fortschritte der Verfahrenstechnik. Abteilung C. Thermische Verfahrenstechnik — Fortschr Verfahrenstech Abt C
Fortschritte der Verfahrenstechnik. Abteilung D. Reaktionstechnik — Fortschr Verfahrenstech Abt D
Fortschritte der Verhaltensforschung — Fortschr Verhaltensforsch
Fortschritte der Veterinaermedizin — Fortschr Veterinaermed
Fortschritte der Wasserchemie und Ihrer Grenzgebiete [*Germany*] — Fortschr Wasserchem Ihrer Grenzgeb
Fortschritte der Wasserchemie und Ihrer Grenzgebiete — Fortschr Wasserchem Ihrer Grenzgebie
Fortschritte der Zoologie — Fortschr Zool
Fortschritte det Physik. Sonderband — Fortschr Phys Sonderb
Fortschritte im Acker- und Pflanzenbau [*Advances in Agronomy and Crop Science*] — FAPBBY
Fortschritte im Acker- und Pflanzenbau — Fortschr Acker Pflanzenb
Fortschritte im Acker- und Pflanzenbau — Fortschr Acker- Pflanzenbau
Fortschritte im Strahlenschutz — Fortschr Strahlenschutz
Fortschritte in der Anorganisch Chemischen Industrie — Fortschr Anorg Chem Ind
Fortschritte in der Arzneimittelforschung. Gesamtkongress der Deutschen Pharmazeutischen Wissenschaften — Fortschr Arzneimittelforsch Gesamtkongr Dtsch Pharm Wiss
Fortschritte in der Atomspektrometrischen Spurenanalytik — Fortschr Atomspektrom Spurenanal
Fortschritte in der Diagnostik und Therapie des Primaeren Glaukoms. Hauptreferate der Essener Fortbildung fuer Augenaerzte — Fortschr Diag Ther Primaeren Glaukoms Hauptref Essener Fortb
Fortschritte in der Geologie von Rheinland und Westfalen — Fortschr Geol Rheinl Westfalen
Fortschritte in der Geologie von Rheinland und Westfalen — Fortschr Geol Rheinland Westfalen
Fortschritte in der Metallographie. Berichte der Internationalen Metallographie-Tagung — Fortschr Metallogr Ber Int Metallogr Tag
Fortschritte in der Tierphysiologie und Tierernaehrung — Fortschr Tierphysiol Tierernaehr
Fortschritte in der Zoologischen Systematik und Evolutionsforschung — Fortschr Zool Syst Evolutionsforsch
Fortschritte in der Zoologischen Systematik und Evolutionsforschung — FZSEDV
Fortschrittliche Betriebsfuehrung und Industrial Engineering — ALD
Fortschrittliche Betriebsfuehrung und Industrial Engineering — FBE
Fortschrittliche Betriebsfuehrung und Industrial Engineering — Fortschr Betriebsfuehr Industr Engin
Fortschrittsberichte der Chemiker-Zeitung — Fortschrittsber Chem Ztg
Fortschrittsberichte der Deutschen Keramischen Gesellschaft — Fortschrittsber Dtsch Keram Ges
Fortschrittsberichte fuer die Landwirtschaft — Fortschrber Landw
Fortschrittsberichte fuer die Landwirtschaft — Fortschrittsber Landwirtsch
Fortschrittsberichte ueber Kolloide und Polymere — Fortschrittsber Kolloide Polym
Fortuna Italiana — Fortuna Ital
Fortune [*New York*] — F
Fortune — FO
Fortune — FOR
Fortune — FORTA
Fortune — FOT
Fortune Special Issue. Investor's Guide — Fortune Sp
Forum — F
Forum — Fo
Forum: A Ukrainian Review (Scranton, Pennsylvania) — ForumS
Forum (Arecibo, Puerto Rico) — FMA
Forum der Brauerei. Beilage — Forum Brau Beil
Forum der Letteren — FdL
Forum der Letteren — FL
Forum der Letteren — Forum Lett
Forum foer Ekonomi och Teknik — FEKTA
Forum foer Ekonomi och Teknik — Forum Ekon Tek
Forum for Applied Biotechnology — Forum Appl Biotechnol
Forum for Death Education and Counseling. Newsletter — FDEC
Forum for Modern Language Studies — FMLS
Forum for Modern Language Studies — Forum Mod L
Forum for the Discussion of New Trends in Education — Forum
Forum for the Discussion of New Trends in Education — Forum Disc New Trends Educ
Forum for the Problems of Zionism — FPZ
Forum (Houston) — ForumH
Forum Italicum — FI
Forum Italicum — FoI
Forum Linguisticum — For L
Forum Linguisticum — For Ling
Forum Mathematicum — Form Math

Forum Medicum (English Edition) — Forum Med Engl Ed
Forum Microbiologicum — Forum Microbiol
Forum Mikrobiologie [*Germany*] — Forum Mikrobiol
Forum Musicum — Forum M
Forum Navale — Forum Nav
Forum of Education — For of Educ
Forum of Education — Forum Ed
Forum of Education — Forum Educ
Forum on Geology of Industrial Minerals. Proceedings — Forum Geol Ind Miner Proc
Forum on Medicine — Forum Med
Forum on Peptides — Forum Pept
Forum on Public Affairs — Forum Pub Aff
Forum Report. Science and Industry Forum. Australian Academy of Science — Forum Rep Sci Ind Forum Aust Acad Sci
Forum Sekolah Pasca Sarjana Institut Pertanian Bogor — Forum Sekolah Pasca Sarjana Inst Pertanian Bogor
Forum Solaire International — Forum Sol Int
Forum Staedte Hygiene — Forum Staedte Hyg
Forum Stress- und Schlafforschung — Forum Stress Schlafforsch
Forum Theologiae Linguisticae — FThL
Forum Theologicum — Forum Theol
Forum Theologicum — FT
Forum Umwelt Hygiene — Forum Umw Hyg
Forum Umwelt Hygiene — Forum Umwelt Hyg
Forum Umwelt Hygiene — FUHYD
Forum (Zagreb) — ForumZ
Forwood Lectures — Forw L
Foseco Developments — Foseco Dev
Fosfororganicheskie Soedineniya i Polimery — Fosfororg Soedin Polim
Foster's Monthly Reference Lists — Foster Mo Ref
Foto Magazin — Foto Mag
Fotoelektricheskie i Opticheskie Yavleniya v Poluprovodnikakh. Trudy Vsesoyuznogo Soveshchaniya po Fotoelektricheskim i Opticheskim Yavleniyam v Poluprovodnikakh — Fotoelektr Opt Yavleniya Poluprovodn Tr Vses Soveshch
Fotograf Polski — Fotogr Pol
Fotografia Italiana — Fotogr Italiana
Fotokemijska Industrija — Fotokem Ind
Fotokhimicheskaya Promyshlennost — Fotokhim Prom
Fotokhimicheskie Protsessy Registratsii Gologramm. Materialy Vsesoyuznogo Seminara Fotokhimicheskie Protsessy Registratsii Gologramm — Fotokhim Protsessy Regist Gologramm Mater Vses Semin
Foto-Kino-Technik — Foto Kino Tech
Fouiles Franco-Suisses — FFS
Fouilles de Delphes — F Delphes
Fouilles de Delphes — FD
Fouilles de Delphes — FdD
Fouilles de Doura-Europos — FDE
Fouilles de Thorikos — Fd Th
Fouilles de Xanthos — Fd X
Fouilles Franco-Polonaises [*Cairo*] — FFP
Fouilles. Institut Francais d'Archeologie Orientale — FIFAO
Fouling and Enhancement Interactions. National Heat Transfer Conference — Fouling Enhancement Interact Natl Heat Transfer Conf
Foundation — FOU
Foundation Facts — Found Facts
Foundation for Biotechnical and Industrial Fermentation Research — Found Biotech Ind Ferment Res
Foundation for Biotechnical and Industrial Fermentation Research. Publication — Found Biotech Ind Ferment Res Publ
Foundation for Fundamental Research on Matter. Yearbook — Found Fundam Res Matter Yearb
Foundation for Life Sciences. Symposium — Found Life Sci Symp
Foundation for Materials Research in the Sea. Report — Found Mater Res Sea Rep
Foundation for Scientific Research in Surinam and the Netherlands Antilles. Publication — Found Sci Research Surinam and Netherlands Antilles Pub
Foundation Institute for Nuclear Research. Yearbook — Found Inst Nucl Res Yearb
Foundation News — Found News
Foundations — Fou
Foundations [*Baptist*] — Foun
Foundations and Philosophy of Science and Technology Series — Found Philos Sci Tech Ser
Foundations in Library and Information Science — Found Lib Inform Sci
Foundations of Communications — Found Comm
Foundations of Computer Science — Found Comput Sci
Foundations of Computing and Decision Sciences — Found Comput Decision Sci
Foundations of Computing Series — Found Comput Ser
Foundations of Control Engineering [*Poland*] — Found Control Eng
Foundations of Language — F Lang
Foundations of Language — FL
Foundations of Language — FoL
Foundations of Language — Found Lang
Foundations of Linguistics Series [*Elsevier Book Series*] — FLS
Foundations of Physics — FNDPA
Foundations of Physics — Found Phys
Foundations of Physics Letters — Found Phys Lett
Foundations of Semiotics — Foundations Semiotics
Foundations of Space Biology and Medicine — Found Space Biol Med
Foundry — FOUNA
Foundry and Metal Treating — Foundry Met Treat
Foundry Industry — Foundry Ind
Foundry Management and Technology — Foundry Manage Technol
Foundry Practice — Foundry Pract
Foundry Processes and Moulding Materials. Proceedings. Annual Conference. British Steel Castings Research Association — Foundry Processes Moulding Mater Proc Annu Conf Br Steel Cas
Foundry (Shenyang, People's Republic of China) — Foundry Shenyang Peoples Repub China
Foundry Trade Journal — Found Trade J
Foundry Trade Journal — Foundry Trade J
Foundry Trade Journal — FUTJA
Fountainwell Drama Series — FDS
Fountainwell Drama Texts — FDT
Four Corners Geological Society. Bulletin — Four Corners Geol Soc Bull
Four Corners Geological Society. Field Conference. Guidebook — Four Corners Geol Soc Field Conf Guideb
Four Decades of Poetry 1890-1930 — FDP
Four Quarters — Four Qt
Four Quarters — Four Quart
Four Quarters — FQ
Fourrages Actualites — Fourrages Actual
Fourth Plan of Economic and Social Development. Summary 1981-1985 (Togo) — (Togo) Plan
Fox Breeders Gazette — Fox Breeders Gaz
Fox Chase Cancer Center. Scientific Report — Fox Chase Cancer Cent Sci Rep
Fox Chase Cancer Center. Scientific Report — SRFCEE
FPRDI [*Forest Products Research and Development Institute*] **Journal** — FPRDI J
Fra det Gamle Gilleleje — Fdg Gil
Fra Frederiksborg Amt — F Fbr A
Fra Fysikkens Verden — Fra Fys Verden
Fra Fysikkens Verden — FYVDA
Fra Himmerland og Kjaer Herred — F Hml
Fra Holbaek Amt — F Hb A
Fra Kobenhavns Amt — F Kbh A
Fra National Museets Arbejdsmark — FNA
Fra Nationalmuseets Arbejdsmark — Fra Natnmus Arbsm
Fra Ny-Carlsberg Glyptoteks Sammlingen — NCGS
Fra Randers Amt — FRA
Fra Ribe Amt — F Rb A
Fra Sundhedsstyrelsen — Fra Sundhedsstyr
Fra Sundhedsstyrelsen — FRSUB
Fra Sundhedsstyrelsen (Copenhagen) — Fra Sundhedsstyr (Copenhagen)
Fra Viborg Amt. Aarbog Udgivet af Historisk Samfund for Viborg Amt — F Vb A
Fracastoro — Frac
Fracastoro — FRACA
Fractal Geometry in Biological Systems. An Analytical Approach [*monograph*] — Fractal Geom Biol Syst
Fractal Reviews in the Natural and Applied Sciences. Proceedings of the IFIP Working Conference on Fractals in the Natural and Applied Sciences — Fractal Rev Nat Appl Sci Proc IFIP Work Conf
Fractals in Engineering. Proceedings of the Conference — Fractals Eng Proc Conf
Fractography of Glasses and Ceramics — Fractogr Glasses Ceram
Fracture Analysis. Proceedings. National Symposium on Fracture Mechanics — Fract Anal Proc Natl Symp Fract Mech
Fracture and Fatigue. Elasto-Plasticity, Thin Sheet, and Micromechanisms Problems. Proceedings. Colloquium on Fracture — Fract Fatigue Elasto Plast Thin Sheet Micromech Probl Proc C
Fracture Mechanics. National Symposium on Fracture Mechanics — Fract Mech Natl Symp Fract Mech
Fracture Mechanics of Ceramics — Fract Mech Ceram
Fracture Mechanics. Proceedings. National Symposium on Fracture Mechanics — Fract Mech Proc Natl Symp
Fracture Mechanics. Symposium — Fract Mech Symp
Fracture Mechanics. Symposium. National Symposium on Fracture Mechanics — Fract Mech Symp Natl Symp Fract Mech
Fracture. Proceedings. International Conference on Fracture — Fract Proc Int Conf
Fraenkische Alb — Fr A
Fraenkische Blaetter fuer Geschichtsforschung und Heimatpflege — FB
Fraenkische Forschungen — FF
Fraenkischer Kourier [*Nuernberg*] — Fraenk Kourier
Fraenkisches Magazin fuer Statistik, Naturkunde, und Geschichte — Fraenk Mag Statist
Fragen der Ernaehrung — Fragen Ernaehr
Fragipans. Their Occurrence, Classification, and Genesis. Proceedings. Symposium — Fragipans Their Occurrence Classif Genesis Proc Symp
Fragmenta Balcanica. Musei Macedonici Scientiarum Naturalium — Fragm Balc Mus Macedonici Sci Nat
Fragmenta Balcanica. Musei Macedonici Scientiarum Naturalium — Fragm Balcan
Fragmenta Balcanica. Prirodonaucen Muzej (Skopje) — Fragm Balcan Prir Muz (Skopje)
Fragmenta Botanica — Fragm Bot
Fragmenta Botanica Musei Historico-Naturalis Hungarici — Fragm Bot Mus Hist Nat Hung
Fragmenta Coleopterologica — Fragm Coleopterol
Fragmenta Coleopterologica Japonica — FCPJA3
Fragmenta Coleopterologica Japonica — Fragm Coleopterol Jpn
Fragmenta Comicorum Graecorum — FCGM
Fragmenta Comicorum Graecorum — Frag Com Graec
Fragmenta Entomologica — Fragm Ent
Fragmenta Entomologica — Fragm Entomol
Fragmenta Faunistica — Fragm Faun
Fragmenta Faunistica Hungarica — Fragm Faun Hung

Fragmenta Faunistica. Polska Akademia Nauk Instytut Zoologii — Fragm Faun Pol Akad Nauk Inst Zool
Fragmenta Faunistica (Warsaw) — Fragm Faun (Warsaw)
Fragmenta Floristica et Geobotanica — Fragm Flor Geobot
Fragmenta Floristica et Geobotanica (Cracow) — Fragm Florist Geobot (Cracow)
Fragmenta Herbologica Jugoslavica — Fragm Herbol Jugosl
Fragmenta Historicorum Graecorum — FHG
Fragmenta Historicorum Graecorum — Frag Hist Graec
Fragmenta Mineralogica et Palaeontologica — Fragm Mineral Palaeontol
Fragmenta Philosophorum Graecorum — FPG
Fragmenta Poetarum Latinorum Epicorum et Lyricorum Praeter Ennium et Lucilium post A. Baehrens — FPEL
Fragmenta Poetarum Latinorum Epicorum et Lyricorum Praeter Ennium et Lucilium post A. Baehrens — FPL
Fragmenta Poetarum Romanorum — FPR
Fragmenta Poetarum Romanorum — Frag Poet Rom
Fragmente der Griechischen Historiker — F Gr H
Fragmente der Griechischen Historiker — FGH
Fragmente der Griechischen Historiker — FGrHist
Fragmente der Vorsokratiker — FV
Fragmente der Vorsokratiker — FVS
Fragmente der Vorsokratiker — Vorsokr
Fragmente, Nachrichten und Abhandlungen zur Befoerderung der Finanz-, Polizey-, Oekonomie- und Naturkunde — Fragm Nachr Abh Befoerd Finanz Naturk
Fragmentos (Venezuela) — FV
Fragments of Attic Comedy after Meineke — F Att Com
Fragrance Journal — Fragrance J
Francais au Nigeria — Fa N
Francais dans le Monde — FDM
Francais dans le Monde — FMonde
Francais dans le Monde — Fr Mo
Francais Moderne — FM
Francais Moderne — Fr M
Francais Moderne — Fr Mod
Francais Moderne — Fran Mod
Francais Moderne — Franc Mod
France Actuelle — Fr Actuelle
France Agricole — Fr Agric
France Alimentaire — FRM
France au Combat — FAC
France. Bureau de Recherches Geologiques et Minieres. Bulletin. Section 2. Geologie des Gites Mineraux — Fr Bur Rech Geol Min Bull Sect 2 Geol Gites Miner
France. Bureau de Recherches Geologiques et Minieres. Bulletin. Serie 2. Section 1. Geologie de la France — Fr Bur Rech Geol Minieres Bull Ser 2 Sect 1
France. Bureau de Recherches Geologiques et Minieres. Bulletin. Serie 2. Section 4 — Fr Bur Rech Geol Minieres Bull Ser 2 Sect 4
France. Bureau de Recherches Geologiques et Minieres. Memoires — Fr Bur Rech Geol Min Mem
France. Bureau de Recherches Geologiques et Minieres. Memoires — Fr Bur Rech Geol Minieres Mem
France. Centre de Recherches sur les Zones Arides. Publications. Serie Geologie — Fr Cent Rech Zones Arides Publ Ser Geol
France. Centre National de la Recherche Scientifique. Colloques Internationaux — Fr Cent Natl Rech Sci Colloq Int
France. Centre National pour l'Exploitation des Oceans. Publications. Resultats des Compagnes a la Mer Brest — Fr Cent Natl Exploit Oceans Publ Result Compagnes Mer
France. Centre National pour l'Exploitation des Oceans. Rapport Annuel — Fr Cent Natl Exploit Oceans Rapp Annu
France. Commissariat a l'Energie Atomique. Note CEA-N — Fr Commis Energ At Note CEA N
France. Commissariat a l'Energie Atomique. Rapport — Fr Commis Energ At Rapp
France d'Outre-Mer — Fr O-Mer
France et Ses Parfums — Fr Ses Parfums
France Franciscaine — FF
France Franciscaine — Fr Fr
France Graphique — Fr Graph
France Illustration — Fr Ill
France Illustration — France Illus
France Illustration. Supplement — France Illus Sup
France. Institut National de la Propriete Industrielle. Bulletin Officiel de la Propriete Industrielle. Abreges — Fr Inst Natl Propr Ind Bull Off Propr Ind Abr
France. Institut National de la Propriete Industrielle. Bulletin Officiel de la Propriete Industrielle. Abreges Descriptifs — Fr Inst Natl Propr Ind Bull Off Propr Ind Abr Descr
France Latine — FrL
France Libre — FL
France Libre — Fr Libre
France Medicale — Fr Med
France. Ministere de l'Agriculture. Bulletin Technique d'Information — Fr Minist Agric Bull Tech Inf
France. Ministere de l'Industrie. Memoires pour Servir a l'Explication de la Carte Geologique. Detaillee de la France — Fr Minist Ind Mem Servir Explication Carte Geol Detaill Fr
France Nouvelle — FrN
France. Office de la Recherche Scientifique et Technique d'Outre-Mer. Cahiers. Serie Geologie — Fr Off Rech Sci Tech Outre-Mer Cah Ser Geol
France. Office de la Recherche Scientifique et Technique d'Outre-Mer. Cahiers. Serie Geophysique — Fr ORSTOM Cah Ser Geophys
France. Office de la Recherche Scientifique et Technique d'Outre-Mer. Cahiers. Serie Hydrologie — Fr ORSTOM Cah Ser Hydrol
France. Office de la Recherche Scientifique et Technique d'Outre-Mer. Cahiers. Serie Pedologie — Fr Off Rech Sci Tech Outre-Mer Cah Ser Pedol
France. Office de la Recherche Scientifique et Technique d'Outre-Mer. Cahiers. Serie Pedologie — Fr ORSTOM Cah Ser Pedol
France. Office de la Recherche Scientifique et Technique d'Outre-Mer. Initiations-Documentations-Techniques — Fr Off Rech Sci Tech Outre-Mer Initiations Doc
France. Office de la Recherche Scientifique et Technique d'Outre-Mer. Monographies Hydrologiques — Fr Off Rech Sci Tech Outre-Mer Monogr Hydrol
France. Office de la Recherche Scientifique et Technique d'Outre-Mer. Monographies Hydrologiques — Fr ORSTOM Monogr Hydrol
France. Patent Document. Brevet d'Invention — Fr Pat Doc Brev Invent
France. Patent Document. Certificat d'Addition — Fr Pat Doc Certif Addit
France. Patent Document. Certificat d'Addition a un Brevet Special Medicament — Fr Pat Doc Certif Addit Brev Spec Med
France. Patent Document. Certificat d'Utilite — Fr Pat Doc Certif Util
France. Patent Document. Demande — Fr Pat Doc Demande
France Pays Bas — CNP
France. Republique. Bureau de Recherches Geologiques et Minieres. Bulletin — Fr Repub Bur Rech Geol Min Bull
France. Republique. Direction des Mines. Publications. Bureau de Recherches Geologiques et Geophysiques et Minieres — Fr Repub Dir Mines Publ Bur Rech Geol Geophys Min
France. Service de la Carte Geologique. Bulletin — Fr Serv Carte Geol Bull
France. Service d'Exploitation Industrielle des tabacs et des Allumettes. Memorial. Serie B. Publications. Institut Experimental des Tabacs de Bergerac — Fr Serv Exploit Ind Tab Allumettes Mem Ser B
France-Amerique — FA
France-Asie — Fr Asie
France-Asie — FrA
France-Asie; Revue de Culture et de Synthese Franco-Asiatique — France As
France-Eurafrique — FE
France-Eurafrique — Fr Eurafr
France-Inde — Fr Ind
France-Indochine — Fr Ind
France-Pharmacie — Fr Pharm
France-Pologne — Fr P
Franchising in the Economy, 1983-1985 — Franchis'g
Franciscaans Leven — FL
Franciscaans Leven — Fr Lev
Franciscaans Leven — Franc Lev
Franciscan Historical Classics — FHC
Franciscan Studies — Fr St
Franciscan Studies — Fran Stds
Franciscan Studies — Fran Stud
Franciscan Studies — Franc S
Franciscan Studies — Franciscan Stud
Franciscan Studies — FranS
Franciscan Studies — FS
Franciscan Studies — FSt
Franciscan Studies Annual — Fr SA
Franciscan Studies. Annual [*St. Bonaventure, New York*] — FrancSt
Franciscana — Franc
Franciscana. Sint-Truiden — Fr
Franciscansch Leven — FL
Franciscanum — FM
Franco Maria Ricci — FMR
Frank Leslie's Popular Monthly — Fr L
Frankenland — Frld
Frankfurter Allgemeine — FrankfAllg
Frankfurter Allgemeine Zeitung — FAZ
Frankfurter Allgemeine Zeitung — FZ
Frankfurter Allgemeine Zeitung fuer Deutschland — FFA
Frankfurter Allgemeine Zeitung fuer Deutschland — Frankf Zt
Frankfurter Althistorische Studien — FAS
Frankfurter Arbeiten aus dem Gebiete der Anglistik und der Amerika-Studien — FAGAAS
Frankfurter Beitraege zur Anglistik und Amerikanistik — FBAA
Frankfurter Beitraege zur Germanistik — FBG
Frankfurter Hefte — FH
Frankfurter Hefte — Fr H
Frankfurter Hefte — Frankfurt H
Frankfurter Hefte — Frankfurter Hft
Frankfurter Hefte — FrHe
Frankfurter Hefte — FRHED
Frankfurter Hefte. Zeitschrift fuer Kultur und Politik — Frankf Hefte
Frankfurter Historische Forschungen — Frankf Hist Forsch
Frankfurter Judaistische Beitraege — FJB
Frankfurter Kakteen-Freund — FKFRD2
Frankfurter Kakteen-Freund — Frankf Kakteen-Freund
Frankfurter Kirchenkalender — FKKal
Frankfurter Medizinische Annalen fuer Aerzte, Wundaerzte, Apotheker, und Denkende Leser aus Allen Staenden — Frankfurter Med Ann Aerzte
Frankfurter Muenzzeitung — FMZ
Frankfurter Muenzzeitung — Frankf Muenzztg
Frankfurter Quellen und Forschungen zur Germanischen und Romanischen Philologie — Frankfurt Quellen u Forsch z German u Roman Philol
Frankfurter Studien zur Religion und Kultur der Antike — FSRKA
Frankfurter Theologische Studien — FTS
Frankfurter Universitaets-Zeitung — FUZg
Frankfurter Verein fuer Geographie und Statistik. Jahresbericht — Frankfurter Ver Geog Jber
Frankfurter Zeitschrift fuer Pathologie — Frankf Z Path
Frankfurter Zeitschrift fuer Pathologie — Frankf Z Pathol

Frankfurter Zeitschrift fuer Pathologie — Frankfurter Z Pathol
Frankfurter Zeitschrift fuer Pathologie — FZP
Franse Boek — FB
Franz-Delitsch-Vorlesungen — FDV
Franziskaner-Missionen — Fr Miss
Franziskanische Forschungen — Fr For
Franziskanische Forschungen — Franz Forsch
Franziskanische Forschungen — Frz F
Franziskanische Lebensbilder — FLB
Franziskanische Quellenschriften — FQS
Franziskanische Studien — F St
Franziskanische Studien — F Stud
Franziskanische Studien — Franz St
Franziskanische Studien — Franzisk St
Franziskanische Studien — Franzisk Stud
Franziskanische Studien [*Padeborn*] — FranzS
Franziskanische Studien — FrSt
Franziskanische Studien — FS
Franziskanische Studien. Beiheft — FSB
Franziskanische Studien (Munster) — FrSM
Franzoesisch Heute — FrH
Fraser of Allander Institute. Quarterly Economic Commentary — Fraser of Allander Inst Q Econ Commentary
Fraser's Magazine — Fraser
Fraser's Magazine — Frasers M
Frate Francesco — FF
Fraternite-Matin [*Abidjan*] — Frt
Frauen und Film — Frauen & F
Fraunhofer-Gesellschaft zur Foerderung der Angewandte Forschung. Institut fuer Chemie der Treib- und Explosivstoffe. Jahrestagung — Fraunhofer Ges Foerd Angew Forsch Inst Chem Treib Explosivst
Fraunhofer-Gesellschaft zur Foerderung der Angewandten Forschung. Beispiele Angewandte Forschung — Fraunhofer Ges Foerd Angew Forsch Beispiele Angew Forsch
Fraunhofer-Institut fuer Betriebsfestigkeit. Bericht — Fraunhofer-Inst Betriebsfestigkeit Ber
Fraunhofer-Institut fuer Chemische Technologie. Internationale Jahrestagung — Fraunhofer-Inst Chem Technol Int Jahrestag
FRB [*Fisheries Research Board, Canada*] **Annual Report** — FRB Annu Rep
Freddo — FREDA
Freds-Bladet — FrBl
Freds-Varden — FrV
Free Association — Free Assoc
Free China Review — FCR
Free China Review — Free China R
Free China Review — GFCR
Free Inquiry — Free Inq
Free Labour World — Free Lab Wld
Free Labour World — Free Lbr Wld
Free Lance — Free L
Free Radical Biology and Medicine — Free Radic Biol Med
Free Radical Copolimerization, Dispersions, Glassy State Relaxation — Free Radical Copolim Dispersions Glassy State Relax
Free Radical Research — Free Radic Res
Free Radicals in Biological Systems. Proceedings. Symposium — Free Radicals Biol Syst Proc Symp
Free Radicals in Biology — Free Radicals Biol
Free Radicals in Digestive Diseases. Proceedings. International Symposium. Free Radicals in Digestive Diseases — Free Radicals Dig Dis Proc Int Symp
Free Radicals in Liver Injury. Proceedings. International Meeting — Free Radicals Liver Inj Proc Int Meet
Free Radicals in Medicine and Biology. Proceedings. Pharmacia Symposium — Free Radicals Med Biol Proc Pharm Symp
Free University Quarterly. A Quarterly of Christian Knowledge and Life [*Amsterdam*] — FUQ
Free University Quarterly. A Quarterly of Christian Knowledge and Life (Amsterdam) — FU (Amst)
Free World — FW
Free World Energy Survey — F Wld Energy
Freedom News — Free News
Freedom Socialist — Free Soc
Freedom Socialist — Freedom Soc
Freeing the Spirit — Free Spir
Free-living and Symbiotic Plathelminthes. Proceedings. International Symposium. Biology of Turbellarians — Free Living Symbiotic Plathelminthes Proc Int Symp Biol Turb
Freeman — Fm
Freiberger Forschungshefte — Freib FH
Freiberger Forschungshefte — Freiberger Forsch H
Freiberger Forschungshefte. Reihe A — Freiberg Forschungsh Reihe A
Freiberger Forschungshefte. Reihe B [*Germany*] — Freiberg Forschungsh B
Freiberger Forschungshefte. Reihe B. Metallurgie — Freiberger Forschungsh B Metall
Freiberger Forschungshefte. Reihe C — Freiberg Forschungsh C
Freiberger Forschungshefte. Reihe C — Freiberg Forschungsh Reihe C
Freiberger Forschungshefte. Reihe D [*Germany*] — Freiberg Forschungsh D
Freiberger Forschungshefte. Series C. Geologie. Geophysik. Mineralogie-Lagerstaettenlehre und Paleontologie — Freiberger Forsch Ser C
Freiburg Colloquium on Reproductive Medicine — Freiburg Colloq Reprod Med
Freiburg Congress on Nephrology — Freiburg Congr Nephrol
Freiburger Diozezesan Archiv — FrD
Freiburger Diozesanarchiv — FDA
Freiburger Forschungen zur Kunst und Literaturgeschichte — FFKL
Freiburger Fortbildungstagung ueber Nephrologie — Freib Fortbildungstag Nephrol
Freiburger Geographische Mitteilungen — Freiburger Geog Mitt
Freiburger Geschichtsblaetter — FG
Freiburger Historische Studien — FHS
Freiburger Katholisches Kirchenblatt — FKKB
Freiburger Rundbrief — Fr Ru
Freiburger Rundbrief [*Freiburg Im Breisgau*] — FreibRu
Freiburger Rundbrief — FRu
Freiburger Symposion an der Medizinischen Universitaets-Klinik — Freib Symp Med Univ Klin
Freiburger Theologische Studien — F Th St
Freiburger Theologische Studien — FreibThSt
Freiburger Universitaetsblaetter — Freiburger Universitaetsbl
Freiburger Universitaetsreden — FUR
Freiburger Veroeffentlichungen aus dem Geebiete von Kirche und Staat — FVKS
Freiburger Zeitschrift fuer Philosophie und Theologie — Frei Z Phil Theol
Freiburger Zeitschrift fuer Philosophie und Theologie — FreibZ
Freiburger Zeitschrift fuer Philosophie und Theologie — FZ Ph Th
Freiburger Zeitschrift fuer Philosophie und Theologie — FZPT
Freie Wirtschaft — Freie Wirtsch
Freie Wirtschaft — FW
Freier Christentum — FrChr
Freies Deutsches Hochstift: Reihe der Schriften — FDHRS
Freies Forum. Nordwestdeutscher Zahnaerzte — Fr For NW Dt Zahn Ae
Freight and Container Transportation — Freight & Container Transp
Freight Management — FM
Freight Management — Freight Mgmt
Fremdenverkehr + das Reiseburo. Tourismus und Kongress — FDA
Fremtiden — Fremt
French American Commerce — Fr Am Commer
French American Review — FAR
French American Review — Fr Am Rev
French American Review — French Am Rev
French CAM [*Certificat d'Addition a un Brevet Special Medicament*]. **Patent Document** — Fr CAM
French Demande. Patent Document — Fr Demande
French Forum — Fr F
French Forum — Fr Forum
French Forum Monographs — FrFM
French Genealogist — French Geneal
French Historical Studies — FHS
French Historical Studies — Fr Hist Stu
French Historical Studies — Fr Hist Stud
French Historical Studies — French Hist St
French Historical Studies — French Hist Stud
French Historical Studies — FrH
French Historical Studies — PFHS
French Journal of Clinical and Biological Research — Fr J Clin Biol Res
French Journal of Water Science — Fr J Water Sci
French Journal of Water Science — RFSEDN
French Literature on Microfiche — Fr LM
French Literature Series [*Columbia, South Carolina*] — FLS
French Literature Series — Fr Lit Ser
French Medicament. Patent Document — Fr M
French Quarterly — FQ
French Railway Techniques — Fr Railw Tech
French Review — FR
French Review — Fr Rev
French Review — French R
French Review — French Rev
French Science News — Fr Sci N
French Studies — F St
French Studies — Fr St
French Studies — French St
French Studies — French Stud
French Studies — FS
French Studies — PFRS
French Studies. A Quarterly Review — Fr Stud
French Studies in Southern Africa — FSSA
French Techniques — Fr Tech
French Techniques. Building, Civil Engineering, and Town Planning — French Tech Building Civ Engng & Town Planning
French Techniques. Electrical Engineering and Electronics Industries — French Tech Electr Engn & Electron Ind
French Techniques. Mechanical, Hydraulic, and Consultant Engineering Industries — French Tech Mech Hydraul & Consult Engng Ind
French Techniques. Metal Industries — French Tech Metal Ind
French Techniques. Miscellaneous Industries and Consumer Goods — French Tech Misc Ind & Consum Goods
French Techniques. Transportation Studies and Research — French Tech Tranp Stud & Res
French West Africa. Inspection de l'Agriculture. Bulletin de la Protection Vegetaux — Fr West Afr Insp Agric Bull Prot Veg
French-American Commerce — French Am Com
Frequences Modulation and Television — FMTV
Frequency Control Symposium. Proceedings — Freq Control Symp Proc
Frequenz — FQNZA
Frequenz — Freq
Fresenius' Zeitschrift fuer Analytische Chemie — Fresenius Z Anal Chem
Fresenius' Zeitschrift fuer Analytische Chemie — Z Anal Chem
Fresenius' Zeitschrift fuer Analytische Chemie — ZACFA
Fresh Water from the Sea. Proceedings. International Symposium — Fresh Water Sea Proc Int Symp
Freshwater Biological Association. Annual Report — FBARAD

Freshwater Biological Association. Annual Report — Freshw Biol Assoc Annu Rep
Freshwater Biological Association. Occasional Publication — OPFAEI
Freshwater Biological Association. Scientific Publication — Freshw Biol Assoc Sci Publ
Freshwater Biology — Freshw Biol
Freshwater Biology — Freshwater Biol
Freshwater Biology — Frsh Wat Biol
Freshwater Biology — FWBLA
Freshwater Biology Association. Annual Report — Freshwater Biol Assoc Annu Rep
Freshwater Biology Association. Scientific Publication — Freshwater Biol Assoc Sci Publ
Freshwater Fisheries Newsletter — Freshwat Fish Newsl
Freshwater Fisheries Newsletter — Freshwater Fish Newsl
Freshwater Invertebrate Biology — FIBID9
Freshwater Invertebrate Biology — Freshwater Invertebr Biol
Fresno Bee — FB
Frets Magazine — Frets Mag
Freude am Leben — Freude Leben
Freunde der Naturwissenschaften in Wien. Berichte ueber die Mittheilungen (W. Haidinger) — Freunde Naturw Ber (Haidinger)
Freywillige Beytraege zu den Hamburgischen Nachrichten aus dem Reiche der Gelehrsamkeit — Freywillige Beytr Hamburg Nachr Gelehrsamk
FRI Bulletin. Forest Research Institute. New Zealand Forest Service — FRI Bull For Res Inst NZ For Serv
FRI [*Fuel Research Institute*] **News** — FRIN
Friction and Wear in Machinery — Frict Wear Mach
Friction and Wear in Machinery (USSR) — Frict Wear Mach (USSR)
Friday Memo — Fri Memo
Friday Report — Fri Report
Fridericiana — FRDCA
Fridericiana. Zeitschrift der Universitaet Karlsruhe — Fridericiana Z Univ Karlsruhe
Fridtjof Nansen Institute. Newsletter — FNIN
Friedberger Geschichtsblaetter — Fried G Bl
Friede ueber Israel — F Ue I
Friedreichs Blaetter fuer Gerichtliche Medizin und Sanitaetspolizei — FriedreichsBl
Friedrich-Schiller-Universitaet Jena. Wissenschaftliche Zeitschrift. Naturwissenschaftliche Reihe — Friedrich Schiller Univ Jena Wiss Z Naturwiss Reihe
Friend. Philadelphia, Pennsylvania — Friend Ph
Friends Historical Association. Bulletin — Friends Hist Assoc Bull
Friends Intelligencer — FI
Friends Journal — FJ
Friends. Library of Trinity College. Dublin. Annual Bulletin — TCD Ann Bull
Friends of the Forest. Rinyu — Friends Forest
Friends of the P. I. Nixon Medical Historical Library — Friends PI Nixon Med Hist Libr
Fries Landbouwblad — FLBWA
Fries Landbouwblad [*Netherlands*] — Fries Landbouwbl
Friesisches Jahrbuch — FJ
Frigisinga — Fris
Frit Danmark. Udgivet af en Kreds af Danske — Frit D
Friuli Medico — Friul Med
Friuli Medico — Friuli Med
FRNM [*Foundation for Research on the Nature of Man*] **Bulletin** — FRNM Bull
Froebel Journal — Froebel J
Frohe Botschaft — Fro Bot
Froid et la Climatisation — Froid Clim
From Imperium to Autoritas — FITA
From Metabolite, to Metabolism, to Metabolon — From Metab Metab Metabolon
From Theoretical Physics to Biology. Proceedings. International Conference — From Theor Phys Biol Proc Int Conf
From Unknown Worlds — FUN
Frommann's Klassiker der Philosophie — Frommanns Klassiker
Fronimo — Fro
Front Nauki i Tekhniki [*Former USSR*] — Front Nauki Tekh
Front og Bro — Fr Br
Front Slobode — Front Sl
Frontier — Front
Frontier Nursing Service. Quarterly Bulletin — Front Nurs Serv Q Bull
Frontier Science (Tokyo) — Front Sci (Tokyo)
Frontiers — FRNTA
Frontiers in Aging Series — FIAS
Frontiers in Aging Series — Front Aging Ser
Frontiers in Applied Mathematics — Frontiers Appl Math
Frontiers in Artificial Intelligence and Applications — Frontiers Artificial Intelligence Appl
Frontiers in Bioscience — Front Biosci
Frontiers in Biotransformation — Front Biotransform
Frontiers in Carbohydrate Research — Front Carbohydr Res
Frontiers in Catecholamine Research. Proceedings. International Catecholamine Symposium — Front Catecholamine Res Proc Int Catecholamine Symp
Frontiers in Cellular Surface Research. Boehringer Ingelheim Ltd. Symposium — Front Cell Surf Res Boehringer Ingelheim Ltd Symp
Frontiers in Chemistry — Front Chem
Frontiers in Computer Science — Frontiers Comput Sci
Frontiers in Diabetes — FDIADJ
Frontiers in Diabetes — Front Diabetes
Frontiers in Headache Research — Front Headache Res
Frontiers in Molecular Biology — Front Mol Biol
Frontiers in Neuroendocrinology — Front Neuroendocrinol
Frontiers in Nuclear Dynamics — Front Nucl Dyn
Frontiers in Particle Physics — Front Part Phys
Frontiers in Physics — Front Phys
Frontiers in Physics — Frontiers in Phys
Frontiers in Systems Research — Frontiers in Systems Res
Frontiers of Biology [*Elsevier Book Series*] — FOB
Frontiers of Biology — Front Biol
Frontiers of Clinical Neuroscience — FCNEEG
Frontiers of Clinical Neuroscience — Front Clin Neurosci
Frontiers of Flavor. Proceedings. International Flavor Conference — Front Flavor Proc Int Flavor Conf
Frontiers of Gastrointestinal Research — Front Gastrointest Res
Frontiers of Health Services Management — Front Health Serv Manage
Frontiers of Hormone Research — Front Horm Res
Frontiers of Internal Medicine. International Congress of Internal Medicine — Front Intern Med Int Congr
Frontiers of Matrix Biology — FMXBAL
Frontiers of Matrix Biology — Fron Matrix Biol
Frontiers of Matrix Biology — Front Matrix Biol
Frontiers of Medical and Biological Engineering — Front Med Biol Eng
Frontiers of Nonequilibrium Statistical Physics — Front Nonequilib Stat Phys
Frontiers of Oral Physiology — Front Oral Physiol
Frontiers of Organosilicon Chemistry. Proceedings. International Symposium on Organosilicon Chemistry — Front Organosilicon Chem Proc Int Symp Organosilicon Chem
Frontiers of Plant Science — Front Plant Sci
Frontiers of Plant Science — Frontiers Plant Sci
Frontiers of Plant Science. Connecticut Agricultural Experiment Station — Frontiers Pl Sci
Frontiers of Plant Science. Connecticut Agricultural Experiment Station (New Haven) — Front Plant Sci Conn Agric Exp Stn (New Haven)
Frontiers of Power Conference. Proceedings — Front Power Conf Proc
Frontiers of Power Technology Conference. Proceedings — Front Power Technol Conf Proc
Frontiers of Radiation Therapy and Oncology — Front Radiat Ther Oncol
Frontsoldat Erzaehlt — Fr
Frost and Sullivan News. American Market — Frost
Frost i Jord/Frost Action in Soils — FRIJ
Frozen and Chilled Foods — Frozen and Chilled Fds
Frozen Food Digest — Frozen Fd Di
Frozen Foods — Frozen Fds
Frozen Foods — Frozen Food
Frozen Foods — FRS
Fruchtfolgeforschung und Fruchtfolgegestaltung. Internationales Symposium — Fruchtfolgeforsch Fruchtfolgegestaltung Int Symp
Fruchtsaft Industrie — Fruchtsaft Ind
Fruehgriechische Sagenbilder — FS
Fruehjahrskolloquium der Universitaet Bremen — Fruehjahrskolloq Univ Bremen
Fruehjahrstagung der Online-Benutzergruppe der DGD — Fruehjahrstag Online Benutzergruppe DGD
Fruehkretischen Siegel — FKS
Fruehmittelalterliche Studien — FM St
Fruehmittelalterliche Studien — FMAS
Fruehmittelalterliche Studien — Fruehma St
Fruehmittelalterliche Studien — Fruehmittelalt Stud
Fruehmittelalterliche Studien. Jahrbuch des Instituts fuer Fruehmittelalterforschung der Universitaet Muenster — Frueh Mit Alt St
Fruehmittelalterliche Studien. Jahrbuch des Instituts fuer Fruehmittelalterforschung der Universitaet Muenster — Frueh Mittelalterl Stud
Fruit and Tropical Products — FTP
Fruit and Vegetable Digest — Fruit Veg Digest
Fruit and Vegetable Juice Processing Technology — Fruit Veg Juice Process Technol
Fruit and Vegetable Review — Fruit & Veg R
Fruit Grower — Fruit Grow
Fruit Grower and Horticulturist. A Monthly Magazine of Practical Horticulture — Fruit Grower Hort
Fruit Notes. Cooperative Extension Service. University of Massachusetts — Fruit Notes Coop Ext Serv Univ Mass
Fruit Processing — Fruit Process
Fruit Products Journal and American Food Manufacturer — Fruit Prod J Am Food Manuf
Fruit Products Journal and American Vinegar Industry — Fruit Prod J Am Vinegar Ind
Fruit Science Reports (Skierniewice) — Fruit Sci Rep (Skierniewice)
Fruit Situation TFS. United States Department of Agriculture. Economic Research Service — Fruit Situat US Dep Agric Econ Res Serv
Fruit Trees/Kwaju — Fruit Trees
Fruit Varieties and Horticultural Digest — Fruit Var Hortic Dig
Fruit Varieties Journal — Fruit Var J
Fruit, Vegetable, and Honey Crop and Market Report — Fruit Veg Honey Crop Mkt Rep
Fruit World and Market Grower — Fruit World Mark Grow
Fruit World Annual — Fruit World Ann
Fruit World Annual and Orchardists' Guide — Fruit World Annu Orchardists' Guide
Fruit Yearbook — Fruit Yb
Fruits — Fru
Fruits — FRUIA
Fruits Agro-Industrie Regions Chaudes [*Database*] — FAIREC
Fruits d'Outre-Mer — Fru O-Mer
Fruits et Primeurs de l'Afrique du Nord — Fruits Prim Afr Nord
Fruitteelt — FRT
Frunzenskii Politekhnicheskii Institut. Trudy — Frunz Politekh Inst Tr

Frustula Entomologica — Frustula Entomol
Frustula Entomologica. Istituto di Entomologia — Frust Entomol Ist Entomol
Frysk Jierboek — FryskJb
Fryske Plaknammen — FPn
FS. Cooperative Extension Service. Cook College — FS Coop Ext Serv Cook Coll
FS. Fact Sheet. Oregon State University. Extension Service — FS Fact Sheet Oreg State Univ Ext Serv
FS. Political Risk Letter — Pol
FS-Berichte — FS Ber
FSC [*Friends Service Council*] **News** — FSC Ne
FSHEB. Cooperative Extension Service. University of Arkansas. Division of Agriculture. US Department of Agriculture, and County Governments Cooperating — FSHEB Coop Ext Serv Univ Arkansas Div Agric US Dep Agric Cty
FSHED. Cooperative Extension Service. University of Arkansas — FSHED Coop Ext Serv Univ Arkansas
FSHEE. Cooperative Extension Service. University of Arkansas. Division of Agriculture. US Department of Agriculture, and County Governments Cooperating — FSHEE Coop Ext Serv Univ Arkansas Div Agric US Dep Agric Cty
FSHEF. University of Arkansas. Cooperative Extension Service — FSHEF Univ Arkansas Coop Ext Serv
FSHEH. University of Arkansas. Division of Cooperative Extension Service — FSHEH Univ Arkansas Div Coop Ext Serv
FSHEI. University of Arkansas. Cooperative Extension Service — FSHEI Univ Arkansas Coop Ext Serv
FSHEL. University of Arkansas. Cooperative Extension Service — FSHEL Univ Arkansas Coop Ext Serv
FSIS Facts. Food Safety and Inspection Service. US Department of Agriculture — FSIS Facts Food Safety Insp Serv US Dep Agric
FSQS. United States Department of Agriculture. Food Safety and Quality Service — FSQS US Dep Agric Food Saf Qual Serve
FSSA (Fertilizer Society of South Africa) Publication — FSSA Publ
FSSA [*Fertilizer Society of South Africa*] **Journal** — FSSA J
Ftiziologia — Ftiziol
Fu Jen Studies — FJS
Fu Jen Studies — FJSTEX
Fu Jen Studies — Fu Jen Stud
Fudan Journal — Fudan J
Fudan Journal (Natural Science) — Fudan J (Nat Sci)
Fuel Abstracts — Fu Abstr
Fuel Abstracts and Current Titles — FACT
Fuel Abstracts and Current Titles — Fuel Abstr Curr Titles
Fuel Abstracts and Current Titles. Institute of Fuel — Fu Abstr Curr Titl
Fuel and Combustion [*Japan*] — Fuel Combust
Fuel and Combustion Engineering — Fuel Combust Eng
Fuel and Energy Abstracts — Fuel & Energy Abstr
Fuel Economist (Watford, England) — Fuel Econ (Watford Engl)
Fuel Economy — Fuel Econ
Fuel Economy. A Seatrade Study — Seatrade S
Fuel Economy Review — Fu Econ Rev
Fuel Economy Review — Fuel Econ Rev
Fuel Efficiency — Fuel Effic
Fuel Efficiency Bulletin — Fuel Eff Bull
Fuel in Science and Practice — Fuel Sci Prac
Fuel in Science and Practice — Fuel Sci Pract
Fuel Oil and Temperature Journal — Fuel Oil Temp J
Fuel Oil Journal — Fuel Oil J
Fuel Oil Journal (Houston) — Fuel Oil J Houston
Fuel Oils by Sulfur Content — Fuel Oils Sulfur Content
Fuel-, Orr-, Gegegyogyaszat — FOGGA
Fuel-, Orr-, Gegegyogyaszat [*Hungary*] — Fuel- Orr- Gegegyogy
Fuel Processing Technology — FPTED
Fuel Processing Technology [*Netherlands*] — Fuel Process Technol
Fuel Processing Technology — Fuel Processing Tech
Fuel Research. Department of Scientific and Industrial Research (Great Britain) — Fuel Res Dep Sci Ind Res GB
Fuel Research Institute of South Africa. Bulletin — Fuel Res Inst S Afr Bull
Fuel Research Institute (Pretoria). Bulletin — Fuel Res Inst (Pretoria) Bull
Fuel Science and Technology — Fuel Sci Technol
Fuel Science and Technology International — Fuel Sci Technol Int
Fuel Society Journal [*England*] — Fuel Soc J
Fuel Technology and Management — Fuel Technol Manage
Fueloil and Oil Heat — FOOHA
Fueloil and Oil Heat and Solar Systems — Fueloil & Oil Heat
Fueloil and Oil Heat and Solar Systems — Fueloil Oil Heat Sol Syst
Fuels and Furnaces — Fuels Furn
Fuentes de Historia Medieval — Fuentes Hist Medieval
Fuer Arbeit und Besinnung — FAB
Fuer Theologie und Philosophie — FTP
Fuggetlen Magyarorszag — Fugg Magyar
Fuji Bank Bulletin [*Tokyo*] — FUJ
Fuji Bank Bulletin — Fuji Bank
Fuji Bank Bulletin — Fuji Bank Bul
Fuji Denki Review — Fuji Denki Rev
Fuji Electric Journal — Fuji Electr J
Fuji Electric Review — Fuji Electr Rev
Fujikura Technical Review — Fujikura Tech Rev
Fujitsu — FUJTA
Fujitsu General — Fujitsu Gen
Fujitsu Scientific and Technical Journal [*Japan*] — Fujitsu Sci Tech J
Fujitsu Scientific and Technical Journal [*Japan*] — FUSTA
Fukien Academy. Research Bulletin — Fukien Acad Res Bull
Fukien Agricultural Journal — Fukien Agric J
Fukien Agriculture/Fu-Chien Nung Yeh — Fukien Agric
Fukien Christian University. Science Journal — Fukien Christ Univ Sci J
Fukien Culture/Fukien Wen Hua — Fukien Cult
Fukui Daigaku Gakugeigakubu Kiyo — FDGK
Fukui Kogyo Daigaku Kenkyu Kiyo — MFITD
Fukuoka Acta Medica — Fukuoka Acta Med
Fukuoka Igaku Zasshi [*Japan*] — FKIZA
Fukuoka Kyoiku Daigaku Kiyo, Dai-3-Bu, Rika-Hen — FKDRA
Fukuoka University Science Reports — Fukuoka Univ Sci Rep
Fukushima Daigaku Gakugei Gakubu Rika Hokoku — FGGHA
Fukushima Igaku Zasshi — FSIZA
Fukushima Journal of Medical Science — FJMSA
Fukushima Journal of Medical Science — Fukush J Med Sci
Fukushima Journal of Medical Science — Fukushima J Med Sci
Fukushima Medical Journal — Fukushima Med J
Fulbright Educational Development Program Grantee Reports — Fulbright Educ Dev Program Grantee Rep
Fulbright Newsletter — FulN
Fulbright University Administrator Program Grantee Reports — Fulbright Univ Adm Program Grantee Rep
Fuldaer Geschichtsblaetter — Fulda Geschbll
Fuldaer Hefte — Fu H
Fulmer Research Institute. Newsletter — Fulmer Res Inst Newsl
Fulmer Research Institute. Special Report — Fulmer Res Inst Spec Rep
Funbericht aus Schwaben — FS
Function and Materials (Tokyo) — Funct Mater Tokyo
Function and Structure of the Immune System — Funct Struct Immune Syst
Functional Analysis and Its Applications — FAA
Functional Analysis and Its Applications — Functional Anal Appl
Functional and Developmental Morphology — Funct Dev Morphol
Functional Aspects of Parasite Surfaces. Symposium. British Society for Parasitology — Funct Aspects Parasite Surf Symp Br Soc Parasitol
Functional Biology and Medicine — Funct Biol Med
Functional Differential Equations. Israel Seminar — Funct Differential Equations Israel Sem
Functional Neurology — Funct Neurol
Functional Orthodontist — Funct Orthod
Functional Photography — Funct Photgr
Functional Photography — Funct Photogr
Functional Polymer — Funct Polym
Functional Units in Protein Biosynthesis. Federation of European Biochemical Societies Meeting — Funct Units Protein Biosynth Fed Eur Biochem Soc Meet
Functiones et Approximatio Commentarii Mathematici — Funct Approx Comment Math
Functiones et Approximatio Commentarii Mathematici — Funct Approximatio Comment Math
Functions — Func
Fund and Wagnalls' Standard Dictionary of Folklore — SDFL
Fund for the Replacement of Animals in Medical Experiments. Technical News — FRAME
Fund Management International — Fund Man Int
Fund Raising Management — FRM
Fund Raising Management — Fund Raising Manage
Fund Raising Management — Fund Raising Mgt
Fundacao Brasileira para a Conservacao da Natureza Boletim Informativo — Fund Bras Conserv Nat Bol Inf
Fundacao de Ciencias Aplicadas. Faculdade de Engenharia Industrial. Revista Pesquisa e Tecnologia FEI — Fund Cienc Apl Fac Eng Ind Rev Pesqui Tecnol FEI
Fundacao Instituto Agronomico do Parana. Boletim Tecnico — Fund Inst Agron Parana Bol Tec
Fundacao Servicos de Saude Publica. Revista (Brazil) — Fund Serv Saude Publica Rev (Braz)
Fundacao Zoobotanica do Rio Grande Do Sul. Publicacoes Avulsas — Fund Zoobot Rio Grande Do Sul Publ Avulsas
Fundacao Zoobotanica do Rio Grande Do Sul. Publicacoes Avulsas — PAFZDW
Fundacion Bariloche. Departamento de Recursos Naturales y Energia. Publicacion (San Carlos De Bariloche, Argentina) — Fund Bariloche Dep Recur Nat Energ Publ (Argent)
Fundacion Bariloche Series — FBASDJ
Fundacion Bariloche Series — Fund Bariloche Ser
Fundacion Juan March. Serie Universitaria — Fund Juan March Ser Univ
Fundacion Miguel Lillo Miscelanea — Fund Miguel Lillo Misc
Fundacion Roux-Ocefa. Archivos — Fund Roux Ocefa Arch
Fundamenta Balneo Bioclimatologica — Fundam Balneo Bioclimatol
Fundamenta Informaticae — Fund Inform
Fundamenta Informaticae — Fund Informat
Fundamenta Mathematicae — Fund Math
Fundamenta Scientiae — Fund Sci
Fundamenta Scientiae — Fundam Sci
Fundamental and Applied Toxicology — FAATD
Fundamental and Applied Toxicology — Fundam Appl Toxicol
Fundamental and Applied Toxicology. Official Journal. Society of Toxicology — Fundam Appl Toxicol Off J Soc Toxicol
Fundamental and Clinical Aspects of Internal Medicine [*Elsevier Book Series*] — FCAIM
Fundamental and Clinical Pharmacology — Fundam Clin Pharmacol
Fundamental Aspects of Heterogeneous Catalysis Studied by Particle Beams — Fundam Aspects Heterog Catal Stud Part Beams
Fundamental Aspects of Pollution Control and Environmental Science [*Elsevier Book Series*] — FAPCES
Fundamental Aspects of Pollution Control and Environmental Science [*Elsevier Book Series*] — FAPSEK

Fundamental Aspects of Pollution Control and Environmental Science — Fundam Aspects Pollut Control Environ Sci
Fundamental Interactions in Physics and Astrophysics. Lectures. Coral Gables Conference on Fundamental Interactions at High Energy — Fundam Interact Phys Astrophys Lect Coral Gables Conf Fundam
Fundamental Interactions in Physics. Proceedings. Coral Gables Conference on Fundamental Interactions — Fundam Interact Phys Proc Coral Gables Conf Fundam Interact
Fundamental Phenomena in the Material Sciences — Fundam Phenom Mater Sci
Fundamental Problems in Statistical Mechanics. Proceedings. International Summer School on Fundamental Problems in Statistical Mechanics — Fundam Probl Stat Mech
Fundamental Radiologica — Fundam Radiol
Fundamental Research in Homogenous Catalysis — Fundam Res Homogenous Catal
Fundamental Studies in Computer Science [*Elsevier Book Series*] — FSCS
Fundamental Studies in Computer Science — Fundamental Stud in Comput Sci
Fundamental Studies in Engineering [*Elsevier Book Series*] — FSE
Fundamental Theories of Physics — Fund Theories Phys
Fundamental'nye Osnovy Opticheskoi Pamyati i Sredy — Fundam Osn Opt Pamyati Sredy
Fundamental'nye Problemy Metrologii. Materialy Vsesoyuznogo Seminara — Fundam Probl Metrol Mater Vses Semin
Fundamentals and Applications of Ternary Diffusion. Proceedings. International Symposium — Fundam Appl Ternary Diffus Proc Int Symp
Fundamentals in Respiratory Diseases — Fundam Respir Dis
Fundamentals of Aerospace Instrumentation — Fundam Aerosp Instrum
Fundamentals of Applied Entomology [*Monograph*] — Fundam Appl Entomol
Fundamentals of Cosmic Physics — Fundam Cosm Phys
Fundamentals of Cosmic Physics — Fundam Cosmic Phys
Fundamentals of Gas Phase Ion Chemistry — Fundam Gas Phase Ion Chem
Fundamentals of Radiation Heat Transfer. National Heat Transfer Conference — Fundam Radiat Heat Transfer Natl Heat Transfer Conf
Fundamentals, Process Design, and Development — Fundamentals Proc Design Dev
Fundberichte aus Baden-Wuerttemberg — Fber Bad Wuert
Fundberichte aus Baden-Wuerttemberg — Fu Ber Bad Wuert
Fundberichte aus Baden-Wuerttemberg — Fundber Baden-Wuerttemberg
Fundberichte aus Hessen — FH
Fundberichte aus Hessen — Fu Ber Hessen
Fundberichte aus Hessen — Fundber Hessen
Fundberichte aus Oesterreich — FO
Fundberichte aus Oesterreich — Fu Ber Oe
Fundberichte aus Oesterreich — Fundber Oesterreich
Fundberichte aus Schwaben — F B Schwaben
Fundberichte aus Schwaben — Fundb Schwaben
Fundberichte aus Schwaben — Fundber Schwaben
Fundicao — FDCOA
Fundicao e Materias-Primas — Fundicao Mater Primas
Fundmuenzen der Roemischen Zeit in Deutschland — FMD
Fundmuenzen der Roemischen Zeit in Deutschland — FMRD
Fungal Genetics and Biology — Fungal Genet Biol
Fungal Spore Morphogenetic Controls. Proceedings. International Fungal Spore Symposium — Fungal Spore Morphogenet Control Proc Int Fungal Spore Symp
Fungal Viruses. International Congress of Microbiology. Mycology Section — Fungal Viruses Int Congr Microbiol Mycol Sect
Fungi Canadenses — Fungi Can
Fungicides, Herbicides, Insecticides — Fung Herb Insect
Funk and Scott Annual Index of Corporations and Industries — Funk Scott Annu Ind
Funk and Scott Index of Corporations and Industries — Funk Scott Index Corp Ind
Funk and Wagnalls Standard Dictionary — F & W
Funkcialaj Ekvaciog — Funkcial Ekvac
Funkcional'nyj Analiz i Ego Prilozenija — Funkc Anal
Funk-Fachhaendler — FUFAB
Funkschau — FUSHA
Funk-Technik — FT
Funk-Technik — Funk T
Funk-Technik — Funk-Tech
Funk-Technik — FUTEA
Funktionelle Biologie und Medizin — Funkt Biol Med
Funktionelle und Morphologische Organisation der Zelle — Funkt Morphol Organ Zelle
Funktionsanalyse Biologischer Systeme — Funktionsanal Biol Syst
Funktsii Organizma v Usloviyakh Izmenennoi Gazovoi Sredy — Funkts Org Usloviyakh Izmen Gazov Sredy
Funktsional'naya Neirokhimiya Tsentral'noi Nervnoi Sistemy. Materialy Vsesoyuznogo Simpoziuma — Funkts Neirokhim Tsentr Nervn Sist Mater Vses Simp
Funktsional'nyi Analiz i ego Prilozheniya. Nauka. Moscow — Funktsional Anal i Prilozhen
Funtai Kogaku — FUKOB
Funtai Kogaku Kaishi — FKKAD
Funtai Oyobi Funmatsuyakin — FOFUA
Fur Trade Journal of Canada — Fur Trade J Can
Furche. Freie Kulturpolitische Wochenschrift — Fu
Furche-Studien — Fur St
Furioso — Fur
Furman Studies — FS
Furman Studies — FurmS
Furman University. Bulletin — FUB
Furnaces. Design, Structural Materials, and Fuels. Industrial Process Heating Symposium. Proceedings — Furn Des Struct Mater Fuels Ind Process Heat Symp Proc
Furnas (C. C.) Memorial Conference — Furnas C C Meml Conf
Furniture Design and Manufacturing — FDM
Furniture Manufacturer — FJA
Furniture Manufacturer — Furn Mfr
Furniture Manufacturer — Furnit Manuf
Furniture Production — Furnit Prod
Furniture Retailer — Furnit Ret
Furniture Workers Press — Furniture Wkrs P
Furniture World and Furniture Buyer and Decorator — FWD
Furrow — FURWA
Furtwaengler und Reichhold, Griechische Vasenmalerei — FR
Furukawa Electric Review — Furukawa Electr Rev
Furukawa Review — Furukawa Rev
Fushoku Boshoku Shinpojumu Shiryo — FBSSD
Fusion Energy Foundation. Newsletter — Fusion Energy Found Newsl
Fusion Energy Update — FENUD
Fusion Engineering and Design — Fusion Eng Des
Fusion/Fission Energy Systems Review Meeting. Proceedings — Fusion Fisssion Energy Syst Rev Meet Proc
Fusion Forefront — FUFOD
Fusion Nucleaire — Fusion Nucl
Fusion Power Associates. Executive Newsletter — ENFAD
Fusion Power Associates. Executive Newsletter — Fusion Power Assoc Exec Newsl
Fusion Power Report — FPORD
Fusion Power Report — Fusion Power Rep
Fusion Technology — Fusion Technol
Fusion Technology. Proceedings. Symposium — Fusion Technol Proc Symp
Fuso Metals — Fuso Met
Fussboden Zeitung — FII
Fussboden Zeitung [*Germany*] — Fussboden Ztg
Fussboden Zeitung — FUZED
Futbol Internacional [*Database*] — FUTB
Future Abstracts — Fut Abstr
Future Computing Systems — Fut Comp Sys
Future Fiction — Fut
Future Gas Consumption of the US — Gas Consum
Future Life — Fut L
Future of Children — Future Child
Future of Nonfuel Minerals in the United States and World. Input-Output Projections, 1980-2030 — Nonfuel M
Future Population and Labour Force of Canada. Projections to the Year 2051 — Cdn P & L
Future Science Fiction — FUTF
Future Survey — Future Sur
Future Trends and Prospects for the Australian Mineral Processing Sector. Bureau of Mines Information Circular — BMIC 8900
Future Trends in Biomedical Applications of Lasers — Future Trends Biomed Appl Lasers
Futures — FUR
Futures — Fut
Futures — FUTU
Futures — FUTUB
Futures Information Service [*Database*] — FUTU
Futures. Michigan State University. Agricultural Experiment Station — Futures Mich State Univ Agric Exp Stn
Futures World News [*Database*] — FWN
Futuribles — FUTUD
Futuribles — NTI
Futurist — FTST
Futurist — FUS
Futurist — Fut
Futurist — FUTUA
Futuristic Stories — FUTS
Fuzzy Mathematics — Fuzzy Math
Fuzzy Sets and Systems — Fuzzy Sets and Syst
FWP [*Founding, Welding, Production Engineering*] **Journal** [*South Africa*] — FWP J
FWP [*Founding, Welding, Production Engineering*] **Journal** — FWPJA
FWS/OBS. United States Fish and Wildlife Service. Office of Biological Services — FWS/OBS US Fish Wildl Serv Off Biol Serv
FWS. Viriginia Polytechnic Institute and State University. School of Forestry and Wildlife Resources — FWS Va Polytech Inst State Univ Sch For Wildl Resour
Fyizika Tverdogo Tyila — Fyiz Tverd Tyila
Fyns Stifts Landburgstidende — F S Lbt
Fynsk Jul — Fy J
Fynske Aarboger — Fy Aa
Fynske Minder — Fyn Mind
Fyra Svenska Reformationskrifter Tryckta i Stockholm Ar 1562 — FSRTS
Fyring — Fyr
Fysiatricky a Reumatologicky Vestnik — Fysiatr Reumatol Vestn
Fysiatricky Vestnik — Fysiatr Vestn
Fysiokjemikeren — FYJKA
Fysisk Tidsskrift — Fys T
Fysisk Tidsskrift — Fys Tidsskr
Fysisk Tidsskrift [*Denmark*] — FYTIA
Fyzikalny Casopis — Fyz Cas
Fyzikalny Casopis. Vydavatel'stvo Slovenskej Akademie Vied — FYCAB

G

G & N Cooperator (Gippsland and Northern Cooperative) — G & N Coop
G. Becks Therapeutischer Almanach — Therap Alm Beck
G Proteins and Signal Transduction. Society of General Physiologists. Annual Symposium — G Proteins Signal Transduction Soc Gen Physiol Annu Symp
G Report. Saskatchewan Research Council. Geology Division — G Rep Sask Res Counc Geol Div
Gaceta Algodonera. Publicacion Defensora de Plantadores e Industriales del Algodon — Gac Algodonera
Gaceta de AVDA — Gac AVDA
Gaceta de Cuba — GC
Gaceta de Cuba — GdC
Gaceta de Granja. Asociacion Argentina Criadores de Aves, Conejos, y Abejas — Gac Granja
Gaceta de la Propriedad Industrial — Gac Propr Ind
Gaceta de las Artes Graficas del Libro y de la Industria del Papel — Gac Artes Graficas Libro Ind Pap
Gaceta de Medicina Zoologica — Gac Med Zool
Gaceta de Sanidad Militar — Gac San Mil
Gaceta del Colmenar — Gac Colmen
Gaceta Farmaceutica — Gac Farm
Gaceta Literaria — GLit
Gaceta Matematica — Gaceta Mat
Gaceta Matematica (Madrid) — Gac Mat (Madrid)
Gaceta Matematica. Primera Serie [*Madrid*] — Gaceta Mat I
Gaceta Medica — Gac Med
Gaceta Medica Boliviana — Gac Med Bol
Gaceta Medica Catalana — Gac Med Catalana
Gaceta Medica de Bilbao — Gac Med Bilbao
Gaceta Medica de Caracas — Gac Med Car
Gaceta Medica de Caracas — Gac Med Caracas
Gaceta Medica de Lima — Gac Med Lima
Gaceta Medica de Mexico — Gac Med Mex
Gaceta Medica de Mexico — GMMEA
Gaceta Medica del Norte Bilbao — Gac Med Norte Bilbao
Gaceta Medica del Sur — Gac Med Del Sur
Gaceta Medica del Uruguay — Gac Med Urug
Gaceta Medica Espanola — Gac Med Esp
Gaceta Medica Espanola — Gac Medica Espan
Gaceta Medica (Guayaquil) Ecuador — Gac Med (Guayaquil)
Gaceta Medico-Quirurgica de Bolivia — Gac Med Quir Bol
Gaceta (Mexico) — GM
Gaceta Numismatica — Gac Num
Gaceta Numismatica — GN
Gaceta Oficial (Caracas) — Gaceta Of Caracas
Gaceta Peruana de Medicina y Cirugia — Gac Per Med Cirug
Gaceta Sanitaria — Gac Sanit
Gaceta. Universidad Autonoma de Mexico — GUAM
Gaceta Veterinaria (Buenos Aires) — Gac Vet (B Aires)
Gadja Mada Journal of the Medical Sciences — Gadja Mada J Med Sci
Gads Danske Magasin — G d Mg
Gads Danske Magasin — GDM
Gaea Norvegica — Gaea Norveg
Gaekwad's Oriental Series — GOS
Gaelic Journal — Gael J
Gaertnerisch-Botanische Briefe — Gaertn Bot Briefe
Gaerungslose Fruechteverwertung — Gaerungslose Fruechteverwert
Gai Saber. Revista de l'Escola Occitana — Gai S
Gaigokugo Gaigoku Bungaku Kenkyu — GGK
GAK. Gummi, Asbest, Kunststoffe — GAK Gummi Asbest Kunstst
Gakujutsu Geppo — GAGEA
Gakujutsu Hokoku. Bulletin. Faculty of Agriculture. Kagoshima University — Gakujutsu Hokoku Bull Fac Agric Kagoshima Univ
Gakujutsu Hokoku. Bulletin of the College of Agriculture. Utsunomiya University — Gakujutsu Hokoku Bull Utsunomiya Univ
Gakujutsu Hokoku Tokushu. Special Bulletin — Gakujutsu Hokoku Tokushu Spec Bull
Gakujutsu Kenkyu Hokoku. Research Bulletin. Obihiro University — Gakujutsu Kenkyu Hokoku Res Bull Obihiro Univ
Gakujutsu Kenkyu Hokoku. Research Reports. Kochi University Nogaku — Gakujutsu Kenkyu Hokoku Res Rep Kochi Univ Nogaku
Galaxy — GAL
Galaxy Book — Gal Bo
Galaxy Science Fiction — GSF
Galaxy Science Fiction Novels — GSFN
Galenica Acta — Gal Act
Galerias de Arte y Salas de Exposiciones [*Database*] — GALE
Galicia Clinica — Gal Clin
Galicia Clinica — Galicia Clin
Galileo — Gali
Gallagher Report — Gallagher
Galleon. Bulletin of the Society for Colonial History — Galleon
Gallerie e Grandi Opere Sotterranee — Gallerie Grandi Opere Sotter
Gallerie Nazionale Italiane — GNI
Gallia Christiana Novissima — GCN
Gallia Cristiana — GC
Gallia. Fouilles et Monuments Archeologiques en France Metropolitaine — Gallia F
Gallia Prehistoire — Gall Preh
Gallia Prehistoire — Gallia Pr Hist
Gallia Prehistoire — Gallia Prehist
Gallica Biologica Acta — Gall Biol Act
Galling Report on Italy — GAR
Gallup Report — Gallup Rep
Gallup Report — Gallup Rept
Gallup Report — Gallup Rpt
Galpin Society. Journal — Galp Soc J
Galpin Society. Journal — Galpin S J
Galpin Society. Journal — Galpin Soc
Galpin Society. Journal — Galpin Soc J
Galpin Society. Journal — GAVEA
Galpin Society. Journal — GSJ
Galvano [*France*] — GALVA
Galvano Tecnica [*Later, Galvanotecnica & Processi al Plasma*] — Galvano Tec
Galvano-Organo-Traitements de Surface — Galvano Organo Trait Surf
Galvanotechnik — GVTKA
Galvanotechnik und Oberflaechenschutz — Galvanotech Oberflaechenschutz
Galvanotechnisches Kolloquium — Galvanotech Kolloq
Galvanotechnisches Symposium. Kurzfassungen der Vortraege — Galvanotech Symp Kurzfassungen Vortr
Galvanotecnica and Nuove Finiture — Galvanotec Nuove Finiture
Galvanotecnica e Processi al Plasma — Galvanotec Processi Plasma
Galvano-Teknisk Tidsskrift — Galvano Tek Tidsskr
Galway Archaeological and Historical Society. Journal — Galway Arch Hist Soc J
GAM. Bulletin du Groupe d'Acoustique Musicale — GAM
Gambia News Bulletin — GNB
Gambit — Gam
Game Conservancy Annual Review — Game Conservancy Annu Rev
Game Research Association. Annual Report — Game Res Assoc Annu Rep
Game Research Report. Colorado Division of Wildlife — Game Res Rep Colo Div Wildl
Games and Economic Behavior — Games Econom Behav
Gamete Quality and Fertility Regulation. Proceedings. Renier de Graaf Symposium — Gamete Qual Fertil Regul Proc Reinier de Graaf Symp
Gamete Research [*United States*] — Gamete Res
Gamma — GAM
Gamma Field Symposia — Gamma Field Symp
Gan To Kagaku Ryoho — GTKRD
Gan Vanof. Garden and Landscape. Israeli Gardeners' Association — Gan Vanof IGA
Ganciclovir Therapy for Cytomegalovirus Infection — Ganciclovir Ther Cytomegalovirus Infect
Gandhi Marg — GM
Ganga Oriental Series — Ga OS
Ganita [*India*] — GNTAA
Ganita Bharat Ganita Parisad [*Lucknow*] — Ganita
Gann Japanese Journal of Cancer Research — Gann
Gann Monograph on Cancer Research — Gann Monogr Cancer Res
Gann Monographs — GANMA
Gann Monographs — Gann Mon
Gann Monographs — Gann Monogr
Gannon College. Chemistry Journal — Gannon Coll Chem J
Ganz-MAVAG Koezlemenyek — Ganz MAVAG Koezl
GAO (General Accounting Office) Review — GAO (Gen Accounting Office) R
GAO [*General Accounting Office*] **Review** — GAO Rev
GAP [*Group for the Advancement of Psychiatry*] **Report** — GAP
GARC [*Graphic Arts Research Center*] **Newsletter** — GARC Newsl
Garcia de Orta — Garc Orta
Garcia de Orta (Lisbon) — Garcia de Orta (Lisb)
Garcia de Orta. Serie de Botanica [*Lisbon*] — Garcia de Orta Ser Bot
Garcia de Orta. Serie de Estudos Agronomicos [*Lisbon*] — Garcia de Orta Ser Estud Agron

Garcia de Orta. Serie de Farmacognosia — Garcia de Orta Ser Farmacogn
Garcia de Orta. Serie de Geografia — Garcia de Orta Geogr
Garcia de Orta. Serie de Geologia — Garcia de Orta Geol
Garcia de Orta. Serie de Geologia — Garcia de Orta Ser Geol
Garcia de Orta. Serie de Zoologia [*Lisbon*] — Garcia de Orta Ser Zool
Garcia Lorca Review — Garcia Lorca Rev
Garcia Lorca Review — GLR
Garden and Forest — Garden & F
Garden and Home Builder — Gard & Home B
Garden Beautiful — Gard Beautiful
Garden Companion and Florists' Guide — Gard Companion Florists Guide
Garden Digest — Gard Digest
Garden History. Journal. Garden History Society — Garden Hist
Garden History Society. Newsletter — Garden History Soc Newsletter
Garden Island — Garden Is
Garden Journal — Gard J
Garden Journal — Garden J
Garden Journal. New York Botanical Garden — Gard J New York Bot Gard
Garden Journal. New York Botanical Garden — Gard J NY Bot Gard
Garden Journal. New York Botanical Garden — Gdn J NY Bot Gdn
Garden. Journal of the Royal Horticultural Society — Garden J R Hortic Soc
Garden Life (London) — Gard Life London
Garden Magazine — Gard M
Garden. New York Botanical Garden — Garden New York
Gardener. A Magazine of Horticulture and Floriculture (Edinburgh) — Gardener Edinburgh
Gardener and Practical Florist — Gard Pract Florist
Gardener's Abstracts — Gard Abstr
Gardeners' and Farmers' Journal — Gard Farmers J
Gardener's and Forester's Record — Gard Foresters Rec
Gardeners' Chronicle and Gardening Illustrated — Gard Chron
Gardeners' Chronicle (London) — Gard Chron (Lond)
Gardeners' Chronicle of America — Gard Chron Am
Gardener's Chronicle of America — Gard Chron Amer
Gardeners' Magazine (London) — Gard Mag London
Gardener's Monthly and Horticulturist — Gard Monthly Hort
Gardening Illustrated — Gard Illustr
Gardening Illustrated — Gdng Ill
Gardening Magazine (Calcium) — Gard Mag Calcium
Gardening World — Gard World
Gardens and Gardening. The Studio Gardening Annual — Gard Gardening
Gardens Bulletin — Gdns Bull
Gardens Bulletin (Singapore) — Gard Bull (Singapore)
Gardens Bulletin (Singapore) — Gdns Bull (Singapore)
Gardens, Fruit, and Flower Guide. Mississippi Cooperative Extension Service. Extension Horticulture Department — Gard Fruit Flower Guide Miss Coop Ext Serv Ext Hortic Dep
Gardens of the Pacific — Gard Pacific
Garden-Work for Villa, Suburban, Town, and Cottage Gardens — Gard Work Villa Gard
Garland Reference Library of the Humanities — Garland Ref Lib Humanities
Garland Reference Library of the Humanities — GRLH
GARP [*Global Atmospheric Research Programme*] **Publications Series** — GARP Publ Ser
Garrett Theological Studies — Gar TS
Garten Landschaft. Landscape Architecture Planning — Gart Landschaft Landscape Archit Plann
Garten und Kleintierzucht. C (Imker) — Garten u Kleintierz C (Imker)
Gartenbau im Reich — Gartenbau Reich
Gartenbau-Forschung — Gartenbau Forsch
Gartenbauwissenschaft — Gartenbauwiss
Gartenbauwissenschaft — GTBWA
Garten-Schoenheit. Illustrierte Schrift fuer den Garten- und Blumenfreund, Liebhaber und Fachmann — Gart Schoenheit
Garten-Zeitschrift fuer Gaertner und Gartenfreunde, Siedler, und Kleingaertner. Illustrierte Flora — Gart Z Gaertn Ill Fl
Gartenzeitschrift Illustrierte Flora — Gartenz Ill Fl
Gartenzeitung der Oesterreichischen Gartenbaugesellschaft in Wien — Gartenzeitung Oesterr Gartenbauges Wien
Gartner Tidende — Grt T
Garyounis Scientific Bulletin — Garyounis Sci Bull
Gas Abstracts — GAABA
Gas Abstracts — Gas Abstr
Gas Age — GAAGA
Gas Age Record and Natural Gas — Gas Age Rec Nat Gas
Gas Age-Record — Gas Age Rec
Gas and Oil Power — Gas Oil Pwr
Gas and Oil Power — GOPOA
Gas + Architecture — AGUSD
Gas Chromatography Abstracts — Gas Chromat Abstr
Gas Chromatography. International Symposium — Gas Chromatogr Int Sym
Gas Chromatography. Proceedings of the International Symposium (Europe) — Gas Chromatogr Proc Int Symp (Eur)
Gas Conditioning Conference. Proceedings — Gas Cond Conf Proc
Gas Council (Great Britain). Research Communication — Gas Counc (Gt Brit) Res Commun
Gas Council (Great Britain). Research Communications — Gas Counc (GB) Res Commun
Gas Digest — Gas Dig
Gas Discharges. International Conference — Gas Discharges Int Conf
Gas Energy Supply Outlook, 1980-2000. American Gas Association — AGA 2000
Gas Engineer — GAENA
Gas Engineer [*England*] — Gas Eng
Gas Engineering — Gas Eng
Gas Engineering and Management — Gas Eng Manage
Gas Engineering and Management — Gas Engine Manage
Gas Engineering and Management — Gas Engng Mgmnt
Gas Engineering and Management — Gas Engng Mgmt
Gas Engineering Magazine — Gas Eng Mag
Gas Facts. American Gas Association — AGA Facts
Gas Heat in Industry — Gas Heat Ind
Gas Heat International — Gas Heat Int
Gas in Canada — Gas Can
Gas Industrie (Leipzig) — Gas Ind (Leipzig)
Gas Industries — Gas Ind
Gas Industry (London) — Gas Ind (London)
Gas Industry. Manufactured Gas Edition — Gas Ind Manuf Gas Ed
Gas Industry. Natural Gas Edition — Gas Ind Nat Gas Ed
Gas Industry. Natural Gas Edition — GINGA
Gas Institute News — Gas Inst News
Gas Journal — Gas J
Gas Journal — GJ
Gas Kinetics and Energy Transfer — Gas Kinet Energy Transfer
Gas. Maandblad voor de Gasindustrie — GAS
Gas Magazine [*United States*] — Gas Mag
Gas Magazine — GMGZA
Gas Measurement Institute — Gas Meas Inst
Gas (Philadelphia) — Gas (Phila)
Gas Processors Association. Annual Convention. Proceedings — Gas Process Assoc Annu Conv Proc
Gas Processors Association. Proceedings — Gas Process Assoc Proc
Gas Record — Gas Rec
Gas Research Board. Communication — Gas Res Board Commun
Gas Research Insights — GR Insights
Gas Research Institute Digest — Gas Res Inst Dig
Gas Review — Gas Rev
Gas Separation and Purification — Gas Sep Purif
Gas Supply Review — Gas Supply Rev
Gas Supply Review — GSRED
Gas Turbine International — Gas Turbine Int
Gas Turbine World — GTWOD
Gas Waerme International — Gas Waerme Int
Gas, Wasser, Abwasser — GWASA
Gas, Wasser, Abwasser. Schweizerische Monatszeitschrift fuer Gasfoerderung und Siedlungswasserwirtschaft — GHA
Gas World — Gas Wld
Gas World — GHT
Gas World and Gas Journal — Gas World Gas J
Gas. Zeitschrift fuer Rationelle Energieanwendung [*Germany*] — Gas Z Ration Energieanwend
Gas. Zeitschrift fuer Rationelle Energieanwendung — GCB
Gaseous Air Pollutants and Plant Metabolism. Proceedings. International Symposium on Gaseous Air Pollutants and Plant Metabolism — Gaseous Air Pollut Plant Metab Proc Int Symp
Gaseous Dielectrics. Proceedings. International Symposium on Gaseous Dielectrics — Gaseous Dielectr Proc Int Symp
Gases in Research and Industry — Gases Res Ind
Gases in Research and Industry. Commonwealth Industrial Gases Ltd. — Gases Res Ind Gas Div CIG
Gasgemeinschaft — GASGB
Gasline Planning Update. Northwest Alaska Pipeline Company. Manpower and Impact Planning Department — GLPU
Gasohol USA — GAUSD
Gasschutz und Luftschutz. Ausgabe B — Gasschutz Luftschutz Ausg B
Gastech Proceedings — Gastech Proc
Gasteknikeren — Gtk
Gastroenterologia — Gastroent
Gastroenterologia — Gastroenterol
Gastroenterologia Acta. Conventus Medicinae Internae Hungarici — Gastroenterol Acta Conv Med Intern Hung
Gastroenterologia Japonica — Gastroenterol Jpn
Gastroenterologia. Supplementum — Gastroenterologia Suppl
Gastroenterologia y Hepatologia — Gastroenterol Hepatol
Gastroenterological Endoscopy — Gastroenterol Endosc
Gastroenterologie Clinique et Biologique — Gastroenterol Clin Biol
Gastroenterologie und Stoffwechsel — Gastroenterol Stoffwechsel
Gastroenterologische Fortbildungskurse fuer die Praxis — Gastroenterol Fortbildungskurse Prax
Gastroenterology — Gastroent
Gastroenterology — Gastroenty
Gastroenterology. Abstracts and Citations — GAAC
Gastroenterology. Abstracts and Citations — Gastroenterol Abstr & Cit
Gastroenterology. Abstracts and Citations — Gastroenterol Abstr Citations
Gastroenterology Annual — Gastroenterol Annu
Gastroenterology Clinics of North America — Gastroenterol Clin North Am
Gastroenterology Nursing — Gastroenterol Nurs
Gastrointestinal Absorption Database — GIABS
Gastrointestinal and Liver Physiology — GLP
Gastrointestinal Endoscopy — Gastroin En
Gastrointestinal Endoscopy — Gastroint Endosc
Gastrointestinal Endoscopy — Gastrointest Endosc
Gastrointestinal Endoscopy Clinics of North America — Gastrointest Endosc Clin N Am
Gastrointestinal Motility. International Symposium — Gastrointest Motil Int Symp
Gastrointestinal Motility. Proceedings. International Symposium on Gastrointestinal Motility — Gastrointest Motil Proc Int Symp
Gastrointestinal Radiology — GARAD
Gastrointestinal Radiology — Gastrointest Radiol
Gastrointestinal Radiology Reviews — Gastrointest Radiol Rev

Gastronomia Espanola [*Database*] — GAST
Gastvrij — HRO
Gateway to Medicine — Gateway Med
GATF [*Graphic Arts Technical Foundation*] **Bulletin** — GATF Bull
GATF [*Graphic Arts Technical Foundation*] **Education Report** — GATF Educ Rep
GATF [*Graphic Arts Technical Foundation*] **Environmental Control Report** — GATF Envir Control Rept
GATF [*Graphic Arts Technical Foundation*] **Research Progress** — GATF Res Progr
GATF [*Graphic Arts Technical Foundation*] **Research Progress Report** — GATF Res Prog Rep
GATF [*Graphic Arts Technical Foundation*] **Research Project Report** — GATF Res Proj Rep
GATF [*Graphic Arts Technical Foundation*] **Technical Service Information** — GATF Tech Serv Inform
[*The*] **Gathering** — Gath
GATN (German-American Trade News) — GATN (German-Am Trade News)
Gatooma Research Station. Annual Report — Gatooma Res Stn Annu Rep
Gattefosse. Bulletin Technique — Gattefosse Bull Tech
Gattefosse. Report — Gattefosse Rep
Gauhati University. Journal — GUJ
Gaule. Societe d'Histoire, d'Archeologie et de Tradition Gauloise — GSHATG
Gauss Gesellschaft eV. (Goettingen). Mitteilungen — Gauss Ges (Goettingen) Mitt
Gavroche — Gav
Gavroche — Gavr
Gay Books Bulletin — GBB
Gay Community News — Gay News
Gay Community News — GCN
Gay Insurgent — Gay Insrg
Gay Liberation — Gay
Gay Literature — Gay L
Gay Sunshine — Gay Sun
Gayana Botanica — Gayana Bot
Gayana Botanica Miscelanea — Gayana Bot Misc
Gayana Miscelanea — Gayana Misc
Gayana Zoologia — Gayana Zool
Gaz Chaleur International — Gaz Chal Int
Gaz d'Aujourd'hui — Gaz Aujourd
Gaz Europe Information — Gaz Eur Inf
Gaz Woda i Technika Sanitarna — Gaz Woda Tech Sanit
Gazdasag es Jogtudomany — Gazdasag es Jogtud
Gazdasagi Lapok — Gazd Lapok
Gazdaszati Koezloeny — Gazd Koezl
Gazelle Review of Literature on the Middle East — Gazelle Rev Lit ME
Gazeta Agricola de Angola — Gazeta Agric Angola
Gazeta Clinica — Gaz Clin
Gazeta Clinica (Sao Paulo) — Gaz Clin (S Paulo)
Gazeta Cukrownicza — Gaz Cukrow
Gazeta Cukrownicza — Gazeta Cukrown
Gazeta da Pharmacia — Gaz Pharm
Gazeta das Aldeias — GA
Gazeta de Matematica — Gaz Mat
Gazeta di Fisica — Gaz Fis
Gazeta do Agricultor (Angola) — Gaz Agr (Angola)
Gazeta Krakowska — GK
Gazeta Literara — GLit
Gazeta Matematica Perfectionare Metodica si Metodologica in Matematica si Informatica — Gaz Mat Mat Inform
Gazeta Matematica Publicatie Lunara pentru Tineret — Gaz Mat Publ Lunara pentru Tineret
Gazeta Medica da Bahia — Gaz Med Bahia
Gazeta Medica Portuguesa — Gaz Med Port
Gazeta Musical — GM
Gazeta Musical e de Todas las Artes — Gaz Mus
Gazeta Zydowska — GZ
Gazette Apicole — Gaz Apic
Gazette Apicole — Gaz Apicole
Gazette Archeologique — GA
Gazette Archeologique — Gaz Arch
Gazette Archeologique — Gaz Archeol
Gazette. Bureau des Brevets — Gaz Bur Brev
Gazette de Lausanne — Gaz Laus
Gazette de Lausanne — GLa
Gazette des Beaux Arts — Gazette BA
Gazette des Beaux-Arts — Gaz BA
Gazette des Beaux-Arts — Gaz Bea-Art
Gazette des Beaux-Arts — Gaz Beaux-Arts
Gazette des Beaux-Arts — GBA
Gazette des Hopitaux Civils et Militaires — Gaz Hop Civ Mil
Gazette des Hopitaux Civils et Militaires — Gaz Hopit Civ
Gazette des Lettres — Gaz Lettres
Gazette des Lettres — GL
Gazette des Mathematiciens — Gaz Math
Gazette d'Israel [*Tunis*] — GI
Gazette du Palais [*France*] — GP
Gazette du Travail — Gaz Trav
Gazette Economique — Gaz Econ
Gazette. Egyptian Paediatric Association — Gaz Egypt Paediatr Assoc
Gazette. Egyptian Society of Gynaecology and Obstetrics — Gaz Egypt Soc Gynaecol Obstet
Gazette Hebdomadaire des Sciences Medicales de Bordeaux — Gaz Hebd Sc Med Bordeaux
Gazette Hebdomadaire des Sciences Medicales de Bordeaux — Gaz Hebd Sci Med Bordeaux
Gazette India — Gaz India
Gazette. Institute of Medical Laboratory Science — Gaz Inst Med Lab Sci
Gazette. Kasr El Aini Faculty of Medicine — Gaz Kasr El Aini Fac Med
Gazette Medicale de France — Gaz Med Fr
Gazette Medicale de l'Algerie — Gaz Med Algerie
Gazette Medicale de Nantes — Gaz Med Nantes
Gazette Medicale de Paris — Gaz Med De Paris
Gazette Medicale de Paris — Gaz Med Paris
Gazette Medicale de Picardie — Gaz Med Picardie
Gazette Medicale d'Orient — Gaz Med Orient
Gazette (Montreal) — Gaz (Montrl)
Gazette Numismatique Suisse — GNS
Gazette Obstetricale — Gaz Obst
Gazette: Official Journal of the Western Australian Institute of Technology — Gaz WA Inst Tech
Gazette. University of Newcastle — Gaz Univ Newcastle
Gazette. University of Newcastle — Newcastle Univ Gaz
Gazette. University of Sydney — Gaz Univ Syd
Gazette. University of the Witwatersrand — Gaz Univ Wits
Gazette. University of Western Australia — Gaz Univ WA
Gazette. University of Western Australia — Gazette Univ WA
Gazettes Medicales — Gaz Med
Gazi Medical Journal — Gazi Med J
Gazi Universitesi Eczacilik Fakultesi Dergisi — Gazi Univ Eczacilik Fak Derg
Gazi University. Faculty of Pharmacy. Journal — Gazi Univ Fac Pharm J
Gazo Shindan — GASHD
Gazodinamika i Teploobmen — Gazodin Teploobmen
Gazovaya Khromatografiya [*Former USSR*] — Gazov Khromatogr
Gazovaya Khromatografiya. Trudy Vsesoyuznoi Konferentsii — Gazov Khromatogr Tr Vses Konf
Gazovaya Promyshlennost — Gazov Promst
Gazovaya Promyshlennost. Seriya. Ispol'zovanie Gaza v Narodnom Khozyaistve. Obzornaya Informatsiya — Gazov Promst Ser Ispolz Gaza Nar Khoz Obz Inf
Gazovaya Promyshlennost. Seriya. Ispol'zovanie Gaza v Narodnom Khozyaistve. Referativnaya Informatsiya — Gazov Promst Ser Ispolz Gaza Nar Khoz Ref Inf
Gazovaya Promyshlennost. Seriya. Podgotovka i Pererabotka Gaza i Gazovogo Kondensata. Obzornaya Informatsiya — Gazov Promst Ser Podgot Pererab Gaza Gazov Kondens Obz Inf
Gazovaya Promyshlennost. Seriya. Podgotovka i Pererabotka Gaza i Gazovogo Kondensata. Referativnaya Informatsiya — Gazov Promst Ser Podgot Pererab Gaza Gazov Kondens Ref Inf
Gazovaya Promyshlennost. Seriya. Transport i Khranenie Gaza. Obzornaya Informatsiya — Gazov Promst Ser Transp Khranenie Gaza Obz Inf
Gazovaya Promyshlennost. Seriya. Transport i Khranenie Gaza. Referativnaya Informatsiya — Gazov Promst Ser Transp Khranenie Gaza Ref Inf
Gazovoe Delo [*Former USSR*] — Gazov Delo
Gaz-Physique-Orsay Database — GAPHYOR
Gazy v Litom Metalle. Doklady Soveshchaniya po Teorii Liteinykh Protsessov — Gazy Litom Met Dokl Soveshch Teor Liteinykh Protsessov
Gazzetta Chimica Italiana — Gaz Chim It
Gazzetta Chimica Italiana — Gaz Chim Ital
Gazzetta Chimica Italiana — Gazz Chim Ital
Gazzetta Clinica dello Spedale Civico di Palermo — Gazz Clin Sped Civ Palermo
Gazzetta Commerciale — Gaz Com
Gazzetta degli Ospedali e delle Cliniche — Gazz Osped Clin
Gazzetta degli Ospitali Milano — Gazz Osp Milano
Gazzetta del Mezzogiorno — GdM
Gazzetta Internazionale di Medicina — Gazz Internaz Med
Gazzetta Internazionale di Medicina e Chirurgia [*Italy*] — Gazz Int Med Chir
Gazzetta Medica Italiana — Gazz Med Ital
Gazzetta Medica Italiana. Archivio per le Scienze Mediche — Gazz Med Ital Arch Sci Med
Gazzetta Medica Italiana. Provincie Venete — Gazz Med Ital Prov Venete
Gazzetta Medica Italo-Argentina — Gazz Med Italo Argent
Gazzetta Medica Napolitana — Gazz Med Napol
Gazzetta Medica Siciliana [*Italy*] — Gazz Med Sicil
Gazzetta Sanitaria — GASAA
Gazzetta Sanitaria — Gazz Sanit
Gazzetta Sanitaria. Edition Francaise — Gazz Sanit Edn Francaise
Gazzetta Sanitaria (English Issue) — Gazz Sanit (Engl Issue)
Gazzetta Siciliana di Medicina e Chirurgia d'Igiene e d'Interessi Professionali — Gazz Sicil Med e Chir
Gazzetta Ufficiale [*Rome*] — GU
Gazzetta Ufficiale della Repubblica Italiana — Gaz Uff
Gazzetta Ufficiale della Repubblica Italiana — Gazz Uff Repub Ital
Gazzetta Ufficiale della Repubblica Italiana — GURID
Gazzettino Numismatico — Gaz Num
GB Digest (Girls' Brigade) — GB Digest
GBF [*Gesellschaft fuer Biotechnologische Forschung*] **Monograph Series** — GBF Monogr Ser
GBF [*Gesellschaft fuer Biotechnologische Forschung*] **Monograph Series** — GMSED
GCCA [*Graduate Careers Council of Australia*] **Newsletter** — GCCA Newsletter
Gdanskie Towarzystwo Naukowe Rozprawy Wydzialu [*Poland*] — Gdansk Tow Nauk Rozpr Wydz
Gdanskie Towarzystwo Naukowe Rozprawy Wydzialu — GTRWA
Gdanskie Towarzystwo Naukowe. Rozprawy Wydzialu 3. Nauk Matematyczno-Przyrodniczych — Gdansk Tow Nauk Rozpr Wydz 3
Gdanskie Zeszyty Humanistyczne — GZH
Gebrauchsgraphik — Gebrauchs
Gebrauchsgraphik Novum — Gebrauchs Novum
Geburtshilfe und Frauenheilkunde — Geburtsh Fr
Geburtshilfe und Frauenheilkunde — Geburtsh Frauenheilkd
Geburtshilfe und Frauenheilkunde — Geburtshilfe Frauenheilkd

Geburtshilfe und Frauenheilkunde — Geburtshilfe Fraunheilkd
Geburtshilflich-Gynaekologische Praxis. Internationales Muensteraner Gespraech ueber Geburtshilflich-Gynaekologische Praxis — Geburtshilflich Gynaekol Prax Int Muensteraner Gespraech
GEC [*General Electric Company*] **Atomic Energy Review** — GEC At Energy Rev
GEC [*General Electric Company*] **Bibliography** — GEC Bibliogr
GEC Engineering — GEC Eng
GEC [*General Electric Company*] **Journal** — GEC J
GEC Journal of Research — GEC J Res
GEC [*General Electric Company*] **Journal of Science and Technology** — GEC J Sci & Technol
GEC [*General Electric Company*] **Telecommunications** — GEC Telecommun
Gedenkschriften. Oudheidkundige Kring voor het Land van Dendermonde — GOKD
Gedrag und Gezondheid — Gedrag & Gezond
Gedrag-Tijdschrift voor Psychologie — Gedrag T P
Gefahrstoffe. Reinhaltung der Luft. Air Quality Control — Gefahrstoffe Reinhalt Luft
Gegenbaurs Morphologisches Jahrbuch — Gegenbaurs Morphol Jahrb
Gegenwart — Ge
Gegenwart der Dichtung — GdD
Gegenwart. Zeitschrift fuer Literatur, Wirtschaftsleben, und Kunst — Geg
Gegenwartsfragen Biblischer Theologie — GB Th
Gegenwartskunde Gesellschaft Staat Erziehung — Geg G S Erz
Geillustreerd Tuinbouwblad — Geill Tuinbouwbl
Geisinger Medical Center. Bulletin — Geisinger Med Cent Bull
Geist und Gestalt — GG
Geist und Leben [*Wuerzburg*] — GeistLeb
Geist und Leben — GL
Geist und Leben der Ostkirche — GLOK
Geist und Tat — GuT
Geist und Werk der Zeiten — GWZ
Geist und Zeit — GuZ
Geistes- und Sozialwissenschaftliche Dissertationen — GSD
Geisteskampf der Gegenwart — GKG
Geisteswissenschaftliche Forschungen — GWF
Geistige Arbeit — GA
Geistige Arbeit — GArb
Geistige Arbeit — Geist Arb
Gekkan Haikibutsu — GEHAD
Gelatin and Glue Research Association — Gel and Glue Res Assoc
Gelatine, Leim, Klebstoffe — Gelatine Leim Klebst
Gelbe Hefte — Gelbe H
Gelbe Hefte — Gelbe Hh
Gelbe Hefte — GH
Geldgeschichtliche Nachrichten — GN
Gelehrte Anzeigen der Baierischen Akademie der Wissenschaften — GABAW
Gelehrte Anzeiger der Bayerischen Akademie der Wissenschaften — Anzeig d Bayer Akd Wiss
Gelehrte Anzeiger der Bayerischen Akademie der Wissenschaften — Gel Anz
Gelehrte Ergoetzlichkeiten und Nachrichten — Gel Ergoetzlichk Nachr
Gelehrte Zeitung. Herausgegeben zu Kiel — Gel Zeitung Kiel
Gelfand Mathematical Seminars — Gelfand Math Sem
Geloof en Vrijheid — Gel Vrij
Gelre. Bijdragen en Mededeelingen — GBM
Geltenden Verfassungsgesetze der Evangelisch-Deutschen Landeskirchen — GVEDL
Geluid en Omgeving — GEG
Gem State News Letter — Gem State News Lett
Gem State RN News Letter [*Idaho*] — Gem State RN News Lett
Gematologiya i Perelivanie Krovi — Gematol Pereliv Krovi
Gematologiya i Perelivanie Krovi Respublikanskoi Mezhvedomstvennyi Sbornik — Gematol Pereliv Krovi Resp Mezhved Sb
Gematologiya i Transfuziologiya — Gematol Transfuziol
Gemeenschap der Kerken — Ge Ke
Gemeente — Gem
Gemeentebestuur Maandschrift der Vereeniging van Nederlandsche Gemeenten — Gmtebest
Gemeentebestuur Tijdschrift van de Vereniging van Nederlandse Gemeenten — G
Gemeentelijk Jaarboek — GJ
Gemeenteraad — GR
Gemeentestem — GS
Gemeentestem; Weekblad, aan de Belangen van de Gemeente in Nederland Gewijd — GMS
Gemeindezeitung fuer Elsass-Lothringen — GzgEL
Gemeinnuetziger Almanach — Gemeinnuetz Alman
Gemeinnuetziges Natur und Kunstmagazin oder Abhandlungen zur Befoerderung der Naturkunde, der Kuenste, Manufacturen und Fabriken — Gemeinnuetz Natur Kunstmag
Gemeinnuetziges Pesther Journal. Zeitung fuer Landwirthschaft, Gartenbau, Handel, Industrie, und Gewerbe — Gemeinnuetz Pesther J
Gemeinsames Amtsblatt. Ausgabe A [*Germany*] — Gemeinsames Amtsbl A
Gemeinsames Amtsblatt. Ausgabe A — GMAMA
Gemeinsames Amtsblatt des Landes Baden-Wuerttemberg. Ausgabe A — Gemeinsames Amtsbl Landes Baden-Wuerttemb A
Gemeinsames Ministerialblatt A — Gemeinsames Ministerialbl A
Gemengde Branche. Vakblad voor de Huishoudelijke en Luxe Artikelen, Glas, Porselein, Aardewerk, en Kunstnijverheid — GBR
Gemmological Society of Japan Journal — Gemmol Soc Jap J
Gemologia. Associacao Brasileira de Gemologia e Mineralogia (Sao Paulo) — Gemol (Sao Paulo)
Gems and Gemology. Gemological Institute of America — Gems Gemol
Gems and Minerals — Gems Miner
GEN (Gastroenterologia, Endocrinologia, Nutricion) (Caracas) — GEN (Gastroenterol Endocrinol Nutr) (Caracas)
GEN. Government Equipment News — GEN
Genava — Gen
Gencho Hiroshima Igaku — GEHIA
Gendai Iryo — GEIRD
Gendai No Shinryo — GNSHD
Genden Shiryo — GESHA
Gene Amplification and Analysis — Gene Amplif Anal
Gene Amplification and Analysis Series [*Elsevier Book Series*] — GAA
Gene Analysis Techniques — Gene Anal T
Gene Analysis Techniques — Gene Anal Tech
Gene Expression — Gene Expr
Gene Expression and Development. Proceedings. International Congress on Isozymes — Gene Expression Dev Proc Int Congr Isozymes
Gene Expression and Its Regulation. Proceedings. International Latin American Symposium — Gene Expression Its Regul Proc Int Lat Am Symp
Gene Geography — Gene Geogr
Gene Therapy — Gene Ther
Gene Transfer and Expression Protocols — Gene Transfer Expression Protoc
Genealogical Magazine — GENEAL MAG
Genealogical Periodical Annual Index — Geneal Per Ind
Genealogical Periodical Annual Index — Genealogical Period Annu Index
Genealogisches Handbuch des Adels — GH d A
Genealogiska Samfundets i Finland Arsskrift — Geneal Samf Finl Arsskr
Genealogists' Magazine — Genealog Mag
Genees-, Natuur- en Huishoudkundig Kabinet — Genees Natuur Huishoudk Kab
Geneeskunde — Geneesk
Geneeskunde — Geneeskd
Geneeskunde en Sport — Geneeskd Sport
Geneeskundig Tijdschrift voor Nederlandsch-Indiee — Geneesk Tijdschr Ned Indie
Geneeskundig Tijdschrift voor Nederlandsch-Indiee — Geneesk Tijdschr Nederl-Indiee
Geneeskundige Bladen uit Kliniek en Laboratorium voor de Praktijk — Geneeskd Bl
Geneeskundige Courant voor het Koningrijk der Nederlanden — Geneesk Courant
Geneeskundige Documentatie — Geneeskd Doc
Geneeskundige Gids — GEGIA
Geneeskundige Gids — Geneeskd Gids
General Acts of Arkansas — Ark Acts
General Agreement on Tariffs and Trade [*Database*] — GATT
General Agreement on Tariffs and Trade Bibliography — GATT
General and Applied Entomology — Gen Appl Entomol
General and Comparative Endocrinology — Gen C Endoc
General and Comparative Endocrinology — Gen Comp Endocr
General and Comparative Endocrinology — Gen Comp Endocrinol
General and Comparative Endocrinology. Supplement — Gen Comp Endocrinol Suppl
General and Diagnostic Pathology — Gen Diagn Pathol
General and Special Laws of the State of Texas — Tex Gen Laws
General Assembly Including the Reports of the Meetings, the Annexes to Those Records, and the Supplements. Official Reports — GAOR
General Conference. European Physical Society — Gen Conf Eur Phys Soc
General Contracting — Gen Contract
General Cytochemical Methods — Gen Cytochem Methods
General Dentistry — GEDED
General Dentistry — Gen Dent
General Economic Conditions in Turkey — Eco Turkey
General Education — General Ed
General Education Review. College of Agriculture and Veterinary Medicine. Nihon University — Gen Ed Rev Coll Agric Vet Med Nihon Univ
General Education Review. Toho University — Gen Ed Rev Toho Univ
General Electric Company Limited. Atomic Review — Gen Electr Co Ltd At Rev
General Electric Company Limited. Journal — Gen Electr Co Ltd J
General Electric Company Limited. Journal of Science and Technology — Gen Electr Co Ltd J Sci Technol
General Electric Company. Power Engineering Limited Bibliography — Gen Electr Co Power Eng Ltd Bibliogr
General Electric Review — Gen El Rev
General Electric Review — Gen Electr Rev
General Electric Review — GEREA
General Electrical Review — Gen Elec R
General Engineer [*United Kingdom*] — Gen Eng
General Engineering Transactions [*Australia*] — Gen Eng Trans
General Fisheries Council for the Mediterranean. Proceedings and Technical Papers — Gen Fish Counc Mediterr Proc Tech Pap
General Fisheries Council for the Mediterranean. Session Report — Gen Fish Counc Mediterr Sess Rep
General Heterocyclic Chemistry Series — Gen Het Cycl Chem Ser
General Heterocyclic Chemistry Series — Gen Heterocycl Chem Ser
General History and Collection of Voyages and Travels, Arranged in Systematic Order. R. Kerr [*Monograph*] — KV
General Hospital Psychiatry — Gen Hosp Psychiatry
General Index — Gen Index
General Index to Published Reports. Mineral Resources Group — Gen Index Publ Reports
General Information Programme-UNISIST [*Universal System for Information in Science and Technology*] **Newsletter** — GIPND
General Laws of Mississippi — Miss Laws
General Laws of Rhode Island — RI Gen Laws
General Laws of the Commonwealth of Massachusetts — Mass Gen L
General Linguistics — Gen Ling
General Linguistics — Gen Linguis

General Linguistics — GL
General Mining Association of the Province of Quebec. Journal — Gen M As Que J
General Motors Corporation. Research Laboratories. Research Publication — Gen Mot Corp Res Lab Res Publ
General Motors Engineering Journal [*United States*] — Gen Mot Eng J
General Motors Research Laboratories. Search — GM Search
General Motors Research Laboratories Symposia Series — Gen Mot Res Lab Symp Ser
General Newsletter. National Research Council (Canada). Division of Mechanical Engineering — Gen Newsl Natl Res Counc (Can) Div Mech Eng
General Newsletter. National Research Council (Canada). Division of Mechanical Engineering — GNNED
General Pathology and Pathological Anatomy — Gen Pathol Pathol Anat
General Pharmacology — Gen Pharm
General Pharmacology — Gen Pharmacol
General Physiology and Biophysics — Gen Physiol Biophys
General Practice — GP
General Practice Adviser — Gen Prac Adv
General Practice Clinics — Gen Pract Clin
General Practitioner (London) — Gen Practnr (Lond)
General Publication — Gen Pub
General Radio Experimenter — Gen Rad Exp
General Relativity and Gravitation — Gen Relat G
General Relativity and Gravitation — Gen Relativ and Gravitation
General Relativity and Gravitation — Gen Relativ Gravitation
General Relativity and Gravitation — Gen Relativity Gravitation
General Report. Department of Architectural Science. University of Sydney — Gen Rep Dep Archit Sci Syd Univ
General Report. Minister of Mines. Province of Quebec — Gen Rep Minist Mines Prov Que
General Report R8-GR. US Department of Agriculture. Forest Service. Southern Region — Gen Rep R8 GR US Dep Agric For Serv South Reg
General Repository — Gen Repos
General Science Index — Gen Sci Index
General Science Quarterly — Gen Sci Q
General Semantics Bulletin — GSB
General Series. Colorado State University. Agricultural Experiment Station — Gen Ser Colo State Agr Exp Sta
General Series. Colorado State University. Experiment Station — Gen Ser Colo State Univ Exp Stn
General Statutes of Connecticut — Conn Gen Stat
General Statutes of North Carolina — NC Gen Stat
General Systems — Gen Syst
General Systems Bulletin — Gen Syst
General Technical Report FPL. United States Department of Agriculture. Forest Service. Forest Products Laboratory — Gen Tech Rep FPL US Dep Agric For Serv For Prod Lab
General Technical Report FPL. United States. Forest Products Laboratory (Madison, Wisconsin) — Gen Tech Rep FPL US For Prod Lab (Madison Wis)
General Technical Report NE. US Department of Agriculture. Forest Service. Northeastern Forest Experiment Station — Gen Tech Rep NE US Dep Agric For Serv Northeast For Exp Stn
General Technical Report PSW. Pacific Southwest Forest and Range Experiment Stat — Gen Tech Rep PSW Pac Southwest For Range Exp Stn
General Technical Report. RM. Rocky Mountain Forest and Range Experiment Station. United States Forest Service — Gen Tech Rep RM Rocky Mt For Range Exp Stn US For Serv
General Technical Report SE. US Department of Agriculture. Forest Service. Southeastern Forest Experiment Station — Gen Tech Rep SE US Dep Agric For Serv Southeast For Exp Stn
General Technical Report SO. US Department of Agriculture. Forest Service. Southern Forest Experiment Station — Gen Tech Rep SO US Dep Agric For Serv South For Exp Stn
General Technical Report. US Department of Agriculture. Forest Service. Intermountain Research Station — Gen Tech Rep US Dep Agric For Serv Intermt Res Stn
General Technical Report WO. United States Forest Service — Gen Tech Rep WO US For Ser
General Telephone and Electronics Corporation. Research and Development Journal — Gen Teleph Electron Corp Res Dev J
General Topology and Its Applications — General Topology and Appl
General-Anzeiger fuer die Gesamten Interessen des Judentums [*Berlin*] — GAJ
Generale Maatschappij van Belgie. Informatieblad — SGH
Generalgouvernement — Gen Gouv
Generals of the Army and the Air Force and Admirals of the Navy — Gen Arm
Generalschematismus der Katholischen Geistlichkeit Deutschlands — GKGD
Generalschematismus der Katholischen Maenner- und Frauenkloester Deutschlands — GKMFD
Genes and Development — Genes Dev
Genes and Genetic Systems — Genes Genet Syst
Genes and Tumor Genes. Workshop Conference Hoechst — Genes Tumor Genes Workshop Conf Hoechst
Genes, Chromosomes, and Cancer — Genes Chromosomes Cancer
Genes to Cells — Genes Cells
Genesis of Precambrian Iron and Manganese Deposits. Proceedings. Kiev Symposium — Genesis Precambrian Iron Manganese Deposits Proc Kiev Symp
Genesis West — GW
Genet Epidemiology. Supplement — Genet Epidemiol Suppl
Genetic Analysis — Genet Anal
Genetic Analysis. Biomolecular Engineering — Genet Anal Biomol Eng
Genetic Analysis, Techniques, and Applications — Genet Anal Tech Appl
Genetic and Cellular Technology — Genet Cell Technol
Genetic Counseling — Genet Couns
Genetic Engineering and Biotechnology Yearbook — Genet Eng Biotechnol Yearb
Genetic Engineering Letter — Genet Eng Lett
Genetic Engineering (London) — Genet Eng (London)
Genetic Engineering (New York). Principles and Methods — Genet Eng (NY)
Genetic Engineering News — Genet Eng News
Genetic Engineering of Animals. Proceedings. Symposium on Genetic Engineering of Animals — Genet Eng Anim Proc Symp
Genetic Engineering. Principles and Methods — Genet Eng Princ Methods
Genetic Epidemiology — Genet Epidemiol
Genetic Hypertension. Proceedings. International Symposium on SHR and Related Studies — Genet Hypertens Proc Int Symp SHR Relat Stud
Genetic Maps — Genet Maps
Genetic Psychology Monographs — Gen Psych Mon
Genetic Psychology Monographs — Genet Psych
Genetic Psychology Monographs — Genet Psychol Mon
Genetic Psychology Monographs — Genet Psychol Monog
Genetic Psychology Monographs — Genet Psychol Monogr
Genetic Psychology Monographs — Genetic Psychol Monog
Genetic Psychology Monographs — GPM
Genetic Psychology Monographs — GPMOA3
Genetic Resources Communication — Genet Resour Commun
Genetic, Social, and General Psychology Monographs — Genet Soc Gen Psychol Monogr
Genetic, Social, and General Psychology Monographs — GSGMEQ
Genetic Technology News — Genet Technol News
Genetic Technology News — GTN
Genetic Technology News — GTNEEA
Genetic Toxicity [*Database*] — GENETOX
Genetica [*The Hague*] — GENEA3
Genetica Agraria — Genet Agr
Genetica Agraria — Genet Agrar
Genetica. Colloqui — Genet Colloq
Genetica Iberica — Gen Iber
Genetica Iberica — Genet Iber
Genetica Polonica — Genet Pol
Genetica Sinica [*Peking*] — Genet Sinica
Genetical Research — Gen Res
Genetical Research — Genet Res
Genetical Research — GENRA8
Genetics — Genet
Genetics — GENTAE
Genetics Abstracts — Genet Abstr
Genetics and Biology of Drosophila — Genet Biol Drosophila
Genetics and Breeding (Sofia) — Genet Breed (Sofia)
Genetics and Physiology Notes — Genet Physiol Notes
Genetics and Physiology Notes. Institute of Paper Chemistry — Genet Physiol Note Inst Paper Chem
Genetics and Plant Breeding — Genet Plant Breed
Genetics and Product Formation in Streptomyces — Genet Prod Form Streptomyces
Genetics, Development, and Evolution. Stadler Genetics Symposium — Genet Dev Evol Stadler Genet Symp
Genetics Lectures — Genet Lect
Genetics of Hearing Impairment — Genet Hear Impairment
Genetics of Hematological Disorders. Selected Papers. International Clinical Genetics Seminar — Genet Hematol Disord Sel Pap Int Clin Genet Semin
Genetics of Industrial Microorganisms. Proceedings. International Symposium on Genetics of Industrial Microorganisms — Genet Ind Microorg Proc Int Symp
Genetics of Kidney Disorders. Proceedings. International Clinical Genetics Seminar — Genet Kidney Disord Proc Int Clin Genet Semin
Genetics of Pattern Formation and Growth Control — Genet Pattern Form Growth Control
Genetics of Sex Determination — Genet Sex Determ
Genetics; Principles and Perspectives — Genet Princ Perspect
Genetics; Principles and Perspectives — GPPEDP
Genetics. Supplement [*United States*] — Genetics Suppl
Genetics. Supplement — GNTSA
Genetik — GNTKAC
Genetika — GNKAA5
Genetika a Slechteni — Genet Slecht
Genetika a Slechteni — Genet Slechteni
Genetika a Slechteni — GESLB
Genetika a Slechteni — GESLBG
Genetika Biokhimiya i Immunokhimiya Osobo Opasnykh Infektsii — Genet Biokhim Immunokhim Osobo Opasnykh Infekts
Genetika Biokhimiya i Immunokhimiya Osobo Opasnykh Infektsii — Genet Biokhim Immunokhim Osobo Opasnykh Infektsii
Genetika Cheloveka — Genet Chel
Genetika i Selektsiia. Genetics and Plant Breeding — Genet Sel Genet Plant Breed
Genetika i Selektsiia v Azerbaidzhan — Genet Sel Azerb
Genetika i Selektsiya — Genet Sel
Genetika i Selektsiya — Genet Selektsiya
Genetika i Selektsiya — GESKAC
Genetika Zhivotnykh i Evolyutsiya. Izbrannye Trudy Mezhdunarodnogo Geneticheskogo Kongressa — Genet Zhivotn Evol Izbr Tr Mezhdunar Genet Kongr
Genetique Humaine — Genet Hum
Genetique, Selection, Evolution — Genet Sel Evol
Genetique, Selection, Evolution — GSEVD8
Geneva Series Commentary — GSC
Geneve-Afrique — GAf
Geneve-Afrique — GeA

Geneve-Afrique — Geneve-Afr
Genezis Boksitov. Trudy Soveshchaniya — Genezis Boksitov Tr Soveshch
Gengo Kenkyu [*Journal. Linguistic Society of Japan*] — Geng Kenk
Gengo Kenkyu [*Journal. Linguistic Society of Japan*] — GK
Gengo Seikatsu — GS
Gengogaku Ronso — GeR
Genie Biologique et Medical — GBQMAL
Genie Biologique et Medical — Genie Biol Med
Genie Chimique [*Chemical Engineering Science*] — Gen Chim
Genie Chimique [*Chemical Engineering Science*] [*France*] — Genie Chim
Genie Civil — Genie Civ
Genie des Reacteurs et des Reactions — Genie React React
Genie du Christianisme — Gen Chr
Genie Industrial [*France*] — Genie Ind
Genie Industrial — GINDB
Genie Rural — GENRB
Genio Rurale — Gen Rur
Genitourinary Medicine — GEMEE2
Genitourinary Medicine — Genitourin Med
Genius der Zeit. Ein Journal — Genius Zeit
Genius Operator Advertising Data Bank — GO
Genome Analysis — Genome Anal
Genome Analysis. From Sequence to Function. European Meeting. Human Genome Organisation — Genome Anal Sequence Funct Eur Meet Hum Genome Organ
Genome Evolution — Genome Evol
Genome Research — Genome Res
Genome Science and Technology — Genome Sci
Genomic Responses to Environmental Stress — Genomic Responses Environ Stress
Genossenschafts Forum. Raiffeisenrundschau und Blaetter fuer Genossenschaftswesen — GNA
Gensan Nenji Taikai Gijiroku — GNTGD
Gensen-Kyo — GEKYA
Genshi Doryoku Kenkyukai Teirei Kenkyukai Nenkai Hokokusho — GDKTA
Genshi Nenryo Kosha Nempo — GNKNA
Genshiryoku Anzen Hakusho — GAHAD
Genshiryoku Anzen Iinkai Geppo — GAIGD
Genshiryoku Heiwa Riyo Kenkyu Seika Hokokusho — GHRKA
Gente Minhota — GM
Gentes Herbarum — GEHEA7
Gentes Herbarum — Gent Herb
Gentes Herbarum — Gentes Herb
Gentleman's Magazine — Gent M
Gentleman's Magazine — GM
Gentleman's Magazine. New Series — Gent M NS
Gentlemen's Quarterly — GQ
Gents Orientalistische Bijdragen — GOB
Gentsche Bijdragen tot de Kunstgeschiedenis — GBKG
Gentse Bijdragen tot de Kunstgeschiedenis en de Ouheidkunde — GBK
Gentse Bijdragen tot de Kunstgeschiedenis en de Ouheidkunde — GBKO
Geo Abstracts and Indexes — Geo Abs & Indexes
Geo Abstracts. B. Climatology and Hydrology — Geo Abstr B Climatol Hydrol
Geo Abstracts. C. Economic Geography — Geo Abstr C Econ Geog
Geo Abstracts. D. Social and Historical Geography — Geo Abstr D Soc Hist Geog
Geo Abstracts. E. Sedimentology — Geo Abstr E Sedimentology
Geo Abstracts. F. Regional and Community Planning — Geo Abstr F Reg Com Plan
Geo Abstracts. G — GAG
Geo Abstracts. G. Remote Sensing, Photogrammetry, and Cartography — Geo Abstr G Remote Sensing Photogram Cartogr
Geo Journal — Geo J
Geo Marine Technology — Geo Mar Technol
Geo-Archeologia. Periodico dell'Associazione Geo-Archeologica Italiana — Geo-Archeologia
Geobios [*Jodhpur*] — GBOSBU
Geobios [*Lyon*] — GEBSAJ
Geobotanicnyj Zbirnyk. Recueil Geobotanique — Geobot Zbirn
Geobotanisches Institut Rubel Veroeffentlichungen — Geobot Inst Rubel Veroeff
Geobotany — GEOBD2
Geochemical Exploration. Proceedings. International Geochemical Exploration Symposium — Geochem Explor Proc Int Geochem Explor Symp
Geochemical Journal — GEJOBE
Geochemical Journal — Geochem J
Geochemical Journal (Geochemical Society of Japan) — Geochem J (Geochem Soc Jap)
Geochemical Journal (Nagoya) — Geochem J (Nagoya)
Geochemical Journal (Tokyo) — Geochem J (Tokyo)
Geochemical News — Geochem News
Geochemical Report. Alaska. Division of Geological and Geophysical Surveys — Geochem Rep Alaska Div Geol Geophys Surv
Geochemical Society of India. Bulletin — Geochem Soc India Bull
Geochemical Society. Special Publication — Geochem Soc Spec Publ
Geochemie. Geochemical Methods and Data — Geochem Geochem Methods Data
Geochemistry — CKNKDM
Geochemistry [*Nagoya*] — GECHB
Geochemistry and the Environment — Geochem Environ
Geochemistry International — Geochem Int
Geochimica [*English Translation*] — GEOCD
Geochimica Brasiliensis — Geochim Bras
Geochimica et Cosmochimica Acta — GCACAK
Geochimica et Cosmochimica Acta — Geoch Cos A
Geochimica et Cosmochimica Acta — Geoch Cosm A
Geochimica et Cosmochimica Acta — Geochim Cosmochim Acta
Geochimica et Cosmochimica Acta — Geochim et Cosmochim Acta
Geochimica et Cosmochimica Acta. Supplement — GCASD
Geochimica et Cosmochimica Acta. Supplement — Geochim Cosmochim Acta Suppl
Geochimie Organique des Sediments Marins Profonds — Geochim Org Sediments Mar Profonds
Geochronique — GECHD
GEOCOME. Geological Congress of the Middle East. Papers — GEOCOME Geol Congr Middle East Pap
Geodaetische und Geophysikalische Veroeffentlichungen. Reihe III — Geodaet Geophys Veroeffentlichungen Reihe III
Geodaetisk Institut (Denmark). Meddelelse — Geod Inst (Den) Medd
Geodaetisk Institut. Meddelelse — Geod Inst Medd
Geodaetisk Institut. Meddelelse — Geodaet Inst Medd
Geodaetisk Institut. Meddelelse — GEOIM
Geodaetisk Institut. Skrifter — Geod Inst Skr
Geodaetisk Institut. Skrifter — GEOIS
Geodaetisk Instituts Skrifter — Geodaet Inst Skrf
Geoderma — GEDMAB
Geodesy and Aerophotography [*Later, Geodesy, Mapping, and Photogrammetry*] **(USSR)** — Geod Aerophotogr (USSR)
Geodesy, Mapping, and Photogrammetry — Geod Mapp Photogramm
Geodesy, Mapping, and Photogrammetry — Geodes Mapp Photogramm
Geodesy, Mapping, and Photogrammetry. English Translation — Geod Mapp Photogramm Engl Transl
Geodetic Society of Japan. Journal — Geod Soc Jap J
Geodeticky a Kartograficky Obzor — Geod Kartogr Obzor
Geodetski List. Glasilo Saveza Geodeyskih Inzenjera i Geometara SFR Jugoslavija (Zagreb) — Geod List (Zagreb)
Geodezia es Kartografia — Geod Kartogr
Geodezia es Kartografia (Budapest) — Geod Kartogr (Budap)
Geodeziia, Kartografiia, i Aerofotos'emka [*Ukrainian SSR*] — Geod Kartogr Aerofotos
Geodeziia, Kartografiia, i Aerofotos'emka — GKAEA
Geodezija i Kartografija — GK
Geodezijos Darbai [*Lithuanian SSR*] — Geod Darb
Geodinamicheskie Issledovaniya — Geodin Issled
Geodynamic Researches — Geodyn Res
Geoexploration — Geoexplor
Geoexploration Monographs — Geoexplor Monogr
Geofisica e Meteorologia — Geofis Met
Geofisica e Meteorologia — Geofis Meteorol
Geofisica International — Geofis Int
Geofisica Pura e Applicata — Geofis Pur Appl
Geofisica Pura e Applicata [*Italy*] — Geofis Pura Appl
Geofizicheskaya Apparatura [*Former USSR*] — Geofiz App
Geofizicheskaya Apparatura — Geofiz Appar
Geofizicheskaya Razvedka — Geofiz Razved
Geofizicheskie Issledovaniya — Geofiz Issled
Geofizicheskie Issledovaniya pri Reshenii Geologicheskikh Zadach v Vostochnoi Sibri — Geofiz Issled Reshenii Geol Zadach Vost Sib
Geofizicheskie Metody Poiskov i Razvedki Rudnykh i Nerudnykh Mestorozhdenii — Geofiz Metody Poiskov Razved Rudn Nerudn Mestorozhd
Geofizicheskie Metody Razvedki v Arktike — Geofiz Metody Razved Arkt
Geofizicheskii Byulleten [*Former USSR*] — Geofiz Byull
Geofizicheskii Byulleten (Budapest) — Geofiz Byull (Budapest)
Geofizicheskii Sbornik — Geofiz Sb
Geofizicheskii Sbornik. Akademiya Nauk Ukrainskoi SSR. Institut Geofiziki [*Ukrainian SSR*] — Geofiz Sb Akad Nauk Ukr SSR Inst Geofiz
Geofizicheskii Sbornik. Akademiya Nauk Ukrainskoi SSR. Institut Geofiziki — GFZSA
Geofizicheskii Sbornik (Kiev) [*Ukrainian SSR*] — Geofiz Sb (Kiev)
Geofizicheskii Sbornik (Sverdlovsk) — Geofiz Sb (Sverdlovsk)
Geofizicheskii Zhurnal [*Ukrainian SSR*] — Geofiz Zh
Geofizicheskii Zhurnal — GEZHD
Geofizicheskoe Priborostroenie — Geofiz Priborostr
Geofizika i Astronomiya Informatsionnyi Byulleten — GEASA
Geofizika i Astronomiya Informatsionnyi Byulleten [*Ukrainian SSR*] — Geofiz Astron Inf Byull
Geofizikai Koeslemenyek — Geofiz Koeslemenyek
Geofizikai Koezlemenyek — Geof Koezl
Geofizikai Koezlemenyek — Geofiz Kozl
Geofizikai Koezlemenyek — Geofiz Kozlemenyek
Geofizyka i Geologia Naftowa [*Poland*] — Geofiz Geol Naft
Geoforum — GEFO
Geoforum — GEOF
Geofysikalni Sbornik — Geofys Sb
Geofysiske Publikasjoner — Geof Publ
Geofysiske Publikasjoner — Geofys Publ
Geognostische Jahreshefte — GeogJh
Geografia — GEOG
Geograficeskij Sbornik — Geogr Sb
Geograficeskij Sbornik — Geogr Sborn
Geograficheskii Ezhegodnik — Geogr Ezheg
Geograficheskii Sbornik Penzenskogo Otdeleniya Geograficheskogo Obshchestva SSSR — Geogr Sb Penz Otd Geogr Ova SSSR
Geograficheskii Sbornik Penzenskogo Otdeleniya Geograficheskogo Obshchestva SSSR — GSPGAF
Geograficheskoe Obshchestvo SSSR Doklady — Geogr Ovo SSSR Dokl
Geografija ir Geologija — Geogr Geol
Geografinis Metrastis — Geogr Metrastis
Geografisch Tijdschrift — Geogr Tijdschr
Geografisch Tijdschrift — Geogr Tjds
Geografisch Tijdschrift. Nieuwe Reeks — GET

Geografisk Tidsskrift — Geog Tidsskr
Geografisk Tidsskrift — Geogr T
Geografisk Tidsskrift — Geogr Tidsskrift
Geografisk Tidsskrift — GETD
Geografisk Tidsskrift — Ggr T
Geografisk Tidsskrift — GGTI-A
Geografisk Tidsskrift — GT
Geografiska Annaler — Geog Annaler
Geografiska Annaler — Geogr A
Geografiska Annaler — Geogr Ann
Geografiska Annaler — Geogr Annlr
Geografiska Annaler. A. Physical Geography — Geogr Ann Phys Geogr
Geografiska Annaler. B. Human Geography — Geogr Ann Hum Geogr
Geografiska Annaler. Series A — GGFA
Geografiska Annaler. Series B. Human Geography — GAHGAJ
Geografiska Annaler. Series B. Human Geography — Geogr Ann B
Geografiska Annaler. Series B. Human Geography — Geogr Ann Ser B Hum Geogr
Geografiske Casopis — Geogr Cas
Geografiya Ezhegodnogo Geograficheskogo Obshchestva Litovskoi SSR — Geogr Ezheg Geogr Ova Lit SSR
Geografiya Raka v Turkmenii — Geogr Raka Turkm
Geografiya v Shkole [*Former USSR*] — Geogr Shk
Geografski Glasnik — Geogr Glas
Geografski Glasnik — Geogr Glasn
Geografski Pregled — Geogr Pregl
Geografski Vestnik — Geogr Vestn
Geographe Canadien — Geogr Can
Geographi Graeci Minores — Geog Gr Min
Geographi Graeci Minores — Geog Graec Min
Geographi Graeci Minores — GGM
Geographi Latini Minores — Geog Lat Min
Geographi Latini Minores — GLM
Geographia — Geogr
Geographia Medica — Geogr Med
Geographia Medica — GMDCB4
Geographia Polonica — Geogr Pol
Geographic Cross-Reference Data [*Database*] — GEOBASE
Geographic Data File [*Database*] — GDF
Geographic Names Information System [*Database*] — GNIS
Geographic Society of Chicago. Bulletin — Geog Soc Chicago B
Geographica — Geogr
Geographica Helvetica — Geogr Helv
Geographica Helvetica — GgHv
Geographica Helvetica — GGHVA4
Geographica Helvetica — GH
Geographica (Lisbon) — GeoL
Geographical Abstracts — GA
Geographical Abstracts — Geo Abstr
Geographical Abstracts — GeoAb
Geographical Abstracts — Geogr Abstr
Geographical Abstracts — Geogrl Abstr
Geographical Analysis — GeAn
Geographical Analysis — Geogr Anal
Geographical Bulletin — Geog Bul
Geographical Bulletin — Geogr B
Geographical Bulletin (Budapest) — Geogr Bull Budapest
Geographical Education — Geogr Educ
Geographical Journal — GegJ
Geographical Journal — GEJO
Geographical Journal — Geog J
Geographical Journal — Geog Jnl
Geographical Journal — Geogr J
Geographical Journal — Geogr Journ
Geographical Journal — Geogrl J
Geographical Journal — GGGJ
Geographical Journal — GGJO-A
Geographical Journal — GJ
Geographical Journal (London) — Geogr J (Lond)
Geographical Journal (London) — Geogr Jour
Geographical Journal. Royal Geographical Society of London — Geogr J London
Geographical Knowledge (Peking) — Geogr Knowl (Peking)
Geographical Magazine — GeM
Geographical Magazine — GEMA
Geographical Magazine — Geog M
Geographical Magazine — Geog Mag
Geographical Magazine — GgMa
Geographical Magazine — GGMA-A
Geographical Magazine — GM
Geographical Magazine — IGMA
Geographical Magazine (London) — Geogr Mag (Lond)
Geographical Observer — GeOb
Geographical Outlook — GO
Geographical Paper. Canada Department of Environment — GEPACDE
Geographical Review — GegR
Geographical Review — Geog R
Geographical Review — Geog Rev
Geographical Review — Geogr R
Geographical Review — Geogr Rev
Geographical Review — Geogrl Rev
Geographical Review — GeoR
Geographical Review — GEORAD
Geographical Review — GR
Geographical Review — PGER
Geographical Review. American Geographical Society — AGS/GR
Geographical Review (New York) — Geogr Rev (New York)
Geographical Review (New York) — Geogr Rev NY
Geographical Review of India — Geog R Ind
Geographical Review of India — Geogr RI
Geographical Review of India — GRI
Geographical Review of India — GRIN-A
Geographical Review of Japan — Geogr Rev Jap
Geographical Section. General Staff. War Office [*London*] — GSGS
Geographical Society of Philadelphia. Bulletin — Geog Soc Phila
Geographical Society of Philadelphia. Bulletin — Geog Soc Phila B
Geographical Studies — Geogr Stud
Geographical Teacher — Geogr Tchr
Geographie et Recherche — Geogr Et Rech
Geographie et Recherche — Georgr et Rech
Geographie Physique et Quaternaire — Geog Phys et Quat
Geographische Berichte — Geogr Ber
Geographische en Geologische Mededelingen, Physiographisch Geologische Reeks, Geographisch Instituut (Utrecht) — Geogr Geol Meded Physiogr Geol Reeks Geogr Inst (Utrecht)
Geographische Gesellschaft in Hamburg. Mitteilungen — Geog Gesell Hamburg Mitt
Geographische Gesellschaft in Hamburg. Mitteilungen — Geogr Ges Hamb Mitt
Geographische Gesellschaft in Muenchen. Jahresbericht — Geog Ges Muenchen Jber
Geographische Gesellschaft in Wien — Geog Gesell In Wien Mitt
Geographische Informationen — Geogr Inf
Geographische Rundschau — Geog Rdsch
Geographische Rundschau — Geog Rund
Geographische Rundschau — Geogr Rdsch
Geographische Rundschau — Geogr Rundsch
Geographische Rundschau — GgRu
Geographische Rundschau — GR
Geographische Schriften — Geogr Schriften
Geographische Wochenschrift (Leipzig) — GWL
Geographische Zeitschrift — Geog Z
Geographische Zeitschrift — Geogr Z
Geographische Zeitschrift — Geogr Ztschr
Geographische Zeitschrift — Ggr Z
Geographische Zeitschrift — GZ
Geographischer Anzeiger — GA
Geographischer Anzeiger — GAnz
Geographischer Anzeiger — Geogr Anz
Geographischer Jahresbericht aus Oesterreich — Geogr Jber Oesterr
Geographisches Jahrbuch — Geogr Jahrb
Geographisches Jahrbuch — Geogr Jb
Geographisches Jahrbuch — GJ
Geographisches Jahrbuch — GJb
Geographisches Jahrbuch aus Oesterreich — Geogr Jb Oester
Geographisches Taschenbuch — Geogr TB
Geography [*London*] — G
Geography — Geogr
Geography — GGHY-A
Geography — GGHYAD
Geography — GY
Geography — PGEO
Geography and Map Division Bulletin [*Special Libraries Association*] — Geog Map Div Bull
Geography of the Hittite Empire — GHE
Geography Teacher — Geogr Teach
Geo-Heat Center. Quarterly Bulletin — GCQBD
Geo-Heat Center. Quarterly Bulletin [*United States*] — Geo Heat Cent Q Bull
Geo-Heat Utilization Center. Quarterly Bulletin [*United States*] — Geo-Heat Util Cent Q Bull
Geo-Heat Utilization Center. Quarterly Bulletin — Geo-Heat Util Center Q Bull
Geojournal — GEOJDQ
Geokhimicheskie Issledovaniya — Geokhim Issled
Geokhimicheskie Metody Poiskov. Nefti i Gaza — Geokhim Metody Poiskov Nefti Gaza
Geokhimicheskie Metody pri Poiskakh i Razvedke Rudnykh Mestorozhdenii — Geokhim Metody Poiskakh Razved Rudn Mestorozhd
Geokhimicheskii Sbornik — Geokhim Sb
Geokhimicheskii Sbornik — GKSBA
Geokhimiya — Geokhim
Geokhimiya Akademiya Nauk (SSSR) — Geokhim Akad Nauk (SSSR)
Geokhimiya Elementov i Soedinenii v Pochvakh — Geokhim Elem Soedin Pochvakh
Geokhimiya i Rudoobrazovanie — Geokhim Rudoobraz
Geokhimiya, Mineralogiya, i Petrologiya — Geokhim Mineral Petrol
Geokhimiya, Mineralogiya, Petrografiya — Geokhim Mineral Petrogr
Geokhimiya Nefti i Neftyanykh Mestorozhdenii — Geokhim Nefti Neft Mestorozhd
Geokhimiya Osadochnykh Porod i Rud. Materialy Vsesoyuznoi Litologicheskoi Konferentsii — Geokhim Osad Porod Rud Mater Vses Litol Konf
Geokhimiya v Chekhoslovakii. Trudy Geokhimicheskoi Konferentsii — Geokhim Chekh Tr Geokhim Konf
Geologi [*Helsinki*] — GEOHAH
Geologia Applicata e Idrogeologia — Geol Appl Idrogeol
Geologia Colombiana — Geol Colomb
Geologia e Metalurgia. Boletim — Geol Metal Bol
Geologia e Metalurgia. Boletim. Escola Politecnica. Universidade de Sao Paulo — Geol Met Bol
Geologia e Metalurgia (Sao Paulo) — Geol Metal (Sao Paulo)
Geologia Sudetica — Geol Sudetica
Geologia Sudetica [*Warsaw*] — GLSDA6
Geologia Sudetica (Warsaw) — Geol Sudetica (Warsaw)

Geologia Tecnica — Geol Tec
Geologia y Metalurgia [*Bolivia*] — Geol Metal
Geologia y Metalurgia (San Luis Potosi) — Geol Metal (San Luis Potosi)
Geologia y Recursos Naturales del Neuquen, Relatorio. Congreso Geologico Argentino — Geol Recur Nat Neuquen Relat Congr Geol Argent
Geologic Atlas of Pennsylvania — Geol Atlas PA
Geologic Index — Geol Ind
Geologic Map and Mineral Resources. Summary (State of Tennessee) — Geol Map Miner Resour Summ (State Tennessee)
Geologic Map. Deputy Ministry for Mineral Resources (Kingdom of Saudi Arabia) — Geol Map Deputy Minist Miner Resour (Saudi Arabia)
Geologic Map GM. Saudi Arabia. Directorate General of Mineral Resources — Geol Map GM Saudi Arabia Dir Gen Miner Resour
Geologic Map. Montana Bureau of Mines and Geology — Geol Map Montana Bur Mines Geol
Geologic Notes. South Carolina Geological Survey — Geol Notes SC Geol Surv
Geologic Report. Alaska — Geol Rep Alaska
Geologic Report. State of Alaska Department of Natural Resources — Geol Rep State Alaska Dep Nat Resour
Geologica Balcanica — GEBAD2
Geologica Balcanica — Geol Balc
Geologica Balcanica. Bulgarska Akademiya ne Naukite (Sofia) — Geol Balc (Sofia)
Geologica Bavarica — GEBAAX
Geologica Bavarica — Geol Bav
Geologica Bavarica — Geol Bavar
Geologica Bavarica — Geol Bavarica
Geologica Carpathica — Geol Carpathica
Geologica et Palaeontologica — Geol Palaeontol
Geologica Hungarica — Geol Hung
Geologica Hungarica. Series Palaeontologica — Geol Hung Ser Palaeontol
Geologica Hungarica. Series Palaeontologica — GHPADP
Geologica Romana — Geol Rom
Geologica Romana — Geol Roman
Geologica Romana — GROMAL
Geologica Ultriectina — Geol Ultriectina
Geological Abstracts — Geol Abstr
Geological and Mining Society of American Universities. Year Book and Directory — G M Soc Am Univ Y Bk
Geological and Mining Survey of Iran. Report — Geol Min Surv Iran Rep
Geological and Scientific Bulletin — G Sc B
Geological Association of Canada — Geol Assoc Can
Geological Association of Canada. Cordilleran Section. Programme and Abstracts — Geol Assoc Can Cordilleran Sect Programme Abstr
Geological Association of Canada. Proceedings — Geol Assoc Can Proc
Geological Association of Canada. Proceedings — Geol Assoc Canada Proc
Geological Association of Canada. Special Paper — GASPBY
Geological Association of Canada. Special Paper — Geol Assoc Can Spec Pap
Geological Bulletin. Florida. Bureau of Geology — Geol Bull Fla Bur Geol
Geological Bulletin. Geological Survey of China — Geol Bull Geol Surv China
Geological Bulletin. National Geological Survey of China [*People's Republic of China*] — Geol Bull Natl Geol Surv China
Geological Bulletin. Punjab University — GBPUA6
Geological Bulletin. Punjab University — Geol Bull Punjab Univ
Geological Bulletin. University of Peshawar — Geol Bull Univ Peshawar
Geological Center. Research Series — Geol Center Research Ser
Geological Circular. Ontario. Department of Mines — Geol Circ Ont Dep Mines
Geological Circular. University of Texas at Austin. Bureau of Economic Geology — Geol Circ Univ Tex Austin Bur Econ Geol
Geological Correlation [*Paris*] — Geol Correl
Geological Investigation Series. Geological Survey of Pakistan. Interim Geological Report — Geol Invest Ser Geol Surv Pak Interim Geol Rep
Geological Journal — Geol J
Geological Journal (Kiev) — Geol J Kiev
Geological Journal (Liverpool) — Geol J (Liverpool)
Geological Journal of Queen Mary College — Geol J Queen Mary Coll
Geological Journal of Universities — Geol J Univ
Geological Magazine — G Mag
Geological Magazine — GEMGA4
Geological Magazine — Geol M
Geological Magazine — Geol Mag
Geological Magazine (London) — GML
Geological Memoirs. Geological Survey of China. Series A — Geol Mem Geol Surv China Ser A
Geological Memoirs. Geological Survey of China. Series B — Geol Mem Geol Surv China Ser B
Geological, Mining, and Metallurgical Society of India. Quarterly Journal — Geol Min Metall Soc India Q J
Geological, Mining, and Metallurgical Society of Liberia. Bulletin — Geol Min Met Soc Liberia Bull
Geological, Mining, and Metallurgical Society of Liberia. Bulletin — Geol Min Metall Soc Liberia Bull
Geological Notes and Local Details for 1:10,000 Sheets. Institute of Geological Sciences [*Keyworth*] — Geol Notes Local Details 1:10000 Sheets Inst Geol Sci
Geological Paper. Carleton University. Department of Geology — Geol Pap Carleton Univ Dep Geol
Geological Paper. Mineral Resources Division (Manitoba) — Geol Pap Miner Resour Div (Manitoba)
Geological Papers. Geological Survey of Malaysia — Geol Pap Geol Surv Malaysia
Geological Report. Hiroshima University — Geol Rep Hiroshima Univ
Geological Report. Hiroshima University — HIRDAP
Geological Report. Mineral Resources Division (Manitoba) — Geol Rep Miner Resour Div (Manitoba)
Geological Report on Coal Fields of Korea — Geol Rep Coal Fields Korea
Geological Report. Quebec. Department of Natural Resources — Geol Rep Que Dep Nat Resour
Geological Reports. Department of Natural Resources (Quebec) — Geol Rep Dep Nat Resour (Queb)
Geological Reports. Shimane University — Geol Rep Shimane Univ
Geological Research and Development Centre. Bulletin (Bandung, Indonesia) — Geol Res Dev Cent Bull Bandung Indones
Geological Review (Beijing) — Geol Rev (Beijing)
Geological Science and Technology Information — Geol Sci Technol Inf
Geological Science (Beijing) — Geol Sci (Beijing)
Geological Section. Bulletin. Libya Ministry of Industry — Geol Sect Bull Libya Minist Ind
Geological Society Miscellaneous Paper (London) — Geol Soc Misc Pap London
Geological Society. Newsletter (London) — Geol Soc (Lond) Newsl
Geological Society of America — Geol Soc Amer
Geological Society of America. Abstracts with Programs — Geol Soc Am Abstr Programs
Geological Society of America. Abstracts with Programs — Geol Soc America Abs with Programs
Geological Society of America. Annual Meeting. Field Trip Guidebook — Geol Soc Am Annu Meet Field Trip Guideb
Geological Society of America. Bulletin — BUGMAF
Geological Society of America. Bulletin — G Soc Am B
Geological Society of America. Bulletin — Geol S Am B
Geological Society of America Bulletin — Geol Soc Am
Geological Society of America. Bulletin — Geol Soc Am Bull
Geological Society of America. Bulletin — Geol Soc Amer Bull
Geological Society of America. Bulletin — Geol Soc Bull
Geological Society of America. Bulletin — IGSA
Geological Society of America. Cordilleran Section. Annual Meeting Guidebook — Geol Soc Am Cordilleran Sect Annu Meet Guideb
Geological Society of America. Engineering Geology Case Histories — Geol Soc Amer Eng Geol Case Hist
Geological Society of America. Map and Chart Series — Geol Soc Am Map Chart Ser
Geological Society of America. Memoir — Geol Soc Am Mem
Geological Society of America. Memoir — Geol Soc Amer Mem
Geological Society of America. Memoir — GSAMAQ
Geological Society of America. Microform Publication — Geol Soc Am Microform Publ
Geological Society of America. Proceedings — Geol Soc Am Proc
Geological Society of America. Proceedings — Geol Soc Proc
Geological Society of America. Southeastern Section Guidebook — Geol Soc Am Southeast Sect Guideb
Geological Society of America. Special Paper — Geol Soc Am Spec Pap
Geological Society of America. Special Paper — Geol Soc Amer Spec Pap
Geological Society of America. Special Paper (Regional Studies) — Geol Soc Am Spec Pap (Reg Stud)
Geological Society of America. Special Paper (Regional Studies) — GSAPAZ
Geological Society of America. Special Papers — Geol Soc America Spec Paper
Geological Society of Australia. Journal — Geol Soc Australia J
Geological Society of Australia. Special Publication — Geol Soc Aust Spec Publ
Geological Society of China. Proceedings — Geol Soc China Proc
Geological Society of Dublin. Journal — G Soc Dublin J
Geological Society of Dublin. Journal — Geol Soc Dublin J
Geological Society of Egypt. Annual Meeting. Abstracts — Geol Soc Egypt Annu Meet Abstr
Geological Society of Finland. Bulletin — Geol Soc Finl Bull
Geological Society of Glasgow. Transactions — G Soc Glas Tr
Geological Society of Greece. Bulletin — Geol Soc Greece Bull
Geological Society of India. Bulletin — Geol Soc India Bull
Geological Society of India. Bulletin — GSIBAX
Geological Society of India. Journal — Geol Soc India J
Geological Society of India. Journal — Geol Soc India Jour
Geological Society of India. Memoir — Geol Soc India Mem
Geological Society of Iraq. Journal — Geol Soc Iraq J
Geological Society of Jamaica. Journal — Geol Soc Jam J
Geological Society of Japan. Journal — Geol Soc Jap J
Geological Society of Japan. Memoir — Geol Soc Jpn Mem
Geological Society of Korea. Journal — Geol Soc Korea J
Geological Society of London. Journal — Geol Soc Lond J
Geological Society of London. Memoirs — Geol Soc London Mem
Geological Society of London. Miscellaneous Paper — Geol Soc Lond Misc Pap
Geological Society of London. Quarterly Journal — Geol Soc Lond Q J
Geological Society of London. Special Publication — Geol Soc London Spec Publ
Geological Society of London. Special Report — Geol Soc Lond Spec Rep
Geological Society of London. Transactions. Proceedings. Quarterly Journal — G Soc London Tr Pr Q J
Geological Society of Malaysia. Bulletin — Geol Soc Malays Bull
Geological Society of Malaysia. Bulletin — GSMBBK
Geological Society of Malaysia. Newsletter — Geol Soc Malays Newsl
Geological Society of Malaysia. Newsletter — GSMNBM
Geological Society of New Jersey. Report — Geol Soc NJ Rept
Geological Society of New Zealand. Newsletter — Geol Soc NZ Newsl
Geological Society of Norfolk. Bulletin — Geol Soc Norfolk Bull
Geological Society of Pennsylvania. Transactions — G Soc PA Tr
Geological Society of South Africa. Congress Abstracts — Geol Soc S Afr Congr Abstr
Geological Society of South Africa. Quarterly News Bulletin — Geol Soc S Afr Q News Bull
Geological Society of South Africa. Quarterly News Bulletin — GSQNA
Geological Society of South Africa. Special Publication — Geol Soc S Afr Spec Publ
Geological Society of South Africa. Transactions — Geol Soc S Afr Trans

Geological Society of South Africa. Transactions and Proceedings — Geol Soc So Africa Trans
Geological Society of the Oregon Country. News Letter — Geol Soc Oregon Country News Letter
Geological Society of the Philippines. Journal — Geol Soc Philipp J
Geological Society of Tokyo. Journal — G Soc Tokyo J
Geological Society of Zimbabwe. Special Publication — Geol Soc Zimbabwe Spec Publ
Geological Society Special Publication — Geol Soc Spec Publ
Geological Survey. Borneo Region. Malaysia. Memoir — Geol Surv Borneo Reg Malays Mem
Geological Survey. Borneo Region. Malaysia. Report — Geol Surv Borneo Reg Malays Rep
Geological Survey Bulletin (United States) — Geol Surv Bull (US)
Geological Survey Circular — Geol Surv Circ
Geological Survey Circular (United States) — Geol Surv Circ US
Geological Survey Department. British Territories in Borneo. Report — Geol Surv Dep Br Territ Borneo Rep
Geological Survey Department. Economic Report (Zambia) — Geol Surv Dep Econ Rep (Zambia)
Geological Survey Department. Federation of Malaya. Memoir — Geol Surv Dep Fed Malaya Mem
Geological Survey Department (Jamaica, West Indies). Bulletin — Geol Surv Dep (Jam) Bull
Geological Survey Department (Jamaica, West Indies). Occasional Paper — Geol Surv Dep (Jam West Indies) Occas Pap
Geological Survey. East Malaysia. Report — Geol Surv East Malays Rep
Geological Survey of Alabama. Circular — Geol Surv Ala Circ
Geological Survey of Alabama. Special Report — Geol Surv Ala Spec Rep
Geological Survey of Botswana. District Memoir — Geol Surv Botswana Dist Mem
Geological Survey of British Guiana. Bulletin — Geol Surv Br Guiana Bull
Geological Survey of Canada. Bulletin — CMGEA
Geological Survey of Canada. Bulletin — CMGEAE
Geological Survey of Canada. Bulletin — Geol Surv Can Bull
Geological Survey of Canada. Bulletin — GSC Bul
Geological Survey of Canada. Bulletin — GSCB
Geological Survey of Canada. Economic Geology Report — Geol Surv Can Ec Geol Rep
Geological Survey of Canada. Economic Geology Report — Geol Surv Can Econ Geol Rep
Geological Survey of Canada. Memoir — Geol Surv Can Mem
Geological Survey of Canada. Memoir — GSCM
Geological Survey of Canada. Paper — CGCPA
Geological Survey of Canada. Paper — CGCPAJ
Geological Survey of Canada. Paper — Geol Surv Can Pap
Geological Survey of Canada. Paper — GSCP
Geological Survey of Ceylon. Memoir — Geol Surv Ceylon Mem
Geological Survey of Denmark. II Series — DGUBAA
Geological Survey of Denmark. II Series — Geol Surv Den II Ser
Geological Survey of Denmark. III Series — DGUCAD
Geological Survey of Denmark. III Series — Geol Surv Den III Ser
Geological Survey of Denmark. Report — DGURBP
Geological Survey of Denmark. Report — Geol Surv Den Rep
Geological Survey of Denmark. Serie A — DGUADA
Geological Survey of Denmark. Serie A — Geol Surv Den Ser A
Geological Survey of Denmark. Serie B — DGUBDD
Geological Survey of Denmark. Serie B — Geol Surv Den Ser B
Geological Survey of Denmark. Yearbook — DGUAB8
Geological Survey of Denmark. Yearbook — Geol Surv Den Yearb
Geological Survey of Egypt. Annals — Geol Surv Egypt Ann
Geological Survey of Fiji. Bulletin — Geol Surv Fiji Bull
Geological Survey of Finland. Bulletin — Geol Surv Finl Bull
Geological Survey of Finland. Bulletin — GSFB
Geological Survey of Finland. Bulletin — GSFNAK
Geological Survey of Georgia. Bulletin — Geol Surv GA Bull
Geological Survey of Georgia. Information Circular — Geol Surv Ga Inf Circ
Geological Survey of Great Britain Bulletin — Geol Surv GB Bull
Geological Survey of Great Britain. Handbooks. British Regional Geology — Geol Surv GB Handb B Reg Geol
Geological Survey of Great Britain. Memoirs. Geological Survey of Great Britain, England, and Wales — Geol Surv GB Mem Geol Surv GB Engl Wales
Geological Survey of Great Britain. Memoirs of the Geological Survey (Scotland) — Geol Surv GB Mem Geol Surv (Scotl)
Geological Survey of Greenland. Report — Geol Surv Greenl Rep
Geological Survey of Greenland. Report — Geol Surv Greenland Rep
Geological Survey of Guyana. Bulletin — Geol Surv Guyana Bull
Geological Survey of India. Bulletins. Series B. Engineering Geology and Ground-Water — Geol Surv India Bull Ser B
Geological Survey of India. Miscellaneous Publication — Geol Surv India Misc Publ
Geological Survey of India. News — Geol Surv India News
Geological Survey of India. Records — Geol Surv India Rec
Geological Survey of India. Special Publication Series — Geol Surv India Spec Publ Ser
Geological Survey of Indonesia. Publikasi Teknik. Seri Geologi Ekonomi — Geol Surv Indones Publ Tek Seri Geol Ekon
Geological Survey of Indonesia. Special Publication — Geol Surv Indones Spec Publ
Geological Survey of Iowa. Water-Supply Bulletin — Geol Surv Iowa Water Supply Bull
Geological Survey of Iran. Report — Geol Surv Iran Rep
Geological Survey of Ireland. Bulletin — Geol Surv Ir Bull
Geological Survey of Ireland. Bulletin — Geol Surv Irel Bull
Geological Survey of Ireland. Information Circular — Geol Surv Ir Info Circular
Geological Survey of Israel. Bulletin — Geol Surv Isr Bull
Geological Survey of Japan. Hydrogeological Maps of Japan — Geol Surv Jap Hydrogeol Maps Jap
Geological Survey of Japan. Report — Geol Surv Jap Rep
Geological Survey of Japan. Report — Geol Surv Jpn Rep
Geological Survey of Japan. Special Report — Geol Surv Jpn Spec Rep
Geological Survey of Kenya. Bulletin — Geol Surv Kenya Bull
Geological Survey of Kenya. Report — Geol Surv Kenya Rep
Geological Survey of Korea. Geological Reports on Coal Fields of Korea — Geol Surv Korea Geol Rep Coal Fields Korea
Geological Survey of Korea. Report of Geophysical and Geochemical Exploration — Geol Surv Korea Rep Geophys Geochem Explor
Geological Survey of Korea. Technical Paper — Geol Surv Korea Tech Pap
Geological Survey of Malaysia. Annual Report — Geol Surv Malays Annu Rep
Geological Survey of Malaysia. Annual Report — MGSACU
Geological Survey of Malaysia. District Memoir — Geol Surv Malays Dist Mem
Geological Survey of Malaysia. District Memoir — GSMMBJ
Geological Survey of Malaysia. Geological Papers — Geol Surv Malays Geol Pap
Geological Survey of Malaysia. Geological Papers — GSMPAR
Geological Survey of New South Wales. Bulletin — Geol Surv NSW Bull
Geological Survey of New South Wales. Department of Mines. The Mineral Industry of New South Wales — Geol Surv of NSW Miner Ind NSW
Geological Survey of New South Wales. Geological Survey Report — Geol Surv NSW Geol Surv Rep
Geological Survey of New South Wales. Geological Survey Report — Geol Surv NSW Rep
Geological Survey of New South Wales. Mineral Resources — Geol Surv NSW Miner Resour
Geological Survey of New South Wales. Records — Geol Surv NSW Rec
Geological Survey of Nigeria. Bulletin — Geol Surv Nigeria Bull
Geological Survey of Ohio. Information Circular — Geol Surv Ohio Inf Circ
Geological Survey of Pakistan. Interim Geological Report — Geol Surv Pak Interim Geol Rep
Geological Survey of Papua New Guinea. Report — Geol Surv Papua New Guinea Rep
Geological Survey of Queensland. Publication — Geol Surv Queensl Pub
Geological Survey of Queensland. Publication — Geol Surv Queensl Publ
Geological Survey of Queensland. Report — Geol Surv Queensl Rep
Geological Survey of Sierra Leone. Bulletin — Geol Surv Sierra Leone Bull
Geological Survey of South Australia. Bulletin — Bull Geol Surv South Aust
Geological Survey of South Australia. Bulletin — Geol Surv South Aust Bull
Geological Survey of South Australia. Report of Investigations — Geol Surv South Aust Rep Invest
Geological Survey of Tanzania. Bulletin — Geol Surv Tanzania Bull
Geological Survey of Tasmania. Bulletin — Bull Geol Surv Tas
Geological Survey of Tasmania. Bulletin — Bull Geol Surv Tasm
Geological Survey of Uganda. Memoir — Geol Surv Uganda Mem
Geological Survey of Uganda. Report — Geol Surv Uganda Rep
Geological Survey of Victoria. Bulletin — Bull Geol Surv Vic
Geological Survey of Victoria. Bulletin — Bull Geol Surv Vict
Geological Survey of Victoria. Bulletin — Geol Surv Victoria Bull
Geological Survey of Victoria. Memoir — Geol Surv Victoria Mem
Geological Survey of Victoria. Memoir — MGSVAN
Geological Survey of West Malaysia. District Memoir — Geol Surv West Malaysia Dist Mem
Geological Survey of West Malaysia. Economic Bulletin — Geol Surv West Malays Econ Bull
Geological Survey of Western Australia. Annual Report — Geol Surv West Aust Annu Rep
Geological Survey of Western Australia. Bulletin — Geol Surv W Aust Bull
Geological Survey of Western Australia. Report — Geol Surv West Aust Rep
Geological Survey of Wyoming. Bulletin — Geol Surv Wyo Bull
Geological Survey of Wyoming. County Resource Series — Geol Surv Wyo C Resour Ser
Geological Survey of Wyoming. Memoir — Geol Surv Wyo Mem
Geological Survey of Wyoming. Preliminary Report — Geol Surv Wyo Prelim Rep
Geological Survey of Wyoming. Public Information Circular — Geol Surv Wyo Public Inf Circ
Geological Survey of Wyoming. Report of Investigations — Geol Surv Wyo Rep Invest
Geological Survey Open-File Report [*United States*] — GSORD
Geological Survey Open-File Report (United States) — Geol Surv Open File Rep (US)
Geological Survey Paper. Department of Mines. Tasmania — Geol Surv Pap Tas Dep Mines
Geological Survey Professional Paper (United States) — Geol Surv Prof Pap (US)
Geological Survey Record. Tasmania — Geol Surv Rec Tasmania
Geological Survey Report. Department of Mines (New South Wales) — Geol Surv Rep Dep Mines (NSW)
Geological Survey. Water-Supply Paper — Geol Surv Water Supply Pap
Geologicheskaya Izuchennost SSR — Geol Izuch SSR
Geologicheskaya Literatura SSSR Bibliograficheskiy Yezhegodnik — Geol Lit SSSR Bibliogr Yezhegodnik
Geologicheskii Sbornik — Geol Sbornik
Geologicheskii Sbornik (Lvov) — Geol Sb (Lvov)
Geologicheskii Sbornik (Moscow) — Geol Sb Moscow
Geologicheskii Sbornik (Tiflis) — Geol Sb (Tiflis)
Geologicheskii Sbornik Vsesoyuznogo Instituta Nauchno Tekhnologicheskoi Informatsii — Geol Sb Vses Inst Nauchno Tekhnol Inf
Geologicheskii Zhurnal [*Kiev*] — Geol Zh
Geologicheskii Zhurnal (Russian Edition) — Geol Zh (Russ Ed)

Geologicheskoe Stroenie i Poleznye Iskopaemye Kalmytskoi ASSR — Geol Str Poleznye Iskop Kalmytskoi ASSR
Geologicheskoe Stroenie i Poleznye Iskopaemye Nizhnego Povolzh'ya — Geol Str Polezn Iskop Nizhnego Povolzhya
Geologichnii Zhurnal (Ukrainian Edition) — Geol Zh (Ukr Ed)
Geologicke Prace — Geol Pr
Geologicke Prace [*Bratislava*] — GEOPA7
Geologicke Prace (Bratislava) — Geol Pr (Bratisl)
Geologicke Prace. Zpravy — Geol Prace Zpr
Geologicky Pricskum — Geol Pricskum
Geologicky Pruzkum — Geol Pruzkum
Geologicky Pruzkum — GEYPA
Geologicky Pruzkum n.p. Ostrava. Sbornik — Geol Pruzkum np Ostrava Sb
Geologicky Sbornik (Bratislava) — Geol Sb Bratislava
Geologicky Zbornik — Geol Zb
Geologicky Zbornik [*Bratislava, Czechoslovakia*] — GESBA
Geologicky Zbornik — GESBAJ
Geologicky Zbornik - Geologica Carpathica — Geol Zb Geol Carpathica
Geologicky Zbornik - Geologica Carpathica. Slovenska Akademia Vied — Geol Zb Slov Akad Vied
Geologicnyj Zurnal/Journal of Geology — Geol Zurn
Geologie — Geol
Geologie Alpine — GALPBX
Geologie Alpine — Geol Alp
Geologie Appliquee et Prospection Miniere — Geol Appl Prospect Miniere
Geologie. Beihefte — Geol Beih
Geologie. Beihefte — Geologie Beih
Geologie. Bulletin de la Societe Belge de Geologie — Geol Bull Soc Belge Geol
Geologie de la France — Geol Fr
Geologie de l'Ingenieur — Geol Ing
Geologie des Gites Mineraux — Geol Gites Miner
Geologie en Mijnbouw — GEMIA
Geologie en Mijnbouw — GEMIAA
Geologie en Mijnbouw — Geol Mijnb
Geologie en Mijnbouw — Geol Mijnbouw
Geologie en Mijnbouw — Geologie Mijnb
Geologie Mediterraneenne — Geol Mediter
Geologie, Paleontologie, Hydrologie (Brussels) — Geol Paleontol Hydrol Brussels
Geologie und Bauwesen — Geol Bauwes
Geologiese Vereniging van Suid-Afrika. Kwartaallikse Nuusbulletin — Geol Ver S-Afr Kwart Nuusbull
Geologija — Geol
Geologija. Razprave in Porocila [*Ljubljana*] — Geol Razpr Porocila
Geologijos Institutas (Vilnius). Darbai — Geol Inst (Vilnius) Darb
Geologikai Anagnoriseis Ekthesis — Geol Anagoriseis Ekthesis
Geologikai kai Geofizikai Meletai — Geol Geofiz Meletai
Geologinen Tutkimuslaitos. Geoteknillisia Julkaisuja — Geol Tutkimuslaitos Geotek Julk
Geologisch Mijnbouwkundige Dienst van Suriname. Mededeling — Geol Mijnbouwkd Dienst Suriname Meded
Geologische Abhandlungen Hessen — GAHEDG
Geologische Abhandlungen Hessen — Geol Abh Hessen
Geologische Blaetter fuer Nordost-Bayern und Angrenzende Gebiete — GBNBA7
Geologische Blaetter fuer Nordost-Bayern und Angrenzende Gebiete — Geol Bl
Geologische Blaetter fuer Nordost-Bayern und Angrenzende Gebiete — Geol Bl Nordost-Bayern
Geologische Blaetter fuer Nordost-Bayern und Angrenzende Gebiete — Geol Bl Nordost-Bayern Angrenzende Geb
Geologische Blaetter fuer Nordost-Bayern und Angrenzende Gebiete — Geol Blaett Nordost Bayern
Geologische Mitteilungen — Geol Mitt
Geologische Reichs-Museum in Leiden. Sammlungen — G Reichs-Mus Leiden Samm
Geologische Rundschau — G Rundschau
Geologische Rundschau — Geol Rdsch
Geologische Rundschau — Geol Rundsch
Geologische Rundschau — Geol Rundschau
Geologische Rundschau — GeolR
Geologische Rundschau — GERUA
Geologische Stichting. Mededelingen. Nieuwe Serie (Netherlands) — Geol Sticht Meded Nieuwe Ser Neth
Geologische und Palaeontologische Abhandlungen — GPAbh
Geologische und Paleontologische Abhandlungen — G Pal Abh
Geologisches Archiv — Geol Arch
Geologisches Jahrbuch — GEJAA
Geologisches Jahrbuch — GEJAA5
Geologisches Jahrbuch — Geol Jahrb
Geologisches Jahrbuch — Geol Jb
Geologisches Jahrbuch. Beihefte — GEJBA8
Geologisches Jahrbuch. Beihefte — Geol Jahrb Beih
Geologisches Jahrbuch Hessen — Geol Jahrb Hessen
Geologisches Jahrbuch Hessen — GJHEDB
Geologisches Jahrbuch. Reihe A. Allgemeine und Regionale Geologie BR Deutschland und Nachbargebiete, Tektonik, Stratigraphie, Palaeontologie — Geol Jahrb Reihe A
Geologisches Jahrbuch. Reihe B. Regionale Geologie Ausland — Geol Jahrb Reihe B
Geologisches Jahrbuch. Reihe C. Hydrogeologie, Ingenieurgeologie [*Germany*] — Geol Jahrb Reihe C
Geologisches Jahrbuch. Reihe D. Mineralogie, Petrographie, Geochemie, Lagerstaettenkunde — Geol Jahrb Reihe D
Geologisches Jahrbuch. Reihe E. Geophysik [*Germany*] — Geol Jahrb Reihe E
Geologisches Jahrbuch. Reihe E. Geophysik — Geol Jahrb Reihe E Geophys
Geologisches Jahrbuch. Reihe F. Bodenkunde — Geol Jahr Reihe F
Geologisches Jahrbuch. Reihe F. Bodenkunde — Geol Jahrb Reihe F Bodenk
Geologisches Jahrbuch. Series A — Geol Jahrbuch Ser A
Geologisches Jahrbuch. Series B — Geol Jahrbuch Ser B
Geologisches Jahrbuch. Series C — Geol Jahrbuch Ser C
Geologisches Jahrbuch. Series D — Geol Jahrbuch Ser D
Geologisches Jarhbuch. Series E — Geol Jahrbuch Ser E
Geologisches Zentralblatt. Anzeiger fuer Geologie, Petrographie, Palaeontologie, und Verwandte Wissenschaften. Revue Geologique/ Geological Review/Rassegna Geologica — Geol Zentralbl
Geologiska Foereningens i Stockholm. Foerhandlingar — G Foeren Stockholm Foerh
Geologiska Foereningens i Stockholm. Foerhandlingar — Geol Foer Stockh Foerh
Geologiska Foereningens i Stockholm. Foerhandlingar — Geol Foeren St Foerh
Geologiska Foereningens i Stockholm. Foerhandlingar — Geol Foeren Stockh Foerh
Geologiska Foereningens i Stockholm. Foerhandlingar — GFF
Geologiska Foereningens i Stockholm. Foerhandlingar — GFSFA
Geologiska Foereningens i Stockholm. Foerhandlingar — GFSFA4
Geologist [*New York*] — GLGSA
Geologists' Association (London). Proceedings — G As (London) Pr
Geologists' Association (London). Proceedings — Geol Assoc (Lond) Proc
Geologists' Association (London). Proceedings — Geologists' Assoc (London) Proc
Geologiya, Gidrogeologiya, Poleznye Iskopaemye Belorussii i Metody Ikh Issledovaniya. Materialy Dokladov Nauchnoi Konferentsii Molodykh Geologov Belorussii — Geol Gidrogeol Polezn Iskop Beloruss Metody Ikh Issled Mater
Geologiya i Geofizika — Geol Geofiz
Geologiya i Geofizika — Geol i Geofiz
Geologiya i Geofizika — GGASA
Geologiya i Geokhimiya — Geol Geokhim
Geologiya i Geokhimiya Goryuchikh Iskopaemykh [*Ukrainian SSR*] — Geol Geokhim Goryuch Iskop
Geologiya i Geokhimiya Goryuchikh Iskopaemykh Akademiya Nauk Ukrain'skoi SSR — Geol Geokhim Goryuch Iskop Akad Nauk Ukr SSR
Geologiya i Geokhimiya Goryuchikh Kopalin — Geol Geokhim Goryuchikh Kopalin
Geologiya i Geokhimiya Goryuchikh Kopalin Akademiya Nauk Ukrain'skoi RSR — Geol Geokhim Goryuch Kopalin Akad Nauk Ukr RSR
Geologiya i Geokhimiya Mestorozhdenii Tverdykh Goryuchikh Iskopaemykh — Geol Geokhim Mestorozhd Tverd Goryuch Iskop
Geologiya i Geokhimiya Neftyanskh i Gazovykh Mestorozhdenii — Geol Geokhim Neft Gazov Mestorozhd
Geologiya i Mineralogiya — Geol Mineral
Geologiya i Neftegazonosnost Turkmenistana — Geol Neftegazonosn Turkm
Geologiya i Neftegazonosnost Turkmenistana — GNTUD
Geologiya i Poleznye Iskopaemye Kalmytskoi ASSR — Geol Polezn Iskop Kalmytskoi ASSR
Geologiya i Poleznye Iskopaemye Urala — Geol Polezn Iskop Urala
Geologiya i Poleznye Iskopaemye Zapadnogo Kazakhstana — Geol Polezn Iskop Zapadn Kaz
Geologiya i Poleznye Iskopaemye Zarubezhnykh Stran — Geol Polezn Iskop Zarub Stran
Geologiya i Razrabotka Gazovykh i Gazokondensatnykh Mestorozhdenii Ukrainy — Geol Razrab Gazov Gazokondens Mestorozhd Ukr
Geologiya i Razvedka — Geol Razved
Geologiya i Razvedka Gazovykh i Gazokondensatnykh Mestorozhdenii — Geol Razved Gazov Gazokondens Mestorozhd
Geologiya i Razvedka Gazovykh i Gazokondensatnykh Mestorozhdenii. Nauchno-Tekhnicheskii Obzor — Geol Razved Gazov Gazokondens Mestorozhd Nauchno Tekh Obz
Geologiya i Razvedka Nedr — Geol Razved Nedr
Geologiya i Rudonosnost Pritashkentskogo Raiona. Zapiski Uzbekistanskogo Otdeleniya Vsesoyuznogo Mineralogicheskogo Obshchestva — Geol Rudonosn Pritashk Raiona Zap Uzb Otd Vses Mineral Ova
Geologiya i Rudonosnost Yuga Ukrainy — Geol Rudonosn Yuga Ukr
Geologiya i Syr'evye Resursy Redkikh Elementov v SSSR. Tezisy Dokladov na Vsesoyuznom Soveshchanii — Geol Syrevye Resur Redk Elem SSSR Tezisy Dokl Vses Soveshch
Geologiya Kazakhstana — Geol Kaz
Geologiya Mestorozhdenii Redkikh Elementov — Geol Mestorozhd Redk Elem
Geologiya Metamorficheskikh Kompleksov — Geol Metamorf Kompleksov
Geologiya. Metodika i Tekhnika Razvedki. Laboratornye Raboty — Geol Metod Tekh Razved Lab Rab
Geologiya Morya — Geol Morya
Geologiya, Nauchnye Doklady, Gertsenovskie Chteniya — Geol Nauchn Dokl Gertsenovskie Chteniya
Geologiya Nefti — Geol Nefti
Geologiya Nefti i Gaza — GENGA
Geologiya Nefti i Gaza — Geol Nefti Gaza
Geologiya Nefti i Gaza — Geol Nefti i Gaza
Geologiya Nefti i Gaza Severo-Vostoka Evropeiskoi Chasti SSSR — Geol Nefti Gaza Sev Vostoka Evr Chasti SSSR
Geologiya Poberezh'ya i Dna Chernogo i Azovskogo Morei v Predelakh Ukrainskoi SSR — Geol Poberezh'ya Dna Chern Azovskogo Morei Predelakh Ukr SSR
Geologiya Poberezh'ya i Dna Chernogo i Azovskogo Morei v Predelakh USSR — Geol Poberezhya Dna Chern Azovskogo Morei Predelakh USSR
Geologiya, Poiski, i Razvedka Nerudnykh Poleznykh Iskopaemykh — Geol Poiski Razved Nerudn Polezn Iskop
Geologiya, Poiski, i Razvedka Nerudnykh Poleznykh Iskopaemykh — GPRID
Geologiya. Razrabotka Gazovykh Mestorozhdenii i Ispol'zovanie Gaza v Srednei Azii — Geol Razrab Gazov Mestorozhd Ispolz Gaza Sredn Azii

Geologiya. Razvedka i Razrabotka Gazovykh i Gazokondensatnykh Mestorozhdenii Severnogo Kavkaza — Geol Razved Razrab Gazov Gazokondens Mestorozhd Sev Kavk
Geologiya Rossypei. Doklady Soveshchaniya — Geol Rossypei Dokl Soveshch
Geologiya Rudnykh Mestorozhdenii — Geol Rud Mestorozhd
Geologiya Rudnykh Mestorozhdenii — Geol Rudn Mestorozhd
Geologiya Rudnykh Mestorozhdenii — GRMAA
Geologiya SSSR — Geol SSSR
Geologiya Tsentral'nogo Kazakhstana — Geol Tsentr Kaz
Geologiya Uzberezhzhya i Dna Chornogo ta Azovs'kogo Moriv u Mezhakh URSR — Geol Uzberezhzhya Dna Chorn Azovskogo Moriv Mezhakh URSR
Geologiya Zakaspiya — Geol Zakaspiya
Geologues — GEOLB
Geology — GGGY
Geology — GLGYB
Geology [*Boulder*] — GLGYBA
Geology and Geophysics. Academy of Sciences (USSR) — GGR
Geology and Geophysics (Novosibirsk) — Geol Geophys (Novosibirsk)
Geology and Ground-Water Resources — Geol Ground Water Resour
Geology and Metallogeny of Copper Deposits. Proceedings. Copper Symposium. Inter — Geol Metallog Copper Deposits Proc Copper Symp Int Geol Congr
Geology and Mineral Resources of the Far East — Geol Miner Resour Far East
Geology and Palaeontology of Southeast Asia — Geol Palaeontol Southeast Asia
Geology and Prospecting — Geol Prospect
Geology Club of Puerto Rico. Bulletin — Geology Club Puerto Rico Bull
Geology. Exploration and Mining in British Columbia — Geol Explor Min BC
Geology from Space — Geol Space
Geology Map and Mineral Resources Summary. North Carolina Geological Survey — Geol Map Miner Resour Summ North Carolina Geol Surv
Geology of Coal Measures and Stratigraphy of the Carboniferous in the USSR — Geol Coal Meas Stratigr Carboniferous USSR
Geology of Kazakhstan — Geol Kaz
Geology of Libya. Symposium on the Geology of Libya — Geol Libya Symp
Geology of Pennsylvania — G PA
Geology of Poland — Geol Pol
Geology of Precambrian — Geol Precambrian
Geology of Tungsten — Geol Tungsten
Geoloogia Instituudi Uurimused. Eesti NSV Teaduste Akadeemia — Geol Inst Uurim Eesti NSV Tead Akad
Geoloski Glasnik [*Yugoslavia*] — Geol Glas
Geoloski Glasnik. Posebna Izdanja — Geol Glas Posebna Izd
Geoloski Glasnik (Sarajevo) — Geol Glas Sarajevo
Geoloski Glasnik (Titograd, Yugoslavia) — Geol Glas (Titograd Yugosl)
Geoloski Vjesnik — GEVJA
Geoloski Vjesnik [*Zagreb*] — GEVJAO
Geoloski Vjesnik (Zagreb) — Geol Vjesn (Zagreb)
Geolshki Anali Balkanskoga Poluostrva — Geol An Balk Poluostrva
Geomagnetic Bulletin. Institute of Geological Sciences — Geomagn Bull Inst Geol Sci
Geomagnetic Series. Earth Physics Branch — Geomagn Ser Earth Phys Branch
Geomagnetism and Aeronomy [*English Translation*] — Geomagn and Aeron
Geomagnetism and Aeronomy [*English Translation*] — GMARA
Geomagnetism and Aeronomy (English Translation) — Geomagn Aeron (Engl Transl)
Geomagnetism and Aeronomy (USSR) — Geomagn Aeron (USSR)
Geomagnetizm i Aeronomiya — GEAEA
Geomagnetizm i Aeronomiya — Geomag Aer
Geomagnetizm i Aeronomiya — Geomagn Aeron
Geo-Marine Letters — Geo-Mar Let
Geomechanics Computing Programme — Geomech Comput Progm
Geometriae Dedicata — Geom Dedicata
Geometric and Functional Analysis — Geom Funct Anal
Geometric Design Publications — Geom Des Publ
Geomicrobiology Journal — GEJODG
Geomicrobiology Journal — Geomicrobiol J
Geomicrobiology Journal — Geomicrobiology J
Geomimet — GEOMD
Geomorphological Abstracts — Geomorph Abstr
Geophysica Norvegica — Geophys Norv
Geophysica Norvegica — GPNOA
Geophysical Abstracts — Geophys Abstr
Geophysical and Astrophysical Fluid Dynamics — Geophys and Astrophys Fluid Dyn
Geophysical and Astrophysical Fluid Dynamics — Geophys Astrophys Fluid Dyn
Geophysical and Astrophysical Fluid Dynamics — Geophys Astrophys Fluid Dynamics
Geophysical Aspects of the Energy Problem. Proceedings. Course — Geophys Aspects Energy Probl Proc Course
Geophysical Bulletin (Moscow) — Geophys Bull Moscow
Geophysical Case Histories — Geophys Case Histories
Geophysical Communications (Kiev) — Geophys Commun (Kiev)
Geophysical Exploration — Geophys Explor
Geophysical Fluid Dynamics — Geophys Fluid Dyn
Geophysical Institute. Faculty of Science. Tokyo University. Geophysical Notes. Supplement — Geophys Inst Fac Sci Tokyo Univ Geophys Notes Suppl
Geophysical Institute. University of Alaska. Contribution Series — GIUAC
Geophysical Institute. University of Alaska. UAG Report Series — GIUAG R
Geophysical Journal — Geophys J
Geophysical Journal — Geophys Jour
Geophysical Journal — GJOUD
Geophysical Journal International — Geophys J I
Geophysical Journal (Moscow) — Geophys J (Moscow)
Geophysical Journal (Oxford) — Geophys J Oxford
Geophysical Journal. Royal Astronomical Society — GEOJA
Geophysical Journal. Royal Astronomical Society — Geophys J R
Geophysical Journal. Royal Astronomical Society — Geophys J R Astr Soc
Geophysical Journal. Royal Astronomical Society — Geophys J R Astron Soc
Geophysical Journal. Royal Astronomical Society — Geophys J R Astronom Soc
Geophysical Magazine [*Tokyo*] — GEOMA
Geophysical Magazine — Geophys Mag
Geophysical Magazine (Tokyo) — Geophys Mag (Tokyo)
Geophysical Memoirs (London) — Geophys Mem (Lond)
Geophysical Monograph — Geophys Monogr
Geophysical Monograph — GPMGAD
Geophysical Monograph. American Geophysical Union — Geophys Monogr Am Geophys Union
Geophysical Note (Tokyo) — Geophys Note (Tokyo)
Geophysical Prospecting — Geophys Prospect
Geophysical Prospecting — Geophys Prospecting
Geophysical Prospecting — GPPRA
Geophysical Prospecting (The Hague) — Geophys Prospect (The Hague)
Geophysical Research Bulletin — Geophys R B
Geophysical Research Bulletin — Geophys Res Bull
Geophysical Research Bulletin — GRBUD
Geophysical Research in Norway — Geophys Res Norw
Geophysical Research Letters — Geophys R L
Geophysical Research Letters — Geophys Res Lett
Geophysical Research Papers — Geophys Res Pap
Geophysical Society of Tulsa. Proceedings — Geophys Soc Tulsa Proc
Geophysical Surveys — Geophys Surv
Geophysical Surveys — GPSVA
Geophysical Transactions (Budapest) — Geophys Trans (Budapest)
Geophysics — Geophys
Geophysics — GPYSA
Geophysics and Astrophysics Monographs — Geophys Astrophys Monogr
Geophysics and Space Data Bulletin — Geophys Space Data Bull
Geophysics and Space Data Bulletin — GSDBA
Geophysics and Tectonics Abstracts — Geophys Tecton Abstr
Geophysics. The Leading Edge of Exploration — Geophys Lead Edge Explor
Geophysik und Geologie — Geophys Geol
Geophysik und Geologie (Leipzig). Karl-Marx-Universitaet. Geophysikalische Veroeffentlichungen. Serie 3 — Geophys Geol (Leipz) Karl-Marx-Univ Ser 3
Geophysikalische Arbeiten sowie Mitteilungen aus Meteorologie und Astrophysik — Geophys Arb Mitt Meteorol Astrophys
Geophytology — GPHTAR
Geoppinger Akademische Beitraege — GAB
Geo-Processing — Geo-Process
George Eliot Fellowship Review — GEFR
George Herbert Journal — GHJ
George Mason University. Law Review — Geo Mason UL Rev
George Mason University. Law Review — GMU L Rev
George Mason University. Law Review — GMU LR
George Washington Journal of International Law and Economics — Geo Wash J Int L
George Washington Journal of International Law and Economics — Geo Wash J Intl L and Econ
George Washington Journal of International Law and Economics — George Washington J Internat Law and Econ
George Washington Journal of International Law and Economics — JIL
George Washington Law Review — Geo Wash L Rev
George Washington Law Review — George Wash
George Washington Law Review — George Wash L Rev
George Washington Law Review — George Washington Law R
George Washington Law Review — GW
George Washington Law Review — GW LR
George Washington Law Review — GWLRA
George Washington University. Bulletin — BGWVAO
George Washington University. Bulletin — George Wash Univ Bull
George Washington University. Bulletin — George Washington Univ Bull
Georgetown Dental Journal — Georgetown Dent J
Georgetown Immigration Law Quarterly — Georgetown Immigr Law Q
Georgetown Law Journal — Geo
Georgetown Law Journal — Geo LJ
Georgetown Law Journal — Georget Law
Georgetown Law Journal — Georget LJ
Georgetown Law Journal — Georgetown Law J
Georgetown Law Journal — Georgetown LJ
Georgetown Law Journal — Gr LJ
Georgetown Medical Bulletin — Georgetown Med Bull
Georgetown Medical Bulletin — GTMBAQ
Georgetown University Law Center Immigration Law Reporter — Georgetown Univ Law Cent Immigr Law Rep
Georgetown University. Monograph Series on Languages and Linguistics — GMSLL
Georgetown University. Monograph Series on Languages and Linguistics — GUMSL
Georgetown University. Papers on Languages and Linguistics — GUP
Georgetown University. Round Table on Languages and Linguistics — GURT
Georgetown University. School of Dentistry. Mirror — Georgetown Univ Sch Dent Mirror
Georgia 4H Cloverleaf. News and Views of Georgia's Future Leaders — Ga 4H Cloverleaf News Views Ga Future Leaders
Georgia. Agricultural Experiment Station. Annual Report — GA Agric Exp Stn Annu Rep
Georgia. Agricultural Experiment Station. Bulletin — GA Agric Exp Stn Bull
Georgia. Agricultural Experiment Station. Circular — GA Agric Exp Stn Circ
Georgia. Agricultural Experiment Station. Leaflet — GA Agric Exp Stn Leafl

Georgia. Agricultural Experiment Station. Mimeograph Series — GA Agric Exp Stn Mimeogr Ser
Georgia. Agricultural Experiment Station. Publications — GA Ag Exp
Georgia. Agricultural Experiment Station. Research Bulletin — GA Agric Exp Stn Res Bull
Georgia. Agricultural Experiment Station. Research Report — GA Agric Exp Stn Res Rep
Georgia. Agricultural Experiment Station. Technical Bulletin — GA Agric Exp Stn Tech Bull
Georgia. Agricultural Experiment Stations. Biennial Report — GA Agric Exp Stn Bienn Rep
Georgia. Agricultural Experiment Stations. Field Crops Variety Trials — GA Agric Exp Stn Field Crops Var Trials
Georgia. Agricultural Experiment Stations. Field Crops Variety Trials — GA Agric Exp Stn Field Crops Variety Trials
Georgia Agricultural Research — GA Agric Res
Georgia Agricultural Research — GEARA
Georgia Agricultural Research. Georgia Experiment Stations — GA Agric Res GA Exp Stn
Georgia Agricultural Research. University of Georgia — GA Agr Res
Georgia Appeals Reports — Ga App
Georgia Bar Association — Ga Bar Assn
Georgia Bar Journal — GA B J
Georgia Bar Journal — GA Bar J
Georgia Bar Journal — GBJ
Georgia Bar Journal — Georgia BJ
Georgia Botanic Journal and College Sentinel — Georgia Bot J Coll Sentinel
Georgia Business — GA Bus
Georgia Business — Georgia Bus
Georgia Cattleman — Ga Cattleman
Georgia Department of Education. Statistical Report — Georgia Dep Educ Stat Rep
Georgia. Department of Mines, Mining, and Geology. Geological Survey. Bulletin — GA Dep Mines Min Geol Geol Surv Bull
Georgia. Department of Mines, Mining, and Geology. Geological Survey. Bulletin — GA Dep Mines Mining Geol Geol Surv Bull
Georgia. Department of Mines, Mining, and Geology. Geological Survey. Circular — GA Dep Mines Min Geol Geol Surv Circ
Georgia. Department of Natural Resources. Geologic and Water Resources Division. Information Circular — GA Dep Nat Resour Geol Water Resour Div Inf Circ
Georgia. Department of Natural Resources. Geological Survey. Information Circular — Ga Dep Nat Resour Geol Surv Inf Circ
Georgia Engineer — GA Engineer
Georgia Entomological Society. Journal — Ga Entomol Soc J
Georgia Farm Bureau News — Ga Farm Bur News
Georgia. Forest Research Council. Annual Report — GA For Res Counc Annu Rep
Georgia. Forest Research Council. Report — GA For Res Counc Rep
Georgia. Forest Research Council. Report — GFRRA
Georgia Forest Research Paper — GA For Res Pap
Georgia Forest Research Paper. Georgia Forest Research Council — GA For Res Pap GA For Res Counc
Georgia Forestry — Ga For
Georgia Genealogical Survey — Georgia Geneal Surv
Georgia Genealogist — Georgia Geneal
Georgia. Geologic and Water Resources Division. Information Circular — GA Geol Water Resour Div Inf Circ
Georgia. Geological Survey. Bulletin — GA Geol Surv Bull
Georgia. Geological Survey. Bulletin — GA GSB
Georgia Geological Survey. Bulletin. Circular — GA Geol Survey Bull Circ
Georgia. Geological Survey. Circular — GA Geol Surv Circ
Georgia. Geological Survey. Information Circular — GA Geol Surv Inf Circ
Georgia Historical Quarterly — GA His Q
Georgia Historical Quarterly — GA Hist Q
Georgia Historical Quarterly — GA Hist Quart
Georgia Historical Quarterly — GAHQ
Georgia Historical Quarterly — GeH
Georgia Historical Quarterly — Georgia Hist Quart
Georgia Historical Quarterly — GHQ
Georgia Historical Society Annals — Ga Hist Soc Annals
Georgia Historical Society. Collections — Ga His S
Georgia Historical Society. Collections — GA Hist Soc Coll
Georgia Institute of Technology. Engineering Experiment Station. Bulletin — GA Inst Technol Eng Exp Sta Bull
Georgia Institute of Technology. Engineering Experiment Station. Circular — GA Inst Technol Eng Exp Stn Circ
Georgia Institute of Technology. Engineering Experiment Station. Report — GA Inst Technol Eng Exp Stn Rep
Georgia Institute of Technology. Engineering Experiment Station. Reprints — GA Inst Technol Eng Exp Stn Repr
Georgia Institute of Technology. Engineering Experiment Station. Special Reports — GA Inst Technol Eng Exp Stn Spec Rep
Georgia Institute of Technology. Engineering Experiment Station. The Research Engineer — Ga Inst Technol Eng Exp Stn Res Eng
Georgia Institute of Technology. Environmental Resources Center. ERC (Report) — GA Inst Technol Environ Resour Cent ERC (Rep)
Georgia Institute of Technology. Series in Nuclear Engineering — GA Inst Technol Ser Nucl Eng
Georgia Journal of International and Comparative Law — GA J Int & Comp L
Georgia Journal of International and Comparative Law — GA J Internat and Comparative Law
Georgia Journal of International and Comparative Law — GA J Int'l & Comp L
Georgia Journal of International and Comparative Law — Georgia J Int Comp L
Georgia Journal of Science — GA J Sci
Georgia Journal of Science — GJSCD
Georgia Journal of Science. Official Publication. Georgia Academy of Science — Ga J Sci Off Publ Ga Acad Sci
Georgia Law Reporter — Georgia Law Rep
Georgia Law Review — GA L
Georgia Law Review — GA L Rev
Georgia Law Review — GA Law R
Georgia Law Review — GA LR
Georgia Law Review — Geo Rev
Georgia Law Review — Georgia L Rev
Georgia Law Review — GLR
Georgia Laws — GA Laws
Georgia Librarian — GA Libn
Georgia Librarian — GA Librn
Georgia Mineral Newsletter — GA Miner Newsl
Georgia Mineral Newsletter — GA Mineral Newsletter
Georgia Museum of Art Bulletin — Georgia Mus Art Bull
Georgia Music News — GN
Georgia Nursing — GA Nurse
Georgia Nutrition Conference for the Feed Industry. Proceedings — Ga Nutr Conf Feed Ind Proc
Georgia Operator — GA Oper
Georgia Practician — Ga Practician
Georgia Reports — GA
Georgia Review — GA R
Georgia Review — GA Rev
Georgia Review — Geo R
Georgia Review — Georgia R
Georgia Review — Georgia Rev
Georgia Review — GeR
Georgia Review — GR
Georgia Review — PGAR
Georgia. School of Technology. State Engineering Experiment Station. Circular — Ga Sch Technol State Eng Exp Stn Circ
Georgia. School of Technology. State Engineering Experiment Station. Reprint — GA Sch Technol State Eng Exp Stn Repr
Georgia School of Technology. State Engineering Experiment Station. Research Engineer — Ga Sch Technol State Eng Exp Stn Res Eng
Georgia. School of Technology. State Engineering Experiment Station. Special Report — Ga Sch Technol State Eng Exp Stn Spec Rep
Georgia State Bar Journal — GA SBJ
Georgia State Bar Journal — GA St BJ
Georgia State Bar Journal — Georgia St BJ
Georgia State Bar Journal — GSB
Georgia State College of Agriculture. Publications — GA Ag Coll
Georgia Veterinarian — GA Vet
Georgia. Water Quality Control Board. Technical Report — GA Water Qual Control Board Tech Rep
Georgian Academy of Sciences. A. Razmadze Mathematical Institute. Memoirs on Differential Equations and Mathematical Physics — Mem Differential Equations Math Phys
Georgian Mathematical Journal — Georgian Math J
Georgikon Deltion — Georgikon Delt
Geos. Canada Department of Energy, Mines, and Resources — GEOQ
Geoscience Abstracts — Geosci Abstr
Geoscience Abstracts — Geoscience Abs
Geoscience and Man — Geosci Man
Geoscience Canada — Geosci Can
Geoscience Canada — GOCA
Geoscience Data Index for Alberta [*Database*] — GEODIAL
Geoscience Documentation — Geosci Doc
Geoscience Documentation [*England*] — GSDCB
Geoscience Information Society. Proceedings — Geoscience Inf Soc Proc
Geoscience Information Society. Proceedings — GISPA
Geoscience Journal — Geosci J
Geoscience Magazine — Geosci Mag
Geoscience Reports of Shizuoka University — Geosci Rep Shizuoka Univ
Geoscience Research Grant Program. Summary of Research — Geosci Res Grant Program Summ Res
Geoscience Studies [*Japan*] — Geosci Stud
Geoscience Study. Ontario. Division of Mines — Geosci Study Ont Div Mines
Geoscope — GEOS
Geostandards Newsletter — Geostand Newsl
Geostandards Newsletter — Geostandards Newsl
Geostatistics Applied to Earth Sciences. Papers. International Geostatistics Congress — Geostat Appl Earth Sci Pap Int Geostat Congr
Geosynthetic Testing for Waste Containment Applications — Geosynth Test Waste Containment Appl
Geosynthetics International — Geosynth Int
Geotechnical Abstracts — GA
Geotechnical Abstracts — Geotech Abstr
Geotechnical and Environmental Aspects of Geopressure Energy. Papers — Geotech Environ Aspects Geopressure Energy Pap
Geotechnical Engineering — Geotech Eng
Geotechnical Testing Journal — Geotech Test J
Geotechnique — Geotechniq
Geotechnique [*England*] — GTNQA
Geotectonics — Geotecton
Geoteknillisia Julkaisuja — Geotek Julk
Geoteknisk Institut. Bulletin — Geoteknisk Inst Bull
Geotektonika — Geotekton
Geotektonika — GTKTA
Geotektonika, Tektonofizika, i Geodinamika — Geotekton Tektonofiz Geodin
Geotektonika, Tektonofizika, i Geodinamika — Geotektonika Tektonofiz Geodinamika

Geotektonische Forschungen — Geotekton Forsch
Geotektonische Forschungen — Geotektonische Forsch
Geotermicheskie Issledovaniya i Ispol'zovanie Tepla Zemli. Trudy Soveshchaniya po Geotermicheskim Issledovaniyam v SSSR — Geoterm Issled Ispolz Tepla Zemli Tr Soveshch
Geothermal Energy — Geotherm Energy
Geothermal Energy Magazine — Geotherm Energy Mag
Geothermal Energy Update — Geotherm Energy Update
Geothermal Hot Line — Geotherm Hot Line
Geothermal Hot Line — GHLID
Geothermal Report — Geotherm Rep
Geothermal Report — GERED
Geothermal Report. Mineral Resources Department (Fiji) — Geotherm Rep Miner Resour Dep (Fiji)
Geothermal Resources Council. Special Report — Geotherm Resour Counc Spec Rep
Geothermal Resources Council. Special Report — RGRCD
Geothermal Resources Council. Transactions [*People's Republic of China*] — Geotherm Resour Counc Trans
Geothermal Technology [*Japan*] — Geotherm Technol
Geothermics — Geotherm
Geothermics — GTMCA
Geotimes — Geot
Geotimes — GEOTA
Geotimes — GEOTAJ
Geowissenschaften in Unserer Zeit — Geowiss Unserer Zeit
Gepgyartastechnologia [*Hungary*] — GEPGA
Geraniums Around the World. International Geranium Society — Geraniums Around Wld
Gerarchia Cattolica e la Famiglia Pontificia — GCFP
Gerber-Zeitung — Gerber Ztg
Gerbil Digest — GEDID2
Gerbil Digest — Gerbil Dig
Gercke und Norden. Einleitung in die Altertumswissenschaft — Gercke Norden
Gereedschap — GRS
Gereformeerd Theologisch Tijdschrift [*Kampen*] — GerefTTS
Gereformeerd Theologisch Tijdschrift [*Kampen*] — GThT
Gereformeerd Theologisch Tijdschrift — GTT
Gerfaut — GRFTAV
Gerfaut. Revue Scientifique Belge d'Ornithologie — Gerfaut Rev Sci Belge Ornithol
Geriatric Clinical Pharmacology — Geriat Clin Pharmacol
Geriatric Medicine — Geriatr Med
Geriatric Nursing — Geriatr Nurs
Geriatric Nursing — Geriatric Nurs
Geriatric Nursing (London) — Geriatr Nurs (Lond)
Geriatrics — GERIA
Geriatrics — GERIAZ
Geriatrics Survey — Geriatr Surv
Gerichtssaal — GS
Gerichtszeitung — Gerichtsztg
Gerlands Beitraege zur Geophysik — BEGOA
Gerlands Beitraege zur Geophysik — Gerlands Beitr Geophys
German American Trade News — German TN
German Canadian Review — GCR
German Chemical Engineering — Ger Chem Eng
German Chemical Engineering — Ger Chem Engng
German Chemical Engineering — German Chem Engng
German Democratic Republic. Patent Document — Ger Democr Repub Pat Doc
German Economic Review — GER
German Economic Review — Ger Econ Re
German Economic Review — German Econ R
German Foreign Policy — Germ Foreign Policy
German Hydrographic Journal — Ger Hydrogr J
German International — German Int
German International — German Internat
German Journal of Cardiology — Ger J Cardiol
German Journal of Gastroenterology — Ger J Gastroenterol
German Journal of Ophthalmology — Ger J Ophthalmol
German Language and Literature Monographs — GLLM
German Life and Letters — Ger L & L
German Life and Letters — Ger Life L
German Life and Letters — Ger Life Lett
German Life and Letters — GL & L
German Life and Letters — GLAL
German Life and Letters — GLL
German Life and Letters. New Series — GLLNS
German Medical Monthly — Ger Med Mon
German Medical Monthly — German Med Monthly
German Medical Monthly — GRMMA
German Medical Research — Ger Med Res
German Medicine — Ger Med
German Medicine — GRMDA
German Mining — GERMD
German Offenlegungschrift. Patent Document — Ger Offen
German Plastics [*Germany*] — Ger Plast
German Plastics — GPLAD
German Quarterly — Ger Q
German Quarterly — Ger Quart
German Quarterly — German Q
German Quarterly — GQ
German Shepherd Quarterly — GSQ
German Solar Energy Forum — Ger Sol Energy Forum
German Studies in America — GSA
German Studies Newsletter — Germ Stud Newsl
German Studies Review — Ger S R
German Studies Review — Ger St Rev
German Trade Directory — Germ Tr Dir
German Tribune — TGT
German Tribune Quarterly Review — Germn Tb Q
German Yearbook of International Law — German Yb Int Law
German-American Studies — GAS
German-Canadian Yearbook [*Deutschkanadisches Jahrbuch*] — GCY
Germania — Ger
Germania [*Berlin*] — Germ
Germania Benedictina — Germ Ben
Germania Judaica — Germ Jud
Germania Judaica. Schriftenreihe — Germ Jud S
Germania. Korrespondenzblatt der Roemisch-Germanischen Kommission des Deutschen Archaeologischen Instituts — Germania Korrbl
Germania Monastica — Germ Mon
Germania Sacra — Germ Sac
Germanic Notes — Ger Note
Germanic Notes — GN
Germanic Review — Ger Rev
Germanic Review — Germ R
Germanic Review — Germ Rev
Germanic Review — GR
Germanic Review — IGRV
Germanica Wratislaviensia — GeW
Germanica Wratislaviensia — GW
Germanische Studien — GSt
Germanisch-Romanische Monatsschrift — Ger Rom Mon
Germanisch-Romanische Monatsschrift — Ger Roman Monatsschr
Germanisch-Romanische Monatsschrift — Germ-Rom Monat
Germanisch-Romanische Monatsschrift — G-R Mon
Germanisch-Romanische Monatsschrift — GRM
Germanisch-Romanische Monatsschrift — GRMS
Germanistica Pragensia — GPrag
Germanistik — Ger
Germanistische Abhandlungen — GA
Germanistische Arbeitshefte — GA
Germanistische Linguistik — GermL
Germanistische Mitteilungen. Zeitschrift des Belgischen Germanisten- und Deutschlehrerverbandes — GMit
Germanistische Studien — GS
Germanistische Texte und Studien — GTS
Germano-Slavica — G
Germano-Slavica — G Slav
Germano-Slavica — Ger Slav
Germano-Slavica — Gsl
Germanskaya Tekhnika — Ger Tekh
Germany. Bundesanstalt fuer Bodenforschung und Geologische Landesaemter. Geologisches Jahrbuch. Beiheft — Ger Bundesanst Bodenforsch Geol Jahrb Beih
Germany (West). Patent Document. Auslegeschrift — Ger (West) Pat Doc Auslegeschr
Germany (West). Patent Document. Offenlegungschrift — Ger West Pat Doc Offen
Germany. Zentrales Geologisches Institut. Abhandlungen — Ger Zent Geol Inst Abh
Germany. Zentrales Geologisches Institut. Jahrbuch fuer Geologie — Ger Zent Geol Inst Jahrb Geol
Germany. Zentrales Geologisches Institut. Wissenschaftlich-Technischer Informationsdienst — Ger Zentrales Geol Inst Wiss-Tech Informationsdienst
German-Yugoslav Meeting on Materials Science and Development — Ger Yugosl Meet Mater Sci Dev
Germplasm Resources Information Network [*Database*] — GRIN
Gerodontology — Gerodontolo
Gerodontology — GRDND6
Gerontologia — GEROA
Gerontologia [*Basel*] GEROAJ
Gerontologia Clinica [*Later, Gerontology*] — Gerontol Clin
Gerontologia Clinica — GRNCA
Gerontologia Clinica — GRNCAK
Gerontological Abstracts — Gerontol Abstr
Gerontologist — Gerontol
Gerontologist — GGGT
Gerontologist — GRNTA
Gerontologiya i Geriatriya — Gerontol Geriatr
Gerontology — GERNDJ
Gerontology and Geriatrics Education — GAGE
Gerontology and Geriatrics Education — Gerontol Geriatr Educ
Gerontology Extension Lectures — Gerontol Ext Lect
Gerontology Extension Lectures — ZKKODY
Gertsinskie Magmaticheskie Kompleksy Vostochnogo Kazakhstana — Gertsinskie Magmat Kompleksy Vost Kaz
Gesammelte Abhandlungen. Deutsches Lederinstitut (Freiberg) — Gesammelte Abh Dtsch Lederinst (Freiberg)
Gesammelte Abhandlungen zur Kenntnis der Kohle — Gesammelte Abh Kenn Kohle
Gesammelte Arbeiten des Weissrussischen Landwirtschaftlichen Instituts — Gesammelte Arb Weissruss Landwirtsch Inst
Gesammelte Aufsaetze zur Kulturgeschichte Spaniens — GAKGS
Gesammelte Aufsaetze zur Kulturgeschichte Spaniens — GAKS
Gesammelte Beitraege der Naturwissenschaftlichen Fakultaet der Palacky Universitaet in Olomouc — Gesammelte Beitr Naturwiss Fak Palacky Univ Olomouc
Gesammelte Berichte aus Betrieb und Forschung der Ruhrgas Aktiengesellschaft [*Germany*] — Gesammelte Ber Betr Forsch Ruhrgas Ag

Gesammelte Schriften — GS
GESAMP (Joint Group of Experts on the Scientific Aspects of Marine Pollution) Reports and Studies — GESAMP Rep Stud
Gesamtbericht Weltkraftkonferenz — Gesamtber Weltkraftkonf
Gesamtkatalog der Wiegendrucke — GKW
Gesamtkommentar Oeffentliches Dienstrecht — GK Oe D
Gesamtkongress der Deutschen Pharmazeutischen Wissenschaften — Gesamtkong Dtsch Pharm Wiss
Gesamtverzeichnis — GAZ
Gesamtverzeichnis Auslaendischer Zeitschriften und Serien — GAZS
Gesamtverzeichnis der Kongressschriften [*Database*] — GKS
Gesamtverzeichnis Oesterreichischer Dissertationen — Gesamtverzeichnis Oesterreichischer Diss
Geschichte der Arabischen Literatur — GAL
Geschichte der Arabischen Literatur — Gesch Arab Lit
Geschichte der Arabischen Litteratur. Supplement — GALS
Geschichte der Griechischen Literatur [*Muenchen*] — G Gr L
Geschichte der Griechischen Literatur [*Bern*] — G Gr L
Geschichte der Griechischen Literatur [*Bern*] — GGL
Geschichte der Griechischen Religion — GGR
Geschichte der Griechischen Religion — GrG
Geschichte der Kirche. Einsiedeln — GDK
Geschichte der Korinthischen Vasen — GKV
Geschichte der Oekumenischen Konzilien — G Oe K
Geschichte der Pfarreien der Erzdioezese Koeln — GPEK
Geschichte der Philosophie in Einzeldarstellungen — GPE
Geschichte der Roemischen Literatur — GRL
Geschichte der Wissenschaft in Deutschland — GWD
Geschichte der Wissenschaften — Ge Wiss
Geschichte des Altertums — GdA
Geschichte des Arabischen Schrifttums — GAS
Geschichte des Byzantinischen Literatur — GBL
Geschichte in der Schule — Gesch Schule
Geschichte in Wissenschaft und Unterricht — Gesch Wiss Unterr
Geschichte in Wissenschaft und Unterricht — Gesch Wiss Unterricht
Geschichte in Wissenschaft und Unterricht — GWU
Geschichte in Wissenschaft und Unterricht. Beiheft — GWUB
Geschichte und Gesellschaft — Gesch Ges
Geschichte und Gesellschaft — Gesch U Ges
Geschichtliche Darstellung der Naturforschenden Gesellschaft in Emden — Gesch Darstellung Naturf Ges Emden
Geschichtliche Darstellung der Verhandlungen der Naturforschenden Gesellschaft in Emden — Gesch Darstellung Verh Naturf Ges Emden
Geschichtliche Studien zur Politik und Gesellschaft — GSPG
Geschichtsblaetter des Deutschen Hugenottenvereins — GBDHV
Geschichtsblaetter fuer Mittelrheinische Bistuemer — GBMRB
Geschichtsblaetter fuer Stadt und Land Magdeburg — GBSLM
Geschichtsblaetter fuer Waldeck und Pyrmont — GW
Geschichtsfreund — Gfd
Geschichtsfreund. Beiheft — G Fd B
Geschichtsschreiber der Deutschen Vorzeit — GDV
Geschiedenis van de Kerk. Hilversum — GKH
Geschiedkundige Bladen — GB
Geschriften van de Vereniging voor Belastingswetenschap — Geschrift
Geschriften van de Vereniging voor Belastingswetenschap — GVB
Gesellschaft der Geologie- und Bergbaustudenten in Oesterreich. Mitteilungen — Ges Geol Bergbaustud Oesterr Mitt
Gesellschaft der Geologie- und Bergbaustudenten in Wien. Mitteilungen — Ges Geol Bergbaustud Wien Mitt
Gesellschaft der Wissenschaften zu Goettingen, Nachrichten. Geschaeftliche Mitteilungen — Ges Wiss Goettingen Nachr Geschaeftliche Mitt
Gesellschaft Deutscher Chemiker. Fachgruppe Analytische Chemie. Mitteilungsblatt — Ges Dtsch Chem Fachgruppe Anal Chem Mitteilungsbl
Gesellschaft Deutscher Chemiker. Fachgruppe Chemie-Information. Vortragstagung. Tagungsbericht — Ges Dtsch Chem Fachgruppe Chem Inf Vortragstag Tagungsber
Gesellschaft Deutscher Metallhuetten- und Bergleute. Schriften — Ges Dtsch Metallhuetten- und Bergleute Schr
Gesellschaft Deutscher Naturforscher und Aerzte. Verhandlungen — Ges Dtsch Naturforsch Aerzte Verh
Gesellschaft Deutscher Naturforscher und Aerzte. Wissenschaftliche Konferenz [*A publication*] — Ges Dtsch Naturforsch Aerzte Wiss Konf
Gesellschaft fuer Aerosolforschung. Conference — Ges Aerosolforsch Conf
Gesellschaft fuer Aerosolforschung. Jahrestagung — Ges Aerosolforsch Jahrestag
Gesellschaft fuer Biologische Chemie. Konferenz — Ges Biol Chem Konf
Gesellschaft fuer Biotechnologische Forschung. Monograph Series — Ges Biotechnol Forsch Monogr Ser
Gesellschaft fuer die Geschichte und Bibliographie des Brauwesens. Jahrbuch [*Berlin*] — Ges Gesch & Bibliog Brauwes Jahrb
Gesellschaft fuer Erdkunde. Verhandlungen (Berlin) — Gesell F Erdk Berlin Verhandl
Gesellschaft fuer Erdkunde. Zeitschrift (Berlin) — Gesell F Erdk Berlin Zeits
Gesellschaft fuer Erdkunde zu Berlin. Verhandlungen. Zeitschrift — Ges Erdk Berlin Verh Zs
Gesellschaft fuer Erdkunde zu Leipzig. Mitteilungen — Gesell Erdk Leipz Mitt
Gesellschaft fuer Fortschritte auf dem Gebiet der Inneren Medizin. Symposion — Ges Fortschr Geb Inn Med Symp
Gesellschaft fuer Kernenergieverwertung in Schiffbau und Schiffahrt. Bericht — Ges Kernenergieverwert Schiffbau Schiffahrt Ber
Gesellschaft fuer Kieler Stadtgeschichte. Mitteilungen — Gesell f Kieler Stadtgesch Mitt
Gesellschaft fuer Kieler Stadtgeschichte. Mitteilungen — Gesell Kieler Stadtgesch Mitt
Gesellschaft fuer Konsumforschung — G f K
Gesellschaft fuer Naturkunde in Wuerttemberg. Jahreshefte — Ges Naturkd Wuerttemb Jahresh
Gesellschaft fuer Oekologie. Jahresversammlung — Ges Oekol Jahresversamml
Gesellschaft fuer Oekologie. Verhandlungen — Ges Oekol Verh
Gesellschaft fuer Reaktorsicherheit. Bericht — Ges Reaktorsicherh Ber
Gesellschaft fuer Reaktorsicherheit. Bericht GRS-S [*Germany*] — Ges Reaktorsicherh Ber GRS-S
Gesellschaft fuer Reaktorsicherheit. Bericht GRS-S — GRGSD
Gesellschaft fuer Reaktorsicherheit. Bericht. GRS-S. Stellungnahmen zu Kernenergiefragen — Ges Reaktorsicherh Ber GRS S Stellungnahmen Kernenergiefragen
Gesellschaft fuer Romanische Literatur — GRL
Gesellschaft fuer Schwerionenforschung. Report — Ges Schwerionenforsch Rep
Gesellschaft fuer Strahlen- und Umweltforschung. Bereich Projekttraegerschaften. BPT-Bericht — Ges Strahlen Umweltforsch Bereich Projekttraegerschaften BPT
Gesellschaft fuer Strahlen- und Umweltforschung. Bericht P — Ges Strahlen Umweltforsch Ber P
Gesellschaft fuer Strahlen- und Umweltforschung. GSF-Bericht BT — Ges Strahlen Umweltforsch GSF Ber BT
Gesellschaft fuer Strahlen- und Umweltforschung. Institut fuer Oekologische Chemie. Bericht O — Ges Strahlen Umweltforsch Inst Oekol Chem Ber O
Gesellschaft fuer Strahlen- und Umweltforschung. Institut fuer Toxikologie und bericht TOX — Ges Strahlen Umweltforsch Inst Toxikol Biochem Abt Toxikol Be
Gesellschaft Naturforschender Freunde zu Berlin. Sitzungsberichte — Ges Naturf Freund Berlin Szb
Gesellschaft pro Vindonissa. Jahresbericht — GPVJ
Gesellschaft und Theologie — GT
Gesellschaft zur Befoerderung der Gesammten Naturwissenschaften zu Marburg. Schriften — Ges Naturw Marburg Schrift
Gesellschaft zur Bekaempfung der Krebskrankheiten Nordrhein-Westfalen. Symposium — Ges Bekaempf Krebskrankh Nordrhein Westfalen Symp
Gesellschaft zur Bekampfung der Krebskrankheiten im Nordrhein-Westfalen. Mitteilungsdienst — GBKMA
Gesellschaft zur Bekampfung der Krebskrankheiten im Nordrhein-Westfalen. Mitteilungsdienst [*Germany*] — Ges Bekampf Krebskr Nordrhein-Westfalen Mitteilungdienst
Gesellschaft zur Foerderung der Wissenschaft des Judentums — GFWJ
Gesetz ueber Kassenarztrecht — GKAR
Gesetz- und Verordnungsblatt fuer das Land Hessen. Teil 1 — Gesetz-Verordnungsbl Land Hessen Teil 1
Gesetz und Zeugnis — Gu Z
Gesetz zur Regelung der Wiedergutmachung Nationalsozialistischen Unrechts fuer Angehoerige des Oeffentlichen Dienstes — Wiederg G
Gesetzblatt der DDR. Teil I [*German Democratic Republic*] — GBl I
Gesetzblatt der DDR. Teil II [*German Democratic Republic*] — GBl II
Gesetzblatt der Deutschen Demokratischen Republik [*Germany*] — Gesetzblatt Dtsch Demokr Repub
Gesetzblatt der Deutschen Demokratischen Republik. Teil 1 — GDDTD
Gesetzblatt der Deutschen Demokratischen Republik. Teil 1 [*German Democratic Republic*] — Gesetzbl DDR Teil I
Gesetzblatt fuer Baden-Wuerttemberg — Gesetzbl Baden-Wuerttemb
Gesneriad Journal — Gesneriad J
Gesnerus — Gesn
Gesnerus Supplement — Gesnerus Suppl
Gespraech der Religionen — Ge Rel
Gespraechskreis Wissenschaft und Wirtschaft — GKWW
Gesta Dei per Francos — GDF
Gestalt und Gedanke — GG
Gestalt und Gedanke. Ein Jahrbuch — GuG
Gestalten und Kraefte Evangelischer Kirchengeschichte — GKEKG
Gestion — Gest
Gestion des Entreprises [*Database*] — DOGE
Gestos (California) — GSC
Gesuido Jigyo Chosahi Hokoku — GJCHD
Gesunde Pflanzen — Gesunde Pfl
Gesunde Pflanzen — Gesunde Pflanz
Gesundheit und Wohlfahrt — Gesun Wohlfahrt
Gesundheit und Wohlfahrt — Gesundh Wohlf
Gesundheits- und Umwelttechnik — Gesund Umwelttechnik
Gesundheitsdienst — Gesundhd
Gesundheitsfuehrung des Deutschen Volkes — Gesundheitsfuehr Dtsch Volkes
Gesundheitsfuersorge — Gesundh Fuers
Gesundheits-Ingenieur — GEINA
Gesundheits-Ingenieur — Ges-Ing
Gesundheits-Ingenieur — Gesundheits-Ing
Gesundheits-Ingenieur — Gesundh-Ing
Gesundheits-Ingenieur — Gesundhtsingenieur
Gesundheits-Ingenieur — Gesund-Ing
Gesundheits-Ingenieur — GI
Gesundheits-Ingenieur. Haustechnik-Bauphysik-Umwelttechnik — Gesund-Ing Haustech-Bauphys-Umwelttech
Gesundheitswesen und Desinfektion — GEDEAL
Gesundheitswesen und Desinfektion — Gesundheitswes Desinfekt
Geterogennyi Kataliz. Materialy Vsesoyuznoi Konferentsii po Mekhanizmu Kataliticheskikh Reaktsii — Geterog Katal Mater Vses Konf Mekh Katal Reakts
Geterogennyi Kataliz. Trudy Mezhdunarodnogo Simpoziuma po Geterogennomu Katalizu — Geterog Katal
Getreide Mehl und Brot — GEMBAN
Getreide Mehl und Brot — Getreide Mehl Brot
Getreide und Mehl — GETMA
Getreide und Mehl — Getreide Mehl
Getriebe Motoren Antriebselemente — Getriebe Mot Antriebselem

Gettysburg Theological Studies — GTS
Getuigenis (Utrecht) — Get
Geuzenpenning Munt- en Penningkundig Nieuws — GP
Gewasbescherming — GEWAD5
Gewerbearchiv — Gew A
Gewerbearchiv — GEWED
Gewerbearchiv. Zeitschrift fuer Gewerbeverwaltungsrecht und Wirtschaftsverwaltungsrecht — GWA
Gewerbesteuergesetz — Gew St G
Gewerbliche Rundschau — Gewerbliche Rdsch
Gewerblicher Rechtsschutz — Gewerbl Rechtsschutz
Gewerblicher Rechtsschutz und Urheberrecht — Gewerbl Rechtsschutz U Urheberr
Gewerblicher Rechtsschutz und Urheberrecht — Gewerbl Rechtsschutz Urheberrecht
Gewerkschaftliche Monatshefte — Gew MH
Gewerkschaftliche Monatshefte — Gew Mon H
Gewerkschaftliche Monatshefte — Gewerk MH
Gewerkschaftliche Monatshefte — Gewerksch Monatsh
Gewerkschaftliche Monatshefte — Gewerkschaftl Mh
Gewerkschaftliche Monatshefte — Gewerkschaftliche Mhefte
Gewerkschaftliche Monatshefte — GMOND
Gewerkschaftliche Monatshefte — GWM
Gewerkschaftliche Praxis — Gewerk Prax
Gewerkschaftliche Rundschau — Gew Rundsch
Gewerkschaftliche Rundschau — Gewerk Rd
Gewerkschaftliche Rundschau — Gewerksch Rundsch
Geyer's Dealer Topics — Geyer DT
Geyer's Office Dealer — Geyer OD
Geyser — GEYSD
Gezetzgebungsstand [*Database*] — GESTA
Gezira Research Station and Substations. Annual Report — Gezira Res Stn Substn Annu Rep
Gezira Research Station and Substations. Annual Report — GZSRAA
Gezondheidsorganisatie TNO [*Nederlands Centrale Organisatie voor Toegepast-Natuurwetenschappelijk Onderzoek*]. Afdeling Gezondheidstechniek. Rapport — Gezondheidsorgan TNO Afd Gezondheidstech Rapp
GFF (Geologiska Foreningen i Stockholm Forhandlingar) — GFF (Geol Foren Stockholm Forhandl)
GFZ-CA [*Grossforschungszentrum Chemieanlagen*] **Mitteilungen** — GFZ-CA Mitt
GHAA [*Group Health Association of America*] **Journal** — GHAA Jnl
Ghana. Animal Research Institute. Annual Report — GARIA7
Ghana. Animal Research Institute. Annual Report — Ghana Anim Res Inst Annu Rep
Ghana Bulletin of Theology — GBT
Ghana Bulletin of Theology — Ghana B Theol
Ghana Bulletin of Theology — Ghana Bull Theol
Ghana Bulletin of Theology — GhB
Ghana. Council for Scientific and Industrial Research. Forest Products Research Institute. Annual Report — GFPIAW
Ghana. Council for Scientific and Industrial Research. Forest Products Research Institute. Annual Report — Ghana CSIR For Prod Res Inst Annu Rep
Ghana. Council for Scientific and Industrial Research. Forest Products Research Institute. Technical Newsletter — GFTNAX
Ghana. Council for Scientific and Industrial Research. Forest Products Research Institute. Technical Newsletter — Ghana Counc Sci Ind Res For Prod Res Inst Tech Newsl
Ghana. Council for Scientific and Industrial Research. Forest Products Research Institute. Technical Newsletter — Ghana CSIR For Prod Res Inst Tech Newsl
Ghana Farmer — Ghana Fmr
Ghana. Fishery Research Unit. Information Report — Ghana Fish Res Unit Inf Rep
Ghana. Fishery Research Unit. Information Report — RGFRD4
Ghana. Fishery Research Unit. Marine Fishery Research — GMFRBP
Ghana. Fishery Research Unit. Marine Fishery Research Reports — Ghana Fish Res Unit Mar Fish Res Rep
Ghana Forestry Journal — Ghana For J
Ghana Journal of Agricultural Science — Ghana J Agric Sci
Ghana Journal of Agricultural Science — GJASA
Ghana Journal of Agricultural Science — GJASAF
Ghana Journal of Science — Ghana J Sci
Ghana Journal of Science — GHJSA
Ghana Journal of Science — GHJSAC
Ghana Journal of Sociology — Ghana J Sociol
Ghana Law Reports — GLR
Ghana Library Journal — Ghana Libr J
Ghana Library Journal — Ghana Library J
Ghana Medical Journal — Ghana Med J
Ghana Medical Journal — GHMJA
Ghana Medical Journal — GHMJAY
Ghana Notes and Queries — Ghana Notes
Ghana Social Science Journal — Ghana Soc S
Ghana Social Science Journal — Ghana Soc Sci J
Ghanaian Nurse — Ghana Nurse
Ghanaian Times — GT
Gl. Gesundheits-Ingenieur-Haustechnik, Bauphysik, Umwelttechnik — GI Gesund Ing Haustech Bauphys Umwelttech
Gl. Haustechnik, Bauphysik, Umwelttechnik — GHBUD
GI Research. Journal of Gastrointeestinal Research — GI Res
Giannini Foundation Research Report — Giannini Found Res Rep
Giannini Information Series. Giannini Foundation of Agricultural Economics — Giannini Inf Ser Giannini Found Agric Econ
Giant Molecular Clouds in the Galaxy. Gregynog Astrophysics Workshop — Giant Mol Clouds Galaxy Gregynog Astrophys Workshop
Giardini. Giornale della Societa Orticola di Lombardia — Giardini Soc Orticola
Giardino Coloniale di Palermo. Lavori — Giardino Colon Palermo Lav
Gibb Memorial Series — GMS
Gibridnye Vychislitel'nye Mashiny i Kompleksy — Gibridnye Vycisl Masiny i Kompleksy
Gibridnye Vychislitel'nye Mashiny i Kompleksy — Gilbrid Vychisl Mashiny Kompleksy
Gibridnye Vychislitel'nye Mashiny i Kompleksy — GVMKD
Gidratatsiya i Tverdenie Tsementov — Gidratatsiya Tverd Tsem
Gidravlicheskie Mashiny — GDVMA
Gidravlika i Gidrotekhnika — Gidravl Gidrotekh
Gidroaeromehanika — GDROA
Gidroaeromehanika i Teorija Uprugosti — Gidroaeromeh i Teor Uprogosti
Gidrobiologiceskij Zurnal SSSR — Gidrobiol Zurn SSSR
Gidrobiologicheskie Issledovaniya — Gidrobiol Issled
Gidrobiologicheskie Issledovaniya Dukshtasskikh Ozer — Gidrobiol Issled Dukshtasskikh Ozer
Gidrobiologicheskii Zhurnal — GBZUA
Gidrobiologicheskii Zhurnal — GBZUAM
Gidrobiologicheskii Zhurnal — Gidrobiol Zh
Gidrobiologicheskii Zhurnal Akademiya Nauk Ukrainskoi SSR — Gidrobiol Zh Akad Nauk Ukr SSR
Gidrobiologicheskii Zhurnal/Hydrobiological Journal — Gidrobiol Zh Hydrobiol J
Gidrodinamika Bol'shikh Skorostei — Gidrodin Bol'shikh Skorostei
Gidrodinamika i Teploobmen — Gidrodin Teploobmen
Gidrogeologicheskii Sbornik — Gidrogeol Sb
Gidrogeologiya i Gidrogeokhimiya — Gidrogeol Gidrogeokhim
Gidrogeologiya i Inzhenernaya Geologiya Aridnoi Zony SSSR — Gidrogeol Inzh Geol Aridnoi Zony SSSR
Gidrogeologiya i Karstovedenie — Gidrogeol Karstoved
Gidrogeologiya. Inzhenernaya Geologiya — Gidrogeol Inzh Geol
Gidrokhimicheskiye Materialy — Gidrokhim Mater
Gidrokhimiya Urala — Gidrokhim Urala
Gidroliznaja i Lesohimiceskaja Promyshlennost — Gidrol Lesohim Prom
Gidroliznaya i Lesokhimicheskaya Promyshlennost — Gidroliz Lesokhim Promysh
Gidroliznaya i Lesokhimicheskaya Promyshlennost — GLKPA
Gidrometeorologiya Azerbaidzhana i Kaspiiskogo. Morya — Gidromet Azerb Kasp Morya
Gidroprivod Gidropnevmoavtomatika — Gidroprivod Gidropnevmoavtomatika
Gidrotekhnicheskoe Stroitel'stvo — Gidrotekh Stroit
Gidrotekhnicheskoe Stroitel'stvo — GTSTA
Gidrotekhnika i Melioratsiya — Gidrotekh Melior
Gidrotekhnika i Melioratsiya v Latviiskoi SSR — Gidrotekh Melior Lat SSR
Gids — G
Gids — GIC
Gids op Maatschappelijk Gebied. Tijdschrift voor Syndicale, Culturele, en Sociale Problemen — GIS
Gids voor Personeelsbeleid. Arbeidsvraagstukken en Sociale Verzekering — SVG
Giervalk — GRFTAV
Giessener Abhandlungen zur Agrar- und Wirtschaftsforschung des Europaeischen Ostens — Giessener Abh Agr WirtForsch Eur Ostens
Giessener Beitraege zur Deutschen Philologie — GBDP
Giessener Beitraege zur Entwicklungsforschung. Reihe 1 — Giessener Beitr Entwicklungsforsch Reihe 1
Giessener Beitraege zur Romanischen Philologie — GBRP
Giessener Geologische Schriften — Giessener Geol Schr
Giessener Naturwissenschaftliche Vortraege — Giessener Naturwiss Vortraege
Giessener Schriftenreihe Tierzucht und Haustiergenetik — Giessener Schriftenr Tierz Haustiergenet
Giessener Schriftenreihe Tierzucht und Haustiergenetik — GSTHA4
Giesserei [*Germany*] — GIESA
Giesserei — Giess
Giesserei. Technisch-Wissenschaftliche Beihefte, Giessereiwesen, und Metallkunde — Giesserei Tech Wiss Beih
Giesserei und Maschinenbau Zeitung — Giesserei Maschinenbau Ztg
Giesserei-Erfahrungsaustausch — Giesserei-Erfah
Giessereiforschung — GSFGB
Giesserei-Praxis — Giesserei Prax
Giessereipraxis — GIPXA
Giesserei-Rundschau — GIERB
Giesserei-Rundschau [*Austria*] — Giesserei-Rundsch
Giessereitechnik — GSRTA
Giesserei-Zeitung — Giessereiztg
Gifford Lectures — Giff L
Gifford Lectures on Natural Religion — GLNR
GIFT (Grupo Interuniversitario de Fisica Teorica) International Seminar on Theoretical Physics — GIFT Int Semin Theor Phys
Gifted Child Quarterly — GICQA
Gifted Child Quarterly — Gift Ch Q
Gifted Child Quarterly — Gift Child
Gifted Child Quarterly — Gifted Child Q
Gifted Child Quarterly — IGCQ
Gifted Child Today — GCT
Gifts and Decorative Accessories — GAB
Gifu College of Agriculture. Research Bulletin — Gifu Coll Agric Res Bull
Gifu College of Education. Annals — Ann Gifu College Ed
Gifu Daigaku Igakubu Kiyo — GDIKAN
Gifu Daigaku Nogakubu Kenkyu Hokoku — GNKEAH
Gifu University. Faculty of General Education. Bulletin — Bull Fac Gen Ed Gifu Univ

Gifu Yakka Daigaku Kiyo [*Annual Proceedings. Gifu Pharmaceutical University*] — GYDKA9
Gigiena i Epidemiologiia — Gig i Epidemiol
Gigiena i Sanitariya — Gig San
Gigiena i Sanitariya — Gig Sanit
Gigiena i Sanitariya — GISAA
Gigiena i Sanitariya — GISAAA
Gigiena i Toksikologiya Novykh Pestitsidov i Klinika Otravlenii. Doklady Vsesoyuznoi Nauchnoi Konferentsii — Gig Toksikol Nov Pestits Klin Otravlenii Dokl Vses Nauchn Ko
Gigiena i Toksikologiya Pestitsidov i Klinika Otravlenii — Gig Toksikol Pestitsi Klin Otravlenii
Gigiena i Toksikologiya Polimernykh Stroitel'nykh Materialov — Gig Toksikol Polim Stroit Mater
Gigiena Naselennykh Mest [*Ukrainian SSR*] — Gig Naselennykh Mest
Gigiena Naselennykh Mest Respublikanskoi Mezhvedomstvennyi Sbornik — Gig Nasel Mest Resp Mezhved Sb
Gigiena Naselennykh Mest Respublikanskoi Mezhvedomstvennyi Sbornik — GNAMAP
Gigiena Primeneiya Polimernykh Materialov v Stroitel'stve. Materialy Vsesoyuznogo Soveshchaniya po Voprosam Sanitarno-Gigienicheskogo Kontrolya Primeneniem Polimernykh Materialov v Stroitel'stve — Gig Primen Polim Mater Stroit Mater Vses Soveshch
Gigiena Primeneniya Polimernykh Materialov i Izdelii iz Nikh — Gig Primen Polim Mater Izdelii Nikh
Gigiena Primeneniya. Toksikologiya, Pestitsidov, i Klinika Otravlenii — Gig Primen Toksikol Pestits Klin Otravlenii
Gigiena. Toksikologiya i Klinika Novykh Insektofungitsidov. Trudy Vsesoyuznoi Nauchnoi Konferentsii po Gigiene i Toksikologii Insektofungitsidov — Gig Toksikol Klin Nov Insektofungits Tr Vses Nauchn Konf
Gigiena Truda [*Ukrainian SSR*] — Gig Tr
Gigiena Truda i Professional'naya Patologiya v Estonskoi SSR [*Estonian SSR*] — Gig Tr Prof Patol Est SSR
Gigiena Truda i Professional'naya Patologiya v Estonskoi SSR — GTPPA
Gigiena Truda i Professional'nye Zabolevaniya — Gig Tr Prof Zabol
Gigiena Truda i Professional'nye Zabolevaniya — GTPZA
Gigiena Truda i Professional'nye Zabolevaniya — GTPZAB
Gigiena Truda Respublikanskii Mezhvedomstvennyi Sbornik — Gig Tr Resp Mezhved Sb
Gigiena Truda Respublikanskii Mezhvedomstvennyi Sbornik — GIGTA7
Gigienicheskie Aspekty Okhrany Okruzhayushchei Sredy — Gig Aspekty Okhr Okruzh Sredy
Gigienicheskii — Gigien
Giho. Research and Development Headquarters. Japan Defense Agency — Giho Res Dev Headquarters Jpn Defense Agency
Gijutsu — GIJUA
Gijutsu Daijesuto — GIDAD
Gijutsu Kenkyusho Shoho — GKSHA
Gijutsu Shiryo. Mitsubishi Sekiyu Kabushiki Kaisha — MSGSB
Gil Vicente — GV
Gila Review — Gila Rev
Gilbert and Sullivan Journal — G & S J
Gildeboek — Gb
Gillett Memorial Lecture — Gillett Mem Lect
Ginecologia Brasileira — Ginecol Bras
Ginecologia Brasileira — GNCBA
Ginecologia Brasileira — GNCBA2
Ginecologia Clinica — GICLDY
Ginecologia Clinica — Ginecol Clin
Ginecologia Pratica — Ginecol Prat
Ginecologia. Revista Pratica. Societa Toscana di Ostetricia e Ginecologia (Florence) — Ginecologia Florence
Ginecologia y Obstetricia de Mexico — Ginecol Obstet Mex
Ginecologia y Obstetricia (Lima) — Ginecol Obstet (Lima)
Ginekologia Polska — Ginekol Pol
Ginekologia Polska — GIPOA
Ginekologia Polska — GIPOA3
Ginekologia Polska. Suplement — Ginekol Pol Supl
Ginekologia Polska. Suplement — GKPSAT
Ginekologija i Opstetricija — Ginekol Opstet
Giornale. Accademia di Medicina di Torino — G Accad Med Torino
Giornale. Associazione Napolitana di Medici e Naturalisti — Giorn Assoc Napol Med
Giornale Botanico Italiano — G Bot Ital
Giornale Botanico Italiano — GBOIA
Giornale Botanico Italiano — Giorn Bot Ital
Giornale Critico della Filosofia Italiana — G Crit Filosof Ital
Giornale Critico della Filosofia Italiana — GCFI
Giornale Critico della Filosofia Italiana — GFI
Giornale Critico della Filosofia Italiana — Giorn Crit d Filos Ital
Giornale Dantesco — GD
Giornale d'Artiglieria e Genio — GAG
Giornale d'Artiglieria e Genio — Giorn Artigl
Giornale de' Letterati (Pisa) — Giorn Letterati Pisa
Giornale de Scienze Naturali ed Economiche di Palermo — Giorn Sci Nat Econ Palermo
Giornale degli Allevatori [*Italy*] — G Allevatori
Giornale degli Economisti e Annali di Economia — G Economisti
Giornale degli Economisti e Annali di Economia — GE
Giornale degli Economisti e Annali di Economia — Giorn Econom Ann Econom
Giornale degli Economisti e Annali di Economia — Giornale Economisti e Ann Econ
Giornale degli Scavi di Pompei — GSP
Giornale dei Congressi Medici — Giorn Cong Med
Giornale dei Poeti — GP
Giornale dei Pollicoltori — G Pollicolt
Giornale dei Pollicoltori — GIPLA
Giornale del Genio Civile — G Genio Civ
Giornale della Arteriosclerosi — G Arterioscler
Giornale della Libreria — GL
Giornale della Lombardia — Gior Lomb
Giornale della Reale Accademia di Medicina di Torino — Gior R Accad Med Torino
Giornale della Reale Accademia Medico-Chirurgica di Torino — G R Accad Med Chir Torino
Giornale della Reale Societa Italiana d'Igiene — Gior R Soc Ital Ig
Giornale della Societa Asiatica Italiana — GSAI
Giornale di Agricoltura — G Agr
Giornale di Agricoltura del Regno d'Italia — Giorn Agric Regno Italia
Giornale di Agricoltura Domenica — G Agr Domen
Giornale di Agricoltura. Societa Agraria Jesina — Giorn Agric Jesi
Giornale di Anestesia Stomatologica — G Anest Stomatol
Giornale di Astronomia — G Astron
Giornale di Batteriologia e Immunologia — G Batteriol Immunol
Giornale di Batteriologia, Virologia, ed Immunologia — G Batteriol Virol Immunol
Giornale di Batteriologia, Virologia, ed Immunologia — GBVID
Giornale di Batteriologia, Virologia, ed Immunologia. Annali dell'Ospedale Maria Vittoria di Torino — G Batteriol Virol Immunol Ann Osp Maria Vittoria Torino
Giornale di Batteriologia, Virologia, ed Immunologia. Annali dell'Ospedale Maria Vittoria di Torino. Parte 1. Sezione Microbiologica — G Batteriol Virol Immunol Microbiol
Giornale di Batteriologia, Virologia, ed Immunologia. Annali dell'Ospedale Maria Vittoria di Torino. Parte 2. Sezione Clinica — G Batteriol Virol Immunol Clin
Giornale di Batteriologia, Virologia, ed Immunologia. Annali dell'Ospedale Maria Vittoria di Torino. Parte I. Sezione Microbiologia — GBVMAC
Giornale di Batteriologia, Virologia, ed Immunologia. Annali dell'Ospedale Maria Vittoria di Torino. Parte II. Sezione Clinica — GBVCAG
Giornale di Biochimica — G Biochim
Giornale di Biochimica — Gi Biochim
Giornale di Biologia Applicata alla Industria Chimica — G Biol Appl Ind Chim
Giornale di Biologia Applicata alla Industria Chimica ed Alimentare — G Biol Appl Ind Chim Aliment
Giornale di Biologia e Medicina Sperimentale — G Biol Med Sper
Giornale di Biologia Industriale Agraria ed Alimentare — G Biol Ind Agrar Aliment
Giornale di Bordo. Mensile di Storia, Letteratura, ed Arte — GdB
Giornale di Chimica Applicata — G Chim Appl
Giornale di Chimica Industriale — G Chim Ind
Giornale di Chimica Industriale ed Applicata — G Chim Ind Appl
Giornale di Chirurgia — G Chir
Giornale di Clinica Medica — G Clin Med
Giornale di Clinica Medica — Gior Clin Med
Giornale di Clinica Medica (Bologna) — G Clin Med (Bologna)
Giornale di Farmacia Chimica e Scienze Affini — G Farm Chim
Giornale di Farmacia Chimica e Scienze Affini — G Farm Chim Sci Affini
Giornale di Farmacia-Chimica e Scienze Accessorie — Giorn Farm Chim Sci Accessorie
Giornale di Fisica — G Fis
Giornale di Fisica. Quaderni — G Fis Quad
Giornale di Fisica Sanitaria e Protezione Contro le Radiazioni — G Fis Sanit
Giornale di Fisica Sanitaria e Protezione Contro le Radiazioni — G Fis Sanit Prot Radiaz
Giornale di Fisica Sanitaria e Protezione Contro le Radiazioni — G Fis Sanit Protez Contro Radiaz
Giornale di Fisica Sanitaria e Protezione Contro le Radiazioni — GFSRA
Giornale di Fisica. Societa Italiana di Fisica [*Italy*] — G Fis Soc Ital Fis
Giornale di Geologia — G Geol
Giornale di Geologia (Bologna) — G Geol (Bologna)
Giornale di Geologia. Museo Geologico di Bologna. Annali — G Geol Mus Geol Bologna Ann
Giornale di Gerontologia — G Gerontol
Giornale di Gerontologia — Gior Geront
Giornale di Gerontologia. Supplemento — G Gerontol Suppl
Giornale di Igiene e Medicina Preventiva — G Ig Med Prev
Giornale di Letterati d'Italia — Gior Lett Italia
Giornale di Malattie Infettive e Parassitarie — G Mal Infett Parassit
Giornale di Matematiche di Battaglini — Giorn Mat Battaglini
Giornale di Matematiche di Battaglini. Serie 6 [*Naples*] — Giorn Mat Battaglini 6
Giornale di Medicina di Laboratorio — G Med Lab
Giornale di Medicina e Tisiologia — G Med Tisiol
Giornale di Medicina Militare — G Med Mil
Giornale di Medicina Practica — Gior Med Prat
Giornale di Medicina Veterinaria — Gior Med Vet
Giornale di Metafisica — G Metaf
Giornale di Metafisica — GdiM
Giornale di Metafisica — GM
Giornale di Microbiologia — G Microbiol
Giornale di Neuropsichiatria dell'Eta Evolutiva — G Neuropsichiatr Eta Evol
Giornale di Ostetricia e Ginecologia — G Ostet Ginecol
Giornale di Pneumologia — G Pneumol
Giornale di Psichiatria e di Neuropatologia — G Psichiatr Neuropatol
Giornale di Ricerca e Medicina di Laboratorio — G R Med Lab
Giornale di Risicoltura — G Risic
Giornale di Scienze ed Arti — Giorn Sci Arti
Giornale di Scienze, Lettere, ed Arti per la Sicilia — Gior Sc Lett ed Arti Sicilia
Giornale di Scienze Mediche — G Sci Med
Giornale di Stomatologia e di Ortognatodonzia — G Stomatol Ortognatodonzia

Giornale di Trasporti Industrali — Gior Trasp Ind
Giornale di Viticoltura e di Enologia, Agricoltura, e Industrie Agrarie — Giorn Vitic Enol
Giornale d'Italia — GdI
Giornale d'Italia Agricola — Giorn Italia Agric
Giornale Economico — Giorn Econ
Giornale Economico — Giornale Econ
Giornale Filologico Ferrarese — GFF
Giornale Filologico Ferrarese — Giorn Fil Ferr
Giornale Fisico-Medico Ossia Raccolta di Osservazioni Sopra la Fisica, Matematica, Chimica, Storia Naturale, Medicina, Chirurgia, Arti, e Agricoltura — Giorn Fis Med
Giornale Internazionale delle Scienze Mediche — Gior Internaz Sc Med
Giornale Italiano della Tubercolosi — G Ital Tuberc
Giornale Italiano della Tubercolosi e delle Malattie del Torace — G Ital Tuberc Mal Torace
Giornale Italiano delle Malattie del Torace — G Ital Mal Torace
Giornale Italiano delle Malattie del Torace. Supplemento — G Ital Mal Torace Suppl
Giornale Italiano delle Malattie Veneree e della Pelle — Gior Ital Mal Ven
Giornale Italiano di Anestesia e di Analgesia — G Ital Anest Analg
Giornale Italiano di Anestesiologia — G Ital Anestesiol
Giornale Italiano di Cardiologia — G Ital Cardiol
Giornale Italiano di Chemioterapia — G Ital Chemioter
Giornale Italiano di Chimica Clinica — G Ital Chim Clin
Giornale Italiano di Chimica Clinica — GICCD7
Giornale Italiano di Chirurgia — G Ital Chir
Giornale Italiano di Dermatologia [*Later, Giornale Italiano di Dermatologia e Venereologia*] — G Ital Dermatol
Giornale Italiano di Dermatologia e Sifilologia — G Ital Dermatol Sifilol
Giornale Italiano di Dermatologia e Venereologia — G Ital Dermatol Venereol
Giornale Italiano di Dermatologia Minerva Dermatologica — G Ital Dermatol Minerva Dermatol
Giornale Italiano di Entomologia — G Ital Entomol
Giornale Italiano di Entomologia — GIENDG
Giornale Italiano di Filologia — GIF
Giornale Italiano di Filologia — Giorn It Fil
Giornale Italiano di Filologia. Biblioteca — GIFB
Giornale Italiano di Filologia (Naples) — Giorn It Fil (Nap)
Giornale Italiano di Gerontologia — G Ital Gerontol
Giornale Italiano di Malattie Esotiche e Tropicali ed Igiene Coloniale — Gior Ital Mal Esot e Trop ed Ig Colon
Giornale Italiano di Medicina del Lavoro — G Ital Med Lav
Giornale Italiano di Medicina del Lavoro — GIMLDG
Giornale Italiano di Nefrologia — G Ital Nefrol
Giornale Italiano di Oftalmologia — G Ital Oftalmol
Giornale Italiano di Patologia e di Scienze Affini — G Ital Patol Sci Affini
Giornale Italiano di Patologia e Scienze Affini — Giorn Ital Patol Sci Affini
Giornale Italiano di Psicologia — GIPSB
Giornale Ligustico di Scienze, Lettere, ed Arti — Giorn Ligustico Sci
Giornale Medico del Regio Esercito e della Regia Marina — Gior Med R Esercito
Giornale. Reale Accademia di Medicina di Torino — G R Accad Med Torino
Giornale. Societa Asiatica Italiana — Gior Soc Asia It
Giornale. Societa Asiatica Italiana — Giorn Soc Asiat Ital
Giornale. Societa d'Incoraggiamento della Scienze e delle Arti Stabilata in Milano — Giorn Soc Incoragg Sci Milano
Giornale Storico della Letteratura Italiana — G Stor Let
Giornale Storico della Letteratura Italiana — Gior Storico
Giornale Storico della Letteratura Italiana — Giorn Stor d Lett Ital
Giornale Storico della Letteratura Italiana — GSLI
Giornale Storico della Letteratura Italiana. Supplement — GSLIS
Giornale Storico della Lunigiana — Giorn Stor Lunig
Giornale Storico delle Lunigiana e del Territorio Lucense — GLL
Giornale Storico e Letterario della Liguria — GSLL
Giornale Svizzero di Farmacia — G Svizz Farm
Giornale Veneto di Scienze Mediche — G Veneto Sci Med
Giornata della Scienza. Consiglio Nazionale della Ricerche. Convegno sulle Vitamine — Giornata Sci Cons Naz Ric Conv Vitam
Giovanni Lorenzini Foundation. Monographs — Giovanni Lorenzini Found Monogr
Giovanni Lorenzini Foundation. Symposia — Giovanni Lorenzini Found Symp
Giperbazitovye Assotsiatsii Skladchatykh Oblastei — Giperbazitovye Assots Skladchatykh Obl
Gipertonicheskaya Bolezn Ateroskleroz i Koronarnaya Nedostatochnost — Giperton Bolezn Ateroskler Koron Nedostatochn
Girl About Town — G
Girls' Own Paper — GOP
Girl's Realm — GR
Gissing Newsletter — Gissing N
GIT [*Glas- und Instrumenten-Technik*] **Fachzeitschrift fuer das Laboratorium** [*West Germany*] — GITEA
GIT [*Glas- und Instrumenten-Technik*] **Fachzeitschrift fuer das Laboratorium. Supplement** — GIT Fachz Lab Suppl
GIT [*Glas- und Instrumenten-Technik*] **Labor-Medizin** — GIT Labor Med
GIT [*Glas- und Instrumenten-Technik*] **Labor-Medizin** — GLMDD
GIT Spezial Chromatographie — GIT Spez Chromatogr
GIT [*Glas- und Instrumenten-Technik*] **Supplement** — GIT Suppl
Gitarre & Laute — G&L
Gitarrefreund — Gf
Gitut'yun ew Texnika — Gitut'yun Texnika
Giurisprudenza Completa della Corte Suprema di Cassazione. Civile — Giur Compl Cass Civ
Giurisprudenza Completa della Corte Suprema di Cassazione. Criminale — Giur Compl Cass Crim
Giurisprudenza Costituzionale — Giur Cost
Giurisprudenza delle Imposte Dirette di Registro e di Negoziazione — Giur Imp Reg Negoz
Giurisprudenza Italiana — Giur Ital
Giustizia Civile — Giust Civ
Giustizia Penale — Giust Pen
Givaudan Flavorist — Givaudan Flavor
Gjurmime Albanologijike — GAlb
Gjurmime Albanologjike [*Prishtina*] — GjA
GKB [*Graz-Koeflacher Eisenbahn und Bergbaugesellschaft*] **Zeitung fuer Eisenbahn und Bergbau** — GKB Zt
Glacier Natural History Association. Special Bulletin — Glacier Nat History Assoc Special Bull
Glaciological Data. World Data Center A — GDWDA
Glaciological Data. World Data Center A — GDWDCA
GLAD [*Greater London Association for Disabled People*] **Journal** — GLAD Jnl
Gladiolus — GLADB
Gladiolus Bulletin. New England Gladiolus Society — Gladiolus Bull
Gladiolus Magazine — Gladiolus Mag
Glahn Samfundet — Gl Smf
Glamorgan Historian — Glamorgan Hist
Glamour — GGLA
Glas. Srpska Akademija Nauka i Umetnosti. Odeljenje Tehnickih Nauka — Glas Srp Akad Nauka Umet Od Teh Nauka
Glas. Srpska Akademija Nauka — GlasSAN
Glas. Srpska Akademija Nauka — GlSAN
Glas. Srpska Akademija Nauka i Umetnosti Odeljenje Medicinskih Nauka — Glas Srp Akad Nauk Umet Od Med Nauk
Glas. Srpska Akademija Nauka i Umetnosti Odeljenje Medicinskih Nauka — Glas Srp Akad Nauka
Glas. Srpska Akademija Nauka i Umetnosti Odeljenje Medicinskih Nauka — Glas Srp Akad Nauka Med
Glas. Srpska Akademija Nauka i Umetnosti Odeljenje Medicinskih Nauka — SUGMAW
Glas. Srpska Akademija Nauka i Umetnosti Odeljenje Prirodno-Matematickikh Nauka — Glas Srp Akad Nauka Umet Od Prir Mat Nauka
Glas. Srpska Akademija Nauka i Umetnosti Odeljenje Prirodno-Matematickih Nauka — Glas Srpska Akad Nauka Umet Od Prir-Mat Nauka
Glas. Srpska Akademija Nauka i Umetnosti Odeljenje Prirodno-Matematickih Nauka — GSAKAK
Glas und Apparat — Glas Appar
Glas- und Hochvakuum Technik — Glas Hochv Techn
Glas- und Hochvakuum Technik — Glas Hochvak Tech
Glas- und Instrumenten Technik Fachzeitschrift fuer das Laboratorium — GIT
Glas- und Instrumenten Technik Fachzeitschrift fuer das Laboratorium — GIT Fachz Lab
Glas- und Instrumenten-Technik Fachzeitschrift fuer das Laboratorium — Glas Instrum Tech Fachz Lab
Glas-Email-Keramo-Technik — Glas Em Ker
Glas-Email-Keramo-Technik [*Germany*] — Glas-Email-Keramo-Tech
Glasers Annalen — Glasers Ann
Glasers Annalen fuer Gewerbe und Bauwesen — Glasers Ann Gewerbe Bauwes
Glasers Annalen fuer Gewerbe und Bauwesen — GlasersAnn
Glasers Annalen ZEV [*Zeitschrift fuer Eisenbahnwesen und Verkehrstechnik*] — Glasers Ann ZEV
Glasgow Archaeological Journal — Glasgow AJ
Glasgow Archaeological Journal — Glasgow Arch J
Glasgow Archaeological Journal — Glasgow Archaeol J
Glasgow Art Gallery and Museums Association. Review — Glasgow Art R
Glasgow Bibliographical Society — GBS
Glasgow Dental Journal — Glasg Dent J
Glasgow Herald — GH
Glasgow Mathematical Journal — Glas Math J
Glasgow Medical Journal — Glasg Med J
Glasgow Medical Journal — Glasgow Med J
Glasgow Naturalist — GGNTAS
Glasgow Naturalist — Glasg Nat
Glasgow Naturalist — Glasgow Nat
Glasgow University. Oriental Society. Transactions [*Glasgow*] — GlasgOrTrans
Glasgow University Oriental Society. Transactions — GUOS
Glasgow University. Publications — Glasg Univ Publ
Glasgow University Publications — GUP
Glashuette und Keramik — Glashuette Keram
Glasilo Zbora Lijecnika Hrvatske — Glasilo Zbora Lijec Hrvat
Glas-Instrument-Technik [*Germany*] — Glas-Instrum-Tech
Glasnik — Gl
Glasnik — Glas
Glasnik — Glasn
Glasnik. Bioloske Sekcije. Hrvatsko Prirodoslovno Drustvo — Glasn Biol Sekc Hrv Prir Dr
Glasnik Casopis za Poljoprivredu Vodoprivredu. Veterinarstvo i Sumarstvo AKMO [*A publication*] — Glas Casop Poljopriv Vodopriv Vet Sumar AKMO
Glasnik Drustva Hemicara i Tehnologa SR Bosne i Hercegovine — Glas Drus Hem Tehnol SR Bosne Hercegovine
Glasnik Drustva Hemicara NR Bosne i Hercegovine — Glas Drus Hem NR Bosne Hercegovine
Glasnik Drzavnog Muzeja u Sarajevu. Prirodne Nauke — Glasn Drzavn Muz U Sarajevu Prir Nauke
Glasnik Hemicara i Technologa Bosne i Hercegovine — Glas Hem Technol Bosne Hercegovine
Glasnik Hemicara i Technologa Bosne i Hercegovine [*Yugoslavia*] — Glas Hemicara Technol Bosne Hercegovine
Glasnik Hemijskog Drustva (Beograd) — Glas Hem Drus (Beograd)
Glasnik Hemijskog Drustva (Beograd) — Glasn Hem Drust (Beogr)
Glasnik Hemijskog Drustva Kraljevine Jugoslavije — Glas Hem Drus Kralj Jugosl

Glasnik Hemijskog Druzstva (Beograd) — Glas Hemij Druz (Beograd)
Glasnik Hrvatskoga Naravoslovnoga Drustva — Glasn Hrvatsk Nar Drustva
Glasnik Khemijskog Drushtva [*Beograd*] — GHDBAX
Glasnik Khemijskog Drushtva (Beograd) — Glas Khem Drush (Beogr)
Glasnik Matematicki — Glas Mat
Glasnik Matematicki. Serija III — Glas Mat Ser III
Glasnik Matematicki. Serija III. Drustvo Matematicara i Fizicara SR Hrvatske. — Glasnik Mat Ser III
Glasnik Matematicko-Fizicki i Astronomski [*Yugoslavia*] — Glas Mat-Fiz Astron
Glasnik Muzeja Kosova i Metohije — GMKM
Glasnik Muzejskega Drustva za Slovenijo [*Ljubljana*] — Gl M Slov
Glasnik Muzejskega Drustva za Slovenijo [*Ljubljana*] — GMDS
Glasnik na Hemicarite i Tehnolozite na Makedonija — Glas Hem Tehnol Maked
Glasnik Pravoslavne Tzrkve u Kraljevini Srbiji — GPTKS
Glasnik Prirodnjackog Muzeja Srpske Zemlje. Bulletin du Museum d'Histoire Naturelle du Pays Serbe. Serija B. Bioloske Nauke — Glasn Prir Muz Srpske Zemlje Ser B Biol Nauke
Glasnik Prirodnjackog Muzeja Srpske Zemlje. Serija A. Mineralogija, Geologija, Paleontologija — Glas Prir Muz Srp Zemlje Ser A
Glasnik Prirodnjackog Muzeja u Beogradu. Serija A. Mineralogija, Geologija, Palentologija [*Yugoslavia*] — Glas Prir Muz Beogradu Serija A
Glasnik Prirodnjackog Muzeja u Beogradu. Serija A. Mineralogija, Geologija, Paleontologija — Glas Prir Muz Beogradu Ser A
Glasnik Republickog Zavoda za Zastitu Prirode i Prirodnjackog Muzeja Titogradu — Glas Repub Zavoda Zast Prir Prir Muz Titogradu
Glasnik Republickog Zavoda za Zastitu Prirode i Prirodnjackog Muzeja Titogradu — GRZZAD
Glasnik Skopskog Naucnog Drustva. Bulletin de la Societe Scientifique de Skopje — Glasn Skopsk Naucn Drustva
Glasnik. Srpska Akademija Nauka i Umetnosti [*Belgrad*] — Glas SAN
Glasnik. Srpska Akademija Nauka i Umetnosti [*Belgrad*] — Glas SANU
Glasnik. Srpska Akademija Nauka i Umetnosti [*Belgrad*] — Glasnik SANU
Glasnik. Srpska Akademija Nauka i Umetnosti [*Belgrad*] — GSAN
Glasnik. Srpska Akademija Nauka i Umetnosti [*Belgrad*] — SAN
Glasnik Sumarskog Fakulteta Univerzitet u Beogradu — Glasnik Sumar Fak Univ Beogradu
Glasnik Tsentralnogo Khigiyenskog Zavoda (Beograd) — Glasnik Tsentral Khig Zavoda (Beograd)
Glasnik za Sumske Pokuse — Glas Sumske Pokuse
Glasnik za Sumske Pokuse — GLSPA8
Glasnik Zemaljskog Muzeja Bosne i Hercegovine u Sarajevu — Bull Sarajevo
Glasnik Zemaljskog Muzeja Bosne i Hercegovine u Sarajevu — Gl Hrv M
Glasnik Zemaljskog Muzeja Bosne i Hercegovine u Sarajevu — Glasnik-Sarajevo
Glasnik Zemaljskog Muzeja Bosne i Hercegovine u Sarajevu — GLM Bosn
Glasnik Zemaljskog Muzeja Bosne i Hercegovine u Sarajevu — GZM
Glasnik Zemaljskog Muzeja Bosne i Hercegovine u Sarajevu — GZMBHS
Glasnik Zemaljskog Muzeja Bosne i Hercegovine u Sarajevu — GZMS
Glasnik Zemaljskog Muzeja Bosne i Hercegovine u Sarajevu. Prirodne Nauke — Glas Zemaljskog Muz Bosne Hercegovine Sarajevu Prir Nauke
Glasnik Zemaljskog Muzeja [*Subseries*] **Etnologija** — GZM
Glasnik Zemaljskog Muzeja u Sarajevu — Gl M Sar
Glasnik Zemaljskog Muzeja u Sarajevu. Bulletin de Musee de la Republique Populaire de Bosnie et Hercegovine a Sarajevo — Glasn Zemaljsk Muz U Sarajevu
Glass and Ceramics — Glass and Ceram
Glass and Ceramics — Glass Ceram
Glass and Ceramics. English Translation — Glass Ceram Engl Transl
Glass and Fine Ceramics. Scientific-Technical Conference — Glass Fine Ceram Sci Tech Conf
Glass Digest — Glass Dig
Glass Hill — GIH
Glass in Australia — Glass Aust
Glass Industry — Glass Ind
Glass Industry — GLI
Glass Industry (Moscow) — Glass Ind Moscow
Glass International — Glass Int
Glass Packaging — Glass Packag
Glass Packer — GLPAAG
Glass Packer/Processor — Glass Packer Process
Glass Physics and Chemistry (Translation of Fizika i Khimiya Stekla) — Glass Phys Chem Transl of Fiz Khim Stekla
Glass Science and Technology [*Elsevier Book Series*] — GST
Glass Technology — Glass Tech
Glass Technology — Glass Technol
Glass Worker — Glass Work
Glass Workers News — Glass Wkrs News
Glasses for Electronic Applications — Glasses Electron Appl
Glasshouse Crops Research Institute. Annual Report — GCRRAE
Glasshouse Crops Research Institute. Annual Report — Glasshouse Crops Res Inst Annu Rep
Glassworks — Glass
Glastechnische Berichte — Glastech Ber
Glastechnische Berichte. Sonderband. 32K — Glastech Ber Sonderb 32K
Glasteknisk Tidskrift [*Sweden*] — Glastek Tidskr
Glasteknisk Tidskrift — Glastek Tidskrift
Glasul Bisericii — Gla Bi
Glaube in der 2 Welt — Glaube 2 Welt
Glaucoma — GLAUD4
Glaucoma. Transactions of the Conference — Glaucoma Trans Conf
Glavnaya Geofizicheskaya Observatoriya imeni. A. I. Voeikova. Trudy — Gl Geofiz Obs im Al Voeikova Tr
Glavno Upravlenie na Stroitelnite Voiski. Nauchno-Tekhnicheska Informat siya (Sofia) — Gl Upr Stroit Voiski Nauchno Tekh Inf Sofia
Glaxo Volume — Glaxo Vol
Glaxo Volume — GLVOAK
Gleanings in Bee Culture — GLBCAK
Gleanings in Bee Culture — Glean Bee Cult
Gleanings in Bee Culture — Gleanings
Gleanings in Bee Culture — Gleanings Bee Cult
Gledaliski List Akademije za Igralsko Umetnost — GLAIU
Gledaliski List Slovenskega Narodnega Gledalisca v Ljubljane — GLSNG-L
Gledaliski List Slovenskega Narodnega Gledalisca v Mariboru — GLSNG-M
Gleistechnik und Fahrbahnbau — Gleistech Fahrbahnbau
Glenbow — GLBO
Glendale Law Review — Glendale L Rev
Glendale Law Review — Glendale Law R
Glens Falls Review — Glens Falls Rev
Gli Archivi Italiani — GAI
Gli Ebrei nell'Alto Medioevo — Ge
Glial and Neuronal Cell Biology. International Congress of Anatomy — Glial Neuronal Cell Biology Int Congr Anat
Glimpses of Kashmir Culture — Glimp Kash Cult
Global 2000. Report to the President. Volume 1 [*United States*] — Global One
Global 2000. Report to the President. Volume 2 [*United States*] — Global Two
Global Analysis Pure and Applied. Advanced — Global Anal Pure Appl Adv
Global Analysis Pure and Applied. Series A — Global Anal Pure Appl Ser A
Global Analysis Pure and Applied. Series B — Global Anal Pure Appl Ser B
Global and Planetary Change — Global Plan
Global Atmospheric Research Programme. Publications Series — Global Atmos Res Programme Publ Ser
Global Biogeochemical Cycles — Global Biogeochem Cycles
Global Church Growth Bulletin — CGB
Global Communications — Global Commun
Global Digest — GD
Global Environment Protection Strategy through Thermal Engineering — Global Environ Prot Strategy Therm Eng
Global Finance Journal — GFJ
Global Impacts of Applied Microbiology. International Conference — Global Impacts Appl Microbiol Int Conf
Global Jewish Database — GJD
Global Journal of Pure and Applied Sciences — Global J Pure Appl Sci
Global Lending and Overseas Banking Evaluator [*Database*] — GLOBE
Global Perspective Country Outlook [*Database*] — GPCO
Global Perspectives — Global Persp
Global Research Notes Series in Mathematics — Global Res Notes Ser Math
Globe — Gl
Globe and Mail Report on Business. Globe and Mail Limited — Globe Mail Rep Bus Globe Mail Ltd
Globus — Gl
Glomerulonephritis. Symposium on Nephrology — Glomerulonephritis Symp Nephrol
Gloria Dei — Gl Dei
Glos Anglii — GA
Glossa — Gl
Glossaire de la Terminologie Acarologique — Glossaire Terminol Acarol
Glossaire des Patois de la Suisse Romande — GPSR
Glossari di Lingua Contemporanea — GLC
Glossaria Interpretum [*Elsevier Book Series*] — Gl
Glossaria Latini — GL
Glossaria Latini — GlL
Glossaria Latini — Gloss Lat
Glossarium Mediae et Infimae Latinitatis Conditum — GMILC
Glossary of Acarological Terminology — Glossary Acarol Terminol
Glossary of Acarological Terminology/Glossaire de la Terminologie Acarologique — GACTD2
Glotta — Gl
Glow International — Glow
Glowny Instytut Elektrotechniki (Warsaw). Biuletyn Informacyjny — Gl Inst Elektrotech (Warsaw) Biul Inf
Gloxinian — GLOXAC
Glubinnoe Stroenie Urala. Trudy Ural'skoi Sessii Nauchnogo Soveta po Kompleksnym Issledovaniyam Zemnoi Kory i Verkhnei Mantii. Akademiya Nauk SS — Glubinnoe Str Urala Tr Ural Sess Nauchn Sov Kompleksn Issled
Glueckauf-Forschungshefte — Glueckauf-Forschungsh
Glutamate, Cell Death, and Memory. Proceedings. Colloque Medecine et Recherche — Glutamate Cell Death Mem Proc Colloq Med Rech
Glutathione. Proceedings. Conference. German Society of Biological Chemistry — Glutathione Proc Conf Germ Soc Biol Ghem
Glutathione S-Transferases and Drug Resistance. International Conference on GST — Glutathione S Transferases Drug Resist Int Conf GST
Glycoconjugate Journal — Glycoconj J
Glycoconjugate Journal — Glycoconjugate J
Glycosylation and Disease — Glycosylation Dis
Glyph. Johns Hopkins Textual Studies — Glyph Jon H
Gmelin Formula Index [*Database*] — GFI
Gmelin's Handbuch der Anorganischen Chemie — GH
GMI Short Paper. Oregon Department of Geology and Mineral Industries — GMI Short Pap Oreg Dep Geol Miner Ind
Gnomon — Gn
GO. Revista de Atualizacao em Ginecologia e Obstetricia — GO Rev Atualizacao Ginecol Obstet
GO. Revista de Atualizacao em Ginecologia e Obstetricia — GORABE
Gobrecht Journal — Gobrecht J
Godey's Lady's Book — Godey
Godisen Zbornik. Bioloski Fakultet na Univerzitetot Kiril i Metodij-Skopje. Biologija — God Zb Biol Fak Univ Kiril Metodij Skopje Biol
Godisen Zbornik. Filozofski Fakultet na Univerzitetot Skopje — Ann Skopje
Godisen Zbornik. Filozofski Fakultet na Univerzitetot Skopje — GZ

Godisen Zbornik ka Zemjodelsko-Sumarskiot. Fakultet na Univerzitetot (Skopje) — God Zbor Zemjodel Sumar Fak Univ (Skopje)
Godisen Zbornik na Filozofski ot Fakultet na Univerzitetot vo Skopje. Prirodno-Matematicki Oddel — God Zb Filoz Fak Univ Skopje Prir Mat Oddel
Godisen Zbornik na Filozofskiot Fakultet na Universitetot vo Skopje — God Zbor Skopje
Godisen Zbornik na Sumarskiot. Fakultet na Univerzitetot (Skopje) — God Zb Sumar Fak Univ (Skopje)
Godisen Zbornik na Zemjodelskiot Fakultet na Univerzitetot vo Skopje — God Zb Zemjod Fak Univ Skopje
Godisen Zbornik na Zemjodelsko-Sumarskiot. Fakultet na Univerzitetot (Skopje) — Godisen Zb Zemjod-Sum Fak Univ (Skopje)
Godisen Zbornik na Zemjodelsko-Sumarskiot. Fakultet na Univerzitetot Skopje Ovostarstvo — Godisen Zb Zemjod-Fak Univ Skopje Ovostarstvo
Godisen Zbornik na Zemjodelsko-Sumarskiot. Fakultet na Univerzitetot Skopje. Sumarstvo — God Zb Zemjod Sumar Fak Univ Skopje Sumar
Godisen Zbornik na Zemjodelsko-Sumarskiot. Fakultet na Univerzitetot Skopje. Zemjodelstvo — God Zb Zemjod Sumar Fak Univ Skopje Zemjod
Godisen Zbornik. Prirodno-Matematicki Fakultet na Univerzitetot Kiril i Metodij-Skopje. Biologija — God Zb Prir Mat Fak Univ Kiril Metodij Skopje Biol
Godisen Zbornik. Prirodno-Matematicki Fakultet na Univerzitetot Kiril i Metodij-Skopje. Sekcija A. Matematika. Fizika i Hemija — God Zb Prir Mat Fak Univ Kiril Metodij Skopje Sek A M
Godisen Zbornik. Prirodno-Matematicki. Fakultet na Univerzitetot (Skopje) — God Zb Prir Mat Fak Univ (Skopje)
Godisen Zbornik. Prirodno-Matematicki. Fakultet na Univerzitetot (Skopje) Matematika, Fizika, i Hemija — God Zb Prir Mat Fak Univ (Skopje) Mat Fiz Hem
Godishen Otchet. Durzhavna Zemledelska Opitna i Kontrolna Stantsiya (Sofia) — God Otchet Durzh Zemled Opitna Kontrolna Stn (Sofia)
Godishen Otchet. Zemledelski Izpitatelen Institut v Sofiya — God Otchet Zemled Izpit Inst Sofiya
Godishen Zbornik Annuaire. Biologie — God Zb Annu Biol
Godishen Zbornik Biologija Bioloshki Fakultet na Univerzitetot Kiril i Metodij Skopje — God Zb Biol Biol Fak Univ Kiril Metod Skopje
Godishen Zbornik Biologija Priridno-Matematichki. Fakultet na Univerzitetot Kiril i Metodij Skopje — God Zb Biol Prir-Mat Fak Univ Kiril Metodij Skopje
Godishen Zbornik Biologija Prirodno-Matematichki Fakultet na Univerzitetot Kirili Metodij Skopje — God Zb Biol Prir Mat Fak Univ Kiril Metod Skopje
Godishen Zbornik na Meditsinskiot. Fakultet vo Skopje — God Zb Med Fak Skopje
Godishni Nauchni Trudove. Vissh Meditsinski Institut (Varna) — God Nauchni Tr Vissh Med Inst Varna
Godishnik na Durzhavna ta Politekhnika (Sofiya) — God Durzh Politekh (Sofiya)
Godishnik na Instituta po Tsvetna Metalurgiya. Plovdiv — God Inst Tsvetna Metal Plovdiv
Godishnik na Inzhenerno-Stroitelniya Institut — God Inzh Stroit Inst
Godishnik na Khimiko Tekhnologicheskiya Institut — God Khim Tekhnol Inst
Godishnik na Khimiko-Tekhnologicheskaya Institut (Burgas, Bulgaria) — God Khim Tekhnol Inst Burgas Bulg
Godishnik na Mashino Elektrotekhnicheskiya Institut — God Mash Elektrotekh Inst
Godishnik na Meditsinkata Akademiya "Vulko Chervenkov" (Sofia) — God Med Akad (Sofia)
Godishnik na Minniya Nauchnoizsledovatelski Institut — God Minniya Nauchnoizsled Inst
Godishnik na Narodniia Arkheologicheski Muzei — God Nar M
Godishnik na Narodniia Arkheologicheski Muzei. Plovdiv — A Mus Plovdiv
Godishnik na Narodniia Arkheologicheski Muzei. Plovdiv — God Muz Plov
Godishnik na Narodniia Arkheologicheski Muzei. Plovdiv — God Muz Plovdiv
Godishnik na Narodniia Arkheologicheski Muzei. Plovdiv — God Plovdiv
Godishnik na Narodniia Arkheologicheski Muzei (Sofia) — Ann (Sofia)
Godishnik na Narodniia Arkheologicheski Muzei (Sofia) — God Muz (Sofia)
Godishnik na Nauchnoizsledovatelskiya i Proektantski Institut za Rudodobiv i Obogatyavane — God Nauchnoizsled Proekt Inst Rudodobiv Obogat
Godishnik na Nauchnoizsledovatelskiya i Proektantski Institut za Rudodobiv i Obogatyavane. Rudodobiv — God Nauchnoizsled Proekt Inst Rudodobiv Obogat Rudodobiv
Godishnik na Nauchnoizsledovatelskiya i Proektno-Konstruktorski Institut po Tavetna Metalurgiya (Plovdiv) — God Nauchnoizsled Proektno Konstr Inst Tavetna Metal Plovdiv
Godishnik na Nauchnoizsledovatelskiya Institut po Khimicheska Promishlennost — God Nauchnoizsled Inst Khim Prom
Godishnik na Nauchnoizsledovatelskiya Institut po Koksokhimiya i Neftoprerabotvane — God Nauchnoizsled Inst Koksokhim Neftoprerab
Godishnik na Nauchnoizsledovatelskiya Institut po Metalurgiya i Obogatyatvane — God Nauchnoizsled Inst Metal Obogat
Godishnik na Nauchnoizsledovatelskiya Institut po Neftoprerabotvane i Neftokhimiya — God Nauchnoizsled Inst Neftoprerab Neftokhim
Godishnik na Nauchnoizsledovatelskiya Institut po Tsvetna Metalurgiya (Plovdiv) [*Bulgaria*] — God Nauchnoizsled Inst Tsvetna Metal (Plovdiv)
Godishnik na Nauchnoizsledovatelskiya Institut za Goriva i Toplotekhnika — God Nauchnoizsled Inst Goriva Toplotekh
Godishnik na Nauchnoizsledovatelskiya Institut za Kamenovuglenata Promishlenost — God Nauchnoizsled Inst Kamenovuglenata Promst
Godishnik na Nauchnoizsledovatelskiya Institut za Tekhnolozhki Izsledovaniya na Gorivata — God Nauchnoizsled Inst Tekhnol Izsled Gorivata
Godishnik na Plovdivskata Narodna Biblioteka i Muzei v Plovdiv — Ann Plovdiv
Godishnik na Plovdivskata Narodna Biblioteka i Muzei v Plovdiv — God Plovdiv
Godishnik na Plovdivskata Narodna Biblioteka i Muzei v Plovdiv — Godisnik Plovdiv
Godishnik na Plovdivskata Narodna Biblioteka i Muzei v Plovdiv — GPNBM
Godishnik na Selskostopanskata Akademiya "Georgi Dimitrov" [*Sofia*] — God Selskostop Akad George Dimitrov
Godishnik na Selskostopanskata Akademiya "Georgi Dimitrov" (Sofia) Agronomicheski Fakultet — God Selskostop Akad (Sofia) Agron Fak
Godishnik na Selskostopanskata Akademiya "Georgi Dimitrov" (Sofia). Lesotekhnicheski Fakultet — God Selskostop Akad (Sofia) Lesotekh Fak
Godishnik na Sofiiskiia Universitet — GNU
Godishnik na Sofiiskiia Universitet — God Sof
Godishnik na Sofiiskiya Tekhnologichen Universitet — God Sofis Tekhnol Univ
Godishnik na Sofiiskiya Universitet — God Sof Un
Godishnik na Sofiiskiya Universitet — God Sof Univ
Godishnik na Sofiiskiya Universitet. Agronomicheski Fakultet — God Sofii Univ Agron Fak
Godishnik na Sofiiskiya Universitet. Agronomo Lesovudski Fakultet — God Sofii Univ Agron Lesovud Fak
Godishnik na Sofiiskiya Universitet. Biologicheski Fakultet — GSBIAJ
Godishnik na Sofiiskiya Universitet. Biologicheski Fakultet. Kniga 1. Zoologiya, Fiziologiya, i Biokhimiya na Zhivotnite — God Sofii Univ Biol Fak Kn I Zool Fiziol Biokhim Zhivotn
Godishnik na Sofiiskiya Universitet. Biologicheski Fakultet. Kniga 1. Zoologiya, Fiziologiya, i Biokhimiya na Zhivotnite — GSBZA2
Godishnik na Sofiiskiya Universitet. Biologicheski Fakultet. Kniga 2. Botanika, Mikrobiologiya, Fiziologiya, i Biokhimiya Rasteniyata — SBGKAT
Godishnik na Sofiiskiya Universitet. Biologo-Geologo-Geografski Fakultet — God Sofii Univ Biol Geol Geogr Fak
Godishnik na Sofiiskiya Universitet. Biologo-Geologo-Geografski Fakultet. Kniga I. Biologiya — God Sofii Univ Biol-Geol-Geogr Fak Kn I Biol
Godishnik na Sofiiskiya Universitet. Biologo-Geologo-Geografski Fakultet. Kniga I. Biologiya — GSBBAW
Godishnik na Sofiiskiya Universitet. Biologo-Geologo-Geografski Fakultet. Kniga I. Biologiya (Botanika) — God Sofii Univ Biol-Geol-Geogr Fak Kn I Biol (Bot)
Godishnik na Sofiiskiya Universitet. Biologo-Geologo-Geografski Fakultet. Kniga I. Biologiya (Zoologiya) — God Sofii Univ Biol-Geol-Geogr Fak Kn I Biol (Zool)
Godishnik na Sofiiskiya Universitet. Fizicheski Fakultet [*Bulgaria*] — God Sofii Univ Fiz Fak
Godishnik na Sofiiskiya Universitet. Fiziko-Matematicheski Fakultet — God Sofii Univ Fiz Mat Fak
Godishnik na Sofiiskiya Universitet. Geologo-Geografski Fakultet — God Sofii Univ Geol Geogr Fak
Godishnik na Sofiiskiya Universitet. Geologo-Geografski Fakultet. Kniga 1. Geologiya — GGKGA
Godishnik na Sofiiskiya Universitet. Khimicheski Fakultet — God Sofii Univ Khim Fak
Godishnik na Sofiiskiya Universitet. Kliment Okhridski Biologicheski Fakultet — God Sofii Univ Kliment Okhridski Biol Fak
Godishnik na Sofiiskiya Universitet. Kliment Okhridski Biologicheski Fakultet — GSUFD6
Godishnik na Sofiiskiya Universitet "Kliment Okhridski". Fakultet po Matematika i Mekhanika — God Sofii Univ Kliment Okhridski Fak Mat Mekh
Godishnik na Sofiiskiya Universitet Kliment Okhridski. Fizika i Tekhn ika na P oluprovodnitsite — God Sofii Univ Kliment Okhridski Fiz Tekh Poluprovodn
Godishnik na Sofiiskiya Universitet "Kliment Okhridski". Geologo-Geogra fski Fakultet — God Sofii Univ Kliment Okhridski Geol Geogr Fak
Godishnik na Sofiiskiya Universitet. Lesovuden Fakultet — God Sofii Univ Lesovud Fak
Godishnik na Sofiiskiya Universitet. Matematicheski Fakultet — God Sofii Univ Mat Fak
Godishnik na Sofiiskiya Universitet. Meditsinski Fakultet — God Sofii Univ Med Fak
Godishnik na Sofiiskiya Universitet. Prirodo-Matematicheski Fakultet — God Sofii Univ Prir Mat Fak
Godishnik na Visshite Tekhnicheski Uchebni Zavedeniya. Fizika — God Vissh Tekh Uchebn Zaved Fiz
Godishnik na Visshite Tekhnicheski Uchebni Zavedeniya. Prilozhna Mekhanika — God Vissh Tekh Uchebn Zaved Prilozh Mekh
Godishnik na Visshite Tekhnicheski Uchebni Zavedeniya. Prilozhna Mekhanika — God Vissh Tekh Uchebni Zaved Mekh
Godishnik na Visshite Tekhnicheski Uchebni Zavedeniya. Seriya Prilozhna Mekhanika — God Vissh Tekh Uchebni Zaved Ser Prilozh Mekh
Godishnik na Visshite Uchebni Zavedeniya. Prilozhna Matematika — God Vissh Uchebn Zaved Prilozh Mat
Godishnik na Visshite Uchebni Zavedeniya. Prilozhna Matematika — Godishnik Vissh Uchebn Zaved Prilozhna Mat
Godishnik na Visshite Uchebni Zavedeniya. Seriya Tekhnicheska Fizika [*Bulgaria*] — God Vissh Uchebn Zaveden Ser Tekh Fiz
Godishnik na Visshite Uchebni Zavedeniya. Seriya Tekhnicheski Fizika — Godishnik Vissh Uchebn Zaved Tekhn Fiz
Godishnik na Visshite Uchebni Zavedeniya. Seriya Tekhnicheski Mekhanika — Godishnik Vissh Uchebn Zaved Tekhn Mekh
Godishnik na Visshite Uchebni Zavedeniya. Tekhnicheska Fizika — God Vissh Uchebni Zaved Tekh Fiz
Godishnik na Visshiya Institut po Arkhitektura i Stroitelstvo (Sofiya) — God Vissh Inst Arkhit Stroit (Sofiya)
Godishnik na Visshiya Inzhenerno-Stroitelen Institut — God Vissh Inzh Stroit Inst
Godishnik na Visshiya Khimikotekhnologicheski Institut [*Bulgaria*] — God Vissh Khimikotekhnol Inst
Godishnik na Visshiya Khimikotekhnologicheski Institut — GVKIA
Godishnik na Visshiya Khimiko-Tekhnologicheski Institut (Burgas, Bulgaria) — God Vissh Khim-Tekhnol Inst (Burgas Bulg)
Godishnik na Visshiya Khimikotekhnologicheski Institut (Burgas, Bulgaria) — Godishnik Vissh Khimikotekhn Inst (Burgas)
Godishnik na Visshiya Khimiko-Tekhnologicheski Institut Prof. d-r As. Zlatarov , Gr. Burgas — God Vissh Khim Tekhnol Inst Prof d r As Zlatarov Gr Burgas

Godishnik na Visshiya Khimiko-Tekhnologicheski Institut. Sofia — God Vissh Khim Tekhnol Inst Sofia
Godishnik na Visshiya Khimikotekhnologicheski Institut (Sofia) — God Vissh Khimikotekhnol Inst (Sofia)
Godishnik na Visshiya Mashino-Elektrotekhnicheski Institut — God Vissh Mash Elektrotekh Inst
Godishnik na Visshiya Minno-Geolozhki Institut (Sofia) — God Vissh Minno-Geol Inst (Sofia)
Godishnik na Visshiya Pedagogicheski Institut v Shumen — God Vissh Podagog Inst Shumen
Godishnik na Visshiya Pedagogicheski Institut v Shumen. Prirodo-Matematicheski Fakultet — Godishnik Vissh Ped Inst Shumen Prirod-Mat Fak
Godisnik na Bioloskog Instituta Univerziteta u Sarajevu — GBISAX
Godisnik na Duchovnata Akademija Sveti Kliment Ochridski — GDA
Godisnik na Ekonomski ot Fakultet (Skopje) — Godis Ekon Fak (Skopje)
Godisnik na Energoproekt — God Energoproekt
Godisnik na Sofijskija Universitet. Bogosloviki Fakultet — GSUB
Godisnik na Sofijskiya Universitet. Biologicheski Fakultet — God Sofii Univ Biol Fak
Godisnik na Sofijskiya Universitet. Fakultet po Slavjanski Filologii — GodSU
Godisnik na Sofijskiya Universitet. Fakultet po Zapadni Filologii — GSUFZF
Godisnik na Sofijskiya Universitet. Filologiceski Fakultet — GSU
Godisnik na Sofijskiya Universitet. Filologiceski Fakultet — GSUF
Godisnik na Sofijskiya Universitet. Istorikofilologiceski Fakultet — God
Godisnik na Vissija Himikotehnologiceski Institut (Burgas) — Godisnik Viss Himikotehn Inst (Burgas)
Godisnik na Vissija Inzerno-Stroitelnija Institut — Godisnik Viss Inz-Stroitel Inst
Godisnik na Vissija Pedagogiceski Institut v Sumen Prirodo-Matematiceski Fakultet — Godisnik Viss Ped Inst Sumen Prirod-Mat Fak
Godisnik na Vissite Tehniceski Ucebni Zavedenija. Fizika — Godisnik Viss Tehn Ucebn Zaved Fiz
Godisnik na Vissite Tehniceski Ucebni Zavedenija. Matematika — Godisnik Viss Tehn Ucebn Zaved Mat
Godisnik na Vissite Tehniceski Ucebni Zavedenija Prilozna Mehanika — Godisnik Viss Tehn Ucebn Zaved Prilozna Meh
Godisnik na Vissite Ucebni Zavedenija. Prilozna Matematika — Godisnik Viss Ucebn Zaved Prilozna Mat
Godisnik na Vissite Ucebni Zavedenija. Tehniceski Fizika — Godisnik Viss Ucebn Zaved Tehn Fiz
Godisnik na Vissite Ucebni Zavedenija Tehniceski Mehanika — Godisnik Viss Ucebn Zaved Tehn Meh
Godisnik. Sumarski Institut — Godisn Sum Inst
Godisnik. Sumarski Institut (Skopje) — God Sumar Inst (Skopje)
Godisnjak Bioloskog Instituta u Sarajevu/Jahrbuch des Biologischen Institutes in Sarajevo/Annuaire de l'Institut Biologique a Sarajevo — God Biol Inst U Sarajevu
Godisnjak Bioloskog Instituta Univerziteta u Sarajevu — God Biol Inst Univ Sarajevu
Godisnjak Centra za Balkanoloska Ispitivanja — GCBI
Godisnjak Centra za Balkanoloska Ispitivanja — God Balk Isp
Godisnjak Filozofskog Fakulteta u Novom Sadu — GFFNS
Godisnjak Filozofskog Fakulteta u Novom Sadu — GodFFNS
Godisnjak Naucnog Drustva Nr Bosne i Hercegovine — GNDBiH
Godisnjak Pomorskog Muzeja u Kotoru — Godisnjak Pomorskog Muz Kotoru
Godisnjak. Srpska Kraljevska Akademija — God Srpska Kral Akad
Godisnjak Vojnomedicinske Akademije [*Beograd*] — God Vojnomed Akad
Godisnjica Nikole Cupica — Godisnjica Nik Cupica
GODORT [*Government Documents Round Table*] **Documents to the People** — GODORT DTTP
Godovoi Otchet Vengerskogo Geologicheskogo Instituta — Godovoi Otchet Veng Geol Inst
Goed Geraakt — GGR
Goedekes Grundriss zur Geschichte der Deutschen Dichtung — GG
Goeppinger Arbeiten zur Germanistik — GAG
Goerres-Bibliothek — Goer Bi
Goeteborger Germanistische Forschungen — GGF
Goeteborgs Handelstidning — GHT
Goeteborgs Hogskolas Arsskrift — GHA
Goeteborgs Kungliga Vetenskaps-och Vitterhets-Samhaelles Handlingar — GKVVH
Goeteborgs Kungliga Vetenskaps-och Vitterhets-Samhaelles Handlingar — Goeteborgs K Vetensk-o Vitterhets Samh Handl
Goeteborgs Universitets Arsskrift — GUA
Goeteborgs Vetenskaps och Vitterhets Samhaelles Handlingar — Goeteborg Vetensk Handlg
Goeteborgs Vetenskaps- och Vitterhetssamhaelles Handlingar — GVSH
Goeteborgs Vetenskaps- och Vitterhetssamhaelles Handlingar. Bihang — GVSHB
Goeteborgs Vetenskaps- och Vitterhetssamhaelles Handlingar. Humanistiska Skrifter — GVSHH
Goethe. Neue Folge des Jahrbuchs der Goethe-Gesellschaft — Goethe NF Jb Goethe Ges
Goethe. Vierteljahresschrift der Goethe-Gesellschaft — Goe
Goethe-Almanach — Goethe-Al
Goetheborgs och Bohuslaens Hushall-Saellskapets Handlingar — Goetheborgs Hush Saellsk Handl
Goethe-Jahrbuch — GJb
Goethe-Jahrbuch — GoeJ
Goethe-Jahrbuch — Goethe-Jahr
Goethe-Jahrbuch — Goethe-Jahrb
Goethe-Kalender — GK
Goettinger Arbeiten zur Geologie und Palaeontologie — Goett Arb Geol Palaeontol
Goettinger Asiatische Forschungen — G As F
Goettinger Floristische Rundbriefe — Goett Florist Rundbriefe
Goettinger Forschungen — Goe F
Goettinger Handkommentar zum Alten Testament (1917-1922) — GHAT
Goettinger Jahrbuch — G Jb
Goettinger Jahrbuch — Goett Jahrb
Goettinger Jahrbuch — Goettinger Jahrb
Goettinger Jahrbuch — GoJ
Goettinger Miszellen. Beitraege zur Aegyptologischen Diskussion — GM
Goettinger Miszellen. Beitraege zur Aegyptologischen Diskussion — GMBAD
Goettinger Miszellen Beitraege zur Aegyptologischen Diskussion — Goett Misz
Goettinger Miszellen. Beitraege zur Aegyptologischen Diskussion — Gott Misz
Goettinger Pflanzenzuechter-Seminar — Goettingor Pflanzanzuechter Semin
Goettinger Predigt-Bibliothek — GPB
Goettinger Predigt-Hefte — GPH
Goettinger Predigtmeditationen — GPM
Goettinger Rechtswissenschaftliche Studien — GRWS
Goettinger Studien zur Rechtsgeschichte — GSR
Goettinger Universitaetsschriften. Series A. Schriften — Goettinger Universitaetsschr Ser A Schr
Goettinger Universitaets-Zeitung — Goettinger Univ Ztg
Goettinger Wirtschafts- und Sozialwissenschaftliche Studien — Goettinger Wirtsch Sozialwissensch Stud
Goettingische Anzeigen von Gelehrten Sachen — GAGS
Goettingische Anzeigen von Gelehrten Sachen unter der Aufsicht der Koeniglichen Gesellschaft der Wissenschaften — Goett Anz Gel Sachen
Goettingische Bibliothek der Neuesten Theologischen Literatur — GBNTL
Goettingische Gelehrte Anzeigen — GG Anz
Goettingische Gelehrte Anzeigen — Goett Anz
Goettingische Gelehrte Anzeigen — Goett G Anz
Goettingische Gelehrte Anzeigen — Goett Gel Anz
Goettingische Gelehrte Anzeigen — Goettg Gel Anzgn
Goettingische Gelehrte Anzeigen — Gott Anz
Goettingische Gelehrte Anzeigen — Gott Gelehrte Anz
Goettingische Gelehrte Anzeiger — GGA
Goettingische Zeitungen von Gelehrten Sachen — Goett Zeitungen Gel Sachen
Goettingische Zeitungen von Gelehrten Sachen — GZGS
Goettingisches Journal der Naturwissenschaften — Goetting J Naturw
Going Down Swinging — GDS
Goinsiday — GOSD
Gold Bulletin — Gold Bull
Gold Bulletin and Gold Patent Digest — Gold Bull Gold Pat Dig
Gold Coast Geological Survey. Bulletin — Gold Coast Geol Surv Bull
Gold Coast Review — Gold Coast R
Gold Placer Deposits at the Foot of the Eastern Cordillera of Bolivia — Gold Placer Deposits Foot East Cordillera Bolivia
Golden Book Magazine — GBM
Golden Book Magazine — Golden Bk
Golden Book Magazine — Golden Bk M
Golden Bough — GB
Golden Fleece — GOF
Golden Fleece — Gold Fleece
Golden Fleece — GOVAD
Golden Gate Law Review — Golden Gate L Rev
Golden Gate University. Law Review — GOL
Golden Gate University. Law Review — Gol Gate LR
Golden Gate University. Law Review — Golden Gate UL Rev
Golden Goose — GG
Goldene Keyt — Gold K
Golden's Diagnostic Radiology — Goldens Diagn Radiol
Goldschmidt Informiert — Goldschmidt Inf
Goldsmiths Journal and Gemmologist — Goldsmiths J Gemm
Goldsmiths Journal and Gemmologist — Goldsmiths J Gemmol
Golf Course Reporter — Golf Course Rep
Golf Digest — GGOD
Golf Digest — Golf Dig
Golf Digest Magazine — Golf Dig Mag
Golf Magazine — GGOM
Golf Magazine — Golf Mag
Goltdammers Archiv fuer Strafrecht und Strafprozess — Goltd Arch
Gomal University. Journal of Research — Gomal Univ J Res
Gomal University. Journal of Research — GUJRD
Gomogennyi Kataliz. Materialy Koordinatsionnogo Soveshchaniya po Gomogennomu Katalizu — Gomogennyi Katal Mater Koord Soveshch
Gonzaga Law Review — Gon LR
Gonzaga Law Review — Gonz L Rev
Gonzaga Law Review — Gonzaga L Rev
Good Apple Newspaper — Good Apple
Good Book Guide — GBG
Good Farming Quarterly — Good Farming Quart
Good Gardening — Good Gard
Good Housekeeping — Gd House
Good Housekeeping — GGOH
Good Housekeeping — GH
Good Housekeeping — Good H
Good Housekeeping — Good House
Good Housekeeping — Good Housekeep
Good Libraries — Good Libr
Good News Broadcaster — GNB
Good Packaging — Good Pkg
Good Roads Magazine — Good Roads Mag
Good Times — Gd Times
Good Weekend — GW
Goodfellow Review of Crafts — Goodfellow
Goodwill — GW
Gopher Music Notes — GM

Gordian. Internationale Zeitschrift fuer Lebensmittel und Lebensmitteltechnologie — GOR
Gordian. Internationale Zeitschrift fuer Lebensmittel und Lebensmitteltechnologie — Gordian Int Z Lebensm Lebensmitteltechnologie
Gordon Review — Gor R
Gordon Review — Gord R
Gorenie i Problemy Tusheniya Pozharov. Materialy Vsesoyuznoi Nauchno-Prakticheskoi Konferentsii — Gorenie Probl Tusheniya Pozharov Mater Vses Nauchno Prak Kon
Gorenie Tverdogo Topliva. Materialy Vsesoyuznoi Konferentsii po Goreniyu Tverdogo Topliva i Grafitov — Gorenie Tverdogo Top Mater Vses Konf
Gorenie Tverdogo Topliva. Trudy Vsesoyuznoi Konferentsii po Goreniyu Tverdogo Topliva — Gorenie Tverd Top Tr Vses Konf
Goriski Letnik Zbornik Goriskega Muzeja — Gor Let
Goriva i Maziva — GOMAB
Gor'kovskii Gosudarstvennyi Nauchno-Issledovatel'skii Institut Gigieny Truda i Profboleznei. Trudy — Gor'k Gos Nauchno Issled Inst Gig Tr Profbolezn Tr
Gor'kovskii Gosudarstvennyi Pedagogicheskii Institut im. M. Gor'kogo. Uchenye Zapiski — Gork Gos Pedagog Inst im M Gorkogo Uch Zap
Gor'kovskii Gosudarstvennyi Universitet im. NI Lobachevskogo. Uchenye Zapiski — Gork Gos Univ im N I Lobachevskogo Uch Zap
Gor'kovskii Gosudarstvennyi Universitet Imeni N. I. Lobacevskogo. Prikladnye Problemy Procnosti i Plasticnosti — Prikl Problemy Proc i Plast
Gor'kovskii Gosudarstvennyi Universitet. Ucenye Zapiski — Gor'kov Gos Univ Ucen Zap
Gor'kovskii Meditsinskii Institut imeni S.M. Kirova. Trudy — Gork Med Inst im S M Kirova Tr
Gor'kovskii Sel'skokhozyaistvennyi Institut. Trudy — Gor'k Skh Inst Tr
Gornaya Elektromekhanika i Avtomatika — Gorn Elektromekh Avtom
Gornictwo Odkrywkowe — Gorn Odkrywkowe
Gornictwo Odkrywkowe — GROKA
Gornoe Davlenie i Kreplenie Gornykh Vyrabotok — Gorn Davlenie Kreplenie Gorn Vyrabotok
Gornoe Delo (Alma-Ata) — Gorn Delo Alma Ata
Gorno-Ekonomicheskie Aspekty Kompleksnogo Razvitiya KMA — Gorno Ekon Aspekty Kompleksn Razvit KMA
Gorno-Obogatitel'noe Delo — Gorno-Obogat Delo
Gorno-Obogatitel'nyi Zhurnal — Gorno-Obogat Zh
Gornye Mashiny i Avtomatika — Gorn Mash Avtom
Gornye, Stroitel'nye i Dorozhnye Mashiny — GSDMA
Gornyi Zhurnal — Gorn Zh
Gornyi Zhurnal (Moscow) — Gorn Zh (Mos)
Gornyi Zhurnal (Sverdlovsk) — Gorn Zh Sverdlovsk
Gorsko Stopanstvo [*Bulgaria*] — Gorsko Stop
Gorsko Stopanstvo — GOSTA
Gorskostopanska Nauka — Gorskostop Nauka
Gorskostopanska Nauka. Forest Science — Gorskostop Nauka For Sci
Gorskostopanska Nauka Izvestiya na Akademiiata na Selskostopankite Nauke — Gorskostop Nauka Izv Akad Selskostop Nauke
Gortania; Atti del Museo Friulano di Storia Naturale — Gortania Atti Mus Friulano Stor Nat
Goryuchie Slantsy. Khimiya i Tekhnologiya [*Estonian SSR*] — Goryuch Slantsy Khim Tekhnol
Goryuchie Slantsy. Khimiya i Tekhnologiya — Goryuchie Slantsy Khim Tekhnol
Goryuchie Slantsy (Moscow) — Goryuch Slantsy (Moscow)
Goryuchie Slantsy (Tallinn) [*Estonian SSR*] — Goryuch Slantsy (Tallinn)
Gospital'noe Delo — Gosp Delo
Gospodarka Miesna — Gospod Miesna
Gospodarka Paliwami i Energia — Gospod Paliwami Energ
Gospodarka Planowa — Gosp Planowa
Gospodarka Wodna — Gospod Wodna
Gosudarstvennyi Gidrologicheskii Institut. Trudy — Gos Gidrol Inst Tr
Gosudarstvennyi Institut po Proektirovaniyu i Issledovatel'skim Rabotam v Neftyanoi Promyshlennosti. Trudy — Gos Inst Proekt Issled Rab Neft Promsti Tr
Gosudarstvennyi Institut po Proektirovaniyu Zavadov Sanitarno-Tekhnicheskogo Oborudovaniya. Sbornik Trudov — Gos Inst Proekt Zavodov Sanit Tekh Oborud Sb Tr
Gosudarstvennyi Institut Prikladnoi Khimii Trudy — Gos Inst Prikl Khim Tr
Gosudarstvennyi Makeevskii Nauchno-Issledovatel'skii Institut po Bezopasnosti Rabot v Gornoi Promyshlennosti. Trudy — Gos Makeev Nauchno Issled Inst Bezop Rab Gorn Prom Tr
Gosudarstvennyi Nauchno-Issledovatel'skii Energeticheskii Institut Imeni G. M. Krzhizhanovskogo Sbornik Trudov — Gos Nauchno Issled Energ Inst Im G M Krzhizhanovskogo Sb Tr
Gosudarstvennyi Nauchno-Issledovatel'skii i Proektnyi Institut Giprotyumenneftegaz. Trudy — Gos Nauchno Issled Proektn Inst Giprotyumenneftegaz Tr
Gosudarstvennyi Nauchno-Issledovatel'skii i Proektnyi Institut Osnovnoi Khimii. Trudy — Gos Nauchno Issled Proektn Inst Osnovn Khim Tr
Gosudarstvennyi Nauchno-Issledovatel'skii i Proektnyi Institut Redkometallicheskoi Promyshlennosti. Nauchnye Trudy — Gos Nauchno Issled Proektn Inst Redkomet Promsti Nauchn Tr
Gosudarstvennyi Nauchno-Issledovatel'skii i Proektnyi Institut Splavov i Obrabotki Tsvetnykh Metallov. Trudy — Gos Nauchno Issled Proektn Inst Splavovg Obrab Tsvetn Met Tr
Gosudarstvennyi Nauchno-Issledovatel'skii Institut Keramicheskoi Promyshlennosti Trudy — Gos Nauchno Issled Inst Keram Promsti Tr
Gosudarstvennyi Nauchno-Issledovatel'skii Institut Ozernogo i Rechnogo Rybnogo Khozyaistva. Sbornik Nauchnykh Trudov — Gos Nauchno Issled Inst Ozern Rechn Rybn Khoz Sb Nauchn Tr
Gosudarstvennyi Nauchno-Issledovatel'skii Institut po Keramzitu. Snornik Nauchnykh Trudov — Gos Nauchno Issled Inst Keramzitu Sb Nauchn Tr
Gosudarstvennyi Nauchno-Issledovatel'skii Institut Stroitel'noi Keramik i. Trudy — Gos Nauchno Issled Inst Stroit Keram Tr
Gosudarstvennyi Nauchno-Issledovatel'skii Institut Tsvetnykh Metallov. Nauchnye Trudy — Gos Nauchno Issled Inst Tsvetn Met Nauchn Tr
Gosudarstvennyi Nauchno-Issledovatel'skii Rentgeno-Radiologicheskii Institut Trudy — Gos Nauchno Issled Rentgeno Radiol Inst Tr
Gosudarstvennyi Nauchno-Issledovatel'skii Tsentr Izucheniya Prirodnykh Resursov. Trudy — Gos Nauchno Issled Tsentr Izuch Prir Resur Tr
Gosudarstvennyi Okeanograficheskii Institut. Trudy — Gos Okeanogr Inst Tr
Gosudarstvennyi Proektno-Izyskatel'skii i Nauchno-Issledovatel'skii Institut Morskogo Transporta. Trudy — Gos Proektno Izyskat Nauchno Issled Inst Morsk Transp Tr
Gosudarstvennyi Proektnyi i Nauchno-Issledovatel'skii Institut "Gipronikel". Sbornik Nauchnykh Trudov — Gos Proektn Nauchno Issled Inst Gipronikel Sb Nauchn Tr
Gosudarstvennyi Proektnyi i Nauchno-Issledovatel'skii Institut Gipronikel. Trudy — Gos Proektn Nauchno Issled Inst Gipronikel Tr
Gosudarstvennyi Vsesoyuznyi Dorozhnyi Nauchno-Issledovatel'skii Institut. Trudy — Gos Vses Dorozhn Nauchno Issled Inst Tr
Gosudarstvennyi Vsesoyuznyi Institut po Proektirovaniyu i Nauchno-Issledovatel'skim Rabotam Yuzhgiprotsement. Trudy — Gos Vses Inst Proekt Nauchno Issled Rab Yuzhgiprotsement Tr
Gosudarstvennyi Vsesoyuznyi Nauchno-Issledovatel'skii Institut Stroitel 'nykh Materialov i Konstruktsii. Sbornik Trudov — Gos Vses Nauchno Issled Inst Stroit Mater Konstr Sb Tr
Gosudarstvennyi Vsesoyuznyi Nauchno-Issledovatel'skii Institut Stroitel 'nykh Materialov i Konstruktsii. VNIIStrom. Sbornik Nauchnykh Trudov — Gos Vses Nauchno Issled Inst Stroit Mater Konstr VNIIStrom S
Gosudarstvennyi Vsesoyuznyi Nauchno-Issledovatel'skii Institut Tsementn oi Promyshlennosti. Trudy — Gos Vses Nauchno Issled Inst Tsem Promsti Tr
Gosudarstvennyi Vsesoyuznyi Nauchno-Issledovatel'skii Institut Tsementnoi Promyshlennosti Nauchnye Soobshcheniya — Gos Vses Nauchno Issled Inst Tsem Promsti Nauchn Soobshch
Gosudarstvennyi Vsesoyuznyi Nauchno-Issledovatel'skii Proektnyi Institut po Asbestovoi Promyshlennosti. Nauchnye Trudy — Gos Vses Nauchno Issled Proektn Inst Astestovoi Prom Nauchn
Gosudarstvennyi Vsesoyuznyi Proektnyi i Nauchno-Issledovatel'skii Institut Tsementnoi Promyshlennosti Trudy — Gos Vses Proektn Nauchno Issled Inst Tsem Promsti Tr
Goteborg Universitet. Naturgeografiska Institutionen. Rapport — Goteborg Univ Naturgeogr Inst Rapp
Goteborgs Ethnographical Museum — Goteb Ethnogr Mus
Goteborgs Kungliga Vetenskaps och Vitter Hets-Samhalles Handlingar Sjatte Foljden. Series B — Goteb K Vetensk Vitter Hets-Samh Handl Sjatte Foljden Ser B
Goteborgs Kungliga Vetenskaps- Och Vitterhets-Samhalles Handlingar. Series B — Goteborgs K Vetensk Vitterhets Samh Handl Ser B
Goteborgs Naturhistoriska Museum Arstryck — Goteb Naturhist Mus Arstryck
Goteborgs Tandlakare-Sallskaps Arsbok — Goteb Tandlak Sallsk Arsb
Goteborgs-Posten — GPT
Gothaer Museumshefte — G Mus
Gothenburg Studies in English — Goth SE
Gothenburg Studies in English — GSE
Gothenburg Studies in Philosophy — GSP
Gothenburg Studies in Physics — Gothenburg Stud Phys
Gotlaendskt Arkiv — Got Ark
Gotlaendskt Arkiv — Gotlaendskt Ark
Gotlaendskt Arkiv — Gotlaendskt Arkiv
Gottesdienst und Kirchenmusik — GK
Gottesdienst und Kirchenmusik — Gottesd u Kir
Gottesdienst und Kirchenmusik — Gottesdienst Km
Goucher College Cuneiform Inscriptions — GCCI
Goucher College Series — Gouc Col Se
Goulcae Journal of Education (Goulburn College of Advanced Education) — Goulcae J Educ
Gould League of Bird Lovers of New South Wales. Notes — Gould League NSW Notes
Gourmet — GGOU
Gouvernement General de l'Afrique Equatoriale Francaise. Bulletin. Direction des Mines et de la Geologie — Gouv Gen Afr Equat Fr Bull Dir Mines Geol
Gouvernement General de l'Algerie. Bulletin du Service de la Carte Geologique de l'Algerie. Serie 1. Paleontologie — Gouv Gen Alger Bull Serv Carte Geol Alger Ser 1
Gouvernement General de l'Algerie. Bulletin du Service de la Carte Geologique del'Algerie. Serie 5. Petrographie — Gouv Gen Alger Bull Serv Carte Geol Alger Ser 5
Gouvernement General de l'Algerie. Bulletin. Service de la Carte Geologique de l'Algerie. Serie 2. Stratigraphie — Gouv Gen Alger Bull Serv Carte Geol Alger Ser 2
Gouvernement General de l'Algerie. Bulletin. Service de la Carte Geologique de l'Algerie. Serie 3. Geologique Appliquee — Gouv Gen Alger Bull Serv Carte Geol Alger Ser 3
Gouvernement General de l'Algerie. Bulletin. Service de la Carte Geologique de l'Algerie. Serie 6. Metallogenie — Gouv Gen Alger Bull Serv Carte Geol Alger Ser 6
Gouvernement General de l'Algerie. Inspection Generale de l'Agriculture Recherche et l'Experimentation Agricole en Algerie — Gouv Gen Alger Insp Gen Agric Rapp Cons Exp Rech Agron Rech
Gouvernementsblad van Suriname — GB
Governing — IGOV
Government [*Boston*] — GOVT
Government Accountants Journal — GAC
Government Agricultural Research Centre. Ghent. Activity Report — Gov Agric Res Cent Ghent Act Rep
Government and Opposition — GAO
Government and Opposition — Govt & Oppos
Government and Opposition — Govt and Opposition

Government and Opposition — Govt Oppos
Government and Opposition — Govt Opposition
Government and Opposition — Gvt and Opposition
Government and Opposition — PGNO
Government Blue Book [*London*] — BB
Government College Economic Journal — Govt Col Econ J
Government Computer News — GCN
Government Computer News — GCNED
Government Contracts Reports. Commerce Clearing House — Govt Cont Rep CCH
Government Data Systems [*United States*] — Gov Data Syst
Government Data Systems — Govt Data Sys
Government Data Systems — GVDSB
Government Employee Relations Report — GERR
Government Employee Relations Report — Gov't Empl Rel Rep
Government Employee Relations Report. Bureau of National Affairs — Govt Empl Rel Rep BNA
Government Executive — GOV
Government Finance Review — Govt Fin R
Government Finance Statistics [*Database*] — GFSY
Government Finance Statistics Yearbook — GFS
Government Gazette. Western Australia — Govt Gaz W Aust
Government Metallurgical Laboratory. Republic of South Africa. Report — Gov Metall Lab Repub S Afr Rep
Government of Alberta Publications [*Database*] — GAP
Government of Victoria Research Project Series. Department of Agriculture — Gov Victoria Res Proj Ser Dep Agric
Government Pest Infestation Laboratory. Annual Report — Gov Pest Infest Lab Annu Rep
Government Publications [*England*] — Govt Publns
Government Publications Review — Gov Pub R
Government Publications Review — Gov Publ Rev
Government Publications Review — Govt Pub R
Government Publications Review — Govt Pub Rev
Government Publications Review — Govt Pubns R
Government Publications Review — Govt Pubns Rev
Government Publications Review (Part A) — Govt Pubns R (Pt A)
Government Relations Note — Gov Relat Note
Government Reports Announcements — Gov Rep Announce
Government Reports Announcements [*United States*] — GVRAA
Government Reports Announcements and Index — Gov Rep Announce Index
Government Reports Announcements and Index — Gov Reports Announce & Index
Government Reports Announcements and Index — Govt Rep Announce Index
Government Reports Announcements and Index — Govt Rept Announc
Government Reports Announcements and Index — GRA and I
Government Reports Announcements (US) — Gov Rep Announce US
Government Research Centers Directory — Gov Res Cent Dir
Government Securities Management System [*Database*] — GSMS
Government Standard — Govt Stand
Government Union Review — Govt Union R
Government Union Review — Govt Union Rev
Government Union Review — GUR
Governmental Accounting. Procedures and Practices — Gov Account Proc Pract
Governmental Finance — GF
Governmental Finance — GOF
Governmental Finance — Gov Finance
Governmental Finance — Governmental Fin
Governmental Finance — Govt Fin
Governmental Research Bulletin (Florida) — Governmental Research Bul (Fla)
Governmental Research Centers Directory — GRCD
Government-Industry Data Exchange Program [*Database*] — GIDEP
Governors Bulletin — Gov Bul
Govind Ballabh Pant University of Agriculture and Technology. Experiment Station. Technical Bulletin — Govind Ballabh Pant Univ Agric Technol Exp Stn Tech Bull
Gower Birds — Gower B
Gower Federal Service [*Database*] — GFS
Goz Klinigi Bulteni — Goz Klin Bul
Gozdarski Vestnik — Gozd Vestn
GP. Journal of the American Academy of General Practice — GEPCA
GP. Journal of the American Academy of General Practice — GP J Am Acad Gen Pract
GPO [*Government Printing Office*] **Newsletter** [*United States*] — GPO Newsl
GPO [*Government Printing Office*] **Newsletter** — GPOND
GPO [*Government Printing Office*] **Sales Publications Reference File** [*Database*] — PRF
GQ. Gentlemens Quarterly — GGQQ
Grace Hospital. Bulletin — Grace Hosp Bull
Grace Log (New York) — Grace Log NY
Grace Theological Journal — Grace Th J
Grace Theological Journal — GTJ
Gradbeni Vestnik [*Yugoslavia*] — Gradbeni Vestn
Grade Teacher — Grade Teach
Grade Teacher (Darien, Connecticut) — GTD
Gradevinski Fakultet. Radovi (Sarajevo) — Gradevin Fak Rad (Sarajevo)
Gradevinski Fakultet (Sarajevo). Radovi — Gradevinski Fak (Sarajevo) Rad
Gradina, via si Livada — Grad Via Livada
Gradinarska i Lozarska Nauka [*Horticulture and Viticultural Science*] — Gradinar Lozar Nauk
Gradinarska i Lozarska Nauka [*Horticulture and Viticultural Science*] — Gradinar Lozar Nauka
Gradinarska i Lozarska Nauka (Horticulture and Viticultural Science) — Gradinar Lozar Nauka (Hortic Vitic Sci)
Gradja za Povijest Knjizevnosti Hrvatske — Gradja
Gradjevinski Fakultet (Sarajevo) Radovi — Gradjevin Fak (Sarajevo) Rad
Graduate — Grad
Graduate [*Canada*] — GRADD
Graduate English Papers — GEP
Graduate Faculty Philosophy Journal — Grad Fac Phil J
Graduate Journal — Grad J
Graduate Research in Education and Related Disciplines — Grad Res Ed
Graduate Seminar Journal — Grad Sem J
Graduate Student of English — GSE
Graduate Student Series in Physics — Grad Student Ser Phys
Graduate Studies in Mathematics — Grad Stud Math
Graduate Studies on Latin American at the University of Kansas — GSLA
Graduate Study. Concordia Theological Seminary. [*St. Louis, MO*] — GSCTS
Graduate Texts in Computer Science — Grad Texts Comput Sci
Graduate Texts in Contemporary Physics — Grad Texts Contemp Phys
Graduate Texts in Mathematical Physics — Grad Texts Math Phys
Graduate Texts in Mathematics — Grad Texts Math
Graduate Texts in Mathematics — Graduate Texts in Math
Graduate Woman — Grad Woman
Graecitas Christianorum Primaeva — GCP
Graecitas et Latinitas Christianorum Primaeva — GLCP
Graecolatina et Orientalia — Ge O
Graecolatina et Orientalia — GLO
Graefes Archiv fuer Klinische und Experimentelle Ophthalmologie — Graefes Arch Klin Exp Ophthalmol
Graefes Archiv fuer Ophthalmologie — Arch Ophthalm
Graefes Archiv fuer Ophthalmologie — Graefes Arch Ophthalmol
Graefe's Archive for Clinical and Experimental Ophthalmology — GACOD
Graefe's Archive for Clinical and Experimental Ophthalmology — Graefe's Arch Clin Exp Ophthalmol
Graensevagten — Grsv
Graezistische Abhandlungen — GA
Graficus; Onafhankelijk Weekblad voor de Grafische Industrie [*Rijswijk*] — GRF
Grafisch Orgaan — GOC
Grafische Technik Dokumentationsdienst — Grafische Tech
Grafisk Aarbog — Graf Aa
Grafisk Arbok — Grafisk Arb
Grafisk Teknik — Graf Tekn
Grafiska Forskningslaboratoriet. Projektrapport — Grafiska Forskningslab Projektrapp
Grafiska Forskningslaboratoriets. Meddelande — Grafiska Forskningslab Medd
Grafiske Hojskoles Smaskrifter — Grafiske Hojskoles Smaskr
Grafiskt Forum — GF
Grafschaft Glatzer Heimatblaetter — GG Hb
Grahamstown Historical Society. Annals — Grahamstown Hist Soc Ann
Grai si Suflet — G & S
Grai si Suflet — GS
Grain and Feed Journals Consolidated — Grain Feed J Consol
Grain and Feed Review — Grain Feed Rev
Grain Boundaries in Semiconductors. Proceedings. Materials Research Society. Annual Meeting — Grain Boundaries Semicond Proc Mater Res Soc Ann Meet
Grain Bulletin — GB
Grain de Sel — Grain
Grain Producer News — Grain Prod News
Grain Trade Buyers Guide and Management Reference — Grain Trade Buyers Guide Manage Ref
Grainger Journal — Grainger J
Grains Journal — Grains J
Gramaphone — Gra
Grammaire Homerique — GH
Grammaticae Romanae Fragmenta — Gramm Rom Frag
Grammatici Graeci — Gr Gr
Grammatici Graeci — Gramm Graec
Grammatici Latini — GL
Grammatici Latini — Gr L
Grammatici Latini — Gr Lat
Grammatici Latini — Gramm Lat
Grammatik des Neutestamentlichen Griechisch — GVG
Gramophone — GR
Grana Palynologica — Grana Palynol
Grand Canyon Natural History Association. Bulletin — Grand Canyon Nat History Assoc Bull
Grand Council of the Cree (of Quebec) Update — GCCU
Grand Dictionnaire Universel du XIX Siecle — GDU
Grand Larousse Encyclopedique — GLE
Grand Street — PGST
Grande Enciclopedia Portuguesa e Brasileira — GE
Grande Enciclopedia Portuguesa e Brasileira — GEPB
Grande Encyclopedie — GE
Grande Revue — GR
Grandes Religions du Monde — GR Mo
Grandi del Cattolicesimo — G Cat
Grands Classiques Gauthier-Villars — Grands Class Gauthier Villars
Grands Ecrivains de la France — Grands Ecr de la Fr
Grands Ecrivains de la France — Grands Ecr de la France
Grands Ecrivains de la France — Grands Ecriv de la Fr
Grands Ecrivains de la France — Grands Ecriv de la France
Grands Ecrivains Francais — GEF
Grands Evenements Litteraires — GEL
Granite Monthly — Gran Mo
Granite Monthly — Granite Mo
Granite State Magazine [*Manchester, NH*] — Gran St M
Granite State Magazine — Granite State M
Granos Semilla Selecta — Granos Semilla Selec

Grants Magazine — Grants Mag
Grantsmanship Center. News — Grantsmanship Cent News
Grantsmanship Center. News — GSCN
Grape Culturist — Grape Cult
Grapevine. University of California. Cooperative Extension Service — Grapevine Univ Calif Coop Ext Serv
Graphic Arts Abstracts — GAA
Graphic Arts Abstracts — Graph Arts Abstr
Graphic Arts Abstracts — Graphic Arts Abstr
Graphic Arts Bulletin — Graphic Arts Bul
Graphic Arts Literature Abstracts — Graphic Arts Lit Abstr
Graphic Arts Monthly — GA
Graphic Arts Monthly — Graphic Arts M
Graphic Arts Monthly and the Printing Industry — Graph Arts Mon Print Ind
Graphic Arts Monthly and the Printing Industry — Graphic Arts Mon
Graphic Arts Monthly and the Printing Industry — Graphic Arts Mon Print Ind
Graphic Arts Progress — Graphic Arts Prog
Graphic Arts Technical Foundation. Research Progress Report — Graphic Arts Tech Found Res Prog Rep
Graphic Arts Technical Foundation. Research Project Report — Graphic Arts Tech Found Res Proj Rep
Graphic Communications Weekly — GC
Graphic Communications Weekly — GCW
Graphic Communications Weekly — Graphic Comm Wk
Graphic Communications World — GCWOD
Graphic Communications World — Graphic Commun World
Graphic Science — Graphic Sci
Graphic Technology — Graphic Technol
GraphiCommunicator — GRPCD
Graphik Visuelles Marketing — GWF
Graphis — GRPHA
Graphischen Kuenste — Graph Kuenste
Graphs and Combinatorics — Graphs Combin
Grasas y Aceites — Grasas Aceit
Grasas y Aceites — Grasas Aceites
Grass and Forage Science — Grass Forage Sci
Grass and Forage Science. Journal. British Grassland Society — Grass Forage Sci J Br Grassl Soc
Grass: The Journal of the British Association of Green Crop Driers — Grass J Br Assoc Green Crop Driers
Grassland Research Institute (Hurley). Annual Report — Grassl Res Inst (Hurley) Annu Rep
Grassland Research Institute (Hurley). Experiments in Progress — Grassl Res Inst (Hurley) Exp Prog
Grassland Research Institute (Hurley). Technical Report — Grassl Res Inst (Hurley) Tech Rep
Grassland Research Institute. Memoir — Grassl Res Inst Mem
Grassland Science — Grassl Sci
Grassland Society of Southern Africa. Proceedings — Grassl Soc South Afr Proc
Grassroots Development. Journal. Inter-American Foundation — Grassroots Dev J Inter Am Found
Gratz College. Annual of Jewish Studies — GCAJS
Gratz College. Annual of Jewish Studies — GratzCAJS
Graver Water Conditioning Company. Technical Reprint — Graver Water Cond Co Tech Repr
Gravida — Gra
Gravitatsiya i Teoriya Otnositel'nosti *[Former USSR]* — Gravitatsiya Teor Otnositel'nosti
Gray Herbarium Contributions — Gray Herb Contr
Gray Panther Network — Gray Pant
Graylands Education News — Graylands Ed News
Graz. Landesmuseum Joanneum. Abteilung fuer Geologie, Palaeontologie, und Bergbau. Mitteilungen — Graz Landesmus Joanneum Abt Geol Palaeontol Bergbau Mitt
Graz. Landesmuseum Joanneum. Abteilung fuer Mineralogie. Mitteilungsblatt — Graz Landesmus Joanneum Abt Mineral Mitteilungsbl
Graz. Landesmuseum Joanneum. Jahresbericht — Graz Landesmus Joanneum Jahresber
Graz. Landesmuseum Joanneum. Museum fuer Bergbau, Geologie, und Technik. Mitteilungen — Graz Landesmus Joanneum Mus Bergbau Geol Tech Mitt
Grazer Beitraege — GB
Grazer Beitraege — Graz Beitr
Grazer Beitraege. Zeitschrift fuer die Klassische Altertumswissenschaft — GBZKA
Grazer Mathematische Berichte — Grazer Math Ber
Grazer Philosophische Studien — Grazer Phil Stud
Grazer Tageblatt — GT
Grazhdanskaya Aviatsiya — Grazhdanskaya Aviats
GRC. Genetic Resources Communication — GRC Genet Resour Commun
Great Barrier Reef Committee. Heron Island Research Station. Papers — Grt Barrier Reef Comm Pap
Great Basin Naturalist — Great Basin Nat
Great Basin Naturalist — Gt Basin Nat
Great Basin Naturalist. Memoirs — Great Basin Nat Mem
Great Britain. Aeronautical Research Council. Current Papers — GB Aeronaut Res Counc Curr Pap
Great Britain. Agricultural Research Council. Letcombe Laboratory. Annual Report — GB Agric Res Counc Letcombe Lab Annu Rep
Great Britain. Agricultural Research Council. Radiobiological Laboratory. ARCRL — GB Agric Res Counc Radiobiol Lab ARCRL
Great Britain and the East — GBE
Great Britain and the East — Gt Brit & East
Great Britain. British Geological Survey. Mineral Assessment Report — Gt Brit Brit Geol Surv Min Assess Rep
Great Britain. British Geological Survey. Report — Gt Brit Brit Geol Surv Rep
Great Britain. British Geological Survey. Seismological Bulletin — Gt Brit Brit Geol Surv Seismol Bull
Great Britain. Central Unit on Environmental Pollution. Pollution Paper — GB Cent Unit Environ Pollut Pollut Pap
Great Britain. Civil Service Department. Report — Gt Brit Civil Serv Dep Rep
Great Britain. Colonial Office — GBCO
Great Britain. Department of Health and Social Security. Reports on Public Health and Medical Subjects — GB Dep Health Soc Secur Rep Public Health Med Subj
Great Britain. Department of Scientific and Industrial Research. Chemical Research. Special Report — GB Dep Sci Ind Res Chem Res Spec Rep
Great Britain. Department of Scientific and Industrial Research. Food Investigation Board. Special Report — GB Dep Sci Ind Res Food Invest Board Spec Rep
Great Britain. Department of Scientific and Industrial Research. Food Investigation Board. Technical Paper — GB Dep Sci Ind Res Food Invest Tech Pap
Great Britain. Department of Scientific and Industrial Research. Food Investigation. Food Science Abstracts — GB Dep Sci Ind Res Food Invest Food Sci Abstr
Great Britain. Department of Scientific and Industrial Research. Forest Products Research — GB Dep Sci Ind Res For Prod Res
Great Britain. Department of Scientific and Industrial Research. Forest Products Research Bulletin — GB Dep Sci Ind Res For Prod Res Bull
Great Britain. Department of Scientific and Industrial Research. Forest Products Research Special Report — GB Dep Sci Ind Res For Prod Res Spec Rep
Great Britain. Department of Scientific and Industrial Research. Forestry Commission. Reports on Forest Research — GB Dep Sci Ind Res For Comm Rep For Res
Great Britain. Department of Scientific and Industrial Research. Fuel Research. Fuel Abstracts — GB Dep Sci Ind Res Fuel Res Fuel Abstr
Great Britain. Department of Scientific and Industrial Research. Fuel Research. Publication — GB Dep Sci Ind Res Fuel Res
Great Britain. Department of Scientific and Industrial Research. Fuel Research. Survey Paper — GB Dep Sci Ind Res Fuel Res Surv Pap
Great Britain. Department of Scientific and Industrial Research. Fuel Research. Technical Paper — GB Dep Sci Ind Res Fuel Res Tech Pap
Great Britain. Department of Scientific and Industrial Research. Index to the Literature of Food Investigation — GB Dep Sci Ind Res Index Lit Food Invest
Great Britain. Department of Scientific and Industrial Research. National Building Studies Research Paper — GB Dep Sci Ind Res Natl Build Stud Res Pap
Great Britain. Department of Scientific and Industrial Research. Overseas Technical Report — GB Dep Sci Ind Res Overseas Tech Rep
Great Britain. Department of Scientific and Industrial Research. Pest Infestation Research Board. Report — GB Dep Sci Ind Res Pest Infest Res Board Rep
Great Britain. Department of Scientific and Industrial Research. Report. Warren Spring Laboratory — GB Dep Sci Ind Res Rep Warren Spring Lab
Great Britain. Department of Scientific and Industrial Research. Road Note — GB Dep Sci Ind Res Road Note
Great Britain. Department of Scientific and Industrial Research. Road Research Laboratory. Report RRL — GB Dep Sci Ind Res Road Res Lab Rep RRL
Great Britain. Department of Scientific and Industrial Research. Road Research Laboratory. Road Research Technical Paper — GB Dep Sci Ind Res Road Res Lab Road Res Tech Pap
Great Britain. Department of Scientific and Industrial Research. Road Research. Road Research Abstracts — GB Dep Sci Ind Res Road Res Road Abstr
Great Britain. Department of Scientific and Industrial Research. Torry Research Station. Annual Report — GB Dep Sci Ind Res Torry Res Stn Annu Rep
Great Britain. Department of Scientific and Industrial Research. Torry Technical Paper — GB Dep Sci Ind Res Torry Tech Pap
Great Britain. Department of Trade and Industry. Laboratory of the Government Chemist. Miscellaneous Report — GB Dep Trade Ind Lab Gov Chem Misc Rep
Great Britain. Department of Trade and Industry. Warren Spring Laboratory. Review — GB Dep Trade Ind Warren Spring Lab Rev
Great Britain. Electricity Council. Annual Report and Accounts — Gt Brit Electr Counc Ann Rep Acc
Great Britain. Explosives Research and Development Establishment. Technical Note — GB Explos Res Dev Establ Tech Note
Great Britain. Explosives Research and Development Establishment. Technical Report — GB Explos Res Dev Establ Tech Rep
Great Britain. Forest Products Research Board. Bulletin — GB For Prod Res Board Bull
Great Britain. Forest Products Research Bulletin — GB For Prod Res Bull
Great Britain. Forest Products Research Special Report — GB For Prod Res Spec Rep
Great Britain. Forestry Commission. Annual Report of the Forestry Commissioners — GB For Comm Annu Rep For Comm
Great Britain. Forestry Commission. Booklet — GB For Comm Bookl
Great Britain. Forestry Commission. Bulletin — GB For Comm Bull
Great Britain. Forestry Commission. Forest Record — GB For Comm For Rec
Great Britain. Forestry Commission. Leaflet — GB For Comm Leafl
Great Britain. Forestry Commission. Occasional Paper — GB For Comm Occas Pap
Great Britain. Forestry Commission. Occasional Paper — OPFCDN

Great Britain. Forestry Commission. Report on Forest Research — GB For Comm Rep For Res
Great Britain. Forestry Commission. Research and Development Paper — GB For Comm Res Dev Pap
Great Britain. Forestry Commission. Research Branch Paper — GB For Comm Res Branch Pap
Great Britain. Institute of Geological Sciences. Annual Report — GB Inst Geol Sci Annu Rep
Great Britain. Institute of Geological Sciences. Geomagnetic Bulletin — GB Inst Geol Sci Geomagn Bull
Great Britain. Institute of Geological Sciences. Mineral Assessment Report — GB Inst Geol Sci Miner Assess Rep
Great Britain. Institute of Geological Sciences. Mineral Resources Consultative Committee. Mineral Dossier — GB Inst Geol Sci Miner Resour Consult Comm Miner Dossier
Great Britain. Institute of Geological Sciences. Overseas Memoir — GB Inst Geol Sci Overseas Mem
Great Britain. Institute of Geological Sciences. Report — GB Inst Geol Sci Rep
Great Britain. Joint Fire Research Organization. Fire Research Technical Paper — GB Jt Fire Res Organ Fire Res Tech Pap
Great Britain. Laboratory of the Government Chemist. Occasional Paper — GB Lab Gov Chem Occas Pap
Great Britain. Land Resources Development Centre. Land Resource Study — GB Land Resour Dev Cent Land Resour Study
Great Britain. Land Resources Development Centre. Land Resource Study — GLRSAC
Great Britain. Land Resources Division. Land Resource Bibliography — GB Land Resour Div Land Resour Bibliogr
Great Britain. Land Resources Division. Land Resource Bibliography — GLRBAT
Great Britain. Land Resources Division. Land Resource Study — GB Land Resour Div Land Resour Study
Great Britain. Mineral Resources Consultative Committee. Mineral Dossier — GB Miner Resour Consult Comm Miner Dossier
Great Britain. Ministry of Agriculture, Fisheries, and Food. Bulletin — GB Minist Agric Fish Food Bull
Great Britain. Ministry of Agriculture, Fisheries, and Food. Directorate of Fisheries Research. Fisheries Research Technical Report — FRTRDJ
Great Britain. Ministry of Agriculture, Fisheries, and Food. Directorate of Fisheries Research. Fisheries Research Technical Report — GB Minist Agric Fish Food Dir Fish Res Fish Res Tech Rep
Great Britain. Ministry of Agriculture, Fisheries, and Food. Directorate of Fisheries Research. Laboratory Leaflet — GB Minist Agric Fish Food Dir Fish Res Lab Leafl
Great Britain. Ministry of Agriculture, Fisheries, and Food. Fisheries Laboratory Leaflet. New Series — GB Ministry Agric Fish Food Fish Lab Leafl New Ser
Great Britain. Ministry of Agriculture, Fisheries, and Food. Fisheries Radiobiological Laboratory. Technical Report — GB Minist Agric Fish Food Fish Radiobiol Lab Tech Rep
Great Britain. Ministry of Agriculture, Fisheries, and Food. National Agricultural Advisory Service. Experimental Husbandry Farms and Experimental Horticulture Stations. Progress Report — GNEHAU
Great Britain. Ministry of Agriculture, Fisheries, and Food. Reference Book — GB Minist Agric Fish Food Ref Book
Great Britain. Ministry of Agriculture, Fisheries, and Food. Technical Bulletin — GB Minist Agric Fish Food Tech Bull
Great Britain. Ministry of Aviation. Aeronautic Research Council. Current Papers — GB Minist Aviat Aeronaut Res Counc Curr Pap
Great Britain. Ministry of Overseas Development. Land Resources Division. Land Resource Bibliography — GB Minist Overseas Dev Land Resour Div Land Resour Bibliogr
Great Britain. Ministry of Overseas Development. Land Resources Division. Progress Report — GB Minist Overseas Dev Land Resour Div Prog Rep
Great Britain. Ministry of Power. Safety in Mines Research Establishment. Research Report — GB Minist Power Saf Mines Res Establ Res Rep
Great Britain. Ministry of Technology. Forest Products Research. Bulletin — GB Minist Technol For Prod Res Bull
Great Britain. Ministry of Technology. Forest Products Research. Special Report — GB Minist Technol For Prod Res Spec Rep
Great Britain. Ministry of Technology. Warren Spring Laboratory. Report — GB Minist Technol Warren Spring Lab Rep
Great Britain. National Building Studies. Research Paper — GB Nat Build Stud Res Pap
Great Britain. National Building Studies. Technical Paper — GB Nat Build Stud Tech Pap
Great Britain. National Engineering Laboratory. NEL Report — GB Natl Eng Lab NEL Rep
Great Britain. Natural Environment Research Council. News Journal — GB Nat Environ Res Counc News J
Great Britain. Natural Environment Research Council. Publications. Series D — GB Nat Environ Res Counc Publ Ser D
Great Britain. Natural Environment Research Council. Report — GB Nat Environ Res Counc Rep
Great Britain. Pest Infestation Research Board. Report — GB Pest Infest Res Board Rep
Great Britain. Road Research Laboratory. Road Note — GB Road Res Lab Road Note
Great Britain. Road Research Laboratory. Road Research Technical Paper — GB Road Res Lab Road Tech Pap
Great Britain. Royal Aircraft Establishment. Technical Report — GB R Aircr Establ Tech Rep
Great Britain. Royal Armament Research and Development Establishment. RARDE Memorandum — GB R Armament Res Dev Establ RARDE Memo
Great Britain. Safety in Mines Research Establishment. Report — GB Saf Mines Res Establ Rep
Great Britain. Safety in Mines Research Establishment. Research Report — GB Saf Mines Res Establ Res Rep
Great Britain. Soil Survey of England and Wales. Annual Report — GB Soil Surv Engl Wales Annu Rep
Great Britain. Soil Survey. Special Survey — GB Soil Surv Spec Surv
Great Britain. Torry Research Station. Torry Technical Paper — GB Torry Res Stn Torry Tech Pap
Great Britain. Tropical Products Institute. Report L — GB Trop Prod Inst Rep L
Great Britain. Warren Spring Laboratory. Mineral Processing Information Note — GB Warren Spring Lab Miner Process Inf Note
Great Britain. Warren Spring Laboratory. Report — GB Warren Spring Lab Rep
Great Britain. Warren Spring Laboratory. Report LR — GB Warren Spring Lab LR
Great Britain. Warren Spring Laboratory. Review — GB Warren Spring Lab Rev
Great Britain. Water Resource Board. Publication — GB Water Resour Board Publ
Great Canadian Sands News — GCOS
Great Lakes Entomologist — Great Lakes Entomol
Great Lakes Entomologist — Gt Lakes Ent
Great Lakes Fishery Commission. Annual Report — Great Lakes Fish Comm Annu Rep
Great Lakes Fishery Commission. Technical Report — Great Lakes Fish Comm Tech Rep
Great Lakes Research Division. University of Michigan. Publication — Great Lakes Res Div Univ Mich Publ
Great Lakes Research Division. University of Michigan. Special Report — Great Lakes Res Div Univ Mich Spec Rep
Great Lakes Review — GLRev
Great Lakes Review — Great Lakes
Great Lakes Review. A Journal of Midwest Culture — GrLR
Great Plains Agricultural Council. Publication — Great Plains Agric Counc Publ
Great Plains Agricultural Council. Publication — Publ Great Plains Agric Coun
Great Plains Journal — GPJ
Great Plains Journal — Gt Plains Jour
Great Plains Quarterly — GPQ
Great Science Fiction Stories — GSFS
Great Speckled Bird — Grt Bird
Great Synagogue Congregational Journal — Great Synag Cong J
Great Texts of the Bible — GT Bi
Greater Baton Rouge Business Report — Baton Rou B
Greater London Association for the Disabled. Quarterly — GLAD
Greater London Intelligence Journal — GLIJ
Greater Milwaukee Dental Bulletin — Greater Milw Dent Bull
Greater St. Louis Dental Society. Bulletin [*US*] — Greater St Louis Dent Soc Bull
Greece and Rome — G a R
Greece and Rome — G & R
Greece and Rome [*Oxford*] — GaR
Greece and Rome [*Oxford*] — Gr and R
Greece and Rome — PGNR
Greece and Rome. New Surveys in the Classics — Greece & Rome New Surv Class
Greece's Weekly for Business and Finance — BUX
Greek and Byzantine Studies — G & BS
Greek and Roman Bronzes — GRB
Greek and Roman Jewellery — GRJ
Greek Anthology. Hellenistic Epigrams — HE
Greek Atomic Energy Commission. Nuclear Research Center Democritus. Report DEM O — Greek AEC Nucl Res Cent Democritus Rep DEMO
Greek Coins in North American Collections — GCNAC
Greek Dark Ages — GDA
Greek Geometric Pottery — GGP
Greek Lyric Poetry from Alcman to Simonides — GLP
Greek Lyric Poetry from Alcman to Simonides — Gr Lyr Poet
Greek Orthodox Theological Review — GOTR
Greek Orthodox Theological Review — Gr Orth Th R
Greek Orthodox Theological Review [*Brookline, MA*] — GrOrthTR
Greek Orthodox Theological Review — GTR
Greek Ostraca in the Bodleian Library at Oxford and Various Other Collections — Ostr Bodl
Greek Ostraca in the University of Michigan Collection — O Mich
Greek Ostraca in the University of Michigan Collection — Ostr Mich
Greek Papyri from the Cairo Museum. Together with Papyri of Roman Egypt from American Collections. Goodspeed — P Goodsp Cair
Greek Papyri in the Library of Cornell University — P Cornell
Greek Particles — GP
Greek, Roman, and Byzantine Monographs — GRB Mon
Greek, Roman, and Byzantine Monographs — GRBM
Greek, Roman, and Byzantine Scholarly Aids — GRBSA
Greek, Roman, and Byzantine Studies — GR & BS
Greek, Roman, and Byzantine Studies — GR Byz S
Greek, Roman, and Byzantine Studies — Gr Rom Byz St
Greek, Roman, and Byzantine Studies — GRBS
Greek, Roman, and Byzantine Studies — Greek Rom & Byz Stud
Greek, Roman, and Byzantine Studies — Greek Rom B
Greek, Roman, and Byzantine Studies — Greek Roman Byz Stud
Greek, Roman, and Byzantine Studies — GrR
Greek, Roman, and Byzantine Studies — PGRB
Greek, Roman, Byzantine Studies — Greek Roman Byzantine Stud
Greek-English Lexikon — GEL
Green Book Album — Green Bk Album
Green Bulletin — Green Bull
Green Mountain — Green Mt
Green Revolution — Green Rev

Green Revolution — Green Revol
Green River Review — GRR
Greenfield Review — Green R
Greenfield Review — Greenfield Rev
Greenkeepers Reporter — Greenkeepers Rep
Greenland Bioscience. Meddelelser om Gronland — GRBSC
Greenland. Geologiske Undersoegelse. Bulletin — Greenland Geol Unders Bull
Greenland. Geologiske Undersoegelse. Rapport — Greenland Geol Unders Rapp
Greenland Geoscience [*Denmark*] — Greenl Geosci
Greenland Geoscience. Meddelelser om Gronland — GRGSC
Greenland Newsletter. Greenland Home Rule Information Service (Tusarliivik) — GRNL
Greensboro News and Record — NCNR
Greenskeeper's Bulletin — Greenskeepers Bull
Greenwich Time Report — Greenwich Time Rep
Gregorianische Rundschau — Gr Rd
Gregorianum — Greg
Gregorianum (Roma) — Gr
Gregorios ho Palamas — GP
Gregorios ho Palamas — Greg Pal
Gregoriusblad — Gregor
Gregoriusblatt — Gregoriusbl
Gregoriusblatt fuer Katholische Kirchenmusik — Gr Bl
Gregorius-Bote fuer Katholische Kirchensaenger — Gr Bo
Greifswald Ernst-Moritz-Arndt-Universitaet. Wissenschaftliche Zeitschrift. Mathematisch-Naturwissenschaftliche Reihe — Wiss Z Greifswald Ernst Moritz Arndt Univ Math Natur-Reihe
Greifswalder Beitraege zur Literatur und Stilforschung — GBLS
Greifswalder Studien zur Lutherforschung und Neuzeitlichen Geistesgeschichte — GSLF
Greifswalder Theologische Forschungen — G Th F
Greinar — GRNR
GREMP [*Geothermal Reservoir Engineering Management Program*] **News** — NGRPD
Grenada Agricultural Department. Report — Grenada Agric Dep Rep
Grenfell Clinical Quarterly — GRCQ
Grenoble. Faculte des Sciences. Laboratoire de Geologie. Memoires — Grenoble Fac Sci Lab Geol Mem
Grenzfragen der Psychologie — GFP
Grenzfragen Zwischen Theologie und Philosophie — GFTP
Grenzgebiete der Medizin — Grenzgeb Med
Grenzgebiete der Psychiatrie — Grenzgeb Psychiatr
Grenzmaerkische Heimatblaetter — Grenzmaerk Heimatbl
GRI [*Gravure Research Institute*] **Newsletter** — GRI Newsl
Gribnye Vrediteli Kul'turnyh i Dikorastusih Poleznyh Rastenij Kavkaza — Gribn Vredit Kult Dikorast Polezn Rast Kavkaza
Griechische Feste — GF
Griechische Grammatik auf der Grundlage von Karl Brugmanns Griechischer Grammatik — SB
Griechische Kriegsschriftsteller — Gr Krieg
Griechische Muenzen. Abhandlungen. Bayerische Akademie der Wissenschaften. Philosophischphilologische Klasse — Gr Muenz
Griechische Mythologie — Gr Myth
Griechische Papyri aus dem Berliner Museum — GPBM
Griechische Papyri im Museum des Oberhessischen Geschichtsvereins zu Giessen — PGiess
Griechische Papyrus der Kaiserlichen Universitaets- und Landesbibliothek zu Strassburg — P Strasb
Griechische Papyrusurkunden der Hamburger Staats- und Universitaetsbibliothek — P Hamb
Griechische Plastik — Gr Pl
Griechische Roman-Papyri und Verwandte Texte — Gr Roman Papyri
Griechische und Griechisch-Demotische Ostraka der Universitaets- und Landesbibliothek zu Strassburg im Elsass — O Stras
Griechische und Griechisch-Demotische Ostraka der Universitaets- und Landesbibliothek zu Strassbourg im Elsass — Ostr Strassb
Griechische und Roemische Portraets — GRP
Griechische Urkunden der Papyrussammlung zu Leipzig — P Leips
Griechische Urkunden des Aegyptischen Museums zu Kairo — GUAMK
Griechische Vasenmalerei — Griech Vas
Griechische Vers-Inschriften — GVI
Griechische Verskunst — GV
Griechische Verskunst — GVK
Griechischen Landschaften — GL
Griechischen Papyrusurkunden Kleineren Formats — P Klein Form
Griechischer Wirtschaftsdienst — GRW
Griechisches Etymologisches Woerterbuch — GEW
Griechisches Etymologisches Woerterbuch — Gr EW
Griefswald-Stralsunder Jahrbuch — GSJb
Griffin's Statistical Monograph Series — Griffin's Statist Monograph Ser
Griffin's Statistical Monographs and Courses — Griffins Statist Monograph Courses
Griffith Gazette — Griffith Gaz
Griffith Observer — Griffith Observ
Griffith Researcher — Griffith Res
Grillparzer Forum Forchtenstein — GFF
Grinding and Finishing — GRFIA
Grinding and Finishing — Grinding Finish
Grindlays Bank Review — Grindlays Bank R
Gripp i Respiratornye Virusnye Infektsii — Gripp Respir Virusn Infektsii
Grits and Grinds (Worcester, Massachusetts) — Grits Grinds (Worcester, Mass)
Grocery and Storekeeping News — Groc & Storekeeping News
Grodnenskii Sel'skokhozyaistvennyi Institut. Sbornik Nauchnykh Trudov — Grodn Skh Inst Sb Nauchn Tr
Groene Amsterdammer — Gr A
Groene Amsterdammer — GRM
Groenlands Geologiske Undersoegelse. Bulletin — GGUB
Groenlands Geologiske Undersoegelse. Bulletin — Groenl Geol Unders Bull
Groenlands Geologiske Undersoegelse. Bulletin — Groenlands Geol Unders Bull
Groenlands Geologiske Undersoegelse. Bulletin — Groenlands Geol Undersoegelse Bull
Groenlands Geologiske Undersoegelse. Miscellaneous Papers — GGUMP
Groenlands Geologiske Undersoegelse. Miscellaneous Papers — Groenlands Geol Unders Misc Pap
Groenlands Geologiske Undersoegelse. Rapport — GGUR
Groenlands Geologiske Undersoegelse. Rapport — Groenl Geol Unders Rap
Groenten en Fruit — GFR
Grond-, Chemiese, en Fisiese Wetenskappe — Grond Chem Fis Wet
Grondboor en Hamer [*Nederlandse Geologische Vereniging Tijdschrift*] — Grondboor Hamer
Groningen Oriental Studies — Groningen Orient Stud
Groningsche Volksalmanach — GVA
Gronlandsposten — Gronpl
Grootkeuken. Voedingsblad voor Instellingen en Bedrijven — VOH
Grope Kunstfuehrer — GKF
Grosse Brockhaus — BG
Grosse Entschluss — Gr Ent
Grosse Herder — GH
Grosse Juedische National-Biographie — GJNB
Grosse Naturforscher — Grosse Naturforsch
Grosses Vollstaendiges Universal Lexikon aller Wissenschaften und Kuenste — GVUL
Grosses Zoologisches Praktikum — Grosses Zool Prakt
Grote Winkler Prins Encyclopedie — GWPE
Grotius Annuaire Internationle — GAI
Grotius Society Transactions — Grotius Soc Trans
Ground Engineering — Ground Eng
Ground Engineering — Ground Engng
Ground Water Age — Ground Wat
Ground Water Bulletin. North Carolina. Division of Ground Water — Ground Water Bull NC Div Ground Water
Ground Water Circular. North Carolina. Division of Ground Water — Ground Water Circ NC Div Ground Water
Ground Water Heat Pump Journal — Ground Water Heat Pump J
Ground Water Heat Pump Journal — GWHJD
Ground Water Management — Ground Water Manage
Ground Water Monitoring Review — Ground Water Monit Rev
Ground Water Report. Oregon. Water Resources Department — Ground Water Rep Oreg Wat Resour Dep
Ground Water Series. Circular. Colorado Water Conservation Board — Ground Water Ser Circ Colo Water Conserv Board
Ground Water Series. Kansas Geological Survey — Ground Water Ser Kans Geol Surv
Grounds Maintenance — Grounds Maint
Groundwater Quality and Treatment. Proceedings. Water Quality Conference — Groundwater Qual Treat Proc Water Qual Conf
Group and Family Therapy — Group Fam Ther
Group and Organization Studies — GOS
Group and Organization Studies — Group Org Stud
Group and Organization Studies — Group Organ Stud
Group for the Advancement of Psychiatry. Report — Group Adv Psychiatry Rep
Group Health Journal — Group Health J
Group Health News — Group Health N
Group of Experts on the Scientific Aspects of Marine Pollution. Reports and Studies — Group Experts Sci Aspects Mar Pollut Rep Stud
Group Practice — Group Pract
Group Practice Journal — Group Pract J
Group Processes. Transactions. Conference — Group Processes Trans Conf
Group Psychotherapy [*Later, Group Psychotherapy, Psychodrama, and Sociometry*] — GRPSB
Group Psychotherapy and Psychodrama [*Later, Group Psychotherapy, Psychodrama, and Sociometry*] — Group Psych
Group Psychotherapy, Psychodrama, and Sociometry — Group Psychother Psychodrama Sociometry
Group Theatre Paper — GTP
Groupe de Recherches sur les Produits Superficiellement Actifs. Colloque — Groupe Rech Prod Superficiellement Actifs Colloq
Groupe Francais de Rheologie. Cahiers — Groupe Fr Rheol Cah
Groupe Francais des Argiles. Bulletin — Groupe Fr Argiles Bull
Groupe International de Recherches sur les Ordures Menageres. Bulletin d'Information — Groupe Int Rech Ordures Menageres Bull Inf
Groupe International d'Etude pour les Recherches sur les Ordures Menageres. Bulletin d'Information — Groupe Int Etude Rech Ordures Menageres Bull Inf
Groupe Linguistique d'Etudes Chamito-Semitiques. Comptes Rendus — GLECS
Groupe Polyphenols. Bulletin de Liaison — Groupe Polyphenols Bull Liaison
Grouped Enterprises Data Base — GRPENT
Groupement Francais pour le Developpement des Recherches Aeronautiques. Bulletin du GRA — Group Fr Dev Rech Aeronaut Bull GRA
Groupement pour l'Avancement de la Mecanique Industrielle — Group Avan Mec Ind
Groupement pour l'Avancement des Methodes d'Analyse Spectrographique des Produits Metallurgiques. Congres — Group Av Methodes Anal Spectrog Prod Metall Congr
Groupements Techniques Veterinaires. Bulletin — Group Tech Vet Bull
Grove Chronology of Music History — Grove Chron Mus Hist
Grove's Dictionary of Music and Musicians — Grove
Grower Annual — Grower Annu
Growers' Directory. Illinois Crop Improvement Association — Growers' Dir Ill Crop Impr Ass

Growers' Handbook and Annual Proceedings. Ohio Vegetable and Potato Growers' Association — Growers' Handb Annu Proc
Growing Point — GP
Growing Points. Central Coast Counties. University of California. Berkeley. Cooperative Extension Service — Grow Points Cent Coast Counties Univ Calif Berkeley Coop Ext
Growth and Change — GAC
Growth and Change — GRC
Growth and Change — Growth Chan
Growth and Change — GRZ
Growth, Development, and Aging — Growth Dev Aging
Growth, Development, and Aging. GDA — Growth Dev Aging GDA
Growth Regulation — Growth Regul
Growth. Supplement — Growth Suppl
Groznenskii Neftyanoi Institut. Trudy — Grozn Neft Inst Tr
Groznenskii Neftyanoi Nauchno-Issledovatel'skii Institut. Trudy — Grozn Neft Nauchno Issled Inst Tr
Groznenskii Neftyznik — Grozn Neft
GRS (Gesellschaft fuer Reaktorsicherheit). Kurz-Information. Reihe A — GRS (Ges Reaktorsicherheit) Kurz-Inf Reihe A
GRS (Gesellschaft fuer Reaktorsicherheit). Kurz-Information. Reihe B — GRS (Ges Reaktorsicherheit) Kurz-Inf Reihe B
GRS (Gesellschaft fuer Reaktorsicherheit). Kurz-Information. Reihe C — GRS (Ges Reaktorsicherheit) Kurz-Inf Reihe C
GRS (Gesellschaft fuer Reaktorsicherheit). Kurz-Information. Reihe D — GRS (Ges Reaktorsicherheit) Kurz-Inf Reihe D
GRS (Gesellschaft fuer Reaktorsicherheit). Kurz-Information. Reihe E — GRS (Ges Reaktorsicherheit) Kurz-Inf Reihe E
GRS (Gesellschaft fuer Reaktorsicherheit). Kurz-Information. Reihe F — GRS (Ges Reaktorsicherheit) Kurz-Inf Reihe F
GRS (Gesellschaft fuer Reaktorsicherheit). Kurz-Information. Reihe G — GRS (Ges Reaktorsicherheit) Kurz-Inf Reihe G
GRS (Gesellschaft fuer Reaktorsicherheit). Kurz-Information. Reihe H — GRS (Ges Reaktorsicherheit) Kurz-Inf Reihe H
GRS (Gesellschaft fuer Reaktorsicherheit). Kurz-Information. Reihe J [*West Germany*] — GRS Kurz-Inf Reihe J
GRS (Gesellschaft fuer Reaktorsicherheit). Kurz-Information. Reihe K — GRS (Ges Reaktorsicherheit) Kurz-Inf Reihe K
GRS (Gesellschaft fuer Reaktorsicherheit) Translations. Safety Codes and Guides — GRS (Ges Reaktorsicherheit) Transl Saf Codes Guides
GRS [*Gesellschaft fuer Reaktorsicherheit*] **Translations. Safety Codes and Guides** — TSCGD
Gruchots Beitraege zur Erlaeuterung des Deutschen Rechts — GruchB
Grudnaya Khirurgiya — GRHKA
Grudnaya Khirurgiya — Grudn Khir
Grudtvig Studier — GStud
Gruene Reihe des Bundesministeriums fuer Gesundheit und Umweltschutz — Gruene Reihe Bundesminist Gesund Umweltschutz
Grund und Boden — Grund u Boden
Grundeigentum — GRUND
Grundig Technische Informationen — Grundig Tech Inf
Grundkurs Mathematik — Grundkurs Math
Grundkurs Physik — Grundkurs Phys
Grundlagen der Exakten Naturwissenschaften — Grundlagen Exakt Naturwiss
Grundlagen der Germanistik — GdG
Grundlagen der Landtechnik — Grundlagen Landtech
Grundlagen der Mathematik und Informatik — Grundlagen Math Inform
Grundlagen der Schaltungstechnik — Grundlagen Schaltungstech
Grundlagen und Fortschritte der Lebensmitteluntersuchung und Lebensmitteltechnologie — Grundlagen Fortschr Lebensmittelunters Lebensmitteltechnolo
Grundlagenstudien aus Kybernetik und Geisteswissenschaft — GKG
Grundlagenstudien aus Kybernetik und Geisteswissenschaft — Grund Kyber Geist
Grundlehren der Mathematischen Wissenschaften — Grundlehren Math Wiss
Grundriss der Akkadischen Grammatik — GAG
Grundriss der Germanischen Philologie — GGP
Grundriss der Germanischen Philologie (Hermann Paul, Editor) — Pauls Grdr
Grundriss der Gesamtwissenschaft des Judentums — GGJ
Grundriss der Geschichtswissenschaft — Gd G
Grundriss der Indo-Arischen Philologie — Grdr Indo Ar Philol
Grundriss der Kirchengeschichte — GKG
Grundriss der Romanische Philologie — Grundriss der Roman Philol
Grundriss der Romanischen Philologie (G. Groeber, Editor) — Groebers Grdr
Grundriss der Slavischen Philologie und Kulturgeschichte — GSPK
Grundriss der Theologischen Wissenschaft — G Th W
Grundrisse zum Neuen Testament — GNT
Grundskyld — Grund
Grundtvig Studier — GrSt
Grundwissen Mathematik — Grundwissen Math
Grune Stadt. Naturschutz in der Grossstadt — Grune Stadt Natur Grosstadt
Gruntovedenie i Inzhenernaya Geologiya — Gruntoved Inzh Geol
Grupo Interuniversitario de Fisica Teorica de Altas Energias. Informe. GIFT — Grupo Interuniv Fis Teor Altas Energ GIFT
Gruppe Deutscher Kolonialwirtschaftlicher Unternehmungen. Mitteilungen — Gruppe Dtsch Kolonialwirtsch Unternehm Mitt
Gruppenpsychotherapie und Gruppendynamik — Gruppenpsyc
Gruyter Lahrbuch — GLB
Gruzinskii Nauchno-Issledovatel'skii Institut Pishchevoi Promyshlennost i. Trudy — Gruz Nauchno Issled Inst Pishch Promsti Tr
Gruzinskii Politehniceskii Institut Imeni V. I. Lenina Trudy — Gruzin Politehn Inst Trudy
Gruzinskii Politekhnicheskii Institut imeni V. I. Lenina. Trudy — Gruz Politekh Inst im V I Lenina Tr
Gruzinskii Politekhnicheskii Institut imeni V.I. Lenina. Nauchnye Trudy — Gruz Politekh Inst im V I Lenina Nauchn Tr
Gruzinskii Sel'skokhozyaistvennyi Institut Nauchnye Trudy — Gruz Skh Inst Nauchn Tr
Gruzinskii Sel'skokhozyaistvennyi Institut Trudy — Gruz Skh Inst Tr
Gruzinskii Zootekhnichesko-Veterinarnyi Uchebno-Issledovatel'skii Institut. Sbornik Trudov — Gruz Zootekh Vet Uchebno Issled Inst Sb Tr
Gruzlica i Choroby Pluc — Gruzl
GS News Technical Report [*Japan*] — GS News Tech Rep
GSA [*Geological Society of America*] **Special Paper (Regional Studies)** — GSA Spec Pap (Reg Stud)
GSF [*Gesellschaft fuer Strahlen- und Umweltforschung*] **Bericht** — GSF Ber
GSF [*Gesellschaft fuer Strahlen- und Umweltforschung*] **Bericht BT** — GSF Ber BT
GSF [*Gesellschaft fuer Strahlen- und Umweltforschung*] **Bericht O** — GSF Ber O
GSF [*Gesellschaft fuer Strahlen- und Umweltforschung*] **Bericht P** — GSF Ber P
GSI [*Gesellschaft fuer Schwerionenforschung*] **Bericht** — GSI Ber
GSI (Gesellschaft fuer Schwerionenforschung) Scientific Report — GSI Sci Rep
G.S.N. Gesneriad Saintpaulia News — GSN
GTA [*Grain Terminal Association*] **Digest** — GTA Dig
GTE [*General Telephone and Electronics Corp.*] **Automatic Electric Technical Journal** [*GTE Automatic Electric World-Wide Communications Journal*] [*Later,*] — GTE Auto
GTE [*General Telephone and Electronics Corp.*] **Automatic Electric Technical Journal** [*GTE Automatic Electric World-Wide Communications Journal*] [*Later,*] — GTE Autom Electr J
GTE [*General Telephone and Electronics Corp.*] **Automatic Electric Technical Journal** [*GTE Automatic Electric World-Wide Communications Journal*] [*Later,*] — GTE Autom Electr Tech J
GTE [*General Telephone and Electronics Corp.*] **Automatic Electric World-Wide Communications Journal** — GTE Autom Electr World-Wide Commun J
GTE (General Telephone and Electronics Corp.) Research and Development Journal — GTE Res Dev J
GTR-WO [*General Technical Report WO*] **United States Forest Service** — GTR WO US For Serv
GUA [*Geologisch Instituut. Universiteit van Amsterdam*] **Papers of Geology** — GUA Pap Geol
Guacamayo y la Serpiente — GYS
Guam Agricultural Experiment Station. Publications — Guam Ag Exp
Guam Civil Code — Guam Civ Code
Guam Code Annotated — Guam Code Ann
Guam Code of Civil Procedure — Guam Civ Proc Code
Guam Government Code — Guam Govt Code
Guam Probate Code — Guam Prob Code
Guam Reports — Guam
Guangxue Xuebao — GUXUD
Guardian — G
Guardian [*London*] — GD
Guardian — GN
Guardian — MGD
Guardian Weekly — GW
Guatemala Indigena — GI
Guatemala Indigena — Guatem Indig
Guatemala Indigena (Guatemala) — Guat Indig Guat
Guelph Dairy Research Report — Guelph Dairy Res Rep
Guertler. Bijouterie und Metallwaren Industrie — Guertler Bijout Metallwaren Ind
Guetersloher Beitraege zur Heimatund Landeskunde — Guetersloher Beitr
Guia Quincenal (Buenos Aires) — Guia Quin BA
Guidance and Special Education Bulletin — Guid Spec Educ Bull
Guidance Information System [*Database*] — GIS
Guide to Indian Periodical Literature — G Indian Per Lit
Guide to Indian Periodical Literature — GInd
Guide to Indian Periodical Literature — Guide Indian Period Lit
Guide to Microforms in Print — GMP
Guide to Religious and Semi-Religious Periodicals — Guide Relig Semi Relig Period
Guide to Religious Periodicals — G Rel Per
Guide to Religious Periodicals — Guide Relig Period
Guide to Reviews of Books from and about Hispanic America — Guide Rev Books Hisp Am
Guide to Scientific Instruments — GUISA
Guide to Social Science and Religion in Periodical Literature — GSSRPL
Guide to Social Science and Religion in Periodical Literature — Guide Soc Sci Relig Period Lit
Guide to the Performing Arts — GPA
Guide to the Performing Arts — GPerfArts
Guide to the Performing Arts — Guide Perform Arts
Guide to Venture Capital Sources — GVCS
Guide to Yeast Genetics and Molecular Biology — Guide Yeast Genet Mol Biol
Guidebook. Annual Field Conference. Montana Geological Society — Guideb Annu Field Conf Mont Geol Soc
Guidebook. Georgia Geological Society — Guideb GA Geol Soc
Guidebook Series. Geological Institute (Bucharest) — Guideb Ser Geol Inst (Bucharest)
Guidebook Series. Illinois State Geological Survey — Guideb Ser Ill St Geol Surv
Guidebook to the Geology of Utah — Guideb Geol Utah
Guidebook. Wyoming Geological Association. Annual Field Conference — Guideb Wyo Geol Assoc Annu Field Conf
Guidelines in Medicine — Guidel Med
Guidelines to Metabolic Therapy — Guidel Metab Ther
Guild Gardener. National Gardens Guild — Guild Gard
Guild Notes — Guild Nts
Guild of Carillonneurs in North America. Bulletin — GCNA
Guild of Pastoral Psychology — GPP
Guild Practitioner — Guild Prac

Guildhall Miscellany — Guildhall Misc
Guildhall Studies in London History — Guidhall Stud London Hist
Guildhall Studies in London History — Guildhall S
Guilford Law and Behavior Series — Guilford Law Behav Ser
Guinea-Pig Newsletter — Guinea-Pig NL
Guion Literario — GLite
Guitar and Lute — GL
Guitar Player — GP
Guitar Player — IGUP
Guitar Review — GTR
Guitar Review — GU
Guitar Review — GuiR
Guitar Review — Guitar R
Guitar Review — Guitar Rev
Guitar Toronto — Guit T
Guitarra Magazine — Guitarra
Gujarat Agricultural University. Research Journal — Gujarat Agric Univ Res J
Gujarat Law Reporter — GLR
Gujarat Law Times — Guj LT
Gujarat Research Society. Journal — GRS
Gujarat Research Society Journal — GRSJ
Gujarat Statistical Review — Gujarat Statist Rev
Gulden Passer — GP
Gulf and Caribbean Fisheries Institute. University of Miami. Proceedings — Gulf Caribb Fish Inst Univ Miami Proc
Gulf Coast Association of Geological Societies. Field Trip Guidebook — GCGGA
Gulf Coast Association of Geological Societies. Transactions — Gulf Coast Assoc Geol Socs Trans
Gulf Coast Cattleman — Gulf Coast Cattlem
Gulf Coast Oil Reporter — GCOR
Gulf Mirror — GLFM
Gulf Research Reports — Gulf Res Rep
Gulf Shores Symposium on Unusual DNA Structures — Gulf Shores Symp Unusual DNA Struct
Gulf States Historical Magazine — Gulf States Hist M
Gulf Times — GLFT
Gummi, Asbest, Kunststoffe [*Later, Gummi, Fasern, Kunststoffe*] — Gummi Asbest Kunstst
Gummi, Asbest, Kunststoffe [*Later, Gummi, Fasern, Kunststoffe*] — Gummi Kunst
Gummi, Asbest, Kunststoffe. Internationale Unabhangige Fachzeitschrift — GUM
Gummi, Fasern, Kunststoffe — Gummi Fasern Kunstst
Gummi, Fasern, Kunststoffe — Gummi Kunst
Gummi- und Asbest. Zeitung — Gummi Asbest Ztg
Gummi. Zeitung. Beilage — Gummi Ztg Beil
Gummi. Zeitung und Kautschuk — Gummi Ztg Kautsch
Gundriss der Sozialoekonomik — Gd S
Gunma Journal of Agricultural Research. A. General — Gunma J Agric Res A
Gunma Journal of Liberal Arts and Science — Gunma J Libr Arts Sci
Gunma Journal of Medical Sciences — Gunma J Med Sci
Gunma Journal of Medical Sciences. Supplementum — Gunma J Med Sci Suppl
Gunma Reports of Medical Sciences — Gunma Rep Med Sci
Gunma Symposia on Endocrinology — Gunma Symp Endocrinol
Gunma Symposia on Endocrinology — GUSYA
Gunton's Magazine — Gunton
Gunton's Magazine — Guntons M
Gunton's Magazine — Guntons Mag
Gure Herria — GH
Gurukula Kangri Vishwavidyalaya. Journal of Scientific Research — Gurukula Kangri Vishwavidyalaya J Sci Res
Gustav Freytag Blaetter — GFB
Gutenberg Jahrbuch — Gut Jb
Gutenberg Jahrbuch — Gutenberg Jahrb
Gutenberg-Jahrbuch — G Jb
Gutenberg-Jahrbuch — GJ
Gutenberg-Jahrbuch — GuJ
Gutenberg-Jahrbuch — Gutenberg Jb
Guthrie Bulletin — Guthrie Bull
Guyana. Geological Survey Department. Report — Guyana Geol Surv Dep Rep
Guyana Journal of Science — Guyana J Sci
Guyana. Ministry of Agriculture and Natural Resources. Agriculture and Land Development Departments. Annual Report — Guyana Minist Agric Nat Resour Agric Land Dev Ann Rep
Guyana. Ministry of Agriculture and Natural Resources. Agriculture and Land Development Departments. Annual Report — Guyana Mist Agric Nat Resourc Agric Land Dev Dep Annu Rep
Guyana. Ministry of Agriculture and Natural Resources. Geological Survey Department. Report — Guyana Minist Agric Nat Resour Geol Surv Dep Rep
Guyana Sugar Experiment Station's Bulletin — Guyana Sugar Exp Stn Bull
Guy's Hospital Gazette — Guy's Hosp Gaz
Guy's Hospital Reports — GHREA
Guy's Hospital Reports — Guy's Hosp Rep
Gwent Local History — GLH
GWF. Das Gas- und Wasserfach — GWF Gas Wasserfach
GWF. Das Gas- und Wasserfach. Gas/Erdgas — GWF Gas Wasserfach Gas Erdgas
GWF. Das Gas- und Wasserfach. Wasser/Abwasser — GWF Gas Wasserfach Wasser Abwasser
GWF. Gas- und Wasserfach: Wasser/Abwasser — GWWAA
Gymnasieskolen — Gymnsk
Gymnasium — Gym
Gymnasium und Wissenschaft — GW
Gymnasium. Zeitschrift fuer Kultur der Antike und Humanistische Bildung — G
Gymnasium. Zeitschrift fuer Kultur der Antike und Humanistische Bildung — Gymn
Gynaekologische Rundschau — Gynaekol Rundsch
Gynaekologische Urologie. Urologisches Symposium — Gynaekol Urol Urol Symp
Gynakologisch-Geburtshilfliche Rundschau — Gynakol Geburtshilfliche Rundsch
Gynecologic and Obstetric Investigation — Gynecol Obstet Invest
Gynecologic Endocrinology. Proceedings. Annual Symposium on Reproductive Medicine — Gynecol Endocrinol Proc Annu Symp Reprod Med
Gynecologic Investigation — Gynecol Inv
Gynecologic Investigation — Gynecol Invest
Gynecologic Oncology — Gynecol Oncol
Gynecologic Oncology — GYNOA
Gynecological Endocrinology — Gynecol Endocrinol
Gynecologie et Obstetrique — Gynecol Obstet
Gynecologie et Obstetrique de Langue Francaise — GYOBA
Gynecologie et Obstetrique. Supplement — Gynecol Obstet Suppl
Gynecologie Pratique — Gynecol Prat
Gynecology and Obstetrics. Proceedings. World Congress of Gynecology and Obstetrics — Gynecol Obstet Proc World Congr
Gyosei Jiken Saibanreishu — Gyoshu
Gyosei Saiban Geppo — Gyosai Geppo
Gyosei Saibansho Hanketsuroku — Gyohan
Gypsy Scholar — Gy S
Gyuemoelcseszeti, Boraszati, es Kerteszeti Ujsag — Gyuemoelcsesz Borasz Kert Ujs
Gyuemoelcseszeti es Konyhakerteszeti Fuezetek — Gyuemoelcsesz Konyhakert Fuez
Gyvulininkystes ir Veterinarijos Instituto Darbai — Gyvulinink Vet Inst Darb

H

H. W. Gillett Memorial Lecture — H W Gillett Meml Lect
H2O. Tijdschrift voor Watervoorziening en Afvalwaterbehandeling — HTW
HAA [*Herpetological Association of Africa*] **Journal** — HAA J
Haagsch Maandblad — HM
Haandarbejdets Fremme — Haa Fr
Haarlemsch Bijdragen — HBd
Haarlemsche Bijdragen — Haarl B
Habana Museo y Biblioteca de Malacologia. Circulares — Habana Mus y Biblioteca Malacologia Circ
Habana Museo y Biblioteca de Zoologia. Circulares — Habana Mus y Biblioteca Zoologia Circ
Habitat — HABI
Habitat — HABT-A
Habitat Australia — Habitat Aust
Habitat et Vie Sociale — Habitat Vie Soc
Habitat International [*England*] — Habitat Int
Habitat International — HINTD
Habiter — HBTF-A
Hacettepe Bulletin of Medicine-Surgery — Hacettepe Bull Med-Surg
Hacettepe Bulletin of Natural Sciences and Engineering — Hacettepe Bull Nat Sci Eng
Hacettepe Bulletin of Social Sciences and Humanities — Hacett B SS
Hacettepe Fen ve Muhendislik Bilimleri Dergisi — Hacettepe Fen Muhendislik Bilimleri Derg
Hacettepe Fen ve Muhendislik Bilimleri Dergisi [*Turkey*] — Hacettepe Muhendislik Bilimleri Derg
Hacettepe Medical Journal — Hacettepe Med J
Hacienda Publica (Asuncion) — Hac Publ Asuncion
Hacienda Publica Espanola — Hacienda Publica Esp
Hadashot Archaeologioth — Hadashot Arch
Hadashot Arke'ologiyot — HA
Hadashot Arke'ologiyot — Had Ark
Hadashot Muzeon Israel — HMI
Hadassah Newsletter [*New York*] — HN
Hadassah Newsletter [*New York*] — HNL
Haderslev Samfundets Aarsskrift — Adersl Samf Aa
Hadronic Journal — Hadronic J
Hadronic Journal Supplement — Hadronic J Suppl
Hadronic Press Collection of Original Articles — Hadronic Press Collect Orig Artic
Hadronic Press Monographs in Applied Mathematics — Hadronic Press Monogr Appl Math
Hadronic Press Monographs in Mathematics — Hadronic Press Monographs Math
Hadronic Press Monographs in Theoretical Physics — Hadronic Press Monographs Theoret Phys
Hadronic Press New Series of Reprints of Historical Value — Hadronic Press New Ser Reprints Hist Value
Hadronic Press Reprint Series in Mathematics — Hadronic Press Reprint Ser Math
Hadtoertenelmi Koezlemenyek — HK
Haematologia Hungarica — Haematol Hung
Haematologica — HAEMA
Haematologica Latina — Haematol Lat
Haematologie und Bluttransfusion [*Haematology and Blood Transfusion*] — Haematol Bluttransfus
Haematology and Blood Transfusion — Haematol Blood Transfus
Ha-Ensiqlopedija Ha-Ibrit — Elb
Ha-Ensiqlopedija Ha-Talmudit — E Tal
Haerterei-Technik und Waermebehandlung — Haerterei-Tech Waermebehandl
Haerterei-Technische Mitteilungen — Haerterei-Tech Mitt
Haerterei-Technische Mitteilungen — Haert-Tech Mitt
Haerterei-Technische Mitteilungen (HTM) [*Germany*] — HTM Haerterei-Tech Mitt
Haffkine Institute. Annual Report — Haffkine Inst Annu Rep
Haffkine Institute. Bulletin — Haffkine Inst Bull
Hagiographischer Jahresberichte — HGJ
Ha-Hinnuk Ham-Musiquali — Ha Hinnuk Ham M
Hahnemann International Symposium on Hypertension — Hahnemann Int Symp Hypertens
Hahnemann Symposium — Hahnemann Symp
Hahnemann Symposium on Salt and Water Retention — Hahnemann Symp Salt Water Retention
Hahnemannian Monthly — Hahnemannian Mon
Hahnenklee-Symposion — Hahnenklee Symp
Hahn-Meitner-Institut fuer Kernforschung Berlin. Berichte — Hahn Meitner Inst Kernforsch Berlin Ber
Haifa Law Reports — HLR
Haikan To Schizai — HKTSA
Haile Selassie I University. Department of Geology. Annual Report — Haile Selassie I Univ Dep Geol Annu Rep
Hair, Trace Elements, and Human Illness. Human Hair Symposium — Hair Trace Elem Hum Illness Hum Hair Symp
Hajkusagi Muzeum Evkoenyve — HME
Hakata Symposium — Hakata Symp
Hakko Kogaku Kaishi — HKOKD
Hakodate Technical College. Research Reports — Hakodate Tech Coll Res Rep
Hakone Symposium. Proceedings — Hakone Symp Proc
Haksul Yonguchi - Chungnam Taehakkyo. Chayon Kwahak Yonguso — HYCYD
Halbmonatliches Literaturverzeichnis der Fortschrifte der Physik — Halbmon Literaturverz Fortschr Phys
Hale Lectures — Hale L
Hale Memorial Lectures — HML
Half-Yearly Journal. Mysore University. Section B. Science Including Medicine and Engineering — Half-Yrly J Mysore Univ Sect B Sci Incl Med Eng
Halle auz Cuirs — Halle Cuirs
Halle Universitaet. Wissenschaftliche Zeitschrift Gesellschafts und Sprachwissenschaftliche Reihe — Halle Univ Wiss Z Gesellsch & Sprachw Reihe
Haller Muenzblaetter — Haller Mb
Hallesches Jahrbuch fuer Geowissenschaften — Hallesches Jahrb Geowiss
Hallesches Jahrbuch fuer Mitteldeutsche Erdgeschichte — Hallesches Jahrb Mitteldtsh Erdgesch
Hallische Monographien — HM
Hallische Universitaetsreden — HUR
Hallisches Winckelmannsprogramme — Ha Wpr
Hallisches Winckelmannsprogramme — Hall W Pr
Hallisches Winckelmannsprogramme — HWPr
Halogen Chemistry — Halogen Chem
Halsbury's Law of England — Halsbury
Halsbury's Law of England — Halsbury L Eng
Halsbury's Law of England — Halsbury's Laws
Halton Business Journal — Halton Bus Jnl
Halve Maen — HalM
Ham Radio Horizons — Ham Rad Horiz
Ham (Walter P.) and Company. Monthly Bulletin — Ham Mo Bul
Hamann Newsletter — HN
Hamburg Geologischen Staatsinstitut. Mitteilungen — Hamburg Geol Staatsinstitut Mitt
Hamburg in Zahlen — HMZA
Hamburg. Institut fuer Asienkunde. Mitteilungen — MIAH
Hamburg. Zoologisches Staatsinstitut und Zoologisches Museum. Mitteilungen — Hamb Zool Staatsinst u Zool Mus Mitt
Hamburger Akademische Rundschau — Hamburger Akad Rdsch
Hamburger Akademische Rundschau — HAR
Hamburger Beitraege zur Angewandten Mineralogie, Kristallphysik, und Petrogenese — Hamb Beitr Angew Mineral Kristallphys Petrog
Hamburger Beitraege zur Archaeologie — Hamb Beitr A
Hamburger Beitraege zur Archaeologie — HBA
Hamburger Beitraege zur Geschichte der Deutschen Juden — HBGDJ
Hamburger Beitraege zur Numismatik — Hamb Beitr Num
Hamburger Beitraege zur Numismatik — HBN
Hamburger Beitraege zur Philosophie des Kritischen Idealismus — HB Kr I
Hamburger Beitraege zur Zeitgeschichte — HBZ
Hamburger Berichte zur Siedlungswasserwirtschaft — Hamb Ber Siedlungswasserwirtsch
Hamburger Fremdenblatt — HF
Hamburger Geophysikalische Einzelschriften — Hamb Geophys Einzelschriften
Hamburger Ibero-Amerikanische Reihe — HIAR
Hamburger Jahrbuch fuer Wirtschafts- und Gesellschaftspolitik — Hamburg Jb Wirtsch- u Ges-Polit
Hamburger Jahrbuch fuer Wirtschafts- und Gesellschaftspolitik — Hamburger Jahrb Wirt Gesellschaftspol
Hamburger Philologische Studien — HPS
Hamburger Romanistische Dissertationen — HRD
Hamburger Rundschau — HR
Hamburger Steuer und Zoll-Nachrichten — Hamb St u Z Nachr
Hamburger Symposion ueber Blutgerinnung — Hamb Symp Blutgerinnung
Hamburger Symposium ueber Tumormarker — Hamb Symp Tumormarker
Hamburger Wirtschaft [*Mitteilungen der Handelskammer Hamburg*] — Hamb Wirtsch
Hamburger Wochenschrift fuer Aerzte und Zahnaerzte — Hamb Wschr Ae Zahn Ae

Hamburgische Berichte von Neuen Gelehrten Sachen — Hamburg Ber Neuen Gel Sachen
Hamburgische Kirche und Ihre Geistlichen seit der Reformation — HKGR
Hamburgischer Garten-Almanach — Hamburg Gart Alman
Hamburgischer Lehrer-Verein fuer Naturkunde. Bericht — Hamburg Lehrer Verein Naturk Ber
Hamburgisches Magazin, oder Gesammlete Schriften, zum Unterricht und Vergnuegen aus der Naturforschung und den Angenehmen Wissenschaften Ueberhaupt — Hamburg Mag
Hamburgisches Verordnungsblatt — HV Bl
Hamdard Islamicus — Hamdard Islam
Hamdard Medical Digest — Hamdard Med Dig
Hamdard Medicus — Hamdard Med
Hamdard Medicus — HMDDAH
Hamilton Association. Journal and Proceedings — Hamilton As J Pr
Hamilton Scientific Association. Journal and Proceedings — Hamilton Sc As J Pr
Hamlet Review — HamletR
Hamlet Studies — H St
Hamline Law Review — Hamline L Rev
Hamline Law Review — Hamline LR
Hammersmith Cardiology Workshop Series — Hammersmith Cardiol Workshop Ser
Hammersmith Cardiology Workshop Series — HCWSEN
Hammurabi's Gesetz — HG
Hampshire Beekeeper — Hamps Beekpr
Hampton Bulletin — Hampton Bul
Hampton's Magazine — Hampton
Hampton's Magazine — Hamptons M
Han Guk Journal of Genetic Engineering — Han Guk J Genet Eng
Han Guk Journal of Genetic Engineering — HYKOE3
Hanauer Geschichtsblaetter — Han G
Hanauisches Magazin — Hanauisches Mag
Hancock Museum. Newcastle upon Tyne. Bulletin — Hancock Mus Newcastle upon Tyne Bull
Hand Book — Hand
Hand Clinics — Hand Clin
Handball Magazine — Handball Mag
Handbok. Norges Byggforskningsinstitutt — Hb Norg Byggforsk Inst
Handbood of Lipids in Human Nutrition — Handbk Lipids Hum Nutr
Handbook. Bureau of Economic Geology. University of Texas at Austin — Handb Bur Econ Geol Univ Tex Austin
Handbook. Institute of Orthopaedics — Hb Inst Orth
Handbook of Advanced Materials Testing — Handb Adv Mater Test
Handbook of Air Pollution Analysis — Handb Air Pollut Anal
Handbook of Amyotrophic Lateral Sclerosis — Handb Amyotrophic Lateral Scler
Handbook of Analysis of Synthetic Polymers and Plastics — Handb Anal Synth Polym Plast
Handbook of Antioxidants — Handb Antioxid
Handbook of Anxiety — Handb Anxiety
Handbook of Applicable Mathematics Guidebook — Handbook Appl Math Guidebook
Handbook of Applied Polymer Processing Technology — Handb Appl Polym Process Technol
Handbook of Auditory and Vestibular Research Methods — Handb Aud Vestibular Res Methods
Handbook of Biochemistry and Molecular Biology — Handb Biochem Mol Biol
Handbook of Biological Physics — Handb Biol Phys
Handbook of Brewing — Handb Brew
Handbook of Chromatography. Lipids — Handb Chromatog Lipids
Handbook of Church History — HCH
Handbook of Composites — Handb Compos
Handbook of Compound Semiconductors. Growth, Processing, Characterization, and Devices — Handb Compd Semicond
Handbook of Crystal Growth — Handb Cryst Growth
Handbook of Deposition Technologies for Films and Coatings. Science, Technology, and Applications — Handb Deposition Technol Films Coat
Handbook of Derivatives for Chromatography — Handb Deriv Chromatogr
Handbook of Disinfectants and Antiseptics — Handb Disinfect Antiseptics
Handbook of Ecotoxicology — Handb Ecotoxicol
Handbook of Electronic Materials — Handb Electr Mat
Handbook of Elemental Abundances in Meteorites — Handb Elem Abundances Meteorites
Handbook of Endocrinology — Handb Endocrinol
Handbook of Endotoxin — HAENE6
Handbook of Endotoxin — Handb Endotoxin
Handbook of Environmental Chemistry — Handb Environ Chem
Handbook of Environmental Isotope Geochemistry [*Elsevier Book Series*] — HEIG
Handbook of Experimental Immunology — Handb Exp Immunol
Handbook of Experimental Pharmacology — Handb Exp Pharmacol
Handbook of Exploration Geochemistry — Handb Explor Geochem
Handbook of Exploration Geochemistry [*Elsevier Book Series*] — HEG
Handbook of Fiberglass and Advanced Plastics Composites — Handb Fiberglass Adv Plast Compos
Handbook of Fillers and Reinforcements for Plastics — Handb Fillers Reinf Plast
Handbook of Food Allergies — Handb Food Allerg
Handbook of Food Analysis — Handb Food Anal
Handbook of Food Engineering — Handb Food Eng
Handbook of Food Preparation — Handb Food Prep
Handbook of Functional Gastrointestinal Disorders — Handb Funct Gastrointest Disord
Handbook of Genotoxic Effects and Fish Chromosomes — Handb Genotoxic Eff Fish Chromosomes
Handbook of Grignard Reagents — Handb Grignard Reagents
Handbook of Heat Transfer — Handb Heat Transfer
Handbook of Highly Toxic Materials Handling and Management — Handb High Toxic Mater Handl Manage
Handbook of Hypertension — Handb Hypertens
Handbook of Industrial Chemistry — Handb Ind Chem
Handbook of Inflammation — Handb Inflammation
Handbook of Inflammation [*Elsevier Book Series*] — HOI
Handbook of Ion Sources — Handb Ion Sources
Handbook of Labor Statistics. BLS Bulletin 2070. US Bureau of Labor Statistics — BLS 2070
Handbook of Labor Statistics. BLS Bulletin 2175. US Bureau of Labor Statistics — BLS 2175
Handbook of Lasers with Selected Data on Optical Technology — Handb Lasers Sel Data Opt Technol
Handbook of Lipid Research — Handb Lipid Res
Handbook of Magnetic Materials — Handb Magn Mater
Handbook of Materials and Processes for Electronics — Handb Mater Processes Electron
Handbook of Metal-Ligand Interactions in Biological Fluids. Bioinorganic Chemistry — Handb Met Ligand Interact Biol Fluids Bioinorg Chem
Handbook of Methodology for the Assessment of Air Pollution Effects on Vegetation — Handb Methodol Assess Air Pollut Eff Veg
Handbook of Methods in Gastrointestinal Pharmacology — Handb Methods Gastrointest Pharmacol
Handbook of Micro/Nano Tribology — Handb Micro Nano Tribol
Handbook of Milk Composition — Handb Milk Compos
Handbook of Molecular Cytology — Handb Mol Cytol
Handbook of Natural Pesticides. Methods — Handb Nat Pestic Methods
Handbook of Natural Toxins — Handb Nat Toxins
Handbook of Naturally Occuring Food Toxicants — Handb Nat Occuring Food Toxicants
Handbook of Neurohypophyseal Hormone Analogs — Handb Neurohypophyseal Hor Analogs
Handbook of Nonmedical Applications of Liposomes — Handb Nonmed Appl Liposomes
Handbook of Nutritional Supplements — Handb Nutr Suppl
Handbook of Optical Properties — Handb Opt Prop
Handbook of Organic Waste Conversion — Handb Org Waste Convers
Handbook of Paper Science [*Elsevier Book Series*] — HPS
Handbook of Pharmacokinetic/Pharmacodynamic Correlation — Handb Pharmacokinet Pharmacodyn Correl
Handbook of Pharmacologic Methodologies for the Study of the Neuroendocrine System — Handb Pharmacol Methodol Study Neuroendocr Syst
Handbook of Phycological Methods. Physiological and Biochemical Methods — Handb Phycol Methods Physiol Biochem Methods
Handbook of Physiology — Handb Physiol
Handbook of Physiology. Section 1. The Nervous System — Handb Physiol Sect 1 Nerv Syst
Handbook of Physiology. Section 2. The Cardiovascular System — Handb Physiol Sect 2 Cardiovasc Syst
Handbook of Physiology. Section 4. Adaptation to the Environment — Handb Physiol Sect 4 Adapt Environ
Handbook of Physiology. Section 5. Adipose Tissue — Handb Physiol Sect 5 Adipose Tissue
Handbook of Physiology. Section 7. Endocrinology — Handb Physiol Sect 7 Endocrinol
Handbook of Physiology. Section 8. Renal Physiology — Handb Physiol Sect 8 Renal Physiol
Handbook of Physiology. Section 9. Reactions to Environmental Agents — Handb Physiol Sect 9 React Environ Agents
Handbook of Plant Cell Culture — Handb Plant Cell Cult
Handbook of Plant Cell Culture — HPCCEY
Handbook of Polymer Composites for Engineers — Handb Polym Compos Eng
Handbook of Polymer-Fibre Composites — Handb Polym Fibre Compos
Handbook of Powder Technology [*Elsevier Book Series*] — HOPT
Handbook of Precision Engineering — Handb Precis Eng
Handbook of Pressure-Sensitive Adhesive Technology — Handb Pressure Sensitive Adhes Technol
Handbook of Psychiatry and Endocrinology — Handb Psychiatry Endocrinol
Handbook of Psychopharmacology — Handb Psychopharmacol
Handbook of Radioimmunoassay — Handb Radioimmunoassay
Handbook of Semiconductor Lasers and Photonic Integrated Circuits — Handb Semicond Lasers Photonic Integr Circuits
Handbook of Separation Techniques for Chemical Engineers — Handb Sep Tech Chem Eng
Handbook of Shock Trauma — Handb Shock Trauma
Handbook of Shock Trauma — HSHTDS
Handbook of Soil Mechanics [*Elsevier Book Series*] — HSM
Handbook of Soy Oil Processing and Utilization — Handb Soy Oil Process Util
Handbook of Starch Hydrolysis Products and their Derivatives — Handb Starch Hydrolysis Prod and their Deriv
Handbook of Statistics [*Elsevier Book Series*] — HS
Handbook of Stereoisomers. Drugs in Psychopharmacology — Handb Stereoisomers Drugs Psychopharmacol
Handbook of Strata-Bound and Stratiform Ore Deposits — Handb Strata Bound Stratiform Ore Depostis
Handbook of Surfaces and Interfaces — Handb Surf Interfaces
Handbook of Teratology — Handb Teratol
Handbook of the Biology of Aging — Handb Biol Aging
Handbook of the Hypothalamus — Handb Hypothal
Handbook of Thermoplastic Elastomers — Handb Thermoplas Elastomers
Handbook of Thick Film Technology — Handb Thick Film Technol
Handbook of Tropical Foods — Handb Trop Foods

Handbook of Vacuum Arc Science and Technology. Fundamentals and Applications — Handb Vac Arc Sci Technol
Handbook of Vitamins. Nutritional, Biochemical, and Clinical Aspects — Handb Vitam
Handbook of Water-Soluble Gums and Resins — Handb Water Soluble Gums Resins
Handbook of X-Ray and Ultraviolet Photoelectron Spectroscopy — Handb X Ray Ultraviolet Photoelectron Spectrosc
Handbook on Bioethanol. Production and Utilization — Handb Bioethanol
Handbook on Continuous Fiber-Reinforced Ceramic Matrix Composites — Handb Contin Fiber Reinf Ceram Matrix Compos
Handbook on Discontinuously Reinforced Ceramic Matrix Composites — Handb Discontin Reinf Ceram Matrix Compos
Handbook on Drug Abuse — Handb Drug Abuse
Handbook on Oral Contraception — Handb Oral Contracept
Handbook on Semiconductors — Handb Semicond
Handbook on the Physics and Chemistry of Rare Earths — Handb Phys Chem Rare Earths
Handbook. South Africa. Geological Survey — Handb S Afr Geol Surv
Handbook. South Australia Department of Mines and Energy — Handb South Aust Dep Mines Energy
Handbook. South Pacific Commission — Handb South Pac Comm
Handbook. United States National Bureau of Standards — Handb US Natn Bur Stand
Handbooks in Economics — Handbooks in Econom
Handbooks in Economics [*Elsevier Book Series*] — HE
Handbooks in Science and Technology — Handbooks Sci Tech
Handbuch der Allgemeinen Pathologie — Handb Allg Pathol
Handbuch der Altchristlichen Epigraphik — HAE
Handbuch der Altertumswissenschaft — Handb Alt
Handbuch der Altertumswissenschaft — HAW
Handbuch der Altertumswissenschaft — Hb AW
Handbuch der Altertumswissenschaft — Hd AW
Handbuch der Altertumswissenschaft — HdA
Handbuch der Archaeologie — Hand d Arch
Handbuch der Archaeologie — HB Arch
Handbuch der Archaeologie — Hd Arch
Handbuch der Archaeologie — HdA
Handbuch der Archaeologie — Hdb Archaeol
Handbuch der Bakteriellen Infektionen bei Tieren — Handb Bakt Infekt Tieren
Handbuch der Bakteriellen Infektionen bei Tieren — HBITDG
Handbuch der Chaldischen Inschriften. Archiv fuer Orientforschung. Beiheft — H Ch I
Handbuch der Deutschen Evangelischen Kirchenmusik — HDEKM
Handbuch der Deutschen Gegenwartsliteratur — Hb d G
Handbuch der Deutschen Literaturgeschichte — HDL
Handbuch der Deutschen Wirtschafts- und Sozialgeschichte — HDWSG
Handbuch der Dogmengeschichte — HDG
Handbuch der Europaeischen Geschichte — HEG
Handbuch der Experimentellen — Handb Exp Pharmak
Handbuch der Experimentellen Pharmakologie — Handb Exp Pharmakol
Handbuch der Gesamten Arbeitsmedizin — Hb d G A
Handbuch der Griechischen Dialekte — HGD
Handbuch der Histochemie — Handb Histochem
Handbuch der Historischen Staetten Deutschlands — Hb Hist St
Handbuch der Infusionstherapie und Klinischen Ernaehrung — Handb Infusionsther Klin Ernaehr
Handbuch der Infusionstherapie und Klinischen Ernaehrung — HIKEEV
Handbuch der Inneren Mission — HIM
Handbuch der Italischen Dialekte — Hdb It Dial
Handbuch der Italischen Dialekte — HID
Handbuch der Katholischen Sittenlehre — HKSL
Handbuch der Kirchengeschichte — Hb KG
Handbuch der Kirchengeschichte fuer Studierende — HKG
Handbuch der Klassischen Altertumswissenschaft — HKAW
Handbuch der Klassischen Altertumswissenschaft (Iwan von Mueller, Editor) — Iwan Mueller
Handbuch der Kulturgeschichte — H Ku G
Handbuch der Kulturgeschichte. Abteilung 1. Geschichte des Deutschen Lebens — H Ku G GD
Handbuch der Kulturgeschichte. Abteilung 2. Geschichte des Voelkerlebens — H Ku G GV
Handbuch der Kulturgeschichte. Neue Abteilung. Abteilung 1. Zeitalter Deutscher Kultur — H Ku G ZD
Handbuch der Kulturgeschichte. Neue Abteilung. Abteilung 2. Kulturen der Voelker — H Ku G KV
Handbuch der Kunstwissenschaft — HKW
Handbuch der Lebensmittelchemie — Handb Lebensmittelchemie
Handbuch der Literaturgeschichte in Einzeldarstellungen. Kroeners Taschenausgabe — HLEKT
Handbuch der Literaturwissenschaft — HLW
Handbuch der Literaturwissenschaft (Herausgegeben von Martimort) — HLWM
Handbuch der Medizinschen Radiologie [*Germany*] — Handb Med Radiol
Handbuch der Messtechnik in der Betriebskontrolle — Handb Messtech Betriebskontrolle
Handbuch der Mineralogie — Handb Mineral
Handbuch der Mittelalterlichen und Neueren Geschichte — HMANG
Handbuch der Mittelalterlichen und Neueren Geschichte. Abteilung 1. Allgemeines — HMANGA
Handbuch der Mittelalterlichen und Neueren Geschichte. Abteilung 2. Politische Geschichte — HMANGP
Handbuch der Mittelalterlichen und Neueren Geschichte. Abteilung 3. Verfassung, Recht, Wirtschaft — HMANGV
Handbuch der Mittelalterlichen und Neueren Geschichte. Abteilung 4. Hilfswissenschaften und Altertuemer — HMANGH
Handbuch der Modernen Datenverarbeitung — HMD
Handbuch der Moraltheologie — HMT
Handbuch der Orientalistik — H Or
Handbuch der Orientalistik — Handb der Or
Handbuch der Orientalistik — HdO
Handbuch der Orientalistik — HO
Handbuch der Ostkirchenkunde — HOK
Handbuch der Paedagogik — H Paed
Handbuch der Palaeozoologie — Hb Palaeozool
Handbuch der Pastoraltheologie — HP Th
Handbuch der Pflanzenanatomie — Handb Pflanzenanat
Handbuch der Pflanzenanatomie — HPANAJ
Handbuch der Pflanzenernahrung und Duengung — Handb Pflernahr Dueng
Handbuch der Philosophie — H Ph
Handbuch der Physik — Handb Phys
Handbuch der Psychologie — H Ps
Handbuch der Psychologie — Hb d Ps
Handbuch der Psychologie — Hb Psych
Handbuch der Psychologie (Herausgegeben von Katz) — H Ps K
Handbuch der Rechtspraxis — HRP
Handbuch der Regionalen Geologie — HRG
Handbuch der Religionsgeschichte — HRG
Handbuch der Religionswissenschaft (Herausgegeben von Leipoldt) — HRW L
Handbuch der Speziellen Pathologischen Anatomie der Haustiere (Ernst Joest) [*A publication*] — Handb Spez Path Anat Haustiere (Ernst Joest)
Handbuch der Staerke in Einzeldarstellungen — Handb Staerke Einzeldarst
Handbuch der Textilhilfsmitte — Handb Textilhilfsm
Handbuch der Tierernaehrung — Handb Tierernaehr
Handbuch der Urologie — Handb Urol
Handbuch der Virusinfektionen bei Tieren — Handb Virusinfekt Tieren
Handbuch der Wirtschaftswissenschaften — Hb d W
Handbuch der Zoologie — Handb Zool
Handbuch des Gesamten Miet und Raumrechts — Hb Miet R
Handbuch des Kathodischen Korrosionsschutzes — Handb Kathod Korrosionsschutzes
Handbuch des Kirchlichen Archivwesens — HKA
Handbuch fuer Rundfunk und Fernsehen [*Database*] — HARU
Handbuch Philosophie — Handbuch Philos
Handbuch Theologischer Grundbegriffe — H Th G
Handbuch zu den Neutestamentlichen Apokryphen — HNTA
Handbuch zum Alten Testament — HAT
Handbuch zum Alten Testament [*Tuebingen*] — HbAT
Handbuch zum Alten Testament [*Tuebingen*] — HbzAT
Handbuch zum Evangelischen Kirchengesangbuch — HEKG
Handbuch zum Neuen Testament — Hb NT
Handbuch zum Neuen Testament — HNT
Handbuch zum Neuen Testament. Supplement — HNTSup
Handbuch zur Deutschen Militaergeschichte — Handb Deutsch Militaerges
Handbuecherei des Christen in der Welt — H Ci W
Handbuecherei fuer Gemeindearbeit — HGA
Handchirurgie, Mikrochirurgie, Plastische Chirurgie — Handchir Mikrochir Plast Chir
Handchirurgie, Mikrochirurgie, Plastische Chirurgie — HMPCD9
Hand-Commentar zum Neuen Testament — HC
Handel en Industrie — Handel Ind
Handel Jahrbuch — H Jb
Handel Jahrbuch — Handel Jb
Handel Wewnetrzny — Hand Wewn
Handel Wewnetrzny — Handel Wewn
Handel Zagraniczy — Handel Zagran
Handel. Zeitschrift fuer Theorie und Praxis des Innenhandels in der Deutschen Demokratischen Republik — VSO
Handelinge. Kollege van Geneeskunde van Suid-Afrika — Handel Koll Geneeskd S-Afr
Handelinge. Kollege van Geneeskunde van Suid-Afrika — TCMDBN
Handelinge van die Kongres van die Weidingsvereniging van Suidelike Afrika — Handel Kongr Weidingsvereniging Suidelike Afr
Handelinge van die Suid-Afrikaanse Instituut van Elektriese Ingenieurs — Handel S Afr Inst Electr Ing
Handelinge Voedingsvereniging van Suidelike Afrika — Handel Voedingsver Suidelike Afr
Handelinge. Voedingvereeniging van Suidelike Afrika — Handel Voeding Ver Suidel
Handelinge. Weidingsvereniging van Suidelike Afrika — Handel Weidingsvereniging Suidelike Afr
Handelingen der Maatschappij voor Geschied- en Oudheidkunde te Gent — Ann Gand
Handelingen der Maatschappij voor Geschiedenis en Oudheidkunde te Gent — Hand Gent
Handelingen der Maatschappij voor Geschiedenis en Oudheidkunde te Gent — HMGOG
Handelingen en Mededeelingen. Maatschappij der Nederlandsche Letterkunde te Leiden — HMMNL
Handelingen. Genootschap voor Geschiedenis Gesticht Onder de Benaming. Societe d'Emulation de Bruges — HGGSEB
Handelingen. Koninklijke Commissie voor Toponymie en Dialectologie — Handelingen Commissie Toponymie & Dialectologie
Handelingen. Koninklijke Commissie voor Toponymie en Dialectologie — HandKonCommTop-Dial
Handelingen. Koninklijke Commissie voor Toponymie en Dialectologie — HKCTD
Handelingen. Koninklijke Gescheiden Oudheidkundige Kring van Kortrijk — HKGOKK
Handelingen. Koninklijke Kring voor Oudheidkunde Letteren en Kunst van Mechelen — Handel Oudheid Mechelen

Handelingen. Koninklijke Kring voor Oudheidkunde. Letteren en Kunst van Mechelen Malines [*Belgium*] — Handel Oudheidkunde Mechelen
Handelingen. Koninklijke Zuidnederlandse Maatschappij voor Taal en Letterkunde en Geschiedenis — HKZM
Handelingen. Nederlands Filologencongres — HandNFc
Handelingen. Nederlands Natuur- en Geneeskundig Congres — Handel Ned Nat Geneeskd Congr
Handelingen. Nederlandse Juristen-Vereeniging — Hand Ned Jur V
Handelingen. Nederlandse Phonologische Werkgemeenschap — Handelingen Ned Phonol Werkgomoonechap
Handelingen. Provinciaal Genootschap van Kunsten en Wetenschappen in Noord Brabant — Handel Prov Genootsch Kunsten N Brabant
Handelingen van de Kring voor Oudheidkunde, Letteren, en Kunst van Mechelen — HKOM
Handelingen van de Nederlands-Belgische Vereeniging van Graanonderzoekers — Handel Ned Belg Ver Graanonderz
Handelingen. Vlaamse Filologencongres — Hand Vl Fc
Handelingen. Zuidnederlandse Maatschappij voor Taal-En Letterkunde en Geschiedenis — HZM
Handelingen. Zuidnederlandse Maatschappij voor Taal-En Letterkunde en Geschiedenis — HZMTLG
Handelingen. Zuidnederlandse Maatschappij voor Taal-En Letterkunde en Geschiedenis — HZnMTL
Handeln und Entscheiden in Komplexen Oekonomischen Situationen — Handeln Entscheid Komplexen Oekon Situat
Handels- og Sofartsmuseet paa Kronborg — H o S Mus
Handels Rundschau — EDK
Handelsblatt [*Information service or system*] — Handelsblt
Handelsblatt [*Information service or system*] — HB
Handelsblatt Databank — HB
Handelsblatt. Wirtschaftzeitung und Finanzzeitung — HAT
Handelspartner. Nederlands Duitse Handelscourant — MKD
Handelsreiziger — HEI
Handelsvidenskabeligt Tidsskrift — Handelsv T
Handelsvoorlichting Bank Mees en Hope — BMH
Handes Amsoreaj/Handes Amsorya — Hand Am
Handes Amsorya — HA
Handes Amsorya. Monatschrift fuer Armenische Philologie — Handes Amsorya
Handicapped Educational Exchange [*Database*] — HEX
Handicapped Rights and Regulations — HRR
Handicapped Users' Database — HUD
Handling and Shipping [*Later, Handling and Shipping Management*] — Handl & Shipp
Handling and Shipping Management — H & S Mgmt
Handling and Shipping Management — Handl & Shipp Mgt
Handling and Shipping Management — Handl Shipp Manage
Handling and Shipping Management — HSM
Handling Chemical Carcinogens in the Laboratory. Problems of Safety — Handl Chem Carcinog Lab Probl Saf
Handling, Conveying, Automation [*Germany*] — Handl Conveying Autom
Handling, Conveying, Automation — HCAUA
Handling of Nuclear Information. Proceedings of the Symposium — Handl Nucl Inf Proc Symp
Handling of Radiation Accidents. Proceedings of a Symposium — Handl Radiat Accid Proc Symp
Handlingar. Carl Johans Foerbundet — Handl C Johans Foerb
Handlingar och Tidskrift. Kungliga Krigsvetenskaps-Akademien — Handl T Kungl Krigsvet Akad
Handlingar. Svenska Forskningsinstitutet foer Cement och Betong vid Kungliga Tekniska Hoegskolan i Stockholm — Handl Sven Forskningsinst Cem Betong K Tek Hoegsk Stockholm
Handlingar. Vitterhets- Historie- och Antikvitets-Akademien — HVHAA
Handlingar. Vitterhets- Historie- och Antikvitets-Akademien. Filologisk-Filosofiska Serien — HVHAA FF
Handweaver and Craftsman — Handweaver
Handwerksordnung — Handw O
Handwierk — HND
Handwoerterbuch der Betriebswirtschaft — Hwb d B
Handwoerterbuch der Betriebswirtschaft — HWBW
Handwoerterbuch der Musikalischen Terminologie — HMT
Handwoerterbuch der Rechtswissenschaft — HWRW
Handwoerterbuch der Sozialwissenschaften — HDStW
Handwoerterbuch der Sozialwissenschaften — Hwb d Sw
Handwoerterbuch der Soziologie — HWS
Handwoerterbuch des Deutschen Maerchens — HDM
Handwoerterbuch des Islam — H Isl
Handwoerterbuch zur Deutschen Rechtsgeschichte — HRG
Handwoerterbuch zur Deutschen Rechtsgeschichte — Hwb Dt RG
Hanes Gweithwyr Cymru [*Welsh Labour History*] — HGC
Hang K'ung Chih Shih — HKCSA
Hanging Loose — Hang L
Hanging Loose — HL
Han'guk Pusik Hakhoechi — HPHAD
Han'guk Sikmul Poho Hakhoe Chi — HSHCA
Han'guk Sikp'un Kwahak Hoechi. Korean Journal of Food Science and Technology — Han'guk Sikp'un Kwhak Hoechi Korea J Food Sci Technol
Han'guk Sikp'un Kwahakhoe Chi — HSKCA
Han'guk T'oyang Bilyo Hakhoe Chi — HTBHA
Han'guk Uikwahak — HAUID
Hannah Dairy Research Institute. Report — Hannah Dairy Res Inst Rep
Hannah Research — Hannah Res
Hannah Research Institute. Report — Hannah Res Inst Rep
Hannover Uni — HAUND
Hannoverische Beytraege zum Nutzen und Vergnuegen — Hannover Beytr Nutzen Vergnuegen
Hannoverisches Magazin worin kleine Abhandlungen, Gesamlet (Gesammelt) und Aufbewahret Sind — Hannover Mag
Hannoversche Geschichtsblaetter — Ha G
Hannoversche Geschichtsblaetter — Hannov Geschbll
Hannoversche Geschichtsblaetter — HG
Hannoversche Rechtspflege — Hann Rpfl
Hanrei Jiho — Hanji
Hanrei Taimuzu — Hanta
Hans Joachim Moser Musik-Lexikon — Moser ML
Hans Pfitzner-Gesellschaft. Mitteilungen — Pfitzner
Hans Selye Symposia on Neuroendocrinology and Stress — Hans Selye Symp Neuroendocrinol Stress
Hansard (Commons) — Hansard (C)
Hansard. House of Commons. Official Report [*Great Britain*] — Hansard House Commons Off Rep
Hansard (Lords) — Hansard (L)
Hansard Oral Questions [*Database*] — HOQ
Hansard Written Questions [*Database*] — HWQ
Hanseatische Gerichtszeitung — HansGZ
Hanseatische Rechts-Zeitschrift — HRZ
Hanseatisches Justizverwaltungsblatt — Hans JV Bl
Hanseniase — HANSB
Hanseniase. Resumos e Noticias — Hanseniase Resumos Not
Hansenologia Internationalis — Hansenol Int
Hanser Literatur-Kommentare — HLK
Hansische Geschichtsblaetter — Hans G Bl
Hansische Geschichtsblaetter — Hans Gesch
Hansische Geschichtsblaetter — Hans Geschbll
Hansische Geschichtsblaetter — Hansische Gesch Bl
Hansische Geschichtsblaetter — HGB
Hansische Geschichtsblaetter — HGH
Hantes Amsoriay — Hant Ams
Hants Field Club and Archaeological Society — HFC
Hanyang Idae Haksuljip — HIHAD
Hanzaigaku Zasshi (Acta Criminologiae et Medicinae Legalis Japonica) — Hanzaigaku Zasshi (Acta Criminol Med Leg Jpn)
Haolam [*Jerusalem*] — H
Hapeol Hatzair [*Tel Aviv*] — HH
Harbin Gongye Daxue Xuebao — HPKYA
Harbor Dental Log — Harbor Dent Log
Harbour and Shipping — Harbour & Shipp
Harburger Jahrbuch — Harburger Jahrb
Hardsyssels Aarbog — Hardsyssels Aarb
Hardsyssels Aarbog — Hds Aa
Hardware Journal — Hardware J
Hardware Retailing — Hardware R
Hardware Today — Hware
Hardware Trade Journal — Hardware Trade J
Hardware Trade Journal — HTJ
Hardwood Record — Hardwood Rec
Hardwood Record — Hdwd Rec
Hare Express. Fort Good Hope — HE
Harefuah — HAREA
Harefuah — Haref
Harker Geological Society. Journal — Harker Geol Soc J
Harlem Hospital Bulletin — Harl Hosp Bull
Harlem Hospital Bulletin (New York) — Harlem Hosp Bull (NY)
Harmonie — Har
Harmonika-Jahrbuch — Harmonika Jb
Harokeach Haivri. The Hebrew Pharmacist (Science Edition) — Harokeach Haivri Heb Pharm (Sci Ed)
Harold L. Lyon Arboretum. Lecture — Harold L Lyon Arbor Lect
Harp News — Harp N
Harper Adams Utility Poultry Journal — Harp Ad Util Poult J
Harper Hospital. Bulletin — Harper Hosp Bull
Harper Hospital. Bulletin — HHBLA
Harper Torchbook — HTB
Harper's — GHAR
Harpers — Ha
Harper's Annotated Bible — HAB
Harper's Bazaar — GHAB
Harper's Bazaar — Harp B
Harper's Bazaar — Harp Baz
Harper's Bible Dictionary — HBD
Harper's Magazine — H
Harper's Magazine — HAMAA
Harper's Magazine — Harp
Harper's Magazine — Harper
Harper's Magazine — HM
Harper's Monthly Magazine — Harp MM
Harper's Monthly Magazine — Harpers Mon Mag
Harper's New Monthly Magazine — Harper's Mag
Harper's Weekly — Harp W
Harpsichord — HD
Harpsichord — HPD
Harris County Physician Newsletter — Harris County Physician
Harris Electronic News [*Database*] — HEN
Harry G. Armstrong Aerospace Medical Research Laboratory. Technical Report AAMRL-TR — Harry G Armstrong Aerosp Med Res Lab Tech Rep AAMRL TR
Hart Crane Newsletter — HCN
Harterei-Technische Mitteilungen [*Germany*] — Hart-Tech Mitt
Hartford Courant — Hartfd Cou
Hartford Hospital. Bulletin — Hartf Hosp Bull
Hartford Hospital. Bulletin — Hartford Hosp Bull

Hartford Quarterly — Hart Q
Hartford Quarterly — HQ
Hartford Seminary Record — Hartf Sem Rec
Hartford Seminary Record — Hartford Sem Rec
Hartford Studies in Linguistics — Hartf Stud Ling
Hartford Studies in Literature — HSL
Hartford's Other Voice [*Superseded by Wild Raspberry*] — HO Voice
Hartman's Tijdschrift ter Beoefening van het Administratieve Recht — Hartm Tds
Hartman's Tijdschrift ter Beoefening van het Administratieve Recht — HT
Hart's Fuel Technology and Management — Harts Fuel Technol Manage
Hartwick Review — Hart R
Harvard Advocate — Harv Ad
Harvard Advocate — Harvard A
Harvard AIDS Institute Series on Gene Regulation of Human Retroviruses — Harv AIDS Inst Ser Gene Regul Hum Retroviruses
Harvard Alumni Bulletin — Har Alum Bull
Harvard Architecture Review — Harvard Archre Review
Harvard Armenian Texts and Studies — HATS
Harvard Books in Biophysics — Harv Books Biophys
Harvard Books in Biophysics — HBBIAD
Harvard Business Review — HABRA
Harvard Business Review — Har Bus R
Harvard Business Review — Harv Bus Re
Harvard Business Review — Harv Bus Rev
Harvard Business Review — Harvard BR
Harvard Business Review — Harvard Bsns R
Harvard Business Review — Harvard Bus R
Harvard Business Review — Harvard Bus Rev
Harvard Business Review — Harvard Busin R
Harvard Business Review — HBR
Harvard Business Review Online — HBR
Harvard Business School. Bulletin — BHBSA
Harvard Civil Rights - Civil Liberties Law Journal — HCRCA
Harvard Civil Rights - Civil Liberties Law Review — Har Civ Ri LR
Harvard Civil Rights - Civil Liberties Law Review — Harv Civ Rights - Civ Liberties Law Rev
Harvard Civil Rights - Civil Liberties Law Review — Harv Civil Rights L Rev
Harvard Civil Rights - Civil Liberties Law Review — Harv CR-CLL
Harvard Civil Rights - Civil Liberties Law Review — Harv CR-CLL Rev
Harvard Civil Rights - Civil Liberties Law Review — Harvard Civil Rights - Civil Liberties Law R
Harvard Civil Rights - Civil Liberties Law Review — Harvard Civil Rights L Rev
Harvard College. Museum of Comparative Zoology. Annual Report — Harvard Coll Mus CZ An Rp
Harvard College. Museum of Comparative Zoology. Bulletin — Harvard Coll Mus C Z B
Harvard College. Museum of Comparative Zoology. Bulletin — Harvard Coll Mus Comp Zoology Bull
Harvard College. Museum of Comparative Zoology. Memoirs — Harvard Coll Mus C Z Mem
Harvard Dental Alumni Bulletin — Harv Dent Alumni Bull
Harvard Divinity Bulletin — Harv Div B
Harvard Divinity Bulletin — HDB
Harvard Divinity School. Annual — HDSA
Harvard Divinity School. Bulletin [*Cambridge, MA*] — HarvDBull
Harvard Divinity School. Bulletin — HDSB
Harvard East Asian Series — Harv East As Ser
Harvard East Asian Series — HEAS
Harvard Educational Review — GHER
Harvard Educational Review — Harv Edu Re
Harvard Educational Review — Harv Educ Rev
Harvard Educational Review — Harvard Ed R
Harvard Educational Review — Harvard Educ R
Harvard Educational Review — HEdR
Harvard Educational Review — HER
Harvard English Studies — Harvard Engl Stud
Harvard English Studies — HES
Harvard Environmental Law Review — Harv Environ Law Rev
Harvard Environmental Law Review — Harv Envtl L Rev
Harvard Environmental Law Review — Harvard Environ Law Rev
Harvard Environmental Law Review — Harvard Environmental Law R
Harvard Forest. Annual Report — Harv For Annu Rep
Harvard Forest. Bulletin — Harv For Bull
Harvard Forest. Bulletin — Harvard Forest Bull
Harvard Forest. Papers — Harv For Pap
Harvard Forest Papers — Harvard Forest Pap
Harvard Germanic Studies — HGS
Harvard Graduate School of Design. News — HGSD News
Harvard Graduates' Magazine — Harv Grad M
Harvard Graduates' Magazine — HGM
Harvard Health Letter — IHHL
Harvard Historical Monographs — HHM
Harvard Historical Studies — Harvard Hist Stud
Harvard Historical Studies — HHS
Harvard International Law Journal — Har Int LJ
Harvard International Law Journal — Harv Int L J
Harvard International Law Journal — Harv Int'l LJ
Harvard International Law Journal — Harvard Int LJ
Harvard International Law Journal — Harvard Internat Law J
Harvard Journal of Asiatic Studies — Harv Asia
Harvard Journal of Asiatic Studies — Harv J Asia
Harvard Journal of Asiatic Studies — Harv J Asiatic Stud
Harvard Journal of Asiatic Studies — Harvard J Asiat Stud
Harvard Journal of Asiatic Studies — HJAS
Harvard Journal of Asiatic Studies — PHAS
Harvard Journal of Law and Public Policy — Harv JL and Pub Poly
Harvard Journal of Law and Public Policy — Harvard J Law and Public Policy
Harvard Journal on Legislation — HAR
Harvard Journal on Legislation — Har J Leg
Harvard Journal on Legislation — Harv J Leg
Harvard Journal on Legislation — Harv J Legis
Harvard Journal on Legislation — Harv J on Legis
Harvard Journal on Legislation — Harvard J Legislation
Harvard Journal on Legislation — Harvard J on Legis
Harvard Landscape Architecture Monographs — Harvard Landscape Architect Monogr
Harvard Law Review — HALRA
Harvard Law Review — Har LR
Harvard Law Review — Harv L Rev
Harvard Law Review — Harv Law R
Harvard Law Review — Harv Law Rev
Harvard Law Review — Harvard L Rev
Harvard Law Review — Harvard Law R
Harvard Law Review — Harvard Law Rev
Harvard Law Review — HLR
Harvard Law School Bulletin — Harv LS Bull
Harvard Library Bulletin — HarL
Harvard Library Bulletin — Harv Lib Bull
Harvard Library Bulletin — Harv Libr B
Harvard Library Bulletin — Harv Libr Bull
Harvard Library Bulletin — Harvard Lib Bul
Harvard Library Bulletin — Harvard Libr Bull
Harvard Library Bulletin — HarvLB
Harvard Library Bulletin — HL
Harvard Library Bulletin — HLB
Harvard Magazine — HAMAD
Harvard Magazine — Harv Mag
Harvard Magazine — Harvard Mag
Harvard Medical Alumni Bulletin — Harv Med Alumni Bull
Harvard Medical Alumni Bulletin — Harvard Med Alumni Bull
Harvard Medical School. Health Letter — Harv Med Sch Health Lett
Harvard Medical School. Health Letter — Harvard Med Sch Health Let
Harvard Memoirs — Harv Mem
Harvard Middle Eastern Studies — MES
Harvard Monographs in Applied Science — Harvard Mon Applied Sci
Harvard Monthly — Harv Mo
Harvard Oriental Series — HOS
Harvard Papers in Theoretical Geography — Harv Pap Theoret Geogr
Harvard Pathophysiology Series — Harv Pathophysiol Ser
Harvard Public Health Alumni Bulletin — Harv Public Health Alumni Bull
Harvard Public Health Alumni Bulletin — Harvard Public Health Alumni Bull
Harvard Public Health Alumni Bulletin — HPHBA
Harvard Review — Harv R
Harvard Review of Psychiatry — Harv Rev Psychiatry
Harvard Semitic Monographs — Harv Sem Mon
Harvard Semitic Monographs — HSM
Harvard Semitic Series [*Cambridge, MA*] — HarSemSer
Harvard Semitic Series — Harv Sem Ser
Harvard Semitic Series — HSS
Harvard Series in Ukrainian Studies — Harv Ser Ukrain Stud
Harvard Slavic Studies — Harvard Slav Stud
Harvard Slavic Studies — HS St
Harvard Slavic Studies — HSLS
Harvard Slavic Studies — HSS
Harvard Studies and Notes in Philology and Literature — HSNPL
Harvard Studies and Notes in Philology and Literature — HSPL
Harvard Studies in Classical Philology — H St Cl Ph
Harvard Studies in Classical Philology — Harv Class Phil
Harvard Studies in Classical Philology — Harv St
Harvard Studies in Classical Philology — Harv St Cl Phil
Harvard Studies in Classical Philology — Harv St Cla
Harvard Studies in Classical Philology — Harv Stud
Harvard Studies in Classical Philology — Harv Stud Class Philol
Harvard Studies in Classical Philology — Harvard Stud Cl Philol
Harvard Studies in Classical Philology — HS Cl Ph
Harvard Studies in Classical Philology — HSCP
Harvard Studies in Classical Philology — HSPh
Harvard Studies in Classical Philology. Supplemental Volume — HSCPS
Harvard Studies in Comparative Literature — HSCL
Harvard Studies in Romance Languages — HSRL
Harvard Studies in World Religions — HSWR
Harvard Theological Review — Har Theol Rev
Harvard Theological Review — HarT
Harvard Theological Review — Harv Th R
Harvard Theological Review — Harv Th Rev
Harvard Theological Review — Harv Theol
Harvard Theological Review — Harv Theol R
Harvard Theological Review — Harv Theol Rev
Harvard Theological Review — Harvard Th R
Harvard Theological Review — Harvard Theol R
Harvard Theological Review — Harvard Theol Rev
Harvard Theological Review [*Cambridge, MA*] — HarvTR
Harvard Theological Review — HThR
Harvard Theological Review — HTR
Harvard Theological Review — PHTR
Harvard Theological Studies — H Th S
Harvard Theological Studies [*Cambridge, MA*] — HThSt
Harvard Theological Studies [*Cambridge, MA*] — HTS
Harvard Ukrainian Studies — HUS

Harvard University. Arnold Arboretum Journal — Arnold Arbor J
Harvard University. Arnold Arboretum. Journal — Harv Univ Arnold Arbor J
Harvard University. Botanical Museum Leaflets — Harvard Univ Bot Mus Leaflets
Harvard University. Bulletin — Harvard Univ B
Harvard University. Department of Engineering. Publications — Harvard Univ Dep Eng Publ
Harvard University. Gray Herbarium. Contributions — Harvard Univ Gray Herbarium Contr
Harvard University. Harvard Soil Mechanics Series — Harvard Univ Harvard Soil Mech Ser
Harvard University. Museum of Comparative Zoology. Bulletin — Harv Univ Mus Comp Zool Bull
Harvard University. Museum of Comparative Zoology. Bulletin — Harvard Univ Mus Comp Zoology Bull
Harvard University. Museum of Comparative Zoology. Memoirs — Museum Comp Zool Memoirs
Harvard University. Museum of Comparative Zoology. Special Occasional Publication — Harv Univ Mus Comp Zool Spec Occas Publ
Harvard University. Papers of the Peabody Museum of Archaeology and Ethnology — HUPPAE
Harvard University. School of Public Health. Dean's Report — Harv Univ Sch Public Health Dean's Rep
Harvard Women's Law Journal — Harv Women LJ
Harvard Women's Law Journal — Harvard Women's Law J
Harvard Women's Law Review — Har Women LR
Harvard-Yenching Institute Studies — HYIS
Harvest Field — HF
Harvest Quarterly — Harvest Q
Harvester in Australia — Harvester in Aust
Harvester Readings in the History of Science and Philosophy [*Brighton*] — Harvester Readings Hist Sci Philos
Harvey Lecture Series — Harvey Lecture Ser
Harvey Lectures — HALEA
Harvey Lectures — Harvey Lect
Haryana Agricultural University. Journal of Research — Haryana Agric Univ J Res
Haryana Agricultural University. Journal of Research — J Res Haryana Agric Univ
Haryana Journal of Agronomy — Haryana J Agron
Haryana Journal of Horticulture Sciences — Haryana J Hort Sci
Harz Zeitschrift — Harz Z
Haskell Lectures on History of Religions — HLHR
Hasler Review — Hasler Rev
Hasler-Mitteilungen — HAMIA
Hasler-Mitteilungen — Hasler Mitt
Hassadeh — HASSA
Hastings and East Sussex Naturalist — Hastings E Suss Nat
Hastings Area Archaeological Papers — Hastings Area Archaeol Pap
Hastings Center Report — GHCR
Hastings Center. Report — Hast Cent Rpt
Hastings Center. Report — Hastings Cent Rep
Hastings Center. Report — Hastings Ctr Rept
Hastings Center. Report — HSCRA
Hastings Center. Studies — Hast Cen St
Hastings Center. Studies — Hast Cent St
Hastings Center. Studies — Hastings Cent Stud
Hastings Center. Studies — HCSTA
Hastings Constitutional Law Quarterly — Has Con LQ
Hastings Constitutional Law Quarterly — Hast Const LQ
Hastings Constitutional Law Quarterly — Hastings Const LQ
Hastings Deering News — Hast Deering News
Hastings International and Comparative Law Review — Has Int and Comp LR
Hastings International and Comparative Law Review — Hastings Intl and Comp L Rev
Hastings International and Comparative Law Review — HICLR
Hastings Law Journal — Has LJ
Hastings Law Journal — Hast Law J
Hastings Law Journal — Hast LJ
Hastings Law Journal — Hastings L J
Hastings Law Journal — HLJ
Haszard and Warburton's Reports. Prince Edward Island [*Canada*] — PEI
Hataassiya (Tel Aviv) — HT
HAU [*Haryana Agricultural University*] **Journal of Research** — HAU J Res
Haunt of Horror — HOH
Hauptvortraege der Jahrestagung des Verbandes Deutscher Physikalischer Gesellschaften — Hauptvortr Jahrestag Verb Dtsch Phys Ges
Hauptvortraege der Tagung der Deutschen Physiologische Gesellschaft — Hauptvortr Tag Dtsch Physiol Ges
Hauptvortraege. Tagung Physik und Elektronik — Hauptvortr Tag Phys Electron
Haus der Technik-Essen-Vortragsveroeffentlichungen — Haus Tech Essen Vortragsveroeff
Haus der Technik-Vortrags-Veroeffentlichungen — Haus Tech-Vortrag-Veroeff
Haus Technik [*Germany*] — Haus Tech
Haus und Wohnung — H u W
Haus und Wohnung — HW
Hausmitteilungen Jos Schneider — Hausmitt Jos Schneider
Hausmusik — Hausm
Hausmusik — Hausmus
Haustechnik, Bauphysik, Umwelttechnik — Haustech Bauphys Umwelttech
Haustechnische Rundschau [*Germany*] — Haustech Rundsch
Haustechnische Rundschau — Ht R
Hauswirtschaft und Wissenschaft — Hauswirtsch U Wiss
Hauswirtschaft und Wissenschaft — HAWIA
Hauszeitschrift der VAW und der Erftwerk AG fuer Aluminium — Hausz VAW Erftwerk AG Alum
Hautarzt [*Austria*] — HAUTA
Havana Biblioteca Nacional. Revista — Havana Bibl Nac R
Havana Universidad. Ciencias. Serie 4. Ciencias Biologicas — Havana Univ Cienc Ser 4 Cienc Biol
Havana Universidad. Ciencias. Serie 7. Geografia — Havana Univ Cienc Ser 7 Geogr
Havana Universidad. Ciencias. Serie 8. Investigaciones Marinas — Havana Univ Cienc Ser 8 Invest Mar
Havana Universidad. Tecnologia. Serie 10. Ingenieria Hidraulica — Havana Univ Tecnol Ser 10 Ing Hidraul
Havekunst — Hvk
Haven. Medlemsblad for de Samvirkende Danske Haveselskaber — Hv
Havsforskningsinstituets Skrift — Havforskningsinst Skr
Havsforskningsinstitutets Skrift (Helsinki) — Havsforskningsinst Skr Helsinki
Hawaii. Agricultural Experiment Station. Agricultural Economics Bulletin — Hawaii Agric Exp Stn Agric Econ Bull
Hawaii Agricultural Experiment Station. Annual Report — Hawaii Agric Exp Sta Annual Rep
Hawaii. Agricultural Experiment Station. Biennial Report — Hawaii Agric Exp Stn Bienn Rep
Hawaii. Agricultural Experiment Station. Bulletin — Hawaii Agric Exp Stn Bull
Hawaii. Agricultural Experiment Station. Circular — Hawaii Agric Exp Stn Circ
Hawaii Agricultural Experiment Station. Departmental Paper — Hawaii Agric Exp Stn Dep Pap
Hawaii. Agricultural Experiment Station. Miscellaneous Publication — HAMPBF
Hawaii. Agricultural Experiment Station. Miscellaneous Publication — Hawaii Agric Exp Stn Misc Pub
Hawaii. Agricultural Experiment Station. Miscellaneous Publication — Hawaii Agric Exp Stn Misc Publ
Hawaii Agricultural Experiment Station. Press Bulletin — Hawaii Agric Exp Sta Press Bull
Hawaii. Agricultural Experiment Station. Progress Notes — Hawaii Agric Exp Stn Prog Notes
Hawaii. Agricultural Experiment Station. Publications — Hawaii Ag Exp
Hawaii. Agricultural Experiment Station. Research Bulletin — Hawaii Agric Exp Stn Res Bull
Hawaii. Agricultural Experiment Station. Research Report — Hawaii Agric Exp Stn Res Rep
Hawaii. Agricultural Experiment Station. Special Publication — Hawaii Agric Exp Stn Spec Publ
Hawaii. Agricultural Experiment Station. Station Progress Notes — Hawaii Agric Exp Stn Stn Prog Notes
Hawaii. Agricultural Experiment Station. Technical Bulletin — Hawaii Agric Exp Stn Tech Bull
Hawaii. Agricultural Experiment Station. Technical Progress Report — Hawaii Agric Exp Stn Tech Prog Rep
Hawaii Agricultural Experiment Station. University of Hawaii College of Agriculture. Circular — Hawaii Agric Exp Stn Univ Hawaii Coll Agric Circ
Hawaii Agricultural Experiment Station. University of Hawaii College of Agriculture. Special Publication — Hawaii Agric Exp Stn Univ Hawaii Coll Agric Spec Publ
Hawaii Agricultural Experiment Station. University of Hawaii College of Agriculture. Station Progress Notes — Hawaii Agric Exp Stn Univ Hawaii Coll Agric Stn Prog Notes
Hawaii Appellate Reports — Haw App
Hawaii Bar Journal — Hawaii B J
Hawaii Business — Hawaii Bsn
Hawaii Business — Hawaii Bus
Hawaii Dairy Newsletter. Hawaii Cooperative Extension Service. US Department of Agriculture — Hawaii Dairy Newsl Hawaii Coop Ext Serv US Dep Agric
Hawaii Dental Journal — Hawaii Dent J
Hawaii. Department of Land and Natural Resources. Division of Water and Land Development. Circular — Hawaii Dep Land Nat Resour Div Water Land Dev Circ
Hawaii. Department of Land and Natural Resources. Division of Water and Land Development. Report — Hawaii Dep Land Nat Resour Div Water Land Dev Rep
Hawaii. Division of Hydrography. Bulletin — Hawaii Div Hydrogr Bull
Hawaii. Division of Water and Land Development. Circular — Hawaii Div Water Land Dev Circ
Hawaii. Division of Water and Land Development. Report — Hawaii Div Water Land Dev Rep
Hawaii Farm Science — Hawaii Farm Sci
Hawaii Farm Science — HAWFA
Hawaii Food Processor. Hawaii University. Cooperative Extension Service — Hawaii Food Process Hawaii Univ Coop Ext Serv
Hawaii Food Technology News. Hawaii Cooperative Extension Service — Hawaii Food Technol News Hawaii Coop Ext Serv
Hawaii Institute of Geophysics. Biennial Report — Hawaii Inst Geophys Bienn Rep
Hawaii Institute of Geophysics (Honolulu). University of Hawaii — HIG (Honolulu) HI
Hawaii Institute of Geophysics. Publication — Hawaii Inst Geophys Publ
Hawaii Institute of Geophysics. Report HIG — Hawaii Inst Geophys Rep HIG
Hawaii Institute of Tropical Agriculture and Human Resources. Research Extension Series — Hawaii Inst Trop Agric Hum Resour Res Ext Ser
Hawaii Journal of History — Hawaii J Hist
Hawaii Library Association. Journal — Hawaii Lib Assn J
Hawaii Library Association. Journal — HLA J
Hawaii Library Association Newsletter — Hawaii Libr Assoc Newsl
Hawaii Medical Journal — Hawaii Med J
Hawaii Medical Journal — HWMJA
Hawaii Medical Journal and Inter-Island Nurses' Bulletin — Hawaii Med J Inter Isl Nurses Bull

Hawaii Orchid Journal — Hawaii Orchid J
Hawaii Reports — Haw
Hawaii Revised Statutes — Haw Rev Stat
Hawaii University. Cooperative Extension Service. Circular — Hawaii Univ Coop Ext Serv Circ
Hawaii University. Institute of Geophysics. Contributions — Hawaii Univ Inst Geophys Contrib
Hawaii University. Institute of Geophysics. Report — Hawaii Univ Inst Geophys
Hawaii University. Look Laboratory of Oceanographic Engineering. Technical Report — Hawaii Univ Look Lab Oceanogr Eng Tech Rep
Hawaii University. Sea Grant Program. Reports — Hawaii Univ Sea Grant Prog Rep
Hawaii University. Water Resources Research Center. Annual Report — Hawaii Univ Water Resour Res Cent Annu Rep
Hawaii University. Water Resources Research Center. Technical Report — Hawaii Uni Water Resour Cent Tech Rep
Hawaii University. Water Resources Research Center. Technical Report — Hawaii Univ Water Resour Res Cent Tech Rep
Hawaiian Forester and Agriculturist — Hawaiian For
Hawaiian Forester and Agriculturist — Hawaiian Forester Agric
Hawaiian Journal of History — Hawaiian J Hist
Hawaiian Planters' Monthly — Hawaii Plant Mon
Hawaiian Planters' Record — Hawaii Plant Rec
Hawaiian Planters' Record — Hawaii Plrs' Rec
Hawaiian Shell News — Hawaii Shell News
Hawaiian Shell News — HWSNAM
Hawaiian Shell News (Honolulu) — Hawaii Shell News (Honolulu)
Hawaiian Sugar Planters' Association. Experiment Station. Annual Report — Hawaii Sugar Plant Assoc Exp Stn Annu Rep
Hawaiian Sugar Technologists Reports — Hawaii Sugar Technol Rep
Hawaiian Volcano Observatory — Hawaiian Vol Obs
Hawaii's Labor Trends — HLT
Hawker Siddeley Technical Review — Hawker Siddeley Tech Rev
Hawthorne Society. Newsletter — HSN
Haydn Yearbook — Haydn Yb
Haydn-Studien — Haydn-Stud
Haygazean Hayagitagan Handes — Haygaz Hayag Handes
Hazard Assessment of Chemicals — Hazard Assess Chem
Hazard Waste Training Bulletin for Supervisors — Hazard Waste Train Bul Sup
Hazardous and Industrial Solid Waste Testing. Symposium — Hazard Ind Solid Waste Test Symp
Hazardous and Industrial Waste Management and Testing. Symposium — Hazard Ind Waste Manage Test Symp
Hazardous and Toxic Substances — Hazard Toxic Subst
Hazardous and Toxic Wastes. Technology, Management, and Health Effects — Hazard Toxic Wastes Technol Manage Health Eff
Hazardous Cargo Bulletin — Hazard Cargo Bull
Hazardous Cargo Bulletin — Hazardous Cargo Bull
Hazardous Chemicals Information and Disposal [*Database*] — HAZINF
Hazardous Materials Management Journal — Hazard Mater Manage J
Hazardous Substances Data Bank — HSDB
Hazardous Waste — Hazard Waste
Hazardous Waste and Hazardous Materials — Hazard Waste Hazard Mater
Hazardous Waste and Pollution Compliance Guidelines — HWPCG
Hazards Bulletin — Haz Bull
Hazards Bulletin — Hazards Bull
Hazards in the Chemical Laboratory — Hazards Chem Lab
Hazards Review — Haz Rev
HBJ [*Hypothec Bank of Japan*] **Monthly** — HBJ Mth
HE. Purdue University. Cooperative Extension Service — HE Purdue Univ Coop Ext Serv
HE Revista. Orgao Oficial do Centro de Estudos do Hospital-Escola da Universidade Federal de Juiz de Fora — HE Rev
Head and Neck. Journal for the Sciences and Specialties of the Head and Neck — Head Neck
Head and Neck Surgery — Head Nec Surg
Head and Neck Surgery — Head Neck Surg
Head Teachers' Review — Head Teachers' R
Headache — HEADA
Headache. Meeting of the Italian Headache Society — Headache Meet Ital Headache Soc
Headline Series — Headline Ser
Headline Series — HeS
Healing Light — Heal Light
Health — GHEA
Health — HEAHB
Health — Hlth
Health [*San Francisco*] — PINH
Health Affairs — HAFFB
Health Affairs — Health Aff
Health Affairs — HFF
Health Affairs (Millwood, Virginia) — Health Aff (Millwood)
Health Affairs (Philadelphia) — Health Aff (Pa)
Health and Hygiene — Health Hyg
Health and Hygiene — HEHYDD
Health and Hygiene in the Home — Hlth Hyg Ho
Health and Medical Care Services Review — Health Med Care Serv Rev
Health and Medical Care Services Review — HMCSR
Health and Medical Libraries Catalogue [*Database*] — HEMLOC
Health and Medicine — Health & Med
Health and Population Perspectives and Issues — Health Popul Perspect Issues
Health and Population Perspectives and Issues — HPPIDE
Health and Safety — H & S
Health and Safety at Work — Health Saf Work
Health and Safety at Work — Hlth Saf at Work
Health and Safety Bulletin — Health Saf Bull
Health and Safety Executive Directorate of Information and Advisory Services. Translations [*England*] — Hlth Saf Exec Direct Inf and Advisory Services Transl
Health and Safety in Industry and Commerce — Health Saf Ind Commer
Health and Safety Laboratories. Technical Paper (United Kingdom) — Health Saf Lab Tech Pap (UK)
Health and Safety Monitor — Hlth Saf Monitor
Health and Safety Science Abstracts [*Database*] — HSSA
Health and Social Service Journal — Health Soc Serv J
Health and Social Service Journal — Health Social Serv J
Health and Social Service Journal — Hlth Soc Serv J
Health and Social Service Journal — HSSJB
Health and Social Work — Health Soc Work
Health and Social Work — Hlth Soc Wrk
Health and Social Work — PHSW
Health and Society — HSY
Health and Strength — H & S
Health and Welfare Statistics — Health Welfare Stat
Health Aspects of Chemical Safety. Interim Document — Health Aspects Chem Saf Interim Doc
Health Audiovisual On-line Catalog [*Database*] — HAVC
Health Bulletin — Health Bul
Health Bulletin — Health Bull
Health Bulletin (Edinburgh) — Health Bull (Edinb)
Health Care Dimensions — Health Care Dimen
Health Care Education — Health Care Educ
Health Care Financing Review — HCFA Rev
Health Care Financing Review — Health Care Financ Rev
Health Care Financing Review — Health Care Financing R
Health Care Financing Trends — Health Care Financ Trends
Health Care for Women, International — Health Care Women Int
Health Care in Canada — Health Care Can
Health Care Instrumentation — HCAIEJ
Health Care Instrumentation — Health Care Instrum
Health Care Law Newsletter — Health Care Law Newsl
Health Care Literature Information Network [*Database*] — HECLINET
Health Care Management Review — HCM
Health Care Management Review — HCMR
Health Care Management Review — Health Care Manage Rev
Health Care Marketer and Target Market — Health Care Mark Target Market
Health Care Newsletter — Health Care Newsl
Health Care Planning and Marketing — Health Care Plan & Mkt
Health Care Planning and Marketing — Health Care Plann Market
Health Care Security and Safety Management — Health Care Secur Saf Manage
Health Care Strategic Management — HCT
Health Care Strategic Management — Health Care Strateg Manage
Health Care Supervisor — HCS
Health Care Supervisor — Health Care Superv
Health Care Systems — Health Care Syst
Health Care Week — Health Care Wk
Health Communications and Informatics — HCIND5
Health Communications and Informatics — Health Commun Inf
Health Communications and Informatics — Health Commun Informatics
Health Congress. Royal Society for the Promotion of Health. Papers — Health Congr R Soc Health Pap
Health Congress. Royal Society of Health. Papers for Discussion — Health Congr R Soc Health Pap Discuss
Health Cost Management — Health Cost Manage
Health Crisis 2000 (United States) — Health (US)
Health Devices — HED
Health Economics — Health Econ
Health Education — Health Ed
Health Education — Health Educ
Health Education [*Ottawa*] — HEDO
Health Education Association of New South Wales. Newsletter — Health Educ Assoc NSW Newsl
Health Education Bulletin — Health Educ Bull
Health Education Journal — Health Ed J
Health Education Journal — Health Educ
Health Education Journal — Health Educ J
Health Education Journal [*London*] — HEDJ
Health Education Monographs — Heal Ed Mon
Health Education Monographs — Health Educ Monogr
Health Education Monographs — HEEMA
Health Education Quarterly — Health Educ Q
Health Education Quarterly — HEDQ
Health Education Quarterly. Supplement — Health Educ Q Suppl
Health Education Reports — Health Educ Rep
Health Education Reports — HERP
Health Education (Washington) — HEDW
Health Educator. Newsletter — HEDU
Health Foods Business — Health Foods Bus
Health Horizon — Hlth Horiz
Health in New South Wales — Health NSW
Health in New South Wales — HNSWA
Health Industry Today — Health Ind
Health Information Digest — Hlth Inf Dig
Health Information Digest for Hot Countries — Hlth Inf Dig Hot Count
Health Instruction Yearbook — Hlth Instr Yb
Health Insurance Statistics [*United States Health, Education, and Welfare Department*] — Health Insur Stat
Health Laboratory Science — Health Lab
Health Laboratory Science — Health Lab Sc
Health Laboratory Science — Health Lab Sci
Health Laboratory Science — HLSCA

Health Laboratory Science — Hlth Lab Sci
Health Law in Canada — Health
Health Law in Canada — Health L Can
Health Law Project Library Bulletin — Health Law Proj Libr Bull
Health Libraries Review — Health Libr Rev
Health Management Forum — Health Manage Forum
Health Management Quarterly — Health Manage Q
Health Manpower Literature — Health Manpow Lit
Health Manpower Report [*Later, Health Planning and Manpower Report*] — Health Manpow Rep
Health Marketing Quarterly — Health Mark Q
Health Marketing Quarterly — Health Mkt Q
Health News — Hlth Ne
Health News — Hlth New
Health of the School Child — Hlth Sch Ch
Health Officers' Journal — Health Officers J
Health Perspectives [*Later, Consumer Health Perspectives*] — Health Perspect
Health Perspectives and Issues — Health Perspect Issues
Health Physics — Health Phys
Health Physics — Hlth Phys
Health Physics — HLTPA
Health Physics Research Abstracts — IHPAB
Health Physics (Tokyo) — Health Phys (Tokyo)
Health Planning and Manpower Report — Health Plann Manpow Rep
Health Planning and Manpower Report — Health Plann Manpower Rep
Health Policy and Education — Health Policy Educ
Health Policy Quarterly — Health Policy Q
Health Policy Quarterly — HPOQ
Health Practitioner. Physician Assistant — Health Pract Physician Assist
Health Progress — Health Prog
Health Promotion Monographs — HPRM
Health Psychology — Health Psychol
Health Psychology — HPSY
Health Reports — Health Rep
Health Rights News — Hlth Rght
Health Risk Analysis. Proceedings. Life Sciences Symposium — Health Risk Anal Proc Life Sci Symp
Health Science Review — Health Sci Rev
Health Service Journal — Health Serv J
Health Service Reports — Health Serv Rep
Health Services — Hlth Serv
Health Services Administration. Publications — HSA
Health Services and Mental Health Administration. Publications — HSM
Health Services and Mental Health Administration (United States). Health Reports — Health Serv Ment Health Adm US Health Rep
Health Services Manager — Health Serv Manager
Health Services Manpower Review — Health Serv Manpow Rev
Health Services Report — Health Serv
Health Services Report — HSRPA
Health Services Research [*Chicago*] — Health Serv Res
Health Services Research — HESEA
Health Services Research — Hlth Serv Res
Health Services Research — HSR
Health Services Research Notes — Health Serv Res Notes
Health Technology — Health Technol
Health Technology Assessment — Health Technol Assess
Health Technology Assessment Reports — Health Technol Assess Rep
Health Topics — Hlth Top
Health Values. Achieving High Level Wellness — HVHW
Health Values. Health Behavior, Education and Promotion — Health Values
Health Visitor — Health Visit
Health Yearbook — Hlth Yb
Healthcare Computing and Communications — Healthc Comput Commun
Healthcare Evaluation System [*Database*] — HES
Healthcare Executive — Healthc Executive
Healthcare Executive — HEE
Healthcare Financial Management — Healthcare Financ Manage
Healthcare Financial Management — HFM
Healthcare Financing Review — HCF
Healthcare Forum Journal — Healthc Forum
Healthcare Marketing Report — Healthcare
Healthcare Online — Healthc Online
Healthcare Protection Management — Healthc Prot Manage
Health-PAC [*Policy Advisory Center*] **Bulletin** — Health-PAC Bull
Health-PAC [*Policy Advisory Center*] **Bulletin** — Hlth PAC
Hearing Aid Journal — Hear Aid J
Hearing Aid Journal — Hear Aid Jnl
Hearing Instruments — Hear Instrum
Hearing News — Hearing N
Hearing Rehabilitation Quarterly — Hear Rehab Quart
Hearing Research — Hear Res
Hearst's International. Cosmopolitan — Hearsts Int Cosmopol
Hearst's Magazine — Hearst's M
Heart and Lung. Journal of Critical Care — Heart and Lung
Heart and Lung. Journal of Critical Care — Heart Lung
Heart and Vessels. Supplement — Heart Vessels Suppl
Heart Bulletin — H Bull
Heart Bulletin — Heart Bull
Heart Bulletin — HEBUA
Heart Center Bulletin. St. Francis Hospital (Roslyn, New York) — Heart Cent Bull St Francis Hosp (Roslyn NY)
Heart Function and Metabolism. Proceedings of the International Meeting of the International Study Group for Research in Cardiac Metabolism — Heart Funct Metab Proc Int Meet Int Study Group Res Card Meta
Heart. Muscle and Pump. Proceedings. Workshop on Contractile Behavior of the Heart — Heart Muscle Pump Proc Workshop Contract Behav Heart
Hearts and Heart-Like Organs — Hearts Heart Like Organs
Heat and Fluid Flow — HTFFA
Heat and Mass Transfer. Australasian Conference — Heat Mass Transfer Australas Conf
Heat and Technology (Bologna) — Heat Technol (Bologna)
Heat Engineering — Heat Eng
Heat Engineering [*Livingston, NJ*] — HEENA
Heat Exchangers. Journees Internationales de l'Institut Francais des Combustibles et de l'Energie — Heat Exch Journ Int Inst Fr Combust Energ
Heat Management and Pollution Control [*Japan*] — Heat Manage Pollut Control
Heat Recovery Systems — Heat Recovery Syst
Heat Recovery Systems and CHP. Combined Heat and Power — Heat Recovery Syst CHP
Heat Technology — Heat Technol
Heat Technology (Dresher, Pennsylvania) — Heat Technol (Dresher Pa)
Heat Transfer and Fluid Flow Digest — Heat Transfer & Fluid Flow Dig
Heat Transfer and Fluid Flow in Rotating Machinery. International Symposium on Transport Phenomena — Heat Transfer Fluid Flow Rotating Mach Int Symp Transp Phenom
Heat Transfer and Fluid Mechanics Institute. Preprints of Papers — Heat Transfer Fluid Mech Inst Prepr Pap
Heat Transfer and Fluid Mechanics Institute. Proceedings — Heat Transfer Fluid Mech Inst Proc
Heat Transfer Engineering — Heat Transfer Eng
Heat Transfer Engineering — Heat Transfer Engng
Heat Transfer in Geophysical Media. National Heat Transfer Conference — Heat Transfer Geophys Media Natl Heat Transfer Conf
Heat Transfer in High Technology and Power Engineering. Proceedings of the Seminar — Heat Transfer High Technol Power Eng Proc Semin
Heat Transfer. International Heat Transfer Conference — Heat Transfer Int Heat Transfer Conf
Heat Transfer. Japanese Research — Heat Transfer Jap Res
Heat Transfer. Japanese Research — Heat Transfer - Japan Res
Heat Transfer. Japanese Research — Heat Transfer Jpn Res
Heat Transfer. Japanese Research — HTJPA
Heat Transfer. Soviet Research — Heat Transfer Sov Res
Heat Treating — Heat Treat
Heat Treating and Forging — Heat Treat Forg
Heat Treatment Journal — Heat Treat J
Heat Treatment of Metals — Heat Treat Met
Heat Treatment of Metals — HTRMB
Heat Treatment of Metals (Beijing) — Heat Treat Met (Beijing)
Heat Treatment of Metals (China) — Heat Treat Met (China)
Heat Treatment. Proceedings of the International Heat Treatment Conference — Heat Treat Proc Int Heat Treat Conf
Heating, Air Conditioning, and Refrigeration — Heat Air Cond Refrig
Heating, Air Conditioning, and Refrigeration — Heat Air Condit Refrig
Heating and Air Conditioning Contractor — HACCA
Heating and Air Conditioning Contractor — Heat Air Cond Contr
Heating and Air Conditioning Journal — HAC
Heating and Air Conditioning Journal — Heat Air Cond J
Heating and Air Conditioning Journal — Heat Air Condit J
Heating and Air Conditioning Journal — Heat and Air Cond J
Heating and Air Conditioning Journal — Heating & Air Conditioning Jnl
Heating and Ventilating — Heat & Vent
Heating and Ventilating — HEVEA
Heating and Ventilating Engineer — Heat
Heating and Ventilating Engineer — Heat and Vent Eng
Heating and Ventilating Engineer — Heat & Vent Engr
Heating and Ventilating Engineer — Heat Vent Eng
Heating and Ventilating Engineer — Heat Vent Engr
Heating and Ventilating Engineer and Journal of Air Conditioning — Heat Vent Eng J Air Cond
Heating and Ventilating Engineer and Journal of Air Conditioning — HVECA
Heating and Ventilating Magazine — Heat Vent Mag
Heating and Ventilating News — Heat Vent News
Heating and Ventilating Review — Heat Vent Rev
Heating and Ventilating Review — HVREA
Heating/Combustion Equipment News — Heat Combust Equip News
Heating, Piping, and Air Conditioning — Heat Pip Air Condit
Heating, Piping, and Air Conditioning — Heat Piping Air Cond
Heating, Piping, and Air Conditioning — Heat Pipng
Heating, Piping, and Air Conditioning — Heating Piping
Heating, Piping and Air Conditioning — HPAOA
Heating Piping and Air Conditioning (Tokyo) — Heat Piping Air Cond (Tokyo)
Heaton Review — HR
Heavy Flavor and Electroweak Theory. Proceedings of the International Symposium — Heavy Flavor Electroweak Theory Proc Int Symp
Heavy Ion Inertial Fusion. Proceedings. International Symposium — Heavy Ion Inertial Fusion Proc Int Symp
Heavy Metals in the Environment — Heavy Met Environ
Heavy Metals in the Environment. International Conference. 4th — Heavy Met Environ Int Conf 4th
Heavy Oil/Enhanced Recovery Index [*Database*] — HERI
Heavy Truck Equipment News — Heavy Truck Equip N
Heavy-Ion Physics Today and Tomorrow. Proceedings. Adriatic International Conference on Nuclear Physics — Heavy Ion Phys Today Tomorrow Proc Adriat Int Conf Nucl Phys
Hebbel-Jahrbuch — Hebbel-Jahrb
Hebbel-Jahrbuch — HJb
Hebdomadaire de la Chimie — Hebd Chim
Hebdomadaire de la Production a la Distribution [*Paris*] — ICU
Hebezeuge und Foerdermittel — HEFOA

Hebraeische Bibliographie [*Berlin*] — HB
Hebraeisches und Aramaeisches Woerterbuch zum Alten Testament — HAWAT
Hebraica (Chicago) — Hebr
Hebrew Annual Review — HAR
Hebrew Computational Linguistics — HCompL
Hebrew Medical Journal — Heb Med J
Hebrew Pharmacist — Heb Pharm
Hebrew Student — Heb St
Hebrew Studies [*Louisville, KY*] — HS
Hebrew Studies — HSt
Hebrew Technical College (Haifa). Scientific Publications — Heb Tech Coll (Haifa) Sci Publ
Hebrew Theological College Journal — HTCJ
Hebrew Union College Annual — Hebrew Union Coll Annu
Hebrew Union College. Annual — HebrUCA
Hebrew Union College. Annual — HUCA
Hebrew University. Geological Department (Jerusalem) — HUJGD
Hebrew University (Jerusalem) — Hebrew Univ (Jerusalem)
Hebrew University (Jerusalem) — HUJ
Hebrew University. Studies in Literature — Hebrew U St
Hebrew University. Studies in Literature — HUSL
Hebridean Naturalist — Hebridean Nat
Hechos y Dichos — HD
Hechos y Dichos — Hy D
Hedendaagsche Letteroefeningen — Hedend Letteroefen
Hedeselskabets Tidsskrift — Hedeselsk Tidsskr
Hedeselskabets Tidsskrift — Hs T
Hefte des Archaeologischen Seminars der Universitaet Bern — HASB
Hefte des Archaeologischen Seminars der Universitaet Bern — Hefte A Bern
Hefte fuer Geschichte, Kunst, und Volkskunde — HGKV
Hefte fuer Literatur und Kritik — HLK
Hefte zum Bibelstudium — HBSt
Hefte zur Christlichen Welt — HCW
Hefte zur Missionskunde — HMK
Hefte zur Unfallheilkunde [*Germany*] — Heft Unfallheilk
Hefte zur Unfallheilkunde — Hefte Unfallheilkd
Hegel-Jahrbuch — Hegel-Jrbh
Hegel-Studien — Hegel-Stud
Heh Hua Hsueh Yu Fang She Hua Hsueh — HHHHD
Heidelberg Science Library — Heidelb Sci Libr
Heidelberger Abhandlungen — HA
Heidelberger Abhandlungen zur Mittleren und Neueren Geschichte — HAMNG
Heidelberger Abhandlungen zur Philosophie und Ihrer Geschichte — HAPG
Heidelberger Akademie der Wissenschaften. Mathematisch-Naturwissenschaftliche Klasse. Sitzungsberichte — HAMSB
Heidelberger Akademie der Wissenschaften. Mathematisch-Naturwissenschaftliche Klasse. Sitzungsberichte [*Germany*] — Heidelberg Akad Wiss Math Naturwiss Kl Sitzungsber
Heidelberger Akademie der Wissenschaften. Sitzungsberichte — Heid Sitzb
Heidelberger Beitraege zur Mineralogie und Petrographie — Heidelb Betr Mineral Petrogr
Heidelberger Beitraege zur Romanistik — HBR
Heidelberger Beitrage zur Mineralogie und Petrographie — Heidelberger Beitr Mineralogie u Petrographie
Heidelberger Colloquium on Spin Glasses. Proceedings of a Colloquium — Heidelb Colloq Spin Glasses Proc Colloq
Heidelberger Forschungen — HF
Heidelberger Gespraeche — Heidelb Gespraeche
Heidelberger Jahrbuch — HeJ
Heidelberger Jahrbuecher — Hd Jb
Heidelberger Jahrbuecher — He Jb
Heidelberger Jahrbuecher — Heidelb Jahrb
Heidelberger Jahrbuecher — Heidelberger Jahrb
Heidelberger Jahrbuecher — HeidJb
Heidelberger Jahrbuecher fuer Literatur — HJL
Heidelberger Rechtswissenschaftliche Abhandlungen — HRWA
Heidelberger Taschenbuecher — Heidelb Taschenb
Heil Gewuerz-Pflanzen — Heil Gewuerz-Pflanz
Heilberufe [*Germany*] — HLBFA
Heilig Land [*Nijmegen, Netherlands*] — H Land
Heilige Land — HeilL
Heilige Land — HL
Heiligenkreuzer Studien — Heil St
Heiliger Dienst — Hl D
Heilpaedagogische Forschung — Heilpaed For
Heilpaedagogische Forschung — Heilpaedagog Forsch
Heilpaedagogische Werkblaetter — HPWBA
Heimarbeitsgesetz — H Arb G
Heimatblaetter des Historischen Vereins Bamberg — H Bl HVB
Heimatbuch der Ostumsiedler — Heimatb Ostumsiedler
Heimatbund der Deutschen aus Russland — Heimatb Dt Russl
Heimatjahrbuch fuer den Kreis Hofgeismar — Hj Kreis Hofgeismar
Heimatliche Kirchenkunst und Kirchengeschichte — HKKG
Heimatstimmen aus dem Kreise Olpe — Hst Kreise Olpe
Heimkehr zur Kirche — HzK
Heine-Jahrbuch — HeineJ
Heine-Jahrbuch — Heine-Jahrb
Heinrich Hertz Institut Geophysical Data — HHI Geophys Data
Heinrich Hertz Institut Solar Data — HHI Sol Data
Heinrich Schliemanns Sammlung Trojanische Altertuemer — SS
Heizen mit Sonne — HESOD
Heizung, Lueftung, Haustechnik [*Later, HLH. Zeitschrift fuer Heizung, Lueftung, Klimatechnik, Haustechnik*] — Heiz Lueft Haustech
Heizung, Lueftung, Haustechnik [*HLH. Zeitschrift fuer Heizung, Lueftung, Klimatechnik, Haustechnik*] [*Germany*] [*Later,*] — Heizung-Lueftung Haustech
Hejnal Mariacki — Hej Mar
Hejnat Mariacki — HM
Hejubian Yu Dengliziti Wuli — HYDWD
Heidelberger Klinische Annalen — Heidelberger Klin Ann
Helgolaender Meeresuntersuchungen — Helgol Meeresunters
Helgolaender Meeresuntersuchungen — HEMEDC
Helgolaender Wissenschaftliche Meeresuntersuchungen — Helg W Meer
Helgolaender Wissenschaftliche Meeresuntersuchungen — Helgol Wiss Meeresunters
Helgolaender Wissenschaftliche Meeresuntersuchungen — HELOA
Helgolaender Wissenschaftliche Meeresuntersuchungen — HWM
Helgolaender Wissenschaftliche Meeresuntersuchungen/Marine Investigations — Helgolander Wiss Meeresunters Mar Invest
Helicon — Hel
Helicopter International — Heli Intnl
Helicopter World — Heli World
Helicopter World — Helicop Wld
Helikon. Revista di Tradizione e Cultura Classica dell'Universita di Messina — Helikon
Helikon. Rivista di Tradizione e Cultura Classica — HIK
Helinium. Revue Consacree a l'Archeologie des Pays-Bas de la Belgique et du Grand Duche de Luxembourg — Helinium
Helium Atom Scattering from Surfaces — Helium At Scattering Surf
Hellas-Jahrbuch — Hel
Hellas-Jahrbuch — HellasJB
Hellenic Armed Forces Medical Review — Hell Armed Forces Med Rev
Hellenic Veterinary Medicine — Hell Vet Med
Hellenica. Paris — Hell P
Hellenika [*Salonika*] — Hellen
Hellenika. Jahrbuch fuer die Freunde Griechenlands — Hellenika Jb
Hellenika. Philogikon, Hisstorikon kai Leographikon Periodikon Syngramma — Hell
Hellenika (Salonika) — Hellenika (S)
Hellenika Stomatologika Chronika — Hell Stomatol Chron
Hellenike Anaisthesiologia — Hell Anaisthesiol
Hellenike Kteniatrike — Hell Kteniatr
Hellenike Mikrobiologike kai Hygieinologike Hetaireia Deltion — Hell Mikrobiol Hygieinol Hetaireia Delt
Hellenikos Philologikos Syllogos — Hell Phil Syll
Hellenis Adelphe — Hell Adelphe
Hellenisme Contemporain — HC
Hellenisme Contemporain — Hellenisme Contemp
Hellweg. Wochenschrift fuer Deutsche Kunst — He
Helmantica. Revista de Humanidades Clasicas — Helm
Helmantica. Salamanca — Helm
Helminthologia — Helminthol
Helminthologia [*Bratislava*] — HMTGA4
Helminthological Abstracts — Helminth Abstr
Helminthological Society of Washington. Proceedings — Helminthol Soc Wash Proc
Helping Person in the Group — Help Person Group
Helps for Bible Translators — HFBT
Helps for Translators Series — He Tr
Helsingin Sanomat — HISAN
Helsingin Sanomat — HSan
Helsingin Teknillinen Korkeakoulu. Radiolaboratorio. Internal Report — Helsingin Tek Korkeakoulu Radiolaboratorio Intern Rep
Helsingin Teknillinen Korkeakoulu Tieteellisia Julkaisuja — Helsingin Tek Korkeakoulu Tiet Julk
Helsinki University of Technology Institute of Mathematics Systems Research Reports — Helsinki Univ Tech Inst Math Syst Res Rep
Helsinki University of Technology. Institution of Process Metallurgy. Report — Helsinki Univ Technol Inst Process Metall Rep
Helsinki University of Technology. Laboratory of Forest Products Chemistry. Reports. Series C — Helsinki Univ Technol Lab For Prod Chem Rep Ser C
Helsinki University of Technology. Laboratory of Materials Processing and Powder Metallurgy. Report TKK-V-B — Helsinki Univ Technol Lab Mater Process Powder Metall Rep TK
Helsinki University of Technology. Laboratory of Physics. Research Report — Helsinki Univ Technol Lab Phys Res Rep
Helsinki University of Technology. Research Papers — Helsinki Univ Technol Res Pap
Helvetia Archaeologica — HA
Helvetia Archaeologica — Helv A
Helvetia Archaeologica — Helvet Arch
Helvetica Archaeologica — Helv Arch
Helvetica Chimica Acta — HCACA
Helvetica Chimica Acta — HChA
Helvetica Chimica Acta — Helv Chim A
Helvetica Chimica Acta — Helv Chim Acta
Helvetica Chirurgica Acta — H Ch A
Helvetica Chirurgica Acta — HCA
Helvetica Chirurgica Acta — HCATA
Helvetica Chirurgica Acta — Helv Chir Acta
Helvetica Chirurgica Acta. Supplementum — Helv Chir Acta Suppl
Helvetica Medica Acta — Helv Med Acta
Helvetica Medica Acta — HMA
Helvetica Medica Acta — HMACA
Helvetica Medica Acta. Series B. Helvetica Chirurgica Acta — Helv Med Acta Ser B
Helvetica Medica Acta. Series C. Helvetica Paediatrica Acta — Helv Med Acta Ser C
Helvetica Medica Acta. Series C. Helvetica Paediatrica Acta. Supplementum — Helv Med Acta Ser C Suppl

Helvetica Medica Acta. Series D. Helvetica Paediatrica Acta — Helv Med Acta Ser D
Helvetica Medica Acta. Series D. Helvetica Paediatrica Acta. Supplementum — Helv Med Acta Ser D Suppl
Helvetica Medica Acta. Supplementum — Helv Med Acta Suppl
Helvetica Odontologica Acta — Helv Odon A
Helvetica Odontologica Acta — Helv Odontol Acta
Helvetica Odontologica Acta — HONAA
Helvetica Odontologica Acta. Supplementum — Helvetica Odontol Acta Suppl
Helvetica Odontologica Acta. Supplementum — HOASAR
Helvetica Paediatrica Acta — Helv Paed A
Helvetica Paediatrica Acta — Helv Paediat Acta
Helvetica Paediatrica Acta — Helv Paediatr Acta
Helvetica Paediatrica Acta — HPA
Helvetica Paediatrica Acta — HPAAA
Helvetica Paediatrica Acta. Supplementum — Helv Paediatr Acta Suppl
Helvetica Physica Acta — Helv Phys A
Helvetica Physica Acta — Helv Phys Acta
Helvetica Physica Acta — HPACA
Helvetica Physica Acta. Supplementum — Helv Phys Acta Suppl
Helvetica Physiologica et Pharmacologica Acta — H Phys Pharm A
Helvetica Physiologica et Pharmacologica Acta — Helv Physiol Pharmac Acta
Helvetica Physiologica et Pharmacologica Acta — Helv Physiol Pharmacol Acta
Helvetica Physiologica et Pharmacologica Acta — HPPAA
Helvetica Physiologica et Pharmacologica Acta. Supplementum — Helv Physiol Pharmacol Acta Suppl
Helvetica Physiologica et Pharmacologica Acta. Supplementum — HPASA
Helvetische Muenzen-Zeitung — HMZ
Hematologic Pathology — Hematol Pathol
Hematologic Reviews — Hematol Rev
Hematological Oncology — Hematol Onc
Hematological Oncology — Hematol Oncol
Hematology [*New York*] — HEMAEZ
Hematology and Cell Therapy — Hematol Cell Ther
Hematology/Oncology Clinics of North America — Hematol Oncol Clin North Am
Hematology. Plenary Sessions. Scientific Contributions. International Congress of Hematology — Hematol Plenary Sess Sci Contrib Int Congr Hematol
Hematopathology and Molecular Hematology — Hematopathol Mol Hematol
Hemel en Dampkring — HEMEA
Hemeroteca Nacional [*Database*] — HENA
Hemijska Industrija — Hem Ind
Hemijska Industrija — Hemijska Ind
Hemijska Industrija - Industrija Secera — Hem Ind Ind Secera
Hemijska Vlakna — Hem Vlakna
Hemingway Newsletter — HNews
Hemingway Notes — Hemingway N
Hemingway Notes — HN
Hemingway Review — HemR
Hemingway Review — PHEM
Hemisphere — Hemis
Hemisphere — Hs
Hemoglobin — HEMOD
Hemostase — HEMOA
Henceforth — He
Hennepin Lawyer — Hennepin Law
Hennepin Reporter — Hennepin Rep
Henry Bradshaw Society — HBS
Henry E. Sigerist Supplements. Bulletin of the History of Medicine — Henry E Sigerist Suppl Bull Hist Med
Henry Ford Hospital. International Symposium — Henry Ford Hosp Int Symp
Henry Ford Hospital. Medical Bulletin — Henry Ford Hosp Med Bull
Henry Ford Hospital. Medical Journal — Henry Ford Hosp Med J
Henry Ford Hospital. Medical Journal — HFHJA
Henry James Review — HJR
Heohragicheskyi Zbirnyk L'vivs'koho Vida Heohraficheskoho Tovarystva Ukrains'koho SSR — Heohr Zb Lviv Vida Heohr Tov Ukr SSR
HEP [*Higher Education Publications*] **Higher Education Directory** — HEP
Hepatic Metabolism and Disposition of Endo- and Xenobiotics. Proceedings. Falk Symposium — Hepatic Metab Dispos Endo Xenobiot Proc Falk Symp
Hepato-Gastroenterology — Hepato-Gastroenterol
Hepatology Research and Clinical Issues — HEPADF
Hepatology. Research and Clinical Issues — Hepatol Res Clin Issues
Hepatotoxicite Medicamenteuse — Hepatotoxic Med
Her Majesty's Stationary Office — HMSO
Her Majesty's Stationery Office Daily Lists — HMSO Daily Lists
Herald Geological — Her Geol
Herald of Christian Science — HCS
Herald of Holiness — H Hol
Herald of Library Science — Her Libr Sci
Herald of Library Science — Herald Lib Sci
Herald of Library Science — HLS
Herald Research Bulletin — Herald Research Bul
Herald Tribune — HT
Heraut van de Christelijke Wetenschap — HCWe
Herb Grower Magazine — Herb Grower Mag
Herb, Spice, and Medicinal Plant Digest — Herb Spice Med Plant Dig
Herba Hungarica — HEHUA
Herba Hungarica — Herba Hung
Herba Polonica — Herba Pol
Herbage Abstracts — Herb Abstr
Herbage Abstracts — Herbage Abstr
Herbage Reviews — Herb Rev
Herbergen der Christenheit — Her Chr
Herbicide Resistance in Weeds and Crops. Long Ashton International Symposium — Herb Resist Weeds Crops Long Ashton Int Symp
Herbier General de l'Amateur, Contenant la Description, l'Histoire, Proprietes et la Culture des Vegetaux Utiles et Agreables — Herb Gen Amateur
Herbs, Spices, and Medicinal Plants — HSMPE8
Herbs, Spices, and Medicinal Plants. Recent Advances in Botany, Horticulture, and Pharmacology — Herbs Spices Med Plants Recent Adv Bot Hortic Pharmacol
Hercules Chemist — Hercules Chem
Hercynia — HERCA
Hercynia fuer die Fachgebiete Botanik-Geographie-Geologie Palaeontologie-Zoologie — Hercynia Fachgeb Bot-Geogr-Geol Palaeontol-Zool
Herder Buecherei — Her Bue
Herder Buecherei. Duenndruckausgaben — Her Bue D
Herder Korrespondenz — HEKOD
Herder Korrespondenz — Her Korr
Herder Korrespondenz — Herder Korresp
Herder Korrespondenz. Beiheft — Her Korr B
Herders Bibelkommentar — HBK
Herder's Konservationslexikon — HKL
Herders Theologische Lehrbuecher — HTL
Herders Theologischer Kommentar zum Neuen Testament — H Th K
Herders Theologischer Kommentar zum Neuen Testament — HTKNT
Here and Now — H & N
Here and Now — HN
Hereditas — HEREA
Hereditas — Hered
Hereditas (Lund, Sweden) — Hereditas Lund Swed
Heredity [*England*] — HDTYA
Heredity — Hered
Hereford Journal of Southern Africa — Hereford J Sthn Afr
Hereford Quarterly — Hereford Q
Hereford Quarterly. Australian Hereford Society — Aust Hereford Soc Q
Herion Informationen — Herion Inf
Heritage. Alberta Department of Culture, Youth, and Recreation — HRTG
Heritage Australia Information System [*Database*] — HERA
Heritage. Monthly Newsletter. Alaska Office of History and Archaeology — HERI
Heritage of Indian Art Series — HIAS
Heritage of Kansas — HK
Heritage West — Heritage W
Heritage West. British Columbia's Leading Heritage Magazine — HEWE
Herlovianeren — Herl
Hermaea. Halle — Herm
Herman Otto Muzeum Evkoenyve — HOME
Hermannsburger Missionsblatt — HMB
Hermanthena — Her
Hermathena — Ha
Hermeneutische Untersuchungen zur Theologie — HU Th
Hermes — Hm
Hermes. Collana di Testi Antichi — Herm
Hermes [*Wiesbaden*] **Einzelschriften** — Hermes E
Hermes. Messager Scientifique et Populaire de l'Antiquite Classique en Russie — HR
Hermes. Revista del Pais Vasco — HRPV
Hermes. Zeitschrift fuer Klassische Philologie — H
Hermes. Zeitschrift fuer Klassische Philologie — Herm
Hermes. Zeitschrift fuer Klassische Philologie — Hermes Z Kl
Hermes. Zeitschrift fuer Klassische Philologie — HZKP
Hermsdorfer Technische Mitteilungen — Hermsdorfer Tech Mitt
Heroes of Islam Series — H Isl S
Heron (English Edition) — Heron (Engl Ed)
Herpetologica — Herpetologi
Herpetologica — HPTGA
Herpetological Review — Herpetol Rev
Herrenjournal International. Fachzeitschrift fuer Herrenmode — KLI
Herrigs Archiv fuer das Studium der Neueren Sprachen und Literaturen — HA
Herterofonia — Het
Hertfordshire Archaeological Review — Hertfordshire Archaeol Rev
Hertfordshire Archaeology — Hertford A
Hertfordshire Archaeology — Hertfordshire Arch
Hertfordshire Archaeology — Hertfordshire Archaeol
Hervormde Teologiese Studies — HTS
Herz Kreislauf — Herz Kreisl
Herz Kreislauf — HZKLA
Herzl Year Book — HYB
Hesdoerffers Monatshefte fuer Blumen- und Gartenfreunde — Hesdoerffers Monatsh Blumen Gartenfreunde
Hesperia — H
Hesperia — Hesp
Hesperis. Archives Berberes et Bulletin. Institut des Hautes Etudes Marocaines — Hesp
Hesperis. Paris — Hes
Hesperis. Tamuda — Hes Ta
Hesperis-Tamuda — H-T
Hesse Landesamt fuer Bodenforschung Notizblatt — Hesse Landesamt Bodenforsch Notizblatt
Hessische Bibliographie [*Database*] — HEBIS-BIB
Hessische Biene — Hess Biene
Hessische Blaetter fuer Volkskunde — HBV
Hessische Blaetter fuer Volkskunde — HBVk
Hessische Chronik — HC
Hessische Floristische Briefe — Hess Florist Briefe
Hessische Landwirtschaftliche Zeitschrift — Hess Landw Z
Hessisches Aerzteblatt — Hess Aerztebl

Hessisches Hebopfer Theologischer und Philologischer Anmerkungen — HHO
Hessisches Jahrbuch fuer Landesgeschichte — HeJL
Hessisches Jahrbuch fuer Landesgeschichte — Hess Jb Landesgesch
Hessisches Jahrbuch fuer Landesgeschichte — HJLG
Hessisches Lagerstaettenarchiv — Hess Lagerstaettenarch
Het Boek — Boek
Het Boek — HB
Het Christelijk Oosten [*Nijmegen*] — ChrOost
Het Christelijk Oosten en Hereniging — Christ Oosten
Het Gildeboek. Tijdschrift voor Kerkelijke Kunst en Oudheidkunde — HGB
Het Jachtbedrijf — J
Het Oude Land van Loon. Jaarboek van de Federatie der Geschied- en Oudheidkundige Kringen van Limburg — Land Loon
Heteroatom Chemistry — Heteroat Chem
Heterocyclic Chemistry — Heterocycl Chem
Heterocyclic Communications — Heterocycl Commun
Heterodoxical Voice — Het Voice
Heterogeneous Catalysis — Heterog Catal
Heterogeneous Catalysis. Proceedings. International Symposium — Heterog Catal Proc Int Symp
Hethiter und Hethitisch — HuH
Hethitisch-Akkadische Bilinguie des Hattusili I. Abhandlungen. Bayerische Akademie der Wissenschaften. Philosophisch-Historische Abteilung — HAB
Hethitische Keilschrifttexte aus Boghazkoei in Umschrift — H Bo
Hethitische Keilschrifttexte aus Boghazkoei in Umschrift — HKT
Hethitischen Totenritual. Deutsches Akademie der Wissenschaften. Institut fuer Orientforschung. Veroeffentlichungen — H Tr
Hethitischen Totenritual. Deutsches Akademie der Wissenschaften. Institut fuer Orientforschung. Veroeffentlichungen — Ht TR
Hethitisches Elementarbuch — HE
Hethitisches Keilschrift-Lesebuch — HKL
Hethitisches Woerterbuch — HW
Heubner Foundation Monograph Series — Heubner Foundation Monograph Ser
Heurtey Bulletin d'Informations. English Edition — Heurtey Bull Inform
Heves Megyei Mueszaki Elet — Heves Megyei Muesz Elet
Hewett Lectures — Hew L
Hewlett-Packard Journal — Hewlett
Hewlett-Packard Journal — Hewlett-Packard J
Heythrop Journal — Hey J
Heythrop Journal — Heythrop
Heythrop Journal — Heythrop J
Heythrop Journal. A Quarterly Review of Philosophy and Theology [*Oxford*] — HeythJ
HF Communication Systems and Techniques. International Conference — HF Commun Syst Tech Int Conf
HIA [*Horological Institute of America*] **Journal of Modern Watchmaking** — HIA J Mod Watchmaking
Hibbert Journal — Hibbert J
Hibbert Journal — HibbJ
Hibbert Journal — HibJ
Hibbert Journal — HJ
Hibbert Journal — HJl
Hibbert Lectures — Hib L
Hibeh Papyri — P Hibeh
Hibernation and Torpor in Mammals and Birds — Hibernation Torpor Mamm Birds
Hibridni Kukuruz Jugoslavie — Hibridni Kukuruz Jugoslav
Hickenia (Boletin del Darwinion) — Hickenia (Bol Darwinion)
Hickory Task Force Report. Southeastern Forest Experiment Station — Hickory Task Force Rep Stheast For Exp Sta
Hid — Hi
Hide and Leather — Hide Leather
Hide and Leather with Shoe Factory — Hide Leather Shoe Fact
Hidrobiologia [*Bucharest*] — HDBLA2
Hidrologiai Koezloeny — HIDRA
Hidrologiai Koezloeny — Hidrol Koezl
Hidrotehnica Gospodarirea Apelor. Meteorologia — HGAMA
Hidrotehnica Gospodarirea Apelor. Meteorologia [*Romania*] — Hidroteh Gospod Apelor Meteorol
Hidrotehnika un Melioracija Latvijas PSR — Hidroteh Melior Latv PSR
Hiei International Symposium on Teratocarcinoma and the Cell Surface — Hiei Int Symp Teratocarcinoma Cell Surf
Hier et Demain — H Dem
Hierglyphes Hittites — HH
Hieroglyphisch-Hethitisches Glossar — Hh Gl
Hierophant — Hiero
Hi-Fi News and Record Review — HFN
Hi-Fi News and Record Review — Hi-Fi News Rec Rev
Hi-Fi News and Record Reviews — HiFi
Hi-Fi/Stereo Buyers' Guide — HFSBG
Hifuka No Rinsho [*Japan*] — HIRIB
Higashi Nippon Dental Journal — Higashi Nippon Dent J
Higginson Journal of Poetry — Higg J Poet
High Energy Chemistry [*English Translation*] — HIECA
High Energy Chemistry — High Energy Chem
High Energy Chemistry (English Translation) — High Energy Chem (Engl Transl)
High Energy Chemistry (Translation of Khimiya Vysokikh Energii) — High Energy Chem Transl of Khim Vys Energ
High Energy Collisions. International Conference — High Energy Collisions Int Conf
High Energy Electromagnetic Interactions and Field Theory. Session — High Energy Electromagn Interact Field Theory Sess
High Energy Nuclear Collisions and Quark Gluon Plasma. International Symposium — High Energy Nucl Collisions Quark Gluon Plasma Int Symp
High Energy Physics and Nuclear Physics — High Energy Phys Nucl Phys
High Energy Physics and Nuclear Physics — High Energy Phys Nuclear Phys
High Energy Physics and Nuclear Structure. Proceedings of the International Conference on High Energy Physics and Nuclear Structure — High Energy Phys Nucl Struct Proc Int Conf
High Energy Physics Index — HEPIA
High Fidelity — GHIF
High Fidelity — HF
High Fidelity — Hi Fi
High Fidelity/Musical America — HF/MA
High Fidelity/Musical America — Hi Fi
High Fidelity/Musical America — Hi Fi/Mus Am
High/Low Report — Hi Lo
High Mountain Ecology Research Station (Finse, Norway) Reports — HMENR
High Performance Fiber Reinforced Cement Composites. Proceedings. International Workshop — High Perform Fiber Reinf Cem Compos Proc Int Workshop
High Performance Textiles — High Per T
High Points — H Points
High Polymers — High Polym
High Polymers — HIPOA
High Polymers (Japan) — High Polym (Jpn)
High Power Laser and Particle Beams — High Power Laser Part Beams
High Pressure and Biotechnology. Proceedings. European Seminar — High Pressure Biotechnol Proc Eur Semin
High Pressure Engineering. International Conference — High Pressure Eng Int Conf
High Purity Materials in Science and Technology. International Symposium. Proceedings — High Purity Mater Sci Technol Int Symp Proc
High School — H Sch
High School Chemistry Teachers' Magazine — High Sch Chem Teach Mag
High School Journal — H Sch J
High School Journal — High Sch J
High School Journal — HSJ
High School Quarterly — H Sch Q
High School Teacher — H Sch Teach
High Solids Coatings — High Solids Coat
High Speed Ground Transportation Journal — High Speed Gr Transpn J
High Speed Ground Transportation Journal — High Speed Ground Transp J
High Speed Ground Transportation Journal — HSGTA
High Speed Ground Transportation Journal — HSGTJ
High Speed Testing — High Speed Test
High Strain Rate Behavior of Refractory Metals and Alloys. Proceedings. Symposium — High Strain Rate Behav Refract Met Alloys Proc Symp
High Technology — High Tech
High Technology [*United States*] — High Technol
High Technology Business — High Technol Bus
High Technology Business — HTN
High Technology Letters — High Technol Lett
High Temperature — High Temp
High Temperature [*English Translation*] — HITEA
High Temperature and Materials Science — High Temp Mater Sci
High Temperature Chemical Processes — High Temp Chem Processes
High Temperature (English Translation) — High Temp (Engl Transl)
High Temperature Liquid-Metal Heat Transfer Technology Meeting. Proceedings — High Temp Liq Met Heat Transfer Technol Meet Proc
High Temperature Materials and Processes — High Temp Mater Processes
High Temperature Materials Data Bank — HTM-DB
High Temperature Reaction Rate Data — High Temp React Rate Data
High Temperature Science — High Temp S
High Temperature Science — High Temp Sci
High Temperature Science — HITSA
High Temperature Superconducting Compounds III. Processing and Microstructure Property Relationships. Proceedings. Symposium — High Temp Supercond Compd III Proc Symp
High Temperature Superconductivity — High Temp Supercond
High Temperature Technology — High Temp Technol
High Temperature (Translation of Teplofizika Vysokikh Temperatur) — High Temp Transl of Teplofiz Vys Temp
High Temperature USSR — High Temp R
High Temperatures-High Pressures — High Temp High Pressures
High Temperatures-High Pressures — HTHPA
High Times — HT
High Voltage Electron Microscopy. Proceedings of the International Conference — High Voltage Electron Microsc Proc Int Conf
Higher Education — High Educ
Higher Education — Higher Ed
Higher Education — Higher Educ
Higher Education Abstracts — High Educ Abstr
Higher Education and Research in the Netherlands — HIC
Higher Education Collective Bargaining — High Educ Col Barg
Higher Education Exchange — High Educ Ex
Higher Education Journal — Higher Ed J
Higher Education Research and Development — High Educ R & D
Higher Education Review — High Educ R
Higher Education Review — High Educ Rev
Higher Education Review — Higher Ed R
Higher Mathematics — Higher Math
Highlights of Agricultural Research. Alabama Agricultural Experiment Station [*A publication*] — Highlights Agr Res
Highlights of Agricultural Research. Alabama Agricultural Experiment Station — Highlights Agric Res Ala Agric Exp Stn
Highlights of Astronomy — Highlights Astron
Highlights of Modern Biochemistry. Proceedings. International Congress of Biochemistry — Highlights Mod Biochem Proc Int Congr Biochem

High-Performance Liquid Chromatography. Advances and Perspectives — High Perform Liq Chromatogr
High-Pressure Science and Technology. AIRAPT [*International Association for the Advancement of High Pressure Science and Technology*] **Conference** — High Pressure Sci Technol AIRAPT Conf
High-Purity Materials in Science and Technology. International Symposium — High Purity Mater Sci Technol Int Symp
High-Resolution Displays and Projection Systems — High Resolut Disp Proj Syst
High-Speed Flight Propulsion Systems — High Speed Flight Propuls Syst
High-Speed Surface Craft — High-Speed Surf Craft
High-Speed Surface Craft, Incorporating Hovering Craft and Hydrofoil — HSSC
High-Strength Materials. Proceedings of the Berkeley International Materials Conference — High Strength Mater Proc Berkeley Int Mater Conf
Highway — Highw
Highway and Heavy Construction — Highw Heavy Constr
Highway and Urban Mass Transportation — Hi Urb Mass Tran
Highway and Urban Mass Transportation [*United States*] — Highw Urban Mass Transp
Highway Engineer — Highw Eng
Highway Engineer — Highw Engr
Highway Engineer — Highway Engr
Highway Engineering in Australia — Highw Eng Aust
Highway Engineering in Australia — Highw Engng Aust
Highway Geology Symposium Proceedings — Highway Geol Symp Proc
Highway Research Abstracts — Highw Res Abstr
Highway Research Abstracts — HwyResAb
Highway Research Board. Bulletin — Highw Res Board Bull
Highway Research Board. Bulletin. Special Reports — Highw Res Board Bull Spec Rep
Highway Research Board. Highway Research Abstracts — Highw Res Board Highw Res Abstr
Highway Research Board. National Cooperative Highway Research Program. Report [*A publication*] — Highw Res Bd Nat Coop Highw Res Program Rep
Highway Research Board. National Cooperative Highway Research Program. Report [*A publication*] — Highw Res Board Natl Coop Highw Res Program
Highway Research Board. Proceedings of the Annual Meeting — Highw Res Board Proc Annu Meet
Highway Research Board. Special Report — Highw Res Board Spec Rep
Highway Research Bulletin [*India*] — Highw Res Bull
Highway Research Bulletin (New Delhi) — Highw Res Bull (New Delhi)
Highway Research Circular — Highw Res Circ
Highway Research Information Service [*Database*] — HRIS
Highway Research News — Highw Res News
Highway Research Record — Highw Res Rec
Highway Research Record — HIRRA
Highway Safety Literature Service [*Database*] — HSL
Highway Transport — Highw Transp
Highway Trust Fund. Annual Report — Highway Tr Fd Ann Rep
Highway User Quarterly — Highway User Q
Highway Vehicle Systems Contractors' Coordination Meeting. Proceedings — Highw Veh Syst Contract Coord Meet Proc
Highways and Public Works — Highw Publ Wks
Highways and Public Works — Highw Public Wks
Highways and Public Works — Highw Public Works
Highways and Road Construction — Highw Rd Constr
Highways and Road Construction — Highw Road Const
Highways and Road Construction — HWRCB
Highways and Road Construction International — Highw Road Constr Int
Highways and Transportation — Highws Transpn
Highways Design and Construction — Highw Des Constr
Highways of Traffic Engineering — Highw Traff Engng
Higiena, Epidemiologiya, i Mikrobiologiya — Hig Epidemiol Mikrobiol
Higiena i Sanitariya — Hig Sanit
Higiena i Zdraveopazvane — Hig Zdraveopaz
Higijena. Casopis za Higijenu, Mikrobiologiju, Epidemiologiju, i Sanitarnu Tehniku — Hig Cas Hig Mikrobiol Epidemiol Sanit
Hijo Prodigo — HP
Hikaku Kagaku [*Japan*] — HIKAA
Hikobia Journal of the Hiroshima Botanical Club — Hikobia J Hiroshima Bot Club
Hikone Ronso — HNR
Hileia Medica — HIMDD3
Hilfe fuers Amt — HfA
Hilfsbuecher fuer den Kirchlichen Unterricht — HKU
Hilgardia — HILGA
Hilgardia. A Journal of Agricultural Science — Hilgardia J Agric Sci
Hilgardia. California Agricultural Experiment Station — Hilgardia Calif Agric Exp Stn
Hilger Journal — Hilger J
Hillsdale Review — Hillsdale Rev
Hillside Journal of Clinical Psychiatry — Hillside J Clin Psychiatry
Hillside Journal of Clinical Psychiatry — HJCPDU
Himachal Journal of Agricultural Research — Himachal J Agric Res
Himalayan Chemical and Pharmaceutical Bulletin — Himalayan Chem Pharm Bull
Himalayan Geology — Himalayan Geol
Himalayan Journal — HmJ
Himalayan Journal. Records. Himalayan Club — Himalayan J
Himalayan Review — Himal R
Himmel und Erde — Himmel u Erde
Hindemith-Jahrbuch [*Annales Hindemith*] — Hindemith Jb
Hindi Review — Hindi R
Hindu Astronomical and Mathematical Text Series — Hindu Astronom Math Text Ser
Hindu Text Information — HTI
Hindu Weekly Review — HWR
Hindustan Antibiotics Bulletin — HINAA
Hindustan Antibiotics Bulletin — Hind Antibiot Bull
Hindustan Antibiotics Bulletin — Hindustan Antibiot Bull
Hindustan Review — Hindu R
Hindustan Review — Hindustan R
Hindustan Review — HR
Hinrichsen's Musical Year Book — HMYB
Hinyokika Kiyo [*Japan*] — HIKYA
Hippokrates — HIPPA
Hippologische Sammlung — HS
Hippologisk Tidsskrift — Hip T
Hiradastechnika [*Hungary*] — HIRAA
Hiradastechnika. Hiradastechnikai Tudomanyos Egyesulet Lapja — Hiradas-Tech
Hiradastechnikai Ipari Kutato Intezet Koezlemenyei — HIKI Koezl
Hiradastechnikai Ipari Kutato Intezet Koezlemenyei — Hiradastech Ipari Kut Intez Koezl
Hiradastechnikai Ipari Kutatointezet Koezlemenyei — Hiradastech Ipari Kutatointez Kozl
Hiram Poetry Review — Hiram Po R
Hirosaki Daigaku Nogakubu Gakujutsu Hokoku — HIROA
Hirosaki Igaku [*Japan*] — HIRIA
Hirosaki Medical Journal — Hirosaki Med J
Hiroshima Chemical Laboratory Report — Hiroshima Chem Lab Rep
Hiroshima Daigaku Bungakubu Kiyo — HiroBK
Hiroshima Daigaku Genbaku Hoshano Igaku Kenkyusho Nenpo — HDGHA
Hiroshima Daigaku Kogakubu Kenkyu Hokoku — HIDKA
Hiroshima Journal of Anesthesia — Hiroshima J Anesth
Hiroshima Journal of Medical Sciences — HIJMA
Hiroshima Journal of Medical Sciences — Hiros J Med
Hiroshima Journal of Medical Sciences — Hiroshima J M Sc
Hiroshima Journal of Medical Sciences — Hiroshima J Med Sci
Hiroshima Mathematical Journal — Hiroshima Math J
Hiroshima Medical Journal [*Japan*] — Hiroshima Med J
Hiroshima Studies in English Language and Literature — HSELL
Hiroshima University Geological Report — Hiroshima Univ Geol Rep
Hiroshima University Journal of Science. Series C. Geology and Mineralogy — Hiroshima Univ J Sci Ser C
Hispalis Medica — Hisp Med
Hispamerica — HARL
Hispamerica. Revista de Literatura — Hispam
Hispania — H
Hispania — Hi
Hispania — Hia
Hispania — His
Hispania [*Madrid*] — Hisp
Hispania — HS
Hispania Antiqua — HAnt
Hispania Antiqua Epigraphica — HA Ep
Hispania Antiqua Epigraphica — HA Epigr
Hispania Antiqua Epigraphica — HAE
Hispania Antiqua Epigraphica — Hisp Ant Epigr
Hispania Antiqua Epigraphica. Suplemento Anual de Archivo Espanol de Arqueologia — Hispania Ant Epigr
Hispania (Baltimore) — HBalt
Hispania (Madrid) — HiM
Hispania (Madrid) — HispM
Hispania (Madrid) — HMad
Hispania Sacra — Hisp Sac
Hispania Sacra — Hisp Sacra
Hispania Sacra — HS
Hispania (Stanford, California) — HCal
Hispania (Stanford, California) — HispCal
Hispania (University of Kansas. Lawrence) — HisK
Hispania (University of Kansas. Lawrence) — HisL
Hispania (USA) — HiUS
Hispanic — GHSP
Hispanic American Arts — HAA
Hispanic American Historical Review — HAHR
Hispanic American Historical Review — HiAH
Hispanic American Historical Review — His Am Hist Rev
Hispanic American Historical Review — Hisp Am Hist R
Hispanic American Historical Review — Hisp Amer Hist Rev
Hispanic American Historical Review — Hispan Am H
Hispanic American Historical Review — Hispan Am Hist R
Hispanic American Historical Review — Hispan Am Hist Rev
Hispanic American Historical Review — Hispanic Am His R
Hispanic American Historical Review — Hispanic Amer Hist Rev
Hispanic American Historical Review — PHAH
Hispanic American Historical Review (Durham, North Carolina) — Hisp Am Hist Rev Durham
Hispanic American Report — Hispan Am Rep
Hispanic American Report (Stanford, California) — Hisp Am Rept Stanford
Hispanic Americans Information Directory — HAID
Hispanic Business — Hispanic B
Hispanic Business — Hispanic Bus
Hispanic Health and Mental Health Data Base — HHMHDB
Hispanic Journal — HisJ
Hispanic Journal (Pennsylvania) — HJP
Hispanic Monitor — Hispan Mon
Hispanic Press Index — Hisp Press Ind
Hispanic Review — GHIR
Hispanic Review — HIR

Hispanic Review — Hisp Rev
Hispanic Review — Hispan R
Hispanic Review — Hispan Rev
Hispanic Review — HR
Hispanic Times — Hispan T
Hispanistische Studien — H Studien
Hispano-American Historical Review — Hispano Amer Hist Rev
Hispanoamericano — HA
Hispanofila [*Madrid*] — Hispano
Hispanofila [*Madrid and Illinois*] — Hispl
Hispanofila — HLE
HISS [*Herpetological Information Search Systems*] **News-Journal** — HISS News-J
Histochemical Journal — Histochem J
Histochemistry — Histochemis
Histochemistry and Cell Biology — Histochem Cell Biol
Histocompatibility Testing — Histocompat Test
Histoire. Academie Royale des Sciences. Avec les Memoires de Physique Tires des Registres de Cette Academie — Hist Acad Roy Sci Mem Phys
Histoire. Academie Royale des Sciences et Belles Lettres (Berlin) — Hist Acad Roy Sci Berlin
Histoire Ancienne de l'Afrique du Nord — HAAN
Histoire. Congregation de Saint-Maur — HCSM
Histoire de Constantinople Depuis le Regne de l'Ancien Justin Jusqua la fin de l'Empire — H Con
Histoire de la Democratie Chretienne — HDC
Histoire de la Spiritualite Chretienne — HSC
Histoire de l'Academie Royale des Sciences — Hist Acad Roy Sc
Histoire de l'Academie Royale des Sciences. Avec les Memoires de Mathematique and de Physique. In Duodecimo (Paris) — Hist Acad Roy Sci Mem Math Phys Paris 12
Histoire de l'Education (Paris) — Hist Educ Paris
Histoire de l'Eglise — HE
Histoire de Lorraine — Hist Lor
Histoire des Cinciles Oecumeniques — HCO
Histoire des Dioceses de France — HDF
Histoire des Dogmes — Hist Dog
Histoire des Idees et Critique Litteraire — HICL
Histoire des Relations Internationales — HRI
Histoire des Sciences Medicales — Hist Sci Med
Histoire des Sciences. Textes et Etudes — Hist Sci Textes Etudes
Histoire du Droit et des Institutions de l'Eglise en Occident — HDIEO
Histoire Ecclesiastique et Civile de Lorraine — HECL
Histoire, Economie et Societe — Hist Econ Soc
Histoire et Archeologie. Dossiers — Doss Arch
Histoire et Archeologie. Dossiers — Doss Archeologie
Histoire et Memoires. Academie Royale des Sciences, Inscriptions, et Belles Lettres de Toulouse — Hist Mem Acad Roy Sci Toulouse
Histoire et Memoires de la Societe des Sciences Physiques de Lausanne — Hist Mem Soc Sci Phys Lausanne
Histoire et Memoires. Institute de France — HMIF
Histoire et Nature. Cahiers de l'Association pour l'Histoire des Sciences de la Nature — Hist Nat
Histoire et Sociologie de l'Eglise — HSE
Histoire Generale des Religions — HGR
Histoire Litteraire de la France — HLF
Histoire Religieuse du Canada — HRC
Histoire Sociale/Social History — HieS
Histoire Sociale/Social History — Hist Soc
Histoire Universelle des Missions Catholiques — HUMC
Histology and Histopathology — Histol Histopathol
Histopathology [*Oxford*] — HISTDD
Historia [*Argentina*] — Hiet
Historia — HIH
Historia [*South Africa*] — His
Historia Agriculturae — Hist Ag
Historia Argentina — HISTA
Historia (Bogota) — Hist Bogota
Historia. Bratislava — Hist B
Historia (Buenos Aires) — Hist BA
Historia de Espana — HE
Historia de Espana — Hist Esp
Historia Ecclesiastica de Espana — Heė
Historia (France) — Hif
Historia Hospitalium. Mitteilungen der Deutschen Gesellschaft fuer Kranken-Hausgeschichte — Hist Hosp
Historia i Teoria Literatury-Studia — HTLStu
Historia. Instituto de Historia (Santiago, Chile) — Hist Santiago
Historia Judaica — Hist Jud
Historia Judaica — HJ
Historia Judaica — HJud
Historia Mathematica — Hist Math
Historia Mathematica — Historia Math
Historia Mathematica — HM
Historia Medicinae Veterinariae — Hist Med Vet
Historia Mexicana — H Mex
Historia Mexicana — HiM
Historia Mexicana — Hist Mex
Historia Mexicana — HM
Historia Mexicana. Colegio de Mexico — Hist Mexicana
Historia. Milano — Hist M
Historia Mundi — Mist Mun
Historia Numorum — HN
Historia Obrera. Centro de Estudios Historicos del Movimiento Obrero Mexicano — CEHSMO
Historia Paraguaya — HP
Historia Paraguaya (Asuncion) — Hist Paraguaya Asuncion
Historia (Paris) — HisP
Historia Religionum. Uppsala — HR U
Historia. Revue d'Histoire Ancienne — Hist
Historia (Rio Piedras, Puerto Rico) — Hist Rio Piedras
Historia Salutis [*Napoli*] — H Sal
Historia Salutis. Napoli. Serie Teologica — H Sal T
Historia Scientiarum — Historia Sci
Historia Scientiarum. International Journal. History of Science Society of Japan — Hist Scientiarum
Historia Scientiarum. Second Series — Historia Sci 2
Historia Societatis Jesu — HSJ
Historia. Wiesbaden — Hist
Historia. Zeitschrift fuer Alte Geschichte — Historia Z
Historia. Zeitschrift fuer Alte Geschichte — Historia Z Alt Gesch
Historia-Augusta-Colloquium [*Bonn*] — HAC
Historiallinen Aikakauskirja — HisA
Historiallinen Aikakauskirja/Historische Zeitschrift — Hist Aik
Historiallinen Arkisto — Hist Arkisto
Historiallinen Arkisto/Historisches Archiv — Hist Ark
Historiallisia Tutkimuksia/Historische Untersuchungen — Hist Tutk
Historiallisia Tutkimuksia. Suomen Historiallinen Seura — Hist Tutkimuksia
Historian — Hisn
Historian — Hist
Historian — Hn
Historian. A Journal of History — PHJH
Historians of India, Pakistan, and Ceylon [*Monograph*] — HIPC
Historic Brass Society Journal — Historic Brass J
Historic Brass Society Newsletter — HBSN
Historic Documents — Hist Doc
Historic Preservation — Hist Pres
Historic Preservation — Hist Preser
Historic Preservation — Hist Preservation
Historic Trials Series — Hi Tr S
Historica — Hist
Historica Iberica — HI
Historica. Praha — Hist P
Historical Abstracts [*Database*] — HA
Historical Abstracts — Hist Abstr
Historical Abstracts — HistAb
Historical Abstracts. Part A. Modern History Abstracts — Hist Abstr Part A Mod Hist Abstr
Historical Abstracts. Part B. Twentieth Century Abstracts — Hist Abstr Part B Twent Century Abstr
Historical and Linguistic Studies in Literature Related to the New Testament — HSLNT
Historical and Philosophical Society of Ohio. Bulletin — HPSO
Historical and Philosophical Society of Ohio. Quarterly Publications — Hist Philos Soc Ohio Q Publ
Historical and Scientific Society of Manitoba. Transactions — Hist Sc Soc Manit Tr
Historical Bulletin — HB
Historical Bulletin — Hist Bull
Historical Commentary on Thucydides — HCT
Historical Journal — Hist J
Historical Journal — Historical J
Historical Journal — HJ
Historical Journal — PHIJ
Historical Journal (Birmingham) — Hist Ju (Birmingham)
Historical Journal of Film, Radio, and Television — Hist J Film
Historical Journal of Film, Radio, and Television — Hist J FR & TV
Historical Journal of Film, Radio, and Television — Hist Jnl F R & TV
Historical Journal of Western Massachusetts — Hist J West Mass
Historical Magazine [*Dawson's*] — Hist M
Historical Magazine of the Protestant Episcopal Church — Hist Mag
Historical Magazine of the Protestant Episcopal Church — Hist Mag PE Ch
Historical Magazine of the Protestant Episcopal Church — Hist Mag Protest Episc Church
Historical Magazine of the Protestant Episcopal Church — HME
Historical Magazine of the Protestant Episcopal Church — HMPEC
Historical Magazine. Protestant Episcopal Church — Hist Mag Prot Epsc Ch
Historical Magazine. Protestant Episcopal Church — HistM
Historical Metallurgical Group. Bulletin — Hist Metall Group Bull
Historical Metallurgy — Hist Metall
Historical Methods — Hist Meth
Historical Methods Newsletter — Hist Methods Newsl
Historical New Hampshire — Hist NH
Historical New Hampshire — HistN
Historical New Hampshire — HNH
Historical News [*New Zealand*] — Hist News
Historical Outlook — His Outlook
Historical Outlook — Hist Outl
Historical Papers — Hist Pap
Historical Papers — Hist Papers
Historical Papers. Lancaster County Historical Society [*Pennsylvania*] — Pap Lanc Co Hist Soc
Historical Papers. Trinity College Historical Society — HPTCHS
Historical Performance — Historical Per
Historical Performance — HP
Historical Records and Studies — HRS
Historical Records of Australia — HRA
Historical Records of Australian Science — Hist Rec Aust Sci
Historical Records of New South Wales — HRNSW
Historical Records Survey — HRS
Historical Reflections. Directions Series — Hist Refl D

Historical Reflections/Reflexions Historiques — Hist Reflec
Historical Reflections/Reflexions Historiques — Hist Reflect
Historical Review (New Zealand) — Hist Rev
Historical Review of Berks County — HistRB
Historical Review of Berks County — HRBC
Historical Series. Canada Department of Agriculture — Hist Ser Can Dep Agric
Historical Series. Reformed Church in America — HSRCA
Historical Society of Montana. Contributions — Hist Soc Mont Contr
Historical Society of Pennsylvania. Archives — Hist Soc Pa Archives
Historical Society of Queensland. Journal — Hist Soc Q J
Historical Society of Queensland. Journal — Hist Soc Qld J
Historical Society of Queensland. Journal — J Hist Soc QD
Historical Society of Queensland. Journal — J Hist Soc Qld
Historical Society of Queensland. News Bulletin — Hist Soc Qld News
Historical Society of Southern California. Quarterly — HSSC
Historical Society of Southern California. Quarterly — HSSCQ
Historical Studies — H St
Historical Studies — Hist Stud
Historical Studies [*Australia*] — HistS
Historical Studies — HS
Historical Studies, Australia and New Zealand — HS
Historical Studies. Biographies — H St B
Historical Studies in the Physical and Biological Sciences — Hist Stud Phys Biol Sci
Historical Studies in the Physical Sciences — Hist Stud Phys Sci
Historical Studies in the Physical Sciences — HSPhS
Historical Studies. Monasteries and Convents — H St M
Historical Studies-Australia and New Zealand — Hist Stud
Historical Studies-Australia and New Zealand — Hist Stud Aust NZ
Historical Studies-Australia and New Zealand — Hist Stud Austral
Historical Studies-Australia and New Zealand — Hist Studies
Historical Wyoming — HW
Historiche Avonden. Uitgegeven door het Historiche Genootschap te Groningen ter Gelegenheid van Zijn Twintigjarig Bestaan — HAHGG
Historici Graeci Minores — HGM
Historicke Studie [*Bratislava*] — Hist St
Historicky Casopis — HC
Historicky Casopis — Hist Cas
Historicky Casopis — Hist Casopis
Historicorum Romanorum Reliquiae — Hist Rom Rel
Historicorum Romanorum Reliquiae — Hist Rom Reliquiae
Historicorum Romanorum Reliquiae — HR Rel
Historicorum Romanorum Reliquiae — HRR
Historielaerarnas Foerenings Aarskrift — Histt
Historielaerarnas Foerenings Aarsskrift — Hist-Laerar Foeren Arsskr
Historijski Zbornik — Hist Zbor
Historijski Zbornik — HZ
Historiografia y Bibliografia Americanistas — HBA
Historiografia y Bibliografia Americanistas. Escuela de Estudios Hispano-Americanos de Sevilla — EEHA/HBA
Historiographia Linguistica — Hist Ling
Historiographia Linguistica — Hist Linguist
Historiographia Linguistica — HistL
Historiographia Linguistica — HL
Historisch-Biographisches Lexikon der Schweiz — HBLS
Historische. Archiv fuer die Erzbistum Koeln — HAEK
Historische Bibliothek — HB
Historische Blaetter — H Bl
Historische Studien (Herausgegeben von Arndt) — HS A
Historische Vierteljahrschrift [*Leipzig*] — Hist Viertel
Historische Vierteljahrschrift — HV
Historische Vierteljahrschrift — HVJ
Historische Vierteljahrschrift — HVJS
Historische Vierteljahrsschrift — HistVjhrschr
Historische Vierteljahrsschrift — HVSchr
Historische Zeitschrift — Hist Z
Historische Zeitschrift — Hist Zeit
Historische Zeitschrift — Hist Zeitschr
Historische Zeitschrift — Hist Ztsch
Historische Zeitschrift — HiZ
Historische Zeitschrift — HZ
Historische Zeitschrift. Beiheft — HZB
Historische Zeitschrift. Sonderheft — HZS
Historischen Personennamen des Griechischen bis zur Kaiserzeit — HPG
Historischen Personennamen des Griechischen bis zur Kaiserzeit — HPN
Historischer Verein fuer die Grafschaft Ravensberg zu Bielefeld. Jahresberichte — Hist Ver f d Grafsch Ravensberg Jahresber
Historischer Verein fuer Mittelfranken. Jahresberichte — Hist Ver f Mittelfranken Jahresber
Historischer Verein fuer Oberpfalz und Regensburg. Verhandlungen — Hist Verein Oberpfalz & Regensburg Verh
Historischer Verein fuer Straubing und Umgebung — Hist Ver Straubing
Historisches Jahrbuch [*Muenster*] — Hist J
Historisches Jahrbuch — Hist Jahrb
Historisches Jahrbuch — Hist Jb
Historisches Jahrbuch — HistoJ
Historisches Jahrbuch — HJ
Historisches Jahrbuch [*Muenster*] — HJB
Historisches Jahrbuch der Goerresgesellschaft — HistJb
Historisches Jahrbuch der Stadt Graz — Hist Jb Graz
Historisches Jahrbuch der Stadt Graz — HJ Graz
Historisches Jahrbuch der Stadt Linz — Hist Jahrb Stadt Linz
Historisches Jahrbuch der Stadt Linz — HJ Linz
Historisches Literaturblatt — HLB
Historisches Taschenbuch — Hist Taschenb
Historisches Taschenbuch — HT
Historisches Woerterbuch der Philosophie — HWP
Historisch-Politische Blaetter fuer das Katholische Deutschland — HPB
Historisch-Politische Blaetter fuer das Katholische Deutschland — HPBKD
Historisch-Politische Blaetter fuer das Katholische Deutschland — HPBL
Historisch-Politisches Buch — HPB
Historisk Aarbog for Skive og Omegn — Skvb
Historisk Aarbog for Thisted Amt — H Aa Th
Historisk Samfund for Praesto Amt — Aarb Pr A
Historisk Tidskrift — Hist Tidskr
Historisk Tidskrift — Historick Tidskr
Historisk Tidskrift [*Finland*] — HistorTf
Historisk Tidskrift — HT
Historisk Tidskrift [*Stockholm*] — HTG
Historisk Tidskrift — HTK
Historisk Tidskrift foer Finland — Hist T Finl
Historisk Tidskrift foer Finland — Hist Tidskr Finl
Historisk Tidskrift foer Finland — HTF
Historisk Tidskrift foer Finland — HTsFi
Historisk Tidskrift foer Skaneland — HTS
Historisk Tidskrift (Oslo) — HTO
Historisk Tidskrift (Stockholm) — Hist T Stockholm
Historisk Tidskrift (Stockholm) — HTS
Historisk Tidskrift utgivet av Svensk Historisk Foerening — SHT
Historisk Tidsskrift — Hist Tidssk
Historisk Tidsskrift [*Sweden*] — HistorTs
Historisk Tidsskrift (Denmark) — HistorTd
Historisk Tidsskrift (Kopenhagen) — Hist T Kopenhagen
Historisk Tidsskrift. Norske Historiske Forening — HTN
Historisk Tidsskrift (Oslo) — Hist T Oslo
Historisk Tidsskrift. Svenska Historiska Foerening — HTS
Historisk Tidsskrift udgivet af det Danske Historiske Forening (Kobenhaven) — Hist Tidsskr Kobenh
Historiska Biblioteket — Hist Biblioth
Historiska Handlingar — Hist Handl
Historiska och Litteraturhistoriska Studier — Hist Litt Hist Stud
Historiska och Litteraturhistoriska Studier — HLS
Historiske Meddelelser om Staden Kobenhavn — HMSK
Historiske Meddelelser om Staden Kobenhavn og dens Borgere — Hist Medd Kobenhavn
Historiske Meddelelser om Staden Kobenhavn og dens Borgere — HM Kbh
Historiske Meddelelser om Staden Kobenhavn og dens Borgere — HMK
Historiske-Philologiske Meddelelser — Hist Philol Meddel
Historisk-Filosofiske Meddelelser. Dansk Videnskabernes Selskab — Dansk Vid Selsk
Historisk-Filosofiske Meddelelser Udgivet af det Kongelinge Danske Videnskabernes Selskab — HFM
Historisk-Filosofiske Meddelelser Udgivet af det Kongelinge Danske Videnskabernes Selskab — HFMKDVS
History — H
History — Hist
History and Philosophy of Logic — Hist Phil Logic
History and Philosophy of Logic — Hist Philos Logic
History and Philosophy of the Life Sciences — Hist Phil Life Sci
History and Philosophy of the Life Sciences (Pubblicazioni della Stazione Zoologica di Napoli. Section II) — Hist Philos Life Sci (Pubbl Stn Zool Napoli Sect II)
History and Philosophy of the Life Sciences. Pubblicazioni della Stazione Zoologica di Napoli. Section II — HPLSDO
History and Social Science Teacher — Hist Soc Sci Teach
History and Technology — Hist and Technol
History and Theory — H & T
History and Theory — H Th
History and Theory — Hist & T
History and Theory — Hist and Theory
History and Theory — Hist Theor
History and Theory — Hist Theory
History and Theory — PHNT
History. Berwickshire Naturalists' Club — Hist Berwickshire Natur Club
History. Berwickshire Naturalists' Club — Hist Berwickshire Naturalists Club
History in Africa — Hist Afr
History in Africa — Hist Africa
History in Christian Perspective — HCP
History (London) — Hist L
History of Anthropology Newsletter — Hist Anthropol Newslett
History of Biochemistry. Comprehensive Biochemistry — Hist Beiochem Compr Biochem
History of Childhood Quarterly — Hist Child Q
History of Childhood Quarterly — Hist Childhood Quart
History of Education — Hist Educ
History of Education Journal — HEJ
History of Education Journal — Hist Educ J
History of Education Journal — Hist Educ Jour
History of Education Quarterly — Hist Educ Q
History of Education Quarterly — Hist Educ Quart
History of Education Society Bulletin — Hist Educ Soc Bull
History of Education Society. Bulletin — History of Ed Soc Bull
History of European Ideas — Hist Eur Id
History of European Ideas — Hist Eur Ideas
History of European Ideas — Hist Euro Ideas
History of Higher Education Annual — Hist High Educ Annu
History of Ideas Newsletter — HINL
History of Ideas Series — HIS
History of Irish Catholicism — HIC
History of Learning and Science in Finland — Hist Learn Sci Finland

History of Logic — Hist Logic
History of Medicine — Hist Med
History of Medicine Series — His Med Ser
History of Medicine Series — Hist Med Ser
History of Medicine Series — HMSEDU
History of Modern Physics and Astronomy — Hist Modern Phys Astronom
History of Photography — Hist of Photogr
History of Photography — Hist Photo
History of Photography — Hist Photog
History of Photography — Hist Photogr
History of Political Economy — Hist Pol Ec
History of Political Economy — Hist Pol Econ
History of Political Economy — Hist Pol Economy
History of Political Economy — Hist Polit
History of Political Economy — Hist Polit Econ
History of Political Economy — HistoryP
History of Political Economy — HIT
History of Political Economy — HOPE
History of Political Economy — HPE
History of Political Economy — PHPE
History of Political Thought — Hist Pol Th
History of Political Thought — Hist Polit Thought
History of Religions — GHRL
History of Religions — H Rel
History of Religions — HiR
History of Religions — Hist Rel
History of Religions — Hist Relig
History of Religions — Hist Religions
History of Religions — HR
History of Science — Hist of Sci
History of Science — Hist Sci
History of Science in America. News and Views — Hist Sci Amer News Views
History of Science Series — Hist Sci Ser
History of Science Series — HSCSBW
History of Technology — Hist Technol
History of the Canadian West — HICW
History of the Canadian West — Hist Can W
History of the Ecumenical Movement — HEM
History of the English Church — HEC
History of the Freedom Movement — HFM
History of the Greek and Roman Theater — GRT
History of the Greek and Roman Theater — HGRT
History of Universities — Hist Univ
History Quarterly — His Q
History Review of New Books — HRN
History. Reviews of New Books — Hist R New Bk
History. Reviews of New Books — History Rev
History. Reviews of New Books — HRNB
History Teacher — Hist Tchr
History Teacher — Hist Teach
History Teachers Association of New South Wales. Newsletter — Hist Teach Assoc NSW Newsl
History Teacher's Magazine — His Teach M
History Teacher's Magazine — Hist Tchr Mag
History Teacher's Magazine — HTM
History. The Journal of the Historical Association — PHIS
History Today — GHIS
History Today — Hist Today
History Today — HistoT
History Today — HT
History Workshop — Hist Worksh
History Workshop — Hist Workshop
History Workshop — History
History Workshop Series — Hist Work S
Histria Archaeologica [*Pula*] — Histria A
Histria Archaeologica [*Pula*] — Histria Arch
Hitachi Metals Technical Review — Hitachi Met Tech Rev
Hitachi Review — Hitachi Rev
Hitachi Technology — Hitachi Technol
Hitachi Zosen Technical Review — Hitachi Zosen Tech Rev
Hititsubashi Review — HiR
Hitotsubashi Academy. Annals — AHA
Hitotsubashi Journal of Arts and Sciences — Hitotsubashi J Arts Sc
Hitotsubashi Journal of Arts and Sciences — Hitotsubashi J Arts Sci
Hitotsubashi Journal of Arts and Sciences — HJAS
Hitotsubashi Journal of Commerce and Management — Hitotsubashi J Com Manag
Hitotsubashi Journal of Commerce and Management — Hitotsubashi J Commer and Mgt
Hitotsubashi Journal of Commerce and Management — Hitotsubashi J Commer Manage
Hitotsubashi Journal of Commerce and Management — HJC
Hitotsubashi Journal of Economics — AHA
Hitotsubashi Journal of Economics — Hitots J Econ
Hitotsubashi Journal of Economics — Hitotsubashi J Econ
Hitotsubashi Journal of Economics — HJE
Hitotsubashi Journal of Law and Politics — Hitotsubashi J Law and Politics
Hitotsubashi Journal of Law and Politics — Hitotsubashi JL & Pol
Hitotsubashi Journal of Social Studies — Hitotsubashi J Soc Stud
Hitotsubashi Journal of Social Studies — Hitotsubashi J Social Studies
Hitotsubashi Journal of Social Studies — HJSS
Hitotsubashi Kenkyu — HitK
Hitotsubashi Ronso — HiR
Hitotsubashi University. Hitotsubashi Academy. Annals — HAA
Hittite Hieroglyphic Monuments — HHM
Hittite Hieroglyphs — HH
Hiyoshi Review of Natural Science — Hiyoshi Rev Natur Sci
Hjaelpskolan — Hjaelp
Hjalmar Bergman Samfundet Arsbok — HBSA
HLA and Disease Registry — HDREDU
HLA and Disease Registry — HLA Dis Regist
Hlas Revoluce — HR
HLH. Heizung, Lueftung, Klimatechnik, Haustechnik — HLHZA
HLH. Zeitschrift fuer Heizung, Lueftung, Klimatechnik, Haustechnik — H & L & H
HLH. Zeitschrift fuer Heizung, Lueftung, Klimatechnik, Haustechnik — HLH Heiz Lueft Klimatech Haustech
HLH. Zeitschrift fuer Heizung, Lueftung, Klimatechnik, Haustechnik — HLH (Heiz Luftung Klimatech Haustech)
HLH. Zeitschrift fuer Heizung, Lueftung, Klimatechnik, Haustechnik — HLH Z Heiz Lueft Klimatech Haustech
HLH. Zeitschrift fuer Heizung, Lueftung, Klimatechnik, Haustechnik — HLH Zeit Heizung Lueftung Klim Haustech
HMW [*Heilmittelwerke*] **Jahrbuch** — HMW Jb
HNO. Hals-, Nasen-, Ohren-Heilkunde — HNO
HNO: Wegweiser fuer die Fachaerztliche Praxis [*Later, HNO. Hals-, Nasen-, Ohren-Heilkunde*] — HNO Weg Fac
Ho Eranistes — HoE
Ho Neos Koubaras — HNK
Hoard's Dairyman — Hoard's D
Hoard's Dairyman — Hoards Dairym
Hobbies — Hob
Hobby Electronics — Hobby Electron
Hoch- und Tiefbau — H u T
Hoch- und Tiefbau — Hoch u Tiefbau
Hoch- und Tiefbau — HTB
Hochfrequenztechnik und Elektroakustik [*Germany*] — Hochfrequenztech Elektroakust
Hochkirche [*Charlottenburg, Germany*] — H Ki
Hochland — Hchl
Hochland — Hl
Hochland — Ho
Hochland — Hochl
Hochschulbuecher fuer Mathematik — Hochschulb Math
Hochschulbuecher fuer Physik — Hochschulb Phys
Hochschulbuecher fuer Physik — Hochschulbuecher fuer Phys
Hochschuldidaktik der Naturwissenschaften — Hochschuldidaktik Naturwiss
Hochschule fuer Architektur und Bauwesen Weimar. Wissenschaftliche Zeitschrift — Hochsch Archit Bauwes Weimar Wiss Z
Hochschule fuer Architektur und Bauwesen Weimar. Wissenschaftliche Zeitschrift. Reihe B — Hochsch Archit Bauwes Weimar Wiss Z Reihe B
Hochschullehrbuecher fuer Biologie — Hochschullehrb Biol
Hochschulnachrichten — Hn
Hochschulpolitische Informationen — HPI
HochschulSammlung Ingenieurwissenschaft Datenverarbeitung — HochschulSammlung Ingenieurwiss Datenverarbeitung
HochschulSammlung Naturwissenschaft Informatik — HochschulSammlung Naturwiss Informat
HochschulSammlung Naturwissenschaft Mathematik — HochschulSammlung Naturwiss Math
Hochschulwissen [*Prag*] — HschW
Hochschulwissen in Einzeldarstelungen — Hw
Hodder Christian Paperbacks — HCPB
Hodowla Roslin — Hodowla Rosl
Hodowla Roslin Aklimatyzacja i Nasiennictwo — Hodowla Rosl Aklim Nasienn
Hoefchen-Briefe fuer Wissenschaft und Praxis — Hoefchenbr Wiss Prax
Hoehenklima und Sein Einfluss auf den Menschen. Gedenkvorlesung — Hoehenklima Sein Einfluss Menschen Gedenkvorlesung
Hoehlankunde Wissenschaftliche Beihefte — Hoehle Wiss Beih
Hoehle Zeitschrift fuer Karst- und Hoehlenkunde — Hoehle Z Karst Hoehlenkunde
Hoelderlin-Jahrbuch — Hoe Jb
Hoelderlin-Jahrbuch — HoJb
Hoelderlin-Jahrbuch — Holderlin-Jahrb
Hoesch. Arbeitskreis Forschung und Entwicklung, Berichte aus Forschung und Entwicklung Unserer Werke — Hoesch Ber Forsch Entwickl Werke
Hoesch. Berichte aus Forschung und Entwicklung Unserer Werke — Hoesch Ber Forsch Entwickl Unserer Werke
Hofmannsthal Blaetter — HBL
Hofstra Law Review — Hof LR
Hofstra Law Review — Hofstra L Rev
Hofstra University. Yearbook of Business — Hofstra Univ Yrbk Bus
Hog Farm Management — Hog Farm Manage
Hog Production — Hog Prod
Hogaku Kenkyu — Hog Kenk
Hogarth Essays — Hogarth Ess
Hogen Kenkyu Nenpo — HKN
Hogg's Instructor — Hogg
Hohenheimer Arbeiten — Hohenheimer Arb
Hohenheimer Umwelttagung — Hohenheimer Umwelttag
Hoja (Costa Rica) — HCR
Hoja Divulgativa. Campo Agricola Experimental (Valle del Fuerte) — Hoja Divulgativa Campo Agric Exp (Valle Fuerte)
Hoja Tecnica INIA [*Instituto Nacional de Investigaciones Agrarias*] — Hoja Tec INIA
Hoja Tecnica. INIA (Instituto Nacional de Investigaciones Agrarias) (Spain) — Hoja Tec (Inst Nac Invest Agrar) (Spain)
Hoja Tisiologica — Hoj Tisiol
Hoja Tisiologica — Hoja Tisiol
Hojas Litararias — HLit
Hojas Universitarias (Bogota) — HJB

Hojskolebladet — HB
Hojskolebladet — Hojskolebl
Hojskolebladet. Tidende for Folkeoplysning — Hskbl
Hoken Butsuri — HOKBA
Hokkaido Daigaku Bungakubu Kiyo — HKDBK
Hokkaido Daigaku Juigaku Bu [*Japanese Journal of Veterinary Research*] — Hokk Daig Juig Bu
Hokkaido Daigaku Kogakubu Kenkyu Hokoku — HDKKA
Hokkaido Daigaku Nogakubu Enshurin Kenkyu Hokoku — HOKDA
Hokkaido Forest Products Research Institute. Monthly Reports — Hokkaido For Prod Res Inst Mon Rep
Hokkaido Forest Products Research Institute. Reports — Hokkaido Forest Prod Res Inst Rept
Hokkaido Geological Survey. Report — Hokkaido Geol Surv Rep
Hokkaido Journal of Medical Science — Hokkaido J Med Sci
Hokkaido Journal of Orthopedic and Traumatic Surgery — Hokkaido J Orthop & Trauma Surg
Hokkaido Journal of Orthopedic and Traumatic Surgery — HSGZA4
Hokkaido Journal of Public Health — Hokkaido J Public Health
Hokkaido Mathematical Journal — Hokkaido Math J
Hokkaido National Agricultural Experiment Station. Data — Hokkaido Natl Agric Exp Stn Data
Hokkaido National Agricultural Experiment Station. Report — Hokkaido Natl Agric Exp Stn Rep
Hokkaido National Agricultural Experiment Station. Soil Survey Report — Hokkaido Natl Agric Exp Stn Soil Surv Rep
Hokkaido National Agricultural Experiment Station. Soil Survey Report — HONKAY
Hokkaido University. Faculty of Science. Journal. Series 4. Geology and Mineralogy — Hokkaido Univ Fac Sci J Ser 4
Hokkaido University. Institute of Low Temperature Science. Low Temperature Science. Series A. Physical Sciences — Hokkaido Univ Inst Low Temp Sci Low Temp Sci Ser A Phys Sci
Hokkaido University. Medical Library Series — Hokkaido Univ Med Libr Ser
Hokkaido-Ritsu Kogyo Shikenjo Hokoku — HOKSA
Hokoku. Aichi-ken Ringyo Shikenjo — Hokoku Aichi-Ken Ringyo Shikenjo
Hokoku. Bulletin. Akita Fruit-Tree Experiment Station/Akita Kaju Shikenjo — Hokoku Bull Akita Fruit Tree Exp Stn/Akita Kaju Shikenjo
Hokoku. Bulletin. Chugoku National Agricultural Experiment Station. Series E. Environment Division — Hokoku Bull Chugoku Natl Agric Exp Stn Ser E Environ Div
Hokoku. Bulletin. Kagoshima Tobacco Experiment Station/Kagoshima Tabako Shikenjo — Hokoku Bull Kagoshima Tob Exp Stn/Kagoshima Tabako Shikenjo
Hokoku. Bulletin. National Institute of Agricultural Sciences. Series A. Physics and Statistics — Hokoku Bull Natl Inst Agric Sci Ser A Phys and Stat
Hokoku. Bulletin. Tohoku Daigaku Nogaku Kenkyujo — Hokoku Bull Tohoku Daigaku Nogaku Kenkyujo
Hokoku, Japan. Tabako Shikenjo Okayama/Bulletin. Okayama Tobacco Experiment Station — Hokoku Jap Tab Shikenjo Okayama/Bull Okayama Tob Exp Stn
Hokuriku Journal of Anesthesiology — Hokuriku J Anesthesiol
Hokuriku Journal of Public Health — Hokuriku J Public Health
Holarctic Ecology — HAEC
Holarctic Ecology — HOECD2
Holarctic Ecology — Holarct Ecol
Holarctic Ecology [*Denmark*] — Holarctic Ecol
Holbert Herald — Holbert H
Holborn Review — Holb Rev
Holdheims Monatsschrift fuer Handelsrecht und Bankwesen. Steuer- und Stempelfragen — HoldhM
Holdheims Monatsschrift fuer Handelsrecht und Bankwesen. Steuer- und Stempelfragen — Mschr Handelsr Bankw
Holistic Health Review — HHRV
Holland in South East Asia — HPI
Holland Info — Holld Info
Holland Quarterly — HFK
Holland Schweiz — HOY
Holland Shipbuilding [*Netherlands*] — Holland Shipbuild
Holland Shipbuilding — HOS
Holland Shipbuilding and Marine Engineering [*Later, Holland Shipbuilding*] — Holland Shipbuild
Holland's Export Magazine. Holland Shipping and Trading [*Rotterdam*] — HST
Hollands Maandblad — Hollands Maandbl
Hollandsch Landbouweekblad. Officieel Orgaan van de Hollandsche Maatschappij van Landbouw — Holl Landbouwweekbl
Hollandsch Weekblad — HW
Hollins Critic — HC
Hollins Critic — Hol Crit
Holloman Symposium on Primate Immunology and Molecular Genetics — Holloman Symp Primate Immunol Mol Genet
Hollow Section [*United Kingdom*] — Hollow Sec
Holly Newsletter. Holly Society of America — Holly Newslett
Holly Society Journal — Holly Soc J
Hollywood Quarterly — Hollywood Q
Holstein-Friesian World — Holstein World
Holy Blossom Men's Bulletin — HBMB
Holy Land Postal History — HLPH
Holy Name Monthly — Holy Name Mo
Holz als Roh- und Werkstoff — Holz Roh We
Holz als Roh- und Werkstoff — Holz Roh- Werkst
Holz als Roh- und Werkstoff — HRW
Holzchemische Industrie — Holzchem Ind
Holzforschung — Holzforsch
Holzforschung und Holzverwertung — H u H
Holzforschung und Holzverwertung — Holzf Holzv
Holzforschung und Holzverwertung — Holzf Holzverwert
Holzforschung und Holzverwertung — Holzforsch Holzverwert
Holz-Kurier — Holz Kur
Holztechnologie — Holztechnol
Holztechnologie — Htg
Holz-Zentralblatt — Holz Zbl
Holz-Zentralblatt — Holz Zentralbl
Holz-Zentralblatt. Unabhangiges Organ fuer die Forstwirtschaft und Holzwirtschaft — HOD
Hombre y Cultura — HC
Hombre y Cultura — Hombre y Cult
Hombres de la Ciencia y Tecnica — Hombres Ci Tec
Home — GHOM
Home and Auto Buyer Guide — Home Auto
Home and Foreign Fields — Home For Fields
Home and Foreign Review — Ho & For R
Home and Garden Bulletin. US Department of Agriculture — Home Gard Bull US Dep Agric
Home and Garden Bulletins — Home Gdn Bull
Home Builders Journal — Home Build Jnl
Home Computer News — Home Com N
Home Economics Bulletin — Home Ec Bul
Home Economics Guide GH. University of Missouri-Columbia. Cooperative Extension Service — Home Econ Guide GH Univ Mo Columbia Coop Ext Serv
Home Economics Information. Kern County. Cooperative Extension. University of California — Home Econ Inf Kern Cty Coop Ext Univ Calif
Home Economics News — Home Econ News
Home Economics Newsletter — Home Econ Newsl
Home Economics. North Carolina Agricultural Extension Service — Home Econ NC Agric Ext Serv
Home Economics Research Journal — HERJ
Home Economics Research Journal — Home Econ Res J
Home Energy Digest and Wood Burning Quarterly — Home Energy Dig Wood Burn Q
Home Fitness and Equipment — Home Fit Equip
Home Garden [*Later, Family Handyman*] — Home Gard
Home Geographic Monthly — Home Geog Mo
Home Geographic Monthly — Home Geogr Mon
Home Health Care Services Quarterly — Home Health Care Serv Q
Home Health Journal — Home Health J
Home Health Review — Home Health Rev
Home Healthcare Nurse — Home Healthc Nurse
Home Improvements Journal — Home Improvements Jnl
Home Mechanix — GHMX
Home Office Library Bulletin — Home Off Lib Bull
Home Office Research Bulletin — Home Off Res Bull
Home Progress — Home Prog
Home Satellite Newsletter — Home Sat Newsl
Home Science — Home Sci
Home Techniques — Home Tech
Home University Library of Modern Knowledge — HULMK
Home Video Publisher — Home Video
Homemakers' Magazine — Home Mag
Homenagem a D. Luis de Hoyos Sainz — HLHS
Homenagem a Fritz Krueger — HFK
Homenagem a Martins Sarmento — HMS
Homenaje a Menendez Pidal — HMP
Home-Office Computing [*Formerly, Family and Home-Office Computing*] — GFHC
Homeowner — GHMR
Homes International — Homes Int
Homicide Statistcs — Homicide Stat
Homilectica et Biblica — He B
Homiletic and Pastoral Review — Hom Past Rev
Homiletic and Pastoral Review — HPR
Homiletic Review — Hom R
Homiletic Review — Homiletic R
Homiletics — Hom
Homines — HUI
Homme et l'Oiseau — Homme Oiseau
Homme et Societe — Homme et Soc
Homme et Societe — Homme Soc
Homme Prehistorique [*Paris*] — Homme Preh
Homme. Revue Francaise d'Anthropologie. La Sorbonne, l'Ecole Pratique des Hautes Etudes — EPHE/H
Hommes d'Outre-Mer — Homm O-Mer
Hommes et Migrations — Hommes et Migr
Hommes et Migrations. Documents — Hommes et Migr Doc
Hommes et Mondes — H & M
Hommes et Mondes — HeM
Hommes et Mondes — HM
Hommes et Mondes — Hom
Hommes et Techniques — Homm Techn
Hommes et Techniques — Hommes et Techn
Hommes et Techniques — Hommes Tech
Homo Dei — HD
Homoeopathic Digest — Homoeopath
Homogeneous Catalysis in Organic and Inorganic Chemistry — Homogeneous Catal Org Inorg Chem
Honam Mathematical Journal — Honam Math J
Honar va Mardom — HvM
Honda Memorial Series on Materials Science — Honda Meml Ser Mater Sci
Honduras Literaria (Tegucigalpa) — Hond Lit Tegucigalpa
Honduras Rotaria (Tegucigalpa) — Hond Rotar Tegucigalpa
Honest Ulsterman — Hon Ulst
Honeybee Science — Honeybee Sci

Honeywell Computer Journal — Honeywell Comput J
Hong Kong Economic Papers — HEP
Hong Kong Economic Papers — HK Econ Pap
Hong Kong Engineer — Hong Kong Eng
Hong Kong Engineer — Hong Kong Engr
Hong Kong Enterprise — TBU
Hong Kong Law Review — HK Law R
Hong Kong Nursing Journal — Hong Kong Nurs J
Hong Kong University. Fisheries Journal — Hong Kong Univ Fish J
Hongik University. Journal [*Republic of Korea*] — Hongik Univ J
Honolulu Advertiser — Honolulu Ad
Honourable Society of Cymmrodorion. Transactions — Cym Trans
Hoofs and Horns — H & H
Hooker's Icones Plantarum. Or Figures, with Brief Descriptive Characters and Remarks of New or Rare Plants — Hookers Icon Pl
Hoosier Folklore — HF
Hoosier Folklore Bulletin — HFB
Hoosier School Libraries — Hoosier Sch Lib
Hope Reports Quarterly — Hope Rep Q
Hopei Agricultural and Forestry Journal/Hopei Nung-Lin Hsueeh-K'an — Hopei Agric Forest J
Hopfen Rundschau — Hopf Rdsch
Hopital — Hop
Hopital Belge — Hop Belge
Hopital d'Aujourd'hui — Hop Aujourd
Hopital et l'Aide Sociale a Paris — Hop Aide Soc Par
Hopkins Quarterly — Hopkins Q
Hopkins Quarterly — HopQ
Hopkins Quarterly — HQ
Hopkins Research Bulletin — HRB
Hopkins Review — Hop R
Hoppe-Seyler's Zeitschrift fuer Physiologische Chemie — Ho Sey Zs
Hoppe-Seyler's Zeitschrift fuer Physiologische Chemie — Hoppe-Seyler's Z Physiol Chem
Hoppe-Seyler's Zeitschrift fuer Physiologische Chemie — Hoppe-Seylers Zs
Hoppe-Seyler's Zeitschrift fuer Physiologische Chemie — Hoppe-Seyler's Ztschr Physiol Chem
Hoppe-Seyler's Zeitschrift fuer Physiologische Chemie — H-S Z Physl
HO-Purdue University. Cooperative Extension Service — HO Purdue Univ Coop Ext Serv
Hora de Poesia — HdP
Hora Medica — Hora Med
Horae Semiticae — H Sem
Horae Soederblomianae — H Soed
Horeca — HRC
Horeca Info — HCR
Horitsu Shinbun — Shinbun
Horizon — GHOR
Horizon — Hor
Horizon — Hrzn
Horizon France Libre — HFrL
Horizons — HORI
Horizons — Horiz
Horizons — HVU
Horizons in Biblical Theology — Horizons Bib Th
Horizons in Biochemistry and Biophysics — Horiz Biochem Biophys
Horizons in Biochemistry and Biophysics — HZBBA
Horizons in Endocrinology — Horiz Endocrinol
Horizons Unlimited — Horiz Unltd
Horizonte. Emuna — Hor
Horizontes Economicos (Buenos Aires) — Horizon Econ BA
Horizontes. Mexico — HORM
Horizontes (Ponce, Puerto Rico) — Horizon Ponce
Horizontes (Puerto Rico) — HPR
Hormel Institute. University of Minnesota. Annual Report — Hormel Inst Univ Minn Annu Rep
Hormon- und Stoffwechselforschung — Horm Stoffwechselforsch
Hormonal Factors in Fertility, Infertility, and Contraception. Proceedings. Meeting. International Study Group for Steroid Hormones — Horm Factors Fertil Infertil Contracept Proc Meet
Hormonal Steroids. Proceedings of the International Congress on Hormonal Steroids — Horm Steroids Proc Int Congr
Hormone and Metabolic Research — Horm Metab Res
Hormone and Metabolic Research — Hormone Met
Hormone and Metabolic Research/Hormon- und Stoffwechselforschung/ Hormones et Metabolisme — Horm Metab Res Horm Stoffwechselforsch Horm Metab
Hormone and Metabolic Research (Supplement) — Horm Metab Res (Suppl)
Hormone and Metabolic Research. Supplement Series — Horm Metab Res Suppl Ser
Hormone Frontier in Gynecology — Horm Front Gynecol
Hormone Perception and Signal Transduction in Animals and Plants — Horm Percept Signal Transduction Anim Plants
Hormone Receptors — Horm Recept
Hormone Research — Horm Res
Hormone Research — Hormone Res
Hormone Research (Basel) — Horm Res (Basel)
Hormones and Behavior — Horm Behav
Hormones and Behavior — Hormone Beh
Hormones and Cancer. Selected Papers and Discussion from the Clinical Cancer Seminar — Horm Cancer Sel Pap Discuss Clin Cancer Semin
Hormones and Cell Regulation — Horm Cell Regul
Hormones and Immunity. Proceedings of the International Conference on Hormones and Immunity — Horm Immun Proc Int Conf
Hormones et Metabolisme — Horm Metab
Horn Book — HB
Horn Book — IHBO
Horn Book Magazine — Horn Bk
Horn Call — HC
Horn of Africa — Horn Afr
Hornicky Vestnik — Horn Vestn
Hornicky Vestnik a Hornicke a Hutnicke Listy — Horn Vestn a Hornicke a Hutnicke Listy
Hornik a Hutnik — Horn Hutn
Horological Institute of America. Journal — Horol Inst Am J
Horological Journal — Horol J
Horse and Rider — GHNR
Horseman — GHRS
Horseman's Abstracts — HorsAb
Horsemen's Journal — GHOJ
Horticulteur Chalonnais — Hort Chalonnais
Horticulteur Francais. Journal des Amateurs et des Interets Horticoles — Horticulteur Franc
Horticulteur Praticien — Hort Praticien
Horticulteur Provencal — Hort Provencal
Horticultura — Hort
Horticultural Abstracts — Hort Abstr
Horticultural Abstracts — Hortic Abstr
Horticultural Advance — Hortic Adv
Horticultural Advance (Sahranpur) — Hortic Adv (Sahranpur)
Horticultural and Viticultural Sciences (Sofia) — Hortic Vitic Sci (Sofia)
Horticultural Bulletin — Hortic Bull
Horticultural Centre Loughgall. Annual Report — Hortic Cent Loughgall Annu Rep
Horticultural Division of Tokai Kinki Agricultural Experiment Station. Reports — Hortic Div Tokai Kinki Agric Exp Stn Rep
Horticultural Education Association. Yearbook — Hortic Educ Assoc Yearb
Horticultural Journal, and Florists' Register, of Useful Information Connected with Floriculture — Hort J Florists Reg
Horticultural Journal and Royal Lady's Magazine — Hort J Roy Ladys Mag
Horticultural Machinery Leaflet — Hort Mach Leafl
Horticultural News — Hort N
Horticultural News. New Jersey State Horticultural Society — Hortic News NJ State Hortic Soc
Horticultural Plan Breeding — Hort Pl Breed
Horticultural Products Review FHORT. US Department of Agriculture. Foreign Agricultural Service — Hortic Prod Rev FHORT US Dep Agric Foreign Agric Serv
Horticultural Register, and General Magazine — Hort Reg Gen Mag
Horticultural Research — Hort Res
Horticultural Research — Hortic Res
Horticultural Research (Edinburgh) — Hort Res (Edinb)
Horticultural Research Institute of Ontario. Report — Hortic Res Inst Ont Rep
Horticultural Research Record. New South Wales Department of Agriculture. Division of Horticulture — Hort Res Rec
Horticultural Review and Botanical Magazine — Hort Rev Bot Mag
Horticultural Reviews — Hortic Rev
Horticultural Science (Calcutta) — Hortic Sci (Calcutta)
Horticultural Science (Stuttgart) — Hortic Sci (Stuttg)
Horticultural Times/Engei Tsushin (Kanagawa) — Hort Times Kanagawa
Horticulture — GHTC
Horticulture — Hort
Horticulture Alsacienne — Hort Alsac
Horticulture and Special Crops — Hortic Spec Crops
Horticulture Digest. University of Hawaii. Cooperative Extension Service — Hortic Dig Univ Hawaii Coop Ext Serv
Horticulture Francaise — Hortic Fr
Horticulture Genevoise. Societe d'Horticulture de Geneve — Hort Genev
Horticulture in New Zealand — Hortic NZ
Horticulture Industry — Hortic Ind
Horticulture Industry — Horticulture Ind
Horticulture News — Hort
Horticulture Tropicale. Taiwan Horticultural Society — Hort Trop
Horticulturist and Journal of Rural Art and Rural Taste — Hort J Rural Art Rural Taste
HortScience — HortSci
Hortus Musicus — HM
Horyzonty — Hor
Hoshasen Kagaku. Appendix [*Japan*] — Hoshasen Kagaku Append
Hoshasen Seibutsu Kenkyu — HSKEA
Hosiery Statistics — Hosiery St
Hosiery Trade Journal — Hosiery Trade J
Hospice Journal — Hosp J
Hospice Journal — Hospice J
Hospitais Portugueses — Hosp Port
Hospital — Hosp
Hospital Abstract Service — Hosp Abstr Serv
Hospital Abstracts — HospAb
Hospital Abstracts — Hospit Abstr
Hospital Administration — Hospital Admin
Hospital Administration (Chicago) — Hosp Adm (Chicago)
Hospital Administration Currents — Hosp Admin Curr
Hospital Administration in Canada — Hosp Adm Can
Hospital Administration (New Delhi) — Hosp Adm (New Delhi)
Hospital Admitting Monthly — Hosp Admitting Mon
Hospital and Community Psychiatry — H and CP
Hospital and Community Psychiatry — Hosp Comm Psych
Hospital and Community Psychiatry — Hosp Commun
Hospital and Community Psychiatry — Hosp Community Psychiat
Hospital and Community Psychiatry — Hosp Community Psychiatr

Hospital and Community Psychiatry — Hosp Community Psychiatry
Hospital and Community Psychiatry — HSCPA
Hospital and Health Management — Hosp Hlth Man
Hospital and Health Services Administration — HHS
Hospital and Health Services Administration — Hosp and Health
Hospital and Health Services Administration — Hosp Health Serv Adm
Hospital and Health Services Administration — Hosp Health Serv Admin
Hospital and Health Services Review — Hosp Health Serv Rev
Hospital Bond Review — Hosp Bond Rev
Hospital Building Bulletin — Hosp Build Bull
Hospital Buyer — Hosp Buyer
Hospital Buyer's Guide — HBG
Hospital Buyer's Guide — Hosp Buyers Guide
Hospital Capital Finance (Chicago) — Hosp Cap Finance (Chicago)
Hospital Care — Hosp Care
Hospital Central Militar (Lomas De Sotelo, Mexico). Publicacion Trimestral — Hosp Cent Mil (Lomas De Sotelo Mex) Publ Trimest
Hospital Colonia. Revista Medica — Hosp Colon Rev Med
Hospital de Hoje — Hosp Hoje
Hospital del Vina Del Mar. Boletin Trimestral — Hosp Vina Del Mar Bol Trimest
Hospital del Vina Del Mar. Publicacion Trimestral — Hosp Vina Del Mar Publ Trimest
Hospital Development — Hosp Dev
Hospital Development — Hosp Develop
Hospital Digest and Buyer — Hosp Dig Buyer
Hospital dos Servidores do Estado. Revista Medica — Hosp Servidores Estado Rev Med
Hospital Employee Health — Hosp Employee Health
Hospital Engineering — Hosp Eng
Hospital Equipment and Supplies — Hosp Equip Supplies
Hospital Financial Management — Hosp Fin Mgt
Hospital Financial Management — Hosp Finan Manage
Hospital Financial Management — Hosp Financ Manage
Hospital Food and Nutrition Focus — Hosp Food Nutr Focus
Hospital for Joint Diseases. Bulletin — Hosp Jt Dis Bull
Hospital Formulary — Hosp Formul
Hospital Formulary Management — Hosp Formul Manage
Hospital Forum — Hosp Forum
Hospital General (Madrid) — Hosp Gen (Madr)
Hospital General. Revista de Medicina y Cirugia — Hosp Gen
Hospital Geral de Santo Antonio-Porto. Boletim — Hosp Geral Santo Antonio Porto Bol
Hospital Gift Shop Management — Hosp Gift Shop Manage
Hospital Health Care Newsletter — Hosp Health Care Newsl
Hospital Highlights — Hosp High
Hospital Infection Control — Hosp Infect Control
Hospital In-Patient Statistics. Western Australia — Hosp Inpat Stat West Aust
Hospital International — Hosp Int
Hospital Italiano de La Plata. Revista Medica — Hosp Ital La Plata Rev Med
Hospital Law Newsletter — Hosp Law Newsletter
Hospital Libraries — Hosp Libr
Hospital Literature Index — HLI
Hospital Literature Index — Hosp Lit Ind
Hospital Literature Index — Hospit Lit Index
Hospital Magazine — Hospital Mag
Hospital Management — Hosp Manag
Hospital Management Communications — Hosp Manage Commun
Hospital Management Quarterly — Hosp Manage Q
Hospital Management Review — Hospit Manage Rev
Hospital Manager — Hosp Manager
Hospital Materials Management — Hosp Mater Manage
Hospital Materiel Management Quarterly — Hosp Mater Manage Q
Hospital Medical Staff — Hosp Med Staff
Hospital Medical Staff Advocate — Hosp Med Staff Advocate
Hospital Medicine — Hosp Med
Hospital Music Newsletter — Hospital Mus News
Hospital Peer Review — Hosp Peer Rev
Hospital Pharmacist — Hosp Pharm
Hospital Pharmacist (Saskatoon, Saskatchewan) — Hosp Pharm (Saskatoon Sask)
Hospital Pharmacy — Hosp Pharm
Hospital Physician — Hosp Physician
Hospital Planning — Hosp Plan
Hospital Practice — Hosp Pract
Hospital Practice — Hosp Practice
Hospital Practice. Office Edition — Hosp Pract Off Ed
Hospital Progress — Hosp Prog
Hospital Progress — Hosp Progr
Hospital Purchasing Management — Hosp Purch Manage
Hospital (Rio De Janeiro) — Hospital (Rio De J)
Hospital Risk Management — Hosp Risk Manage
Hospital Security and Safety Management — Hosp Secur Saf Manage
Hospital Social Service — Hosp Social Serv
Hospital Statistics. American Hospital Association — AHA Stat
Hospital Supervision — Hosp Superv
Hospital Supervisors Bulletin — Hosp Superv Bull
Hospital Technology Series — Hosp Technol Ser
Hospital Therapeutics — Hosp Ther
Hospital Topics — Hosp Top
Hospital Topics — HOTOA
Hospital Topics and Buyer — Hosp Top Buyer
Hospital Tribune — Hosp Trib
Hospital Trustee — Hosp Trustee
Hospital Week — Hosp Week
Hospital-Hygiene — Hosp-Hyg
Hospital-Hygiene, Gesundheitswesen, und Desinfektion — Hosp Hyg Gesundheitswes Desinfekt
Hospitalia — Hosp
Hospitalis — Hosp
Hospitality — Hos
Hospitality — Hosp
Hospitality Educator — Hospitality Educ
Hospitality Management — HM
Hospitality Yukon. Yukon Visitors Association — HOYU
Hospitals — HOSIA
Hospitals — Hosp
Hospitals — HSP
Hospitals and Health Networks — Hosp Health Netw
Hospitals' Association. Journal — Hosp Assoc J
Hospitium Ecclesiae — Hos Ec
Hospodarsky Zpravodaj — Hospos Zpr
Host Defense — Host Def
Hot Isostatic Pressing. Theory and Applications. Proceedings. International Conference — Hot Isostatic Pressing Theory Appl Proc Int Conf
Hot Laboratories and Equipment Conference. Proceedings — Hot Lab Equip Conf Proc
Hot Rod — IHRO
Hotel and Catering Review — HCR
Hotel and Motel Management — H & M Mgmt
Hotel and Motel Management — HMM
Hotel and Motel Management — Hotel & Motel Mgt
Hotel and Motel Management — Hotel Motel Manage
Hotel Gazette of South Australia — Hotel Gaz SA
Hotel Revue. Beroepstijdschrift op Managementniveau — HTL
Hotel Revue. Wochenzeitung fuer Hotellerie und Tourismus — SHR
Hotelgewerbe und Gastgewerbe Rundschau. Unabhangiges Fachorgan fuer Gastronomie, Betriebstechnische, und Kuhltechnische Praxis und Gemeinschaftsverpflegung — HGG
Hotels and Restaurants International — H & RI
Hotels and Restaurants International — Hotel Rest
Hotels and Restaurants International — SWW
Houches. Ecole d'Ete de Physique Theoretique — Houches Ec Ete Phys Theor
Houille Blanche — Houil Blanc
Houille Blanche — Houille Bl
HO-University of Kentucky. College of Agriculture. Cooperative Extension Service — HO Univ KY Coll Agr Coop Ext Serv
House and Garden — GHNG
House and Garden — H & G
House and Garden — House & G
House and Garden — House & Gard
House and Garden — Hse and Garden
House and Garden Building Guide [*United States*] — House Garden Build Guide
House and Home — H & Home
House Beautiful — GHBE
House Beautiful — House B
House Beautiful's Gardening and Outdoor Living [*United States*] — House Beautiful's Gard Outdoor Living
House Builder — House Bldr
House Builder — Hse Builder
House of Lords. Select Committee on the European Communities. Reports — Hse of Lords Select Commit Eur Commun Rep
Household and Personal Products Industry — Household
Household and Personal Products Industry — Household Pers Prod Ind
Household Words — House Words
Householder Commentaries — Hous Com
Housesmiths Journal — Housesmith Jnl
Housing Abstracts — Housing Abs
Housing and Construction Technical Bulletin — Housing & Constr Tech Bull
Housing and Development Reporter. Bureau of National Affairs — Hous & Dev Rep BNA
Housing and Planning References — Housing and Planning Refs
Housing and Planning References — Housing Plann Refs
Housing and Planning References — HousP
Housing and Planning Review — Housing Plann Rev
Housing and Society — Housing Soc
Housing and Urban Development Trends — Hous Urb Dev Tr
Housing, Building, and Planning — Hous Build Pl
Housing Europe — Housing Eur
Housing Finance Review — HFE
Housing Finance Review — Housing Fin R
Housing Finance Review — Housing Fin Rev
Housing Industry, 1980-2000 — Housing 80
Housing Magazine — Housing Mag
Housing Monthly — Housing Mo
Housing Monthly — Housing Mthly
Housing Research Papers — Hous Res Pap
Housing Review — Housing Rev
Housman Society. Journal — HSJ
Houston Business Journal — Houston BJ
Houston Chronicle — Houstn Chr
Houston Geological Society. Bulletin — Houston Geol Soc Bull
Houston Journal of International Law [*Also, an information service or system*] — HJIL
Houston Journal of International Law — Hou J Intl L
Houston Journal of International Law — Hous J Intl L
Houston Journal of International Law — Houston J Int'l L
Houston Journal of Mathematics — Houston J M
Houston Journal of Mathematics — Houston J Math
Houston Law Review — Hou LR
Houston Law Review — Hous L Rev

Houston Law Review — Houst L Rev
Houston Law Review — Houston L Rev
Houston Law Review — Houston Law
Houston Law Review — HUL
Houston Living — Houston Liv
Houston Magazine — Houstn Mag
Houston Magazine — Houston Mag
Houston Symphony. Program Notes — Houston Sym
Houthandel en Houtnijverheid. Algemeen Vakblad voor de Houthandel en de Houtnijverheid — HHN
Houtim — HUTMA
Houtinstituut TNO. Circulaire — Houtinst TNO Circ
Houtwereld Vakblad Gewijd aan de Belangen van de Houthandel en van de Houtverwerkende Industrie — HOH
Hovercraft World — Hovercr Wld
Hovering Craft and Hydrofoil — HCHY
Hovering Craft and Hydrofoil — Hov Craft Hydrof
How to Evaluate Health Programs — How Eval Health Programs
Howaldtswerke Deutsche Werft. Aktiengesellschaft. Hamburg und Kiel. Werkzeitung — HDW Werkztg
Howard Journal of Penology and Crime Prevention — How J Pen
Howard Journal of Penology and Crime Prevention — Howard J Penology Crime Prev
Howard Journal of Penology and Crime Prevention — Howard Journal
Howard Law Journal — How Law J
Howard Law Journal — How LJ
Howard Law Journal — Howard L J
Howard Law Journal — Howard Law J
Howard Review — Howard R
Howard Ruff's Financial Success Report — Ruff Fin Suc Rep
Howard University Record — Howard Univ Rec
Howard University Reviews of Science — Howard Univ Rev Sci
Howard University Studies in History — Howard Univ Stud Hist
Howitt's Journal — Howitt
HP [*Heilpraktiker*] **Journal** — HPJ
HP [*Hewlett-Packard*] **Journal** — HPJ
HP [*Heilpraktiker*] **Kurier** — HP Kurier
HPA [*Hospital Physicists Association*] **Bulletin** [*England*] — HPA Bull
HPB Surgery — HPB Surg
HPLC (High Performance Liquid Chromatography) in the Pharmaceutical Industry — HPLC Pharm Ind
HPN. Hospital Purchasing News — HPN Hosp Purch News
HRAF [*Human Relations Area Files*] **Newsletter** — HRAF Newsl
Hrana i Ishrana — Hrana Ishr
HRC. Journal of High Resolution Chromatography — HRC J High
HRC. Journal of High Resolution Chromatography — HRC J High Resolut Chromatogr
HRF [*National College for Heating, Ventilating, Refrigeration, and Fan Engineering*] **Bulletin** — HRF Bull
HRIN [*Human Resource Information Network*] **Special Reports Library** [*Database*] — SRL
Hristianskoe Ctenie — HC
HRLSD [*Health and Rehabilitative Library Services Division*] **Journal** — HRLSD J
Hrvatska Revija — HR
Hrvatski Dijalektoloski Zbornik — HDZ
Hrvatski Dijalektoloski Zbornik — HDZb
Hrvatski Geografski Glasnik — Hrv Geogr Glasn
Hrvatsko Kolo — HK
Hrvatsko Kolo — Hrv Kolo
HSI. Hungarian Scientific Instruments — HSI Hung Sci Instrum
Hsien-Tai Fo-Hsueh — HFH
Hsin-Ya Shu-Yuan Hsueh-Shy Nien-K'an — HYHN
HSL [*Health and Safety Executive Library*] **Abstract** [*England*] — HSL Abs
HSMHA [*Health Services and Mental Health Administration*] **Health Report** — HSHRA
HSMHA [*Health Services and Mental Health Administration*] **Health Report** — HSMHA Health Rep
HSRI (Highway Safety Research Institute) Research Review — HSRI (High Saf Res Inst) Res Rev
HSRI [*Highway Safety Research Institute*] **Report** — HSRI Rep
HSRI [*Highway Safety Research Institute*] **Research Review** — HSRI Res Rev
HSTC [*History of Canadian Sciences, Technology, and Medicine*] **Bulletin** — HSTC Bull
Hsueh Tsung Quarterly — HTQ
Hua Hsueh [*Taiwan*] — HUSHA
Hua Hsueh Hsueh Pao — HHHPA
Hua Hsueh Shih Chieh — HUAKA
Hua Hsueh Tung Pao [*China*] — HHTPA
Hua-T'ung Normal University Journal. Natural Science Series/Hua-T'ung Shih ta Hsueeh Pao. Tzu Jan K'o Hsueeh — Hua Tung Norm Univ J Nat Sci Ser
Hub. Hay River — HB
Huber Law Survey — Huber Law Surv
HUD [*Department of Housing and Urban Development*] **Challenge** — HUD Chal
HUD [*Department of Housing and Urban Development*] **International Bulletin** — HUD Intl Bull
HUD [*Department of Housing and Urban Development*] **International Information Series** — HUD Intl Information Series
HUD [*Department of Housing and Urban Development*] **Newsletter** — HNL
HUD [*Department of Housing and Urban Development*] **Newsletter** — HUD News
HUD [*US Department of Housing and Urban Development*] **Newsletter** — HUD Newsl
Hudebni Nastroje — Hud Nastroje
Hudebni Revue — H R
Hudebni Rozhledy — H Ro
Hudebni Rozhledy — Hud R
Hudebni Rozhledy — Hud Rozhl
Hudebni Veda — Hud Veda
Hudebni Veda — HV
HudebXXX Veda — HV
Hudeiba Research Station. Annual Report — Hudeiba Res Stn Annu Rep
Hudobny Zivot — Hud Zivot
Hudrobioloogilised Uurimused — Hudrobiol Uurim
Hudson Review — HR
Hudson Review — Hud R
Hudson Review — Hudson
Hudson Review — Hudson R
Hudson Review — Hudson Rev
Hudson Review — HuR
Hudson Review — HuRe
Hudson Review — PHUD
Huebner International Series on Risk, Insurance, and Economic Security — Huebner Internat Ser Risk Insur Econom Secur
Huelva Arqueologica — Huelva A
Huenefeld Report [*United States*] — Huenefeld Rep
Hueso Humero — HH
Huguenot Society of South Africa. Bulletin — Huguenot Soc S Afr Bull
Huis en Hof. Maandblad voor Liefhebbers van Bloem en Plant — Huis Hof
Huisarts en Wetenschap — Huisarts Wet
Huit Colloques de Biologie Clinique — Huit Colloq Biol Clin
Hule Mexicano y Plasticos — Hule Mex Plast
Hull University. Occasional Papers in Geography — Hull Univ Occas Pap Geogr
Hulsean Lectures — Hul L
Human and Ecological Risk Assessment — Hum Ecol Risk Assess
Human and Experimental Toxicology — Hum Exp Toxicol
Human Antibodies and Hybridomas — Hum Antibodies Hybridomas
Human Behavior — HB
Human Behavior — Hum Behav
Human Biology — HUBIA
Human Biology — Hum Biol
Human Biology — Human Biol
Human Biology — PHBI
Human Biology in Oceania — Hum Biol Oceania
Human Biology. Official Publication. Human Biology Council. Wayne State University. School of Medicine — WSU/HB
Human Cancer Immunology [*Elsevier Book Series*] — HCI
Human Cancer Immunology — Hum Cancer Immunol
Human Cell — Hum Cell
Human Chromosome Newsletter — Hum Chrom Newsl
Human Communication Research — Hum Commun Res
Human Communication Research — IHCR
Human Communications — Hum Commun
Human Communications Research — HCRE
Human Communications Research — Human Comm Res
Human Context — Hum Context
Human Context — Human Cont
Human Development — HD
Human Development — HUDEA
Human Development — Hum Dev
Human Development — Human Dev
Human Ecology — Hum Ecol
Human Ecology — Hum Ecology
Human Ecology — Human Ecol
Human Ecology — PHEC
Human Ecology and Race Hygiene — Hum Ecol Race Hyg
Human Ecology Forum — Hum Ecol Forum
Human Ecology Forum — PHEF
Human Environment in Sweden [*United States*] — Hum Environ Swed
Human Events — HE
Human Events — Hum Ev
Human Factors — HUFAA
Human Factors — Hum Fact
Human Factors — Hum Factors
Human Factors — Human Fact
Human Fertility — Hum Fertil
Human Gene Therapy — Hum Gene Ther
Human Genetics — Hum Genet
Human Genetics. Supplement — Hum Genet Suppl
Human Hair Symposium. Papers — Hum Hair Symp Pap
Human Heredity — HH
Human Heredity — HUHEA
Human Heredity — Hum Hered
Human Heredity — Hum Heredity
Human Heredity — Human Hered
Human Immunology — Hum Immunol
Human Intelligence International Newsletter — Human Intel Int Newsl
Human Life Review — Human Life R
Human Lymphocyte Differentiation — Hum Lymphocyte Differ
Human Mind; a Discussion at the Nobel Conference — Hum Mind Discuss Nobel Conf
Human Molecular Genetics — Hum Mol Genet
Human Movement Science — HMSCDO
Human Movement Science — Hu Move Sci
Human Movement Science — Hum Mov Sci
Human Mutation — Hum Mutat
Human Needs — Hum Needs
Human Neurobiology — Hum Neurob
Human Neurobiology — Hum Neurobiol
Human Neurobiology — HUNEDR
Human Nutrition. A Comprehensive Treatise — Hum Nutr Compr Treatise
Human Nutrition. Applied Nutrition — HNAND8

Human Nutrition. Applied Nutrition — Hum Nutr Appl Nutr
Human Nutrition. Applied Nutrition and Clinical Practice — Hum Nutr Appl Nutr Clin Pract
Human Nutrition. Clinical Nutrition — HNCNDI
Human Nutrition. Clinical Nutrition — Hum Nutr Cl
Human Nutrition. Clinical Nutrition — Hum Nutr Clin Nutr
Human Nutrition. Food Sciences and Nutrition — Hum Nutr Food Sci Nutr
Human Organization — HO
Human Organization — Hum Org
Human Organization — Hum Organ
Human Organization — Human Org
Human Organization — Human Organ
Human Organization — HUORAY
Human Organization — ORG
Human Organization Clearinghouse Bulletin — Hum Organ Clgh Bull
Human Organization. Society for Applied Anthropology — SAA/HO
Human Pathology — HPCQA
Human Pathology — Hum Path
Human Pathology — Hum Pathol
Human Pathology — Human Path
Human Pharmacology and Drug Research — Hum Pharmacol Drug Res
Human Physiology — Hum Physiol
Human Physiology [*English Translation of Fiziologiya Cheloveka*] — HUPHD
Human Physiology (English Translation of Fiziologiya Cheloveka) — Hum Physiol (Engl Transl Fiziol Chel)
Human Potential — Hum Potential
Human Psychopharmacology — Hum Psychopharmacol
Human Psychopharmacology. Clinical and Experimental — Hum Psychop
Human Relations — HR
Human Relations — HRL
Human Relations — Hum Rel
Human Relations — Hum Relat
Human Relations — Hum Relations
Human Relations — Human Rel
Human Relations — Human Relat
Human Relations — HUR
Human Reproduction — Hum Reprod
Human Reproduction [*Oxford*] — HUREEE
Human Reproduction (Oxford) — Hum Reprod (Oxford)
Human Reproduction. Proceedings of World Congress — Hum Reprod Proc World Congr
Human Reproductive Medicine [*Elsevier Book Series*] — HRM
Human Reproductive Medicine — Hum Reprod Med
Human Reproductive Medicine — Human Reprod Med
Human Resource Development — Human Resource Dev
Human Resource Management — HRM
Human Resource Management — Hum Resour Manage
Human Resource Management — Hum Resource Mgt
Human Resource Management — Human Resource Mgt
Human Resource Management (Australia) — Hum Resour Manage (Aust)
Human Resource Planning — HRP
Human Resource Planning — Hum Resour Plann
Human Resource Report — Hum Res Rep
Human Resources Abstracts — HRA
Human Resources Abstracts — Hum Resour Abstr
Human Resources Abstracts — Human Resour Abstr
Human Resources Administration — HRA
Human Resources Forum [*United States*] — Hum Resour Forum
Human Rights — Hum Rights
Human Rights — PHRI
Human Rights Journal — HRJ
Human Rights Journal — Hum Rights J
Human Rights Journal — Human Rights J
Human Rights Quarterly — Human Rights Q
Human Rights Quarterly — PHRQ
Human Rights Review — Hum Rights Rev
Human Rights Review — Human Rights Rev
Human Science [*Inkan Kwahak*] [*Republic of Korea*] — Hum Sci
Human Science (Seoul) — Hum Sci (Seoul)
Human Sciences Research Council Newsletter — HSRC Newsletter
Human Settlements — Hum Settlements
Human Studies — Hum Stud
Human Studies — Human S
Human Systems Management — HSM
Human Systems Management — HUM
Human Systems Management — Hum Syst Manage
Human Toxicology — HT
Human Toxicology — Hum Toxicol
Human Vision, Visual Processing, and Digital Display — Hum Vision Visual Process Digital Disp
Human World — Hum Wld
Humana Studia — Hum Stud
Humane Education — Humane Educ
Humane Review — Humane R
Humangenetik — Humangenet
Humanidades — HES
Humanidades — Hum
Humanidades (Buenos Aires) — Hum(BA)
Humanidades. Comillas — Hum C
Humanidades. Facultad de Humanidades. Universidad de los Andes (Merida, Venezuela) — Human Merida
Humanidades (Guatemala) — Human Guat
Humanidades (Mexico) — Human Mex
Humanidades Publicacion Universitaria — HPU
Humanidades. Serie 4. Logica Matematica [*Havana*] — Human Ser 4 Logica Mat
Humanidades. Serie 4. Logica Matematica — Humanidades Ser 4 Logica Mat
Humaniora Norvegica — HNorv
Humanisme Contemporain — Hum Contemp
Humanisme et Entreprise — Human et Entr
Humanisme et Renaissance — H & R
Humanisme et Renaissance — He R
Humanisme et Renaissance — HR
Humanisme et Renaissance — HRen
Humanisme et Renaissance — Hum et Ren
Humanisme et Renaissance — Humanisme Renaiss
Humanisme et Renaissance — HuR
Humanismus und Technik — Hum Tech
Humanist — GTHU
Humanist — Hum
Humanistica Lovaniensia — HL
Humanistica Lovaniensia — Hum Lov
Humanistische Gymnasium — H Gym
Humanistische Gymnasium — Hum Gymn
Humanistisches Gymnasium — HG
Humanistiska Vetenskaps-Samfundet i Lund Arsberattelse — Hum Vetensk Samf i Lund Arsberatt
Humanitas — Hum
Humanitas. Boletin Ecuatoriano de Antropologia (Quito) — Hum (Q)
Humanitas (Brescia) — Hum (Br)
Humanitas (Brescia) — HumB
Humanitas Christiana — Hum C
Humanitas: La Nouvelle Revue des Humanites — Hum(NRH)
Humanitas (Monterrey) — HumM
Humanitas (Nuevo Leon) — HumNL
Humanitas. Revue Internationale de Philologie Classique et Humanites — Hum (RIPh)
Humanitas (Tucuman, Argentina) — HumT
Humanitas. Universidad de Nuevo Leon. Centro de Estudios Humanisticos — UNL/H
Humanites Chretiennes — Hum Chr
Humanites Chretiennes — Human Chr
Humanites. Revue d'Enseignement Secondaire et d'Education — Hum (RES)
Humanities Association. Bulletin — HAB
Humanities Association of Canada. Bulletin — Hum Ass Bull
Humanities Association. Review — HAR
Humanities Association. Review — Hum Assoc Rev
Humanities Association. Review/Revue. Association des Humanites — Hum Assoc R
Humanities in Society — HIS
Humanities in Society — Hum Soc
Humanities in Society — Human Soc
Humanities in the South — HS
Humanities Index — HI
Humanities Index — Hum Ind
Humanities Index — Humanit Index
Humanities Review — Hum Rev
Humanizacja Pracy — Human Pracy
Humantias Christiana. Lateinische Reihe — Hum C L
Humble Way [*Exxon Corporation*] — HWAY
Humboldt Universitaet Berichte — Humboldt Univ Ber
Humboldt-Taschenbuecher — HT
Hume Studies — Hume Stud
Humpty Dumpty's Magazine — Humpty D
Humus — Hum
Hunan Annals of Mathematics — Hunan Ann Math
Hunden — Hnd
Hundred Years of the University of Calcutta [*Monograph*] — HYUC
Hungarian Academy of Sciences. Central Research Institute for Physics. Report KFKI [*Kozponti Fizikai Kutato Intezet*] — Hung Acad Sci Cent Res Inst Phys KFKI
Hungarian Agricultural Review — Hung Agr Rev
Hungarian Agricultural Review — Hung Agric Rev
Hungarian Annual Meeting for Biochemistry. Proceedings — Hung Annu Meet Biochem Proc
Hungarian Building Bulletin — Hung Build Bull
Hungarian Digest — HUD
Hungarian Economy — HUG
Hungarian Economy — Hung Econ
Hungarian Foreign Trade — HUF
Hungarian Foreign Trade — Hung For Tr
Hungarian Forest Scientifical Review — Hung For Sci Rev
Hungarian Halasztott [*Patent Document*] — Hung Halasztott
Hungarian Heavy Industries — Hung Heavy Ind
Hungarian Journal of Chemistry — Hung J Chem
Hungarian Journal of Chemistry — MGKFA3
Hungarian Journal of Industrial Chemistry — Hung J Ind Chem
Hungarian Journal of Industrial Chemistry — Hung J Indus Chem
Hungarian Journal of Industrial Chemistry (Vesprem) — Hungarian J Indust Chem (Vesprem)
Hungarian Journal of Metallurgy — Hung J Metall
Hungarian Journal of Mining and Metallurgy — Hung J Min Metall
Hungarian Journal of Mining and Metallurgy. Mining — Hung J Min Metall Min
Hungarian Law Review — Hung L Rev
Hungarian Machinery — Hung Mach
Hungarian Medical Archives — Hung Med Arch
Hungarian Medical Bibliography — Hung Med Biblio
Hungarian Medical Journal — Hung Med J
Hungarian Mining Journal — Hung Min J
Hungarian Music Quarterly — HMQ
Hungarian Musical Guide — Hung Mus G

Hungarian News Agency. Weekly Bulletin — WEH
Hungarian Patent Document — Hung
Hungarian Pharmacological Society. Congress — Hung Pharmacol Soc Congr
Hungarian Quarterly — Hungar Quart
Hungarian Quarterly — Hungarian Q
Hungarian Quarterly [*New York*] — HunQ
Hungarian Review — Hung R
Hungarian Review of Agricultural Sciences — Hung Rev Agric Sci
Hungarian Scientific Instruments — Hung Sci Instrum
Hungarian Scientific Instruments — HUSIA
Hungarian Studies in English — HSE
Hungarian Studies in English — Hung St Engl
Hungarian Studies Review — HSR
Hungarian Survey — Hung S
Hungarian Tanner — Hung Tanner
Hungarian Technical Abstracts — Hung Tech Abstr
Hungarian Teljes (Patent Document) — Hung Teljes
Hungarian Veterinary Journal — Hung Vet J
Hungarica Acta Biologica — Hung A Biol
Hungarica Acta Biologica — Hung Acta Biol
Hungarica Acta Chimica — Hung A Chim
Hungarica Acta Chimica — Hung Acta Chim
Hungarica Acta Mathematica — Hung A Math
Hungarica Acta Medica — Hung A Med
Hungarica Acta Medica — Hung Acta Med
Hungarica Acta Physica — Hung A Phys
Hungarica Acta Physica — Hung Acta Phys
Hungarica Acta Physiologica — Hung A Physiol
Hungarica Acta Physiologica — Hung Acta Physiol
Hungarofilm Bulletin — HUFB
Hungarofilm Bulletin [*Budapest*] — Hungarofilm Bull
Hungarologiai Intezet Tudomanyos Kozlemenyei — HITK
Hungaropress — HUN
Hungaropress — Hung Press
Hungary. Foeldtani Intezet. Evkoenyve — Hung Foeldt Intez Evk
Hungary. Magyar Allami Foeldtani Intezet. Evkoenyve — Hung Magy Allami Foeldt Intez Evk
Hungary. Orszagos Talalmanyi Hivatal. Szabadalmi Kozlony es Vedjegyertesito — Hung Orsz Talalmanyi Hivatal Szabad Kozl Vedjegyert
Hungary. Patent Document. Szabadalmi Leiras — Hung Pat Doc Szabad Leiras
Hunger Notes. World Hunger Education Service — Hung Notes World Hung Educ Serv
Hungry Mind Review — HMR
Hunick Zoo. Monthly Publication of Tanana Chiefs Conference — HZOO
Hunter Natural History — Hunter Nat Hist
Hunter Valley Research Foundation. Journal — Hunter Res Found J
Hunter Valley Research Foundation. Monograph — Hunter Valley Res Fdn Monograph
Hunter Valley Research Foundation. Special Report — Hunter Valley Res Found Spec Rep
Hunting Group Review — Hunt Gr Rev
Hunting Group Review — Hunting Group Rev
Huntington Historical Society. Quarterly — Huntington Hist Soc Quart
Huntington Library. Bulletin — HLB
Huntington Library. Bulletin — Hunt Lib Bull
Huntington Library. Quarterly — HLQ
Huntington Library. Quarterly — Hunt Lib Q
Huntington Library. Quarterly — Hunt Libr Q
Huntington Library. Quarterly — Huntington Libr Q
Huntington Library Quarterly — PHUN
Hunt's Merchants' Magazine — Hunt
Huntsville Letter — Huntsville Let
Huron Historical Notes — Huron Hist N
Huron Institute. Papers — Huron Inst Pap
Hushallnings Sallskapens Tidskrift — Hushall Sallsk Tidskr
Husky Fever (The Musher's Monthly News. Insert in Northern News Report) — HF
Husson Review [*Bangor, ME*] — HussR
Hutni Projekt Praha. Technicko-Ekonomicky Zpravodaj — Hutni Proj Praha Tech Ekon Zpr
Hutnicke Aktuality [*Czechoslovakia*] — Hutn Aktual
Hutnicke Listy — Hutn Listy
Hutnik (Katowice) — Hutn (Katowice)
Huyck Felt Bulletin — Huyck Felt Bull
Hvalradets Skrifter — Hvalradets Skr
Hvem er Hvem — HEH
Hyacinth Control Journal — Hyacinth Control J
Hyatt's PC News Report — Hyatt's PC
Hydraulic and Air Engineering — Hydraul & Air Engng
Hydraulic Engineering — Hydraul Eng
Hydraulic Engineering (Budapest) — Hydraul Eng (Budapest)
Hydraulic Pneumatic Mechanical Power — Hydraul Pneum Mech Power
Hydraulic Pneumatic Power [*Later, Hydraulic Pneumatic Mechanical Power*] — Hydraul Pneum Power
Hydraulic Pneumatic Power [*Later, Hydraulic Pneumatic Mechanical Power*] — Hydraul Pneum Pwr
Hydraulic Pneumatic Power and Controls — Hydraul Pneum Power Controls
Hydraulic Power Transmission — Hydr Pow Transm
Hydraulics and Pneumatics — Hydr Pneum
Hydraulics and Pneumatics — Hydra Pneum
Hydraulics and Pneumatics — Hydraul & Pneum
Hydraulics Research — Hydr Res
Hydrazine and Water Treatment. Proceedings of the International Conference — Hydrazine Water Treat Proc Int Conf
Hydride Symposium — Hydride Symp
Hydro Electric Power [*Japan*] — Hydro Electr Power
Hydro Research News — Hydro Res News
Hydrobiologia — Hydrobiol
Hydrobiological Bulletin — Hydrobiol Bull
Hydrobiological Journal — Hydrobiol J
Hydrobiological Journal (English Translation of Gidrobiologicheskii Zhurnal) [*A publication*] — Hydrobiol J (Engl Transl Gidrobiol Zh)
Hydrobiological Studies — Hydrobiol Stud
Hydrocarbon Processing — Hydroc Proc
Hydrocarbon Processing — Hydrocarbn
Hydrocarbon Processing — Hydrocarbon Process
Hydrocarbon Processing and Petroleum Refiner [*Later, Hydrocarbon Processing*] — HPPRA
Hydrocarbon Processing and Petroleum Refiner [*Later, Hydrocarbon Processing*] — Hydrocarbon Process Pet Refiner
Hydrocarbon Processing. International Edition — Hydrocarbon Process Int Ed
Hydrocarbure — HYDCA
Hydrochemische Materialien — Hydrochem Mater
Hydrochemische und Hydrogeologische Mitteilungen — Hydrochem Hydrogeol Mitt
Hydrocyclones. Papers Presented at the International Conference — Hydrocyclones Pap Int Conf
Hydroelectric Power — Hydroelectr Power
Hydrogen Energy — Hydrogen E
Hydrogen in Metals — Hydrogen Met
Hydrogen Progress [*United States*] — Hydrogen Prog
Hydrogene et Materiaux. Congres International — Hydrogene Mater Congr Int
Hydrogeologicke Informace (Czechoslovakia. Ustav Geologickeho Inzenyrstvi) — Hydrogeol Inf (Czech)
Hydrographic Bulletin — Hydrog Bull
Hydrographic Office. Publication — HO Publ
Hydrographic Review — Hydrog Rev
Hydro-Lab Journal — Hydro Lab J
Hydrologic Bulletin. Rhode Island. Water Resources Board — Hydrol Bull RI Water Resour Board
Hydrologic Report. New Mexico. Bureau of Mines and Mineral Resources — Hydrol Rep NM Bur Mines Miner Resour
Hydrologic Reports. State Bureau of Mines and Mineral Resources (New Mexico) — Hydrol Rep St Bur Mines Miner Resour (New Mexico)
Hydrological Journal — Hydrol J
Hydrological Sciences Bulletin [*England*] — Hydrol Sci Bull
Hydrological Sciences. Bulletin des Sciences Hydrologiques — Hydrol Sci Bull Sci Hydrol
Hydrological Sciences Bulletin. International Association of Hydrological Sciences — Hydrol Sci Bull Int Assoc Hydrol Sci
Hydrological Sciences Journal — Hydro Sci J
Hydrological Series. Australian Water Resources Council — Hydrol Ser Aust Wat Resour Coun
Hydrological Series. Australian Water Resources Council — Hydrol Ser Aust Water Resour Counc
Hydrologinen Vuosikirja — Hydrol Vuosik
Hydrologische Abteilung der Dortmunder Stadtwerke. Veroeffentlichungen — Hydrol Abt Dortm Stadtwerke Veroeff
Hydrologische Bibliographie — Hydrol Bibl
Hydrology and Water Resources in Arizona and the Southwest — Hydrol Water Resour Ariz Southwest
Hydrology for the Water Management of Large River Basins. Proceedings. International Symposium — Hydrol Water Manage Large River Basins Proc Int Symp
Hydrology Papers — Hydrol Pap
Hydrology Symposium — Hydrol Symp
Hydrology Symposium. Proceedings (Ottawa) — Hydrol Symp Proc (Ottawa)
Hydrolysis and Wood Chemistry USSR — Hydrolysis Wood Chem USSR
Hydromechanics and Hydraulic Engineering Abstracts — Hydromech & Hydraul Engng Abstr
Hydrotechnical Construction — Hydrotech Constr
Hydrotechnical Construction (English Translation) — Hydrotech Constr (Engl Transl)
Hydrotechnical Transactions — Hydrotech Trans
Hygiea. Supplement — Hygiea Suppl
Hygiene — Hyg
Hygiene and Sanitation — Hyg Sanit
Hygiene and Sanitation — HYSAA
Hygiene and Sanitation (USSR) — Hyg Sanit (USSR)
Hygiene de la Viande et du Lait — Hyg Viande Lait
Hygiene Mentale — Hyg Ment
Hygiene Mentale — HYMEA
Hygiene Mentale. Supplement de l'Encephale — Hyg Ment Suppl Encephale
Hygiene und Medizin — Hyg Med
Hygienische Rundschau — Hyg Rundschau
Hygienische Rundschau — HygR
Hygienisches Zentralblatt — Hyg Zentralbl
Hygienisk Revy — Hyg Revy
Hymn — Hy
Hymnologische Beitraege — Hy B
Hymnologiske Meddelelser. Vaerkstedsblad om Salmer — Hymn M
Hyogo Journal of Medical Sciences — Hyogo J Med Sci
Hyogo Natural History/Hyogo Hakubutsugakkai Kaiho — Hyogo Nat Hist
Hyogo Noka Daigaku Kiyo — HNDKB
Hyogo University Journal — Hyogo Univ J
Hyogo University of Teacher Education. Journal. Series 3. Natural Sciences, Practical Life Studies — Hyogo Univ Teach Educ J Ser 3
Hyogo-Ken Gan Senta Nenpo — HYGNA
Hyogo-Ken Journal of Natural History/Hyogo-Ken Chuto Kyoiku Hakubutsugaku Zasshi — Hyogo Ken J Nat Hist

Hyogo-Kenritsu Nogyo Shikenjo Kenkyu Hokoku — HYKMA
Hyomen — HYMNB
Hypatia — IHYP
Hyperbaric Oxygen Review — Hyperbaric Oxy Rev
Hyperfine Interactions [*Netherlands*] — Hyperfine Interact
Hypersonic Flow Research — Hypersonic Flow Res
Hypertension, Atherosclerosis, and Lipids. Proceedings. Workshop — Hypertens Atheroscler Lipids Proc Workshop
Hypertension Research — Hypertens Res
Hypertension Supplement — Hypertens Suppl
Hyperthermia and Oncology — Hyperthermia Oncol
Hypomnemata. Geottingen — Hyp

I

I and L. Ideologies and Literature — I L Ideol L
I Ch'uan Hsueh Pao. Acta Genetica Sinica — I Ch'uan Hsueh Pao Acta Genet Sin
I Mech E Conference Publications — I Mech E Conf Publ
IACP [*International Association of Chiefs of Police*] **Law Enforcement Legal Review** — IACP Law Enforce Leg Rev
IACP [*International Association of Chiefs of Police*] **Legal Points** — IACP Leg Pt
IADC [*International Association of Dredging Companies*] **Newsletter** — IADC Newsl
IAE (Institute of Atomic Engineers) Journal — IAE J
IAEA (International Atomic Energy Agency) Symposium on Neutron Inelastic Scattering. Proceedings. Symposium — IAEA Symp Neutron Inelastic Scattering Proc Symp
IAEA-NPPCI Specialists' Meeting on New Instrumentation of Water Cooled Reactors. Proceedings — IAEA NPPCI Spec Meet New Instrum Water Cooled React Proc
IAG [*Institute of Applied Geology*] **Bulletin** — IAG Bull
IAG [*International Federation for Information Processing. Administrative Data Processing Group*] **Journal** — IAG J
IAG [*International Federation for Information Processing. Administrative Data Processing Group*] **Literature on Automation** — IAG Lit Auto
IAGOD (International Association of the Genesis of Ore Deposits) Symposium — IAGOD Symp
IAHS (International Association of Hydrological Sciences) Publication — IAHS Publ
IAHS-AISH (Association International des Sciences Hydrologiques) Publication — IAHS AISH Publ
IAJE (International Association of Jazz in Education) Jazz Research Papers — IAJE Res
IAJRC [*International Association of Jazz Record Collectors*] **Journal** — IAJRC
IAL Boletim. Instituto Adolfo Lutz — IAL Bol Inst Adolfo Lutz
Iambi et Elegi Graeci ante Alexandrum Cantati — IEGAC
IAMP [*International Association of Meteorology and Atmospheric Physics*] **News Bulletin** — IAMP News Bull
IAMS (International Association of Microbiolobical Societies) Monograph — IAMS Monogr
IANR (Institute of Agriculture and Natural Resources) Quarterly — IANR (Inst Agric Nat Resour) Q
IAPAR (Fundacao Instituto Agronomico do Parana) Boletim Tecnico — IAPAR (Fund Inst Agron Parana) Bol Tec
IAPAR (Fundacao Instituto Agronomico do Parana) Circular — IAPAR (Fund Inst Agron Parana) Circ
IAPL (Indian Association for Programmed Learning) Newsletter — IAPL Newsl
IARC (International Agency for Research on Cancer) Monographs on the Evaluation of Carcinogenic Risk of Chemicals to Man — IARC Monogr Eval Carcinog Risk Chem Man
IARC (International Agency for Research on Cancer) Monographs. Supplement — IARC Monogr Suppl
IARC (International Agency for Research on Cancer) Publications — IARC (Int Agency Res Cancer) Publ
IARC [*International Agency for Research on Cancer*] **Monographs** — IARC Monogr
IARC [*International Agency for Research on Cancer*] **Monographs. Evaluation of the Carcinogenic Risk of Chemicals to Humans** — IARC Monogr Eval Carcinog Risk Chem Hum
IARC [*International Agency for Research on Cancer*] **Monographs. Evaluation of the Carcinogenic Risk of Chemicals to Humans. Supplement** — IARC Monogr Eval Carcinog Risk Chem Hum Suppl
IARC [*International Agency for Research on Cancer*] **Publications** — IARC Publ
IARC [*International Agency for Research on Cancer*] **Scientific Publications** — IARC Sci Publ
IARC [*International Agency for Research on Cancer*] **Scientific Publications** — IARCC
Iasi Universitatea. Analele Stiintifice. Sectiunea 2-B. Geologie. Serie Noua — Iasi Univ An Stiint Sect 2 B Ser Noua
IASLIC [*Indian Association of Special Libraries and Information Centres*] **Bulletin** — IASLIC Bull
Iasul Literar — I Lit
Iatrikai Athenai — Iatr Ath
IAVCEI (International Association of Volcanology and Chemistry of the Earth's Interior) Proceediings in Volcanology — IAVCEI Proc Volcanol
IAWA [*International Association of Wood Anatomists*] **Bulletin** — IAWA Bull
IAWPRC (International Association on Water Pollution Research and Control) Workshop — IAWPRC Wrkshp
Iazyk i Literatura — I & L
IBA [*Independent Broadcasting Authority*] **Technical Review** — IBA Tech Rev
Ibadan Review — Ibadan
Ibadan Review — Ibadan Rev
Ibadan Social Sciences Series — Ibadan Soc Sci Ser
Ibadan Studies in English — ISE
Ibadan University. Department of Forestry. Bulletin — Ibadan Univ Dep For Bull
Ibaraki Daigaku Kogakubu Kenkyu Shuho — IDKSA
Ibaraki Daigaku Nogakubu Gakujutsu Hokoku — IDNGA
IBBD [*Instituto Brasileiro de Bibliografia e Documentacao*] **Boletim Informativo** — IBBD Bol Inf
IBBD [*Instituto Brasileiro de Bibliografia e Documentacao*] **Noticias Diversas** — IBBD Not Diversas
IBEC Research Institute. Bulletin — IBEC Res Inst Bull
Iberica (New York) — IbNY
Iberiul-K'avk'asiuri Enatmecniereba — IKE
Ibero-American Pragensia. Anuario. Centro de Estudios de la Universidad Carolina — IAP
Ibero-Americana — Ibero Am
Ibero-Amerikanische Archiv (Berlin) — Ibero Am Arch Berlin
Iberoamerikanische Studien — IAS
Ibero-Amerikanisches Archiv — IAA
Ibero-Amerikanisches Archiv — Iberoamer Archiv
Ibero-Romania — Ib
Ibero-Romania — Ibero
Ibis [*London*] — Ib
IBM [*International Business Machines Corp.*] **Journal of Research and Development** — IBM J
IBM [*International Business Machines Corp.*] **Journal of Research and Development** — IBM J R D
IBM [*International Business Machines Corp.*] **Journal of Research and Development** — IBM J Res
IBM [*International Business Machines Corp.*] **Journal of Research and Development** — IBM J Res and Dev
IBM [*International Business Machines Corp.*] **Journal of Research and Development** — IBM J Res Dev
IBM [*International Business Machines Corp.*] **Journal of Research and Development** — IBM J Res Develop
IBM [*International Business Machines Corp.*] **Journal of Research and Development** — IBM Jrl
IBM [*International Business Machines Corp.*] **Nachrichten** — IBM Nachr
IBM [*International Business Machines Corp.*] **System User** — IBM User
IBM [*International Business Machines Corp.*] **Systems Journal** — IBM Syst J
IBM [*International Business Machines Corp.*] **Systems Journal** — IBM Systems J
IBM [*International Business Machines Corp.*] **Systems Journal** — ISY
IBM [*International Business Machines Corp.*] **Technical Disclosure Bulletin** — IBM Tech Discl Bull
IBM [*International Business Machines Corp.*] **Technical Disclosure Bulletin** — IBM Tech Disclosure Bull
IBP (International Biological Programme) Handbook — IBP (Int Biol Programme) Handb
IBP (International Biological Programme) i Norden — IBP (Int Biol Programme) Norden
IBRO Handbook Series — IBRO Handb Ser
IBRO (International Brain Research Organisation) Handbook Series. Methods in the Neurosciences — IBRO (Int Brain Res Org) Handb Ser Methods Neurosci
IBRO (International Brain Research Organization) Monograph Series — IBRO Monogr Ser
Ibsen Yearbook — Ibsen Yearb
Ibsen-Aarboken — IA
IC [*International Combustion Products Limited*] **Publications** — IC Publ
ICA [*Instituto Colombiano Agropecuario*] **Informa** — ICA Inf
ICA Informa. Instituto Colombiano Agropecuario — ICA Informa Inst Colomb Agropecu
ICA (Instituto Colombiano Agropecuario) Boletin Tecnico — ICA (Inst Colomb Agropecu) Bol Tec
ICACH. Organo del Instituto de Ciencias y Artes de Chiapas. Tuxtla Gutierrez (Chiapas, Mexico) — ICACH Tuxtla Gutierrez
ICAITI [*Instituto Centro Americano de Investigacion y Tecnologia Industrial*] **Boletin Informativo** — ICAITI Bol Inform
ICAITI (Instituto Centroamericano de Investigacion y Tecnologia Industrial) Informe Tecnico — ICAITI (Inst Centroam Invest Tecnol Ind) Inf Tec
ICALEO (International Conress oon Applications of Lasers and Electro-Optics) Proceedings — ICALEO Proc
ICAO [*International Civil Aviation Organization*] **Bird Strike Information System** [*Database*] — IBIS
ICAO [*International Civil Aviation Organization*] **Bulletin** [*Canada*] — ICAO Bull
ICC [*International Chamber of Commerce*] **Business World** — ICC Bus World
ICC (International Computation Centre) Bulletin — ICC Bull

ICC [*Interstate Commerce Commission*] **Practitioners' Journal** — ICC Prac J
ICC [*Interstate Commerce Commission*] **Practitioners' Journal** — ICC Pract J
ICC [*Interstate Commerce Commission*] **Practitioners' Journal** — PJ
ICD [*International College of Dentists*] **Scientific and Educational Journal** — ICD Sci Educ J
Ice Abstracts — Ice Abs
Ice and Refrigeration — Ice Refrig
Ice Cap News. American Society of Polar Philatelists — ICNS
Ice Cream Field and Ice Cream Trade Journal — Ice Cream Field Ice Cream Trade J
Ice Cream Review — Ice Cream R
Ice Cream Review — Ice Cream Rev
Ice Cream Trade Journal — Ice Cream Trade J
ICE (Internal Combustion Engine Division, ASME) American Society of Mechanical Engineers — ICE Am Soc Mech Eng
Ice (London) — ICEL
Ice News. Artec, Inc. — ICEN
ICEA [*Institut Canadien d'Education des Adultes*] **Cahiers** — ICEA Cah
ICEA [*International Childbirth Education Association*] **News** — ICEN
ICEA [*International Childbirth Education Association*] **Review** — ICER
Iceberg Research. Scott Polar Research Institute — ICBR
Iceland Review — ICRE
Icelandic Canadian — IC
Icelandic Fisheries Laboratories. Annual Report — Icel Fish Lab Annu Rep
ICFTU [*International Confederation of Free Trade Unions*] **Economic and Social Bulletin** — ICFTU Econ & Social Bul
ICHCA [*International Cargo Handling Coordination Association*] **Journal** — ICHCA J
ICHCA [*International Cargo Handling Coordination Association*] **Monthly Journal** — ICHCA Mon J
Ichthyologica: The Aquarium Journal — Ichthyol Aquarium J
Ichthyological Bulletin. J. L. B. Smith Institute of Ichthyology — Ichthyol Bull JLB Smith Inst Ichthyol
Ichthyological Series. Department of Biology. College of Science. Tunghai University — Ichthyol Ser Dep Biol Coll Sci Tunghai Univ
ICI [*Imperial Chemical Industries Ltd.*] **Engineering Plastics** — ICI Engng Plast
ICI [*Imperial Chemical Industries Ltd.*] **Magazine** — ICI Mag
ICIA [*International Center of Information on Antibiotics*] **Information Bulletin** — ICIA Inf Bull
ICID [*International Commission on Irrigation and Drainage*] **Bulletin** — ICID Bull
ICID Bulletin. International Commission on Irrigation and Drainage — ICID Bull Int Comm Irrig Drain
ICIDCA [*Instituto Cubano de Investigaciones de los Derivados de la Cana de Azucar*] **Boletin** — ICIDCA Bol
ICL [*International Combustion Limited*] **Publications** — ICL Publ
ICL [*International Computers Limited*] **Technical Journal** — ICL Tech J
ICM-90 Satellite Conference Proceedings — ICM 90 Satell Conf Proc
ICMC [*International Catholic Migration Commission*] **News** — ICMC Ne
ICME [*International Committee for Museum of Ethnography*] **News** — ICME N
ICMR (International Center for Medical Research) Annals — ICMR (Int Cent Med Res) Ann
ICMR (International Center for Medical Research) Seminar. Proceedings — ICMR Semin Proc
ICN-UCLA (International Chemical and Nuclear Corp. - University of California at Los Angeles) Symposium on Molecular Biology — ICN UCLA Symp Mol Biol
ICN-UCLA [*International Chemical and Nuclear Corp. - University of California at Los Angeles*] **Symposia on Molecular and Cellular Biology** — ICN-UCLA Symp Mol Cell Biol
ICO [*Institute of Chemist-Opticians*] **Journal** — ICOJ
ICOL Meeting — ICOL Meet
Iconclass [*Elsevier Book Series*] — IC
Icones Florae Alpinae Plantarum — Icon Fl Alpinae Pl
Icones Fungorum Malayensium — Icon Fungorum Malayensium
Icones Plantarum Africanarum — Icon Pl Afr
Icones Plantarum Formosanarum nec non et Contributiones ad Floram Formosanam — Icon Pl Formosan
Icones Plantarum Sinicarum — Icon Pl Sin
Iconographia Dermatologica, Syphilidologica, et Urologica — Iconogr Dermatol
Iconographia Medica — Icon Med
Iconographia Mycologica — Iconogr Mycol
Iconographia Plantarum Asiae Orientalis — Icon Pl As Or
Iconographie de la Faune et de la Flore Mediterraneennes — Icon Fau Fl Medit
Iconographie Medicale du Praticien — Icon Med Prat
ICP [*International Computer Programs, Inc.*] **Business Software Review** — ICB
ICP [*International Computer Programs*] **Directory** — ICP Dir
ICP (Inductively Coupled Plasma) Information Newsletter — ICP Inf Newsl
ICP [*International Computer Programs, Inc.*] **Interface Administrative and Accounting** — ICP Admin
ICP [*International Computer Programs, Inc.*] **Interface Banking Industry** — ICP Bank Indus
ICP [*International Computer Programs, Inc.*] **Interface Data Processing Management** — ICP DP Mgmt
ICP [*International Computer Programs, Inc.*] **Journal of Information Products and Services** — ICP J Inf Prod and Serv
ICP [*International Computer Programs, Inc.*] **Journal of Software Products and Services** — ICP J Software Prod and Serv
ICP [*International Computer Programs, Inc.*] **Software Business Review** — ICP Soft Bus Rev
ICP [*International Computer Programs*] **Software Information Database** — SID
ICP [*International Computer Programs, Inc.*] **Software Journal** — ICP Software J
ICR (Institute for Chemical Research) Annual Report — ICR Annu Rep
ICR Report. University of Tokyo. Institute for Cosmic Ray Research — ICR Rep Univ Tokyo Inst Cosmic Ray Res
ICRISAT [*International Crops Research Institute for the Semi-Arid Tropics*] **Annual Report** — ICRISAT Annu Rep
ICRISAT (International Crops Research Institute for the Semi-Arid Tropics) Research Bulletin — ICRISAT (Int Crops Res Inst Semi-Arid Trop) Res Bull
ICRP (International Commission on Radiological Protection) Annals — ICRP Ann
ICRP [*International Commission on Radiological Protection*] **Publication** — ICRP Publ
ICRS [*Institute of Contemporary Russian Studies*] **Medical Reports. Monographs in Soviet Medical Science** — ICRS Med Rep Monogr Sov Med Sci
ICRU [*International Commission on Radiological Units*] **Report** [*A publication*] — ICRU Rep
ICSSR [*Indian Council of Social Science Research*] **Research Abstracts Quarterly** — ICSSR Res Abstr Q
ICSU (International Council of Scientific Unions) Press Symposium — ICSU Press Symp
ICSU [*International Council of Scientific Unions*] **Review of World Science** — ICSU Rev World Sci
ICSU [*International Council of Scientific Unions*] **Short Reports** — ICSU Short Rep
ICT [*International Computers and Tabulators Limited*] **Data Processing Journal** — ICTD Pr
ICTP College on Theoretical and Computational Plasma Physics. Selected Lectures (International Center for Theoretical Physics) — ICTP Coll Theor Comput Plasma Phys Sel Lect
ICUIS [*Institute on the Church in Urban-Industrial Society*] **Abstract Service** [*A publication*] — ICUIS Abstr Service
ID. University of Kentucky. Cooperative Extension Service — ID Univ Ky Coop Ext Serv
IDA [*International Desalination Association*] **Journal** — IDA Jnl
IDA [*International Desalination Association*] **Magazine** — IDA Mag
Idaho. Agricultural Experiment Station. Current Information Series — Curr Inf Ser Idaho Agric Exp Stn
Idaho. Agricultural Experiment Station. Publications — Idaho Ag Exp
Idaho. Agricultural Experiment Station. Research Bulletin — Idaho Agric Exp Stn Res Bull
Idaho Agricultural Research Progress Report. University of Idaho. College of Agriculture — Idaho Agr Res Progr Rep
Idaho Agricultural Science. University of Idaho. College of Agriculture — Idaho Agr Sci
Idaho. Bureau of Mines and Geology. Bulletin — Idaho Bur Mines Geol Bull
Idaho. Bureau of Mines and Geology. County Report — Idaho Bur Mines Geol County Rep
Idaho. Bureau of Mines and Geology. Earth Sciences Series — Idaho Bur Mines and Geology Earth Sci Ser
Idaho. Bureau of Mines and Geology. Information Circular — Idaho Bur Mines Geol Inf Circ
Idaho. Bureau of Mines and Geology. Mineral Resources Report — Idaho Bur Mines Geol Miner Resour Rep
Idaho. Bureau of Mines and Geology. Pamphlet — Idaho Bur Mines Geol Pam
Idaho Citizen — Idaho Cit
Idaho. Department of Fish and Game. Wildlife Bulletin — Idaho Dep Fish Game Wildl Bull
Idaho. Department of Reclamation. Water Information Bulletin — Idaho Dep Reclam Water Inf Bull
Idaho. Department of Reclamation. Water Information Bulletin — Idaho Dept Reclamation Water Inf Bull
Idaho. Department of Water Administration. Water Information Bulletin — Idaho Dep Water Adm Water Inf Bull
Idaho. Department of Water Resources. Basic Data Release — Idaho Dep Water Resour Basic Data Release
Idaho. Department of Water Resources. Water Information Bulletin — Idaho Dep Water Resour Water Inf Bull
Idaho. Division of Environment. Department of Health and Welfare. Water Quality Series — Idaho Div Environ Dep Health Welfare Water Qual Ser
Idaho. Forest, Wildlife, and Range Experiment Station. Bulletin — Idaho For Wildl Range Exp Stn Bull
Idaho. Forest, Wildlife, and Range Experiment Station. Information Series — Idaho For Wildl Range Exp Stn Inf Ser
Idaho. Forest, Wildlife, and Range Experiment Station. Note — Idaho For Wildl Range Exp Stn Note
Idaho. Forest, Wildlife, and Range Experiment Station. Paper — Idaho For Wildl Range Exp Stn Pap
Idaho. Forest, Wildlife, and Range Experiment Station. Station Note — Idaho For Wildl Range Exp Stn Stn Note
Idaho. Forest, Wildlife, and Range Experiment Station. Technical Report — Idaho For Wildl Range Exp Stn Tech Rep
Idaho Law Review — ID LR
Idaho Law Review — Ida LR
Idaho Law Review — Idaho L Rev
Idaho Librarian — Idaho Libn
Idaho Librarian — Idaho Librn
Idaho Mining Industry. Annual Report — Idaho Min Industry Ann Rept
Idaho Power Company. Bulletin — Idaho Power Co Bull
Idaho Reports — Idaho
Idaho. State Horticultural Association. Proceedings of the Annual Convention — Idaho State Hortic Assoc Proc Annu Conv
Idaho Statesman — Idaho Stat
Idaho University. Agricultural Experiment Station. Current Information Series [*A publication*] — Idaho Univ Agric Exp Stn Curr Inf Ser
Idaho University. Current Information Series — Idaho Univ Curr Inf Ser
Idaho University. Engineering Experiment Station. Bulletin — Idaho Univ Eng Exp Sta Bull
Idaho University. Forest, Range, and Wildlife Experiment Station. Research Note — Idaho Univ For Range Wildl Exp Stn Res Note
Idaho University. Water Resources Research Institute. Research Technical Completion Report — Idaho Univ Water Resour Res Inst Res Tech Completion Rep

Idaho Yesterdays — Idaho Yest
Idaho Yesterdays — IY
Idea Personal Trainer — Idea Personal Train
Idea. The Journal of Law and Technology — IDE
Idea. The Journal of Law and Technology — Idea
Idealistic Studies — Ideal Stud
Idealistische Neuphilologie — Idealist Neuphilol
Idealistische Neuphilologie — INPh
Ideas en Ciencias Sociales — ICS
Ideas for Management — Ideas for Mgmt
Ideas for Management — Ideas Manage
Ideas/Idees. Department of Indian and Northern Affairs — IDEA
Ideas in Modern Biology. Proceedings. International Congress of Zoology — Ideas Mod Biol Proc Int Congr Zool
Ideas y Valores — I & V
Ideas y Valores — IV
Ideggyogyaszati Szemle — Ideggyogy Sz
Ideggyogyaszati Szemle — Ideggyogy Szle
Idemitsu Petroleum Journal [*Japan*] — Idemitsu Pet J
Idengaku Zasshi. Supplement [*Japan*] — Idengaku Zasshi Suppl
Identification and Analysis of Organic Pollutants in Water. Chemical Congress. North American Continent — Identif Anal Org Pollut Water Chem Congr North Am Cont
Identification and System Parameter Estimation. Proceedings. IFAC (International Federation of Automatic Control) Symposium — Identif Syst Parameter Estim Proc IFAC Symp
Ideologies and Literature — I & L
Ideology and Consciousness — I and C
IDF [*International Diabetes Federation*] **Bulletin** — IDF Bul
IDF Bulletin (Brussels) (International Diabetes Federation) — IDF Bull Brussels
IDIA [*Informativo de Investigaciones Agricolas*]. Suplemento — IDIA Supl
Idische (Buenos Aires) — IBA
Idler — I
IDMA [*Indian Drug Manufacturers' Association*] **Bulletin** — IDMA Bull
IDOC [*International Documentation*] **Bulletin** — IDOC Bul
Idojaras — Idoj
Idojaras — IDOJA
IDP [*Information and Data Base Publishing*] **Report** [*United States*] — IDP Rep
IDR Industrial Diamond Review — IDR Ind Diamond Rev
IDRC (International Development Research Centre) TS — IDRC (Int Dev Res Cent) TS
IDRC [*International Development Research Centre*] **Reports** — IDRC Rep
IDS [*Institute of Development Studies*] **Bulletin** — IDS Bulletin
IDSA [*Institute for Defense Studies and Analyses*] **Journal** [*India*] — IDSA J
IE. Industrial Engineering — IE Ind Eng
IEA (International Energy Agency) Coal Research. Report ICTIS/ER — IEA Coal Res Rep ICTIS ER
IEA (International Energy Agency) Coal Research. Report ICTIS/TR — IEA Coal Res Rep ICTIS TR
IEC [*International Electrotechnical Commission*] **Bulletin** — IEC Bull
IECI [*Industrial Electronics and Control Instrumentation Group*] **Annual Conference Proceedings** [*United States*] — IECI Annu Conf Proc
IEE Conference on Telecommunications — IEE Conf Telecommun
IEE [*Institution of Electrical Engineers*] **Conference Publication (London)** — IEE Conf Publ (Lond)
IEE [*Institution of Electrical Engineers*] **Control Engineering Series** — IEE Control Engrg Ser
IEE [*Institution of Electrical Engineers*] **Electromagnetic Waves Series** — IEE Electromagn Waves Ser
IEE [*Institute of Electrical Engineers*] **Energy Series** — IEE Energy Ser
IEE (Institution of Electrical Engineers) National Conference on UK Telecommunications Networks-Present and Future — IEE Natl Conf UK Telecommun Networks Present Future
IEE (Institution of Electrical Engineers) Proceedings. Part A. Physical Science, Measurement and Instrumentation, Management and Education — IEE Proc Part A Phys Sci Meas Instrum Manage Educ
IEE [*Institution of Electrical Engineers*] **Journal on Computers and Digital Techniques** — IEE J Comput and Digital Tech
IEE [*Institution of Electrical Engineers*] **Journal on Computers and Digital Techniques** — IEE J Comput Digital Tech
IEE [*Institution of Electrical Engineers*] **Journal on Electric Power Applications** — IEE J Electr Power Appl
IEE [*Institution of Electrical Engineers*] **Journal on Electronic Circuits and Systems** — IEE J Electron Circuits and Syst
IEE [*Institution of Electrical Engineers*] **Journal on Electronic Circuits and Systems** — IEE J Electron Circuits Syst
IEE [*Institution of Electrical Engineers*] **Journal on Microwaves, Optics, and Acoustics** — IEE J Microwaves Opt Acoust
IEE [*Institution of Electrical Engineers*] **Journal on Solid-State and Electron Devices** — IEE J Solid-State and Electron Devices
IEE [*Institution of Electrical Engineers*] **Journal on Solid-State and Electron Devices** — IEE J Solid-State Electron Devices
IEE [*Institution of Electrical Engineers*] **Monograph Series** — IEE Monogr Ser
IEE [*Institution of Electrical Engineers*] **Proceedings. A. Physical Science, Measurement and Instrumentation, Management and Education** — IEE Proc A Phys Sci Meas Instrum Manage Educ
IEE [*Institution of Electrical Engineers*] **Proceedings. J. Optoelectronics** — IEE Proc J Optoelectron
IEE [*Institution of Electrical Engineers*] **Proceedings. Part 1. Solid-State and Electron Devices** — IEE Proc Pt 1 Solid State Electron
IEE [*Institution of Electrical Engineers*] **Proceedings. Part A** — IEE Proc A
IEE [*Institution of Electrical Engineers*] **Proceedings. Part B. Electric Power Applications** — IEE Proc B Elect Pwr Applics
IEE [*Institution of Electrical Engineers*] **Proceedings. Part B. Electric Power Applications** — IEE Proc B Electr Power Appl
IEE [*Institution of Electrical Engineers*] **Proceedings. Part C. Generation, Transmission, and Distribution** — IEE Proc C
IEE [*Institution of Electrical Engineers*] **Proceedings. Part C. Generation, Transmission, and Distribution** — IEE Proc C Gener Transm Distrib
IEE [*Institution of Electrical Engineers*] **Proceedings. Part C. Generation, Transmission, and Distribution** — IEE Proc Generation Transm Distrib
IEE [*Institution of Electrical Engineers*] **Proceedings. Part C. Generation, Transmission, and Distribution** [*England*] — IEE Proc Part C
IEE [*Institution of Electrical Engineers*] **Proceedings. Part D. Control Theory and Applications** — IEE Proc D
IEE [*Institution of Electrical Engineers*] **Proceedings. Part D. Control Theory and Applications** — IEE Proc D Control Theory Applics
IEE [*Institution of Electrical Engineers*] **Proceedings. Part D. Control Theory and Applications** [*England*] — IEE Proc Part D
IEE [*Institution of Electrical Engineers*] **Proceedings. Part E. Computers and Digital Techniques** — IEE Proc E
IEE [*Institution of Electrical Engineers*] **Proceedings. Part E. Computers and Digital Techniques** — IEE Proc E Comput Digit Tech
IEE [*Institution of Electrical Engineers*] **Proceedings. Part E. Computers and Digital Techniques** [*England*] — IEE Proc Part E
IEE [*Institution of Electrical Engineers*] **Proceedings. Part E. Computers and Diigital Techniques** — IEE Proc E Computers Digit Techniques
IEE [*Institution of Electrical Engineers*] **Proceedings. Part F. Communications, Radar, and Signal Processing** — IEE Proc F
IEE [*Institution of Electrical Engineers*] **Proceedings. Part F. Communications, Radar, and Signal Processing** — IEE Proc F Commun Radar Signal Process
IEE [*Institution of Electrical Engineers*] **Proceedings. Part F. Communications, Radar, and Signal Processing** [*England*] — IEE Proc Part F
IEE [*Institution of Electrical Engineers*] **Proceedings. Part G. Electronic Circuits and Systems** — IEE Proc G
IEE [*Institution of Electrical Engineers*] **Proceedings. Part G. Electronic Circuits and Systems** — IEE Proc G Electron Circuits Syst
IEE [*Institution of Electrical Engineers*] **Proceedings. Part G. Electronic Circuits and Systems** [*England*] — IEE Proc Part G
IEE [*Institution of Electrical Engineers*] **Proceedings. Part H. Microwaves, Optics, and Antennas** — IEE Proc H
IEE [*Institution of Electrical Engineers*] **Proceedings. Part H. Microwaves, Optics, and Antennas** — IEE Proc H Microwaves Opt Antennas
IEE [*Institution of Electrical Engineers*] **Proceedings. Part H. Microwaves, Optics, and Antennas** [*England*] — IEE Proc Part H
IEE [*Institution of Electrical Engineers*] **Proceedings. Part I. Solid-State and Electron Devices** — IEE Proc I
IEE [*Institution of Electrical Engineers*] **Proceedings. Part I. Solid-State and Electron Devices** — IEE Proc I Solid-State Electron Devices
IEE [*Institution of Electrical Engineers*] **Proceedings. Part I. Solid-State and Electron Devices** [*England*] — IEE Proc Part I
IEE Proceedings-A. Science, Measurement, and Technology — IEE Proc A Sci Meas Technol
IEE [*Institution of Electrical Engineers*] **Reviews** — IEE Rev
IEE [*Institution of Electrical Engineers*] **Reviews** — IERWA
IEE Topics in Control Series — IEE Topics Control Ser
IEEE Aerospace and Electronic Systems Magazine — IEEE Aerosp Electron Syst Mag
IEEE. Annual Textile Industry Technical Conference — IEEE Annu Text Ind Tech Conf
IEEE. Annual Textile Industry Technical Conference. Proceedings [*United States*] — IEEE Annu Text Ind Tech Conf Proc
IEEE [*Institute of Electrical and Electronics Engineers*] **Cement Industry** — IEEE Cem Ind
IEEE. Cement Industry Technical Conference Paper — IEEE Cem Ind Tech Conf Pap
IEEE. Circuits and Systems Magazine [*United States*] — IEEE Circuits Syst Mag
IEEE CIT Conference — IEEE CIT Conf
IEEE. Communications Magazine — IEEE Commun Mag
IEEE. Communications Society. Magazine [*Later, IEEE. Communications Magazine*] — IEEE Commun Soc Mag
IEEE. Computer Graphics and Applications — ICGAD
IEEE. Computer Graphics and Applications — IEEE Comput Graphics and Appl
IEEE. Computer Group News — IEEE Comput Group News
IEEE Computer Society Press Reprint Collections — IEEE Comput Soc Press Reprint Collect
IEEE Computer Society Press Technology Series — IEEE Comput Soc Press Tech Ser
IEEE Computer Society Press Tutorial — IEEE Comput Soc Press Tutor
IEEE. Conference Record. Annual Conference of Electrical Engineering Problems in the Rubber and Plastics Industries — IEEE Conf Rec Annu Conf Electr Eng Probl Rubber Plast Ind
IEEE [*Institute of Electrical and Electronics Engineers*] **Conference Record. Annual Pulp and Paper Industry Technical Conference** — IEEE Conf Rec Ann Pulp Pap Ind Tech Conf
IEEE Conference Record. IEEE International Symposium on Electrical Insulation — IEEE Conf Rec IEEE Int Symp Electr Insul
IEEE. Conference Record. Industrial and Commercial Power Systems. Technical Conference — IEEE Conf Rec Ind Commer Power Syst Tech Conf
IEEE Conference Record of Annual Meeting. IEEE Industry Applications Society — IEEE Conf Rec Annu Meet IEEE Ind Appl Soc
IEEE Conference Record (Rocky Mountain Bioengineering Symposium) — IEEE Conf Rec Rocky Mt Bioeng Symp
IEEE. Conference Records. Thermionic Conversion Specialist Conference — IEEE Conf Rec Thermion Convers Spec Conf
IEEE. Control Systems Magazine — IEEE Control Syst Mag
IEEE. Electromagnetic Compatibility Symposium. Record — IEEE Electromagn Compat Symp
IEEE. Electron Device Letters [*United States*] — IEEE Electron Device Lett

IEEE. Electronics and Aerospace Systems. Convention Record [*United States*] — IEEE Electron Aerosp Syst Conv Rec
IEEE Electrotechnology Review — IEEE Electrotech Rev
IEEE. Engineering in Medicine and Biology Magazine — IEEE Eng Med and Biol Mag
IEEE. Engineering Management — IEEE Trans Engng Man
IEEE. Engineering Management Review — IEEE Eng Manage Rev
IEEE. Intercon Technical Papers — IEEE Intercon Tech Pap
IEEE. International Conference on Magnetics. Proceedings of the Intermag Conference — IEEE Proc Intermag Conf
IEEE. International Convention. Digest — IEEE Int Conv Dig
IEEE. International Convention. Record — IEEE Int Conv Rec
IEEE International Electron Devices — IEEE Int Electron Devices
IEEE International Symposium on Applications of Ferroelectrics — IEEE Int Symp Appl Ferroelectr
IEEE International Symposium on Electrical Insulation. Conference Record — IEEE Int Symp Electr Insul Conf Rec
IEEE International Symposium on Electromagnetic Compatibility. Proceedings — IEEE Int Symp Electromagn Compat Proc
IEEE. Journal of Oceanic Engineering — IEEE J Ocean Eng
IEEE. Journal of Oceanic Engineering — IEEE J Oceanic Eng
IEEE. Journal of Oceanic Engineering — IEEE Journal of Oceanic Engineering
IEEE. Journal of Quantum Electronics — IEEE J Q El
IEEE. Journal of Quantum Electronics — IEEE J Quantum Electron
IEEE Journal of Selected Topics in Quantum Electronics — IEEE J Sel Top Quantum Electron
IEEE. Journal of Solid-State Circuits — IEEE J Soli
IEEE. Journal of Solid-State Circuits — IEEE J Solid-State Circuits
IEEE. Journal on Selected Areas in Communications — IEEE J Sel
IEEE. Journal on Selected Areas in Communications — IEEE J Sel Areas Commun
IEEE MTT-S [*Microwave Theory and Techniques Society*] **International Microwave Symposium Digest** — IEEE MTT S Int Microwave Symp Dig
IEEE/NPSS (Nuclear and Plasma Science Society) Symposium on Fusion Engineering — IEEE/NPSS Symp Fusion Eng
IEEE. Photovoltaic Specialists Conference. Conference Record [*United States*] — IEEE Photovoltaic Spec Conf Conf Rec
IEEE. Power Engineering Review — IEEE Power Eng Rev
IEEE Power Engineering Society. Special Publication — IEEE Power Eng Soc Spec Publ
IEEE Press Selected Reprint Series — IEEE Press Selected Reprint Ser
IEEE Press Series on Electromagnetic Waves — IEEE Press Ser Electromagnet Waves
IEEE. Proceedings — IEEE Proc
IEEE. Proceedings. Annual Symposium on Reliability — IEEE Proc Annu Symp Rel
IEEE. Proceedings. Conference on Electrical Applications for the Textile Industry — IEEE Proc Conf Elec Appl Text Ind
IEEE. Proceedings. Conference on Engineering in Medicine and Biology — IEEE Proc Conf Eng Med Biol
IEEE Proceedings D. Control Theory and Applications — IEEE Proc D Control Theory Appl
IEEE. Proceedings. Electronic Components Conference — IEEE Proc Electron Components Conf
IEEE. Proceedings. National Aerospace and Electronics Conference — IEEE Proc Nat Aerosp Electron Conf
IEEE. Proceedings. National Aerospace and Electronics Conference — IEEE Proc Natl Aerosp Electron Conf
IEEE. Region Six (Western USA). Conference Record — IEEE Reg Six (West USA) Conf Rec
IEEE. Spectrum — IEEE S
IEEE. Spectrum — IEEE Spectr
IEEE. Spectrum — IEEE Spectrum
IEEE. Spectrum — SPC
IEEE. Standards Publications — IEEE Stand Publ
IEEE. Student Papers — IEEE Stud Pap
IEEE Symposium on Fusion Engineering. Proceedings — IEEE Symp Fusion Eng Proc
IEEE. Technical Activities Guide [*United States*] — IEEE Tech Act Guide
IEEE. Transactions on Acoustics, Speech, and Signal Processing — IEEE Acoust
IEEE. Transactions on Acoustics, Speech, and Signal Processing — IEEE Trans Acoust Speech Signal Process
IEEE. Transactions on Acoustics, Speech, and Signal Processing — IEEE Trans ASSP
IEEE. Transactions on Acoustics, Speech, and Signal Processing — IETAB
IEEE. Transactions on Aerospace [*Later, IEEE. Transactions on Aerospace and Electronic Systems*] — IEEE Trans Aerosp
IEEE. Transactions on Aerospace and Electronic Systems — IEEE Aer El
IEEE. Transactions on Aerospace and Electronic Systems — IEEE Trans Aerosp and Electron Syst
IEEE. Transactions on Aerospace and Electronic Systems — IEEE Trans Aerosp Electron Syst
IEEE. Transactions on Aerospace and Electronic Systems — IEEE Trans Aerospace and Electron Systems
IEEE. Transactions on Aerospace and Electronic Systems — IEEE Trans Aerospace Electron Systems
IEEE. Transactions on Aerospace and Navigational Electronics — IEEE Trans Aerosp Navig Electron
IEEE. Transactions on Antennas and Propagation — IEEE Antenn
IEEE. Transactions on Antennas and Propagation — IEEE Trans Antennas and Propagation
IEEE. Transactions on Antennas and Propagation — IEEE Trans Antennas Propag
IEEE. Transactions on Antennas and Propagation — IEEE Trans Antennas Propagat
IEEE. Transactions on Applications and Industry — IEEE Trans Appl Ind
IEEE. Transactions on Applications and Industry — IEEE Trans Applic Ind
IEEE. Transactions on Audio — IEEE Trans Audio
IEEE. Transactions on Audio — IEEUA
IEEE. Transactions on Audio and Electroacoustics — IEEE Trans Audio and Electroacoust
IEEE. Transactions on Audio and Electroacoustics — IEEE Trans Audio Electroacoust
IEEE. Transactions on Automatic Control — IEEE Auto C
IEEE. Transactions on Automatic Control — IEEE Trans Autom Control
IEEE. Transactions on Automatic Control — IEEE Trans Automat Contr
IEEE. Transactions on Automatic Control — IEEE Trans Automat Control
IEEE. Transactions on Automatic Control — IEEE Trans Automatic Control
IEEE. Transactions on Bio-Medical Electronics — IEEE Trans Bio Med Electron
IEEE. Transactions on Biomedical Engineering — IEBEA
IEEE. Transactions on Biomedical Engineering — IEEE Biomed
IEEE. Transactions on Biomedical Engineering — IEEE Trans Biomed Eng
IEEE. Transactions on Broadcast and Television Receivers — IEEE Trans Broadcast and Telev Receivers
IEEE. Transactions on Broadcast and Television Receivers — IEEE Trans Broadcast Telev Receivers
IEEE. Transactions on Broadcasting — IEEE Broadc
IEEE. Transactions on Broadcasting — IEEE Trans Broadcast
IEEE. Transactions on Cable Television — IEEE Trans Cable Telev
IEEE. Transactions on Cable Television — IEEE Trans CATV
IEEE. Transactions on Circuit Theory — IEEE Trans Circuit Theory
IEEE. Transactions on Circuits and Systems — IEEE Circ S
IEEE. Transactions on Circuits and Systems — IEEE Trans CAS
IEEE. Transactions on Circuits and Systems — IEEE Trans Circuits and Syst
IEEE. Transactions on Circuits and Systems — IEEE Trans Circuits and Systems
IEEE. Transactions on Circuits and Systems — IEEE Trans Circuits Syst
IEEE Transactions on Circuits and Systems. I. Fundamental Theory and Applications — IEEE Trans Circuits Systems I Fund Theory Appl
IEEE. Transactions on Communication and Electronics — IEEE Trans Commun Electron
IEEE. Transactions on Communication Technology [*Later, IEEE. Transactions on Communications*] — IEEE Trans Com Tech
IEEE. Transactions on Communication Technology [*Later, IEEE. Transactions on Communications*] — IEEE Trans Commun Technol
IEEE. Transactions on Communications — IECMB
IEEE. Transactions on Communications — IEEE Commun
IEEE. Transactions on Communications — IEEE Trans Com
IEEE. Transactions on Communications — IEEE Trans Comm
IEEE. Transactions on Communications — IEEE Trans Commun
IEEE. Transactions on Communications Systems — IEEE Trans Commun Syst
IEEE. Transactions on Component Parts — IEEE Trans Component Parts
IEEE. Transactions on Components, Hybrids, and Manufacturing Technology — IEEE Trans Components Hybrids and Manuf Technol
IEEE. Transactions on Components, Hybrids, and Manufacturing Technology — IEEE Trans Components Hybrids Manuf Technol
IEEE. Transactions on Computer-Aided Design of Integrated Circuits and Systems — IEEE Trans Comput-Aided Des Integrated Circuits and Syst
IEEE. Transactions on Computers — IEEE Comput
IEEE. Transactions on Computers — IEEE Trans
IEEE. Transactions on Computers — IEEE Trans Comput
IEEE. Transactions on Computers — IEEE Trans Computers
IEEE. Transactions on Consumer Electronics — IEEE Cons E
IEEE. Transactions on Consumer Electronics — IEEE Trans CE
IEEE. Transactions on Consumer Electronics — IEEE Trans Consum Electron
IEEE. Transactions on Education — IEEE Educat
IEEE. Transactions on Education — IEEE Trans Educ
IEEE. Transactions on Electrical Insulation — IEEE El Ins
IEEE. Transactions on Electrical Insulation — IEEE Trans Elec Insul
IEEE. Transactions on Electrical Insulation — IEEE Trans Electr Insul
IEEE. Transactions on Electromagnetic Compatibility — IEEE Elmagn
IEEE. Transactions on Electromagnetic Compatibility — IEEE Trans Electromagn Compat
IEEE. Transactions on Electron Devices — IEEE Device
IEEE. Transactions on Electron Devices — IEEE T El Dev
IEEE. Transactions on Electron Devices — IEEE Trans Electron Devices
IEEE. Transactions on Electronic Computers — IEECA
IEEE. Transactions on Electronic Computers [*United States*] — IEEE Trans Electron Comput
IEEE. Transactions on Engineering Management — IEEE Manage
IEEE. Transactions on Engineering Management — IEEE Trans Eng Manag
IEEE. Transactions on Engineering Management — IEEE Trans Eng Manage
IEEE. Transactions on Engineering Writing and Speech — IEEE Trans Eng Writ and Speech
IEEE. Transactions on Engineering Writing and Speech — IEEE Trans Eng Writing Speech
IEEE. Transactions on Engineering Writing and Speech — IEEE Trans Engng Wrtg Speech
IEEE. Transactions on Geoscience and Remote Sensing — IEEE Trans Geosci and Remote Sensing
IEEE. Transactions on Geoscience and Remote Sensing [*United States*] — IEEE Trans Geosci Remote Sens
IEEE. Transactions on Geoscience and Remote Sensing — IEEE Trans Geosci Remote Sensing
IEEE. Transactions on Geoscience Electronics — IEEE Geosci
IEEE. Transactions on Geoscience Electronics — IEEE Trans Geosci Electron
IEEE. Transactions on Geoscience Electronics — IEEE Trans Geosci Electronics
IEEE. Transactions on Human Factors in Electronics [*United States*] — IEEE Trans Hum Factors Electron

IEEE. Transactions on Human Factors in Electronics — IEHFA
IEEE. Transactions on Industrial Electronics — IEEE Trans Ind Electron
IEEE. Transactions on Industrial Electronics and Control Instrumentation [*Later, IEEE. Transactions on Industrial Electronics*] — IEEE Ind El
IEEE. Transactions on Industrial Electronics and Control Instrumentation [*Later, IEEE. Transactions on Industrial Electronics*] — IEEE Trans Ind Electron and Control Instrum
IEEE. Transactions on Industrial Electronics and Control Instrumentation [*Later, IEEE. Transactions on Industrial Electronics*] — IEEE Trans Ind Electron Control Instrum
IEEE. Transactions on Industry and General Applications [*Later, IEEE. Transactions on Industry Applications*] — IEEE Trans Ind and Gen Appl
IEEE. Transactions on Industry and General Applications [*Later, IEEE. Transactions on Industry Applications*] — IEEE Trans Ind Gen Appl
IEEE. Transactions on Industry Applications — IEEE Ind Ap
IEEE. Transactions on Industry Applications — IEEE Trans Ind Appl
IEEE. Transactions on Information Theory — IEEE Info T
IEEE. Transactions on Information Theory — IEEE Trans Inf Theory
IEEE. Transactions on Information Theory — IEEE Trans Inform Theory
IEEE. Transactions on Information Theory — IEEE Trans Information Theory
IEEE. Transactions on Instrumentation and Measurement — IEEE Instr
IEEE. Transactions on Instrumentation and Measurement — IEEE Trans Instrum and Meas
IEEE. Transactions on Instrumentation and Measurement — IEEE Trans Instrum Meas
IEEE. Transactions on Magnetics — IEEE Magnet
IEEE. Transactions on Magnetics — IEEE Trans Magn
IEEE. Transactions on Man-Machine Systems — IEEE Trans Man-Mach Syst
IEEE. Transactions on Manufacturing Technology — IEEE Trans Manuf Technol
IEEE. Transactions on Manufacturing Technology — IETMB
IEEE. Transactions on Medical Imaging — IEEE Med Im
IEEE. Transactions on Medical Imaging — IEEE Trans Med Imaging
IEEE. Transactions on Microwave Theory and Techniques — IEEE Micr T
IEEE. Transactions on Microwave Theory and Techniques — IEEE Trans Microwave Theory and Tech
IEEE. Transactions on Microwave Theory and Techniques — IEEE Trans Microwave Theory Tech
IEEE. Transactions on Military Electronics — IEEE Trans Mil Electron
IEEE Transactions on Neural Networks — IEEE Neural
IEEE. Transactions on Nuclear Science — IEEE Nucl S
IEEE. Transactions on Nuclear Science — IEEE T Nucl Sci
IEEE. Transactions on Nuclear Science — IEEE Trans Nucl Sci
IEEE Transactions on Parallel and Distributed Sustems — IEEE Parall
IEEE. Transactions on Parts, Hybrids, and Packaging — IEEE Parts
IEEE. Transactions on Parts, Hybrids, and Packaging — IEEE Trans Parts Hybrids and Packag
IEEE. Transactions on Parts, Hybrids, and Packaging — IEEE Trans Parts Hybrids Packag
IEEE. Transactions on Parts, Materials, and Packaging — IEEE Trans Parts Mater and Packag
IEEE. Transactions on Parts, Materials, and Packaging — IEEE Trans Parts Mater Packag
IEEE. Transactions on Pattern Analysis and Machine Intelligence — IEEE Trans Pattern Anal and Mach Intell
IEEE. Transactions on Plasma Science — IEEE Plas S
IEEE. Transactions on Plasma Science — IEEE T Pl Sci
IEEE. Transactions on Plasma Science — IEEE Trans Plasma Sci
IEEE. Transactions on Plasma Science — IEEE Trans PS
IEEE. Transactions on Plasma Science — ITPSB
IEEE. Transactions on Power Apparatus and Systems — IEEE Power
IEEE. Transactions on Power Apparatus and Systems — IEEE Trans Power App Syst
IEEE. Transactions on Power Apparatus and Systems — IEEE Trans Power Appar and Syst
IEEE. Transactions on Product Engineering and Production — IEEE Trans Prod Eng Prod
IEEE. Transactions on Professional Communications — IEEE Prof C
IEEE. Transactions on Professional Communications — IEEE Trans Prof Commun
IEEE Transactions on Radio Frequency Interference — IEEE Trans Radio Freq Interference
IEEE Transactions on Rehabilitation Engineering — IEEE Trans Rehabil Eng
IEEE. Transactions on Reliability — IEEE Reliab
IEEE. Transactions on Reliability — IEEE Trans Rel
IEEE. Transactions on Reliability — IEEE Trans Reliab
IEEE. Transactions on Reliability — IEEE Trans Reliability
IEEE [*Institute of Electrical and Electronics Engineers*] **Transactions on Signal Processing** — IEEE Signal
IEEE. Transactions on Software Engineering — IEEE Trans SE
IEEE. Transactions on Software Engineering — IEEE Trans Software Eng
IEEE. Transactions on Software Engineering — IEEE Trans Software Engrg
IEEE. Transactions on Software Engineering — Soft Eng
IEEE. Transactions on Sonics and Ultrasonics — IEEE Son Ul
IEEE. Transactions on Sonics and Ultrasonics — IEEE Trans Sonics & Ultrason
IEEE. Transactions on Sonics and Ultrasonics — IEEE Trans Sonics Ultrason
IEEE. Transactions on Space Electronics and Telemetry — IEEE Trans Space Electron Telem
IEEE. Transactions on Systems, Man, and Cybernetics — IEEE Syst M
IEEE. Transactions on Systems, Man, and Cybernetics — IEEE Trans Syst Man and Cybern
IEEE. Transactions on Systems, Man, and Cybernetics — IEEE Trans Syst Man Cybern
IEEE. Transactions on Systems, Man, and Cybernetics — IEEE Trans System
IEEE. Transactions on Systems, Man, and Cybernetics — IEEE Trans Systems Man Cybernet
IEEE. Transactions on Systems, Science, and Cybernetics — IEEE Trans Syst Sci and Cybern
IEEE. Transactions on Systems, Science, and Cybernetics — IEEE Trans Syst Sci Cybern
IEEE. Transactions on Ultrasonics Engineering — IEEE Trans Ultrason Eng
IEEE. Transactions on Ultrasonics Engineering — IEEE Trans Ultrasonics Eng
IEEE. Transactions on Vehicular Communications — IEEE Trans Veh Commun
IEEE. Transactions on Vehicular Communications — IEVCA
IEEE. Transactions on Vehicular Technology — IEEE Trans Veh Technol
IEEE. Transactions on Vehicular Technology — IEEE Veh T
IEEE Ultrasonics Symposium — IEEE Ultrason Symp
IEEE VLSI Multilevel Interconnection Conference — IEEE VLSI Multilevel Interconnect Conf
IEEE. Wescon Convention Record — IEEE Wescon Conven Rec
IEEE. Wescon Technical Papers — IEEE Wescon Tech Pap
IEE-IERE [*Institution of Electrical Engineers-Institution of Electronic and Radio Engineers*] **Proceedings (India)** — IEE-IERE Proc (India)
Iemootsies — TMB
IERE [*Institution of Electronic and Radio Engineers*] **Conference Proceedings (London)** — IERE Conf Proc (Lond)
IES Data Collections [*Database*] — IES-DC
IES [*Illuminating Engineering Societies of Australia*] **Lighting Review** — IES Light Rev
IES [*Illuminating Engineering Societies of Australia*] **Lighting Review** — IES Lighting Rev
IES [*Illuminating Engineering Societies of Australia*] **Lighting Review** — IES Ltg Rev
IES [*Illuminating Engineering Society*] **Monograph** — IES Mon
IET: Zeitschrift fuer Elektrische Informations- und Energietechnik — IET Z Elektr Inf Energietech
IF. Industrialization Forum — IFSRD
IF. Informatore Fitopatologico — IF Inf Fitopatol
IFA (International Fiscal Association) News — IFA News
IFA [*Institutul de Fizica Atomica*] **Monograph Series** — IFA Monogr Ser
IFAC (International Federation of Automatic Control) Proceedings Series — IFAC Proc Ser
IFAC (International Federation of Automatic Control) Series for Graduates, Research Workers, and Practising Engineers — IFAC Ser Grad Res Work Practising Engr
IFAC (International Federation of Automatic Control) Symposia Series — IFAC Symp Ser
IFAC (International Federation of Automatic Control) Symposia Series — IFAC Sympos Ser
IFAC Symposium on Identification and System Parameter Estimation (International Federation of Automatic Control) — IFAC Symp Identif Syst Parameter Estim
IFAC Symposium. Proceedings (International Federation of Automatic Control) — IFAC Symp Proc
IFAC Workshop (International Federation of Automatic Control) — IFAC Wrkshp
IFAC Workshop on Adaptive Control of Chemical Processes (International Federation of Automatic Control) — IFAC Workshop Adapt Control Chem Processes
IFAC Workshop on Modelling and Control of Biotechnical Processes (International Federation of Automatic Control) — IFAC Workshop Modell Control Biotech Processes
I.F.C.C. Bulletin. Institut Francais du Cafe et du Cacao — IFCC Bull
IFCC (International Federation of Clinical Chemistry) Workshop — IFCC Workshop
Ife African Studies — Ife Afr Stud
IFF [*Institut fuer Festkoerperforschung*] **Bulletin** — IFF Bull
IFF [*Institut fuer Festkoerperforschung*] **Bulletin** — IFFBB
IFFA. International Flavours and Food Additives — IFFA Int Flavours Food Addit
IFIP [*International Federation for Information Processing*] **Congress Series** [*Elsevier Book Series*] — IFIPC
IFIP [*International Federation for Information Processing*] **Information Bulletin** — IFIP Inf Bul
IFIP (International Federation for Information Processing) Medical Informatics Monograph Series — IFIP (Int Fed Inf Process) Med Inf Monogr Ser
IFIP (International Federation for Information Processing) World Conference Series on Medical Informatics — IFIP (Int Fed Inf Process) World Conf Ser Med Inf
IFIP [*International Federation for Information Processing*] **Medical Informatics Monograph Series** — IFIP Med Inf Monogr Ser
IFIP [*International Federation for Information Processing*] **World Conference Series on Medical Informatics** [*Elsevier Book Series*] — IFIPW
IfL [*Institut fuer Leichtbau und Oekonomische Verwendung von Werkstoffen*] **Mitteilung** [*Germany*] — IfL Mitt
IFLA [*International Federation of Library Associations and Institutions*] **Journal** — IFJOD
IFOC. International Fiber Optics and Communications — IFOC Int Fiber Opt
Ifo-Schnelldienst — Ifo
IFSCC (International Federation of Societies of Cosmetic Chemists) Congress — IFSCC Congr
IFT [*International Foundation for Telemetering*] **Journal** — IFT Jnl
IFTA [*Institut Francais de Transport Aerien*] **Research Papers** — IFTA Res Pap
IG [*Industrial Group, United Kingdom Atomic Energy Authority*] **Information Series** — IG Inf Ser
Igaku No Ayumi [*Japan*] — IGAYA
Igalaaq. Nortext [*Ottawa*] — IGLQ
IGG [*Instituto Geografico e Geologico de Sao Paulo*] **Revista** — IGG
Igiena, Microbiologie, si Epidemiologie — Ig Microb Epidem
Igiena, Microbiologie, si Epidemiologie — Ig Microbiol Epidemiol
Igiene e Sanita Pubblica — Ig San Pubbl
Igiene e Sanita Pubblica — Ig Sanita Pubblica
Igiene Moderna — Ig Mod

Iglesia de Espana en el Peru — IEP
IGT [*Instituut voor Grafische Techniek*] **Nieuws** — IGT Nie
IGU [*International Geographical Union*] **Newsletter** — IGU Newsl
IGW [*Institut fuer Gesellschaft und Wissenschaft*] **Informationen zur Wissenschaftsentwicklung** — IGW Inf
IGY [*International Geophysical Year*] **Bulletin** — IGY Bull
IGY [*International Geophysical Year*] **General Report Series** — IGY Gen Rep Ser
IGY [*International Geophysical Year*] **Oceanography Report** — IGY Oc Rep
IGY [*International Geophysical Year*] **Rocket Report** — IGY Rocket Rep
IGY [*International Geophysical Year*] **Satellite Report Series** — IGY Sat Rep Ser
IH Review [*New Zealand Society for the Intellectually Handicapped*] — IH Rev
Iheringia. Botanica. Museo Rio-Grandense de Ciencias Naturais — Iheringia Bot
Iheringia. Serie Antropologia — Iheringia Ser Antropol
Iheringia. Serie Botanica — Iheringia Ser Bot
Iheringia. Serie Divulgacao — Iheringia Ser Divulg
Iheringia. Serie Geologia — Iheringia Ser Geol
Iheringia. Serie Miscelanea — Iheringia Ser Misc
Iheringia. Serie Zoologia — Iheringia Ser Zool
IHI [*Ishikawajima-Harima Heavy Industries*] **Engineering Review** — IHI Eng Rev
IHVE [*Institution of Heating and Ventilating Engineers*] **Journal** — IHVE J
IHW [*Institut fuer Handwerkswirtschaft*] **Berichte** — IHW Ber
Il Movimento di Liberazione in Italia — Mov Liberaz Ital
IIASA Collaborative Proceedings Series (International Institute for Applied Systems Analysis) — IIASA Collab Proc Ser
IIASA Conference on Energy Resources (International Institute for Applied Systems Analysis) — IIASA Conf Energy Resour
IIASA Conference on Energy Resources. Proceedings (International Institute for Applied Systems Analysis) — IIASA Conf Energy Resour Proc
IIASA (International Institute for Applied Systems Analysis) Collaborative Proceedings Series — IIASA (Int Inst Appl Syst Anal) Collab Proc Ser
IIASA (International Institute for Applied Systems Analysis) Executive Report [*A publication*] — IIASA (Int Inst Appl Syst Anal) Exec Rep
IIASA [*International Institute for Applied Systems Analysis*] **Proceedings Series** — IIASA Proc Ser
IIASA [*International Institute for Applied Systems Analysis*] **Reports** — IIASA Rep
IIC [*International Institute for the Conservation of Museum Objects*] **Abstracts** — IIC Abstr
IIC. International Review of Industrial Property and Copyright Law — IIC Int R Ind Prop Cop Law
IICA (Instituto Interamericano de Ciencias Agricolas) Serie Publicaciones Miscelaneas — IICA (Inst Interam Cienc Agric) Ser Publ Misc
IID [*Institut International de Documentation*] **Communications** — IID Comm
IIE [*Institute of Industrial Engineers, Inc.*] **Transactions** — IIE Trans
IIF-IIR (Institut International du Froid - International Institute of Refrigeration) Commissions. Proceedings — IIF IIR Comm Proc
IIHR [*Iowa Institute of Hydraulic Research*] **Report** — IIHR Rep
IIRB. Revue de l'Institut International de Recherches Betteravieres — IIRB Rev Inst Int Rech Better
IJS [*Institut "Jozef Stefan"*] **Report R** — IJS Rep R
IKA. Zeitschrift fuer Internationalen Kulturaustausch — IKA Z fuer Int Kulturaustausch
IKO. Innere Kolonisation Land und Gemeinde — IKO Inn Kolonisation Land Gemeinde
Ikon — Ik
Ikonomicheska Mis'l — IKMLA
Ikonomika i Mekhanizatsiya na Selskoto Stopanstvo — Ikon Mekh Selsk Stop
Ikonomika na Selskoto Stopanstvo. Rural Economics — Ikon Selskoto Stop Rural Econ
Ikushugaku Zasshi/Japanese Journal of Breeding — Ikushugaku Zasshi/Jap J Breed
Ikuska. Instituto Vasco de Investigaciones — IVI
Il Bolletino — Il Boll
Il Bollettino delle Cliniche — Boll Clin
Il Dottore in Scienze Agrarie Forestali — Dottore Sci Agrar For
Il Hagalgal (Jerusalem) — HJ
Il Medico Veterinario (Torino) — Medico Vet (Torino)
Il Mondo — ILMN
Il Politico — Po
Il Polo. Istituto Geografico Polare — ILPO
Il Ponte — ILP
Il Progresso Medico — Prog Med
Il Tesaur — ILT
ILAFA. Congreso Latinoamericano de Siderurgia. Memoria Tecnica (Instituto Latinoamericano del Fierro y el Acero) — ILAFA Congr Latinoam Sider Mem Tec
Ilahiyat Fakueltesi Dergisi [*Ankara*] — I Fa De
Ilahiyat Fakultesi Dergisi — IFD
ILCA (International Livestock Centre for Africa) Research Report — ILCA (Int Livest Centr Afr) Res Rep
Ilerda — Ile
Iliff Review — Iliff R
Iliff Review — IR
Illawarra Historical Society. Monthly Notice — Illaw Hist Soc M Notice
Illawarra Historical Society. Newsletter — Illawarra Hist Soc Newsletter
Illini Horticulture. Illinois State Horticultural Society — Illini Hort
Illinois Administrative Code — Ill Admin Code
Illinois Agricultural Economics — Ill Agr Econ
Illinois Agricultural Economics — Ill Agric Econ
Illinois Agricultural Economics. Department of Agricultural Economics. Illinois University. Agricultural Experiment Station — Ill Agric Econ Dep Agric Econ Ill Univ Agric Exp Stn
Illinois. Agricultural Experiment Station. Bulletin — Ill Agric Exp Stn Bull
Illinois. Agricultural Experiment Station. Circular — Ill Agric Exp Stn Circ
Illinois. Agricultural Experiment Station. Department of Forestry. Forestry Research Report — Ill Agric Exp Stn Dep For For Res Rep
Illinois. Agricultural Experiment Station. Forestry Note — Ill Agric Exp Stn For Note
Illinois. Agricultural Experiment Station. Publications — Ill Ag Exp
Illinois Air Quality Report — Ill Air Qual Rep
Illinois Appellate Court Reports — Ill App
Illinois Banker — IBK
Illinois Bar Journal — IBJ
Illinois Bar Journal — Ill B J
Illinois Bar Journal — Ill Bar J
Illinois Biological Monographs — Ill Biol Mon
Illinois Biological Monographs — Ill Biol Monogr
Illinois Business — Ill Bus
Illinois Business Education Association. Reports — IBEA Reports
Illinois Business Review — ILB
Illinois Business Review — Ill Bus R
Illinois Catholic Historical Review — ICHR
Illinois Catholic Historical Review — Ill Cath His R
Illinois Classical Studies — ICS
Illinois Classical Studies — Ill Class Stud
Illinois Classical Studies — Ill Classic Stud
Illinois Coal Mining Investigations. Cooperative Agreement. Bulletin — Ill Coal M Investigations B
Illinois Coal. Proceedings. Annual Illinois Energy Conference — Ill Coal Proc Annu Ill Energy Conf
Illinois Continuing Legal Education — Ill CLE
Illinois Continuing Legal Education — Ill Cont Legal Ed
Illinois Court of Claims Reports — Ill Ct Cl
Illinois Dental Journal — Ill Dent J
Illinois. Department of Conservation. Technical Bulletin — Ill Dep Conserv Tech Bull
Illinois Department of Energy and Natural Resources. Document — Ill Dep Energy Nat Resour Doc
Illinois. Division of Fisheries. Special Fisheries Report — Ill Div Fish Spec Fish Rep
Illinois. Division of Industrial Planning and Development. Atlas of Illinois Resources — Ill Div Indus Plan and Devel Atlas Ill Res
Illinois Education — Ill Educ
Illinois Energy Conference — Ill Energy Conf
Illinois Energy Notes — Ill Energy Notes
Illinois. Environmental Protection Agency. Lake Michigan Water Quality Report — Ill Environ Prot Agency Lake Mich Water Qual Rep
Illinois Farmer — Illinois F
Illinois Geographical Society. Bulletin — Ill Geogr Soc Bull
Illinois. Geological Survey. Oil and Gas Drilling in Illinois. Monthly Report — Ill Geol Surv Oil Gas Drill Ill Mon Rep
Illinois Government Research — Ill Gov Res
Illinois Health News — Ill Hlth Ne
Illinois Horizons — Ill Horiz
Illinois Institute for Environmental Quality Document — Ill Inst Environ Qual Doc
Illinois Institute of Natural Resources Document — Ill Inst Nat Resour Doc
Illinois Institute of Technology. Research Publications — Ill Inst Technol Res Publ
Illinois Issues — Ill Issues
Illinois Journal of Health, Physical Education, and Recreation — ILHP
Illinois Journal of Mathematics — ILJM
Illinois Journal of Mathematics — Ill J Math
Illinois Journal of Mathematics — Illinois J Math
Illinois Labor Bulletin — Ill Labor Bull
Illinois Law Review — Ill L Rev
Illinois Law Review — Ill Law R
Illinois Law Review — Ill Law Rev
Illinois Law Review — Illinois Law Rev
Illinois Legislative Service (West) — Ill Legis Serv (West)
Illinois Libraries — Ill Lib
Illinois Libraries — Ill Libr
Illinois Library Association. Record — ILA Rec
Illinois Medical and Dental Monographs — Ill Med Dent Monogr
Illinois Medical Bulletin — Ill Med Bull
Illinois Medical Journal — Ill Med J
Illinois Medical Journal — Illinois Med J
Illinois Medical Journal — Illinois MJ
Illinois Medical Journal — IMJ
Illinois Mineral Notes — Illinois Miner Notes
Illinois Monographs in Medical Sciences — Ill Monogr Med Sci
Illinois Monthly Magazine — Ill Mo
Illinois Music Educator — IL
Illinois Music Educator — IME
Illinois Natural History Society. Transactions — Ill N H Soc Tr
Illinois Natural History Survey. Biological Notes — Ill Nat Hist Surv Biol Notes
Illinois Natural History Survey. Bulletin — Ill Nat Hist Surv Bull
Illinois Natural History Survey. Circular — Ill Nat Hist Surv Circ
Illinois Petroleum — Ill Pet
Illinois Petroleum Monitor — Ill Pet Mon
Illinois Publications in Language and Literature — IPLL
Illinois Quarterly — Ill Q
Illinois Rail System Plan. Annual Update — IRSPAU
Illinois Register — Ill Reg
Illinois Reports — Ill
Illinois Research — Ill Res
Illinois Research. Illinois Agricultural Experiment Station — Ill Res Agric Exp Stn
Illinois Research. Illinois Agricultural Experiment Station — Ill Res Ill Agric Exp Stn
Illinois Research. University of Illinois Agricultural Experiment Station — Illinois Res

Illinois Resource Network [*Database*] — IRN
Illinois Revised Statutes — Ill Rev Stat
Illinois Schools Journal — Ill Sch J
Illinois Society of Engineers and Surveyors — Ill Soc Eng
Illinois State Academy of Science. Transactions — Ill St Ac Sc Tr
Illinois State Academy of Science. Transactions — Ill State Acad Sci Trans
Illinois State Academy of Science. Transactions — Illinois Acad Sci Trans
Illinois State Academy of Science. Transactions — Trans Illinois State Acad Sci
Illinois State Florists Association. Bulletin — Ill State Florists Assoc Bull
Illinois State Geological Survey. Bulletin — Ill G S B
Illinois State Geological Survey. Bulletin — Ill State Geol Surv Bull
Illinois State Geological Survey. Circular — ILGCA
Illinois State Geological Survey. Circular — Ill State Geol Surv Circ
Illinois State Geological Survey. Circular — Illinois Geol Survey Circ
Illinois. State Geological Survey. Cooperative Ground-Water Report — Ill State Geol Surv Coop Ground Water Rep
Illinois. State Geological Survey. Cooperative Resources Report — Ill State Geol Surv Coop Resour Rep
Illinois State Geological Survey. Guide Leaflet — Ill Geol Surv Guide Leafl
Illinois State Geological Survey. Guidebook Series — IGSSA
Illinois State Geological Survey. Guidebook Series — Ill State Geol Surv Guideb Ser
Illinois State Geological Survey. Illinois Minerals Note — Ill State Geol Surv Ill Miner Note
Illinois State Geological Survey. Illinois Petroleum — ILGPA
Illinois State Geological Survey. Illinois Petroleum — Ill State Geol Surv Ill Petrol
Illinois State Geological Survey. Industrial Minerals Notes — Ill State Geol Surv Ind Miner Notes
Illinois. State Geological Survey. Report of Investigations — Ill State Geol Surv Rep Invest
Illinois State Geological Survey. Review of Activities — Ill Geol Surv Rev Act
Illinois State Historical Library. Collections — Ill His Col
Illinois State Historical Library. Collections — Ill Hist Coll
Illinois State Historical Library. Publications — Ill His L
Illinois State Historical Society. Journal — Ill His J
Illinois State Historical Society. Journal — Ill State Hist Soc Jour
Illinois State Historical Society. Journal — ISHS
Illinois State Historical Society. Journal — ISHSJ
Illinois State Historical Society. Transactions — Ill His S Trans
Illinois State Historical Society. Transactions — Ill His Trans
Illinois State Historical Society. Transactions — Ill State Hist Soc Trans
Illinois State Horticultural Society. Newsletter — Ill State Hort Soc N L
Illinois State Laboratory of Natural History. Bulletin — Ill St Lab N H B
Illinois State Museum of Natural History. Bulletin — Ill St Mus N H B
Illinois State Museum. Popular Science Series. Scientific Papers. Story of Illinois Series — Ill State Mus Pop Sci Ser Sci Paper Story Ill Ser
Illinois State Museum. Reports of Investigations — Ill State Mus Rep Invest
Illinois State University. Journal — Ill State Univ Jour
Illinois. State Water Survey and State Geological Survey. Cooperative Ground-Water Report — Ill State Water Surv State Geol Surv Coop Ground Water Rep
Illinois State Water Survey and State Geological Survey. Cooperative Resources Report — Ill State Water Surv State Geol Surv Coop Resour Rep
Illinois State Water Survey. Bulletin — Ill State Water Surv Bull
Illinois State Water Survey. Circular — Ill State Water Surv Circ
Illinois State Water Survey. Cooperative Ground-Water Report — Ill State Water Survey Cooperative Ground-Water Rept
Illinois State Water Survey. Division Bulletin. Circular. Reports of Investigations — Ill State Water Survey Div Bull Circ Rept Inv
Illinois. State Water Survey. Illinois. State Geological Survey. Cooperative Resources Report — Ill State Water Surv Ill State Geol Surv Coop Resour Rep
Illinois State Water Survey. Reports of Investigations — Ill State Water Surv Rep Invest
Illinois State Water Survey. Reports of Investigations — Illinois Water Survey Rept Inv
Illinois Student Lawyer — Ill Stud Law
Illinois Studies in Anthropology — Ill Stud Anthropol
Illinois Studies in Anthropology — ISA
Illinois Studies in Language and Literature — ISLL
Illinois Teacher — Ill Teach
Illinois Teacher of Home Economics — Ill Teach Home Econ
Illinois. University. Agricultural Experiment Station. Bulletin — Ill Univ Agric Exp Stn Bull
Illinois. University Agricultural Experiment Station. Forestry Note — Ill Univ Agric Exp Stn For Note
Illinois University. Bulletin. University Studies — Ill Univ B Univ Studies
Illinois University (Chicago Circle). Department of Geological Sciences. Technical Report — Ill Univ (Chicago Circle) Dep Geol Sci Tech Rep
Illinois University. Civil Engineering Studies. Construction Research Series — Ill Univ Civ Eng Stud Constr Res Ser
Illinois University. Civil Engineering Studies. Hydraulic Engineering Series — Ill Univ Civ Eng Stud Hydraul Eng Ser
Illinois University. Civil Engineering Studies. Soil Mechnanics Series — Ill Univ Civ Eng Stud Soil Mech Ser
Illinois University. Civil Engineering Studies. Structural Research Series — Ill Univ Civ Eng Stud Struct Res Ser
Illinois University. Cooperative Extension Service. Circular — Ill Univ Coop Ext Serv Circ
Illinois University. Department of Civil Engineering. Structural Research Series — Ill Univ Dep Civ Eng Struct Res Ser
Illinois University. Department of Electrical Engineering. Aeronomy Laboratory. Aeronomy Report — Ill Univ Dep Electr Eng Aeron Lab Aeron Rep
Illinois University. Department of Theoretical and Applied Mechanics. TAM Report — Ill Univ Dep Theor Appl Mech TAM Rep
Illinois University. Department of Theoretical and Applied Mechanics. TAM Report — Ill Univ TAM Rep
Illinois University. Engineering Experiment Station. Bulletin — Ill U Eng Exp Sta Bul
Illinois University. Engineering Experiment Station. Bulletin — Ill Univ Eng Exp Sta Bull
Illinois. University. Engineering Experiment Station. Bulletin — Ill Univ Eng Exp Stn Bull
Illinois University. Engineering Experiment Station. Bulletin. Circulars — Ill Univ Eng Expt Sta Bull Circ
Illinois University. Engineering Experiment Station. Circular — Ill U Eng Exp Sta Circ
Illinois. University. Engineering Experiment Station. Circular — Ill Univ Eng Exp Stn Circ
Illinois. University. Engineering Experiment Station. Reprint Series — Ill Univ Eng Exp Stn Repr Ser
Illinois University. Engineering Experiment Station. Technical Report — Ill Univ Eng Exp Stn Tech Rep
Illinois University. Proceedings of the Sanitary Engineering Conference — Ill Univ Proc Sanit Eng Conf
Illinois University. Water Resources Center. Research Report — Ill Univ Water Resour Cent Res Rep
Illinois Vegetable Growers' Bulletin. Illinois State Vegetable Growers' Association — Illinois Veg Growers Bull
Illinois Veterinarian — Ill Vet
Illiterati — Ill
Illuminare — Im
Illuminating Engineer (London) — Illum Eng (London)
Illuminating Engineering [*Later, Illuminating Engineering Society. Journal*] — IE
Illuminating Engineering [*Later, Illuminating Engineering Society. Journal*] — Ill Eng
Illuminating Engineering [*Later, Illuminating Engineering Society. Journal*] — Illum Eng
Illuminating Engineering (New York) — Illum Eng (NY)
Illuminating Engineering Society. Journal — Illum Eng Soc J
Illuminating Engineering Society. Transactions — Illum Eng Soc Trans
Illustrated American — Il Am
Illustrated Archaeologist — Illus Archaeol
Illustrated Broadcast Equipment Encyclopedia — IBEE
Illustrated London News — Ill London News
Illustrated London News — Illus Lond N
Illustrated London News — Illus Lond News
Illustrated London News — Illus London News
Illustrated London News — ILN
Illustrated Video Equipment Reference Catalog — IVERC
Illustrated Weekly of India — Illus W Ind
Illustrated Weekly of India. Annual — Illus W Ind A
Illustrated World — IW
Illustration — ILL
Illustration Horticole — Ill Hort
Illustrations of Greek Drama — IGD
Illustratori di Libri per Ragazzi — Illust Libri Rag
Illustrazione Biellese — IBi
Illustrazione Italiana — II
Illustrazione Pubblicitaria — Illust Pubb
Illustrazione Scientifica — Illne Scient
Illustrazione Vaticana — Ill Vat
Illustrazione Vaticana — IV
Illustrazione Vaticana — IVat
Illustrerad Motor Sport — Illus Motor Sp
Illustrerad Teknisk Tidning — Illus Tek Tidn
Illustrierte Flora — Ill Fl
Illustrierte Landwirtschaftliche Zeitung — Illus Landwirtsch Ztg
Illustrierte Monatshefte fuer die Gesammten Interessen des Judentums — IMJ
Illustrierte Monatsschrift der Aerztlichen Polytechnik — Ill Mschr Aerztl Polytechn
Illustrierte Zeitschrift fuer Entomologie — IZEnt
Illustrierte Zeitschrift fuer Tierfreunde. Organ des Oesterreichischen Bundes der Vogelfreunde in Graz — Ill Zs Tierfrde
Illustriertes Jahrbuch der Naturkunde — Ill Jahrb Naturk
Illustrirter Rosengarten — Ill Rosengart
Illyrici Sacri — Il Sac
Ilmenau, Technische Hochschule, Wissenschaftliche Zeitschrift — Ilmenau Tech Hochsch Wiss Z
Il'menskii Zapovednik. Trudy — Ilmenskii Zapov Tr
Ilmij Asarlari. V. I. Lenin Monidagi Toskent Davlat Universiteti — IlATos
ILO [*International Labour Organisation*] **Yearbook** — ILO Yb
Ilocos Fisheries Journal — Ilocos Fish J
Ilocos Review — Ilocos R
ILRI [*International Institute for Land Reclamation and Improvement*] **Publication** — ILRI Publ
ILRI Publication. International Institute for Land Reclamation and Improvement — ILRI Publ Int Inst Land Reclam Improv
Ilustracao Moderna [*Porto*] — IM
Ilustracao Trasmontana — IT
Ilustracion Cubana — ICub
Ilustracion del Clero — Ilu Cle
ILZRO [*International Lead Zinc Research Organization*] **Annual Review** — ILZRO Ann Rev
IM. Industrial Minerals — IM Ind Miner
Im Kampf und den Alten Orient — KAO
Im Lande der Bibel — Ld Bi
IMA (Institute of Mathematics and Its Applications) Journal of Mathematics Applied in Medicine and Biology — IMA (Inst Math Appl) J Math Appl Med Biol

IMA (Institute of Mathematics and Its Applications) Symposia — IMA Symp
IMA [*Institute of Mathematics and Its Applications*] **Journal of Applied Mathematics** — IMA J Appl Math
IMA Journal of Mathematical Control and Information — IMA J Math Control Inform
IMA Journal of Mathematics Applied in Business and Industry — IMA J Math Appl Bus Indust
IMA Journal of Mathematics Applied in Medicine and Biology — IMA J Math Appl Med Biol
IMA Journal of Mathematics in Management — IMA J Math Management
IMA [*Institute of Mathematics and Its Applications*] **Journal of Numerical Analysis** [*London*] — IMA J Numer Anal
IMA Volumes in Mathematics and its Applications — IMA Vol Math Appl
Image and Vision Computing — Image Vis C
Image Dynamics in Science and Medicine — Image Dyn Sci Med
Image et Son — Image & S
Image. Journal of Nursing Scholarship — Image J Nurs Sch
Image Processing Algorithms and Techniques — Image Process Algorithms Tech
Image Storage and Retrieval Systems — Image Storage Retr Syst
Image Technology — Image Technol
Imagen — IN
Images. Marquette University Dental Reflections — Images Marquette Univ Dent Reflections
Imagination — Im
Imagination, Cognition, and Personality — IC
Imagination Science Fiction — ISF
Imagines Inscriptionum Atticarum — Imag
Imagines Inscriptionum Atticarum — Imag Inscr Attic
Imagines Inscriptionum Graecarum Antiquissimarum — Imag IGA
Imago — Im
Imago Mundi — IM
Imago Mundi — Im M
IMC [*International Micrographic Congress*] **Journal** — IMC J
IMC [*International Information Management Congress*] **Journal** — IMC Jrnl
IMD [*Institute of Metal Division. American Institute of Mining, Metallurgical, and Petroleum Engineers*] **Special Report Series** — IMD Spec Rep Ser
IMechE Conference. Proceedings. Institution of Mechanical Engineers — IMechE Conf Proc Inst Mech Eng
IMechE Conference Transactions — IMechE Conf Trans
IMechE Seminar — IMechE Semin
IMEKO Symposium on Photon Detectors (Internationale Messtechnische Konfoderation) — IMEKO Symp Photon Detect
IMEKO Technical Committee on Metrology-TC8. Symposium (Internationale Messtechische Konfoderation) — IMEKO Tech Comm Metrol TC8 Symp
IMF [*International Monetary Fund*] **Survey** — IFU
IMF [*International Monetary Fund*] **Survey** — IMF Svy
IMF [*Institute of Metal Finishing*] **Symposium. Publication** — IMF Symp Publ
Imkerfreund — IMKRA3
IMLS [*Institute of Medical Laboratory Sciences*] **Current Topics in Medical Laboratory Sciences** — ICTSDI
IMLS (Institute of Medical Laboratory Sciences) Current Topics in Medical Laboratory Sciences — IMLS (Inst Med Lab Sci) Curr Top Med Lab Sci
IMM [*Institute of Mining and Metallurgy*] **Abstracts** — IMM Abstr
Immergruene Blaetter — IGBLBZ
Immergruene Blaetter — Immergrune Bl
Immigration Journal — Imm J
Immobilized Enzyme Engineering. Proceedings. National Seminar — Immobilized Enzyme Eng Proc Natl Semin
Immok Yukchong Yonku-So Yongu Pogo — IYYYA8
Immune Mechanisms in Cutaneous Disease — Immune Mech Cutaneous Dis
Immune Regulators in Transfer Factor. Proceedings. International Symposium on Transfer Factor — Immune Regul Transfer Factor Proc Int Symp
Immune System and Infectious Diseases. International Convocation on Immunology — Immune Syst Infect Dis Int Convoc Immunol
Immune System. Functions and Therapy of Dysfunction — Immune Syst Funct Ther Dysfunct
Immune System. Genes, Receptors, Signals. ICN-UCLA Symposium on Molecular Biology — Immune Syst Genes Recept Signals ICN UCLA Symp Mol Biol
Immunitaet und Infektion — IMIND
Immunitaet und Infektion — IMINDI
Immunitaet und Infektion — Immun Infekt
Immunitet i Pokoi Rastenii — Immun Pokoi Rast
Immunitet Sel'skokhozyaistvennykh Rastenii k Boleznyam i Vreditelyam — Immun Skh Rast Bolezn Vred
Immunity and Tolerance in Oncogenesis — Immun Tolerance Oncog
Immunity Bulletin — Immun Bull
Immunity, Cancer, and Chemotherapy. Basic Relationships on the Cellular Level. Symposium [*monograph*] — Immun Cancer Chemother Symp
Immunity to Parasites. Symposium. British Society for Parasitology — Immun Parasites Symp Br Soc Parasitol
Immunization for Japanese Encephalitis. Conference — Immun Jpn Encephalitis Conf
Immunoassay Technology — Immunoassay Technol
Immunoassay Technology — IMTCE7
Immunoassays in Food Analysis. Proceedings of a Symposium — Immunoassays Food Anal Proc Symp
Immunobiology — IMMND4
Immunobiology and Immunotherapy of Cancer — Immunobiol Immunother Cancer
Immunobiology of Proteins and Peptides — Immunobiol Proteins Pept
Immunobiology Supplement — Immunobiol Suppl
Immunochemical Protocols — Immunochem Protoc
Immunochemistry — IMCHAZ
Immunochemistry — Immunochem
Immunochemistry of Proteins — Immunochem Proteins
Immunochemistry of the Extracellular Matrix — Immunochem Extracell Matrix
Immunodiagnosis of Cancer [*Monograph*] — Immunodiagn Cancer
Immunoenzymatic Techniques. Proceedings. International Symposium on Immunoenzymatic Techniques — Immunoenzym Tech Proc Int Symp
Immunofluorescence and Related Staining Techniques. Proceedings. International Conference in Immunoflourescence and Related Staining Techniques — Immunofluoresc Relat Staining Tech Proc Int Conf
Immunogenetics — Immunogenet
Immunogenetics — IMNGBK
Immunologia Clinica — Immunol Clin
Immunologia Clinica e Sperimentale — ICSPD4
Immunologia Clinica e Sperimentale — Immunol Clin Sper
Immunologia Polska — Immunol Pol
Immunologia Polska — IMPODM
Immunologic Research — Immunol Res
Immunologic Research — IMRSEB
Immunological Communications — IMLCA
Immunological Communications — IMLCAV
Immunological Communications — Immun Commun
Immunological Communications — Immunol Com
Immunological Communications — Immunol Commun
Immunological Investigations — IMINEJ
Immunological Investigations — Immunol Invest
Immunological Methods — Immunol Methods
Immunological Reviews — Immunol Rev
Immunological Reviews — IMRED2
Immunologicheskie Aspekty Biologii Razvitiya. Materialy Rabochego Soveshchaniya Immunologicheskie Aspekty Biologii Razvitiya — Immunol Aspekty Biol Razvit Mater Rab Soveshch
Immunologiya — IMMLDW
Immunologiya — IMNGA
Immunologiya i Bakteriologiya Khronicheskogo Infektsionnogo Protsessa — Immunol Bakteriol Khronicheskogo Infekts Protsessa
Immunologiya Razmnozheniya. Trudy Mezhdunarodnogo Simpoziuma — Immunol Razmnozheniya Tr Mezhdunar Simp
Immunology — IMMUAM
Immunology — Immun
Immunology and Aging — Immunol Aging
Immunology and Allergy Clinics of North America — Immunol Allergy Clin North Am
Immunology and Cell Biology — Immunol Cell Biol
Immunology and Hematology Research. Monograph — Immunol Hematol Res Monogr
Immunology and Infectious Diseases — Immunol Infect Dis
Immunology in Medical Practice [*Monograph*] — Immunol Med Pract
Immunology Letters — IMLED
Immunology Letters — IMLED6
Immunology Letters — Immunol Lett
Immunology of Cardiovascular Disease — Immunol Cardiovasc Dis
Immunology of Milk and the Neonate — Immunol Milk Neonate
Immunology of Reproduction. Proceedings. International Symposium — Immunol Reprod Proc Int Symp
Immunology of the Bacterial Cell Envelope — Immunol Bact Cell Envelope
Immunology Series — Immunol Ser
Immunology Series — Immunology Ser
Immunology Series — IMSED7
Immunology Today — Immunol Today
Immunology Today — IMTOD8
Immunoparasitology Today. A Combined Issue of Immunology Today and Parasitology Today — Immunop Tod
Immunopathology. International Convocation on Immunology — Immunopathol Int Convoc Immunol
Immunopharmacology — IMMUDP
Immunopharmacology and Immunotoxicology — Immunopharmacol Immunotoxicol
Immunotoxicology and Immunopharmacology — Immunotoxicol Immunopharmacol
Imono. Journal of the Japan Foundrymen's Society — Imono J Japan Foundrymen's Soc
Impact — Imp
Impact. Agricultural Research in Texas. Annual Report — Impact Agric Res Tex Annu Rep
Impact. Agricultural Research in Texas. Annual Report — IPCTAO
Impact des Projets sur l'Environnement. Congres AQTE [*Association Quebecoise des Techniques de l'Eau*] — Impact Proj Environ Congr AQTE
Impact of Acid Rain and Deposition on Aquatic Biological Systems. Symposium — Impact Acid Rain Deposition Aquat Biol Syst Symp
Impact of Biology on Modern Psychiatry. Proceedings. Symposium — Impact Biol Mod Psychiatry Proc Symp
Impact of Science on Society — Imp Sci Soc
Impact of Science on Society — Impact Sci
Impact of Science on Society — Impact Sci Soc
Impact of Science on Society — IMS
Impact of Science on Society [*English Edition*] — ISSOA8
Impact of Science on Society — PISC
Impact of Science on Society (English Edition) — Impact Sci Soc (Engl Ed)
Impact of Toxicology on Food Processing. Symposium — Impact Toxicol Food Process Symp
Impact of VLBI (Viking Lander Biological Instrument) on Astrophysics and Geophysics. Proceedings. Symposium. International Astronomical Union — Impact VLBI Astrophys Geophys Proc Symp Int Astron Union
Impacto Socialista — Impact Soc

Impacts de la Structure des Paysages Agricoles sur la Protection des Cultures. Colloque France-Pologne — Impacts Struct Paysages Agric Prot Cult Colloq Fr Pol
Impacts of Nuclear Releases into the Aquatic Environment. Proceedings. International Symposium — Impacts Nucl Releases Aquat Environ Proc Int Symp
Impacts of Radionuclide Releases into the Marine Environment. Proceedings. International Symposium — Impacts Radionuclide Releases Mar Environ Proc Int Symp
Imperial and Asiatic Quarterly Review — EAQR
Imperial and Asiatic Quarterly Review — IAQR
Imperial and Asiatic Quarterly Review — Imp Asiat Q Rev
Imperial and Colonial Magazine — ICM
Imperial Bureau of Animal Health. Review Series — Imp Bur Anim Health Rev Ser
Imperial Bureau of Dairy Science. Technical Communication — Imp Bur Dairy Sci Tech Commun
Imperial Bureau of Fruit Production (Great Britain). Technical Communication — Imp Bur Fruit Prod GB Tech Commun
Imperial Bureau of Soil Science, Soils, and Fertilizers — Imp Bur Soil Sci Soils Fert
Imperial Bureau of Soil Science. Technical Communication — Imp Bur Soil Sci Tech Commun
Imperial Chemical Industries Review — ICI Rev
Imperial College of Science and Technology. Applied Geochemistry Research Group. Technical Communication — Imp Coll Sci Technol Appl Geochem Res Group Tech Commun
Imperial College of Science and Technology. Geochemical Prospecting Research Centre. Technical Communication — Imp Coll Sci Technol Geochem Prospect Res Cent Tech Commun
Imperial College of Science and Technology. Rock Mechanics Research Report — Imp Coll Sci Technol Rock Mech Res Rep
Imperial College of Tropical Agriculture (Trinidad). Circular — Imp Coll Trop Agric (Trinidad) Circ
Imperial College of Tropical Agriculture (Trinidad). Low Temperature Research Station. Memoirs — Imp Coll Trop Agric (Trinidad) Low Temp Res Stn Mem
Imperial College of Tropical Agriculture (Trinidad). Memoirs. Mycological Series — Imp Coll Trop Agric (Trinidad) Mem Mycol Ser
Imperial Earthquake Investigation Committee. Bulletin — Imp Earthquake Investigation Com B
Imperial Ethiopian Government Institute of Agricultural Research. Report — IEGRBU
Imperial Ethiopian Government Institute of Agricultural Research. Report — Imp Ethiop Gov Inst Agric Res Rep
Imperial Institute Bulletin — Imp Inst B
Imperial Institute of Agricultural Research (Pusa). Bulletin — Imp Inst Agric Res (Pusa) Bull
Imperial Oil Review — IMOR
Imperial Oil Review — Imp Oil R
Imperial Oil Review — Imperial Oil R
Imperial Review — Imp Rev
Imperial Zootechnical Experiment Station. Bulletin — Imp Zootech Exp Stn Bull
Impetus. Magazine Supplement of the Financial Post — IMPE
Impianti — IMPID
Implantation of the Ovum. Papers — Implant Ovum Pap
Implement and Tractor — Imp & Tractr
Implement and Tractor Red Book — Imp & Trac RB
Import/Export News — Imp Exp
Import Statistical Schedule (Japan) — Jpn Import
Importance of Vitamins to Human Health. Proceedings. Kellogg Nutrition Symposium — Importance Vitam Hum Health Proc Kellogg Nutr Symp
Important Advances in Oncology — Important Adv Oncol
Imprensa Medica — Impr Med
Impresa Pubblica — Impr Pubbl
Imprimerie et Industries Graphiques — Imprim Ind Graphiques
Imprimerie Nationale — Impr Nat
Improving Catheter Site Care. Proceedings. Symposium — Improv Catheter Site Care Proc Symp
Improving College and University Teaching — ICUNA5
Improving College and University Teaching — ICUT
Improving College and University Teaching — Improv Coll & Univ Teach
Improving College and University Teaching — Improv Coll Univ Teach
Improving College and University Teaching — Improving Coll & Univ Teach
Improving College and University Teaching Yearbook — Improv Coll Univ Teach Ybk
Improving Human Performance — Impr Hum P
Impulse — Imp
Impulse zur Entwicklung Metallurgischer Verfahren. Vortraege beim Metallurgischen Seminar — Impulse Entwickl Metall Verfahren Vortr Metall Semin
Impul'snaya Fotometriya — Impul'snaya Fotom
Impulstechniken — Impulstech
IMR. Industrial Management Review — IMR Ind Manage Rev
Imre Nagy Institute Review — Imre Nagy Inst Rev
IMS [*Industrial Management Society*] **Clinical Proceedings** — IMS Clin Proc
IMZ [*Internationales Musikzentrum*] **Bulletin** — IMZ Bul
In Business — In Bus
In Business — INB
In Gerardagum — InGerar
In Health — PINH
In Practice — In Pract
In Practice — IPRCDH
In Review. Canadian Books for Young People — In Rev
In Search/En Quete [*Canada*] — In Search
In Situ. Oil-Coal-Shale-Minerals — In Situ Oil Coal Shale Miner
In Tema di Medicina e Cultura — In Tema Med Cult
In the Grade School — In Grade Sch
In Theory Only — INTGA
In Theory Only — ITO
In These Times — ITT
In Touch with the Dutch — IUH
In Vitro [*Rockville*] — ITCSAF
In Vitro Cellular and Developmental Biology — In Vitro Cell Dev Biol
In Vitro Cellular and Developmental Biology. Animal — In Vitro Cell Dev Biol Anim
In Vitro Cellular and Developmental Biology. Journal. Tissue Cultural Association — In Vitro Cell Dev Biol J Tissue Cult Assoc
In Vitro Effects of Mineral Dusts. International Workshop — In Vitro Eff Miner Dusts Int Workshop
In Vitro Immunology — In Vitro Immunol
In Vitro. Journal of the Tissue Culture Association — In Vitro J Tissue Cult Assoc
In Vitro. Journal of the Tissue Culture Association — ITCSA
In Vitro Monograph — In Vitro Monogr
In Vitro Monograph — IVMOD2
In Vitro Toxicology — In Vitro Toxicol
In Vitro Toxicology. Mechanisms and New Technology — In Vitro Toxicol Mech New Technol
In Vitro v CSSR — IVTRBA
In Vivo. The Business and Medicine Report — In Vivo Bus Med Rep
Inadvertent Modification of the Immune Response. Proceedings. FDA [*US Food and Drug Administration*] **Science Symposium** — Inadvertent Modif Immune Response Proc FDA Sci Symp
Inaugural Lectures. University of Oxford — ILUO
Inbound Traffic Guide — ITG
Inc. — INO
Incentive Marketing — IMK
Incentive Marketing — Incntv Mkt
Incentive Marketing — IVM
InCider — GINC
Inclusion Compounds — Inclusion Compd
Income Tax Act Regulations [*Database*] — ITA
Income Tax Decisions of Australasia — ITDA
Income Tax Decisions of Australasia (Ratcliffe and McGrath) — R & McG
Income Tax Reporter — Income Tax Rep
Incomes Data Services Ltd. International Report — IDS Report
Incompatibility Newsletter — Incompat Newsl
Incontri Linguistici — ILing
Incontri Linguistici — InLi
Incontri Musicali — IM
Incontro di Studio su le Possibilita delle Colture e degli Allevamenti nei Territori Alpini — Incontro Stud Possibilita Colt Allevamenti Territ Alp
Incorporated Australian Insurance Institute. Journal — Inc Aust Insurance Inst J
Incorporated Linguist — Inc Linguist
Incorporated Linguist [*London*] — IncL
Incorporated Linguist — Incorp Ling
Incorporating Your Business — Incorp Bus
INCRA [*International Copper Research Association, Inc.*] **Research Report** — INCRA Res Rep
Increasing Understanding of Public Problems and Policies — Increasing Understanding Public Probl Policies
Incremental Motion Control Systems and Devices. Newsletter — Incremental Motion Control Syst Devices Newsl
Incunable. Salamanca — Inc
Incunable Short Title Catalogue [*Database*] — ISTC
Indagationes Mathematicae — Indag Math
Indagationes Mathematicae. New Series — Indag Math NS
Indagini e Problemi — Ind Probl
Indent. Journal of International Dentistry. English Edition — Indent Engl
Independent — IND
Independent — INDEP
Independent Agent — IndA
Independent Banker — IBA
Independent Baptist Missionary Messenger — Indep Bap Mis Mess
Independent Broadcasting [*United Kingdom*] — Ind Bcasting
Independent Broadcasting — Indep Broadcast
Independent Coal Operator [*United States*] — Indep Coal Oper
Independent Education — Indep Ed
Independent Education — Indep Educ
Independent Film Journal — Indep F J
Independent Investor — Indep Invest
Independent Investors Forum [*Database*] — IIF
Independent Journal of Philosophy — Indep J Philos
Independent Journal of Philosophy — Independ J Phil
Independent Petroleum Association of America. Monthly — Indep Pet Assoc Am Mon
Independent Petroleum Association of America. Monthly — Independent Petroleum Assoc America Monthly
Independent Restaurants — Inde Rest
Independent School Bulletin — Ind Sch Bull
Independent School Bulletin — ISB
Independent Shavian — I Sh
Independent Shavian — I Shaw
Independent Shavian — IndS
Independent Voice — Indep Voice
Independent Woman — Ind Woman
Index 81 [*Eighty-One*] **Congress Papers** — Index 81 Eighty One Congr Pap
Index Aeronauticus — Ind Aeron
Index Analyticus Cancerologiae — Ind Analyt Canc
Index Analyticus Cancerologiae — Index Anal Cancerol

Index Aureliensis — Ind Aurel
Index Bibliographicus — Ind Bibl
Index Bibliographicus Societatis Jesu — IBSJ
Index Catalog of Medical and Veterinary Zoology — Index Cat Med Vet Zool
Index Chemicus — Index Chem
Index Chemicus Registry System [*Database*] — ICRS
Index Ethnographicus — Ind Ethn
Index Generaux du Lineaire — IGLB
Index Hepaticarum — INHEES
Index Horti Botanici Universitatis Budapestinensis — Index Horti Bot Univ Budapest
Index India — IIn
Index India — Ind India
Index Islamicus — Ind Isl
Index Islamicus — Ind Islam
Index Islamicus — Index Islam
Index Library — IL
Index Librorum Prohibitorum — ILP
Index Medicus — IM
Index Medicus — IMed
Index Medicus — Ind Med
Index Medicus — Index Med
Index Odontologicus — Ind Odont
Index of American Periodical Verse — Ind Amer Per Verse
Index of American Periodical Verse — Index Am Period Verse
Index of Articles on Jewish Studies — IAJS
Index of Articles on Jewish Studies — IJewAr
Index of Catholic Biographies — ICB
Index of Conference Proceedings Received by the British Library Lending Division — Index Conf Proc Received by BLLD
Index of Economic Articles — IEc
Index of Economic Articles in Journals and Collective Volumes — Index Econ Artic J Collect Vols
Index of Economic Journals — Ind Econ J
Index of Economic Journals — Index Econ J
Index of Indian Medical Periodicals — Ind Ind Med Per
Index of Mathematical Papers — Index Math Pap
Index of Potters' Stamps on Terra Sigillata — IPSTS
Index of Psychoanalytic Writings — Index Psychoanal Wr
Index of Transactions and Journal. Society of Motion Picture Engineers — Index JSMPE
Index of Veterinary Specialities — IVS
Index on Censorship — I on C
Index on Censorship — Index Censor
Index on Censorship. Writers and Scholars International — INDEX
Index. Park Practice Program — Index Park Pract Prog
Index Quaderni Camerti di Studi Romanistici — Index Quad
Index Romanus — Ind Rom
Index Romanus — IR
Index Society Publications — Index Soc Pub
Index Specifications and Standards — Index Specif Stand
Index to American Doctoral Dissertations — IADD
Index to Book Reviews in the Humanities — IBk
Index to Book Reviews in the Humanities — Index Book Rev Humanit
Index to Canadian Legal Periodical Literature — Index Can Leg Period Lit
Index to Canadian Securities Cases — ICSC
Index to Chinese Periodicals — ICP
Index to Commonwealth Legal Periodicals — Index Commonw Leg Period
Index to Commonwealth Little Magazines — ICLM
Index to Current Information — ICI
Index to Current Urban Documents — Ind Curr Urb Doc
Index to Current Urban Documents — Index Curr Urban Doc
Index to Current Urban Documents — Index Current Urban Docs
Index to Dental Literature — IDL
Index to Dental Literature — Index Dent Lit
Index to Educational Videotapes — Ind Educ Vid
Index to Federal Tax Articles. Supplement — Index Fed Tax Artic Supp
Index to Foreign Legal Periodicals — IFLP
Index to Foreign Legal Periodicals — Index Foreign Leg Per
Index to Foreign Legal Periodicals and Collections of Essays — Index Foreign Leg Per Collect Essays
Index to Free Periodicals — IFP
Index to Free Periodicals — Index Free Period
Index to Government Orders — Index Gov Orders
Index to Health and Safety Education — Ind Hlth Saf Educ
Index to IEEE [*Institute of Electrical and Electronic Engineers*] **Publications** — Index IEEE Publ
Index to Indian Periodical Literature — Index Indian Period Lit
Index to International Statistics — IIS
Index to Jewish Periodicals — IJewPer
Index to Jewish Periodicals — Ind Jew Per
Index to Jewish Periodicals — Index Jew Period
Index to Latin American Periodicals — LatAm
Index to Legal Periodicals — ILP
Index to Legal Periodicals — Ind Leg Per
Index to Legal Periodicals — Index Leg Period
Index to Legal Periodicals [*United States*] — Index Legal Period
Index to Legal Periodicals — LegPer
Index to Literature on the American Indian — Ind Lit Amer Indian
Index to Literature on the American Indian — Index Lit Am Indian
Index to Little Magazines — Ind Little Mag
Index to Little Magazines — LMags
Index to New England Periodicals — Index New Engl Period
Index to New England Periodicals — INEP
Index to New Zealand Periodicals — Ind NZ Per
Index to New Zealand Periodicals — Index New Z Period
Index to Park Practice — Index Park Pract
Index to Periodical Articles by and about Blacks — Ind Per Blacks
Index to Periodical Articles by and about Blacks — Index Period Artic Blacks
Index to Periodical Articles by and about Negroes [*Later, Index to Periodical Articles by and about Blacks*] — Ind Per Negroes
Index to Periodical Articles by and about Negroes [*Later, Index to Periodical Articles by and about Blacks*] — Index Period Artic Negroes
Index to Periodical Articles by and about Negroes [*Later, Index to Periodical Articles by and about Blacks*] — INeg
Index to Periodical Articles on Aging — Index Period Lit Aging
Index to Periodical Articles Related to Law — Ind Per Art Relat Law
Index to Periodical Articles Related to Law — Index Period Artic Relat Law
Index to Periodical Articles Related to Law — IPARL
Index to Philippine Periodicals — Index Philip Period
Index to Plant Chromosome Numbers — Index Pl Chromosome Numbers
Index to Publications. American Society of Mechanical Engineers — Index Publ Am Soc Mech Eng
Index to Religious Periodical Literature — Index to Relig Period Lit
Index to Religious Periodical Literature — IRPL
Index to Scientific and Technical Proceedings — IS & TP
Index to Scientific Reviews [*Institute for Scientific Information*] [*Information service or system*] — Ind Sci Rev
Index to Scientific Reviews — Index Sci Rev
Index to Scientific Reviews [*Database*] — ISR
Index to Selected Periodicals — Ind Sel Per
Index to Social Sciences and Humanities Proceedings — Index Soc Sci Humanit Proc
Index to South African Periodicals — Ind SA Per
Index to South African Periodicals — Index South Afr Period
Index to the Journal of the Society of Motion Picture and Television Engineers — Index JSMPTE
Index to the Literature of Food Investigation — Index Lit Food Invest
Index to United States Government Periodicals — Ind US Gov Per
Index to United States Government Periodicals — Index US Gov Period
Index Veterinarius — Ind Vet
Index Veterinarius — Index Vet
India. Articles in Economic History — IAEH
India. Atomic Energy Commission. Bhabha Atomic Research Centre. Report — India AEC Bhabha At Res Cent Rep
India. Coffee Board. Annual Report — ICBRAO
India. Coffee Board. Annual Report — India Coffee Board Annu Rep
India. Coffee Board. Research Department. Annual Detailed Technical Report — ICOAB5
India. Coffee Board. Research Department. Annual Detailed Technical Report — India Coffee Bd Res Dep Annu Detailed Tech Rep
India. Coffee Board. Research Department. Annual Detailed Technical Report — India Coffee Board Res Dep Annu Detailed Tech Rep
India. Coffee Board. Research Department. Annual Report — AINCAR
India. Coffee Board. Research Department. Annual Report — India Coffee Board Res Dep Annu Rep
India. Coffee Board. Research Department. Bulletin — India Coffee Board Res Dep Bull
India. CSIR [*Council of Scientific and Industrial Research*] **Zoological Memoir** [*A publication*] — India CSIR Zool Mem
India Cultures Quarterly — Ind Cult Q
India. Directorate of Plant Protection, Quarantine, and Storage. Plant Protection Bulletin — India Dir Plant Prot Quar Storage Plant Prot Bull
India Economic Bulletin — IAE
India. Geological Survey. Bulletins. Series A. Economic Geology — India Geol Surv Bull Ser A
India. Geological Survey. Bulletins. Series B. Engineering Geology and Ground-Water — India Geol Surv Bull Ser B
India. Geological Survey. Memoirs — India Geol Surv Mem
India. Geological Survey. Memoirs. Palaeontologia Indica. New Series — India Geol Surv Mem Palaeontol Indica New Ser
India. Geological Survey. Miscellaneous Publication — India Geol Surv Misc Publ
India. Geological Survey. News — India Geol Surv News
India International Centre Quarterly — India Int Centre Quart
India Library Association Bulletin — ILAB
India. National Academy of Science. Proceedings. Section B — India Natl Acad Sci Proc Sect B
India Office Records. Marine Journal — IORMJ
India. Oil and Natural Gas Commission. Bulletin — India Oil Nat Gas Comm Bull
India Quarterly — Ind Q
India Quarterly — Ind Quart
India Quarterly — India Q
India Quarterly — India Quar
India Quarterly — India Quart
India Quarterly — IQ
India Rubber Journal — Ind Rub J
India Rubber Review — India Rubb R
India Rubber World — Ind Rub Wd
India Rubber World — India Rubb Wld
India Rubber World (New York) — India Rub World NY
Indian Academy of Geoscience. Journal — Indian Acad Geosci J
Indian Academy of Mathematics. Journal — J Indn Acad Math
Indian Academy of Medical Sciences. Annual — Indian Acad Med Sci Ann
Indian Academy of Sciences. Proceedings — Indian Acad Sci Pro
Indian Academy of Sciences. Proceedings. Plant Sciences — Indian Acad Sci Proc Plant Sci
Indian Academy of Sciences. Proceedings. Section A. Earth and Planetary Sciences — Indian Acad Sci Proc Sect A

Indian Academy of Sciences. Proceedings. Section A. Earth and Planetary Sciences — PISAA7
Indian Academy of Sciences. Proceedings. Section A. Earth and Planetary Sciences — Proc Indian Acad Sci Sect A Earth Planetary Sci
Indian Academy of Sciences. Proceedings. Section B — Indian Acad Sci Proc Sect B
Indian Academy of Sciences. Proceedings. Section B — PISBAA
Indian Advocate — Ind Adv
Indian Affairs — InAf
Indian Affairs Record — IAR
Indian Agricultural Research Institute [*New Delhi*]. Annual Report — IRIABC
Indian Agricultural Research Institute [*New Delhi*]. Annual Scientific Report — IRISAV
Indian Agricultural Research Institute (New Delhi). Annual Report — Indian Agric Res Inst (New Delhi) Annu Rep
Indian Agricultural Research Institute (New Delhi). Annual Scientific Report — Indian Agric Res Inst (New Delhi) Annu Sci Rep
Indian Agriculturist — INAGAT
Indian Agriculturist — Indian Agr
Indian Agriculturist — Indian Agric
Indian America — INAM
Indian and Eastern Engineer — Ind East Eng
Indian and Eastern Engineer — Indian East Eng
Indian and Foreign Review — I & FR
Indian and Inuit Supporter. A Newsletter of the Indian and Inuit Support Group of Newfoundland and Labrador — IAIS
Indian and Northern Affairs Backgrounder — INAB
Indian and Northern Affairs Communique — INAC
Indian Anthropologist — Ind Anthro
Indian Antiquary — I Aq
Indian Antiquary — IA
Indian Antiquary — IAn
Indian Antiquary — Ind Ant
Indian Antiquary — Indian Ant
Indian Archaeology — Ind Ar
Indian Architect — Indian Archt
Indian Archives — Ind Arch
Indian Art and Letters — IAL
Indian Art Sketch Book — IASB
Indian Association for the Cultivation of Science. Proceedings — Indian Assoc Cultiv Sci Proc
Indian Bee Journal — IBEJA8
Indian Bee Journal — Indian Bee J
Indian Behavioural Sciences Abstracts — IBSA
Indian Behavioural Sciences Abstracts — Indian Behav Sci Abstr
Indian Biologist — INBID9
Indian Biologist — Indian Biol
Indian Botanical Contactor — IBCOEH
Indian Botanical Contactor — Indian Bot Contactor
Indian Botanical Reporter — IBREDR
Indian Botanical Reporter — Indian Bot Rep
Indian Bureau of Mines. Mineral Economics Division. Market Survey Series — Indian Bur Mines Miner Econ Div Mark Surv Ser
Indian Cases — Indian Cas
Indian Central Jute Committee. Annual Report of the Jute Agricultural Research Institute — ICJRAU
Indian Central Jute Committee. Annual Report of the Jute Agricultural Research Institute — Indian Cent Jute Comm Annu Rep Jute Agric Res Inst
Indian Ceramic Society. Transactions — Indian Ceram Soc Trans
Indian Ceramic Society. Transactions — Indian Ceramic Soc Trans
Indian Ceramics [*India*] — Indian Ceram
Indian Chemical Engineer — Indian Chem Engr
Indian Chemical Journal — Indian Chem J
Indian Chemical Journal. Annual Number [*India*] — Indian Chem J Ann Number
Indian Chemical Manufacturer — ICMFA
Indian Chemical Manufacturer — Indian Chem Manuf
Indian Chemical Manufacturer. Annual Number — Indian Chem Manuf Annu Number
Indian Church Commentaries — Ind CC
Indian Church History Review — ICHR
Indian Church History Review — Ind Ch HR
Indian Church History Review — Ind Chur Hist R
Indian Church History Review — Indian Church Hist R
Indian Coconut Journal — ICOJAV
Indian Coconut Journal — Indian Coconut J
Indian Coffee — ICOFAJ
Indian Coffee — Indian Cof
Indian Concrete Journal — Indian Concr J
Indian Cooperative Review — Ind Coop R
Indian Cotton Growing Review — ICGRAF
Indian Cotton Growing Review — Ind Cott Grow Rev
Indian Cotton Growing Review — Indian Cott Grow Rev
Indian Cotton Growing Review — Indian Cotton Grow Rev
Indian Cotton Growing Review. Indian Central Cotton Committee — Indian Cotton Growing Rev
Indian Cotton Journal — Indian Cott J
Indian Cotton Textile Industry — Ind Cott Text Ind
Indian Council of Agricultural Research. Animal Husbandry Series — IAAHA9
Indian Council of Agricultural Research. Animal Husbandry Series — Indian Counc Agric Res Anim Husb Ser
Indian Council of Agricultural Research. Annual Technical Report — IAARA5
Indian Council of Agricultural Research. Annual Technical Report — Indian Counc Agric Res Annu Tech Rep
Indian Council of Agricultural Research. Cereal Crop Series — IACEAA
Indian Council of Agricultural Research. Cereal Crop Series — Indian Counc Agric Res Cereal Crop Ser
Indian Council of Agricultural Research. Entomological Monographs — IAEMAA
Indian Council of Agricultural Research. Entomological Monographs — Indian Counc Agric Res Entomol Monogr
Indian Council of Agricultural Research. Miscellaneous Bulletin — ICARAJ
Indian Council of Agricultural Research. Miscellaneous Bulletin — Indian Counc Agric Res Misc Bull
Indian Council of Agricultural Research. Monograph — IAMOAM
Indian Council of Agricultural Research. Monograph — Indian Counc Agric Res Monogr
Indian Council of Agricultural Research. Report Series — IARTAS
Indian Council of Agricultural Research. Report Series — Indian Counc Agric Res Rep Ser
Indian Council of Agricultural Research. Research Series — ICRRA2
Indian Council of Agricultural Research. Research Series — Indian Counc Agric Res Res Ser
Indian Council of Agricultural Research. Review Series — Indian Counc Agric Res Rev Ser
Indian Council of Agricultural Research. Review Series — IRRSA8
Indian Council of Agricultural Research. Technical Bulletin — ICATAP
Indian Council of Agricultural Research. Technical Bulletin — Indian Counc Agric Res Tech Bull
Indian Council of Medical Research. Annual Report — Indian Counc Med Res Annu Rep
Indian Council of Medical Research. Technical Report Series — IMRSB8
Indian Council of Medical Research. Technical Report Series — Indian Counc Med Res Tech Rep Ser
Indian Culture — IC
Indian Culture — Ind Cult
Indian Dental Journal — Ind Dent J
Indian Dental Review — Ind Dent Rev
Indian Drugs — INDRBA
Indian Ecclesiastical Studies — Ind E St
Indian Ecclesiastical Studies — Ind Eccl St
Indian Ecclesiastical Studies — Ind ES
Indian Ecclesiastical Studies [*Belgium*] — IndEcSt
Indian Ecologist — Indian Ecol
Indian Economic and Social History Review — IESH
Indian Economic and Social History Review — IESHR
Indian Economic and Social History Review — Ind Econ Soc Hist R
Indian Economic and Social History Review — IndE
Indian Economic and Social History Review — India Econ Soc Hist R
Indian Economic and Social History Review — Indian Econ Soc Hist Rev
Indian Economic Journal — I Econ J
Indian Economic Journal — IEE
Indian Economic Journal — IEJ
Indian Economic Journal — Ind Econ J
Indian Economic Journal — Ind EJ
Indian Economic Review — IER
Indian Economic Review — Ind Econ R
Indian Economic Review — Indian Econ R
Indian Education Newsletter [*Vancouver, British Columbia*] — INEN
Indian Educational Review — Ind Educ R
Indian Educational Review — Indian Ed Rev
Indian Educator — Indian Educ
Indian Engineer — Indian Eng
Indian Evangelical Review — IEvR
Indian Export Trade Journal — Indian Export Trade J
Indian Farm Mechanization — Indian Farm Mech
Indian Farming — Ind F
Indian Farming — Ind Farm
Indian Farming — Indian Fmg
Indian Farming — INFAA2
Indian Folklore — F
Indian Folklore — IFL
Indian Food Packer — IFPAAU
Indian Food Packer — Indian Food Pack
Indian Foreign Policy Annual Survey — Indian For Pol Ann Surv
Indian Forest Bulletin — IFOBAS
Indian Forest Bulletin — Indian For Bull
Indian Forest Bulletin. Entomology. Forest Research Institute (Dehra) — Indian For Bull For Res Inst (Dehra)
Indian Forest Leaflets — FRILAB
Indian Forest Leaflets — Ind For Leafl
Indian Forest Leaflets — Indian For Leafl
Indian Forest Records — Ind For Rec
Indian Forest Records — Indian For Rec
Indian Forest Records. Botany — IFRBA9
Indian Forest Records. Botany — Indian For Rec Bot
Indian Forest Records. Botany. Forest Research Institute — Indian Forest Rec Bot
Indian Forest Records. Entomology — IFREAI
Indian Forest Records. Entomology — Indian For Rec Entomol
Indian Forest Records. Forest Management and Mensuration — IFREDL
Indian Forest Records. Forest Management and Mensuration — Indian For Rec For Manage & Mensuration
Indian Forest Records. Forest Pathology — IFFPAP
Indian Forest Records. Forest Pathology — Indian For Rec For Pathol
Indian Forest Records. Mycology — IFRMA8
Indian Forest Records. Mycology — Indian For Rec Mycol
Indian Forest Records. Silvics — IFRSDT
Indian Forest Records. Silvics — Indian For Rec Silvics
Indian Forest Records. Silviculture — IFRSAQ

Indian Forest Records. Silviculture — Indian For Rec Silvic
Indian Forest Records. Statistical — IFRSBR
Indian Forest Records. Statistical — Indian For Rec Stat
Indian Forest Records. Timber Mechanics — IFRTAT
Indian Forest Records. Timber Mechanics — Indian For Rec Timber Mech
Indian Forest Records. Wild Life and Recreation — Indian For Rec Wild Life Recreat
Indian Forest Records. Wild Life and Recreation — Indian For Rec Wild Life Recreation
Indian Forest Records. Wild Life and Recreation — IWLRAA
Indian Forest Records. Wood Anatomy — IFRAA6
Indian Forest Records. Wood Anatomy — Indian For Rec Wood Anat
Indian Forest Records. Wood Preservation — Indian For Rec Wood Preserv
Indian Forest Records. Wood Seasoning — Indian For Rec Wood Seas
Indian Forest Records. Wood Technology — Indian For Rec Wood Technol
Indian Forester — IFORA8
Indian Forester — Ind For
Indian Forester — Indian For
Indian Foundry Journal — Indian Foundry J
Indian Geographer — IG
Indian Geographer — Ind Geogr
Indian Geographical Journal [*Madras*] — IGJ
Indian Geographical Journal — Ind Geog J
Indian Geographical Journal — Ind Geogr J
Indian Geohydrology — Indian Geohydrol
Indian Geological Index — Indian Geol Index
Indian Geologists Association. Bulletin — Indian Geol Assoc Bull
Indian Geotechnical Journal — IGTJA
Indian Geotechnical Journal — Indian Geotech J
Indian Heart Journal — IHEJAG
Indian Heart Journal — Ind Heart J
Indian Heart Journal — Indian Heart J
Indian Heart Journal. Teaching Series — Indian Heart J Teach Ser
Indian Highways — Indian Highw
Indian Historian — I Hist
Indian Historian — IndH
Indian Historian — Indian Hist
Indian Historical Quarterly — IHQ
Indian Historical Quarterly — Ind Hist Q
Indian Historical Quarterly — Indian Hist Q
Indian Historical Records Commission. Proceedings — IHRC
Indian History Congress. Proceedings — IHCP
Indian Homoeopathic Review — Ind Hom Rev
Indian Horizons — I Horizons
Indian Horizons — Ind Hor
Indian Horizons — Ind Horizons
Indian Horticulture — Indian Hort
Indian Horticulture — Indian Hortic
Indian Horticulture — INHOAK
Indian Industries — Indian Ind
Indian Institute of Architects. Journal — Indian Inst of Archts Jnl
Indian Institute of Metals. Transactions — Indian Inst Met Trans
Indian Institute of Technology. Bombay Series — Indian Inst Technol Bombay Ser
Indian Journal of Acarology — IJACDQ
Indian Journal of Acarology — Indian J Acarol
Indian Journal of Adult Education — Ind J Ad Ed
Indian Journal of Adult Education — Indian J Adult Ed
Indian Journal of Agricultural and Veterinary Education — IJVEAW
Indian Journal of Agricultural and Veterinary Education — Ind J Agric Vet Educ
Indian Journal of Agricultural and Veterinary Education — Indian J Agric Vet Educ
Indian Journal of Agricultural Chemistry — IJACB
Indian Journal of Agricultural Chemistry — IJACBO
Indian Journal of Agricultural Chemistry — Indian J Agric Chem
Indian Journal of Agricultural Economics — IJAE
Indian Journal of Agricultural Economics — Ind J Agr Econ
Indian Journal of Agricultural Economics — Ind J Agric Econ
Indian Journal of Agricultural Economics — Indian J Agr Econ
Indian Journal of Agricultural Economics — Indian J Agric Econ
Indian Journal of Agricultural Research — IJARC
Indian Journal of Agricultural Research — IJARC2
Indian Journal of Agricultural Research — Indian J Agric Res
Indian Journal of Agricultural Science — I J Agr Sci
Indian Journal of Agricultural Science — IJASA3
Indian Journal of Agricultural Science — Ind J Ag Sci
Indian Journal of Agricultural Science — Ind J Agric Sci
Indian Journal of Agricultural Science — Indian J Agr Sci
Indian Journal of Agricultural Science — Indian J Agric Sci
Indian Journal of Agronomy — IJAGAZ
Indian Journal of Agronomy — Indian J Agron
Indian Journal of Air Pollution Control [*India*] — Indian J Air Pollut Control
Indian Journal of American Studies — IJAS
Indian Journal of Anaesthesia — IJANBN
Indian Journal of Anaesthesia — Ind J Anesth
Indian Journal of Anaesthesia — Indian J Anaesth
Indian Journal of Animal Health — IJAHA4
Indian Journal of Animal Health — Indian J Anim Health
Indian Journal of Animal Health — Indian J Animal Health
Indian Journal of Animal Research — IALRB
Indian Journal of Animal Research — IALRBR
Indian Journal of Animal Research — Indian J Anim Res
Indian Journal of Animal Sciences — IJLAA4
Indian Journal of Animal Sciences — Indian J Anim Sci
Indian Journal of Applied Chemistry — Indian J Appl Chem
Indian Journal of Applied Psychology — IJAPBT
Indian Journal of Applied Psychology — Indian J Appl Psychol
Indian Journal of Biochemistry [*Later, Indian Journal of Biochemistry and Biophysics*] — IJBCAS
Indian Journal of Biochemistry [*Later, Indian Journal of Biochemistry and Biophysics*] — Indian J Biochem
Indian Journal of Biochemistry and Biophysics — I J Bioch B
Indian Journal of Biochemistry and Biophysics — Indian J Biochem Biophys
Indian Journal of Botany — IJBODX
Indian Journal of Botany [*India*] — Indian J Bot
Indian Journal of Cancer — IJCAAR
Indian Journal of Cancer — Indian J Cancer
Indian Journal of Cancer Chemotherapy — Indian J Cancer Chemother
Indian Journal of Chemical Education — IJCEA
Indian Journal of Chemical Education — Indian J Chem Educ
Indian Journal of Chemical Sciences — Indian J Chem Sci
Indian Journal of Chemistry — I J Chem
Indian Journal of Chemistry — IJOCAP
Indian Journal of Chemistry — Indian J Chem
Indian Journal of Chemistry. Section A. Inorganic, Physical, Theoretical, and Analytical — IJCADU
Indian Journal of Chemistry. Section A. Inorganic, Physical, Theoretical, and Analytical — Indian J Chem A
Indian Journal of Chemistry. Section A. Inorganic, Physical, Theoretical, and Analytical — Indian J Chem Sect A
Indian Journal of Chemistry. Section A. Inorganic, Physical, Theoretical, and Analytical — Indian J Chem Sect A Inorg Phys Theor Anal
Indian Journal of Chemistry. Section B. Organic Chemistry, Including Medicinal Chemistry — IJSBDB
Indian Journal of Chemistry. Section B. Organic Chemistry, Including Medicinal Chemistry — Indian J Chem B
Indian Journal of Chemistry. Section B. Organic Chemistry, Including Medicinal Chemistry — Indian J Chem Sect B
Indian Journal of Chemistry. Section B. Organic Chemistry, Including Medicinal Chemistry — Indian J Chem Sect B Org Chem Incl Med Chem
Indian Journal of Chest Diseases [*Later, Indian Journal of Chest Diseases and Allied Sciences*] — IJCDA2
Indian Journal of Chest Diseases [*Later, Indian Journal of Chest Diseases and Allied Sciences*] — Indian J Chest Dis
Indian Journal of Chest Diseases and Allied Sciences — ICDSD6
Indian Journal of Chest Diseases and Allied Sciences — Indian J Chest Dis Allied Sci
Indian Journal of Child Health — IJCHA
Indian Journal of Child Health [*India*] — Indian J Child Health
Indian Journal of Commerce [*Chandigarh*] — IJC
Indian Journal of Commerce — Ind J Commer
Indian Journal of Comparative Animal Physiology — ICAPDG
Indian Journal of Comparative Animal Physiology — Indian J Comp Anim Physiol
Indian Journal of Criminology — Indian J Criminol
Indian Journal of Cryogenics — IJCRD
Indian Journal of Cryogenics — Indian J Cryog
Indian Journal of Dairy Science — IJDSAI
Indian Journal of Dairy Science — Indian J Dairy Sci
Indian Journal of Dermatology [*Later, Indian Journal of Dermatology, Venereology, and Leprology*] — IJDEAA
Indian Journal of Dermatology [*Later, Indian Journal of Dermatology, Venereology, and Leprology*] — Indian J Dermatol
Indian Journal of Dermatology and Venereology [*Later, Indian Journal of Dermatology, Venereology, and Leprology*] — IJDVAR
Indian Journal of Dermatology and Venereology [*Later, Indian Journal of Dermatology, Venereology, and Leprology*] — Indian J Dermatol Venereol
Indian Journal of Dermatology, Venereology, and Leprology — IJDLDY
Indian Journal of Dermatology, Venereology, and Leprology — Indian J Dermatol Venereol Leprol
Indian Journal of Earth Sciences — IJEAB
Indian Journal of Earth Sciences — IJEAB4
Indian Journal of Earth Sciences — Indian J Earth Sci
Indian Journal of Ecology — IJECDC
Indian Journal of Ecology — Indian J Ecol
Indian Journal of Economics — IJE
Indian Journal of Economics — Ind J Econ
Indian Journal of Educational Administration and Research — Indian J Ed Adm & Res
Indian Journal of Engineering Mathematics — Indian J Engrg Math
Indian Journal of English Studies [*Calcutta*] — IJES
Indian Journal of Entomology — IJENA8
Indian Journal of Entomology — Indian J Ent
Indian Journal of Entomology — Indian J Entomol
Indian Journal of Environmental Health — IJEHB
Indian Journal of Environmental Health — IJEHBP
Indian Journal of Environmental Health — Indian J Environ Health
Indian Journal of Environmental Protection [*India*] — Indian J Environ Prot
Indian Journal of Experimental Biology — I J Ex Biol
Indian Journal of Experimental Biology — IJEBA6
Indian Journal of Experimental Biology — Indian J Exp Biol
Indian Journal of Experimental Biology — Indian J Expl Biol
Indian Journal of Experimental Psychology — IJEPAE
Indian Journal of Experimental Psychology — Indian J Exp Psychol
Indian Journal of Extension Education — Indian J Ext Educ
Indian Journal of Farm Chemicals — Indian J Farm Chem
Indian Journal of Farm Sciences — IJFSBT
Indian Journal of Farm Sciences — Indian J Farm Sci
Indian Journal of Fisheries — IJFIAW
Indian Journal of Fisheries — Indian J Fish

Indian Journal of Forestry — IJFODJ
Indian Journal of Forestry — Ind J Forest
Indian Journal of Forestry — Indian J For
Indian Journal of Gastroenterology — Indian J Gastroenterol
Indian Journal of Genetics and Plant Breeding — I J Genet P
Indian Journal of Genetics and Plant Breeding — IJGBAG
Indian Journal of Genetics and Plant Breeding — Indian J Genet Pl Breed
Indian Journal of Genetics and Plant Breeding — Indian J Genet Plant Breed
Indian Journal of Helminthology — IJHEAU
Indian Journal of Helminthology — Indian J Helminthol
Indian Journal of Heredity — Indian J Hered
Indian Journal of Heredity — INJHA
Indian Journal of Heredity — INJHA9
Indian Journal of Heterocyclic Chemistry — Indian J Heterocycl Chem
Indian Journal of History of Medicine — Indian J Hist Med
Indian Journal of History of Science — Indian J Hist Sci
Indian Journal of History of Science. National Institute of Sciences of India [*New Delhi*] — Indian J History Sci
Indian Journal of Horticulture — IJHOAQ
Indian Journal of Horticulture — Indian J Hort
Indian Journal of Horticulture — Indian J Hortic
Indian Journal of Hospital Pharmacy — IJHPBU
Indian Journal of Hospital Pharmacy — Indian J Hosp Pharm
Indian Journal of Industrial Medicine — IJIDAW
Indian Journal of Industrial Medicine — Indian J Ind Med
Indian Journal of Industrial Relations — I J Ind Rel
Indian Journal of Industrial Relations — Ind J Indus Rel
Indian Journal of Industrial Relations — Ind J Industr Relat
Indian Journal of Industrial Relations — Indian J Ind Rel
Indian Journal of International Law — IJIL
Indian Journal of International Law — Ind J Int L
Indian Journal of International Law — Indian J Int Law
Indian Journal of International Law — Indian J Int'l L
Indian Journal of International Law — Indian J of Internat L
Indian Journal of Leprosy — Indian J Lepr
Indian Journal of Linguistics/Praci-Bhasha-Vijnan — IJL
Indian Journal of Malariology — IJMAA9
Indian Journal of Malariology — Indian J Malariol
Indian Journal of Marine Sciences — IJMNB
Indian Journal of Marine Sciences — Indian J Mar Sci
Indian Journal of Mathematics — Indian J Math
Indian Journal of Mechanics and Mathematics — Indian J Mech Math
Indian Journal of Medical Research — I J Med Res
Indian Journal of Medical Research — Indian J Med Res
Indian Journal of Medical Research — Indian J Med Research
Indian Journal of Medical Research. Section A — Indian J Med Res Sect A
Indian Journal of Medical Research. Section A. Infectious Diseases — I J Med R A
Indian Journal of Medical Research. Section B — Indian J Med Res Sect B
Indian Journal of Medical Sciences — Indian J Med Sci
Indian Journal of Medicine and Surgery — Indian J Med Surg
Indian Journal of Meteorology and Geophysics [*Later, Mausam*] — Indian J Meteorol and Geophys
Indian Journal of Meteorology and Geophysics [*Later, Mausam*] — Indian J Meteorol Geophys
Indian Journal of Meteorology, Hydrology, and Geophysics [*Later, Mausam*] — Indian J Meteorol Hydrol and Geophys
Indian Journal of Meteorology, Hydrology, and Geophysics [*Later, Mausam*] — Indian J Meteorol Hydrol Geophys
Indian Journal of Microbiology — IJMBA
Indian Journal of Microbiology — Indian J Microbiol
Indian Journal of Mycological Research — Indian J Mycol Res
Indian Journal of Mycology and Plant Pathology — Indian J Mycol Plant Pathol
Indian Journal of Natural Products — Indian J Nat Prod
Indian Journal of Natural Rubber Research — Indian J Nat Rubber Res
Indian Journal of Nematology — Indian J Nematol
Indian Journal of Nutrition and Dietetics — I J Nutr D
Indian Journal of Nutrition and Dietetics — Indian J Nutr Diet
Indian Journal of Occupational Health — Ind J Occup Hlth
Indian Journal of Occupational Health — Indian J Occup Health
Indian Journal of Ophthalmology — Indian J Ophthalmol
Indian Journal of Orthopaedics [*India*] — Indian J Orthop
Indian Journal of Otolaryngology — Ind J Otol
Indian Journal of Otolaryngology — Indian J Otolaryngol
Indian Journal of Parasitology — Indian J Parasitol
Indian Journal of Pathology and Bacteriology [*Later, Indian Journal of Pathology and Microbiology*] — Indian J Pathol Bacteriol
Indian Journal of Pathology and Microbiology — Indian J Pathol Microbiol
Indian Journal of Pediatrics — Indian J Pediatr
Indian Journal of Pharmaceutical Education — Indian J Pharm Educ
Indian Journal of Pharmaceutical Sciences — Indian J Pharm Sci
Indian Journal of Pharmacology — Indian J Pharmacol
Indian Journal of Pharmacy — Indian J Pharm
Indian Journal of Philosophy — IJP
Indian Journal of Physical and Natural Sciences — Indian J Phys Nat Sci
Indian Journal of Physical Anthropology and Human Genetics — Indian J Phys Anthropol Hum Genet
Indian Journal of Physics — I J Physics
Indian Journal of Physics — Indian J Phys
Indian Journal of Physics. B — Indian J Phys B
Indian Journal of Physics. Part A — Indian J Phys Part A
Indian Journal of Physics. Part B — Indian J Phys Part B
Indian Journal of Physiology and Allied Sciences — Indian J Physiol Allied Sci
Indian Journal of Physiology and Pharmacology — Indian J Physiol Pharmacol
Indian Journal of Plant Pathology — Indian J Plant Pathol
Indian Journal of Plant Physiology — Indian J Plant Physiol
Indian Journal of Plant Protection — Indian J Plant Prot
Indian Journal of Political Science — IJPS
Indian Journal of Political Science — Ind J Pol Sci
Indian Journal of Political Science — Ind J Polit Sci
Indian Journal of Political Science — India J Pol Sci
Indian Journal of Politics — Ind J Polit
Indian Journal of Poultry Science — Indian J Poult Sci
Indian Journal of Poultry Science. Official Journal. Indian Poultry Science Association — Indian J Poult Sci Off J Indian Poult Sci Assoc
Indian Journal of Power and River Valley Development — Indian J Power and River Val Dev
Indian Journal of Power and River Valley Development — Indian J Power River Val Dev
Indian Journal of Power and River Valley Development — Indian J Power River Val Develop
Indian Journal of Psychiatry — Ind J Psych
Indian Journal of Psychiatry — Indian J Psychiatry
Indian Journal of Psychological Medicine — Indian J Psychol Med
Indian Journal of Psychology — I J Psychol
Indian Journal of Psychology — Indian J Psychol
Indian Journal of Psychology — INJPA
Indian Journal of Public Administration — IJPA
Indian Journal of Public Administration — Ind J Publ Adm
Indian Journal of Public Administration — Indian J of Publ Adm
Indian Journal of Public Administration — Indian J Pub Admin
Indian Journal of Public Health — Indian J Publ Health
Indian Journal of Public Health — Indian J Public Health
Indian Journal of Pure and Applied Mathematics — Indian J Pure and Appl Math
Indian Journal of Pure and Applied Mathematics — Indian J Pure Appl Math
Indian Journal of Pure and Applied Physics — I J PA Phys
Indian Journal of Pure and Applied Physics — Indian J Pure and Appl Phys
Indian Journal of Pure and Applied Physics — Indian J Pure Appl Phys
Indian Journal of Pure and Applied Science — Indian J Pure Appl Sci
Indian Journal of Radio and Space Physics — IJRSA
Indian Journal of Radio and Space Physics — Indian J Radio and Space Phys
Indian Journal of Radio and Space Physics — Indian J Radio Space Phys
Indian Journal of Radiology — Indian J Radiol
Indian Journal of Radiology and Imaging — Indian J Radiol Imag
Indian Journal of Regional Science — Indian J Reg Sci
Indian Journal of Science and Industry — Indian J Sci Ind
Indian Journal of Science and Industry. Section A. Agricultural and Animal Sciences — Indian J Sci Ind Sect A Agric Anim Sci
Indian Journal of Science and Industry. Section A. Agricultural Sciences [*Later, Indian Journal of Agricultural Research*] — IJIAA
Indian Journal of Science and Industry. Section A. Agricultural Sciences [*Later, Indian Journal of Agricultural Research*] — Indian J Sci Ind Sect A
Indian Journal of Science and Industry. Section B. Animal Sciences [*Later, Indian Journal of Animal Research*] — Indian J Sci Ind Sect B Anim Sci
Indian Journal of Sericulture — IJSEA
Indian Journal of Sericulture — Indian J Seric
Indian Journal of Social Research — I J Soc Res
Indian Journal of Social Research — Ind J Soc Res
Indian Journal of Social Work — IJSW
Indian Journal of Social Work — Ind J Soc Wk
Indian Journal of Social Work — Indian J Social Work
Indian Journal of Soil Conservation — Indian J Soil Conser
Indian Journal of Statistics — Ind J Stat
Indian Journal of Sugar Cane Research and Development — Indian J Sugar Cane Res Dev
Indian Journal of Surgery — Indian J Surg
Indian Journal of Technology — I J Techn
Indian Journal of Technology — Indian J Tech
Indian Journal of Technology — Indian J Technol
Indian Journal of Textile Research — Indian J Text Res
Indian Journal of the History of Medicine — IJHM
Indian Journal of Theology — IJT
Indian Journal of Theology — Ind J Th
Indian Journal of Theology [*Serampore*] — IndJT
Indian Journal of Theoretical Physics — I J Theor P
Indian Journal of Theoretical Physics — Indian J Theor Phys
Indian Journal of Tuberculosis — IJTBAD
Indian Journal of Tuberculosis — Indian J Tuberc
Indian Journal of Tuberculosis — Indian J Tuberculosis
Indian Journal of Veterinary Medicine — IJVMDP
Indian Journal of Veterinary Medicine — Indian J Vet Med
Indian Journal of Veterinary Pathology — Indian J Vet Pathol
Indian Journal of Veterinary Science — Ind J Vet Sci
Indian Journal of Veterinary Science and Animal Husbandry — Ind J Vet Sci An Hus
Indian Journal of Veterinary Science and Animal Husbandry — Indian J Vet Sci
Indian Journal of Veterinary Science and Animal Husbandry — Indian J Vet Sci Anim Husb
Indian Journal of Veterinary Surgery — IJVSD9
Indian Journal of Veterinary Surgery — Indian J Vet Surg
Indian Journal of Virology — IJVIEE
Indian Journal of Virology — Indian J Virol
Indian Journal of Weed Science — Indian J Weed Sci
Indian Journal of Zoology — Indian J Zool
Indian Journal of Zootomy — Indian J Zootomy
Indian Labour Gazette — ILG
Indian Labour Journal — Ind Lab J
Indian Lac Research Institute. Annual Report — Indian Lac Res Inst Annu Rep
Indian Lac Research Institute. Bulletin — Indian Lac Res Inst Bull
Indian Lac Research Institute. Research Notes — Indian Lac Res Inst Res Notes

Indian Lac Research Institute. Technical Notes — Indian Lac Res Inst Tech Note
Indian Law Institute. Journal — ILI
Indian Law Reporter. American Indian Lawyers Training Program — Indian L Rep Am Indian Law Training Program
Indian Law Review — ILR
Indian Law Review — Ind LR
Indian Law Review — Indian L Rev
Indian Librarian — I Lib
Indian Librarian — IL
Indian Librarian — ILn
Indian Librarian — Ind Lib
Indian Librarian — Indian Librn
Indian Library Association. Bulletin — Indian Libr Ass Bull
Indian Library Association. Journal — ILA
Indian Library Association. Journal — Indian Lib Assn J
Indian Library Science Abstracts — Indian Lib Sci Abstr
Indian Library Science Abstracts — Indian Libr Sci Abstr
Indian Linguistics — I Lg
Indian Linguistics — IL
Indian Linguistics — ILin
Indian Linguistics — Ind Ling
Indian Linguistics — Ind Linguist
Indian Literature — I Lit
Indian Literature — IL
Indian Literature — Ind L
Indian Literature — IndLit
Indian Literature — InL
Indian Medical Forum — Ind Med For
Indian Medical Forum — Indian Med Forum
Indian Medical Gazette — IMG
Indian Medical Gazette — Ind Med Gaz
Indian Medical Gazette — Indian M Gaz
Indian Medical Gazette — Indian Med Gaz
Indian Medical Journal — Ind Med J
Indian Medical Journal (Calcutta) — Indian Med J (Calcutta)
Indian Medical Record — Ind Med Rec
Indian Medical Research Memoirs — Ind Med Res Mem
Indian Medical Research Memoirs — Indian Med Res Mem
Indian Medical Review — Indian Med R
Indian Medical Service — Ind Med Serv
Indian Medical Service News — Ind Med Serv N
Indian Medical World — Ind Med Wld
Indian Mineralogist — Indian Mineral
Indian Minerals — Indian Miner
Indian Minerals Yearbook — Indian Miner Yearb
Indian Mining and Engineering Journal — Indian Min Engng J
Indian Mining Journal — Ind Min J
Indian Museum. Bulletin — Indian Mus Bull
Indian Museum Notes — Ind Mus Not
Indian Museum. Records — Indian Mus Rec
Indian Music Journal — Indian MJ
Indian Music Quarterly — Indian Mus Q
Indian Musician — IPOGA
Indian Musicological Society. Journal — Indian M S
Indian National Science Academy. Bulletin — Indian Nat Sci Acad Bull
Indian National Science Academy. Bulletin — INSA Bull
Indian National Science Academy. Mathematical Tables — Ind Natl Sci Acad Math Table
Indian National Science Academy. Monographs — Indian Natl Sci Acad Monogr
Indian National Science Academy. Proceedings. Part A. Physical Sciences — Indian Natl Sci Acad Proc Part A
Indian National Science Academy. Transactions — Indian Natl Sci Acad Trans
Indian Natural Resources — Indian Nat Resour
Indian News — INDN
Indian Notes — Indn Notes
Indian Notes and Monographs — Indn Notes Monogr
Indian Numismatic Chronicle — INC
Indian Paediatrics — Indian Paediatr
Indian Pediatrics — Indian Pediatr
Indian PEN — InPEN
Indian PEN — IPEN
Indian Perfumer — Indian Perfum
Indian Perfumer — IPERAS
Indian Periodical Literature — Ind Per Lit
Indian Pharmacist — Ind Pharm
Indian Philosophical Annual — Ind Philo A
Indian Philosophical Quarterly — Indian Phil Quart
Indian Philosophy and Culture — Indian Phil Cult
Indian Philosophy and Culture. Quarterly — IPC
Indian Physician — Ind Phyc
Indian Physico-Mathematical Journal — Ind Phys Math J
Indian Physico-Mathematical Journal — Indian Phys Math J
Indian Physiologist — Ind Phys
Indian Phytopathology — Indian Phytopathol
Indian Phytopathology — IPHYA
Indian Planting and Gardening — Indian Pl Gard
Indian Police Journal — Ind Pol J
Indian Political Science Review — I Polit Sci
Indian Political Science Review — Ind Pol Sci R
Indian Political Science Review — Ind Polit Sci R
Indian Political Science Review — India Pol Sci R
Indian Potash Journal — Indian Potash J
Indian Potato Journal — Indian Potato J
Indian Poultry Gazette [*India*] — Indian Poult Gaz
Indian Poultry Review — Indian Poult Rev
Indian Practitioner — Indian Pract
Indian Practitioner — IPRAA
Indian Psychological Abstracts — Indian Psychol Abstr
Indian Psychological Review — I Psychol R
Indian Psychological Review — Ind Psych R
Indian Psychological Review — Indian Psychol R
Indian Public Health and Municipal Journal — Ind Publ Hlth Munic J
Indian Pulp and Paper — Indian Pulp Pap
Indian Pulp and Paper Technical Association. Journal — IPPTA
Indian Record — Indian Rec
Indian Record — INRE
Indian Refractory Makers Association. Journal — Indian Refract Makers Assoc J
Indian Research Series — IRS
Indian Review — Ind R
Indian Review — Indian R
Indian Review — IR
Indian Review of Life Sciences — Indian Rev Life Sci
Indian Rubber Manufacturers Research Association. Technical Seminar. Proceedings — Indian Rubber Manuf Res Assoc Tech Semin Proc
Indian Science Abstracts — Ind Sci Abstr
Indian Science Abstracts — Indian Sci Abstr
Indian Science Abstracts — Indian Sci Abstracts
Indian Science Abstracts (New Delhi) — Indian Sci Abstr New Delhi
Indian Science Congress Association. Proceedings — Indian Sci Cong Assoc Proc
Indian Science Congress Association. Proceedings — Indian Sci Congr Assoc Proc
Indian Science Cruiser — Indian Sci Cruiser
Indian Science Index — Indian Sci Ind
Indian Science Index — Indian Sci Index
Indian Scientific Agriculturist — Ind Sci Agric
Indian Soap Journal — Ind Soap J
Indian Social Studies Quarterly — India Soc Stud Q
Indian Society for Nuclear Techniques in Agriculture and Biology. Newsletter — Indian Soc Nucl Tech Agric Biol Newsl
Indian Society for Nuclear Techniques in Agriculture and Biology. Newsletter — Indian Soc Nuclear Tech Agric Biol Newsl
Indian Society for Nuclear Techniques in Agriculture and Biology. Newsletter — ISNTAW
Indian Society of Desert Technology and University Centre of Desert Studies. Transactions — Indian Soc Desert Technol Univ Cent Desert Stud Trans
Indian Society of Soil Science. Bulletin — Indian Soc Soil Sci Bull
Indian Society of Soil Science. Journal — Indian Soc Soil Sci J
Indian Sociological Bulletin — Ind Soc B
Indian Sociological Review — Ind Soc Rev
Indian Sociologist — Ind Soc
Indian Studies — Ind Stud
Indian Studies: Past and Present — Ind S
Indian Studies Past and Present — ISPP
Indian Sugar — Indian Sug
Indian Tea Association. Proceedings of the Annual Conference — Indian Tea Assoc Proc Annu Conf
Indian Tea Association. Scientific Department. Tocklai Experimental Station. Annual Report — Indian Tea Assoc Sci Dep Tocklai Exp Stn Annu Rep
Indian Tea Association. Scientific Department. Tocklai Experimental Station. Memorandum — Indian Tea Assoc Sci Dep Tocklai Exp Stn Memo
Indian Tea Association. Tocklai Experimental Station. Annual Report — Indian Tea Assoc Tocklai Exp Stn Annu Rep
Indian Tea Association. Tocklai Experimental Station. Memorandum — Indian Tea Assoc Tocklai Exp Stn Memo
Indian Tea Association. Tocklai Experimental Station. Memorandum — Indian Tea Assoc Tocklai Exp Stn Memor
Indian Territory Reports — Indian Terr
Indian Textile Journal — Indian Text J
Indian Tobacco Journal — Indian Tob J
Indian Truth — INTU
Indian Veterinary Journal — Indian Vet J
Indian Veterinary Medical Journal — Indian Vet Med J
Indian Veterinary Medical Journal — IVMJDL
Indian Voice — INVO
Indian Welding Journal — Indian Weld J
Indian World — INWO
Indian Writing Today — IWT
Indian Year Book of International Affairs — IYBIA
Indian Yearbook of International Affairs — Ind Yb Int Aff
Indian Yearbook of International Affairs — Ind YBIA
Indian Yearbook of International Affairs — Indian Yb of Internat Aff
Indian Yearbook of International Affairs — IYIA
Indian Zoological Memoirs — Indian Zool Mem
Indian Zoologist — Indian Zool
Indiana Academy of Science. Monograph — Indiana Acad Sci Monogr
Indiana Academy of Science. Proceedings — Ind Acad Sci Proc
Indiana Administrative Code — Ind Admin Code
Indiana Aeronautics Commission. Annual Report — Ind Aeron Com Ann Rep
Indiana. Agricultural Experiment Station. Inspection Report — Indiana Agric Exp Stn Insp Rep
Indiana. Agricultural Experiment Station. Research Progress Report — Indiana Agric Exp Stn Res Prog Rep
Indiana. Beitraege zur Voelker- und Sprachenkunde, Archaeologie, und Anthropologie des Indianischen Amerika. Ibero-Amerikanisches Institut — IAI/I
Indiana Business — Indiana Bs
Indiana Business Review — Indiana Bus R
Indiana Business Review — Indiana Busin R
Indiana Code — Ind Code

Indiana Court of Appeals Reports — Ind App
Indiana. Department of Conservation. Geological Survey. Bulletin — Indiana Dep Conserv Geol Surv Bull
Indiana. Division of Water. Bulletin — Indiana Div Water Bull
Indiana. Division of Water Resources. Bulletin — Ind Div Water Res Bull
Indiana English Journal — IEJ
Indiana Folklore — IndF
Indiana. Geological Survey. Bulletin — Indiana Geol Surv Bull
Indiana. Geological Survey. Mineral Economics Series — Indiana Geol Surv Miner Econ Ser
Indiana. Geological Survey. Mineral Economics Series — Indiana Geol Surv Mineral Econ Ser
Indiana. Geological Survey. Mineral Economics Series — Indiana Geol Survey Mineral Economics Ser
Indiana. Geological Survey. Miscellaneous Map — Indiana Geol Surv Misc Map
Indiana. Geological Survey. Occasional Paper — Indiana Geol Surv Occas Pap
Indiana. Geological Survey. Report of Progress — Indiana Geol Surv Rep Prog
Indiana. Geological Survey. Special Report — Indiana Geol Surv Spec Rep
Indiana Historical Commission. Collections — Ind His Col
Indiana Historical Society. Prehistory Research Series — IHSPRS
Indiana Historical Society. Publications — IHSP
Indiana Historical Society. Publications — Ind His S
Indiana Historical Society. Publications — Ind Hist Soc Publ
Indiana Historical Society. Publications — Indiana Hist Soc Publ
Indiana History Bulletin — IHB
Indiana History Bulletin — Ind Hist Bull
Indiana History Bulletin — Indiana Hist Bull
Indiana Journal. Indiana Association for Health, Physical Education, and Recreation — INHP
Indiana Law Journal — ILJ
Indiana Law Journal — IN LJ
Indiana Law Journal — Ind L J
Indiana Law Journal — Ind Law Jour
Indiana Law Journal — Indiana Law
Indiana Law Journal — Indiana LJ
Indiana Law Review — IN LR
Indiana Law Review — Ind L Rev
Indiana Law Review — Ind LR
Indiana Law Review — Indiana L Rev
Indiana Legal Forum — IN LF
Indiana Legal Forum — Ind Legal F
Indiana Legal Forum — Indiana Leg Forum
Indiana Magazine of History — IMH
Indiana Magazine of History — Ind M
Indiana Magazine of History — Ind Mag Hist
Indiana Magazine of History — Indiana M Hist
Indiana Magazine of History — Indiana Mag Hist
Indiana Medical Journal. A Quarterly Record. Medical Sciences of the South and West (Evansville) — Indiana Med J Evansville
Indiana Medicine — Indiana Med
Indiana Military History Journal — Indiana Mil Hist Jnl
Indiana Musicator — IN
Indiana Names [*Indiana State University*] — IN
Indiana Register — Ind Reg
Indiana Reports — Ind
Indiana Slavic Studies — Ind Slav St
Indiana Slavic Studies — Indiana Slav Stud
Indiana Slavic Studies — ISS
Indiana Social Studies Quarterly — Indn
Indiana Speech Journal — Indiana Sp J
Indiana State Bar Association — Indiana State Bar Assn
Indiana State University. Department of Geography and Geology. Professional Paper — Indiana State Univ Dep Geogr Geol Prof Pap
Indiana Theory Review — Indiana Theory R
Indiana University. Art Museum. Bulletin — Ind Un Art B
Indiana University Art Museum. Publications — Indiana Univ Art Mus Publ
Indiana University Bookman — IUB
Indiana University. Extension Division Bulletin — Ind Univ Extension Division Bull
Indiana University. Folklore Institute. Monograph Series — In Univ Fol
Indiana University. Folklore Series — IUFS
Indiana University Humanities Series — Indiana Univ Hum Ser
Indiana University. Humanities Series — IUHS
Indiana University. Mathematics Journal — Indi Math J
Indiana University. Mathematics Journal — Indiana Univ Math J
Indiana University Publications. African Series — Indiana Univ Publ Afr Ser
Indiana University Publications. Anthropology and Linguistics — IUPAL
Indiana University Publications. Folklore Series — IUPFS
Indiana University Publications. Humanistic Series — IUPHS
Indiana University Publications. Language Science Monographs — IUPLSM
Indiana University Publications. Slavic and East European Series — IUPSEES
Indiana University Publications. Uralic and Altaic Series — IUPUAS
Indiana University. Research Center in Anthropology, Folklore, and Linguistics — IURCAFL
Indiana University. School of Education. Bulletin — Ind Univ Sch Ed B
Indiana University. School of Education. Bulletin — Indiana Univ Ed Bul
Indiana University Studies in the History and Theory of Linguistics — IUSHTL
Indiana Writing Today — IWT
Indianapolis Business Journal — Indianpl B
Indianapolis Star — Indianpl S
Indian-Ed. University of Alberta — INED
Indians of Quebec. Confederation of Indians of Quebec — INQU
India's Urban Future [*Monograph*] — IUF
Indicadores Economicos (Mexico) — Indicadores Econs (Mexico)
Indicadores Economicos (Rio Grande Do Sul) — Indicadores Econs (RS)
Indicateurs de l'Economie du Centre — Indicateurs Econ Centre
Indicatore Cartotecnico — Indic Cartotec
Indicatore Grafico — Indic Grafico
Indice — IE
Indice Agricola de America Latina y el Caribe — Indice Agricola Am Lat Caribe
Indice Agricole de America Latina y el Caribe — Ind Agri Am Lat Caribe
Indice Bibliografico de Lepra — Indice Bibliogr Lepra
Indice Bibliografico. UNAM (Universidad Nacional Autonoma de Mexico) — IBU
Indice Cultural Espanol — ICE
Indice Cultural Espanol — Ind Cult Esp
Indice Cultural Espanol — Indice Cult Espan
Indice de Arte y Letras — Ind
Indice de Artes y Letras — IAL
Indice de Artes y Letras — INDAL
Indice de la Literatura Dental en Castellano — Ind Lit Dent
Indice de la Literatura Dental en Castellano — Indice Lit Dent Castellano
Indice de la Literatura Dental Periodica en Castellano — Indice Lit Dent Period Castellano
Indice Generale degli Incunabuli delle Biblioteche d'Italia — IGI
Indice (Havanna) — IndiceH
Indice Historico Espanol — IHE
Indice Historico Espanol — Ind Hist Esp
Indice Medico Espanol — Ind Med Esp
Indice Medico Espanol — Indice Med Esp
Indice Taxonomico. Asociacion Sudamericana de Fitotaxonomistos — Indice Taxon
Indices de Revista de Bibliotecologia — IREBI
Indices. Monographs in Philosophical Logic and Formal Linguistics — Indices Monographs Philos Logic Formal Linguistics
Indices zum Altdeutschen Schrifttum — Indices Altdeutsch Schrift
Indien und die Buddhistische Welt — IBW
Indirections [*Ontario Council of Teachers of English*] — Indirect
Indisch Genootschap — Indisch Genoot
Indisch Tijdschrift van het Recht — Ind TvhR
Indisch Tijdschrift van het Recht — IT
Indisch Tijdschrift van het Recht — ITR
Indisch Tijdschrift van het Recht — ITvhR
Indisch Tijdschrift van het Recht — T
Indische Gids — IG
Indische Gids — Ind Gids
Indische Post — IP
Indische Studien — Ind St
Indium Phosphide and Related Materials. International Conference — Indium Phosphide Relat Mater Int Conf
Indium Phosphide and Related Materials. Processing, Technology, and Devices — Indium Phosphide Relat Mater Process Technol Devices
Individual Instruction — Indiv Inst
Individual Onsite Wastewater Systems — Individ Onsite Wastewater Syst
Individual Psychologist — Indiv Psych
Individual Psychologist — IPSYA
Individual Psychology — INPS
Indo-Asia — Indo-As
Indo-Asian Culture — IAC
Indo-Asian Culture — Ind As Cult
Indo-Asian Culture — Indo Asian Cult
Indochina Chronicle — Indochina
Indogaku Bukkuogaku Kenkyu — IBK
Indogaku Bukkyogaku Kenkyu — Ind Buk Kenk
Indogermanische Bibliothek — IB
Indogermanische Bibliothek — Idg B
Indogermanische Forschungen — Idg Forsch
Indogermanische Forschungen — IF
Indogermanische Forschungen — Ig F
Indogermanische Forschungen — IGForsch
Indogermanische Forschungen — Ind Forsch
Indogermanische Forschungen — Indo Germ Forsch
Indogermanische Forschungen — Indog Forsch
Indogermanische Forschungen — Indogerm F
Indogermanische Forschungen — Indogerm Forschgg
Indogermanische Forschungen — InF
Indogermanische Grammatik — Idg Gr
Indogermanische Jahrbuch — I Jahrb
Indogermanische Jahrbuch — IJ
Indogermanische Jahrbuch — IJb
Indogermanisches Etymologisches Woerterbuch — IEW
Indogermanisches Etymologisches Woerterbuch — Indogerm Etymol Woert
Indogermanisches Jahrbuch — Idg Jb
Indogermanisches Jahrbuch — IGJ
Indogermanisches Jahrbuch — Indogerm Jb
Indo-Iranian Journal — IIJ
Indo-Iranian Journal — Indo Iran J
Indo-Iranian Monographs — IIM
Indo-Iranica — II
Indoiranische Quellen und Forschungen — IIQF
Indonesia — Indo
Indonesia — INO
Indonesia Development News — Indones Dev News
Indonesia. Directorate of Higher Education. Research Journal — Indon Dir Higher Educ Res J
Indonesia. Direktorat Geologi. Publikasi Chusus — Indones Dir Geol Publ Chusus
Indonesia. Direktorat Geologi. Publikasi Teknik. Seri Geofisika — Indones Dir Geol Publ Tek Ser Geofis
Indonesia. Direktorat Geologi. Publikasi Teknik. Seri Paleontologi — Indones Dir Geol Publ Tek Ser Paleontol

Indonesia. Direktorat Geologi. Publikasi Teknik. Serie Geologi Ekonomi — Indones Dir Geol Publ Tek Ser Geol Ekon
Indonesia Letter — ILN
Indonesia. News and Views — Indonesia New
Indonesia Tourist Statistics — Indonesia Tour Stat
Indonesian Abstracts — Indones Abstr
Indonesian Commercial Newsletter — ICN
Indonesian Institute of Marine Research. Oceanographical Cruise Report — Indones Inst Mar Res Oceanogr Cruise Rep
Indonesian Journal of Crop Science — IJCSEH
Indonesian Journal of Crop Science — Indones J Crop Sci
Indonesian Journal of Geography — Indo J Geog
Indonesian Journal of Geography — Indones J Geogr
Indonesian Journal of Geography — Indonesian J G
Indonesian Journal of Pharmacy — Indones J Pharm
Indonesian Petroleum Association. Annual Convention. Proceedings — Indones Pet Assoc Annu Conv Proc
Indonesian Quarterly — Indo Q
Indonesian Quarterly — Indones Quart
Indonesie — In
Indoor + Built Environment — Indoor Environ
Indoor Environment — Indoor Environ
Indo-Pacific Fisheries Council. Occasional Papers — Indo-Pac Fish Counc Occas Pap
Indo-Pacific Fisheries Council. Proceedings — Indo-Pac Fish Counc Proc
Indo-Pacific Fisheries Council. Regional Studies — Indo-Pac Fish Counc Reg Stud
Indo-Pacific Fisheries Council. Special Publications — Indo-Pac Fish Counc Spec Publ
Indo-Pacific Mollusca — Indo-Pac Mollusca
Indo-Soviet Symposium on Crystal Growth — Indo Soviet Symp Cryst Growth
Induction of Flowering. Some Case Histories [*monograph*] — Induct Flowering
Industri og Miljoe — Ind Miljoe
Industria — INDUA
Industria Alimentara — INALA
Industria Alimentara (Bucharest) — Ind Aliment (Bucharest)
Industria Alimentara. Produse Animale — Ind Aliment Prod Anim
Industria Alimentara. Produse Vegetale — IAPVA
Industria Alimentara. Produse Vegetale [*Romania*] — Ind Aliment Prod Veg
Industria Alimentara. Produse Vegetale — Ind Aliment Veget
Industria Alimentaria — Ind Aliment
Industria Alimenticia (Havana) — Ind Aliment (Havana)
Industria Azucarera — Ind Azucar
Industria Chimica, Mineraria, e Metallurgica — Ind Chim Min Metall
Industria Chimica (Rome) — Ind Chim (Rome)
Industria Chimica (Turin) — Ind Chim Turin
Industria Conserve — ICOPA
Industria Conserve [*Parma*] — ICOPAF
Industria Conserve — Ind Conserve
Industria Conserve (Parma) — Ind Conserve (Parma)
Industria Constructiilor si a Materialelor de Constructii — Ind Constr Mater Constr
Industria degli Olii Minerali i dei Grassi — Ind Olii Miner Grassi
Industria dei Farmaci — Ind Farm
Industria del Gas e degli Acquedotti — Ind Gas Acquedotti
Industria della Carta — ICAMA
Industria della Carta — Ind Carta
Industria della Carta e delle Arti Grafiche — Ind Carta Arti Grafiche
Industria della Ceramica e Silicati — Ind Ceram Silicat
Industria della Gomma [*Italy*] — Ind d Gomma
Industria della Gomma. Minsiledi Economia e Tenica Degil Elastomeri — Ind Gomma
Industria della Vernice — Ind Vernice
Industria do Norte de Portugal — Ind Norte Port
Industria Farmaceutica y Bioquimica — IFBQA8
Industria Farmaceutica y Bioquimica — Ind Farm Bioquim
Industria Italiana dei Laterizi — Ind Ital Laterizi
Industria Italiana del Cemento — IICEA
Industria Italiana del Cemento — IICEW
Industria Italiana del Cemento — Ind Ital Cem
Industria Italiana del Freddo — Ind Ital Freddo
Industria Italiana delle Conserve — Ind Ital Conserve
Industria Italiana delle Conserve Alimentari — Ind Ital Conserve Aliment
Industria Italiana Elettrotecnica [*Italy*] — Ind Ital Elettrotec
Industria Italiana Elettrotecnica ed Elettronica — Ind Ital Elettrotec & Elettron
Industria Lattiera e Zooteenia — Ind Latt Zootee
Industria Lechera — Ind Leche
Industria Lemnului — Ind Lemnului
Industria Lemnului — Industr Lemn
Industria Lemnului Celulozei si Hirtiei — Ind Lemnului Celul Hirtiei
Industria Minera — INMID
Industria Minera (Madrid) — Ind Min (Madrid)
Industria Mineraria — INMRA
Industria Mineraria (Rome) — Ind Min (Rome)
Industria Oggi — Ind Oggi
Industria Portuguesa — Ind Port
Industria Saccarifera Italiana [*Italy*] — Ind Sacc Ital
Industria Saccarifera Italiana — Ind Saccarif Ital
Industria Saccarifera Italiana — INSIA
Industria Saponiera e degli Olii. Steariniera. Profumiera — Ind Sapon Olii Stearin Profum
Industria Textila (Bucharest) — Ind Text Bucharest
Industria Usoara [*Romania*] — Ind Usoara
Industria Usoara — INUSA
Industria Usoara Pielarie — Ind Usoara Piel
Industria Usoara. Textile, Tricotaje, Confectii Textile — Ind Usoara Text Tricotaje Confectii Text
Industria y Quimica (Buenos Aires) — Ind Quim (Buenos Aires)
Industrial Accident Law Bulletin — Ind Accid Law Bul
Industrial Air Pollution. Assessment and Control — Ind Air Pollut
Industrial and Commercial Gas — Ind Comm Gas
Industrial and Commercial Photographer — Ind Commer Photogr
Industrial and Commercial Photographer — Ind Commercial Photographer
Industrial and Commercial Photography — IDPGA
Industrial and Commercial Training — ICT
Industrial and Commercial Training — Ind & Coml Training
Industrial and Commercial Training — Ind Commerc Train
Industrial and Engineering Chemistry — I & EC
Industrial and Engineering Chemistry — IEC
Industrial and Engineering Chemistry — IECHA
Industrial and Engineering Chemistry — Ind & Eng Chem
Industrial and Engineering Chemistry — Ind Eng Chem
Industrial and Engineering Chemistry — Indus and Eng Chemistry
Industrial and Engineering Chemistry. Analytical Edition [*United States*] — Ind Eng Chem Anal Ed
Industrial and Engineering Chemistry. Analytical Edition — Ind Eng Chem Analyt Ed
Industrial and Engineering Chemistry. Analytical Edition — Ind Engng Chem Analyt Edn
Industrial and Engineering Chemistry. Fundamentals — IECFA
Industrial and Engineering Chemistry. Fundamentals — Ind & Eng Chem Fundamentals
Industrial and Engineering Chemistry. Fundamentals — Ind & Engng Chem Fundam
Industrial and Engineering Chemistry. Fundamentals — Ind Eng Chem Fundam
Industrial and Engineering Chemistry. Fundamentals — Ind Eng Chem Fundamentals
Industrial and Engineering Chemistry. Fundamentals — Ind Eng F
Industrial and Engineering Chemistry (International Edition) — Industr Engng Chem (Int Ed)
Industrial and Engineering Chemistry. News Edition [*United States*] — Ind Eng Chem News Ed
Industrial and Engineering Chemistry. Process Design and Development — IEC Process Des Dev
Industrial and Engineering Chemistry. Process Design and Development — IEPDA
Industrial and Engineering Chemistry. Process Design and Development — Ind and Eng Chem Process Des and Dev
Industrial and Engineering Chemistry. Process Design and Development — Ind & Eng Chem Process Design
Industrial and Engineering Chemistry. Process Design and Development — Ind & Engng Chem Process Des & Dev
Industrial and Engineering Chemistry. Process Design and Development — Ind Eng Chem Process Design Develop
Industrial and Engineering Chemistry. Process Design and Development — Ind Eng PDD
Industrial and Engineering Chemistry. Product Research and Development — IEC Prod Res Dev
Industrial and Engineering Chemistry. Product Research and Development — IEPRA
Industrial and Engineering Chemistry. Product Research and Development — Ind and Eng Chem Prod Res and Dev
Industrial and Engineering Chemistry. Product Research and Development — Ind Eng Chem Prod Res Dev
Industrial and Engineering Chemistry. Product Research and Development — Ind Eng PRD
Industrial and Intellectual Property in Australia — IIP
Industrial and Intellectual Property in Australia — IIPA
Industrial and Intellectual Property in Australia — Ind & Int Prop Aus
Industrial and Labor Relations Forum — Ind and Labor Relations Forum
Industrial and Labor Relations Forum — Indus & Lab Rel F
Industrial and Labor Relations Report — Ind and Labor Relations Rept
Industrial and Labor Relations Report — Ind Lab Rel Rep
Industrial and Labor Relations Review — ILR
Industrial and Labor Relations Review — ILRR
Industrial and Labor Relations Review — Ind & L Rel Rev
Industrial and Labor Relations Review — Ind & Lab Rel Rev
Industrial and Labor Relations Review — Ind & Labor Rel R
Industrial and Labor Relations Review — Ind and Labor Relations R
Industrial and Labor Relations Review — Ind and Labor Rels Rev
Industrial and Labor Relations Review — Ind & Lbr Rel R
Industrial and Labor Relations Review — Ind Lab Rel
Industrial and Labor Relations Review — Ind Labor Relat Rev
Industrial and Labor Relations Review — Indus & Lab Rel Rev
Industrial and Labor Relations Review — Indust & L Rel Rev
Industrial and Labor Relations Review — Industr Lab Relat R
Industrial and Labor Relations Review — Industrial & Labor Rel Rev
Industrial and Labour Information — Indust Labour Information
Industrial and Mining Review — Ind & Min R
Industrial and Mining Standard — Ind & Min S
Industrial and Mining Standard — Ind & Min Standard
Industrial and Process Heating — Ind Process Heat
Industrial and Process Heating — IPRHA
Industrial and Production Engineering — Ind Prod Eng
Industrial and Scientific Instruments — Ind Sci Instrum
Industrial Applications for Isotopic Power Generators. Joint UKAEA-ENEA International Symposium — Ind Appl Isot Power Gener Jt UKAEA ENEA Int Symp
Industrial Applications of Holographic and Speckle Measuring Techniques — Ind Appl Hologr Speckle Meas Tech

Industrial Arbitration Cases [*Western Australia*] — IC
Industrial Arbitration Reports [*New South Wales*] — AR
Industrial Arbitration Reports (New South Wales) — AR(NSW)
Industrial Arbitration Reports (New South Wales). New South Wales Reports — NSWR
Industrial Arbitration Service — IAS
Industrial Arbitration Service. Current Review — IAS Current Review
Industrial Archaeology — Ind Archaeol
Industrial Archaeology Review — Ind Archaeol Rev
Industrial Architecture — Ind Arch
Industrial Arts and Vocational Education/Technical Education — Ind Arts & Voc Ed
Industrial Arts Index — Ind A Ind
Industrial Arts Index — Ind Arts Index
Industrial Arts Initiative — Initiative
Industrial Australian and Mining Standard — Ind Aust & Min Standard
Industrial Australian and Mining Standard — Ind Austr Min Stand
Industrial Bulletin — Ind Bull
Industrial Bulletin (Bombay) — Ind Bull Bombay
Industrial Bulletin. New York State Department of Labor — Ind Bull NY State Dep Labor
Industrial Bulletin of Arthur D. Little, Incorporated — Ind Bull Arthur D Little Inc
Industrial Canada — Ind Can
Industrial Chemical News — Ind Chem N
Industrial Chemist — Ind Chem
Industrial Chemist — INDCA
Industrial Chemistry Bulletin — Ind Chem Bull
Industrial Chemistry Library — Ind Chem Libr
Industrial Design — Ind Des
Industrial Design — Ind Design
Industrial Development — IDS
Industrial Development — Ind Dev
Industrial Development — Ind Devel
Industrial Development Abstracts [*Database*] — IDA
Industrial Development Abstracts — Ind Dev Abstr
Industrial Development Abstracts — Ind Develop Abstr
Industrial Development and Manufacturers Record [*Later, Industrial Development*] [*A publication*] — Ind Dev
Industrial Development and Manufacturers Record [*Later, Industrial Development*] [*A publication*] — Ind Dev Manuf Rec
Industrial Development News Asia and the Pacific — Ind Dev N Asia Pac
Industrial Development of Western Australia — Ind Development of WA
Industrial Development Officers — Ind Dev Officers
Industrial Diamond Abstracts — Ind Diamond Abstr
Industrial Diamond Development — Ind Diam Dev
Industrial Diamond Review — Ind Diam Re
Industrial Diamond Review — Ind Diam Rev
Industrial Diamond Review — Ind Diamond Rev
Industrial Diamond Review — INDRA
Industrial Diamond Review — Indus Diamond Rev
Industrial Distribution — IND
Industrial Distribution — Ind Distr
Industrial Distribution — Ind Distrib
Industrial Economics Review — Ind Ec Rev
Industrial Education Council. Newsletter — Ind Ed News
Industrial Education Magazine — Ind Ed M
Industrial Education Magazine — Ind Educ
Industrial Education Magazine — Ind Educ M
Industrial Egypt — EGI
Industrial Electronics — Ind Elect
Industrial Electronics [*England*] — Ind Electron
Industrial Engineer — Ind Eng
Industrial Engineer — Indust Engr
Industrial Engineering — IDLEB
Industrial Engineering — IEN
Industrial Engineering — ILENDP
Industrial Engineering — Ind Eng
Industrial Engineering — Ind Engng
Industrial Engineering — Indus Eng
Industrial Engineering — Indust Engineering
Industrial Environmental Research Laboratory [*Research Triangle Park*]. Annual Report — ARIADS
Industrial Environmental Research Laboratory (Research Triangle Park). Annual Report — Ind Environ Res Lab (Research Triangle Park) Annu Rep
Industrial Equipment Materials and Services — Ind Equip Mater & Serv
Industrial Equipment News — IEN
Industrial Equipment News — Ind Equip News
Industrial Equipment Selector — Ind Equip Sel
Industrial Explosives [*Japan*] — Ind Explos
Industrial Finishing — Ind Fin
Industrial Finishing — Ind Finish
Industrial Finishing and Surface Coatings — Ind Finish & Surf Coatings
Industrial Finishing and Surface Coatings — Ind Finish Surf Coat
Industrial Finishing (Wheaton, Illinois) — IFIIA
Industrial Finishing (Wheaton, Illinois) — Ind Finish (Wheaton Ill)
Industrial Finishing Yearbook — Ind Finish Yearb
Industrial Fishery Products Market Review and Outlook — Indus Fish Prod Mark Rev & Outl
Industrial Gas — Ind Gas
Industrial Gas — INGNA
Industrial Gas and Energy [*United States*] — Ind Gas Energy
Industrial Gas (Duluth) — Ind Gas (Duluth)
Industrial Gerontology — IDGEAH
Industrial Gerontology — Ind Geront
Industrial Gerontology — Ind Gerontol
Industrial Gerontology — Industr Gerontol
Industrial Health — Ind Health
Industrial Health — INHEA
Industrial Health — INHEAO
Industrial Health and Hazards Update [*Database*] — IH & HU
Industrial Health Foundation Symposia — Ind Health Found Symp
Industrial Health (Kawasaki) — Ind Health (Kawasaki)
Industrial Health Review — Ind Health Rev
Industrial Heating — Ind Heat
Industrial Heating — INHTA
Industrial Heating Engineer — Ind Heat Eng
Industrial Heating (Pittsburg) — Ind Heat (Pittsburg)
Industrial Heating (Tokyo) — Ind Heat (Tokyo)
Industrial Hygiene [*Japan*] — Ind Hygiene
Industrial Hygiene Bulletin — Ind Hyg Bull
Industrial Hygiene Digest — Ind Hyg Dig
Industrial Hygiene Foundation of America. Legal Series. Bulletin — Ind Hyg Found Am Leg Ser Bull
Industrial Hygiene Foundation of America. Medical Series. Bulletin — Ind Hyg Found Am Med Ser Bull
Industrial Hygiene Foundation of America. Transactions. Bulletin — Ind Hyg Found Am Trans Bull
Industrial Hygiene Highlights — IHYHA
Industrial Hygiene Highlights [*United States*] — Ind Hyg Highlights
Industrial Hygiene News — Ind Hyg Ne
Industrial Hygiene Review — IHYRB
Industrial Hygiene Review [*United States*] — Ind Hyg Rev
Industrial India — Ind India
Industrial India — ININA
Industrial Information Bulletin — Ind Information Bul
Industrial Laboratories [*Chicago*] — Ind Lab
Industrial Laboratory [*English Translation*] — INDLA
Industrial Laboratory (United States) — Ind Lab (US)
Industrial Laboratory (USSR) — Ind Lab (USSR)
Industrial Law Journal — Ind Law J
Industrial Law Journal — Indus LJ
Industrial Law Journal — Indust LJ
Industrial Law Review Quarterly — Indust L Rev Q
Industrial Law Review Quarterly — Industrial L Rev Q
Industrial Lubrication — Ind Lubric
Industrial Lubrication and Technology — Ind Lubr & Technol
Industrial Lubrication and Tribology — Ind Lubr Tribol
Industrial Lubrication and Tribology — Ind Lubric Tribology
Industrial Machinery [*Japan*] — Ind Mach
Industrial Maintenance and Plant Operation — Ind Main Pl Op
Industrial Management [*London*] — BUS
Industrial Management — IDMGB
Industrial Management — IM
Industrial Management [*Canada (already exists in GUS II database)*] — IMT
Industrial Management — Ind Manage
Industrial Management [*New York*] — Ind Management
Industrial Management [*New York*] — Ind Mgt
Industrial Management — Indust Man
Industrial Management — Indust Management
Industrial Management — INM
Industrial Management and Data Systems — Ind Manage and Data Syst
Industrial Management and Data Systems — Ind Mgt & Data Syst
Industrial Management (London) — Ind Management (London)
Industrial Management Review — Ind Management R
Industrial Management Review — Ind Mgt R
Industrial Marketing [*Later, Business Marketing*] — IMARD
Industrial Marketing [*Later, Business Marketing*] — IMK
Industrial Marketing [*Later, Business Marketing*] — IN
Industrial Marketing [*Later, Business Marketing*] — Ind Mark
Industrial Marketing [*Later, Business Marketing*] — Ind Market
Industrial Marketing [*Later, Business Marketing*] — Ind Mkt
Industrial Marketing [*Later, Business Marketing*] — Ind Mktg
Industrial Marketing [*Later, Business Marketing*] — Ind Mktng
Industrial Marketing Digest — III
Industrial Marketing Digest — Ind Market Dig
Industrial Marketing Management — IMD
Industrial Marketing Management — IMM
Industrial Marketing Management — Ind Mark Manage
Industrial Marketing Management — Ind Mkt Man
Industrial Marketing Management — Ind Mkt Mgt
Industrial Mathematics — Ind Math
Industrial Mathematics — Indust Math
Industrial Medicine — Ind Med
Industrial Medicine and Surgery — IMS
Industrial Medicine and Surgery — IMSUA
Industrial Medicine and Surgery — IMSUAI
Industrial Medicine and Surgery — Ind Med
Industrial Medicine and Surgery — Ind Med & Surg
Industrial Medicine and Surgery — Ind Med Surg
Industrial Medicine and Surgery — Indust Med
Industrial Minerals — ILM
Industrial Minerals — IM
Industrial Minerals — Ind Min
Industrial Minerals — Ind Miner
Industrial Minerals — Indus Minerals
Industrial Minerals and Rocks — Ind Miner Rocks
Industrial Minerals (London) — Ind Miner (London)
Industrial Obst- und Gemueseverwertung — Ind Obst- Gemueseverwert
Industrial Organisation and Health — Ind Org Hlth
Industrial Pharmacology — Ind Pharmacol

Industrial Philippines — Ind Philippines
Industrial Photography — Ind Phot
Industrial Photography — Ind Photogr
Industrial Photography — Industrial Phot
Industrial Photography — INPHA
Industrial Physicist — Ind Phys
Industrial Planning and Development — Ind Plann Dev
Industrial Power and Mass Production — Ind Power Mass Prod
Industrial Power, Steam Heat, Light, and Air and the Fuel Economist — Ind Power Steam Heat Light Air Fuel Econ
Industrial Process Design for Pollution Control. Proceedings. Workshop — Ind Process Des Pollut Control
Industrial Production. Historical Statistics — IPHS
Industrial Products Magazine — Ind Prod Mag
Industrial Products Magazine — IPM
Industrial Progress and Development — Ind Progress
Industrial Progress and Development — Ind Progress and Development
Industrial Progress and Development — Indust Progress
Industrial Progress and Development — Industr Progr
Industrial Property Law Annual — Indust Prop Law Ann
Industrial Property Quarterly — Ind Prop Quart
Industrial Property Seminar (Monash University, 1972) — Ind Prop Sem
Industrial Psychology — Indust Psychol
Industrial Quality Control — Ind Quality Control
Industrial Radiography and Non-Destructive Testing — Ind Radiogr
Industrial Radiography and Non-Destructive Testing — Ind Radiogr Non Destr Test
Industrial Rare Metals [*Japan*] — Ind Rare Met
Industrial Relations — IDR
Industrial Relations — Ind Rel
Industrial Relations — Ind Relat
Industrial Relations — Ind Relations
Industrial Relations — Indus Rel
Industrial Relations — Industr Relat
Industrial Relations [*Canada*] — INR
Industrial Relations — IR
Industrial Relations (Berkeley) — Ind Relations (Berkeley)
Industrial Relations (Berkeley) — Industr Relat Berkeley
Industrial Relations Briefing — Ind Rel Briefing
Industrial Relations (Calcutta) — Industr Relat Calcutta
Industrial Relations Guide. Prentice-Hall — Indus Rel Guide P-H
Industrial Relations Journal — Ind Rel J
Industrial Relations Journal — Industr Relat J
Industrial Relations Journal — IRJ
Industrial Relations Journal of South Africa — Ind Relat J S Afr
Industrial Relations Law Journal — Ind Rel Law J
Industrial Relations Law Journal — Ind Rel LJ
Industrial Relations Law Journal — Indus Rel LJ
Industrial Relations Law Journal — Indust Rel LJ
Industrial Relations Law Journal — IRJ
Industrial Relations Law Journal — IRL
Industrial Relations Legal Information Bulletin — IRLIB
Industrial Relations News — Ind Rel News
Industrial Relations (Quebec) — Ind Relations (Quebec)
Industrial Relations Research Association. Proceedings — IRR
Industrial Relations Research Association. Proceedings — IRRA
Industrial Relations Review and Report — Ind Rel Rev Rep
Industrial Relations Review and Report — Ind Relat Rev Rep
Industrial Relations Review and Report — IR
Industrial Relations Society. Proceedings of Convention — Ind Rel Soc Proc
Industrial Research — IDRSA
Industrial Research — Ind Res
Industrial Research and Development — Ind Res
Industrial Research and Development — Ind Res & Devel
Industrial Research and Development [*United States*] — Ind Res/Dev
Industrial Research and Development News — IRDN
Industrial Research/Kung Yeh Chung Hsin — Industr Res
Industrial Research (London) — Ind Res (Lond)
Industrial Research News [*Australia*] — Ind Res News
Industrial Research News. Commonwealth Scientific and Industrial Research Organisation — Ind Res News CSIRO
Industrial Research Study. Timber Research and Development Association — Industr Res Study Timb Res Developm Ass
Industrial Review and Mining Year Book — Ind R & Mining Yrbk
Industrial Review of Japan — Ind Review Jap
Industrial Robot — Ind Robot
Industrial Safety — Ind Saf
Industrial Safety — Ind Safety
Industrial Safety — ISAFA
Industrial Safety and Health Bulletin — Ind Saf Hlth Bull
Industrial Safety Chronicle — Ind Saf Chron
Industrial Safety Data File — Ind Saf Data File
Industrial Safety Survey — Ind Saf Surv
Industrial Science and Engineering — Ind Sci Eng
Industrial Science and Technology [*Japan*] — Ind Sci Technol
Industrial Short-Term Trends — Ind Short-Term Trends
Industrial Situation in India — Indus Sit Ind
Industrial Society — INS
Industrial Society — IS
Industrial Specification — Ind Spec
Industrial Standardization — Ind Stand
Industrial Standardization and Commercial Standards. Monthly — Ind Stand Commer Stand Mon
Industrial Supervisor — Ind Sup
Industrial Technology Research Institute. Chungnam University — Ind Technol Res Inst Chungnam Univ
Industrial Utilisation of Sugar and Mill By-Products — Ind Util Sugar Mill By-Prod
Industrial Vegetation Turf and Pest Management — Ind Veg Turf Pest Manage
Industrial Victoria — Ind Vic
Industrial Waste. Advanced Water and Solid Waste Conference. Proceedings — Ind Waste Adv Water Solid Waste Conf Proc
Industrial Waste Conference Proceedings — Ind Waste Conf Proc
Industrial Wastes — Ind Wastes
Industrial Wastes — INWAB
Industrial Wastes (Chicago) — Ind Wastes (Chicago)
Industrial Water and Wastes — Ind Water Wastes
Industrial Water and Wastes — INWWAH
Industrial Water Engineering — Ind Water Eng
Industrial Water Engineering — IWEGA
Industrial Water Engineering — IWEGAA
Industrial Water Treatment — Ind Water Treat
Industrial Worker — Ind Wrkr
Industrial-Arts Magazine — Ind-Arts M
Industrialisation et Productivite — Industrial et Productiv
Industrialised Building — Ind Bldg
Industrialization Forum [*Canada*] — IF
Industrias de la Alimentacion (Mexico City) — Ind Aliment (Mexico City)
Industrias de Transformacao — Ind de Transformacao
Industrie — Ind
Industrie — IUS
Industrie Agrarie — IDTAA
Industrie Agrarie [*Italy*] — Ind Agr
Industrie Agrarie — Industrie Agr
Industrie Alimentari — INALB
Industrie Alimentari — Industrie Aliment
Industrie Alimentari (Pinerolo, Italy) — Ind Aliment (Pinerolo Italy)
Industrie Ceramique — IDCQA
Industrie Ceramique — Ind Ceram
Industrie Chimique — Ind Chim
Industrie Chimique Belge — ICBEA
Industrie Chimique Belge — Ind Chim Belge
Industrie Chimique, le Phosphate — Ind Chim Phosph
Industrie Chimique (Paris) — Ind Chim (Paris)
Industrie de la Parfumerie — Ind Parf
Industrie dei Silicati — Ind Silic
Industrie delle Bevande — Ind Bevande
Industrie des Plastiques — Ind Plast
Industrie des Plastiques Modernes — Ind Plast Mod
Industrie des Plastiques Modernes et Elastomeres [*Later, Plastiques Modernes et Elastomeres*] — Ind Plast Mod Elastomeres
Industrie Diamanten Rundschau — IDR
Industrie Diamanten Rundschau — Ind Diamanten Rundsch
Industrie du Petrole [*France*] — Ind Pet
Industrie du Petrole — Ind Petr
Industrie du Petrole — Industr Petrole
Industrie du Petrole — IPETA
Industrie du Petrole dans le Monde. Gaz-Chimie [*France*] — Ind Pet Monde Gaz-Chim
Industrie du Petrole dans le Monde. Gaz-Chimie — IPMCD
Industrie du Petrole en Europe. Gaz-Chimie — Ind Pet Eur Gaz Chim
Industrie du Petrole en Europe. Gaz-Chimie — IPEUB
Industrie du Petrole et Energies Industrielles — Ind Pet Energ Ind
Industrie du Petrole. Gaz-Chimie — Ind Pet Gaz Chim
Industrie du Petrole. Gaz-Chimie — Ind Petrol Gaz-Chim
Industrie Francaise du Coton et des Fibres Alliees — Industr Franc Coton Fibres Alliees
Industrie Hoteliere — IHA
Industrie Lackier-Betrieb — ILBEA
Industrie Lackier-Betrieb — Ind Lackier-Betr
Industrie Lackier-Betrieb — Ind Lackier-Betrb
Industrie Lackier-Betrieb. Zentralblatt fuer Lackiertechnik und Beschichtungstechnik — ISL
Industrie Minerale — Ind Miner
Industrie Minerale. Mine — Ind Miner Mine
Industrie Minerale. Mineralurgie — Ind Miner Mineralurgie
Industrie Minerale. Mines et Carrieres — Ind Miner Mines Carr
Industrie Minerale. Mines et Carrieres. Les Techniques — Ind Miner Mines Carr Tech
Industrie Minerale (Paris) — Ind Miner (Paris)
Industrie Minerale. Serie Mine — IMMNB
Industrie Minerale. Serie Mineralurgie — IMMLC
Industrie Minerale. Serie Mineralurgie [*France*] [*Industrie Minerale. Serie Techniques*] [*Later,*] — Ind Miner Ser Mineralurgie
Industrie Minerale. Serie Techniques [*St. Etienne, France*] — Ind Miner Ser Tech
Industrie Minerale. Serie Techniques — Ind Miner Tech
Industrie Minerale (St. Etienne) [*France*] — Ind Miner (St Etienne)
Industrie Minerale (St. Etienne, France) — Ind Miner (St Etienne Fr)
Industrie Minerale. Supplement. Les Techniques (St. Etienne) [*France*] — Ind Miner Suppl Techniques (St Etienne)
Industrie Miniere du Quebec — Ind Min Quebec
Industrie Siderurgique en Europe — Ind Sid Eur
Industrie Textile — Ind Text
Industrie Textile — Ind Textil
Industrie Textile en Europe — Ind Text Eur
Industrie Textile. Revue Mensuelle Internationale Technique et Economique Textile — INM
Industrie und Handel — IDHAA
Industrie und Handel — Ind Handel

Industrie und Handelskammer — IHK
Industrie- und Handelsrevue — MSR
Industrie und Umwelt — Ind Umwelt
Industrie und Umwelt. Massnahmen und Planungen zum Umweltschutz in Oesterreich. Vortragsreihen — Ind Umwelt Massnahmen Plan Umweltschutz Oesterr Vortragsr
Industrie-Anzeiger — IANZA
Industrie-Anzeiger — IAZ
Industrie-Anzeiger — Ind-Anz
Industrieblatt — Ind Bl
Industrieel Eigendom — IE
Industrieel Eigendom — INE
Industrie-Elektrik und Elektronik — Ind-Elektr Elektron
Industrie-Elektronik in Forschung und Fertigung — IEFFA
Industrie-Elektronik in Forschung und Fertigung [*Germany*] — Ind-Elektron Forsch Fertigung
Industriefeuerung — IFRGA
Industriele Eigendom — Ind Eigendom
Industriell Datateknik — Ind Datatek
Industriell Teknik — IDTKA
Industriell Teknik [*Sweden*] — Ind Tek
Industrielle Obst- und Gemueseverwertung — INOGA
Industrielle Obst- und Gemueseverwertung — INOGAV
Industrielle Organisation — Ind Org
Industriemagazin. Management, Marketing, Technologie — IDW
Industries Alimentaires et Agricoles — IAL
Industries Alimentaires et Agricoles — IALAA
Industries Alimentaires et Agricoles — Ind Aliment Agr
Industries Alimentaires et Agricoles (Paris) — Ind Aliment Agric (Paris)
Industries Atomiques — INATA
Industries Atomiques — Ind At
Industries Atomiques et Spatiales — IAQSB
Industries Atomiques et Spatiales — Ind At & Spat
Industries Atomiques et Spatiales — Ind At Spatiales
Industries de la Parfumerie et de la Cosmetique — Ind Parf Cosm
Industries de la Parfumerie et de la Cosmetique — Ind Parfum Cosmet
Industries de l'Alimentation Animale — Ind Aliment Anim
Industries de l'Habillement — Inds Habillement
Industries des Cereales — Ind Cereales
Industries des Corps Gras — Ind Corps Gras
Industries des Plastiques (Paris) — Ind Plast (Paris)
Industries du Bois en Europe — I d B
Industries Electriques et Electroniques — Electrique
Industries Electriques et Electroniques — Ind Electr Electron
Industries Electroniques — Ind Electron
Industries et Techniques — Ind Tech
Industries et Techniques — INDTA
Industries et Travaux d'Outre-Mer — Ind Trav O-Mer
Industries et Travaux d'Outre-Mer — Inds et Trav Outremer
Industries et Travaux d'Outre-Mer — Industr Trav O-Mer
Industries et Travaux d'Outre-Mer — ITOMA
Industries Francaises d'Equipement [*France*] — Ind Fr Equip
Industries Francaises du Telephone, du Telegraphe, et de Leurs Applications Telematiques — Fr Telephn
Industries Thermiques — Ind Therm
Industries Thermiques et Aerauliques — Ind Therm Aerauliques
Industrija Secera — HIISAP
Industrija Secera — Ind Secera
Industry 2000. New Perspectives — Ind 2000
Industry and Development — IOE
Industry and Electricity (Osaka) [*Japan*] — Ind Electr (Osaka)
Industry and Environment [*Japan*] — Ind Environ
Industry and Health Care — Ind Health Care
Industry and Health Care (Cambridge, Massachusetts) — Ind Health Care (Cambridge MA)
Industry and Power [*United States*] — Ind Power
Industry and Welding — Ind Weld
Industry Applications Society. Annual Meeting. Conference Record [*United States*] — IAS Annu Meet Conf Rec
Industry, Commerce, Development — Ind Comm Dev
Industry Data Sources [*Database*] — IDS
Industry File Index System [*Database*] — IFIS
Industry International — Ind Int
Industry of Free China — IFB
Industry of Free China [*Taipei*] — IFC
Industry of Free China — Indus Free China
Industry of Free China — Industry Free China
Industry Report. Chemicals — Ind Rept Chemicals
Industry Report. Containers and Packaging — Ind Rept Containers Pkg
Industry Report. Pulp, Paper, and Board — Ind Rept Pulp Pbd
Industry Today — Ind Today
Industry Week — IDW
Industry Week — Ind W
Industry Week — Ind Week
Industry Week — Indus Week
Industry Week — IW
Industry Week — IWEEA
Industry-University Cooperative Chemistry Program — Ind Univ Coop Chem Program
Inequality in Education — Inequal Educ
INF [*Inventario Nacional Forestal*] **Informacion Tecnica** — INF Inf Tec
INF (Inventario Nacional Forestal) Nota — INF (Inventario Nac For) Nota
Infancia y Adolescencia (Caracas) — Infan Adol Caracas
Infant Behavior and Development — IBD
Infant Behavior and Development — IBDEDP
Infant Behavior and Development — Infant Behav & Dev
Infant Nutrition, Development, and Disease. Symposium — Infant Nutr Dev Dis Symp
Infantry Magazine — Infantry
Infection and Immunity — Infec Immun
Infection and Immunity — Infect Immun
Infection and Immunity — INFIB
Infection Control [*Thorofare*] — IICODV
Infection Control — Infect Cont
Infection Control — Infect Control
Infection Control and Hospital Epidemiology — Infect Control Hosp Epidemiol
Infection Control and Urological Care — Infect Control Urol Care
Infection Control Digest — Infect Control Dig
Infection Control Rounds — Infect Control Rounds
Infection Control (Thorofare) — Infect Control (Thorofare)
Infection, Inflammation, and Immunity — Infect Inflammation & Immun
Infection, Inflammation, and Immunity — KEMEDB
Infectious Agents and Disease — Infect Agents Dis
Infectious Disease and Therapy — Infect Dis Ther
Infectious Disease Clinics of North America — Infect Dis Clin North Am
Infectious Disease Reviews — Infect Dis Rev
Infectious Diseases and Antimicrobial Agents — IDAADC
Infectious Diseases and Antimicrobial Agents — Infect Dis Antimicrob Agents
Infectologia [*Mexico*] — INFTET
Infektion, Blutgerinnung und Haemostase. Hamburger Symposion ueber Blutgerinnung — Infekt Blutgerinnung Haemostase Hamb Symp Blutgerinnung
Infektionskrankheiten und Ihre Erreger — Infektionskr Ihre Erreger
Infektionsprophylaxe in der Intensivmedizin. Die Selektive Darmdekontamination (SDD) — Infektionsprophyl Intensivmed Sel Darmdekontam SDD
Infektsionnye Gepatit Respublikanskoi Mezhvedomstvennyi Sbornik — Infekts Gepatit Resp Mezhved Sb
Infektsionnye Zabolevaniya Kul'turnykh Rastenii Moldavii — Infekts Kult Rast Mold
Infektsionnyi Gepatit — Infekts Gepatit
Infinity Science Fiction — Inf
Infirmiere Auxiliaire — Infirm Aux
Infirmiere Canadienne — Infirm Can
Infirmiere Francaise — Infirm Fr
Infirmiere Haitienne — Infirm Haiti
Inflammation and Drug Therapy Series — Inflammation Drug Ther Ser
Inflammation Research — Inflamm Res
Inflammation Research — Inflammation Res
Inflammatory Disease and Therapy — Inflammatory Dis Ther
Influence of Polymer Additives on Velocity and Temperature Fields. Symposium. Proceedings — Influence Polym Addit Velocity Temp Fields Symp Proc
Infobrief Research and Technology [*Germany*] — Infobrief Res Technol
Infodoc Aerospace and Military Equipment — Infodoc
INFOR. Canadian Journal of Operational Research and Information Processing — INFOR Canad J Oper Res Inform Process
INFOR. Canadian Journal of Operational Research and Information Processing — INFOR Canad J Operational Res and Information Processing
INFOR. Canadian Journal of Operational Research and Information Processing — INFOR J
Informacao Cultural Portugues — ICP
Informacao Social — Info Soc
Informacije Rade Koncar — Inf Rade Koncar
Informacio-Elektronika — Inf-Elektron
Informacio-Elektronika — Informac-Elektron
Informacio-Elektronika — Inform-Elektron
Informacion Agricola — Inf Agric
Informacion Arqueologica — Inf A
Informacion Arqueologica — Inf Arqu
Informacion Bibliografica. Caja Nacional de Ahorro Postal (Buenos Aires) — Inform Bibliogr BA
Informacion Comercial Espanola — IBS
Informacion Comercial Espanola — ICE
Informacion Comercial Espanola — Info Comer Esp
Informacion Comercial Espanola — Inform Com Esp
Informacion de Quimica Analitica — IFQAA
Informacion de Quimica Analitica — Inf Quim Anal
Informacion de Quimica Analitica — Informac Quim Analit
Informacion de Quimica Analitica (Madrid) — Inf Quim Anal (Madrid)
Informacion de Quimica Analitica, Pura, y Aplicada a la Industria — Inf Quim Anal Pura Apl Ind
Informacion de Quimica Analitica, Pura, y Aplicada a la Industria — IQAPA
Informacion Dental — Inf Dent
Informacion Economica de la Argentina — Info Econ Argentina
Informacion Economica Mundial — Inform Econ Mund
Informacion Juridica. Comision de Legislacion Extranjera del Ministerio de Justicia — Inf Juridica
Informacion Senal Serie. Pecuaria — Inform Senal Ser Pecu
Informacion Tecnica. Argentine Republic. Estacion Experimental Agropecuaria Manfredi — Inf Tec Argent Repub Estac Exp Agropecu Manfredi
Informacion Tecnologica — Inf Tecnol
Informaciones Cientificas — Inf Cient
Informaciones Cientificas Francesas. Association pour la Diffusion de la Pensee Francaise — Inform Ci Franc
Informaciones Culturales — InC
Informaciones Geograficas. Universidad de Chile — UC/IG
Informaciones Medicas (Havana) — Inf Med (Havana)
Informaciones Psiquiatricas — Inf Psiquiat
Informaciones sobre Grasas y Aceites — Inf Grasas Aceites
Informaciones sobre Grasas y Aceites — Inform Grasas Aceites

Informaciones Sociales (Lima) — Inf Soc (L)
Informaciones Sociales (Lima) — Inform Soc Lima
Informaciones y Memorias. Sociedad de Ingenieros del Peru — Inf Mem Soc Ing Peru
Informacni Bulletin pro Otazky Jazykovedne — IBOJ
Informacni Publikace. Stredisko Technickych Informacni Potravinarskeho Prumyslu — Inf Publ Stredisko Tech Inf Potravin Prum
Informacni Zpravodaj VLIS [*Vojenska Lekarska Informacni Sluzba*] — Inf Zp VLIS
Informacoes Economicas. Instituto de Economia Agricola — Inf Econ Inst Econ Agric
Informacoes sobre a Industria Cinematografica Brasileira. Anuario — Inform Ind Cinemat Bras
Informador Apicola — Inform Apic
Informador Universitario — IU
Informant — INFTD
Informare si Documentare Selectiva. Tehnica Nucleara — Inf Doc Sel Teh Nucl
Informatica e Diritto — Inf e Diritto
Informatics in Pathology — Inform Pathol
Informatie [*Netherlands*] — INR
Informatie Bulletin — IFV
Informatie- en Documentatiebulletin. Sociaal-Economische Raad — IDBu
Informatie. Maandblad voor Informatieverwerking — ISQ
Informatieblad van het Economisch en Sociaal Instituut voor de Middenstand — Infbl
Informatieblad voor Bezoekers — Inform Bezoekers
Informatienieuws — IMF
Informatik — IIDWA
Informatik Berichte — Inform Ber
Informatik - Kybernetik - Rechentechnik — Inform Kybernet Rechentech
Informatik und Recht — Inform Recht
Informatik-Berichte (Bonn) — Informatik-Ber (Bonn)
Informatik-Fachberichte — Inf-Fachber
Informatik-Fachberichte — Informatik-Fachber
Informatik-Spektrum — Inf-Spektrum
Information — IML
Information — Info
Information Access Series — Inform Access Ser
Information Age — Inf Age
Information Age — Info Age
Information Age in Perspective — Inf Age Perspect
Information Agricole (Paris) — Inf Agric (Paris)
Information America — Inform Am
Information and Computation — Inform and Comput
Information and Control — IFCNA
Information and Control — Inf and Control
Information and Control — Inf C
Information and Control — Inf Contr
Information and Control — Inf Control
Information and Control — Inform and Control
Information and Control — Inform Contr
Information and Control. Xinxi yu Kongzhi (Shenyang) — Inform and Control Shenyang
Information and Liaison Bulletin. Association of African Geological Surveys [*A publication*] — Inf Liaison Bull Ass Afr Geol Surv
Information and Management [*Netherlands*] — IFM
Information and Management — INF
Information and Management — Inf and Manage
Information and Management — Inf Manage
Information and Management — Info & Mgmt
Information and Records Management — I & R Mgmt
Information and Records Management — Info and Record Managem
Information and Records Management — Info Rec Mgmt
Information and Records Management — IRM
Information and Referral — Info and Referral
Information and Referral. Journal of the Alliance of Information and Referral Systems — Inf and Referral J Alliance Inf Referral Syst
Information and Software Technolgy — Inf Softw Technol
Information and Word Processing Report — Info WP Rep
Information Battelle Frankfurt — Inf Battelle Frankfurt
Information Bienenwirtschaft — Inf Bienenw
Information Bienenzucht — Inf Bienenzucht
Information Bulletin — IB
Information Bulletin: Appendices on Provisional Nomenclature, Symbols, Terminology, and Conventions (International Union of Pure and Applied Chemistry) — Inf Bull Append Prov Nomencl Symb Terminol Conv (IUPAC)
Information Bulletin: Appendices on Provisional Nomenclature, Symbols, Terminology, and Conventions (International Union of Pure and Applied Chemistry) — Inf Bull: Append Provis Nomencl Symb Terminol Conv (IUPAC)
Information Bulletin: Appendices on Provisional Nomenclature, Symbols, Units, and Standards (International Union of Pure and Applied Chemistry) — Inf Bull Append Provis Nomencl Symb Units Stand (IUPAC)
Information Bulletin. Bituminous Coal Research — Inf Bull Bitum Coal Res
Information Bulletin. Cooperative Extension. New York State College of Agriculture and Life Sciences — Inf Bull Coop Ext NY St Coll Agric Life Sci
Information Bulletin. Division of Animal Production. Commonwealth Scientific and Industrial Research Organisation — Inf Bull Div Anim Prodn CSIRO
Information Bulletin. International Center of Information on Antibiotics — Inf Bull Int Cent Inf Antibiot
Information Bulletin. International Geological Correlation Programme. Project Number 61. Sealevel — Information Bulletin IGCP Project No 61 Sealevel
Information Bulletin. International Scientific Radio Union — Inf Bull Int Scient Rad Un
Information Bulletin. International Union of Pure and Applied Chemistry. Appendices on Provisional Nomenclature, Symbols, Units, and Standards — Inf Bull IUPAC Append Provis Nomencl Symb Units Stand
Information Bulletin. International Union of Pure and Applied Chemistry. Technical Reports — Inf Bull IUPAC Tech Rep
Information Bulletin. ISWA (International Solid Wastes Public Cleansing Association) — Inf Bull ISWA (Int Solid Wastes Public Clean Assoc)
Information Bulletin. Library Automated Systems Information Exchange — Inf Bull Libr Autom Syst Inf Exch
Information Bulletin. Library Automated Systems Information Exchange — LASIE
Information Bulletin. New York State College of Agriculture — Inf Bull NY St Coll Agric
Information Bulletin. New York State College of Agriculture. Cooperative Extension Service — Inf Bull NY State Coll Agric Coop Ext Serv
Information Bulletin of Australian Criminology — IBAC
Information Bulletin on Isotopic Generators — IBIGB
Information Bulletin on Isotopic Generators [*France*] — Inf Bull Isot Generators
Information Bulletin on Variable Stars — Inf Bull Variable Stars
Information. Bulletin. Scientific Research Council — Inf B Scient Res Coun
Information Bulletin. Timber Research and Development Association — Inform Bull Timb Res Developm Ass
Information Card. Clemson Agricultural College. Extension Service — Inform Card Clemson Agr Coll Ext Serv
Information Card. Clemson University. Cooperative Extension Service — Inf Card Clemson Univ Coop Ext Serv
Information Centre on the Chemical Industry. Bulletin — Inf Cent Chem Ind Bull
Information. Chilean Nitrate Agricultural Service — Inf Chil Nitrate Agric Serv
Information Chimie — Info Chimie
Information Circular. Arkansas Geological Commission — Inf Circ Arkans Geol Comm
Information Circular. BHP [*Broken Hill Proprietary Ltd.*] **Central Research Laboratories** — Inf Circ BHP Central Res Lab
Information Circular. Bureau of Mines and Geo-Sciences (Philippines) — Inf Circ Bur Mines Geosci (Philipp)
Information Circular. Division of Fisheries and Oceanography. Commonwealth Scientific and Industrial Research Organisation — Inf Circ Div Fish Oceanogr CSIRO
Information Circular. Economic Geology Research Unit. University of the Witwatersrand — Inf Circ Econ Geol Res Unit Univ Witwaters
Information Circular. Geology and Physiography Section. Nature Conservancy Council — Inf Circ Geol Physiogr Sect Nat Conserv Counc
Information Circular. Georgia Geologic and Water Resources Division — Inf Circ GA Geol Water Resour Div
Information Circular. Kentucky Geological Survey — Inf Circ Kentucky Geol Surv
Information Circular. Minnesota Geological Survey — Inf Circ Minn Geol Surv
Information Circular. Newfoundland and Labrador Mineral Resources Division — Inf Circ Newfoundland Labrador Miner Resour Div
Information Circular. Newfoundland Mineral Resources Division — Inf Circ Newfoundland Miner Resour Div
Information Circular. Philippines Bureau of Mines — Inf Circ Philipp Bur Mines
Information Circular. South Pacific Commission — Inf Circ South Pac Comm
Information Circular. Tennessee Division of Geology — Inf Circ Tenn Div Geol
Information Circular. United States Bureau of Mines — Inf Circ US Bur Mines
Information Circular. United States Bureau of Mines — XIMIA
Information. Commission des Communautes Europeennes — Information Commun Europ
Information Community. An Alliance for Progress — Inf Community Alliance Prog
Information Cuttings Service on World Mining Industry — Inf Cuttings Serv World Min Ind
Information Dentaire — INDEA
Information Dentaire — Inf Dent
Information der Internationalen Treuhand AG — IIT
Information des Cours Complementaires — ICC
Information d'Histoire de l'Art — IHA
Information Digest — Inf Digest
Information Display — Inf Disp
Information Display — Inf Display
Information Dynamics — Inf Dyn
Information Economics and Policy — IEP
Information Economique Africaine — IAK
Information Economique Africaine — Info Econ Afr
Information et Documentation — Inf & Doc
Information Executive — Info Exec
Information fuer die Fischwirtschaft — INFID
Information Geographique — Inf Geogr
Information Geographique — Inform Geogr
Information Historique — IH
Information Historique — Inf Hist
Information Historique — InfH
Information Historique — Inform Hist
Information Hotline — IH
Information Hotline [*United States*] — Inf Hotline
Information in Chemistry, Pharmacology, and Patents — Inf Chem Pharmacol Pat
Information in Science Extension [*Database*] — ISE
Information Industry Directory — IID
Information Industry Market Place — IIMP
Information Intelligence Online Newsletter — Inf Int Online Newsletter
Information Intelligence Online Newsletter — Inf Intell Online Newsl
Information Jouets — Inf Jou
Information Litteraire — IL
Information Litteraire — Inf Litt
Information Management — Info Mgmt
Information Management — IRM
Information Manager — Info Manager
Information Manager — Info Mgr

Information Medicale Roumaine — Inf Med Roum
Information News [*England*] — Inf News
Information News and Sources — Inf News & Sources
Information. Nitrate Corporation of Chile. Chilean Nitrate Agricultural Service — Inf Nitrate Corp Chile Chil Nitrate Agric Serv
Information North. AINA [*Arctic Institute of North America*] **Newsletter** — INFN
Information North Quebec. Bulletin de Liaison des Centres de Recherches Nordique de Quebec — INQB
Information Numismatique — Inf Num
Information on Education — Inform Educ
Information on Research in Baden-Wuerttemberg [*Database*] — INFORBW
Information on Roads [*Database*] — INROADS
Information Paper. Australian Atomic Energy Commission — Inf Pap Aust AEC
Information: Part 1: News/Sources/Profiles — Inf: Pt 1
Information: Part 2: Reports/Bibliographies — Inf: Pt 2
Information Pipeline. Norman Wells Project Review — INPI
Information Privacy — Inf Privacy
Information Processing and Management — Inf Pr Man
Information Processing and Management — Inf Proc Man
Information Processing and Management — Inf Process and Manage
Information Processing and Management — Inf Process Manage
Information Processing and Management — Inf Processing & Mgt
Information Processing and Management — IPM
Information Processing and Management — ISR
Information Processing in Japan — Inform Process Japan
Information Processing Journal — InfP
Information Processing Letters — IFPLA
Information Processing Letters — Inf Process Lett
Information Processing Letters — Inform Process Lett
Information Processing Letters — Information Processing Lett
Information Processing Machines — Inf Process Mach
Information Processing Machines — Inform Process Mach
Information Processing Society of Japan (Joho Shori) — Inf Process Soc Jpn (Joho Shori)
Information Psychiatrique — Inf Psychiat
Information Psychiatrique — Inf Psychiatr
Information Release. Geological Survey of Pakistan — Inf Release Geol Surv Pak
Information Report BC-X. Canadian Forestry Service. Pacific Forestry Centre — Inf Rep BC X Can For Serv Pac For Cent
Information Report. Chemical Control Research Institute (Canada) — Inf Rep Chem Control Res Inst (Can)
Information Report. Chemical Control Research Institute. Environment Canada Forestry Service — Inf Rep Chem Control Res Inst Envir Can For Serv
Information Report DPC-X — Inf Rep DPC X
Information Report E-X. Canadian Forestry Service. Policy, Analysis, and Program Development Branch — Info Rep EX Can For Serv Policy Anal Program Dev Branch
Information Report FMR-X. Forest Management Institute — Inf Rep FMR-X For Manage Inst
Information Report. Forest Fire Research Institute (Ottawa) — Inform Rep For Fire Res Inst (Ottawa)
Information Report. Forest Management Institute (Ottawa) — Inform Rep For Mgmt Inst (Ottawa)
Information Report. Forest Products Laboratory (Vancouver) — Inform Rep For Prod Lab (Vancouver)
Information Report. Forest Research Laboratory (Calgary) — Inform Rep For Res Lab (Calgary)
Information Report. Forest Research Laboratory (Quebec) — Inform Rep For Res Lab (Quebec)
Information Report. Forest Research Laboratory (Victoria, British Columbia) — Inform Rep For Res Lab (Victoria BC)
Information Report FPM-X. Forest Pest Management Institute — Inf Rep FPM-X For Pest Manage Inst
Information Report M-X. Maritimes Forest Research Centre. Canadian Forestry Service — Inf Rep M X Marit For Res Cent Can For Serv
Information Report M-X. Maritimes Forest Research Centre. Canadian Forestry Service — Info Rep M-X Mar For Res Cent
Information Report NOR-X. Northern Forest Research Centre — Inf Rep NOR-X North For Res Cent
Information Report NOR-X. Northern Forest Research Centre. Canadian Forestry Service — Info Rep NOR X North For Res Cen Can For Serv
Information Report N-X. Canadian Forestry Service. Newfoundland Forest Research Centre — Inf Rep N X Can For Serv Newfoundland For Res Cent
Information Report O-X. Canadian Forestry Service. Great Lakes Forestry Centre — Inf Rep O X Can For Serv Great Lakes For Cent
Information Report Series. Fisheries — Inf Rep Ser Fish
Information Report. Washington Researches [*United States*] — Inf Rep Washington Res
Information Reports and Bibliographies — Inf Rep Bibliogr
Information Reports and Bibliographies — Inf Rept Bibliog
Information Resources Annual — Inform Res
Information Resources Annual — IRA
Information Retrieval and Library Automation — IRLA
Information Retrieval and Library Automation Letter — Inf Retr Libr Automn
Information Science Abstracts — Inform Sci
Information Science Abstracts — InfSciAb
Information Science Abstracts — ISA
Information Sciences — Inf Sci
Information Sciences — Inf Sciences
Information Sciences — Inform Sci
Information Sciences — Information Sci
Information Sciences — InfoS
Information Scientist — Inf Scient
Information Scientist — Inf Scientist
Information Series. Colorado Geological Survey — Inf Ser Colorado Geol Surv
Information Series. Colorado State University. Environmental Resources Center — Inf Ser Colo State Univ Environ Resour Cent
Information Series in Agricultural Economics. University of California. Agricultural Extension Service — Inform Ser Agr Econ Univ Calif Agr Ext Serv
Information Series. New Zealand Department of Scientific and Industrial Research — Inf Ser Dep Scient Ind Res NZ
Information Series. New Zealand Department of Scientific and Industrial Research — Inf Ser NZ Dep Sci Ind Res
Information Series. New Zealand Forest Service — Inf Ser NZ For Serv
Information Series. New Zealand Forest Service — Inform Ser NZ For Serv
Information Series. University of Idaho. Forest Wildlife and Range Experiment Station — Inf Ser Univ Idaho For Wildl Range Exp Stn
Information Service Leaflet. Central Information, Library, and Editorial Section. Commonwealth Scientific and Industrial Research Organisation — Inf Serv Leafl CILES CSIRO
Information Service Leaflet. Division of Mechanical Engineering. Commonwealth Scientific and Industrial Research Organisation — Info Serv Leafl Div Mech Eng CSIRO
Information Service Sheet. Division of Building Research. Commonwealth Scientific and Industrial Research Organisation — Inf Serv Sheet Div Build Res CSIRO
Information Service Sheet. Division of Mechanical Engineering. Commonwealth Scientific and Industrial Research Organisation — Inf Serv Sheet Div Mech Eng CSIRO
Information Services and Use — INF
Information Services and Use [*Netherlands*] — Inf Serv Use
Information Services and Use — ISU
Information Services and Use — ISUDX
Information Sheet. Agricultural Experiment Station. Mississippi State University — Inf Sh Miss Agric Exp Stn
Information Sheet. Mississippi Agricultural Experiment Station — Inform Sheet Miss Agr Exp Sta
Information Sheet. Mississippi State University. Cooperative Extension Service — Inf Sheet Miss State Univ Coop Ext Serv
Information Sheet. Yukon Territory. Bureau of Statistics — YIS
Information Society — Inf Soc
Information Society — TSO
Information Standards Quarterly — ISQ
Information Storage and Retrieval — IFSRA
Information Storage and Retrieval — Inf Stor Retr
Information Storage and Retrieval — Inf Storage
Information Storage and Retrieval — Inf Storage & Retr
Information Storage and Retrieval — Inf Storage Retr
Information Storage and Retrieval — Inform Stor Retrieval
Information Strategy. The Executive's Journal — IFS
Information (Swedish Pulp and Paper Association) — Inform (Swed)
Information System for Hazardous Organics in Water [*Database*] — ISHOW
Information System Language Studies — ISLS
Information System on Food, Agriculture, and Forestry [*Database*] — ELFIS
Information Systems — Inf Syst
Information Systems [*Elmsford, NY*] — Info Systems
Information Systems — Information Syst
Information Systems News — Info Sys New
Information Technology — Info Technol
Information Technology and Libraries — Inf Technol and Libr
Information Technology and Libraries — Inf Technol Libr
Information Technology and Libraries — Info Tech
Information Technology and Libraries — ITL
Information Technology and People — Inf Tech People
Information Technology. Research and Development — Inf Technol Res and Dev
Information Technology Series — Inform Tech Ser
Information Technology Training — Inform Technol Train
Information Text Series. College of Tropical Agriculture and Human Resources. University of Hawaii. Cooperative Extension Service — Inf Text Ser Coll Trop Agric Hum Resour Univ Hawaii Coop Ext
Information Times — Info Times
Information Today — IT
Information ueber Steuer und Wirtschaft — Inf
Information ueber Steuer und Wirtschaft — Inform Steuer Wirtsch
Information Washington — Info Wash
Information World — IWWDD
Information World (Abingdon) [*England*] — Inf World (Abingdon)
Information World Review — Inf World Rev
Information World (Washington, DC) — Inf World (Washington DC)
Information Zukunfts- und Friedensforschung — Inf Zukunfts-Friedensforsch
Informationen aus der Orthodoxen Kirche — IOK
Informationen aus Orthodontie und Kieferorthopaedie mit Beitraegen aus der Internationalen Literatur — Inf Orthod Kieferorthop
Informationen Bildung Wissenschaft — Inf Bild Wiss
Informationen der Abteilung fuer Geschichte der Imperialistischen Ostforschung an der Humboldt-Universitaet — Inform Imperialist Ostforsch
Informationen fuer die Fischwirtschaft — Inf Fischwirtsch
Informationen Kerntechnische Normung — Inf Kerntech Normung
Informationen zu Naturschutz und Landschaftspflege in Nordwestdeutschland — Inf Naturschutz Landschaftspflege Nordwestdeutschl
Informationen zu Naturschutz und Landschaftspflege in Nordwestdeutschland — INLND6
Informationen zur Erziehungs- und Bildungshistorischen Forschung — Inform Erzieh Bildungshist Forsch
Informationen zur Raumentwicklung — Inf Raumentwickl
Informationen zur Raumentwicklung — Inform Raumentwicklung
Informations Aerauliques et Thermiques — IATHA
Informations Aerauliques et Thermiques — Inf Aerauliques Therm

Informations Agricoles (Algiers) — Inform Agric Algiers
Informations and Documents — Inform Doc
Informations Catholiques Internationales — ICI
Informations Catholiques Internationales — Inf Cath Int
Informations Catholiques Internationales — Inform Cathol Int
Informations Constitutionnelles et Parlementaires — Inform Constit Parl
Informations Cooperatives — Inform Coop
Informations Economiques — IE
Informations Economiques et Syndicales — Info Econ Synd
Informations Economiques (Tunis) — IFT
Informations et Documentation Agricoles — Inform Doc Agr
Informations et Documents — Info et Docs
Informations et Documents — Inform et Doc
Informations Scientifiques — Inf Sci
Informations Sociales [*Paris*] — Inf Soc
Informations Sociales (Paris) — Inf Soc (P)
Informations Sociales (Paris) — Inform Soc (Paris)
Informations. Societe Francaise de Photographie — Inf Soc Franc Photogr
Informations sur l'Irradiation des Denrees — Inf Irradiat Denrees
Informations Techniques. Centre Technique Interprofessionnel des Oleagineux Metropolitains — Inf Tech Cent Tech Interprof Ol Metrop
Informations Techniques. Centre Technique Interprofessionnel des Oleagineux Metropolitains — Inf Techn CETIOM
Informations Techniques des Services Veterinaires — Infs Tech Serv Vet
Informations UFOD [*Union Francaise des Organismes de Documentation*] — Inf UFOD
Informations Universitaires en Relations Internationales et Etudes Etrangeres — Info Univ Rel Inter Etud Etran
Informations Universitaires et Professionnelles Internationales — Inform Univ Profes Int
Informationsberichte des Bayerischen Landesamtes fuer Wasserwirtschaft — Informationsber Bayer Landesamtes Wasserwirtsch
Informationsblatt fuer de Gemeinden in den Niederdeutschen Lutherischen Landeskirchen — INLL
Informationsblatt fuer die Gemeinden in den Niederdeutschen Lutherischen Landeskirchen [*Hamburg*] — InfBl
Informations-Chimie — INFCA
Informations-Chimie — Inf-Chim
Informations-Chimie — ISV
Informationsdienst. Arbeitsgemeinschaft fuer Pharmazeutische Verfahrenstechnik — Informationsdienst Arbeitsgem Pharm Verfahrenstech
Informationsdienst der Stadt (Wien) — Stadt (Wien)
Informationsdienst West-Ost — IWO
Informationzentrum Haut — Inform Haut
Informatique et Gestion [*France*] — IAG
Informatique et Gestion — Inf & Gestion
Informatique et Gestion — Informat et Gestion
Informatique et Sciences Humaines — Inform Sci Hum
Informatique et Sciences Humaines — Inform Sci Humaines
Informatique Geologique. Sciences de la Terre — Inf Geol Sci Terre
Informatique/Intelligence Artificielle — Inform Intelligence Artificielle
Informativo Bibliografico (Rosario, Argentina) — Informativo Bibliogr Rosario
Informativo de Investigaciones Agricolas — IDIA
Informativo do INT [*Instituto Nacional de Tecnologia*] [*Brazil*] — Inf INT
Informatologia Yugoslavica — Inform Yugoslav
Informatore Agrario — Inform Agr
Informatore Agrario — Inftore Agr
Informatore Botanico Italiano — IBOLB
Informatore Botanico Italiano — Inf Bot Ital
Informatore del Giovane Entomologo — Inf Giovane Entomol
Informatore del Marmista — Inf Marmista
Informatore di Ortoflorofrutticoltura — Inf Ortoflorofruttic
Informatore Fitopatologico — Inf Fitopatol
Informatore Fitopatologico — Inform Fitopatol
Informatore Fitopatologico — Inftore Fitopatol
Informatore Medico — Inf Med
Informatore Medico (Genoa) — Inf Med (Genoa)
Informatore Odonto-Stomatologico — Inf Odontostomatol
Informatore Zootecnico — Inf Zootec
Informatore Zootecnico — Inform Zootec
Informatsionnyi Byulleten' Instituta Geologii Arktiki — Inf Byull Inst Geol Arkt
Informatsionnyi Byulleten' Instituta Geologii Arktiki — Inf Byull Inst Geol Arktiki
Informatsionnyi Byulleten' Mezhvedomstvennyi Geofizicheskii Komitet pri Prezidiume Akademii Nauk Ukrainskoi SSR — Inf Byull Mezhved Geofiz Kom Prezidiume Akad Nauk Ukr SSR
Informatsionnyi Byulleten' Mikroelementy Sibirii — Inf Byull Mikroelem Sib
Informatsionnyi Byulleten' Moskovskogo Nauchno Issledovatel'skogo Instituta Sanitarii i Gigieny — Inf Byull Mosk Nauchno Issled Inst Sanit Gig
Informatsionnyi Byulleten' Nauchnyi Sovet po Problemam Radiobiologii Akademiya Nauk SSSR — Inf Byull Nauchn Sov Probl Radiobiol Akad Nauk SSSR
Informatsionnyi Byulleten Orgenergostroi — Inf Byull Orgenergostroi
Informatsionnyi Byulleten' Sibirskii Institut Fiziologii i Biokhimii Rastenii — Inf Byull Sib Inst Fiziol Biokhim Rast
Informatsionnyi Byulleten' Sovetskoi Antarkticheskoi Ekspeditsii — Inf Byull Sov Antarkt Eksped
Informatsionnyi Byulleten' Vsesoyuznyi Institut po Proektirovaniyu Organizatsii Energeticheskogo Stroitel'stva — Inf Byull Vses Inst Proekt Organ Energ Stroit
Informatsionnyi Byulleten' Vsesoyuznyi Nauchno Issledovatel'skii Institut po Mashinam dlya Promyshlennosti Stroitel'nykh Materialov — Inf Byull Vses Nauchno Issled Inst Mash Promsti Stroit Mater
Informatsionnyi Sbornik Institut Zemnoi Kory Sibirskoe Otdelenie Akademiya Nauk SSSR — Inf Sb Inst Zemnoi Kory Sib Otd Akad Nauk SSSR
Informatsionnyi Sbornik Trudov Vychislitel'nogo Tsentra Irkutskii Gosudarstvennyi Universitet — Inf Sb Tr Vychisl Tsentra Irkutsk Gos Univ
Informatsionnyi Sbornik Vsesoyuznyi Nauchno-Issledovatel'skii Geologicheskii Institut — Inf Sb Vses Nauchno Issled Geol Inst
Informatsiya o Nauchno-Issledovatel'skikh Rabotakh Filial Vsesoyuznogo Instituta Nauchnoi i Tekhnicheskoi Informatsii — Inf Nauchno Issled Rab Fil VIN i TI
Informatsiya o Nauchno-Issledovatel'skikh Rabotakh Institut Tekhniko-Ekonomicheskoi Informatsii — Inf Nauchno Issled Rab Inst Tekh Ekon Inf
Informazione Elettronica — Inf Elettron
Informazioni e Studi Vivaldiani — Inf Studi Vivaldiani
Informazioni e Studi Vivaldiani — Info Stud Vivaldiani
Informazioni Seriche. Rivista dell' Industria Bacologica e Serica — Inform Seriche
Informazioni Soimet — Inf So
Informe Agropecuario [*Agricultural Report*]. Empresa de Pesquisa Agropecuaria de Minas Gerais — Inf Agropecu Empresa Pesqui Agropecu Minas Gerais
Informe Anual de Labores. Costa Rica. Ministerio de Agricultura y Ganaderia — Informe Anu Labores Costa Rica Min Agr Ganad
Informe de Investigacion Agricola (Mexico) — Inf Invest Agric (Mexico)
Informe de Investigacion. Centro de Investigaciones Tecnologicas (Pando, Uruguay) — Inf Invest Cent Invest Tecnol (Pando Urug)
Informe Economico — IEP
Informe Economico — Info Econ
Informe Economico (Argentina) — Arg Inform
Informe. Estacion Experimental Agricola de "La Molina" (Lima) — Inf Estac Exp Agric La Molina (Lima)
Informe. Estacion Experimental Agricola La Molina (Lima) — Informe Est Exper La Molina Lima
Informe Mensual. Estacion Experimental Agricola de "La Molina" [*Lima*] — Infme Mens Estac Exp Agric La Molina
Informe Mensual. Estacion Experimental Agricola de "La Molina" (Lima) — Inf Mens Estac Exp Agric La Molina (Lima)
Informe Mensual. Estacion Experimental Agricola de "La Molina" (Lima) — Informe Mens Estac Exp Agr "La Molina" (Lima)
Informe Relaciones Mexico-Estados Unidos — Info Relaciones Mex-Estados Unidos
Informe Tecnico. Estacion Experimental Agropecuaria (Pergamino) — Informe Tec Estac Exp Agropecuar (Pergamino)
Informe Tecnico. Estacion Experimental Regional Agropecuaria [*Pergamino*]. Instituto Nacional de Tecnologia Agropecuaria — Infme Tec Estac Exp Agropec
Informe Tecnico. Estacion Experimental Regional Agropecuaria (Pergamino) — Inf Tec Estac Exp Reg Agropecu (Pergamino)
Informe Tecnico. Instituto Centroamericano de Investigacion y Tecnologia Industrial — Inf Tec ICAITI
Informe Tecnico. Instituto Centroamericano de Investigacion y Tecnologia Industrial — Inf Tec Inst Centroam Invest Tecnol Ind
Informe Tecnico. Instituto Forestal [*Chile*] — Informe Tec
Informe Tecnico. Instituto Forestal (Santiago, Chile) — Inf Tec Inst For (Santiago Chile)
Informe Tecnico (Provincia de Buenos Aires). Ministerio de Asuntos Agrarios. Direccion de Agricultura — Infme Tec Minst Asuntos Agrarios (Buenos Aires)
Informes Cientificos y Tecnicos. Universidad Nacional de Cuyo — Infmes Cient Tec Univ Nac Cuyo
Informes de la Construccion — Inf Constr
Informes de Pro Mundi Vita America Latina — Informes PMV Am Lat
Informes. Provincia de Buenos Aires. Comision de Investigaciones Cientificas — Inf Prov Buenos Aires Com Invest Cient
Informes Tecnicos. Instituto de Investigaciones Pesqueras — Inf Tec Inst Invest Pesq
Informes Tecnicos. Instituto de Investigaciones Pesqueras — ITIPD5
Informes y Memorias de la Comisaria General de Excavaciones Arqueologicas — IM
Informes y Memorias. Servicio Nacional de Excavaciones Arqueologicas — IM
Informes y Memorias. Servicio Nacional de Excavaciones Arqueologicas — Informes y Mem
Infortunistica e Traumatologia del Lavoro — Infort Traum Lav
Infosystems [*Wheaton, IL*] — Infosys
InfoWorld in Review. Special Report from InfoWorld — Info Wld Rv
Infraestructura Teatral [*Database*] — ITEA
Infrared Fiber Optics — Infrared Fiber Opt
Infrared Focal Plane Array Producibility and Related Materials — Infrared Focal Plane Array Prod Relat Mater
Infrared Physics — INFPA
Infrared Physics — Infrar Phys
Infrared Physics — Infrared Phys
Infrared Search System [*Database*] — IRSS
Infrared Sensors. Detectors, Electronics, and Signal Processing — Infrared Sens Detect Electron Signal Process
Infusionstherapie und Klinische Ernaehrung — Infusionsther Klin Ernaehr
Infusionstherapie und Klinische Ernaehrung. Forschung und Praxis — Infusionsther Klin Ernaer Forsch Prax
Infusionstherapie und Klinische Ernaehrung. Sonderheft — Infusionsther Klin Ernaehr Sonderh
Infusionstherapie und Transfusionsmedizin — Infusionsther Transfusionsmed
Ingegneria — IGGEA
Ingegneria Ambientale [*Italy*] — Ing Ambientale
Ingegneria Chimica — ICHIA
Ingegneria Chimica Italiana — Ing Chim Ital
Ingegneria Chimica (Milan) — Ing Chim (Milan)
Ingegneria Ferroviaria — INFEA
Ingegneria Ferroviaria — Ing Ferrov
Ingegneria Meccanica — IGMEA
Ingegneria Meccanica — Ing Mecc
Ingegneria Nucleare — Ing Nucl

Ingegneria Nucleare — INNUA
Ingegneria Sanitaria — Ing Sanit
Ingegneria Sanitaria — INSAA
Ingenieria Aeronautica y Astronautica [*Spain*] — Ing Aeronaut Astronaut
Ingenieria Agronomica — Ing Agron
Ingenieria Agronomica [*Caracas*] — INGAB8
Ingenieria Agronomica (Caracas) — Ing Agron (Caracas)
Ingenieria Civil — Ing Civil
Ingenieria Civil (Havana) — Ing Civ (Havana)
Ingenieria e Industria (Argentina) — IGINA
Ingenieria Electrica y Mecanica — Ing Electr & Mec
Ingenieria. Escuela Nacional de Ingenieros (Mexico) — Ing Mex
Ingenieria Forestal — Ingen For
Ingenieria Hidraulica en Mexico — Ing Hidraul Mexico
Ingenieria Hidraulica en Mexico — Ingenieria Hidraul Mex
Ingenieria Hidraulica en Mexico (Mexico) — Ing Hidraul Mex
Ingenieria Mecanica y Electrica — Ing Mec y Electr
Ingenieria Naval (Madrid) — Ing Nav (Madrid)
Ingenieria Petrolera [*Mexico*] — Ing Pet
Ingenieria Quimica e Industrias — Ing Quim Ind
Ingenieria Quimica (Madrid) — Ing Quim Madrid
Ingenieria Quimica (Medellin, Colombia) — Ing Quim (Medellin Colombia)
Ingenieria Quimica (Mexico City) — Ing Quim (Mexico City)
Ingenieria Textil (Barcelona) — Ing Text (Barcelona)
Ingenieria y Arquitectura — Ing Arquit
Ingenieria y Arquitectura (Bogota) — Ing Arquitec Bogota
Ingenieur — Ing
Ingenieur — INGRA
Ingenieur Chimiste (Brussels) — Ing Chim (Brussels)
Ingenieur der Deutschen Bundespost — Ing Dt Bu Po
Ingenieur in Nederlandsch Indie — Ing Ned Indie
Ingenieur (Montreal) — INMOA
Ingenieur-Archiv. Gesellschaft fuer Angewandte Mathematik und Mechanik — INARA
Ingenieur-Archiv. Gesellschaft fuer Angewandte Mathematik und Mechanik [*West Germany*] — Ing-Arch
Ingenieur-Digest — IGDGA
Ingenieur-Digest — Ing-Dig
Ingenieur-Journal — Ing Journ
Ingenieurs. Arts et Metiers — Ing Arts Metiers
Ingenieurs de l'Automobile — IAUTA
Ingenieurs de l'Automobile — Ing Auto
Ingenieurs de l'Ecole Superieure de Physique et de Chimie Industrielles — Ing Ec Super Phys Chim Ind
Ingenieurs de l'Ecole Superieure de Physique et de Chimie Industrielles — Ing EPCI
Ingenieurs des Villes de France — Ingen Villes France
Ingenieurs et Techniciens — IGNTA
Ingenieurs et Techniciens — Ing & Tech
Ingenieursblad — INBLA
Ingenieursblad — TWT
Ingenieur-Zeitung — IngZg
Ingenioer- og Bygningsvaesen [*Denmark*] — Ing Bygningsvaes
Ingenioer- og Bygningsvaesen Ugeoversigt [*Denmark*] — Ing Bygningsv Ugeovers
Ingenioeren (1892-1966) — INGEA
Ingenioeren-Forskning [*Denmark*] — Ing-Forsk
Ingenioerens Ugeblad — Ing Ugebl
Ingenioer-Magasinet [*Denmark*] — Ing-Mag
Ingenioer-Nytt — IGNTB
Ingenioersvetenskapsakademien. Handlingar — Ingenioersvetenskapsakad Handl
Ingenioervidenskabelige Skrifter — Ingenioervidensk Skr
Ingenioervidenskabelige Skrifter. Series A — Ingenioervidensk Skr Ser A
Ingenioervidenskabelige Skrifter. Series B — Ingenioervidensk Skr Ser B
Ingenior- og Bygningsvaesen — Ing o B
Ingenioren — Ing
Ingeniors Vetenskaps Akademien. Meddelande — Ing Vetenskaps Akad Medd
Inha University IIR — Inha Univ IIR
Inhalation Therapy — Inhal Ther
Inhaled Particles — Inhaled Part
Inheemsche Nijverheid op Java, Madoera, Bali en Lombok — Inheemsche Nijverh Java
Inheritance, Estate, and Gift Tax Reports (Commerce Clearing House) — CCH Inh Est & Gift Tax Rep
Iniciacao a Matematica — Iniciacao Mat
INIREB Informa. Instituto de Investigaciones sobre Recursos Bioticos — INIREB Informa Inst Invest Recur Bioticos
INIS [*International Nuclear Information System*] **Atomindex** — INIS
INIS [*International Nuclear Information System*] **Newsletter** — INNLA
Initiation a la Linguistique — I Ling
Initiation a l'Epigraphie Mycenienne — Ep Myc
Initiation a l'Islam — Ini Isl
Inititatives in Population — Initiatives Popul
Iniziative — Iniz
Injectable Contraceptives Newsletter — Injectable Contraceptives Newsl
Injury Prevention — Inj Prev
Ink and Print — TBI
Inka Corporate Authorities [*Database*] — INKACORP
Inland Architect — Inland Archt
Inland Bird-Banding News — Inl Bird-Banding News
Inland Printer — Inland Ptr
Inland Printer/American Lithographer — Inland P
Inland Printer/American Lithographer — Inland Printer Am Lithogr
Inland Seas — InS
Inland Waters Directorate. Report Series (Canada) — Inland Waters Dir Rep Ser Can
Inlandsch Reglement — IR
Inlichitingsblad van de Christelijke Centrale der Metaalbewerkers van Belgie — Inlichitingsblad CCMB
Inmersion y Ciencia — Inmersion Cienc
Inmun Kwahak — IKw
Innere Medizin — Innere Med
Innere Mission — I Mis
Innere Mission im Evangelischen Deutschland — IMED
Innere Reich — IR
Innerrhoder Geschichtsfreund — IG
Innes Review — In R
Innes Review — Innes Rev
Innes Review — InnR
Innovatie Informatiebulletin ter Bevordering van de Industriele Vernieuwing in Ons Land — INQ
Innovations in Materials Research — Innovations Mater Res
Innovative Higher Education — Innov High Educ
Innovator's Digest [*Database*] — ID
Innsbrucker Beitraege zur Kulturwissenschaft — IBK
Innsbrucker Beitraege zur Kulturwissenschaft — IBKW
Innsbrucker Beitraege zur Kulturwissenschaft. Sonderheft — IBKWS
Innsbrucker Beitraege zur Sprachwissenschaft — IBS
Inorganic and Nuclear Chemistry Letters — Inorg and Nucl Chem Lett
Inorganic and Nuclear Chemistry Letters — Inorg Nucl
Inorganic and Nuclear Chemistry Letters — Inorg Nucl Chem Lett
Inorganic and Nuclear Chemistry Letters — INUCA
Inorganic Chemistry — INOCA
Inorganic Chemistry — Inorg Chem
Inorganic Chemistry of the Main Group Elements — Inorg Chem Main Group Elem
Inorganic Chemistry of the Transition Elements — Inorg Chem Transition Elem
Inorganic Crystal Structure Database — ICSD
Inorganic Ion Exchangers in Chemical Analysis [*Monograph*] — Inorg Ion Exch Chem Anal
Inorganic Macromolecules Reviews — Inorg Macromol Rev
Inorganic Materials [*English Translation*] — INOMA
Inorganic Materials — Inorg Mater
Inorganic Materials (Tokyo) — Inorg Mater Tokyo
Inorganic Materials (Translation of Neorganicheskie Materialy) — Inorg Mater Transl of Neorg Mater
Inorganic Materials (USSR) — Inorg Mater (USSR)
Inorganic Perspectives in Biology and Medicine — Inorg Perspect Biol Med
Inorganic Reaction Mechanisms — Inorg React Mech
Inorganica Chimica Acta — ICHAA
Inorganica Chimica Acta — Inorg Chim
Inorganica Chimica Acta — Inorg Chim Acta
Inorganica Chimica Acta. Reviews — Inorg Chim Acta Rev
Inostrannaya Literatura [*Moscow*] — InL
Inostrannye Jazyki v Skole — IJaS
Inostrannye Jazyki v Skole — IJS
Inostrannye Jazyki v Skole — InostrJazyki
Inostrannye Jazyki v Skole — IYaSh
Inozemna Filologia — In Fil
Inozemna Filologiya [*L'vov*] — InF
Inozemna Filolohiji — InozF
INPADOC [*International Patent Documentation Center*] **Data Base** — IDB
In-Plant Reproductions [*United States*] — In-Plant Reprod
In-Plant Reproductions — IRPRD
INPO [*Institute of Nuclear Power Operations*] **Impact** [*United States*] — INPO Impact
INPO [*Institute of Nuclear Power Operations*] **Review** [*United States*] — INPO Rev
Inqueritos Nacional de Precos (Capitais) — Inqueritos Nac de Precos (Capitais)
Inqueritos Nacional de Precos (Unidades da Federacao) — Inqueritos Nac de Precos (Unidades da Federacao)
Inquiry — Inq
Inquiry — INQYA
Inquiry — IQY
Inquiry — PINQ
Inquiry Magazine — Inquiry Mag
Insatsu Zasshi — INZAA
Inschriften der Altassyrischen Koenige — IAK
Inschriften Griechischer Bildhauer — IGB
Inschriften von Erythrai und Klazomenai — IEK
Inschriften von Magnesia am Maeander — I Magn
Inschriften von Magnesia am Maeander — I Magnesia
Inschriften von Magnesia am Maeander — IvM
Inschriften von Olympia — I Olympia
Inschriften von Olympia — Inscr Olymp
Inschriften von Olympia — Iv Ol
Inschriften von Olympia — IvO
Inschriften von Pergamon — I Pergamon
Inschriften von Pergamon — Inscr Perg
Inschriften von Pergamon — IvP
Inschriften von Priene — I Priene
Inschriften von Priene — Insv Priene
Inschriften von Priene — Iv Pr
Inscripciones Cristianas de la Espana Romana y Visigoda — ICERV
Inscripciones Hispanias en Verso — IHV
Inscripciones Latinas de la Espana Romana — ILER
Inscripciones Romanas de Galicia — Inscr Rom Gal
Inscripciones Romanas de Galicia — IRG
Inscriptiile Daciei Romane — IDR

Inscriptiile Grecesti si Latine din Secolele IV-XII Descoperite in Romania — IGLR
Inscriptiones Antiquae Orae Septentrionalis Ponti Euxini — Insc Pont Euxini
Inscriptiones Antiquae Orae Septentrionalis Ponti Euxini — Inscr Or Sept Pon Eux
Inscriptiones Antiquae Orae Septentrionalis Ponti Euxini — IOSPE
Inscriptiones Antiquae Orae Septentrionalis Ponti Euxini — IPE
Inscriptiones Bavariae Romanae — IBR
Inscriptiones Britanniae Christianae — IBC
Inscriptiones Britanniae Christianae — Inscr Brit Christ
Inscriptiones Christianae Latinae Veteres — ICLV
Inscriptiones Christianae Urbis Romae. Nova Series — ICUR
Inscriptiones Creticae — ICr
Inscriptiones Creticae Opera et Consilio Friderici Halbherr Collectae — I Creticae
Inscriptiones Creticae Opera et Consilio Friderici Halbherr Collectae — IC
Inscriptiones Creticae Opera et Consilio Friderici Halbherr Collectae — ICret
Inscriptiones Creticae Opera et Consilio Friderici Halbherr Collectae — Inscript Cret
Inscriptiones Cuneiformes du Kultepe — ICK
Inscriptiones Graecae — IG
Inscriptiones Graecae [*Berlin*] — Inscr Gr
Inscriptiones Graecae [*Berlin*] — Inscr Graec
Inscriptiones Graecae ad Inlustrandas Dialectos Selectae — IG Dial
Inscriptiones Graecae ad Res Romanas Pertinentes — IGROM
Inscriptiones Graecae ad Res Romanas Pertinentes — IGRR
Inscriptiones Graecae ad Res Romanas Pertinentes — Inscr Graec ad Res Rompert
Inscriptiones Graecae Antiquissimae — IGA
Inscriptiones Graecae Antiquissimae Praeter Atticas in Attica Repertas — IA
Inscriptiones Graecae Antiquissimae Praeter Atticas in Attica Repertas — IGA
Inscriptiones Graecae Antiquissimae Praeter Atticas in Attica Repertas — Inscr Gr Antiq
Inscriptiones Graecae Consilio et Auctoritate Academiae Literarum Regiae Borussicae Editae — I G
Inscriptiones Graecae. Editio Minor — IGE Mi
Inscriptiones Graecae in Bulgaria Repertae — I Gr B
Inscriptiones Graecae in Bulgaria Repertae — IG Bulg
Inscriptiones Graecae in Bulgaria Repertae — IGB
Inscriptiones Graecae in Bulgaria Repertae — IGBR
Inscriptiones Graecae in Bulgaria Repertae — Inscr Bulg
Inscriptiones Graecae Septentrionalis — IG Sept
Inscriptiones Graecae Septentrionalis — IGS
Inscriptiones Graecae Siciliae et Infimae ad Ius Pertinentes — IGS
Inscriptiones Graecae Siciliae et Infimae Italiae — IGSI
Inscriptiones Graecae Urbis Romae — IG Urbis Romae
Inscriptiones Graecae Urbis Romae — IGUR
Inscriptiones Graecarum Insularum — IGIns
Inscriptiones Hispaniae Christianae — IHC
Inscriptiones Hispaniae Christianae — IHCS
Inscriptiones Italiae — II
Inscriptiones Italiae — IIt
Inscriptiones Italiae — Inscr Ital
Inscriptiones Italiae et Siciliae — IIS
Inscriptiones Italiae Inferioris Dialecticae — IIID
Inscriptiones Latinae Christianae Veteres — IL Ch V
Inscriptiones Latinae Christianae Veteres — ILCV
Inscriptiones Latinae Christianae Veteres — Inscr Lat Christ Vet
Inscriptiones Latinae Liberae Rei Publicae — ILLR
Inscriptiones Latinae Liberae Rei Publicae — Inscr Lat Librei Publicae
Inscriptiones Latinae quae in Iugoslavia Inter Annos MCMXL et MCMLX Repertae et Edita Sunt — I Iug
Inscriptiones Latinae quae in Iugoslavia Inter Annos MCMXL et MCMLX Repertae et Edita Sunt — Inscr Iug
Inscriptiones Latinae Selectae — ILS
Inscriptiones Latinae Selectae — Inscr Lat Sel
Inscriptiones Pyliae ad Mycenaeum Aetatem Pertinentes — Inscr Pyliae Mycen Aet Pert
Inscriptiones Pyliae ad Mycenaeum Aetatem Pertinentes — IP
Inscriptiones Regni Neopolitani — IRN
Inscriptions Chretiennes de la Gaule Anterieures au VIIIe Siecle — Inscr Christ
Inscriptions de Delos — I Delos
Inscriptions de Delos — ID
Inscriptions de Delos — In Del
Inscriptions de Delos — Inscr de Delos
Inscriptions de la Mesie Superieure — IMS
Inscriptions Grecques de Philae — I Philae
Inscriptions Grecques de Philae — Inscr Philae
Inscriptions Grecques et Latines de la Syrie — IGLS
Inscriptions Grecques et Latines de la Syrie — IGLSyr
Inscriptions Grecques et Latines de la Syrie — Inscr Gr Lat Syrie
Inscriptions Grecques et Latines de la Syrie — Inscr Grec Lat la Syrie
Inscriptions Hittites Hieroglyphiques — IHH
Inscriptions in the Minoan Linear Script of Class A — ILA
Inscriptions Latines d'Afrique — IL Afr
Inscriptions Latines d'Afrique — ILAf
Inscriptions Latines d'Afrique — Inscr Lat Afr
Inscriptions Latines d'Algerie — IL Al
Inscriptions Latines d'Algerie — IL Alg
Inscriptions Latines d'Algerie — ILA
Inscriptions Latines d'Algerie — Inscr Lat Alg
Inscriptions Latines de la Gaule [*Narbonnaise, France*] — ILG
Inscriptions Latines de la Gaule (Narbonnaise) — ILG (Narb)
Inscriptions Latines de la Gaule (Narbonnaise) — Inscr Lat Gaule
Inscriptions Latines des Trois Gaules — IL de Gaule
Inscriptions Latines des Trois Gaules — ILTG
Inscriptions Latines du Maroc — I Maroc
Inscriptions Latines du Maroc — IL Mar
Inscriptions Latines du Maroc — IL Maroc
Inscriptions Latines du Maroc — ILM
Inscriptions Latins de la Tunisie — Inscr Tunisie
Inscriptions of Cos — I Cos
Inscriptions of Cos — Inscr Cos
Inscriptions of Kourion — I Kourion
Inscriptions of Kourion — Inscr Kourion
Inscriptions Romaines d'Algerie — IRA
Inscrizioni Antico-Ebraiche Palestinesi — IAP
Insect Answers. Cooperative Extension Service. Washington State University — Insect Answers Coop Ext Serv Wash St Univ
Insect Biochemistry — Insect Bioc
Insect Biochemistry — Insect Biochem
Insect Biochemistry and Molecular Biology — Insect Biochem Mol Biol
Insect Disease Report. United States Forest Service. Northern Region — Insect Dis Rep US For Serv North Reg
Insect Ecology — Insect Ecol
Insect Molecular Biology — Insect Bol Biol
Insect Science and Its Application — Insect Sci Appl
Insect Science and Its Application — Insect Sci Its Applica
Insect Science and Its Application — ISIADL
Insect World Digest — Insect Wld Dig
Insecta Matsumurana — Insecta Matsum
Insecta Matsumurana. Supplement — Insecta Matsumurana Suppl
Insectes Sociaux [*Social Insects*] — Insect Soc
Insectes Sociaux — Insectes Soc
Insectes Sociaux [*Social Insects*] — INSOA7
Insectes Sociaux/Social Insects — Insects Soc Soc Insects
Insecticide and Acaricide Tests — Insectic Acaricide Tests
Insect-Plant Interactions — Insect Plant Interact
Insects of Micronesia — Insects Micronesia
Insel-Almanach — IA
Insel-Almanach — In A
Insemnari Stiintifice — ISt
INSERM [*Institut National de la Sante et de la Recherche Medicale*] **Colloque** — INSERM Colloq
INSERM [*Institut National de la Sante et de la Recherche Medicale*] **Symposia** — INSERM Symp
INSERM [*Institut National de la Sante et de la Recherche Medicale*] **Symposia** [*Elsevier Book Series*] — IS
Inside Canberra — Inside Canb
Inside Education — Inside Educ
Inside Print. The Voice of Print Advertising — Inside Prt
Insiders' Chronicle — Insiders' Chr
Insight — IINS
Insight — INS
Insight — INSI
Inspection and Advice — Insp Adv
Inspection Report. Purdue University. Agricultural Experiment Station — Insp Rep Purdue Univ Agric Exp Stn
INSPEL. International Journal of Special Libraries — INSPEL
Insriptiones Christianae Urbis Romae. Nova Series — ICURNS
Installatie — VLF
Installatie Journaal — ERN
Installatore Italiano — INITB
Installatore Italiano [*Italy*] — Install Ital
Installatore Italiano — Installatore Ital
Instant Research on Peace and Violence — Instant Res
Instant Research on Peace and Violence — Instant Res Peace Violence
Instant Update [*Database*] — IU
Instellingen — TGI
Institut Archeologique Liegeois. Bulletin — IALBull
Institut Atomnoi Energii Imeni I. V. Kurchatova. Raport IAE — Inst At Energ I V Kurchatova Rap IAE
Institut Belge pour l'Amelioration de la Betterave. Publication — Inst Belge Amelior Betterave Publ
Institut Belge pour l'Amelioration de la Betterave. Publication Trimestrielle — Inst Belge Amelior Betterave Publ Trimest
Institut Belles-Lettres Arabes. Revue [*Tunis*] — IBLA
Institut Colonial International — Inst Col Int
Institut de Botanique. Universite de Geneve — Inst Bot Univ Geneve
Institut de France. Academie des Inscriptions et Belles-Lettres. Memoires — Mem Acad des Inscript
Institut de France. Academie des Sciences Morales et Politiques. Memoires — AMPM
Institut de France (Paris). Academie des Inscriptions et Belles-Lettres. Monuments et Memoires — Acad Inscr (Paris) Mon et Mem
Institut de Geologie du Bassin d'Aquitaine. Bulletin — Inst Geol Bassin Aquitaine Bull
Institut de Geologie du Bassin d'Aquitaine. Memoires — Inst Geol Bassin Aquitaine Mem
Institut de Medecine Legale et de Medecine Sociale. Archives — Inst Med Leg Med Soc Arch
Institut de Recherches des Ressources Hydrauliques (Budapest). Communications en Langues Etrangeres — Inst Rech Ressour Hydraul (Budapest) Commun Lang Etrang
Institut de Recherches Entomologiques et Phytopathologiques d'Evine. Departement de Botanique — Inst Rech Entomol Phytopathol Evine Dep Bot
Institut de Recherches pour les Huiles et Oleagineux (IRHO). Rapport Annuel — Inst Rech Huiles Oleagineux (IRHO) Rapp Annu
Institut de Recherches pour les Huiles et Oleagineux [*IRHO*]. **Rapport Annuel** — IHUOA9

Institut de Recherches pour les Huiles et Oleagineux [*IRHO*]. Rapport Annuel — Inst Rech Huiles Ol Rapp Annu
Institut d'Egypte Bulletin — Inst d'Egypte Bull
Institut d'Elevage et de Medecine Veterinaire des Pays Tropicaux. Rapport d'Activite — Inst Elev Med Vet Pays Trop Rapp Act
Institut d'Elevage et de Medecine Veterinaire des Pays Tropicaux. Rapport d'Activite — RIETDJ
Institut des Hautes Etudes Scientifiques. Publications Mathematiques — Inst Hautes Etudes Sci Publ Math
Institut des Parcs Nationaux du Congo Belge. Exploration du Parc National Albert — Inst Parcs Nationaux Congo Belge Explor Parc Natl Albert
Institut des Parcs Nationaux du Congo Belge. Exploration du Parc National Albert — Inst Parcs Nationaux Congo Explor Parc Natl Albert
Institut des Peches Maritimes. Bulletin — Inst Peches Mar Bul
Institut des Peches Maritimes. Revue des Travaux — Inst Peches Marit Rev Trav
Institut des Recherches sur le Caoutchouc au Viet-Nam. Archive — Inst Rech Caoutch Viet Nam Arch
Institut des Recherches sur le Caoutchouc au Viet-Nam Laikhe. Rapports Annuels — Inst Rech Caoutch Viet Nam Laikhe Rapp Annu
Institut des Sciences Agronomiques du Burundi (ISABU). Rapport Annuel et Notes Annexes — Inst Sci Agron Burundi (ISABU) Rapp Annu Notes Annexes
Institut des Sciences Agronomiques du Burundi [*ISABU*]. Rapport Annuel et Notes Annexes — RANBDM
Institut d'Estudis Catalans — IEC
Institut d'Estudis Catalans — Inst Est Catalanes
Institut Elektroniki i Vycislitel'noi Tehniki. Akademija Nauk Latviiskoi SSR. Teorija Konecnyh. Avtomatov i Ee Prilozenja — Teor Konecn Avtomatov i Prilozen
Institut Elie Cartan — Inst Elie Cartan
Institut Federal de Recherches Forestieres. Memoires — Inst Fed Rech For Mem
Institut foer Eskimologi. Kobenhavns Universitet — IEKU
Institut Fondamental d'Afrique Noire. Bulletin. Serie A. Sciences Naturelles [*Dakar*] — Inst Fondam Afr Noire Bull Ser A
Institut Francais d'Archeologie Orientale. Bibliotheque d'Etude — IFAOBE
Institut Francais de Recherche pour l'Exploitation de la Mer. Actes de Colloques — Inst Fr Rech Exploit Mer Actes Colloq
Institut Francais d'Etudes Andines. Bulletin — Inst Fr Etud Andines
Institut Francais d'Haiti. Memoires — Inst Francais d'Haiti Mem
Institut Francais du Cafe et du Cacao. Bulletin — Inst Fr Cafe Cacao Bull
Institut Francais du Petrole. Revue et Annales des Combustible Liquides [*Later, Institut Francais du Petrole. Revue*] — Inst Fr Pet Rev
Institut Francais du Petrole. Revue et Annales des Combustible Liquides [*Later, Institut Francais du Petrole. Revue*] — Inst Francais Petrole Rev
Institut fuer Auslandsbeziehungen — IAB
Institut fuer Auslandsbeziehungen. Mitteilungen — Inst Auslandsbezieh Mitt
Institut fuer Bauwissenschaftliche Forschung. Publikation [*Switzerland*] — Inst Bauwissensch Forsch Publ
Institut fuer Bauwissenschaftliche Forschung. Publikation — Inst Bauwissenschaftliche Forsch Publ
Institut fuer Ernaehrungsforschung (Rueschlikon-Zuerich). Schriftenreihe — Inst Ernaehrungsforsch (Rueschlikon-Zuerich) Schriftenr
Institut fuer Hydromechanik und Wasserwirtschaft. Eidgenoessische Technische Hochschule Zuerich — Inst Hydromech Wasserwirtsch Eidg Tech Hochsch Zuerich
Institut fuer Kernphysik der Johann-Wolfgang-Goethe-Universitaet (Frankfurt) — IKF
Institut fuer Kerntechnik der Technischen Universitaet (Berlin). Bericht — Inst Kerntech Tech Univ (Berlin) Ber
Institut fuer Marxistische Studien und Forschungen — IMSF
Institut fuer Oesterreichische Geschichtsforschung. Mitteilungen (Vienna) — Mitt Oesterr Ges (Vienna)
Institut fuer Strahlenhygiene Berichte — Inst Strahlenhyg Ber
Institut fuer Textil- und Faserforschung. Stuttgart. Berichte — Inst Text Faserforsch Stuttgart Ber
Institut fuer Wasserforschung Dortmund. Veroeffentlichungen — Inst Wasserforsch Dortmund Veroeff
Institut Goryuchikh Iskopaemykh Trudy — Inst Goryuch Iskop Tr
Institut Grand-Ducal de Luxembourg. Section des Sciences Naturelles. Physiques et Mathematiques. Archives — Inst Grand Ducal Luxemb Sect Sci Nat Phys Math Arch
Institut Indochinois pour l'Etude de l'Homme. Bulletin et Travaux — IIEH
Institut Intermediare International. Bulletin — Inst Interm Int Bul
Institut International de Recherches Betteravieres. Compte Rendu Definitif de l'Assemblee — Inst Int Rech Better CR Definitif Assem
Institut International de Recherches Betteravieres. Congres d'Hiver. Compte Rendu — Inst Int Rech Better Congr Hiver CR
Institut International de Recherches Betteravieres. Revue — Inst Int Rech Better Rev
Institut International de Statistique. Revue — Inst Int Stat R
Institut Interuniversitaire des Sciences Nucleaires. Monographie — Inst Interuniv Sci Nucl Monogr
Institut Interuniversitaire des Sciences Nucleaires. Rapport Annuel — Inst Interuniv Sci Nucl Rapp Annu
Institut Jazykoznanija. Doklady i Soobscenija — I Ja DS
Institut. Journal des Sciences et des Societes Savantes en France et a l'Etranger. Section 1 — Inst Sect 1
Institut Jozef Stefan. IJS Porocilo — Inst Jozef Stefan IJS Porocilo
Institut Jozef Stefan. IJS Report — Inst Jozef Stefan IJS Rep
Institut Khimii Akademiya Nauk Tadzhikskoi SSR Trudy — Inst Khim Akad Nauk Tadzh SSR Tr
Institut Matematiki i Estestvoznanija pri Severo-Kavkazskom Gosudarstvennom Universitete/Institute of Mathematics and Natural Sciences to the North Caucasus State University/Institut des Mathematiques et des Science Naturelles — Inst Mat Estestv Severo Kavkazsk Gosud Univ
Institut Mathematique. Publications. Nouvelle Serie (Belgrade) — Publ Inst Math (Belgrad) NS
Institut Mehaniki Moskovskogo Gosudarstvennogo Universiteta Naucnye Trudy — Inst Meh Moskov Gos Univ Naucn Trudy
Institut Michel Pacha. Annales — Inst Michel Pacha Ann
Institut Napoleon. Revue — Inst Napoleon R
Institut National de la Recherche Agronomique au Service des Industries Agricoles et Alimentaires — Inst Natl Rech Agron Serv Ind Agric Aliment
Institut National de la Recherche Agronomique de Tunisie — Inst Nat Rech Agron Tunisie
Institut National de la Recherche Agronomique de Tunisie. Annales — Inst Natl Rech Agron Tunis Ann
Institut National de la Recherche Agronomique de Tunisie. Documents Techniques — Inst Natl Rech Agron Tunis Doc Tech
Institut National de la Recherche Agronomique de Tunisie. Documents Techniques — Inst Natl Rech Agron Tunisie Doc Tech
Institut National de la Recherche Agronomique de Tunisie. Laboratoire d'Arboriculture Fruitiere. Rapport d'Activite — Inst Natl Rech Agron Tunis Lab Aboriculture Fruit Rapp Act
Institut National de la Recherche Agronomique de Tunisie. Laboratoire d'Arboriculture Fruitiere. Rapport d'Activite — Inst Natl Rech Agron Tunisie Lab Arboric Fruit Rapp Act
Institut National de la Recherche Agronomique (Paris) — Inst Nat Rech Agron (Paris)
Institut National de l'Industrie Charbonniere. Bulletin Technique - Mines — Inst Nat Ind Charbonniere Bull Tech-Mines
Institut National des Industries Extractives. Bulletin Technique. Mines et Carrieres [*Liege*] — Inst Nat Ind Extr Bull Tech-Mines Carrieres
Institut National des Industries Extractives (Liege). Bulletin Technique. Mines et Carrieres — Inst Natl Ind Extr (Liege) Bull Tech Mines Carrieres
Institut National des Radioelements (Belgium). Rapport — Inst Natl Radioelem (Belg) Rapp
Institut National Genevois. Bulletin — Inst Natl Genevois Bull
Institut National Genevois. Bulletin. New Series — Inst Natl Genevois Bull NS
Institut National pour l'Amelioration des Conserves de Legumes. Bulletin Bimestriel (Belgium) — Inst Natl Amelior Conserves Legumes Bull Bimest (Belg)
Institut National pour l'Amelioration des Conserves de Legumes. Bulletin Trimestriel (Belgium) — Inst Nat Amelior Conserves Legumes Bull Trimest (Belg)
Institut Neorganicheskoi Khimii i Elektrokhimii Akademiya Nauk Gruzinskoi SSR Sbornik — Inst Neorg Khim Elektrokhim Akad Nauk Gruz SSR Sb
Institut Oceanographique. Annales — Inst Oceanogr Ann
Institut Oceanographique de Nha Trang — Inst Oceanogr Nha Trang
Institut Pasteur Bangui. Rapport Annuel — Inst Pasteur Bangui Rapp Annu
Institut Pasteur de la Guyane et du Territoire de l'Inini. Publications — Inst Past Guy Ter L In
Institut Pasteur de la Republique Unie du Cameroun. Rapport sur le Fonctionnement Technique — Inst Pasteur Repub Unie Cameroun Rapp Fonct Tech
Institut po Ribna Promishlenost. Filial po Sladkovodno Ribarstvo (Plovdiv). Izvestiya — Inst Ribna Prom Fil Sladkovodno Ribar (Plovdiv) Izv
Institut po Ribni Resursi (Varna). Izvestiya — Inst Ribni Resur (Varna) Izv
Institut po Tsvetna Metalurgiya (Plovdiv). Godishnik — Inst Tsvetna Metal (Plovdiv) God
Institut Rastenievodstva — Inst Rasteniev
Institut Royal Colonial Belge. Bulletin des Seances — BICB
Institut Royal Colonial Belge. Bulletin des Seances — Inst R Colon Belge Bull Seances
Institut Royal Colonial Belge. Compte Rendu des Seances — ICB
Institut Royal Colonial Belge. Section des Sciences Naturelles et Medicales. Memoires. Collection in Quarto — Inst R Colon Belge Sect Sci Nat Med Mem Collect 4o
Institut Royal Colonial Belge. Section des Sciences Naturelles Medicales. Memoires. Collection in Octavo — Inst R Colon Belge Sect Sci Nat Med Mem Collect 8
Institut Royal des Sciences Naturelles de Belgique. Bulletin — Inst R Sci Nat Belg Bull
Institut Royal des Sciences Naturelles de Belgique. Bulletin — Inst Roy Sci Natur Belgique Bul
Institut Royal des Sciences Naturelles de Belgique. Bulletin. Sciences de la Terre — Inst R Sci Nat Belg Bull Sci Terre
Institut Royal des Sciences Naturelles de Belgique. Documents de Travail — Inst R Sci Nat Belg Doc Trav
Institut Royal des Sciences Naturelles de Belgique. Memoires — Inst R Sci Nat Belg Mem
Institut Royal des Sciences Naturelles de Belgique. Memoires. Deuxieme Serie — Inst R Sci Nat Belg Mem Deuxieme Ser
Institut Royal Meteorologique de Belgique. Bulletin Trimestriel. Observations d'Ozone — Inst R Meteorol Belg Bull Trimest Obs Ozone
Institut Russkogo Jazyka i Slovesnosti pri Akademii Nauk SSSR — IRJaSl
Institut Scientifique Cherifien. Travaux. Serie Generale — Inst Sci Cherifien Trav Ser Gen
Institut Scientifique Cherifien. Travaux. Serie Sciences Physiques — Inst Sci Cherifien Trav Ser Sci Phys
Institut Suisse de Recherches Forestieres. Memoires — Inst Suisse Rech For Mem
Institut Suisse de Recherches Forestieres. Memoires — MSAVAH
Institut Technique du Batiment et des Travaux Publics. Annales — Inst Tech Batim Trav Pub Ann

Institut Textile de France. Bulletin — Inst Textile Fr Bul
Institut Textile de France-Nord. Bulletin d'Information — Inst Text Fr Nord Bull Inf
Institut za Alatne Masine i Alate. Monografije — Inst Alatne Masine Alate Monogr
Institut za Alatne Masine i Alate. Saopstenja — Inst Alatne Masine Alate Saopstenja
Institut za Oceanografiju i Ribarstvo (Split). Biljeske — Inst Oceanogr Ribar (Split) Biljeske
Institut za Zastitu Bilja. Posebna Izdanja — Inst Zast Bilja Posebna Izd
Institut Zoologii i Parazitologii Akademiya Nauk Tadzhikskoi SSR Trudy — Inst Zool Parazitol Akad Nauk Tadzh SSR Tr
Institute d'Architecture et de Genie Civil Sofia. Annuaire. Fascicule II. Mathematiques — Ann Inst Archit Genie Civil Sofia Fasc II Math
Institute for Applied Research on Natural Resources (Abu-Ghraib, Iraq). Technical Report — Inst Appl Res Nat Resour (Abu Ghraib Iraq) Tech Rep
Institute for Applied Research on Natural Resources. Technical Report (Bulletin) — Inst Appl Res Nat Resour Tech Rep (Bull)
Institute for Cancer Research (Philadelphia). Scientific Report — Inst Cancer Res (Phila) Sci Rep
Institute for Defence Studies and Analyses. Journal [*India*] — IDSFA
Institute for Defence Studies and Analyses. Journal — Inst Def Stud Anal J
Institute for Defense Analyses. Paper — Inst Def Anal Pap
Institute for Fermentation Research Communications (Osaka) — Inst Ferment Res Commun (Osaka)
Institute for Marine Environmental Research. Report — Inst Mar Environ Res Rep
Institute for Mining and Mineral Research. University of Kentucky. Technical Report — Inst Min Miner Res Univ K Tech Rep
Institute for Nonlinear Science — Inst Nonlinear Sci
Institute for Nuclear Study. University of Tokyo. Reports — Inst Nucl Study Univ Tokyo Rep
Institute for Physics and Nuclear Engineering Report (Romania) — Inst Phys Nucl Eng Rep (Rom)
Institute for Public Service and Vocational Training. Bulletin — Inst Public Serv Vocat Train Bull
Institute for Research in Construction. Publications [*Database*] — IRCPUBS
Institute for Research into Mental Retardation. Monograph [*Oxford*] — IRMNA2
Institute for Research into Mental Retardation. Monograph (Oxford) — Inst Res Ment Retard Monogr (Oxford)
Institute for Research into Mental Retardation (Oxford). Symposium — Inst Res Ment Retard (Oxford) Symp
Institute for Socioeconomic Studies. Journal — Inst Socioeconomic Studies J
Institute for Studies in American Music. Newsletter — News ISAM
Institute for Water Resources. University of Alaska. Report — IWRUAR
Institute Forum — Inst Forum
Institute fuer Auslandsbeziehungen. Mitteilungen — Mitt Inst Auslandsbezieh
Institute Mexicano del Petroleo. Revista — Inst Mex Petrol Rev
Institute of African Studies — Inst Afr Stud
Institute of African Studies. Occasional Publications — IASOP
Institute of Agricultural Research. Annual Report (Addis Ababa) — Inst Agric Res Annu Rep (Addis Ababa)
Institute of Agricultural Research. Annual Research Seminar. Proceedings (Addis Ababa) — Inst Agric Res Annu Res Semin Proc (Addis Ababa)
Institute of Agricultural Research. Progress Report (Addis Ababa) — Inst Agric Res Prog Rep (Addis Ababa)
Institute of Agricultural Research. Samaru. Annual Report — Inst Agric Res Samaru Annu Rep
Institute of Agricultural Sciences. University of Alaska. Bulletin — IASUAB
Institute of Agricultural Sciences. University of Alaska. Research Reports — IASURR
Institute of Animal Physiology. Report — Inst Anim Physiol Rep
Institute of Arctic and Alpine Research. Occasional Papers — IAAROP
Institute of Arctic and Alpine Research. University of Colorado. Occasional Paper — Inst Arct Alp Res Univ Colo Occas Pap
Institute of Arctic and Alpine Research. University of Colorado. Occasional Paper — OPURD7
Institute of Australian Foundrymen. Annual Proceedings — Inst Aust Foundrymen Annu Proc
Institute of Australian Foundrymen. New South Wales Division. Annual Proceedings — Inst Aust Foundrymen NSW Div Annu Proc
Institute of Bankers. Journal — Inst Bankers J
Institute of Biology [*London*]. **Journal** — Inst Biol J
Institute of Biology (London). Symposium — Inst Biol (Lond) Symp
Institute of Biology. Symposia (London) — Inst Biol Symp (Lond)
Institute of Biology's Studies in Biology — Inst Biol Stud Biol
Institute of Botany. Academia Sinica Monograph Series — Inst Bot Acad Sin Monogr Ser
Institute of Brewing (Australia and New Zealand Section). Proceedings of the Convention — Inst Brew (Aust NZ Sect) Proc Conv
Institute of British Geographers (Liverpool). Transactions and Papers — Trans Papers (L) Brit G
Institute of British Geographers. Transactions — Inst Br Geogr Trans
Institute of British Geographers. Transactions — Inst Br Geographers Trans
Institute of Chemistry of Ireland. Journal — Inst Chem Irel J
Institute of Clerks of Works. Journal — Inst of Clerks of Works Jnl
Institute of Corn and Agricultural Merchants. Journal — ICAM J
Institute of Dental Research. Biennial Report (Sydney) — Inst Dent Res Bienn Rep (Syd)
Institute of Dental Research. United Dental Hospital of Sydney. Annual Report — Inst Dent Res United Dent Hosp Sydney Annu Rep
Institute of Development Studies. Bulletin [*England*] — Inst Dev Stud Bull
Institute of Electrical and Electronics Engineers. Proceedings — Inst Elect & Electronics Eng Proc
Institute of Electrical and Electronics Engineers. Transactions on Industry Application — Inst Elect & Electronics Eng Trans IA
Institute of Electrical and Electronics Engineers. Transactions on Power Apparatus and Systems — Inst Elect & Electronics Eng Trans PAS
Institute of Electronics and Communication Engineers of Japan. Transactions. Section E. English — Inst Electron Commun Eng Jpn Trans Sect E
Institute of Electronics, Information, and Communication Engineers. Transactions. Section E. English — Inst Electron Inf Commun Eng Trans Sect E
Institute of Environmental Sciences. Annual Technical Meeting. Proceedings — Inst Environ Sci Annu Tech Meet Proc
Institute of Environmental Sciences. Proceedings — IESPAF
Institute of Environmental Sciences. Proceedings — Inst Environ Sci Proc
Institute of Environmental Sciences. Technical Meeting. Proceedings — Inst Environ Sci Tech Meet Proc
Institute of Ethnomusicology. Selected Reports — Inst Ethmus Sel Repts
Institute of Forest Products. College of Forest Resources. University of Washington. Contribution — Inst For Prod Colleg For Resour Univ Wash Contrib
Institute of Forest Zoology. Research Notes — Inst For Zool Res Notes
Institute of Foresters of Australia. Newsletter — Inst For Aust Newslett
Institute of Foresters of Australia. Newsletter — Inst Foresters Aust Newsl
Institute of Foresters of Australia. Newsletter — Inst Foresters Aust Newslett
Institute of Foresters of Australia. Newsletter — Newsl Inst Foresters Aust
Institute of Freshwater Research (Drottningholm). Report — Inst Freshw Res (Drottningholm) Rep
Institute of Freshwater Research (Drottningholm). Report — Inst Freshwater Res (Drottningholm) Rep
Institute of Freshwater Research (Drottningholm). Report — RIFRAF
Institute of Fuel (London). Bulletin — Inst Fuel (London) Bull
Institute of Fuel (London). Wartime Bulletin — Inst Fuel (London) Wartime Bull
Institute of Fuel. Symposium Series (London) — Inst Fuel Symp Ser (London)
Institute of Gas Technology — Inst Gas Technol
Institute of Gas Technology (Chicago). Research Bulletin — Inst Gas Technol (Chicago) Res Bull
Institute of Gas Technology (Chicago). Technical Report — Inst Gas Technol (Chicago) Tech Rep
Institute of Geological Science. Charles University. Report on Research — Inst Geol Sci Charles Univ Rep Res
Institute of Geological Sciences (London). Report — Inst Geol Sci (London) Rep
Institute of Geological Sciences. Overseas Memoir — Inst Geol Sci Overseas Mem
Institute of Geological Sciences. Report [*England*] — Inst Geol Sci Rep
Institute of Gerontology Series — Inst Gerontol Ser
Institute of Historical Research. Bulletin — IHRB
Institute of Historical Research. Bulletin — Inst Hist Res Bull
Institute of International Education. News Bulletin — IIENB
Institute of International Education. News Bulletin — Inst Int Educ N Bul
Institute of International Relations. Proceedings — Inst Int Rel Proc
Institute of Low Temperature Science. Contributions (Japan) — ILTSJ
Institute of Marine Engineers. Annual Report — Inst Mar Eng Annu Rep
Institute of Marine Engineers. Annual Volume — Inst Mar Eng Annu Vol
Institute of Marine Engineers. Transactions — Inst Mar Eng Trans
Institute of Marine Engineers. Transactions. Series C — Inst Mar Eng Trans Ser C
Institute of Marine Research. Lysekil Series Biology Report — Inst Mar Res Lysekil Ser Biol Rep
Institute of Marine Science. Notes. University of Alaska — IMSN
Institute of Marine Science. Publications — Inst Marine Sci Pub
Institute of Marine Science. Report. University of Alaska — Inst Mar Sci Rep Univ Alaska
Institute of Mathematical Statistics. Bulletin — Inst Math Statist Bull
Institute of Mathematical Statistics Lecture Notes. Monograph Series — IMS Lecture Notes Monograph Ser
Institute of Mathematics and Its Applications. Bulletin — Inst Math Its Appl Bull
Institute of Mathematics and its Applications Conference Series. New Series — Inst Math Appl Conf Ser New Ser
Institute of Mathematics and its Applications Monograph Series — IMA Monogr Ser
Institute of Mathematics and its Applications Monograph Series — IMA Monograph Ser
Institute of Medical Laboratory Sciences. Gazette — IMLS Gaz
Institute of Mennonite Studies Series — IMSS
Institute of Metallurgical Technicians. Conference Papers (London) — Inst Metall Tech Conf Pap (London)
Institute of Metals. Journal — Inst Metals J
Institute of Metals. Monograph and Report Series — Inst Met Monogr Rep Ser
Institute of Microbiology. Rutgers University. Annual Report — Inst Microbiol Rutgers Univ Annu Rep
Institute of National Language. Lecture Series — Inst Nat Lang Lect Ser
Institute of Natural Sciences. Nanyang University. Technical Report — Inst Nat Sci Nanyang Univ Tech Rep
Institute of Nomads. Petroleum Exposition Symposium — Inst Nomads Pet Expo Symp
Institute of Nuclear Chemistry and Technology. Report INCT — Inst Nucl Chem Technol Rep INCT
Institute of Nuclear Physics (Cracow). Report — Inst Nucl Phys (Cracow) Rep
Institute of Nuclear Research (Warsaw). Report — Inst Nucl Res (Warsaw) Rep
Institute of Ocean Sciences. Patricia Bay. Contractor Report — IOSCR
Institute of Oceanographic Sciences. Annual Report — ARISDE
Institute of Oceanographic Sciences. Annual Report — Inst Oceanogr Sci Annu Rep
Institute of Oceanographic Sciences. Collected Reprints — Inst Oceanogr Sci Col Repr
Institute of Oceanographic Sciences. Data Report — IOS Data Report
Institute of Oceanographic Sciences. Report — IOS Report
Institute of Personnel Management. Digest — Inst Personnel Mgmt Dig

Institute of Petroleum. Abstracts — Inst Pet Abstr
Institute of Petroleum. Journal — Inst Pet J
Institute of Petroleum (London). Papers — Inst Pet (Lond) Pap
Institute of Petroleum. Review — Inst Petroleum Rev
Institute of Petroleum. Review — IPREA
Institute of Petroleum. Technical Paper IP — Inst Pet Tech Pap IP
Institute of Petroleum. Technical Papers — Inst Petrol Tech Pap
Institute of Phonetics. Report — Inst Phonet Rep
Institute of Physical and Chemical Research. Rikagaku Kenkyusho. Scientific Papers — Inst Phys Chem Res Rikagaku Kenkyusho Sci Pap
Institute of Physics. Conference Digest — Inst Phys Conf Dig
Institute of Physics. Conference Series — Inst Phys Conf Ser
Institute of Physics. Conference Series — IPHSA
Institute of Physics Short Meetings Series — Inst Phys Short Meet Ser
Institute of Phytopathology Research. Annual Report — Inst Phytopathol Res Annu Rep
Institute of Plasma Physics. Nagoya University. Report IPPJ-REV — Inst Plasma Phys Nagoya Univ Rep IPPJ REV
Institute of Polar Studies (Ohio). Contribution Series — IPSOCS
Institute of Polar Studies (Ohio). Reports — ISPOR
Institute of Printed Circuits. Technical Report — Inst Printed Circuits Tech Rep
Institute of Professional Librarians of Ontario. Newsletter — Inst Prof Librn Ont Newsl
Institute of Psychiatry. Maudsley Monographs — Inst Psychiatry Maudsley Monogr
Institute of Public Affairs. Review — IPA
Institute of Public Affairs (Victoria). Review — IPA (VIC) R
Institute of Radio Engineers. Proceedings — Inst Radio Eng Proc
Institute of Radio Engineers. Transactions on Information Theory — IRE Trans Inform Theory
Institute of Refrigeration London. Proceedings — Inst Refrig London Proc
Institute of Science Magazine — Inst Sci Mag
Institute of Sewage Purification. Journal and Proceedings — Inst Sewage Purif J Proc
Institute of Social, Economic, and Government Research. University of Alaska. Occasional Papers — ISEGROP
Institute of Social, Economic, and Government Research. University of Alaska. Report — ISEGRR
Institute of Social, Economic, and Government Research. University of Alaska. Research Notes — ISEGRN
Institute of Social, Economic, and Government Research. University of Alaska. Research Summary — ISEGRS
Institute of Social Studies. The Hague Research Report Series — Inst Soc Stud Hague Res Rep Ser
Institute of Soil Science. Academia Sinica. Soil Research Report — Inst Soil Sci Acad Sin Soil Res Rep
Institute of Soil Science. Academia Sinica. Soil Research Report — SRREEC
Institute of Sound and Vibration — Inst Sound Vib
Institute of Space and Aeronautical Science. University of Tokyo. Report — Inst Space Aeronaut Sci Univ Tokyo Rep
Institute of the Aeronautical Sciences. Sherman M. Fairchild Publication Fund. Preprint — Inst Aeronaut Sci Sherman M. Fairchild Publ Fund Prepr
Institute of Traditional Cultures. Bulletin — ITC
Institute of Vitreous Enamellers. Bulletin — Inst Vitreous Enamellers Bull
Institute of World Affairs. Proceedings — Inst World Affairs Proc
Institute on Estate Planning — Inst Estate Plan
Institute on Lake Superior Geology. Technical Sessions, Abstracts, and Field Guides — Inst Lake Super Geol Tech Sess Abstr Field Guides
Institute on Mineral Law — Inst Min L
Institute on Oil and Gas Law and Taxation — Inst Oil & Gas L & Taxation
Institute on Planning, Zoning, and Eminent Domain. Proceedings — Inst on Plan Zon and Eminent Domain Proc
Institute on Private Investments Abroad and Foreign Trade — Inst Private Investments
Institute on Private Investments and Investors Abroad. Proceedings — Inst on Priv Invest and Investors Abroad Proc
Institute on Securities Regulation — Inst on Sec Reg
Institute on Securities Regulation — Inst Securities Reg
Institute on the Church in Urban-Industrial Society. Bibliography Series — ICUIS Biblio
Institute on the Church in Urban-Industrial Society. Occasional Papers — ICUIS Occ Paper
Institute on the Church in Urban-Industrial Society. Occasional Papers — ICUIS Occasional Paper
Institutes of Education of the Universities of Newcastle Upon Tyne and Durham. Journal — Newcastle Inst Ed J
Institutes of Gaius [*Roman law*] — G Inst
Institutes of Justinian [*Roman law*] — J Inst
Institutet foer Vatten- och Luftvaardsforskning. Publikation B — Inst Vatten Luftvaardsforsk Publ B
Institutet fuer Verkstadsteknisk Forskning. IVF Resultat — Inst Verkstadstek Forsk IVF Resultat
Instituti Geographici Universitatis Turkuensis. Publications — IGUTP
Institution of Automotive and Aeronautical Engineers, Australia and New Zealand. Journal — IAAE Journal
Institution of Automotive and Aeronautical Engineers, Australia and New Zealand. Journal — IAAEJ
Institution of Certificated Mechanical and Electrical Engineers. South Africa. Arthur Hallet Memorial Lectures — Inst Certif Mech Electr Eng S Afr Arthur Hallet Mem Lect
Institution of Chemical Engineers. Quarterly Bulletin — Inst Chem Eng Q Bull
Institution of Chemical Engineers. Symposium Series — Inst Chem Eng Symp Ser
Institution of Chemical Engineers. Transactions — Inst Chem Eng Trans
Institution of Civil Engineers. Proceedings — Inst Civ Engr Proc
Institution of Civil Engineers. Proceedings. Part 1. Design and Construction — Inst Civ Engrs Proc Part 1
Institution of Civil Engineers. Proceedings. Part 2. Research and Theory — Inst Civ Engrs Proc Part 2
Institution of Electrical Engineers. Conference Publication — Inst Elec Eng Conf Publ
Institution of Electrical Engineers. Journal — Inst E E J
Institution of Electrical Engineers. Journal — Inst Elec Eng J
Institution of Electrical Engineers. Proceedings — Inst E E Proc
Institution of Electrical Engineers. Proceedings. A — Proc IEE-A
Institution of Electrical Engineers Proceedings. A. Science, Measurement, and Technology — Inst Electr Eng Proc A Sci Meas Technol
Institution of Electrical Engineers. Proceedings. B — Proc IEE-B
Institution of Electrical Engineers. Proceedings. C — Proc IEE-C
Institution of Electrical Engineers. Proceedings. D — Proc IEE D
Institution of Electrical Engineers. Proceedings. F — Proc IEE F
Institution of Electrical Engineers. Proceedings. G — Proc IEE G
Institution of Electrical Engineers Proceedings. Part I. Solid-State and Electron Devices — Inst Electr Eng Proc Part I Solid State Electron Devices
Institution of Electrical Engineers. Student Quarterly Journal — Student Q J Instn Elec Engrs
Institution of Electronic and Radio Engineers. Conference Proceedings — Inst Electron Radio Eng Conf Proc
Institution of Electronics and Telecommunication Engineers. Journal — Inst Electron Telecommun Eng J
Institution of Engineers. Australia. Mechanical and Chemical Engineering. Transactions — Inst Eng Aust Mech Chem Eng
Institution of Engineers. Australia. Transactions. Electrical Engineering — Inst Eng Aust Trans Electr Eng
Institution of Engineers (Ceylon). Transactions — Inst Eng (Ceylon) Trans
Institution of Engineers of Australia. Chemical Engineering in Australia — Inst Eng Aust Chem Eng Aust
Institution of Engineers of Australia. Chemical Engineering Transactions — Inst Eng Aust Chem Eng Trans
Institution of Engineers of Australia. Civil Engineering Transactions — Inst Eng Aust Civ Eng Trans
Institution of Engineers of Australia. Electrical and Mechanical Engineering Transactions — Elect Mech Engng Trans
Institution of Engineers of Australia. Electrical Engineering Transactions — Inst Eng (Aust) Elec Eng Trans
Institution of Engineers of Australia. Electrical Engineering Transactions — Inst Eng Aust Electr Eng Trans
Institution of Engineers of Australia. General Engineering Transactions — Inst Eng (Aust) Gen Eng Trans
Institution of Engineers of Australia. Journal — Inst Eng Aust J
Institution of Engineers of Australia. Journal — Inst Engineers Aust J
Institution of Engineers of Australia. Mechanical and Chemical Engineering Transactions — Inst Eng Aust Mech and Chem Eng Trans
Institution of Engineers of Australia. Mechanical and Chemical Engineering Transactions — Inst Eng Aust Mech & Chem Trans
Institution of Engineers of Australia. Mechanical and Chemical Engineering Transactions — Inst Eng (Aust) Mech Chem Eng Trans
Institution of Engineers of Australia. Mechanical Engineering Transactions — Inst Eng (Aust) Mech Eng Trans
Institution of Engineers of Australia. Queensland Division. Technical Papers — Inst Eng Aust Queensland Div Tech Pap
Institution of Engineers of Australia. South Australia Division. Bulletin — Inst Eng Aust South Aust Div Bull
Institution of Engineers of Australia. Tasmania Division. Bulletin — Inst Engrs Tas Bul
Institution of Engineers of Australia. Tasmania Division. Bulletin — Tas Div Bul
Institution of Fire Engineers. Quarterly — Inst Fire Eng Q
Institution of Gas Engineers. Communications — IGECB
Institution of Gas Engineers. Communications [*Finland*] — Inst Gas Eng
Institution of Gas Engineers. Communications — Inst Gas Eng Commun
Institution of Gas Engineers. Journal — Inst Gas Eng J
Institution of Highway Engineers. Journal — Inst Highw Engrs J
Institution of Locomotive Engineers. Journal — Inst Locomotive Eng J
Institution of Mechanical Engineers Conference Transactions — Inst Mech Eng Conf Trans
Institution of Mechanical Engineers. Journal and Proceedings — Inst Mech Eng J & Proc
Institution of Mechanical Engineers (London). Proceedings — Inst Mech Eng (Lond) Proc
Institution of Mechanical Engineers. Proceedings — Inst Mech Eng Proc
Institution of Mechanical Engineers. Proceedings. Part 3 — Inst Mech Eng Proc Part 3
Institution of Mechanical Engineers. Railway Division. Journal [*London*] — Inst Mech Eng Ry Div J
Institution of Mechanical Engineers. Railway Division. Journal — J Rly Div Instn Mech Engrs
Institution of Mechanical Engineers. Seminar — Inst Mech Eng Semin
Institution of Mechanical Engineers. War Emergency Proceedings — Inst Mech Eng War Emerg Proc
Institution of Metallurgists. Autumn Review Course. Series 3 (London) — Inst Metall Autumn Rev Course Ser 3 (London)
Institution of Metallurgists. Course Volume. Series 3 (London) — Inst Metall Course Vol Ser 3 (London)
Institution of Metallurgists. Series 3 (London) — Inst Metall Ser 3 (London)
Institution of Metallurgists. Spring Residential Course. Series 3 (London) — Inst Metall Spring Resid Course Ser 3 (London)
Institution of Mining and Metallurgy. Bulletin — Inst Min Metall Bull
Institution of Mining and Metallurgy. Transactions — Inst Min & Met Trans
Institution of Mining and Metallurgy. Transactions. Section A. Mining Industry — Inst Min Metall Trans Sect A

Institution of Mining and Metallurgy. Transactions. Section A. Mining Industry — Inst Min Metall Trans Sect A Min Ind
Institution of Mining and Metallurgy. Transactions. Section B. Applied Earth Science — Inst Min Metall Trans Sect B
Institution of Mining and Metallurgy. Transactions. Section B. Applied Earth Science — Inst Mining Met Trans Sect B
Institution of Mining and Metallurgy. Transactions. Section C. Mineral Processing and Extractive Metallurgy — Inst Min Metall Trans Sect C
Institution of Mining Engineers. Transactions — Inst M Eng Tr
Institution of Municipal Engineers. Journal — Inst Munic Engrs J
Institution of Municipal Engineers. South African District. Annual Journal — Inst Munic Eng S Afr Dist Annu J
Institution of Petroleum Technologists. Journal — Inst Petroleum Tech J
Institution of Plant Engineers. Journal [*England*] — Inst Plant Eng J
Institution of Post Office Electrical Engineers. Paper — Inst Post Office Elec Eng Paper
Institution of Public Health Engineers. Journal — Inst Public Health Eng J
Institution of Public Health Engineers Yearbook — Inst Pub Hlth Eng Yearb
Institution of Radio and Electronics Engineers of Australia. Proceedings — Inst Radio & Electron Engrs Aust Proc
Institution of Radio and Electronics Engineers of Australia. Proceedings — Inst Radio Electron Eng Aust Proc
Institution of Water and Environmental Management. Journal — Inst Water Environ Manage J
Institution of Water Engineers and Scientists. Journal — Inst Water Eng Sci J
Institution of Water Engineers. Journal [*Later, Institution of Water Engineers and Scientists. Journal*] — Inst Water Eng J
Institutional Distribution — ID
Institutional Distribution — Inst Distrib
Institutional Investor — II
Institutional Investor — IIN
Institutional Investor — Inst Invest
Institutional Investor — Inst Investor
Institutional Investor — Inst Invst
Institutional Investor. International Edition — III
Institutionen foer Internationell Pedagogik. Report — Inst Internat Pedagog Report
Institutionen foer Skoglig Matematisk Statistik Rapporter och Uppsatser — Inst Skoglig Mat Stat Rapp Uppsatser
Institutionen foer Skoglig Matematisk Statistik Rapporter och Uppsatser — SMSRAH
Institutionen foer Skogsforyngring Rapporter och Uppsatser — Inst Skogsforyngring Rapp Uppsatser
Institutionen foer Skogsforyngring Rapporter och Uppsatser — SIRRBJ
Institutionen foer Skogszoologi Rapporter och Uppsatser — Inst Skogszool Rapp Uppsatser
Institutionen foer Skogszoologi Rapporter och Uppsatser — SISRBO
Institutionendokumentation zur Arbeitsmarkt- und Berufsforschung [*Database*] — InstDokAB
Institutionenverzeichnis fuer Internationale Zusammenarbeit [*Database*] — IVIZ
Institutiones Biblicae Scholis Accomodatae — IBSA
Institutiones Mathematicae — Institutiones Math
Institutiones Philosophicae Scholasticae — IPS
Institutions — Inst
Institutions/Volume Feeding — Inst Vol Feed
Institutions/Volume Feeding Management [*Later, Institutions/Volume Feeding*] — Inst/Vol Feeding Mgt
Instituto Agricola Catalan de San Isidro. Revista — Inst Agric Cat San Isidro Rev
Instituto Antartico Argentino. Contribuciones — Inst Antart Argent Contrib
Instituto Antartico Chileno. Boletin — Inst Antart Chileno Bol
Instituto Archeologico e Geographico Pernambucano. Revista — Inst Archeol E Geog Pernamb R
Instituto Biologico da Bahia. Boletim — Inst Biol Bahia Bol
Instituto Caro y Cuervo — ICC
Instituto Centro Americano de Investigacion y Tecnologia Industrial. Publicaciones Geologicas — Inst Cent Am Investig Tecnol Ind Publ Geol
Instituto Coimbra — IC
Instituto Colombiano Agropecuario. Boletin Tecnico — Inst Colomb Agropecu Bol Tec
Instituto Cubano de Investigaciones Tecnologicas. Serie de Estudios sobre Trabajos de Investigacion — ICITA
Instituto Cubano de Investigaciones Tecnologicas. Serie de Estudios sobre Trabajos de Investigacion [*Cuba*] — Inst Cubano Invest Tecnol Ser Estud Trab Invest
Instituto de Biologia Aplicada. Publicaciones (Barcelona) — Inst Biol Apl Publ (Barcelona)
Instituto de Biologia e Pesquisas Tecnologicas (Curitiba). Boletim — Inst Biol Pesqui Tecnol (Curitiba) Bol
Instituto de Biologia Marina (Mar Del Plata). Contribucion — Inst Biol Mar (Mar Del Plata) Contrib
Instituto de Biologia Marina (Mar Del Plata). Memoria Anual — Inst Biol Mar (Mar Del Plata) Mem Anu
Instituto de Biologia Marina (Mar Del Plata). Serie Contribuciones — Inst Biol Mar (Mar Del Plata) Ser Contrib
Instituto de Botanica "Dr. Goncalo Sampaio." Faculdade de Ciencias. Universidade do Porto. Publicacoes — Inst Bot "Dr Goncalo Sampaio" Fac Cien Univ Porto Publ
Instituto de Ciencias Naturales y Matematicas. Universidad de El Salvador. Comunicaciones — Inst Cienc Nat Mat Univ El Salvador Comun
Instituto de Economia y Producciones Ganaderas del Ebro. Comunicaciones — Inst Econ Prod Ganad Ebro Comun
Instituto de Estudios Alicantinos. Revista — Inst Estud Alicantinos Rev
Instituto de Estudos Brasileiros — Inst E B
Instituto de Fomento Algodonero (Bogota) — Inst Fom Algod (Bogota)
Instituto de Fomento Pesquero. Boletin Cientifico — Inst Fom Pesq Bol Cient
Instituto de Fomento Pesquero. Publicacion — Inst Fom Pesq Publ
Instituto de Geologia y Mineria. Revista. Universidad Nacional de Tucuman — Inst Geol Min Rev Univ Nac Tucuman
Instituto de Investigacao Agronomica (Angola). Serie Cientifica — Inst Invest Agron (Angola) Ser Cient
Instituto de Investigacao Agronomica (Angola). Serie Tecnica — Inst Invest Agron (Angola) Ser Tec
Instituto de Investigacao Agronomica (Mocambique). Serie Memorias — Inst Invest Agron (Mocambique) Ser Mem
Instituto de Investigacao Cientifica (Angola). Relatorios e Comunicacoes [*A publication*] — Inst Invest Cient (Angola) Relat Comun
Instituto de Investigacion de los Recursos Marinos (Callao). Informe — Inst Invest Recur Mar (Callao) Inf
Instituto de Investigaciones Biomedicas. Universidad Nacional Autonoma de Mexico. Informe — Inst Invest Biomed Univ Nac Auton Mex Inf
Instituto de Investigaciones Geologicas. Boletin (Chile) — Inst Invest Geol Bol Chile
Instituto de Materiales y Modelos Estructurales. Boletin Tecnico. Universidad Central de Venezuela — Inst Mater Modelos Estruct Bol Tec Univ Cent Venez
Instituto de Nutricion de Centro America y Panama. Informe Anual — INCIBC
Instituto de Nutricion de Centro America y Panama. Informe Anual — Inst Nutr Cent Am Panama Inf Anu
Instituto de Orientacion y Asistencia Tecnica del Oeste. Anuario — Inst Orientac Asist Tec Oeste Anu
Instituto de Pesquisa Agropecuaria do Norte [*IPEAN*]. Boletim Tecnico — BTIPAR
Instituto de Pesquisa Agropecuaria do Norte (IPEAN). Boletim Tecnico — Inst Pesqui Agropecu Norte (IPEAN) Bol Tec
Instituto de Pesquisas Agronimicas (Recife). Boletim Tecnico — Inst Pesqui Agron (Recife) Bol Tec
Instituto de Pesquisas Agronomicas. Boletim Tecnico — BIPADB
Instituto de Pesquisas Agronomicas. Boletim Tecnico — Inst Pesqui Agron Bol Tec
Instituto de Pesquisas Agronomicas de Pernambuco. Boletim Tecnico — Inst Pesqui Agron Pernambuco Bol Tec
Instituto de Pesquisas Agronomicas de Pernambuco. Circular — Inst Pesqui Agron Pernambuco Circ
Instituto de Pesquisas Agronomicas de Pernambuco. Publicacao — Inst Pesqui Agron Pernambuco Publ
Instituto de Pesquisas Agropecuarias do Norte. Boletim Tecnico — Inst Pesqui Agropecu Norte Bol Tec
Instituto de Pesquisas Agropecuarias do Sul. Boletim Tecnico — Inst Pesqui Agropecu Sul Bol Tec
Instituto de Pesquisas e Experimentacao Agropecuarias do Norte (Belem). Boletim Tecnico — Inst Pesqui Exp Agropecu Norte (Belem) Bol Tec
Instituto de Pesquisas e Experimentacao Agropecuarias do Norte (IPEAN) (Belem). Boletim Tecnico — Inst Pesqui Exp Agropecu Norte (IPEAN) (Belem) Bol Tec
Instituto de Pesquisas e Experimentacao Agropecuarias do Norte (IPEAN). Serie Botanica e Fisiologia Vegetal — Inst Pesqui Exp Agropecu Norte (IPEAN) Ser Bot Fisiol Veg
Instituto de Pesquisas e Experimentacao Agropecuarias do Norte (IPEAN). Serie Botanica e Fisiologia Vegetal — Inst Pesqui Exp Agropecu Norte Ser Bot Fisiol Veg
Instituto de Pesquisas e Experimentacao Agropecuarias do Norte (IPEAN). Serie Culturas da Amazonia — Inst Pesqui Exp Agropecu Norte (IPEAN) Ser Cult Amazonia
Instituto de Pesquisas e Experimentacao Agropecuarias do Norte (IPEAN). Serie Culturas da Amazonia — Inst Pesqui Exp Agropecu Norte Ser Cult Amazonia
Instituto de Pesquisas e Experimentacao Agropecuarias do Norte (IPEAN). Serie Estudos e Ensaios — Inst Pesqui Exp Agropecu Norte (IPEAN) Ser Estud Ens
Instituto de Pesquisas e Experimentacao Agropecuarias do Norte (IPEAN). Serie Estudos e Ensaios — Inst Pesqui Exp Agropecu Norte (IPEAN) Ser Estud Ensaios
Instituto de Pesquisas e Experimentacao Agropecuarias do Norte (IPEAN). Serie Estudos e Ensaios — Inst Pesqui Exp Agropecu Norte Ser Estud Ens
Instituto de Pesquisas e Experimentacao Agropecuarias do Norte (IPEAN). Serie Estudos sobre Bovinos — Inst Pesqui Exp Agropecu Norte (IPEAN) Ser Estud Bovinos
Instituto de Pesquisas e Experimentacao Agropecuarias do Norte (IPEAN). Serie Estudos sobre Bovinos — Inst Pesqui Exp Agropecu Norte Ser Estud Bovinos
Instituto de Pesquisas e Experimentacao Agropecuarias do Norte (IPEAN). Serie Estudos sobre Bubalinos — Inst Pesqui Exp Agropecu Norte (IPEAN) Ser Estud Bubalinos
Instituto de Pesquisas e Experimentacao Agropecuarias do Norte (IPEAN). Serie Estudos sobre Bubalinos — Inst Pesqui Exp Agropecu Norte Ser Estud Bubalinos
Instituto de Pesquisas e Experimentacao Agropecuarias do Norte (IPEAN). Serie Estudos sobre Forrageiras na Amazonia — IPFABH
Instituto de Pesquisas e Experimentacao Agropecuarias do Norte (IPEAN). Serie Fertilidade de Solos — Inst Pesqui Exp Agropecu Norte (IPEAN) Ser Fertil Solos
Instituto de Pesquisas e Experimentacao Agropecuarias do Norte (IPEAN). Serie Fertilidade de Solos — Inst Pesqui Exp Agropecu Norte Ser Fertil Solos
Instituto de Pesquisas e Experimentacao Agropecuarias do Norte (IPEAN). Serie Fitotecnia — Inst Pesqui Agropecu Norte (IPEAN) Ser Fitotec
Instituto de Pesquisas e Experimentacao Agropecuarias do Norte (IPEAN). Serie Fitotecnia — Inst Pesqui Exp Agropecu Norte (IPEAN) Ser Fitotec
Instituto de Pesquisas e Experimentacao Agropecuarias do Norte (IPEAN). Serie Fitotecnia — Inst Pesqui Exp Agropecu Norte Ser Fitotec

Instituto de Pesquisas e Experimentacao Agropecuarias do Norte (IPEAN). Serie Quimica de Solos — Inst Pesqui Exp Agropecu Norte (IPEAN) Ser Quim Solos
Instituto de Pesquisas e Experimentacao Agropecuarias do Norte (IPEAN). Serie Quimica de Solos — Inst Pesqui Exp Agropecu Norte Ser Quim Solos
Instituto de Pesquisas e Experimentacao Agropecuarias do Norte (IPEAN). Serie Solos da Amazonia — Inst Pesqui Exp Agropecu Norte (IPEAN) Ser Solos Amazonia
Instituto de Pesquisas e Experimentacao Agropecuarias do Norte (IPEAN). Serie Solos da Amazonia — Inst Pesqui Exp Agropecu Norte Ser Solos Amazonia
Instituto de Pesquisas e Experimentacao Agropecuarias do Norte (IPEAN). Serie Tecnologia — Inst Pesqui Exp Agropecu Norte (IPEAN) Ser Tecnol
Instituto de Pesquisas e Experimentacao Agropecuarias do Norte (IPEAN). Serie Tecnologia — Inst Pesqui Exp Agropecu Norte Ser Tecnol
Instituto de Pesquisas e Experimentacao Agropecuarias do Sul. Circular — Inst Pesqui Exp Agropecu Sul Circ
Instituto de Pesquisas Tecnologicas (Sao Paulo). Boletim — Inst Pesqui Tecnol (Sao Paulo) Boletim
Instituto de Pesquisas Tecnologicas (Sao Paulo). Publicacao — Inst Pesqui Tecnol (Sao Paulo) Publ
Instituto de Pesquisas Veterinarias Desiderio Finamor. Arquivos — Inst Pesqui Vet Desiderio Finamor Arq
Instituto de Quimica Agricola (Rio De Janeiro). Memoria — Inst Quim Agric (Rio De Janeiro) Mem
Instituto de Quimica Aplicada a la Farmacia (Lima). Boletim Informativo — Inst Quim Apl Farm (Lima) Bol Inf
Instituto de Tecnologia de Alimentos. Boletin — Inst Tecnol Alimentos Bol
Instituto de Tecnologia Industrial. Estado de Minas Gerais. Avulso — Inst Tecnol Ind Estado Minas Gerais Avulso
Instituto de Tecnologia Industrial. Estado de Minas Gerais. Boletim — Inst Tecnol Ind Estado Minas Gerais Boletim
Instituto de Zootecnia. Boletim Tecnico [*Sao Paulo*] — IZBTBM
Instituto de Zootecnia. Boletim Tecnico (Sao Paulo) — Inst Zootec Bol Tec (Sao Paulo)
Instituto del Hierro y del Acero (Madrid). Publicaciones — Inst Hierro Acero (Madrid) Publ
Instituto del Mar del Peru (Callao). Informe — Inst Mar Peru (Callao) Inf
Instituto Ecuatoriano de Ciencias Naturales. Contribucion — Inst Ecuat Cienc Nat Contrib
Instituto Eduardo Torroja de la Construccion y del Cemento. Monografias — Inst Eduardo Torroja Constr Cem Monogr
Instituto Espanol de Oceanografia. Notas y Resumenes — Inst Esp Oceanogr Notas Resumenes
Instituto Experimental de Investigacion y Fomento Agricola-Ganadero (Santa Fe). Publicacion Tecnica — Inst Exp Invest Fom Agric Ganad (St Fe) Publ Tec
Instituto Fisico-Geografico Nacional de Costa Rica. Anales — Inst Fisico-Geog Nac Costa Rica An
Instituto Florestal Boletim Tecnico — Inst Flor Bol Tecn
Instituto Florestal. Boletim Tecnico (Sao Paulo) — Inst Florest Bol Tec (Sao Paulo)
Instituto Florestal. Publicacao (Sao Paulo) — Inst Florest Publ (Sao Paulo)
Instituto Forestal de Investigaciones y Experiencias [*Madrid*]. Comunicacion — Inst For Invest Exp Comun
Instituto Forestal de Investigaciones y Experiencias (Madrid). Anales — Inst For Invest Exper (Madrid) An
Instituto Forestal de Investigaciones y Experiencias (Madrid). Boletin — Inst For Invest Exper (Madrid) Bol
Instituto Forestal de Investigaciones y Experiencias (Madrid). Comunicacion [*A publication*] — Inst For Invest Exper (Madrid) Comun
Instituto Forestal de Investigaciones y Experiencias (Madrid). Trabajos — Inst For Invest Exper (Madrid) Trab
Instituto Forestal Nacional. Folleto Tecnico Forestal — Inst For Nac Foll Tec For
Instituto Gemologico Espanol. Boletin — Inst Gemol Esp Bol
Instituto Geofisico de los Andes Colombianos. Publicacion. Serie A. Sismologia — Inst Geofis Andes Colomb Publ Ser A
Instituto Geografico e Geologico. Estado de Sao Paulo. Boletim — Ins Geog Geol Estado Sao Paulo Bol
Instituto Geografico e Geologico. Estado de Sao Paulo. Boletim — Inst Geogr Geol Estado Sao Paulo Bol
Instituto Geografico Nacional. Boletin Geologico (Guatemala) — Inst Geog Nac Bol Geol (Guatemala)
Instituto Geografico Nacional (Guatemala). Boletin Geologico — Inst Geogr Na (Guatem) Bol Geol
Instituto Geographico e Historico da Bahia. Revista — Inst Geog E Hist Da Bahia R
Instituto Geologico del Uruguay. Boletin — Inst Geol Urug Bol
Instituto Geologico y Minero de Espana. Mapa Geologico de Espana — Inst Geol Min Esp Mapa Geol Esp
Instituto Historico e Geographico Brasileiro. Revista — Inst Hist E Geog Bras R
Instituto Interamericano del Nino. Boletin — Inst Interam Nino Bol
Instituto Mexicano de Minas y Metalurgia. Informes y Memorias — Inst Mex Minas Met Inf
Instituto Mexicano de Recursos Naturales Renovables. Serie de Mesas Redondas — Inst Mex Recur Nat Renov Ser Mesas Redondas
Instituto Mexicano del Petroleo. Publicacion — Inst Mex Pet Publ
Instituto Municipal de Ciencias Naturales Miscelanea. Zoologica — Inst Munic Cienc Nat Misc Zool
Instituto Nacional de Investigacion y Fomento Mineros (Peru). Serie Memorandum — Inst Nac Invest Fom Min (Peru) Ser Memo
Instituto Nacional de Investigaciones Agrarias. Anales. Serie. Tecnologia Agraria (Spain) — Inst Nac Invest Agrar An Ser Technol Agrar Spain
Instituto Nacional de Investigaciones Agrarias. Comunicaciones. Serie: Proteccion Vegetal (Spain) — Inst Nac Invest Agrar Comun Ser Prot Veg (Spain)
Instituto Nacional de Investigaciones Agricolas. Secretaria de Agricultura y Ganaderia (Mexico). Folleto Tecnico — Inst Nac Invest Agric SAG (Mex) Foll Tec
Instituto Nacional de Investigaciones Agricolas. Secretaria de Agricultura y Ganaderia (Mexico). Folleto Tecnico — Inst Nac Invest Agric Secr Agric Ganad (Mex) Foll Tec
Instituto Nacional de Investigaciones Agronomicas. Boletin [*Spain*] — Inst Nac Invest Agron Bol
Instituto Nacional de Investigaciones Agronomicas (Madrid). Conferencias — Inst Nac Invest Agron (Madr) Conf
Instituto Nacional de Investigaciones Agronomicas (Spain). Cuaderno — Inst Nac Invest Agron (Spain) Cuad
Instituto Nacional de Investigaciones Forestales. Boletin Divulgativo — Inst Nac Inv For Bol Divulg
Instituto Nacional de Investigaciones Forestales. Boletin Tecnico — Inst Nac Invest For Bol Tec
Instituto Nacional de Investigaciones Forestales. Catalogo — Inst Nac Invest For Cat
Instituto Nacional de Investigaciones Forestales. Publicacion Especial — Inst Nac Invest For Publ Esp
Instituto Nacional de la Pesca (Cuba). Centro de Investigaciones Pesqueras. Boletin de Divulgacion Tecnica — Inst Nac Pesca (Cuba) Cent Invest Pesq Bol Divulg Tec
Instituto Nacional de la Pesca (Cuba). Centro de Investigaciones Pesqueras. Contribucion — Inst Nac Pesca (Cuba) Cent Invest Pesq Contrib
Instituto Nacional de Medicina Legal de Colombia. Revista — Inst Nac Med Leg Colomb Rev
Instituto Nacional de Nutricion. Caracas. Publicacion — Inst Nac Nutr Caracas Publ
Instituto Nacional de Pesca. Boletin Cientifico y Tecnico — Inst Nac Pesca Bol Cient Tec
Instituto Nacional de Pesca [*Ecuador*]. Boletin Informativo — IBIFAG
Instituto Nacional de Pesca. Boletin Informativo (Guayaquil) — Inst Nac Pesca Bol Inf (Guayaquil)
Instituto Nacional de Pesca (Ecuador). Boletin Informativo — Inst Nac Pesca (Ecuador) Bol Inf
Instituto Nacional de Pesca. Informativo Especial — Inst Nac Pesca Inf Espec
Instituto Nacional de Pesca. Serie Informes Pesqueros — Inst Nac Pesca Ser Inf Pesq
Instituto Nacional de Pesqui Amazonia. Publicacao Quimica — Inst Nac Pesqui Amazonia Publ Quim
Instituto Nacional de Tecnologia Agropecuaria. Boletin Informativo — Inst Nac Tecnol Agropecu Bol Inf
Instituto Nacional de Tecnologia Agropecuaria. Suelos Publicacion — Inst Nac Tecnol Agropecu Suelos Publ
Instituto Nacional de Tecnologia. Boletim — Inst Nac Tecnol Bol
Instituto Nacional de Tecnologia Industrial. Boletin Tecnico (Argentina) — Inst Nac Tecnol Ind Bol Tec (Argentina)
Instituto Nacional del Carbon (Oviedo, Spain). Boletin Informativo — Inst Nac Carbon (Oviedo Spain) Bol Inf
Instituto Nacional del Carbon y Sus Derivados "Francisco Pintado Fe." Publicacion INCAR — Inst Nac Carbon Sus Deriv "Francisco Pintado Fe" Publ INCAR
Instituto Nacional do Livro — Inst N L
Instituto Nacional para la Conservacion de la Naturaleza. Naturalia Hispanica [*A publication*] — Inst Nac Conserv Nat Nat Hisp
Instituto Nacional para la Conservacion de la Naturaleza. Naturalia Hispanica — NAHID3
Instituto Nacional para la Conservacion de la Natureleza. Estacion Central de Ecologia. Boletin (Spain) — Inst Nac Conserv Nat Estac Cent Ecol Bol (Spain)
Instituto Peruano-Norte Americano — IPNA
Instituto Provincial Agropecuario (Mendoza). Boletin Tecnica — Inst Prov Agropecuar (Mendoza) Bol Tec
Instituto Provincial de Paleontologia de Sabadell. Boletin Informativo — Inst Prov Paleontol Sabadell Bol Inf
Instituto Tecnologico de Monterrey. Division de Ciencias Agropecuarias y Maritimas. Informe de Investigacion — Inst Tec Monterrey Div Cienc Agropecu Marit Inf Invest
Instituto Tecnologico de Monterrey. Division de Ciencias Agropecuarias y Maritimas. Informe de Investigacion — Inst Tecnol Monterrey Div Cien Agropecu Marit Inf Invest
Instituto Tecnologico de Monterrey. Division de Ciencias Agropecuarias y Maritimas. Informe de Investigacion — ITMIB2
Instituto Tecnologico do Rio Grande Do Sul. Boletim — Inst Tecnol Rio Grande Sul Bol
Instituto Tecnologico y de Estudios Superiores de Monterrey. Departamento de Quimica. Boletin — Inst Tecnol Estud Super Monterrey Dep Quim Bol
Instituto Universitario Pedagogico de Caracas. Monografias Cientificas "Augusto Pi Suner" — Inst Univ Pedagog Caracas Monogr Cient Augusto Pi Suner
Instituto Universitario Pedagogico de Caracas. Monografias Cientificas "Augusto Pi Suner" — MCASDZ
Instituts Mitteilungen — IMA
Institutt foer Husdyrernaering og Foringslaere Norges Landbrukshogskole Beretning — IHFLBS
Institutt foer Husdyrernaering og Foringslaere Norges Landbrukshogskole Beretning — Inst Husdyrernaer Foringslaere Nor Landbrukshogsk Beret
Institutt foer Husdyrernaering og Foringslaere Norges Landbrukshogskole Beretning — Inst Husdyrernaering Foringslaere Nor Landbrukshogsk Beret
Institutul Agronomic "Dr. Petru Groza" (Cluj). Lucrari Stiintifice. Seria Agricultura — Inst Agron Dr Petru Groza (Cluj) Lucr Stiint Ser Agric
Institutul Agronomic "Dr. Petru Groza" (Cluj). Lucrari Stiintifice. Seria Medicina Veterinara — Inst Agron Dr Petru Groza (Cluj) Lucr Stiint Ser Med Vet

Institutul Agronomic "Dr. Petru Groza" (Cluj). Lucrari Stiintifice. Seria Medicina Veterinara si Zootehnie — IALMAB
Institutul Agronomic "Dr. Petru Groza" (Cluj). Lucrari Stiintifice. Seria Zootehnie — Inst Agron Dr Petru Groza (Cluj) Lucr Stiint Ser Zooteh
Institutul Agronomic "Ion Ionescu de la Brad" (Iasi). Lucrari Stiintifice — Inst Agron Ion Ionescu de la Brad (Iasi) Lucr Stiint
Institutul Agronomic "Ion Ionescu de la Brad" (Iasi). Lucrari Stiintifice. Seria Agronomie — Inst Agron Ion Ionescu de la Brad Iasi Lucr Stiint Ser Agron
Institutul Agronomic Nicolae Balcescu. Bucuresti. Lucrari Stiintifice. Seria B. Horticultura — Inst Agron Nicolae Balcescu Bucuresti Lucr Stiint Ser B
Institutul Agronomic Timisoara Lucrari Stiintifice. Seria Agronomie — Inst Agron Timisoara Lucr Stiint Ser Agron
Institutul Agronomic Timisoara Lucrari Stiintifice. Seria Medicina Veterinara [*A publication*] — Inst Agron Timisoara Lucr Stiint Ser Med Vet
Institutul Agronomic Timisoara Lucrari Stiintifice. Seria Zootehnie — Inst Agron Timisoara Lucr Stiint Ser Zooteh
Institutul Agronomic Timisoara Lucrari Stiintifice. Seria Zootehnie — LSSZB7
Institutul de Cercetari pentru Cereale si Plante Tehnice Fundulea Probleme de Genetica Teoretica si Aplicata — IGTAAN
Institutul de Cercetari pentru Industrie si Chimie Alimentara. Lucrari de Cercetare — Inst Cercet Ind Chim Aliment Lucr Cercet
Institutul de Cercetari Veterinare si Biopreparate Pasteur. Lucrarile — Inst Cercet Vet Bioprep Pasteur Lucr
Institutul de Chimie Alimentara. Lucrari de Cercetare — Inst Chim Aliment Lucr Cercet
Institutul de Fizica Atomica. Report (Romania) — Inst Fiz At Rep (Rom)
Institutul de Fizica si Inginerie Nucleara. Report (Romania) — Inst Fiz Ing Nucl Rep (Rom)
Institutul de Geologie si Geofizica. Bucharest. Studii Tehnice si Economice. Seria E. Hidrogeologie — Inst Geol Geofiz Bucharest Stud Teh Econ Ser E
Institutul de Geologie si Geofizica. Studii Tehnice si Economice. Seria E. Hidrogeologie — Inst Geol Geofiz Stud Teh Econ Ser E
Institutul de Geologie si Geofizica. Studii Tehnice si Economice. Seria I. Mineralogie-Petrografie — Inst Geol Geofiz Stud Teh Econ Ser I
Institutul de Meteorologie si Hidrologie. Culegere de Lucrari de Meteorologie — Inst Meteorol Hidrol Culegere Lucr Meteorol
Institutul de Meteorologie si Hidrologie. Studii si Cercetari. Partea 1. Meteorologie — Inst Meteorol Hidrol Stud Cercet Partea 1
Institutul de Meteorologie si Hidrologie. Studii si Cercetari. Partea 2. Hidrologie — Inst Meteorol Hidrol Stud Cercet Partea 2
Institutul de Mine Petrosani. Lucrarile Stiintifice — Inst Mine Petrosani Lucr Stiint
Institutul de Pathologie si Igiena Animala. Colectia Indrumari (Bucharest) [*A publication*] — Inst Pathol Ig Anim Colect Indrumari (Buchar)
Institutul de Pathologie si Igiena Animala. Probleme de Epizootologie Veterinara (Bucharest) — Inst Pathol Ig Anim Probl Epizootol Vet (Buchar)
Institutul de Petrol si Gaze din Bucuresti. Studii — Inst Pet Gaze Bucuresti Stud
Institutul de Studii si Proiectari Energetice. Buletinul [*Romania*] — Inst Stud Proiect Energ Bul
Institutul Geologic al Romaniei. Anuarul — Inst Geol Rom Anu
Institutul Geologic. Studii Tehnice si Economice. Seria E. Hidrogeologie — Inst Geol Stud Teh Econ Ser E
Institutul Geologic. Studii Tehnice si Economice. Seria I. Mineralogie-Petrografie — Inst Geol Stud Teh Econ Ser I
Institutul Politehnic Bucuresti. Buletinul. Seria Metalurgie — Inst Politeh Bucuresti Bul Ser Metal
Institutul Politehnic din Iasi. Buletinul. Sectia 1. Matematica, Mecanica Teoretica, Fizica [*Romania*] — Inst Politeh Iasi Bul Sect 1
Institutul Politehnic din Iasi. Buletinul. Sectia 5. Constructii-Arhitectura [*A publication*] — Inst Politeh Iasi Bul Sect 5
Institutul Politehnic din Iasi. Buletinul. Sectia 7. Textile, Pielarie — Inst Politeh Iasi Bul Sect 7
Institutul Politehnic "Gheorghe Gheorghiu-Dej" Bucuresti. Buletinul. Seria Chimie — Inst Politeh Gheorghe Gheorghiu Dej Bucuresti Bul Ser Chim
Institutul Politehnic "Gheorghe Gheorghiu-Dej" Bucuresti. Buletinul. Seria Mecanica — Inst Politeh Gheorghe Gheorghiu Dej Bucuresti Bul Ser Mec
Institutul Politehnic "Traian Vuia." Seminarul di Matematica si Fizica. Lucrarile — Inst Politeh Traian Vuia Semin Mat Fiz Lucr
Institutului Politehnic (Cluj). Buletinul Stiintific. Seria Constructii — Bul Stiint Inst Politehn (Cluj) Ser Construc
Institutului Politehnic Cluj-Napoca. Buletinul Stiintific. Seria Arhitectura-Constructii — Bul Stiint Inst Politehn Cluj-Napoca Ser Arhitect-Construc
Institutului Politehnic Cluj-Napoca. Buletinul Stiintific. Seria Chimie-Metalurgie — Bul Stiint Inst Politehn Cluj-Napoca Ser Chim Metal
Institutului Politehnic Cluj-Napoca. Buletinul Stiintific. Seria Constructii de Masini — Bul Stiint Inst Politehn Cluj-Napoca Ser Construc Mas
Institutului Politehnic Cluj-Napoca. Buletinul Stiintific. Seria Matematica-Fizica-Mecanica Aplicata — Bul Stiint Inst Politehn Cluj-Napoca Ser Mat-Fiz-Mec Apl
Institutului Politehnic din Iasi. Buletinul. Sectia I [*Iasi*] — Bul Inst Politehn Iasi Sect I
Institutului Politehnic Gheorghe Gheorghiu Dej Bucuresti. Buletinul. Seria Mecanica [*Bucharest*] — Bul Inst Politehn Bucuresti Ser Mec
Institutului Politehnic Traian Vuia Timisoara. Lucrarile Seminarului de Matematica si Fizica — Inst Politehn Traian Vuia Timisoara Lucrar Sem Mat Fiz
Instituut voor Biologisch en Scheikundig Onderzoek van Landbouwgewassen (Wageningen). Jaarboek — Inst Biol Scheikd Onderz Landbouwgewassen (Wageningen) Jaarb
Instituut voor Biologisch en Scheikundig Onderzoek van Landbouwgewassen (Wageningen). Jaarverslag — IBSJBB
Instituut voor Biologisch en Scheikundig Onderzoek van Landbouwgewassen (Wageningen). Mededeling — Inst Biol Scheikd Onderz Landbouwgewassen (Wageningen) Meded
Instituut voor Bodemvruchtbaarheid Haren-Groningen. Jaarverslag — Inst Bodemvruchtbaarheid Haren-Gr Jaarversl
Instituut voor Bodemvruchtbaarheid Haren-Groningen. Rapport — Inst Bodemvruchtbaarheid Haren-Gr Rapp
Instituut voor Bodemvruchtbaarheid. Jaarverslag — Inst Bodemvruchtbaarheid Jaarversl
Instituut voor Bodemvruchtbaarheid. Rapport — Inst Bodemvruchtbaarheid Rapp
Instituut voor de Pluimveeteelt "Het Spelderholt." Mededeling — Inst Pluimveeteelt "Het Spelderholt" Meded
Instituut voor de Pluimveeteelt "Het Spelderholt." Mededeling — IPLMAE
Instituut voor Gezondheidstechniek TNO [*Toegepast-Natuurwetenschappelijk Onderzoek*]. Rapport — Inst Gezondheidstech TNO Rapp
Instituut voor Pluimveeonderzoek "Het Spelderholt." Jaarverslag — Inst Pluimveeonderz "Het Spelderholt" Jaarversl
Instituut voor Pluimveeonderzoek "Het Spelderholt." Mededeling — Inst Pluimveeonderz "Het Spelderholt" Meded
Instituut voor Toegepast Biologisch Onderzoek in de Natuur [*Institute for Biological Field Research*]. Mededeling — Inst Toegepast Biol Onderzoek Meded
Instituut voor Toegepast Biologisch Onderzoek in de Natuur [*Institute for Biological Field Research*]. Mededeling — MIBNAU
Instituut voor Toegepast Biologisch Onderzoek in de Natuur [*Institute for Biological Field Research*]. Medeling — Inst Toegepast Biol Onderz Nat Meded
Instruction Sheet. Central Experimental Farm (Ottawa) — Instr Sh Cent Exp Fm (Ottawa)
Instructional Course Lectures — Instr Course Lect
Instructional Innovator — Instr Innov
Instructional Innovator — Instr Innovator
Instructional Resources — Instr Res
Instructional Resources Information System [*Database*] — IRIS
Instructional Science — Instr Sci
Instructions Nautiques — Instr Naut
Instructor — IINT
Instructor — Inst
Instructor — Instr
Instructor and Teacher — Instr Teach
Instrument Abstracts — Instrum Abstr
Instrument and Control Engineering — Instrum Control Engng
Instrument Construction (USSR) — Instrum Constr (USSR)
Instrument Engineer — Instrum Eng
Instrument Maintenance Management — Instrum Maint Manage
Instrument Maker — Instrum Maker
Instrument Manufacturing — Instrum Manuf
Instrument News — Instrum News
Instrument Practice — INPAA
Instrument Practice — Instrum Pract
Instrument Review [*England*] — Instrum Rev
Instrument Revue (Leiden) — Instrum Rev (Leiden)
Instrument Society of America. Conference Preprint — Instrum Soc Amer Conf Preprint
Instrument Society of America. Instrumentation Index — Instrum Soc Am Instrum Index
Instrument Society of India. Journal — Instrum Soc India J
Instrument und Forschung — Instrum Forsch
Instrumenta Patristica — IP
Instrumenta Rationis. Sources for the History of Logic in the Modern Age — Instrum Rationis Sources Hist Logic Modern Age
Instrumentalist — IN
Instrumentalist — Ins
Instrumentalist — Instrument
Instrumentalist — ISMTB
Instrumental'nye Metody Analiza v Ekologii — Instrum Metody Anal Ekol
Instrumentation — INSRAG
Instrumentation and Automation — Instrum Autom
Instrumentation Bulletin — Instrum Bull
Instrumentation for Planetary and Terrestrial Atmospheric Remote Sensing — Instrum Planet Terr Atmos Remote Sens
Instrumentation in Medicine [*England*] — Instrum Med
Instrumentation in the Aerospace Industry — Instrum Aerosp Ind
Instrumentation in the Chemical and Petroleum Industries — INCPA
Instrumentation in the Chemical and Petroleum Industries — Instrum Chem Pet Ind
Instrumentation in the Cryogenic Industry — Instrum Cryog Ind
Instrumentation in the Food and Beverage Industry — Instrum Food Beverage Ind
Instrumentation in the Iron and Steel Industry — Instrum Iron Steel Ind
Instrumentation in the Metals Industries — Instrum Met Ind
Instrumentation in the Mining and Metallurgy Industries — IMIDB
Instrumentation in the Mining and Metallurgy Industries — Instrum Min Metall Ind
Instrumentation in the Power Industry — Instrum Power Ind
Instrumentation in the Power Industry — IPWIA
Instrumentation in the Pulp and Paper Industry [*United States*] — Instrum Pulp Pap Ind
Instrumentation in the Pulp and Paper Industry — IPPIC
Instrumentation Nucleaire [*France*] — Instrum Nucl
Instrumentation Technology — Inst Tech
Instrumentation Technology — Instr Tech
Instrumentation Technology — Instrn Technol
Instrumentation Technology — Instrum Tech
Instrumentation Technology — Instrum Technol
Instrumentation Technology — Instrumentation Tech
Instrumentation Technology — IRTCA4
Instrumentation Test Report. Bureau of Meteorology — Instrum Test Rep Bur Meteor
Instrumentenbau Musik International — INAUA
Instrumentenbau Zeitschrift — Instrum Zeit

Instrumentenbau-Zeitschrift — Instrumentenbau Z
Instrumentenbau-Zeitschrift — IZ
Instrumentenbau-Zeitschrift. Music International — IB
Instruments and Automation — INAUA3
Instruments and Automation — Instr & Autom
Instruments and Automation — Instrum Automat
Instruments and Control Systems — Instr Contr
Instruments and Control Systems — Instrum and Control Syst
Instruments and Control Systems — Instrum Contr Syst
Instruments and Control Systems — Instrum Control Syst
Instruments and Electronics Developments — Instrum Electr Dev
Instruments and Experimental Techniques — Instr Exp Techn
Instruments and Experimental Techniques — Instrum and Exp Tech
Instruments and Experimental Techniques — Instrum Exp Tech
Instruments et Laboratoires — ILABAY
Instruments et Laboratoires — Instrum Lab
Instruments India — Instrum India
Instruments India — ISIDB
Instytut Badan Literackick Polskiej Akademii Nauk — IBL
Instytut Celulozowo-Papierniczego. Prace — Inst Celul Papier Pr
Instytut Energetyki. Biuletyn — Inst Energ Biul
Instytut Farb i Lakierow. Biuletyn Informacyjny — Inst Farb Lakierow Biul Inf
Instytut Filozofii i Socjologii Pan — IFiS
Instytut Geolgiczny (Warsaw). Prace — Inst Geol (Warsaw) Pr
Instytut Krajowych Wlokien Naturalnych. Prace — Inst Krajowych Wlok Nat Pr
Instytut Lekow. Biuletyn Informacyjny — Inst Lekow Biul Inf
Instytut Materialow Ogniotrwalych. Biuletyn Informacyjny — Inst Mater Ogniotrwalych Biul Inf
Instytut Metali Niezelaznych. Biuletyn — Inst Met Niezelazn Biul
Instytut Metali Niezelaznych Biuletyn — Instytut Met Niezel Biul
Instytut Metali Niezelaznych Prace — Inst Niezel Pr
Instytut Metalurgii Zelaza. Prace — Inst Metal Zelaza Pr
Instytut Niskich Temperatur i Badan Strukturalnych PAN Prace. Seria. Prace Komitetu Krystalografii — Inst Nisk Temp Badan Strukt PAN Pr Ser Pr Kom Krystalogr
Instytut Ochrony Roslin. Materialy Sesji Naukowej — Inst Ochr Rosl Mater Ses Nauk
Instytut Przemyslu Organicznego. Prace — Inst Przem Org Pr
Instytut Przemyslu Tworzyw i Farb. Biuletyn Informacyjny — Inst Przem Tworzyw Farb Biul Inf
Instytut Przemyslu Wiazacych Materialow Budowlanych. Krakow. Biuletyn Informacyjny — Inst Przem Wiazacych Mater Budow Krakow Biul Inf
Instytut Techniki Budowlanej. Prace — Inst Tech Budow Pr
Instytut Technologii Materialow Elektronicznych. Prace — Inst Technol Mater Elektron Pr
Instytut Wlokiennictwa. Prace — Inst Wlok Pr
Instytut Zootechnik. Biuletyn Informacyjny — BIIZDH
Instytut Zootechniki. Biuletyn Informacyjny — Inst Zootech Biul Inf
Instytut Zootechniki w Polsce Wydawnictwa Wlasne — Inst Zootech Pol Wydawn Wlasne
Instytut Zootechniki w Polsce Wydawnictwa Wlasne — IZWWAX
Instytut Zootechniki w Polsce Wyniki Oceny Wartosci Hodowlanej Buhajow — Inst Zootech Pol Wyniki Oceny Wartosci Hodowlanej Buhajow
Instytut Zootechniki w Polsce Wyniki Oceny Wartosci Hodowlanej Buhajow — WOWBDG
Instytutow Hutniczych. Prace — Inst Hutn Pr
Insula — In
Insula — Ins
Insula Fulcheria. Museo Civico — IF
Insula (Havanna) — InsulaH
Insulana — Insul
Insulation — Insul
Insulation — Insulatn
Insulation/Circuits — Insul/Circuits
Insulation Journal — Insulation J
Insulation Journal — Insulatn
Insulation Materials. Testing and Applications — Insul Mater Test Appl
Insulin Receptors. Part A. Methods for the Study of Structure and Function — Insulin Recept Part A Methods Study Struct Funct
Insurance — INS
Insurance Advocate — IA
Insurance Asia [*Manila*] — IA
Insurance Counsel Journal — ICJ
Insurance Counsel Journal — Ins Coun J
Insurance Counsel Journal — Ins Counsel J
Insurance Counsel Journal — Insur Couns J
Insurance Decisions — Insurance D
Insurance Economics Surveys — Ins Econ Surv
Insurance Facts — Insurance F
Insurance Field (Fire and Casualty Edition) — Ins Field (Fire Ed)
Insurance Field (Life Edition) — Ins Field (Life Ed)
Insurance Forum — IF
Insurance Law Journal — ILJ
Insurance Law Journal — Ins L J
Insurance Law Journal — Ins Law J
Insurance Law Journal — Insur Law J
Insurance Law Journal — Insur LJ
Insurance Law Reports. Commerce Clearing House — Ins L Rep CCH
Insurance Lines — Insur Lines
Insurance Litigation Reporter — Ins LR
Insurance Magazine — IM
Insurance, Mathematics, and Economics — IME
Insurance, Mathematics, and Economics — Insurance Math Econom
Insurance Periodicals Index [*Database*] — IPI
Insurance Sales — IRS
Insurance Salesman — IS
Insurance Worker — Ins Wkr
Insurgent Sociologist — Insrg Soc
Insurgent Sociologist — Insurg Soc
INTA [*Instituto Nacional de Tecnologia Agropecuaria*] **Coleccion Cientifica** — CCAODF
INTA/CONIE [*Instituto Nacional de Tecnica Aeroespacial/Comision Nacional de Investigacion del Espacio*] **Informacion Aeroespacial** [*Spain*] — INTA/CONIE Inf Aeroesp
INTA [*Instituto Nacional de Tecnologia Agropecuaria*] **Divulgacion Tecnica** — DTIMD9
INTA [*Instituto Nacional de Tecnologia Agropecuaria*] **Estacion Experimental Agropecuaria Concordia. Serie Notas Tecnicas** — SNTCDL
INTA [*Instituto Nacional de Tecnologia Agropecuaria*]. Estacion Experimental Manfredi. Informacion Tecnica — INTA Estac Exp Manfredi Inf Tec
INTA [*Instituto Nacional de Tecnologia Agropecuaria*]. Estacion Experimental Regional Agropecuaria . Informe Tecnico [*Pergamino*] — EAPTA8
INTA [*Instituto Nacional de Tecnologia Agropecuaria*]. Estacion Experimental Regional Agropecuaria (Parana). Serie Tecnica — INTA Estac Exp Reg Agropecu (Parana) Ser Tec
INTA [*Instituto Nacional de Tecnologia Agropecuaria*]. Estacion Experimental Regional Agropecuaria (Pergamino). Informe Tecnico — INTA Estac Exp Reg Agropecu Pergamino Inf Tec
INTA [*Instituto Nacional de Tecnologia Agropecuaria*]. Estacion Experimental Regional Agropecuaria (Pergamino). Publicacion Tecnica — INTA Estac Exp Reg Agropecu Pergamino Publ Tec
INTA [*Instituto Nacional de Tecnologia Agropecuaria*]. Estacion Experimental Regional Agropecuaria . Publicacion Tecnica [*Pergamino*] — ITXPA9
INTA [*Instituto Nacional de Tecnologia Agropecuaria*]. Estacion Experimental Regional Agropecuaria . Serie Tecnica [*Parana*] — ITEAA5
INTA (Instituto Nacional de Tecnologia Agropecuaria) Coleccion Cientifica — INTA (Inst Nac Tecnol Agropecu) Colecc Cient
INTA (Instituto Nacional de Tecnologia Agropecuaria) Divulgacion Tecnica — INTA (Inst Nac Tecnol Agropecu) Divulg Tec
INTA (Instituto Nacional de Tecnologia Agropecuaria) Manual Agropecuario — INTA (Inst Nac Tecnol Agropecu) Man Agropecu
INTA (Instituto Nacional de Tecnologia Agropecuaria). Serie Tecnia — INTA (Inst Nac Tecnol Agropecu) Ser Tec
INTA [*Instituto Nacional de Tecnologia Agropecuaria*]. Manual Agropecuario — AMAABJ
InTech (Instrumentation Technology) — InTech (Instrum Technol)
Integracion Latinoamericana — IDT
Integracion Latinoamericana — IL
Integracion Latinoamericana — Integr Latinoamer
Integracion Latinoamericana. Instituto para la Integracion de America Latina — INTAL/IL
Integral Industrial [*Colombia*] — Integr Ind
Integral Transformations and Special Functions. An International Journal — Integral Transform Spec Funct
Integrated Circuit Metrology, Inspection, and Process Control — Integr Circuit Metrol Insp Process Control
Integrated Circuits International — Integrated Circuits Int
Integrated Control of Weeds. Proceedings — Integr Control Weeds Proc
Integrated Crop-Livestock-Fish Farming — Integr Crop Livest Fish Farming
Integrated Education — Integ Educ
Integrated Education — Integrated Educ
Integrated Education: Race and Schools — Integ Ed
Integrated Ferroelectrics — Integr Ferroelectr
Integrated Instructional Information Resource [*Database*] — IIIR
Integrated Optical Circuit Engineering — Integr Opt Circuit Eng
Integrated Optical Circuit Engineering. International Conference — Integr Opt Circuit Eng Int Conf
Integrated Optoelectronics for Communication and Processing — Integr Optoelectron Commun Process
Integrated Pollution Control through Clean Technology — Integr Pollut Control Clean Technol
Integrative Control Functions of the Brain [*Elsevier Book Series*] — ICFB
Integrative Physiological and Behavioral Science — Integr Physiol Behav Sci
Integrative Psychiatry — Int Psych
Integratsionnye Virusy [*Monograph*] — Integr Virusy
Integrierte Konzepte der Abfallentsorgung. Muelltechnisches Seminar — Integr Konzepte Abfallentsorgung Muelltech Semin
Integriertes Statistisches Informationssystem [*Database*] — ISIS
Intellectual Observer — Intel Obs
Intellectual Property Law Review — Intell Prop L Rev
Intellectual Property Reports [*Australia*] — IPR
Intellectual Repository and New Jerusalem Magazine — IRNJM
Intellectual Repository for the New Church — IRNC
Intelligence — NTLLDT
Intelligence Digest — Intell Dig
Intelligent Instruments and Computers — Intell Instrum Comput
Intelligent Robots and Computer Vision — Intell Rob Comput Vision
Intelligent Vehicle Highway Systems — Intell Veh Highw Syst
Intensivbehandlung — NTNSDQ
Intensive Agriculture — Inten Agric
Intensive Agriculture — Intensive Agr
Intensive Care Medicine — Intensive Care Med
Intensive Care Nursing — Intensive Care Nurs
Intensivmedizin — ITMZBJ
Intensivmedizin, Notfallmedizin, Anaesthesiologie — Intensivmed Notfallmed Anaesthesiol
Intensivmedizin und Diagnostik — Intensivmed Diagn
Intensivmedizin und Notfallmedizin — Intensivmed Notfallmed
Intensivmedizinische Praxis — Intensivmed Prax
Intensivmedizinische Praxis — IPRADB

Inter American Scene — IS
Inter Dependent — Inter Depend
Inter Electronique [*France*] — Inter Electron
Inter Regions — Inter Reg
Interaction — INTA
Interaction of Mechanics and Mathematics Series — Interact Mech Math Ser
Interaction of Mechanics and Mathematics Series — Interaction Mech Math Ser
Interactions Among Cell Signalling Systems — Interact Cell Signalling Syst
Interactive Computing — Int Comp
Interagency Rehabilitation Research Information System [*Database*] — IRRI
Interagency Workshop on In-Situ Water Quality Sensing. Biological Sensors — Interagency Workshop In Situ Water Qual Sens Biol Sens
Inter-American — Inter-Am
Inter-American Bibliographical Review (Washington, DC) — Inter Am Bibliogr Rev Wash
Inter-American Cacao Conference. Proceedings — Inter Am Cacao Conf Proc
Inter-American Conference on Congenital Defects. Papers and Discussions — Inter Am Conf Congenital Defects Pap Discuss
Interamerican Conference on Materials Technology. Proceedings — Interam Conf Mater Technol Proc
Inter-American Conference on Radiochemistry. Proceedings — Inter Am Conf Radiochem Proc
Inter-American Congress on Brucellosis. Papers — Inter Am Congr Brucell Pap
Inter-American Economic Affairs [*Washington*] — IAA
Inter-American Economic Affairs — IAMEA
Inter-American Economic Affairs — Inter-Am Econ Affairs
Inter-American Economic Affairs — Inter-Amer Econ Aff
Inter-American Institute for Musical Research. Yearbook — Intam Inst Mus Res
Inter-American Institute of Agricultural Sciences of the OAS. Tropical Center for Research and Graduate Training. Report — Inter Am Inst Agric Sci OAS Trop Cent Res Grad Train Rep
Interamerican Journal of Psychology — Interam J P
Inter-American Law Review — Int-Am L Rev
Inter-American Law Review — Inter-Am L Rev
Inter-American Music Bulletin — Inter Amer M Bul
Inter-American Music Bulletin (English Edition) — Intam Mus B (Eng Ed)
Inter-American Music Bulletin (Washington, DC) — Inter Am Music Bull Wash
Inter-American Music Review — Intam Mus R
Inter-American Music Review — Inter Am M
Inter-American Music Review — Inter-Amer M R
Inter-American Musical Research. Yearbook — Intam Mus Res Yrbk
Inter-American Quarterly — Inter Amer Q
Inter-American Quarterly — Inter-Am Q
Inter-American Quarterly (Washington, DC) — Inter Am Quart Wash
Inter-American Review of Bibliography — IARB
Inter-American Review of Bibliography — IntA
Inter-American Review of Bibliography — Interam Rev Bibliogr
Inter-American Review of Bibliography/Revista Interamericana de Bibliografia — R Inter Am Bibliogr
Inter-American Symposium on the Peaceful Application of Nuclear Energy. Papers — Inter Am Symp Peaceful Appl Nucl Energy Pap
Inter-American Symposium on the Peaceful Application of Nuclear Energy. Proceedings — Inter Amer Symp Peaceful Appl Nucl Energy Proc
Inter-American Tropical Tuna Commission. Bulletin — BTTCA9
Inter-American Tropical Tuna Commission. Bulletin — Inter-Am Trop Tuna Comm Bull
Inter-American Tropical Tuna Commission. Special Report — Inter-Am Trop Tuna Comm Spec Rep
Inter-American Tropical Tuna Commission. Special Report — SRICDS
Interavia Aerospace Review [*database*] — IAR
Interavia (English Edition) — Interavia (Engl Ed)
Interavia. Revue Internationale Aeronautique, Astronautique, Electronique — ITA
Interavia Space Markets [*database*] — ISM
Intercellular and Intracellular Communication — IINCEH
Intercellular and Intracellular Communication — Intercell Intracell Commun
Interchemical Review — Interchem Rev
Interchurch News — Interchurch N
Interciencia — ITRCDB
Interciencia. Asociacion Interciencia [*Caracas*] — AI/I
Inter-City Cost of Living Indicators — ICLI
Inter-Clinic Information Bulletin — Int Clin Inf Bul
Intercollegiate Law Journal — Intercol Law J
Intercollegiate Review — Intercoll Rev
Intercollegiate Socialist — Intercol Socialist
Intercolonial Medical Journal of Australasia — Intercolon Med J Australas
Interconnections in the Ancient Near-East — IANE
Intercontinental Press — Intercont
Intercontinental Press — Intercontinental Pr
Inter-Corporate Ownership [*Database*] — CLRA
Interdepartmental Committee for Atmospheric Sciences. ICAS. Report. (US) — Interdep Comm Atmos Sci ICAS Rep US
Interdepartmental Committee for Atmospheric Sciences. Report. United States — Interdep Comm Atmos Sci Rep US
Interdisciplinary Applied Mathematics — Interdiscip Appl Math
Interdisciplinary Center for European Studies. Newsletter [*Montreal*] — Interdis Center Eur Stud Newslett
Interdisciplinary Essays — IE
Interdisciplinary Information Sciences — Interdiscip Inform Sci
Interdisciplinary Mathematics — Interdiscip Math
Interdisciplinary Mathematics — Interdisciplinary Math
Interdisciplinary Neuroendocrinology. International Meeting — Interdiscip Neuroendocrinol Int Meet
Interdisciplinary Science Reviews — Interdis Sci Rev
Interdisciplinary Science Reviews — Interdiscip Sci Rev
Interdisciplinary Science Reviews — Interdisciplinary Sci Rev
Interdisciplinary Science Reviews — ISR
Interdisciplinary Seminars on Tachyons and Related Topics. Proceedings — Interdisc Semin Tachyons Relat Top Proc
Interdisciplinary Statistics — Interdiscip Statist
Interdisciplinary Systems Research — Interdisciplinary Systems Res
Interdisciplinary Topics in Gerontology — Interdiscip Top Gerontol
Interdisciplinary Topics in Gerontology — ITGEA
Interdisciplinary Topics in Gerontology — ITGEAR
Interdisziplinaere Gerontologie — Interdiszip Gerontol
Interdisziplinaror Sonderbereich Umweltschutz. Mitteilungen — ISU Mitt
Intereconomics — Interecon
Intereconomics. Monthly Review of International Trade and Development — WSA
Interface Age/Computing for Business — INA
Interface. Data Processing Management — INF
Interface. The Computer Education Quarterly — Interface Comput Educ Q
Interfaces — INFAC
Interfaces — INT
Interfaces in Computing [*Later, Computer Standards and Interfaces*] — IC
Interfaces in Computing [*Later, Computer Standards and Interfaces*] — Interfaces Comput
Interfaces in New Materials. Proceedings. Workshop — Interfaces New Mater Proc Workshop
Interfacial Phenomena in Biological Systems — Interfacial Phenom Biol Syst
Interferon — INRFDC
Interferon y Biotecnologia — INTBEB
Interferon y Biotecnologia — Interferon Biotecnol
Intergovernmental Oceanographic Commission. Technical Series — Intergov Oceanogr Comm Tech Ser
Intergovernmental Oceanographic Commission. Technical Series — IOCTAH
Intergovernmental Oceanographic Commission. Workshop Report — Intergov Oceanogr Comm Workshop Rep
Intergovernmental Perspective — Intergov Persp
Interim Document. Health Aspects of Chemical Safety — Interim Doc Health Aspects Chem Saf
Interior Ballistics of Guns — Inter Ballist Guns
Interior Design — Int Des
Interior Design — Inter Des
Interior Design — Interior Des
Interior Landscape International — Interior Landscape Intl
Interior Textiles — Int Text
Interiors — Inter
Interlending and Document Supply — Interlend and Doc Supply
Interlending Review — Interlending Rev
Intermediair. Informatie voor Leidinggevende Functionarissen — ITI
Intermediaire des Chercheurs et Curieux — Interm des Cherch et Curieux
Intermediaire des Chercheurs et des Curieux — I d CC
Intermediaire des Chercheurs et des Curieux — ICC
Intermediaire des Chercheurs et des Curieux — Intermed Chercheurs
Intermediaire des Genealogistes — IG
Intermediate Science Curriculum Study. Newsletter — Intermed Sci Curric Study Newsl
Intermediate Teacher — Int Teach
Intermountain Association of Geologists. Annual Field Conference. Guidebook [*A publication*] — Intermt Assoc Geol Annu Field Conf Guideb
Intermountain Association of Petroleum Geologists. Annual Field Conference. Guidebook — Intermt Assoc Pet Geol Annu Field Conf Guideb
Intermountain Economic Review — Intermountain Econ R
Intermountain Economic Review — Intermt Econ Rev
Internacia Pedagogia Recuo — IPR
Internal Auditor — Auditor
Internal Auditor — IAU
Internal Auditor — Int Aud
Internal Auditor — Int Auditor
Internal Auditor — Intern Audit
Internal Combustion Engine [*Japan*] — Intern Combust Eng
Internal Medicine — Intern Med
Internal Medicine — NAIKAB
Internal Medicine Adviser — Intern Med Adv
Internal Medicine (Amsterdam) — Intern Med (Amsterdam)
Internal Medicine News — Intern Med News
Internal Medicine (Tokyo) — Intern Med (Tokyo)
Internal Report. Division of Mechanical Engineering. Commonwealth Scientific and Industrial Research Organisation — Int Rep Div Mech Eng CSIRO
Internal Report. Mineral Policy Sector. Department of Energy, Mines, and Resources (Canada) — Intern Rep Miner Policy Sector Dep Energy Mines Resour (Can)
Internal Report. Technical University of Helsinki. Radio Laboratory — Intern Rep Tech Univ Helsinki Radio Lab
Internal Report. University of Oxford. Department of Engineering Science — Intern Rep Univ Oxford Dep Eng Sci
Internal Spin Structure of the Nucleon. Symposium — Intern Spin Struct Nucleon Symp
Internasjonal Politikk [*Oslo*] — Internas Polit
Internasjonal Politikk [*Norway*] — Internasjonal Polit
Internasjonal Politikk (Bergen) — Int Polit (Bergen)
Internasjonal Politikk (Oslo) — Int Polit (O)
Internasjonal Politikk (Oslo) — Int Politikk (Oslo)
Internationaal Opereren — IBD
Internationaal Tijdschrift voor Brouwertj en Mouterij — Int Tijdschr Brouw Mout
International Abstracts in Operations Research — IAOP
International Abstracts in Operations Research — IAOR
International Abstracts in Operations Research — Int Abstr Oper Res
International Abstracts of Biological Sciences — IABS

International Abstracts of Biological Sciences — Int Abstr Biol Sci
International Abstracts of Surgery — Int Abstr Surg
International Abstracts of Surgery — Internat Abstr Surg
International Academy for Biomedical and Drug Research — Int Acad Biomed Drug Res
International Academy of Pathology. Monograph — IAPMAV
International Academy of Pathology. Monograph — Int Acad Pathol Monogr
International Actuarial Congress Transactions — Int Act Congr Trans
International Advances in Nondestructive Testing — Int Adv Nondestr Test
International Advances in Surgical Oncology — IASODL
International Advances in Surgical Oncology — Int Adv Surg Oncol
International Advertiser — Int Advertiser
International Advertiser — Intnl Advt
International Aerospace Abstracts [*Database*] — IAA
International Aerospace Abstracts — Int Aerosp Abstr
International Aerospace Abstracts — IntAe
International Affairs — IA
International Affairs — IAI
International Affairs — INA
International Affairs — Int Aff
International Affairs [*England*] — Int Affairs
International Affairs — Internat Aff
International Affairs — PINA
International Affairs. Bulletin — Int Aff Bull
International Affairs (London) — Int Aff (London)
International Affairs (London) — Internat Affairs (London)
International Affairs (Moscow) — IAM
International Affairs (Moscow) — Int Aff Moscow
International Affairs (Moscow) — Internat Affairs (Moscow)
International Affairs. Royal Institute of International Affairs — RIIA/IA
International Affairs. Studies — Int Aff Stud
International African Bibliography — Int Afr Bibliogr
International Agency for Research on Cancer. Monographs on the Evaluation of Carcinogenic Risk of Chemicals to Man — Int Agency Res Cancer Monogr Eval Carcinog Risk Chem Man
International Agriculture Publications. General Series — Int Agric Publ Gen Ser
International Analyst — Int Anal
International and Comparative Law Quarterly — I & CLQ
International and Comparative Law Quarterly — ICLQ
International and Comparative Law Quarterly — Int & Comp
International and Comparative Law Quarterly — Int & Comp L Q
International and Comparative Law Quarterly — Int Comp Law Q
International and Comparative Law Quarterly — Int Comp Law Quart
International and Comparative Law Quarterly — Internat Comp LQ
International and Comparative Law Quarterly — Int'l & Comp LQ
International and Comparative Law Quarterly — LQ
International and Comparative Law Quarterly. Fourth Series — Internat and Comparative Law Q 4th Ser
International and Comparative Law Quarterly. Supplement — ICLQS
International and Comparative Public Policy — Int Comp Pub Pol
International Anesthesiology Clinics — Anesthesiol Clin
International Anesthesiology Clinics — IACLAV
International Anesthesiology Clinics — Int Anesthesiol Clin
International Anesthesiology Clinics — Internat Anesth Clin
International Angiology — Int Angiol
International Annals of Criminology — Internat Annals Criminology
International Anthropological and Linguistic Review — IALR
International Applied Mechanics — Internat Appl Mech
International Architect — Int Archit
International Architect — Intl Archt
International Archives of Allergy and Applied Immunology — IAAAAM
International Archives of Allergy and Applied Immunology — IAOHD
International Archives of Allergy and Applied Immunology — Int A Aller
International Archives of Allergy and Applied Immunology — Int Arch Allergy Appl Immunol
International Archives of Allergy and Applied Immunology — Int Archs Allergy Appl Immun
International Archives of Allergy and Applied Immunology — Internat Arch Allergy
International Archives of Allergy and Immunology — Int Arch Allergy Immunol
International Archives of Ethnography — Int Archs Ethnogr
International Archives of Occupational and Environmental Health — IAEHD
International Archives of Occupational and Environmental Health — IAEHDW
International Archives of Occupational and Environmental Health — Int A Occup
International Archives of Occupational and Environmental Health — Int Arch Occup Environ Health
International Archives of Occupational Health [*Later, International Archives of Occupational and Environmental Health*] — Int Arch Occup Health
International Archives of Photogrammetry — Int Arch Photogramm
International Archives of the History of Ideas — IAHI
International Art Market — IAM
International Asbestos-Cement Review — Intl Asbestos Cement Review
International Association — Int Ass
International Association for Bridge and Structural Engineering. Publications — Int Ass Bridge Struct Eng Publ
International Association for Hydraulic Research. Congress. Proceedings — Int Assoc Hydraul Res Congr Proc
International Association for Mathematical Geology. Journal — Int Assoc Math Geol J
International Association of Agricultural Librarians and Documentalists. Quarterly Bulletin — IAALD Q Bull
International Association of Dairy and Milk Inspectors. Annual Report — Int Assoc Dairy Milk Insp Annu Rep
International Association of Dental Students. Newsletter — IADS Newsl
International Association of Dentistry for Children. Journal — Int Assoc Dent Child J
International Association of Engineering Geology. Bulletin — Int Assoc Eng Geol Bull
International Association of Engineering Geology. Bulletin — Int Assoc Engng Geol Bull
International Association of Hydrogeologists. Memoirs — Int Assoc Hydrogeol Mem
International Association of Hydrological Sciences - Association Internationale des Sciences Hydrologiques. Publication — Int Assoc Hydrol Sci Assoc Int Sci Hydrol Publ
International Association of Hydrological Sciences. Hydrological Sciences Bulletin — Int Assoc Hydrol Sci Hydrol Sci Bull
International Association of Hydrological Sciences. Publication — Int Assoc Hydrol Sci Publ
International Association of Hydrological Sciences Special Publication — Int Assoc Hydrol Sci Spec Publ
International Association of Medical Museums. Bulletin and Journal of Technical Methods — Internat Ass Med Mus Bull
International Association of Scientific Hydrology. Bulletin — Int Assoc Sci Hydrol Bull
International Association of Scientific Hydrology. Bulletin — Internat Assoc Sci Hydrology Bull
International Association of Scientific Hydrology. Bulletin. Publication — Internat Assoc Sci Hydrology Bull Pub
International Association of Scientific Hydrology. Publications — Internat Assoc Sci Hydrology Pub
International Association of Technological University Libraries. Proceedings [*A publication*] — IATUL Proc
International Association of Theoretical and Applied Limnology. Communication [*Germany*] — Int Assoc Theor Appl Limnol Commun
International Association of Theoretical and Applied Limnology. Proceedings [*A publication*] — Int Assoc Theor Appl Limnol Proc
International Association of Theoretical and Applied Limnology. Proceedings [*A publication*] — IVTLAP
International Association of Universities. Papers and Reports — Int Assoc Univ Pap Rep
International Association of Volcanology and Chemistry of the Earth's Interior. Special Series — Int Assoc Volcanol Chem Earth's Inter Spe Ser
International Association of Wood Anatomists. Bulletin — IAWABV
International Association of Wood Anatomists. Bulletin — Int Assoc Wood Anat Bull
International Associations/Associations Internationales — Int Assoc/Assoc Int
International Astronautical Congress. Proceedings — Int Astronaut Congr Proc
International Astronomical Union. Circular — IAU Circ
International Astronomical Union Colloquium — Int Astron Union Colloq
International Astronomical Union. Symposium — IAUSA
International Astronomical Union. Symposium — Int Astron Union Symp
International Atlantic Salmon Foundation. Special Publication Series — IASFAP
International Atlantic Salmon Foundation. Special Publication Series — Int Atl Salmon Found Spec Publ Ser
International Atomic Energy Agency. Bibliographical Series — IAEA Bibliogr Ser
International Atomic Energy Agency. Bibliographical Series — Int At Energy Ag Bibliogr Ser
International Atomic Energy Agency. Bulletin — IAEA Bull
International Atomic Energy Agency. Bulletin — IAY
International Atomic Energy Agency. Bulletin — Int At Energy Agency Bull
International Atomic Energy Agency. Proceedings Series — IAEA Proc Ser
International Atomic Energy Agency. Proceedings Series — Int At Energy Ag Proc Ser
International Atomic Energy Agency. Safety Series — IAEA Saf Ser
International Atomic Energy Agency. Safety Series — Int At Energy Agency Saf Ser
International Atomic Energy Agency. Technical Report Series — IAEA Tech Rep Ser
International Atomic Energy Agency. Technical Report Series — Int At Energy Agency Tech Rep Ser
International Automotive Review — IAR
International Bank Note Society. Quarterly Magazine — IBNS
International Banking and Financial Law Bulletin — Int Bank Fin Law Bul
International Bauxite Association. Quarterly Review — Int Bauxite Assoc Q Rev
International Beekeeping Congress. Preliminary Scientific Meeting — Int Beekeep Congr Prelim Sci Meet
International Beekeeping Congress. Summaries of Papers — Int Beekeep Congr Summ
International Beekeeping Congress. Summaries Supplement — Int Beekeep Congr Summ Suppl
International Behavioural Scientist — Int Behav Scientist
International Beverage News — IBG
International Bibliography — IB
International Bibliography — Int Bibliogr
International Bibliography, Information, and Documentation — IBID
International Bibliography of Book Reviews — Int Bibliogr Book Rev
International Bibliography of Book Reviews of Scholarly Literature — Int Bibliogr Book Rev Schol Lit
International Bibliography of Economics — IBE
International Bibliography of Historical Sciences — IBHS
International Bibliography of Periodical Literature — Int Bibliogr Period Lit
International Bibliography of Political Science — IBPS
International Bibliography of Social and Cultural Anthropology — IBSCA
International Bibliography of Sociology — IBS
International Bibliography of the History of Relgions — IBHR
International Bibliography of the History of Religions — Int Bibliogr Hist Relig
International Bibliography of the Social Sciences — IBSS

International Bibliography of the Social Sciences — Int Bibl Soc Sci
International Bibliography of the Social Sciences, Economics, and Sociology [*Database*] — IBS
International Biodeterioration and Biodegradation — Int Biodeterior Biodegrad
International Biodeterioration Bulletin — IBDBAD
International Biodeterioration Bulletin — INBIEA
International Biodeterioration Bulletin — Int Biod B
International Biodeterioration Bulletin — Int Biodeterior
International Biodeterioration Bulletin — Int Biodeterior Bull
International Biodeterioration Bulletin. Reference Index — Intern Biodet Bull
International Bio-Energy Directory and Handbook — IBEDH
International Bioindicators Symposium — Int Bioindic Symp
International Biological Programme. Handbook — Int Biol Programme Handb
International Biological Programme Series — IBPRDM
International Biological Programme Series — Int Biol Programme
International Bioscience Monographs — IBMOEX
International Bioscience Monographs — Int Biosci Monogr
International Boat Industry — IBI
International Botanical Congress. Papers — Int Bot Congr
International Botanical Congress. Recent Advances in Botany — Int Bot Congr Recent Advan Bot
International Bottler and Packer — IBB
International Brain Research Organization. Bulletin — IBRO Bull
International Brain Research Organization. Monograph Series — IBRSDZ
International Brain Research Organization. Monograph Series — Int Brain Res Organ Monogr Ser
International Broadcast Engineer — Int Broadc Engr
International Broadcast Engineer — Int Broadcast Eng
International Broadcasting Systems and Operation — Int Broadcast Syst and Oper
International Buddhist News Forum — IBNF
International Building Services Abstracts — Int Build Serv Abstr
International Bulletin for Research on Law in Eastern Europe — Int Bull Res E Eur
International Bulletin for Research on Law in Eastern Europe — Int'l Bull Research E Eur
International Bulletin of Bacteriological Nomenclature and Taxonomy — IBBNA5
International Bulletin of Bacteriological Nomenclature and Taxonomy — Int Bull Bacteriol Nomencl Taxon
International Bulletin of Bibliography on Education — Int Bull Bibliogr Educ
International Bulletin of Missionary Research — InB
International Bulletin of Missionary Research — Int B Miss R
International Bulletin of Missionary Research — Int Bul Miss R
International Bulletin of Missionary Research — PBMR
International Bulletin of Plant Protection — Int Bull Pl Protect
International Bulletin on Information on Refrigeration — Int Bull Inf Refrig
International Bureau of Education. Bulletin — Int Bur Ed B
International Business — Internat Bus
International Business Database — IBD
International Business Equipment — Int Bus Equip
International Business Lawyer — Intl Bus Law
International Business Men's Magazine — IBMM
International Business Opportunities. Egypt — Int Bus Opp Egy
International Business Opportunities. Oil and Gas in Africa — Int Bus Opp Oil Gas Afr
International Business Research Series — Int Bus Res Ser
International Cadmium Conference — Int Cadmium Conf
International Canada — Int Can
International Canadian Studies News — Int Can Stud N
International Cancer Congress. Abstracts — Int Cancer Congr Abstr
International Cancer Research Foundation. Report of Activities — Int Cancer Res Found Rep Act
International Cast Metals Journal — ICMJD
International Cast Metals Journal — Int Cast Met J
International Cataloguing — Int Cataloguing
International Catholic Migration — ICMC
International Cellular Plastics Conference. Proceedings — Int Cell Plast Conf Proc
International Cement Seminar Proceedings — Int Cem Semin Proc
International Center for Arid and Semi-Arid Land Studies. Publication — Int Cent Arid Semi-Arid Land Stud Publ
International Center for Medical Research. Seminar Proceedings — Int Cent Med Res Semin Proc
International Centre for Mechanical Sciences. Courses and Lectures — Int Cent Mech Sci Courses Lect
International Chemical and Export Industry — Int Chem Export Ind
International Chemical Engineering — Int Chem En
International Chemical Engineering — Int Chem Eng
International Chemical Engineering — Int Chem Engng
International Chemical Engineering — Internat Chem Engng
International Chemical Engineering and Processing Industries — Int Chem Eng Process Ind
International Child Welfare Review — Int Child Welfare Rev
International Children's Center. Courrier — Int Child Cent Cour
International Civil Engineering Monthly — Int Civ Eng Mon
International Classification — INCLD
International Classification — Int Classif
International Classification — Int Classification
International Clearinghouse on Science and Mathematics. Curricular Developments Report — ICSMAQ
International Clearinghouse on Science and Mathematics. Curricular Developments Report — Int Clgh Sci Math Curricular Dev Rep
International Clinical Genetics Seminar — Int Clin Genet Semin
International Clinical Products Review — ICPR
International Clinical Psychopharmacology — Int Clin Psychopharmacol
International Clinics — Internat Clin
International Coal Report [*England*] — Int Coal Rep
International Coal Trade [*Bureau of Mines*] — ICT
International CODATA (Committee on Data for Science and Technology) Conference Proceedings — Int CODATA Conf Proc
International Colloquium on Diffractive Optical Elements — Int Colloq Diffr Opt Elem
International Colloquium on Lecithin. Phospholipids. Biochemical, Pharmaceutical, and Analytical Considerations — Int Colloq Lecithin Phospholipids
International Colloquium on Role of Chemistry in Archaeology — Int Colloq Role Chem Archaeol
International Comet Quarterly — Int Comet Q
International Commerce — Int Com
International Commerce — Int Comm
International Commerce — Int Commer
International Commercial Bank of China. Economic Review — Internat Commer Bank China Econ R
International Commission for the Northwest Atlantic Fisheries. Annual Proceedings — ICNFAE
International Commission for the Northwest Atlantic Fisheries. Annual Proceedings — Int Comm Northwest Atl Fish Annu Proc
International Commission for the Northwest Atlantic Fisheries. Annual Report — ARIFD9
International Commission for the Northwest Atlantic Fisheries. Annual Report — Int Comm Northwest Atl Fish Annu Rep
International Commission for the Northwest Atlantic Fisheries. Redbook. Part III — ICNWAV
International Commission for the Northwest Atlantic Fisheries. Redbook. Part III — Int Comm Northwest Atl Fish Redb Part III
International Commission for the Northwest Atlantic Fisheries. Research Bulletin — IAFBAG
International Commission for the Northwest Atlantic Fisheries. Research Bulletin — ICNAF
International Commission for the Northwest Atlantic Fisheries. Research Bulletin — Int Comm Northwest Atl Fish Res Bull
International Commission for the Northwest Atlantic Fisheries. Selected Papers — Int Comm Northwest Atl Fish Sel Pap
International Commission for the Northwest Atlantic Fisheries. Selected Papers — SPIFDN
International Commission for the Northwest Atlantic Fisheries. Special Publication — IAFPAO
International Commission for the Northwest Atlantic Fisheries. Special Publication — ICNAFSP
International Commission for the Northwest Atlantic Fisheries. Special Publication — Int Comm Northwest Atl Fish Spec Publ
International Commission for the Northwest Atlantic Fisheries. Statistical Bulletin — ICNABY
International Commission for the Northwest Atlantic Fisheries. Statistical Bulletin — Int Comm Northwest Atl Fish Stat Bull
International Commission of Jurists. Review — Internat Comm Jurists R
International Commission of Jurists. Review — Intl Comm Jurists Rev
International Commission on Illumination. Proceedings — Int Comm Illum Proc
International Commission on Radiological Protection. Annals — Int Comm Radiol Prot Ann
International Commission on Radiological Protection. Publication — Int Comm Radiol Prot Publ
International Commission on Whaling. Report — ICWRBS
International Commission on Whaling. Report — Int Comm Whaling Rep
International Committee for Bird Preservation. Pan American Section. Research Report — Int Comm Bird Preserv Pan Am Sect Res Rep
International Committee for Bird Preservation. Pan American Section. Research Report — PSBRA9
International Committee for Coal Petrology. Proceedings — Internat Comm Coal Petrology Proc
International Committee on the History of Geological Sciences. Newsletter — Int Comm Hist Geol Sci Newsl
International Communications in Heat and Mass Transfer — Int Commun Heat and Mass Transfer
International Communications News — Int Com News
International Computer Science Series — Internat Comput Sci Ser
International Computer Symposium Proceedings — Intl Comp Symp
International Conciliation — InC
International Conciliation — Int Concil
International Conciliation — Internat Conciliation
International Conference. Center for High Energy Forming. Proceedings — Int Conf Cent High Energy Form Proc
International Conference in Organic Coatings Science and Technology. Proceedings (Technomic Publication) — Int Conf Org Coat Sci Technol Proc (Technomic Publ)
International Conference on Antennas and Propagation — Int Conf Antennas Propag
International Conference on Atomic Spectroscopy — Int Conf At Spectrosc
International Conference on Biomass for Energy, Industry, and Environment — Int Conf Biomass Energy Ind Environ
International Conference on Circulating Fluidized Beds — Int Conf Circ Fluid Beds
International Conference on Composite Structures — Int Conf Compos Struct
International Conference on Computers in Chemical Research, Education, and Technology — Int Conf Comput Chem Res Educ Technol
International Conference on Developments in Power System Protection — Int Conf Dev Power Syst Prot
International Conference on Die Casting — Int Conf Die Cast
International Conference on Electrophotography — Int Conf Electrophotogr

International Conference on Electrorheological Fluids — Int Conf Electrorheol Fluids
International Conference on Fire Safety. Proceedings — Int Conf Fire Saf Proc
International Conference on Fluid Sealing. Proceedings — Int Conf Fluid Sealing Proc
International Conference on Fluidized Bed Combustion. Proceedings — Int Conf Fluid Bed Combust Proc
International Conference on Food Safety and Quality Assurance. Applications of Immunoassay Systems — Int Conf Food Saf Qual Assur Appl Immunoassay Syst
International Conference on Food Science. Refrigeration and Air Conditioning — Int Conf Food Sci Refrig Air Cond
International Conference on Frequency Control and Synthesis — Int Conf Freq Control Synth
International Conference on Genetics — Int Conf Genet
International Conference on Heavy Crude and Tar Sands — Int Conf Heavy Crude Tar Sands
International Conference on High Energy Physics. Proceedings — Int Conf High Energy Phys Proc
International Conference on High Energy Rate Fabrication. Proceedings — Int Conf High Energy Rate Fabr Proc
International Conference on Hyperbaric Medicine. Proceedings — Int Conf Hyperbaric Med Proc
International Conference on Image Processing and its Applications — Int Conf Image Process Its Appl
International Conference on Indium Phosphide and Related Materials — Int Conf Indium Phosphide Relat Mater
International Conference on Insect Pathology and Biological Control — Int Conf Insect Path Biol Control
International Conference on Internal Friction and Ultrasonic Attenuation in Solids — Int Conf Intern Frict Ultrason Attenuation Solids
International Conference on Large Electric Systems. Proceedings [*France*] — Int Conf Large Electr Syst Proc
International Conference on Lattice Dynamics. Proceedings — Int Conf Lattice Dyn Proc
International Conference on Lymphatic Tissues and Germinal Centres in Immune Reactions — Int Conf Lymphatic Tissues Germinal Cent Immune React
International Conference on Natural Glasses — Int Conf Nat Glasses
International Conference on Noise Control Engineering. Proceedings — Int Conf Noise Control Eng Proc
International Conference on Nuclear Structure at High Angular Momentum — Int Conf Nucl Struct High Angular Momentum
International Conference on Photosynthesis — Int Conf Photosynth
International Conference on Plasma Source Mass Spectrometry — Int Conf Plasma Source Mass Spectrom
International Conference on Protein Engineering — Int Conf Protein Eng
International Conference on Quarantine and Plant Protection Against Pests and Diseases. Report of the Soviet Delegation — Int Conf Quar Plant Prot Pests Dis Rep Soviet Deleg
International Conference on Research in Thermochemical Biomass Conversion — Int Conf Res Thermochem Biomass Convers
International Conference on Reye's Syndrome. Proceedings — Int Conf Reyes Syndr Proc
International Conference on Sarcoidosis and Other Granulomatous Diseases. Proceedings — Int Conf Sarcoidosis Other Granulomatous Dis Proc
International Conference on Sarcoidosis. Proceedings — Int Conf Sarcoidosis Proc
International Conference on Separations Science and Technology — Int Conf Sep Sci Technol
International Conference on Silicon Carbide — Int Conf Silicon Carbide
International Conference on Software Engineering for Telecommunication Switching Systems — Int Conf Software Eng Telecommun Switching Syst
International Conference on Software Engineering for Telecommunication Systems and Services — Int Conf Software Eng Telecommun Syst Serv
International Conference on Soil Mechanics and Foundation Engineering. Proceedings — Int Conf Soil Mech Found Eng Proc
International Conference on Solid State Nuclear Track Detectors — Int Conf Solid State Nucl Track Detect
International Conference on Solid Surfaces — Int Conf Solid Surf
International Conference on Solidification. Proceedings — Int Conf Solidif Proc
International Conference on Solid-Solid Phase Transformations — Int Conf Solid Solid Phase Transform
International Conference on Spectroscopy. Proceedings — Int Conf Spectrosc Proc
International Conference on Sputtering and Its Applications — Int Conf Sputtering Its Appl
International Conference on Stable Isotopes. Proceedings — Int Conf Stable Isot Proc
International Conference on Strontium Metabolism. Papers — Int Conf Strontium Metab Pap
International Conference on Sulphur in Construction — Int Conf Sulphur Constr
International Conference on Superlattices, Microstructures, and Microdevices — Int Conf Superlattices Microstruct Microdevices
International Conference on Superoxide and Superoxide Dismutase — Int Conf Superoxide Superoxide Dismutase
International Conference on Surface Engineering — Int Conf Surf Eng
International Conference on Surface Modification Technology — Int Conf Surf Modif Technol
International Conference on Surface Waves in Plasmas and Solids — Int Conf Surf Waves Plasmas Solids
International Conference on Tetanus. Proceedings — Int Conf Tetanus Proc
International Conference on Texture. Proceedings — Int Conf Texture Proc
International Conference on Textures of Materials. Proceedings — Int Conf Textures Mater Proc
International Conference on the Biotechnology of Microbial Products — Int Conf Biotechnol Microb Prod
International Conference on the Effect of Hydrogen on the Behavior of Materials — Int Conf Eff Hydrogen Behav Mater
International Conference on the Microscopy of Oxidation — Int Conf Microsc Oxid
International Conference on the Physics of Semiconductors. Proceedings — Int Conf Phys Semicond Proc
International Conference on the Strength of Metals and Alloys. Conference. Proceedings — Int Conf Strength Met Alloys Conf Proc
International Conference on Theoretical Physics and Biology — Int Conf Theor Phys Biol
International Conference on Thermal Analysis. Proceedings — Int Conf Therm Anal Proc
International Conference on Thermal Conductivity. Proceedings — Int Conf Therm Conduct Proc
International Conference on Thermal Insulation. Proceedings — Int Conf Therm Insul Proc
International Conference on Thermally Stable Polymers. Invited and Main Lectures — Int Conf Therm Stable Polym Invited Main Lect
International Conference on Thermoelectric Properties of Metallic Conductors. Proceedings — Int Conf Thermoelectr Prop Met Conduct Proc
International Conference on Thermoplastic Elastomer Markets and Products — Int Conf Thermoplast Elastomer Markets Prod
International Conference on Thrombosis and Embolism. Proceedings — Int Conf Thromb Embolism Proc
International Conference on Toxic Dinoflagellate Blooms — Int Conf Toxic Dinoflagellate Blooms
International Conference on Toxic Dinoflagellates — Int Conf Toxic Dinoflagellates
International Conference on Transfer of Water Resources Knowledge. Proceedings — Int Conf Transfer Water Resour Knowl Proc
International Conference on Transmutation Doping in Semiconductors — Int Conf Transmutat Doping Semicond
International Conference on Trichinellosis — Int Conf Trichinellosis
International Conference on Ultrastructure Processing of Ceramics, Glasses, and Composites — Int Conf Ultrastruct Process Ceram Glasses Compos
International Conference on Uranium Mine Waste Disposal. Proceedings — Int Conf Uranium Mine Waste Disposal Proc
International Conference on Vacuum Metallurgy — Int Conf Vac Metall
International Conference on Vibrations at Surfaces — Int Conf Vib Surf
International Conference on Water Pollution Research. Proceedings — Int Conf Water Pollut Res
International Conference on Water Pollution Research. Proceedings — WPRCDZ
International Conference on X-Ray Optics and Microanalysis. Proceedings — Int Conf X Ray Opt Microanal Proc
International Conference on Zeolites — Int Conf Zeolites
International Conference on Zinc Coated Steel Sheet — Int Conf Zinc Coated Steel Sheet
International Conference. Trends in Quantum Electronics — Int Conf Trends Quantum Electron
International Congress and Symposium Series. Royal Society of Medicine Services Limited — Int Congr Symp Ser R Soc Med Serv Ltd
International Congress. European Association of Poison Control Centers — Int Congr Eur Assoc Poison Control Cent
International Congress for Electron Microscopy — Int Congr Electron Microsc
International Congress for Hygiene and Preventive Medicine. Proceedings — Int Congr Hyg Prev Med Proc
International Congress for Microbiology. Symposia — Int Congr Microbiol Symp
International Congress for Microbiology. Symposia — SICMAU
International Congress for Stereology. Proceedings — Int Congr Stereol Proc
International Congress in Scandinavia on Chemical Engineering. Proceedings — Int Congr Scand Chem Eng Proc
International Congress in Vitreous Enamelling. Proceedings — Int Congr Vitreous Enamelling Proc
International Congress. International Solid Wastes and Public Cleansing Association. Proceedings — Int Congr Int Solid Wastes Public Clean Assoc Proc
International Congress. International Union for the Study of Social Insects — Int Congr Int Union Study Soc Insects
International Congress. IUSSI [*International Union for the Study of Social Insects*] — Int Congr IUSSI
International Congress of Acarology — Int Congr Acarol
International Congress of Anatomy — Int Congr Anat
International Congress of Angiology — Int Congr Angiol
International Congress of Animal Production. Proceedings — Int Congr Anim Prod Proc
International Congress of Applications of Lasers and Electro-Optics. Proceedings — Int Congr Appl Lasers Electro-Opt Proc
International Congress of Biochemistry — Int Congr Biochem
International Congress of Biochemistry. Abstracts — ICBCBE
International Congress of Biochemistry. Abstracts — Int Congr Biochem Abstr
International Congress of Biochemistry. Proceedings — Int Congr Biochem Proc
International Congress of Biogenetics — Int Congr Biogenet
International Congress of Chemical Engineering, Chemical Equipment Design, and Automation. Proceedings — Int Congr Chem Eng Chem Equip Des Autom Proc
International Congress of Chemotherapy. Proceedings — Int Congr Chemother Proc
International Congress of Child Neurology. Proceedings — Int Congr Child Neurol Proc
International Congress of Clinical Pathology. Eight Colloquia on Pathology — Int Congr Clin Pathol Eight Colloq Pathol

International Congress of Comparative Physiology and Biochemistry — Int Congr Comp Physiol Biochem
International Congress of Cybernetics and Systems — Int Congr Cybern Syst
International Congress of Endocrinology — Int Congr Endocrinol
International Congress of Entomology. Proceedings — ICEPAX
International Congress of Entomology. Proceedings — Int Congr Entomol Proc
International Congress of Essential Oils, Fragrances, and Flavours — Int Congr Essent Oils Fragrances Flavours
International Congress of Food Science and Technology — Int Congr Food Sci Technol
International Congress of Fruit Juices — Int Congr Fruit Juices
International Congress of Gastroenterology — Int Congr Gastroenterol
International Congress of Genetics. Selected Papers — Int Congr Genet Sel Pap
International Congress of Gerontology. Condensations of Papers — Int Congr Gerontol Condens Pap
International Congress of Hematology. Lectures — Int Congr Hematol Lect
International Congress of Heterocyclic Chemistry — Int Congr Heterocycl Chem
International Congress of Historical Sciences. Proceedings — Internatl Cong Hist Sci Proc
International Congress of Immunology — Int Congr Immunol
International Congress of Immunology Satellite Workshop — Int Congr Immunol Satell Workshop
International Congress of Industrial Chemistry — Int Congr Industr Chem
International Congress of Infectious Pathology. Communications — Int Congr Infect Pathol Commun
International Congress of Inflammation — Int Congr Inflammation
International Congress of Internal Medicine. Proceedings — Int Congr Intern Med Proc
International Congress of Linguists. Proceedings — ICL
International Congress of Liver Diseases — Int Congr Liver Dis
International Congress of Man Made Textiles. Economic and Technological Reports — Int Congr Man Made Text Econ Technol Rep
International Congress of Microbiology — Int Congr Microbiol
International Congress of Military Medicine and Pharmacy — Int Congr Mil Med Pharm
International Congress of Nephrology. Proceedings — Int Congr Nephrol Proc
International Congress of Neuropathology. Rapports et Discussions — Int Congr Neuropathol Rapp Discuss
International Congress of Nutrition — Int Congr Nutr
International Congress of Ophthalmology — Int Congr Ophthalmol
International Congress of Parasitology — Int Congr Parasitol
International Congress of Pesticide Chemistry — Int Congr Pest Chem
International Congress of Pharmaceutical Sciences of FIP [*Federation of Internationale Pharmacutique*]. Proceedings — Int Congr Pharm Sci FIP Proc
International Congress of Pharmacology. Proceedings — Int Congr Pharmacol Proc
International Congress of Physiological Sciences — Int Congr Physiol Sci
International Congress of Plant Pathology — Int Congr Plant Pathol
International Congress of Plant Protection — Int Congr Pl Prot
International Congress of Plant Protection. Proceedings. Conference — Int Congr Plant Prot Proc Conf
International Congress of Plant Tissue and Cell Culture. Proceedings — Int Congr Plant Tissue Cell Cult Proc
International Congress of Protozoology — Int Congr Protozool
International Congress of Protozoology. Proceedings. Congress — Int Congr Protozool Proc Congr
International Congress of Pure and Applied Chemistry — Int Congr Pure Appl Chem
International Congress of Quantum Chemistry — Int Congr Quantum Chem
International Congress of Quantum Chemistry. Proceedings — Int Congr Quantum Chem Proc
International Congress of Reproductive Immunology — Int Congr Reprod Immunol
International Congress of Soil Science — Int Congr Soil Sci
International Congress of Speleology. Abhandlungen — Int Congr Speleol Abh
International Congress of Systematic and Evolutionary Biology — Int Congr Syst Evol Biol
International Congress of Theoretical and Applied Mechanics — Int Congr Theor Appl Mech
International Congress of Unitas Malacologica Europaea — Int Congr Unitas Malacol Eur
International Congress of Zoology. Proceedings — Int Cong Zool Pr
International Congress on Amino Acid Research — Int Congr Amino Acid Res
International Congress on Animal Reproduction and Artificial Insemination — Int Congr Anim Reprod Artif Insemin
International Congress on Applied Mineralogy in the Minerals Industry — Int Congr Appl Mineral Miner Ind
International Congress on Astronautics. Proceedings — Int Congr Astronaut Proc
International Congress on Bioceramics and the Human Body — Int Congr Bioceram Hum Body
International Congress on Catalysis — Int Congr Catal
International Congress on Catalysis. Preprints — Int Congr Catal Prepr
International Congress on Catalysis. Proceedings — Int Congr Catal Proc
International Congress on Cataract Surgery — Int Congr Cataract Surg
International Congress on Combustion Engines. Proceedings — Int Congr Combust Engines Proc
International Congress on Diet and Nutrition — Int Congr Diet Nutr
International Congress on Diseases of Cattle — Int Congr Dis Cattle
International Congress on Diseases of the Chest — Int Congr Dis Chest
International Congress on Electro-Heat. Proceedings — Int Congr Electro Heat Proc
International Congress on Electron Microscopy. Proceedings — Int Congr Electron Micros Proc
International Congress on Engineering and Food — Int Congr Eng Food
International Congress on Glass — Int Congr Glass
International Congress on Glass Fibre Reinforced Cement. Proceedings — Int Congr Glass Fibre Reinf Cem Proc
International Congress on Glass. Technical Papers — Int Congr Glass Tech Pap
International Congress on Hair Research — Int Congr Hair Res
International Congress on Heat Treatment of Materials — Int Congr Heat Treat Mater
International Congress on High-Speed Photography and Photonics — Int Congr High Speed Photogr Photonics
International Congress on Hydrogen and Materials — Int Congr Hydrogen Mater
International Congress on Hydrogen in Metals — Int Congr Hydrogen Met
International Congress on Instrumentation in Aerospace Simulation Facilities — Int Congr Instrum Aerosp Simul Facil
International Congress on Instrumentation in Aerospace Simulation Facilities. Record — Int Congr Instrum Aerosp Simul Facil Rec
International Congress on Large Dams — Int Congr Large Dams
International Congress on Marine Corrosion and Fouling — Int Congr Mar Corros Fouling
International Congress on Medicinal Plant Research — Int Congr Med Plant Res
International Congress on Metallic Corrosion. Proceedings — Int Congr Met Corros Proc
International Congress on Neuromuscular Diseases — Int Congr Neuromuscular Dis
International Congress on Nitrogen Fixation — Int Congr Nitrogen Fixation
International Congress on Obesity. Proceedings — Int Congr Obes Proc
International Congress on Occupational Health — Int Congr Occup Health
International Congress on Phosphorus Compounds. Proceedings — Int Congr Phosphorus Compd Proc
International Congress on Photobiology — Int Congr Photobiol
International Congress on Photosynthesis. Proceedings — Int Congr Photosynth Proc
International Congress on Placental Proteins — Int Congr Placental Proteins
International Congress on Polymer Concretes — Int Congr Polym Concr
International Congress on Pteridines. Handbook — Int Congr Pteridines Handb
International Congress on Pteridines. Handbook — IPTHA5
International Congress on Reprography and Information — Int Congr Reprogr Inf
International Congress on Rheology — Int Congr Rheol
International Congress on Rock Mechanics — Int Congr Rock Mech
International Congress on Sedimentology — Int Congr Sedimentology
International Congress on Soilless Culture. Proceedings — Int Congr Soilless Cult Proc
International Congress on Static Electricity — Int Congr Static Electr
International Congress on Surface Active Substances — Int Congr Surf Act Subst
International Congress on the Chemistry of Cement — Int Congr Chem Cem
International Congress on the Chemistry of Cement. Proceedings — Int Cong Chem Cem Proc
International Congress on the Chemistry of Cement. Proceedings — Int Congr Chem Cem Proc
International Congress on the History of Oceanography — Int Congr Hist Oceanogr
International Congress on Toxicology — Int Congr Toxicol
International Congress on Ultra Low Doses — Int Congr Ultra Low Doses
International Congress on Waves and Instabilities in Plasmas — Int Congr Waves Instab Plasmas
International Congress. Precast Concrete Industry. Proceedings. Main and Supplementary Papers — Int Congr Precast Concr Ind Proc Main Suppl Pap
International Congress Series [*Elsevier Book Series*] — ICS
International Congress Series. Excerpta Medica — EXMDA
International Congress Series. Excerpta Medica [*Netherlands*] — Int Congr Ser Excerpta Med
International Congress. Society for the Advancement of Breeding Researches in Asia and Oceania — Int Congr Soc Advanc Breed Res Asia Oceania
International Congress. The Role of Viruses in Human Cancer — Int Congr Role Viruses Hum Cancer
International Construction — Int Constr
International Consumer Reports [*Database*] — ICR
International Contract — Internat Contract
International Controlled Release Pesticide Symposium. Proceedings — Int Controlled Release Pest Symp Proc
International Convocation on Immunology. Proceedings — Int Convoc Immunol Proc
International Copper Information Bulletin — Int Copper Inf Bull
International Copper Research Association Research Report — Int Copper Res Assoc Res Rep
International Corbicula Symposium — Int Corbicula Symp
International Correspondence Schools. Serial — Internat Correspondence Schools Serial
International Corrosion Conference Series — Int Corros Conf Ser
International Cosmic Ray Conference. Conference Papers — Int Cosmic Ray Conf Conf Pap
International Cotton Bulletin — Int Cotton Bull
International Council for the Exploration of the Sea. Cooperative Research Report — ICEXBO
International Council for the Exploration of the Sea. Cooperative Research Report — Int Counc Explor Sea Coop Res Rep
International Council for the Exploration of the Sea. Cooperative Research Report. Series A — Int Counc Explor Sea Coop Res Rep Ser A
International Council for the Exploration of the Sea. Cooperative Research Report. Series A — IXSAAZ
International Council for the Exploration of the Sea. Cooperative Research Report. Series B — Int Counc Explor Sea Coop Res Rep Ser B
International Council for the Exploration of the Sea. Cooperative Research Report. Series B — IXSBB5

International Council of Scientific Unions — Int Counc Sci Unions
International Council of Scientific Unions. Committee on Data for Science and Technology. CODATA Special Report — ICSU Comm Data Sci Technol CODATA Spec Rep
International Council of Scientific Unions. Inter-Union Commission on Geodynamics. Report — Int Counc Sci Unions Inter-Union Comm Geodynamics Rep
International Council of Scientific Unions. Inter-Union Commission on Geodynamics Scientific Report — ICSU Inter Union Comm Geodyn Sci Rep
International Council of Scientific Unions. Review — ICSU Rev
International Council of Scientific Unions. Scientific Committee on Problems of the Environment. SCOPE Report — ICSU Sci Comm Probl Environ SCOPE Rep
International Course on Materials Science — Int Course Mater Sci
International Course on New Methods in the Study of Transport across the Cell Membrane — Int Course New Methods Study Transp Cell Membr
International Course on Peritoneal Dialysis — Int Course Peritoneal Dial
International Court of Justice. Reports of Judgements, Advisory Opinions, and Orders — Rep ICJ
International Court of Justice. Yearbook — ICJYB
International Criminal Police Review — Int Crim Police Rev
International Critical Commentary — ICC
International Critical Commentary of the Holy Scriptures — ICC
International Cryogenic Engineering Conferences — Int Cryog Eng Conf
International Currency Report — ICR
International Currency Review — ICP
International Currency Review — Int Curr Rev
International Currency Review — Int Currency R
International Currency Review — Internat Currency R
International Current Meter Group. Report — Int Curr Meter Group Rep
International Cystic Fibrosis Congress — Int Cystic Fibrosis Congr
International Dairy Congress. Congress Report — Int Dairy Congr Congr Rep
International Dairy Congress. Proceedings — Int Dairy Congr Proc
International Dairy Federation. Annual Bulletin — IDABAC
International Dairy Federation. Annual Bulletin — Int Dairy Fed Annu Bull
International Dairy Federation. Bulletin — Int Dairy Fed Bull
International DATA Series. Series A — Int DATA Ser Ser A
International Defense Intelligence — IDI
International Defense Intelligence — Int Def Intell
International Defense Review [*Database*] — IDR
International Defense Review — Intnl Def R
International Demographics — Int Demogr
International Demographics — Intnl Demo
International Dental Journal — IDJOAS
International Dental Journal — Int Dent J
International Desalination and Water Reuse Quarterly — Int Desalin Water Reuse Q
International Development Abstracts — Int Dev Abstr
International Development Research Centre. Publication IDRC — IDCIDC
International Development Research Centre. Publication IDRC — Int Dev Res Cent Publ IDRC
International Development Research Centre. Technical Report. IDRC — Int Dev Res Cent Tech Rep IDRC
International Development Research Centre. Technical Studies IDRC-TS — IDRCE2
International Development Research Centre. Technical Studies IDRC-TS — Int Dev Res Cent Tech Stud IDRC-TS
International Development Review — Int Dev Rev
International Development Review — Int Develop R
International Development Review — Internat Development R
International Die Casting Exposition and Congress. Transactions — Int Die Cast Expos Congr Trans
International Digest — Int Dig
International Digest — Int'l Dig
International Digest of Health Legislation — IDHLA9
International Digest of Health Legislation — Int Dig Health Legis
International Directory of Executive Recruiters — Int Dir Exec Recruit
International Directory of the Nonwoven Fabrics Industry — Nonwn Fabr
International Dissolving Pulps Conference. Conference Papers — Int Dissolving Pulps Conf Conf Pap
International Dissolving Pulps Conference. Preprints — Int Dissolving Pulps Conf Prepr
International District Heating Association. Official Proceedings — Int Dist Heat Assoc Off Proc
International Dostoevsky Society. Bulletin — IDSB
International Dredging Abstracts — Int Dredg Abstr
International Dredging Review — Int Dredging Rev
International Drug Regulatory Monitor — Int Drug Regul Monit
International Drying Symposium — Int Drying Symp
International Dun's Market Identifiers [*Database*] — IDMI
International Dyer, Textile Printer, Bleacher, and Finisher — Int Dyer
International Dyer, Textile Printer, Bleacher, and Finisher — Int Dyer Text Printer Bleacher Finish
International Dyke Conference — Int Dyke Conf
International Economic Appraisal [*Database*] — IEAS
International Economic Indicators — Internat Econ Indicators
International Economic Indicators and Competitive Trends — Inter Econ Indic & Comp Tr
International Economic Indicators Database — IEIDATA
International Economic Review — IEC
International Economic Review — IER
International Economic Review — Int Ec R
International Economic Review — Int Econ R
International Economic Review — IntER
International Economic Review — Internat Econ R
International Economic Review — Internat Econom Rev
International Educational and Cultural Exchange [*Washington, DC*] — IECE
International Educational and Cultural Exchange — Int Ed & Cul Exch
International Educational and Cultural Exchange — Inter Ed & Cul Ex
International Electric Vehicle Symposium — Int Electr Veh Symp
International Electrodeposition Conference — Int El Dep Conf
International Electron Devices Meeting. Technical Digest — Int Electron Devices Meet Tech Dig
International Electronics Packaging Conference — Int Electron Packag Conf
International Electrotechnical Commission. Publications — Int Electrotech Comm Publ
International Enamelist — Int Enamelist
International Encyclopedia of Pharmacology and Therapeutics — IEPT
International Encyclopedia of the Social Sciences — IESS
International Endodontic Journal — Int Endod J
International Endothelial Cell Symposium — Int Endothelial Cell Symp
International Environment and Safety — Int Env Saf
International Environment and Safety — Int Environ Saf
International Environment Reporter — INER
International Erlangen-Nuremberg Symposium on Experimental Gerontology — Int Erlangen Nuremberg Symp Exp Gerontol
International Estuarine Research Conference — Int Estuarine Res Conf
International Executive — Int Exec
International Executive Transfers — Int Exec Trans
International Export Chemist — Int Export Chem
International Fabric Alternatives Forum. Proceedings — Int Fabr Altern Forum Proc
International Fair and Technical Meetings of Nuclear Industries — Int Fair Tech Meet Nucl Ind
International Family Planning Digest — Int Fam Plann Dig
International Family Planning Perspectives — Int Fam Plann Perspect
International Family Planning Perspectives — Internat Family Planning Perspectives
International Family Planning Perspectives and Digest — Internat Family Planning Perspectives and Dig
International Federation for Modern Languages and Literatures — IFMLL
International Federation of Agricultural Producers. News — IFAP Ne
International Federation of Automatic Control. Proceedings Series — Int Fed Autom Control Proc Ser
International Federation of Automatic Control Workshop on Modelling and Control of Biotechnical Processes — Int Fed Autom Control Workshop Modell Control Biotech Process
International Federation of Fruit Juice Producers. Scientific-Technical Commission. Reports — Int Fed Fruit Juice Prod Sci Tech Comm Rep
International Federation of Library Associations. News — IFLA News
International Federation of Societies of Cosmetic Chemists Congress — Int Fed Soc Cosmet Chem Congr
International Fermentation Symposium — Int Ferment Symp
International Fertilizer Congress. Papers of Foreign Participants — Int Fert Congr Pap Foreign Participants
International Fertilizer Development Center. Special Publication — Int Fert Dev Cent Spec Publ
International Fiber Optics and Communications — IFOC
International Fiber Optics and Communications Exposition in the US Papers — Int Fiber Opt Commun Expos US Pap
International Fiction Review — IFR
International Fiction Review — Int Fict R
International Field Emission Symposium — Int Field Emiss Symp
International Field Year for the Great Lakes. Bulletin — IFYGL Bull
International Field Year for the Great Lakes. Technical Manual Series — Int Field Year Great Lakes Tech Man Ser
International Film Guide — Interntl F G
International Finance Alert [*Database*] — IFA
International Finance. Chase Manhattan Bank — Internat Fin Chase
International Financial Law Review — IFL
International Financial Law Review — TIC
International Financial News Survey — IFNS
International Financial Statistics [*Database*] — IFS
International Fire Chief — Int Fire Chief
International Fire Fighter — Int Fire Fighter
International Flame Research Foundation. Members Conference — Int Flame Res Found Members Conf
International Flavours and Food Additives — Int Flavours Food Addit
International Fluidized-Bed-Combustion and Applied-Technology Symposium — Int Fluid Bed Combust Appl Technol Symp
International Folk Music Council. Journal — IFMCJ
International Folk Music Council. Journal — Int Folk Mus Council Jl
International Folk Music Council. Yearbook — IFMCY
International Folklore Bibliography — Int Folk Bibliogr
International Food Industries Congress. Proceedings — Int Food Ind Congr Proc
International Forging Conference — Int Forg Conf
International Forum for Logotherapy — Int Forum Logotherapy
International Forum on Information and Documentation — Int Forum Inf and Doc
International Forum on Information and Documentation — Int Forum Inf Docum
International Foundry Conference. Papers — Int Foundry Conf Pap
International Foundry Congress. Congress Papers — IFCPD
International Foundry Congress. Congress Papers [*Switzerland*] — Int Foundry Cong Congr Pap
International Free Trade Union News — Int Free Trade Un
International Freighting Weekly — In Freight
International Freighting Weekly — Int Freight
International Fruit World — Int Fruit World
International Fundamental Research Symposium — Int Fund Res Symp
International GABA B Symposium — Int GABA B Symp

International Galvanizing Conference. Edited Proceedings — Int Galvanizing Conf Ed Proc
International Gas Conference. Transactions and Papers — Int Gas Conf Trans Pap
International Gas Technology Highlights — Int Gas Technol Highlights
International Geochemical Exploration Symposium — Int Geochem Explor Symp
International Geochemical Exploration Symposium. Proceedings — Int Geochem Explor Symp Proc
International Geographical Congress — Int Geogr Congr
International Geographical Congress. Papers - Congres International de Geographie. Communications — Int Geogr Congr Pap - Congr Int Geogr Commun
International Geographical Congress. Report. Verhandlungen — Int Geog Cong Rp Verh
International Geological Congress — Int Geol Congr
International Geological Congress. Abstracts. Congres Geologique International. Resumes — Int Geol Congr Abstr Congr Geol Int Resumes
International Geological Congress. Report of the Session — Int Geol Congr Rep Sess
International Geology Review — Int Geol Rev
International Geology Review — Internat Geology Rev
International Geophysical Year. Rocket Report — Int Geophys Year Rocket Rep
International Geophysical Year. World Data Center. A. General Report Series — IGY World Data Center A Gen Rept Ser
International Geophysical Year. World Data Center. A. Glaciological Report Series — IGY World Data Center A Glaciolog Rept Ser
International Geophysics Series: A Series of Monographs — Int Geophys Ser
International Giessener Symposium on Experimental Gerontology — Int Giessener Symp Exp Gerontol
International Glaciospeleological Survey. Bulletin — Int Glaciospeleological Surv Bull
International Glass Review — Int Glass Rev
International Goat and Sheep Research — INRSDH
International Goat and Sheep Research — Int Goat Sheep Res
International Goat and Sheep Research — Internatl Goat Sheep Res
International Gothenburg Symposium on Chemical Treatment — Int Gothenburg Symp Chem Treat
International Gothenburg Symposium on Chemical Water and Wastewater Treatment — Int Gothenburg Symp Chem Water Wastewater Treat
International Grassland Congress — Int Grassl Congr
International Grassland Congress. Proceedings — Int Grassl Congr Proc
International Green Crop Drying Congress — Int Green Crop Drying Congr
International Gstaad Symposium. Proceedings — Int Gstaad Symp Proc
International Guide to Classical Studies — IGCS
International Guide to Classical Studies — Int G Class Stud
International Guide to Classical Studies — Int Guide Classical Stud
International Guide to Classical Studies — IntGuC
International Guide to Medieval Studies — IGMS
International Gymnast — GING
International Gymnast — Int Gym
International Haarmann and Reimer Symposium on Fragrance and Flavor Substances — Int Haarmann Reimer Symp Fragrance Flavor Subst
International Health News — Int Health News
International Health Physics Data [*Database*] — IHPD
International Heat Pipe Conference. Papers — Int Heat Pipe Conf Pap
International Heat Transfer Conference — Int Heat Transfer Conf
International Heat Treatment Conference. Proceedings — Int Heat Treat Conf Proc
International Henry Miller Letter — IHML
International Herald Tribune — IHT
International Herald Tribune — NHT
International Histological Classification of Tumors — IHCTA2
International Histological Classification of Tumors — Int Histol Classif Tumors
International History Review — Int Hist R
International Horn Society Newsletter — IHSN
International Horticulture Congress — Int Hort Congr
International Hospital Equipment — IHE
International Hotel Review — IHR
International Humanism Magazine [*Netherlands*] — IH
International Hydrocarbon Processing — Int Hydrocarbon Process
International Hydrographic Conference — Int Hydrogr Conf
International Hydrographic Review — Int Hyd Rev
International Hydrographic Review — Int Hydrogr Rev
International Hydrological Decade. Newsletter — Int Hydrol Decade Newsl
International Hydrology Symposium — Int Hydrol Symp
International Hyperbaric Congress Proceedings — Int Hyperbaric Congr Proc
International Hypersonics Conference — Int Hypersonics Conf
International IEEE VLSI [*Very-Large-Scale Integration*] **Multilevel Interconnection Conference** — Int IEEE VLSI Multilevel Interconnect Conf
International IGT Symposium on Gas, Oil, Coal, and Environmental Biotechnolgoy — Int IGT Symp Gas Oil Coal Environ Biotechnol
International Immunobiological Symposium. Proceedings — Int Immunobiol Symp Proc
International Immunology — Int Immunol
International Index — Int Ind
International Index — Int Index
International Index. Annual Cumulation — Int Index Annu Cumu
International Index to Film Periodicals — IIFP
International Index to Film Periodicals — Int Ind Film
International Index to Film Periodicals — Int Index Film Period
International Index to Multi-Media Information — IIMMI
International Index to Multi-Media Information — Int Index Multi Media Inf
International Index to Periodicals — Int Index Period
International Industrial Biotechnology — Int Ind Biotechnol
International Industrial Diamond Symposium — Int Ind Diamond Symp
International Industry — Int Ind
International Info — Intnl Info
International Information System of the Agricultural Sciences and Technology [*Database*] — AGRIS
International Institute for Applied Systems Analysis. Collaborative Proceedings Series — Int Inst Appl Syst Anal Collab Proc Ser
International Institute for Applied Systems Analysis. Collaborative Publications — IIASA Collab Publ
International Institute for Applied Systems Analysis. Proceedings Series — Int Inst Appl Syst Anal Proc Ser
International Institute for Applied Systems Analysis. Professional Paper — IIASA Prof Pap
International Institute for Applied Systems Analysis. Professional Paper — Int Inst Appl Syst Anal Prof Pap
International Institute for Applied Systems Analysis. Research Memorandum — IIASA Res Memo
International Institute for Applied Systems Analysis. Research Memorandum — Int Inst Appl Syst Anal Res Mem
International Institute for Applied Systems Analysis. Research Reports — IIASA Res Rep
International Institute for Applied Systems Analysis. Research Reports — IIASA Research Reports
International Institute for Conservation of Historic and Artistic Works. Abstracts — Int Inst Conserv Hist Artistic Works Abstr
International Institute for Labour Studies Bulletin — Int Inst Labour Stud Bull
International Institute for Land Reclamation and Improvement. Annual Report [*A publication*] — Int Inst Land Reclam Improv Annu Rep
International Institute for Land Reclamation and Improvement. Bulletin — Int Inst Land Reclam Improv Bull
International Institute for Land Reclamation and Improvement. ILRI Publication — Int Inst Land Reclam Improv ILRI Publ
International Institute for Land Reclamation and Improvement (Netherlands). Bibliography — Int Inst Land Reclam Impr (Netherlands) Bibliogr
International Institute for Land Reclamation and Improvement (Netherlands). Bulletin — Int Inst Land Reclam Impr (Netherlands) Bull
International Institute for Land Reclamation and Improvement (Netherlands). Publication — Int Inst Land Reclam Impr (Netherlands) Publ
International Institute for Land Reclamation and Improvement (Netherlands). Publication — Int Inst Land Reclam Improv (Neth) Pub
International Institute for Land Reclamation and Improvement. Publication — Int Inst Land Reclam Improv Publ
International Institute for Land Reclamation and Improvement. Publication — Int Inst Ld Reclam Improv
International Institute for Sugar Beet Research. Journal — Int Inst Sugar Beet Res J
International Institute of Philosophy. Symposia — Int Inst Ph
International Institute of Refrigeration. Bulletin [*Paris*] — Bull Int Inst Ref
International Institute of Refrigeration. Bulletin — Int Inst Refrig Bull
International Institute of Refrigeration. Bulletin. Annexe — Int Inst Refrig Bull Annexe
International Institute of Seismology and Earthquake Engineering. Bulletin — Int Inst Seismol Earthquake Eng Bull
International Institute of Seismology and Earthquake Engineering. Individual Studies by Participants — Int Inst Seismol Earthquake Eng Individ Stud
International Institute of Synthetic Rubber Producers. Annual Meeting Proceedings — Int Inst Synth Rubber Prod Annu Meet Proc
International Institute on the Prevention and Treatment of Alcoholism. Papers — Int Inst Prev Treat Alcohol Pap
International Institution for Production Engineering Research Annals — Int Inst Prod Eng Res Ann
International Instrumentation Symposium. Proceedings — Int Instrum Symp Proc
International Insurance Monitor — IIM
International Insurance Monitor — IMO
International Interest and Exchange Rate Database — FXBASE
International Interpreter — Int Interp
International Intertrade Index [*Database*] — III
International Investment Monitor [*Database*] — IIM
International Iron and Steel Congress. Proceedings — Int Iron Steel Congr Proc
International Iron and Steel Institute. Annual Meeting and Conference. Panel Discussion Speeches — Int Iron Steel Inst Annu Meet Conf Panel Discuss Speeches
International IUPAP [*International Union of Pure and Applied Physics*] **Conference on Few Body Problems in Physics** — Int IUPAP Conf Few Body Probl Phys
International Journal — IJ
International Journal — Int J
International Journal — Internat J
International Journal — Internatl Jour
International Journal — Int'l J
International Journal. Academy of Ichthyology — IJAIDA
International Journal. Academy of Ichthyology — Int J Acad Ichthyol
International Journal. Computers and Fluids — Internat J Comput and Fluids
International Journal for Development Technology — Int J Dev Technol
International Journal for Housing Science and Its Applications — Int J Hous Sci Appl
International Journal for Housing Science and Its Applications — Int J Housing Sc Applications
International Journal for Hybrid Microelectronics — Int J Hybrid Microelectron
International Journal for Numerical and Analytical Methods in Geomechanics [*A publication*] — IJNGD
International Journal for Numerical and Analytical Methods in Geomechanics [*A publication*] — Int J Num Anal Meth Geomech
International Journal for Numerical and Analytical Methods in Geomechanics [*A publication*] — Int J Numer Anal Methods Geomech

International Journal for Numerical and Analytical Methods in Geomechanics — Int J Numer and Anal Methods Geomech
International Journal for Numerical and Analytical Methods in Geomechanics [*A publication*] — Internat J Numer Analyt Methods Geomech
International Journal for Numerical Methods in Engineering — Int J Num Meth Eng
International Journal for Numerical Methods in Engineering — Int J Num Meth Engng
International Journal for Numerical Methods in Engineering — Int J Numer Methods Eng
International Journal for Numerical Methods in Engineering — Int J Numer Methods Engng
International Journal for Numerical Methods in Engineering — Internat J Numer Methods Engrg
International Journal for Numerical Methods in Fluids — Int J Numer Methods Fluids
International Journal for Numerical Methods in Fluids — Internat J Numer Methods Fluids
International Journal for Parasitology — Int J Paras
International Journal for Parasitology — Int J Parasitol
International Journal for Philosophy of Religion — Int J Ph Rel
International Journal for Philosophy of Religion — Int J Phil
International Journal for Philosophy of Religion — Int J Phil Relig
International Journal for Philosophy of Religion — Int J Philos Relig
International Journal for Philosophy of Religion [*The Hague*] — IntJPhilRel
International Journal for Philosophy of Religion — PIPR
International Journal for Quality in Health Caree — Int J Qual Health Care
International Journal for Radiation Physics and Chemistry [*Later, Radiation Physics and Chemistry*] — Int J Rad P
International Journal for Radiation Physics and Chemistry [*Later, Radiation Physics and Chemistry*] — Int J Radiat Phys and Chem
International Journal for Radiation Physics and Chemistry [*Later, Radiation Physics and Chemistry*] — Int J Radiat Phys Chem
International Journal for the Advancement of Counselling — Int J Adv Couns
International Journal for the Study of Animal Problems — Int J Stud Anim Probl
International Journal for the Study of Animal Problems — Int J Study Anim Probl
International Journal for Vitamin and Nutrition Research — Int J Vit N
International Journal for Vitamin and Nutrition Research — Int J Vitam Nutr Res
International Journal for Vitamin and Nutrition Research. Supplement — Int J Vitam Nutr Res Suppl
International Journal. Japan Society for Precision Engineering — Int J Jpn Soc Precis Eng
International Journal of Acarology — IJOADM
International Journal of Acarology — Int J Acarol
International Journal of Accounting — Internat J Accounting
International Journal of Adaptive Control and Signal Processing — Internal J Adapt Control Signal Process
International Journal of Adhesion and Adhesives [*England*] — Int J Adhes Adhes
International Journal of Adhesion and Adhesives — Int J Adhesion & Adhesives
International Journal of Adolescent Medicine and Health — IJAHE8
International Journal of Adolescent Medicine and Health — Int J Adolesc Med Health
International Journal of Adult and Youth Education — Int J Adult Youth Ed
International Journal of Adult Orthodontics and Orthognathic Surgery — Int J Adult Orthodon Orthognath Surg
International Journal of Advertising — IJA
International Journal of Advertising — Int Jnl Adv
International Journal of African Historical Studies — IJAHS
International Journal of African Historical Studies — Int J Afr H
International Journal of African Historical Studies — Int J Afr Hist Stud
International Journal of African Historical Studies — Int J Afr Stud
International Journal of African Historical Studies — Int J Afric Hist Stud
International Journal of African Historical Studies — IntJA
International Journal of African Historical Studies — PIAH
International Journal of Aging and Human Development — AGHDAK
International Journal of Aging and Human Development — IAHD
International Journal of Aging and Human Development — Int J Aging
International Journal of Aging and Human Development — Int J Aging Hum Dev
International Journal of Agrarian Affairs — Int J A Aff
International Journal of Agrarian Affairs — Int J Ag Affairs
International Journal of Agrarian Affairs — Int J Agr Aff
International Journal of Air and Water Pollution — IAPWA
International Journal of Air and Water Pollution [*England*] — Int J Air Water Pollut
International Journal of Air Pollution — IJAPA
International Journal of Air Pollution — Int J Air Pollut
International Journal of Algebra and Computation — Internal J Algebra Comput
International Journal of Ambient Energy — Int J Amb Energy
International Journal of Ambient Energy [*England*] — Int J Ambient Energy
International Journal of Ambient Energy — Intl Jnl of Ambient Energy
International Journal of American Linguistics — IJAL
International Journal of American Linguistics — Int J Am Ling
International Journal of American Linguistics — Int J Amer
International Journal of American Linguistics — PIAL
International Journal of American Linguistics. Memoir — IJALM
International Journal of American Linguistics. Supplement — IJALS
International Journal of Andrology — IJA
International Journal of Andrology — IJANDP
International Journal of Andrology — Int J Androl
International Journal of Andrology — Int J Andrology
International Journal of Andrology. Supplement — IJSPDJ
International Journal of Andrology. Supplement — Int J Androl Suppl
International Journal of Anesthesia — Int J Anesth
International Journal of Animal Sciences — Int J Anim Sci
International Journal of Antimicrobial Agents — Int J Antimicrob Agents
International Journal of Applied Radiation and Isotopes — IJARAY
International Journal of Applied Radiation and Isotopes — Int J A Rad
International Journal of Applied Radiation and Isotopes — Int J Appl Radiat
International Journal of Applied Radiation and Isotopes — Int J Appl Radiat and Isot
International Journal of Applied Radiation and Isotopes — Int J Appl Radiat Isot
International Journal of Applied Radiation and Isotopes — Int J Appl Radiat Isotopes
International Journal of Applied Science and Computations — Internat J Appl Sci Comput
International Journal of Approximate Reasoning — Internat J Approx Reason
International Journal of Artificial Organs — IJAOD
International Journal of Artificial Organs — IJAODS
International Journal of Artificial Organs — Int J Artif Organs
International Journal of Arts Medicine — IJAM
International Journal of Bank Marketing — IJB
International Journal of Behavioral Development — IJBDDY
International Journal of Behavioral Development — Int J Behav Dev
International Journal of Behavioral Geriatrics — Int J Behav Geriatrics
International Journal of Bifurcation and Chaos in Applied Sciences and Engineering — Internat J Bifur Chaos Appl Sci Engrg
International Journal of Biochemistry — IJBOBV
International Journal of Biochemistry — Int J Bioch
International Journal of Biochemistry — Int J Biochem
International Journal of Biochemistry and Cell Biology — Int J Biochem Cell Biol
International Journal of Bio-Chromatography — Int J Bio Chromatogr
International Journal of Bioclimatology and Biometeorology — Int J Bioclim
International Journal of Bioclimatology and Biometeorology — Int J Bioclim Biomet
International Journal of Bioclimatology and Biometeorology — Int J Bioclimatol Biometeorol
International Journal of Biological Macromolecules — IJBMDR
International Journal of Biological Macromolecules — Int J Biol Macromol
International Journal of Biological Markers — Int J Biol Markers
International Journal of Biological Research in Pregnancy — IJBPD2
International Journal of Biological Research in Pregnancy — Int J Biol Res Pregnancy
International Journal of Biomedical Computing — IJBCB
International Journal of Bio-Medical Computing — IJBCBT
International Journal of Bio-Medical Computing — Int J Bio-M
International Journal of Biomedical Computing — Int J Biomed Comp
International Journal of Bio-Medical Computing — Int J Bio-Med Comput
International Journal of Bio-Medical Computing — Internat J Bio-Med Comput
International Journal of Biomedical Engineering — IJBEAY
International Journal of Biomedical Engineering — Int J Biomed Eng
International Journal of Biometeorology — IJBMAO
International Journal of Biometeorology — Int J Biom
International Journal of Biometeorology — Int J Biometeorol
International Journal of Cancer — IJCNAW
International Journal of Cancer — Int J Canc
International Journal of Cancer — Int J Cancer
International Journal of Cancer Control and Prevention — ICCPDQ
International Journal of Cancer Control and Prevention — Int J Cancer Control Prev
International Journal of Cancer. Supplement — Int J Cancer Suppl
International Journal of Cardiac Imaging — Int J Card Imaging
International Journal of Cardiology — IJCDD5
International Journal of Cardiology — Int J Cardiol
International Journal of Cast Metals Research — Int J Cast Met Res
International Journal of Cell Cloning — IJCCE3
International Journal of Cell Cloning — Int J Cell Cloning
International Journal of Cement Composites — Int J Cement Composites
International Journal of Cement Composites and Lightweight Concrete — Int J Cem Compos Lightweight Concr
International Journal of Chemical Kinetics — IJCKBO
International Journal of Chemical Kinetics — Int J Ch K
International Journal of Chemical Kinetics — Int J Chem Kinet
International Journal of Child Psychotherapy — Int J Child
International Journal of Chronobiology — IJCBA
International Journal of Chronobiology — IJCBAU
International Journal of Chronobiology — Int J Chronobiol
International Journal of Circuit Theory and Applications — Int J Circuit Theory and Appl
International Journal of Circuit Theory and Applications — Int J Circuit Theory Appl
International Journal of Circuit Theory and Applications — Internat J Circuit Theory Appl
International Journal of Climatology — Int J Clim
International Journal of Clinical and Experimental Hypnosis — IJEHA
International Journal of Clinical and Experimental Hypnosis — IJEHAO
International Journal of Clinical and Experimental Hypnosis — Int J C E Hy
International Journal of Clinical and Experimental Hypnosis — Int J Clin & Exp Hypnosis
International Journal of Clinical and Experimental Hypnosis — Int J Clin Exp Hypn
International Journal of Clinical and Experimental Hypnosis — Int J Clin Exp Hypnos
International Journal of Clinical and Laboratory Research — Int J Clin Lab Res
International Journal of Clinical Monitoring and Computing — IJMCEJ
International Journal of Clinical Monitoring and Computing — Int J Clin Monit Comput
International Journal of Clinical Neuropsychology — IJCNF2
International Journal of Clinical Neuropsychology — Int J Clin Neuropsychol

International Journal of Clinical Pharmacology and Biopharmacy — IJCBD
International Journal of Clinical Pharmacology and Biopharmacy — IJCBDX
International Journal of Clinical Pharmacology and Biopharmacy — Int J Clin
International Journal of Clinical Pharmacology and Biopharmacy — Int J Clin Pharmacol Biopharm
International Journal of Clinical Pharmacology and Therapeutics — Int J Clin Pharmacol Ther
International Journal of Clinical Pharmacology Research — CPHRDE
International Journal of Clinical Pharmacology Research — Int J Clin Pharm Res
International Journal of Clinical Pharmacology Research — Int J Clin Pharmacol Res
International Journal of Clinical Pharmacology, Therapy, and Toxicology — IJCPB5
International Journal of Clinical Pharmacology, Therapy, and Toxicology — Int J Clin Pharm
International Journal of Clinical Pharmacology, Therapy, and Toxicology — Int J Clin Pharmacol Ther Toxicol
International Journal of Coal Geology — IJCGD
International Journal of Coal Geology [*Netherlands*] — Int J Coal Geol
International Journal of Colorectal Disease — Int J Colorectal Dis
International Journal of Community Psychiatry and Experimental Psychotherapy — Int J Com P
International Journal of Comparative and Applied Criminal Justice — Intl J Comp and App Crim Just
International Journal of Comparative Sociology — IJCS
International Journal of Comparative Sociology — Int J Comp
International Journal of Comparative Sociology — Int J Comp Soc
International Journal of Comparative Sociology — Int J Comp Sociol
International Journal of Comparative Sociology — Int J Comp Sociology
International Journal of Comparative Sociology — Int J Compar Sociol
International Journal of Comparative Sociology — Internat J Comp Sociol
International Journal of Comparative Sociology — PICS
International Journal of Comparative Sociology. York University. Department of Sociology and Anthropology [*Toronto, Canada*] — YU/IJCS
International Journal of Computational Geometry and Applications — Internat J Comput Geom Appl
International Journal of Computer and Information Sciences — IJC
International Journal of Computer and Information Sciences — IJCIS
International Journal of Computer and Information Sciences — Int J C Inf
International Journal of Computer and Information Sciences — Int J Comput & Inf Sci
International Journal of Computer and Information Sciences — Internat J Comput Inform Sci
International Journal of Computer and Information Sciences — Internat J Comput Information Sci
International Journal of Computer Mathematics — Int J Com M
International Journal of Computer Mathematics — Int J Comput Math
International Journal of Computer Mathematics. Section A. Programming Languages. Theory and Methods — Int J Comput Math Sect A
International Journal of Computer Mathematics. Section A. Programming Languages. Theory and Methods — Internat J Comput Math
International Journal of Computer Mathematics. Section B. Computational Methods — Int J Comput Math Sect B
International Journal of Contemporary Sociology — Int J Con S
International Journal of Contemporary Sociology — Int J Contemp Sociol
International Journal of Contemporary Sociology — Int J Contemporary Sociol
International Journal of Control — Int J Contr
International Journal of Control — Int J Control
International Journal of Control — Internat J Control
International Journal of Cosmetic Science — IJCMDW
International Journal of Cosmetic Science — Int J Cosmet Sci
International Journal of Criminology and Penology — Int J Criminology Penology
International Journal of Crude Drug Research — IJCREE
International Journal of Crude Drug Research — Int J Crude Drug Res
International Journal of Dermatology — IJDEBB
International Journal of Dermatology — Int J Dermatol
International Journal of Developmental Biology — Int J Dev Biol
International Journal of Developmental Neuroscience — IJDN
International Journal of Developmental Neuroscience — IJDND6
International Journal of Developmental Neuroscience — Int J Dev Neurosci
International Journal of Dravidian Linguistics — IJDL
International Journal of Dravidian Linguistics — Int J Dravid Ling
International Journal of Earthquake Engineering and Structural Dynamics — Int J Earthquake Eng Struct Dyn
International Journal of Eating Disorders — INDIDJ
International Journal of Eating Disorders — Int J Eat Disor
International Journal of Eating Disorders — Int J Eating Disord
International Journal of Ecology and Environmental Sciences — IJESDQ
International Journal of Ecology and Environmental Sciences — Int J Ecol Environ Sci
International Journal of Electrical Engineering Education — Int J El En
International Journal of Electrical Engineering Education — Int J Elec Eng Educ
International Journal of Electrical Engineering Education — Int J Elec Engng Educ
International Journal of Electrical Engineering Education — Int J Electr Eng Educ
International Journal of Electrical Power Amp Energy Systems [*England*] — Int J Electr Power Energy Syst
International Journal of Electronics — Int J Elect
International Journal of Electronics — Int J Electron
International Journal of Electronics — Internat J Electron
International Journal of Energy Research — IJERD
International Journal of Energy Research — Int J Energy Res
International Journal of Energy Systems — Int J Energy Syst
International Journal of Engineering Fluid Mechanics — Int J Eng Fluid Mech
International Journal of Engineering Science — Int J Eng S
International Journal of Engineering Science — Int J Eng Sci
International Journal of Engineering Science — Int J Engng Sci
International Journal of Engineering Science — Internat J Engng Science
International Journal of Engineering Science — Internat J Engrg Sci
International Journal of Entomology — IJENEC
International Journal of Entomology — Int J Entomol
International Journal of Environmental Analytical Chemistry — IJEAA3
International Journal of Environmental Analytical Chemistry — Int J Environ Anal Chem
International Journal of Environmental Health Research — Int J Environ Health Res
International Journal of Environmental Pollution — Int J Environ Pollut
International Journal of Environmental Studies — IJES
International Journal of Environmental Studies — IJEVAW
International Journal of Environmental Studies — Int J Env S
International Journal of Environmental Studies — Int J Environ Stud
International Journal of Environmental Studies — Int J Environ Studies
International Journal of Environmental Studies — Internat J Environmental Studies
International Journal of Environmental Studies — Int'l J Envir Stud
International Journal of Epidemiology — IJEPBF
International Journal of Epidemiology — Int J Epid
International Journal of Epidemiology — Int J Epidemiol
International Journal of Equilibrium Research — Int J Equilib Res
International Journal of Ethics — IJE
International Journal of Ethics — Int J Ethics
International Journal of Experimental Medicine — Int J Exp Med
International Journal of Experimental Pathology — Int J Exp Pathol
International Journal of Family Psychiatry — IJFPDM
International Journal of Family Psychiatry — Int J Fam Psychiatry
International Journal of Fatigue — Int J Fatigue
International Journal of Fertility — INJFA3
International Journal of Fertility — Int J Fert
International Journal of Fertility — Int J Fertil
International Journal of Fertility — Internat J Fertil
International Journal of Fertility and Menopausal Studies — Int J Fertil Menopausal Stud
International Journal of Finance — IJOF
International Journal of Food Microbiology — IJFMDD
International Journal of Food Microbiology — Int J F Mic
International Journal of Food Microbiology — Int J Food Microbiol
International Journal of Food Science and Technology — Int J Food Sci Technol
International Journal of Food Sciences and Nutrition — Int J Food Sci Nutr
International Journal of Food Technology and Food Process Engineering — Int J Food Technol Food Process Eng
International Journal of Forensic Dentistry — Int J Forensic Dent
International Journal of Forensic Document Examiners — Int J Forensic Doc Exam
International Journal of Foundations of Computer Science — Internat J Found Comput Sci
International Journal of Fracture — Int J Fract
International Journal of Fracture — Internat J Fracture
International Journal of Fracture Mechanics — Int J Fract Mech
International Journal of Fusion Energy — Int J Fusion Energy
International Journal of Game Theory — Int J Game Theory
International Journal of Game Theory — Internat J Game Theory
International Journal of General Systems — IJGSAX
International Journal of General Systems — Int J Gen S
International Journal of General Systems — Int J Gen Syst
International Journal of General Systems — Internat J Gen Syst
International Journal of General Systems — Internat J Gen Systems
International Journal of Genome Research — Int J Genome Res
International Journal of Geriatric Psychiatry — Int J Geriatr Psychiatry
International Journal of Government Auditing — IGA
International Journal of Group Psychotherapy — IJGPA
International Journal of Group Psychotherapy — IJGPAO
International Journal of Group Psychotherapy — Int J Group Psychother
International Journal of Group Psychotherapy — Int J Grp P
International Journal of Group Tensions — Int J Group Tensions
International Journal of Group Tensions — Int J Grp T
International Journal of Gynaecology and Obstetrics — IJGOAL
International Journal of Gynaecology and Obstetrics — Int J Gynaecol Obstet
International Journal of Gynecological Pathology — IJGPDR
International Journal of Gynecological Pathology — Int J Gynecol Pathol
International Journal of Health Education — IJHE
International Journal of Health Education — Int J Healt
International Journal of Health Education — Int J Health Educ
International Journal of Health Planning and Management — Int J Health Plann Manage
International Journal of Health Services — HS
International Journal of Health Services — IJUSC3
International Journal of Health Services — Int J He Se
International Journal of Health Services — Int J Health Serv
International Journal of Health Services — Int J Hlth Serv
International Journal of Heat and Fluid Flow [*England*] — Int J Heat Fluid Flow
International Journal of Heat and Fluid Flow — Internat J Heat Fluid Flow
International Journal of Heat and Mass Transfer — IJHMA
International Journal of Heat and Mass Transfer — Int J Heat
International Journal of Heat and Mass Transfer — Int J Heat & Mass Transfer
International Journal of Heat and Mass Transfer — Int J Heat Mass Transfer
International Journal of Heat and Mass Transfer — Internat J Heat Mass Transfer
International Journal of Hematology — Int J Hematol

International Journal of High Technology Ceramics — Int J High Technol Ceram
International Journal of Hospitality Management — Int J Hosp Manage
International Journal of Hydrogen Energy — Int J Hydrogen Energy
International Journal of Hygiene and Environmental Medicine — Int J Hyg Environ Med
International Journal of Hyperthermia — IJHYEQ
International Journal of Hyperthermia — Int J Hyperthermia
International Journal of Immunochemistry [*England*] — Int J Immunochem
International Journal of Immunopathology and Pharmacology — Int J Immunopathol Pharmacol
International Journal of Immunopharmacology — IJIMDS
International Journal of Immunopharmacology — Int J Immunopharmacol
International Journal of Immunotherapy — IJIMET
International Journal of Immunotherapy — Int J Immunother
International Journal of Impotence Research — Int J Impot Res
International Journal of Industrial Medicine and Surgery — Int J Ind Med Surg
International Journal of Industrial Organization — IJI
International Journal of Information and Management Sciences — Internat J Inform Management Sci
International Journal of Infrared and Millimeter Waves [*United States*] — Int J Infrared Millim Waves
International Journal of Infrared and Millimeter Waves — Int J Infrared Millimeter Waves
International Journal of Insect Morphology and Embryology — IJIMBQ
International Journal of Insect Morphology and Embryology — Int J Insect Morph Embryol
International Journal of Insect Morphology and Embryology — Int J Insect Morphol Embryol
International Journal of Institutional Management in Higher Education — Int J Inst Mangt in Higher Educ
International Journal of Instructional Media — IM
International Journal of Instructional Media — Int J Instr Media
International Journal of Intercultural Relations — IJIR
International Journal of Invertebrate Reproduction — IJIRD9
International Journal of Invertebrate Reproduction — Int J Invertebr Reprod
International Journal of Invertebrate Reproduction and Development — IJIDE2
International Journal of Invertebrate Reproduction and Development — Int J Invertebr Reprod Dev
International Journal of Language and Philosophy. Foundations of Language — Found Language
International Journal of Law and Psychiatry — Int J Law Psychiatry
International Journal of Law and Psychiatry — Intl J L and Psych
International Journal of Law and Science — Int J Law Sci
International Journal of Law Libraries — IJLL
International Journal of Law Libraries — Int J Law Lib
International Journal of Law Libraries — Int J Law Libr
International Journal of Law Libraries — Int J Law Librs
International Journal of Law Libraries — Intl JL Lib
International Journal of Legal Information — Intl J Legal Info
International Journal of Legal Information — Int'l J Legal Infor
International Journal of Legal Medicine — Int J Legal
International Journal of Legal Medicine — Int J Legal Med
International Journal of Leprosy [*Later, International Journal of Leprosy and Other Mycobacterial Diseases*] — IJLEAG
International Journal of Leprosy [*Later, International Journal of Leprosy and Other Mycobacterial Diseases*] — Int J Lepr
International Journal of Leprosy [*Later, International Journal of Leprosy and Other Mycobacterial Diseases*] — Internat J Leprosy
International Journal of Leprosy and Other Mycobacterial Diseases — Int J Lepr Other Mycobact Dis
International Journal of Lifelong Education — Int J Life Educ
International Journal of Machine Tool Design and Research — Int J Mach
International Journal of Machine Tool Design and Research — Int J Mach Tool Des Res
International Journal of Magnetism — Int J Magn
International Journal of Mammalian Biology — Int J Mamm Biol
International Journal of Man-Machine Studies — Int J Man-M
International Journal of Man-Machine Studies — Int J Man-Mach Stud
International Journal of Man-Machine Studies — Internat J Man-Mach Stud
International Journal of Man Machine Studies — Internat J Man-Machine Studies
International Journal of Manpower — IJM
International Journal of Manpower — Int J Manpower
International Journal of Masonry Construction — Int J Masonry Constr
International Journal of Mass Spectrometry and Ion Physics [*Later, International Journal of Mass Spectrometry and Ion Processes*] — Int J Mass
International Journal of Mass Spectrometry and Ion Physics [*Later, International Journal of Mass Spectrometry and Ion Processes*] — Int J Mass Spectrom and Ion Phys
International Journal of Mass Spectrometry and Ion Physics [*Later, International Journal of Mass Spectrometry and Ion Processes*] — Int J Mass Spectrom Ion Phys
International Journal of Mass Spectrometry and Ion Processes — Int J Mass Spectrom Ion Processes
International Journal of Materials and Product Technology — Int J Mater Prod Technol
International Journal of Materials Engineering Research — Int J Mater Eng Res
International Journal of Materials in Engineering Applications — Int J Mater Eng Appl
International Journal of Mathematical and Statistical Sciences — Internat J Math Statist Sci
International Journal of Mathematical Education in Science and Technology — Int J Math Educ Sci and Technol
International Journal of Mathematical Education in Science and Technology — Int J Math Educ Sci Technol
International Journal of Mathematical Education in Science and Technology — Internat J Math Ed Sci Tech
International Journal of Mathematics — Internat J Math
International Journal of Mathematics and Mathematical Sciences — Internat J Math Math Sci
International Journal of Mechanical Engineering Education — Int J Mech Engng Educ
International Journal of Mechanical Sciences — Int J Mech
International Journal of Mechanical Sciences — Int J Mech Sci
International Journal of Mechanochemistry and Mechanical Alloying — Int J Mechanochem Mech Alloying
International Journal of Medical Microbiology — Int J Med Microbiol
International Journal of Medical Microbiology, Virology, Parasitology, and Infectious Diseases — Int J Med Microbiol Virol Parasitol Infect Dis
International Journal of Mental Health — Int J Ment
International Journal of Mental Health — Int J Ment Health
International Journal of Mental Health — Internat J Mental Health
International Journal of Microbiology and Hygiene. Abt. 1. Originale A. Medical Microbiology, Infectious Diseases, Parasitology — Int J Microbiol Hyg Abt 1 Orig A
International Journal of Microbiology and Hygiene. Abteilung 1. Originale B. Environmental Hygiene, Hospital Hygiene, Industrial Hygiene, Preventive Medicine — Int J Microbiol Hyg Abt 1 Orig B
International Journal of Microbiology and Hygiene. Series A. Medical Microbiology, Infectious Diseases, Virology, Parasitology — Int J Microbiol Hyg Ser A
International Journal of Microbiology and Hygiene. Series B. Environmental Hygiene, Hospital Hygiene, Industrial Hygiene, Preventive Med — Int J Microbiol Hyg Ser B
International Journal of Microcirculation. Clinical and Experimental — Int J Microcirc Clin Exp
International Journal of Micrographics and Video Technology — Int J Microgr and Video Technol
International Journal of Middle East Studies — IJMES
International Journal of Middle East Studies — Int J M E St
International Journal of Middle East Studies — Int J Mid E Stud
International Journal of Middle East Studies — Int J Mid East Stud
International Journal of Middle East Studies — Int J Middle East Stud
International Journal of Middle East Studies — Internat J Middle East Studies
International Journal of Middle East Studies — IntJM
International Journal of Middle East Studies — PMES
International Journal of Mine Water — Int J Mine Water
International Journal of Mineral Processing — Int J Miner Process
International Journal of Mineral Processing — Internat J Mineral Proc
International Journal of Mini and Microcomputers — Int J Mini and Microcomput
International Journal of Mining Engineering — Int J Min Eng
International Journal of Modern Physics. A — Internat J Modern Phys A
International Journal of Modern Physics. B — Internat J Modern Phys B
International Journal of Modern Physics C. Computational Physics. Physical Computation — Internat J Modern Phys C
International Journal of Modern Physics. D. Gravitation, Astrophysics, Cosmology — Internat J Modern Phys D
International Journal of Modern Physics. E. Nuclear Physics — Internat J Modern Phys E
International Journal of Multiphase Flow — Int J Multiph Flow
International Journal of Multiphase Flow — Int J Multiphase Flow
International Journal of Multiphase Flow — Internat J Multiphase Flow
International Journal of Mushroom Sciences — Int J Mushroom Sci
International Journal of Music Education — Int J Mus Ed
International Journal of Mycology and Lichenology — IJMLEC
International Journal of Mycology and Lichenology — Int J Mycol Lichenol
International Journal of Nautical Archaeology and Underwater Exploration — IJNA
International Journal of Nautical Archaeology and Underwater Exploration — Int J Naut
International Journal of Nautical Archaeology and Underwater Exploration — Int J Naut Archaeol Underwater Explor
International Journal of Nautical Archaeology and Underwater Exploration [*London*] — Int JNA
International Journal of Nautical Archaeology and Underwater Exploration — J Naut Arch
International Journal of Nephrology, Urology, Andrology — Int J Nephrol Urol Androl
International Journal of Neural Systems — Int J Neural Syst
International Journal of Neurology — Int J Neuro
International Journal of Neurology — Int J Neurol
International Journal of Neuropharmacology — Int J Neuropharmacol
International Journal of Neuropsychiatry — Int J Neuropsychiatr
International Journal of Neuropsychiatry — Int J Neuropsychiatry
International Journal of Neuropsychiatry — Internat J Neuropsychiat
International Journal of Neuropsychiatry. Supplement — Int J Neuropsychiatry Suppl
International Journal of Neuroscience — IJN
International Journal of Neuroscience — IJNUB
International Journal of Neuroscience — Int J Neurosci
International Journal of Neuroscience — Int J Neurs
International Journal of Nondestructive Testing — Int J Nondestr Test
International Journal of Nondestructive Testing — Int J Nondestruct Test
International Journal of Non-Linear Mechanics — Int J Non-Linear Mech
International Journal of Non-Linear Mechanics — Internat J Non-Linear Mech
International Journal of Nonlinear Optical Physics — Int J Nonlinear Opt Phys
International Journal of Nuclear Medicine and Biology — IJNMC
International Journal of Nuclear Medicine and Biology — Int J Nuc M
International Journal of Nuclear Medicine and Biology — Int J Nucl Med & Biol
International Journal of Nuclear Medicine and Biology — Int J Nucl Med Biol

International Journal of Numerical Methods for Heat and Fluid Flow — Int J Numer Methods Heat Fluid Flow
International Journal of Numerical Methods for Heat and Fluid Flow — Internat J Numer Methods Heat Fluid Flow
International Journal of Numerical Modelling. Electronic Networks, Devices, and Fields — Internat J Numer Modelling
International Journal of Nursing Studies — Int J Nurs
International Journal of Nursing Studies — Int J Nurs Stud
International Journal of Obesity — Int J Obes
International Journal of Obesity — Int J Obesity
International Journal of Obesity and Related Metabolic Disorders — Int J Obes Relat Metab Disord
International Journal of Occupational Health and Safety — Int J Occ H
International Journal of Occupational Health and Safety — Int J Occup Health and Saf
International Journal of Occupational Health and Safety — Int J Occup Health Saf
International Journal of Occupational Health and Safety — IOHSA
International Journal of Occupational Medicine and Environmental Health — Int J Occup Med Environ Health
International Journal of Occupational Medicine and Toxicology — Int J Occup Med Toxicol
International Journal of Oceanology and Limnology — Int J Oceanol Limnol
International Journal of Offender Therapy [*Later, International Journal of Offender Therapy and Comparative Criminology*] — Int J Offen
International Journal of Offender Therapy and Comparative Criminology — Int J Offend Therapy
International Journal of Offender Therapy and Comparative Criminology — Intl J Offend Ther and Comp Criminology
International Journal of Oncology — Int J Oncol
International Journal of Operations and Production Management — IJO
International Journal of Operations and Production Management — IJOPM
International Journal of Operations and Production Management — Int J Oper and Prod Manage
International Journal of Operations and Production Management — IOP
International Journal of Opinion and Attitude Research — IJOAR
International Journal of Oral and Maxillofacial Implants — Int J Oral Maxillofac Implants
International Journal of Oral and Maxillofacial Surgery — Int J Oral Maxillofac Surg
International Journal of Oral History [*Canada (already exists in GUS II database)*] — IJOH
International Journal of Oral History — Int J Oral
International Journal of Oral Myology — Int J Oral Myol
International Journal of Oral Surgery — Int J Or Su
International Journal of Oral Surgery — Int J Oral Surg
International Journal of Orofacial Myology — Int J Orofacial Myology
International Journal of Orthodontia and Dentistry for Children — Int J Orthod Dent Child
International Journal of Orthodontics — Int J Orthod
International Journal of Orthodontics — Int J Orthodont
International Journal of Pancreatology — Int J Pancreatol
International Journal of Parallel Programming — Internat J Parallel Programming
International Journal of Parapsychology — IJP
International Journal of Partial Hospitalization — Int J Partial Hosp
International Journal of Pediatric Nephrology — Int J Pediatr Nephrol
International Journal of Pediatric Otorhinolaryngology — Int J Pediatr Otorhinolaryngol
International Journal of Peptide and Protein Research — IJPPC
International Journal of Peptide and Protein Research — Int J Pept
International Journal of Peptide and Protein Research — Int J Pept Protein Res
International Journal of Peptide and Protein Research — Int J Peptide Prot Res
International Journal of Peptide and Protein Research — Int J Peptide Protein Res
International Journal of Periodontics and Restorative Dentistry — Int J Periodontics Restorative Dent
International Journal of Periodontics and Restorative Dentistry — Int'l J of PRD
International Journal of Pharmaceutical Advances — Int J Pharm Adv
International Journal of Pharmaceutical Technology and Product Manufacture — Int J Pharm Technol Prod Manuf
International Journal of Pharmaceutics — Int J Pharm
International Journal of Pharmaceutics (Amsterdam) — Int J Pharm (Amst)
International Journal of Pharmacognosy — Int J Pharmacogn
International Journal of Physical Distribution and Materials Management — IJP
International Journal of Physical Distribution and Materials Management — IJPDMM
International Journal of Physical Distribution and Materials Management — Internat J Physical Distribution and Materials Mgt
International Journal of Physical Distribution and Materials Management — IPD
International Journal of Physical Distribution and Materials Management — IVR
International Journal of Physical Distribution [*Later, International Journal of Physical Distribution and Materials Management*]. Journal Series — Int J Phys Distrib J Ser
International Journal of Physical Distribution [*Later, International Journal of Physical Distribution and Materials Management*]. Monograph Series — Int J Phys Distrib Monogr Ser
International Journal of Physical Education — Int J PE
International Journal of Physical Education — Int J Phys Educ
International Journal of Plant Physiology — Int J Plant Physiol
International Journal of Plant Physiology (Stuttgart) — Int J Plant Physiol (Stuttgart)
International Journal of Policy Analysis and Information Systems [*United States*] — Int J Policy Anal Inf Syst
International Journal of Policy Analysis and Information Systems — Internat J Policy Anal Inform Systems
International Journal of Political Education — IJPE
International Journal of Politics — Int J Polit
International Journal of Politics — Int'l J Pol
International Journal of Polymer Analysis and Characterization — Int J Polym Anal Charact
International Journal of Polymeric Materials — Int J Polym Mat
International Journal of Polymeric Materials — Int J Polym Mater
International Journal of Powder Metallurgy — Int J Powd
International Journal of Powder Metallurgy — Int J Powder Metall
International Journal of Powder Metallurgy and Powder Technology — Int J Powder Metall & Powder Tech
International Journal of Powder Metallurgy and Powder Technology — Int J Powder Metall Powder Technol
International Journal of Powder Metallurgy and Powder Technology — Int J Powder Metall Technol
International Journal of Powder Metallurgy and Powder Technology — IPMPC
International Journal of Pressure Vessels and Piping — Int J Pressure Vessels Piping
International Journal of Primatology — Int J Primatol
International Journal of Production Research — IJPR
International Journal of Production Research — Int J Prod Res
International Journal of Prosthodontics — Int J Prosthod
International Journal of Protein Research — Int J Protein Res
International Journal of Psychiatry — IJP
International Journal of Psychiatry — Int J Psychiat
International Journal of Psychiatry — Int J Psychiatry
International Journal of Psychiatry — Int J Psyci
International Journal of Psychiatry in Medicine — Int J Psy M
International Journal of Psychiatry in Medicine — Int J Psychiatry Med
International Journal of Psychiatry in Medicine — PM
International Journal of Psychoanalysis — IJPsa
International Journal of Psychoanalysis — Int J Psych
International Journal of Psychoanalysis — Int J Psychoanal
International Journal of Psychoanalytic Psychotherapy — Int J Ps Ps
International Journal of Psychoanalytic Psychotherapy — Int J Psychoanal Psychother
International Journal of Psychobiology — Int J Psychobiol
International Journal of Psychology — Int J Psychol
International Journal of Psychology — Int J Psyco
International Journal of Psychophysiology — Int J Psychophysiol
International Journal of Psychosomatics — Int J Psychosom
International Journal of Public Administration — IJP
International Journal of Public Administration — IPA
International Journal of Public Health — Int J Publ Hlth
International Journal of Quantum Chemistry — Int J Quant
International Journal of Quantum Chemistry — Int J Quant Chem
International Journal of Quantum Chemistry — Int J Quantum Chem
International Journal of Quantum Chemistry. Quantum Biology Symposium [*United States*] — Int J Quant Chem Quant Biol Symp
International Journal of Quantum Chemistry. Quantum Biology Symposium — Int J Quantum Chem Quantum Biol Symp
International Journal of Quantum Chemistry. Quantum Chemistry Symposia — Int J Quantum Chem Quantum Chem Symp
International Journal of Quantum Chemistry. Symposium — Int J Quant Chem Symp
International Journal of Quantum Chemistry. Symposium — Int J Quantum Chem Sym
International Journal of Quantum Chemistry. Symposium — Int J Quantum Chem Symp
International Journal of Radiation Applications and Instrumentation. Part A. Applied Radiation and Isotopes — Int J Rad Appl Instrum A
International Journal of Radiation Applications and Instrumentation. Part A. Applied Radiation and Isotopes — Int J Radiat Appl Instrum Part A Appl Radiat Isot
International Journal of Radiation Applications and Instrumentation. Part B. Nuclear Medicine and Biology — Int J Rad Appl Instrum B
International Journal of Radiation Applications and Instrumentation. Part C — Int J Radiat Appl Instrum Part C
International Journal of Radiation Applications and Instrumentation. Part E — Int J Radiat Appl Instrum Part E
International Journal of Radiation Biology — Int J Rad B
International Journal of Radiation Biology — Int J Radiat Biol
International Journal of Radiation Biology and Related Studies in Physics, Chemistry, and Medicine — Int J Radiat Biol
International Journal of Radiation Biology and Related Studies in Physics, Chemistry, and Medicine — Int J Radiat Biol Relat Stud Phys Chem Med
International Journal of Radiation Engineering — IJRED
International Journal of Radiation Engineering [*Israel*] — Int J Radiat Eng
International Journal of Radiation: Oncology-Biology-Physics — Int J Rad O
International Journal of Radiation: Oncology-Biology-Physics — Int J Radiat Oncol-Biol-Phys
International Journal of Radiation: Oncology-Biology-Physics — Int J Radiat Oncology Biol Phys
International Journal of Radiation Sterilization — IJRSD
International Journal of Radiation Sterilization [*Israel*] — Int J Radiat Steril
International Journal of Radioactive Materials Tansport — Int J Radioact Mater Transp
International Journal of Rapid Solidification — Int J Rap S
International Journal of Refractory and Hard Metals — Int J Refract and Hard Met
International Journal of Refractory and Hard Metals — Int J Refract Hard Met
International Journal of Refractory Metals and Hard Materials — Int J Refract Met Hard Mater

International Journal of Refrigeration — Int J Refrig
International Journal of Rehabilitation Research — Int J Rehabil Res
International Journal of Reliability, Quality, and Safety Engineering — Int J Reliab Qual Saf Eng
International Journal of Religious Education — IJRE
International Journal of Religious Education — Int J Relig Ed
International Journal of Religious Education — Intl Jnl Rel Ed
International Journal of Remote Sensing — Int J Remot
International Journal of Remote Sensing — Int J Remote Sens
International Journal of Research in Marketing — IJR
International Journal of Research in Physical Chemistry and Chemical Physics — Int J Res Phys Chem Chem Phys
International Journal of Research Management [*United States*] — Int J Res Manage
[*The*] **International Journal of Robotics Research** — IJRR
International Journal of Robotics Research — Int J Robot Res
International Journal of Robust and Nonlinear Control — Internat J Robust Nonlinear Control
International Journal of Rock Mechanics — Int J Rock
International Journal of Rock Mechanics and Mining Sciences [*Later, International Journal of Rock Mechanics and Mining Sciences and Geomechanics Abstracts*] — Int J Rock Mech Min Sci
International Journal of Rock Mechanics and Mining Sciences [*Later, International Journal of Rock Mechanics and Mining Sciences and Geomechanics Abstracts*] — Int J Rock Mech Mining Sci
International Journal of Rock Mechanics and Mining Sciences [*Later, International Journal of Rock Mechanics and Mining Sciences and Geomechanics Abstracts*] — Internat Jour Rock Mechanics and Mining Sci
International Journal of Rock Mechanics and Mining Sciences and Geomechanics Abstracts — Int J Rock Mech and Min Sci and Geomech Abstr
International Journal of Rock Mechanics and Mining Sciences and Geomechanics Abstracts — Int J Rock Mech Min Sci Geomech Abstr
International Journal of Rock Mechanics and Mining Sciences and Geomechanics Abstracts — Int J Rock Mech Mining Sci Geomech Abstr
International Journal of Rumanian Studies — IJRS
International Journal of Sexology — IJS
International Journal of Sexology — Int J Sex
International Journal of Slavic Linguistics and Poetics — IJSLP
International Journal of Social Economics — IJS
International Journal of Social Economics — IJSE
International Journal of Social Economics — Int J Soc Econ
International Journal of Social Economics — Internat J Social Econ
International Journal of Social Economics — ISE
International Journal of Social Economics (Bradford) — IHB
International Journal of Social Psychiatry — IJSPA
International Journal of Social Psychiatry — Int J Soc P
International Journal of Social Psychiatry — Int J Soc Psych
International Journal of Social Psychiatry — Int J Soc Psychiatr
International Journal of Social Psychiatry — Int J Soc Psychiatry
International Journal of Social Psychiatry — Int J Social Psych
International Journal of Social Psychiatry — Int J Social Psychiat
International Journal of Social Psychiatry — ISPY
International Journal of Sociology — Int J Sociol
International Journal of Sociology — Internat J Sociol
International Journal of Sociology and Social Policy — Int J Sociol Soc Policy
International Journal of Sociology of the Family — Int J Soc F
International Journal of Sociology of the Family — Int J Sociol Family
International Journal of Soil Dynamics and Earthquake Engineering — Int J Soil Dyn and Earthquake Eng
International Journal of Solar Energy — Int J Sol Energy
International Journal of Solar Energy — Int J Solar Energy
International Journal of Solids and Structures — Int J Solids and Struct
International Journal of Solids and Structures — Int J Solids Struct
International Journal of Solids and Structures — Internat J Solids and Structures
International Journal of Speleology — Int J Speleol
International Journal of Sport Nutrition — Int J Sport Nutr
International Journal of Sport Nutrition — Int J Sport Nutrition
International Journal of Sport Psychology — Int J Sp Ps
International Journal of Sport Psychology — Int J Sport Psy
International Journal of Sport Psychology — Int J Sport Psychol
International Journal of Sports Medicine — Int J Sports Med
International Journal of STD and AIDS — Int J STD AIDS
International Journal of Sulfur Chemistry — IJSCC
International Journal of Sulfur Chemistry — Int J Sulfur Chem
International Journal of Sulfur Chemistry. Part A. Original Experimental — Int J Sulfur Chem Part A
International Journal of Sulfur Chemistry. Part B. Quarterly Reports on Sulfur Chemistry — Int J Sulfur Chem Part B
International Journal of Sulfur Chemistry. Part C. Mechanisms of Reactions of Sulfur Compounds — Int J Sulfur Chem Part C
International Journal of Symbology — IJSym
International Journal of Symbology — Int J Symb
International Journal of Systematic Bacteriology — Int J Sy B
International Journal of Systematic Bacteriology — Int J Syst Bacteriol
International Journal of Systematic Bacteriology — Intern J System Bacteriol
International Journal of Systems Science — Int J Syst
International Journal of Systems Science — Int J Syst Sci
International Journal of Systems Science — Internat J Systems Sci
International Journal of Technology Advances — Int J Technol Adv
International Journal of Technology Assessment in Health Care — Int J Technol Assess Health Care
International Journal of the Addictions — IJOA
International Journal of the Addictions — INJABN
International Journal of the Addictions — Int J Addic
International Journal of the Addictions — Int J Addict
International Journal of the History of Sport — Int J Hist Sport
International Journal of the Sociology of Language — IJSL
International Journal of the Sociology of Language — Int J Soc L
International Journal of the Sociology of Language — Int J Soc Lang
International Journal of the Sociology of Language — Int J Sociol Lang
International Journal of the Sociology of Law — Int J Sociol Law
International Journal of the Sociology of Law — Intl J Soc L
International Journal of Theoretical Physics — Int J Theor
International Journal of Theoretical Physics — Int J Theor Phys
International Journal of Theoretical Physics — Internat J Theoret Phys
International Journal of Thermophysics — Int J Therm
International Journal of Thermophysics — Int J Thermophys
International Journal of Toxicology, Occupational, and Environmental Health — Int J Toxicol Occup Environ Health
International Journal of Transport Economics — IJT
International Journal of Transport Economics — Int J Transp Econ
International Journal of Tropical Agriculture — Int J Trop Agric
International Journal of Tropical Plant Diseases — Int J Trop Plant Dis
International Journal of Turkish Studies — IJTS
International Journal of Uncertainty, Fuzziness, and Knowledge-Based Systems — Internat J Uncertain Fuzziness Knowledge Based Systems
International Journal of Urban and Regional Research — Int J Urban Reg Res
International Journal of Urban and Regional Research — Internat J Urban and Regional Research
International Journal of Urology — Int J Urol
International Journal of Vehicle Design — Int J Veh Des
International Journal of Water Resources Development — Int J Water Resour Dev
International Journal of Women's Studies — IJWS
International Journal of Women's Studies — Int J Womens Stud
International Journal of Wood Preservation — Int J Wood Preserv
International Journal of Zoonoses — Int J Zoonoses
International Journal on Gas Utilization — Int J Gas Util
International Journal on Policy and Information — Int J Policy and Inf
International Journal on Tissue Reactions — Int J Tissue React
International Journal. Toronto — IJT
International Kimberlite Conference. Proceedings — Int Kimberlite Conf Proc
International Kongress der Volkserzaehlungsforscher — IKV
International Kupffer Cell Symposium — Int Kupffer Cell Symp
International Labmate — Int Labmate
International Labor and Working Class History — Int Labor W
International Labor Organization. Occupational Safety and Health Series — Int Labor Organ Occup Saf Health Ser
International Laboratory — Int Lab
International Labour Documentation — ILD
International Labour Documentation — ILL
International Labour Documentation — Int Labour Doc
International Labour Office. Legislative Series [*London, England*] — Int'l Lab Off Leg S
International Labour Office. Occupational Safety and Health Series — Int Labour Off Occup Saf Health Ser
International Labour Review — BOU
International Labour Review — ILR
International Labour Review — INLR-A
International Labour Review — Int Lab R
International Labour Review — Int Lab Rev
International Labour Review — Int Labour R
International Labour Review — Int Labour Rev
International Labour Review — Int Lbr R
International Labour Review — Int LR
International Labour Review — Internat Labour R
International Labour Review — Int'l Lab Rev
International Labour Review. Statistical Supplement — ILRSS
International Labour Review. Statistical Supplement — Int Labour R Stat Sup
International Language Reporter — ILR
International Law News — Int L News
International Law News — Intl L News
International Law Quarterly — ILQ
International Law Quarterly — Int LQ
International Law Quarterly — Internat LQ
International Law Quarterly — Int'l LQ
International Lawyer — Int Law
International Lawyer — Int Lawyer
International Lawyer — Intl Law
International Lawyer — Int'l Lawyer
International Lawyer. Quarterly Publication of the Section of International and Comparative Law of the American Bar Association — Internat Lawyer
International League of Women Composers Journal — ILWCJ
International Lecture Series in Computer Science — Internat Lecture Ser Comput Sci
International Legal Materials — ILM
International Legal Materials — Internat Legal Materials
International Legal Materials — Intl Legal Mat
International Legal Materials — Int'l Legal Materials
International Library of Anthropology — Internat Lib Anthropol
International Library of Economics — Internat Lib Econom
International Library of Philosophy — Int Lib Ph
International Library of Psychology, Philosophy, and Scientific Method — ILPP
International Library Review — Int Lib R
International Library Review — Int Libr Re
International Library Review — Int Libr Rev
International Lichenological Newsletter — Int Lichenol Newslett
International Lighting Review — Int Lighting Rev
International Lighting Review — Int Ltg Rev
International Lighting Review — Intl Lighting Review

International Literary Annual [*London*] — ILA
International Literature [*Former USSR*] — IL
International Logic Review — Int Log Rev
International Logic Review — Internat Logic Rev
International Logo Exchange — ILE
International Loss Prevention Symposium — Int Loss Prev Symp
International Magazine — Internat M
International Management — IM
International Management — IMG
International Management — Int Manag
International Management — Int Manage
International Management — Int Mgmt
International Management — Int Mgt
International Management — Internat Mgt
International Management — MGH
International Management Africa — Int Manage Afr
International Management. Asia/Pacific — Int Manage Asia Pac
International Management Association. Special Report — IMA Spec Rep
International Management Digest — Int Man Dig
International Management Information — IMI
International Management Information — Int Man Inf
International Management Series — Int Man Ser
International Marine and Air Catering — IMAC
International Marine Science [*IOC*] — IMS
International Mathematical News — Internat Math News
International Mathematics Research Notices — Internat Math Res Notices
International Medical Abstracts and Reviews — Int Med Abstr Rev
International Medical and Surgical Survey — Int Med Surg Surv
International Medical Congress. Transactions — Int Med Cong Trans
International Medical Digest — Int Med Dig
International Medical Magazine — Int Med M
International Medical Magazine — Int Med Mag
International Medical Newsletter — Int Med Newsl
International Medieval Bibliography — IMB
International Medieval Bibliography — Int Medieval Bibliogr
International Meeting. Italian Society of Endocrinology — Int Meet Ital Soc Endocrinol
International Meeting of Anaesthesiology and Resuscitation — Int Meet Anaesthesiol Resusc
International Meeting on Cholinesterases — Int Meet Cholinesterases
International Meeting on Polymer Science and Technology. Rolduc Polymer Meeting — Int Meet Polym Sci Technol Rolduc Polym Meet
International Mental Health Research Newsletter — Int Ment Heal Res Newsl
International Metallurgical Reviews — IMRVB
International Metallurgical Reviews — Int Metall Rev
International Metallurgical Reviews — Int Metall Revs
International Metals Reviews — Int Met Rev
International Microchemical Symposium — Int Microchem Symp
International Microelectronic Symposium. Proceedings — Int Microelectron Symp Proc
International Migration — INMI
International Migration — Internat Migration
International Migration — RMP
International Migration Review — IMR
International Migration Review — Int Migr Re
International Migration Review — Int Migration R
International Migration Review — Int Migration Rev
International Migration Review — Internat Migration R
International Migration Review. Center for Migration Studies — CMS/IMR
International Migration Review. IMR — PIMR
International Mineral Processing Congress. Technical Papers — Int Miner Process Congr Tech Pap
International Minerals Scene — Int Miner Scene
International Mining — Int Min
International Mining Equipment — Int Min Equip
International Missionary Council — Int Mis Council
International Modern Foundry — Int Mod Foundry
International Modern Language Series — Intern Mod Language Series
International Molders' Journal — Int Molders J
International Monetary Fund. Finance and Development — IMF F & D
International Monetary Fund. Staff Papers — IMF
International Monetary Fund. Staff Papers — IMF Staff Pa
International Monetary Fund. Staff Papers — Int Monet Fund Staff Pap
International Monetary Fund. Staff Papers — Int Monetar
International Monetary Fund. Staff Papers — Int Monetary Fund Staff Pa
International Monetary Fund Staff Papers — Int Monetary Fund Staff Paps
International Monetary Fund. Staff Papers — Internat Monetary Fund Staff Pas
International Monetary Market Year Book — IMMYB
International Monographs on Obesity Series — Int Monogr Obesity Ser
International Monthly — Int Mo
International Monthly — Inter M
International Monthly — Internat Mo
International Music Educator — Int Mus Ed
International Music Guide — IMG
International Musician — IM
International Musician — Int Mus
International Musician — Intm
International Musicological Society. Report of the Congress — IMS
International Nannoplankton Association. Newsletter — INA
International Nematology Network Newsletter — Int Nematol Network Newsl
International Newsletter on Chemical Education — Int Newsl Chem Educ
International Nickel — Int Nickel
International North Pacific Fisheries Commission. Annual Report — Int North Pac Fish Comm Annu Rep
International North Pacific Fisheries Commission. Bulletin — INPFCB
International North Pacific Fisheries Commission. Bulletin — Int North Pac Fish Comm Bull
International NOTAMS [*Notices to Airmen*] — IN
International Nuclear Information System [*Database*] — INIS
International Nuclear News Service — INNS
International Nursing Index — INI
International Nursing Index — Int Nurs Index
International Nursing Index — IntNurl
International Nursing Review — Int Nurs Re
International Nursing Review — Int Nurs Rev
International Nutrition Policy Series — Int Nutr Policy Ser
International Oceanographic Foundation. Bulletin — Internat Oceanog Found Bull
International Office of Cocoa and Chocolate. Periodic Bulletin — Int Off Cocoa Choc Period Bull
International Oil Scouts Association. Yearbook — Int Oil Scouts Assoc Yearb
International Ophthalmology — INOPD
International Ophthalmology — Int Ophthalmol
International Ophthalmology Clinics — Int Ophthalmol Clin
International Ophthalmology Clinics — IOPCA
International Optical Computing Conference Proceedings — Int Opt Comp Conf Proc
International Organization — Int Org
International Organization — Int Organ
International Organization — Internat Org
International Organization — Internatl Organ
International Organization — Intl Org
International Organization — IOG
International Organization — PIOR
International Organization (Boston) — Intern Organ Boston
International Organization for the Study of Human Development. International Congress — Int Organ Study Hum Dev Int Congr
International Orthopaedics — Int Orthop
International Pacific Halibut Commission. Annual Report — Int Pac Halibut Comm Annu Rep
International Pacific Halibut Commission. Scientific Report — Int Pac Halibut Comm Sci Rep
International Pacific Halibut Commission. Scientific Report — IPHCSR
International Pacific Halibut Commission. Technical Report — Int Pac Halibut Comm Tech Rep
International Pacific Halibut Commission. Technical Report — IPHCTR
International Pacific Salmon Fisheries Commission. Annual Report — Int Pac Salmon Fish Comm Annu Rep
International Pacific Salmon Fisheries Commission. Bulletin — Int Pac Salmon Fish Comm Bull
International Pacific Salmon Fisheries Commission. Progress Report — Int Pac Salmon Fish Comm Prog Rep
International Pacific Salmon Fisheries Commission. Progress Report — IPSFCPR
International Packaging Abstracts — Int Packag Abs
International Packaging Abstracts — Int Packag Abstr
International Paper Board Industry [*European Edition*] — Intern Pbd Ind
International Paper Board Industry. Corrugated Manufacture and Conversion — IPE
International Peat Congress. Proceedings — Int Peat Congr Proc
International Peat Society. Bulletin — Int Peat Soc Bull
International Pediatric Association. Bulletin — Int Pediatr Assoc Bull
International Perspectives — Int Perspect
International Perspectives — Int Perspectives
International Perspectives (Canada) — Internat Perspectives (Can)
International Perspectives in Urology — Int Perspect Urol
International Pest Control — I Pest Cntrl
International Pest Control — Int Pest Contr
International Pest Control — Int Pest Control
International Petroleum Abstracts — Int Pet Abstr
International Petroleum Annual — Int Petrol Annu
International Petroleum Annual [*Database*] — IPA
International Petroleum Quarterly — IPQ
International Petroleum Technology — Int Pet Technol
International Petroleum Times — Int Pet Times
International Petroleum Times — Int Petr Tms
International Petroleum Times — Int Petrol Times
International Pharmaceutical Abstracts — Int Pharm Abstr
International Pharmaceutical Abstracts [*American Society of Hospital Pharmacists*] [*Bibliographic database*] — IPA
International Pharmaceutical Technology and Product Manufacture — Int Pharm Technol Prod Manuf Abstr
International Pharmaceutical Technology Symposium — Int Pharm Technol Symp
International Pharmacopsychiatry — Int Pharmac
International Pharmacopsychiatry — Int Pharmacopsychiatry
International Philosophical Quarterly — Int Phil Q
International Philosophical Quarterly — Int Phil Quart
International Philosophical Quarterly — Int Philo Q
International Philosophical Quarterly — Int Philos Q
International Philosophical Quarterly — IPQ
International Philosophical Quarterly — PIPQ
International Phonetic Association Journal — IPAJ
International Photobiological Congress — Int Photobiol Congr
International Photographer — Int Photogr
International Photographer — Internl Photogr
International Photography — Intern Phot
International Photography Index — Int Photo Ind
International Photography Techniques — Intern Phot Tech
International Photo-Technik — Int Photo Tech

International Physics Workshop Series — Int Phys Workshop Ser
International Pipe Line Industry — Int Pipe Ln
International Pipe Line Industry — Pipeln Ind
International Pipeline Technology Convention — Int Pipeline Technol Conv
International Pipes and Pipelines — Int Pipes Pipelines
International Planned Parenthood Federation. Medical Bulletin — Int Plann Parent Fed Med Bull
International Planning Glossaries [*Elsevier Book Series*] — IPG
International Political Science Abstracts — Int Polit Sci Abstr
International Political Science Abstracts — IntPolSc
International Polymer Science and Technology — Int Polym Sci & Technol
International Post — IP
International Potash Institute. Bulletin — Int Potash Inst Bull
International Potash Institute. Colloquium. Proceedings — Int Potash Inst Colloq Proc
International Potash Institute. Research Topics — Int Potash Inst Res Top
International Power Generation [*England*] — Int Power Generation
International Power Sources Symposium (London) — Int Power Sources Symp London
International Power Sources Symposium. Proceedings — Int Power Sources Symp Proc
International President's Bulletin — Int Presidents Bul
International Pressure Die Casting Conference. Conference Papers — Int Pressure Die Cast Conf Conf Pap
International Problems — Int Problems
International Problems — Internat Problems
International Problems (Belgrade) — Int Probl (Belgrade)
International Problems (Tel-Aviv) — Int Probl (Tel-Aviv)
International Problems (Tel-Aviv) — Internat Problems (Tel-Aviv)
International Progress in Urethanes — Int Prog Urethanes
International Projectionist [*United States*] — Int Proj
International Property Investment Journal — Int Prop Invest Jnl
International Property Review — Int Prop Rev
International Psoriasis Bulletin — Int Psoriasis Bull
International Psychiatry Clinics — Int Psychiatry Clin
International Psycho-Analytical Association. Monograph — Int Psycho Anal Assoc Mono
International Psycho-Analytical Association. Monograph Series — Int Psycho-Anal Assoc Monogr Ser
International Psychogeriatrics — Int Psychogeriatr
International Quarterly — Int Q
International Quarterly — Internat
International Quarterly of Analytical Chemistry — Int Q Anal Chem
International Quarterly of Community Health Education — IQ
International Quarterly of Community Health Education — IQCH
International Quarterly of Entomology — Int Q Entomol
International Railway Gazette — Int Railw Gaz
International Railway Journal — Int Railw J
International Reading Association Conference. Papers — Int Read Assn Conf Pa
International Reading Association Convention. Papers — Int Read Assn Conv Pa
International Record. Medicine and General Practice Clinics — Int Rec Med Gen Pract Clin
International Record of Medicine — Int Rec Med
International Record of Medicine — Internat Rec Med
International Reference Service — Int Ref Serv
International Reformed Bulletin — IRB
International Regional Science Review [*United States*] — Int Reg Sci Rev
International Register of Potentially Toxic Chemicals [*Database*] — IRPTC
International Rehabilitation Medicine — Int Rehabil Med
International Rehabilitation Review — Int Rehab Rev
International Reinforced Plastics Conference. Papers — Int Reinf Plast Conf Pap
International Relations — Int Rel
International Relations — IR
International Relations. Journal. David Davies Memorial Institute of International Studies — Int Relations
International Relations (London) — Int Relat (London)
International Relations (Prague) — Int Relat (Prague)
International Relations (Teheran) — Int Relat (Teheran)
International Repertory of the Literature of Art [*Database*] — RILA
International Rescuer — Int Rescuer
International Research and Evaluation-Information and Technology Transfer Database — IRE-ITTD
International Research Centers Directory — IRCD
International Research Communications System Medical Science. Library Compendium — Int Res Commun Syst Med Sci Libr Compend
International Research Group on Refuse Disposal Information. Bulletin — Int Res Group Refuse Disposal Inf Bull
International Review — Int R
International Review — Int Rv
International Review — Internat R
International Review for Business Education — Inter Rev for Bus Ed
International Review for the Sociology of Sport — Int Rev Soc Sport
International Review of Administrative Sciences — IAS
International Review of Administrative Sciences — Int R Adm Sci
International Review of Administrative Sciences — Int R Admin Sci
International Review of Administrative Sciences — Internat R Admin Sciences
International Review of Administrative Sciences — IRA
International Review of Administrative Sciences (Brussels) — Internat R Admin Science (Brussels)
International Review of Administrative Sciences. International Institute of Administrative Sciences — IIAS/IRAS
International Review of Agricultural Economics — Int R Ag Econ
International Review of Agricultural Economics — Int R Agric Econ
International Review of Agriculture — Int R Ag
International Review of American Linguistics — IRAL
International Review of Applied Linguistics in Language Teaching — IRAL
International Review of Biochemistry — Int Rev Biochem
International Review of Chiropractic — Int Rev Chiro
International Review of Community Development — Int R Com Dev
International Review of Community Development — Int R Comm Dev
International Review of Community Development — Int R Community Develop
International Review of Community Development — IRCD-A
International Review of Connective Tissue Research — ICOTA
International Review of Connective Tissue Research — Int Rev Connect Tissue Res
International Review of Criminal Policy — Internat R Criminal Policy
International Review of Cytology — Int Rev Cyt
International Review of Cytology — Int Rev Cytol
International Review of Cytology — IRCYA
International Review of Cytology. Supplement — ICYSB
International Review of Cytology. Supplement — Int Rev Cytol Suppl
International Review of Education — Int R Ed
International Review of Education — Int R Educ
International Review of Education — Int Rev Edu
International Review of Education — Int Rev Educ
International Review of Education — International R Ed
International Review of Education — IRE
International Review of Education. United Nations Educational, Scientific, and Cultural Organization. Institute for Education — UNESCO/IRE
International Review of Educational Cinematography — Int R Ed Cinemat
International Review of Experimental Pathology — Int Rev Exp Pathol
International Review of Forestry Research — Int Rev For Res
International Review of Forestry Research — Int Rev Forest Res
International Review of General and Experimental Zoology — Int Rev Gen Exp Zool
International Review of History and Political Science — Int R Hist Pol Sci
International Review of History and Political Science — Int R Hist Polit Sci
International Review of History and Political Science — Int Rev His
International Review of Industrial Property and Copyright Law — IIC
International Review of Industrial Property and Copyright Law — Int'l Rev Ind Prop & C'right L
International Review of Industrial Property and Copyright Law — Int'l Rev Ind Prop'y & Copyr
International Review of Law and Economics — Intl Rev L and Econ
International Review of Medicine and Surgery — Int Rev Med Surg
International Review of Mission — Int Rev Mission
International Review of Mission — PIRM
International Review of Missions — Int R Miss
International Review of Missions — Int R Missions
International Review of Missions — Int Rev Miss
International Review of Missions — Int Rev Missions
International Review of Missions — Internat Rev Missions
International Review of Missions — IRM
International Review of Modern Sociology — Int R Mod Sociol
International Review of Modern Sociology — Int Rev Mod
International Review of Music Aesthetics and Sociology [*Later, International Review of the Aesthetics and Sociology of Music*] — IRMAS
International Review of Neurobiology — Int Rev Neurobiol
International Review of Neurobiology. Supplement — Int Rev Neurobiol Suppl
International Review of Physiology — Int Rev Physiol
International Review of Physiology — IRPHD
International Review of Poultry Science — Int Rev Poult Sci
International Review of Psychoanalysis — Int Rev Psychoanal
International Review of Publications in Sociology [*Database*] — IRPS
International Review of Slavic Linguistics — IRSL
International Review of Social History — Int R Scl Hist
International Review of Social History — Int R Soc Hist
International Review of Social History — Int Rev S H
International Review of Social History — Int Rev Soc Hist
International Review of Social History — Internat Rev Soc Hist
International Review of Social History — IntR
International Review of Social History — IRSH
International Review of Sport Sociology — Int R Sport Sociol
International Review of Sport Sociology — Int Rev Sport Soc
International Review of the Aesthetics and Sociology of Music — Int R Aesthetics Sociology M
International Review of the Aesthetics and Sociology of Music — Int R Aesthetics & Soc
International Review of the Aesthetics and Sociology of Music — Int R Aesthetics & Soc Mus
International Review of the Aesthetics and Sociology of Music — Int Rev Aes
International Review of the Aesthetics and Sociology of Music — IRAMD
International Review of the Aesthetics and Sociology of Music — IRASM
International Review of the Army, Navy, and Air Force Medical Services — Int Rev Army Navy Air Force Med Serv
International Review of the Science and Practice of Agriculture — Int R Sci & Prac Ag
International Review of Trachoma — Int Rev Trach
International Review of Tropical Medicine — Int Rev Trop Med
International Review of Tropical Medicine — Internat Rev Trop Med
International Review Service [*United States*] — Int Rev Serv
International Reviews in Aerosol Physics and Chemistry — Int Rev Aerosol Phys Chem
International Reviews in Physical Chemistry [*England*] — Int Rev Phys Chem
International Reviews of Immunology — Int Rev Immunol
International Revue [*London*] — IR
International Rice Commission. Newsletter — Int Rice Comm Newsl

International Rice Research Institute (Los Banos). Annual Report — Int Rice Res Inst (Los Banos) Annu Rep
International Rice Research Institute (Los Banos). Technical Bulletin — Int Rice Res Inst (Los Banos) Tech Bull
International Rice Research Institute. Research Paper Series — Int Rice Res Inst Res Pap Ser
International Rice Research Institute. Technical Bulletin — Int Rice Res Inst Techn Bull
International Rice Research Newsletter — Int Rice Res Newsl
International Road Research Documentation [*Database*] — IRRD
International Ropeway Review — Int Ropeway Rev
International Rubber Digest — Int Rubb Dig
International Salzburg Conference — Int Salzburg Conf
International SAMPE (Society for the Advancement of Material and Process Engineering) Environmental Conference — Int SAMPE Environ Conf
International School of Atmospheric Physics. Proceedings. Course — Int Sch Atmos Phys Proc Course
International School of Neuroscience — Int Sch Neurosci
International School on Laser Surface Microprocessing — Int Sch Laser Surf Microprocess
International School on Physical Problems in Microelectronics — Int Sch Phys Probl Microelectron
International Schools for Computer Scientists — Internat Schools Comput Sci
International Science — Int Sci
International Science and Technology — Int Sci Technol
International Science and Technology — Inter Sci Techn
International Science and Technology — Intern Sci Technol
International Science Fiction — INT
International Science Research News — Int Sci Res News
International Science Review Series — Int Sci Rev Ser
International Scientific Council for Trypanosomiasis Research and Control. Publication — Int Sci Counc Trypanosomiasis Res Control Publ
International Scientific Council for Trypanosomiasis. Research Publication — Int Sci Counc Trypanosomiasis Res Publ
International Sculpture — Int Sculp
International Security — Int Sec
International Security — Int Secur
International Security — Internat Security
International Security — Intnl Sec
International Security — PSEC
International Security Review — Int Secur Rev
International Security Review — Internat Security R
International Sedimentary Petrographical Series — Int Sed Petrograph Ser
International Seismological Centre. Bulletin — Int Seismol Cent Bull
International Seminar on High Energy Physics Problems — Int Semin High Energy Phys Probl
International Seminar on Magnetism — Int Semin Magn
International Seminar on Non-Destructive Examination in Relation to Structural Integrity — Int Semin Non Destr Exam Relat Struct Integr
International Seminar on Reproductive Physiology and Sexual Endocrinology — Int Semin Reprod Physiol Sex Endocrinol
International Seminars — Int Sem
International Series in Experimental Psychology — Int Ser Exp Psychol
International Series in Experimental Psychology — ISEPDC
International Series in Management Science/Operations Research — Internat Ser Management Sci Oper Res
International Series in Modern Applied Mathematics and Computer Science — Internat Ser Mod Appl Math Comput Sci
International Series in Natural Philosophy — Internat Ser Natural Philos
International Series in Nonlinear Mathematics. Theory, Methods, and Application — Internat Ser Nonlinear Math Theory Methods Appl
International Series in Operations Research and Management Science — Internat Ser Oper Res Management Sci
International Series in Pure and Applied Mathematics — Internat Ser Pure Appl Math
International Series of Monographs in Analytical Chemistry — Int Ser Monogr Anal Chem
International Series of Monographs in Experimental Psychology — Int Ser Monogr Exp Psychol
International Series of Monographs in Natural Philosophy — Int Ser Monogr Nat Philos
International Series of Monographs in Natural Philosophy — Internat Ser Monographs in Natural Philos
International Series of Monographs in Oral Biology — Int Ser Monogr Oral Biol
International Series of Monographs in Pure and Applied Mathematics — Internat Ser Monographs Pure Appl Math
International Series of Monographs in the Science of the Solid State — Int Ser Monogr Sci Solid State
International Series of Monographs in the Science of the Solid State — Int Ser Sci Solid State
International Series of Monographs on Chemistry — Inter Ser Monogr Chem
International Series of Monographs on Chemistry — Internat Ser Monogr Chem
International Series of Monographs on Chemistry — ISMCEE
International Series of Monographs on Computer Science — Internat Ser Monographs Comput Sci
International Series of Monographs on Nuclear Energy — Int Ser Monogr Nucl Energy
International Series of Monographs on Nuclear Energy. Division 7. Reactor Engineering — Int Ser Monogr Nucl Energy Div 7
International Series of Monographs on Physics — Internat Ser Monographs Phys
International Series of Monographs on Pure and Applied Biology. Division Biochemistry — Int Ser Monogr Pure Appl Biol Div Biochem
International Series of Monographs on Pure and Applied Biology. Division Botany — Int Ser Monogr Pure Appl Biol Div Bot
International Series of Monographs on Pure and Applied Biology. Modern Trends in Physiological Sciences — Int Ser Monogr Pure Appl Biol Mod Trends Physiol Sci
International Series of Monographs on Pure and Applied Biology. Zoology Division — Int Ser Pure Appl Biol Zool Div
International Series of Numerical Mathematics — Internat Ser Numer Math
International Series on Applied Systems Analysis — Internat Ser Appl Systems Anal
International Series on Biomechanics — Int Ser Biomech
International Series on Biomechanics — ISEBD4
International Series on Computational Engineering — Internat Ser Comput Engrg
International Series on Materials Science and Technology — Int Ser Mater Sci Technol
International Series on Sport Sciences — Int Ser Sport Sci
International Shade Tree Conference. Proceedings — Int Shade Tree Conf Proc
International Ship Painting and Corrosion Conference. Proceedings — Int Ship Painting Corros Conf Proc
International Shipbuilding Progress — Int Shipbldg Progr
International Shipbuilding Progress — Int Shipbuild Prog
International Shipbuilding Progress — Int Shipbuild Progress
International Shipping and Shipbuilding Directory — Int Ship Shipbuild Dir
International Social Development Review — Int Soc Dev
International Social Development Review — Int Soc Dev Rev
International Social Science Bulletin — Int Soc Sc Bull
International Social Science Bulletin — ISSB
International Social Science Bulletin (Paris) — Intern Soc Sc Bull Paris
International Social Science Journal — Int Soc Sc J
International Social Science Journal [*UNESCO*] — Int Soc Sci
International Social Science Journal [*UNESCO*] — Int Soc Sci J
International Social Science Journal [*UNESCO*] — Int Social Sci J
International Social Science Journal [*UNESCO*] — Internat Social Science J
International Social Science Journal [*UNESCO*] — ISSJ
International Social Science Journal [*UNESCO*] — IXS
International Social Science Journal — PSSJ
International Social Science Journal (Paris) — Intern Soc Sc Jour Paris
International Social Sciences Bulletin — Internat Soc Sci Bull
International Social Sciences Journal — Internat Soc Sci J
International Social Security Review — Int Soc Secur R
International Social Security Review — Int Soc Secur Rev
International Social Security Review — Int Soc Security Rev
International Social Work — Int Soc Work
International Socialist — IS
International Socialist Review — I S Revw
International Socialist Review — Int Social R
International Society for Biochemical Endocrinology. Meeting — Int Soc Biochem Endocrinol Meet
International Society for Heart Research. Annual Meeting — Int Soc Heart Res Annu Meet
International Society for Rock Mechanics. Congress Proceedings — Int Soc Rock Mech Congr Proc
International Society of Bassists. Newsletter — ISB
International Society of Bassists Newsletter — ISBN
International Society of Petroleum Industry Biologists. Annual Meeting — Int Soc Pet Ind Biol Annu Meet
International Solar Energy Society. American Section. Proceedings of the Annual Meeting — Int Sol Energy Soc Am Sect Proc Annu Meet
International Solar Energy Society Congress — Int Sol Energy Soc Congr
International Solid Wastes and Public Cleansing Association. Information Bulletin — Int Solid Wastes Public Clean Assoc Inf Bull
International Sourcebook. Corrosion in Marine Environment — Int Sourceb Corros Mar Environ
International Spectator — Int Spectator
International Standard Bible Encyclopedia — ISBE
International Statistical Institute. Review — RSIR
International Statistical Review — Int St Rvw
International Statistical Review — Int Stat R
International Statistical Review — Int Stat Rev
International Statistical Review — Internat Statist Rev
International Studies — Int St
International Studies [*New Delhi*] — Int Stud
International Studies — IS
International Studies. East Asian Series Research Publication — Int St E As
International Studies in Economics and Econometrics — Internat Stud Econom Econometrics
International Studies in Philosophy — Int Stud Phil
International Studies in Philosophy [*Turin*] — IS Ph
International Studies in the Philosophy of Science — Internat Stud Philos Sci
International Studies (New Delhi) — Int Stud (New Delhi)
International Studies (New Delhi) — Internat Studies (New Delhi)
International Studies of Management and Organization — Int Stud Manage Org
International Studies of Management and Organization — ISM
International Studies on Sparrows — Int Stud Sparrows
International Studies Quarterly — Int Stud Q
International Studies Quarterly — Int Stud Quart
International Studies Quarterly — PISQ
International Studio — Int Studio
International Sugar Confectionery Manufacturers' Association. Periodic Bulletin — Int Sugar Confect Manuf Assoc Period Bull
International Sugar Journal — Int Sug J
International Sugar Journal — Int Sugar J
International Sugar Journal — ISU
International Summer School on Fundamental Problems in Statistical Mechanics — Int Summer Sch Fundam Probl Stat Mech

International Summer School on Low-Level Measurements of Man-Made Radionuclides in the Environment — Int Summer Sch Low Level Meas Man Made Radionuclides Environ
International Superconductivity Technology Center. Journal — Int Supercond Technol Cent J
International Surgery — Int Surg
International Symposia in Economic Theory and Econometrics — Internat Sympos Econom Theory Econometrics
International Symposium. Canadian Society for Immunology — Int Symp Can Soc Immunol
International Symposium Chemical Oxidation. Technologies for the Nineties — Int Symp Chem Oxid
International Symposium devoted to Tests on Bitumens and Bituminous Materials — Int Symp Tests Bitumens Bitum Mater
International Symposium for Survival in the Cold — Int Symp Survival Cold
International Symposium. Hosei University — Int Symp Hosei Univ
International Symposium of Mass Spectrometry in Biochemistry and Medicine — Int Symp Mass Spectrom Biochem Med
International Symposium on Adjuvants for Agrochemicals — Int Symp Adjuvants Agrochem
International Symposium on Advanced Structural Materials — Int Symp Adv Struct Mat
International Symposium on Agricultural and Food Processing Wastes. Proceedings — Int Symp Agric Food Process Wastes Proc
International Symposium on Alcohol Fuels — Int Symp Alcohol Fuels
International Symposium on Amyloidosis — Int Symp Amyloidosis
International Symposium on Antibiotic Resistance — Int Symp Antibiot Resist
International Symposium on Batteries. Proceedings — Int Symp Batteries Proc
International Symposium on Bioluminescence and Chemiluminescence — Int Symp Biolumin Chemilumin
International Symposium on Boron Steels — Int Symp Boron Steels
International Symposium on Carotenoids — Int Symp Carotenoids
International Symposium on Carotenoids Other than Vitamin A. Abstracts of Communications — Int Symp Carotenoids Other than Vitam A Abstr Commun
International Symposium on Cationic Polymerization — Int Symp Cationic Polym
International Symposium on Cells of the Hepatic Sinusoid — Int Symp Cells Hepatic Sinusoid
International Symposium on Chemotherapy — Int Symp Chemother
International Symposium on Clinical Enzymology — Int Symp Clin Enzymol
International Symposium on Combination Therapies — Int Symp Comb Ther
International Symposium on Combustion. Papers — Int Symp Combust Pap
International Symposium on Contamination Control. Proceedings — Int Symp Contam Control Proc
International Symposium on Corals and Coral Reefs. Proceedings — Int Symp Corals Coral Reefs Proc
International Symposium on Crop Protection. Papers — Int Symp Crop Prot Pap
International Symposium on Cyclodextrins — Int Symp Cyclodextrins
International Symposium on Electrometallurgical Plant Practice — Int Symp Electrometall Plant Pract
International Symposium on Electron Beam Ion Sources and Their Applications — Int Symp Electron Beam Ion Sources Their Appl
International Symposium on Equine Medication Control — Int Symp Equine Med Control
International Symposium on Far-From-Equilibrium Dynamics of Chemical Systems — Int Symp Far From Equilib Dyn Chem Syst
International Symposium on Fish Oil and Blood-Vessel Wall Interactions — Int Symp Fish Oil Blood Vessel Wall Interact
International Symposium on Flammability and Fire Retardants. Proceedings — Int Symp Flammability Fire Retard Proc
International Symposium on Forest Hydrology (Pennsylvania) — Int Symp Forest Hydrol (Pennsylvania)
International Symposium on Foundations of Plasticity — Int Symp Found Plast
International Symposium on Fresh Water from the Sea. Proceedings — Int Symp Fresh Water Sea Proc
International Symposium on Gas Flow and Chemical Lasers — Int Symp Gas Flow Chem Lasers
International Symposium on Gaseous Dielectrics — Int Symp Gaseous Dielectr
International Symposium on Gonorrhea. Proceedings — Int Symp Gonorrhea Proc
International Symposium on Heterogeneous Catalysis. Proceedings — Int Symp Heterog Catal Proc
International Symposium on High-Temperature Oxidation and Sulphidation Processes — Int Symp High Temp Oxid Sulphidation Processes
International Symposium on Humidity and Moisture — Int Symp Humidity and Moisture
International Symposium on Immunopathology — Int Symp Immunopathol
International Symposium on Isolation, Characterization, and Use of Hepatocytes — Int Symp Isol Charact Use Hepatocytes
International Symposium on Landslide Control. Proceedings — Int Symp Landslide Control Proc
International Symposium on Lymphology — Int Symp Lymphol
International Symposium on Macromolecule-Metal Complexes — Int Symp Macromol Met Complexes
International Symposium on Metalworking Lubrication — Int Symp Metalwork Lubr
International Symposium on Microbial Drug Resistance — Int Symp Microb Drug Resist
International Symposium on Molecular Beams. Proceedings — Int Symp Mol Beams Proc
International Symposium on Nephrotoxicity — Int Symp Nephrotoxic
International Symposium on Nerves and the Gut — Int Symp Nerves Gut
International Symposium on New Polymerization Reactions and Reaction Mechanisms — Int Symp New Polym React React Mech
International Symposium on Nuclear Induced Plasmas and Nuclear Pumped Lasers. Papers — Int Symp Nucl Induced Plasmas Nucl Pumped Lasers Pap
International Symposium on Passivity — Int Symp Passivity
International Symposium on Pharmacology of Cerebral Ischemia — Int Symp Pharmacol Cereb Ischemia
International Symposium on Plasticity and Its Current Applications — Int Symp Plast Its Curr Appl
International Symposium on Polynuclear Aromatic Hydrocarbons — Int Symp Polynucl Aromat Hydrocarbons
International Symposium on Production, Refining, Fabrication, and Recycling of Light Metals — Int Symp Prod Refin Fabr Recycl Light Met
International Symposium on Quality Control — Int Symp Qual Control
International Symposium on Radiosensitizers and Radioprotective Drugs — Int Symp Radiosensitizers Radioprot Drugs
International Symposium on Rarefied Gas Dynamics — Int Symp Rarefied Gas Dyn
International Symposium on Regulated Streams — Int Symp Regul Streams
International Symposium on Remote Sensing of Environment. Proceedings — Int Symp Remote Sensing Environ Proc
International Symposium on Solar-Terrestrial Physics. Proceedings — Int Symp Sol Terr Phys Proc
International Symposium on Specialty Polymers — Int Symp Spec Polym
International Symposium on Structure and Dynamics of Nucleic Acids and Proteins — Int Symp Struct Dyn Nucleic Acids Proteins
International Symposium on Subscriber Loops and Services — Int Symp Subscriber Loops Serv
International Symposium on Sub-Tropical and Tropical Horticulture — Int Symp Sub Trop Trop Hortic
International Symposium on Sulphur in Agriculture. Proceedings — Int Symp Sulphur Agric Proc
International Symposium on Superheavy Metals. Proceedings — Int Symp Superheavy Elem Proc
International Symposium on Surface Phenomena and Additives in Water-Based Coatings and Printing Technology — Int Symp Surf Phenom Addit Water Based Coat Print Technol
International Symposium on Surfactants in Solution — Int Symp Surfactants Solution
International Symposium on Taurine — Int Symp Taurine
International Symposium on Technical Diagnostics — Int Symp Tech Diagn
International Symposium on the Decontamination of Nuclear Installations — Int Symp Decontam Nucl Install
International Symposium on the Interface between Microbiology and Analytical Chemistry — Int Symp Interface Microbiol Anal Chem
International Symposium on the Metallurgy and Applications of Superalloys 718, 625, and Various Derivatives — Int Symp Metall Appl Superalloys 718 625 Var Deriv
International Symposium on the Phylogeny of T and B Cells. Proceedings — Int Symp Phylog T B Cells Proc
International Symposium on the Structure and Functioning of Plant Populations — Int Symp Struct Funct Plant Popul
International Symposium on the Structure of the Eye — Int Symp Struct Eye
International Symposium on the Synthesis and Applications of Isotopically Labeled Compounds — Int Symp Synth Appl Isot Labeled Compd
International Symposium on the Use of Isotopes and Radiation in Research on Soil-Plant Relationships — Int Symp Use Isot Radiat Res Soil Plant Relat
International Symposium on Theory and Practice in Affinity Techniques — Int Symp Theory Pract Affinity Tech
International Symposium on Thermodynamics of Nuclear Materials — Int Symp Thermodyn Nucl Mater
International Symposium on Topical Problems in Orthopedic Surgery — Int Symp Top Probl Orthop Surg
International Symposium on Topics in Surface Chemistry. Proceedings — Int Symp Top Surf Chem Proc
International Symposium on Toxicology of Carbon Disulphide. Proceedings — Int Symp Toxicol Carbon Disulphide Proc
International Symposium on Trace Analysis and Technological Development — Int Symp Trace Anal Technol Dev
International Symposium on Trace Element Metabolism in Animals — Int Symp Trace Elem Metab Anim
International Symposium on Trace Elements in Man and Animals — Int Symp Trace Elem Man Anim
International Symposium on Transfer Factor — Int Symp Transfer Factor
International Symposium on Transition Radiation of High Energy Particles — Int Symp Transition Radiat High Energy Part
International Symposium on Transport Phenomena — Int Symp Transp Phenom
International Symposium on Tumor Pharmacotherapy — Int Symp Tumor Pharmacother
International Symposium on Tumor Viruses — Int Symp Tumor Viruses
International Symposium on Turbulent Shear Flows — Int Symp Turbul Shear Flows
International Symposium on Uranium Evaluation and Mining Techniques — Int Symp Uranium Eval Min Tech
International Symposium on Urolithiasis and Related Clinical Research — Int Symp Urolithiasis Relat Clin Res
International Symposium on Urolithiasis Research — Int Symp Urolithiasis Res
International Symposium on Vascular Neuroeffector Mechanisms — Int Symp Vasc Neuroeff Mech
International Symposium on Viral Hepatitis — Int Symp Viral Hepatitis
International Symposium on Viruses and Wastewater Treatment — Int Symp Viruses Wastewater Treat
International Symposium on Water Chemistry and Corrosion Problems of Nuclear Reactor Systems and Components — Int Symp Water Chem Corros Probl Nucl React Syst Compon
International Symposium on Water-Rock Interaction — Int Symp Water Rock Interact
International Symposium on Water-Rock Interaction. Proceedings — Int Symp Water Rock Interact Proc

International Symposium on Weak and Electromagnetic Interactions in Nuclei — Int Symp Weak Electromagn Interact Nucl
International Symposium on Winter Concreting — Int Symp Winter Concreting
International Symposium on Yeast and Other Protoplasts — Int Symp Yeast Other Protoplasts
International Symposium on Yeasts — Int Symp Yeasts
International Symposium Pollen Physiology and Fertilization — Int Symp Pollen Physiol Fert
International Symposium. Princess Takamatsu Cancer Research Fund — Int Symp Princess Takamatsu Cancer Res Fund
International Symposium Synergetics and Cooperative Phenomena in Solids and Macromolecules — Int Symp Synergetics Coop Phenom Solids Macromol
International Symposium. Technical Committee on Photon-Detectors. International Measurement Confederation. Proceedings — Int Symp Tech Comm Photon Detect Int Meas Confed Proc
International Symposium. Technical Committee on Photonic Measurement (Photon-Detectors). Proceedings — Int Symp Tech Comm Photonic Meas Photon Detect Proc
International Symposium. Weathering of Plastics and Rubbers — Int Symp Weathering Plast Rubbers
International Symposium Workshop on Particulate and Multiphase Processes — Int Symp Workshop Part Multiphase Processes
International Synthetic Rubber Symposium. Lectures — Int Synth Rubber Symp Lect
International Tailing Symposium. Proceedings — Int Tailing Symp Proc
International Tax Journal — Int Tax J
International Tax Journal — Internat Tax J
International Tax Journal — Intl Tax J
International Tax Journal — ITJ
International Teamster — Int Teamster
International Technical Conference on Toxic Air Contaminants — Int Tech Conf Toxic Air Contam
International Technical Cooperation Centre Review — Int Tech Coop Cent Rev
International Telemetering Conference. Proceedings — Int Telem Conf Proc
International Telemetering Conference. Proceedings [*United States*] — Int Telemetering Conf Proc
International Television Almanac — ITA
International Textile Bulletin. Dyeing/Printing/Finishing [*World Edition*] — Int Text Bull Dyeing Print Finish
International Textile Machinery — Int Text Mach
International Textile Review — Int Text Rev
International Textiles — INT
International Theoretical School on High Energy Physics for Experimentalists — Int Theor Sch High Energy Phys Exp
International Thermal Expansion Symposium — Int Therm Expans Symp
International Thermal Spraying Conference — Int Therm Spraying Conf
International Thyroid Conference. Proceedings — Int Thyroid Conf Proc
International Thyroid Conference. Transactions — Int Thyroid Conf Trans
International Thyroid Symposium — Int Thyroid Symp
International Timber Magazine — Int Timber Mag
International Tin Research and Development Council. Bulletin — Int Tin Res Dev Counc Bull
International Tin Research and Development Council. General Report — Int Tin Res Dev Counc Gen Rep
International Tin Research and Development Council. Information Circular — Int Tin Res Dev Counc Inf Circ
International Tin Research and Development Council. Miscellaneous Publications — Int Tin Res Dev Counc Misc Publ
International Tin Research and Development Council. Statistical Bulletin — Int Tin Res Dev Counc Stat Bull
International Tin Research and Development Council. Technical Publication. Series A — Int Tin Res Dev Counc Tech Publ Ser A
International Tin Research and Development Council. Technical Publication. Series D — Int Tin Res Dev Counc Tech Publ Ser D
International Tin Research Council. Reports — Int Tin Res Counc Rep
International Tin Research Institute Publication — Int Tin Res Inst Publ
International Tinplate Conference — Int Tinplate Conf
International Titanium Casting Seminar — Int Titanium Cast Semin
International TNO Conference on Biotechnology. Proceedings — Int TNO Conf Proc
International TNO Meeting on the Biology of the Interferon System — Int TNO Meet Biol Interferon Syst
International Topical Conference on High Power Electron and Ion Beam Research and Technology. Proceedings — Int Top Conf High Power Electron Ion Beam Res Technol Proc
International Topical Conference on Kinetics of Aggregation and Gelation — Int Top Conf Kinet Aggregation Gelation
International Topical Conference on Meson-Nuclear Physics — Int Top Conf Meson Nucl Phys
International Topical Conference on the Physics of MOS Insulators — Int Top Conf Phys MOS Insul
International Topical Conference on the Physics of SiO2 and Its Interfaces. Proceedings — Int Top Conf Phys SiO2 Its Interfaces Proc
International Topical Meeting on Reactor Thermal Hydraulics — Int Top Meet React Therm Hydraul
International Tourism Quarterly — INTQ
International Tourism Quarterly — IQT
International Tracts in Computer Science and Technology and Their Application — Int Tracts Comput Sci Technol Their Appl
International Trade Administration Report — ITA
International Trade and Resource Information System [*Database*] — ITRIS
International Trade Documentation — IDV
International Trade Forum — Forum
International Trade Forum — IGB
International Trade Forum — Int Trade Forum
International Trade Forum — Internat Trade Forum
International Trade Forum — ITF
International Trade Law and Practice — Internat Trade Law and Practice
International Trade Law and Practice — Int'l Trade L & Prac
International Trade Law Journal — Intl Trade LJ
International Trade Reporter — ITR
International Trade Reporter. Bureau of National Affairs — Intl Trade Rep BNA
International Trade Reporter's US Export Weekly — Int Trade Rep US Exp W
International Trade Union News — Int Trade Union N
International Transplutonium Element Symposium — Int Transplutonium Elem Symp
International Travel Catering — ITC
International Tree Crops Journal — Int Tree Crops J
International Tree Crops Journal — ITRJDW
International Trombone Association. Journal — ITA J
International Trombone Association. Newsletter — ITA N
International Trumpet Guild. Journal — ITG
International Trumpet Guild. Journal — ITG J
International Trumpet Guild. Newsletter — IT
International Trumpet Guild. Newsletter — ITG N
International Tug Convention (Proceedings) — Int Tug Conv (Proc)
International Tungsten Symposium — Int Tungsten Symp
International Turfgrass Research Conference — Int Turfgrass Res Conf
International Turtle and Tortoise Society. Journal — Int Turtle Tortoise Soc J
International UFO Reporter [*Center for Unidentified Flying Object Studies*] — IUR
International Union Against Cancer. Monograph Series — Int Union Cancer Monogr Ser
International Union Against Cancer. Technical Report Series — Int Union Cancer Tech Rep Ser
International Union Against Cancer. UICC [*Union Internationale Contre le Cancer*] **Technical Report Series** — Int Union Cancer UICC Tech Rep Ser
International Union for Conservation of Nature and Natural Resources. Annual Report — Int Union Conserv Nat Nat Resour Annu Rep
International Union for Conservation of Nature and Natural Resources. Technical Meeting — IUCN
International Union for Quaternary Research — Int Union Quat Res
International Union for the Conservation of Nature and Natural Resources. Proceedings and Papers. Technical Meeting — Int Union Conserv Nat Nat Resour Proc Pap
International Union for the Study of Social Insects. International Congress — Int Union Study Soc Insects Int Congr
International Union of Air Pollution Prevention Associations. International Clean Air Congress. Papers — Int Union Air Pollut Prev Assoc Int Clean Air Congr Pap
International Union of Biochemistry Symposium — Int Union Biochem Symp
International Union of Biochemistry Symposium Series — Int Union Biochem Symp Ser
International Union of Biological Sciences. Series B — Int Union Biol Sci Ser B
International Union of Biological Sciences. Series D. Newsletter — Int Union Biol Sci Ser D Newsl
International Union of Crystallography. Commission on Crystallographic Apparatus. Bibliography — Int Union Crystallogr Comm Crystallogr Appar Bibliogr
International Union of Crystallography. Crystallographic Symposia — Int Union Crystallogr Crystallogr Symp
International Union of Crystallography Crystallographic Symposia — Internat Union Cryst Cryst Sympos
International Union of Forestry Research Organizations Conference on Wood Quality and Utilization of Tropical Species — Int Union For Res Organ Conf Wood Qual Util Trop Spec
International Union of Geodesy and Geophysics. Newsletter — IUGG Newsl
International Union of Geological Sciences. International Subcommission on Stratigraphic Classification. Circular — Int Union Geol Sci Int Subcomm Stratigr Cl Circ
International Union of Geological Sciences. Series A — Int Union Geol Sci Ser A
International Union of Pure and Applied Chemistry — Int Union Pure Appl Chem
International Union of Pure and Applied Chemistry. Information Bulletin — IUPAC Inf Bull
International Union of Pure and Applied Chemistry. Information Bulletin. Appendices on Provisional Nomenclature, Symbols, Terminology, and Conventions — IUPAC Inf Bull Append Provis Nomencl Symb Terminol Conv
International Union of Pure and Applied Chemistry. Information Bulletin. Appendices on Tentative Nomenclature, Symbols, Units, and Standards — IUPAC Inf Bull Append Tentative Nomencl Symb Units Stand
International Urinary Stone Conference — Int Urinary Stone Conf
International Urogynecology Journal and Pelvic Floor Dysfunction — Int Urogynecol J Pelvic Floor Dysfunct
International Urology and Nephrology — Int Urol Nephrol
International Velsicol Symposium. Proceedings — Int Velsicol Symp Proc
International Vereinigung fuer Theoretische und Angewandte Limnologie. Mitteilungen [*Germany*] — Int Ver Theor Angew Limnol Mitt
International Veterinary Bulletin — Int Vet Bull
International Veterinary News — Int Vet News
International Virology — Int Virol
International Visual Field Symposium — Int Visual Field Symp
International Washington Spring Symposium — Int Wash Spring Symp
International Water Conference. Annual Meeting. Engineers' Society of Western Pennsylvania — Int Water Conf Annu Meet Eng Soc West Pa
International Water Conservancy Exhibition — Int Water Conservancy Exhib
International Water Pollution Research Conference. Papers — Int Water Pollut Res Conf Pap
International Water Power and Dam Construction — Int Water Power & Dam Constr
International Water Power and Dam Construction — Int Water Power Dam
International Water Power and Dam Construction — IWPCD

International Water Supply Association. Congress — Int Water Supply Assoc Congr
International Water Supply Congress. Proceedings — Int Water Supply Congr Proc
International Waterfowl Research Bureau Bulletin — Int Waterfowl Res Bur Bull
International Whaling Commission. Report of the Commission — Int Whaling Comm Rep Comm
International Whaling Commission. Report of the Commission — RCICDE
International Whaling Commission. Reports — Int Whaling Comm Rep
International Whaling Commission. Reports — IWCR
International Whaling Commission. Reports. Special Issue — IWCRSI
International Wheat Genetics Symposium — Int Wheat Genet Symp
International Who's Who — IWW
International Wildlife — GINW
International Wildlife — Int Wildl
International Wildlife — Int Wildlife
International Wildlife — INWI
International Williston Basin Symposium. Papers — Int Williston Basin Symp Pap
International Williston Basin Symposium. Proceedings — Int Williston Basin Symp Proc
International Winter Meeting on Fundamental Physics — Int Winter Meet Fundam Phys
International Winter School on Crystallographic Computing — Int Winter Sch Crystallogr Comput
International Wire and Cable Symposium. Proceedings — Int Wire Cable Symp Proc
International Wire and Machinery Association. International Conference — Int Wire Mach Assoc Int Conf
International Woodworker — Int Woodworker
International Wool Textile Research Conference. Proceedings — Int Wool Text Res Conf Proc
International Working Conference on Stored-Product Entomology — Int Work Conf Stored Prod Entomol
International Workshop High Performance Fiber Reinforced Cement Composites — Int Workshop High Perform Fiber Reinf Cem Compos
International Workshop. Lessons from Animal Diabetes — Int Workshop Lessons Anim Diabetes
International Workshop on Adenosine and Xanthine Derivatives — Int Workshop Adenosine Xanthine Deriv
International Workshop on Articular Cartilage and Osteoarthritis — Int Workshop Articular Cartilage Osteoarthritis
International Workshop on Ascorbic Acid in Domestic Animals — Int Workshop Ascorbic Acid Domest Anim
International Workshop on Basic Properties and Clinical Applications of Transfer Factor — Int Workshop Basic Prop Clin Appl Transfer Factor
International Workshop on Behavioral Effects of Nicotine — Int Workshop Behav Eff Nicotine
International Workshop on Bone Histomorphometry — Int Workshop Bone Histomorphom
International Workshop on Cold Neutron Sources — Int Workshop Cold Neutron Sources
International Workshop on Condensed Matter Physics — Int Workshop Condens Matter Phys
International Workshop on Coordinated Regulation of Gene Expression — Int Workshop Coord Regul Gene Expression
International Workshop on Cysticercosis — Int Workshop Cysticercosis
International Workshop on Ecological Physical Chemistry — Int Workshop Ecol Phys Chem
International Workshop on Electroweak Physics beyond the Standard Model — Int Workshop Electroweak Phys Stand Model
International Workshop on Fetal Brain Development — Int Workshop Fetal Brain Dev
International Workshop on Fundamental Research in Homogeneous Catalysis — Int Workshop Fundam Res Homogeneous Catal
International Workshop on Geometry and Interfaces — Int Workshop Geom Interfaces
International Workshop on Hemopoiesis in Culture — Int Workshop Hemopoiesis Cult
International Workshop on Human Gene Mapping — Int Workshop Hum Gene Mapp
International Workshop on Human Leukocyte Differentiation Antigens — Int Workshop Hum Leukocyte Differ Antigens
International Workshop on Iloprost — Int Workshop Iloprost
International Workshop on Immune-Deficient Animals in Experimental Research — Int Workshop Immune Defic Anim Exp Res
International Workshop on Industrial Biofouling and Biocorrosion — Int Workshop Ind Biofouling Biocorros
International Workshop on Intrauterine Contraception. Advances and Future Prospects — Int Workshop Intrauterine Contracept Adv Future Prospects
International Workshop on Light Absorption by Aerosol Particles — Int Workshop Light Absorpt Aerosol Part
International Workshop on Low Temperature Detectors for Neutrinos and Dark Matter — Int Workshop Low Temp Detect Neutrinos Dark Matter
International Workshop on Male Contraception. Advances and Future Prospects — Int Workshop Male Contracept Adv Future Prospects
International Workshop on Membrane Bioenergetics — Int Workshop Membr Bioenerg
International Workshop on Methods of Structural Analysis of Modulated Structures and Quasicrystals — Int Workshop Methods Struct Anal Modulated Struct Quasicryst
International Workshop on MeV and keV Ions and Cluster Interactions with Surfaces and Metals — Int Workshop MeV keV Ions Cluster Interact Surf Met
International Workshop on NK Cells — Int Workshop NK Cells
International Workshop on Nude Mice. Proceedings — Int Workshop Nude Mice Proc
International Workshop on Oxygen Free Radicals in Shock — Int Workshop Oxygen Free Radicals Shock
International Workshop on Photoinduced Self-Organization Effects in Optical Fiber. Quebec — Int Workshop Photoinduced Self Organ Eff Opt Fiber
International Workshop on Physics and Engineering of Computerized Multidimensional Imaging and Processing — Int Workshop Phys Eng Comput Multidimens Imaging Process
International Workshop on Physiology and Biochemistry of Stressed Plants — Int Workshop Physiol Biochem Stressed Plants
International Workshop on Positron and Positronium Chemistry — Int Workshop Positron Positronium Chem
International Workshop on QSAR [*Quantitative Structure-Activity Relationship*] **in Environmental Toxicology** — Int Workshop QSAR Environ Toxicol
International Workshop on Rare-Earth Magnets and Their Applications — Int Workshop Rare Earth Magnets Their Appl
International Workshop on Relativistic Aspects of Nuclear Physics — Int Workshop Relativ Aspects Nucl Phys
International Workshop on Research Frontiers in Fertility Regulation — Int Workshop Res Front Fertil Regul
International Workshop on Scale-Up of Water and Wastewater Treatment Processes — Int Workshop Scale Up Water Wastewater Treat Processes
International Workshop on Take-All of Cereals — Int Workshop Take All Cereals
International Workshop on the Biological Properties of Peptidoglycan — Int Workshop Biol Prop Peptidoglycan
International Workshop on the Determination of Antiepileptic Drugs on Body Fluids — Int Workshop Determ Antiepileptic Drugs Body Fluids
International Workshop on the Physics of Semiconductor Devices — Int Workshop Phys Semicond Devices
International Workshop on Transfer Factor — Int Workshop Transfer Factor
International Workshop on Weak Interactions and Neutrinos — Int Workshop Weak Interact Neutrinos
International Yearbook of Agricultural Legislation — Int Yearbook Ag Leg
International Yearbook of Cartography — Int Yearb Cartogr
International Yearbook of Education — Int Yearbook of Ed
International Yearbook of Education — Int Yrbk Ed
International Year-Book of Game Theory and Applications — Internat Year Book Game Theory Appl
International Yearbook of Nephrology — Int Yb Neph
International Yeast Symposium — Int Yeast Symp
International Zeolite Conference — Int Zeolite Conf
International Zoo Yearbook — Int Zoo Yearb
International Zoological Congress — Int Zool Cong
Internationale Beitraege zur Pathologie und Therapie der Ernaehrungsstoerungen, Stoffwechsel- und Verdauungskrankheiten — Intern Beitr Ernaehrgsstoer
Internationale Bergwirtschaft und Bergtechnik — Int Bergwirtsch Bergtech
Internationale Bibliographie der Rezensionen — Int Bibl Rezen
Internationale Bibliographie der Rezensionen Wissenschaftlicher Literatur — Int Bibl Rezen Wiss Lit
Internationale Bibliographie der Zeitschriftenliteratur [*International Index to Periodicals*] — IBZ
Internationale Bibliographie der Zeitschriftenliteratur aus Allen Gebieten des Wissens — Int Bibliogr Zeitschriftenliteratur Allen Gebieten Wissens
Internationale Bibliothek fuer Psychologie und Soziologie — IBP
Internationale Bildungs- und Informations-Datenbank — IBD
Internationale Dialog Zeitschrift — Int Dialog Z
Internationale Dichtungstagung — Int Dichtungstag
Internationale Elektronische Rundschau — Int Elektr
Internationale Elektronische Rundschau — Int Elektron Rundsch
Internationale Entwicklung — Internat Entwicklung
Internationale Fachmesse und Fachtagungen fuer die Kerntechnische Industrie. Vortraege — Int Fachmesse Fachtag Kerntech Ind Vortr
Internationale Fachschrift fuer die Schokoladen-Industrie — Int Fachschr Schok Ind
Internationale Fruchtsaftunion. Wissenschaftlich-Technische Kommission. Berichte — Int Fruchtsaftunion Wiss-Tech Komm Ber
Internationale Gesellschaft fuer Getreidechemie. Berichte — Int Ges Getreidechem Ber
Internationale Hefte der Widerstandsbewegung — IHW
Internationale Kamer van Koophandel — IKK
Internationale Katholische Zeitschrift — Int Kath Z
Internationale Kirchliche Zeitschrift — IKZ
Internationale Kirchliche Zeitschrift — Internat Kirchl Z
Internationale Kirchliche Zeitschrift [*Bern*] — IntKiZ
Internationale Maschinenrundschau — IMR
Internationale Mitteilungen fuer Bodenkunde — Int Mitt Bodenkd
Internationale Mitteilungen fuer Bodenkunde — Intern Mitt Bodenkde
Internationale Monatschrift fuer Wissenschaft, Kunst, und Technik — IMW
Internationale Monatsschrift — IMS
Internationale Monatsschrift fuer Wissenschaft, Kunst, und Technik — IM
Internationale Monatsschrift fuer Wissenschaft, Kunst, und Technik — IMWKT
Internationale Oekumenische Bibliographie — IOB
Internationale Revue der Gesamten Hydrobiologie — Int R Gesam
Internationale Revue der Gesamten Hydrobiologie — Int Rev Gesamten Hydrobiol
Internationale Revue der Gesamten Hydrobiologie. Systematische Beihefte — Int Rev Gesamten Hydrobiol Syst Beih
Internationale Revue der Gesamten Hydrobiologie und Hydrographie — Int Rev Gesamten Hydrobiol Hydrogr
Internationale Richard-Strauss-Gesellschaft. Mitteilungen — Strauss
Internationale Roehrenindustrie — Int Roehrenind
Internationale Rundschau der Arbeit — IRA

Internationale Schriftenreihe zur Numerischen Mathematik — Internat Schriftenreihe Numer Math
Internationale Spectator — Int Sp
Internationale Spectator — Int Spect
Internationale Spectator — Internat Spectator
Internationale Spectator — ISB
Internationale Tagung fuer das Studium der Brennstoffzellenbatterien. Tagungsbericht — Int Tag Stud Brennstoffzellenbatterien Tagungsber
Internationale Tagung ueber die Restlose Vergasung von Gefoerderter Kohle — Int Tag Restlose Vergasung Gefoerderter Kohle
Internationale Tagung ueber Elektrische Kontakte — Int Tag Elektr Kontakte
Internationale Tagung ueber Elektrische Kontakte. Vortraege — Int Tag Elektr Kontakte Vortr
Internationale Vereinigung fuer Theoretische und Angewandte Limnologie und Verhandlungen — Int Ver Theor Angew Limnol Verh
Internationale Wirtschaft mit den Mitteilungen der Bundeswirtschaftskammer [*A publication*] — IVL
Internationale Wissenschaftliche Korrespondenz zur Geschichte der Deutschen Arbeiterbewegung — IWK
Internationale Wochenschrift fuer Wissenschaft, Kunst, und Technik — OWW
Internationale Wolltextil-Forschungskonferenz. Proceedings — Int Wolltext Forschungskonf Proc
Internationale Zeitschrift der Landwirtschaft — Int Z Landwirtsch
Internationale Zeitschrift der Landwirtschaft — Internat Z Landw
Internationale Zeitschrift fuer Aerztliche Psychoanalyse — Intern Zs Aerztl Psychoanal
Internationale Zeitschrift fuer Angewandte Physiologie — IZAPA
Internationale Zeitschrift fuer Angewandte Physiologie Einschliesslich Arbeitsphysiologie — Int Z Angew Phsyiol Einschl Arbeitsphysiol
Internationale Zeitschrift fuer Angewandte Physiologie Einschliesslich Arbeitsphysiologie [*Germany*] — Int Z Angew Physiol
Internationale Zeitschrift fuer Bohrtechnik, Erdoelbergbau, und Geologie — Int Z Bohrtech Erdoelbergbau Geol
Internationale Zeitschrift fuer Elektrowaerme — Int Z Elektrowaerme
Internationale Zeitschrift fuer Erziehungswissenschaft — Int Z Erzieh
Internationale Zeitschrift fuer Erziehungswissenschaft — IZEW
Internationale Zeitschrift fuer Gas Waerme — Int Z Gas Waerme
Internationale Zeitschrift fuer Haematologie — Int Z Haematol
Internationale Zeitschrift fuer Klinische Pharmakologie, Therapie, und Toxicologie — Int Z Klin Pharmakol Ther Toxicol
Internationale Zeitschrift fuer Klinische Pharmakologie, Therapie, und Toxikologie — IZKPAK
Internationale Zeitschrift fuer Lebensmittel-Technologie und -Verfahrenstechnik — Int Z Lebensm Technol Verfahrenstech
Internationale Zeitschrift fuer Metallographie — Int Z Metallogr
Internationale Zeitschrift fuer Physikalisch Chemische Biologie — Int Z Phys Chem Biol
Internationale Zeitschrift fuer Rehabilitationsforschung — IJRRDK
Internationale Zeitschrift fuer Rehabilitationsforschung — Int Z Rehabilitationsforsch
Internationale Zeitschrift fuer Theoretische und Angewandte Genetik — Int Z Theor Angew Genet
Internationale Zeitschrift fuer Theorie und Praxis. Statistische Hefte — Int Z Theorie U Praxis Statists
Internationale Zeitschrift fuer Vitamin und Ernaehrungsforschung — Int Z Vitam-Ernaehrungsforsch
Internationale Zeitschrift fuer Vitamin- und Ernaehrungsforschung. Beiheft — Int Z Vitam Ernaehrungsforsch Beih
Internationale Zeitschrift fuer Vitaminforschung — Int Z Vitamforsch
Internationale Zeitschrift fuer Vitaminforschung — Int Z Vitaminforsch
Internationale Zeitschrift fuer Vitaminforschung. Beiheft — Int Z Vitaminforsch Beih
Internationale Zeitschrift fuer Vitaminforschung. Beiheft — IZVBA
Internationale Zeitschriftenschau fuer Bibelwissenschaft und Grenzgebiete — Int Z Bibelwiss
Internationale Zeitschriftenschau fuer Bibelwissenschaft und Grenzgebiete — Int Zeitschriftenschau Bibelwissenschaft Grenzgeb
Internationale Zeitschriftenschau fuer Bibelwissenschaft und Grenzgebiete [*Stuttgart/Duesseldorf*] — IZBG
Internationale Zeitschriftenschau fuer Bibelwissenschaft und Grenzgebiete [*Stuttgart/Duesseldorf*] — IZSch
Internationaler Betriebswirtschaftlicher Zeitschriftenreport — Internat Betriebswirt Zeitschriftenreport
Internationaler Emailkongress — Int Emailkongr
Internationaler Fruchtsaft-Kongress. Kongress-Hauptbericht — Int Fruchtsaft Kongr Kongr Hauptber
Internationaler Giessereikongress — Int Giessereikongr
Internationaler Glaskongress. Fachvortraege — Int Glaskongr Fachvortr
Internationaler Holzmarkt — IH
Internationaler Holzmarkt — Int Holzmarkt
Internationaler Holzmarkt — ITH
Internationaler Kongress fuer Byzantinische Studien — IKBS
Internationaler Kongress fuer Elektronenmikroskopie. Verhandlungen — Int Kongr Elektronenmikrosk Verh
Internationaler Kongress fuer Lutherforschung — IKLF
Internationaler Kongress fuer Orientalisten — IKO
Internationaler Kongress fuer Papyrologie — IKP
Internationaler Kongress fuer Pastorallliturgie — IKPL
Internationaler Kongress fuer Religionsgeschichte — IKRG
Internationaler Kongress fuer Religionssoziologie — IKRS
Internationaler Kongress fuer Roentgenoptik und Mikroanalyse — Int Kongr Roentgenoptik Mikroanal
Internationaler Kongress ueber die Tierische Fortpflanzung und die Kuenstliche Besamung — Int Kongr Tier Fortpflanz Kuenstliche Besamung
Internationaler Verband fuer Materialpruefung. Kongress — Int Verb Materialpruef Kongr
Internationaler Wasserversorgungskongress der International Water Supply Association — Int Wasserversorgungskongr Int Water Supply Assoc
Internationaler Wasserversorgungskongress der International Water Supply Association. IWSA — Int Wasserversorgungskongr Int Water Supply Assoc IWSA
Internationaler Wasserversorgungskongress der IWSA (International Water Supply Association) — Int Wasserversorgungskongr IWSA
Internationales Afrikaforum — AKB
Internationales Afrikaforum — Int Afr Forum
Internationales Afrikaforum — Int Afrikaforum
Internationales Afrikaforum — Internat Afrikaforum
Internationales Archiv fuer Arbeits- und Umweltmedizin — Int Arch Arb Umweltmed
Internationales Archiv fuer Arbeits- und Umweltmedizin — Int Arch Arbeits-Umweltmed
Internationales Archiv fuer Arbeitsmedizin — IAANBS
Internationales Archiv fuer Arbeitsmedizin — Int Arch Arbeitsmed
Internationales Archiv fuer Ethnographie — AE
Internationales Archiv fuer Ethnographie — IAE
Internationales Archiv fuer Ethnographie — Inst Arch Ethnog
Internationales Archiv fuer Ethnographie — Int Archiv Ethnog
Internationales Archiv fuer Ethnographie — Int Archiv Ethnogr
Internationales Archiv fuer Ethnologie — Internat Archiv f Ethno
Internationales Archiv fuer Gewerbepathologie und Gewerbehygiene — Int Arch Gewerbepathol Gewerbehyg
Internationales Archiv fuer Gewerbepathologie und Gewerbehygiene — IRGGA
Internationales Archiv fuer Gewerbepathologie und Gewerbehygiene — IRGGAJ
Internationales Archiv fuer Photogrammetrie — IAPhgr
Internationales Archiv fuer Sozialgeschichte der Deutschen Literatur — IASL
Internationales Asienforum — IAQ
Internationales Asienforum — Int As For
Internationales Asienforum — Int Asien Forum
Internationales Asienforum — Int Asienf
Internationales Asienforum — Internat Asienforum
Internationales Energie-Forum — Int Energie Forum
Internationales Gewerbearchiv — Int Gewerbearchiv
Internationales Gewerbearchiv der Kleinbetrieb und Mittelbetrieb in der Modernen Wirtschaft — IGW
Internationales Hydromikrobiologisches Symposium. Verhandlungen — Int Hydromikrobiol Symp Verh
Internationales Jahrbuch der Politik — I Jb Pol
Internationales Jahrbuch der Politik — Int Jb Pol
Internationales Jahrbuch der Sozialpolitik — IJS
Internationales Jahrbuch der Tribologie — Int Jahrb Tribol
Internationales Jahrbuch fuer Geschichts- und Geographie-Unterricht — Int Jb Gesch und Geogr Unterr
Internationales Jahrbuch fuer Geschichtsunterricht — IJGU
Internationales Jahrbuch fuer Geschichtsunterricht — Internat Jb Gesch Unterricht
Internationales Jahrbuch fuer Religionssoziologie — IJ Rel Soz
Internationales Jahrbuch fuer Religionssoziologie — IJRS
Internationales Jahrbuch fuer Religionssoziologie — Int Jb Relig Soziol
Internationales Jahrbuch fuer Soziologie — IJSoz
Internationales Journal fuer Prophylaktische Medizin und Sozialhygiene — Int J Prophyl Med Sozialhyg
Internationales Recht und Diplomatie — Int Recht u Diplom
Internationales Recht und Diplomatie — Internat Recht und Diplomatie
Internationales Spektrochemisches Colloquium. Berichte — Int Spektrochem Colloq Ber
Internationales Symposium ueber Struktur und Funktion der Erythrozyten — Int Symp Strukt Funkt Erythrozyten
Internationales Symposium ueber Systemfungizide — Int Symp Systemfungiz
Internationales Symposium ueber Wasserunkraeuter — Int Symp Wasserunkraeuter
Internationales Veredler-Jahrbuch — Int Veredler Jahrb
Internationales Verkehrswesen — Int Verkehrswesen
Internationales Verkehrswesen; Fachzeitschrift fuer Information und Kommunikation in Verkehr — INJ
Internationales Wissenschaftliches Kolloquium. Technische Hochschule Ilmenau — Int Wiss Kolloq Tech Hochsch Ilmenau
Internationales Wissenschaftliches Kolloquium ueber Kaffee — Int Wiss Kolloq Kaffee
Internationelle Studier (Stockholm) — Int Stud (Stockholm)
Internazionale Wissenschaftliche Korrespondenz zur Geschichte der Deutschen Arbeiterbewegung — Int Wiss Korresp Gesch Dtsch Arb-Bew
Internist — INTEAG
Internistische Praxis — INPXAJ
Internistische Praxis — Internist Prax
Internistische Welt — Internist Welt
Inter-Nord — INNO
Inter-Parliamentary Bulletin — Inter Parliamentary Bull
Inter-Parliamentary Bulletin — Inter-Parliamentary Bul
Interpersonal Development — Interpers D
Interpretation — GITP
Interpretation — In
Interpretation — Interp
Interpretation — Interpretat
Interpretation — ITPTBG
Interpretation. A Journal of Bible and Theology [*Richmond, VA*] — Int
Interpretation. A Journal of Bible and Theology [*Richmond, VA*] — Interpr
Interpretation. A Journal of Bible and Theology — Intpr
Interpretation. A Journal of Political Philosophy — IJPP

Interpretation (Richmond) — Int (R)
Interpreter — IN
Interpreter — Int
Interpreter — INTR
Interpreter's Bible — Int B
Interpreter's Dictionary of the Bible — IDB
Interpublic Group of Companies, Incorporated. News Release — Intrpub NR
Interracial Books for Children. Bulletin — Inter B C
Interracial Books for Children. Bulletin — Interracial Bks Child Bull
Interracial Review — Interracial Rev
Interregional Symposium on the Iron and Steel Industry. Papers — Interreg Symp Iron Steel Ind Pap
Interscholastic Athletic Administration — Intersch Ath Adm
Interscholastic Athletic Administration — Intersch Athl Adm
Interscience Conference on Antimicrobial Agents and Chemotherapy — Intersci Conf Antimicrob Agents Chemother
Interscience Conference on Antimicrobial Agents and Chemotherapy. Proceedings — Intersci Conf Antimicrob Agents Chemother Proc
Interscience Library of Chemical Engineering and Processing — Interscience Libr Chem Eng Process
Interscience Monographs and Texts in Physics and Astronomy — Intersci Monogr Texts Phys Astron
Interscience Publication — Intersci Publ
Intersectum — INSMD4
Intersekcijski Sestanek Medicinskih Biokemikov SR Slovenije in SR Hrvatske. Clanki — Intersekc Sestanek Med Biokem SR Slov SR Hrvat Clanki
Inter-Society Color Council Newsletter — ISCC Newsl
Intersociety Cryogenics Symposium — Intersoc Cryog Symp
Intersociety Energy Conversion Engineering Conference. Proceedings — Intersoc Energy Convers Eng Conf Proc
INTERSOL 85. Proceedings. Biennial Congress. International Solar Energy Society — INTERSOL 85 Proc Bienn Congr Int Sol Energy Soc
Interstate Conference of Headmistresses of Australian Girls' Schools. Report — Interstate Conf of Headmistresses
Interstate Oil and Gas Compact Commission. Committee Bulletin — Oil Gas Compact Bull
Interstate Oil Compact Commission. Committee Bulletin — Interstate Oil Compact Comm Comm Bull
Interstate Oil Compact. Quarterly Bulletin — Interstate Oil Compact Quart Bull
Interstitial Nephropathies. Symposium on Nephrology — Interstitial Nephropathies Symp Nephrol
Intertax — FMC
Inter-Union Commission on Geodynamics. Scientific Report — Inter-Union Comm Geodyn Sci Rep
Interuniversitair Instituut voor Kernwetenschappen. Monografie — Interuniv Inst Kernwet Monogr
Inter-University Electronics Series — Inter-Univ Electron Ser
Inter-University Faculty Work Conference — Interuniv Fac Work Conf
Interview — GINT
Interview — Interv
Intervirology — Intervirolo
Intervirology — IVRYA
Intervirology — IVRYAK
Intestinal Toxicology — Intest Toxicol
Intracellular Calcium-Dependent Proteolysis [*Monograph*] — Intracell Calcium Depend Proteolysis
Intracellular Messengers — Intracell Messengers
Intracellular Transfer of Lipid Molecules — Intracell Transfer Lipid Mol
Intramolecular and Nonlinear Dynamics — Intramol Nonlinear Dyn
Intramural Law Review of American University — Intra L Rev (Am U)
Intramural Law Review of New York University — Intra L Rev (NYU)
Intramural Law Review of University of California at Los Angeles — Intra L Rev UCLA
Intra-Science Chemistry Reports — Intra-Sci Chem Rep
Introduction a la Bible — IB
Introduction aux Etudes d'Histoire Ecclesiastique Locale — IEHEL
Introduction to Glass Integrated Optics — Introd Glass Integr Opt
Introduction to the Molecular Genetics of Cancer — Introd Mol Genet Cancer
Introduktsiya ta Aklimatizatsiya Roslin na Ukraini — Introd Aklim Rosl Ukr
Introduktsiya ta Eksperimental'na Ekologiya Roslin — Introd Eksp Ekol Rosl
INTSOY [*International Soybean Program*] **Series** — INTSOY Ser
INTSOY [*International Soybean Program*] **Series. University of Illinois. College of Agriculture** — INTSOY Ser Univ Ill Coll Agric
Inuit Art Quarterly — INAQ
Inuit. Inuit Circumpolar Conference [*Greenland*] — IICC
Inuit Nipingat. Baker Lane. Northwest Territory — IP
Inuit North [*Nortext, Ottawa*] — INUN
Inuit Okakheet. Kitikmeot Inuit Association — INOK
Inuit Tapirisat of Canada. Press Release — ITPR
Inuit Today — INUI
Inuit Today Newsletter. Inuit Ublumi Tusagatsangit — INTN
Inukshuk. Frobisher Bay — IK
Inulirijut. Department of Indian and Northern Affairs. Education Section. Social Development Division [*Canada*] — INUL
Inummarit — INUM
Inuttitut — INUT
Inuvialuit — INUV
Inuvialuit — INVL
Invasion and Metastasis — INVMDJ
Inventaire des Inscriptions de Palmyre — INV
Inventaire des Maladies des Plantes au Canada — Inventaire Mal Plantes Can
Inventaire des Mosaiques de la Gaule et de l'Afrique — IMGA
Inventaire des Mosaiques de la Gaule et de l'Afrique — Inv Mos
Inventaire des Mosaiques de la Gaule et de l'Afrique — Inv Mos Afrique
Inventaire des Mosaiques de la Gaule et de l'Afrique — Inv Mosaiques
Inventaire Mineralogique de la France — Inventaire Mineral Fr
Inventaire Sommaire de la Collection Waddington — Inv Waddington
Inventaire Sommaire de la Collection Waddington — ISCW
Inventaire Sommaire de la Collection Waddington — Wad
Inventaire Sommaire de la Collection Waddington — Waddington
Inventaria Archaeologica — Inventaria
Inventaria Archaeologica — Invt Arch
Inventario — Inv
Inventario del Patrimonio Arquitectonico Espanol [*Database*] — IPAA
Inventario del Patrimonio Historico-Artistico Espanol [*Database*] — IPAT
Inventario Musical [*Database*] — IMUS
Invention Intelligence [*India*] — Invent Intell
Invention Intelligence — Invention
Invention Management — INMAD
Invention Management [*United States*] — Invent Manage
Inventiones Mathematicae — Invent Math
Inventors' and Patenting Sourcebook — IPS
Inventory Locator Service [*Database*] — ILS
Inventory of Canadian Agri-Food Research [*Database*] — ICAR
Inventory of Greek Coin Hoards — IGCH
Inventory of Marriage and Family Literature — IMFL
Inventory of Sources for History of Twentieth Century Physics [*Database*] — ISHTCP
Inverse and Ill-posed Problems Series — Inverse Ill posed Probl Ser
Inverse Problems — Inverse Pr
Inverse Problems in Engineering — Inverse Probl Eng
Invertebrate Endocrinology — INENE6
Invertebrate Endocrinology — Invertebr Endocrinol
Invertebrate Models for Biomedical Research — Invertebr Models Biomed Res
Invertebrate Neuroscience — Invert Neurosci
Invertebrate Neuroscience — Invertebr Neurosci
Invertebrate Reproduction and Development — Invertebr R
Invertebrate Reproduction and Development — Invertebr Reprod Dev
Invertebrate Taxonomy — Invertebr Taxon
Invertebrate Tissue Culture. Applications in Medicine, Biology, and Agriculture. Proceedings. International Conference on Invertebrate Tissue Culture — Invertebr Tissue Cult Appl Med Biol Agric Proc Int Conf
Invertebrate Tissue Cultures. Research Applications. Extended Proceedings. United States-Japan Seminar — Invertebr Tissue Cult Res Appl Ext Proc US Jpn Semin
Investigacion Agraria. Produccion y Proteccion Vegetales — Invest Agrar Prod Prot Veg
Investigacion Agricola [*Santiago*] — IAGRD4
Investigacion Agricola — Investigacion Agric
Investigacion Agricola. Consejo Nacional de Investigaciones Agricolos — Invest Agric
Investigacion Agricola (Santiago) — Invest Agric (Santiago)
Investigacion Clinica [*Maracaibo*] — ICLIAD
Investigacion Clinica — Invest Clin
Investigacion Clinica (Maracaibo) — Invest Clin (Maracaibo)
Investigacion Clinica. Suplemento — Invest Clin Supl
Investigacion e Informacion Textil — Invest Inf Text
Investigacion e Informacion Textil y de Tensioactivos — Invest Inf Text Tens
Investigacion e Informacion Textil y de Tensioactivos — Invest Inf Text Tensioactivos
Investigacion Economica — Invest Econ
Investigacion Economica — Investigacion Econ
Investigacion en la Clinica y en el Laboratorio — Invest Clin Lab
Investigacion en la Clinica y en el Laboratorio — RCLADN
Investigacion Medica Internacional — IMEIDH
Investigacion Medica Internacional — Invest Med Int
Investigacion Operacional [*Havana*] — Investigacion Oper
Investigacion Pediatrica — Invest Pediatr
Investigacion Pesquera — Inv Pesq
Investigacion Pesquera — Invest Pesq
Investigacion Pesquera — Investigacion Pesq
Investigacion Pesquera — IPESAV
Investigacion Pesquera. Suplemento. Resultados Expediciones Cientificas — Invest Pesq Supl Result Exped Cient
Investigacion y Progreso — IP
Investigacion y Progreso Agricola — Invest Prog Agric
Investigacion y Progreso Agricola — IPAGBA
Investigacion y Tecnica del Papel — Invest Tec Papel
Investigaciones Agropecuarias [*Lima, Peru*] — IAGPBU
Investigaciones Agropecuarias (Lima, Peru) — Invest Agropecu (Lima)
Investigaciones Agropecuarias (Lima, Peru) — Invest Agropecu (Peru)
Investigaciones de Campo — Invest Campo
Investigaciones Historicas (Mexico) — Invest Hist Mex
Investigaciones. Laboratorio de Quimica Biologica. Universidad Nacional de Cordoba — Invest Lab Quim Biol Univ Nac Cordoba
Investigaciones Linguisticas — IL
Investigaciones Marinas CICIMAR (Centro Interdisciplinario de Ciencias Marinas) — Invest Mar CICIMAR
Investigaciones Marinas. Universidad Catolica de Valparaiso — IMCVA9
Investigaciones Marinas. Universidad Catolica de Valparaiso — Invest Mar Univ Catol Valparaiso
Investigaciones Zoologicas Chilenas — Inv Zool Chilenas
Investigaciones Zoologicas Chilenas — Invest Zool Chil
Investigaciones Zoologicas Chilenas — IZOCAZ
Investigacoes (Sao Paulo) — Invest S Paulo
Investigation and Utilization of Clays and Clay Minerals. Proceedings. Symposium — Invest Util Clays Clay Miner Proc Symp
Investigation of Air Pollution - Deposit Gauge and Lead Dioxide Candle — Investigation Air Pollut-Deposit Gauge Lead Diox Candle

Investigation of Air Pollution - Smoke and Sulphur Dioxide Survey — Investigation Air Pollut Smoke Sulph Diox Surv
Investigation of Rates and Mechanisms of Reactions — Invest Rates Mech React
Investigation of the Geothermal Potential of the UK. British Geological Survey — Invest Geotherm Potential UK Br Geol Surv
Investigation of the Geothermal Potential of the UK. Institute of Geological Sciences — Invest Geotherm Potential UK Inst Geol Sci
Investigation Report. Commonwealth Scientific and Industrial Research Organization. Institute of Earth Resources — Investigation Report-CSIRO Institute of Earth Resources
Investigation Report. Division of Mineral Chemistry. Commonwealth Scientific and Industrial Research Organisation — Invest Rep Div Miner Chem CSIRO
Investigation Report. Division of Mineral Physics. Commonwealth Scientific and Industrial Research Organisation — Invest Rep Div Miner Phys CSIRO
Investigation Report. Division of Mineralogy. Commonwealth Scientific and Industrial Research Organisation — Invest Rep Div Miner CSIRO
Investigation Report. Minerals Research Laboratories. Commonwealth Scientific and Industrial Research Organisation — Invest Rep Miner Res Lab CSIRO
Investigation Report. Mines Branch. Canada — Invest Rep Mines Branch Can
Investigation Reports. Commonwealth Scientific and Industrial Research Organisation (Australia) — Invest Rep CSIRO (Aust)
Investigational New Drugs — INNDDK
Investigational New Drugs — Invest New Drugs
Investigations in Fish Control — Invest Fish Control
Investigations in Ophthalmology and Visual Science — INOPA
Investigations of Indiana Lakes and Streams — IILSAH
Investigations of Indiana Lakes and Streams — Inv Ind Lakes and Streams
Investigations of Indiana Lakes and Streams — Invest Indiana Lakes Streams
Investigations on Cetacea — Invest Cetacea
Investigations on Cetacea — IVNCDN
Investigations on Pesticide Residues — Invest Pestic Residues
Investigative and Cell Pathology — ICPADC
Investigative and Cell Pathology — Invest Cell Pathol
Investigative Microtechniques in Medicine and Biology — Invest Microtech Med Biol
Investigative Ophthalmology [*Later, Investigative Ophthalmology and Visual Science*] — INOPAO
Investigative Ophthalmology [*Later, Investigative Ophthalmology and Visual Science*] — Inv Ophth
Investigative Ophthalmology [*Later, Investigative Ophthalmology and Visual Science*] — Invest Ophth
Investigative Ophthalmology [*Later, Investigative Ophthalmology and Visual Science*] — Invest Ophthalmol
Investigative Ophthalmology and Visual Science — Invest Ophthal Visual Sci
Investigative Ophthalmology and Visual Science — Invest Ophthalmol Vis Sci
Investigative Ophthalmology and Visual Science — Invest Ophthalmol Visual Sci
Investigative Ophthalmology and Visual Science — IOVSDA
Investigative Radiology — Inv Radiol
Investigative Radiology — Invest Radiol
Investigative Radiology — INVRAV
Investigative Urology — INURAQ
Investigative Urology — Inv Urol
Investigative Urology — Invest Urol
Investitionshilfegesetz — IHG
Investment Analysts Journal — Invest Anal J
Investment Appraisals for Chemical Engineers — Investment Appraisals Chem Eng
Investment Bankers Association of America. Bulletin — IBA of A
Investment Banking — Inv Banking
Investment Dealers' Digest — Inv DD
Investment Dealers' Digest — Investment Dealers Dig
Investment Decisions — Invest Dec
Investment Forum — Invest For
Investment Letter — Invest Let
Investment Management World — Invest Man Wld
Investment Monthly — Invest Mon
Investment Quality Trends — IQ
Investment Review — INV
Investment Statistics — Invest Stats
Investment Trust Year Book — ITYB
Investor-Owned Hospital Review — Investor Owned Hosp Rev
Investors Chronicle — IC
Investors Chronicle — Investors Chron
Investors Chronicle and Financial World — Investors Chronicle
Investors Chronicle and Stock Exchange Gazette — Inv Chron
Invited Lectures and Contributed Papers. International Conference on Clustering Phenomena — Invited Lect Contrib Pap Int Conf Clustering Phenom Nucl
Invited Papers. European Conference on Controlled Fusion and Plasma Physics — Invited Pap Eur Conf Controlled Fusion Plasma Phys
Invited Papers. International Conference on Multiphoton Processes — Invited Pap Int Conf Multiphoton Processes
Invited Papers. International Conference on Phenomena in Ionized Gases — Invited Pap Int Conf Phenom Ioniz Gases
Invited Papers. International Symposium on Discharges and Electrical Insulation in Vacuum — Invited Pap Int Symp Discharges Electr Insul Vac
Invited Papers. National Conference on Atomic Spectroscopy — Invited Pap Natl Conf At Spectrosc
Invited Papers presented at the European Solid State Circuits Conference — Invited Pap Eur Solid State Circuits Conf
Inwestycje i Budownictwo — Inwest i Budown
Inzenerno-Fiziceskii Zurnal — Inz-Fiz Z
Inzenernyi Zurnal Mehanika Tverdogo Tela — Inz Z Meh Tverd Tela
Inzenyrske Stavby — Inz Stavby
Inzhenerna Geologiya i Khidrogeologiya — Inzh Geol Khidrogeol
Inzhenernaya Geologiya — Inzh Geol
Inzhenerno Fizicheskii Zhurnal — Inzhenerno Fizicheskii Zh
Inzhenerno-Fizicheskii Zhurnal — Inzh-Fiz Zh
Inzhenerno-Fizicheskii Zhurnal Akademiya Nauk Beloruskoi SSR — Inzh-Fiz Zh Akad Nauk Belorus SSR
Inzhenernyi Sbornik [*Former USSR*] — Inzh Sb
Inzhenernyi Sbornik — INZSA
Inzhenernyi Zhurnal [*Former USSR*] — Inzh Zh
Inzhenernyi Zhurnal. Mekhanika Tverdogo Tela — Inzh Zh Mekh Tverd Tela
Inzynieria Chemiczna — Inz Chem
Inzynieria Chemiczny i Procesowa — Inz Chem i Proc
Inzynieria i Aparatura Chemiczna [*Poland*] — Inz Apar Chem
Inzynieria i Aparatura Chemiczna — Inz i Aparat Chem
Inzynieria i Budownictwo — Inz Budownictwo
Inzynieria Materialowa — Inz Materialowa
IO Management-Zeitschrift — IIOOD
Iodine Abstracts and Reviews — Iodine Abstr Rev
Ion and Plasma Assisted Techniques. International Conference — Ion Plasma Assisted Tech Int Conf
Ion Channels of Vascular Smooth Muscle Cells and Endothelial Cells. Proceedings. International Society for Heart Research — Ion Channels Vasc Smooth Muscle Cells Endothelial Cells Proc
Ion Exchange and Adsorption — Ion Exch Adsorpt
Ion Exchange and Membranes — IEXMBW
Ion Exchange and Membranes — Ion Exch
Ion Exchange and Membranes — Ion Exch and Membranes
Ion Exchange and Membranes — Ion Exch Membr
Ion Exchange and Solvent Extraction — IESEB
Ion Exchange and Solvent Extraction — Ion Exch Solvent Extr
Ion Exchange Progress — Ion Exch Prog
Ion Formation from Organic Solids. Proceedings. International Conference — Ion Form Org Solids Proc Int Conf
Ion Implantation in Semiconductors and Other Materials. Proceedings. International Conference — Ion Implant Semicond Other Mater Proc Int Conf
Ionizing Radiation (Tokyo) — Ioniz Radiat (Tokyo)
Ionosfernye Issledovaniya — IISSA
Ionosfernye Issledovaniya [*Former USSR*] — Ionos Issled
Ionospheric Data — ID
Ionospheric Researches — Ionos Res
Ion-Selective Electrode Reviews — Ion-Sel Electrode Rev
Ion-Selective Electrode Reviews — Ion-Selective Electrode Rev
Ion-Selective Electrodes in Analytical Chemistry — Ion Sel Electrodes Anal Chem
Ion-Selective Electrodes. Symposium — Ion Sel Electrodes Symp
IOP (Institute of Physics) Short Meetings Series — IOP Short Meet Ser
Iowa Academy of Science. Journal — Iowa Acad Sci J
Iowa Academy of Science. Proceedings — Iowa Ac Sc Pr
Iowa Academy of Science. Proceedings — Iowa Acad Sci Proc
Iowa Administrative Bulletin — Iowa Admin Bull
Iowa Administrative Code — Iowa Admin Code
Iowa. Agricultural Experiment Station. Research Bulletin — IERBA2
Iowa Agricultural Experiment Station. Research Bulletin — Iowa Agric Exp Sta Res Bull
Iowa. Agricultural Experiment Station. Research Bulletin — Iowa Agric Exp Stn Res Bull
Iowa Agricultural Experiment Station. Special Report — Iowa Agric Exp Sta Special Rep
Iowa. Agriculture and Home Economics Experiment Station. Research Bulletin — Iowa Agric Home Econ Exp Stn Res Bull
Iowa. Agriculture and Home Economics Experiment Station. Research Bulletin — IWRBBR
Iowa. Agriculture and Home Economics Experiment Station. Soil Survey Reports [*A publication*] — Iowa Agric Home Econ Exp Stn Soil Surv Rep
Iowa. Agriculture and Home Economics Experiment Station. Special Report — Iowa Agric Home Econ Exp Stn Spec Rep
Iowa. Agriculture and Home Economics Experiment Station. Special Report — IWSRBC
Iowa Bird Life — IOBLAM
Iowa Bureau of Labor. Biennial Report — Iowa Bur Lab Bien Rep
Iowa Code, Annotated (West) — Iowa Code Ann (West)
Iowa Conservationist — ICNSAJ
Iowa Conservationist — Iowa Conserv
Iowa Dental Bulletin — Iowa Dent Bull
Iowa Dental Journal — Iowa Dent J
Iowa Drug Information Service — Iowa Drug Inf Serv
Iowa Engineering Experiment Station. Engineering Report — Iowa Eng Exp Stn Eng Rep
Iowa English Bulletin. Yearbook — IEBY
Iowa English Yearbook — IEY
Iowa Farm Science — Iowa Farm Sci
Iowa Foreign Language Bulletin — IFLB
Iowa Geological Survey. Annual Report — Iowa Geol Surv Annu Rep
Iowa. Geological Survey. Report of Investigations — Iowa Geol Surv Rep Invest
Iowa. Geological Survey. Technical Paper — Iowa Geol Surv Tech Pap
Iowa Geological Survey Water Atlas — Iowa Geol Surv Water Atlas
Iowa. Geological Survey. Water Atlas — Iowa Geol Survey Water Atlas
Iowa. Geological Survey. Water-Supply Bulletin — Iowa Geol Survey Water-Supply Bull
Iowa Historical Record — Iowa Hist Rec
Iowa Institute of Hydraulic Research. Report — IIHR Report
Iowa Journal of History — IJH
Iowa Journal of History and Politics — IA J
Iowa Journal of History and Politics — Ia J Hist Pol

Iowa Journal of History and Politics — IJHP
Iowa Journal of History and Politics — Iowa Jour Hist and Pol
Iowa Journal of Research in Music Education — IR
Iowa Law Bulletin — Ia Law Bul
Iowa Law Review — IA L Rev
Iowa Law Review — Ia Law R
Iowa Law Review — IA Law Rev
Iowa Law Review — IA LR
Iowa Law Review — ILR
Iowa Law Review — Iowa L Rev
Iowa Law Review — Iowa Law R
Iowa Legislative Service (West) — Iowa Legis Serv (West)
Iowa Library Quarterly — Iowa Lib Q
Iowa Medical Journal — Iowa Med J
Iowa Medicine — Iowa Med
Iowa Music Educator — IO
Iowa Naturalist — Iowa Nat
Iowa Orthopaedic Journal — Iowa Orthop J
Iowa Reports — Iowa
Iowa Review — IowaR
Iowa State Bar Association. News Bulletin — Iowa St BA News Bull
Iowa State College. Engineering Experiment Station. Engineering Report. Project — Iowa State Coll Eng Expt Sta Eng Rept Proj
Iowa State College. Iowa Engineering Experiment Station. Engineering Report — Iowa State Coll Iowa Eng Exp Stn Eng Rep
Iowa State College. Journal of Science — Iowa State Coll J Sci
Iowa State College of Agriculture and Mechanical Arts. Agricultural Experiment Station. Publications — IA Ag Exp
Iowa State College of Agriculture and Mechanical Arts. Engineering Experiment Station. Bulletin — Iowa State Coll Agric Mech Arts Eng Exp Stn Bull
Iowa State College of Agriculture and Mechanical Arts. Engineering Experiment Station. Engineering Report — Iowa State Coll Agric Mech Arts Eng Exp Stn Eng Rep
Iowa State College Veterinarian — Iowa State Coll Vet
Iowa State Institutions. Bulletin — Iowa Institutions B
Iowa State Journal of Research — Iowa State J Res
Iowa State Journal of Research — ISJR
Iowa State Journal of Research — ISJRA
Iowa State Journal of Research — ISJRA6
Iowa State Journal of Science — Iowa St J Sci
Iowa State Journal of Science — Iowa State J Sci
Iowa State Journal of Science — ISJSA9
Iowa State University (Ames). Engineering Research Institute. Report — Iowa State Univ (Ames) Eng Res Inst Rep
Iowa State University Bulletin. Engineering Report. Iowa Engineering Experiment Station — Iowa State Univ Bull Eng Rep Iowa Eng Exp Stn
Iowa State University. Department of Earth Sciences. Publication — Iowa State Univ Dept Earth Sci Pub
Iowa State University. Engineering Research Institute. Technical Report ISU-ERI-AMES — Iowa State Univ Eng Res Inst Tech Rep ISU-ERI-AMES
Iowa State University. Laboratories of Natural History. Bulletin — Iowa Univ Lab N H B
Iowa State University of Science and Technology. Doctoral Dissertations. Abstracts and References — IDD
Iowa State University of Science and Technology. Engineering Experiment Station. Bulletin [*Ames, IA*] — Iowa State Univ Eng Exp Sta Bull
Iowa State University of Science and Technology. Engineering Experiment Station. Bulletin — Iowa State Univ Sci and Technology Eng Expt Sta Bull
Iowa State University of Science and Technology. Engineering Experiment Station. Bulletin — Iowa State Univ Sci Technol Eng Exp Stn Bull
Iowa State University of Science and Technology. Engineering Experiment Station. Engineering Report — Iowa State Univ Sci Technol Eng Exp Stn Eng Rep
Iowa State University Press Series in the History of Technology and Science — Iowa State Univ Press Ser Hist Tech Sci
Iowa State University. Statistical Laboratory. Annual Report — Iowa State Univ Stat Lab Annu Rep
Iowa State University. Statistical Laboratory. Annual Report — IUSRAV
Iowa State University Veterinarian — Iowa State Univ Vet
Iowa State Water Resources Research Institute. Annual Report — Iowa State Water Resour Res Inst Annu Rep
Iowa Studies in Clasical Philology — ISCP
Iowa Symposium on Toxic Mechanisms. Proceedings — Iowa Symp Toxic Mech Proc
IPA [*Instituto Provincial Agropecuario Mendoza, Argentina*] **Boletin Tecnico** — IPA Bol Tec
IPA [*International Pharmaceutical Abstracts*] **Review** — IPA Rev
IPA [*Institute of Public Affairs*] **Review** — IPA Rev
IPA [*Institute of Public Affairs*] **Review** — IPAR
Ipargazdasagi Szemle — Ipargazd Szle
Ipari Energiagazdalkodas — Ip Energiagazd
Ipari Energiagazdalkodas — Ipari Energiagazd
Iparmueveszeti Muzeum es a Hopp Ferenc Keletazssiai Mueveszeti Muzeum Evkoenyve — Ipar ME
Iparmueveszeti Muzeum Evkoenyvei — IME
Iparmueveszeti Muzeum Evkoenyvei — Iparmuveszeti Muz Ev
IPC [*Institute of Philippine Culture*] **Monographs** — IPC Mg
IPC [*Institute of Philippine Culture*] **Papers** — IPC Pap
IPCR (Institute of Physical and Chemical Research) Cyclotron Progress Report — IPCR Cyclotron Prog Rep
IPE. Industrial and Production Engineering — IPE Ind Prod Eng
IPE [*Industrial and Production Engineering*] **International** — IPE Int
IPE International Industrial and Production Engineering — IPE Int Ind Prod Eng
IPEF. Instituto de Pesquisas e Estudos Florestais — IPEF Inst Pesqui Estud Florest
IPEF. Instituto de Pesquisas e Estudos Florestais — IPEF Inst Pesqui Estud Florestais
IPEF [*Instituto de Pesquisas e Estudos Florestais*] **Publicacao Semestral** — IPEF Publ Semest
IPI [*International Potash Institute*] **Bulletin** — IPI Bull
IPI [*International Potash Institute*] **Bulletin** — IPIBD3
IPI [*International Potash Institute*] **Research Topics** — IPI Res Top
IPI [*International Potash Institute*] **Research Topics** — IRTOD9
IPLO [*Institute of Professional Librarians of Ontario*] **Quarterly** — IPLO Q
IPP [*Max Planck Institut fuer Plasmaphysik*] **Presseinformationen** — IPP Presseinf
IPPF [*International Planned Parenthood Federation*] **Medical Bulletin** — IPPF Med Bull
IPPF [*International Planned Parenthood Federation*] **Medical Bulletin (English Edition)** — IPPF Med Bull (Engl Ed)
IPW [*Institut fuer Internationale Politik und Wirtschaft der Deutschen Demokratischen Republik*] **Berichte** — IPW Ber
IPW [*Institut fuer Internationale Politik und Wirtschaft der Deutschen Demokratischen Republik*] **Forschungshefte** — IPW Forsch-H
IPW (Institut fuer Internationale Politik und Wirtschaft der Deutschen Demokratischen Republik) Forschungshefte — IPW Forschungshefte
IQ [*Series*] **Society of Manufacturing Engineers** — IQ Soc Manuf Eng
Iqbal [*Lahore*] — I
Iqbal Review — Iqbal R
Iqbal Review — IqR
IR and T Nuclear Journal [*United States*] — IRT Nucl J
Ir Genes and Ia Antigens. Proceedings. Ir Gene Workshop — Ir Genes Ia Antigens Proc Ir Gene Workshop
IR Research Reports — IR Research Repts
Iran. Departement de Botanique. Ministere de l'Agriculture et du Developpement Rural — Iran Dep Bot Minist Agric Dev Rural
Iran Geological Survey. Report — Iran Geol Surv Rep
Iran Journal. British Institute of Persian Studies — Iran
Iran Journal of Public Health — IJPHC
Iran Plant Pests and Diseases Research Institute. Department of Botany. Publication — Iran Plant Pests Dis Res Inst Dep Bot Publ
Iran. Plant Pests and Diseases Research Institute. Department of Botany. Publication — PPPBDD
Iran Service — IRS
Iranian Journal of Agricultural Research — IJAGC3
Iranian Journal of Agricultural Research — Iran J Agric Res
Iranian Journal of Agricultural Sciences — Iran J Agric Sci
Iranian Journal of Agricultural Sciences — IRJADJ
Iranian Journal of Chemistry and Chemical Engineering — Iran J Chem Chem Eng
Iranian Journal of Medical Sciences — Iran J Med Sci
Iranian Journal of Plant Pathology — IJPLBO
Iranian Journal of Plant Pathology — Iran J Plant Pathol
Iranian Journal of Polymer Science and Technology (English Edition) — Iran J Polym Sci Technol Engl Ed
Iranian Journal of Public Health — IJPHCD
Iranian Journal of Public Health — Iran J Public Health
Iranian Journal of Science and Technology — IJSTBT
Iranian Journal of Science and Technology — Iran J Sci and Technol
Iranian Journal of Science and Technology — Iran J Sci Technol
Iranian Journal of Science and Technology — Iranian J Sci Tech
Iranian Polymer Journal — Iran Polym J
Iranian Review of International Relations — Iran R Int Relat
Iranian Review of International Relations — Iranian R Internat Relations
Iranian Studies — Ira Stud
Iranian Studies — Iran Stud
Iranian Studies — IranS
Iranian Studies — IrS
Iranica Antiqua — IA
Iranica Antiqua [*Leiden*] — Iran Ant
Iranica Antiqua — Iran Antiq
Iranica Antiqua — Iranica Ant
Iranica Antiqua [*Leiden*] — IrAnt
Iranica Antiqua. Supplements — IRAS
Iranica Antique. Supplements — Iranica Ant Suppl
Iranische Texte und Hilfsbuecher — ITH
Iraq Natural History Museum. Publication — Iraq Nat Hist Mus Publ
Iraq Natural History Museum. Publication — PINHA3
Iraq Natural History Museum. Report — Iraq Nat Hist Mus Rep
Iraq Natural History Museum. Report — IRNRAJ
Iraq Times — IT
Iraqi Academy. Journal — Iraqi Acad J
Iraqi Chemical Society. Journal — Iraqi Chem Soc J
Iraqi Dental Journal — Iraqi Dent J
Iraqi Geographical Journal — Iraqi Geogr J
Iraqi Journal of Science — Iraqi J Sci
Iraqi Journal of Science — IRJSD5
IRAT (Institut de Recherches Agronomiques Tropicales et Cultures Vivrieres) Bulletin Agronomique — IRAT Bull Agron
IRC [*Indian Roads Congress*] **Bulletin** — IRC Bull
IRC [*Indian Roads Congress*] **Highway Research Board. Highway Research Bulletin** — IRC Highw Res Board Highw Res Bull
IRCS (International Research Communications System) Library Compendium — IRCS Libr Compend
IRCS (International Research Communications System) Medical Science — IRCS (Int Res Commun Syst) Med Sci
IRCS [*International Research Communications System*] **Medical Science** — IMSCE2

IRCS [*International Research Communications System*] **Medical Science** — IRCS Med Sci
IRCS [*International Research Communications System*] **Medical Science. Library Compendium** — IRCS Med Sci-Libr Compend
IRCS [*International Research Communications System*] **Medical Science. Library Compendium** — IRLCAW
IRCS [*International Research Communications System*] **Medical Science. Library Compendium** — IRLCD
IRCS [*International Research Communications System*] **Research on Clinical Pharmacology and Therapeutics** — IRCTD
IRE (Institute of Radio Engineers) Transactions on Antennas and Propagation — IRE Trans Antennas Propag
IRE (Institute of Radio Engineers) Transactions on Electron Devices — IRE Trans Electron Devices
IRE (Institute of Radio Engineers) Transactions on Radio Frequency Interference — IRE Trans Radio Freq Interference
IRE (Institute of Radio Engineers) Transactions on Space Electronics and Telemetry — IRE Trans Space Electron Telem
IRE [*Institute of Radio Engineers*] **International Convention Record** — IRE Int Conv Rec
IRE [*Institute of Radio Engineers*] **National Convention Record** — IRE Natl Conv Rec
IRE [*Institute of Radio Engineers*] **Rapport. Institut National des Radioelements. Belgium** — IRE Rapp Inst Natl Radioelem Belg
IRE [*Institute of Radio Engineers*] **Transactions on Aeronautical and Navigational Electronics** — IRE Trans Aeronaut Navig Electron
IRE [*Institute of Radio Engineers*] **Transactions on Aerospace and Navigational Electronics** — IRE Trans Aerosp Navig Electron
IRE [*Institute of Radio Engineers*] **Transactions on Audio** — IRE Trans Audio
IRE [*Institute of Radio Engineers*] **Transactions on Automatic Control** — IRE Trans Autom Control
IRE [*Institute of Radio Engineers*] **Transactions on Bio-Medical Electronics** — IRE Trans Bio Med Electron
IRE [*Institute of Radio Engineers*] **Transactions on Broadcast and Television Receivers** — IRE Trans Broadcast Telev Receivers
IRE [*Institute of Radio Engineers*] **Transactions on Broadcast Transmission Systems** — IRE Trans Broadcast Transm Syst
IRE [*Institute of Radio Engineers*] **Transactions on Broadcasting** — IRE Trans Broadcast
IRE [*Institute of Radio Engineers*] **Transactions on Circuit Theory** — IRE Trans Circuit Theory
IRE [*Institute of Radio Engineers*] **Transactions on Communications Systems** — IRE Trans Commun Syst
IRE [*Institute of Radio Engineers*] **Transactions on Component Parts** — IRCPA
IRE [*Institute of Radio Engineers*] **Transactions on Component Parts** — IRE Trans Component Parts
IRE [*Institute of Radio Engineers*] **Transactions on Electronic Computers** — IRE Trans Electron Comput
IRE [*Institute of Radio Engineers*] **Transactions on Engineering Management** — IRE Trans Eng Manage
IRE [*Institute of Radio Engineers*] **Transactions on Industrial Electronics** — IRE Trans Ind Electron
IRE [*Institute of Radio Engineers*] **Transactions on Instrumentation** — IRE Trans Instrum
IRE [*Institute of Radio Engineers*] **Transactions on Medical Electronics** — IRE Trans Med Electron
IRE [*Institute of Radio Engineers*] **Transactions on Microwave Theory and Techniques** — IRE Trans Microwave Theory Tech
IRE [*Institute of Radio Engineers*] **Transactions on Military Electronics** — IRE Trans Mil Electron
IRE [*Institute of Radio Engineers*] **Transactions on Military Electronics** — IRMLA
IRE [*Institute of Radio Engineers*] **Transactions on Nuclear Science** — IRE Trans Nucl Sci
IRE [*Institute of Radio Engineers*] **Transactions on Nuclear Science** — IRNSA
IRE [*Institute of Radio Engineers*] **Transactions on Production Techniques** — IRE Trans Prod Tech
IRE [*Institute of Radio Engineers*] **Transactions on Reliability and Quality Control** — IRE Trans Reliab Qual Control
IRE [*Institute of Radio Engineers*] **Transactions on Telemetry and Remote Control** — IRE Trans Telem Remote Control
IRE [*Institute of Radio Engineers*] **Transactions on Ultrasonics Engineering** — IRE Trans Ultrason Eng
IRE [*Institute of Radio Engineers*] **Transactions on Vehicular Communications** — IRE Trans Veh Commun
IRE [*Institute of Radio Engineers*] **WESCON Convention Record** [*Western Electronics Show and Convention*] — IRE WESCON Conv Rec
IRE [*Institute of Radio Engineers*] **Western Electronic Show and Convention. Convention Record** — IRE West Electron Show Conv Conv Rec
IREBI. Indices de Revista de Bibliotecologia — Indice Rev Bibliotecol
Ireland. A Journal of Irish Studies — Eire
Ireland Administration. Yearbook and Diary — Ireld Yrbk
Ireland. Department of Agriculture and Fisheries. Fishery Leaflet — Ir Dept Agric Fish Fish Leaflet
Ireland. Department of Agriculture and Fisheries. Journal — Irel Dep Agric Fish J
Ireland. Department of Agriculture. Journal — Ir Dept Agric J
Ireland. Department of Fisheries and Forestry. Trade and Information Section. Fishery Leaflet — FLDSD2
Ireland. Department of Fisheries and Forestry. Trade and Information Section. Fishery Leaflet — Irel Dep Fish For Trade Inf Sect Fish Leafl
Ireland. Geological Survey. Bulletin — Irel Geol Surv Bull
Ireland. National Soil Survey. Soil Survey Bulletin — Irel Natl Soil Surv Soil Surv Bull
Ireland of the Welcomes — Ir Wel
Ireland Today — Ir Today
Irenikon — Iren
Iris Hibernia — Ir Hib
Irish Agricultural and Creamery Review — Irish Agr Creamery Rev
Irish Agricultural Magazine — Irish Agric Mag
Irish Ancestor — Ir Ancest
Irish and International Fibres and Fabrics Journal — Ir Int Fibres Fabr J
Irish Archaeological Research Forum — Ir Archaeol Res Forum
Irish Archaeological Research Forum — Irish Arch Res For
Irish Archival Bulletin — Ir Arch Bull
Irish Astronomical Journal — Irish Astr
Irish Astronomical Journal — Irish Astron J
Irish Banking Review — IHG
Irish Banking Review — Irish Banking R
Irish Beekeeper — Irish Beekpr
Irish Bibliographical Pamphlets — Ir Bibliog Pamph
Irish Birds — IBIRDL
Irish Birds — Ir Birds
Irish Book [*Bibliographical Society of Ireland*] — IB
Irish Book — Ir Book
Irish Book Lover — Ir Book Lov
Irish Booklore — Ir Booklore
Irish Broadcasting Review [*Republic of Ireland*] — Irish Bcasting R
Irish Builder — Ir Bld
Irish Builder and Engineer — Ir Bld Engineer
Irish Builder and Engineer — Irish Bldr & Engineer
Irish Catholic Historical Committee Proceedings — Ir Cath Hist Comm Proc
Irish Chemical Association Journal — Ir Chem Assoc J
Irish Committee of Historical Sciences. Bulletin — Ir Comm Hist Sci Bull
Irish Company Profiles [*Database*] — ICP
Irish Computer — Ir Comput
Irish Defence Journal [*An Cosantoir*] — Ir Def J
Irish Dental Journal — Ir Dent J
Irish Digest — ID
Irish Ecclesiastical Gazette — Ir Eccles Gaz
Irish Ecclesiastical Record — IER
Irish Ecclesiastical Record — Ir Eccles Rec
Irish Ecclesiastical Record — IrEccRec
Irish Ecclesiastical Record [*Dublin*] — IrERec
Irish Ecclesiastical Review — IER
Irish Economic and Social History — Ir Econ Soc Hist
Irish Economic and Social History — Irish Econ Soc Hist
Irish Economist — Irish Econ
Irish Engineers — Ir Eng
Irish Farmers' Journal and Weekly Intelligencer — Irish Farmers J Weekly Intelligencer
Irish Fisheries Investigations. Series A. Freshwater — IFIFAA
Irish Fisheries Investigations. Series A. Freshwater — Ir Fish Invest Ser A Freshwater
Irish Fisheries Investigations. Series B. Marine — IFIMAV
Irish Fisheries Investigations. Series B. Marine — Ir Fish Invest Ser B Mar
Irish Folk Music Studies — Irish Folk M Stud
Irish Folk Song Society Journal — Ir Folk Song Soc J
Irish Forestry — Ir For
Irish Forestry — IRFOA4
Irish Forestry — Irish For
Irish Genealogist — Ir Geneal
Irish Geographical Bulletin — Ir Geogr B
Irish Geography — Ir Geog
Irish Georgian Society. Bulletin — Irish Georgian Soc Bull
Irish Georgian Society. Quarterly Bulletin — Ir Georg Soc Qtr Bull
Irish Georgian Society. Quarterly Bulletin — Irish Georgian Soc Qly Bull
Irish Historical Studies — IHS
Irish Historical Studies — Ir Hist St
Irish Historical Studies — Ir Hist Stud
Irish Historical Studies — IrH
Irish Historical Studies — Irish Hist
Irish Historical Studies — Irish Hist Stud
Irish Independent — II
Irish Journal of Agricultural and Food Research — Ir J Agric Food Res
Irish Journal of Agricultural Economics and Rural Sociology — Ir J Agric Econ Rural Sociol
Irish Journal of Agricultural Economics and Rural Sociology — Irish J Agric Econ and Rural Sociol
Irish Journal of Agricultural Research — IJALAG
Irish Journal of Agricultural Research — Ir J Agr Res
Irish Journal of Agricultural Research — Ir J Agric Res
Irish Journal of Agricultural Research — Irish J Agr
Irish Journal of Agricultural Research — Irish J Agr Res
Irish Journal of Agricultural Research — Irish J Agric Res
Irish Journal of Earth Sciences — Ir J Earth Sci
Irish Journal of Education — Ir J Ed
Irish Journal of Education — Irish J Ed
Irish Journal of Environmental Science — IESCDD
Irish Journal of Environmental Science — Ir J Environ Sci
Irish Journal of Environmental Science — Irish J Environ Sci
Irish Journal of Food Science and Technology — IFSTD
Irish Journal of Food Science and Technology — IFSTD3
Irish Journal of Food Science and Technology — Ir J Food Sci Technol
Irish Journal of Food Science and Technology — Irish J Food Sci Technol
Irish Journal of Medical Science — IJMSAT
Irish Journal of Medical Science — Ir J Med Sci
Irish Journal of Medical Science — Irish J Med
Irish Journal of Psychiatric Nursing — Irish Jnl Psych Nurs
Irish Journal of Psychological Medicine — Ir J Psychol Med
Irish Journal of Psychology — Ir J Psychol

Irish Journal of Psychology — Irish J Psy
Irish Journal of Psychology — IRJPAR
Irish Journal of Psychotherapy — Ir J Psychother
Irish Journal of Psychotherapy — IRJPDU
Irish Journal of Psychotherapy and Psychosomatic Medicine — Ir J Psychother Psychosom Med
Irish Jurist — IJ
Irish Jurist — Ir Jur
Irish Jurist — Ir Jurist
Irish Jurist — Irish Jur
Irish Jurist. New Series [*1856-67*] — Ir Jur NS
Irish Jurist Reports — Ir Jur R
Irish Law Reports Monthly — ILRM
Irish Law Times — ILT
Irish Law Times — Ir L T
Irish Law Times — Ir Law T
Irish Law Times — Irish LT
Irish Law Times and Solicitors' Journal — ILT & SJ
Irish Law Times and Solicitors' Journal — Ir LT Journal
Irish Law Times and Solicitors' Journal — Ir LTJ
Irish Law Times and Solicitors' Journal. A Weekly Gazette of Legal News and Information — Ir L Times and Solicitors' J
Irish Library Bulletin — Ir Lib Bull
Irish Library Bulletin — Irish Lib Bul
Irish Literary Inquirer — Ir Lit Inquirer
Irish Literary Studies — Irish Lit S
Irish Magazine — Ir Mag
Irish Mathematical Society Bulletin — Irish Math Soc Bull
Irish Medical Journal — IMDJBD
Irish Medical Journal — Ir Med J
Irish Medical Journal — Irish Med J
Irish Medical Times — Irish Med Times
Irish Monthly — Ir Mon
Irish Monthly — Ir Mthl
Irish Monthly — Irish Mo
Irish Monthly — IrM
Irish Naturalist — Ir Nat
Irish Naturalists' Journal — INAJA4
Irish Naturalists' Journal — Ir Nat J
Irish Numismatics — Irish Num
Irish Numismatist — Ir Num
Irish Nurses' Journal — Ir Nurse J
Irish Nursing and Hospital World — Ir Nurs Hosp W
Irish Nursing and Hospital World — Ir Nurs Hosp World
Irish Nursing News — Ir Nurs News
Irish Offshore Review — Ir Offshore Rev
Irish Quarterly Review — Ir Qtr Rev
Irish Quarterly Review — Irish Q
Irish Railway Record Society Journal — Ir Rail Rec Soc J
Irish Reports — IR
Irish Review — Ir R
Irish Spelaeology — Ir Spelaeol
Irish Speleology — Ir Spel
Irish Statesman — IS
Irish Statistical Bulletin — Irish Stat
Irish Statistical Bulletin — Irish Statis Bul
Irish Sword — Ir Sword
Irish Sword — Irish S
Irish Textile Journal — Ir Text J
Irish Theological Quarterly — I Th Q
Irish Theological Quarterly — Ir Theol Qtr
Irish Theological Quarterly — Irish Theol Quart
Irish Theological Quarterly [*Maynooth*] — IrishThQ
Irish Theological Quarterly [*Maynooth*] — IrTQ
Irish Theological Quarterly — ITQ
Irish Times — Ir Times
Irish Times — IRT
Irish University Review — Ir Univ Rev
Irish University Review — Irish U Rev
Irish University Review — IUR
Irish Veterinary Journal — Ir Vet J
Irish Wildfowl Committee. Publication [*Ireland*] — Irish Wildfowl Comm Publ
Irish Writing — Ir Writing
Irish-American Genealogist — Irish Am Geneal
Irisleabhar Mha Nuad — IMN
Irkutskii Gosudarstvennyi Nauchno-Issledovatel'skii Institut Redkikh i Tsvetnykh Metallov. Nauchnye Trudy — Irkutsk Gos Nauchno Issled Inst Redk Tsvetn Met Nauchn Tr
Irkutskii Nauchno-Issledovatel'skii Institut Epidemiologii i Mikrobiologii. Trudy — Irkutsk Nauchno Issled Inst Epidemiol Mikrobiol Tr
Irkutskii Politehniceskii Institut Trudy — Irkutsk Politehn Inst Trudy
IRMA [*Indian Refractory Makers Association*] **Journal** — IRMA J
IRMMH [*Institute for Research into Mental and Multiple Handicap*] **Monograph** — IRMMD2
IRMMH [*Institute for Research into Mental and Multiple Handicap*] **Monograph** — IRMMH Monogr
IRMR [*Institute for Research into Mental Retardation*] **Study Group** — IRMR Study Group
IRMRA (India Rubber Manufacturers Research Association) Rubber Conference. Programme and Papers — IRMRA Rubber Conf Programme Pap
Irodalmi Szemle — I Sz
Irodalmi Szemle — Irod Szle
Irodalomtoertenet — Irtoert
Irodalomtoertenet — It
Irodalomtorteneti Fuzetek — Irodal F
Irodalomtorteneti Kozlemenyek — IK
Iron Age — IRA
Iron Age. Metal Producing Management Edition — Iron Age
Iron Age Metalworking International [*Later, Chilton's IAMI Iron Age Metalworking International*] — IAMI
Iron Age Metalworking International [*Later, Chilton's IAMI Iron Age Metalworking International*] — Ir Age Int
Iron Age Metalworking International [*Later, Chilton's IAMI Iron Age Metalworking International*] — Iron Age Metalwork Int
Iron and Coal Trades Review — ICTRA
Iron and Coal Trades Review [*England*] — Iron Coal Trades Rev
Iron and Steel — Iron St
Iron and Steel — Iron Steel
Iron and Steel Castings. Current Industrial Reports — Iron Steel Cast Curr Ind Rep
Iron and Steel Engineer — Iron and Steel Eng
Iron and Steel Engineer — Iron Steel Eng
Iron and Steel Industry — Iron Steel Ind
Iron and Steel Industry in China — Iron Steel Ind China
Iron and Steel Industry Profiles — ISIP
Iron and Steel Institute. Carnegie Scholarship Memoirs — Iron Steel Inst Carnegie Scholarship Mem
Iron and Steel Institute (London). Bibliographical Series — Iron Steel Inst (London) Bibliogr Ser
Iron and Steel Institute. London. Carnegie Scholarship Memoirs — Iron Steel Inst London Carnegie Scholarship Mem
Iron and Steel Institute (London). Publication — Iron Steel Inst (London) Publ
Iron and Steel Institute (London). Special Report — Iron Steel Inst (London) Spec Rep
Iron and Steel Institute of Japan. Special Report — Iron Steel Inst Jpn Spec Rep
Iron and Steel International — Iron and Steel Int
Iron and Steel International — Iron St Int
Iron and Steel International — Iron Steel Int
Iron and Steel Review (Kao-hsiung, Taiwan) — Iron Steel Rev (Kao hsiung Taiwan)
Iron and Steel Society of AIME. Transactions — Iron Steel Soc AIME Trans
Iron and Steel Society. Transactions — Iron Steel Soc Trans
Iron in Biochemistry and Medicine [*monograph*] — Iron Biochem Med
Iron Metabolism and Its Disorders. Proceedings. Workshop Conference Hoechst — Iron Metab Its Disord Proc Workshop Conf Hoechst
Iron Nutrition and Interactions in Plants. Proceedings. International Symposium — Iron Nutr Interact Plants Proc Int Symp
Iron Trade Review — Iron Tr R
Iron Trade Review — Iron Trade R
Ironmaking and Steelmaking — Ironmkg Steelmkg
Ironmaking Conference Proceedings — Ironmaking Conf Proc
Ironmaking Proceedings — Ironmaking Proc
Ironmaking Proceedings. Metallurgical Society of AIME. Iron and Steel Division — Ironmaking Proc AIME
Ironwood — Iron
IRPA European Congress on Radiation Protection — IRPA Eur Congr Radiat Prot
Irradiation des Aliments [*English Edition*] — FOIRA8
Irradiation des Aliments — Irradiat Aliments
Irradiation des Aliments (English Edition) — Irradiat Aliments (Engl Ed)
Irreversible Processes and Selforganization. Proceedings. International Conference on Irreversible Processes and Selforganization — Irreversible Processes Selforgan Proc Int Conf
IRRI [*International Rice Research Institute*] **Research** — IRPSDZ
IRRI [*International Rice Research Institute*] **Research Paper Series** — IRRI Res Pap Ser
IRRI Research Paper Series. International Rice Research Institute — IRRI Res Pap Ser Int Rice Res Inst
Irrigacion en Mexico. Mexico. Comicion Nacional de Irrigacion — Irrig Mexico
Irrigated Winter Wheat. Technical Publication — Irrig Winter Wheat Tech Publ
Irrigation Age — Irr Age
Irrigation Age — Irrig Age
Irrigation and Drainage Paper — Irrig Drain Pap
Irrigation and Drainage Paper (Food and Agriculture Organization of the United Nations) — Irrig Drain Pap (FAO)
Irrigation and Drainage Systems. An International Journal — Irrig Drain Syst Int J
Irrigation and Power — IRPWA
Irrigation and Power — Irrig Power
Irrigation and Power Abstracts — Irrig & Power Abstr
Irrigation Association. Technical Conference Proceedings — Irrig Assoc Tech Conf Proc
Irrigation Engineering and Maintenance — Irrig Eng Maint
Irrigation Farmer — Irrig Farmer
Irrigation Farmer — Irrig Fmr
Irrigation Journal — Irrig J
Irrigation Science — Irrig Sci
Irrigation Science — IRSCD2
IRS [*Institut fuer Reaktorischerheit der Technischen Ueberwachungs-Vereine*] **Kurz-Information. Reihe A** [*Germany*] — IRS Kurz-Inf Reihe A
IRS [*Institut fuer Reaktorischerheit der Technischen Ueberwachungs-Vereine*] **Kurz-Information. Reihe B** [*Germany*] — IRS Kurz-Inf Reihe B
IRS [*Institut fuer Reaktorischerheit der Technischen Ueberwachungs-Vereine*] **Kurz-Information. Reihe C** [*Germany*] — IRS Kurz-Inf Reihe C
IRS [*Institut fuer Reaktorischerheit der Technischen Ueberwachungs-Vereine*] **Kurz-Information. Reihe D** [*Germany*] — IRS Kurz-Inf Reihe D
IRS [*Institut fuer Reaktorischerheit der Technischen Ueberwachungs-Vereine*] **Mitteilungen** [*Germany*] — IRS Mitt
IRSIA. [*Institute pour l'Encouragement de la Recherche Scientifique dans l'Industrie et l'Agriculture*] **Comptes Rendus de Recherches** — IRSIA CR Rech

IRSID. Institut de Recherches de la Siderurgie Francaise. Rapport — IRSID Inst Rech Sider Fr Rapp
Irving Trust Company. Economic View from One Wall Street — Irving View
Irwin Strasburger Memorial Seminar on Immunology. Proceedings — Irwin Strasburger Meml Semin Immunol Proc
Is Lietuviu Kulturos Istorijos — LKI
ISA [*Instrument Society of America*] **Conference Preprint** — ISA Prepr
ISA (Instrument Society of America) Proceedings. Annual Instrument-Automation Conference and Exhibit — ISA Proc Annu Instrum Autom Conf Exhib
ISA [*Instrument Society of America*] **Journal** — ISA J
ISA [*Instrument Society of America*] **Journal** — ISAJA
ISA [*Instrument Society of America*] **Proceedings. International Power Instrumentation Symposium** — ISA Proc Int Power Instrum Symp
ISA [*Instrument Society of America*] **Proceedings. National Aerospace Instrumentation Symposium** [*United States*] — ISA Proc Natl Aerosp Instrum Symp
ISA [*Instrument Society of America*] **Proceedings. National Power Instrumentation Symposium** [*United States*] — ISA Proc Natl Power Instrum Symp
ISA [*Instrument Society of America*] **Transactions** — ISA Trans
ISA [*Instrument Society of America*] **Transactions** — ISATA
ISA [*Instrument Society of America*] **Transactions** — ISATAZ
Isaac Asimov's Science Fiction Magazine — IASF
Isaac Newton Institute Series of Lectures — Isaac Newton Inst Ser Lectures
Isaac Pitblado Lectures on Continuing Legal Education — Pitblado Lect
ISATA [*International Symposium on Autommotive Technology and Automation*] **Proceedings** — ISATA Proc
ISCA [*International Society of Copier Artists*] **Quarterly** — ISCA Quart
Iscrizioni delle Chiese e d'Altri Edifici di Roma — ICR
Iscrizioni delle Chiese e Degli Altri Edifici di Milano — ICM
Iscrizioni Greche e Latine. Catalogue General des Antiquites d'Egyptiennes du Musee d'Alexandrie — Inscr Mus Alex
Iscrizioni Greche Lapidarie del Museo di Palermo — IGLMP
Iscrizioni Greche Lapidarie del Museo di Palermo — IMP
Iscrizioni Latine della Sardegna — I Sardegna
Iscrizioni Latine della Sardegna — IL Sard
Iscrizioni Latine della Sardegna — Inscr Sardegna
Iscrizioni Latine Lapidarie del Museo di Palermo — ILLP
Iscrizioni Preeleniche di Hagia Triada in Creta e della Grecia Peninsulare — HT
Iscrizioni Preeleniche di Hagia Triada in Creta e della Grecia Peninsulare — IPHTCGP
ISD (Institut fuer Statik und Dynamik) -Bericht — ISD Ber
ISDO [*Industrial Services Centre. Documentation and Publication Branch*] **Bulletin** — ISDO Bul
ISGE [*International Society for Geothermal Engineering*] **Transactions and Geothermal World Journal** [*United States*] — ISGE Trans Geotherm World J
ISGE [*International Society for Geothermal Engineering*] **Transactions and the Geothermal Journal** [*United States*] — ISGE Trans Geotherm J
ISH (Institut fuer Strahlenhygiene) Berichte — ISH Ber
Ishikawajima-Harima Engineering Review — Ishikawajima-Harima Eng Rev
Ishikawajima-Harima Giho — ISHGA
Ishikawajima-Harima Heavy Industries Company. Engineering Review — Ishikawajima Harima Heavy Ind Co Eng Rev
Ishikawa-Ken Nogyo Shikenjo Kenkyu Hokoku — ISKHDI
ISHM [*International Society for Hybrid Microelectronics*] **Journal** — ISHM J
ISHM [*International Society for Hybrid Microelectronics*] **Proceedings** — ISHM Proc
ISI [*Institute for Scientific Information*] **Atlas of Science. Animal and Plant Sciences** — ISI Atlas Sci Anim Plant Sci
ISI [*Institute for Scientific Information*] **Atlas of Science. Biochemistry** — ISI Atlas Sci Biochem
ISI [*Institute for Scientific Information*] **Atlas of Science. Immunology** — ISI Atlas Sci Immunol
ISI [*Indian Standards Institution*] **Bulletin** — ISI Bull
ISI [*Institute for Scientific Information*] **Index to Scientific and Technical Proceedings and Books** [*Database*] — ISI/ISTP & B
ISI (Institute for Scientific Information) Atlas of Science. Pharmacology — ISI Atlas Sci Pharmacol
ISIJ (Iron and Steel Institute of Japan) International — ISIJ Int
Isis — I
Isis — Is
Isis — PSIS
Iskopaemye Rify i Metodika Ikh Izucheniya. Trudy Paleoekologo-Litologicheskoi Sessii — Iskop Rify Metod Ikh Izuch Tr Paleoekol Litol Sess
Iskusstvennoe Volokno — Iskusstv Volokno
Iskusstvennye Materialy — Iskusstv Mater
Iskusstvennye Sputniki Zemli — Iskusstv Sputniki Zemli
Iskusstvennye Sputniki Zemli Akademiya Nauk SSSR [*Former USSR*] — Iskusstv Sputniki Zemli Akad Nauk SSSR
Iskusstvo Kino — IK
Iskusstvo Kino — Iskus K
Iskusstvo Kino — Iskusstvo K
Islam — Isl
Islam and the Modern Age — IMAg
Islam and the Modern Age — Islam Mod Age
Islam Ansiklopedisi — IA
Islam Ansiklopedisi — Isl Ans
Islam d'Hier et Aujourd'hui — IHA
Islam (Zuerich) — Islam Z
Islamabad Journal of Sciences — IJSCDE
Islamabad Journal of Sciences. Journal of Mathematics and Sciences — Islamabad J Sci
Islamic Academy Patrika — IAP
Islamic Culture — IC
Islamic Culture — Islam Cult
Islamic Culture — IslC
Islamic Literature — IL
Islamic Literature — Is Lit
Islamic Quarterly — IQ
Islamic Quarterly — Islamic Quart
Islamic Quarterly [*London*] — IslQ
Islamic Quarterly — IsQ
Islamic Research Asociation Miscellany — IRAM
Islamic Research Association Series — IRAS
Islamic Review — Isl R
Islamic Studies — IS
Islamic Studies — Isl St
Islamic Studies — Islam Stud
Islamic Surveys — Isl S
Islamic World — IW
Islamic World Defence — Islm Wld D
Islamic World Review — IWR
Islamica [*Leipzig*] — Isl
Island — I
Island Arc — Isl Arc
Islas (Santa Clara, Cuba) — Islas S Clara
Islenzk Tunga — IT
Islenzkar Landbunadarrannsoknir [*Journal of Agricultural Research in Iceland*] [*A publication*] — Isl Landbunadarrannsoknir
Islenzkar Landbunadarrannsoknir [*Journal of Agricultural Research in Iceland*] [*A publication*] — ISLRBH
ISLIC International Conference on Information Science. Proceedings — ISLIC Int Conf Inf Sci Proc
Islote (Hormigueros, Puerto Rico) — IEH
Ismaili Society Series — ISS
Ismaili Society Series. Monographs and Collections of Articles — ISSM
Ismaili Society Series. Texts and Translations — ISST
ISME [*International Society for Music Education*] **Yearbook** — ISME Yb
ISMEC [*Information Service in Mechanical Engineering*] **Bulletin** — ISMEC Bull
Ismertetoe Oesszmueveszetben, Gazdasagban es Kereskedesben — Ismert Oesszmuev Gazd Keresk
Isokinetics and Exercise Science — Isokinetics & Ex Sci
Isolation. Revetements et Architecture Evolutive — Isol Revetements Archit Evol
Isotope and Radiation Research [*Egypt*] — Isot Radiat Res
Isotope and Radiation Research on Animal Diseases and Their Vectors. Proceedings — Isot Radiat Res Anim Dis Vec
Isotope Geoscience — IG
Isotope Geoscience — Isot Geosci
Isotope in Industrie und Landwirtschaft — Isot Ind Landwirtsch
Isotope News [*Japan*] — Isot News
Isotopen Technik — Isot Tech
Isotopenpraxis — Isotopenprax
Isotopes and Radiation [*Japan*] — Isot Radiat
Isotopes and Radiation in Parasitology — Isot Radiat Parasitol
Isotopes and Radiation Technology — Isot Radiat Technol
Isotopes and Radiation Technology — Isotop Radiat Technol
Isotopes and Radiation Technology — ISRTAI
Isotopes in Environmental and Health Studies — Isot Environ Health Stud
Isotopes in Organic Chemistry [*Elsevier Book Series*] — IOC
Isotopes in the Physical and Biomedical Sciences — Isot Phys Biomed Sci
Isotopes Radiation — Isotopes Radiat
Isotopic Generator Information Centre. Gif-sur-Yvette. Newsletter — Isot Gener Inf Cent Gif sur Yvette News
Isotopic Generator Information Centre (Gif-Sur-Yvette). Newsletter — Isot Generator Inf Cent (Gif Sur Yvettte) Newsl
Isotriko-Astronomicheskie Issledovaniia — Istor Astron Issled
Isozymes. Current Topics in Biological and Medical Research — ICTPDF
Isozymes. Current Topics in Biological and Medical Research — Isozymes Curr Top Biol Med Res
Ispol'zovanie Gaza v Narodnom Khozyaistve — IGNKB
Ispol'zovanie Gaza v Narodnom Khozyaistve [*Former USSR*] — Ispol'z Gaza Nar Khoz
Ispol'zovanie Mikroorganizmov v Narodnom Khozyaistve — Ispolz Mikroorg Nar Khoz
Ispol'zovanie Neorganicheskikh Resursov Okeanicheskoi Vody — Ispol'z Neorg Resur Okeanicheskoi Vody
Ispol'zovanie Tverdykh Topliv Sernistykh Mazutov i Gaza [*Former USSR*] — Ispol'z Tverd Topl Sernistykh Mazutov Gaza
Ispol'zovanie Tverdykh Topliv Sernistykh Mazutov i Gaza — ITSMA
ISR. Interdisciplinary Science Reviews — ISR Interdiscip Sci Rev
ISR Interdisciplinary Systems Research — ISR Interdisciplinary Systems Res
Israel. Agricultural Research Organization. Division of Forestry. Triennial Report of Research — Isr Agric Res Org Div For Trienn Rep Res
Israel. Agricultural Research Organization. Division of Forestry. Triennial Report of Research — TRRFDP
Israel. Agricultural Research Organization. Special Publication — Isr Agric Res Organ Spec Publ
Israel. Agricultural Research Organization. Special Publication — SPACD8
Israel. Agricultural Research Organization. Volcani Center. Bet Dagan. Special Publication — Isr Agric Res Organ Volcani Cent Bet Dagan Spec Publ
Israel. Agricultural Research Organization. Volcani Center. Pamphlet — Isr Agric Res Organ Volcani Cent Pam
Israel. Agricultural Research Organization. Volcani Center. Preliminary Report — Isr Agric Res Organ Volcani Cent Prelim Rep
Israel Agricultural Research Station. Rehovot. Records — Isr Agric Res Stn Rehovot Rec
Israel Alternative Energy Review — Isr Altern En Rev
Israel Annals of Psychiatry — Israel Ann Psychiat
Israel Annals of Psychiatry and Related Disciplines — IPRDAH
Israel Annals of Psychiatry and Related Disciplines — Isr Ann Psy

Israel Annals of Psychiatry and Related Disciplines — Isr Ann Psychiatry
Israel Annals of Psychiatry and Related Disciplines — Isr Ann Psychiatry Relat Discip
Israel. Atomic Energy Commission. IA Report — Isr AEC IA Rep
Israel. Atomic Energy Commission. LS Report — Isr AEC LS Rep
Israel Business — Israel Bus
Israel Business and Investors' Report — ILR
Israel Business and Investors' Report — Israel Inv
Israel Economist — IET
Israel Economist — Israel E
Israel Exploration Journal — IEJ
Israel Exploration Journal — Isr Ex J
Israel Exploration Journal — Isr Expl J
Israel Exploration Journal [*Jerusalem*] — IsrEJ
Israel Exploration Journal. Jerusalem — I Ex J
Israel Exploration Journal. Jerusalem — Israel Explor Journal
Israel Exploration Society. Bulletin — IESB
Israel Export and Trade Journal — ISJ
Israel Forum — IF
Israel. Geological Society. Annual Meeting — AMISEE
Israel Geological Society. Annual Meeting — Isr Geol Soc Annu Meet
Israel. Geological Survey. Bulletin — ISGBBC
Israel. Geological Survey. Bulletin — Isr Geol Surv Bull
Israel. Geological Survey. Geological Data Processing Unit. Report — Isr Geol Surv Geol Data Process Unit Rep
Israel. Geological Survey. Report — Isr Geol Surv Rep
Israel Goldstein Lectures — IGL
Israel. Hydrological Service. Report — Isr Hydrol Serv Rep
Israel. Institute for Technology and Storage of Agricultural Products. Scientific Activities — Isr Inst Technol Storage Agric Prod Sci Act
Israel. Institute of Agricultural Engineering. Scientific Activities — Isr Inst Agric Eng Sci Act
Israel. Institute of Agricultural Engineering. Scientific Activities — SAIEDH
Israel. Institute of Animal Science. Scientific Activities — Isr Inst Anim Sci Sci Act
Israel. Institute of Animal Science. Scientific Activities — SAISDP
Israel. Institute of Field and Garden Crops. Scientific Activities — Isr Inst Field Gard Crops Sci Act
Israel. Institute of Field and Garden Crops. Scientific Activities — SAICDB
Israel. Institute of Horticulture. Scientific Activities — Isr Inst Hortic Sci Act
Israel. Institute of Horticulture. Scientific Activities — SAIHDO
Israel. Institute of Plant Protection. Scientific Activities — Isr Inst Plant Prot Sci Act
Israel. Institute of Soils and Water. Scientific Activities — Isr Inst Soils Water Sci Act
Israel Journal of Agricultural Research — IJAR
Israel Journal of Agricultural Research — IJOAAJ
Israel Journal of Agricultural Research — Isr J Agric Res
Israel Journal of Agricultural Research — Israel J Agr Res
Israel Journal of Agricultural Research — Israel J Agric Res
Israel Journal of Botany — IJB
Israel Journal of Botany — IJBOAU
Israel Journal of Botany — Isr J Bot
Israel Journal of Botany — Israel J Bot
Israel Journal of Chemistry — ISJCAT
Israel Journal of Chemistry — Isr J Chem
Israel Journal of Chemistry — Israel J Chem
Israel Journal of Dental Medicine — IJDMAY
Israel Journal of Dental Medicine — Isr J Dent Med
Israel Journal of Earth-Sciences — IJERAK
Israel Journal of Earth-Sciences — IJES
Israel Journal of Earth-Sciences — Isr J Earth
Israel Journal of Earth-Sciences — Isr J Earth-Sci
Israel Journal of Earth-Sciences — Israel J Earth Sci
Israel Journal of Entomology — IJENB9
Israel Journal of Entomology — Isr J Entomol
Israel Journal of Entomology — Israel J Ent
Israel Journal of Experimental Medicine — IJEMA5
Israel Journal of Experimental Medicine — Isr J Exp Med
Israel Journal of Mathematics — Isr J Math
Israel Journal of Mathematics — Israel J Math
Israel Journal of Medical Sciences — IJMDAI
Israel Journal of Medical Sciences — IJMS
Israel Journal of Medical Sciences — Isr J Med S
Israel Journal of Medical Sciences — Isr J Med Sci
Israel Journal of Medical Sciences — Israel J Med Sc
Israel Journal of Psychiatry and Related Sciences — IJPR
Israel Journal of Psychiatry and Related Sciences — IPRSDV
Israel Journal of Psychiatry and Related Sciences — Isr J Psychiatr Relat Sci
Israel Journal of Psychiatry and Related Sciences — Isr J Psychiatry Relat Sci
Israel Journal of Technology — ISJTAC
Israel Journal of Technology — Isr J Tech
Israel Journal of Technology — Isr J Technol
Israel Journal of Technology — Israel J Tech
Israel Journal of Technology — Israel J Technol
Israel Journal of Veterinary Medicine — IJVMEQ
Israel Journal of Veterinary Medicine — Isr J Vet Med
Israel Journal of Zoology — IJZ
Israel Journal of Zoology — IJZOAE
Israel Journal of Zoology — Isr J Zool
Israel Journal of Zoology — Israel J Zool
Israel Law Review — ILR
Israel Law Review — Is LR
Israel Law Review — Isr Law Rev
Israel Law Review — Israel L Rev
Israel Law Review — Israel Law R
Israel Life and Letters [*New York*] — IsrLLetters
Israel Mathematical Conference Proceedings — Israel Math Conf Proc
Israel Medical Journal — ISMJAV
Israel Medical Journal — Isr Med J
Israel. Minhal Ha-Mechkar Ha-Chaklai. Merkaz Volkani. Buletin — Isr Minhal Ha Mechkar Ha Chaklai Merkaz Volkani Bul
Israel. Ministry of Agriculture. Extension Service Publication — Publ Ext Serv Israel Min Agric
Israel. Ministry of Agriculture. Water Commission. Hydrological Service. Hydrological Paper — Isr Min Agr Water Comm Hydrol Serv Hydrol Paper
Israel Museum News — Isr Mus N
Israel. National Council for Research and Development. Report — Isr Natl Counc Res Dev Rep
Israel. National Council for Research and Development. Report NCRD — Isr Natl Counc Res Dev Rep NCRD
Israel Numismatic Bulletin — INB
Israel Numismatic Journal — INJ
Israel Numismatic Journal — Isr Num J
Israel Oceanographic and Limnological Research. Annual Report — IOLRAM
Israel Oceanographic and Limnological Research. Annual Report — Isr Oceanogr Limnol Res Annu Rep
Israel Oriental Studies — Isr Orient Stud
Israel. Patent Document — Isr Pat Doc
Israel. Patent Office. Patents and Designs Journal — Isr Pat Off Pat Des J
Israel Pharmaceutical Journal — IPHJAJ
Israel Pharmaceutical Journal — Isr Pharm J
Israel Philatelist — IP
Israel Philatelist (Chur) — IP(Ch)
Israel Physical Society. Annals — Isr Phys Soc Ann
Israel Quarterly of Economics — IQE
Israel Science and Technology Digest — Isr Sci Technol Dig
Israel Securities Review — Isr Sec Rev
Israel Society of Special Libraries and Information Centers. Bulletin — ISLIC Bull
Israel Society of Special Libraries and Information Centers. Bulletin — Isr Soc Spec Libr Inf Cent Bull
Israel Society of Special Libraries and Information Centres. International Conference on Information Science. Proceedings — Isr Soc Spec Libr Inf Cent Int Conf Inf Sci Proc
Israel Symposium on Desalination — Isr Symp Desalin
Israel Tax Law Letter — Isr Tax Law Let
[*The*] **Israel Year Book** — IYB
Israel Yearbook on Human Rights — Israel Yb on Human Rights
Israel Yearbook on Human Rights — IYHR
Israel Youth Horizon [*Jerusalem*] — IYH
Israeli Annals of Psychiatry — IPRDA
Israeli Chemist — Isr Chem
Israeli Journal of Aquaculture Bamidgeh — Isr Aquacult Bamidgeh
Israeli Journal of Mathematics — ISJM
Israelite [*Cincinnati*] — Ist
Israelitische Monatsschrift — Isr Mschr
Israelitische Rundschau [*Berlin*] — IR
Israelitische Rundschau — Isr Rd
Israelitische Wochenschrift [*Breslau/Magdeburg*] — ISWOS
Israelitische Wochenschrift (Klausner) — IWK
Israelitisches Familienblatt [*Hamburg*] — ISFAM
Israelitisches Wochenblatt — IW
Israelitisches Wochenblatt (Berlin) — IWB
ISRRT [*International Society of Radiographers and Radiological Technicians*] **Newsletter** [*England*] — ISRRT Newsl
ISSCT [*International Society of Sugarcane Technologists*] **Entomology Newsletter** — ENTND2
ISSCT (International Society of Sugarcane Technologists) Entomology Newsletter — ISSCT (Int Soc Sugarcane Technol) Entomol Newsl
Issledovanie Dinamicheskikh Protsessov v Verkhnei Atmosfere — Issled Din Protsessov Verkhn Atmos
Issledovanie Ekosistemy Baltiiskogo Morya. Sovetsko-Shvedskaya Kompleksnaya Ekspeditsiya v Baltiiskom More — Issled Ekosist Balt Morya
Issledovanie i Optimizatsiya Protsessov Tekstil'noi Tekhnologii — Issled Optim Protsessov Tekst Tekhnol
Issledovanie Konstruktsii s Primeneniem Plastmass — Issled Konstr Primen Plastmass
Issledovanie Kosmicheskogo Prostranstva — Issled Kosm Prostranstva
Issledovanie Operacii i Statisticeskoe Modelirovanie — Issled Operacii i Statist
Issledovanie Plazmennykh Sgustkov — Issled Plazmennykh Sgustkov
Issledovanie Protsessov Obrabotki Metallov Davleniem — Issled Protsessov Obrab Met Davleniem
Issledovanie Sistem — Issled Sist
Issledovanie Solntsa i Krasnykh Zvezd — Issled Solntsa Krasnykh Zvezd
Issledovanie Splavov Tsvetnykh Metallov — Issled Splavov Tsvetn Met
Issledovaniia po Tekhnologii Stroitel'nykh Materialov — Issled Tekhnol Stroit Mater
Issledovanija Nekotoryh Voprosov Matematiceskoi Kibernetiki — Issled Nekotoryh Voprosov Mat Kibernet
Issledovaniya Dal'nevostochnykh Morei SSSR — Issled Dalnevost Morei SSSR
Issledovaniya Fauny Morei — Issled Fauny Morei
Issledovaniya po Betonu i Zhelezobetonu — Issled Betonu Zhelezobetonu
Issledovaniya po Bionike — Issled Bionike
Issledovaniya po Elektrokhimii Magnetokhimii i Elektrokhimicheskim Metodam Analiza — Issled Elektrokhim Magnetokhim Elektrokhim Metodam Anal
Issledovaniya po Fizike Atmosfery Akademiya Nauk Estonskoi SSR [*Estonian SSR*] — Issled Fiz Atmos Akad Nauk Est SSR
Issledovaniya po Fizike Kipeniya [*Former USSR*] — Issled Fiz Kipeniya
Issledovaniya po Genetike — ISGEA

Issledovaniya po Genetike — Issled Genet
Issledovaniya po Geomagnetizmii, Aeronomii, i Fizike Solntsa — Issled Geomagn Aeron Fiz Solntsa
Issledovaniya po Ispol'zovaniyu Solnechnoi Energii — Issled Ispolz Soln Energ
Issledovaniya po Khimicheskoi Pererabotke Rud — Issled Khim Pererab Rud
Issledovaniya po Kvantovoi Teorii Sistem Mnogikh Chastits — Issled Kvantovoi Teor Sist Mnogikh Chastits
Issledovaniya po Mekhanike Stroitel'nykh Materialov i Konstruktsii — Issled Mekh Stroit Mater Konstr
Issledovaniya po Mikrobiologii — Issled Mikrobiol
Issledovaniya po Stroitel'stvu [*Estonian SSR*] — Issled Stroit
Issledovaniya po Stroitel'stvu. Tekhnologiya i Dolgovechnost Avtoklavnykh Betonov — Issled Stroit Tekhnol Dolgovechnost Avtoklavn Betonov
Issledovaniya po Tekhnologii Rybnykh Produktov — Issled Tekhnol Rybn Prod
Issledovaniya po Teorii Plastin i Obolochek — Issled Teor Plastin Obolochek
Issledovaniya po Uprugosti i Plastichnosti — IDUPA
Issledovaniya po Uprugosti i Plastichnosti — Issled Uprug Plast
Issledovaniya po Uprugosti i Plastichnosti — Issled Uprugosti Plast
Issledovaniya po Vodopodgotovke — Issled Vodopodgot
Issledovaniya po Zashchite Metallov ot Korrozii v Khimicheskoi Promyshlennosti — Issled Zashch Met Korroz Khim Prom
Issledovaniya po Zharoprochnym Splavam [*Former USSR*] — Issled Zharoproch Splavam
Issledovaniya po Zharoprochnym Splavam — Issled Zharoprochn Splavam
Issledovaniya Strukturnogo Sostoyaniya Neorganicheskikh Veshchestv — Issled Strukt Sostoyaniya Neorg Veshchestv
Issledovaniya Tsentral'no-Amerikanskikh Morei — Issled Tsentr Am Morei
Issledovaniya v Oblasti Fiziki i Khimii Kauchukov i Rezin — Issled Obl Fiz Khim Kauch Rezin
Issledovaniya v Oblasti Fiziki i Khimii Tverdogo Tela — Issled Obl Fiz Khim Tverd Tela
Issledovaniya v Oblasti Fiziki Tverdogo Tela — Issled Obl Fiz Tverd Tela
Issledovaniya v Oblasti Genezisa Pochv — Issled Obl Genezisa Pochv
Issledovaniya v Oblasti Khimicheskikh i Fizicheskikh Metodov Analiza Mineral'nogo Syr'ya — Issled Obl Khim Fiz Metodov Anal Miner Syrya
Issledovaniya v Oblasti Khimicheskikh Istochnikov Toka — Issled Obl Khim Istochnikov Toka
Issledovaniya v Oblasti Khimii Drevesiny. Tezisy Dokladov. Konferentsiya Molodykh Uchenykh — Issled Obl Khim Drev Tezisy Dokl Konf Molodykh Uch
Issledovaniya v Oblasti Khimii i Khimicheskoi Tekhnologii Drevesiny — Issled Obl Khim Khim Tekhnol Drev
Issledovaniya v Oblasti Khimii i Tekhnologii Produktov Pererabotki Goryuchikh Iskopaemykh — Issled Obl Khim Tekhnol Prod Pererab Goryuch Iskop
Issledovaniya v Oblasti Khimii Silikatov i Okislov — Issled Obl Khim Silik Okislov
Issledovaniya v Oblasti Kinetiki Modelirovaniya i Optimizatsii Khimicheskikh Protsessov — Issled Obl Kinet Model Optim Khim Protsessov
Issledovaniya v Oblasti Kompleksnogo Ispol'zovaniya Topliv [*Former USSR*] — Issled Obl Kompleksn Ispol'z Topl
Issledovaniya v Oblasti Neorganicheskoi i Fizicheskoi Khimii — Issled Obl Neorg Fiz Khim
Issledovaniya v Oblasti Plastichnosti i Obrabotki Metallov Davleniem — Issled Obl Plast Obrab Met Davleniem
Issledovaniya v Oblasti Sinteza i Kataliza Organicheskikh Soedinenii — Issled Obl Sint Katal Org Soedin
Issledovaniya v Oblasti Tekhniki i Tekhnologii Lakokrasochnykh Pokrytii — Issled Obl Tekh Tekhnol Lakokras Pokrytii
Issledovaniya v Oblasti Tekhnologii Mineral'nykh Udobrenii — Issled Obl Tekhnol Miner Udobr
Issledovaniya Vyazhushchikh Veshchestv i Izdelii na Ikh Osnove — Issled Vyazhushchikh Veshchestv Izdelii Ikh Osn
Issledovatel'skaja Kafedra Botaniki. Cabinet Botanique — Issl Kafedra Bot
Issue Briefing Paper. United States Department of Agriculture. Office of Governmental and Public Affairs — Issue Briefing Pap USDA Off Gov Pub Aff
Issues and Commentary [*Alaska*] — ISAC
Issues and Policy Summaries [*United States*] — Issues Policy Summ
Issues and Reviews in Teratology — Issues Rev Teratol
Issues and Studies — Iss Stud
Issues and Studies — Issues and Stud
Issues and Studies — Issues Stud
Issues and Studies. National Research Council (United States) — Issues Stud Natl Res Counc (US)
Issues Bulletin — Issues Bul
Issues in Accounting Education — Issues Account Educ
Issues in Ancient Philosophy — Issues Anc Philos
Issues in Bank Regulation — IRG
Issues in Bank Regulation — Issues Bank Regul
Issues in Canadian Science Policy — ICSP
Issues in Comprehensive Pediatric Nursing — Issues Compr Pediatr Nurs
Issues in Criminology — Issues Crim
Issues in Engineering [*United States*] — Issues Eng
Issues in Engineering. Journal of Professional Activities. Proceedings of the American Society of Civil Engineers — Issues Engng J Prof Activities Proc ASCE
Issues in Health Care of Women — Issues Health Care Women
Issues in Health Care Technology — Issues Hlth Care Tech
Issues in Law and Medicine — Issues Law Med
Issues in Mental Health Nursing — Issues Ment Health Nurs
Issues in Radical Therapy — Rad Ther
Issues in Radical Therapy — Rad Thera
Issues in Science and Technology — GIST
Issues in Science and Technology — Issues Sci Technol
Istanbul Arkeolji Muezeleri Yiligi — A Arch Mus
Istanbul Arkeolji Muezeleri Yiligi — IAM
Istanbul Arkeolji Muezeleri Yiligi — IAMY
Istanbul Arkeolji Muezeleri Yiligi — Istamb A Muez Yil
Istanbul Arkeologi Muzeleri Yilligi — Istanbul Ark Muz Yilligi
Istanbul Asariatika Muzeleri Nesriyati — IAM
Istanbul Contribution to Clinical Science — Istanbul Contrib Clin Sci
Istanbul Goz Klinigi Bulteni — Istanbul Goz Klin Bul
Istanbul Medical Faculty. Medical Bulletin. Istanbul University — Istanbul Med Fac Med Bull Istanbul Univ
Istanbul Teknik Universitesi Bulteni [*Bulletin of the Technical University of Istanbul*] — Bulteni Istanbul Tek Univ
Istanbul Teknik Universitesi Bulteni [*Bulletin of the Technical University of Istanbul*] — Istanbul Tek Univ Bul
Istanbul Teknik Universitesi Dergisi — Istanbul Tek Univ Derg
Istanbul Teknik Universitesi Nukleer Enerji Enstitusu. Bulten — Istanbul Tek Univ Nukl Enerji Enst Bul
Istanbul Tip Fakultesi Mecmuasi — Istanbul Tip Fak Mecm
Istanbul Universitesi Dishekimligi Fakultesi Dergisi — Istanbul Univ Dishekim Fak Derg
Istanbul Universitesi Eczacilik Fakultesi Mecmuasi — Istanbul Univ Eczacilik Fak Mecm
Istanbul Universitesi Edebiyat Fakultesi Turk ve Edebiyat Dergisi — Istanbul Univ Edebiyat Fak Turk ve Edebiyat Dergisi
Istanbul Universitesi Edegiyat Fakultesi Turk Dili ve Edebiyati Dergisi — TDED
Istanbul Universitesi fen Fakueltesi Mecmuasi — Istanb Univ fen Fak Mecm
Istanbul Universitesi Fen Fakultesi Hidrobiologi Arastirma Enstitusu Yayinlari — Istanbul Univ Fen Fak Hidrobiol Arastirma Enst Yayin
Istanbul Universitesi. Fen Fakultesi. Matematik Dergisi — Istanbul Univ Fen Fak Mat Derg
Istanbul Universitesi Fen Fakultesi Mecmuasi — Istanbul Univ Fen Fak Mecm
Istanbul Universitesi Fen Fakultesi Mecmuasi. Seri A — IFMAA
Istanbul Universitesi Fen Fakultesi Mecmuasi. Seri A — Istanbul Univ Fen Fak Mecm Ser A
Istanbul Universitesi Fen Fakultesi Mecmuasi. Seri B — IFMBA
Istanbul Universitesi Fen Fakultesi Mecmuasi. Seri B. Tabii Ilimler — Istanbul Univ Fen Fak Mecm Ser B
Istanbul Universitesi Fen Fakultesi Mecmuasi. Seri B. Tabii Ilimler — Istanbul Univ Fen Fak Mecm Seri B Tabii Ilimler
Istanbul Universitesi Fen Fakultesi Mecmuasi. Seri C. Astronomi-Fizik-Kimya — IFMCA
Istanbul Universitesi Fen Fakultesi Mecmuasi. Seri C. Astronomi-Fizik-Kimya — Istanbul Univ Fen Fak Mecm Ser C
Istanbul Universitesi Observatuari Yazilari — Istanbul Univ Obs Yazilari
Istanbul Universitesi Orman Fakultesi Dergisi — Istanb Univ Orman Fak Derg
Istanbul Universitesi Orman Fakultesi Dergisi. Seri A — Istanbul Univ Orman Fak Derg Seri A
Istanbul Universitesi Tip Fakultesi Mecmuasi — Istanbul Univ Tip Fak Mecm
Istanbul Universitesi Tip Fakultesi Mecmuasi — IUTFAY
Istanbul Universitesi Veteriner Fakultesi Dergisi — Istanbul Univ Vet Fak Derg
Istanbul Universitesi Veteriner Fakultesi Dergisi/Journal of the Faculty of Veterinary Medicine. University of Istanbul — Istanbul Univ Vet Fak Derg J Fac Vet Med Univ Istanbul
Istanbul Universitesi Yaymlam (Orman Fakultesi) — Istanbul Univ Yay (Orm Fak)
Istanbul University. Medical Bulletin — Istanbul Univ Med Bull
Istanbul University. Medical Faculty. Medical Bulletin — Istanbul Univ Med Fac Med Bull
Istanbul University. Review of the Geographical Institute. International Edition — Istanbul Univ Rev Geog Inst Internat Ed
Istanbuler Beitrage zur Klinischen Wissenschaft — Istanbuler Beitr Klin Wiss
Istanbuler Forschungen — IF
Istanbuler Forschungen — Ist Forsch
Istanbuler Forschungen — Istanb Forsch
Istanbuler Forschungen. Deutsches Archaeologisches Institut — IFDAI
Istanbuler Mitteilungen — I Mitt
Istanbuler Mitteilungen — Ist Mit
Istanbuler Mitteilungen — Ist Mitt
Istanbuler Mitteilungen. Beiheft — Ist Mitt Bh
Istanbuler Mitteilungen. Deutsches Archaeologisches Institut — IMDAI
Istanbuler Mitteilungen. Deutsches Archaeologisches Institut — Ist Mitt
Istanbuler Mitteilungen. Deutsches Archaeologisches Institut — Istanbuler Mitt
Istanbuler Schriften — Ist Schr
ISTFA (International Symposium for Testing and Failure Analysis) Proceedings. International Symposium for Testing and Failure Analysis — ISTFA Proc Int Symp Test Failure Anal
Istina [*Boulogne-sur-Seine*] — Ist
Istituto Botanico dell' Universita. Laboratorio Crittogamico (Pavia). Atti — Ist Bot Univ Lab Crittogam (Pavia) Atti
Istituto Botanico di Palermo. Lavori — Ist Bot Palermo Lav
Istituto Carlo Erba per Ricerche Terapeutiche. Raccolta di Pubblicazioni Chimiche, Biologiche, e Mediche — Ist Carlo Erba Ric Ter Racc Pubbl Chim Biol Med
Istituto Centrale per la Patologia del Libro Alfonso Gallo. Bollettino — Ist Cent Patol Libro Alfonso Gallo Boll
Istituto Chimico Agrario Sperimentale di Gorizia. Nuovi Annali. Pubblicazione — Ist Chim Agrar Sper Gorizia Nuovi Ann Pubbl
Istituto Chimico Agrario Sperimentale di Gorizia. Nuovi Annali. Pubblicazione — Ist Chim Agrar Sper Gorizia Nuovi Anna Pubbl
Istituto Coloniale Italiano. Memorie e Monografie. Serie Politica — Ist Col Ital Mem E Mon Ser Pol
Istituto de Bologna. Reale Accademia delle Scienze. Classe di Scienze Fisiche. Memorie — Ist Bologna R Ac Sc Cl Sc Fis Mem
Istituto di Agronomia e Coltivazioni Erbacee. Esperienzi e Ricerche. Universita di Pisa — Ist Agron Esper Ric
Istituto di Automatica. Universita di Roma Notiziario — Ist Autom Univ Roma Not

Istituto di Fisica Tecnica e Impianti Termotecnici dell'Universita di Genova. Relazione FTR — Ist Fis Tec Impianti Termotec Univ Genova Relaz FTR
Istituto di Geologia, Paleontologia, e Geografia Fisica. Universita di Milano. Pubblicazione. Serie G — Ist Geol Paleontol Geogr Fis Univ Milano Pubbl Ser G
Istituto di Geologia. Universita di Milano. Pubblicazione. Serie G — Is Geol Univ Milano Pubbl Ser G
Istituto di Geologia. Universita di Milano. Pubblicazione. Serie G — Ist Geol Univ Milano Pubbl Ser G
Istituto di Patologia del Libro. Bollettino — Ist Patologia Libro Boll
Istituto di Ricerca sulle Acque. Quaderni — Ist Ric Acque Quad
Istituto di Ricerca sulle Acque. Rapporti Tecnici — Ist Ric Acque Rapp Tec
Istituto di Sanita Pubblica. Rendiconti — Ist Sanita Pubblica Rend
Istituto d'Incoraggiamento di Napoli. Atti — Ist Incoraggiamento Napoli Atti
Istituto Federale di Ricerche Forestali. Memorie — Ist Fed Ric For Mem
Istituto Geofisico (Trieste). Pubblicazione — Ist Geof (Trieste) Pubbl
Istituto Giangiacomo Feltrinelli. Annali — Ann Ist Feltrinelli
Istituto Italiano di Idrobiologia Dottore Marco de Marchi. Memorie — Ist Ital Idrobiol Dott Marco de Marchi Mem
Istituto Italo-Latino Americano. Noticiero — Ist It Lat Am Not
Istituto Italo-Latino Americano. Pubblicazione — Ist Italo Lat Am Pubbl
Istituto Lombardo. Accademia di Scienze e Lettere. Memorie della Classe di Lettere — ILML
Istituto Lombardo. Accademia di Scienze e Lettere. Rendiconti — Ist Lombardo Accad Sci e Lettere Rend
Istituto Lombardo. Accademia di Scienze e Lettere. Rendiconti. A. Scienze Matematiche, Fisiche, Chimiche, e Geologiche — Ist Lomb Accad Sci Lett Rend A Sci Mat Fis Chim Geol
Istituto Lombardo. Accademia di Scienze e Lettere. Rendiconti. A. Scienze Matematiche, Fisiche, Chimiche, e Geologiche — Istit Lombardo Accad Sci Lett Rend A
Istituto Lombardo. Accademia di Scienze e Lettere. Rendiconti. B. Scienze Biologiche e Mediche — ILRBBI
Istituto Lombardo. Accademia di Scienze e Lettere. Rendiconti. B. Scienze Biologiche e Mediche — Ist Lomb Accad Sci Lett Rend B
Istituto Lombardo. Accademia di Scienze e Lettere. Rendiconti. Classe de Lettere — ILRL
Istituto Lombardo. Accademia di Scienze e Lettere. Rendiconti. Parte Generale e Atti Ufficiali — Ist Lomb Accad Sci Lett Rend Parte Gen Atti Uffic
Istituto Lombardo. Accademia di Scienze e Lettere. Rendiconti. Scienze Biologiche e Mediche. B — Ist Lombardo Accad Sci Lett Rend Sci Biol Med B
Istituto Lombardo. Accademia di Scienze e Lettere. Rendiconti. Scienze Matematiche, Fisiche, Chimiche, e Geologiche. A — Ist Lombardo Accad Sci Lett Rend A
Istituto Nazionale di Genetica per la Cerealicoltura Nazareno Strampelli [*A publication*] — Ist Naz Genet Cerealicolt Nazareno Strampelli
Istituto per la Ricerca di Base. Series of Monographs in Advanced Mathematics — Istit Ric Base Ser Monogr Adv Math
Istituto Sperimentale dei Metalli Leggeri. Memorie e Rapport — Ist Sper Met Leggeri Mem Rapp
Istituto Sperimentale per il Tabacco. Annali — Ist Sper Tab Ann
Istituto Sperimentale per la Cerealicoltura. Annali — Ist Sper Cerealic Ann
Istituto Sperimentale per la Nutrizione delle Piante. Annali — Ist Sper Nutr Piante Ann
Istituto Sperimentale per la Valorizzazione Tecnologica dei Prodotti Agricoli (Milano). Annali — Ist Sper Valorizzazione Tecnol Prod Agric (Milano) Ann
Istituto Sperimentale per la Viticoltura (Conegliano, Italy). Annali — Ist Sper Vitic (Conegliano Italy) Ann
Istituto Sperimentale per la Zootecnia. Annali — Ist Sper Zootec Ann
Istituto Sperimentale per l'Olivicoltura. Annali. Numero Speciale — Ist Sper Olivic Ann Numero Spec
Istituto Sperimentale Talassografico (Trieste). Pubblicazione — Ist Sper Talassogr (Trieste) Pubbl
Istituto Superiore di Sanita. Laboratori di Fisica. Lectures ISS L (Rome) — Ist Super Sanita Lab Fis Lect ISS L (Rome)
Istituto Superiore di Sanita. Laboratori di Fisica. Preprints ISS P (Rome) — Ist Super Sanita Lab Fis Prepr ISS P (Rome)
Istituto Superiore di Sanita. Laboratori di Fisica. Reports and Reviews ISS R (Rome) — Ist Super Sanita Lab Fis Rep Rev ISS R (Rome)
Istituto Superiore di Sanita. Laboratori di Fisica. Technical Notes ISS T (Rome) — Ist Super Sanita Lab Fis Tech Notes ISS T (Rome)
Istituto Superiore di Sanita. Laboratorio delle Radiazioni. Preprints. ISS P (Rome) — Ist Super Sanita Lab Radiaz Prepr ISS P (Rome)
Istituto Superiore di Sanita. Laboratorio delle Radiazioni. Reports and Reviews ISS R (Rome) — Ist Super Sanita Lab Radiaz Rep Rev ISS R (Rome)
Istituto Superiore di Sanita. Laboratorio delle Radiazioni. Technical Notes ISS T (Rome) — Ist Super Sanita Lab Radiaz Tech Notes ISS T (Rome)
Istituto Superiore di Sanita. Laboritori di Fisica. Rapporti — Ist Super Sanita Lab Fis Rapp
Istituto Superiore di Sanita. Rapporti — Ist Super Sanita Rapp
Istituto Svizzero di Ricerche Forestali. Memorie — Ist Svizz Ric For Mem
Istituto Talassografico (Trieste). Pubblicazione — Ist Talassogr (Trieste) Pubbl
Istituto Tecnico Agrario Statale (Macerata) — Ist Tec Agr Stat (Macerata)
Istituto Tecnico Statale Commerciale e per Geometri Roberto Valturio [*Rimini*] — IRV
Istituto Universitario di Bergamo. Studi Archeologici — Ist Univ Bergamo Studi Arch
Istituto Universitario Navale (Napoli). Annali — Ist Univ Nav (Napoli) Ann
Istituto Universitario Orientale di Napoli. Annali. Sezione Germanica — Ist Univ Orient Nap Ann Sez Ger
Istituto Veneto di Scienze, Lettere, ed Arti. Atti. Classe di Scienze Fisiche, Matematiche, e Naturali — Ist Veneto Sci Lett Arti Atti Cl Sci Fis Mat Nat
Istituto Veneto di Scienze, Lettere, ed Arti. Atti. Classe di Scienze Matematiche e Naturali — Ist Veneto Sci Lett Arti Atti Cl Sci Mat Nat
Istituto Veneto di Scienze, Lettere, ed Arti. Venezia. Atti. Classe di Scienze Matematiche e Naturali — Ist Veneto Sci Lett Arti Atti Cl Sci Mat Natur
Istituto Veneto di Scienze, Lettere, ed Arti. Venezia. Atti. Classe di Scienze Matematiche e Naturali — Istit Veneto Sci Lett Arti Atti Cl Sci Mat Natur
Istochniki Rudnogo Veshchestva Endogonnykh Mestorozhdenii — Istochniki Rudn Veshchestva Endog Mestorozhd
Istoriceski Pregled — Ist Pr
Istoriceskii Zapiski — IstZap
Istoriceskii Zapiski Akademii Nauk SSSR — IZ
Istoriceskij Sbornik Instituta Istorii, Arheologii, i Etnografii — Ist Sb Inst Ist Arheol Etnogr
Istoriceskij Zurnal — Ist Zurn
Istoriceskij Zurnal — IZ
Istoricheski Pregled — IP
Istoricheski Pregled — Ist Preg
Istoricheski Prehled — IstP
Istoricheskii Zhurnal — Ist Zhurn
Istoriia, Arkheologiia, i Etnografiia Srednei Azii — Ist Ark Etnog Sred Azii
Istoriia Material-noj Kul'tury Uzbekistana — Ist Mat Kul't Uzbek
Istorija SSSR — Ist SSSR
Istorija SSSR — Istor SSSR
Istorijski Glasnik — IstG
Istoriko-Astronomiceskie Issledovanija — Istor-Astronom Issled
Istoriko-Filologiceskij Sbornik Syktyvbar — IFSSykt
Istoriko-Filologiceskij Zurnal — IFZ
Istoriko-Filologiceskij Zurnal — Ist-Filol Z
Istoriko-Filologicheskii Zhurnal — IFZ Arm
Istoriko-Filologicheskii Zhurnal — Ist Filol Zh
Istoriko-Filologicheskii Zhurnal. Akademia Nauk Armianskoi — Ist Fil Zhur A N Armian
Istoriko-Matematiceskie Issledovanija — Istor-Mat Issled
Istoriski Casopis — IC
Istoriski Casopis — Ist Cas
Istoriski Glasnik — Ist Gl
Istoritcheskii Viestnik — IV
Istoriya i Metodologiya Estestvennykh Nauk — Istor Metodol Estestv Nauk
Istorya SSSR — IsS
Istorycni Dzerela ta ich Vykorystannja — Ist Dzerela Vykorystannja
Istvan Kiraly Muzeum Koezlemenyei — IKM Koezl
Istvan Kiraly Muzeum Koezlemenyei — IKMK
ISWA [*International Solid Wastes and Public Cleansing Association*] **Information Bulletin** — ISWA Inf Bull
ISWS Bulletin. Illinois Water Survey — ISWS Bull Ill Water Surv
It Beaken — ItB
Ita Humanidades — IH
Italamerican — Italamer
Italia Agricola — It Agr
Italia Agricola — Ital Agr
Italia Agricola — Ital Agric
Italia Agricola — Italia Agric
Italia Antichissima — IA
Italia Che Scrive — ICS
Italia Che Scrive — It
Italia Dialettale — ID
Italia Dialettale. Rivista di Dialettologia Italiana — It Dial
Italia e i Cereali — Ital Cereali
Italia Forestale e Montana — It For Montan
Italia Forestale e Montana — Ital For Mont
Italia Francescana — IFr
Italia Francescana — It Fr
Italia Intellettuale — II
Italia Medica — Ital Med
Italia Medioevale e Umanistica — IMU
Italia Medioevale e Umanistica — Italia Medioevale Uman
Italia Militare — Ital Milit
Italia Nostra — IN
Italia Numismatica — IN
Italia Real Comitato Geologico. Bollettino — Italia R Comitato G B
Italia Sacra — IS
Italia Sacra — It Sac
Italia Vinicola ed Agraria — Ital Vinic Agrar
Italia-America Latina (Naples) — Italia Am Lat Napoli
Italian Americana — Ital A
Italian Americana — Ital Am
Italian Books and Periodicals — IBP
Italian Culture — It Cult
Italian Culture — ItC
Italian Economic Survey — It Econ Surv
Italian Expeditions to the Karakorum [K^2] **and Hindu Kush. Scientific Reports** — Ital Exped Karakorum Hindu Kush Sci Rep
Italian General Review of Dermatology — Ital Gen Rev Derm
Italian General Review of Dermatology — Ital Gen Rev Dermatol
Italian General Review of Oto-Rhino-Laryngology — Ital Gen Rev Oto-Rhino-Laryng
Italian Journal of Biochemistry — Ital J Bioc
Italian Journal of Biochemistry — Ital J Biochem
Italian Journal of Biochemistry (English Edition) — Ital J Biochem (Engl Ed)
Italian Journal of Chest Diseases — GIMTB4
Italian Journal of Chest Diseases — Ital J Chest Dis
Italian Journal of Food Science — Ital J Food Sci
Italian Journal of Gastroenterology — Ital J Gastroenterol
Italian Journal of Gastroenterology — IYJGDH
Italian Journal of Medicine — IJMEEP
Italian Journal of Medicine — Ital J Med
Italian Journal of Neurological Sciences — IJNSD3

Italian Journal of Neurological Sciences — Ital J Neurol Sci
Italian Journal of Ophthalmology — Ital J Ophthalmol
Italian Journal of Orthopaedics and Traumatology — Ital J Orthop Traumatol
Italian Journal of Orthopaedics and Traumatology. Supplementum — Ital J Orthop Traumatol Suppl
Italian Journal of Sports Traumatology — IJSTDV
Italian Journal of Sports Traumatology — Ital J Sports Traumatol
Italian Journal of Surgical Sciences — IJSSET
Italian Journal of Surgical Sciences — Ital J Surg Sci
Italian Journal of Zoology — Ital J Zool
Italian Linguistics — Ital L
Italian. Patent Document — Ital
Italian Quarterly — IQ
Italian Quarterly — Ital Q
Italian Quarterly — Ital Quart
Italian Quarterly — ItQ
Italian Review of Orthopaedics and Traumatology — Ital Rev Orthop Traumatol
Italian Studies — IS
Italian Studies — ISt
Italian Studies — It St
Italian Trends. Banco Lavoro — Bnc Lavoro
Italian-American Business — Italian-Am Bus
Italian-Australian Bulletin of Commerce — Ital Aust Bul Commerce
Italianistica. Revista di Letteratura Italiana — IRLI
Italianistica. Revista di Letteratura Italiana — Ital
Italica — I
Italica — It
Italica — Ital
Italienische Studien — IS
Italienische Weine — Ital Weine
Italy. Comitato Nazionale per l' Energia Nucleare. CNEN-RT/CHI — Italy Com Naz Energ Nucl CNEN RT CHI
Italy. Comitato Nazionale per l' Energia Nucleare. CNEN-RT/FIMA — Italy Com Naz Energ Nucl CNEN RT FIMA
Italy. Comitato Nazionale per l'Energia Nucleare. CNEN-RT/ING — Italy Com Naz Energ Nucl CNEN RT ING
Italy. Comitato Nazionale per l'Energia Nucleare. Rapporto Tecnico CNEN-RT/BIO — Italy Com Naz Energ Nucl Rapp Tec CNEN RT BIO
Italy. Comitato Nazionale per l'Energia Nucleare. Rapporto Tecnico CNEN-RT/DISP — Italy Com Naz Energ Nucl Rapp Tec CNEN RT DISP
Italy. Comitato Nazionale per l'Energia Nucleare. Rapporto Tecnico CNEN-RT/FARE-SDI — Italy Com Naz Energ Nucl Rapp Tec CNEN RT FARE SDI
Italy. Comitato Nazionale per l'Energia Nucleare. Rapporto Tecnico CNEN-RT/FARE-SIN — Italy Com Naz Energ Nucl Rapp Tec CNEN RT FARE SIN
Italy. Comitato Nazionale per l'Energia Nucleare. Rapporto Tecnico CNEN-RT/FI — Italy Com Naz Energ Nucl Rapp Tec CNEN RT FI
Italy. Comitato Nazionale per l'Energia Nucleare. Rapporto Tecnico CNEN-RT/MET — Italy Com Naz Energ Nucl Rapp Tec CNEN RT MET
Italy. Comitato Nazionale per l'Energia Nucleare. Rapporto Tecnico CNEN-RT/PROT — Italy Com Naz Energ Nucl Rapp Tec CNEN RT PROT
Italy. Comitato Nazionale per l'Energia Nucleare. Rapporto Tecnico RT/AI — Italy Com Naz Energ Nucl Rapp Tec RT AI
Italy. Comitato Nazionale per l'Energia Nucleare. Rapporto Tecnico RT/BIO — Italy Com Naz Energ Nucl Rapp Tec RT BIO
Italy. Comitato Nazionale per l'Energia Nucleare. Rapporto Tecnico RT/CHI — Italy Com Naz Energ Nucl Rapp Tec RT CHI
Italy. Comitato Nazionale per l'Energia Nucleare. Rapporto Tecnico RT/DISP — Italy Com Naz Energ Nucl Rapp Tec RT DISP
Italy. Comitato Nazionale per l'Energia Nucleare. Rapporto Tecnico RT/EC — Italy Com Naz Energ Nucl Rapp Tec RT EC
Italy. Comitato Nazionale per l' Energia Nucleare. Rapporto Tecnico RT/EL — Italy Com Naz Energ Nucl Rapp Tec RT EL
Italy. Comitato Nazionale per l'Energia Nucleare. Rapporto Tecnico RT/FI — Italy Com Naz Energ Nucl Rapp Tec RT FI
Italy. Comitato Nazionale per l'Energia Nucleare. Rapporto Tecnico RT/FIMA — Italy Com Naz Energ Nucl Rapp Tec RT FIMA
Italy. Comitato Nazionale per l'Energia Nucleare. Rapporto Tecnico RT/GEN — Italy Com Naz Energ Nucl Rapp Tec RT GEN
Italy. Comitato Nazionale per l'Energia Nucleare. Rapporto Tecnico RT/GEO — Italy Com Naz Energ Nucl Rapp Tec RT GEO
Italy. Comitato Nazionale per l'Energia Nucleare. Rapporto Tecnico RT/GIU — Italy Com Naz Energ Nucl Rapp Tec RT GIU
Italy. Comitato Nazionale per l'Energia Nucleare. Rapporto Tecnico RT/ING — Italy Com Naz Energ Nucl Rapp Tec RT ING
Italy. Comitato Nazionale per l'Energia Nucleare. Rapporto Tecnico RT/MET — Italy Com Naz Energ Nucl Rapp Tec RT MET
Italy. Comitato Nazionale per l'Energia Nucleare. Rapporto Tecnico RT/PROT — Italy Com Naz Energ Nucl Rapp Tec RT PROT
Italy. Documents and Notes — Italy Doc Notes
Italy. Documents and Notes — Italy Docs and Notes
Italy. Documents and Notes — ITF
Italy. Istituto Superiore delle Poste e delle Telecomunicazioni. Note Recensioni e Notizie — Italy Ist Super Poste Telecomun Note Recens Not
Italy. Ministero dell'Agricoltura e delle Foreste Collana Verde — Italy Minist Agric For Collana Verde
Italy. Patent Document — Italy Pat Doc
Italy. Servizio Geologico. Bollettino — Italy Serv Geol Boll
Italy. Servizio Geologico. Memorie per Servire alla Descrizione della Carta Geologica d'Italia — Italy Serv Geol Mem
Italy. Ufficio Centrale Brevetti. Bollettino dei Brevetti per Invenzioni, Modelli, e Marchi — Italy Uffic Cent Brev Boll Brev Invenz Modelli Marchi
Italyan Filolojisi — ItF
ITC [*International Training Centre for Aerial Survey*] **Journal** — ITC J
ITCC [*International Technical Cooperation Centre*] **Review** [*Israel*] — ITCC Rev
ITCC [*International Technical Cooperation Centre*] **Review** — ITCCC
ITD. Izotoptechnika, Diagnosztika — ITD Izotoptech Diagn
ITE [*Institute of Transportation Engineers*] **Journal** [*United States*] — ITE J
ITEME [*Institution of Technician Engineers in Mechanical Engineering*] **Newsletter** — ITEME Newsl
ITG [*Informationstechnische Gesellschaft*] **Fachberichte** — ITG Fachber
Itim Mizrah News Agency. Bulletin on Palestinian Organizations — IMO
Itim Mizrah News Agency Hadashot. Current Comment — IMH
Itinerari — Itin
Itinerari dei Musei e Monumenti d'Italia — IMMI
Itineraria Romana. Roemisiche Reisewege an der Hand der Tabula Peutingeriana — It R
Itinerario — IO
Itinerarium [*Buenos Aires*] — Itin
Itogi Eksperimental'nykh Rabot Molodykh Issledovatelei po Voprosam Sel'skogo Khozyaistva — Itogi Eksp Rab Molodykh Issled Vopr Sel'sk Khoz
Itogi Nauki Astronomiya — Itogi Nauki Astron
Itogi Nauki Biologicheskaya Khimiya — Itogi Nauki Biol Khim
Itogi Nauki Biologicheski Osnovy Rastenievodstva — Itogi Nauki Biol Osn Rastenievod
Itogi Nauki Biologicheskie Nauki — Itogi Nauki Biol Nauki
Itogi Nauki Biologicheskie Ul'trastruktury — Itogi Nauki Biol Ultrastrukt
Itogi Nauki Elektrokhimiya — Itogi Nauki Elektrokhim
Itogi Nauki Embriologiya — Itogi Nauki Embriol
Itogi Nauki Farmakologiya. Khimioterapevticheskie Sredstva — Itogi Nauki Farmakol Khimioter Sredstva
Itogi Nauki Farmakologiya. Toksikologiya — Itogi Nauki Farmakol Toksikol
Itogi Nauki Fizicheskaya Khimiya — Itogi Nauki Fiz Khim
Itogi Nauki Fiziko-Matematicheskie Nauki — Itogi Nauki Fiz Mat Nauki
Itogi Nauki Fiziologiya, Cheloveka, i Zhivotnykh — Itogi Nauki Fiziol Chel Zhivotn
Itogi Nauki Geofizika — Itogi Nauki Geofiz
Itogi Nauki Geokhimiya Mineralogiya Petrografiya — Itogi Nauki Geokhim Mineral Petrogr
Itogi Nauki i Tekhniki Atomnaya Energetika — Itogi Nauki Tekh At Energ
Itogi Nauki i Tekhniki Biofizika — Itogi Nauki Tekh Biofiz
Itogi Nauki i Tekhniki Elektrokhimiya — Itogi Nauki Tekh Elektrokhim
Itogi Nauki i Tekhniki Farmakologiya Khimioterapevticheski Sredstva Toksikolog iya — Itogi Nauki Tekh Farmakol Khimioter Sredstva Toksikol
Itogi Nauki i Tekhniki Fizicheskaya Khimiya Kinetika — Itogi Nauki Tekh Fiz Khim Kinet
Itogi Nauki i Tekhniki Fiziologiya Cheloveka i Zhivotnykh — Itogi Nauki Tekh Fiziol Chel Zhivotn
Itogi Nauki i Tekhniki Fiziologiya Rastenii — Itogi Nauki Tekh Fiziol Rast
Itogi Nauki i Tekhniki Genetika Cheloveka — Itogi Nauki Tekh Genet Chel
Itogi Nauki i Tekhniki Geokhimiya Mineralogiya Petrografiya — Itogi Nauki Tekh Geokhim Mineral Petrogr
Itogi Nauki i Tekhniki Gidrogeologiya, Inzhenernaya Geologiya — Itogi Nauki Tekh Gidrogeol Inzh Geol
Itogi Nauki i Tekhniki Gornoe Delo — Itogi Nauki Tekh Gorn Delo
Itogi Nauki i Tekhniki Issledovanie Kosmicheskogo Prostranstva — Itogi Nauki Tekh Issled Kosm Prostranstva
Itogi Nauki i Tekhniki Khimicheskaya Termodinamika i Ravnovesiya — Itogi Nauki Tekh Khim Termodin Ravnovesiya
Itogi Nauki i Tekhniki Khimiya i Tekhnologiya Vysokimolekulyarnykh Soedinenii — Itogi Nauki Tekh Khim Tekhn Vysokimol Soedin
Itogi Nauki i Tekhniki Korroziya i Zashchita ot Korrozii — IKZKA
Itogi Nauki i Tekhniki Korroziya i Zashchita ot Korrozii [*Former USSR*] — Itogi Nauki Tekh Korroz Zashch Korroz
Itogi Nauki i Tekhniki Kristallokhimiya — Itogi Nauki Tekh Kristallokhim
Itogi Nauki i Tekhniki Mestorozhdeniya Goryuchikh Poleznykh Iskopaemykh — IMGIA
Itogi Nauki i Tekhniki Mestorozhdeniya Goryuchikh Poleznykh Iskopaemykh [*Former USSR*] [*A publication*] — Itogi Nauki Tekh Mestorozhd Goryuch Polezn Iskop
Itogi Nauki i Tekhniki Metallovedenie i Termicheskaya Obrabotka — IMTOA
Itogi Nauki i Tekhniki Metallovedenie i Termicheskaya Obrabotka — Itogi Nauki Tekh Metalloved Term Obrab
Itogi Nauki i Tekhniki Metallurgiya Tsvetnykh i Redkikh Metallov — Itogi Nauki Tekh Metall Tsvetn Redk Met
Itogi Nauki i Tekhniki Mikrobiologiya — Itogi Nauki Tekh Mikrobiol
Itogi Nauki i Tekhniki Molekulyarnaya Biologiya — Itogi Nauki Tekh Mol Biol
Itogi Nauki i Tekhniki Nemetallicheskie Poleznye Iskopaemye — Itogi Nauki Tekh Nemet Polezn Iskop
Itogi Nauki i Tekhniki Neorganicheskaya Khimiya — Itogi Nauki Tekh Neorg Khim
Itogi Nauki i Tekhniki Obogashchenie Poleznykh Iskopaemykh — IOPIA
Itogi Nauki i Tekhniki Obogashchenie Poleznykh Iskopaemykh — Itogi Nauki Tekh Obogashch Polezn Iskop
Itogi Nauki i Tekhniki Obshchaya Ekologiya, Biotsenologiya — Itogi Nauki Tekh Obshch Ekol Biotsenol
Itogi Nauki i Tekhniki Obshchaya Geologiya — Itogi Nauki Tekh Obshch Geol
Itogi Nauki i Tekhniki Onkologiya — Itogi Nauki Tekh Onkol
Itogi Nauki i Tekhniki Pozharnaya Okhrana — Itogi Nauki Tekh Pozharnaya Okhr
Itogi Nauki i Tekhniki Proizvodstvo Chuguna i Stali — Itogi Nauki Tekh Proizvod Chuguna Stali
Itogi Nauki i Tekhniki Razrabotka Mestorozhdenii Tverdykh Poleznykh Iskopaemykh — ITRID
Itogi Nauki i Tekhniki Razrabotka Neftyanykh i Gazovykh Mestorozhdenii — IRNGA
Itogi Nauki i Tekhniki Rudnye Mestorozhdeniya — Itogi Nauki Tekh Rudn Mestorozhd
Itogi Nauki i Tekhniki Seriya Astronomiya — Itogi Nauki Tekh Ser Astron
Itogi Nauki i Tekhniki Seriya Atomnaya Energetika — Itogi Nauki Tekh Ser At Energ

Itogi Nauki i Tekhniki Seriya Biofizika — Itogi Nauki Tekh Ser Biofiz
Itogi Nauki i Tekhniki Seriya Biologicheskaya Khimiya — Itogi Nauki Tekh Ser Biol Khim
Itogi Nauki i Tekhniki Seriya Biotekhnologiya — Itogi Nauki Tekh Ser Biotekhnol
Itogi Nauki i Tekhniki Seriya Diagrammy Sostoyaniya Nemetallicheskikh Sistem — Itogi Nauki Tekh Ser Diagrammy Sostoyaniya Nemet Sist
Itogi Nauki i Tekhniki Seriya Elektrokhimiya — Itogi Nauki Tekh Ser Elektrokhim
Itogi Nauki i Tekhniki Seriya Elektronika i Ee Primenenie — Itogi Nauki Tekh Ser Elektron Ee Primen
Itogi Nauki i Tekhniki Seriya Farmakologiya, Khimioterapeuticheskie Sredstva — Itogi Nauki Tekh Ser Farmakol Khimioter Sredstva
Itogi Nauki i Tekhniki Seriya Fizicheskaya Rastenii — Itogi Nauki Tekh Ser Fiz Rast
Itogi Nauki i Tekhniki Seriya Fiziki Zemli — Itogi Nauki Tekh Ser Fiz Zemli
Itogi Nauki i Tekhniki Seriya Fiziologiya Cheloveka i Zhivotnykh — Itogi Nauki Tekh Ser Fiziol Chel Zhivotn
Itogi Nauki i Tekhniki Seriya Fiziologiya, Khimiya, Kinetika — Itogi Nauki Tekh Ser Fiziol Khim Kinet
Itogi Nauki i Tekhniki Seriya Genetika Cheloveka — Itogi Nauki Tekh Ser Genet Chel
Itogi Nauki i Tekhniki Seriya Geokhimiya, Mineralogiya, Petrografiya — Itogi Nauki Tekh Ser Geokhim Mineral Petrogr
Itogi Nauki i Tekhniki Seriya Gidrogeologiya, Inzhenernaya Geologiya — Itogi Nauki Tekh Ser Gidrogeol Inzh Geol
Itogi Nauki i Tekhniki Seriya Gidrologiya Sushi — Itogi Nauki Tekh Ser Gidrol Sushi
Itogi Nauki i Tekhniki Seriya Gornoe Delo — Itogi Nauki Tekh Ser Gorn Delo
Itogi Nauki i Tekhniki Seriya Immunologiya — Itogi Nauki Tekh Ser Immunolo
Itogi Nauki i Tekhniki Seriya Issledovanie Kosmicheskogo Prostranstva — Itogi Nauk & Tekh Ser Issled Kosm Prostranstva
Itogi Nauki i Tekhniki Seriya Issledovanie Kosmicheskogo Prostranstva — Itogi Nauki Tekh Ser Issled Kosm Prostranstva
Itogi Nauki i Tekhniki Seriya Khimicheskaya Termodinamika i Ravnovesiya — Itogi Nauki Tekh Ser Khim Termodin Ravnovesiya
Itogi Nauki i Tekhniki Seriya Khimicheskoe, Neftepererabatyvayushchee i Polimernoe Mashinostroenie — Itogi Nauki Tekh Ser Khim Neftepererab Polim Mashinostr
Itogi Nauki i Tekhniki Seriya Khimiya i Tekhnologiya Vysokomolekulyarnykh Soedinenii — Itogi Nauki Tekh Ser Khim Tekhnol Vysokomol Soedin
Itogi Nauki i Tekhniki Seriya Khimiya Tverdogo Tela — Itogi Nauki Tekh Ser Khim Tverd Tela
Itogi Nauki i Tekhniki Seriya Khromatografiya — Itogi Nauki Tekh Ser Khromatogr
Itogi Nauki i Tekhniki Seriya Kinetika i Kataliz — Itogi Nauki Tekh Ser Kinet Katal
Itogi Nauki i Tekhniki Seriya Korroziya i Zashchita ot Korrozii — Itogi Nauki Tekh Ser Korroz Zashch Korroz
Itogi Nauki i Tekhniki Seriya Kristallokhimiya — Itogi Nauki Tekh Ser Kristallokhim
Itogi Nauki i Tekhniki Seriya Mekhanika Zhidkosti i Gaza — Itogi Nauki Tekh Ser Mekh Zhidk Gaza
Itogi Nauki i Tekhniki Seriya Mestorozhdeniya Goryuchikh Poleznykh Iskopaemykh — Itogi Nauki Tekh Ser Mestorozhd Goryuch Polezn Iskop
Itogi Nauki i Tekhniki Seriya Metallovedenie i Termicheskaya Obrabotka — Itogi Nauki Tekh Ser Metalloved Term Obrab
Itogi Nauki i Tekhniki Seriya Metallurgiya Tsvetnykh i Redkikh Metallov — Itogi Nauki Tekh Ser Metall Tsvetn Redk Met
Itogi Nauki i Tekhniki Seriya Mikrobiologiya — Itogi Nauki Tekh Ser Mikrobiol
Itogi Nauki i Tekhniki Seriya Molekulyarnaya Biologiya — Itogi Nauki Tekh Ser Mol Biol
Itogi Nauki i Tekhniki Seriya Morfologiya Cheloveka i Zhivotnykh — Itogi Nauki Tekh Ser Morfol Chel Zhivotn
Itogi Nauki i Tekhniki Seriya Nemetallicheskie Poleznye Iskopaemye — Itogi Nauki Tekh Ser Nemet Polezn Iskop
Itogi Nauki i Tekhniki Seriya Neorganicheskaya Khimiya — Itogi Nauki Tekh Ser Neorg Khim
Itogi Nauki i Tekhniki Seriya Obogashchenie Poleznykh Iskopaemykh — Itogi Nauki Tekh Ser Obogashch Polezn Iskop
Itogi Nauki i Tekhniki Seriya Obshchaya Ekologiya, Biotsenologiya, Gidrobiologiya — Itogi Nauki Tekh Ser Obshch Ekol Biotsenol Gidrobiol
Itogi Nauki i Tekhniki Seriya Obshchaya Genetika — Itogi Nauki Tekh Ser Obshch Genet
Itogi Nauki i Tekhniki Seriya Obshchaya Geologiya — Itogi Nauki Tekh Ser Obshch Geol
Itogi Nauki i Tekhniki Seriya Obshchie Problemy Fiziko-Khimicheskoi Biologii — Itogi Nauki Tekh Ser Obshch Probl Fiz Khim Biol
Itogi Nauki i Tekhniki Seriya Obshchie Voprosy Patologii — Itogi Nauki Tekh Ser Obshch Vopr Patol
Itogi Nauki i Tekhniki Seriya Okeanologiya — Itogi Nauki Tekh Ser Okeanol
Itogi Nauki i Tekhniki. Seriya. Okeanologiya — ITSOD
Itogi Nauki i Tekhniki Seriya Onkologiya — Itogi Nauki Tekh Ser Onkol
Itogi Nauki i Tekhniki Seriya Organicheskaya Khimiya — Itogi Nauki Tekh Ser Org Khim
Itogi Nauki i Tekhniki Seriya Pochvovedenie i Agrokhimiya — Itogi Nauki Tekh Ser Pochvoved Agrokhim
Itogi Nauki i Tekhniki Seriya Pozharnaya Okhrana — Itogi Nauki Tekh Ser Pozharnaya Okhr
Itogi Nauki i Tekhniki Seriya Proizvodstvo Chuguna i Stali — Itogi Nauki Tekh Ser Proizvod Chuguna Stali
Itogi Nauki i Tekhniki Seriya Prokatnoe i Volochil'noe Proizvodstvo — Itogi Nauki Tekh Ser Prokatnoe Volochil'noe Proizvod
Itogi Nauki i Tekhniki Seriya Protsessy i Apparaty Khimicheskoi Tekhnologii — Itogi Nauki Tekh Ser Protsessy Appar Khim Tekhnol
Itogi Nauki i Tekhniki. Seriya. Puchki Zaryazhennykh Chastits i Tverdoe Telo — Itogi Nauki Tekh Ser Puchki Zaryazhennykh Chastits Tverd Telo
Itogi Nauki i Tekhniki Seriya Radiatsionnaya Biologiya — Itogi Nauki Tekh Ser Radiats Biol
Itogi Nauki i Tekhniki Seriya Rastvory, Rasplavy — Itogi Nauki Tekh Ser Rastvory Rasplavy
Itogi Nauki i Tekhniki Seriya Razrabotka Mestorozhdenii Tverdykh Poleznykh Iskopaemykh — Itogi Nauki Tekh Ser Razrab Mestorozhd Tverd Polezn Iskop
Itogi Nauki i Tekhniki Seriya Razrabotka Neftyanykh i Gazovykh Mestorozhdenii — Itogi Nauki Tekh Ser Razrab Neft Gazov Mestorozhd
Itogi Nauki i Tekhniki Seriya Rudnye Mestorozhdeniya — Itogi Nauki Tekh Ser Rudn Mestorozhd
Itogi Nauki i Tekhniki Seriya Stroenie Molekul i Khimicheskaya Svyaz — Itogi Nauki Tekh Ser Str Mol Khim Svyaz
Itogi Nauki i Tekhniki Seriya Svarka — Itogi Nauki Tekh Ser Svarka
Itogi Nauki i Tekhniki Seriya Svetotekhnika i Infrakrasnaya Tekhnika — Itogi Nauki Tekh Ser Svetotekh Infrakrasnaya Tekh
Itogi Nauki i Tekhniki Seriya Tekhnicheskii Analiz v Metallurgii — Itogi Nauki Tekh Ser Tekh Anal Metall
Itogi Nauki i Tekhniki. Seriya. Tekhnologiya Mashinostroeniya — Itogi Nauki Tekh Ser Tekhnol Mashinostr
Itogi Nauki i Tekhniki Seriya Tekhnologiya Organicheskikh Veshchestv — Itogi Nauki Tekh Ser Tekhnol Org Veshchestv
Itogi Nauki i Tekhniki Seriya Tekhnologiya Razrabotki Mestorozhdenii — Itogi Nauki Tekh Ser Tekhnol Razrab Mestorozhd
Itogi Nauki i Tekhniki Seriya Teoriya Metallurgicheskikh Protsessov — Itogi Nauki Tekh Ser Teor Metall Protsessov
Itogi Nauki i Tekhniki Seriya Toksikologiya — Itogi Nauki Tekh Ser Toksikol
Itogi Nauki i Tekhniki Seriya Virusologiya — Itogi Nauki Tekh Ser Virusol
Itogi Nauki i Tekhniki Seriya Zashchita Rastenii — Itogi Nauki Tekh Ser Zashch Rast
Itogi Nauki i Tekhniki Seriya Zhivotnovodstvo i Veterinariya — Itogi Nauki Tekh Ser Zhivotnovod Vet
Itogi Nauki i Tekhniki Svarka — Itogi Nauki Tekh Svarka
Itogi Nauki i Tekhniki Svetotekhnika i Infrakrasnaya Tekhniki — Itogi Nauki Tekh Svetotekh Infrakrasnaya Tekh
Itogi Nauki i Tekhniki Tekhnologiya Mashinostroeniya — Itogi Nauki Tekh Tekhnol Mashinostr
Itogi Nauki i Tekhniki Teoriya Metallurgicheskikh Protsessov — Itogi Nauki Tekh Teor Metall Protsessov
Itogi Nauki i Tekhniki Toksikologiya — Itogi Nauki Tekh Toksikol
Itogi Nauki i Tekhniki Virusologiya — Itogi Nauki Tekh Virusol
Itogi Nauki i Tekhniki Zhivotnovodstvo i Veterinariya — Itogi Nauki Tekh Zhivotnovod Vet
Itogi Nauki Khimicheskie Nauki — Itogi Nauki Khim Nauki
Itogi Nauki Khimiya i Tekhnologiya Vysokomolekulyarnykh Soedinenii — Itogi Nauki Khim Tekhnol Vysokomol Soedin
Itogi Nauki Korroziya i Zashchita ot Korrozii — Itogi Nauki Korroz Zashch Korroz
Itogi Nauki Kristallokhimiya — Itogi Nauki Kristallokhim
Itogi Nauki. Nemetallicheskie Poleznye Iskopaemye — Itogi Nauki Nemet Polezn Iskop
Itogi Nauki Neorganicheskaya Khimiya — Itogi Nauki Neorg Khim
Itogi Nauki Obshchaya Genetika — Itogi Nauki Obshch Genet
Itogi Nauki Obshchie Voprosy Patologii — Itogi Nauki Obshch Vopr Patol
Itogi Nauki Onkologiya — Itogi Nauki Onkol
Itogi Nauki Rudnye Mestorozhdeniya — Itogi Nauki Rudn Mestorozhd
Itogi Nauki Tekhnicheskie Nauki — Itogi Nauki Tekh Nauki
Itogi Nauki Tekhnologiya Organicheskikh Veshchestv — Itogi Nauki Tekhnol Org Veshchestv
Itogi Nauki Tsitologiya Obshchaya Genetika. Genetika Cheloveka — Itogi Nauki Tsitol Obshch Genet Genet Chel
Itogi Nauki Veterinariya — Itogi Nauki Vet
Itogi Nauki Virusologiya i Mikrobiologiya — Itogi Nauki Virusol Mikrobiol
Itogi Nauki Vysokomolekulyarnye Soedineniya — Itogi Nauki Vysokomol Soedin
Itogi Nauki Zashchita Rastenii — Itogi Nauki Zashch Rast
Itogi Polevyh Rabot Instituta Etnografii — Itogi Polev Rabot Inst Etnogr
Itogi Voronezskaja Stancii Zascity Rastenij — Itogi Voronezsk Stancii Zasc Rast
Iton Rishmi [*Official Gazette*] — IR
IUB (International Union of Biochemistry) Symposium Series — IUB (Int Union Biochem) Symp Ser
IUCC [*Inter-University Committee on Computing*] **Bulletin** — IUCC Bull
IUCC [*Inter-University Committee on Computing*] **Newsletter** — IUCC Newsl
IUCN [*International Union for Conservation of Nature and Natural Resources*] **Annual Report** — IUCN Ann Rep
IUCN [*International Union for Conservation of Nature and Natural Resources*] **Bulletin** — IUCN Bull
IUCN (International Union for Conservation of Nature and Natural Resources) Otter Specialist Group Bulletin — IUCN OSG Bull
IUCN [*International Union for Conservation of Nature and Natural Resources*] **Publications. New Series** — IUCN Publ New Ser
IUCN [*International Union for Conservation of Nature and Natural Resources*] **Yearbook** — IUCN Yearb
IUCr (International Union of Crystallography) Crystallographic Symposia — IUCr Crystallogr Symp
IUGG [*International Union of Geodesy and Geophysics*] **Chronicle** — IUGG Chron
Iugoslavica Physiologica Pharmacologica Acta — Iugosl Physiol Pharmacol Acta
IUPAC [*International Union of Pure and Applied Chemistry*] **Chemical Data Series** — IUPAC Chem Data Ser
IUPAC (International Union of Pure and Applied Chemistry) Symposium on Macromolecules — IUPAC Symp Macromol
IVA (Ingenjoersvetenskapsakademien) Meddelande — IVA (Ingenjoersvetenskapsakad) Medd
IVA [*Ingenjoersvetenskapsakademien*] **och des Laboratorien** — IVA
IVA [*Ingenjoersvetenskapsakademien*] **Tidskrift foer Teknisk-Vetenskaplig Forskning** — IVA
IVA [*Ingenjoersvetenskapsakademien*] **Tidskrift foer Teknisk-Vetenskaplig Forskning** [*Sweden*] — IVA Tidskr Tek Vetensk Forsk

IVA [*Ingenjoersvetenskapsakademien*] **Tidskrift foer Teknisk-Vetenskaplig Forskning** — IVA Tidskr Tek-Vetenskaplig Forsk
IVA [*Ingenjoersvetenskapsakademien*] **Tidskrift foer Teknisk-Vetenskaplig Forskning** — IVAAA
Ivano-Frankivs'kii Derzhavnii Medichnii Institut Naukovi Zapiski — Ivano Frankivs'kii Derzh Med Inst Nauk Zap
Ivanovskii Gosudarstvennyi Pedagogiceskii Institut Imeni D. A. Furmanova Ivanovskoe Matematiceskoe Obscestvo Ucenye Zapiski — Ivanov Gos Ped Inst Ucen Zap
Ivanovskii Gosudarstvennyi Universitet Ucenye Zapiski — Ivanov Gos Univ Ucen Zap
IVF. Journal of In Vitro Fertilization and Embryo Transfer — IVF J In Vitro Fert Embryo Transfer
IVL [*Instituet foer Vatten och Luftvardsforskning*] **Bulletin** — IVL Bull
IVL (Institutet foer Vatten och Luftvaardsforskning) Publikation B — IVL Publ B
IVL (Institutet foer Vatten och Luftvaardsforskning) Report — IVL Rep
Ivor's Art Review — IAR
Ivor's Art Review — Ivor's Art R
Ivory Coast. Direction des Mines et de la Geologie. Bulletin — Ivory Coast Dir Mines Geol Bull
IVT [*Instituut voor de Veredeling van Tuinbouwgewassen*] **Jaarverslag** — IVT Jaarversl
IVT [*Instituut voor de Veredeling van Tuinbouwgewassen*] **Mededeling** — IVT An Mededel
IVTAN [*Institut Vysokikh Temperatur Akademiya Nauk*] **Reviews** — IVTAN Rev
IVTAN [*Institut Vysokikh Temperatur Akademiya Nauk*] **Reviews of the High Temperature Institute Academy of Sciences of the USSR** — IVTAN Rev High Temp Inst Acad Sci USSR
Iwata Institute of Plant Biochemistry. Publication — Iwata Inst Plant Biochem Publ
Iwata Tob Shikenjo Hokoku/Bulletin. Iwata Tobacco Experimental Station — Iwata Tob Shikenjo Hokoku Bull Iwata Tob Exp Stn
Iwate Daigaku Kyoikugakubu Kenkyu Nenpo — IDKKB
Iwate Daigaku Nogakubu Hokoku — IDNHA
Iwate University. Faculty of Engineering. Technology Reports — Iwate Univ Technol Rep
Iwate-Ken Eisei Kenkyusho Nenpo — IKEND
IWGIA [*International Work Group for Indigenous Affairs*] **Document** — IWGIAD
IWGIA [*International Work Group for Indigenous Affairs*] **Newsletter** — IWGIAN
IWS (Institut fuer Wassergefaehrdende Stoffe) Schriftenreihe — IWS Schriftenr
IWSA (International Water Supply Association) International Water Supply Conference and Exhibition — IWSA Int Water Supply Conf Exhib
IXe Congres International des Sciences Historiques. Rapports — Rapp IXe Congr Internat Sci Hist
Iz Istorii Biologii — Iz Ist Biol
Iz Istorii Biologii — Iz Istor Biol
Iz Istorii Estestvoznaniia i Tekhniki i Pribaltiki — Iz Ist Estestvozn TekhbPribaltiki
Iz Istorii Kul'tury Narodov Uzbekistana — I Ist Kul't Narod Uzbek
Izdanija Severo-Kavkazskoj Kraevoj Stancii Zascity Rastenij. Ser. A. Naucnye i Organizacionnye Raboty — Izd Severo Kavkazsk Kraev Stancii Zasc Rast Ser A Naucn Organ
Izdanija. Zavod za Ribarstvo na SR Makedonija — Izd Zavod Ribar SR Maked
Izdanja Zavod za Hidrotehniku Gradevinskog Fakulteta u Sarajevu — Izd Zavod Hidroteh Gradevinskog Fak Sarajevu
Izhevskii Meditsinskii Institut Trudy — Izhevsk Med Inst Tr
Izhevskii Sel'skokhozyaistvennyi Institut. Trudy — Izhevsk Skh Inst Tr
Izkustvo — Izk
Izmenenie Pochvy pri Okyl'turivanii Ikh Klassifikatsiya i Diagnostika "Kolos" — Izmen Pochv Okyl't Klassif Diagnostika "Kolos"
Izmerital'naja Technika — Izmer Techn
Izmeritel'naya Tekhnika — Izmer Tekh
Izmeritel'naya Tekhnika i Proverochnoe Delo — Izmer Tekh Proverochn Delo
Iznos i Zashchita Konstruktsu Promyshlennykh Zdanii — Iznos Zashch Konstr Prom Zdanii
Izobretatel i Ratsionalizator [*Former USSR*] — Izobret Ratsion
Izobreteniya Promyshlennye Obraztsy Tovarnye Znaki — IPOTA
Izobreteniya Promyshlennye Obraztsy Tovarnye Znaki — Izobret Prom Obraztsy Tovarnye Znaki
Izoliatsiya Elektricheskikh Mashin. Sbornik Sostavlen po Materialam Konferentsii Sozvannoi Leningradskim Otdelenium Nauchno-Tekhnicheskogo Obshchestva Energetekii — IEMSA
Izolyatsiya Elektricheskikh Mashin — Izol Elektr Mash
Izotoptechnika, Diagnosztika — Izotoptech Diagn
Izotopy v SSSR — ISOBA
Izotopy v SSSR — Izot SSSR
Izraelita Magyar Irodalmi Tarsulat Evkonyv — IMIT
Izsledvaniya po Biologichnata Borba s Vreditelite na Rasteniyata — Izsled Biol Borba Vred Rast
Izuchenie Mirchinskoi Biologii — Izuch Mirchinskoi Biol
Izuchenie Prichin Avarii i Povrezhdenii Stroitel'nykh Konstruktsii — Izuch Prichin Avarii Povrezhdenii Stroit Konstr
Izvanredna Izdanja Farmakoloskog Instituta Zagrebu — Izvanredna Izd Farmakol Inst Zagrebu
Izvanredna Izdanja Instituta za Farmakologiju i Toksikologiju u Zagrebu — Izvanredna Izd Inst Farmakol Toksikol Zagrebu
Izvanredna Izdanja Zavoda za Farmakologiju i Toksikologiju Medicinskog Fakulteta u Zagrebu — Izvanredna Izd Zavoda Farmakol Toksikol Med Fak Zagrebu
Izvesca o Razpravama Matematicko-Prirodoslovnoga Razreda Jugoslavenska Akademia Znanosti i Umjetnosti. Bulletin des Travaux. Classe des Sciences Mathematiques et Naturelles. Academie Jougoslave des Sciences et des Beaux-Arts — Izv Razpr Mat Prir Razr Jugoslav Akad Znan
Izvestiia Akademii Nauk Azerbaidzhanskoi SSR [*Soviet Socialist Republic*] — IAA
Izvestiia Akademii Nauk Azerbaidzhanskoi SSR [*Soviet Socialist Republic*] — IANA
Izvestiia Akademii Nauk Azerbaidzhanskoi SSR — Izv Azerb
Izvestiia Akademii Nauk BSSR. Seriia Selskokhoziaistvennykh Navuk — Izv Akad Nauk BSSR Ser S-Kh Navuk
Izvestiia Akademii Nauk Estonskoi SSR. Biologiia — Izv Akad Nauk Est SSR Biol
Izvestiia Akademii Nauk Estonskoi SSR Khimiia Eesti NSV Teaduste Akadeemia Toimetised Keemia — Izv Akad Nauk Est SSR Khim Eesti NSV Tead Akad Toim Keem
Izvestiia Akademii Nauk Estonskoi SSR Seriia Fiziko-Matematicheskikh i Tekhnicheskikh Nauk [*Estonian SSR*] — Izv Akad Nauk Est SSR Ser Fiz Mat Tekh Nauk
Izvestiia Akademii Nauk. Seriia Biologicheskaia — Izv Akad Nauk Ser Biol
Izvestiia Akademiia Nauk Kazakhskoi. Seriia Arkheologicheskaia — IANKSA
Izvestiia Akademiia Nauk Kazakhskoi. Seriia Arkheologicheskaia — Izv Kaz
Izvestiia Gosudarstvennoi Rossiiskoi Arkheologicheskoi Kommissii — IAK
Izvestiia Gosudarstvennoi Rossiiskoi Arkheologicheskoi Kommissii — IRAO
Izvestiia Gosudarstvennoi Rossiiskoi Arkheologicheskoi Kommissii — Izv Arch Comm
Izvestiia Gosudarstvennoi Rossiiskoi Arkheologicheskoi Kommissii — Izv Gosud Ross Arkh Kom
Izvestiia. Institut za Zhivotnovudstvo Bulgarska Akademiia na Naukite — Izv Inst Zhivotn Bulg Akad Nauk
Izvestiia na Arkheologicheskiia Institut. Bulgarska Akademiia na Naukite — ABAI
Izvestiia na Arkheologicheskiia Institut. Bulgarska Akademiia na Naukite — B Inst Arch Bulg
Izvestiia na Arkheologicheskiia Institut. Bulgarska Akademiia na Naukite — BAB
Izvestiia na Arkheologicheskiia Institut. Bulgarska Akademiia na Naukite — Bull Inst Bulg
Izvestiia na Arkheologicheskiia Institut. Bulgarska Akademiia na Naukite — IAIBAN
Izvestiia na Arkheologicheskiia Institut. Bulgarska Akademiia na Naukite — Izv Bulg A
Izvestiia na Arkheologicheskiia Institut. Bulgarska Akademiia na Naukite — Izv Inst Arch Bulg
Izvestiia na Arkheologicheskiia Institut. Bulgarska Akademiia na Naukite — Izvestiia-Institut
Izvestiia na Balgarskite Muzei — Iz Balg Muz
Izvestiia na B'lgarskoto Istorichesko Druzestvo — IzBID
Izvestiia na Bulgarskoto Istorichesko Druzhestvo — Izv Bulg Ist Druz
Izvestiia na Instituta po Fiziologiia (Sofia) — Izv Inst Fiziol (Sofia)
Izvestiia na Mikrobiologicheskiia Institut (Sofia) — Izv Mikrobiol Inst (Sofia)
Izvestiia na Narodniia Muzei Burgas — Izv Narod Muz Burgas
Izvestiia na Narodniia Muzei (Rousse) — Iz Narod Muz (Rousse)
Izvestiia na Narodniia Muzei Ruse — INMR
Izvestiia na Narodniia Muzei Varna — INMV
Izvestiia na Narodniia Muzei (Varna) — Iz Narod Muz (Varna)
Izvestiia na Narodniia Muzei Varna — Izvestia-Varna
Izvestiia na Narodniia Muzei Varna — Izvestija Varna
Izvestiia na Okrazhniia Istoricheski Muzei — Izv Okra Istor Muz
Izvestiia na Okrazhniia Istoricheski Muzei — Izv Okraz Istor Muz
Izvestiia Narodni Muzefa Sumen Bulgaria — Iz Narod Muz Sumen
Izvestiia Otdeleniia Obshchestvennykh Nauk Akademiia Nauk Tadzhikskoi SSR — Izv Otdel Obshchest Nauk A N Tadzh
Izvestiia Rossiiskoi Akademii Nauk — IRAN
Izvestiia Rossiiskoi Akademii Nauk — Izvest Ross Akad Nauk
Izvestiia Tavricheskogo Obshchestva Istorii. Arkheologii i Ethografii — ITOIAE
Izvestiia Tavricheskoi Uchenoi Arkhivnoi Kommissii — ITUAK
Izvestiia. Vestnik Obshchestvennykh Nauk. Akademia Nauk Armianskoi SSR [*Soviet Socialist Republic*] — IANA
Izvestiia. Vestnik Obshchestvennykh Nauk. Akademia Nauk Armianskoi SSR [*Soviet Socialist Republic*] — IVONANA
Izvestija Abhazskogo Instituta Jazyka, Literatury, i Istorii — Izv Abhaz Inst Jaz Lit Ist
Izvestija Akademii Nauk Armjanskoi SSR Serija Fizika — Izv Akad Nauk Armjan SSR Ser Fiz
Izvestija Akademii Nauk Armjanskoi SSR Serija Matematika — Izv Akad Nauk Armjan SSR Ser Mat
Izvestija Akademii Nauk Armjanskoi SSR Serija Mehanika — Izv Akad Nauk Armjan SSR Ser Meh
Izvestija Akademii Nauk Armjanskoi SSR Serija Tehniceskih Nauk — Izv Akad Nauk Armjan SSR Ser Tehn Nauk
Izvestija Akademii Nauk Armjanskoj SSR — Izv Ak N Armj SSR
Izvestija Akademii Nauk Azerbaidzanskoi SSR Serija Fiziko-Tehniceskih i Matematiceskih Nauk — Izv Akad Nauk Azerbaidzan SSR Ser Fiz Tehn Mat Nauk
Izvestija Akademii Nauk Azerbajdzanskogo SSR Serija Literatury, Jazyka, i Iskusstva — Izv Akad Nauk Azerb SSR Ser Lit Jaz Isk
Izvestija Akademii Nauk Azerbajdzanskoj SSR. Serija Biologiceskih i Sel'skohozjajstvennyh Nauk. Azaerbajgan SSR Elmlaer Akademijasynyn Haebaerlae — Izv Akad Nauk Azerbajdzansk SSR Ser Biol Selskohoz Nauk
Izvestija Akademii Nauk Estonskoj SSR Obscestvennye Nauki — Izv Akad Nauk Eston SSR Obsc Nauki
Izvestija Akademii Nauk Estonskoj SSR. Serija Biologii, Sel'skohozjajstvennyh Nauk i Medicinskih Nauk — Izv Akad Nauk Estonsk SSR Ser Biol
Izvestija Akademii Nauk Kazahskoj SSR — Izv Ak N Kaz
Izvestija Akademii Nauk Kazahskoj SSR. Serija Botaniceskaja. Kazak SSR Gylym Akademijasynyn Habarlary — Izv Akad Nauk Kazahsk SSR Ser Bot
Izvestija Akademii Nauk Kazahskoj SSR Serija Fiziko-Matematiceskaja — Izv Akad Nauk Kazah SSR Ser Fiz-Mat
Izvestija Akademii Nauk Kazahskoj SSR Serija Obscestvennyh Nauk — Izv Akad Nauk Kazah SSR Ser Obsc Nauk
Izvestija Akademii Nauk Latvijskoj SSR. Latvijas PSR Zinatnu Akademijas Vestis — Izv Akad Nauk Latvijsk SSR

Izvestija Akademii Nauk Moldavskoj SSR — Izv Ak N Mold SSR
Izvestija Akademii Nauk Moldavskoj SSR Serija Fiziko-Tehniceskih i Matematiceskih Nauk — Izv Akad Nauk Moldav SSR Ser Fiz-Tehn Mat Nauk
Izvestija Akademii Nauk Moldavskoj SSR Serija Obscestvennyh Nauk — Izv Akad Nauk Mold SSR Ser Obsc Nauk
Izvestija Akademii Nauk Otdelenie Chimiceskich Nauk — Izv ANO Ch N
Izvestija Akademii Nauk SSSR — Izv Ak N SSSR
Izvestija Akademii Nauk SSSR Mehanika Tverdogo Tela — Izv Akad Nauk SSSR Meh Tverd Tela
Izvestija Akademii Nauk SSSR Mehanika Zidkosti i Gaza — Izv Akad Nauk SSSR Meh Zidk Gaza
Izvestija Akademii Nauk SSSR. Otdelenie Matematiceskih i Estestvennyh Nauk. Serija Biologiceskaja/Bulletin. Academie des Sciences de l'URSS. Classe des Sciences Mathematiques et Naturelles. Serie Biologique — Izv Akad Nauk SSSR Otd Mat Nauk Ser Biol
Izvestija Akademii Nauk SSSR Serija Ekonomiceskaja — Izv Akad Nauk SSSR Ser Ekon
Izvestija Akademii Nauk SSSR Serija Fizika Atmosfery i Okeana — Izv Akad Nauk SSSR Ser Fiz Atmosfer i Okeana
Izvestija Akademii Nauk SSSR Serija Fizika Zemli — Izv Akad Nauk SSSR Ser Fiz Zemli
Izvestija Akademii Nauk SSSR Serija Geograficeskaja 1 Geofiziceskaja — Izv Ak N SSSR Ser Geogr
Izvestija Akademii Nauk SSSR Tekhniceskaja Kibernetika — Izv Akad Nauk SSSR Tehn Kibernet
Izvestija Akademii Nauk Tadzikiskoj SSR Otdelenie Obscestvennyh Nauk — Izv Akad Nauk Tadz SSR Otdelenie Obsc Nauk
Izvestija Akademii Nauk Tadzikskoi SSR Otdelenie Fiziko-Matematiceskih i Geologo-Himiceskih Nauk — Izv Akad Nauk Tadzik SSR Otdel Fiz-Mat i Geolog-Him Nauk
Izvestija Akademii Nauk Turkmenskoi SSR Serija Fiziko-Tehniceskih Himiceskih i Geologiceskih Nauk — Izv Akad Nauk Turkmen SSR Ser Fiz-Tehn Him Geol Nauk
Izvestija Akademii Nauk Turkmenskoj SSR Serija Obscestvennyh Nauk — Izv Akad Nauk Turkm SSR Ser Obsc Nauk
Izvestija Akademii Nauk Turkmenskoj SSR. Turkmenistan SSRnin Ylymlar Akademijasnyn Habarlary — Izv Akad Nauk Turkmensk SSR
Izvestija Akademii Nauk Uzbekskoj SSR. Uzbekiston SSR Fanlar Akademijasining Ahboroti — Izv Akad Nauk Uzbeksk SSR
Izvestija Akademii Nauk UzSSR. Serija Fiziko-Matematiceskih Nauk — Izv Akad Nauk UzSSR Ser Fiz-Mat Nauk
Izvestija Akademija Nauk Kirgizskoi SSR — Izv Akad Nauk Kirgiz SSR
Izvestija Batumskogo Subtropiceskogo Botaniceskogo Sada — Izv Batumsk Subtrop Bot Sada
Izvestija. Biologiceskie Nauki. Telekagir. Biologiakan Gitouthjounner — Izv Biol Nauki
Izvestija Biologiceskogo Naucno-Issledovatel'skogo Instituta pri Permskom Gosudarstvennom Universitete imeni A.M. Gor'kogo. Bulletin de l'Institut des Recherches Biologiques de Perm — Izv Biol Naucno Issl Inst Permsk Gosud Univ Gorkogo
Izvestija Biologo-Geograficeskogo Naucno-Issledovatel'skogo Instituta pri Vostocno-Sibirskom Gosudarstvennom Universitete. Bulletin de l'Institut Scientifique de Biologie et de Geographie a l'Universite d'Irkoutsk — Izv Biol Geogr Naucno Issl Inst Vost Sibirsk Gosud Univ
Izvestija Estestvenno-Naucnogo Instituta pri Molotovskom Universitete imeni A. A. Gor'kogo — Izv Estestv Naucn Inst Molotovsk Univ Gorkogo
Izvestija. Estestvennye Nauki. Telekagir. Bnakan Gitouthjounner/Bulletin. Academy of Sciences. Armenian SSR — Izv Estestv Nauki
Izvestija Glavnogo Botaniceskogo Sada SSSR. Bulletin du Jardin Botanique Principal de l'URSS — Izv Glavn Bot Sada SSSR
Izvestija Imperatorskago Botaniceskago Sada Petra Velikago — Izv Imp Bot Sada Petra Velikago
Izvestija Imperatorskago Kazanskago Universiteta — Izv Imp Kazansk Univ
Izvestija Instituta Pocvovedenija i Geobotaniki Sredne-Aziatskogo Gosudarstvennogo Universiteta. Bulletin. Institut de Pedologie et de Geobotanique. Universite de l'Asie Centrale — Izv Inst Pocvov Sredne Aziatsk Gosud Univ
Izvestija Jakutskago Otdela Imperatorskago Russkago Geograficeskago Obscestva — Izv Jakutsk Otd Imp Russk Geogr Obsc
Izvestija Jugo-Osetinskogo Instituta Kraevedenija — I Jug Os I K
Izvestija Jugo-Osetinskogo Naucno-Issledovatelskogo Instituta Akademii Nauk Gruzinskoj SSR — Izv Jugo Oset Nauc-Issled Inst Akad Nauk Gruz SSR
Izvestija Juzno-Ussurijskogo Otdela Gosudarstvennogo Russkogo Geograficeskogo Obscestva/Bulletin. Southern Ussuri Branch. Russian Geographical Society — Izv Juzno Ussurijsk Otd Gosud Russk Geogr Obsc
Izvestija Karelo-Finskogo Filiala Akademii Nauk SSSR — Izv Karelo Finsk Fil Akad Nauk SSSR
Izvestija Karel'skogo i Kol'skogo Filialov Akademii Nauk — IKKF
Izvestija Kazahskogo Filiala Akademii Nauk SSSR. KSRO Gylym Akademijasynyn Kazak Filialynyn Habarlary — Izv Kazahsk Fil Akad Nauk SSSR
Izvestija Kazanskogo Filiala Akademii Nauk SSSR Serija Fiziko-Matematiceskih i Tehniceskih Nauk — Izv Kazan Fil Akad Nauk SSSR Ser Fiz-Mat i Tehn Nauk
Izvestija Kievskogo Botaniceskogo Sada. Visnyk Kyjivsk'kogo Botanicnogo Sadu. Bulletin de Jardin Botanique de Kieff — Izv Kievsk Bot Sada
Izvestija Komi Filiala Geograficeskogo Obscestva SSSR — Izv Komi Fil Geogr Obsc SSSR
Izvestija Krasnojarskago Pododtela Vostocno-Sibirskago Otdela Imperatorskago Russkago Geograficeskago Obscestva — Izv Krasnojarsk Pododt Vost Sibirsk Otd Imp Russk Geogr Obsc
Izvestija Krasnojarskogo Otdela Russkogo Geograficeskogo Obscestva — Izv Krasnojarsk Otd Russk Geogr Obsc
Izvestija Lisicanskogo Muzeja — I Lis M
Izvestija na Archeologiceskija Institut — Izv Arch Inst
Izvestija na Archeoogiceskija Institut. Otdelenie za Istorija, Archeologija i Filosofija — IAIOI
Izvestija na Balgarskoto Istoricesko Druzestvo — IBID
Izvestija na Biologiceskija Institut. Bulgarska Akademija na Naukite, Otdelenie za Biologicne I Medicinski Nauki — Izv Biol Inst
Izvestija na Botaniceskija Institut — Izv Bot Inst
Izvestija na Bulgarskija Archeologiceski Institut — IAI
Izvestija na Bulgarskija Archeologiceski Institut — IBAI
Izvestija na Bulgarskoto Archeologicesko Druzestvo — IBAD
Izvestija na Bulgarskoto Botanicesko Druzestvo. Bulletin de la Societe Botanique de Bulgarie — Izv Bulg Bot Druz
Izvestija na Centralnata Chelmintologicna Laboratorija — Izv Cent Chelmint Lab
Izvestija na Instituta po Biologi Metodij Popov/Bulletin. Methodi Popoff Institute of Biology — Izv Inst Biol Metodij Popov
Izvestija na Instituta za Muzyka pri Bulgarskata Akademija na Naukite — Izvestija Inst MBAN
Izvestija na Istoriceskoto Druzestvo — IIDS
Izvestija na Muzeite ot Juzna Balgarija [*Bulletin des Musees de la Bulgarie du Sud*] — Izv Muz Juz Balg
Izvestija na Narodnija Muzej Burgas — Izv Burgas
Izvestija na Narodnija Muzej Varna — Izv Varna
Izvestija na Seminara po Slavjanska Filologija — ISSF
Izvestija na Varnenskoto Archeologicesko Druzestvo — IVAD
Izvestija Naucnogo Instituta imeni P. F. Lesgafta. Bulletin. Institut Scientifique Lesshaft — Izv Naucn Inst Lesgafta
Izvestija Obscestva Izucenija Vostocno-Sibirskogo Kraja — Izv Obsc Izuc Vost Sibirsk Kraja
Izvestija Otdelenija Estestvennyh Nauk — Izv Otd Estestv Nauk
Izvestija Permskogo Biologiceskogo Naucno-Issledovatel'skogo Instituta. Bulletin de l'Institut des Recherches Biologiques de Perm — Izv Permsk Biol Naucno Issl Inst
Izvestija Petrogradskoj Oblastnoj Stancii Zascity Rastenij ot Vreditelej. Bulletin. Station Regionale Protectrice des Plantes a Petrograd — Izv Petrogradsk Obl Stancii Zasc Rast Vredit
Izvestija Rostovskoj Stancii Zascity Rastenij — Izv Rostovsk Stancii Zasc Rast
Izvestija Sapropelevogo Komiteta. Bulletin du Comite pour l'Etude des Sapropelites — Izv Sapropel Komiteta
Izvestija Severo-Kavkazskogo Naucnogo Centra Vyssej Skoly Serija Estestvennye Nauki [*Rostov-On-Don*] — Izv Severo-Kavkaz Naucn Centra Vyss Skoly Ser Estestv Nauk
Izvestija Severo-Kavkazskogo Naucnogo Centra Vyssei Skoly Serija Obscestvennyh Nauk — Izv Sev-Kavk Nauc Centra Vyss Skoly Ser Obsc Nauk
Izvestija Severo-Kavkazskogo Naucnogo Centra Vyssei Skoly Serija Tehniceskie Nauki — Izv Severo-Kavkaz Naucn Centra Vyss Skoly Ser Tehn Nauk
Izvestija Sibirskago Otdela Imperatorskago Russkago Geograficeskago Obscestva — Izv Sibirsk Otd Imp Russk Geogr Obsc
Izvestija Sibirskogo Otdelenija Akademii Nauk SSSR Serija Biologiceskih Nauk — Izv Sibir Otdel Akad Nauk SSSR Ser Biol Nauk
Izvestija Sibirskogo Otdelenija Akademii Nauk SSSR Serija Obscestvennyh Nauk — Izv Sib Otdel Akad Nauk SSSR Ser Obsc Nauk
Izvestija Sibirskogo Otdelenija Akademija Nauk SSSR — Izv Sibirsk Otdel Akad Nauk SSSR
Izvestija Sibirskogo Otdelenija Akademija Nauk SSSR Serija Tehniceskih Nauk — Izv Sibirsk Otdel Akad Nauk SSSR Ser Tehn Nauk
Izvestija Sibirskoj Kraevoj Stancii Zascity Rastenij ot Vreditelej — Izv Sibirsk Kraev Stancii Zasc Rast Vredit
Izvestija S.-Peterburgskoj Biologiceskoj Laboratorii. Bulletin du Laboratoire Biologique de Saint-Petersbourg — Izv S Peterburgsk Biol Lab
Izvestija Sredne-Aziatskogo Otdela Godusarstvennogo Russkogo Geograficeskogo Obscestva — Izv Sredne Aziatsk Otd Gosud Russk Geogr Obsc
Izvestija Tavreiceskogo Obscestva Istorii, Archeologii, Etnografii — ITOIAE
Izvestija Tihookeanskogo Naucnogo Instituta Rybnogo Hozjajstva — Izv Tihookeansk Naucn Inst Rybn Hoz
Izvestija Tihookeanskoj Naucno-Promyslovoj Stancii/Bulletin. Pacific Scientific Research Station — Izv Tihookeansk Naucno Promysl Stancii
Izvestija Tomskago Universiteta — Izv Tomsk Univ
Izvestija Tomskogo Ordena Trudovogo Krasnogo Znameni Politehniceskogo Instituta Imeni S. M. Kirova — Izv Tomsk Politehn Inst
Izvestija Tomskogo Otdelenija Vsesojuznogo Botaniceskogo Obscestva — Izv Tomsk Otd Vsesojuzn Bot Obsc
Izvestija Turkestanskogo Otdela Russkogo Geograficeskogo Obscestva — ITORGO
Izvestija Uzbekistanskogo Filiala Akademii Nauk SSSR. Uzbekiston Filialining Ahboroti — Izv Uzbekistansk Fil Akad Nauk SSSR
Izvestija Voronezskogo Gosudarstvennogo Pedagogiceskogo Instituta — Izv Voronez Gos Ped Inst
Izvestija Voronezskogo Pedagogiceskogo Instituta — Izv Voronez Pedag Inst
Izvestija Voronezskoj Stancii po Bor'be s Vrediteljami Rastenij — Izv Voronezsk Stancii Borbe Vredit Rast
Izvestija Vostocno-Sibirskago Otdela Imperatorskago Russkago Geograficeskago Obscestva. Isvestija der Ost-Sibirischen Abtheilung der Kaiserlich-Russischen Geographischen Gesellschaft — Izv Vost Sibirsk Otd Imp Russk Geogr Obsc
Izvestija Vostocno-Sibirskogo Otdela Imperatorskogo Russkogo Geograficeskogo Obscestva — IVSOIRGO
Izvestija Vostocno-Sibirskogo Otdela Russkogo Geograficeskogo Obscestva — IVSORGO
Izvestija Vsesojuznogo Geograficeskogo Obscestva — IVGO
Izvestija Vsesojuznogo Geograficeskogo Obscestva — Izv Vsesojuz Geogr Obsc
Izvestija Vsesojuznogo Geograficeskogo Obscestva/Izvestia de la Societe de Geographie de l'URSS/Bulletin. USSR Geographical Society — Izv Vsesojuzn Geogr Obsc

Izvestija Vyssih Ucebnyh Zavedenii Aviacionnaja Tehnika — Izv Vyss Ucebn Zaved Aviacion Tehn
Izvestija Vyssih Ucebnyh Zavedenii Elektromehanika — Izv Vyss Ucebn Zaved Elektromehanika
Izvestija Vyssih Ucebnyh Zavedenii Fizika — Izv Vyss Ucebn Zaved Fizika
Izvestija Vyssih Ucebnyh Zavedenii Geodezija i Aerofotos Emka — Izv Vyss Ucebn Zaved Geod i Aerofot
Izvestija Vyssih Ucebnyh Zavedenii Matematika — Izv Vyss Ucebn Zaved Matematika
Izvestija Vyssih Ucebnyh Zavedenii Radiofizika — Izv Vyss Ucebn Zaved Radiofizika
Izvestija Zapadno-Sibirskogo Otdela Russkogo Geograficeskogo Obscestva — IZSORGO
Izvestija Zapadno-Sibirskoj Kraevoj Stancii Zascity Rastenij — Izv Zapadno Sibirsk Kraev Stancii Zasc Rast
Izvestiya [*Moscow*] — Iz
Izvestiya. Academy of Sciences USSR. Atmospheric and Oceanic Physics — Izv Acad Sci USSR Atmos and Oceanic Phys
Izvestiya. Academy of Sciences USSR. Atmospheric and Oceanic Physics — Izv Acad Sci USSR Atmos Oceanic Phys
Izvestiya. Academy of Sciences USSR. Atmospheric and Oceanic Physics — Izv Acad Sci USSR Atmospher Ocean Phys
Izvestiya. Academy of Sciences USSR. Geologic Series — Izv Acad Sci USSR Geol Ser
Izvestiya. Academy of Sciences USSR. Physics of the Solid Earth — Izv Acad Sci USSR Phys Solid Earth
Izvestiya Akademii Krupnogo Sotsialisticheskogo Sel'skogo Khozyaistva — Izv Akad Krupnogo Sots Selsk Khoz
Izvestiya Akademii Latviiskoi SSR Seriya Fizicheskikh i Tekhnicheskikh Nauk [*Latvian SSR*] — Izv Akad Latv SSR Ser Fiz Tekh Nauk
Izvestiya Akademii Nauk — Izv Akad Nauk
Izvestiya Akademii Nauk Armenii. Fizika — Izv Akad Nauk Arm Fiz
Izvestiya Akademii Nauk Armenii. Nauki o Zemle — Izv Akad Nauk Arm Nauki Zemle
Izvestiya Akademii Nauk Armjanskoj SSR Obscestvennyh Nauk — IzvANArm
Izvestiya Akademii Nauk Armyanskoi SSR — Izv Akad Nauk Arm SSR
Izvestiya Akademii Nauk Armyanskoi SSR Biologicheskie i Sel'skokhozyaistvennye Nauki — Izv Akad Nauk Arm SSR Biol S-Kh Nauki
Izvestiya Akademii Nauk Armyanskoi SSR Biologicheskie Nauki — IABNA
Izvestiya Akademii Nauk Armyanskoi SSR Biologicheskie Nauki — Izv Akad Nauk Arm SSR Biol Nauki
Izvestiya Akademii Nauk Armyanskoi SSR Estestvennye Nauki — Izv Akad Nauk Arm SSR Estestv Nauki
Izvestiya Akademii Nauk Armyanskoi SSR Fizika — Izv Akad Nauk Arm SSR Fiz
Izvestiya Akademii Nauk Armyanskoi SSR Fiziko Matematicheskie Estestvennye i T ekhnicheskie Nauki — Izv Akad Nauk Arm SSR Fiz Mat Estest Tekh Nauki
Izvestiya Akademii Nauk Armyanskoi SSR Geologicheskie i Geograficheskie Nauki — IAGGA
Izvestiya Akademii Nauk Armyanskoi SSR Geologicheskie i Geograficheskie Nauki [*Armenian SSR*] — Izv Akad Nauk Arm SSR Geol Geogr Nauki
Izvestiya Akademii Nauk Armyanskoi SSR Khimicheskie Nauki — IARKA
Izvestiya Akademii Nauk Armyanskoi SSR Khimicheskie Nauki [*Armenian SSR*] — Izv Akad Nauk Arm SSR Khim Nauki
Izvestiya Akademii Nauk Armyanskoi SSR Meditsinskie Nauki — Izv Akad Nauk Arm SSR Med Nauki
Izvestiya Akademii Nauk Armyanskoi SSR Mekhanika — Izv Akad Nauk Arm SSR Mekh
Izvestiya Akademii Nauk Armyanskoi SSR Nauki po Zemle [*Armenian SSR*] — Izv Akad Nauk Arm SSR Nauki Zemle
Izvestiya Akademii Nauk Armyanskoi SSR Seriya Fiziko-Matematicheskikh Nauk — IAMNA
Izvestiya Akademii Nauk Armyanskoi SSR Seriya Fiziko-Matematicheskikh Nauk [*Armenian SSR*] — Izv Akad Nauk Arm SSR Ser Fiz-Mat Nauk
Izvestiya Akademii Nauk Armyanskoi SSR Seriya Khimicheskikh Nauk — Izv Akad Nauk Arm SSR Ser Khim Nauk
Izvestiya Akademii Nauk Armyanskoi SSR Seriya Matematika [*Armenian SSR*] — Izv Akad Nauk Arm SSR Ser Mat
Izvestiya Akademii Nauk Armyanskoi SSR Seriya Mekhanika [*Armenian SSR*] — Izv Akad Nauk Arm SSR Ser Mekh
Izvestiya Akademii Nauk Armyanskoi SSR Seriya Mekhanika — Izv Akad Nauk Armyan SSR Ser Mekh
Izvestiya Akademii Nauk Armyanskoi SSR Seriya Tekhnicheskikh Nauk [*Armenian SSR*] — Izv Akad Nauk Arm SSR Ser Tekh Nauk
Izvestiya Akademii Nauk Armyanskoi SSR Seriya Tekhnicheskikh Nauk — Izv Akad Nauk Armyan SSR Ser Tekhn Nauk
Izvestiya Akademii Nauk Azerbaidzhanskoi SSR — IANAB
Izvestiya Akademii Nauk Azerbaidzhanskoi SSR — Izv Akad Nauk Az SSR
Izvestiya Akademii Nauk Azerbaidzhanskoi SSR — Izv Akad Nauk Azerb SSR
Izvestiya Akademii Nauk Azerbaidzhanskoi SSR Seriya Biologicheskikh i Meditsinskikh Nauk — Izv Akad Nauk Az SSR Ser Biol Med Nauk
Izvestiya Akademii Nauk Azerbaidzhanskoi SSR Seriya Biologicheskikh i Sel'skokhozyaistvennykh Nauk — Izv Akad Nauk Az SSR Ser Biol Skh Nauk
Izvestiya Akademii Nauk Azerbaidzhanskoi SSR Seriya Biologicheskikh Nauk — IABLA
Izvestiya. Akademii Nauk Azerbaidzhanskoi SSR Seriya Biologicheskikh Nauk — Izv Akad Nauk Az SSR Ser Biol Nauk
Izvestiya Akademii Nauk Azerbaidzhanskoi SSR Seriya Biologicheskikh Nauk — Izv Akad Nauk Azerb SSR Ser Biol Nauk
Izvestiya Akademii Nauk Azerbaidzhanskoi SSR Seriya Fiziko-Matematicheskikh i Tekhnicheskikh Nauk — Izv Akad Nauk Az SSR Ser Fiz Mat Tekh Nauk
Izvestiya Akademii Nauk Azerbaidzhanskoi SSR Seriya Fiziko-Tekhnicheskikh i Khimicheskikh Nauk — Izv Akad Nauk Az SSR Ser Fiz Tekh Khim Nauk
Izvestiya Akademii Nauk Azerbaidzhanskoi SSR Seriya Fiziko-Tekhnicheskikh i Matematicheskikh Nauk — Izv Akad Nauk Az SSR Ser Fiz-Tekh i Mat Nauk
Izvestiya Akademii Nauk Azerbaidzhanskoi SSR Seriya Fiziko-Tekhnicheskikh i Matematicheskikh Nauk [*Azerbaidzhan SSR*] — Izv Akad Nauk Az SSR Ser Fiz-Tekh Mat Nauk
Izvestiya Akademii Nauk Azerbaidzhanskoi SSR Seriya Geologo-Geograficheskikh Nauk — Izv Akad Nauk Az SSR Ser Geol Geogr Nauk
Izvestiya Akademii Nauk Azerbaidzhanskoi SSR Seriya Nauk i Zemle — Izv Akad Nauk Az SSR Ser Nauk Zemle
Izvestiya Akademii Nauk Azerbajdzhanskoj SSR Seriya Nauk i Zemle — Izv Akad Nauk Azerb SSR Ser Nauk Zemle
Izvestiya Akademii Nauk Azerbajdzhanskoj SSR Seriya Obscestvennych Nauk — IzvANAzerb
Izvestiya Akademii Nauk Belarusi. Seriya Biologicheskikh Nauk — Izv Akad Nauk Belarusi Ser Biol Nauk
Izvestiya Akademii Nauk Belarusi. Seriya Fiziko-Energeticheskikh Nauk — Izv Akad Nauk Belarusi Ser Fiz Energ Nauk
Izvestiya Akademii Nauk Belarusi. Seriya Fiziko-Tekhnicheskikh Nauk — Izv Akad Nauk Belarusi Ser Fiz Tekh Nauk
Izvestiya Akademii Nauk Belarusi. Seriya Khimicheskikh Nauk — Izv Akad Nauk Belarusi Ser Khim Nauk
Izvestiya Akademii Nauk Belorusskoi SSR — Izv Akad Nauk B SSR
Izvestiya Akademii Nauk Belorusskoi SSR Seriya Biologicheskikh Nauk — Izv Akad Nauk B SSR Ser Biol Nauk
Izvestiya Akademii Nauk Belorusskoi SSR. Seriya Biologicheskikh Nauk — Izv Akad Nauk Beloruss SSR Ser Biol Nauk
Izvestiya Akademii Nauk Belorusskoi SSR Seriya Sel'skokhozyaistvennykh Nauk — Izv Akad Nauk B SSR Ser S Kh Nauk
Izvestiya Akademii Nauk Belorusskoi SSR. Seriya Sel'skokhozyaistvennykh Nauk — Izv Akad Nauk Beloruss SSR Ser Skh Nauk
Izvestiya Akademii Nauk BSSR Seriya Fiziko-Energeticheskikh Nauk — Izv Akad Nauk BSSR Ser Fiz Energ Nauk
Izvestiya Akademii Nauk BSSR Seriya Fiziko-Matematicheskikh Nauk [*Belorussian S SR*] — Izv Akad Nauk BSSR Ser Fiz-Mat Nauk
Izvestiya Akademii Nauk BSSR Seriya Fiziko-Tekhnicheskikh Nauk — Izv Akad Nauk BSSR Ser Fiz Tekh Nauk
Izvestiya Akademii Nauk BSSR Seriya Khimicheskikh Nauk — Izv Akad Nauk BSSR Ser Khim Nauk
Izvestiya Akademii Nauk Ehstonskoj SSR Geologiya — Izv Akad Nauk Ehst SSR Geol
Izvestiya Akademii Nauk Ehstonskoj SSR Khimiya i Geologiya — Izv Akad Nauk Ehst SSR Khim Geol
Izvestiya Akademii Nauk Estonii. Biologiya — Izv Akad Nauk Est Biol
Izvestiya Akademii Nauk Estonii. Fizika, Matematika — Izv Akad Nauk Est Fiz Mat
Izvestiya Akademii Nauk Estonskoi SSR — Izv Akad Nauk Est SSR
Izvestiya Akademii Nauk Estonskoi SSR Fizika Matematika [*Estonian SSR*] — Izv Akad Nauk Est SSR Fiz Mat
Izvestiya Akademii Nauk Estonskoi SSR. Geologiya — Izv Akad Nauk Est SSR Geol
Izvestiya Akademii Nauk Estonskoi SSR. Khimiya — Izv Akad Nauk Est SSR Khim
Izvestiya Akademii Nauk Estonskoi SSR Seriya Biologicheskaya — Izv Akad Nauk Est SSR Ser Biol
Izvestiya Akademii Nauk Estonskoi SSR Seriya Biologicheskaya — Izv Akad Nauk Eston SSR Ser Biol
Izvestiya Akademii Nauk Estonskoi SSR Seriya Fizichesko. Matematicheskaya — Izv Akad Nauk Estonskoi SSR Fiz Mat
Izvestiya Akademii Nauk Estonskoi SSR Seriya Khimicheskaya — Izv Akad Nauk Estonskoi SSR Khim
Izvestiya Akademii Nauk Estonskoi SSR Seriya Tekhnicheskikh i Fiziko-Matematicheskikh Nauk — Izv Akad Nauk Est SSR Ser Tekh Fiz Mat Nauk
Izvestiya Akademii Nauk. Fizika Atmosfery i Okeana — Izv Akad Nauk Fiz Atmos Okeana
Izvestiya Akademii Nauk Gruzii. Seriya Khimicheskaya — Izv Akad Nauk Gruz Ser Khim
Izvestiya Akademii Nauk Gruzinskoi SSR Seriya Biologicheskaya [*Georgian SSR*] — Izv Akad Nauk Gruz SSR Ser Biol
Izvestiya Akademii Nauk Gruzinskoi SSR Seriya Khimicheskaya — IGSKD
Izvestiya Akademii Nauk Gruzinskoi SSR Seriya Khimicheskaya — Izv Akad Nauk Gruz SSR Ser Khim
Izvestiya Akademii Nauk Kazakhskoi SSR — Izv Akad Nauk Kazakh SSR
Izvestiya Akademii Nauk Kazakhskoi SSR Seriya Astronomicheskaya i Fizicheskaya — Izv Akad Nauk Kaz SSR Ser Astron Fiz
Izvestiya Akademii Nauk Kazakhskoi SSR Seriya Astronomii, Fiziki, Matematiki , Mekhaniki — Izv Akad Nauk Kaz SSR Ser Astron Fiz Mat Mekh
Izvestiya Akademii Nauk Kazakhskoi SSR Seriya Biologicheskaya — Izv Akad Nauk Kaz SSR Ser Biol
Izvestiya Akademii Nauk Kazakhskoi SSR Seriya Biologicheskaya — Izv Akad Nauk Kazakh SSR Ser Biol
Izvestiya Akademii Nauk Kazakhskoi SSR Seriya Biologicheskikh Nauk — Izv Akad Nauk Kaz SSR Ser Biol Nauk
Izvestiya Akademii Nauk Kazakhskoi SSR Seriya Botanicheskaya — Izv Akad Nauk Kaz SSR Ser Bot
Izvestiya Akademii Nauk Kazakhskoi SSR Seriya Botaniki i Pochvovedeniya — Izv Akad Nauk Kaz SSR Ser Bot Pochvoved
Izvestiya Akademii Nauk Kazakhskoi SSR Seriya Botaniki i Pochvovedeniya — Izv Akad Nauk Kazakh SSR Ser Bot Pochvoved
Izvestiya Akademii Nauk Kazakhskoi SSR Seriya Energeticheskaya — Izv Akad Nauk Kaz SSR Ser Energ
Izvestiya Akademii Nauk Kazakhskoi SSR Seriya Filologii i Iskusstvovedeniya [*A publication*] — IzvANKaz
Izvestiya Akademii Nauk Kazakhskoi SSR Seriya Fiziko-Matematicheskaya — Izv Akad Nauk Kaz SSR Ser Fiz-Mat

Izvestiya Akademii Nauk Kazakhskoi SSR Seriya Fiziko-Matematicheskikh Nauk — IAKFA
Izvestiya Akademii Nauk Kazakhskoi SSR Seriya Fiziko-Matematicheskikh Nauk [*Kazakh SSR*] — Izv Akad Nauk Kaz SSR Ser Fiz-Mat Nauk
Izvestiya Akademii Nauk Kazakhskoi SSR Seriya Fiziologicheskaya — Izv Akad Nauk Kaz SSR Ser Fiziol
Izvestiya Akademii Nauk Kazakhskoi SSR Seriya Fiziologii i Biokhimii Rastenii — Izv Akad Nauk Kaz SSR Ser Fiziol Biokhim Rast
Izvestiya Akademii Nauk Kazakhskoi SSR Seriya Fiziologii i Meditsiny — Izv Akad Nauk Kaz SSR Ser Fiziol Med
Izvestiya Akademii Nauk Kazakhskoi SSR Seriya Geologicheskaya — Izv Akad Nauk Kaz SSR Ser Geol
Izvestiya Akademii Nauk Kazakhskoi SSR Seriya Gornogo Dela — Izv Akad Nauk Kaz SSR Ser Gorn Dela
Izvestiya Akademii Nauk Kazakhskoi SSR Seriya Gornogo Dela Metallurgii Stroitel'stva i Stroimaterialov — Izv Akad Nauk Kaz SSR Ser Gorn Dela Metall Stroit Stroimat
Izvestiya Akademii Nauk Kazakhskoi SSR Seriya Khimicheskaya — Izv Akad Nauk Kaz SSR Ser Khim
Izvestiya Akademii Nauk Kazakhskoi SSR Seriya Matematiki i Mekhaniki — Izv Akad Nauk Kaz SSR Ser Mat Mekh
Izvestiya Akademii Nauk Kazakhskoi SSR Seriya Meditsinskikh Nauk — Izv Akad Nauk Kaz SSR Ser Med Nauk
Izvestiya Akademii Nauk Kazakhskoi SSR Seriya Meditsiny i Fiziologii — Izv Akad Nauk Kaz SSR Ser Med Fiziol
Izvestiya Akademii Nauk Kazakhskoi SSR Seriya Metallurgii. Obogashcheniya i Ogneuporov — Izv Akad Nauk Kaz SSR Ser Metall Obogashch Ogneuporov
Izvestiya Akademii Nauk Kazakhskoi SSR Seriya Mikrobiologicheskaya — Izv Akad Nauk Kaz SSR Ser Mikrobiol
Izvestiya Akademii Nauk Kazakhskoi SSR Seriya Tekhnicheskikh Khimicheskikh Nauk — Izv Akad Nauk Kaz SSR Ser Tekh Khim Nauk
Izvestiya Akademii Nauk Kazakhskoi SSR Seriya Zoologicheskaya — Izv Akad Nauk Kaz SSR Ser Zool
Izvestiya Akademii Nauk Kirgizskoi SSR — Izv Akad Nauk Kirg SSR
Izvestiya Akademii Nauk Kirgizskoi SSR Fiziko-Tekhnicheskie i Matematicheskie Nauki — Izv Akad Nauk Kirg SSR Fiz Tekh Mat Nauki
Izvestiya Akademii Nauk Kirgizskoi SSR Khimiko-Tekhnologicheskie Nauki — Izv Akad Nauk Kirg SSR Khim Tekhnol Nauki
Izvestiya Akademii Nauk Kirgizskoi SSR Seriya Biologicheskikh Nauk — Izv Akad Nauk Kirg SSR Ser Biol Nauk
Izvestiya Akademii Nauk Kirgizskoi SSR Seriya Biologicheskikh Nauk — Izv Akad Nauk Kirgiz SSR Ser Biol Nauk
Izvestiya Akademii Nauk Kirgizskoi SSR Seriya Estestvennykh i Tekhnicheskikh Nauk [*Kirgiz SSR*] — Izv Akad Nauk Kirg SSR Ser Estestv Tekh Nauk
Izvestiya Akademii Nauk Latviiskoi SSR — Izv Akad Nauk Latv SSR
Izvestiya Akademii Nauk Latviiskoi SSR — Izv Akad Nauk Latvii SSR
Izvestiya Akademii Nauk Latviiskoi SSR Seriya Fizicheskikh i Tekhnicheskikh Nauk — Izv Akad Nauk Latv SSR Ser Fiz Tekh Nauk
Izvestiya Akademii Nauk Latviiskoi SSR Seriya Khimicheskaya — Izv Akad Nauk Latv SSR Ser Khim
Izvestiya Akademii Nauk Latviiskoi SSR Seriya Khimicheskikh Nauk — Izv Akad Nauk Latv SSR Khim
Izvestiya Akademii Nauk. Mekhanika Zhidkosti i Gaza — Izv Akad Nauk Mekh Zhidk Gaza
Izvestiya Akademii Nauk Moldavskoi SSR — Izv Akad Nauk Mold SSR
Izvestiya Akademii Nauk Moldavskoi SSR — Izv Akad Nauk Moldav SSR
Izvestiya Akademii Nauk Moldavskoi SSR Seriya Biologicheskaya — Izv Akad Nauk Mold SSR Ser Biol
Izvestiya Akademii Nauk Moldavskoi SSR Seriya Biologicheskikh i Khimicheskikh Nauk — Izv Akad Nauk Mold SSR Ser Biol Khim Nauk
Izvestiya Akademii Nauk Moldavskoi SSR Seriya Biologicheskikh i Sel'skokhozyaistvennykh Nauk — Izv Akad Nauk Mold SSR Ser Biol S-Kh Nauk
Izvestiya Akademii Nauk Moldavskoi SSR Seriya Fiziko-Tekhnicheskikh i Matematicheskikh Nauk — IZFMB
Izvestiya Akademii Nauk Moldavskoi SSR Seriya Fiziko-Tekhnicheskikh i Matematicheskikh Nauk — Izv Akad Nauk Mold SSR Ser Fiz-Tekh Mat Nauk
Izvestiya Akademii Nauk Respubliki Kazakhstan. Seriya Fiziko-Matematicheskaya — Izv Akad Nauk Resp Kaz Ser Fiz Mat
Izvestiya Akademii Nauk Respubliki Kazakhstan. Seriya Geologicheskaya — Izv Akad Nauk Resp Kaz Ser Geol
Izvestiya Akademii Nauk Respubliki Kyrgyzstan. Fiziko-Tekhnicheskie, Matematicheskie, i Gorno-Geologicheskie Nauki — Izv Akad Nauk Resp Kyrg Fiz Tekh Mat Gorno Geol Nauki
Izvestiya Akademii Nauk Respubliki Kyrgyzstan. Khimiko-Tekhnologicheskie i Biologicheskie Nauki — Izv Akad Nauk Resp Kyrg Khim Tekhnol Biol Nauki
Izvestiya Akademii Nauk Seriya Fizicheskaya — IANFA
Izvestiya Akademii Nauk. Seriya Fizicheskaya — Izv Akad Nauk Ser Fiz
Izvestiya Akademii Nauk. Seriya Geologicheskaya — Izv Akad Nauk Ser Geol
Izvestiya Akademii Nauk SSR Moldova. Biologicheskie i Khimicheskie Nauki — Izv Akad Nauk SSR Mold Biol Khim Nauki
Izvestiya Akademii Nauk SSSR — IAKSA
Izvestiya Akademii Nauk SSSR — Izv Akad Nauk SSSR
Izvestiya Akademii Nauk SSSR Energetika i Transport — Izv Akad Nauk SSSR Energ Transp
Izvestiya Akademii Nauk SSSR Fizika Atmosfery i Okeana — IFAOA
Izvestiya Akademii Nauk SSSR Fizika Atmosfery i Okeana — Izv Akad Nauk SSSR Fiz Atmos i Okeana
Izvestiya Akademii Nauk SSSR Fizika Atmosfery i Okeana — Izv Akad Nauk SSSR Fiz Atmos Okeana
Izvestiya Akademii Nauk SSSR Fizika Zemli — Izv Akad Nauk SSSR Fiz Zemli
Izvestiya Akademii Nauk SSSR Mekhanika — Izv Akad Nauk SSSR Mekh
Izvestiya Akademii Nauk SSSR Mekhanika i Mashinostroenie — Izv Akad Nauk SSSR Mekh Mashinostr
Izvestiya Akademii Nauk SSSR Mekhanika Tverdogo Tela — Izv Akad Nauk SSSR Mekh Tverd Tela
Izvestiya Akademii Nauk SSSR Mekhanika Zhidkosti i Gaza — Izv Akad Nauk SSSR Mekh Zhidk Gaza
Izvestiya Akademii Nauk SSSR Mekhanika Zhidkosti i Gaza — Izv Akad Nauk SSSR Mekh Zhidk Gaza
Izvestiya Akademii Nauk SSSR Mekhanika Zhidkosti i Gaza — Izv Akad Nauk SSSR Mekh Zhidk i Gaza
Izvestiya Akademii Nauk SSSR Mekhanika Zhidkosti i Gaza — Izv Akad Nauk SSSR Mekh Zhidkosti Gaza
Izvestiya Akademii Nauk SSSR Metallurgiya i Gornoe Delo — Izv Akad Nauk SSSR Metall Gorn Delo
Izvestiya Akademii Nauk SSSR Metally — Izv Akad Nauk SSSR Met
Izvestiya Akademii Nauk SSSR Metally — Izv Akad Nauk SSSR Metally
Izvestiya Akademii Nauk SSSR Neorganicheskie Materialy — Izv Akad Nauk SSSR Neorg Mater
Izvestiya Akademii Nauk SSSR Otdelenie Fiziko-Matematicheskikh Nauk — Izv Akad Nauk SSSR Otd Fiz Mat Nauk
Izvestiya Akademii Nauk SSSR Otdelenie Khimicheskikh Nauk — Izv Akad Nauk SSSR Otd Khim Nauk
Izvestiya Akademii Nauk SSSR Otdelenie Literatury i Jazyka — IzvAN
Izvestiya Akademii Nauk SSSR Otdelenie Literatury i Jazyka — Izvestiya Akad Nauk SSSR
Izvestiya Akademii Nauk SSSR Otdelenie Matematicheskikh i Estestvennykh Nauk [*A publication*] — Izv Akad Nauk SSSR Otd Mat Estestv Nauk
Izvestiya Akademii Nauk SSSR Otdelenie Matematicheskikh i Estestvennykh Nauk. Seriya Biologicheskaya — Izv Akad Nauk SSSR Otd Mat Estest Nauk Ser Biol
Izvestiya Akademii Nauk SSSR Otdelenie Matematicheskikh i Estestvennykh Nauk. Seriya Fizicheskaya — Izv Akad Nauk SSSR Otd Mat Estest Nauk Ser Fiz
Izvestiya Akademii Nauk SSSR Otdelenie Matematicheskikh i Estestvennykh Nauk. Seriya Geograficheskaya i Geofizicheskaya — Izv Akad Nauk SSSR Otd Mat Estest Nauk Ser Geogr Geofiz
Izvestiya Akademii Nauk SSSR Otdelenie Matematicheskikh i Estestvennykh Nauk. Seriya Geologicheskaya — Izv Akad Nauk SSSR Otd Mat Estest Nauk Ser Geol
Izvestiya Akademii Nauk SSSR Otdelenie Matematicheskikh i Estestvennykh Nauk. Seriya Khimicheskaya — Izv Akad Nauk SSSR Otd Mat Estest Nauk Ser Khim
Izvestiya Akademii Nauk SSSR Otdelenie Tekhnicheskikh Nauk — IANTA
Izvestiya Akademii Nauk SSSR Otdelenie Tekhnicheskikh Nauk [*Former USSR*] — Izv Akad Nauk SSSR Otd Tekh Nauk
Izvestiya Akademii Nauk SSSR Otdelenie Tekhnicheskikh Nauk Energetika i Avtomatika [*Former USSR*] — Izv Akad Nauk SSSR Otd Tekh Nauk Energ Avtom
Izvestiya Akademii Nauk SSSR Otdelenie Tekhnicheskikh Nauk Energetika i Transport — Izv Akad Nauk SSSR Otd Tekh Nauk Energ Transp
Izvestiya Akademii Nauk SSSR Otdelenie Tekhnicheskikh Nauk Mekhanika i Mashinostroenie — IANSA
Izvestiya Akademii Nauk SSSR Otdelenie Tekhnicheskikh Nauk Mekhanika i Mashinostroenie [*Former USSR*] — Izv Akad Nauk SSSR Otd Tekh Nauk Mekh Mashinstr
Izvestiya Akademii Nauk SSSR Otdelenie Tekhnicheskikh Nauk Mekhanika i Mashinostroenie — Izv Akad Nauk SSSR Otd Tekh Nauk Mekh Masinostr
Izvestiya Akademii Nauk SSSR Otdelenie Tekhnicheskikh Nauk Metallurgiya i Gornoe Delo — Izv Akad Nauk SSSR Otd Tekh Nauk Metall Gorn Delo
Izvestiya Akademii Nauk SSSR Otdelenie Tekhnicheskikh Nauk Metallurgiya i Toplivo — IANMA
Izvestiya Akademii Nauk SSSR Otdelenie Tekhnicheskikh Nauk Metallurgiya i Toplivo [*Former USSR*] — Izv Akad Nauk SSSR Otd Tekh Nauk Metall Topl
Izvestiya Akademii Nauk SSSR Otdelenie Tekhnicheskikh Nauk Tekhnicheskaya Kibernetika — Izv Akad Nauk SSSR Otd Tekh Nauk Tekh Kibern
Izvestiya Akademii Nauk SSSR Otdeleniya Gumanitarnykh Nauk — IAN-OGN
Izvestiya Akademii Nauk SSSR Otdeleniya Literatury i Jazyka — IAN-OLJa
Izvestiya Akademii Nauk SSSR Otdeleniya Obscestvennykh Nauk — IAN OON
Izvestiya Akademii Nauk SSSR Otdeleniya Russkogo Jazyka i Slavesnosti Akademii Nauk — IAN ORJaSL
Izvestiya Akademii Nauk SSSR Seriya Biologicheskaya — IAN SSS Bio
Izvestiya Akademii Nauk SSSR Seriya Biologicheskaya — Izv Akad Nauk SSSR Biol
Izvestiya Akademii Nauk SSSR Seriya Biologicheskaya — Izv Akad Nauk SSSR Ser Biol
Izvestiya Akademii Nauk SSSR Seriya Ekonomicheskaia — IZSEA
Izvestiya Akademii Nauk SSSR Seriya Fizicheskaya — IAN SSS Fiz
Izvestiya Akademii Nauk SSSR Seriya Fizicheskaya — Izv Akad Nauk SSSR Fiz
Izvestiya Akademii Nauk SSSR Seriya Fizicheskaya — Izv Akad Nauk SSSR Ser Fiz
Izvestiya Akademii Nauk SSSR Seriya Fizika Atmosfery i Okeana — IAN SSS FAO
Izvestiya Akademii Nauk SSSR Seriya Geofizicheskaya — IAGFA
Izvestiya Akademii Nauk SSSR Seriya Geofizicheskaya [*Former USSR*] — Izv Akad Nauk SSSR Ser Geofiz
Izvestiya Akademii Nauk SSSR Seriya Geograficheskaya — Izv Akad Nauk SSSR Ser Geogr
Izvestiya Akademii Nauk SSSR Seriya Geograficheskaya i Geofizicheskaya — IAGYA
Izvestiya Akademii Nauk SSSR Seriya Geograficheskaya i Geofizicheskaya — Izv Akad Nauk SSSR Ser Geogr Geofiz
Izvestiya Akademii Nauk SSSR Seriya Geologicheskaya — Izv Akad Nauk SSSR Ser Geol
Izvestiya Akademii Nauk SSSR Seriya Geologicheskaya (Translated Abstracts) — Izv Akad Nauk SSSR Ser Geol (Transl Abstr)

Izvestiya Akademii Nauk SSSR Seriya Khimicheskaya — Izv Akad Nauk SSSR Khim
Izvestiya Akademii Nauk SSSR Seriya Khimicheskaya — Izv Akad Nauk SSSR Ser Khim
Izvestiya Akademii Nauk SSSR Seriya Literatury i Jazyka [*Moscow*] — IAN
Izvestiya Akademii Nauk SSSR Seriya Matematicheskaya — Izv Akad Nauk SSSR Ser Mat
Izvestiya Akademii Nauk SSSR Tekhnicheskaya Kibernetika — Izv Akad Nauk SSSR Tekh Kibern
Izvestiya Akademii Nauk SSSR Tekhnicheskaya Kibernetika — Izv Akad Nauk SSSR Tekhn Kibernet
Izvestiya Akademii Nauk Tadzhikskoi SSR Otdelenie Biologicheskikh Nauk — Izv Akad Nauk Tadzh SSR Otd Biol Nauk
Izvestiya Akademii Nauk Tadzhikskoi SSR Otdelenie Biologicheskikh Nauk — Izv Akad Nauk Tadzhik SSR Otd Biol Nauk
Izvestiya Akademii Nauk Tadzhikskoi SSR Otdelenie Estestvennykh Nauk — Izv Akad Nauk Tadzh SSR Otd Estestv Nauk
Izvestiya Akademii Nauk Tadzhikskoi SSR Otdelenie Fizichesko-Tekhnicheskikh i Khimicheskikh Nauk — Izv Akad Nauk Tadzhik SSR Otd Fiz-Tekh Khim Nauk
Izvestiya Akademii Nauk Tadzhikskoi SSR Otdelenie Fiziko-Matematicheskikh i Geologo-Khimicheskikh Nauk [*Later, Izvestiya Akademi Nauk Tadzhikskoi SSR Otdelenie Fiziko-Matematicheskikh, Khimicheskikh, i Geologicheskikh Nauk*] — Izv Akad Nauk Tadzh SSR Otd Fiz-Mat Geol-Khim Nauk
Izvestiya Akademii Nauk Tadzhikskoi SSR Otdelenie Fiziko-Matematicheskikh, Khimicheskikh, i Geologicheskikh Nauk — Izv Akad Nauk Tadzh SSR Otd Fiz Mat Khim Geol Nauk
Izvestiya Akademii Nauk Tadzhikskoi SSR Otdelenie Fiziko-Matematicheskikh, Khimicheskikh, i Geologicheskikh Nauk — Izv Akad Nauk Tadzhik SSR Otdel Fiz-Mat Khim i Geol Nauk
Izvestiya Akademii Nauk Tadzhikskoi SSR Otdelenie Fiziko-Tekhnicheskikh i Khimicheskikh Nauk [*Tadzhik SSR*] — Izv Akad Nauk Tadzh SSR Otd Fiz-Tekh Khim Nauk
Izvestiya Akademii Nauk Tadzhikskoi SSR Otdelenie Geologo-Khimicheskikh i Tekhnicheskikh Nauk — Izv Akad Nauk Tadzh SSR Otd Geol Khim Tekh Nauk
Izvestiya Akademii Nauk Tadzhikskoi SSR Otdelenie Obscestvennych Nauk — IzvANTadz
Izvestiya Akademii Nauk Tadzhikskoi SSR Otdelenie Sel'skokhozyaistvennykh i Biologicheskikh Nauk — Izv Akad Nauk Tadzh SSR Otd S-Kh Biol Nauk
Izvestiya Akademii Nauk Turkmenistana — Izv Akad Nauk Turkm
Izvestiya Akademii Nauk Turkmenistana. Seriya Biologicheskikh Nauk — Izv Akad Nauk Turkm Ser Biol Nauk
Izvestiya Akademii Nauk Turkmenistana. Seriya Fiziko-Matematicheskikh. Tekhnicheskikh. Khimicheskikh i Geologicheskikh Nauk — Izv Akad Nauk Turkm Ser Fiz Mat Tekh Khim Geol Nauk
Izvestiya Akademii Nauk Turkmenskoi SSR — Izv Akad Nauk Turkm SSR
Izvestiya Akademii Nauk Turkmenskoi SSR Seriya Biologicheskikh Nauk — Izv Akad Nauk Turkm SSR Ser Biol Nauk
Izvestiya Akademii Nauk Turkmenskoi SSR Seriya Biologicheskikh Nauk — Izv Akad Nauk Turkmen SSR Ser Biol Nauk
Izvestiya Akademii Nauk Turkmenskoi SSR Seriya Fiziko-Tekhnicheskikh, Khimicheskikh, i Geologicheskikh Nauk — ITUFA
Izvestiya Akademii Nauk Turkmenskoi SSR Seriya Fiziko-Tekhnicheskikh, Khimicheskikh, i Geologicheskikh Nauk — Izv Akad Nauk Turkm SSR Ser Fiz-Tekh Khim Geol Nauk
Izvestiya Akademii Nauk Turkmenskoi SSSR Seriya Obshchestvennych Nauk — IAT
Izvestiya Akademii Nauk Turkmenskoi SSSR Seriya Obshchestvennych Nauk — IzvANTurkm
Izvestiya Akademii Nauk Turkmenskoi SSSR Seriya Obshchestvennykh Nauk — Izv Akad Nauk Turkm SSSR Ser Obshchestv Nauk
Izvestiya Akademii Nauk Uzbekistanskoj SSSR — IANUz
Izvestiya Akademii Nauk Uzbekskoi SSR — Izv Akad Nauk Uzb SSR
Izvestiya Akademii Nauk Uzbekskoi SSR — Izv Akad Uzb SSR
Izvestiya Akademii Nauk Uzbekskoi SSR Seriya Biologicheskaya — Izv Akad Nauk Uzb SSR Ser Biol
Izvestiya Akademii Nauk Uzbekskoi SSR Seriya Fiziko-Matematicheskikh Nauk — Izv Akad Nauk Uzb SSR Ser Fiz-Mat Nauk
Izvestiya Akademii Nauk Uzbekskoi SSR Seriya Fiziko-Matematicheskikh Nauk — Izv Akad Uzb SSR Fiz-Mat
Izvestiya Akademii Nauk Uzbekskoi SSR Seriya Geologicheskaya — Izv Akad Nauk Uzb SSR Ser Geol
Izvestiya Akademii Nauk Uzbekskoi SSR Seriya Khimicheskikh Nauk — Izv Akad Nauk Uzb SSR Ser Khim Nauk
Izvestiya Akademii Nauk Uzbekskoi SSR Seriya Meditsinskaya — Izv Akad Nauk Uzb SSR Ser Med
Izvestiya Akademii Nauk Uzbekskoi SSR Seriya Tekhnicheskikh Nauk — Izv Akad Nauk Uzb SSR Ser Tekh Nauk
Izvestiya Akademii Nauk Uzbekskoi SSR Seriya Tekhnicheskikh Nauk — Izv Akad Nauk UzSSR Ser Tekh Nauk
Izvestiya Akademii Nauk UzSSR Seriya Biologicheskaya — Izv Akad Nauk UzSSR Ser Biol
Izvestiya Akademii Nauk UzSSR Seriya Geologicheskaya — Izv Akad Nauk UzSSR Ser Geol
Izvestiya Akademii Nauk UzSSR Seriya Khimicheskikh Nauk — Izv Akad Nauk UzSSR Ser Khim Nauk
Izvestiya Akademii Nauk UzSSR Seriya Meditsinskaya — Izv Akad Nauk UzSSR Ser Med
Izvestiya Akademii Pedagogicheskikh Nauk RSFSR — Izv Akad Pedagog Nauk RSFSR
Izvestiya Akademii Stroitel'stva i Arkhitektury SSSR — Izv Akad Stroit Arkhit SSSR
Izvestiya Akademiya Nauk Armyanskoi SSR Biologicheskie Nauk — Izv Akad Nauk Armyan SSR Biol Nauk
Izvestiya Altaiskogo Otdela Geograficheskogo Obscestva SSSR — Izv Altai Otd Geogr O-Va SSSR
Izvestiya Armyanskogo Filiala Akademii Nauk SSSR — Izv Arm Fil Akad Nauk SSSR
Izvestiya Armyanskogo Filiala Akademii Nauk SSSR Estestvennye Nauki — Izv Arm Fil Akad Nauk SSSR Estestv Nauki
Izvestiya Armyanskogo Gosudarstvennogo Zaocnogo Pedagogiceskogo Instituta — IzvArmZPI
Izvestiya Astrofizicheskogo Instituta Akademiya Nauk Kazakhskoi SSR — Izv Astrofiz Inst Akad Nauk Kaz SSR
Izvestiya Azerbaidzhanskogo Filiala Akademii Nauk SSSR — Izv Azerb Fil Akad Nauk SSSR
Izvestiya Batumskogo Botanicheskogo Sada — Izv Batum Bot Sada
Izvestiya Batumskogo Botanicheskogo Sada Akademii Nauk Gruzinskoi SSR — Izv Batum Bot Sada Akad Nauk Gruz SSR
Izvestiya Biologicheskogo Nauchno-Issledovatel'skogo Instituta i Biologicheskoi Stantsii pri Permskom Gosudarstvennom Universitete — Izv Biol Nauchno-Issled Inst Biol Stn Permsk Gos Univ
Izvestiya Biologicheskogo Nauchno-Issledovatel'skogo Instituta pri Molotovskom Gosudarstvennom Universitete — Izv Biol Nauchno Issled Inst Molotov Gos Univ
Izvestiya Biologicheskogo Nauchno-Issledovatel'skogo Instituta pri Permskom Gosudarstvennom Universitete — Izv Biol Nauchno Issled Inst Permsk Gos Univ
Izvestiya Biologo-Geograficheskogo Nauchno-Issledovatel'skogo Instituta pri Irkutskom Gosudarstvennom Universitete — Izv Biol Geogr Nauchno Issled Inst Irkutsk Gos Univ
Izvestiya Byuro po Evgenike. Akademiya Nauk SSSR — Izv Byuro Evgen Akad Nauk SSSR
Izvestiya Byuro po Genetike. Akademiya Nauk SSSR — Izv Byuro Genet Akad Nauk SSSR
Izvestiya Byuro po Genetike i Evgenike. Akademiya Nauk SSSR — Izv Byuro Genet Evgen Akad Nauk SSSR
Izvestiya Ceceno-Ingusskogo Naucno-Issledovatel-Skogo Instituta Istorii, Jazyka, i Literatury — IzvCIngNII
Izvestiya Dnepropetrovskogo Gornogo Instituta — Izv Dnepropetr Gorn Inst
Izvestiya Ekaterinoslavskogo Gornogo Instituta — Izv Ekaterinosl Gorn Inst
Izvestiya Ekaterinoslavskogo Vysshago Gornago Uchilishcha — Izv Ekaterinosl Vyssh Gorn Uchil
Izvestiya Elektrotekhnicheskogo Instituta (Leningrad) — Izv Elektrotekh Inst (Leningrad)
Izvestiya Energeticheskogo Instituta Akademiya Nauk SSSR — IEKNA
Izvestiya Energeticheskogo Instituta Akademiya Nauk SSSR — Izv Energ Inst Akad Nauk SSSR
Izvestiya Erevanskogo Meditsinskogo Instituta i Meditsinskogo Obshchestva Armenii — Izv Erevan Med Inst Med Ova Arm
Izvestiya Estestvenno-Nauchnogo Instituta Imeni P. S. Lesgafta — Izv Estestv Nauchn Inst Im P S Lesgafta
Izvestiya Estestvenno-Nauchnogo Instituta pri Molotovskom Gosudarstvennom Universiteta Imeni M. Gor'kogo — Izv Estestv-Nauchn Inst Molotov Gos Univ Im M Gor'kogo
Izvestiya Estestvennonauchnogo Instituta pri Molotovskom Gosudarstvennom Universitete — Izv Estestvennonauchn Inst Molotov Gos Univ
Izvestiya Estestvennonauchnogo Instituta pri Permskom Gosudarstvennom Universitet [*Former USSR*] — Izv Estestvennonauchn Inst Permsk Gos Univ
Izvestiya Fakul'teta Sel'skokhozyaistvennykh Nauk Moshonmad'yarovar Vengriya — Izv Fak S kh Nauk Moshonmad'yarovar Vengriya
Izvestiya Fiziko-Khimicheskogo Nauchno-Issledovatel'skogo Instituta pri Irkutskom Gosudarstvennom Universitete — Izv Fiz-Khim Nauchno-Issled Inst Irkutsk Gos Univ
Izvestiya Geologicheskogo Obshchestva Gruzii — Izv Geol Ova Gruz
Izvestiya Glavnoi Astronomicheskoi Observatorii v Pulkove — IGOPA
Izvestiya Glavnoi Astronomicheskoi Observatorii v Pulkove — Izv Gl Astron Obs Pulkove
Izvestiya Glavnoi Rossiiskoi Astronomicheskoi Observatorii — Izv Gl Ross Astron Obs
Izvestiya Gorskogo Sel'skokhozyaistvennogo Instituta — Izv Gorskogo S'kh Inst
Izvestiya Gosudarstvennogo Nauchno-Issledovatel'skogo Instituta Kolloidnoi Khimii — Izv Gos Nauchno-Issled Inst Kolloidn Khim
Izvestiya Gosudarstvennogo Nauchno-Issledovatel'skogo Instituta Ozernogo i Rechnogo Rybnogo Khozyaistva — Izv Gos Nauchno-Issled Inst Ozern Rechn Rybn Khoz
Izvestiya Gruzinskogo Nauchno-Issledovatel'skogo Instituta Gidrotekhniki i Melioratsii — Izv Gruz Nauchno Issled Inst Gidrotekh Melior
Izvestiya i Trudy Kharbinskogo Politekhnicheskogo Instituta — Izv Tr Kharb Politekh Inst
Izvestiya i Trudy Russko-Kitaiskogo Politekhnicheskogo Instituta — Izv Tr Russ Kitaiskogo Politekh Inst
Izvestiya i Uchenyya Zapiski Imperatorskago Kazanskago Universiteta — Izv Uch Zap Imp Kazan Univ
Izvestiya Imperatorskago Lesnago Instituta — Izv Imp Lesn Inst
Izvestiya Imperatorskoi Akademii Nauk — Izv Imp Akad Nauk
Izvestiya Imperatorskoi Akademii Nauk (St. Petersburg) — Izvest Imp Akad Nauk (S Petersburg)
Izvestiya. Institut po Furazhite. Pleven — Izv Inst Furazhite Pleven
Izvestiya. Institut po Pshenitsata i Slunchogleda (Tolbukhin) — Izv Inst Pshenitsata Slunchogleda (Tolbukhin)
Izvestiya. Institut po Sladkovodno Ribovudstvo (Plovdiv) — Izv Inst Sladkovodno Ribovud (Plovdiv)
Izvestiya. Institut Ribni Resursov (Varna) — Izv Inst Ribni Resur (Varna)
Izvestiya. Institut Rukopisej Akademii Nauk Gruzinskoj SSR — IzvIRGruz
Izvestiya. Institut Rybnykh Resursov (Varna) — Izv Inst Rybn Resur
Izvestiya Instituta Chistykh Khimicheskikh Reaktivov — Izv Inst Chist Khim Reakt

Izvestiya Instituta Fiziko-Khimicheskogo Analiza. Akademiya Nauk SSSR — Izv Inst Fiz Khim Anal Akad Nauk SSSR
Izvestiya Instituta Nauk i Iskusstv SSR Armenii — Izv Inst Nauk Iskusstv SSR Arm
Izvestiya Irkutskogo Gosudarstvennogo Pedagogicheskogo Instituta — Izv Irkutsk Gos Pedagog Inst
Izvestiya Irkutskogo Nauchno-Issledovatel'skogo Protivochumnogo Instituta Sibiri i Dal'nego Vostoka — Izv Irkutsk Nauchno-Issled Protivochumn Inst Sib Dal'n Vost
Izvestiya Irkutskogo Sel'skokhozyaistvennogo Instituta — Izv Irkutsk Skh Inst
Izvestiya Ivanovo-Voznesenskogo Politekhnicheskogo Instituta — Izv Ivanovo Voznesensk Politekh Inst
Izvestiya Ivanovskogo Sel'skokhozyaistvennogo Instituta — Izv Ivanov Skh Inst
Izvestiya Jugo-Osetinskogo Naucno-Issledovatel'skogo Instituta — IzvJOsNII
Izvestiya Jugo-Osetinskogo Naucno-Issledovatel'skogo Instituta Akademii Nauk-Gruzinskoj SSR — Izvestiya Jugo-Oset Nauc-Issl Inst
Izvestiya Jugo-Osetinskogo Naucno-Issledovatel'skogo Instituta Akademii Nauk-Gruzinskoj SSR — IzvJuOsI
Izvestiya Kalininskogo Gosudarstvennogo Pedagogicheskogo Instituta — Izv Kalinin Gos Pedagog Inst
Izvestiya Karel'skogo i Kol'skogo Filialov Akademii Nauk SSSR — Izv Karel Kolsk Fil Akad Nauk SSSR
Izvestiya Kazakhskogo Filiala Akademii Nauk SSSR. Seriya Biologicheskaya — Izv Kaz Fil Akad Nauk SSSR Ser Biol
Izvestiya Kazakhskogo Filiala Akademii Nauk SSSR. Seriya Botanicheskaya — Izv Kaz Fil Akad Nauk SSSR Ser Bot
Izvestiya Kazakhskogo Filiala Akademii Nauk SSSR. Seriya Energeticheskaya — Izv Kaz Fil Akad Nauk SSSR Ser Energ
Izvestiya Kazakhskogo Filiala Akademii Nauk SSSR. Seriya Fiziologii i Biokhimii Rastenii — Izv Kaz Fil Akad Nauk SSSR Ser Fiziol Biokhim Rast
Izvestiya Kazakhskogo Filiala Akademii Nauk SSSR. Seriya Gornogo Dela — Izv Kaz Fil Akad Nauk SSSR Ser Gorn Dela
Izvestiya Kazakhskogo Filiala Akademii Nauk SSSR. Seriya Zoologicheskaya — Izv Kaz Fil Akad Nauk SSSR Ser Zool
Izvestiya Kazanskogo Filiala Akademii Nauk SSR — Izv Kazan Fil Akad Nauk SSR
Izvestiya Kazanskogo Filiala Akademii Nauk SSSR Seriya Biologicheskikh i Sel's kokhozyaistvennykh Nauk — Izv Kazan Fil Akad Nauk SSSR Ser Biol Skh Nauk
Izvestiya Kazanskogo Filiala Akademii Nauk SSSR Seriya Biologicheskikh Nauk — Izv Kazan Fil Akad Nauk SSSR Ser Biol Nauk
Izvestiya Kazanskogo Filiala Akademii Nauk SSSR Seriya Fiziko-Matematicheskikh i Tekhnicheskikh Nauk — Izv Kazan Fil Akad Nauk SSSR Ser Fiz Mat Tekh Nauk
Izvestiya Kazanskogo Filiala Akademii Nauk SSSR Seriya Geologicheskikh Nauk — Izv Kazan Fil Akad Nauk SSSR Ser Geol Nauk
Izvestiya Kazanskogo Filiala Akademii Nauk SSSR Seriya Khimicheskikh Nauk — Izv Kazan Fil Akad Nauk SSSR Ser Khim Nauk
Izvestiya Kazanskogo Lesotekhnicheskogo Instituta — Izv Kazan Lesotekh Inst
Izvestiya Khlopchatobumazhnoi Promyshlennosti — Izv Khlopchatobum Prom
Izvestiya Khlopchatobumazhnoi Promyshlennosti — Izv Khlopchatobum Promsti
Izvestiya Kievskogo Politekhnicheskogo Instituta — Izv Kiev Politekh Inst
Izvestiya Kirgizskogo Filiala Akademii Nauk SSSR — Izv Kirg Fil Akad Nauk SSSR
Izvestiya Kirgizskogo Filiala Akademii Nauk SSSR — Izvestiya Kirgiz Filiala Akad Nauk SSSR
Izvestiya Kirgizskogo Filiala Vsesoyuznogo Obshchestva Pochvovedov — Izv Kirg Fil Vses Ova Pochvovedov
Izvestiya Kirgizskogo Geograficheskogo Obshchestva — Izv Kirg Geogr Ova
Izvestiya Komi Filiala Geograficheskogo Obshchestva SSSR — Izv Komi Fil Geogr Ova SSSR
Izvestiya Komi Filiala Vsesoyuznogo Geograficheskogo Obshchestva — Izv Komi Fil Vses Geogr Obshch
Izvestiya Komi Filiala Vsesoyuznogo Geograficheskogo Obshchestva SSSR — Izv Komi Fil Vses Geogr Ova
Izvestiya Komi Filiala Vsesoyuznogo Geograficheskogo Obshchestva SSSR — Izv Komi Fil Vses Geogr O-Va SSSR
Izvestiya Komissii po Fizike Planet Akademiya Nauk SSSR — Izv Kom Fiz Planet Akad Nauk SSSR
Izvestiya Krymskogo Otdela Geograficheskogo Obshchestva SSSR — Izv Krym Otd Geogr Ova SSSR
Izvestiya Krymskogo Otdela Geograficheskogo Obshchestva SSSR — Izv Krymsk Otd Geog Obshch Soyuza SSR
Izvestiya Krymskogo Pedagogicheskogo Instituta — Izv Krym Pedagog Inst
Izvestiya Krymskoi Astrofizicheskoi Observatorii — IKAOA
Izvestiya Krymskoi Astrofizicheskoi Observatorii — Izv Krym Astrofiz Obs
Izvestiya Kubanskogo Pedagogicheskogo Instituta — Izv Kuban Pedagog Inst
Izvestiya Kuibyshevskogo Inzhenerno-Meliorativnogo Instituta — Izv Kuibyshev Inzh Melior Inst
Izvestiya Kuibyshevskogo Sel'skokhozyaistvennogo Instituta — Izv Kuibyshev Sel'khoz Inst
Izvestiya Kuibyshevskogo Sel'skokhozyaistvennogo Instituta — Izv Kuibyshev S-Kh Inst
Izvestiya Kurganskogo Mashinostroitel'nogo Instituta — Izv Kurgan Mashinostroit Inst
Izvestiya Latviiskoi Akademii Nauk — Izv Latv Akad Nauk
Izvestiya Leningradskogo Elektrotekhnicheskogo Instituta — ILEUA
Izvestiya Leningradskogo Elektrotekhnicheskogo Instituta — Izv Leningr Elektrotekh Inst
Izvestiya Leningradskogo Elektrotekhnicheskogo Instituta Imeni V. I. Ul'yanova — Izv Leningr Elektrotekh Inst Im V I Ul'yanova
Izvestiya Leningradskogo Gosudarstvennogo Universiteta — ILGU
Izvestiya Leningradskogo Lesnogo Instituta — Izv Leningr Lesn Inst
Izvestiya Lesotekhnicheskoi Akademii — Izv Lesotekh Akad
Izvestiya Ministerstvo Proizvodstva i Zagotovok Sel'skokhozyaistvennykh Productov Armyanskoi SSR — Izv Minist Proizvod Zagotovok S-Kh Prod Arm SSR
Izvestiya Ministerstvo Sel'skogo Khozyaistva Armyanskoi SSR — Izv Minist Selsk Khoz Arm SSR
Izvestiya Ministerstvo Sel'skogo Khozyaistva Armyanskoi SSR — Izv Minist Skh Arm SSR
Izvestiya Ministerstvo Sel'skogo Khozyaistva Armyanskoi SSR Sel'skokhozyaistvennye Nauki — Izv Minist Sel'sk Khoz Arm SSR S-Kh Nauki
Izvestiya Moldavskogo Filiala Akademii Nauk SSSR — Izv Mold Fil Akad Nauk SSSR
Izvestiya Moskovskii Tekstil'nyi Institut — Izv Mosk Tekst Inst
Izvestiya Moskovskogo Selskokhozyaistvennogo Instituta — Izv Mosk Skh Inst
Izvestiya na Akademiyata na Selskostopanskite Nauki. Gorskostopanski Nauka — Izv Akad Selskostop Nauki Gorskostop Nauka
Izvestiya na Akademiyata na Selskostopanskite Nauki. Gradinarska i Lozarska Nauka — Izv Akad Selskostop Nauki Gradinar Lozar Nauka
Izvestiya na Akademiyata na Selskostopanskite Nauki. Rastenievudni Nauki — Izv Akad Selskostop Nauki Rastenievud Nauki
Izvestiya na Akademiyata na Selskostopanskite Nauki. Veterinarno Meditsinski Nauki — Izv Akad Selskostop Nauki Vet Med Nauki
Izvestiya na Akademiyata na Selskostopanskite Nauki. Zhivotnovudni Nauki — Izv Akad Selskostop Nauki Zhivotnovud Nauki
Izvestiya na Balgarskiya Archeologiceski Institut — IzvBAI
Izvestiya na Biologicheskiya Institut. Bulgarska Akademiya na Naukite — Izv Biol Inst Bulg Akad Nauk
Izvestiya na Botanicheskiya Institut. Bulgarska Akademiya na Naukite — Izv Bot Inst Bulg Akad Nauk
Izvestiya na Botanicheskiya Instituta B'lgarska Akademiya na Naukite — Izv Bot Inst B'lg Akad Nauk
Izvestiya na Botanicheskiya Instituta B'lgarska Akademiya Naukite Otdelenie za Biologichni Nauki — Izv Bot Inst B Akad Nauk Otd Biol Nauki
Izvestiya na Bulgarskata Akademiya na Naukite. Otdelenie za Fiziko-Matematicheski i Tekhnicheski Nauki Seriya Fizicheska — Izv Bulg Akad Nauk Otd Fiz Mat Tekh Nauki Ser Fiz
Izvestiya na Dobrudzhanskiya Selskostopanski Nauchnoizsledovatelski Institut Tolbukhin — Izv Dobruzhan Selskostop Nauchnoizsled Inst Tolbukhin
Izvestiya na Druzestovoto na Filolozite-Slavisti v Balgarija (Sofija) — IDS
Izvestiya na Druzestovoto na Filolozite-Slavisti v Balgarija (Sofija) — IzvDS
Izvestiya na Durzhavniya Institut za Kontrol na Lekarstvenite Sredstva — Izv Durzh Inst Kontrol Lek Sredstva
Izvestiya na Etnografskija Institut Muzej — IEIM
Izvestiya na Filiala po Sladkovodno Ribarstvo (Plovdiv). Institut po Ribna Promishlenost — Izv Fil Sladkovodno Ribar (Plovdiv) Inst Ribna Promst
Izvestiya na Fizicheskiya Instituta ANEB. Bulgarska Akademiya na Naukite — IFABA
Izvestiya na Fizicheskiya Instituta ANEB. Bulgarska Akademiya na Naukite — Izv Fiz Inst ANEB Bulg Akad Nauk
Izvestiya na Geofizichniya Institut — Izv Geofiz Inst
Izvestiya na Geofizichniya Institut. Bulgarska Akademiya na Naukite — IGBMA
Izvestiya na Geofizichniya Institut. Bulgarska Akademiya na Naukite [*Bulgaria*] — Izv Geofiz Inst Bulg Akad Nauk
Izvestiya na Geologicheskiya Institut. Bulgarska Akademiya na Naukite — Izv Geol Inst Bulg Akad Nauk
Izvestiya na Geologicheskiya Institut. Bulgarska Akademiya na Naukite. Seriya Geokhimiya, Mineralogiya, i Petrografiya — IGGMA
Izvestiya na Geologicheskiya Institut. Bulgarska Akademiya na Naukite. Seriya Geokhimiya, Mineralogiya, i Petrografiya [*Bulgaria*] — Izv Geol Inst Bulg Akad Nauk Ser Geokhim Mineral Petrogr
Izvestiya na Geologicheskiya Institut. Bulgarska Akademiya na Naukite. Seriya Geotektonika — Izv Geol Inst Bulg Akad Nauk Ser Geotekton
Izvestiya na Geologicheskiya Institut. Bulgarska Akademiya na Naukite. Seriya Geotektonika, Stratigrafiya, i Litologiya — Izv Geol Inst Bulg Akad Nauk Ser Geotekton Stratigr Litol
Izvestiya na Geologicheskiya Institut. Bulgarska Akademiya na Naukite. Seriya Geotektonika, Stratigrafiya, i Litologiya — Izv Geol Inst Bulg Akad Nauk Ser Geotektonika Stratigr Litol
Izvestiya na Geologicheskiya Institut. Bulgarska Akademiya na Naukite. Seriya Inzhenerna Geologiya i Khidrogeologiya — Izv Geol Inst Bulg Akad Nauk Ser Inzh Geol Khidrogeol
Izvestiya na Geologicheskiya Institut. Bulgarska Akademiya na Naukite. Seriya Neftena i Vuglishtna Geologiya [*Bulgaria*] — IGNVB
Izvestiya na Geologicheskiya Institut. Bulgarska Akademiya na Naukite. Seriya Neftena i Vuglishtna Geologiya — Izv Geol Inst Bulg Akad Nauk Ser Neft Vuglishtna Geol
Izvestiya na Geologicheskiya Institut. Bulgarska Akademiya na Naukite. Seriya Neftena i Vuglishtna Geologiya — Izv Geol Inst Bulg Akad Nauk Ser Neftena Vuglishtna Geol
Izvestiya na Geologicheskiya Institut. Bulgarska Akademiya na Naukite. Seriya Paleontologiya — Izv Geol Inst Bulg Akad Nauk Ser Paleontol
Izvestiya na Geologicheskiya Institut. Bulgarska Akademiya na Naukite. Seriya Prilozhna Geofizika — Izv Geol Inst Bulg Akad Nauk Ser Prilozh Geofiz
Izvestiya na Geologicheskiya Institut. Bulgarska Akademiya na Naukite. Seriya Prilozhna Geofizika — Izv Geol Inst Bulg Akad Nauk Ser Prilozhna Geof
Izvestiya na Geologicheskiya Institut. Bulgarska Akademiya na Naukite. Seriya Stratigrafiya i Litologiya — Izv Geol Inst Bulg Akad Nauk Ser Stratigr Litol
Izvestiya na Geologicheskiya Institut. Seriya Paleontologiya (Sofia) — Izv Geol Inst Ser Paleontol (Sofia)
Izvestiya na Geologicheskiya Institut. Seriya Prilozhna Geofizika — Izv Geol Inst Ser Prilozh Geofiz
Izvestiya na Instituta Khidrotekhnika i Melioratsii. Akademiya Selskostopanskite Nauki v Bulgariya — Izv Inst Khidrotekh Melior Akad Selskostop Nauki Bulg
Izvestiya na Instituta po Biokhimiya. Bulgarska Akademiya na Naukite — Izv Inst Biokhim Bulg Akad Nauk

Izvestiya na Instituta po Biologiya. Bulgarska Akademiya na Naukite — Izv Inst Biol Bulg Akad Nauk
Izvestiya na Instituta po Biologiya "Metodii Popov." Bulgarskoi Akademii Nauk — Izv Inst Biol "Metod Popov" Bulg Akad Nauk
Izvestiya na Instituta po Eksperimentalna Meditsina. Bulgarska Akademiya na Naukite — Izv Inst Eksp Med Bulg Akad Nauk
Izvestiya na Instituta po Eksperimentalna Veterinarna Meditsina. Bulgarska Akademiya na Naukite — Izv Inst Eksp Vet Med Bulg Akad Nauk
Izvestiya na Instituta po Elektronika — Izv Inst Elektron
Izvestiya na Instituta po Elektronika. Bulgarska Akademiya na Naukite — IIEBB
Izvestiya na Instituta po Elektronika. Bulgarska Akademiya na Naukite — Izv Inst Elektron Bulg Akad Nauk
Izvestiya na Instituta po Energetika. Bulgarska Akademiya na Naukite — Izv Inst Energ Bulg Akad Nauk
Izvestiya na Instituta po Fizikokhimiya. Bulgarska Akademiya na Naukite — Izv Inst Fizikokhim Bulg Akad Nauk
Izvestiya na Instituta po Fiziologiya. B'lgarska Akademiya na Naukite — Izv Inst Fiziol B'lg Akad Nauk
Izvestiya na Instituta po Fiziologiya. Bulgarska Akademiya na Naukite — Izv Inst Fiziol Bulg Akad Nauk
Izvestiya na Instituta po Fiziologiya na Rasteniyata. Bulgarska Akademiya na Naukite — IFRPA
Izvestiya na Instituta po Fiziologiya na Rasteniyata. Bulgarska Akademiya na Naukite [*Bulgaria*] — Izv Inst Fiziol Rast Bulg Akad Nauk
Izvestiya na Instituta po Fiziologiya na Rasteniyata "Metodii Popov." Bulgarska Akademiya na Naukite — Izv Inst Fiziol Rast "Metodii Popov" Bulg Akad Nauk
Izvestiya na Instituta po Fiziologiya na Rasteniyata "Metodii Popov." Bulgarskoi Akademii Nauk — Izv Inst Fiziol Rast "Metod Popov" Bulg Akad Nauk
Izvestiya na Instituta po Izucheniya Platiny i Drugikh Blagorodnykh Metallov. Akademiya Nauk SSSR — Izv Inst Izuch Platin Drugikh Blagorodn Met Akad Nauk SSSR
Izvestiya na Instituta po Khidrologiya i Meteorologiya. Bulgarska Akademiya na Naukite — IIKMA
Izvestiya na Instituta po Khidrologiya i Meteorologiya. Bulgarska Akademiya na Naukite — Izv Inst Khidrol Meteor
Izvestiya na Instituta po Khidrologiya i Meteorologiya. Bulgarska Akademiya na Naukite [*Bulgaria*] — Izv Inst Khidrol Meteorol Bulg Akad Nauk
Izvestiya na Instituta po Khranene. Bulgarska Akademiya na Naukite — Izv Inst Khranene Bulg Akad Nauk
Izvestiya na Instituta po Lozarstvo i Vinarstvo (Pleven). Akademiya na Selskostopanskite Nauki v Bulgariya — Izv Inst Lozar Vinar (Pleven) Akad Selskostop Nauki Bulg
Izvestiya na Instituta po Morfologiya. Bulgarska Akademiya na Naukite — IMBMA
Izvestiya na Instituta po Morfologiya. Bulgarska Akademiya na Naukite [*Bulgaria*] — Izv Inst Morfol Bulg Akad Nauk
Izvestiya na Instituta po Morfologiya. Bulgarska Akademiya na Naukite za Meditsinski Nauki — Izv Inst Morfol B'lg Akad Nauk Med Nauki
Izvestiya na Instituta po Obshcha i Sravnitelna Patologiya. Bulgarska Akademiya na Naukite [*Bulgaria*] — Izv Inst Obshch Sravn Patol Bulg Akad Nauk
Izvestiya na Instituta po Obshcha i Sravnitelna Patologiya. Bulgarska Akademiya na Naukite — Izv Inst Obshcha Sravn Patol B'lg Akad Nauk
Izvestiya na Instituta po Obshcha i Sravnitelna Patologiya. Bulgarska Akademiya na Naukite — Izv Inst Obshcha Sravn Patol Bulg Akad Nauk
Izvestiya na Instituta po Obshta i Neorganichna Khimiya. Bulgarska Akademiya na Naukite — IOBKA
Izvestiya na Instituta po Obshta i Neorganichna Khimiya. Bulgarska Akademiya na Naukite — Izv Inst Obshta Neorg Khim Bulg Akad Nauk
Izvestiya na Instituta po Obshta i Neorganichna Khimiya i po Organichna Khimiya. Bulgarska Akademiya na Naukite — Izv Inst Obshta Neorg Khim Org Khim Bulg Akad Nauk
Izvestiya na Instituta po Obshta i Sravnitelna Patologiya. Bulgarska Akademiya na Naukite — Izv Inst Obshta Sravn Patol Bulg Akad Nauk
Izvestiya na Instituta po Obshta i Sravnitelna Patologiya. Bylgarska Akademiya na Naukite — Izv Inst Obshta Sravn Patol Bylg
Izvestiya na Instituta po Okeanografiya i Ribno Stopanstvo. Bulgarska Akademiya na Naukite — Izv Inst Okeanogr Ribno Stop Bulg Akad Nauk
Izvestiya na Instituta po Organichna Khimiya. Bulgarska Akademiya na Naukite [*Bulgaria*] — IOKKA
Izvestiya na Instituta po Organichna Khimiya. Bulgarska Akademiya na Naukite — Izv Inst Org Khim Bulg Akad Nauk
Izvestiya na Instituta po Ovoshcharstvo. Gara Kostinbrod — Izv Inst Ovoshcharstvo
Izvestiya na Instituta po Pamuka (Chirpan) — Izv Inst Pamuka (Chirpan)
Izvestiya na Instituta po Rastenievudstvo. Akademiya na Selskostopanskite Nauki v Bulgariya — Izv Inst Rastenievud Akad Selskostop Nauki Bulg
Izvestiya na Instituta po Rastenievudstvo. Bulgarska Akademiya na Naukite — Izv Inst Rast Bulg Akad Nauk
Izvestiya na Instituta po Ribovudstvo i Ribolov (Varna). Bulgarska Akademiya na Naukite — Izv Inst Ribovud Ribolov (Varna) Bulg Akad Nauk
Izvestiya na Instituta po Sravnitelna Patologiya na Zhivotnite — Izv Inst Sravn Patol Zhivotn
Izvestiya na Instituta po Sravnitelna Patologiya na Zhivotnite. Bulgarska Akademiya na Naukite [*Bulgaria*] — Izv Inst Srav Patol Zhivotn Bulg Akad Nauk
Izvestiya na Instituta po Sravnitelna Patologiya na Zhivotnite. Bulgarska Akademiya na Naukite — Izv Inst Sravn Patol Zhivotn Bulg Akad Nauk
Izvestiya na Instituta po Sravnitelna Patologiya na Zhivotnite. Bulgarska Akademiya na Naukite Otdelenie za Biologichni Nauki — Izv Inst Sravn Patol Zhivotn B'lg Akad Nauk Otd Biol Nauki
Izvestiya na Instituta po Sravnitelna Patologiya na Zhivotnite. Bylgarska Akademiya na Naukite — Izv Inst Sravn Patol Zhivotn Bylg
Izvestiya na Instituta po Tekhnicheska Kibernetika — Izv Inst Tekh Kibern
Izvestiya na Instituta po Tekhnicheska Kibernetika. Bulgarska Akademiya na Naukite — Izv Inst Tekh Kibern Bulg Akad Nauk
Izvestiya na Instituta po Tekhnicheska Mekhanika. Bulgarska Akademiya na Naukite — Izv Inst Tekh Mekh Bulg Akad Nauk
Izvestiya na Instituta po Tsarevitsata-Knezha — Izv Inst Tsarevitsata-Knezha
Izvestiya na Instituta po Tyutyuna (Plovdiv). Akademiya na Selskostopanskite Nauki v Bulgariya — Izv Inst Tyutyuna (Plovdiv) Akad Selskostop Nauki Bulg
Izvestiya na Instituta po Vodni Problemi. Bulgarska Akademiya na Naukite — Izv Inst Vodni Probl Bulg Akad Nauk
Izvestiya na Instituta po Vodni Problemi. Bulgarska Akademiya na Naukite. Otdelenie za Tekhnicheskij Nauki — Izv Inst Vodn Probl Bulg Akad Nauk
Izvestiya na Instituta po Vodno Stopanstvo i Stroitelstvo. Bulgarska Akademiya na Naukite — Izv Inst Vodno Stop Stroit Bulg Akad Nauk
Izvestiya na Instituta po Zhivotnovudstvo. Bulgarska Akademiya na Naukite — Izv Inst Zhivotnovud Bulg Akad Nauk
Izvestiya na Instituta po Zhivotnovudstvo (Kostinbrod). Akademiya na Selskostopanskite Nauki v Bulgariya — Izv Inst Zhivotnovud (Kostinbrod) Akad Selskostop Nauki Bulg
Izvestiya na Instituta za Belgarska Literatura — IIBL
Izvestiya na Instituta za Belgarski Ezik — IIBE
Izvestiya na Instituta za Belgarski Ezik — IzvIBE
Izvestiya na Instituta za Gorata. Akademiya na Selskostopanskite Nauki v Bulgariya — Izv Inst Gorata Akad Selskostop Nauki Bulg
Izvestiya na Instituta za Klinichna i Obshchestvena Meditsina. Bulgarska Akademiya na Naukite — Izv Inst Klin Obshchest Med Bulg Akad Nauk
Izvestiya na Instituta za Muzika — IIM
Izvestiya na Instituta za Pochvoznanie i Agrotekhnika. Akademiya na Selskostopanskite Nauki v Bulgariya — Izv Inst Pochvozn Agrotekh Akad Selskostop Nauki Bulg
Izvestiya na Istoriceskoto Druzestvo — IID
Izvestiya na Kamarata na Narodnata Kultura. Seriya Biologiya Zemedelie i Lesovudstvo — Izv Kamarata Nar Kult Ser Biol Zemed Lesovud
Izvestiya na Khidravlicheskata Laboratoriya. Inzhenerno-Stroitelen Institut — Izv Khidravl Lab Inzh Stroit Inst
Izvestiya na Khidravlicheskata Laboratoriya Vissh Inzhenerno-Stroitelen Institut — Izv Khidravl Lab Vissh Inzh Stroit Inst
Izvestiya na Khimicheskiya Institut. Bulgarska Akademiya na Naukite — IKBKA
Izvestiya na Khimicheskiya Institut. Bulgarska Akademiya na Naukite [*Bulgaria*] — Izv Khim Inst Bulg Akad Nauk
Izvestiya na Kompleksniya Selskostopanski Nauchnoizsledvatelski Institut (Karnobat) — Izv Kompleks Selskostop Nauchnoizsled Inst (Karnobat)
Izvestiya na Meditsinskite Institut. Bulgarska Akademiya na Naukite — Izv Med Inst Bulg Akad Nauk
Izvestiya na Mikrobiologicheskiya Institut. Bulgarska Akademiya na Naukite — IMNSA
Izvestiya na Mikrobiologicheskiya Institut. Bulgarska Akademiya na Naukite — Izv Mikrobiol Inst Bulg Akad Nauk
Izvestiya na Mikrobiologicheskiya Institut Sofiya — Izv Mikrobiol Inst Sof
Izvestiya na Nauchnoizsledovatelski Institut po Lozarstvo i Vinarstvo (Pleven) — Izv Nauchnoizsled Inst Lozar Vinar (Pleven)
Izvestiya na Nauchnoizsledovatelski Institut po Ovoshtarstvo. Gara Kostinbrod — Izv Nauchnoizsled Inst Ovoshtarstvo Gara Kostinbrod
Izvestiya na Nauchnoizsledovatelski Institut za Gorata — Izv Nauchnoizsled Inst Gorata
Izvestiya na Nauchnoizsledovatelskiya Geolozhki Institut (Sofia) — Izv Nauchnoizsled Geol Inst (Sofia)
Izvestiya na Nauchnoizsledovatelskiya Institut po Kinematografiya i Radio — Izv Nauchnoizsled Inst Kinematogr Radio
Izvestiya na Nauchnoizsledovatelskiya Institut po Okeanografiya i Ribno Stopanstvo (Varna) — Izv Nachnoizsled Inst Okeanogr Ribno Stop (Varna)
Izvestiya na Nauchnoizsledovatelskiya Institut po Pochvoznanie i Agrotekhnika — Izv Nauchnoizsled Inst Pochvozn Agrotekh
Izvestiya na Nauchnoizsledovatelskiya Institut po Rastenievudstvo — Izv Nauchnoizsled Inst Rastenievud
Izvestiya na Nauchnoizsledovatelskiya Institut po Zhivotnovudstvo. Kostinbrod — Izv Nauchnoizsled Inst Zhivotnovud Kostinbrod
Izvestiya na Nauchnoizsledovatelskiya Institut za Ribno Stopanstvo i Okeanografiya (Varna) — Izv Nauchnoizsled Inst Ribno Stop Okeanogr (Varna)
Izvestiya na Nauchnoizsledovatelskiya Institut za Zashtita na Rasteniyata — Izv Nauchnoizsled Inst Zasht Rast
Izvestiya na Otdelenieto za Biologicheski i Meditsinski Nauki. Bulgarska Akademiya na Naukite — Izv Otd Biol Med Nauki Bulg Akad Nauk
Izvestiya na Otdelenieto za Khimicheski Nauki. Bulgarska Akademiya na Naukite — IOKNA
Izvestiya na Otdelenieto za Khimicheski Nauki. Bulgarska Akademiya na Naukite — Izv Otd Khim Nauki Bulg Akad
Izvestiya na Otdelenieto za Khimicheski Nauki. Bulgarska Akademiya na Naukite — Izv Otd Khim Nauki Bulg Akad Nauk
Izvestiya na Pochveniya Institut. Bulgarska Akademiya na Naukite — Izv Pochv Inst Bulg Akad Nauk
Izvestiya na Sektsiyata po Astronomiya. Bulgarska Akademiya na Naukite — IBASB
Izvestiya na Sektsiyata po Astronomiya. Bulgarska Akademiya na Naukite — Izv Sekts Astron Bulg Akad Nauk
Izvestiya na Tekhnicheskiya Institut. Bulgarska Akademiya na Naukite — Izv Tekh Inst Bulg Akad Nauk
Izvestiya na Tsentralnata Biokhimichna Laboratoriya. Bulgarska Akademiya na Naukite — Izv Tsentr Biokhim Lab Bulg Akad Nauk
Izvestiya na Tsentralnata Khelmintologichna Laboratoriya. Bulgarska Akademiya na Naukite — ITKBA
Izvestiya na Tsentralnata Khelmintologichna Laboratoriya. Bulgarska Akademiya na Naukite — Izv Tsentr Khelmintol Lab B'lg Akad Nauk
Izvestiya na Tsentralnata Laboratoriya po Biokhimiya. Bulgarska Akademiya na Naukite — Izv Tsentr Lab Biokhim Bulg Akad Nauk

Izvestiya na Tsentralnata Laboratoriya po Energetika. Bulgarska Akademiya na Naukite — Izv Tsentr Lab Energ Bulg Akad Nauk
Izvestiya na Tsentralnata Nauchnoizsledovatelska Laboratoriya za Khidravlichni Izsledvaniya — Izv Tsentr Nauchnoizsled Lab Khidravl Izsled
Izvestiya na Tsentralniya Nauchnoizsledovatelski Institut po Lozarstvo i Vinarstro. Pleven — Izv Tsentr Nauchnoizsled Inst Lozar Vinar Pleven
Izvestiya na Tsentralniya Nauchnoizsledovatelski Institut po Nezarazni Bolesti i Zookhigiena — Izv Tsentr Nauchnoizsled Inst Nezarazni Boles Zookhig
Izvestiya na Tsentralniya Nauchnoizsledovatelski Institut po Pochvoznanie i Agrotekhnika — Izv Tsentr Nauchnoizsled Inst Pochvozn Agrotekh
Izvestiya na Tsentralniya Nauchnoizsledovatelski Institut po Rastenievudstvo — Izv Tsentr Nauchnoizsled Inst Rastenievudrotekh
Izvestiya na Tsentralniya Nauchnoizsledovatelski Institut po Ribovudstvo i Ribolov, Varna, Bulgarska Akademiya na Naukite — Izv Tsentr Nauchnoizsled Inst Ribovud Ribolov Varna Bulg Aka
Izvestiya na Tsentralniya Nauchnoizsledovatelski Institut po Tyutyuna. Plovdiv — Izv Tsentr Nauchnoizsled Inst Tyutyuna Plovdiv
Izvestiya na Tsentralniya Nauchnoizsledovatelski Institut po Zhivotnovudstvo "Georgi Dimitrov" — Izv Tsent Nauchnoizsled Inst Zhivotnovud "Georgi Dimitrov"
Izvestiya na Tsentralniya Nauchnoizsledovatelski Institut po Zhivotnovudstvo. Kostinbrod — Izv Tsentr Nauchnoizsled Inst Zhivotnovud Kostinbrod
Izvestiya na Tsentralniya Nauchnoizsledovatelski Institut za Gorata — Izv Tsentr Nauchnoizsled Inst Gorata
Izvestiya na Tsentralniya Nauchnoizsledovatelski Institut za Zashnita na Rasteniyata — Izv Tsent Nauchnoizsled Inst Zasht Rast
Izvestiya na Tsentralniya Nauchnoizsledovatelski Veterinaren Institut po Virusologiya — Izv Tsentr Nauchnoizsled Vet Inst Virusol
Izvestiya na Tsentralniya Veterinaren Institut za Zarazni i Parazitni Bolesti — Izv Tsentr Vet Inst Zarazni Parazit Boles
Izvestiya na Tsentralniya Veterinarniya Nauchnoizsledovatelski Institut za Nezarazni Bolesti i Zookhigiena — Izv Tsentr Vet Nauchnoizsled Inst Nezarazni Boles Zookhig
Izvestiya na Veterinarniya Institut po Virusologiya. Akademiya na Selskostopanskite Nauki v Bulgaria — Izv Vet Inst Virusol Akad Selskostop Nauki Bulg
Izvestiya na Veterinarnokhigienniya Institut za Zhivotinski Produkti. Akademiya na Selskostopanskie Nauki v Bulgaria — Izv Veterinarnokhig Inst Zhivotin Prod Akad Selskostop Nauki
Izvestiya na Visshiya Mashinno-Elektrotekhnicheski Institut Lenin [*Bulgaria*] [*A publication*] — Izv Vissh Mash-Elektrotekh Inst Lenin
Izvestiya na Vmei "Lenin" — Izv Vmei "Lenin"
Izvestiya na Zoologicheskiya Institut s Muzei. Bulgarska Akademiya na Naukite — Izv Zool Inst Muz Bulg Akad Nauk
Izvestiya Natsional'noi Akademii Nauk Respubliki Kazakhstan. Seriya Geologicheskaya — Izv Nats Akad Nauk Resp Kaz Ser Geol
Izvestiya Nauchno-Issledovatel'skogo Geologicheskogo Instituta (Sofia) — Izv Nauchno Issled Geol Inst (Sofia)
Izvestiya Nauchno-Issledovatel'skogo Instituta Gidrotekhniki — Izv Nauchno Issled Inst Gidrotekh
Izvestiya Nauchno-Issledovatel'skogo Instituta Mashinostroeniya i Metalloobrabotki — Izv Nauchno Issled Inst Mashinostr Metalloobrab
Izvestiya Nauchno-Issledovatel'skogo Instituta Nefte- i Uglekhimicheskogo Sinteza pri Irkutskom Universitete — INEUB
Izvestiya Nauchno-Issledovatel'skogo Instituta Nefte- i Uglekhimicheskogo Sinteza pri Irkutskom Universitete — Izv Nauchno-Issled Inst Nefte Uglekhim Sint Irkutsk Univ
Izvestiya Nauchno-Issledovatel'skogo Instituta Ozernogo i Rechnogo Rybnogo Khozyaistva — Izv Nauchno Issled Inst Ozern Rechn Rybn Khoz
Izvestiya Nauchno-Issledovatel'skogo Instituta Postoyannogo Toka — IIPTA
Izvestiya Nauchno-Issledovatel'skogo Instituta Postoyannogo Toka [*Former USSR*] — Izv Nauchno-Issled Inst Postoyan Toka
Izvestiya Nauchno-Issledovatel'skogo Instituta Uglya (Prague) — Izv Nauchno Issled Inst Uglya (Prague)
Izvestiya Nikolaevskoi Glavnoi Astronomicheskoi Observatorii — Izv Nikolaev Gl Astron Obs
Izvestiya Omskogo Otdeleniya Geograficheskogo Obshchestva SSR — Izv Omsk Otd Geogr O-Va SSR
Izvestiya Osetinskogo Nauchno-Issledovatel'skogo Instituta Kraevedeniya — Izv Oset Nauchno Issled Inst Kraeved
Izvestiya Otdeleniya Estestvennykh Nauk. Akademiya Nauk Tadzhikskoi SSR — Izv Otd Estestv Nauk Akad Nauk Tadzh SSR
Izvestiya Permskogo Biologicheskogo Nauchno-Issledovatel'skogo Instituta — Izv Permsk Biol Nauchno-Issled Inst
Izvestiya Petrogradskogo Lesnogo Instituta — Izv Petrograd Lesn Inst
Izvestiya Petrovskoi Sel'skokhozyaistvennoi Akademii — Izv Petrovsk Skh Akad
Izvestiya Petrovskoi Sel'skokhozyaistvennoi Akademii — Izv Petrovskoi Skh Akad
Izvestiya Petrovskoi Zemledel'cheskoi i Lesnoi Akademii — Izv Petrovsk Zemled Lesn Akad
Izvestiya Petrovskoi Zemledel'cheskoi i Lesnoi Akademii — Izv Petrovskoi Zemled Lesn Akad
Izvestiya. Physics of the Solid Earth — Izv Phys Solid Earth
Izvestiya po Khimiya — Izv Khim
Izvestiya Povolzhskogo Lesotekhnicheskogo Instituta — Izv Povolzh Lesotekh Inst
Izvestiya Rossiiskogo Instituta Prikladnoi Khimii — Izv Ross Inst Prikl Khim
Izvestiya Rossiiskoi Akademii Nauk — Izv Ross Akad Nauk
Izvestiya Rossiiskoi Akademii Nauk. Energetika — Izv Ross Akad Nauk Energ
Izvestiya Rossiiskoi Akademii Nauk. Mekhanika Zhidkosti i Gaza — Izv Ross Akad Nauk Mekh Zhidk Gaza
Izvestiya Rossiiskoi Akademii Nauk. Seriya Biologicheskaya — Izv Ross Akad Nauk Ser Biol
Izvestiya Rostovskogo na Donu Nauchno-Issledovatel'skogo Instituta Epidemiologii Mikrobiologii i Gigieny — Izv Rostov Donu Nauchno-Issled Inst Epidemiol Mikrobiol Gig
Izvestiya Sakhalinskogo Otdela Geograficheskogo Obshchestva SSSR — Izv Sakhalin Otd Geogr Ova SSSR
Izvestiya Samarskogo Sel'skokhozyaistvennogo Instituta — Izv Samar Skh Inst
Izvestiya Sankt-Peterburgskago Lesnago Instituta — Izv St Peterb Lesn Inst
Izvestiya Saratovskogo Obshchestva Estestvoispytatelei — Izv Sarat Ova Estestvoispyt
Izvestiya Sektora Fiziko-Khimicheskogo Analiza Institut Obshchei i Neorganicheskoi Khimii Akademiya Nauk SSSR — Izv Sekt Fiz-Khim Anal Inst Obshch Neorg Khim Akad Nauk SSSR
Izvestiya Sektora Fiziko-Khimicheskogo Analiza Institut Obshchei i Neorganicheskoi Khimii Imeni N. S. Kurnakova Akademiya Nauk SSSR — IFKKA
Izvestiya Sektora Platiny i Drugikh Blagorodnykh Metallov Institut Obshchei i Neorganicheskoi Khimii Akademiya Nauk SSSR — IPBKA
Izvestiya Sektora Platiny i Drugikh Blagorodnykh Metallov Institut Obshchei i Neorganicheskoi Khimii Akademiya Nauk SSSR [*Former USSR*] — Izv Sekt Platiny Drugikh Obshch Neorg Khim Akad Nauk SSSR
Izvestiya Sel'skokhozyaistvennoi Akademii Imeni K. A. Timiryazeva — Izv Skh Akad Im K A Timiryazeva
Izvestiya Sel'skokhozyaistvennoi Nauki.Ministerstvo Sel'skogo Khozyaistva Armya nskoi SSR — Izv Sel'-Khoz Nauki Minist Sel' Khoz Armyan SSR
Izvestiya. Sel'skokhozyaistvennye Nauki. Ministerstvo Proizvodstva i Zagotovok Sel'skokhozyaistvennykh Produktov Armyanskoi SSR — Izv Skh Nauki Minist Proizvod Zagotovok Skh Prod Arm SSR
Izvestiya. Sel'skokhozyaistvennye Nauki. Ministerstvo Sel'skogo Khozyaistva Armyanskoi SSR — Iav Skh Nauki Minist Selsk Khoz Arm SSR
Izvestiya Sel'skokhozyaistvennykh Nauk — Izv Sel'khoz Nauk
Izvestiya Sel'skokhozyaistvennykh Nauk — Izv S-Kh Nauk
Izvestiya Seminara po Slavjanske Filologija — IzvSLF
Izvestiya Severo-Kavkazskogo Nauchnogo Tsentra Vysshei Shkoly Seriya Estestvennye Nauki — Izv Sev-Kavk Nauchn Tsentra Vyssh Shk Estestv Nauki
Izvestiya Severo-Kavkazskogo Nauchnogo Tsentra Vysshei Shkoly Seriya Estestvennye Nauki [*Former USSR*] — Izv Sev-Kavk Nauchn Tsentra Vyssh Shk Ser Estestv Nauk
Izvestiya Severo-Kavkazskogo Nauchnogo Tsentra Vysshei Shkoly Seriya Tekhnicheskie Nauki — Izv Severo-Kavkaz Nauchn Tsentra Vyssh Shkoly Ser Tekhn Nauk
Izvestiya Severo-Kavkazskogo Nauchnogo Tsentra Vysshei Shkoly. Tekhnicheskie Nauki — Izv Sev Kavk Nauchn Tsentra Vyssh Shk Tekh Nauki
Izvestiya Severo-Osetinskogo Nauchno-Issledovatel'skogo Instituta — Izv Sev Oset Nauchno Issled Inst
Izvestiya Severo-Osetinskogo Nauchno-Issledovatel'skogo Instituta — IzvSOsNII
Izvestiya Sibirskogo Mekhaniko-Mashinostroitel'nogo Instituta — Izv Sib Mekh-Mashinostroit Inst
Izvestiya Sibirskogo Otdeleniya Akademii Nauk SSSR — Izv Sib Otd Akad Nauk SSSR
Izvestiya Sibirskogo Otdeleniya Akademii Nauk SSSR — Izv Sibir Otd Akad Nauk SSSR
Izvestiya Sibirskogo Otdeleniya Akademii Nauk SSSR Geologiya i Geofizika — Izv Sib Otd Akad Nauk SSSR Geol Geofiz
Izvestiya Sibirskogo Otdeleniya Akademii Nauk SSSR Seriya Biologicheskikh Nauk — Izv Sib Otd Akad Nauk SSSR Ser Biol Nauk
Izvestiya Sibirskogo Otdeleniya Akademii Nauk SSSR Seriya Biologicheskikh Nauk — Izv Sib Otdel Akad Nauk SSSR Ser Biol Nauk
Izvestiya Sibirskogo Otdeleniya Akademii Nauk SSSR Seriya Biologo-Meditsinskikh Nauk — Izv Sib Otd Akad Nauk SSSR Ser Biol-Med Nauk
Izvestiya Sibirskogo Otdeleniya Akademii Nauk SSSR Seriya Biologo-Meditsinskikh Nauk — Izv Sib Otdel Akad Nauk SSSR Ser Biol-Med Nauk
Izvestiya Sibirskogo Otdeleniya Akademii Nauk SSSR Seriya Khimicheskikh Nauk — Izv Sib Otd Akad Nauk SSSR Ser Khim Nauk
Izvestiya Sibirskogo Otdeleniya Akademii Nauk SSSR Seriya Khimicheskikh Nauk — Izv Sibir Otd Akad Nauk SSSR Khim
Izvestiya Sibirskogo Otdeleniya Akademii Nauk SSSR Seriya Khimicheskikh Nauk — Izv Sibir Otd Akad Nauk SSSR Ser Khim Nauk
Izvestiya Sibirskogo Otdeleniya Akademii Nauk SSSR Seriya Obshchestvennykh Nauk — ISOOA
Izvestiya Sibirskogo Otdeleniya Akademii Nauk SSSR Seriya Obshchestvennykh Nauk [*Former USSR*] — Izv Sib Otd Akad Nauk SSSR Ser Obshchestv Nauk
Izvestiya Sibirskogo Otdeleniya Akademii Nauk SSSR Seriya Tekhnicheskikh Nauk [*A publication*] — Izv Sib Otd Akad Nauk SSSR Ser Tekh Nauk
Izvestiya Sibirskogo Otdeleniya Akademii Nauk SSSR Seriya Tekhnicheskikh Nauk [*A publication*] — Izv Sibir Otd Akad Nauk SSSR Ser Tekh Nauk
Izvestiya Sibirskogo Otdeleniya Akademii Nauk SSSR Seriya Tekhnicheskikh Nauk [*A publication*] — Izv Sibir Otd Akad Nauk SSSR Tekh
Izvestiya Sibirskogo Otdeleniya Akademii Nauk SSSR. Sibirskii Biologicheskii Zhurnal — Izv Sib Otd Akad Nauk SSSR Sib Biol Zh
Izvestiya Sibirskogo Otdeleniya Akademii Nauk SSSR. Sibirskii Fiziko-Technicheskii Zhurnal — Izv Sib Otd Akad Nauk SSSR Sib Fiz Tekh Zh
Izvestiya Sibirskogo Otdeleniya Geologicheskogo Komiteta — ISOKD
Izvestiya Sibirskogo Otdeleniya Geologicheskogo Komiteta [*Former USSR*] — Izv Sib Otd Geol Kom
Izvestiya Sibirskogo Tekhnologicheskogo Instituta — Izv Sib Tekhnol Inst
Izvestiya Tadzikskogo Filiala Akademii Nauk — IzvTadzikAN
Izvestiya Tbilisskogo Nauchno-Issledovatel'skogo Instituta Sooruzhenii i Gidroenergetiki — Izv Tbilis Nauchno Issled Inst Sooruzh Gidroenerg
Izvestiya Tekstil'noi Promyshlennosti i Torgovli — Izv Tekst Promsti Torg
Izvestiya Teplotekhnicheskogo Instituta (Moscow) — Izv Teplotekh Inst (Moscow)
Izvestiya Tikhookeanskogo Nauchnogo Instituta Rybnogo Khozyaistva — Izv Tikhookean Nauchn Inst Rybn Khoz

Izvestiya Tikhookeanskogo Nauchno-Issledovatel'skogo Instituta Rybnogo Khozyaistva i Okeanografii — Izv Tikhookean Nauchno-Issled Inst Rybn Khoz Okeanogr
Izvestiya Tikhookeanskoi Nauchno-Promyslovoi Stantsii — Izv Tikhookean Nauchno Promysl Stn
Izvestiya Timiryazevskoi Sel'skokhozyaistvennoi Akademii — Izv Timiryazev Sel'-Khoz Akad
Izvestiya Timiryazevskoi Sel'skokhozyaistvennoi Akademii — Izv Timiryazev S-Kh Akad
Izvestiya Timiryazevskoi Sel'skokhozyaistvennoi Akademii — Izv Timiryazevsk Skh Akad
Izvestiya Tomskogo Gosudarstvennogo Universiteta — Izv Tomsk Gos Univ
Izvestiya Tomskogo Industrial'nogo Instituta — Izv Tomsk Ind Inst
Izvestiya Tomskogo Otdeleniya Russkogo Botanicheskogo Obshchestva — Izv Tomsk Otd Russ Bot Ova
Izvestiya Tomskogo Otdeleniya Vsesoyuznogo Botanicheskogo Obshchestva — Izv Tomsk Otd Vses Bot Ova
Izvestiya Tomskogo Politekhnicheskogo Instituta Imeni S. M. Kirova — Izv Tomsk Politekh Inst
Izvestiya Tomskogo Politekhnicheskogo Instituta Mekhanika i Mashinostroenia — Izv Tomsk Politekh Inst Mekh Mashinostr
Izvestiya Tsentral'nogo Instituta po Razvitiyu Gornoi Promyshlennosti — Izv Tsentr Inst Razvit Gorn Promsti
Izvestiya Tsentral'nogo Nauchno-Issledovatel'skogo Biokhimicheskogo Instituta Pishchevoi i Vkusovoi Promyshlennosti SSSR — Izv Tsentr Nauchno Issled Biokhim Inst Pishch Vkusovoi Proms
Izvestiya Tsentral'nogo Nauchno-Issledovatel'skogo Instituta Kozhevennoi Promyshlennosti — Izv Tsentr Nauchno Issled Inst Kozh Promsti
Izvestiya Turkmenskogo Filiala Akademii Nauk SSR — Izv Turkm Fil Akad Nauk SSR
Izvestiya Turkmenskogo Filiala Akademii Nauk SSSR — Izvestiya Turkm Filiala Akad Nauk SSSR
Izvestiya Ural'skogo Gornogo Instituta v Ekaterinburge — Izv Ural Gorn Inst Ekaterinburge
Izvestiya Ural'skogo Politekhnicheskogo Instituta — Izv Ural Politekh Inst
Izvestiya Uzbekistanskogo Filiala Geograficheskogo Obshchestva SSSR — Izv Uzb Fil Geogr Ova SSSR
Izvestiya Uzbekskogo Geograficheskogo Obshchestva — Izv Uzb Geogr Ova
Izvestiya Vengerskikh Sel'skokhozyaistvennykh Nauchno-Issledovatel'skikh Institutov. B. Zhivotnovodstvo — Izv Veng Skh Nauchno Issled Inst B
Izvestiya Vengerskikh Sel'skokhozyaistvennykh Nauchno-Issledovatel'skikh Institutow A. Rastenievodstvo — Izv Veng S'kh Nauchno-Issled Inst A
Izvestiya Vengerskikh Sel'skokhozyaistvennykh Nauchno-Issledovatel'skikh Institutow C. Sadovodstvo — Izv Veng S kh Nauchno-Issled Inst C
Izvestiya Vengerskogo Gorno-Issledovatel'skogo Instituta — Izv Veng Gorno Issled Inst
Izvestiya VNIIG [*Vsesoiuznyi Nauchno-Issledovatel'ski Institut Gidrotekhniki*] **imeni B.E. Vedeneeva** — Izv VNIIG im BE Vedeneeva
Izvestiya Voronezhskogo Gosudarstvennogo Pedagogicheskogo Instituta — Izv Voronezh Gos Ped Inst
Izvestiya Voronezhskogo Gosudarstvennogo Pedagogicheskogo Instituta — Izv Voronezh Gos Pedagog Inst
Izvestiya Voronezskogo Gosudarstvennego Pedagogiceskogo Instituta — Izvestiya Voronezskogo Gos Ped Inst
Izvestiya Voronezskogo Gosudarstvennogo Pedagogiceskogo Instituta — IVGPI
Izvestiya Voronezskogo Gosudarstvennogo Pedagogiceskogo Instituta — IzvVorPI
Izvestiya Vostochno-Sibirskogo Otdela Geograficheskogo Obshchestva SSSR — Izv Vost Sib Otd Geogr Ova SSSR
Izvestiya Vostochnosibirskogo Sel'skokhozyaistvennogo Instituta — Izv Vostochnosib Skh Inst
Izvestiya Vostochnykh Filialov Akademii Nauk SSSR — Izv Vost Fil Akad Nauk SSSR
Izvestiya Vostochnykh Filialov Akademii Nauk SSSR [*Former USSR*] — Izv Vost Filial Akad Nauk SSSR
Izvestiya Vsesoyuznogo Geograficheskogo Obshchestva — IVGOA
Izvestiya Vsesoyuznogo Geograficheskogo Obshchestva — Izv Vses Geogr Obshch
Izvestiya Vsesoyuznogo Geograficheskogo Obshchestva — Izv Vses Geogr O-Va
Izvestiya Vsesoyuznogo Nauchno-Issledovatel'skogo Instituta Gidrotekhniki [*Former USSR*] — Izv Vses Nauchno-Issled Inst Gidrotekh
Izvestiya Vsesoyuznogo Nauchno-Issledovatel'skogo Instituta Gidrotekhniki imeni B.E. Vedeneeva — Izv Vses Nauchno Issled Inst Gidrotekh im BE Vedeneeva
Izvestiya Vsesoyuznogo Nauchno-Issledovatel'skogo Instituta Ozernogo i Rechnogo Rybnogo Khozyaistva — Izv Vses Nauchno Issled Inst Ozern Rechn Rybn Khoz
Izvestiya Vsesoyuznogo Teplotekhnicheskogo Instituta — Izv Vses Teplotekh Inst
Izvestiya Vuzov Mashinostroenie — IIBDA
Izvestiya Vuzov Mashinostroenie [*Former USSR*] — Izv Vuzov Mashinostr
Izvestiya VUZOV Stroitel'stvo i Arkhitektura — Izv VUZOV Stroit Arkhit
Izvestiya Vysshego Uchebnogo Zavedeniya Agrarnykh Nauk v Moshonmadyarovare (Vengriya) — Izv Vyssh Uchebn Zaved Agrar Nauk Moshonmadyarovare Vengriya
Izvestiya Vysshikh Uchebnykh Zavedenii Aviatsionnaya Tekhnika — IVUAA
Izvestiya Vysshikh Uchebnykh Zavedenii Aviatsionnaya Tekhnika — Izv VUZ Aviats Tekh
Izvestiya Vysshikh Uchebnykh Zavedenii Aviatsionnaya Tekhnika — Izv Vyssh Uchebn Zaved Aviats Tekh
Izvestiya Vysshikh Uchebnykh Zavedenii Chernaya Metallurgiya — IVUMA
Izvestiya Vysshikh Uchebnykh Zavedenii Chernaya Metallurgiya — Izv VUZ Chernaya Metall
Izvestiya Vysshikh Uchebnykh Zavedenii Chernaya Metallurgiya — Izv Vyssh Ucheb Zaved Chern Met
Izvestiya Vysshikh Uchebnykh Zavedenii Chernaya Metallurgiya — Izv Vyssh Uchebn Zaved Chern Metall
Izvestiya Vysshikh Uchebnykh Zavedenii Ehlektromekhanika — Izv Vyssh Uchebn Zaved Ehlektromekh
Izvestiya Vysshikh Uchebnykh Zavedenii Ehnergetika — Izv Vyssh Uchebn Zaved Ehnerg
Izvestiya Vysshikh Uchebnykh Zavedenii Elektromekhanika — Izv VUZ Elektromekh
Izvestiya Vysshikh Uchebnykh Zavedenii Elektromekhanika — Izv Vyssh Ucheb Zaved Elektromekh
Izvestiya Vysshikh Uchebnykh Zavedenii Energetika — IVZEA
Izvestiya Vysshikh Uchebnykh Zavedenii Energetika — Izv VUZ Energ
Izvestiya Vysshikh Uchebnykh Zavedenii Energetika — Izv Vyssh Ucheb Zaved Energ
Izvestiya Vysshikh Uchebnykh Zavedenii Fizika — IVUZ Fiz
Izvestiya Vysshikh Uchebnykh Zavedenii Fizika — Izv VUZ Fiz
Izvestiya Vysshikh Uchebnykh Zavedenii Geodeziya i Aerofotos'emka [*Former USSR*] — Izv Vyssh Uchebn Zaved Geod Aerofotos'emka
Izvestiya Vysshikh Uchebnykh Zavedenii Geologiya i Razvedka — IVUGA
Izvestiya Vysshikh Uchebnykh Zavedenii Geologiya i Razvedka — Izv Vyssh Ucheb Zaved Geol i Razved
Izvestiya Vysshikh Uchebnykh Zavedenii Geologiya i Razvedka — Izv Vyssh Ucheb Zavedenii Geol Razvedka
Izvestiya Vysshikh Uchebnykh Zavedenii Geologiya i Razvedka — Izv Vyssh Uchebn Zaved Geol Razved
Izvestiya Vysshikh Uchebnykh Zavedenii Gornyi Zhurnal — Izv VUZ Gornyi Zh
Izvestiya Vysshikh Uchebnykh Zavedenii Gornyi Zhurnal — Izv Vyssh Ucheb Zaved Gorn Zh
Izvestiya Vysshikh Uchebnykh Zavedenii i Energeticheskikh Ob'edinenii SNG. Energetika — Izv Vyssh Uchebn Zaved Energ Obedin SNG Energ
Izvestiya Vysshikh Uchebnykh Zavedenii Khimiya i Khimicheskaya — Izv Vyssh Ucheb Zaved Khim i Khim
Izvestiya Vysshikh Uchebnykh Zavedenii Khimiya i Khimicheskaya Tekhnologiya — IVUKA
Izvestiya Vysshikh Uchebnykh Zavedenii Khimiya I Khimicheskaya Tekhnologiya — Izv VUZ Kh i Kh Tekh
Izvestiya Vysshikh Uchebnykh Zavedenii Khimiya i Khimicheskaya Tekhnologiya — Izv VUZ Khim i Khim Tekhnol
Izvestiya Vysshikh Uchebnykh Zavedenii Khimiya i Khimicheskaya Tekhnologiya — Izv Vyssh Uchebn Zaved Khim Khim Tekhnol
Izvestiya Vysshikh Uchebnykh Zavedenii Lesnoi Zhurnal — Izv VUZ Lesnoi Zh
Izvestiya Vysshikh Uchebnykh Zavedenii Lesnoi Zhurnal — Izv Vyssh Uchebn Zaved Lesn Zh
Izvestiya Vysshikh Uchebnykh Zavedenii Mashinostroenie — Izv VUZ Mashinostr
Izvestiya Vysshikh Uchebnykh Zavedenii Mashinostroenie — Izv Vyssh Uchebn Zaved Mashinostr
Izvestiya Vysshikh Uchebnykh Zavedenii Matematika — Izv VUZ Mat
Izvestiya Vysshikh Uchebnykh Zavedenii Neft' i Gaz — IVUNA
Izvestiya Vysshikh Uchebnykh Zavedenii Neft' i Gaz — Izv Vyssh Ucheb Zaved Neft i Gaz
Izvestiya Vysshikh Uchebnykh Zavedenii Neft' i Gaz — Izv Vyssh Uchebn Zaved Neft' Gaz
Izvestiya Vysshikh Uchebnykh Zavedenii Pishchevaya Tekhnologiya — IVUPA
Izvestiya Vysshikh Uchebnykh Zavedenii Pishchevaya Tekhnologiya — IVUPA8
Izvestiya Vysshikh Uchebnykh Zavedenii Pishchevaya Tekhnologiya — Izv VUZ Pishch Tekhnol
Izvestiya Vysshikh Uchebnykh Zavedenii Pishchevaya Tekhnologiya — Izv Vyssh Uchebn Zaved Pishch Tekhnol
Izvestiya Vysshikh Uchebnykh Zavedenii Priborostroenie — Izv VUZ Priborostr
Izvestiya Vysshikh Uchebnykh Zavedenii Priborostroenie — Izv Vyssh Uchebn Zaved Priborostr
Izvestiya Vysshikh Uchebnykh Zavedenii. Prikladnaya Nelineinaya Dinamika — Izv Vyssh Uchebn Zaved Prikl Nelinein Dinamika
Izvestiya Vysshikh Uchebnykh Zavedenii Radioelektronika — Izv VUZ Radioelektron
Izvestiya Vysshikh Uchebnykh Zavedenii Radioelektronika — Izv Vyssh Uchebn Zaved Radioelektron
Izvestiya Vysshikh Uchebnykh Zavedenii Radiofizika — Izv VUZ Radiofiz
Izvestiya Vysshikh Uchebnykh Zavedenii Radiotekhnika — Izv Vyssh Uchebn Zaved Radiotekh
Izvestiya Vysshikh Uchebnykh Zavedenii Seriya Pishchevaya Tekhnologiya — Izv Vyssh Ucheb Zaved Ser Pishch Tekhnol
Izvestiya Vysshikh Uchebnykh Zavedenii. Severo-Kavkazskii Region. Estestvennye Nauki — Izv Vyssh Uchebn Zaved Severo Kavkaz Reg Estestv Nauk
Izvestiya Vysshikh Uchebnykh Zavedenii. Stroitel'stvo — Izv Vyssh Uchebn Zaved Stroit
Izvestiya Vysshikh Uchebnykh Zavedenii Stroitel'stvo i Arkhitektura — Izv Vyssh Uchebn Zaved Stroit Arkhit
Izvestiya Vysshikh Uchebnykh Zavedenii Tekhnologiya Legkoi Promyshlennosti — Izv VUZ Tekh Leg Prom
Izvestiya Vysshikh Uchebnykh Zavedenii Tekhnologiya Legkoi Promyshlennosti — Izv VUZ Tekhnol Legkoi Prom-St
Izvestiya Vysshikh Uchebnykh Zavedenii Tekhnologiya Legkoi Promyshlennosti — Izv Vyssh Ucheb Zaved Tekh Legk
Izvestiya Vysshikh Uchebnykh Zavedenii Tekhnologiya Legkoi Promyshlennosti — Izv Vyssh Uchebn Zaved Tekhnol Legk Promsti
Izvestiya Vysshikh Uchebnykh Zavedenii Tekhnologiya Tekstil'noi Promyshlennosti — Izv VUZ Tekhnol Tekstil Prom
Izvestiya Vysshikh Uchebnykh Zavedenii Tekhnologiya Tekstil'noi Promyshlennosti — Izv Vyssh Uchebn Zaved Tekhnol Tekst Promsti

Izvestiya Vysshikh Uchebnykh Zavedenii Tsvetnaya Metallurgiya — Izv VUZ Tsvetn Metall

Izvestiya Vysshikh Uchebnykh Zavedenii Tsvetnaya Metallurgiya — Izv Vyssh Ucheb Zaved Tsvet Met

Izvestiya Vysshikh Uchebnykh Zavedenii Tsvetnaya Metallurgiya — Izv Vyssh Uchebn Zaved Tsvetn Metall

Izvestiya Vysshikh Uchebnykh Zavedenij Fizika — Izv Vyssh Uchebn Zaved Fiz

Izvestiya Vysshikh Uchebnykh Zavedenij Gornyj Zhurnal — Izv Vyssh Uchebn Zaved Gorn Zh

Izvestiya Vysshikh Uchebnykh Zavedenij Radiofizika — Izv Vyssh Uchebn Zaved Radiofiz

Izvestiya Vysshikh Uchebnykh Zavedenij. Tsvetnaya Metallurgiya — Izv Vyssh Uchebn Zaved Tsvetn

Izvestiya Vysshikh Uchebnykh Zavednii — Izv Vyssh Uchebn Zaved

Izvestiya Zabaikal'skogo Filiala Geograficheskogo Obshchestva SSSR [*Former USSR*] — Izv Zabaik Fil Geogr O-Va SSSR

Izvjesca. Institut za Oceanografiju i Ribarstvo u Splitu — Izvjesca Inst Oceanogr Ribar Splitu

J

J. L. B. Smith Institute of Ichthyology. Special Publication — JLB Smith Inst Ichthyol Spec Publ
J. N. Banerjea Memorial Volume [*Calcutta University*] — JNB
J. Paul Getty Museum Journal — Getty Mus
J. Paul Getty Museum. Journal — Getty Mus J
J. Stefan Institute of Physics. Reports — J Stefan Inst Phys Rep
JAAMI. Journal. Association for the Advancement of Medical Instrumentation [*A publication*] — AMIJAH
JAAMI. Journal. Association for the Advancement of Medical Instrumentation — JAAMI J Assoc Adv Med Instrum
Jaarbeericht. Vooraziatisch - Egyptisch Genootschap Ex Oriente Lux — Jaarber Ex Oriente Lux
Jaarbeericht. Vooraziatisch - Egyptisch Genootschap Ex Oriente Lux — Jber EOL
Jaarbericht. Vooraziatische-Egyptisch Genootschap "Ex Oriente Lux" — JbEOL
Jaarbericht. Vooraziatische-Egyptisch Genootschap "Ex Oriente Lux" — JEOL
Jaarbericht. Vooraziatische-Egyptisch Genootschap "Ex Oriente Lux" — JVEG
Jaarblad. Botaniese Vereniging van Suid-Afrika — Jaarbl Bot Ver S-Afr
Jaarboek. Akademie te Amsterdam — Jaarb Ak Amst
Jaarboek der Nederlandse Akademie van Wetenschappen — JNAW
Jaarboek der Roomisch-Katholieke Universiteit te Nijmegen — JRKUN
Jaarboek en Discussies. Voordrachten Werkgenootschap van Katholieke Theologen in Nederland — JWKTN
Jaarboek. Instituut voor Biologisch en Scheikundig Onderzoek van Landbouwgewassen — Jaarb Inst Biol Scheik Onderz LandbGewass
Jaarboek. Karakul Breeders Society of South Africa — Jaarb Karakul Breeders Soc S Afr
Jaarboek. Koninklijke Academie van Wetenschappen (Amsterdam) — JKAWA
Jaarboek. Koninklijke Academie voor Overzeese Wetenschappen (Brussels) — Jaarb K Acad Overzeese Wet (Brussels)
Jaarboek. Koninklijke Museum voor Schone Kunsten Antwerpen — Jb K Mus Schon Kunst Antwerp
Jaarboek. Koninklijke Nederlandsche Academie — JKNA
Jaarboek. Koninklijke Nederlandsche Academie van Wetenschappen — JbKNA
Jaarboek. Koninklijke Vlaamse Academie voor Taal-en Letterkunde — JbKVA
Jaarboek. Koninklijke Vlaamse Academie voor Wetenschappen — JbKVAW
Jaarboek. Koninklijke Vlaamse Academie voor Wetenschappen, Letteren en Schone Kunsten van Belgie — Jaarb K Vlaam Acad Wet Lett Schone Kunsten Belg
Jaarboek. Koninklijke Vlaamse Academie voor Wetenschappen. Letteren en Schone Kunsten van Belgie — JKVA
Jaarboek. Koninklijke Vlaamse Academie voor Wetenschappen, Letteren, en Schone Kunsten van Belgiee — Jaarb Kon Vlaamse Acad Wetensch Belgiee
Jaarboek. Maatschappij der Nederlandsche Letterkunde te Leiden — JbMNL
Jaarboek. Nederlandse Natuurkundige Vereniging [*Netherlands*] — Jaarb Ned Natuurk Ver
Jaarboek. Nederlandse Natuurkundige Vereniging — JNNVA
Jaarboek. Proefstation voor de Boomkwekerij te Boskoop — Jaarb Proefstat Boomkwekerij Boskoop
Jaarboek. Rijksinstituut voor het Onderzoek der Zee — Jaarb Rijksinst Onderz Zee
Jaarboek. Rijksuniversiteit te Utrecht — Jaarb Rijksuniv Utrecht
Jaarboek. Stichting voor Fundamenteel Onderzoek der Materie en Stichting Instituut voor Kernphysisch Onderzoek — Jaarb Sticht Fundam Onderz Mater Sticht Inst Kernphys Onderz
Jaarboek Suid-Afrikaanse Buro vir Rasse-Aangeleenthede — Jaarb Suid Afr Buro Rasse Aangeleenthede
Jaarboek van de Geschieden Oudheidkundige Kring van stad en land van Breda de Oranjeboom — Jb Oranjeboom
Jaarboek van de Koninklijke Akademie van Wetenschappen, Gevestigd te Amsterdam — Jaarb Kon Akad Wetensch Amsterdam
Jaarboek van de Maatschappij der Nederlandsche Letterkunde te Leiden — Jb Mij Nederl Letterkde
Jaarboek van de Natuurwetenschappelijke Studiekring voor Suriname en Curacao — Jaarb Natuurw Studiekring Suriname Curacao
Jaarboek van het Centraal Bureau voor Genealogie — Jb Centr Bureau Geneal
Jaarboek van het Genootschap Amstelodamum — Jb Genootschap Amstelodamum
Jaarboek van het Koninklijk Nederlandsch Genootschap voor Munt-en Penningkunde — J Ned Gen
Jaarboek van het Ministerie van Buitenlandse Zaken — Jaarboek BZ
Jaarboek van het Vlaams Rechtsgenootschap — Jaarb VRG
Jaarboek van het Vlaams Rechtsgenootschap — JVR
Jaarboek van Kankeronderzoek en Kankerbestrijding in Nederland [*Netherlands*] — Jaarb Kankeronderz Kankerbestrijding Ned
Jaarboek van Kankeronderzoek en Kankerbestrijding in Nederland — JKKNA
Jaarboek. Vereeniging Amstelodanum — JVA
Jaarboek. Vereeniging voor Nederlandsche Muziekgeschiedenis — J V N M
Jaarboek. Vereniging voor de Vergelijkende Studie van het Recht van Belgie en Nederland — Jb Belg Ned
Jaarboek. Vereniging voor de Vergelijkende Studie van het Recht van Belgie en Nederland — Jb Ver Vgl St R B Nedl
Jaarboek. Vereniging voor de Vergelijkende Studie van het Recht van Belgie en Nederland — JVVS
Jaarboek voor de Eredienst — JED
Jaarboek. Werkgenootschap van Katholieke Theologen in Nederland [*Hilversum*] [*A publication*] — JbWerkKaTNed
Jaarboekje van de Koninklijke Algemeene Vereeniging von Bloembollencultuur — Jaarb Kon Alg Ver Bloembollencult
Jaarboekje van de Vergelijkende van Directeuren van Hypotheekbanken — Jb H
Jaarboekje van J. A. Alberdingk-Thym — JAT
Jaarboekje van Oud-Utrecht — JOU
Jaarboekje voor Geschiedenis en Oudheidkunde van Leiden en Omstreken — JGOL
Jaarboekje voor Geschiedenis en Oudheidkunde van Leiden en Rijnland — JGOLR
Jaarsverlag van de Vereeniging voor Terpenonderzoek over de Vereenigingsjaren — JVT
Jaarsverlag van de Vereeniging voor Terpenonderzoek over de Vereenigingsjaren Groningen — Jaars Terpen Groningen
Jaarverslag. Institut voor Graan, Meel, en Brood (Wageningen) — Jaarversl Inst Graan Meel Brood (Wageningen)
Jaarverslag. Instituut voor Bodemvruchtbaarheid — Jaarversl Inst Bodemvruchtbaarheid
Jaarverslag. Laboratorium voor Bloembollenonderzoek Lisse — Jaarversl Lab Bloembollenonderz Lisse
Jaarverslag. TNO [*Toegepast Natuurwetenschappelijk Onderzoek*] — Jaarversl TNO
JACC. Journal. American College of Cardiology — JACC J Am Coll Cardiol
JACEP. Journal of the American College of Emergency Physicians — JACEB
Jack London Newsletter — JLN
Jackson Journal of Business — Jack Journl
Jackson Memorial Hospital Bulletin — Jackson Meml Hosp Bull
Jacksonville Monthly — Jacksonville M
Jacob Boehme Society Quarterly — JBSQ
Jacobean Drama Studies — JDS
JACT (Japanese Association of Casting Technology) News — JACT News
Jadavpur Journal of Comparative Literature — Jadav J Comp Lit
Jadavpur Journal of Comparative Literature — JJCL
Jaderna Energie — Jad Energ
Jaderna Energie — JADEA
Jadernaja Fizika — Jadernaja Fiz
Jadranski Zbornik. Prilozi za Povjest Istre, Rijeke i Hrvatskog Primorja — Jad Zborn
Jadranski Zbornik. Prolozi za Povijest Istre, Rijeke, i Hrvatskog Primorja — Jadr Zbor
JAG [*Judge Advocate General, US Air Force*] **Bulletin** — JAG
JAG [*Judge Advocate General, US Navy*] **Journal** — JAG J
Jagd- und Forst-Neuigkeiten — Jagd Forst Neuigk
Jagger Journal — Jagger J
Jagt og Fiskeri — Jgt o Fsk
Jahangirnagar Review Part A. Science — Jahangirnagar Rev Part A Sci
Jahrbuch 1939 der Deutsch-Bulgarischen Gesellschaft e. V. Leipzig — Jb Dt Bulg Ges 1939
Jahrbuch. Akademie der Wissenschaften in Goettingen — Jahrb Akad Wiss Gottingen
Jahrbuch. Akademie der Wissenschaften in Goettingen — JB Goett
Jahrbuch. Akademie der Wissenschaften in Goettingen — JbAWG
Jahrbuch. Akademie der Wissenschaften und der Literatur [*Mainz*] — JbAWL
Jahrbuch. Akademie der Wissenschaften und der Literatur (Mainz) — Jahrb Akad Wiss Lit (Mainz)
Jahrbuch. Akademie der Wissenschaften und der Literatur. Mainz — JAWM
Jahrbuch. Akademie der Wissenschaften und der Literatur (Mainz) — Jb (Mainz)
Jahrbuch. Albertus Universitaet zu Koenigsberg — JAUK
Jahrbuch. Arbeitsgemeinschaft der Rheinischen Geschichtsvereine — JARGV
Jahrbuch. Arbeitsgemeinschaft fuer Fuetterungsberatung — Jahrb Arbeitsgem Fuetterungsberat
Jahrbuch. Arbeitsgemeinschaft fuer Fuetterungsberatung — Jahrb Arbeitsgemein Futterungsberat

Jahrbuch. Barlach-Gesellschaft — JBG
Jahrbuch. Bayerische Akademie der Wissenschaften — Jahrb Bayer Akad Wiss
Jahrbuch. Bayerische Akademie der Wissenschaften — JBAW
Jahrbuch. Bayerische Akademie der Wissenschaften — JbBAW
Jahrbuch. Bayerische Akademie der Wissenschaften (Muenchen) — JB (Muenchen)
Jahrbuch. Berliner Museen — J Berl M
Jahrbuch. Berliner Museen — Jahr Berliner Mus
Jahrbuch. Berliner Museen — Jahrb Ber M
Jahrbuch. Berliner Museen — Jb Berl Mus
Jahrbuch. Berliner Museen — JBM
Jahrbuch. Bernisches Historische Museum — JB Bern Hist Mus
Jahrbuch. Bernisches Historische Museum — JBM
Jahrbuch. Biblische Wissenschaften — JhBW
Jahrbuch. Bodendenkmalpflege in Mecklenburg — Jahrb Bodenden Meck
Jahrbuch. Bodendenkmalpflege in Mecklenburg — JB Meck
Jahrbuch. Bundesanstalt fuer Pflanzenbau und Samenpruefung — Jahrb Bundesanst Pflanzenbau Samenpruf
Jahrbuch. Bundesanstalt fuer Pflanzenbau und Samenpruefung (Wien) — Jahrb Bundesanst Pflanzebau Samenpruef (Wien)
Jahrbuch Chemische Industrie — Jahrb Chem Ind
Jahrbuch. Coburger Landesstiftung — Jahrb Coburg Landesstift
Jahrbuch. Coburger Landesstiftung — Jb Coburg Landesst
Jahrbuch. Coburger Landesstiftung — JCL
Jahrbuch. Dante Gesellschaft — JbDG
Jahrbuch der Absatz- und Verbrauchsforschung — Jb Absatz und Verbrauchsforsch
Jahrbuch der Absatz- und Verbrauchsforschung — MVB
Jahrbuch der Akademie der Wissenschaften. Goettingen — JAWG
Jahrbuch der Akademie der Wissenschaften und der Literatur in Mainz — JAWL
Jahrbuch der Albertus-Universitaet zu Koenigsberg — Jb Albertus Univ Koenigsberg
Jahrbuch der Albertus-Universitat zu Konigsberg — JaA
Jahrbuch der Asiatischen Kunst — JAK
Jahrbuch der Asiatischen Kunst — Jb Asiat Kunst
Jahrbuch der Bayerischen Missionskonferenz — JBMK
Jahrbuch der Berliner Museen — Jb Berliner Mus
Jahrbuch der Berliner Museen — JbBM
Jahrbuch der Biblischen Wissenschaft — JBW
Jahrbuch der Bodendenkmalpflege in Mecklenburg — Bod Denkm Pfl Mecklenb
Jahrbuch der Brennkrafttechnischen Gesellschaft — Jahrb Brennkrafttech Ges
Jahrbuch der Charakterologie — JdCh
Jahrbuch der Chemisch-Technologischen Hochschule Prof. Dr. A. Zlatarov. Burgas — Jahrb Chem Technol Hochsch Prof Dr A Zlatarov Burgas
Jahrbuch der Deutschen Akademie der Wissenschaften — JDAW
Jahrbuch der Deutschen Akademie der Wissenschaften zu Berlin — D Ad W
Jahrbuch der Deutschen Akademie der Wissenschaften zu Berlin — Jahrb Deutsch Akad Wiss Berlin
Jahrbuch der Deutschen Akademie der Wissenschaften zu Berlin — Jb Berlin
Jahrbuch der Deutschen Kakteen-Gesellschaft in der Deutschen Gesellschaft fuer Gartenkultur — Jahrb Deutsch Kakteen Ges
Jahrbuch der Deutschen Mikrologischen Gesellschaft — Jahrb Deutsch Mikrol Ges
Jahrbuch der Deutschen Shakespeare-Gesellschaft — JbSh
Jahrbuch der Deutschen Shakespeare-Gesellschaft — JDSG
Jahrbuch der Dioezese Augsburg — JDA
Jahrbuch der Dissertationen der Philosophisches Fakultaet der Friedrich-Wilhelm Universitaet zu Berlin — Jahrbuch d Diss d Philos Fak Berlin
Jahrbuch der Drahtlosen Telegraphie — Jb Drahtl Telegr
Jahrbuch der Drahtlosen Telegraphie — JdlT
Jahrbuch der Elektrochemie — Jb Elektrochem
Jahrbuch der Entscheidungen der Freiwilligen Gerichtsbarkeit und des Grundbuchwesens — Jahrb FrG
Jahrbuch der Gehe-Stiftung — Jb Gehestiftg
Jahrbuch der Geologischen Bundesanstalt (Austria) — Jahrb Geol Bundesanst Austria
Jahrbuch der Geologischen Landesanstalt — J d g L A
Jahrbuch der Geologischen Landesanstalt (Austria) — Jahrb Geol Landesanst (Austria)
Jahrbuch der Geologischen Reichsanstalt Wien — Jb Geol Reichsanst Wien
Jahrbuch der Geologischen Staatsanstalt — Jahrb Geol Staatsanst
Jahrbuch der Geologischen Staatsanstalt (Austria) — Jahrb Geol Staatsanst Austria
Jahrbuch der Gesellschaft fuer die Geschichte des Protestantismus in Oesterreich — JGGPOe
Jahrbuch der Gesellschaft fuer die Geschichte des Protestantismus in Oesterreich — JGPr Oe
Jahrbuch der Gesellschaft fuer die Geschichte des Protestantismus in Oesterreich. Sonderheft — JGPr Oe S
Jahrbuch der Gesellschaft fuer Lothringische Geschichte und Altertumskunde — Jahrb der Ges fuer Lothring Geschichte
Jahrbuch der Gesellschaft fuer Lothringische Geschichte und Altertumskunde — JGLG
Jahrbuch der Gesellschaft fuer Niedersaechsische Kirchengeschichte — JaG
Jahrbuch der Gesellschaft fuer Niedersaechsische Kirchengeschichte — JGNKG
Jahrbuch der Gesellschaft fuer Niedersaechsische Kirchengeschichte. Beiheft — JGNKG B
Jahrbuch der Gesellschaft Oesterreichischer Volkswirte — Jb Ges Oester Volkswirte
Jahrbuch der Hafenbautechnischen Gesellschaft — Jb Hafenbautechn Ges
Jahrbuch der Hafenbautechnischen Gesellschaft — JHbG
Jahrbuch der Hamburger Kunstsammlungen — JHK
Jahrbuch der Hamburger Wissenschaftlichen Anstalten — JHWA
Jahrbuch der Hessischen Kirchengeschichtliche Vereinigung — JaHK
Jahrbuch der Hessischen Kirchengeschichtlichen Vereinigung — JHKGV
Jahrbuch der Historischen Forschung in der Bundesrepublik Deutschland — Jahrb Hist Forsch Bundesrepub Deut
Jahrbuch der Hochschule fuer Chemische Technologie. Burgas, Bulgaria — Jahrb Hochsch Chem Technol Burgas Bulg
Jahrbuch der Imkers — Jb Imkers
Jahrbuch der Internationalen Vereinigung fuer Gewerblichen Rechtsschutz — IVGewRSchutz
Jahrbuch der Internationalen Vereinigung fuer Gewerblichen Rechtsschutz — Jb Intern Vereing Gewerbl Rschutz
Jahrbuch der Internationalen Vereinigung fuer Gewerblichen Rechtsschutz — JV Gew R Schutz
Jahrbuch der K. K. Geologischen Reichsanstalt (Austria) — Jahrb KK Geol Reichsanst Austria
Jahrbuch der Kirchengeschichtlichen Vereinigung in Hessen und Nassau — JKGVH
Jahrbuch der Koeniglich Preussischen Kunstsammlungen — Jb Kgl Preuss Kunstsamml
Jahrbuch der Koeniglich Saechsischen Akademie fuer Forst- und Landwirte zu Tharandt — Jahrb Koenigl Saechs Akad Forst Landwirte Tharandt
Jahrbuch der Kunsthistorischen Sammlung in Wien. Beilage — JKSWB
Jahrbuch der Kunsthistorischen Sammlungen [*Vienna*] — Jahrb Kunsth Samml
Jahrbuch der Liturgiewissenschaft — Jb Liturgwiss
Jahrbuch der Maenner von Morgenstern, Heimatbund and Elb- und Wesermuendung — JMM
Jahrbuch der Max-Planck-Gesellschaft zur Foerderung der Wissenschaften — Jahrb Max Planck Ges Foerd Wiss
Jahrbuch der Musik Bibliothek Peters — Jb P
Jahrbuch der Musikbibliothek Peters — Jb M P
Jahrbuch der Musikbibliothek Peters — Jb Musikbibl Peters
Jahrbuch der Musikwelt — JDM
Jahrbuch der Neuen Freien Presse — NFP Jb
Jahrbuch der Neuesten und Wichtigsten Erfindungen und Entdeckungen — Jahrb Neuesten Wichtigsten Erfind Entdeck
Jahrbuch der Oesterreichischen Byzantinischen Gesellschaft — Jb Oesterr Byzant Ges
Jahrbuch der Oesterreichischen Byzantinistik — Jahrb Oesterr Byzantinistik
Jahrbuch der Oesterreichischen Byzantinistik — Jahrb Oesterreich Byzantinistik
Jahrbuch der Oesterreichischen Byzantinistik — Jb Oe Byz
Jahrbuch der Oesterreichischen Byzantinistik — JOEB
Jahrbuch der Oesterreichischen Byzantinistik — JOEByz
Jahrbuch der Oesterreichischen Byzantinistik Gesellschaft — Jahrb Oesterreich Byzant Gesell
Jahrbuch der Oesterreichischen Byzantinistik Gesellschaft — JbOeBG
Jahrbuch der Oesterreichischen Byzantinistik Gesellschaft — JOB
Jahrbuch der Oesterreichischen Byzantinistik Gesellschaft — JOEBG
Jahrbuch der Oesterreichischen Leo-Gesellschaft — JOeLG
Jahrbuch der Organischen Chemie — Jahrb Org Chem
Jahrbuch der Ostasiatischen Kunst — Jb Ostas Kunst
Jahrbuch der Ostasiatischen Kunst — JOK
Jahrbuch der Philosophischen Fakultaet. 2. Universitaet Bern — Jahrb Philos Fak 2 Univ Bern
Jahrbuch der Philosophischen Fakultaet 2. Zweite der Universitaet Bern — Jahrb Philos Fak 2 Zweite Univ Bern
Jahrbuch der Philosophischen Fakultaet Bonn — JPFB
Jahrbuch der Philosophischen Fakultaet. Universitaet zu Goettingen — JFG
Jahrbuch der Philosophischen Fakultaet zu Leipzig — Jahrbuch d Philos Fak Leipzig
Jahrbuch der Philosophischen Gesellschaft an der Universitaet Wien — J Ph GUW
Jahrbuch der Preussischen Akademie der Wissenschaften — JPAW
Jahrbuch der Preussischen Kunstsammlung — Jb Pr Ks
Jahrbuch der Preussischen Kunstsammlung — JPK
Jahrbuch der Preussischen Kunstsammlungen — JPrK
Jahrbuch der Radioaktivitaet und Elektronik — Jahrb Radioakt Elektron
Jahrbuch der Reichsstelle fuer Bodenforschung (Germany) — Jahrb Reichsstelle Bodenforsch (Ger)
Jahrbuch der Reisen und Neuesten Statistik — Jahrb Reisen Neuesten Statist
Jahrbuch der Rheinischen Denkmalpflege — JRD
Jahrbuch der Rheinischen Denkmalpflege — JRDP
Jahrbuch der Saechsischen Akademie der Wissenschaften — JSAW
Jahrbuch der Saechsischen Missionskonferenz — JSMK
Jahrbuch der Schiffbautechnischen Gesellschaft — Jb Schiffbautechn Ges
Jahrbuch der Schlesischen Friedrich-Wilhelms-Universitaet zu Breslau — Jahrb Schlesischen Friedrich Wilhelms Univ
Jahrbuch der Schlesischen Friedrich-Wilhelms-Universitaet zu Breslau — Jb Schles Univ Breslau
Jahrbuch der Schlesischen Friedrich-Wilhelms-Universitaet zu Breslau. Beiheft — JSFWUB
Jahrbuch der Schule der Weisheit — Jb Schule Weisht
Jahrbuch der Schweizerischen Gesellschaft fuer Urgeschichte — Jahrb Schweiz Ges Urgesch
Jahrbuch der Schweizerischen Gesellschaft fuer Urgeschichte — Jahrb Schweiz Gesell Urgesch
Jahrbuch der Schweizerischen Gesellschaft fuer Urgeschichte — Jahresb Schweiz Urgesch
Jahrbuch der Schweizerischen Gesellschaft fuer Urgeschichte — Jahresber Schweiz Ges Urgesch
Jahrbuch der Schweizerischen Gesellschaft fuer Urgeschichte — Jb Schw Ges Urgesch
Jahrbuch der Schweizerischen Gesellschaft fuer Urgeschichte — Jb SGU
Jahrbuch der Schweizerischen Naturforschenden Gesellschaft. Wissenschaftlicher Teil — Jahrb Schweiz Naturforsch Ges Wiss Teil
Jahrbuch der Schweizerischen Philosophischen Gesellschaft — JSPG

Jahrbuch der Staatlichen Akademie fuer Kirchen- und Schulmusik — JSAKM
Jahrbuch der Staatlichen Kunstsammlungen (Dresden) — JKD
Jahrbuch der Staatlichen Kunstsammlungen in Baden-Wuerttemberg — Jahrb d Staatl Kunstsammlungen Bad Wuertt
Jahrbuch der Staatlichen Kunstsammlungen in Baden-Wuerttemberg — JKBW
Jahrbuch der Stadt Linz — JbSL
Jahrbuch der Stiftung Preussischer Kulturbesitz — Jb Stift Preuss Kul Bes
Jahrbuch der Studiengesellschaft zur Foerderung der Kernenergieverwertung in Schiffbau und Schiffahrt e. V — Jahrb Studienges Foerd Kernenergieverwert Schiffbau Schiffahr
Jahrbuch der Synodalkommission und des Vereins fuer Ostpreussische Kirchengeschichte — JSOPK
Jahrbuch der Technik — JT
Jahrbuch der Theologischen Schule Bethel — J Th SB
Jahrbuch der Vereinigung Freunde der Universitaet Mainz — Jahrb Ver Freunde Univ Mainz
Jahrbuch der Vereins fuer Schlesische Kirchengeschichte — JVSKG
Jahrbuch der Weltpolitik — Jb Weltpolit
Jahrbuch der Weltpolitik. Band 1. Jahrbuch fuer Politik und Auslandskunde — Jb Politik Auslandskde
Jahrbuch der Wirtschaft Osteuropas — Jb Wirtsch Osteuropas
Jahrbuch der Wissenschaftlichen Gesellschaft fuer Luftfahrt — JWGL
Jahrbuch der Wissenschaftlichen und Praktischen Tierzucht — JWPTZ
Jahrbuch der Wittheit zu Bremen — JWB
Jahrbuch der Zeit- und Kulturgeschichte — JZKg
Jahrbuch der Zentralkommission fuer Erhaltung des Deutschtums — Jb Ztrkomm Erhaltg Dttums
Jahrbuch des Akademischen Missionsbundes der Universitaet Freiburg — JAMBF
Jahrbuch des Baltischen Deutschtums — Jb Balt Deutschtum
Jahrbuch des Bernischen Historischen Museums — Jahrb Hist Mus Bern
Jahrbuch des Bernischen Historischen Museums — Jb Bernischen Hist Mus
Jahrbuch des Bernischen Historischen Museums — Jb BHM
Jahrbuch des Caritasverbandes — JCV
Jahrbuch des Deutschen Archaeologischen Instituts [*Berlin*] — Arch Jahrb
Jahrbuch des Deutschen Archaeologischen Instituts [*Berlin*] — DAIJ
Jahrbuch des Deutschen Archaeologischen Instituts [*Berlin*] — Deutsch Archaeol Ins Jahrb
Jahrbuch des Deutschen Archaeologischen Instituts [*Berlin*] — Jahrb DAI
Jahrbuch des Deutschen Archaeologischen Instituts [*Berlin*] — Jahrbd Arch Inst
Jahrbuch des Deutschen Archaeologischen Instituts [*Berlin*] — Jahrbuch Deut Arch Inst
Jahrbuch des Deutschen Archaeologischen Instituts [*Berlin*] — JAI
Jahrbuch des Deutschen Archaeologischen Instituts [*Berlin*] — Jb Arch I
Jahrbuch des Deutschen Archaeologischen Instituts — Jb Dt Archaeol Inst
Jahrbuch des Deutschen Archaeologischen Instituts [*Berlin*] — JD Arch Inst
Jahrbuch des Deutschen Archaeologischen Instituts. Ergaenzungsheft — JDAIE
Jahrbuch des Deutschen Saengerbundes — Jb Deutschen Saengerbundes
Jahrbuch des Eisenbahnwesens [*Germany*] — Jahrb Eisenbahnwes
Jahrbuch des Emslaendischen Heimatvereins [*Meppen*] — JEHV
Jahrbuch des Evangelischen Bundes — JEB
Jahrbuch des Evangelischen Vereins fuer Westfaelische Kirchengeschichte — JEVWKG
Jahrbuch des Freien Deutschen Hochstifts — Jahrb Freien Deut Hochstifts
Jahrbuch des Historischen Vereins des Kantons Glarus — JHVG
Jahrbuch des Historischen Vereins Dillingen — Jahrb Hist Ver Dilling
Jahrbuch des Historischen Vereins Dillingen — Jahresber Hist Ver Dillingen
Jahrbuch des Historischen Vereins Dillingen — JHVDill
Jahrbuch des Historischen Vereins fuer das Fuerstentum Liechtenstein — Jahrb Hist Ver Liechten
Jahrbuch des Historischen Vereins fuer das Fuerstentum Liechtenstein — Jb HVFL
Jahrbuch des Historischen Vereins fuer das Fuerstentum Liechtenstein — JHVL
Jahrbuch des Historischen Vereins fuer des Fuerstentum Liechtenstein — Jb Liechtenstein
Jahrbuch des Historischen Vereins fuer Mittelfranken — JHVM
Jahrbuch des Historischen Vereins fuer Wuerttembergisch Franken — JHVF
Jahrbuch des Historischen Vereins fuer Wuerttembergisch Franken — KJ
Jahrbuch des Instituts fuer Brennstoffe und Waermetechnik — Jahrb Inst Brennst Waermetech
Jahrbuch des Instituts fuer Christliche Sozialwissenschaften der Westfaelischen Wilhelms-Universitaet — JICSW
Jahrbuch des Instituts fuer Deutsche Geschichte — Jahrb Inst Deut Gesch
Jahrbuch des Instituts fuer Deutsche Ostarbeit (Kraukau) — Jb Inst Dt Ostarbeit Krakau
Jahrbuch des Instituts fuer Grenz- und Auslandsstudien — Jb Inst Grenz U Auslandsstud
Jahrbuch des Kaiserlichen Archaeologischen Instituts — JAI
Jahrbuch des Kaufmannsgerichts Berlin — Berl KfmG J
Jahrbuch des Koelner Geschichtsvereins — Jb Koeln Geschver
Jahrbuch des Marburger Universitaetsbundes — JMUB
Jahrbuch des Martin-Luther-Bundes — JMLB
Jahrbuch des Musealvereines Wels — Jb Wels
Jahrbuch des Musealvereins Wels — JMW
Jahrbuch des Museums fuer Voelkerkunde zu Leipzig — Jb Mus Voelkerkunde zu Leipzig
Jahrbuch des Museums fuer Voelkerkunde zu Leipzig — Jb Museum Voelkerkde Leipzig
Jahrbuch des Museums fuer Voelkerkunde zu Leipzig — JMVK
Jahrbuch des Nordfriesischen Instituts — JNFI
Jahrbuch des Oberoesterreichischen Musealvereins — Jahrb Oberoesterr Musealvereins
Jahrbuch des Oberoesterreichischen Musealvereins — Jahresber Oberoesterr Musealver
Jahrbuch des Oberoesterreichischen Musealvereins — Jb OOe MV
Jahrbuch des Oberoesterreichischen Musealvereins — JOOEM
Jahrbuch des Oeffentlichen Rechts — Jb Oeffentl R
Jahrbuch des Oeffentlichen Rechts — JOeffR
Jahrbuch des Oeffentlichen Rechts der Gegenwart — Jb Oeff Recht
Jahrbuch des Oeffentlichen Rechts der Gegenwart — Jb Oeff Rechts
Jahrbuch des Oesterreichischen Volksliedwerkes — JOV
Jahrbuch des Osteuropa-Instituts zu Breslau — Jb Osteur Inst Breslau
Jahrbuch des Reichsamts fuer Bodenforschung — Jahrb Reichsamts Bodenf
Jahrbuch des Reichsamts fuer Bodenforschung — Jahrb Reichsamts Bodenforsch
Jahrbuch des Roemisch-Germanischen Zentral Museums Mainz — Jb RGZ
Jahrbuch des Roemisch-Germanischen Zentral Museums Mainz — JRGZM
Jahrbuch des Siebenbuergischen Karpathen-Vereins — Jahrb Siebenbuerg Karpathen Vereins
Jahrbuch des Staedtischen Museums fuer Voelkerkunde [*Leipzig*] — Jb Staedt Mus Voelkerkde
Jahrbuch des Staedtischen Museums fuer Voelkerkunde (Leipzig) — JMVL
Jahrbuch des Staedtischen Museums fuer Voelkerkunde zu Leipzig — Jb Staedt Mus Volk Lpz
Jahrbuch des Staedtischen Museums fuer Voelkerkunde zu Leipzig — JSMVK
Jahrbuch des Stiftes Klosterneuburg — JSK
Jahrbuch des Ungarischen Forschungsinstituts fuer Fleischwirtschaft — Jahrb Ung Forschungsinst Fleischwirtsch
Jahrbuch des Ungarischen Karpathen-Vereines — Jahrb Ung Karpathen Vereines
Jahrbuch des Verbandes der Vereine Katholischer Akademiker — JVVKA
Jahrbuch des Vereins fuer Augsburger Bistumgeschichte — JVABG
Jahrbuch des Vereins fuer Christliche Erziehungswissenschaft — JVCEW
Jahrbuch des Vereins fuer die Evangelische Kirchengeschichte Westfalens — JVEKGW
Jahrbuch des Vereins fuer die Evangelische Kirchengeschichte Westfalens — JVevKW
Jahrbuch des Vereins fuer Evangelische Kirchengeschichte der Grafschaft Mark — JVEKGM
Jahrbuch des Vereins fuer Geschichte der Stadt Wien — Jahrb Ver Gesch Stadt Wien
Jahrbuch des Vereins fuer Geschichte der Stadt Wien — Jb Ver Gesch Wein
Jahrbuch des Vereins fuer Geschichte der Stadt Wien — Jb VGSW
Jahrbuch des Vereins fuer Geschichte der Stadt Wien — JVGW
Jahrbuch des Vereins fuer Niederdeutsche Sprachforschung — Jb V f Niederd Sprachf
Jahrbuch des Vereins fuer Niederdeutsche Sprachforschung — Jb Ver Niederdt Sprachforsch
Jahrbuch des Vereins fuer Niederdeutsche Sprachforschung — Niederdt Jb
Jahrbuch des Vereins fuer Wissenschaftliche Paedagogik — JVWP
Jahrbuch des Vereins zum Schutz der Bergwelt — Jahrb Ver Schutz Bergwelt
Jahrbuch des Vereins zum Schutze der Alpenpflanzen — Jahrb Vereins Schutze Alpenpfl
Jahrbuch des Vereins zum Schutze der Alpenpflanzen und Tiere — Jahrb Ver Schutze Alpenpflanz Tiere
Jahrbuch des Vereins zum Schutze der Alpenpflanzen und -tiere — Jahrb Vereins Schutze Alpenpfl Alpentiere
Jahrbuch des Vorarlberger Landesmuseumsvereins — Jb Vorarlberg
Jahrbuch des Wissenschaftlichen Forschungs-, Proektierungs-, und Konstruktionsinstitut fuer Ne-Metallurgie (Plovdiv) — Jahrb Wiss Forsch Proekt Konstruktionsinst Ne Metall Plovdiv
Jahrbuch des Wissenschaftlichen Forschungs- und Projektierungsinstituts fuer Erzbergbau und Aufbereitung — Jahrb Wiss Forsch Projektierungsinst Erzbergbau Aufbereit
Jahrbuch des Wissenschaftlichen Forschungsinstitut fuer Chemische Industrie. (Sofia) — Jahrb Wiss Forschungsinst Chem Ind Sofia
Jahrbuch des Wissenschaftlichen Forschungsinstituts fuer Bergbau. Stara Zagora, Bulgaria — Jahrb Wiss Forschungsinst Bergbau Stara Zagora Bulg
Jahrbuch. Deutsche Akademie der Landwirtschaftswissenschaften (Berlin) — Jahrb Deut Akad Landwirt Wiss (Berlin)
Jahrbuch. Deutsche Akademie der Wissenschaften zu Berlin — JbDAW
Jahrbuch. Deutsche Akademie fuer Sprache und Dichtung in Darmstadt — JDASD
Jahrbuch. Deutsche Gesellschaft fuer Chronometrie — Jahrb Dtsch Ges Chronom
Jahrbuch. Deutsche Schiller-Gesellschaft — JDSG
Jahrbuch. Deutsche Shakespeare-Gesellschaft — JDSh
Jahrbuch. Deutsche Shakespeare-Gesellschaft Ost — SJO
Jahrbuch Deutscher Bibliophilen — JDB
Jahrbuch. Deutsches Archaeologische Institut — Jahr Deutsch Archaeol Inst
Jahrbuch. Deutsches Archaeologische Institut [*Berlin*] — JbDAI
Jahrbuch. Deutsches Archaeologische Institut — JDAI
Jahrbuch. Deutsches Archaeologische Institut — JdI
Jahrbuch. Deutsches Archaeologische Institut. Archaeologischer Anzeiger [*Berlin*] — JbDAI ArAnz
Jahrbuch. Deutsches Archaeologische Institut. Ergaenzungsheft — JDI-EH
Jahrbuch. Diplomatische Akademie (Wien) — Jb Diplom Akad (Wien)
Jahrbuch. Droste-Gesellschaft — JDG
Jahrbuch Evangelischer Mission — J Ev Miss
Jahrbuch. Evangelischer Verein fuer Westfaelische Kirchengeschichte — JEVWK
Jahrbuch. Freies Deutsche Hochstift — JFDH
Jahrbuch fuer Aesthetik und Allgemeine Kunstwissenschaft — JAAK
Jahrbuch fuer Aesthetik und Allgemeine Kunstwissenschaft — JAe
Jahrbuch fuer Aesthetik und Allgemeine Kunstwissenschaft — JAeAK
Jahrbuch fuer Aesthetik und Allgemeine Kunstwissenschaft — JfAaK
Jahrbuch fuer Altbayerische Kirchengeschichte — JABKG

Jahrbuch fuer Altbayerische Kirchengeschichte — Jb Altbayer Kirchengesch
Jahrbuch fuer Altertumskunde [*Vienna*] — Jahrb Altkde
Jahrbuch fuer Altertumskunde [*Vienna*] — JAK
Jahrbuch fuer Altertumskunde [*Vienna*] — Jb Alt Kde
Jahrbuch fuer Altertumskunde — Jb Altertskde Wien
Jahrbuch fuer Amerikastudien — J Am St
Jahrbuch fuer Amerikastudien — JA
Jahrbuch fuer Amerikastudien — JahAs
Jahrbuch fuer Amerikastudien — Jahrb Amerikastud
Jahrbuch fuer Amerikastudien — JAS
Jahrbuch fuer Amerikastudien — Jb AS
Jahrbuch fuer Antike und Christentum — JAC
Jahrbuch fuer Antike und Christentum — JACh
Jahrbuch fuer Antike und Christentum — JbAC
Jahrbuch fuer Antike und Christentum — JbAChr
Jahrbuch fuer Antike und Christentum. Ergaenzungsband — JACE
Jahrbuch fuer Auswaertige Politik — Jb Ausw Politik
Jahrbuch fuer Bergbau Energie Mineraloel und Chemie — Jahrb Bergbau Energ Mineraloel Chem
Jahrbuch fuer Berlin-Brandenburgische Kirchengeschichte — JBBKG
Jahrbuch fuer Brandenburgische Kirchengeschichte — J Br KG
Jahrbuch fuer Brandenburgische Kirchengeschichte — Jb Brandbg Kirchgesch
Jahrbuch fuer Brandenburgische Kirchengeschichte — JBKG
Jahrbuch fuer Brandenburgische Landesgeschichte — Jahrb Brandenburg Landesgesch
Jahrbuch fuer Brandenburgische Landesgeschichte — JBL
Jahrbuch fuer Brandenburgische Landesgeschichte — JBLG
Jahrbuch fuer Caritaswissenschaft und Caritasarbeit — JCW
Jahrbuch fuer Christliche Kunst — JCK
Jahrbuch fuer Christliche Sozialwissenschaften der Westfaelischen Wilhelms-Universitaet Muenster — JCSW
Jahrbuch fuer das Bistum (Mainz) — JBM
Jahrbuch fuer das Bistum Mainz — JBMz
Jahrbuch fuer das Oldenburger Muensterland — Jb Oldenburger Muensterland
Jahrbuch fuer den Internationalen Rechtsverkehr — JbIR
Jahrbuch fuer Deutsche Kirchengeschichte — JDKG
Jahrbuch fuer die Geschichte der Juden — JGJ
Jahrbuch fuer die Geschichte der Juden und des Judentums — JGJJ
Jahrbuch fuer die Geschichte des Herzogtums Oldenburg — JGO
Jahrbuch fuer die Geschichte Mittel- und Ostdeutschlands — Jahrb Gesch Mittel Ostdeut
Jahrbuch fuer die Geschichte Mittel- und Ostdeutschlands — Jahrb Gesch Mittel Ostdtschl
Jahrbuch fuer die Geschichte Mittel- und Ostdeutschlands — Jb Gesch Mittel U Ostdtl
Jahrbuch fuer die Geschichte Mittel- und Ostdeutschlands — JbG
Jahrbuch fuer die Geschichte Mittel- und Ostdeutschlands — JGMOD
Jahrbuch fuer die Geschichte Mittel- und Ostdeutschlands. Band 1. Jahrbuch fuer die Geschichte des Deutschen Ostens — Jb Gesch des Deutschen Ostens
Jahrbuch fuer die Geschichte Osteuropas [*Wiesbaden*] — Jb G Ost
Jahrbuch fuer die Geschichte von Staat, Wirtschaft, und Gesellschaft Lateinamerikas — JGSLA
Jahrbuch fuer die Gewaesserkunde Norddeutschlands — Jb Gewaesserkde Norddtld
Jahrbuch fuer Erziehungswissenschaft und Jugendkunde — Jb Erziehgswiss Jugendkde
Jahrbuch fuer Erziehungswissenschaft und Jugendkunde — JEJ
Jahrbuch fuer Fraenkische Landesforschung — Jahrb Fraenk Landesforsch
Jahrbuch fuer Fraenkische Landesforschung — JbFL
Jahrbuch fuer Fraenkische Landesforschung — JFL
Jahrbuch fuer Fraenkische Landesforschung — JFLF
Jahrbuch fuer Friedens- und Konfliktforschung — Jb Friedens- u Konfliktforsch
Jahrbuch fuer Geschichte der Deutsch-Slawischen Beziehungen und Geschichte Ost- und Mitteleuropas — Jb Gesch Ost U Mitteleur
Jahrbuch fuer Geschichte der Socialistischen Laender Europas — Jahrb Gesch Soz Laender Eur
Jahrbuch fuer Geschichte der Sozialistischen Lander Europas — Jb Gesch Sozial Land Europas
Jahrbuch fuer Geschichte der UdSSR und der Volksdemokratischen Laender Europas — Jb Gesch UdSSR
Jahrbuch fuer Geschichte des Deutschen Ostens — JGDO
Jahrbuch fuer Geschichte Osteuropas — JbGO
Jahrbuch fuer Geschichte und Kultur Kunst des Mittelrheins und Seiner Nachbargebiete — JGKMR
Jahrbuch fuer Geschichte und Kunst des Mittelrheins und Seiner Nachbargebiete — Jahrb Gesch & Kunst Mittelrheins & Nachbargeb
Jahrbuch fuer Geschichte und Kunst des Mittelrheins und Seiner Nachbargebiete — JGKM
Jahrbuch fuer Geschichte von Staat, Wirtschaft, und Gesellschaft Lateinamerikas — JGSWGL
Jahrbuch fuer Gesetzgebung, Verwaltung und Rechtspflege des Deutschen Reichs — Jb Gesetzg Verw
Jahrbuch fuer Internationale Germanistik — JIG
Jahrbuch fuer Internationales Recht — Jb Int Recht
Jahrbuch fuer Internationales und Auslaendisches Oeffentliches Recht — J f IR
Jahrbuch fuer Juedische Geschichte und Literatur — JGL
Jahrbuch fuer Juedische Geschichte und Literatur [*Berlin*] — JJGL
Jahrbuch fuer Juedische Volkskunde — JJV
Jahrbuch fuer Juedische Volkskunde — JJVK
Jahrbuch fuer Junge Kunst — Jb Junge Kunst
Jahrbuch fuer Kinderheilkunde und Physische Erziehung — Jahrb Kinderh
Jahrbuch fuer Kinderheilkunde und Physische Erziehung — Jahrb Kinderheilkd Phys Erzieh
Jahrbuch fuer Kleinasiatische Forschung — Jb Kl F
Jahrbuch fuer Kleinasiatische Forschung — JbKAF
Jahrbuch fuer Kleinasiatische Forschung — JKF
Jahrbuch fuer Kleinasiatische Forschung. Internationale Orientalistische Zeitschrift — JKAF
Jahrbuch fuer Kunstsammler — JfKs
Jahrbuch fuer Kunstwissenschaft — Jb Kunstwiss
Jahrbuch fuer Kunstwissenschaft [*Leipzig*] — JbKW
Jahrbuch fuer Kunstwissenschaft — JKW
Jahrbuch fuer Landeskunde von Niederdonau — Jahrbuch Niederdonau
Jahrbuch fuer Landeskunde von Niederoesterreich — Jb LKNOe
Jahrbuch fuer Landeskunde von Niederoesterreich — JbLN
Jahrbuch fuer Landeskunde von Niederoesterreich — JbNo
Jahrbuch fuer Landeskunde von Niederoesterreich — JLKNO
Jahrbuch fuer Landeskunde von Niederoesterreich — JLN
Jahrbuch fuer Landeskunde von Nieder-Oesterreich — JLN Oe
Jahrbuch fuer Litergiewissenschaft — JbLW
Jahrbuch fuer Litergiewissenschaft — JfLW
Jahrbuch fuer Liturgiewissenschaft — J Li W
Jahrbuch fuer Liturgiewissenschaft — JLW
Jahrbuch fuer Liturgik und Hymnologie — Jahrb Liturg & Hymnol
Jahrbuch fuer Liturgik und Hymnologie — Jb Liturgik Hymnologie
Jahrbuch fuer Liturgik und Hymnologie [*Kassel*] — JbLitHymn
Jahrbuch fuer Liturgik und Hymnologie — JLH
Jahrbuch fuer Mikroskopiker — Jahrb Mikroskop
Jahrbuch fuer Mineralogie, Geognosie, Geologie, und Petrefaktenkunde — Jb Miner
Jahrbuch fuer Mineralogie und Geologie — J f MG
Jahrbuch fuer Mission [*Nurnberg*] — Jb Miss
Jahrbuch fuer Morphologie und Mikroskopische Anatomie. Abteilung 2 — Jahrb Morphol Mikrosk Anat Abt 2
Jahrbuch fuer Musikalische Volks- und Voelkerkunde — Jb Fuer Musikalische Volks und Voelkerkunde
Jahrbuch fuer Musikalische Volks- und Voelkerkunde — Jb M Volks Volkerkunde
Jahrbuch fuer Musikalische Volks- und Voelkerkunde — Jb Musik Volks-u Voelkerk
Jahrbuch fuer Mystische Theologie — J My Th
Jahrbuch fuer Niederdeutsche Sprachforschung — Jb f Niederdeut Spr
Jahrbuch fuer Niederdeutsche Sprachforschung — Jb f Niederdt Spr
Jahrbuch fuer Numismatik und Geldgeschichte — J f Num
Jahrbuch fuer Numismatik und Geldgeschichte — Jahrb Numism Geldgesch
Jahrbuch fuer Numismatik und Geldgeschichte — Jb NG
Jahrbuch fuer Numismatik und Geldgeschichte — Jb Num
Jahrbuch fuer Numismatik und Geldgeschichte — JfNG
Jahrbuch fuer Numismatik und Geldgeschichte — JNG
Jahrbuch fuer Numismatik und Geldgeschichte — JNGG
Jahrbuch fuer Oesterreichische Kulturgeschichte — Jb Osterreich Kultur Gesch
Jahrbuch fuer Opernforschung — Opernforschung
Jahrbuch fuer Optik und Feinmechanik — Jahrb Opt Feinmech
Jahrbuch fuer Ostasienmission — JOAM
Jahrbuch fuer Ostdeutsche Volkskunde — Jb Ostdt Volkskde
Jahrbuch fuer Ostdeutsche Volkskunde — JOV
Jahrbuch fuer Ostpreussische Kirchengeschichte — JOPKG
Jahrbuch fuer Ostrecht — Jb Ostrecht
Jahrbuch fuer Philologie — JfPhil
Jahrbuch fuer Philologie — JP
Jahrbuch fuer Philosophie und Phaenomenologische Forschungen — JPPF
Jahrbuch fuer Philosophie und Phaenomenologische Forschungen. Ergaenzungsband — JPPFE
Jahrbuch fuer Philosophie und Spekulative Theologie — J Ph ST
Jahrbuch fuer Philosophie und Spekulative Theologie — Jb Philos Spekul Theol
Jahrbuch fuer Philosophie und Spekulative Theologie — JPST
Jahrbuch fuer Philosophie und Spekulative Theologie — JPT
Jahrbuch fuer Philosophie und Spekulative Theologie. Ergaenungsheft — J Ph ST E
Jahrbuch fuer Photographie und Reproduktionstechnik — Jahrb Photogr Reproduktionstech
Jahrbuch fuer Praehistorische und Ethnographische Kunst — IPEK
Jahrbuch fuer Praehistorische und Ethnographische Kunst — JPEK
Jahrbuch fuer Psychiatrie und Neurologie — Jb Psychiatr Neurol
Jahrbuch fuer Psychiatrie und Neurologie — JbPsN
Jahrbuch fuer Psychologie, Psychotherapie, und Medizinische Anthropologie — JPPMB
Jahrbuch fuer Salesianische Studien — Jb Sal St
Jahrbuch fuer Schlesische Kirche und Kirchengeschichte — Jb Schles Kirche Kirchengesch
Jahrbuch fuer Schlesische Kirchengeschichte — JSKG
Jahrbuch fuer Schweizerische Geschichte — JSG
Jahrbuch fuer Sexuelle Zwischenstufen — JSexZ
Jahrbuch fuer Solothurnische Geschichte — J Sol G
Jahrbuch fuer Solothurnische Geschichte — JSoG
Jahrbuch fuer Sozialwissenschaft — Jahrb Sozia
Jahrbuch fuer Sozialwissenschaft — Jb Soz -Wiss
Jahrbuch fuer Sozialwissenschaft — Jb Sozialwiss
Jahrbuch fuer Sozialwissenschaft — JSW
Jahrbuch fuer Sozialwissenschaft. Zeitschrift fuer Wirtschaftswissenschaften — JAZ
Jahrbuch fuer Staudenkunde — Jahrb Staudenk
Jahrbuch fuer Technische Physik — JT Ph
Jahrbuch fuer Verkehrswissenschaft — Jb Verkehrswiss
Jahrbuch fuer Verkehrswissenschaft — JfVw
Jahrbuch fuer Volkskunde der Heimatvertriebenen — Jb Volkskde Heimatvertriebenen
Jahrbuch fuer Volkskunde der Heimatvertriebenen — JbVH

Jahrbuch fuer Volkskunde der Heimatvertriebenen — JVH
Jahrbuch fuer Volkskunde und Kulturgeschichte — Jb Volksk Kulturgesch
Jahrbuch fuer Volksliedforschung — Jahrb Volks
Jahrbuch fuer Volksliedforschung — Jb Volksliedf
Jahrbuch fuer Volksliedforschung — JV
Jahrbuch fuer Volksliedforschung — JVF
Jahrbuch fuer Wirtschafts und Sozialpaedagogik — JW u S
Jahrbuch fuer Wirtschafts und Sozialpaedagogik — JWS
Jahrbuch fuer Wirtschaftsgeschichte — Jb Wirtsch -Gesch
Jahrbuch fuer Wirtschaftsgeschichte — Jb Wirtschaftsgesch
Jahrbuch fuer Wirtschaftsgeschichte — JbW
Jahrbuch fuer Wirtschaftsgeschichte — JWG
Jahrbuch fuer Wissenschaftliche und Praktische Tierzucht — Jb Wiss Prakt Tierzucht
Jahrbuch fuer Wissenschaftliche und Praktische Zuechtungskunde — Jb Wiss Prakt Zuechtgskde
Jahrbuch fuer Wissenschaftliche und Praktische Zuechtungskunde — JWPZK
Jahrbuch fuer Zuckerruebenbau — Jahrb Zuckerruebenbau
Jahrbuch. Geologische Bundesanstalt — Jahrb Geol Bundesanst
Jahrbuch. Geologische Bundesanstalt. Sonderband — Jahrb Geol Bundesanst Sonderb
Jahrbuch. Gesellschaft fuer die Geschichte des Protestantismus in Oesterreich — JGGPO
Jahrbuch. Gesellschaft fuer die Geschichte des Protestantismus in Oesterreich — JGGPOes
Jahrbuch. Gesellschaft fuer Geschichte der Juden in der Cechoslovakischen Republik [*Prague*] — JGGJC
Jahrbuch. Gesellschaft fuer Geschichte der Juden in der Cechoslovakischen Republik [*Prague*] — JGJC
Jahrbuch. Gesellschaft fuer Lothringische Geschichte und Altertumskunde — JGLGA
Jahrbuch. Gesellschaft fuer Lothringische Geschichte und Altertumskunde — JGLGAK
Jahrbuch. Gesellschaft fuer Niedersaechsische Kirchengeschichte — JGNSKG
Jahrbuch. Gesellschaft fuer Wiener Theater-Forschung — Jb Ges Wiener Theater F
Jahrbuch. Gesellschaft fuer Wiener Theater-Forschung — JGWT
Jahrbuch. Goethe-Gesellschaft — JGG
Jahrbuch. Grillparzer-Gesellschaft — JGG
Jahrbuch. Grillparzer-Gesellschaft — JGrG
Jahrbuch. Hafenbautechnische Gesellschaft [*Germany*] — Jahrb Hafenbautech Ges
Jahrbuch. Hamburger Kunstsammlungen — Jahr Hamburger Kunstsam
Jahrbuch. Hamburger Kunstsammlungen — Jahrbuch Hamburger Kunstsam
Jahrbuch. Hamburger Kunstsammlungen — Jb Hamb Ku Samml
Jahrbuch. Heidelberger Akademie der Wissenschaften — Jbuch Heidelberger Akad Wiss
Jahrbuch. Heidelberger Akademie der Wissenschaften — JHAW
Jahrbuch. Historischer Verein Dillingen — JHVD
Jahrbuch. Historischer Verein fuer das Fuerstbistum Bamberg — JHVFB
Jahrbuch. Institut fuer Ne-Metallurgie (Plovdiv) — Jahrb Inst Ne-Metall (Plovdiv)
Jahrbuch. Jean-Paul-Gesellschaft — JJPG
Jahrbuch. Juedisch-Literarische Gesellschaft [*Frankfurt Am Main*] — JJLG
Jahrbuch. Juedisch-Literarische Gesellschaft [*Frankfurt Am Main*] — JLG
Jahrbuch. K. K. Heraldische Gesellschaft, "Adler" — JHGA
Jahrbuch. Karl-May-Gesellschaft — JKMG
Jahrbuch. Kleist-Gesellschaft — JKG
Jahrbuch. Koelnischer Geschichtsverein — JKGV
Jahrbuch. Koenigliche Tieraerztliche und Landwirtschaftliche Universitaet (Copenhagen) — Jahrb K Tieraerztl Landwirtsch Univ (Copenhagen)
Jahrbuch. Kunsthistorische Sammlungen — JKS
Jahrbuch. Kunsthistorische Sammlungen des Allerhoechsten Kaiserhauses — Jahrb d Kunsthist Samml d Kaiserhauses
Jahrbuch. Kunsthistorische Sammlungen des Allerhoechsten Kaiserhauses — Jahrb Kunsth Samml Kaiserh
Jahrbuch. Kunsthistorische Sammlungen (Wien) — Jahr Kunsthist Sam (Wien)
Jahrbuch. Kunsthistorische Sammlungen (Wien) — Jb KS (Wien)
Jahrbuch. Kunsthistorische Sammlungen (Wien) — Jb Kunsthist Samml (Wien)
Jahrbuch. Kunsthistorische Sammlungen (Wien) — JKSW
Jahrbuch. Kunsthistorische Sammlungen (Wien) — JW
Jahrbuch. Lederwirtschaft Oesterreich — Jahrb Lederwirtsch Oesterr
Jahrbuch. Leipziger Bienenzeitung — Jb Leipzig Bienenztg
Jahrbuch. Marburger Universitaetsbund — JbMu
Jahrbuch. Max-Planck-Gesellschaft — Jahrb Max Planck Ges
Jahrbuch. Max-Planck-Gesellschaft zur Foerderung der Wissenschaften — Jb Max Planck Ges Foerd Wiss
Jahrbuch. Museum fuer Voelkerkunde zu Leipzig — JMVL
Jahrbuch. Nordfriesisches Institut — JNI
Jahrbuch. Nordrhein Westfalen Landesamt fuer Forschung — Jahrb Nordrh Westfal Landesamt Forsch
Jahrbuch Oberflaechentechnik [*Germany*] — Jahrb Oberflaechentech
Jahrbuch. Oberoesterreichischer Musealverein — Jahrb Oberoesterr Musealver
Jahrbuch. Oberoesterreichischer Musealverein — JOMV
Jahrbuch. Oesterreichische Byzantinische Gesellschaft — JOBG
Jahrbuch. Oesterreichische Byzantinische Gesellschaft [*Vienna*] — JOstByzGes
Jahrbuch Peters — Jb Peters
Jahrbuch. Preussische Geologische Landesanstalt — Jahrb Preuss Geol Landesanst
Jahrbuch. Preussische Kunstsammlungen — Jahrb d Preuss Kunstsamml
Jahrbuch. Preussische Kunstsammlungen — Jahrb Preuss Kunstsamml
Jahrbuch. Preussische Kunstsammlungen — JPKS
Jahrbuch. Preussische Kunstsammlungen — JPrKS
Jahrbuch. Raabe-Gesellschaft — JRG
Jahrbuch. Roemisch-Germanisches Zentralmuseum [*Mainz*] — JRGZ
Jahrbuch. Roemisch-Germanisches Zentralmuseum (Mainz) — Jb Z Mus (Mainz)
Jahrbuch. Roemisch-Germanisches Zentralmuseum (Mainz) — JRGZMainz
Jahrbuch. Saechsische Akademie der Wissenschaften zu Leipzig — JbSAW
Jahrbuch. Sammlung Kippenberg Duesseldorf — JSK
Jahrbuch. Schiffbautechnische Gesellschaft — Jahrb Schiffbautech Ges
Jahrbuch. Schiller-Gesellschaft — JSG
Jahrbuch. Schlesische Friedrich-Wilhelm Universitaet zu Breslau — JSFWUB
Jahrbuch. Schlesische Friedrich-Wilhelm Universitaet zu Breslau — JSUB
Jahrbuch. Schweizerische Gesellschaft fuer Ur- und Fruehgeschichte — Jb Schw Ges Urgesch
Jahrbuch. Schweizerische Gesellschaft fuer Ur- und Fruehgeschichte — Jb Schweiz Ges Ur Fruehgesch
Jahrbuch. Schweizerische Gesellschaft fuer Urgeschichte — JSGU
Jahrbuch. Shakespeare Gesellschaft — JbShG
Jahrbuch. Staatliche Kunstsammlungen (Dresden) — Jb St Kunstsamml (Dresden)
Jahrbuch. Staatlichen Kunstsammlungen in Baden-Wuerttemberg — Jb Ku Samml Bad Wuert
Jahrbuch. Staatliches Museum fuer Mineralogie und Geologie zu Dresden — Jahrb Staatl Mus Mineral Geol Dresden
Jahrbuch. Stiftung Preussischer Kulturbesitz — JSPK
Jahrbuch. Technische Universitaet Muenchen — Jahrb Tech Univ Muenchen
Jahrbuch ueber die Fortschritte der Mathematik — Jbuch
Jahrbuch Ueberlicke Mathematik — Jahrb Uberblicke Math
Jahrbuch. Ungarische Archaeologische Gesellschaft — JUAG
Jahrbuch. Universitaet Duesseldorf — JUD
Jahrbuch. Verein fuer Juedische Geschichte und Literatur — JVJGL
Jahrbuch. Verein fuer Landeskunde und Heimatpflege im Gau Oberdonau — JVLHOD
Jahrbuch. Verein fuer Niederdeutsche Sprachforschung — JVNS
Jahrbuch. Verein fuer Westfaelische Kirchengeschichte — JVWK
Jahrbuch. Verein Schweizerischer Gymnasial-Lehrer — JVSch
Jahrbuch. Verein von Altertumsfreunden im Rheinland — JVA
Jahrbuch. Verein von Altertumsfreunden im Rheinland — JVARh
Jahrbuch. Vereinigung Juedischer Exportakademiker — JVJE
Jahrbuch. Versuch und Lehranstalt fuer Brauerei in Berlin — Jahrb Vers Lehranst Brau Berlin
Jahrbuch vom Zuerichsee — Jahrb Zuerichsee
Jahrbuch. Vorarlberger Landesmuseums Vereins — JVL
Jahrbuch. Vorarlberger Landesmuseums Vereins — JVLV
Jahrbuch Weichsel-Warthe — Jb Weichsel Warthe
Jahrbuch. Wiener Goethe-Verein — JWGV
Jahrbuch. Wissenschaftliches Forschungsinstitut fuer Buntmetallurgie (Plovdiv) — Jahrb Wiss Forschungsinst Buntmetall (Plovdiv)
Jahrbucher fuer Geschichte Osteuropas — JbxO
Jahrbuecher der Akademie Gemeinnuetziger Wissenschaften — JAGW
Jahrbuecher der Gewaechskunde — Jahrb Gewaechsk
Jahrbuecher der Koeniglichen Akademie Gemeinnuetziger Wissenschaften zu Erfurt — Jahrb Koenigl Akad Gemeinnuetz Wiss Erfurt
Jahrbuecher der Literatur. Verhandlungen des Naturhistorisch-Medicinischen Vereins zu Heidelberg — Jbb Lit Heidelbg
Jahrbuecher der Nationaloekonomie und Statistik — Jbb Nationaloek Statist
Jahrbuecher der Theologie und Theologischer Nachrichten — JTTN
Jahrbuecher des Kaiserlich Koeniglichen Polytechnischen Instituts in Wien — Jahrb K K Polytechn Inst Wien
Jahrbuecher des Nassauischen Vereins fuer Naturkunde — Jahrb Nassauischen Vereins Naturk
Jahrbuecher des Saechsischen Oberverwaltungsgerichts — Jbb Saechs Oberverwaltgsger
Jahrbuecher des Vereins fuer Mecklenburgische Geschichte und Altertumskunde — JVMG
Jahrbuecher des Vereins fuer Naturkunde im Herzogthum Nassau — Jahrb Ver Naturkd Herzogthum Nassau
Jahrbuecher des Vereins von Altertumsfreunden im Rheinlande — JVAFR
Jahrbuecher fuer Classische Philologie — JC Ph
Jahrbuecher fuer Classische Philologie. Supplement — JC Ph S
Jahrbuecher fuer Deutsche Theologie [*Stuttgart/Gotha*] — JDT
Jahrbuecher fuer Deutsche Theologie [*Stuttgart/Gotha*] — JDTh
Jahrbuecher fuer die Deutsche Armee und Marine — Jbb Dt Armee
Jahrbuecher fuer die Landeskunde der Herzogtuemer Schleswig, Holstein und Lauenburg — JLKHS
Jahrbuecher fuer Geschichte der Slaven — JGSl
Jahrbuecher fuer Geschichte Osteuropas — Jahrb Gesch
Jahrbuecher fuer Geschichte Osteuropas — Jahrb Gesch Osteur
Jahrbuecher fuer Geschichte Osteuropas — Jahrb Gesch Osteurop
Jahrbuecher fuer Geschichte Osteuropas — Jahrb Gesch Osteuropas
Jahrbuecher fuer Geschichte Osteuropas — Jb Gesch Osteur
Jahrbuecher fuer Geschichte Osteuropas — JGO
Jahrbuecher fuer Geschichte Osteuropas — JGOE
Jahrbuecher fuer Juedische Geschichte und Literatur — JaJGL
Jahrbuecher fuer Kultur und Geschichte der Slaven — Jb Kult Gesch Slaven
Jahrbuecher fuer Kultur und Geschichte der Slaven — JKGS
Jahrbuecher fuer Nationaloekonomie und Statistik — J f N St
Jahrbuecher fuer National-Oekonomie und Statistik — Jahrb N St
Jahrbuecher fuer Nationaloekonomie und Statistik — Jb Nationaloekon Statist
Jahrbuecher fuer Nationaloekonomie und Statistik — Jb Nationaloekon und Statis
Jahrbuecher fuer National-Oekonomie und Statistik — Jb'r Nat-Oekon Statist
Jahrbuecher fuer Nationaloekonomie und Statistik — JNOS
Jahrbuecher fuer Nationaloekonomie und Statistik — JNS
Jahrbuecher fuer Nationaloekonomie und Statistik — JNSt
Jahrbuecher fuer Philologie — Jbb Philol
Jahrbuecher fuer Philologie und Paedagogik — JPP
Jahrbuecher fuer Protestantische Theologie — JP Th

Jahrbuecher fuer Protestantische Theologie [*Leipzig/Braunschweig*] — JPT
Jahrbuecher fuer Psychiatrie und Neurologie — Jahrb Psychiatr Neurol
Jahrbuecher fuer Psychiatrie und Neurologie — Jb f Psych
Jahrbuecher fuer Theoogie und Christliche Philosophie — JTCP
Jahrbuecher fuer Wissenschaftliche Botanik — Jahrb Wiss Bot
Jahrbuecher fuer Wissenschaftliche Botanik — Jbb Wiss Bot
Jahrbuecher fuer Wissenschaftliche Kritik. Herausgegeben von der Societaet fuer Wissenschaftliche Kritik zu Berlin — Jahrb Wiss Krit
Jahrbuecher fuer Wissenschaftliche Kritik zu Berlin — Berlin Jahrb f Wiss Kritik
Jahrbuecher. Nassauischer Verein fuer Naturkunde — Jahrb Nassau Ver Naturkd
Jahrbuechlein der Detuschen Theologischen Literatur — JDTL
Jahresbericht. Bischoefliches Gymnasium und Dioezesanseminar. Kollegium Petrinum in Urfar — Jb Bischof Gymnas Kolleg Petrinum
Jahresbericht. Botanischer Verein zu Hamburg EV — Jahresber Bot Verein Hamb EV
Jahresbericht. Chemisch Technische Reichsanstalt — Jahresber Chem Tech Reichsanst
Jahresbericht der Bayerischen Bodendenkmalpflege — Jahresber Bayer Bodendenkmal
Jahresbericht der Bayerischen Bodendenkmalpflege — JBB
Jahresbericht der Bundesanstalt fuer Materialpruefung — Jahresber Bundesanst Materialpruef
Jahresbericht der Deutschen Geschichte — Jber Dt Gesch
Jahresbericht der Geographischen Gesellschaft in Hamburg — Jahresber Geogr Ges Hamburg
Jahresbericht der Geographischen Gesellschaft in Muenchen — JGGM
Jahresbericht der Geschichtswissenschaft — JBG
Jahresbericht der Gesellschaft von Freunden der Naturwissenschaft zu Gera — JbGFNG
Jahresbericht der Goerresgesellschaft — JGG
Jahresbericht der Historisch-Antiquarischen Gesellschaft von Graubuenden — JHAGG
Jahresbericht der Instituts fuer Geschichte der Naturwissenschaft — Jahresber Inst Gesch Naturwiss
Jahresbericht der Israelitisch-Theologischen Lehranstalt — JITL
Jahresbericht der Landesanstalt fuer Immissions- und Bodennutzungsschutz des Landes Nordrhein-Westfalen — Jahresber Landesanst Immissions Bodennutzungsschutz Landes N
Jahresbericht der Naturforschenden Gesellschaft zu Freiburg — Jahresber Naturf Ges Freiburg
Jahresbericht der Naturforschenden Gesellschaft zu Halle — Jahresber Naturf Ges Halle
Jahresbericht der Naturhistorischen Gesellschaft Nuernberg — Jahresb Naturhist Ges Nuernberg
Jahresbericht der Naturhistorischen Kantonal-Gesellschaft in Solothurn — Jahresber Naturhist Kantonal Ges Solothurn
Jahresbericht der Naturwissenschaftlichen Gesellschaft zu Elberfeld — Jahresber Naturwiss Ges Elberfeld
Jahresbericht der Pharmazie — Jahresber Pharm
Jahresbericht der Rheinischen Mission — JRM
Jahresbericht der Schlesichen Gesellschaft fuer Vaterlaendische Kultur — Jber Schles Ges Vaterld Kult
Jahresbericht der Schlesichen Gesellschaft fuer Vaterlaendische Kultur — JSs
Jahresbericht der Schlesischen Gesellschaft fuer Vaterlaendische Kultur — JSGVK
Jahresbericht der Schlesischen Gesellschaft fuer Vaterlandische Kultur — Jahresber der Schles Gesellschaft fuer Vaterland Kultur
Jahresbericht der Schweizer Gesellschaft fuer Urgeschichte — Jahresber Schweiz Urgesch
Jahresbericht der Vereinigung der Vertreter der Angewandten Botanik — Jahresber Vereinigung Vertreter Angew Bot
Jahresbericht der Vereinigung fuer Angewandte Botanik — Jber Vereing Angew Bot
Jahres-Bericht der Westphaelischen Gesellschaft fuer Vaterlaendische Cultur — Jahres Ber Westphael Ges Vaterl Cult
Jahresbericht der Zuercherischen Botanischen Gesellschaft — Jahresber Zuecherischen Bot Ges
Jahresbericht des Allgemeinen Evngelisch-Protestantischen Missionsvereins — JAEPM
Jahresbericht des Bernischen Historischen Museums in Bern — Jahresber Hist Mus Bern
Jahresbericht des Botanischen Vereines am Mittel- und Niederrheine — Jahresber Bot Vereines Mittel Niederrheine
Jahresbericht des Gartenbauvereins in Mainz — Jahresber Gartenbauvereins Mainz
Jahresbericht des Geographischen Vereins zu Frankfurt — Jahresber Geogr Vereins Frankfurt
Jahresbericht des Historischen Museums Schloss Thun — JHMT
Jahresbericht des Historischen Vereins fuer die Grafschaft Ravensberg — JHVGR
Jahresbericht des Historischen Vereins fuer Straubing und Ungebung — Jahresber Hist Ver Straubing
Jahresbericht des Historischen Vereins fuer Straubing und Ungebung — JHVS
Jahresbericht des Instituts fuer Vorgeschichte der Universitaet Frankfurt — Jber Inst Vg Frankf
Jahresbericht des Literarischen Zentralblatts — Jber Lit Zbl
Jahres-Bericht des Naturhistorischen Vereins in Passau — Jahres Ber Naturhist Vereins Passau
Jahresbericht des Naturwissenschaftlichen Vereins in Halle — Jahresber Naturwiss Vereins Halle
Jahresbericht des Naturwissenschaftlichen Vereins zu Magdeburg. Nebst den Sitzungsberichten — Jahresber Naturwiss Vereins Magdeburg Sitzungsber
Jahresbericht des Niedersaechsischen Botanischen Vereins/Botanische Abteilung der Naturhistorischen Gesellschaft zu Hannover — Jahresber Niedersaechs Bot Vereins
Jahresbericht des Niedersaechsischen Geologischen Vereins — JbNsGV
Jahresbericht des Nordoberfraenkischen Vereins fuer Natur-, Geschichts-, Landes-, und Familienkunde in Hof A.D.S — Jahresber Nordoberfraenk Vereins Natur Familienk Hof
Jahresbericht des Philologischen Vereins — JPhV
Jahresbericht des Physikalischen Vereins zu Frankfurt am Main — Jahresber Phys Vereins Frankfurt
Jahresbericht des Sonnblick-Vereins — Jahresber Sonnblick Vereins
Jahresbericht des Thueringer Gartenbau Vereins zu Gotha — Jahresber Thueringer Gartenbau Vereins Gotha
Jahresbericht des Thueringisch-Saechsischen Vereins fuer Erforschung des Vaterlaendischen Altertums — JTSV
Jahresbericht des Vereins fuer Naturkunde an der Unterweser — Jahresber Vereins Naturk Unterweser
Jahresbericht des Vereins fuer Naturkunde zu Zwickau in Sachsen — Jahresber Vereins Naturk Zwickau
Jahresbericht des Vereins zur Erforschung der Regensburger Domgeschichte — JVRDG
Jahresbericht des Vereins zur Unterstutzung der Armen Negerkinder — JVUN
Jahresbericht des Vorarlberger Museum-Vereins — Jber Vorarlbg Museum Ver
Jahresbericht. Deutsche Forschungs- und Versuchsanstalt fuer Luft- und Raumfahrt — Jahresber DFVLR
Jahresbericht. Deutsche Mathematiker-Vereinigung — Jber Deutsch Math-Verein
Jahresbericht. Deutsches Hydrographische Institut (Hamburg) — Jahresber Dtsch Hydrogr Inst (Hamburg)
Jahresbericht fuer Geschichtswissenschaft — JGW
Jahresbericht fuer Neuere Deutsche Literaturgeschichte — Jber Neuer Dt Litgesch
Jahresbericht. Gesellschaft pro Vindonissa — Jber Pro Vindon
Jahresbericht. Gesellschaft pro Vindonissa. Basel — Jahresber GPV
Jahresbericht. Gesellschaft pro Vindonissa. Basel — Jb GPV
Jahresbericht. Historisch-Antiquarische Gesellschaft von Graubuenden — Jahresbericht Grabunden
Jahresbericht. Historisch-Antiquarische Gesellschaft von Graubuenden — Jber Hist Ges Graub
Jahresbericht. Historisch-Antiquarische Gesellschaft von Graubuenden — JHAG
Jahresbericht. Historischer Verein fuer Mittelfranken — JBHVMF
Jahresbericht. Institut fuer Strahlen- und Kernphysik. Universitaet Bonn — Jahresber Inst Strahlenphys Kernphys Univ Bonn
Jahresbericht. Kernforschungsanlage Juelich — Jahresber Kernforschungsanlage Juelich
Jahresbericht Kestner-Museum (Hannover) — Jber Mus (Han)
Jahresbericht. Kurashiki-Zentralhospital — Jahresber Kurashiki-Zentralhosp
Jahresbericht. Max-Planck-Institut fuer Plasmaphysik. Garching bei Muenchen — Jahresber MPI Plasmaphys Garching
Jahresbericht. Medizinisches Institut fuer Umwelthygiene — Jahresber Med Inst Umwelthyg
Jahresbericht. Naturforschende Gesellschaft Fraubuendens — Jber Naturf Ges Fraubuendens
Jahresbericht. Naturwissenschaftlicher Verein zu Wuppertal — Jber Naturw Ver Wuppertal
Jahresbericht. Philologischer Verein — JPhV
Jahresbericht. Philologischer Verein zu Berlin — Jahresb PVB
Jahresbericht. Philologischer Verein zu Berlin — PVB
Jahresbericht. Schweizerische Akademie der Medizinischen Wissenschaften — Jahresber Schweiz Akad Med Wiss
Jahresbericht. Schweizerische Gesellschaft fuer Vererbungsforschung — Jahresber Schweiz Ges Vererbungsforsch
Jahresbericht. Schweizerisches Landesmuseum — Sch L
Jahresbericht. Schweizerisches Landesmuseum (Zuerich) — Jahresber Schweiz Landesmus Zuerich
Jahresbericht. Schweizerisches Landesmuseum (Zuerich) — Jahresbericht (Zuerich)
Jahresbericht. Schweizerisches Landesmuseum (Zuerich) — Jber (Zuerich)
Jahresbericht ueber den Botanischen Garten in Bern — Jahresber Bot Gart Bern
Jahresbericht ueber den Naturwissenschaftlichen Verein des Fuerstenthums Luneberg — Jahresber Naturwiss Verein Fuerstenth Luneburg
Jahres-Bericht ueber den Verein fuer Kunde der Natur und der Kunst im Fuerstenthum Hildesheim und in der Stadt Goslar — Jahres Ber Verein Kunde Natur Fuerstenth Hildesheim
Jahresbericht ueber die Fortschritte auf dem Gesamtgebiete der Agrikulturchemie — Jahresber Fortschr Gesamtgeb Agrikulturchem
Jahresbericht ueber die Fortschritte der Animalischen Physiologie — Jahresber Fortschr Anim Physiol
Jahresbericht ueber die Fortschritte der Chemie und Verwandter Theile Anderer Wissenschaften — Jahresber Fortschr Chem Verw Theile Andrer Wiss
Jahresbericht ueber die Fortschritte der Inneren Medizin im In- und Auslande — Jber Inn M
Jahresbericht ueber die Fortschritte der Klassischen Altertumswissenschaft [*A publication*] — JFA
Jahresbericht ueber die Fortschritte der Klassischen Altertumswissenschaft [*A publication*] — JFKA
Jahresbericht ueber die Fortschritte der Klassischen Altertumswissenschaft — JKAW
Jahresbericht ueber die Fortschritte der Pharmakognosie, Pharmacie, und Toxicologie — Jahresber Fortschr Pharmakogn
Jahresbericht ueber die Fortschritte der Physiologie — Jahresber Fortschr Physiol

Jahresbericht ueber die Fortschritte der Tierchemie — Jahresber Fortschr Tierchm
Jahresbericht ueber die Fortschritte der Tierchemie — Jber Fortschr Tierchem
Jahresbericht ueber die Fortschritte in der Lehre von den Pathogenen Mikroorganismen Umfassend Bacterien, Pilze, und Protozoeen — Jahresb Fortschr Lehre Path Mikroorganism
Jahresbericht ueber die Fortschritte in der Pharmacie in Allen Laendern — Jahresber Fortschr Pharm in Allen Laendern
Jahresbericht ueber die Gesamte Tuberkulose-Forschung — Jber Ges Tuberkforsch
Jahresbericht ueber die Leistungen und Fortschritte im Gebiete der Ophthalmologie — Jber Ophth
Jahresbericht ueber die Leistungen und Fortschritte in der Anatomie und Physiologie — Jber Leistg Fortschr Anat
Jahresbericht ueber die Liestungen auf dem Gebiete der Veterinaer-Medizin — Jahresb Leistung Vet-Med
Jahresbericht ueber die Verbreitung von Tierseuchen im Deutschen Reiche — Jber Tierseuch
Jahresbericht ueber Germanische Philologie — Jber Germ Philol
Jahresbericht und Abhandlungen des Naturwissenschaftlichen Vereins in Magdeburg — Jahresber Abh Naturwiss Vereins Magdeburg
Jahresbericht und Mittheilungen des Gartenbau-Vereins fuer Neuvorpommern und Rugen — Jahresber Mitth Gartenbau Vereins Neuvorpommern
Jahresbericht und Mittheilungen des Gartenbau-Vereins im Grossherzogthum Hessen — Jahresber Mitth Gartenbau Vereins Grossherzogth Hessen
Jahresbericht. Universitaet Wuerzburg — Jahresber Univ Wuerzb
Jahresbericht. Verein fuer Geschichte der Stadt Nuernberg — VGN
Jahresbericht. Vereins fuer Heimatgeschichte — JVH
Jahresbericht Veterinaer-Medizin — Jahresb Vet Med
Jahresbericht von der Gesellschaft fuer Natur- und Heil-Kunde zu Dresden — Jahresber Ges Natur Heil Kunde Dresden
Jahresbericht zur Geschichte der Slaven — JbGSl
Jahresberichte. Berliner Literatur Gesellschaft — JBLG
Jahresberichte der Deutschen Mathematiker-Vereinigung — Jahresber Deut Math Ver
Jahresberichte der Geschichtswissenschaft. Herausgegeben von der Historischen Gesellschaft — JGHHG
Jahresberichte der Historischen Vereinigung Seetal — JHVSe
Jahresberichte der Koeniglichen Ungarischen Geologischen Anstalt — Jahresber K Ung Geol Anst
Jahresberichte der Naturhistorischen Gesellschaft zu Hannover — Jahresber Naturhist Ges Hannover
Jahresberichte der Wetterauischen Gesellschaft fuer die Gesamte Naturkunde zu Hanau — Jahresber Wetterauischen Ges Gesamte Naturkd Hanau
Jahresberichte des Deutschen Pflanzenschutzdienstes — Jahresber Dtsch Pflanzenschutzdienstes
Jahresberichte des Literarischen Zentralblattes — JLZ
Jahres-Berichte des Naturwissenschaftlichen Vereins in Elberfeld — Jahres Ber Naturwiss Vereins Elberfeld
Jahresberichte des Vereins fuer Mecklenburgische Geschichte — Jberr Ver Mecklenb Gesch
Jahresberichte. Juedisch-Theologisches Seminar "Frankelsche Stiftung" — JbJTS
Jahresberichte. Schlesische Gesellschaft fuer Vaterlaendische Kultur — Jahresb Schles Gesellsch Vaterl Kult
Jahresberichte ueber das Hoehre Schulwesen — JHSch
Jahresberichte ueber die Erscheinungen auf dem Gebiete der Germanischen Literaturgeschichte — Jb u Ersch Ger Lit
Jahresberichte ueber die Fortschritte der Anatomie und Entwicklungsgeschichte — Jber Anat
Jahresberichte ueber die Fortschritte der Klassischen Altertumswissenschaft — JAW
Jahresberichte ueber die Fortschritte der Klassischen Altertumswissenschaft — JFKAW
Jahresberichte ueber die Veraenderungen und Fortschritte im Militaerwesen — VFM
Jahresberichte und Mitteilungen. Oberrheinischer Geologische Verein — Jahresber Mitt Oberrheinischen Geol Ver
Jahresberichte und Rechnungen. Historisches Museum (Basel) [*Switzerland*] — Jb Rechnung Hist Mus (Basel)
Jahresbibliographie. Bibliothek fuer Zeitgeschichte, Weltkriegsbuecherei — J Bibliogr Bibl Zeitgesch
Jahresbriefe des Berneuchener Kreises — JBK
Jahresheft. Gemeinschaft der Selbstverwirklichung — JGSV
Jahresheft. Geologisches Landesamt in Baden Wuerttemberg — Jahresh Geol Landesamtes Baden Wuerttemb
Jahresheft. Verein fuer Vaterlaendische Naturkunde in Wuerttemberg — J Ver Vaterl Naturk Wuertt
Jahreshefte des Oesterreichischen Archaeologischen Institutes in Wien — J Ost Arch Inst
Jahreshefte des Oesterreichischen Archaeologischen Institutes in Wien — Jahrbd Oesterreich Inst
Jahreshefte des Oesterreichischen Archaeologischen Institutes in Wien — Jahresh
Jahreshefte des Oesterreichischen Archaeologischen Institutes in Wien — Jahresh Oesterr Arch Inst
Jahreshefte des Oesterreichischen Archaeologischen Institutes in Wien — JOAIW
Jahreshefte des Oesterreichischen Archaeologischen Institutes in Wien — OeJhh
Jahreshefte des Oesterreichischen Archaeologischen Institutes in Wien — Oest Jahrh
Jahreshefte des Oesterreichischen Archaeologischen Institutes in Wien — Oesterr Archaeol Inst Jahresh
Jahreshefte des Oesterreichischen Archaeologischen Institutes in Wien — OJ
Jahreshefte des Oesterreichischen Archaeologischen Institutes in Wien — Ost Jahrh
Jahreshefte des Oesterreichischen Archaeologischen Instituts — Jhh Oester Archaeol Inst
Jahreshefte des Oesterreichischen Archaeologischen Instituts — OesterrJh
Jahreshefte des Vereins fuer Mathematik und Naturwissenschaften in Ulm — Jahresh Vereins Math Ulm
Jahreshefte. Gesellschaft fuer Naturkunde in Wuerttemberg — Jahresh Ges Naturkd Wuerttemb
Jahreshefte. Oesterreichisches Archaeologische Institut. Beiblatt — Oe Jh Beibl
Jahreshefte. Oesterreichisches Archaeologische Institut in Wien — JdOI
Jahreshefte. Oesterreichisches Archaeologische Institut in Wien — JhOAI
Jahreshefte. Oesterreichisches Archaeologische Institut in Wien — JOEAI
Jahreshefte. Oesterreichisches Archaeologische Institut in Wien — Oe Jh
Jahreshefte. Verein fuer Vaterlaendische Naturkunde in Wuerttemberg — Jahresh Ver Vaterl Naturkd Wuerttemb
Jahreskatalog der Wiener Botanischen Tauschvereins — Jahreskat Wiener Bot Tauschvereins
Jahreskolloquium des Sonderforschungsbereichs 270 der Universitaet Stuttgart — Jahreskolloq Sonderforschungsbereichs 270 Univ Stuttgart
Jahreskurse fuer Aerztliche Fortbildung — Jahreskurse Aerztl Fortbild
Jahresmappe der Deutschen Gesellschaft fuer Christliche Kunst — JDGCK
Jahresschrift des Kreismuseums Haldensleben — JKH
Jahresschrift des Salzburger Museums Carolino-Augusteum — JSMCA
Jahresschrift des Salzburger Museums Carolino-Augusteum — JSMCCA
Jahresschrift fuer die Vorgeschichte der Saechsisch-Thueringischen Laender — Jschr Vorgesch Saechs Thuer Laender
Jahresschrift fuer Mitteldeutsche Vorgeschichte — JMV
Jahresschrift fuer Mitteldeutsche Vorgeschichte — Jschr Mitteldtsch Vorgesch
Jahresschrift fuer Mitteldeutsche Vorgeschichte (Halle) — J Schr Vg (Halle)
Jahrestagung der Gesellschaft zur Erforschung der Makromolekularen Organo- und Immunotherapie. Kongressberichte — Jahrestag Ges Erforsch Makromol Organo Immunother Kongressbe
Jahrestagung des Fachverbandes fuer Strahlenschutz — Jahrestag Fachverb Strahlenschutz
Jahrestagung. Institut fuer Chemie der Treib- und Explosivstoffe der Fraunhofer-Gesellschaft — Jahrestag Inst Chem Treib Explosivst Fraunhofer Ges
Jahrestreffen der Katalytiker der DDR. Programm und Tagungsbericht — Jahrestreffen Katal DDR Programm Tagungsber
Jahresversammlung der Deutschen Arbeitsgemeinschaft fuer Blutgerinnungsforschung — Jahresversamml Dtsch Arbeitsgem Blutgerinnungsforsch
Jahresversammlung. Gesellschaft fuer Oekologie — Jahresversamml Ges Oekol
Jahresverzeichnis der Deutschen Hochschulschriften — JVH
Jahrliche Zeitschrift fuer Physiatrie und Prophylaxie — Jahrliche Z Physiatr Prophyl
Jahrs-Bericht des Naturwissenschaftlichen Vereins in Hamburg — Jahrs Ber Naturwiss Vereins Hamburg
Jahrsschriften fuer Theologie und Kirchenrecht der Katholiken — J Th KR
Jain Journal — Jain J
Jaina Antiquary — Jaina Antiq
JAMA. Journal. American Medical Association — JAMA J Am Med Assoc
JAMA. The Journal of the American Medical Association — GJAM
Jamaica Agricultural Society. Journal — Jamaica Ag Soc J
Jamaica Architect — Jamaica Archt
Jamaica Bauxite Institute Digest — Jam Bauxite Inst Dig
Jamaica. Department of Agriculture. Bulletin — Jam Dep Agric Bull
Jamaica. Department of Science and Agriculture. Bulletin — Jam Dep Sci Agric Bull
Jamaica Exports. Complimentary Guide to Trade and Investment Opportunities — JAM
Jamaica. Geological Survey Department. Annual Report — Jamaica Geol Survey Dept Ann Rept
Jamaica. Geological Survey Department. Bulletin — Jamaica Geol Survey Dept Bull
Jamaica. Geological Survey Department. Economic Geology Report — Jam Geol Surv Dep Econ Geol Rep
Jamaica. Geological Survey Department. Occasional Paper — Jamaica Geol Survey Dept Occ Pap
Jamaica. Geological Survey Department. Publication — Jamaica Geol Survey Pub
Jamaica. Geological Survey Department. Short Paper — Jamaica Geol Survey Dept Short Pap
Jamaica Handbook — Jamaica Handb
Jamaica Journal — JJ
Jamaica Journal. Institute of Jamaica — IJ/JJ
Jamaica Library Association Bulletin — JLAB
Jamaica Medical Review — Jam Med Rev
Jamaica. Mines and Geology Division. Special Publication — Jam Mines Geol Div Spec Publ
Jamaica. Ministry of Agriculture and Fisheries. Bulletin — Jam Minist Agric Fish Bull
Jamaica. Ministry of Agriculture and Lands. Annual Report — Jam Minist Agric Lands Annu Rep
Jamaica. Ministry of Agriculture and Lands. Bulletin — Jam Minist Agric Lands Bull
Jamaica. Ministry of Agriculture. Bulletin — Jam Minist Agric Bull
Jamaica Physical Journal — Jamaica Phys J
Jamaican Association of Sugar Technologists. Journal — Jam Assoc Sugar Technol J
Jamaican Association of Sugar Technologists. Quarterly — Jam Assoc Sugar Technol Q
Jamaican Historical Review — Jam Hist Rev

James Arthur Lecture on the Evolution of the Human Brain — James Arthur Lect Evol Hum Brain
James Cook University of North Queensland. Department of Tropical Veterinary Science. Veterinary Reviews and Monographs — James Cook Univ North Queensl Dep Trop Vet Sci Vet Rev Monog
James Joyce Quarterly — J J Qtr
James Joyce Quarterly — James Joy Q
James Joyce Quarterly — James Joyce Q
James Joyce Quarterly — JJQ
James Joyce Quarterly — PJJQ
James Joyce Review — JJR
James Madison Journal — James Madison J
James Sprunt Historical Publications — James Sprunt Hist Publ
James Sprunt Historical Studies — James Sprunt Hist Stud
Jamia Educational Quarterly — Jamia Ed Q
JAMM. Journal for Australian Music and Musicians — JAMM
Jammu and Kashmir University Review — JKUR
Jan Liao Hsueh Pao — JLHPA
Jane Austen Society. Report — JASR
Jane's Defence Review — Jn D Rv
Jane's Defence Weekly — Janes Def W
Jane's Fighting Ships — JFS
Janssen Chimica Acta — Janssen Chim Acta
Janssen Research Foundation Series — Janssen Res Found Ser
Janssen Research Foundation Series [*Elsevier Book Series*] — JRFS
Janua Linguarum — JanL
January — JA
Janus — J
Janus. Archives Internationales pour l'Histoire de la Medecine — Jan
Janus Pannonius Muezeum Evkoenyve — JPM
Janus Pannonius Muezeum Evkoenyve — JPME
Janus Pannonius Muzeum Evkoenyve — Jan Pan Evk
Janus Pannonius Muzeum Evkoenyve — Janus Pannon Muz Evk
Janus. Supplements — JS
JAOCS. Journal. American Oil Chemists' Society — JAOCS J Am Oil Chem Soc
JAP. Respiratory, Environmental, and Exercise Physiology — JAP Respir Environ Exercise Physiol
Japan Academy. Proceedings — Jap Acad Proc
Japan Agricultural Research Quarterly — Jap Agr Res Q
Japan Agricultural Research Quarterly — Jpn Agric Res Q
Japan Analyst — Jpn Analyst
Japan and America — Jap Am
Japan Annual of Law and Politics — Ja Ann Law Pol
Japan Annual of Law and Politics — JALP
Japan Annual of Law and Politics — Jap Ann of Law & Pol
Japan Annual Reviews in Electronics, Computers, and Telecommunications — Jpn Annu Rev Electron Comput Telecommun
Japan Architect — JA
Japan Architect — Japan Arch
Japan Architect — Japan Archt
Japan Architect — Jpn Archit
Japan Association of Ion Exchange. Journal — Jpn Assoc Ion Exch J
Japan Association of Language Teachers. Journal — Jap Assoc Lang Teach Jnl
Japan. Atomic Energy Research Institute. Annual Report and Account — ARJID
Japan. Atomic Energy Research Institute. Annual Report and Account — Jpn At Energy Res Inst Annu Rep Acc
Japan Atomic Energy Research Institute. Report JAERI-M — Jpn At Energy Res Inst Rep JAERI-M
Japan. Atomic Energy Research Institute. Report. Research Report — Jpn At Energy Res Inst Rep Res Rep
Japan Baptist Annual — JBA
Japan Bibliographical Annual — JBGA
Japan Biographical Encyclopedia — JBE
Japan Business — Jap Bus
Japan Chemical Analysis Center. Report — Jpn Chem Anal Cent Rep
Japan Chemical Annual — J Chem An
Japan Chemical Annual — Jpn Chem Annu
Japan Chemical Industry — Jpn Chem Ind
Japan Chemical Industry Association Monthly — Jpn Chem Ind Assoc Mon
Japan Chemical Quarterly — JCHQA
Japan Chemical Quarterly — Jpn Chem Q
Japan Chemical Review — Jpn Chem Rev
Japan Chemical Review. Japan Chemical Week Supplement — J Chem Rev
Japan Chemical Week — Jap Chem Week
Japan Chemical Week — Japan Chem
Japan Chemical Week — JCW
Japan Chemical Week. Supplement. Where Is Great Change in Chemical Industry's Scope Leading — J Chem S
Japan Chemistry — Jap Chem
Japan Christian Quarterly — Ja Christ Q
Japan Christian Quarterly — Jap Chr Q
Japan Christian Quarterly — JCQ
Japan Christian Year Book — JCY
Japan Computers — Jap Comp
Japan Conference on Liquid Atomisation and Spray System — Jpn Conf Liq Atomisation Spray Syst
Japan Directory of Professional Associations [*Database*] — JDPA
Japan Echo — Ja Echo
Japan Economic Almanac — Jpn Eco A
Japan Economic Journal — JEF
Japan Economic Journal — JEJ
Japan Economic Journal — Jpn Econ J
Japan Economic Newswire [*Database*] — JEN
Japan Electron Optics Laboratory. JEOL News — Jpn Electro Opt Lab JEOL News
Japan Electronic Engineering — JEE
Japan Electronic Engineering — Jpn Electron Eng
Japan Electronics Buyers' Guide — J Elec Buy
Japan Electronics Industry — JEI
Japan Electronics Industry — Jpn Elec I
Japan Electronics (Washington) — Jap Electron (Wash)
Japan Energy — Jap En
Japan Energy and Technology Intelligence — Jpn Energy Technol Intell
Japan English Publications in Print [*Database*] — JEPP
Japan Evangelist — Jap Ev
Japan Fertilizer News/Nihon Hiryo Shinbun — Japan Fertilizer News
Japan Finishing — Jpn Finish
Japan Food Science — Jpn Food Sci
Japan Foundation Newsletter — Ja Found Newsl
Japan Fudo Saiensu — Jpn Fudo Saiensu
Japan Gas Association. Journal — Jpn Gas Assoc J
Japan Geological Survey. Bulletin — Jap Geol Surv Bull
Japan Geological Survey. Report — Jap Geol Surv Rep
Japan Geothermal Energy Association. Journal — Jap Geotherm Energy Assoc J
Japan Hospitals — Jpn Hosp
Japan Industrial and Technological Bulletin — Jpn Ind Technol Bull
Japan Industrial Technology Association Nyusu — Jpn Ind Technol Assoc Nyusu
Japan Information Exchange [*Database*] — JIE
Japan. Institute of Navigation. Journal — Jap Inst Nav J
Japan Interpreter — Ja Interp
Japan Interpreter — Jap Inter
Japan Interpreter — Japan Inter
Japan Interpreter — JI
Japan Investment Service [*Database*] — JIS
Japan Journal of Applied Mathematics — Japan J Appl Math
Japan Journal of Burn Injuries — Jpn J Burn Inj
Japan Journal of Nurses' Education — Jap J Nurses Educ
Japan Journal of Thermophysical Properties — Jpn J Thermophys Prop
Japan Journal of Water Pollution Research — Jpn J Water Pollut Res
Japan Labor Bulletin — Ja Labor B
Japan Labor Bulletin — Japan Lbr Bul
Japan Letter — IDR
Japan Light Metal Welding — Jpn Light Met Weld
Japan (London) — JAL
Japan Manufacturing — Jap Man
Japan Materials — Jap Mat
Japan Medical Congress — JMC
Japan Medical Gazette — Japan Med Gaz
Japan Medical Research Foundation. Publication — JMRPDC
Japan Medical Research Foundation. Publication — Jpn Med Res Found Publ
Japan Medical World — Japan Med World
Japan Medical World — Jpn Med World
Japan Meteorological Agency. Volcanological Bulletin — Jap Meteorol Agency Volcanol Bull
Japan Missionary Bulletin — Ja Mission B
Japan Missionary Bulletin [*Tokyo*] — JMB
Japan National Congress for Applied Mechanics — Jpn Natl Congr Appl Mech
Japan. National Institute of Polar Research. Memoirs. Special Issue — JNIPRMSI
Japan National Laboratory for High Energy Physics. Report KEK — Jpn Natl Lab High Energy Phys KEK
Japan Nickel Review — Jpn Nickel Rev
Japan. Patent Document. Kokai Tokkyo Koho — Jpn Pat Doc Kokai Tokkyo Koho
Japan Pesticide Information — Jap Pestic Inf
Japan Pesticide Information — Japan Pestic Inf
Japan Pesticide Information — JPIFAN
Japan Pesticide Information — Jpn Pestic Inf
Japan Petroleum and Energy Weekly — Jpn Petrol
Japan Plastics — Jpn Plast
Japan Plastics Age — J Plas Age
Japan Plastics Age — Jap Plast Age
Japan Plastics Age — Jpn Plast Age
Japan Plastics Age News — Jpn Plast Age News
Japan Plastics Industry Annual — J Plast An
Japan Price Indexes Annual, 1984 — Jpn P Indx
Japan Printer — Jpn Printer
Japan Public Works Research Institute. Report. Ministry of Construction — Jap Public Works Res Inst Rep (Minist Constr)
Japan Publishers Directory [*Database*] — JPD
Japan Pulp and Paper — IPF
Japan Pulp and Paper — Jap Pulp Pap
Japan Quarterly — GJAQ
Japan Quarterly — Ja Q
Japan Quarterly — Jap Q
Japan Quarterly — Jap Quart
Japan Quarterly — Japan Q
Japan Quarterly — Japan Quart
Japan Quarterly — Jpn Quart
Japan Quarterly — JQ
Japan Science Review. Biological Sciences — Jpn Sci Rev Biol Sci
Japan Science Review. Humanistic Studies — JSRHS
Japan Science Review. Literature, Philosophy, and History — JSR LPH
Japan Science Review. Medical Sciences — Jpn Sci Rev Med Sci
Japan Semiconductor Technology Reports — Jpn Semicond Technol Rep
Japan Shipbuilding and Marine Engineering — Jap Shipbldg Mar Eng

Japan Shipbuilding and Marine Engineering — Jap Shipbuild & Mar Engng
Japan Socialist Review — Ja Socialist R
Japan Socialist Review — JSR
Japan Society Bulletin — Japan Soc B
Japan Society for Aeronautical and Space Sciences. Transactions — Jpn Soc Aeronaut Space Sci Trans
Japan Society for Composite Materials. Transactions — Jpn Soc Compos Mater Trans
Japan Society for the Promotion of Science. Sub-Committee for Physical Chemistry of Steelmaking. Special Report — Jap Soc Promot Sci Sub-Comm Phys Chem Steelmaking Spec Rep
Japan Society of London. Bulletin — Ja Soc Lond B
Japan Society of London. Bulletin — JSLB
Japan Society of Lubrication Engineers. International Tribology Conference — Jpn Soc Lubr Eng Int Tribol Conf
Japan Society of Mechanical Engineers. Bulletin — Bull Jap Soc Mech E
Japan Society of Mechanical Engineers. Bulletin — Jpn Soc Mech Eng Bull
Japan Society of Mechanical Engineers. International Journal. Series 1. Solid Mechanics, Strength of Materials — Jpn Soc Mech Eng Int J Ser 1
Japan Society of Mechanical Engineers. International Journal. Series 2. Fluids Engineering, Heat Transfer, Power, Combustion, Thermophysical Properties — Jpn Soc Mech Eng Int J Ser 2
Japan Society of Precision Engineering. Bulletin — Jpn Soc Precis Eng Bull
Japan Spectroscopic Company. Application Notes — JASCO Appl Notes
Japan Spectroscopic Company. Application Notes — Jpn Spectros Co Appl Notes
Japan Statistical Yearbook — Japan Stat
Japan Steel and Tube Technical Review — Jpn Steel Tube Tech Rev
Japan Steel Bulletin — Jpn Steel Bull
Japan Steel Works — Jpn Steel Works
Japan Steel Works. Technical News — Jpn Steel Works Tech News
Japan Steel Works. Technical Review — Jpn Steel Works Tech Rev
Japan Steel Works. Technical Review (English Edition) — Jpn Steel Works Tech Rev (Engl Ed)
Japan Symposium on Thermophysical Properties — Jpn Symp Thermophys Prop
Japan TAPPI [*Technical Association of the Pulp and Paper Industry*] — Jpn TAPPI
Japan Technology Information and Evaluation Service [*Database*] — J-TIES
Japan Telecommunications Review — Jap Telecom
Japan Telecommunications Review — Jpn Telecommun Rev
Japan Textile News — Jpn Text News
Japan. The Economic and Trade Picture [*London*] — JAN
Japan Trade Directory — JTD
Japan Transportation — Jap Transport
Japan Views Quarterly — JVQ
Japan Welding Society. International Symposium — Jpn Weld Soc Int Symp
Japan Welding Society. Transactions — Jap Weld Soc Trans
Japanese Agricultural Research Quarterly — Jap Agric Res Q
Japanese Annals of Social Psychology — Japan A Soc Psychol
Japanese Annual Bibliography of Economics — Jap Ann Bib Econ
Japanese Annual of International Law — Ja Ann Int Law
Japanese Annual of International Law — JAIL
Japanese Annual of International Law — Japan Annu Int Law
Japanese Annual of International Law — Japanese An Internat Law
Japanese Antarctic Research Expedition. Data Reports — Jpn Antarct Res Exped Data Rep
Japanese Antarctic Research Expedition. Scientific Reports. Series C. Geology — Jpn Antarct Res Exped Sci Rep Ser C
Japanese Archives of Histology — Jpn Arch Histol
Japanese Archives of Internal Medicine — Jap Arch Int Med
Japanese Archives of Internal Medicine — Jpn Arch Intern Med
Japanese Association for Animal Cell Technology. Annual Meeting — Jpn Assoc Anim Cell Technol Annu Meet
Japanese Association of Fire Science and Engineering. Journal — Jpn Assoc Fire Sci Eng J
Japanese Association of Mineralogists, Petrologists, and Economic Geologists. Journal — Jap Assoc Mineral Petrol Econ Geol J
Japanese Association of Petroleum Technologists. Journal — Jap Assoc Pet Technol J
Japanese Bee Journal — Jap Bee J
Japanese Cancer Association. Gann Monograph — Jpn Cancer Assoc Gann Monogr
Japanese Chemical Pharmaceutical Journal — Jpn Chem Pharm J
Japanese Circulation Journal — Jap Circ J
Japanese Circulation Journal [*English edition*] — JCIRA
Japanese Circulation Journal — Jpn Circ J
Japanese Clinics — Jpn Clin
Japanese Dental Journal — Jpn Dent J
Japanese Economic Studies — Ja Econ Stud
Japanese Economic Studies — Jap Econ St
Japanese Economic Studies — Japan Econ Stud
Japanese Economic Studies — Japanese Econ Studies
Japanese Economic Studies. A Journal of Translations — JES
Japanese Fantasy Film Journal — JFFJ
Japanese Finance and Industry — Japanese Fin and Industry
Japanese Finance and Industry — SJF
Japanese Fruits/Kajitsu Nihon — Jap Fruits
Japanese Heart Journal — Jap Heart J
Japanese Heart Journal — Jpn Heart J
Japanese Invasion of America's Personal Computer Market — Jpn P Comp
Japanese Journal for the Midwife — Jap J Midwife
Japanese Journal for the Midwife — Jpn J Midwife
Japanese Journal of Aerospace and Environmental Medicine — Jpn J Aerosp Environ Med
Japanese Journal of Aerospace Medicine and Psychology — Jpn J Aerosp Med Psychol
Japanese Journal of Aerospace Medicine and Psychology — KUISA
Japanese Journal of Alcohol Studies and Drug Dependence — Jpn J Alcohol Stud & Drug Depend
Japanese Journal of Allergology — Jpn J Allergol
Japanese Journal of Allergy — Jap J Allergy
Japanese Journal of Allergy — Jpn J Allergy
Japanese Journal of Anaesthesiology — Jap J Anaesth
Japanese Journal of Anesthesiology — Jpn J Anesthesiol
Japanese Journal of Animal Reproduction — Jpn J Anim Reprod
Japanese Journal of Antibiotics — Jpn J Antibiot
Japanese Journal of Applied Entomology and Zoology — Jap J Appl Ent Zool
Japanese Journal of Applied Entomology and Zoology — Jap J Appl Entomol Zool
Japanese Journal of Applied Entomology and Zoology — Jpn J Appl Entomol Zool
Japanese Journal of Applied Physics — Jap J A Phy
Japanese Journal of Applied Physics — Jap J Appl Phys
Japanese Journal of Applied Physics — Jpn J Appl Phys
Japanese Journal of Applied Physics. Part 1 — Jpn J Appl Phys 1
Japanese Journal of Applied Physics. Part 1. Regular Papers and Short Notes [*A publication*] — JAPND
Japanese Journal of Applied Physics. Part 1. Regular Papers and Short Notes [*A publication*] — Jpn J Appl Phys Part 1
Japanese Journal of Applied Physics. Part 2. Letters — JAPLD
Japanese Journal of Applied Physics. Part 2. Letters — Jpn J Appl Phys 2 Lett
Japanese Journal of Applied Physics. Part 2. Letters — Jpn J Appl Phys Part 2
Japanese Journal of Applied Physics. Supplement — Jap J Appl Phys Suppl
Japanese Journal of Applied Physics. Supplement — Jpn J Appl Phys Suppl
Japanese Journal of Applied Zoology — Jap J Appl Zool
Japanese Journal of Astronomy — Jap J Astr
Japanese Journal of Astronomy — Jpn J Astron
Japanese Journal of Astronomy and Geophysics — Jap J Astr Geophys
Japanese Journal of Astronomy and Geophysics — Jpn J Astron Geophys
Japanese Journal of Bacteriology — Jpn J Bacteriol
Japanese Journal of Biochemistry of Exercise — Jpn J Biochem Exercise
Japanese Journal of Botany — Jap J Bot
Japanese Journal of Botany — Jap J Botan
Japanese Journal of Botany — Jpn J Bot
Japanese Journal of Brain Physiology — Jpn J Brain Physiol
Japanese Journal of Breeding — Jap J Breed
Japanese Journal of Breeding — Jpn J Breed
Japanese Journal of Cancer Clinics — Jpn J Cancer Clin
Japanese Journal of Cancer Research — Jap J Canc Res
Japanese Journal of Cancer Research — Jpn J Cancer Res
Japanese Journal of Cancer Research (Gann) — Jpn J Cancer Res (Gann)
Japanese Journal of Chemistry — Jpn J Chem
Japanese Journal of Chemotherapy — Jpn J Chemother
Japanese Journal of Chest Diseases — Jpn J Chest Dis
Japanese Journal of Child and Adolescent Psychiatry — Jpn J Child Adoles Psychiatry
Japanese Journal of Child Psychiatry — Jap J Child
Japanese Journal of Clinical and Experimental Medicine — Jpn J Clin Exp Med
Japanese Journal of Clinical Electron Microscopy — Jpn J Clin Electron Microsc
Japanese Journal of Clinical Hematology — Jpn J Clin Hematol
Japanese Journal of Clinical Medicine — Jap J Clin Med
Japanese Journal of Clinical Medicine — Jpn J Clin Med
Japanese Journal of Clinical Oncology — Jpn J Clin Oncol
Japanese Journal of Clinical Ophthalmology — Jpn J Clin Ophthalmol
Japanese Journal of Clinical Pathology — Jap J Clin Path
Japanese Journal of Clinical Pathology — Jpn J Clin Pathol
Japanese Journal of Clinical Pathology. Supplement — Jpn J Clin Pathol Suppl
Japanese Journal of Clinical Pharmacology — Jpn J Clin Pharmacol
Japanese Journal of Clinical Pharmacology and Therapeutics — Jpn J Clin Pharmacol Ther
Japanese Journal of Clinical Radiology — JJCRA
Japanese Journal of Clinical Radiology — Jpn J Clin Radiol
Japanese Journal of Clinical Urology — Jpn J Clin Urol
Japanese Journal of Constitutional Medicine — Jpn J Const Med
Japanese Journal of Crop Science — Jpn J Crop Sci
Japanese Journal of Dairy and Food Science — Jpn J Dairy Food Sci
Japanese Journal of Dairy Science — Jpn J Dairy Sci
Japanese Journal of Dental Health — Jpn J Dent Health
Japanese Journal of Dermatology — Jpn J Dermatol
Japanese Journal of Dermatology and Urology — Jpn J Dermatol Urol
Japanese Journal of Dermatology and Venereology — Jpn J Dermatol Venereol
Japanese Journal of Dermatology. Series B (English Edition) — Jpn J Dermatol Ser B (Engl Ed)
Japanese Journal of Ecology — Jap J Ecol
Japanese Journal of Ecology — Jpn J Ecol
Japanese Journal of Educational Psychology — Jap J Edu P
Japanese Journal of Endocrinology — Jpn J Endocrinology
Japanese Journal of Engineering. Abstracts — Jpn J Eng Abstr
Japanese Journal of Ergonomics — Jpn J Ergonomics
Japanese Journal of Ethnology — JJE
Japanese Journal of Ethnology — Jpn J Ethnol
Japanese Journal of Experimental Medicine — Jap J Exp M
Japanese Journal of Experimental Medicine — Jap J Exp Med
Japanese Journal of Experimental Medicine — Jpn J Exp Med
Japanese Journal of Experimental Morphology — Jpn J Exp Morphol
Japanese Journal of Fertility and Sterility — Jpn J Fertil Steril
Japanese Journal of Food Chemistry — Jpn J Food Chem
Japanese Journal of Food Microbiology — Jpn J Food Microbiol
Japanese Journal of Forensic Toxicology — Jpn J Forensic Toxicol

Japanese Journal of Freezing and Drying — Jpn J Freezing Drying
Japanese Journal of Fuzzy Theory and Systems — Japanese J Fuzzy Theory Systems
Japanese Journal of Gastroenterology — Jpn J Gastroenterol
Japanese Journal of Genetics — Jap J Gen
Japanese Journal of Genetics — Jap J Genet
Japanese Journal of Genetics — Jpn J Genet
Japanese Journal of Genetics. Supplement — Jpn J Genet Suppl
Japanese Journal of Geology and Geography — Jap J Geol Geogr
Japanese Journal of Geology and Geography — Japan J Geol & Geog
Japanese Journal of Geology and Geography — Japanese Jour Geology and Geography
Japanese Journal of Geology and Geography — Jpn J Geol Geogr
Japanese Journal of Geophysics — Jap J Geophys
Japanese Journal of Geophysics — Jpn J Geophys
Japanese Journal of Geriatrics — Jpn J Geriatr
Japanese Journal of Herpetology — Jpn J Herpetol
Japanese Journal of Human Genetics — Jap J Hum G
Japanese Journal of Human Genetics — Jap J Hum Gen
Japanese Journal of Human Genetics — Jpn J Hum Genet
Japanese Journal of Hygiene — Jpn J Hyg
Japanese Journal of Ichthyology — Jap J Ichthyol
Japanese Journal of Ichthyology — Jpn J Ichthyol
Japanese Journal of Industrial Health — Jpn J Ind Health
Japanese Journal of Leprosy — Jpn J Lepr
Japanese Journal of Limnology — Jap J Limnol
Japanese Journal of Limnology — Jpn J Limnol
Japanese Journal of Lymphology — Jpn J Lymphol
Japanese Journal of Magnetic Resonance in Medicine — Jpn J Magn Reson Med
Japanese Journal of Malacology — Jpn J Malacol
Japanese Journal of Mathematics — Japan J Math
Japanese Journal of Mathematics — Jpn J Math
Japanese Journal of Mathematics. New Series — Japan J Math NS
Japanese Journal of Medical Eelctronics and Biological Engineering — Jpn J Med Electron Biol
Japanese Journal of Medical Electronics and Biological Engineering — Jap J Med Electron & Biol Eng
Japanese Journal of Medical Electronics and Biological Engineering — Jpn J Med Electron and Biol Eng
Japanese Journal of Medical Electronics and Biological Engineering — Jpn J Med Electron Biol Eng
Japanese Journal of Medical Mycology — Jpn J Med Mycol
Japanese Journal of Medical Progress — Jpn J Med Prog
Japanese Journal of Medical Science and Biology — Jap J Med S
Japanese Journal of Medical Science and Biology — Jap J Med Sci Biol
Japanese Journal of Medical Science and Biology — Jpn J Med Sci Biol
Japanese Journal of Medical Sciences. Part 1. Anatomy — Jpn J Med Sci 1
Japanese Journal of Medical Sciences. Part 2. Biochemistry — Jpn J Med Sci 2
Japanese Journal of Medical Sciences. Part 3. Biophysics — Jpn J Med Sci 3
Japanese Journal of Medical Sciences. Part 4. Pharmacology — Jap J Med Sci Pt 4 Pharmacol
Japanese Journal of Medical Sciences. Part 4. Pharmacology — Japan J Med Sc Pt 4 Pharmacol
Japanese Journal of Medical Sciences. Part 4. Pharmacology — Jpn J Med Sci 4
Japanese Journal of Medical Sciences. Part 5. Pathology — Jpn J Med Sci 5
Japanese Journal of Medical Sciences. Part 6. Bacteriology and Parasitology [*A publication*] — Jpn J Med Sci 6
Japanese Journal of Medical Sciences. Part 7. Social Medicine and Hygiene — Jpn J Med Sci 7
Japanese Journal of Medical Sciences. Part 8. Internal Medicine, Pediatry, and Psychiatry — Jpn J Med Sci 8
Japanese Journal of Medical Sciences. Part 9. Surgery, Orthopedy, and Odontology — Jpn J Med Sci 9
Japanese Journal of Medical Sciences. Part 10. Ophthalmology — Jpn J Med Sci 10
Japanese Journal of Medical Sciences. Part 11. Gynecology and Tocology — Jpn J Med Sci 11
Japanese Journal of Medical Sciences. Part 12. Oto-Rhino-Laryngology — Jpn J Med Sci 12
Japanese Journal of Medical Sciences. Part 13. Dermatology and Urology — Jpn J Med Sci 13
Japanese Journal of Medicine — Jap J Med
Japanese Journal of Medicine — Jpn J Med
Japanese Journal of Michurin Biology — Jpn J Michurin Biol
Japanese Journal of Michurin Biology — MSKEDJ
Japanese Journal of Microbiology — Jap J Micro
Japanese Journal of Microbiology — Jap J Microb
Japanese Journal of Microbiology — Jpn J Microbiol
Japanese Journal of Microbiology. Japan Bacteriological Society — Jap J Microbiol
Japanese Journal of Mutagenicity Tests on Chemicals — Jpn J Mutagen Tests Chem
Japanese Journal of Nephrology — Jpn J Nephrol
Japanese Journal of Neurology and Psychiatry — Jpn J Neurol Psychiatry
Japanese Journal of Nuclear Medicine — Jpn J Nucl Med
Japanese Journal of Nuclear Medicine — KAIGBZ
Japanese Journal of Nuclear Medicine Technology — Jpn J Nucl Med Technol
Japanese Journal of Nursing — Jap J Nurs
Japanese Journal of Nursing — Jpn J Nurs
Japanese Journal of Nursing Art — Japan J Nurs Art
Japanese Journal of Nursing Research — Jap J Nurs Res
Japanese Journal of Nursing Research — Jpn J Nurs Res
Japanese Journal of Nutrition — Jap J Nutr
Japanese Journal of Nutrition — Jpn J Nutr
Japanese Journal of Obstetrics and Gynecology — Jpn J Obstet Gynecol
Japanese Journal of Ophthalmology — Jap J Ophthal
Japanese Journal of Ophthalmology — JJOPA7
Japanese Journal of Ophthalmology — Jpn J Ophthalmol
Japanese Journal of Optics — Jpn J Opt
Japanese Journal of Oral Biology — Jpn J Oral Biol
Japanese Journal of Palynology — Jap J Palynol
Japanese Journal of Palynology — Jpn J Palynol
Japanese Journal of Paper Technology — Jpn J Pap Technol
Japanese Journal of Parasitology — Jap J Parasit
Japanese Journal of Parasitology — Jpn J Parasitol
Japanese Journal of Parasitology — KISZAR
Japanese Journal of Pediatric Surgery and Medicine — Jpn J Pediat Surg Med
Japanese Journal of Pediatrics — Jpn J Pediat
Japanese Journal of Pediatrics — Jpn J Pediatr
Japanese Journal of Pharmacognosy — Jap J Pharmacogn
Japanese Journal of Pharmacognosy — Jpn J Pharm
Japanese Journal of Pharmacognosy — Jpn J Pharmacogn
Japanese Journal of Pharmacognosy — Jpn J Pharmacognosy
Japanese Journal of Pharmacognosy — SHZAAY
Japanese Journal of Pharmacology — Jap J Pharm
Japanese Journal of Pharmacology — Jap J Pharmac
Japanese Journal of Pharmacology — JJPAA
Japanese Journal of Pharmacology — JJPAAZ
Japanese Journal of Pharmacology — Jpn J Pharmacol
Japanese Journal of Pharmacy and Chemistry — Jpn J Pharm Chem
Japanese Journal of Pharmacy and Chemistry — YKKKA8
Japanese Journal of Phycology — JJPHDP
Japanese Journal of Phycology — Jpn J Phycol
Japanese Journal of Phycology (Japanese Edition) — Jpn J Phycol Jpn Ed
Japanese Journal of Physical Education — Jpn J Phys Educ
Japanese Journal of Physical Education — TAKEAZ
Japanese Journal of Physical Fitness and Sports Medicine — Jpn J Phys Fitness Sports Med
Japanese Journal of Physical Fitness and Sports Medicine — TAKAAN
Japanese Journal of Physics — Jpn J Phys
Japanese Journal of Physiology — Jap J Phys
Japanese Journal of Physiology — Jap J Physi
Japanese Journal of Physiology — Jap J Physiol
Japanese Journal of Physiology — JJPHA
Japanese Journal of Physiology — JJPHAM
Japanese Journal of Physiology — Jpn J Physiol
Japanese Journal of Plastic and Reconstructive Surgery — Jpn J Plast Reconstr Surg
Japanese Journal of Plastic and Reconstructive Surgery — KEGEAC
Japanese Journal of Proctology — Jpn J Proctol
Japanese Journal of Psychiatry and Neurology — Jpn J Psychiatry Neurol
Japanese Journal of Psychology — Jap J Psych
Japanese Journal of Psychology — Jap J Psychol
Japanese Journal of Psychology — Jpn J Psychol
Japanese Journal of Psychology — SHKEA5
Japanese Journal of Psychopharmacology — Jpn J Psychopharmacol
Japanese Journal of Psychopharmacology — YSKOD8
Japanese Journal of Psychosomatic Medicine — Jpn J Psychosom Med
Japanese Journal of Psychosomatic Medicine — SHIGD4
Japanese Journal of Public Health — Jpn J Public Health
Japanese Journal of Public Health — NKEZA4
Japanese Journal of Radiological Technology — Jpn J Radiol Technol
Japanese Journal of Religious Studies — Ja J Rel Stud
Japanese Journal of Religious Studies — Jpn J Relig
Japanese Journal of Sanitary Zoology — Jap J Sanit Zool
Japanese Journal of Sanitary Zoology — Jpn J Sanit Zool
Japanese Journal of Smooth Muscle Research — Jpn J Smooth Muscle Res
Japanese Journal of Smooth Muscle Research — NHEIAY
Japanese Journal of Soil Science and Plant Nutrition — Jpn J Soil Sci Plant Nutr
Japanese Journal of Studies on Alcohol — JJSAAG
Japanese Journal of Studies on Alcohol — Jpn J Stud Alcohol
Japanese Journal of Surgery — JJSGA
Japanese Journal of Surgery — JJSGAY
Japanese Journal of Surgery — Jpn J Surg
Japanese Journal of Surgical Metabolism and Nutrition — Jpn J Surg Metab Nutr
Japanese Journal of the Nation's Health — Jpn J Nations Health
Japanese Journal of the Neurosciences Research Association — Jpn J Neurosci Res Assoc
Japanese Journal of Thoracic Diseases — Jpn J Thorac Dis
Japanese Journal of Thoracic Diseases — NKYZA2
Japanese Journal of Toxicology — Jpn J Toxicol
Japanese Journal of Toxicology and Environmental Health — Jpn J Toxicol Environ Health
Japanese Journal of Tropical Agriculture — Jap J Trop Agr
Japanese Journal of Tropical Agriculture — Jpn J Trop Agric
Japanese Journal of Tropical Agriculture — NENOA8
Japanese Journal of Tropical Medicine and Hygiene — Jpn J Trop Med Hyg
Japanese Journal of Tuberculosis — Jpn J Tuberc
Japanese Journal of Tuberculosis — JPTUAL
Japanese Journal of Tuberculosis and Chest Diseases — JJTCAR
Japanese Journal of Tuberculosis and Chest Diseases — Jpn J Tuberc Chest Dis
Japanese Journal of Urology — Jpn J Urol
Japanese Journal of Veterinary Research — Jap J Vet R
Japanese Journal of Veterinary Research — Jap J Vet Res
Japanese Journal of Veterinary Research — JJVRA

Japanese Journal of Veterinary Research — JJVRAE
Japanese Journal of Veterinary Research — Jpn J Vet R
Japanese Journal of Veterinary Research — Jpn J Vet Res
Japanese Journal of Veterinary Science — Jap J Vet S
Japanese Journal of Veterinary Science — Jap J Vet Sci
Japanese Journal of Veterinary Science — Jpn J Vet Sci
Japanese Journal of Veterinary Science — NJUZA9
Japanese Journal of Veterinary Science/Nigon Juigaku Zasshi — Jap J Vet Sci Nigon Juigaku Zasshi
Japanese Journal of Zoology — Jap J Zool
Japanese Journal of Zoology — JJZOAP
Japanese Journal of Zoology — Jpn J Zool
Japanese Journal of Zootechnical Science — Jap J Zootech Sci
Japanese Journal of Zootechnical Science — Jpn J Zootech Sci
Japanese Journal of Zootechnical Science — NICKA3
Japanese Literature Today — Ja Lit Today
Japanese Medical Journal — Jpn Med J
Japanese Medical Literature — Jpn Med Lit
Japanese Military Technology. Procedures for Transfers to the United States — Japanese MT
Japanese National Railways. Railway Technical Research — Jap Nat Ry Ry Tech Res
Japanese Nuclear Medicine — JANMA
Japanese Nuclear Medicine — Jpn Nucl Med
Japanese Periodicals Index — Jap Per Ind
Japanese Pharmacology and Therapeutics — Jpn Pharmacol Ther
Japanese Poultry Science — Jap Poult Sci
Japanese Poultry Science — Jap Poultry Sci
Japanese Poultry Science — Jpn Poult Sci
Japanese Poultry Science — NKKGAB
Japanese Progress in Climatology — Jap Prog Climatol
Japanese Psychological Research — Jap Psy Res
Japanese Psychological Research — Jpn Psychol Res
Japanese Psychological Research — JPREA
Japanese Psychological Research — JPREAV
Japanese Railway Engineering — JAREB
Japanese Railway Engineering — Jpn Railw Eng
Japanese Religions — Ja Rel
Japanese Religions — Jap R
Japanese Religions — Jap Rel
Japanese Review of Clinical Ophthalmology — Jpn Rev Clin Ophthalmol
Japanese Safety Forces Medical Journal — Jpn Saf Forces Med J
Japanese Science Review. Mining and Metallurgy — Jpn Sci Rev Min Metall
Japanese Scientific Monthly — Jpn Sci Mon
Japanese Semiconductor Technology News — Jap Semicond Tech N
Japanese Society for Tuberculosis. Annual Report — ARJSAG
Japanese Society for Tuberculosis. Annual Report — Jpn Soc Tuberc Annu Rep
Japanese Society of Grassland Science Journal/Nihon Sochi Gakkai Shi — Jap Soc Grassland Sci J
Japanese Sociological Review — JSR
Japanese Studies — Japan Stud
Japanese Studies in German Language and Literature — JSGLL
Japanese Studies in the History of Science — Ja Stud Hist Sci
Japanese Studies in the History of Science — Jap Stud Hist Sci
Japanese Studies in the History of Science — Japan Stud Hist Sci
Japanese Studies in the History of Science — Jpn Stud Hist Sci
Japanese Symposium on Plasma Chemistry. Proceedings — Jpn Symp Plasma Chem Proc
Japanese-Chinese Symposium on Coagulation, Fibrinolysis, and Platelets — Jpn Chin Symp Coagulation Fibrinolysis Platelets
Japan-France Seminar on Composite Materials — Jpn Fr Semin Compos Mater
Japan-Germany Medical Reports — Jpn-Ger Med Rep
Japanisch-Deutsche Medizinische Berichte — Jpn Dtsch Med Ber
Japanisch-Deutsche Zeitschrift — JDZ
Japanisch-Deutsche Zeitschrift fuer Wissenschaft und Technik — Jap Dt Zs Wiss Techn
Japan-Italy Joint Symposium on Heavy Ion Physics — Jpn Italy Jt Symp Heavy Ion Phys
Japan-Soviet Symposium on Mechanochemistry — Jpn Sov Symp Mechanochem
Japan-US Conference on Composite Materials — Jpn US Conf Compos Mater
Japan-US Seminar on HTGR [*High-Temperature Gas-Cooled Reactor*] **Safety Technology. Proceedings** — Jpn US Semin HTGR Saf Technol Proc
Japan-U.S. Seminar on Polymer Synthesis — Jpn US Semin Polym Synth
Japan-USSR Polymer Symposium. Proceedings — Jpn USSR Polym Symp Proc
JAPCA. The Journal of the Air and Waste Management Association — JAPCA J Air
Jardin Botanico/Secretaria de Agricultura y Fomento — Jard Bot
Jardinier Portatif — Jard Portatif
Jardins de France — Jard Fr
JARE [*Japanese Antarctic Research Expedition*] **Data Reports** — JARE Data Rep
JARE (Japanese Antarctic Research Expedition) Data Reports — JARE (Jpn Antarct Res Exped) Data Rep
JARE (Japanese Antarctic Research Expedition) Scientific Reports. Series C. Earth Sciences — JARE Sci Rep Ser C
JARE [*Japanese Antarctic Research Expedition*] **Scientific Reports. Series E. Biology** — JARE Sci Rep Ser E Biol
JARE [*Japanese Antarctic Research Expedition*] **Scientific Reports. Special Issue** — JSRSA
Jarmuevek, Mezoegazdasagi Gepek [*Hungary*] — Jarmuevek Mezoegazd Gepek
Jaroslavskii Gosudarstvennyi Pedagogiceskii Institut Doklady na Naucnyh Konferencijah — Jaroslav Gos Ped Inst Dokl Naucn Konfer
Jaroslavskii Gosudarstvennyi Pedagogiceskii Institut Imeni K. D. Usinskogo Ucenye Zapiski — Jaroslav Gos Ped Inst Ucen Zap
Jaroslavskii Tehnologiceskii Institut Fiziko-Matematiceskie Nauki Sbornik Naucnyh Trudov — Jaroslav Tehn Inst Fiz-Mat Nauk Sb Naucn Trudov
JARQ. Japan Agricultural Research Quarterly — JARQ
JARQ. Japan Agricultural Research Quarterly — JARQ Jap Agric Res Q
JARQ. Japan Agricultural Research Quarterly — JARQ Jpn Agric Res Q
Jarrow Lecture — Jar L
JASCO [*Japan Spectroscopic Company*] **Report** — JARED
JASCO [*Japan Spectroscopic Company*] **Report** — JASCO Rep
JASSA. Journal of the Australian Society of Security Analysts — JASSA
JAST (Jamaican Association of Sugar Technologists) Journal — JAST J
Jaszberenyi Jaszmuseum Evkoenyve — JJE
JAT. Journal of Applied Toxicology — JAT J Appl Toxicol
Jauna Gaita — J Ga
Jaunakais Mezsaimnieciba — Jaunakais Mezsaimn
Jaundice. Proceedings. International Symposium. Canadian Hepatic Foundation — Jaundice Proc Int Symp Can Hepatic Found
Java Gazette (Jakarta) — JGJ
Jazyk i Literatura — JaiL
Jazykovedny Aktuality — JAk
Jazykovedny Aktuality. Zpravodaj Jazykovedneho Sdruzeni pri Ceskoslovenske Akademii Ved — JazA
Jazykovedny Casopis — JC
Jazykovedny Sbornik — JazSb
Jazykovedny Sbornik — JS
Jazykovedny Studie — JazS
Jazykovedny Studie — JS
Jazykovedny Zbornik — JZ
Jazz di Ieri e di Oggi — Jazz Ieri
Jazz Educators Journal — Jazz Ed J
Jazz Educators Journal — JEJ
Jazz Journal [*Later, Jazz Journal International*] — Jazz J
Jazz Journal [*Later, Jazz Journal International*] — Jazz Jl
Jazz Journal International — Jazz J Int
Jazz Journal International — JJI
Jazz Magazine — Jazz Mag
Jazz Magazine — Jz
Jazz Magazine (United States) — Jazz Mag (US)
Jazz Monthly — Jazz Mo
Jazz Report — Jazz Rept
Jazz Research — Jazz Res
Jazz Review — Jazz R
Jazz Rytm i Piosenka — Jazz Rytm
Jazz Times — Jazz T
Jazzforschung — Jazzf
JBI (Jamaica Bauxite Institute) Digest — JBI Dig
JBIC. Journal of Biological Inorganic Chemistry — JBIC J Biol Inorg Chem
JBM. Jornal Brasileiro de Medicina — JBM J Bras Med
JCPT. Journal of Canadian Petroleum Technology — JCPT J Can Pet Technol
JCU. Journal of Clinical Ultrasound — JCU J Clin Ultrasound
JDC Digest — JDCD
JDC Review — JDCR
JDR. Journal for Drugtherapy and Research — JDR J Drugther Res
JDR. Journal of Drug Research — JDR J Drug Res
Je Sais, Je Crois — JSJC
Jealott's Hill Bulletin — Jealott's Hill Bull
Jean-Paul-Gesellschaft. Jahrbuch — Jean-Paul-Gesellsch Jahrb
Jeddah Journal of Marine Research — Jeddah J Mar Res
JEE [*Japan Electronic Engineering*] **Japan Electronic Engineering** — JEE Jpn Electron Eng
JEE. Journal of Electronic Engineering — JEE
JEE. Journal of Electronic Engineering [*Japan*] — JEE J Electron Eng
JEE. Journal of Electronic Engineering — JEEND
Jefferson Business — Jeffrsn B
JEGP. Journal of English and Germanic Philology — PJEG
JEI. Japan Electronic Industry — JEI Jpn Electron Ind
JEI. Journal of the Electronics Industry — JEI J Electron Ind
Jeju University Journal. Natural Sciences — Jeju Univ J Nat Sci
JEMF [*John Edwards Memorial Foundation*] **Quarterly** — JEMF Quart
JEMF [*John Edwards Memorial Foundation*] **Quarterly** — JEMFA
JEMF [*John Edwards Memorial Foundation*] **Quarterly** — JEMFQ
JEMIC [*Japan Electric Meters Inspection Corporation*] **Technical Report** — JEMIC Tech Rep
Jemna Mechanika a Optika — Jemna Mech a Opt
Jemna Mechanika a Optika — Jemna Mech Opt
Jemna Mechanika a Optika — JMKOA
Jena Review — Jena Rev
Jena Review. Supplement [*Germany*] — Jena Rev Suppl
Jena Review. Supplement — JRVSB
Jenaer Germanistische Forschungen — JGF
Jenaer Harnsteinsymposium — Jenaer Harnsteinsymp
Jenaer Jahrbuch — Jenaer Jahrb
Jenaer Rundschau — Jena Rundsch
Jenaer Rundschau — Jenaer Rundsch
Jenaer Zeiss-Jahrbuch — Jen Zeiss Jb
Jenaische Zeitschrift fuer Medizin Herausgegeben von der Medicinisch-Naturwissenschaftlichen Gesellschaft zu Jena — Jenaische Z Med
Jenaische Zeitschrift fuer Medizin und Naturwissenschaft [*Germany*] — Jena Z Med Naturwiss
Jenaische Zeitschrift fuer Medizin und Naturwissenschaft — Jena Zs Med
Jenaische Zeitschrift fuer Medizin und Naturwissenschaft — Jena Zs Med Naturw
Jenaische Zeitschrift fuer Medizin und Naturwissenschaft — Jenaische Zeitschrift
Jenaische Zeitschrift fuer Medizin und Naturwissenschaft — Jenaische Ztschr Med u Naturw

Jenaische Zeitschrift fuer Naturwissenschaft — Jena Z Naturw
Jenaische Zeitschrift fuer Naturwissenschaft — Jena Z Naturwiss
Jenaische Zeitschrift fuer Naturwissenschaft — Jenaische Ztschr Naturw
Jenaische Zeitschrift fuer Naturwissenschaft Herausgegeben von der Medicinisch-Naturwissenschaftlichen Gesellschaft zu Jena — Jenaische Z Naturwiss
JENER [*Joint Establishment for Nuclear Energy Research. Netherlands and Norway*] **Publication** — JENER Publ
JENER [*Joint Establishment for Nuclear Energy Research. Netherlands and Norway*] **Report** — JENER Rep
Jennings Magazine — Jennings Mag
Jen-Sal Journal — Jen-Sal J
Jentgen's Artificial Silk Review — Jentgens Artif Silk Rev
Jentgen's Rayon Review — Jentgens Rayon Rev
Jeofizik — JEOFD
JEOL (Japan Electron Optics Laboratory) News — JEOL (Jpn Electron Opt Lab) News
JEOL [*Japan Electron Optics Laboratory*] **News. Series Analytical Instrumentation** — JEOL News Ser Anal Instrum
Jernal Antropoloji dan Sosioloji — J Antro Sos
Jernal Sains Malaysia — J Sains Malays
Jernal Sains Nuklear — J Sains Nukl
Jernal Sejarah — J Sej
Jernkontorets Annaler — Jernkon Ann
Jernkontorets Annaler — Jernkontorets Ann
Jernkontorets Annaler. Edition A — Jernkontorets Ann Ed A
Jernkontorets Annaler. Edition B — Jernkontorets Ann Ed B
Jerome Biblical Commentary — JBC
Jeronimo Zurita. Cuadernos de Historia. Institucion Fernando el Catolico — J Zurita
Jersey Bulletin — Jersey Bul
Jersey Bulletin and Dairy World — Jersey B
Jersey Journal — Jersey J
Jerusalem Journal of International Relations — Jerus J Int Rel
Jerusalem Journal of International Relations — Jerusalem J Int Relat
Jerusalem Post — JP
Jerusalem Post Magazine — JPM
Jerusalem Post Weekly — JPW
Jerusalem Quarterly — Je Q
Jerusalem Quarterly — Jerusalem Q
Jerusalem Quarterly — JQ
Jerusalem Studies in Arabic and Islam — JSAI
Jerusalem Symposia on Quantum Chemistry and Biochemistry — Jerus Symp Quantum Chem Biochem
Jerusalem Winter School for Theoretical Physics — Jerusalem Winter School Theoret Phys
Jeschurun (Berlin) — Jesch
Jessie and John Danz Lectures. University of Washington Press — J and J Danz Lectures
Jesuit Missions — JM
Jesuiten [*Graz*] — Jesu
Jesuites Missionnaires — Jes Miss
Jet — GJET
JET. Journal of Education for Teaching — JET J Educ Teach
Jet Propulsion [*United States*] — Jet Propul
Jet Propulsion — JETPA
Jet Propulsion Laboratory. Publication — Jet Propul Lab Publ
Jet Propulsion Laboratory. Publication 78 — JPL Publ 78
Jet Propulsion Laboratory. Quarterly Technical Review — Jet Propul Lab Q Tech Rev
Jet Propulsion Laboratory. Space Programs Summary — JPL Space Programs Summ
Jet Propulsion Laboratory. Special Publication JPL SP — Jet Propul Lab Spec Publ JPL SP
Jet Propulsion Laboratory. Technical Memorandum — Jet Propul Lab Tech Memo
Jeta e Re — J e R
JETI. Japan Energy and Technology Intelligence — JETI
JETP Letters [*English Translation of JETP Pis'ma v Redaktsiyu*] — JETP Lett
Jeune Afrique — JA
Jeune Afrique [*Paris*] — JEU
Jeune Afrique — JeuneA
Jeune Afrique Economie — JAE
Jeune Cinema — Jeune C
Jeune Scientifique [*Canada*] — Jeune Sci
Jeunes Travailleurs — Jeunes Trav
Jeunesse — J
Jeunesse et Orgue — JeO
Jeunesse et Orgue — Jeunesse
Jewel of Africa [*Zambia*] — JoA
Jewish Advocate [*Bombay*] — JA
Jewish Affairs — JA
Jewish Affairs — JAf
Jewish Affairs — JAff
Jewish Affairs — Jew Aff
Jewish Affairs (Johannesburg) — JAJ
Jewish Affairs (London) — JAL
Jewish Affairs (New York) — JAN
Jewish Apocryphal Literature — JAL
Jewish Audio-Visual Review — JAVR
Jewish Book Annual [*New York*] — JBA
Jewish Chronicle [*London*] — JC
Jewish Chronicle [*London*] — JChr
Jewish Chronicle — Jew Chr
Jewish Chronicle [*London*] — JewChron
Jewish Civilization — Je Ci
Jewish Commentary — Jew Com
Jewish Currents — Je C
Jewish Currents — Jewish Cu
Jewish Daily Bulletin — JDB
Jewish Daily Forward — JDF
Jewish Education — J Ed
Jewish Education — Jewish Ed
Jewish Education — Jewish Educ
Jewish Encyclopedia — JE
Jewish Family Living — JFL
Jewish Family Name File [*Database*] — JFNF
Jewish Forum — Jew For
Jewish Frontier — J Fron
Jewish Frontier — Jew Fron
Jewish Frontier — JF
Jewish Historical Society of England. Miscellanies — JHSEM
Jewish Historical Society of England. Transactions — Jew Hist Soc Engl Trans
Jewish Historical Society of England. Transactions — Jewish Hist Soc of England Trans
Jewish Historical Society of England. Transactions — JHSET
Jewish History Series — JHS
Jewish Intelligencer — J Int
Jewish Journal of Sociology — Jew J Socio
Jewish Journal of Sociology — Jewish J Sociology
Jewish Journal of Sociology [*London*] — JewJSoc
Jewish Journal of Sociology — JJ Soc
Jewish Journal of Sociology — JJS
Jewish Journal of Sociology — JJSO
Jewish Language Review — JLR
Jewish Life [*New York*] — JewL
Jewish Life — JLi
Jewish Memorial Hospital Bulletin — Jew Meml Hosp Bull
Jewish Monthly — JM
Jewish Monuments in Bohemia and Moravia — JMBM
Jewish Newsletter — JN
Jewish Observer and Middle East Review [*London*] — JO
Jewish Observer and Middle East Review — JOMER
Jewish Palestine Exploration Society. Bulletin — JPESB
Jewish Quarterly — JQ
Jewish Quarterly Review — Jew Q R
Jewish Quarterly Review — Jew Q Rev
Jewish Quarterly Review — Jew Quart R
Jewish Quarterly Review — JewQ
Jewish Quarterly Review — JQR
Jewish Review [*London*] — JewRev
Jewish Social Research Series — JSRS
Jewish Social Service Quarterly — JSSQ
Jewish Social Studies — J Soc S
Jewish Social Studies — JeSS
Jewish Social Studies — Jew Soc Stu
Jewish Social Studies — Jew Soc Stud
Jewish Social Studies — Jewish Soc Stud
Jewish Social Studies [*New York*] — JewSocSt
Jewish Social Studies — JSS
Jewish Spectator — J Spec
Jewish Student Review — JSR
Jewish Telegraphic Agency. Daily News Bulletin — JDNB
Jewish Tribune [*Bombay*] — JT
Jewish Universal Encyclopedia — JUE
[*The*] **Jewish Week** — JW
Jewish Year Book — JYB
Jewish Yearbook — JY
Jew's College Publications — JCP
Jezik — J
Jezik in Slovstvo — JiS
Jezyk Polski — JP
Jezyk Polski — JPol
Jezyk Rosyjski — JR
Jezyki Obce w Szkole — JOS
Jezykoznawca — Jz
JFCC (Japan Fine Ceramics Center) Review — JFCC Rev
JFE. Journal du Four Electrique — JFE J Four Electr
JFE. Journal du Four Electrique et des Industries Electrochimiques — JFE J Four Electr Ind Electrochim
JFE. Journal du Four Electrique et des Industries Electrochimiques — JJFED
JGR. Journal of Geophysical Research — JGR J Geophys Res
JGR. Journal of Geophysical Research. Planets — JGR J Geophys Res Planets
JGR. Journal of Geophysical Research. Series A. Space Physics — JGR J Geophys Res A
JGR. Journal of Geophysical Research. Series C. Oceans and Atmospheres — JGR J Geophys Res C Oceans Atmos
JGR. Journal of Geophysical Research. Series D. Atmospheres — JGR J Geophys Res D Atmos
JGR. Journal of Geophysical Research. Solid Earth and Planets — JGR J Geophys Res Solid Earth Planets
Jiangsu Journal of Traditional Chinese Medicine — Jiangsu J Tradit Chin Med
Jiangsu Medical Journal — Jiangsu Med J
Jianzhu Xuebao — CCHPA
Jibi To Rinsho — JIRIA
Jichi Medical School Journal — Jichi Med Sch J
JICST [*Japan Information Center of Science and Technology*] **File on Current Science and Technology Research in Japan** [*Database*] — JICST File CS
JICST [*Japan Information Center of Science and Technology*] **File on Medical Science in Japan** [*Database*] — JICST File MS

JICST [*Japan Information Center of Science and Technology*] **File on Science and Technology** [*Database*] — JICST File ST
JICST [*Japan Information Center of Science and Technology*] **File on Science, Technology, and Medicine in Japan** [*Database*] — JICST File STM
Jidische Kultur Gezelschaft [*Argentina*] — JKG
Jido Seigyo — JDSEA
Jihocesky Sbornik Historicky — JcSH
Jihocesky Sbornik Historicky — JSH
JiJi Securities Data Service [*Database*] — JSD
Jikeikai Medical Journal — Jikeikai Med J
Jikken Keitaigakushi — JIKEA
Jinbun Gakuho [*Journal of Social Science and Humanities*] — JBGH
Jinbun Kenkyu [*Studies in Humanities*] — JBKK
Jinbungaku [*Studies in Humanities*] — JBG
Jinetsu Energi — JIEND
Jinko Zoki — JNZKA
Jinruigaku Zasshi [*Anthropological Journal*] — JZ
Jinsen Medical Journal — Jinsen Med J
JIP/Areal Marketing Database — JIP/AMD
Jishou University Journal. Natural Science Edition — J Jishou Univ Nat Sci Ed
JJATS. Journal. Japanese Association for Thoracic Surgery — JJATS J Jpn Assoc Thorac Surg
JkA. Jernkontorets Annaler — JkA Jernkontorets Ann
JMCI. Journal of Molecular and Cellular Immunology — JMCI J Mol Cell Immunol
JNCI. Journal of the National Cancer Institute — JJIND
JNCI. Journal of the National Cancer Institute — JNCI
JNCI. Journal of the National Cancer Institute — JNCI J Natl Cancer Inst
JNKVV [*Jawaharlal Nehru Krishi Vishwa Vidyalaya*] **Research Journal** — JNKVV Res J
JNM. Journal of Nuclear Medicine — JNM
JNMM. Journal. Institute of Nuclear Materials Management — JNMM
Job Outlook for College Graduates through 1990 — Job Outlk
Job Safety and Health — Job Safe & H
Job Safety and Health [*Database*] — JOSH
Job Safety Consultant — JSCOD
Jobless Newsletter — Jobless Newsl
Jobson's Investment Digest — Jobsons Invest Dig
Jobson's Investment Digest — Jobsons Investment D
Jobson's Mining Yearbook [*Australia*] — Jobsons Min Yearb
Joekull (Reykjavik) — JOKUA
Joenkoepings Laens Hushallningssaellskaps. Tidskrift — Joenkoepings Laens Hushallningssaellsk Tidskr
Joensuun Korkeakoulun Julkaisuja. Sarja B1 — Joensuun Korkeakoulun Julk Sar B1
Joensuun Korkeakoulun Julkaisuja. Sarja B2 — Joensuun Korkeakoulun Julk Sar B2
Joensuun Korkeakoulun Julkaisuja. Sarja B11 — Joensuun Korkeakoulun Julk Sar B11
Joernaal van die Suid-Afrikaanse Chemiese Instituut — J S Afr Chem Inst
JOGN [*Journal of Obstetric, Gynecologic, and Neonatal Nursing*] **Nursing** — JOGN Nurs
JOGN [*Journal of Obstetric, Gynecologic, and Neonatal Nursing*] **Nursing** — JOGNB
Jogtudomanyi Koezloeny — Jogtud Koezl
Johann-Gottfried-Herder Institut Marburg/Lahn. Wissenschaftlicher Dienst — Wiss Dienst
John Alexander Monograph Series on Various Phases of Thoracic Surgery — John Alexander Monogr Ser Var Phases Thorac Surg
John and Mary's Journal. Dickinson College Friends of the Library — John Mary J
John Coffin Memorial Lectures — JCML
John Dewey Society. Yearbook — John Dewey Soc Yrbk
John Donne Journal. Studies in the Age of Donne — JDJ
John Herron Art Institute. Bulletin [*Indianapolis*] — John Herron Art Inst Bul
John Innes Bulletin — John Innes Bull
John Innes Horticultural Institution. Annual Report — John Innes Hortic Inst Annu Rep
John Innes Institute. Annual Report — John Innes Inst Annu Rep
John Innes Symposium — John Innes Symp
John Jacob Abel Symposium on Drug Development. Proceedings — John Jacob Abel Symp Drug Dev Proc
John Lawrence Interdisciplinary Symposium on the Physical and Biomedical Sciences — John Lawrence Interdiscip Symp Phys Biomed Sci
John Lee Pratt International Symposium on Nutrient Management of Food Animals toEmbrace and Protect the Environment — John Lee Pratt Int Symp Nutr Manage Food Anim Enhance Prot En
John Marshall Journal of Practice and Procedure — J Mar J Prac & Proc
John Marshall Journal of Practice and Procedure — J Marshall J
John Marshall Journal of Practice and Procedure — JMJ
John Marshall Journal of Practice and Procedure — John Mar J Prac & Proc
John Marshall Journal of Practice and Procedure — John Marshall J
John Marshall Journal of Practice and Procedure — John Marshall Jr
John Marshall Law Review — J Mar L Rev
John Marshall Law Review — J Mar LR
John Marshall Law Review — JMLR
John Marshall Law Review — John Marsh L Rev
John O'Hara Journal — JOHJ
John Rylands Library. Bulletin — Bull John Ryl Libr
John Rylands Library. Bulletin — John Rylands Lib Bul
John Rylands Library. Bulletin — JRL
John Rylands Library. Bulletin — JRLB
John Updike Newsletter — John Updike Newsl
Johns Hopkins Applied Physics Laboratory. Technical Digest — Johns Hopkins Appl Phys Lab Tech Dig
Johns Hopkins Center for Alternatives to Animal Testing. Newsletter — Johns Hopkins Cent Alternatives Anim Test Newsl
Johns Hopkins Hospital Bulletin — Johns Hopkins Hosp Bul
Johns Hopkins Hospital. Bulletin — Johns Hopkins Hosp Bull
Johns Hopkins Magazine — JHMa
Johns Hopkins Magazine — Johns Hopkins M
Johns Hopkins Magazine — Johns Hopkins Mag
Johns Hopkins Medical Journal — Johns H Med
Johns Hopkins Medical Journal — Johns Hopkins Med J
Johns Hopkins Medical Journal. Supplement — Johns Hopkins Med J Suppl
Johns Hopkins Oceanographic Studies — Johns Hopkins Oceanogr Stud
Johns Hopkins Series in the Mathematical Sciences — Johns Hopkins Ser in Math Sci
Johns Hopkins Studies in Romance Language and Literature — JHSRLL
Johns Hopkins Studies in the Mathematical Sciences — Johns Hopkins Stud Math Sci
Johns Hopkins University. Applied Physics Laboratory. Special Report — Johns Hopkins Univ Appl Phys Lab Spec Rep
Johns Hopkins University. Applied Physics Laboratory. Technical Digest [*United States*] — Johns Hopkins APL Tech Dig
Johns Hopkins University. Applied Physics Laboratory. Technical Digest — Johns Hopkins APL Technical Digest
Johns Hopkins University. Applied Physics Laboratory. Technical Digest — Johns Hopkins Univ Appl Phys Lab Tech Dig
Johns Hopkins University. Chesapeake Bay Institute. Technical Report — Johns Hopkins Univ Chesapeake Bay Inst Tech Rept
Johns Hopkins University. Circular — Johns Hopkins Univ Cir
Johns Hopkins University. McCollum Pratt Institute. Contribution — Johns Hopkins Univ McCollum Pratt Inst Contrib
Johns Hopkins University Studies — Johns Hopkins Univ Studies
Johns Hopkins University. Studies in Geology — Johns Hopkins Univ Studies in Geology
Johns Hopkins University. Studies in Historical and Political Science — Hop U Stud
Johns Hopkins University. Studies in Historical and Political Science — J H U Studies
Johns Hopkins University. Studies in Historical and Political Science — Johns H U Stud
Johns Hopkins University. Studies in Historical and Political Science — Johns Hopkins Univ Stud
Johns Hopkins Workshop on Current Problems in Particle Theory. Proceedings — Johns Hopkins Workshop Curr Probl Part Theory Proc
Johnson Society. Transactions — JST
Johnsonian News Letter — JN
Johnsonian News Letter — JNL
Joho Kagaku Gijutsu Kenkyu Shukai Happyo Ronbunshu — JKGKA
Joho Shori — JOSHA
Joides Journal — Joides J
Joining and Materials — Joining Mater
Joining Sciences — Joining Sci
Joint Army-Navy-Air Force Thermochemical Tables [*Database*] — JANAF
Joint Automatic Control Conference. Preprints of Technical Papers — Joint Automat Contr Conf Prepr Tech Pap
Joint Center Report — JCR
Joint Commission Journal on Quality Improvement — Jt Comm J Qual Improv
Joint Commission on Rural Reconstruction in China (United States and Republic of China). Plant Industry Series — J Comm Rural Reconstr China (US Repub China) Plant Ind Ser
Joint Commission on Rural Reconstruction in China (United States and Republic of China). Plant Industry Series — Jt Comm Rural Reconstr China US Repub China Plant Ind Ser
Joint Conference. Chemical Institute of Canada/American Chemical Society. Abstracts of Papers — J Conf Chem Inst Can Am Chem Soc Abstr Pap
Joint Conference. Chemical Institute of Canada/American Chemical Society. Abstracts of Papers — J Conf CIC/ACS Abstr Pap
Joint Conference. Chemical Institute of Canada and the American Chemical Society. Abstracts of Papers — Jt Conf Chem Inst Can Am Chem Soc Abstr Pap
Joint Conference CIC/ACS. Abstracts of Papers — Jt Conf CIC ACS Abstr Pap
Joint Conference on Cholera — Jt Conf Cholera
Joint Conference on Cholera. Proceedings — Jt Conf Cholera Proc
Joint Conference Proceedings. Ferrous Division/Pacific Coast Meeting. Wire Association International — Jt Conf Proc Ferrous Div Pac Coast Meet Wire Assoc Int
Joint Conference Proceedings. Wire Association International. Nonfererous/Electrical Divisions — Jt Conf Proc Wire Assoc Int Nonferrous Electr Div
Joint Conference. US-Japan Cooperative Medical Science Program. Cholera Panel — Jt Conf US Jpn Coop Med Sci Program Cholera Panel
Joint Congress. European Tissue Culture Society and the European Reticuloendothelial Society — Jt Congr Eur Tissue Cult Soc Eur Reticuloendothel Soc
Joint Corrosion Conference — Jt Corros Conf
Joint Establishment for Nuclear Energy Research (Netherlands and Norway). Publication — Jt Establ Nucl Energy Res Neth Norway Publ
Joint European Torus. Report. JET-R — Jt Eur Torus Rep JET R
Joint Group of Experts on the Scientific Aspects of Marine Pollution — J Group Experts Sci Aspects Mar Pollut
Joint Group of Experts on the Scientific Aspects of Marine Pollution. Reports and Studies — Jt Group Experts Sci Aspects Mar Pollut Rep Stud
Joint Institute for Laboratory Astrophysics. Information Center. Report — JILA Inf Cent Rep
Joint Institute for Laboratory Astrophysics. Information Center. Report — Jt Inst Lab Astrophys Inf Cent Rep
Joint Institute for Laboratory Astrophysics. Report — JILA Rep
Joint Institute for Laboratory Astrophysics. Report — Jt Inst Lab Astrophy Rep

Joint Institute for Nuclear Research. Dubna, USSR. Preprint — Jt Inst Nucl Res Dubna USSR Prepr
Joint Institute for Nuclear Research-CERN School of Physics — Jt Inst Nucl Res CERN Sch Phys
Joint International Conference on Creep. Papers — Jt Int Conf Creep Pap
Joint Oceanographic Institutions for Deep Earth Sampling. Journal — JOIDES Journal
Joint Polytechnics Symposium on Manufacturing Engineering — Jt Polytech Symp Manuf Eng
Joint Publication. Imperial Agricultural Bureaux — Joint Publ Imp Agric Bur
Joint Publications Research Service — JPRS
Joint Symposium. Scaling-Up of Chemical Plant and Processes. Proceedings — Jt Symp Scaling Up Chem Plant Processes Proc
Jokull — JOKU
JOM. Journal. Minerals, Metals, and Materials Society — JOM J Min
JOM. Journal of Occupational Medicine — JJOMD
JOM. Journal of Occupational Medicine [*United States*] — JOM J Occup Med
Jongleur — JG
Jonxis Lectures — Jonxis Lect
Jonxis Lectures [*Elsevier Book Series*] — TJL
Jony Metali Przejsciowych w Ukladach Biologicznych. Seminarium Instytutu Biologii Molekularnej UJ — Jony Met Przejsciowych Ukladach Biol Semin Inst Biol Mol UJ
Jord och Skog — Jord Skog
Jord og Myr. Tidsskrift foer det Norske Jord og Myselskap — JOGM
Jordan Dental Journal — Jordan Dent J
Jordan Lectures in Comparative Religion — JLCR
Jordan Medical Journal — Jordan Med J
Jordan. Ministry of Agriculture. Annual Report (English Edition) — Jordan Minist Agric Annu Rep (Eng Ed)
Jordbruksekonomiska Meddelanden — Jordbruksekon Meddel
Jordbruksekonomiska Meddelanden — Jord-Ekon Medd
Jordbruksekonomiska Meddelanden. Statens Jordbruksnamned — Jordbruksekon Medd Statens Jordbruksnamned
Jordbrukstekniska Institutet. Cirkulaer — Jordbrukstek Inst Cirk
Jordburgs-Teknik — Jdb T
Jorden Runt — JoR
Jornada Medica — Jorn Med
Jornadas Agronomicas. Trabajos — Jornadas Agron Trab
Jornadas Agronomicas y Veterinarias. Universidad de Buenos Aires. Facultad de Agronomia y Veterinaria — Jornadas Agron Vet Univ Buenos Aires Fac Agron Vet
Jornadas Metalurgicas Hispano-Francesas — Jorn Metal Hisp Fr
Jornadas Nacionales de Farmaceuticos Analistas Clinicos. Trabajos — Jorn Nac Farm Anal Clin Trab
Jornadas Tecnicas Papeleras. Trabajos — Jorn Tec Papeleras Trab
Jornal Brasileiro de Doencas Toracicas — J Bras Doencas Torac
Jornal Brasileiro de Ginecologia — J Bras Ginecol
Jornal Brasileiro de Medicina — J Bras Med
Jornal Brasileiro de Medicina — JBRMA
Jornal Brasileiro de Nefrologia — J Bras Nefrol
Jornal Brasileiro de Neurologia — J Bras Neurol
Jornal Brasileiro de Neurologia — JBRNA
Jornal Brasileiro de Patologia — J Bras Patol
Jornal Brasileiro de Psicologia — Jorn Bras Psicol
Jornal Brasileiro de Psiquiatria — J Bras Psiquiatr
Jornal Brasileiro de Psiquiatria — JBPSA
Jornal Brasileiro de Urologia — J Bras Urol
Jornal. Clube de Mineralogia — J Clube Mineral
Jornal de Estomatologia — J Estomat
Jornal de Filologia — JF
Jornal de Letras — JdL
Jornal de Letras — JL
Jornal de Letras e Artes — JLA
Jornal de Medicina de Pernambuco — J Med Pernambuco
Jornal de Mineralogia — J Mineral
Jornal de Noticas — JN
Jornal de Pediatria — J Ped
Jornal de Sciencias Mathematicas, Physicas, e Naturaes — J Sci Math Phys Nat
Jornal de Sciencias Naturais — Jorn Sci Nat
Jornal de Turismo — JT
Jornal do Commercio — J Commercio
Jornal do Commercio — J Do Comm
Jornal do Medico — J Med
Jornal do Medico (Porto) — J Med (Porto)
Jornal do Sindicato Nacional dos Farmaceuticos. Sociedade Farmaceutica Lusitana — J Sind Nac Farm Soc Farm Lusit
Jornal dos Clinicos — JCLIA
Jornal dos Farmaceuticos — J Farm
Jornal o Medico [*Porto*] — JOM
Jornal Portugues de Economia e Financas — J Port Econ e Fins
Jornal. Sociedade das Ciencias Medicas de Lisboa — J Soc Cienc Med Lisb
Jornal Sul-Americano de Biociencias — J Sul-Am Biocienc
Jornal Sul-Americano de Medicina — J Sul-Am Med
JOS. Journal of Official Statistics — JOS J Off Stat
Josa Andras Muzeum Evkoenyve — Josa Andras Muz Ev
Josai Jinbun Kenkyu [*Studies in the Humanities*] — JJK
Josai Shika Daigaku Kiyo. Bulletin of the Josai — Jos Shik Daig Kiyo
Josanpu Zasshi. Japanese Journal for Midwives — Josan Zass
Joseph Quincy Adams Memorial Studies — AMS
JOT. Journal fuer Oberflaechentechnik — JOT J Oberflaechentech
Journal A. Presses Academiques Europeennes — J A
Journal. A Quarterly Journal of Automatic Control — JA Quart J Automat Control
Journal. Aberystwyth Agriculture Society — JAAS
Journal. Academy of General Dentistry — J Acad Gen Dent
Journal. Academy of Natural Sciences of Philadelphia — J Acad Nat Sci Phila
Journal. Academy of Natural Sciences of Philadelphia — J Acad Nat Sci Philadelphia
Journal. Academy of Socialist Agriculture. Moscow — J Acad Soc Agric Moscow
Journal. Acoustical Society of America — J Acoust So
Journal. Acoustical Society of America — J Acoust Soc Am
Journal. Acoustical Society of America — J Acoust Soc Amer
Journal. Acoustical Society of America — J Acoustical Soc Am
Journal. Acoustical Society of America — JAcS
Journal. Acoustical Society of America — JAS
Journal. Acoustical Society of America — JASA
Journal. Acoustical Society of America — JASMA
Journal. Acoustical Society of America — JASMAN
Journal. Acoustical Society of America — Jour Acoust Soc
Journal. Acoustical Society of America. Supplement — J Acoust Soc Am Suppl
Journal. Acoustical Society of India — J Acoust Soc India
Journal. Acoustical Society of Japan — J Acoust Soc Jap
Journal. Acoustical Society of Japan — J Acoust Soc Jpn
Journal. Addiction Research Foundation — J Addict Res Found
Journal. Addiction Research Foundation — JARF
Journal. Adelaide Botanic Gardens — J Adelaide Bot Gard
Journal. Adelaide Botanic Gardens — JABGDP
Journal. Adhesion Society of Japan — J Adhes Soc Jpn
Journal. Adhesive and Sealant Council [*United States*] — J Adhes Sealant Counc
Journal. Aero Medical Society of India — AMSJAX
Journal. Aero Medical Society of India — J Aero Med Soc India
Journal. Aeronautical Sciences — J Aeronaut Sci
Journal. Aeronautical Society of India — J Aeronaut Soc India
Journal. Aeronautical Society of South Africa — J Aeronaut Soc S Afr
Journal. Aerospace Transport Division. American Society of Civil Engineers — J Aerosp Transp Div Am Soc Civ Eng
Journal Africain de Science et Technologie. Serie A. Technologie — J Afr Sci Technol Ser A
Journal. African Society — J Afr S
Journal. African Society — J Afr Soc
Journal. African Society — J African Soc
Journal. African Society — Journ Afric Soc
Journal. Agricultural and Horticultural Society of Western Australia — J Agric Soc Western Australia
Journal. Agricultural Association of China — J Agr Ass China
Journal. Agricultural Association of China — J Agric Ass China
Journal. Agricultural Association of China — J Agric Assoc China
Journal. Agricultural Association of China. New Series — CHNHAN
Journal. Agricultural Association of China. New Series — J Agric Assoc China New Ser
Journal. Agricultural Association of China (Taipei) — J Agric Assoc China Taipei
Journal. Agricultural Chemical Society of Japan — J Agr Che J
Journal. Agricultural Chemical Society of Japan — J Agr Chem Soc Jap
Journal. Agricultural Chemical Society of Japan — J Agric Chem Soc Japan
Journal. Agricultural Chemical Society of Japan — J Agric Chem Soc Jpn
Journal. Agricultural Chemical Society of Japan — NNKKAA
Journal. Agricultural Engineering Society of Japan — J Agr Eng Soc Jap
Journal. Agricultural Experiment Station. Government General Chosen/Noji Shikenjo Kenkyu Hokoku — J Agric Exp Sta Gov Gen Chosen
Journal. Agricultural Experiment Station of Chosen — J Agr Exp Sta Chosen
Journal. Agricultural Laboratory — J Agr Lab
Journal. Agricultural Laboratory [*Chiba*] — NDKSBX
Journal. Agricultural Laboratory (Chiba) — J Agric Lab (Chiba)
Journal. Agricultural Research Centre (Vantaa, Finland) — J Agric Res Cent (Vantaa Finl)
Journal. Agricultural Researches in Tokai-Kinki Region/Tokai Kinki Nogy Kenkyu — J Agric Res Tokai Kinki Region
Journal. Agricultural Society of Japan — J Agric Soc Jpn
Journal. Agricultural Society of Trinidad and Tobago — J Agr Soc Trinidad Tobago
Journal. Agricultural Society of Trinidad and Tobago — J Agric Soc Trin
Journal. Agricultural Society of Trinidad and Tobago — J Agric Soc Trin & Tobago
Journal. Agricultural Society of Trinidad and Tobago — J Agric Soc Trin Tob
Journal. Agricultural Society of Trinidad and Tobago — J Agric Soc Trinidad Tobago
Journal. Agricultural Society of Trinidad and Tobago — JASTAA
Journal. Agricultural Society. University College of Wales — J Agr Soc Wales
Journal. Agricultural Society. University College of Wales — J Agric Soc Univ Coll Wales
Journal. Agricultural Society. University College of Wales (Aberystwyth) — J Agric Soc Univ Coll Wales (Aberyst)
Journal. Aichi Medical University Association — J Aichi Med Univ Assoc
Journal. Air and Waste Management Association — J Air Waste Manag Assoc
Journal. Air Pollution Control Association — J Air Pollu
Journal. Air Pollution Control Association — J Air Pollut Contr Ass
Journal. Air Pollution Control Association — J Air Pollut Control Assoc
Journal. Air Pollution Control Association — J Air Pollution Control Assoc
Journal. Air Pollution Control Association — JAPCA
Journal. Air Pollution Control Association — JPCAAC
Journal. Air Transport Division. American Society of Civil Engineers — J Air Transp Div Am Soc Civ Eng
Journal. Alabama Academy of Science — J Ala Acad Sci
Journal. Alabama Academy of Science — J Alab Acad Sci
Journal. Alabama Academy of Science — J Alabama Acad Sci
Journal. Alabama Academy of Science — JAASAJ
Journal. Alabama Dental Association — ALDJA
Journal. Alabama Dental Association — J Ala Dent Assoc
Journal. Alaska Geological Society — JAG

Journal. Albert Einstein Medical Center — J Albert Einstein Med Cent
Journal. Albert Einstein Medical Center — JAEMA
Journal. Albert Einstein Medical Center [*Philadelphia*] — JAEMAL
Journal. Albert Einstein Medical Center (Philadelphia) — J Albert Einstein Med Cent (Phila)
Journal. Alberta Society of Petroleum Geologists — J Alberta Soc Pet Geol
Journal. All India Dental Association — J All India Dent Assoc
Journal. All India Institute of Medical Sciences — J All India Inst Med Sci
Journal. All India Institute of Medical Sciences — JAISDS
Journal. All India Institute of Mental Health — J All India Inst Ment Health
Journal. All India Ophthalmological Society — J All India Ophthalmol Soc
Journal. Allied Dental Societies — J Allied Dent Soc
Journal. All-India Ophthalmological Society — J All Ind Ophth Soc
Journal. Alumni Association. College of Physicians and Surgeons (Baltimore) [*A publication*] — J Alumni Ass Coll Phys and Surg (Baltimore)
Journal. American Academy of Applied Nutrition — J Am Acad Appl Nutr
Journal. American Academy of Audiology — J Am Acad Audiol
Journal. American Academy of Child and Adolescent Psychiatry — ICAP
Journal. American Academy of Child and Adolescent Psychiatry — J Am Acad Child Adolesc Psychiatry
Journal. American Academy of Child Psychiatry — J Am A Chil
Journal. American Academy of Child Psychiatry — J Am Acad Child Psych
Journal. American Academy of Child Psychiatry — J Am Acad Child Psychiatry
Journal. American Academy of Child Psychiatry — J Am Academy Child Psychiatry
Journal. American Academy of Child Psychiatry — JACPA
Journal. American Academy of Dermatology — J Am Acad Dermatol
Journal. American Academy of Dermatology — JAADDB
Journal. American Academy of Gnathologic Orthopedics — J Am Acad Gnathol Orthop
Journal. American Academy of Gold Foil Operators — J Am Acad Gold Foil Oper
Journal. American Academy of Psychoanalysis — J Am Acad P
Journal. American Academy of Psychoanalysis — J Am Acad Psychoanal
Journal. American Academy of Psychoanalysis — J Amer Acad Psychoanal
Journal. American Academy of Psychoanalysis — JAAP
Journal. American Academy of Psychoanalysis — JAAPCC
Journal. American Academy of Religion — J Am A Rel
Journal. American Academy of Religion — J Am Acad Rel
Journal. American Academy of Religion — J Am Acad Relig
Journal. American Academy of Religion — J Am Acad Religion
Journal. American Academy of Religion — JAAR
Journal. American Academy of Religion [*Brattleboro, VT*] — JAmAcRel
Journal. American Academy of Religion — PJAA
Journal. American Academy of Religion. Thematic Studies — JAAR Thematic St
Journal. American Analgesia Society — J Am Analg Soc
Journal. American Animal Hospital Association — J Am Anim Hosp Assoc
Journal. American Animal Hospital Association — JAAHBL
Journal. American Association for Hygiene and Baths — J Am Assoc
Journal. American Association for Hygiene and Baths — J Am Assoc Hyg Baths
Journal. American Association for Promoting Hygiene and Public Baths — J Am Assoc Promot Hyg Public Baths
Journal. American Association for the Promotion of Science, Literature, and the Arts — J Amer Assoc Promot Sci
Journal. American Association of Cereal Chemists — J Am Assoc Cereal Chem
Journal. American Association of Medical Record Librarians — J Am Ass Med Rec Libr
Journal. American Association of Nephrology Nurses and Technicians — J AANNT
Journal. American Association of Nephrology Nurses and Technicians — J Am Assoc Nephrol Nurses Tech
Journal. American Association of Nurse Anesthetists — J Am Assoc Nurse Anesth
Journal. American Association of Teacher Educators in Agriculture — J Am Assoc Teach Educ Agric
Journal. American Association of Variable Star Observers — J Am Assoc Variable Star Obs
Journal. American Audiology Society — J Am Audiol Soc
Journal. American Audiology Society — JAASD
Journal. American Auditory Society — J Am Aud Soc
Journal. American Bakers Association and American Institute of Baking — J Am Bakers Assoc Am Inst Baking
Journal. American Board of Family Practice — J Am Board Fam Pract
Journal. American Ceramic Society — J Am Cer Soc
Journal. American Ceramic Society — J Am Ceram
Journal. American Ceramic Society — J Am Ceram Soc
Journal. American Ceramic Society — J Amer Ceram Soc
Journal. American Ceramic Society — JACTA
Journal. American Ceramic Society Incorporating Advanced Ceramic Materials and Communications — J Am Ceram Soc Adv Ceram Mater Commun
Journal. American Ceramic Society with Communications — J Am Ceram Soc Commun
Journal. American Chamber of Commerce of the Philippines — JAACP
Journal. American Chemical Society — Amer Chem Soc J
Journal. American Chemical Society — J Am Chem S
Journal. American Chemical Society — J Am Chem Soc
Journal. American Chemical Society — J Amer Chem Soc
Journal. American Chemical Society — JACS
Journal. American Chemical Society — JACSA
Journal. American Chemical Society — JACSAT
Journal. American College Health Association — J Am Coll H
Journal. American College Health Association — J Am Coll Health Assn
Journal. American College Health Association — J Am Coll Health Assoc
Journal. American College Health Association — JAHAA
Journal. American College Health Association — JAHAAY
Journal. American College of Cardiology — J Am Coll Cardiol
Journal. American College of Cardiology — JACCDI
Journal. American College of Dentists — J Am Coll Dent
Journal. American College of Dentists — J Amer Coll Dent
Journal. American College of Dentists — JACDA
Journal. American College of Emergency Physicians — JACEP
Journal. American College of Emergency Physicians and the University Association for Emergency Medical Services — JACEP
Journal. American College of Nutrition — J Am Coll Nutr
Journal. American College of Nutrition — JONUDL
Journal. American College of Surgeons — J Am Coll Surg
Journal. American College of Toxicology — J Am Coll Toxicol
Journal. American College of Toxicology — JACT
Journal. American College of Toxicology — JACTDZ
Journal. American College of Toxicology. Part B — J Amer Coll Toxicol Part B
Journal. American Concrete Institute — J Am Concr Inst
Journal. American Concrete Institute — JACI
Journal. American Concrete Institute — JACIA
Journal. American Dental Association — J Am Dent A
Journal. American Dental Association — J Am Dent Assoc
Journal. American Dental Association — JADSA
Journal. American Dental Association — JADSAY
Journal. American Dental Association and the Dental Cosmos — J Am Dent Assoc Dent Cosmos
Journal. American Dental Hygienists' Association — J Am Dent Hyg Assoc
Journal. American Dental Hygienists' Association — JAHYA4
Journal. American Dental Society of Anesthesiology — J Am Dent Soc Anesthesiol
Journal. American Dietetic Association — GADA
Journal. American Dietetic Association — J Am Diet A
Journal. American Dietetic Association — J Am Diet Assoc
Journal. American Dietetic Association — J Am Dietet A
Journal. American Dietetic Association — J Amer Diet Ass
Journal. American Dietetic Association — JADAA
Journal. American Dietetic Association — JADAAE
Journal. American Dietetic Association — JOAD
Journal. American Geographical and Statistical Society — JAGS
Journal. American Geriatrics Society — J Am Ger So
Journal. American Geriatrics Society — J Am Geriat Soc
Journal. American Geriatrics Society — J Am Geriatr Soc
Journal. American Geriatrics Society — J Am Geriatrics Soc
Journal. American Geriatrics Society — JAGSA
Journal. American Geriatrics Society — JAGSAF
Journal. American Health Care Association — J Am Health Care Assoc
Journal. American Helicopter Society — J Am Helicopter Soc
Journal. American Helicopter Society — J Amer Heli
Journal. American Industrial Hygiene Association — J Am Ind Hyg Assoc
Journal. American Institute of Architecture — Jour Am Inst Archit
Journal. American Institute of Electrical Engineers — J Am Inst Electr Eng
Journal. American Institute of Homeopathy — J Am Inst Homeop
Journal. American Institute of Homeopathy — J Am Inst Homeopath
Journal. American Institute of Homeopathy — J Am Inst Homeopathy
Journal. American Institute of Homeopathy — JAIHA
Journal. American Institute of Homeopathy — JAIHAQ
Journal. American Institute of Metals — J Am Inst Met
Journal. American Institute of Planners — AIPJA
Journal. American Institute of Planners — J Am Inst P
Journal. American Institute of Planners — J Am Inst Plann
Journal. American Institute of Planners — J Amer Inst Planners
Journal. American Intraocular Implant Society — AIIJD
Journal. American Intraocular Implant Society — J Am Intraocul Implant Soc
Journal. American Judicature Society — Am Jud Soc'y
Journal. American Judicature Society — J Am Jud Soc
Journal. American Judicature Society — Jour Am Jud Soc
Journal. American Judicature Society — Judicature
Journal. American Killifish Association — AKAJAV
Journal. American Killifish Association — J Am Killifish Assoc
Journal. American Leather Chemists' Association — J Am Leath
Journal. American Leather Chemists' Association — J Am Leath Chem Ass
Journal. American Leather Chemists' Association — J Am Leather Chem Assoc
Journal. American Leather Chemists' Association — J Amer Leather Chem Ass
Journal. American Leather Chemists' Association — JALCA
Journal. American Leather Chemists' Association — JALCAQ
Journal. American Leather Chemists' Association. Supplement — J Am Leather Chem Assoc Suppl
Journal. American Leather Chemists' Association. Supplement — JLCSA4
Journal. American Liszt Society — J ALS
Journal. American Liszt Society — JL
Journal. American Medical Association — J Am Med A
Journal. American Medical Association — J Am Med Ass
Journal. American Medical Association — J Am Med Assoc
Journal. American Medical Association — J Amer Med Ass
Journal. American Medical Association — JAMA
Journal. American Medical Association — JAMAA
Journal. American Medical Association — JAMAAP
Journal. American Medical Informatics Association — J Am Med Inform Assoc
Journal. American Medical Record Association — J Am Med Rec Assoc
Journal. American Medical Technologists — J Am Med Technol
Journal. American Medical Technologists — JAMDAY
Journal. American Medical Women's Association — J Am Med Wom Ass
Journal. American Medical Women's Association — J Am Med Wom Assoc
Journal. American Medical Women's Association — J Am Med Women Assoc
Journal. American Medical Women's Association — J Am Med Women's Assoc
Journal. American Medical Women's Association — JAMWA
Journal. American Medical Women's Association — JAMWAN

Journal. American Mosquito Control Association — J Am Mosq Control Assoc
Journal. American Mosquito Control Association — JAMAET
Journal. American Mosquito Control Association. Supplement — J Am Mosq Control Assoc Suppl
Journal. American Musical Instrument Society — J Am Mus In
Journal. American Musical Instrument Society — JI
Journal. American Musical Society — JAMS
Journal. American Musicological Society — J Am Music
Journal. American Musicological Society — J Amer Musicol Soc
Journal. American Musicological Society — JA
Journal. American Musicological Society — JAMS
Journal. American Musicological Society — JMUSA
Journal. American Musicological Society — PAJM
Journal. American Oil Chemists' Society — J Am Oil Ch
Journal. American Oil Chemists' Society — J Am Oil Chem Soc
Journal. American Oil Chemists' Society — J Amer Oil
Journal. American Oil Chemists' Society — J Amer Oil Chem Soc
Journal. American Oil Chemists' Society — JAOCA
Journal. American Oil Chemists' Society — JAOCA7
Journal. American Oil Chemists' Society — JAOCS
Journal. American Optometric Association — J Am Optom Assoc
Journal. American Optometric Association — JAOPB
Journal. American Optometric Association — JAOPBD
Journal. American Oriental Society — Amer Orient Soc J
Journal. American Oriental Society — J Am Or Soc
Journal. American Oriental Society — J Am Orient
Journal. American Oriental Society — J Am Orient Soc
Journal. American Oriental Society — J Amer Orient Soc
Journal. American Oriental Society — JAOS
Journal. American Oriental Society — PJOS
Journal. American Oriental Society. Supplement — JAOSS
Journal. American Osteopathic Association — J Am Osteopath A
Journal. American Osteopathic Association — J Am Osteopath Assoc
Journal. American Osteopathic Association — JAOA
Journal. American Osteopathic Association — JAOAA
Journal. American Osteopathic Association — JAOAAZ
Journal. American Paraplegia Society — J Am Paraplegia Soc
Journal. American Peanut Research and Education Association — J Am Peanut Res Educ Assoc
Journal. American Peanut Research and Education Association — JAMPB3
Journal. American Peat Society — J Am Peat Soc
Journal. American Pharmaceutical Association — J Am Pharm
Journal. American Pharmaceutical Association — J Am Pharm Ass
Journal. American Pharmaceutical Association — J Am Pharm Assoc
Journal. American Pharmaceutical Association — J Amer Pharm Assoc
Journal. American Pharmaceutical Association — Journ Amer Pharm Assoc
Journal. American Pharmaceutical Association — JPHAA
Journal. American Pharmaceutical Association — JPHAA3
Journal. American Pharmaceutical Association. Practical Pharmacy Edition — J Am Phar
Journal. American Pharmaceutical Association. Practical Pharmacy Edition — J Am Pharm Assoc Pract Pharm Ed
Journal. American Pharmaceutical Association. Scientific Edition — J Am Pharm Assoc Sci Ed
Journal. American Pharmaceutical Association. Scientific Edition — J Amer Pharm Ass Sci Ed
Journal. American Pharmaceutical Association. Scientific Edition — JAPMA8
Journal. American Physical Therapy Association — JAPTB
Journal. American Planning Association — AIP
Journal. American Planning Association — J Am Plann Assoc
Journal. American Planning Association — J Amer Plann Assoc
Journal. American Planning Association — JAIP
Journal. American Planning Association — JAM
Journal. American Planning Association — JAPA
Journal. American Podiatric Medical Association — J Am Podiatr Med Assoc
Journal. American Podiatric Medical Association — JAPAEA
Journal. American Podiatry Association — J Am Podiatry Assoc
Journal. American Podiatry Association — JPDAAH
Journal. American Portuguese Society — JAPS
Journal. American Psychoanalytic Association — J Am Psycho
Journal. American Psychoanalytic Association — J Am Psychoanal Ass
Journal. American Psychoanalytic Association — J Am Psychonal Assoc
Journal. American Psychoanalytic Association — J Amer Psychoanal Ass
Journal. American Psychoanalytic Association — JAPOA
Journal. American Psychoanalytic Association — JAPOAE
Journal. American Real Estate and Urban Economics Association — J Am Real Estate Urban Econ Assoc
Journal. American Research Center in Egypt — JARCE
Journal. American Research Center in Egypt — Jnl Am Res Cent Egypt
Journal. American Rocket Society — J Am Rocket Soc
Journal. American Scientific Affiliation — J Amer Scient Affil
Journal. American Scientific Affiliation — JASA
Journal. American Society for Geriatric Dentistry — J Am Soc Geriatr Dent
Journal. American Society for Horticultural Science — J Am S Hort
Journal. American Society for Horticultural Science — J Am Soc Hort Sci
Journal. American Society for Horticultural Science — J Am Soc Hortic Sci
Journal. American Society for Horticultural Science — J Amer Soc Hort Sci
Journal. American Society for Horticultural Science — JOSHB
Journal. American Society for Horticultural Science — JOSHB5
Journal. American Society for Information Science — AISJB
Journal. American Society for Information Science — Am Soc Info Science J
Journal. American Society for Information Science — J Am S Infor
Journal. American Society for Information Science — J Am Soc Inf Sci
Journal. American Society for Information Science — J Amer Soc Inform Sci
Journal. American Society for Information Science — JAS
Journal. American Society for Information Science — JASIS
Journal. American Society for Information Science — JSI
Journal. American Society for Preventive Dentistry — J Am Soc Prev Dent
Journal. American Society for Psychical Research — J Am S Psyc
Journal. American Society for Psychical Research — J Am Soc Psych Res
Journal. American Society for Psychical Research — JASPR
Journal. American Society for the Study of Orthodontics — J Am Soc Study Orthod
Journal. American Society of Agronomy — J Am Soc Agron
Journal. American Society of Agronomy — J Amer Soc Agron
Journal. American Society of Agronomy — Jour Am Soc Agron
Journal. American Society of Brewing Chemists — J Am Soc Brew Chem
Journal. American Society of Brewing Chemists — JSBCD3
Journal. American Society of Chartered Life Underwriters — J Am Soc CLU
Journal. American Society of Echocardiography — J Am Soc Echocardiogr
Journal. American Society of Farm Managers and Rural Appraisers — J Amer Soc Farm Manage Rural Appraisers
Journal. American Society of Heating and Ventilating Engineers — J Am Soc Heat Vent Eng
Journal. American Society of Mechanical Engineers — J Am Soc Mech Eng
Journal. American Society of Naval Engineers — J Am Soc Nav Eng
Journal. American Society of Nephrology — J Am Soc Nephrol
Journal. American Society of Psychosomatic Dentistry — JSPDA5
Journal. American Society of Psychosomatic Dentistry and Medicine — J Am Soc Psychosom Dent
Journal. American Society of Psychosomatic Dentistry and Medicine — J Am Soc Psychosom Dent Med
Journal. American Society of Psychosomatic Dentistry and Medicine — JPDMBK
Journal. American Society of Safety Engineers — J Am Soc Saf Eng
Journal. American Society of Safety Engineers — J Amer Soc Safety Eng
Journal. American Society of Safety Engineers — JSSEA
Journal. American Society of Sugar Beet Technologists — J Am Soc Sug Beet Technol
Journal. American Society of Sugar Beet Technologists — J Am Soc Sugar Beet Technol
Journal. American Society of Sugar Beet Technologists — J Amer Soc Sugar Beet Tech
Journal. American Society of Sugar Beet Technologists — J Amer Soc Sugar Beet Technol
Journal. American Society of Sugar Beet Technologists — JASBA
Journal. American Society of Sugar Beet Technologists — JASBAO
Journal. American Statistical Association — J Am Stat A
Journal. American Statistical Association — J Am Stat Assoc
Journal. American Statistical Association — J Amer Statist Assoc
Journal. American Statistical Association — JASA
Journal. American Statistical Association — JSTNA
Journal. American Steel Treaters' Society — J Am Steel Treaters' Soc
Journal. American Studies Association of Texas — JASAT
Journal. American Venereal Disease Association — J Am Vener Dis Assoc
Journal. American Venereal Disease Association — JAVAD5
Journal. American Veterinary Medical Association — J Am Vet Me
Journal. American Veterinary Medical Association — J Am Vet Med Ass
Journal. American Veterinary Medical Association — J Am Vet Med Assoc
Journal. American Veterinary Medical Association — J Amer Vet Med Ass
Journal. American Veterinary Medical Association — JAVMA
Journal. American Veterinary Medical Association — JAVMA4
Journal. American Veterinary Radiology Society — J Am Vet Ra
Journal. American Veterinary Radiology Society — J Am Vet Radiol Soc
Journal. American Veterinary Radiology Society — JAVRAJ
Journal. American Viola Society — J Am Voila S
Journal. American Water Works Association — J Am Water
Journal. American Water Works Association — J Am Water Works Assoc
Journal. American Water Works Association — J Amer Water Works Ass
Journal. American Water Works Association — JAWWA
Journal. American Welding Society — J Am Weld Soc
Journal. American Wine Society — J Am Wine Soc
Journal. American Zinc Institute — J Am Zinc Inst
Journal. Anatomical Society of India — J Anat Soc Ind
Journal. Anatomical Society of India — J Anat Soc India
Journal. Anatomical Society of India — JAINAA
Journal. Ancient Near East Society of Columbia University — J Anc Near East Soc
Journal. Ancient Near Eastern Society — JANES
Journal. Ancient Near Eastern Society. Columbia University — J Anc Near East Soc Columbia Univ
Journal and Proceedings. Arts and Crafts Society of Ireland — J Proc Arts Crafts Soc Ir
Journal and Proceedings. Asiatic Society of Bengal — J Proc Asiat Soc Bengal
Journal and Proceedings. Asiatic Society of Bengal — JASB
Journal and Proceedings. Australian Jewish Historical Society — JAJHS
Journal and Proceedings. Institute of Chemistry of Great Britain and Ireland — J Proc Inst Chem GB Irel
Journal and Proceedings. Institute of Road Transport Engineers — J Proc Inst Rd Transp Engrs
Journal and Proceedings. Institute of Sewage Purification — J Proc Inst Sewage Purif
Journal and Proceedings. Institution of Chemists (India) — J Proc Inst Chem (India)
Journal and Proceedings. Institution of Chemists (India) — J Proc Instn Chem (India)
Journal and Proceedings. Institution of Mechanical Engineers. London — J Proc Inst Mech Eng London
Journal and Proceedings. Oil Technologists' Association — J Proc Oil Technol Assoc

Journal and Proceedings. Royal Asiatic Society of Bengal — JPASB
Journal and Proceedings. Royal Institute of Chemistry — J Proc R Inst Chem
Journal and Proceedings. Royal Society of New South Wales — J Proc R Soc NSW
Journal and Proceedings. Royal Society of New South Wales — J Proc Roy Soc NSW
Journal and Proceedings. Royal Society of New South Wales — JPRSA
Journal and Proceedings. Royal Society of Western Australia — J Proc R Soc West Aust
Journal and Proceedings. Sydney Technical College. Chemical Society — J Proc Sydney Tech Coll Chem Soc
Journal and Transactions. Harbin Polytechnic Institute. Manchuria, China — J Trans Harbin Polytech Inst Manchuria China
Journal and Transactions. Society of Engineers (London) — J Trans Soc Eng (London)
Journal. Andhra Historical Research Society — J Andhra Hist Res Soc
Journal. Andhra Historical Research Society — JAHRS
Journal. Anglo-Mongolian Society — J Anglo-Mongol Soc
Journal. Animal Technicians Association — J Anim Tech Ass
Journal. Animal Technicians Association — J Anim Tech Assoc
Journal. Animal Technicians Association — JATAAQ
Journal. Annamalai University — J Annamalai Univ
Journal. Annamalai University. Part B — J Annamalai Univ Part B
Journal. Anthropological Institute — JAI
Journal. Anthropological Institute of Great Britain and Ireland — J Anthropol Inst
Journal. Anthropological Institute of Great Britain and Ireland — Journ Anthr Inst
Journal. Anthropological Society of Bombay — J Anthrop Soc Bombay
Journal. Anthropological Society of Bombay — JASB
Journal. Anthropological Society of Nippon — J Anthr S N
Journal. Anthropological Society of Nippon — J Anthropol Soc Nippon
Journal. Anthropological Society of Nippon — JIZAAA
Journal. Anthropological Society of Nippon/Jinruigaku Zasshi (Tokyo) — J Anthrop Soc Tokyo
Journal. Anthropological Society of Oxford — J Anthrop Soc Oxford
Journal. Anthropological Society of Oxford — J Anthropol Soc Oxford
Journal. AOAC [Association of Official Analytical Chemists] International — J AOAC Inst
Journal. Aoyama Gakuin Woman's Junior College — J Aoyama Gakuin Woman's Jr Coll
Journal. Arab Maritime Transport Academy — MIZ
Journal. Arab Veterinary Medical Association — J Arab Vet Med Assoc
Journal. Archaeological Institute of America — JAIA
Journal. Arizona Academy of Science — J Ariz Acad Sci
Journal. Arizona-Nevada Academy of Science — J Ariz Nev Acad Sci
Journal. Arkansas Medical Society — J Ark Med Soc
Journal. Arkansas Medical Society — J Arkansas Med Soc
Journal. Arkansas Medical Society — JAMSA
Journal. Arms and Armour Society — J Arms Armour Soc
Journal. Arnold Arboretum — J Arn Arb
Journal. Arnold Arboretum — J Arn Arbor
Journal. Arnold Arboretum — Jour Arnold Arboretum
Journal. Arnold Arboretum — Journ Arn Arb
Journal. Arnold Arboretum. Harvard University — J Arnold Arbor
Journal. Arnold Arboretum. Harvard University — J Arnold Arbor Harv Univ
Journal. Arnold Arboretum (Harvard University) — J Arnold Arboretum Harvard Univ
Journal. Arnold Schoenberg Institute — J A Schoenb
Journal. Arnold Schoenberg Institute — J Arnold Schoenberg Inst
Journal. Arnold Schoenberg Institute — JASI
Journal. Arnold Schoenberg Institute — JS
Journal. Asahikawa National College of Technology — J Asahikawa Natl Coll Technol
Journal. Asahikawa Technical College — J Asahikawa Tech Coll
Journal. Asahikawa Technical College — J Asahikawa Tech College
Journal. Asian Pacific Dental Student Association (Tokyo) — J APDSA (Tokyo)
Journal. Asiatic Society — J Asiat Soc
Journal. Asiatic Society. Bengal (Letters) — JASB(L)
Journal. Asiatic Society. Letters — JASL
Journal. Asiatic Society of Bangladesh — ASBJ
Journal. Asiatic Society of Bangladesh — J Asiat Soc Bangla
Journal. Asiatic Society of Bangladesh. Science — J Asiat Soc Bangladesh Sci
Journal. Asiatic Society of Bengal — J As Soc Beng
Journal. Asiatic Society of Bengal — J Asiat Soc Bengal
Journal. Asiatic Society of Bengal — JASB
Journal. Asiatic Society of Bengal — Jour As Soc Nat Hist Bengal
Journal. Asiatic Society of Bengal — Journ Asiat
Journal. Asiatic Society of Bengal. Letters — J Asiat Soc Bengal Lett
Journal. Asiatic Society of Bengal. Science — J Asiat Soc Bengal Sci
Journal. Asiatic Society of Bombay — J Asiat Soc Bombay
Journal. Asiatic Society of Bombay — JAS B
Journal. Asiatic Society of Bombay — JASBo
Journal. Asiatic Society of Bombay. Supplement — JASBoS
Journal. Asiatic Society of Calcutta — JAS Calcutta
Journal. Asiatic Society of Calcutta — JASC
Journal. Asiatic Society of Great Britain and Ireland — JAS
Journal. Asiatic Society of Pakistan — JASP
Journal. Asiatic Society. Science — J Asiat Soc Sci
Journal Asiatique — J Asiat
Journal Asiatique — J Asiatique
Journal Asiatique — JA
Journal Asiatique [*Paris*] — JAs
Journal. Assam Research Society — J Assam Res Soc
Journal. Assam Research Society — JARS
Journal. Assam Science Society — J Assam Sci Soc
Journal. ASSE (American Society of Safety Engineers) — J ASSE
Journal. Association Canadienne des Radiologistes — J Assoc Can Radiol
Journal. Association for Academic Minority Physicians — J Assoc Acad Minor Phys
Journal. Association for Computing Machinery — J Ass Comput Mach
Journal. Association for Computing Machinery — J Assoc Comput Mach
Journal. Association for Computing Machinery — JACM
Journal. Association for Education by Radio-Television — JAERT
Journal. Association for Hospital Medical Education — J Assoc Hosp Med Educ
Journal. Association for Physical and Mental Rehabilitation [*United States*] [*A publication*] — J Assoc Phys Ment Rehabil
Journal. Association for the Advancement of Agricultural Sciences in Africa — J Assoc Adv Agric Sci Afr
Journal. Association for the Advancement of Medical Instrumentation — J Ass Advan Med Instrum
Journal. Association for the Advancement of Medical Instrumentation — J Assoc Adv Med Instrum
Journal. Association for the Care of Children in Hospitals — J Assoc Care Child Hosp
Journal. Association for the Care of Children's Health — J Assoc Care Child Health
Journal. Association for the Study of Perception — J As Stud P
Journal. Association for the Study of Perception — J Assoc Study Percept
Journal. Association Medicale Canadienne — J Assoc Med Can
Journal. Association Medicale Mutuelle — Journ Ass Med Mut
Journal. Association of American Medical Colleges — J Assoc Am Med Coll
Journal. Association of Engineering Societies — J Assoc Eng Soc
Journal. Association of Engineers and Architects in Israel — J Assoc Eng Archit Isr
Journal. Association of Engineers and Architects in Palestine — J Assoc Eng Archit Palest
Journal. Association of Engineers (Calcutta) — J Assoc Eng (Calcutta)
Journal. Association of Engineers (India) — J Assoc Eng (India)
Journal. Association of Lunar and Planetary Observers. Strolling Astronomer [*A publication*] — J Assoc Lunar and Planet Obs Strolling Astron
Journal. Association of Medical Illustrators — J Assoc Med Illus
Journal. Association of Military Surgeons. United States — J Assn Mil Surg US
Journal. Association of Nurses in AIDS Care — J Assoc Nurses AIDS Care
Journal. Association of Official Agricultural Chemists — J Ass Off Agric Chem
Journal. Association of Official Agricultural Chemists — J Assoc Off Agric Chem
Journal. Association of Official Analytical Chemists — J AOAC
Journal. Association of Official Analytical Chemists — J Ass Off Analyt Chem
Journal. Association of Official Analytical Chemists — J Ass Offic Anal Chem
Journal. Association of Official Analytical Chemists — J Assoc Off Anal Chem
Journal. Association of Official Analytical Chemists — J Assoc Offic Anal Chem
Journal. Association of Pediatric Oncology Nurses — J Assoc Pediatr Oncol Nurses
Journal. Association of Personal Computers for Chemists — J Assoc Pers Comput Chem
Journal. Association of Physicians of India — J Assoc Physicians India
Journal. Association of Public Analysts — J Ass Public Analysts
Journal. Association of Public Analysts — J Assoc Public Anal
Journal. Association of Teachers of Italian — JATI
Journal. Association of Teachers of Japanese — J Asso Teach Ja
Journal. Association of Veterinary Anaesthetists — J Assoc Vet Anaesth
Journal. Association Scientifique de l'Ouest Africain — J Assoc Sci Ouest Afr
Journal. Astronomical Society of Victoria — J Astronomical Soc VIC
Journal. Atlantic Provinces Linguistic Association/Revue. Association de Linguistique des Provinces Atlantiques — JAPLA
Journal. Atomic Energy Commission (Japan) — J At Energy Comm (Jpn)
Journal. Atomic Energy Society of Japan — J At Energy Soc Jap
Journal. Atomic Energy Society of Japan — J At Energy Soc Jpn
Journal. Audio Engineering Society — ADIOA
Journal. Audio Engineering Society — J Aud Eng S
Journal. Audio Engineering Society — J Aud Eng Soc
Journal. Audio Engineering Society — J Audio Eng Soc
Journal. Audio Engineering Society — JAES
Journal. Australasian Ceramic Society — J Australas Ceram Soc
Journal. Australasian Commercial Teachers' Association — JACTA
Journal. Australasian Institute of Metals — J Australas Inst Met
Journal. Australasian Universities Modern Language Association — JAUMLA
Journal. Australian Catholic Historical Society — J Aust Cath Hist Soc
Journal. Australian Ceramic Society — J Aust Ceram Soc
Journal. Australian Ceramic Society — J Aust Ceramic Soc
Journal. Australian College of Speech Therapists — J Aust Coll Speech Ther
Journal. Australian Entomological Society — J Aust Ent Soc
Journal. Australian Entomological Society — J Aust Entomol Soc
Journal. Australian Institute of Agricultural Science — J Aus I Agr
Journal. Australian Institute of Agricultural Science — J Aust Inst Ag Science
Journal. Australian Institute of Agricultural Science — J Aust Inst Agr Sci
Journal. Australian Institute of Agricultural Science — J Aust Inst Agric Sci
Journal. Australian Institute of Agricultural Science — J Austral Inst Agric Sci
Journal. Australian Institute of Agricultural Science — JAIAS
Journal. Australian Institute of Horticulture — J Aust Inst Hort
Journal. Australian Institute of Horticulture — J Aust Inst Hortic
Journal. Australian Institute of Metals — J Aus I Met
Journal. Australian Institute of Metals — J Aust Inst Met
Journal. Australian Institute of Metals — J Aust Inst Metals
Journal. Australian Institute of Surgical and Dental Technicians — J Aust Inst Surg Dent Tech
Journal. Australian Mathematical Society — J Aust Math Soc
Journal. Australian Mathematical Society — JAUMA
Journal. Australian Mathematical Society. Series A — J Austral Math Soc Ser A

Journal. Australian Mathematical Society. Series A. Pure Mathematics and Statistics — J Aus Mat A
Journal. Australian Mathematical Society. Series B — J Austral Math Soc Ser B
Journal. Australian Mathematical Society. Series B. Applied Mathematics — J Aus Mat B
Journal. Australian Mathematical Society. Series B. Applied Mathematics — JAMMD
Journal. Australian Planning Institute — J Aust Planning Inst
Journal. Australian Rhododendron Society — J Austral Rhododendron Soc
Journal. Australian Stipendiary Magistrates' Association — ASMA
Journal. Baltimore College of Dental Surgery — J Baltimore Coll Dent Surg
Journal. Bangladesh Academy of Sciences — J Bangladesh Acad Sci
Journal. Baoji College of Arts and Science. Natural Science — J Baoji College Arts Sci Nat Sci
Journal. Bar Association of the District of Columbia — J BADC
Journal. Bar Association of the District of Columbia — JBA Dist Colum
Journal. Bar Association of the State of Kansas — J BA Kan
Journal. Bar Association of the State of Kansas — JB Assn St Kan
Journal. Bar Association of the State of Kansas — JBK
Journal. Bar Council of India — Jnl Bar Cound India
Journal. Barbados Museum and Historical Society — BMHS/J
Journal. Barbados Museum and Historical Society — J Barb Mus Hist Soc
Journal. Beijing Institute of Technology — J Beijing Inst Tech
Journal Belge de Medecine Physique et de Rehabilitation — J Belge Med Phys Rehabil
Journal Belge de Medecine Physique et de Rhumatologie — J Belge Med Phys Rhumatol
Journal Belge de Neurologie et de Psychiatrie — J Belge Neurol Psychiatr
Journal Belge de Neurologie et de Psychiatrie — Journ Be Neur Psych
Journal Belge de Radiologie — J Belg Rad
Journal Belge de Radiologie — J Belge Radiol
Journal Belge de Radiologie — Jl Belge Radiol
Journal Belge de Radiologie — Journ Be Radiol
Journal Belge de Radiologie. Monographie [*Belgium*] — J Belge Radiol Monogr
Journal Belge de Rhumatologie et de Medecine Physique — J Belge Rhumatol Med Phys
Journal Belge d'Urologie — Journ Be Urol
Journal. Bergen County Dental Society — J Bergen Cty Dent Soc
Journal. Bethune University of Medical Sciences — J Bethune Univ Med Sci
Journal. Beverly Hills Bar Association — J Bev Hills BA
Journal. Beverly Hills Bar Association — J Beverly Hills Ba
Journal. Bharati Research Institute — Jnl Bharati Res Inst
Journal. Bihar Agricultural College — J Bihar Agric Coll
Journal. Bihar and Orissa Research Society [*Later, Journal. Bihar Research Society*] — JBORS
Journal. Bihar Puravid Parishad — J Bihar Pur Par
Journal. Bihar Research Society — J Bihar RS
Journal. Bihar Research Society — JBIRS
Journal. Bihar Research Society — JBRS
Journal. Biological Board of Canada — J Biol Board Can
Journal. Biological Institute — J Biol Inst
Journal. Biological Institute (Seoul, Korea) — Journ Biol Inst Univ Seoul Korea
Journal. Biological Photographic Association — J Biol Phot
Journal. Biological Photographic Association — J Biol Phot Assn
Journal. Biological Photographic Association — J Biol Photogr Ass
Journal. Biological Photographic Association — J Biol Photogr Assoc
Journal. Biological Photographic Association — JBPAA
Journal. Biophysical Society of Japan — J Biophys Soc Jpn
Journal. Birla Institute of Technology and Science — BITJA
Journal. Birla Institute of Technology and Science — J Birla Inst Technol and Sci
Journal. Birla Institute of Technology and Science — J Birla Inst Technol Sci
Journal. Birla Institute of Technology and Science (Pilani) — J Birla Inst Tech and Sci (Pilani)
Journal. Birmingham Metallurgical Society — J Birmingham Metall Soc
Journal. Board of Agriculture [*Great Britain*] — J Bd Ag
Journal. Board of Agriculture — JBA
Journal. Board of Agriculture. British Guiana — J Bd Agric Br Gui
Journal. Board of Agriculture (Great Britain) — J Board Agric (GB)
Journal. Board of Agriculture (London) — J Bd Agric (London)
Journal. Board of Direction. American Society of Civil Engineers — J Board Dir Am Soc Civ Eng
Journal. Board of Greenkeeping Research — J Board Greenkeeping Res
Journal. Board of Trade of Metropolitan Toronto — Bd Trade Metropolitan Toronto J
Journal. Bombay Branch. Royal Asiatic Society — JBBAS
Journal. Bombay Branch. Royal Asiatic Society — JBBRAS
Journal. Bombay Branch. Royal Asiatic Society — JBRAS
Journal. Bombay Branch. Royal Asiatic Society — JRAS Bombay
Journal. Bombay Historical Society — JBHS
Journal. Bombay Natural History Society — J Bom Natur Hist Soc
Journal. Bombay Natural History Society — J Bombay Nat Hist Soc
Journal. Bombay Natural History Society — JBNHS
Journal. Bombay Natural History Society — Jour Bombay Nat Hist Soc
Journal. Bombay University — JUB
Journal. Bombay University. Arts — JBUA
Journal. Boston Society of Civil Engineers — J Boston Soc Civ Eng
Journal. Boston Society of Civil Engineers Section. American Society of Civil Engineers — J Boston Soc Civ Eng Sect ASCE
Journal. Botanical Society of South Africa — J Bot Soc S Afr
Journal. Botanical Society of South Africa — J Bot Soc South Africa
Journal Botanique. Academie des Sciences. RSS d'Ukraine — J Bot Acad Sci RSS Ukr
Journal Botanique de l'URSS — J Bot URSS
Journal. Bowman Gray School of Medicine. Wake Forest College — J Bowman Gray Sch Med Wake For Coll
Journal. Brewing Society of Japan — J Brew Soc Jpn
Journal. British Archaeological Association — J Br A Ass
Journal. British Archaeological Association — J Brit Arch Ass
Journal. British Archaeological Association — JAA
Journal. British Archaeological Association — JBAA
Journal. British Archaeological Association. Series 3 — J Brit Archaeol Ass 3 Ser
Journal. British Association of Malaysia — JBAM
Journal. British Association of Teachers of the Deaf — Jr Br Assoc Teach Deaf
Journal. British Astronomical Association — J Br Astron Assoc
Journal. British Astronomical Association — J Brit Astron Ass
Journal. British Astronomical Association — Journ Br Astr Ass
Journal. British Boot and Shoe Institution — J Br Boot Shoe Instn
Journal. British Ceramic Society — J Brit Ceram Soc
Journal. British Ceramic Society — JBCSA
Journal. British Dental Association — J Br Dent Assoc
Journal. British Dental Association — J Brit Dental Assoc
Journal. British Endodontic Society — J Br Endod Soc
Journal. British Fire Services Association — J Br Fire Serv Assoc
Journal. British Grassland Society — J Br Grassl
Journal. British Grassland Society — J Br Grassl Soc
Journal. British Grassland Society — J Br Grassld Soc
Journal. British Institute of International Affairs — J Brit Inst Int Affairs
Journal. British Institute of International Affairs — JBIIA
Journal. British Institution of Radio Engineers — J Br Inst Radio Eng
Journal. British Interplanetary Society — J Brit Interplanet Soc
Journal. British Interplanetary Society — JBIS
Journal. British Nuclear Energy Society — J Br Nucl E
Journal. British Nuclear Energy Society — J Br Nucl Energy Soc
Journal. British Nuclear Energy Society — J Brit Nucl Energy Soc
Journal. British Nuclear Energy Society — JBNSA
Journal. British Ship Research Association — J Brit Ship Res Ass
Journal. British Society for Phenomenology — J Br Soc Ph
Journal. British Society for Phenomenology — J Brit Soc Phenomenol
Journal. British Society of Master Glass Painters — J Brit Soc Master Glass Paint
Journal. British Society of Master Glass-Painters — JBSMGP
Journal. British Sociological Association — BSA/J
Journal. British Thoracic and Tuberculosis Association — BTTA
Journal. British Waterworks Association — J Br Waterworks Assoc
Journal. British Wood Preserving Association — J Br Wood Preserv Assoc
Journal. Bromeliad Society — J Bromeliad Soc
Journal. Buddhist Text and Anthropological Society — JBTS
Journal. Buddhist Text Society — Journ Buddh Text Soc
Journal. Burma Research Society — JBRS
Journal. Busan Medical College — J Busan Med Coll
Journal. Butler Society — J Butler Soc
Journal. Cactus and Succulent Society of America — J Cact Succ Soc Amer
Journal. California Dental Association — J Calif Dent Assoc
Journal. California Horticultural Society — J Calif Hort Soc
Journal. California Horticultural Society — J Calif Hortic Soc
Journal. California Rare Fruit Growers — J Calif Rare Fruit Grow
Journal. California State Dental Association — J Calif State Dent Assoc
Journal. California State Dental Association — JCDEA
Journal. Cama Oriental Institute — JCOI
Journal. Camborne School of Mines — J Camborne Sch Mines
Journal. Camera Club (London) — J Camera Club (London)
Journal. Canadian Association for Music Therapy — JAMTD
Journal. Canadian Association for Young Children — J CAYC
Journal. Canadian Association of Radiologists — J Can Assoc Radiol
Journal. Canadian Association of Radiologists — JCARA
Journal. Canadian Athletic Therapists Association — J Can Ath Ther Assoc
Journal. Canadian Bar Association — Can Bar AJ
Journal. Canadian Bar Association — J Can B Ass'n
Journal. Canadian Bar Association — J Can Ba
Journal. Canadian Ceramic Society — J Can Ceram Soc
Journal. Canadian Ceramic Society — JCCS
Journal. Canadian Ceramic Society — JCCSA
Journal. Canadian Chiropractic Association — J Can Chiro Assoc
Journal. Canadian Church Historical Society — J Can Ch H
Journal. Canadian Church Historical Society — JCCHS
Journal. Canadian Dental Association — J Can Dent Assoc
Journal. Canadian Dental Association — J Canad Dent A
Journal. Canadian Dental Association — JCDAA
Journal. Canadian Dietetic Association — J Can Diet Ass
Journal. Canadian Dietetic Association — J Can Diet Assoc
Journal. Canadian Institute of Food Science and Technology — J Can Inst Food Sci Technol
Journal. Canadian Linguistic Association [*Edmonton*] — JCLA
Journal. Canadian Mining Institute — J Can Min Inst
Journal. Canadian Psychiatric Association — J Can Psychiatr Assoc
Journal. Canadian Society of Forensic Science — J Can Soc Forensic Sci
Journal Canadien d'Anesthesie — J Can Anesth
Journal Canadien de Biochimie — J Can Biochim
Journal Canadien de Botanique — J Can Bot
Journal Canadien de Chimie — J Can Chim
Journal Canadien de Chirurgie — J Can Chir
Journal Canadien de Genetique et de Cytologie — J Can Genet Cytol
Journal Canadien de la Pharmacie Hospitaliere — J Can Pharm Hosp
Journal Canadien de la Recherche Forestiere — J Can Rech For
Journal Canadien de Microbiologie — J Can Microbiol
Journal Canadien de Physiologie et Pharmacologie — J Can Physiol Pharmacol
Journal Canadien de Physique — J Can Phys

Journal Canadien de Zoologie — J Can Zool
Journal Canadien des Sciences Appliquees au Sport — J Can Sci Appl Sport
Journal Canadien des Sciences de la Terre — J Can Sci Terre
Journal Canadien des Sciences Halieutiques et Aquatiques — J Can Sci Halieutiques Aquat
Journal Canadien des Sciences Neurologiques — J Can Sci Neurol
Journal Canadien d'Ophtalmologie — J Can Ophtalmol
Journal Canadien d'Otolaryngologie — J Can Otolaryngol
Journal. Cancer Center. Niigata Hospital [*Japan*] — J Cancer Cent Niigata Hosp
Journal. Cancer Research Committee. University of Sydney — J Cancer Res Comm Univ Sydney
Journal. Canterbury Botanical Society — J Cant Bot Soc
Journal. Capital Institute of Medicine — J Cap Inst Med
Journal. Catch Society of America — JCSA
Journal. Catgut Society — JCAS
Journal. Catholic Medical College — J Cathol Med Coll
Journal. Catholic Nurses Guild of England and Wales — J Cathol Nurses Guild Engl Wales
Journal. Cellulose Institute (Tokyo) — J Cellul Inst (Tokyo)
Journal. Central Agricultural Experiment Station — J Cent Agr Exp Sta
Journal. Central Agricultural Experiment Station — J Cent Agric Exp Stn
Journal. Central Bureau for Animal Husbandry and Dairying in India — J Cent Bur Anim Husb Dairy India
Journal. Central China Normal University. Natural Sciences — J Cent China Norm Univ Nat Sci
Journal. Central China Teachers College. Natural Sciences Edition — J Cent China Teach Coll Nat Sci Ed
Journal. Central Mississippi Valley American Studies Association — JCMVASA
Journal. Central-South Institute of Mining and Metallurgy — J Cent South Inst Min Metall
Journal. Centre of Islamic Legal Studies — JCILS
Journal. Ceramic Association of Japan — J Ceram Assoc Jpn
Journal. Ceramic Society of Japan — J Cer Soc Jap
Journal. Ceramic Society of Japan — J Ceram Soc Jpn
Journal. Ceramic Society of Japan (Japanese Edition) — J Ceram Soc Jpn (Jpn Ed)
Journal. Ceylon Branch. British Medical Association — J Ceylon Br Brit Med Ass
Journal. Ceylon Branch. British Medical Association — J Ceylon Branch Brit Med Assoc
Journal. Ceylon Branch. Royal Asiatic Society — JCBAS
Journal. Ceylon Branch. Royal Asiatic Society — JCRAS
Journal. Ceylon Obstetric and Gynaecological Association — Journ Ceyl Obstet Gyn Ass
Journal. Changchun College of Geology — J Changchun Coll Geol
Journal. Changchun Geological Institute — J Changchun Geol Inst
Journal. Changchun University of Earth Science — J Changchun Univ Earth Sci
Journal. Changsha Normal University of Water Resources and Electric Power. Natural Sciences Edition — J Changsha Norm Univ Water Res Electr Power Nat Sci Ed
Journal. Charles H. Tweed International Foundation — J Charles H. Tweed Int Found
Journal. Chartered Institute of Transport — J Chart Inst Transp
Journal. Chartered Institution of Building Services — J Chart Inst Bld Serv
Journal. Chartered Institution of Building Services [*England*] — J Chart Inst Build Serv
Journal. Chartered Institution of Building Services — Jrl Bldg S
Journal. Chekiang Provincial Library/Che Chiang T'u Shu Kuan Pao — J Chekiang Prov Libr
Journal. Chekiang University — J Chekiang Univ
Journal. Chemical and Metallurgical Society of South Africa — J Chem Metall Soc S Afr
Journal. Chemical, Metallurgical, and Mining Society of South Africa — J Chem Metall Min Soc S Afr
Journal. Chemical Society — J Chem Soc
Journal. Chemical Society — JCS
Journal. Chemical Society — Journ Chem Soc
Journal. Chemical Society. A. Inorganic, Physical, Theoretical — J Chem Soc A
Journal. Chemical Society. A. Inorganic, Physical, Theoretical — J Chem Soc A Inorg Phys Theor
Journal. Chemical Society. Abstracts — J Chem Soc Abstr
Journal. Chemical Society. Abstracts — JCSA
Journal. Chemical Society. B. Physical, Organic — J Chem Soc B
Journal. Chemical Society. B. Physical Organic — J Chem Soc B Phys Org
Journal. Chemical Society. C. Organic — J Chem Soc C
Journal. Chemical Society. C. Organic — J Chem Soc C Org
Journal. Chemical Society. Chemical Communications — J Chem S Ch
Journal. Chemical Society. Chemical Communications — J Chem Soc Chem Commun
Journal. Chemical Society. Chemical Communications — JCS Chem Comm
Journal. Chemical Society. D. Chemical Communications — J Chem Soc D Chem Commun
Journal. Chemical Society. Dalton Transactions — J Chem S Da
Journal. Chemical Society. Dalton Transactions — J Chem Soc Dalton Trans
Journal. Chemical Society. Dalton Transactions — JCDTBI
Journal. Chemical Society. Dalton Transactions. Inorganic Chemistry — JCS Dalton
Journal. Chemical Society. Faraday Transactions — J Chem Soc Faraday Trans
Journal. Chemical Society. Faraday Transactions. I — J Chem S F I
Journal. Chemical Society. Faraday Transactions. I — J Chem Soc Faraday Trans I
Journal. Chemical Society. Faraday Transactions. I. Physical Chemistry — JCS Faraday I
Journal. Chemical Society. Faraday Transactions. II — J Chem S F II
Journal. Chemical Society. Faraday Transactions. II — J Chem Soc Faraday Trans II
Journal. Chemical Society. Faraday Transactions. II. Chemical Physics — JCS Faraday II
Journal. Chemical Society (London) — J Chem Soc (London)
Journal. Chemical Society (London). Dalton Transactions — J Chem Soc (London) Dalton Trans
Journal. Chemical Society (London). Faraday Transactions. I — J Chem Soc (London) Faraday Trans I
Journal. Chemical Society (London). Faraday Transactions. II — J Chem Soc (London) Faraday Trans II
Journal. Chemical Society (London). Perkin Transactions. I — J Chem Soc (London) Perkin Trans I
Journal. Chemical Society (London). Perkin Transactions. II — J Chem Soc (London) Perkin Trans II
Journal. Chemical Society (London). Section A. Inorganic, Physical, Theoretical — J Chem Soc (London) A Inorg Phys Theor
Journal. Chemical Society (London). Section B. Physical, Organic — J Chem Soc (London) B Phys Org
Journal. Chemical Society (London). Section C. Organic Chemistry — J Chem Soc (London) C Org
Journal. Chemical Society (London). Section D. Chemical Communications — J Chem Soc (London) Chem Commun
Journal. Chemical Society (London). Section D. Chemical Communications — J Chem Soc (London) D Chem Commun
Journal. Chemical Society of Japan — J Chem Soc Jpn
Journal. Chemical Society of Japan. Chemistry and Industrial Chemistry — J Chem Soc Jpn Chem Ind Chem
Journal. Chemical Society of Japan. Industrial Chemistry Section — J Chem Soc Jap Ind Chem Sect
Journal. Chemical Society of Japan. Pure Chemistry Section — J Chem Soc Jpn Pure Chem Sect
Journal. Chemical Society of Pakistan — J Chem Soc Pak
Journal. Chemical Society. Perkin Transactions. I — J Chem S P I
Journal. Chemical Society. Perkin Transactions. I — J Chem Soc Perkin Trans
Journal. Chemical Society. Perkin Transactions. I — J Chem Soc Perkin Trans I
Journal. Chemical Society. Perkin Transactions. I. Organic and Bioorganic Chemistry — JCS Perkin I
Journal. Chemical Society. Perkin Transactions. II — J Chem S P II
Journal. Chemical Society. Perkin Transactions. II — J Chem Soc Perkin Trans II
Journal. Chemical Society. Perkin Transactions. II. Physical Organic Chemistry — JCS Perkin II
Journal. Chemical Society [*London*] **Section C. Organic Chemistry** — J Che Soc Sect C Org Chem
Journal. Chemical Society. Section D. Chemical Communications — CCJDA
Journal. Chemical Society. Transactions — J Chem Soc Trans
Journal. Chemical Society. Transactions — JCST
Journal. Cheng Kung University. Science and Engineering — J Cheng Kung Univ Sci Eng
Journal. Cheng Kung University. Science, Engineering, and Medicine — J Cheng Kung Univ Sci Eng Med
Journal. Chester Archaeological Society — J Chester Arch Soc
Journal. Chester Archaeological Society — J Chester Archaeol Soc
Journal. Chiba Medical Society — J Chiba Med Soc
Journal Chimique de l'Ukraine — J Chim Ukr
Journal. China Coal Society [*People's Republic of China*] — J China Coal Soc
Journal. China Coal Society (Beijing) — J China Coal Soc (Beijing)
Journal. China Medical University (Chinese Edition) — J China Med Univ (Chin Ed)
Journal. China Pharmaceutical University — J China Pharm Univ
Journal. China Society of Chemical Industry — J China Soc Chem Ind
Journal. China Textile Engineering Association — J China Text Eng Assoc
Journal. China University of Science and Technology — J China Univ Sci Technol
Journal. Chinese Agricultural Chemical Society — J Chin Agri Chem Soc
Journal. Chinese Association of Refrigeration — J Chin Assoc Refrig
Journal. Chinese Biochemical Society — J Chin Biochem Soc
Journal. Chinese Ceramic Society — J Chin Ceram Soc
Journal. Chinese Chemical Society — J Chin Chem
Journal. Chinese Chemical Society — J Chin Chem Soc
Journal. Chinese Chemical Society — Journ Chin Chem Soc
Journal. Chinese Chemical Society (Peking) — J Chin Chem Soc (Peking)
Journal. Chinese Chemical Society (Taipei) — J Chin Chem Soc (Taipei)
Journal. Chinese Colloid and Interface Society — J Chin Colloid Interface Soc
Journal. Chinese Environmental Protection Society — J Chin Environ Prot Soc
Journal. Chinese Foundrymen's Association — J Chin Foundrymen's Assoc
Journal. Chinese Institute of Chemical Engineers — J Chin Inst Chem Eng
Journal. Chinese Institute of Chemical Engineers — J Chinese Inst Chem Engrs
Journal. Chinese Institute of Engineers — J Chin Inst Eng
Journal. Chinese Institute of Engineers [*Taipei*] — J Chinese Inst Engrs
Journal. Chinese Institute of Industrial Engineers — J Chinese Inst Indust Engrs
Journal. Chinese Language Teachers Association — J Chin Lang Teach Asso
Journal. Chinese Language Teachers Association — JCLTA
Journal. Chinese Rare Earth Society — J Chin Rare Earth Soc
Journal. Chinese Silicate Society — J Chin Silic Soc
Journal. Chinese Silicate Society — J Chin Silicates Soc
Journal. Chinese Society of Veterinary Science — CKSCDN
Journal. Chinese Society of Veterinary Science — J Chin Soc Vet Sci
Journal. Chinese Society of Veterinary Science (Taipei) — J Chin Soc Vet Sci (Taipei)
Journal. Chinese University of Hong Kong — J Chin U HK
Journal. Chinese University of Hong Kong — J Chin Univ Hong Kong
Journal. Ching Hua University [*People's Republic of China*] — J Ching Hua Univ
Journal. Chongqing University — J Chongqing Univ

Journal. Chosen Agricultural Society/Chosen Nokai Ho. Keijo — J Chosen Agric Soc
Journal. Chosen Medical Association — J Chosen Med Assoc
Journal. Christian Medical Association of India — J Christ Med Assoc India
Journal. Chromatography Library — J Chromatogr Libr
Journal. Chromatography Library [*Elsevier Book Series*] — JCL
Journal. Chromatography Library [*Elsevier Book Series*] — JCLIDR
Journal. Chromatography Library (Amsterdam) — J Chromatogr Libr (Amsterdam)
Journal. Chulalongkorn Hospital Medical School (Bangkok) — J Chulalongkorn Hosp Med Sch (Bangkok)
Journal Citation Reports — JCR
Journal. City Planning Division. American Society of Civil Engineers — J City Plann Div Am Soc Civ Eng
Journal. Civil War Token Society — JCWTS
Journal. Clay Products Institute of America — J Clay Prod Inst Am
Journal. Clay Research Group of Japan — J Clay Res Group Jpn
Journal. Clay Science Society of Japan — J Clay Sci Soc Jpn
Journal. Clerks of Works Association of Great Britain — J Clerks Works Assoc GB
Journal. Cleveland Engineering Society — J Cleveland Eng Soc
Journal. Clinical Electron Microscopy Society of Japan — J Clin Electron Microsc Soc Jpn
Journal. Coal Mining Engineers Association of Kyushu — J Coal Min Eng Assoc Kyushu
Journal. Coal Research Institute (Tokyo) — J Coal Res Inst (Tokyo)
Journal. College and University Personnel Association — J Coll & Univ Personnel Assn
Journal. College and University Personnel Association — J Coll Univ
Journal. College of Agriculture. Hokkaido Imperial University — J Coll Agric Hokkaido Imp Univ
Journal. College of Agriculture. Tohoku Imperial University — J Coll Agric Tohoku Imp Univ
Journal. College of Agriculture. Tokyo Imperial University — J Coll Ag Tokyo
Journal. College of Agriculture. Tokyo Imperial University — J Coll Agric Tokyo Imp Univ
Journal. College of Arts and Sciences. Chiba University — J Coll Arts Sci Chiba Univ
Journal. College of Arts and Sciences. Chiba University/Chiba Daigaku Bunri Gakubu Kiyo. Shizen Kagaku — J Coll Arts Chiba Univ
Journal. College of Arts and Sciences. Chiba University. Natural Science [*Japan*] — J Coll Arts Sci Chiba Univ Nat Sci
Journal. College of Ceramic Technology. University of Calcutta — J Coll Ceram Technol Univ Calcutta
Journal. College of Dairy Agriculture — J Coll Dairy Agr
Journal. College of Dairy Agriculture — J Coll Dairy Agric
Journal. College of Dairy Agriculture (Ebetsu, Japan) — J Coll Dairy Agri (Ebetsu Japan)
Journal. College of Dairy Agriculture (Ebetsu, Japan) — J Coll Dairy Agric (Ebetsu Jpn)
Journal. College of Dairy Agriculture (Nopporo) — J Coll Dairy Agric (Nopporo)
Journal. College of Dairying (Ebetsu, Japan) — J Coll Dairy (Ebetsu Japan)
Journal. College of Dairying. Natural Science (Ebetsu) — J Coll Dairy Nat Sci (Ebetsu)
Journal. College of Dairying (Nopporo) — J Coll Dairy (Nopporo)
Journal. College of Education. Seoul National University — J Coll Educ Seoul Natl Univ
Journal. College of Engineering and Technology. Jadavpur University — J Coll Eng Technol Jadavpur Univ
Journal. College of Engineering. Nihon University — J Coll Eng Nihon Univ
Journal. College of Engineering. Tokyo Imperial University — J Coll Eng Tokyo Imp Univ
Journal. College of General Practitioners — J Coll Gen Pract
Journal. College of Industrial Technology. Nihon University [*Japan*] — J Coll Ind Technol Nihon Univ
Journal. College of Industrial Technology. Nihon University. Series A — J Coll Ind Technol Nihon Univ A
Journal. College of Industrial Technology. Nihon University. Series B — J Coll Ind Technol Nihon Univ B
Journal. College of Liberal Arts and Sciences. University of the East — J Col Lib Arts
Journal. College of Liberal Arts. Toyama University. Natural Sciences — J Coll Lib Arts Toyama Univ Nat Sci
Journal. College of Marine Science and Technology. Tokai University [*A publication*] — J Coll Mar Sci Technol Tokai Univ
Journal. College of Radiologists of Australasia — J Coll Radiol Australas
Journal. College of Radiologists of Australasia — J Coll Radiol Australasia
Journal. College of Radiologists of Australia — J Coll Radiol Aust
Journal. College of Science and Engineering. National Chung Hsing University — J Coll Sci Eng Natl Chung Hsing Univ
Journal. College of Science. Imperial University of Tokyo — J Coll Sci Imp Univ Tokyo
Journal. College of Science. King Saud University — J Coll Sci King Saud Univ
Journal. College of Science. University of Riyadh — J Coll Sci Univ Riyadh
Journal. College of Science. University of Riyadh — J College Sci Univ Riyadh
Journal. College of Surgeons of Australasia — J Coll Surgeons Australasia
Journal. Colorado Dental Association — J Colo Dent Assoc
Journal. Colorado-Wyoming Academy of Science — J Colo-Wyo Acad Sci
Journal. Colour Society — J Colour Soc
Journal. Community Development Society — J Community Dev Soc
Journal. Comparative Education Society in Europe (British Section) — Compare
Journal Complementaire du Dictionaire des Sciences Medicales — J Complem Dict Sci Med
Journal. Computer Society of India — J Comput Soc India
Journal. Connecticut State Dental Association — J Conn State Dent Assoc
Journal. Connecticut State Medical Society — J Conn State Med Soc
Journal. Construction Division. American Society of Civil Engineers — Jnl Constr Div Am Soc Civ Eng
Journal. Construction Division. Proceedings of the American Society of Civil Engineers — J Cons ASCE
Journal. Construction Division. Proceedings of the American Society of Civil Engineers — J Const Div Proc ASCE
Journal. Construction Division. Proceedings of the American Society of Civil Engineers — J Constr Div Am Soc Civ Eng
Journal. Construction Division. Proceedings of the American Society of Civil Engineers — J Constr Div Amer Soc Civil Eng Proc
Journal. Cooling Tower Institute — J Cooling Tower Inst
Journal. Copyright Society of the USA — J Copyright Socy USA
Journal. Cork Historical and Archaeological Society — J Cork Hist Archaeol Soc
Journal. Cork Historical and Archaeological Society — JCHAS
Journal. Cork Historical and Archaeological Society — Journal Cork Hist Soc
Journal. Cornish Methodist Historical Association — JCMHA
Journal. Corrosion Science Society of Korea — J Corros Sci Soc Korea
Journal. Council for Scientific and Industrial Research (Australia) — J Coun Scient Ind Res (Aust)
Journal. Council for Scientific and Industrial Research (Australia) — J Counc Sci Ind Res (Australia)
Journal. County Kildare Archaeological Society — J Co Kildare Archaeol Soc
Journal. Crystallographic Society of Japan — J Crystallogr Soc Jap
Journal d'Agriculture, de Medecine, et des Sciences Accessoires — J Agric Med
Journal d'Agriculture, d'Economie Rurale, et des Manufactures du Royaume des Pays-Bas — J Agric Pays Bas
Journal d'Agriculture du Sud-Ouest/Societe d'Horticulture de la Haute-Garonne — J Agric Sud Ouest
Journal d'Agriculture Pratique — J Ag Pratique
Journal d'Agriculture Pratique — J Agr Prat
Journal d'Agriculture Pratique — J Agric Prat
Journal d'Agriculture Traditionnelle et de Botanique Appliquee — J Agr Trad Bot Appl
Journal d'Agriculture Traditionnelle et de Botanique Appliquee. Travaux d'Ethnobotanique et d'Ethnozoologie — J Agric Tradit Bot Appl Trav Ethnobot Ethnozool
Journal d'Agriculture Traditionnelle et de Botanique Appliquee. Travaux d'Ethnobotanique et d'Ethnozoologie — JATADT
Journal d'Agriculture Tropicale — J Agric Trop
Journal d'Agriculture Tropicale et de Botanique Appliquee [*Later, Journal d'Agriculture Traditionnelle et de Botanique Appliquee*] — J Agr Trop Bot Appl
Journal d'Agriculture Tropicale et de Botanique Appliquee [*Later, Journal d'Agriculture Traditionnelle et de Botanique Appliquee*] — J Agric Trop Bot Appl
Journal d'Agriculture Tropicale et de Botanique Appliquee [*Later, Journal d'Agriculture Traditionnelle et de Botanique Appliquee*] — J Agric Trop Botan Appl
Journal d'Agriculture Tropicale et de Botanique Appliquee [*Later, Journal d'Agriculture Traditionnelle et de Botanique Appliquee*] — JATBAT
Journal. Dalian Engineering Institute — J Dalian Eng Inst
Journal. Dalian Institute of Technology — J Dalian Inst Technol
Journal d'Analyse Mathematique — J Anal Math
Journal d'Analyse Mathematique [*Jerusalem*] — J Analyse Math
Journal d'Analyse Mathematique [*Jerusalem*] — JAM
Journal d'Analyse Mathematique [*Jerusalem*] — JdAM
Journal de Biologie Buccale — J Biol Bucc
Journal de Biologie Buccale — J Biol Buccale
Journal de Biologie et de Medecine Nucleaires — J Biol Med Nucl
Journal de Biologie et de Medecine Nucleaires — JBMNA
Journal de Biologie (Moscow) — J Biol Moscow
Journal de Biomateriaux Dentaires — J Biomater Dent
Journal de Biophysique et de Biomecanique — J Biophys Biomec
Journal de Biophysique et Medecine Nucleaire — J Biophys Med Nucl
Journal de Botanique [*L. Morot, Editor*] — Jour De Bot
Journal de Botanique, Appliquee a l'Agriculture, a la Pharmacie, a la Medecine, et aux Arts — J Bot Agric
Journal de Botanique, Appliquee a l'Agriculture, a la Pharmacie, a la Medecine, et aux Arts — Journ Bot Appl Agric
Journal de Botanique, Appliquee a l'Agriculture, a la Pharmacie, a la Medecine, et aux Arts — Journ de Bot
Journal de Botanique (L. Morot, Editor) — Morot J Bot
Journal de Botanique Neerlandaise — Jour Bot Neerl
Journal de Botanique Neerlandaise — Journ Bot Neerland
Journal de Botanique (Paris) (Edited by L. Morot) — Journ Bot Paris
Journal de Botanique. Redige par une Societe de Botanistes (Desvaux, Editor) — Desv Journ
Journal de Botanique. Redige par une Societe de Botanistes (Desvaux, Editor) — Journ De Bot Desv
Journal de Botanique, Redige par une Societe de Botanistes (Edited by Desvaux) — Jour Bot Desvaux
Journal de Botanique, Redige par une Societe de Botanistes (Edited by Desvaux) — Jour de Bot
Journal de Chimie Appliquee — J Chim Appl
Journal de Chimie Generale — J Chim Gen
Journal de Chimie Medicale, de Pharmacie, et de Toxicologie — J Chim Med Pharm Toxicol
Journal de Chimie Physique [*France*] — J Chim Phys
Journal de Chimie Physique — JCPQA
Journal de Chimie Physique et de Physico-Chimie Biologique — J Chim Phys
Journal de Chimie Physique et de Physico-Chimie Biologique — J Chim Phys et Phys-Chim Biol
Journal de Chimie Physique et de Physico-Chimie Biologique — J Chim Phys Phys-Chim Biol

Journal de Chimie Physique et de Physico-Chimie Biologique — Journ Chim Phys Chim
Journal de Chimie Physique et Revue Generale des Colloides [*France*] — J Chim Phys Rev Gen Colloides
Journal de Chimie Physique et Revue Generale des Colloides — JPRGA
Journal de Chirurgie — J Chir
Journal de Chirurgie — Journ Chir
Journal de Conchyliologie — J Conchyl
Journal de Conchyliologie — J Conchyliol
Journal de Conchyliologie — Jour Conchyliologie
Journal de Droit Africain — J Droit Afr
Journal de Genetique Humaine — J Genet Hum
Journal de Geneve — J De Geneve
Journal de Geneve — J Gen
Journal de Geneve — JG
Journal de Gynecologie, Obstetrique, et Biologie de la Reproduction [*Paris*] — J Gynecol Obstet Biol Reprod
Journal de Gynecologie, Obstetrique, et Biologie de la Reproduction [*Paris*] — JGOBA
Journal de la France Agricole — J Fr Agric
Journal de la France Agricole — JLFAA
Journal de la Marine Marchande — J Mar March
Journal de la Marine Marchande et de la Navigation Aerienne — JMM
Journal de la Marine Marchande et de la Navigation Aerienne — JMMNA
Journal de la Paix — J Paix
Journal de la Planification du Developpement — J Planif Develop
Journal de l'Agriculture Experimentale — J Agric Exp
Journal de l'Anatomie et de la Physiologie Normales et Pathologiques de l'Homme et des Animaux — J Anat Physiol Norm Pathol Homme Anim
Journal de l'Anatomie et de la Physiologie Normales et Pathologiques de l'Homme et des Animaux — J De L Anat Et De La Physiol
Journal de l'Association pour l'Avancement en Afrique des Sciences de l'Agriculture — J Assoc Av Afr Sci Agric
Journal de l'Enregistrement et du Notariat — JEN
Journal de l'Equipement Electrique et Electronique — J Equip Electr et Electron
Journal de l'Evangelisation — J Ev
Journal de l'Exploitation des Corps Gras Industriels — J Exploit Corps Gras Ind
Journal de l'Industrie des Colorants — J Ind Color
Journal de l'Institut Historique — JI Hist
Journal de Mathematiques et de Physique Appliquees — J Math Phys Appl
Journal de Mathematiques Pures et Appliquees — J Math P A
Journal de Mathematiques Pures et Appliquees — J Math Pures Appl
Journal de Mathematiques Pures et Appliquees. Neuvieme Serie — J Math Pures Appl 9
Journal de Mecanique — J Mec
Journal de Mecanique — J Mecanique
Journal de Mecanique Appliquee — J Mec Appl
Journal de Mecanique Appliquee — JMAPD
Journal de Mecanique et Physique de l'Atmosphere [*France*] — J Mec Phys Atmos
Journal de Mecanique et Physique de l'Atmosphere — J Mecan Phys Atm
Journal de Mecanique Theorique et Appliquee [*Journal of Theoretical and Applied Mechanics*] — J Mec Theor Appl
Journal de Mecanique Theorique et Appliquee [*Journal of Theoretical and Applied Mechanics*] — J Mec Theor et Appl
Journal de Medecine, Chirurgie, Pharmacie (Paris) — J Med Chir Pharm (Paris)
Journal de Medecine de Besancon — J Med Besancon
Journal de Medecine de Bordeaux — J Med Bord
Journal de Medecine de Bordeaux — J Med Bordeaux
Journal de Medecine de Bordeaux — JMBXA
Journal de Medecine de Bordeaux et du Sud-Ouest — J Med Bord Sud-Ouest
Journal de Medecine de Bordeaux et du Sud-Ouest — J Med Bordeaux Sud Ouest
Journal de Medecine de Caen — J Med Caen
Journal de Medecine de Caen — Jnl Med Caen
Journal de Medecine, de Chirurgie, et de Pharmacie Militaires — J Med Chir Pharm Militaires
Journal de Medecine de Lyon — J Med Lyon
Journal de Medecine de Montpellier — J Med Montp
Journal de Medecine de Montpellier — J Med Montpellier
Journal de Medecine de Paris — J Med Pa
Journal de Medecine de Poitiers — J Med Poitiers
Journal de Medecine de Strasbourg — J Med Strasb
Journal de Medecine de Strasbourg [*France*] — J Med Strasbourg
Journal de Medecine et de Chirurgie — J Med Chir
Journal de Medecine et de Chirurgie Pratiques — J Med Chir Prat
Journal de Medecine et de Chirurgie Pratiques — J Med et Chir Prat
Journal de Medecine Legale. Droit Medical — J Med Leg Droit Med
Journal de Medecine Legale Psychiatrique et d'Anthropologie Criminelle — J Med Leg Psych Anthr
Journal de Medecine Nucleaire et Biophysique — J Med Nucl Biophys
Journal de Medecine Veterinaire et Comparee — J Med Vet et Comp
Journal de Medecine Veterinaire et de Zootechnie (Lyon) — J Med Vet et Zootech (Lyon)
Journal de Medecine Veterinaire (Lyon) — J Med Vet (Lyon)
Journal de Medecine Veterinaire Militaire — J Med Vet Mil
Journal de Micrographie — J Microg
Journal de Microscopie [*France*] — J Microsc
Journal de Microscopie — J Microscopie
Journal de Microscopie et de Biologie Cellulaire — J Microsc B
Journal de Microscopie et de Biologie Cellulaire — J Microsc Biol Cell
Journal de Microscopie et de Biologie Cellulaire — JMBCD
Journal de Microscopie et de Spectroscopie Electroniques — J Microsc et Spectrosc Electron
Journal de Microscopie et de Spectroscopie Electroniques — J Microsc Spectrosc Electron
Journal de Microscopie et de Spectroscopie Electroniques — JMSED
Journal de Microscopie et de Spectroscopie Electroniques (France) — J Microsc Spectrosc Electron (France)
Journal de Microscopie (Paris) — J Microsc (Paris)
Journal de Microscopie/Societe Francaise de Microscopie Electronique — J Microscop
Journal de Parodontologie — J Parodontol
Journal de Pharmacie — J Pharm
Journal de Pharmacie (Antwerp) — J Pharm (Antwerp)
Journal de Pharmacie Clinique — J Pharm Clin
Journal de Pharmacie de Belgique — J Pharm Belg
Journal de Pharmacie de Belgique — JPBEA
Journal de Pharmacie et de Chimie — J Pharm Chim
Journal de Pharmacie et des Sciences Accessoires — J Pharm Sci Accessoires
Journal de Pharmacie et des Sciences Accessoires (Paris) — J Pharm (Paris)
Journal de Pharmacologie — J Pharmacol
Journal de Pharmacologie Clinique — J Pharmacol Clin
Journal de Pharmacologie (Paris) — J Pharmacol (Paris)
Journal de Physiologie — JOPHA
Journal de Physiologie et de Pathologie Generale — J Physiol et Path Gen
Journal de Physiologie et de Pathologie Generale — J Physiol Pathol Gen
Journal de Physiologie Experimentale et Pathologique — J Physiol Exper
Journal de Physiologie (Paris) — J Physiol (Paris)
Journal de Physiologie (Paris) — J Physl (Par)
Journal de Physiologie (Paris). Supplement [*France*] — J Physiol (Paris) Suppl
Journal de Physiologie (Paris). Supplement — JOPPA
Journal de Physique — J Phys
Journal de Physique — J Physique
Journal de Physique 1. Physique Generale, Physique Statistique, Matiere Condensee, Domaines Interdisciplinaires — J Phys 1 Phys Gen Phys Stat
Journal de Physique 2. Physique Atomique et Moleculaire, Physico-Chimie, Mecanique et Hydrodynamique — J Phys 2 Phys At Mol Phys Chim
Journal de Physique 3. Physique Applique, Science des Materiaux, Fluides, Plasmas et Instrumentation — J Phys 3 Phys Appl Sci Mater
Journal de Physique. Colloque — J Phys Colloq
Journal de Physique. Colloque — JPQCA
Journal de Physique, de Chimie, d'Histoire Naturelle, et des Arts — J Phy
Journal de Physique, de Chimie, d'Histoire Naturelle, et des Arts — J Phys Chim Hist Nat Arts
Journal de Physique et le Radium — J Phys Rad
Journal de Physique et le Radium [*France*] — J Phys Radium
Journal de Physique I. General Physics, Statistical Physics, Condensed Matter, Cross-Disciplinary Physics — J Phys I
Journal de Physique. I. Physique Generale, Physique Statistique, Matiere Condensee Domaines Interdisciplinaires — J Physique I
Journal de Physique II. Atomic, Molecular and Cluster Physics, Chemical Physics, Mechanics, and Hydrodynamics — J Phys II
Journal de Physique IV — J Phys IV
Journal de Physique IV — J Physique IV
Journal de Physique (Les Ulis, France) — J Phys (Les Ulis Fr)
Journal de Physique. Lettres — J Phys Lett
Journal de Physique. Lettres (Paris) — J Phys (Paris) Lett
Journal de Physique (Orsay, France) — J Phys (Orsay Fr)
Journal de Physique (Paris) — J Phys (Paris)
Journal de Physique (Paris). Colloque — J Phys (Paris) Colloq
Journal de Physique (Paris). Supplement — J Phys (Paris) Suppl
Journal de Physique (Societe Francaise de Physique). Colloque — J Phys (Soc Fr Phys) Colloq
Journal de Physique. Supplement — JPQSA
Journal de Physique Theorique et Appliquee — J Phys Theor Appl
Journal de Psychiatrie Biologique et Therapeutique — J Psychiatr Biol Ther
Journal de Psychologie Normale et Pathologique — J Psychol Norm Path
Journal de Psychologie Normale et Pathologique — JP
Journal de Psychologie Normale et Pathologique — JPNP
Journal de Psychologie Normale et Pathologique — JPNPA
Journal de Psychologie Normale et Pathologique — JPsNP
Journal de Psychologie Normale et Pathologique — JPsych
Journal de Psychologie Normale et Pathologique (Paris) — J Psychol Norm Pathol (Paris)
Journal de Radiologie — J Radiol
Journal de Radiologie [*Paris*] — JORADF
Journal de Radiologie (Brussels) — J Radiol Brussels
Journal de Radiologie, d'Electrologie, et de Medecine Nucleaire [*Later, Journal de Radiologie*] — J Radiol Electrol Med Nucl
Journal de Radiologie et d'Electrologie — J Radiol Electrol
Journal de Radiologie et d'Electrologie et Archives d'Electricite Medicale — J Radiol Electrol Arch Electr Med
Journal de Radiologie (Paris) — J Radiol (Paris)
Journal de Recherche Oceanographique — J Rech Oceanogr
Journal de Recherches Atmospheriques — J Rech Atmos
Journal de Stomatologie — J Stomat
Journal de Stomatologie de Belgique — J Stomatol Belg
Journal de Theorie des Nombres de Bordeaux — J Theor Nombres Bordeaux
Journal de Toxicologie Clinique et Experimentale — J Toxicol Clin Exp
Journal de Toxicologie Medicale — J Toxicol Med
Journal de Vulgarisation de l'Horticulture — J Vulg Hort
Journal Dentaire du Quebec — J Dent Que
Journal. Dental Association of South Africa — DASJA
Journal. Dental Association of South Africa — J Dent Assoc S Afr
Journal. Dental Association of Thailand — J Dent Assoc Thai
Journal. Dental Association of Thailand — J Dent Assoc Thailand
Journal. Dental Guidance Council on the Handicapped — J Dent Guid Counc Handicap

Journal. Department of Agriculture and Fisheries (Dublin) — J Dept Agr Fish (Dublin)
Journal. Department of Agriculture and Fisheries (Republic of Ireland) — J Dep Agric Fish (Irel)
Journal. Department of Agriculture (Ireland) — J Dep Agric (Irel)
Journal. Department of Agriculture. Kyushu Imperial University — J Dep Agric Kyushu Imp Univ
Journal. Department of Agriculture. Kyushu Imperial University — J Dept Agric Kyushu Imp Univ
Journal. Department of Agriculture of (Puerto Rico) — J Dep Agric (PR)
Journal. Department of Agriculture (Puerto Rico) — J Dept Ag (Puerto Rico)
Journal. Department of Agriculture. Republic of Ireland — J Dep Agric Repub Irel
Journal. Department of Agriculture. South Africa — J Dept Ag S Africa
Journal. Department of Agriculture. South Australia — J Dep Agric S Aust
Journal. Department of Agriculture. South Australia — J Dept Ag S Australia
Journal. Department of Agriculture. South Australia — J Dept Ag SA
Journal. Department of Agriculture. South Australia — J Dept Agr S Aust
Journal. Department of Agriculture. Union of South Africa — J Dep Agric Un S Afr
Journal. Department of Agriculture (Union of South Africa) — J Dep Agric (Union S Afr)
Journal. Department of Agriculture. Victoria [*Australia*] — J Dep Agric Vict
Journal. Department of Agriculture. Victoria — J Dept Ag VIC
Journal. Department of Agriculture. Victoria — J Dept Ag Victoria
Journal. Department of Agriculture. Victoria — J Dept Agr Victoria
Journal. Department of Agriculture. Victoria, Australia — J Dep Agric Victoria Aust
Journal. Department of Agriculture. Western Australia — J Dep Agric W Aust
Journal. Department of Agriculture. Western Australia — J Dep Agric West Aust
Journal. Department of Agriculture. Western Australia — J Dept Agr W Aust
Journal. Department of Agriculture. Western Australia — J Dept Agric W Aust
Journal. Department of English. Calcutta University — JDECU
Journal. Department of Geography. National University of Malaysia — J Dep Geogr Natl Univ Malaysia
Journal. Department of Lands and Agriculture (Ireland) — J Dep Lands Agric (Irel)
Journal. Department of Letters. Calcutta University — JDLC
Journal der Chemischen Industrie (Moscow) — J Chem Ind (Moscow)
Journal der Erfindungen, Theorien, und Widerspruche in der Natur- und Arzneiwissenschaft — J Erfind Natur Arzneiwiss
Journal der Moden — J Moden
Journal der Pharmazie von Elsass-Lothringen — J Pharm Els Lothr
Journal der Russischen Physikalisch-Chemischen Gesellschaft — J Russ Phys Chem Ges
Journal des Administrations Communales — Journ Adm Com
Journal des Agreges — J Agreges
Journal des Agreges — JAGGAD
Journal des Associations Patronales — JAS
Journal des Beaux-Arts et des Sciences — J Beaux Arts Sci
Journal des Caisses d'Epargne — J Caisses Epargne
Journal des Communautes — Jd Co
Journal des Connaissances Medico-Chirurgicales — J Conn Med Chir
Journal des Connaissances Usuelles et Pratiques — J Connaissances Usuelles Prat
Journal des Debats — J Debats
Journal des Debats [*Paris*] — JD
Journal des Debats — Journ Deb
Journal des Debats Politiques et Litteraires — JDPL
Journal des Economistes — J Ec
Journal des Economistes — J Econ
Journal des Economistes — J Economistes
Journal des Etudes Anciennes — JEA
Journal des Fabricants de Sucre — J Fabr Sucre
Journal des Industries du Gaz — J Ind Gaz
Journal des Ingenieurs — J Ing
Journal des Ingenieurs de l'URTB [*Union des Revues Techniques Belges*] — J Ing URTB
Journal des Juges de Paix — JJP
Journal des Juges de Paix — Journ J Paix
Journal des Juges de Paix — JPaix
Journal des Maladies Vasculaires — J Mal Vasc
Journal des Materiaux Nucleaires — J Mater Nucl
Journal des Mines et de la Metallurgie — J Mines Metall
Journal des Missions Evangeliques — J D Mis Evang
Journal des Missions Evangeliques — JME
Journal des Observateurs — J Obs
Journal des Poetes — JdP
Journal des Poetes (Brussels) — JPB
Journal des Recherches. Centre National de la Recherche Scientifique [*France*] — J Rech CNRS
Journal des Recherches. Centre National de la Recherche Scientifique. Laboratoires de Bellevue (Paris) — J Rech Cent Natl Rech Sci Lab Bellevue (Paris)
Journal des Savants — J des Savants
Journal des Savants — J Savants
Journal des Savants — JdS
Journal des Savants — Journ Sav
Journal des Savants — JS
Journal des Savants — JSav
Journal des Scavans (Amsterdam) — J Scavans Amsterdam
Journal des Sciences, Arts, et Metiers. Par Une Societe de Gens de Lettres et d'Artistes — J Sci Arts Metiers
Journal des Sciences de la Nutrition — J Sci Nutr
Journal des Sciences de la Nutrition. Supplementum — J Sci Nutr Suppl
Journal des Sciences et Techniques de la Tonnellerie — J Sci Tech Tonnellerie
Journal des Sciences Hydrologiques — J Sci Hydrol
Journal des Sciences Medicales de Lille — J Sci Med Lille
Journal des Sciences Militaires — Journ Sciences Milit
Journal des Societes — JS
Journal des Tribunaux — J Trib
Journal des Tribunaux — Journ Trib
Journal des Tribunaux — JT
Journal des Tribunaux d'Outre-Mer — Journ Trib Outr
Journal des Tribunaux d'Outre-Mer — JTO
Journal des Tribunaux d'Outre-Mer — JTOM
Journal des Usines a Gaz [*France*] — J Usines Gaz
Journal des Veterinaires du Midi — J Vet Midi
Journal. Devon Trust for Nature Conservation — J Devon Trust Nat Conserv
Journal d'Horticulture Pratique et de Jardinage — J Hort Prat Jard
Journal d'Horticulture Suisse — J Hort Suisse
Journal d'Hygiene Clintologie (Paris) — J Hyg (Paris)
Journal. Diabetic Association of India — J Diabetic Assoc India
Journal. Dietetic Association (Victoria) — J Diet Assoc (Victoria)
Journal d'Informations Techniques des Industries de la Fonderie — J Inf Tech Ind Fonderie
Journal. District of Columbia Dental Society — J DC Dent Soc
Journal d'Oto-Rhino-Laryngologie — J Oto-Rhino-Laryngol
Journal d'Oto-Rhino-Laryngologie — JOTODX
Journal du Conseil — J Conseil
Journal du Conseil — Jour Conseil
Journal du Conseil. Conseil International pour l'Exploration de la Mer — J Cons Cons Int Explor Mer
Journal du Conseil. Conseil International pour l'Exploration de la Mer — J Cons Int Explor Mer
Journal du Conseil. Conseil Permanent International pour l'Exploration de la Mer — J Cons Cons Perm Int Explor Mer
Journal du Cycle de Physique et de Chimie. Academie des Sciences d'Ukraine — J Cycle Phys Chim Acad Sci Ukr
Journal du Droit International — J Dr Int
Journal du Droit International — J Droit Int
Journal du Droit International — J Droit Internat
Journal du Droit International — J du Droit Int'l
Journal du Four Electrique — J Four Elec
Journal du Four Electrique — J Four Electr
Journal du Four Electrique et des Industries Electrochimiques — J Four Electr Ind Electrochim
Journal du Frottement Industriel [*France*] — J Frottement Ind
Journal du Ministere Public — J du MP
Journal du Textile [*Paris*] — JLT
Journal. Durham School of Agriculture — J Durham Sch Agr
Journal. Durham University — JDU
Journal d'Urologie et de Nephrologie — J Urol Neph
Journal d'Urologie et de Nephrologie — J Urol Nephrol
Journal d'Urologie et de Nephrologie. Supplement — J Urol Nephrol Suppl
Journal d'Urologie Medicale et Chirurgicale — J Urol Med Chir
Journal d'Urologie (Paris) — J Urol Paris
Journal. East Africa Natural History Society — J Ea Afr Nat Hist Soc
Journal. East Africa Natural History Society and National Museum — J East Afr Nat Hist Soc Natl Mus
Journal. East African Swahili Committee — JEAfrSC
Journal. East China Institute of Chemical Technology — J East China Inst Chem Technol
Journal. East China Institute of Textile Science and Technology — J East China Inst Text Sci Technol
Journal. East China Petroleum Institute — J East China Petrol Inst
Journal. East India Association — J E India Assoc
Journal. East India Association — J East India Assn
Journal. East India Association — JEIA
Journal. Ecole Polytechnique — J Ec Polytech
Journal. Ecole Polytechnique (Paris) — J Ec Polytech (Paris)
Journal. Education Department. Niigata University — J Educ Dept Niigata Univ
Journal. Egyptian and Oriental Society — J Eg Or Soc
Journal. Egyptian Medical Association — J Egypt Med Ass
Journal. Egyptian Medical Association — J Egypt Med Assoc
Journal. Egyptian Medical Association — J Egyptian MA
Journal. Egyptian Medical Association — JEMAA
Journal. Egyptian Medical Society — J Egypt Med Soc
Journal. Egyptian Public Health Association — J Egypt Public Health Assoc
Journal. Egyptian Public Health Association — JEGPA
Journal. Egyptian Society of Obstetrics and Gynecology — J Egypt Soc Obstet Gynecol
Journal. Egyptian Society of Parasitology — J Egypt Soc Parasitol
Journal. Egyptian Veterinary Medical Association — J Egypt Vet Med Ass
Journal. Eighteen Nineties Society — JENS
Journal. Electric Engineering Society (Tokyo) — J Electr Eng Soc (Tokyo)
Journal. Electrical Communications Laboratory — J Electr Commun Lab
Journal. Electrochemical Association of Japan — J El Ass J
Journal. Electrochemical Society — J El Chem Soc
Journal. Electrochemical Society — J El Soc
Journal. Electrochemical Society — J Elchem So
Journal. Electrochemical Society — J Electrochem Soc
Journal. Electrochemical Society [*United States*] — JESOA
Journal. Electrochemical Society of India — J Electrochem Soc India
Journal. Electrochemical Society of India — JESIA
Journal. Electrochemical Society of Japan — J Electrochem Soc Japan
Journal. Electrodepositors' Technical Society — J Electrodepositors Tech Soc
Journal. Electroplater's and Depositors' Technical Society — J Electroplat Depositors Tech Soc
Journal. Elisha Mitchell Scientific Society — J Elisha Mitch Sci Soc

Journal. Elisha Mitchell Scientific Society — J Elisha Mitchell Sci Soc
Journal. Elisha Mitchell Scientific Society — J Elisha Mitchell Scient Soc
Journal. Elisha Mitchell Scientific Society — JEMSA
Journal. Energy Division. American Society of Civil Engineers — J Energy Div Am Soc Civ Eng
Journal. Energy Division. American Society of Civil Engineers — J Energy Div ASCE
Journal. Energy Division. American Society of Civil Engineers. Proceedings — J Energy Div Proc ASCE
Journal. Engineering Mechanics Division. Proceedings of the American Society of Civil Engineers — J Eng Mech Div Am Soc Civ Eng
Journal. Engineering Mechanics Division. Proceedings of the American Society of Civil Engineers — J Eng Mech Div Amer Soc Civil Eng Proc
Journal. Engineering Mechanics Division. Proceedings of the American Society of Civil Engineers — J Engng Mech Div Proc ASCE
Journal. English Agricultural Society — J Engl Agric Soc
Journal. English Folk Dance and Song Society — JEFDS
Journal. English Folk Dance and Song Society — JEFDSS
Journal. English Folk Dance and Song Society — JEFS
Journal. English Institute — JEI
Journal. English Place-Name Society — J Engl Place-Name Soc
Journal. Entomological Society of Australia — J Ent Soc Aust
Journal. Entomological Society of Australia — J Entomol Soc Aust
Journal. Entomological Society of Australia (New South Wales) — J Entomol Soc Aust (NSW)
Journal. Entomological Society of Australia (New South Wales Branch) — J Ent Soc Aust (NSW)
Journal. Entomological Society of British Columbia — J Ent Soc BC
Journal. Entomological Society of British Columbia — J Entomol Soc BC
Journal. Entomological Society of Queensland — J Ent Soc Qd
Journal. Entomological Society of Southern Africa — J Ent Soc South Afr
Journal. Entomological Society of Southern Africa — J Ent Soc Sth Afr
Journal. Entomological Society of Southern Africa — J Entomol Soc S Afr
Journal. Entomological Society of Southern Africa — J Entomol Soc South Afr
Journal. Entomological Society of Southern Africa — J Entomol Soc Sthn Afr
Journal. Envangelical Theological Society — J Ev Th S
Journal. Environmental Engineering Division. American Society of Civil Engineers — J Envir Eng
Journal. Environmental Engineering Division. American Society of Civil Engineers — J Environ Eng Div Am Soc Civ Eng
Journal. Environmental Engineering Division. American Society of Civil Engineers — J Environ Eng Div ASCE
Journal. Environmental Engineering Division. American Society of Civil Engineers — JEEGA
Journal. Environmental Engineering Division. Proceedings of the American Society of Civil Engineers — J Environ Engng Div Proc ASCE
Journal. Environmental Engineering Division. Proceedings of the American Society of Civil Engineers — JEED
Journal. Environmental Laboratories Association — J Environ Lab Assoc
Journal. Environmental Protection Society (Republic of China) — J Environ Prot Soc (Repub China)
Journal. European Ceramic Society — J Eur Ceram Soc
Journal Europeen de Cancerologie — J Eur Cancerol
Journal Europeen de la Pharmacie Hospitaliere — J Eur Pharm Hosp
Journal Europeen de Pathologie Forestiere — J Eur Pathol For
Journal Europeen de Radiotherapie, Oncologie, Radiophysique, Radiobiologie — J Eur Radiother
Journal Europeen de Toxicologie — J Eur Toxicol
Journal Europeen de Toxicologie. Supplement — J Eur Toxicol Suppl
Journal Europeen des Steroides [*France*] — J Eur Steroides
Journal Europeen des Steroides — JEPSB
Journal. Evangelical Theological Society — ETS
Journal. Evangelical Theological Society — J Evang Th S
Journal. Evangelical Theological Society — JETS
Journal. Ewha Medical Association — J Ewha Med Assoc
Journal. Faculty of Agriculture. Hokkaido Imperial University — J Fac Agric Hokkaido Imp Univ
Journal. Faculty of Agriculture. Hokkaido University — J Fac Agric Hokkaido Univ
Journal. Faculty of Agriculture. Hokkaido University. Series Entomology — J Fac Agric Hokkaido Univ Ser Entomol
Journal. Faculty of Agriculture. Iwate University — J Fac Agr Iwate Univ
Journal. Faculty of Agriculture. Iwate University — J Fac Agric Iwate Univ
Journal. Faculty of Agriculture. Kyushu University — J Fac Agr Kyushu Univ
Journal. Faculty of Agriculture. Kyushu University — J Fac Agric Kyushu Univ
Journal. Faculty of Agriculture. Kyushu University — JFAKA
Journal. Faculty of Agriculture. Shinshu University — J Fac Agr Shinshu Univ
Journal. Faculty of Agriculture. Shinshu University — J Fac Agric Shinshu Univ
Journal. Faculty of Agriculture. Tottori University — J Fac Agr Tottori Univ
Journal. Faculty of Agriculture. Tottori University — J Fac Agric Tottori Univ
Journal. Faculty of Applied Biological Science. Hiroshima University — J Fac Appl Biol Sci Hiroshima Univ
Journal. Faculty of Arts. Royal University of Malta — J Faculty Arts Roy Univ Malta
Journal. Faculty of Education. Natural Sciences. Tottori University [*Japan*] — J Fac Educ Nat Sci Tottori Univ
Journal. Faculty of Education. Saga University — J Fac Ed Saga Univ
Journal. Faculty of Education. Saga University. Part 1 — J Fac Ed Saga Univ Part 1
Journal. Faculty of Education. Tottori University. Natural Science — J Fac Educ Tottori Univ Nat Sci
Journal. Faculty of Engineering. Chiba University — J Fac Eng Chiba Univ
Journal. Faculty of Engineering. Chiba University — J Fac Engrg Chiba Univ
Journal. Faculty of Engineering. Ibaraki University [*Japan*] — J Fac Eng Ibaraki Univ
Journal. Faculty of Engineering. Shinshu University — J Fac Eng Shinshu Univ
Journal. Faculty of Engineering. Tokyo Imperial University — J Fac Eng Tokyo Imp Univ
Journal. Faculty of Engineering. University of Tokyo — J Fac Eng Univ Tokyo
Journal. Faculty of Engineering. University of Tokyo — J Fac Engng Univ Tokyo
Journal. Faculty of Engineering. University of Tokyo. Series A. Annual Report — J Fac Eng Univ Tokyo Ser A
Journal. Faculty of Engineering. University of Tokyo. Series A. Annual Report — JETAA
Journal. Faculty of Engineering. University of Tokyo. Series B — J Fac Eng Univ Tokyo Ser B
Journal. Faculty of Engineering. University of Tokyo. Series B — J Fac Engrg Univ Tokyo Ser B
Journal. Faculty of Engineering. University of Tokyo. Series B — JETBA
Journal. Faculty of Fisheries and Animal Husbandry. Hiroshima University — J Fac Fish Anim Husb Hir Univ
Journal. Faculty of Fisheries and Animal Husbandry. Hiroshima University — J Fac Fish Anim Husb Hiroshima Univ
Journal. Faculty of Fisheries. Prefectural University of Mie — J Fac Fish Prefect Univ Mie
Journal. Faculty of International Studies of Culture. Kyushu Sangyo University — J Fac Internat Stud Cult Kyushu Sangyo Univ
Journal. Faculty of Liberal Arts and Sciences. Shinshu University — J Fac Lib Arts Sci Shinshu Univ
Journal. Faculty of Liberal Arts. Shinshu University. Part II. Natural Sciences — J Fac Lib Arts Shinshu Univ Part II Nat Sci
Journal. Faculty of Liberal Arts. Yamaguchi University — J Fac Liberal Arts Yamaguchi Univ
Journal. Faculty of Liberal Arts. Yamaguchi University. Natural Sciences — J Fac Liberal Arts Yamaguchi Univ Natur Sci
Journal. Faculty of Marine Science and Technology. Tokai University [*A publication*] — J Fac Mar Sci Technol Tokai Univ
Journal. Faculty of Marine Science. King Abdulaziz University — J Fac Mar Sci King Abdulaziz Univ
Journal. Faculty of Medicine (Baghdad) — J Fac Med (Baghdad)
Journal. Faculty of Medicine. Chulalongkorn University (Bangkok) — J Fac Med Chulalongkorn Univ (Bangkok)
Journal. Faculty of Medicine. Shinshu University — J Fac Med Shin Univ
Journal. Faculty of Medicine. University of Ankara — J Fac Med Univ Ankara
Journal. Faculty of Medicine. University of Ankara. Supplement — J Fac Med Univ Ankara Suppl
Journal. Faculty of Oceanography. Tokai University — J Fac Oceanogr Tokai Univ
Journal. Faculty of Pharmacy. Ankara University — J Fac Pharm Ankara Univ
Journal. Faculty of Pharmacy. Gazi University — J Fac Pharm Gazi Univ
Journal. Faculty of Pharmacy. Istanbul University — J Fac Pharm Istanbul Univ
Journal. Faculty of Political Science and Economics. Tokai University — J Fac Polit Sci Econ Tokai Univ
Journal. Faculty of Radiologists — J Fac Rad
Journal. Faculty of Radiologists (London) — J Fac Radiol (Lond)
Journal. Faculty of Science and Technology. Kinki University — J Fac Sci Technol Kinki Univ
Journal. Faculty of Science. Ege University. Series A — J Fac Sci Ege Univ Ser A
Journal. Faculty of Science. Hokkaido Imperial University. Ser V. Botany/ Rigaku-Bu Kiyo — J Fac Sci Hokkaido Imp Univ Ser 5 Bot
Journal. Faculty of Science. Hokkaido Imperial University. Series 4. Geology and Mineralogy — J Fac Sci Hokkaido Imp Univ Ser 4
Journal. Faculty of Science. Hokkaido Imperial University. Series 5. Botany — J Fac Sci Hokkaido Imp Univ Ser 5
Journal. Faculty of Science. Hokkaido University — J Fac Sci Hokkaido Univ
Journal. Faculty of Science. Hokkaido University. Series I. Mathematics — J Fac Sci Hokkaido Univ Ser I
Journal. Faculty of Science. Hokkaido University. Series IV. Geology and Mineralogy — J Fac Sci Hokkaido Univ Ser IV
Journal. Faculty of Science. Hokkaido University. Series IV. Geology and Mineralogy — J Fac Sci Hokkaido Univ Ser IV Geol Mineral
Journal. Faculty of Science. Hokkaido University. Series V. Botany — J Fac Sci Hokkaido Univ Ser V Bot
Journal. Faculty of Science. Hokkaido University. Series VI. Zoology — J Fac Sci Hokkaido Univ Ser VI
Journal. Faculty of Science. Hokkaido University. Series VI. Zoology — J Fac Sci Hokkaido Univ Ser VI Zool
Journal. Faculty of Science. Hokkaido University. Series VI. Zoology — J Fac Sci Hokkaido Univ VI
Journal. Faculty of Science. Hokkaido University. Series VII. Geophysics — J Fac Sci Hokkaido Univ Ser VII
Journal. Faculty of Science. Imperial University of Tokyo. Section II. Geology, Mineralogy, Geography, Seismology — J Fac Sci Imp Univ Tokyo Sect II
Journal. Faculty of Science. Imperial University of Tokyo. Section IV. Zoology — J Fac Sci Imp Univ Tokyo Sect IV Zool
Journal. Faculty of Science. Imperial University of Tokyo. Section V. Anthropology — J Fac Sci Imp Univ Tokyo Sect V
Journal. Faculty of Science. Nigata University — J Fac Sci Nigata Univ
Journal. Faculty of Science. Niigata University. Series II. Biology, Geology, and Mineralogy — J Fac Sci Niigata Univ Ser II Biol Geol Mineral
Journal. Faculty of Science. Series A. Ege University — J Fac Sci Ser A Ege Univ
Journal. Faculty of Science. Series B. Ege University — J Fac Sci Ser B Ege Univ
Journal. Faculty of Science. Shinshu University — J Fac Sci Shinshu Univ
Journal. Faculty of Science. Tokyo University — J Fac Sci Tokyo Univ
Journal. Faculty of Science. University of Tokyo — J Fac Sci Univ Tokyo
Journal. Faculty of Science. University of Tokyo. Section I. Mathematics, Astronomy, Physics, and Chemistry — J Fac Tok I

Journal. Faculty of Science. University of Tokyo. Section IA. Mathematics — J Fac Sci Univ Tokyo Sect IA
Journal. Faculty of Science. University of Tokyo. Section IA. Mathematics — J Fac Sci Univ Tokyo Sect IA Math
Journal. Faculty of Science. University of Tokyo. Section II. Geology, Mineralogy, Geography, and Geophysics — J Fac Sci Univ Tokyo Sect II Geol Mineral Geogr Geophys
Journal. Faculty of Science. University of Tokyo. Section III. Botany — J Fac Sci Univ Tokyo Sect III Bot
Journal. Faculty of Science. University of Tokyo. Section IV. Zoology [*Japan*] — J Fac Sci Univ Tokyo Sect IV
Journal. Faculty of Science. University of Tokyo. Section IV. Zoology — J Fac Sci Univ Tokyo Sect IV Zool
Journal. Faculty of Science. University of Tokyo. Section V. Anthropology — J Fac Sci Univ Tokyo Sect V
Journal. Faculty of Science. University of Tokyo. Section V. Anthropology — J Fac Sci Univ Tokyo Sect V Anthropol
Journal. Faculty of Textile Science and Sericulture. Shinshu University. Series A. Biology — J Fac Text Seric Shinshu Univ Ser A
Journal. Faculty of Textile Science and Sericulture. Shinshu University. Series A. Biology — J Fac Text Sericu Shinshu Univ Ser A Biol
Journal. Faculty of Textile Science and Sericulture. Shinshu University. Series B. Textile Engineering — J Fac Text Seric Shinshu Univ Ser B
Journal. Faculty of Textile Science and Sericulture. Shinshu University. Series C. Chemistry — J Fac Text Seric Shinshu Univ Ser C
Journal. Faculty of Textile Science and Sericulture. Shinshu University. Series D. Arts and Sciences — J Fac Text Seric Shinshu Univ Ser D
Journal. Faculty of Textile Science and Sericulture. Shinshu University. Series E. Sericulture — J Fac Text Seric Shinshu Ser E Seric
Journal. Faculty of Textile Science and Sericulture. Shinshu University. Series E. Sericulture — J Fac Text Seric Shinshu Univ Ser E
Journal. Faculty of Textile Science and Technology. Shinshu University. Series A. Biology — J Fac Text Sci Technol Shinshu Univ Ser A
Journal. Faculty of Textile Science and Technology. Shinshu University. Series A. Biology — J Fac Text Sci Technol Shinshu Univ Ser A Biol
Journal. Faculty of Textile Science and Technology. Shinshu University. Series B. Textile Engineering — J Fac Text Sci Technol Shinshu Univ Ser B
Journal. Faculty of Textile Science and Technology. Shinshu University. Series C. Chemistry — J Fac Text Sci Technol Shinshu Univ Ser C
Journal. Faculty of Textile Science and Technology. Shinshu University. Series D. Arts — J Fac Text Sci Technol Shinshu Univ Ser D
Journal. Faculty of Textile Science and Technology. Shinshu University. Series E. Agriculture and Sericulture — J Fac Text Sci Technol Shinshu Univ Ser E
Journal. Faculty of Textile Science and Technology. Shinshu University. Series E. Agriculture and Sericulture — J Fac Text Sci Technol Shinshu Univ Ser E Agric Seric
Journal. Faculty of Textile Science and Technology. Shinshu University. Series F. Physics and Mathematics — J Fac Text Sci Technol Shinshu Univ Ser F
Journal. Faculty of Veterinary Medicine. University of Ankara — J Fac Vet Med Univ Ankara
Journal. Faculty of Veterinary Medicine. University of Firat — J Fac Vet Med Univ Firat
Journal. Faculty of Veterinary Medicine. University of Istanbul — J Fac Vet Med Univ Istanbul
Journal. Farmers' Club — J Farmers' Club
Journal. Farnham Museum Society — J Farnham Mus Soc
Journal. Federal Home Loan Bank Board — JHLB
Journal. Feng Chia University — J Feng Chia Univ
Journal. Fengchia College of Engineering and Business — J Fengchia Coll Eng Bus
Journal. Fermentation Association of Japan — J Ferment Assoc Jpn
Journal. Fisheries Research Board of Canada — J Fish Res
Journal. Fisheries Research Board of Canada — J Fish Res Board Can
Journal. Fisheries Research Board of Canada — J Fish Res Board Canada
Journal. Fisheries Research Board of Canada — J Fisheries Res Board Can
Journal. Fisheries Research Board of Canada — JFRB
Journal. Fisheries Research Board of Canada — JFRBA
Journal. Fisheries Society of Taiwan — J Fish Soc Taiwan
Journal. Flemish Association of Gastro-Enterology — J Flemish Assoc Gastro Enterol
Journal. Flintshire Historical Society — JFHS
Journal. Florida Academy of General Practice — J Fla Acad Gen Pract
Journal. Florida Anti-Mosquito Association — J Fla Anti Mosq Assoc
Journal. Florida Engineering Society — J FL Eng Soc
Journal. Florida Engineering Society — J Fla Eng Soc
Journal. Florida Medical Association — J Fla Med Ass
Journal. Florida Medical Association — J Fla Med Assoc
Journal. Florida Medical Association — J Florida MA
Journal. Florida Medical Association — JFMA
Journal. Florida State Dental Society — J Fla State Dent Soc
Journal. Fluorescent Mineral Society — J Floresc Miner Soc
Journal foer Litteraturen og Theatern — J Litt Theatern
Journal. Folk Song Society — JFSS
Journal. Folklore Institute — J Folk Inst
Journal. Folklore Institute — J Folkl Inst
Journal. Folklore Institute — J Folklore Inst
Journal. Folklore Institute — JFI
Journal. Folklore Institute — JFLI
Journal. Folklore Institute — Jour Folklore Inst
Journal. Folklore Society of Greater Washington — JFSGW
Journal. Food Hygienic Society of Japan — J Fd Hyg Soc Jap
Journal. Food Hygienic Society of Japan — J Food Hyg Soc Jap
Journal. Food Hygienic Society of Japan — J Food Hyg Soc Jpn
Journal. Food Hygienic Society of Japan — J Food Hygienic Soc Jap
Journal for Drugtherapy and Research — J Drugther Res
Journal for General Philosophy of Science — J Gen Philos Sci
Journal for Hawaiian and Pacific Agriculture — J Hawaii Pac Agric
Journal for Language Teaching — J Lang Teach
Journal for Medicaid Management — J Medicaid Manage
Journal for Medicaid Management — J Medicaid Mgt
Journal for Research in Mathematics Education — J Res Math Educ
Journal for Scientific Agricultural Research — J Sci Agr Res
Journal for Scientific Agricultural Research — J Sci Agric Res
Journal for Scientific and Technical Agricultural Essays — J Sci Tech Agric Essays
Journal for Special Educators — J Sp Educators
Journal for Special Educators of the Mentally Retarded [*Later, Journal for Special Educators*] — J Sp Educ Men Retard
Journal for Special Educators of the Mentally Retarded [*Later, Journal for Special Educators*] — J Spec Ed Men Retard
Journal for Starch and Its Related Carbohydrates and Enzymes — J Starch Its Relat Carbohyd Enzymes
Journal for Studies in Economics and Econometrics — J Stud Econ Economet
Journal for Studies in Economics and Econometrics — J Studies Econ and Econometrics
Journal for Study of Iron Metallurgy — J Study Iron Metall
Journal for Technical and Vocational Education in South Africa — J Tech Vocat Educ S Afr
Journal for the History of Arabic Science — J Hist Arabic Sci
Journal for the History of Astronomy — J Hist Astron
Journal for the History of Astronomy — J Hist Astronom
Journal for the Humanities and Technology — J Hum Technol
Journal for the Scientific Study of Religion — J Sci St Re
Journal for the Scientific Study of Religion — J Sci Stud Rel
Journal for the Scientific Study of Religion — J Sci Stud Relig
Journal for the Scientific Study of Religion — J Scient Stud Relig
Journal for the Scientific Study of Religion [*New Haven, CT*] — JScStRel
Journal for the Scientific Study of Religion — JSSR
Journal for the Scientific Study of Religion — JSSRel
Journal for the Scientific Study of Religion — PJSR
Journal for the Study of Judaism [*Later, Journal for the Study of Judaism in the Persian, Hellenistic, and Roman Periods*] — J St Jud
Journal for the Study of Judaism [*Later, Journal for the Study of Judaism in thePersian, Hellenistic, and Roman Periods*] — JSJ
Journal for the Study of Judaism in the Persian, Hellenistic, and Roman Periods [*Leiden*] — JStJu
Journal for the Study of the New Testament — J St N T
Journal for the Study of the New Testament — JSNT
Journal for the Study of the Old Testament — J St OT
Journal for the Study of the Old Testament — JSOT
Journal for the Theory of Social Behavior — J T S Behav
Journal for the Theory of Social Behavior — J Theor Soc Behav
Journal for the Theory of Social Behavior — J Theory Soc Behav
Journal for Theology and the Church — JTC
Journal for Theology and the Church — JTCh
Journal for Town and Regional Planning — J Town Reg Plann
Journal for Water and Wastewater Research — J Water Wastewater Res
Journal for Water and Wastewater Research — JWABAQ
Journal. Forensic Science Society — J For Sci Socy
Journal. Forensic Science Society — J Forensic Sci Soc
Journal. Forensic Science Society of India — J Forensic Sci Soc India
Journal. Forest Products Research Society — J For Prod Res Soc
Journal Forestier Suisse — J For Suisse
Journal Forestier Suisse/Schweizerische Zeitschrift fuer Forstwesen — J For Suisse Schweiz Z Forstwes
Journal. Forestry Commission — J For Comm
Journal. Formosan Medical Association — J Formosan Med Assoc
Journal Francais de Biophysique et Medecine Nucleaire — J Fr Biophys Med Nucl
Journal Francais de Biophysique et Medecine Nucleaire — JFBND
Journal Francais de Medecine et Chirurgie Thoraciques — J Fr Med Chir Thorac
Journal Francais d'Hydrologie — J Fr Hydrol
Journal Francais d'Ophtalmologie — J Fr Ophtalmol
Journal Francais d'Oto-Rhino-Laryngologie — JFORL
Journal Francais d'Oto-Rhino-Laryngologie, Audio-Phonologie, et Chirurgie Maxillo-Faciale — J Fr Oto Rhino Laryngol Audio Phonol Chir Maxillo Fac
Journal Francais d'Oto-Rhino-Laryngologie, Audio-Phonologie, et Chirurgie Maxillo-Faciale — JFOAB
Journal Francais d'Oto-Rhino-Laryngologie et Chirurgie Maxillo-Faciale — J Fr Oto Rhino Laryngol Chir
Journal Francais d'Oto-Rhino-Laryngologie et Chirurgie Maxillo-Faciale [*Later, Journal Francias d'Oto-Rhino-Laryngologie*] — J Fr Oto Rhino Laryngol Chir Maxillo Fac
Journal Francais d'Oto-Rhino-Laryngologie et Chirurgie Maxillo-Faciale [*Later, Journal Francais d'Oto-Rhino-Laryngologie*] — J Fr Oto-Rhino-Laryngol
Journal. Franklin Institute — J Frankl I
Journal. Franklin Institute — J Franklin Inst
Journal. Franklin Institute — JFI
Journal. Franklin Institute — JFINA
Journal. Franklin Institute. Monograph — J Franklin Inst Monogr
Journal. Friends' Historical Society — JFHS
Journal. Friends' Historical Society. Supplement — JFHSS
Journal. Fudan University. Natural Science — J Fudan Univ Nat Sci
Journal. Fuel Society of Japan [*Nenryo Kyokai-Shi*] — J Fuel Soc Jap
Journal fuer Angewandte Chemie — J Ang Chem
Journal fuer Auserlesene Theologische Literatur — JATL
Journal fuer Betriebswirtschaft — OBW
Journal fuer Chemie und Physik — J Chem Phys

Journal fuer die Botanik (Goettingen) (Edited by H. A. Schrader) — J Bot Schrader
Journal fuer die Botanik (Goettingen) (Edited by H. A. Schrader) — J fuer Bot Schrader
Journal fuer die Botanik (Goettingen) (Edited by H. A. Schrader) — Schrad Journ Bot
Journal fuer die Botanik (H. A. Schrader, Editor) — Schrader Journ Botan
Journal fuer die Gartenkunst — J Gartenkunst
Journal fuer die Neueste Hollaendische Medizinische und Naturhistorische Literatur — J Neueste Holl Med Naturhist Lit
Journal fuer die Neuesten Land- und Seereisen und das Interessanteste aus der Voelker- und Laenderkunde — J Neuesten Land Seereisen
Journal fuer die Reine und Angewandte Mathematik — J Rein Math
Journal fuer die Reine und Angewandte Mathematik — J Reine Angew Math
Journal fuer Fabrik, Manufactur, und Handlungen — J Fabrik
Journal fuer Gasbeleuchtung und Verwandte Beleuchtungsarten sowie fuer Wasserversorgung — J Gasbeleucht Verw Beleuchtungsarten Wasserversorg
Journal fuer Hirnforschung — J Hirnforsch
Journal fuer Landwirthschaft und Gartenbau — J Landw Gartenbau
Journal fuer Landwirtschaft — J Landwirtsch
Journal fuer Landwirtschaft — Journ Landwirtsch
Journal fuer Landwirtschaftliche Wissenschaft — J Landwirtsch Wiss
Journal fuer Literatur, Kunst, und Geselliges Leben — J Lit Kunst Geselliges Leben
Journal fuer Makromolekulare Chemie — J Makromol Chem
Journal fuer Marktforschung — J Marktforsch
Journal fuer Medizinische Kosmetik — J Med Kosmet
Journal fuer Ornithologie — J Ornithol
Journal fuer Ornithologie — Journ Ornithol
Journal fuer Praktische Chemie — J Prak Chem
Journal fuer Praktische Chemie — J Prakt Chem
Journal fuer Praktische Chemie — Journ Pr Chem
Journal fuer Praktische Chemie — Journ Prakt Chem
Journal fuer Praktische Chemie — JPCh
Journal fuer Psychologie und Neurologie — J Psychol Neurol
Journal fuer Psychologie und Neurologie — J Psychol u Neurol
Journal fuer Psychologie und Neurologie — Jour f Psychol u Neurol
Journal fuer Reine und Angewandte Mathematik — JRAM
Journal fuer Religion, Wahrheit, und Litteratur — JRWL
Journal fuer Signalaufzeichnungsmaterialien — J Signalaufzeichnungsmater
Journal fuer Signalaufzeichnungsmaterialien — J Signalaufzeichnungsmaterialien
Journal fuer Theologische Literatur — JTL
Journal. Fujian Agricultural College — J Fujian Agric Coll
Journal. Fujian Teachers University. Natural Science Edition — J Fujian Teach Univ Nat Sci Ed
Journal. Fukuoka Dental College — J Fukuoka Dent Col
Journal. Gakugei Tokushima University. Natural Science — J Gakugei Tokushima Univ Nat Sci
Journal. Galway Archaeological and Historical Society — J Galway Archaeol Hist Soc
Journal. Ganganatha Jha Kendriya Sanskrit Vidyapeetha — J Gan Jha Kend Sans Vid
Journal. Ganganatha Jha Research Institute — JGJRI
Journal. Ganganatha Jha Research Institute — JGRI
Journal. Gansu Teachers' University. Natural Science Edition — J Gansu Teach Univ Nat Sci Ed
Journal. Gemmological Society of Japan — J Gemmol Soc Jpn
Journal General de la Litterature Etrangere, ou Indicateur Bibliographique et Raisonne des Livres Nouveaux — J Gen Litt Etrangere
Journal General de Medecine, de Chirurgie, et de Pharmacie — J Gen Med Chir et Pharm
Journal General de Medecine, de Chirurgie, et de Pharmacie, Francaises et Etrangeres — J Gen Med Franc Etrangeres
Journal General. Societes et Travaux Scientifiques de la France et de l'Etranger. Section 1. Sciences Mathematiques, Physiques, et Naturelles — J Gen Soc Trav Sci France Etranger Sect 1 Sci Math
Journal. Geochemical Society of India — J Geochem Soc India
Journal Geographica — J Geog
Journal. Geological Society — Geol Soc J
Journal. Geological Society [*London*] — J Geol S
Journal. Geological Society of Australia — J Geol Soc Aust
Journal. Geological Society of Australia — J Geol Soc Australia
Journal. Geological Society of India — J Geol S In
Journal. Geological Society of India — J Geol Soc India
Journal. Geological Society of Iraq — J Geol Soc Iraq
Journal. Geological Society of Jamaica — J Geol Soc Jam
Journal. Geological Society of Japan — J Geol Soc Jpn
Journal. Geological Society of Korea — J Geol Soc Korea
Journal. Geological Society of London — J Geol Soc London
Journal. Geological Society of London — JGSLA
Journal. Geological Society of Thailand — J Geol Soc Thailand
Journal. Geological Society of the Philippines — J Geol Soc Philipp
Journal. Geological Society of Tokyo — J Geol Soc Tokyo
Journal. Geological Society (Seoul) — J Geol Soc (Seoul)
Journal. Georgia Dental Association — GDAJA
Journal. Georgia Dental Association — J GA Dent Assoc
Journal. Georgia Entomological Society — GENSA
Journal. Georgia Entomological Society — J GA Ent Soc
Journal. Georgia Entomological Society — J GA Entomol Soc
Journal. Geotechnical Engineering Division. American Society of Civil Engineers — J Geotech Engng Div ASCE
Journal. Geotechnical Engineering Division. Proceedings of the American Society of Civil Engineers — J Geotech Eng Div Am Soc Civ Eng
Journal. Geotechnical Engineering Division. Proceedings of the American Society of Civil Engineers — J Geotech Eng Div Amer Soc Civil Eng Proc
Journal. Geotechnical Engineering Division. Proceedings of the American Society of Civil Engineers — J Geotech Engng Div Proc ASCE
Journal. Geothermal Energy Research and Development Company, Limited — J Geotherm Energy Res Dev Co Ltd
Journal. Graduate Music Students. Ohio State University — J GMS OSU
Journal. Graduate Research Center — J Grad Res Cent
Journal. Graduate Research Center. Southern Methodist University — J Grad Res Cent South Methodist Univ
Journal. Greater India Society — JGIS
Journal. Greater India Society — Journal Greater India Soc
Journal. Gujarat Research Society [*India*] — J Guj Res Soc
Journal. Gujarat Research Society [*India*] — J Gujarat Res Soc
Journal. Gujarat Research Society [*India*] — JGRS
Journal. Gujarat Research Society [*India*] — Journal Gujarat Research Soc
Journal. Gyeongsang National University. Natural Sciences [*Republic of Korea*] [*A publication*] — J Gyeongsang Natl Univ Nat Sci
Journal. Gyeongsang National University. Natural Sciences — NKTAD
Journal. Gyeongsang National University. Science and Technology — J Gyeongsang Natl Univ Sci Technol
Journal. Gyeongsang National University. Science and Technology — JGSTD
Journal. Gypsy Lore Society — JGLS
Journal. Gypsy Lore Society — JGyLS
Journal. Hangzhou University. Natural Science Edition — J Hangzhou Univ Nat Sci Ed
Journal. Hanyang Medical College [*South Korea*] — J Hanyang Med Coll
Journal. Harbin Industrial College — J Harbin Ind Coll
Journal. Harbin Institute of Technology — J Harbin Inst Technol
Journal. Harbin University of Science and Technology — J Harbin Univ Sci Technol
Journal. Hattori Botanical Laboratory — J Hattori Bot Lab
Journal. Hawaii Dental Association — J Hawaii Dent Assoc
Journal. Hawaii Dental Association — JHDA
Journal. Hawaii State Dental Association — J Hawaii State Dent Assoc
Journal Hebdomadaire de Medecine — J Hebd Med
Journal Hebdomadaire des Progres des Sciences Medicales — J Hebd Progr Sci Med
Journal. Hebei Academy of Sciences — J Hebei Acad Sci
Journal. Hebei College of Geology — J Hebei Coll Geol
Journal. Hebei Institute of Technology — J Hebei Inst Technol
Journal. Hebei Normal University. Natural Science Edition — J Hebei Norm Univ Nat Sci Ed
Journal. Hebei University. Natural Science Edition — J Hebei Univ Nat Sci Ed
Journal. Hebrew Union College [*Cincinnati*] — JHUC
Journal Helvetique — J Helv
Journal. Heraldic and Genealogical Society of Wales — JHGSW
Journal. Herpetological Association of Africa — J Herpetol Assoc Afr
Journal. High Pressure Gas Safety Institute of Japan — J High Pressure Gas Saf Inst Jpn
Journal. High Temperature Society [*Japan*] — J High Temp Soc
Journal. High Temperature Society (Japan) — J High Temp Soc (Jpn)
Journal. High Temperature Society (Suita, Japan) — J High Temp Soc (Suita Jpn)
Journal. Highway Division. American Society of Civil Engineers — J Highw Div Am Soc Civ Eng
Journal. Hillside Hospital — J Hillside Hosp
Journal. Hiroshima Botanical Club — J Hiroshima Bot Club
Journal. Hiroshima Medical Association [*Japan*] — J Hiroshima Med Assoc
Journal. Hiroshima University. Dental Society — J Hiroshima Univ Dent Soc
Journal. Historical Firearms Society of South Africa — J Hist Firearms Soc S Afr
Journal. Historical Metallurgy Society — J Hist Metall Soc
Journal. Historical Metallurgy Society [*London*] — JHMS
Journal. Historical Society of Nigeria — J Hist Soc Nig
Journal. Historical Society of Nigeria — J Hist Soc Nigeria
Journal. Historical Society of Sierra Leone — J Hist Soc Sierra Leone
Journal. Historical Society of South Australia — JHSSA
Journal. Historical Society of the Church in Wales — J Hist Soc Church Wales
Journal. Historical Society of the Church in Wales — JHSCW
Journal. Historical Society of the Presbyterian Church of Wales — JHSPCW
Journal. History of Ideas — JHId
Journal. Hokkaido Dental Association — J Hokkaido Dent Assoc
Journal. Hokkaido Fisheries Experimental Station — J Hokkaido Fish Exp Stn
Journal. Hokkaido Fisheries Scientific Institution — J Hokkaido Fish Sci Inst
Journal. Hokkaido Forest Products Research Institute — J Hokkaido Forest Prod Res Inst
Journal. Hokkaido Gakugei University — J Hokkaido Gakugei Univ
Journal. Hokkaido Gakugei University. Section B [*Japan*] — J Hokkaido Gakugei Univ Sect B
Journal. Hokkaido Gynecology and Obstetrical Society — J Hokkaido Gynecol Obstet Soc
Journal. Hokkaido University of Education — J Hokkaido Univ Educ
Journal. Hokkaido University of Education. Section II-A — J Hokkaido Univ Ed Sect IIA
Journal. Hokkaido University of Education. Section II-A [*Japan*] — J Hokkaido Univ Educ Sect II A
Journal. Hokkaido University of Education. Section II-B — J Hokkaido Univ Educ IIB
Journal. Hokkaido University of Education. Section II-B — J Hokkaido Univ Educ Sect II-B
Journal. Hokkaido University of Education. Section II-C [*Japan*] — J Hokkaido Univ Educ Sect II C
Journal. Hokuto Technical Junior College — J Hokuto Tech Jr Coll
Journal. Hong Kong Branch. Royal Asiatic Society — J HK Br Roy Asiat Soc
Journal. Hong Kong Branch. Royal Asiatic Society — J Hong Kong Branch Roy Asiatic Soc
Journal. Hongkong Fisheries Research Station — J Hongkong Fish Res Sta

Journal. Hongkong University. Geographical, Geological, and Archaeological Society — JGGAS
Journal. Hopeh University. Natural Science [*People's Republic of China*] — J Hopeh Univ Nat Sci
Journal. Horological Institute of Japan — J Horol Inst Jpn
Journal. Horticultural Association of Japan/Engei Gakkai Zasshi — J Hort Assoc Japan
Journal. Horticulture Association of Japan — J Hortic Assoc Jpn
Journal. Horticulture Association of London — J Hortic Assoc London
Journal. Hotel Dieu de Montreal — J Hotel Dieu de Montreal
Journal. Houston [*Texas*] **District Dental Society** — J Houston Dist Dent Soc
Journal. Huazhong (Central China) University of Science and Technology — J Huazhong (Cent China) Univ Sci Technol
Journal. Huazhong Institute of Technology [*People's Republic of China*] — J Huazhong Inst Technol
Journal. Huazhong Institute of Technology. English Edition — J Huazhong Inst Tech
Journal. Huazhong Institute of Technology. English Edition — J Huazhong Inst Technol Engl Ed
Journal. Huazhong [*Central China*] **University of Science and Technology. English Edition** — J Huazhong Univ Sci Tech
Journal. Hunan Normal University. Natural Science Edition — J Hunan Norm Univ Nat Sci Ed
Journal. Hunan Science and Technology University — J Hunan Sci Technol Univ
Journal. Hunan University — J Hunan Univ
Journal. Hungarian Chemical Society — J Hung Chem Soc
Journal. Hungarian Society of Engineers and Architects — J Hung Soc Eng Archit
Journal. Hungarian Veterinary Surgeons — J Hung Vet Surg
Journal. Hunter Valley Research Foundation — J Hunter Valley Research Foundation
Journal. Hyderabad Archaeological Society — JHAS
Journal. Hyderabad Geological Survey — J Hyderabad Geol Surv
Journal. Hydraulic Division. Proceedings of the American Society of Civil Engineers — J Hydraul Div Proc ASCE
Journal. Hydraulics Division. American Society of Civil Engineers — J Hydr-ASCE
Journal. Hydraulics Division. American Society of Civil Engineers — J Hydraul Div Am Soc Civ Eng
Journal. Hydraulics Division. Proceedings of the American Society of Civil Engineers — J Hydraul Div Amer Soc Civil Eng Proc
Journal. Hydraulics Division. Proceedings of the American Society of Civil Engineers — JYCE-A
Journal. Hygienic Chemical Society of Japan — J Hyg Chem Soc Japan
Journal. Hyogo College of Medicine — J Hyogo Coll Med
Journal. IARI [*Indian Agricultural Research Institute*]. Post-Graduate School — J IARI Post-Grad Sch
Journal. Idaho Academy of Science — J Idaho Acad Sci
Journal. Idaho Academy of Science — JIDSDP
Journal. Illinois State Historical Society — J Ill Hist Soc
Journal. Illinois State Historical Society — J Ill State Hist Soc
Journal. Illinois State Historical Society — J Illinois State Hist Soc
Journal. Illinois State Historical Society — JIHS
Journal. Illinois State Historical Society — JILLHS
Journal. Illinois State Historical Society — JISHS
Journal. Illuminating Engineering Institute of Japan — J Illum Eng Inst Jap
Journal. Illuminating Engineering Society — J Illum Eng Soc
Journal. Illuminating Engineering Society — J Illum Engng Soc
Journal. Imperial Agricultural Experiment Station. Nishigahara, Tokyo/Noji Shikenjo Iho — J Imp Agric Exp Sta Nishigahara Tokyo
Journal. Imperial Agricultural Experiment Station (Tokyo) — J Imp Agr Exp Sta (Tokyo)
Journal. Imperial College. Chemical Engineering Society — J Imp Coll Chem Eng Soc
Journal. Imperial College. Chemical Society — J Imp Coll Chem Soc
Journal. Imperial Fisheries Institute (Japan) — J Imp Fish Inst (Jpn)
Journal. Incorporated Australian Insurance Institute — J Inc Aust Insurance Inst
Journal. Incorporated Brewers' Guild — J Inc Brew Guild
Journal. Incorporated Clerks of Works Association of Great Britain — J Inc Clerks Works Assoc GB
Journal. India Society of Engineers — J India Soc Eng
Journal. Indian Academy of Dentistry — J Indian Acad Dent
Journal. Indian Academy of Forensic Sciences — J Indian Acad Forensic Sci
Journal. Indian Academy of Forensic Sciences — JIFSA
Journal. Indian Academy of Geoscience — J Indian Acad Geosci
Journal. Indian Academy of Philosophy — J Ind Acad Philo
Journal. Indian Academy of Philosophy — J Indian Acad Phil
Journal. Indian Academy of Philosophy — JIAP
Journal. Indian Academy of Sciences — J Indian Acad Sci
Journal. Indian Academy of Wood Science — J Indian Acad Wood Sci
Journal. Indian Anthropological Institute — JIAI
Journal. Indian Anthropological Society — J Ind Anthropol Soc
Journal. Indian Anthropological Society — J Indian Anthropol Soc
Journal. Indian Anthropological Society — JIAS
Journal. Indian Association for Communicable Diseases — J Indian Assoc Commun Dis
Journal. Indian Botanical Society — J Ind Bot Soc
Journal. Indian Botanical Society — J Indian Bot Soc
Journal. Indian Ceramic Society — J Indian Ceram Soc
Journal. Indian Chemical Society — J Ind Ch S
Journal. Indian Chemical Society — J Indian Chem Soc
Journal. Indian Chemical Society. Industrial and News Edition [*India*] — J Indian Chem Soc Ind News Ed
Journal. Indian Chemical Society. Industrial and News Edition — JINEA
Journal. Indian Council of Chemists — J Indian Counc Chem
Journal. Indian Dental Association — J Indian Dent Assoc
Journal. Indian Geophysical Union — J Indian Geophys Union
Journal. Indian Geoscience Association — J Indian Geosci Assoc
Journal. Indian Institute of Bankers — Indian Inst Bankers J
Journal. Indian Institute of Bankers — JIIB
Journal. Indian Institute of Science — J Indian I
Journal. Indian Institute of Science — J Indian Inst Sci
Journal. Indian Institute of Science. Section A — J Indian Inst Sci Sect A
Journal. Indian Institute of Science. Section B — J Indian Inst Sci Sect B
Journal. Indian Institute of Science. Section C — J Indian Inst Sci Sect C
Journal. Indian Institute of Science. Section C. Biological Sciences — J Indian Inst Sci Sect C Biol Sci
Journal. Indian Law Institute — J Indian Law Inst
Journal. Indian Law Institute — JILI
Journal. Indian Leather Technologists Association — J Indian Leather Technol Assoc
Journal. Indian Mathematical Society — J Indian Math Soc
Journal. Indian Mathematical Society — JIMS
Journal. Indian Medical Association — J Indian Med A
Journal. Indian Medical Association — J Indian Med Ass
Journal. Indian Medical Association — J Indian Med Assoc
Journal. Indian Musicological Society — J Ind Musicol Soc
Journal. Indian Musicological Society — J Indian Musicol Soc
Journal. Indian National Society of Soil Mechanics and Foundation Engineering — J Indian Nat Soc Soil Mech Found Eng
Journal. Indian Pediatric Society — J Indian Pediatr Soc
Journal. Indian Plywood Industries Research Institute — J Indian Plywood Ind Res Inst
Journal. Indian Potato Association — J Indian Potato Assoc
Journal. Indian Potato Association — JIPA
Journal. Indian Refractory Makers Association — J Indian Refract Makers Assoc
Journal. Indian Roads Congress — J Indian Roads Congr
Journal. Indian Roads Congress — JIRC
Journal. Indian Society of Agricultural Statistics — J Indian Soc Agr Statist
Journal. Indian Society of Agricultural Statistics — J Indian Soc Agric Stat
Journal. Indian Society of Oriental Art — JISOA
Journal. Indian Society of Pedodontics and Preventive Dentistry — J Indian Soc Pedod Prev Dent
Journal. Indian Society of Soil Science — J Indian Soc Soil Sci
Journal. Indian Society of Statistics and Operations Research — J Indian Soc Statist Oper Res
Journal. Indian Sociological Society — JISS
Journal. Indian Statistical Association — J Indian Statist Assoc
Journal. Indian Statistical Association — J Indn St A
Journal. Indiana Dental Association — J Indiana Dent Assoc
Journal. Indiana State Dental Association — J Indiana State Dent Assoc
Journal. Indiana State Medical Association — J Indiana MA
Journal. Indiana State Medical Association — J Indiana State Med Assoc
Journal. Indiana State Medical Association — JIDXA
Journal. Indianapolis District Dental Society — J Indianap Dist Dent Soc
Journal. Indonesian Atomic Energy Agency — J Indones At Energy Agency
Journal. Indonesian Atomic Energy Agency — Jnl Indones Atom Energ Agency
Journal. Industrial Explosives Society. Explosion and Explosives (Japan) — J Ind Explos Soc (Jap)
Journal. Industrial Explosives Society (Japan) — J Ind Explos Soc (Jpn)
Journal. Information Processing Society of Japan — J Inf Process Soc Jap
Journal. Information Processing Society of Japan — J Inf Process Soc Jpn
Journal. Information Science and Technology Association (Japan) — J Inf Sci Technol Assoc (Jpn)
Journal. Inland Fisheries Society of India — J Inl Fish Soc India
Journal. Inland Fisheries Society of India — J Inland Fish Soc India
Journal. Institut Canadien de Science et Technologie Alimentaire — J Inst Can Sci Technol Aliment
Journal. Institut Canadien de Technologie Alimentaire — J Inst Can Technol Aliment
Journal. Institut des Renseignements Scientifiques et Techniques. Academie Tchecoslovaque de l'Agriculture — J Inst Renseign Tech Acad Tchecoslovaque Agric
Journal. Institute for Agricultural Resources Utilization. Chinju Agricultural College — J Inst Agric Resour Utiliz Chinju Agric Coll
Journal. Institute for Defence Studies and Analyses — J Inst Def Stud Anal
Journal. Institute for Scientific and Technical Information. Czechoslovak Academy of Agriculture — J Inst Sci Tech Inf Czech Acad Agric
Journal. Institute for Socioeconomic Studies [*United States*] — J Inst Socioecon Stud
Journal. Institute for Socioeconomic Studies — J Institute Socioecon Stud
Journal. Institute for Socioeconomic Studies — JIS
Journal. Institute for Socioeconomic Studies — JISSD
Journal. Institute for Socioeconomic Studies — JSC
Journal. Institute of Actuaries — Inst Actuaries J
Journal. Institute of Animal Technicians — J Inst Anim Tech
Journal. Institute of Armament Studies [*Poona, India*] — Jnl Inst Armament Stud
Journal. Institute of Armament Studies (Poona, India) — J Inst Armament Stud (Poona India)
Journal. Institute of Armament Technology (Poona, India) — J Inst Armament Technol (Poona India)
Journal. Institute of Bankers — JIB
Journal. Institute of Biology — J Inst Biol
Journal. Institute of Brewing — J I Brewing
Journal. Institute of Brewing — J Inst Brew
Journal. Institute of Brewing — JINBA
Journal. Institute of Brewing. Supplement — J Inst Brew Suppl
Journal. Institute of British Foundrymen — J Inst Br Foundrymen
Journal. Institute of Chemistry (India) — J Inst Chem (India)
Journal. Institute of Chemistry of Ireland — J Inst Chem Irel

Journal. Institute of Clerks of Works of Great Britain — J Inst Clerks Works G Bt
Journal. Institute of Clerks of Works of Great Britain — J Inst Clerks Works GB
Journal. Institute of Draftsmen — J Inst Draftsmen
Journal. Institute of Electrical Communication Engineers of Japan [*Later, Journal. Institute of Electronics and Communication Engineers of Japan*] — J Inst Electr Commun Eng Jap
Journal. Institute of Electrical Engineers [*South Korea*] — J Inst Electr Eng
Journal. Institute of Electronics and Communication Engineers of Japan — J Inst Electron and Commun Eng Jpn
Journal. Institute of Electronics and Communication Engineers of Japan — J Inst Electron Commun Eng Jap
Journal. Institute of Electronics and Communication Engineers of Japan — J Inst Electron Commun Eng Jpn
Journal. Institute of Energy [*United Kingdom*] — J Inst Energy
Journal. Institute of Enology and Viticulture. Yamanashi University — J Inst Enol Viti Yamanashi Univ
Journal. Institute of Fuel — J I Fuel
Journal. Institute of Fuel — J Inst Fuel
Journal. Institute of Fuel — JIFUA
Journal. Institute of Fuel. Supplement — J Inst Fuel Suppl
Journal. Institute of Geology. Vikram University — J Inst Geol Vikram Univ
Journal. Institute of Highway Engineers — J Inst Highw Eng
Journal. Institute of Jamaica — J Inst Jamaica
Journal. Institute of Mathematics and Computer Sciences (Computer Science Series) — J Inst Math Comput Sci Comput Sci Ser
Journal. Institute of Mathematics and Computer Sciences (Mathematics Series) — J Inst Math Comput Sci Math Ser
Journal. Institute of Mathematics and Its Applications — J I Math Ap
Journal. Institute of Mathematics and Its Applications — J Inst Math and Appl
Journal. Institute of Mathematics and Its Applications — J Inst Math Appl
Journal. Institute of Mathematics and Its Applications — J Inst Math Applic
Journal. Institute of Mathematics and Its Applications — J Inst Math Its Appl
Journal. Institute of Mathematics and Its Applications — JMTAA
Journal. Institute of Metals — JIMEA
Journal. Institute of Metals (London) — J Inst Met (Lond)
Journal. Institute of Metals. Metallurgical Abstracts — JIMMA
Journal. Institute of Metals. Supplement — J Inst Met Suppl
Journal. Institute of Mine Surveyors of South Africa — J Inst Min Surv S Afr
Journal. Institute of Mine Surveyors of South Africa — J Inst Mine Surv S Afr
Journal. Institute of Muslim Minority Affairs — JIMMA
Journal. Institute of Navigation — J Inst Navig
Journal. Institute of Nuclear Materials Management — J Inst Nucl Mater Manage
Journal. Institute of Petroleum — J Inst Pet
Journal. Institute of Petroleum — JIPEA
Journal. Institute of Petroleum. Abstracts — J Inst Pet Abstr
Journal. Institute of Polytechnics. Osaka City University — J Inst Polytech Osaka Cy Univ
Journal. Institute of Polytechnics. Osaka City University. Series C. Chemistry — J Inst Polytech Osaka City Univ Ser C
Journal. Institute of Polytechnics. Osaka City University. Series D. Biology [*A publication*] — J Inst Polytech Osaka City Univ Ser D
Journal. Institute of Polytechnics. Osaka City University. Series E. Engineering — J Inst Polytech Osaka City Univ Ser E
Journal. Institute of Polytechnics. Osaka City University. Series G. Geoscience — J Inst Polytech Osaka City Univ Ser G
Journal. Institute of Safety of High Pressure Gas Engineering [*Japan*] — J Inst Saf High Pressure Gas Eng
Journal. Institute of Science Technology — J Inst Sci Technol
Journal. Institute of Sewage Purification — J Inst Sewage Purif
Journal. Institute of Television Engineers of Japan — J Inst Telev Eng Jpn
Journal. Institute of Transport — J Inst Transp
Journal. Institute of Transport (Australian Section) — J Inst Transport
Journal. Institute of Wood Science — J I Wood Sc
Journal. Institute of Wood Science — J Inst Wood Sci
Journal. Institute of Wood Science — JIWSA
Journal. Institution of Automobile Engineers (London) — J Inst Automob Eng (London)
Journal. Institution of Automotive and Aeronautical Engineers — J Inst Auto & Aero Engrs
Journal. Institution of Automotive and Aeronautical Engineers — J Inst Automot Aeronaut Eng
Journal. Institution of Automotive and Aeronautical Engineers — J Inst Automotive & Aeronautical Eng
Journal. Institution of Automotive and Aeronautical Engineers — J Inst Automotive & Aeronautical Engrs
Journal. Institution of Certificated Engineers (South Africa) — J Inst Certif Eng (S Afr)
Journal. Institution of Chemists — JOICA
Journal. Institution of Chemists (India) — J Inst Chem (India)
Journal. Institution of Civil Engineers — J Inst Civ Eng
Journal. Institution of Computer Sciences — J Inst Comput Sci
Journal. Institution of Electrical Engineers [*England*] — J Inst Electr Eng
Journal. Institution of Electrical Engineers of Japan — J Inst Electr Eng Jpn
Journal. Institution of Electrical Engineers. Part 1. General — J Inst Electr Eng Part 1
Journal. Institution of Electrical Engineers. Part 2. Power Engineering — J Inst Electr Eng Part 2
Journal. Institution of Electrical Engineers. Part 3. Radio and Communication Engineering — J Inst Electr Eng Part 3
Journal. Institution of Electronics and Telecommunication Engineers — J Inst Electron Telecommun Eng
Journal. Institution of Electronics and Telecommunication Engineers (New Delhi) — J Inst Electron Telecommun Eng (New Delhi)
Journal. Institution of Engineers (Australia) — J Inst Eng (Aust)
Journal. Institution of Engineers (Australia) — J Inst Engrs (Aust)
Journal. Institution of Engineers (Australia) — J Inst Engrs (Australia)
Journal. Institution of Engineers (Australia) — J Instn Engrs (Aust)
Journal. Institution of Engineers (Australia) — JISGA
Journal. Institution of Engineers (Bangladesh) — J Inst Eng (Bangladesh)
Journal. Institution of Engineers (Federation of Malaysia) — Jnl Inst Eng (Fed Malaysia)
Journal. Institution of Engineers (India) — J Inst Eng (India)
Journal. Institution of Engineers (India) — J Inst Engrs (India)
Journal. Institution of Engineers (India). Chemical Engineering Division — J Inst Eng (India) Chem Eng Div
Journal. Institution of Engineers (India). Chemical Engineering Division — JECEA
Journal. Institution of Engineers (India). Civil Engineering Division — J Inst Eng (India) Civ Eng Div
Journal. Institution of Engineers (India). Civil Engineering Division — JECVA
Journal. Institution of Engineers (India). Electrical Engineering Division — J Inst Eng (India) Elec Eng Div
Journal. Institution of Engineers (India). Electrical Engineering Division — JEELA
Journal. Institution of Engineers (India). Electronics and Telecommunication Engineering Division — J Inst Eng (India) Electron and Telecommun Eng Div
Journal. Institution of Engineers (India). Electronics and Telecommunication Engineering Division — J Inst Eng (India) Electron Telecommun Eng Div
Journal. Institution of Engineers (India). Electronics and Telecommunication Engineering Division — J Inst (India) Electron Telecommun Eng Div
Journal. Institution of Engineers (India). Environmental Engineering Division [*A publication*] — J Inst Eng (India) Environ Eng Div
Journal. Institution of Engineers (India). General Engineering Division — J Inst Eng (India) Gen Eng Div
Journal. Institution of Engineers. (India) Hindi Division — J Inst Eng India Hindi Div
Journal. Institution of Engineers (India). Industrial Development and General Engineering Division — J Inst Eng (India) Ind Dev Gen Eng Div
Journal. Institution of Engineers (India). Interdisciplinary and General Engineering — J Inst Eng (India) Interdisciplinary and Gen Eng
Journal. Institution of Engineers (India). Mechanical Engineering Division — J Inst Eng (India) Mech Eng Div
Journal. Institution of Engineers (India). Mining and Metallurgy Division — J Inst Eng (India) Min and Metall Div
Journal. Institution of Engineers (India). Mining and Metallurgy Division — J Inst Eng (India) Min Metall Div
Journal. Institution of Engineers (India). Mining and Metallurgy Division — J Inst Eng (India) Mining Met Div
Journal. Institution of Engineers (India). Part CH. Chemical Engineering Division — J Inst Eng (India) Part CH
Journal. Institution of Engineers. (India) Part CH. Chemical Engineering Division — J Inst Eng India Part CH Chem
Journal. Institution of Engineers (India). Part CI — J Inst Engrs (India) Part CI
Journal. Institution of Engineers (India). Part GE. General Engineering — J Inst Eng (India) Part GE
Journal. Institution of Engineers (India). Part IDGE [*Industrial Development and General Engineering*] — J Inst Eng (India) Part IDGE
Journal. Institution of Engineers (India). Part ME — J Inst Engrs (India) Part ME
Journal. Institution of Engineers. (India) Part MM. Mining and Metallurgy Division — J Inst Eng India Part MM Min
Journal. Institution of Engineers (India). Part MM. Mining and Metallurgy Division — J Inst Eng (India) Part MM Min Metall Div
Journal. Institution of Engineers (India). Public Health Engineering Division — J Inst Eng (India) Pub Health Eng Div
Journal. Institution of Engineers (India). Public Health Engineering Division — J Inst Eng (India) Public Health Eng Div
Journal. Institution of Engineers (Malaysia) — J Inst Eng (Malaysia)
Journal. Institution of Gas Engineers — J Inst Gas Eng
Journal. Institution of Gas Engineers — J Instn Gas Engrs
Journal. Institution of Heating and Ventilating Engineers — J Inst Heat Vent Eng
Journal. Institution of Heating and Ventilating Engineers — J Instn Heat Vent Engrs
Journal. Institution of Heating and Ventilating Engineers — JIHVE
Journal. Institution of Highway Engineers — J Instn Highw Engrs
Journal. Institution of Locomotive Engineers — J Instn Loco Engrs
Journal. Institution of Locomotive Engineers — JILEA
Journal. Institution of Mechanical Engineers (London) — J Inst Mech Eng (London)
Journal. Institution of Municipal Engineers — J Inst Munic Eng
Journal. Institution of Municipal Engineers — J Instn Munic Engrs
Journal. Institution of Nuclear Engineers — J I Nucl En
Journal. Institution of Nuclear Engineers — J Inst Nucl Eng
Journal. Institution of Nuclear Engineers — J Instn Nucl Engrs
Journal. Institution of Petroleum Technologists [*England*] — J Inst Pet Technol
Journal. Institution of Production Engineers — J Inst Prod Eng
Journal. Institution of Public Health Engineers — J Inst Public Health Eng
Journal. Institution of Sanitary Engineers — J Inst Sanit Eng
Journal. Institution of Telecommunication Engineers — J Inst Telecommun Eng
Journal. Institution of Telecommunication Engineers — JITE
Journal. Institution of Telecommunication Engineers (New Delhi) — J Inst Telecommun Eng (New Delhi)
Journal. Institution of the Rubber Industry — J Inst Rubber Ind
Journal. Institution of the Rubber Industry — J Instn Rubb Ind
Journal. Institution of Water and Environmental Management — J Inst Water Environ Manage
Journal. Institution of Water Engineers — J Inst Water Eng
Journal. Institution of Water Engineers — J Instn Wat Engrs
Journal. Institution of Water Engineers and Scientists — J Inst Water Eng Sci

Journal. Institution of Water Engineers and Scientists — J Inst Water Engrs & Sci
Journal. Institution of Water Engineers and Scientists — J Instn Wat Engrs Scientists
Journal. Institution of Water Engineers and Scientists — J Instn Water Engnrs Sci
Journal. Instrument Society of America — J Instrum Soc Am
Journal. Instrument Society of India — J Instrum Soc India
Journal. Interdenominational Theological Center — J Int Th C
Journal. International Academy of Preventive Medicine — J Int Acad Prev Med
Journal. International Arthur Schnitzler Research Association — JIASRA
Journal. International Association for Mathematical Geology — J Int A Mat
Journal. International Association for Mathematical Geology — J Int Ass Math Geol
Journal. International Association for Mathematical Geology — J Int Assoc Math Geol
Journal. International Association for Mathematical Geology — J Internat Assoc Math Geol
Journal. International Association for Mathematical Geology — J Internat Assoc Mathematical Geol
Journal. International Association of Dentistry for Children — J Int Assoc Dent Child
Journal. International Association of Dentistry for Children — Jnl Int Ass Dent Child
Journal. International Association on the Artificial Prolongation of the Human Specific Lifespan — J Int Assoc Artif Prolongation Hum Specific Lifespan
Journal. International College of Dentists. Japan Section — J Int Coll Dent Jpn
Journal. International College of Surgeons [*United States*] — J Int Coll Surg
Journal. International College of Surgeons — J Internat Coll Surgeons
Journal. International Commission of Jurists — J Int Comm Jurists
Journal. International Council for Health, Physical Education, and Recreation — J ICHPER-SD
Journal International d'Archeologie Numismatique — J Arch Num
Journal International d'Archeologie Numismatique — J Int Ar Num
Journal International d'Archeologie Numismatique — J Int Num
Journal International d'Archeologie Numismatique — JAN
Journal International d'Archeologie Numismatique — JIAN
Journal International d'Archeologie Numismatique — JIN
Journal International d'Archeologie Numismatique — Journ Int Arch Num
Journal International d'Archeologie Numismatique — Journal Intern d'Archeol Numism
Journal International de Medecine Experimentale — J Int Med Exp
Journal International de Psychologie — J Int Psychol
Journal International de Vitaminologie — J Int Vitaminol
Journal International de Vitaminologie et de Nutrition — J Int Vitaminol Nutr
Journal International de Vitaminologie et de Nutrition. Supplement — J Int Vitaminol Nutr Suppl
Journal International des Sciences de la Vigne et du Vin — J Int Sci Vigne Vin
Journal. International Desalination Association — J Int Desalin Assoc
Journal International d'Hematologie — J Int Hematol
Journal. International Double Reed Society — IDRSJ
Journal. International Double Reed Society — JIDRS
Journal International du Cancer — J Int Cancer
Journal. International Federation of Gynaecology and Obstetrics — J Int Fed Gynaecol Obstet
Journal. International Folk Music Council — J Int Folk Mus Coun
Journal. International Folk Music Council — JIFC
Journal. International Folk Music Council — JIFM
Journal. International Folk Music Council — JIFMC
Journal. International Institute for Aerial Survey and Earth Sciences — J Int Inst Aerial Surv Earth Sci
Journal. International Institute for Sugar Beet Research — J Int Inst Sugar Beet Res
Journal. International Phonetic Association — J Int Phonetic Assoc
Journal. International Phonetic Association — JIPA
Journal. International Society of Leather Trades' Chemists — J Int Soc Leather Trades Chem
Journal. International Union of Bricklayers and Allied Craftsmen — J BAC
Journal. Iowa Academy of Science — J Iowa Acad Sci
Journal. Iowa Academy of Science. JIAS — J Iowa Acad Sci JIAS
Journal. Iowa Medical Society — J Iowa Med Soc
Journal. Iowa State Medical Society — J Iowa State Med Soc
Journal. Iraqi Academy — J Iraqi Acad
Journal. Iraqi Chemical Society — J Iraqi Chem Soc
Journal. Irish Baptist Historical Society — JIBHS
Journal. Irish Colleges of Physicians and Surgeons — Ir Coll Phys Surg J
Journal. Irish Colleges of Physicians and Surgeons — J Ir Coll Physicians Surg
Journal. Irish Colleges of Physicians and Surgeons — J Irish C P
Journal. Irish Dental Association — J Ir Dent Assoc
Journal. Irish Free State Department of Agriculture — J Dept Ag Ireland
Journal. Irish Medical Association — J Ir Med Assoc
Journal. Irish Medical Association — J Irish MA
Journal. Irish Medical Association — JIMSA
Journal. Iron and Steel Association — J Iron Steel Assoc
Journal. Iron and Steel Institute — J Iron St Inst
Journal. Iron and Steel Institute (London) — J Iron Steel Inst (London)
Journal. Iron and Steel Institute of Japan — J Iron Steel Inst Jpn
Journal. Iron and Steel Institute of West Scotland — J Iron Steel Inst West Scotl
Journal. Irrigation and Drainage Division. Proceedings of the American Society of Civil Engineers — J Irrig & Drain Div Proc ASCE
Journal. Irrigation and Drainage Division. Proceedings of the American Society of Civil Engineers — J Irrig Drain Div Am Soc Civ Eng
Journal. Irrigation and Drainage Division. Proceedings of the American Society of Civil Engineers — J Irrig Drain Div ASCE
Journal. Irrigation and Drainage Division. Proceedings of the American Society of Civil Engineers — JRCE-A
Journal. Islamic Medical Association of the United States and Canada — J IMA
Journal. Israel Medical Association — J Isr Med Assoc
Journal. Israel Oriental Society — JIOS
Journal. Italian Astronomical Society — J Ital Astron Soc
Journal. Italian Dairy Science Association — J Ital Dairy Sci Assoc
Journal. Iwate Daigaku Nogaku-Bu — J Iwate Daigaku Nogaku
Journal. Iwate Medical Association — J Iwate Med Assoc
Journal. Jamaica Agricultural Society — J Jam Agric Soc
Journal. Jamaica Bauxite Institute — J Jamaica Bauxite Inst
Journal. Japan Academy of Surgical Metabolism and Nutrition — J Jpn Acad Surg Metab Nutr
Journal. Japan Accident Medical Association — J Jpn Accident Med Assoc
Journal. Japan Air Cleaning Association — J Jpn Air Clean Assoc
Journal. Japan Aromatic Industry Association — J Jpn Aromat Ind Assoc
Journal. Japan Association for Philosophy of Science — J Jap Assoc Philos Sci
Journal. Japan Association of Automatic Control Engineers — J Jap Assoc Autom Control Eng
Journal. Japan Association of Automatic Control Engineers — J Jpn Assoc Automat Control Eng
Journal. Japan Atherosclerosis Society — J Jpn Atherosclerosis Soc
Journal. Japan Boiler Association — J Jpn Boiler Assoc
Journal. Japan Broncho-Esophagological Society — J Jpn Broncho-Esophagol Soc
Journal. Japan Contact Lens Society — J Jpn Contact Lens Soc
Journal. Japan Copper and Brass Research Association — J Jpn Copper Brass Res Assoc
Journal. Japan Dental Association — J Jpn Dent Assoc
Journal. Japan Dental Society of Anesthesiology — J Jpn Dent Soc Anesthesiol
Journal. Japan Diabetes Society — J Jpn Diabetes Soc
Journal. Japan Diabetic Society — J Jpn Diabetic Soc
Journal. Japan Electric Association — J Jpn Electr Assoc
Journal. Japan Epilepsy Society — J Jpn Epilepsy Soc
Journal. Japan Foundrymen's Society — J Jpn Foundrymens Soc
Journal. Japan Gas Association — J Jpn Gas Assoc
Journal. Japan General Foundry Center — J Jpn Gen Foundry Cent
Journal. Japan Geothermal Energy Association — J Jpn Geotherm Energy Assoc
Journal. Japan Health Physics Society — J Jpn Health Phys Soc
Journal. Japan Hospital Association — J Jpn Hosp Assoc
Journal. Japan Hydraulic and Pneumatic Society — J Japan Hydraul & Pneum Soc
Journal. Japan Institute of Light Metals — J Jap Inst Light Metals
Journal. Japan Institute of Light Metals — J Jap Inst Met
Journal. Japan Institute of Light Metals — J Jpn Inst Light Met
Journal. Japan Institute of Metals — J Jpn Inst Met
Journal. Japan Institute of Metals (Sendai) — J Jpn Inst Met (Sendai)
Journal. Japan Institute of Navigation — J Jpn Inst Navig
Journal. Japan Medical Association — J Jpn Med Assoc
Journal. Japan Medical College — J Jpn Med Coll
Journal. Japan Oil Chemists Society — J Jpn Oil Chem Soc
Journal. Japan Pancreas Society — J Jpn Pancreas Soc
Journal. Japan Paper and Pulp Association — J Jpn Pap Pulp Assoc
Journal. Japan Perfumery Flavouring Association — J Jpn Perfum Flavour Assoc
Journal. Japan Petroleum Institute — J Jpn Pet Inst
Journal. Japan Pharmaceutical Association — J Jpn Pharm Assoc
Journal. Japan Pharmaceutical Association — NYZZA3
Journal. Japan Plating Society — J Jpn Plat Soc
Journal. Japan Research Association for Textile End-Uses — J Jpn Res Assoc Text End-Uses
Journal. Japan Sewage Works Association — J Jpn Sewage Works Assoc
Journal. Japan Society for Aeronautical and Space Sciences — J Jpn Soc Aeronaut and Space Sci
Journal. Japan Society for Cancer Therapy — J Jpn Soc Cancer Ther
Journal. Japan Society for Dental Apparatus and Materials — J Jpn Soc Dent Appar Mater
Journal. Japan Society for Food Science and Technology — J Jpn Soc Food Sci Technol
Journal. Japan Society for Heat-Treatment — J Jpn Soc Heat Treat
Journal. Japan Society for Safety Engineering — J Jpn Soc Saf Eng
Journal. Japan Society for Simulation Technology — J Jpn Soc Simulation Technol
Journal. Japan Society for Technology of Plasticity — J Jap Soc Technol Plast
Journal. Japan Society for Technology of Plasticity — J Jpn Soc Technol Plast
Journal. Japan Society of Air Pollution — J Jap Soc Air Pol
Journal. Japan Society of Air Pollution — J Jpn Soc Air Pollut
Journal. Japan Society of Blood Transfusion — J Jpn Soc Blood Transfus
Journal. Japan Society of Civil Engineers — J Jap Soc Civ Eng
Journal. Japan Society of Colo-Proctology — J Jpn Soc Colo-Proctol
Journal. Japan Society of Colo-Proctology — NDKGAU
Journal. Japan Society of Colour Material — J Jpn Soc Colour Mater
Journal. Japan Society of Composite Materials — J Jpn Soc Compos Mater
Journal. Japan Society of Fluid Mechanics — J Jpn Soc Fluid Mech
Journal. Japan Society of Infrared Science and Technology — J Jpn Soc Infrared Sci Technol
Journal. Japan Society of Lubrication Engineers — J Jap S Lub
Journal. Japan Society of Lubrication Engineers — J Japan Soc Lubr Engrs
Journal. Japan Society of Lubrication Engineers — J Jpn Soc Lubr Eng
Journal. Japan Society of Lubrication Engineers. International Edition — J Japan Soc Lubr Enrs Int Edn
Journal. Japan Society of Mechanical Engineers — J Jap Soc Mech Eng
Journal. Japan Society of Mechanical Engineers — J Jpn Soc Mech Eng

Journal. Japan Society of Powder and Powder Metallurgy — J Jap Soc Powder Met
Journal. Japan Society of Powder and Powder Metallurgy — J Jpn Soc Powder Metall
Journal. Japan Society of Powder and Powder Metallurgy — J Jpn Soc Powder Powder Metall
Journal. Japan Society of Precision Engineering — J Jap Soc Precis Eng
Journal. Japan Society of Precision Engineering — J Japan Soc Precis Engng
Journal. Japan Society of Precision Engineering — J Jpn Soc Precis Eng
Journal. Japan Society of the Reticuloendothelial System — J Jpn Soc Reticuloendothel Syst
Journal. Japan Society of Waste Management Experts — J Jpn Soc Waste Manage Experts
Journal. Japan Soy Sauce Research Institute — J Jpn Soy Sauce Res Inst
Journal. Japan Statistical Society — J Japan Statist Soc
Journal. Japan Stomatological Society — J Jpn Stomatol Soc
Journal. Japan Tar Industry Association — J Jpn Tar Ind Assoc
Journal. Japan Thermal Spraying Society — J Jpn Therm Spraying Soc
Journal. Japan Turfgrass Research Association — J Jap Turfgrass Res Assoc
Journal. Japan Turfgrass Research Association — J Jpn Turfgrass Res Assoc
Journal. Japan Veterinary Medical Association — J Jap Vet Med Ass
Journal. Japan Veterinary Medical Association — J Jpn Vet Med Assoc
Journal. Japan Water Works Association — J Jpn Water Works Assoc
Journal. Japan Water Works Association — JWWJA
Journal. Japan Welding Society — J Jpn Weld Soc
Journal. Japan Wood Research Society — J Jap Wood Res Soc
Journal. Japan Wood Research Society — J Japan Wood Res Soc
Journal. Japan Wood Research Society — J Jpn Wood Res Soc
Journal. Japanese Anodizing Association — J Jpn Anodizing Assoc
Journal. Japanese Association for Dental Science — J Jpn Assoc Dent Sci
Journal. Japanese Association for Infectious Diseases — J Jap Assoc Infect Dis
Journal. Japanese Association for Infectious Diseases — J Jpn Assoc Infect Dis
Journal. Japanese Association for Thoracic Surgery — J Jpn Assoc Thorac Surg
Journal. Japanese Association of Crystal Growth — J Japan Assoc Cryst Growth
Journal. Japanese Association of Mineralogists, Petrologists, and Economic Geologists — J Jap Ass Mineral Petrol Econ Geol
Journal. Japanese Association of Mineralogists, Petrologists, and Economic Geologists — J Jpn Assoc Mineral Pet Econ Geol
Journal. Japanese Association of Mineralogists, Petrologists, and Economic Geologists — J Jpn Assoc Mineral Petrol Econ Geol
Journal. Japanese Association of Periodontology — J Jpn Assoc Periodontol
Journal. Japanese Association of Petroleum Technologists — J Jpn Assoc Pet Technol
Journal. Japanese Association of Physical Medicine, Balneology, and Climatology — J Jpn Assoc Phys Med Balneol Climatol
Journal. Japanese Balneo-Climatological Association — J Jpn Balneo Climatol Assoc
Journal. Japanese Biochemical Society — J Jap Biochem Soc
Journal. Japanese Biochemical Society — J Jpn Biochem Soc
Journal. Japanese Ceramic Association — J Jpn Ceram Assoc
Journal. Japanese Ceramic Society — J Jpn Ceram Soc
Journal. Japanese College of Angiology — J Jpn Coll Angiol
Journal. Japanese Cosmetic Science Society — J Jpn Cosmet Sci Soc
Journal. Japanese Crystallographical Society — J Jpn Crystallogr Soc
Journal. Japanese Dental Anesthesia Society — J Jpn Dent Anesth Soc
Journal. Japanese Dermatological Association — J Jpn Dermatol Assoc
Journal. Japanese Forestry Society — J Jap For Soc
Journal. Japanese Forestry Society — J Jpn For Soc
Journal. Japanese Forestry Society/Nippon Ringaku Kaishi — J Jap Forest Soc
Journal. Japanese Horticultural Society/Journal. Societe d'Horticulture du Japon / Zeitschrift der Japanischen Gartenbau-Gesellschaft / Nippon Engeikai Zasshi — J Jap Hort Soc
Journal. Japanese Institute of Landscape Architects — J Jpn Inst Landscape Archit
Journal. Japanese Medical Society for Biological Interface — J Jpn Med Soc Biol Interface
Journal. Japanese Obstetrical and Gynecological Society — JJOGA
Journal. Japanese Obstetrical and Gynecological Society (English Edition) — J Jpn Obstet Gynecol Soc (Engl Ed)
Journal. Japanese Obstetrical and Gynecological Society (Japanese Edition) — J Jpn Obstet Gynecol Soc (Jpn Ed)
Journal. Japanese Obstetrics and Gynecology — J Jpn Obstet Gynecol
Journal. Japanese Orthopaedic Association — J Jpn Orthop Assoc
Journal. Japanese Psychosomatic Society — J Jpn Psychosom Soc
Journal. Japanese Society for Biomaterials — J Jpn Soc Biomater
Journal. Japanese Society for Cutaneous Health — J Jpn Soc Cutaneous Health
Journal. Japanese Society for Dental Materials and Devices — J Jpn Soc Dent Mater Devices
Journal. Japanese Society for Horticultural Science — J Jpn Soc Hortic Sci
Journal. Japanese Society for Hypothermia — J Jpn Soc Hypothermia
Journal. Japanese Society for Magnesium Research — J Jpn Soc Magnesium Res
Journal. Japanese Society for Strength and Fracture of Materials — J Jpn Soc Strength Fract Mater
Journal. Japanese Society of Clinical Nutrition — J Jpn Soc Clin Nutr
Journal. Japanese Society of Food and Nutrition — J Jap Soc Fd Nutr
Journal. Japanese Society of Food and Nutrition — J Jap Soc Food Nutr
Journal. Japanese Society of Food and Nutrition — J Jpn Soc Food Nutr
Journal. Japanese Society of Grassland Science — J Jap Soc Grassland Sci
Journal. Japanese Society of Grassland Science — J Jap Soc Grassld Sci
Journal. Japanese Society of Grassland Science — J Jpn Soc Grassl Sci
Journal. Japanese Society of Herbage Crops and Grassland Farming — J Jpn Soc Herb Crops Grassl Farming
Journal. Japanese Society of Hospital Pharmacists — J Jpn Soc Hosp Pharm
Journal. Japanese Society of Internal Medicine — J Jpn Soc Intern Med
Journal. Japanese Society of Irrigation, Drainage, and Reclamation Engineering — J Jpn Soc Irrig Drain Reclam Eng
Journal. Japanese Society of Nutrition and Food Science — J Jpn Soc Nutr Food Sci
Journal. Japanese Society of Starch Science — J Jpn Soc Starch Sci
Journal. Japanese Society of Tribologists — J Jpn Soc Tribol
Journal. Japanese Society of Veterinary Science — J Japan Soc Vet Sc
Journal. Japanese Society of X-Ray Technicians — J Jpn Soc X-Ray Tech
Journal. Japanese Society on Poultry Diseases — J Jpn Soc Poult Dis
Journal. Japanese Surgical Society — J Jpn Surg Soc
Journal. Japanese Technical Association of the Pulp and Paper Industry — J Jpn Tech Assoc Pulp Pap Ind
Journal. Jewish Palestine Exploration Society [*Jerusalem*] — JJPES
Journal. Jinan University. Natural Science and Medicine Edition — J Jinan Univ Nat Sci Med Ed
Journal. Jiwaji University — J Jiwaji Univ
Journal. Jiwaji University — JJWUA
Journal. Jiwaji University. Science, Technology, and Medicine — J Jiwaji Univ Sci Technol Med
Journal. JJ Group of Hospitals and Grant Medical College — J JJ Group Hosp Grant Med Coll
Journal. Johannesburg Historical Foundation — J Johannesburg Hist Found
Journal. Joint Panel on Nuclear Marine Propulsion — J Joint Panel Nucl Mar Propul
Journal. Joint Panel on Nuclear Marine Propulsion [*England*] — J Jt Panel Nucl Mar Propul
Journal. JSLE (Japan Society of Lubrication Engineers). International Edition — J JSLE (Jpn Soc Lubr Eng) Int Ed
Journal. Jundi Shapur Medical School — J Jundi Shapur Med Sch
Journal. Junior Institution of Engineers (London) — J Jr Inst Eng (London)
Journal. Just Intonation Network — Just Intonation
Journal. Juzen Medical Society — J Juzen Med Soc
Journal. Kagawa Nutrition College — J Kagawa Nutr Coll
Journal Kajian Kejuruteraan — J Kajian Kejuruteraan
Journal. Kanagawa Odontological Society — J Kanagawa Odontol Soc
Journal. Kanagawa Prefectural Junior College of Nutrition — J Kanagawa Prefect J Coll Nutr
Journal. Kanazawa Medical University — J Kanazawa Med Univ
Journal. Kansai Medical School [*Japan*] — J Kansai Med Sch
Journal. Kansai Medical University — J Kansai Med Univ
Journal. Kansas Bar Association — J Kan BA
Journal. Kansas Dental Association — J Kans Dent Assoc
Journal. Kansas Entomological Society — J Kans Ent Soc
Journal. Kansas Entomological Society — J Kans Entomol Soc
Journal. Kansas Geological Survey — J Kansas Geol Surv
Journal. Kansas Medical Society — J Kan Med Soc
Journal. Kansas Medical Society — J Kans Med Soc
Journal. Kansas Medical Society — J Kansas Med Soc
Journal. Kansas Medical Society — JKMSA
Journal. Kansas State Dental Association — J Kans State Dent Assoc
Journal. Kanto Tosan Agricultural Experiment Station/Kanto Tosan Nogyo Shikenjo Kenkyu Hokoku — J Kanto Tosan Agric Exp Sta
Journal. Kanto-Tosan Agricultural Experiment Station — J Kanto-Tosan Agr Exp Sta
Journal Karadeniz University. Faculty of Arts and Sciences. Series of Mathematics-Physics — J Karadeniz Univ Fac Arts Sci Ser Math Phys
Journal. Karnatak University — J Karnatak Univ
Journal. Karnatak University — JKAUA
Journal. Karnatak University [*Dharwar*] — JKU
Journal. Karnatak University. Humanities — J Karnatak U Hum
Journal. Karnatak University. Science — J Karnatak Univ Sci
Journal. Karnatak University. Social Sciences — J Karnatak U Soc Sci
Journal. Keio Medical Society [*Japan*] — J Keio Med Soc
Journal. Kentucky Dental Association — Jnl KY Dent Assoc
Journal. Kentucky Medical Association — J KY Med Assoc
Journal. Kentucky State Medical Association — J Ky State Med Assoc
Journal. Kerala Academy of Biology — J Kerala Acad Biol
Journal. Kerry Archaeological and Historical Society — J Kerry Archaeol Hist Soc
Journal. Kerry Archaeological and Historical Society — JKAHS
Journal. Khedivial Agricultural Society — J Khediv Agric Soc
Journal. King Saud University. Engineering Science — J King Saud Univ Eng Sci
Journal. King Saud University. Science — J King Saud Univ Sci
Journal. Kirin University. Natural Science — J Kirin Univ Nat Sci
Journal. Kongju National Teacher's College [*Republic of Korea*] — J Kongju Natl Teach Coll
Journal. Kongju National Teacher's College — JKNCD
Journal. Korea Electric Association [*Republic of Korea*] — J Korea Electr Assoc
Journal. Korea Information Science Society — J Korea Inf Sci Soc
Journal. Korea Institute of Electronics Engineers — J Korea Inst Electron Eng
Journal. Korea Institute of Electronics Engineers — JKHHA
Journal. Korea Merchant Marine College. Natural Sciences Series [*Republic of Korea*] — J Korea Merch Mar Coll Nat Sci Ser
Journal. Korea Merchant Marine College. Natural Sciences Series — JMMSD
Journal. Korea Military Academy [*Republic of Korea*] — J Korea Mil Acad
Journal. Korea Military Academy — JKMAD
Journal. Korean Academy of Maxillofacial Radiology — CHPAD
Journal. Korean Academy of Maxillofacial Radiology [*Republic of Korea*] — J Korean Acad Maxillofac Radiol
Journal. Korean Academy of Periodontology — J Korean Acad Periodontol
Journal. Korean Agricultural Chemical Society [*Republic of Korea*] — J Korean Agric Chem Soc

Journal. Korean Association for Radiation Protection — J Korean Assoc Radiat Prot
Journal. Korean Astronomical Society — J Korean Astron Soc
Journal. Korean Cancer Research Association — J Korean Cancer Res Assoc
Journal. Korean Ceramic Society [*Republic of Korea*] — J Korean Ceram Soc
Journal. Korean Chemical Society — J Korean Chem Soc
Journal. Korean Dental Association [*Republic of Korea*] — J Korean Dent Assoc
Journal. Korean Fiber Society — J Korean Fiber Soc
Journal. Korean Forestry Society [*Republic of Korea*] — J Korean For Soc
Journal. Korean Forestry Society — JKFSD
Journal. Korean Infectious Diseases — J Korean Infect Dis
Journal. Korean Institute of Chemical Engineers [*Republic of Korea*] — J Korean Inst Chem Eng
Journal. Korean Institute of Electrical Engineers [*Republic of Korea*] — J Korean Inst Electr Eng
Journal. Korean Institute of Electrical Engineers [*Republic of Korea*] — JKIEA
Journal. Korean Institute of Electronics Engineers — J Korean Inst Electron Eng
Journal. Korean Institute of Metals [*Republic of Korea*] — J Korean Inst Met
Journal. Korean Institute of Metals [*Republic of Korea*] — KUHCA
Journal. Korean Institute of Mineral and Mining Engineers [*Republic of Korea*] — J Korean Inst Miner Mining Eng
Journal. Korean Institute of Mining [*Republic of Korea*] — J Korean Inst Min
Journal. Korean Institute of Mining Engineers — J Korean Inst Min Eng
Journal. Korean Institute of Mining Geology [*Republic of Korea*] — J Korean Inst Min Geol
Journal. Korean Institute of Rubber Industry — J Korean Inst Rubber Ind
Journal. Korean Institute of Surface Engineering — J Korean Inst Surf Eng
Journal. Korean Mathematical Society — J Korean Math Soc
Journal. Korean Mathematical Society — JKMSD
Journal. Korean Medical Association [*Republic of Korea*] — J Korean Med Assoc
Journal. Korean Meteorological Society [*Republic of Korea*] — J Korean Meteorol Soc
Journal. Korean Nuclear Society [*Republic of Korea*] — J Korean Nucl Soc
Journal. Korean Nuclear Society — KNSJA
Journal. Korean Operations Research Society — JKORS
Journal. Korean Ophthalmological Society — J Korean Ophthalmol Soc
Journal. Korean Oriental Medical Society — J Korean Orient Med Soc
Journal. Korean Physical Society — J Korean Phys Soc
Journal. Korean Physical Society [*Republic of Korea*] — KPSJA
Journal. Korean Preventive Medicine Society — J Korean Prev Med Soc
Journal. Korean Radiological Society [*Republic of Korea*] — J Korean Radiol Soc
Journal. Korean Research Institute for Better Living — J Korean Res Inst Better Living
Journal. Korean Research Society for Dental Hypnosis — J Korean Res Soc Dent Hypn
Journal. Korean Research Society of Radiological Technology [*Republic of Korea*] — J Korean Res Soc Radiol Technol
Journal. Korean Society for Horticultural Science — J Korean Soc Hort Sci
Journal. Korean Society for Horticultural Science — J Korean Soc Hortic Sci
Journal. Korean Society for Microbiology — J Korean Soc Microbiol
Journal. Korean Society of Agricultural Engineers — J Korean Soc Agric Eng
Journal. Korean Society of Agricultural Machinery — J Korean Soc Agric Mach
Journal. Korean Society of Civil Engineers [*Republic of Korea*] — J Korean Soc Civ Eng
Journal. Korean Society of Crop Science [*Republic of Korea*] — J Korean Soc Crop Sci
Journal. Korean Society of Food and Nutrition — J Korean Soc Food Nutr
Journal. Korean Society of Mechanical Engineers [*Republic of Korea*] — J Korean Soc Mech Eng
Journal. Korean Society of Nutrition and Food — J Korean Soc Nutr Food
Journal. Korean Society of Soil Science and Fertilizer — J Korean Soc Soil Sci Fert
Journal. Korean Society of Textile Engineers and Chemists [*Republic of Korea*] — J Korean Soc Text Eng Chem
Journal. Korean Statistical Society — J Korean Statist Soc
Journal. Korean Surgical Society — J Korean Surg Soc
Journal. Koyasan University — J Koyasan Univ
Journal. Kumamoto Medical Society — J Kumamoto Med Soc
Journal. Kumamoto Women's University — J Kumamoto Women's Univ
Journal. Kumasi University of Science and Technology — J Kumasi Univ Sci Technol
Journal. Kurume Medical Association — J Kurume Med Assoc
Journal. Kuwait Medical Association — J Kuwait Med Assoc
Journal. Kyorin Medical Society — J Kyorin Med Soc
Journal. Kyoto Medical Association — J Kyoto Med Assoc
Journal. Kyoto Prefectural Medical University [*Japan*] — J Kyoto Prefect Med Univ
Journal. Kyoto Prefectural University of Medicine — J Kyoto Prefect Univ Med
Journal. Kyungpook Engineering [*Republic of Korea*] — J Kyungpook Eng
Journal. Kyungpook Engineering. Kyungpook National University — J Kyungpook Eng Kyungpook Natl Univ
Journal. Kyushu Coal Mining Technicians Association — J Kyushu Coal Min Tech Assoc
Journal. Kyushu Dental Society [*Japan*] — J Kyushu Dent Soc
Journal. Kyushu Hematological Society — J Kyushu Hematol Soc
Journal. Lancashire Dialect Society — JLDS
Journal. Lanchow University. Natural Sciences — J Lanchow Univ Nat Sci
Journal. Language Association of Eastern Africa — J Language Ass East Afr
Journal. Language Association of Eastern Africa — JLAEA
Journal. Lanzhou University. Natural Sciences — J Lanzhou Univ Nat Sci
Journal. Law Society of Scotland — J L Socy Scot
Journal. Law Society of Scotland — J Law Soc Sc
Journal. Law Society of Scotland — J Law Soc Scot
Journal. Law Society of Scotland — J of the L Soc of Scotl
Journal. Law Society of Scotland — JL Soc Scotland
Journal. Law Society of Scotland — JL Soc'y
Journal. Law Society of Scotland — JLS
Journal. Leather Industries Research Institute of South Africa — J Leather Ind Res Inst S Afr
Journal. Leeds University Textile Association — J Leeds Univ Text Assoc
Journal. Leeds University Textile Students' Association — J Leeds Univ Text Stud Assoc
Journal. Leeds University Union Chemical Society — J Leeds Univ Union Chem Soc
Journal. Leeds University Union Chemical Society — J LUU Chem Soc
Journal. Lepidopterists' Society — J Lepid Soc
Journal. Lepidopterists Society — J Lepidopt Soc
Journal. Library of Rutgers University — JLRU
Journal. Limnological Society of South Africa — J Limnol Soc South Afr
Journal. Linguistic Association of the Southwest — JLAS
Journal. Linnean Society of London. Botany — J Linn Soc Lond Bot
Journal. Linnean Society of London. Zoology — J Linn Soc Lond Zool
Journal. London Mathematical Society — J Lond Math
Journal. London Mathematical Society — J London Math Soc
Journal. London Mathematical Society — JLMS
Journal. London Mathematical Society. Second Series — J London Math Soc (2)
Journal. London School of Tropical Medicine — J London School Trop Med
Journal. London Society — J Lond Soc
Journal. Louisiana Dental Association — J LA Dent Assoc
Journal. Louisiana State Medical Society — J LA Med Soc
Journal. Louisiana State Medical Society — J LA State Med Soc
Journal. Louisiana State Medical Society — J Louis St Med Soc
Journal. Louisiana State Medical Society — JLSMA
Journal. Luoyang University — J Luoyang Univ
Journal. Lute Society of America — J Lute
Journal. Lute Society of America — J Lute Soc Amer
Journal. Macomb Dental Society — J Macomb Dent Soc
Journal. Madras Agricultural Students' Union — J Madras Agric Stud Union
Journal. Madras Institute of Technology — J Madras Inst Technol
Journal. Madras University — J Madras Univ
Journal. Madras University. Section B. Contributions in Mathematics, Physical and Biological Science — J Madras Univ B
Journal. Madras University. Section B. Contributions in Mathematics, Physical and Biological Science — J Madras Univ Sect B
Journal. Madurai Kamaraj University — J Madurai Kamaraj Univ
Journal. Magnetics Society of Japan — J Magn Soc Jpn
Journal. Maha-Bodhi Society — JMBS
Journal. Maharaja Sayajirao University of Baroda — J Maharaja Sayajirao Univ Baroda
Journal. Maharaja Sayajirao University of Baroda — JMSUB
Journal. Maharaja Sayayira University of Baroda — J Mahar Sayayira Univ Baroda
Journal. Maharashtra Agricultural Universities — J Maharashtra Agric Univ
Journal. Maine Dental Association — J Maine Dent Assoc
Journal. Maine Medical Association — J Maine Med Assoc
Journal. Maine Medical Association — JMMAA
Journal. Malacological Society of Australia — J Malac Soc Aust
Journal. Malacological Society of Australia — J Malacol Soc Aust
Journal. Malaria Institute of India — J Malar Inst India
Journal. Malayan Branch. British Medical Association — J Mal Br Brit Med Ass
Journal. Malayan Branch. British Medical Association — J Malaya Branch Br Med Assoc
Journal. Malayan Branch. Royal Asiatic Society — JMBAS
Journal. Malayan Branch. Royal Asiatic Society — JMBRAS
Journal. Malayan Branch. Royal Asiatic Society — JMRAS
Journal. Malayan Veterinary Medical Association — J Mal Vet Med Ass
Journal. Malaysian Branch. Royal Asiatic Society — J Mal Br Roy Asiat Soc
Journal. Malaysian Branch. Royal Asiatic Society — J Malay Br Roy Asia
Journal. Malaysian Branch. Royal Asiatic Society — J Malay Branch Roy Asiatic Soc
Journal. Malaysian Branch. Royal Asiatic Society — J Malays Branch R Asiat Soc
Journal. Mammalogical Society of Japan — J Mammal Soc Jpn
Journal. Mammillaria Society — J Mammillaria Soc
Journal. Manchester Egyptian and Oriental Society — JMEOS
Journal. Manchester Geographical Society — J Manch Geogr Soc
Journal. Manchester Geographical Society — J Manchester Geogr Soc
Journal. Manchester Geographical Society — JMGS
Journal. Manchester Geological Association — J Manch Geol Ass
Journal. Manchester Oriental Society — JMOS
Journal. Manchester University Egyptian and Oriental Scoiety — J Manch
Journal. Manchester University. Egyptian and Oriental Society — JMUEOS
Journal. Manchester University Egyptian and Oriental Society — JMUES
Journal. Manitoba Elementary Teachers' Association — JMETA
Journal. Manx Museum — J Manx Mus
Journal. Manx Museum — JMM
Journal. Marine Biological Association [*United Kingdom*] — J Marine Bi
Journal. Marine Biological Association (India) — J Mar Biol Assoc (India)
Journal. Marine Biological Association of India — J Mar Biol Ass India
Journal. Marine Biological Association (United Kingdom) — J Mar Biol Ass (UK)
Journal. Marine Biological Association (United Kingdom) — J Mar Biol Assoc (UK)
Journal. Marine Biological Association (United Kingdom) — J Marine Biol Ass (United Kingdom)
Journal. Marine Engineering Society in Japan — J Mar Eng Soc Jpn
Journal. Marine Technology Society — J Mar Technol Soc
Journal. Maritime Safety Academy. Part 2 [*Japan*] — J Marit Saf Acad Part 2
Journal. Market Research Society — J Market Res Soc
Journal. Market Research Society — JMRS
Journal. Market Research Society — JRS

Journal. Market Research Society — Market Research Soc J
Journal. Market Research Society (London) — J Market (L)
Journal. Market Research Society of Victoria — J Market Research Society Vic
Journal. Maryland Academy of Sciences — J MD Acad Sci
Journal. Maryland State Dental Association — J MD State Dent Assoc
Journal. Massachusetts Dental Society — J Mass Dent Soc
Journal. Material Testing Research Association [*Japan*] — J Mater Test Res Assoc
Journal. Materials Science Research Institute. Dongguk University — J Mater Sci Res Inst Dongguk Univ
Journal. Materials Science Research Institute. Dongguk University — JKYND
Journal. Materials Science Society of Japan — J Mater Sci Soc Jpn
Journal. Mathematical Society of Japan — J Math Jap
Journal. Mathematical Society of Japan — J Math Soc Japan
Journal. Mathematical Society of Japan — J Math Soc Jpn
Journal. Mathematical Society of Japan — JMSJ
Journal. Matsumoto Dental College Society — J Matsumoto Dent Coll Soc
Journal. Maulana Azad College of Technology [*India*] — J MACT
Journal. Maulana Azad College of Technology — J Maulana Azad College Tech
Journal. Maulana Azad College of Technology — J of MACT
Journal. Mechanical Engineering Laboratory [*Japan*] — J Mech Eng Lab
Journal. Mechanical Engineering Laboratory — J Mech Engng Lab
Journal. Mechanical Engineering Laboratory (Tokyo) — J Mech Eng Lab (Tokyo)
Journal. Mechanical Engineers Association of Witwatersrand — J Mech Eng Assoc Witwatersrand
Journal. Mechanical Laboratory of Japan — J Mech Lab Jap
Journal. Mechanical Laboratory of Japan — J Mech Lab Jpn
Journal. Mechanical Laboratory (Tokyo) — J Mech Lab (Tokyo)
Journal. Medical and Dental Association of Botswana — J Med Dent Assoc Botswana
Journal. Medical and Pharmaceutical Society for Wakan-Yaku — J Med Pharm Soc Wakan Yaku
Journal. Medical Association of Croatia — J Med Assoc Croat
Journal. Medical Association of Eire — J Med Ass Eire
Journal. Medical Association of Eire — J Med Assoc Eire
Journal. Medical Association of Formosa — J Med Ass Form
Journal. Medical Association of Georgia — J Med Assn GA
Journal. Medical Association of Georgia — J Med Assoc GA
Journal. Medical Association of Israel — J Med Assoc Isr
Journal. Medical Association of Iwate Prefectural Hospital [*Japan*] — J Med Assoc Iwate Prefect Hosp
Journal. Medical Association of Jamaica — J Med Assoc Jam
Journal. Medical Association of Okayama — J Med Ass Ok
Journal. Medical Association of South Africa — J Med Ass South Africa
Journal. Medical Association of South Africa — J Med Assoc S Afr
Journal. Medical Association of Taiwan — J Med Assoc Taiwan
Journal. Medical Association of Thailand — J Med Ass Thail
Journal. Medical Association of Thailand — J Med Assoc Thai
Journal. Medical Association of Thailand — J Med Assoc Thail
Journal. Medical Association of Thailand — J Med Assoc Thailand
Journal. Medical Association of the State of Alabama — J Med A Alabama
Journal. Medical Association of the State of Alabama — J Med Assoc State Ala
Journal. Medical Association of the State of Alabama — J Med Assoc State Alabama
Journal. Medical College in Keijo — J Med Coll Keijo
Journal. Medical Colleges of PLA [*Peoples Liberation Army*] — J Med Coll PLA
Journal Medical de Bruxelles — J Med Brux
Journal Medical de la Gironde — J Med Gironde
Journal Medical Francais — J Med Franc
Journal Medical Haitien — J Med Hait
Journal Medical Libanais — J Med Liban
Journal. Medical Professions Association — J Med Prof Ass
Journal. Medical School. Jundi Shapur University — J Med Sch Jundi Shapur Univ
Journal. Medical Society of New Jersey — J Med Soc New Jers
Journal. Medical Society of New Jersey — J Med Soc New Jersey
Journal. Medical Society of New Jersey — J Med Soc NJ
Journal. Medical Society of New Jersey — JMSNA
Journal. Medical Society of Toho University — J Med Soc Toho Univ
Journal. Medical Women's Federation — J Med Wom Fed
Journal Medicale (Ukraine) — J Med (Ukr)
Journal Medico-Chirurgical — J Med Chir
Journal. Meikai University School of Dentistry — J Meikai Univ Sch Dent
Journal Mensuel de Psychiatrie et de Neurologie — J Mens Psychiatr Neurol
Journal. Mental Health Administration — J Ment Health Adm
Journal. Mercer Dental Society — J Mercer Dent Soc
Journal. Merioneth Historical Record Society — J Merioneth Hist Rec Soc
Journal. Metal Finishing Society of Japan — J Met Finish Soc Jap
Journal. Metal Finishing Society of Japan — J Met Finish Soc Jpn
Journal. Metal Finishing Society of Korea — J Met Finish Soc Korea
Journal. Metal Finishing Society of Korea — J Metal Finish Soc Korea
Journal. Metallurgical Club. Royal College of Science and Technology — J Metall Club R Coll Sci Technol
Journal. Metallurgical Club. University of Strathclyde — J Metall Club Univ Strathclyde
Journal. Metallurgical Society of Japan — J Metall Soc Jpn
Journal. Meteorological Society of Japan — J Met Soc Jap
Journal. Meteorological Society of Japan — J Meteorol Soc Jpn
Journal. Michigan Dental Association — J Mich Dent Assoc
Journal. Michigan State Dental Association — J Mich State Dent Assoc
Journal. Michigan State Dental Society — J Mich State Dent Soc
Journal. Michigan State Medical Society — J Mich Med Soc
Journal. Michigan State Medical Society — J Mich St Med Soc
Journal. Michigan State Medical Society — J Mich State Med Soc
Journal. Michigan Teachers of English — JMTE
Journal. Middle East Society [*Jerusalem*] — JMES
Journal. Mie Medical College — J Mie Med Coll
Journal. Military Service Institution — J Mil Serv Inst
Journal. Minami Osaka Hospital — J Minami Osaka Hosp
Journal. Mine Ventilation Society of South Africa — J Mine Vent Soc S Afr
Journal. Mineralogical Society of Japan — J Mineral Soc Jpn
Journal. Mining and Materials Processing Institute of Japan — J Min Mat Process Inst Jpn
Journal. Mining and Metallurgical Institute of Japan — J Min Metall Inst Jap
Journal. Mining and Metallurgical Institute of Japan — J Mining Met Inst Jap
Journal. Mining College. Akita University. Series A. Mining Geology — J Min Coll Akita Univ Ser A
Journal. Mining Institute of Japan — J Min Inst Jpn
Journal. Mining Institute of Kyushu [*Japan*] — J Min Inst Kyushu
Journal. Ministere de l'Instruction Publique en Russie — JMIR
Journal. Ministry of Agriculture (Great Britain) — J Minist Agric (GB)
Journal. Ministry of Education. Malaysia — J Kementerian Pelajaran Min Ed Malay
Journal. Ministry of Health — J Minist Hlth
Journal. Minnesota Academy of Science — J Minn Acad Sci
Journal. Mississippi Academy of Sciences — J Miss Acad Sci
Journal. Mississippi State Medical Association — J Miss Med Ass
Journal. Mississippi State Medical Association — J Miss St Med Ass
Journal. Mississippi State Medical Association — J Miss State Med Assoc
Journal. Mississippi State Medical Association — J Mississippi Med Ass
Journal. Missouri Bar — J MO B
Journal. Missouri Bar — J MO Bar
Journal. Missouri Dental Association — J Missouri Dent Assoc
Journal. Missouri Dental Association — J MO Dent Assoc
Journal. Missouri State Medical Association — J Mo State Med Assoc
Journal. Missouri Water and Sewage Conference — J MO Water Sewage Conf
Journal. Missouri Water and Sewerage Conference — J Mo Water Sewerage Conf
Journal Mondial de Pharmacie — J Mond Pharm
Journal. Moscow Physical Society — J Moscow Phys Soc
Journal. Motion Picture Society of India — J Motion Pict Soc India
Journal. Mount Sinai Hospital — J Mt Sinai Hosp
Journal. Mount Sinai Hospital (New York) — J Mt Sinai Hosp (NY)
Journal. Music Academy (Madras) — JMAM
Journal Musical Francais — J Mus Francais
Journal. Mysore Agricultural and Experimental Union — J Mysore Agr Exp Union
Journal. Mysore Medical Association — J Mysore Med Assoc
Journal. Mysore State Education Federation — J Mysore State Ed Fed
Journal. Mysore University. Section A. Arts — J Mysore U Arts
Journal. Mysore University. Section B. Science — HJMSA
Journal. Mysore University. Section B. Science — J Mysore Univ Sect B
Journal. Mysore University. Section B. Science [*India*] — J Mysore Univ Sect B Sci
Journal. Mysore University. Section B. Science — JMYUAP
Journal. Nagari Pracarini Sabha — JNPS
Journal. Nagasaki Earth Science Association — J Nagasaki Earth Sci Assoc
Journal. Nagasaki Public Health Society — J Nagasaki Public Health Soc
Journal. Nagoya City University Medical Association [*Japan*] — J Nagoya City Univ Med Assoc
Journal. Nagoya Medical Association — J Nagoya Med Assoc
Journal. Nakanihon Automotive Junior College — J Nakanihon Automot Jr Coll
Journal. Nanjing Agricultural College — J Nanjing Agric Coll
Journal. Nanjing Agricultural University — J Nanjing Agric Univ
Journal. Nanjing College of Pharmacy — J Nanjing Coll Pharm
Journal. Nanjing Forestry University — J Nanjing For Univ
Journal. Nanjing Institute of Forestry — J Nanjing Inst For
Journal. Nanjing Institute of Technology — J Nanjing Inst Technol
Journal. Nanjing Technological College of Forest Products — J Nanjing Technol Coll For Prod
Journal. Nanjing University. Natural Science Edition — J Nanjing Univ Nat Sci Ed
Journal. Nanking Engineering Institute — J Nanking Eng Inst
Journal. Nara Gakugei University [*Japan*] — J Nara Gakugei Univ
Journal. Nara Gakugei University. Natural Science — J Nara Gakugei Univ Nat Sci
Journal. Nara Medical Association — J Nara Med Ass
Journal. Nara Medical Association — J Nara Med Assoc
Journal. National Academy of Administration [*India*] — JNAA
Journal. National Academy of Sciences [*Republic of Korea*] — J Natl Acad Sci
Journal. National Academy of Sciences (Republic of Korea). Natural Sciences Series — J Natl Acad Sci (Repub Korea) Nat Sci Ser
Journal. National Agricultural Experiment Station. Nishigahara, Tokyo/Noji Shikenjo Iho — J Natl Agric Exp Sta Nishigahara Tokyo
Journal. National Agricultural Society of Ceylon — J Nat Agric Soc Ceylon
Journal. National Agricultural Society of Ceylon — J Natl Agric Soc Ceylon
Journal. National Analgesia Society [*US*] — J Natl Analg Soc
Journal. National Association for Hospital Development [*US*] — J Natl Assoc Hosp Dev
Journal. National Association for Staff Development in Further and Higher Education — NASD J
Journal. National Association for Women Deans, Administrators, and Counselors — J Natl Assn Women Deans Adm & Counsel
Journal. National Association for Women Deans, Administrators, and Counselors — J NAWDAC
Journal. National Association of Biblical Instructors — JNABI
Journal. National Association of College Admissions Counselors — J Nat Assn Col Adm Counsel
Journal. National Association of College Admissions Counselors — J Natl Assn Coll Adm Counsel

Journal. National Association of Private Psychiatric Hospitals [*US*] — J Natl Assoc Priv Psychiatr Hosp
Journal. National Association of Private Psychiatric Hospitals — JNAPPH
Journal. National Cancer Institute — J Nat Canc
Journal. National Cancer Institute — J Nat Cancer Inst
Journal. National Cancer Institute — J Natl Cancer Inst
Journal. National Cancer Institute — J Natn Cancer Inst
Journal. National Cancer Institute — JNC
Journal. National Chemical Laboratory for Industry [*Japan*] — J Nat Chem Lab Ind
Journal. National Chemical Laboratory for Industry [*Japan*] — J Natl Chem Lab Ind
Journal. National Chemical Laboratory for Industry — JNCLA
Journal. National Chiao Tung University — J Natl Chiao Tung Univ
Journal. National Defense Medical College — J Natl Def Med Coll
Journal. National Dental Association [*US*] — J Nat Dent Assoc
Journal. National Education Association (New York) — NEA Jour NY
Journal. National Education Society of Ceylon — J Nat Ed Soc Ceylon
Journal. National Institute for Personnel Research. South African Council for Scientific and Industrial Research — J Natl Inst Pers Res S Afr CSIR
Journal. National Institute of Agricultural Botany — J Natl Inst Agric Bot
Journal. National Institute of Agricultural Botany — J Natn Inst Agric Bot
Journal. National Institute of Agricultural Botany (United Kingdom) — J Nat Inst Agric Bot (UK)
Journal. National Institute of Hospital Administration — J Nat Inst Hospital Adm
Journal. National Institute of Social Sciences — J Nat Inst Soc Sci
Journal. National Intravenous Therapy Association — NITA
Journal. National Intravenous Therapy Association — NITAJ
Journal. National Malaria Society [*US*] — J Nat Malar Soc
Journal. [*US*] **National Medical Association** — J Natl Med Assoc
Journal. National Research Council of Thailand — J Nat Res Coun Thai
Journal. National Research Council of Thailand — J Natl Res Counc Thail
Journal. National Research Council of Thailand — J Natl Res Counc Thailand
Journal. National Science Council of Sri Lanka — J Nat Sci Counc Sri Lanka
Journal. National Science Council of Sri Lanka — J Natl Sci Counc Sri Lanka
Journal. National Sun Yat-sen University — J Nat Sun Yat-sen Univ
Journal. National Technical Association — J Nat Tech Assoc
Journal. National Technical Association [*United States*] — J Natl Tech Assoc
Journal. National Technical Association — JNTAD
Journal. National University of Defense Technology [*China*] — J Natl Univ Def Technol
Journal. National Volleyball Coaches Association — J NVCA
Journal. Natural History and Science Society of Western Australia — J Nat Hist Sci Soc Western Australia
Journal. Natural Science Research Institute. Yonsei University [*Republic of Korea*] — J Nat Sci Res Inst
Journal. Natural Science Research Institute. Yonsei University — J Nat Sci Res Inst Yonsei Univ
Journal. Natural Scientific Society. Ichimura Gakuen Junior College — J Nat Sci Soc Ichimura Gakuen J Coll
Journal. Natural Scientific Society. Ichimura Gakuen University and Ichimura Gakuen Junior College — J Nat Sci Soc Ichimura Gakuen Univ Ichimura Gakuen J Coll
Journal. Nautical Society of Japan — J Naut Soc Jpn
Journal. Nebraska Dental Association — J Nebr Dent Assoc
Journal. Nepal Chemical Society — J Nepal Chem Soc
Journal. Nepal Pharmaceutical Association — J Nepal Pharm Assoc
Journal. Nepal Pharmaceutical Association — J NPA
Journal. Neurological Society of India — J Neurol Soc India
Journal. New African Literature and the Arts — J New Afr Lit Arts
Journal. New Brunswick Museum — J NB Mus
Journal. New Brunswick Museum — JNBMDW
Journal. New England Water Pollution Control Association — J N Engl Water Pollut Control Assoc
Journal. New England Water Works Association — J N Engl Water Works Assoc
Journal. New England Water Works Association — J New Engl Water Works Ass
Journal. New England Water Works Association — J New Engl Water Works Assoc
Journal. New Hampshire Dental Society — J NH Dent Soc
Journal. New Jersey Dental Association — J NJ Dent Assoc
Journal. New Jersey Dental Hygienists Association — J NJ Dent Hyg Assoc
Journal. New Jersey State Dental Society — J NJ State Dent Soc
Journal. New South Wales Council for the Mentally Handicapped — J NSW Council for Mentally Handicapped
Journal. New York Botanical Garden — J NY Bot Gdn
Journal. New York Entomological Society — J NY Ent So
Journal. New York Entomological Society — J NY Entomol Soc
Journal. New York Entomological Society — Jl NY Ent Soc
Journal. New York Medical College. Flower and Fifth Avenue Hospitals — J NY Med Coll Flower and Fifth Ave Hosp
Journal. New York Medical College. Flower and Fifth Avenue Hospitals — J NY Med Coll Flower Fifth Ave Hosp
Journal. New York State Nurses Association — J NY State Nurses Assoc
Journal. New York State School Nurse Teachers Association — J NY State Sch Nurse Teach Assoc
Journal. New Zealand Association of Bacteriologists — J NZ Assoc Bacteriol
Journal. New Zealand Dietetic Association — J NZ Diet Assoc
Journal. New Zealand Dietetic Association — Jl NZ Diet Ass
Journal. New Zealand Federation of Historical Societies — J NZ Fed Hist Soc
Journal. New Zealand Institute of Chemistry — J NZ Inst Chem
Journal. New Zealand Institute of Medical Laboratory Technology — J NZ Inst Med Lab Technol
Journal. New Zealand Society of Periodontology — J NZ Soc Periodontol
Journal. Newark Beth Israel Hospital — J Newark Beth Isr Hosp
Journal. Newark Beth Israel Hospital [*United States*] — J Newark Beth Israel Hosp
Journal. Newark Beth Israel Hospital — JNBIA
Journal. Newark Beth Israel Medical Center — J Newark Beth Isr Med Cent
Journal. Nigeria Association of Dental Students — J Niger Assoc Dent Stud
Journal. Nigerian Institute for Oil Palm Research — J Nigerian Inst Oil Palm Res
Journal. Nihon University Medical Association — J Nihon Univ Med Assoc
Journal. Nihon University Medical Association — NICHAS
Journal. Nihon University School of Dentistry — J Nihon Univ Sch Dent
Journal. Niigata Agricultural Experiment Station — J Niigata Agric Exp Stn
Journal. Nippon Dental Association — J Nippon Dent Assoc
Journal. Nippon Dental College — J Nippon Dent Coll
Journal. Nippon Hospital Pharmacists Association. Scientific Edition — J Nippon Hosp Pharm Assoc Sci Ed
Journal. Nippon Medical School — J Nippon Med Sch
Journal. Nippon Medical School — NIDZAJ
Journal. Nippon University School of Dentistry — J Nippon Univ Sch Dent
Journal. Nissei Hospital [*Japan*] — J Nissei Hosp
Journal. North Carolina Dental Society — J NC Dent Soc
Journal. North Carolina Section of the American Water Works Association and North Carolina Water Pollution Control Association — J NC Sect Am Water Works Assoc NC Water Pollut Control Assoc
Journal. North China Branch. Royal Asiatic Society — J N Ch R A S
Journal. North China Branch. Royal Asiatic Society — JNCB
Journal. North China Branch. Royal Asiatic Society — JNCBRAS
Journal. Northampton Museum and Art Gallery — J Northampton Mus
Journal. Northamptonshire Natural History Society and Field Club — J Northamptonshire Natur Hist Soc Fld Club
Journal. Northwest University. Natural Science Edition — J Northwest Univ Nat Sci Ed
Journal. Norwegian Medical Association — J Norw Med Assoc
Journal. Numismatic Society of India — JNSI
Journal. Numismatic Society of Madhya Pradesh — JNSMP
Journal Numismatique — JN
Journal. Ocean University of Qingdao — J Ocean Univ Qingdao
Journal. Oceanographical Society of Japan — J Oceanogr Soc Jpn
Journal. Oceanological Society of Korea [*South Korea*] — HHHCA
Journal. Oceanological Society of Korea — J Oceanol Soc Korea
Journal of Abdominal Surgery — J Abdom Surg
Journal of Abdominal Surgery — JABSBP
Journal of Abnormal and Social Psychology — J Ab Social Psychol
Journal of Abnormal and Social Psychology — J Abnorm Soc Psychol
Journal of Abnormal and Social Psychology — JASP
Journal of Abnormal and Social Psychology — JASPAW
Journal of Abnormal Child Psychology — IACP
Journal of Abnormal Child Psychology — J Abnorm Child Psychol
Journal of Abnormal Child Psychology — JABCAA
Journal of Abnormal Psychology — GABP
Journal of Abnormal Psychology — J Abn Psych
Journal of Abnormal Psychology — J Abnorm Psychol
Journal of Abnormal Psychology — JAbP
Journal of Abnormal Psychology — JAP
Journal of Abnormal Psychology — JAPCA
Journal of Abnormal Psychology — JAPCAC
Journal of Abnormal Psychology and Social Psychology — J Abnorm Psychol Soc Psychol
Journal of Abnormal Psychology. Monograph — J Abnorm Psychol Monogr
Journal of Abnormal Psychology. Monograph — JABPAF
Journal of Abstracts. British Ship Research Association — J Abstr Br Ship
Journal of Abstracts. British Ship Research Association — Jnl Abstr Brit Ship Res Assoc
Journal of Abstracts in International Education — J Abstr Int Educ
Journal of Academic Librarianship — J Acad Libnship
Journal of Academic Librarianship — J Acad Libr
Journal of Academic Librarianship — J Acad Librarianship
Journal of Academic Librarianship — JAL
Journal of Accelerator Science and Technology — J Accel Sci Technol
Journal of Accident and Emergency Medicine — J Accid Emerg Med
Journal of Accidental Medicine [*Japan*] — J Accidental Med
Journal of Accountancy — J Account
Journal of Accountancy — J Accountancy
Journal of Accountancy — J Acctcy
Journal of Accountancy — J Accy
Journal of Accountancy — JAC
Journal of Accounting and Economics [*Netherlands*] — JAE
Journal of Accounting and Public Policy — JAT
Journal of Accounting Auditing and Finance — J Account Audit Finance
Journal of Accounting Auditing and Finance — JAA
Journal of Accounting Auditing and Finance — Jrl Audit
Journal of Accounting Research — J Account Res
Journal of Accounting Research — J Accountin
Journal of Accounting Research — J Accounting Res
Journal of Accounting Research — J Acct Res
Journal of Accounting Research — JAR
Journal of Acetylene Lighting — J Acetylene Light
Journal of Acoustic Emission — J Acoust Emiss
Journal of Acquired Immune Deficiency Syndromes — J Acquired Immune Defic Syndr
Journal of Acquired Immune Deficiency Syndromes and Human Retrovirology — J Acquir Immune Defic Syndr Hum Retrovirol
Journal of Acquired Immune Deficiency Syndromes and Human Retrovirology — J Acquired Immune Defic Syndr Hum Retrovirol
Journal of Active Oxygens and Free Radicals — J Act Oxygens Free Radicals
Journal of Addictive Diseases — J Addict Dis
Journal of Adhesion — J Adhes

Journal of Adhesion — J Adhesion
Journal of Adhesion Science and Technology — J Adhes Sci
Journal of Adhesion Science and Technology — J Adhes Sci Technol
Journal of Administration Overseas — J Adm Overs
Journal of Administration Overseas — J Adm Overseas
Journal of Administration Overseas — J Admin Overseas
Journal of Administration Overseas — JADO
Journal of Adolescence — IADL
Journal of Adolescence — J Adolesc
Journal of Adolescence — J Adolescence
Journal of Adolescence — JOADE8
Journal of Adolescent Health — J Adolesc Health
Journal of Adolescent Health Care — J Adolesc Health Care
Journal of Adolescent Health Care — JAHCD9
Journal of Adolescent Research — J Adolescent Res
Journal of Adult Education — J Adult Ed
Journal of Advanced Education — J Adv Educ
Journal of Advanced Nursing — J Adv Nurs
Journal of Advanced Science — J Adv Sci
Journal of Advanced Transportation [*United States*] — J Adv Transp
Journal of Advanced Transportation — J Advanced Transp
Journal of Advanced Zoology — J Adv Zool
Journal of Advanced Zoology — JAZODX
Journal of Advertising — J Adv
Journal of Advertising — J Advert
Journal of Advertising — J Advertising
Journal of Advertising — JA
Journal of Advertising — JOA
Journal of Advertising — Jrl Advtg
Journal of Advertising Research — ADR
Journal of Advertising Research — J Adv Res
Journal of Advertising Research — J Advert Res
Journal of Advertising Research — JAD
Journal of Advertising Research — JAI
Journal of Advertising Research — JAR
Journal of Advertising Research — Jrl Ad Res
Journal of Aerosol Research (Japan) — J Aerosol Res Jpn
Journal of Aerosol Science — J Aerosol Sci
Journal of Aerosol Science — J Aerosol Science
Journal of Aerospace Science — JAS
Journal of Aesthetic Education — J Aes Ed
Journal of Aesthetic Education — J Aes Educ
Journal of Aesthetic Education — J Aesth Educ
Journal of Aesthetic Education — J Aesthet E
Journal of Aesthetic Education — J Aesthetic Educ
Journal of Aesthetic Education — JAE
Journal of Aesthetic Education — JAEDB
Journal of Aesthetic Education — JAesE
Journal of Aesthetics and Art Criticism — J Aes Art C
Journal of Aesthetics and Art Criticism — J Aes Art Crit
Journal of Aesthetics and Art Criticism — J Aesth
Journal of Aesthetics and Art Criticism — J Aesth & Art C
Journal of Aesthetics and Art Criticism — J Aesthet Art Crit
Journal of Aesthetics and Art Criticism — J Aesthetics
Journal of Aesthetics and Art Criticism — JA
Journal of Aesthetics and Art Criticism — JAAC
Journal of Aesthetics and Art Criticism — JArC
Journal of Aesthetics and Art Criticism — JARCA
Journal of Aesthetics and Art Criticism — Jl Aesthetics
Journal of Aesthetics and Art Criticism — Jnl Aesthetics
Journal of Aesthetics and Art Criticism — Jnl Aesthetics & Art Crit
Journal of Aesthetics and Art Criticism — Jour Aesthetics and Art Crit
Journal of Aesthetics and Art Criticism — PAAC
Journal of Affective Disorders — J Affect Disord
Journal of Affective Disorders — J Affective Disord
Journal of Affective Disorders — JADID7
Journal of African Administration — J Afr Adm
Journal of African Administration — JAA
Journal of African and Comparative Literature — JACL
Journal of African Earth Sciences — J Afr Earth Sci
Journal of African Earth Sciences — JAES
Journal of African Earth Sciences and the Middle East — J Afr Earth Sci Middle East
Journal of African History — J Afr Hist
Journal of African History — J Afric Hist
Journal of African History — J African Hist
Journal of African History — JAf H
Journal of African History — JAfrH
Journal of African History — JAH
Journal of African History — PJAH
Journal of African Languages — J Afr Lang
Journal of African Languages — J Afr Langs
Journal of African Languages — J Afr Languages
Journal of African Languages — JAfrL
Journal of African Languages — JAL
Journal of African Languages and Linguistics — JALL
Journal of African Law — J Afr L
Journal of African Law — J Afr Law
Journal of African Law — J African Law
Journal of African Law — JAf L
Journal of African Law — JAL
Journal of African Studies — J Afr Stud
Journal of African Studies — J African Studies
Journal of African-Afro-American Affairs — Jnl Afr Afro Am Aff
Journal of Aging and Physical Activity — J Aging & Phys Act
Journal of Agricultural and Food Chemistry — J Ag & Food Chem
Journal of Agricultural and Food Chemistry — J Agr Food
Journal of Agricultural and Food Chemistry — J Agr Food Chem
Journal of Agricultural and Food Chemistry — J Agri Food Chem
Journal of Agricultural and Food Chemistry — J Agric Fd Chem
Journal of Agricultural and Food Chemistry — J Agric Food Chem
Journal of Agricultural and Food Chemistry — J Agricultural Food Chem
Journal of Agricultural and Food Chemistry — JA & FC
Journal of Agricultural and Food Chemistry — JAFCAU
Journal of Agricultural and Scientific Research — J Agric Sci Res
Journal of Agricultural and Scientific Research — JASRE8
Journal of Agricultural Economics — J Ag Econ
Journal of Agricultural Economics — J Agr Econ
Journal of Agricultural Economics — J Agric Econ
Journal of Agricultural Economics — JAE
Journal of Agricultural Economics and Development — J Agr Econ Dev
Journal of Agricultural Economics and Development — J Agric Econ Dev
Journal of Agricultural Economics Research — J Agric Econ Res
Journal of Agricultural Engineering — J Agric Eng
Journal of Agricultural Engineering Research — J Agr Eng R
Journal of Agricultural Engineering Research — J Agr Eng Res
Journal of Agricultural Engineering Research — J Agric Eng Res
Journal of Agricultural Engineering Research — J Agric Engin Res
Journal of Agricultural Engineering Research — J Agric Engng Res
Journal of Agricultural Engineering Research — JAERA2
Journal of Agricultural Entomology — J Agric Entomol
Journal of Agricultural Entomology — JAENES
Journal of Agricultural Ethics — J Agric Ethics
Journal of Agricultural Faculty of Ege University — J Agric Fac Ege Univ
Journal of Agricultural Meteorology [*Tokyo*] — J Agric Meteorol
Journal of Agricultural Meteorology — NOKIAB
Journal of Agricultural Meteorology (Japan) — J Agr Meteorol (Japan)
Journal of Agricultural Meteorology (Tokyo) — J Agric Met (Tokyo)
Journal of Agricultural Research — J Ag Res
Journal of Agricultural Research — J Agr Res
Journal of Agricultural Research — J Agric Res
Journal of Agricultural Research — JAGRA
Journal of Agricultural Research (Alexandria) — J Agric Res (Alexandria)
Journal of Agricultural Research in Iceland [*Islenzkar Landbunadar Rannsoknir*] — J Agric Res Icel
Journal of Agricultural Research in Iceland [*Islenzkar Landbunadar Rannsoknir*] — JARI
Journal of Agricultural Research in the Tokai-Kinki Region — J Agr Res Tokai-Kinki Reg
Journal of Agricultural Research (Lahore) — J Agric Res Lahore
Journal of Agricultural Research of China — CHNCDB
Journal of Agricultural Research of China — J Agric Res China
Journal of Agricultural Research (Punjab) — J Agric Res Punjab
Journal of Agricultural Research (Riyadh, Saudi Arabia) — J Agric Res (Riyadh Saudi Arabia)
Journal of Agricultural Science — J Agr Sci
Journal of Agricultural Science — J Agric Sci
Journal of Agricultural Science — JASIAB
Journal of Agricultural Science (Beijing) — J Agric Sci Beijing
Journal of Agricultural Science (Cambridge) — J Agric Sci (Camb)
Journal of Agricultural Science (Helsinki) — J Agric Sci Helsinki
Journal of Agricultural Science in Finland — J Agric Sci Finl
Journal of Agricultural Science in Finland — JASFE6
Journal of Agricultural Science in Finland. Maataloustieteellinen Aikakauskirja — J Agric Sci Finl Maataloustieteellinen Aikak
Journal of Agricultural Science. Tokyo Nogyo Daigaku — J Agr Sci Tokyo Nogyo Daigaku
Journal of Agricultural Science. Tokyo Nogyo Daigaku — J Agric Sci Tokyo Nogyo Daigaku
Journal of Agricultural Science. Tokyo Nogyo Daigaku — TNDNAG
Journal of Agricultural Science/Tokyo Nogyo Daigaku Nogyo Shuho (Tokyo) — J Agric Sci Tokyo
Journal of Agricultural Science. Tokyo Nogyo Daigaku. Supplement — J Agric Sci Tokyo Nogyo Daigaku Suppl
Journal of Agricultural Taxation and Law — AGR
Journal of Agricultural Taxation and Law — J Ag T and L
Journal of Agriculture — J Agric
Journal of Agriculture [*Victoria*] — JAGVAO
Journal of Agriculture and Forestry — J Agric For
Journal of Agriculture and Forestry (National Chung Hsing University) — J Agric For Natl Chung Hsing Univ
Journal of Agriculture and Industry of South Australia — J Agric Ind South Aust
Journal of Agriculture and Industry of South Australia. Agricultural Bureau — J Agric Industr South Australia
Journal of Agriculture and Water Resources Research — J Agric Water Resour Res
Journal of Agriculture and Water Resources Research — JAWRES
Journal of Agriculture (Department of Agriculture. Victoria) — J Ag (VIC)
Journal of Agriculture (Department of Agriculture. Victoria) — J Agric (VIC)
Journal of Agriculture (Department of Agriculture. Western Australia) — J A (WA)
Journal of Agriculture (Department of Agriculture. Western Australi (West Aust)
Journal of Agriculture (Edinburgh) — J Agric Edinburgh
Journal of Agriculture (Melbourne) — J Agr (Melbourne)
Journal of Agriculture of Western Australia — J Agr W
Journal of Agriculture of Western Australia — JAWAA7
Journal of Agriculture (South Australia) — J Ag (SA)
Journal of Agriculture (South Australia) — J Agr (S Aust)
Journal of Agriculture (South Australia) — J Agric (S Aust)

Journal of Agriculture (South Australia) — J Agric (South Aust)
Journal of Agriculture (South Perth, Australia) — J Agric (South Perth Aust)
Journal of Agriculture. University of Puerto Rico — J Ag Univ Puerto Rico
Journal of Agriculture. University of Puerto Rico — J Agr Univ PR
Journal of Agriculture. University of Puerto Rico — J Agric Univ PR
Journal of Agriculture. University of Puerto Rico — J Agric Univ Puerto Rico
Journal of Agriculture. University of Puerto Rico — JAUPA
Journal of Agriculture. University of Puerto Rico — JAUPA8
Journal of Agriculture. University of Puerto Rico — Jour Agr Univ Puerto Rico
Journal of Agriculture. University of Puerto Rico — Journ Agr Univ Puerto Rico
Journal of Agriculture. University of Puerto Rico (Rio Piedras) — Jour Agr Univ P R Rio Piedras
Journal of Agriculture (Victoria) — J Agric (Vict)
Journal of Agriculture (Victoria) — J Agric (Victoria)
Journal of Agriculture (Victoria, Australia) — J Agric Victoria Aust
Journal of Agriculture. Victoria Department of Agriculture — J Agric Vict Dep Agric
Journal of Agronomic Education — J Agron Educ
Journal of Agronomy and Crop Science — J Agron Crop Sci
Journal of Agronomy and Crop Science — JASCEV
Journal of Air Law and Commerce — J Air L
Journal of Air Law and Commerce — J Air L and Com
Journal of Air Law and Commerce — J of Air L & Commerce
Journal of Air Traffic Control — JATC
Journal of Aircraft — J Aircr
Journal of Aircraft — J Aircraft
Journal of Alcohol and Drug Education — J Alc Drug
Journal of Alcohol and Drug Education — J Alcohol & Drug Educ
Journal of Alcohol and Drug Education — JADE
Journal of Alcoholism — J Alc
Journal of Alcoholism — J Alcohol
Journal of Alcoholism — JALCBR
Journal of Algebra — J Algebra
Journal of Algebraic Combinatorics — J Algebraic Combin
Journal of Algebraic Geometry — J Algebraic Geom
Journal of Algorithms — J Algorithms
Journal of Allergy — J All
Journal of Allergy [*Later, Journal of Allergy and Clinical Immunology*] — J Allergy
Journal of Allergy [*Later, Journal of Allergy and Clinical Immunology*] — JOALAS
Journal of Allergy and Clinical Immunology — J Allerg Cl
Journal of Allergy and Clinical Immunology — J Allergy Clin Immun
Journal of Allergy and Clinical Immunology — J Allergy Clin Immunol
Journal of Allergy and Clinical Immunology — JACIBY
Journal of Allergy and Clinical Immunology. Official Publication of American Academy of Allergy — J Allergy Clin Immunol Off Publ Am Acad Allergy
Journal of Allied Health — J Allied Health
Journal of Allied Health — JAHEDF
Journal of Alloy Phase Diagrams — J Alloy Phase Diagrams
Journal of Alloys and Compounds — J Alloys Compd
Journal of Altered States of Consciousness — J Altered States Conscious
Journal of Altered States of Consciousness — JACODK
Journal of Alternative and Complementary Medicine — JACM
Journal of Ambulatory Care Management — J Ambul Care Manage
Journal of Ambulatory Care Management — J Ambulatory Care Manage
Journal of American College Health — J Am Coll Health
Journal of American College Health — JACH
Journal of American College Health — JACHEY
Journal of American Culture — J Am Cult
Journal of American Culture — J Amer Cult
Journal of American Culture — PJAC
Journal of American Ethnic History — JAEH
Journal of American Ethnic History — PJEH
Journal of American Folklore — GFOK
Journal of American Folklore — J Am F-Lore
Journal of American Folklore — J Am Folk
Journal of American Folklore — J Am Folkl
Journal of American Folklore — J Am Folklo
Journal of American Folklore — J Am Folklore
Journal of American Folklore — JAF
Journal of American Folklore — JAFL
Journal of American Folklore — Jnl Am Folklore
Journal of American Folklore — Jour Am Folklore
Journal of American Folklore. American Folklore Society — AFS/JAF
Journal of American Folklore. Supplement — JAFS
Journal of American History — GJAH
Journal of American History — J Am His
Journal of American History — J Am Hist
Journal of American History — J Amer Hist
Journal of American History — JAH
Journal of American History — Jnl Am Hist
Journal of American History — JoAH
Journal of American Humor — JAHum
Journal of American Indian Education — J Am Indian Ed
Journal of American Insurance — AMI
Journal of American Insurance — J Am Ins
Journal of American Insurance — J Am Insur
Journal of American Insurance — JAI
Journal of American Musicology — JAM
ournal of American Photography — JAP
urnal of American Studies — GJAS
rnal of American Studies — J Am St
nal of American Studies — J Am Stud
al of American Studies — J Am Studies
l of American Studies — J Amer Stud
f American Studies — JAmS
Journal of American Studies — JAS
Journal of American Studies — JAStud
Journal of American Studies — JoAm
Journal of American Studies — Jour Am Studies
Journal of Analysis — J Anal
Journal of Analytical and Applied Pyrolysis — J Anal Appl Pyrolysis
Journal of Analytical and Applied Pyrolysis — JAAPD
Journal of Analytical and Applied Pyrolysis — JAAPDD
Journal of Analytical Atomic Spectrometry — J Anal At Spectrom
Journal of Analytical Chemistry of the USSR — J Anal Chem
Journal of Analytical Chemsitry (Translation of Zhurnal Analiticheskoi Khimii) — J Anal Chem Transl of Zh Anal Khim
Journal of Analytical Psychology — J Anal Psych
Journal of Analytical Psychology — J Anal Psychol
Journal of Analytical Psychology — JANPA7
Journal of Analytical Science — J Anal Sci
Journal of Analytical Toxicology — J Anal Toxicol
Journal of Analytical Toxicology — JATOD3
Journal of Anatomy — J Anat
Journal of Anatomy — JOANAY
Journal of Anatomy and Physiology — J Anat Phys
Journal of Anatomy and Physiology — J Anat Physiol
Journal of Ancient Indian History — J Anc Ind Hist
Journal of Ancient Indian History — JAIH
Journal of Andrology — J Androl
Journal of Andrology — JA
Journal of Andrology — JOAND3
Journal of Anesthesia — J Anesth
Journal of Anhui Medical College — J Anhui Med Coll
Journal of Animal Behavior — J Anim Behav
Journal of Animal Breeding and Genetics — J Anim Breed Genet
Journal of Animal Breeding and Genetics — JABAE8
Journal of Animal Ecology — J Anim Ecol
Journal of Animal Ecology — J Animal Ecol
Journal of Animal Ecology — J Animal Ecology
Journal of Animal Ecology — JAECAP
Journal of Animal Morphology and Physiology — J Anim Morph Physiol
Journal of Animal Morphology and Physiology — J Anim Morphol Physiol
Journal of Animal Morphology and Physiology — JAMPA2
Journal of Animal Physiology and Animal Nutrition — J Anim Physiol Anim Nutr
Journal of Animal Physiology and Animal Nutrition — JAPNEF
Journal of Animal Production of the United Arab Republic — J Anim Prod UAR
Journal of Animal Production of the United Arab Republic — J Anim Prod Un Arab Repub
Journal of Animal Production Research — J Anim Prod Res
Journal of Animal Production Research — JAPRDQ
Journal of Animal Science — J Anim Sci
Journal of Animal Science — J Animal Sci
Journal of Animal Science — JANSA
Journal of Animal Science — JANSAG
Journal of Anthropological Archaeology — JAA
Journal of Anthropological Research — J Anthr Res
Journal of Anthropological Research — J Anthro Res
Journal of Anthropological Research — J Anthrop Res
Journal of Anthropological Research — J Anthropol Res
Journal of Anthropological Research — JAPRCP
Journal of Anthropological Research — JAR
Journal of Anthropological Research — PJAR
Journal of Anthropological Research. University of New Mexico. Department of Anthropology — UNM/JAR
Journal of Anthropology — J Anthr
Journal of Anthropology — J Anthrop
Journal of Antibacterial and Antifungal Agents. Japan — J Antibact Antifungal Agents Jpn
Journal of Antibiotics [*Tokyo*] — J Antibiot
Journal of Antibiotics [*Tokyo*] — JANTAJ
Journal of Antibiotics. Series A — J Antibiot Ser A
Journal of Antibiotics. Series A [*Tokyo*] — JAJAAA
Journal of Antibiotics. Series B — J Antibiot Ser B
Journal of Antibiotics. Series B (Japan) — J Antibiot Ser B (Japan)
Journal of Antibiotics (Tokyo) — J Antibiot (Tokyo)
Journal of Antibiotics (Tokyo). Series A — J Antibiot (Tokyo) Ser A
Journal of Antimicrobial Chemotherapy — J Antimicrob Chemother
Journal of Antimicrobial Chemotherapy — JACHD
Journal of Antimicrobial Chemotherapy — JACHDX
Journal of Anxiety Disorders — J Anxiety Disord
Journal of Apicultural Research — J Apic Res
Journal of Apicultural Research — J Apicult R
Journal of Apicultural Research — JACRAQ
Journal of Apocrypha — JA
Journal of Applied Analysis — J Appl Anal
Journal of Applied Animal Research — J Appl Anim Res
Journal of Applied Bacteriology — J App Bact
Journal of Applied Bacteriology — J App Bacteriol
Journal of Applied Bacteriology — J Appl Bact
Journal of Applied Bacteriology — J Appl Bacteriol
Journal of Applied Bacteriology — JABAA4
Journal of Applied Behavior Analysis — J App Behav Anal
Journal of Applied Behavior Analysis — J App Behavior Anal
Journal of Applied Behavior Analysis — J Appl Be A
Journal of Applied Behavior Analysis — J Appl Behav Anal
Journal of Applied Behavior Analysis — JAB
Journal of Applied Behavior Analysis — JABA
Journal of Applied Behavior Analysis — JOABAW
Journal of Applied Behavioral Science — J Ap Behav Sci

Journal of Applied Behavioral Science — J App Behav Sci
Journal of Applied Behavioral Science — J App Behavioral Sci
Journal of Applied Behavioral Science — J Appl Beh
Journal of Applied Behavioral Science — J Appl Behav Sci
Journal of Applied Behavioral Science — JAB
Journal of Applied Behavioral Science — JABS
Journal of Applied Behavioral Science — JBS
Journal of Applied Biochemistry — J Appl Biochem
Journal of Applied Biochemistry — JAB
Journal of Applied Biochemistry — JABIDV
Journal of Applied Biology — J Appl Biol
Journal of Applied Biomaterials — J Appl Biomater
Journal of Applied Biomechanics — J Appl Bio
Journal of Applied Cardiology — J Appl Cardiol
Journal of Applied Chemistry — J Appl Chem
Journal of Applied Chemistry. Abstracts — J Appl Chem Abstr
Journal of Applied Chemistry and Biotechnology — J Appl Ch B
Journal of Applied Chemistry and Biotechnology — J Appl Chem and Biotechnol
Journal of Applied Chemistry and Biotechnology — J Appl Chem Biotechnol
Journal of Applied Chemistry and Biotechnology — JACBB
Journal of Applied Chemistry and Biotechnology. Abstracts — J Appl Chem Biotechnol Abstr
Journal of Applied Chemistry (London) — J Appl Chem (London)
Journal of Applied Chemistry of the USSR — J Appl Chem
Journal of Applied Chemistry of the USSR — J Appl Chem USSR
Journal of Applied Chemistry of the USSR — J Appld Chem USSR
Journal of Applied Chemistry. USSR. English Translation — J Appl Chem USSR Engl Transl
Journal of Applied Communication Series — JACS
Journal of Applied Corporate Finance — JACF
Journal of Applied Cosmetology — J Appl Cosmetol
Journal of Applied Crystallography — J Appl Crys
Journal of Applied Crystallography — J Appl Crystallogr
Journal of Applied Developmental Psychology — J Appl Dev Psychol
Journal of Applied Developmental Psychology — JADPDS
Journal of Applied Ecology — J Ap Ecol
Journal of Applied Ecology — J App Ecol
Journal of Applied Ecology — J Appl Ecol
Journal of Applied Ecology — J Applied Ecology
Journal of Applied Ecology — JAPEAI
Journal of Applied Ecology (Shenyang, People's Republic of China) — J Appl Ecol Shenyang Peoples Repub China
Journal of Applied Educational Studies — J Appl Educ Stud
Journal of Applied Educational Studies — J Applied Ednl Studies
Journal of Applied Electrochemistry — J Appl Elec
Journal of Applied Electrochemistry — J Appl Electrochem
Journal of Applied Entomology — J Appl Entomol
Journal of Applied Entomology — JOAEEB
Journal of Applied Fire Science — J Appl Fire Sci
Journal of Applied Gerontology — J Appl Gerontol
Journal of Applied Ichthyology — J Appl Ichthyol
Journal of Applied Management — J Appl Manage
Journal of Applied Management — JAM
Journal of Applied Mathematics and Mechanics — J Appl Math Mech
Journal of Applied Mathematics and Mechanics — J Appld Math Mech
Journal of Applied Mathematics and Mechanics (English Translation) — J Appl Math Mech (Engl Transl)
Journal of Applied Mathematics and Physics — J Appl Math Phys
Journal of Applied Mathematics and Simulation — J Appl Math Simulation
Journal of Applied Mechanics — J App Mech
Journal of Applied Mechanics and Technical Physics — J Appl Mech and Tech Phys
Journal of Applied Mechanics and Technical Physics — J Appl Mech Tech Phys
Journal of Applied Mechanics and Technical Physics — J Appld Mech Tech Physics
Journal of Applied Mechanics. Transactions. ASME [*American Society of Mechanical Engineers*] — J Appl Mech
Journal of Applied Mechanics. Transactions. ASME [*American Society of Mechanical Engineers*] — J Appl Mech Trans ASME
Journal of Applied Medicine — J Appl Med
Journal of Applied Metalworking — J Appl Metalwork
Journal of Applied Metalworking — JAMLD
Journal of Applied Meteorology — J Ap Meterol
Journal of Applied Meteorology — J App Meteor
Journal of Applied Meteorology — J Appl Met
Journal of Applied Meteorology — J Appl Meteorol
Journal of Applied Microscopy and Laboratory Methods — J Appl Microscop Lab Meth
Journal of Applied Microscopy (Rochester, New York) — J Applied Micr (Rochester NY)
Journal of Applied Mycology — J Appl Mycol
Journal of Applied Mycology. Hokkaido University/Oyo Kinkagu (Japan) — Journ Appl Mycol Japan
Journal of Applied Non-Classical Logics — J Appl Non Classical Logics
Journal of Applied Nutrition — J Ap Nutrition
Journal of Applied Nutrition — J App Nutr
Journal of Applied Nutrition — J Appl Nutr
Journal of Applied Nutrition — JOAN
Journal of Applied Photographic Engineering — J Appl Photogr Eng
Journal of Applied Photographic Engineering — Jl Appl Photogr Engin
Journal of Applied Physics — J Appl Phys
Journal of Applied Physics — J Applied Physics
Journal of Applied Physics — JAP
Journal of Applied Physics. Japan — J Appl Phys Jpn
Journal of Applied Physics (Moscow) — J Appl Phys (Moscow)
Journal of Applied Physiology [*Later, Journal of Applied Physiology: Respiratory, Environmental, and Exercise Physiology*] — J App Physiol
Journal of Applied Physiology [*Later, Journal of Applied Physiology: Respiratory, Environmental, and Exercise Physiology*] — J Appl Physiol
Journal of Applied Physiology [*Later, Journal of Applied Physiology: Respiratory, Environmental, and Exercise Physiology*] — JAPYA
Journal of Applied Physiology: Respiratory, Environmental, and Exercise Physiology — J Appl Physiol Respir Environ Exerc Physiol
Journal of Applied Physiology: Respiratory, Environmental, and Exercise Physiology — J Appl Physiol Respir Environ Exercise Physiol
Journal of Applied Plant Sociology — J Appl Pl Sociol
Journal of Applied Pneumatics — J Appl Pneum
Journal of Applied Polymer Science — J Appl Poly
Journal of Applied Polymer Science — J Appl Polym Sci
Journal of Applied Polymer Science — J Appld Polymer Science
Journal of Applied Polymer Science. Applied Polymer Symposium — J Appl Polym Sci Appl Polym Symp
Journal of Applied Probability — J App Prob
Journal of Applied Probability — J Appl Probab
Journal of Applied Probability — J Appl Probability
Journal of Applied Psychology — J Ap Psychol
Journal of Applied Psychology — J App Psy
Journal of Applied Psychology — J App Psychol
Journal of Applied Psychology — J Appl Psyc
Journal of Applied Psychology — J Appl Psychol
Journal of Applied Psychology — JAP
Journal of Applied Psychology — JAPs
Journal of Applied Psychology — JAPSA
Journal of Applied Psychology — JAY
Journal of Applied Psychology — JOAP
Journal of Applied Science and Computations — J Appl Sci Comput
Journal of Applied Science and Engineering. Section A. Electrical Power and Information Systems — J Appl Sci Eng A
Journal of Applied Science and Engineering. Section A. Electrical Power and Information Systems — J Appl Sci Eng Sect A Electr
Journal of Applied Sciences — J Appl Sci
Journal of Applied Social Psychology — IASP
Journal of Applied Social Psychology — J App Soc Psychol
Journal of Applied Social Psychology — J Appl So P
Journal of Applied Social Psychology — JASP
Journal of Applied Sociology — J Ap Sociol
Journal of Applied Spectroscopy — J Appl Spectrosc
Journal of Applied Spectroscopy (English Translation) — J Appl Spectrosc Engl Transl
Journal of Applied Spectroscopy (USSR) — J Appl Spectrosc (USSR)
Journal of Applied Sport Psychology — J Appl Sport Psy
Journal of Applied Statistical Sciences — J Appl Statist Sci
Journal of Applied Statistics — J Appl Statist
Journal of Applied Systems Analysis — J Appl Syst Anal
Journal of Applied Systems Analysis — J Appl Systems Analysis
Journal of Applied Therapeutics — J Appl Ther
Journal of Applied Toxicology — J Appl Toxicol
Journal of Applied Toxicology — JAT
Journal of Applied Toxicology. JAT — J Appl Toxicol JAT
Journal of Approximation Theory — J Approx Th
Journal of Approximation Theory — J Approx Theory
Journal of Approximation Theory — J Approximation Theory
Journal of Approximation Theory — JAPT
Journal of Aquariculture — J Aquaric
Journal of Aquariculture and Aquatic Sciences — J Aquaric & Aquat Sci
Journal of Aquatic Food Product Technology — J Aquat Food Prod Technol
Journal of Aquatic Plant Management — J Aquat Pl
Journal of Aquatic Plant Management — J Aquat Plant Manage
Journal of Aquatic Plant Management — J Aquatic Pl Management
Journal of Arab Affairs — J Arab Affairs
Journal of Arab Literature — JAL
Journal of Arabic Literature — J Ar L
Journal of Arabic Literature — J Arab Lit
Journal of Arabic Literature — JArabL
Journal of Arachnology — J Arachnol
Journal of Arboriculture — J Arboric
Journal of Archaeological Chemistry — J Archaeol Chem
Journal of Archaeological Science — J A Scien
Journal of Archaeological Science — J Arch Sci
Journal of Archaeological Science — J Archaeol Sci
Journal of Archaeological Science — JAS
Journal of Architectural Education — Jnl of Archtl Education
Journal of Architectural Research — JARR
Journal of Architectural Research — Jnl of Archtl Research
Journal of Area Studies — Jnl Area Stud
Journal of Arid Environments — J Arid Environ
Journal of Arizona History — J Ariz Hist
Journal of Arizona History — J Arizona Hist
Journal of Arizona History — JArizH
Journal of Arizona History — Jr A
Journal of Armament Studies — J Armament Stud
Journal of Arthroplasty — J Arthroplasty
Journal of Artificial Intelligence Research — J Artificial Intelligence Res
Journal of Arts Management and Law — J Art Mgmt L
Journal of Arts Management and Law — J Arts Mgt and L
Journal of Asian Affairs — J As Aff
Journal of Asian and African Studies — J Asian Afr
Journal of Asian and African Studies — J Asian Afr Stud
Journal of Asian and African Studies — J Asian & Afric Stud
Journal of Asian and African Studies — JAAS

Journal of Asian and African Studies — PJAS
Journal of Asian and African Studies (Tokyo) — J As Afr Stud (T)
Journal of Asian Art — JAA
Journal of Asian Culture — J As Cult
Journal of Asian History — J As Hist
Journal of Asian History — J Asian His
Journal of Asian History — J Asian Hist
Journal of Asian History — JAH
Journal of Asian History — PJAY
Journal of Asian Martial Arts — J Asian Martial Arts
Journal of Asian Studies — GASU
Journal of Asian Studies — J Asia Stud
Journal of Asian Studies — J Asian St
Journal of Asian Studies — J Asian Stud
Journal of Asian Studies — JaAS
Journal of Asian Studies — JAS
Journal of Asian Studies — JASt
Journal of Asian Studies — Jnl Asian Stu
Journal of Asian-Pacific and World Perspectives — J As Pac World
Journal of Asiatic Studies — J Asiat Stud
Journal of Assisted Reproduction and Genetics — J Assist Reprod Genet
Journal of Asthma — J Asthma
Journal of Asthma Research [*Later, Journal of Asthma*] — J Asthma Res
Journal of Astronomy (Peiping) — J Astron (Peiping)
Journal of Astrophysics and Astronomy — J Astrophys and Astron
Journal of Astrophysics and Astronomy — J Astrophys Astron
Journal of Astrophysics and Astronomy — JAA
Journal of Atherosclerosis Research — J Atheroscler Res
Journal of Atherosclerosis Research — J Atherosclerosis Res
Journal of Athletic Training — J Ath Train
Journal of Atmospheric and Terrestrial Physics — J Atm Ter P
Journal of Atmospheric and Terrestrial Physics — J Atmos and Terr Phys
Journal of Atmospheric and Terrestrial Physics — J Atmos Terr Phys
Journal of Atmospheric and Terrestrial Physics — J Atmospher Terrestr Phys
Journal of Atmospheric and Terrestrial Physics — Journ Atmos Terr Phys
Journal of Atmospheric and Terrestrial Physics. Supplement — J Atmos Terr Phys Suppl
Journal of Atmospheric Chemistry — J Atmos Chem
Journal of Audiovisual Media in Medicine — J Audiov Media Med
Journal of Auditory Research — J Aud Res
Journal of Auditory Research — JAURA
Journal of Auditory Research. Supplement — J Aud Res Suppl
Journal of Australian Political Economy — J Aust Polit Econ
Journal of Australian Political Economy — JAPE
Journal of Australian Studies — J Austral Stud
Journal of Australian Studies — JAS
Journal of Austronesian Studies — J Austronesian Stud
Journal of Austronesian Studies — JAS
Journal of Autism and Childhood Schizophrenia — J Autism & Child Schizo
Journal of Autism and Childhood Schizophrenia — J Autism Ch
Journal of Autism and Childhood Schizophrenia — J Autism Child Schizophrenia
Journal of Autism and Childhood Schizophrenia — JAUCB
Journal of Autism and Developmental Disorders — J Autism & Devel Dis
Journal of Autism and Developmental Disorders — J Autism Dev Disord
Journal of Autism and Developmental Disorders — J Autism Dev Disorders
Journal of Autoimmunity — J Autoimmun
Journal of Automated Reasoning — J Automat Reason
Journal of Automatic Chemistry [*England*] — J Autom Chem
Journal of Automation and Information Sciences — J Automat Inform Sci
Journal of Automotive Engineering — J Automot Eng
Journal of Automotive Engineering — JAUEA
Journal of Autonomic Pharmacology — J Auton Pharmacol
Journal of Aviation Medicine — J Aviat Med
Journal of Aviation Medicine — J Aviation Med
Journal of Bacteriology — J Bact
Journal of Bacteriology — J Bacteriol
Journal of Ballistics — J Ballist
Journal of Baltic Studies — J Bal Stud
Journal of Baltic Studies — J Baltic St
Journal of Baltic Studies — JBalS
Journal of Band Research — J Band Res
Journal of Band Research — JB
Journal of Band Research — JBASB
Journal of Bank Research — J Bank Res
Journal of Bank Research — J Bank Research
Journal of Bank Research — JBR
Journal of Banking and Finance — J Bank Finance
Journal of Banking and Finance — J Banking and Fin
Journal of Banking and Finance — J Banking Finance
Journal of Banking and Finance [*Netherlands*] — JBA
Journal of Banking and Finance — JBF
Journal of Banking and Finance — JBK
Journal of Baoji College of Arts and Science. Natural Science — J Baoji Coll Arts Sci Nat Sci
Journal of Basic and Clinical Physiology and Pharmacology — J Basic Clin Physiol Pharmacol
Journal of Basic Engineering — J Basic Eng
Journal of Basic Engineering. Transactions. ASME [*American Society of Mechanical Engineers*] — J Basic Eng Trans ASME
Journal of Basic Engineering. Transactions. ASME [*American Society of Mechanical Engineers*]. Series D — J Basic Eng Trans ASME Ser D
Journal of Basic Microbiology — J Basic Microbiol
Journal of Basic Sciences. Hanyang Institute of Basic Science — J Basic Sci Hanyang Inst Basic Sci
Journal of Basque Studies — J Bas S
Journal of Basque Studies — Jnl Basque Stud
Journal of Beckett Studies — J Beck S
Journal of Beckett Studies — J Beckett S
Journal of Beckett Studies — J Beckett Stud
Journal of Behavior Therapy and Experimental Psychiatry — J Behav Exp
Journal of Behavior Therapy and Experimental Psychiatry — J Behav Ther Exp Psychiatry
Journal of Behavioral Assessment — J Behav Assess
Journal of Behavioral Assessment — Jnl Behav Asses
Journal of Behavioral Economics — JBE
Journal of Behavioral Medicine — J Behav Med
Journal of Behavioral Medicine — JOBM
Journal of Behavioural Science — J Behav Sci
Journal of Behavioural Science — J Behavioural Sci
Journal of Beijing Forestry College — J Beijing For Coll
Journal of Beijing Forestry University — J Beijing For Univ
Journal of Beijing Institute of Chemical Technology. Natural Science — J Beijing Inst Chem Technol Nat Sci
Journal of Beijing Medical College — J Beijing Med Coll
Journal of Beijing Medical University — J Beijing Med Univ
Journal of Beijing Polytechnic University — J Beijing Polytech Univ
Journal of Beijing University of Aeronautics and Astronautics — J Beijing Univ Aeronaut Astronaut
Journal of Beijing University of Iron and Steel Technology — J Beijing Univ Iron Steel Technol
Journal of Belizean Affairs — JBA
Journal of Bethune Medical University — J Bethune Med Univ
Journal of Bible and Religion — JBR
Journal of Biblical Literature — J Bib Lit
Journal of Biblical Literature — J Bibl Lit
Journal of Biblical Literature — JBL
Journal of Biblical Literature — Journ Bib Lit
Journal of Biblical Literature — Journ Biblical Lit
Journal of Biblical Literature — PJBL
Journal of Biblical Literature. Monograph Series — JBLMS
Journal of Bioactive and Compatible Polymers — J Bioact Compat Polym
Journal of Biochemical and Biophysical Methods — J Biochem and Biophys Methods
Journal of Biochemical and Biophysical Methods — JBBMD
Journal of Biochemical and Microbiological Technology and Engineering — J Biochem Microbiol Tech Eng
Journal of Biochemical and Microbiological Technology and Engineering — J Biochem Microbiol Technol Eng
Journal of Biochemical and Microbiological Technology and Engineering — Journ Biochem Micr Tech Eng
Journal of Biochemical Toxicology — J Biochem Toxicol
Journal of Biochemistry — J Biochem
Journal of Biochemistry — Journ Biochem
Journal of Biochemistry and Molecular Biology — J Biochem Mol Biol
Journal of Biochemistry (Tokyo) — J Biochem (Tokyo)
Journal of Biocommunication — J Biocommun
Journal of Biocommunication — JBIC
Journal of Bioelectricity — J Bioelectr
Journal of Bioenergetics [*Later, Journal of Bioenergetics and Biomembranes*] — J Bioenerg
Journal of Bioenergetics and Biomembranes — J Bioenerg Biomembr
Journal of Bioengineering — J Bioeng
Journal of Bioethics — J Bioeth
Journal of Biogeography — J Biogeogr
Journal of Biological Chemistry — J Biol Chem
Journal of Biological Chemistry — Jour Biol Chem
Journal of Biological Chemistry — Journ Biol Chem
Journal of Biological Education — J Biol Educ
Journal of Biological Education — J Biological Ed
Journal of Biological Inorganic Chemistry — J Biol Inorg Chem
Journal of Biological Photography — J Biol Photogr
Journal of Biological Physics — J Biol Phys
Journal of Biological Physics — JBPHB
Journal of Biological Psychology — J Biol Psychol
Journal of Biological Regulators and Homeostatic Agents — J Biol Regul Homeost Agents
Journal of Biological Regulators and Homeostatic Agents — J Biol Regul Homeostatic Agents
Journal of Biological Research — J Biol Res
Journal of Biological Research (Naples) — J Biol Res Naples
Journal of Biological Response Modifiers — J Biol Response Mod
Journal of Biological Response Modifiers — J Biol Response Modif
Journal of Biological Response Modifiers — JBRM
Journal of Biological Rhythms — J Biol Rhythms
Journal of Biological Sciences — J Biol Sci
Journal of Biological Sciences (Baghdad) — J Biol Sci (Baghdad)
Journal of Biological Sciences (Bombay) — J Biol Sci (Bombay)
Journal of Biological Sciences Research — J Biol Sci Res
Journal of Biological Sciences Research — JBSREF
Journal of Biological Sciences Research Publication — J Biol Sci Res Publ
Journal of Biological Sciences Research Publication — JBSPE9
Journal of Biological Standardization — J Biol Stan
Journal of Biological Standardization — J Biol Stand
Journal of Biological Standardization — JBSTB
Journal of Biological Systems — J Biol Systems
Journal of Biology (Bronx, NY) — J Biol (Bronx NY)
Journal of Biology (Bucharest) — J Biol Bucharest
Journal of Biology. Osaka City University — J Biol Osaka City Univ
Journal of Bioluminescence and Chemiluminescence — J Biolumin Chemilumin
Journal of Biomaterials Applications — J Biomat Appl

Journal of Biomaterials Applications — J Biomater Appl
Journal of Biomaterials Science. Polymer Edition — J Biomater Sci Polym Ed
Journal of Biomathematics — J Biomath
Journal of Biomechanical Engineering — J Biomech Eng
Journal of Biomechanical Engineering. Transactions. ASME [*American Society of Mechanical Engineers*] — J Biomech Eng Trans ASME
Journal of Biomechanics — J Biomech
Journal of Biomechanics — J Biomechan
Journal of Biomedical Engineering — J Biomed Eng
Journal of Biomedical Materials Research — J Biomed Mat Res
Journal of Biomedical Materials Research — J Biomed Mater Res
Journal of Biomedical Materials Research — J Biomed MR
Journal of Biomedical Materials Research. Biomedical Materials Symposium — J Biomed Mater Res Biomed Mater Symp
Journal of Biomedical Materials Research Symposium — J Biomed Mater Res Symp
Journal of Biomedical Optics — J Biomed Opt
Journal of Biomedical Systems — J Biomed Syst
Journal of Biomolecular NMR [Nuclear Magnetic Resonance] — J Biomol NMR
Journal of Biomolecular Screening — J Biomol Screening
Journal of Biomolecular Structure and Dynamics — J Biomol Struct & Dyn
Journal of Biomolecular Structure and Dynamics — J Biomol Struct Dyn
Journal of Biomolecular Structure and Dynamics — JBSDD6
Journal of Biopharmaceutical Statistics — J Biopharm Stat
Journal of Biophysical and Biochemical Cytology — J Biophys Biochem Cytol
Journal of Biophysical and Biochemical Cytology — Journ Biophys Biochem Cytol
Journal of Biophysics (Tokyo) — J Biophys (Tokyo)
Journal of Biosciences — J Biosci
Journal of Biosciences [*Bangalore*] — JOBSDN
Journal of Biosciences (Bangalore) — J Biosci (Bangalore)
Journal of Biosocial Science — J Biosoc
Journal of Biosocial Science — J Biosoc Sc
Journal of Biosocial Science — J Biosoc Sci
Journal of Biosocial Science — J Biosocial Sci
Journal of Biosocial Science. Supplement — J Biosoc Sci Suppl
Journal of Biosocial Science. Supplement — J Biosocial Sci Suppl
Journal of Biotechnology — J Biotech
Journal of Biotechnology — J Biotechnol
Journal of Biotechnology — JBITD4
Journal of Black Poetry — J Black Poetry
Journal of Black Poetry — JnlOBP
Journal of Black Studies — GJBS
Journal of Black Studies — J Black St
Journal of Black Studies — J Black Stud
Journal of Black Studies — J Black Studies
Journal of Black Studies — J of Black Stud
Journal of Black Studies — JBlackS
Journal of Bone and Joint Surgery — J Bone Joint Surg
Journal of Bone and Joint Surgery — J Bone Jt Surg
Journal of Bone and Joint Surgery (American Volume) — J Bone (Am V)
Journal of Bone and Joint Surgery (American Volume) — J Bone Joint Surg (Am)
Journal of Bone and Joint Surgery (American Volume) — J Bone Jt Surg (Am Vol)
Journal of Bone and Joint Surgery (British Volume) — J Bone (Br V)
Journal of Bone and Joint Surgery (British Volume) — J Bone Joint Surg (Br)
Journal of Bone and Joint Surgery (British Volume) — J Bone Jt Surg (Br Vol)
Journal of Bone and Mineral Metabolism — J Bone Miner Metab
Journal of Bone and Mineral Research — J Bone Miner Res
Journal of Botanical Analysis/Chih-Wu Fen-Liu Hsueh-Pao — Chih Wu Fen Liu Hsueeh Pao
Journal of Botany [*W. J. Hooker, Editor*] — Journ Bot
Journal of Botany. British and Foreign — J Bot Br Foreign
Journal of Botany. British and Foreign — Journ Bot Brit For
Journal of Botany, British and Foreign (London) — J Bot Lond
Journal of Botany, British and Foreign (London) — Seeman Journ Bot
Journal of Botany. United Arab Republic — J Bot UAR
Journal of Botany (W. J. Hooker, Editor) — Hook J Bot
Journal of Botany (W. J. Hooker, Editor) — J Bot Hooker
Journal of Botany (W. J. Hooker, Editor) — Jour Bot Hooker
Journal of Brain Science — J Brain Sci
Journal of Brewing — J Brew
Journal of British Studies — J Br Stud
Journal of British Studies — J Brit Stud
Journal of British Studies — JBS
Journal of British Studies — JoB
Journal of British Studies — Jour Brit Studies
Journal of British Studies — PJBS
Journal of Broadcasting [*Later, Journal of Broadcasting and Electronic Media*] — J Broadcast
Journal of Broadcasting [*Later, Journal of Broadcasting and Electronic Media*] — J Broadcasting
Journal of Broadcasting [*Later, Journal of Broadcasting and Electronic Media*] — J of Bcasting
Journal of Broadcasting [*Later, Journal of Broadcasting and Electronic Media*] — JB
Journal of Broadcasting [*Later, Journal of Broadcasting and Electronic Media*] — JOB
Journal of Broadcasting and Electronic Media — GBEM
Journal of Broadcasting and Electronic Media — J Broadcst
Journal of Bryology — J Bryol
Journal of Burn Care and Rehabilitation — J Burn Care Rehabil
Journal of Business — IBU
Journal of Business — J Bsns
Journal of Business — J Bus
Journal of Business — J Busin
Journal of Business — JB
Journal of Business — JBU
Journal of Business — JOB
Journal of Business — Jnl Bus
Journal of Business Administration — JBA
Journal of Business Administration — Jnl Bus Adm
Journal of Business Administration — JOB
Journal of Business and Economic Statistics — J Bus Econom Statist
Journal of Business Communication — J Bus Commun
Journal of Business Communication — J Bus Communic
Journal of Business Communication — JBC
Journal of Business Education — J Bsns Ed
Journal of Business Education — J Bsns Educ
Journal of Business Education — J Bus Ed
Journal of Business Education — JBE
Journal of Business Education — Jnl Business Ed
Journal of Business Ethics — J Bus Ethics
Journal of Business Ethics — JBE
Journal of Business Ethics — JBT
Journal of Business Finance and Accounting — JBF
Journal of Business Finance and Accounting — JBFA
Journal of Business Finance and Accounting — Jl Bus Fin
Journal of Business Forecasting — JFC
Journal of Business Law [*British*] — J Bus L
Journal of Business Law [*British*] — JBL
Journal of Business Logistics — JBG
Journal of Business Research — J Bus Res
Journal of Business Research — J Bus Research
Journal of Business Research — JBS
Journal of Business Research — JBU
Journal of Business Strategy — J Bus Strategy
Journal of Business Strategy — Jl Bus Strat
Journal of Business Strategy — JST
Journal of Buyouts and Acquisitions — JAQ
Journal of Buyouts and Acquisitions — JBO
Journal of Byelorussian Studies — JBS
Journal of Byelorussian Studies — JByelS
Journal of Canadian Art History — J Can Art Hist
Journal of Canadian Art History — Jnl of Canadian Art History
Journal of Canadian Culture — Jnl Can Cult
Journal of Canadian Fiction — J Can Fic
Journal of Canadian Fiction — J Can Fict
Journal of Canadian Fiction — JCF
Journal of Canadian Petroleum Technology — J Can Pet T
Journal of Canadian Petroleum Technology — J Can Pet Technol
Journal of Canadian Petroleum Technology — J Can Petrol Technol
Journal of Canadian Petroleum Technology — JCPT
Journal of Canadian Studies — J Can Stud
Journal of Canadian Studies — J Can Studies
Journal of Canadian Studies — JCanS
Journal of Canadian Studies — PJCS
Journal of Cancer Education — J Cancer Educ
Journal of Cancer Research — J Cancer Res
Journal of Cancer Research and Clinical Oncology — J Cancer Res Clin Oncol
Journal of Capacity Management — J Cap Mgmt
Journal of Capillary Electrophoresis — J Capillary Electrophor
Journal of Carbohydrate Chemistry — J Carbohydr Chem
Journal of Carbohydrate Chemistry — JCACDM
Journal of Carbohydrate Chemistry — JCC
Journal of Carbohydrates-Nucleosides-Nucleotides — J Carb-Nucl
Journal of Carbohydrates-Nucleosides-Nucleotides — J Carbohyd-Nucl-Nucl
Journal of Carbohydrates-Nucleosides-Nucleotides — J Carbohydr-Nucleosides-Nucleotides
Journal of Cardiac Failure — J Card Fail
Journal of Cardiac Rehabilitation — J Cardiac Rehab
Journal of Cardiac Rehabilitation — Jnl Cardiac Rehab
Journal of Cardiography — J Cardiogr
Journal of Cardiology — J Cardiol
Journal of Cardiopulmonary Rehabilitation — J Cardiopul Rehab
Journal of Cardiopulmonary Rehabilitation — J Cardpulm Rehabil
Journal of Cardiothoracic and Vascular Anesthesia — J Cardiothorac Vasc Anesth
Journal of Cardiovascular Electrophysiology — J Cardiovasc Electrophysiol
Journal of Cardiovascular Medicine — J Cardiovasc Med
Journal of Cardiovascular Medicine — JCMEDK
Journal of Cardiovascular Medicine — Jnl Cardiovasc Med
Journal of Cardiovascular Nursing — J Cardiovasc Nurs
Journal of Cardiovascular Pharmacology — J Cardiovasc Pharmacol
Journal of Cardiovascular Pharmacology and Therapeutics — J Cardiovasc Pharmacol Ther
Journal of Cardiovascular Risk — J Cardiovasc Risk
Journal of Cardiovascular Surgery — J Card Surg
Journal of Cardiovascular Surgery — J Cardiovas Surg
Journal of Cardiovascular Surgery — J Cardiovasc Surg
Journal of Cardiovascular Surgery (Torino) — J Cardiovasc Surg (Torino)
Journal of Cardiovascular Ultrasonography — J Cardiovasc Ultrason
Journal of Cardiovascular Ultrasonography — JCAUD8
Journal of Career Education — J Car Ed
Journal of Caribbean History — JCH
Journal of Caribbean History. University of the West Indies. Department of History and Caribbean Universities Press — UWI/JCH
Journal of Caribbean Studies — JC St
Journal of Caribbean Studies — JCS

Journal of Caribbean Studies (Florida) — JCSF
Journal of Cataloging and Classification — J Cat & Class
Journal of Catalysis — J Catal
Journal of Catalysis — J Catalysis
Journal of Catalysis (Dalian) — J Catal (Dalian)
Journal of Cataract and Refractive Surgery — J Cataract Refract Surg
Journal of Cataract and Refractive Surgery — J Cataract Refractive Surg
Journal of Cell Biology — J Cell Biol
Journal of Cell Science — J Cell Sci
Journal of Cell Science. Supplement — J Cell Sci Suppl
Journal of Cellular and Comparative Physiology [*Later, Journal of Cellular Physiology*] — J Cell Comp Physiol
Journal of Cellular Biochemistry — J Cell Biochem
Journal of Cellular Biochemistry — JCEBD
Journal of Cellular Biochemistry. Supplement — J Cell Biochem Suppl
Journal of Cellular Biochemistry. Supplement — JCBSD7
Journal of Cellular Engineering incorporating Molecular Engineering — J Cell Eng incorporating Mol Eng
Journal of Cellular Pharmacology — J Cell Pharmacol
Journal of Cellular Physiology — J Cell Phys
Journal of Cellular Physiology — J Cell Physiol
Journal of Cellular Physiology. Supplement — J Cell Physiol Suppl
Journal of Cellular Physiology. Supplement — JCPSB
Journal of Cellular Plastics — J Cell Plast
Journal of Cellular Plastics — J Cellular Plastics
Journal of Cellulose Science and Technology — J Cellul Sci Technol
Journal of Celtic Studies — JC St
Journal of Celtic Studies — JCeltS
Journal of Celtic Studies — JCS
Journal of Central Asia — J Cent Asia
Journal of Central China Normal University. Natural Sciences — J Central China Normal Univ Natur Sci
Journal of Central European Affairs — J Cent Eur Aff
Journal of Central European Affairs — J Cent Eur Affairs
Journal of Central European Affairs — J Centr Eur Aff
Journal of Central European Affairs — JCEA
Journal of Central South University of Technology (Chinese Edition) — J Cent South Univ Technol Chin Ed
Journal of Central South University of Technology (English Edition) — J Cent South Univ Technol Engl Ed
Journal of Cereal Science — J Cereal Sci
Journal of Cereal Science — JCS
Journal of Cereal Science — JCSCDA
Journal of Cerebral Blood Flow and Metabolism — J Cereb Blood Flow Metab
Journal of Cerebral Blood Flow and Metabolism — JCBF
Journal of Cerebral Blood Flow and Metabolism — JCBMDN
Journal of Changsha Communications Institute — J Changsha Comm Inst
Journal of Changsha Railway Institute — J Changsha Railway Inst
Journal of Changsha University of Electric Power. Natural Science Edition — J Changsha Univ Electr Power Nat Sci Ed
Journal of Chemical and Biochemical Kinetics — J Chem Biochem Kinet
Journal of Chemical and Engineering Data — J Chem En D
Journal of Chemical and Engineering Data — J Chem Eng Data
Journal of Chemical and Engineering Data — JC & ED
Journal of Chemical Documentation — J Chem Doc
Journal of Chemical Documentation — J Chem Docum
Journal of Chemical Ecology — J Chem Ecol
Journal of Chemical Education — ICHE
Journal of Chemical Education — J Chem Ed
Journal of Chemical Education — J Chem Educ
Journal of Chemical Education. Software — J Chem Educ Software
Journal of Chemical Engineering (Beijing) — J Chem Eng (Beijing)
Journal of Chemical Engineering Data — J Chem Engng Data
Journal of Chemical Engineering Education — J Chem Eng Educ
Journal of Chemical Engineering of Japan — J Chem Eng Jap
Journal of Chemical Engineering of Japan — J Chem Eng Jpn
Journal of Chemical Engineering of Japan — J Chem Engng Japan
Journal of Chemical Engineering (Tientsin) — J Chem Eng (Tientsin)
Journal of Chemical Industry and Engineering — J Chem Ind Eng
Journal of Chemical Industry and Engineering (China, Chinese Edition) — J Chem Ind Eng (China Chin Ed)
Journal of Chemical Industry (Budapest) — J Chem Ind (Budapest)
Journal of Chemical Industry (Japan) — J Chem Ind Jpn
Journal of Chemical Industry (Moscow) — J Chem Ind (Moscow)
Journal of Chemical Information and Computer Science — J Chem Inform Comput Sci
Journal of Chemical Information and Computer Sciences — J Chem Inf
Journal of Chemical Information and Computer Sciences — J Chem Inf and Comput Sci
Journal of Chemical Information and Computer Sciences — J Chem Inf Comp Sci
Journal of Chemical Information and Computer Sciences — J Chem Inf Comput Sci
Journal of Chemical Information and Computer Sciences — JCICS
Journal of Chemical Information and Computer Sciences — JCISD
Journal of Chemical Neuroanatomy — J Chem Neur
Journal of Chemical Neuroanatomy — J Chem Neuroanat
Journal of Chemical Physics — J Chem Phys
Journal of Chemical Physics — J Chem Physics
Journal of Chemical Physics — JCPSA
Journal of Chemical Physics — Jour Chem Physics
Journal of Chemical Physics — Journ Chem Phys
Journal of Chemical Research. Miniprint — J Chem Res Miniprint
Journal of Chemical Research. Part M — J Chem Res M
Journal of Chemical Research. Part S. Synopses — J Chem Res Part S
Journal of Chemical Research. Part S. Synopses — J Chem Res S
Journal of Chemical Research. Part S. Synopses [*England*] — J Chem Res Synop
Journal of Chemical Sciences — J Chem Sci
Journal of Chemical Software — J Chem Software
Journal of Chemical Technology and Biotechnology — J Chem Tech Biotech
Journal of Chemical Technology and Biotechnology — J Chem Tech Biotechnol
Journal of Chemical Technology and Biotechnology — J Chem Technol and Biotechnol
Journal of Chemical Technology and Biotechnology — J Chem Technol Biotechnol
Journal of Chemical Technology and Biotechnology. A. Chemical Technology — J Chem Technol Biotechnol A
Journal of Chemical Technology and Biotechnology. A. Chemical Technology — J Chem Technol Biotechnol A Chem Technol
Journal of Chemical Technology and Biotechnology. A. Chemical Technology — J Chem Technol Biotechnol Chem Technol
Journal of Chemical Technology and Biotechnology. A. Chemical Technology — JCTTDW
Journal of Chemical Technology and Biotechnology. B. Biotechnology — J Chem Technol Biotechnol B
Journal of Chemical Technology and Biotechnology. B. Biotechnology — J Chem Technol Biotechnol B Biotechnology
Journal of Chemical Technology and Biotechnology. B. Biotechnology — JTBBD7
Journal of Chemical Thermodynamics — J Chem Ther
Journal of Chemical Thermodynamics — J Chem Thermodyn
Journal of Chemical Thermodynamics and Thermochemistry — J Chem Thermodyn Thermochem
Journal of Chemical Vapor Deposition — J Chem Vap Deposition
Journal of Chemistry (United Arab Republic) — J Chem (UAR)
Journal of Chemometrics — J Chemom
Journal of Chemotherapy — J Chemother
Journal of Chemotherapy and Advanced Therapeutics — J Chemother Adv Ther
Journal of Chemotherapy (Florence) — J Chemother (Florence)
Journal of Chemotherapy (Philadelphia) — J Chemother (Philadelphia)
Journal of Chengdu Institute of Technology — J Chengdu Inst Technol
Journal of Chengdu University. Natural Sciences — J Chengdu Univ Natur Sci
Journal of Chengdu University of Science and Technology — J Chengdu Univ Sci Tech
Journal of Child and Adolescent Psychopharmacology — J Child Adolesc Psychopharmacol
Journal of Child Development — JCDVA
Journal of Child Language — J Ch L
Journal of Child Language — J Child Lang
Journal of Child Language — J Child Language
Journal of Child Language — JCLa
Journal of Child Neurology — J Child Neurol
Journal of Child Neurology — JOCNEE
Journal of Child Psychology and Psychiatry — J Child Psy
Journal of Child Psychology and Psychiatry — J Child Psych & Psychiatry
Journal of Child Psychology and Psychiatry — J Child Psychol
Journal of Child Psychology and Psychiatry — J Child Psychol Psychiat
Journal of Child Psychology and Psychiatry and Allied Disciplines [*Later, Journal of Child Psychology and Psychiatry*] — J Child Psychol & Psych
Journal of Child Psychology and Psychiatry and Allied Disciplines [*Later, Journal of Child Psychology and Psychiatry*] — J Child Psychol Psychiatry
Journal of Child Psychology and Psychiatry and Allied Disciplines [*Later, Journal of Child Psychology and Psychiatry*] — J Child Psychol Psychiatry Allied Discipl
Journal of Child Psychology and Psychiatry and Allied Disciplines [*Later, Journal of Child Psychology and Psychiatry*] — JPPDA
Journal of Child Psychology and Psychiatry. Book Supplement — J Child Psychol Psychiatry Book Suppl
Journal of Child Psychotherapy — J Child Psychotherapy
Journal of Children in Contemporary Society — J Child Contemp Soc
Journal of China University of Geosciences (Chinese Edition) — J China Univ Geosci Chin Ed
Journal of China University of Science and Technology — J China Univ Sci Tech
Journal of Chinese and American Engineers — J Chin Amer Engin
Journal of Chinese Linguistics — J Chin Ling
Journal of Chinese Linguistics — J Chinese Ling
Journal of Chinese Linguistics — JChinL
Journal of Chinese Pharmaceutical Sciences — J Chin Pharm Sci
Journal of Chinese Philosophy — J Chin Phil
Journal of Chinese Philosophy — J Chin Philo
Journal of Chinese Philosophy — JChinP
Journal of Chiropractic — J Chiro
Journal of Christian Camping — JCC
Journal of Christian Education — J Chr Ed
Journal of Christian Education — J Christ Educ
Journal of Christian Education — J Christian Ed
Journal of Christian Education — J Christian Educ
Journal of Christian Education — JCE
Journal of Christian Jurisprudence — J Christ Juris
Journal of Christian Jurisprudence — J Christian Juris
Journal of Christian Nursing — J Christ Nurs
Journal of Christian Nursing — J Christ Nurse
Journal of Christian Philosophy — J Chr Philos
Journal of Christian Reconstruction — JCR
Journal of Chromatographic Science — J Chrom Sci
Journal of Chromatographic Science — J Chromat Sci
Journal of Chromatographic Science — J Chromatogr Sci
Journal of Chromatography — J Chromat

Journal of Chromatography — J Chromatogr
Journal of Chromatography. A — J Chromatogr A
Journal of Chromatography. B. Biomedical Applications — J Chromatogr B Biomed Appl
Journal of Chromatography. Biomedical Applications — J Chromat Biomed Appl
Journal of Chromatography. Biomedical Applications — J Chromatogr Biomed Appl
Journal of Chromatography. Chromatographic Reviews — J Chromat Chromat Rev
Journal of Chromatography. Supplementary Volume — J Chromatogr Suppl Vol
Journal of Chronic Diseases — J Chron Dis
Journal of Chronic Diseases — J Chronic Dis
Journal of Church and State — J C St
Journal of Church and State — J Ch S
Journal of Church and State — J Ch St
Journal of Church and State — J Church & State
Journal of Church and State — J Church St
Journal of Church and State — J Church State
Journal of Church and State — JCS
Journal of Church and State — JoC
Journal of Church and State — Jour Church and State
Journal of Church and State — PJCH
Journal of Church Music — J Church M
Journal of Church Music — J Church Mus
Journal of Church Music — JC
Journal of Church Music — JChM
Journal of Church Music — JCM
Journal of Circuits, Systems, and Computers — J Circuits Systems Comput
Journal of Civil and Hydraulic Engineering (Taipei) — J Civ Hydraul Eng (Taipei)
Journal of Civil Defense — J Civ D
Journal of Civil Engineering Design [*United States*] — J Civ Eng Des
Journal of Civil Engineering (Taipei) — J Civ Eng (Taipei)
Journal of Classical and Sacred Philology — JCSP
Journal of Classical Studies [*Kyoto University*] — JCS
Journal of Classical Studies. Classical Society of Japan — JCIS
Journal of Classification — Classif
Journal of Classification — J Classif
Journal of Classification — J Classification
Journal of Clean Technology and Environmental Sciences — J Clean Technol Environ Sci
Journal of Clean Technology, Environmental Toxicology, and Occupational Medicine — J Clean Technol Environ Toxicol Occup Med
Journal of Climate — J Clim
Journal of Climate and Applied Meteorology — J Clim and Appl Meteorol
Journal of Climate and Applied Meteorology — J Clim App Meteorol
Journal of Climatology — J Climatol
Journal of Clinical and Experimental Gerontology — J Clin Exp Gerontol
Journal of Clinical and Experimental Gerontology — JCEG
Journal of Clinical and Experimental Hypnosis — J Clin Exp Hypn
Journal of Clinical and Experimental Medicine — J Clin Exp Med
Journal of Clinical and Experimental Medicine (Tokyo) — J Clin Exp Med (Tokyo)
Journal of Clinical and Experimental Neuropsychology — J Clin Exp Neuropsychol
Journal of Clinical and Experimental Psychopathology — J Clin Exp Psychopathol
Journal of Clinical and Experimental Psychopathology and Quarterly Review of Psychiatry and Neurology — J Clin Exp Psychopathol Q Rev Psychiatry Neurol
Journal of Clinical and Hospital Pharmacy — J Clin Hosp Pharm
Journal of Clinical and Laboratory Immunology — J Clin Lab Immunol
Journal of Clinical Anesthesia — J Clin Anesth
Journal of Clinical Apheresis — J Clin Apheresis
Journal of Clinical Biochemistry and Nutrition — J Clin Biochem Nutr
Journal of Clinical Chemistry and Clinical Biochemistry — J Clin Chem Clin Biochem
Journal of Clinical Chemistry and Clinical Biochemistry — JCCBD
Journal of Clinical Child Psychology — ICCP
Journal of Clinical Child Psychology — J Clin Chil
Journal of Clinical Child Psychology — J Clin Child Psychol
Journal of Clinical Computing — J Clin Comput
Journal of Clinical Dentistry — J Clin Dent
Journal of Clinical Dermatology [*Japan*] — J Clin Dermatol
Journal of Clinical Dysmorphology — J Clin Dysmorphol
Journal of Clinical Electron Microscopy — J Clin Electron Microsc
Journal of Clinical Endocrinology — J Clin Endocr
Journal of Clinical Endocrinology — J Clin Endocrinol
Journal of Clinical Endocrinology and Metabolism — J Clin Endocrinol
Journal of Clinical Endocrinology and Metabolism — J Clin Endocrinol Metab
Journal of Clinical Endocrinology and Metabolism — JCEM
Journal of Clinical Engineering — J Clin Eng
Journal of Clinical Engineering — JCEND
Journal of Clinical Epidemiology — J Clin Epidemiol
Journal of Clinical Ethics — J Clin Ethics
Journal of Clinical Gastroenterology — J Clin Gast
Journal of Clinical Gastroenterology — J Clin Gastroenterol
Journal of Clinical Hematology and Oncology — J Clin Hematol Oncol
Journal of Clinical Hematology and Oncology — JCHOD
Journal of Clinical Hypertension — J Clin Hypertens
Journal of Clinical Immunoassay — J Clin Immunoassay
Journal of Clinical Immunology — J Clin Immunol
Journal of Clinical Immunology — JCIMD
Journal of Clinical Investigation — J Clin Inv
Journal of Clinical Investigation — J Clin Invest
Journal of Clinical Laboratory Analysis — J Clin Lab Anal
Journal of Clinical Laboratory Automation — J Clin Lab Autom
Journal of Clinical Laboratory Work (Peking) — J Clin Lab Work (Peking)
Journal of Clinical Medicine — J Clin Med
Journal of Clinical Microbiology — J Clin Micr
Journal of Clinical Microbiology — J Clin Microbiol
Journal of Clinical Microbiology — JCMID
Journal of Clinical Monitoring — J Clin Monit
Journal of Clinical Neuro-Ophthalmology — J Clin Neuro-Ophthalmol
Journal of Clinical Neuro-Ophthalmology — JCNOD
Journal of Clinical Neurophysiology — J Clin Neurophysiol
Journal of Clinical Neuropsychology — J Clin Neuropsychol
Journal of Clinical Nutrition — J Clin Nutr
Journal of Clinical Nutrition and Gastroenterology — J Clin Nutr Gastroenterol
Journal of Clinical Nutrition (Tokyo) — J Clin Nutr (Tokyo)
Journal of Clinical Oncology — J Clin Oncol
Journal of Clinical Ophthalmology — Journ Clin Ophthal
Journal of Clinical Orthodontics — J Clin Orthod
Journal of Clinical Pathology [*London*] — J Clin Path
Journal of Clinical Pathology — J Clin Pathol
Journal of Clinical Pathology — Journ Clin Path
Journal of Clinical Pathology. Clinical Molecular Pathology — J Clin Pathol Clin Mol Pathol
Journal of Clinical Pathology (London) — J Clin Pathol (Lond)
Journal of Clinical Pathology (Supplement) — J Clin Pathol (Suppl)
Journal of Clinical Pathology. Supplement. Royal College of Pathologists — J Clin Pathol Suppl R Coll Pathol
Journal of Clinical Pediatrics (Sapporo) — J Clin Pediatr (Sapporo)
Journal of Clinical Periodontology — J Clin Periodontol
Journal of Clinical Pharmacology — J Clin Phar
Journal of Clinical Pharmacology — J Clin Pharmacol
Journal of Clinical Pharmacology and the Journal of New Drugs — J Clin Pharmacol
Journal of Clinical Pharmacology and the Journal of New Drugs — J Clin Pharmacol J New Drugs
Journal of Clinical Pharmacology and the Journal of New Drugs — J Clin Pharmacol New Drugs
Journal of Clinical Pharmacy — J Clin Pharm
Journal of Clinical Pharmacy and Therapeutics — J Clin Pharm Ther
Journal of Clinical Psychiatry — J Clin Psychiatry
Journal of Clinical Psychology — ICPS
Journal of Clinical Psychology — J Clin Psyc
Journal of Clinical Psychology — J Clin Psychol
Journal of Clinical Psychology — JCP
Journal of Clinical Psychology — JCPs
Journal of Clinical Psychology — JCPYA
Journal of Clinical Psychology — Journ Clin Psychol
Journal of Clinical Psychopharmacology — J Clin Psychopharmacol
Journal of Clinical Science — J Clin Sci
Journal of Clinical Stomatology Conferences — J Clin Stomatol Conf
Journal of Clinical Surgery — J Clin Surg
Journal of Clinical Ultrasound [*United States*] — J Clin Ultrasound
Journal of Clinical Ultrasound — JCLTB
Journal of Clinical Ultrasound — JCU
Journal of Coal Quality — J Coal Qual
Journal of Coastal Research — Coastal Res
Journal of Coastal Research — J Coastal Res
Journal of Coated Fabrics — J Coated Fabr
Journal of Coated Fabrics — J Coated Fabrics
Journal of Coated Fibrous Materials — J Coated Fibrous Mater
Journal of Coatings Technology — J Coat Technol
Journal of Coatings Technology — J Coatings Technol
Journal of Coatings Technology — JCTED
Journal of Coatings Technology — JOT
Journal of Coatings Technology — Jrl Coatng
Journal of Coconut Industries — J Coconut Ind
Journal of Coconut Industries — J Coconut Industr
Journal of Coffee Research — J Coffee Res
Journal of Coffee Research — JCFRB
Journal of Collective Negotiations in the Public Sector — J Col Negot
Journal of Collective Negotiations in the Public Sector — J Collect Negotiations Public Sect
Journal of Collective Negotiations in the Public Sector — JCN
Journal of Collective Negotiations in the Public Sector — JCNPS
Journal of Collective Negotiations in the Public Sector — JPS
Journal of College and University Law — J Coll and U L
Journal of College and University Law — J Coll & Univ L
Journal of College and University Law — JC and UL
Journal of College Placement — J Col Placement
Journal of College Placement — J Coll Placement
Journal of College Placement — J College Place
Journal of College Science Teaching — J Coll Sci Teach
Journal of College Student Personnel — J Col Stud Personnel
Journal of College Student Personnel — J Coll Stud
Journal of College Student Personnel — J Coll Stud Personnel
Journal of College Student Personnel — J Coll Student Personnel
Journal of Colloid and Interface Science — J Coll I Sc
Journal of Colloid and Interface Science — J Colloid and Interface Sci
Journal of Colloid and Interface Science — J Colloid Interface Sci
Journal of Colloid and Interface Science — J Colloid Interface Science
Journal of Colloid Science [*Later, Journal of Colloid and Interface Science*] — J Colloid Sci
Journal of Colloid Science [*Later, Journal of Colloid and Interface Science*] — JCSCA
Journal of Colloid Science. Supplement — J Colloid Sci Suppl
Journal of Color and Appearance — J Color

Journal of Color and Appearance — J Color Appearance
Journal of Color and Appearance — JCA
Journal of Combinatorial Designs — J Combin Des
Journal of Combinatorial Mathematics and Combinatorial Computing — J Combin Math Combin Comput
Journal of Combinatorial Theory — J Comb Theory
Journal of Combinatorial Theory. Series A — J Comb Th A
Journal of Combinatorial Theory. Series A — J Comb Theory Ser A
Journal of Combinatorial Theory. Series A — J Combin Theory Ser A
Journal of Combinatorial Theory. Series A — J Combinatorial Theory Ser A
Journal of Combinatorial Theory. Series B — J Comb Th B
Journal of Combinatorial Theory. Series B — J Comb Theory Ser B
Journal of Combinatorial Theory. Series B — J Combin Theory Ser B
Journal of Combinatorial Theory. Series B — J Combinatorial Theory Ser B
Journal of Combinatorics, Information, and System Sciences [*Delhi*] — J Combin Inform System Sci
Journal of Combinatorics, Information, and System Sciences — J Combinatorics Information Syst Sci
Journal of Combustion Science and Technology — J Combust Sci Technol
Journal of Combustion Toxicology — J Combust Toxic
Journal of Combustion Toxicology — J Combust Toxicol
Journal of Combustion Toxicology — J Combustion Toxicol
Journal of Combustion Toxicology — JCTOD
Journal of Commerce — J Commer
Journal of Commerce — Jnl Com
Journal of Commerce — Jrl Comm
Journal of Commerce. European Edition — JCG
Journal of Commerce Import Bulletin — Jnl Com Import Bul
Journal of Commercial Bank Lending — CBL
Journal of Commercial Bank Lending — J Comm Bank Lending
Journal of Commercial Bank Lending — J Commer Bank Lending
Journal of Commercial Bank Lending — JCB
Journal of Common Market Studies — J Com Mkt S
Journal of Common Market Studies — J Comm Market Studs
Journal of Common Market Studies — J Comm Mkt Stud
Journal of Common Market Studies — J Common Mark Stud
Journal of Common Market Studies — J Common Market Stud
Journal of Common Market Studies — J Common Market Studies
Journal of Common Market Studies — J Common Mkt Stud
Journal of Common Market Studies — JCS
Journal of Common Market Studies — JCT
Journal of Commonwealth and Comparative Politics — J Commonw Comp Pol
Journal of Commonwealth and Comparative Politics — J Commonw Comp Polit
Journal of Commonwealth and Comparative Politics — J Commonwealth Comp Polit
Journal of Commonwealth and Comparative Politics — JCCP
Journal of Commonwealth and Comparative Politics. University of London. Institute of Commonwealth Studies — ICS/JCCP
Journal of Commonwealth Literature — J Commonw Lit
Journal of Commonwealth Literature — J Commonwealth Lit
Journal of Commonwealth Literature — JCL
Journal of Commonwealth Literature — JComLit
Journal of Commonwealth Literature — PJCL
Journal of Commonwealth Political Studies — J Comm Pol Studs
Journal of Commonwealth Political Studies — J Commonw Polit Stud
Journal of Commonwealth Political Studies — JCPS
Journal of Communicable Diseases — J Commun Dis
Journal of Communication — GJOC
Journal of Communication — J Comm
Journal of Communication — J Commun
Journal of Communication — J Communication
Journal of Communication — JC
Journal of Communication — JCMNA
Journal of Communication — JCP
Journal of Communication — Jl Commun
Journal of Communication — JOC
Journal of Communication Disorders — J Comm Dis
Journal of Communication Disorders — J Commun Disord
Journal of Communication Disorders — JCDIA
Journal of Communication Management — JOC
Journal of Community Action — J Community Action
Journal of Community Communications — Com Com
Journal of Community Education — J Community Educ
Journal of Community Health — GCOH
Journal of Community Health — J Commun Health
Journal of Community Health — J Community Health
Journal of Community Health — JOCH
Journal of Community Health Nursing — J Community Health Nurs
Journal of Community Psychology — J Community Psychol
Journal of Community Psychology — JCPSD
Journal of Comparative Administration — J Comp Adm
Journal of Comparative and Physiological Psychology [*1947-1982*] — J Com Physl
Journal of Comparative and Physiological Psychology [*1947-1982*] — J Comp & Physiol Psychol
Journal of Comparative and Physiological Psychology [*1947-1982*] — J Comp Physiol Psychol
Journal of Comparative and Physiological Psychology [*1947-1982*] — JCPP
Journal of Comparative and Physiological Psychology [*1947-1982*] — JCPPA
Journal of Comparative Business and Capital Market Law — JCW
Journal of Comparative Corporate Law and Securities Regulation — J Comp Corp L and Sec
Journal of Comparative Corporate Law and Securities Regulation — J Comp Corp L and Sec Reg
Journal of Comparative Economics — J Comp Econ
Journal of Comparative Economics — J Comparative Econ
Journal of Comparative Economics — JCE
Journal of Comparative Economics — PJCE
Journal of Comparative Ethology — J Comp Ethol
Journal of Comparative Family Studies — J Comp Fam Stud
Journal of Comparative Family Studies — J Comp Family Stud
Journal of Comparative Family Studies — JCFS
Journal of Comparative Family Studies — PCFS
Journal of Comparative Legislation and International Law — J Comp Leg & Int Law
Journal of Comparative Legislation and International Law — J Comp Legis
Journal of Comparative Legislation and International Law — J Comp Legis Int Law
Journal of Comparative Legislation and International Law — JCL & IL
Journal of Comparative Legislation and International Law and the Review of Legislation — JCL
Journal of Comparative Literature and Aesthetics — JCLA
Journal of Comparative Medicine and Surgery — J Comp Med Surg
Journal of Comparative Medicine and Veterinary Archives — J Comp Med and Vet Arch
Journal of Comparative Neurology — J Comp Neur
Journal of Comparative Neurology — J Comp Neurol
Journal of Comparative Neurology — JCNEA
Journal of Comparative Neurology and Psychology — J Comp Neurol Psychol
Journal of Comparative Pathology — J Comp Path
Journal of Comparative Pathology — J Comp Pathol
Journal of Comparative Pathology and Therapeutics — J Comp Path and Therap
Journal of Comparative Pathology and Therapeutics — J Comp Pathol Ther
Journal of Comparative Physical Education and Sport — J Compar PE & Sport
Journal of Comparative Physiology — J Comp Phys
Journal of Comparative Physiology — J Comp Physiol
Journal of Comparative Physiology. A. Sensory, Neural, and Behavioral Physiology — J Comp Physiol A
Journal of Comparative Physiology. A. Sensory, Neural, and Behavioral Physiology — J Comp Physiol A Sens Neural Behav Physiol
Journal of Comparative Physiology. B. Biochemical, Systemic, and Environmental Physiology — J Comp Physiol B
Journal of Comparative Physiology. B. Biochemical, Systemic, and Environmental Physiology — J Comp Physiol B Biochem Syst Environ Physiol
Journal of Comparative Physiology. B. Metabolic and Transport Functions — J Comp Physiol B Metab Transp Funct
Journal of Comparative Psychology — J Comp Psychol
Journal of Comparative Psychology — JCP
Journal of Comparative Psychology — PJCP
Journal of Compliance in Health Care — J Compliance Health Care
Journal of Composite Materials — J Compos Ma
Journal of Composite Materials — J Compos Mater
Journal of Composite Materials — J Composite Mat
Journal of Composites Technology and Research — J Compos Technol Res
Journal of Computational Acoustics — J Comput Acoust
Journal of Computational and Applied Mathematics — J Comput Appl Math
Journal of Computational and Graphical Statistics — J Comput Graph Statist
Journal of Computational Biology — J Comput Biol
Journal of Computational Chemistry — J Comput Chem
Journal of Computational Chemistry — JCC
Journal of Computational Mathematics — J Comput Math
Journal of Computational Neuroscience — J Comput Neurosci
Journal of Computational Physics — J Comput Ph
Journal of Computational Physics — J Comput Phys
Journal of Computational Physics — J Computational Phys
Journal of Computed Tomography — CT
Journal of Computed Tomography — J Comput Tomogr
Journal of Computer and System Sciences — J Comput and Syst Sci
Journal of Computer and System Sciences — J Comput Sy
Journal of Computer and System Sciences — J Comput Syst Sci
Journal of Computer and System Sciences — J Comput System Sci
Journal of Computer and System Sciences — JCSS
Journal of Computer and Systems Sciences International — J Comput Systems Sci Internat
Journal of Computer Science and Technology (English Edition) — J Comput Sci Tech English Ed
Journal of Computer-Aided Molecular Design — J Comput Aided Mol Des
Journal of Computer-Assisted Tomography — J Comput Assist Tomogr
Journal of Computer-Assisted Tomography — J Comput Assisted Tomogr
Journal of Computer-Assisted Tomography — JCATD
Journal of Computer-Based Instruction — J Comput Based Instr
Journal of Computers in Mathematics and Science Teaching — J Comput Math and Sci Teach
Journal of Computing and Information — J Comput Inform
Journal of Computing in Higher Education — JCHE
Journal of Conchology — J Conchol
Journal of Conchology — JC
Journal of Confict Resolution — PJCR
Journal of Conflict Resolution — J Conf Res
Journal of Conflict Resolution — J Confl Res
Journal of Conflict Resolution — J Conflict Resol
Journal of Conflict Resolution — J Conflict Resolu
Journal of Conflict Resolution — J Conflict Resolution
Journal of Conflict Resolution — JCfR
Journal of Conflict Resolution — JCR
Journal of Conflict Resolution — Jour Conflict Resolution
Journal of Constitutional and Parliamentary Studies — J Const Parl Stud
Journal of Constitutional and Parliamentary Studies [*India*] — JCPS
Journal of Constructional Steel Research — J Constr Steel Res

Journal of Consulting and Clinical Psychology — GCCP
Journal of Consulting and Clinical Psychology — J Cons Clin
Journal of Consulting and Clinical Psychology — J Consult & Clin Psychol
Journal of Consulting and Clinical Psychology — J Consult Clin Psychol
Journal of Consulting and Clinical Psychology — JCLPB
Journal of Consulting Psychology — J Consult Psychol
Journal of Consulting Psychology — J Consulting Psychol
Journal of Consulting Psychology — JCPHA
Journal of Consumer Affairs — J Con A
Journal of Consumer Affairs — J Cons Affairs
Journal of Consumer Affairs — J Consum Af
Journal of Consumer Affairs — J Consum Aff
Journal of Consumer Affairs — J Consumer Aff
Journal of Consumer Affairs — J Consumer Affairs
Journal of Consumer Affairs — JCA
Journal of Consumer Marketing — Jl Con Mkt
Journal of Consumer Policy — J Consum Policy
Journal of Consumer Policy — J Consumer Policy
Journal of Consumer Product Flammability — J Consum Prod Flamm
Journal of Consumer Product Flammability — J Consum Prod Flammability
Journal of Consumer Product Flammability — J Consumer Prod Flamm
Journal of Consumer Product Flammability — J Consumer Prod Flammability
Journal of Consumer Product Flammability — JCPFD
Journal of Consumer Research — J Consum Res
Journal of Consumer Research — J Consumer Res
Journal of Consumer Research — JCR
Journal of Consumer Research — Jl Consmr R
Journal of Consumer Studies and Home Economics — J Consum Stud Home Econ
Journal of Consumer Studies and Home Economics — J Consumer Studies and Home Econ
Journal of Contaminant Hydrology — J Contam Hydrol
Journal of Contemporary African Studies — J Contemp Afr Stud
Journal of Contemporary Asia — J Contemp
Journal of Contemporary Asia — J Contemp Asia
Journal of Contemporary Asia — JCA
Journal of Contemporary Asia — PJCA
Journal of Contemporary Business — BPT
Journal of Contemporary Business — J Cont Bus
Journal of Contemporary Business — J Contemp Bus
Journal of Contemporary Business — J Contemp Busin
Journal of Contemporary Business — J Contemporary Bus
Journal of Contemporary Business — JCB
Journal of Contemporary Business — Jl Cont B
Journal of Contemporary Ethnography — PJET
Journal of Contemporary Health Law and Policy — J Contemp Health Law Policy
Journal of Contemporary History — GJCH
Journal of Contemporary History — J Cont Hist
Journal of Contemporary History — J Contemp Hist
Journal of Contemporary History — J Contemporary Hist
Journal of Contemporary History — JCH
Journal of Contemporary History — JCHi
Journal of Contemporary History — JoCH
Journal of Contemporary History — Jour Contemp Hist
Journal of Contemporary Law — J Cont L
Journal of Contemporary Law — J Contemp L
Journal of Contemporary Mathematical Analysis — J Contemp Math Anal
Journal of Contemporary Psychotherapy — J Cont Psyt
Journal of Contemporary Puerto Rican Thought — JCPT
Journal of Contemporary Studies — J Contemp Stud
Journal of Contemporary Studies — J Contemporary Studies
Journal of Contemporary Studies — JCSTD
Journal of Continuing Education in Nursing — J Cont Ed Nurs
Journal of Continuing Education in Nursing — J Contin Educ Nurs
Journal of Continuing Education in Nursing — JCEN
Journal of Continuing Education in Obstetrics and Gynecology — J Contin Educ Obstet Gynecol
Journal of Continuing Education in Psychiatry — J Contin Educ Psychiatry
Journal of Contraception — J Contracept
Journal of Controlled Release — J Controlled Release
Journal of Convex Analysis — J Convex Anal
Journal of Cooperage Sciences and Techniques — J Cooperage Sci Tech
Journal of Cooperative Education — J Coop Educ
Journal of Coordination Chemistry — J Coord Ch
Journal of Coordination Chemistry — J Coord Chem
Journal of Coordination Chemistry — JCCMB
Journal of Corporate Taxation — J Corp Tax
Journal of Corporate Taxation — J Corporate Taxation
Journal of Corporate Taxation — JCT
Journal of Corporation Law — J Corp L
Journal of Corporation Law — J Corp Law
Journal of Corporation Law — J Corpn L
Journal of Corporation Law — JCL
Journal of Corrosion Science and Engineering [*Electronic Publication*] — J Corros Sci Eng Electronic Publication
Journal of Counseling and Development — J Counsel & Devt
Journal of Counseling and Development. JCD — GCND
Journal of Counseling Psychology — GCPS
Journal of Counseling Psychology — J Coun Psyc
Journal of Counseling Psychology — J Couns Psych
Journal of Counseling Psychology — J Counsel Ply
Journal of Counseling Psychology — J Counsel Psychol
Journal of Counseling Psychology — JCP
Journal of Counseling Psychology — JLCPA
Journal of Counseling Psychology — Jnl Counsel Psych
Journal of Country Music — J Country M
Journal of Country Music — J Country Mus
Journal of Country Music — J Ctry Mus
Journal of Country Music — JCM
Journal of Craniofacial Genetics and Developmental Biology — J Craniofac Genet Dev Biol
Journal of Craniofacial Genetics and Developmental Biology — J Craniofacial Genet Dev Biol
Journal of Craniofacial Genetics and Developmental Biology. Supplement — J Craniofac Genet Dev Biol Suppl
Journal of Craniofacial Genetics and Developmental Biology. Supplement — J Craniofacial Genet Dev Biol Suppl
Journal of Cranio-Mandibular Practice — J Craniomandibular Pract
Journal of Cranio-Mandibular Practice — Jnl Cranio Mandib Pract
Journal of Cranio-Maxillo-Facial Surgery — J Craniomaxillofac Surg
Journal of Creative Behavior — J Creat Beh
Journal of Creative Behavior — J Creative Behavior
Journal of Creative Behavior — JCB
Journal of Criminal Justice — J Crim Jus
Journal of Criminal Justice — J Crim Just
Journal of Criminal Justice — J Criminal Justice
Journal of Criminal Justice — PJCJ
Journal of Criminal Law — J Crim L
Journal of Criminal Law — JCL
Journal of Criminal Law and Criminology — J Crim L
Journal of Criminal Law and Criminology — J Crim L and Criminology
Journal of Criminal Law and Criminology — J Crim Law
Journal of Criminal Law and Criminology — J Crim Law & Criminol
Journal of Criminal Law and Criminology — J Criminal Law and Criminology
Journal of Criminal Law and Criminology — Jour Crim L
Journal of Criminal Law and Criminology — PCLC
Journal of Criminal Law, Criminology, and Police Science [*Later, Journal of Criminal Law and Criminology*] — J Crim Law Criminol Police Sci
Journal of Criminal Law, Criminology, and Police Science [*Later, Journal of Criminal Law and Criminology*] — J Crim LC & PS
Journal of Criminal Law, Criminology, and Police Science [*Later, Journal of Criminal Law and Criminology*] — JCLCPS
Journal of Criminal Law, Criminology, and Police Science [*Later, Journal of Criminal Law and Criminology*] — Jour Crim Law
Journal of Criminal Law (English) — J Crim L (Eng)
Journal of Critical Analysis — J Crit Anal
Journal of Critical Care — J Crit Care
Journal of Croatian Studies — J Croat Stud
Journal of Croatian Studies — J Croatian Studies
Journal of Croatian Studies — JCS
Journal of Cross-Cultural Psychology — J Cross-Cul
Journal of Cross-Cultural Psychology — J Cross-Cult Psych
Journal of Cross-Cultural Psychology — J Cross-Cult Psychol
Journal of Cross-Cultural Psychology — JCCP
Journal of Cross-Cultural Psychology — JCPGB
Journal of Crustacean Biology — J Crust Biol
Journal of Crustacean Biology — J Crustacean Biol
Journal of Crustacean Biology — Jnl Crustacean Biol
Journal of Cryosurgery — J Cryosurg
Journal of Cryptology — J Cryptology
Journal of Crystal and Molecular Structure — J Cryst and Mol Struct
Journal of Crystal and Molecular Structure — J Cryst Mol
Journal of Crystal and Molecular Structure — J Cryst Mol Struct
Journal of Crystal and Molecular Structure — JCMS
Journal of Crystal Growth — J Cryst Gr
Journal of Crystal Growth — J Cryst Growth
Journal of Crystallographic and Spectroscopal Research — J Crystallogr and Spectrosc Res
Journal of Cuneiform Studies — J Cun S
Journal of Cuneiform Studies — J Cun St
Journal of Cuneiform Studies — J Cuneiform St
Journal of Cuneiform Studies — J Cuneiform Stud
Journal of Cuneiform Studies — JCS
Journal of Current Biosciences — J Curr Biosci
Journal of Current Laser Abstracts — J Curr Laser Abstr
Journal of Current Social Issues — J Cur Soc Issues
Journal of Current Social Issues [*United States*] — J Curr Soc Issues
Journal of Current Social Issues — J Current Social Issues
Journal of Current Social Issues — JSISD
Journal of Curriculum Studies — J Curr Stud
Journal of Curriculum Studies — J Curric St
Journal of Curriculum Studies — JCS
Journal of Cutaneous and Veneral Diseases — J Cutan Veneral Dis
Journal of Cutaneous Diseases including Syphilis — J Cutan Dis
Journal of Cutaneous Pathology — J Cut Path
Journal of Cutaneous Pathology — J Cutan Pathol
Journal of Cutaneous Pathology — J Cutaneous Pathol
Journal of Cybernetics — J Cyb
Journal of Cybernetics — J Cybern
Journal of Cybernetics — J Cybernet
Journal of Cybernetics and Information Science — J Cybern and Inf Sci
Journal of Cybernetics and Information Science — J Cybern Inf Sci
Journal of Cycle Research — J Cycle Res
Journal of Cyclic Nucleotide and Protein Phosphorylation Research — J Cyclic Nucleotide Protein Phosphor Res
Journal of Cyclic Nucleotide and Protein Phosphorylation Research — J Cyclic Nucleotide Protein Phosphorylation Res
Journal of Cyclic Nucleotide Research — J Cycl Nucl
Journal of Cyclic Nucleotide Research — J Cyclic Nucleotide Res
Journal of Cyclic Nucleotide Research — JCNRD

Journal of Cytology and Genetics — J Cytol Genet
Journal of Dairy Research — J Dairy Res
Journal of Dairy Science — J Dairy Sci
Journal of Dalian Institute of Technology — J Dalian Inst Tech
Journal of Dalian University of Technology — J Dalian Univ Tech
Journal of Data Education — J Data Ed
Journal of Data Management — J Data Manage
Journal of Data Management — J Data Mgt
Journal of Data Management — JDM
Journal of Defense and Diplomacy — Jrl Def & D
Journal of Defense Research — JDR
Journal of Delinquency — J Delinq
Journal of Dendrology — J Dendrol
Journal of Dental Education — J Dent Educ
Journal of Dental Engineering — DE
Journal of Dental Engineering — J Dent Eng
Journal of Dental Health — J Dent Health
Journal of Dental Health (Tokyo) — J Dent Health (Tokyo)
Journal of Dental Medicine — J Dent Med
Journal of Dental Practice Administration — J Dent Pract Adm
Journal of Dental Research — J Dent Res
Journal of Dental Technics — J Dent Tech
Journal of Dental Technology — J Dent Technol
Journal of Dentistry — J Dent
Journal of Dentistry for Children — J Dent Chil
Journal of Dentistry for Children — J Dent Child
Journal of Dentistry for Children — JDCHA
Journal of Dentistry for Children — JODC
Journal of Dentistry for the Handicapped — J Dent Handicap
Journal of Dermatologic Surgery — J Dermatol Surg
Journal of Dermatologic Surgery and Oncology — J Dermatol Surg Oncol
Journal of Dermatological Science — J Dermatol Sci
Journal of Dermatology — J Dermatol
Journal of Dermatology (Tokyo) — J Dermatol (Tokyo)
Journal of Design Automation and Fault-Tolerant Computing — J Des Autom and Fault-Tolerant Comput
Journal of Design Automation and Fault-Tolerant Computing — J Des Autom Fault Tolerant Comput
Journal of Design Automation and Fault-Tolerant Computing — J Design Automat Fault-Tolerant Comput
Journal of Detergents — J Deterg
Journal of Detergents and Collective Chemistry — J Deterg Collect Chem
Journal of Deuterium Science — J Deuterium Sci
Journal of Developing Areas — J Dev Areas
Journal of Developing Areas — J Devel Areas
Journal of Developing Areas — J Develop Areas
Journal of Developing Areas — J Developing Areas
Journal of Developing Areas — JDA
Journal of Developing Areas — JDD
Journal of Developing Areas — JoD
Journal of Development — JOD
Journal of Development Economics — J Dev Econ
Journal of Development Economics — J Devel Econ
Journal of Development Economics — J Develop Econ
Journal of Development Economics — J Development Econ
Journal of Development Economics — JDE
Journal of Development Planning — J Dev Planning
Journal of Development Planning — J Develop Plan
Journal of Development Planning — J Development Planning
Journal of Development Studies — J Dev Stud
Journal of Development Studies — J Dev Studies
Journal of Development Studies — J Devel Stud
Journal of Development Studies — J Develop Stud
Journal of Development Studies — J Development Studies
Journal of Development Studies — J Development Studs
Journal of Development Studies — JDP
Journal of Development Studies — JDS
Journal of Developmental and Behavioral Pediatrics — J Dev Behav Pediatr
Journal of Developmental and Behavioral Pediatrics — JDBP
Journal of Developmental Areas — Jour Devel Areas
Journal of Developmental Biology — J Dev Biol
Journal of Developmental Physiology — J Dev Physiol
Journal of Developmental Physiology (Oxford) — J Dev Physiol (Oxf)
Journal of Developmental Reading — J Develop Read
Journal of Dharma — J Dharma
Journal of Diabetes and Its Complications — J Diabetes Complications
Journal of Diabetic Complications — J Diabet Complications
Journal of Dialysis — J Dial
Journal of Dialysis — JDIAD
Journal of Diarrhoeal Diseases Research — J Diarrhoeal Dis Res
Journal of Dietetics and Home Economics [*South Africa*] — J Diet Home Econ
Journal of Dietetics and Home Economics — Jnl Diet Home Ec
Journal of Difference Equations and Applications — J Differ Equations Appl
Journal of Differential Equations — J Diff Equa
Journal of Differential Equations — J Differ Equations
Journal of Differential Equations — J Differential Equations
Journal of Differential Geometry — J Differential Geom
Journal of Differential Geometry — J Differential Geometry
Journal of Digital Imaging — J Digit Imaging
Journal of Digital Systems — J Digital Syst
Journal of Digital Systems — J Digital Systems
Journal of Dispersion Science and Technology — J Dispersion Sci Technol
Journal of Distribution [*Japan*] — J Distrib
Journal of Diverse Unsung Miracle Plants for Healthy Evolution among People — DUMP HEAP
Journal of Divorce — J Divorce
Journal of Divorce — JODV
Journal of Documentary Reproduction — J Doc Reprod
Journal of Documentation — J Doc
Journal of Documentation — J Docum
Journal of Documentation — J Document
Journal of Documentation — J Documentation
Journal of Documentation — JD
Journal of Documentation [*London*] — JOD
Journal of Domestic Wastewater Treatment Research — J Domest Wastewater Treat Res
Journal of Drug Development — J Drug Dev
Journal of Drug Development and Clinical Practice — J Drug Dev Clin Pract
Journal of Drug Education — DE
Journal of Drug Education — J Drug Educ
Journal of Drug Education — JODE
Journal of Drug Issues — GJDI
Journal of Drug Issues — J Drug Iss
Journal of Drug Issues — J Drug Issues
Journal of Drug Issues — JODI
Journal of Drug Research (Cairo) — J Drug Res (Cairo)
Journal of Drug Research. JDR — J Drug Res JDR
Journal of Drug Targeting — J Drug Target
Journal of Dynamic Systems, Measurement, and Control — J Dyn Syst Meas Control
Journal of Dynamical and Control Systems — J Dynam Control Systems
Journal of Dynamics and Differential Equations — J Dynam Differential Equations
Journal of Early Adolescence — J Early Adolescence
Journal of Earth Sciences — J Earth Sci
Journal of Earth Sciences (Dublin) — J Earth Sci (Dublin)
Journal of Earth Sciences (Leeds, England) — J Earth Sci (Leeds Engl)
Journal of Earth Sciences. Nagoya University — J Earth Sci Nagoya Univ
Journal of Earth Sciences. Royal Dublin Society — J Earth Sci R Dublin Soc
Journal of Earth Sciences. Royal Dublin Society — Jnl Earth Sci R Dublin Soc
Journal of East and West Studies — J East West Stud
Journal of East Asian Affairs — J East Asian Affairs
Journal of East Asiatic Studies — JEAS
Journal of East Asiatic Studies — Jl E Asiat Stud
Journal of East China Institute of Metallurgy — J East China Inst Metall
Journal of East China Normal University. Natural Science — J East China Norm Univ Nat Sci
Journal of East China Normal University. Natural Science Edition — J East China Norm Univ Natur Sci Ed
Journal of Eastern African Research and Development — J East Afr Res Dev
Journal of Eastern African Research and Development — J East Afr Res Develop
Journal of Eastern Asia — J E Asia
Journal of Ecclesiastical History — J Eccl H
Journal of Ecclesiastical History — J Eccl Hist
Journal of Ecclesiastical History — J Eccles Hist
Journal of Ecclesiastical History — J Ecclesiast Hist
Journal of Ecclesiastical History — JEcH
Journal of Ecclesiastical History — JEH
Journal of Ecclesiastical History — JoE
Journal of Ecclesiastical History — Jour Eccl Hist
Journal of Ecclesiastical History — PECC
Journal of Ecology — J Ecol
Journal of Ecology — J Ecology
Journal of Ecology — Jour Ecology
Journal of Ecology — PJEC
Journal of Econometrics — J Econom
Journal of Econometrics — J Economet
Journal of Econometrics — J Econometrics
Journal of Econometrics — JEC
Journal of Econometrics — JECMB
Journal of Econometrics — JRE
Journal of Economic Abstracts — J Econ Abstr
Journal of Economic Affairs — J Econ Aff
Journal of Economic and Business History — J Econ Bus Hist
Journal of Economic and Business History — JEBH
Journal of Economic and Business History — Jour Econ and Bus Hist
Journal of Economic and Social Measurement — J Econ Soc Meas
Journal of Economic and Taxonomic Botany — J Econ Taxon Bot
Journal of Economic Behavior — JEB
Journal of Economic Behavior and Organization — J Econom Behavior Organization
Journal of Economic Behavior and Organization — JBO
Journal of Economic Biology — J Econ Biol
Journal of Economic Dynamics and Control — J Econ Dyn and Control
Journal of Economic Dynamics and Control — J Econ Dynam Control
Journal of Economic Dynamics and Control — J Econom Dynamics Control
Journal of Economic Dynamics and Control — JED
Journal of Economic Education — J Econ Ed
Journal of Economic Education — J Econ Educ
Journal of Economic Entomology — J Ec Ent
Journal of Economic Entomology — J Econ Ent
Journal of Economic Entomology — J Econ Entom
Journal of Economic Entomology — J Econ Entomol
Journal of Economic History — J Econ H
Journal of Economic History — J Econ Hist
Journal of Economic History — JEH
Journal of Economic History — Jnl Econ Hist
Journal of Economic History — JoEH
Journal of Economic History — Jour Econ Hist

Journal of Economic History — PEHI
Journal of Economic History. Supplement — J Econ Hist S
Journal of Economic History/Supplement — JEH/S
Journal of Economic Issues — J Econ Iss
Journal of Economic Issues — JEI
Journal of Economic Literature [*Information service or system*] — J Econ Liter
Journal of Economic Literature [*Information service or system*] — JEB
Journal of Economic Literature [*Information service or system*] — JEconLit
Journal of Economic Literature [*Information service or system*] — JEL
Journal of Economic Psychology — JEP
Journal of Economic Studies — J Econ Studies
Journal of Economic Studies — JES
Journal of Economic Theory — J Econ Theo
Journal of Economic Theory — J Econ Theory
Journal of Economic Theory — J Econom Theory
Journal of Economic Theory — JET
Journal of Economics and Business — J Econ and Bus
Journal of Economics and Business — J Econ Bus
Journal of Economics and Business — JEB
Journal of Economics and Sociology — JES
Journal of Economics Issues — J Econ Issues
Journal of Ecoonomic Research — J Econ Res
Journal of Ecumenical Studies — J Ec St
Journal of Ecumenical Studies — J Ecum Stud
Journal of Ecumenical Studies — J Ecumen Stud
Journal of Ecumenical Studies — J Ecumenical Stud
Journal of Ecumenical Studies — JES
Journal of Ecumenical Studies — PECM
Journal of Education — IJED
Journal of Education — J Ed
Journal of Education — J Educ
Journal of Education — JE
Journal of Education and Psychology — J Ed & Psychol
Journal of Education and Psychology — J Educ Psych
Journal of Education (Boston University School of Education) — JEB
Journal of Education. Department of Education (Nova Scotia) — J of Ed (NS)
Journal of Education. Faculty of Education. University of Natal — J Educ Univ Natal
Journal of Education Finance — J Educ Fin
Journal of Education for Librarianship — J Educ Libr
Journal of Education for Librarianship — J Educ Librarianship
Journal of Education for Library and Information Science — JELIS
Journal of Education for Social Work — J Educ Soc
Journal of Education for Social Work — J Educ Soc Work
Journal of Education for Teaching — J Educ for Teach
Journal of Education for Teaching — JOET
Journal of Education (London) — J Ed (London)
Journal of Education (London) — J Educ (Lond)
Journal of Education. University of Hong Kong — J Ed Univ HK
Journal of Educational Administration — J Ed Admin
Journal of Educational Administration — J Educ Adm
Journal of Educational Administration and History — J Ednl Admin and History
Journal of Educational Administration and History — J Educ Adm Hist
Journal of Educational Administration and History — J Educ Admin Hist
Journal of Educational Computing Research — EC
Journal of Educational Data Processing — J Ed Data Process
Journal of Educational Data Processing — J Educ D P
Journal of Educational Data Processing — J Educ Data Proc
Journal of Educational Measurement — J Ed M
Journal of Educational Measurement — J Educ M
Journal of Educational Media Science — J Educ Media Science
Journal of Educational Method — J Educ Method
Journal of Educational Modules for Materials Science and Engineering — J Educ Modules Mater Sci Eng
Journal of Educational Psychology — GESY
Journal of Educational Psychology — J Ed Psychol
Journal of Educational Psychology — J Educ Psyc
Journal of Educational Psychology — J Educ Psychol
Journal of Educational Psychology — JEP
Journal of Educational Psychology — JEPs
Journal of Educational Research — J Ed Res
Journal of Educational Research — J Educ Res
Journal of Educational Research — J Educ Research
Journal of Educational Research — JER
Journal of Educational Research — JOERA
Journal of Educational Sociology — J Ed Soc
Journal of Educational Sociology — J Educ Soc
Journal of Educational Sociology — J Educ Social
Journal of Educational Sociology — J Educ Sociol
Journal of Educational Statisics — J Ed Stat
Journal of Educational Technology — ET
Journal of Educational Technology — J Ednl Technology
Journal of Educational Technology Systems — J Educ Tech Syst
Journal of Educational Technology Systems — J Educ Technol Syst
Journal of Educational Thought — J Ed Thought
Journal of Educational Thought — J Educ Th
Journal of Egyptian Archaeology — J Eg Arch
Journal of Egyptian Archaeology — J Egypt Arch
Journal of Egyptian Archaeology — J Egypt Archaeol
Journal of Egyptian Archaeology — JE Arch
Journal of Egyptian Archaeology — JEA
Journal of Egyptian Archaeology — Journ Eg Arch
Journal of Egyptian Archaeology — Journ Egypt Arch
Journal of Egyptian Archaeology — Journ of Egypt Archaeol
Journal of Egyptian Archaeology — Journal of Eg Arch
Journal of Egyptian Pharmacy — J Egypt Pharm
Journal of Elasticity — J Elast
Journal of Elasticity — J Elasticity
Journal of Elastomers and Plastics — J Elastomers Plast
Journal of Elastomers and Plastics — JEPLA
Journal of Elastoplastics [*Later, Journal of Elastomers and Plastics*] — J Elastoplast
Journal of Electrical and Electronics Engineering (Australia) — J Electr Electron Eng (Aust)
Journal of Electrical Engineering — J Electr Eng
Journal of Electricity — J Elec
Journal of Electricity — J Electr
Journal of Electricity and Western Industry — J Electr West Ind
Journal of Electricity, Power, and Gas — J Electr Power Gas
Journal of Electroanalytical Chemistry [*Netherlands*] — J Electroanal Chem
Journal of Electroanalytical Chemistry. Abstract Section — J Electroanal Chem Abstr Sect
Journal of Electroanalytical Chemistry and Interfacial Electrochemistry — J Elec Chem
Journal of Electroanalytical Chemistry and Interfacial Electrochemistry — J Electroanal Chem Interfacial Electrochem
Journal of Electrocardiology [*San Diego*] — J Elcardiol
Journal of Electrocardiology — J Electrocardiol
Journal of Electrocardiology — JECAB
Journal of Electrocardiology (San Diego) — J Electrocardiol (San Diego)
Journal of Electromyography and Kinesiology — J Electromyo & Kines
Journal of Electron Microscopy — J Elec Micr
Journal of Electron Microscopy — J Electr Microsc
Journal of Electron Microscopy — J Electron Microsc
Journal of Electron Microscopy — J Electron Micry
Journal of Electron Microscopy Technique — J Electron Microsc Tech
Journal of Electron Microscopy (Tokyo) — J Electron Microsc (Tokyo)
Journal of Electron Spectroscopy and Related Phenomena — J Elec Spec
Journal of Electron Spectroscopy and Related Phenomena — J Elect Spectrosc
Journal of Electron Spectroscopy and Related Phenomena — J Electr Spectr
Journal of Electron Spectroscopy and Related Phenomena — J Electron Spectrosc and Relat Phenom
Journal of Electron Spectroscopy and Related Phenomena — J Electron Spectrosc Relat Phenom
Journal of Electronic Defense — J Elec Def
Journal of Electronic Engineering — J Elec E
Journal of Electronic Engineering — J Electron Eng
Journal of Electronic Materials — J Elec Mat
Journal of Electronic Materials — J Electron Mater
Journal of Electronic Materials — JECMA
Journal of Electronics — J Electron
Journal of Electronics and Control [*England*] — J Electron Control
Journal of Electronics (Beijing) — J Electron (Beijing)
Journal of Electronics Manufacturing — J Electron Manuf
Journal of Electrophysiological Techniques — J Electroph
Journal of Electrophysiology — Jnl Electrophysiol
Journal of Electrostatics — J Electrost
Journal of Electrostatics — J Electrostat
Journal of Embryology and Experimental Morphology — J Emb Exp M
Journal of Embryology and Experimental Morphology — J Embr Exp Morph
Journal of Embryology and Experimental Morphology — J Embryol Exp Morphol
Journal of Emergency Medical Services. JEMS — J Emerg Med Serv JEMS
Journal of Emergency Medicine — J Emerg Med
Journal of Emergency Nursing — J Emerg Nurs
Journal of Emergency Nursing — J Emergency Nurs
Journal of Emergency Nursing — JEN
Journal of Emergency Services — J Emerg Services
Journal of Emotional Education — JOEEA
Journal of Employment Counseling — J Empl Coun
Journal of Employment Counseling — J Employ Counsel
Journal of Employment Counseling — JEY
Journal of Endocrinological Investigation — J Endocrinol Invest
Journal of Endocrinological Investigation — JEIND
Journal of Endocrinology — J Endocr
Journal of Endocrinology — J Endocrinol
Journal of Endocrinology — JOENA
Journal of Endodontics — J Endod
Journal of Endodontics — J Endodont
Journal of Endourology — J Endourol
Journal of Endovascular Surgery — J Endovasc Surg
Journal of Energetic Materials — J Energ Mater
Journal of Energy — J Energy
Journal of Energy and Development — IEX
Journal of Energy and Development — J Energy and Development
Journal of Energy and Development — J Energy Dev
Journal of Energy and Development — J Energy Develop
Journal of Energy and Development — JENDD
Journal of Energy Engineering — EY
Journal of Energy Engineering — J Energy Eng
Journal of Energy Law and Policy — J Energy L & Pol'y
Journal of Energy Law and Policy — J Energy L P
Journal of Energy Law and Policy — J Energy Law and Policy
Journal of Energy Resources Technology — J Energy Resour Technol
Journal of Energy Resources Technology — J Energy Resources Technol
Journal of Energy Resources Technology. Transactions of the American Society of Mechanical Engineers — J Energy Resour Technol Trans ASME
Journal of Energy Resources Techology — JERTD
Journal of Engineering and Applied Sciences (Peshawar) — J Eng Appl Sci Peshawar
Journal of Engineering Education — J Eng Ed

Journal of Engineering Education — J Eng Educ
Journal of Engineering Education — JEE
Journal of Engineering for Gas Turbines and Power — J Eng Gas Turbines Power
Journal of Engineering for Industry — J Eng Ind
Journal of Engineering for Industry. Transactions of the American Society of Mechanical Engineers — J Eng Ind Tran ASME
Journal of Engineering for Industry. Transactions of the American Society of Mechanical Engineers — J Eng Ind Trans ASME
Journal of Engineering for Power — J Eng Power
Journal of Engineering for Power — Jrl Eng Pwr
Journal of Engineering for Power. Transactions of the American Society of Mechanical Engineers — J Eng Power Trans ASME
Journal of Engineering Materials and Technology — J Eng Mat & Tech
Journal of Engineering Materials and Technology — J Eng Mater
Journal of Engineering Materials and Technology — J Eng Mater Technol
Journal of Engineering Materials and Technology — J Eng Materials & Tech
Journal of Engineering Materials and Technology. Transactions of the American Society of Mechanical Engineers — J Eng Mater Technol Trans ASME
Journal of Engineering Mathematics — J Eng Math
Journal of Engineering Mathematics — J Engng Math
Journal of Engineering Mathematics — J Engrg Math
Journal of Engineering Mathematics — JLEMA
Journal of Engineering Mechanics — EM
Journal of Engineering Mechanics — J Eng Mech
Journal of Engineering. National Chung-hsing Univeristy — J Eng Natl Chung Hsing Univ
Journal of Engineering Physics — J Eng Phys
Journal of Engineering Physics — J Engn Phys
Journal of Engineering Physics — J Engrg Phys
Journal of Engineering Physics and Thermophysics — J Engrg Phys Thermophys
Journal of Engineering Physics (Belgrade) — J Eng Phys (Belgrade)
Journal of Engineering Physics (English Translation of Inzhenerno-Fizicheskii Zhurnal) [*Belorussian SSR*] — J Eng Phys (Engl Transl)
Journal of Engineering Physics (Minsk) — J Eng Phys (Minsk)
Journal of Engineering Psychology — J Eng Psychol
Journal of Engineering Science and Technology (Seoul) — J Eng Sci Technol Seoul
Journal of Engineering Sciences — J Eng Sci
Journal of Engineering Sciences (Saudi Arabia) — J Eng Sci (Saudi Arabia)
Journal of Engineering Thermophysics — J Eng Thermophy
Journal of English — J En
Journal of English and German Philology — J Engl Ger Philol
Journal of English and Germanic Philology — J Eng and Germ Philol
Journal of English and Germanic Philology — J Eng Ger Philol
Journal of English and Germanic Philology — J Engl & Germ Philol
Journal of English and Germanic Philology — J Engl Ger
Journal of English and Germanic Philology — JEG Ph
Journal of English and Germanic Philology — JEG Phil
Journal of English and Germanic Philology — JEGP
Journal of English and Germanic Philology — Jnl Engl Ger Philol
Journal of English and Germanic Philology (Urbana) — Journ Engl Germ Philol Urbana
Journal of English Linguistics — J Eng L
Journal of English Linguistics — JEL
Journal of English Literary History — ELH
Journal of English Studies — J Eng S
Journal of English Studies — JES
Journal of Enterostomal Therapy — J Enterostom Ther
Journal of Enterprise Management — JEM
Journal of Enterprise Management — JEN
Journal of Enterstomal Therapy — J Enteros Ther
Journal of Entomological Research — J Entomol Res
Journal of Entomological Research (New Delhi) — J Entomol Res (New Delhi)
Journal of Entomological Science — J Entomol Sci
Journal of Entomological Science — JES
Journal of Entomology — J Ent
Journal of Entomology and Zoology — J Ent Zool
Journal of Entomology and Zoology — J Entomol Zool
Journal of Entomology. Series A. General Entomology — J Entomol A
Journal of Entomology. Series A. General Entomology — J Entomol Ser A
Journal of Entomology. Series A. General Entomology — J Entomol Ser A Gen Entomol
Journal of Entomology. Series A. Physiology and Behaviour — J Entomol Ser A Physiol Behav
Journal of Entomology. Series B. Taxonomy — J Entomol B
Journal of Entomology. Series B. Taxonomy — J Entomol Ser B Taxon
Journal of Entomology. Series B. Taxonomy and Systematics — J Entomol Ser B Taxon Syst
Journal of Environmental Biology — J Environ Biol
Journal of Environmental Conservation Technology — J Environ Conserv Technol
Journal of Environmental Economics and Management — J Envir Econ Man
Journal of Environmental Economics and Management — J Environ Econ Manage
Journal of Environmental Economics and Management — J Environmental Econ and Mgt
Journal of Environmental Economics and Management — JEE
Journal of Environmental Economics and Management — JEEMD
Journal of Environmental Economics and Management — JEM
Journal of Environmental Education — J Env Educ
Journal of Environmental Education — J Environ Educ
Journal of Environmental Education — JEVEB
Journal of Environmental Engineering — EE
Journal of Environmental Engineering (Los Angeles) — J Environ Eng (Los Angeles)
Journal of Environmental Health — J Environ Health
Journal of Environmental Health — PENV
Journal of Environmental Horticulture — J Environ Hortic
Journal of Environmental Management — J Envir Mgm
Journal of Environmental Management — J Environ Manage
Journal of Environmental Pathology and Toxicology — J Environ Pathol Toxicol
Journal of Environmental Pathology, Toxicology, and Oncology — J Environ Pathol Toxicol Oncol
Journal of Environmental Planning and Pollution Control — J Environ Plann Pollut Control
Journal of Environmental Pollution Control (Tokyo) — J Environ Pollut Control (Tokyo)
Journal of Environmental Psychology — Jnl of Environmental Psychology
Journal of Environmental Quality — J Envir Q
Journal of Environmental Quality — J Envir Qual
Journal of Environmental Quality — J Envir Quality
Journal of Environmental Quality — J Environ Qual
Journal of Environmental Quality — JEVQA
Journal of Environmental Radioactivity — J Environ Radioact
Journal of Environmental Science and Health — J Envir Sci Hlth
Journal of Environmental Science and Health. Part A. Environmental Science and Engineering — J Environ Sci Health Part A
Journal of Environmental Science and Health. Part A. Environmental Science and Engineering — J Environ Sci Health Part A Environ Sci Eng
Journal of Environmental Science and Health. Part A. Environmental Science and Engineering and Toxic and Hazardous Substance Control — J Environ Sci Health Part A Environ Sci Eng Toxic Hazard
Journal of Environmental Science and Health. Part B. Pesticides, Food Contaminants, and Agricultural Wastes — J Environ Sci Health B
Journal of Environmental Science and Health. Part B. Pesticides, Food Contaminants, and Agricultural Wastes — J Environ Sci Health Part B
Journal of Environmental Science and Health. Part B. Pesticides, Food Contaminants, and Agricultural Wastes — J Environ Sci Health Part B Pestic Food Contam Agric Wastes
Journal of Environmental Science and Health. Part C — J Environ Sci Health Part C
Journal of Environmental Science and Health. Part C. Environmental Carcinogenesis and Ecotoxicolgy Reviews — J Environ Sci Health Part C Environ Carcinog Ecotoxicol Rev
Journal of Environmental Science and Health. Part C. Environmental Carcinogenesis Reviews — J Environ Sci Health Part C Environ Carcinog Rev
Journal of Environmental Science and Health. Part C. Environmental Health Sciences — J Environ Sci Health (C)
Journal of Environmental Science and Health. Part C. Environmental Health Sciences — J Environ Sci Health Part C Environ Health Sci
Journal of Environmental Sciences — J Envir Sci
Journal of Environmental Sciences — J Environ Sci
Journal of Environmental Sciences (Beijing, China) — J Environ Sci (Beijing)
Journal of Environmental Systems — ES
Journal of Environmental Systems — J Environ Syst
Journal of Environmental Systems — J Environ Systems
Journal of Environmental Systems — JET
Journal of Environmental Systems — JEVSB
Journal of Enzyme Inhibition — J Enzyme Inhib
Journal of Epidemiology — J Epidemiol
Journal of Epidemiology and Community Health — J Epidemiol Community Health
Journal of Equine Medicine and Surgery — J Equine Med Surg
Journal of Equine Veterinary Science — J Equine Vet Sci
Journal of Essential Oil Research — J Essent Oil Res
Journal of Essential Oil Research. JEOR — J Essent Oil Res JEOR
Journal of Ethiopian Law — J Ethiop Law
Journal of Ethiopian Law — J Ethiopian Law
Journal of Ethiopian Studies — J Et S
Journal of Ethiopian Studies — J Ethiop Stud
Journal of Ethiopian Studies — J Ethiop Studs
Journal of Ethiopian Studies — J Ethiopian Stud
Journal of Ethiopian Studies [*Addis Ababa/London*] — JESt
Journal of Ethiopian Studies [*Addis Ababa/London*] — JEthiopSt
Journal of Ethiopian Studies — JEthS
Journal of Ethnic Studies — GESU
Journal of Ethnic Studies — J Eth S
Journal of Ethnic Studies — J Ethnic Stud
Journal of Ethnic Studies — JETCA
Journal of Ethnic Studies — JoEtS
Journal of Ethnobiology — J Ethnobiol
Journal of Ethnopharmacology — J Ethnopharmacol
Journal of Ethology — J Ethol
Journal of Eukaryotic Microbiology — J Eukaryot Microbiol
Journal of European Economic History — J Eur Econ Hist
Journal of European Economic History — J Europ Econ Hist
Journal of European Economic History — JoEuE
Journal of European Economic History — PEEH
Journal of European Industrial Training — J Eur Ind Train
Journal of European Industrial Training — J Eur Ind Training
Journal of European Industrial Training — JEU
Journal of European Industrial Training — JTR
Journal of European Studies — J Eur Stud
Journal of European Studies — JES
Journal of European Studies — JoES
Journal of European Studies — PEUS
Journal of European Training — J Eur Train

Journal of European Training — J Europ Training
Journal of Evolutionary Biochemistry and Physiology — J Evol Bioc
Journal of Evolutionary Biochemistry and Physiology — J Evolut Biochem Physiol
Journal of Evolutionary Biochemistry and Physiology (English Translation of Zhurnal Evolyutsionnoi Biokhimii i Fiziologii) — J Evol Biochem Physiol (Engl Transl Zh Evol Biokhim Fiziol)
Journal of Evolutionary Biochemistry and Physiology (USSR) — J Evol Biochem Physiol (USSR)
Journal of Evolutionary Biology — J Evol Biol
Journal of Evolutionary Psychology — JEP
Journal of Exceptional Children — J Excep Child
Journal of Existentialism — J Existent
Journal of Existentialism — JETXA
Journal of Experimental and Clinical Cancer Research — J Exp Clin Cancer Res
Journal of Experimental and Theoretical Artificial Intelligence — JETAI
Journal of Experimental and Theoretical Physics — J Experiment Theoret Phys
Journal of Experimental and Theoretical Physics — JETP
Journal of Experimental Animal Science — J Exp Anim
Journal of Experimental Animal Science — J Exp Anim Sci
Journal of Experimental Biology — J Exp Biol
Journal of Experimental Biology — J Exper Biol
Journal of Experimental Biology and Medicine — J Exp Biol Med
Journal of Experimental Botany — J Exp Bot
Journal of Experimental Botany — J Exper Bot
Journal of Experimental Botany — JEB
Journal of Experimental Child Psychology — IECP
Journal of Experimental Child Psychology — J Exp C Psy
Journal of Experimental Child Psychology — J Exp Child Psy
Journal of Experimental Child Psychology — J Exp Child Psychol
Journal of Experimental Child Psychology — J Exper Child Psychol
Journal of Experimental Child Psychology — JECPA
Journal of Experimental Education — J Exp Ed
Journal of Experimental Education — J Exp Educ
Journal of Experimental Education — J Exper Educ
Journal of Experimental Education — JEE
Journal of Experimental Marine Biology and Ecology — J Exp Mar B
Journal of Experimental Marine Biology and Ecology — J Exp Mar Biol Ecol
Journal of Experimental Marine Biology and Ecology — J Exper Marine Biol & Ecol
Journal of Experimental Medical Sciences — J Exp Med Sci
Journal of Experimental Medicine — J Exp M
Journal of Experimental Medicine — J Exp Med
Journal of Experimental Medicine — J Exper Med
Journal of Experimental Medicine — Journ of Exp Med
Journal of Experimental Pathology — J Exp Pathol
Journal of Experimental Pathology (New York) — J Exp Pathol NY
Journal of Experimental Psychology — J Exp Psych
Journal of Experimental Psychology — J Exp Psychol
Journal of Experimental Psychology — JEPSA
Journal of Experimental Psychology — JExP
Journal of Experimental Psychology: Animal Behavior Processes — J Exp Psy A
Journal of Experimental Psychology. Animal Behavior Processes — J Exp Psychol Anim Behav Process
Journal of Experimental Psychology: Animal Behavior Processes — J Exp Psychol Anim Behav Processes
Journal of Experimental Psychology: Animal Behavior Processes — J Exp Psychol Animal Behav Proc
Journal of Experimental Psychology: Animal Behavior Processes — JPAPD
Journal of Experimental Psychology. Animal Behavior Processes — PXPA
Journal of Experimental Psychology: General — J Exp Psy G
Journal of Experimental Psychology: General — J Exp Psychol Gen
Journal of Experimental Psychology: General — JPGED
Journal of Experimental Psychology. General — PXPG
Journal of Experimental Psychology: Human Learning and Memory — J Ex P L
Journal of Experimental Psychology: Human Learning and Memory — J Exp Psy H
Journal of Experimental Psychology: Human Learning and Memory — J Exp Psychol Hum Learn Mem
Journal of Experimental Psychology: Human Learning and Memory — J Exper Psychol Human Learn Mem
Journal of Experimental Psychology: Human Learning and Memory — JPHMD
Journal of Experimental Psychology: Human Perception and Performance — J Ex P H P
Journal of Experimental Psychology: Human Perception and Performance — J Exp Psy P
Journal of Experimental Psychology: Human Perception and Performance — J Exp Psychol Hum Perc Perf
Journal of Experimental Psychology: Human Perception and Performance — J Exp Psychol Hum Percept Perform
Journal of Experimental Psychology: Human Perception and Performance — J Exper Psychol Human Percept & Perf
Journal of Experimental Psychology: Human Perception and Performance — JPHPD
Journal of Experimental Psychology. Human Perception and Performance — PXPH
Journal of Experimental Psychology: Learning, Memory, and Cognition — J Exp Psychol Learn Mem Cogn
Journal of Experimental Psychology. Learning, Memory, and Cognition — PXPL
Journal of Experimental Psychology: Monograph — J Exp Psychol Monogr
Journal of Experimental Research in Personality — J Exp Res Pers
Journal of Experimental Social Psychology — IESP
Journal of Experimental Social Psychology — J Exp S Psy
Journal of Experimental Social Psychology — J Exp Soc Psych
Journal of Experimental Social Psychology — J Exp Soc Psychol
Journal of Experimental Social Psychology — J Exper Soc Psychol
Journal of Experimental Social Psychology — J Exper Social Psychol
Journal of Experimental Therapeutics — J Exp Ther
Journal of Experimental Therapeutics and Oncology — J Exp Ther Oncol
Journal of Experimental Zoology — J Exp Zool
Journal of Experimental Zoology — J Exper Zool
Journal of Experimental Zoology. Supplement — J Exp Zool Suppl
Journal of Explosives and Propellants. R.O.C. — J Explos Propellants ROC
Journal of Exposure Analysis and Environmental Epidemiology — J Expo Anal Environ Epidemiol
Journal of Extension — J Ext
Journal of Extra-Corporeal Technology — J Extra Corpor Technol
Journal of Extra-Corporeal Technology — J Extra Corporeal Technol
Journal of Family Counseling — J Fam Couns
Journal of Family History — J Fam Hist
Journal of Family History — PJFH
Journal of Family History. Studies in Family, Kinship, and Demography — JOFH
Journal of Family Issues — J Fam Issues
Journal of Family Issues — PJFI
Journal of Family Law — J Fam L
Journal of Family Law — J Fam Law
Journal of Family Law — J Family L
Journal of Family Practice — J Fam Pract
Journal of Family Welfare — J Fam Wel
Journal of Family Welfare — J Fam Welf
Journal of Farm Animal Science — J Farm Anim Sci
Journal of Farm Economics — J Farm Econ
Journal of Farm Economics — JFE
Journal of Farm History — Jour Farm Hist
Journal of Feminist Studies in Religion — PFSR
Journal of Fermentation and Bioengineering — J Ferm Bioe
Journal of Fermentation and Bioengineering — J Ferment Bioeng
Journal of Fermentation Industries — J Ferment Ind
Journal of Fermentation Technology — J Ferm Tech
Journal of Fermentation Technology — J Ferment Techn
Journal of Fermentation Technology — J Ferment Technol
Journal of Fermentation Technology — JFTED
Journal of Fermentation Technology (Osaka) [*Japan*] — J Ferment Technol (Osaka)
Journal of Ferrocement — J Ferrocem
Journal of Ferrocement [*New Zealand*] — J Ferrocement
Journal of Fertilizer Issues — Fert Issues
Journal of Fertilizer Issues — J Fert Issues
Journal of Fibrinolysis — J Fibrinolysis
Journal of Field Archaeology — J Field A
Journal of Field Archaeology — J Field Arch
Journal of Field Archaeology — J Field Archaeol
Journal of Field Archaeology — JFA
Journal of Field Archaeology. Boston University Association for Field Archaeology — AFA/JFA
Journal of Field Ornithology — J Field Ornithol
Journal of Finance — J Fin
Journal of Finance — J Finance
Journal of Finance — JF
Journal of Finance — JFI
Journal of Finance — JOF
Journal of Financial and Quantitative Analysis — J Fin Qu An
Journal of Financial and Quantitative Analysis — J Financ Quant Anal
Journal of Financial and Quantitative Analysis — JFQ
Journal of Financial and Quantitative Analysis — JFQA
Journal of Financial Economics — J Financ Econ
Journal of Financial Economics — JFE
Journal of Financial Economics — JFEC
Journal of Financial Education — JFED
Journal of Financial Intermediation — JFI
Journal of Financial Planning [*Later, Journal of Financial Planning Today*] — J Fin Planning
Journal of Financial Planning Today — JFP
Journal of Financial Research — JFR
Journal of Financial Services Research — JFSR
Journal of Fire and Flammability — J Fire Flamm
Journal of Fire and Flammability — J Fire Flammability
Journal of Fire and Flammability/Combustion Toxicology. Supplement — J Fire Flammability Combust Toxicol Suppl
Journal of Fire and Flammability/Consumer Product Flammability. Supplement — J Fire Flammability Consum Prod Flammability Suppl
Journal of Fire and Flammability/Fire Retardant Chemistry. Supplement — J Fire Flammability Fire Retard Chem Suppl
Journal of Fire Retardant Chemistry — J Fire Retard Chem
Journal of Fire Retardant Chemistry — J Fire Retardant Chem
Journal of Fire Retardant Chemistry — JFRCD
Journal of Fire Sciences — J Fire Sc
Journal of Fire Sciences — J Fire Sci
Journal of Fish Biology — J Fish Biol
Journal of Fish Diseases [*England*] — J Fish Dis
Journal of Fish Sausage — J Fish Sausage
Journal of Fisheries/Nippon Suisangaku Zasshi — J Fish
Journal of Flour and Animal Feed Milling — F & A Feed
Journal of Flour and Animal Feed Milling — J Flour Anim Feed Milling
Journal of Flow Injection Analysis — J Flow Injection Anal
Journal of Fluency Disorders — J Fluency Dis
Journal of Fluency Disorders — J Fluency Disord

Journal of Fluid Mechanics — J Fluid Mec
Journal of Fluid Mechanics — J Fluid Mech
Journal of Fluids Engineering. Transactions of the American Society of Mechanical Engineers — J Fluid Eng Trans ASME
Journal of Fluids Engineering. Transactions of the American Society of Mechanical Engineers — J Fluids Eng
Journal of Fluorescence — J Fluoresc
Journal of Fluorine Chemistry — J Fluorine
Journal of Fluorine Chemistry — J Fluorine Chem
Journal of Foetal Medicine — J Foctal Med
Journal of Folklore Research — Folk Res
Journal of Folklore Research — JFR
Journal of Food and Agriculture [*Nigeria*] — J Food Agric
Journal of Food and Nutrition (Canberra) — J Food Nutr (Canberra)
Journal of Food Biochemistry — J Food Biochem
Journal of Food Composition and Analysis — J Food Compos Anal
Journal of Food Distribution Research — J Food Distrib Res
Journal of Food Engineering — J Food Eng
Journal of Food Process Engineering — J Food Process Eng
Journal of Food Processing and Preservation — J Food Process Preserv
Journal of Food Protection — J Food Prot
Journal of Food Protection — J Food Protect
Journal of Food Protection — JFPRD
Journal of Food Quality — J Food Qual
Journal of Food Resources Development — J Food Resour Dev
Journal of Food Resources Development — JFRDD
Journal of Food Safety — J Food Saf
Journal of Food Safety — J Food Safety
Journal of Food Science — J Fd Sci
Journal of Food Science — J Food Sci
Journal of Food Science — PJFS
Journal of Food Science. An Official Publication. Institute of Food Technologists — J Food Sci Off Publ Inst Food Technol
Journal of Food Science and Technology — J Fd Sci Technol
Journal of Food Science and Technology — J Food Sci Tech
Journal of Food Science and Technology — J Food Sci Technol
Journal of Food Science and Technology (Mysore) — J Food Sci Technol (Mysore)
Journal of Food Science and Technology (Tokyo) — J Food Sci Technol (Tokyo)
Journal of Food Science. Kyoto Women's University — J Food Sci Kyoto Women's Univ
Journal of Food Service Systems — J Food Serv Syst
Journal of Food Technology — J Fd Technol
Journal of Food Technology — J Food Technol
Journal of Foot and Ankle Surgery — J Foot Ankle Surg
Journal of Foot Surgery — J Foot Surg
Journal of Foot Surgery — JFSUB
Journal of Foraminiferal Research — J Foraminiferal Res
Journal of Forecasting — J Forecasting
Journal of Forecasting — JOF
Journal of Forensic Medicine — J For Med
Journal of Forensic Medicine — J Forensic Med
Journal of Forensic Medicine (Istanbul) — J Forensic Med Istanbul
Journal of Forensic Odonto-Stomatology — J Forensic Odontostomatol
Journal of Forensic Sciences — J For Sci
Journal of Forensic Sciences — J Foren Sci
Journal of Forensic Sciences — J Forensic Sci
Journal of Forest History — J For Hist
Journal of Forest History — J Forest Hist
Journal of Forest Science (Chittagong, Bangladesh) — J For Sci (Chittagong Bangladesh)
Journal of Forestry — J For
Journal of Forestry — J Forest
Journal of Forestry (Budapest) — J For (Budapest)
Journal of Forestry (United States) — JFUS
Journal of Forestry (Washington, DC) — J Forest Washington
Journal of Formosan Forestry/Taiwan Sanrinkai Kaiho — J Formosan Forest
Journal of Forms Management — J Forms Man
Journal of Forms Management — JFM
Journal of Fourier Analysis and Applications — J Fourier Anal Appl
Journal of Fractional Calculus — J Fract Calc
Journal of Free Radicals in Biology and Medicine — J Free Radic Biol Med
Journal of Free Radicals in Biology and Medicine — J Free Radicals Biol Med
Journal of Freshwater — J Freshwater
Journal of Freshwater Ecology — J Freshw Ec
Journal of Freshwater Ecology — J Freshwater Ecol
Journal of Freshwater Ecology — JFE
Journal of Fudan University. Natural Science — J Fudan Univ Natur Sci
Journal of Fuel and Heat Technology — J Fuel Heat Technol
Journal of Fuel Chemistry and Technology (Taiyuan, People's Republic of China) — J Fuel Chem Technol (Taiyuan Peoples Repub China)
Journal of Functional Analysis — J Funct Ana
Journal of Functional Analysis — J Funct Anal
Journal of Functional Analysis — J Functional Analysis
Journal of Functional and Logic Programming — J Funct Logic Programming
Journal of Functional Materials — J Funct Mater
Journal of Functional Programming — J Funct Programming
Journal of Further and Higher Education — J Fur Higher Educ
Journal of Fushun Petroleum Institute — J Fushun Pet Inst
Journal of Fusion Energy — J Fusion Energy
Journal of Fusion Energy — JFE
Journal of Fusion Energy — JFEND
Journal of Futures Markets — J Futures Markets
Journal of Futures Markets — JFM
Journal of Futures Markets — JFU
Journal of Fuzhou University. Natural Science Edition — J Fuzhou Univ Nat Sci Ed
Journal of Fuzzy Mathematics — J Fuzzy Math
Journal of Gakugei. Tokushima University — J Gakugei Tokushima Univ
Journal of Garden History — J Gard Hist
Journal of Garden History — J Garden Hist
Journal of Garden History — Jnl of Garden History
Journal of Gas Chromatography — J Gas Chromatogr
Journal of Gas Chromatography — JGCRA
Journal of Gas Lighting — J Gas Lighting
Journal of Gas Lighting, Water Supply, and Sanitary Improvement — J Gas Light Water Supply Sanit Improv
Journal of Gastroenterology — J Gastroenterol
Journal of Gastroenterology and Hepatology — J Gastroenterol Hepatol
Journal of Gastrointestinal Research — J Gastrointest Res
Journal of Gemmmology and Proceedings of the Gemmological Association of Great Britain — J Gemmol
Journal of Gemmology — J Gemmol
Journal of Gemmology and Proceedings of the Gemmological Association of Great Britain — Jour Gemmology
Journal of General and Applied Microbiology — J Gen A Mic
Journal of General and Applied Microbiology — J Gen Appl Microbiol
Journal of General Biology (Moscow) — J Gen Biol (Moscow)
Journal of General Chemistry — J Gen Chem
Journal of General Chemistry — JGC
Journal of General Chemistry of the USSR — J Gen Chem USSR
Journal of General Chemistry of the USSR (English Translation) — J Gen Chem USSR (Engl Transl)
Journal of General Education — J Gen Ed
Journal of General Education — J Gen Educ
Journal of General Education — J of Gen Educ
Journal of General Education — JGE
Journal of General Education — Jnl Gen Ed
Journal of General Education. Tokyo Nogyo Daigaku — J Gen Ed Tokyo Nogyo Daigaku
Journal of General Internal Medicine — J Gen Intern Med
Journal of General Management — J Gen Manag
Journal of General Management — J Gen Mgt
Journal of General Management — JEP
Journal of General Management [*United Kingdom*] — JGM
Journal of General Management — JGMAA
Journal of General Microbiology — J Gen Micro
Journal of General Microbiology — J Gen Microbiol
Journal of General Physiology — J Gen Physiol
Journal of General Physiology — J Gen Physl
Journal of General Psychology — J Gen Psych
Journal of General Psychology — J Gen Psychol
Journal of General Psychology — JGP
Journal of General Psychology — JGPs
Journal of General Psychology — JGPSA
Journal of General Psychology — PJGP
Journal of General Virology — J Gen Virol
Journal of Genetic Psychology — J Gen Ps
Journal of Genetic Psychology — J Genet Psy
Journal of Genetic Psychology — J Genet Psychol
Journal of Genetic Psychology — JGEPs
Journal of Genetic Psychology — JGP
Journal of Genetic Psychology — JGPYA
Journal of Genetic Psychology — PJGS
Journal of Genetics — J Genet
Journal of Genetics and Breeding — J Genet & Breed
Journal of Geobotany — J Geobot
Journal of Geochemical Exploration — J Geochem E
Journal of Geochemical Exploration — J Geochem Explor
Journal of Geochemical Exploration — JGCEA
Journal of Geodynamics — J Geodyn
Journal of Geography — J Geog
Journal of Geography — J Geogr
Journal of Geography — JG
Journal of Geography — JOGG A
Journal of Geography (Chicago) — Jour Geogr Chicago
Journal of Geography in Higher Education — J Geogr Higher Educ
Journal of Geography. National Council of Geographic Education — NCGE/J
Journal of Geography (Tokyo) — J Geogr (Tokyo)
Journal of Geological Education — J Geol Educ
Journal of Geological Education — Jour Geol Education
Journal of Geological Sciences. Applied Geophysics — J Geol Sci Appl Geophys
Journal of Geological Sciences. Economic Geology, Mineralogy — J Geol Sci Econ Geol Mineral
Journal of Geological Sciences. Geology — J Geol Sci Geol
Journal of Geological Sciences. Palaeontology — J Geol Sci Palaeontol
Journal of Geological Sciences. Technology, Geochemistry (Prague) — J Geol Sci Technol Geochem (Prague)
Journal of Geology — J Geo
Journal of Geology — J Geol
Journal of Geology [*Chicago*] — JG
Journal of Geology. Ukrainian Academy of Sciences. Institute of Geology — J Geol Ukr Acad Sci Inst Geol
Journal of Geology. United Arab Republic — J Geol UAR
Journal of Geomagnetism and Geoelectricity — J Geomagn & Geoelectr
Journal of Geomagnetism and Geoelectricity — J Geomagn G
Journal of Geomagnetism and Geoelectricity — J Geomagn Geoelec
Journal of Geometric Analysis. Mathematics — J Geom Anal
Journal of Geometry — J Geom

Journal of Geometry — J Geometry
Journal of Geometry and Physics — J Geom Phy
Journal of Geometry and Physics — J Geomet Phys
Journal of Geophysical Prospecting — J Geophys Prospect
Journal of Geophysical Research — J Geoph Res
Journal of Geophysical Research — J Geophys Res
Journal of Geophysical Research — JGR
Journal of Geophysical Research. A. Space Physics — J Geophys Res A Space Phys
Journal of Geophysical Research. Atmospheres — J Geophys Res Atmos
Journal of Geophysical Research. Planets — J Geophys Res Planets
Journal of Geophysical Research. Series B — J Geophys Res B
Journal of Geophysical Research. Series C. Oceans — J Geophys Res C Oceans
Journal of Geophysical Research. Series C. Oceans — J Geophys Res Oceans
Journal of Geophysical Research. Series C. Oceans and Atmospheres — J Geo R-O A
Journal of Geophysical Research. Series C. Oceans and Atmospheres — J Geophys Res C Oceans Atmos
Journal of Geophysical Research. Series C. Oceans and Atmospheres — JGR C
Journal of Geophysical Research. Series D. Atmospheres — J Geophys Res
Journal of Geophysical Research. Series D. Atmospheres — J Geophys Res D Atmos
Journal of Geophysical Research. Solid Earth and Planets — J Geophys Res Solid Earth Planets
Journal of Geophysical Research. Space Physics — J Geo R-S P
Journal of Geophysical Research. Space Physics — J Geophys Res Space Phys
Journal of Geophysics — J Geophys
Journal of Geophysics — JGEOD
Journal of Geophysics (Kiev) — J Geophys (Kiev)
Journal of Geophysics (Moscow) — J Geophys (Moscow)
Journal of Geophysics/Zeitschrift fuer Geophysik — J Geophys Zeitschr Geophys
Journal of Geosciences. Osaka City University — J Geosci Osaka City Univ
Journal of Geotechnical Engineering — GT
Journal of Geriatric Psychiatry — J Geriat Ps
Journal of Geriatric Psychiatry — J Geriatr Psychiatry
Journal of Geriatric Psychiatry and Neurology — J Geriatr Psychiatry Neurol
Journal of German-American Studies — Jnl Ger Am Stud
Journal of Gerontological Nursing — J Gerontol Nurs
Journal of Gerontological Social Work — J Gerontol Soc Work
Journal of Gerontological Social Work — JGSW
Journal of Gerontological Social Work — PGSW
Journal of Gerontology — J Geront
Journal of Gerontology — J Gerontol
Journal of Gerontology — J Gerontology
Journal of Gerontology — JOGEA
Journal of Gesamte Oberflaechentechnik — J Gesamte Oberflaechentech
Journal of Glaciology — J Glaciol
Journal of Glaciology — JOGL
Journal of Glaciology — Jour Glaciology
Journal of Glass Studies — J Glass Stud
Journal of Glass Studies — JGS
Journal of Glaucoma — J Glaucoma
Journal of Global Optimization — J Global Optim
Journal of Gnathology — J Gnathol
Journal of Government Mechanical Laboratory (Japan) — J Gov Mech Lab (Jpn)
Journal of Graph Theory — J Graph Theory
Journal of Great Lakes Research — J Great Lakes Res
Journal of Great Lakes Research — JGLRD
Journal of Group Theory in Physics. An International Journal Devoted to Applications of Group Theory to Physical Problems — J Group Theory Phys
Journal of Growth — J Growth
Journal of Guangdong Institute of Technology — J Guangdong Inst Technol
Journal of Guangdong Non-Ferrous Metals — J Guangdong Non Ferrous Met
Journal of Guidance and Control — J Guid and Control
Journal of Guidance and Control [*United States*] — J Guid Control
Journal of Guidance and Control — J Guidance & Control
Journal of Guidance and Control — J Guidance Control
Journal of Guidance, Control, and Dynamics — J Guid Control and Dyn
Journal of Guilin College of Geology — J Guilin Coll Geol
Journal of Guilin Institute of Technology — J Guilin Inst Technol
Journal of Guizhou Institute of Technology — J Guizhou Inst Tech
Journal of Gunma-ken Nuclear Medicine Forum — J Gunma Ken Nucl Med Forum
Journal of Gynaecological Endocrinology — Gynaecol Endocr
Journal of Gynaecological Endocrinology — J Gynaecol Endocr
Journal of Gynaecological Endocrinology — J Gynaecol Endocrinol
Journal of Gynecologic Surgery — J Gynecol S
Journal of Gynecological Practice [*Japan*] — J Gynecol Pract
Journal of Hand Surgery — J Hand Surg
Journal of Hand Surgery — JHSUD
Journal of Hand Surgery. American Volume — J Hand Surg Am
Journal of Hand Surgery. British Volume — J Hand Surg Br
Journal of Hand Therapy — J Hand Ther
Journal of Harbin Institute of Technology — J Harbin Inst Tech
Journal of Hard Materials — J Hard Mater
Journal of Haryana Studies — J Haryana Stud
Journal of Hazardous Materials — J Hazard Mater
Journal of Hazardous Materials — J Hazard Materials
Journal of Hazardous Materials — J Hazardous Mat
Journal of Health Administration Education — J Health Adm Educ
Journal of Health and Human Behavior — J Health Hum Behav
Journal of Health and Human Resources Administration — J Health Hum Resour Adm
Journal of Health and Human Resources Administration — J Health Hum Resources Admin
Journal of Health and Human Resources Administration — JHH
Journal of Health and Social Behavior — J Health & Soc Behav
Journal of Health and Social Behavior — J Health & Social Behavior
Journal of Health and Social Behavior — J Health So
Journal of Health and Social Behavior — J Health Soc Behav
Journal of Health and Social Behavior — J of H and SB
Journal of Health and Social Behavior — JHSB
Journal of Health and Social Behavior — PHSB
Journal of Health Care Finance — J Health Care Finance
Journal of Health Care for the Poor and Underserved — J Health Care Poor Underserved
Journal of Health Care Marketing — J Health Care Mark
Journal of Health Care Marketing — J Health Care Market
Journal of Health Care Marketing — J Health Care Mkt
Journal of Health Care Marketing — JHCM
Journal of Health Care Technology — J Health Care Technol
Journal of Health Care Technology — Jnl Health Care Tech
Journal of Health Economics — J Health Econ
Journal of Health Economics — JOHE
Journal of Health Education — J Health Ed
Journal of Health, Physical Education, Recreation — J Health Phys Ed Rec
Journal of Health, Physical Education, Recreation — JOHPER
Journal of Health Physics and Radiation Protection — J Health Phys Radiat Prot
Journal of Health Politics, Policy, and Law — J Health Pol
Journal of Health Politics, Policy, and Law — J Health Pol Poly and L
Journal of Health Politics, Policy, and Law — J Health Polit Policy Law
Journal of Health Politics, Policy, and Law — JHPLD
Journal of Health Politics, Policy, and Law — JHPP
Journal of Health Toxicology — J Health Toxicol
Journal of Health Toxicology — J Toxicol
Journal of Healthcare Education and Training — J Healthc Educ Train
Journal of Healthcare Materiel Management — J Healthc Mater Manage
Journal of Healthcare Protection Management — J Healthc Prot Manage
Journal of Heart and Lung Transplantation — J Heart Lung Transplant
Journal of Heart Valve Disease — J Heart Valve Dis
Journal of Heat Recovery Systems [*England*] — J Heat Recovery Syst
Journal of Heat Recovery Systems — J Heat Recovery Systems
Journal of Heat Transfer. Transactions of the American Society of Mechanical Engineers — J Heat Tran
Journal of Heat Transfer. Transactions of the American Society of Mechanical Engineers — J Heat Transfer Trans ASME
Journal of Heat Transfer. Transactions of the American Society of Mechanical Engineers. Series C — J Heat Transfer
Journal of Heat Treating [*United States*] — J Heat Treat
Journal of Heating Technics — J Heat Tech
Journal of Hebei University of Technology — J Hebei Univ Technol
Journal of Hebraic Studies [*New York*] — JHebrSt
Journal of Hellenic Studies — J Hel Stud
Journal of Hellenic Studies — J Hell St
Journal of Hellenic Studies — J Hell Stud
Journal of Hellenic Studies — J Hellen St
Journal of Hellenic Studies — J Hellen Stud
Journal of Hellenic Studies — J Hellenic Stud
Journal of Hellenic Studies — JH St
Journal of Hellenic Studies — JHEL
Journal of Hellenic Studies — JHS
Journal of Hellenic Studies — JoHS
Journal of Hellenic Studies — Journ Hell St
Journal of Hellenic Studies — Journ Hell Stud
Journal of Hellenic Studies — PJHS
Journal of Hellenic Studies. Archaeological Reports — JHS-AR
Journal of Hellenic Studies. Supplement — JHSS
Journal of Helminthology — J Helminth
Journal of Helminthology — J Helminthol
Journal of Hematotherapy — J Hematother
Journal of Hepatology — J Hepatol
Journal of Hepatology — Jnl Hepatol
Journal of Hepatology [*Amsterdam*] — JOHEEC
Journal of Hepatology (Amsterdam) — Hepatol (Amst)
Journal of Hepatology (Amsterdam) — J Hepatol (Amst)
Journal of Hepatology. Supplement — J Hepatol Suppl
Journal of Heredity — J Hered
Journal of Heredity — J Heredity
Journal of Heredity — JOHEA
Journal of Heredity — PHER
Journal of Herpetology — J Herpetol
Journal of Heterocyclic Chemistry — J Hetero Ch
Journal of Heterocyclic Chemistry — J Heterocycl Chem
Journal of High Polymers (Shanghai) — J High Polym (Shanghai)
Journal of High Resolution Chromatography and Chromatography Communications [*West Germany*] — HRC CC J High Resolut Chromatogr Chromatogr Commun
Journal of High Resolution Chromatography and Chromatography Communications [*West Germany*] — J High Resolut Chromatogr Chromatogr Commun
Journal of High Temperature Chemical Processes — J High Temp Chem Processes
Journal of Higher Education — IJHE
Journal of Higher Education — J Hi E
Journal of Higher Education — J High Educ
Journal of Higher Education — J Higher Educ

Journal of Higher Education — Jnl Higher Ed
Journal of Hispanic Philology — J Hispan Ph
Journal of Hispanic Philology — JHP
Journal of Hispanic Politics — Jnl Hisp Pol
Journal of Histochemistry and Cytochemistry — J Hist Cyto
Journal of Histochemistry and Cytochemistry — J Histochem Cytochem
Journal of Historical Geography — J Hist G
Journal of Historical Geography — J Hist Geog
Journal of Historical Geography — J Hist Geogr
Journal of Historical Geography — PJHG
Journal of Historical Geography (England) — JHE
Journal of Historical Research — J Hist Res
Journal of Historical Research — JHR
Journal of Historical Studies — J Hist Stud
Journal of Historical Studies — JHS
Journal of Historical Studies — JHSt
Journal of Historical Studies — JHStud
Journal of History — HJH
Journal of History [*Independence, Missouri*] — J His
Journal of History — JH
Journal of History and Political Science — JHPS
Journal of History for Senior Students — JHSS
Journal of Histotechnology [*United States*] — J Histotechnol
Journal of Hohai University — J Hohai Univ
Journal of Hokkaido Society of Grassland Science — J Hokkaido Soc Grassl Sci
Journal of Holistic Health — JHH
Journal of Holistic Health — JOHH
Journal of Holistic Medicine — J Holistic Med
Journal of Holistic Medicine — JHMEDL
Journal of Holistic Nursing — J Holistic Nurs
Journal of Home Economics — J Ho E
Journal of Home Economics — J Home Econ
Journal of Home Economics — JHE
Journal of Home Economics — Jnl Home Econ
Journal of Home Economics Education — J of Home Ec Ed
Journal of Home Economics of Japan — J Home Econ Jpn
Journal of Homosexuality — J Homosex
Journal of Homosexuality — J Homosexuality
Journal of Homosexuality — JOHX
Journal of Homosexuality — PJHX
Journal of Horticultural Science — J Hort Sci
Journal of Horticultural Science — J Hortic Sci
Journal of Horticulture — J Hortic
Journal of Horticulture and Practical Gardening — J Hort Pract Gard
Journal of Hospital Dental Practice — J Hosp Dent Pract
Journal of Hospital Infection — J Hosp Infect
Journal of Hospital Infection — JHINDS
Journal of Hospital Supply, Processing, and Distribution — J Hosp Supply Process Distrib
Journal of Hospitality & Leisure Marketing — J Hosp & Leisure Market
Journal of Hospitality Education — J Hospitality Educ
Journal of Housing — J Housing
Journal of Housing — JHO
Journal of Housing — JOH
Journal of Housing — JOHOA
Journal of Housing for the Elderly — J Housing Elderly
Journal of Huazhong (Central China) Agricultural University — J Huazhong Cent Chiha Agric Univ
Journal of Human Behavior and Learning — J Hum Behav Learn
Journal of Human Behavior and Learning — JHBLEM
Journal of Human Ecology — J Hum Ecol
Journal of Human Ergology — J Hum Ergol
Journal of Human Ergology (Tokyo) — J Hum Ergol (Tokyo)
Journal of Human Evolution — J Hum Evol
Journal of Human Evolution — J Hum Evolution
Journal of Human Hypertension — J Hum Hypertens
Journal of Human Movement Studies — J Hu Move Stud
Journal of Human Movement Studies — J Hum Mov Stud
Journal of Human Movement Studies — JHMSDT
Journal of Human Nutrition — J Hum Nutr
Journal of Human Nutrition and Dietetics — J Hum Nutr Diet
Journal of Human Relations — J Hum Relat
Journal of Human Relations — J Hum Relations
Journal of Human Relations — J of Human Rela
Journal of Human Relations — JHR
Journal of Human Relations — JHuR
Journal of Human Relations — Jour Human Rel
Journal of Human Resources — J Hum Resources
Journal of Human Resources — J Human Resources
Journal of Human Resources — JHR
Journal of Human Services Abstracts — J Hum Serv Abstr
Journal of Human Stress — J Hum Stress
Journal of Human Stress — J Human Stress
Journal of Humanistic Psychology — J Hum Psy
Journal of Humanistic Psychology — J Hum Psychol
Journal of Humanistic Psychology — J Humanist Psychol
Journal of Humanistic Psychology — J Humanistic Psychol
Journal of Hydraulic Engineering — HY
Journal of Hydraulic Engineering (Peking) — J Hydraul Eng (Peking)
Journal of Hydraulic Research — J Hydraul Res
Journal of Hydraulic Research/Journal de Recherches Hydrauliques — J Hydraul Res J Rech Hydraul
Journal of Hydrodynamics. Series B (English Edition) — J Hydrodyn Ser B English Ed
Journal of Hydrogeology — J Hydrogeol
Journal of Hydrological Sciences [*Poland*] — J Hydrol Sci
Journal of Hydrology [*New Zealand*] — J Hydrol
Journal of Hydrology [*Amsterdam*] — JHYDA7
Journal of Hydrology [*Dunedin*] — JLHYAD
Journal of Hydrology (Amsterdam) — J Hydrol (Amst)
Journal of Hydrology and Hydromechanics — J Hydrol Hydromech
Journal of Hydrology (Dunedin) — J Hydrol (Dunedin)
Journal of Hydrology (Netherlands) — J Hydrol (Neth)
Journal of Hydronautics — J Hydronaut
Journal of Hygiene — J Hyg
Journal of Hygiene — J Hygiene
Journal of Hygiene (Ankara) — J Hyg (Ankara)
Journal of Hygiene (Cambridge) — J Hyg (Camb)
Journal of Hygiene, Epidemiology, Microbiology, and Immunology — J Hyg Ep Mi
Journal of Hygiene, Epidemiology, Microbiology, and Immunology — J Hyg Epidemiol Microbiol Immunol
Journal of Hygiene, Epidemiology, Microbiology, and Immunology (Prague) — J Hyg Epidemiol Microbiol Immunol (Prague)
Journal of Hygiene (London) — J Hyg (Lond)
Journal of Hygiene. Supplement — J Hyg Suppl
Journal of Hygienic Chemistry — J Hyg Chem
Journal of Hypertension — J Hypertens
Journal of Hypertension. Supplement — J Hypertens Suppl
Journal of Ichthyology — J Ichthyol
Journal of Ichthyology [*English Translation of Voprosy Ikhtiologii*] — JITHA
Journal of Ichthyology (English Translation of Voprosy Ikhtiologii) — J Ichthyol (Engl Trans Vopr Ikhtiol)
Journal of Ichthyology (USSR) [*English Translation of Voprosy Ikhtiologii*] — J Ichthyol (USSR)
Journal of Imaging Science — J Imaging Sci
Journal of Imaging Technology — J Imaging Technol
Journal of Immunoassay — J Immunoassay
Journal of Immunogenetics — J Immunogen
Journal of Immunogenetics — J Immunogenet
Journal of Immunogenetics — JIMGA
Journal of Immunogenetics (Oxford) — J Immunogenet (Oxf)
Journal of Immunological Methods — J Immunol M
Journal of Immunological Methods — J Immunol Methods
Journal of Immunology — J Immun
Journal of Immunology — J Immunol
Journal of Immunology — JI
Journal of Immunology, Virus Research, and Experimental Chemotherapy — J Immunol Virus Res Exp Chemother
Journal of Immunopharmacology — J Immunopharmacol
Journal of Immunotherapy — J Immunother
Journal of Immunotherapy with Emphasis on Tumor Immunology — J Immunother Emphasis Tumor immunol
Journal of Imperial and Commonwealth History — J Imp Com H
Journal of Imperial and Commonwealth History — J Imp Common Hist
Journal of Imperial and Commonwealth History — J Imp Commonw Hist
Journal of Imperial and Commonwealth History — JICH
Journal of In Vitro Fertilization and Embryo Transfer — J In Vitro Fert Embryo Transfer
Journal of Inclusion Phenomena — J Incl Phen
Journal of Inclusion Phenomena — J Inclusion Phenom
Journal of Inclusion Phenomena and Molecular Recognition in Chemistry — J Inclusion Phenom Mol Recognit Chem
Journal of Indian and Buddhist Studies — JIBS
Journal of Indian Art — Journ Ind Art
Journal of Indian Art and Industry — JIA
Journal of Indian Art and Industry — Jour of Indian Art and Ind
Journal of Indian Botany — J Indian Bot
Journal of Indian History — J Ind Hist
Journal of Indian History — J Indian Hist
Journal of Indian History — JIH
Journal of Indian History — JoIH
Journal of Indian Industries and Labour — J Indian Ind Labour
Journal of Indian Philosophy — J Ind Philo
Journal of Indian Philosophy — J Indian P
Journal of Indian Philosophy — J Indian Phil
Journal of Indian Philosophy — JIP
Journal of Indian Textile History — JITH
Journal of Indian Writing in English — JIWE
Journal of Individual Psychology — J Indiv Psy
Journal of Individual Psychology — J Individ Psychol
Journal of Indo-European Studies — J Indo-Eur
Journal of Indo-European Studies — J Indo-European Stud
Journal of Indo-European Studies — JIES
Journal of Indoor Air International — J Indoor Air Int
Journal of Industrial Aerodynamics — J Ind Aero
Journal of Industrial Aerodynamics — J Ind Aerodyn
Journal of Industrial and Engineering Chemistry [*United States*] — J Ind Eng Chem
Journal of Industrial and Engineering Chemistry — J Ind Engng Chem
Journal of Industrial and Engineering Chemistry — JIECA
Journal of Industrial and Engineering Chemistry (Seoul) — J Ind Eng Chem Seoul
Journal of Industrial Archaeology — JIA
Journal of Industrial Arts Education — J Ind Arts Ed
Journal of Industrial Chemistry — J Ind Chem
Journal of Industrial Economics — J Ind Econ
Journal of Industrial Economics — J Industr Econ
Journal of Industrial Economics — JIE
Journal of Industrial Economics (Oxford) — JIO

Journal of Industrial Engineering — J Ind Eng
Journal of Industrial Engineering — JLIEA
Journal of Industrial Fabrics — J Ind Fabr
Journal of Industrial Hygiene — J Ind Hyg
Journal of Industrial Hygiene — J Indust Hyg
Journal of Industrial Hygiene and Toxicology — J Ind Hyg
Journal of Industrial Hygiene and Toxicology — J Ind Hyg Toxicol
Journal of Industrial Hygiene and Toxicology — J Indust Hyg Toxicol
Journal of Industrial Hygiene and Toxicology — JIHTA
Journal of Industrial Irradiation Technology — J Ind Irrad Tech
Journal of Industrial Irradiation Technology — J Ind Irradiat Technol
Journal of Industrial Irradiation Technology — JIIT
Journal of Industrial Microbiology — J Ind Microbiol
Journal of Industrial Microbiology — JIM
Journal of Industrial Microbiology. Supplement — J Ind Microbiol Suppl
Journal of Industrial Pollution Control — J Ind Pollut Control
Journal of Industrial Relations — J Ind Rel
Journal of Industrial Relations — J Ind Relations
Journal of Industrial Relations — J Indus Rel
Journal of Industrial Relations — J Indust Relations
Journal of Industrial Relations — J Industr Relat
Journal of Industrial Relations — JIR
Journal of Industrial Teacher Education — J Ind Teach Educ
Journal of Industrial Teacher Education — J Industr Teacher Educ
Journal of Industrial Technology [*South Korea*] — J Ind Technol
Journal of Industrial Technology. Daegu University — JITUD
Journal of Industrial Technology. Myong-Ji University [*Republic of Korea*] — J Ind Technol Myong-Ji Univ
Journal of Industrial Technology. Myong-Ji University — JINTD
Journal of Industry — J Ind
Journal of Industry — J Indust
Journal of Industry — J Industry
Journal of Industry and Trade — J Ind Trade
Journal of Infection — J Infect
Journal of Infection and Chemotherapy — J Infect Chemother
Journal of Infectious Diseases — J Infect Dis
Journal of Inferential and Deductive Biology — J Inferential Deductive Biol
Journal of Inflammation — J Inflamm
Journal of Inflammation — J Inflammation
Journal of Information and Image Management — J Inf Image Manage
Journal of Information and Image Management — JIIM
Journal of Information and Image Management — JMG
Journal of Information and Optimization Sciences — J Inf and Optimiz Sci
Journal of Information and Optimization Sciences — J Inform Optim Sci
Journal of Information and Optimization Sciences — JIOS
Journal of Information Management — J Info Mgmt
Journal of Information Management — JIM
Journal of Information Processing — J Info Process
Journal of Information Processing — J Inform Process
Journal of Information Processing — J Information Processing
Journal of Information Processing and Cybernetics — J Inform Process Cybernet
Journal of Information Processing and Management — J Inf Process Manage
Journal of Information Recording — J Inf Rec
Journal of Information Recording Materials — J Inf Rec Mat
Journal of Information Recording Materials — J Inf Rec Mater
Journal of Information Science [*Netherlands*] — J Inf Sci
Journal of Information Science — JISCD
Journal of Information Science. Principles and Practice — J Inf Sci Princ and Pract
Journal of Information Science. Principles and Practice — J Info Sci
Journal of Information Systems Management — J Info Sys Mgmt
Journal of Information Systems Management — JIF
Journal of Infusional Chemotherapy — J Infus Chemother
Journal of Inherited Metabolic Disease — J Inherit Metab Dis
Journal of Inherited Metabolic Disease — J Inherited Metab Dis
Journal of Inorganic and Nuclear Chemistry — J Inorg and Nucl Chem
Journal of Inorganic and Nuclear Chemistry — J Inorg Nuc
Journal of Inorganic and Nuclear Chemistry — J Inorg Nucl Chem
Journal of Inorganic and Nuclear Chemistry — Jour Inorganic and Nuclear Chemistry
Journal of Inorganic and Nuclear Chemistry. Supplement — J Inorg Nucl Chem Suppl
Journal of Inorganic and Organometallic Polymers — J Inorg Organomet Polym
Journal of Inorganic Biochemistry — J Inorg Biochem
Journal of Inorganic Chemistry (Nanjing, People's Republic of China) — J Inorg Chem (Nanjing Peoples Repub China)
Journal of Inorganic Chemistry (Nanjing, People's Republic of China) — Jnl Inorg Chem (Nanjing PRC)
Journal of Inorganic Chemistry (USSR) — J Inorg Chem (USSR)
Journal of Inorganic Materials — J Inorg Mat
Journal of Inorganic Materials — J Inorg Mater
Journal of Insect Behavior — J Insect Behav
Journal of Insect Pathology — J Insect Path
Journal of Insect Pathology — J Insect Pathol
Journal of Insect Physiology — J Insect Ph
Journal of Insect Physiology — J Insect Physiol
Journal of Insect Physiology — JIPHA
Journal of Inspectors of Schools of Australia and New Zealand — J Insp Sch
Journal of Instructional Psychology — J Instr Psychol
Journal of Instrument Materials — J Instrum Mater
Journal of Insurance — J Ins
Journal of Insurance — JI
Journal of Insurance — JIS
Journal of Integral Equations — J Integral Equations
Journal of Integral Equations and Applications — J Integral Equations Appl
Journal of Integral Equations and Mathematical Physics — J Integral Equations Math Phys
Journal of Intellectual Disability Research — J Intellect Disabil Res
Journal of Inter American Studies and World Affairs — J Inter Amer Stud World Affairs
Journal of Interamerican Studies — JIAS
Journal of Interamerican Studies and World Affairs — J Intam St
Journal of Interamerican Studies and World Affairs — J Interam Stud
Journal of Interamerican Studies and World Affairs — J Interam Stud World Aff
Journal of Interamerican Studies and World Affairs — J Interamer Stud
Journal of Interamerican Studies and World Affairs — JIS
Journal of Inter-American Studies and World Affairs — JoIS
Journal of Interamerican Studies and World Affairs — Jour Interam Studies
Journal of Interamerican Studies and World Affairs — PISW
Journal of Interamerican Studies and World Affairs. Sage Publication for the Center for Advanced International Studies. University of Miami — Sage/JIAS
Journal of Inter-American Studies (Gainesville, Florida; Coral Gables, Florida) — Jour Inter Am Stud Gainesville Coral Gables
Journal of Intercultural Studies — J Intercult Stud
Journal of Intercultural Studies — J Intercultural Stud
Journal of Interdisciplinary Cycle Research — J Interd Cy
Journal of Interdisciplinary Cycle Research — J Interdiscip Cycle Res
Journal of Interdisciplinary Cycle Research — J Interdiscipl Cycle Res
Journal of Interdisciplinary History — J Interd H
Journal of Interdisciplinary History — J Interdis H
Journal of Interdisciplinary History — J Interdis Hist
Journal of Interdisciplinary History — J Interdiscip Hist
Journal of Interdisciplinary History — Joly
Journal of Interdisciplinary History — PIHI
Journal of Interdisciplinary Modeling and Simulation — J Interdiscip Model Simul
Journal of Interdisciplinary Modeling and Simulation — J Interdisciplinary Modeling Simulation
Journal of Interdisciplinary Modeling and Simulation — JIMSD2
Journal of Interferon and Cytokine Research — J Interferon Cytokine Res
Journal of Interferon Research — J Interferon Res
Journal of Interferon Research — JIREDJ
Journal of Intergroup Relations — J Intergroup Rel
Journal of Intergroup Relations — J of Intergroup Rela
Journal of Internal Medicine — J Intern Med
Journal of Internal Medicine — JIM
Journal of Internal Medicine. Supplement — J Intern Med Suppl
Journal of International Affairs — J Int Aff
Journal of International Affairs — J Int Affairs
Journal of International Affairs — J Internat Affairs
Journal of International Affairs — J Intl Aff
Journal of International Affairs — JIA
Journal of International Affairs — Jour of Int Affairs
Journal of International Affairs — PJIA
Journal of International Affairs. Columbia University. School of International Affairs — CU/JIA
Journal of International Biomedical Information and Data — J Int Biomed Inf Data
Journal of International Business Studies — J Int Bus Stud
Journal of International Business Studies — J Internat Bus Studies
Journal of International Business Studies — JIB
Journal of International Business Studies — Jrl Int B
Journal of International Economics — J Int Econ
Journal of International Economics — J Internat Econ
Journal of International Economics — JIE
Journal of International Economics — JIN
Journal of International Law and Economics — J Int L and Ec
Journal of International Law and Economics — J Int Law & Econ
Journal of International Law and Economics — J Int Law E
Journal of International Law and Economics — J Internat Law and Econ
Journal of International Law and Economics — J Intl L and Econ
Journal of International Law and Economics — J of Internat L and Econ
Journal of International Medical Research — J Int Med R
Journal of International Medical Research — J Int Med Res
Journal of International Money and Finance — JIMF
Journal of International Money and Finance — JMF
Journal of International Numismatics — J Int Num
Journal of International Relations — J Int Relations
Journal of International Relations — J Intern Rel
Journal of International Relations — J Internat Rel
Journal of International Research Communications — J Int Res Commun
Journal of Inverse and Ill-Posed Problems — J Inverse Ill Posed Probl
Journal of Invertebrate Pathology — J Inver Pat
Journal of Invertebrate Pathology — J Invert Path
Journal of Invertebrate Pathology — J Invertebr Pathol
Journal of Invertebrate Pathology — JIVPAZ
Journal of Investigational Allergology and Clinical Immunology — J Invest Allergol Clin Immunol
Journal of Investigational Allergology and Clinical Immunology — J Investig Allergol Clin Immunol
Journal of Investigative Dermatology — J Inves Der
Journal of Investigative Dermatology — J Invest Dermat
Journal of Investigative Dermatology — J Invest Dermatol
Journal of Investigative Dermatology Symposium Proceedings — J Invest Dermatol Symp Proc
Journal of Investigative Medicine — J Investig Med
Journal of Investigative Surgery — J Invest Surg
Journal of Ion Exchange — J Ion Exch

Journal of Iran Society — JIS
Journal of Irish Genealogy — JIG
Journal of Irish Literature — J Ir Lit
Journal of Irish Literature — J Irish Lit
Journal of Irish Literature — JIL
Journal of Iron and Steel Engineering — J Iron & Steel Eng
Journal of Irreproducible Results — Jrl Irrep
Journal of Irrigation and Drainage — IR
Journal of Irrigation and Drainage Engineering — J Irrig Drain Eng
Journal of Islamic and Comparative Law — J Islamic Comp Law
Journal of Isotopes — J Isot
Journal of Israel Numismatics — JIN
Journal of Italian Linguistics — Jnl Ital Ling
Journal of Japan Foundry Engineering Society — J Jpn Foundry Eng Soc
Journal of Japan Society for Atmospheric Environment — J Jpn Soc Atmos Environ
Journal of Japan Society for the Study of Obesity — J Jpn Soc Study Obes
Journal of Japan Women's University. Faculty of Science — J Jpn Womens Univ Fac Sci
Journal of Japanese Botany — J Jap Bot
Journal of Japanese Botany — J Jpn Bot
Journal of Japanese Chemistry — J Jap Chem
Journal of Japanese Chemistry — J Jpn Chem
Journal of Japanese Chemistry. Supplement — J Jpn Chem Suppl
Journal of Japanese Foundry Engineering Society — J Jpn Foundry Eng Soc
Journal of Japanese Studies — J Ja Stud
Journal of Japanese Studies — J Jpn Stud
Journal of Japanese Studies — JJS
Journal of Japanese Studies — PJJS
Journal of Japanese Trade and Industry — J Japanese Trade and Industry
Journal of Jazz Studies — J Jazz Stud
Journal of Jazz Studies — J Jazz Studies
Journal of Jazz Studies — JJ
Journal of Jazz Studies — JJS
Journal of Jewish Communal Service — J Jew Commun Serv
Journal of Jewish Communal Service — J Jewish Communal Service
Journal of Jewish Communal Service — JJCS
Journal of Jewish Communal Service — JJeCoS
Journal of Jewish Lore and Philosophy [*New York*] — JJewLorePh
Journal of Jewish Lore and Philosophy — JJLP
Journal of Jewish Music and Liturgy — Jewish Mus & Lit
Journal of Jewish Studies — J Jewish St
Journal of Jewish Studies — JJewS
Journal of Jewish Studies — JJS
Journal of Jewish Studies [*London*] — JJSt
Journal of Jewish Studies — Jo Je S
Journal of Jianghan Petroleum Institute — J Jianghan Pet Inst
Journal of Jinsen Medical Sciences — J Jinsen Med Sci
Journal of Jishou University. Natural Science Edition — J Jishou Univ Nat Sci Ed
Journal of Juristic Papyrology — J Jur P
Journal of Juristic Papyrology — J Jur Pap
Journal of Juristic Papyrology — JJP
Journal of Juristic Papyrology — Journ of Jur Pap
Journal of Juvenile Law — J Juv L
Journal of Juvenile Research — J Juvenile Res
Journal of Karyopathology; Especially Tumor and Tumorvirus — J Karyopathol Espec Tumor Tumorvirus
Journal of Karyopathology; Especially Tumor and Tumorvirus — J Karyopathol Tumor Tumorvirus
Journal of Knot Theory and its Ramifications — J Knot Theory Ramifications
Journal of Korea Forestry Energy — J Korea For Energy
Journal of Korean Medical Science — J Korean Med Sci
Journal of Korean Pharmaceutical Sciences — J Korean Pharm Sci
Journal of Kukem — J Kukem
Journal of Labelled Compounds [*Later, Journal of Labelled Compounds and Radiopharmaceuticals*] — J Label Com
Journal of Labelled Compounds [*Later, Journal of Labelled Compounds and Radiopharmaceuticals*] — J Labelled Compd
Journal of Labelled Compounds and Radiopharmaceuticals — J Label Compound Radiopharm
Journal of Labelled Compounds and Radiopharmaceuticals — J Labelled Compd Radiopharm
Journal of Labelled Compounds and Radiopharmaceuticals — JLCRD
Journal of Labor Economics — JLB
Journal of Labor Research — J Labor Research
Journal of Labor Research — J Lbr Res
Journal of Labor Research — JLR
Journal of Laboratory and Clinical Medicine — J La Cl Med
Journal of Laboratory and Clinical Medicine — J Lab Clin Med
Journal of Labour Hygiene in Iron and Steel Industry — J Labour Hyg Iron Steel Ind
Journal of Land and Public Utility Economics — J Land & PU Econ
Journal of Land and Public Utility Economics — J Land & Pub Util Econ
Journal of Land and Public Utility Economics — Jour Land Public Utility Econ
Journal of Lanzhou Railway College — J Lanzhou Railway College
Journal of Lanzhou Railway Institute — J Lanzhou Railway Inst
Journal of Laparoendoscopic Surgery — J Laparoendosc Surg
Journal of Laryngology and Otology — J Lar Otol
Journal of Laryngology and Otology — J Laryng
Journal of Laryngology and Otology — J Laryng Ot
Journal of Laryngology and Otology — J Laryngol Otol
Journal of Laryngology and Otology — JLOTA
Journal of Laryngology and Otology. Supplement — J Laryngol Otol Suppl
Journal of Latin American Lore — J Lat Am L
Journal of Latin American Lore — JLAL
Journal of Latin American Lore. University of California. Latin American Center — UCLA/JLAL
Journal of Latin American Studies — GLAS
Journal of Latin American Studies — J Lat Am St
Journal of Latin American Studies — J Lat Am Stud
Journal of Latin American Studies — J Latin Amer Stud
Journal of Latin American Studies — JLAS
Journal of Law and Commerce — J L and Com
Journal of Law and Economic Development — J L & Econ Develop
Journal of Law and Economic Development — J Law & Econ Dev
Journal of Law and Economic Development — JL & Econ Dev
Journal of Law and Economic Development — Jour Law and Econ
Journal of Law and Economics — J L and Ec
Journal of Law and Economics — J L & Econ
Journal of Law and Economics — J Law & Econ
Journal of Law and Economics — J Law Econ
Journal of Law and Economics — JLE
Journal of Law and Economics — Jol
Journal of Law and Education — J L and Ed
Journal of Law and Education — J L & Educ
Journal of Law and Education — J Law & Educ
Journal of Law and Information Science — JLIS
Journal of Law and Society — J Law Soc
Journal of Learning Disabilities — J Lear Disabil
Journal of Learning Disabilities — J Learn Di
Journal of Learning Disabilities — J Learn Dis
Journal of Learning Disabilities — J Learn Disab
Journal of Learning Disabilities — J Learn Disabil
Journal of Learning Disabilities — JLD
Journal of Learning Disabilities — JLDIA
Journal of Leather Research — J Leather Res
Journal of Legal Education — J Leg Ed
Journal of Legal Education — J Leg Educ
Journal of Legal Education — J Legal Ed
Journal of Legal Education — J Legal Educ
Journal of Legal Education — Jour Legal Ed
Journal of Legal History — J Leg Hist
Journal of Legal Medicine — J L Med
Journal of Legal Medicine — J Leg Med
Journal of Legal Medicine — J Legal Med
Journal of Legal Pluralism and Unofficial Law — J Leg Plur
Journal of Legal Studies — J L Studies
Journal of Legal Studies — J Leg Stud
Journal of Legal Studies — J Legal Stud
Journal of Legislation [*United States*] — J Legis
Journal of Legislation — J Legislation
Journal of Leisurability — J Leisur
Journal of Leisurability — J Leisurability
Journal of Leisure Research — J Leis Res
Journal of Leisure Research — J Leisure
Journal of Leisure Research — J Leisure Res
Journal of Leisure Research — JLER
Journal of Leisure Research — PLEI
Journal of Leukocyte Biology — J Leukoc Biol
Journal of Leukocyte Biology — J Leukocyte Biol
Journal of Leukocyte Biology. Supplement — J Leukoc Biol Suppl
Journal of Liaoning Normal University (Natural Science) — J Liaoning Norm Univ Nat Sci
Journal of Liberal Arts and Natural Sciences. Sapporo Medical College — J Lib Arts Nat Sci Sapporo Med Coll
Journal of Liberal Arts and Sciences. Kitasato University — J Lib Arts Sci Kitasato Univ
Journal of Liberal Arts and Sciences. Sapporo Medical College — J Lib Arts Sci Sapporo Med Coll
Journal of Libertarian Studies — J Liber Stud
Journal of Libertarian Studies — J Libertar Stud
Journal of Librarianship — J Libnship
Journal of Librarianship — J Libr
Journal of Librarianship — J Librarianship
Journal of Library Administration — J Lib Admin
Journal of Library and Information Science — J Lib and Info Science
Journal of Library and Information Science — J Lib Inf Sci
Journal of Library and Information Science — J Libr Inf Sci
Journal of Library Automation — J Lib Automation
Journal of Library Automation — J Libr Aut
Journal of Library Automation — J Libr Auto
Journal of Library Automation — J Libr Autom
Journal of Library Automation — J Libr Automn
Journal of Library Automation — JOLA
Journal of Library History [*Later, Journal of Library History, Philosophy, and Comparative Librarianship*] — J Lib Hist
Journal of Library History [*Later, Journal of Library History, Philosophy, and Comparative Librarianship*] — J Libr Hist
Journal of Library History [*Later, Journal of Library History, Philosophy, and Comparative Librarianship*] — JLH
Journal of Library History [*Later, Journal of Library History, Philosophy, and Comparative Librarianship*] — Jnl Lib Hist
Journal of Library History — JoL
Journal of Library History [*Later, Journal of Library History, Philosophy, and Comparative Librarianship*] — Jour Lib Hist
Journal of Library History, Philosophy, and Comparative Librarianship — J Lib Hist
Journal of Library History, Philosophy, and Comparative Librarianship — J Libr Hist

Journal of Library History, Philosophy, and Comparative Librarianship — JLH
Journal of Lie Theory — J Lie Theory
Journal of Life Sciences — J Life Sci
Journal of Life Sciences — Jnl Life Sci
Journal of Life Sciences. Royal Dublin Society — J Life Sci R Dublin Soc
Journal of Light and Visual Environment — J Light Visual Environ
Journal of Light Metal Welding and Construction — J Light Met Weld Constr
Journal of Lightwave Technology — J Lightwave Technol
Journal of Linguistic Research — JLR
Journal of Linguistics — J Lg
Journal of Linguistics — J Ling
Journal of Linguistics — J Linguist
Journal of Linguistics — J Linguistics
Journal of Linguistics — JL
Journal of Linguistics — PJLN
Journal of Lipid Mediators — J Lipid M
Journal of Lipid Mediators — J Lipid Mediators
Journal of Lipid Mediators and Cell Signalling — J Lipid Mediat Cell Signal
Journal of Lipid Research — J Lipid Res
Journal of Lipid Research — J Lipid Research
Journal of Liposome Research — J Liposome Res
Journal of Liquid Chromatography — J Liq Chromatogr
Journal of Liquid Chromatography — J Liquid Chromatogr
Journal of Liquid Chromatography and Related Technologies — J Liq Chromatogr Relat Technol
Journal of Literary Semantics — J Lit Sem
Journal of Literary Semantics — JLS
Journal of Local Administration Overseas — J Local Adm Ov
Journal of Logic and Computation — J Logic Comput
Journal of Logic, Language, and Information — J Logic Lang Inform
Journal of Logic Programming — J Logic Programming
Journal of Long Island History — JoLI
Journal of Long-Term Care Administration — J Long Term Care
Journal of Long-Term Care Administration — J Long Term Care Adm
Journal of Long-Term Care Administration — J Long Term Care Admin
Journal of Long-Term Effects of Medical Implants — J Long Term Eff Med Implants
Journal of Low Frequency Noise and Vibration — J Low Freq Noise Vib
Journal of Low Temperature Physics — J L Temp Ph
Journal of Low Temperature Physics — J Low Temp Phys
Journal of Low-Temperature Plasma Chemistry — Jnl Low Temp Plas Chem
Journal of Lubrication Technology — J Lubr Tech
Journal of Lubrication Technology — J Lubr Technol
Journal of Lubrication Technology. Transactions of the American Society of Mechanical Engineers — J Lub Tech
Journal of Lubrication Technology. Transactions of the American Society of Mechanical Engineers — J Lubr Technol Trans ASME
Journal of Lubrication Technology. Transactions of the American Society of Mechanical Engineers — J Lubric Technol Trans ASME
Journal of Luminescence — J Lumin
Journal of Luminescence — J Luminesc
Journal of Lymphology — J Lymphol
Journal of Macroeconomics — JMA
Journal of Macromarketing — JMM
Journal of Macromolecular Chemistry — J Macromol Chem
Journal of Macromolecular Science. Chemistry — J Macromol Sci Chem
Journal of Macromolecular Science. Chemistry. Supplement — J Macromol Sci Chem Suppl
Journal of Macromolecular Science. Part A. Chemistry — J Macr S Ch
Journal of Macromolecular Science. Part A. Chemistry — J Macromol Sci A
Journal of Macromolecular Science. Part A. Chemistry — J Macromol Sci Chem A
Journal of Macromolecular Science. Part A. Chemistry — J Macromol Sci Part A
Journal of Macromolecular Science. Part A. Chemistry — J Macromol Sci Part A Chem
Journal of Macromolecular Science. Part B. Physics — J Macr S Ph
Journal of Macromolecular Science. Part B. Physics — J Macromol Sci B
Journal of Macromolecular Science. Part B. Physics — J Macromol Sci Part B
Journal of Macromolecular Science. Part B. Physics — J Macromol Sci Phys
Journal of Macromolecular Science. Part C. Reviews in Macromolecular Chemistry — J Macr S Rm
Journal of Macromolecular Science. Part C. Reviews in Macromolecular Chemistry — J Macromol Sci C
Journal of Macromolecular Science. Part C. Reviews in Macromolecular Chemistry — J Macromol Sci Part C
Journal of Macromolecular Science. Part C. Reviews in Macromolecular Chemistry — J Macromol Sci Rev Macromol Chem
Journal of Macromolecular Science. Part D. Reviews in Polymer Technology — J Macromol Sci Part D
Journal of Macromolecular Science. Part D. Reviews in Polymer Technology — J Macromol Sci Rev Polym Technol
Journal of Macromolecular Science. Pure and Applied Chemistry — J Macromol Sci Pure Appl Chem
Journal of Macromolecular Science. Reviews in Macromolecular Chemistry and Physics — J Macromol Sci Rev Macromol Chem Phys
Journal of Magic History — J Magic Hist
Journal of Magnetic Resonance — J Magn Res
Journal of Magnetic Resonance — J Magn Reson
Journal of Magnetic Resonance — J Magn Resonance
Journal of Magnetic Resonance Imaging — J Magn Reson Imaging
Journal of Magnetic Resonance. Series B — J Magn Reson B
Journal of Magnetism and Magnetic Materials — J Magn and Magn Mater
Journal of Magnetism and Magnetic Materials — J Magn Magn Mater
Journal of Magnetism and Magnetic Materials — JMMMD
Journal of Magnetohydrodynamics and Plasma Research — J Magnetohydrodyn Plasma Res
Journal of Malacology — J Mal
Journal of Malaysian and Comparative Law — J Mal & Comp L
Journal of Maltese Studies — JMS
Journal of Mammalogy — J Mammal
Journal of Mammalogy — JMAM
Journal of Mammalogy — Jour Mammal
Journal of Mammalogy — PJMA
Journal of Management — J Manage
Journal of Management — J Mgt
Journal of Management — JOM
Journal of Management Consulting — JCS
Journal of Management Consulting — JMG
Journal of Management Development — JMD
Journal of Management Studies — J Manag Stu
Journal of Management Studies — J Manage Stud
Journal of Management Studies — J Mgt Stud
Journal of Management Studies — J Mgt Studies
Journal of Management Studies — JMN
Journal of Management Studies — JMS
Journal of Manipulative and Physiological Therapeutics — J Manip Physiol Ther
Journal of Manipulative and Physiological Therapeutics — J Manipulative Physiol Ther
Journal of Manipulative and Physiological Therapeutics — JMPT
Journal of Manufacturing and Operations Management — J Manuf Oper Management
Journal of Marine Environmental Engineering — J Mar Environ Eng
Journal of Marine Research — J Mar Res
Journal of Marine Research — J Marine Re
Journal of Marine Research — J Marine Res
Journal of Marine Science — J Mar Sci
Journal of Marital and Family Therapy — J Marital Fam Ther
Journal of Marital and Family Therapy — PJMF
Journal of Maritime Law and Commerce — J Mar L and Com
Journal of Maritime Law and Commerce — J Mar Law & Com
Journal of Maritime Law and Commerce — J Marit Law
Journal of Maritime Law and Commerce — J Maritime L
Journal of Maritime Law and Commerce — J Maritime Law and Commer
Journal of Maritime Law and Commerce — J of Marit L and Commerce
Journal of Maritime Law and Commerce — Mar L and Com
Journal of Marketing — J Mark
Journal of Marketing — J Market
Journal of Marketing — J Marketing
Journal of Marketing — J Mkt
Journal of Marketing — J Mktg
Journal of Marketing — J Mkting
Journal of Marketing — JM
Journal of Marketing — JMK
Journal of Marketing — Jnl Marketing
Journal of Marketing — Jrl Market
Journal of Marketing and Public Policy — JMPPD
Journal of Marketing for Professions — J Mark Prof
Journal of Marketing Research — J Mark Res
Journal of Marketing Research — J Market R
Journal of Marketing Research — J Marketing Res
Journal of Marketing Research — J Mkt Res
Journal of Marketing Research — J Mktg Res
Journal of Marketing Research — J Mkting Res
Journal of Marketing Research — JMR
Journal of Marketing Research — Jrl Mkt R
Journal of Marriage and the Family GMNF
Journal of Marriage and the Family — J Mar Fam
Journal of Marriage and the Family — J Marr & Fam
Journal of Marriage and the Family — J Marriage
Journal of Marriage and the Family — J Marriage & Fam
Journal of Marriage and the Family — J Marriage Family
Journal of Marriage and the Family — JMF
Journal of Marriage and the Family — Jnl Marr & Fam
Journal of Marriage and the Family — JOMF
Journal of Mass Spectrometry and Ion Physics — J Mass Sp Ion P
Journal of Mass Spectrometry and Ion Physics — J Mass Spectrom
Journal of Mass Spectrometry and Ion Physics — J Mass Spectrom Ion Phys
Journal of Materials — J Mater
Journal of Materials Chemistry — J Mat Chem
Journal of Materials Engineering — J Mater Eng
Journal of Materials Engineering and Performance — J Mater Eng Perform
Journal of Materials for Energy Systems — J Mater Energy Syst
Journal of Materials for Energy Systems — JMSMD
Journal of Materials in Civil Engineering — J Mater Civ Eng
Journal of Materials Research — J Mater Res
Journal of Materials Science — J Mat Sci
Journal of Materials Science — J Mater Sci
Journal of Materials Science — J Materials Sci
Journal of Materials Science. Letters — J Mat Sci Lett
Journal of Materials Science. Letters — J Mater Sci Lett
Journal of Materials Science. Materials in Electronics — J Mater Sci Mater Electron
Journal of Materials Science. Materials in Medicine — J Mater Sci Mater Med
Journal of Materials Shaping Technology — J Mater Shaping Technol
Journal of Materials Technology — J Mater Technol
Journal of Maternal-Fetal Medicine — J Matern Fetal Med
Journal of Mathematical Analysis and Applications — J Math Anal
Journal of Mathematical Analysis and Applications — J Math Anal and Appl
Journal of Mathematical Analysis and Applications — J Math Anal Appl

Journal of Mathematical and Physical Sciences — J Math and Phys Sci
Journal of Mathematical and Physical Sciences — J Mathematical and Physical Sci
Journal of Mathematical and Physical Sciences — JMPSB
Journal of Mathematical Biology — J Math Biol
Journal of Mathematical Chemistry — J Math Chem
Journal of Mathematical Economics — J Math Econom
Journal of Mathematical Economics — JME
Journal of Mathematical Imaging and Vision — J Math Imaging Vision
Journal of Mathematical Modelling for Teachers — J Math Modelling Teach
Journal of Mathematical Physics — J Math Phys
Journal of Mathematical Physics — J Mathematical Phys
Journal of Mathematical Physics (New York) — J Math Phys (NY)
Journal of Mathematical Psychology — J Math Psyc
Journal of Mathematical Psychology — J Math Psych
Journal of Mathematical Psychology — J Math Psychol
Journal of Mathematical Psychology — J Mathematical Psychology
Journal of Mathematical Research and Exposition — J Math Res Exposition
Journal of Mathematical Sciences — J Math Sci
Journal of Mathematical Sciences. University of Tokyo — J Math Sci Univ Tokyo
Journal of Mathematical Sociology — J Math Soci
Journal of Mathematical Sociology — J Math Sociol
Journal of Mathematical Sociology — J Mathematical Sociology
Journal of Mathematical Study — J Math Study
Journal of Mathematical Systems, Estimation, and Control — J Math Systems Estim Control
Journal of Mathematics and Mechanics — J Math Mech
Journal of Mathematics and Mechanics — JOMMA
Journal of Mathematics and Physics — J Math & Phys
Journal of Mathematics and Physics — J Math Phys
Journal of Mathematics and Physics (Cambridge, Massachusetts) — J Math Phys (Cambridge Mass)
Journal of Mathematics and Sciences — J Math Sci
Journal of Mathematics (Jabalpur) — J Math (Jabalpur)
Journal of Mathematics. Kyoto University — J Math Kyoto Univ
Journal of Mathematics. Kyoto University — JMKU
Journal of Mathematics. New Series — J Math NS
Journal of Mathematics. Tokushima University — J Math Tokushima Univ
Journal of Maxillofacial Orthopedics — J Maxillofac Orthop
Journal of Maxillofacial Surgery — J Maxillofac Surg
Journal of Mayan Linguistics — JM Ling
Journal of Mechanical Design [*United States*] — J Mech Des
Journal of Mechanical Design. Transactions of the American Society of Mechanical Engineers — J Mech Des Trans ASME
Journal of Mechanical Engineering Science — J Mech E
Journal of Mechanical Engineering Science — J Mech Eng
Journal of Mechanical Engineering Science — J Mech Eng Sci
Journal of Mechanical Engineering Science — J Mech Engng Sci
Journal of Mechanical Working Technology — J Mech Work Technol
Journal of Mechanical Working Technology — J Mech Working Technol
Journal of Mechanisms — J Mech
Journal of Mechanochemistry and Cell Motility — J Mechanochem & Cell Motility
Journal of Mechanochemistry and Cell Motility — J Mechanochem Cell Motil
Journal of Mechanochemistry and Cell Motility — J Mechanochem Cell Motility
Journal of Medical and Veterinary Mycology — J Med Vet Mycol
Journal of Medical Education — J M Educ
Journal of Medical Education — J Med Ed
Journal of Medical Education — J Med Educ
Journal of Medical Education — JMEDA
Journal of Medical Electronics — J Med El
Journal of Medical Electronics — J Med Electron
Journal of Medical Engineering and Technology — J Med Eng and Technol
Journal of Medical Engineering and Technology — J Med Eng Technol
Journal of Medical Entomology — J Med Ent
Journal of Medical Entomology — J Med Entomol
Journal of Medical Entomology. Supplement — J Med Entomol Suppl
Journal of Medical Enzymology — J Med Enzymol
Journal of Medical Ethics — J Med Ethic
Journal of Medical Ethics — J Med Ethics
Journal of Medical Ethics — PJME
Journal of Medical Genetics — J Med Genet
Journal of Medical Genetics — JM Genet
Journal of Medical Humanities and Bioethics — J Med Hum Bioeth
Journal of Medical Humanities and Bioethics — J Med Humanit Bioethics
Journal of Medical Laboratory Technology — J Med Lab Technol
Journal of Medical Microbiology — J Med Micro
Journal of Medical Microbiology — J Med Microbiol
Journal of Medical Primatology — J Med Prim
Journal of Medical Primatology — J Med Primatol
Journal of Medical Primatology — JMPMA
Journal of Medical Research — J Med Res
Journal of Medical Sciences — J Med Sci
Journal of Medical Sciences. Banaras Hindu University — J Med Sci Banaras Hindu Univ
Journal of Medical Sciences (Taipei) — J Med Sci Taipei
Journal of Medical Screening — J Med Screen
Journal of Medical Systems — J Med Syst
Journal of Medical Technology — J Med Technol
Journal of Medical Technology (Tokyo) — J Med Technol (Tokyo)
Journal of Medical Virology — J Med Virol
Journal of Medicinal and Aromatic Plant Sciences — J Med Aromat Plant Sci
Journal of Medicinal and Pharmaceutical Chemistry — J Med Pharm Chem
Journal of Medicinal Chemistry — J Med Chem
Journal of Medicinal Chemistry — JMC
Journal of Medicinal Plant Research. Planta Medica — J Med Plant Res
Journal of Medicine — J Med
Journal of Medicine and International Medical Abstracts and Reviews — J Med Int Med Abstr Rev
Journal of Medicine and Pharmaceutical Science — J Med Pharm Sci
Journal of Medicine and Philosophy — J Med Phil
Journal of Medicine and Philosophy — J Med Philos
Journal of Medicine and Philosophy — PJMP
Journal of Medicine (Cincinnati) — J Med (Cincinnati)
Journal of Medicine. Experimental and Clinical — J Med Exp Clin
Journal of Medicine. Experimental and Clinical (Basel) — J Med (Basel)
Journal of Medicine. Mie Prefectural University — J Med Mie Prefect Univ
Journal of Medicine (Westbury, New York) — J Med (Westbury NY)
Journal of Medieval and Renaissance Studies — J Mediev R
Journal of Medieval and Renaissance Studies — J Mediev Renaissance Stud
Journal of Medieval and Renaissance Studies — J Medieval Renaiss Stud
Journal of Medieval and Renaissance Studies — JMRS
Journal of Medieval and Renaissance Studies — JoMa
Journal of Medieval and Renaissance Studies — PJMR
Journal of Medieval History — J Mediev Hi
Journal of Medieval History — J Medieval Hist
Journal of Medieval History — JMeH
Journal of Medieval History — JMH
Journal of Mediterranean Anthropology and Archaeology — J Mediterr Anthropol Archaeol
Journal of Membrane Biology — J Membr Bio
Journal of Membrane Biology — J Membr Biol
Journal of Membrane Biology — J Membrane Biol
Journal of Membrane Science — J Membr Sci
Journal of Membrane Science — J Membrane Sci
Journal of Mental Deficiency Research — J Ment Def
Journal of Mental Deficiency Research — J Ment Defic Res
Journal of Mental Deficiency Research — J Mental Def Research
Journal of Mental Health — J Ment Health
Journal of Mental Science — J Ment Sc
Journal of Mental Science — J Ment Sci
Journal of Mental Science — JMSCA
Journal of Mental Subnormality — J Ment Subnorm
Journal of Mental Subnormality — JMSBA
Journal of Metabolic Research — J Metab Res
Journal of Metal Finishing — J Met Finish
Journal of Metallurgy — J Metall
Journal of Metals — J Met
Journal of Metals — J Metals
Journal of Metals — JOM
Journal of Metals — Jrl Metals
Journal of Metals (Tokyo) — J Met (Tokyo)
Journal of Metamorphic Geology — J Metamorph Geol
Journal of Metamorphic Geology — JMG
Journal of Meteorological Research [*Japan*] — J Meteorol Res
Journal of Meteorology — J Met
Journal of Meteorology [*United States*] — J Meteorol
Journal of Meteorology — JOMYA
Journal of Methods-Time Measurement — MTM
Journal of Mexican American History — J Mex Am Hist
Journal of Microbial Biotechnology — J Microb Biotechnol
Journal of Microbiological Methods — J Microbiol Methods
Journal of Microbiological Methods — JMM
Journal of Microbiology — J Microbiol
Journal of Microbiology and Serology — J Microbiol Serol
Journal of Microbiology (Chaoyang, People's Republic of China) — J Microbiol (Chaoyang Peoples Repub China)
Journal of Microbiology, Epidemiology, and Immunobiology — J Microbiol Epidem Immunobiol
Journal of Microbiology, Epidemiology, and Immunobiology. English Translation — J Microbiol Epidemiol Immunobiol Engl Transl
Journal of Microbiology, Epidemiology, and Immunobiology (USSR) — J Microbiol Epidemiol Immunobiol (USSR)
Journal of Microbiology of the United Arab Republic — J Microbiol UAR
Journal of Microbiology (Seoul) — J Microbiol Seoul
Journal of Microcolumn Separations — J Microcolumn Sep
Journal of Microcomputer Applications — J Microcomput Appl
Journal of Microelectromechanical Systems — J Microelectromech Syst
Journal of Microencapsulation — J Microencapsul
Journal of Microencapsulation — J Microencapsulation
Journal of Micrographics — J Microgr
Journal of Micrographics — J Micrographics
Journal of Micrographics — JMG
Journal of Micronutrient Analysis — J Micronutr Anal
Journal of Microorganisms and Fermentation — J Microorg Ferment
Journal of Microphotography — J Microphotogr
Journal of Microscopy — J Microsc
Journal of Microscopy — J Microscopy
Journal of Microscopy and Natural Science — J Micr and Nat Sc
Journal of Microscopy (Oxford) — J Microsc (O)
Journal of Microscopy (Oxford) — J Microsc (Oxf)
Journal of Microsurgery — J Microsurg
Journal of Microwave Power — J Microwave Power
Journal of Microwave Power — J Microwave Pwr
Journal of Microwave Power — JLMPA
Journal of Microwave Power — JMPO
Journal of Microwave Power and Electromagnetic Energy — J Microw Power Electromagn Energy
Journal of Microwave Power and Electromagnetic Energy. A Publication. International Microwave Power Institute — J Microwave Power Elctromagn Energy Publ Int Microwave Power

Journal of Military Assistance — JOMA
Journal of Military History — PJMH
Journal of Milk and Food Technology [*Later, Journal of Food Protection*] — J Milk & Food Tech
Journal of Milk and Food Technology [*Later, Journal of Food Protection*] — J Milk Food
Journal of Milk and Food Technology [*Later, Journal of Food Protection*] — J Milk Food Technol
Journal of Milk and Food Technology [*Later, Journal of Food Protection*] — JMFT
Journal of Milk Technology — J Milk Tech
Journal of Milk Technology — J Milk Technol
Journal of Mineralogy, Petrology, and Economic Geology — J Mineral Petrol Econ Geol
Journal of Mines, Metals, and Fuels — J Mines Met Fuels
Journal of Mines, Metals, and Fuels [*Calcutta*] — J Mines Metals Fuels
Journal of Mines, Metals, and Fuels (Calcutta) — J Mines Met Fuels (Calcutta)
Journal of Mining and Geology [*Nigeria*] — J Min Geol
Journal of Mining and Metallurgy. Foundry — J Min Metall Foundry
Journal of Mining and Metallurgy. Metallurgy — J Min Metall Metall
Journal of Minnesota Public Law — Jnl Minn Pub Law
Journal of Missile Defense Research — JMDR
Journal of Mississippi History — J Miss Hist
Journal of Mississippi History — JMH
Journal of Mississippi History — JMiH
Journal of Mississippi History — JMissH
Journal of Mississippi History — JoM
Journal of Mississippi History — Jour Miss Hist
Journal of Mithraic Studies — JMS
Journal of Mithraic Studies — Jnl Mithraic Stud
Journal of Modern African Studies — J Mod Afr S
Journal of Modern African Studies — J Mod Afr Stud
Journal of Modern African Studies — J Mod Afr Studs
Journal of Modern African Studies — J Mod Afric Stud
Journal of Modern African Studies — JMAS
Journal of Modern African Studies — JoMAS
Journal of Modern African Studies — PJST
Journal of Modern Greek Studies — JMGS
Journal of Modern History GMHI
Journal of Modern History — J Mod Hist
Journal of Modern History — JMH
Journal of Modern History — Jnl Mod Hist
Journal of Modern History — JoMH
Journal of Modern History — Jour Mod Hist
Journal of Modern Literature — GMLI
Journal of Modern Literature — J Mod Lit
Journal of Modern Literature — JML
Journal of Modern Optics — J Mod Opt
Journal of Modern Optics — J Modern Opt
Journal of Modern Watchmaking — J Mod Watchmaking
Journal of Molecular and Applied Genetics — J Mol Appl Genet
Journal of Molecular and Applied Genetics — JMAG
Journal of Molecular and Applied Genetics — Jnl Mol Appl Genet
Journal of Molecular and Cellular Cardiology — J Mol Cel C
Journal of Molecular and Cellular Cardiology — J Mol Cell Cardiol
Journal of Molecular and Cellular Immunology — J Mol Cell Immunol
Journal of Molecular and Cellular Immunology — JMCI
Journal of Molecular Biology — J Mol Biol
Journal of Molecular Biology — J Molec Biol
Journal of Molecular Biology — JMB
Journal of Molecular Catalysis — J Mol Catal
Journal of Molecular Catalysis — JMCAD
Journal of Molecular Catalysis A. Chemical — J Mol Catal A Chem
Journal of Molecular Catalysis B. Enzymatic — J Mol Catal B Enzym
Journal of Molecular Catalysis (China) — J Mol Catal (China)
Journal of Molecular Electronics — J Mol Electron
Journal of Molecular Endocrinology — J Mol Endoc
Journal of Molecular Endocrinology — J Mol Endocrinol
Journal of Molecular Evolution — J Mol Evol
Journal of Molecular Graphics — J Mol Graph
Journal of Molecular Graphics — J Mol Graphics
Journal of Molecular Graphics — JMG
Journal of Molecular Liquids — J Mol Liq
Journal of Molecular Medicine — J Mol Med
Journal of Molecular Medicine (Berlin) — J Mol Med Berlin
Journal of Molecular Modeling [*Electronic Publication*] — J Mol Model Electronic Publication
Journal of Molecular Neuroscience — J Mol Neuro
Journal of Molecular Neuroscience — J Mol Neurosci
Journal of Molecular Recognition — J Mol Recognit
Journal of Molecular Recognition — JMR
Journal of Molecular Science — J Mol Sci
Journal of Molecular Science. International Edition — J Mol Sci Int Ed
Journal of Molecular Spectroscopy — J Mol Spect
Journal of Molecular Spectroscopy — J Mol Spectrosc
Journal of Molecular Structure — J Mol Struct
Journal of Molecular Structure — JMS
Journal of Molluscan Studies — J Molluscan Stud
Journal of Molluscan Studies. Supplement — J Molluscan Stud Suppl
Journal of Monetary Economics — J Monet Econ
Journal of Monetary Economics — J Monetary Econ
Journal of Monetary Economics — JME
Journal of Money, Credit, and Banking — J Money Cred & Bank
Journal of Money, Credit, and Banking — J Money Cred Bank
Journal of Money, Credit, and Banking — J Money Credit & Banking
Journal of Money, Credit, and Banking — J Money Credit Bank
Journal of Money, Credit, and Banking — JMB
Journal of Money, Credit, and Banking — JMCB
Journal of Moral Education — J Moral Ed
Journal of Moral Education — J Moral Educ
Journal of Mormon History — J Mormon Hist
Journal of Morphology — J Morph
Journal of Morphology — J Morphol
Journal of Morphology and Physiology — J Morph and Physiol
Journal of Morphology and Physiology — J Morphol Physiol
Journal of Morphology. Supplement — J Morphol Suppl
Journal of Moscow Patriarchate — JMP
Journal of Motor Behavior — J Mot Behav
Journal of Motor Behavior — J Motor Beh
Journal of Multivariate Analysis — J Multivar Anal
Journal of Multivariate Analysis — J Multivariate Anal
Journal of Multivariate Analysis — JMultiAn
Journal of Muscle Research and Cell Motility — J Muscle Res Cell Motil
Journal of Muscle Research and Cell Motility — Jnl Muscle Res Cell Motil
Journal of Music Teacher Education — JMTE
Journal of Music Theory — J Mus Theory
Journal of Music Theory — J Music Theory
Journal of Music Theory — J Music Thr
Journal of Music Theory — JM
Journal of Music Theory — JMTheory
Journal of Music Theory — JMUTB
Journal of Music Theory Pedagogy — J Mus Theory Pedagogy
Journal of Music Therapy — J Mus Ther
Journal of Music Therapy — J Mus Therapy
Journal of Music Therapy — J Music Ther
Journal of Music Therapy — JMT
Journal of Music Therapy — JMTherapy
Journal of Music Therapy — JMUTA
Journal of Music Therapy — JT
Journal of Musicological Research — J Mus Res
Journal of Musicological Research — J Music Res
Journal of Musicology — Jl Musicology
Journal of Musicology — JMus
Journal of Musicology — PJMU
Journal of Mycology — J Mycol
Journal of Nagano-ken Junior College — J Nagano-ken Jr Coll
Journal of Nagasaki Medical Association — J Nagasaki Med Assoc
Journal of NAL Associates — J NAL Assoc
Journal of Nanjing Institute of Chemical Technology — J Nanjing Inst Chem Technol
Journal of Nanjing Institute of Technology — J Nanjing Inst Tech
Journal of Nanjing Institute of Technology (English Edition) — J Nanjing Inst Tech English Ed
Journal of Nanjing University of Aeronautics and Astronautics — J Nanjing Univ Aeronaut Astronaut
Journal of Nanjing University of Science and Technology — J Nanjing Univ Sci Technol
Journal of Narrative Technique — J Narr Tech
Journal of Narrative Technique — JNT
Journal of Natal and Zulu History — J Natal Zulu Hist
Journal of National Academy of Mathematics. India — J Nat Acad Math India
Journal of National Science and Mathematics — J Nat Sci and Math
Journal of Natural Geometry — J Natur Geom
Journal of Natural History — J Nat Hist
Journal of Natural History — J Natur Hist
Journal of Natural History — J Natural Hist
Journal of Natural Philosophy, Chemistry, and the Arts — J Nat Philos
Journal of Natural Physical Sciences — J Natur Phys Sci
Journal of Natural Products — J Nat Prod
Journal of Natural Products — JNPRD
Journal of Natural Products (Lloydia) — J Nat Prod (Lloydia)
Journal of Natural Resources Management and Interdisciplinary Studies — JNRM
Journal of Natural Rubber Research — J Nat Rubber Res
Journal of Natural Rubber Research — JNRREQ
Journal of Natural Science. Beijing Normal University — J Nat Sci Beijing Norm Univ
Journal of Natural Science. Chonnam National University — J Nat Sci Chonnam Natl Univ
Journal of Natural Science. Chonnam National University — JNCUD
Journal of Natural Science. College of Science. Korea University — J Nat Sci Coll Sci Korea Univ
Journal of Natural Sciences [*Malaysia*] — J Nat Sci
Journal of Natural Sciences and Mathematics — J Nat Sci Math
Journal of Natural Sciences and Mathematics — J Natur Sci and Math
Journal of Natural Sciences and Mathematics — J Natur Sci Math
Journal of Natural Sciences and Mathematics (Lahore) — J Nat Sci Math (Lahore)
Journal of Natural Sciences. College of General Studies. Seoul National University — J Nat Sci Coll Gen Stud Seoul Natl Univ
Journal of Natural Sciences (Seoul) — J Nat Sci Seoul
Journal of Natural Sciences. Yeungnam University — J Nat Sci Yeungnam Univ
Journal of Navigation — J Navig
Journal of NDI [*Japan*] — J NDI
Journal of Near Eastern Studies — J Near E St
Journal of Near Eastern Studies — J Near E Stud
Journal of Near Eastern Studies — J Near East
Journal of Near Eastern Studies — J Near East St
Journal of Near Eastern Studies — J Near East Stud
Journal of Near Eastern Studies — J Near Eastern Stud
Journal of Near Eastern Studies — JNE

Journal of Near Eastern Studies — JNES
Journal of Near Eastern Studies [*Chicago*] — Journal Near East Stud
Journal of Near Eastern Studies — PJNE
Journal of Negro Education — J Negro Ed
Journal of Negro Education — J Negro Educ
Journal of Negro Education — J of Neg Ed
Journal of Negro Education — J of Negro Educ
Journal of Negro Education — JNE
Journal of Negro Education — JNEEA
Journal of Negro Education — Jnl Negro Ed
Journal of Negro History — J Neg Hist
Journal of Negro History — J Negro His
Journal of Negro History — J Negro Hist
Journal of Negro History — J of Negro Hist
Journal of Negro History — JNH
Journal of Negro History — Jnl Negro Hist
Journal of Negro History — JoN
Journal of Negro History — Jr N H
Journal of Nematology — J Nematol
Journal of Nephrology Nursing — J Nephrol Nurs
Journal of Nervous and Mental Disease — J Nerv Ment
Journal of Nervous and Mental Disease — J Nerv Ment Dis
Journal of Nervous and Mental Disease — JNMD
Journal of Nervous and Mental Disease — JNMDA
Journal of Neural Transmission — J Neural Tr
Journal of Neural Transmission — J Neural Transm
Journal of Neural Transmission. General Section — J Neur Tr-G
Journal of Neural Transmission. General Section — J Neural Transm Gen Sect
Journal of Neural Transmission. Parkinson's Disease and Dementia Section — J Neur Tr-P
Journal of Neural Transmission. Parkinsons Disease and Dementia Section — J Neural Transm Park Dis Dement Sect
Journal of Neural Transmission Parkinson's Disease and Dementia Section — J Neural Transm Parkinson's Dis Dementia Sect
Journal of Neural Transmission. Supplementum — J Neural Transm Suppl
Journal of Neural Transplantation and Plasticity — J Neural Transplant Plast
Journal of Neurobiology — J Neurobiol
Journal of Neurochemistry — J Neurochem
Journal of Neurocytology — J Neurocyt
Journal of Neurocytology — J Neurocytol
Journal of Neurocytology — JNCYA
Journal of Neuroendocrinology — J Neuroendo
Journal of Neuroendocrinology — J Neuroendocrinol
Journal of Neurogenetics — J Neurogen
Journal of Neurogenetics — J Neurogenet
Journal of Neuroimaging — J Neuroimaging
Journal of Neuroimmunology — J Neuroimmunol
Journal of Neuroimmunology — Jnl Neuroimmunol
Journal of Neuroimmunology. Supplement — J Neuroimmunol Suppl
Journal of Neurology — J Neurol
Journal of Neurology (Berlin) — J Neurol (Berlin)
Journal of Neurology, Neurosurgery, and Psychiatry — J Ne Ne Psy
Journal of Neurology, Neurosurgery, and Psychiatry — J Neurol Neurosurg Psychiat
Journal of Neurology, Neurosurgery, and Psychiatry — J Neurol Neurosurg Psychiatry
Journal of Neurology, Neurosurgery, and Psychiatry — JNNPA
Journal of Neuro-Oncology — J Neuro-Oncol
Journal of Neuro-Ophthalmology — J Neuroophthalmol
Journal of Neuropathology and Experimental Neurology — J Ne Exp Ne
Journal of Neuropathology and Experimental Neurology — J Neuropath Exp Neurol
Journal of Neuropathology and Experimental Neurology — J Neuropath Exper Neurol
Journal of Neuropathology and Experimental Neurology — J Neuropathol Exp Neurol
Journal of Neurophysiology — J Neurophysiol
Journal of Neurophysiology — J Neurphysl
Journal of Neurophysiology — JONEA
Journal of Neurophysiology (Bethesda) — J Neurophysiol (Bethesda)
Journal of Neuropsychiatry — J Neuropsychiat
Journal of Neuropsychiatry — J Neuropsychiatry
Journal of Neuropsychiatry and Clinical Neurosciences — J Neuropsychiatry Clin Neurosci
Journal of Neuropsychiatry. Supplement — J Neuropsychiatr Suppl
Journal of Neuroradiology — J Neuroradiol
Journal of Neuroscience — J Neurosci
Journal of Neuroscience — JN
Journal of Neuroscience Methods — J Neurosci Methods
Journal of Neuroscience Methods — JNMED
Journal of Neuroscience Nursing — J Neurosci Nurs
Journal of Neuroscience Research — J Neurosci Res
Journal of Neurosurgery — J Neurosurg
Journal of Neurosurgical Anesthesiology — J Neurosurg Anesthesiol
Journal of Neurosurgical Nursing — J Neurosurg Nurs
Journal of Neurosurgical Nursing — JNSNA
Journal of Neurosurgical Sciences — J Neurosurg Sci
Journal of Neurosurgical Sciences — JNSSB
Journal of Neurotrauma — J Neurotrauma
Journal of Neurovirology — J Neurovirol
Journal of Neuro-Visceral Relations — J Neuro-Visc Relat
Journal of Neuro-Visceral Relations. Supplementum — J Neuro Visc Relat Suppl
Journal of Neutron Research — J Neutron Res
Journal of New Drugs — J New Drugs
Journal of New Drugs — JNDRA
Journal of New Energy — J New Energy
Journal of New Generation Computer Systems — J New Generation Comput Systems
Journal of New Jersey Poets — JnlONJP
Journal of New Music Research — J New Mus Res
Journal of New Remedies and Clinics — J New Rem Clin
Journal of New World Archaeology — Jnl New Wld Archaeol
Journal of NMR [*Nuclear Magnetic Resonance*] **Medicine** — J NMR Med
Journal of Non-Classical Logic — J Non Classical Logic
Journal of Non-Crystalline Solids — J Non-Cryst
Journal of Non-Crystalline Solids — J Non-Cryst Solids
Journal of Nondestructive Evaluation [*United States*] — J Nondestr Eval
Journal of Non-Destructive Inspection — J Non-Destr Insp
Journal of Non-Equilibrium Thermodynamics — J Non-Equilib Thermodyn
Journal of Non-Equilibrium Thermodynamics — JNETD
Journal of Nonlinear Mathematical Physics — J Nonlinear Math Phys
Journal of Nonlinear Optical Physics and Materials — J Nonlinear Opt Phys Mater
Journal of Nonlinear Science — J Nonlinear Sci
Journal of Nonmetals [*Later, Semiconductors and Insulators*] — J Nonmet
Journal of Nonmetals [*Semiconductors and Insulators*] [*England*] [*Later,*] — JNMTA
Journal of Nonmetals and Semiconductors [*Later, Semiconductors and Insulators*] [*A publication*] — J Nonmet and Semicond
Journal of Nonmetals and Semiconductors [*Later, Semiconductors and Insulators*] [*A publication*] — J Nonmet Semicond
Journal of Non-Newtonian Fluid Mechanics — J Non-Newtonian Fluid Mech
Journal of Nonparametric Statistics — J Nonparametr Statist
Journal of Nonverbal Behavior — J Nonverbal Behav
Journal of Nonverbal Behavior — JNVBDV
Journal of Nonverbal Behavior — PJNB
Journal of Northeast Asian Studies — J Northeast Asian Studies
Journal of Northeast University of Technology — J Northeast Univ Tech
Journal of Northeastern University. Natural Science — J Northeast Univ Nat Sci
Journal of Northern Luzon — J No Luzon
Journal of Northern Luzon — JNL
Journal of Northern Studies — JONS
Journal of Northwest Atlantic Fishery Science — J Northwest Atl Fish Sci
Journal of Northwest Atlantic Fishery Science — JNAFS
Journal of Northwest Atlantic Fishery Science — JNFS
Journal of Northwest University. Natural Sciences — J Northwest Univ
Journal of Nuclear Agriculture and Biology — J Nucl Agric Biol
Journal of Nuclear Agriculture and Biology — JNABD
Journal of Nuclear and Radiochemistry (Peking) — J Nucl Radiochem (Peking)
Journal of Nuclear Biology and Medicine — J Nucl Biol
Journal of Nuclear Biology and Medicine — J Nucl Biol Med
Journal of Nuclear Cardiology — J Nucl Cardiol
Journal of Nuclear Energy — J Nucl Energ
Journal of Nuclear Energy — J Nucl Energy
Journal of Nuclear Energy [*New York*] [*1954-59*] — JNUCA
Journal of Nuclear Energy. Part A. Reactor Science — J Nucl Energy Part A
Journal of Nuclear Energy. Part B. Reactor Technology — J Nucl Energy Part B
Journal of Nuclear Energy. Part C. Plasma Physics, Accelerators, Thermonuclear Research — J Nucl Energy Part C
Journal of Nuclear Energy. Parts A/B. Reactor Science and Technology — J Nucl Energy Parts A/B
Journal of Nuclear Materials — J Nucl Mat
Journal of Nuclear Materials — J Nucl Mater
Journal of Nuclear Materials Management — J Nucl Mater Manage
Journal of Nuclear Medicine — J Nucl Med
Journal of Nuclear Medicine — J Nuclear Med
Journal of Nuclear Medicine and Allied Sciences — J Nucl Med Allied Sci
Journal of Nuclear Medicine and Allied Sciences — JNMSD
Journal of Nuclear Medicine. Pamphlet — J Nucl Med Pam
Journal of Nuclear Medicine. Supplement — J Nucl Med Suppl
Journal of Nuclear Medicine Technology — J Nucl Med Technol
Journal of Nuclear Physics (Moscow) — J Nucl Phys (Moscow)
Journal of Nuclear Science and Technology — J Nuc Sci T
Journal of Nuclear Science and Technology — J Nucl Sci and Technol
Journal of Nuclear Science and Technology — J Nucl Sci Technol
Journal of Nuclear Science and Technology — J Nuclear Sci Tech
Journal of Nuclear Sciences (Seoul) — J Nucl Sci (Seoul)
Journal of Number Theory — J Number Th
Journal of Number Theory — J Number Theory
Journal of Numismatic Fine Arts — JNFA
Journal of Nurse Midwifery — J Nurs Midwife
Journal of Nurse Midwifery — J Nurse Midwife
Journal of Nurse-Midwifery — J Nurse Midwifery
Journal of Nursery Education — J Nurs Ed
Journal of Nursing Administration — J Nurs Adm
Journal of Nursing Administration — J Nurs Admin
Journal of Nursing Care — J Nurs Care
Journal of Nursing Care Quality — J Nurs Care Qual
Journal of Nursing Education — J Nurs Ed
Journal of Nursing Education — J Nurs Educ
Journal of Nursing Education — JNE
Journal of Nursing Ethics — J Nurs Ethics
Journal of Nursing History — J Nurs Hist
Journal of Nursing Measurement — J Nurs Meas
Journal of Nursing Staff Development — J Nurs Staff Dev
Journal of Nursing (Taipei) — J Nurs (Taipei)
Journal of Nutrition — J Nutr
Journal of Nutrition and Dietetics — J Nutr Diet
Journal of Nutrition Education — J Nutr Educ
Journal of Nutrition Education — JNE

Journal of Nutrition Education — JONE
Journal of Nutrition Education — PJNU
Journal of Nutrition for the Elderly — J Nutr Elderly
Journal of Nutrition for the Elderly — JNELDA
Journal of Nutrition, Growth, and Cancer — J Nutr Growth Cancer
Journal of Nutrition. Supplement [*United States*] — J Nutr Suppl
Journal of Nutrition (Tokyo) — J Nutr (Tokyo)
Journal of Nutritional and Environmental Medicine — J Nutr Environ Med
Journal of Nutritional Assessment — J Nutr Assess
Journal of Nutritional Biochemistry — J Nutr Biochem
Journal of Nutritional Science and Vitaminology — J Nutr Sc V
Journal of Nutritional Science and Vitaminology — J Nutr Sci Vitaminol
Journal of Nutritional Sciences — J Nutr Sci
Journal of Nutritional Sciences. Supplementum — J Nutr Sci Suppl
Journal of Obesity and Weight Regulation — J Obes Weight Regul
Journal of Obesity and Weight Regulation — J Obesity Weight Regul
Journal of Obesity and Weight Regulation — JOWRDN
Journal of Obstetric, Gynecologic, and Neonatal Nursing — J Obstet Gynecol Neonatal Nurs
Journal of Obstetric, Gynecologic, and Neonatal Nursing — JOGNN
Journal of Obstetrics and Gynaecology — J Obstet Gynaecol
Journal of Obstetrics and Gynaecology. British Empire — J Obstet Gynaecol Brit Empire
Journal of Obstetrics and Gynaecology of India — J Obstet Gynaecol India
Journal of Obstetrics and Gynaecology of the British Commonwealth — J Obstet Gynaec Br Commonw
Journal of Obstetrics and Gynaecology of the British Commonwealth — J Obstet Gynaec Brit Cmwlth
Journal of Obstetrics and Gynaecology of the British Commonwealth — J Obstet Gynaec Brit Common
Journal of Obstetrics and Gynaecology of the British Commonwealth — J Obstet Gynaecol Br Commonw
Journal of Obstetrics and Gynaecology of the British Empire — J Obst and Gynaec Brit Emp
Journal of Obstetrics and Gynaecology of the British Empire — J Obstet Gynaec Brit Emp
Journal of Obstetrics and Gynaecology of the British Empire — J Obstet Gynaecol Br Emp
Journal of Obstetrics and Gynaecology Research — J Obstet Gynaecol Res
Journal of Obstetrics and Gynaecology (Tokyo) — J Obstet Gynaecol Tokyo
Journal of Occupational Accidents — J Occup Accid
Journal of Occupational Accidents — J Occupational Accidents
Journal of Occupational and Environmental Medicine — J Occup Environ Med
Journal of Occupational Behaviour — J Occ Bhvr
Journal of Occupational Behaviour — J Occup Behav
Journal of Occupational Behaviour — JOB
Journal of Occupational Health — J Occup Health
Journal of Occupational Medicine — J Occ Med
Journal of Occupational Medicine — J Occup Med
Journal of Occupational Medicine — J Occupa Med
Journal of Occupational Medicine — J Occupat Med
Journal of Occupational Medicine — JOCMA
Journal of Occupational Medicine — JOM
Journal of Occupational Medicine — JOOM
Journal of Occupational Medicine and Toxicology — J Occup Med Toxicol
Journal of Occupational Psychology — J Occ Psy
Journal of Occupational Psychology — J Occup Psychol
Journal of Occupational Psychology — J Occupa Psychol
Journal of Occupational Psychology — JOP
Journal of Ocean Technology — J Ocean Technol
Journal of Ocular Pharmacolgy and Therapeutics — J Ocul Pharmacol Ther
Journal of Ocular Pharmacology — J Ocul Pharmacol
Journal of Ocular Therapy and Surgery — J Ocul Ther Surg
Journal of Ocular Therapy and Surgery — Jnl Ocular Ther Surg
Journal of Odontology. Osaka University — J Odontol Osaka Univ
Journal of Odor Control — J Odor Control
Journal of Offender Counseling, Services, and Rehabilitation — JOCS
Journal of Oil and Fat Industries — J Oil Fat Ind
Journal of Oil and Fat Industries — Jnl Oil Fat Ind
Journal of Oilseeds Research — J Oilseeds Res
Journal of Oilseeds Research — JOREES
Journal of Okayama Prefectural Agricultural Experiment Station/Okayama-Kenritsu Nogyo Shikenjo Jiho — J Okayama Prefect Agric Exp Sta
Journal of Oncology Pharmacy Practice — J Oncol Pharm Pract
Journal of Oncology. Tianjin Medical Journal. Supplement — J Oncol Tianjin Med J Suppl
Journal of Operational Psychiatry — J Operational Psychiatr
Journal of Operator Theory — J Operator Theory
Journal of Ophthalmic Nursing and Technology — J Ophthalmic Nurs Technol
Journal of Optical Communications — J Opt Commun
Journal of Optics — J Opt
Journal of Optimization Theory and Applications — J Optim Th
Journal of Optimization Theory and Applications — J Optim Theory Appl
Journal of Optimization Theory and Applications — J Optimiz Theory and Appl
Journal of Optimization Theory and Applications — J Optimization Theory Appl
Journal of Oral and Maxillofacial Surgery — J Oral Maxillofac Surg
Journal of Oral and Maxillofacial Surgery — JOMS
Journal of Oral and Maxillofacial Surgery — JOMSD
Journal of Oral Implant and Transplant Surgery — J Oral Implant Transplant Surg
Journal of Oral Implantology — J Oral Implantol
Journal of Oral Medicine — J Oral Med
Journal of Oral Pathology — J Oral Pathol
Journal of Oral Pathology and Medicine — J Oral Pathol Med
Journal of Oral Rehabilitation — J Oral Rehabil
Journal of Oral Surgery — J Oral Surg
Journal of Oral Surgery, Anesthesia, and Hospital Dental Service — J Oral Surg Anesth Hosp Dent Serv
Journal of Oral Therapeutics and Pharmacology — J Oral Ther Pharmacol
Journal of Oral Therapeutics and Pharmacology — J Oral Therap Pharmacol
Journal of Oral Therapeutics and Pharmacology — JOTPA
Journal of Organic Chemistry — J Org Chem
Journal of Organic Chemistry of the USSR — J Org Chem USSR
Journal of Organizational Behavior Management — J Orgl Bhvr Mgt
Journal of Organizational Behavior Management — JBM
Journal of Organizational Behavior Management — JOR
Journal of Organizational Communication — J Orgl Com
Journal of Organometallic Chemistry — J Organomet Chem
Journal of Organometallic Chemistry — J Organometal Chem
Journal of Organometallic Chemistry — J Organometallic Chem
Journal of Organometallic Chemistry — J Orgmet Ch
Journal of Oriental Literature — JOL
Journal of Oriental Medicine/Manshu Igaku Zasshi — J Orient Med
Journal of Oriental Research — JOR
Journal of Oriental Research. Madras — JORM
Journal of Oriental Studies — J Or Stud
Journal of Oriental Studies — J Orient Stud
Journal of Oriental Studies — JOS
Journal of Orthomolecular Psychiatry — J Orthomol Psychiatry
Journal of Orthomolecular Psychiatry — Jnl Orthomol Psych
Journal of Orthopaedic and Sports Physical Therapy — J Ortho and Sports Phys Ther
Journal of Orthopaedic and Sports Physical Therapy — J Orthop Sports Phys Ther
Journal of Orthopaedic Research — J Orthop R
Journal of Orthopaedic Research — J Orthop Res
Journal of Orthopaedic Research — JOREDR
Journal of Orthopaedic Trauma — J Orthop Trauma
Journal of Otolaryngology — J Otolaryngol
Journal of Otolaryngology — JOTOD
Journal of Otolaryngology of Japan — J Otolaryngol Jpn
Journal of Otolaryngology of Japan — JOJAA
Journal of Otolaryngology. Supplement — J Otolaryngol Suppl
Journal of Pacific History — J Pac Hist
Journal of Pacific History — J Pacif Hist
Journal of Pacific History — J Pacific Hist
Journal of Pacific History — Jour Pac Hist
Journal of Pacific History — JPH
Journal of Pacific History — PJPH
Journal of Paediatric Dentistry — J Paediatr Dent
Journal of Paediatrics and Child Health — J Paediatr Child Health
Journal of Pain and Symptom Management — J Pain Symptom Manage
Journal of Paint Technology — J Paint Tec
Journal of Paint Technology — J Paint Technol
Journal of Paleontology — J Paleont
Journal of Paleontology — J Paleontol
Journal of Palestine Studies — J Pales Stu
Journal of Palestine Studies — J Palestine Stud
Journal of Palestine Studies — J Palestine Studies
Journal of Palestine Studies — JPS
Journal of Palliative Care — J Palliat Care
Journal of Palynology — J Palynol
Journal of Palynology — J Palynology
Journal of Palynology — Jour Palynology
Journal of Palynology. Palynological Society of India — J Palynol Palynol Soc India
Journal of Parallel and Distributed Computing — J Par Distr
Journal of Parapsychology — J Parapsych
Journal of Parapsychology — J Parapsychol
Journal of Parapsychology — JP
Journal of Parapsychology — PJPA
Journal of Parasitic Diseases — J Parasit Dis
Journal of Parasitology — J Parasit
Journal of Parasitology — J Parasitol
Journal of Parasitology — J Parasitology
Journal of Parasitology and Applied Animal Biology — J Parasitol Appl Anim Biol
Journal of Parenteral and Enteral Nutrition — J Parenter Enteral Nutr
Journal of Parenteral and Enteral Nutrition — JPEN
Journal of Parenteral Science and Technology — J Parenter Sci Technol
Journal of Park and Recreation Administration — J Park Rec Adm
Journal of Parliamentary Information — J Parlia Info
Journal of Partial Differential Equations — J Partial Differential Equations
Journal of Partial Differential Equations. Series A — J Partial Differential Equations Ser A
Journal of Partnership Taxation — JPT
Journal of Pastoral Care — J Past Care
Journal of Pastoral Care — J Pastoral Care
Journal of Pastoral Care — JPC
Journal of Pastoral Counseling — J Past Coun
Journal of Pastoral Practice — JPP
Journal of Pathology — J Pathol
Journal of Pathology — J Pathology
Journal of Pathology and Bacteriology — J Path and Bacteriol
Journal of Pathology and Bacteriology — J Path Bact
Journal of Pathology and Bacteriology — J Pathol Bacteriol
Journal of Patient Account Management — J Patient Acc Manage
Journal of Peace Research — J Peace Res
Journal of Peace Research — J Peace Research
Journal of Peace Research — JPR

Journal of Peace Research — JPRe
Journal of Peace Research — PJPR
Journal of Peace Science — J Peace Sci
Journal of Peasant Studies — J Peas Stud
Journal of Peasant Studies — J Peasant Stud
Journal of Peasant Studies — J Peasant Studies
Journal of Peasant Studies — JPS
Journal of Pediatric and Adolescent Gynecology — J Pediatr Adolesc Gynecol
Journal of Pediatric and Perinatal Nutrition — J Pediatr Perinat Nutr
Journal of Pediatric Endocrinology — J Podiatr Encodrinol
Journal of Pediatric Endocrinology — J Pediatr Endocr
Journal of Pediatric Endocrinology and Metabolism — J Pediatr Endocrinol Metab
Journal of Pediatric Gastroenterology and Nutrition — J Pediatr Gastroenterol Nutr
Journal of Pediatric Hematology/Oncology — J Pediatr Hematol Oncol
Journal of Pediatric Nursing. Nursing Care of Children and Families — J Pediatr Nurs
Journal of Pediatric Oncology Nursing — J Pediatr Oncol Nurs
Journal of Pediatric Ophthalmology — J Pediatr Ophthalmol
Journal of Pediatric Ophthalmology and Strabismus — J Pediatr Ophthalmol Strabismus
Journal of Pediatric Orthopaedics. Part B — J Pediatr Orthop B
Journal of Pediatric Orthopedics — J Pediatr Orthop
Journal of Pediatric Psychology — J Pediat Psychol
Journal of Pediatric Psychology — J Pediatr Psychol
Journal of Pediatric Surgery — J Ped Surg
Journal of Pediatric Surgery — J Pediat Surg
Journal of Pediatric Surgery — J Pediatr Surg
Journal of Pediatrics — J Ped
Journal of Pediatrics — J Pediat
Journal of Pediatrics — J Pediatr
Journal of Pediatrics — J Pediatrics
Journal of Pediatrics — JOPDA
Journal of Pediatrics (Berlin) — J Pediatr Berlin
Journal of Pediatrics (St. Louis) — J Pediatr (St Louis)
Journal of Pedodontics — J Pedod
Journal of Penicillin — J Penicillin
Journal of Pension Planning and Compliance — J Pen Pl and Comp
Journal of Pension Planning and Compliance — J Pension Plan and Compliance
Journal of Pension Planning and Compliance — J Pension Planning and Compliance
Journal of Pension Planning and Compliance — PPC
Journal of Pension Planning and Compliance — PPL
Journal of Perinatal Medicine — J Perinat Med
Journal of Perinatology — J Perinat
Journal of Perinatology — J Perinatol
Journal of Periodontal Research — J Period Re
Journal of Periodontal Research — J Periodontal Res
Journal of Periodontal Research. Supplement — J Periodontal Res Suppl
Journal of Periodontology — J Periodont
Journal of Periodontology — J Periodontol
Journal of Periodontology - Periodontics — J Periodontol-Periodontics
Journal of Periodontology - Periodontics — JPDPA
Journal of Personal Selling and Sales Management — JPN
Journal of Personal Selling and Sales Management — JPS
Journal of Personality — J Personal
Journal of Personality — JPer
Journal of Personality — JPers
Journal of Personality — PJPY
Journal of Personality and Social Psychology — GPSP
Journal of Personality and Social Psychology — J Pers Soc
Journal of Personality and Social Psychology — J Pers Soc Psychol
Journal of Personality and Social Psychology — J Person Soc Psychol
Journal of Personality and Social Psychology — J Personality & Social Psychol
Journal of Personality and Social Psychology — JPSP
Journal of Personality and Social Psychology — JPSPB
Journal of Personality and Social Systems — JPSS
Journal of Personality Assessment — J Pers Asse
Journal of Personality Assessment — J Pers Assess
Journal of Personality Assessment — JNPAB
Journal of Personality Disorders — J Personal Disord
Journal of Pesticide Reform. A Publication. Northwest Coalition for Alternatives to Pesticides — J Pestic Reform Publ Northwest Coalition Alternatives Pestic
Journal of Pesticide Science — J Pestic Sci
Journal of Pesticide Science (International Edition) — J Pestic Sci Int Ed
Journal of Pesticide Science (Nihon Noyakugaku Kaishi) — J Pestic Sci (Nihon Noyakugaku Kaishi)
Journal of Petroleum Geology [*England*] — J Pet Geol
Journal of Petroleum Geology — J Petrol Geol
Journal of Petroleum Science and Engineering — J Pet Sci Eng
Journal of Petroleum Technology — J Pet Tech
Journal of Petroleum Technology — J Pet Technol
Journal of Petroleum Technology — J Petro Tec
Journal of Petroleum Technology — J Petrol Techn
Journal of Petroleum Technology — J Petrol Technol
Journal of Petroleum Technology — JPET
Journal of Petroleum Technology — JPT
Journal of Petroleum Technology — Jrl Petro
Journal of Petrology — J Petrol
Journal of Pharmaceutical and Biomedical Analysis — J Pharm B
Journal of Pharmaceutical and Biomedical Analysis — J Pharm Biomed Anal
Journal of Pharmaceutical Research and Development — J Pharm Res Dev
Journal of Pharmaceutical Science and Technology (Japan) — J Pharm Sci Technol Jpn
Journal of Pharmaceutical Sciences — J Pharm Sc
Journal of Pharmaceutical Sciences — J Pharm Sci
Journal of Pharmaceutical Sciences — JPMSA
Journal of Pharmaceutical Sciences (Ankara) — J Pharm Sci (Ankara)
Journal of Pharmaceutical Sciences. Mahidol University — J Pharm Sci Mahidol Univ
Journal of Pharmaceutical Sciences of the United Arab Republic — J Pharm Sci UAR
Journal of Pharmaceutical Society. Pilani — J Pharm Soc Pilani
Journal of Pharmacobio-Dynamics — J Pharmacobio-Dyn
Journal of Pharmacokinetics and Biopharmaceutics — J Phar Biop
Journal of Pharmacokinetics and Biopharmaceutics — J Pharmacokinet Biopharm
Journal of Pharmacokinetics and Biopharmaceutics — JPBPB
Journal of Pharmacological and Toxicological Methods — J Pharmacol Toxicol Methods
Journal of Pharmacological Methods — J Pharmacol Methods
Journal of Pharmacology and Experimental Therapeutics — J Pharm Exp
Journal of Pharmacology and Experimental Therapeutics — J Pharm Exp Ther
Journal of Pharmacology and Experimental Therapeutics — J Pharmacol Exp Ther
Journal of Pharmacology and Experimental Therapeutics — J Pharmacol Exper Therap
Journal of Pharmacy and Pharmacology — J Pharm Pha
Journal of Pharmacy and Pharmacology — J Pharm Pharmac
Journal of Pharmacy and Pharmacology — J Pharm Pharmacol
Journal of Pharmacy and Pharmacology. Supplement — J Pharm Pharmacol Suppl
Journal of Pharmacy and Pharmacology. Supplement — JPPSA
Journal of Pharmacy (Lahore) — J Pharm (Lahore)
Journal of Pharmacy of University of Marmara — J Pharm Univ Marmara
Journal of Pharmacy Technology — J Pharm Technol
Journal of Pharmacy. University of Karachi — J Pharm Univ Karachi
Journal of Phase Equilibria — J Phase Equilibr
Journal of Phenomenological Psychology — J Phenomen
Journal of Philippine Development — J Phil Dev
Journal of Philippine Development — J Philippine Development
Journal of Philippine Statistics — J Phil Stat
Journal of Philippine Statistics — J Philippine Statis
Journal of Philology [*London*] — Journ of Phil
Journal of Philology — JP
Journal of Philology [*London*] — JPh
Journal of Philosophical Logic — J Phil Log
Journal of Philosophical Logic — J Phil Logic
Journal of Philosophical Logic — J Philos Lo
Journal of Philosophical Logic — J Philos Logic
Journal of Philosophical Logic — JPL
Journal of Philosophical Studies — J Phil Stud
Journal of Philosophy — IJPH
Journal of Philosophy — J Phil
Journal of Philosophy — J Philos
Journal of Philosophy — Jnl Philos
Journal of Philosophy — Jour Philos
Journal of Philosophy — JP
Journal of Philosophy — JPh
Journal of Philosophy of Education — J Phil Educ
Journal of Philosophy, Psychology, and Scientific Methods — J Ph P
Journal of Phonetics — JPh
Journal of Phonetics — JPhon
Journal of Photoacoustics — J Photoacoust
Journal of Photoacoustics — Jnl Photoacoust
Journal of Photochemical Etching — J Photochem Etching
Journal of Photochemistry — J Photochem
Journal of Photochemistry — JPCMA
Journal of Photochemistry and Photobiology. A. Chemistry — J Photochem Photobiol A
Journal of Photochemistry and Photobiology. B. Biology — J Photochem Photobiol B
Journal of Photographic Science — J Phot Sci
Journal of Photographic Science — J Photogr Sci
Journal of Photopolymer Science and Technology — J Photopolym Sci Technol
Journal of Photoscience — J Photosci
Journal of Phycology — J Phycol
Journal of Phycology — J Phycology
Journal of Physical and Chemical Reference Data — J Ph Ch Ref Data
Journal of Physical and Chemical Reference Data — J Phys & Chem Ref Data
Journal of Physical and Chemical Reference Data — J Phys Chem Ref Data
Journal of Physical and Chemical Reference Data — JPCRB
Journal of Physical and Chemical Reference Data — JPCRD
Journal of Physical and Chemical Reference Data. Supplement — J Phys Chem Ref Data Suppl
Journal of Physical and Chemical Reference Data. Supplement — JPCSC
Journal of Physical and Colloid Chemistry — J Phys & Colloid Chem
Journal of Physical and Colloid Chemistry — J Phys Coll Chem
Journal of Physical and Colloid Chemistry — JPCCA
Journal of Physical Chemistry — J Phys Chem
Journal of Physical Chemistry — J Physical Chem
Journal of Physical Chemistry (Moscow) — J Phys Chem Moscow
Journal of Physical Chemistry (Washington, DC) — J Phys Chem (Wash)
Journal of Physical Education — J Phys Ed
Journal of Physical Education — J Phys Educ
Journal of Physical Education and Program — J PE

Journal of Physical Education and Recreation [*Later, Journal of Physical Education, Recreation, and Dance*] — J Phys Educ & Rec
Journal of Physical Education and Recreation [*Later, Journal of Physical Education, Recreation, and Dance*] — J Phys Educ Recr
Journal of Physical Education & Sport Sciences — J PE and Sport Sci
Journal of Physical Education New Zealand — J PE NZ
Journal of Physical Education, Recreation, and Dance — GPRD
Journal of Physical Education, Recreation, and Dance — J PERD
Journal of Physical Education, Recreation, and Dance — J Phys Educ Rec & Dance
Journal of Physical Oceanography — J Phys Ocea
Journal of Physical Oceanography — J Phys Oceanogr
Journal of Physical Organic Chemistry — J Phys Org Chem
Journal of Physics — J Phys
Journal of Physics. A: General Physics — J Phys A Gen Phys
Journal of Physics. A: General Physics (London) — J Phys A (London)
Journal of Physics. A: Mathematical and General [*Bristol*] — J Phys A
Journal of Physics. A: Mathematical and General — JPHAC
Journal of Physics. A: Mathematical and General (London) — J Phys A (London) Math Gen
Journal of Physics. A: Mathematical, Nuclear, and General — J Phys A Math Nucl Gen
Journal of Physics. A: Proceedings. Physical Society. General (London) — J Phys A (London) Proc Phys Soc Gen
Journal of Physics and Chemistry of Niigata — J Phys Chem Niigata
Journal of Physics and Chemistry of Solids — J Phys and Chem Solids
Journal of Physics and Chemistry of Solids — J Phys Ch S
Journal of Physics and Chemistry of Solids — J Phys Chem Sol
Journal of Physics and Chemistry of Solids — J Phys Chem Solids
Journal of Physics and Chemistry of Solids. Letters Section — J Phys Chem Solids Lett Sect
Journal of Physics and Chemistry of Solids. Supplement [*England*] — J Phys Chem Solids Suppl
Journal of Physics and Chemistry of Solids. Supplement — JPCSB
Journal of Physics. B: Atomic and Molecular Physics — J of Phys B At Mol Phys
Journal of Physics. B: Atomic and Molecular Physics — J Phys B
Journal of Physics. B: Atomic and Molecular Physics (London) — J Phys B (London)
Journal of Physics. B. Proceedings. Physical Society. Atomic and Molecular Physics — J Phys B Proc Phys Soc At Mol
Journal of Physics (Bangalore, India) — J Phys Bangalore India
Journal of Physics. C. Proceedings. Physical Society. Solid State Physics — J Phys C Proc Phys Soc Solid
Journal of Physics. C: Solid State Physics — J Phys C
Journal of Physics. C: Solid State Physics — J Phys C Solid State Phys
Journal of Physics. C: Solid State Physics (London) — J Phys C (London)
Journal of Physics. C. Solid State Physics. Supplement — J Phys C Suppl
Journal of Physics, Chemistry, and Earth Science — J Phys Chem Earth Sci
Journal of Physics. Condensed Matter — J Phys Condens Matter
Journal of Physics. Condensed Matter — J Phys-Cond
Journal of Physics. D: Applied Physics — J Phys D Appl Phys
Journal of Physics. D: Applied Physics (London) — J Phys D (London)
Journal of Physics. E: Scientific Instruments — J Phys E
Journal of Physics. E: Scientific Instruments — J Phys E Sci Instrum
Journal of Physics. E: Scientific Instruments — Sci Instrum
Journal of Physics. E: Scientific Instruments (London) — J Phys E (London) Sci Instrum
Journal of Physics Education — JPEDD
Journal of Physics. F: Metal Physics — J Phys F
Journal of Physics. F: Metal Physics — J Phys F Met Phys
Journal of Physics. F: Metal Physics — JPFMA
Journal of Physics. G. Nuclear and Particle Physics — J Phys G Nucl Part Phys
Journal of Physics. G: Nuclear Physics — J Phys G
Journal of Physics. G: Nuclear Physics — J Phys G Nu
Journal of Physics. G. Nuclear Physics — J Phys G Nucl Phys
Journal of Physics. G: Nuclear Physics — JPHGB
Journal of Physics (Moscow) [*Former USSR*] — J Phys (Moscow)
Journal of Physics of the Earth — J Phys Earth
Journal of Physics of Uzbekistan — J Phys Uzb
Journal of Physics (USSR) — J Phys (USSR)
Journal of Physiology — J Ph
Journal of Physiology — J Phys
Journal of Physiology — J Physiol
Journal of Physiology — JPHYA
Journal of Physiology and Biochemistry — J Physiol Biochem
Journal of Physiology and Pharmacology — J Physiol Pharmacol
Journal of Physiology (Cambridge, United Kingdom) — J Physiol Cambridge UK
Journal of Physiology (London) — J Physiol (Lond)
Journal of Physiology (London) — J Physiol (London)
Journal of Physiology (London) — J Physl (Lon)
Journal of Physiology. Paris — J Physiol Paris
Journal of Phytopathology — J Phytopathol
Journal of Phytopathology (Berlin) — J Phytopathol (Berl)
Journal of Phytopathology (UAR) — J Phytopathol (UAR)
Journal of Pineal Research — J Pineal Res
Journal of Pipelines — J Pipelines
Journal of Pipelines — JOPID
Journal of Planar Chromatography — JPC
Journal of Planar Chromatography. Modern TLC — J Planar Chromatogr Mod TLC
Journal of Plankton Research [*England*] — J Plankton Res
Journal of Planning and Environment Law — J Plan & Environ L
Journal of Planning and Environment Law — J Plan Envir Law
Journal of Planning and Environment Law — J Plann Environ Law
Journal of Planning and Environment Law — J Planning and Environment Law
Journal of Planning and Environment Law — Jnl of Planning & Environment Law
Journal of Planning and Environment Law — JPEL
Journal of Planning and Property Law — J Plan & Prop L
Journal of Planning and Property Law — J Plann Property Law
Journal of Planning and Property Law — JPPL
Journal of Planning Law — J P L
Journal of Planning Law — J Pl L
Journal of Plant Anatomy and Morphology (Jodhpur) — J Plant Anat Morphol (Jodhpur)
Journal of Plant Breeding — J Plant Breed
Journal of Plant Diseases and Protection — J Plant Dis Prot
Journal of Plant Foods — J Plant Foods
Journal of Plant Growth Regulation — J Plant Growth Regul
Journal of Plant Growth Regulation — JPGR
Journal of Plant Nutrition — J Plant Nut
Journal of Plant Nutrition — J Plant Nutr
Journal of Plant Nutrition and Soil Science — J Plant Nutr Soil Sci
Journal of Plant Physiology — J Plant Physiol
Journal of Plant Protection — J Plant Prot
Journal of Plant Protection in the Tropics — J Plant Prot Trop
Journal of Plant Protection (Suwon, Korea) — J Plant Prot Suwon Korea
Journal of Plantation Crops — J Plant Crops
Journal of Plantation Crops — J Plantn Crops
Journal of Plantation Crops — J Platn Crops
Journal of Plasma Physics — J Plasma Ph
Journal of Plasma Physics — J Plasma Phys
Journal of Plastic and Reconstructive Surgical Nursing — J Plast Reconstr Surg Nurs
Journal of Podiatric Medical Education — J Podiatr Med Educ
Journal of Police Science and Administration — J Polic Sci
Journal of Police Science and Administration — J Police Sci Adm
Journal of Police Science and Administration — J Police Sci and Ad
Journal of Police Science and Administration — J Police Sci & Adm
Journal of Police Science and Admnistration — PJPS
Journal of Policy Analysis and Management — J Policy Anal Manage
Journal of Policy Analysis and Management — J Policy Analysis and Mgt
Journal of Policy Analysis and Management — J Policy Analysis Manage
Journal of Policy Analysis and Management — JPA
Journal of Policy Analysis and Management — JPAMD
Journal of Policy Analysis and Management — PJPM
Journal of Policy Modeling — J Pol Modeling
Journal of Policy Modeling — J Policy Model
Journal of Political and Military Sociology — J Mil Soc
Journal of Political and Military Sociology — J Pol and Military Sociol
Journal of Political and Military Sociology — J Pol Mil Sociol
Journal of Political and Military Sociology — J Polit Mil
Journal of Political and Military Sociology — J Polit Milit Sociol
Journal of Political Economy — J Pol Econ
Journal of Political Economy — J Pol Economy
Journal of Political Economy — J Polit Ec
Journal of Political Economy — J Polit Econ
Journal of Political Economy — Jnl Polit Econ
Journal of Political Economy — Jour Pol Econ
Journal of Political Economy — JPE
Journal of Political Economy — JPY
Journal of Political Studies — J Pol Stud
Journal of Political Studies — J Polit Stud
Journal of Politics — J Polit
Journal of Politics — J Politics
Journal of Politics — Jnl Politics
Journal of Politics — JoPo
Journal of Politics — Jour Politics
Journal of Politics — JP
Journal of Politics — JPol
Journal of Politics — PJPL
Journal of Politics and Economics — JPE
Journal of Pollution Control (Tokyo) — J Pollut Control (Tokyo)
Journal of Polymer Engineering — J Polym Eng
Journal of Polymer Materials — J Polym Mater
Journal of Polymer Research — J Polym Res
Journal of Polymer Science — J Pol Sci
Journal of Polymer Science — J Polym Sci
Journal of Polymer Science — JPS
Journal of Polymer Science. Macromolecular Reviews — J Polym Sci Macromol Rev
Journal of Polymer Science. Part A. General Papers — J Polym Sci Part A Gen Pap
Journal of Polymer Science. Part A. Polymer Chemistry — J Polym Sci Part A Polym Chem
Journal of Polymer Science. Part A-1: Polymer Chemistry — J Polym Sci A-1
Journal of Polymer Science. Part A-1. Polymer Chemistry — J Polym Sci Part A1
Journal of Polymer Science. Part A-1: Polymer Chemistry — J Polym Sci Part A-1: Polym Chem
Journal of Polymer Science. Part A-2: Polymer Physics — J Polym Sci A-2
Journal of Polymer Science. Part A-2. Polymer Physics — J Polym Sci Part A2
Journal of Polymer Science. Part A-2: Polymer Physics — J Polym Sci Part A-2: Polym Phys
Journal of Polymer Science. Part B: Polymer Letters — J Polym Sci B
Journal of Polymer Science. Part B: Polymer Letters — J Polym Sci Part B: Polym Lett
Journal of Polymer Science. Part B. Polymer Letters — J Polym Sci Part C Polym Lett

Journal of Polymer Science. Part B. Polymer Physics. Polymer Physics and Physical Chemistry — J Polym Sci Part B Polym Phys
Journal of Polymer Science. Part C: Polymer Symposia [*Later, Journal of Polymer Science. Polymer Symposia Edition*] — J Pol Sci C
Journal of Polymer Science. Part C: Polymer Symposia [*Later, Journal of Polymer Science. Polymer Symposia Edition*] — J Polym Sci Part C
Journal of Polymer Science. Part C: Polymer Symposia [*Later, Journal of Polymer Science. Polymer Symposia Edition*] — J Polym Sci Part C: Polym Symp
Journal of Polymer Science. Part C. Polymer Symposia [*Later, Journal of Polymer Science. Polymer Symposia Edition*] — JPSCD
Journal of Polymer Science. Part D: Macromolecular Reviews — J Polym Sci Part D
Journal of Polymer Science. Part D: Macromolecular Reviews — J Polym Sci Part D: Macromol Rev
Journal of Polymer Science. Polymer Chemistry Edition — J Pol Sc PC
Journal of Polymer Science. Polymer Chemistry Edition — J Polym Sci Polym Chem
Journal of Polymer Science. Polymer Chemistry Edition — J Polym Sci Polym Chem Ed
Journal of Polymer Science. Polymer Letters Edition — J Pol Sc PL
Journal of Polymer Science. Polymer Letters Edition — J Polym Sci Polym Lett
Journal of Polymer Science. Polymer Letters Edition — J Polym Sci Polym Lett Ed
Journal of Polymer Science. Polymer Letters Edition — JPYBA
Journal of Polymer Science. Polymer Physics Edition — J Pol Sc PP
Journal of Polymer Science. Polymer Physics Edition — J Polym Sci Polym Phys
Journal of Polymer Science. Polymer Physics Edition — J Polym Sci Polym Phys Ed
Journal of Polymer Science. Polymer Symposia Edition — J Polym Sci Polym Symp
Journal of Polymer Science. Polymer Symposia Edition — JPYCA
Journal of Pomology — J Pomol
Journal of Pomology and Horticultural Science — J Pomol Hort Sci
Journal of Pomology and Horticultural Science — J Pomol Hortic Sci
Journal of Pomology and Horticultural Science — J Pomology
Journal of Popular Culture — GJPC
Journal of Popular Culture — J Pop Cul
Journal of Popular Culture — J Pop Cult
Journal of Popular Culture — J Pop Culture
Journal of Popular Culture — JnlOPC
Journal of Popular Culture — JoPop
Journal of Popular Culture — JPC
Journal of Popular Culture — JPOCB
Journal of Popular Film [*Later, Journal of Popular Film and Television*] — JPF
Journal of Popular Film and Television — GPFT
Journal of Popular Film and Television — J Pop F & TV
Journal of Popular Film and Television — J Pop Fi TV
Journal of Popular Film and Television — J Pop Film & TV
Journal of Popular Film and Television — J Popular F
Journal of Population — J Popul
Journal of Population. Behavioral, Social, and Environmental Issues — J Popul Behav Soc Environ Issues
Journal of Population Research — J Pop Res
Journal of Porous Materials — J Porous Mater
Journal of Portfolio Management — J Portf Manage
Journal of Portfolio Management — J Portfolio Mgt
Journal of Portfolio Management — JPM
Journal of Portfolio Management — JPO
Journal of Portfolio Management — Jrl P Mgmt
Journal of Post Anesthesia Nursing — J Post Anesth Nurs
Journal of Post Keynesian Economics — J Post Keynes Econ
Journal of Post Keynesian Economics — JKE
Journal of Postgraduate Medicine (Bombay) — J Postgrad Med (Bombay)
Journal of Postgraduate Pharmacy. Hospital Edition — J Postgrad Pharm Hosp Ed
Journal of Powder and Bulk Solids Technology — J Powder Bulk Solids Tech
Journal of Powder and Bulk Solids Technology — J Powder Bulk Solids Technol
Journal of Power Sources — J Power Sources
Journal of Practical Approaches to Developmental Handicap — J of Prac App
Journal of Practical Nursing — J Pract Nurs
Journal of Practical Pharmacy — J Pract Pharm
Journal of Pragmatics — J Prag
Journal of Pre-Medical Course. Sapporo Medical College — J Pre-Med Course Sapporo Med Coll
Journal of Pre-Raphaelite Studies — J Pre-Raph
Journal of Presbyterian Historical Society of England — JPHSE
Journal of Presbyterian Historical Society of England. Special Publication — JPHSESP
Journal of Presbyterian History — J Pres H
Journal of Presbyterian History — J Presby H
Journal of Presbyterian History — J Prsbyt Hist
Journal of Presbyterian History — JoPr
Journal of Presbyterian History — Jour Presby Hist
Journal of Presbyterian History — JPH
Journal of Pressure Vessel Technology — J Pressure Vessel Technol
Journal of Pressure Vessel Technology — JPVTA
Journal of Pressure Vessel Technology. Transaction. ASME [*American Society of Mechanical Engineers*] — J Pressure Vessel Technol Trans ASME
Journal of Prevention — J Prev
Journal of Preventive Dentistry — J Prev Dent
Journal of Preventive Dentistry — JPVDA
Journal of Preventive Psychiatry — J Prev Psychiatry
Journal of Primary Prevention — JOPP
Journal of Prison and Jail Health — J Prison Jail Health
Journal of Prison Health — JPRH
Journal of Proceedings. American Horticultural Society — J Proc Am Hort Soc
Journal of Proceedings. Mueller Botanic Society of Western Australia — J Proc Mueller Bot Soc Western Australia
Journal of Process Control — J Process Control
Journal of Product Innovation Management — JPI
Journal of Production Agriculture — J Prod Agric
Journal of Products Law — J Prod Law
Journal of Products Liability — J Prod Liab
Journal of Products Liability — J Prod Liability
Journal of Products Liability — JPL
Journal of Professional Activities. American Society of Civil Engineers — J Prof Act Am Soc Civ Eng
Journal of Professional Issues in Engineering — EI
Journal of Professional Nursing — J Prof Nurs
Journal of Professional Services Marketing — J Prof Serv Mark
Journal of Projective Techniques — J Proj Tech
Journal of Projective Techniques [*Later, Journal of Personality Assessment*] — JPTEA
Journal of Projective Techniques and Personality Assessment [*Later, Journal of Personality Assessment*] — J Project Techniques
Journal of Property Management — J Prop Manage
Journal of Property Management — J Prop Mgt
Journal of Property Management — J Property Mgt
Journal of Property Management — JPM
Journal of Property Management — JYM
Journal of Propulsion and Power — J Propul P
Journal of Propulsion and Power — J Propul Power
Journal of Propulsion Technology — J Propul Technol
Journal of Prosthetic Dentistry — J Pros Dent
Journal of Prosthetic Dentistry — J Prosthet Dent
Journal of Prosthetic Dentistry — JPDEA
Journal of Protein Chemistry — J Protein Chem
Journal of Protozoology — J Protozool
Journal of Psychedelic Drugs — J Psychedel Drugs
Journal of Psychedelic Drugs — J Psychedelic Drugs
Journal of Psychiatric Nursing and Mental Health Services — J Psychiatr Nurs
Journal of Psychiatric Nursing and Mental Health Services — JPNNB
Journal of Psychiatric Research — J Psych Res
Journal of Psychiatric Research — J Psychiatr Res
Journal of Psychiatric Treatment and Evaluation — J Psychiatr Treat Eval
Journal of Psychiatry and Law — J P and L
Journal of Psychiatry and Law — J Psych and L
Journal of Psychiatry and Law — J Psych & Law
Journal of Psychiatry and Law — J Psych Law
Journal of Psychiatry and Law — J Psychiatr Law
Journal of Psychiatry and Law — J Psychiatry & L
Journal of Psychiatry and Neuroscience — J Psychiatry Neurosci
Journal of Psychoactive Drugs — J Psychoact Drugs
Journal of Psychoactive Drugs — JOPD
Journal of Psychoanalytic Anthropology — J Psychoanal Anthropol
Journal of Psychoanalytic Anthropology — JPANDA
Journal of Psychohistory — J Psychohist
Journal of Psycholinguistic Research — J Psycholin
Journal of Psycholinguistic Research — J Psycholing Res
Journal of Psycholinguistic Research — J Psycholinguist Res
Journal of Psycholinguistic Research — JPR
Journal of Psycholinguistic Research — JPRLB
Journal of Psycholinguistic Research — JPsyR
Journal of Psychological Researches — J Psychol Res
Journal of Psychological Researches — JPSRB
Journal of Psychology — IPSY
Journal of Psychology — J Ps
Journal of Psychology — J Psychol
Journal of Psychology — JOPSA
Journal of Psychology — JP
Journal of Psychology — JPs
Journal of Psychology — JPsy
Journal of Psychology and Judaism — JPJu
Journal of Psychology and Theology — J Psych Th
Journal of Psychology and Theology — J Psychol T
Journal of Psychology and Theology — JPT
Journal of Psychology of the Blind — JPSBA
Journal of Psychopathology and Behavioral Assessment — J Psychopathol Behav Assess
Journal of Psychopathology and Behavioral Assessment — JPBAEB
Journal of Psychopharmacology (Margate, New Jersey) — J Psychopharmacol (Margate NJ)
Journal of Psychopharmacology (Oxford) — J Psychopharmacol (Oxford)
Journal of Psychosocial Nursing and Mental Health Services — J Psychosoc Nurs
Journal of Psychosocial Nursing and Mental Health Services — J Psychosoc Nurs Ment Healt Serv
Journal of Psychosocial Nursing and Mental Health Services — J Psychosocial Nurs
Journal of Psychosocial Oncology — J Psychosoc Oncol
Journal of Psychosocial Oncology — JPONED
Journal of Psychosocial Oncology — JPSO
Journal of Psychosomatic Obstetrics and Gynaecology — J Psychosom Obstet Gynaecol
Journal of Psychosomatic Obstetrics and Gynaecology — JPOGDP
Journal of Psychosomatic Research — J Psychosom
Journal of Psychosomatic Research — J Psychosom Res
Journal of Psychotherapy and the Family — J Psychother & Fam

Journal of Psychotherapy and the Family — JPFAEV
Journal of Psychotherapy Practice and Research — J Psychother Pract Res
Journal of Public and International Affairs — J Public and Internat Affairs
Journal of Public Economics — J Publ Econ
Journal of Public Economics — J Public Econ
Journal of Public Economics — JPU
Journal of Public Health — J Public Health
Journal of Public Health — RSPUB9
Journal of Public Health and Medical Technology. Korea University — J Public Health Med Technol Korea Univ
Journal of Public Health Dentistry — J Public Health Dent
Journal of Public Health Dentistry — JPHD
Journal of Public Health Medicine — J Public Health Med
Journal of Public Health Policy — J Public Health Policy
Journal of Public Health Policy — JPHP
Journal of Public Health Practice [*Japan*] — J Public Health Pract
Journal of Public Law — J Pub L
Journal of Public Law — Jour Pub Law
Journal of Public Nuisance (Tokyo) — J Public Nuisance Tokyo
Journal of Public Policy — J Public Policy
Journal of Public Policy and Marketing — JMP
Journal of Pulp and Paper Science — J Pulp and Pap Sci
Journal of Purchasing [*Later, Journal of Purchasing and Materials Management*] — J Purch
Journal of Purchasing and Materials Management — J Purch Mater Manage
Journal of Purchasing and Materials Management — J Purchasing & Materials Mgt
Journal of Purchasing and Materials Management — JPM
Journal of Purchasing and Materials Management — JPR
Journal of Pure and Applied Algebra — J Pure Appl Algebra
Journal of Pure and Applied Sciences — J Pure Appl Sci
Journal of Pure and Applied Sciences (Ankara) — J Pure Appl Sci (Ankara)
Journal of Pure Mathematics — J Pure Math
Journal of Pyrotechnics — J Pyrotech
Journal of Qingdao Institute of Chemical Technology — J Qingdao Inst Chem Technol
Journal of Qingdao University. Engineering and Technology Edition — J Qingdao Univ Eng Technol Ed
Journal of Qingdao University. Natural Science Edition — J Qingdao Univ Nat Sci Ed
Journal of Quality in Clinical Practice — J Qual Clin Pract
Journal of Quality Technology — J Qual Tech
Journal of Quality Technology — J Qual Technol
Journal of Quality Technology — J Quality Tech
Journal of Quality Technology — JQT
Journal of Quantitative Spectroscopy and Radiative Transfer — J Quan Spec
Journal of Quantitative Spectroscopy and Radiative Transfer — J Quant Spectrosc and Radiat Transfer
Journal of Quantitative Spectroscopy and Radiative Transfer — J Quant Spectrosc Radiat Transfer
Journal of Quantitative Trait Loci — J Quant Trait Loci
Journal of Quantum Electronics — JQE
Journal of Race Development — J Race Dev
Journal of Race Development — J Race Development
Journal of Racial Affairs — J Racial Aff
Journal of Racial Affairs — J Racial Affairs
Journal of Radiation Curing — J Radiat Curing
Journal of Radiation Curing — JRDCA
Journal of Radiation Research — J Radiat Res
Journal of Radiation Research — JRARA
Journal of Radiation Research and Radiation Processing — J Radiat Res Radiat Process
Journal of Radiation Research (Tokyo) — J Radiat Res (Tokyo)
Journal of Radioanalytical and Nuclear Chemistry — J Radioanal Nucl Chem
Journal of Radioanalytical and Nuclear Chemistry — JRNCDM
Journal of Radioanalytical Chemistry [*Later, Journal of Radioanalytical and Nuclear Chemistry*] — J Rad Chem
Journal of Radioanalytical Chemistry [*Later, Journal of Radioanalytical and Nuclear Chemistry*] — J Radioanal Chem
Journal of Radiological Protection — J Radiol Prot
Journal of Radiology — JRADA
Journal of Radiology and Physical Therapy. University of Kanazawa — J Radiol Phys Ther Univ Kanazawa
Journal of Raman Spectroscopy — J Raman Sp
Journal of Raman Spectroscopy — J Raman Spectrosc
Journal of Range Management — J Range Man
Journal of Range Management — J Range Manage
Journal of Range Management — J Range Mgt
Journal of Reading — IRED
Journal of Reading — J Read
Journal of Reading Behavior — J Read Beh
Journal of Reading Behavior — J Read Behav
Journal of Reading Behavior — J Read Behavior
Journal of Reading, Writing, and Learning Disabilities International — J Read Writ Learn Disabil Int
Journal of Real Estate Education — JREE
Journal of Real Estate Finance and Economics — JREFEC
Journal of Real Estate Research — JRER
Journal of Real Estate Taxation — J Real Est Tax
Journal of Real Estate Taxation — JET
Journal of Real Estate Taxation — JRE
Journal of Real Estate Taxation — Jrl RE Tax
Journal of Recent Advances in Applied Sciences — J Recent Adv Appl Sci
Journal of Receptor and Signal Transduction Research — J Recept Signal Transduct Res
Journal of Receptor and Signal Transduction Research — J Recept Signal Transduction Res
Journal of Receptor Research — J Recept Res
Journal of Receptor Research — JRERDM
Journal of Reconstructive Dietics and Alimentation — J Reconstr Diet Aliment
Journal of Reconstructive Microsurgery — J Reconstr Microsurg
Journal of Reconstructive Microsurgery — JRMIE2
Journal of Recreational Mathematics — J Recreational Math
Journal of Recreational Mathematics — PJRM
Journal of Recreational Mathematics — RM
Journal of Reform Judaism — JRJ
Journal of Refractive and Corneal Surgery — J Refract Corneal Surg
Journal of Refractive Surgery — J Refract Surg
Journal of Refrigeration — J Refrig
Journal of Regional Cultures — J Reg Cult
Journal of Regional Science — J Reg Sc
Journal of Regional Science — J Reg Sci
Journal of Regional Science — J Region Sci
Journal of Regional Science — J Regional Science
Journal of Regional Science — JRES-A
Journal of Regional Science — JRG
Journal of Regional Science — JRS
Journal of Rehabilitation — J Rehab
Journal of Rehabilitation — J Rehabil
Journal of Rehabilitation — JOREA
Journal of Rehabilitation — PJRE
Journal of Rehabilitation in Asia — J Rehabil Asia
Journal of Rehabilitation of the Deaf — J Rehabil D
Journal of Rehabilitation R and D [*Research and Development*] — J Rehabil R D
Journal of Rehabilitation Research and Development — J Rehabil Res Dev
Journal of Rehabilitation Research and Development — PJHB
Journal of Rehabilitation Research and Development. Clinical Supplement — J Rehabil Res Dev Clin Suppl
Journal of Reinforced Plastics and Composites — J Reinf Plast Comp
Journal of Reinforced Plastics and Composites — J Reinf Plast Compos
Journal of Religion — J Rel
Journal of Religion — J Relig
Journal of Religion — Jnl Relig
Journal of Religion — Jour of Relig
Journal of Religion — JR
Journal of Religion — JRe
Journal of Religion — PJRL
Journal of Religion and Health — J Rel Health
Journal of Religion and Health — J Relig H
Journal of Religion and Health — J Religion Health
Journal of Religion and Health — JR He
Journal of Religion and Psychical Research — J Rel Psych Res
Journal of Religion in Africa — J Rel Africa
Journal of Religion in Africa — J Relig Afr
Journal of Religion in Africa — J Relig Africa
Journal of Religion in Africa — JRA
Journal of Religious Education — J Relig Educ
Journal of Religious Ethics — J Rel Ethics
Journal of Religious Ethics — J Relig Ethics
Journal of Religious Ethics — JRE
Journal of Religious Ethics — PJRS
Journal of Religious History — J Rel H
Journal of Religious History — J Rel Hist
Journal of Religious History — J Relig His
Journal of Religious History — J Relig Hist
Journal of Religious History — J Religious History
Journal of Religious History — JoR
Journal of Religious History — Jour Relig Hist
Journal of Religious History — JRH
Journal of Religious Psychology — JRP
Journal of Religious Studies — J Re S
Journal of Religious Studies — J Rel St
Journal of Religious Thought — J of Rel Thought
Journal of Religious Thought — J of Relig Thought
Journal of Religious Thought — J R Th
Journal of Religious Thought — J Rel Thot
Journal of Religious Thought — J Rel Thought
Journal of Religious Thought — JRT
Journal of Remote Sensing — J Remote Sensing
Journal of Renaissance and Baroque Music — J Ren & Bar Mus
Journal of Renaissance and Baroque Music — JRBM
Journal of Reproduction and Development — J Reprod Dev
Journal of Reproduction and Fertility — J Repr Fert
Journal of Reproduction and Fertility — J Reprd & Fert
Journal of Reproduction and Fertility — J Reprod Fertil
Journal of Reproduction and Fertility — JRPFA
Journal of Reproduction and Fertility. Abstract Series — J Reprod Fertil Abstr Ser
Journal of Reproduction and Fertility. Supplement — J Reprod Fertil Suppl
Journal of Reproductive Biology and Comparative Endocrinology — J Reprod Biol Comp Endocrinol
Journal of Reproductive Biology and Comparative Endocrinology — JRBED2
Journal of Reproductive Fertility — J Reprod Fertil
Journal of Reproductive Immunology — J Reprod Immunol
Journal of Reproductive Immunology — JRIMD
Journal of Reproductive Medicine — J Reprod Med
Journal of Reproductive Medicine. Lying-In — J Reprod Med Lying-In
Journal of Research and Development in Education — J Res & Devel Educ
Journal of Research and Development in Education — J Res Dev E
Journal of Research and Development in Education — J Res Develop Educ

Journal of Research and Laboratory Medicine (Milan) — J Res Lab Med Milan
Journal of Research APAU [*Andhra Pradesh Agricultural University*] — JRAPDU
Journal of Research APAU (Andhra Pradesh Agricultural University) — J Res APAU (Andhra Pradesh Agric Univ)
Journal of Research. Assam Agricultural University — J Res Assam Agric Univ
Journal of Research Communication Studies — J Res Commun Stud
Journal of Research in Crime and Delinquency — J Res Crime
Journal of Research in Crime and Delinquency — J Res Crime & Del
Journal of Research in Crime and Delinquency — J Res Crime & Delinq
Journal of Research in Crime and Delinquency — PJRC
Journal of Research in Indian Medicine — J Res Indian Med
Journal of Research in Indian Medicine, Yoga, and Homoeopathy — J Res Indian Med Yoga Homoeopathy
Journal of Research in Indian Medicine, Yoga, and Homoeopathy — JRIHDC
Journal of Research in Music Education — J Res Mus Ed
Journal of Research in Music Education — J Res Mus Educ
Journal of Research in Music Education — J Res Music
Journal of Research in Music Education — J Res Music Educ
Journal of Research in Music Education — J Research M Education
Journal of Research in Music Education — Jl of Research
Journal of Research in Music Education — JRM
Journal of Research in Music Education — JRME
Journal of Research in Music Education — JRMEA
Journal of Research in Personality — J Res Pers
Journal of Research in Reading — J Res Read
Journal of Research in Science. Agra University — J Res Sci Agra Univ
Journal of Research in Science Teaching — J Res Sci Teach
Journal of Research in Singing — J Res Singing
Journal of Research in Singing — JRS
Journal of Research in Singing and Applied Vocal Pedagogy — J Res Singing
Journal of Research (Japan) — J Res (Jpn)
Journal of Research (Ludhiana) [*India*] — J Res (Ludhiana)
Journal of Research. [*US*] **National Bureau of Standards** — J Res Nat Bur Stand
Journal of Research. [*US*] **National Bureau of Standards** — J Res Nat Bur Standards
Journal of Research. [*US*] **National Bureau of Standards** — J Res NBS
Journal of Research. [*US*] **National Bureau of Standards** — JRNBA
Journal of Research. National Bureau of Standards. A. Physics and Chemistry — J Res Natl Bur Stand A Phys Chem
Journal of Research. National Bureau of Standards. B. Mathematics and Mathematical Physics — J Res Natl Bur Stand B Math Math
Journal of Research. National Bureau of Standards. C. Engineering and Instrumentation — J Res Natl Bur Stand C Eng
Journal of Research. [*US*] **National Bureau of Standards. Section A. Physics and Chemistry** — J Res Nat Bur Stand Sect A Phys Chem
Journal of Research. [*US*] **National Bureau of Standards. Section A. Physics and Chemistry** — J Res Natl Bur Stand A
Journal of Research. [*US*] **National Bureau of Standards. Section A. Physics and Chemistry** — J Res NBS A
Journal of Research. [*US*] **National Bureau of Standards. Section B. Mathematical Sciences** — J Res Nat Bur Stand Sect B Math Sci
Journal of Research. [*US*] **National Bureau of Standards. Section B. Mathematical Sciences** — J Res NBS B
Journal of Research. [*US*] **National Bureau of Standards. Section B. Mathematics and Mathematical Physics** — J Res Natl Bur Stand B
Journal of Research. [*US*] **National Bureau of Standards. Section C. Engineering and Instrumentation** — J Res Nat Bur Stand Sect C
Journal of Research. [*US*] **National Bureau of Standards. Section C. Engineering and Instrumentation** — J Res Nat Bur Stand Sect C Eng Instrum
Journal of Research. [*US*] **National Bureau of Standards. Section C. Engineering and Instrumentation** — J Res Natl Bur Stand C
Journal of Research. [*US*] **National Bureau of Standards. Section D. Radio Science** — J Res Nat Bur Stand Sect D
Journal of Research. National Bureau of Standards (United States) — J Res Natl Bur Stand (US)
Journal of Research. National Institute of Standards and Technology — J Res Nat I
Journal of Research. National Institute of Standards and Technology [*US*] — J Res Natl Inst Stand Tehcnol
Journal of Research. National Institute of Standards. C. Technology — J Res Natl Inst Stand Technol
Journal of Research of the Chichibu Onoda Cement Corporation — J Res Chichibu Onoda Cem Corp
Journal of Research on the Lepidoptera — J Res Lepid
Journal of Research. Onoda Cement Co. — J Res Onoda Cem Co
Journal of Research. Punjab Agricultural University — J Res Punjab Agr Univ
Journal of Research. Punjab Agricultural University — J Res Punjab Agric Univ
Journal of Research. Punjab Agricultural University — JRPUA
Journal of Research. United States Geological Survey — J Res US G S
Journal of Research. United States Geological Survey — J Res US Geol Surv
Journal of Research. Visva-Bharati — J Res Visva Bharati
Journal of Resource Management and Technology — J Res M & T
Journal of Resources and Environment — J Resour Environ
Journal of Retail Banking — J Retail Bank
Journal of Retail Banking — J Retail Banking
Journal of Retail Banking — JRB
Journal of Retailing — J Retail
Journal of Retailing — J Retailing
Journal of Retailing — JRL
Journal of Retailing — Jrl Retail
Journal of Retailing — JRT
Journal of Rheology — J Rheol
Journal of Rheology — J Rheology
Journal of Rheumatology — J Rheumatol
Journal of Rheumatology. Supplement — J Rheumatol Suppl
Journal of Risk and Insurance — J Risk & Insur
Journal of Risk and Insurance — J Risk Ins
Journal of Risk and Insurance — J Risk Insur
Journal of Risk and Insurance — JRI
Journal of Risk and Uncertainty — JRU
Journal of Roman Studies — J Rom S
Journal of Roman Studies — J Rom Stud
Journal of Roman Studies — J Roman Stud
Journal of Roman Studies [*London*] — Journ of Rom Stud
Journal of Roman Studies [*London*] — Journ Rom St
Journal of Roman Studies — Journ Rom Stud
Journal of Roman Studies — JRS
Journal of Roman Studies — PJRO
Journal of Root Crops — J Root Crops
Journal of Rural Cooperation — J Rur Coop
Journal of Rural Cooperation. International Research Center on Rural Cooperative Communities — J Rural Coop Int Res Cent Rural Coop Communities
Journal of Rural Development — J Rur Develop
Journal of Rural Development — J Rural Dev
Journal of Rural Economics and Development — J Rur Econ Dev
Journal of Rural Economics and Development — J Rural Econ and Development
Journal of Rural Education — J Rural Educ
Journal of Rural Engineering and Development — J Rural Eng Dev
Journal of Rural Engineering and Development — ZKUFAK
Journal of Rural Studies — J Rural Stud
Journal of Russian Studies — JRS
Journal of Russian Studies — JRuS
Journal of Sacred and Classical Philology — JSCP
Journal of Sacred Literature and Biblical Record — JSL
Journal of Safety Research — J Saf Res
Journal of Safety Research — J Safe Res
Journal of Saitama Institute of Technology — J Saitama Inst Technol
Journal of Saitama Medical School — J Saitama Med Sch
Journal of Saitama University. Mathematics and Natural Science — J Saitama Univ Math Nat Sci
Journal of SCCJ [*Society of Cosmetic Chemists of Japan*] — J SCCJ
Journal of School Health — IJSH
Journal of School Health — J Sch Healt
Journal of School Health — J Sch Health
Journal of School Health — J Sch Hlth
Journal of School Health — JOSH
Journal of School Health — JSHEA
Journal of School Psychology — J Sch Psych
Journal of School Psychology — J Sch Psychol
Journal of Science — J Sci
Journal of Science, and Annals of Astronomy, Biology, Geology, Industrial Arts, Manufactures, and Technology — J Sci Ann Astron
Journal of Science and Engineering (National Chung Hsing University) — J Sci Eng Natl Chung Hsing Univ
Journal of Science and Engineering Research [*India*] — J Sci Eng Res
Journal of Science and Engineering Research — J Sci Engrg Res
Journal of Science and Technology — J Sci and Technol
Journal of Science and Technology — J Sci Tech
Journal of Science and Technology — J Sci Technol
Journal of Science and Technology — JST
Journal of Science and Technology (London) — J Sci Technol (London)
Journal of Science and Technology (Peshawar) — J Sci Technol (Peshawar)
Journal of Science and Technology (Peshawar, Pakistan) — JSTPD
Journal of Science. Busan National University — J Sci Busan Natl Univ
Journal of Science. Busan National University — JOUSD
Journal of Science. College of General Education. University of Tokushima — J Sci Coll Gen Educ Univ Tokushima
Journal of Science Education and Technology — J Sci Educ Technol
Journal of Science Education. Chonnam National University — J Sci Educ Chonnam Natl Univ
Journal of Science Education. Chungbuk National University — J Sci Educ Chungbuk Natl Univ
Journal of Science Education. Chungbuk National University — JSCUD
Journal of Science Education. Jeonbug National University — J Sci Educ Jeonbug Natl Univ
Journal of Science Education (Jeonju) — J Sci Educ (Jeonju)
Journal of Science Education. Science Education Research Institute Teacher's College. Kyungpook University — J Sci Educ Sci Educ Res Inst Teach Coll Kyungpook Univ
Journal of Science. Gakugei Faculty. Tokushima University — J Sci Gakugei Fac Tokushima Univ
Journal of Science. Hiroshima University — J Sci Hiroshima Univ
Journal of Science. Hiroshima University. Series A. Mathematics, Physics, Chemistry — J Sci Hiroshima Univ Ser A Math Phys Chem
Journal of Science. Hiroshima University. Series A. Physics and Chemistry — J Sci Hiroshima Univ A
Journal of Science. Hiroshima University. Series A. Physics and Chemistry — J Sci Hiroshima Univ Ser A
Journal of Science. Hiroshima University. Series A. Physics and Chemistry — J Sci Hiroshima Univ Ser A Phys
Journal of Science. Hiroshima University. Series A. Physics and Chemistry — J Sci Hiroshima Univ Ser A Phys Chem
Journal of Science. Hiroshima University. Series A-II — J Sci Hiroshima Univ Ser A-II
Journal of Science. Hiroshima University. Series B. Division 1. Zoology — J Sc Hiroshima Univ S B Div 1 Zool
Journal of Science. Hiroshima University. Series B. Division 1. Zoology — J Sci Hiroshima Univ Ser B Div 1 Zool

Journal of Science. Hiroshima University. Series B. Division 2. Botany — J Sci Hiroshima Univ Ser B Div 2 Bot
Journal of Science. Hiroshima University. Series C. Geology and Mineralogy — J Sci Hiroshima Univ Ser C
Journal of Science. Hiroshima University. Series C. Geology and Mineralogy — J Sci Hiroshima Univ Ser C (Geol Mineral)
Journal of Science (Karachi) — J Sci (Karachi)
Journal of Science (Katmandu, Nepal) — J Sci (Katmandu Nepal)
Journal of Science. National University of Shantung/Kuo-li Shantung ta Hsueeh K'o Hsueeh Ts'ung K'an — J Sci Natl Univ Shantung
Journal of Science of Labor [*Japan*] — J Sci Labor
Journal of Science of Labour. Part 1 (in Japanese) — J Sci Labour Part 1 (Jpn)
Journal of Science of Labour. Part 2 — J Sci Labour Part 2
Journal of Science Technology (Aberdeen, Scotland) — J Sci Technol (Aberdeen Scotl)
Journal of Sciences. Islamic Republic of Iran — J Sci Islamic Repub Iran
Journal of Scientific Agricultural Society (Tokyo) — J Sci Agric Soc Tokyo
Journal of Scientific Agriculture — J Sci Agric
Journal of Scientific and Industrial Research — J Sci and Ind Res
Journal of Scientific and Industrial Research — J Sci Ind R
Journal of Scientific and Industrial Research — J Sci Ind Res
Journal of Scientific and Industrial Research — J Scient Ind Res
Journal of Scientific and Industrial Research. C. Biological Sciences — J Sci Industr Res C Biol Sci
Journal of Scientific and Industrial Research (India) — J Sci Ind Res (India)
Journal of Scientific and Industrial Research. Section A. General — J Sci Ind Res Sect A
Journal of Scientific and Industrial Research. Section B — J Sci Ind Res Sect B
Journal of Scientific and Industrial Research. Section C. Biological Sciences — J Sci Ind Res Sect C
Journal of Scientific and Industrial Research. Section D. Technology — J Sci Ind Res Sect D
Journal of Scientific Computing — J Sci Comput
Journal of Scientific Instruments — J Sci Instr
Journal of Scientific Instruments — J Sci Instrum
Journal of Scientific Instruments — J Scient Instrum
Journal of Scientific Instruments and Physics in Industry — J Sci Instrum Phys Ind
Journal of Scientific Instruments. Supplement — J Sci Instrum Suppl
Journal of Scientific Medicine of Jundi Shapur University — J Sci Med Jundi Shapur Univ
Journal of Scientific Research — J Sci Res
Journal of Scientific Research. Banaras Hindu University — J Sci Res Banaras Hindu Univ
Journal of Scientific Research. Banaras Hindu University — JSRBA
Journal of Scientific Research (Bhopal) — J Sci Res (Bhopal)
Journal of Scientific Research (Bhopal, India) — J Sci Res Bhopal India
Journal of Scientific Research (Hardwar, India) — J Sci Res (Hardwar)
Journal of Scientific Research (Hardwar, India) — J Sci Res (Hardwar India)
Journal of Scientific Research in Plants and Medicines — J Sci Res Plants & Med
Journal of Scientific Research (Indonesia) — J Sci Res (Indones)
Journal of Scientific Research (Lahore) — J Sci Res (Lahore)
Journal of Sea Research — J Sea Res
Journal of Secondary Education — J Sec Ed
Journal of Sedimentary Petrology — J Sed Petrol
Journal of Sedimentary Petrology — J Sediment Petrol
Journal of Sedimentary Petrology — J Sediment Petrology
Journal of Sedimentary Research — J Sediment Res
Journal of Sedimentary Research. Section A. Sedimentary Petrology and Processes — J Sediment Res Sect A
Journal of Seed Technology — J Seed Technol
Journal of Semitic Studies — J Sem St
Journal of Semitic Studies — J Semitic S
Journal of Semitic Studies — J Semitic Stud
Journal of Semitic Studies [*Manchester*] — JSemS
Journal of Semitic Studies [*Manchester*] — JSeS
Journal of Semitic Studies — JSS
Journal of Semitic Studies — JSSt
Journal of Semitic Studies. Monograph — JS St M
Journal of Separation and Process Technology — J Separ Proc Technol
Journal of Separation Process Technology — J Sep Process Technol
Journal of Sericultural Science of Japan — J Seric Sci Jpn
Journal of Sex and Marital Therapy — J Sex Marital Ther
Journal of Sex Education and Therapy — JSET
Journal of Sex Research — J Sex Res
Journal of Sex Research — PJSX
Journal of Shaanxi Normal University. Natural Science Edition — J Shaanxi Norm Univ Nat Sci Ed
Journal of Shanghai Jiaotong University/Shanghai Jiaotong Daxue Xuebao — J Shanghai Jiaotong Univ
Journal of Shanghai Second Medical University — J Shanghai Second Med Univ
Journal of Shanghai University. Natural Science — J Shanghai Univ Nat Sci
Journal of Shanghai University of Science and Technology — J Shanghai Univ Sci Technol
Journal of Shanghai University of Technology — J Shanghai Univ Technol
Journal of Shansi Normal College/Shan Hsi Sze Fan Hsueeh Yuan Hsueeh Pao — J Sanshi Norm Coll
Journal of Shanxi University. Natural Science Edition — J Shanxi Univ Natur Sci Ed
Journal of Shellfish Research — J Shellfish Res
Journal of Shenyang Institute of Chemical Technology — J Shenyang Inst Chem Technol
Journal of Shenyang Pharmaceutical University — J Shenyang Pharm Univ
Journal of Ship Research — J Ship Res
Journal of Shoreline Management — J Shoreline Manage
Journal of Shoulder and Elbow Surgery — J Shoulder Elbow Surg
Journal of Signal Recording Materials — J Signal Rec Mater
Journal of Sleep Research — J Sleep Res
Journal of Small Animal Medicine — J Small Anim Med
Journal of Small Animal Practice — J Sm Anim P
Journal of Small Animal Practice — J Small Anim Pract
Journal of Small Business Canada — J Small Bus Can
Journal of Small Business Management — J Small Bus Manage
Journal of Small Business Management — J Small Bus Mgt
Journal of Small Business Management — JSB
Journal of Smooth Muscle Research — J Smooth Muscle Res
Journal of Social and Economic Studies — J Social and Econ Studies
Journal of Social and Political Ideas in Japan — JSPIJ
Journal of Social and Political Studies — J Soc Polit Stud
Journal of Social and Political Studies — J Social and Pol Studies
Journal of Social Casework — J Social Casework
Journal of Social Forces — J Social Forces
Journal of Social History — J Soc Hist
Journal of Social History — JoSoc
Journal of Social History — Jour Soc Hist
Journal of Social History — JSH
Journal of Social History — JSHY
Journal of Social History — PJSH
Journal of Social Hygiene — J Soc Hygiene
Journal of Social Hygiene — J Social Hyg
Journal of Social Issues — GSOI
Journal of Social Issues — J Soc Iss
Journal of Social Issues — J Soc Issue
Journal of Social Issues — J Social Issues
Journal of Social Issues — Jour of Soc Issues
Journal of Social Issues — JSI
Journal of Social Philosophy — J Soc Phil
Journal of Social Philosophy — Jour Soc Philos
Journal of Social Philosophy and Jurisprudence — JSPH
Journal of Social Policy — J Soc Pol
Journal of Social Policy — J Soc Polic
Journal of Social Policy — J Soc Policy
Journal of Social Policy — J Social Policy
Journal of Social Policy — PJSP
Journal of Social, Political, and Economic Studies — J Social Pol and Econ Studies
Journal of Social, Political, and Economic Studies — PJSS
Journal of Social Psychology — ISPS
Journal of Social Psychology — J Soc Psych
Journal of Social Psychology — J Soc Psychol
Journal of Social Psychology — J Social Psychol
Journal of Social Psychology — JSP
Journal of Social Psychology — JSPs
Journal of Social Psychology — JSPSA
Journal of Social Research — J Soc Res
Journal of Social Research — JSR
Journal of Social Science — J Social Sci
Journal of Social Sciences — J Soc Sci
Journal of Social Sciences — Jour Soc Sci
Journal of Social Sciences — JSS
Journal of Social Sciences and Humanities — J Soc Sci Hum
Journal of Social Services Research — JSSR
Journal of Social Therapy — J Soc Ther
Journal of Social Welfare Law — J Soc Welfare L
Journal of Social Welfare Law — JSWL
Journal of Social Work and Human Sexuality — J Soc Work & Hum Sex
Journal of Social Work and Human Sexuality — JSWS
Journal of Societal Issues — J Soc Issues
Journal of Societal Issues — JSI
Journal of Sociologie Medicine — J Sociol Med
Journal of Soil and Water Conservation — J Soil & Water Conser
Journal of Soil and Water Conservation [*US*] — J Soil Wat
Journal of Soil and Water Conservation [*US*] — J Soil Water Conserv
Journal of Soil and Water Conservation — JSWC
Journal of Soil and Water Conservation in India — J Soil Water Conserv India
Journal of Soil Biology and Ecology — J Soil Biol & Ecol
Journal of Soil Contamination — J Soil Contam
Journal of Soil Science — J Soil Sci
Journal of Soil Science of the United Arab Republic — J Soil Sci UAR
Journal of Soil Science of the United Arab Republic — J Soil Sci Un Arab Repub
Journal of Soil Science (Shenyang, People's Republic of China) — J Soil Sci Shenyang Peoples Repub China
Journal of Solar Energy Engineering [*United States*] — J Sol Energy Eng
Journal of Solar Energy Engineering — Jrl Solar
Journal of Solar Energy Research — J Sol Energy Res
Journal of Solar Energy Science and Engineering — J Sol En Sci
Journal of Solar Energy Science and Engineering [*United States*] — J Sol Energy Sci Eng
Journal of Solid Lubrication — J Solid Lubr
Journal of Solid State Chemistry — J Sol St Ch
Journal of Solid State Chemistry — J Solid State Chem
Journal of Solid Waste Technology and Management — J Solid Waste Technol Manage
Journal of Solid Wastes — J Solid Wastes
Journal of Solid Wastes Management [*Japan*] — J Solid Wastes Manage
Journal of Solid-Phase Biochemistry — J Solid-Phase Biochem
Journal of Solid-State Circuits [*IEEE*] — JSSC
Journal of Solution Chemistry — J Sol Chem

Journal of Solution Chemistry — J Soln Chem
Journal of Solution Chemistry — J Solut Chem
Journal of Solution Chemistry — J Solution Chem
Journal of Solution Chemistry — JSLCA
Journal of Somatic Experience — J Somat Exp
Journal of Soochow University. College of Arts and Sciences/Tung-Wu Hsueeh-Pao — J Soochow Univ Coll Arts
Journal of Sound and Vibration — J Sound and Vib
Journal of Sound and Vibration — J Sound Vib
Journal of Sound and Vibration — J Sound Vibration
Journal of Sound and Vibration — JSVIA
Journal of South African Botany — J S Afr Bot
Journal of South African Botany — Jl S Afr Bot
Journal of South African Botany. Supplementary Volume — J S Afr Bot Suppl Vol
Journal of South Asian Languages — JSAL
Journal of South Asian Literature — J S Asia L
Journal of South Asian Literature — J So AL
Journal of South Asian Literature — J South As Lit
Journal of South Asian Literature — J South Asian Lit
Journal of South China Normal University. Natural Science Edition — J South China Normal Univ Natur Sci Ed
Journal of South China Normal Univesity. Natural Science Edition — J South China Norm Univ Nat Sci Ed
Journal of South-East Asia and the Far East — JSAFE
Journal of Southeast Asian History — J SE Asian Hist
Journal of Southeast Asian History — JSAH
Journal of South-East Asian History — JSEAH
Journal of Southeast Asian Studies — J Se As Stud
Journal of Southeast Asian Studies — J SE Asia S
Journal of Southeast Asian Studies — J SE Asian Stud
Journal of Southeast Asian Studies — J Southeast Asian Stud
Journal of Southeast Asian Studies — JoSos
Journal of Southeast Asian Studies — JSAS
Journal of Southeast Asian Studies — PJSE
Journal of Southern African Affairs — J South Afr Aff
Journal of Southern African Studies — J South Afr Stud
Journal of Southern African Studies — J Sth Afr Stud
Journal of Southern History — J S Hist
Journal of Southern History — J So Hist
Journal of Southern History — J South His
Journal of Southern History — J South Hist
Journal of Southern History — J Southern Hist
Journal of Southern History — JoSou
Journal of Southern History — JSH
Journal of Southern History — PJSN
Journal of Southern Research — J South Res
Journal of Soviet Cardiovascular Research — J Sov Cardiovasc Res
Journal of Soviet Cardiovascular Research — Jnl Sov Cardiovasc Res
Journal of Soviet Laser Research — J Sov Laser Res
Journal of Soviet Mathematics — J Soviet Math
Journal of Soviet Oncology — J Sov Oncol
Journal of Space Law — J Space L
Journal of Space Law — J Space Law
Journal of Spacecraft and Rockets — J Spac Rock
Journal of Spacecraft and Rockets — J Spacecr and Rockets
Journal of Spacecraft and Rockets — J Spacecr Rockets
Journal of Spacecraft and Rockets — JSR
Journal of Spanish Studies. Twentieth Century — J Span Stud
Journal of Spanish Studies. Twentieth Century — JSS
Journal of Spanish Studies. Twentieth Century — JSSTC
Journal of Special Education — J Sp Educ
Journal of Special Education — J Spec Ed
Journal of Special Education — J Spec Educ
Journal of Special Education — JSPEB
Journal of Spectroscopy — J Spectrosc
Journal of Speech and Hearing Disorders — ISHD
Journal of Speech and Hearing Disorders — J Sp Disorders
Journal of Speech and Hearing Disorders — J Speech & Hear Dis
Journal of Speech and Hearing Disorders — J Speech & Hear Disord
Journal of Speech and Hearing Disorders — J Speech D
Journal of Speech and Hearing Disorders — J Speech Hear Disord
Journal of Speech and Hearing Disorders — J Speech Hearing Dis
Journal of Speech and Hearing Disorders — JSHD
Journal of Speech and Hearing Disorders — JSHDA
Journal of Speech and Hearing Research — J Speech & Hear Res
Journal of Speech and Hearing Research — J Speech He
Journal of Speech and Hearing Research — J Speech Hear Res
Journal of Speech and Hearing Research — JSHR
Journal of Speech and Hearing Research — JSPHA
Journal of Speech Disorders — Jour Speech Disorders
Journal of Spinal Cord Medicine — J Spinal Cord Med
Journal of Spinal Disorders — J Spinal Disord
Journal of Sport & Exercise Psychology — J Sport & Ex Psy
Journal of Sport and Social Issues — J Sport and Soc Iss
Journal of Sport and Social Issues — J Sport Soc Iss
Journal of Sport Behavior — J Sport Beh
Journal of Sport Behavior — J Sport Behav
Journal of Sport History — J Sport Hist
Journal of Sport Management — J Sport Management
Journal of Sport Psychology — J Sport Psy
Journal of Sport Psychology — J Sport Psychol
Journal of Sport Rehabilitation — J Sport Rehab
Journal of Sports Medicine — J Sports Med
Journal of Sports Medicine and Physical Fitness — J Sport Med
Journal of Sports Medicine and Physical Fitness — J Sports Med and P Fit
Journal of Sports Medicine and Physical Fitness — J Sports Med Phys Fit
Journal of Sports Medicine and Physical Fitness — J Sports Med Phys Fitness
Journal of Sports Sciences — J Sport Sci
Journal of Sports Sciences — J Sports Sci
Journal of Sports Sciences — JSS
Journal of Sports Traumatology — J Sports Trauma
Journal of Starch Technology. Research Society of Japan — J Starch Technol Res Soc Jpn
Journal of State Government — PJSG
Journal of State Medicine — J St Med
Journal of State Medicine — J State Med
Journal of Statistical Computation and Simulation — J Stat Comput Simul
Journal of Statistical Computation and Simulation — J Statist Comp and Simulation
Journal of Statistical Computation and Simulation — J Statist Comput Simulation
Journal of Statistical Computation and Simulation — JSCSA
Journal of Statistical Physics — J Stat Phys
Journal of Statistical Physics — J Statist Phys
Journal of Statistical Planning and Inference — J Stat Plann and Inference
Journal of Statistical Planning and Inference — J Stat Plann Inference
Journal of Statistical Planning and Inference — J Statist Plann Inference
Journal of Statistical Planning and Inference — JSP
Journal of Statistical Research — J Stat Rsr
Journal of Statistical Research — J Statist Res
Journal of Sterile Services Management — J Sterile Serv Manage
Journal of Steroid Biochemistry — J Ster Biochem
Journal of Steroid Biochemistry — J Steroid B
Journal of Steroid Biochemistry — J Steroid Biochem
Journal of Steroid Biochemistry and Molecular Biology — J Steroid Biochem Mol Biol
Journal of Stored Products Research — J Stored Pr
Journal of Stored Products Research — J Stored Prod Res
Journal of Strain Analysis — J Strain Anal
Journal of Strain Analysis — J Strain Analysis
Journal of Strain Analysis for Engineering Design — J Strain Anal Eng Des
Journal of Strain Analysis for Engineering Design — J Strain Anal Engng Des
Journal of Strain Analysis for Engineering Design — JSAED
Journal of Strength and Conditioning Research — J Streng & Con Res
Journal of Structural Biology — J Struct Biol
Journal of Structural Chemistry — J Struct Ch
Journal of Structural Chemistry — J Struct Chem
Journal of Structural Chemistry — JSC
Journal of Structural Chemistry (English Translation) — J Struct Chem (Engl Transl).
Journal of Structural Engineering — ST
Journal of Structural Geology — J Struct Geol
Journal of Structural Learning — J Struct Le
Journal of Structural Learning — J Structural Learning
Journal of Structural Mechanics — J Struc Mec
Journal of Structural Mechanics — J Struct Mech
Journal of Structural Mechanics — J Structural Mech
Journal of Studies on Alcohol — GSAL
Journal of Studies on Alcohol — J Stud Alc
Journal of Studies on Alcohol — J Stud Alcohol
Journal of Studies on Alcohol — J Studies Alcohol
Journal of Studies on Alcohol — JSALO
Journal of Studies on Alcohol (Supplement) — J Stud Alcohol (Suppl)
Journal of Submicroscopic Cytology — J Submic Cy
Journal of Submicroscopic Cytology — J Submicrosc Cytol
Journal of Submicroscopic Cytology and Pathology — J Submicrosc Cytol Pathol
Journal of Substance Abuse — J Subst Abuse
Journal of Substance Abuse Treatment — J Subst Abuse Treat
Journal of Sugarcane Research — J Sugarcane Res
Journal of Superconductivity — J Supercond
Journal of Supercritical Fluids — J Supercrit Fluids
Journal of Supervision and Training in Ministry — J Supervision
Journal of Supervision and Training in Ministry — J Supervision Tr Min
Journal of Supramolecular Structure [*Later, Journal of Cellular Biochemistry*] — J Supram St
Journal of Supramolecular Structure [*Later, Journal of Cellular Biochemistry*] — J Supramol Struct
Journal of Supramolecular Structure [*Later, Journal of Cellular Biochemistry*] — J Supramolecular Struct
Journal of Supramolecular Structure [*Later, Journal of Cellular Biochemistry*] — JSPMA
Journal of Supramolecular Structure and Cellular Biochemistry [*Later, Journal of Cellular Biochemistry*] — J Supramol Struct Cell Biochem
Journal of Supramolecular Structure (Supplement) — J Supramol Struct (Suppl)
Journal of Surgical Oncology — J Surg Oncol
Journal of Surgical Oncology. Suppplement — J Surg Oncol Suppl
Journal of Surgical Research — J Surg Res
Journal of Swimming Research — J Swim Res
Journal of Symbolic Anthropology — J Symb Anthropol
Journal of Symbolic Logic — J Sym Log
Journal of Symbolic Logic — J Symb Log
Journal of Symbolic Logic — J Symb Logic
Journal of Symbolic Logic — J Symbol Logic
Journal of Symbolic Logic — J Symbolic Logic
Journal of Symbolic Logic — JSL
Journal of Symbolic Logic. Quarterly — JSLQ
Journal of Synagogue Music — JSM
Journal of Synthetic Crystals — J Synth Cryst

Journal of Synthetic Lubrication — J Synth Lubr
Journal of Synthetic Organic Chemistry (Japan) — J Syn Org (J)
Journal of Synthetic Organic Chemistry (Japan) — J Synth Org Chem (Jpn)
Journal of Synthetic Rubber Industry (Lanzhou, People's Republic of China) — J Synth Rubber Ind (Lanzhou People's Repub China)
Journal of Systems and Software — J Sys and Soft
Journal of Systems and Software — J Syst and Software
Journal of Systems and Software — J Systems Software
Journal of Systems and Software — JSS
Journal of Systems Engineering — J Syst Eng
Journal of Systems Engineering — J Syst Engng
Journal of Systems Engineering — J Systems Engrg
Journal of Systems Management — J Sys Mgmt
Journal of Systems Management — J Sys Mgt
Journal of Systems Management — J Syst Man
Journal of Systems Management — J Syst Manage
Journal of Systems Management — J Syst Mgt
Journal of Systems Management — J Systems Mgt
Journal of Systems Management — JSM
Journal of Systems Science and Mathematical Sciences — J Systems Sci Math Sci
Journal of Taiwan Agricultural Research — J Taiwan Agr Res
Journal of Taiwan Agricultural Research — J Taiwan Agric Res
Journal of Tamil Studies — J Tam S
Journal of Tamil Studies — J Tamil Stud
Journal of Tamil Studies — JTS
Journal of Taxation — J Tax
Journal of Taxation — J Taxation
Journal of Taxation — J Tax'n
Journal of Taxation — JOT
Journal of Taxation — JTX
Journal of Taxation of Investments — JTI
Journal of Tea Science — J Tea Sci
Journal of Teacher Education — GTEA
Journal of Teacher Education — J Teach Ed
Journal of Teacher Education — J Teach Educ
Journal of Teacher Education — JTE
Journal of Teaching and Learning — J Teach Learn
Journal of Teaching in Physical Education — J Teaching PE
Journal of Technical Methods and Bulletin. International Association of Medical Museums — J Techn Meth
Journal of Technical Physics — J Tech Phys
Journal of Technical Physics (Warsaw) — J Tech Phys Warsaw
Journal of Technical Sciences — J Tech Sci
Journal of Technical Topics in Civil Engineering — TC
Journal of Technical Writing and Communication — J Tech Writ Commun
Journal of Technical Writing and Communication — TW
Journal of Technological Researches. College of Engineering. Kanto Gakuin University — J Technol Res Coll Eng Kanto Gakuin Univ
Journal of Technology — J Techn
Journal of Technology — J Technol
Journal of Technology and Education. Electrochemical Society of Japan — J Technol Educ Electrochem Soc Jpn
Journal of Technology and Engineering — J Technol Eng
Journal of Technology. Bengal Engineering College — J Tech Bengal Engrg College
Journal of Technology. Bengan Engineering College — J Technol Bengal Eng Coll
Journal of Teflon — J Teflon
Journal of Telecommunication Networks — J Telecom Net
Journal of Telecommunication Networks — J Telecommun Networks
Journal of Telemedicine and Telecare — J Telemed Telecare
Journal of Terramechanics — J Terramech
Journal of Terramechanics — J Terramechanics
Journal of Tertiary Educational Administration — J Tertiary Educ Adm
Journal of Testing and Evaluation — J Test and Eval
Journal of Testing and Evaluation — J Test Eval
Journal of Testing and Evaluation — Jl Test Eval
Journal of Testing and Evaluation — JTEVA
Journal of Textile Engineering (Taichung, Taiwan) — J Text Eng Taichung Taiwan
Journal of Textile Research (Shanghai) — J Text Res Shanghai
Journal of Textile Science — J Text Sci
Journal of Texture Studies — J Text Stud
Journal of Texture Studies — J Texture Stud
Journal of Thanatology — J Thanatol
Journal of the Aero/Space Sciences [*Later, American Institute of Aeronautics and Astronautics. Journal*] — J Aero/Space Sci
Journal of the Aeronautical Sciences — J Aero Sci
Journal of the Air and Waste Management Association — J Air Waste Manage Assoc
Journal of the American Association of Gynecologic Laparoscopists — J Am Assoc Gynecol Laparosc
Journal of the American Mathematical Society — J Amer Math Soc
Journal of the Asahikawa National College of Technology — J Asahikawa Nat College Tech
Journal of the Astronautical Sciences — J Astronaut
Journal of the Astronautical Sciences — J Astronaut Sci
Journal of the Atmospheric Sciences — J Atmos Sci
Journal of the Atmospheric Sciences — J Atmospheric Sci
Journal of the Autonomic Nervous System — J Auton Nerv Syst
Journal of the Bihar Mathematical Society — J Bihar Math Soc
Journal of the Chartered Institution of Water and Environmental Management — J Chart Inst Water Environ Manage
Journal of the Chemical Fertilizer Industry — J Chem Fert Ind
Journal of the Chinese Institute of Environmental Engineering — J Chin Inst Environ Eng
Journal of the Chinese Nutrition Society — J Chin Nutr Soc
Journal of the Dental Auxiliaries — J Dent Aux
Journal of the Dental School. National University of Iran — J Dent Sch Natl Univ Iran
Journal of the Early Republic — J Early Repub
Journal of the Early Republic — PJER
Journal of the Earth and Space Physics (Tehran) — J Earth Space Phys (Tehran)
Journal of the Economic and Social History of the Orient — J Econ Soc Hist Or
Journal of the Economic and Social History of the Orient — J Econ Soc Hist Orient
Journal of the Economic and Social History of the Orient — JESHO
Journal of the Egyptian Mathematical Society — J Egyptian Math Soc
Journal of the Electronics Industry — Jrl Elec I
Journal of the European Optical Society. Part B — J Eur Opt Soc Part B
Journal of the Experimental Analysis of Behavior — IXAB
Journal of the Experimental Analysis of Behavior — J Ex An Beh
Journal of the Experimental Analysis of Behavior — J Exp Anal Behav
Journal of the Experimental Analysis of Behavior — J Exp Analysis Behav
Journal of the Experimental Analysis of Behavior — J Exper Anal Behav
Journal of the Experimental Analysis of Behavior — JEAB
Journal of the Eye — J Eye
Journal of the Faculty of Human Life Sciences. Prefectural University of Kumamoto — J Fac Hum Life Sci Prefect Univ Kumamoto
Journal of the Faculty of Science and Technology. Kinki University — J Fac Sci Tech Kinki Univ
Journal of the Faculty of Science. Ege University. Series A-B — J Fac Sci Ege Univ Ser A B
Journal of the Faculty of Science. University of Tokyo. Section 2. Geology, Mineralogy, Geography, Geophysics — J Fac Sci Univ Tokyo Sect 2
Journal of the Fourth Military Medical University — J Fourth Mil Med Univ
Journal of the Franklin Institute. B. Engineering and Applied Mathematics — J Franklin Inst B
Journal of the Heat Transfer Society of Japan — J Heat Transfer Soc Jpn
Journal of the Hellenic Diaspora — JHD
Journal of the Historical Society of Nigeria — JtH
Journal of the History of Biology — J Hist Biol
Journal of the History of Ideas — GHII
Journal of the History of Ideas — J Hist Id
Journal of the History of Ideas — J Hist Idea
Journal of the History of Ideas — J Hist Ideas
Journal of the History of Ideas — JHI
Journal of the History of Ideas — Jnl Hist Ideas
Journal of the History of Ideas — Jour Hist Ideas
Journal of the History of Ideas — JtHI
Journal of the History of Medicine — JHM
Journal of the History of Medicine — Jour Hist Med
Journal of the History of Medicine and Allied Sciences — J Hist Med
Journal of the History of Medicine and Allied Sciences — J Hist Med Allied Sci
Journal of the History of Medicine and Allied Sciences [*New York*] — JHM
Journal of the History of Medicine and Allied Sciences — JtHM
Journal of the History of Philosophy — J Hist Phil
Journal of the History of Philosophy — J Hist Philos
Journal of the History of Philosophy [*Berkeley*] — JHP
Journal of the History of Philosophy — JHPh
Journal of the History of Philosophy — Jour Hist Phil
Journal of the History of Philosophy — PJHP
Journal of the History of Science (Japan) — J Hist Sci (Jpn)
Journal of the History of Sociology — J Hist Sociol
Journal of the History of the Behavioral Sciences — J Hist Beh
Journal of the History of the Behavioral Sciences — J Hist Beh Sci
Journal of the History of the Behavioral Sciences — J Hist Behav Sci
Journal of the History of the Behavioral Sciences — JHBSA
Journal of the History of the Behavioral Sciences — Journ Hist Behavioral Sci
Journal of the History of the Behavioral Sciences — JtHB
Journal of the Hydrogen Energy Systems Society of Japan — J Hydrogen Energy Syst Soc Jpn
Journal of the IES (Institute of Environmental Sciences) — J IES
Journal of the IETE (Institution of Electronics and Telecommunication Engineers) — J IETE
Journal of the Illinois State Historical Society — JtI
Journal of the Indian Medical Profession — J Indian Med Prof
Journal of the Indian Society of Agricultural Statistics — J Indian Soc Agricultural Statist
Journal of the Institute of Environmental Sciences — J Inst Environ Sci
Journal of the Institute of Nuclear Materials Management — JNMM
Journal of the Institution of Engineers (India). Metallurgy and Material Science Division — J Inst Eng India Metall Mater Sci Div
Journal of the Institution of Water and Environmental Management — J Inst Water Environ Manage
Journal of the Interest Group in Pure and Applied Logics — J IGPL
Journal of the International Federation of Clinical Chemistry — J Int Fed Clin Chem
Journal of the International Neuropsychological Society — J Int Neuropsychol Soc
Journal of the Iraqi Medical Professions — J Iraqi Med Prof
Journal of the Japanese Society of Computational Statistics — J Japanese Soc Comput Statist
Journal of the Lancaster County Historical Society — JtL
Journal of the Legal Profession — J Legal Prof
Journal of the Less-Common Metals — J Less Common Met
Journal of the Less-Common Metals — J Less-C Met
Journal of the Malaysian Branch. Royal Asiatic Society — JtM

Journal of the Mechanics and Physics of Solids — J Mech Phys
Journal of the Mechanics and Physics of Solids — J Mech Phys Solids
Journal of the Methodist Historical Society of South Africa — J Methodist Hist Soc of S Afr
Journal of the Microscopy Society of America — J Microsc Soc Am
Journal of the Moscow Patriarchate — J Moscow Patr
Journal of the Neurological Sciences — J Neur Sci
Journal of the Neurological Sciences — J Neurol Sci
Journal of the Neurological Sciences — JNSCA
Journal of the New African Literature and the Arts — JNALA
Journal of the Nigerian Mathematical Society — J Nigerian Math Soc
Journal of the Northwest Semitic Languages — J Nw SL
Journal of the Northwest Semitic Languages [*Leiden*] — JNSEL
Journal of the Northwest Semitic Languages [*Leiden*] — JNSL
Journal of the Northwest Semitic Languages [*Leiden*] — JNWSemL
Journal of the Pakistan Historical Society — JtP
Journal of the Philosophy of Sport — J Phil Sport
Journal of the Philosophy of Sport — J Philos Sport
Journal of the Presbyterian Historical Society of England — JtPHS
Journal of the Ramanujan Mathematical Society — J Ramanujan Math Soc
Journal of the Remount and Veterinary Corps — J Remount Vet Corps
Journal of the Retail Traders' Association of New South Wales — J Retail Traders Assn NSW
Journal of the Retail Traders' Association of New South Wales — J Retail Traders Assoc NSW
Journal of the Royal Artillery — J Roy Artil
Journal of the Royal Artillery — J Roy Arty
Journal of the Royal Australian Historical Society — JtR
Journal of the Royal Society of Antiquaries of Ireland — JtRSA
Journal of the Rutgers University Library — JtRU
Journal of the Science Club — J Sci Club
Journal of the Science of Food and Agriculture — J Sc Food Agriculture
Journal of the Science of Food and Agriculture — J Sci Fd Agric
Journal of the Science of Food and Agriculture — J Sci Food
Journal of the Science of Food and Agriculture — J Sci Food Agr
Journal of the Science of Food and Agriculture — J Sci Food Agric
Journal of the Science of Food and Agriculture — JSFA
Journal of the Science of Food and Agriculture. Abstracts — J Sci Food Agric Abstr
Journal of the Science of Soil and Animal Fertilizers (Japan) — J Sci Soil Anim Fert (Jpn)
Journal of the Science of Soil and Manure (Japan) — J Sci Soil Manure (Jap)
Journal of the Society for Gynecologic Investigation — J Soc Gynecol Investig
Journal of the Society of Architectural Historians — JtSAH
Journal of the Society of Electrical Materials Engineering — J Soc Electr Mater Eng
Journal of the Speculative Philosophy — J Spec Philos
Journal of the Sports Turf Research Institute — J Sports Turf Res Inst
Journal of the Textile Institute. Part 1. Fibre Science and Textile Technology — J Text Inst Part 1
Journal of the Theory and Criticism of the Visual Arts — J Theor Crit Vis Art
Journal of the Victorian Teachers' Union — J Vic Teachers Union
Journal of the West — J West
Journal of the West — Jour of West
Journal of the West — JtW
Journal of the West — JW
Journal of the West — PJWT
Journal of the Wuxi Institute of Light Industry — J Wuxi Inst Light Ind
Journal of the Wuxi University of Light Industry — J Wuxi Univ Light Ind
Journal of Theological Studies — J Th St
Journal of Theological Studies — J Theol St
Journal of Theological Studies — Journ Theol Stud
Journal of Theological Studies — JThS
Journal of Theological Studies — JTS
Journal of Theological Studies — PJTS
Journal of Theology for Southern Africa — J Th So Africa
Journal of Theology for Southern Africa — J Theol Sthn Afr
Journal of Theoretical and Applied Mechanics — J Theoret Appl Mech
Journal of Theoretical Biology — J Theor Bio
Journal of Theoretical Biology — J Theor Biol
Journal of Theoretical Biology — J Theoret Biol
Journal of Theoretical Biology — JTB
Journal of Theoretical Neurobiology — J Theor N
Journal of Theoretical Probability — J Theoret Probab
Journal of Theoretical Science — J Theor Sci
Journal of Therapy — J Ther
Journal of Thermal Analysis — J Therm Ana
Journal of Thermal Analysis — J Therm Anal
Journal of Thermal Analysis — J Thermal Anal
Journal of Thermal Analysis — JTA
Journal of Thermal Biology — J Therm Bio
Journal of Thermal Biology — J Therm Biol
Journal of Thermal Engineering — J Therm Eng
Journal of Thermal Engineering — J Therm Engng
Journal of Thermal Insulation — J Therm Insul
Journal of Thermal Insulation — J Thermal Insulation
Journal of Thermal Stresses — J Therm Stresses
Journal of Thermal Stresses — J Thermal Stresses
Journal of Thermophysics and Heat Transfer — J Thermophys Heat Transfer
Journal of Thermoplastic Composite Materials — J Thermoplast Compos Mater
Journal of Thermosetting Plastics (Japan) — J Thermosetting Plast (Jpn)
Journal of Thoracic and Cardiovascular Surgery — J Thor Surg
Journal of Thoracic and Cardiovascular Surgery — J Thora Cardiovasc Surg
Journal of Thoracic and Cardiovascular Surgery — J Thorac Cardiov Surg
Journal of Thoracic and Cardiovascular Surgery — J Thorac Cardiovasc Surg
Journal of Thoracic and Cardiovascular Surgery — J Thoracic Cardiovas Surg
Journal of Thoracic Imaging — J Thorac Imaging
Journal of Thoracic Surgery — J Thorac Surg
Journal of Thoracic Surgery — J Thoracic Surg
Journal of Thought — J Thought
Journal of Thrombosis and Thrombolysis — J Thromb Thrombolysis
Journal of Time Series Analysis — J Time Ser Anal
Journal of Tissue Culture Methods — J Tissue Cult Methods
Journal of Tissue Culture Methods — JTCMD
Journal of Town Planning Institute — J Town Pl I
Journal of Toxicological Sciences — J Toxicol Sci
Journal of Toxicology and Environmental Health — J Tox Env H
Journal of Toxicology and Environmental Health — J Toxicol Environ Health
Journal of Toxicology. Clinical Toxicology — J Toxicol Clin Toxicol
Journal of Toxicology. Cutaneous and Ocular Toxicology — J Toxicol Cutaneous Ocul Toxicol
Journal of Toxicology. Toxin Reviews — J Toxicol Toxin Rev
Journal of Toxicology. Toxin Reviews — JTTRD9
Journal of Trace and Microprobe Techniques — J Trace Microprobe Tech
Journal of Trace and Microprobe Techniques — JTMTDE
Journal of Trace Elements and Electrolytes in Health and Disease — J Trace Elem Electrolytes Health Dis
Journal of Trace Elements in Experimental Medicine — J Trace Elem Exp Med
Journal of Trace Elements in Medicine and Biology — J Trace Elem Med Biol
Journal of Traditional Chinese Medicine — J Tradit Chin Med
Journal of Traditional Chinese Medicine — JTCMEC
Journal of Traditional Sino-Japanese Medicine — J Tradit Sino Jpn Med
Journal of Traffic Medicine — Jnl Traf Med
Journal of Transactions. Society for Promoting the Study of Religions — JSPSR
Journal of Transactions. Victoria Institute — JTVI
Journal of Transpersonal Psychology — J Transpers Psych
Journal of Transpersonal Psychology — J Transpersonal Psychol
Journal of Transport Economics and Policy — J Transp Ec
Journal of Transport Economics and Policy — J Transp Econ Policy
Journal of Transport Economics and Policy — J Transport Econ and Policy
Journal of Transport Economics and Policy — J Transport Econ Pol
Journal of Transport Economics and Policy — JTE
Journal of Transport Economics and Policy — JTEP
Journal of Transport Economics and Policy — JTP
Journal of Transport History — J Transp Hist
Journal of Transport History — J Transport Hist
Journal of Transportation Engineering — TE
Journal of Transportation Engineering. Proceedings. American Society of Civil Engineers — JTCE
Journal of Transportation Medicine [*Japan*] — J Transp Med
Journal of Trauma — J Trauma
Journal of Trauma. Injury, Infection, and Critical Care — J Trauma Inj Infect Crit Care
Journal of Traumatic Stress — J Trauma Stress
Journal of Travel Research — JTR
Journal of Tribology — J Tribol
Journal of Tropical and Subtropical Botany — J Trop Subtrop Bot
Journal of Tropical Ecology — J Trop Ecol
Journal of Tropical Forestry — J Trop For
Journal of Tropical Geography — J Trop Geog
Journal of Tropical Geography — J Trop Geogr
Journal of Tropical Geography — J Tropical Geography
Journal of Tropical Geography — JTG
Journal of Tropical Geography — JTGG-A
Journal of Tropical Geography — JTGGAA
Journal of Tropical Medicine and Hygiene — J Trop Med
Journal of Tropical Medicine and Hygiene — J Trop Med Hyg
Journal of Tropical Medicine and Hygiene — JTMH
Journal of Tropical Medicine and Hygiene (London) — J Trop Med and Hyg (London)
Journal of Tropical Medicine (London) — J Trop Med (London)
Journal of Tropical Pediatrics — J Trop Ped
Journal of Tropical Pediatrics — J Trop Pediat
Journal of Tropical Pediatrics — J Trop Pediatr
Journal of Tropical Pediatrics and African Child Health — J Trop Pediatr Afr Child Health
Journal of Tropical Pediatrics and Environmental Child Health — J Trop Pediatr Environ Child Health
Journal of Tropical Pediatrics and Environmental Child Health. Monograph — J Trop Pediatr Environ Child Health Monogr
Journal of Tropical Veterinary Science — J Trop Vet Sc
Journal of Tuberculosis and Leprosy [*Japan*] — J Tuberc Lepr
Journal of Turkish Phytopathology — J Turk Phytopathol
Journal of Typographic Research — J Typogr Res
Journal of Typographic Research — JTR
Journal of Ukrainian Graduate Studies — JUKGS
Journal of Ukrainian Studies — J Ukr Stud
Journal of Ultrasound in Medicine — J Ultrasound Med
Journal of Ultrastructure and Molecular Structure Research — J Ultrastruct Mol Struct Res
Journal of Ultrastructure Research — J Ultra Res
Journal of Ultrastructure Research — J Ultrastruct Res
Journal of Ultrastructure Research. Supplement — J Ultrastruct Res Suppl
Journal of Undergraduate Psychological Research — JUPOA
Journal of University of Fisheries — J Univ Fish
Journal of University of Science and Technology Beijing — J Univ Sci Technol Beijing
Journal of University Studies — J Univ Stud

Journal of UOEH [*University of Occupational and Environmental Health*] [*Japan*] — J UOEH
Journal of Urban Affairs — J Urban Affairs
Journal of Urban Analysis — J Urban Anal
Journal of Urban Analysis — J Urban Analysis
Journal of Urban Economics — J Urban Ec
Journal of Urban Economics — J Urban Econ
Journal of Urban Economics — JUE
Journal of Urban History — J Urban H
Journal of Urban History — J Urban His
Journal of Urban History — J Urban Hist
Journal of Urban History — PJUH
Journal of Urban Law — J Urban
Journal of Urban Law — J Urban L
Journal of Urban Law — J Urban Law
Journal of Urban Law — JUL
Journal of Urban Planning and Development — UP
Journal of Urology — J Urol
Journal of Urology — JUr
Journal of Urology (Baltimore) — J Urol (Baltimore)
Journal of Utilization of Agricultural Products — J Utiliz Agr Prod
Journal of Vacuum Science and Technology — J Vac Sci and Technol
Journal of Vacuum Science and Technology — J Vac Sci T
Journal of Vacuum Science and Technology — J Vac Sci Tech
Journal of Vacuum Science and Technology — J Vac Sci Technol
Journal of Vacuum Science and Technology. A. Vacuum, Surfaces, and Films — J Vac Sci and Technol A
Journal of Vacuum Science and Technology. B. Micro-Electronics Processing and Phenomena — J Vac Sci and Technol B
Journal of Value Engineering — J Value Eng
Journal of Value Inquiry — J Value Inq
Journal of Vascular and Interventional Radiology — J Vasc Interv Radiol
Journal of Vascular Research — J Vasc Res
Journal of Vascular Surgery — J Vasc Surg
Journal of Vascular Surgery — JVSUES
Journal of Venereal Disease Information — J Vener Dis Inf
Journal of Verbal Learning and Verbal Behavior — J Verb Learn
Journal of Verbal Learning and Verbal Behavior — J Verb Learn Verb Behav
Journal of Verbal Learning and Verbal Behavior — J Verbal Learn
Journal of Verbal Learning and Verbal Behavior — JVLBA
Journal of Verbal Learning and Verbal Behavior — JVLVB
Journal of Vertebrate Paleontology — J Vertebr Paleontol
Journal of Vertebrate Paleontology — JVP
Journal of Vertebrate Paleontology — JVPADK
Journal of Vestibular Research — J Vestib Res
Journal of Veterinary Anaesthesia — J Vet Anaesth
Journal of Veterinary and Animal Husbandry Research (India) — J Vet Anim Husb Res (India)
Journal of Veterinary Diagnostic Investigation — J Vet Diagn Invest
Journal of Veterinary Internal Medicine — J Vet Intern Med
Journal of Veterinary Medical Education — J Vet Med Educ
Journal of Veterinary Medical Science — J Vet Med Sci
Journal of Veterinary Medicine [*Japan*] — J Vet Med
Journal of Veterinary Medicine. Series A — J Vet Med Ser A
Journal of Veterinary Medicine. Series A — JVMAE6
Journal of Veterinary Medicine. Series B — J Vet Med Ser B
Journal of Veterinary Medicine. Series B — JVMBE9
Journal of Veterinary Medicine (Teheran) — J Vet Med Teheran
Journal of Veterinary Orthopedics — Jnl Vet Orthoped
Journal of Veterinary Pharmacology and Therapeutics — J Vet Pharm Ther
Journal of Veterinary Pharmacology and Therapeutics — J Vet Pharmacol Ther
Journal of Veterinary Pharmacology and Therapeutics — JVPTD9
Journal of Veterinary Science of the United Arab Republic — J Vet Sci UAR
Journal of Vibration and Control — J Vib Control
Journal of Vinyl and Additive Technology — J Vinyl Addit Technol
Journal of Vinyl Technology — J Vinyl Technol
Journal of Viral Hepatitis — J Viral Hepat
Journal of Virological Methods — J Virol Methods
Journal of Virological Methods — JVMED
Journal of Virology — J Virol
Journal of Virology — J Virology
Journal of Virology (Tokyo) — J Virol (Tokyo)
Journal of Visual Impairment and Blindness — J Visual Impairment & Blind
Journal of Visual Impairment and Blindness — JVIBDM
Journal of Vitaminology — J Vitaminol
Journal of Vitaminology (Kyoto) — J Vitaminol (Kyoto)
Journal of VLSI and Computer Systems — J VLSI Comput Systems
Journal of Vocational Behavior — J Voc Behav
Journal of Vocational Behavior — J Vocat Beh
Journal of Vocational Behavior — J Vocat Behav
Journal of Voice — J Voice
Journal of Volcanology and Geothermal Research — J Volcanol Geotherm Res
Journal of Voluntary Action Research — J Volun Act
Journal of Voluntary Action Research — J Volun Action Res
Journal of Volunteer Administration — J Volunteer Adm
Journal of Volunteer Administration — JVA
Journal of Water and Solid Wastes Management — J Water Solid Wastes Manage
Journal of Water and Waste [*Japan*] — J Water Waste
Journal of Water Borne Coatings — J Water Borne Coat
Journal of Water Resources — J Water Resour
Journal of Water Resources — JWREEG
Journal of Water Resources Planning and Management — WR
Journal of Water Re-use Technology — J Water Reuse Technol
Journal of Water Science — J Water Sci
Journal of Waterway, Port, Coastal, and Ocean Engineering — WW
Journal of Weavers, Spinners, and Dyers — J Weavers Spinners Dyers
Journal of Wellness Perspectives — J Well Perspect
Journal of West African Languages — J W Afr Langs
Journal of West African Languages — JWAfrL
Journal of West African Languages — JWAL
Journal of Western Speech — JWS
Journal of Wildlife Diseases — J Wildl Dis
Journal of Wildlife Diseases — JWIDA
Journal of Wildlife Management — J Wildl Man
Journal of Wildlife Management — J Wildl Manage
Journal of Wildlife Management — J Wildlife Mgt
Journal of Wildlife Management — JWIM
Journal of Wildlife Management — PJWM
Journal of Wildlife Management. Supplement — J Wildlife Manage Suppl
Journal of Wind Engineering and Industrial Aerodynamics — J Wind Eng and Ind
Journal of Wind Engineering and Industrial Aerodynamics — J Wind Engng & Ind Aerodyn
Journal of Wind Engineering and Industrial Aerodynamics — J Wind Engng Ind Aerodynam
Journal of Women's Health — J Womens Health
Journal of Women's Studies in Literature — JWSL
Journal of Wood Chemistry and Technology — J Wood Chem Technol
Journal of Wood Chemistry and Technology — JWCTD
Journal of Wood Chemistry and Technology — JWCTDJ
Journal of World Forest Resource Management — J World For Resour Manage
Journal of World History — J Wld Hist
Journal of World History — J World Hist
Journal of World History — JWH
Journal of World Trade Law — J Wld Trade Law
Journal of World Trade Law — J World Tr
Journal of World Trade Law — J World Tr L
Journal of World Trade Law — J World Trade L
Journal of World Trade Law — J World Trade Law
Journal of World Trade Law — JWT
Journal of World Trade Law — JWTL
Journal of World Trade Law — WTN
Journal of Wuhan Institute of Technology — J Wuhan Inst Tech
Journal of Wuhan University. Natural Sciences Edition — J Wuhan Univ Natur Sci Ed
Journal of Xi'an Medical University — J Xian Med Univ
Journal of Xi'an Petroleum Institute — J Xian Pet Inst
Journal of X-Ray Technology — J X-Ray Technol
Journal of Yiyang Teachers' College — J Yiyang Teachers College
Journal of Youth and Adolescence — J Youth Ado
Journal of Youth and Adolescence — J Youth Adolesc
Journal of Youth and Adolescence — J Youth & Adolescence
Journal of Youth and Adolescence — JOYA
Journal of Youth and Adolescence — JYADA6
Journal of Youth and Adolescence — PJYA
Journal of Youth Services in Libraries — JOYS
Journal of Yugoslav Pomology — J Yugosl Pomol
Journal of Zhejiang Institute of Technology — J Zhejiang Inst Technol
Journal of Zoo and Wildlife Medicine — J Zoo Wild
Journal of Zoo and Wildlife Medicine — J Zoo Wildl Med
Journal of Zoo Animal Medicine — J Zoo Anim Med
Journal of Zoological Research — J Zool Res
Journal of Zoological Research [*Aligarh*] — JZRED2
Journal of Zoological Research (Aligarh) — J Zool Res (Aligarh)
Journal of Zoology — J Zool
Journal of Zoology [*London*] — JZOOAE
Journal of Zoology (London) — J Zool (Lond)
Journal of Zoology. Proceedings. Zoological Society of London — J Zool Proc Zool Soc Lond
Journal of Zoology. Series A — J Zool Ser A
Journal of Zoology. Series A — JZSAEU
Journal of Zoology. Series B — J Zool Ser B
Journal of Zoology. Series B — JZSBEX
Journal. Office des Recherches sur les Pecheries du Canada — J Off Rech Pech Can
Journal Officiel. Communaute Europeenne du Charbon et de l'Acier — JOCECA
Journal Officiel de la Republique Francaise — J Off Repub Fr
Journal Officiel de la Republique Francaise — JOOFA
Journal Officiel de la Republique Francaise — JORF
Journal Officiel de la Republique Francaise. Recueil Dalloz — JO
Journal Officiel des Communautes Europeennes — JO
Journal Officiel. Republique Algerienne Democratique et Populaire — J Off Repub Alger Democr Pop
Journal. Ohio Herpetological Society — J Ohio Herpetol Soc
Journal. Oil and Colour Chemists' Association — J OCCA
Journal. Oil and Colour Chemists' Association — J Oil Col C
Journal. Oil and Colour Chemists' Association — J Oil Colour Chem Ass
Journal. Oil and Colour Chemists' Association — J Oil Colour Chem Assoc
Journal. Oil Technologists' Association of India — J Oil Technol Assoc India
Journal. Oil Technologists' Association of India (Bombay) — J Oil Technol Assoc India (Bombay)
Journal. Oil Technologists' Association of India (Kanpur, India) — J Oil Technol Assoc India (Kanpur India)
Journal. Okayama Dental Society — J Okayama Dent Soc
Journal. Okayama Medical Society [*Japan*] — J Okayama Med Soc
Journal. Okayama Medical Society. Supplement [*Japan*] — J Okayama Med Soc Suppl
Journal. Oklahoma Dental Association — J Okla Dent Assoc

Journal. Oklahoma State Dental Association — J Okla State Dent Assoc
Journal. Oklahoma State Medical Association — J Okla State Med Assoc
Journal. Old Athlone Society — J Old Athlone Soc
Journal. Old Wexford Society — J Old Wexford Soc
Journal. Old Wexford Society — Old Wexford Soc J
Journal on Numerical Methods and Computer Applications — J Numer Methods Comput Appl
Journal. Ontario Dental Association [*Canada*] — J Ont Dent Assoc
Journal. Open Education Association of Queensland — J Open Educ Assoc Qld
Journal. Operating Room Research Institute — JORRI
Journal. Operation Research Society of America — J Oper Res Soc Am
Journal. Operational Research Society — J Op Res Soc
Journal. Operational Research Society — J Oper Res Soc
Journal. Operational Research Society — JORS
Journal. Operations Research Society of Japan — J Op Res So
Journal. Operations Research Society of Japan — J Oper Res Soc Jap
Journal. Operations Research Society of Japan — J Operations Res Soc Japan
Journal. Operations Research Society of Japan — JORSJ
Journal. Operative Brewers' Guild — J Oper Brew Guild
Journal. Optical Society of America — J Opt Soc
Journal. Optical Society of America — J Opt Soc Am
Journal. Optical Society of America — J Opt Soc Amer
Journal. Optical Society of America — JOSA
Journal. Optical Society of America — JOSAA
Journal. Optical Society of America. A. Optics and Image Science — J Opt Soc Am A
Journal. Optical Society of America and Review of Scientific Instruments — J Opt Soc Am Rev Sci Instrum
Journal. Optical Society of America. B. Optical Physics — J Opt Soc Am B Opt Phys
Journal. Optical Society of America. Cumulative Index — J Opt Soc Cum Ind
Journal. Oregon Dental Association — J Oreg Dent Assoc
Journal. Organ Historical Society — JOHS
Journal. Organometallic Chemistry Library — J Organomet Chem Libr
Journal. Organometallic Chemistry Library [*Elsevier Book Series*] — JOML
Journal. Oriental Institute — J Or Inst
Journal. Oriental Institute [*Baroda*] — JOI
Journal. Oriental Institute (Baroda) — J Orient Inst (Baroda)
Journal. Oriental Institute (Baroda) — JOIB
Journal. Oriental Society of Australia — J Or Soc Aust
Journal. Oriental Society of Australia — J Oriental Soc Aust
Journal. Oriental Society of Australia — JOSA
Journal. Orissa Botanical Society — J Orissa Bot Soc
Journal. Orissa Botanical Society — JOBSEO
Journal. Orissa Mathematical Society — J Orissa Math Soc
Journal. Osaka City Medical Center — J Osaka City Med Cent
Journal. Osaka Dental University — J Osaka Dent Univ
Journal. Osaka Industrial University. Natural Sciences — J Osaka Ind Univ Nat Sci
Journal. Osaka Institute of Science and Technology. Part 1 — J Osaka Inst Sci Technol Part 1
Journal. Osaka Medical College [*Japan*] — J Osaka Med Coll
Journal. Osaka Odontological Society — J Osaka Odontol Soc
Journal. Osaka Sangyo University. Natural Ssciences — J Osaka Sangyo Univ Nat Sci
Journal. Osaka University Dental School — J Osaka Univ Dent Sch
Journal. Osaka University Dental Society [*Japan*] — J Osaka Univ Dent Soc
Journal. Oslo City Hospital — J Oslo City Hosp
Journal. Osmania University — J Osmania Univ
Journal. Oto-Laryngological Society of Australia — J Oto-Laryngol Soc Aust
Journal. Oto-Rhino-Laryngological Society of Japan — J Oto-Rhino-Laryngol Soc Jpn
Journal. Otto Rank Association — J Otto Rank
Journal. Otto Rank Association — J Otto Rank Assoc
Journal Ouest-Africain de Pharmacologie et de Recherche sur les Medicaments — J Ouest Afr Pharmacol Rech Med
Journal. Pakistan Historical Society — J Pak Hist Soc
Journal. Pakistan Historical Society — J Pak HS
Journal. Pakistan Medical Association — J Pak Med Ass
Journal. Pakistan Medical Association — J Pak Med Assoc
Journal. Palaeographical Society — J Palaegr Soc
Journal. Palestine Arab Medical Association — J Palest Arab Med Ass
Journal. Palestine Oriental Society — JPaOrS
Journal. Palestine Oriental Society — JPOS
Journal. Pali Text Society — JPTS
Journal. Pangasinan Medical Society — J Pang Med Soc
Journal. Panjab Historical Society — J Pan HS
Journal. Panjab University Historical Society — JPUHS
Journal. Papua and New Guinea Society — J Papua NG Society
Journal. Parenteral Drug Association — J Parenter Drug Assoc
Journal. Parenteral Drug Association — JPDADK
Journal. Patent Office Society — J Pat Of So
Journal. Patent Office Society — J Pat Off Soc'y
Journal. Patent Office Society — J POS
Journal. Patent Office Society — Jrl P
Journal. Pattern Recognition Society — Pattern Recognition
Journal. PCA (Portland Cement Association, Chicago) Research and Development Laboratories — J PCA Res Dev Lab
Journal. Peking National University/Kuo Li Pei-p'ing Ta Hsueeh Hsueeh Pao — J Peking Natl Univ
Journal. Pennsylvania Academy of Science — J PA Acad Sci
Journal. Pennsylvania Water Works Operators' Association — J PA Water Works Oper Assoc
Journal. Perth Hospital — J Perth Hosp
Journal. Pharmaceutical Association of Siam — J Pharm Assoc Siam
Journal. Pharmaceutical Association of Thailand — J Pharm Assoc Thailand
Journal. Pharmaceutical Society of Hyogo — J Pharm Soc Hyogo
Journal. Pharmaceutical Society of Japan — J Pharm Soc Jap
Journal. Pharmaceutical Society of Japan — J Pharm Soc Japan
Journal. Pharmaceutical Society of Japan — J Pharm Soc Jpn
Journal. Pharmaceutical Society of Korea — J Pharm Soc Korea
Journal. Philadelphia Association for Psychoanalysis — J Phila Assoc Psychoanal
Journal. Philadelphia College of Pharmacy — J Philadelphia Coll Pharm
Journal. Philadelphia County Dental Society — J Phila Cty Dent Soc
Journal. Philadelphia General Hospital — J Philadelphia Gen Hosp
Journal. Philippine Dental Association — J Philipp Dent Assoc
Journal. Philippine Federation of Private Medical Practitioners — J Philipp Fed Priv Med Pract
Journal. Philippine Islands Medical Association — J Philipp Isl Med Assoc
Journal. Philippine Medical Association — J Philipp Med Assoc
Journal. Philippine Medical Association — J Philippine MA
Journal. Philippine Medical Association — JPMEA
Journal. Philippine Pharmaceutical Association — J Philipp Pharm Assoc
Journal. Philippine Veterinary Medical Association — J Philipp Vet Med Assoc
Journal. Photographic Society of America — J Phot Soc Amer
Journal. Photographic Society of America — J Photogr Soc Am
Journal. Photographic Society of America — JPSA
Journal. Photomicrographic Society — J Photomicrogr Soc
Journal. Physical Society of Japan — J Phys Jap
Journal. Physical Society of Japan — J Phys Soc Jap
Journal. Physical Society of Japan — J Phys Soc Jpn
Journal. Physical Society of Japan — JUPSA
Journal. Physical Society of Japan. Supplement — J Phys Soc Jpn Suppl
Journal. Physiological Society of Japan — J Physiol Soc Jpn
Journal. Pipeline Division. American Society of Civil Engineers — J Pipeline Div Am Soc Civ Eng
Journal. Polarographic Society [*England*] — J Polarogr Soc
Journal. Polarographic Society — JPLSA
Journal. Polynesian Society — J Pol Soc
Journal. Polynesian Society — J Polyn Soc
Journal. Polynesian Society — J Polynes Soc
Journal. Polynesian Society — J Polynesia
Journal. Polynesian Society — J Polynesian Soc
Journal. Polynesian Society — JPS
Journal Polytechnique — J Polytech
Journal. Poona University — JPU
Journal. Post Graduate School. Indian Agricultural Research Institute — J Post Grad Sch Indian Agric Res Inst
Journal pour le Transport International — Trans Intl
Journal pour le Transport International — Trans Intnl
Journal pour les Materiaux d'Enregistrement des Signaux — J Mater Enregistrement Signaux
Journal. Power Division. American Society of Civil Engineers — J Power Div Am Soc Civ Eng
Journal Pratique de Droit Fiscal et Financier — Dr Fisc
Journal Pratique de Droit Fiscal et Financier — J Prat de Droit Fiscal
Journal Pratique de Droit Fiscal et Financier — JDF
Journal Pratique de Droit Fiscal et Financier — JDFisc
Journal Pratique de Droit Fiscal et Financier — Journ Fisc
Journal Pratique de Droit Fiscal et Financier — Journ Prat Dr Fisc et Fin
Journal Pratique de Droit Fiscal et Financier — JPDF
Journal Pratique de Droit Fiscal et Financier — JPFF
Journal. Predental Faculty. Gifu College of Dentistry — J Predent Fac Gifu Coll Dent
Journal. Presbyterian Historical Society — J Presby Hist Soc
Journal. Presbyterian Historical Society — JPHS
Journal. Prestressed Concrete Institute — J Pre Concr
Journal. Prestressed Concrete Institute — J Prestressed Concr Inst
Journal. Printing Historical Society — J Print Hist Soc
Journal. Proceedings. Winchester and Hampshire Scientific and Literary Society — J Proc Winchester Hampshire Sci Soc
Journal. Public Service of Papua and New Guinea — J Public Service Papua & NG
Journal. Pusan Medical College — J Pusan Med Coll
Journal. Qing Hua University — J Qing Hua Univ
Journal. Quekett Microscopical Club — J Quekett Microsc Club
Journal. Quekett Microscopical Club — J Quekett Microscop Club
Journal. Radio Research Laboratories [*Japan*] — J Rad Res L
Journal. Radio Research Laboratories [*Japan*] — J Radio Res Lab
Journal. Radio Research Laboratories [*Tokyo*] — JRRLA
Journal. Rajasthan Institute of Historical Research — J Raj Inst Hist Res
Journal. Rakuno Gakuen University. Natural Science — J Rakuno Gakuen Univ Nat Sci
Journal. Rama Varma Research Institute — JRVRI
Journal Refractories — J Refract
Journal. Regional College of Education (Bhopal) — J Reg Col Ed Bhopal
Journal. Regional Cultural Institute — JRCI
Journal. Research and Development Laboratories. Portland Cement Association — J Res Dev Lab Portland Cem Assoc
Journal. Research Association of Powder Technology (Japan) — J Res Assoc Powder Technol (Jpn)
Journal. Research Institute for Catalysis. Hokkaido University — J Res Inst Catal Hokkaido Univ
Journal. Research Institute for Catalysis. Hokkaido University — J Res Inst Catalysis Hokkaido Univ
Journal. Research Institute for Catalysis. Hokkaido University — JRINA
Journal. Research Institute of Medical Science of Korea [*Republic of Korea*] — J Res Inst Med Sci Korea

Journal. Research Institute of Science and Technology. Nihon University — J Res Inst Sci and Technol Nihon Univ
Journal. Research Institute of Science and Technology. Nihon University [*Japan*] — J Res Inst Sci Technol Nihon Univ
Journal. Research Society of Pakistan — J Res Soc Pak
Journal. Research Society of Pakistan — JRSP
Journal. Reticuloendothelial Society — J Retic Soc
Journal. Reticuloendothelial Society — J Reticuloendothel Soc
Journal. Reticuloendothelial Society — JRSOD
Journal. Rhode Island State Dental Society — J RI State Dent Soc
Journal. Rio Grande Valley Horticulture Society — J Rio Grande Val Hortic Soc
Journal. Rocky Mountain Medieval and Renaissance Association — JRMMRA
Journal. ROK (Republic of Korea) Naval Medical Corps — J ROK Nav Med Corps
Journal. Rossica Society of Russian Philately — J Rossica Soc
Journal. Royal Aeronautical Society [*England*] — J R Aeronaut Soc
Journal. Royal African Society — J R Afr Soc
Journal. Royal African Society — JAf S
Journal. Royal African Society — JRAfS
Journal. Royal Agricultural Society — J R Agric Soc
Journal. Royal Agricultural Society of England — J R Agric Soc Engl
Journal. Royal Agricultural Society of England — J Roy Agr S
Journal. Royal Agricultural Society of England — J Roy Agric Soc England
Journal. Royal Agricultural Society of England — Jl R Agric Soc
Journal. Royal Agricultural Society of England — JRAGAY
Journal. Royal Agricultural Society of England — Royal Agric Soc England J
Journal. Royal Anthropological Institute — J Roy Anthropol Inst
Journal. Royal Anthropological Institute of Great Britain and Ireland — J Anthr Inst
Journal. Royal Anthropological Institute of Great Britain and Ireland — J R Anthropol Inst GB Irel
Journal. Royal Anthropological Institute of Great Britain and Ireland — J Roy Anthrop Inst Gt Br Ire
Journal. Royal Anthropological Institute of Great Britain and Ireland — J Roy Anthropol Inst Gr Brit
Journal. Royal Anthropological Institute of Great Britain and Ireland — JAI
Journal. Royal Anthropological Institute of Great Britain and Ireland — JAIB
Journal. Royal Anthropological Institute of Great Britain and Ireland — JAnthrI
Journal. Royal Anthropological Institute of Great Britain and Ireland — Jl R Anthrop Inst
Journal. Royal Anthropological Institute of Great Britain and Ireland — Journ of the Ant Inst
Journal. Royal Anthropological Institute of Great Britain and Ireland — JRAI
Journal. Royal Archaeological Institute — JAI
Journal. Royal Army Medical Corps — J R Army Med Corps
Journal. Royal Army Medical Corps — JRAMA
Journal. Royal Army Veterinary Corps — J R Army Vet Corps
Journal. Royal Artillery — Journ Royal Artill
Journal. Royal Asiatic Society — J Roy Asiat Soc
Journal. Royal Asiatic Society — J Roy Asiatic Soc
Journal. Royal Asiatic Society. Bombay Branch — JRASBB
Journal. Royal Asiatic Society. Ceylon Branch — JRASCB
Journal. Royal Asiatic Society. Hong Kong Branch — JRASHKB
Journal. Royal Asiatic Society. Malayan Branch — JRASM
Journal. Royal Asiatic Society. Malayan Branch — JRASMB
Journal. Royal Asiatic Society of Bengal — JASBe
Journal. Royal Asiatic Society of Bengal — JRASBengal
Journal. Royal Asiatic Society of Bengal. London Edition — JASBeL
Journal. Royal Asiatic Society of Bengal. Part 1. History, Antiquities — JASBeH
Journal. Royal Asiatic Society of Bengal. Part 2. Natural History — JASBeN
Journal. Royal Asiatic Society of Bengal. Part 3. Anthropology — JASBeA
Journal. Royal Asiatic Society of Bengal. Pirated Edition — JASBeP
Journal. Royal Asiatic Society of Bengal. Science — J R Asiat Soc Bengal Sci
Journal. Royal Asiatic Society of Great Britain and Ireland — J Roy Asia
Journal. Royal Asiatic Society of Great Britain and Ireland — Journ Asiat Soc
Journal. Royal Asiatic Society of Great Britain and Ireland — JR Asiat Soc GB Irel
Journal. Royal Asiatic Society of Great Britain and Ireland — JRAS
Journal. Royal Astronomical Society of Canada — J R Astron Soc Can
Journal. Royal Astronomical Society of Canada — J Roy Astro
Journal. Royal Astronomical Society of Canada — J Roy Astron Soc Can
Journal. Royal Astronomical Society of Canada — JRASA
Journal. Royal Australian Historical Society — J R Aust Hist Soc
Journal. Royal Australian Historical Society — J Roy Aust
Journal. Royal Australian Historical Society — J Royal Aust Hist Soc
Journal. Royal Australian Historical Society — JRAHS
Journal. Royal Central Asian Society — J Roy Centr Asian Soc
Journal. Royal Central Asian Society — JCAS
Journal. Royal Central Asian Society — JRCAS
Journal. Royal Central Asian Society — RCAS
Journal. Royal College of General Practitioners — J R Coll Gen Pract
Journal. Royal College of General Practitioners — J Roy Coll Gen Pract
Journal. Royal College of General Practitioners. Occasional Paper — J R Coll Gen Pract Occas Pap
Journal. Royal College of Physicians of London — J R Coll Physicians
Journal. Royal College of Physicians of London — J R Coll Physicians Lond
Journal. Royal College of Physicians of London — J Roy Col P
Journal. Royal College of Physicians of London — J Roy Coll Phys London
Journal. Royal College of Surgeons in Ireland — J R Coll Surg Irel
Journal. Royal College of Surgeons in Ireland — RSIJA
Journal. Royal College of Surgeons of Edinburg — J R Coll Surg Edinburg
Journal. Royal College of Surgeons of Edinburgh — J R Coll Surg Edinb
Journal. Royal College of Surgeons of Edinburgh — JRCSA
Journal. Royal Commonwealth Society — J Roy Commonw Soc
Journal. Royal Egyptian Medical Association — J R Egypt Med Assoc
Journal. Royal Electrical and Mechanical Engineers [*England*] — J R Electr Mech Eng
Journal. Royal Electrical and Mechanical Engineers — JR Electr and Mech Eng
Journal. Royal Geographical Society — Journ Roy Geog Soc
Journal. Royal Geographical Society — JRGS
Journal. Royal Horticultural Society — J Roy Hort Soc
Journal. Royal Horticulture Society — J R Hortic Soc
Journal. Royal Horticulture Society — Jl R Hort Soc
Journal. Royal Institute of British Architects — J R Inst Br Archit
Journal. Royal Institute of British Architects — J Roy Inst Br Archit
Journal. Royal Institute of British Architects — JRBA-A
Journal. Royal Institute of British Architects — JRIBA
Journal. Royal Institute of British Architects — RIBA Journal
Journal. Royal Institute of Chemistry — J R Inst Chem
Journal. Royal Institute of International Affairs — JRIIA
Journal. Royal Institute of Public Health [*England*] — J R Inst Public Health
Journal. Royal Institute of Public Health and Hygiene — J R Inst Public Health Hyg
Journal. Royal Institution of Cornwall — J Roy Inst Cornwall
Journal. Royal Institution of Cornwall. New Series — J Roy Inst Cornwall N Ser
Journal. Royal Meteorological Society — JRMS
Journal. Royal Microscopical Society — J Microsc Soc
Journal. Royal Microscopical Society — J R Microsc Soc
Journal. Royal Microscopical Society — J Roy Micr Soc
Journal. Royal Microscopical Society — J Roy Microscop Soc
Journal. Royal Microscopical Society — Jl R Microsc Soc
Journal. Royal Military College of Australia — J Royal Military College Aust
Journal. Royal Naval Medical Service — J R Nav Med Serv
Journal. Royal Naval Medical Service — JRNMA
Journal. Royal Netherlands Chemical Society — J R Neth Chem Soc
Journal. Royal New Zealand Institute of Horticulture — J Roy New Zealand Inst Hort
Journal. Royal Photographic Society — Journal of RPS
Journal. Royal Sanitary Institute [*England*] — J R Sanit Inst
Journal. Royal School of Mines — Jr Sch Mines
Journal. Royal Signals Institution — JR Signals Inst
Journal. Royal Society for the Encouragement of Arts, Manufactures, and Commerce — J R Soc Encour Arts Manuf Commer
Journal. Royal Society of Antiquaries of Ireland — J Ant Ire
Journal. Royal Society of Antiquaries of Ireland — J Roy Soc Antiq Ir
Journal. Royal Society of Antiquaries of Ireland — Journal Soc Antiq
Journal. Royal Society of Antiquaries of Ireland — Journal Soc Antiqu Ireland
Journal. Royal Society of Antiquaries of Ireland — JRSAI
Journal. Royal Society of Antiquaries of Ireland — JRSAntI
Journal. Royal Society of Antiquaries of Ireland — JSAI
Journal. Royal Society of Antiquaries of Ireland. Supplement — JSAIS
Journal. Royal Society of Arts [*England*] — J R Soc Arts
Journal. Royal Society of Arts — J Roy Soc Arts
Journal. Royal Society of Arts — Jl R Soc Arts
Journal. Royal Society of Arts — JRSA
Journal. Royal Society of Arts — JRSAA
Journal. Royal Society of Health — J R Soc Health
Journal. Royal Society of Health — J R Soc Hlth
Journal. Royal Society of Health — JRSHDS
Journal. Royal Society of Medicine — J R Soc Med
Journal. Royal Society of Medicine — J Roy Soc Med
Journal. Royal Society of New Zealand — J R Soc NZ
Journal. Royal Society of New Zealand — J Royal Soc New Zeal
Journal. Royal Society of New Zealand — J RSNZ
Journal. Royal Society of New Zealand — Jl R Soc NZ
Journal. Royal Society of Western Australia — J R Soc West Aust
Journal. Royal Society of Western Australia — J Royal Soc WA
Journal. Royal Society of Western Australia — JRSUA
Journal. Royal Statistical Society [*England*] — J R Stat Soc
Journal. Royal Statistical Society — J Roy Statis
Journal. Royal Statistical Society — J Roy Statist Soc
Journal. Royal Statistical Society — JRSS
Journal. Royal Statistical Society. A Journal of Verbal Learning and Verbal Behavior — J Roy Stat Soc A J Verb Learn Verb Beh
Journal. Royal Statistical Society. Series A. General — J Roy Sta A
Journal. Royal Statistical Society. Series A. General — J Roy Statist Soc Ser A
Journal. Royal Statistical Society. Series A. General — JSTAA
Journal. Royal Statistical Society. Series A. General — Royal Statis Soc J Ser A Gen
Journal. Royal Statistical Society. Series B. Methodological — J Roy Sta B
Journal. Royal Statistical Society. Series B. Methodological — J Roy Statist Soc Ser B
Journal. Royal Statistical Society. Series B. Methodological — JSTBA
Journal. Royal Statistical Society. Series C. Applied Statistics — J Roy Sta C
Journal. Royal Statistical Society. Series C. Applied Statistics — J Roy Statist Soc Ser C
Journal. Royal Statistical Society. Series C. Applied Statistics — J Roy Statist Soc Ser C Appl Statist
Journal. Royal Statistical Society. Series C. Applied Statistics — RSSJA
Journal. Royal Swedish Academy of Agriculture — J R Swed Acad Agric
Journal. Royal Swedish Academy of Agriculture and Forestry — J R Swed Acad Agric For
Journal. Royal Swedish Academy of Agriculture and Forestry. Supplement — J R Swed Acad Agric For Suppl
Journal. Royal Swedish Academy of Forestry and Agriculture — J R Swed Acad For Agric
Journal. Royal Television Society — JR Telev Soc
Journal. Royal United Service Institution [*Later, Journal. Royal United Services Institute for Defence Studies*] — J R United Serv Inst

Journal. Royal United Service Institution — JRUSI
Journal. Royal United Service Institutions — J Roy United Serv Instn
Journal. Royal United Services Institute for Defence Studies — RUSI
Journal. Royal United Services Institution — J Roy Un Serv Instn
Journal RPF — J RPF
Journal. Rubber Industry (Moscow) — J Rubber Ind Moscow
Journal. Rubber Research Institute of Malaya — J Rubb Res Inst Malaya
Journal. Rubber Research Institute of Malaya — J Rubber Res Inst Malaya
Journal. Rubber Research Institute of Malaysia — J RRI Malaysia
Journal. Rubber Research Institute of Malaysia — J Rubber Res Inst Malays
Journal. Rubber Research Institute of Malaysia — JRRIAN
Journal. Rubber Research Institute of Sri Lanka — J RRI Sri Lanka
Journal. Rubber Research Institute of Sri Lanka — J Rubber Res Inst Sri Lanka
Journal. Russian Physical-Chemical Society — J Russ Phys Chem Soc
Journal. Rutgers University Library — J Rutgers Univ Libr
Journal. Rutgers University Library — JRUL
Journal. Sadul Rajasthani Research Institute — Journal Sadul Rajasthani Research Inst
Journal. Sagami Women's University — J Sagami Womens Univ
Journal. Saint Barnabas Medical Center — J St Barnabas Med Cent
Journal. Saitama Medical Society — J Saitama Med Soc
Journal. Saitama University. Faculty of Education. Mathematics and Natural Science — J Saitama Univ Fac Ed Math Natur Sci
Journal. Saitama University. Natural Science [*Japan*] — J Saitama Univ Nat Sci
Journal. San Antonio District Dental Society — J San Antonio Dent Soc
Journal. Sanitary Engineering Division. American Society of Civil Engineers — J Sanit Eng Div Am Soc Civ Eng
Journal. Sanitary Engineering Division. Proceedings. American Society of Civil Engineers — J Sanit Eng Div Proc Am Soc Civ Eng
Journal. San'yo Association for Advancement of Science and Technology [*Japan*] — J San'yo Assoc Adv Sci Technol
Journal. Sapporo Municipal General Hospital [*Japan*] — J Sapporo Munic Gen Hosp
Journal. Sapporo Society of Agriculture and Forestry — J Sapporo Soc Agric For
Journal. Sapporo Society of Agriculture and Forestry/Sapporo Noringakkai-Ho — J Sapporo Soc Agric
Journal. School Library Association of Queensland — J Sch Lib Ass Q
Journal. School Library Association of Queensland — J Sch Lib Assoc Qld
Journal. School Library Association of Queensland — J Sch Libr Assoc Qld
Journal. School of Languages — JSL
Journal. School of Pharmacy. University of Tehran — J Sch Pharm Univ Tehran
Journal. Science Association. Maharajah's College — J Sci Assoc Maharajah's Coll
Journal. Science Faculty of Chiangmai University — J Sci Fac Chiangmai Univ
Journal. Science Society of Thailand — J Sci Soc Thailand
Journal. Scientific Agricultural Society of Finland — J Sci Agric Soc Finl
Journal. Scientific Agricultural Society of Finland — J Scient Agric Soc Finl
Journal. Scientific Laboratories. Denison University — J Sci Lab D
Journal. Scientific Laboratories. Denison University — J Sci Lab Denison Univ
Journal. Scientific Research Council of Jamaica — J Sci Res Counc Jam
Journal. Scientific Research Institute — J Sci Res Inst
Journal. Scientific Research Institute (Tokyo) — J Sci Res Inst (Tokyo)
Journal. Scientific Research Institutes. Ministry of Agriculture (Bulgaria) — J Sci Res Inst Ministr Agric Bulg
Journal Scientifique de la Meteorologie — J Sci Meteorol
Journal. Scottish Association of Geography Teachers — J Scott Assoc Geogr Teach
Journal. Scunthorpe Museum Society — J Scunthorpe Mus Soc
Journal. Seattle-King County Dental Society — J Seattle King Cty Dent Soc
Journal. Seismological Society of Japan — J Seismol Soc Jpn
Journal. Seoul Woman's College — J Seoul Woman's Coll
Journal. Serbian Chemical Society — J Serb Chem Soc
Journal. Severance Union Medical College — J Severance Union Med Coll
Journal. Seychelles Society — J Seychelles Soc
Journal. Shandong College of Oceanology — J Shandong Coll Oceanol
Journal. Shandong University. Natural Science Edition — J Shandong Univ Nat Sci Ed
Journal. Shanghai College of Textile Technology — J Shanghai Coll Text Technol
Journal. Shanghai First and Second Medical College — J Shanghai First Second Med Coll
Journal. Shanghai Institute of Chemical Technology — J Shanghai Inst Chem Technol
Journal. Shanghai Institute of Railway Technology — J Shanghai Inst Railway Tech
Journal. Shanghai Science Institute — J Shanghai Sci Inst
Journal. Shanghai Science Institute. Section 1. Experimental Biology and Medicine — J Shanghai Sci Inst Sect 1
Journal. Shanghai Science Institute. Section 1. Mathematics, Astronomy, Physics, Geophysics, Chemistry, and Allied Sciences — J Shanghai Sci Inst Sect 1
Journal. Shanghai Science Institute. Section 2. Geology, Palaeontology, Mineralogy, and Petrology — J Shanghai Sci Inst Sect 2
Journal. Shanghai Science Institute. Section 3. Systematic and Morphological Biology — J Shanghai Sci Inst Sect 3
Journal. Shanghai Science Institute. Section 4. Experimental Biology and Medicine — J Shanghai Sci Inst Sect 4
Journal. Shanghai Science Institute. Section 5. General — J Shanghai Sci Inst Sect 5
Journal. Shanxi University. Natural Science Edition — J Shanxi Univ Nat Sci Ed
Journal. Sheffield University Metallurgical Society — J Sheffield Univ Met Soc
Journal. Shenyang College of Pharmacy — J Shenyang Coll Pharm
Journal. Shiga Prefectural Junior College. Series A — J Shiga Prefect Jr Coll Ser A
Journal. Shikoku Public Health Society — J Shikoku Public Health Soc
Journal. Shimane Medical Association [*Japan*] — J Shimane Med Assoc
Journal. Shimonoseki College of Fisheries — J Shimonoseki Coll Fish
Journal. Shimonoseki University of Fisheries — J Shimonoseki Univ Fish
Journal. Shivaji University — J Shivaji Univ
Journal. Shivaji University (Science) — J Shivaji Univ Sci
Journal. Showa Medical Association [*Japan*] — J Showa Med Assoc
Journal. Showa University Dental Society — J Showa Univ Dent Soc
Journal. Siam Society — J Siam Soc
Journal. Siam Society [*Bangkok*] — JSS
Journal. Siam Society (Bangkok) — JSSB
Journal. Siam Society. Natural History Supplement — J Siam Soc Nat Hist Suppl
Journal. Siamese Veterinary Association — J Siamese Vet Assoc
Journal. Sichuan University. Natural Science Edition — J Sichuan Univ Nat Sci Ed
Journal. Sigenkagaku Kenkyusyo/Shigen Kagaku Kenkyusho Obun Hokoku — J Sigenkagaku Kenkyusyo
Journal. Singapore National Academy of Science — J Singapore Nat Acad Sci
Journal. Singapore National Academy of Science — J Singapore Natl Acad Sci
Journal. Singapore Paediatric Society — J Singapore Paediatr Soc
Journal. SMPTE [*Society of Motion Picture and Television Engineers*] [*A publication*] — J SMPTE
Journal. Societas Internationalis Odonatologica — J Soc Int Odonatologica
Journal. Societe Canadienne des Anesthesistes — J Soc Can Anesth
Journal. Societe Canadienne des Sciences Judiciaires — J Soc Can Sci Judiciaires
Journal. Societe des Africanistes — J Soc Afr
Journal. Societe des Africanistes — J Soc African
Journal. Societe des Africanistes — J Soc Africanistes
Journal. Societe des Africanistes — JSA
Journal. Societe des Africanistes — JSAf
Journal. Societe des Africanistes — JSAfr
Journal. Societe des Americanistes — J Soc Am
Journal. Societe des Americanistes — J Soc Amer
Journal. Societe des Americanistes — JSA
Journal. Societe des Americanistes — SA/J
Journal. Societe des Americanistes de Paris — J Soc Am Paris
Journal. Societe des Americanistes de Paris — JSAm
Journal. Societe des Americanistes de Paris — JSAmP
Journal. Societe des Americanistes de Paris — JSAP
Journal. Societe des Americanistes (Paris) — Jour Soc Am Paris
Journal. Societe des Ingenieurs de l'Automobile — J Soc Ing Automob
Journal. Societe des Oceanistes — J Soc Ocean
Journal. Societe des Oceanistes — J Soc Oceanistes
Journal. Societe des Oceanistes — JSO
Journal. Societe des Oceanistes — JSOc
Journal. Societe Finno-Ougrienne — Journal Soc Finno-Ougr
Journal. Societe Finno-Ougrienne — JSFOu
Journal. Societe Internationale des Chimistes des Industries du Cuir — J Soc Int Chim Ind Cuir
Journal. Societe Physico-Chimique Russe — J Soc Phys Chim Russe
Journal. Societe Regionale d'Horticulture du Nord de la France — J Soc Regionale Hort N France
Journal. Societe Statistique de Paris — J Soc Statist Paris
Journal. Society for Army Historical Research — J Soc Army Hist Res
Journal. Society for Health Systems — J Soc Health Syst
Journal. Society for International Numismatics — JSIN
Journal. Society for Mass Media and Resource Technology — JSMMART
Journal. Society for Non-Destructive Testing — J Soc Non-Destr Test
Journal. Society for Psychical Research — J Soc Psych Res
Journal. Society for Psychical Research — JSPR
Journal. Society for Radiological Protection — J Soc Radiol Prot
Journal. Society for Research in Asiatic Music — J Res Asiatic
Journal. Society for the Bibliography of Natural History — J Soc Bibliogr Nat Hist
Journal. Society for the Bibliography of Natural History — J Soc Bibliogr Natur Hist
Journal. Society for the Study of State Governments [*Varanasi*] — JSSSG
Journal. Society for Underwater Technology — J Soc Underwater Technol
Journal. Society for Water Treatment and Examination — J Soc Water Treat Exam
Journal. Society of Air-Conditioning and Refrigerating Engineers of Korea [*Republic of Korea*] — J Soc Air-Cond Refrig Eng Korea
Journal. Society of Archer-Antiquaries — J Soc Archer-Antiq
Journal. Society of Architectural Historians — J S Archit
Journal. Society of Architectural Historians — J Soc Arch H
Journal. Society of Architectural Historians — J Soc Arch Hist
Journal. Society of Architectural Historians — J Soc Architect Hist
Journal. Society of Architectural Historians — JASAH
Journal. Society of Architectural Historians — Jour Society Archit Historians
Journal. Society of Architectural Historians — JSAH
Journal. Society of Archivists — J Soc Arch
Journal. Society of Archivists — JSA
Journal. Society of Arts — J Soc Arts
Journal. Society of Automotive Engineers — J Soc Automot Eng
Journal. Society of Automotive Engineers of Japan — J Soc Automot Eng Jpn
Journal. Society of Automotive Engineers of Japan, Incorporated — J Soc Automot Eng Jpn Inc
Journal. Society of Biblical Literature — JSBL
Journal. Society of Brewing (Japan) — J Soc Brew (Japan)
Journal. Society of Brewing (Tokyo) — J Soc Brew (Tokyo)
Journal. Society of Chemical Industry (Japan) — J Soc Chem Ind (Jpn)
Journal. Society of Chemical Industry (Japan) — JSCJA
Journal. Society of Chemical Industry (London) — J Soc Chem Ind (Lond)
Journal. Society of Chemical Industry (London) — J Soc Chem Ind (London)

Journal. Society of Chemical Industry (London). Abstracts — J Soc Chem Ind (London) Abstr
Journal. Society of Chemical Industry (London). Review Section — J Soc Chem Ind (London) Rev Sect
Journal. Society of Chemical Industry (London). Transactions and Communications — J Soc Chem Ind (London) Trans Commun
Journal. Society of Chemical Industry of Victoria — J Soc Chem Ind Vic
Journal. Society of Comparative Legislation — J Soc Comp Leg
Journal. Society of Comparative Legislation — J Soc Comp Legis
Journal. Society of Comparative Legislation — JSCL
Journal. Society of Cosmetic Chemists — J S Cosm Ch
Journal. Society of Cosmetic Chemists — J Soc Cosmet Chem
Journal. Society of Dairy Technology — J Soc Dairy Technol
Journal. Society of Dairy Technology — Soc Dairy Technol J
Journal. Society of Domestic and Sanitary Engineering — J Soc Domest Sanit Eng
Journal. Society of Dyers and Colourists — J S Dye Col
Journal. Society of Dyers and Colourists — J Soc Dy Colour
Journal. Society of Dyers and Colourists — J Soc Dyers
Journal. Society of Dyers and Colourists — J Soc Dyers Colour
Journal. Society of Dyers and Colourists — J Soc Dyers Colourists
Journal. Society of Dyers and Colourists — JSDC
Journal. Society of Engineers for Mineral Springs [*Japan*] — J Soc Eng Miner Springs
Journal. Society of Engineers for Mineral Springs. Japan — J Soc Eng Miner Springs Jpn
Journal. Society of Engineers (London) — J Soc Eng (Lond)
Journal. Society of Environmental Engineers — J Soc Env Engrs
Journal. Society of Environmental Engineers — J Soc Environ Eng
Journal. Society of Environmental Engineers — J Soc Environ Engrs
Journal. Society of Experimental Agriculturists — J Soc Exp Agric
Journal. Society of Fiber Science and Technology. Japan — J Soc Fiber Sci Technol Jpn
Journal. Society of Forestry/Ringakukai Zasshi — J Soc Forest
Journal. Society of Glass Technology — J Soc Glass Technol
Journal. Society of Heating, Air Conditioning, and Sanitary Engineers of Japan — J SHASE
Journal. Society of High Polymers of Japan — J Soc High Polym Jpn
Journal. Society of High Pressure Gas Industry — J Soc High Pressure Gas Ind
Journal. Society of Industrial and Applied Mathematics [*United States*] — J Soc Ind Appl Math
Journal. Society of Industrial and Applied Mathematics — JSIAM
Journal. Society of Instrument and Control Engineers — J Soc Instrum and Control
Journal. Society of Instrument and Control Engineers — J Soc Instrum Control Eng
Journal. Society of Leather Technologists and Chemists — J Soc Leath Technol Chem
Journal. Society of Leather Trades Chemists — J Soc Leath Trades Chem
Journal. Society of Materials Science (Japan) — J Soc Mater Sci (Jpn)
Journal. Society of Motion Picture and Television Engineers — J Soc Mot Pict Tel Eng
Journal. Society of Motion Picture and Television Engineers — J Soc Motion Pict and Telev Eng
Journal. Society of Motion Picture and Television Engineers — J Soc Motion Pict Telev Eng
Journal. Society of Motion Picture and Television Engineers — Jl Soc Mot Pict Telev Engin
Journal. Society of Motion Picture Engineers — J Soc Mot Pict Eng
Journal. Society of Motion Picture Engineers — J Soc Motion Pict Eng
Journal. Society of Motion Picture Engineers — JSMPE
Journal. Society of Naval Architects of Japan — J Soc Nav Arch Japan
Journal. Society of Naval Architects of Japan — J Soc Nav Archit Jpn
Journal. Society of Occupational Medicine — J Soc Occup Med
Journal. Society of Organic Synthetic Chemistry — J Soc Org Synth Chem
Journal. Society of Organic Synthetic Chemistry (Japan) — J Soc Org Syn Chem (Jpn)
Journal. Society of Oriental Research — JSOR
Journal. Society of Osteopaths (London) — J Soc Osteopaths (Lond)
Journal. Society of Petroleum Engineers — J Soc Pet Eng
Journal. Society of Photographic Science and Technology of Japan — J Soc Photogr Sci and Technol Jpn
Journal. Society of Photographic Science and Technology of Japan — Jl Soc Photogr Sci
Journal. Society of Photographic Science and Technology of Japan — Jl Soc Photogr Sci Technol Japan
Journal. Society of Photographic Scientists and Engineers — JSPSE
Journal. Society of Photo-Optical Instrumentation Engineers — J Soc Photo Opt Instrum Eng
Journal. Society of Powder Technology (Japan) — J Soc Powder Technol Jpn
Journal. Society of Public Teachers of Law — J Soc Pub T L
Journal. Society of Public Teachers of Law — J Socy Pub Tchrs L
Journal. Society of Public Teachers of Law — JSPTL
Journal. Society of Public Teachers of Law. New Series — J Soc Pub Teach Law N S
Journal. Society of Research Administrators — JRA
Journal. Society of Research Administrators — Soc Research Administrators J
Journal. Society of Research Administrators — SRA
Journal. Society of Resource Geology — J Soc Resour Geol
Journal. Society of Rheology. Japan — J Soc Rheol Jpn
Journal. Society of Rubber Industry (Japan) — J Soc Rubber Ind (Jpn)
Journal. Society of Scientific Photography of Japan — J Soc Sci Photogr Jpn
Journal. Society of Tropical Agriculture/Nettai Nogaku Kwaishi — J Soc Trop Agric
Journal. Society of Tropical Agriculture. Taihoku Imperial Univeristy — J Soc Trop Agric Taihoku Imp Univ
Journal. Soil Conservation Service of New South Wales — J Soil Conserv NSW
Journal. Soil Conservation Service of New South Wales — J Soil Conserv Serv NSW
Journal. Soil Conservation Service of New South Wales — J Soil Conserv Service NSW
Journal. Soil Conservation Service of New South Wales — J Soil Conservation Serv NSW
Journal. Soil Mechanics and Foundations Division. American Society of Civil Engineers — J Soil Mech Found Div Am Soc Civ Eng
Journal. Soil Science Society of America — J Soil Sci Soc Am
Journal. Soil Science Society of the Philippines — J Soil Sci Soc Philipp
Journal. Solar Energy Society of Korea [*Republic of Korea*] — J Sol Energy Soc Korea
Journal. Somerset Mines Research Group — J Somerset Mines Res Group
Journal. Soonchunhyang College — J Soonchunhyang Coll
Journal. South African Association of Analytical Chemists — J S Afr Assoc Anal Chem
Journal. South African Biological Society — J S Afr Biol Soc
Journal. South African Chemical Institute — J S Afr Chem Inst
Journal. South African Chemical Institute — J S African Chem Inst
Journal. South African Chemical Institute — J SA Chem I
Journal. South African Chemical Institute — J South Afr Chem Inst
Journal. South African Chemical Institute — JSACA
Journal. South African Forestry Association — J S Afr For Assoc
Journal. South African Forestry Association — J SA For Assoc
Journal. South African Forestry Association — JSAFA4
Journal. South African Institute of Mining and Metallurgy — J S Afr Inst Min Metall
Journal. South African Institute of Mining and Metallurgy — J S Afr Inst Mining Met
Journal. South African Institute of Mining and Metallurgy — J SA I Min
Journal. South African Institute of Mining and Metallurgy — JSAMA
Journal. South African Institution of Engineers — J S Afr Inst Eng
Journal. South African Speech and Hearing Association — J S Afr Speech Hear Assoc
Journal. South African Speech and Hearing Association — JSHABP
Journal. South African Veterinary Association — J S Afr Vet Assoc
Journal. South African Veterinary Association — J South Afr Vet Assoc
Journal. South African Veterinary Association — JAVTA
Journal. South African Veterinary Medical Association [*Later, South African Veterinary Association. Journal*] — J S Afr Vet Med Assoc
Journal. South African Veterinary Medical Association [*Later, South African Veterinary Association. Journal*] — J South Afr Vet Med Ass
Journal. South African Veterinary Medical Association [*Later, South African Veterinary Association. Journal*] — J Sth Afr Vet Med Ass
Journal. South Carolina Medical Association — J SC Med Assoc
Journal. South Carolina Medical Association — JSCMA
Journal. South China Institute of Technology — J South China Inst Technol
Journal. South China Institute of Technology. Natural Sciences — J South China Inst Technol Nat Sci
Journal. South China University of Technology. Natural Science — J South China Univ Technol Nat Sci
Journal. South West African Scientific Society — J South West Afr Sci Soc
Journal. South West African Scientific Society — J SWA Sci Soc
Journal. Southeast University (China) — J Southeast Univ (China)
Journal. South-Eastern Agricultural College (Wye) [*Kent*] — Jl S-East Agric Coll (Wye)
Journal. Southeastern Agricultural College (Wye, England) — J Southeast Agric Coll (Wye England)
Journal. Southeastern Section. American Water Works Association — J Southeast Sect Am Water Works Assoc
Journal. Southern African Wildlife Management Association — J South Afr Wildl Manage Assoc
Journal. Southern California Dental Assistants Association — J South Calif Dent Assistants Assoc
Journal. Southern California Dental Association — J South Calif Dent Assoc
Journal. Southern California Dental Association — J South California Dent A
Journal. Southern California Meter Association — J South Calif Meter Assoc
Journal. Southern California State Dental Association — J South Calif State Dent Assoc
Journal. Southern Orthopaedic Association — J South Orthop Assoc
Journal. Southwest Scotland Grassland Society — J Southw Scotland Grassland Soc
Journal. Southwest-China Teachers College. Series B. Natural Science — J Southwest China Teach Coll Ser B
Journal. Spectroscopical Society of Japan — J Spectros Soc Jpn
Journal. Spray Coating Society of Japan — J Spray Coat Soc Jpn
Journal. Starch Sweetener Technological Research Society of Japan — J Starch Sweet Technol Res Soc Japan
Journal. Statistical Society — J Statis Soc
Journal. Steward Anthropological Society — J Steward Anthro Soc
Journal. Steward Anthropological Society — J Steward Anthropol Soc
Journal. Stomatological Society (Japan) — J Stomatol Soc (Jpn)
Journal. Straits Branch. Royal Asiatic Society — J Straits Branch Roy Asiat Soc
Journal. Straits Branch. Royal Asiatic Society — JSBAS
Journal. Straits Branch. Royal Asiatic Society — JSBRAS
Journal. Structural Division. Proceedings of the American Society of Civil Engineers — J Struct Di
Journal. Structural Division. Proceedings of the American Society of Civil Engineers — J Struct Div Amer Soc Civil Eng Proc
Journal. Structural Division. Proceedings of the American Society of Civil Engineers — J Struct Div Proc ASCE
Journal. Student American Medical Association — J Stud Amer Med Ass

Journal. Suffolk Academy of Law — J Suffolk Acad L
Journal. Sugar Industry — J Sugar Ind
Journal Suisse d'Apiculture — J Suisse Apic
Journal Suisse de Chimie et Pharmacie — J Suisse Chim Pharm
Journal Suisse de Medecine — J Suisse Med
Journal Suisse de Pharmacie — J Sui Pharm
Journal Suisse de Photographie — J Suisse Photogr
Journal Suisse d'Horlogerie — J Suisse Horlog
Journal Suisse d'Horlogerie et de Bijouterie — J Suisse Horlog Bijout
Journal. Sulfuric Acid Association of Japan — J Sulfuric Acid Assoc Jpn
Journal. Surface Finishing Society of Japan — J Surf Finish Soc Jpn
Journal. Surveying and Mapping Division. Proceedings of the American Society of Civil Engineers — J Surv & Mapp Div Proc ASCE
Journal. Surveying and Mapping Division. Proceedings of the American Society of Civil Engineers — J Surv Mapp
Journal. Surveying and Mapping Division. Proceedings of the American Society of Civil Engineers — J Surv Mapping Div Amer Soc Civil Eng Proc
Journal. SWA (South West Africa) Scientific Society — J SWA (South West Afr) Sci Soc
Journal. SWA Wissenschaftliche Gesellschaft — J SWA Wiss Ges
Journal. Tachikawa College of Tokyo — J Tachikawa Coll Tokyo
Journal. Taiwan Museum — J Taiwan Mus
Journal. Taiwan Pharmaceutical Association — J Taiwan Pharm Assoc
Journal. Taiyuan Institute of Technology — J Taiyuan Inst Technol
Journal. Taiyuan University of Technology — J Taiyuan Univ Technol
Journal. Takeda Research Laboratories — J Takeda Res Lab
Journal. Takeda Research Laboratories [*Japan*] — J Takeda Res Labs
Journal. Technical Association of Pulp and Paper Industry of Korea — J Tech Assoc Pulp Pap Ind Korea
Journal. Technical Association of the Fur Industry — J Tech Assoc Fur Ind
Journal. Technical Councils of ASCE. Proceedings of the American Society of Civil Engineers — J Tech Councils ASCE Proc ASCE
Journal. Technical Laboratory (Tokyo) — J Tech Lab (Tokyo)
Journal. Technological Society of Starch — J Technol Soc Starch
Journal. Tennessee Academy of Science — J Tenn Acad Sci
Journal. Tennessee Academy of Science — J Tennessee Acad Sci
Journal. Tennessee Academy of Science — JTASA
Journal. Tennessee Dental Association — J Tenn Dent Assoc
Journal. Tennessee Dental Association — JTDAA
Journal. Tennessee Medical Association — J Tenn Med Ass
Journal. Tennessee Medical Association — J Tenn Med Assoc
Journal. Tennessee Medical Association — J Tennesee Med Assoc
Journal. Tennessee Medical Association — JTMMA
Journal. Tennessee State Dental Association — J Tenn State Dent Assoc
Journal. Texas Dental Hygienists Association — J Texas Dent Hyg Assoc
Journal. Textile Association — J Text Assoc
Journal. Textile Institute — J Text Inst
Journal. Textile Institute — J Textile Inst
Journal. Textile Institute. Abstracts — J Text Inst Abstr
Journal. Textile Institute. Proceedings — J Text Inst Proc
Journal. Textile Institute. Proceedings and Abstracts — J Text Inst Proc Abstr
Journal. Textile Institute. Transactions — J Text Inst Trans
Journal. Textile Machinery Society of Japan — J Text Mach Soc Jap
Journal. Textile Machinery Society of Japan (Japanese Edition) — J Text Mach Soc Jpn Jpn Ed
Journal. Thai Veterinary Medical Association — J Thai Vet Med Assoc
Journal. Thailand Research Society — JTRS
Journal. Tianjin University — J Tianjin Univ
Journal. Timber Development Association of India — J Timber Dev Assoc India
Journal. Timber Dryers' and Preservers' Association of India — J Timber Dryers Preserv Assoc India
Journal. Tohoku Dental University — J Tohoku Dent Univ
Journal. Tohoku Mining Society [*Japan*] — J Tohoku Min Soc
Journal. Tokyo Agricultural College/Tokyo Nogyo Daigaku Kiyo — J Tokyo Agric Coll
Journal. Tokyo Chemical Society — J Tokyo Chem Soc
Journal. Tokyo College of Fisheries — J Tokyo Coll Fish
Journal. Tokyo Dental College Society — J Tokyo Dent Coll Soc
Journal. Tokyo Medical Association — J Tokyo Med Assoc
Journal. Tokyo Medical College — J Tokyo Med Coll
Journal. Tokyo Society of Veterinary Science and Animal Science — J Tokyo Soc Vet Sci Anim Sci
Journal. Tokyo University of Fisheries — J Tokyo Univ Fish
Journal. Tokyo University of Fisheries — JTUFA
Journal. Tokyo University of Fisheries. Special Edition — J Tokyo Univ Fish Spec Ed
Journal. Tokyo Women's Medical College — J Tokyo Women's Med Coll
Journal. Tongji Medical University — J Tongji Med Univ
Journal. Tosoh Research — J Tosoh Res
Journal. Tottori Daigaku Nogaku-Buo — J Tottori Daigaku Nogaku
Journal. Toyo University. General Education. Natural Science — J Toyo Univ Gen Educ Nat Sci
Journal. Toyota National Technical College — J Toyota Natl Tech Coll
Journal. Transactions. Victoria Institute — JTV
Journal. Transportation Engineering Division. American Society of Civil Engineers. Proceedings — J Transp Eng Div Amer Soc Civil Eng Proc
Journal. Transvaal Institute of Mechanical Engineers — J Transvaal Inst Mech Eng
Journal. Travis County Medical Society [*Michigan*] — J Travis County Med Soc
Journal. Trevithick Society — J Trevithick Soc
Journal. Tsing Hua University — J Tsing Hua Univ
Journal. Tsinghua University and Peking University. Science and Technology — J Tsinghua Univ Peking Univ Sci Technol
Journal. Tsinghua University. Science and Technology — J Tsinghua Univ Sci Technol
Journal. Tsuda College — J Tsuda College
Journal. Tung-Chi University — J Tung-Chi Univ
Journal. Turkish Medical Society — J Turk Med Soc
Journal Typographique et Bibliographique — J Typogr Bibliogr
Journal. Union des Proprietaires d'Appareils a Acetylene — J Union Propr Appar Acetylene
Journal. United Provinces Historical Society — JUPHS
Journal. United Service Institution of India — J United Ser Inst Ind
Journal. United Service Institution of India — J United Serv Inst India
Journal. United Service Institution of India — JUSII
Journal. United States Artillery — J US Artillery
Journal. United States National Committee — JUSNC
Journal. Universalist Historical Society — JUHS
Journal. University Film Association — J U Film As
Journal. University Film Association [*Carbondale*] — J Univ F Assoc
Journal. University Geological Society (Nagpur) — J Univ Geol Soc (Nagpur)
Journal. University of Agriculture. Prague. Agronomy. Series B. Livestock Production — J Univ Agric Prague Agron Ser B
Journal. University of Bombay — J Univ Bombay
Journal. University of Bombay. New Series — J Univ Bombay NS
Journal. University of Durban-Westville — J Univ Durban-Westville
Journal. University of Gauhati — J Univ Gauhati
Journal. University of Gauhati — JUG
Journal. University of Gauhati. Arts — JUGA
Journal. University of Gauhati. Science — JUGS
Journal. University of Kuwait (Science) — J Univ Kuwait (Sci)
Journal. University of Occupational and Environmental Health — J Univ Occup Environ Health
Journal. University of Peshawar — J Univ Peshawar
Journal. University of Peshawar — JUP
Journal. University of Poona — J Univ Poona
Journal. University of Poona. Humanities Section — JUP
Journal. University of Poona. Science and Technology — J Univ Poona Sci Technol
Journal. University of Poona. Science and Technology — JUPOA
Journal. University of Saugar — J Univ Saugar
Journal. University of Saugar. Part 2. Section A. Physical Sciences — J Univ Saugar Part 2 Sect A
Journal. University of Sheffield. Geological Society — J Univ Sheffield Geol Soc
Journal. University of Sydney. Medical Society — J Univ S Med Soc
Journal. Urban Living and Health Association [*Japan*] — J Urban Living Health Assoc
Journal. Urban Planning and Development Division. American Society of Civil Engineers — J Urban Plann Dev Div Am Soc Civ Eng
Journal. Urban Planning and Development Division. Proceedings of the American Society of Civil Engineers — J Urban Pla
Journal. Urban Planning and Development Division. Proceedings of the American Society of Civil Engineers — J Urban Planning & Dev Div Proc ASCE
Journal. Urban Planning and Development Proceedings. American Society of Civil Engineers — JUPD-A
Journal. Urusvati Himalayan Research Institute of Roerich Museum — J Urusvati Himalayan Res Inst Roerich Mus
Journal. Uttar Pradesh Government Colleges Academic Society — J Uttar Pradesh Gov Colleges Acad Soc
Journal. Vacuum Society of Japan — J Vac Soc Jpn
Journal. Veterinary Association of Thailand — J Vet Assoc Thailand
Journal. Veterinary Faculty. University of Tehran — J Vet Fac Univ Tehran
Journal. Victoria University of Manchester — J Victoria Univ Manchester
Journal. Viola da Gamba Society of America — J Viola da Gamba Soc Amer
Journal. Violin Society of America — J Violin S
Journal. Violin Society of America — J Violin Soc Amer
Journal. Violin Society of America — JV
Journal. Visva-Bharati Study Circle — JVSC
Journal. Vitamin Society of Japan — J Vitam Soc Jpn
Journal. Wakayama Medical Society — J Wakayama Med Soc
Journal. Walters Art Gallery — J Walters Art Gal
Journal. Walters Art Gallery — JWAG
Journal. Walters Art Gallery — JWalt
Journal. Warburg and Courtauld Institute — J Warburg and Courtauld Inst
Journal. Warburg and Courtauld Institute — J Warburg C
Journal. Warburg and Courtauld Institute — J Warburg Courtauld Inst
Journal. Warburg and Courtauld Institute — JWarb
Journal. Warburg and Courtauld Institute — JWCI
Journal. Warburg and Courtauld Institute [*London*] — JWI
Journal. Warburg and Courtauld Institutes — Journ Warburg Inst
Journal. Washington Academy of Sciences — J Wash Acad Sci
Journal. Washington Academy of Sciences — J Washington Acad Sci
Journal. Washington Academy of Sciences — JWAS
Journal. Washington Academy of Sciences — JWASA
Journal. Water Pollution Control Federation — J Water P C
Journal. Water Pollution Control Federation — J Water Pollut Contr Fed
Journal. Water Pollution Control Federation — J Water Pollut Control Fed
Journal. Water Pollution Control Federation — JWPCF
Journal. Water Pollution Control Federation — JWPFA
Journal. Water Resources Planning and Management Division. Proceedings of the American Society of Civil Engineers — J Water Resour Plann Manage Div Am Soc Civ Eng
Journal. Water Resources Planning and Management Division. Proceedings of the American Society of Civil Engineers — J Water Resour Plann Manage Div ASCE
Journal. Water Resources Planning and Management Division. Proceedings of the American Society of Civil Engineers — J Water Resour Planning & Manage Div Proc ASCE
Journal. Water Works Association [*Japan*] — J Water Works Assoc

Journal. Waterways and Harbors Division. American Society of Civil Engineers — J Waterw Harbors Div Am Soc Civ Eng
Journal. Waterways, Harbors, and Coastal Engineering Division. American Society of Civil Engineers — J Waterway
Journal. Waterways, Port, Coastal, and Ocean Division. American Society of Civil Engineers — J Waterw Port Coastal Ocean Div ASCE
Journal. Waterways, Port, Coastal, and Ocean Division. American Society of Civil Engineers. Proceedings — J Waterway Port Coastal Ocean Div Amer Soc Civil Eng Proc
Journal. Waterways, Port, Coastal, and Ocean Division. Proceedings. American Society of Civil Engineers — J Waterway Port Coastal & Ocean Div Proc ASCE
Journal. Waterworks and Sewerage Association — J Waterworks Sewerage Assoc
Journal. Wednesday Society — J Wednesday Soc
Journal. Welding Society — J Weld Soc
Journal. Welsh Bibliographic Society — JWBS
Journal. Welsh Bibliographical Society — J Welsh Bibliog Soc
Journal. West African Institute for Oil Palm Research — J West Afr Inst Oil Palm Res
Journal. West African Science Association — J West Afr Sci Assoc
Journal. West African Science Association — JW Afr Sci Ass
Journal. West Australian Nurses — J West Aust Nurses
Journal. West China Border Research Society — J W China Border Res Soc
Journal. West China Border Research Society — JWCBRS
Journal. West China University of Medical Sciences — J West China Univ Med Sci
Journal. West of Scotland Iron and Steel Institute — J West Scot Iron Steel Inst
Journal. West Virginia Philosophical Society — J W Vir Phil Soc
Journal. Western Australian Nurses Association — J WA Nurses
Journal. Western Society of Engineers — J West Soc Eng
Journal. Western Society of Periodontology — J West Soc Periodont
Journal. Western Society of Periodontology — J West Soc Periodontol
Journal. William Morris Society — JWMS
Journal. Wisconsin Association for Health, Physical Education, and Recreation — WIHP
Journal. Wisconsin Dental Association — J Wis Dent Assoc
Journal. Wisconsin Dental Association — J Wisc Dent Assoc
Journal. Wisconsin State Dental Society — J Wis State Dent Soc
Journal. Won Kwang Public Health Junior College — J Won Kwang Public Health Jr Coll
Journal. World Mariculture Society — J World Maric Soc
Journal. World Mariculture Society — J World Maricult Soc
Journal. Wuhan University. Natural Sciences Edition — J Wuhan Univ Nat Sci Ed
Journal. Wuhan University of Technology — J Wuhan Univ Technol
Journal. Xiamen University. Natural Science — J Xiamen Univ Nat Sci
Journal. Xi'an Jiaotong University — J Xian Jiaotong Univ
Journal Xinjiang University. Natural Science — J Xinjiang Univ Natur Sci
Journal. Yamagata Agriculture and Forestry Society — J Yamagata Agric For Soc
Journal. Yamashina Institute for Ornithology — J Yamashina Inst Ornithol
Journal. Yokohama City University. Chemical and Physical Series — J Yokohama City Univ Chem Phys Ser
Journal. Yokohama City University. Series C. Natural Science — J Yokohama City Univ Ser C
Journal. Yokohama Municipal University — J Yokohama Munic Univ
Journal. Yokohama Municipal University. Series C. Natural Sciences/ Yokohama Shiritsu Daigaku Kiyo — J Yokohama Munic Univ Ser C Nat Sci
Journal. Yonago Medical Association — J Yonago Med Assoc
Journal. Yunnan University. Series A/Yun Nan Ta Hsueeh Hsueeh Pao. Lui — J Yunnan Univ Ser A
Journal. Zhejiang Engineering Institute — J Zhejiang Eng Inst
Journal. Zhejiang Medical University — J Zhejiang Med Univ
Journal. Zhejiang Medical University — ZYDXDM
Journal. Zhejiang University — J Zhejiang Univ
Journal. Zhejiang University. Natural Science Edition — J Zhejiang Univ Nat Sci Ed
Journal. Zoological Society of India — J Zool Soc India
Journalism Conference and Workshop — J Conf Workshop
Journalism Conference and Workshop. American Dental Association Council on Journalism and American Association of Dental Editors — Journalism Conf Workshop ADA
Journalism Educator — Journalism Educ
Journalism History — PJOU
Journalism Quarterly — J'ism Quart
Journalism Quarterly — JmQ
Journalism Quarterly — Journ Q
Journalism Quarterly — Journal Q
Journalism Quarterly — Journalism Q
Journalism Quarterly — Journalism Quart
Journalism Quarterly — JQ
Journalism Quarterly. Association for Education in Journalism — AEJ/JQ
Journalist. Orgaan van de Nederlandse Vereniging van Journalisten — JNL
Journalistbladet — Journbl
Journalisten — Journ
Journal-Lancet — J-Lancet
Journal-Lancet — JOLAB
Journal-Newsletter. Association of Teachers of Japanese — JATJ
Journals of Gerontology — PGNY
Journals of Gerontology. Series A. Biological Sciences and Medical Sciences — J Gerontol A Biol Sci Med Sci
Journals of Gerontology. Series A. Biological Sciences and Medical Sciences — J Gerontol Ser A
Journals of Gerontology. Series B. Psychological Sciences and Social Sciences — J Gerontol B Psychol Sci Soc Sci
Journee d'Etudes sur les Flammes. Rapports — Journ Etud Flammes Rapp
Journee d'Etudes sur les Pollutions Marines en Mediterranee — Journ Etud Pllut Mar Mediterr
Journee du Depoussierage des Fumees et Gaz Industriels. Compte Rendu — Journ Depoussierage Fumees Gaz Ind CR
Journee Vinicole Export — Journ Vinic Export
Journees Angeiologiques de Langue Francaise — Journ Angeiol Lang Fr
Journees Annuelles de Diabetologie Hotel-Dieu — Journ Annu Diabetol Hotel-Dieu
Journees Biochimiques Latines. Rapports — Journ Biochim Lat Rapp
Journees de Calorimetrie et d'Analyse Thermique — Journ Calorim Anal Therm
Journees de Calorimetrie et d'Analyse Thermique. Preprints — Journ Calorim Anal Therm Prepr
Journees de Diabetologie de Vals. Comptes Rendus — Journ Diabetol Vals CR
Journees de Diabetologie. Hotel-Dieu — Journ Diabetol Hotel Dieu
Journees de la Recherche Ovine et Caprine — Journ Rech Ovine Caprine
Journees de la Recherche Porcine en France — Journ Rech Porcine Fr
Journees de la Recherche Porcine en France. Compte Rendu — Journ Rech Porcine Fr CR
Journees de Printemps de la Mecanique Industrielle — Journ Printemps Mec Ind
Journees de Travail INSERM [*Institut National de la Sante et de la Recherche Medicale*]-DPHM — J Trav INSERM-DPHM
Journees d'Electronique — Journ Electron
Journees d'Etudes. Societe Thomiste — JEST
Journees d'Information. Institut des Corps Gras — Journ Inf Inst Corps Gras
Journees d'Information sur les Corps Gras Animaus. Compte Rendu — Journ Inf Corps Gras Anim CR
Journees Internationales de Siderurgie — Journ Int Sider
Journees Internationales d'Etude. Groupe Polyphenols et Assemblee Generale — Journ Int Etude Groupe Polyphenols Assem Gen
Journees Internationales. Groupe Polyphenols — Journ Int Groupe Polyphenols
Journees Internationales Huiles Essentielles — Journ Int Huiles Essent
Journees Medicales Annuelles de Broussais-La Charite — Journ Med Annu Broussais La Charite
Journees Medicales de France et de l'Union Francaise — Journ Med Fr
Journees Metallurgiques Hispano-Francaises — Journ Metall Hisp Fr
Journees Nationales de Biologie. Comptes-Rendus — Journ Natl Biol CR
Journees Pharmaceutiques Francaises — Journ Pharm Fr
Journees Scientifiques. Centre National de Coordination des Etudes et Recherches sur la Nutrition et l'Alimentation — Journ Sci Cent Natl Coord Etud Rech Nutr Aliment
Journey-to-Work Database — JTW
Joven Cuba — JC
JPEN. Journal of Parenteral and Enteral Nutrition — JPEN J Parent Enteral Nutr
JPL (Jet Propulsion Laboratory) Publication — JPL Publ
JPL [*Jet Propulsion Laboratory*] **Quarterly Technical Review** — JPL Q Tech Rev
JPL [*Jet Propulsion Laboratory*] **Technical Memorandum** — JPL Tech Memo
JPL [*Jet Propulsion Laboratory*] **Technical Report** — JPL Tech Rep
JPMA. Journal. Pakistan Medical Association — JPMA J Pak Med Assoc
JPO. Journal of Practical Orthodontics — JPO J Prac Orthod
JPT. Journal of Petroleum Technology — JPT J Pet Technol
JQ. Journalism Quarterly — GJQQ
JRS. Journal of Raman Spectroscopy — JRS J Raman Spectrosc
JSME [*Japan Society of Mechanical Engineers*] **International Journal** — JSME Int J
JSME (Japan Society of Mechanical Engineers) International Journal — JSME Internat J
JSME (Japan Society of Mechanical Engineers) International Journal. Series 2. Fluids Engineering, Heat Transfer, Power, Combusion, and Themophysical Properties — JSME Int J Ser 2
JSME (Japan Society of Mechanical Engineers) International Journal. Series C. Dynamics, Control, Robotics, Design, and Manufacturing — JSME Int J Ser C
JSS [*Japanese, Swiss, Swedish*] **Project. Technical Report** — JSS Proj Tech Rep
JSSP [*Junior Secondary Science Project*] **Newsletter** — JSSP News
JST [*Japan. Semiconductor Technology*] **Reports** — JST Rep
JSW [*Japan Steel Works*] **Technical Review** — JSW Tech Rev
Jubilee Geological Volume — Jubilee Geol Vol
JUCO [*National Junior College Athletic Association*] **Review** — JUCO Rev
JUCS. Journal of Universal Computer Science — JUCS
Judaic Studies — JS
Judaica [*Zurich*] — Jud
Judaica Bohemiae — JB
Judaica Bohemiae — Jud Boh
Judaica Book News — JBN
Judaic-Christian Research Symposium — JCRS
Judaism — GJUD
Judaism — Jdm
Judaism — Ju
Judaism — Jud
Judaism — JUM
Judaism and Christianity — Ja C
Judenfrage in Politik, Recht, Kultur, und Wirtschaft — Judenfrage
Judge Advocate General of the Navy. Journal [*US*] — JAG Journal
Judge Advocate Journal — Ja J
Judge Advocate Journal — Judge Advo J
Judges' Journal — Jud J
Judges' Journal — Judges J
Judicature — Judic
Judicature. Journal of the American Judicature Society — Judicature J Am Jud Soc'y
Judicial Discipline and Disability Digest [*Database*] — JDDD
Judiciary — J

Juedische Buch Vereinigung [*Berlin*] — JBV
Juedische Familien Forschung — JFF
Juedische Gemeinde Luzern — JGL
Juedische Kulturgemeinschaft — JKG
Juedische Nachrichten — JUNA
Juedische Presse — Jued Pr
Juedische Presse. Literaturblatt — Jued Pr L
Juedische Rundschau [*Berlin*] — JR
Juedische Rundschau [*Berlin*] — JRd
Juedische Rundschau — Jued Rd
Juedische Rundschau. Literaturblatt — Jued Rd L
Juedische Rundschau. Schriftenreihe — Jued Rd S
Juedische Volkszeitung [*Oberingelheim/Leipzig*] — JVZ
Juedische Weltrundschau — JWR
Juedische Wochenzeitung — JWZ
Juedische Zeitschrift fuer Wissenschaft und Leben — JZWL
Juedische Zeitung — JZ
Juedische Zeitung fuer Ostdeutschland [*Breslau*] — JZO
Juedischer Altestenrat — JAR
Juedischer Ordnungsdienst — JOD
Juedisches Echo [*Munich*] — JE
Juedisches Gemeinde — JG
Juedisches Lexikon — JL
Juedisches Literaturblatt — JLBl
Juedisches Literaturblatt — Jued Litbl
Juedisches Litteratur-Blatt — JLB
Juedisches Volksblatt (Breslau) — JV(B)
Juedisches Zentralblatt — JCBl
Juedisches Zentralblatt — Jued Zbl
Juedisches Zentralblatt — JZ Bl
Jugement du Tribunal Civil de Bruxelles — Civ Brux
Jugement du Tribunal Correctionnel de Bruxelles — Corr Brux
Jugement du Tribunal de Commerce de Bruxelles — Comm Brux
Jugend Film Fernsehen — JFF
Jugobanka. Economic News — IVA
Jugoslavenska Ginekologija I Perinatologija — Jugosl Ginekol Perinatol
Jugoslavenska Medicinska Biokemija — Jugosl Med Biokem
Jugoslavenske Akademije Znanosti i Umjetnosti — JAZU
Jugoslavensko Drustvo za Primjenu Goriva i Maziva. Strucna Izdanja — Jugosl Drus Primjenu Goriva Maziva Strucna Izd
Jugoslovanski Mednarodni Simpozij o Aluminiju. Clanki — Jugosl Mednar Simp Alum Clanki
Jugoslovanski Simpozij za Hmeljarstvo Referati — Jugosl Simp Hmeljarstvo Ref
Jugoslovanski Simpozij za Hmeljarstvo Referati — RJSHDQ
Jugoslovenska Ginekologija i Opstetricija — JGNOAC
Jugoslovenska Ginekologija i Opstetricija — Jugosl Ginekol Opstet
Jugoslovenska Medicinska Biohemija — Jugosl Med Biohem
Jugoslovenska Pedijatrija — JPPIAX
Jugoslovenska Pedijatrija — Jugosl Pedijatr
Jugoslovenski Istorijski Casopis — Jug Ist Cas
Jugoslovenski Istoriski Casopis — JIC
Jugoslovenski Medjunarodni Simpozij o Aluminiju — Jugos Medjunar Simp Alum
Jugoslovenski Pregled — Jugosl Pregl
Jugoslovenski Veterinarski Glasnik — Jugosl Vet Glasn
Jugoslovensko Drustvo za Mehaniku. Teorijska i Primenjena Mehanika — Teor Primen Meh
Jugoslovensko Drustvo za Proucavanje Zemljista. Posebne Publikacije — Jugosl Drus Prouc Zemljista Posebne Publ
Jugoslovensko Pcelarstvo — Jugosl Pcelarstvo
Jugoslovensko Pronalazastvo — Jugosl Pronalazastvo
Jugoslovensko Vinogradarstvo i Vinarstvo — Jugosl Vinograd Vinar
Jugoslovensko Vocarstvo — Jugosl Vocarstvo
Juhasz Gyula Tanarkepzo Foiskola Tudomanyos Kozlemenyei — Juhasz Gyula Tanarkepzo Foiskola Tud Kozl
Juilliard News Bulletin — JN
Juilliard Review — Juilliard R
Juilliard Review. Annual — JU
Jul i Roskilde — Jul i Ro
Jul i Skive — Jul i Sk
Jul i Vejle — Jul i Ve
Jul i Vestjylland — Jul i Vestj
Jul paa Bornholm — Jul p B
Julkaisuja-Oulu Yliopisto. Ydintekniikkan Laitos — Julk Oulu Yliopisto Ydintek Laitos
Julliard News Bulletin — JNB
July — JL
June — JE
Juneau Report — JURT
Junge Destillateur und Brenner — Junge Destill Brenner
Junge Kirche — JK
Junge Wirtschaft — Jung Wirt
Junior Bookshelf — JB
Junior Bookshelf — Jr Bkshelf
Junior College Journal — Jr Coll J
Junior College Journal — Jr Coll Jnl
Junior College Journal — Jun Col J
Junior College Journal — Junior Coll J
Junior High Clearing House — J H Clearing House
Junior Institution of Engineers (London). Journal and Record of Transactions — Junior Inst Eng (London) J Rec Trans
Junior Libraries — Jr Lib
Junior Philippine Scientist — Jr Philipp Sci
Junior Scholastic — Jr Schol
Junior Scholastic — JS
Junior-Senior High School Clearing House — J-S H Sch Clearing House
Junkatsu — JUNKA
Junta de Ciencias Naturals — Junta Ci Nat
Junta de Energia Nuclear. Report. JEN (Spain) — Junta Energ Nucl Rep JEN Spain
Junta de Energia Nuclear. Report (Spain) — Junta Energ Nucl Rep (Spain)
Junta de Investigacoes Cientificas do Ultramar. Estudos, Ensaios, e Documentos (Portugal) — Junta Invest Cient Ultramar Estud Ensaios Doc (Port)
Junta de Investigacoes do Ultramar. Estudos, Ensaios, e Documentos — JIUEAV
Junta de Investigacoes do Ultramar. Estudos, Ensaios, e Documentos — Junta Invest Ultramar Estud Ens Doc
Junta de Investigacoes do Ultramar. Portugal. Estudos, Ensaios, e Documentos — Junta Invest Ultramar Port Estud Ensaios Doc
Juntendo Medical Journal — Juntendo Med J
Junyj Chudoznik — Ju Ch
Jura. Rivista Internazionale di Diritto Romano e Antico — Jura Riv
Juridical Review — JR
Juridical Review — JUR R
Juridical Review — Jur Rev
Juridical Review — Jurid R
Juridical Review — Jurid Rev
Juridical Review — Juridical Rev
Juridiska Foereningen i Finland. Tidskrift — Jur Foeren I Finl T
Jurimetrics Journal — Juri J
Jurimetrics Journal — Jurimetrics
Jurimetrics Journal — Jurimetrics J
Juris Doctor — JD
Juris Ecclesiastici Graecorum Hisoria et Monumenta — JEGH
Jurisprudence Commerciale de Belgique — J Comm B
Jurisprudence Commerciale de Bruxelles — JCB
Jurisprudence Commerciale de Bruxelles — Jur B
Jurisprudence Commerciale de Bruxelles — Jur Com Brux
Jurisprudence Commerciale de Flandres — Jur Fl
Jurisprudence Commerciale de Verviers — JCV
Jurisprudence Commerciale de Verviers — Jur V
Jurisprudence Commerciale des Flandres — JCF
Jurisprudence Commerciale des Flandres — JCFl
Jurisprudence Commerciale des Flandres — Jr Com Fl
Jurisprudence Commerciale des Flandres — Jr Comm Fl
Jurisprudence de la Cour d'Appel de Liege — JAL
Jurisprudence de la Cour d'Appel de Liege — JCAL
Jurisprudence de la Cour d'Appel de Liege — Jur L
Jurisprudence de l'Etat Independant du Congo — Jur Etat
Jurisprudence de Louage d'Ouvrage — JLO
Jurisprudence de Louage d'Ouvrage — Jur Ouv
Jurisprudence des Tribunaux de l'Arrondissement de Nivelles — Jp Niv
Jurisprudence du Divorce et de la Separation de Corps — Jur Div
Jurisprudence du Port D'Anvers — JA
Jurisprudence du Port D'Anvers [*Belgium*] — JPA
Jurisprudence du Port D'Anvers — Jur A
Jurisprudence du Port D'Anvers — Jur Anv
Jurisprudence du Port D'Anvers — Jur Port Anv
Jurisprudence du Tribunal de Commerce de Verviers — Jur Comm Verviers
Jurisprudence et Droit du Congo — Jur & Dr du Congo
Jurisprudence et Droit du Congo — Jur Congo
Jurisprudencia Argentina — JA
Jurisprudentie van het Hof van Justitie van de Europese Gemeenschappen — Jur
Jurist. Quarterly Journal of Jurisprudence — Jur
Juristen — Jur
Juristenblad [*Antwerpen*] — Jb
Juristenzeitung — JZ
Juristische Abhandlungen — Jur Abh
Juristische Blaetter — JBl
Juristische Blaetter — Jur Bl
Juristische Monatsschrift fuer Posen, West- und Ostpreussen und Pommern — PosMSchr
Juristische Papyri — Jur Pap
Juristische Praxis — JP
Juristische Rundschau — Jur R
Juristische Rundschau — Jur Rd
Juristische Schulung — Ju S
Juristische Schulung — Jurist Sch
Juristische Vierteljahresschrift — Jur Vjschr
Juristische Zeitschrift fuer das Reichsland Elsass-Lothringen — Jur Zs Els Lothr
Juristisches Literaturblatt — Jur Litbl
Jurnal Fizik Malaysia — J Fiz Malays
Jurnal Pendidikan. Universiti Kebangsaan Malaysia [*Kuala Lumpur*] — J Pendid UKM
Jurnal Pendidikan. University of Malaya — J Pendid UM
Jurnal Sains Institut Penyelidikan Getah Malaysia — J Sains Inst Penyelidikan Getah Malays
Jurnal Sains Malaysia. Series A. Life Sciences — J Sains Malays Ser A
Jurnal Sains Malaysia. Series B. Physical and Earth Sciences — J Sains Malays Ser B
Jurnal Sains Nuklear Malaysia — J Sains Nukl Malays
Jus Canonicum — JC
Jus Documentacao (Rio de Janeiro) — Jus Doc Rio
Jus Ecclesiasticum — Jus Ecc
Jus Ecclesiasticum — Jus Eccl
Jus; Rivista di Scienze Giuridiche — Jus
Jus Romanum Medii Aevi — Jus Rom MA

Just Economics — Just Econ
Just Seventeen — J17
Justice of the Peace — Just P
Justice of the Peace (New South Wales) — JP (NSW)
Justice of the Peace Reports [*United Kingdom*] — JP
Justice of the Peace (Western Australia) — JP (WA)
Justice System Journal — J System J
Justice System Journal — Just Sys J
Justice System Journal — Just Syst J
Justice System Journal — Justice System J
Justitia — J
Justiz und Verwaltung — Ju V
Justizverwaltungsblatt — JV Bl
Justus Liebigs Annalen der Chemie — JLACBF
Justus Liebigs Annalen der Chemie — Ju Lieb Ann Chem
Justus Liebigs Annalen der Chemie — Just Lieb Ann Chem
Justus Liebigs Annalen der Chemie — Justus Liebigs Ann Chem
Jute Abstracts — Jute Abstr
Jute and Jute Fabrics. Bangladesh Newsletter — Jute Jute Fabr Bangladesh Newsl
Jute Bulletin — Jute Bull
Jutendo Medicine [*Japan*] — Jutendo Med
Juvenile and Family Court Journal — Juv and Fam Courts J
Juvenile and Family Court Journal — Juv & Fam Ct J
Juvenile Court Judges Journal — Juv Ct JJ
Juvenile Court Judges Journal — Juv Ct Judges J
Juvenile Justice — Juven Just
Juventude Evangelica — Juv Ev
Juzen Igakkai Zasshi — JUZIAG
Juznoslovenski Filolog — JF
Juznoslovenski Filolog — JslF
Juznoslovenski Filolog. Povremeni Spis za Slovensku Filologiju i Lingvistiku — Juz Fil
Jydsk Landbrug — J Ldb
Jyske Samlinger — Jy Saml

K

K (Rapor) TC Atom Enerjisi Komisyonu — K Rap TC At Enerj Kom
Kabar Sebarang. Sulating Maphilindo — Kab Seb
Kabardino-Balkarskaya Opytnaya Stantsiya Sadovodstva. Trudy — Kabard Balkar Opytn Stn Sadovod Tr
Kabardino-Balkarskii Gosudarstvennyi Universitet. Sbornik Nauchnykh Rabot Aspirantov — Kabard Balkar Gos Univ Sb Nauchn Rab Aspir
Kabardino-Balkarskii Gosudarstvennyi Universitet. Ucenyi Zapiski — Kabardino-Balkarsk Gos Univ Ucen Zap
Kabel'naya Tekhnika — Kabel Tekh
Kabel'naya Tekhnika — Kabeln Tekh
Kabelvisie Onafhankelijk Tijdschrift voor Kabel en Lokale Televisie — KVS
Kabinet der Natuurlijke Historien, Wetenschappen, Konsten en Handwerken — Kab Natuurl Hist
Kabul University. Faculty of Agriculture. Research Notes — Kabul Univ Fac Agric Res Note
Kabul University. Faculty of Agriculture. Technical Bulletin — Kabul Univ Fac Agric Tech Bull
Kachestva na Promishlenite Zelenchukovu Sortove — Kach Prom Zelenchukovu Sortove
Kachestvennaya Stal — Kach Stal
Kachestvo Poverkhnosti Detalei Mashin — Kach Poverkhn Detalei Mash
Kachiku Hanshokugaku Zasshi — KHZAD
Kadelpian Review — Kadel R
Kadmos. Supplement — KadmosS
Kadry Sel'sko Khoziaistva — Kadry Selsk Khoz
Kaelte und Klimatechnik — Kaelte Klimatech
Kaelte-Industrie — Kaelte Ind
Kaelte-Industrie (Moscow) — Kaelte Ind Moscow
Kaelte-Klima-Praktiker — Kaelte-Klima-Prakt
Kaeltetechnik-Klimatisierung — Kaeltetech-Klim
Kaeltetechnischer Anzeiger — Kaeltetech Anz
Kaernbraenslesaekerhet. Teknisk Rapport — Kaernbraenslesaekerhet Tek Rapp
Kaffee und Tee Markt — GKT
Kaffee- und Tee-Markt — Kaffee Tee Markt
Kagaku Keisatsu Kenkyusho Hokoku, Hokagaku Hen — KKHKA
Kagaku Keizai — KAKZA
Kagaku Kogaku — Kag Kog
Kagaku Kogyo — KAKOA
Kagaku Kogyo. Supplement — KKOSB
Kagaku Kojo — KAJKA
Kagaku (Kyoto) — KAKYA
Kagaku To Seibutsu — KASEA
Kagoshima Daigaku Bunka Hokoku [*Cultural Science Reports. Kagoshima University*] — KagoBH
Kagoshima Daigaku Kogakubu Kenkyu Hokoku — KDKKB
Kagoshima Daigaku Suisangakubu Kiyo — KDSGA
Kahtou: a Publication of the Native Communications Society of British Columbia — KATO
Kainai News — KN
Kairos. Religionswissenschaftliche Studien [*Salzburg*] — KairosSt
Kairos. Zeitschrift fuer Religionswissenschaft und Theologie — Kair
Kaiser Foundation Medical Bulletin — Kaiser Fdn Med Bull
Kaiser Foundation Medical Bulletin — Kaiser Found Med Bull
Kaiser Foundation Medical Bulletin. Abstract Issue — Kaiser Found Med Bull Abstr Issue
Kaiserlich-Deutsches Archaeologisches Institut. Jahrbuch — Kais-Deutsch Archaol Inst Jahrb
Kaiserliche Akademie der Wissenschaften in Wien. Philosophisch-Historische Klasse. Denkschriften — Kais Akad d Wiss Denksch Philos-Hist Kl
Kaiserliche Akademie der Wissenschaften in Wien. Philosophisch-Historische Klasse. Sitzungsberichte — Kais Akad d Wissensch Sitzungsb Philos-Hist Klasse
Kaiserliche Akademie der Wissenschaften. Mathematische-Naturwissenschaftliche Klasse. Sitzungsberichte — K Ak Wiss Mat-Nat Kl Szb
Kaiserlich-Koenigliche Geographische Gesellschaft in Wien. Mitteilungen — K-K Geog Ges Wien Mitt
Kaiserlich-Koenigliche Geologische Reichsanstalt. Verhandlungen. Jahrbuch — K-Kg Reichsanstalt Verh Jb
Kaiserlich-Koenigliche Naturhistorische Hofmuseum. Annalen — K-K Naturh Hofmus An
Kaiser-Traktate — KT
Kajian Ekonomi Malaysia — Kaj Ekon Mal
Kajian Veterinaire — Kajian Vet
Kaju Shikenjo Hokoku. Bulletin of the Fruit Tree Research Station. Series A. Yatabe — Kaju Shikenjo Hokoku Bull Fruit Tree Res Stn Ser A Yatabe
Kakao und Zucker — Kakao Zuck
Kakatiya Journal of English Studies — Kakatiya J Eng Stud
Kakteen und Andere Sukkulenten — Kakteen Sukkulenten
Kakteen und Andere Sukkulenten. Organ der Deutschen Kakteen — Kakteen Sukk
Kakteen und Orchideen Rundschau — Kakteen Orchideen Rundsch
Kakuriken Kenkyu Hokoku — KKYHB
Kakuriken Kenkyu Hokoku. Supplement [*Japan*] — Kakuriken Kenkyu Hokoku Suppl
Kakuyugo Kenkyu — KAKEA
Kakyu Saibansho Keiji Saibanreishu — Kakeishu
Kakyu Saibansho Minji Saibanreishu — Kaminshu
Kalamazoo Medicine — Kalamazoo Med
Kaleidoscope. Current World Data [*Database*] — KCWD
Kaleidoscope Insert — Kal Inser
Kaleidoscope-Madison — Kal-Mad
Kaleidoscope-Milwaukee — Kal-Mil
Kalender der Detuschen Volksgemeinschaft fuer Rumaenien — KDV
Kalender des Schweizer Imkers — Kal Schweiz Imkers
Kalender foer Sveriges Berghandtering — Kal Sver Bergh
Kalevalaseuran Vuosikirja — KSVK
Kalevalaseuran Vuosikirja — KV
Kalikaq Yugnek. Bethel Regional High School — KQYK
Kaliningradskii Gosudarstvennyi Pedagogiceskii Institut Ucenye Zapiski — Kaliningrad Gos Ped Inst Ucen Zap
Kaliningradskii Gosudarstvennyi Universitet. Kafedra Teoreticheskoi i Eksperimental'noi Fiziki. Trudy — Kaliningr Gos Univ Kafedra Teor Eksp Fiz Tr
Kaliningradskii Gosudarstvennyi Universitet Trudy Kafedry Teoreticeskoi i Eksperimental'noi Fiziki — Kaliningrad Gos Univ Trudy Kaf Teoret i Eksper Fiz
Kaliningradskii Gosudarstvennyi Universitet Ucenye Zapiski — Kaliningrad Gos Univ Ucen Zap
Kaliningradskii Tekhnicheskii Institut Rybnoi Promyshlennosti i Khozyaistva. Trudy — Kaliningr Tekh Inst Rybn Promsti Khoz Tr
Kaliningradskogo Gosudarstvennogo Universitet Differencial'naja Geometrija Mnogoobrazii Figur — Kaliningrad Gos Univ Differencial'naja Geom Mnogoobraz Figur
Kalininskii Gosudarstvennyi Pedagogiceskii Institut Imeni M. I. Kalinina Ucenye Zapiski — Kalinin Gos Ped Inst Ucen Zap
Kalininskii Politekhnicheskii Institut. Trudy — Kalinin Politekh Inst Tr
Kalium Symposium — Kalium Symp
Kalk-, Gips-, und Schamottezeitung — Kalk Gips Schamotteztg
Kalmytskii Nauchno-Issledovatel'skii Institut Myasnogo Skotovodstva. Nauchnye Trudy — Kalmytskii Nauchno-Issled Inst Myasn Skotovod Nauchn Tr
Kamena — Kam
Kamer van Koophandel en Fabrieken te Paramaribo. Bulletin — KKA
Kamloops Forest Region Newsletter — Kamloops For Reg Newsl
Kammer der Technik Suhl. Tagungsband — Kammer Tech Suhl Tagungsband
Kampeer + Caravan Kampioen — KPK
Kamper Almanak — Kamper Alm
Kampioen — KAP
Kamp's Paedagogische Taschenbuecher — Kamp's Paed Tb
Kampuchea Bulletin — Kampuchea Bull
Kanaanaeische und Araemaische Inschriften — KAI
Kanagawa Prefectural Museum. Bulletin — Kanagawa Prefect Mus Bull
Kanagawa University. Faculty of Engineering. Reports — Rep Fac Engrg Kanagawa Univ
Kanagawa University. Faculty of Technology. Reports — Rep Fac Tech Kanagawa Univ
Kanagawa-Ken Kogyo Shikenjo Kenkyu Hokoku — KKSKA
Kanazawa Daigaku Hobungakubu Ronshu. Bungakuhen [*Studies and Essays. Faculty of Law and Literature. Kanazawa University. Literature*] — KanazHB
Kanazawa Daigaku Kyoyobu Ronshu. Jinbunkagakuhen [*Studies in Humanities. College of Liberal Arts. Kanazawa University*] — KanazJK
Kanazawa Ika Daigaku Zasshi — KIDZD
Kanazawa University. Research Institute of Tuberculosis. Annual Report — Kanazawa Univ Res Inst Tuberc Annu Rep
Kanbum Gakkai Kaiho [*Journal. Sinological Society*] — KGH
Kangaku Kenkyu [*Sinological Studies*] — KGKK
Kanina — KA
Kano Studies [*Nigeria*] — Kano S
Kano Studies — Kano Stud
Kanonistische Studien und Texte — K St T
Kansai Gaidai Kenkyu Ronshu [*Journal. Kansai University of Foreign Studies*] — KGKR
Kansai Society of Naval Architects. Journal — Kansai Soc NA Jnl

Kansallis-Osake-Pankki. Economic Review — Kansallis-Osake-Pankki Econ R
Kansallis-Osake-Pankki. Economic Review — KOP
Kansallis-Osake-Pankki. Economic Review — KOS
Kansantaloudellinen Aikakauskirja — Kansantal Aikakausk
Kansas Academy of Science. Transactions — Kan Acad Sci Trans
Kansas Academy of Science. Transactions — Kans Ac Sc Tr
Kansas Academy of Science. Transactions — Kans Acad Sci Trans
Kansas Academy of Science. Transactions — Kansas Acad Sci Trans
Kansas Administrative Regulations — Kan Admin Regs
Kansas Agricultural Experiment Station. Biennial Report of the Director — Kans Agric Exp Stn Bienn Rep Dir
Kansas Agricultural Experiment Station. Bulletin — Kans Agric Exp Stn Bull
Kansas Agricultural Experiment Station. Circular — Kans Agric Exp Stn Circ
Kansas Agricultural Experiment Station. Research Publication — Kans Agric Exp Stn Res Publ
Kansas Agricultural Experiment Station. Technical Bulletin — Kans Agric Exp Stn Tech Bull
Kansas Agricultural Situation. Kansas State University of Agriculture and Applied Science. Extension Service — Kans Agr Situation
Kansas Bar Association. Journal — Kan B Ass'n J
Kansas Bar Association. Journal — Kan BAJ
Kansas Business Teacher — Kansas Bus Tchr
Kansas City Business Journal — KC Bsns Jl
Kansas City Medical Journal — Kans Ci Med J
Kansas City Medical Journal — Kans Cy Med J
Kansas City Philharmonic Program Notes — KC Phil
Kansas City Review — Kansas R
Kansas City Review of Science and Industry — Kansas City Rv Sc
Kansas City Star — KC Star
Kansas City Times — KC Times
Kansas Court of Appeals Reports — Kan App
Kansas Court of Appeals Reports. Second Series — Kan App 2d
Kansas Engineering Experiment Station. Bulletin — Kans Eng Exp Stn Bull
Kansas. Engineering Experiment Station (Manhattan, Kansas). Special Report — Kans Eng Exp Stn (Manhattan Kans) Spec Rep
Kansas Environmental Health Services Bulletin — Kans Environ Health Serv Bull
Kansas Geological Survey. Basic Data Series. Ground-Water Release — Kans Geol Surv Basic Data Ser Ground Water Release
Kansas Geological Survey. Bulletin — Kans Geol Surv Bull
Kansas Geological Survey. Chemical Quality Series — Kans Geol Surv Chem Qual Ser
Kansas Geological Survey. Ground-Water Series — Kans Geol Surv Ground Water Ser
Kansas Geological Survey. Map — Kansas Geol Survey Map
Kansas Geological Survey. Series on Spatial Analysis — Kans Geol Surv Ser Spat Anal
Kansas Geological Survey. Short Papers in Research — Kan Geol Surv Short Pap Res
Kansas Ground Water. Basic-Data Release — Kans Ground Water Basic-Data Release
Kansas Historical Quarterly — KaH
Kansas Historical Quarterly — Kan Hist Quar
Kansas Historical Quarterly — Kans Hist Q
Kansas Historical Quarterly — KHQ
Kansas Journal of Sociology — Kansas J Sociol
Kansas Judicial Council. Bulletin — JCB
Kansas Judicial Council. Bulletin — Kan Jud Council Bull
Kansas Law Review — Kan L Rev
Kansas Law Review — Kan Law Rev
Kansas Law Review — KS LR
Kansas Library Bulletin — Kan Lib Bull
Kansas Library Bulletin — Kan Libr Bull
Kansas Library Bulletin — Kansas Lib Bul
Kansas Magazine — KM
Kansas Medicine — Kans Med
Kansas Music Review — KA
Kansas Nurse — Kans Nurse
Kansas Quarterly — KanQ
Kansas Quarterly — KaQ
Kansas Quarterly — KQ
Kansas Quarterly — KsQ
Kansas Register — Kan Reg
Kansas Reports — Kan
Kansas School Naturalist — Kans Sch Nat
Kansas State Agricultural College. Agricultural Experiment Station. Bulletin — Kansas Agric Exp Sta Bull
Kansas State Agricultural College. Agricultural Experiment Station Circular — Kansas Agric Exp Sta Circ
Kansas State Agricultural College. Agricultural Experiment Station Progress Report — Kansas Agric Exp Sta Progr Rep
Kansas State Agricultural College. Agricultural Experiment Station. Publications — Kan Ag Exp
Kansas State Agricultural College. Agricultural Experiment Station Technical Bulletin — Kansas Agric Exp Sta Techn Bull
Kansas State Board of Agriculture. Division of Entomology. Activities — Kans State Board Agric Div Entomol Act
Kansas State Board of Agriculture. Transactions. Annual Report. Biennial Report — Kans St Bd Agr Tr An Rp Bien Rp
Kansas State Department of Health. Environmental Health Services. Bulletin — Kans State Dep Health Environ Health Serv Bull
Kansas State Geological Survey. Bulletin — Kans State Geol Surv Bull
Kansas State Geological Survey. Computer Contribution — Kans State Geol Surv Comput Contrib
Kansas State Geological Survey. Computer Contribution — Kans State Geol Surv Computer Contrib
Kansas State Geological Survey. Ground-Water Series — Kans State Geol Surv Ground Water Ser
Kansas State Geological Survey. Special Distribution Publication — Kans State Geol Surv Spec Distrib Publ
Kansas State Geological Survey. Special Distribution Publication — Kans State Geol Surv Spec Distribution Publication
Kansas State Historical Society. Collections — Kan State Hist Soc Coll
Kansas State Historical Society. Collections — Kas His S
Kansas State Historical Society. Transactions — Kansas State Hist Soc Trans
Kansas State Horticultural Society. Transactions — Kans State Hortic Soc Trans
Kansas State University. Bulletin — Kans State Univ Bull
Kansas State University Bulletin. Kansas Engineering Experiment Station. Bulletin — Kans State Univ Bull Kans Eng Exp Sta Bull
Kansas State University. Center for Energy Studies. Report — Kans State Univ Cent Energy Stud Rep
Kansas State University. Engineering Experiment Station. Bulletin — Kans State Univ Eng Exp Stn Bull
Kansas State University. Engineering Experiment Station. Reprint — Kans State Univ Eng Exp Stn Repr
Kansas State University. Engineering Experiment Station. Special Report — Kans State Univ Eng Exp Stn Spec Rep
Kansas State University. Institute for Systems Design and Optimization. Report — Kan State Univ Inst Syst Des Optim Rep
Kansas State University. Institute for Systems Design and Optimization. Report — Kans State Univ Inst Syst Des Optim Rep
Kansas State Water Resources Board. Bulletin — Kansas Water Resources Board Bull
Kansas Statutes Annotated — Kan Stat Ann
Kansas Stockman — Kans Stockman
Kansas Teacher and Western School Journal — Kans Teach
Kansas University. Bulletin of Education — Kans Univ B Ed
Kansas University. Kansas Studies in Education — Kan Univ Kan Studies Ed
Kansas University Lawyer — Kansas Univ Lawyer
Kansas University. Museum of Natural History. Miscellaneous Publication — Kansas Univ Mus Nat History Misc Pub
Kansas University. Museum of Natural History. Publications. Paleontological Contributions. Science Bulletin — Kans Univ Mus Nat History Pub Paleont Contr Sci Bull
Kansas University. Paleontological Contributions — Kansas Univ Paleont Contr
Kansas University. Paleontology Contribution Paper — Kans Univ Paleontol Contrib Pap
Kansas University. Quarterly — Kans Univ Q
Kansas University. Science Bulletin — Kans Univ Sc B
Kansas University. Science Bulletin — Kans Univ Sci Bull
Kansas University Science Bulletin — Kansas Univ Sci Bull
Kansas Water and Sewage Works Association. Report — Kans Water Sewage Works Assoc Rep
Kansas Water Resources Board. Bulletin — Kans Water Res Board Bull
Kansas Water Resources Research Institute. Contribution — Kans Water Resour Res Inst Contrib
Kansas Wheat Quality. Kansas State Board of Agriculture [*Kansas Wheat Commission*] — Kans Wheat Qual Kans State Board Agr
Kansatieteellinen Arkisto — K Ar
Kanto Journal of Orthopedics and Traumatology [*Japan*] — Kanto J Orthop Traumatol
Kantoor en Efficiency — KEE
Kant-Studien — Kant-Stud
Kant-Studien — KS
Kant-Studien — KSt
Kao Fen Tzu T'ung Hsun — KFTTA
Kaohsiung Journal of Medical Sciences — Kaohsiung J Med Sci
Kapala Cruise Report — Kapala Cruise Rep
Kapala Cruise Report — KCREEN
Kapitalistate — Kapital
Kapitalistate — Kapitalis
Kappa Beta Pi Quarterly — KBP Q
Kapper — KAC
Kappersbondsnieuws — BOW
Karachi Law Journal — Kar LJ
Karachi University Gazette — Karachi Univ Gaz
Karachi University. Journal of Science — Karachi Univ J Sci
Karada No Kagaku — KARKA
Karakulevodstvo i Zverovodstvo — Karakulevod Zverovod
Karakulevodstvo i Zverovodstvo — KZ
Karate and Oriental Arts — KOA
Karbo-Energochemia-Ekologia — Karbo Energochem Ekol
Karcher Symposium — Karcher Symp
Kardiologia Polska — Kardiol Pol
Kardiologia Polska. Towarzystwo Internistow Polskich. Sekeja Kardiologiczna — Kardiol Pol Tow Internistow Pol Sek Kardiol
Karger Biobehavioral Medicine Series — Karger Biobehav Med Ser
Karger Biobehavioral Medicine Series — KBMEDO
Karger Continuing Education Series — Karger Contin Educ Ser
Karger Continuing Education Series — KCESDX
Kariba Studies — Kariba Stud
Karjantuote — KARJA
Karl-August-Forster-Lectures — Karl-August-Forster-Lect
Karlovarsky Lazensky Casopis — Karlov Laz Cas
Karlsburg Symposium — Karlsburg Symp
Karlsruher Beitraege zur Entwicklungsphysiologie der Pflanzen — Karlsruher Beitr Entwicklungsphysiol Pflanz
Karlsruher Berichte zur Ingenieurbiologie — Karlsruher Ber Ingenieurbiol
Karlsruher Geographische Hefte — Karlsruher Geogr Hefte
Karnatak University. Journal — KU
Karnatak University. Journal of Science — Karnatak Univ J Sci

Karnataka Medical Journal — Karnataka Med J
Karolinska Foerbundets Arsbok — Karolinska Foerb Arsb
Karolinska Institute. Laboratory for Clinical Stress Research. Reports — Karolinska Inst Lab Clin Stress Res Rep
Karolinska Institute Nobel Conference — Karolinska Inst Nobel Conf
Karolinska Symposia on Research Methods in Reproductive Endocrinology — Karolinska Symp Res Methods Reprod Endocrinol
Karpatenjahrbuch — Karpaten Jb
Karpato-Balkanskaya Geologicheskaya Assotsiatsiya. Materialy Komissii Mineralogii i Geokhimii — Karpato Balk Geol Assots Mater Kom Mineral Geokhim
Karszt- es Barlangkutatas — Karszt Barlangkut
Kartellzeitung Akademisch-Theologischer Vereine — KZATV
Karthago. Revue d'Archeologie Africaine — Kart
Karthago. Revue d'Archeologie Africaine — Karth
Kartoffel-Tagung, Vortraege Anlaesslich der Fachtagung der Arbeitsgemeinschaft Kartoffelforschung e. V — Kartoffel Tag Vortr Anlaesslich Fachtag Arbeitsgem Kartoffelf
Kartograficeskaja Letopis — Kartogr Let
Kartograficky Prehled — Kartogr Pr
Kartographische Nachrichten — Kartogr Nachr
Kartographische Nachrichten (Stuttgart) — Kartogr Nachr (Stuttg)
Kartographische und Schulgeographische Zeitschrift — Kartogr Schulgeogr Zs
Kartonagen und Papierwaren-Zeitung — Kartonagen Papierwaren-Ztg
Kartoplya Ovochevi ta Bashtanni Kul'turi — Kartoplya Ovochevi Bashtanni Kult
Kartvelur Enata St'rukt'uris Sak'itxebi — KESS
Kasaner Medizinisches Journal — Kasan Med J
Kaseigaku Zasshi. Journal of Home Economics of Japan — Kaseigaku Zasshi J Home Econ Jap
Kasetsart Journal — Kasetsart J
Kasetsart University. Fishery Research Bulletin — Kasetsart Univ Fish Res Bull
Kashi Sanskrit Series — KSS
Kashmir Science — Kashmir Sci
Kashmir University. Faculty of Science. Research Journal — Kashmir Univ Fac Sci Res J
Kasr El-Aini Journal of Surgery — Kasr El-Aini J Surg
Kasseler Arbeiten zur Sprache und Literatur. Anglistik-Germanistik-Romanistik — KASL
Kassenzahnarzt. Colloquium Med Dent — Kassenzahnarzt Colloq Med Dent
Kataliticheskaya Konversiya Uglevodorodov — Katal Konvers Uglevodorodov
Kataliticheskaya Pererabotka Uglevodorodnogo Syr'ya — Katal Pererab Uglevodorodnogo Syr'ya
Kataliticheskie Prevrascheniya Uglevodorodov — Katl Prevrashch Uglevodorodov
Kataliticheskie Reaktsii v Zhidkoi Faze. Materialy Vsesoyuznoi Konferentsii po Kataliticheskim Reaktsiyam v Zhidkoi Faze — Katal Reakts Zhidk Faze Mater Vses Konf
Kataliticheskie Reaktsii v Zhidkoi Faze. Trudy Vsesoyuznoi Konferentsii — Katal Reakts Zhidk Faze Tr Vses Konf
Kataliz i Katalizatory [*Former USSR*] — Katal Katal
Katallagete — Katal
Katalog Fauny Polski — Kat Fauny Pol
Katalog over Datamateriale for Norges Berggrunn — Kat Datamater Nor Berggrunn
Katalog Rekopisow Orientalnych ze Zbirorow Polskich — KROZP
Katechetische Blaetter — Kat Bl
Katechetische Monatsschrift — Kat Mschr
Katechetische Zeitschrift — Kat Zs
Katei Saiban Geppo — Kasai Geppo
Katholiek — Kat
Katholiek — Kath
Katholiek Archief — Kath Ar
Katholiek Cultureel Tijdschrift — Kath Cult Tijdsch
Katholiek Cultureel Tijdschrift — KCT
Katholiek Cultureel Tijdschrift Streven — KCTS
Katholiek Cultureel Tijdschrift Streven — Streven
Katholiek Sociaal Tijdschrift — KST
Katholiek Staatskundig Maandschrift — KSM
Katholieke Encyclopaedie — KE
Katholieke Universiteit te Leuven. Landbouwinstituut. Verhandelingen — Kathol Univ Leuven Landbouwinst Verh
Katholik — Kath
Katholische Gedanken — KG
Katholische Jahrbuch — Kath Jb
Katholische Kirche im Wandel der Zeiten und Voelker — KKWZ
Katholische Kirchenzeitung — KKZ
Katholischen Missionen — KM
Katholischer Digest — Kath Dig
Katholischer Glaube und Wissenschaft in Oesterreich — KGWOe
Katholisches Leben und Kaempfen — KLK
Katholisches Missionsjahrbuch der Schweiz — Kath MJS
Katholisches Missionsjahrbuch der Schweiz — KMJS
Katilolehti. Tidskrift foer Barnmorskor — Katilolehti
Katimavik. Faculty of Physical Education. University of Alberta — KTMK
Katolikus Szemle. Budapest — KSB
Katolikus Szemle. Roma. Kis Koenyvtara — KSKK
Kauchuk i Rezina — Kauch i Rezina
Kauno Politechnikos Instituto Darbai — Kauno Politech Inst Darb
Kauno Politechnikos Instituto Jubiliejines Mokslines-Technines Konferencijos. Darbai — Kauno Politech Inst Jubiliejines Mokslines Tech Konf Darb
Kauno Valstibinio Universiteto Technikos Fakulteto Darbai — Kauno Valstibinio Univ Tech Fak Darb
Kauno Valstybinio Medicinos Instituto Darbai — Kauno Valstybinio Med Inst Darb
Kauppalehti — KAUP
Kautschuk und Gummi. Kunststoffe — Kaut Gum Ku
Kautschuk und Gummi. Kunststoffe — Kaut Gummi
Kautschuk und Gummi. Kunststoffe — Kaut u Gummi Kunst
Kautschuk und Gummi. Kunststoffe — Kautsch Gummi Kunstst
Kautschuk und Gummi. Kunststoffe. Asbest — Kautch Gummi Kunstst Asbest
Kautschuk und Gummi. Kunststoffe, Asbest — Kautsch Gummi Kunstst Asbest
Kautschuk und Gummi. Kunststoffe. Plastomere, Elastomere, Duromere — Kautsch Gummi Kunstst Plastomere Elastomere Duromere
Kautschuk und Gummi (Moscow) — Kautsch Gummi Moscow
Kavkazskii Institut Mineral'nogo Syr'ya. Trudy — Kavk Inst Miner Syrya Tr
Kavkazskij Etnograficeskij Sbornik — Kavk Etnogr Sb
Kavkazsko-Blizhnevostochnyi Sbornik — KBS
Kawamata Chemical Bulletin of Leather Technology — Kawamata Chem Bull Leather Technol
Kawasaki Medical Journal — KAMJD
Kawasaki Medical Journal — Kawasaki Med J
Kawasaki Review — Kawasaki Rev
Kawasaki Rozai Technical Report — Kawasaki Rozai Tech Rep
Kawasaki Steel Technical Bulletin — Kawasaki Steel Tech Bull
Kawasaki Steel Technical Report [*Japan*] — Kawasaki Steel Tech Rep
Kawasaki Steelmaking Technical Report [*Japan*] — Kawasaki Steelmaking Tech Rep
Kawasaki Technical Review [*Japan*] — Kawasaki Tech Rev
Kazak SSR Gylym Akademijasynyn Habarlary. Izvestija Akademii Nauk Kazachskoj SSR — Kazak Ak Habarlary
Kazakhskii Gosudarstvennyi Pedagogiceskii Institut Imeni Abaja Ucenye Zapiski — Kazah Gos Ped Inst Ucen Zap
Kazakhskii Nauchno-Issledovatel'skii Institut Lesnogo Khozyaistva i Agrolesomelioratsii Trudy — Kaz Nauchno-Issled Inst Lesn Khoz Agrolesomelio Tr
Kazakhskii Nauchno-Issledovatel'skii Institut Lesnogo Khozyaistva Trudy — Kaz Nauchno-Issled Inst Lesn Khoz Tr
Kazakhskii Nauchno-Issledovatel'skii Institut Zashchity Rastenii. Trudy — Kaz Nauchno Issled Inst Zashch Rast Tr
Kazakhskii Regional'nyi Nauchno-Issledovatel'skii Institut. Trudy — Kaz Reg Nauchno Issled Inst Tr
Kazakhskii Sel'skokhozyaistvennyi Institut. Trudy — Kaz Skh Inst Tr
Kazakhstanskoe Petrograficheskoe Soveshchanie — Kaz Petrogr Soveshch
Kazanskii Gosudarstvennyi Meditsinskii Institut. Nauchnye Trudy — Kazan Gos Med Inst Nauchn Tr
Kazanskii Gosudarstvennyi Pedagogicheskii Institut. Uchenye Zapiski — Kazan Gos Pedagog Inst Uch Zap
Kazanskii Gosudarstvennyi Veterinarnyi Institut imeni N.E. Baumana. Nauchnye Trudy — Kazan Gos Vet Inst im NE Baumana Nauchn Tr
Kazanskii Meditsinskii Zhurnal — Kazan Med Z
Kazanskii Meditsinskii Zhurnal — Kazan Med Zh
Kazanskii Meditsinskii Zhurnal — Kazan Med Zhurnal
Kazanskii Ordena Trudovogo Krasnogo Znameni Gosudarstvennyi Universitet Imeni V. I. Ul'janova-Lenina Ucenye Zapiski — Kazan Gos Univ Ucen Zap
Kazanskii Universitet Issledovanija po Prikladnoi Matematike — Issled Prikl Mat
Kazanskii Universitet Issledovaniya po Teorii Plastin i Obolochek — Issled Teor Plastin i Obolochek
KBS [*Kaernbraenslesaekerhet*] **Technical Report** — KBS Tech Rep
KBS [*Kaernbraenslesaekerhet*] **Teknisk Rapport** — KBS Tek Rapp
KDD Technical Journal — KDD Tech J
Keats-Shelley Journal — Keats-Shell
Keats-Shelley Journal — Keats-Shelley J
Keats-Shelley Journal — KSJ
Keats-Shelley Journal. Annual Bibliography — Keats-Shelley J Ann Bibl
Keats-Shelley Memorial Association. Bulletin — Keats Sh M
Keats-Shelley Memorial Bulletin [*Rome*] — KSMB
Keats-Shelley Memorial Bulletin (Rome) — KSMB(R)
Keel ja Kirjandus — KjK
Keele ja Kirjanduse Instituudi Uurimused — KKIU
Keemia Teated — Keem Teated
Keeping Abreast. Journal of Human Nurturing — Keep Abreast J
Keeping Abreast. Journal of Human Nurturing — Keep Abreast J Hum Nurt
Keeping Posted for Teachers [*New York*] — KPT
Keeping Up with Orff Schulwerk in the Clasroom — KUO
Keesings Archiv der Gegenwart — KAG
Keesing's Contemporary Archives — KCA
Keesings Historisch Archief — KHA
Keewatin Echo — KE
Kehutanan Indonesia — Kehutanan Indones
Keidanren Review of Japanese Economy — KEI
Keiji Saiban Geppo — Keisai Geppo
Keiji Soshoho — Keisoho
Keikinzoku — KEIKA
Keilalphabetischen Texte aus Ugarit — KTU
Keilschriftliche Bibliothek — KB
Keilschrifttexte aus Assur. Historischen Inhalts — KAH
Keilschrifttexte aus Assur. Juristischen Inhalts — KAJ
Keilschrifttexte aus Assur. Religioesen Inhalts — KAR
Keilschrifttexte aus Assur Vverschiedenen Inhalts — KAV
Keilschrifttexte aus Boghazkoei — KBO
Keilschrifturkunden aus Boghazkoei — KUB
Keio Business Review — KBR
Keio Business Review [*Tokyo*] — Keio Bus R
Keio Economic Studies — Keio Econ S
Keio Economic Studies [*Tokyo*] — Keio Econ Stud
Keio Economic Studies — KES
Keio Engineering Reports — Keio Eng Rep
Keio Engineering Reports — Keio Engrg Rep
Keio Gijuku University [*Tokyo*]. Annual Report. Economics — An Rep Econ Keio Gijuku Univ

Keio Journal of Medicine — Keio J Med
Keio Journal of Politics — Keio J Polit
Keio Mathematical Seminar. Reports — Keio Math Sem Rep
Keio Science and Technology Reports — Keio Sci Tech Rep
Keiryo Kokugogaku [*Mathematical Linguistics*] — Ke K
Keith Shipton Developments. Special Study — Keith Shipton Dev Spec Study
KEK Annual Report (National Laboratory for High Energy Physics) — KEK Annu Rep (Natl Lab High Energy Phys)
Keleti Szemle — Kel Sz
Keleti Szemle — KS
Keleti Szemle — KSz
Kellogg Foundation International Food Research Symposium — Kellogg Found Int Food Res Symp
Kellogg Nutrition Symposium — Kellogg Nutr Symp
Kellogg Nutrition Symposium. Proceedings — Kellogg Nutr Symp Proc
KEM. Konstruktion, Elemente, Methoden — KEM Konstr Elem Methoden
KEMA [*Keuring van Elektrotechnische Materialen Arnhem*] **Publikaties** — KEMA Publ
KEMA [*Keuring van Elektrotechnische Materialen Arnhem*] **Scientific and Technical Reports** — KEMA Sci Tech Rep
Kemerovskii Gosudarstvennyi Pedagogiceskii Institut Ucenye Zapiski — Kemerov Gos Ped Inst Ucen Zap
Kemi. Revue de Philologie et d'Archeologie Egyptiennes et Coptes — Ke
Kemiai Kozlemenyek — Kem Kozl
Kemiai Kozlemenyek — Kem Kozlem
Kemia-Kemi — Kem-Kemi
Kemian Teollisuus [*Finland*] — Kem Teollisuus
Kemia-Talajtani Tanszek — Kem-Talajt
Kemija u Industriji [*Yugoslavia*] — Kem Ind
Kemikusok Lapja — Kem Lapja
Kemio Internacia — Kem Int
Kemisk Maandesblad. Nordisk Handelsblad foer Kemisk Industri — Kem Maandesbl Nord Handelsbl Kem Ind
Kemisk Maanedsblad og Nordisk Handelsblad for Kemisk Industri — Kem M
Kemisk Tidskrift — Kem Tidskr
Kemiska Vaextskyddsmedel — Kem Vaextskyddsmedel
Kenana Research Station. Annual Report — Kenana Res Stn Annu Rep
Kendall's Library of Statistics — Kendalls Lib Statist
Kenkyu Hokoku. Bulletin. Faculty of Agriculture. Tamagawa University — Kenkyu Hokoku Bull Fac Agric Tamagawa Univ
Kenkyu Hokoku. Journal. Faculty of Education. Tottori University. Natural Science — Kenkyu Hokoku J Tottori Univ Nat Sci
Kenkyu Hokoku. Journal. Niigata Agricultural Experiment Station — Kenkyu Hokoku J Niigata Agricultural Experiment Station
Kenkyu Hokoku. Research Bulletin. Hokkaido National Agricultural Experiment Station — Kenkyu Hokoku Res Bull Hokkaido Natl Agric Exp Stn
Kenkyu Hokoku. Scientific Papers. Central Research Institute. Japan Tobacco and Salt Public Corporation — Kenkyu Hokoku Sci Pap Cent Res Inst Jap Tob Salt Public Corp
Kenkyu Nempo Tokyo Daigaku Kyoiku-gabuku — KeN
Kenley Abstracts — Kenley Abstr
Kenritsu Gan Senta Niigata Byoin Ishi — KGNBA
Kent Archaeological Review — Kent A R
Kent Archaeological Review — Kent Archaeol Rev
Kent Messenger — KM
Kent Review — Kent Rev
Kent Technical Review — Kent Tech Rev
Kentucky Academy of Science. Transactions — Kentucky Acad Sci Trans
Kentucky Acts — KY Acts
Kentucky Administrative Register — KY Admin Reg
Kentucky Administrative Regulations Service — KY Admin Regs
Kentucky Agri-Business Quarterly — KY Agri-Bus Q
Kentucky Agri-Business Spotlight — KY AgriBus Spotlight
Kentucky. Agricultural Experiment Station. Annual Report — KY Agric Exp Stn Annu Rep
Kentucky. Agricultural Experiment Station. Bulletin — KY Agric Exp Stn Bull
Kentucky. Agricultural Experiment Station. Miscellaneous Publications — KY Agric Exp Stn Misc Pubs
Kentucky. Agricultural Experiment Station. Progress Report — KY Agric Exp Stn Prog Rep
Kentucky. Agricultural Experiment Station. Publications — KY Ag Exp
Kentucky. Agricultural Experiment Station. Regulatory Bulletin — KY Agric Exp Stn Regul Bull
Kentucky. Agricultural Experiment Station. Regulatory Series. Bulletin — Ky Agric Exp Stn Regul Ser Bull
Kentucky. Agricultural Experiment Station. Results of Research — KY Agric Exp Stn Results Res
Kentucky. Agricultural Extension Service. Leaflet — KY Agric Ext Serv Leafl
Kentucky Bar Journal — KBJ
Kentucky Bar Journal — KY B J
Kentucky Bench and Bar — KBB
Kentucky Bench and Bar — KY Bench and B
Kentucky Business Education Association. Journal — KBEA J
Kentucky Business Ledger — KY Bus Led
Kentucky Coal Journal — Ky Coal J
Kentucky Dental Journal — KY Dent J
Kentucky. Department of Fish and Wildlife Resources. Fisheries Bulletin — KY Dep Fish Wildl Resour Fish Bull
Kentucky. Department of Mines and Minerals. Geological Division. Bulletin — KY Dep Mines Miner Geol Div Bull
Kentucky. Department of Mines and Minerals. Geological Division. Series 8. Bulletin — KY Dep Mines Miner Geol Div Ser 8 Bull
Kentucky. Department of Mines and Resources. Geological Division. Bulletin — KY Dep Mines Resour Geol Div Bull
Kentucky Economic Information System [*Database*] — KEIS
Kentucky Economy — KY Economy
Kentucky Farm and Home Science — KY Farm Home Sci
Kentucky Folklore Record — KFR
Kentucky Folklore Record — KY Folk Rec
Kentucky Folklore Record — KY Folkl Rec
Kentucky Folklore Series — KFS
Kentucky Foreign Language Journal (Lexington) — Kentucky For Lang Jour Lexington
Kentucky Foreign Language Quarterly — KFLQ
Kentucky. Geological Survey. Bulletin — Kentucky Geol Surv Bull
Kentucky. Geological Survey. Bulletin — Kentucky Geol Survey Bull
Kentucky. Geological Survey. Bulletin — KY Geol Surv Bull
Kentucky. Geological Survey. Bulletin. Information Circular. Report of Investigations. Special Publication — KY Geol Survey Bull Inf Circ Rept Inv Special Pub
Kentucky. Geological Survey. County Report — Kentucky Geol Survey County Rept
Kentucky. Geological Survey. County Report — KY Geol Surv Cy Rep
Kentucky. Geological Survey. Information Circular — Kentucky Geol Survey Inf Circ
Kentucky. Geological Survey. Information Circular — KY Geol Surv Inf Circ
Kentucky. Geological Survey. Report of Investigations — Kentucky Geol Survey Rept Inv
Kentucky. Geological Survey. Report of Investigations — KY Geol Surv Rep Invest
Kentucky. Geological Survey. Report of Progress. Bulletin — KY G S Rp Prog B
Kentucky. Geological Survey. Series 9. Bulletin — KY Geol Surv Ser 9 Bull
Kentucky. Geological Survey. Series 9. Report of Investigation — KY Geol Surv Ser 9 Rep Invest
Kentucky. Geological Survey. Series 9. Special Publication — KY Geol Surv Ser 9 Spec Publ
Kentucky. Geological Survey. Series 10. County Report — KY Geol Surv Ser 10 Cty Rep
Kentucky. Geological Survey. Series 10. Information Circular — KY Geol Surv Ser 10 Inf Circ
Kentucky. Geological Survey. Series 10. Report of Investigation — KY Geol Surv Ser 10 Rep Invest
Kentucky. Geological Survey. Special Publication — Kentucky Geol Survey Spec Pub
Kentucky. Geological Survey. Special Publication — Ky Geol Surv Spec Publ
Kentucky. Geological Survey. Thesis Series — KY Geol Surv Thesis Ser
Kentucky Historical Society. Register — KHS
Kentucky Historical Society. Register — KHSR
Kentucky Historical Society. Register — KY Hist Soc Reg
Kentucky Historical Society. Register — KYHS
Kentucky Law Journal — Kentucky LJ
Kentucky Law Journal — KLJ
Kentucky Law Journal — KY L J
Kentucky Law Journal — KY Law J
Kentucky Law Reporter — KY L Rptr
Kentucky Library Association. Bulletin — KY Lib Assn Bull
Kentucky Library Association. Bulletin — KY Libr Ass Bull
Kentucky Medical Journal — Kentucky Med J
Kentucky Medical Journal — KY Med J
Kentucky. Nature Preserves Commission. Technical Report — KY Nat Preserv Comm Tech Rep
Kentucky Nurse — KY Nurse
Kentucky Nurses' Association. Newsletter — KY Nurses Assoc News Lett
Kentucky Nurses' Association. Newsletter — KY Nurses Assoc Newsl
Kentucky Opinions — KY Op
Kentucky Philological Association. Bulletin — KPAB
Kentucky Reports — KY
Kentucky Review — KRev
Kentucky Review — KYR
Kentucky Revised Statutes and Rules Service (Baldwin) — KY Rev Stat & R Serv (Baldwin)
Kentucky Revised Statutes, Annotated. Official Edition (Michie/Bobbs-Merrill) — KY Rev Stat Ann (Michie/Bobbs-Merrill)
Kentucky Romance Quarterly — KRQ
Kentucky Romance Quarterly — KY Roman Q
Kentucky School Journal — KY Sch J
Kentucky State Historical Society. Register — KSHSR
Kentucky State Historical Society. Register — KY Reg
Kentucky State Historical Society. Register — Ky State Hist Soc Reg
Kentucky. University. College of Agriculture. Cooperative Extension Service. Report — KY Univ Coll Agric Coop Ext Serv Rep
Kentucky University. Office of Research and Engineering Services. Bulletin — KY Univ Off Res Eng Serv Bull
Kentucky University. Office of Research and Engineering Services. Bulletin — KY Univ Office Res Eng Services Bull
Kentucky Warbler — KY Warbler
Kenya and East African Medical Journal — Kenya and East African Med J
Kenya. Colony and Protectorate. Department of Agriculture. Bulletin — Kenya Colony Prot Dep Agric Bull
Kenya. Colony and Protectorate. Geological Survey. Memoir — Kenya Colony Prot Geol Surv Mem
Kenya. Colony and Protectorate. Mining and Geological Department. Geological Survey of Kenya. Report — Kenya Colony Prot Min Geol Dep Geol Surv Kenya Rep
Kenya. Department of Agriculture. Annual Report — KARRAA
Kenya. Department of Agriculture. Annual Report — Kenya Dep Agric Annu Rep
Kenya Farmer — Kenya Fmr
Kenya. Geological Survey of Kenya. Bulletin — Kenya Geol Surv Kenya Bull
Kenya. Geological Survey of Kenya. Memoir — Kenya Geol Surv Kenya Mem

Kenya. Geological Survey of Kenya. Report — Kenya Geol Surv Kenya Rep
Kenya Historical Review — Kenya Hist Rev
Kenya Information Services. Bulletin — Kenya Inform Serv Bull
Kenya Institute of Administration — Kenya Inst Admin
Kenya Journal of Science and Technology. Series B. Biological Sciences — Kenya J Sci Technol Ser B Biol Sci
Kenya Journal of Science and Technology. Series B. Biological Sciences — KSTSDG
Kenya Medical Journal — Kenya Med J
Kenya. Mines and Geological Department. Report — Kenya Mines Geol Dep Rep
Kenya Nursing Journal — Kenya Nurs J
Kenya Regional Studies — Kenya Reg Stud
Kenya Review — Kenya R
Kenya Tuberculosis and Respiratory Diseases Research Centre. Annual Report — ARKCEB
Kenya. Tuberculosis and Respiratory Diseases Research Centre. Annual Report — Kenya Tuberc Respir Dis Res Cent Ann Rep
Kenya Tuberculosis Investigation Centre. Annual Report — ARKCDA
Kenya. Tuberculosis Investigation Centre. Annual Report — Kenya Tuberc Invest Cent Annu Rep
Kenyon Review — KenR
Kenyon Review — Kenyon R
Kenyon Review — Kenyon Rev
Kenyon Review — KR
Kenyon Review — PKEN
Kep- es Hangtechnika — Kep es Hangtech
Kerala Journal of Veterinary Science — Kerala J Vet Sci
Kerala Journal of Veterinary Science — KJVSA
Kerala Law Times — Ker LT
Kerala Law Times — KLT
Keramicheskaya Promyshlennost. Promyshlennost Stroitel'nykh Materialov — Keram Promst Promst Stroit Mater
Keramicheskaya Promyshlennost. Referativnaya Informatsiya — Keram Promst Ref Inf
Keramicheskii Sbornik — Keram Sb
Keramik Magazin — Keram Mag
Keramik und Glas (Moscow) — Keram Glas (Moscow)
Keramika i Steklo — Keram Steklo
Keramisch Instituut TNO. Mededelingen — Keram Inst TNO Meded
Keramische Rundschau — Keram Rundsch
Keramische Rundschau und Kunst-Keramik — Keram Rundsch Kunst-Keram
Keramische Zeitschrift — Keram Z
Keramische Zeitschrift. Beilage — Keram Z Beil
Kerk en Theologie [*Wageningen*] — KTh
Kerk en Theologie [*Wageningen*] — KTheol
Kerk en Wereld Reeks — KWR
Kerkehistoriske Samlinger — KHS
Kerkhistorisch Archief — KHAr
Kerkhistorische Studien — KH St
Kerkyraika Chronika — KerC
Kermisgids — UTD
Kern — KER
Kern Citrus. Cooperative Extension. University of California — Kern Citrus Coop Ext Univ Calif
Kern Cotton. University of California. Cooperative Extension Service — Kern Cotton Univ Calif Coop Ext Serv
Kern Irrigation. Cooperative Extension. University of California — Kern Irrig Coop Ext Univ Calif
Kernenergie — Kernenerg
Kernenergie. Beilage [*Germany*] — Kernenerg Beil
Kernenergie. Beilage — Kernenergie Beil
Kernenergie-Ingenieur — Kernenerg Ing
Kernforschungsanlage Juelich. Berichte Juel — Kernforschungsanlage Juelich Ber Juel
Kernforschungsanlage Juelich. Jahresbericht — Kernforschungsanlage Juelich Jahresber
Kernforschungsanlage Juelich. Spezielle Berichte — Kernforschungsanlage Juelich Spez Ber
Kernforschungszentrum Karlsruhe. Bericht — Kernforschungsz Karlsruhe Ber
Kernforschungszentrum Karlsruhe. Bericht KfK — Kernforschungszent Karlsruhe Ber KfK
Kernforschungszentrum Karlsruhe. Externer Bericht — Kernforschungszent Karlsruhe Externer Ber
Kernforschungszentrum Karlsruhe. Nachrichten — Kernforschungszent Karlsruhe Nachr
Kerngetallen van Nederlandse Effecten (Amsterdam) — AKG
Kernontwikkelingskorporasie van Suid-Afrika. Verslag PEL — Kernontwikkelingskorporasie S Afr Versl PEL
Kernontwikkelingskorporasie van Suid-Afrika. Verslag PER — Kernontwikkelingskorporasie S Afr Versl PER
Kerntechnik, Isotopentechnik, und Chemie — Kerntech Isotopentech Chem
Kerntechnik, Isotopentechnik, und Chemie — Kerntechnik Isotopentech Chem
Kerntechnik und Isotopentechnik — Kerntech Isotopentech
Kerntechnik Vereinigt mit Atompraxis — Kerntech Atomprax
Kerntechnische Normung Informationen [*Germany*] — Kerntech Normung Inf
Kerry Archaeological and Historical Society. Journal — Kerry Arch Hist Soc J
Kerry Archaeological Magazine — Kerry Arch Mag
Kerteszet es Szoeleszet — Kert Szoelesz
Kerteszeti Egyetem Kozlemenyei — Kert Egy Kozl
Kerteszeti Egyetem Kozlemenyei — Kertesz Egyet Kozl
Kerteszeti es Szoeleszeti Foeiskola Evkoenyve. Annales Academiae Horti- et Viticulturae — Kert Szoelesz Foeisk Evk
Kerteszeti es Szoleszeti Foiskola Evkoryve — Kert Szolesz Foiskola Evk
Kerteszeti es Szoleszeti Foiskola Evkoryve — Kertesz Szolesz Foisk
Kerteszeti es Szoleszeti Foiskola Kozlemenyei — Kert Szolesz Foiskola Kozl
Kerteszeti es Szoleszeti Foiskola Kozlemenyei — Kertesz Szolesz Foisk Kozl
Kerteszeti Fuezetek — Kert Fuez
Kerteszeti Irodalmi Tajekoztato — Kert Irod Tajekozt
Kerteszgazda Nep Kertesze — Kerteszgazda Nep Kert
Kerygma und Dogma — K D
Kerygma und Dogma — Ke Do
Kerygma und Dogma — KerDo
Kerygma und Dogma [*Goettingen*] — KuD
Kerygma und Dogma. Beiheft — Ku D B
Kerygma und Mythos — Ku M
Keston News Service — Keston News
Keszthelyi Mezoegazdasagi Akademia Koezlemenyei — Keszthelyi Mezoegazd Akad Koezlem
Keszthelyi Mezogazdasagi Akademia Kiadvanyai — Keszthelyi Mezogazd Akad Kiad
Keszthelyi Mezogazdasagtudomanyi Kar Kozlemenyei — Keszthelyi Mezogazdasagtud Kar Kozl
Kettering International Symposium on Nitrogen Fixation — Kettering Int Symp Nitrogen Fixation
Keukenkompas. Vakblad voor Inbouwkeukens, Inbouwapparatuur, en Accessoires — KOK
Keuring van Elektrotechnische Materialen. Scientific and Technical Reports — Keuring Elektrotech Mater Sci Tech Rep
Kevo Notes — KEVN
Kevo Subarctic Research Station. Reports — KSRS
Kew Bulletin — KB
Kew Bulletin — Kew Bull
Kew Bulletin. Additional Series — Kew Bull Addit Ser
Kew Bulletin. Royal Botanic Gardens — Kew Bull R Bot Gard
Kew Magazine — Kew Mag
Kexue Shiyan — KHSYA
Kexue Tongbao [*Foreign Language Edition*] — KHTPBU
Kexue Tongbao (Chinese Edition) — Kexue Tongbao (Chin Ed)
Kexue Tongbao (Foreign Language Edition) — Kexue Tongbao (Foreign Lang Ed)
Key British Enterprises [*Database*] — KBE
Key Engineering Materials — Key Eng Mater
Key Notes Donemus — Key Notes
Key Texts. Classic Studies in the History of Ideas — Key Texts Classic Stud Hist Ideas
Key to Christian Education — Key
Key to Economic Science — ERB
Key to Economic Science — Key Econ Sci
Key to Economic Science and Managerial Sciences — Key Econ Sci Manage Sci
Key to Oceanographic Records Documentation — Key Oceanogr Rec Doc
Key to Oceanographic Records Documentation — KORADQ
Key Word Index of Wildlife Research — Key Word Index Wildl Res
Keyboard — K
Keyboard — KEYRA
Keyboard Classics — KC
Keyboard Magazine — Key
Keyboard Magazine — Keybd Mag
Keynotes — KeN
Keystone Folklore Quarterly — KFQ
Keystone News Bulletin [*United States*] — Keystone News Bull
Keyword Index for the Medical Literature — Keyword Index Med Lit
Keyword Index in Internal Medicine — Keyword Index Intern Med
KFA (Kernforschungsanlage) Jahresbericht — KFA Jahresber
KFAS [*Kuwait Foundation for the Advancement of Sciences*] **Proceedings Series** — KFAS Proc Ser
KFK [*Kernforschungszentrum Karlsruhe*] **Hausmitteilungen** — KFK Hausmitt
KFK [*Kernforschungszentrum Karlsruhe*] **Nachrichten** — KFK Nachr
KFKI [*Kozponti Fizikai Kutato Intezet*] **Kozlemenyek** — KFKI Kozl
KFKI [*Kozponti Fizikai Kutato Intezet*] **Report** — KFKI Rep
KFT. Kraftfahrzeugtechnik — KFT
KFT. Kraftfahrzeugtechnik — KFT Kraftfahrztech
KFT. Kraftfahrzeugtechnik — KKRTD
KGS-NCIC [*Kentucky Geological Survey. National Cartographic Information Center*] **Newsletter** — KGS NCIC Newsl
Khadi Gramodyong [*India*] — Khadi Gram
Khaleej Times — KT
Kharchova Promyslovist — Kharchova Promst
Khar'kovskii Institut Mekhanizatsii i Elektrifikatsii Sel'skogo Khozyaistva Nauchnye Zapiski — Khar'k Inst Mekh Elektrif Sel'sk Khoz Nauchn Zap
Khar'kovskii Meditsinskii Institut Trudy — Khar'k Med Inst Tr
Khar'kovskii Ordena Trudovogo Krasnogo Znameni Gosudarstvennyi Universitet Imeni A. M. Gor'kogo Teoriya Funktsii Funktsional'nyi Analiz i Ikh Prilozheniya — Teor Funktsii Funktsional Anal i Prilozhen
Khar'kovskii Ordena Trudovogo Krasnogo Znameni Gosudarstvennyi Universitet Imeni A.M. Gor'kogo Radiotekhnika — Radiotekhn
Khayats Oriental Reprints — Kor
Khayats Oriental Translations — KOT
Kheberleri Izvestiya [*Former USSR*] — Kheberleri Izv
Khematologiya i Kruvoprelivane — Khematol Kruvoprelivane
Khersonesskii Sbornik. Materialy po Arkheologii Khersonesa Tavricheskogo — KhSB
KHI [*Kawasaki Heavy Industries*] **Technical Review** [*Japan*] — KHI Tech Rev
Khidrologiya i Meteorologiya — Khidrol Met
Khidrologiya i Meteorologiya — Khidrol Meteorol
Khidrologiya i Meteorologiya — KHMEA
Khigiena. Epidemiologiya i Mikrobiologiya — Khig Epidemiol Mikrobiol
Khigiena i Zdraveopazvane — Khig Zdraveopaz
Khigiena i Zdraveopazvane — Khig Zdraveopazvane
Khimicheskaia Tekhnologiia — Khim Tekhnol
Khimicheskaya Geografiya i Gidrogeokhimiya — Khim Geogr Gidrogeokhim

Khimicheskaya i Mekhanicheskaya Pererabotka Drevesiny i Drevesnykh Otkhodov — Khim Mekh Pererab Drev Drev Otkhodov
Khimicheskaya Nauka i Promyshlennost — Khim Nauka Prom-St
Khimicheskaya Pererabotka Drevesiny — Khim Pererab Drev
Khimicheskaya Pererabotka Drevesiny Nauchno-Tekhnicheskii Sbornik [*Former USSR*] — Khim Pererab Drev Nauchno-Tekh Sb
Khimicheskaya Promyshlennost — Khim Prom
Khimicheskaya Promyshlennost (Moscow) — Khim Promst (Moscow)
Khimicheskaya Promyshlennost Seriya Anilinokrasochnaya Promyshlennost — Khim Promst Ser Anilinokras Promst
Khimicheskaya Promyshlennost Seriya Avtomatizatsiya Khimicheskikh Proizvodstv. Nauchno-Tekhnicheskii Referativnyi Sbornik — Khim Promst Ser Avtom Khim Proizvod
Khimicheskaya Promyshlennost Seriya Azotnaya Promyshlennost. Nauchno-Tekhnicheskii Referativnyi Sbornik — Khim Promst Ser Azotn Promst
Khimicheskaya Promyshlennost Seriya Fosfornaya Promyshlennost — Khim Promst Ser Fosfornaya Promst
Khimicheskaya Promyshlennost Seriya Fosfornaya Promyshlennost. Nauchno-Tekhnicheskii Referativnyi Sbornik — Khim Promst Ser Fosfornaya Promst
Khimicheskaya Promyshlennost Seriya Kaliinaya Promyshlennost. Nauchno-Tekhnicheskii Referativnyi Sbornik — Khim Promst Ser Kaliinaya Promst
Khimicheskaya Promyshlennost Seriya Khimiya i Tekhnologiya Izotopov i Mechenykh Soedinenii — Khim Promst Ser Khim Tekhnol Izot Mechenykh Soedin
Khimicheskaya Promyshlennost Seriya Khimiya i Tekhnologiya Lyuminoforov i Chistykh Neorganicheskikh Materialov. Nauchno-Tekhnicheskii Referativnyi Sbornik — Khim Promst Ser Khim Tekhnol Lyuminoforov Chist Neorg Mater
Khimicheskaya Promyshlennost Seriya Khlornaya Promyshlennost. Nauchno-Tekhnicheskii Referativnyi Sbornik — Khim Promst Ser Khlornaya Promst
Khimicheskaya Promyshlennost Seriya Kislorodnaya Promyshlennost. Nauchno-Tekhnicheskii Referativnyi Sbornik — Khim Promst Ser Kislorodn Promst
Khimicheskaya Promyshlennost. Seriya. Okhrana Okruzhayushchei Sredy i Ratsional'noe Ispol'zovanie Prirodnykh Resursov — Khim Promst Ser Okhr Okruzh Sredy Ratsion Ispol'z Prir Resur
Khimicheskaya Promyshlennost Seriya Proizvodstvo i Pererabotka Plastmass i Sinteticheskikh Smol. Nauchno-Tekhnicheskii Referativnyi Sbornik — Khim Promst Ser Proizvod Pererab Plastmass Sint Smol
Khimicheskaya Promyshlennost Seriya Promyshlennost Gornokhimicheskogo Syr'ya. Nauchno-Tekhnicheskii Referativnyi Sbornik — Khim Promst Ser Promst Gornokhim Syrya
Khimicheskaya Promyshlennost Seriya Promyshlennost Khimicheskikh Volokon. Nauchno-Tekhnicheskii Referativnyi Sbornik — Khim Promst Ser Promst Khim Volokon
Khimicheskaya Promyshlennost Seriya Promyshlennost Mineral'nykh Udobrenii i Sernoi Kosloty. Nauchno-Tekhnicheskii Referativnyi Sbornik — Khim Promst Ser Promst Miner Udobr Sernoi Kosloty
Khimicheskaya Promyshlennost Seriya Promyshlennost Tovarov Bytovoi Khimii. Nauchno-Tekhnicheskii Referativnyi Sbornik — Khim Promst Ser Promst Tovarov Bytovoi Khim
Khimicheskaya Promyshlennost Seriya Reaktivy i Osobo Chistye Veshchestva. Nauchno-Tekhnicheskii Referativnyi Sbornik — Khim Promst Ser Reakt Osobo Chist Veshchestva
Khimicheskaya Promyshlennost Seriya Sistemy i Sredstva Avtomatizatsii Khimicheskikh Proizvodstv — Khim Promst Ser Sist Sredstva Avtom Khim Proizvod
Khimicheskaya Promyshlennost Seriya Stekloplastiki i Steklovokno, Obzornaya Informatsiya — Khim Promst Ser Stekloplast Steklovokno Obz Inf
Khimicheskaya Promyshlennost Seriya Toksikologiya i Sanitarnaya Khimiya Plastmass. Nauchno-Tekhnicheskii Referativnyi Sbornik — Khim Promst Ser Toksikol Sanit Khim Plastmass
Khimicheskaya Promyshlennost' Ukrainy — Khim Prom-St' Ukr
Khimicheskaya Promyshlennost za Rubezhom — Khim Promst Rubezhom
Khimicheskaya Svyaz' v Kristallakh i Ikh Fizicheskie Svojstva — Khim Svyaz' Krist Fiz Svoj
Khimicheskaya Tekhnologiya Biologicheski Aktivnykh Soedinenii — Khim Tekhnol Biol Akt Soedin
Khimicheskaya Tekhnologiya i Khimiya — Khim Tekhnol Khim
Khimicheskaya Tekhnologiya (Kharkov) [*Ukrainian SSR*] — Khim Tekhnol (Kharkov)
Khimicheskaya Tekhnologiya (Kiev) [*Ukrainian SSR*] — Khim Tekhnol (Kiev)
Khimicheskaya Tekhnologiya. Nauchno-Proizvodstvennyi Sbornik — Khim Tekhnol Nauchno Proizvod Sb
Khimicheskaya Tekhnologiya Pererabotki Nefti i Gaza — Khim Tekhnol Pererab Nefti Gaza
Khimicheskaya Tekhnologiya. Respublikanskii Mezhvedomstvennyi Nauchno-Tekhnicheskii Sbornik — Khim Tekhnol Resp Mezhved Nauchno Tekh Sb
Khimicheskaya Tekhnologiya Svoistva i Primenenie Plastmass — Khim Tekhnol Svoistva Primen Plastmass
Khimicheskaya Tekhnologiya Voloknistykh Materialov — Khim Tekhnol Voloknistykh Mater
Khimicheskaya Termodinamika i Ravnovesiya — Khim Termodin Ravnovesiya
Khimicheskie Ochistki Teploenergeticheskogo Oborudovaniya — Khim Ochistki Teploenerg Oborud
Khimicheskie Produkty Koksovaniya Uglei Vostoka SSSR — Khim Prod Koksovaniya Uglei Vostoka SSSR
Khimicheskie Reaktivy i Preparaty — Khim Reakt Prep
Khimicheskie Signaly Zhivotnykh — Khim Signal Zhivotn
Khimicheskie Sredstva Zashchity Rastenii — Khim Sredstva Zashch Rast
Khimicheskie Volokna — Khim Volokna
Khimicheskie Volokna. Seriya Monografii — Khim Volokna Ser Monogr
Khimicheskii Referativnyi Zhurnal — Khim Ref Zh
Khimicheskii Zhurnal. Seriya A — Khim Zh Ser A
Khimicheskii Zhurnal. Seriya B — Khim Zh Ser B
Khimicheskii Zhurnal. Seriya G — Khim Zh Ser G
Khimicheskii Zhurnal. Seriya V — Khim Zh Ser V
Khimicheskoe i Neftyanoe Mashinostroenie — Khim i Neft Mashinostr
Khimicheskoe i Neftyanoe Mashinostroenie — Khim Neft Mashinostr
Khimicheskoe Mashinostroenie — KMMRA
Khimicheskoe Mashinostroenie (Kiev) — Khim Mashinostr (Kiev)
Khimicheskoe Mashinostroenie (Moscow) — Khim Mashinostr (Moscow)
Khimicheskoe Mashinostroenie. Moskovskii Institut Khimicheskogo Mashinostroeniya — Khim Mash Mosk Inst Khim Mash
Khimicheskoe Mashinostroenie Moskovskii Institut Khimicheskogo Mashinostroeniya — Khim Mashinostr Mosk Inst Khim Mashinostr
Khimicheskoe, Neftepererabatyvayushchee i Polimernoe Mashinostroenie — Khim Neftepererab Polim Mashinostr
Khimichna Promislovist (Kiev) — Khim Promst (Kiev)
Khimichna Promislovist. Naukovo-Tekhnichnii Zbirnik — Khim Promst Nauk Tekh Zb
Khimichna Promislovist Ukraini — Khim Promst Ukr
Khimichnii Zbirnik. L'vivs'kii Derzhavnii Universitet — Khim Zb Lviv Derzh Univ
Khimiko Farmatsevticheskaya Promyshlennost — Khim Farm Promst
Khimiko-Farmatsevticheskii Zhurnal — Khim-Far Zh
Khimiko-Farmatsevticheskii Zhurnal — Khim-Farm Zh
Khimiko-Okeanologicheskie Issledovaniya. Materialy Vsesoyuznoi Konferentsii po Khimii Morei i Okeanov — Khim Okeanol Issled Mater Vses Konf Khim Morei Okeanov
Khimiko-Termicheskaya Obrabotka Stali i Splavov — Khim Term Obrab Stali Splavov
Khimiya Belka — Khim Belka
Khimiya Drevesiny — Khim Drev
Khimiya Elementoorganicheskikh Soedinenii — Khim Elementoorg Soedin
Khimiya Geterotsiklicheskikh Soedinenii — Khim Geterotsikl Soedin
Khimiya Geterotsiklicheskikh Soedinenii — Khim Geterotsiklich Soedin
Khimiya Geterotsiklicheskikh Soedinenii Akademiya Nauk Latviiskoi SSR [*Latvian SSR*] — Khim Geterotsikl Soedin Akad Nauk Latv SSR
Khimiya Geterotsiklicheskikh Soedinenii. Sbornik — Khim Geterot Soed
Khimiya Geterotsiklicheskikh Soedinenii Sbornik — Khim Geterotsikl Soedin Sb
Khimiya Geterotsiklicheskikh Soedineniya — Khim Getero
Khimiya i Fiziko-Khimiya Prirodnykh i Sinteticheskikh Polimerov — Khim Fiz-Khim Prir Sint Polim
Khimiya i Industriya — Khim Ind
Khimiya i Industriya (Sofia) — Khim Ind (Sofia)
Khimiya i Khimicheskaya Tekhnologiya (Alma-Ata) — Khim Khim Tekhnol (Alma-Ata)
Khimiya i Khimicheskaya Tekhnologiya (Cheboksary, USSR) — Khim Khim Teknol (Cheboksary USSR)
Khimiya i Khimicheskaya Tekhnologiya (Drevesiny) [*Former USSR*] — Khim Khim Tekhnol (Drev)
Khimiya i Khimicheskaya Tekhnologiya (Ivanovo, USSR) — Khim Khim Tekhnol (Ivanovo USSR)
Khimiya i Khimicheskaya Tekhnologiya (Lvov) — Khim Khim Tekhnol (Lvov)
Khimiya i Khimicheskaya Tekhnologiya (Minsk) — Khim Khim Tekhnol (Minsk)
Khimiya i Khimicheskaya Tekhnologiya (Tomsk) — Khim Khim Tekhnol (Tomsk)
Khimiya i Meditsina — Khim Med
Khimiya i Oborona — Khim Oborona
Khimiya i Pererabotka Topliv — Khim Pererab Topl
Khimiya i Prakticheskoe Primenenie Kremneorganicheskikh Soedinenii. Trudy Konferentsii — Khim Prakt Primen Kremneorg Soedin Tr Konf
Khimiya i Primenenie Elementoorganicheskikh Soedinenii — Khim Primen Elementoorg Soedin
Khimiya i Primenenie Fosfororganicheskikh Soedinenii. Trudy Konferentsii — Khim Primen Fosfororg Soedin Tr Konf
Khimiya i Primenenie Fosfororganicheskikh Soedinenii. Trudy Yubileinoi Konferentsii — Khim Primen Fosfororg Soedin Tr Yubileinoi Konf
Khimiya i Tekhnologiya Bumagi — Khim Tekhnol Bum
Khimiya i Tekhnologiya Drevesiny Tsellyulozy i Bumagi — Khim Tekhnol Drev Tsellyul Bum
Khimiya i Tekhnologiya Elementoorganicheskikh Soedinenii i Polimerov — Khim Tekhnol Elementoorg Soedin Polim
Khimiya i Tekhnologiya Goryuchikh Slantsev i Produktov Ikh Pererabotki [*Former USSR*] — Khim Tekhnol Goryuch Slantsev Prod Ikh Pererab
Khimiya i Tekhnologiya Izotopov i Mechenykh Soedinenii. Referativnyi Sbornik — Khim Tekhnol Izot Mechenykh Soedin
Khimiya i Tekhnologiya Kondensirovannykh Fosfatov. Trudy Vsesoyuznogo Soveshchaniya po Fosfatam (Kondensirovannym) — Khim Tekhnol Kondens Fosfatov Tr Vses Soveshch
Khimiya i Tekhnologiya Krasheniya, Sinteza Krasitelei, i Polimernykh Materialov — Khim Tekhnol Krasheniya Sint Krasitelei Polim Mater
Khimiya i Tekhnologiya Molibdena i Vol'frama — Khim Tekhnol Molbdena Vol'frama
Khimiya i Tekhnologiya Neorganicheskikh Proizvodstv — Khim Tekhnol Neorg Proizvod
Khimiya i Tekhnologiya Oksidnykh Magnitnykh Materialov — Khim Tekhnol Oksidnykh Magn Mater
Khimiya i Tekhnologiya Organicheskikh Proizvodstv — Khim Tekhnol Org Proizvod
Khimiya i Tekhnologiya Produktov Organicheskogo Sinteza, Poluprodukty dlya Sinteza Poliamidov — Khim Tekhnol Prod Org Sint Poluprod Sint Poliamidov
Khimiya i Tekhnologiya Topliv i Masel — Khim i Tekhnol Topliv i Masel
Khimiya i Tekhnologiya Topliv i Masel [*Former USSR*] — Khim Tekhnol Top Masel
Khimiya i Tekhnologiya Topliv i Masel — Khim Tekhnol Topl Masel
Khimiya i Tekhnologiya Topliva — Khim Tekhnol Topl
Khimiya i Tekhnologiya Topliva i Produktov Ego Pererabotki — Khim Tekhnol Topl Prod Ego Pererab
Khimiya i Tekhnologiya Tsellyulozy — Khim Tekhnol Tsellyul

Khimiya i Tekhnologiya Tsellyulozy i Volokna — Khim Tekhnol Tsellyul Volokna
Khimiya i Tekhnologiya Vody — Khim Tekhnol Vody
Khimiya i Tekhnologiya Vysokomolekulyarnykh Soedinenii — Khim Tekhnol Vysokomol Soedin
Khimiya i Termodinamika Rastvorov — Khim Termodin Rast
Khimiya i Termodinamika Rastvorov — Khim Termodin Rastvorov
Khimiya i Zhizn — Khim Zhizn
Khimiya, Nauchnye Doklady, Gertsenovskie Chteniya — Khim Nauchn Dokl Gertsenovskie Chteniya
Khimiya Nepredel'nykh Soedinenii — Khim Nepredelnykh Soedin
Khimiya Plazmy — Khim Plazmy
Khimiya Plazmy Sbornik Statej — Khim Plazmy
Khimiya Prirodnykh Soedinenii — Khim Prir S
Khimiya Prirodnykh Soedinenii — Khim Prir Soedin
Khimiya Prirodnykh Soedinenii — Khim Prirod Soed
Khimiya Prirodnykh Soedinenii (Tashkent) — Khim Prir Soedin (Tashk)
Khimiya. Proizvodstvu — Khim Proizvod
Khimiya Rastvorov — Khim Rastvorov
Khimiya Rastvorov Redkozemel'nykh Elementov — Khim Rastvorov Redkozem Elem
Khimiya Redkikh Elementov — Khim Redk Elem
Khimiya Sera- i Azotorganicheskikh Soedinenii Soderzhashchikhsiya v Neftyakh i Nefteproduktakh — Khim Sera Azotorg Soedin Soderzh Neftyakh Nefteprod
Khimiya Seraorganicheskikh Soedinenii, Soderzhashchikhsya v Neftyakh i Nefteproduktakh [*Former USSR*] — Khim Seraorg Soedin Soderzh Neftyakh Nefteprod
Khimiya Trudyashchimsya — Khim Trudyashchimsya
Khimiya Tverdogo Tela — Khim Tverd Tela
Khimiya Tverdogo Topliva (Leningrad) — Khim Tverd Topl (Leningrad)
Khimiya Tverdogo Topliva (Moscow) — Khim Tverd Topl (Moscow)
Khimiya v Interesakh Ustoichivogo Razvitiya — Khim Interesakh Ustoich Razvit
Khimiya v Sel'skom Khozyaistve — Khim Sel'Khoz
Khimiya v Sel'skom Khozyaistve — Khim Sel'sk Khoz
Khimiya v Shkole — Khim Shk
Khimiya Vysokikh Ehnergij — Khim Vys Ehnerg
Khimiya Vysokikh Energij — Khim Vys Energ
Khimizatsiya Sel'skogo Khozyaistva — Khim Selsk Khoz
Khimizatsiya Sel'skogo Khozyaistva Bashkirii — Khim Sel'sk Khoz Bashk
Khimizatsiya Sotsialisticheskogo Zemledeliya — Khim Sots Zemled
Khirurgicheskaia Lietopis — Khir Lietop
Khirurgiya — KHIGA
Khirurgiya [*Moscow*] — KHIRAE
Khirurgiya Zhelchevyvodyashchikh Putei — Khir Zhelchevyvodyashchikh Putei
Khlebopekarnaya i Konditerskaya Promyshlennost — Khlebopek Konditer Promst
Khlebopekarnaya i Konditerskaya Promyshlennost — Khlebopek Kondter Promst
Khlebopekarnaya i Konditerskaya Promyshlennost — Khlebopekar Konditer Prom
Khlebopekarnaya Promyshlennost — Khlebopek Promst
Khlopehatobumazhnaya Promyshlennost — Khlopehatobuma Promst
Khlopkovaya Promyshlennost — Khlopk Promst
Khlopkovodstvo — Khlopkovod
Khlopkovoe Delo — Khlopk Delo
Khlopkovuyu Nezavisimost, Za — Khlopk Nezavisimost Za
Kholodil'naya Promyshlennost — Kholod Promst
Kholodil'naya Tekhnika [*Former USSR*] — Kholod Tekh
Kholodil'naya Tekhnika — Kholod Tekhn
Kholodil'naya Tekhnika i Tekhnologiya [*Ukrainian SSR*] — Kholod Tekh Tekhnol
Khranitelna Promishlenost — Khranit Prom
Khranitelna Promishlenost — Khranit Prom-St
Khranitelna Promishlenost — Khranitelna Prom-St
Khranitelnopromishlena Nauka — Khranitelnoprom Nauka
Khristianskoe Chtenie — Kh Ch
Khristianskoe Tchtenie — KT
Khronika VOZ [*Vsemirnoj Organisatsij Zdravookhraneniya*] — Khron VOZ
Ki, Klima, Kaelte, Heizung — Ki Klima Kaelte Heiz
Ki, Klima, und Kaelte-Ingenieur — Ki Klima Kaelte Ing
Ki, Klima, und Kaelte-Ingenieur — KLKIA
Kiangsi Journal of Traditional Chinese Medicine — Kiangsi J Tradit Chin Med
Kibernetika i Avtomatika — Kibern Avtom
Kibernetika i Sistemnyi Analiz — Kibernet Sistem Anal
Kibernetika i Vychislitel'naya Tekhnika — Kibern i Vychisl Tekh
Kibernetika i Vychislitel'naya Tekhnika [*Ukrainian SSR*] — Kibern Vychisl Tekh
Kibernetika i Vychislitel'naya Tekhnika — Kibernet i Vychisl Tekhn
Kibernetika i Vycislitel'naya Tehnika — Kibernet i Vycisl Tehn
Kidma. Israel Journal of Development — Kidma Isr J Dev
Kidney and Blood Pressure Research — Kidney Blood Pressure Res
Kidney Disease — KIDID6
Kidney Disease — Kidney Dis
Kidney International — Kidney Int
Kidney International. Supplement — Kidney Int Suppl
Kieferchirurgie — Kieferchir
Kieler Beitraege — Kieler Beitr
Kieler Beitraege zur Anglistik und Amerikanistik — KBAA
Kieler Blaetter — Kieler Bl
Kieler Blaetter — Kieler Blaett
Kieler Meeresforschungen — Kiel Meeresforsch
Kieler Meeresforschungen — KM
Kieler Meeresforschungen, Sonderheft — Kiel Meeresforsch Sonderh
Kieler Milchwirtschaftliche Forschungsberichte — Kiel Milchwirtsch Forschungsber
Kieler Milchwirtschaftliche Forschungsberichte — KMFB
Kieler Notizen zur Pflanzenkunde in Schleswig Holstein — Kiel Not Pflanzenkd Schleswig Holstein
Kieler Rechtswissenschaftliche Abhandlungen — Kieler Rechtswiss Abh
Kieler Studien zur Deutschen Literaturgeschichte — Kieler Studien
Kieler Studien zur Deutschen Literaturgeschichte — KSDL
Kieler Zeitschriftenverzeichnis — KIZV
KIER [*Korea Institute of Energy and Resources*] **Miscellaneous Report** — KIER Misc Rep
Kierkegaardiana — Kie
Kierunki — Ki
Kiev Universitet Visnik Seriya Geografi — Kiev Univ Visn Ser Geogr
Kievski Politekhnicheskii Institut Adaptivnye Sistemy Avtomaticheskogo Upravleniya — Adapt Sistemy Avtomat Upravleniya
Kievskii Gosudarstvennyi Universitet Mezhvedomstvennyi Nauchnyi Sbornik Vychislitel'naya i Prikladnaya Matematika — Vychisl Prikl Mat
Kiewskia Uniwersitetskia Izwestia — Kiewsk Univers Izwestia
KIGAM [*Korea Research Institute of Geoscience and Mineral Resources*] **Bulletin** [*A publication*] — KIGAM Bull
Kiito Kensajo Kenkyu Hokoku. Research Reports of the Silk Conditioning Houses — Kiito Kensajo Kenkyu Hokoku Res Rep Silk Cond
Kiivs'kii Derzhavnii Universitet Imeni T. G. Shevchenka Naukovi Shchorichnik — Kiiv Derzh Univ Im T G Shevchenka Nauk Shchorichnik
Kiivs'kii Derzhavnii Universitet. Naukovi Zapiski — Kiiv Derzh Univ Nauk Zap
Kiivs'kii Derzhavnii Universitet Students'ki Naukovi Pratsi — Kiiv Derzh Univ Stud Nauk Pr
Kilkenny and South-East of Ireland Archaeological Society. Journal — Kilkenny SE Ir Arch Soc J
Kilobaud Microcomputing — Kilobaud Microcomput
Kimball's Dairy Farmer — Kimball's D F
Kimiya, Handasa Kimit — Kim Handasa Kim
Kimya Annali — Kim Ann
Kimya Muhendisligi [*Turkey*] — Kim Muhendisligi
Kimya ve Sanayi [*Turkey*] — Kim Sanayi
Kinatuinamot Illengajuk — KI
Kinderaerztliche Praxis — Kinderaerztl Prax
Kindergarten and First Grade — Kind and First Grade
Kindergarten Primary Magazine — Kind M
Kindler Taschenbuecher Geist und Psyche — Kindler Tb
Kindlers Literatur Lexikon — KLL
Kindling Symposium — Kindling Symp
Kinematika i Fizika Nebesnykh Tel — Kinemat Fiz Nebesn Tel
Kinematika i Fizika Nebesnykh Tel — Kinematika Fiz Nebesnykh Tel
Kinesitherapie Scientifique — Kinesither Sci
Kinetics and Catalysis — Kinet Catal
Kinetics and Catalysis (English Translation) — Kinet Catal (Engl Transl)
Kinetics and Catalysis in Microheterogeneous Systems — Kinet Catal Microheterog Syst
Kinetics and Catalysis (Translation of Kinetika i Kataliz) — Kinet Catal Transl of Kinet Katal
Kinetics and Mechanisms of Polymerization — Kinet Mech Polym
Kinetika Goreniya Iskopaemykh Topliv — Kinet Goreniya Iskop Topl
Kinetika i Kataliz — Kinet Katal
Kinetika i Kataliz. Itogi Nauki i Tekhniki — Kinet Katal Itogi Nauki Tekh
King Abdulaziz Medical Journal — King Abdulaziz Med J
King Abdulaziz University. Faculty of Earth Sciences. Bulletin — King Abdulaziz Univ Fac Earth Sci Bull
King Abdulaziz University. Faculty of Marine Sciences. Journal — King Abdulaziz Univ Fac Mar Sci J
King Abdulaziz University. Faculty of Science. Bulletin — King Abdulaziz Univ Fac Sci Bull
King Abdulaziz University. Institute of Applied Geology. Bulletin — King Abdulaziz Univ Inst Appl Geol Bull
King Faisal Specialist Hospital. Medical Journal — King Faisal Spec Hosp Med J
King Saud University. College of Science. Journal — King Saud Univ Coll Sci J
King Saud University. Engineering Science. Journal — King Saud Univ Eng Sci J
King Saud University. Journal. Science — King Saud Univ J Sci
King Saud University. Science. Journal — King Saud Univ Sci J
Kingdom Come — K
King's Gazette — Kings Gaz
Kingston Geology Review [*British*] — Kingston Geol Rev
Kingston Law Review — Kingston L Rev
Kingston Law Review — Kingston LR
Kingston (Ontario) Historical Society. Proceedings — Kingston Ont Hist Soc Proc
Kingston-On-Hull Museums. Bulletin — Kingston-On-Hull Mus Bull
Kininy i Kininovaya Sistema Krovi. Biokhimiya, Farmakologiya, Patfiziologiya, Metody Issledovaniya. Rol V. Patologii — Kininy Kininovaya Sist Krovi
Kinki Chugoku Agricultural Research — Kinki Chugoku Agric Res
Kinki Daigaku Genshiryoku Kenkyusho Nenpo — KDGNB
Kino-Foto-Khimpromyshlennost — Kino Foto Khimpromst
Kino-Photo Industry — Kino Photo Ind
Kinotechnik — Kinotech
Kino-Technik (Berlin) — Kino Tech (Berlin)
Kinotechnik und Filmtechnik. Ausgabe A — Kinotech Filmtech Ausg A
Kinotechnik und Filmtechnik. Ausgabe B — Kinotech Filmtech Ausg B
Kintyre Antiquarian and Natural History Society. Magazine — Kintyre Antiqu Nat Hist Soc Mag
Kinyu Keizai — Kin Kei
Kinzoku Zairyo — KIZRA
Kinzoku Zairyo Gijutsu Kenkyusho Kenkyu Hokoku — KZGKA
Kipenie i Kondensatsiya — Kipenie Kondens
Kipling Journal — KJ
Kiplinger's Personal Finance Magazine [*Formerly, Changing Times*] — GCHT
Kirche fuer die Welt — KfW
Kirche im Angriff — KiA
Kirche im Osten — K i O

Kirche im Osten — K Ost
Kirche im Osten — KO
Kirche im Osten. Beiheft — KOB
Kirche im Osten. Monographienreihe — KOM
Kirche in Bewegung und Entscheidung — KBE
Kirche in der Welt — K i W
Kirche in Ihrer Geschichte — KIG
Kirche und Gesellschaft — KuG
Kirchen der Welt — KW
Kirchenblatt fuer die Reformierte Schweiz [*Basel*] — KBl Ref
Kirchenblatt fuer die Reformierte Schweiz — Kbl RS
Kirchenblatt fuer die Reformierte Schweiz — KBRS
Kirchenchor — Kirchor
Kirchenfreund — Kchfd
Kirchengeschichte — KG
Kirchengeschichtliche Abhandlungen — KGA
Kirchengeschichtliche Studien [*Berlin*] — KG St
Kirchenlexikon — KL
Kirchenmusikalische Nachrichten — Km Nachrichten
Kirchenmusikalisches Jahrbuch — K Jb
Kirchenmusikalisches Jahrbuch — Kirchenmusik Jb
Kirchenmusikalisches Jahrbuch — Km J
Kirchenmusikalisches Jahrbuch — Km Jb
Kirchenmusiker — Kirmus
Kirchenmusiker — Km
Kirchenrechtliche Abhandlungen — KRA
Kirchenreform [*Stuttgart*] — KR
Kirchliche Dogmatik — KD
Kirchliche Korrespondenz des Evangelischen Bundes zur Wahrung der Deutsch-Protestantischen Interessen — KKEB
Kirchliche Mitteilungen aus und Ueber Nord-Amerika — KMNA
Kirchliche Monatsschrift — K Ms
Kirchliche Verwaltungslehre — KVL
Kirchliche Zeitschrift — KZ
Kirchliches Handbuch fuer das Katholische Deutschland — KH
Kirchliches Jahrbuch fuer die Evangelischen Landeskirchen Deutschlands — KJ
Kirchner, Prosopographia Attica — Kirch PA
Kirgizkii Nauchno-Issledovatel'skii Institut Zhivotnovodstva i Veterinarii. Trudy — Kirg Nauchno Issled Inst Zhivotnovod Vet Tr
Kirgizskii Gosudarstvennyi Meditsinskii Institut. Sbornik Nauchnykh Trudov — Kirg Gos Med Inst Sb Nauchn Tr
Kirgizskii Gosudarstvennyi Meditsinskii Institut. Trudy — Kirg Gos Med Inst Tr
Kirgizskii Gosudarstvennyi Meditsinskii Institut. Trudy. Seriya Khimicheskikh Nauk — Kirg Gos Med Inst Tr Ser Khim Nauk
Kirgizskii Nauchno-Issledovatel'skii Institut Pochvovedeniya. Trudy — Kirg Nauchno Issled Inst Pochvoved Tr
Kirin University Journal. Natural Sciences [*People's Republic of China*] — Kirin Univ J Nat Sci
Kirjallisuudentutkijain Seuran Vuosikirja — KSV
Kirjath Sepher [*Jerusalem*] — KS
Kirke og Kultur — Ki o Ku
Kirke og Kultur — Kirke og Kult
Kirke og Kultur — KK
Kirke og Kultur — KoK
Kirkehistoriske Samlinger — Kirk Saml
Kirkehistoriske Samlinger — Kirkh Saml
Kirkehistoriske Studier (Kobenhavn) — KHSK
Kirke-Leksikon for Norden — KLN
Kirken og Tiden — Ko T
Kirkens Front — Kirk F
Kirkens Verden — KV
Kirkia. Journal. Federal Herbarium — Kirkia Jnl
Kirk-Othmer Encyclopedia of Chemical Technology — Encycl Chem Technol
Kirkus Reviews — Kirkus R
Kirkus Reviews — KR
Kirovskii Gosudarstvennyi Pedagogiceskii Institut Imeni V. I. Lenina. Ucenye Zapiski — Kirov Gos Ped Inst Ucen Zap
Kirovskii Gosudarstvennyi Pedagogicheskii Institut. Uchenye Zapiski — Kirov Gos Pedagog Inst Uch Zap
Kirton Agricultural Journal — Kirton Agric J
Kiserletes Orvostudomany — Kiserl Orvostud
Kiserletuegyi Koezlemenyek — Kiserl Koezlem
Kiserletugyi Koezlemenyek — Kiserl Kozl
Kiserletugyi Koezlemenyek — Kiserletugyi Koezlem
Kiserletugyi Koezlemenyek. A Kotet. Novenytermesztes — Kiserletugyi Kozl A
Kiserletugyi Koezlemenyek. B Kotet. Allattenyesztes — Kiserletugyi Kozl B
Kiserletugyi Koezlemenyek. C Kotet. Kerteszet — Kiserletugyi Kozl C
Kiserletugyi Koezlemenyek. Erdogazdasag — Kiserl Koezl Erdogazdasag
Kiserletugyi Koezlemenyek. Melleklet — Kiserletugyi Kozl Mellek
Kishechnye Infektsii — Kishechnye Infekts
Kishinevskii Politekhnicheskii Institut. Trudy — Kishinev Politekh Inst Tr
Kishinevskii Sel'skokhozyaistvennyi Institut Imeni M. V. Frunze. Trudy — Kishinev Skh Inst Im M V Frunze
Kisinevskii Gosudarstvennyi Universitet. Ucenye Zapiski — Kisinev Gos Univ Ucen Zap
Kislorodnaya Promyshlennost — Kislorodn Promst
Kiso To Rinsho — KSRNA
Kitakanto Medical Journal — Kitakanto Med J
Kitano Hospital Journal of Medicine — Kitano Hosp J Med
Kitasato Archives of Experimental Medicine — Kit Arch Exp Med
Kitasato Archives of Experimental Medicine — Kitasato Arch Exp Med
Kitasato Igaku — KIIGD
Kitasato Jikken Igaku [*Kitasato Archives of Experimental Medicine*] — Kit Jik Igaku
Kitasato Medicine — Kitasato Med
Kitto's Journal of Sacred Literature — Kitto
Kiyo. Journal of the Faculty of Science. Hokkaido University. Series VI. Zoology — Kiyo J Fac Sci Hokkaido Univ Ser VI Zool
Kjobenhavns Universitets Journal — Kjobenhavns Univ J
KLA (Korean Library Association) Bulletin — KLA Bul
Klank en Weerklank — Klank
Klasicni Naucn. Spisi. Matematicki Institut (Beograd) — Klasicni Naucn Spisi Mat Inst (Beograd)
Klassich-Philologische Studien — KPS
Klassiker der Religion — KlRel
Klassiker des Protestantismus — Kl Prot
Klassisch-Philologische Studien — Klass Phil Stud
Klassizismus und Kulturverfall — KuKv
Klaus-Groth-Gesellschaft. Jahresgabe — KGGJ
Kleberg Studies in Natural Resources — Kleberg Stud Nat Resour
Klei en Keramiek [*Netherlands*] — Klei Keram
Klei en Keramiek — KLY
Klein Placaatboek — K Pl B
Klein, Schanzlin, und Becker Aktiengesellschaft. Technische Berichte [*Berlin*] [*A publication*] — KSB Tech Ber
Kleinasiatische Forschungen — KAF
Kleinasiatische Forschungen — KF
Kleinasiatische Forschungen [*Weimar*] — KLF
Kleinasiatische Forschungen [*Weimar*] — KLFO
Kleinasiatische Forschungen [*Weimar*] — KlForsch
Kleinasiatische Personennamen — KPN
Kleine Aegyptische Texte — KAeT
Kleine Allgemeine Schriften zur Philosophie, Theologie, und Geschichte — KASP
Kleine Allgemeine Schriften zur Philosophie, Theologie, und Geschichte. Geschichtliche Reihe — KASPG
Kleine Allgemeine Schriften zur Philosophie, Theologie, und Geschichte. Philosophische Reihe — KASPP
Kleine Allgemeine Schriften zur Philosophie, Theologie, und Geschichte. Theologische Reihe — KASPT
Kleine Beltraege zur Droste-Forschung [*Munster*] — KBDF
Kleine Deutsche Prosadenkmaeler des Mittelalters — KDPM
Kleine Ergaenzungsreihe zu den Hochschulbuechern fuer Mathematik — Kleine Ergaenzungsreihe Hochschulbuechern Math
Kleine Marianische Buecherei — KMB
Kleine Naturwissenschaftliche Bibliothek — Kleine Naturwiss Bibliothek
Kleine Pauly. Lexikon der Antike — Kl Pauly
Kleine Pauly. Lexikon der Antike — KlP
Kleine Pauly. Lexikon der Antike — KP
Kleine Schriften der Naturforshenden Gesellschaft in Emden — Kleine Schriften Naturf Ges Emden
Kleine Schriften. Gesellschaft fuer Theatergeschichte — KSGT
Kleine Schriften zur Theologie — KSTh
Kleine Texte fuer Vorlesungen und Uebungen — KIT
Kleine Texte fuer Vorlesungen und Uebungen — KTVU
Kleine Vandenhoeck-Reihe — KVR
Kleinen Kirchenfuehrer — Kl KF
Kleiner Kirchenfuehrer — KKF
Kleinere Sanskrit Texte — KST
Kleinheubacher Berichte [*Germany*] — Kleinheubacher Ber
Kleintier-Praxis — Kleintier Prax
Kleintier-Praxis — KLEPA
Kleio — Kl
Klepzig Fachberichte fuer die Fuehrungskraefte aus Industrie und Praxis — Klepzig Fachber Fuehrungskraefte Ind Prax
Klepzig Fachberichte fuer die Fuehrungskraefte aus Industrie und Technik — Klepzig Fachber Fuehrungskraefte Ind Tech
Klepzig Fachberichte fuer die Fuehrungskraefte aus Maschinenbau und Huettenwesen — KFFMA
Klepzig Fachberichte fuer die Fuehrungskraefte aus Maschinenbau und Huettenwesen — Klepzig Fachber
Klepzig's Textil-Zeitschrift — Klepzigs Text Z
Klerenomia [*Thessaloniki*] — Kl
Klerusblatt [*Muenchen*] — Kl Bl
Klerus-Blatt (Salzburg) — Kl Bl S
Klett Studienbuecher Mathematik — Klett Studienbuecher Math
Kliatt Paperback Book Guide — Kliatt
Kliatt Paperback Book Guide — KPG
Klima, Kaelte, Heizung — Klima Kaelte Heiz
Klima und Kaelte Ingenieur — Klima Kaelte Ing
Klima und Kaelte-Ingenieur — Klim Kaelte Ing
Klima und Kaelteingenieur — Klima Kaelteing
Klima-Kaelte-Technik — KKATD
Klima-Kaelte-Technik — Klima-Kaelte-Tech
Klima-Schnellmeldedienst — Klima Schn D
Klima-Technik — Klima-Tech
Klimatisacija Grejanje Hladenje — Klim Grej Hlad
Kline Guide to the Chemical Industry — Kline Chem
Klinicheskaia Khirurgiia — Klin Khir
Klinicheskaia Laboratornaia Diagnostika — Klin Lab Diagn
Klinicheskaya Khirurgiya [*Kiev*] — Klin Khir
Klinicheskaya Khirurgiya — KLKHA
Klinicheskaya Meditsina — KLMIA
Klinicheskaya Meditsina (Moscow) — Klin Med (Mosc)
Klinicheskaya Meditsina (Moscow) — Klin Med (Moscow)
Klinicheskaya Onkologiya — Klin Onkol
Klinicheskii — Klinich
Klinicheskoi Rentgenologii Respublikanskoi Mezhvedomstvennyi Sbornik — Klin Rentgenol Resp Mezhved Sb
Klinichna Khirurhiia — Klin Khir

Klinicka Biochemie a Metabolismus — Klin Biochem Metab
Klinik und Praxis — Klin Prax
Klinika i Lechenie Zlokachestvennykh Novoobrazovanii — Klin Lech Zlokach Novoobraz
Klinika Oczna — Klin Oczna
Klinika Oczna — KOAOA
Klinikus — Klin
Klinische Anaesthesiologie und Intensivtherapie — Klin Anaesthesiol Intensivther
Klinische Medizin (Moscow) — Klin Med (Moscow)
Klinische Medizin. Oesterreichische Zeitschrift fuer Wissenschaftliche und Praktische Medizin — Klin Med Osterr Z Wiss Prakt Med
Klinische Medizin (Vienna) — Klin Med (Vienna)
Klinische Monatsblaetter fuer Augenheilkunde — Klin Monats
Klinische Monatsblaetter fuer Augenheilkunde — Klin Monatsbl Augenheilkd
Klinische Monatsblaetter fuer Augenheilkunde — KlMb
Klinische Monatsblaetter fuer Augenheilkunde — KMAUA
Klinische Monatsblaetter fuer Augenheilkunde. Beihefte — Klin Monatsbl Augenheilkd Beih
Klinische Padiatrie — Klin Padiatr
Klinische Paediatrie — Klin Paediat
Klinische Paediatrie — Klin Paediatr
Klinische Physiologie — Klin Physiol
Klinische und Experimentelle Urologie — Klin Exp Urol
Klinische Wochenschrift — Kl Ws
Klinische Wochenschrift — Klin Wchnschr
Klinische Wochenschrift — Klin Woch
Klinische Wochenschrift — Klin Wochenschr
Klinische Wochenschrift — Klin Ws
Klinische Wochenschrift — Klin Wschr
Klinische Wochenschrift — KLWOA
Klinisches Jahrbuch — Klin Jahrb
Klinisches Jahrbuch — Klin Jb
Klinisches Labor. Zeitschrift fuer Klinische Laboratorien und Transfusionsserologische Diagnostik — Klin Labor
Klinisch-Radiologisches Seminar — Klin Radiol Semin
Klinisch-Therapeutische Wochenschrift — Klin Therap Wchnschr
Kliniska un Eksperimentala Medicina — Klin Eksp Med
Klio. Beitraege zur Alten Geschichte — K
Klio. Beitraege zur Alten Geschichte — Kl
Klio. Beitraege zur Alten Geschichte — Klio
Klosterarchive, Tegesten, und Urkunden — KARU
Klucze do Oznaczania Bezkregowcow Polski — Klucze Oznaczania Bezkregowcow Pol
Klucze do Oznaczania Bezkregowcow Polski — KOBPDP
Klucze do Oznaczania Owadow Polski — Klucze Oznaczania Owadow Pol
Klucze do Oznaczania Owadow Polski — PTEKAA
Kluwer International Series in Engineering and Computer Science — Kluwer Internat Ser Engrg Comput Sci
Kluwer International Series in Engineering and Computer Science. VLSI, Computer Architecture and Digital Signal Processing — Kluwer Internat Ser Engrg Comput Sci VLSI Comput Archit
Kluwer Texts in the Mathematical Sciences — Kluwer Texts Math Sci
KMS Lecture Notes in Mathematics. Korean Math — KMS Lecture Notes Math
Knaur Taschenbuecher — Knaur Tb
Knaur Visuell — Knaur Vis
Knee Surgery, Sports Traumatology, Arthroscopy — Knee Surg Sports Traumatol Arthrosc
Knickerbocker Magazine — Knick
Knickerbocker Weekly — Knick Wkly
Kniga i Proletarskaya Revolyutsiya — KPR
Kniga i Revoljucija — KiR
Knight's Local Government Reports [*United Kingdom*] — Knight's Local Govt R
Knihovna Geologickeho Ustavu pro Cechy a Moravu — Knih Geol Ustavu Cechy Moravu
Knihovna Statniho Geologickeho Ustavu Ceskoslovenske Republiky — Knih Statniho Geol Ustavu Cesk Repub
Knihovna Ustredniho Ustavu Geologickeho — Knih Ustred Ust Geol
Knihovna Ustredniho Ustavu Geologickeho — Knih Ustred Ustavu Geol
Knihovna Ustredniho Ustavu Geologickeho — Knih UUG
Knitter's Circular and Monthly Record — Knitters Circ Mon Rec
Knitting International — Knitting Int
Knitting Times — Knit Times
Knizhnaya Letopis. Dopolnitel'nyi Vypusk [*Former USSR*] — Kn Letopis Dop Vyp
Knizhnaya Letopis. Dopolnitel'nyi Vypusk — Knizhnaya Letopis Dopl Vyp
Knizhnaya Letopis Ukazatel Seriinykh Izdanii — Knizhnaya Letopis Ukazatel Ser Izdanii
Kniznaja Letopis — Kn Let
Kniznaja Letopis Dopolnitelnyi Vypusk — Kniznaja Letopis Dopl Vyp
Kniznica Epsilon — Kn Epsil
Kniznice a Vedecke Informacie — Kniznice & Ved Inf
Kniznice Odbornych a Vedeckych Spisu Vysokeho Uceni Technickeho v Brne [*Czechoslovakia*] — Kniznice Odb Ved Spisu Vys Uceni Tech Brne
Kniznice Odbornych a Vedeckych Spisu Vysokeho Uceni Technickeho v Brne — Kniznice Odborn Ved Spisu Vysoke Uceni Tech v Brne
Kniznice Odbornych a Vedeckych Spisu Vysokeho Uceni Technickeho v Brne. Rada A — Kniznice Odb Ved Spisu Vys Uceni Tech Brne A
Kniznice Odbornych a Vedeckych Spisu Vysokeho Uceni Technickeho v Brne. Rada B [*Czechoslovakia*] — Kniznice Odb Ved Spisu Vys Uceni Tech Brne B
Knjizevna Istorija — KnjIst
Knjizevna Kritika. Casopis za Estetiku Knjizevnosti — KnjiK
Knjizevne Novine — KnjiNov
Knjizevne Novine — KnN
Knjizevnost — K
Knjizevnost — Knji
Knjizevnost — Knjiz
Knjizevnost i Jezik — KiJ
Knjizevnost i Jezik — KJ
Knjizevnost i Jezik — Knj J
Knjizevnost i Jezik u Skoli — KJS
Knjizica Sigma — Knjiz Sigma
Knochenverarbeitung und Leim — Knochenverarb Leim
Knossos Tablets — KT
Knowing Christianity Series — KCS
Knowledge — K
Knowledge — Knowl
Knowledge and Practice of Mathematics — Knowledge Practice Math
Knowledge and Society. Studies in the Sociology of Culture Past and Present — Knowl Soc
Knowledge of Plant Pathology (Peking) — Knowl Plant Pathol (Peking)
Knowledge-Based Control of Solidification Processes' Symposium — Knowl Based Control Solidif Processes Symp
Knox and Fitzhardinge's Reports [*New South Wales*] — Knox & Fitz
Knox's Supreme Court Reports — Kn
Knox's Supreme Court Reports (New South Wales) — Kn (NSW)
Knox's Supreme Court Reports (New South Wales) — Knox (NSW)
K'o Hsueh Chi Lu — KHCLA
K'o Hsueh T'Ung PAO (Foreign Language Edition) — K'o Hsueh T'Ung PAO (Foreign Lang Ed)
Koatsu Gasu — KOGAA
Kobayashi Rigaku Kenkyusho Hokoku — KKEHA
Kobe Economic and Business Review — KEBR
Kobe Economic and Business Review — Kobe Econ Bus R
Kobe Gaidai Ronso [*Kobe City University Journal*] — KGR
Kobe Journal of Mathematics — Kobe J Math
Kobe Journal of Medical Sciences — KJMDA
Kobe Journal of Medical Sciences — Kobe J Med Sci
Kobe Kogyo Technical Report [*Japan*] — Kobe Kogyo Tech Rep
Kobe Research Development — Kobe Res Dev
Kobe Shosen Daigaku Kiyo. Dai-2-Rui. Kokai, Kikan, Rigaku-Hen — KSDKA
Kobe Steel Report — Kobe Steel Rep
Kobe University. Economic Review — Kobe U Econ R
Kobe University. Economic Review — Kobe Univ Econ R
Kobe University. Economic Review — KUA
Kobe University. Economic Review — KUER
Kobe University. Law Review — Kobe U Law R
Kobe University. Law Review — Kobe Univ L Rev
Kobe University. Law Review — Kobe Univ Law R
Kobe University. Mathematics Seminar Notes. Second Edition — Math Sem Notes Kobe Univ Second Ed
Kobelco Technical Bulletin — Kobelco Tech Bull
Kobstadforeningens Tidsskrift — Kbf T
Kobunshi Kagaku — KOKAA
Kobunshi Kako — KOKAB
Kobunshi Ronbunshu — Kobunsh Ron
Kobunshi Ronbunshu — Kobunshi Ronbun
Kochi University. Faculty of Science. Memoirs. Series A. Mathematics — Mem Fac Sci Kochi Univ Ser A Math
Kodai Mathematical Journal — Kodai Math J
Kodai Mathematical Seminar Reports — Kodai Math Sem Rep
Kodaikanal Observatory Bulletin. Series A — Kodaikanal Obs Bull A
Kodaikanal Observatory Bulletin. Series A [*India*] — Kodaikanal Obs Bull Ser A
Kodaikanal Observatory Bulletin. Series B — Kodaikanal Obs Bull B
Kodak Data Book of Applied Photography — Kodak Data Book of Applied Phot
Kodak International Fotografie — Kodak Internat Fotogr
Kodak Laboratory Chemicals Bulletin — Kodak Lab Chem Bull
Kodak Publication. G-47 — Kodak Publ G 47
Kodak Publication. G-49 — Kodak Publ G 49
Kodak Publication. G-102 — Kodak Publ G 102
Kodak Research Laboratories. Monthly Abstract Bulletin — Kodak Res Lab Mon Abstr Bull
Kodaly Envoy — Kodaly
Koedoe Monograph — Koedoe Monogr
Koehler, Ludwig und Walter Baumgartner. Lexicon in Veteris Testamenti Libros — KBL
Koeln. Vierteljahreschrift fuer Freunde der Stadt — Koeln
Koeln. Vierteljahrsschrift fuer Freunde der Stadt — Koln Vierteljahr Freunde
Koelner Anglistische Arbeiten — KAA
Koelner Blaetter fuer Berufserziehung — K Bl BE
Koelner Domblatt — KDB
Koelner Domblatt — Koe D Bl
Koelner Domblatt — Koeln Dombl
Koelner Geographische Arbeiten — Koe Geogr Arb
Koelner Geographische Arbeiten — Koeln Geogr Arb
Koelner Geologische Hefte — Koeln Geol H
Koelner Germanistische Studien — KGS
Koelner Historische Abhandlungen — HAb
Koelner Jahrbuch fuer Vor- und Fruehgeschichte — K Jb
Koelner Jahrbuch fuer Vor- und Fruehgeschichte — KJVFG
Koelner Jahrbuch fuer Vor- und Fruehgeschichte — Koeln JB V Frueh Gesch
Koelner Jahrbuch fuer Vor- und Fruehgeschichte — Koln Jb Vor Fruh Gesch
Koelner RAST [*Radio-Allergo-Sorbens-Tests*] **Symposion** — Koeln RAST Symp
Koelner Romanistische Arbeiten — KRA
Koelner Sozialpolitische Vierteljahresschrift — KSPV
Koelner Sozialpolitische Vierteljahrshefte — Koeln Sozialpolit Vjhh
Koelner Tageblatt — Koe T
Koelner Viertaljahrshefte fuer Sozialwissenschaft — KVjhS
Koelner Vierteljahrshefte fuer Sozialwissenschaften — KVSW
Koelner Vierteljahrshefte fuer Sozialwissenschaften. Soziologische Hefte — KVSWS

Koelner Vierteljahrshefte fuer Sozialwissenschaften. Soziolpolitische Hefte — KVSWSP
Koelner Vierteljahrshefte fuer Sozioogie — KVS
Koelner Zeitschrift fuer Soziologie — KZS
Koelner Zeitschrift fuer Soziologie. N.F. der Koelner Vierteljahrshefte fuer Soziologie — Koelner Z Soziol
Koelner Zeitschrift fuer Soziologie und Sozial-Psychologie — Koe Z Soz Soz Psych
Koelner Zeitschrift fuer Soziologie und Sozial-Psychologie — Koelner Z
Koelner Zeitschrift fuer Soziologie und Sozialpsychologie — Koelner Z fuer Soziologie und Sozialpsychol
Koelner Zeitschrift fuer Soziologie und Sozial-Psychologie — Koelner Z Soz
Koelner Zeitschrift fuer Soziologie und Sozialpsychologie — Koelner Z Soziol Sozialpsych
Koelner Zeitschrift fuer Soziologie und Sozialpsychologie — Koelner Z Soziol Sozialpsychol
Koelner Zeitschrift fuer Soziologie und Sozial-Psychologie — Koelner Z Soziol u Soz-Psychol
Koelner Zeitschrift fuer Soziologie und Sozial-Psychologie — KZSS
Koelnisches Encyclopedisches Journal — Koeln Encycl J
Koeltechniek/Klimaatregeling — NVK
Koeniglich-Bayerische Akademie der Wissenschaften zu Muenchen. Mathematisch-Physikalische Klasse. Sitzungsberichte. Abhandlungen — K-Bayer Ak Wiss Muenchen Mat-Phys Kl Szb Abh
Koeniglich-Boehmische Gesellschaft der Wissenschaften in Prag. Mathematisch-Naturwissenschaftliche Klasse. Sitzungsberichte — K-Boehm Ges Wiss Mat-Nat Kl Szb
Koenigliche Akademie der Wissenschaften (Berlin). Sitzungsberichte — Koen Akad D Wiss Berlin Sitzungsb
Koenigliche Akademie der Wissenschaften (Wien). Denkschriften — AWWDs
Koenigliche Gesellschaft der Wissenschaften zu Goettingen. Abhandlungen — K Ges Wiss Goettingen Abh
Koenigliche Landesanstalt fuer Wasserhygiene zu Berlin-Dahlem. Mitteilungen — K Landesanst Wasserhyg Berlin Dahlem Mitt
Koenigliche Pruefungsanstalt fuer Wasserversorgung und Abwaesserbeseitigung zu Berlin. Mittellungen — K Pruefungsanst Wasserversorg Abwaesserbeseit Berlin Mitt
Koenigliche Tieraerztliche und Landwirtschaftliche Universitaet. Jahrbuch. Copenhagen — K Tieraerztl Landwirtsch Univ Jahrb Copenhagen
Koeniglichen Akademie der Wissenschaften in Paris. Physische Abhandlungen — Koenigl Akad Wiss Paris Phys Abh
Koeniglich-Preussische Akademie der Wissenschaften (Berlin). Abhandlungen — AWBAbh
Koeniglich-Preussische Akademie der Wissenschaften (Berlin). Sitzungsberichte — AWBSb
Koeniglich-Saechsische Gesellschaft der Wissenschaften zu Leipzig. Mathematisch-Physische Klasse. Berichte ueber die Verhandlungen — K-Saechs Ges Wiss Leipzig Mat-Phys Kl Ber
Koenigsberg Universitaet. Jahrbuch — Konigsberg Univ Jahrb
Koenigsberger Archiv fuer Naturwissenschaft und Mathematik — Koenigsberger Arch Naturwiss Math
Koenigsberger Deutsche Forschungen — KDF
Koenigsberger Gelehrten Gesellschaft. Naturwissenschaftliche Klasse. Schriften — Koenigsb Gelehrten Ges Naturwiss Kl Schr
Koenigsberger Hartungsche Zeitung — KHZ
Koenigsberger Hartungsche Zeitung — Koenigsbg Hartung Ztg
Koenigsberger Historische Forschungen — KHF
Koenigsberger Naturwissenschaftliche Unterhaltungen — Koenigsberger Naturwiss Unterhalt
Koenigsteiner Blaetter — Koenigsteiner Bl
Koeroesi Csoma-Archivum — KCsA
Koerperschaftssteuergesetz — Koerp St G
Koezgazdasagi Szemle — Koezgazd Szle
Koezlekedes Tudomanyi Szemle — Koezlekedes Tud Sz
Koezlekedestudomanyi Szemle — Koezlek Sz
Koezlemenyei. Agrartudomanyok Osztalyanak. Magyar Tudomanyos Akademia — Kozlem Agrartud Oszt Magy Tud Akad
Koezlemenyei Magyar Tudomanyos Akademia Muszaki Fizikai Kutato Intezetenek — Koezl Magy Tud Akad Musz Fiz Kut Intez
Koezlemenyei. Mosonmagyoarovari Agrartudomanyi Foiskola — Kozlem Mosonmagyoarovari Agrartud Foiskola
Koezlemenyek az Erdelyi Nemzeti Muzeum Erem es Regisegtarabal — KENMER
Koezlemenyek az Erdelyi Nemzeti Muzeum Erem es Regisegtarabal — Koezl Erdel Nem Muz Er Reg
Koezlemenyek-MTA Szamitastechnikai es Automatizalasi Kutato Intezet (Budapest) — Koezlemenyek-MTA Szamitastechn Automat Kutato Int (Budapest)
Koezlemenyek-MTA Szamitastechnikai es Automatizalasi Kutato Intezet (Budapest) — Koezl-MTA Szamitastech Automat Kutato Int (Budapest)
Koezlemenyek-MTA Szamitastechnikai es Automatizalasi Kutato Intezet (Budapest) — Kozlemenyek-MTA Szamitastechn Automat Kutato Int (Budapest)
Koezneveles — Koezn
Kogyo Gijutsu — KOGJA
Kogyo Gijutsuin. Hakko Kenkyusho Kenkyu Hokoku — KGHKA
Kogyo Kagaku Zasshi — KGKZA
Kogyo Zairyo — KZAIA
Kohaszati Lapok [*Hungary*] — Kohasz Lapok
Kohle und Heizoel — KOHED
Koinonia [*Essen*] — Koin
Koinonike Epitheoresis — Koinonike Epitheor
Kokalos Studi Pubblicati. Istituto di Storia Antica. Universita di Palermo — Kokalos
Kokka Gakkai Zassi [*Journal. Association of Political and Social Science*] — Kok Gak Zas
Koks i Khimiya — KOKKA
Koks i Khimiya [*Former USSR*] — Koks Khim
Koks, Smola, Gaz — KSMGA
Koks und Chemie — Koks Chem
Koksnes Kimija — Koksnes Kim
Koku Igaku Jikkentai Hokoku — KJNNA
Kokugo Kokubun No Kenkyu [*Studies in Japanese Language and Literature*] — KKK
Kokugo To Kokubungaku [*Japanese Language and Literature*] — KK
Kokugo To Kokubungaku [*Japanese Language and Literature*] — KtoK
Kokusai Shukyo Nyuzu — KSN
Kokyu To Junkan — KOJUA
Kolchoznoe Proizvodstvo — Kolch Proizv
Koleopterologische Rundschau — Koleopterol Rundsch
Koleopterologische Rundschau — KR
Kolhospnyk Ukrainy — Kolhospnyk Ukr
Kolkhoznoe Proizvodstvo — Kolkhoz Proizvod
Kolkhozno-Sovkhoznoe Proizvodstvo — Kolkhoz-Sovkhoz Proizvod
Kolkhozno-Sovkhoznoe Proizvodstvo Kirgizii — Kolkhoz-Sovkhoz Proizvod Kirgizii
Kolkhozno-Sovkhoznoe Proizvodstvo Moldavii — Kolkhoz-Sovkhoz Proizvod Mold
Kolkhozno-Sovkhoznoe Proizvodstvo RSFSR — Kolkhoz-Sovkhoz Proizvod RSFSR
Kolkhozno-Sovkhoznoe Proizvodstvo Turkmenistana — Kolkhozno-Sovkhoznoe Proizod Turkm
Kollasuyo (La Paz) — Kollas La Paz
Kollektsioner Azerbaidzhana — Koll Azerb
Kolloid-Beihefte — Kolloid Beih
Kolloidchemische Beihefte — Kolloidchem Beih
Kolloidchemische Beihefte — Kolloidchem Beihh
Kolloidkemiai Konferencia — Kolloidkem Konf
Kolloidnyi Zhurnal — KO
Kolloidnyi Zhurnal — Koll Z
Kolloidnyi Zhurnal — Koll Zh
Kolloidnyi Zhurnal — Kolloid Zh
Kolloidnyi Zhurnal — Kolloidn Zh
Kolloidnyi Zhurnal — Kolloidnyi Zh
Kolloidnyi Zhurnal — KOZHA
Kolloid-Zeitschrift [*Germany*] — Kolloid-Z
Kolloid-Zeitschrift. Beihefte — Kolloid Z Beih
Kolloid-Zeitschrift und Zeitschrift fuer Polymere — Kolloid-Z & Z Polym
Kolloid-Zeitschrift und Zeitschrift fuer Polymere — KZZPA
Kolloid-Zeitschrift und Zeitschrift fuer Polymere. Supplementum — Kolloid Z Z Polym Suppl
Kolloquium fuer Klinische Pharmakologie und Experimentelle Therapie — Kolloq Klin Pharmakol Exp Ther
Kolloquium ueber Technische Anwendung und Verarbeitung von Kunststoffen — Kolloq Tech Anwend Verarb Kunstst
Kolokvium o Nizkych Radioaktivitach. Zbornik Referatov — Kolok Nizk Radioakt Zb Ref
Kolomenskii Pedagogiceskii Institut Ucenye Zapiski — Kolomen Ped Inst Ucen Zap
Koloniaal Instituut te Amsterdam. Afdeeling Handelsmuseum. Mededeeling — Kolon Inst Amsterdam Afd Handelsmus Meded
Koloniaal Tijdschrift — Kol T
Koloniaal Tijdschrift — KT
Koloniaal Verslag — KV
Koloniaal Weekblad — KW
Koloniale Abhandlungen — Kol Abhandl
Koloniale Rundschau — Kol Rundschau
Koloniale Rundschau — KolR
Koloniale Rundschau — KR
Koloniale Studien — Kol St
Koloniale Studien — KS
Koloniales Jahrbuch — KJ
Kolonialforstliche Mitteilungen — Kolonialforstl Mitt
Koloristicheskie Izvestiya — Kolor Izv
Koloristische Rundschau — Kolor Rundsch
Kolorisztikai Ertesito — KOERA
Kolorisztikai Ertesito — Kolor Ert
Kolozsvari Ferenc Jozsef Tudomanyegyetem Evkoenyve — Kolozsvari Ferenc Jozsef Tudomanyegyet Evk
Komarom Megyei Muzeumok Koezlemenei — Komarom Meg Muz Koz
Komarom Megyei Muzeumok Koezlemenyei — Komarom MK
Komarovskie Chteniya Botanicheskogo Instituta Academii Nauk SSSR — Komarovskie Chteniya Bot Inst Akad Nauk SSSR
Kombinatornyi Analiz — Kombin Anal
Kombinatornyi Analiz — Kombinatornyi Anal
Komeet — KGI
Komisja Krystalogradfii PAN [*Polska Akademia Nauk*]. Biuletyn Informacyjny — Kom Krystalogr PAN Biul Inf
Kommentar zum Neuen Testament — KNT
Kommentare und Beitraege zum Alten und Neuen Testament — KBANT
Kommentare zum Arzneibuch der Deutschen Demokratischen Republik — Komment Arzneib DDR
Kommission der Europaeischen Gemeinschaften — CECED9
Kommission der Europaeischen Gemeinschaften — Komm Eur Gem
Kommission fuer Wasserforschung. Mitteilung. Deutsche Forschungsgemeinschaft — Komm Wasserforsch Mitt Dtsch Forschungsgem
Kommission zur Erforschung der Luftverunreinigung. Deutsche Forschungsgemeinschaft. Mitteilung — Komm Erforsch Luftverunreinig Dtsch Forschungsgem Mitt
Kommunal Aarbog — Kom Aa
Kommunal Statistisk DataBank — KSDB

Kommunalabgabengesetz — K Abg G
Kommunalabgabengesetz — Komm Abg G
Kommunale Steuer-Zeitschrift — Komm St Z
Kommunal-Kassen-Zeitschrift — Komm Kass Z
Kommunal'nvoe Khozyaistvo — Kommunal'n Khoz
Kommunalwirtschaft — KMLWA
Kommunalwirtschaft. Sonderheft — Kommunalwirtschaft Sonderh
Kommunismus und Klassenkampf — Kommun u Klassenkampf
Kommunist Azerbajdzana — Kommunist Azerbajd
Kommunist Sovetskoj Latvii — Komm Sov Latv
Kommunist Sovetskoj Latvii — Kommunist Sov Latvii
Kommunist Ukrainy — Kom Ukr
Komparatistische Hefte — KompH
Kompleksnoe Ispol'zovanie Mineral'nogo Syr'ya — Kompleksn Ispol'z Miner Syr'ya
Kompleksnoe Ispol'zovanie Rud Chernykh Metallov — Kompleksn Ispolz Rud Chern Met
Kompleksnoe Razvitie KMA — Kompleksn Razvit KMA
Kompleksnye Issledovaniya Kaspiiskogo Morya — Kompleksn Issled Kasp Morya
Kompleksnye Issledovaniya Prirody Okeana — KIPOB
Kompleksnye Issledovaniya Prirody Okeana — Kompleksn Issled Prir Okeana
Kompleksnye Issledovaniya Vodokhranilishch — Kompleksn Issled Vodokhran
Kompozitsionnye Polimernye Materialy — Kompoz Polim Mater
Komsomol'skaja Pravda — Ko Pr
Komunikaty Mazursko-Warminskie — KoM
Komunikaty Mazursko-Warminskie — Kom Mazur-Warmin
Komunist (Belgrade) — KB
Konan Women's College. Researches — Konan Women's Coll Res
Koncar Strucne Informacije — Koncar Strucne Inf
Kondordanz zu den Qumrantexten — KQT
Konepajamies — KNPJB
Konference Ceskoslovenskych Fyziku. Sbornik Prednasek — Konf Cesk Fyz Sb Prednasek
Konference o Keramice pro Elektroniku. Prace — Konf Keram Elektron Pr
Konferencia o Lepeni Kovov Intermetalbond. Prace — Konf Lepeni Kovov Intermetalbond Pr
Konferencia o Termickej Analyze. Zbornik — Konf Term Anal Zb
Konferencia so Zahranicnou Ucastou Celostatne Dni Tepelneho Spracovania — Konf Zahr Ucastou Celostatne Dni Tepelneho Spracovania
Konferencja Komisji Biologii Nowotworow Polskiej Akademii Nauk — Konf Kom Biol Nowotworow Pol Akad Nauk
Konferencja Metaloznawcza. Materialy Konferencyjne — Konf Metalozn Mater Konf
Konferencja Metalurgii Proszkow. Materialy Konferencyjne — Konf Metal Proszkow Mater Konf
Konferencja Metalurgii Proszkow w Polsce. Materialy Konferencyjne — Konf Metal Proszkow Pol Mater Konf
Konferencja Mikroskopii Elektronowej Ciala Stalego — Konf Mikrosk Elektron Ciala Stalego
Konferencja na temat Metody Badan Odpornosci Materialow na Pekanie, Zbior Prac — Konf Metody Badan Odpornosci Mater Pekanie Zbior Pr
Konferencja Naukowa Sekcji Wenerologicznej Polskiego Towarzystwa Dermatologicznego — Konf Nauk Sekc Wenerol Pol Tow Dermatol
Konferencja Naukowo-Techniczna Elektrostatyka w Przemysle, ELSTAT-80 Osiemdziesiat — Konf Nauk Tech Electrost Przem ELSTAT 80 Osiemdziesiat
Konferencja Naukowo-Techniczna. Rozwoj Stali Odpornych na Korozje — Konf Nauk Tech Rozwoj Stali Odpornych Koroz
Konferencja Naukowo-Techniczna Technologia Robot Antykorozyjnych — Konf Nauk Tech Technol Rob Antykoroz
Konferencja Teoretyczna Chemikow Polskich — Konf Teor Chem Pol
Konferentsiya Molodykh Nauchnykh Rabotnikov Instituta Neorganicheskoi Khimii. Akademiya Nauk Latviiskoi SSR — Konf Molodykh Nauchn Rab Inst Neorg Khim Akad Nauk Latv SSR
Konferentsiya Molodykh Spetsialistov po Mekhanike Polimerov. Tezisy Dokladov — Konf Molodykh Spets Mekh Polim Tezisy Dokl
Konferentsiya Molodykh Uchenykh Eksperiment v Sovremennoi Biologii i Meditsine Materialy — Konf Molodykh Uch Eksp Sovrem Biol Med Mater
Konferentsiya Molodykh Uchenykh i Spetsialistov po Biologii, Meditsine i Biomeditsinskoi Tekhnicke — Konf Molodykh Uch Spets Biol Med Biomed Tekh
Konferentsiya Molodykh Uchenykh. Institut Problem Kompleksnogo Osvoeniya Nedr — Konf Molodykh Uch Inst Probl Kompleksn Osvoeniya Nedr
Konferentsiya Molodykh Uchenykh Laboratorii Monitoringa Prirodnoi Sredy i Klimata — Konf Molodykh Uch Lab Monit Prir Sredy Klim
Konferentsiya Molodykh Uchenykh Moldavii — Konf Molodykh Uch Mold
Konferentsiya Molodykh Uchenykh-Onkologov. Tezisy Dokladov — Konf Molodykh Uch Onkol Tezisy Dokl
Konferentsiya po Poverkhnostnym Silam. Sbornik Dokladov — Konf Poverkhn Silam Sb Dokl
Konferentsiya po Poverkhnostnym Yavleniyam v Zhidkostyakh. Materialy — Konf Poverkhn Yavleniyam Zhidk Mater
Konferentsiya po Radioelektronike — Konf Radioelektron
Konferentsiya po Svarke Legkikh, Tsvetnykh i Tugoplavkikh Metallov i Splavov — Konf Svarke Legk Tsvetn Tugoplavkikh Met Splavov
Konferentsiya po Teplofizicheskim Svoistvam Veshchestv — Konf Teplofiz Svoistvam Veshchestv
Konferentsiya po Voprosam Tsito- i Gistokhimii. Doklady — Konf Vopr Tsito Gistokhim Dokl
Konferentsiya po Zharostoikim Betonam — Konf Zharostoikim Betonam
Konferenz der Gesellschaft fuer Biologische Chemie — Konf Ges Biol Chem
Konferenz der Gesellschaft fuer Biologische Chemie. Papers — Konf Ges Biol Chem Pap
Konferenz der Internationalen Gesellschaft fuer Biologische Rhythmusforschung — Konf Int Ges Biol Rhythm Forsch
Konferenz fuer Schweisstechnik — Konf Schweisstech
Konferenz ueber Aktuelle Probleme der Tabakforschung — Konf Aktuel Probl Tabakforsch
Konferenz ueber die Menschliche Schilddruese — Konf Menschl Schilddruese
Konferenz ueber Feuerbetone — Konf Feuerbetone
Konferenz ueber N-Nitroso-Verbindungen und Lactone — Konf N Nitroso Verbind Lactone
Konferenz ueber Sicherheitstechnik der Landwirtschaftlichen Chemisierung. Vortraege — Konf Sicherheitstech Landwirtsch Chem Vortr
Konferenz ueber Tribologie. Vortraege — Konf Tribol Vortr
Konfessionskundliche Schriften des Johann Adam Moehler Instituts — KKSMI
Konfessionskundliche Schriftenreihe — KKS
Konfessionskundliche und Kontroverstheologische Studien — KKTS
Kongelige Danske Videnskabernes Selskab. Biologiske Skrifter — BSVSAQ
Kongelige Danske Videnskabernes Selskab. Biologiske Skrifter — K Dan Vidensk Selsk Biol Skr
Kongelige Danske Videnskabernes Selskab. Historisk-Filosofiske Meddelelser [*Copenhagen*] — KDVS
Kongelige Danske Videnskabernes Selskab. Matematisk-Fysisk Meddelelser [*Denmark*] — K Dan Vidensk Selsk Mat Fys Medd
Kongelige Danske Videnskabernes Selskab. Matematisk-Fysisk Meddelelser — KDVSA
Kongelige Danske Videnskabernes Selskab. Matematisk-Fysisk Skrifter [*Denmark*] [*A publication*] — K Dan Vidensk Selsk Mat Fys Skr
Kongelige Danske Videnskabernes Selskab. Matematisk-Fysisk Skrifter — KVMFA
Kongelige Danske Videnskabernes Selskab. Oversigt Selskabets Virksomhed — K Dan Vidensk Selsk Over Selsk Virksomhed
Kongelige Danske Videnskabernes Selskab. Oversigt Selskabets Virksomhed — Kgl Danske Vidensk Selsk Oversigt
Kongelige Danske Videnskabernes Selskab. Skrifter — K Danske Vidensk Selsk Skr
Kongelige Danske Videnskabernes Selskab. Skrifter. Naturvidenskabelig og Mathematisk Afdeling — K Dan Vidensk Selsk Skr Naturvidensk Mat Afd
Kongelige Danske Videnskabernes Selskabs Bekiendtgiorelse — Kongel Danske Vidensk Selsk Bekiendtg
Kongelige Danske Videnskabernes Selskabs Skrifter — Danske Vid Selsk Skrift
Kongelige Norske Videnskabers Selskab — KNVS
Kongelige Norske Videnskabers Selskab. Foerhandlinger — K Nor Vidensk Selsk Foerhandl
Kongelige Norske Videnskabers Selskab. Foerhandlinger — K Nor Vidensk Selsk Forh
Kongelige Norske Videnskabers Selskab. Foerhandlinger — KNSFA2
Kongelige Norske Videnskabers Selskab. Foerhandlinger (Trondheim) — Norske Vid Selsk Forh (Trondheim)
Kongelige Norske Videnskabers Selskab Museet. Botanisk Avdeling Rapport — K Nor Vidensk Selsk Mus Bot Avd Rapp
Kongelige Norske Videnskabers Selskab. Museet. Botanisk Avdeling Rapport — RNVSDY
Kongelige Norske Videnskabers Selskab. Museet. Miscellanea — K Nor Vidensk Selsk Mus Misc
Kongelige Norske Videnskabers Selskab Museet. Rapport Botanisk Serie — K Nor Vidensk Selsk Mus Rapp Bot Ser
Kongelige Norske Videnskabers Selskab. Skrifter — K Nor Vidensk Selsk Skr
Kongelige Norske Videnskabers Selskab. Skrifter (Trondheim) — Norske Vid Selsk Skr (Trondheim)
Kongelige Norske Videnskabers Selskabs Museet. Arsbok — Kongel Norske Vidensk Selsk Mus Arsbok
Kongelige Veterinaer og Landbohojskole Institut foer Sterilitetsforskning Arsberetning — K Vet Landbohojsk Inst Sterilitetsforsk Arsberet
Kongelige Veterinaer-og Landbohojskole Arsskrift — K Vet-Landbohojsk Arsskr
Kongo-Overzee. Tijdschrift voor en Over Belgisch-Kongo en Andere Overzeese Gewesten — KO
Kongres na Bulgarskite Mikrobiolozi. Materiali — Kongr Bulg Mikrobiol Mater
Kongres po Mikrobiologiya. Materiali ot Kongres na Mikrobiolozite v Bulgariya — Kongr Mikrobiol Mater Kongr Mikrobiol Bulg
Kongres van de Europese Federatie van de Corrosie. Voordrukken — Kongr Eur Fed Corros Voordrukken
Kongress der Deutschen Gesellschaft fuer Allergie- und Immunitaetsforschung — Kongr Dtsch Ges Allerg Immunitaetsforsch
Kongress der Deutschen Gesellschaft fuer Biologische Psychiatrie — Kongr Dtsch Ges Biol Psychiatr
Kongress der Europaeischen Foederation Korrosion. Vordrucke — Kongr Eur Foed Korros Vordrucke
Kongress der Europaeischen Gesellschaft fuer Haematologie. Verhandlungen — Kongr Eur Ges Haematol Verh
Kongress der Europaeischen Gesellschaft fuer Zuechtungsforschung — Kongr Eur Ges Zuechtungsforsch
Kongress der Pharmazeutischen Wissenschaften, Vortraege und Originalmitteilungen — Kongr Pharm Wiss Vortr Originalmitt
Kongress fuer Thrombose und Blutstillung — Kongr Thromb Blutstillung
Kongress Khimiya v Sel'skom Khozyaistve — Kongr Khim Selsk Khoz
Kongress und Ausstellung Wasser — Kongr Ausstellung Wasser
Kongress- und Tagungsberichte der Martin-Luther-Universitaet Halle-Wittenberg — Kongr Tagungsber Martin Luther Univ Halle Wittenberg
Kongress-Bericht. Internationaler Fruchtsaft-Kongress — Kongr Ber Int Fruchtsaft Kongr
Kongresszentralblatt fuer die Gesamte Innere Medizin und Ihre Grenzgebiete — Kong Zentralbl Ges Innere Med
Kongresszentralblatt fuer die Gesamte Innere Medizin und Ihre Grenzgebiete [*A publication*] — Kongr Zbl Ges Inn Med
Koninklijk Academie van Belgie. Jaarboek — ARBQA4
Koninklijk Academie van Belgie. Jaarboek — K Acad Belg Jaarb
Koninklijk Belgisch Instituut tot Verbetering van de Biet. Driemaandelijkse Publikatie — K Belg Inst Verbetering Biet Driemaand Publ

Koninklijk Belgisch Instituut voor Natuurwetenschappen. Studiedocumenten — IRSNAW
Koninklijk Belgisch Instituut voor Natuurwetenschappen. Studiedocumenten — K Belg Inst Natuurwet Studiedoc
Koninklijk Belgisch Instituut voor Natuurwetenschappen. Verhandelingen — K Belg Inst Natuurwet Verh
Koninklijk Belgisch Instituut voor Natuurwetenschappen. Verhandelingen — MIRNA8
Koninklijk Belgisch Koloniaal Instituut. Afdeeling der Natuur- en Geneeskundige Wetenschappen. Verhandelingen in 4 — K Belg Kolon Inst Afd Nat Geneeskd Wet Verh 4
Koninklijk Belgisch Koloniaal Instituut. Bulletijn der Zittingen — K Belg Kolon Inst Bull Zittingen
Koninklijk Instituut voor de Tropen. Afdeling Tropische Producten. Mededeling — K Inst Trop Afd Trop Prod Meded
Koninklijk Instituut voor de Tropen. Centrale Bibliotheek. Aanwinstenlijst — KIT
Koninklijk Instituut voor de Tropen. Mededeling. Afdeling Tropische Producten — K Inst Tropen Meded Afd Tropische Producten
Koninklijk Instituut voor Taals-Land- en Volkenkunde. Translation Series — KITLVTS
Koninklijk Museum voor Midden-Afrika [*Tervuren, Belgie*]. Annalen. Reeks in Octavo. Geologische Wetenschappen — KBGWAB
Koninklijk Museum voor Midden-Afrika (Tervuren, Belgie) Annalen. Reeks in Octavo. Geologische Wetenschappen — K Mus Midden Afr (Tervuren Belg) Ann Reeks 8 Geol Wet
Koninklijk Museum voor Midden-Afrika (Tervuren, Belgie). Annalen. Reeks in Octavo. Geologische Wetenschappen — K Mus Midden-Afr (Tervuren Belg) Ann Reeks 8o Geol Wet
Koninklijk Museum voor Midden-Afrika (Tervuren, Belgie). Annalen. Reeks in Octavo. Geologische Wetenschappen — K Mus Midden-Afr (Tervuren Belg) Ann Reeks Octavo Geol Wet
Koninklijk Museum voor Midden-Afrika (Tervuren, Belgie). Annalen. Reeks in Octavo. Zoologische Wetenschappen — K Mus Midden-Afr (Tervuren Belg) Ann Reeks Octavo Zool Wet
Koninklijk Museum voor Midden-Afrika (Tervuren, Belgie). Rapport Annuel. Departement de Geologie et de Mineralogie — K Mus Midden-Afr (Tervuren Belg) Rapp Annu Dep Geol Mineral
Koninklijk Museum voor Midden-Afrika (Tervuren, Belgie). Zoologische Documentatie — K Mus Midden-Afr (Tervuren Belg) Zool Doc
Koninklijk Museum voor Midden-Afrika [*Tervuren, Belgie*]. Zoologische Documentatie — MADZAK
Koninklijk Nederlands Geologisch Mijnbouwkundig Genootschap. Verhandelingen — K Ned Geol Mijnbouwkd Genoot Verh
Koninklijk Nederlandsch Aardrijkskundig Genootschap. Tijdschrift — K Nederlandsch Aardrijkskundig Genootschap Tijdschrift
Koninklijk Nederlandsch Geologisch-Mijnbouwkundig Genootschap Verhandelingen. Geologische Serie — K Nederlandsch Geol-Mijn Genootschap Verh Geol Ser
Koninklijk Nederlandsch Meteorologisch Instituut — KNMI
Koninklijke Academie van Belgie. Klasse der Wetenschappen, Verhandelingen. Verzameling in 8 — K Acad Belg Kl Wet Verh Verzamel 8
Koninklijke Academie voor Koloniale Wetenschappen. Mededelingen der Zittingen — K Acad Kolon Wet Meded Zittingen
Koninklijke Academie voor Overzeese Wetenschappen. Klasse voor Technische Wetenschappen. Verhandelingen in 8 (Brussels) — K Acad Overzeese Wet Kl Tech Wet Verh 8 Brussels
Koninklijke Academie voor Overzeese Wetenschappen. Mededelingen der Zittingen — K Acad Overzeese Wet Meded Zittingen
Koninklijke Belgische Commissie voor Volkskunde, Vlaamse Afdeling Jaarboek — KBCJ
Koninklijke Belgische Vereniging der Electrotechnici. Bulletin — K Belg Ver Electrotech Bull
Koninklijke Nederlandsche Heidemaatschappij. Tijdschrift — K Ned Heidemaatsch Tijdschr
Koninklijke Nederlandsche Reedersvereeniging — KNR
Koninklijke Nederlandsche Reedersvereeniging — KNRV
Koninklijke Nederlandsche Stoomboot Maatschappij — KNSM
Koninklijke Nederlandse Akademie van Wetenschappen. Afdeling Natuurkunde. Verhandelingen. Proceedings — K Nederlandse Akad Wetensch Afd Natuurk Verh Proc
Koninklijke Nederlandse Akademie van Wetenschappen, Afdeling Natuurkunde, Verhandelingen, Tweede Reeks — K Ned Akad Wet Afd Natuurkd Verh Tweede Reeks
Koninklijke Nederlandse Akademie van Wetenschappen. Indagationes Mathematicae ex Actis Quibus Titulus — Nederl Akad Wetensch Indag Math
Koninklijke Nederlandse Akademie van Wetenschappen. Proceedings — K Ned Akad Wet Proc
Koninklijke Nederlandse Akademie van Wetenschappen. Proceedings — Koninkl Nederlandse Akad Wetensch Proc
Koninklijke Nederlandse Akademie van Wetenschappen. Proceedings. Series A. Mathematical Sciences [*Netherlands*] — K Ned Akad Wet Proc Ser A
Koninklijke Nederlandse Akademie van Wetenschappen. Proceedings. Series A. Mathematical Sciences — K Ned Akad Wet Proc Ser A Math Sci
Koninklijke Nederlandse Akademie van Wetenschappen. Proceedings. Series A. Mathematical Sciences — KNWAA
Koninklijke Nederlandse Akademie van Wetenschappen. Proceedings. Series A. Mathematical Sciences — Nederl Akad Wetensch Proc Ser A
Koninklijke Nederlandse Akademie van Wetenschappen. Proceedings. Series B. Palaeontology, Geology, Physics, and Chemistry — K Ned Akad Wet Proc Ser B Palaeontol Geol Phys Chem
Koninklijke Nederlandse Akademie van Wetenschappen. Proceedings. Series B. Physical Sciences [*Koninklijke Nederlandse Akademie van Wetenschappen. Proceedings. Series B. Palaeontology, Geology, Physics, and Chemistry*] [*Netherlands*] [*Later,*] — K Ned Akad Wet Proc Ser B Phys Sci
Koninklijke Nederlandse Akademie van Wetenschappen. Proceedings. Series B. Physical Sciences [*Later, Koninklijke Nederlandse Akademie van Wetenschappen. Proceedings. Series B. Palaeontology, Geology, Physics, and Chemistry*] — Nederl Akad Wetensch Proc Ser B
Koninklijke Nederlandse Akademie van Wetenschappen. Proceedings. Series C. Biological and Medical Sciences [*Netherlands*] — K Ned Akad Wet Proc Ser C
Koninklijke Nederlandse Akademie van Wetenschappen. Proceedings. Series C. Biological and Medical Sciences — KNWCA
Koninklijke Nederlandse Akademie van Wetenschappen. Verhandelingen. Afd Natuurkunde Eerste Reeks — Konink Nederl Akad Wetensch Verh Afd Natuurk Eerste Reeks
Koninklijke Nederlandse Akademie van Wetenschappen. Verhandelingen. Afdeling Natuurkunde — Koninkl Nederlandse Akad Wetensch Verh Afd Natuurk
Koninklijke Nederlandse Akademie van Wetenschappen. Verhandelingen. Afdeling Natuurkunde. Tweede Reeks — K Ned Akad Wet Verh Afd Natuurkd Tweede Reeks
Koninklijke Nederlandse Akademie van Wetenschappen. Verhandelingen. Afdeling Natuurkunde. Tweede Reeks — VNAWAG
Koninklijke Nederlandse Akademie van Wetenschappen. Verslag van de Gewone Vergadering van de Afdeling Natuurkunde — K Ned Akad Wet Versl Gewone Vergad Afd Natuurkd
Koninklijke Nederlandse Akademie van Wetenschappen. Verslag van de Gewone Vergadering van de Afdeling Natuurkunde — Nederl Akad Wetensch Verslag Afd Natuurk
Koninklijke Nederlandse Middenstandsbond — KNMB
Koninklijke Nederlandse Natuurhistorische Vereniging. Uitgave — K Ned Natuurhist Ver Uitg
Koninklijke Nederlandse Natuurhistorische Vereniging. Uitgave — KNNUDP
Koninklijke Nederlandse Vereniging van Transportondernemingen — KNVTO
Koninklijke Vereeniging Indische Instituut — Kon Veren Indische Inst
Koninklijke Vereeniging Koloniaal Instituut, Afdeeling Handelsmuseum. Mededeeling — K Ver Kolon Inst Afd Handelsmus Meded
Koninklijke Vereeniging Koloniaal Instituut. Afdeeling Tropische Hygiene. Mededeeling — K Ver Kolon Inst Afd Trop Hyg Meded
Koninklijke Vereeniging Koloniaal Instituut Gids in het Volkenkundig Museum — Kon Veren Kol Inst G
Koninklijke Vereniging Indisch Instituut, Afdeling Tropische Hygiene. Mededeling — K Ver Indisch Inst Afd Trop Hyg Mededed
Koninklijke Vlaamsche Academie voor Wetenschappen. Letteren en Schone Kunsten van Belgie. Verslagen en Mededeelingen — K Vlaam Acad Wet Lett Schone Kunsten Belg Versl Meded
Koninklijke Vlaamse Academie voor Taal- en Letterkunde — KVATL
Koninklijke Vlaamse Academie voor Wetenschappen. Letteren en Schone Kunsten van Belgie. Jaarboek — K Vlaam Acad Wet Lett Schone Kunsten Belg Jaarb
Koninklijke Vlaamse Chemische Vereniging Tijdingen — K Vlaam Chem Ver Tijd
Koninklijke Zuidnederlandse Maatschappij voor Taal- en Letterkunde en Geschiedenis — KZMTLG
Konjunkturberichte — KONJD
Konjunkturberichte — Konjunkturber
Konjunkturpolitik — Konj Pol
Konjunkturpolitik — Konjunkturpol
Konjunkturpolitik. Zeitschrift fuer Angewandte Konjunkturforschung — KOJ
Konjunkturpolitik. Zeitschrift fuer Angewandte Konjunkturforschung. Beihefte — KOH
Konkurito Janaru — KOJAA
Konserven-Industrie. Allgemeine Deutsche Konserven-Zeitung — Konserv Ind Allg Dtsch Konserv Ztg
Konserven-Industrie (Moscow) — Konserv Ind Moscow
Konserves and Dybfrost — Konserv Dybfrost
Konservnaya i Ovoshchesushil'naya Promyshlennost' — Konserv Ovoshchesush Prom
Konservnaya i Ovoshchesushil'naya Promyshlennost' — Konservn Ovoshchesush Prom-St
Konservnaya i Ovoshchesushil'naya Promyshlennost' — KOPRA
Konservnaya i Plodoovoshchchnaya Promyshlennost — Konservn Plodoovoschchn Prom
Konservnaya i Plodoovoshchnaya Promyshlennost — Konservn Plodoovoshchn Promst
Konservnaya Promyshlennost — Konservn Promst
Konstanzer Blaetter fuer Hochschulfragen — Konstanz Bl Hochschulfr
Konsthistorisk Tidskrift — KHT
Konsthistorisk Tidskrift — Konsthist T
Konsthistorisk Tidskrift — Konsthist Tid
Konsthistorisk Tidskrift — Konsthist Tidskrift
Konsthistorisk Tidskrift — Konsthist Ts
Konsthistorisk Tidskrift — KoTi
Konsthistorisk Tidskrift — KT
Konstitution und Klinik — Konst Klin
Konstitutionelle Medizin — Konstit Med
Konstitutionelle Medizin und Neuraltherapie — Konstit Med Neur Ther
Konstitutsiya i Svoistva Mineralov — Konst Svoistva Miner
Konstitutsiya i Svoistva Mineralov — Konst Svoj Miner
Konstruieren mit Kunststoffen. Vortraege vom Konstruktions-Symposion der DECHEMA [*Deutsche Gesellschaft fuer Chemisches Apparatewesen, Chemische Technik, und Biotechnologie eV*] — Konstr Kunstst Vortr Konstr Symp DECHEMA
Konstruieren und Giessen [*Germany*] — Konstr Giessen
Konstruktion, Elemente, Methoden — Konstr Elem Methoden
Konstruktion im Maschinen-, Apparate-, und Geraetebau — KMAGA
Konstruktion im Maschinen-, Apparate-, und Geraetebau — Konstr Masch App Geraetebau

Konstruktion im Maschinen-, Apparate-, und Geraetebau — Konstr Masch-Appar- Geraetebau
Konstruktiver Ingenieurbau Berichte — KIBBA
Konstruktiver Ingenieurbau Berichte — Konstr Ingenieurbau Ber
Konstruktorskii — Konstrukt
Konstruktsionnye Materialy na Osnove Grafita — Konstr Mater Osn Grafita
Konstruktsionnye Materialy na Osnove Ugleroda — Konstr Mater Osn Ugleroda
Konstruktsionnye Uglegrafitovye Materialy Sbornik Trudov — Konstr Uglegrafitovye Mater Sb Tr
Konsultatsionnye Materialy Ukrainskii Gosudarstvennyi Institut Eksperimental'noi Farmatsii — Konsult Mater Ukr Gos Inst Eksp Farm
Konsument. Test Magazine der Konsumenteninformation — KAZ
Kontakblad van de Historische Vereniging van het Land van Maas en Waal — KVMW
Kontakt und Studium — Kontakt Stud
Kontexte — Kont
Kontrol i Tekhnologiya Protsessov Obogashcheniya Poleznykh Iskopaemykh — Kontrol Tekhnol Protsessov Obogashch Polezn Iskop
Kontrol'no Izmeritel'naya Tekhnika — Kontrol'no Izmer Tekh
Kontrol'nyi — Kontr
Konyv es Neveles — KoN
Konyvtari Figyelo — Konyvtari Figy
Konzepte der Sprack- und Literaturwissenschaft — KDSL
Konzepte eines Zeitgemaessen Physikunterrichts — Konzepte Zeitgemaess Physikunterrichts
Konzertzeitung. Blaetter der Philharmonie — Bll Philharm
Konzerv- es Paprikaipar — KONPA
Konzerv- es Paprikaipar — Konzerv-Paprikaip
Konzervipari Higieniai Napok — Konzervipari Hig Napok
Konzil von Chalkedon — Kon Chal
Kooperationen — Koop
Kooperativno Zemedelie — Kooper Zemed
Koopkracht. Blad voor de Konsument — CBJ
Koopman — KMA
Koordinatsionnaya Khimiya — Koord Khim
Kopalnictwo Naftowe w Polsce — Kopalnictwo Naft Pol
Kopenhagener Beitraege zur Germanistischen Linguistik — KBGL
Kopenhagener Germanistische Studien — KopGS
Koranyi Sandor Tarsasag Tudomanyos Ulesei — Koranyi Sandor Tarsasag Tud Ulesei
Korea and World Affairs — Kor World Aff
Korea Exchange Bank. Monthly Review — KRE
Korea. Geological and Mineral Institute. Report of Geological and Mineral Exploration — Korea Geol and Miner Inst Rep of Geol Miner Explor
Korea. Geological Survey. Geology and Ground-Water Resources — Korea Geol Surv Geol Ground Water Resour
Korea. Institute of Energy and Resources. Bulletin — KIER Bulletin
Korea Institute of Energy and Resources. Report on Geoscience and Mineral Resources — Korea Inst Energy Resour Rep Geosci Miner Resour
Korea. Institute of Forest Genetics. Research Reports — Korea Inst Forest Genet Res Rept
Korea Journal — KJ
Korea Journal — KoJ
Korea Journal [*Republic of Korea*] — Kor J
Korea Journal — Korea J
Korea Journal of Comparative Law [*Republic of Korea*] — Kor J Comp Law
Korea Journal of International Studies [*Republic of Korea*] — Kor J Int Stud
Korea Medical Journal — Korea Med J
Korea Observer — KO
Korea Observer [*Republic of Korea*] — Kor Obs
Korea Research Institute of Geoscience and Mineral Resources. KIGAM Bulletin — Korea Res Inst Geosci Miner Resour KIGAM Bull
Korea Studies Forum [*Pittsburg*] — Kor Stud Forum
Korea Trade Report — KTR
Korea University. Medical Journal — Korea Univ Med J
Korea World Affairs — Korea Wld Aff
Korean Affairs — KA
Korean Applied Physics — Korean Appl Phys
Korean Arachnology — KOARER
Korean Arachnology — Korean Arachnol
Korean Bee Journal — Korean Bee J
Korean Biochemical Journal — Korean Biochem J
Korean Business Review — KBE
Korean Central Journal of Medicine — Korean Cent J Med
Korean Chemical Society. Bulletin — Korean Chem Soc Bull
Korean Frontier — KF
Korean Institute of Mineral and Mining Engineers. Journal [*Republic of Korea*] — Korean Inst Miner Min Eng J
Korean Journal of Agricultural Economics — Korean J Agric Econ
Korean Journal of Animal Sciences — Korean J Anim Sci
Korean Journal of Applied Entomology — Korean J Appl Entomol
Korean Journal of Applied Microbiology and Bioengineering [*Republic of Korea*] — Korean J Appl Microbiol Bioeng
Korean Journal of Applied Statistics — Korean J Appl Statist
Korean Journal of Biochemistry — Korean J Biochem
Korean Journal of Botany — Korean J Bot
Korean Journal of Breeding [*Republic of Korea*] — Korean J Breed
Korean Journal of Ceramics — Korean J Ceram
Korean Journal of Chemical Engineering — Korean J Chem Eng
Korean Journal of Computational and Applied Mathematics — Korean J Comput Appl Math
Korean Journal of Dairy Science — Korean J Dairy Sci
Korean Journal of Dermatology — Korean J Dermatol
Korean Journal of Entomology — Korean J Entomol
Korean Journal of Environmental Health Society [*Republic of Korea*] — Korean J Environ Health Soc
Korean Journal of Food Science and Technology — Korean J Fd Sci Technol
Korean Journal of Food Science and Technology — Korean J Food Sci Technol
Korean Journal of Genetics — KJGEDG
Korean Journal of Genetics — Korean J Genet
Korean Journal of Hematology — Korean J Hematol
Korean Journal of Horticultural Science [*South Korea*] — Korean J Hort Sci
Korean Journal of Horticultural Science — Korean J Hortic Sci
Korean Journal of Internal Medicine — Korean J Intern Med
Korean Journal of International Studies — KJIS
Korean Journal of International Studies — Korean J Ind Stud
Korean Journal of Medicinal Chemistry — Korean J Med Chem
Korean Journal of Microbiology — Korean J Microbiol
Korean Journal of Mycology — HKCHDD
Korean Journal of Mycology — Korean J Mycol
Korean Journal of Nuclear Medicine — Korean J Nucl Med
Korean Journal of Nutrition — Korean J Nutr
Korean Journal of Obstetrics and Gynecology — Korean J Obstet Gynecol
Korean Journal of Ophthalmology — Korean J Ophthalmol
Korean Journal of Parasitology — Korean J Parasitol
Korean Journal of Pharmacognosy — Korean J Pharmacogn
Korean Journal of Pharmacology — Korean J Pharmacol
Korean Journal of Physiology [*South Korea*] — Korean J Physiol
Korean Journal of Plant Pathology — Korean J Plant Pathol
Korean Journal of Plant Protection [*South Korea*] — Korean J Plant Prot
Korean Journal of Preventive Medicine — Korean J Prev Med
Korean Journal of Public Health — Korean J Public Health
Korean Journal of Radiology — Korean J Radiol
Korean Journal of Sericultural Science — Korean J Seric Sci
Korean Journal of Urology [*Republic of Korea*] — Korean J Urol
Korean Journal of Veterinary Research [*Republic of Korea*] — Korean J Vet Res
Korean Journal of Zoology — Korean J Zool
Korean Medical Abstracts — KOMAB
Korean Medicine — Kor Med
Korean Research Institute of Geoscience and Mineral Resources. Report on Geoscience and Mineral Resources — Korean Res Inst Geosci Miner Resour Rep Geosci Miner Resour
Korean Review — Korean R
Korean Scientific Abstracts [*South Korea*] — Korean Sci Abstr
Korean Scientific Abstracts — Korean Sci Abstracts
Korean Scientific Abstracts — KOSAB
Korean Scientific Abstracts — KSABD
Korean Society of Animal Nutrition and Feedstuffs — Korean Soc Anim Nutr & Feedstuffs
Korean Studies Forum [*Republic of Korea*] — Korean Stud For
Korean Survey — KS
Koreana Quarterly — Koreana Quart
Koreana Quarterly — KQ
Korhaz- es Orvostechnika [*Hungary*] — Korh Orvostech
Korma i Kormlenie Sel'skokhozyaitvennykh Zhivotnykh — Korma Korml Skh Zhivotn
Korma i Produkty Zhivotnovodstva — Korma Prod Zhivotnovod
Kormi ta Godivlya Sil's'kogospodars'kikh Tvarin — Kormi Godivlya Sil's'kogospod Tvarin
Kormlenie Sel'skokhozyaistvennykh Zhivotnykh — Korml Skh Zhivotn
Kormoproizvodstvo Sbornik Nauchnykh Rabot — Kormoproizvod Sb Nauchn Rab
Korn Magasinet — Korn Mag
Koronarinsuffizienz. Symposium der Deutschen Gesellschaft fuer Fortschritte auf dem Gebiet der Inneren Medizin — Koronarinsuffizienz Symp Dtsch Ges Fortschr Geb Inn Med
Korose a Ochrana Materialu — Korose Ochr Mater
Koroze a Ochrana Materialu — KOCMA
Koroze a Ochrana Materialu — Koroze Ochr Mater
Korozija i Zastita — Koroz Zast
Korpus Bosporskikh Nadpisei — KBN
Korpuskularphotographie. Vortraege und Diskussionen auf dem Internationalen Kolloquium ueber Korpuskularphotographie — Korpuskularphotogr Vortr Diskuss Int Kolloq
Korrelyatsiya Endogennykh Protsessov Dal'nego Vostoka SSSR — Korrel Endog Protsessov Dalnego Vostoka SSSR
Korrespondenz Abwasser — Korresp Abwasser
Korrespondenzblaetter des Allgemeinen Aerztlichen Vereins von Thueringen — Korr Bl Thuering
Korrespondenzblaetter des Archivs fuer Anthropologie und Urgeschichte — Ko Bl A f A
Korrespondenzblaetter des Archivs fuer Anthropologie und Urgeschichte — Korrbll Arch Anthropol
Korrespondenzblatt der Aerztlichen Kreis- und Bezirksvereine in Sachsen — Korrbl Aerztl Kreisver Sachs
Korrespondenzblatt der Deutschen Anthropologischen Gesellschaft — Ko Bl DAG
Korrespondenzblatt der Deutschen Gesellschaft fuer Anthrolopogie, Ethnologie, und Urgeschichte — Korr Blatt
Korrespondenzblatt der Deutschen Gesellschaft fuer Anthrolopogie, Ethnologie, und Urgeschichte — Korrbl Dt Ges Anthr Eth Urgesch
Korrespondenzblatt der Deutschen Gesellschaft fuer Anthropologie — KBlAnthr
Korrespondenzblatt der Deutschen Gesellschaft fuer Anthropologie — Korrbl Dt Ges Anthropol
Korrespondenzblatt der Deutschen Gesellschaft fuer Anthropologie, Ethnologie, und Urgeschichte — KDGA
Korrespondenzblatt der Westdeutschen Zeitschrift fuer Geschichte und Kunst — Korrbl Westdn Zeitschr

Korrespondenzblatt der Westdeutschen Zeitschrift fuer Geschichte und Kunst — Korrbl Westdt Zs Gesch
Korrespondenzblatt der Westdeutschen Zeitschrift fuer Geschichte und Kunst — KWZ
Korrespondenzblatt des Gesamtvereins der Deutschen Geschichts- und Altertumsvereine — KGVDG
Korrespondenzblatt des Gesamt-Vereins der Deutschen Geschichts- und Altertumsvereine — Korrbl Gesamtver Dt Geschver
Korrespondenzblatt des Vereins fuer Niederdeutsche Sprachforschung — Korr Bl Nd S
Korrespondenzblatt des Vereins fuer Niederdeutsche Sprachforschung — Korrbl Ver Niederdt Sprachforsch
Korrespondenzblatt des Vereins fuer Niederdeutsche Sprachforschung — Nd Kbl
Korrespondenzblatt des Vereins fuer Niederdeutsche Sprachforschung — Niederdt Kbl
Korrespondenzblatt des Vereins fuer Siebenbuergische Landeskunde — Ko Bl VSL
Korrespondenzblatt des Vereins zur Gruendung und Erhaltung einer Akademie fuer die Wissenschaft des Judentums — KVAWJ
Korrespondenzblatt fuer die Hoeheren Schulen Wuerttembergs — KBW
Korrespondenzblatt fuer die Hoeheren Schulen Wuerttembergs — Korrespondenzbl Wuertt
Korrespondenzblatt. Gesamtverein der Deutschen Geschichte und Altertumsvereine — KBDA
Korrespondenzblatt. Verein fuer Niederdeutsche Sprachforschung — Kbl
Korrespondenzblatt. Verein fuer Niederdeutsche Sprachforschung — KVNS
Korrespondenzblatt. Verein fuer Niederdeutsche Sprachforschung — Nd Kbl
Korrespondenzblatt. Verein fuer Niederdeutsche Sprachforschung — Nd Ko Bl
Korrespondenzbriefe fuer Zuckerfabriken — Korrespondenzbriefe Zuckerfabr
Korrosion och Ytskydd — Korros Ytskydd
Korrosion und Ihre Bekaempfung — Korros Ihre Bekaempf
Korrosion und Metallschutz — Korros Metallschutz
Korrosionsinstitutet. Bulletin — Korrosionsinst Bull
Korrosionsinstitutet. Rapport — KI Rapp
Korrosionsinstitutet. Rapport — Korrosionsinst Rapp
Korrozios Figyelo — Korroz Figyelo
Korroziya i Bor'ba s Nei — Korroz Borba Nei
Korroziya i Zashchita Konstruktsionnykh Metallicheskikh Materialov — Korroz Zashch Konstr Met Mater
Korroziya i Zashchita ot Korrozii — Korroz Zashch Korroz
Korroziya i Zashchita v Neftegazovoi Promyshlennosti [*Former USSR*] — Korroz Zashch Neftegazov Prom-St
Korroziya i Zashchita v Neftegazovoi Promyshlennosti Nauchno-Tekhnicheskii Sbornik — Korroz Zashch
Korroziya Metallov i Splavov [*Former USSR*] — Korroz Met Splavov
Korroziya Tsementov i Mery Bor'by s Nei — Korroz Tsem Mery Borby Nei
Korroziya v Khimicheskikh Proizvodstvakh i Sposoby Zashchity — Korroz Khim Proizvod Sposoby Zashch
Korsakov Journal of Neurology and Psychiatry — Kors J Neur Psych
Korsakov Journal of Neurology and Psychiatry — Korsakov J Neurol Psychiatry
Korte Berichten over Buitenlandse Projecten — PFA
Korte Berichten over Handel, Ambacht, Dienstverlening, Toerisme, Middenbedrijf, en Kleinbedrijf — LDG
Korte Berichten voor de Chemiebranche — KCH
Korte Berichten voor de Kledingbranche — KBK
Korte Berichten voor de Machinebranche en Apparatenbranche — KBA
Korte Berichten voor de Meubelbranche en Stofferingsbranche — KBM
Korte Berichten voor de Verfbranche — KBV
Korte Berichten voor de Verpakkingsbranche — KBP
Korte Berichten Voor Landbouw, Nijverheid en Handel — Korte Ber Landb
Korte Berichten voor Milieu — MIN
Korte Mededeeling van het Landbouwproefstation in Suriname — Korte Meded Landbouwproefstat Suriname
Korte Mededeling Stichting Bosbouwproefstation "De Dorschkamp" — Korte Meded Bosbouwproefsta
Korte Mededelingen Stichting Bosbouwproefstation "De Dorschkamp" — Korte Meded Sticht Bosbproefstn Dorschkamp
Korte Verklaring der Heilige Schrift [*Kampen*] — KV
Korte Verklaring der Heilige Schrift — KVHS
Koseisho Gan Kenkyu Joseikin Ni Yoru Kenkyu Hokoku — KKJHD
Koshu Eiseiin Kenkyu Hokoku — KEKHA
Kosmetiek — PAR
Kosmetik Journal — Kosmet J
Kosmetik-Parfum-Drogen Rundschau — Kosmet Parfum Drogen Rundsch
Kosmetische Chemie, Kongress der Internationalen Foederation der Gesellschaften der Kosmetik-Chemikev. Vortraege und Diskussionen — Kosmet Chem Kongr Int Foed Ges Kosmet Chem Vortr Diskuss
Kosmetologie. Zeitschrift fuer Kosmetik in Wissenschaft und Praxis — Kosmetol
Kosmiceskie Issledovanija — Kosmic Issled
Kosmiceskie Issledovanija — Kosmices Issled
Kosmicheskaya Biologiya i Aviakosmicheskaya Meditsina — KBAMA
Kosmicheskaya Biologiya i Aviakosmicheskaya Meditsina — Kosm B Av M
Kosmicheskaya Biologiya i Aviakosmicheskaya Meditsina — Kosm Biol Aviakosm Med
Kosmicheskaya Biologiya i Meditsina — KBMEA
Kosmicheskaya Biologiya i Meditsina — Kosm Biol Med
Kosmicheskaya Mineralogiya, Materialy S'ezda MMA — Kosm Mineral Mater Sezda MMA
Kosmicheskie Issledovaniya — KOISA
Kosmicheskie Issledovaniya — Kosm Issled
Kosmicheskie Issledovaniya na Ukraine [*Ukrainian SSR*] — Kosm Issled Ukr
Kosmicheskie Issledovaniya Zemnykh Resursov Metody i Sredstva Izmerenii i ObrAabotki Informatsii — Kosm Issled Zemnykh Resur
Kosmicheskie Luchi — Kosm Luchi
Kosmicheskie Luchi i Problemy Kosmofiziki. Trudy Vsesoyuznogo Soveshchaniya po Kosmofizicheskomu Napravleniyu Issledovanii Kosmicheskikh Luchei — Kosm Luchi Probl Kosmofiz Tr Vses Soveshch
Kosmicheskii — Kosmich
Kosmichni Izsledvaniya v Bulgariya — Kosm Izsled Bulg
Kosmokhimiya i Meteoritika. Materialy Vsesoyuznogo Simpoziuma — Kosmokhim Meteorit Mater Vses Simp
Kosmos [*Stuttgart*] — KSMSA
Kosmos Bibliothek — Kosmos Bibl
Kosmos. Seria A. Biologia (Warsaw) — KOSBA
Kosmos. Seria A. Biologia (Warsaw) — Kosmos Sor A Biol (Warsaw)
Kosmos. Seria A. Biologia (Warsaw) — Kosmos Ser A (Warsaw)
Kosmos. Seria B. Przyroda Nieozywiona (Warsaw) — Kosmos (Warsaw) Ser B
Kosmos-Baendchen — Kosm Bd
Kostnicke Jiskry — Ko Jis
Kostromskoi Gosudarstvennyi Pedagogiceskii Institut Imeni N. A. Nekrasova UcenyEe Zapiski — Kostrom Gos Ped Inst Ucen Zap
Koto Saibansho Keiji Hanreishu — Kokeishu
Koto Saibansho Minji Hanreishu — Kominshu
Kovcezic — Ko
Kovcezic — Kov
Kovodelny Prumysl — Kovodelny Prum
Kovove Materialy — KOMAA
Kovove Materialy — Kovove Mater
Kozarstvi — KOZAA
Kozgazdasagi Szemle — Kozgazd Szle
Kozhevenno-Obuvnaya Promyshlennost — KOOPA
Kozhevenno-Obuvnaya Promyshlennost [*Former USSR*] — Kozh-Obuvn Promst
Kozhevenno-Obuvnaya Promyshlennost SSSR — Kozh Obuvn Prom SSSR
Kozhevenno-Obuvnaya Promyshlennost SSSR — Kozh Obuvn Promst SSSR
Kozponti Fizikai Kutato Intezet Kozlemenyek — Kozp Fiz Kut Intez Kozl
Kozponti Fizikai Kutato Intezet. Report KFKI — Kozp Fiz Kut Intez Rep KFKI
Kraevedceskie Zapiski Kamcatskaja Oblastnajakraevedceskaja Muzeja — Kraeved Zap Kamc Obl Kraeved Muzeja
Kraevedcheskie Zapiski Oblastnoi Kraevedcheskoi Muzei Upravleniya Magadanskogo Oblispolkoma — Kraeved Zap Obl Kraeved Muz Upr Magadan Oblispolkoma
Kraevye Zadachi dlya Differentsial'nykh Uravnenij — Kraev Zadachi Differ Uravn
Kraftfahrtechnische Forschungsarbeiten — Kraftfahrtech Forschungsarb
Kraftfahrzeugtechnik — KFZTA
Kraftfutter — KFFUA
Krajowa Konferencja Kalorymetrii i Analizy Termicznej. Prace — Krajowa Konf Kalorym Anal Term Pr
Krajowa Szkola na Temat Mikroskopii Elektronowej — Krajowa Szk Temat Mikrosk Elektron
Krajowe Sympozjum Badania Nieniszczace w Budownictwie — Krajowe Symp Badania Nieniszczace Budow
Krajowe Sympozjum Podstawy Teorii Wyladowan Elektrycznych w Gazach. Prace — Krajowe Symp Podstawy Teor Wyladowan Elektr Gazach Pr
Krajowe Sympozjum Zastosowan Izotopow w Technice. Referaty — Krajowe Symp Zastosow Izot Tech Ref
Krajowy Zjazd Endokrynologow Polskich — Krajowy Zjazd Endokrynol Pol
Kraks Blaa Bog — KBB
Kralovska Ceska Spolecnost Nauk — KCSN
Kralupsky Vlastivedny Sbornik — Kralupsky Vlastiv Sborn
Krankenhaus — Krank Hs
Krankenhaus-Apotheke — Krankenhaus Apoth
Krankenhausarzt — Kr Hs A
Krankenhaus-Umschau — Kr Hs Umsch
Krankenhaus-Umschau — KRKHB
Krankenpflege Journal — Krankenpfl
Krankenpflege. Soins Infirmiers — Krankenpfl Soins Infirm
Krasnaja Nov' — KN
Krasnodarskii Gosudarstvennyi Pedagogicheskii Institut. Trudy — Krasnodar Gos Pedagog Inst Tr
Krasnodarskii Politekhnicheskii Institut. Trudy — Krasnodar Politekh Inst Tr
Krasnojarskii Politehniceskii Institut. Sbornik Naucnyh Trudov Mehaniceskogo Fakul'teta — Krasnojarsk Politehn Inst Sb Naucn Trudov Meh Fak
Krasnoyarskii Gosudarstvennyi Meditsinskii Institut. Trudy — Krasnoyarsk Gos Med Inst Tr
Krasnoyarskii Institut Tsvetnykh Metallov. Sbornik Trudov — Krasnoyarsk Inst Tsvetn Met Sb Tr
Kratka Bulgarska Enciklopedija — KBE
Kratkaia Evreiskaia Entsiklopediia — KEE
Kratkaja Literaturnaja Enciklopedija — KLE
Kratkie Soderzhaniya Dokladov. Vsesoyuznaya Simpozium po Vtorichnoi i Fotoelektronmoi Emissii — Kratk Soderzh Dokl Vses Simp Vtorichnoi Fotoelektron Emissii
Kratkie Soobscenija Instituta Arheologii — Kr Soobsc Inst Arheol
Kratkie Soobscenija o Doklakach i Polevych Issledovanijach Instituta Archeologii — Kra Soob
Kratkie Soobshcheniia — KS
Kratkie Soobshcheniia. Akademiia Nauk SSSR. Institut Arkheologii — KKSANIA
Kratkie Soobshcheniia. Akademiia Nauk SSSR. Institut Arkheologii — Kra Soob
Kratkie Soobshcheniia. Akademiia Nauk SSSR. Institut Arkheologii — Kra Soob Inst A
Kratkie Soobshcheniia. Akademiia Nauk SSSR. Institut Arkheologii — Krat Soob Akad Nauk Inst Arkh
Kratkie Soobshcheniia. Akademiia Nauk SSSR. Institut Arkheologii — Krat Soob Akad Nauk SSSR Inst Ark
Kratkie Soobshcheniia Institut Etnografii Akademiia Nauk SSSR — Krat Soob Inst Etnogr
Kratkie Soobshcheniia Institut Istorii Material'noi Kul'tury Akademiia Nauk SSSR — Krat Soob Inst Ist Mater Kul't

Kratkie Soobshcheniia Instituta Arkheologii Akademii Nauk SSSR — Krat Soob Inst Ark A N SSSR
Kratkie Soobshcheniia Instituta Arkheologii. Akademiia Nauk URSR — KC
Kratkie Soobshcheniia Instituta Arkheologii. Akademiia Nauk URSR — Kra Soob Inst A
Kratkie Soobshcheniia Instituta Arkheologii. Akademiia Nauk URSR — KSI AAN USSR
Kratkie Soobshcheniia Instituta Arkheologii. Akademiia Nauk URSR — KSIA
Kratkie Soobshcheniia Instituta Arkheologii. Akademiia Nauk URSR (Kiev) — KS Kiev
Kratkie Soobshcheniia Instituta Arkheologii. Akademiia Nauk URSR (Kiev) — Ksia Kiev
Kratkie Soobshcheniia o Polevykh Arkheologicheskikh Issledovaniiakh Odesskogo Gosudarotvennogo Arkheologicheskogo Muzeia — KS Odessa
Kratkie Soobshcheniia o Polevykh Arkheologicheskikh Issledovaniiakh Odesskogo Gosudarotvennogo Arkheologicheskogo Muzeia — KSOGAM
Kratkie Soobshcheniia o Polevykh Arkheologicheskikh Issledovaniiakh Odesskogo Gosudarstvennogo Arkheologicheskogo Muzeia — Krat Soob OGAM
Kratkie Soobshcheniya. Akademiya Nauk SSSR. Institut Arkheologii — KSIA
Kratkie Soobshcheniya. Akademiya Nauk SSSR. Institut Etnografii imeni N. N. Miklucho-Maklaja — KSIE
Kratkie Soobshcheniya Buryatskogo Kompleksnogo Nauchno-Issledovatel'skogo Instituta — Kratk Soobshch Buryat Kompleksn Nauchno-Issled Inst
Kratkie Soobshcheniya po Fizike — Kratk Soobshch Fiz
Kratkije Soobscenija Breves Communications de l'Institute d'Archeologie (Kiev) — KrSoob(Kiev)
Kratkije Soobscenija Instituta Ethnografiji Akademiji Nauk SSSR — Kratkije Soobscenija Inst Eth
Kratkije Soobscenija Instituta Narodov Azii — KSINA
Kratkije Soobscenija Instituta Slajanovednija Akademija Nauk SSSR — KSISL
Kratkije Soobscenija Instituta Vostokovedenija Akademija Nauk SSSR — KSIV
Kratkir Soobscenija Burjatskogo Kompleksnogo Naucnoissledovatel'skogo Instituta Serija Storiko-Filologiceskaja — KSBurNII
Krebsarzt — Krebs A
Krebsforschung — Krebsforsch
Krebsforschung und Krebsbekaempfung [*Germany*] — Krebsforsch Krebsbekaempf
Kredietbank. Weekberichten — KRB
Kredietbank. Weekly Bulletin — Kredietbank W Bul
Kredietwaardigheden — DCD
Kredit und Kapital — Kredit U Kapital
Kresge Art Center. Bulletin — Kresge Art Bull
Kresge Eye Institute. Bulletin — Kresge Eye Inst Bull
Krestanska Revue — Kr R
Krestanska Revue [*Prague*] — KrestR
Krestanska Revue [*Prague*] — KrK
Krestanska Revue. Theologicka Priloha [*Prague*] — KrestRTPril
Krestanska Revue. Theologicka Priloha [*Prague*] — KrRThPr
Krete, Mykene, Troy — KMT
Kretika Chronika — K Chr
Kretika Chronika — KChron
Kretika Chronika — Kr Ch
Kretika Chronika — Kret Chron
Kretika Chronika — Krit Chron
Kriegsopferversorgung — KOV
Kriegstechnische Zeitschrift (Berlin) — Kriegst Zs Berlin
Kriegsvortraege der Rheinischen Friedrich-Wilhelms-Universitaet Bonn am Rhein — KRFWU
Kriminalistik — KRMNA
Kriminalistik und Forensische Wissenschaften — Krim Forensische Wiss
Kriogennaya i Vakuumnaya Tekhnika [*Ukrainian SSR*] — Kriog Vak Tekh
Kriogennye Mashiny — Kriog Mash
Kris Study Group of the New York Psychoanalytic Institute. Monograph — Kris Study Group NY Psychoanal Inst Monogr
Kristall und Technik — Krist Tech
Kristall und Technik — Krist und Tech
Kristall und Technik — Kristall Tech
Kristall und Technik — KRTEA
Kristallizatsiya i Svoistva Kristallov — Krist Svoistva Krist
Kristallizatsiya Zhidkosti — Krist Zhidk
Kristallografiya — KRISA
Kristallografiya — Kristallogr
Kristallographie. Grundlagen und Anwendung — Kristallogr Grundl Anwend
Kristallokhimiya Neorganicheskikh Soedinenii — Kristallokhim Neorg Soedin
Kristeligt Dagblad — KD
Kristen Gemenskap — Kr Ge
Kriterii Prognoznoi Otsenki Territorii na Tverdye Poleznye Iskopaemye — Kriter Prognoznoi Otsenki Territ Tverd Polezn Iskop
Kriterion — Krit
Kritik (Copenhagen) — KritC
Kritik des Oeffentlichen Lebens — K d Oe L
Kritika Burzhuaznykh Kontseptsii Vseobshchei Istorii — KKI
Kritika Chronika — K Ch
Kritika Chronika — KC
Kritika Chronika — Kr Chron
Kritika Phylla — KP
Kritikas Gadagramata — K Gad
Kritische Berichte zur Kunstgeschichtlichen Literatur — KBKL
Kritische Blaetter der Boersenhalle — Krit Blaett Boersenhalle
Kritische Blaetter der Forst- und Jagdwissenschaft — Krit Blaett Forst Jagdwiss
Kritische Blaetter zur Literatur der Gegenwart — KBLG
Kritische Justiz — Krit Justiz
Kritische Justiz — KRJUD
Kritische Vierteljahresschrift — KVJS
Kritische Vierteljahresschrift fuer Gesetzgebung — KVG
Kritische Vierteljahresschrift fuer Gesetzgebung und Rechtswissenschaft — Krit Viertel Ges Recht
Kritische Vierteljahresschrift fuer Gesetzgebung und Rechtswissenschaft — KVGR
Kritische Vierteljahrsschrift fuer Gesetzgebung und Rechtswissenschaft — Krit VJSchr
Kritische Vierteljahrsschrift fuer Gesetzgebung und Rechtswissenschaft — KritVj
Kritisches Journal der Neuesten Theologischen Literatur — KJNTL
Kritisches Journal fuer das Katholische Deutschland — KJKD
Kritisch-Exegetischer Kommentar ueber das Neue Testament — KEK
Kroc Foundation Series — Kroc Found Ser
Kroc Foundation Symposia — Kroc Found Symp
Kroeber Anthropological Society. Papers — Kroeber Anthro Soc Pap
Kroeber Anthropological Society Papers — Kroeber Anthropol Soc Pap
Kroeners Taschenausgabe — KTA
Krokodil — Kr
Krolikovodstvo i Zverovodstvo — Krolikovod Zverovod
Kroniek — Kr
Kroniek van Afrika — Kroniek van Afr
Kroniek van het Ambacht/Kleinbedrijf en Middenbedrijf — KRA
Kroniek van Kunst en Kultur — KVKEK
Kronika — Kr
Kronika — Kron
Kronobergsboken Arsbok foer Hylten-Cavallius Foereningen — Kronobergsboken
KRS Jugoslavije/Carsus Iugoslaviae — KRS Jugosl/Carsus Iugosl
Krupp Technical Review [*English Translation*] — KRTRA
Krupp Technical Review (English Translation) [*Germany*] — Krupp Tech Rev (Engl Transl)
Kruppsche Monatsheft — Kruppsche Monatsh
Krymskii Gosudarstvennyi Meditsinskii Institut Trudy — Krym Gos Med Inst Tr
Krystalizacja Przemyslowa. Krajowe Sympozjum. Materialy Konferencyjne — Kryst Przem Krajowe Symp Mater Konf
Krzepniecie Metali i Stopow — Krzepniecie Met Stopow
KSB [*Klein, Schanzlin, Becker*] **Technische Berichte** [*Germany*] — KSB Tech Ber
Ksiazka i Wiedza — KiW
KSU (Kyoto Sangyo University). Economic and Business Review — KSU (Kyoto Sangyo Univ) Econ and Bus R
Ktavim Records of the Agricultural Research Station — Ktavim Rec Agric Res Stn
KTMF. Tudomanyos Koezlemenyei — KTMF Tud Koezl
K'uang Yeh — KNGYA
K'uang Yeh Chi Shu — KYCSA
Kubanskii Gosudarstvennyi Universitet Naucnyi Trudy — Kuban Gos Univ Naucn Trudy
Kubanskoe Otdelenie Vsesoyuznogo Obshchestva Genetikov i Selektsionerov. Trudy — Kuban Otd Vses Ova Genet Sel Tr
Kubota Technical Reports — Kubota Tech Rep
Kuchurganskii Liman - Okhladitel Moldavskoi GRES [*Gosudarstvennaya Raionnaya Elektro-Stantsiya*] — Kuchurganskii Liman Okhladitel Mold GRES
Kuehlungsborner Kolloquium — Kuehlungsborner Kolloq
Kuehn-Archiv — Kuehn-Arch
Kuelfoeldi Agrarirodalmi Roevid Kivonatai. Kerteszet, Szoeleszet, Boraszat — Kuelf Agrarirod Roevid Kivonatai Kert
Kuelfoeldi Agrarirodalmi Roevid Kivonatai. Noevenyvedelem — Kuelf Agrarirod Roevid Kivonatai Noevenyved
Kuelfoeldi Agrarirodalmi Szemle. Noevenyvedelem — Kuelf Agrarirod Szemle Noevenyved
Kuelfoeldi Agrarirodalom Szemleje. Kerteszet es Szoeleszet — Kuelf Agrarirod Szemleje Kert Szoelesz
Kuelfoeldi es Hazai Agrarirodalmi Szemle. Erdeszet — Kuelf Hazai Agrarirod Szemle Erdesz
Kuelfoeldi es Hazai Agrarirodalmi Szemle. Noevenyvedelem — Kuelf Hazai Agrarirod Szemle Noevenyved
Kuelfoeldi Meheszeti Szemle — Kuelfoeldi Mehesz Szemle
Kuerchners Deutscher Gelehrtenkalender — KDGK
Kugellager-Zeitschrift — Kugellager-Z
Kuhns Zeitschrift fuer Vergleichende Sprachforschung — Zs Vglde Sprachforsch
Kuibysevskii Gosudarstvennyi Pedagogiceskii Institut Naucnyi Trudy — Kuibysev Gos Ped Inst Naucn Trudy
Kuibyshevskaya Nauchno-Issledovatel'skaya Veterinarnaya Stantsiya. Sbornik Nauchnykh Trudov — Kuibyshev Nauchno Issled Vet Stn Sb Nauchn Tr
Kuibyshevskaya Neft — Kuibyshev Neft
Kuibyshevskii Aviatsionnyi Institut imeni Akademika S.P. Koroleva. Trudy — Kuibyshev Aviats Inst im Akad SP Koroleva Tr
Kuibyshevskii Gosudarstvennyi Pedagogicheskii Institut imeni V.V. Kuibysheva. Nauchnye Trudy — Kuibyshev Gos Pedagog Inst im VV Kuibysheva Nauchn Tr
Kuibyshevskii Inzhenerno-Stroitel'nyi Institut Trudy — Kuibyshev Inzh Stroit Inst Tr
Kuibyshevskii Meditsinskii Institut imeni D. I. Ul'yanova. Trudy — Kuibyshev Med Inst im DI Ulyanova Tr
Kukem Dergisi — Kukem Derg
Kuki Seijo — KUSEB
Kukuruza — KUKUA
Kulliyat al-Ulum, Majallah — Kulliyat Ulum Maj
Kultur — K
Kultur in Literatur — KL
Kultur og Folkeminder — KOF
Kultur og Klasse — Ku Kl
Kultur und Katholizismus — Kul Kath

Kultur und Leben — Kult u Leben
Kultur und Natur in Niederoesterreich — KNNOe
Kultura — KA
Kultura es Jozosseg — Kult es Jozosseg
Kul'tura i Iskusstvo Antichnogo Mira i Vostoka — KIAM
Kultura i Spoleczenstwo — KiS
Kultura i Spoleczenstwo — Kult i Spolecz
Kultura Slova — KS
Kultura Slova — KSl
Kultura (Warsaw) — KulturaW
Kulturarbeit — KA
Kulturas Biroja Biletins [*Bulletin. Cultural Bureau of the American Latvian Association in the US*] — KBB
Kulturen Arsbok till Medlemmerna av Kulturhistoriska Foerening foer Soedra Sverige — Kulturen
Kultur-Fronten — KuFr
Kulturgeografi — Kultggr
Kulturgeschichtliche Forschungen — KGF
Kulturhistorische Liebhaberbibliothek — KLB
Kulturhistorisk Leksikon foer Nordisk Middelalder [*Kobenhavn*] — KLNMD
Kulturhistorisk Leksikon foer Nordisk Middelalder [*Oslo*] — KLNMN
Kulturhistoriskt Lexsikon foer Nordisk Medeltid [*Malmoe*] — KLNMS
Kulturminder — Kultm
Kulturni Politika — KP
Kulturny Zivot [*Bratislava*] — KZ
Kulturos Barai — KB
Kulturpflanze Beiheft — Kulturpflanze Beih
Kultuurpatronen. Bulletin Etnografisch Museum (Delft) — KBEMD
Kumamoto Daigaku Kogakubu Kenkyu Hokoku — KUDKA
Kumamoto Daigaku Taishitsu Igaku Kenkyusho Hokoku — KDTIA
Kumamoto Journal of Mathematics — Kumamoto J Math
Kumamoto Journal of Science — Kumamoto J Sci
Kumamoto Journal of Science. Biology — Kumamoto J Sci Biol
Kumamoto Journal of Science. Geology — Kumamoto J Sci Geol
Kumamoto Journal of Science. Mathematics — Kumamoto J Sci Math
Kumamoto Journal of Science. Sect 2. Biology — Kumamoto J Sci Sect 2 Biol
Kumamoto Journal of Science. Series A. Mathematics, Physics, and Chemistry — KJSAA
Kumamoto Journal of Science. Series A. Mathematics, Physics, and Chemistry — Kumamoto J Sci Ser A
Kumamoto Journal of Science. Series A. Mathematics, Physics, and Chemistry — Kumamoto Jour Sci Ser A Mathematics Physics and Chemistry
Kumamoto Journal of Science. Series B. Section 1. Geology — Kumamoto J Sci Ser B Sect 1
Kumamoto Journal of Science. Series B. Section 2. Biology — KJSBA
Kumamoto Journal of Science. Series B. Section 2. Biology — Kumamoto J Sci Ser B Sect 2 Biol
Kumamoto Medical Journal — Kumamoto Med J
Kumamoto Medical Journal — KUMJA
Kumamoto Pharmaceutical Bulletin — Kumamoto Pharm Bull
Kumamoto University. Faculty of Education. Memoirs. Natural Science — Mem Fac Ed Kumamoto Univ Natur Sci
Kun Chung Hseuh Pao. Acta Entomologica Sinica — Kun Chung Hseuh Pao Acta Entomol Sin
K'ung Meng Msueh-Pao [*Journal. Confucius Mencius Society*] — KMHP
Kungl Skogs- och Lantbruksakademiens Tidskrift. Supplement — K Skogs Lantbruksakad Tidskr Suppl
Kungl Skytteanska Samfundets Handlingar — KSSH
Kungliga Fysiografiska Saelleskapets i Lund. Foerhandlingar — KFSLAW
Kungliga Fysiografiska Saellskapets i Lund. Arsbok — K Fysiogr Sallsk Lund Arsb
Kungliga Fysiografiska Saellskapets i Lund. Arsbok — KFSAAX
Kungliga Fysiografiska Saellskapets i Lund. Foerhandlingar — K Fysiogr Sallsk Lund Forh
Kungliga Fysiografiska Sallskapets i Lund. Handlingar — K Fysiogr Sallsk Lund Handl
Kungliga Gustav Adolfs Akademiens. Minnesbok — KGAAM
Kungliga Humanistika Vetenskaps-Samfundets Arsbok — Arsb Kungl Humanist Vet Samf
Kungliga Humanistiska Vetenskapssamfundet i Lund. Arsberattelse — AHVsLund
Kungliga Humanistiska Vetenskapssamfundet i Uppsala — KHVSU
Kungliga Humanistiska Vetenskapssamfundet i Uppsala. Arsbok — AHVsUppsala
Kungliga Krigsvetenskapsakademiens. Handlingar och Tidskrift — K Krigsvetenskapakad Handlingar Tidskr
Kungliga Krigsvetenskapsakademiens Tidskrift — Kungl Krigsvetenskapsakad T
Kungliga Lantbruksakademien. Ekonomiska Avdelning. Meddelande — K Lantbruksakad Ekon Avd Medd
Kungliga Lantbruksakademien. Tekniska Avdelning. Meddelande — K Lantbruksakad Tek Avd Medd
Kungliga Lantbruksakademien. Traedgaardsavdelning. Meddelande — K Lantbruksakad Traedgaardsavd Medd
Kungliga Lantbruksakademien. Vetenskapsavdelning. Meddelande — K Lantbruksakad Vetenskapsavd Medd
Kungliga Lantbruks-Akademiens. Handlingar och Tidskrift — K Lantbruks Akad Handl Tidskr
Kungliga Lantbruksakademiens. Tidskrift — K Lantbruksakad Tidskr
Kungliga Lantbruksakademiens. Tidskrift — KLATA8
Kungliga Lantbrukshoegskolan och Statens Lantbruksfoersoek. Statens Husdjursforsok Meddelande — KLSSAR
Kungliga Lantbrukshoegskolan och Statens Lantbruksfoersoek. Statens Jordbruksfoersoek Meddelande — K Lantbrukshoegsk Statens Lantbruksfoers Jordbruksfoers Medd
Kungliga Lantbrukshoegskolans. Annaler — K Lantbrhogsk Annlr
Kungliga Lantbruks-Hoegskolans Annaler — K Lantbruks Hoegsk Ann
Kungliga Lantbrukshoegskolans. Annaler — K Lantbrukshogsk Ann
Kungliga Lantbrukshoegskolans. Annaler — KLHAAK
Kungliga Lantbruksstyrelsen. Meddelande — K Lantbruksstyr Medd
Kungliga Skogs- och Lantbruksakademiens. Tidskrift — K Skogs o Lantbr Akad Tidskr
Kungliga Skogs- och Lantbruksakademiens. Tidskrift — KSLTA
Kungliga Svenska Vetenskapsakademiens. Avhandlingar i Naturskyddsarenden — K Sven Vetenskapsakad Avh Naturskyddsarenden
Kungliga Svenska Vetenskapsakademiens. Handlingar — K Sven Vetenskapsakad Handl
Kungliga Svenska Vetenskaps-Akademiens. Handlingar. Oefversigt til Handlingar — K Svenska Vet-Ak Hdl Oefv
Kungliga Svenska Vetenskapsakademiens. Skrifter i Naturskyddsarenden — K Sven Vetenskapsakad Skr Naturskyddsarenden
Kungliga Tekniska Hoegskolans. Handlingar [*Sweden*] — K Tek Hoegsk Handl
Kungliga Vetenskapsakademien. Nobelinstitut. Meddelanden — K Vetenskapsakad Nobelinst Medd
Kungliga Vetenskaps-Akademiens. Handlingar — K Vetensk Akad Handl
Kungliga Vetenskaps-Akademiens. Nya Handlingar (Stockholm) — K Vetensk Akad N Handl (Stockholm)
Kungliga Vetenskapssamhaellets i Uppsala. Arsbok — K Vetenskapssamh Uppsala Arsb
Kungliga Vetenskaps-Societetens. Arsbok — K Vetensk-Soc Arsb
Kungliga Vitterhets Historie och Antikvitets Akademiens. Handlingar — KVHAAH
Kunst der Nederlanden — KN
Kunst der Welt in den Berliner Museen — Ku Welt Berl Mus
Kunst des Orients — KdO
Kunst des Orients — KO
Kunst des Orients — Ku Or
Kunst des Orients — Kunst Or
Kunst en Cultuur — K & C
Kunst fuer Alle — KfA
Kunst in Hessen und am Mittelrhein — KHM
Kunst in Hessen und am Mittelrhein — KHMR
Kunst und Antiquariat — KuA
Kunst und Antiquariat — Kunst u Antiq
Kunst und Kirche — KuKi
Kunst und Kuenstler — K & K
Kunst und Kultur der Hethiter — KKH
Kunst und Kunsthandwerk — KuKh
Kunst und Literatur — KL
Kunst und Literatur — KuL
Kunst und Literatur. Sowjetwissenschaft Zeitschrift zur Verbreitung Sowjetischer Erfahrungen — Kunst u Lit
Kunst und Sprache — K & S
Kunstblatt der Jugend — Kunstbl Jugend
Kunstchronik — KC
Kunstchronik — Kunstchr
Kunstduenger- und Leim-Industrie — Kunstduenger Leim Ind
Kunstgeschichte in Bildern — KB
Kunstgeschichte in Bildern — KIB
Kunstgeschichtliche Anzeigen — KAnz
Kunstgeschichtliche Anzeigen — KGA
Kunstgeschichtliches Jahrbuch der Zentralkommission fuer Erforschung und Erhaltung der Kunst- und Historischen Denkmale — KgJ
Kunstharz-Nachrichten — Kunstharz Nachr
Kunstliteratur — KI
Kunstmuseets Aarskrift — Knstm Aa
Kunstmuseets Arsskrift — KA
Kunststof en Rubber — Kunstof Rub
Kunststof en Rubber — Kunstst Rubber
Kunststof en Rubber — PTA
Kunststoff Journal — Kunstst J
Kunststoff und Gummi — Kunstst Gummi
Kunststoff-Berater — KUBEA
Kunststoff-Berater — Kunst-Ber
Kunststoff-Berater — Kunstst-Berat
Kunststoffberater, Rundschau, und Technik — Kunststoffberat Rundsch Tech
Kunststoff-Berater Vereinigt mit Kunststoff-Rundschau und Kunststoff-Technik — Kunstst-Berat Rundsch Tech
Kunststoffe — K
Kunststoffe — KUN
Kunststoffe — Kunstst
Kunststoffe Fortschrittsberichte — Kunstst Fortschrittsber
Kunststoffe. German Plastics — Kunstst Ger Plast
Kunststoffe. German Plastics, Including Kunststoffe im Bau — Kunststoff
Kunststoffe im Bau — Kunstst Bau
Kunststoffe in der Medizin — Kunstst Med
Kunststoffe. Organ der Deutschen Kunststoff-Fachverbaende — KUNSA
Kunststoffe-Plasticos (Munich) — Kunstst Plast Munich
Kunststoffe-Plastics — Kunstst-Plast
Kunststoffe-Plastics — KUPLA
Kunststoffe-Plastics; Schweizerische Fachzeitschrift fuer Herstellung, Verarbeitung, und Anwendung von Kunststoffen — KUP
Kunststoffe-Plastics (Solothurn, Switzerland) — Kunstst Plast Solothurn Switz
Kunststoff-Rundschau — Kunstst-Rundsch
Kunststoff-Rundschau — KURUA
Kunststoff-Technik und Kunststoff-Anwendung — Kunstst Tech Kunstst Anwend
Kunststoff-Verarbeitung — Kunstst Verarb
Kunstwissenschaftliches Jahrbuch. Gorresgesellschaft — KJG
Kuo-Hsueh Chi-K'an — KHCK
Kuo-li Taiwan Shih-fan Ta-hsueeh Li-shih Hsueeh-pao — KuSh
Kupfer-Mitteilungen — Kupfer Mitt

Kuratorium fuer Technik in der Landwirtschaft. Berichte ueber Landtechnik [*A publication*] — KTL Ber Landtech
Kuratorium fuer Technik in der Landwirtschaft. Flugschrift — Kurator Tech Landwirt Flugschr
Kurganskii Sel'skokhozyaistvennyi Institut. Sbornik Nauchnykh Rabot — Kurgan Skh Inst Sb Nauchn Rab
Kurme Medical Journal — KRMJA
Kurme Medical Journal — Kurme Med J
Kurortologiya i Fizioterapiya [*Bulgaria*] — Kurortol Fizioter
Kurortologiya i Fizioterapiya (Tbilisi) — Kurortol Fizioter Tbilisi
Kurortoloogilised Uurimused — Kurortol Uurim
Kuroshi 4 (Four). Proceedings. Symposium for the Co-operative Study of the Kuroshio and Adjacent Regions — Kuroshi 4 (Four) Proc Symp Coop Stud Kuroshio Adjacent Reg
Kurskii Gosudarstvennyi Meditsinskii Institut. Sbornik Trudov — Kursk Gos Med Inst Sb Tr
Kurskii Gosudarstvennyi Pedagogiceskii Institut. Ucenye Zapiski — Kursk Gos Ped Inst Ucen Zap
Kurskii Gosudarstvennyi Pedagogicheskii Institut. Nauchnye Trudy — Kursk Gos Pedagog Inst Nauchn Tr
Kurt Weill Newsletter — Kurt Weill N
Kurt Weill Newsletter — KWN
Kurtrierisches Jahrbuch — KJb
Kurtrierisches Jahrbuch — Kurtrier Jb
Kurtrierisches Jahrbuch — Kut
Kurume Medical Journal — Kurume Med J
Kurume University. Journal — Kurume Univ J
Kurzberichte aus dem Papyrussammlungen. Universitaets Bibliothek. Giessen — KPG
Kurze Uebersicht der Verhandlungen der Allgemeinen Schweizerischen Gesellschaft fuer die Gesammten Naturwissenschaften — Kurze Uebers Verh Allg Schweiz Ges Gesammten Naturwiss
Kurzer Grundriss der Germanischen Philologie — KGGP
Kurzer Hand-Commentar zum Alten Testament — KHAT
Kurzer Hand-Commentar zum Alten Testament — KHC
Kurzfassungen der Vortraege des Galvanotechnischen Symposiums — Kurzfassungen Vortr Galvanotech Symp
Kurzgefasster Kommentr zu den Heiligen Schriften Alten und Neuen Testamentes — KK
Kurzgefasstes Exegetisches Handbuch — KEH
Kurzgefasstes Exegetisches Handbuch zum Alten Testament — KEH
Kurzmitteilungen Deutsche Dendrologische Gesellschaft — Kurzmitt Dtsch Dendrol Ges
Kurznachrichten. Akademie der Wissenschaften in Goettingen [*Germany*] — Kurznachr Akad Wiss Goettingen
Kurznachrichten. Akademie der Wissenschaften in Goettingen. Sammelheft — Kurznachr Akad Wiss Goettingen Sammelh
Kuwait Bulletin of Marine Science — Kuwait Bull Mar Sci
Kuwait Foundation for the Advancement of Sciences Proceedings Series — Kuwait Found Adv Sci Proc Ser
Kuwait Institute for Scientific Research. Annual Research Report — Kuwait Inst Sci Res Annu Res Rep
Kuwait Journal of Science and Engineering — Kuwait J Sci Eng
Kuwait Journal of Science and Engineering. An International Journal of Kuwait University — Kuwait J Sci Engrg
Kuwait Medical Association. Journal — Kuwait Med Assoc J
Kuwait Times — KWT
Kuznechno-Shtampovochnoe Proizvodstvo — KSPRA
Kuznechno-Shtampovochnoe Proizvodstvo — Kuznechno Shtampovochnoe Proizvod
Kuznechno-Shtampovochnoe Proizvodstvo — Kuznechno-Shtampov
Kuznica — Kuz
Kvantovaya Ehlektronika — Kvantovaya Ehlektron
Kvantovaya Elektronika — Kvan Elektr
Kvantovaya Elektronika (Kiev) — Kvantovaya Elektron (Kiev)
Kvantovaya Elektronika (Moskva) — Kvantovaya Elektron (Moskva)
Kvartal'nyi Zhurnal Istorii Nauki i Tekhniki (Warsaw) — Kvart Zh Istor Nauki Tekh Warsaw
Kvartalsskrift. Bergen Bank — KBEBD
Kvartalsskrift (Stockholm) — Kvartalsskrift (Stockh)
Kvasny Prumysl [*Czechoslovakia*] — Kvasny Prum
Kvasny Prumysl — KVPRA
Kvinden og Samfundet — Kv o S
Kwandur Newsletter. Council for Yukon Indians — KWDR
Kwangju Teachers College. Science Education Center. Review — Kwangju Teach Coll Sci Educ Cent Rev
Kwangsan Hakhoe Chi — KWHCA
Kwangsi Agriculture/Kuang Hsi Nung Yeh — Kwangsi Agric
Kwansei Gakuin University — KGU
Kwansei Gakuin University. Annual Studies — KGUAS
Kwansei Gakuin University. Annual Studies — Kwansei Gakuin U Ann Stud
Kwansei Gakuin University. Annual Studies — Kwansei Gakuin Univ Annual Stud
Kwansei Gakuin University. Sociology Department Studies — Kwansei Gakuin Sociol Dept Stud
Kwartaalfacetten. Informatie over Krediet en Financiering — KTF
Kwartaalreeks over Informatie en Informatie Beleid — KII
Kwartalnik Geologiczny — Kwart Geol
Kwartalnik Geologiczny — Kwartalnik Geol
Kwartalnik Geologiczny — KWGEA
Kwartalnik Geologiczny (Poland. Instytut Geologiczny) — Kwart Geol (Pol Inst Geol)
Kwartalnik Historii Kultury — Kwart Hist Kult
Kwartalnik Historii Kultury Materialnej — Kwar Hist Kul Mat
Kwartalnik Historii Kultury Materialnej — Kwart Hist Kul Mater
Kwartalnik Historii Kultury Materialnej — Kwart Hist Kult Mater
Kwartalnik Historii Nauki i Techniki — Kwart Hist Nauk Tech
Kwartalnik Historii Nauki i Techniki — Kwart Hist Nauki i Tech
Kwartalnik Historii Nauki i Techniki — Kwart Hist Nauki Tech
Kwartalnik Historyczny — KH
Kwartalnik Historyczny — Kw Hist
Kwartalnik Historyczny — Kwartalnik Hist
Kwartalnik Historyczny — KwH
Kwartalnik Institutu Polsko-Radzieckiego — KIPR
Kwartalnik Klasyczny — KK
Kwartalnik Klasyczny — KKL
Kwartalnik Klasyczny — Kw Kl
Kwartalnik Muzyczny — KM
Kwartalnik Naucyziela Opolskiego — KNO
Kwartalnik Neofilologiczny — KN
Kwartalnik Neofilologiczny — KNf
Kwartalnik Opolski — Kwart Opolski
Kwartalnik Opolski — KwO
Kwartalnik Prasoznawczy — KP
KWU [*Kraftwerk Union AG, Muehlheim*] **Report** — KWU Rep
KWU [*Kraftwerk Union AG, Muehlheim*] **Report** — KWURA
Kybernetik — Kyb
Kybernetik. Informationsverarbeitung — Kybernet Informationsverarbeitung
Kybernetika — Kyb
Kybernetika — KYBNA
Kybernetika. Supplement — Kybernetika Suppl
Kyklos — KS
Kyklos — Kyk
Kyklos. Internationale Zeitschrift fuer Sozialwissenschaften — PKYK
Kyklos. Internationale Zeitschrift fuer Sozialwissenschaften. Revue International des Sciences Sociales. International Review for Social Sciences — Kyklos Int Z Sozialwiss Int Rev Soc Sci
Kylteknisk Tidskrift — Kyltek Tidskr
Kyorin Journal of Medicine and Medical Technology — Kyorin J Med Med Technol
Kyoto Daigaku Kogaku Kenkyusho Iho — KDKIA
Kyoto Daigaku Kogyo Kyoin Yoseijo Kenkyu Hokoku — KDKHB
Kyoto Daigaku Nogaku-Bu Enshurin Hokoku/Bulletin. Kyoto University Forests — Kyoto Daigaku Nogaku-Bu Enshurin Hokoku Bull Kyoto Univ For
Kyoto Furitsu Ika Daigaku Zasshi — KFIZA
Kyoto Prefectural University. Scientific Reports. Natural Science and Living Science — Sci Rep Kyoto Pref Univ Natur Sci Living Sci
Kyoto Prefectural University. Scientific Reports. Natural Science and Living Science — Sci Rep Kyoto Prefect Univ Natur Sci Living Sci
Kyoto University. African Studies — Kyoto Univ Afr Stud
Kyoto University. Economic Review — Kyo
Kyoto University. Economic Review — Kyoto Univ Econ R
Kyoto University. Faculty of Science. Memoirs. Series of Geology and Mineralogy — Kyoto Univ Fac Sci Mem Ser Geol Mineral
Kyoto University. Geophysical Research Station. Reports — Kyoto Univ Geophys Res Stn Rep
Kyoto University. Institute for Chemical Research. Annual Report — Kyoto Univ Inst Chem Res Annu Rep
Kyoto University. Jimbun Kagaku Kenkyu-sho. Silver Jubilee Volume — SJV
Kypriaka Chronika — KyC
Kypriakai Spoudai — KS
Kypriakai Spoudai — KSp
Kypriakai Spoudai — Kypr Spud
Kypriakai Spoudai — KyS
Kypriakos Logos — KL
Kyrkohistorisk Arsskrift — KA
Kyrkohistorisk Arsskrift — KHA
Kyrkohistorisk Arsskrift — Kyrkohist Arsskr
Kyung Hee University. Oriental Medical Journal — Kyung Hee Univ Orient Med J
Kyungpook Education Forum — Kyungpook Educ Forum
Kyungpook Mathematical Journal — Kyungpook Math J
Kyungpook University. Medical Journal — KUMJB
Kyungpook University. Medical Journal — Kyungpook Univ Med J
Kyushu Agricultural Research — Kyushu Agr Res
Kyushu American Literature [*Fukuoka, Japan*] — KAL
Kyushu Chugokugakkaiho [*Journal of the Sinological Society of Kyushu*] — KSCGH
Kyushu Daigaku Kogaku Shuho — KDKSB
Kyushu Journal of Mathematics — Kyushu J Math
Kyushu Journal of Medical Science — Kyush J Med Sci
Kyushu Journal of Medical Science — Kyushu J Med Sci
Kyushu Ketsueki Kenkyu Dokokaishi — KKKDB
Kyushu Memoirs of Medical Sciences — Kyushu Mem Med Sci
Kyushu University. College of General Education. Reports on Earth Science — Kyushu Univ Coll Gen Educ Rep Earth Sci
Kyushu University. Department of Geology. Science Reports — Kyushu Univ Dep Geol Sci Rep
Kyushu University. Faculty of Agriculture. Science Bulletin — Kyushu Univ Fac Agr Sci Bull
Kyushu University. Faculty of Science. Memoirs — Kyushu Univ Faculty Sci Mem
Kyushu University. Faculty of Science. Memoirs. Series D. Geology — Kyushu Univ Fac Sci Mem Ser D
Kyushu University. Reports of Research Institute for Applied Mechanics — Kyushu Univ Rep Res Inst Appl Mech
Kyushu University. Research Institute of Fundamental Information Science. Research Report — Res Inst Fund Inform Sci Res Rep

L

L. B. Case's Botanical Index. An Illustrated Quarterly Botanical Magazine — L B Cases Bot Index
L. Cooperative Extension Service. Kansas State University — L Coop Ext Serv Kans State Univ
(La) Antigua (Panama) — LAAP
La Bas — La B
La Belgique Horticole. Annales de Botanique et d'Horticulture — Belgique Hort
La Ciencia Tomista [*Salamanca*] — CiTom
(La) Ciudad de Dios Revista Agustiniana — LCD
La Civilta Cattolica [*Rome*] — CivCatt
La Crosse City Business — La Cros Bsn
(La) Educacion (Washington, D. C.) — LEW
La Educacion (Washington, DC) — Educ Wash
La France Apicole — France Apic
La Geographie — La Geog
La Giustizia — LaG
La Hacienda — Hac
La Lettura — Lal
La Ley. Revista Juridica Argentina — LL
La Literatura Argentina (Buenos Aires) — Lit Arg BA
LA. Los Alamos National Laboratory — LA Los Alamos Nat Lab
La Maison-Dieu — LMD
La Maison-Dieu — Mais D
La Maison-Dieu — Mais Dieu
La Medicine Eclairee par les Sciences Physiques, ou Journal des Decouvertes Relatives aux Differentes Parties de l'Art de Guerir — Med Eclairee Sci Phys
La Meunerie Francaise — Meunerie Franc
La Molina Peru Estacion Experimental Agricola. Informe — La Molina Peru Estac Exp Agric Inf
La Monda Lingvo-Problemo — LMLP
(La) Nacion — LN
(La) Nacion (Costa Rica) — LNCR
La Nature — LN
La Nouvelle Bigarure — Nouv Bigarure
La Nouvelle Clio [*Brussels*] — NClio
La Nouvelle Clio — Nouv Clio
La Nueva Democracia [*New York*] — ND
La Nuova Italia — LNI
(La) Palabra — LP
La Parisienne — LaPar
La Parola del Passato — LPP
(La) Prensa (Argentina) — LPA
La Rassegna — LaR
La Rassegna Nazionale (Florence) — RNF
La Recherche — LRE
La Recherche Aerospatiale — Recherche Aerospat
La Recherche Aerospatiale. English Edition — Rech Aerospat English
(La) Revista Catolica — LRC
La Revue Bibliographique — LRB
La Revue du Caire [*Cairo*] — RC
La Revue Scientifique du Limousin — Rev Sci Limousin
La Sainte Bible — LSB
La Sainte Bible. Traduit en Francais sous la Direction de l'Ecole Biblique de Jerusalem — BJ
La Semaine Juridique (Juris-Classeur Periodique) [*France*] — JCP
La Table Ronde [*Paris*] — TableR
La Table Ronde [*Paris*] — TabR
La Torre — LaT
La Torre — LT
La Tour de l'Orle d'Or — TOO
La Trobe Historical Studies — LTHS
La Trobe Library Journal — La Trobe Library J
La Trobe Library Journal — LTLJ
La Trobe University. School of Agriculture. Seminar Paper — La Trobe Univ Sch Agric Semin Pap
(La) Universidad — LUD
La Universidad (San Salvador) — Univ S Salvador
La Vanguardia [*Spain*] — LV
La Vie Spirituelle [*Paris*] — VS
La Vie Wallonne. Revue Mensuelle Illustree — Vie Wallonne
Lab Animal — Lab Anim
Lab Instrumenten — Lab Instrum
Lab Management Today — Lab Manage Today
Labdev Journal of Science and Technology — Labdev J Sci Technol
Labdev Journal of Science and Technology. Part A. Physical Sciences — Labdev J Sci & Technol A
Labdev Journal of Science and Technology. Part A. Physical Sciences — Labdev J Sci Tech Part A
Labdev Journal of Science and Technology. Part A. Physical Sciences — Labdev Part A
Labdev Journal of Science and Technology. Part B. Life Sciences — Labdev J Sci & Technol B
Labdev Journal of Science and Technology. Part B. Life Sciences — Labdev J Sci Technol Part B Life Sci
Labdev Journal of Science and Technology. Part B. Life Sciences — Labdev Part B
Labelled Comppounds. Part A-B — Labelled Compd Part AB
Labeo. Rassegna di Diritto Romano — Lab
Labo-Pharma. Problemes et Techniques — Labo Pharma Probl Tech
Labor and Employment Law — Lab and Empl L
Labor and Material Requirements for Private Multi-Family Housing Construction. BLS Bulletin 1892. US Bureau of Labor Statistics — BLS 1892
Labor Arbitration Information System [*Database*] — LAIS
Labor Arbitration Reports. Bureau of National Affairs — Lab Arb BNA
Labor History — La H
Labor History — Lab Hist
Labor History — Labor His
Labor History — Labor Hist
Labor History — PLAH
Labor History (United States) — Lbr Hist (US)
Labor Hygiene and Occupational Diseases (English Translation) — Labor Hyg Occup Dis (Engl Transl)
Labor Hygiene and Occupational Diseases (USSR) — Labor Hyg Occup Dis (USSR)
Labor Law Guide — LLG
Labor Law Journal — Lab L J
Labor Law Journal — Labor L J
Labor Law Journal — Labor Law J
Labor Law Journal — LBLJA
Labor Law Journal — Lbr Law J
Labor Law Journal — LLJ
Labor Law Reports. Commerce Clearing House — Lab L Rep CCH
Labor Medica [*Mexico*] — Lab Med
Labor News — Lab N
Labor Notes — Labor Nts
Labor Relations and Employment News — Lab Rel and Empl News
Labor Relations Reference Manual. Bureau of National Affairs — LRRM BNA
Labor Relations Reporter — Lab Rel Rep
Labor Relations Reporter [*Bureau of National Affairs*] — LRR
Labor Relations Reporter. Bureau of National Affairs — Lab Rel Rep BNA
Labor Relations Week [*Database*] — LRW
Labor Relations Yearbook — Lab Rel Ybk
Labor Statistics [*Database*] — LABSTAT
Labor Studies Journal — Lbr Studies J
Labor Studies Journal — LSJ
Labor Today — ILTO
Labor Today — Labor Tdy
Labor Today — Lbr Today
Laboratoire Central des Fabricants de Peintures, Vernis, et Encres d'Imprimerie. Bulletin du Laboratoire Professionnel — Lab Cent Fabr Peint Vernis Encres Impr Bull Lab Prof
Laboratoire Central des Ponts et Chaussees. Bulletin de Liaison des Laboratoires des Ponts et Chaussees — Lab Cent Ponts Chaussees Bull Liaison Lab Ponts Chaussees
Laboratoire Central des Ponts et Chaussees. Note d'Information Technique — Lab Cent Ponts Chaussees Note Inf Tech
Laboratoire Central des Ponts et Chaussees. Note d'Information Technique — LCPC Note Inf Tech
Laboratoire Central des Ponts et Chaussees. Rapport de Recherche — Lab Cent Ponts Chaussees Rapp Rech
Laboratoire Central des Ponts et Chaussees. Rapport de Recherche LPC — Lab Cent Ponts Chaussees Rapp Rech LPC
Laboratoire de Biochimie de la Nutrition. Publication. Universite Catholique de Louvain. Faculte des Sciences Agronomiques — Lab Biochim Nutr Publ Univ Cathol Louvain Fac Sci Agron
Laboratoire de la Profession des Peintures (Vitry-Thiais, France). Bulletin de Liaison du Laboratoire — Lab Prof Peint (Vitry Thiais Fr) Bull Liaison Lab
Laboratoire de Recherches et de Controle du Caoutchouc. Rapport Technique — Lab Rech Controle Caoutch Rapp Tech
Laboratoire des Ponts et Chaussees. Bulletin de Liaison — Lab Ponts Chaussees Bull Liaison

Laboratoire des Ponts et Chaussees. Rapport de Recherche — Lab Ponts Chaussees Rapp Rech
Laboratoire des Produits Forestiers de l'Est (Canada). Rapport — Lab Prod For Est (Can) Rapp
Laboratoire des Produits Forestiers de l'Est. Rapport Technique. Forintek Canada Corporation — Lab Prod For Est Rapp Tech Forintek Can Corp
Laboratoire d'Etude et de Controle de l'Environnement Siderurgique. Publication P — Lab Etude Controle Environ Sider Publ P
Laboratoire d'Etude et de Controle de l'Environnement Siderurgique. Rapport Exterieur RE — Lab Etude Controle Environ Sider Rapp Exter RE
Laboratoire et Technique — Lab Tech
Laboratoire Federal d'Essai des Materiaux et Institut de Recherches. Industrie, Genie Civil, Arts et Metiers — Lab Fed Essai Mater Inst Rech Ind Genie Civ Arts Metiers
Laboratoire Maritime de Dinard. Bulletin — Lab Marit Dinard Bull
Laboratoire Maritime de Museum National d'Histoire Naturelles a l'Arsenal de Saint Servan — Lab Marit Mus Natl Hist Nat Arsenal Saint Servan
Laboratoire Medical (Stuttgart) — Lab Med (Stuttgart)
Laboratoires des Sciences de la Terre (Saint Jerome, Marseille). Travaux. Serie B — Lab Sci Terre (St Jerome Marseille) Trav Ser B
Laborator Radiologicke Dozimetrie. Ceskoslovenska Akademie Ved. Report — Lab Radiol Dozim Cesk Akad Ved Report
Laboratorio — Lab
Laboratorio 2000 Duemila — Lab 2000 Duemila
Laboratorio Central de Ensayo de Materiales de Construccion. Madrid. Publicacion — Lab Central Ensayo Mater Constr Madrid Publ
Laboratorio Clinico — Lab Clin
Laboratorio de Ensaio de Materiales. Escola Polytechnica (Sao Paulo). Boletim — Lab Ens Mater Esc Polytech (Sao Paulo) Bol
Laboratorio de Ensayo de Materiales e Investigaciones Tecnologicas. Anales [*A publication*] — Lab Ensayo Mater Invest Tecnol An
Laboratorio de Ensayo de Materiales e Investigaciones Tecnologicas de la Provincia de Buenos Aires. Publicaciones. Serie 1. Memorias — Lab Ensayo Mater Invest Tecnol Prov Buenos Aires Publ Ser 1
Laboratorio de Ensayo de Materiales e Investigaciones Tecnologicas de la Provincia de Buenos Aires. Publicaciones. Serie 2 — Lab Ensayo Mater Invest Tecnol Prov Buenos Aires Publ Ser 2
Laboratorio de Ensayo de Materiales e Investigaciones Tecnologicas de la Provincia de Buenos Aires. Publicaciones. Serie 4. Informes Generales — Lab Ensayo Mater Invest Tecnol Prov Buenos Aires Publ Ser 4
Laboratorio di Patologia Clinica — Lab Patol Clin
Laboratorio Nacional de Engenharia Civil (Portugal). Memoria — Lab Nac Eng Civ (Port) Mem
Laboratorio nella Diagnosi Medica — Lab Diagn Med
Laboratorio Scientifico — Lab Sci
Laboratorios Nacionales de Fomento Industrial Tecnologia LANFI — Lab Nac Fom Ind Tecnol LANFI
Laboratorium et Museum et Clinicum — Laborat et Museum
Laboratorium voor Tuinbouwplantenteelt Landbouwhogeschool Wageningen Publikatie — Lab Tuinbouwplantenteelt Landbouwhogesch Wageningen Publ
Laboratoriumi Diagnosztika — Lab Diagn
Laboratoriums Medizin (Mainz) — Lab Med (Mainz)
Laboratoriums-Blaetter — Lab-Bl
Laboratoriums-Blaetter — LABLD
Laboratoriumsblaetter fuer die Medizinische Diagnostik E. V. Behring — Laboratoriumsbl Med Diagn E Behring
Laboratoriumspraxis — Lab Prax
Laboratoriya Biogeokhimii Pustyn. Trudy — Lab Biogeokhim Pustyn Tr
Laboratornaya Praktika — Lab Prakt
Laboratornoe Delo — Lab Del
Laboratornoe Delo — Lab Delo
Laboratornoe Delo — LABDA
Laboratory and Research Methods in Biology and Medicine — Lab Res Methods Biol Med
Laboratory Animal Care — Lab Anim Care
Laboratory Animal Data Bank [*Database*] — LADB
Laboratory Animal Handbooks — Lab Anim Handb
Laboratory Animal in Drug Testing. Symposium. International Committee on Laboratory Animals — Lab Anim Drug Test Symp Int Comm Lab Anim
Laboratory Animal in the Study of Reproduction. Symposium. International Committee on Laboratory Animals — Lab Anim Study Reprod Symp Int Comm Lab Anim
Laboratory Animal Science — Lab Anim Sc
Laboratory Animal Science — Lab Anim Sci
Laboratory Animal Science — LBASA
Laboratory Animal Symposia — Lab Anim Symp
Laboratory Animals — Lab Anim
Laboratory Animals — LBANA
Laboratory Automation and Information Management — Lab Autom Inf Manage
Laboratory Digest — Lab Dig
Laboratory Equipment Digest — Lab Equip Dig
Laboratory for Clinical Stress Research. Karolinska Institute. Reports — Lab Clin Stress Res Karolinska Inst Rep
Laboratory for Clinical Stress Research. Karolinska Sjukhuset. Reports — Lab Clin Stress Res Karolinska Sjukhuset Rep
Laboratory Hazards Bulletin [*Database*] — LHB
Laboratory Instrumentation and Techniques Series — Lab Instrum Tech Ser
Laboratory Investigation — Lab Inv
Laboratory Investigation — Lab Invest
Laboratory Investigation — LAINA
Laboratory Journal of Australasia — Lab J Australas
Laboratory Management — Lab Manage
Laboratory Management — LABMA
Laboratory Medicine — Lab Med
Laboratory Microcomputer — Lab Microcomput
Laboratory of Forest Products Chemistry. Reports. Series C — Lab For Prod Chem Rep Ser C
Laboratory of the Government Chemist (Great Britain). Miscellaneous Report — Lab Gov Chem (GB) Misc Rep
Laboratory of the Government Chemist (Great Britain). Occasional Paper — Lab Gov Chem (GB) Occas Pap
Laboratory Practice — Lab Pract
Laboratory Practice — Lab Practice
Laboratory Practice — LABPA
Laboratory Report. Franklin Institute — Lab Rep Franklin Inst
Laboratory Report. Transport and Road Research Laboratory [*Crowthorne*] — Lab Rep Transp Road Res Lab
Laboratory Technical Report. Division of Mechanical Engineering. National Research Council of Canada — Lab Tech Rep Div Mech Eng Natl Res Counc Can
Laboratory Technical Report. LTR-UA National Research Council. Canada. Unsteady Aerodynamics Laboratory — Lab Tech Rep LTR UA Nat Res Counc Can Unsteady Aerodyn Lab
Laboratory Technical Report. National Research Council. Canada. Division of Me chanical Engineering — Lab Tech Rep Nat Res Counc of Can Div Mech Eng
Laboratory Techniques in Biochemistry and Molecular Biology — Lab Tech Biochem Mol Biol
Laboratory Techniques in Biochemistry and Molecular Biology [*Elsevier Book Series*] — LTB
Laboratory Waste Treatment Plant Bulletin — Lab Waste Treat Plant Bull
Labor-Medizin — Labor Med
LaborPraxis in der Medizin — LaborPraxis Med
Labour and Employment Gazette — Lab and Emp
Labour and Employment Gazette — Lab and Empl
Labour and Employment Gazette — Labour and Employment Gaz
Labour and Society — Lab Soc
Labour and Society — Labour Soc
Labour and Society — LBS
Labour Arbitration Cases [*Database*] — LAC
Labour Gazette — Lab Gaz
Labour Gazette — Labour Gaz
Labour History — Lab Hist
Labour History — Labour Hist
Labour History — Labr Hist
Labour History — LH
Labour History (Australia) — Lbr Hist (Australia)
Labour Information Database — LABORINFO
Labour Information Record — Lab Inf Rec
Labour/Le Travailleur — Labour
Labour Monthly — Lab Mo
Labour Monthly — Labour Mo
Labour Monthly — LM
Labour Research — Labour Res
Labour Research Bulletin — Labour Research Bul
Labour Statistics Bulletin — Lab Stat Bull
Labour Weekly — Labour Wkly
Labrador Nor-Eastern — LANE
Labrador. Resources Advisory Council. Newsletter — LRAC
Labyrinthe — Lab
L'Acclimatation des Animaux et des Plantes — Acclim Anim Et Plantes
Lack- und Farben-Chemie — Lack Farben Chem
Lack- und Farben-Zeitschrift — Lack Farben Z
Lackawanna Institute of History and Science. Proceedings and Collections — Lackawanna Inst Pr
Lackawanna Jurist — Lac Jur
Lackawanna Jurist — Lack Jur
Lackawanna Jurist — Lack Jurist
Lactation Review — Lactation Rev
LACUNY [*Library Association. City University of New York*] **Journal** — LACUNY J
Ladelund Elevforenings Aarskrift — La Aa
Ladenschlussgesetz — Lad Schl G
Ladewig Forschung Aktuell. Reihe IV. Informatik, Statistik, Mathematik — Ladewig Forschung Aktuell Reihe IV Inform Statist Math
Ladies' Home Journal — GLHJ
Ladies' Home Journal — Lad HJ
Ladies' Home Journal — Ladies' H J
Ladies' Home Journal — Ladies Home J
Ladies' Home Journal — LHJ
Lady's Magazine — LM
Laekartidningen — LAKAA
Laerde Selskabs Skrifter — LSSk
Laerde Selskabs Skrifter. Teologiske Skrifter — LSSkT
LAES Mimeo Series. Louisiana Agricultural Experiment Station — LAES Mimeo Ser La Agric Exp Stn
Laesning foer Allmogen i Kronobergs Laen. Hushallssaellskapet — Laesn Allmogen Kronobergs Laen
Lafayette Clinic. Studies on Schizophrenia — Lafayette Clin Stud Schizophr
Lag Bulletin — Lag Bull
Lagina Ephemeris Aegyptiaca et Universa — LE
Lagos Notes and Records — Lagos Notes Rec
Lagrange Lectures — Lagr L
L'Agriculteur Belge et Etranger — Agric Belge Etranger
Lahey Clinic Foundation. Bulletin — Lahey Clin Found Bull
Lahey Clinic Foundation. Bulletin — LCFBA
Laiterie Belge — Lait Belge
Laiterie et les Industries de la Ferme — Lait Ind Ferme
Laits et Produits Latiers. Vache, Brebis, Chevre — Laits Prod Lait
Laka Industrija — Laka Ind
Lake Michigan Water Quality Report — Lake Mich Water Qual Rep

Lake Superior Mining Institute. Proceedings — L Sup M Inst Pr
Lake Superior Mining Institute. Proceedings — Lake Superior Min Inst Proc
Lakes Letter [*United States*] — Lakes Lett
Lakeside Leader [*Slave Lake, Alberta*] — LL
Lakeside Monthly — Lakeside
Lakokrasochnye Materialy i Ikh Primenenie — Lakokras Mater Ikh Primen
Lakokrasochnye Materialy i Ikh Primenenie — LAMAA
Lalahan Zootekni Arastirma Enstitusu Dergisi — Lalahan Zootek Arastirma Enst Derg
Lamar Journal of the Humanities — L J Hum
Lampas. Tijdschrift voor Nederlandse Classici — Lam
L'Analyse Numerique et la Theorie de l'Approximation — Anal Numer Theor Approx
Lanbauforschung Volkenrode — Lanbau Vol
Lancashire and Cheshire Antiquarian Notes — LCAN
Lancaster County Historical Society. Papers — Lancaster Co Hist Soc Pap
Lancaster County Historical Society. Papers — LCHP
Lancaster County Historical Society. Papers — LCHS
Lancaster Series on the Mercersburg Theology — LSMT
Lancet — GLAN
Lancet [*London*] — L
Lancet — LANCA
Lancette Francaise — Lancette Fr
Lanchow University Journal. Natural Sciences [*People's Republic of China*] — Lanchow Univ J Nat Sci
Land and Environment Notes — LEN
Land and Land News — Land
Land and Minerals Surveying [*London*] — Land Miner Surv
Land and Valuation Court Reports [*New South Wales*] — LVR
Land and Water Law Review — L and W LR
Land and Water Law Review — Land & Water L Rev
Land and Water Law Review — Land & Water LR
Land and Water Law Review — LWLR
Land and Water Law Review — LWLRD
Land and Water Law Review — LWR
Land Appeal Court Cases [*New South Wales*] — Land App Ct Cas
Land Appeal Court Cases (New South Wales) — LCC (NSW)
Land Appeal Court Cases (New South Wales) — NSW Land App Cas
Land. Bureau of Land Management [*Alaska*] — Land
Land Conservation Series. Department of the Northern Territory — Land Conserv Ser Dep NT
Land Economics — LAECA
Land Economics — Land Econ
Land Economics — LE
Land Economics — LEC
Land en Tuinbouw Jaarboek — Land-Tuinbouw Jaarb
Land Issues and Problems. Virginia Polytechnic Institute and State University. Cooperative Extension Service — Land Issues Probl VA Polytech Inst State Univ Coop Ext Serv
Land Laws Service — Land L Serv
Land Laws Service [*Australia*] — LLS
Land Newsletter — Land Newsl
Land. Newsletter. Lands Directorate. Environment Canada — LANC
Land of Sunshine — Land of Sun
Land Reform [*Italy*] — LNDR
Land Reform, Land Settlement, and Cooperatives — Land Reform
Land Reformer — LaRe
Land Research Series. Commonwealth Scientific and Industrial Research Organisation — Land Res Ser CSIRO
Land Research Series. Commonwealth Scientific and Industrial Research Organisation (Australia) — Land Res Ser CSIRO (Aust)
Land Research Series. Commonwealth Scientific and Industrial Research Organisation (Melbourne, Australia) — Land Res Ser Commonw Sci Industr Res Organ (Aust)
Land Resource Study. Land Resources Division. Directorate of Overseas Surveys — Land Resour Stud Land Resour Div Dir Overseas Surv
Land Resources Development Centre. Project Record (Surbiton, United Kingdom) — Land Resour Dev Cent Proj Rec (Surbiton UK)
Land Resources Development Centre. Technical Bulletin — Land Resour Dev Cent Tech Bull
Land Resources Division. Directorate of Overseas Surveys. Land Resource Study — Land Resour Div Dir Overseas Surv Land Resour Study
Land Resources Division. Directorate of Overseas Surveys. Technical Bulletin [*A publication*] — Land Resour Div Dir Overseas Surv Tech Bull
Land Resources Management Series. Division of Land Resources Management. Commonwealth Scientific and Industrial Research Organisation — Land Resour Manage Ser Div Land Resour Manage CSIRO
Land Resources Management Series. Division of Land Resources Management. Commonwealth Scientific and Industrial Research Organisation — Land Resour Mgmt Ser Div Land Resour Mgmt CSIRO
Land Subsidence. Proceedings. International Symposium on Land Subsidence — Land Subsidence Proc Int Symp
Land- und Forstwirtschaftliche Forschung in Oesterreich — Land Forstwirtsch Forsch Oesterr
Land Use and Environment Law Review — Land Use and Env L Rev
Land Use Built Form Studies. Information Notes — Land Use Built Form Stud Inf Notes
Land Use Built Form Studies. Reports — Land Use Built Form Stud Reps
Land Use Built Form Studies. Technical Notes — Land Use Built Form Tech Notes
Land Use Built Form Studies. Working Papers — Land Use Built Form Stud Wking Paps
Land Use in Canada Series — LUCS
Land Use Law and Zoning Digest — Land Use Law and Zoning Dig
Land van Aalst — L Aalst
Land van Herle — L Herle
Landarbeit — Landarb
Landarbeit und Technik — Landarb Tech
Landarzt — La A
Landarzt — Land A
Landarzt — LANZA
Landbauforschung Voelkenrode — Landbauforsch Voelkenrode
Landbauforschung Voelkenrode. Sonderheft — Landbauforsch Voelkenrode Sonderh
Landbode; Hollands Landbouwweekblad — HLW
Landbouw Courant — Landb Courant
Landbouw Wereldnieuws. Nederlands Ministerie van Landbouw, Visserij en Voedselvoorziening — Landb Wereldnieuws
Landbouwdocumentatie — MDL
Landbouwetenskap in Suid-Afrika. Agroanimalia — Landbouwet S Afr Agroanimalia
Landbouwetenskap in Suid-Afrika. Agrochemophysica — Landbouwet S Afr Agrochemophysica
Landbouwetenskap in Suid-Afrika. Agroplantae — Landbouwet S Afr Agroplantae
Landbouwetenskap in Suid-Afrika. Phytophylactica — Landbouwet S Afr Phytophylactica
Landbouwhogeschool Wageningen. Mededelingen — Landbouwhogesch Wageningen Meded
Landbouwhogeschool Wageningen. Miscellaneous Papers — Landbouwhogesch Wageningen Misc Pap
Landbouwkundig Tijdschrift — Landbouwkd Tijdschr
Landbouwkundig Tijdschrift — LATIA
Landbouwkundig Tijdschrift — LBT
Landbouwkundig Tijdschrift. Nederlandsch Genootschap voor Landbouwwetenschap (The Hague) — Landbouwk Tijdschr The Hague
Landbouwkundig Tijdschrift (Wageningen and Groningen) — Landbouwk Tijdschr Wageningen Groningen
Landbouwmechanisatie — Landbouwmechan
Landbouwmechanisatie — LDBMA
Landbouwproefstation Suriname. Bulletin — Landbouwproefstn Suriname Bull
Landbouwproefstation Suriname. Mededeling — Landbouwproefstn Suriname Meded
Landbouwvoorlichting — Landbouwvoorl
Landbouwwereldnieuws — LWN
Landbrugsokonomiske. Studier. Copenhagen Veterinaer. Og Landbohojskole. Okonomisk Institut — Landbrugsokonomiske Stud Copenh Vet Landbohojsk Okon Inst
Landburgsraadets Meddelelser. Faellesrepraesentation for det Danske Landburgs Hovedorganisationer — Lbr M
Landerbank Economic Bulletin — Landerbank
Landesanstalt fuer Immissions- und Bodennutzungsschutz des Landes Nordrhein-Westfalen. Jahresbericht — Landesanst Immissions Bodennutzungsschutz Landes Nordrhein
Landesanstalt fuer Immissions- und Bodennutzungsschutz des Landes Nordrhein-Westfalen. Schriftenreihe — Landesanst Immissions Bodennutzungsschutz Landes Nordrhein
Landesanstalt fuer Immissionsschutz Nordrhein-Westfalen. Schriftenreihe — Landesanst Immissionsschutz Nordrhein Westfalen Schriftenr
Landesanstalt fuer Wasser-, Boden-, und Lufthygiene zu Berlin-Dahlen. Mitteilungen — Landesanst Wasser Boden Lufthyg Berlin Dahlem Mitt
Landesanstalt fuer Wasserhygiene zu Berlin-Dahlem. Mitteilungen — Landesanst Wasserhyg Berlin Dahlem Mitt
Landesjagdgesetz — LJG
Landesplanungsgesetz — L Pl G
Landinspektoren — Lsp
Landis and Gyr Review — Landis & Gyr Rev
Landmaschinen-Markt — Landmasch-Markt
Landmaschinen-Rundschau — Landmasch Rundsch
Landmaschinen-Rundschau [*Germany*] — Landmasch-Rundschau
Landmaschinen-Rundschau — LRVSA
Landoekonomisk Forsogslaboratorium Aarbog (Copenhagen) — Landoekonom Forsoglab Aarbog (Copenhagen)
Landoekonomisk Forsogslaboratoriums Efterarsmode — Landokon Forsogslab Efterars
Landowning in Scotland — Landowning in Scot
Landpachtgesetz — LPG
Landscape — L'scape
Landscape Architecture — Land Arch
Landscape Architecture — Landsc Arch
Landscape Architecture — Landscape Arch
Landscape Architecture — Landscape Archre
Landscape Architecture — LSARA
Landscape Design — Landscape Des
Landscape International — Landscape Intl
Landscape Journal — Landscape J
Landscape Planning — Landscape Plann
Landscape Planning — LAPLD
Landscape Research — Landscape Res
Landschaftsdenkmale der Musik — LD
Landslides. Journal. Japan Landslide Society — Landslides J Jpn Landslide Soc
Landtechnik — Landtech
Landtechnik — LTECA
Landtechnische Forschung — Landtech Forsch
Landtmannen. Svenskt Land — Landtmannen Sven Land
Landwirthschaftliche Annalen des Mecklenburgischen Patriotischen Vereins — Landw Ann Mecklenburg Patriot Vereins
Landwirthschaftliche Berichte aus Mitteldeutschland — Landw Ber Mitteldeutschl

Landwirthschaftliche Blaetter, den Zoeglingen der Bildungs-Anstalt in Ungarisch-Altenburg Gewidmet — Landw Blaett Zoegl Bildungs Anst Ungarisch Altenburg
Landwirthschaftliche Zeitung (Augsburg) — Landw Zeitung Augsburg
Landwirtschaft — Landwirt
Landwirtschaft-Angewandte Wissenschaft — Landwirtsch Angew Wiss
Landwirtschaft-Angewandte Wissenschaft. Bundesministerium fuer Ernaehrung, Landwirtschaft, und Forsten — Landwirt-Angew Wiss Bundesmin Ernahr Landwirt Forsten
Landwirtschaftlich-Chemische Bundesversuchsanstalt (Linz). Veroeffentlichungen — Landwirtsch Chem Bundesversuchsanst (Linz) Veroeff
Landwirtschaftliche Brennerei-Zeitung — Landwirtsch Brennerei Ztg
Landwirtschaftliche Forschung — Landw Fo
Landwirtschaftliche Forschung — Landw Forsch
Landwirtschaftliche Forschung — Landwirtsch Forsch
Landwirtschaftliche Forschung — LAWFA
Landwirtschaftliche Forschung. Sonderheft — Landwirt Forsch Sonderh
Landwirtschaftliche Forschung. Sonderheft — Landwirtsch Forsch Sonderh
Landwirtschaftliche Jahrbuecher — Landw Jahrb
Landwirtschaftliche Jahrbuecher — Landwirtsch Jahrb
Landwirtschaftliche Schriftenreihe. Boden, Pflanze, Tier — Landwirtsch Schriftenr Boden Pflanze Tier
Landwirtschaftliche Schriftenreihe. Boden und Pflanze — Landwirt Schriftenr Boden Pflanze
Landwirtschaftliche Zeitschrift fuer das Oesterreichische Schlesien — Landw Z Oesterr Schlesien
Landwirtschaftliche Zeitung (Fuehlings) — Landwirtsch Ztg (Fuehlings)
Landwirtschaftliche-Monatshefte — Landw Mh
Landwirtschaftlichen Versuchs-Stationen — Landwirtsch Ver Stn
Landwirtschaftlichen Versuchs-Stationen — Landwirtsch Vers Stn
Landwirtschaftliches Jahrbuch der Schweiz — Landw Jb Schweiz
Landwirtschaftliches Jahrbuch der Schweiz — Landwirtsch Jahrb Schweiz
Landwirtschaftliches Jahrbuch fuer Bayern — Landw Jb Bay
Landwirtschaftliches Jahrbuch fuer Bayern — Landwirtsch Jahrb Bayern
Landwirtschaftliches Jahrbuch fuer Bayern — Ldwirtsch Jb Bayern
Landwirtschaftliches Jahrbuch fuer Bayern — LwJB
Landwirtschaftliches Wochenblatt — Ldwirtsch Wbl
Landwirtschaftliches Wochenblatt fuer Kurhessen-Waldeck — Landw Wbl Kurhessen-Waldeck
Landwirtschaftliches Wochenblatt fuer Westfalen und Lippe — Landw Wbl Westf Lippe
Landwirtschaftliches Wochenblatt (Muenchen) — Landw Wbl (Muenchen)
Landwirtschaftliches Zentralblatt — Landwirt Zentralbl
Landwirtschaftsgesetz — Landw G
Langages [*Paris*] — Lang
Langages. Litteratures. Linguistique — LLL
Lange Reihen zur Wirtschaftsentwicklung — Wirt Reihe
Langenbecks Archiv fuer Chirurgie — LAACB
Langenbecks Archiv fuer Chirurgie — Langenbeck
Langenbecks Archiv fuer Chirurgie — Langenbecks Arch Chir
Langenbecks Archiv fuer Chirurgie. Supplement — Langenbecks Arch Chir Suppl
Langenbecks Archiv fuer Chirurgie. Supplement. Kongressband — Langenbecks Arch Chir Suppl Kongressbd
Langenbecks Archiv fuer Klinische Chirurgie — Langenbecks Arch Klin Chir
Language — L
Language — LAN
Language — Lang
Language — LE
Language — Lg
Language — PLNG
Language and Automation — Lang Autom
Language and Automation — LangA
Language and Communication — L and C
Language and Communication — Lang and Commun
Language and Culture [*Hokkaido University*] — Lang and C
Language and Language Behavior Abstracts — LangAb
Language and Language Behavior Abstracts. LLBA — Lang Lang Behav Abstr
Language and Linguistics in Melanesia — L and Lin M
Language and Literature — Lang & L
Language and Literature Series — Lang Literature Series
Language and Speech [*England*] — L and S
Language and Speech — La S
Language and Speech — Lang & Speech
Language and Speech — Lang Speech
Language and Speech — LS
Language and Speech — LSp
Language and Style — La S
Language and Style — Lang & S
Language and Style — Lang S
Language and Style — Lang Style
Language and Style — LSty
Language Arts — ILAR
Language Arts — LA
Language Arts — Lang Arts
Language Association of Eastern Africa. Journal — Lang Assoc East Afr Jnl
Language Dissertations — LD
Language in Society [*London*] — Lang Soc
Language in Society — Language Soc
Language in Society — LIS
Language in Society — LS
Language in Society — LSoc
Language. Journal of the Linguistic Society of America — LSA/L
Language Learning — Lang Learn
Language Learning — LangL
Language Learning — LL
Language Learning and Communication — LL and C
Language. Linguistics Society of America — LANG
Language. Linguistics Society of America — Lg
Language Monographs — LangMono
Language Monographs — LM
Language Monographs. Linguistic Society of America — LMLSA
[*The*] **Language of Poetry** — TLOP
Language Problems and Language Planning — LPLP
Language Quarterly — LangQ
Language Research — Lang R
Language Sciences — LangS
Language Sciences — LSci
Language, Speech, and Hearing Services in Schools — Lang Speech & Hearing Serv Sch
Language, Speech, and Hearing Services in Schools — Lang Speech Hear Serv Sch
Language, Speech, and Hearing Services in Schools — LGSHA
Language Teaching — Lang Teach
Language Teaching Abstracts [*Later, Language Teaching and Linguistics Abstracts*] [*A publication*] — LangTAb
Language Teaching and Linguistics Abstracts — Lang Teach & Ling Abstr
Language Teaching and Linguistics Abstracts — Lang Teach Linguist Abstr
Language Teaching and Linguistics Abstracts — LTLA
Langue Francaise — LaF
Langue Francaise — Lang Fr
Langue Francaise — LFr
Langue, Raisonnement, Calcul — Langue Raison Calc
Langues et Lettres Modernes — LLM
Langues et Linguistique — Langues et L
Langues Modernes — L Mod
Langues Modernes — LaM
Langues Modernes — Lang Mod
Langues Modernes — LanM
Langues Modernes — LM
Langues Neo-Latines — LNL
L'Annee Epigraphique — AnnEp
L'Annee Philologique [*Paris*] — AnPh
Lansing's Reports [*New York*] — Lans
Lantbruksakademien. Ekonomiska Avdelning. Meddelande — Lantbruksakad Ekon Avd Medd
Lantbruksakademien. Tekniska Avdelning. Meddelande — Lantbruksakad Tek Avd Medd
Lantbruksakademien. Traedgaardsavdelning. Meddelande — Lantbruksakad Traedgaardsavd Medd
Lantbruksakademien. Vetenskapsavdelning. Meddelande — Lantbruksakad Vetenskapsavd Medd
Lantbrukshoegskolan, Husdjursfoersoeksanstalten. Meddelande — Lantbrukshoegsk Husdjursfoersoeksanst Medd
Lantbrukshoegskolan Jordbruksfoersoeksanstalten Meddelands — Lantbrukshoegsk Jordbruksfoersoeksanst Medd
Lantbrukshoegskolans Annaler — Lantbrhoegsk Ann
Lantbruks-Hoegskolans Annaler — Lantbruks-Hoegsk Ann
Lantbrukshogskolan Husdjursforsoksanstalten Meddelande — Lantbrukshogsk Husdjursforsoksanst Medd
Lantbrukshogskolan. Institutionen foer Vaextodling. Rapporter och Avhandlingar — Lantbrukshogsk Inst Vaextodling Rapp Avh
Lantbrukshogskolan Vaxtskyddsrapporter Jordbruk — Lantbrukshogsk Vaxtskyddsrapp Jordbruk
Lantbrukshogskolan Vaxtskyddsrapporter Jordbruk — VAJODH
Lantbrukshogskolan. Vaxtskyddsrapporter Jordbruk (Uppsala) — Lantbrukshogsk Vaxtskyddsrapp Jordbruk (Uppsala)
Lantbrukshogskolan Vaxtskyddsrapporter Tradgard — Lantbrukshogsk Vaxtskyddsrapp Tradg
Lantbrukshogskolans Annaler — Lantbrhogsk Annlr
Lantbrukshogskolans Annaler — Lantbrukshogsk Ann
Lantbrukshogskolans Meddelanden — Lantbrhogsk Meddn
Lantbrukshogskolans Meddelanden — Lantbrukshogsk Meddel
Lantbrukshogskolans Meddelanden. Series A — Lantbrukshogsk Medd Ser A
Lantbrukshogskolans Meddelanden. Series B — Lantbrukshogsk Medd Ser B
Lantbruksstyrelsen. Meddelanden — Lantbruksstyr Medd
Lantbrukstidskrift foer Dalarne. Kopparbergs Laens Hushallningssaellskap — Lantbrukstidskr Dalarne
Lantbrukstidskrift foer Jaemtland och Haerjedalen — Lantbrukstidskr Jaemtland Haerjedalen
Lantbrukstidskrift foer Stockholms Lan och Stad — Lantbrukstidskr Stockholms Lan Stad
Lanterne Medicale — Lanterne Med
Lanthanide and Actinide Research — Lanthanide Actinide Res
Lantman och Andelsfolk — Lantm Andelsfolk
Lantmannen (Sweden) — LMSLA
Lanzas y Letras — LyL
Laographia — La
Laographia [*Athenai*] — Laogr
Laos — La
Lapidarium Septentrionale — Lap Sept
Lapidarium Septentrionale — LS
Lapidary Journal — ILAP
Lapidary Journal — Lapidary J
Lapidary Journal — Lapidary Jour
Lapin Tutkimusseura Vuosikirja [*Research Society of Lapland. Yearbook*] — LPTV
Laporan. Lembaga Metallurgi Nasional (Indonesia) — Laporan Lembaga Metall Nas (Indones)
Laporan. Lembaga Penelitian Hasil Hutan — LPHLA

Laporan. Lembaga Penelitian Kehutanan — Lap Lemb Penelit Kehutanan
L'Approdo Musicale — LAM
LARC [*Lille, Amiens, Rouen, Caen*] **Medical** — LARC Med
LARC Reports — LARC Rep
Large Open Pit Mining Conference — Large Open Pit Min Conf
Large Scale Systems — Large Scale Syst
Large Scale Systems. Theory and Applications — Large Scale Syst Theory and Appl
Larousse du XX Siecle — LVS
Larousse Mensuel — Lar Mens
Larousse Mensuelle — LM
Laryngo- Rhino- Otologie — Laryngo-Rhino-Otol
Laryngologie, Rhinologie, Otologie — Laryngol Rhinol Otol
Laryngologie, Rhinologie, Otologie — LROTD
Laryngologie, Rhinologie, Otologie (Stuttgart) — Laryngol Rhinol Otol (Stuttg)
Laryngologie, Rhinologie, Otologie, und Ihre Grenzgebiete — Laryngol Rhinol Otol Ihre Grenzgeb
Laryngoscope — LARYA
Laryngoscope — Laryngoscop
Las Ciencias — LC
Las Vegas Review. Journal — Las Vegas Rev J
Laser Ablation for Materials Syntheseis. Symposium — Laser Ablation Mater Synth Symp
Laser Ablation of Electronic Materials. Basic Mechanisms and Applications — Laser Ablation Electron Mater
Laser Advances and Applications. Proceedings. National Quantum Electronics Conference — Laser Adv Appl Proc Nat Quantum Electron Conf
Laser and Particle Beam Chemical Processing for Microelectronics. Symposium — Laser Part Beam Chem Process Microelectron Symp
Laser and Particle Beams — Laser Part
Laser and Particle Beams — Laser Part Beams
Laser and Particle Beams — LPB
Laser and Unconventional Optics Journal — Laser & Unconv Opt J
Laser Applications — Laser Appl
Laser Applications in Medicine and Biology — Laser Appl Med Biol
Laser Chemistry — Laser Chem
Laser Diode Technology and Applications — Laser Diode Technol Appl
Laser Focus — LAFOA
Laser Focus Buyers Guide — Laser Foc
Laser Focus Including Electro-Optics Magazine — Laser Focus Electro Opt Mag
Laser Focus (Littleton, Massachusetts) — Laser Focus (Littleton Mass)
Laser Focus (Newton, Massachusetts) — Laser Focus (Newton Mass)
Laser Focus with Fiberoptic Communications — Laser Focus Fiberopt Commun
Laser Focus with Fiberoptic Communications — Laser Focus Fiberoptic Commun
Laser Focus with Fiberoptic Technology — Laser Focus Fiberopt Technol
Laser Focus with Fiberoptic Technology — Laser Focus Fiberoptic Technol
Laser Focus with Fiberoptic Technology — LFFTD
Laser Focus World — Laser F Wld
Laser Focus World — Laser Foc W
Laser Handbook — Laser Handb
Laser Institute of America. LIA — Laser Inst Am LIA
Laser Interaction and Related Plasma Phenomena — Laser Interact Relat Plasma Phenom
Laser Journal — Laser J
Laser Microtechnology and Laser Diagnostics of Surfaces. International Workshop — Laser Microtechnol Laser Diagn Surf Int Workshop
Laser Physics — Laser Phys
Laser Physics. Proceedings. New Zealand Summer School in Laser Physics — Laser Phys Proc NZ Summer Sch Laser Phys
Laser Physics. Proceedings. New Zealand Symposium on Laser Physics — Laser Phys Proc NZ Symp Laser Phys
Laser Report — Laser Rep
Laser Review — Laser Rev
Laser Review — LASRB
Laser Spectroscopy. International Conference — Laser Spectrosc Int Conf
Laser Spectroscopy. Proceedings. International Conference — Laser Spectros Proc Int Conf
Laser Technical Bulletin. Spectra Physics — Laser Tech Bull Spectra Phys
Laser und Angewandte Strahlentechnik — Laser und Angew Strahlentech
Laser und Elektro-Optik — Laser Elektro-Opt
Laser und Elektro-Optik — Laser und Elektro-Opt
Laser und Optoelektronik — Laser Optoelektron
Laser und Optoelektronik — Laser und Optoelektron
Laser-Induced Damage in Optical Materials. Annual Boulder Damage Symposium — Laser Induced Damage Opt Mater Annu Boulder Damage Symp
Lasers and Applications. A High Tech Publication — Lasers & App
Lasers et Optique Non Conventionnelle — Lasers Opt Non Conv
Lasers in Medical Science — Lasers Med Sci
Lasers in Medical Science — LMSCEZ
Lasers in Microelectronic Manufacturing — Lasers Microelectron Manuf
Lasers in Physical Chemistry and Biophysics. Proceedings. International Meeting. Societe de Chimie Physique — Lasers Phys Chem Biophys Proc Int Meet Soc Chim Phys
Lasers in Surgery and Medicine — Laser Surg
Lasers in Surgery and Medicine — Lasers Surg Med
Lasers in Surgery and Medicine — LSMEDI
Lasers in Surgery and Medicine. Supplement — Lasers Surg Med Suppl
Lasers. Proceedings. International Conference — Lasers Proc Int Conf
L'Asie Francaise — AF
Last Days of the Palace at Knossos — LDPK
Last Generation of the Roman Republic — LGRR
Last Mycenaeans and Their Successors — LMS
Lastenausgleich — LA
Late Roman Bronze Coinage — LRBC
Lateinamerika Anders — Lateinam Anders
Lateinamerika Heute — LatH
Lateinamerika-Berichte — Lateinamer Ber
Lateinamerika-Studien — Lateinam-Studien
Lateinische Grammatik — LG
Lateinische Hymnen des Mittelalters — LHMA
Lateinisches Etymologisches Woerterbuch — Et W
Lateinisches Etymologisches Woerterbuch — LEW
Lateranum [*Roma*] — Lat
Latimer Monographs — Lat M
Latin America — Lat Am
Latin America Commodities Report — LACR
Latin America Economic Report — LAER
Latin America in Books — LAB
Latin America (London) — LAL
Latin America Newsletters — LAN
Latin America Political Report — LAPR
Latin America Regional Reports — LAT
Latin America Weekly Report — LAWR
Latin America Weekly Report — LEP
Latin American Applied Research — Lat Am Appl Res
Latin American Economy and Business — Lat Am Econ Bus
Latin American Executive Report — Latin Amer Exec Rep
Latin American Indian Literature Journal — LALJ
Latin American Indian Literatures — LAIL
Latin American Indian Literatures — Lat Am Ind
Latin American Indian Literatures — Lat Am Ind Lit
Latin American Indian Literatures. University of Pittsburgh. Department of Hispanic Languages and Literatures — UP/LAIL
Latin American Journal of Chemical Engineering and Applied Chemistry — Lat Am J Chem Eng Appl Chem
Latin American Journal of Chemical Engineering and Applied Chemistry — Lat Am J Chem Engng Appld Chem
Latin American Journal of Heat and Mass Transfer — Lat Am J Heat Mass Transfer
Latin American Literary Review — LALR
Latin American Literary Review — Lat Am Lit
Latin American Literary Review — PLAL
Latin American Literature and Arts Review — RLAL
Latin American Mining Letter — Lat Am Min Lett
Latin American Monographs — Lat Amer Mg
Latin American Monthly Economic Indicators — Lat Am Mon Econ Indic
Latin American Music Review — LAMR
Latin American Music Review — Lat Am Mus
Latin American Music Review — Lat Am Mus R
Latin American Newsletters [*Database*] — LAN
Latin American Perspectives — LAP
Latin American Perspectives — Lat Amer
Latin American Perspectives — Latin Am Perspectives
Latin American Perspectives — Latin Amer P
Latin American Perspectives — Latin Amer Perspect
Latin American Perspectives — PLAP
Latin American Research Review — LaA
Latin American Research Review — LARR
Latin American Research Review — Lat Am Res
Latin American Research Review — Lat Am Res R
Latin American Research Review — Latin Am Res R
Latin American Research Review — Latin Am Research R
Latin American Research Review — Latin Amer Res R
Latin American Research Review — Latin Amer Res Rev
Latin American Research Review — PLAR
Latin American Research Review (Austin, Texas) — Lat Am Res Rev Austin
Latin American School of Physics — Lat Am Sch Phys
Latin American Shipping — LA Ship
Latin American Special Reports — Lat Am Spec Rep
Latin American Theater Review — Lat Am Thea
Latin American Theater Review — LATR
Latin American Times — Latin Am Times
Latin Teaching — LatT
Latina et Graeca — L & G
Latin-American Symposium on Surface Physics — Lat Am Symp Surf Phys
Latinitas [*Citta del Vaticano*] — Lati
Latinitas Christianorum Primaeva — LCP
Latino America. Anuario de Estudios Latinoamericanos (Mexico) — LAM
Latinoamericana (Argentina) — LAA
Latinskaia Amerika — LatA
Latinskaja Amerika — Latin Amer
Latinskaja Amerika — Latinsk Amer
Latomus — L
Latomus — Lat
Latomus; Revue d'Etudes Latines — Latomus
Latoratory Robotics and Automation — Lab Rob Autom
Latte, Latticini, e Conserve Animali — Latte Latticini Conserve Anim
Lattice Defects in Crystals. International Summer School on Defects — Lattice Defects Cryst Int Summer Sch Defects
Lattice Defects in Crystals. Proceedings. International Summer School on Lattice Defects in Crystals — Lattice Defects Dryst Proc Int Summer Sch
Latvian Journal of Chemistry — Latv J Chem
Latvian Journal of Physics and Technical Sciences — Latv J Phys Tech Sci
Latviesu Valodas Kulturas Jautajumi — LVKJ
Latviiskii Filial Vsesoyuznogo Obshchestva Pochvovedov Sbornik Trudov — Latv Fil Vses Ova Pochvovedov Sb Tr
Latviiskii Gosudarstvennyi Universitet Imeni Petra Stucki Latviiskii Matematicheskii Ezhegodnik — Latv Mat Ezhegodnik

Latviiskii Gosudarstvennyi Universitet Imeni Petra Stucki Ucenyi Zapiski — Latviisk Gos Univ Ucen Zap
Latviiskii Matematiceskii Ezegodnik — Latviisk Mat Ezegodnik
Latvijas Augstskolas Raksti — Latv Augstsk Raksti
Latvijas Entomologs — Latv Ent
Latvijas Fizikas un Tehnisko Zurnals — Latv Fiz Teh Z
Latvijas Kimijas Zurnals — Latv Kim Z
Latvijas Lauksaimniecibas Akademija. LLA Raksti — Latv Lauksaimn Akad LLA Raksti
Latvijas Lauksaimniecibas Akademijas Raktsi — Latv Lauksaimn Akad Raktsi
Latvijas Lopkopibas un Veterinarijas Zinatniski Petnieciska Instituta Raksti [*A publication*] — Latv Lopkopibas Vet Inst Raksti
Latvijas Lopkopibas un Veterinarijas Zinatniski Petnieciska Instituta Raksti [*A publication*] — Latv Lopkopibas Vet Zinat Petnieciska Inst Raksti
Latvijas PSR Zinatnu Akademija. Biologijas Instituta Raksti — Latv PSR Zinat Akad Biol Inst Raksti
Latvijas PSR Zinatnu Akademija. Biologijas Instituts. Dzivnieku Fiziologijas Sektora Raksti — Latv PSR Zinat Akad Biol Inst Dzivnieku Fiziol Sekt Raksti
Latvijas PSR Zinatnu Akademija Fizikas Instituta Raksti — Latv PSR Zinat Akad Fiz Inst Raksti
Latvijas PSR Zinatnu Akademija Geologijas un Geografijas Instituta Raksti — Latv PSR Zinat Akad Geol Geogr Inst Raksti
Latvijas PSR Zinatnu Akademija. Kimijas Instituta Zinatniskie Raksti — Latv PSR Zinat Akad Kim Inst Zinat Raksti
Latvijas PSR Zinatnu Akademija Mezsaimniecibas Problemu Instituta Raksti — Latv PSR Zinat Akad Mezsaimn Probl Inst Raksti
Latvijas PSR Zinatnu Akademija. Mezsaimniecibas Problemu un Koksnes Kimijas Instituta Raksti — Latv PSR Zinat Akad Mezsaimn Probl Koksnes Kim Inst Raksti
Latvijas PSR Zinatnu Akademija Zootechnikas un Zoohigienas Instituta Raksti — Latv PSR Zinat Akad Zootech Zoohig Inst Raksti
Latvijas PSR Zinatnu Akademijas. Vestis [*Riga*] — Latv PSR Zinat Akad Vestis
Latvijas PSR Zinatnu Akademijas. Vestis — Latvijas PSR Zinatn Akad Vestis
Latvijas PSR Zinatnu Akademijas. Vestis [*Riga*] — LZAV
Latvijas PSR Zinatnu Akademijas. Vestis. Fizikas un Tehnisko Zinatnu Serlja — Latv PSR Zinat Akad Vestis Fiz Teh Ser
Latvijas PSR Zinatnu Akademijas. Vestis. Fizikas un Tehnisko Zinatnu Serija — Latv PSR Zinat Akad Vestis Fiz Teh Zinat Ser
Latvijas PSR Zinatnu Akademijas. Vestis. Fizikas un Tehnisko Zinatnu Serija — Latvijas PSR Zinatn Akad Vestis Fiz Tehn Zinatn Ser
Latvijas PSR Zinatnu Akademijas. Vestis. Kimijas Serija — Latv PSR Zinat Akad Vestis Kim Ser
Latvijas Universitates Botaniska Darza Raksti — Latv Univ Bot Darza Raksti
Latvijas Universitates Raksti — Latv Univ Raksti
Latvijas Universitates Raksti. Kimijas Fakultates Serijas — Latv Univ Raksti Kim Fak Ser
Latvijas Universitates Raksti. Lauksaimniecibas Fakultates Serija — Latv Univ Raksti Lauksaimn Fak Ser
Latvijas Universitates Raksti. Matematikas un Dabas Zinatnu. Fakultates Serija — Latv Univ Raksti Mat Dabas Zinat Fak Ser
Latvijas Universitates Raksti. Medicinas Fakultates Serija — Latv Univ Raksti Med Fak Ser
Latvijas Universitates Zinatniskie Raksti — Latv Univ Zinat Raksti
Latvijas Valsts Universitate. Zinatniskie Raksti — Latv Valsts Univ Zinat Raksti
Latvijas Valsts Universitates Botaniska Darza Raksti — Latv Valsts Univ Bot Darza Raksti
Latvijas Zinatnu Akademijas Vestis — Latv Zinat Akad Vestis
Latvijskij Matematicheskij Ezhegodnik — Latv Mat Ezheg
Launceston Examiner — L Exr
Launceston Examiner (Newspaper) (Tasmania) — L Exr (Newspr) (Tas)
Laundry and Dry Cleaning Journal of Canada — Laundry Dry Clean J Can
Laundry News — Laund News
Laureae Aquincenses — Laur Aqu
Laurel Review — Lau R
Laurentianum [*Roma*] — Laur
Lausizische Monatsschrift — Lausiz Monatsschr
Lautbibliothek der Deutschen Mundarten — LdM
L'Auvergne Litteraire, Artistique, et Historique — Auvergne Litt
Laval Medical — LAMEA
Laval Medical — Laval Med
Laval Theologique et Philosophique — Laval Theol
Laval Theologique et Philosophique — Laval Theol Phil
Laval Theologique et Philosophique — LavTP
Laval Theologique et Philosophique — LThPh
Laval Theologique et Philosophique — LTP
Laval University Forest Research Foundation. Contributions — Laval Univ For Res Found Contrib
L'Avenir Illustre [*Casablanca*] — AI
Lavori. Istituto Botanico Giardino Coloniale di Palermo — Lav Ist Bot Giardino Colon Palermo
Lavori. Istituto Botanico. Reale Universita di Cagliari — Lav Ist Bot Reale Univ Cagliari
Lavori. Istituto di Anatomia e Istologia Patologica. Universita degli Studi (Perugia) — Lav Ist Anat Istol Patol (Perugia)
Lavori. Istituto di Anatomia e Istologia Patologica. Universita degli Studi (Perugia) — Lav Ist Anat Istol Patol Univ Studi (Perugia)
Lavori. Istituto di Anatomia e Istologia Patologica. Universita degli Studi (Perugia) [*Italy*] — Lavori Ist Anat Istol Patol Univ Studi (Perugia)
Lavoro e Medicina — Lav Med
Lavoro e Medicina — LAVMA
Lavoro Neuropsichiatrico — Lav Neuropsichiatr
Lavoro Umano — Lav Um
Lavoro Umano. Supplemento [*Italy*] — Lav Um Suppl
Lavoura Arrozeira — Lav Arroz
Law and Computer Technology [*Later, Law/Technology*] — L & Comp Tech
Law and Computer Technology [*Later, Law/Technology*] — L & Comp Technol
Law and Computer Technology [*Later, Law/Technology*] — Law & Comp Tech
Law and Computer Technology [*Later, Law/Technology*] — Law & Comput Tech
Law and Computer Technology [*Later, Law/Technology*] — Law & Comput Technol
Law and Contemporary Problems — L & Contemp Prob
Law and Contemporary Problems — L and Contemp Probl
Law and Contemporary Problems — Law and Con Pr
Law and Contemporary Problems — Law & Contemp Prob
Law and Contemporary Problems — Law Cont Pr
Law and Contemporary Problems — Law Contemp Probl
Law and Contemporary Problems — LCP
Law and Contemporary Problems — PLCP
Law and Contemporary Problems Series — Law Contemp Probl Ser
Law and Housing Journal — Law and Housing J
Law and Human Behavior — L & Human Behav
Law and Human Behavior — Law and Hum Behav
Law and Human Behavior — Law Hum Behav
Law and Human Behavior — LHBEDM
Law and International Affairs — Law & Int Aff
Law and Justice — L & Just
Law and Justice — Law and Just
Law and Philosophy — Law Phil
Law and Policy in International Business — L & Pol Int'l Bus
Law and Policy in International Business — Law and Pol Int Bus
Law and Policy in International Business — Law & Pol Int'l Bus
Law and Policy in International Business — Law and Policy Internat Bus
Law and Policy in International Business — Law and Poly Intl Bus
Law and Policy in International Business — LPI
Law and Policy Quarterly — Law and Poly Q
Law and Psychology Review — L Psy R
Law and Psychology Review — Law and Psych Rev
Law and Social Problems [*Pondicherry*] — Law Soc Prob
Law and Society Review — L and Soc Rev
Law and Society Review — Law & Soc R
Law and Society Review — Law & Soc Rev
Law and Society Review — Law and Society R
Law and Society Review — Law and Socy Rev
Law and Society Review — Law Soc R
Law and Society Review — PLSR
Law and State — Law State
Law and the Social Order — L & Soc Order
Law and the Social Order — Law & Soc Ord
Law and the Social Order — Law & Soc Order
Law Book Company Ltd. Newsletter — LBC News
Law Book Company's Industrial Arbitration Service — LB Cos Indust Arb Serv
Law Book Company's Practical Forms and Precedents — LB Cos Practical Forms
Law Book Company's Taxation Service — LB Cos Tax Serv
Law Bulletin — Law Bul
Law Council Newsletter — Law Council Newsl
Law Council Newsletter — LCN
Law Digest — Law Dig
Law in Japan — L in Japan
Law in Japan — Law Ja
Law in Transition — L in Trans
Law Institute Journal — L Inst J
Law Institute Journal — Law Inst J
Law Institute Journal — LIJ
Law Institute Journal of Victoria — L Inst J Vict
Law Journal — Law Jour
Law Journal. New Series — LJ
Law Journal Reports. King's Bench. New Series [*United Kingdom*] — LJKB
Law Journal Reports. King's Bench. Old Series [*United Kingdom*] — LJKBOS
Law Librarian — L Lib
Law Librarian — Law Lib
Law Librarian — Law Libn
Law Librarian — Law Librn
Law Library Journal — L Lib J
Law Library Journal — L Libr J
Law Library Journal — Law Lib J
Law Library Journal — Law Libr J
Law Library Journal — LLJ
Law Magazine and Review — Law M R
Law, Medicine, and Health Care — ILMH
Law, Medicine, and Health Care — L Med and Health
Law, Medicine, and Health Care — Law Med & Health Care
Law, Medicine, and Health Care — Law Med Health Care
Law Notes — Law N
Law Notes — LN
Law Notes (New York) — L Notes (NY)
Law Office Economics and Management — L Off Ec and Mgmt
Law Office Economics and Management — L Off Econ & Man
Law Office Economics and Management — Law Off Econ & Management
Law Office Economics and Management — Law Off Econ and Mgt
Law Office Information Service — Law Off Information Service
Law Quarterly Review — L Q Rev
Law Quarterly Review — Law Q
Law Quarterly Review — Law Q R
Law Quarterly Review — Law Q Rev
Law Quarterly Review — Law Quar Rev
Law Quarterly Review — Law Quart
Law Quarterly Review — Law Quart R
Law Quarterly Review — Law Quart Rev
Law Quarterly Review — LQR

Law Reports — LR
Law Reports. Criminal Appeal Reports [*United Kingdom*] — Crim App
Law Reports. English and Irish Appeals [*United Kingdom*] — LR E & I App
Law Reports (New South Wales) — LR (NSW)
Law Reports (New South Wales). Bankruptcy and Probate — LR (NSW) B & P
Law Reports (New South Wales). Divorce — LR (NSW) D
Law Reports (New South Wales). Equity — LR (NSW) Eq
Law Reports (New South Wales). Equity — NSW Eq
Law Reports (New South Wales). Vice-Admiralty — LR (NSW) Vice-Adm
Law Reports (New South Wales). Vice-Admiralty — NSW Ad
Law Reports (New South Wales). Vice-Admiralty — NSW Adm
Law Reports, Privy Council, Indian Appeals — I App
Law Reports (South Australia) — LR(SA)
Law Review — L Rev
Law Review — Law R
Law Review — Law Rev
Law Review — LR
Law Review Digest — Law Rev Dig
Law Society. Bulletin [*South Australia*] — Law Soc Bull
Law Society. Bulletin (South Australia) — LSB (SA)
Law Society. Gazette — Gazette
Law Society. Gazette — L Soc'y Gaz
Law Society. Gazette — Law Socy Gaz
Law Society. Gazette — LSG
Law Society. Journal — L Soc J
Law Society. Journal — Law Soc J
Law Society. Journal — Law Socy J
Law Society. Journal — LSJ
Law Society Judgement Scheme [*South Australia*] — LS Judg Sch
Law Society Judgement Scheme [*South Australia*] — LSJS
Law Society's Gazette — L Soc Gaz
Law Society's Gazette — Law Soc Gaz
Law Society's Gazette — LS Gaz
Law Teacher — L Teach
Law Teacher — Law Tcher
Law Teacher. Journal of the Association of Law Teachers, London — L Teacher
Law/Technology — Law Tech
Law/Technology — Law/Technol
Law Times — L T
Law Times — LT Jo
Law Times — LT Jour
Law Times Reports [*United Kingdom*] — LTR
Law Times Reports. Old Series [*United Kingdom*] — LTROS
LAWASIA [*Law Association for Asia and the Pacific*] **Commercial Law Bulletin** — LAWASIA CLB
LAWASIA [*Law Association for Asia and the Pacific*] **(New Series)** — LAWASIA (NS)
Lawn and Garden Marketing — Lawn Gard Mark
Lawn and Garden Marketing — Lawn Gardn
Lawrence Livermore Laboratory. Report — Lawrence Livermore Lab Rep
Lawrence Review of Natural Products — Lawrence Rev Nat Prod
Lawrence Review of Natural Products — LRNPDF
Lawrence Review of Natural Products. Monograph System — Lawrence Rev Nat Prod Monogr Syst
Lawrence Review of Natural Products. Monograph System — LRNSEP
Laws of Delaware — Del Laws
Laws of Florida — Fla Laws
Laws of Illinois — Ill Laws
Laws of Maryland — Md Laws
Laws of Minnesota — Minn Laws
Laws of Missouri — Mo Laws
Laws of Montana — Mont Laws
Laws of Nebraska — Neb Laws
Laws of New Jersey — NJ Laws
Laws of New Mexico — NM Laws
Laws of New York — NY Laws
Laws of North Dakota — ND Laws
Laws of Pennsylvania — Pa Laws
Laws of Puerto Rico — PR Laws
Laws of South Dakota — SD Laws
Laws of the State of Maine — ME Laws
Laws of the State of New Hampshire — NH Laws
Laws of Utah — Utah Laws
Laws of Vermont — Vt Laws
Laws of Washington — Wash Laws
Laws of Wisconsin — Wis Laws
Lawyer and Law Notes — Law & L N
Lawyer and Law Notes — Lawy & LN
Lawyer of the Americas — Law Am
Lawyer of the Americas — Law Amer
Lawyer of the Americas — Law Americas
Lawyers Guild Review — Law Guild Rev
Lawyers Journal — Law J
Lawyers Liberation Bulletin — LLB
Lawyers' Manual on Professional Conduct. American Bar Association/Bureau of National Affairs — Law Man on Prof Conduct ABA/BNA
Lawyer's Medical Journal — Law Med J
Lawyer's Medical Journal — Lawy Med J
Lawyer's Medical Journal — Lawyers Med J
Lawyers Title Guaranty Funds News — Law Title Guar Funds News
La-Ya'aran/The Forester. Israel Forestry Association — La-Yaaran For Israel For Assoc
Layman's Bible Series — Lay BS
LBL [*Lawrence Berkeley Laboratory*] **Computer Center Newsletter** — LBL Comput Cent Newsl
LBL [*Lawrence Berkeley Laboratory*] **Newsmagazine** [*United States*] — LBL Newsmag
LBMRC [*Louis Braille Memorial Research Centre*] **Research Newsletter** — LBMRC Res Newl
LC [*Liquid Chromatography*] **in Practice** — LC Pract
LC. Listy Cukrovarnicke — LC Listy Cukrov
LCA [*Lawyers for the Creative Arts*] **Quarterly** — LCA Q
LDRC [*Libel Defense Resource Center*] **Bulletin** — LDRC Bulletin
Le Arti — LA
Le Commerce du Levant [*Beirut*] — CDL
Le Figaro — LF
Le Globe (Geneva) — GG
Le Journal des Scavans (Leipzig) — J Scavans Leipzig
Le Lingue Estere — LEst
Le Matin [*Morocco*] — LEM
Le Mois en Afrique — Mois Afr
Le Monde — LM
Le Monde et la Foi — Me F
Le Monde Francais — LMF
Le Monde Juif — MJ
Le Moyen Age — LMA
Le Naturaliste Canadien. Bulletin de Recherches, Observations et Decouvertes se Rapportant a l'Histoire Naturelle du Canada — Naturaliste Canad
Le Nouvelliste Oeconomique et Litteraire — Nouvelliste Oecon Litt
Le Soir — LS
Le Soleil [*Dakar*] — LS
Le Temps — Let
Lea Transit Compendium — LEAT
Lead Abstracts — Lead Abstr
Lead Production (Washington, D.C.) — Lead Prod (Washington DC)
Lead Research Digest — Lead Res Dig
Leaders of Religion — Lea Rel
Leadership — LDS
Leadership — Lea
Leadership and Organization Development Journal — LOD
Leadership and Organization Development Journal — LOT
Leaflet. Agricultural Experiment Station. Alabama Polytechnic Institute — Leafl Agric Exp Stn Ala Polytech Inst
Leaflet. Alabama Agricultural Experiment Station. Alabama Polytechnic Institute — Leafl Ala Agric Exp Stn Ala Polytech Inst
Leaflet. Alabama Agricultural Experiment Station. Auburn University — Leafl Ala Agric Exp Stn Auburn Univ
Leaflet. Amateur Entomologist's Society — Leafl Amat Ent Soc
Leaflet. Animal Production Division. Kenya Ministry of Agriculture — Leafl Anim Prod Div Kenya Minist Agric
Leaflet. British Isles Bee Breeders' Association — Leafl Br Isles Bee Breeders Ass
Leaflet. California Agricultural Experiment Station — Leafl Calif Agric Exp Stn
Leaflet. California Agricultural Experiment Station. Extension Service — Leafl Calif Agric Exp Stn Ext Serv
Leaflet. Commonwealth Forestry and Timber Bureau (Canberra) — Leafl Commonw For Timb Bur (Canberra)
Leaflet. Cooperative Extension Service. Cook College. Rutgers. The State University of New Jersey — Leafl Coop Ext Serv Cook Coll Rutgers State Univ NJ
Leaflet. Cooperative Extension Service. Montana State University — Leafl Coop Ext Serv Mont State Univ
Leaflet. Cooperative Extension Service. Pennsylvania State University — Leafl PA State Univ Ext Serv
Leaflet. Cooperative Extension Service. University of Georgia — Leafl Coop Ext Serv Univ GA
Leaflet. Cooperative Extension. University of California — Leafl Coop Ext Univ Calif
Leaflet. Department of Agriculture and Fisheries (Irish Republic) — Leafl Dep Agric Fish (Ire)
Leaflet. Department of Agriculture and Technical Instruction for Ireland — Leafl Dep Agric Tech Instruct Ire
Leaflet. Department of Agriculture (Ceylon) — Leafl Dep Agric (Ceylon)
Leaflet. Division of Agricultural Sciences. University of California — Leafl Div Agric Sci Univ Calif
Leaflet. Division of Engineering Research and Development. University of Rhode Island — Leafl Div Eng Res Dev Univ RI
Leaflet. Extension Service. Utah State University — Leafl Ext Serv Utah St Univ
Leaflet. Forest Department. Trinidad and Tobago — Leafl Forest Dept Trinidad Tobago
Leaflet. Forestry and Timber Bureau — Leafl For Timb Bur
Leaflet. Forestry Commission (United Kingdom) — Leafl For Comm (UK)
Leaflet. Forests Department. Western Australia — Leafl Forests Dep West Aust
Leaflet. Israel Agricultural Research Organization. Division of Forestry (Ilanot) — Leafl Israel Agric Res Organ Div For (Ilanot)
Leaflet L. Texas Agricultural Experiment Station — Leafl L Tex Agric Exp Stn
Leaflet L. Texas Agricultural Extension Service. Texas A & M University System — Leafl L Tex Agric Ext Serv Tex AM Univ Syst
Leaflet. Ministry of Agriculture (Northern Ireland) — Leafl Minist Agric (Nth Ire)
Leaflet. Montreal Botanical Garden — Leafl Montreal Bot Gdn
Leaflet. Oklahoma State University of Agriculture and Applied Science. Agricultural Extension Service — Leafl Okla State Univ Agr Appl Sci Agr Ext Serv
Leaflet. Pennsylvania State University. Cooperative Extension Service — Leafl Pa State Univ Coop Ext Serv
Leaflet. Purdue University. Department of Agricultural Extension — Leafl Purdue Univ Dep Agric Ext

Leaflet. Rutgers State University. College of Agriculture and Environmental Science. Extension Service — Leafl Rutgers State Univ Coll Agr Environ Sci Ext Serv
Leaflet Series. Florida Department of Natural Resources. Marine Research Laboratory — Leafl Ser Fla Dep Nat Resour Mar Res Lab
Leaflet. Texas Agricultural Experiment Station — Leafl Tex Agric Exp Stn
Leaflet. Tin Research Institute — Leafl Tin Res Inst
Leaflet. United States Department of Agriculture — Leafl US Dep Agric
Leaflet. United States Department of Agriculture — Leaflet US Dep Agric
Leaflet. University of California. Cooperative Extension Service — Leafl Univ Calif Coop Ext Serv
Leaflet. University of Hawaii. Cooperative Extension Service — Leafl Univ Hawaii Coop Ext Serv
Leaflet. University of Kentucky. Agricultural Extension Service — Leafl Univ Ky Agric Ext Serv
Leaflet. University of Kentucky. College of Agriculture. Cooperative Extension Service — Leafl Univ Ky Coll Agric Coop Ext Serv
Leaflet. Vermin and Noxious Weeds Destruction Board [*Victoria*] — Verm Nox Weeds Destr Board Leafl
Leaflet. Village Bee Breeders Association — Leafl VBBA
Leaflet YANR. Auburn University. Alabama Cooperative Extension Service — Leafl YANR Auburn Univ Ala Coop Ext Serv
Leaflet YCRD. Alabama Cooperative Extension Service. Auburn University — Leafl YCRD Ala Coop Ext Serv Auburn Univ
Leaflet YEX. Auburn University Extension Service — Leafl YEX Auburn Univ Ext Serv
Leaflet YF. Alabama Cooperative Extension Service. Auburn University — Leafl YF Ala Coop Ext Serv Auburn Univ
Leaflet YHE. Alabama Cooperative Extension Service. Auburn University — Leafl YHE Ala Coop Ext Serv Auburn Univ
Leaflet YM. Alabama Cooperative Extension Service. Auburn University — Leafl YM Ala Coop Ext Serv Auburn Univ
Leaflets of Botanical Observation and Criticism — Leafl Bot Observ Crit
Leaflets of Western Botany — Leafl W Bot
Leaflets of Western Botany — Leafl West Bot
League Exchange — League Exch
League for International Food Education. Newsletter — League Int Food Educ Newsl
League of Arab States. Arab Petroleum Congress. Collection of Papers — League Arab States Arab Pet Congr Collect Pap
League of Nations. Bulletin of the Health Organization — League Nations Bull Health Org
League of Nations Journal — L Nations J
Learning — Learn
Learning and Motivation — ILMM
Learning and Motivation — Learn & Motiv
Learning and Motivation — Learn Motiv
Learning and Motivation — LNMVA
Learning Exchange — LE
Learning Exchange — Learn Exch
Learning Resources Bulletin — Learn Res Bull
Learning Today — Learn Today
Leather and Shoes — HLS
Leather and Shoes — Leath Shoe
Leather Chemicals (Dandong, People's Republic of China) — Leather Chem Dandong Peoples Repub China
Leather Chemistry [*Japan*] — Leather Chem
Leather Industries — Leather Ind
Leather Industries Research Institute of South Africa. Journal — Leather Ind Res Inst S Afr J
Leather. International Journal of the Industry — LTR
Leather Manufacturer — Leather Manuf
Leather Science — Leath Sci
Leather Science and Engineering — Leather Sci Eng
Leather Science and Technology — Leather Sci Technol
Leather Science (Madras) — Leather Sci (Madras)
Leather Trades Circular and Review — Leather Trades Circ Rev
Leathergoods — LEA
Leaves from a Paint Research Notebook — Leaves Paint Res Noteb
Lebanese Medical Journal — Leban Med J
Lebanese Pharmaceutical Journal — Leb Pharm J
Lebanese Pharmaceutical Journal — Leban Pharm J
Leben und Ausgewaehlte Schriften der Vaeter und Begruender der Lutherischen Kirche — LASLK
Leben und Ausgewaehlte Schriften der Vaeter und Begruender der Reformierten Kirche — LASRK
Leben und Umwelt (Aarau) — Leben Umwelt (Aarau)
Leben und Umwelt (Aarau, Switzerland) — Leben Umwelt (Aarau Switz)
Leben und Umwelt (Wiesbaden) — Leben Umwelt (Wiesb)
Lebende Sprachen — L Spr
Lebende Sprachen — LSp
Lebende Sprachen. Zeitschrift fuer Fremde Sprachen in Wissenschaft und Praxis — LSA
Lebendige Erde — Leben Erde
Lebendige Schule — LS
Lebendige Seelsorge — LS
Lebendiges Zeugnis — Leb Zeug
Lebensgeschichten aus der Wissenschaft — Legensgesch Wiss
Lebensmittel Praxis. Unabhangiges Fachmagazin fuer Unternehmensfuehrung, Werbung, und Verkauf im Lebensmittelhandel — NWH
Lebensmittel- und Biotechnologie — Lebensm Biotechnol
Lebensmittel und Ernaehrung — Lebensm Ernaehrung
Lebensmittelchemie, Lebensmittelqualitaet — Lebensmittelchem Lebensmittelqual
Lebensmittelchemie und Gerichtliche Chemie — Lebensmittelchem Gerichtl Chem
Lebensmittelchemie und Gerichtliche Chemie — Lebensmittelchemie u Gerichtl Chemie
Lebensmittel-Industrie — Lebensm Ind
Lebensmittel-Industrie — Lebensmittel-Ind
Lebensmittelindustrie und Milchwirtschaft — Lebensmittelind Milchwirtsch
Lebensmittel-Wissenschaft Technologie — Lebensm-Wiss Technol
Lebensmittel-Wissenschaft und Technologie/Food Science and Technology — Lebensm Wiss Technol Food Sci Technol
Lebensmittelzeitung — LMH
Lebensversicherungs Medizin — Lebensversicher Med
Leber Magen Darm — Leber Mag D
Lebertagung der Sozialmediziner — Lebertag Sozialmed
Lecciones Ilustradas — Lec Ilus
Lecciones Populares de Matematicas — Lecciones Popular Mat
Lechebnoe i Diagnosticheskoe Primenenie Radioaktivnykh Izotopov. Trudy Ukrainskoi Konferentsii — Lech Diagn Primen Radioakt Izot Tr Ukr Konf
Lechenie na Kurortakh Zabaikal'ya — Lech Kurortakh Zabaik
Lechenie na Kurortakh Zabaikal'ya — Lech Kurortakh Zabaikalya
L'Economie et la Finance de la Syrie et de Pays Arabes [*Damascus*] — EFSPA
Lectio Divina — Le Div
Lector — LR
Lecturas — Lect
Lecturas de Economia — Lecturas Econ
Lecturas Matematicas — Lect Mat
Lecture et Bibliotheques — Lect Biblioth
Lecture Hall for Chemistry and Pharmacology [*Japan*] — Lect Hall Chem Pharmacol
Lecture Notes and Supplements in Physics — Lect Notes Suppl Phys
Lecture Notes and Supplements in Physics — Lecture Notes and Suppl in Phys
Lecture Notes Division. Technical Conference. Society of Plastics Engineers. Vinyl Plastics Divisions — Lect Notes Div Tech Conf Soc Plast Eng Vinyl Plast Div
Lecture Notes in Biomathematics — Lect Notes Biomath
Lecture Notes in Biomathematics — Lecture Notes in Biomath
Lecture Notes in Chemistry — Lect Notes Chem
Lecture Notes in Chemistry [*Berlin*] — Lecture Notes in Chem
Lecture Notes in Computer Science — Lect Notes Comput Sci
Lecture Notes in Computer Science — Lecture Notes in Comput Sci
Lecture Notes in Control and Information Sciences — Lecture Notes in Control and Information Sci
Lecture Notes in Earth Sciences — Lecture Notes Earth Sci
Lecture Notes in Economics and Mathematical Systems — Lecture Notes in Econom and Math Systems
Lecture Notes in Engineering — Lecture Notes in Engrg
Lecture Notes in Logic — Lecture Notes Logic
Lecture Notes in Mathematics — Lect Notes Math
Lecture Notes in Mathematics — Lecture Notes in Math
Lecture Notes in Medical Informatics — Lecture Notes in Med Inform
Lecture Notes in Numerical and Applied Analysis — Lecture Notes Numer Appl Anal
Lecture Notes in Physics — Lect Notes Phys
Lecture Notes in Physics — Lecture Notes in Phys
Lecture Notes in Physics — LNP
Lecture Notes in Physics. New Series M. Monographs — Lecture Notes in Phys New Ser M Monogr
Lecture Notes in Pure and Applied Mathematics — Lecture Notes in Pure and Appl Math
Lecture Notes in Statistics — Lecture Notes in Statist
Lecture Notes of the Science University of Tokyo — Lecture Notes Sci Univ Tokyo
Lecture Notes on Coastal and Estuarine Studies — Lect Notes Coastal Estuarine Stud
Lecture Notes on Coastal and Estuarine Studies — LNCSEA
Lecture Notes on Particles and Fields — Lecture Notes Particles Fields
Lecture Notes Series on Computing — Lecture Notes Ser Comput
Lecture Series. Division of Applied Geomechanics. Commonwealth Scientific and Industrial Research Organisation — Lec Ser Div Appl Geomech CSIRO
Lecture to Central Association of Bee-Keepers — Lect Cent Ass Beekrps
Lectures and Contributed Papers. Symposium on Plasma Heating in Toroidal Devices — Lect Contrib Pap Symp Plasma Heat Toroidal Devices
Lectures. Colloquium on Environmental Protection in Mechanical Engineering — Lect Colloq Environ Prot Mech Eng
Lectures. Conference on Tribology — Lect Conf Tribol
Lectures. Congress on Material Testing — Lect Congr Mater Test
Lectures. Czech-Polish Colloquium on Chemical Thermodynamics and Physical Organic Chemistry — Lect Czech Pol Colloq Chem Thermodyn Phys Org Chem
Lectures. DECHEMA Annual Meeting of Biotechnologists — Lect DECHEMA Annu Meet Biotechnol
Lectures from the Coral Gables Conference on Fundamental Interactions at High Energy — Lect Coral Gables Conf Fundam Interact High Energy
Lectures in Applied Mathematics — LAPMAU
Lectures in Applied Mathematics — Lect Appl Math
Lectures in Applied Mathematics — Lectures in Appl Math
Lectures in Economics. Theory, Institutions, Policy [*Elsevier Book Series*] — LIE
Lectures in Heterocyclic Chemistry — Lect Heterocycl Chem
Lectures in Mathematics [*Tokyo*] — Lectures in Math
Lectures in Mathematics ETH Zuerich — Lectures Math ETH Zuerich
Lectures in Theoretical Physics — Lect Theor Phys
Lectures in Theoretical Physics — LTHPA
Lectures. International Symposium on Migration — Lect Int Symp Migr
Lectures, Monographs, and Reports. Royal Institute of Chemistry — Lect Monogr Rep R Inst Chem

Lectures on High Energy Physics. Lectures Delivered. Summer Meeting of Nuclear Physicists — Lect High Energy Phys Lect Summer Meet Nucl Phys
Lectures on Mathematics in the Life Sciences — Lect Math Life Sci
Lectures on Mathematics in the Life Sciences — Lectures Math Life Sci
Lectures on the History of Religions — LHR
Lectures on the Scientific Basis of Medicine — Lect Sci Basis Med
Lectures on Thermodynamics and Statistical Mechanics. Winter Meeting on Statistical Physics — Lect Thermodyn Stat Mech Winter Meet Stat Phys
Lectures Presented. Anniversary Symposium. Institute of Mathematical Sciences. Madras — Lect Anniv Symp Inst Math Sci Madras
Lectures Presented at the Chania Conference — Lect Chania Conf
Lectures Presented at the FAO/SIDA Training Course on Marine Pollution in Relation to Protection of Living Resources — Lect FAO/SIDA Train Course Mar Pollut Relat Prot Living Res
Leder. Beilage — Leder Beil
Leder- und Schuhwarenindustrie der UdSSR — Leder Schuhwarind UdSSR
Lederbladet — Lederbl
Lederindustrie. Technische Beilage — Lederindustrie Tech Beil
Lederle Bulletin — Lederle Bull
Ledermarkt und Hautemarkt mit Gerbereiwissenschaft und Praxis. Das Wochenjournal fuer die Lederindustrie, den Hautegrosshandel und Ledergrosshandel — LUH
Ledertechnische Rundschau (Berlin) — Ledertech Rundsch (Berlin)
Ledertechnische Rundschau (Zurich) — Ledertech Rundsch (Zurich)
Lederwaren Zeitung — LWZ
L'Educatore Israelita — El
Lee Foundation for Nutritional Research. Report — Lee Found Nutr Res Rep
Leeds and Northrup Technical Journal — Leeds Northr Tech J
Leeds and Northrup Technical Journal — Leeds Northrup Tech J
Leeds Dental Journal — Leeds Dent J
Leeds Geological Association. Transactions — Leeds G As Tr
Leeds Philosophical and Literary Society. Literary and History Section. Proceedings — Leeds Phil Lit Soc Lit Hist Sec Proc
Leeds Studies in English — LeedsSE
Leeds Studies in English and Kindred Languages — LSE
Leeds Texts and Monographs — LTM
Leeds University Oriental Society. Annual — ALUOS
Leeds-Lyon Symposium on Tribology. Proceedings — Leeds Lyon Symp Tribol Proc
Leefmilieu — LEE
Leerblad. Vakblad voor de Lederwarenbranche en Reisartikelenbranche in de Beneluxlanden — LWK
Leeuwenhoek Nederlandsch Tijdschrift — Leeuwenhoek Ned Tijdschr
Left Review — LR
Legal Aid Brief Case — Brief Case
Legal Aid Clearinghouse. Bulletin — LACB
Legal Aid Review — Leg Aid Rev
Legal Aid Review — Legal Aid Rev
Legal Aspects of Medical Practice — Leg Aspects Med Pract
Legal Aspects of Medical Practice — Legal Aspects Med Prac
Legal Bulletin — Legal Bul
Legal Bulletin — Legal Bull
Legal Contents. LC — Leg Contents LC
Legal Economics — Leg Ec
Legal Economics — Leg Econ
Legal Economics — Legal Econ
Legal Education Newsletter — Legal Educ Newsl
Legal Executive — Leg Exec
Legal Information Management Index — Leg Inf Manage Index
Legal Information Service. Reports. Native Law Centre. University of Saskatchewan — LISR
Legal Intelligencer — Leg Int
Legal Issues of European Integration — LIE
Legal Journals Index [*Database*] — LJI
Legal Malpractice Reporter — Legal Malpract Rep
Legal Medical Quarterly — L Med Q
Legal Medical Quarterly — Legal Med Q
Legal Medical Quarterly — LMQ
Legal Medicine — Leg Med
Legal Medicine Annual [*Later, Legal Medicine*] — Leg Med Annu
Legal Medicine Annual — Leg Med Annual
Legal Medicine Annual — Legal Med Ann
Legal Medicine Quarterly — Leg Med Q
Legal Notes and Viewpoints Quarterly — Leg Notes and View Q
Legal Periodical Digest — Leg Period Dig
Legal Reference Services Quarterly — Leg Ref Serv Q
Legal Research Journal — Leg Res J
Legal Research Journal — Legal Res J
Legal Resource Index — Leg Resour Index
Legal Service Bulletin — Leg Ser B
Legal Service Bulletin — Leg Serv Bull
Legal Service Bulletin — Legal Serv Bull
Legal Service Bulletin — Legal Service Bul
Legal Service Bulletin — LSB
Legal Services Bulletin — Legal Services Bul
Legal Studies — Legal Stud
Legal Systems Letter — Legal Sys Let
Legal Times of Washington — Legal Times Wash
Leges Graecorum Sacrae e Titulis Collectae — Leg Sacr
Leges Graecorum Sacrae e Titulis Collectae — LGS
Legge's Supreme Court Cases — Legge
Legionella. Proceedings. International Symposium — Legionella Proc Int Symp
Legislative Digest. Forecast and Review [*Anchorage, AK*] — LD
Legislative Network for Nurses — Legisl Netw Nurses
Legislative Roundup — Legis Roundup
Legislative Studies Quarterly — Leg Stud Q
Legislative Studies Quarterly — Legisl Stud Quart
Legka i Tekstilna Promislovist — Legka Tekst Promst
Legka Promislovist — Legka Promst
Legkaya i Pishchevaya Promyshlennost Podmoskov'ya — Legk Pishch Promst Podmoskov'ya
Legkaya i Tekstil'naya Promyshlennost — Legk Tekst Promst
Legkaya Promyshlennost (Kazakhstana) — Legk Promst (Kaz)
Legkaya Promyshlennost (Kiev) — Legk Promst (Kiev)
Legkaya Promyshlennost (Moscow) — Legk Promst (Moscow)
Legkie Metally — Legk Met
Legkie Splavy Metallovedenie Termicheskaya Obrabotka. Lit'e i Obrabotka Davleniem. Materialy Vsesoyuznoi Konferentsii — Legk Splavy Metalloved Term Obrab Lite Obrab Davleniem Mater
L'Eglise en Priere — EeP
Legon Journal of the Humanities — Legon J Humanities
Legon Journal of the Humanities — LJH
Legume Research — Legume Res
Legume Research — LRESDD
L'Egypte Industrielle [*Cairo*] — EI
Lehigh Alumni Bulletin — Lehigh Alumni Bull
Lehr- und Handbuecher der Ingenieurwissenschaften — Lehrb Handb Ingenieurwiss
Lehrbuch der Allgemeinen Geographie — Lehrb Allg Geogr
Lehrbuch der Anthropologie — Lehrb Anthropol
Lehrbuch der Philosophie — L Ph
Lehrbuch der Speziellen Zoologie — Lehrb Spez Zool
Lehrbuch der Speziellen Zoologie — LSZODB
Lehrbuch Mathematik — Lehrbuch Math
Lehrbuecher und Monographien aus dem Gebiete der Exakten Wissenschaften [*LMW*]. Mathematische Reihe — Lehrbuecher Monograph Geb Exakten Wissensch Math Reihe
Lehrbuecher und Monographien zur Didaktik der Mathematik — Lehrbuecher Monogr Didakt Math
Lehrbuecher und Monographien zur Didaktik der Mathematik — Lehrbuecher Monograph Didakt Math
Lehre und Symbol — Lu S
Lehre und Wehre — Lu W
Lehrproben und Lehrgaenge — L & L
Lehrprogrammbuecher Hochschulstudium. Chemie — Lehrprogrammb Hochschulstud Chem
Leica Fotografie (English Edition) — Leica Fotogr (Engl Ed)
Leica Fotographie — Leica Fot
Leicester Chemical Review — Leicester Chem Rev
Leichhardt Historical Journal — Leichhardt Hist J
Leiden Botanical Series — LBSEDV
Leiden Botanical Series — Leiden Bot Ser
Leidsche Geologische Mededeelingen [*Later, Leidse Geologische Mededelingen*] — Leidsche Geol Meded
Leidse Geologische Mededelingen — Leidse Geol Meded
Leipziger Aegyptologische Studien — LAeS
Leipziger Aegyptologische Studien — LAS
Leipziger Aegyptologische Studien — Lpz Aeg Stud
Leipziger Bienenzeitung — Leipzig Bienenzt
Leipziger Bienenzeitung — Leipzig Bienenztg
Leipziger Bienenzeitung — Lpz Bien Zt
Leipziger Faerber-Zeitung — Leipz Faerber Ztg
Leipziger Gelehrte Zeitungen — Leipziger Gel Zeitungen
Leipziger Historische Abhandlungen — Leipz Hist Abhandl
Leipziger Juedische Zeitung — LJZ
Leipziger Kommentar das Reichsstrafgesetzbuch — LK
Leipziger Lehrerzeitung — LL Zt
Leipziger Lehrerzeitung — LLZg
Leipziger Magazin zur Naturkunde, Mathematik, und Oekonomie — Leipziger Mag Naturk Math
Leipziger Messe Journal — LPM
Leipziger Monatsschrifter fuer Textil-Industrie — Leipz Monatsschr Text Ind
Leipziger Namenkundliche Beitraege — LNB
Leipziger Neueste Nachrichten — LNN
Leipziger Rechtswissenschaftliche Studien — LRS
Leipziger Rechtswissenschaftliche Studien — LRWS
Leipziger Romanischen Studien — Leipz Roman Studien
Leipziger Romanistischer Studien — LRS
Leipziger Semitische Studien — Leipz Semit St
Leipziger Semitistische Studien — LS St
Leipziger Studien zur Classischen Philologie — LSt
Leipziger Uebersetzungen und Abhandlungen zum Mittelalter — LUeAMA
Leipziger Vierteljahrsschrift fuer Suedosteuropa — Leipziger Vjschr Suedosteur
Leipziger Zeitschrift fuer Deutsches Recht — Leipz Zs Dt R
Leipziger Zeitung. Wissenschaftliche Beilage — Leipz Ztg Wiss Beil
Leistung in Zahlen — Leistung
Leisure and Movement — Leis and Move
Leisure Hour — Leis Hour
Leisure Management — Leisure Mgmt
Leisure Monthly Magazine — LM
Leisure, Recreation, and Tourism Abstracts — Leis Rec Tourism Abs
Leisure, Recreation, and Tourism Abstracts — Leis Recreat Tour Abstr
Leisure Studies — Leis Stud
Leisure Studies — Leisure Stud
Leisure Studies Centre. Review — Leis Stud Centre Rev
Leisure Time Electronics — Leisure Ele
Leitfaeden der Angewandten Mathematik und Mechanik — Leitfaeden Angew Math Mech
Leitfaeden der Elektrotechnik — Leitfaden Elektrotech
Leitfaeden der Informatik — Leitfaeden Inform

Leitfaeden fuer Angewandte Mathematik und Mechanik — LAMM
Leitfaeden und Monographien der Informatik — Leitfaeden Monogr Inform
Leitfaeden und Monographien der Informatik — Leitfaeden Monographien Inform
Leitores e Livros (Rio de Janeiro) — Leit Livr Rio
Leitsaetze fuer die Preisermittlung — LSP
Leitura — Lei
Leiturgia [*Kassel*] — Leit
Leitz Scientific and Technical Information — Leitz Sci and Tech Inf
Leitz-Mitteilungen fuer Wissenschaft und Technik — Leitz Mitt Wiss Tech
Leitz-Mitteilungen fuer Wissenschaft und Technik — Leitz-Mitt Wiss & Tech
Leitz-Mitteilungen fuer Wissenschaft und Technik — Leitz-Mitt Wissen Technik
Lejeunia. Revue de Botanique. Memoire — Lejeunia Mem
Leka Promishlenost — Leka Promst
Leka Promishlenost. Tekstil — Leka Promst Tekst
Lekarnicke Listy — Lekarn Listy
Lekarska Veda v Zahranici — Lek Veda Zahr
Lekarske Listy — Lek Listy
Lekarske Prace — Lek Pr
Lekarske Zpravy Lekarske Fakulty Karlovy University v Hradci Kralove — Lek Zpr Lek Fak Karlovy Univ Hradci Kralove
Lekarski — Lekarsk
Lekarsky Obzor — Lek Obz
Lekarsky Zpravy — Lek Zpr
Lekarstvena Informatsiya — Lek Inf
Lekarstvennye i Syrevye Resursy Irkutskoi Oblasti — Lek Syrevye Resur Irkutsk Obl
Lekarstvennye Rasteniya — Lek Rast
Lekarstvennye Sredstva Dal'nego Vostoka — Lek Sredstva Dal'nego Vostoka
Lekarz Wojskowy [*Poland*] — Lek Wojsk
Lekovite Sirovine — Lek Sirovine
Leksikograficeskij Sbornik — LS
Leksikograficeskij Sbornik — LSb
Leksykohraficny j Bjuleten — LBj
Leksykolohiia ta Leksykohrafiia Mizhvidomchyi Zbirnyk — Lt L
Lektsii Mezhdunarodnoi Shkoly po Voprosam Ispol'zovaniya EVM v Yadernykh Issledovaniyakh — Lektsii Mezhdunar Shk Vopr Ispolz EVM Yad Issled
Leland Stanford Junior University. Publications — Leland Stanford Jr Univ Pub
Lembaga Ilmu Pengetahuan Indonesia. Lembaga Metallurgi Nasional. Laporan — Lembaga Ilmu Pengetahuan Indones Lembaga Metall Nas Laporan
Lembaga Metallurgi Nasional. Laporan — Lembaga Metall Nas Laporan
Lembaran Publikasi Lemigas — Lembaran Publ Lemigas
LEMIT [*Laboratorio de Ensayo de Materiales e Investigaciones Tecnologicas*] **Anales** — LEMIT An
LEMIT [*Laboratorio de Ensayo de Materiales e Investigaciones Tecnologicas*] **Anales. Serie 2** — LEMIT An Ser 2
Len i Konopliya — Len Konop
Lenau Almanach — LenauA
Lenau Forum — Lenauf
Lend a Hand — Lend a H
Lending Law Forum — Lend LF
Lending Law Forum — Lending LF
Lenguaje y Ciencias — LenC
Lenguaje y Ciencias — LyC
Lenguas Modernas — LengM
Lenin Academy of Agricultural Science. Agro-Soil Institute. Proceedings. Leningrad Laboratory — Lenin Acad Agric Sci Agro Soil Inst Proc Leningrad Lab
Lenin Academy of Agricultural Sciences. Gedroiz Institute of Fertilizers and Agro-Soil Science. Proceedings. Leningrad Department — Lenin Acad Agric Sci Gedroiz Inst Fert Agro Soil Sci Proc
Leninabadskii Gosudarstvennyi Pedagogiceskii Institut Ucenye Zapiski — Leninabad Gos Ped Inst Ucen Zap
Leningrad Gornyy Institut Zapiski — Leningrad Gorn Inst Zap
Leningrad Mathematical Journal — LMJ
Leningrad Pedagogical Institute of Foreign Languages. Transactions — LGPIT
Leningrad State University. Philology Series. Transactions — LGU
Leningradskaya Lesotekhnicheskaya Akademiya Imeni S. M. Kirova. Nauchnye Trudy — Leningr Lesotekh Akad Im S M Kirova Nauchn Tr
Leningradskii Elektrotekhnicheskii Institut Imeni V. I. Ul'yanova. Izvestiya — Leningr Elektrotekh Inst Im VI Ulyanova Izv
Leningradskii Gidrometeorologicheskii Institut. Sbornik Nauchnykh Trudov — Leningr Gidrometeorol Inst Sb Nauchn Tr
Leningradskii Gidrometeorologicheskii Institut. Trudy — Leningr Gidrometeorol Inst Tr
Leningradskii Gosudarstvennyi Institut Usovershenstvovaniya Vrachei Imeni S. M. Kirova. Nauchnye Trudy — Leningr Gos Inst Usoversh Vrachei Im SM Kirova Nauchn Tr
Leningradskii Gosudarstvennyi Ordena Lenina Universitet Imeni A. A. Zdanova Ucenye Zapiski — Leningrad Gos Univ Ucen Zap
Leningradskii Gosudarstvennyi Ordena Lenina Universitet Imeni A. A. Zdanova Ucenye Zapiski Serija Matematiceskih Nauk — Leningrad Gos Univ Ucen Zap Ser Mat Nauk
Leningradskii Gosudarstvennyi Pedagogiceskii Institut Imeni A. I. Gercena Ucenye Zapiski — Leningrad Gos Ped Inst Ucen Zap
Leningradskii Gosudarstvennyi Pedagogicheskii Institut Imeni M. N. Pokrovskogo. Uchenye Zapiski — Leningr Gos Pedagog Inst Im M N Pokrovskogo Uch Zap
Leningradskii Gosudarstvennyi Universitet Avtomatizirovannye Sistemy Upravlenija — Avtomat Sistemy Upravlen
Leningradskii Gosudarstvennyi Universitet Imeni A. A. Zhdanova. Uchenye Zapiski. Seriya Fizicheskikh i Geologicheskikh Nauk — Leningr Gos Univ Im A A Zhdanova Uch Zap Ser Fiz Geol Nauk
Leningradskii Gosudarstvennyi Universitet Vychislitel'nyi Tsentr Moskovskii Gosudarstvennyi Universitet Vychislitel'nyi Tsentr Vychislitel'naya Tekhnika i Voprosy Kibernetiki — Vychisl Tekhn i Voprosy Kibernet
Leningradskii Institut Aviatsionnogo Priborostroeniya. Trudy — Leningr Inst Aviats Priborostr Tr
Leningradskii Institut Gigieny Truda i Tekhniki Bezopasnosti. Byulleten — Leningr Inst Gig Tr Tekh Bezop Byull
Leningradskii Institut Gigieny Trudy i Tekhniki Bezopasnosti. Trudy i Materialy — Leningr Inst Gig Tr Tekh Bezop Tr Mater
Leningradskii Institut Sovetskoi Torgovli Sbornik Trudov — Leningr Inst Sov Torg Sb Tr
Leningradskii Institut Tochnoi Mekhaniki i Optiki Trudy — Leningr Inst Tochn Mekh Opt Tr
Leningradskii Institut Usovershenstvovaniya Veterinarnykh Vrachei. Sbornik Nauchnykh Trudov — Leningr Inst Usoversh Vet Vrachei Sb Nauchn Tr
Leningradskii Inzenerno-Ekonomiceskii Institut Imeni Pal'miro Tol'jatti Trudy [*A publication*] — Leningrad Inz-Ekonom Inst Trudy
Leningradskii Inzhenerno-Stroitel'nyi Institut Mezhvuzovskii Tematicheskii Sbornik — Leningr Inzh Stroit Inst Mezhvuz Temat Sb
Leningradskii Inzhenerno-Stroitel'nyi Institut Mezhvuzovskii Tematicheskii Sbornik Trudov — Leningr Inzh Mezhvuz Temat Sb Tr
Leningradskii Inzhenerno-Stroitel'nyii Institut Sbornik Trudov — Leningr Inzh Stroit Inst Sb Tr
Leningradskii Inzhenerno-Stroitel'skii Institut Sbornik Trudov — Leningrad Inz-Stroitel Inst Sb Trudov
Leningradskii Korablestroitel'nyi Institut. Trudy — Leningr Korablestroit Inst Tr
Leningradskii Mekhanicheskii Institut Sbornik Trudov — Leningr Mekh Inst Sb Tr
Leningradskii Mekhanicheskii Institut Sbornik Trudov (LMI) — Leningrad Meh Inst Sb Trudov (LMI)
Leningradskii Metallicheskii Zavod Trudy — Leningr Met Zavod Tr
Leningradskii Mezhdunarodnyi Seminar — Leningr Mezhdunar Semin
Leningradskii Nauchno-Issledovatel'skii i Konstruktorskii Institut Khimicheskogo Mashinostroeniya Trudy — Leningr Nauchno Issled Konstr Inst Khim Mashinostr Tr
Leningradskii Nauchno-Issledovatel'skii Institut Gematologii i Perelivaniya Krovi Sbornik Trudov — Leningr Nauchno Issled Inst Gematol Pereliv Krovi Sb Tr
Leningradskii Nauchno-Issledovatel'skii Institut Lesnogo Khozyaistva Sbornik Nauchnykh Trudov — Leningr Nauchno Issled Inst Lesn Khoz Sb Nauchn Tr
Leningradskii Ordena Lenina Gosudarstvennyi Imeni A. A. Zhdanova Metody Vychislenii — Metody Vychisl
Leningradskii Ordena Lenina Gosudarstvennyi Universitet Imeni A. A. Zdanova. Kafedra i Laboratorija Ekonomiko-Matematiceskih Metodov. Primenenie Matematikii v Ekonomike — Primenen Mat Ekonom
Leningradskii Politehniceskii Institut Imeni M. I. Kalinina Trudy LPI — Leningrad Politehn Inst Trudy
Leningradskii Politekhnicheskii Institut imeni M. I. Kalinina. Trudy — Leningr Politekh Inst im M I Kalinina Tr
Leningradskii Sanitarno-Gigienicheskii Meditsinskii Institut. Trudy LSGMI — Leningr Sanit Gig Med Inst Tr LSGMI
Leningradskii Sel'skokhozyaistvennyi Institut. Nauchnye Trudy — Leningr Skh Inst Nauchn Tr
Leningradskii Seminar po Kosmofizike. Materialy — Leningr Semin Kosmofiz Mater
Leningradskii Tekhnologicheskii Institut Tsellyulozno-Bumazhnoi Promyshlennosti Trudy — Leningr Tekhnol Inst Tsellyul Bum Promsti Tr
Leningradskii Universitet Vestnik Geologiya i Geografiya — Leningrad Univ Vestn Geol Geogr
Leningradskii Universitet Voprosy Teorii Sistem Avtomaticheskogo Upravleniya — Voprosy Teor Sistem Avtomat Upravleniya
Leningradskii Veterinarnyi Institut. Sbornik Nauchnykh Rabot — Leningr Vet Inst Sb Nauchn Rab
Leningradskij Universitet Vestnik Serija Istorii, Literatury, i Jazyka — LV
Leningradskoe Obshchestvo Estestvoispytatelei. Trudy — Leningr Ovo Estestvoispyt Tr
Lens and Eye Toxicity Research — Lens Eye Toxic Res
Lens Research — Lens Res
L'Enseignement Secondaire — E Sec
Lenzburger Neujahrsblaetter — Lenz N
Lenzinger Berichte — Lenzinger Ber
Leo Baeck Institute of Jews from Germany. Yearbook — Leo Baeck Inst Jews Germ Yrbk
Leo Baeck Institute. Year Book — LBIYB
Leo Baeck Institute Yearbook — LeB
Leo Baeck Institute Yearbook — Leo Baeck Inst Yearb
Leo Baeck Memorial Lecture — LBML
Leodium — L
Leodium [*Liege*] — Leod
Leonardo — L
Leonardo — Leo
Leonardo — Leon
Leonharki Euleri Opera Omnia. Series Secunda — Leonhar Eul Opera Omnia Ser 2
Lepidoptera [*Copenhagen*] — LEPDAV
Leprosy in India — Lepr India
Leprosy Review — Lep Rev
Leprosy Review — Lepr Rev
Leprosy Review — Leprosy Rev
Leprosy Review — LEREA
Lepton-Photon Interactions. International Symosium — Lepton Photon Interact Int Symosium
Lerindustrien — Ler
LERS (Laboratoires d'Etudes et de Recherches Synthelabo) Monograph Series — LERS (Lab Etud Rech Synthelabo) Monogr Ser
LERS [*Laboratoires d'Etudes et de Recherches Synthelabo*] **Monograph Series** — LERS Monogr Ser
Les Echos — LE

Les Etudes Classiques [*Namur*] — EClass
Les Etudes Classiques — LEC
Les Houches Summer School Proceedings [*Elsevier Book Series*] — LHSSP
Les Informations Politiques et Sociales — LIPES
Les Lettres Francaises — LLF
Les Lettres Romanes — LR
Les Nouvelles Litteraires — LNL
Lesbian Tide — Lesbian T
Leshonenu La'am — LLA
Lesnaja Promyslennost — Lesn Prom
Lesnaja Promyslennost — LP
Lesnaya Bumazhnaya i Derevoobrabatyvayushchaya Promyshlennost (Kiev) — Lesn Bum Derevoobrab Promst (Kiev)
Lesnaya Industriya — Lesn Ind
Lesnaya Promyshlennost — Les Prom
Lesnaya Promyshlennost [*Former USSR*] — Lesn Prom-St
Lesnaya Promyshlennost — Lesnaya Prom
Lesnicka Prace — Lesn Pr
Lesnicka Prace — Lesn Prace
Lesnicka Prace — LP
Lesnicky Casopis — Lesn Cas
Lesnictvi. Ceskoslovenska Akademie Zemedelska Ustav Vedeckotechnickych Informaci pro Zemedelstvi — Lesnictvi Cesk Akad Zemed Ustav Vedeckotech Inf Zemed
Lesnictvi v Zahranici — Lesn Zahr
Lesnoe Hozjajstvo — Lesn Hoz
Lesnoe Khozyaistvo — Les Khoz
Lesnoe Khozyaistvo — Lesn Khoz
Lesnoe Khozyaistvo — Lesnoe Khoz
Lesnoe Khozyaistvo — LKHOAW
Lesnoe Khozyaistvo i Agrolesomelioratsiya v Kazakhstane — Lesn Khoz Agrolesomelior Kaz
Lesnoe Khozyaistvo, Lesnaya, Bumazhnaya i Derevoobrabatyvayushchaya Promyshlennost — Lesn Khoz Lesn Bum Derevoobrab Promst
Lesnoi Zhurnal — Les Zh
Lesnoi Zhurnal (Archangel, USSR) — Lesn Zh (Archangel USSR)
Lesokhimicheskaya Promyshlennost — Lesokhim Promst
Lesokhimiya i Podsochka — Lesokhim Podsochka
Lesonenu. Quarterly of Hebrew — Les
Lesopromyshlennoe Delo — Lesoprom Delo
Lesotho Notes and Records — Lesotho Notes Recs
Lesovedenie — Lesoved
Lesovedenie i Lesnoe Khozyaistvo — Lesoved Lesn Khoz
Lesovodstvenno-Nauchnye Soobshcheniya — Lesovod Nauchn Soobshch
Lesovodstvo i Agrolesomelioratsiia — Lesovod Agrolesomelior
Lesovodstvo i Agrolesomelioratsiya Respublikanskii Mezhvedomstvennyi Tematicheskii Sbornik — Lesovod Agrolesomelior Resp Mezhved Temat Sb
L'Esplorazione Commerciale e l'Esploratore — ECE
L'Esprit Createur — L'Esprit
Lessico Ittito — LI
Lessing Yearbook — LY
Lessons in Islam Series — LIS
Letnija Raboty. Travaux des Vacances. Station Biologique du Wolga — Letn Raboty
Letopis — Lp
Letopis Doma Literatorov — LDL
Letopis Instituta za Serbski ludospyt w Budysinje pri Nemskej Akademiji Wedo-Moscow w Berlinje Rjad A Rec A Literatura — LISL
Letopis Jahresschrift des Instituts fuer Serbische Volksforschung — Letopis Jschr Serb Volksforsch
Letopis Matice Srpske — Let Mat Srp
Letopis Matice Srpske — LetMs
Letopis Matice Srpske. Novi Sad — LMS
Letopis Naucnih Radova. Poljoprivredni Fakultet. Novi Sad — Letop Nauc Rad Poljopriv Fak Novi Sad
Letopis. Slovenska Akademija Znanosti in Umetnosti v Ljubljani — Vest LU
Letopis' Zurnal'nych Statej — Ls S
Letopisi na Khigienno-Epidemiologichnata Sluzhba [*Bulgaria*] — Letopisi Khig-Epidemiol Sluzhba
Letopisi na Khigienno-Epidemiologichnite Instituti — Letopisi Khig-Epidemiol Inst
Letras (Argentina) — LSA
Letras (Caracas) — LetrasC
Letras (Curitiba, Brazil) — Letr Curitiba
Letras de Deusto — LdD
Letras de Deusto — LetD
Letras de Mexico (Mexico) — Letr Mex Mex
Letras del Azuay — LDA
Letras del Ecuador — LetE
Letras Femeninas — L Fem
Letras Femeninas — LF
Letras (Lima) — Letr Lima
Letras (Lima) — LL
Letras Nacionales — LetNa
Letras Nacionales (Bogota) — Letr Nac Bogota
Letras Nuevas — LsNs
Letras (Peru) — LSP
Letras y Artes (Maracaibo) — Letr Art Maracaibo
Lettera di Sociologia Religiosa — LSR
Letteratura — La
Letteratura — Let
Letteratura — Lett
Letteratura ed Arte Contemporanea — LAC
Letteratura Italiana Laterza — LItL
Letterature Contemporanea — LC
Letterature Moderne — LeMo
Letterature Moderne — Lett Mod
Letterature Moderne — LM
Lettere al Nuovo Cimento — Lett Nuov C
Lettere al Nuovo Cimento — Lett Nuovo Cim
Lettere al Nuovo Cimento — Lett Nuovo Cimento
Lettere al Nuovo Cimento. Societa Italiana di Fisica [*Italy*] — Lett Nuovo Cimento Soc Ital Fis
Lettere Italiane — Let It
Lettere Italiane — Lett Ital
Lettere Italiane — LI
Lettere Italiane — LIt
Lettere Italiane — LItal
Letters and Papers on Agriculture, Planting, etc. Selected from the Correpondence-Book. Bath and West and Southern Counties Society — Lett Pap Agric Bath Soc
Letters in Applied and Engineering Sciences — Lett Appl and Eng Sci
Letters in Applied and Engineering Sciences — Lett Appl Eng Sci
Letters in Applied Microbiology — LAMIE7
Letters in Applied Microbiology — Lett Appl Microbiol
Letters in Heat and Mass Transfer — Lett Heat and Mass Transfer
Letters in Heat and Mass Transfer — Lett Heat Mass Transf
Letters in Heat and Mass Transfer — Lett Heat Mass Transfer
Letters in Mathematical Physics — Lett Math Phys
Letters on Brewing — Lett Brew
Lettore de Provincia — LdProv
Lettre aux Communautes de la Mission de France — LCMF
Lettre d'Information — Lettre Inf
Lettre d'Information. Bureau de Recherches Geologiques et Minieres [*Paris*] [*A publication*] — Lett Inf Bur Rech Geol Min
Lettre Medicale de Tours — Lett Med Tours
Lettre Pharmaceutique — Lett Pharm
Lettres Botaniques — Lett Bot
Lettres du Scolasticat de Vals — LSV
Lettres Francaises — LetF
Lettres Francaises — Lettres Fr
Lettres Francaises — LF
Lettres Francaises — LFS
Lettres Francaises. Buenos-Aires — Lettres Fr BA
Lettres Francaises. Montevideo — Lettres Fr Mo
Lettres Modernes — LetM
Lettres Modernes — LMod
Lettres Nouvelles — LeNo
Lettres Nouvelles — LetN
Lettres Nouvelles — LN
Lettres Nouvelles — LNouv
Lettres Romanes — Let Rom
Lettres Romanes — Lett Roman
Lettres Romanes — Lettres Rom
Lettura Oftalmologica — Lettura Oft
Leucocyte Culture Conference. Proceedings — Leucocyte Cult Conf Proc
Leukaemia and Lymphoma Research — Leuk Lymphoma Res
Leukemia Abstracts — Leukemia Abstr
Leukemia and Lymphoma — Leuk Lymphoma
Leukemia Research — Leuk Res
Leukemia Society of America Research, Inc. Annual Scholar Fellow Meeting — Leuk Soc Am Res Inc Annu Scholar Fellow Meet
Leukocytes and Host Defense. Proceedings. Meeting. International Leukocyte Culture Conference — Leukocytes Host Def Proc Meet Int Leukocyte Cult Conf
Leuvense Bijdragen [*Bijblad*] — LB
Leuvense Bijdragen — Leu Bij
Leuvense Bijdragen — Leuv Bijdr
Leuvense Bijdragen (Bijblad) — LBB
Levant Trade Review — LTR
Levantamento de Recursos Naturais. Projecto Radam (Brasil) — Levant Recursos Nat Proj Radam (Bras)
Leveltari Kozlemenyei — Leveltari Kozlem
Leveltari Szemle — Leveltari Sz
Levende Billeder — LB
Levende Natuur — Levende Nat
Levende Talen — LevT
Levende Talen — LT
Levensmiddelenmarkt — NWK
Levensverzekering — LV
Leviathan — LEVID
Levnedsmiddelstyrelsen Publikation — Levnedsmiddelstyr Publ
L'Evolution de l'Humanite — Ev Hum
LEW [*Lokomotivbau-Elektrotechnische Werke*] **Nachrichten** — LEW Nachr
Lex et Scientia — Lex Sci
Lex Orandi — LO
Lexica Graeca Minora — LGM
Lexicon Capuccinum — Lex Cap
Lexicon Iconographicum Mythologiae Classicae — LIMC
Lexicon Vindobonense — Lex Vindob
Lexikalischen Tafelserien der Babylonier und Assyrer — LTBA
Lexikographikon Deltion Akademias Athenon — LDAA
Lexikon der Aegyptologie — LA
Lexikon der Aegyptologie — LAe
Lexikon der Alten Welt — LAW
Lexikon der Alten Welt — Lex AW
Lexikon der Christlichen Ikonographie — L Chr I
Lexikon der Marienkunde — LM
Lexikon der Marienkunde — LMK
Lexikon der Paedagogik der Gegenwart — LPG
Lexikon der Paedagogik (Freiburg) — L Paed (F)

Lexikon der Paedagogik. Herausgegeben von Maximilian Roloff — L Paed R
Lexikon der Psychologie — L Ps
Lexikon der Weltliteratur im 20. Jahrhundert — LWL
Lexikon des Fruegriechischen Epos — L Fgr E
Lexikon des Fruegriechischen Epos — LFE
Lexikon des Gesamten Buchwesens — LGBW
Lexikon des Judentums — Lex Jud
Lexikon des Mittelalters — LdM
Lexikon des Mittelalters — LMA
Lexikon fuer Paedagogik (Bern) — L Paed (B)
Lexikon fuer Theologie und Kirche — L Th K
Lexikon fuer Theologie und Kirche — LTK
Lexikon Paepstlicher Weisungen — LPW
Lexikon Strassenverkehrsrechtlicher Entscheidungen — LSE
Lexikon zur Geschichte und Politik des 20. Jahrhunderts — LGP
Lexington Historical Society. Proceedings — Lexington Hist Soc Proc
Lexington Theological Quarterly — Lex Th Q
Lexington Theological Quarterly — Lex TQ
Lexington Theological Quarterly — LTQ
Lexique Stratigraphique International — LSI
Lexis — Lex
Ley Federal de Trabajo [*Mexico*] — LFT
Leybold Polarographische Berichte — Leybold Polarogr Ber
Leyes Nacionales [*Argentina*] — LN
Leyte-Samar Studies — Leyte-Samar Stud
Leyte-Samar Studies — LSS
LGC [*Laboratory of the Government Chemist*] **Occasional Paper** — LGC Occas Pap
Lgoru Information Bulletin — Lgoru Inf Bull
Lia Fail — LF
Liaison and Services Note. Forest Research Laboratory (Winnipeg) — Liais Serv Note For Res Lab (Winnipeg)
Liaison Report. Commonwealth Geological Liaison Office — Liaison Rep Commonw Geol Liaison Off
Liaisons Sociales — Liaisons Soc
Liaudies Kuryba — LiK
Liber Annualis. Pontificia Universitas Gregoriana — LAPUG
Liber Diurnus Romanorum Pontificum — LDRP
Liber Lovaniensis — LL
Liber Pontificalis — LP
Liber Pontificalis, Prout Exstat in Codice Manuscripto Dertusensi — LPM
Libera Cattedra di Storia della Civilta Fiorentina — LCSCF
Liberaal Reveil — LR
Liberal and Fine Arts Review — LFAR
Liberal Arts Journal. Natural Science. Tottori University — Lib Arts J Nat Sci Tottori Univ
Liberal Arts Journal. Tottori University/Tottori Daigaku Gakugeibu Kenkyu Hokoku — Liberal Arts J Tottori Univ
Liberal Education — LE
Liberal Education — Lib Educ
Liberal Education — Liberal Ed
Liberal Education — Liberal Educ
Liberal Geological Society. Cross Sections. Type Log — Liberal Geol Soc Cross Sec Type Log
Liberal Opinion — Lib Opinion
Liberal Party of Australia. New South Wales Division. Research Bulletin — Lib Pty Aust NSW Div Res Bull
Liberal Party of Australia. New South Wales Division. Research Bulletin — Research Bul
Liberation — Liber
Liberation Bulletin — Liberation Bull
Liberation Support Movement News — LSM News
Liberia Bulletin — Liberia Bull
Liberia Law Journal — LLJ
Liberian Economic and Management Review — Liberian Econ Mgmt Rev
Liberian Law Journal — Liberian LJ
Liberian Studies Journal — Liber Stud J
Liberian Studies Journal — Liberian Stud J
Liberian Studies Journal — LiberianSJ
Libertarian Education: A Magazine for the Liberation of Learning — LIB ED
Libertas Mathematica — Libertas Math
Libertas Mathematica. American Romanian Academy of Arts and Sciences — Libert Math
Liberte Chretienne — LCh
Liberty Bell — LB
Librairie de l'Universite de Fribourg — LUF
Librairie Universelle de France — LUF
Librarian and Book World — Libn & Bk W
Librarians' Browser — Lib Brow
Librarians for Social Change. Journal — LfSC
Librarians' Newsletter [*United States*] — Libr Newsl
Librarie du Bicentenaire de la Revolution Francaise — Lib Bicentenaire Revolution Francaise
Library — LIB
Library Acquisitions. Practice and Theory — Libr Acquis Pract and Theory
Library Administration Quarterly — LAQ
Library and Information Bulletin — Libr Inf Bull
Library and Information Network [*Database*] — LINK
Library and Information Science — Lib Inf Sci
Library and Information Science — Libr and Inf Sci
Library and Information Science Abstracts — Libr Inf Sci Abstr
Library and Information Science Abstracts — LibSciAb
Library and Information Science Abstracts [*Library Association Publishing Ltd.*] [*Bibliographic database England*] — LISA
Library Association of Alberta. Bulletin — L A of Alta Bul
Library Association of Alberta. Bulletin — Lib Assn Alta Bull
Library Association of Australia. University and College Libraries Section. News Sheet — LAA Univ & Coll Lib Sec News
Library Association of Australia. University and College Libraries Section. News Sheet — Libr Ass Aust Univ Coll Libr Sect News Sh
Library Association of Australia. University Libraries Section. News Sheet — LAA Univ Lib Sec News
Library Association of Australia. University Libraries Section. News Sheet — LAA Univ Lib Sec News Sheet
Library Association of the United Kingdom. Monthly Notes — Brit Lib Assoc
Library Association. Record — LAR
Library Association Rocord — LAsR
Library Association. Record — Lib Assn R
Library Association. Record — Lib Assn Rec
Library Association. Record — Lib Assoc Rec
Library Association. Record — Libr AR
Library Association. Record — Libr Ass Rec
Library Association. Record — Libr Assoc Rec
Library Association. University and Research Section. Colleges, Institutes, and Schools of Education Subsection. Newsletter — CISE Newsl
Library Association. Yearbook — Lib Assn Yrbk
Library Association. Youth Libraries Group News — YLG News
Library Binder — Lib Binder
Library Binder — Libr Binder
Library Bulletin. University of London — Libr Bull Univ Lond
Library Chronical. University of Texas at Austin — Libr Chron UTA
Library Chronicle — LC
Library Chronicle — Lib Chron
Library Chronicle — LibC
Library Chronicle — Libr Chron
Library Chronicle. University of Pennsylvania — LCP
Library Chronicle. University of Pennsylvania — LCUP
Library Chronicle. University of Texas — LCUT
Library Chronicle. University of Texas — Libr Chron Univ Tex
Library College Journal — Lib Coll J
Library College Journal — Libr Coll J
Library Computer Equipment Review — Libr Comput Equip Rev
Library Herald — Libr Her
Library History — Lib Hist
Library History — Libr Hist
Library Information Bulletin — Lib Inf Bull
Library Information System [*Database*] — LIBRIS
Library Jottings — Lib Jot
Library Journal — GLJJ
Library Journal — LibJ
Library Journal — Libr J
Library Journal — Library J
Library Journal — LJ
Library Journal (New York) — Libr Jour NY
Library Journal/School Library Journal — LJ/SLJ
Library Leaves from the Library of Long Island University — Lib Leaves
Library Literature — LibLit
Library Literature — Libr Lit
Library Literature — LL
Library (London) — Lib (London)
Library Magazine — Library Mag
Library Management — LMT
Library Management Bulletin — Lib Manage Bul
Library Materials on Africa — Libr Mater Afr
Library Materials on Africa — Libr Mater Africa
Library News Bulletin — Lib News Bul
Library News Bulletin — Libr News Bull
Library Notes — LibN
Library Notes — LN
Library Notes. Royal Commonwealth Society — Libr Notes R Commonw Soc
Library Occurrent — Lib Occurrent
Library of Anglo-Catholic Theology — LACT
Library of Christian Classics — LCC
Library of Congress Acquisitions. Manuscript Division — Libr Congr Acquis Manuscr Div
Library of Congress. Information Bulletin — Lib Cong Inf Bull
Library of Congress. Information Bulletin — Libr Congr Inf Bull
Library of Congress. Quarterly Journal — Lib Cong Q J
Library of Congress. Quarterly Journal of Current Acquisitions — LCQJCA
Library of Congress. Quarterly Journal of Current Acquisitions — Lib Cong Q J Cur Acq
Library of Congress Rule Interpretations — LCRI
Library of Contemporary Theology — LCT
Library of Ecumenical Studies — LES
Library of Engineering Mathematics — Lib Engrg Math
Library of Fathers of the Holy Catholic Church — LoF
Library of History and Doctrine — LHD
Library of Living Theology — LLT
Library of Modern Religious Thought — LMRT
Library of Orthodox Theology — LOT
Library of Philosophy and Theology — LP Th
Library of Protestant Thought — LPT
Library of Religion and Culture — LRC
Library of the University of Chicago — Univ Chic
Library of Theology — L Th
Library Opinion — Lib Op
Library Opinion — Lib Opinion
Library Opinion — Library Op
Library. Palestine Pilgrims Text Society — LPPTS

Library Periodicals Round Table. Newsletter — Lib Period Round Table Newsletter
Library Quarterly — ILIQ
Library Quarterly — Lib Q
Library Quarterly — Lib Qtr
Library Quarterly — Libr Q
Library Quarterly — Libr Quart
Library Quarterly — LQ
Library Record of Australasia — LRA
Library Research — Lib Res
Library Resources and Technical Services — Lib Res Tec
Library Resources and Technical Services — Lib Resources & Tech Serv
Library Resources and Technical Services — Lib Resources and Tech Services
Library Resources and Technical Services — Libr Resour and Tech Serv
Library Resources and Technical Services — Libr Resour Tech Serv
Library Resources and Technical Services — Libr Resources Tech Serv
Library Resources and Technical Services — Libr Resources Tech Servs
Library Resources and Technical Services — LRTS
Library Review — Lib R
Library Review — Lib Rev
Library Review — Libr Rev
Library Review — LR
Library Review. Forestry Commission (London) — Libr Rev For Comm (Lond)
Library Scene — Lib Scene
Library Science — Lib Sci
Library Science Abstracts — Libr Sci Abstr
Library Science (Japan) — Library Sci (Japan)
Library Science Update — Lib Sci Update
Library Science with a Slant to Documentation — Lib Sci Slant Doc
Library Science with a Slant to Documentation — Libr Sci Slant Doc
Library Science with a Slant to Documentation — Libr Sci Slant Docum
Library Technology Reports — ILTR
Library Technology Reports — Lib Tech Rep
Library Technology Reports — Libr Technol Rep
Library Technology Reports — LTR
Library Trends — ILIT
Library Trends — Lib Trends
Library Trends — Libr Trends
Library Trends — LibT
Library World — Lib W
Library World — Libr W
Library World — Libr Wld
Libre Service Actualites — LSA
Libre Service Actualites — LSC
Libri — Li
Libri Coloniarum — Lib Colon
Libri Confirmationum ad Beneficia Ecclesiastica Pragensem per Archidiocesim — LCBEP
Libri del Giorno — Lib Giorn
Libri e Riviste d'Italia — LRI
Libri Erectionum Archidioecesis Pragensis — LEAP
Libri Oncologici [*Yugoslavia*] — Libri Oncol
Libro Anual. Facultad de Teologia. Universidad Pontificia y Civil [*Lima, Peru*] — LAFacTLima
Libro de Actas. Congreso Nacional de Medicina, Higiene, y Seguridad del Trabajo — Libro Actas Congr Nac Med Hig Segur Trab
Libro Italiano — Ll
Libro Italiano — Llt
Libro y Pueblo — LyP
Libros Cubanos — LCub
Libya — Lib
Libya Antiqua — LibAnt
Libya Antiqua — Libya Ant
Libya. Ministry of Industry. Geological Section. Bulletin — Libya Minist Ind Geol Sec Bull
Libya. Ministry of Industry. Geological Section. Bulletin — Libya Minist Ind Geol Sect Bull
Libyan Journal of Agriculture — Libyan J Agric
Libyan Journal of Earth Science — Libyan J Earth Sci
Libyan Journal of Science — Libyan J Sci
Libyca [*Alger*]. Anthropologie, Prehistoire, Ethnographie — Lib APE
Libyca [*Alger*]. Archeologie, Epigraphie — Lib AE
Libyca. Serie Archeologie-Epigraphique — Libica Archeol
Licensing International — Licens Int
Licensing Law and Business Report — Licensing L and Bus Rep
Licentiate All-India Monthly Journal of Medicine and Surgery — Licentiate All-India Mon J Med Surg
Liceo de la Habana — LH
Liceus de Portugal — LicP
Lichenologist [*Oxford*] — LCHNB8
Lichenologist — LICH
Lichenology. Progress and Problems. Proceedings. International Symposium — Lichenol Prog Probl Proc Int Symp
Licht-Forschung — Licht-Forsch
Lichttechnik — Lichttech
Lick Observatory Bulletin — Lick Obs Bull
Lidoflazin. Clinium. Internationales Lidoflazin Symposion — Lidoflazin Int Lidoflazin Symp
Lie Groups and their Applications — Lie Groups Appl
Lie Groups. History. Frontiers and Applications — Lie Groups Hist Frontiers and Appl
Lie Groups. History, Frontiers, and Applications. Series A — Lie Groups Hist Frontiers and Appl Ser A
Lie Groups. History, Frontiers, and Applications. Series B. Systems Information and Control — Lie Groups Hist Frontiers and Appl Ser B Systems Inform Contr
Liebigs Annalen der Chemie — LACHD
Liebigs Annalen der Chemie — Liebigs Ann Chem
Liebigs Annalen. Organic and Bioorganic Chemistry — Liebigs Ann
Lietuviu Kalbotyros Klausimai — LKK
Lietuvos Fizikos Rinkinys — Liet Fiz Rink
Lietuvos Fizikos Rinkinys [*Lithuanian SSR*] — Liet Fiz Rinkinys
Lietuvos Fizikos Zurnalas — Liet Fiz Z
Lietuvos Geologijos Mokslinio Tyrimo Institutas Darbai — Liet Geol Mokslinio Tyrimo Inst Darb
Lietuvos Geologu Mokslines Konferencijos Medziaga — Liet Geol Mokslines Konf Medziaga
Lietuvos Gyvulininkystes ir Veterinarijos Mokslinio Tyrimo Instituto Darbai — Liet Gyvulinink Vet Mokslinio Tyrimo Inst Darb
Lietuvos Gyvulininkystes Mokslinio Tyrimo Instituto Darbai — Liet Gyvulinink Mokslinio Tyrimo Inst Darb
Lietuvos Hidrotechnikos ir Melioracijos Mokslinio Tyrimo Instituto Darbai — Liet Hidrotech Melior Mokslinio Tyrimo Inst Darb
Lietuvos Hidrotechnikos ir Melioracijos Mokslinio Tyrimo Instituto Mokslines Konferencijos Sutrumpintu Pranesimu Medziaga — Liet Hidrotech Melior Mokslinio Tyrimo Inst Mokslines Konf
Lietuvos Matematikos Rinkinys — Liet Mat Rink
Lietuvos Mechanikos Rinkinys — Liet Mech Rinkinys
Lietuvos Misku Ukio Mokslinio Tyrimo Instituto Darbai — Liet Misku Ukio Mokslinio Tyrimo Inst Darb
Lietuvos Mokslu Akademija. Ekologija — Liet Mokslu Akad Ekol
Lietuvos Mokslu Akademija. Eksperimentine Biologija — Liet Mokslu Akad Eksp Biol
Lietuvos TSR Aukstuju Mokyklu Moksliniai Darbai. Radioelektronika — Liet TSR Aukst Mokyklu Moksliniai Darb Radioelektron
Lietuvos TSR Aukstuju Mokyklu Mokslo Darbai. Biologija — Liet TSR Aukst Mokyklu Mokslo Darb Biol
Lietuvos TSR Aukstuju Mokyklu Mokslo Darbai. Chemija ir Chemine Technologija [*Lithuanian SSR*] — Liet TSR Aukst Mokslo Darb Chem Chem Technol
Lietuvos TSR Aukstuju Mokyklu Mokslo Darbai. Chemija ir Chemine Technologija [*A publication*] — Liet TSR Aukst Mokyklu Mokslo Darb Chem Chem Technol
Lietuvos TSR Aukstuju Mokyklu Mokslo Darbai. Elektrotechnika ir Automatika — Liet TSR Aukst Mokyklu Mokslo Darb Elektrotech Autom
Lietuvos TSR Aukstuju Mokyklu Mokslo Darbai. Elektrotechnika ir Mechanika — Liet TSR Aukst Mokyklu Mokslo Darb Elektrotech Mech
Lietuvos TSR Aukstuju Mokyklu Mokslo Darbai. Geografija — Liet TSR Aukst Mokyklu Mokslo Darb Geogr
Lietuvos TSR Aukstuju Mokyklu Mokslo Darbai. Geografija ir Geologija — Liet TSR Aukst Mokyklu Mokslo Darb Geogr Geol
Lietuvos TSR Aukstuju Mokyklu Mokslo Darbai. Geologija — Liet TSR Aukst Mokyklu Mokslo Darb Geol
Lietuvos TSR Aukstuju Mokyklu Mokslo Darbai. Mechanika — Liet TSR Aukst Mokyklu Mokslo Darb Mech
Lietuvos TSR Aukstuju Mokyklu Mokslo Darbai. Mechanine Technologija — Liet TSR Aukst Mokyklu Mokslo Darb Mech Technol
Lietuvos TSR Aukstuju Mokyklu Mokslo Darbai. Medicina — Liet TSR Aukst Mokyklu Mokslo Darb Med
Lietuvos TSR Aukstuju Mokyklu Mokslo Darbai. Statyba ir Architektura — Liet TSR Aukst Mokyklu Mokslo Darb Statyba Archit
Lietuvos TSR Aukstuju Mokyklu Mokslo Darbai. Tekstiles ir Odos Technologija — Liet TSR Aukst Mokyklu Mokslo Darb Tekst Odos Technol
Lietuvos TSR Aukstuju Mokyklu Mokslo Darbai. Ultragarsas — Liet TSR Aukst Mokyklu Moksl Darb Ultragarsas
Lietuvos TSR Aukstuju Mokyklu Mokslo Darbai. Ultragarsas — Liet TSR Aukst Mokyklu Mokslo Darb Ultragarsas
Lietuvos TSR Aukstuju Mokyklu Mokslo Darbai. Vibrotechnika — Liet TSR Aukst Mokyklu Mokslo Darb Vibrotech
Lietuvos TSR Chemiku Analitiku Mokslines Konferencijos Darbai — Liet TSR Chem Anal Mokslines Konf Darb
Lietuvos TSR Geografine Draugija. Geografinis Metrastis — Liet TSR Geogr Draugija Geogr Metrastis
Lietuvos TSR Mokslu Akademija Botanikos Institutas Straipsniu Rinkinys — Liet TSR Mokslu Akad Bot Inst Straipsniu Rinkinys
Lietuvos TSR Mokslu Akademija Geografijos Skyrius Moksliniai Pranesimai — Liet TSR Mokslu Akad Geogr Skyrius Moksliniai Pranesimai
Lietuvos TSR Mokslu Akademija Geologijos Geografijos Instituta Moksliniai Pranesimai — Liet TSR Mokslu Akad Geol Geogr Inst Moksliniai Pranesimai
Lietuvos TSR Mokslu Akademija Melioracijos Institutas Darbai — Liet TSR Mokslu Akad Melior Inst Darb
Lietuvos TSR Mokslu Akademijos Darbai — Liet
Lietuvos TSR Mokslu Akademijos Darbai — Liet TSR Mokslu Akad Darb
Lietuvos TSR Mokslu Akademijos Darbai — Lietuvos Mok Akad Darbai
Lietuvos TSR Mokslu Akademijos Darbai. Serija A [*Vilnius*] — LMAD
Lietuvos TSR Mokslu Akademijos Darbai. Serija B — Liet TSR Mokslu Akad Darb Ser B
Lietuvos TSR Mokslu Akademijos Darbai. Serija B — Liet TSR Mokslu Akad Darbai B
Lietuvos TSR Mokslu Akademijos Darbai. Serija C — Liet TSR Mokslu Akad Darb Ser C
Lietuvos TSR Mokslu Akademijos Darbai. Serija C. Biologijos Mokslai — Liet TSR Mokslu Akad Darb Ser C Biol Mokslai
Lietuvos TSR Mokslu Akademijos Eksperimentines Medicinos Instituto Darbai — Liet TSR Mokslu Akad Eksp Med Inst Darb
Lietuvos TSR Mokslu Akademijos Zinynas — Liet TSR Mokslu Akad Zinynas
Lietuvos TSR Mokslu Akademiya Botanikos Institutas. Botanikos Klausimai — Liet TSR Mokslu Akad Bot Inst Bot Klausimai

Lietuvos Veterinarijos Akademijos Darbai — Liet Vet Akad Darb
Lietuvos Veterinarijos Mokslinio Tyrimo Instituto Darbai — Liet Vet Mokslinio Tyrimo Inst Darb
Lietuvos Zemdirbystes Mokslinio Tyrimo Instituto Darbai — Liet Zemdir Moks Tyrimo Inst Darb
Lietuvos Zemdirbystes Mokslinio Tyrimo Instituto Darbai — Liet Zemdirbystes Mokslinio Tyrimo Inst Darb
Lietuvos Zemes Ukio Akademija Mokslo Darbai — Liet Zemes Ukio Akad Mokslo Darb
Lietuvos Zemes Ukio Akademija Mokslo Darbu Rinkiniai — Liet Zemes Ukio Akad Mokslo Darbu Rinkiniai
Lietuvos Zemes Ukio Akademijos Moksliniai Darbai — Liet Zemes Ukio Akad Moksliniai Darb
Life — GLIF
Life and Environment [*Japan*] — Life Environ
Life and Letters — Life & Lett
Life and Letters — LL
Life Association News — LAN
Life Association News — LAS
Life Australia — Life Aust
Life Chemistry Reports — Life Chem Rep
Life Chemistry Reports. Supplement Series — Life Chem Rep Suppl Ser
Life Digest — Life D
Life Digest — Life Dig
Life, Health, and Accident Insurance Cases. Second. Commerce Clearing House — Life Health & Accid Ins Cas 2d CCH
Life Insurance Courant — Life Ins Courant
Life Insurance in Canada — LIC
Life Insurance Index — Life Insur Index
Life Insurance Selling — LIS
Life Magazine (Chicago) — LMC
Life of Spirit — LoS
Life Science Advances — Life Sci Adv
Life Science Advances — LSADDN
Life Science Advances. Biochemistry — Life Sci Adv Biochem
Life Science Institute Kivo/Jochi Daigaku Seimei Kagaku Kenkyusho — Life Sci Inst Kivo Jochi Daigaku Seimei Kagaku Kenkyusho
Life Sciences — Life Sci
Life Sciences — LIFSA
Life Sciences and Agriculture Experiment Station. Technical Bulletin (Maine) [*A publication*] — Life Sci Agric Exp Stn Tech Bull (Maine)
Life Sciences and Space Research — Life Sci Sp Res
Life Sciences and Space Research [*Netherlands*] — Life Sci Space Res
Life Sciences Collection — Life Sci Collect
Life Sciences Monographs — Life Sci Monogr
Life Sciences. Part I. Physiology and Pharmacology — Life Sci Part I
Life Sciences. Part I. Physiology and Pharmacology — Life Sci Part I Physiol Pharmacol
Life Sciences. Part I. Physiology and Pharmacology — LSPPA
Life Sciences. Part II. Biochemistry. General and Molecular Biology — Life Sci Part II
Life Sciences. Part II. Biochemistry. General and Molecular Biology — Life Sci Part II Biochem Gen Mol Biol
Life Sciences Research in Space. Proceedings. European Symposium — Life Sci Res Space Proc Eur Symp
Life Sciences Research Reports — Life Sci Res Rep
Life Sciences Symposium — Life Sci Symp
Life Sciences Symposium. Environment and Solid Wastes — Life Sci Symp Environ Solid Wastes
Life Support Systems — Life Support Syst
Life Support Systems — LSSYD6
Life with Music — Life with Mus
Lifelong Learning — Lifelong Learn
Lifelong Learning: The Adult Years — Lifelong Learn Adult Years
Lifelong Learning: The Adult Years — LL
Lifescience and Biotechnology (Tokyo) — Lifesci Biotechnol (Tokyo)
Lifeskills Teaching Magazine — Lifeskills Teach Mag
Life-Span Development and Behavior — Life Span Dev Behav
Life-Threatening Behavior — Life-Threat
Lifetime Data Analysis — Lifetime Data Anal
Lift, Elevator Lift, and Ropeway Engineering — Lift Elevator Lift Ropeway Eng
Ligand Quarterly — Ligand Q
Ligand Quarterly — LQUADW
Ligand Review — Ligand Rev
Light and Dark — LD
Light and Lighting — Light and Light
Light and Lighting — Light Light
Light and Lighting — Lt Ltg
Light and Lighting and Environmental Design — Light and Light and Environ Des
Light and Lighting and Environmental Design — Light Light Environ Des
Light and Plant Development. Proceedings. University of Nottingham Easter School in Agricultural Science — Light Plant Dev Proc Univ Nottingham Easter Sch Agric Sci
Light and the Flowering Process. Proceedings. International Symposium. British Photobiology Society — Light Flowering Process Proc Int Symp Br Photobiol Soc
Light in Biology and Medicine. Proceedings. Congress. European Society for Photobiology — Light Biol Med Proc Congr Eur Soc Photobiol
Light Industry — Light Ind
Light Metal Age — Light Met Age
Light Metal Age — Light Mtl
Light Metals and Metal Industry [*England*] — Light Met Met Ind
Light Metals Bulletin — Light Met Bull
Light Metals (London) — Light Met (London)
Light Metals (Moscow) — Light Met (Moscow)
Light Metals (New York) — Light Met (NY)
Light Metals: Proceedings of Sessions. American Institute of Mining, Metallurgical, and Petroleum Engineers. Annual Meeting (New York) — Light Met (New York)
Light Metals Research — Light Met Res
Light Metals Review — Light Met Rev
Light Metals (Tokyo) — Light Met (Tokyo)
Light Metals (Warrendale, Pennsylvania) Proceedings. Technical Sessions. — Light Met (Warrendale Pa)
Light of Buddha — Lo B
Light of Dharma — Lo D
Light Production Engineering — Lt Prod Engng
Light Steam Power — Lit Steam Pwr
Lighting Design and Application — Light Des Appl
Lighting Design and Application — Lighting Des Applic
Lighting Design and Application — Lighting Design & Appl
Lighting Design and Application — Ltg Des Appl
Lighting Equipment News — Light Equip News
Lighting Equipment News — Lighting Equip News
Lighting Equipment News — Ltg Equip News
Lighting in Australia — Light Aust
Lighting Journal — Light J
Lighting Journal (Thorn) — Ltg J (Thorn)
Lighting Research and Technology — Light Res and Technol
Lighting Research and Technology — Light Res Technol
Lighting Research and Technology — Lighting Res Tech
Lighting Research and Technology — Ltg Res Tech
Light-Rail Transit Planning and Technology. Proceedings. Conference — Light Rail Transit Plann Technol Proc Conf
Lightwood Research Conference. Proceedings — Lightwood Res Conf Proc
Lightwood Research Coordinating Council. Proceedings — Lightwood Res Coord Counc Proc
Lignite Symposium. Proceedings — Lignite Symp Proc
Ligue des Bibliotheques Europeennes de Recherche. Bulletin — LIBER Bull
Ligues Ouvrieres Feminines Chretiennes [*Bruessel*] — LOFC
Liiketaloudellinen Aikakauskirja [*Journal of Business Economics*] — Liiketal Aikakausk
Lijecnicki Vjesnik — Lijec Vjesn
Lijecnicki Vjesnik — LIVJA5
Lijecnicki Vjesnik [*English translation*] — MEJOAB
Lijecnicki Vjesnik (English Translation) — Lijec Vjesn (Engl Transl)
Lijecnicki Vjesnik u Zagrebu — Lijec Vjesn Zagrebu
Likvatsionnye Yavleniya v Steklakh. Trudy Vsesoyuznogo Simpoziuma — Likvatsionnye Yavleniya Steklakh Tr Vses Simp
Lillabulero — Lilla
Lille Chirurgical — Lille Chir
Lille Medical — Lille Med
Lille Medical. Actualites — Lille Med Actual
Lille Medical Supplement — Lille Med Suppl
L'Illustration (Paris) — IP
Lilly Scientific Bulletin — Lilly Sci Bull
Lily Yearbook. North American Lily Society — Lily Yearb North Am Lily Soc
Lima Bean Bulletin. California Lima Bean Growers' Association — Lima Bean Bull
Limba Romana — L Rom
Limba Romana [*Bucuresti*] — LbR
Limba Romana [*Bucuresti*] — LimR
Limba Romana [*Bucuresti*] — LiR
Limba Romina — LR
Limba si Literatura — L si L
Limba si Literatura — LiL
Limba si Literatura — LL
Limba si Literatura — LsL
Limba si Literatura Moldoveneasca — LMold
Limba si Literatura Moldoveneasca Chisinau — LLM
Limburg's Jaarboek — LJ
Limen (Argentina) — LNA
Limerick Field Club Journal — Limerick Fld Cl J
Limes u Jugoslaviji — LJ
Limes u Jugoslaviji — LuJ
Limesforschungen — LF
Limia — Li
Limits of Life. Proceedings. College Park Colloquium on Chemical Evolution — Limits Life Proc College Park Colloq Chem Evol
Limnological Society of Southern Africa. Journal — Limnol Soc South Afr J
Limnologicheskie Issledovaniya Dunaya. Doklady Mezhdunarodnoi Konferentsii po Limnologicheskomu Izucheniyu Dunaya — Limnol Issled Dunaya Dokl Mezhdunar Konf Limnol Izuch Dunaya
Limnologie der Donau — Limnol Donau
Limnologische Donauforschungen Berichte der Internationalen Konferenz zur Limnologie der Donau — Limnol Donauforschungen Ber Int Konf Limnol Donau
Limnologische Flussstation Freudenthal. Berichte — Limnol Flussstn Freudenthal Ber
Limnology and Oceanography — Limn Ocean
Limnology and Oceanography — Limnol & Oceanog
Limnology and Oceanography — Limnol & Oceanogr
Limnology and Oceanography — Limnol Oceanogr
Limnology and Oceanography — LO
Limnology and Oceanography. Supplement — Limnol Oceanogr Suppl
Linacre Quarterly — Linacre
Linacre Quarterly — Linacre Q
Lincoln Annex — LA
Lincoln College. Farmers' Conference. Proceedings — Linc Farm Conf Proc
Lincoln Herald — LH

Lincoln Law Review — Linc LR
Lincoln Law Review — Lincoln L Rev
Lincoln Record Society — Lincoln Rec Soc
Lincoln Record Society — LRS
Lincolnshire Architectural and Archaeological Society. Reports and Papers — Lincs AA Soc Rep
Lincolnshire History and Archaeology — Lincolnshire Hist Arch
Lincolnshire Notes and Queries — LNQ
Lincolnshire Population — Lincolnshire Pop
Lindane Supplement — Lindane Suppl
Lindbergia. A Journal of Bryology — Lindbergia J Bryol
Linde Reports on Science and Technology — Linde Rep Sci and Technol
Linde Reports on Science and Technology — Linde Rep Sci Technol
Linde Reports on Science and Technology — Linde Reports Sci & Technol
Linde-Berichte aus Technik und Wissenschaft — Linde-Ber Tech Wiss
Linden Lane Magazine — LLM
Lindische Tempelchronik — Chron Lind
Lindische Tempelchronik — Lind Temp Chron
L'Industria Italiana del Cemento — L'Ind Ital del Cemento
Linea de Pensamiento de la Reduccion — LPR
Linear Algebra and Its Applications — Lin Alg App
Linear Algebra and Its Applications — Linear Algebra and Appl
Linear Algebra and Its Applications — Linear Algebra Appl
Linear Algebra and Its Applications — Linear Algebra Its Appl
Linear and Multilinear Algebra — Linear Multilin Algebra
Linear Topological Spaces and Complex Analysis — Linear Topol Spaces Complex Anal
Lineinye Uskoriteli — Lineinye Uskorit
Linen Supply News — Linen News
Lines Review — Lines Rev
Lingnan Science Journal — Lingnan Sci J
Lingnan University Science Bulletin — Lingnan Univ Sci Bull
Lingua — Li
Lingua — LIN
Lingua Bella — L Bella
Lingua e Cultura — LeC
Lingua e Literatura — L & L
Lingua e Literatura — Ling e L
Lingua e Stile — L & S
Lingua e Stile [*Bologna*] — LeS
Lingua e Stile — Ling Stile
Lingua e Stile — LS
Lingua Islandica — LIs
Lingua Nostra — LN
Lingua Nostra — LNo
Lingua Nostra — LNos
Lingua Portuguesa — LP
Lingua Posnaniensis — LP
Lingua Posnaniensis — LPosn
Lingue del Mondo — LDM
Lingue del Mondo — LiM
Lingue Estere — Ling Est
Lingue Straniere — LS
Lingue Straniere — LSt
Linguistic Analysis — Ling A
Linguistic Analysis — Linguist An
Linguistic and Literary Studies in Eastern Europe — Lin Lit S
Linguistic and Literary Studies in Eastern Europe — LLSEE
Linguistic Atlas of New England — LANE
Linguistic Atlas of the Gulf States — LAGS
Linguistic Atlas of the Middle and South Atlantic States — LAMSAS
Linguistic Atlas of the North Central States — LANCS
Linguistic Atlas of the Upper Midwest — LAUM
Linguistic Calculation — Ling Cal
Linguistic Circle of Canberra. Publications — LCCP
Linguistic Circle of Manitoba and North Dakota. Proceedings — Linguistic Circle Manitoba and N Dak Proc
Linguistic Communications — LingC
Linguistic Inquiry — LIn
Linguistic Inquiry — Ling Inq
Linguistic Inquiry — Ling Inquiry
Linguistic Inquiry — LingI
Linguistic Inquiry — Linguist In
Linguistic Notes from La Jolla — LNLJ
Linguistic Reporter — Ling R
Linguistic Society of America. Bulletin — LSAB
Linguistic Survey Bulletin — LSB
Linguistica — Ling
Linguistica Antverpiensia — LA
Linguistica Biblica — LB
Linguistica Biblica — LBIB
Linguistica Biblica — Ling Bibl
Linguistica Biblica [*Bonn*] — LingBib
Linguistica et Litteraria — L & L
Linguistica et Litteraria — Ling Litt
Linguistica Extranea — LE
Linguistica Slovaca — LS
Linguistica Slovaca — LSl
Linguisticae Investigationes — Ling Inv
Linguisticae Investigationes. Supplementa. Studies in French and General Linguistics — Lin Invest
Linguisticae Investigationes. Supplementa. Studies in French and General Linguistics — LIS
Linguistics and International Review — LIR
Linguistics and Language Behavior Abstracts [*Sociological Abstracts, Inc.*] [*San Diego, CA Bibliographic database*] — LLBA
Linguistics and Language Behavior Abstracts. LLBA — Linguist Lang Behav Abstr
Linguistics and Philosophy — Ling & P
Linguistics and Philosophy — Ling Phil
Linguistics and Philosophy — Ling Philos
Linguistics in Documentation — Ling Doc
Linguistics in Literature — Ling Lit
Linguistics of the Tibeto-Burman Area — LTBA
Linguistics (The Hague) — LingH
Linguistik Aktuell — L Akt
Linguistik und Didaktik — LuD
Linguistique — Ling
Linguistique (Paris) — LingP
Linguistische Arbeiten — L Arb
Linguistische Arbeiten — LA
Linguistische Berichte — LBer
Linguistische Berichte — LingB
Linguistische Berichte — Linguist Ber
Linguistische Reihe — LRe
Lingvisticeskij Sbornik — Lingv Sb
Lingvisticeskij Sbornik. Petrozavodsk — LSP
Lingvisticheskie Problemy Funktsional'nogo Modelirovaniia Rechevoi Deiatel'nosti — LPFMRD
Linkoeping Studies in Science and Technology. Dissertations — Linkoeping Stud Sci Tech Diss
Linkoping Studies in Arts and Sciences — Linkoping Stud Arts Sci
Linnaean Fern Bulletin — Linn Fern Bull
Linnaean Society. Journal of Botany — LSJB
Linnaean Society. Journal of Zoology — LSJZ
Linnean Society. Biological Journal — Linnean Soc Biol J
Linnean Society. Journal. Zoology — Linn Soc J Zool
Linnean Society of London. Biological Journal — Linn Soc Lond Biol J
Linnean Society of London. Zoological Journal — Linn Soc Lond Zool J
Linnean Society of New South Wales. Proceedings — Linn Soc NSW Proc
Linnean Society. Symposium Series — Linn Soc Symp Ser
Linneana Belgica — Linn Belg
Linneana Belgica — Linneana Belg
Linzer Archaeologische Forschungen — LAF
Linzer Archaeologische Forschungen — Linz AF
Linzer Biologische Beitraege — Linzer Biol Beitr
Liofilizzazione Criobiologia Applicazioni Criogeniche — Liofilizzazione Criobiol Appl Criog
Lion and the Unicorn — L & U
Lion and the Unicorn — Lion Unicor
Lipid Metabolism. Comprehensive Biochemistry — Lipid Metab Compr Biochem
Lipid Review — Lipid Rev
Lipids and Lipid Metabolism — Lipids Lipid Metab
Lipidyui Obmen u Sel'skokhozyaistvennykh Zhivotnykh Sbornik Dokladov Vsesoyuznogo Simpoziuma po Lipidnomu Obmenu u Sel'skokhozyaistvennykh Zhivo — Lipidnyi Obmen Skh Zhivotn Sb Dokl Vses Simp
Lippay Janos Tudomanyos Ulesszak Eloadasai — Lippay Janos Tud Ulesszak Eloadasai
Lippincott's Magazine — Lippinc
Lippincott's Magazine — Lippincotts M
Lippincott's Medical Science — Lippincott's Med Sci
Lippincott's Monthly — LIPP
Lippincott's Monthly Magazine — Lippincotts Mo M
Lippische Mitteilungen aus Geschichte und Landeskunde — LMGL
Liquefied Natural Gas — Liquefied Nat Gas
Liquid Chromatography and HPLC Magazine — Liq Chromatogr HPLC Mag
Liquid Chromatography in Biomedical Analysis — Liq Chromatogr Biomed Anal
Liquid Crystal Materials, Devices, and Applications — Liq Cryst Mater Devices Appl
Liquid Crystals — Liq Cryst
Liquid Crystals and Ordered Fluids — Liq Cryst Ordered Fluids
Liquid Fuels Technology — Liq Fuels Tech
Liquid Metals. Invited and Contributed Papers. International Conference on Liquid Metals — Liq Met Invited Contrib Pap Int Conf
Liquid Scintillation Counting — Liq Scintill Count
Liquid Scintillation Counting — Liq Scintill Counting
Liquor Control Law Reports. Commerce Clearing House — Liquor Cont L Rep CCH
Liquor Handbook — Liquor Hbk
Lisan Al-'Arabi — LA
LIS-Berichte — LIS Ber
Li-Shih Lun-Ts'ung [*Collection of Articles on History*] — LSLT
Li-shih Yen-chiu — LY
List of Australian Subject Headings — LASH
List of Australian Subject Headings. First Edition — FLASH
List of Books Accessioned and Periodical Articles Indexed. Columbus Memorial Library. Pan American Union (Washington, DC) — List Bks Access Pd Art Index Wash
List of Greek Verse Inscriptions down to 400 BC — LGVI
List of Statutory Instruments — List of Stat Instr
List of Unlocated Research Books — LURB
List Sdruzeni Moravskych Spisovatelu — List
List Taschenbuecher der Wissenschaft — LTW
Liste d'Abbreviations de Mots des Titres de Periodiques — Liste Abbrev Mots Titres
Listener — L
Listener — Li
Listener — Lis

Listener — List
Listener — LST
Listener and BBC (British Broadcasting Corporation) Television Review — Listener BBC Telev Rev
Listin Diario — LD
Listoprokatnoe Proizvodstvo — Listprokatnoe Proizvod
Listvennitsa i Ee Ispol'zovanie v Narodnom Khozyaistve — Listvennitsa Ee Ispolz Nar Khoz
Listy Cukrovarnicke — Listy Cukrov
Listy Cukrovarnicke a Reparske — Listy Cukrov Reparske
Listy Filologicke — LF
Listy Filologicke — LFil
Listy Filologicke — Listy Fil
Listy Filologicke. Supplement. Revue Archeologique — LF(RA)
Listy Filologike — Lis Fil
Listy Pomologicke — Listy Pomol
Listy z Teatru — LzT
Listy Zahradnicke — Listy Zahradn
LITA [*Library and Information Technology Association*] **Information Technology and Libraries** — LITA ITAL
Litaunus — Lit
Liteinoe Proizvodstvo [*Former USSR*] — Liteinoe Proizvod
Liteinoe Proizvodstvo — Liteinoe Prozvod
Literacy Discussion — Litcy Disc
Literacy Discussion — Liter Discussion
Literarische Anzeiger — LA
Literarische Blaetter der Boersenhalle — Lit Blaett Boersenhalle
Literarische Rundschau — LR
Literarische Rundschau fuer das Katholische Deutschland — Lit Rdsch
Literarische Rundschau fuer das Katholische Deutschland — LRKD
Literarische Wochenschrift — Lit Wschr
Literarische Wochenschrift — LW
Literarische Zeitung (Berlin) — Lit Zeitung Berlin
Literarischer Anzeiger fuer Christliche Theologie und Wissenschaft Ueberhaupt — LACTW
Literarischer Handweiser — LH
Literarischer Handweiser — LHW
Literarischer Handweiser — Lit Hdweiser
Literarischer Handweiser Zunaechst fuer das Katholische Deutschland — Lit Hw
Literarisches — Lit
Literarisches Echo — LE
Literarisches Wochenblatt der Boersenhalle — Lit Wochenbl Boersenhalle
Literarisches Zentralblatt — Lit ZentB
Literarisches Zentralblatt — Lit Zentralbl
Literarisches Zentralblatt — LZ
Literarisches Zentralblatt fuer Deutschland — Lit C
Literarisches Zentralblatt fuer Deutschland — LZ
Literarisches Zentralblatt fuer Deutschland — LZB
Literarisches Zentralblatt fuer Deutschland — LZD
Literarium — Lit
Literarni Archiv Pamatniku Narodniho Pisemnictvi — LitAP
Literarni Listy — LitL
Literarni Mesicnik — LitM
Literarni Noviny [*Praha*] — LitN
Literarnohistoricky Sbornik — LHSb
Literary and Historical Society of Quebec. Transactions — Lit Hist Soc Quebec Tr
Literary and Philosophical Society of New York. Transactions — Lit Ph Soc NY Tr
Literary and Theological Review — Lit & Theo R
Literary Criterion [*Mysore*] — LCrit
Literary Criterion — Lit Criterion
Literary Criterion (Mysore) — LCM
Literary Criticism Register. LCR — Lit Crit Regist
Literary Digest — LD
Literary Digest — Lit D
Literary Digest — Lit Dig
Literary Digest — Lit Digest
Literary Digest International Book Review — Lit Digest Intern Book Revw
Literary Endeavour — Lit E
Literary Guide — LG
Literary Half-Yearly — LHY
Literary Half-Yearly — Lit Half
Literary Journal. A Review of Literature, Sciences, Manners, Politics (London) — Lit J London
Literary Letter — Lit Letter
Literary Onomastics Studies — LOS
Literary Perspectives — Lit Per
Literary Research Newsletter — Lit Res New
Literary Research Newsletter — LRN
Literary Review — LiRe
Literary Review — Lit R
Literary Review — Lit Rev
Literary Review — LR
Literary Review — LT
Literary Review — PLIR
Literary Sketches — LiSk
Literary Society of Bombay. Transactions — LSBT
Literary World (Boston) — Lit W (Bost)
Literatur — Lit
Literatur als Kunst — LaK
Literatur als Kunst — LK
Literatur als Sprache. Literaturtheorie-Interpretation-Sprachkritik — Lit AS
Literatur im Dialog — LiD
Literatur in der Gesellschaft — LiG
Literatur in Wissenschaft und Unterricht — LWU
Literatur og Kritik — L K
Literatur und Geschichte. Eine Schriftenreihe — LuG
Literatur und Kritik — Lit Krit
Literatur und Kritik — LK
Literatur und Kritik [*Wien*] — LUK
Literatur und Leben — LL
Literatur und Leben — LuL
Literatur und Wirklichkeit — LuW
Literatura Chilena. Creacion y Critica — LC
Literatura Chilena en el Exilio — LCE
Literatura i Marksizm — LiM
Literatura i Mastatsva — LiM
Literatura i Mystectvo — Lit Mys
Literatura i Sucanist — LitS
Literatura ir Kalba — LiK
Literatura ir Kalba — LK
Literatura ir Menas — Li Men
Literatura Ludowa — LitL
Literatura Ludowa — LLud
Literatura na Jazykach Stran Azii i Afriki — LJSAA
Literatura o Stranach Azii i Afriki — LSAA
Literatura Sovietica — LitS
Literatura un Maksla — LuM
Literatura v Shkole — LS
Literatura v Shkole [*Moscow*] — LSh
Literatura v Shkole — LvS
Literatura v Shkole — LvSK
Literatura (Warsaw, Poland) — LitW
Literaturanzeiger fuer das Allgemeine Wissenschaftliche Schrifttum — LA
Literaturbericht ueber Neue Veroeffentlichungen auf dem Gebiete der Dentalmedizin — Lit Ber Dent Med
Literaturberichte ueber Wasser, Abwasser, Luft, und Boden — Literaturber Wasser
Literaturblatt fuer Germanische und Romanische Philologie — LBGRPh
Literaturblatt fuer Germanische und Romanische Philologie — LBL
Literaturblatt fuer Germanische und Romanische Philologie — LGRP
Literaturblatt fuer Germanische und Romanische Philologie — LGRPh
Literaturblatt fuer Germanische und Romanische Philologie — Litbl f Germ u Rom Phil
Literaturblatt fuer Orientalische Philologie — Litbl Or Philol
Literaturblatt fuer Orientalische Philologie — LOPh
Literaturblatt fuer Romanische und Germanische Philologie — Literaturbl
Literaturdokumentation zur Arbeitsmarkt- und Berufsforschung [*Database*] — LitDokAB
Literature Analysis System on Road Safety [*Database*] — LASORS
Literature and Art [*Russia*] — LI
Literature and Belief — L & B
Literature and History — L & H
Literature and History — Lit Hist
Literature and Ideology — L & I
Literature and Medicine — L & M
Literature and Medicine — L and M
Literature and Psychology — L & P
Literature and Psychology — Lit & Psychol
Literature and Psychology — Lit Psych
Literature and Psychology — Lit Psychol
Literature and Psychology — LitP
Literature and Psychology — LP
Literature and Psychology — PLNP
Literature East and West — LE & W
Literature East and West — LEW
Literature East and West — Literature
Literature East and West — LitEW
Literature/Film Quarterly — LFQ
Literature/Film Quarterly — Lit/F Q
Literature/Film Quarterly — Lit/F Quarterly
Literature/Film Quarterly — Lit/Film Q
Literature/Film Quarterly — PLFQ
Literature in Performance — LPer
Literature in Perspective — LitP
Literature, Meaning, Culture — LMC
Literature, Music, Fine Arts — Lit Mus Fin
Literature Music Fine Arts — LMFA
Literature Review on Oils and Fats — Lit Rev Oils Fats
Literature und Reflexion — LuR
Literaturen Front — L Front
Literaturen Front [*Sofia*] — LF
Literaturen Zbor — LZ
Literaturna Misel [*Sofia*] — LMi
Literaturna Ukrajina — Lit U
Literaturnaia Armeniia. Ezhemesiachnyi Literaturno-Khudozhestvennyi i Obshchestvenno-Politicheskii Zhurnal — LArm
Literaturnaia Entsiklopediia — LE
Literaturnaja Gazeta — Lit Gaz
Literaturnaja Rossija — Li R
Literaturnaya Armeniya [*Erevan*] — LitA
Literaturnaya Gazeta — LG
Literaturnaya Gruziya [*Tbilisi*] — LGr
Literaturnaya Mysl — LitM
Literaturnaya Rossiya — LR
Literaturnoe Nasledstvo — LN
Literaturnoe Obozrenie — LO
Literaturny Sovremennik — LS

Literaturnye Zapiski — LZ
Literaturnyj Kritik — LK
Literaturwissenschaft und Linguistik — Lit Wiss Ling
Literaturwissenschaftliches Jahrbuch der Goerres-Gesellschaft — LJb
Literaturwissenschaftliches Jahrbuch der Goerres-Gesellschaft — LJGG
Literaturwissenschaftliches Jahrbuch der Goerres-Gesellschaft — LWJ
Literatuurinformatie Wetenschapsbeleid — IWB
Literatuuroverzicht Medezeggenschap — LED
Lithologicheskie Issledovanniya v Kazakhstane [*Former USSR*] — Lithol Issled Kaz
Lithology and Mineral Resources — Lith Min Resour
Lithology and Mineral Resources — Lithol Miner Resour
Litho-Printer Magazine [*British*] — LP
Lithuanian Days — LD
Lithuanian Journal of Physics — Lith J Phys
Lithuanian Mathematical Journal — Lithuanian Math J
Lithuanian Mathematical Transactions — Lithuanian Math Trans
Litigation — Lit
Litodinamika, Litologiya i Geomorfologiya Shel'fa. 1976 — Litodin Litol Geomorfol Shelfa 1976
Litologiya, Geokhimiya, i Paleogeografiya Neftegazonosn Osadochnykh Formatsii Uzbekistana — Litol Geokhim Paleogeogr Neftegazonosn Osad Form Uzb
Litologiya, Geokhimiya i Poleznye Iskopaemye Osadochnykh Obrazovanii Tyan-Shanya — Litol Geokhim Polezn Iskop Osad Obraz Tyan Shanya
Litologiya i Poleznye Iskopaemye — Litol i Polez Iskop
Litologiya Paleozoiskikh Otlozhenii Estonii — Litol Paleozoiskikh Otlozh Est
Litovskii Fizicheskii Sbornik — Litov Fiz Sb
Litovskii Fizicheskii Zhurnal — Litov Fiz Zh
Litovskii Matematiceskii Sbornik — Lit Mat Sb
Litovskii Matematiceskii Sbornik — Litovsk Mat Sb
Litovskii Mekhanicheskii Sbornik — Litov Mekh Sb
Litovskii Nauchno-Issledovatel'skii Institut Tekstil'noi Promyshlennosti. Nauchno-Issledovatel'skie Trudy — Litov Nauchno Issled Inst Tekst Promsti Nauchno Issled Tr
Littell's Living Age — Liv Age
Litterae (Kuemmerle) — LittK
Litterae Societatis Jesu — LSJ
Litteraire — Lit
Litteraria — Litt
Litteraria Historica Slovaca — LHSl
Litteraria; Studie a Dokumenty — LSD
Litterarische Denkwuerdigkeiten oder Nachrichten von Neuen Buechern und Kleinen Schriften Besonders der Chursaechsischen Universitaeten, Schulen, und Lande — Litt Denkwuerdigk
Litterarisches Centralblatt fuer Deutschland — LCD
Litterarisches Magazin fuer Katholiken und deren Freunde — LMKF
Litteratur des Katholischen Deutschland — LKD
Litteratur og Samfund — Li Sa
Litterature [*University of Paris*] — Lit
Litteratures — Litt
Litteratures Anciennes du Proche-Orient — LAPO
Litteratur-Journal (Altona) — Litt J Altona
Litteris — Lit
Litteris — Litt
Little Magazine — Little M
Little Magazine — Little Mag
Little Mathematics Library — Little Math Lib
Little Review — LittleR
Lituanistikos Darbai [*Chicago*] — LD
Liturgia — Lit
Liturgia (Burgos) — Lit B
Liturgia (Mainz) — Lit M
Liturgia (Torino) — Lit T
Liturgiarum Orientalium Collectio — LOC
Liturgical Arts — Lit A
Liturgical Arts — Lit Arts
Liturgical Arts — Liturg Arts
Liturgical Library — LL
Liturgical Review — Liturgical Rev
Liturgie und Moenchtum — Lu m
Liturgiegeschichtliche Forschungen — LF
Liturgiegeschichtliche Quellen — LQ
Liturgiegeschichtliche Quellen und Forschungen [*Muenster*] — LQF
Liturgiewissenschaftliche Quellen und Forschungen — LWQF
Liturgische Zeitschrift — LitZs
Liturgisches Jahrbuch — Lit Jb
Liturgisches Jahrbuch — LJ
Liturgy (Elsberry, MO) — Lit E
Livable Winter Newsletter — LVWN
Live Lines — Lv Lns
Live Stock Bulletin — Live Stock Bul
Live Stock Journal and Fancier's Gazette — Live Stock J and Fancier's Gaz
Liver Annual — LIANEI
Liver Annual — Liver Ann
Liver Cirrhosis. Proceedings. Falk Symposium — Liver Cirrhosis Proc Falk Symp
Liver: Quantitative Aspects of Structure and Function. Proceedings of the International Gstaad Symposium — Liver Quant Aspects Struct Func
Liverpool and Manchester Geological Journal — Liverp Manch Geol J
Liverpool and Manchester Geological Journal — Liverpool and Manchester Geol Jour
Liverpool and Manchester Geological Journal — Liverpool Manchester Geol J
Liverpool Annuals of Archaeology and Anthropology — LAAA
Liverpool Classical Monthly — LCM
Liverpool Echo — LVE
Liverpool Geographical Society. Transactions and Annual Report of the Council — Liverpool Geog Soc Tr An Rp
Liverpool Geological Association. Transactions. Journal — Liverpool G As Tr J
Liverpool Geological Society. Proceedings — Liverpool G Soc Pr
Liverpool Law Review — Liverpool L Rev
Liverpool Medical Institution. Transactions and Reports — Liverpool Med Inst Trans Rep
Liverpool Medico-Chirurgical Journal — Liv Med Chir J
Liverpool Monographs in Archaeology and Oriental Studies — LMA
Liverpool Monographs in Archaeology and Oriental Studies — LMAOS
Liverpool School of Tropical Medicine. Memoirs — Liverpool School Trop Med Mem
Lives of Women in Science — Lives Women Sci
Livestock Adviser — Livest Advis
Livestock International — LIINEO
Livestock International — Livest Int
Livestock Producers' Day. Louisiana Agricultural Experiment Station. Animal Science Department — Livest Prod Day La Agric Exp Stn Anim Sci Dep
Livestock Production Science — Livest Prod Sci
Living Age — LA
Living Bird Quarterly — LBQUDZ
Living Bird Quarterly — Living Bird Q
Living Blues — LB
Living Blues — LBl
Living Blues — Liv Blues
Living Cell in Four Dimensions. International Conference — Living Cell Four Dimens Int Conf
Living Church — LC
Living Church — Liv Church
Living Conditions and Health — Liv Condit Hlth
[*The*] **Living Daylights** — TLD
Living for Young Homemakers — Liv for Young Home
Living in the Cold. International Symposium — Living Cold Int Symp
Living Museum — Living Mus
Living Places — LIPL
Living Religion Series — LRS
Living Wilderness — Liv Wild
Living Wilderness — Liv Wildn
Living Wilderness — LW
Living World Commentary — LWC
Livre de l'Etudiant — Livre de l Et
Livre de l'Etudiant — Livre de l Etud
Livre des Rois d'Egypte — LdR
Livre Slovene [*Yugoslavia*] — LSlov
Livres Disponibles — LD
Livres et Auteurs Quebecois — LAQ
Livres et Lectures — LL
Livres Hebdomadaires — LH
Livros de Portugal — LdP
LJ [*Library Journal*] **Special Report** — LJ Spec Rep
Ljetopis Jugoslavenske Akademije — LJA
Ljudska Republika Slovenije — LRS
Llen Cymru — LlC
Lloydia [*Cincinnati*] — LLOYA2
Lloydia. Journal of Natural Products — Lloydia J Nat Prod
Lloydia. Lloyd Library and Museum — Lloydia
Lloyd's Aviation Economist — Lloyds AE
Lloyds Bank Review — LBR
Lloyds Bank Review — Lloyds Bank R
Lloyds Bank Review — Lloyds Bk
Lloyd's Corporate Security International — Lloyd's Corp Secur Int
Lloyd's List — LL
Lloyd's Maritime and Commercial Law Quarterly — Lloyds Mar and Com LQ
Lloyd's Mexican Economic Report — Lloyds Mex
LMG [*Library Management Group*] **Report on Data and Word Processing for Libraries** — LMG Rep Data and Word Process Libr
Lno Penko-Dzhutovaya Promyshlennost — Lno Penko-Dzhutovaya Promst
Local Area Networks. A Harris Perspective — LAN Harris
Local Currents and Their Applications. Proceedings. Informal Conference — Local Curr Their Appl Proc Informal Conf
Local Finance — Loc Finance
Local Finance — Local Fin
Local Finance (The Hague) — Local Fin (The Hague)
Local Government — Local Govt
Local Government Administration — Local Gov Adm
Local Government Administration — Local Govt Adm
Local Government Administration — Local Govt Admin
Local Government Appeals Tribunal Reports — LGATR
Local Government Appeals Tribunal Reports (New South Wales) — LGATR (NSW)
Local Government Bulletin — LGB
Local Government Bulletin [*Manila*] — Local Govt B
Local Government Chronicle — Local Govt Chron
Local Government Engineer — Local Govt Eng
Local Government Forum — Local Govt Forum
Local Government in South Australia — Local Gov in South Aust
Local Government in South Australia — Local Gov South Aust
Local Government in Southern Africa — Local Gov in Sthn Afr
Local Government Information Network [*Database*] — LOGIN
Local Government - IULA [*International Union of Local Authorities*] **Newsletter** [*A publication*] — Local Govt IULA Newsl
Local Government Journal of Western Australia — Local Gov J of Western Aust
Local Government Law and Practice [*Gifford*] — LGL & P
Local Government Law Reports (New South Wales) — LGR (NSW)
Local Government Manpower — Local Govt Manpower

Local Government News — Local Govt News
Local Government Officer — LGO
Local Government Ordinances — LGO
Local Government Policy Making — Local Govt Policy Making
Local Government Quarterly [*Dacca*] — Local Govt Q
Local Government Reports of Australia — LGRA
Local Government Reports of Australia — Local Govt R Austl
Local Government Review — LG Rev
Local Government Review — LGRED
Local Government Review — Loc Gov Rev
Local Government Review — Loc Govt Rev
Local Government Review [*United Kingdom*] — Local Gov Rev
Local Government Review — Local Govt Rev
Local Government Review in Japan — Local Govt R Japan
Local Government Studies — Local Gov Stud
Local Government Studies — Local Govt Stud
Local Historian — Local Hist
Local Population Studies — Local Pop Stud
Local Population Studies Magazine and Newsletter — Local Popul Stud
Local Scripts of Archaic Greece — LS
Local Scripts of Archaic Greece — LSAG
Local Self-Government — Loc Self Gov
Local Self-Government Institute. Quarterly Journal — LSGI
Locate in Europe Information Retrieval System [*Database*] — EUROLOC
Location Report. Division of Mineral Chemistry. Commonwealth Scientific and Industrial Research Organisation — Locat Rep Div Miner Chem CSIRO
Loccumer Protokolle — Locc Prot
Locgov Digest — Locgov Dig
Lochlann — Lo
Lock Haven Bulletin — LHB
Lock Haven Review — LHR
Locke Newsletter — Locke News
Lockheed Georgia Quarterly — Lockheed GA Q
Lockheed Horizons — Lockheed Horiz
Lockheed Symposia on Magnetohydrodynamics — Lockheed Symp Magnetohydrodyn
Lockwood's Directory of the Paper and Allied Trades — Lockwood Dir
Locomotive Engineers' Journal — Locomotive Eng J
Locomotive Journal — Loco J
Locus — Loc
Locust Newsletter. FAO. Plant Production and Protection Division — Locust Newsl FAO Plant Prod Prot Div
Lodging Hospitality — LH
Lodzki Numizmatyk — Lodzki Num
Lodzkie Studia Etnograficzne — Lodz Stud Etnogr
Lodzkie Studia Etnograficzne — Lodzk Stud Etnogr
Lodzkie Towarzystwo Naukowe Prace Wydzialu 3. Nauk Matematyczno-Przyrodniczych — Lodz Tow Nauk Pr Wydz 3
Lodzkie Towarzystwo Naukowe Prace Wydzialu 3. Nauk Matematyczno-Przyrodniczych — Lodz Tow Nauk Pr Wydz 3 Nauk Mat-Przyr
Lodzkie Towarzystwo Naukowe Prace Wydzialu 4. Nauk Lekarskich — Lodz Tow Nauk Pr Wydz 4
Loeb Classical Library — LCL
Loeb Classical Library — Loeb Class Libr
Log Analyst — Log Anal
Loggers Handbook. Pacific Logging Congress — Loggers Handb Pac Logging Congr
Logging and Sawmilling Journal — Log & Saw
Logic and Computation in Philosophy — Logic Comput Philos
Logic and Logical Philosophy — Logic Log Philos
Logica y Teoria de la Ciencia — Logic Teor Ci
Logik und Grundlagen der Mathematik — Logik Grundlagen Math
Logiko-Informatsionnye Resheniya Geologicheskikh Zadach — Logiko Inf Resheniya Geol Zadach
Logique et Analyse — Log Anal
Logique et Analyse — Logique Anal
Logique et Analyse. Nouvelle Serie — Logique et Anal NS
Logique. Mathematiques. Informatique — Logique Math Inform
Logistics and Transportation Review — LGTRA
Logistics and Transportation Review — Logist & Transp Rev
Logistics and Transportation Review — LTR
Logistics Spectrum — Log Spec
Logistics Spectrum — Logist Spectrum
Logos. Internationale Zeitschrift fuer Philosophie und Kultur — Log
Logos Journal — Logos
Logos. Revista de Humanidades — LRH
Logos. Rivista Internazionale di Filosofia — LRIF
Logotechnika Chronika — LChr
Lohnunternehmen in Land- und Forstwirtschaft — Lohnuntern Land-Forstwirt
Lois Sacrees de l'Asie Mineure — LSAM
Lois Sacrees des Cites Grecques — LSCG
Loisir et Societe — Loisir et Soc
Lolland-Falsters Historiske Samfunds Aarbog — LF Aa
Lollipops, Ladybugs, and Lucky Stars — Lollipops
L'Oltremare — LO
LOMA. Literature on Modern Art — Lit Mod Art
L'Ondes Electronique — L'Ondes Electr
London and Edinburgh Philosophical Magazine and Journal of Science — London Edinburgh Philos Mag J Sci
London and Middlesex Archaeological Society. Special Papers — London Middlesex Archaeol Soc Spec Pap
London Aphrodite — LnA
London Archaeologist — Lond A
London Archaeologist — London Archaeol
London Architect — London Archit
London Architect — London Archt
London Bus Magazine — London Bus Mag
London Business School. Journal — London Bus School J
London Clinic Medical Journal — Lond Clin Med J
London Community Work Service Newsletter — London Commun Wk Serv Newsl
London Daily News — LDN
London Divinity Series — LDS
London Divinity Series. New Testament Series — LDSNT
London Divinity Series. Old Testament Series — LDSOT
London Docklands Development Newsletter — London Docklands Dev Newsl
London, Edinburgh, and Dublin Philosophical Magazine and Journal of Science — LEPMJS
London, Edinburgh, and Dublin Philosophical Magazine and Journal of Science — London Edinburgh Dublin Philos Mag J Sci
London Educational Review — London Ednl R
London Evening Standard — LES
London Gallery Bulletin — LB
London Gazette — LG
London Gazette — Lond Gaz
London Health News — London Hlth News
London Industrial Centre News — London Ind Centre News
London Journal — Lond J
London Journal — London J
London Journal — London Jnl
London Labour Briefing — London Labour Brief
London Law Magazine — L Mag
London Law Magazine — Law
London Law Magazine — LM
London Lesbian Newsletter — London Lesbian Newsl
London Magazine — L Mag
London Magazine — LM
London Magazine — LOMa
London Magazine — Lon Mag
London Magazine — Lond M
London Magazine — Lond Mag
London Magazine — London Mag
London Magazine — LonM
London Mathematical Society. Lecture Note Series — Lond Math Soc Lect Note Ser
London Mathematical Society. Lecture Note Series — London Math Soc Lecture Note Ser
London Mathematical Society. Monographs — London Math Soc Monogr
London Mathematical Society. Monographs — London Math Soc Monographs
London Mathematical Society Student Texts — London Math Soc Stud Texts
London Measured Rates and Materials Prices — London Meas Rates Mat Prices
London Mediaeval Studies — LMS
London Mediaeval Studies — Lond Med St
London Medical and Surgical Journal — Lond Med Surg J
London Medical Gazette — Lond Med Gaz
London Medical Journal — London Med J
London Medical Repository — London Med Repos
London Mercury — L Mer
London Mercury — LM
London Mercury — LnM
London Mercury — Lond Mercury
London Mercury — Merc
London Missionary Society. Chronicle — Lond Mis Soc Chr
London Naturalist — Lond Nat
London Naturalist — London Natur
London Oriental Series — LOS
London Passenger Transport — London Passenger Transp
London Physiological Journal — London Physiol J
London Property Register [*Database*] — LPR
London Quarterly — LQ
London Quarterly and Holborn Review — Lond Q R
London Quarterly and Holborn Review — Lond QHR
London Quarterly and Holborn Review — LondQHolbR
London Quarterly and Holborn Review — LQHR
London Quarterly of World Affairs — London Quart Wld Aff
London Quarterly Review — Ld QR
London Quarterly Review — Lond Q
London Quarterly Review — LQR
London Recusant — Ld Rec
London Review — Ld R
London Review of Books — Lon R Bks
London Review of Public Administration — London Rev Public Admin
London School of Economics. Monographs on Social Anthropology — LSEMSA
London School of Tropical Medicine. Research Memoir Series — Lond School Trop Med Research Mem Ser
London Shellac Research Bureau. Bulletin — London Shellac Res Bur Bull
London Shellac Research Bureau. Technical Paper — London Shellac Res Bur Tech Pap
London Society. Journal — London Soc Jnl
London State Information Bank [*Database*] — LSIB
London Studies — London Stud
London Studio — Lond Studio
London Theological Library — LTL
London Times Literary Supplement — LTLS
London Times Literary Supplement — LTS
London Topographical Record — Lond Topog Rec
London Transactions. International Congress of Orientalists — LTCO
London Voluntary News — London Volunt News
London's Australian Magazine — LAM

Lone Hand — LH
Lone Star Review — LSR
Long Ashton International Symposium — Long Ashton Int Symp
Long Ashton Research Station. Report — Long Ashton Res Stn Rep
Long Beach Free Press — LB Free P
Long Island Agronomist — Long Island Agron
Long Island Business — Long Isl B
Long Island Forum — Long Isl Forum
Long Island Historical Society. Memoirs — LI Hist Soc Memoirs
Long Island Horticulture News — Long Isl Hortic News
Long Island Journal of Philosophy. And Cabinet of Variety — Long Island J Philos
Long Point Bird Observatory. Annual Report — Long Point Bird Obs Annu Rep
Long Term Care and Health Services Administration. Quarterly — Long Term Care Health Serv Adm Q
Long-Distance Letter — Long Dst L
Longest Revolution — Long Rev
Longest Revolution — Longest R
Longevita — Longev
Longman's Magazine — Longm
Long-Range Planning — Long Range Plan
Long-Range Planning — Long Range Plann
Long-Range Planning — Long-Rang P
Long-Range Planning — LOR
Long-Range Planning — LRP
Long-Term Care Quarterly — Long Term Care Q
Long-Term Projections [*Database*] — LTP
Loodusuurijate Selts Tappisteaduste Sektsiooni Toimetised — Loodusuurijate Selts Tappistead Sekts Toim
Loodusuurijate. Seltsi Aastaraaman — Loodusuur Seltsi Aastar
Look at Finland — LOAF
Look Japan — Look Jpn
Look Laboratory (Hawaii) — Look Lab (Hawaii)
Looking Ahead and Projection Highlights — Look Ahead Proj Highlights
Loonbedrijf in Land- en Tuinbouw — Loonb Land-Tuinbouw
Lopatochnye Mashiny i Struinye Apparaty — Lopatochnye Mash Struinye Appar
Loquela Mirabilis — LQ
Lore and Language — Lore & L
L'Orient [*Damascus*] — OT
L'Orient Philatelique — OP
Los Angeles Bar Bulletin — LAB
Los Angeles Bar Bulletin — LAB Bull
Los Angeles Bar Bulletin — LABB
Los Angeles Bar Bulletin — Los Angeles B Bull
Los Angeles Bar Journal — LABJ
Los Angeles Business and Economics — Los Angeles Bus and Econ
Los Angeles Business Journal — LA Bsns Jl
Los Angeles Council of Engineers and Scientists. Proceedings Series — LACSD
Los Angeles Council of Engineers and Scientists. Proceedings Series — Los Angeles Counc Eng Sci Proc Ser
Los Angeles County Museum. Bulletin of the Art Division — Los Angeles Mus Art Bull
Los Angeles County Museum. Bulletin of the Art Division — Los Angeles Mus Bul
Los Angeles County Museum. Contributions in Science — Los Ang Cty Mus Contrib Sci
Los Angeles County Museum. Contributions in Science — Los Angeles County Mus Contr Sci
Los Angeles County Museum of History, Science, and Art. Quarterly — Los Angeles Mus Q
Los Angeles County Museum of Natural History. Quarterly — Los Angeles County Mus Nat History Quart
Los Angeles Daily Journal — LA Daily J
Los Angeles Educational Research Bulletin — Los Angeles Ed Res B
Los Angeles Free Press — LA Free P
Los Angeles Lawyer — LA Law
Los Angeles Magazine — ILAM
Los Angeles Medical Journal — L Ang
Los Angeles Philharmonic Orchestra. Symphony Magazine — LA Phil Sym Mag
Los Angeles Philharmonic. Program Notes — LA Phil
Los Angeles Times — ANGE
Los Angeles Times — LA Times
Los Angeles Times — LAT
Los Angeles Times Book Review — LATBR
Los Ensayistas — LES
Losbladig Fiscaal Weekblad FED [*Formerly, Fiscaal Economische Documentatie*] — FED
Loss Prevention — Loss Pre
Loss Prevention: A CEP Technical Manual — Loss Prev
Loss Prevention and Safety Promotion in the Process Industries. Proceedings. International Symposium on Loss Prevention and Safety Promotio the Process Industries — Loss Prev Saf Promot Process Ind Proc Int Symp
Lost Generation Journal — LGJ
Loteria — LA
Loteria. Loteria Nacional de Beneficencia — LNB
Loteria. Loteria Nacional de Beneficencia [*Panama*] — LNB/L
Lotta Antiparassitaria — Lotta Antiparass
Lotta Contro la Tubercolosi — Lotta Contro Tuberc
Lotta Contro la Tubercolosi — Lotta Tuberc
Lotta Contro la Tubercolosi e le Malattie Polmonari Sociali — Lotta Contro Tuberc Mal Polm Soc
Lotta Contro la Tubercolosi e le Malattie Polmonari Sociali — Lotta Tuberc Mal Polm Soc
Lotus. Afro-Asian Writings — LAAW
Lotus International — Lotus Int
L'Ouest Apicole — Ouest Apic
Loughborough University of Technology. Chemical Engineering Journal — Loughborough Univ Technol Chem Eng J
Loughborough University of Technology. Chemical Engineering Society. Journal [*A publication*] — Loughborough Univ Technol Chem Eng Soc J
Loughborough University of Technology. Department of Transport Technology. TT Report — Loughborough Univ Technol Dep Transp Technol TT Rep
Louisiana Academy of Sciences. Proceedings — La Acad Sci Proc
Louisiana Administrative Code — La Admin Code
Louisiana. Agricultural Experiment Station. Bulletin — LA Agric Exp Stn Bull
Louisiana Agricultural Experiment Station. Horticultural Research Circular — Louisiana Agric Exp Sta Hort Res Circ
Louisiana Agricultural Experiment Station. North Louisiana Experiment Station. Annual Report — Louisiana Agric Exp Sta N Louisiana Exp Sta Annual Rep
Louisiana. Agricultural Experiment Station. Publications — LA Ag Exp
Louisiana Agriculture — LA Agr
Louisiana Agriculture — LA Agric
Louisiana Agriculture. Louisiana Agricultural Experiment Station — La Agric La Agric Exp Stn
Louisiana Annual Reports — La Ann
Louisiana Bar Journal — LA B J
Louisiana Bar Journal — LA Bar J
Louisiana. Bureau of Scientific Research and Statistics. Geological Bulletin — La Bur Sci Res Stat Geol Bull
Louisiana. Bureau of Scientific Research. Geological Bulletin — La Bur Sci Res Geol Bull
Louisiana Business Review — LA Bus R
Louisiana Business Survey — LA Bus Survey
Louisiana Business Survey — LA Bus Svy
Louisiana Conservationist — La Conserv
Louisiana Courts of Appeal Reports — La App
Louisiana Dental Association. Journal — LDA J
Louisiana. Department of Conservation. Biennial Report — LA Dept Conserv Bienn Rept
Louisiana. Department of Conservation. Bureau of Scientific Research and Statistics. Geological Bulletin — La Dep Conserv Bur Sci Res Stat Geol Bull
Louisiana. Department of Conservation. Bureau of Scientific Research. Minerals Division. Geological Bulletin — La Dep Conserv Bur Sci Res Miner Div Geol Bull
Louisiana. Department of Conservation. Geological Bulletin — La Dep Conserv Geol Bull
Louisiana. Department of Conservation. Geological Survey and Department of Public Works. Water Resources Pamphlet — La Dep Conserv Geol Surv Dep Public Works Water Resour Pam
Louisiana. Department of Conservation. Geological Survey. Mineral Resources Bulletin — LA Dep Conserv Geol Surv Miner Resour Bull
Louisiana. Department of Public Works. Basic Records Report — LA Dep Public Works Basic Rec Rep
Louisiana. Department of Public Works. Technical Report — LA Dep Public Works Tech Rep
Louisiana. Department of Public Works. Water Resources Pamphlet — LA Dept Public Works Water Res Pamph
Louisiana. Department of Public Works. Water Resources Special Report — La Dep Public Works Water Resour Spec Rep
Louisiana Economy — LA Economy
Louisiana Engineer — LA Eng
Louisiana. Geological Survey and Department of Public Works. Water Reources Bulletin — La Geol Surv Dep Public Works Water Resour Bull
Louisiana. Geological Survey and Department of Public Works. Water Resources Bulletin — LA Geol Surv Water Resour Bull
Louisiana. Geological Survey and Department of Public Works. Water Resources Pamphlet — LA Geol Surv Water Resour Pam
Louisiana. Geological Survey. Bulletin — Louisiana Geol Surv Bull
Louisiana. Geological Survey. Clay Resources Bulletin — LA Geol Surv Clay Resour Bull
Louisiana. Geological Survey. Geological Bulletin — LA Geol Surv Geol Bull
Louisiana. Geological Survey. Mineral Resources Bulletin — LA Geol Surv Miner Resour Bull
Louisiana Historical Quarterly — LA His Q
Louisiana Historical Quarterly — LA Hist Quar
Louisiana Historical Quarterly — LHQ
Louisiana Historical Society. Publications — LA His S
Louisiana History — LA Hist
Louisiana History — LaH
Louisiana History — LoH
Louisiana Journal — Louisiana Jnl
Louisiana Law Review — LA L Rev
Louisiana Law Review — LA Law Rev
Louisiana Law Review — LA LR
Louisiana Law Review — Lou L Rev
Louisiana Law Review — Louisiana L Rev
Louisiana Library Association. Bulletin — LA Lib Assn Bull
Louisiana Library Association. Bulletin — LA Lib Bul
Louisiana Musician — LO
Louisiana. Office of Public Works. Water Resources Basic Records Report — LA Off Public Works Water Resour Basic Rec Rep
Louisiana. Office of Public Works. Water Resources Special Report — La Off Public Works Water Resour Spec Rep
Louisiana. Office of Public Works. Water Resources Technical Report — La Off Public Works Water Resour Tech Rep
Louisiana. Planter and Sugar Manufacturer — LA Plant Sugar Manuf
Louisiana Register — LA Reg

Louisiana Reports — La
Louisiana Rural Economist. Louisiana State University. Department of Agriculture and Agribusiness — LA Rural Econ
Louisiana Session Law Service (West) — LA Sess Law Serv (West)
Louisiana State Board of Health. Quarterly Bulletin — La State Bd Health Q Bul
Louisiana State Department of Conservation. Geological Bulletin — LA State Dep Conserv Geol Bull
Louisiana. State Department of Conservation. Geological Survey and Department of Public Works. Water Resources Bulletin — La State Dep Conserv Geol Surv Dep Public Works Water Resour
Louisiana State Experiment Stations. Geology and Agriculture of Louisiana — LA St Exp Sta G Agr LA
Louisiana State Medical Society — La State Med Soc
Louisiana State Medical Society. Journal — LA State Med Soc J
Louisiana State University and Agricultural and Mechanical College. Division of Engineering Research. Bulletin — La State Univ Agric Mech Coll Div Eng Res Bull
Louisiana State University and Agricultural and Mechanical College. Engineering Experiment Station. Bulletin — La State Univ Agric Mech Coll Eng Exp Stn Bull
Louisiana State University and Agricultural and Mechanical College. Engineering Experiment Station. Reprint Series — LA State Univ Agric Mech Coll Eng Exp Stn Repr Ser
Louisiana State University and Agricultural and Mechanical College. Engineering Experiment Station. Reprint Series — La State Univ Eng Exp Stn Repr Ser
Louisiana State University and Agricultural and Mechanical College. Technical Reports — LA State Univ and Agr Mech Coll Tech Rept
Louisiana State University. Annual Report of the Superintendent — LA St Univ An Rp Sup
Louisiana State University. Division of Engineering Research. Bulletin — LA State Univ Div Eng Res Bull
Louisiana State University. Division of Engineering Research. Engineering Research Bulletin — LA State Univ Div Eng Res Eng
Louisiana State University. Division of Engineering Research. Engineering Research Bulletin. — LA State Univ Div Eng Res Eng Res Bull
Louisiana State University. Engineering Experiment Station. Bulletin. Studies. Physical Science Series — LA State Univ Eng Expt Sta Bull Studies Phys Sci Ser
Louisiana State University. Humanistic Series — LSUHS
Louisiana State University. Proceedings. Annual Forestry Symposium — LA State Univ Proc Annu For Symp
Louisiana State University Studies — LSUS
Louisiana State University. Studies. Biological Science Series — LA State Univ Stud Biol Sci Ser
Louisiana State University. Studies. Coastal Studies Series — LA State Univ Stud Coastal Stud Ser
Louisiana State University Studies. Humanities Series — LSUSH
Louisiana State University. Studies. Humanities Series — LSUSHS
Louisiana State University Studies. Social Science Series — LSUSS
Louisiana Studies — LA Stud
Louisiana Studies — LaS
Louisiana Studies — LoS
Louisiana University and Agricultural and Mechanical College. Forestry Department. The Annual Ring — Louisiana Univ Agric Coll Forest Dept Annual Ring
Louisiana Water Resources Research Institute. Bulletin — LA Water Resour Res Inst Bull
Louisiana Water Resources Research Institute. Bulletin — Louisiana Water Resources Research Inst Bull
Louisville Lawyer — Louisville Law
Louisville Magazine — Louisvl Mg
Louisville Medical News — Louisville Med News
Louisville Medicine — Louisville Med
Louisville Orchestra Program Notes — Lsvl Orch
Louvain Medical — Louv Med
Louvain Studies — Louvain Stds
Louvain Studies [*Leuven*] — LouvSt
Louvain Universite. Institut Geologique. Memoires — Louv Univ Inst Geol Mem
Louvain Universite. Institut Geologique. Memoires — Louvain Univ Inst Geol Mem
Low Countries History. Yearbook [*Acta Historiae Neerlandicae*] — Low Count H
Low Jet Routes — LJR
Low Pay Bulletin — Low Pay Bull
Low Pay Review — Low Pay Rev
Low Temperature Physics (Kiev) — Low Temp Phys (Kiev)
Low Temperature Physics. Proceedings. Summer School — Low Temp Phys Proc Summer Sch
Low Temperature Research Station (Cambridge). Annual Report — Low Temp Res Stn (Camb) Annu Rep
Low Temperature Science. Series A. Physical Sciences — Low Temp Sci Ser A
Low Temperature Science. Series B. Biological Sciences — Low Temp Sci Ser B Biol Sci
Low Temperature Science. Series B. Biological Sciences — LTSB
Low-Level Radioactive Waste Technology Newsletter — Low-Level Radioact Waste Technol Newsl
Low-Rank Fuels Symposium — Low Rank Fuels Symp
Low-Temperature Electric Generator Cooling — Low Temp Electr Gener Cool
Loyola Law Review — Lo LR
Loyola Law Review — Loy L Rev
Loyola Law Review — Loy LR
Loyola Law Review — Loy R
Loyola Law Review — Loyola L Rev
Loyola of Los Angeles. International and Comparative Law Annual — Loy LA Int'l and Comp L Ann
Loyola of Los Angeles. International and Comparative Law Annual — Loyola Los Ang Int'l & Comp L Ann
Loyola of Los Angeles. International and Comparative Law Journal — Loy LA Int'l & Comp LJ
Loyola of Los Angeles. Law Review — Loy LR LA
Loyola of Los Angeles. Law Review — Loyola Los A L Rev
Loyola of Los Angeles. Law Review — Loyola of Los Angeles L Rev
Loyola University Law Journal (Chicago) — Loyola ULJ (Chicago)
Loyola University of Chicago. Law Journal — Loy Chi LJ
Loyola University of Chicago. Law Journal — Loy U Chi LJ
Loyola University of Chicago. Law Journal — Loyola U Chi LJ
Loyola University of Chicago. Law Journal — Loyola Univ of Chicago LJ
Loyola University of Los Angeles [*later, Loyola Marymount University*]. **Law Review** — Loy LA L Rev
Loyola University of Los Angeles [*later, Loyola Marymount University*]. **Law Review** — Loyola UL Rev (LA)
Loyola University of Los Angeles [*later, Loyola Marymount University*]. **Law Review** — Loyola ULA L Rev
Lozarstvo Vinarstvo — Lozar Vinar
Lraber Hasarakakan Gitutyunneri — Lrab Hasarakakan Gitutyun
LSA [*Life Sciences and Agricultural*] **Experiment Station. Technical Bulletin (Maine)** — LSA Exp Stn Tech Bull (Maine)
LSE [*Laurence, Scott, & Electromotors Ltd.*] **Engineering Bulletin** — LSE Eng Bull
LSE [*Laurence, Scott, & Electromotors Ltd.*] **Engineering Bulletin** — LSEBA
LSE [*London School of Economics*] **Quarterly** — LSE Quart
LSI [*Lunar Science Institute*] **Contribution** — LSI Contrib
LSU [*Louisiana State University*] **Forestry Notes. Louisiana Agricultural Experiment Station** — LSU For Notes LA Agric Exp Stn
LSU Forestry Notes. Louisiana Agricultural Experiment Station — LSU Forest Notes
LSU Forestry Notes. Louisiana State University. School of Forestry and Wildlife Management — LSU For Note LA Sch For
LSU Wood Utilization Notes. Agricultural Experiment Station Research Release. Louisiana State University and A & M College — LSU Wood Util Notes Agric Exp Stn Res Release La State Univ
LSU Wood Utilization Notes. Louisiana State University. School of Forestry and Wildlife Management — LSU Wood Util Note LA Sch For
LTF [*Lithographic Technical Foundation*] **Research Progress** — LTF Res Progr
LTSR Medicina — LTSR Med
LUAC [*Life Underwriters Association of Canada*] **Monitor** — LUAC Mon
Lubrication Engineering — Lubr Eng
Lubrication Engineering — Lubric Eng
Lubrication Engineering — Lubric Engng
Lucas Engineering Review — Lucas Eng Rev
Lucas Engineering Review — Lucas Engng Rev
Luce Intellettuale — Ll
Luceafarul — Luc
Lucrari de Cercetare. Institutul de Cercetari pentru Industrie si Chimie Alimentara — Lucr Cercet Inst Cercet Ind Chim Aliment
Lucrari de Cercetare. Institutul de Cercetari si Projectari Alimentare — Lucr Cercet Inst Cercet Project Aliment
Lucrari de Cercetare. Institutul de Chimie Alimentara — Lucr Cercet Inst Chim Aliment
Lucrari de Muzicologie — L de Muz
Lucrari de Muzicologie — LM
Lucrari de Muzicologie — Lucrari Muzicol
Lucrari Stiintifice ale Institutului Agronomic N. Balcescu. Bucuresti. Seria C — Lucr Stiint Inst Agron N Balcescu
Lucrari Stiintifice ale Institutului Agronomic "Nicolae Balcescu" (Bucuresti). Seria C — LSBCA
Lucrari Stiintifice ale Institutului Agronomic "Nicolae Balcescu" (Bucuresti). Seria C — Lucr Stiint Inst Agron N Balcescu (Bucur) Ser C
Lucrari Stiintifice ale Institutului Agronomic "Nicolae Balcescu" (Bucuresti). Seria C [*Romania*] — Lucr Stiint Inst Agron N Balcescu (Bucuresti) Ser C
Lucrari Stiintifice. Centrul Experimental de Ingrasaminte Bacteriene (Bucharest) — Lucr Stiint Cent Exp Ingrasaminte Bact (Bucharest)
Lucrari Stiintifice. Institutul Agronomic "Dr. Petru Groza" (Cluj) — Lucr Sti Inst Agron Dr Petru Groza (Cluj)
Lucrari Stiintifice. Institutul Agronomic "Dr. Petru Groza" (Cluj) — Lucr Stiint Inst Agron (Cluj)
Lucrari Stiintifice. Institutul Agronomic "Dr. Petru Groza" (Cluj). Seria Agricultura — IALAB
Lucrari Stiintifice. Institutul Agronomic "Dr. Petru Groza" (Cluj). Seria Agricultura — Lucr Sti Inst Agron Dr Petru Groza (Cluj) Ser Agr
Lucrari Stiintifice. Institutul Agronomic "Dr. Petru Groza" (Cluj). Seria Agricultura — Lucr Stiint Inst Agron (Cluj) Ser Agric
Lucrari Stiintifice. Institutul Agronomic "Dr. Petru Groza" (Cluj). Seria Medicina Veterinara si Zootehnie — Lucr Stiint Inst Agron (Cluj) Ser Med Vet Zooteh
Lucrari Stiintifice. Institutul Agronomic "Dr. Petru Groza" (Cluj). Seria Medicina Veterinari — Lucr Stiint Inst Agron (Cluj) Ser Med Vet
Lucrari Stiintifice. Institutul Agronomic "Dr. Petru Groza" (Cluj). Seria Zootehnie — Lucr Stiint Inst Agron (Cluj) Ser Zooteh
Lucrari Stiintifice. Institutul Agronomic "Ion Ionescu de la Brad" (Iasi) — Lucr Sti Inst Agron Ion Ionescu de la Brad (Iasi)
Lucrari Stiintifice. Institutul Agronomic "Nicolae Balcescu" (Bucuresti). Seria A. Agronomie [*Romania*] — Lucr Stiint Inst Agron (Bucuresti) Ser A
Lucrari Stiintifice. Institutul Agronomic "Nicolae Balcescu" (Bucuresti). Seria A, B, C — Lucr Sti Inst Agron N Balcescu (Bucuresti) Ser A B C
Lucrari Stiintifice. Institutul Agronomic "Nicolae Balcescu" (Bucuresti). Seria B. Horticultura — Lucr Stiint Inst Agron (Bucuresti) Ser B
Lucrari Stiintifice. Institutul Agronomic "Nicolae Balcescu" (Bucuresti). Seria C. Zootehnie si Medicina Veterinara — Lucr Stiint Inst Agron (Bucuresti) Ser C

Lucrari Stiintifice. Institutul Agronomic "Nicolae Balcescu" (Bucuresti). Seria D. Zootehnie — Lucr Stiint Inst Agron (Bucuresti) Ser D Zooteh
Lucrari Stiintifice. Institutul Agronomic "Nicolae Balcescu." Horticultura — Lucr Stiint Inst Agron "Nicolae Balcescu" Hortic
Lucrari Stiintifice. Institutul Agronomic "Nicolae Balcescu." Imbunatatiri Funciare — Lucr Stiint Inst Agron "Nicolae Balcescu" Imbunatatiri Fun
Lucrari Stiintifice. Institutul Agronomic "Nicolae Balcescu." Medicina Veterinara — Lucr Stiint Inst Agron "Nicolae Balcescu" Med Vet
Lucrari Stiintifice. Institutul Agronomic "Nicolae Balcescu." Seria A. Agronomie — Lucr Stiint Inst Agron "Nicolae Balcescu" Agron
Lucrari Stiintifice. Institutul Agronomic "Nicolae Balcescu." Seria D. Zootehnie — Lucr Stiint Inst Agron "Nicolae Balcescu" Zooteh
Lucrari Stiintifice. Institutul Agronomic "Professor Ion Ionescu de la Brad" — Lucr Sti Inst Agron Professor Ion Ionescu de la Brad
Lucrari Stiintifice. Institutul Agronomic "T. Vladimirescu" (Craiova) — Lucr Sti Inst Agron "T Vladimirescu" (Craiova)
Lucrari Stiintifice. Institutul Agronomic Timisoara (Bucuresti) — Lucr Sti Inst Agron Timisoara (Bucuresti)
Lucrari Stiintifice. Institutul Agronomic (Timisoara). Seria Agronomie — Lucr Stint Inst Agron (Timisoara) Ser Agron
Lucrari Stiintifice. Institutul Agronomic (Timisoara). Seria Medicina Veterinara — Lucr Stiint Inst Agron (Timisoara) Ser Med Vet
Lucrari Stiintifice. Institutul Agronomic (Timisoara). Seria Medicina Veterinara — Lucr Stiint Inst Agron (Timisoara) Seri Medna Vet
Lucrari Stiintifice. Institutul Agronomic (Timisoara). Seria Zootehnie — Lucr Stiint Inst Agron (Timisoara) Ser Zooteh
Lucrari Stiintifice. Institutul Pedagogic din Oradea. Seria Matematica, Fizica, Chimie — Lucr Stiint Inst Pedagog Oradea Ser Mat Fiz Chim
Lucrari Stiintifice. Institutul Pedagogic Galati — Lucrari Sti Inst Ped Galati
Lucrari Stiintifice. Institutul Politehnic (Galati) — Lucr Stiint Inst Politeh (Galati)
Lucrari Stiintifice. Seria B. Horticultura — Lucr Stiint Ser B Hortic
Lucrari Stiintifice. Seria C VII. Zootehnie si Medicina Veterinara [*Bucuresti*] — Lucr Stiint Ser C VII
Lucrari Stiintifice. Seria Zootehnie si Medicina Veterinara — Lucr Stiint Ser Zooteh Med Vet
Lucrari Stiintifice. Statiunea Centrala de Cercetari pentru Sericicultura si Apicultura — Lucr Stiint Stn Cent Cercet Sericic Apic
Lucrarile Gradinii Botanice (Bucuresti) — Lucr Grad Bot (Bucuresti)
Lucrarile Gradinii Botanice (Bucuresti) — Lucr Gradinii Bot (Bucur)
Lucrarile ICPE [*Institutul de Cercetare si Proiectare pentru Industria Electrotehnica*] [*Romania*] — Lucr ICPE
Lucrarile Institutului de Cercetari Alimentare — Lucr Inst Cercet Alim
Lucrarile Institutului de Cercetari Alimentare — Lucr Inst Cercet Aliment
Lucrarile Institutului de Cercetari Veterinare si Biopreparate Pasteur — Lucr Inst Cercet Vet Bioprep Pasteur
Lucrarile Institutului de Petrol, Gaze, si Geologie din Bucuresti — Lucr Inst Pet Gaz Geol Bucuresti
Lucrarile Institutului de Petrol si Gaze din Bucuresti — Lucr Inst Pet Gaze Bucuresti
Lucrarile Prezentate la Conferinta Nationala de Farmacie — Lucr Conf Natl Farm
Lucrarile Seminarului de Matematica si Fizica. Institutului Politehnic "Traian Vuia" (Timisoara) — Lucr Semin Mat Fiz Inst Politeh "Traian Vuia" (Timisoara)
Lucrarile Sesiunii Stiintifice. Institutul Agronomic "Nicolae Balcescu" — Lucr Ses Stiint Inst Agron Nicolae Balcescu
Lucrarile Sesiunii Stiintifice. Institutul Agronomic "Nicolae Balcescu" (Bucuresti). Seria C. Zootehnie si Medicina Veterinara — Lucr Ses Stiint Inst Agron Nicolae Balcescu Ser C
Lucrarile. Simpozion de Biodeteriorare si Climatizare — Lucr Simp Biodeterior Clim
Lucrarile. Simpozion de Climatizare si Biodeteriorare — Lucr Simp Clim Biodeterior
Lucrarile Stiintifice. Institutul Agronomic "Professor Ion Ionescu de la Brad" (Iasi) — Lucr Stiint Inst Agron (Iasi)
Lucrarile Stiintifice. Institutul Agronomic "Professor Ion Ionescu de la Brad" (Iasi) [*Romania*] — Lucr Stiint Inst Agron Ion Ionescu de la Brad (Iasi)
Lucrarile Stiintifice. Institutul Politehnic (Cluj) — Lucr Stiint Inst Politeh (Cluj)
Lucrarile Stiintifice. Institutului de Cercetari Zootehnice — Lucr Sti Inst Cercet Zooteh
Lucrarile Stiintifice. Institutului de Cercetari Zootehnice — Lucr Stiint Inst Cerc Zooteh
Lucrarile Stiintifice. Institutului de Cercetari Zootehnice — Lucr Stiint Inst Cercet Zooteh
Lucrarile Stiintifice. Institutului de Mine Petrosani — Lucr Stiint Inst Mine Petrosani
Lucrarile Stiintifice. Institutului de Mine Petrosani. Seria 4. Stiinte de Cultura Tehnica Generala — Lucr Stiint Inst Mine Petrosani Ser 4
Lucrarile Stiintifice. Institutului de Mine Petrosani. Seria 5. Geologie — Lucr Stiint Inst Mine Petrosani Ser 5
Lucrarile Stiintifice. Institutului de Mine Petrosani. Seria 6. Stiinte Sociale — Lucr Stiint Inst Mine Petrosani Ser 6
Lucrarile Stiintifice. Institutului de Patologie si Igiena Animala — Lucr Stiint Inst Patol Ig Anim
Lucrarile Stiintifice. Institutului de Seruri si Vaccinuri Pasteur (Bucuresti) — Lucr Stiint Inst Seruri Vacc Pasteur (Bucur)
Ludoviciana. Contributions de l'Herbier Louis-Marie. Faculte d'Agriculture. Universite Laval — Ludoviciana Contr Herb
Ludowa Spoldzielnia Wydawnicza — LSW
Ludus Magistralis — LM
Lueneburger Blaetter — Lue B
Lueneburger Blaetter — Lueneburger B
Lueneburger Museumsblaetter — LM Bl
Lueneburger Museumsblaetter — Lueneberger Musbl
Luft- und Kaeltetechnik — Luft- Kaeltetech
Luft- und Kaltetechnik — Luft und Kaeltetech
Luftfahrt und Wissenschaft — LuW
Luftfahrttechnik, Raumfahrttechnik — Luftfahrttech Raumfahrttech
Luggage and Travelware — LLG
Lumen [*Vitoria*] — Lum
Lumen Vitae — Lumen
Lumen Vitae [*Brussels*] — LumVit
Lumen Vitae — LV
Lumen Vitae. Edition Francaise — LVF
Lumen Vitae. English Edition — LVE
Lumiere — Lum
Lumiere et Vie — Lumiere
Lumiere et Vie [*Lyons*] — LumVie
Lumiere et Vie [*Lyons*] — LV
Lumiere et Vie (Bruges) — LVB
Lumiere et Vie (Lyon) — LVL
Lumiere et Vie. Supplement Biblique — LumViSup
Luminescence of Crystals, Molecules, and Solutions. Proceedings. International Conference on Luminescence — Lumin Cryst Mol Solutions Proc Int Conf
Luminescence Techniques in Chemical and Biochemical Analysis — Lumin Tech Chem Biochem Anal
Luna Monthly — LM
Lunar and Planetary Bibliography [*Database*] — LPB
Lunar and Planetary Exploration Colloquium. Proceedings — Lunar and Planetary Explor Colloquium Proc
Lunar and Planetary Institute. Contribution — LPI Contribution
Lunar and Planetary Institute. Technical Report — LPI Technical Report
Lunar Science Institute. Contribution — Lunar Sci Inst Contrib
Lund Studies in English — LSE
Lundastudier i Nordisk Sprakvetenskap — LNS
Lundastudier i Nordisk Sprakvetenskap — LSNS
Lundberg Survey Share of Market [*Database*] — SOM
Lunder Germanistische Forschungen — LGF
Lunder Germanistische Forschungen — Lun Ger For
Lunds Universitet. Arsskrift — LUA
Lunds Universitet. Arsskrift. Avdelningen 2. Kungliga Fysiografiska Salskapets i Lund. Handlinger — Lunds Univ Arsskr Avd 2
Lung Biology in Health and Disease — Lung Biol Health Dis
Lung Cancer. Progress in Therapeutic Research — Lung Cancer Progr Ther Res
Lung Perspectives — Lung Perspect
Lunker Gazette — Lunker Gaz
Luonnon Tutkija — Luonnon Tutk
Lusa [*Viana do Castelo*] — L
Lusiada — Lu
Lusitania. Revista de Estudos Portugueses — Lu
Lusitania Sacra — LS
Lusitania Sacra — LSa
Lusitania Sacra — Lus Sac
Luso Journal of Science and Technology — Luso J Sci Tech
Luso-Brazilian Review — LBR
Luso-Brazilian Review — LusB
Luso-Brazilian Review (Madison, Wisconsin) — Luso Braz Rev Madison
Lute Society. Journal — LSJ
Lute Society. Journal — Lute Soc J
Lute Society of America. Journal — LS
Lute Society of America Newsletter — LSAN
Lute Society of America Quarterly — LSAQ
Luther Jahrbuch — Lu J
Luther. Mitteilungen der Luthergesellschaft — LMLG
Luther. Vierteljahresschrift der Luthergesellschaft — LVLG
Lutheran — Luth
Lutheran Church Quarterly — LChQ
Lutheran Church Quarterly — LCQ
Lutheran Church Quarterly — LuthChQ
[*The*] **Lutheran Church Review** — LChR
Lutheran Church Review — LCR
Lutheran Church Review — Luth Church R
Lutheran Churches of the World — LCW
Lutheran Education — Luth Educ
Lutheran Forum — Luth For
Lutheran Historical Conference. Essays and Reports — Luth H Conf
Lutheran News Service [*Database*] — LNS
Lutheran Quarterly — LQ
Lutheran Quarterly — LuQ
Lutheran Quarterly — LuthQ
Lutheran Standard — Luth S
Lutheran Studies Series — LSSS
Lutheran Theological Journal — Luth Th J
Lutheran Witness — Luth W
Lutheran World — LuthW
Lutheran World — LW
Lutheran World — LWorld
Lutheran World. Supplement — LWS
Lutherische Monatshefte — LM
Lutherische Monatshefte [*Hamburg*] — LuthMonh
Lutherische Rundschau — LR
Lutherische Rundschau [*Stuttgart*] — LRsch
Lutherische Rundschau [*Geneva*] — LuthRu
Lutherische Rundschau. Beiheft — Lr B
Lutherischer Rundblick — L Rb
Lutherisches Missions Jahrbuch — LMJ
Lutherisches Missions-Jahrbuch fuer die Jahre (Berlin) — LMJ B
Luther-Jahrbuch — LJ
Luther-Jahrbuch — L-Jb
Luther-Jahrbuch — Luther-Jahrb
Luther-Jahrbuch [*Hamburg*] — LuthJB

Luther-Jahrbuch — LutJ
Luther-Studien — Luth St
Luthertum. Erlangen — Luth
Lutte Contre le Cancer [*France*] — Lutte Cancer
Luttenberg's Chronologische Verzameling — CV
Lutterworth Library — Lutt L
Luttrell Society. Reprints — LSR
Luvische Texte in Umschrift — LTU
Luxemburgische Bienen-Zeitung — Luxemb Bienenztg
Luzac's Oriental List and Book Review — LOL
Luzac's Oriental Religions Series — LORS
Luzerne Legal Register — LLR
Luzerne Legal Register — Luz Leg Reg
Luzerne Legal Register — Luz LR
Luzerne Legal Register [*Pennsylvania*] — Luzerne Leg Reg (PA)
LVI-Saatotekniikan Tutkimusseminaari — LVI Saatotek Tutkimussemin
L'vivskii Zootekhnichno-Veterinarnii Institut. Naukovi Pratsi — L'viv Zootekh Vet Inst Nauk Pr
L'vovskii Gosudarstvennyi Universitet. Teoreticheskaya Elektrotekhnika — Teoret Elektrotekhn
L'vovskii Politehniceskii Institut. Naucnye Zapiski. Serija Fiziko-Matematiceskaja — L'vov Politehn Inst Naucn Zap Ser Fiz-Mat
L'vovskii Torgovo-Ekonomicheskii Institut. Nauchnye Zapiski — L'vov Torg Ekon Inst Nauchn Zap
LWF [*Lutheran World Federation*] **Documentation** — LWF Doc
LWF [*Lutheran World Federation*] **Report** — LWF Rep
Lyceum of Natural History of New York. Annals. Proceedings — Lyc N H NY An Pr
Lychnos — Ly
Lychnos Lardomshistoriska Samfundets Arsbok — Lychnos Lardomshist Samf Arsb
Lydgate Newsletter — LydgN
Lydisches Woerterbuch — LW
Lydisches Woerterbuch — Lyd Wb
Lying-In Journal of Reproductive Medicine — Lying-In J Reprod Med
Lykisch und Hittitisch — LH
Lymphokine and Cytokine Research — Lymph Cyt R
Lymphokine and Cytokine Research — Lymphokine Cytokine Res
Lymphokine Research — Lymphokine Res
Lymphokines and Thymic Hormones. Their Potential Utilization in Cancer Therapeutics — Lymphokines Thymic Horm Their Potential Util Cancer Ther
Lynx Supplementum (Prague) — Lynx Suppl (Prague)
Lyon Chirurgical — Lyon Chir
Lyon Medical — Lyon Med
Lyon Pharmaceutique — Lyon Pharm
Lyons. Faculte des Sciences. Laboratoires de Geologie. Documents — Lyons Fac Sci Lab Geol Doc
Lyric Opera News — LyON
Lysistrata — LS
Lysosomes in Biology and Pathology — Lysosomes Biol Pathol
Lyuminestsentnye Materialy i Osobo Chistye Veshchestva. Sbornik Nauchnykh Trudov — Lyumin Mater Osobo Chist Veshchestva

M

M. Agricultural Extension Service. University of Minnesota — M Agric Ext Serv Univ Minn
M and B [*May and Baker*] **Laboratory Bulletin** — MB Lab Bull
M and B Pharmaceutical Bulletin — MB Pharm Bull
M. Gentle Men for Gender Justice — M
M Inc — IMMM
M; the Civilized Man — M
M3 Archaeology [*England*] — M3 Archaeol
MAA [*Mathematical Association of America*] **Studies in Mathematics** — MAA Stud Math
Maal og Minne — MM
Maal og Minne — MoM
Maandblad. Centraal Bureau Statistiek — MCS
Maandblad de Pacht — DeP
Maandblad de Pacht — DP
Maandblad de Pieper — Maandbl Pieper
Maandblad de Praktijkgids — Praktijkg
Maandblad der Vereniging van Inspecteurs van Financien — MVI
Maandblad Gemeente-Administratie — MGA
Maandblad N. Samson. Gewijd aan de Belangen der Gemeenteadministratie — MS
Maandblad. Uitgegeven Door Het Natuurhistorisch Genootschap in Limburg — Maandbl Natuurhist Genootsch Limburg
Maandblad van de Centrale Raad van Beroep — Mbl
Maandblad van de Vlaamse Bieenbond — Maandbl Vlaam Bieenb
Maandblad van de Vlaamse Imkersbond — Maandbl Vlaam Imkersb
Maandblad van Financien — MF
Maandblad van Oud-Utrecht — Maandbl Oud Utrecht
Maandblad voor Accountancy en Bedrijfshuishoudkunde — MA
Maandblad voor Accountancy en Bedrijfshuishoudkunde — MAB
Maandblad voor Bedrijfsadministratie en Organisatie — MBO
Maandblad voor Beeldende Kunsten — MBK
Maandblad voor Belastingrecht — M Bel R
Maandblad voor Belastingrecht — MB
Maandblad voor Belastingrecht — Mbl Bel Recht
Maandblad voor Belastingrecht — MvB
Maandblad voor Berechtiging en Reclassering — MvB en R
Maandblad voor Berechtiging en Reclassering van Volwassenen en Kinderen — MB en R
Maandblad voor Berechtiging en Reclassering van Volwassenen en Kinderen — MBR
Maandblad voor de Geestelijke Volksgezondheid — MGV
Maandblad voor de Landbouwvoorlichtingsdienst (Netherlands) — Maandbl Landbouwvoorlichtingsdienst (Neth)
Maandblad voor de Vereniging van Deurwaarders — MvDeurw
Maandblad voor Handelswetenschappen en Administratieve Praktijk — MHW
Maandblad voor het Boekhouden — MB
Maandblad voor het Handelsonderwijs — MHO
Maandblad voor Naturwetenschappen. Genootschap ter Bevordering van Natuur-, Genees- en Heelkunde te Amsterdam — Maandbl Natuurw
Maandblad voor Sociaal Economiese. Wetenschappen — MSE
Maandnotities Betreffende de Economische Toestand — MAQ
Maandschrift Economie — ERK
Maandschrift Economie — Maandschr Econ
Maandschrift Economie — ME
Maandschrift van de Nederlandsche Maatschappij voor Tuinbouw en Plantkunde — Maandschr Ned Maatsch Tuinb
Maandschrift van het Centraal Bureau voor de Statistiek — MCB
Maandschrift voor Bijenteelt — Maandschr Bijent
Maandschrift voor Kindergeneeskunde — Maandschr Kindergeneeskd
Maandschrift voor Kindergeneeskunde — MAKIA
Maandschrift voor Liturgie — MVL
Maandschrift voor Tuinbouw — Maandschr Tuinb
Maandstatistiek Bouwnijverheid — BYB
Maandstatistiek Financiewezen — CSO
Maandstatistiek van Bevolking en Volksgezondheid — CBA
Maandstatistiek van de Binnenlandse Handel en Dienstverlening — MBV
Maandstatistiek van de Brijzen — MRI
Maandstatistiek van de Buitenlandse Handel per Land — MHD
Maandstatistiek van de Industrie — MYV
Maandstatistiek van de Landbouw — MLD
Maandstatistiek Verkeer en Vervoer — MSV
Maanedsskrift for Dyrlaeger — M Dl
Maanedsskrift for Praktisk Laegegerning og Social Medicin — M Pr Lg
Maasbode — M
Maasgouw [*Maastrich*] — Maasg
Maatalouden Tutkimuskeskuksen Aikakauskirja — Maatalouden Tutkimuskeskuksen Aikak
Maatalouden Tutkimuskeskus. Maantutkimuslaitos. Agrogeologisia Julkaisuja — Maatalouden Tutkimuskeskus Maantutkimuslaitos Agrogeol Julk
Maatalouden Tutkimuskeskus. Maantutkimuslaitos. Agrogeologisia Karttoja — Maatalouden Tutkimuskeskus Maantutkimuslaitos Agrogeol Kart
Maatalous ja Koetoiminta — Maatalous Koetoim
Maataloushallinon Aikakauskirja — Maataloushal Aikakausk
Maataloustieteelinen Aikakauskirja — Maatalousst Aikakausk
Maataloustieteelinen Aikakauskirja — Maataloustiet Aikak
Maataloustieteelinen Aikakauskirja — Maataloustieteelinen Aikak
Maatschappijbelangen — MAA
MAC [*Media Agencies Clients*]/Western Advertising — MAC
MAC [*Media Agencies Clients*]/Western Advertising — MAC/WA
Macabre — MAC
Macallat al-Macma al-Limi al-Arabi Dimasq — MMAD
Macaroni Journal — Macaroni J
Macaulay Institute for Soil Research. Annual Report — Macaulay Inst Soil Res Annu Rep
Macaulay Institute for Soil Research. Collected Papers — Macaulay Inst Soil Res Collect Pap
Macchine e Motori Agricoli — Macch Motori Agr
Macedoniae Acta Archaeologica — Mac Acta A
Macedonian Review — Mac R
Machine and Tool Blue Book — Mach Tool Blue Book
Machine Building Industry [*India*] — Mach Build Ind
Machine Design — Mach Des
Machine Design — Mach Design
Machine Design — Machine D
Machine Intelligence and Pattern Recognition — Mach Intell Pattern Recogn
Machine Moderne — Mach Mod
Machine Outil Francaise — Mach Outil Fr
Machine Outil Francaise — MCOFA
Machine Shop — Mach Shop
Machine Shop and Engineering Manufacture [*England*] — Mach Shop Eng Manuf
Machine Tool Engineering — Mach Tool Eng
Machine Tool Review — Mach Tool R
Machine Translation — MT
Machinery [*Later, Machinery and Production Engineering*] — Mach
Machinery [*Later, Machinery and Production Engineering*] — MCNYA
Machinery and Equipment for Food Industry — Mach Equip Food Ind
Machinery and Production Engineering — Mach and Prod Eng
Machinery and Production Engineering — Mach & Prod Engng
Machinery and Production Engineering — Mach Prod E
Machinery and Production Engineering — Mach Prod Eng
Machinery and Production Engineering — Machinery Prod Engng
Machinery Business — Mach Bus
Machinery Korea — Mach Korea
Machinery Korea — MKO
Machinery Lloyd. International Review of Engineering Equipment — Mach Lloyd Int Rev Eng Equip
Machinery Market — Mach Market
Machinery Market — MAM
Machines and Tooling [*English Translation of Stanki i Instrument*] — Mach and Tool
Machines and Tooling [*English Translation of Stanki i Instrument*] — Mach Tool
Machines and Tooling. English Translation of Stanki i Instrument — Mach Tool Engl Transl
Machines et Techniques de Construction — Mach Tech Constr
Machinisme Agricole et Equipement Rural [*France*] — Mach Agric Equip Rural
Machinisme Agricole Tropical — Mach Agr Trop
Machinisme Agricole Tropical — Mach Agric Trop
Mackenzie Delta Research Project [*Canada*] — MDRP
Mackenzie Drift [*Canada*] — MD
Mackenzie News — MA
Mackenzie Pilot [*Canada*] — MP
Mackenzie Times — MK
Maclean's — GMAC
Maclean's — Mac
Maclean's Magazine — Macl Mag
Maclean's Magazine — MM
Maclurean Lyceum. Contributions — Maclurean Lyc Contr
Macmillan's Magazine — Mac
Macmillan's Magazine — Macm M
Macmillan's Magazine — Macmil
Macmillan's Magazine — MM

Macromolecular Chemistry and Physics. Supplement — Macromol Chem Phys Suppl
Macromolecular Physics — Macromol Phys
Macromolecular Reviews — Macromol Rev
Macromolecular Reviews. Part D. Journal of Polymer Science — Macromol R
Macromolecular Specificity and Biological Memory [*Monograph*] — Macromol Specif Biol Mem
Macromolecular Syntheses — Macromol Synth
Macromolecules — Macromolec
Macromolecules — Macromols
Macromolecules and Behavior — Macromol Behav
Macromolecules. Synthesis, Order, and Advanced Properties — Macromol Synth Order Adv Prop
Macuser — IMCU
Macworld — IMCW
Mad River Review — MRR
Madagascar. Direction de l'Industrie et des Mines. Rapports d'Activite. Geologie — Madagascar Dir Ind Mines Rapp Act Geol
Madagascar. Revue de Geographie — Madagascar Rev Geogr
Madagascar. Revue de Geographie — Madagascar Revue de Geogr
Madagascar. Service des Mines. Annales Geologiques — Madagascar Serv Mines Ann Geol
Madamina — Mad
Made in Mexico — Made in Mex
Mademoiselle — GMAD
Mademoiselle — Madem
Mademoiselle — Mlle
Maden Tetkik ve Arama Enstitusu Mecmuasi — Maden Tetkik Arama Enst Mecm
Maden Tetkik ve Arama Enstitusu Yayinlarindan — Maden Tetkik Arama Enst Yayin
Maden Tetkik ve Arama Enstitusu Yayinlarindan [*Turkey*] — Maden Tetkik Arama Enst Yayinlarindan
Maden Tetkik ve Arama Enstitusu Yayinlarindan. Seri A. Bildirigler — Maden Tetkik Arama Enst Yayin Seri A
Maden Tetkik ve Arama Enstitusu Yayinlarindan. Seri B. Irdeller — Maden Tetkik Arama Enst Yayin Seri B
Maden Tetkik ve Arama Enstitusu Yayinlarindan. Seri C. Monografiler — Maden Tetkik Arama Enst Yayin Seri C
Maden Tetkik ve Arama Enstitusu Yayinlarindan. Seri D. Jeolojik Harta Materye-Leri — Maden Tetkik Arama Enst Yayin Seri D
Madhya Bharati. Journal of the University of Saugar. Part 2. Section B. Natural Sciences — Madhya Bharati J Univ Saugar Part 2 Sect B Nat Sci
Madhya Bharati. Part 2. Section A. Physical Sciences — Madhya Bharati Part 2 Sect A Phys
Madhya Bharati. Part 2. Section A. Physical Sciences — Madhya Bharati Pt 2 Sect A
Madison Avenue — MA
Madison Avenue — Madison Av
Madison Avenue — Madison Ave
Madison Avenue — MAV
Madison Quarterly — Mad Q
Madjalah Institut Teknologi Bandung Proceedings [*Indonesia*] — Madjalah Inst Tek Bandung Proc
Madjalah Persatuan Dokter Gigi Indonesia — Madj Persat Dokt Gigi Indones
Madjelis Ilmu Pengetahuan Indonesia Penerbitan — Madjelis Ilmu Pengetahuan Indones Penerbitan
Madness Network News — Madness
Madoqua. Series I — Madoqua Ser I
Madras Agricultural Journal — Madras Agr J
Madras Agricultural Journal — Madras Agric J
Madras Journal of Literature and Science — Madras J Lit Sci
Madras Journal of Literature and Science — MJLS
Madras Law Journal — Mad LJ
Madras Law Journal — Madras LJ
Madras Law Journal — MLJ
Madras Medical Journal — Madras Med J
Madras Review — Mad R
Madras University Islamic Series — MUIS
Madras University. Journal — MUJ
Madras University. Journal. Section A. Humanities — MUJA
Madras University. Journal. Section B. Science — MUJB
Madras University Sanskrit Series — MUSS
Madras Veterinary College. Annual — Madras Vet Coll Annu
Madras Veterinary Journal — Madras Vet J
Madrid Universidad. Facultad de Medicina. Archivos — Madrid Univ Fac Med Arch
Madrider Beitraege. Deutsches Archaeologisches Institut. Abteilung Madrid — MB
Madrider Mitteilungen — MM
Madrider Mitteilungen. Deutsches Archaeologisches Institut. Madrider Abteilung — DAIMM
Madrider Mitteilungen. Deutsches Archaeologisches Institut. Madrider Abteilung — Madrider Mitt
Madrider Mitteilungen. Deutsches Archaeologisches Institut. Madrider Abteilung — MDAI(M)
Madrono. West American Journal of Botany — Madrono West Am J Bot
Madurai University. Journal — J Madurai Univ
Maedchenbildung auf Christlicher Grundlage — MBChrG
Maehrisch-Schlesische Heimat — Maehr Schles Heimat
Maelkeritidende — Mlkt
Maerisch-Schlesische Heimat. Vierteljahresschrift fuer Kultur und Wirtschaft — Maerisch-Schlesische Heimat
Maerkische Forschungen — Maerk F
Maerkische Naturschutz — Maerk Naturschutz
Maeventec Employers Rated Almanac [*Database*] — MERA
Maeventec Travel Information [*Database*] — MTI
MAFES Research Highlights. Mississippi Agricultural and Forestry Experiment Station — MAFES Res Highlights Miss Agric For Exp Stn
Magadanskii Zonal'nyi Nauchno-Issledovatel'skii Institut Sel'skogo Khozyaistva Severo-Vostoka. Trudy — Magadan Zon Nauchno Issled Inst Selsk Khoz Sev Vostoka Tr
Magazijn van Handelsrecht — Mag v H
Magazijn van Handelsrecht — MvH
Magazijn voor Landbouw en Kruidkunde — Mag Landb Kruidk
Magazin aller Neuen Erfindungen, Entdeckungen, und Verbesserungen — Mag Nouen Erfind
Magazin der Auslaendischen Literatur der Gesammten Heilkunde, und Arbeiten des Aerztlichen Vereins zu Hamburg — Mag Ausl Lit Gesammten Heilk
Magazin der Neuesten Erfindungen, Entdeckungen, und Verbesserungen — Mag Neuesten Erfind
Magazin der Neuesten und Interessantesten Reisebeschreibungen — Mag Neuesten Interessantesten Reisebeschreib
Magazin fuer Arbeitsrecht, Sozialpolitik, und Verwandte Gebiete — M Arb R
Magazin fuer Arbeitsrecht, Sozialpolitik, und Verwandte Gebiete — Mag Arbeitsr
Magazin fuer Christliche Dogmatik und Moral — MCDM
Magazin fuer Datenverarbeitung — Mag Datenverarb
Magazin fuer die Geographie, Staatenkunde, und Geschichte — Mag Geogr
Magazin fuer die Gesammte Heilkunde (Von J. N. Rust) — Rusts Magaz
Magazin fuer die Naturkunde Helvetiens — Mag Naturk Helv
Magazin fuer die Neueste Geschichte der Evangelischen Missions- und Bibelgesellschaften — Mag Neueste Gesch Evang Missions Bibelges
Magazin fuer die Neuesten Entdeckungen in der Gesammten Naturkunde — Mag N Entdeck Ges Naturk
Magazin fuer die Neuesten Erfahrungen. Entdeckungen und Berichtigungen im Gebiete der Pharmacie — Mag Neuesten Erfahr Entdeckungen Berichtigungen Geb Pharm
Magazin fuer die Neuste Geschichte der Protestantischen Missions- und Bibelgesellschaft — MNGPM
Magazin fuer die Wissenschaft des Judentums — MagWJ
Magazin fuer die Wissenschaft des Judentums — MWJ
Magazin fuer Freunde der Naturlehre und Naturgeschichte, Scheidekunst, Land- und Stadtwirthschaft, Volks- und Staatsarznei — Mag Freunde Naturl
Magazin fuer Juedische Geschichte und Literatur — MJGL
Magazin fuer Pharmacie und die Dahin Einschlagenden Wissenschaften — Mag Pharm
Magazin fuer Religionsphilosophie, Exegese, und Kirchengeschichte — MRP
Magazin fuer Westphalen — Mag Westphalen
Magazin Istoric — Mag Istor
Magazin Litteraire et Scientifique — Mag Litter Scientif
Magazin von und fuer Dortmund — Mag Dortmund
Magazin zum Gebrauch der Staaten und Kirchengeschichte — MGSKG
Magazine Age — Mag Age
Magazine Age — Magazin Ag
Magazine Antiques — GANT
Magazine Article Guide — MAG
Magazine Article Summaries — MAS
Magazine. Bihar Agricultural College — Mag Bihar Agr Coll
Magazine. College of Agriculture — Mag Coll Agric
Magazine fuer Evangelische Theologie und Kirche — ME Th K
Magazine Index — Mag I
Magazine Index — Mag Index
Magazine Litteraire — Mag Litt
Magazine. London (Royal Free Hospital) School of Medicine for Women — Mag Lond (Roy Free Hosp) School Med Women
Magazine Maclean — Mag Macl
Magazine. Nagpur Agricultural College — Mag Nagpur Agr Coll
Magazine of American History — M Am H
Magazine of American History — M Am Hist
Magazine of American History — Mag Am Hist
Magazine of Antiques — Mag Antiq
Magazine of Art [*Cassell's*] — M of Art
Magazine of Art — MA
Magazine of Art — Mag Art
Magazine of Art — Mag of Art
Magazine of Art — MArt
Magazine of Bank Administration — BAD
Magazine of Bank Administration — Bank Admin
Magazine of Bank Administration — M Bank Admin
Magazine of Bank Administration — MAB
Magazine of Bank Administration — Mag Bank Adm
Magazine of Building — Mag Bldg
Magazine of Building — MB
Magazine of Building Equipment [*Japan*] — Mag Build Equip
Magazine of Business — Mag of Business
Magazine of Christian Literature — M Chr Lit
Magazine of Concrete Research — Mag Concr R
Magazine of Concrete Research — Mag Concr Res
Magazine of Concrete Research — Mag Concrete Res
Magazine of Direct Marketing — Direct Mkt
Magazine of Fantasy and Science Fiction — FSF
Magazine of Fantasy and Science Fiction — IMFS
Magazine of Fantasy and Science Fiction — Mag Fantasy & Sci Fict
Magazine of Fantasy and Science Fiction — MFSF
Magazine of History [*Tarrytown, New York*] — M His
Magazine of History — M of Hist
Magazine of History — Mag of Hist
Magazine of History with Notes and Queries — Mag Hist
Magazine of Horror — MOH

Magazine of Horticulture, Botany, and All Useful Discoveries and Improvements in Rural Affairs — Mag Hort Bot
Magazine of Intelligent Personal Systems — MIPS
Magazine of Mining Health and Safety. MESA [*Mining Enforcement and Safety Administration*] [*United States*] — Mag Min Health Saf MESA
Magazine of Natural History [*London*] — Mag N H
Magazine of Natural History — Mag Nat Hist
Magazine of Natural History and Naturalist — Mag Nat Hist Naturalist
Magazine of Popular Science and Journal of the Useful Arts — Mag Popular Sci J Useful Arts
Magazine of Standards — Mag of Stand
Magazine of Standards — Mag Stand
Magazine of Standards — Mag Std
Magazine of Wall Street — Mag of Wall St
Magazine of Wall Street — Mag Wall St
Magazine of Wall Street — Mag Wall Street
Magazine of Western History — M West Hist
Magazine of Western History — Mag Western Hist
Magazine. Society of Military Medical Science — Mag Soc Milit Med Sci
Magazine. Texas Commission on Alcoholism — MTCA
Magazzino Italiano Che Contiene Storia — Mag Ital
Magdeburger Zeitung — MZ
Magellanic Clouds. Proceedings. Symposium. International Astronomical Union — Magellanic Clouds Proc Symp Int Astron Union
Maghreb Developpement — Maghreb Develop
Maghreb Mathematical Review — Maghreb Math Rev
Maghreb Review — Maghreb Rev
Maghreb-Machrek — Maghreb
Maghrib Studies Group. Newsletter — MSG News
Magic Carpet Magazine — MCM
Magistratuur — M
Magistratuur — Mag
Magmatizm i Glubinnoe Stroenie Zemnoi Kory Srednei Azii — Magmat Glubinnoe Str Zemnoi Kory Sredn Azii
Magmatizm i Poleznye Iskopaemye Severo-Vostochnoi Korei i Yuga Primor'ya — Magmat Polezn Iskop Sev Vost Korei Yuga Primorya
Magna Graecia — Mag Gr
Magna Graecia — MG
Magnes Lecture Series — Magnes Lecture Ser
Magnesium. A Relevant Ion. European Congress on Magnesium — Magnesium Relevant Ion Eur Congr Magnesium
Magnesium. Bulletin — Magnesium Bull
Magnesium Monthly Review — Magnesium Mon Rev
Magnesium Research — Magnes Res
Magnesium Review and Abstracts — Magnesium Rev Abstr
Magnetic and Electrical Separation — Magn Electr Sep
Magnetic Ceramics — Magn Ceram
Magnetic Resonance Annual — Magn Reson Annu
Magnetic Resonance Imaging — Magn Reson Imaging
Magnetic Resonance Imaging Clinics of North America — Magn Reson Imaging Clin N Am
Magnetic Resonance in Chemistry and Biology. Based on Lectures at the Ampere International Summer School — Magn Reson Chem Biol Lect Ampere Int Summer Sch
Magnetic Resonance in Food Science — Magn Reson Food Sci
Magnetic Resonance in Medicine — Magn Reson Med
Magnetic Resonance Quarterly — Magn Reson Q
Magnetic Resonance Review — Magn Reson Rev
Magnetic Resonance Review — Magn Resonance Rev
Magnetics Society of India. Newsletter — Magn Soc India Newsl
Magnetics Society of India. Transactions — Magn Soc India Trans
Magnetische Eigenschaften von Festkoerpern. Vortraege gehalten auf der Metalltagung der DDR — Magn Eigenschaften Festkoerpern Vortr Metalltag DDR
Magnetism and Magnetic Materials Digest — Magn Magn Mater Dig
Magnetism Letters — Magn Lett
Magnetohydrodynamics — Magn Hydrodyn
Magnetohydrodynamics — Magnetohydrodyn
Magnetohydrodynamics in Process Metallurgy. Proceedings. Symposium — Magnetohydrodyn Process Metall Proc Symp
Magnetospheric Phenomena in Astrophysics — Magnetos Phenom Astrophys
Magnitnaya Gidrodinamika — Magn Gidrodin
Magnitnaya i Opticheskaya Spektroskopiya Mineralov i Gornykh Porod — Magn Opt Spektrosk Miner Gorn Porod
Magnitnye Lovushki — Magn Lovushki
Magnitogidrodinamicheskii Metod Polucheniya Elektroenergii — Magnitogidrodin Metod Poluch Elektroenergii
Magnitogidrodinamicheskii Metod Preobrazovaniya Energii [*Former USSR*] — Magnitogidrodin Metod Preobraz Energ
Magnum Oecumenicum Constantiense Concilium — MOCC
Magon Institut de Recherches Agronomiques. Publication. Serie Scientifique — Magon Inst Rech Agron Publ Ser Sci
Magon Institut de Recherches Agronomiques. Publication. Serie Technique — Magon Inst Rech Agron Publ Ser Tech
Magristrates of the Roman Republic — MRR
Magyar Academiai Ertesitoe — Magyar Akad Ertes
Magyar Allami Eoetvoes Lorand Geofizikai Intezet. Evi Jelentese — MAGJB
Magyar Allami Eoetvoes Lorand Geofizikai Intezet. Evi Jelentese — Magy All Eotvos Lorand Geofiz Intez Evi Jel
Magyar Allami Eoetvoes Lorand Geofizikai Intezet. Evi Jelentese — Magy Allami Eoetvoes Lorand Geofiz Intez Evi Jelentese
Magyar Allami Foldtani Intezet. Evi Jelentese — Magy All Foldt Intez Evi Jel
Magyar Allami Foldtani Intezet. Evi Jelentese — MGAJA
Magyar Allami Foldtani Intezet. Evkoenyve — Magy All Foldt Intez Evk
Magyar Allami Foldtani Intezet. Modszertani Koezlemenyek — Magy All Foldt Intez Modszertani Kozl
Magyar Allatorvosok Lapja — Magy Allatorv Lap
Magyar Allatorvosok Lapja — Magy Allatorv Lapja
Magyar Allatorvosok Lapja Kueloenszama — Magy Allatorv Lap Kueloenszama
Magyar Aluminium — Magy Alum
Magyar Asvanyolaj-es Foeldgazkiserleti Intezet Koezlemenyei — Magy Asvanyolaj-Foeldgazkiserl Intez Koezl
Magyar Asvanyolaj-es Foldgaz Kiserleti Intezet Kiadvanyai [*Hungary*] — Magy Asvanyolaj Foldgaz Kiserl Intez Kiadv
Magyar Asvanyolaj-es Foldgaz Kiserleti Intezet Koezlemenyei — Mag Asvanyolaj Foldgaz Kiserl Intez Kozl
Magyar Asvanyolaj-es Foldgaz Kiserleti Intezet Koezlemenyei [*Hungary*] — Magy Asvanyolaj Foldgaz Kiserl Intez Kozl
Magyar Belorvosi Archivum — Magy Belorv Arch
Magyar Belorvosi Archivum es Ideggyogyaszati Szemle — Mag Belorv Arch Ideggyogy Sz
Magyar Biologiai Kutato Intezet Munkai — Magy Biol Kutato Intezet Munkai
Magyar Biologiai Kutatointezet Munkai — Mag Biol Kutatointez Munkai
Magyar Biologiai Kutatointezet Munkai/Arbeiten des Ungarischen Biologischen Forschungsinstituts — Magyar Biol Kutatoint Munkai
Magyar Bor es Gyuemoelcs — Magyar Bor Gyuem
Magyar Chemiai Folyoirat [*Hungary*] — Magy Chem Folyoirat
Magyar Epitoeipar — Magy Epitoeipar
Magyar Filozofiai Szemle — Mag Fil Sz
Magyar Filozofiai Szemle — Magyar Fil Szemle
Magyar Filozofiai Szemle — Magyar Filoz Szle
Magyar Fizikai Folyoirat — Magy Fiz Foly
Magyar Fizikai Folyoirat — Magyar Fiz Foly
Magyar Geofizika — Magy Geofiz
Magyar Gyogyszereszudomanyi Tarsasag Ertesitoje — Mag Gyogyszeresztud Tarsasag Ert
Magyar Kemiai Folyoira [*Hungarian Journal of Chemistry*] — Mag Ke'm Foly
Magyar Kemiai Folyoirat — Magy Kem Fo
Magyar Kemiai Folyoirat — Magy Kem Foly
Magyar Kemiai Folyoirat — Magy Kem Folyoirat
Magyar Kemikusok Lapja — Mag Kem Lapja
Magyar Kemikusok Lapja — Magy Kem Lapja
Magyar Kemikusok Lapja — Magyar Kem Lapja
Magyar Kertesz (Budapest) — Magyar Kert Budapest
Magyar Kir. Szolo es Borgazdasagi Kozponti Kiserleti Allomas (Ampelologiai Intezet) Evkonyve — Mag Kir Szolo Borgazd Kozp Kiserl Allomas Ampelol Intez Evk
Magyar Kir. Szolo es Borgazdasagi Kozponti Kiserleti Allomas. Ampelologiai Intezet Evkonyve — Magy Kir Szolo Borgazd Kozp Kiserl Allomas Ampelol Intez Evk
Magyar Kiralyi Kerteszeti Akademia Koezlemenyei/Mitteilungen der Koeniglichen Ungarischen Gartenbau-Akademie/Bulletin. Academie Royale Hongroise d'Horticulture/Bulletin. Royal Hungarian Horticultural College — Magyar Kir Kert Akad Koezlem
Magyar Koenyvszemle — M Kszle
Magyar Koenyvszemle — Magy Koenyvszle
Magyar Koenyvszemle — Magyar Koenyvsz
Magyar Koenyvszemle — MK
Magyar Koezloeny — Magy Koezl
Magyar Kozlekedes. Mely es Vizepites — Mag Kozlekedes Mely Vizepites
Magyar Mernok es Epitesz Egylet Koezloenye — Mag Mern Epitesz Egylet Kozl
Magyar Mezoegazdasag — Magy Mezoegazd
Magyar Muzeum — M Muzeum
Magyar Muzeum — MM
Magyar Noeorvosok Lapja — Magy Noeorv Lap
Magyar Noeorvosok Lapja — Magy Noeorv Lapja
Magyar Noevenytani Lapok — Magyar Noevenyt Lapok
Magyar Numizmatikai Tarsulat Evkoenyve — Magyar Num Tars Ev
Magyar Nyelv — MNy
Magyar Nyelvjarasok — MNy
Magyar Nyelvjarasok — MNyj
Magyar Nyelvoer — M Nyor
Magyar Nyelvor — MagN
Magyar Nyelvor — MaNy
Magyar Nyelvor — Nyr
Magyar Onkologia — Magy Onkol
Magyar Orvosi Bibliografia — Magy Orv Bibliogr
Magyar Orvosok es Termeszetvizsgalok Nagy Gyuelesemek Munkalatai. Die Versammlung Ungarischer Aerzte und Naturforscher — Magyar Orv Termesz Nagy Gyuel Munk
Magyar Pszichologiai Szemle — Mag Psz Sz
Magyar Pszichologiai Szemle — Magy Pszichol Szle
Magyar Pszichologiai Szemle — Magyar Pszichol Szle
Magyar Pszichologiai Szemle — MPSZA
Magyar Radiologia — Magy Radiol
Magyar Reumatologia — Magy Reumatol
Magyar Sebeszet — Magy Sebesz
Magyar Textiltechnika [*Hungary*] — Magy Textiltech
Magyar Textiltechnika — Magyar Textiltech
Magyar Traumatologia, Orthopaedia, es Helyreallito-Sebeszet — Mag Traumatol Orthop Helyreallito Sebesz
Magyar Traumatologia, Orthopaedia, es Helyreallito-Sebeszet — Magy Traumatol Orthop
Magyar Traumatologia, Orthopaedia, es Helyreallito-Sebeszet — Magy Traumatol Orthop Helyreallito Sebesz
Magyar Traumatologia, Ortopedia, Kezsebeszet, Plasztikai Sebeszet — Magy Traumatol Ortop Kezseb Plasztikai Seb
Magyar Tudomany — M Tud
Magyar Tudomany — Magy Tud

Magyar Tudomanyos Akademia. 3. Osztalyanak Fizikai Kozlemenyei — Magy Tud Akad 3 Oszt Fiz Kozl
Magyar Tudomanyos Akademia. 5 Otodik Orvosi Tudomanyok Osztalyanak Koezlemenyei — Mag Tud Akad 5 Otodik Orv Tud Oszt Kozl
Magyar Tudomanyos Akademia. Acta Historiae Artium — Acta Hist Art
Magyar Tudomanyos Akademia. Agrartudomanyok Osztalyanak Koezlemenyei — Mag Tud Akad Agrartud Oszt Kozl
Magyar Tudomanyos Akademia. Agrartudomanyok Osztalyanak Koezlemenyei — Magy Tud Akad Agrartud Osztal Kozl
Magyar Tudomanyos Akademia Almanachja — Ak Alm
Magyar Tudomanyos Akademia Almanachja — Akad Alm
Magyar Tudomanyos Akademia Atommag Kutato Intezet. Kozlemenyek — Magy Tud Akad Atommag Kut Intez Kozl
Magyar Tudomanyos Akademia Biologiai Csoportjanak Koezlemenyei — Magyar Tud Akad Biol Csoport Koezlem
Magyar Tudomanyos Akademia. Biologiai Csoportjanak Koezlemenyei (Budapest) — Magy Tud Akad Biol Csoportjanak Kozlem (Budapest)
Magyar Tudomanyos Akademia. Biologiai es Orvosi Tudomanyok Osztalyanak Koezlemenyei — Magy Tud Akad Biol Orv Tud Oszt Kozl
Magyar Tudomanyos Akademia. Biologiai Osztalyanak Koezlemenyei — Magy Tudom Akad Biol Osztal Kozl
Magyar Tudomanyos Akademia. Biologiai Tudomanyok Osztalyanak Koezlemenyei — Mag Tud Akad Biol Tud Oszt Kozl
Magyar Tudomanyos Akademia. Biologiai Tudomanyok Osztalyanak Koezlemenyei — Magy Tud Akad Biol Tud Oszt Koezl
Magyar Tudomanyos Akademia Filozofiai es Tortenettudomanyi. Osztalyanak Koezlemenyei — Magy Tud Osz Koez
Magyar Tudomanyos Akademia Filozofiai es Tortenettudomanyi. Osztalyanak Koezlemenyei — MTA
Magyar Tudomanyos Akademia Filozofiai es Tortenettudomanyi. Osztalyanak Koezlemenyei — MTAFTO
Magyar Tudomanyos Akademia Filozofiai es Tortenettudomanyi. Osztalyanak Koezlemenyei — MTAFTOK
Magyar Tudomanyos Akademia Filozofiai es Tortenettudomanyi. Osztalyanak Koezlemenyei — MTAII Oszt Koezl
Magyar Tudomanyos Akademia Filozofiai es Tortenettudomanyi. Osztalyanak Koezlemenyei — MTAK
Magyar Tudomanyos Akademia. Filozofiai-Torteneti Osztalyanak Koezlemenyei — Magyar Tud Akad Filoz-Tort Oszt Kozlem
Magyar Tudomanyos Akademia. Kemiai Tudomanyok Osztalyanak Koezlemenyei — Mag Tud Akad Kem Tud Oszt Kozl
Magyar Tudomanyos Akademia. Kemiai Tudomanyok Osztalyanak Koezlemenyei [*Hungary*] — Magy Tud Akad Kem Tud Oszt Kozlem
Magyar Tudomanyos Akademia. Kemiai Tudomanyok Osztalyanak Koezlemenyei — MGTOA
Magyar Tudomanyos Akademia. Kozponti Fizikai Kutato Intezetenek Koezlemenyei — Mag Tud Akad Kozp Fiz Kut Intez Kozl
Magyar Tudomanyos Akademia Kozponti Fizikai Kutato Intezetenek Kozlemenyei — Magy Tud Akad Kozp Fiz Kut Intez Kozl
Magyar Tudomanyos Akademia. Kozponti Kemiai Kutato Intezetenek Koezlemenyei — Mag Tud Akad Kozp Kem Intez Kozl
Magyar Tudomanyos Akademia. Matematikai es Fizikai Tudomanyok Osztalyanak Koezlemenyei — Mag Tud Akad Mat Fiz Tud Oszt Kozl
Magyar Tudomanyos Akademia. Matematikai es Fizikai Tudomanyok Osztalyanak Koezlemenyei [*Hungary*] — Magy Tud Akad Mat Fiz Tud Oszt Kozlem
Magyar Tudomanyos Akademia. Matematikai es Fizikai Tudomanyok Osztalyanak Koezlemenyei — Magyar Tud Akad Mat Fiz Oszt Koezl
Magyar Tudomanyos Akademia. Matematikai Kutato Intezetenek Koezlemenyei [*Hungary*] — Magy Tud Akad Mat Kut Intez Kozlem
Magyar Tudomanyos Akademia. Mueszaki Fizikai Kutato Intezetenek Koezlemenyei — Magy Tud Akad Muesz Fiz Kut Intez Koezl
Magyar Tudomanyos Akademia. Mueszaki Tudomanyok Osztalyanak Koezlemenyei — Mag Tud Akad Musz Tud Oszt Kozl
Magyar Tudomanyos Akademia. Mueszaki Tudomanyok Osztalyanak Koezlemenyei [*Hungary*] — Magy Tud Akad Muszaki Tud Oszt Kozlem
Magyar Tudomanyos Akademia Nyelv es Irodalomtudomanyi Osztalyanak Koezlemenyei — MTA Nyelv Irod OK
Magyar Tudomanyos Akademia Nyelv es Irodalomtudomanyi Osztalyanak Koezlemenyei — MTAI Oszt Koezl
Magyar Tudomanyos Akademia Nyelv es Irodalomtudomanyi Osztalyanak Koezlemenyei — MTANIOK
Magyar Tudomanyos Akademia. Nyelv-es Irodalomtudomanyi Osztalyanak. Koezlemenyei — MTA
Magyar Tudomanyos Akademia. Nyelv-es Irodalomtudomanyi Osztalyanak. Koezlemenyei — MTAK
Magyar Tudomanyos Akademia Regeszeti Intezetenek Koezlemenyei — Magy Tud Int Koez
Magyar Tudomanyos Akademia Regeszeti Intezetenek Koezlemenyei — MAI
Magyar Tudomanyos Akademia. Tihanyi Biologiai Kutatointezet Evkoenyve — Magy Tud Akad Tihanyi Biol Kutatointez Evk
Magyar Tudomanyos Akademia Tihanyi Biologiai Kutatointezetenek Evkoenyve. Annales Instituti Biologici Tihany Hungaricae Academiae Scientiarum — Magyar Tud Akad Tihanyi Biol Kutatoint Evk
Magyar Tudomanyos Akademia. Veszpremi Akademiai Bizottsaganak Ertesitoje [*Hungary*] — Magy Tud Akad Veszpremi Akad Bizottsaganak Ert
Magyar Villamos Muevek Troeszt Koezlemenyei — Magy Villamos Muevek Troeszt Koezl
Magyarorszag Allatvilaga — Magyarorsz Allatvilaga
Magyarorszag Kulturfloraja — Magy Kult
Magyarorszag Kulturfloraja — Magy Kulturfloraja
Magyarorszag Regeszeti Topografiaja — MRT
Magyarorszag Viragtalan Noeveneinek Meghatarozo Kezikoenyve — Magyarorsz Viragtalan Noeven Meghat Kezikoenyve
Magyarorzag Bortermeszteset 's Kesziteset Targyazo Folyoiras/Z Weinbau Weinbereitung Ungarn. Z Weinbau Weinbereitung Ungarn Siebenbuergen — Magyarorsz Borterm Keszit Targyazo Folyoir
Maha-Bohdi and the United Buddhist World — MBUBW
Maharaja Sajajirao. University of Baroda. Oriental Institute Journal — MSUBOIJ
Maharaja Sayajirao Memorial Lectures — Maharaja Sayajirao Mem Lect
Maharaja Sayajirao University of Baroda. Oriental Institute. Journal — MSUB
Maharashtra Cooperative Quarterly — Maharashtra Coop Q
Maharashtra Cooperative Quarterly — Maharastra Coop Quart
Maharashtra Medical Journal — Mah Med J
Maharastra Sahitya Parisad Patrika — MSPP
Mahatma Phule Agricultural University. Research Journal — Mahatma Phule Agric Univ Res J
Mail on Sunday — MS
Main Currents in Modern Thought — Main Curr M
Main Currents in Modern Thought — Main Curr Mod Thought
Main Currents in Modern Thought — MCMT
Main Group Chemistry — Main Group Chem
Main Roads — Main Rds
Mainake Estudios de Arqueologia Malaguena — MEAM
Maine Agricultural Experiment Station. Abstracts of Recent Publications — Maine Agric Exp Sta Abstr Recent Publ
Maine. Agricultural Experiment Station. Bulletin — Maine Agric Exp Stn Bull
Maine Agricultural Experiment Station. Mimeographed Report — Maine Agric Exp Sta Mimeogr Rep
Maine. Agricultural Experiment Station. Miscellaneous Publication — Maine Agric Exp Stn Misc Publ
Maine. Agricultural Experiment Station. Miscellaneous Report — Maine Agric Exp Stn Misc Rep
Maine. Agricultural Experiment Station. Official Inspections — Maine Agric Exp Stn Off Inspect
Maine. Agricultural Experiment Station. Official Inspections — Maine Agric Exp Stn Official Inspect
Maine. Agricultural Experiment Station. Publications — Maine Ag Exp
Maine. Agricultural Experiment Station. Technical Bulletin — Maine Agric Exp Stn Tech Bull
Maine. Basic-Data Reports. Ground-Water Series — Maine Basic Data Rep Ground Water Ser
Maine. Board of Agriculture. Annual Report — ME Bd Agr An Rp
Maine. Department of Agriculture. Quarterly Bulletin — Maine Ag Dept B
Maine Department of Marine Resources. Fisheries Bulletin — Maine Dept Mar Res Fish Bull
Maine Department of Marine Resources. Fisheries Circulars — Maine Dept Mar Res Fish Circ
Maine Department of Marine Resources. Research Bulletin — Maine Dept Mar Res Res Bull
Maine Farm Research — Maine Farm Res
Maine Farm Research — ME Fm Res
Maine Field Naturalist — Maine Field Nat
Maine. Geological Survey. Special Economic Series — Maine Geol Surv Spec Econ Ser
Maine. Geological Survey. Special Economic Studies Series. Bulletin — Maine Geol Surv Spec Econ Stud Ser Bull
Maine Geology — Maine Geol
Maine Historical Society. Collections — Maine Hist Soc Coll
Maine Historical Society. Collections — ME His S
Maine Law Review — Maine L R
Maine Law Review — Maine L Rev
Maine Law Review — ME L Rev
Maine Legislative Service — Me Legis Serv
Maine Library Association. Bulletin — Maine Lib Assn Bul
Maine Life Magazine — Maine Life Mag
Maine. Life Sciences and Agricultural Experiment Station. Bulletin — Maine Life Sci Agric Exp Stn Bull
Maine. Life Sciences and Agricultural Experiment Station. Official Inspections — Maine Life Sci Agric Exp Stn Off Inspect
Maine. Life Sciences and Agricultural Experiment Station. Technical Bulletin [*A publication*] — Maine Life Agric Exp Stn Tech Bull
Maine. Life Sciences and Agricultural Experiment Station. Technical Bulletin [*A publication*] — Maine Life Sci Agric Exp Stn Tech Bull
Maine Potato Yearbook — Maine Potato Yearb
Maine Reports — ME
Maine Revised Statutes Annotated — Me Rev Stat Ann
Maine State Bar Association. Proceedings — Maine State Bar Assn Proc
Maine. State Water Storage Commission. Annual Report — ME St Water Storage Comm An Rp
Maine. Technology Experiment Station. Bulletin. Papers — Maine Technology Expt Sta Bull Paper
Maine. Technology Experiment Station. University of Maine. Paper — Maine Technol Exp Stn Univ Maine Pap
Mainfraenkisches Jahrbuch fuer Geschichte und Kunst — M Jb
Mainfraenkisches Jahrbuch fuer Geschichte und Kunst — Mainfr Jb
Mainfraenkisches Jahrbuch fuer Geschichte und Kunst — Mainfraenk Jahrb
Mainfraenkisches Jahrbuch fuer Geschichte und Kunst — Mainfraenk Jb Gesch Kunst
Mainfraenkisches Jahrbuch fuer Geschichte und Kunst — MJGK
Maintenance Engineering — Maint Eng
Maintenance Engineering (London) — Maint Eng (London)
Maintenance Management International — Maint Mgmt Internat
Maintenance Management International — MMI
Maintenant — Maint
Mainzer Geowissenschaftliche Mitteilungen — Mainzer Geowiss Mitt
Mainzer Naturwissenschaftliches Archiv — Mainzer Naturwiss Arch
Mainzer Philosophische Forschungen — Ma PF
Mainzer Reihe — MR

Mainzer Romanistische Arbeiten — MRA
Mainzer Studien zur Amerikanistik — MSzA
Mainzer Zeitschrift — Mainz Z
Mainzer Zeitschrift — Mainz Zs
Mainzer Zeitschrift — Mainzer Zeitschr
Mainzer Zeitschrift — MZ
Mainzer Zeitschrift — Mz Zts
Maipu, Chile. Estacion Experimental Agronomica. Boletin Tecnico — Maipu Chile Estac Exp Agron Bol Tec
Mairena — MA
Maison-Dieu — MD
Maitland Mercury — MM
Maitre Phonetique — MaitrePhon
Maitre Phonetique — MP
Maitre Phonetique — MPh
Maitre Phonetique — MPhon
Maitres de la Spiritualite Chretienne — MSC
Maitres Spirituels — Mait Sp
Maize — MAE
Maize for Biological Research [*Monograph*] — Maize Biol Res
Maize Genetics Cooperation. News Letter — Maize Genet Coop News Lett
Majalah Batan — Maj Batan
Majalah Demografi Indonesia — Maj Demog Indo
Majalah Farmasi Indonesia — Maj Farm Indones
Majalah Kedokteran Surabaya — Majalah Kedokt Surabaya
Majallah. Daneshgah- e Tehran. Daneshkade- ye Darusazi — Maj Daneshgah e Tehran Daneshkade ye Darusazi
Majallat al-Majma al-Limi al-Iraqi — MMLI
Majallat Kulliyat al-Adab, al-Iskandariyyah — MKAI
Majallat Majma al-Lughah al-Arabiyah [*Cairo*] — MMLA
Majalle(H)-Ye Daneshkade(H)-Ye Adabiyyat Va Olun-E Ensanie-Ye (Tehran) — MDA (Tehran)
Majalle(H)-Ye Daneshkade(H)-Ye Adabiyyat-E Mashhad — MDAM
Major American Universities Ph.D. Qualifying Questions and Solutions — Major Amer Univ PhD Qualif Questions Solut
Major Appliance Industry Facts Book. Association of Home Appliance Manufacturers — AHAM Facts
Major Biogeochemical Cycles and Their Interactions — Major Biogeochem Cycles Their Interact
Major Companies of the Arab World — MCAW
Major Hazard Incident Data Service [*Database*] — MHIDAS
Major Problems in Clinical Pediatrics — Major Probl Clin Pediatr
Major Problems in Clinical Surgery — Major Probl Clin Surg
Major Problems in Internal Medicine — Major Probl Intern Med
Major Problems in Internal Medicine — MJIMB
Major Problems in Obstetrics and Gynecology — Major Probl Obstet Gynecol
Major Problems in Pathology — Major Probl Pathol
Majority Report — Majority
Makedonika [*Thessalonike*] — Mak
Makedonika — Maked
Makedonika [*Thessalonike*]. Paratema — Mak P
Makedonska Akademija na Naukite i Umetnostite Oddelenie za Matematichki-Tehnichki Nauki. Prilozi — Makedon Akad Nauk Umet Oddel Mat-Tehn Nauk Prilozi
Makedonska Akademija na Naukite i Umetnostite Oddelenie za Prirodo-Matematicki Nauki Prilozi — Makedon Akad Nauk Umet Oddel Prirod-Mat Nauk Prilozi
Makedonski Folklor — Maked Folkl
Makedonski Folklor — MF
Makedonski Jazik — MJ
Makedonski Medicinski Pregled — Maked Med Pregl
Makedonski Medicinski Pregled — Makedon Med Pregl
Makedonski Pregled — Ma P
Makerere Historical Journal — Makerere Hist J
Makerere Historical Journal — Makerere Hist Jnl
Makerere Journal — Makerere J
Makerere Journal — MJ
Makerere Law Journal — Mak LJ
Makerere Law Journal — Makerere LJ
Makerere Law Journal — MLJ
Makerere Medical Journal — Makerere Med J
Making Films in New York — Mak F NY
Making Music — Making Mus
Makromolekulare Chemie — Makr Ch
Makromolekulare Chemie — Makrom Chem
Makromolekulare Chemie — Makromol Chem
Makromolekulare Chemie. Rapid Communications — Makromol Chem Rapid Commun
Makromolekulare Chemie. Supplement — Makromol Chem Suppl
Makromolekulare Chemie. Theory and Simulations — Makromol Chem Theory Simul
Makromolekuly na Granitse Razdela Faz — Makromol Granitse Razdela Faz
Maktab-i-Tasiju' — Mak Tas
Mal Kwa Kul [*Speech and Language*] — MKK
Malacologia. International Journal of Malacology — Malacol Int J Malacol
Malacological Review — Malacol Rev
Malacological Society of Australia. Journal — Malacol Soc Aust J
Malacological Society of London. Proceedings — Malacol Soc L Pr
Malacological Society of London. Proceedings — Malacolog Soc London Proc
Malagasy. Rapport Annuel du Service Geologique — Malagasy Rapp Annu Serv Geol
Malahat Review — Mal R
Malahat Review — Malahat Rev
Malahat Review — MalaR
Malahat Review — MHRev
Malaja Sovetskaja Enciklopedija — MSE
Malakologische Abhandlungen (Dresden) — Malakol Abh (Dres)
Malaria e Malattie dei Paesi Caldi (Roma) — Malaria (Roma)
Malaria. International Archives (Leipzig) — Malaria Internat Arch (Leipzig)
Malattie Cardiovascolari — Mal Cardiovasc
Malattie da Infezione — Mal Infez
Malawi. Annual Report of the Department of Agriculture — Malawi Annu Rep Dep Agric
Malawi. Department of Agriculture and Fisheries. Annual Report. Fisheries Research. Part 2 — Malawi Dep Agric Fish Annu Rep Fish Part 2
Malawi Forest Research Institute. Research Record — Malawi For Res Inst Res Rec
Malawi. Geological Survey Department. Bulletin — Malawi Geol Surv Dep Bull
Malawi. Geological Survey Department. Memoir — Malawi Geol Surv Dep Mem
Malawi Journal of Science and Technology — Malawi J Sci Technol
Malawi National Bibliography — Malawi Nat Bib
Malawi News — MN
Malawian Geographer — Malawian Geogr
Malay Report on Forest Administration — Malay Rep For Admin
Malaya. Department of Agriculture. Bulletin — Malay Dep Agric Bull
Malaya. Department of Agriculture. Bulletin — Malaya Dep Agric Bull
Malaya. Forest Research Institute. Research Pamphlet — Malaya For Res Inst Res Pam
Malaya. Geological Survey Department. Memoir — Malaya Geol Surv Dep Mem
Malaya Law Review — Mal Law R
Malaya Law Review — Malaya L Rev
Malaya Law Review — Malaya Law R
Malaya Law Review — Malaya LR
Malayan Agricultural Journal — Malay Agric J
Malayan Agricultural Journal — Malayan Ag J
Malayan Agricultural Journal — Malayan Agr J
Malayan Agricultural Journal — Malayan Agric J
Malayan Economic Review — Mal Econ R
Malayan Economic Review — Mala Econ R
Malayan Economic Review — Malayan Econ R
Malayan Economic Review — Malayan Econ Rev
Malayan Economic Review — MER
Malayan Forest Records — Malay For Rec
Malayan Forester — Malay For
Malayan Garden Plants — Malayan Gard Pl
Malayan Historical Journal — MHJ
Malayan Journal of Tropical Geography — Malayan J Tr Geog
Malayan Journal of Tropical Geography — Malayan J Trop Geogr
Malayan Journal of Tropical Geography — MJTG
Malayan Law Journal — Mal LJ
Malayan Law Journal — Malayan LJ
Malayan Law Journal — MLJ
Malayan Law Journal. Supplement — MLJ Supp
Malayan Library Journal — Malayan Lib J
Malayan Nature Journal — Malay Nat J
Malayan Pharmaceutical Journal — Mal Pharm J
Malayan Science Bulletin — Malayan Sci Bull
Malayan Tin and Rubber Journal — Malay Tin Rubber J
Malaysia. Annual Report. Institute for Medical Research — Malays Annu Rep Inst Med Res
Malaysia. Borneo Region. Annual Report of the Geological Survey — Malays Borneo Reg Annu Rep Geol Surv
Malaysia. Division of Agriculture. Bulletin — Malays Div Agric Bull
Malaysia. Forest Research Institute. Kepong Research Pamphlet — Malays For Res Inst Kepong Res Pam
Malaysia. Geological Survey. Annual Report — Malays Geol Surv Annu Rep
Malaysia. Geological Survey. Borneo Region. Annual Report — Malays Geol Surv Borneo Reg Annu Rep
Malaysia. Geological Survey. Borneo Region. Bulletin — Malays Geol Surv Borneo Reg Bull
Malaysia. Geological Survey. Borneo Region. Memoir — Malays Geol Surv Borneo Reg Mem
Malaysia. Geological Survey. Borneo Region. Report — Malays Geol Surv Borneo Reg Rep
Malaysia. Geological Survey. District Memoir — Malays Geol Surv Dist Mem
Malaysia. Geological Survey. Map Bulletin — Malays Geol Surv Map Bull
Malaysia. Geological Survey. Report — Malays Geol Surv Rep
Malaysia in History — Mal Hist
Malaysia in History — Malaysia Hist
Malaysia Industrial Digest — MLT
Malaysia Institiut Penylidikan Perubatan Lapuran Tahunan — Malays Inst Penylidikan Perubatan Lapuran Tahunan
Malaysia Institute for Medical Research. Annual Report — Malays Inst Med Res Annu Rep
Malaysia. Ministry of Agriculture and Co-Operatives. Bulletin — Malays Minist Agric Co-Op Bull
Malaysia. Ministry of Agriculture and Fisheries. Bulletin — Malays Minist Agric Fish Bull
Malaysia. Ministry of Agriculture and Lands. Bulletin — Malays Minist Agric Lands Bull
Malaysia. Ministry of Agriculture and Lands. Technical Leaflet — Malays Minist Agric Lands Tech Leafl
Malaysia. Ministry of Agriculture and Rural Development. Bulletin — Malays Minist Agric Rural Dev Bull
Malaysia. Ministry of Agriculture and Rural Development. Fisheries Bulletin [*A publication*] — Malays Minist Agric Rural Dev Fish Bull
Malaysia. Ministry of Agriculture and Rural Development. Risalah Penerangan — Malays Minist Agric Rural Dev Risalah Penerangan
Malaysia. Ministry of Agriculture and Rural Development. Risalah Penerangan [*A publication*] — RPMDDQ

Malaysia. Ministry of Agriculture. Technical Leaflet — Malays Minist Agric Tech Leafl
Malaysia. Ministry of Agriculture. Technical Leaflet — TLMMDD
Malaysia. Ministry of Lands and Mines. Annual Report of the Geological Survey of Malaysia — Malays Minist Lands Mines Annu Rep Geol Surv Malays
Malaysia. Report on Forest Administration in West Malaysia [*Malaysia. Penyata Tahunan Perhutanan Di-Malaysia Barat Tahun*] — Malays Rep For Admin West Malaysia
Malaysia. Report on Forest Administration in West Malaysia [*Malaysia. Penyata Tahunan Perhutanan Di-Malaysia Barat Tahun*] — MRFWA4
Malaysian Agricultural Journal — Malays Agric J
Malaysian Agricultural Research — Malaysian Agric Res
Malaysian Applied Biology — Malays Appl Bio
Malaysian Applied Biology/Biologi Gunaan Malaysia — Malays Appl Biol Biol Gunaan Malays
Malaysian Business — MBM
Malaysian Forester — Malays For
Malaysian Journal of Education — Malay J Ed
Malaysian Journal of Pathology — Malays J Pathol
Malaysian Journal of Reproductive Health — Malays J Reprod Health
Malaysian Journal of Science — Malays J Sci
Malaysian Journal of Science. Series A. Life Sciences — Malays J Sci Ser A
Malaysian Journal of Science. Series B. Physical and Earth Sciences — Malays J Sci Ser B
Malaysian Rubber Developments — Mal Rub Dv
Malaysian Rubber Review — Mal Rub R
Malaysian Rubber Review — Malaysian Rubb Rev
Malaysian Veterinary Journal — Malays Vet J
Malaysian Veterinary Journal — MVEJDP
Malcolm Lowry Newsletter — M L New
Malerei und Zeichnung der Griechen — Mu Z
Malerei und Zeichnung der Griechen — MZ
Malerei und Zeichnung der Klassischen Antike — MZ
Malgache Republique. Annales Geologiques de Madagascar — Malgache Repub Ann Geol Madagascar
Malgache Republique. Rapport Annuel. Service Geologique — Malgache Repub Rapp Annu Serv Geol
Malignant Hyperthermia. Current Concepts — Malig Hyperthermia Curr Concepts
Mal-i-Mic News. Metis and Non-Statute Indians in New Brunswick [*Canada*] — MLMN
Mallee Horticulture Digest — Mallee Hort Dig
Mallee Horticulture Digest — Mallee Hortic Dig
Malmoehus Laens Hushallningssaellskaps Kvartallsskrift — Malmohus Lans Hushallningssallsk Kvartallsskr
Malone Society. Reprints — MSR
Malpractice Digest — Malpract Dig
Malt Research Institute. Publication — Malt Res Inst Publ
Malta Guidelines for Progress Development Plan, 1980-1985 — Malta Plan
Maltese Folklore Review [*Balzan*] — MFR
Malting, Brewing, and Allied Processes — Malting Brew Allied Processes
Malvern Physics Series — Malvern Phys Ser
Mammal Review — Mammal Rev
Mammal Review — MMLRAI
Mammalia — MAMLAN
Mammalia Depicta — Mamm Depicta
Mammalia Depicta — MMDPB7
Mammalia Depicta. Beihefte zur Zeitschrift fuer Saeugetierkunde — Mamm Depicta Beih Z Saeugetierkd
Mammalia. Morphologie, Biologie, Systematique des Mammiferes — Mamm
Mammalian Cell Culture — Mamm Cell Cult
Mammalian Genome — Mamm Genome
Mammalian Reproduction — Mamm Reprod
Mammalian Species — Mamm Species
Mammalian Species — MLNSBP
Mammalogical Informations — Mammal Inf
Mammalogical Informations — STKMBC
Man — MN
Man — PMAN
Man: A Monthly Record of Anthropological Science — Man Mon Rec Anthropol Sci
Man: A Monthly Record of Anthropological Science — MANAAT
Man and His Environment — Man His Environ
Man and Medicine — Man Med
Man and Medicine — MMEDDC
Man and Nature — Man Nat
Man and Nature — MNNTB8
MAN [*Maschinenfabrik Augsburg-Nuernberg*] **Forschen, Planen, Bauen** — MAN Forsch Planen Bauen
Man in Community — MiC
Man in India — Man Ind
Man in India — MANIAJ
Man in India — MI
Man in India — MII
Man. Journal of the Royal Anthropological Institute — Man J R Anthropol Inst
Man (London) — ML
MAN [*Maschinenfabrik Augsburg-Nuernberg*] **Research, Engineering, Manufacturing** [*A publication*] — MAN Res Eng Manuf
Man/Society/Technology — Man/Soc/Tech
Manage — MAN
Managed Accounts Report — MAR
Management — Manag
Management — MNGMD
Management Abstracts — MA
Management Abstracts — Manage Abstr
Management Accounting — CCL
Management Accounting — M Accounting
Management Accounting — MAA
Management Accounting — MAC
Management Accounting — Manage Account
Management Accounting — Mgmt Acct
Management Accounting — Mgt Accounting
Management Accounting — Mgt Acct
Management Accounting — MMA
Management Accounting — NAC
Management Adviser — Manage Advis
Management Adviser — Mgt Adviser
Management and Marketing Abstracts — Manage Market Abstr
Management and Marketing Abstracts [*Database*] — MMA
Management Assessment of Peat as an Energy Resource. Executive Conference Proceedings — Manage Assess Peat Energy Resour Exec Conf Proc
Management by Objectives — Manag Objectives
Management by Objectives — Manage Objectives
Management Contents — Manage Contents
Management Contents [*Database*] — MC
Management Controls — Manage Controls
Management Controls — Mgt Controls
Management Datamatics — Manage Datamatics
Management Decision — Manage Decis
Management Decision — MDE
Management Decision — Mgmt Dec
Management Decision — Mgt Decision
Management Decision — Mngmt Dec
Management Decision — MTD
Management Digest — Management D
Management e Informatica — Manage e Inf
Management, Education, and Development — Mgt Educ & Dev
Management Experten-Nachweis [*Database*] — MANEX
Management Facetten — BAX
Management Focus — MAN
Management Focus — Manage Focus
Management Focus — Mgmt Focus
Management Focus — Mgt Focus
Management in Government — Manage Gov
Management in Government — Mgmt in Govt
Management in Government — Mgt in Govt
Management in Government — MIG
Management in Government — OMB
Management in Printing — Mgmt Printing
Management Index — Manage Index
Management Index — MI
Management Informatics — Manage Inf
Management Information Service Report — Mgt Info Service Rept
Management Information Services — Management Inf Serv
Management Information Systems — Manage Inf Syst
Management Information Systems Quarterly — Manage Inf Syst Q
Management Information Systems Quarterly — MIS
Management International Review — Manag Int R
Management International Review — Manage Int Rev
Management International Review — Mgt Int R
Management International Review — Mgt Internat R
Management International Review — MIR
Management International Review — MUY
Management Japan — Manag Japan
Management Japan — MJP
Management Methods — Mgt Methods
Management. New Zealand Institute of Management — Management NZ
Management News — Manage News
Management of Information Analysis Centers. Proceedings. Forum — Manage Inf Anal Cent Proc Forum
Management of Uncontrolled Hazardous Waste Sites — Manage Uncontrolled Hazard Waste Sites
Management of World Waste — Wld Wast
Management Practice — Mgmt Prac
Management Quarterly — Mgt Q
Management Quarterly — MMQ
Management Quarterly — MQU
Management Record — Mgt Rec
Management Research — Manage Res
Management Research News — Mgmt Res News
Management Review — Manage Rev
Management Review — Mgmt Rev
Management Review — Mgt R
Management Review — MRE
Management Review and Digest — Manage Rev Dig
Management Review and Digest — Mgmt Rev Dig
Management Review and Digest — MR & D
Management Science — Man Sci
Management Science — Manag Sci
Management Science — Manage Sci
Management Science — Management Sci
Management Science — Mgmt Sci
Management Science — MGQ
Management Science — Mgt Sci
Management Science — MSC
Management Science. Series A. Theory — Manag Sci A
Management Science. Series B. Application — Manag Sci B
Management Services — Manage Serv
Management Services — Management Servs
Management Services — Mgmt Serv

Management Services — Mgt Ser
Management Services — Mgt Services
Management Services in Government — Manage Serv Gov
Management Services in Government — Mgmt Serv Govt
Management Services in Government — Mgt Services in Govt
Management Team — MTM
Management Technology — MMT
Management Today — IDI
Management Today — Manag Today
Management Today — Manage Today
Management Today — Mangt Today
Management Today — Mgmt Today
Management Today — Mgt Today
Management Today — MT
Management Today — MTO
Management Totaal — OEF
Management World — Manage World
Management World — Mgmt World
Management World — Mgt World
Management World — MWL
Management Zeitschrift — IOR
Management's Bibliographic Data — Management's Bibliog Data
Management-Zeitschrift [*Switzerland*] — MGZ
Manager Magazin [*Germany*] — MAMAD
Manager Magazin — Man Mag
Manager Magazin — MMG
Manager Magazin — MRF
Managerial and Decision Economics — Managerial and Decision Econ
Managerial and Decision Economics [*England*] — Managerial Decis Econ
Managerial Finance — Managerial Fin
Managerial Finance — MFI
Managerial Planning — Manage Plann
Managerial Planning — Manage Plng
Managerial Planning — Managerial Plan
Managerial Planning — Mgrl Plan
Managerial Planning — MPL
Manager's Magazine — MAG
Manager's Magazine — MAZ
Managing — MAA
Managing — MAG
Managing the Modern Laboratory — Managing Mod Lab
Manchester Association of Engineers. Transactions — Manchester Assoc Eng Trans
Manchester Cuneiform Studies — Mc St
Manchester Cuneiform Studies — MCS
Manchester Evening News — MN
Manchester Geological Society. Transactions — Manchester G Soc Tr
Manchester Guardian — MG
Manchester Guardian (Manchester) — MGM
Manchester Guardian Weekly — Manch Guard
Manchester Guardian Weekly — MGW
Manchester Literary and Philosophical Society. Memoirs and Proceedings — Manch Lit Phil Soc Mem Proc
Manchester Literary and Philosophical Society. Memoirs and Proceedings — Manchester Lit Ph Soc Mem
Manchester Literary and Philosophical Society. Memoirs and Proceedings — Manchester Lit Phil Soc Mem Proc
Manchester Literary Club. Papers — Manch
Manchester Medical Gazette — Manch Med Gaz
Manchester Medical Gazette [*England*] — Manchester Med Gaz
Manchester Mining Society. Transactions — Manchester M Soc Tr
Manchester Quarterly — Man Q
Manchester Quarterly — Manch Q
Manchester Review — Manchester Rev
Manchester Review — Manchr Rev
Manchester Review — ManR
Manchester School of Economic and Social Studies — Manchester
Manchester School of Economic and Social Studies — Manchester Sch Econ Soc Stud
Manchester School of Economic and Social Studies — Manchester School
Manchester School of Economic and Social Studies — MS
Manchester School of Economic and Social Studies — MSESS
Manchester School of Economic and Social Studies — MSL
Manchester School of Economic and Social Studies — PMSE
Manchester Unity Oddfellows' Magazine — MU Oddfellows Mag
Manchester University. Medical School. Gazette — Manch Univ Med Sch Gaz
Mandaeische Grammatik — MG
Mandens Blad — MB
Mandschrift voor Kindergeneeskunde — Mandschr Kindergeneeskd
Manedsskrift foer Praktisk Laegegerning — Manedsskr Prakt Laegegern
Man-Environment Systems — MENS
Manganese Dioxide Symposium. Proceedings — Manganese Dioxide Symp Proc
Manganese Literature Review — Manganese Lit Rev
Manganese Nodules. Dimensions and Perspectives — Manganese Nodules Dimens Perspect
Manhattan — Manhat
Manitoba Association of Confluent Education. Journal — MACEJ
Manitoba Association of Resource Teachers. Journal — MART J
Manitoba Association of School Trustees. Journal — MAST J
Manitoba Bar News — Man B New
Manitoba Bar News — Man Bar News
Manitoba Business — MAN
Manitoba Business — Manitoba B
Manitoba Co-Operator — Manit CoOp
Manitoba Counsellor — Man Couns
Manitoba. Department of Mines and Natural Resources. Mines Branch. Publication — Manit Dep Mines Nat Resour Mines Branch Publ
Manitoba. Department of Mines and Natural Resources. Mines Branch. Publication — Manitoba Dep Mines Natur Resour Mines Br Publ
Manitoba. Department of Mines and Natural Resources. Mines Branch. Publication — MMNPAM
Manitoba. Department of Mines, Natural Resources, and Environment. Wildlife Research MS Reports [*Canada*] — MMNRW
Manitoba. Department of Natural Resources. Library Service Manuscripts [*Canada*] — MNRLSM
Manitoba. Department of Renewable Resources and Transportation Services. Research Branch. Reports [*Canada*] — MRRTS
Manitoba Educational Research Council. Research Bulletins — Man Ed Res C Res B
Manitoba Elementary Teachers' Association. Journal — META J
Manitoba Entomologist — Manit Entomol
Manitoba Entomologist — Manitoba Ent
Manitoba Entomologist — MNEMA9
Manitoba Geographical Series [*Canada*] — MNGS
Manitoba Home Economics Teachers' Association. Journal — MHETA J
Manitoba Law Journal — Man L J
Manitoba Law Journal — Mani LJ
Manitoba Law Journal — Manitoba LJ
Manitoba Law Journal — MLJ
Manitoba Law School. Journal — Man LSJ
Manitoba Math Teacher — Man Math T
Manitoba Medical Review — Manit Med Rev
Manitoba Metis Federation News [*Canada*] — MMFN
Manitoba Modern Language Journal — Man MLJ
Manitoba Music Educator — Man Mus Ed
Manitoba Nature — MANADW
Manitoba Nature — Manit Nat
Manitoba Nature [*Canada*] — MNNA
Manitoba Physical Education Teachers' Association. Journal — MPETA J
Manitoba Reports [*Database*] — MANR
Manitoba School Library Audio-Visual Association. Journal — MSLAVA J
Manitoba Science Teacher — Man Sci Teach
Manitoba Social Science Teacher — Man Soc Sci T
Manitoba Spectra — Man Spectra
Manitoba Teacher — Man Teach
Manizales (Colombia) — MSC
Mankato State College [*later Mankato State University*] **Studies** — MSCS
Mankind — M
Mankind — Man
Mankind — PMNK
Mankind Monographs — Mankind Monogr
Mankind Monographs — MNKMA5
Mankind Quarterly — Mankind Q
Mankind Quarterly — Mankind Quart
Mankind Quarterly — MaQ
Mankind Quarterly — MKQUA4
Man-Made Textiles in India — Man-Made T
Mannesmann Forschungsberichte — Mannesmann Forschungsber
Mannichfaltigkeiten aus dem Gebiete der Literatur, Kunst, und Natur — Mannichfaltigk Lit
Mannus. Zeitschrift fuer Vorgeschichte — Man
Mannus-Buecherei — Man B
Manpower and Applied Psychology — Manp App Psychol
Manpower and Unemployment Research in Africa: A Newsletter — Manpower Unempl Res Afr
Manpower and Unemployment Research in Africa. Newsletter — Manpower Unemployment Res Afr Newsl
Manpower Journal — Manpower J
Mansfelder Blaetter — MansBl
Manson Memorial Lecture — Man ML
Mansoura Science Bulletin — Mansoura Sci Bull
Mansoura Science Bulletin. A. Chemistry — Mansoura Sci Bull A Chem
Mantech Analysis — Mantech Anal
ManTech Journal. US Army — ManTech
ManTech Journal. US Army — ManTech J
Mantova Medica — Mant Med
Manual Arts Bulletin for Teachers in Secondary Schools — Manual Arts Bul
Manual. California Agricultural Experiment Station — Manual Calif Agr Exp Sta
Manual Farmaceutico — Man Farm
Manual. Instituto Forestal (Santiago De Chile) — Manual Inst For (Chile)
Manual of the Textile Industry of Canada — Man Text Ind Can
Manual Training Magazine [*Peoria, IL*] — Man Tr
Manual Training Magazine — Manual Train
Manual. University of California. Agricultural Extension Service — Man Univ Calif Agric Ext Serv
Manuale di Eteo Geroglifico — Man EG
Manuales y Textos Universitarios. Ciencias — Man Textos Univ Cienc
Manuali del Pensiere Cattolico — MPC
Manuali per l'Universita — Man Univ
Manuel d'Archeologie Egyptienne — VMAE
Manuel des Questions Actuelles — MQA
Manuels et Precis de Theologie — MPT
Manuels Informatiques Masson — Manuels Inform Masson
Manufacture — Mfr
Manufactured Milk Products Journal — Manuf Milk Prod J
Manufactured Milk Products Journal — MMPJAE
Manufacturer — Manufact
Manufacturers' Bulletin — Manuf Bul
Manufacturers Hanover Economic Report — MHE
Manufacturers Hanover Trust Co. Financial Digest — MHT Financ

Manufacturers' Monthly — Manuf Mo
Manufacturers' Monthly — Manuf Mon
Manufacturers' Monthly — MM
Manufacturers' Record — Manuf Rec
Manufacturing — Mfg
Manufacturing and Management — Manuf & Management
Manufacturing and Materials Management — Manuf Mat Manage
Manufacturing Applications of Lasers — Manuf Appl Lasers
Manufacturing Chemist [*England*] — Manuf Chem
Manufacturing Chemist — Manuf Chemist
Manufacturing Chemist — MCHMDI
Manufacturing Chemist — Mfg Chem
Manufacturing Chemist and Aerosol News — Manuf Ch Ae
Manufacturing Chemist and Aerosol News — Manuf Chem
Manufacturing Chemist and Aerosol News — Mfg Chem Aerosol News
Manufacturing Chemist and Aerosol News — MfrChemAer
Manufacturing Chemist and Pharmaceutical and Fine Chemical Trade Journal — Man Chem
Manufacturing Chemist, Incorporating Chemical Age — MFC
Manufacturing Chemists' Association. Chemical Safety Data Sheet — Manuf Chem Assoc Chem Saf Data Sheet
Manufacturing Confectioner — Manuf Confect
Manufacturing Engineering — Manuf Eng
Manufacturing Engineering — Mfg Eng
Manufacturing Engineering — MFGEB
Manufacturing Engineering and Management [*Later, Manufacturing Engineering*] — Manuf Eng & Mgt
Manufacturing Engineering and Management [*Later, Manufacturing Engineering*] — Manuf Eng Manage
Manufacturing Engineering and Management [*Later, Manufacturing Engineering*] — MFEMA
Manufacturing Engineering and Management [*Later, Manufacturing Engineering*] — Mfg Eng Manage
Manufacturing Engineering Transactions — Manf Eng Trans
Manufacturing Industries — Manuf Ind
Manufacturing Industries — Manufacturing Ind
Manufacturing Industry — Manufact Ind
Manufacturing Management — Manuf Manage
Manufacturing Perfumer — Manuf Perfum
Manufacturing Resource Planning — Manuf Res Plann
Manufacturing Systems — MFS
Manufacturing Technology Horizons — Manuf Technol Horiz
Manufacturing Technology Horizons — Mfg Tech H
Manufacturing Week — Manuf Week
Manuscript Dissertation — MS Diss
Manuscript Report. McGill University (Montreal). Marine Sciences Centre — Manuscr Rep McGill Univ (Montreal) Mar Sci Cent
Manuscripta — Man
Manuscripta — Manuscr
Manuscripta Geodaetica — Manuscr Geod
Manuscripta Mathematica — Manusc Math
Manuscripta Mathematica — Manuscripta Math
Manuscripts — M
Manuscripts — MSS
Manusia dan Masharakat — MDM
Manx Journal of Agriculture — Manx J Agr
Manx Journal of Agriculture — Manx J Agric
Many-Body Problem. Proceedings. Mallorca International School of Physics — Many Body Probl Proc Mallorca Int Sch Phys
Map Reader — Map Read
Maple Syrup Digest — Maple Syrup Dig
Maquinas & Metais — Maquinas
Mar del Sur — Mar
Mar del Sur — MS
Mar del Sur (Lima) — Mar Sur Lima
Mar y Pesca — MPESA7
Marathwada University. Journal of Science — Marathwada Univ J Sci
Marathwada University. Journal of Science — MUNSDM
Marathwada University. Journal of Science. Section A. Physical Sciences — Marathwada Univ J Sci Sect A Phys Sci
Marathwada University. Journal of Science. Section A. Physical Sciences — MUJSAX
Marathwada University. Journal of Science. Section B. Biological Sciences — Marathwada Univ J Sci Sect B Biol Sci
Marathwada University. Journal of Science. Section B. Biological Sciences — MUJSBY
Marbacher Magazin — Mar M
Marburger Akademische Reden — M Ak R
Marburger Beitraege zur Germanistik — MBG
Marburger Geographische Schriften — Marb Geogr Schr
Marburger Jahrbuch fuer Kunstwissenschaft — Marb Jb
Marburger Jahrbuch fuer Kunstwissenschaft — Marb Jb Kunstwiss
Marburger Jahrbuch fuer Kunstwissenschaft — Marb Jb Kw
Marburger Ostforschungen — MOstf
Marburger Studien zur Aelteren Deutschen Geschichte — MSAeDG
Marburger Theologische Studien — M Th St
Marburger Universitaetsreden — MUR
Marburger Winckelmann-Programm — Marb W Pr
Marburger Winckelmann-Programm — Marb Winck Prog
Marburger Winckelmann-Programm — MWP
Marburger Winckelmann-Programm — MWPr
Marcellia — MRCLBP
March — MR
March of Dimes Birth Defects Foundation. Birth Defects Original Article Series — March Dimes Birth Defects Found Birth Defects Orig Artic Ser
March of India — Mar I
March of India — March India
March of India — Mo I
Marche. L'Hebdomadaire du Dirigeant — MCG
Marche Romane — MR
Marche Romane — MRo
Marche Romane — MRom
Marche Romane. Cahiers de l'ARULg. Association des Romanistes de l'Universite de Liege — Marche Romane
Marches Tropicaux et Mediterraneens — MarTropMed
Marches Tropicaux et Mediterraneens — MCO
Marches Tropicaux et Mediterraneens — MTM
Marching Band Director — MBD
Marconi Instrumentation — Marconi Instrum
Marconi Review — Marconi Rev
MARDATA [*Maritime Data Network*] **Ship Casualty Library** [*Database*] — SC
MARDATA [*Maritime Data Network*] **Ship Library** [*Database*] — SL
MARDATA [*Maritime Data Network*] **Ship Movement Library** [*Database*] — SM
MARDATA [*Maritime Data Network*] **Ships-on-Order Library** [*Database*] — SO
Mare Balticum — MB
Mare Balticum — MBal
Marginalia Dermatologica — Marginalia Dermatol
Maria et Ecclesia — Me E
Marian Library Studies — Marian Libr Stud
Marian Library Studies — MLS
Marian Studies — Mar St
Marian Studies — Marian Stds
Marian Studies [*New York*] — MarS
Marianne Moore Newsletter — Mar Moore N
Marianne Moore Newsletter — MMN
Marianum — Mar
Mariiskii Gosudarstvennyi Pedagogiceskii Institut. Ucenye Zapiski — Mari Gos Ped Inst Ucen Zap
Marina Italiana — Marina Ital
Marine Affairs Journal — Marine Aff Jnl
Marine and Freshwater Research — Mar Freshwater Res
Marine and Petroleum Geology — Mar Pet Geol
Marine Behaviour and Physiology — Mar Behav and Physiol
Marine Behaviour and Physiology — Mar Behav Physiol
Marine Behaviour and Physiology — MBPHAX
Marine Biological Association Journal — Marine Biol Assoc J
Marine Biological Association of India. Journal — Mar Biol Assoc India J
Marine Biological Association of the United Kingdom. Journal — Marine Biol Assn UK J
Marine Biology — Marine Bio
Marine Biology [*Berlin*] — MBIOAJ
Marine Biology [*New York*] — MRBOAS
Marine Biology (Berlin) — Mar Biol (Berl)
Marine Biology. International Journal of Life in Oceans and Coastal Waters [*A publication*] — Mar Biol
Marine Biology Letters — Mar Biol Lett
Marine Biology Letters — MBLED
Marine Biology Letters — MBLED7
Marine Biology (New York) — Mar Biol (NY)
Marine Biology (Vladivostok) — Mar Biol (Vladivostok)
Marine Chemistry — Mar Chem
Marine Chemistry — MRCHB
Marine Chemistry — MRCHBD
Marine Chemistry (Netherlands) — Mar Chem (Neth)
Marine Coatings Conference. Proceedings — Mar Coat Conf Proc
Marine Corps Gazette — Mar Crp G
Marine Corrosion on Offshore Structures. Papers Presented. Symposium — Mar Corros Offshore Struct Pap Symp
Marine Ecology. Progress Series — Mar Ecol Prog Ser
Marine Ecology. Progress Series — MESEDT
Marine Ecology. Pubblicazioni della Stazione Zoologica di Napoli. I — MAECDR
Marine Ecology (Pubblicazioni Stazione Zoologica di Napoli. I) — Mar Ecol (Pubbl Stn Zool Napoli I)
Marine Engineer and Naval Architect — Mar Eng Nav Architect
Marine Engineering [*Japan*] — Mar Eng
Marine Engineering — Marine Eng
Marine Engineering/Log — Mar Eng
Marine Engineering/Log — Mar Eng/Log
Marine Engineering/Log — Mar Engng/Log
Marine Engineering/Log — Marine Eng/Log
Marine Engineering/Log — Mr Eng/Log
Marine Engineering/Log. Catalog and Buyer's Guide — Mar Eng Cat
Marine Engineering/Log. Yearbook and Maritime Review — Mar Eng Yrb
Marine Engineers Journal — Mar Engrs J
Marine Engineers Review — Mar Eng Rev
Marine Engineers Review — Mar Engrs Rev
Marine Engineers Review — MRERB
Marine Environmental Research — Mar Environ Res
Marine Environmental Research — MERSDW
Marine Fisheries Abstracts — Mar Fish Abstr
Marine Fisheries Review — MAFR
Marine Fisheries Review — Mar Fish Re
Marine Fisheries Review — Marine Fisheries R
Marine Food Chains. Proceedings. Symposium — Mar Food Chains Proc Symp
Marine Forest Review — Maine For Rev
Marine Geology — Mar Geol
Marine Geophysical Researches — Mar Geophys Res
Marine Geotechnology — Mar Geotech
Marine Geotechnology — Mar Geotechnol

Marine Geotechnology — Marine Geotech
Marine Geotechnology — Marine Geotechnol
Marine Geotechnology — MRGTAY
Marine Invertebrates of Scandinavia — MAISBP
Marine Invertebrates of Scandinavia — Mar Invertebr Scand
Marine Mammal Science — MAMS
Marine Mammal Science — Mar Mamm Sci
Marine Mammal Science — MMSCEC
Marine Marchande — Marine March
Marine Micropaleontology — MAMIDH
Marine Micropaleontology — Mar Micropaleontol
Marine Mining — Mar Min
Marine Mining — Mar Mining
Marine Mining — MARMDK
Marine News — Mar News
Marine Observer — MAOB
Marine Observer — Mar Obs
Marine Policy [*England*] — Mar Policy
Marine Policy and Management [*England*] — Mar Policy Manage
Marine Policy. The International Journal of Ocean Affairs — MPO
Marine Pollution Bulletin — Mar Pollut Bull
Marine Pollution Bulletin — MPNBAZ
Marine Pollution Research Titles [*Plymouth*] — Mar Pollut Res Titles
Marine Products Month/Shui Ch'an Yueeh K'an (Fu Kan) — Mar Prod Month
Marine Research. Department of Agriculture and Fisheries for Scotland — Mar Res Dep Agric Fish Scotl
Marine Research. Department of Agriculture and Fisheries for Scotland — MARRDZ
Marine Research in Indonesia — Mar Res Indones
Marine Research in Indonesia — MRINAQ
Marine Research Laboratory. Educational Series (St. Petersburg, Florida) — Mar Res Lab Educ Ser (St Petersburg FL)
Marine Research Laboratory. Investigational Report [*South-West Africa*] — MRLAA2
Marine Research Laboratory. Investigational Report (South-West Africa) — Mar Res Lab Invest Rep (S-W Afr)
Marine Research Laboratory. Professional Papers Series (St. Petersburg, Florida) — Mar Res Lab Prof Pap Ser (St Petersburg Florida)
Marine Research Laboratory. Special Scientific Report (St. Petersburg, Florida) — Mar Res Lab Spec Sci Rep (St Petersburg FL)
Marine Research Laboratory. Technical Series (St. Petersburg, Florida) — Mar Res Lab Tech Ser (St Petersburg FL)
Marine Research Series. Scottish Home Department — Mar Res Ser Scott Home Dep
Marine Research Series. Scottish Home Department — MRSHAO
Marine Science [*New York*] — MARSD4
Marine Science Communications — Mar Sci Commun
Marine Science Contents Tables — Mar Sci Cont Tab
Marine Science Contents Tables — Mar Sci Contents Tables
Marine Science Contents Tables — MSCT
Marine Science (New York) — Mar Sci (NY)
Marine Sciences Branch. Manuscript Report Series. Canada Department of Energy, Mines, and Resources — MSBMRS
Marine Sciences Centre. Manuscript Report. McGill University (Montreal) — Mar Sci Cent Manuscr Rep McGill Univ (Montreal)
Marine Sciences. Comtex — Mar Sci Comtex
Marine Sciences Instrumentation — Mar Sci Instrum
Marine Sciences Research Center [*Stony Brook*]. Special Report — SRMBDB
Marine Sciences Research Center. Special Report (Stony Brook) — Mar Sci Res Cent Spec Rep (Stony Brook)
Marine Sciences Research Center (Stony Brook). Technical Report — Mar Sci Res Cent (Stony Brook) Tech Rep
Marine Sciences Research Center [*Stony Brook*]. Technical Report — NYTRAH
Marine Studies of San Pedro Bay, California — Mar Stud San Pedro Bay Calif
Marine Studies of San Pedro Bay, California — MSBCD2
Marine Technology — Mar Technol
Marine Technology Series [*Elsevier Book Series*] — MTS
Marine Technology Society. Annual Conference. Preprints — Mar Technol Soc Annu Conf Prepr
Marine Technology Society. Annual Conference. Preprints — MTCPCI
Marine Technology Society. Annual Conference. Proceedings — Mar Technol Soc Annu Conf Proc
Marine Technology Society. Journal — Mar Tech S J
Marine Technology Society. Journal — Mar Technol Soc J
Marine Technology Society. Journal — Marine Tech Soc J
Marine Technology Society. Journal — MTSJBB
Marine Week — Mar Week
Marine Week — MRWKA
Marine Zoologist — Mar Zool
Marine Zoologist — MAZOAT
Mariner's Mirror — Mar Mirror
Mariner's Mirror — Mariner Mir
Mariner's Mirror — Mariners Mir
Mariner's Mirror — MM
Mariner's Mirror — MMr
Marine-Rundschau — Mar Rd
Marine-Rundschau — Marine Rdsch
Marine-Rundschau — MR
Marine-Verordnungsblatt — Marineverordgsbl
Mariologische Studien — M St
Mariologische Studien — Mariol St
Marion County Medical Society. Bulletin [*Indiana*] — Marion County Med Soc Bull
Marisia. Muzeul Judetean Mures — Mar Muz Jud Mur
Marisia. Muzeul Judetean Mures — MMJM
Marisia Studii si Materiale Arheologice. Istorie. Etnografie — Marisia
Maritime Defence. The Journal of International Naval Technology — Mar D Int
Maritime Industries. Massachusetts Institute of Technology — MAIN
Maritime Law Association of Australia and New Zealand. Newsletter — MLAANZ Newsletter
Maritime Law Book Key Number Data Base — MLB
Maritime Lawyer — Mar Law
Maritime Policy and Management — Marit Policy & Manage
Maritime Research Information Service [*Database*] — MRIS
Maritime Sediments [*Later, Maritime Sediments and Atlantic Geology*] — Marit Sediments
Maritime Sediments [*Later, Maritime Sediments and Atlantic Geology*] — MARSB2
Maritime Sediments and Atlantic Geology — Marit Sediments & Atl Geol
Maritime Sediments and Atlantic Geology — Marit Sediments Atl Geol
Maritime Sediments and Atlantic Geology — Maritime Sediments Atlantic Geol
Maritime Sediments and Atlantic Geology — MSAGD9
Maritimes — MRTMBB
Mark og Montre fra Sydvestjydske Museer — Mark og Montre
Mark Twain Journal — Mark
Mark Twain Journal — Mark Twain
Mark Twain Journal — MTJ
Mark Twain Quarterly — MTQ
Markenartikel. Zeitschrift fuer die Markenartikelindustrie — MAL
Market Adjusted Wood. New Approaches in Forestry and Sawmills. Elmia Wood 81 — Mark Adjust Wood
Market Analysis and Information Database — MAID
Market Bulletin. Florida Department of Agriculture — Market Bull
Market Grower's Journal — Mark Grow J
Market Grower's Journal — MGJOAP
Market Intelligence Europe — Market Intell Eur
Market Research Abstracts — Mark Res Abstr
Market Research Europe — EUS
Market Research Europe — Market Eur
Market Research Europe — MKE
Market Research Great Britain — MRR
Market Research Report — Market Res Rep
Market Review — Market Rev
Market Trends Digest — MTD
Marketing — M
Marketing — MAR
Marketing — MKTG
Marketing Advertising Research Newsletter — Market Adv Res Newsl
Marketing and Advertising General Information Centre [*Database*] — MAGIC
Marketing and Distribution Abstracts — MDA
Marketing and Distributive Education Today — Mktg and DE Today
Marketing and Distributive Educators' Digest — MDE Digest
Marketing and Media Decisions — Mark Media Decis
Marketing and Media Decisions — MED
Marketing and Media Decisions — Mkt & Media Decisions
Marketing and Media Decisions — Mktg Dec
Marketing and Media Decisions. Special Seasonal Edition — Mktg Dec S
Marketing Bulletin. US Department of Agriculture — Mark Bull US Dep Agric
Marketing Communications — Mark Commun
Marketing Communications — Market Com
Marketing Communications — MC
Marketing Communications — MCM
Marketing Communications Report — Market Comm Rep
Marketing Demonstration Leaflet. Ministry of Agriculture and Fisheries [*United Kingdom*] — Mktg Demonst Leafl Minist Agric
Marketing Educator's News — Mktg Educator's N
Marketing Guide. Ministry of Agriculture [*United Kingdom*] — Minist Agric Mktg Guide
Marketing in Europe — ME
Marketing in Europe — MEX
Marketing in Europe — Mktg Eur
Marketing in Hungary — Mark Hung
Marketing in Hungary — MHU
Marketing in Hungary — Mktg Hung
Marketing in Ungarn — Mktg Ungarn
[*The*] **Marketing Information Guide** — Mkt Inform Guide
[*The*] **Marketing Information Guide** — TMIG
Marketing Insights — MI
Marketing Intelligence and Planning — MIP
Marketing Journal — Market J
Marketing Journal — MJL
Marketing Leaflet. Ministry of Agriculture and Fisheries [*United Kingdom*] — Mktg Leafl Minist Agric
Marketing Magazine — Marketing
Marketing Mix — Mark Mix
Marketing News — Mark News
Marketing News — Mktg News
Marketing News — MNW
Marketing Research Report. United States Department of Agriculture — Mark Res Rep US Dep Agric
Marketing Research Report. United States Department of Agriculture — Marketing Res Rep USDA
Marketing Review — Mktg Revw
Marketing Science — MKS
Marketing Series. Agricultural Marketing Adviser (India) — Marketing Ser Agr Marketing Adv (India)
Marketing Times — MKT
Marketing Times — Mktg Times
Marketing Times — MTM
Marketing (United Kingdom) — Mktg (UK)
Marketing Week — Mktg Week
Marketing Week — MKTW

Marketing. Zeitschrift fuer Forschung und Praxis — MRK
Markeur. Marketing Magazine voor Universiteit en Bedrijfsleven — MAR
Markgraefler Jahrbuch — Markgr Jb
Markham Review — Markham R
Markham Review — Markham Rev
Markham Review — MarkR
Markov Processes and Related Fields — Markov Process Related Fields
Marktforschung — GFM
Marktforschung — MRKTD
Marmara Universitesi Eczacilik Dergisi — Marmara Univ Eczacilik Derg
Maroc Antique — MA
Maroc Medical — Mar Med
Maroc Medical — Maroc Med
Maroc. Service Geologique. Notes et Memoires du Service Geologique — Maroc Serv Geol Notes Mem Serv Geol
Marquette Business Review — Marquette Bus R
Marquette Business Review — Marquette Busin R
Marquette Geologists Association. Bulletin — Marquette Geologists Assoc Bull
Marquette Law Review — Marq L Rev
Marquette Law Review — Marq LR
Marquette Law Review — Marquette L Rev
Marquette Law Review — Marquette Law R
Marquette Law Review — Mq L
Marquette Law Review — Mq LR
Marquette Slavic Studies — Marquette Slav Stud
Marquette University. Slavic Institute. Papers — MUSIP
Marquis Who's Who [*Database*] — MWW
Marriage and Family Living — Marr Fam Liv
Marriage and Family Living — Marriage
Marriage and Family Review — MAFR
Marriage and Family Review — Marriage Fam Rev
Marriage and Family Review — PMFR
Marseille Chirurgical — Mars Chir
Marseille Medical — Marseille Med
Mart Magazine — Mart
Martin Centre for Architectural and Urban Studies. Transactions — Martin Centre for Archtl & Urban Studies Trans
Martin Centre for Architectural and Urban Studies. Transactions — Martin Ctr Archit Urban Stud
Martin Classical Lectures — MCL
Martinsreid Institute for Protein Sequence Data [*Database*] — MIPS
Martinus Nijhoff Philosophy Library — Martinus Nijhoff Philos Lib
Marvel Science Fiction — MSF
Marvel Science Stories — MSS
Marvel Tales — MT
Marxism Today — Ma T
Marxism Today — Marx Td
Marxism Today — MT
Marxist Quarterly — Marxist Quar
Marxistische Blaetter — Marx Bl
Marxistische Blaetter fuer Probleme der Gesellschaft — Marxist Blaet Probl Ges
Marxistische Blaetter fuer Probleme der Gesellschaft, Wirtschaft, und Politik — Marxistische Bl
Maryland Academy of Sciences. Bulletin — MD Acad Sci Bull
Maryland Academy of Sciences. Transactions — MD Ac Sc Tr
Maryland Agricultural College. Nature Study Bulletin — Maryland Agric Coll Nat Stud Bull
Maryland. Agricultural Experiment Station. Annual Report — Md Agric Exp Stn Annu Rep
Maryland. Agricultural Experiment Station. Bulletin — MD Agric Exp Stn Bull
Maryland Agricultural Experiment Station. Miscellaneous Publication — Maryland Agric Exp Sta Misc Publ
Maryland. Agricultural Experiment Station. MP — MD Agric Exp Stn MP
Maryland Agricultural Experiment Station. Popular Bulletin — Maryland Agric Exp Sta Popular Bull
Maryland. Agricultural Experiment Station. Publications — MD Ag Exp
Maryland Appellate Reports — Md App
Maryland Bar Journal — Mar BJ
Maryland Bar Journal — MD BJ
Maryland. Board of Natural Resources. Department of Geology, Mines, and Water Resources. Bulletin — Md Board Nat Resour Dep Geol Mines Water Resour Bull
Maryland. Bureau of Mines. Annual Report — MD Bur Mines Ann Rept
Maryland Conservationist — MD Conserv
Maryland. Department of Geology. Mines and Water Resources Bulletin — MD Dep Geol Mines Water Resour Bull
Maryland. Department of Geology. Mines and Water Resources Bulletin. County Reports — MD Dept Geology Mines and Water Res Bull County Rept
Maryland. Department of Natural Resources. Geological Survey. Information Circular — Md Dep Nat Resour Geol Surv Inf Circ
Maryland Energy Saver — MD Energy Saver
Maryland Entomologist — Md Entomol
Maryland. Geological Survey. Basic Data Report — MD Geol Surv Basic Data Rep
Maryland. Geological Survey. Bulletin — MD Geol Surv Bull
Maryland. Geological Survey. County Geologic Map — Maryland Geol Survey County Geol Map
Maryland. Geological Survey. Guidebook — MD Geol Surv Guideb
Maryland. Geological Survey. Information Circular — MD Geol Surv Inf Circ
Maryland. Geological Survey. Quadrangle Atlas — MD Geol Surv Quadrangle Atlas
Maryland. Geological Survey. Report of Investigations — Maryland Geol Survey Rept Inv
Maryland. Geological Survey. Report of Investigations — MD Geol Surv Rep Invest
Maryland. Geological Survey. Special Publication — MD G S Sp Pub
Maryland. Geological Survey. Water Resources Basic Data Report — Md Geol Surv Water Resour Basic Data Rep
Maryland Grapevine — Md Grapevine
Maryland Historian — Mah
Maryland Historian — MD Hist
Maryland Historical Magazine — MaH
Maryland Historical Magazine — Maryland Hist Mag
Maryland Historical Magazine — MD His M
Maryland Historical Magazine — MD Hist M
Maryland Historical Magazine — MD Hist Mag
Maryland Historical Magazine — MdHM
Maryland Historical Magazine — MHM
Maryland Historical Society. Fund-Publications — MD Hist Soc Fund-Publ
Maryland Law Forum — MD LF
Maryland Law Review — Mar L Rev
Maryland Law Review — Mary L Rev
Maryland Law Review — Maryland L Rev
Maryland Law Review — MD L Rev
Maryland Law Review — MD Law R
Maryland Law Review — MD LR
Maryland Libraries — MD Libr
Maryland Magazine — MD Mag
Maryland Medical Journal — Maryland Med J
Maryland Medical Journal — MD Med J
Maryland Music Educator — Ma
Maryland Naturalist — MD Nat
Maryland Naturalist — MD Naturalist
Maryland Nurse — MD Nurse
Maryland Pharmacist — MD Pharm
Maryland Poultryman — MD Poultryman
Maryland Poultryman. Cooperative Extension Service. University of Maryland — Md Poultryman Coop Ext Serv Univ Md
Maryland Psychiatric Quarterly — Mar Psyiat Q
Maryland Register — MD Reg
Maryland Reports — Md
Maryland Researcher — Maryland Res
Maryland State Medical Journal — Maryl St Med J
Maryland State Medical Journal — Maryl St MJ
Maryland State Medical Journal — Maryland MJ
Maryland State Medical Journal — MD State Med J
Maryland. University. Agricultural Experiment Station. Bulletin — Md Univ Agric Exp Stn Bull
Maryland. Water Resources Research Center. Technical Report — Md Water Resour Res Cent Tech Rep
Mary's Own Paper — MOP
Masalah Bangunan — MSBG-A
MASCA Journal. Museum Applied Science Center for Archaeology. University Museum [*Philadelphia*] — MASCA Journ
MASCA [*Museum Applied Science Center for Archaeology*] **Journal. University of Pennsylvania** — MASCA J
MASCA [*Museum Applied Science Center for Archaeology*] **Research Papers in Science and Archaeology** — MASCA Res Pap Sci Archaeol
Maschine und Werkzeung [*Germany*] — Masch Werkzeung
Maschinenbau der Betrich — Maschinenbau Betr
Maschinenbautechnik — Maschintec
Maschinenmarkt — MAX
Maschinenwelt Elektrotechnik — Masch Elektrotech
Mashinostroiteli dlya Khimicheskoi i Metalloobrabatyvayushchei Promyshlennosti — Mashinostroit Khim Metalloobrab Promsti
Mashiny i Apparaty Khimicheskoi Tekhnologii — Mash Appar Khim Tekhnol
Mashiny i Tekhnologiya Pererabotki Polimerov — Mash Tekhnol Pererab Polim
Masinnyj Perevod i Prikladnaja Lingvistika — MP i PL
Masinnyj Perevod i Prikladnaja Lingvistika — MPiKL
Masinnyj Perevod Trudy Instituta Tocnoj Mechaniki i Vycislitel Hoj Techniki Akademiy Nauk SSR — MP
Masino-Traktornaja Stancija — Mas Trakt St
Masinsko-Tehnicki Glasnik — Mas Teh Glas
Maske und Kothurn — Mask Koth
Maske und Kothurn — MuK
Maskinjournalen — Maskin J
Maslo Sapunena Promyshlennost — Maslo Sapunena Promst
Masloboino Zhirovaya Promyshlennost [*Later, Maslozhirovaya Promyshlennost*] — Masl Zhir Prom
Masloboino Zhirovaya Promyshlennost [*Later, Maslozhirovaya Promyshlennost*] — Maslob Zhir Promst
Masloboino Zhirovaya Promyshlennost [*Later, Maslozhirovaya Promyshlennost*] — Maslob Zhirov Prom
Masloboino Zhirovaya Promyshlennost — Maslob Zir Prom
Masloboino Zhirovoe Delo — Maslob Zhir Delo
Maslozhirovaya Promyshlennost [*Formerly, Masloboino Zhirovaya Promyshlennost*] — Maslo Zhir Promst
Masquerade — M
Mass Comm Review — PMCR
Mass Communications Review — MCR
Mass Education Bulletin — Mass Educ B
Mass Loss from Stars. Proceedings. Trieste Colloquium on Astrophysics — Mass Loss Stars Proc Trieste Colloq Astrophys
Mass Media Newsletter — Mass Med Newsl
Mass Production — Mass Prod
Mass Spectrometry Bulletin — Mass Spect Bull
Mass Spectrometry Bulletin [*England*] — Mass Spectrom Bull
Mass Spectrometry Bulletin [*Database*] — MSB
Mass Spectrometry New Instruments and Techniques — Mass Spectrom New Instrum Tech

Mass Spectrometry. Part A-B — Mass Spectrom Part A B
Mass Spectrometry Reviews — Mass Spectrom Rev
Mass Spectroscopy — Mass Spectrosc
Mass Transportation — Mass Transp
Massachusetts Agricultural Experiment Station. Biennial Report — Mass Agric Exp Sta Bienn Rep
Massachusetts Agricultural Experiment Station. Bulletin — Mass Agric Exp Stn Bull
Massachusetts Agricultural Experiment Station Bulletin. Circular — Mass Agric Exp Sta Bull Circ
Massachusetts Agricultural Experiment Station. Control Series. Bulletin — Mass Agric Exp Stn Control Ser Bull
Massachusetts Agricultural Experiment Station. Extension Service Publication — Mass Agric Exp Stn Ext Serv Publ
Massachusetts Agricultural Experiment Station. Monograph Series — Mass Agric Exp Stn Monogr Ser
Massachusetts Agricultural Experiment Station. Publications — Mass Ag Exp
Massachusetts Appeals Court Reports — Mass App Ct
Massachusetts Basic Data Report. Ground Water Series — Mass Basic Data Rep Ground Water Ser
Massachusetts CPA [*Certified Public Accountant*] **Review** — MCP
Massachusetts Dental Society. Journal — Mass Dent Soc J
Massachusetts Department of Natural Resources. Division of Marine Fisheries. Monographs Series — Mass Dep Nat Resour Div Mar Fish Monogr Ser
Massachusetts. Division of Marine Fisheries. Technical Series — Mass Div Mar Fish Tech Ser
Massachusetts Foreign Language Bulletin — MFLB
Massachusetts Fruit Growers' Association. Report of the Annual Meeting — Mass Fruit Grow Assoc Rep Annu Meet
Massachusetts General Laws Annotated (West) — Mass Gen Laws Ann (West)
Massachusetts Health Journal — Mass Hlth J
Massachusetts Historical Society. Collections — Mass Hist Soc Coll
Massachusetts Historical Society. Proceedings — Mass Hist Soc Proc
Massachusetts House of Representatives — Mass H R
Massachusetts Hydrologic Data Report — Mass Hydrol Data Rep
Massachusetts Institute of Technology. Abstracts of Theses — Mass Inst Technology Abs Theses
Massachusetts Institute of Technology and Woods Hole Oceanographic Institution. Papers — Mass Inst Technology and Woods Hole Oceanog Inst Paper
Massachusetts Institute of Technology. Department of Naval Architecture and Marine Engineering. Report — Mass Inst Tech Dep Nav Architect Mar Eng Rep
Massachusetts Institute of Technology. Fluid Mechanics Laboratory. Publication — Mass Inst Tech Fluid Mech Lab Publ
Massachusetts Institute of Technology. Fluid Mechanics Laboratory. Publication — MIT Fluid Mech Lab Publ
Massachusetts Institute of Technology. Research Laboratory of Electronics. Technical Report — Mass Inst Tech Res Lab Electron Tech Rep
Massachusetts Institute of Technology. Research Laboratory of Electronics. Technical Report — Mass Inst Technol Res Lab Electron Tech Rep
Massachusetts Institute of Technology. School of Engineering. Department of Civil Engineering. Hydrodynamics Laboratory. Report — Mass Inst Tech Dep Civ Eng Hydrodyn Lab Rep
Massachusetts Institute of Technology. School of Engineering. Department of Civil Engineering. Research in Earth Physics. Research Report — Mass Inst Tech Dep Civ Eng Res Earth Phys Res Rep
Massachusetts Institute of Technology. School of Engineering. Department of Civil Engineering. Soils Publication — Mass Inst Tech Dep Civ Eng Soils Publ
Massachusetts Institute of Technology. School of Engineering. Ralph M. Parsons Laboratory for Water Resources and Hydrodynamics. Report — MIT Ralph M Parsons Lab Water Resour Hydrodyn Rep
Massachusetts Law Quarterly — Mass L Q
Massachusetts Law Quarterly — MQ
Massachusetts Law Review — Mass L Rev
Massachusetts Law Review — Mass LR
Massachusetts Library Association. Bulletin — Mass Lib Assn Bul
Massachusetts Magazine — Mass M
Massachusetts Medical Journal — Mass Med J
Massachusetts Medicine — Mass Med
Massachusetts Music News — MM
Massachusetts Nurse — Mass Nurse
Massachusetts Quarterly Review — Mass Q
Massachusetts Register — Mass Reg
Massachusetts Reports — Mass
Massachusetts Researcher — Mass Res
Massachusetts Review — Mass R
Massachusetts Review — Mass Rev
Massachusetts Review — MR
Massachusetts Review — PMAR
Massachusetts State Board of Education — Mass St Bd Educ
Massachusetts Studies in English — Mass Stud E
Massachusetts Studies in English — Massachusetts Stud Engl
Massachusetts Studies in English — MSE
Massachusetts University. College of Food and Natural Resources. Agricultural Experiment Station. Research Bulletin — Mass Univ Coll Food Nat Resour Agric Exp Stn Res Bull
Massachusetts University. Department of Geology and Mineralogy. Special Department Publication — Mass Univ Dept Geology and Mineralogy Special Dept Pub
Massachusetts University. Department of Geology. Contribution — Mass Univ Dep Geol Contrib
Masses and Mainstream — MM
Masses Ouvrieres — Mass Ouvr
Masses Ouvrieres — Masses Ouvr
Massey Agricultural College. Dairyfarming Annual — Massey Agric Coll Dairyfarm Annu
Massey Agricultural College. Sheepfarming Annual — Massey Agric Coll Sheepfarm Annu
Massey-Ferguson Review — Massey-Ferguson R
Massimario Tributario — Mass Tribut
Massoobmennye Protsessy i Apparaty Khimicheskoi Tekhnologii — Massoobmennye Protsessy Appar Khim Tekhnol
Massoobmennye Protsessy Khimicheskoi Tekhnologii [*Former USSR*] — Massoobmennye Protsessy Khim Tekhnol
Massorah Magna — MG
Master Builder — Master Bldr
Master Carriers of New South Wales — Master Carriers NSW
Master Drawings — Mast Draw
Master Drawings — Master Draw
Master Painter of Australia — Master Painter Aust
Master Plumber of South Australia — Master Plumber of SA
Master Water Data Index [*Database*] — MWDI
Masterkey. Southwest Museum (Los Angeles, California) — MSMC
Masters Abstracts — MA
Masters Abstracts — MAb
Masters Abstracts — Masters Abstr
Masters in Art — Mast in Art
Masters in Music — Mast in Music
Masters of Modern Physics — Masters Modern Phys
Masyarakat Indonesia — Masya Indo
Matar'jaly da Vyvucen'nja Fleery i Fauny Belarusi/Beitraege zur Erforschung der Flora und Fauna Weissrusslands — Matarj Vyvuc Fleery Fauny Belarusi
Matej Bel University. Acta. Natural Science Series. Series Mathematics — Acta Univ Mathaei Belii Nat Sci Ser Ser Math
Matematica Aplicada e Computacional — Mat Apl Comput
Matematica Contemporanea — Mat Contemp
Matematica Ensenanza Universitaria [*Bogota*] — Mat Ensenanza Univ
Matematicas y Ensenanza — Mat Ensenanza
Matematiceskaja Fizika i Funkcional'nyi Analiz — Mat Fiz i Funkcional Anal
Matematiceskii Sbornik (Novaja Serija) — Mat Sb (NS)
Matematiceskii Sbornik (Tomsk) — Mat Sb (Tomsk)
Matematicheskaya Fizika i Nelineinaya Mekhanika — Mat Fiz Nelinein Mekh
Matematicheskaya Logika i ee Premeneniya — Mat Logika Primenen
Matematicheskie Issledovaniya — Mat Issled
Matematicheskie Metody dlya Issledovaniya Polimerov, Materialy Vsesoyuznogo Soveshehaniya — Mat Metody Issled Polim Mater Vses Soveshch
Matematicheskie Metody i Fiziko-Mekhanicheskie Polya — Mat Metody Fiz Mekh Polya
Matematicheskie Metody v Biologii, Trudy Respublikanskoi Konferentsii — Mat Metody Biol Tr Resp Konf
Matematicheskie Metody v Dinamike Kosmicheskikh Apparatov Akademiya Nauk SSSR Vychislitel'nyi Tsentr [*Former USSR*] — Mat Metody Din Kosm App Akad Nauk SSSR Vychisl Tsentr
Matematicheskie Metody v Khimii, Materialy Vsesoyuznoi Konferentsii — Mat Metody Khim Mater Vses Konf
Matematicheskie Problemy Geofiziki [*Former USSR*] — Mat Probl Geofiz
Matematicheskie Sbornik — Mat Sb
Matematicheskie Voprosy Kibernetiki i Vychislitel'noi Tekhniki — Mat Voprosy Kibernet Vychisl Tekhn
Matematicheskie Zametki — Mat Zametki
Matematicheskoe Modelirovanie i Elektricheskie Tsepi — Mat Model Elektr Tsepi
Matematicheskoe Modelirovanie i Teoriya Elektricheskikh Tsepei [*Former USSR*] — Mat Model Teor Elektr Tsepei
Matematicheskoe Modelirovanie. Rossiiskaya Akademiya Nauk — Mat Model
Matematichki Vesnik. Nova Seriya [*Yugoslavia*] — Mat Vesn Nova Ser
Matematicka Biblioteka — Mat Bibl
Matematicki Bilten — Mat Bilten
Matematicki Fakultet Univerzitetot Kiril i Metodij (Skopje). Godisen Zbornik [*A publication*] — Mat Fak Univ Kiril Metodij (Skopje) Godisen Zb
Matematicki Vesnik — Mat Vesnik
Matematicko Fizicki List za Ucenike Srednjih Skola — Mat Fiz List Ucenike Srednjih Sk
Matematicko-Fyzikalny Casopis — Mat Fyz Cas
Matematicko-Fyzikalny Casopis. Slovenskej Akademie Vied [*Czechoslovakia*] — Mat-Fyz Cas Slov Akad Vied
Matematicky Casopis — Mat Cas
Matematicky Casopis Slovenskej Akademie Vied — Mat Casopis Sloven Akad Vied
Matematika. Periodiceskii Sbornik Perevodov Inostrannyh Statei — Matematika Period Sb Perevodov Inostran Statei
Matematikai es Termeszettudomanyi Ertesitoe — Mat Termeszettud Ertes
Matematikai Lapok — Mat Lapok
Matematisk Tidsskrift — Mat T
Matematisk Tidsskrift — MT
Matematisk-fysiske Meddelelser. Det Kongelige Danske Videnskabernes Selskab — Mat Medd Danske Vid Selsk
Matematisk-Fysiske Meddelelser - Kongelige Danske Videnskabernes Selskab — Mat Fys Medd K Dan Vidensk Selsk
Matematisk-Fysiske Meddelelser. Kongelige Danske Videnskabernes Selskab — Mat-Fys Med
Matematisk-Fysiske Meddelelser. Kongelige Danske Videnskabernes Selskab — Mat-Fys Medd Dan Vidensk Selsk
Matematisk-Fysiske Meddelelser. Kongelige Danske Videnskabernes Selskab — Mat-Fys Medd Danske Vid Selsk
Matematyka dla Politechnik — Mat Politech
Matematyka, Fizyka, Astronomia — Mat Fiz Astron
Matematyka, Fizyka, Chemia — Mat Fiz Chem

Matematyka Stosowana — Mat Stos
Materia Medica Nordmark — Mater Med Nordmark
Materia Medica Polona — Mater Med Pol
Materia Therapeutica — Mater Ther
Material and Design — Mat Des
Material and Technik (Duebendorf, Switzerland) — Mater Tech Duebendorf Switz
Material Flow — Mater Flow
Material Handling Engineering — Mater Handl Eng
Material Handling Engineering — Matrl Hand
Material Handling Engineering Package/Material Handling Interaction. Special Issue — Material H
Material Management Journal and Review — Mater Manage J Rev
Material Reports. University Museum. University of Tokyo — Mater Rep Univ Mus Univ Tokyo
Material Safety Data Sheets [*Database*] — MSDS
Material Science and Engineering — Mater Sci and Eng
Material Sciences in Space. Proceedings. European Symposium on Material Sciences in Space — Mater Sci Space Proc Eur Symp
Material und Organismen — Mater Org
Material und Organismen — Mater Organ
Material und Organismen — Mater u Organ
Material und Organismen (Berlin) — Mater Org (Berl)
Material Yield and Improved Technology. A Summary. Proceedings. Conference on Forging — Mater Yield Improved Technol Summ Proc Conf Forg
Materialdienst des Konfessionskundlichen Institts — Md Kl
Materiale de Constructs (Bucharest) — Mater Constr (Bucharest)
Materiale de Istorie si Muzeografie — Mat Ist Muz
Materiale de Istorie si Muzeografie (Bucuresti) — Mat Ist Muz (Bucuresti)
Materiale Plastice — Mat Plast
Materiale Plastice (Bucharest) — Mater Plast (Bucharest)
Materiale Plastice ed Elastomeri — Mater Plast Elastomeri
Materiale Plastice, Elastomeri, Fibre Sintetice — Mater Plast Elastomeri Fibre Sint
Materiale si Cercetari Arheologice — M C Arh
Materiale si Cercetari Arheologice — MA
Materiale si Cercetari Arheologice — Mat Arh
Materiale si Cercetari Arheologice — Mat si Cerce Arh
Materiale si Cercetari Arheologice — Materiale
Materiale si Cercetari Arheologice — MCA
Materiales de Construccion (Madrid) — Mater Constr (Madrid)
Materiales en Marcha — MeM
Materiales Maquinaria y Metodos para la Construccion — Mater Maquinaria Metodos Constr
Materiali e Contributi per la Storia della Narrativa Greco-Latina — MCSN
Materiali e Discussioni per l'Analisi dei Testi Classici — Mat Testi Cl
Materiali per il Vocabolario Neosumerico — MVN
Materialien aus der Arbeitsmarkt und Berufsforschung — Mat AB
Materialien der Komission fuer Mineralogie und Geochemie. Karpato-Balkanische Geologische Assoziation — Mater Kom Mineral Geochem Karpato Balk Geol Assoz
Materialien des Internationalen Symposiums Biokybernetik — Mater Int Symp Biokybern
Materialien - Umweltbundesamt (Germany) — Mater Umweltbundesamt (Ger)
Materialien zur Bibelgeschichte und Religioesen Volkskunde des Mittelalters — MBGRV
Materialien zur Deutschen Literatur — MDL
Materialien zur Kunde des Buddhismus — MKB
Materialien zur Politischen Bildung — Mater Polit Bildung
Materialkundliche-Technische Reihe — Materialkd-Tech Reihe
Material'naia Kul'tura Tadzhikistana — Mat Kul't Tadzh
Material'no Tekhnicheskoe Snabzhenie [*Former USSR*] — Mater Tekh Snabzhenie
Materialovy Sbornik Statni Vyzkumny Ustav Materialu — Mater Sb Statni Vyzk Ustav Mater
Materialoznavie i Tekhnologiya (Sofia) [*Bulgaria*] — Mater Teknol (Sofia)
Materialpruefengsamt fuer das Bauwesen der Technischen Hochschule Muenchen. Bericht — Materpruefengsamt Bauw Tech Hochsch Muenchen Ber
Materialpruefung — Materialpruef
Materialpruefung/Materials Testing — Mater Pruef Mat Test
Materials and Components in Fossil Energy Applications — Mater Compon Fossil Energy Appl
Materials and Components Newsletter — Mater Compon Newsl
Materials and Contamination Control. Papers Presented. Symposium — Mater Contam Control Pap Symp
Materials and Corrosion — Mater Corros
Materials and Design (Surrey) — Mater Des (Surrey)
Materials and Molecular Research Division. Newsletter [*United States*] — Mater Mol Res Div Newsl
Materials and Process Technology — Mater Process Technol
Materials and Processes for Microelectronic Systems — Mater Processes Microelectron Syst
Materials and Society — Mater Soc
Materials and Structures — Mater Struct
Materials and Structures — Mats Struct
Materials Associated with Direct Energy Conversion. Proceedings. Symposium — Mater Assoc Direct Energy Convers Proc Symp
Materials at High Temperatures — Mater High Temp
Materials Australasia — Mater Australas
Materials Business File [*Database*] — MBF
Materials Characterization — Mater Charact
Materials Characterization by Thermomechanical Analysis — Mater Charact Thermomech Anal
Materials Characterization for Systems Performance and Reliability — Mater Charact Syst Perform Reliab
Materials Chemistry — Mater Chem
Materials Chemistry and Physics — Mater Chem and Phys
Materials Chemistry and Physics — MCP
Materials Engineering — Mat Engng
Materials Engineering — Mater Eng
Materials Engineering — Materials Eng
Materials Engineering — Matrl Eng
Materials Engineering — MTA
Materials Engineering (Cleveland) — Mater Eng (Cleveland)
Materials Evaluation — Mat Eval
Materials Evaluation — Mater Eval
Materials Evaluation — Mater Evaluation
Materials Evaluation — Materials Eval
Materials for Mechanical Engineering — Mater Mech Eng
Materials for the Assyrian Dictionary — MAD
Materials for the Sumerian Lexicon — MSL
Materials Forum — Mater Forum
Materials Handling and Management — Mater Handl Mgmt
Materials Handling and Packaging — MHP
Materials Handling and Storage — Mater Handl & Storage
Materials Handling in Pyrometallurgy. Proceedings. International Symposium — Mater Handl Pyrometall Proc Int Symp
Materials Handling News — Mater Handl News
Materials Handling News — MEH
Materials in Design Engineering — Mater Des Eng
Materials in Engineering (Surrey) — Mater Eng (Surrey)
Materials Journal. SAMPE [*Society for the Advancement of Material and Process Engineering*] **Quarterly** — Mater J SAMPE Quart
Materials Letters — Mater Lett
Materials Life — Mater Life
Materials News International — Mat News Int
Materials Performance — Mater Perf
Materials Performance — Mater Perform
Materials Performance — Mater Performance
Materials Performance — Matrl Perf
Materials Performance — Mats Perf
Materials Performance Maintenance. Proceedings. International Symposium — Mater Perform Maint Proc Int Symp
Materials Processing. Theory and Practices — Mater Process Theory Pract
Materials Processing. Theory and Practices [*Elsevier Book Series*] — MPTP
Materials Protection [*Later, Materials Performance*] — Mater Prot
Materials Protection and Performance [*Later, Materials Performance*] — Mater Prot Perform
Materials Protection and Performance [*Later, Materials Performance*] — Mater Prot Performance
Materials Protection (Wuhan, People's Republic of China) — Mater Prot Wuhan Peoples Repub China
Materials Reclamation Weekly — Mats Reclam Wkly
Materials Reclamation Weekly — WTW
Materials Research and Standards — Mater Res and Stand
Materials Research and Standards — Mater Res Stand
Materials Research Bulletin — Mater Res Bull
Materials Research Bulletin. Special Issue — Mater Res Bull Spec Issue
Materials Research in AECL [*Atomic Energy of Canada Limited*] — Mater Res AECL
Materials Research in Atomic Energy of Canada Limited — Mater Res At Energy Can Ltd
Materials Research Laboratory. Technical Note. MRL-TN (Australia) — Mater Res Lab Tech Note MRL TN Aust
Materials Research Laboratory Technical Report. MRL-TR — Mater Res Lab Tech Rep MRL TR
Materials Research Society. Symposia. Proceedings — Mater Res Soc Symp Proc
Materials Research Society. Symposia. Proceedings [*Elsevier Book Series*] — MRS
Materials Research Society. Symposia. Proceedings — MRSPD
Materials Science [*Poland*] — Mater Sci
Materials Science — Matls Sci
Materials Science and Engineering — Mater Sci E
Materials Science and Engineering — Mater Sci Eng
Materials Science and Engineering. A. Structural Materials. Properties, Microstructure, and Processing — Mater Sci Eng A
Materials Science and Engineering. A. Structural Materials. Properties, Microstructure, and Processing — Mater Sci Eng A Struct Mater
Materials Science and Engineering. B. Solid State Materials for Advanced Technology — Mater Sci Eng B Solid State Mater
Materials Science and Physics of Non-Conventional Energy Sources — Mater Sci Phys Non Conv Energy Sources
Materials Science and Technology — Mater Sci T
Materials Science and Technology (Sofia) — Mater Sci Technol (Sofia)
Materials Science in Energy Technology — Mater Sci Energy Technol
Materials Science Monographs — Mater Sci Monogr
Materials Science Monographs [*Elsevier Book Series*] — MSM
Materials Science of Concrete — Mater Sci Concr
Materials Science of High Temperature Polymers for Microelectronics. Symposium — Mater Sci High Temp Polym Microelectron Symp
Materials Science Reports — Mater Sci Rep
Materials Science Research — Mater Sci Res
Materials Science Research International — Mater Sci Res Int
Materials Science Research Studies Series — Mat Sci Res Stud Ser
Materials Symposium. National SAMPE [*Society for the Advancement of Material and Process Engineering*] **Symposium** — Mater Symp Natl SAMPE Symp
Materials Testing — Mater Test
Materials Today — Mater Today
Materials Transactions. JIM (Japan Institute of Metals) — Mater Trans JIM

Materials und Organismen Beihefte — Mater Org Beih
Materialy Archeologiczne — Mat A
Materialy Archeologiczne — Mat Arch
Materialy Archeologiczne — Materialy Arch
Materialy Badaqcze Instytut Gospodarki Wodnej — Mater Badaq Inst Gospod Wodnej
Materialy Badawcze. Seria. Gospodarka Wodna i Ochrona Wod — Mater Badaw Ser Gospod Wodna Ochr Wod
Materialy Budowlane — Mater Budow
Materialy dlja Izucenija Estestvennyh Proizvoditel'nyh sil Rossii/Materiaux pour l'Etude des Ressources Naturelles de la Russie — Mater Izuc Estestv Priozv Sil Rossii
Materialy do Fizjografii Kraju. Documenta Physiographica Polonica — Mater Fizjogr Kraju
Materialy do Historii Filozofii Sredniowiecznej w Polsce — MHF
Materialy Florystyczne i Geobotaniczne — Mater Floryst Geobot
Materialy i Doslidzhenniia z Arkheologi i Prykarpattia i Volyni — MDAPV
Materialy i Issledovaniia po Arkheologii Latviiskoi (Riga) — Mat (Riga)
Materialy i Issledovaniia po Arkheologii SSSR [*Soyuz Sovetskikh Sotsialisticheskikh Respublik*] — Mat Iss
Materialy i Issledovaniia po Arkheologii SSSR — Mati Iss
Materialy i Issledovanija po Arkheologii SSSR — MIA
Materialy i Issledovanija po Istorii Russkogo Jazyka — MatIRJa
Materialy i Issledovanija po Russkoj Dialektologii — MatRD
Materialy i Issledovanija po Russkoj Dialektologii — MIRD
Materialy i Issledovanija Smolenskoj Oblasti — MISO
Materialy i Podzespoly Magnetyczne. Konferencja — Mater Podzespoly Magn Konf
Materialy i Prace Antropologiczne — Mater Pr Antropol
Materialy i Prace. Instytut Geofizyki. Polska Akademia Nauk — Mater Pr Inst Geofiz Pol Akad Nauk
Materialy i Prace. Polska Akademia Nauk. Instytut Geofizyki — Mater Pr Pol Akad Nauk Inst Geofiz
Materialy i Prace. Zaklad Geofizyki Polska Akademia Nauk — Mater Pr Zakl Geofiz Pol Akad Nauk
Materialy i Tezisy VI Konferentsii po Khimizatsii Sel'skogo Khozyaistva — Mater Tezisy VI Konf Khim Sel' Khoz
Materialy Issledovanii v Pomoshch Proektirovaniyu i Stroitelstvu Karakumskogo Kanala — Mater Issled Pomoshch Proekt Stroit Karakum Kanala
Materialy k Biobibliografii Ucenyh SSSR. Serija Biologiceskih Nauk. Botanika — Mater Biobibliogr Ucen SSSR Ser Biol Nauk Bot
Materialy k Izucheniyu Zhen'shenya i Drugikh Lekarstvennykh Sredstv Dal'nego Vostoka — Mater Izuch Zhen'shenya Drugikh Lek Sredstv Dal'nego Vostoka
Materialy k Poznaniju Fauny i Flory Rossijskoj Imperii. Otdel Botaniceskij — Mater Pozn Fauny Fl Rossijsk Imperii Otd Bot
Materialy k Poznaniyu Fauny i Flory SSSR Otdel Botanicheskii — Mater Poznaniyu Fauny Flory SSSR Otd Bot
Materialy k Poznaniyu Fauny i Flory SSSR Otdel Zoologicheskii — Mater Poznaniyu Fauny Flory SSSR Otd Zool
Materialy k Pribaltiiskoi Nauchnoi Konferentsii po Zashchite Rastenii — Mater Pribalt Nauchn Konf Zashch Rast
Materialy k Respublikanskoi Konferentsii po Poroshkovoi Metallurgii — Mater Resp Konf Poroshk Metall
Materialy k Soveshchaniyu Rabotnikov Laboratorii Geologicheskikh Organizatsii — Mater Soveshch Rab Lab Geol Organ
Materialy k Ucheniyu o Merzlykh Zonakh Zemnoi Kory — Mater Uch Merzlykh Zonakh Zemnoi Kory
Materialy Khar'kovskogo Otdela Geograficheskogo Obshchestva Ukrainy — Mater Khar'k Otd Geogr Ova Ukr
Materialy Komissii Ekspedicionnyh Issledovanij — Mater Komiss Eksped Issl
Materialy Komissii Mineralogii i Geokhimii Karpato-Balkanskaya Geologicheskaya Assotsiatsiya — Mater Kom Mineral Geokhim Karpato Balk Geol Assots
Materialy Komissii po Izuceniju Jakutskoj Avtonomnoj SSR/Materiaux de la Commission pour l'Etude de la Republique Autonome Sovietique Socialiste Jakoute — Mater Komiss Izuc Jakutsk Avton SSR
Materialy Konferentsii Molodykh Biologov Kirgizii — Mater Konf Molodykh Biol Kirg
Materialy Konferentsii Molodykh Uchenykh i Spetsialistov. Akademiya Nauk Armyanskoi SSR — Mater Konf Molodykh Uch Spets Akad Nauk Arm SSR
Materialy Konferentsii Rabotnikov Vuzov i Zavodskikh Laboratorii Yugo-Vostoka SSSR po Voprosam Obshchei Khimii. Khimicheskoi Tekhnologii i Khimiko-Analiticheskogo Kontrolya Proizvodstva — Mater Konf Rab Vuzov Zavod Lab Yugo Vostoka SSSR Vopr Obshch
Materialy Krajowego Seminarium na temat Magnetycznych Materialow Amorficznych — Mater Krajowego Semin Magn Mater Amorficznych
Materialy Mezhrespublikanskogo Soveshchaniya po Koordinatsii Nauchno-Issledovatel'skikh Rabot po Khlopkovodstvu — Mater Mezhresp Soveshch Koord Nauchno Issled Rab Khlopkovod
Materialy Mongol'skoj Kommissii — MMK
Materialy Moskovskoi Gorodskoi Konferentsii Molodykh Uchenykh — Mater Mosk Gor Konf Molodykh Uch
Materialy na Sympozjum Paliw Plynnych i Produktow Smarowych w Gospodarce Morskiej — Mater Symp Paliw Plynnych Prod Smarowych Gospod Morsk
Materialy Nauchnoi Konferentsii Molodykh Uchenykh. Kubanskii Gosudarstvennyi Meditsinskii Institut — Mater Nauchn Konf Molodykh Uch Kuban Gos Med Inst
Materialy Nauchnoi Konferentsii po Sel'skomu Khozyaistvu — Mater Nauchn Konf Selsk Khoz
Materialy Nauchnoi Konferentsii Posvyashchennoi 50-Letiyu Velikoi Oktyabr'skoi Sotsialisticheskoi Revolyutsii. Gruzinskii Zootekhnichesko-Veterinarnyi Uchebno-Issledovatel'skii Institut — Mater Nauchn Konf Gruz Zootekh Vet Uchebno Issled Inst
Materialy Nauchnoi Konferentsii Voronezhskii Sel'skokhozyaistvennyi Institut — Mater Nauchn Konf Voronezh Skh Inst
Materialy Nauchnoi Studencheskoi Konferentsii, Posvyashchennoi 50-letiyu Smolenskogo Gosudarstvennogo Meditsinskogo Instituta — Mater Nauchn Stud Konf Smolensk Gos Med Inst
Materialy Nauchno-Prakticheskoi Konferentsii Oftal'mologov Severnogo Kavkaza — Mater Nauchno Prakt Konf Oftalmol Sev Kavk
Materialy Nauchno-Tekhnicheskoi Konferentsii Leningradskogo Elektrotekhnicheskogo Instituta Svyazi — Mater Nauchno Tekh Konf Leningr Elektrotekh Inst Svyazi
Materialy Naucnoi Konferencii Aspirantov Posvjascennoj Poluvekovomu Jubileju Azerbajdzanskogo Pedagogiceskogo Instituta Imeni V. I. Lenina — Mater Nauc Konfer Aspir Azerb Pedag Inst Im Lenina
Materialy Naukowe Krajowego Zjazdu Endokrynologow Polskich — Mater Nauk Krajowego Zjazdu Endokrynol Pol
Materialy Oblastnoi Konferentsii NTO (Nauchno-Tekhnicheskoe Obshchestva) Sel'skogo Khoyvaistva — Mater Obl Konf NTO Selsk Khoz
Materialy Ogniotrwale [*Poland*] — Mater Ogniotrwale
Materialy Ogniotrwale — MYOGA
Materialy Osobogo Komiteta po Issledovaniju Sojuznyh i Avtonomnyh Respublik — Mater Osob Komiteta Issl Sojuzn Avton Respubl
Materialy Otraslevoi Konferentsii po Pererabotke Vysokosernistykh Neftei — Mater Otrasl Konf Pererab Vysokosernistykh Neftei
Materialy po Archeologii Rossii — MAR
Materialy po Archeologii Severnogo Pricernomor'ja — Mat A Sev Pric
Materialy po Arkheologii BSSR [*Byelorussian Soviet Socialist Republic*] **(Minsk)** — Mat (Minsk)
Materialy po Arkheologii Gruzii i Kavkaza — Mat Ark Gruz Kav
Materialy po Arkheologii i Drevnei Istorii Severnoi Osetii — Mat Arkh SO
Materialy po Arkheologii i Drevnei Istorii Severnoi Osetii — Mat po Arkh
Materialy po Arkheologii Kavkaza — MAK
Materialy po Arkheologii Pivnichnoho Prychornomor'ia — MAPP
Materialy po Arkheologii Rossii — MAP
Materialy po Arkheologii Rossii (Petrograd) — Mat (Petrograd)
Materialy po Arkheologii Severnogo Prichernomor'ia — MASP
Materialy po Ekologii i Fiziologii Rastenii Ural'skoi Flory — Mater Ekol Fiziol Rast Ural Flory
Materialy po Etnografii Gruzii — Mat Etn Gruz
Materialy po Evolyutsionnoi Fiziologii — Mater Evol Fiziol
Materialy po Faune i Ekologii Pochvoobitayushchikh Bespozvonochnykh — Mater Faune Ekol Pochvoobitayushchikh Bespozvon
Materialy po Geneticheskoi i Eksperimental'noi Mineralogii — Mater Genet Eksp Miner
Materialy po Geologii i Metallogenii Kol'skogo Poluostrova — Mater Geol Metallog Kol'sk Poluostrova
Materialy po Geologii i Poleznym Iskopaemym Buryatskoi ASSR — Mater Geol Polezn Iskop Buryat ASSR
Materialy po Geologii i Poleznym Iskopaemym Chitinskoi Oblasti — Mater Geol Polezn Iskop Chit Obl
Materialy po Geologii i Poleznym Iskopaemym Dal'nevostochnogo Kraya — Mater Geol Polezn Iskop Dal'nevost Kraya
Materialy po Geologii i Poleznym Iskopaemym Irkutskoi Oblasti — Mater Geol Polezn Iskop Irkutsk Obl
Materialy po Geologii i Poleznym Iskopaemym Kazakhstana — Mater Geol Polezy Iskop Kaz
Materialy po Geologii i Poleznym Iskopaemym Krasnoyarskogo Kraya — Mater Geol Polezn Iskop Krasnoyarsk Kraya
Materialy po Geologii i Poleznym Iskopaemym Severo Vostoka Evropeiskoi Chasti SSSR — Mater Geol Polezn Iskop Sev Vostoka Evr Chasti SSSR
Materialy po Geologii i Poleznym Iskopaemym Severo-Zapada RSFSR — Mater Geol Polezn Iskop Sev Zapada RSFSR
Materialy po Geologii i Poleznym Iskopaemym Severo-Zapada SSSR — Mater Geol Polezn Iskop Sev Zapada SSSR
Materialy po Geologii i Poleznym Iskopaemym Tsentral'nykh Raionov Evropeiskoi Chasti SSSR — Mater Geol Polezn Iskop Tsentr Raionov Evr Chasti SSSR
Materialy po Geologii i Poleznym Iskopaemym Urala — Mater Geol Polezn Iskop Urala
Materialy po Geologii i Poleznym Iskopaemym Vostochnoi Sibiri — Mater Geol Polezn Iskop Vost Sib
Materialy po Geologii i Poleznym Iskopaemym Yakutskoi ASSR — Mater Geol Polezn Iskop Yakutsk ASSR
Materialy po Geologii i Poleznym Iskopaemym Yuzhnogo Kazakhstana — Mater Geol Polezn Iskop Yuzhn Kaz
Materialy po Geologii i Poleznym Iskopaemym Yuzhnogo Urala — Mater Geol Polezn Iskop Yuzhn Urala
Materialy po Geologii i Poleznym Iskopaemym Zapadnogo Kazakhstana — Mater Geol Polezn Iskop Zapadn Kaz
Materialy po Geologii Mestorozhdenii Redkikh Elementov v Zarubezhnykh Stranakh — Mater Geol Mestorozhd Redk Elem Zarub Stranakh
Materialy po Geologii Tsentral'nogo Kazakhstana — Mater Geol Tsentr Kaz
Materialy po Geologii Tuvinskoi ASSR — Mater Geol Tuvinskoi ASSR
Materialy po Geologii Tyan-Shanya — Mater Geol Tyan Shanya
Materialy po Geologii Zapadno Sibirskoi Nizmennosti — Mater Geol Zapadno Sib Nizmennosti
Materialy po Geologii Zapadnoi Sibiri — Mater Geol Zapadn Sib
Materialy po i Zuceniju Vostoka — MIV
Materialy po Istorii Zemledeliya SSSR — Mater Istor Zemled SSSR
Materialy po Izucheniyu Lechebnykh Mineral'nykh Vod i Gryazei i Bal'neotekhnike — Mater Izuch Lech Miner Vod Gryazei Balneotekh
Materialy po Izucheniyu Stavropol'skogo Kraya — Mater Izuch Stavrop Kraya

Materialy po Jafeticeskomu Jazykoznaniju — MJJ
Materialy po Kompleksnomu Izucheniyu Belogo Morya — Mater Kompleksn Izuch Belogo Morya
Materialy po Matematiceskoj Lingvistike i Masinnomu Perevodu — MMLMP
Materialy po Metallicheskim Konstruktsiyam — Mater Met Konstr
Materialy po Metodike i Tekhnike Geologorazved Rabot — Mater Metod Tekh Geologorazved Rab
Materialy po Mikologii i Fitopatologii Rossii — Mater Mikol Fitopatol Rossii
Materialy po Mineralogii, Geokhimii, i Petrografii Zabaikal'ya — Mater Mineral Geokhim Petrogr Zabaik
Materialy po Mineralogii, Geokhimii, i Petrografii Zabaikal'ya — Mater Mineral Geokhim Petrogr Zabaikal'ya
Materialy po Mineralogii Kol'skogo Poluostrova — Mater Mineral Kol'sk Poluostrova
Materialy po Mineralogii, Petrografii, i Poleznym Iskopaemym Zapadnoi Sibiri — Mater Mineral Petrogr Polezn Iskop Zapadn Sib
Materialy po Nacional'no - Kolonial'nym Problemam — MNKP
Materialy po Obmenu Opytom i Nauchnymi Dostizheniyami v Meditsinskoi Promyshlennosti — Mater Obmenu Opytom Nauchn Dostizh Med Promsti
Materialy po Obmenu Peredovym Opytom i Nauchnymi Dostizheniyamiv Meditsinskoi Promyshlennosti — Mater Obmenu Peredovym Opytom Nauchn Dostizh Med Promsti
Materialy po Obshchemu Merzlotovedeniyu, Mezhduvedomstvennoe Soveshchanie po Merzlotovedeniyu — Mater Obshch Merzlotoved Mezhduved Soveshch Merzlotoved
Materialy po Proizvoditel'nym Silam Uzbekistana — Mater Proizvod Silam Uzb
Materialy po Stal'nym Konstruktsiyam — Mater Stalnym Konstr
Materialy po Tatarskoj Dialektologii — MTatD
Materialy po Toksikologii Radioaktivnykh Veshchestv — Mater Toksikol Radioakt Veshchestv
Materialy po Voprosam Promyshlennoi Toksikologii i Kliniki Professional'nykh Boleznei — Mater Vopr Prom Toksikol Klin Prof Bolezn
Materialy, Povolzhskaya Konferentsiya Fiziologov s Uchastiem Biokhimikov, Farmakologov, i Morfologov — Mater Povolzh Konf Fiziol Uchastiem Biokhim Farmakol Morfol
Materialy Pribaltiiskoi Nauchno-Koordinatsionnoi Konferentsii po Voprosam Parazitologii — Mater Pribalt Nauchno Koord Konf Vopr Parazitol
Materialy Rabochego Soveshchaniya po Statisticheskoi Fizike — Mater Rab Soveshch Stat Fiz
Materialy Resplublikanskoi Nauchno-Prakticheskoi Konferentsii po Probleme Termicheskikh Porazhenii — Mater Resp Nauchno Prakt Konf Probl Term Porazhenii
Materialy Respublikanskogo Seminara po Dinamike Teplovykh Protsessov — Mater Resp Semin Din Tepl Protsessov
Materialy Respublikanskogo S'ezda Gematologov i Transfuziologov Belorussii — Mater Resp Sezda Gematol Transfuziol Beloruss
Materialy Respublikanskogo Soveshchaniya po Neorganicheskoi Khimii — Mater Resp Soveshch Neorg Khim
Materialy Respublikanskoi Konferentsii Elektrokhimikov Litovskoi SSR — Mater Resp Konf Elektrokhim Lit SSR
Materialy Respublikanskoi Konferentsii Molodykh Uchenykh po Fizike — Mater Resp Konf Molodykh Uch Fiz
Materialy Respublikanskoi Konferentsii po Okhrane Prirody — Mater Resp Konf Okhr Prir
Materialy Respublikanskoi Konferentsii po Tekstil'noi Khimii — Mater Resp Konf Tekst Khim
Materialy Respublikanskoi Nauchnoi Konferentsii Agrokhimikov Gruzii — Mater Resp Nauchn Konf Agrokhim Gruz
Materialy Respublikanskoi Nauchnoi Konferentsii Fiziologov Vysshikh Uchebnykh Zavedenii Gruzii — Mater Resp Nauchn Konf Fiziol Vyssh Uchebn Zaved Gruz
Materialy Respublikanskoi Nauchno-Proizvodstvennoi Konferentsii po Zashchite Rastenii v Kazakhstane — Mater Resp Nauchno Proizvod Konf Zashch Rast Kaz
Materialy Respublikanskoi Nauchno-Tekhnicheskoi Konferentsii po Primeneniyu Polimernykh Materialov v Promyshlennosti — Mater Resp Nauchno Tekh Konf Primen Polim Mater Promsti
Materialy Respublikanskoi Rasshirennoi Konferentsii Farmakologov Gruzii — Mater Resp Rasshir Konf Farmakol Gruz
Materialy Rybokhozyaistvennykh Issledovanii Severnogo Basseina — Mater Rybokhoz Issled Sev Basseina
Materialy Seminara po Kibernetike — Mater Semin Kibern
Materialy Seminara po Kibernetike — Materialy Sem Kibernet
Materialy Sesji Naukowej Instytutu Ochrony Roslin (Poznan) — Mater Ses Nauk Inst Ochr Rosl (Poznan)
Materialy Sessii. Ob'edinennaya Sessiya Nauchno-Issledovatel'skikh Institutov Zakavkayskikh Republik Stroitel'stvu — Mater Sess Obedin Sess Nauchno Issled Inst Zakavk Resp Stroit
Materialy S'ezda Farmatsevtov Kazakhstana — Mater Sezda Farm Kaz
Materialy S'ezda Karpato-Balkanskoi Geologicheskoi Assotsiatsii — Mater Sezda Karpato Balk Geol Assots
Materialy S'ezda Karpato-Balkanskoi Geologicheskoi Assotsiatsii. Doklady Sovetskikh Geologov — Mater Sezda Karpato Balk Geol Assots Dokl Sov Geol
Materialy S'ezda Vsesoyuznogo Entomologicheskogo Obshchestva — Mater Sezda Vses Entomol Ova
Materialy Simpoziuma Biokhimicheskie Funktsii v Sisteme Kletochnykh Organell — Mater Simp Biokhim Funkts Sist Kletochnykh Organell
Materialy Simpoziuma Mikologov i Likhenologov Pribaltiiskikh Respublik — Mater Simp Mikol Likhenologov Pribalt Resp
Materialy Simpoziuma po Biokhimii Mitokhondrii — Mater Simp Biokhim Mitokhondrii
Materialy Simpoziuma po Solyanoi Tektonike — Mater Simp Solyanoi Tekton
Materialy Simpoziuma po Spektroskopii Kristallov — Mater Simp Spektrosk Krist
Materialy Soveshchaniya po Mekhanizmu Ingibirovaniya Tsepnykh Gazovykh Reaktsii — Mater Soveshch Mekh Ingib Tsepnykh Gazov Reakts
Materialy Soveshchaniya po Parenteral'nomu Pitaniyu — Mater Soveshch Parenter Pitan
Materialy Soveshchaniya po Probleme Gisto-Gematicheskikh Bar'erov — Mater Soveshch Prob Gisto Gematicheskikh Barerov
Materialy Soveshchaniya po Spektroskopii — Mater Soveshch Spektrosk
Materialy Sovetskoi Antarkticheskoi Ekspeditsii — Mater Sov Antarkt Eksped
Materialy Starozytne — Mat Star
Materialy Starozytne. Panstwowe Muzeum Archeologiczne — Mat Star
Materialy Studencheskogo Nauchnogo Obshchestva. Khar'kovskii Politekhnicheskii Institut — Mater Stud Nauchn Ova Khar'k Politekh Inst
Materialy Teoreticheskoi i Klinicheskoi Meditsiny — Mater Teor Klin Med
Materialy Tikhookeanskogo Nauchnogo Kongressa. Sektsiya Morskaya Biologiya — Mater Tikhookean Nauchn Kongr Sekts Morsk Biol
Materialy Tsentral'nogo Nauchno-Issledovatel'skogo Instituta Bumazhnoi Promyshlennosti — Mater Tsentr Nauchno Issled Inst Bum Promsti
Materialy Tsentral'nogo Nauchno-Issledovatel'skogo Instituta Tekstil'noi Promyshlennosti — Mater Tsentr Nauchno Issled Inst Tekst Promsti
Materialy Tsentral'nogo Nauchno-Issledovatel'skogo Instituta Tsellyuloznoi i Bumazhnoi Promyshlennosti — Mater Tsentr Nauchno Issled Inst Tsellyul Bum Promsti
Materialy Ural'skogo Soveshchaniya po Spektroskopii — Mater Ural Soveshch Spektrosk
Materialy. Vsesoyuznaya Mezhvuzovskaya Konferentsiya po Ozonu — Mater Vses Mezhvuz Konf Ozonu
Materialy Vsesoyuznogo Litologicheskogo Soveshchaniya — Mater Vses Litol Soveshch
Materialy Vsesoyuznogo Nauchno-Issledovatel'skogo Geologicheskogo Instituta — Mater Vses Nauchno Issled Geol Inst
Materialy Vsesoyuznogo Nauchno-Issledovatel'skogo Instituta Bumazhnoi i Tsellyuloznoi Promyshlennosti — Mater Vses Nauchno Issled Inst Bum Tsellyul Promsti
Materialy Vsesoyuznogo Reologicheskogo Simpoziuma — Mater Vses Reol Simp
Materialy Vsesoyuznogo Seminara po Teorii i Tekhnologii Pressovaniya Poroshkov — Mater Vses Semin Teor Tekhnol Pressovaniya Poroshk
Materialy Vsesoyuznogo Simpoziuma Okeanograficheskie Aspekty Okhrany Vod ot Khimicheskikh Zagryaznenii — Mater Vses Simp Okeanogr Aspekty Okhr Vod Khim Zagryaz
Materialy Vsesoyuznogo Simpoziuma po Goreniyu i Vzryvu — Mater Vses Simp Goreniyu Vzryvu
Materialy Vsesoyuznogo Simpoziuma po Khimioprofilaktike i Khimioterapii Grippa — Mater Vses Simp Khimioprofil Khimioter Grippa
Materialy Vsesoyuznogo Simpoziuma po Mekhanoemissii i Mekhanokhimii Tverdykh Tel — Mater Vses Simp Mekhanoemiss Mekhanokhim Tverd Tel
Materialy Vsesoyuznogo Simpoziuma po Problemam Gistofiziologii Soedinitel'noi Tkani — Mater Vses Simp Probl Gistofiziol Soedin Tkani
Materialy Vsesoyuznogo Simpoziuma po Rasprostraneniyu Uprugikh i Uprugoplasticheskikh Voln — Mater Vses Simp Rasprostr Uprugikh Uprugoplast Voln
Materialy Vsesoyuznogo Simpoziuma po Tsitoplazmaticheskoi Nasledstvennosti — Mater Vses Simp Tsitoplazmaticheskoi Nasledstvennosti
Materialy Vsesoyuznogo Simpoziuma. Posvyashchennogo Strukturnoi i Funktsional'noi Organizatsii Mozzhechka — Mater Vses Simp Strukt Funkts Organ Mozzhechka
Materialy Vsesoyuznogo Simpoziuma Struktura i Funktsii Kletochnogo Yadra — Mater Vses Simp Strukt Funkts Kletochnogo Yadra
Materialy Vsesoyuznogo Soveshchaniya po Biokhimicheskoi Genetike Ryb — Mater Vses Soveshch Biokhim Genet Ryb
Materialy Vsesoyuznogo Soveshchaniya po Biologicheskomu Deistviyu Ul'trafioletovogo Izlucheniya — Mater Vses Soveshch Biol Deistviyu Ultrafiolet Izluch
Materialy Vsesoyuznogo Soveshchaniya po Diagrammam Sostoyaniya — Mater Vses Soveshch Diagrammam Sostoyaniya
Materialy Vsesoyuznogo Soveshchaniya po Elektrolyuminestsentsii — Mater Vses Soveshch Elektrolyumin
Materialy Vsesoyuznogo Soveshchaniya po Izucheniyu Chetvertichnogo Perioda — Mater Vses Soveshch Izuch Chetvertichn Perioda
Materialy Vsesoyuznogo Soveshchaniya po Khimii Karbenov i Ikh Analogov — Mater Vses Soveshch Khim Karbenov Ikh Analogov
Materialy Vsesoyuznogo Soveshchaniya po Pnevmoavgomatike — Mater Vses Soveshch Pnevmoavgomatike
Materialy Vsesoyuznogo Soveshchaniya po Psevdoozhizhennomu Sloyu — Mater Vses Soveshch Psevdoozhizhennomu Sloyu
Materialy Vsesoyuznogo Soveshchaniya po Relaksatsionnym Yavleniyam v Polimerakh — Mater Vses Soveshch Relaks Yavleniyam Polim
Materialy Vsesoyuznogo Soveshchaniya po Rostu i Nesovershenstvam Metallicheskikh Kristallov — Mater Vses Soveshch Rostu Nesoversh Met Krist
Materialy Vsesoyuznogo Soveshchaniya po Svarke Raznorodnykh, Kompozitsionnykh, i Mnogosloinykh Materialov — Mater Vses Soveshch Svarke Raznorodnykh Kompoz Mnogosloinykh
Materialy Vsesoyuznogo Soveshchaniya po Tseolitam — Mater Vses Soveshch Tseolitam
Materialy Vsesoyuznogo Soveshchaniya po Tverdym Goryuchim Iskopaemym — Mater Vses Soveshch Tverd Goryuch Iskop
Materialy Vsesoyuznogo Soveshchaniya po Voprosam Primeneniya Mikroelementov v Sel'skom Khozyaistve i Meditsine — Mater Vses Soveshch Vopr Primen Mikroelem Selsk Khoz Med
Materialy Vsesoyuznogo Soveshchaniya Spektroskopistov-Analitikov Tsvetnoi Metallurgii — Mater Vses Soveshch Spektrosk Anal Tsvetn Metall
Materialy Vsesoyuznogo Vulkanologicheskogo Soveshchaniya — Mater Vses Vulkanol Soveshch
Materialy Vsesoyuznoi Konferentsii Farmakologiya Protivoluchevykh Preparatov — Mater Vses Konf Farmakol Protivoluchevykh Prep

Materialy Vsesoyuznoi Konferentsii Farmatsevtov — Mater Vses Konf Farm
Materialy Vsesoyuznoi Konferentsii po Dinamicheskoi Stereokhimii i Konformatsionnomu Analizu — Mater Vses Konf Din Stereokhim Konform Anal
Materialy Vsesoyuznoi Konferentsii po Elektronnoi Mikroskopii — Mater Vses Konf Elektron Mikrosk
Materialy Vsesoyuznoi Konferentsii po Elektronnoluchevoi Svarke — Mater Vses Konf Elektronnoluchevoi Svarke
Materialy Vsesoyuznoi Konferentsii po Fiziologicheskim i Biokhimicheskim Osnovam Povysheniya Produktivnosti Sel'skokhozyaistvennykh Zhivotnykh — Mater Vses Konf Fiziol Biokhim Osn Povysh Prod Skh Zhivotn
Materialy Vsesoyuznoi Konferentsii po Issledovaniyu Stroeniya Organicheskikh Soedinenii Fizicheskimi Metodami — Mater Vses Konf Issled Str Org Soedin Fiz Metodami
Materialy Vsesoyuznoi Konferentsii po Khimii i Biokhimii Uglevodov — Mater Vses Konf Khim Biokhim Uglevodov
Materialy Vsesoyuznoi Konferentsii po Neitronnoi Fizike — Mater Vses Konf Neitr Fiz
Materialy Vsesoyuznoi Konferentsii po Plazmennym Uskoritelyam — Mater Vses Konf Plazmennym Uskorit
Materialy Vsesoyuznoi Konferentsii po Poroshkovoi Metallurgii — Mater Vses Konf Poroshk Metall
Materialy Vsesoyuznoi Konferentsii po Primeneniyu Tunnel'nykh Diodov v Vychislitel'noi Tekhnike — Mater Vses Konf Primen Tunnelnykh Diodov Vychisl Tekh
Materialy Vsesoyuznoi Konferentsii po Voprosam Metodiki i Tekhniki Ul'trazvukovoi Spektrosopii — Mater Vses Konf Vopr Metod Tekh Ultrazvuk Spektrosk
Materialy Vsesoyuznoi Konferentsii po Voprosam Pozharnoi Zashchity Narodnogo Khozyaistva Strany — Mater Vses Konf Vopr Pozharnoi Zashch Nar Khoz Strany
Materialy Vsesoyuznoi Konferentsii Sovremennye Problemy Biokhimii Dykhaniya i Klinika — Mater Vses Konf Sovrem Probl Biokhim Dykhaniya Klin
Materialy Vsesoyuznoi Litologicheskoi Konferentsii — Mater Vses Litol Konf
Materialy Vsesoyuznoi Nauchnoi Konferentsii po Mekhanike Gornykh Porod — Mater Vses Nauchn Konf Mekh Gorn Porod
Materialy Vsesoyuznoi Nauchnoi Konferentsii Sudebnykh Medikov — Mater Vses Nauchn Konf Sud Med
Materialy Vsesoyuznoi Nauchnoi Studencheskoi Konferentsii Student i Nauchno-Tekhnicheskii Progress. Khimiya — Mater Vses Nauchn Stud Konf Stud Nauchno Tekh Prog Khim
Materialy Vsesoyuznoi Nauchno-Tekhnicheskoi Geofizicheskoi Konferentsii — Mater Vses Nauchno Tekh Geofiz Konf
Materialy Vsesoyuznoi Nauchno-Tekhnicheskoi Konferentsii Kompozitsionnye Materialy — Mater Vses Nauchno Tekh Konf Kompoz Mater
Materialy Vsesoyuznoi Shkoly po Fizike Elementarnykh Chastits i Vysokikh Energii — Mater Vses Shk Fiz Elem Chastits Vys Energ
Materialy Vsesoyuznoi Shkoly po Golografii — Mater Vses Shk Gologr
Materialy Vsesoyuznoi Teplofizicheskoi Konferentsii — Mater Vses Teplofiz Konf
Materialy Vsesoyuznoi Teplofizicheskoi Konferentsii po Svoistvamveshchestv pri Vysokikh Temperaturakh — Mater Vses Teplofiz Konf Svoistvamveshchestv pri Vys Temp
Materialy z Polsko-Czechoslowackiej Szkoly Stereochemii Peptydow — Mater Pol Czech Szk Stereochem Pept
Materialy Zachodnio-Pomorskie — Mat Zachodnio-Pomorskie
Materialy Zachodniopomorskie. Muzeum Pomorza Zachodniego — Mater Zachodniopomorskie Muz Pomorza Zachodniego
Materialy Zimnei Shkoly LIYaF (Leningradskii Institut Yadernoi Fiziki) po Fizike Yadra i Elementarnykh Chastits — Mater Zimnei Shk LIYaF Fiz Yadra Elem Chastits
Materialy Zimnei Shkoly po Fizike Poluprovodnikov — Mater Zimnei Shk Fiz Poluprovodn
Materialy Zrodlowe do Dziejow Kosciola w Polsce — MZDKP
Materiaux et Constructions/Materials and Structures — Mater Constr Mater Struct
Materiaux et Constructions (Paris) — Mater Constr (Paris)
Materiaux et Organismes. Supplement — Mater Org Suppl
Materiaux et Techniques — Mater Tech
Materiaux et Techniques (Paris) — Mater Tech (Paris)
Materiaux Nouveaux pour l'Aeronautique. Compte Rendu des Travaux. Congres International Aeronautique — Mater Nouv Aeronaut CR Trav Congr Int Aeronaut
Materiaux pour la Geologie de la Suisse. Geophysique — Mater Geol Suisse Geophys
Materiaux pour le Leve Geobotanique de la Suisse — Mater Leve Geobot Suisse
Materiaux pour l'Histoire Primitive et Naturelle de l'Homme — Mat Hist Primet Nat Homme
Materiaux pour Servir a l'Etude de la Flore et de la Geographie Botanique de l'Orient. Missions du Ministere de l'Instruction Publique en 1904 et en 1906 — Mater Etude Fl Geogr Bot Orient
Materie Plastiche ed Elastomeri — Mat Plast Elast
Materie Plastiche ed Elastomeri — Plastiche
Materie Plastiche (Milan) — Mater Plast Milan
Materiels Nouveaux et Techniques Mondiales — Mater Nouv Tech Mond
Maternal-Child Nursing Journal — Mat-Child Nurs J
Maternal-Child Nursing Journal — Matern Child Nurs J
Maternal-Child Nursing Journal — Maternal-Child Nurs J
Maternal-Child Nursing Journal — MCNJA
Maternidade e Infancia — Matern Infanc
Maternita ed Infanzia — Matern Inf
Mathematica Balkanica — Math Balk
Mathematica Balkanica — Math Balkanica
Mathematica Balkanica. New Series — Math Balkanica NS
Mathematica Bohemica — Math Bohem
Mathematica Japonicae — Math Japon
Mathematica Montisnigri — Math Montisnigri
Mathematica Numerica Sinica — Math Numer Sin
Mathematica Numerica Sinica — Math Numer Sinica
Mathematica Pannonica — Math Pannon
Mathematica Scandinavica — Math Scand
Mathematica Slovaca — Math Slovaca
Mathematicae Notae — Math Notae
Mathematical Algorithms — Math Algorithms
Mathematical and Computer Modelling — Math Comput Modelling
Mathematical and Dynamical Astronomy Series — Math Dynam Astronom Ser
Mathematical Applications in Political Science — Math Appl Polit Sci
Mathematical Approaches to Geophysics — Math Approaches Geophys
Mathematical Biosciences — Math Biosci
Mathematical Centre. Tracts [*Amsterdam*] — Math Centre Tracts
Mathematical Chemistry Series — Math Chem Ser
Mathematical Chronicle — Math Chronicle
Mathematical Chronicle. University of Auckland — Math Chron
Mathematical Concepts and Methods in Science and Engineering — Math Concepts and Methods in Sci and Engrg
Mathematical Concepts and Methods in Science and Engineering — Math Concepts Methods Sci Eng
Mathematical Concepts and Methods in Science and Engineering — Math Concepts Methods Sci Engrg
Mathematical Ecology — Math Ecol
Mathematical Education for Teaching — Math Ed for Teaching
Mathematical Education for Teaching — Math Educ Teach
Mathematical Engineering in Industry — Math Engrg Indust
Mathematical Finance — Math Finance
Mathematical Forum — Math Forum
Mathematical Gazette — Math Gazette
Mathematical Geology — Math Geol
Mathematical Intelligencer — Math Intellig
Mathematical Intelligencer — Math Intelligencer
Mathematical Intelligencer — PMIN
Mathematical Journal. Okayama University — Math J Okayama Univ
Mathematical Logic Quarterly — Math Logic Quart
Mathematical Medley — Math Medley
Mathematical Methods in the Applied Sciences — Math Methods Appl Sci
Mathematical Methods of Operations Research — Math Methods Oper Res
Mathematical Methods of Statistics — Math Methods Statist
Mathematical Modeling — Math Model
Mathematical Modeling and Computational Experiment — Math Modeling Comput Experiment
Mathematical Modelling — Math Modelling
Mathematical Modelling and Scientific Computing — Math Modelling Sci Comput
Mathematical Modelling of Systems — Math Model Systems
Mathematical Models and Methods in Applied Sciences — Math Models Methods Appl Sci
Mathematical Monographs of the University of Cape Town — Math Monographs Univ Cape Town
Mathematical Monthly — Math Mo
Mathematical Notes — Math Notes
Mathematical Notes. Academy of Sciences (USSR) — Math Notes Acad Sci (USSR)
Mathematical Physics and Applied Mathematics — Math Phys Appl Math
Mathematical Physics and Physical Mathematics. Proceedings. International Symposium — Math Phys Phys Math Proc Int Symp
Mathematical Physics Electronic Journal — Math Phys Electron J
Mathematical Physics Monograph Series — Math Phys Monogr Ser
Mathematical Physics Monograph Series — Math Phys Monograph Ser
Mathematical Physics Studies — Math Phys Stud
Mathematical Population Studies — Math Population Stud
Mathematical Problems in Theoretical Physics. Proceedings. International Conference on Mathematical Physics — Math Probl Theor Phys Proc Int Conf
Mathematical Proceedings. Cambridge Philosophical Society — Math Proc C
Mathematical Proceedings. Cambridge Philosophical Society — Math Proc Camb Philos Soc
Mathematical Proceedings. Cambridge Philosophical Society — Math Proc Cambridge Phil Soc
Mathematical Proceedings. Cambridge Philosophical Society — Math Proc Cambridge Philos Soc
Mathematical Proceedings. Cambridge Philosophical Society — MPCPC
Mathematical Programming — Math Prog
Mathematical Programming — Math Progr
Mathematical Programming — Math Program
Mathematical Programming — Math Programming
Mathematical Programming Studies — Math Program Stud
Mathematical Programming Studies — Math Programming Stud
Mathematical Programming Studies [*Elsevier Book Series*] — MPS
Mathematical Publications — Math Publ
Mathematical Reports — Math Rep
Mathematical Reports. College of General Education. Kyushu University — Math Rep College General Ed Kyushu Univ
Mathematical Reports. College of General Education. Kyushu University — Math Rep Kyushu Univ
Mathematical Research — Math Res
Mathematical Research — Math Research
Mathematical Research Letters — Math Res Lett
Mathematical Reviews — Math Rev
Mathematical Reviews — MathR
Mathematical Reviews — MR
Mathematical Reviews Sections — Math Rev Sect
Mathematical Sciences — Math Sci
Mathematical Sciences Reference Series — Math Sci Ref Ser

Mathematical Sciences Research Institute Publications — Math Sci Res Inst Publ
Mathematical Sciences (Washington, DC) — Math Sci Washington DC
Mathematical Scientist — Math Sci
Mathematical Scientist — Math Scientist
Mathematical Social Sciences — Math Soc Sci
Mathematical Social Sciences — Math Social Sci
Mathematical Social Sciences — MSOSD
Mathematical Society [*Banaras Hindu University*] — Math Soc
Mathematical Spectrum — Math Spectrum
Mathematical Structures in Computer Science — Math Structures Comput Sci
Mathematical Studies in Economics and Statistics in the USSR and Eastern Europe — MSE
Mathematical Surveys — Math Surveys
Mathematical Surveys and Monographs — Math Surveys Monogr
Mathematical Surveys and Monographs — Math Surveys Monographs
Mathematical Systems in Economics — Math Syst Econom
Mathematical Systems in Economics — Math Systems in Econom
Mathematical Systems Theory — Math Syst T
Mathematical Systems Theory — Math Systems Theory
Mathematical Topics — Math Top
Mathematical Transactions (English Translation of Matematicheskii Sbornik) — Math Trans (Engl Transl)
Mathematical World — Math World
Mathematics Abstracts [*Database*] — MATH
Mathematics and CAD — Math CAD
Mathematics and Computer Education — Math and Comput Educ
Mathematics and Computer Education — Math Comput Ed
Mathematics and Computers in Simulation — Math and Comp in Simulation
Mathematics and Computers in Simulation — Math and Comput Simulation
Mathematics and Computers in Simulation — Math Comput Simul
Mathematics and Computers in Simulation — Math Comput Simulation
Mathematics and its Application (East European Series) — Math Appl East European Ser
Mathematics and Its Applications — Math Appl
Mathematics and its Applications (Japanese Series) — Math Appl Japanese Ser
Mathematics and its Applications (Soviet Series) — Math Appl Soviet Ser
Mathematics and Mathematical Physics (Washington, DC) — Math Math Phys (Washington DC)
Mathematics and Mechanics of Solids — Math Mech Solids
Mathematics Bulletin — Math Bul
Mathematics Bulletin for Teachers in Secondary Schools — Maths Bul
Mathematics Colloquium. University of Cape Town — Math Colloq Univ Cape Town
Mathematics Department Report — Math Dept Rep
Mathematics Education — Math Education
Mathematics Education Library — Math Ed Lib
Mathematics in Biology — Math Biol
Mathematics in Practice and Theory — Math Practice Theory
Mathematics in School — Math in School
Mathematics in Science and Engineering — Math Sci Eng
Mathematics in Science and Engineering — Math Sci Engrg
Mathematics Journal of Toyama University — Math J Toyama Univ
Mathematics Lecture Note Series — Math Lecture Note Ser
Mathematics Lecture Series — Math Lecture Ser
Mathematics Magazine — GMAT
Mathematics Magazine — Math Mag
Mathematics of Computation — Math Comp
Mathematics of Computation — Math Comput
Mathematics of Computation — Math of Comput
Mathematics of Control, Signals, and Systems — Math Control Signals Systems
Mathematics of Mathematical Science — Math Math Sci
Mathematics of Operations Research — Math Oper Res
Mathematics of Operations Research — MOR
Mathematics of the USSR. Izvestiya — Math USSR Izv
Mathematics of the USSR. Sbornik — Math USSR Sb
Mathematics Seminar [*Delhi*] — Math Sem
Mathematics Seminar — Math Seminar
Mathematics Seminar. Notes. Kobe University — Math Sem Notes Kobe Univ
Mathematics Series — Math Ser
Mathematics Student — Math Student
Mathematics Teacher — Math Teach
Mathematics Teacher — Math Teacher
Mathematics Teaching — Math Teach
Mathematics Teaching — Math Teaching
Mathematics. Theory and Applications — Math Theory Appl
Mathematics Today — Math Today
Mathematik. Didaktik und Unterrichtspraxis — Math Didaktik Unterrichtspraxis
Mathematik fuer die Lehrerausbildung — Mat Lehrerausbildung
Mathematik fuer Ingenieure — Math Ingen
Mathematik fuer Ingenieure, Naturwissenschaftler, Oekonomen, und Landwirte — Math Ing Naturwiss Okon Landwirte
Mathematik fuer Ingenieure, Naturwissenschaftler, Oekonomen, und Landwirte — Math Ingen Naturwiss Oekonom Landwirte
Mathematik fuer Ingenieure, Naturwissenschaftler, Oekonomen, und Sonstige Anwendungsorientierte Berufe — Math Ingen Naturwiss Okonom Sonstige Anwendungsorient Berufe
Mathematik fuer Ingenieure und Naturwissenschaftler — Math Ingen Naturwiss
Mathematik fuer Lehrer — Math Lehrer
Mathematik fuer Naturwissenschaft und Technik — Math Naturwiss Tech
Mathematik fuer Physiker — Math Phys
Mathematik fuer Physiker — Math Physiker
Mathematik fuer Studienanfaenger — Math Studienanfaenger
Mathematik fuer Wirtschaftswissenschaftler — Math Wirtschaftswiss
Mathematik und Ihre Anwendungen in Physik und Technik — Math Anwendungen Phys Tech
Mathematikai es Termeszettudomanyi Ertesitoe — Math Termeszettud Ertes
Mathematik-Arbeitspapiere — Math-Arbeitspapiere
Mathematik-Arbeitspapiere. Universitaet Bremen — Math Arbeitspap Univ Bremen
Mathematike Agoge — Math Agoge
Mathematikuri Kibernetikis Zogierthi Sakithxis Gamokwewa — Math Kibernet Zogierth Sakith Gamokw
Mathematiques et Civilisation — Math Civilis
Mathematiques et Sciences Humaines — Math Sci Hum
Mathematiques Informatique et Sciences Humaines — Math Inform Sci Humaines
Mathematiques pour la Physique — Math Phys
Mathematisch Centrum Amsterdam Rekenafdeling — Math Cent Amsterdam Rekenafd
Mathematisch-Astronomische Blaetter. Neue Folge — Math Astronom Blaetter NF
Mathematische Annalen — Math Ann
Mathematische Annalen — Math Annal
Mathematische Forschungsberichte — Math Forschungsber
Mathematische Grundlagen fuer Mathematiker, Physiker, und Ingenieure — Math Grundlagen Math Phys Ingen
Mathematische Keilschrifttexte — MKT
Mathematische Lehrbuecher und Monographien. I. Abteilung. Mathematische Lehrbuecher — Math Lehrb Monogr I
Mathematische Lehrbuecher und Monographien. I. Abteilung. Mathematische Lehrbuecher — Math Lehrbuecher Monogr I Abt Math Lehrbuecher
Mathematische Lehrbuecher und Monographien. II. Abteilung. Mathematische Monographien — Math Lehrbuecher Monogr II Abt Math Monogr
Mathematische Leitfaeden — Math Leitfaeden
Mathematische Methoden in der Technik — Math Methoden Tech
Mathematische Miniaturen — Math Miniaturen
Mathematische Monographien — Math Monograph
Mathematische Nachrichten — Math Nachr
Mathematische Operationsforschung und Statistik — Ma Opf & St
Mathematische Operationsforschung und Statistik — Math Operationsforsch Stat
Mathematische Operationsforschung und Statistik — Math Operationsforsch Statist
Mathematische Operationsforschung und Statistik — Math Operationsforsch und Stat
Mathematische Operationsforschung und Statistik. Series Optimization — Math Operationsforsch Statist Ser Optim
Mathematische Operationsforschung und Statistik. Series Optimization — Math Operationsforsch Statist Ser Optimization
Mathematische Operationsforschung und Statistik. Series Optimization — Math Operationsforsch und Stat Ser Optimiz
Mathematische Operationsforschung und Statistik. Series Optimization — Optimization
Mathematische Operationsforschung und Statistik. Series Statistik — Math Operationsforsch Statist Ser Statist
Mathematische Operationsforschung und Statistik. Series Statistik — Math Operationsforsch und Stat Ser Stat
Mathematische Reihe — Math Reihe
Mathematische Schuelerbuecherei — Math Schuelerbuecherei
Mathematische Semesterberichte — Math Semesterber
Mathematische Texte — Math Texte
Mathematische und Naturwissenschaftliche Berichte aus Ungarn — Math Naturwiss Ber Ung
Mathematische und Naturwissenschaftliche Berichte aus Ungarn — Math Naturwiss Ber Ungarn
Mathematische und Naturwissenschaftliche Unterricht — Math Naturw Unterr
Mathematische und Naturwissenschaftliche Unterricht — Math Naturwiss Unterr
Mathematische Zeitschrift — Math Z
Mathematischer und Naturwissenschaftlicher Anzeiger der Ungarischen Akademie der Wissenschaften — Math Naturwiss Anz Ung Akad Wiss
Mathematisch-Naturwissenschaftliche Bibliothek — Math-Naturwiss Bibliothek
Mathematisch-Naturwissenschaftliche Blaetter — Math Natwiss Bll
Mathematisch-Naturwissenschaftliche Blaetter — MN Bl
Mathematisch-Naturwissenschaftliche Taschenbuecher — Math-Naturwiss Taschenb
Mathematisch-Physikalische Semesterberichte — Math-Phys Semesterber
Mathematisch-Physikalische Semesterberichte — Mat-Phys Semesterber
Mathesis di Cosenza. Quaderni — Quad Mathesis Cosenza
Mathware and Soft Computing — Mathware Soft Comput
Matica Slovenska — MatSl
Matica Srpska. Zbornik za Prirodne Nauke — Matica Srp Zb Prir Nauke
Matiere Mal Condensee. Ecole d'Ete de Physique Theorique — Matiere Mal Condens Ec Ete Phys Theor
Matieres Medicales — Matieres Med
Matieres Plastiques en Medecine — Matieres Plast Med
Matimyas Matematika — Matimyas Mat
Matrices et Fibres Polymeres. Nouveaux Aspects Chimiques et Physiques. Colloque — Matrices Fibres Polym Nouv Aspects Chim Phys Colloq
Matricularum Regni Poloniae Summaria — MRPS
Matrix — Mat
Matrix and Tensor Quarterly — Matr Tens Q
Matrix and Tensor Quarterly — Matrix and Tensor Q
Matrix and Tensor Quarterly [*London*] — Matrix Tensor Quart
Matrix Biology — Matrix Biol
Matrix Supplement — Matrix Suppl
Matscience Report [*Madras*] — Matscience Rep
Matscience Symposia on Theoretical Physics — Matscience Symp Theor Phys
Matsushita Electric Works. Technical Report — Matsushita Electr Works Tech Rep

Matsushita Medical Journal — Matsushita Med J
Matter of Fact [*A*] [*Database*] — AMOF
MATYC [*Mathematics Association of Two-Year Colleges*] **Journal** — MATYC J
Maulana Abul Kalam Azad. A Memorial Volume [*Monograph*] — MAKA
Mauretania — Maur
Maurice Ewing Series — Maurice Ewing Ser
Mauritius. Department of Agriculture. Annual Report — Mauritius Dep Agric Annu Rep
Mauritius. Department of Agriculture. Bulletin — Mauritius Dep Agric Bull
Mauritius. Department of Agriculture. Scientific Series. Bulletin — Mauritius Dep Agric Sci Ser Bull
Mauritius. Department of Agriculture. Sugar Cane Research Station. Annual Report — Mauritius Dep Agric Sugar Cane Res Stn Annu Rep
Mauritius Economic Bulletin — Mauritius Econ Bull
Mauritius Institute. Bulletin — Mauritius Inst Bull
Mauritius. Ministry of Agriculture and Natural Resources. Annual Report — Mauritius Ministr Agric Nat Resour Annu Rep
Mauritius. Sugar Cane Research Station. Annual Report — Mauritius Sugar Cane Res Stn Annu Rep
Mauritius Sugar Industry Research Institute. Annual Report — Mauritius Sugar Ind Res Inst Annu Rep
Mauritius Sugar Industry Research Institute. Bulletins — Mauritius Sugar Ind Res Inst Bull
Mauritius Sugar Industry Research Institute. Leaflet — Mauritius Sugar Ind Res Inst Leafl
Mauritius Sugar Industry Research Institute. Occasional Paper — Mauritius Sugar Ind Res Inst Occas Pap
Mauritius Sugar Industry Research Institute. Technical Circular — Mauritius Sugar Ind Res Inst Tech Circ
MAW- und HTR-BE-Versuchseinlagerung in Bohrloechern, Statusbericht — MAW HTR BE Versuchseinlagerung Bohrloechern Statusber
Mawdsley Memoirs — MAME
Mawdsley Memoirs — Mawdsley Mem
Maxima Bibliotheca Veterum Patrum et Antiquorum Scriptorum Ecclesiasticorum — MBP
Max-Planck-Gesellschaft. Berichte und Mitteilungen — Max-Planck-Ges Ber Mitt
Max-Planck-Gesellschaft. Jahrbuch — Max-Planck-Ges Jahrb
Max-Planck-Gesellschaft zur Foerderung der Wissenschaften. Projektgruppe fuer Laserforschung. Bericht PLF — Max Planck Ges Foerd Wiss Projektgruppe Laserforsch Ber PLF
Max-Planck-Institut fuer Aeronomie. Mitteilungen — Max Planck Inst Aeron Mitt
Max-Planck-Institut fuer Kernphysik. Report MPI H — Max Planck Inst Kernphys Rep MPI H
Max-Planck-Institut fuer Plasmaphysik. Garching bei Muenchen. Bericht IPP-JET — Max Planck Inst Plasmaphys Garching Muenchen Ber IPP JET
Max-Planck-Institut fuer Plasmaphysik. Presseinformation — Max-Planck-Inst Plasmaphys Presseinf
Max-Planck-Institut fuer Quantenoptik. Bericht MPQ — Max Planck Inst Quantenop Ber MPQ
Max-Planck-Institut fuer Stroemungsforschung. Bericht — Max Planck Inst Stroemungsforsch Ber
Max-Von-Pettenkofer-Institut. Berichte — Max Von Pettenkofer Inst Ber
Maxwell Review — Maxwell R
May — MY
May and Baker Laboratory Bulletin — May Baker Lab Bull
May and Baker Pharmaceutical Bulletin — May Baker Pharm Bull
Maya Research (New Orleans) — Maya Res New Orleans
Maynooth Review — May Rev
Mayo Clinic Health Letter — IMCH
Mayo Clinic. Proceedings — Mayo Clin P
Mayo Clinic. Proceedings — Mayo Clin Proc
Mazda Research Bulletin — Mazda Res Bull
Mazda Technical Review — Mazda Tech Rev
Mazingira. The World Forum for Environment and Development — MFE
Mazungumzo — Maz
Mazungumzo Student Journal of African Studies — Mazungumzo
MBA/Masters in Business Administration — MBA
MBB [*Messerschmitt-Boelkow-Blohm*] **WF-Information** [*German Federal Republic*] — MBB WF-Inf
MBI. Medico-Biologic Information — MBI
MBL (Marine Biology Laboratory) Lectures in Biology (Woods Hole) — MBL (Mar Biol Lab) Lect Biol (Woods Hole)
MBMG. Montana Bureau of Mines and Geology Special Publication — MBMG Mont Bur Mines Geol Spec Publ
McBride's Magazine — McBride's
McCall's — GMCC
McCann-Erickson, Inc. News Release — McCann-E NR
McClure's Magazine [*New York*] — McCl
McClure's Magazine [*New York*] — McClure
McClure's Magazine — McClure's
McClure's Magazine — McClures M
McCollum-Pratt Institute. Johns Hopkins University. Contribution — McCollum Pratt Inst Johns Hopkins Univ Contrib
McCormick Quarterly — McCQ
McGill Dental Review — McGill Dent Rev
McGill Journal of Education — McGill J Educ
McGill Law Journal — McG LJ
McGill Law Journal — McGill L J
McGill Medical Journal — McGill Med J
McGill Medical Journal — McGill Med Jnl
McGill Reporter — McGill Rep
McGill Sub-Arctic Research Laboratory. Research Paper — MSARLRP
McGill University. Axel Heiberg Island Research Reports. Glaciology — McGill Univ Axel Heiberg Isl Res Rep Glaciol
McGill University. Marine Sciences Centre. Manuscript — McGill Univ Mar Sci Cent Manuscr
McGill University [*Montreal*]. Marine Sciences Centre. Manuscript Report — MUMSCMR
McGill University (Montreal). Marine Sciences Centre. Manuscript Report — McGill Univ (Montreal) Mar Sci Cent Manuscr Rep
McGill University [*Montreal*]. Peter Redpath Museum — McGill Univ Peter Redpath Mus
McGloin's Louisiana Courts of Appeal Reports — McGl
McGraw-Hill American Economy Prospects for Growth through 2000 — McGraw 2000
McGraw-Hill Annual Pollution Control Expenditures — McGraw Pol
McGraw-Hill Annual Survey of Business Plans for New Plants and Equipment — McGraw PE
McGraw-Hill Annual Survey of Research and Development Expenditures — McGraw RD
McGraw-Hill Overseas Operations of United States Industrial Companies — McGraw Ove
McGraw-Hill Publications. US Business Outlook. Short Term — McGraw ST
McGraw-Hill Series in Electrical Engineering. Circuits and Systems — McGraw Hill Ser Electr Engrg Circuits Systems
McGraw-Hill Series in Electrical Engineering. Communications and Information Theory — McGraw Hill Ser Electr Engrg Commun Inform Theory
McGraw-Hill Series in Quantitative Methods for Management — McGraw Hill Ser Quantitative Methods Management
McGraw-Hill United States Business Outlook. Long Term — McGraw US
McGraw-Hill's Medicine and Health [*Washington*] — McGraw Hill Med Health
McGraw-Hill's Washington Report on Medicine and Health — McGraw Hill Wash Rep Med Health
MCIC [*Metals and Ceramics Information Center*] **Report** — MCIC Rep
McKee-Pedersen Instruments Applications Notes — McKee Pedersen Instrum Appl Notes
McKinney's Consolidated Laws. New York — NY Law (McKinney)
McKinsey Quarterly — McKinsey Q
McKinsey Quarterly — McKinsey Quart
MCLC (Molecular Crystals and Liquid Crystals) Science and Technology. Section B. Nonlinear Optics — MCLC S&T Sect B Nonlinear Opt
McLean Foraminiferal Laboratory. Reports — McLean Foram Lab Rept
McLean Hospital Journal — McLean Hosp J
McLean Paleontological Laboratory. Reports — McLean Paleont Lab Rept
McMaster University. Symposium on Iron and Steelmaking. Proceedings — McMaster Symp Iron Steelmaking Proc
McMurray Courier — MC
MCN. American Journal of Maternal Child Nursing — MCN Am J Matern Child Nurs
McNair Lectures — McN L
McNeese Review — McN R
MCVQ. Medical College of Virginia. Quarterly — MCVQ Med Coll VA Q
M.D. Anderson Symposium on Fundamental Cancer Research — MD Anderson Symp Fundam Cancer Res
MD Computing — MD Comput
MD: Medical Newsmagazine — MD
MD Medical Newsmagazine — Med Newsmag
MDA [*Missouri Dental Association*] **Journal (Jefferson City, Missouri)** — MDA J (Jefferson City)
ME Proceedings. Conference on Materials Engineering — ME Proc Conf Mater Eng
Mead Johnson Symposium on Perinatal and Developmental Medicine — Mead Johnson Symp Perinat Dev Med
Meander — Me
Meander — Mea
Meander — Mr
Meaning — Me
Meaning and Art [*Elsevier Book Series*] — MART
Meanjin Quarterly [*University of Melbourne*] — Meanjin
Meanjin Quarterly — Meanjin Q
Measure — Meas
Measurement and Automation News — Meas & Autom News
Measurement and Control — Meas and Control
Measurement and Control — Meas Contr
Measurement and Control — Measmt Control
Measurement and Evaluation in Guidance — M & Eval Guid
Measurement and Evaluation in Guidance — Meas Eval G
Measurement and Evaluation in Guidance — Measmt & Eval in Guid
Measurement and Inspection Technology — Meas and Insp Technol
Measurement and Inspection Technology — Meas Insp Technol
Measurement and Instrument Review [*England*] — Meas Instrum Rev
Measurement Focus — Meas Focus
Measurement for Progress in Science and Technology. Proceedings. IMEKO Congress. International Measurement Confederation — Meas Prog Sci Technol Proc IMEKO Congr Int Meas Confed
Measurement Science and Technolgy — Meas Sci Technol
Measurement Techniques [*Former USSR*] — Meas Tech
Measurement Techniques (English Translation) — Meas Tech Engl Transl
Measurement Techniques (USSR) — Meas Tech R
Meat Facts. A Statistical Summary about America's Largest Food Industry — Meat Facts
Meat Industry — Meat Ind
Meat Industry Bulletin — Meat Ind Bul
Meat Industry Journal — Meat Ind J
Meat Industry Journal of Queensland — Meat Ind J Q
Meat Industry Research Conference (New Zealand) — Meat Ind Res Conf (NZ)
Meat Industry Research Institute of New Zealand. Report MIRINZ — Meat Ind Res Inst NZ Rep MIRINZ
Meat Marketing in Australia — Meat Marketing in Aust

Meat Outlook — Meat Outlk
Meat Processing — Meat Proc
Meat Processing — Meat Process
Meat Producer and Exporter — Meat Prod & Exp
Meat Research Institute. Memorandum — Meat Res Inst Memo
Meat Research News Letter — Meat Res News Lett
Meat Science — Meat Sci
Meat Science Institute. Proceedings — Meat Sci Inst Proc
Meat. Situation and Outlook — Meat Situat Outlook
Meat Trades Journal of Australia — Meat Trades J Aust
Meatworks Extension News — MEN
Mecanique des Roches — Mec Roches
Mecanique Electricite — Mec Elec
Mecanique Electricite — Mec Electr
Mecanique Electricite — MQELA
Mecanique- Materiaux- Electricite — Mec Mater Electr
Mecanique- Materiaux- Electricite — Mec-Mat-Elec
Mecanique-Physique — Mec Phys
Mecanismes des Pneumopathies Professionelles. Conference GERP — Mec Pneumopathies Prof Conf GERP
Mecanizarea si Electrificarea Agriculturii — Mecan Electrif Agr
Meccanica Italiana — Mecc Ital
Meccanica. Journal of the Italian Association of Theoretical and Applied Mechanics — Meccanica J Ital Assoc Theoret Appl Mech
Meccanizzacione Agricola — Mecc Agr
Mechanical and Chemical Engineering Transactions — MCHEB
Mechanical and Chemical Engineering Transactions [*Australia*] — Mech Chem Eng Trans
Mechanical and Chemical Engineering Transactions. Institution of Engineers (Australia) — Mech Chem Eng Trans Inst Eng (Aust)
Mechanical and Chemical Engineering Transactions. Institution of Engineers (Australia) — Mech Chem Engng Trans Instn Engrs (Aust)
Mechanical and Corrosion Properties A. Key Engineering Materials — Mech Corros Prop A Key Eng Mater
Mechanical and Corrosion Properties B. Single Crystal Properties — Mech Corros Prop B Single Cryst Prop
Mechanical Behavior of Electromagnetic Solid Continua. Proceedings. IUTAM (International Union of Theoretical and Applied Mechanics) IUPAP Symposium — Mech Behav Electromagn Solid Continua Proc IUTAM IUPAP Symp
Mechanical Behavior of Materials — Mech Behav Mater
Mechanical Behavior of Materials and Structures in Microelectronics. Symposium — Mech Behav Mater Struct Microelectron Symp
Mechanical Behavior of Materials. Proceedings. International Conference on Mechanical Behavior of Materials — Mech Behav Mater Proc Int Conf
Mechanical Behavior of Materials. Proceedings. Symposium on Mechanical Behavior of Materials — Mech Behav Mat Proc Symp
Mechanical Contractor — Mech Contract
Mechanical Design [*Japan*] — Mech Des
Mechanical Engineer (Tokyo) — Mech Eng Tokyo
Mechanical Engineering — GMEE
Mechanical Engineering — Mech Eng
Mechanical Engineering — Mech Engng
Mechanical Engineering — Mech Engrg
Mechanical Engineering Bulletin — Mech Eng Bull
Mechanical Engineering Bulletin — Mech Engng Bull
Mechanical Engineering Journal — Mech Engng J
Mechanical Engineering News — Mech Eng News
Mechanical Engineering News — Mech Engng News
Mechanical Engineering News (Washington, DC) — Mech Eng News (Washington DC)
Mechanical Engineering Note. Australia. Aeronautical Research Laboratories — Mech Eng Note Aust Aeronaut Res Lab
Mechanical Engineering Report (Australia). Aeronautical Research Laboratories [*A publication*] — Mech Eng Rep Aust Aeronaut Res Lab
Mechanical Engineering Report MP. National Research Council of Canada. Division of Mechanical Engineering — Mech Eng Rep MP Natl Res Counc Can Div Mech Eng
Mechanical Engineering Research Studies — Mech Engrg Res Stud
Mechanical Engineering Science Monograph. Institution of Mechanical Engineers [*London*] — Mech Eng Sci Monogr
Mechanical Engineering Series — Mech Engrg Ser
Mechanical Engineering Technology [*England*] — Mech Eng Technol
Mechanical Engineering (Tokyo) — Mech Eng (Tokyo)
Mechanical Engineering Transactions. Institution of Engineers (Australia) — Mech Eng Trans Inst Eng (Aust)
Mechanical Engineer's Contribution to Clean Air. Proceedings. Conference — Mech Eng Contrib Clean Air Proc Conf
Mechanical Failures Prevention Group. Meeting — Mech Failures Prev Group Meet
Mechanical Handling — Mech Handl
Mechanical Music — Mechanical Mus
Mechanical Properties at High Rates of Strain. Proceedings. Conference. Mechanical Properties of Materials at High Rates of Strain — Mech Prop High Rates Strain Proc Conf
Mechanical Properties of Cast Metal. Works. Conference on the Theory of Casting — Mech Prop Cast Met Works Conf Theory Cast
Mechanical Properties of Engineering Ceramics. Proceedings. Conference — Mech Prop Eng Ceram Proc Conf
Mechanical Sciences — Mech Sci
Mechanical Sciences. Mashinovdeniye — Mech Sci
Mechanical Tests for Bituminous Mixes. Characterization, Design, and Quality Control. Proceedings. International Symposium — Mech Tests Bitum Mixes Proc Int Symp
Mechanical Topics — Mech Top
Mechanical Translation — MT
Mechanical Working and Steel Processing. Conference Proceedings — Mech Work Steel Process Conf Proc
Mechanical World and Engineering Record [*England*] — Mech World Eng Rec
Mechanical World and Engineering Record — MWERA
Mechanics: Analysis — Mech Anal
Mechanics and Chemistry of Solid Propellants. Proceedings. Symposium on Naval Structural Mechanics — Mech Chem Solid Propellants Proc Symp Nav Struct Mech
Mechanics and Mathematical Methods. Series of Handbooks. Series I. Computational Methods in Mechanics — Mech Math Methods Ser Handbooks Ser I Comput Methods Mech
Mechanics and Mathematical Methods. Series of Handbooks. Series III. Acoustic, Electromagnetic, and Elastic Wave Scattering — Mech Math Methods Ser Handbooks Ser III Acoust Electromagnet
Mechanics and Practice. Lixue Yu Shijian — Mech Practice
Mechanics: Computational Mechanics — Mech Comput Mech
Mechanics: Dynamical Systems — Mech Dynam Systems
Mechanics of Cohesive-Frictional Materials — Mech Cohesive Frict Mater
Mechanics of Composite Materials — Mech Compos Mater
Mechanics of Composite Materials. Proceedings. Symposium on Naval Structural Mechanics — Mech Compos Mater Proc Symp Nav Struct Mech
Mechanics of Crack Growth. Proceedings. National Symposium on Fracture Mechanics — Mech Crack Growth Proc Natl Symp Fract Mech
Mechanics of Elastic Stability — Mech Elastic Stability
Mechanics of Fluids and Transport Processes — Mech Fluids Transp Process
Mechanics of Fracture — Mech of Fracture
Mechanics of Materials — Mech Mater
Mechanics of Materials — MSMSD
Mechanics of Solids — Mech Solids
Mechanics of Solids (English Translation) — Mech Solids Engl Transl
Mechanics of Structures and Machines — Mech Structures Mach
Mechanics of Surface Structures — Mech Surface Structures
Mechanics Research Communications — Mech Res Comm
Mechanics Research Communications — Mech Res Commun
Mechanics Research Communications — MRCOD
Mechanik Miesiecznik Naukowo-Techniczny — Mech Mies Nauk Tech
Mechanik Miesiecznik Naukowo-Techniczny — Mech Miesiecznik Nauk-Tech
Mechanik Miesiecznik Naukowo-Techniczny — Mechanik
Mechanika (Bydgoszcz, Poland) — Mechanika Bydgoszcz Pol
Mechanika (Opole, Poland) — Mechanika Opole Pol
Mechanika Polimerov — Mech Polim
Mechanika, Technologia Budowy Maszyn (Bydgoszcz, Poland) — Mech Technol Budowy Masz (Bydgoszcz Pol)
Mechanika Teoretyczna i Stosowana — Mech Teor i Stoso
Mechanika Teoretyczna i Stosowana — Mech Teor i Stosow
Mechanika, Zeszyty Naukowe Politechniki Krakowskiej — Mech Zesz Nauk Politech Krakow
Mechanisation Leaflet. Great Britain Ministry of Agriculture, Fisheries, and Food — Mech Leafl GB Min Agr Fish Food
Mechanism and Machine Theory — Mech Mach T
Mechanism of Photosynthesis. Proceedings. International Congress of Biochemistry — Mech Photosynth Proc Int Congr Biochem
Mechanism of Toxic Action on Some Target Organs. Proceedings. European Society of Toxicology Meeting — Mech Tox Action Some Target Organs Proc Eur Soc Toxicol Meet
Mechanisms and Recent Advances in Therapy of Hypertension. International Symposium on Nephrology — Mech Recent Adv Ther Hypertens Int Symp Nephrol
Mechanisms in Fibre Carcinogenesis — Mech Fibre Carcinog
Mechanisms in Symptom Formation. Proceedings. Congress. International College of Psychosomatic Medicine — Mech Symptom Form Proc Congr Int Coll Psychosom Med
Mechanisms of Ageing and Development — MAGDA
Mechanisms of Ageing and Development — Mech Age D
Mechanisms of Ageing and Development — Mech Ageing Dev
Mechanisms of Development — Mech Dev
Mechanisms of Intestinal Adaptation. Proceedings. International Conference on Intestinal Adaptation — Mech Intest Adapt Proc Int Conf
Mechanisms of Lymphocyte Activation and Immune Regulation 3. Developmmental Biology of Lymphocytes — Mech Lymphocyte Act Immune Regul 3
Mechanisms of Lymphocyte Activation. Proceedings. International Leucocyte Conference — Mech Lymphocyte Act Proc Int Leucocyte Conf
Mechanisms of Molecular Migrations — Mech Mol Migr
Mechanisms of Reactions of Sulfur Compounds — Mech React Sulfur Comp
Mechanisms of Reactions of Sulfur Compounds — Mech React Sulfur Compd
Mechanisms of Toxicity and Metabolism — Mech Tox Metab
Mechanisms of Tumor Promotion — Mech Tumor Promot
Mechanix Illustrated — Mech Illus
Mechanizace Automatizace Administrativy — Mech Autom Adm
Mechanizace v Chemickem Prumyslu — Mech Chem Prum
Mechanizacja Rolnictwa — Mech Roln
Mechenye Atomy v Issledovaniyakh Pitaniya Rastenii i Primeneniya Udobrenii Trudy Soveshchaniya [*Moscow*] — Mechenye At Issled Pitan Rast Primen Udobr Tr Soveshch
Mechenye Biologicheski Atkivnye Veshchestva — Mechenye Biol Atk Veshchestva
Mecklenburger Jahrbuch Schwerin — MbJb
Mecklenburgische Zeitschrift fuer Rechtspflege und Rechtswissenschaft — Meckl Z
Mecmuasi Universite. Fen Fakulte (Istanbul) — Mecmuasi Univ Fen Fak (Istanbul)
Mecon Journal — Mecon J
MED. Media in Education and Development — MED Media Educ and Dev

Medal Collector — MC
Medan Ilmu Pengetahuan Madjalak Filsafat, Ilmu, Ilmu Sosial, Budaja, Pasti dan Alam — Medan Ilmu Pengetahuan Madj Filsafat
Meddelande fraan Kungliga Lantbruksakademiens Ekonomiska Avdelning — Medd K Lantbruksakad Ekon Avd
Meddelande fraan Kungliga Lantbruksakademiens Traedgaardsavdelning — Medd K Lantbruksakad Traedgaardsavd
Meddelande fraan Kungliga Lantbruksstyrelsen — Medd K Lantbruksstyr
Meddelande fraan Statens Provningsanstalt. Stockholm — Medd Statens Provningsanst Stockholm
Meddelande fran Alnarpsinstitutets Mejeriavdelning och Statens Mejerifoersoek — Medd Alnarpsinst Mejeriavd Statens Mejerifoers
Meddelande fran Centralstyrelsen foer Malmoehus Laens Foersoeksoch Vaxtskyddsringar — Medd Centralstyr Malmohus Lans Forsoks-Vaxtskyddsringar
Meddelande fran Havsfiskelaboratoriet Lysekil — Medd Havsfiskelab Lysekil
Meddelande fran Institutet foer Maltdrycksforskning — Medd Inst Maltdrycksforsk
Meddelande fran Kvismare Fagelstation — Medd Kvismare Fagelstn
Meddelande fran Lunds Universitet Historiska Museum — Medd Lunds Univ Hist Mus
Meddelande fran Lunds Universitet Historiska Museum — Meddel Lund
Meddelande fran Lunds Universitet Historiska Museum — Meddel Lund U Hist Mus
Meddelande fran Statens Forskningsanst Lantmannabyggnader — Medd Stat Forskningsanst Lantmannabyggnader
Meddelande fran Statens Mejerifoersoek (Sweden) — Medd Statens Mejerifoers (Swed)
Meddelande fran Svenska Textilforskninginstitutet — Medd Sven Text
Meddelande. Grafiska Forskningslaboratoriet — Medd Grafiska Forskningslab
Meddelande. Lantbruksakademiens Traedgardsavdelningen — Meddeland Lantbruksakad Traedgardsavd
Meddelande. Statens Lantbrukskemiska Laboratorium — Medd Statens Lantbrukskem Lab
Meddelande. Statens Vaextskyddsanstalt — Meddeland Statens Vaextskyddsanst
Meddelande. Svenska Mejeriernas Riksfoerening. Produkttekniska Avdelningen — Medd Sven Mejeriernas Riksfoeren Produkttek Avd
Meddelande Svenska Tekniska Vetenskapsakademien i Finland — Medd Svenska Tek Vetenskapsakad Finl
Meddelande-Jordbruksteknisk Institutet — Medd Jordbrukste Inst
Meddelanden fra Dansk Geologiske Forendlingen — Medd Dansk Geol Forend
Meddelanden fraan Institutionen foer Teknisk Kemi. Aabo Akademi — Medd Inst Tek Kemi Aabo Akad
Meddelanden fraan Kungliga Vetenskapsakademiens Nobelinstitut — Medd K Vetenskapsakad Nobelinst
Meddelanden fran Abo Akademis Geologisk-Mineralogiska Institut — Medd Abo Akad Geol Mineral Inst
Meddelanden fran Avdelningen foer Ekologisk Botanik Lunds Universitet — MAEUDD
Meddelanden fran Avdelningen foer Ekologisk Botanik Lunds Universitet — Medd Avd Ekol Bot Lunds Univ
Meddelanden fran Goeteborgs Botaniska Traedgaard — Medd Goeteborgs Bot Traedg
Meddelanden fran Industrins Centrallaboratorium., Helsinki — Medd Ind Centrallab Helsinki
Meddelanden fran Kungliga Lantbrukshogskolan och [*Statens*] **Lantbruksforsok Jordbruksforsok** [*Statens*] — Meddn K Lantbrhogsk Lantbrfors Jordbrfors
Meddelanden fran Kyrkohistoriska Arkivet i Lund — MKHA
Meddelanden fran Lunds Botaniska Museum — Meddeland Lunds Bot Mus
Meddelanden fran Lunds Geologisk-Mineralogiska Institut — Medd Lunds Geol Mineral Inst
Meddelanden fran Lunds Mineralogisk-Geologiska Institution — Medd Lunds Mineral Geol Inst
Meddelanden fran Lunds Universitets Historiska Museum — Meddel Lund
Meddelanden fran Lunds Universitets Historiska Museum de Lund — MLUHM
Meddelanden fran Malmoe Luftfoersvarsfoerening — Medd Luftfoersvarsfoeren Malmoe
Meddelanden fran Seminarierna foer Slaviska Sprak, Jamforande Sprakforskning och Finsk-Ugriska Sprak vis Lunds Universitet — MSLund
Meddelanden fran Statens Kommitte foer Byggnadsforskning — Meddel Komm Byggn
Meddelanden fran Statens Skeppsprovningsanstalt — Medd Statens Skeppsprovningsanst
Meddelanden fran Statens Skogsfoersoeksanstalt — Meddel Skogsfoers Anst
Meddelanden fran Statens Skogsforskningsinstitut — Medd Statens Skogsforskningsinst
Meddelanden fran Statens Skogsforskningsinstitut (Stockholm) — Meddn St Skogsforskinst (Stockholm)
Meddelanden fran Statens Skogsforskningsinstitut (Sweden) — Medd Statens Skogsforskningsinst (Swed)
Meddelanden fran Statens Traedgaardsfoersoek — Medd Statens Traedgaardsfoers
Meddelanden fran Stiftelsen foer Rasforadling av Skogstrad — Medd Stift Rasforadl Skogstrad
Meddelanden fran Strindbergssaellskapet — MFS
Meddelanden fran Svenska Textilforskningsinstitutet — Medd Sven Textilforskningsinst
Meddelanden fran Svenska Traforskningsinstitutet (Trakemi och Pappersteknik) — Medd Svenska Traforskn Inst (Trakem PappTekn)
Meddelanden fran Svenska Traskyddsinstitutet — Medd Sven Traskyddsinst
Meddelanden fran Sveriges Froeodlarefoerbund — Meddn Sverig FroeodlFoerb
Meddelanden fran Sveriges Kemiska Industrikontor — Medd Sver Kem Industrikontor
Meddelanden fran Traedgaardsfoersoek — Medd Traedgaardsfoers
Meddelanden fran Vaextekologiska Institutionen Lunds Universitet — Medd Vaextekol Inst Lund Univ
Meddelanden. Kungliga Lantbruksstyrelsen. Serie A. Allmaent — Medd K Lantbruksstyr Ser A
Meddelanden. Kungliga Lantbruksstyrelsen. Serie B. Landbruksavdelningen — Medd K Lantbruksstyr Ser B
Meddelanden - Lantbruksstyrelsen — Medd Lantbruksstyr
Meddelanden. Statens Vaextskyddsanstalt — Medd Statens Vaextskyddsanst
Meddelanden. Svenska Forskningsinstitutet foer Cement och Betong vid Kungliga Tekniska Hoegskolan i Stockholm — Medd Sven Forskningsinst Cem Betong K Tek Hoegsk Stockholm
Meddelelse fra Hermetikkindustriens Laboratorium — Medd Hermetikkind Lab
Meddelelse fra Papirindustriens Forskningsinstitutt — Medd Papirind Forskningsinst
Meddelelse. Geodaetisk Institut (Denmark) — Medd Geod Inst (Den)
Meddelelse Norsk Treteknisk Institutt — Medd Norsk Tretekn Inst
Meddelelse Statens Planteavlsforsog — Medd Statens Planteavsforsog
Meddelelser fra Carlsberg Laboratoriet — M Cb L
Meddelelser fra Carlsberg Laboratorium — Medd Carlsberg Lab
Meddelelser fra Carlsberg Latoratoriet — Meddel Carlsberg Lab
Meddelelser fra Danmarks Fiskfri-og Havundersogelser — Medd Dan Fisk Havunders
Meddelelser fra Dansk Geologisk Forening — M Gl F
Meddelelser fra Dansk Geologisk Forening — Medd Dan Geol Foren
Meddelelser fra Danskiaererforeningen — MDan
Meddelelser fra det Norske Myrselskap — Medd Nor Myrselsk
Meddelelser fra det Norske Myrselskap — Meddr Norske Myrselsk
Meddelelser fra det Norske Skogforsoeksvesen — Medd Nor Sk
Meddelelser fra det Norske Skogforsoeksvesen — Medd Nor Skogforsoksves
Meddelelser fra det Norske Skogforsoeksvesen — Meddr Norske Skogsfors Ves
Meddelelser fra det Norske Skogforsoeksvesen — MNSKA
Meddelelser fra Historisk-Topografisk Selskab for Gjentofte Kommune — M HT Gjen
Meddelelser fra Kommissionen for Danmarks Fiskeri- og Havundersoegelser. Serie Fiskeri — Medd Komm Dan Fisk Havunders Ser Fisk
Meddelelser fra Kommissionen for Danmarks Fiskeri- og Havundersoegelser. Serie Plankton — Medd Komm Dan Fisk Havunders Ser Plankton
Meddelelser fra Kommissionen for Havundersoegelser. Serie Fiskeri — Medd Komm Havunders Ser Fisk
Meddelelser fra Kommissionen for Havundersoegelser. Serie Hydrografti — Medd Komm Havunders Ser Hydrogr
Meddelelser fra Krigs-Archiverne — Meddelels Krigsarch
Meddelelser fra Norsk Farmaceutisk Selskap — Medd Nor Farm Selsk
Meddelelser fra Norsk Farmaceutisk Selskap — MNFSA
Meddelelser fra Norsk Forening foer Sprog-Videnskap — MNFS
Meddelelser fra Norsk Forening foer Sprog-Videnskap — MNSV
Meddelelser fra Norsk Institute foer Skogforskning — Medd Nor Inst Skogforsk
Meddelelser fra Norsk Viltforskning — Medd Nor Viltforsk
Meddelelser fra Norsk Viltforskning — MFNV
Meddelelser fra Ny Carlsberg Glyptotek — Med NC
Meddelelser fra Ny Carlsberg Glyptotek — Meddelelser NCG
Meddelelser fra Statens Viltundersokelser [*Papers. Norwegian State Game Research Institute*] — Medd Statens Viltunders
Meddelelser fra Statens Viltundersokelser [*Papers. Norwegian State Game Research Institute*] — MFSV
Meddelelser fra Statens Viltundersokelser (Papers. Norwegian State Game Research Institute) — Medd Statens Viltunders (Pap Norw State Game Res Inst)
Meddelelser fra Thorvaldsens Museum — M Thorv Mus
Meddelelser fra Thorvaldsens Museum — Medd Thorvaldsen Mus
Meddelelser fra Thorvaldsens Museum — MThM
Meddelelser fra Vejlaboratoriet — M Vej
Meddelelser fra Vestlandets Forstlige Forsoeksstasjon — Medd Vestl Forstl Forsoeksstn
Meddelelser fra Vestlandets Forstlige Forsoeksstasjon — Medd Vestland Forstl Forsoksta
Meddelelser fra Vestlandets Forstlige Forsoeksstasjon — MFVFF
Meddelelser om Groenland — Medd Groenl
Meddelelser om Groenland — Medd Groenland
Meddelelser om Groenland — Medd Gronl
Meddelelser om Groenland — Meddel om Gronland
Meddelelser om Groenland — MOGR
Meddelelser om Groenland. Geoscience — Medd Groenl Geosci
Meddelelser om Groenland. Man and Society — MOGMS
Medecin de France — Med Fr
Medecin Veterinaire du Quebec — Med Vet Que
Medecin Veterinaire du Quebec — MVEQDC
Medecine — MEDEA
Medecine Actuelle — Med Actuelle
Medecine Aeronautique — Med Aero
Medecine Aeronautique — Med Aeronaut
Medecine Aeronautique et Spatiale, Medecine Subaquatique et Hyperbare — Med Aeronaut Spat Med Subaquat Hyperbare
Medecine Aeronautique et Spatiale, Medecine Subaquatique et Hyperbare — MSMHD
Medecine, Biologie, Environnement — Med Biol Environ
Medecine Clinique et Experimentale — Med Clin Exp
Medecine d'Afrique Noire — Med Afr Noire
Medecine dans le Monde — Med Monde
Medecine du Sport — Med Sport
Medecine du Sport [*Paris*] — MNSPBL
Medecine du Sport (Paris) — Med Sport (Paris)
Medecine et Armees — MDARC
Medecine et Armees — Med Armees
Medecine et Audiovision [*France*] — Med Audiovision

Medecine et Biologie — Med Biol
Medecine et Chirurgie Digestives — Med Chir Dig
Medecine et Hygiene — Med Hyg
Medecine et Hygiene (Geneve) — Med Hyg (Geneve)
Medecine et Informatique — Med Inf
Medecine et Informatique — MINFDZ
Medecine et Informatique (London) — Med Inf (Lond)
Medecine et Nutrition — Med Nutr
Medecine Experimentale (Kharkov) — Med Exp (Kharkov)
Medecine Infantile — Med Infant
Medecine Interne — Med Interne
Medecine Interne [*Paris*] — MEITAL
Medecine Interne (Paris) — Med Interne (Paris)
Medecine Legale a l'Hopital. Congres. Academie Internationale de Medecine Legale et de Medecine Sociale — Med Leg Hop Congr Acad Int Med Leg Med Soc
Medecine Legale et Dommage Corporel — Med Leg Dommage Corpor
Medecine Legale. Toxicologie — Med Leg Toxicol
Medecine Moderne — Med Moderne
Medecine Moderne du Canada — Med Mod Can
Medecine Moderne (Paris) — Med Mod (Paris)
Medecine Nucleaire — Med Nucl
Medecine Nucleaire. Supplementum — Med Nucl Suppl
Medecine Praticienne — Med Prat
Medecine Sociale et Preventive — Med Soc Prev
Medecine Sociale et Preventive — SZPMAA
Medecine Tropicale — Med Trop
Medecine Tropicale (Marseille) — Med Trop (Marseille)
Medecine Tropicale (Marseilles) — Med Trop (Mars)
Medecine Veterinaire Hellenique — Med Vet Hell
Mededeeling. Koloniaal Instituut te Amsterdam. Afdeeling Tropische Hygiene — Meded Kolon Inst Amsterdam Afd Trop Hyg
Mededeeling Koninklijke Vereeniging Indisch Instituut — Meded Kon Veren Indisch Inst
Mededeeling. Koninklijke Vereeniging Koloniaal Instituut. Afdeeling Handelsmuseum — Meded K Ver Kolon Inst Afd Handelsmus
Mededeeling. Koninklijke Vereeniging Koloniaal Instituut. Afdeeling Tropische Hygiene — Meded K Ver Kolon Inst Afd Trop Hyg
Mededeeling. Laboratorium voor Scheikundig Onderzoek te Buitenzorg — Meded Lab Scheikd Onderz Buitenzorg
Mededeelingen. Akademie van Wetenschappen — MAW
Mededeelingen. Algemeen Proefstation der AVROS [*Algemeene Vereeniging van Rubberplanters ter Oostkust van Sumatra*] — Meded Alg Proefstn AVROS
Mededeelingen. Algemeen Proefstation op Java — Meded Alg Proefstat Java
Mededeelingen. Botanisch Instituut. Rijksuniversiteit te Gent — Meded Bot Inst Rijksuniv Gent
Mededeelingen. Centraal Rubberstation — Meded Cent Rubberstn
Mededeelingen der Koninklijke Akademie van Wetenschappen Afdeeling Letterkunde — Meded Kon Akad Wetensch Afd Lettk
Mededeelingen der Koninklijke Nederlandse Akademie van Wetenschappen. Afdeeling Letterkunde — Med Ak Wet
Mededeelingen der Koninklijke Nederlandse Akademie van Wetenschappen. Afdeeling Letterkunde — Mededeelingen
Mededeelingen der Koninklijke Nederlandse Akademie van Wetenschappen. Afdeeling Letterkunde — MNAWA
Mededeelingen. Directeur van de Tuinbouw — Meded Directeur Tuinb
Mededeelingen en Verhandelingen Ex Oriente Lux — MVEOL
Mededeelingen. Encyclopaedisch Bureau — MEB
Mededeelingen Ex Oriente Lux — MEOL
Mededeelingen. Geschied- en Oudheidkundige Kring voor Leuven en Omgeving — MGOKL
Mededeelingen. Geschied- en Oudheidkundige Kring voor Leuven en Omgeving — MGOKLeuven
Mededeelingen. Indonesisch Instituut voor Rubberonderzoek — Meded Indones Inst Rubberonderz
Mededeelingen. Koninklijke Nederlandsche Akademie van Wetenschappen — Meded Kon Nederl Ak Wetensch
Mededeelingen. Koninklijke Nederlandsche Akademie van Wetenschappen. Afdeling Letterkunde — MKAW
Mededeelingen. Koninklijke Nederlandsche Akademie van Wetenschappen. Afdeling Letterkunde — MKNA
Mededeelingen. Koninklijke Nederlandsche Akademie van Wetenschappen. Afdeling Letterkunde — MKNAL
Mededeelingen. Koninklijke Nederlandsche Akademie van Wetenschappen. Afdeling Letterkunde — MKNAWL
Mededeelingen. Koninklijke Nederlandsche Akademie van Wetenschappen. Afdeling Letterkunde — MNAWL
Mededeelingen. Koninklijke Nederlandsche Akademie van Wetenschappen te Amsterdam — MAA
Mededeelingen. Koninklijke Vlaamse Akademie van Wetenschappen — Meded Kon Vl Ak Wetensch
Mededeelingen. Koninklijke Vlaamse Akademie van Wetenschappen, Letteren en Schone Kunsten v Belgie — MKVAB
Mededeelingen. Kunst- en Oudheidkundigen Kring van Herenthals — MKOH
Mededeelingen. Laboratorium voor Bloembollenonderzoek — Meded Lab Bloembollenonderz
Mededeelingen. Nederlandsch-Historisch Institut le Rome — MNHIR
Mededeelingen. Nederlandsch-Historisch Institut le Rome — MNIR
Mededeelingen. Nijmeegse Centrale voor Dialecten Naamkunde — MNCDN
Mededeelingen over Rubber — Meded Rubber
Mededeelingen. Proefstation voor de Java Suikerindustrie — Meded Proefstat Java Suikerindustr
Mededeelingen. Proefstation voor de Java-Suikerindustrie — Meded Proefstn Java Suikerind
Mededeelingen. Proefstation voor Rubber — Meded Proefstat Rubber
Mededeelingen. Rijks Hoogere Land-, Tuin-, en Boschbouwschool — Meded Rijks Hoogere Land Boschbouwsch
Mededeelingen. Rijks Landbouwhoogeschool en de Daaraan Verbonden Instituten — Meded Rijks Landbouwhoogeschool
Mededeelingen. Rijksmuseum voor Volkenkunde — Meded Rijksmus Volk
Mededeelingen uit het Gebied van Natuur, Wetenschapen, en Kunst — Meded Natuur
Mededeelingen Uitgegeven. Vlaamse Toponymische Vereniging — Meded Vl Topon Ver
Mededeelingen Uitgeven. Departement van Landbouw in Nederlandsch-Indiee — Meded Dept Landb Ned Indioo
Mededeelingen van de Afdeeling Rubber Research van het Proefstation West-Java — Meded Afd Rubber Res Proefstn West Java
Mededeelingen van de Landbouwhogeschool — Meded Landbouwhogeschool
Mededeelingen van de Landbouwhoogeschool en de Onderzoekingstations van den Staat te Gent — Meded Landbouwhoogeschool Onderzoekingstat Staat Gent
Mededeelingen van de Rijksvoorlichtingsdienst ten behoeve van den Rubberhandel en de Rubbernijverheid te Delft — Meded Rijksvoorlichtingsdienst Rubberhandel Rubbernijverheid
Mededeelingen van de Vlaamsche Academie voor Wetenschappen, Letteren en Schoone Kunsten van Belgie. Klasse der Letteren — MVAW L
Mededeelingen van de Vlaamsche Academie voor Wetenschappen, Letteren en Schoone Kunsten van Belgie. Klasse der Schoone Kunsten — MVAW SK
Mededeelingen van den Dienst der Volksgezondheid in Nederlandsch-Indie — Meded Dienst Volksgezond Ned Indie
Mededeelingen van het Algemeen Proefstation der Algemeene Rubberplanters ter Oostkust van Sumatra, Algemeene Serie — Meded Alg Proefstn Alg Rubberplant Oostkust Sumatra Alg Ser
Mededeelingen van het Algemeen Proefstation der AVROS, Rubber Serie — Meded Alg Proefstn AVROS Rubber Ser
Mededeelingen van het Proefstation voor het Boschwezen — Meded Proefstat Boschw
Mededeelingen van het Proefstation voor Rijst — Meded Proefstat Rijst
Mededeelingen van het Proefstation voor Rubber — Meded Proefstn Rubber
Mededeelingen van het Proefstation voor Vorstenlandsche Tabak — Meded Proefstn Vorstenl Tab
Mededeelingen. Vereniging Naamkunde te Leuven en Commissie Naamkunde te Amsterdam — MVN
Mededeelingen. Vereniging Naamkunde te Leuven en Commissie Naamkunde te Amsterdam — MVNLA
Mededeelingen. Vlaamsche Academie voor Wetenschappen, Letteren, en Schoone Kunsten van Belgie — MVAW
Mededeelingen. Zuid-Nederlandsche Dialect Centrale — Meded Zuid-Nederl Dial Centr
Mededeling. Geologishe Mijnbouwkundige Dienst van Suriname — Meded Geol Mijnbouwkd Dienst Suriname
Mededeling. Instituut voor Graan. Meel en Brood TNO [*Toegepast Natuurwetenschappelijk Onderzoek*] **(Wageningen)** — Meded Inst Graan Meel Brood TNO (Wageningen)
Mededeling. Instituut voor Moderne Veevoeding "De Schothorst" te Hoogland bij Amersfoorst — Meded Inst Mod Veevoeding De Schothorst Hoogland Amersfoorst
Mededeling. Koninklijk Instituut voor de Tropen. Afdeling Tropische Producten — Meded K Inst Trop Afd Trop Prod
Mededeling. Koninklijke Vereniging Indisch Instituut. Afdeling Handelsmuseum — Meded K Ver Indisch Inst Afd Handelsmus
Mededeling. Koninklijke Vereniging Indisch Instituut. Afdeling Tropische Hygiene — Meded K Ver Indisch Inst Afd Trop Hyg
Mededeling. Proefstation foor de Akker- en Weidebouw — Meded Proefstn Akker Weidebouw
Mededeling. Proefstation voor de Groenteteelt in de Vollegrond in Nederland — Meded Proefstn Groenteteelt Vollegrond Ned
Mededeling. Rijksproefstation voor Zaadcontrole (Wageningen) — Meded Rijksproefstat Zaadcontr (Wageningen)
Mededeling. Stichting Nederlands Graan-Centrum — Meded Stichting Nederl Graan-Cent
Mededeling Vakgroep Landbouwplantenteelt en Graslandkunde — Meded Vakgroep Landbouwplantenteelt Graslandkd
Mededeling. Vezelinstituut TNO [*Toegepast Natuurwetenschappelijk Onderzoek*] — Meded Vezelinst TNO
Mededelingen. Centraal Instituut voor Landbouwkundig Onderzoek — Meded Centr Inst Landbouwk Onderz
Mededelingen der Nederlandse Akademie van Wetenschappen — MNAW
Mededelingen der Zittingen. Koninklijke Academie voor Overzeese Wetenschappen (Brussels) — Meded Zittingen K Acad Overzeese Wet (Brussels)
Mededelingen. Directeur van de Tuinbouw — Med Dir Tuinb
Mededelingen. Directeur van de Tuinbouw — Meded Dir Tuinb
Mededelingen. Directie Tuinbouw (Netherlands) — Meded Dir Tuinbouw (Neth)
Mededelingen en Verhandelingen van het Voor-Aziatisch-Egyptisch Genootschap — MEOL
Mededelingen. Faculteit Diergeneeskunde Rijksuniversiteit (Gent) — Meded Fac Diergeneeskd Rijksuniv (Gent)
Mededelingen. Faculteit Landbouwwetenschappen. Rijksuniversiteit (Gent) — Meded Fac Landbouwwet Rijksuniv (Gent)
Mededelingen. Faculteit Landbouwwetenschappen. Rijksuniversiteit (Gent) — Meded Fac LandWet (Gent)
Mededelingen. Faculteit Landbouwwetenschappen. Rijksuniversiteit (Gent) — MFLRA
Mededelingen. Geologische Stichting — Meded Geol Sticht
Mededelingen. Geologische Stichting. Nieuwe Serie — MGESA
Mededelingen. Geologische Stichting. Nieuwe Serie (Netherlands) — Meded Geol Sticht Nieuwe Ser (Neth)

Mededelingen. Geologische Stichting. Serie C. Uitkomsten van het Geologie-Palaeontologie. Onderzoek van de Ondergrond van Nederland — Meded Geol Stichting Ser C
Mededelingen. Historische Kring Kesteren en Omstreken — MHKK
Mededelingen. Instituut voor Biologisch en Scheikundig Onderzoek van Landbouwgewassen — Meded Inst Biol Scheik Onderz LandbGewass
Mededelingen. Instituut voor Biologisch en Scheikundig Onderzoek van Landbouwgewassen (Wageningen) — Meded Inst Biol Scheik Onderz Landbougewassen (Wageningen)
Mededelingen. Instituut voor Rationele Suikerproductie — Meded Ins Ratio Suikerprod
Mededelingen. Instituut voor Rationele Suikerproductie — Meded Inst Rat Suik Prod
Mededelingen. Instituut voor Rationele Suikerproductie — Meded Inst Ration Suikerprod
Mededelingen. Instituut voor Toegepast Biologisch Onderzoek in der Natuur — Meded Inst Toegep Biol Onderz Nat
Mededelingen. Koninklijke Academie voor Geneeskunde van Belgie — Meded K Acad Geneeskd Belg
Mededelingen. Koninklijke Academie voor Wetenschappen. Letteren en Schone Kunsten van Belgie — Meded K Acad Wet Lett en Schone Kunsten Belg
Mededelingen. Koninklijke Academie voor Wetenschappen. Letteren en Schone Kunsten van Belgie. Klasse der Wetenschappen — Meded K Acad Wet Lett Schone Kunsten Belg Kl Wet
Mededelingen. Koninklijke Academie voor Wetenschappen. Letteren en Schone Kunsten van Belgie. Klasse der Wetenschappen — MKAWA
Mededelingen. Koninklijke Nederlandse Academie van Wetenschappen. Afdeling Letterkunde [*Elsevier Book Series*] — MKL
Mededelingen. Koninklijke Vlaamse Academie voor Wetenschappen. Letteren en Schone Kunsten van Belgie. Klasse der Wetenschappen — Meded K Vlaam Acad Wet Lett Schone Kunsten Belg Kl Wet
Mededelingen. Koninklijke Vlaamse Academie voor Wetenschappen. Letteren en Schone Kunsten van Belgie. Klasse der Wetenschappen — Meded L Vlaam Acad Wet Belg Kl Wet
Mededelingen. Koninklijke Vlaamse Academie voor Wetenschappen. Letteren en Schone Kunsten van Belgie. Klasse der Wetenschappen — MWBWA
Mededelingen. Laboratorium voor Fysiologische Chemie. Universiteit van Amsterdam — Meded Lab Fysiol Chem Univ Amsterdam
Mededelingen. Laboratorium voor Houttechnologie. Rijkslandbouwhogeschool (Gent) — Meded Lab Houttechnol Rijkslandbouwhogesch (Gent)
Mededelingen. Laboratorium voor Physiologische Chemie. Universiteit van Amsterdam — Meded Lab Physiol Chem Univ Amsterdam
Mededelingen. Laboratorium voor Physiologische Chemie. Universiteit van Amsterdam et Nederlands Instituut voor Volksvoeding — Meded Lab Physiol Chem Univ Amsterdam Ned Inst Volksvoed
Mededelingen. Landbouwhogeschool en Opzoekingsstations (Ghent) — Meded Landbouwhogesch Opzoekingssta (Ghent)
Mededelingen. Landbouwhogeschool en Opzoekingsstations van de Staat te Gent — Meded LandbHogesch OpzoekStns Gent
Mededelingen. Landbouwhogeschool en Opzoekingsstations van de Staat te Gent — Meded Landbouwhogesch Opzoekingsstn Staat Gent
Mededelingen. Landbouwhogeschool en Opzoekingsstations van de Staat te Gent — MLOSA
Mededelingen. Landbouwhogeschool (Ghent) — Meded Landbouwhogesch (Ghent)
Mededelingen. Landbouwhogeschool te Wageningen — Meded Landbhogesch Wageningen
Mededelingen. Landbouwhogeschool te Wageningen — Meded Landbouwhogesch Wageningen
Mededelingen. Landbouwproefstation in Suriname — Meded LandProefstn Suriname
Mededelingen. Lederinstituut TNO [*Toegepast Natuurwetenschappelijk Onderzoek*] [*A publication*] — Meded Lederinst TNO
Mededelingen mit de Leidse Verzameling van Spijkerschrift Inscripties — MLVS
Mededelingen. Nationale Cooperatieve Aan- en Verkoopvereniging voor de Landbouw Central Bureau — Meded Nat Coop Aan- Verkoopver Landbouw Cen Bur
Mededelingen. Nederlande Vereniging voor Koeltechniek — Meded Ned Ver Koeltech
Mededelingen. Nederlandsch Historisch Institut te Rome — Med Nl Rome
Mededelingen. Nederlandsch Historisch Institut te Rome — Meded
Mededelingen. Nederlandsch Historisch Institut te Rome — Mededel Neder Inst Rom
Mededelingen. Nederlandsch Historisch Institut te Rome — Nederlands Hist Ins Rome Med
Mededelingen. Nederlandse Algemene Keuringsdienst voor Landbouwzaden en Aardappelpootgoed — Meded Ned Alg Keuringsdienst Landbouwz
Mededelingen. Proefstation voor de Akker- en Weidebouw — Meded Proefstn Akker- en Weideb
Mededelingen. Rijks Geologische Dienst — Meded Rijks Geol Dienst
Mededelingen. Rijks Geologische Dienst. Nieuwe Serie (Netherlands) — Meded Rijks Geol Dienst Nieuwe Ser (Neth)
Mededelingen. Rijks Instituut voor Pharmaco-Therapeutisch Onderzoek — Meded Rijks Inst Pharm Ther Onderz
Mededelingen. Rijksfaculteit Landbouwwetenschappen te Gent — Meded Rijksfac Landbouwwet Gent
Mededelingen. Rijksfaculteit Landbouwwetenschappen te Gent (Belgium) — MRLAB
Mededelingen. Rubber-Stichting (Delft) — Meded Rubber-Sticht (Delft)
Mededelingen. Stichting voor Plantenveredeling (Wageningen) — Meded Stichting Plantenveredeling (Wageningen)
Mededelingen van Belgische Natuurkundige Vereniging — Meded Belg Naturrkd Ver
Mededelingen van de Koninklijke Academie voor Wetenschappen, Letteren, en Schone Kunsten van Belgie. Klasse der Wetenschappen — Meded Kon Akad Wetensch Lett Sch Kunst Belgie Kl Wetensch
Mededelingen van de Nederlandse Vereniging voor Internationaal Recht — Med Ned Ver Int R
Mededelingen van de Rubber-Stichting, Amsterdam — Meded Rubber Sticht Amsterdam
Mededelingen van de Schoolraad voor de Scholen met de Bijbel — MSB
Mededelingen van de Stichting Nederlands Graancentrum — Meded Stichting Ned Graancentrum
Mededelingen van het Biologisch Station te Wijster — Meded Biol Stat Wijster
Mededelingen van het Instituut voor Plantenziektenkundig Onderzoek — Meded Inst Plantenziekten Onderz
Mededelingen van het Kadaster — MK
Mededelingen van het Nederlands Historisch Instituut te Rome — Meded Rom
Mededelingen van het Nederlandsch Historisch Institut te Rome — Med Nederl Hist Inst Rom
Mededelingen van het Rijksstation voor Zeevisserij (Oostende, Belgium) — Meded Rijksstn Zeeviss Oostende Belg
Mededelingen van het Verbond der Belgische Nijverheid — Med VBN
Mededelingen van het Wiskundig Genootschap — Meded Wiskd Genoot
Mededelingen van Wege het Spinozahuis — Med Spin
Mededelingen. Veeartsenijschool. Rijksuniversiteit te Gent — Meded Veeartsenijsch Rijksuniv Gent
Mededelingen. Verbond van Belgische Ondernemingen — BEL
Mededelingen. Vlaamse Chemische Vereniging — Meded Vlaam Chem Ver
Mededelingen. Vlaamse Chemische Vereniging — MVLCA
Mededelingenblad Bedrijfsorganisatie — Mb Bo
Mededelingenblad Bedrijfsorganisatie — Mbl Bdorg
Mededelingenblad Bedrijfsorganisatie — MDM
Mededelingenblad Landbouwschap — Mb Lbs
Mededelingenblad. Nederlandse Vacuumvereniging — Meded Ned Vacuumver
Mededelingenblad. Nederlandse Vacuumvereniging — MNVAD
Mededelingenblad. Vereniging van Vrieden van het Allard Pierson Museum — VVAP
Medelhavsmuseet Bulletin [*Stockholm*] — Medelhavs Mus B
Medellin. Revista. Instituto Pastoral del Celam — MRIR
Medi Science — Medi Sci
Media, Agencies, Clients [*Later, Adweek*] — Mac
Media and Consumer — M & C
Media and Methods — MeMeth
Media, Culture, and Society [*United Kingdom*] — Media, C & S
Media, Culture, and Society — Media Culture Soc
Media, Culture, and Society — PMCS
Media Decisions — MD
Media Ecology Review — Media Eco
Media in Education and Development — Media Educ and Dev
Media in Education and Development — Media in Educ Dev
Media Industry Newsletter — Media Ind N
Media Info — MEI
Media Information Australia — Media Inf Aust
Media Information Australia — MIA
Media Law Notes — Media L Notes
Media Law Reporter. Bureau of National Affairs — Media L Rep BNA
Media Management Journal — Media Manage Jnl
Media Perspektiven — Media Per
Media Report to Women — Media Rpt
Media Reporter [*United Kingdom*] — Media Rep
Media Review — Media Rev
Media Review Digest — Media Rev Dig
Media Review Digest — MRD
Media/Scope — M/S
Mediaeval Academy Publications — MAP
Mediaeval and Renaissance Classics — MRC
Mediaeval and Renaissance Studies — M & R
Mediaeval and Renaissance Studies — M & RS
Mediaeval and Renaissance Studies — Med Ren
Mediaeval and Renaissance Studies — Med Ren St
Mediaeval and Renaissance Studies — MRS
Mediaeval and Renaissance Studies. Warburg Institute — Mediaeval Renaiss Stud Warburg Inst
Mediaeval Philosophical Texts in Translation — Mediaeval Philos Texts Transl
Mediaeval Scandinavia — MScan
Mediaeval Studies — Med St
Mediaeval Studies — Mediaev St
Mediaeval Studies — Mediaev Stud
Mediaeval Studies — Mediaeval Stud
Mediaeval Studies — MedS
Mediaeval Studies — MS
Mediaevalia Bohemica — MB
Mediaevalia et Humanistica — M & H
Mediaevalia et Humanistica — Med et Hum
Mediaevalia et Humanistica — Med Hum
Mediaevalia et Humanistica — Mediev et Hum
Mediaevalia et Humanistica — MetH
Mediaevalia et Humanistica — MH
Mediaevalia et Humanistica — MHum
Mediaevalia Philosophica Polonorum — Mediaev Philos Pol
Mediaevalia Philosophica Polonorum — Mediaevalia Phil Polonorum
Mediaevalia Philosophica Polonorum — MPhP
Mediaevalia Philosophica Polonorum — MPP
Mediafile — Media
Mediators of Inflammation — Mediators Inflammation
Medica — Med
Medica Mundi — Med Mundi

Medica Physica — ABMPEG
Medica Physica — Med Phys
Medical Abbreviations Handbook — MAH
Medical Abstract Service — Med Abstr
Medical Abstracts Journal — Med Abstr J
Medical Advisory Services for Travellers Abroad [*Database*] — MASTA
Medical Affairs — Med Aff
Medical Age — Med Age
Medical and Agricultural Register — Med Agric Reg
Medical and Biological Application of Mass Spectrometry. Proceedings. Symposium — Med Biol Appl Mass Spectrom Proc Symp
Medical and Biological Effects of Light — Med Biol Eff Light
Medical and Biological Engineering [*Later, Medical and Biological Engineering and Computing*] — MBENA
Medical and Biological Engineering [*Later, Medical and Biological Engineering and Computing*] — Med and Biol Eng
Medical and Biological Engineering [*Later, Medical and Biological Engineering and Computing*] — Med Bio Eng
Medical and Biological Engineering [*Later, Medical and Biological Engineering and Computing*] — Med Biol Eng
Medical and Biological Engineering [*Later, Medical and Biological Engineering and Computing*] — Med Biol Engng
Medical and Biological Engineering and Computing — Med and Biol Eng and Comput
Medical and Biological Engineering and Computing — Med Biol Eng Comput
Medical and Biological Illustration — Med Bio Ill
Medical and Biological Illustration — Med Biol Illus
Medical and Nutritional Research Communications — Med Nutr Res Commun
Medical and Other Applications. Proceedings. International Congress on Isozymes — Med Other Appl Proc Int Congr Isozymes
Medical and Pediatric Oncology — Med Pediatr Oncol
Medical and Pediatric Oncology. Supplement — Med Pediatr Oncol Suppl
Medical and Philosophical Commentaries — Med and Phil Comment
Medical and Physical Journal — Med Phys J
Medical and Professional Woman's Journal — Med Prof Womans J
Medical and Psychological Previews [*Database*] — PREV
Medical and Surgical Monitor — Med and Surg Monit
Medical and Surgical Pediatrics — Med Surg Pediatr
Medical and Surgical Reporter — Med Surg Rep
Medical and Technical Publishing Company. International Review of Science. Biochemistry — Med Tech Publ Co Int Rev Sci Biochem
Medical and Veterinary Entomology — Med Vet Entomol
Medical Annals — Med Ann
Medical Annals of the District of Columbia — Med Ann DC
Medical Annals of the District of Columbia — Med Ann Distr Columbia
Medical Annual — MA
Medical Annual [*England*] — Med Annu
Medical Anthropology — Med Anthro
Medical Anthropology — Med Anthropol
Medical Anthropology Newsletter — Med Anthro Newsl
Medical Anthropology Newsletter — Med Anthropol Newsletter
Medical Anthropology Quarterly — Med Anthropol Q
Medical Art — Med Art
Medical Arts and Sciences — Med Arts Sci
Medical Aspects of Drug Abuse — Med Aspects Drug Abuse
Medical Aspects of Exercise Testing and Training [*Monograph*] — Med Aspects Exercise Test Train
Medical Aspects of Human Sexuality — Med Aspects Hum Sex
Medical Association of the State of Alabama. Journal — Med Assoc State Ala J
Medical Association. State of Alabama. Transactions — Med Assn State Ala Trans
Medical Biology — Med Biol
Medical Biology (Helsinki) — Med Biol (Helsinki)
Medical Biology Illustrations — Med Biol Illustr
Medical Brief — Med Brief
Medical Bulletin [*New York*] — Med Bull
Medical Bulletin. Exxon Corporation and Affiliated Companies — Med Bull Exxon Corp Affil Co
Medical Bulletin. Fukuoka University — Med Bull Fukuoka Univ
Medical Bulletin. Istanbul Faculty of Medicine. Istanbul University — Med Bull Istanbul Fac Med Istanbul Univ
Medical Bulletin. Istanbul Medical Faculty — Med Bull Istanbul Med Fac
Medical Bulletin. Istanbul Medical Faculty. Istanbul University — Med Bull Istanbul Med Fac Istanbul Univ
Medical Bulletin. Istanbul University — Med Bull Istanbul Univ
Medical Bulletin. National Medical Center (Seoul) — Med Bull Natl Med Cent (Seoul)
Medical Bulletin of Northern Virginia — Med Bull No Virginia
Medical Bulletin. Providence Hospital (Southfield, Michigan) — Med Bull Providence Hosp (Southfield Mich)
Medical Bulletin. Standard Oil Company (New Jersey) and Affiliated Companies [*A publication*] — Med Bull Stand Oil Co (NJ) Affil Co
Medical Bulletin (United States Army) — Med Bull (US Army)
Medical Bulletin (United States Army, Europe) — M Bull (US Army Europe)
Medical Bulletin. University of Cincinnati — Med Bull Univ Cincinnati
Medical Bulletin. US Army (Europe) — Med Bull US Army (Eur)
Medical Bulletin. Veterans Administration — Med Bull Vet Adm
Medical Care — Med Care
Medical Care Research and Review — MCR and R
Medical Care Research and Review — Med Care Res Rev
Medical Care Review — Med Care Rev
Medical Center Journal. University of Michigan — Med Cent J Univ Mich
Medical Chronicle [*Manchester*] — MC
Medical Clinics of Chicago — Med Clin Chicago
Medical Clinics of North America — M Clin North America
Medical Clinics of North America — Med Clin N Am
Medical Clinics of North America — Med Clin NA
Medical Clinics of North America — Med Clin North Am
Medical Clinics of North America — Med Clinics No Am
Medical College of Virginia. Quarterly — Med C Virg
Medical Communications — MCOM
Medical Communications — Med Commun
Medical Computer Journal — Med Comp J
Medical Consultation and New Remedies — Med Consult New Remedies
Medical Cosmetology — Med Cosmetol
Medical Counterpoint — Mod Counterpoint
Medical Decision Making — Med Decis Making
Medical Decision Making — Med Decision Making
Medical/Dental Journal — Med Dent J
Medical Device and Diagnostic Industry — MDIIDI
Medical Device and Diagnostic Industry — Med Device & Diagn Ind
Medical Devices, Diagnostics, and Instrumentation Reports: the Gray Sheet — MDD
Medical Digest (Bombay) — Med Dig Bombay
Medical Dimensions — Med Dimensions
Medical Documentation — Med Doc
Medical Dosimetry — Med Dosim
Medical Economics — ME
Medical Economics — Med Econ
Medical Economics — MES
Medical Economics for Surgeons — Med Econ Surgeons
Medical Education — Med Educ
Medical Education [*Oxford*] — MEDUD2
Medical Education Briefing — Medic Educ Brief
Medical Education Newsletter — Medic Educ Newsl
Medical Education (Oxford) — Med Educ (Oxf)
Medical Electronics — Med Elec
Medical Electronics — Med Electron
Medical Electronics and Biological Engineering — MEBEA
Medical Electronics and Biological Engineering — Med Electron Biol Eng
Medical Electronics and Data — Med Elec
Medical Electronics and Data — Med Electron Data
Medical Electronics (Tokyo) — Med Electron (Tokyo)
Medical Entomology and Zoology — Med Entomol Zool
Medical Era (St. Louis) — Med Era (St Louis)
Medical Essays and Observations (Edinburgh) — Med Essays and Obs (Edinb)
Medical Group Management — Med Group Manage
Medical Group News — Med Group News
Medical Gynaecology and Sociology — Med Gynaecol Sociol
Medical Gynaecology, Andrology, and Sociology — Med Gynaecol Androl Sociol
Medical Heritage — Med Her
Medical History — Med Hist
Medical History — MedH
Medical History. Supplement — Med Hist Suppl
Medical Hypnoanalysis — Med Hypnoanal
Medical Hypnoanalysis — MHYPDB
Medical Hypotheses — Med Hypotheses
Medical Imaging — Med Imaging
Medical Imaging and Instrumentation — Med Imaging Instrum
Medical Imaging VI. Image Capture, Formatting, and Display — Med Imaging VI Image Capture Formatting Disp
Medical Immunology — Med Immunol
Medical Informatics — Med Inf
Medical Informatics — MINFDZ
Medical Instrumentation — Med Instrum
Medical Instrumentation [*Arlington, VA*] — MLISB
Medical Instrumentation (Arlington, VA) — Med Instrum (Arlington)
Medical Internal Radiation Dose Committee, Pamphlets — Med Intern Radiat Dose Comm Pam
Medical Journal and Record — Med J Rec
Medical Journal. Armed Forces (India) — Med J Armed Forces (India)
Medical Journal. Cairo University — Med J Cairo Univ
Medical Journal. Chulalongkorn Hospital Medical School (Bangkok) — Med J Chulalongkorn Hosp Med Sch (Bangkok)
Medical Journal. Emilio Aguinaldo College of Medicine — Med J EAC
Medical Journal. Emilio Aguinaldo College of Medicine — Med J Emilio Aguinaldo Coll Med
Medical Journal (English Translation of Lijecnicki Vjesnik) — Med J (Engl Transl Lijec Vjesn)
Medical Journal for Communication — Med J Commun
Medical Journal for the Netherlands Indies — Med J Neth Indies
Medical Journal. Fraternity Memorial Hospital — Med J Fraternity Mem Hosp
Medical Journal. Han-Il Hospital — Med J Han-Il Hosp
Medical Journal. Hiroshima Prefectural Hospital — Med J Hiroshima Prefect Hosp
Medical Journal. Hiroshima University — HDIZA
Medical Journal. Hiroshima University [*Japan*] — Med J Hiroshima Univ
Medical Journal. Kagoshima University — Med J Kagoshima Univ
Medical Journal. Kinki University — Med J Kinki Univ
Medical Journal. Kobe University — Med J Kobe Univ
Medical Journal. Medical Association of Siam — Med J Med Assoc Siam
Medical Journal. Minami Osaka Hospital [*Japan*] — Med J Minami Osaka Hosp
Medical Journal. Mutual Aid Association [*Japan*] — Med J Mutual Aid Assoc
Medical Journal. National Hospitals and Sanatoriums of Japan — Med J Natl Hosp Sanat Jpn
Medical Journal of Australia — Med J Aust
Medical Journal of Australia — Med J Austral
Medical Journal of Australia — Medical J Aust
Medical Journal of Australia — MJ Australia
Medical Journal of Australia — MJA

Medical Journal of Australia — MJAUA
Medical Journal of Australia. Supplement — Med J Aust Supp
Medical Journal of Malaya [*Later, Medical Journal of Malaysia*] — Med J Malaya
Medical Journal of Malaysia — Med J Malays
Medical Journal of Malaysia — Med J Malaysia
Medical Journal of Malaysia — MJMLAI
Medical Journal of South Africa — Med J So Africa
Medical Journal of Zambia — Med J Zambia
Medical Journal. Osaka University — Med J Osaka Univ
Medical Journal. Osaka University (English Edition) — Med J Osaka Univ (Engl Ed)
Medical Journal. Osaka University (Japanese Edition) — Med J Osaka Univ (Jpn Ed)
Medical Journal. Shimane Central Hospital — Med J Shimane Cent Hosp
Medical Journal. Shinshu University — Med J Shinshu Univ
Medical Journal. Siamese Red Cross — Med J Siamese Red Cross
Medical Journal. South West — Med J South West
Medical Journal. Sumitomo Hospital — Med J Sumitomo Hosp
Medical Journal (Ukraine) — Med J (Ukr)
Medical Laboratory Advisory Service — Med Laboratory Advisory
Medical Laboratory Observer — Med Lab Observer
Medical Laboratory Observer — MLO
Medical Laboratory Sciences — Med Lab Sci
Medical Laboratory Technology — Med Lab Tec
Medical Laboratory Technology — Med Lab Technol
Medical Laboratory World — Med Lab World
Medical Lasers and Systems — Med Lasers Syst
Medical Letter on Drugs and Therapeutics — Med Lett Drugs Ther
Medical Liability Advisory Service — Med Liability Advisory
Medical Liability Reporter — Med Liab R
Medical Libraries — Med Libr
Medical Library Association. Bulletin — Med Lib Assn Bul
Medical Library Association. Bulletin — Med Lib Assn Bull
Medical Malpractice Cost Containment Journal — Med Malpract Cost Containment J
Medical Malpractice Lawsuit Filings [*Database*] — MEDMAL
Medical Marketing and Media — Med Mark Media
Medical Marketing and Media — Med Market Media
Medical Marketing and Media — Med Markt
Medical Marketing and Media — Med Mkt
Medical Marketing and Media — MMM
Medical Meetings — Med Meetings
Medical Mentor — Med Mentor
Medical Microbiology — Med Microbiol
Medical Microbiology and Immunology — Med Microbi
Medical Microbiology and Immunology — Med Microbiol Immunol
Medical Microbiology and Immunology — MMI
Medical News — Med News
Medical Officer — Med Off
Medical Officer [*England*] — Med Officer
Medical Oncology — Med Oncol
Medical Oncology and Tumor Pharmacotherapy — Med Oncol Tumor Pharmacother
Medical Opinion and Review — Med Opin Rev
Medical Pharmacy — Med Pharm
Medical Physics — Med Phys
Medical Physics Bulletin — Med Phys Bull
Medical Physics Handbooks — Med Phys Handb
Medical Physics Handbooks — MPHAE6
Medical Physiology — Med Physiol
Medical Post [*Canada*] — Med Post
Medical Practice Letter — Med Pract Let
Medical Press — Med Press
Medical Press and Circular — Med Press and Circ
Medical Press and Circular — MP
Medical Press and Circular — MPC
Medical Press of Egypt — Med Press Egypt
Medical Principles and Practice — Med Princ Pract
Medical Problems of Performing Artists — Med Probl Performing Artists
Medical Problems of Performing Artists — MPPA
Medical Problems of Performing Artists — MPPAEC
Medical Proceedings — Med Proc
Medical Products Sales — Med Prod Sales
Medical Products Salesman — Med Prod Salesman
Medical Profession — Med Prof
Medical Progress (New York) — Med Prog (NY)
Medical Progress through Technology — MDPTB
Medical Progress through Technology — Med Pr Tech
Medical Progress through Technology — Med Prog Technol
Medical Psychiatry — Med Psychiatry
Medical Quarterly. Indiana University. School of Medicine — Med Q Indiana Univ Sch Med
Medical Quarterly Review — Med Quart Rev
Medical Radiography and Photography — Med Radiogr Photogr
Medical Radiology (USSR) — Med Radiol (USSR)
Medical Record — Med Rec
Medical Record and Annals — Med Rec Ann
Medical Record and Health Care Information Journal — Med Rec Health Care Inf J
Medical Record (New York) — Med Rec (NY)
Medical Record News — Med Rec News
Medical Record of Mississippi — Med Rec Mississippi
Medical Reference Services Quarterly — Med Ref Serv Q
Medical Reference Services Quarterly — MRSQ
Medical Reports. Charles University Medical Faculty at Hradec Kralove — Med Rep Charles Univ Med Fac Hradec Kralove
Medical Reports. Showa Medical School — Med Rep Showa Med Sch
Medical Repository — Med Reposit
Medical Research Centre (Nairobi). Annual Report — Med Res Cent (Nairobi) Annu Rep
Medical Research Council. Clinical Research Centre Symposium (United Kingdom) — Med Res Counc Clin Res Cent Symp (UK)
Medical Research Council (Great Britain). Annual Report — Med Res Counc (GB) Annu Rep
Medical Research Council (Great Britain). Industrial Health Research Board Report — Med Res Counc (GB) Ind Health Res Board Rep
Medical Research Council (Great Britain). Laboratory Animals Centre. Manual Series — Med Res Counc (GB) Lab Anim Cent Man Ser
Medical Research Council (Great Britain). Laboratory Animals Centre. Manual Series — MSMCDN
Medical Research Council (Great Britain). Laboratory Animals Centre. Symposia — Med Res Counc (GB) Lab Anim Cent Symp
Medical Research Council (Great Britain). Memorandum — Med Res Counc (GB) Memo
Medical Research Council (Great Britain). Monitoring Report — Med Res Counc (GB) Monit Rep
Medical Research Council (Great Britain). Special Report Series — Med Res Counc (GB) Spec Rep Ser
Medical Research Council. Monthly Bulletin — Med Res Counc Mon Bull
Medical Research Council. Special Report Series — MRCSA
Medical Research Engineering — Med Res Eng
Medical Research Index — Med Res Index
Medical Research Institute. Tokyo Medical and Dental University. Annual Report — Med Res Inst Tokyo Med Dent Univ Annu Rep
Medical Research Projects — Med Res Proj
Medical Researches for Photosensitizing Dyes — Med Res Photosensit Dyes
Medical School Rounds — Med Schl
Medical Science — Med Sci
Medical Science Research — Med Sci Res
Medical Self-Care — MDSC
Medical Self-Care — Medical
Medical Service — Med Serv
Medical Service Journal [*Canada*] — MDSJA
Medical Service Journal (Canada) — Med Serv J (Can)
Medical Services Journal (Canada) — Med Services J (Canada)
Medical Society of New Jersey. Journal — Med Soc New Jersey J
Medical Society of Tennessee. Transactions — Med Soc Tenn Trans
Medical Society of the State of Pennsylvania. Transactions — Med Soc PA Tr
Medical Society of Virginia. Transactions — Med Soc Va Trans
Medical Socioeconomic Research Sources — Med Socioecon Res Source
Medical Socioeconomic Research Sources — MSRS
Medical Socioeconomic Research Sources. American Medical Association — MedS
Medical Socioeconomic Research Sources. American Medical Association — MEDSOC
Medical Teacher — Med Teach
Medical Technicians Bulletin — Med Tech Bull
Medical Technology — Med Technol
Medical Technology in Australasia — Med Technol Aust
Medical Technology in Australasia — Med Technol Australas
Medical Technology in Australia — Med Technol Aust
Medical Technology Review — Med Technol Rev
Medical Technology Series — Med Technol Ser
Medical Technology (Tokyo) — Med Technol (Tokyo)
Medical Times — Med Times
Medical Times — METIA
Medical Times and Gazette [*London*] — MT
Medical Times and Gazette [*London*] — MTG
Medical Times and Gazette (London) — Med Times and Gaz (London)
Medical Times (London) — Med Times (London)
Medical Times (New York) — Med Times (NY)
Medical Toxicology — Med Toxicol
Medical Toxicology and Adverse Drug Experience — Med Toxicol Adverse Drug Exper
Medical Toxicology. Proceedings. EUROTOX Congress Meeting — Med Toxicol Proc EUROTOX Congr Meet
Medical Treatment (Tokyo) — Med Treat (Tokyo)
Medical Trial Technique Quarterly — Med Tr TQ
Medical Trial Technique Quarterly — Med Trial Tech Q
Medical Trial Technique Quarterly — Med Trial Technique Q
Medical Trial Technique Quarterly — MTTQ
Medical Tribune — Med Trib
Medical Tribune and Medical News — Med Trib Med N
Medical Ultrasound — Med Ultrasound
Medical Utilization Review — Med Utilization Rev
Medical View — Med View
Medical Virology. Proceedings. International Symposium — Med Virol Proc Int Symp
Medical Weekly — Med Wkly
Medical Woman's Journal — Med Womans J
Medical World — MEWOA
Medical World News — GMWN
Medical World News — Med World
Medical World News — Med World News
Medical World News — MWN
Medical World News for Psychiatrists — Med Wld N Psychiat
Medical-Dental Journal — Med Dent Jnl
Medicamenta (Edicion para el Farmaceutico) — Medicamenta (Ed Farm)

Medicamenta. Revista Mensual de Estudios y Trabajos Profesionales. Edicion para el Farmaceutico — Med Rev Mens Estud Trab Prof Ed Farm
Medicamentos de Actualidad — Med Actual
Medicenter Management — Medicent Man
Medichnii Zhurnal (Kiev) — Med Zh (Kiev)
Medichnii Zhurnal (Ukraine) — Med Zh (Ukr)
Medicina and Cirurgia (Lisbon) — Med Cir Lisbon
Medicina (Bogota) — Med (B)
Medicina, Cirugia, Farmacia — Med Cir Farm
Medicina, Cirugia, Pharmacia — Med Cirugia Pharm
Medicina Clinica — Med Clin
Medicina Clinica (Barcelona) — Med Clin Barcelona
Medicina Clinica e Sperimentale — Med Clin Sper
Medicina Colonial (Madrid) — Med Colon (Madr)
Medicina Contemporanea — Med Cont
Medicina Contemporanea — Med Contemp
Medicina Contemporanea (Lisbon) — Med Contemp (Lisbon)
Medicina Contemporanea (Naples) — Med Contemp Naples
Medicina Contemporanea (Turin) — Med Contemp Turin
Medicina Cutanea [*Later, Medicina Cutanea Ibero-Latino-Americana*] — Med Cut
Medicina Cutanea [*Later, Medicina Cutanea Ibero-Latino-Americana*] — Med Cutanea
Medicina Cutanea Ibero-Latino-Americana — Med Cutan Iber Lat Am
Medicina de Hoje — Med Hoje
Medicina de los Paises Calidos — Med Paises Calidos
Medicina de Occidente — Med Occidente
Medicina del Lavoro — Med Lav
Medicina del Lavoro — MELAA
Medicina dello Sport (Turin) — Med Sport (Turin)
Medicina do Esporte — Med Esporte
Medicina e Cultura — Med Cult
Medicina e Cultura (Milan) — Med Cult (Milan)
Medicina e Morale — Med Morale
Medicina Espanola — Med Esp
Medicina Espanola — Med Espan
Medicina Espanola — Medna Esp
Medicina et Pharmacologia Experimentalis — Med Pharmacol Exp
Medicina et Pharmacologia Experimentalis. International Journal of Experimental Medicine — Med Pharmacol Exp Int J Exp Med
Medicina Experimentalis — Med Exp
Medicina Experimentalis. International Journal of Experimental Medicine — Med Exp Int J Exp Med
Medicina Fisica y Rehabilitacion — Med Fis Rehabil
Medicina Geriatrica — Med Geriatr
Medicina Geriatrica — MGRCAT
Medicina Hupe-UERJ [*Brazil*] — Med Hupe UERJ
Medicina Interna — Med Interna
Medicina Interna (Bucharest) — Med Interna (Buchar)
Medicina Italiana. Rivista di Pediatria e Malattie Infettive — Med Ital
Medicina Legale e delle Assicurazioni — Med Leg Assicur
Medicina (Lisbon) — Med (L)
Medicina Moderna — Med Mod
Medicina nei Secoli — MDSCAD
Medicina nei Secoli — Med Secoli
Medicina Nucleare. Radiobiologica Latina — Med Nucl Radiobiol Lat
Medicina Nucleare. Radiobiologica Latina. Supplement [*Italy*] — Med Nucl Radiobiol Lat Suppl
Medicina Panamericana — Med Panam
Medicina (Parma) — Med (P)
Medicina Philosophica — Med Philos
Medicina Pratica (Napoli) — Med Prat (Napoli)
Medicina Psicosomatica — Med Psicosom
Medicina. Revista do CARL [*Centro Academico Rocha Lima*] — Med Rev CARL
Medicina. Revista do Centro Academico Rocha Lima [*CARL*]. Hospital das Clinicas da Faculdade de Medicina de Ribeirao Preto. Universidade de Sao Paulo — MDCNAY
Medicina. Revista do Centro Academico Rocha Lima [*CARL*] **(Sao Paulo)** — Med Rev Cent Acad Rocha Lima (Sao Paulo)
Medicina Revista Mexicana — Med Rev Mex
Medicina Revuo (Chiba, Japan) — Med Rev (Chiba Jpn)
Medicina (Rijeka, Yugoslavia) — Medicina (Rijeka Yugosl)
Medicina. Rivista della Enciclopedia Medica Italiana — Med Riv Encicl Med Ital
Medicina Sociale — Med Soc
Medicina Sociale (Turin) — Med Soc (Turin)
Medicina Sperimentale — Med Sper
Medicina Sperimentale. Archivio Italiano — Med Sper Arch Ital
Medicina Sportiva — Med Sportiva
Medicina Strucni Casopis Zlh Podruznica Rijeka — Med Strucni Cas Zlh Podruznica Rijeka
Medicina Termale e Climatologia — Med Term Climatol
Medicina Thoracalis — MDTHA
Medicina Thoracalis — Med Thorac
Medicina Tradicionale — Med Tradic
Medicina Tropical (Madrid) — Med Trop (Madr)
Medicina Tropical (Madrid) — Med Trop (Madrid)
Medicina Universal — Med Univers
Medicina y Cirugia — Med Cir
Medicina y Cirugia de Guerra — Med Cir Gu
Medicina y Cirurgia Zootechnicas — Med Cir Zootech
Medicina y Seguridad del Trabajo (Madrid) — Med Segur Trab (Madr)
Medicinal Chemistry — Med Chem
Medicinal Chemistry: A Series of Monographs — Med Chem Ser Monogr
Medicinal Chemistry: A Series of Reviews — Med Chem Ser Rev
Medicinal Chemistry (Academic Press). A Series of Monographs — Med Chem (Academic Press)
Medicinal Chemistry Advances. Proceedings. International Symposium on Medicinal Chemistry — Med Chem Adv Proc Int Symp
Medicinal Chemistry. Proceedings. International Symposium on Medicinal Chemistry — Med Chem Proc Int Symp
Medicinal Chemistry Research — Med Chem Res
Medicinal Chemistry. Special Contributions. International Symposium on Medicinal Chemistry — Med Chem Spec Contrib Int Symp
Medicinal Chemistry (Wiley) — Med Chem (Wiley)
Medicinal Research — Med Res
Medicinal Research: A Series of Monographs — Med Res Ser Monogr
Medicinal Research Reviews — Med Res Rev
Medicinal Research Reviews — MRREDD
Medicine and Biology (Tokyo) — Med Biol (Tokyo)
Medicine and Computer — Med and Comp
Medicine and Law — Med & Law
Medicine and Law — Med Law
Medicine and Law — MELADG
Medicine and Science in Sports — Med Sci Sports
Medicine and Science in Sports — Med Sci Spt
Medicine and Science in Sports and Exercise — Med and Sci Sport
Medicine and Science in Sports and Exercise — Med Sci Sports Exerc
Medicine and Sport (Basel) — Med Sport (Basel)
Medicine and Sport Science — Med Sport Sci
Medicine and Sport Science — MSSCEK
Medicine and Surgery — Med Surg
Medicine and War — Med War
Medicine International [*Great Britain*] — Med Int
Medicine on the Midway — Med Midway
Medicine Publishing Foundation Symposium Series — Med Publ Found Symp Ser
Medicine, Science, and the Law — Med Sci & L
Medicine, Science, and the Law — Med Sci Law
Medicinhistorisk Arsbok — MediA
Medicinisch-Chirurgische Zeitung — Med Chir Zeitung
Medicinisches Archiv von Wien und Oesterreich unter der Enns — Med Arch Wien Oesterreich Unter Der Enns
Medicinisches Wochenblatt fuer Aerzte, Wundaerzte, und Apotheker — Med Wochenbl Aerzte
Medicinsk Arbog — Med Arb
Medicinsk Forum — Med Forum
Medicinsk Revue (Bergen) — Med Rev (Bergen)
Medicinska Istrazivanja — Med Istraz
Medicinska Istrazivanja. Supplementum — Med Istraz Suppl
Medicinska Revija (Belgrade) — Med Rev (Belgr)
Medicinski Anali — Med An
Medicinski Arhiv — Med Arh
Medicinski Arhiv — Med Arhiv
Medicinski Glasnik — Med Glas
Medicinski Podmladak — Med Podmladak
Medicinski Pregled — Med Pregl
Medicinski Problemi [*Bulgaria*] — Med Probl
Medicinski Razgledi — Med Razgledi
Medicinski Vjesnik — Med Vjesnik
Medicinski Zbornik (Sarajevo) — Med Zb (Sarajevo)
Medicinskij Archiv — Med Arch
Medico — Med
Medico Bohringer. Europa — Med Bohringer Eur
Medico Condotto — Med Cond
Medico Condotto — Med Condotto
Medico-Chirurgical Journal and Review — Med Chir J R
Medico-Legal and Criminological Review — Med Leg & Crim Rev
Medico-Legal and Criminological Review — Med-Leg Criminol Rev
Medico-Legal Bulletin — Med Leg Bull
Medicolegal Digest — Medicolegal Dig
Medico-Legal Journal — Med Leg J
Medico-Legal Journal — Med LJ
Medico-Legal Journal — Medico Legal J
Medico-Legal Journal (London) — Med-Leg J (London)
Medico-Legal Journal (New York) — Med-Leg J (NY)
Medicolegal Library — Medicoleg Libr
Medico-Legal News — Med Leg N
Medicolegal News — Medicoleg News
Medico-Legal Society of Victoria. Proceedings — Medico-Legal Soc VIC Proc
Medico-Legal Society. Proceedings — Medico-Legal Soc Proc
Medicus Universalis — Med Universalis
Medien Journal — Medien Jnl
Medien und Erziehung — Medien
Mediese Bydraes — Med Bydr
Mediese Bydraes — Med Bydraes
Medieval and Renaissance Studies. University of North Carolina — Medieval Renaiss Stud Univ N Carolina
Medieval Archaeology — M Ar
Medieval Archaeology — MArch
Medieval Archaeology — Med Arch
Medieval Archaeology — Mediev A
Medieval Archaeology — Medieval Arch
Medieval Archaeology — Medieval Archaeol
Medieval Ceramics — Medieval Ceram
Medieval India Quarterly — MIQ
Medieval Studies in Memory of Gertrude Schoepperle Loomis — GSL
Medievalia et Humanistica — Mediev Humanist
Medievalia et Humanistica — MeH
Medievalia et Humanistica. Studies in Medieval and Renaissance Culture — Medievalia Hum
Medii Aevi Bibliotheca Patristica — MABP

Medikamentoese Immunsuppression, Arbeitstagung — Med Immunsuppr Arbeitstag
Mediko Biologicheskaya Informatsiya — Med Biol Inf
Mediko-Biologichni Problemi — MBLPA3
Mediko-Biologichni Problemi — Med Biol Probl
Medioevo Romanzo — Med R
Medioevo Romanzo — MedRom
Medisch Contact — MDC
Medisch Contact [*Netherlands*] — Med Contact
Medisch Maandblad — Med Maandbl
Medisinske Avhandlinger. Universitet i Bergen — Med Avh Univ Bergen
Mediterranean Congress of Rheumatology — Mediterr Congr Rheumatol
Mediterranean Naturalist. A Monthly Journal of Natural Science — Medit Naturalist
Mediterranean Review — MedR
Mediterranean Review — MRev
Mediterranee Medicale — Mediterr Med
Mediterraneo — Med
Mediterraneo — Medit
Meditsinska Tekhnika (Sofia) — Med Tekh (Sofia)
Meditsinskaia Mysl Uzbekistana — Med Mysl Uzbekistana
Meditsinskaia Radiologiia (Moskva) — Med Radiol (Mosk)
Meditsinskaya Parazitologiya i Parazitarnye Bolezni — Med Parazitol
Meditsinskaya Parazitologiya i Parazitarnye Bolezni — Med Parazitol Parazit Bolezni
Meditsinskaya Parazitologiya i Parazitarnye Bolezni — Medskaya Parazit
Meditsinskaya Promyshlennost SSSR — Med Prom-St SSSR
Meditsinskaya Promyshlennost SSSR — MPSSA
Meditsinskaya Radiologiya — Med Radiol
Meditsinskaya Sestra — Med Sestra
Meditsinskaya Tekhnika — Med Tekh
Meditsinskaya Tekhnika (Moscow) — Med Tekh (Moscow)
Meditsinski Arkhiv [*Bulgaria*] — Med Arkh
Meditsinskii Biulleten — Med Biul
Meditsinskii Referatinynyi Zhurnal — Meditsin Referat Zh
Meditsinskii Zhurnal Uzbekistana — Med Zh Uzb
Meditsinskoe Obozrainie — Med Obozr
Meditsinskoe Obozrienio Sprimona — Med Obozr
Medium Aevum — MA
Medium Aevum — MAE
Medium Aevum — MAev
Medium Aevum — MedAe
Medium Aevum — MedAev
Medium Aevum — Medium Aev
Medium Aevum — PMAE
Medium Aevum Monographs — MAeM
Medium Aevum. Philologische Studien — MAPS
Medium-Energy Antiprotons and the Quark-Gluon Structure of Hadrons — Medium Energy Antiprotons Quark Gluon Struct Hadrons
Medizin Aktuell — Med Aktuell
Medizin in Unserer Zeit — Med Unserer Zeit
Medizin und Chemie (Leverkusen, Germany) — Med Chem (Leverkusen Ger)
Medizin und Ernaehrung — Med Ernaehr
Medizin und Gesellschaft — Med Ges
Medizin und Sport [*Berlin*] — MESPBQ
Medizin und Sport (Berlin) — Med Sport (Berl)
Medizin und Sport (Berlin) — Med Sport (Berlin)
Medizin von Heute (Osaka) — Med Heute Osaka
Medizinal-Markt/Acta Medicotechnica — Med Markt Acta Medicotech
Medizinhistorisches Journal — Medizinhist J
Medizin-Historisches Journal — MHJ
Medizinische Blaetter — Med Bl
Medizinische Blaetter. Wochenschrift fuer die Gesamte Heilkunde (Wien) — Med Bl Wien
Medizinische Dokumentation — Med Dok
Medizinische Folge der Berichte des Osteuropa-Institut an der Freien Universitaet Berlin — Med Folge Ber Osteur Inst Freien Univ Berlin
Medizinische Grundlagenforschung — Med Grundlagenforsch
Medizinische Informatik und Statistik — Med Inform Statist
Medizinische Klinik — M Kl
Medizinische Klinik — Med Klin
Medizinische Klinik — MEKLA
Medizinische Klinik — MK
Medizinische Klinik (Berlin) — Med Klin (Berlin)
Medizinische Klinik (Muenchen) — Med Klin (Muenchen)
Medizinische Klinik (Muenchen) — Medsche Klin (Muenchen)
Medizinische Klinik. Norddeutsche Ausgabe — Med Klin Norddtsch Ausg
Medizinische Klinik. Sueddeutsche Ausgabe — Med Klin Sueddtsch Ausg
Medizinische Klinik. Supplement — Med Klin Suppl
Medizinische Kosmetik — Med Kosmet
Medizinische Laboratorium [*Germany*] — Med Lab
Medizinische Laboratorium (Stuttgart) — Med Lab (Stuttg)
Medizinische Monatsschrift — M Ms
Medizinische Monatsschrift — Med Monatsschr
Medizinische Monatsschrift — MEMOA
Medizinische Monatsschrift fuer Pharmazeuten — Med Monatsschr Pharm
Medizinische Monatsschrift (Stuttgart) — Medsche Mschr (Stuttg)
Medizinische Physik in Forschung und Praxis. Wissenschaftliche Tagung der Deutschen Gesellschaft fuer Medizinische Physik — Med Phys Forsch Prax Wiss Tag Dtsch Ges Med Phys
Medizinische Prisma — Med Prisma
Medizinische (Stuttgart) — Med (S)
Medizinische Technik [*Germany*] — Med Tech
Medizinische Technik [*Database*] — MEDITEC
Medizinische und Paedagogische Jugendkunde — Med Paedagog Jugendkd
Medizinische Welt — Med Welt
Medizinische Welt — MEWEA
Medizinische Welt (Stuttgart) — Medsche Welt (Stuttg)
Medizinische Woche — Med W
Medizinische Zeitung — Med Ztg
Medizinische Zeitung. Russlands — Med Ztg Russlands
Medizinischen Versuche und Bemerkungen (Edinburgh) — Med Versuche u Bemerk (Edinb)
Medizinischer Monatsspiegel — Med Monatssp
Medizinischer Monatsspiegel — Med Monatsspiegel
Medizinisches Conversationsblatt — Med Convers Bl
Medizinisches Correspondenz-Blatt Bayerischer Aerzte — Med Cor-Bl Bayer Aerzte
Medizinisches Correspondenz-Blatt Rheinischer und Westfaelischer Aerzte — Med Cor-Bl Rhein u Westfael Aerzte
Medizinisches Correspondenz-Blatt. Wuerttembergischer Aerztliche Landesverein [*A publication*] — Med Cor-Bl Wuerttemb Aerztl Landesver
Medizinisches Correspondenz-Blatt. Wuerttembergischer Aerztliche Verein — Med Cor-Bl Wuerttemb Aerztl Ver
Medizinisches Institut fuer Lufthygiene und Silikoseforschung. Jahresbericht — Med Inst Lufthyg Silikoseforsch Jahresber
Medizinisch-Naturwissenschaftliche Gesellschaft zu Jena. Denkschriften — Med Naturw Gesell Zu Jena Denks
Medizinisch-Naturwissenschaftliches Archiv — Med Naturwiss Arch
Medizinisch-Naturwissenschaftliches Archiv — MNA
Medizinisch-Orthopaedische Technik — Med Orthop Tech
Medizinishes Journal von Aserbaidshan — Med J Aserb
Medlemsblad den Norske Veterinaerforening — Medlemsbl Nor Veterinaerforen
Medlemsblad foer den Danske Dyrlaegeforening — Medlemsbl Dan Dyrlaegeforen
Medlemsblad for den Danske Dyrlaegeforening — M Dlf
Medlemsblad for Soransk Samfund — Sor Bl
Medlemsblad. Sveriges Veterinaerfoerbund — Medlemsbl Sver Veterinaerfoerb
Medlemsskrift. Stiftelsen Glasinstitutet (Vaexjoe, Sweden) — Medlemsskr Stiftelsen Glasinst (Vaexjoe Swed)
Medullary Thyroid Carcinoma. Proceedings. European Congress on Medullary Thyroid Carcinoma — Medullary Thyroid Carcinoma Proc Eur Congr
Medunarodni Problemi — Medun Probl
Medycyna Doswiadczalna i Mikrobiologia — Med Dosw Mikrobiol
Medycyna Doswiadczalna i Mikrobiologia (Translation) — Med Dosw Mikrobiol (Transl)
Medycyna Doswiadczalna i Spoleczna — Med Dosw Spoleczna
Medycyna Pracy — Med Pr
Medycyna Weterynaryjna — Med Weter
Medycyna Weterynaryjna — Medycyna Wet
Medzinarodna Konferencia o Organickych Povlakoch. Prace — Medzinar Konf Org Povlakoch Pr
Medzinarodna Konferencia o Praskovej Metalurgii. Zbornik Prednasok — Medzinar Konf Praskovej Metal Zb Prednasok
Medzinarodna Konferencia o Preduprave Materialov. Prace — Medzinar Konf Preduprave Mater Pr
Medzinarodna Konferencia Textilnych Chemikov — Medzinar Konf Text Chem
Medzinarodne Sympozium Metrologie — Medzinar Symp Metrol
Medzinarodne Sympozium o Klznom Ulozeni. Zbornik Prednasok — Medzinar Symp Klznom Ulozeni Zb Prednasok
MEEC. Mississippi State University. Cooperative Extension Service — MEEC Miss State Univ Coop Ext Serv
Meerestechnik — mt
Meerestechnik/Marine Technology — Meerestech Mar Tech
Meerestechnik/Marine Technology — Meerestech Mar Technol
Meerestechnik/Marine Technology — Meerestechnik Mar Technol
Meet the Press — IMTP
Meeting. American Psychopathological Association — Meet Am Psychopathol Assoc
Meeting. Eastern African Sub-Committee for Soil Correlation and Land Evaluation — Meet East Afr Sub Comm Soil Correl Land Eval
Meeting. EULAR Standing Committee on International Clinical Studies — Meet EULAR Standing Comm Int Clin Stud
Meeting. Japanese Association for Animal Cell Technology — Meet Jpn Assoc Anim Cell Technol
Meeting News — Meeting Nw
Meeting on Adrenergic Mechanisms. Proceedings — Meet Adrenergic Mech Proc
Meeting Papers. Annual Convention. Gas Processors Association — Meet Pap Annu Conv Gas Process Assoc
Meeting Place Journal. Royal Ontario Museum — Meet Place J R Ont Mus
Meeting. Plasma Protein Group — Meet Plasma Protein Group
Meetings on Atomic Energy — MAEQA
MEGA. Membrany, Ekologie, Geologie, Analytika — MEGA Membr Ekol Geol Anal
Megafon (Argentina) — MNA
Megale Hellenike Enkyklopaideia — MEE
Megiddo Tombs — MT
Mehanika. Periodiceskii Sbornik Perevodov Inostrannyh Statei — Mehanika Period Sb Perevodov Inostran Statei
Mehanika Tverdogo Tela — Meh Tverd Tela
Mehanizacija i Automatizacija — Meh Autom
Mehran University. Research Journal of Engineering and Technology — Mehran Univ Res J Eng and Technol
Meiden Review (International Edition) — Meiden Rev (Int Ed)
Meidensha Review [*later, Meiden Review*] **(International Edition)** — Meidensha Rev (Int Ed)
Meijerbergs Arkiv foer Svensk Ordforskning — MASO
Meijeritieteellinen Aikakauskirja — Meijeritiet Aikak

Meijeritieteellinen Aikakauskirja/Finnish Journal of Dairy Science — Meijertiet Aikak Finn J Dairy Sci
Meisterwerke der Griechischen Plastik — MW
Meisterwerke Griechischer Kunst — Mw
Mejeritekniska Meddelanden — Mejeritek Medd
Mekedonski Pregled. Spisanie za Nauka. Literatura i Obsteostven Zivot — MeP
Mekhanicheskaya Obrabotka. Drevesiny — Mekh Obrab Drev
Mekhanicheskaya Ustalost Metallov. Materialy Mezhdunarodnogo Kollokviuma — Mekh Ustalost Met Mater Mezhdunar Kollok
Mekhanicheskie I Teplovye Svoistva i Stroenie Neorganicheskikh Stekol. Materialy Vsesoyuznogo Simpoziuma — Mekh Tepl Svoistva Str Neorg Stekol Mater Vses Simp
Mekhanika Armirovannykh Plastikov — Mekh Armir Plast
Mekhanika Deformiruemykh Tverdykh Tel [*Former USSR*] — Mekh Deform Tverd Tel
Mekhanika Kompozitnykh Materialov [*Latvian SSR*] — Mekh Kompoz Mater
Mekhanika Kompozitnykh Materialov — Mekh Kompozitnykh Mater
Mekhanika Kompozitnykh Materialov. Rizhskii Politekhnicheskii Institut — Mekh Kompoz Mater Rizh Politekh Inst
Mekhanika Kompozitnykh Materialov (Zinatne) — Mekh Kompoz Mater (Zinatne)
Mekhanika Polimerov — Mekh Polim
Mekhanika Tverdogo Tela — Mekh Tverd Tela
Mekhanika Tverdogo Tela. Trudy Vsesoyuznogo S'ezda po Teoreticheskoi i Prikladnoi Mekhanike — Mekhanika Tverd Tela Tr Vses Sezda Teor Prikl Mekh
Mekhanika Zhidkosti i Gaza [*Former USSR*] — Mekh Zhidk Gaza
Mekhanika Zhidkosti i Gaza. Itogi Nauki i Tekhniki — Mekh Zhidk Gaza Itogi Nauki Tekh
Mekhanizahriya i Avtomahzatsiya Upravleniya — Mekh i Avtom Upr
Mekhanizatsiia i Elektrifikatsiia Sel'skogo Khoziaistva — Mekh Elektrif Sel'sk Khoz
Mekhanizatsiia Sil's'koho Hospodarstva — Mekh Silsk Hospod
Mekhanizatsiya Elektrifikatsiya Sotsialisticheskogo Sel'skogo Khozyaistva — Mekhan Elektrif Sots Sel'Khoz
Mekhanizatsiya i Avtomatizatsiya Proizvodstva — Mekh & Avtom Proiz
Mekhanizatsiya i Avtomatizatsiya Proizvodstva — Mekh Avtom Proizvod
Mekhanizatsiya i Avtomatizatsiya Proizvodstva — Mekh i Avtom Proizvod
Mekhanizatsiya i Avtomatizatsiya Upravleniya — Mekh Avtom Upr
Mekhanizatsiya Khlopkovodstva — Mekh Khlopkovod
Mekhanizm Kataliticheskikh Reaktsii. Materialy Vsesoyuznoi Konferentsii — Mekh Katal Reakts Mater Vses Konf
Mekhanizm Razrusheniya Metallov Akademiya Nauk Ukrainskoi SSR Republikanskii Mezhvedomstvennyi Sbornik — Mekh Razrusheniya Metal Nauk Ukr SSR Repub Mezhvedom Sb
Mekhanizmy Nekotorykh Patologicheskikh Protsessov — Mekh Nek Patol Protsessov
Mekhanizmy Patologicheskikh Protsessov — Mekh Patol Protsessov
Mekhanizmy Prirodnoi i Modifitsirovannoi Radiochuvstvitel'nosti — Mekh Prir Modif Radiochuvstvitel'nosti
Mekhanoemissiya i Mekhanokhimiya Tverdykh Tel. Doklady Vsesoyuznogo Simpoziuma po Mekhanoemissii i Mekhanokhimii Tverdykh Tel — Mekhanoemiss Mekhanokhim Tverd Tel Dokl Vses Simp
Mekong Bulletin — Mekong Bull
Melanesian Law Journal — Melanesian Law J
Melanesian Law Journal — Melanesian LJ
Melanges — Mel
Melanges Asiatiques — M As
Melanges Baldensperger — MB
Melanges Biologiques Tires du Bulletin Physico-Mathematique. Academie Imperiale des Sciences de Saint-Petersbourg — Melanges Biol Bull Phys Math Acad Imp Sci Saint Petersbourg
Melanges. Casa de Velazquez — MCV
Melanges. Casa de Velazquez — Mel Casa Velazquez
Melanges Chinois et Bouddhiques — MCB
Melanges d'Archeologie Egyptienne et Assyrienne [*Paris*] — MdA
Melanges d'Archeologie et d'Histoire — MAH
Melanges d'Archeologie et d'Histoire. Ecole Francaise de Rome — MEFR
Melanges d'Archeologie et d'Histoire. Ecole Francaise de Rome — Mel Arch Hist
Melanges d'Archeologie et d'Histoire. Ecole Francaise de Rome — Mel d Arch
Melanges d'Archeologie et d'Histoire. Ecole Francaise de Rome — Mel del' Ec Fr de Rom
Melanges d'Archeologie et d'Histoire. Ecole Francaise de Rome — Mel Rom
Melanges d'Archeologie et d'Histoire. Ecole Franciase de Rome — Mel Archeol et Hist
Melanges d'Archeologie et d'Histoire. Ecole Franciase de Rome — Melanges
Melanges d'Archeologie et d'Histoire. Ecole Franciase de Rome — Melanges Archeol Hist
Melanges de Linguistique et de Litterature Romanes Offerts a Mario Roques [*A publication*] — Melanges Roques
Melanges de l'Institut Orthodoxe Francais de Paris — MIOFP
Melanges de Philologie Romane et de Litterature Medievale Offerts a Ernest Hoepffner — Melanges Hoepffner
Melanges de Philosophie, d'Histoire, de Morale, et de Litterature — MPHML
Melanges de Philosophie et de Litterature Juives — M Ph LJ
Melanges de Philosophie et de Litterature Juives [*Paris*] — MelPHLJ
Melanges de Philosophie et de Litterature Juives — MPLJ
Melanges de Science Religieuse — M Sci Rel
Melanges de Science Religieuse — MelScR
Melanges de Science Religieuse [*Lille*] — MScRel
Melanges de Science Religieuse — MSR
Melanges de Science Religieuse. Cahier Supplement — MSR C
Melanges d'Histoire Litteraire de la Renaissance Offerts a Henri Chamard — Melanges Chamard
Melanges d'Histoire Sociale — MHS
Melanges d'Histoire Sociale — MHSo
Melanges. Ecole Francaise de Rome. Antiquite — MEFRA
Melanges. Ecole Francaise de Rome. Moyen Age. Temps Modernes — MEFRM
Melanges. Ecole Francaise de Rome. Moyen Age, Temps Modernes — Melang Ecole Fr Rome Moyen Age
Melanges. Ecole Roumaine en France — MERF
Melanges. Faculte Orientale de Beyrouth — MFOB
Melanges. Faculte Orientale. Universite de St. Joseph [*Beyrouth*] — MFOUJ
Melanges. Faculte Orientale. Universite de St. Joseph [*Beyrouth*] — MUJ
Melanges Greco-Romains. Tire du Bulletin Historico-Philologique. Academie Imperiale des Sciences de St. Petersbourg — Mel Gr
Melanges. Institut Dominicain d'Etudes Orientales — MIDEO
Melanges Islamologiques — M Isl
Melanges Malraux Miscellany — MMM
Melanges Syriens Offerts a Monsieur Rene Dussaud — MS
Melanges Theologiques — MT
Melanges. Universite Saint Joseph — Mel Univ St Joseph
Melanges. Universite Saint Joseph — MelUSJ
Melanges. Universite Saint Joseph — MUSJ
Melanges. Universite Saint Joseph (Beyrouth) — Mel (Beyrouth)
Melanges. Universite Saint Joseph (Beyrouth) — MU(B)
Melanges. Universite Saint-Joseph — Mel St J
Melanges. Universite Saint-Joseph — Mel St Joseph
Melanges. Universite Saint-Joseph — Melanges Univ SJ
Melanges. Universite Saint-Joseph — MFO
Melanges. Universite Saint-Joseph Beyrouth — Melanges Univers Saint-Joseph Beyrouth
Melanoma Research — Melanoma Res
Melbourne Chamber of Commerce. Yearbook — Melb Chamber of Commerce Yrbk
Melbourne City Mission Record — Melb City Mission Rec
Melbourne Critical Review [*University of Melbourne*] — MCR
Melbourne Critical Review — Melb Crit R
Melbourne Critical Review — Melb Critical R
Melbourne Critical Review — Melbourne Critical Rev
Melbourne Graduate — Melb Grad
Melbourne Graduate — Melb Graduate
Melbourne Harbour Trust Port Gazette — Port Gazette
Melbourne Historical Journal — Melb Hist J
Melbourne Historical Journal — Melbourne Hist J
Melbourne Historical Journal — Melbourne Hist Jnl
Melbourne Historical Journal — MelH
Melbourne Historical Journal — MHJ
Melbourne Journal of Politics — Melbourne J Politics
Melbourne Legacy Week. Bulletin — Melb Legacy Week Bul
Melbourne Monographs in Germanic Studies — MMGS
Melbourne Monthly Magazine — Melb Mon Mag
Melbourne Papers on Australian Defence — Melbourne Pap Aust Def
Melbourne Review — Melb Rev
Melbourne Slavonic Studies — Melbourne Slavon Stud
Melbourne Slavonic Studies — MelbSS
Melbourne Studies in Education — Melb Stud Educ
Melbourne Studies in Education — Melb Studies in Educ
Melbourne Studies in Education — Melbourne Stud Educ
Melbourne Studies in Education — Melbourne Stud in Educ
Melbourne University. Circular to Schools — Melb Univ Circ to Sch
Melbourne University. Gazette — Melb Univ Gaz
Melbourne University. Gazette — MU Gazette
Melbourne University. Law Review — Melb UL Rev
Melbourne University. Law Review — Melb Univ L Rev
Melbourne University. Law Review — Melb Univ Law R
Melbourne University. Law Review — Melb Univ Law Rev
Melbourne University. Law Review — Melb Univ LR
Melbourne University. Law Review — Melbourne ULR
Melbourne University. Law Review — Melbourne Univ L Rev
Melbourne University. Law Review — Melbourne Univ Law Rev
Melbourne University. Law Review — MU Law R
Melbourne University. Law Review — MULR
Melbourne University. Magazine — Melb Univ Mag
Melbourne University. Magazine — MUM
Melbourne University. Science Review — MU Sci R
Melbourne Walker — Melb Walker
Melbourne Zoological Gardens. Annual Report — Melb Zool Gard Annu Rep
Melding fra Hermetikkindustriens Laboratorium — Meld Hermetikkind Lab
Melding Statens Forsoksgard Kvithamar — Meld St ForsGard Kvithamar
Meldinger fra Norges Landbrukshogskole — Meld Nor Landbrukshogsk
Meldinger fra Norges Landbrukshogskole — Meld Norg Landbrukshogsk
Melding-Landbruksteknisk Institut — Meld Landbruksteknisk Inst
Melding-Meieriinstituttet. Norges Landbrukshogskole — Meld Meieriinst Nor Landbrukshogsk
Melding-Norges Landbrukshogskole. Institutt foer Blomsterdyrking og Veksthusforsok — Meld Nor Landbrukshogsk Inst Blomsterdyrk Veksthusforsok
Melekesskii Gosudarstvennyi Pedagogiceskii Institut. Ucenye Zapiski — Melekess Gos Ped Inst Ucen Zap
Melhoramento e Producao de Sementes de Algumas Hortalicas — Melhor Prod Sementes Hort
Meliorace. Prehled Literatury Zemedelskych a Lesnickych Melioraci — Meliorace Prehl Lit Zemed Lesn Melior
Melioration Acker- und Pflanzenbau — Meliorat Acker- Pflanzenbau
Melioratsiya i Ispol'zovaniya Osushennykh Zemel — Melior Ispol'z Osushennykh Zemel
Melioratsiya Vodnoe Khozyaistva — Melior Vodn Khoz
Melissokomike Ellas — Meliss Ellas
Melita Historica — Mel Hist
Melita Theologica — M Th

Melita Theologica. The Reviews of the Royal University Students' Theological Association [*La Valetta, Malta*] — MeliT
Melita Theologica. The Reviews of the Royal University Students' Theological Association [*La Valetta, Malta*] — MelitaT
Melittologists' Bulletin — Melittologists' Bull
Melk — MEK
Melliand International — Melliand Int
Melliand Textilberichte — Mell Textil
Melliand Textilberichte — Melliand TextBer
Melliand Textilberichte — Melliand Textilber
Melliand Textilberichte International — Melliand Textilber
Melliand Textilberichte International — Melliand Textilber Int
Melliand Textilberichte/International Textile Reports. German Edition — Melliand Textilber Int Text Rep Ger Ed
Melliand Textilchemie — Melliand Textilchem
Melliand Textile Monthly — Melliand Text Mon
Melliands Textil-Berichte — TextB
Melody Maker — GMEM
Melody Maker — Mel Maker
Melody Maker — MLDMA
Melody Maker — MM
Melos/Neue Zeitschrift fuer Musik — Me/NZ
Melos. Neue Zeitschrift fuer Musik — Melos NeueZM
Melsheimer Entomological Series — Melsheimer Ent Ser
Melsheimer Entomological Series — Melsheimer Entomol Ser
Melsunger Medizinisch Pharmazeutische Mitteilungen aus Wissenschaft und Praxis — Melsunger Med Pharm Mitt Wiss Prax
Melsunger Medizinisch Pharmazeutische Mitteilungen aus Wissenschaft und Praxis. Supplement — Melsunger Med Pharm Mitt Wiss Prax Suppl
Melsunger Medizinische Mitteilungen — Melsunger Med Mitt
MELUS — PMEL
Melville Society. Extracts — M S Ex
Melyepitestudomanyi Szemle — Melyepitestud Sz
Member's Update. Canadian Arctic Resources Committee — MEUP
Membrane Biochemistry — Membr Biochem
Membrane Biochemistry — Membrane Biochem
Membrane Defenses against Attack by Complement and Perforins — Membr Def Attack Complement Perforins
Membrane Proteins — Membr Proteins
Membrane Science and Technology — Membr Sci Technol
Membrane Science and Technology Series — Membr Sci Technol Ser
Membrane Separations. Science and Technology — Membr Sep Sci Technol
Membrane Transport Processes — Membr Transp Processes
Membranes. Structure and Function. Federation of European Biochemical Societies Meeting — Membr Struct Funct Fed Eur Biochem Soc Meet
Memminger Geschichtsblaetter — MG
Memoir. American Association of Petroleum Geologists — Mem Am Assoc Pet Geol
Memoir. Botanical Survey of South Africa — Mem Bot Surv S Afr
Memoir. Bureau of Mines and Geology. Montana — Mem Bur Mines Geol Mont
Memoir. Canadian Society of Petroleum Geologists — Mem Can Soc Pet Geol
Memoir. Cyprus. Geological Survey Department — Mem Cyprus Geol Surv Dep
Memoir. Department of Geological Sciences. Virginia Polytechnic Institute and State University — Mem Dep Geol Sci Va Polytech Inst State Univ
Memoir. Fiji. Geological Survey Department — Mem Fiji Geol Surv Dep
Memoir. Geological Society of America — Mem Geol Soc Am
Memoir. Geological Society of China — Mem Geol Soc China
Memoir. Geological Society of India — Mem Geol Soc India
Memoir. Geological Survey of Korea — Mem Geol Surv Kenya
Memoir. Geological Survey of Northern Ireland — Mem Geol Surv North Irel
Memoir. Geological Survey of South West Africa — Mem Geol Surv South West Afr
Memoir. Geological Survey of Victoria — Mem Geol Surv Victoria
Memoir. Geological Survey of Wyoming — Mem Geol Surv Wyo
Memoir. Grassland Research Institute (Hurley, England) — Mem Grassl Res Inst (Hurley Engl)
Memoir. Malaysia Geological Survey. Borneo Region — Mem Malaysia Geol Surv Borneo Region
Memoir. Montana Bureau of Mines and Geology — Mem Mont Bur Mines Geol
Memoir. New Mexico Bureau of Mines and Mineral Resources — Mem NM Bur Mines Miner Resour
Memoir. New Mexico Bureau of Mines and Mineral Resources — NMMMA
Memoir. New York Agricultural Experiment Station — Mem NY Agr Exp Sta
Memoir Series. Calcutta Mathematical Society — Mem Ser Calcutta Math Soc
Memoir. Soil Research Institute (Kumasi, Ghana) — Mem Soil Res Inst (Kumasi Ghana)
Memoir. South Africa Geological Survey — Mem S Afr Geol Surv
Memoir. Virginia Polytechnic Institute and State University. Department of Geological Sciences — Mem Va Polytech Inst State Univ Dep Geol Sci
Memoire. Accademia delle Scienze. Istituto di Bologna — MASIB
Memoire. Accademia delle Scienze. Istituto di Bologna. Classe di Scienze Morali — MASIBM
Memoire. Departement de Mineralogie. Universite de Geneve — Mem Dep Mineral Univ Geneve
Memoire et Travaux Publies par les Facultes Catholiques de Lille — MFCL
Memoire Hors-Serie. Societe Geologique de France — Mem Hors Ser Soc Geol Fr
Memoire. Mission Archeologique Francaise au Caire — MissionArchFrMem
Memoire. Sciences Geologiques. Institut de Geologie. Universite Louis Pasteur de Strasbourg — Mem Sci Geol Inst Geol Univ Louis Pasteur Strasbourg
Memoire. Service Geologique de Belgique — Mem Serv Geol Belg
Memoire. Societe Mathematique de France. Nouvelle Serie — Mem Soc Math France NS
Memoires. Academie Celtique — MA Celt
Memoires. Academie de Chirurgie [*France*] — Mem Acad Chir
Memoires. Academie de Medecine (Paris) — Mem Acad Med (Paris)
Memoires. Academie de Metz — M Ac M
Memoires. Academie de Metz — MAM
Memoires. Academie de Nimes — Mem Acad Nimes
Memoires. Academie de Stanislas — M Ac S
Memoires. Academie des Inscriptions et Belles Lettres — Mem Acad Inscr
Memoires. Academie des Inscriptions et Belles Lettres. Institut de France — MAIBLIF
Memoires. Academie des Inscriptions et Belles-Lettres — MAIBL
Memoires. Academie des Sciences, Arts, et Belles Lettres de Dijon — ASD
Memoires. Academie des Sciences, Arts, et Belles Lettres de Dijon — M Ac Dijon
Memoires. Academie des Sciences, Arts, et Belles Lettres de Dijon — Mem Dijon
Memoires. Academie des Sciences, Arts, et Belles-Lettres de Dijon — Mem Acad Sci Arts Belles Lett Dijon
Memoires. Academie des Sciences, Belles-Lettres, et Arts d'Angers — M Ac A
Memoires. Academie des Sciences, Belles-Lettres, et Arts d'Angers — Mem Angers
Memoires. Academie des Sciences, Belles-Lettres, et Arts de Clermont-Ferrand — MASCF
Memoires. Academie des Sciences, Belles-Lettres, et Arts de Savoie — M Ac Savoie
Memoires. Academie des Sciences de l'Institut de France — MASIF
Memoires. Academie des Sciences de Turin — Mem Acad Sci Turin
Memoires. Academie des Sciences, des Arts, et des Belles-Lettres de Dijon — MAD
Memoires. Academie des Sciences et Belles-Lettres d'Angers — Mem Acad Sci Angers
Memoires. Academie des Sciences, Inscriptions, et Belles-Lettres de Toulouse — MAT
Memoires. Academie des Sciences, Inscriptions, et Belles-Lettres de Toulouse — Mem Acad Sci Inscr B-Lett Toulouse
Memoires. Academie des Sciences, Inscriptions et Belles-Lettres de Toulouse — Mem Acad Sci Inscript Belles Lett Toulouse
Memoires. Academie des Sciences, Inscriptions, et Belles-Lettres de Toulouse — Mem Acad Sci Inscriptions B L Toulouse
Memoires. Academie des Sciences, Inscriptions, et Belles-Lettres de Toulouse [*France*] — Mem Acad Sci Toulouse
Memoires. Academie des Sciences, Inscriptions, et Belles-Lettres de Toulouse — Mem Toulouse
Memoires. Academie des Sciences, Inscriptions, et Belles-Lettres de Toulouse — MSBTA
Memoires. Academie des Sciences. Institut de France — Mem Acad Sci
Memoires. Academie des Sciences. Institut de France — Mem Acad Sci Inst Fr
Memoires. Academie des Sciences Morales et Politiques — MASMP
Memoires. Academie des Vaucluse — MAV
Memoires. Academie d'Histoire de la Culture de Leningrad — MACL
Memoires. Academie Imperiale des Sciences de Saint-Petersbourg. Sixieme Serie. Sciences Mathematiques, Physiques, et Naturelles. Seconde Part Sciences Naturelles — Mem Acad Imp Sci Saint Petersbourg Ser 6 Sci Math Seconde Pt
Memoires. Academie Imperiale des Sciences de St. Petersbourg. Avec l'Histoire de l'Academie — Mem Acad Imp Sci St Petersbourg Hist Acad
Memoires. Academie Imperiale des Sciences de St-Petersbourg — Mem St Petersbourg
Memoires. Academie Malgache — Mem Acad Malgache
Memoires. Academie Polonaise des Sciences et des Lettres. Classe des Sciences Mathematiques et Naturelles. Serie A. Sciences Mathematiques — Mem Acad Pol Sci Lett Cl Sci Math Nat Ser A
Memoires. Academie Polonaise des Sciences et des Lettres. Classe des Sciences Mathematiques et Naturelles. Serie B. Sciences Naturelles — Mem Acad Pol Sci Lett Cl Sci Math Nat Ser B
Memoires. Academie Roumaine — MAR
Memoires. Academie Royale de Belgique — Ac R Belg
Memoires. Academie Royale de Belgique — MAB
Memoires. Academie Royale de Belgique — MARB
Memoires. Academie Royale de Belgique. Classe des Beax-Arts — MABBA
Memoires. Academie Royale de Belgique. Classe des Lettres et des Sciences Morales et Politiques — MABL
Memoires. Academie Royale de Belgique. Classe des Sciences. Collection in Quarto — Mem Acad R Belg Cl Sci Collect 4o
Memoires. Academie Royale de Belgique. Classe des Sciences. Collection in Quarto. Deuxieme Serie — Mem Acad R Belg Cl Sci 4o Ser II
Memoires. Academie Royale de Belgique. Lettres — MARBL
Memoires. Academie Royale de Langue et de Litterature Francaises de Belgique — MALFB
Memoires. Academie Royale de Medecine de Belgique — Mem Acad R Med Belg
Memoires. Academie Royale de Prusse. Concernant l'Anatomie, la Physiologie, la Physique, l'Histoire Naturelle, la Botanique, la Mineralogie (Avignon) — Mem Acad Roy Prusse Anat Avignon
Memoires. Academie Royale des Sciences Coloniales. Classe des Sciences Naturelles et Medicales. Verhandelingen. Koninklike Academie voor Koloniale Wetenschappen. Klasse der Natuur- en Geneeskundige Wetenschappen — Mem Acad Roy Sci Colon Cl Sci Nat
Memoires. Academie Royale des Sciences, des Lettres, et des Beaux-Arts de Belgique — Mem Acad Roy Sci Lett Belg
Memoires. Academie Royale des Sciences d'Outre-Mer (Brussels) — Mem Acad Roy Sci Outre-Mer (Brussels)
Memoires. Academie Royale des Sciences d'Outre-Mer. Classe des Sciences Techniques. Collection in 8 (Brussels) — Mem Acad R Sci Outr Mer Cl Sci Tech Collect (Brussels)

Memoires. Academie Royale des Sciences et des Lettres de Danemark. Section des Sciences — Mem Acad R Sci Lett Dan Sect Sci
Memoires. Academie Royale des Sciences (Paris) — Mem Acad Roy Sci Paris
Memoires. American Folklore Society — MAFLS
Memoires. Association Internationale des Hydrogeologues — Mem Assoc Int Hydrogeol
Memoires. Association Internationale des Hydrogeologues. Reunion d'Istanbul [*A publication*] — Mem Assoc Int Hydrogeol Reunion Istanbul
Memoires. Bibliotheque de la Sorbonne — MBS
Memoires. Bureau de Recherches Geologiques et Minieres [*France*] — Mem BRGM
Memoires. Bureau de Recherches Geologiques et Minieres [*France*] — Mem Bur Rech Geol Minieres
Memoires. Centre de Recherches Anthropologique, Prehistorique, et Ethnologique — MCRAPE
Memoires. Centre National de Recherches Metallurgiques. Section du Hainaut — Mem Cent Nat Rech Metall Sect Hainaut
Memoires. Centre National de Recherches Metallurgiques. Section du Hainaut — Mem Cent Natl Rech Metall Sect Hainaut
Memoires. Cercle Historique et Archeologique de Courtrai — MCHAC
Memoires. Cercle Royal Historique et Archeologique de Courtrai — MCRHAC
Memoires. Classe des Sciences. Academie Royale de Belgique. Collection in 4 — Mem Cl Sci Acad R Belg Collect 4
Memoires. Classe des Sciences. Academie Royale de Belgique. Collection in 8 — Mem Cl Sci Acad R Belg Coll 8
Memoires. Classe des Sciences. Academie Royale de Belgique. Collection in Octavo — Mem Cl Sci Acad R Belg Collect 8o
Memoires. Classe des Sciences Mathematiques et Physiques. Institut National de France — Mem Cl Sci Math Inst Natl France
Memoires. Collection in Octavo. Institut Royal Colonial Belge. Classe des Sciences Techniques — Mem Collect 8 Inst R Colon Belg Cl Sci Tech
Memoires. Commission Departementale des Monuments Historiques du Pas-de-Calais — MCDPC
Memoires. Commission des Antiquites de la Cote-D'Or — MCACO
Memoires. Commission des Antiquites du Departement de la Cote d'Or — MCA Cote d'Or
Memoires. Commission des Antiquites du Departement de la Cote d'Or — Mem CACO
Memoires. Commission des Antiquites du Departement de la Cote d'Or — Mem Dep Cote d'Or
Memoires. Commission des Antiquites du Departement de la Cote-D'Or — Mem Cote D'Or
Memoires. Congres International sur le Gaz Naturel Liquefie — Mem Congr Int Gaz Nat Liquefie
Memoires. Congres Mondial du Petrole — Mem Congr Mond Pet
Memoires Couronnes — Mem Couronnes
Memoires Couronnes et Autres Memoires. Academie Royale des Sciences, Lettres et Beaux-Arts de Belgique — Mem Couronnes Autres Mem Acad Roy Sci Belgique
Memoires Couronnes et Memoires des Savants Etrangers. Academie Royale des Sciences et Belles-Lettres de Bruxelles. In Octavo — Mem Couronnes Mem Savants Etrangers Acad Roy Sci Bruxelles 8
Memoires d'Agriculture, d'Economie Rurale et Domestique. Societe Centrale d'Agriculture de France — Mem Agric Soc Centr Agric France
Memoires d'Agriculture, d'Economie Rurale et Domestique. Societe Royale d'Agriculture de Paris — Mem Agric Soc Roy Agric Paris
Memoires de Athenee Oriental Fonde en 1864 — Mem Athenee Orient
Memoires de la Societe d'Emulation du Department du Doubs — Mem de la Soc d Emul du Doubs
Memoires de la Societe des Lettres, Sciences, et Arts et d'Agriculture de Metz — Mem Soc Lett Metz
Memoires de la Societe des Sciences et Lettres de Loir-et-Cher — Mem Soc Sci Loir Et Cher
Memoires de la Societe des Sciences Naturelles de Seine-et-Oise — Mem Soc Sci Nat Seine Et Oise
Memoires de la Societe d'Histoire Naturelle du Departement de la Moselle — Mem Soc Hist Nat Dep Moselle
Memoires de la Societe Geologique du Nord — Mem Soc Geol Nord
Memoires de la Societe Linneenne de Provence — Mem Soc Linn Provence
Memoires de l'Academie de Stanislas — Mem Acad Stanislas
Memoires de l'Academie des Sciences, Arts et Belles-Lettres de Dijon — Mem Acad Sci Dijon
Memoires de l'Academie Nationale de Metz — Mem Acad Nat Metz
Memoires de l'Academie Royale de Metz. Lettres, Sciences, Arts, Agriculture — Mem Acad Roy Metz
Memoires de l'Academie Royale des Sciences et Belles Lettres Depuis l'Avenement de Frederic Guillaume II au Throne. Avec l'Histoire (Berlin) — Mem Acad Roy Sci Hist Berlin
Memoires de l'Academie Royale des Sciences (Turin) — Mem Acad Roy Sci Turin
Memoires de l'Institut Francais d'Afrique Noire — Mem Inst Franc Afrique Noire
Memoires de l'Institut National de France. Academie des Inscriptions et Belles-Lettres — Mem Inst Nat France
Memoires de l'Institut National des Sciences et Arts. Sciences Mathematiques et Physiques — Mem Inst Natl Sci Sci Math
Memoires de l'Universite de Neuchatel — MUN
Memoires de Mathematique et de Physique. Presentes a l'Academie Royale des Sciences par Divers Scavans — Mem Math Phys Acad Roy Sci Divers Scavans
Memoires de Physique — Mem Phys
Memoires de Physique et de Chimie. Societe d'Arcueil — Mem Phys Chim Soc Arcueil
Memoires de Physique Ukrainiens — Mem Phys Ukr
Memoires de Sciences Physiques — Mem Sci Phys
Memoires. Delegation Archeologique Francaise d'Afghanistan — DAFA
Memoires. Delegation Archeologique Francaise de Afghanistan — MDAFA
Memoires. Delegation en Perse [*Paris*] — MDP
Memoires du Museum d'Histoire Naturelle — Mem Mus Hist Nat
Memoires et Bulletins. Institut Historique de Provence — MIHP
Memoires et Compte Rendu des Travaux. Societe des Ingenieurs Civils de France — Mem CR Trav Soc Ing Civ Fr
Memoires et Comptes Rendus. Societe Royale du Canada — Mem C R Soc R Can
Memoires et Dissertations sur les Antiquites Nationales et Etrangeres — MDAN
Memoires et Documents. Academie des Sciences, Belles-Lettres, et Arts de Besancon — Mem Doc Acad Sci Besancon
Memoires et Documents Publies par l'Academie Chablaisienne — MDAC
Memoires et Documents Publies par l'Academie Faucigny — MDAF
Memoires et Etudes Scientifiques de la Revue de Metallurgie — Mem Etud Sci Rev Metall
Memoires et Observations Recueilles. Societe Oeconomique de Berne — Mem Observ Soc Oecon Berne
Memoires et Publications. Societe des Sciences, des Arts, et des Lettres du Hainaut — Mem Publ Soc Sci Arts Lett Hainaut
Memoires et Publications. Societe des Sciences, des Arts et des Lettres du Heimat — MSALH
Memoires et Travaux. Facultes Catholiques de Lille — Mem Trav Fac Cath
Memoires et Travaux. Societe Hydrotechnique de France — Mem Trav Soc Hydrot France
Memoires. Geological Survey of India — MGSI
Memoires ICF [*Societe des Ingenieurs Civils de France*] — Mem ICF
Memoires. Institut Agronomique et Forestier d'Etat de la Belarussie — Mem Inst Agron For Etat Belarussie
Memoires. Institut de France — MIF
Memoires. Institut de Geologie du Bassin d'Aquitaine — Mem Inst Geol Bassin Aquitaine
Memoires. Institut de Metrologie et de Standardisation de l'URSS Presentes au Comite International des Poids et Mesures — Mem Inst Metrol Stand URSS Presentes Com Int Poids Mes
Memoires. Institut de Recherche Scientifique de Madagascar — M Inst Rech Sci Mad
Memoires. Institut de Recherche Scientifique de Madagascar. Serie A. Biologie Animale — Mem Inst Rech Sci Madagascar Ser A Biol Anim
Memoires. Institut de Recherche Scientifique de Madagascar. Serie B. Biologie — Mem Inst Sci Madagascar Ser B
Memoires. Institut de Recherche Scientifique de Madagascar. Serie B. Biologie Vegetale — Mem Inst Rech Sci Madagascar Ser B Biol Veg
Memoires. Institut de Recherche Scientifique de Madagascar. Serie D. Sciences de la Terre — Mem Inst Sci Madagascar Ser D
Memoires. Institut de Recherche Scientifique de Madagascar. Serie F. Oceanographie — Mem Inst Rech Sci Madagascar Ser F Oceanogr
Memoires. Institut d'Egypte — Mem Inst Egypt
Memoires. Institut d'Egypte — Mem Inst Egypte
Memoires. Institut d'Egypte — MIE
Memoires. Institut Francais d'Afrique Noire — MIFAN
Memoires. Institut Francais d'Archeologie Orientale — IFAO
Memoires. Institut Francais d'Archeologie Orientale — Mem IFAO
Memoires. Institut Francais d'Archeologie Orientale — Mem Inst
Memoires. Institut Francais d'Archeologie Orientale — Mem Inst Franc
Memoires. Institut Francais d'Archeologie Orientale — Mem Inst Francais Arch Or
Memoires. Institut Geodesique de Danemark — Mem Inst Geod Dan
Memoires. Institut Geologique (Romania) — Mem Inst Geol (Rom)
Memoires. Institut Geologique. Universite de Louvain — Mem Inst Geol Univ Louv
Memoires. Institut National de France — Mem Inst Nat Fr
Memoires. Institut National de France — MINF
Memoires. Institut National de France. Academie des Inscriptions et Belles-Lettres — MAI
Memoires. Institut National Polonais d'Economie Rurale — Mem Inst Natl Pol Econ Rurale
Memoires. Institut Oceanographique (Monaco) — Mem Inst Oceanogr (Monaco)
Memoires. Institut Royal Colonial Belge. Section des Sciences Naturelles et Medicales. Verhandelingen. Koninklijk Belgisch Koloniaal Instit Afdeeling der Natuur- en Geneeskundige Wetenschappen. In Quarto — Mem Inst Roy Colon Belge Sect Sci Nat 4
Memoires. Institut Scientifique de Madagascar. Serie B. Biologie Vegetale — Mem Inst Sci Madagascar Ser B Biol Veg
Memoires. Institut Scientifuge de Madagascar — MIMS
Memoires. Institut Suisse de Recherches Forestieres — Mem Inst Suisse Rech For
Memoires. Mission Archeologique en Iran — MMAI
Memoires. Mission Archeologique en Perse — MMAP
Memoires. Mission Archeologique Francaise au Caire [*Paris*] — MMAF
Memoires. Mission Archeologique Francaise au Caire [*Paris*] — MMAFC
Memoires. Museum National d'Histoire Naturelle — Mem Mus Natl Hist Nat
Memoires. Museum National d'Histoire Naturelle (Paris) — Mem Mus Natn Hist Nat (Paris)
Memoires. Museum National d'Histoire Naturelle (Paris). Serie C. Sciences de la Terre — Mem Mus Hist Nat (Paris) Ser C
Memoires. Museum National d'Histoire Naturelle. Serie A. Zoologie — Mem Mus Natl Hist Nat Ser A Zool
Memoires. Museum National d'Histoire Naturelle. Serie A. Zoologie (Paris) — Mem Mus Natl Hist Nat Ser A (Paris)
Memoires. Museum National d'Histoire Naturelle. Serie B. Botanique — Mem Mus Natl Hist Nat Ser B Bot
Memoires. Museum National d'Histoire Naturelle. Serie C. Geologie — Mem Mus Natl Hist Nat Ser C Geol

Memoires. Museum National d'Histoire Naturelle. Serie C. Sciences de la Terre — Mem Mus Natl His Nat Ser C Sci Terre
Memoires. Museum National d'Histoire Naturelle. Serie C. Sciences de la Terre — Mem Mus Natl Hist Nat Ser C Sci Terre
Memoires. Museum National d'Histoire Naturelle. Serie C. Sciences de la Terre — MMNCAH
Memoires. Museum National d'Histoire Naturelle. Serie C. Sciences de la Terre (Paris) — Mem Mus Natl Hist Nat Ser C (Paris)
Memoires. Museum National d'Histoire Naturelle. Serie D. Sciences Physico-Chimiques (Paris) — Mem Mus Natl Hist Nat Ser D (Paris)
Memoires. Office de la Recherche Scientifique et Technique d'Outre-Mer — Mem Off Rech Sci Tech Outre-Mer
Memoires. Office de la Recherche Scientifique et Technique d'Outre-Mer — Mem ORSTOM
Memoires. Osaka Kyoiku University — Mem Osaka Kyoiku Univ
Memoires pour Servir a l'Explication de la Carte Geologique Detaillee de la France — Mem Servir Explication Carte Geol Detaill Fr
Memoires pour Servir a l'Explication des Cartes Geologiques et Minieres de la Belgique — Mem Explic Cartes Geol Min Belg
Memoires pour Servir a l'Explication des Cartes Geologiques et Minieres de la Belgique — Mem Servir Explication Cartes Geol Min Belg
Memoires pour Servir a l'Histoire Naturelle des Animaux et des Plantes — Mem Hist Nat Anim Pl
Memoires pour Servir de Preuves a l'Histoire Ecclesiastique et Civile de Bretagne — MPHEB
Memoires Presentes a la Section de Chimie Minerale. Congres International de Chimie Pure et Appliquee — Mem Sect Chim Miner Congr Int Chim Pure Appl
Memoires Presentes a l'Institut des Sciences, Lettres, et Arts par Divers Savans, et lus dans ses Assemblees. Sciences Mathematiques et Physiques — Mem Inst Sci Divers Savans Sci Math
Memoires Presentes par Divers Savants a l'Academie des Inscriptions et Belles Lettres — Mem Ac Inscr
Memoires Presentes par Divers Savants a l'Academie des Inscriptions et Belles-Lettres [*Paris*] — MDS
Memoires Presentes par Divers Savants a l'Academie des Inscriptions et Belles-Lettres [*Paris*] — MDSAI
Memoires Presentes par Divers Savants. Academie des Inscriptions et Belles-Lettres — MAIBL
Memoires Presentes par Divers Savants. Academie des Inscriptions et Belles-Lettres. Antiquites de la France — MAIBLA
Memoires Presentes par Divers Savants. Academie des Inscriptions et Belles-Lettres. Institut de France — AIBS
Memoires Presentes par Divers Savants. Academie des Inscriptions et Belles-Lettres. Institut de France — Mem del'Acad d Inscr
Memoires Presentes par Divers Savants. Academie des Inscriptions et Belles-Lettres. Sujets Divers d'Erudition — MAIBLE
Memoires Publies. Institut pour la Protection des Plantes — Mem Publies Inst Prot Plant
Memoires Publies. Institut pour la Protection des Plantes — MPIPEM
Memoires Publies. Membres. Institut Francais d'Archeologie Orientale au Caire — Mem Inst Franc Archeol Or Caire
Memoires Publies. Membres. Mission Archeologique Francaise au Caire — MMAF
Memoires Publies par l'Academie de Marseille — Mem Acad Marseille
Memoires Publies par les Membres de la Mission Archeologique Francaise au Caire — Mem Miss Caire
Memoires Publies par les Membres de l'Institut Francais d'Archeologie Orientale du Caire — MIFAO
Memoires Publies par les Membres de l'Institut Francais d'Archeologie Orientale du Caire — MIFAOC
Memoires Publies par les Membres. Mission Archeologique Francaise au Caire — MMFC
Memoires. Research Dept. Toyo Bunko (Tokio) — Mem Res Dept Tokio
Memoires Scientifiques de la Revue de Metallurgie — Mem S R Met
Memoires Scientifiques de la Revue de Metallurgie — Mem Sci Rev Met
Memoires Scientifiques de la Revue de Metallurgie — Mem Sci Rev Metall
Memoires. Section des Orientalistes. Socite Imperiale Russe d'Archeologie — MSO
Memoires. Section Historique. Academie Roumaine — MHAR
Memoires. Service de la Carte Geologique d'Alsace et de Lorraine — Mem Serv Carte Geol Alsace Lorraine
Memoires. Service Geologique et Geophysique (Belgrade) — Mem Serv Geol Geophys (Belgrade)
Memoires. Societe Academique d'Archeologie, Sciences, et Arts du Departement de l'Oise — Mem Soc Acad Archeol Dep Oise
Memoires. Societe Academique des Sciences, Arts, et Belles-Lettres de Falaise — Mem Soc Acad Sci Falaise
Memoires. Societe Archeologique de Midi de la France — Mem Soc A Midi
Memoires. Societe Archeologique de Touraine — Mem Touraine
Memoires. Societe Archeologique du Midi de la France — Mem Midi
Memoires. Societe Archeologique du Midi de la France — MSAMF
Memoires. Societe Archeologique et Historique de la Charente — MSA Charente
Memoires. Societe Archeologique Imperiale Russe — MSAR
Memoires. Societe Belge de Geologie, de Paleontologie — Mem Soc Belge Geol
Memoires. Societe Belge de Geologie, de Paleontologie, et d'Hydrologie. Serie in Octavo — Mem Soc Belge Geol Paleontol Hydrol Ser 8
Memoires. Societe Botanique de France — Mem Soc Bot Fr
Memoires. Societe Centrale d'Agriculture de France — Mem Soc Centr Agric France
Memoires. Societe Centrale de Medecine Veterinaire — Mem Soc Centr Med Vet
Memoires. Societe d'Agriculture, Commerce, Sciences, et Arts du Departement de la Marne — MSA Marne
Memoires. Societe d'Agriculture, Commerce, Sciences, et Arts du Departement de la Marne — MSM
Memoires. Societe d'Agriculture, Commerce, Sciences, et Arts du Departement de la Marne — MSMarne
Memoires. Societe d'Agriculture, Commerce, Sciences, et Arts du Departement de la Marne (Chalons Sur Marne) — Mem Soc Agric Commer Sci Arts (Marne)
Memoires. Societe d'Agriculture, des Sciences, et des Arts de l'Arrondissement de Valenciennes — Mem Soc Agric Arrondissement Valenciennes
Memoires. Societe de Geographie d'Egypte — MSGE
Memoires. Societe de l'Histoire de Paris et de l'Ile-de-France — MSHP
Memoires. Societe de Linguistique de Paris — Mem S Ling
Memoires. Societe de Linguistique de Paris — Mem Soc de Ling de Paris
Memoires. Societe de Linguistique de Paris — Mem Soc Ling
Memoires. Societe d'Emulation de Cambrai — MSEC
Memoires. Societe d'Emulation de Roubaix — MSER
Memoires. Societe d'Emulation du Doubs — MSED
Memoires. Societe des Antiquaires de la Morinie — MSAM
Memoires. Societe des Antiquaires de l'Ouest — MSAO
Memoires. Societe des Antiquaires de Picardie — Mem Soc Ant Picardie
Memoires. Societe des Antiquaires de Picardie — MSAP
Memoires. Societe des Arts et des Sciences de Carcassonne — MSAC
Memoires. Societe des Etude Japonaises, Chinoises, Tartares, et Indochinoises a Paris — MSEJ
Memoires. Societe des Etudes Juives — MSEJ
Memoires. Societe des Ingenieurs Civils de France — Mem Soc Ing Civ Fr
Memoires. Societe des Naturalistes de Kiev — Mem Soc Nat Kiev
Memoires. Societe des Sciences, Agriculture, et Arts de Strasbourg — Mem Soc Sci Strasbourg
Memoires. Societe des Sciences de Nancy — Mem Soc Sci Nancy
Memoires. Societe des Sciences et Lettres de Loir-et-Cher — MSSLC
Memoires. Societe des Sciences Naturelles de Cherbourg — Mem Soc Sci Nat Cherbourg
Memoires. Societe des Sciences Naturelles de Strasbourg — Mem Soc Sci Nat Strasbourg
Memoires. Societe des Sciences Naturelles du Maroc — Mem Soc Sci Nat Maroc
Memoires. Societe des Sciences Naturelles et Archeologiques de la Creuse — Mem Creuse
Memoires. Societe des Sciences Naturelles et Archeologiques de la Creuse — MSSNC
Memoires. Societe des Sciences Naturelles et Physiques du Maroc. Botanique — Mem Soc Sci Nat Phys Maroc Bot
Memoires. Societe des Sciences Naturelles et Physiques du Maroc. Zoologie — Mem Soc Sci Nat Phys Maroc Zool
Memoires. Societe des Sciences Physiques et Naturelles de Bordeaux — Mem Soc Sci Phys Nat Bordeaux
Memoires. Societe d'Histoire et d'Archeologie de Bretagne — MSHAB
Memoires. Societe d'Histoire et d'Archeologie de Chalon-sur-Saone — Mem Chalon S
Memoires. Societe d'Histoire et d'Archeologie de Chalon-Sur-Saone — Mem Soc Chalon
Memoires. Societe d'Histoire et d'Archeologie de Chalon-sur-Saone — MSH Chalon
Memoires. Societe d'Histoire Naturelle de l'Afrique du Nord — Mem Soc Hist Nat Afr Nord
Memoires. Societe d'Histoire Naturelle de l'Afrique du Nord — Mem Soc Hist Natur Afr Nord
Memoires. Societe d'Histoire Naturelle de l'Afrique du Nord. Hors Serie — Mem Soc Hist Nat Afrique N Hors Ser
Memoires. Societe Eduenne — Mem Soc Eduenne
Memoires. Societe Eduenne — MSE
Memoires. Societe Entomologique du Canada — Mem Soc Entomol Can
Memoires. Societe Entomologique du Canada — MESCAK
Memoires. Societe Entomologique du Quebec — Mem Soc Entomol Que
Memoires. Societe Finno-Ougrienne — MSFO
Memoires. Societe Finno-Ougrienne — MSFOu
Memoires. Societe Fribourgeoise des Sciences Naturelles. Bacteriologie — Mem Soc Frib Sci Nat Bacteriol
Memoires. Societe Fribourgeoise des Sciences Naturelles. Botanique — Mem Soc Frib Sci Nat Bot
Memoires. Societe Fribourgeoise des Sciences Naturelles. Chimie — Mem Soc Frib Sci Nat Chim
Memoires. Societe Fribourgeoise des Sciences Naturelles. Geologie et Geographie — Mem Soc Frib Sci Nat Geol Geogr
Memoires. Societe Fribourgeoise des Sciences Naturelles. Mathematique et Physique — Mem Soc Frib Sci Nat Math Phys
Memoires. Societe Fribourgeoise des Sciences Naturelles. Physiologie, Hygiene, Bacteriologie — Mem Soc Frib Sci Nat Physiol Hyg Bacteriol
Memoires. Societe Fribourgeoise des Sciences Naturelles. Zoologie — Mem Soc Frib Sci Nat Zool
Memoires. Societe Geologique de Belgique — Mem Soc Geol Belg
Memoires. Societe Geologique de Belgique — Mem Soc Geol Belgique
Memoires. Societe Geologique de France — Mem Soc Geol Fr
Memoires. Societe Geologique de France. Nouvelle Serie — Mem Soc Geol Fr Nouv Ser
Memoires. Societe Geologique et Mineralogique de Bretagne — Mem Soc Geol Mineral Bretagne
Memoires. Societe Helvetique des Sciences Naturelles — Mem Soc Helv Sci Nat
Memoires. Societe Historique et Archeologique de Langres — MSHAL
Memoires. Societe Imperiale de Mineralogie — Mem Soc Imp Mineral
Memoires. Societe Linguistique de Paris — MSL
Memoires. Societe Linguistique de Paris — MSLP
Memoires. Societe Linneenne de Calvados — Mem Soc Linn Calvados
Memoires. Societe Litteraire de Grenoble — Mem Soc Litt Grenoble

Memoires. Societe Nationale d'Agriculture de France — Mem Soc Natl Agric France
Memoires. Societe Nationale d'Agriculture, Sciences, et Arts d'Angers — Mem Soc Natl Agric Angers
Memoires. Societe Nationale des Antiquaires de France — M Ant Fr
Memoires. Societe Nationale des Antiquaires de France — MAF
Memoires. Societe Nationale des Antiquaires de France — Mem Soc AF
Memoires. Societe Nationale des Antiquaires de France — Mem Soc Ant
Memoires. Societe Nationale des Antiquaires de France — Mem Soc Nat Antiqu France
Memoires. Societe Nationale des Antiquaires de France — Mem Soc Nationale Antiq Fr
Memoires. Societe Nationale des Antiquaires de France — MSAF
Memoires. Societe Nationale des Antiquaires de France — MSNAF
Memoires. Societe Nationale des Antiquaires de France — MSNAFr
Memoires. Societe Nationale des Sciences Naturelles et Mathematiques de Cherbourg — Mem Soc Natl Sci Nat Math Cherbg
Memoires. Societe Nationale des Sciences Naturelles et Mathematiques de Cherbourg — MNMCA
Memoires. Societe Neophilologique de Helsinki — MSNH
Memoires. Societe Neuchateloise des Sciences Naturelles — Mem Soc Neuchatel Sci Nat
Memoires. Societe pour l'Histoire de Droit et des Institutions des Anciens Pays Bourguignons, Comtois et Romands — MSHD
Memoires. Societe pour l'Histoire du Droit et des Institutions des Anciens Pays Bourguignons, Comtois, et Romands — MSHDI
Memoires. Societe Royale Academique de Savoie — Mem Soc Roy Acad Savoie
Memoires. Societe Royale Belge d'Entomologie — Mem Soc R Belge Entomol
Memoires. Societe Royale d'Arras pour l'Encuragement des Sciences, des Lettres, et des Arts — Mem Soc Roy Arras
Memoires. Societe Royale de Botanique de Belgique — Mem Soc R Bot Belg
Memoires. Societe Royale des Sciences de Liege — Mem Soc R Sci Liege
Memoires. Societe Royale des Sciences de Liege. Collection in Octavo — Mem Soc R Sci Liege 8o
Memoires. Societe Royale des Sciences de Liege. Collection in Octavo — Mem Soc R Sci Liege Collect 8
Memoires. Societe Royale des Sciences de Liege. Collection in Octavo — Mem Soc Roy Sci Liege Coll in-8o
Memoires. Societe Royale des Sciences de Liege. Collection in Octavo — MRSLA2
Memoires. Societe Royale des Sciences de Liege. Collection in Quarto — Mem Soc R Sci Liege 4o
Memoires. Societe Royale des Sciences de Liege. Volume Hors Serie [*Belgium*] [*A publication*] — Mem Soc R Sci Liege Vol Hors Ser
Memoires. Societe Royale des Sciences et Belles-Lettres de Nancy — Mem Soc Roy Sci Nancy
Memoires. Societe Royale du Canada — Mem Soc R Can
Memoires. Societe Royale du Canada — MSRC
Memoires. Societe Royale Entomologique de Belgique — Mem Soc R Ent Belg
Memoires. Societe Russe de Mineralogie — Mem Soc Russe Mineral
Memoires. Societe Vaudoise des Sciences Naturelles — Mem Soc Vaudoise Sci Nat
Memoires. Societe Zoologique de France — Mem Soc Zool Fr
Memoires. Societe Zoologique Tchecoslovaque de Prague — Mem Soc Zool Tchec Prague
Memoires Suisses de Paleontologie — Mem Suisses Paleontol
Memoires Suisses de Paleontologie — SPAAAX
Memoires Techniques. Centre Technique des Industries Mecaniques — Mem Tech Cent Tech Ind Mec
Memoires Techniques. CETIM [*Centre Technique des Industries Mecaniques*] — Mem Tech CETIM
Memoires. Universite d'Etat a l'Extreme-Orient — Mem Univ Etat Extreme Orien
Memoirs. Academy of Sciences. Ukrainian SSR [*Soviet Socialist Republic*] — Mem Acad Sci Ukr SSR
Memoirs. Agricultural Experiment Station (Ithaca, New York) — Mem Agric Exp Stn (Ithaca NY)
Memoirs. Akita University — Mem Akita Univ
Memoirs. American Academy at Rome — MAAR
Memoirs. American Academy in Rome — Amer Acad Rome
Memoirs. American Academy in Rome — M Am Acad Rome
Memoirs. American Academy in Rome — Mem AAR
Memoirs. American Academy in Rome — Mem Am Ac
Memoirs. American Academy in Rome — Mem Am Ac Rome
Memoirs. American Academy in Rome — Mem Am Acad Rome
Memoirs. American Academy in Rome — Mem Amer Acad Rome
Memoirs. American Academy of Arts and Sciences — Mem Am Acad Arts Sci
Memoirs. American Anthropological Association — MAAA
Memoirs. American Association for the Advancement of Science — Mem Amer Assoc Advancem Sci
Memoirs. American Entomological Institute (Ann Arbor) — Mem Am Entomol Inst (Ann Arbor)
Memoirs. American Entomological Institute (Gainesville) — Mem Am Entomol Inst (Gainesville)
Memoirs. American Entomological Society — Mem Am Entomol Soc
Memoirs. American Mathematical Society — Mem Am Math
Memoirs. American Mathematical Society — Mem Amer Math Soc
Memoirs. American Philosophical Society — MAPS
Memoirs. American Philosophical Society — Mem Am Philos Soc
Memoirs. American Philosophical Society — Mem Amer Philos Soc
Memoirs and Proceedings. Manchester Literary and Philosophical Society — Mem Proc Manchester Lit Philos Soc
Memoirs and Proceedings. Manchester Literary and Philosophical Society — MMLS
Memoirs and Proceedings. Manchester Literary and Philosophical Society — MPMLPS
Memoirs. Archaeological Survey of Egypt — ASE
Memoirs. Archaeological Survey of India — MASI
Memoirs. Asiatic Society of Bengal — MASB
Memoirs. Asiatic Society of Bengal — Mem Asiat Soc Bengal
Memoirs. Astronomical Society of India — Mem Astron Soc India
Memoirs. Australian Museum — Mem Aust Mus
Memoirs. Bernice Pauahi Bishop Museum of Polynesian Ethnology and Natural History — Mem Bernice Pauahi Bishop Mus
Memoirs. Boston Society of Natural History — Mem Boston Soc Nat Hist
Memoirs. Botanical Survey of South Africa — Mem Botan Surv S Afr
Memoirs. Botaniese Opname van Suid-Afrika — Mem Bot Opname S-Afr
Memoirs. Caledonian Horticultural Society — Mem Caledonian Hort Soc
Memoirs. California Academy of Sciences — Mem Calif Acad Sci
Memoirs. Chubu Electric Power Company Limited [*Japan*] — Mem Chubu Electr Power Co Ltd
Memoirs. Chubu Institute of Technology — Mem Chubu Inst Technol
Memoirs. Chubu Institute of Technology. Series A — Mem Chubu Inst Technol A
Memoirs. Chukyo Women's College. Chukyo Women's Junior College — Mem Chukyo Women's Coll Chukyo Women's J Coll
Memoirs. College of Agriculture. Ehime University — Mem Coll Agric Ehime Univ
Memoirs. College of Agriculture. Kyoto University — Mem Coll Agr Kyoto Univ
Memoirs. College of Agriculture. Kyoto University — Mem Coll Agric Kyoto Univ
Memoirs. College of Agriculture. Kyoto University — MKUBA
Memoirs. College of Agriculture. Kyoto University. Agricultural Economy Series — Mem Coll Agric Kyoto Univ Agric Econ Ser
Memoirs. College of Agriculture. Kyoto University. Animal Science Series — Mem Coll Agric Kyoto Univ Anim Sci Ser
Memoirs. College of Agriculture. Kyoto University. Botanical Series — Mem Coll Agric Kyoto Univ Bot Ser
Memoirs. College of Agriculture. Kyoto University. Chemical Series — Mem Coll Agric Kyoto Univ Chem Ser
Memoirs. College of Agriculture. Kyoto University. Entomological Series — Mem Coll Agric Kyoto Univ Entomol Ser
Memoirs. College of Agriculture. Kyoto University. Fisheries Series — Mem Coll Agric Kyoto Univ Fish Ser
Memoirs. College of Agriculture. Kyoto University. Food Science and Technology Series — Mem Coll Agric Kyoto Univ Food Sci Technol Ser
Memoirs. College of Agriculture. Kyoto University. Genetical Series — Mem Coll Agric Kyoto Univ Genet Ser
Memoirs. College of Agriculture. Kyoto University. Horticultural Series — Mem Coll Agric Kyoto Univ Hortic Ser
Memoirs. College of Agriculture. Kyoto University. Phytopathological Series — Mem Coll Agric Kyoto Univ Phytopathol Ser
Memoirs. College of Agriculture. Kyoto University. Plant Breeding Series — Mem Coll Agric Kyoto Univ Plant Breed Ser
Memoirs. College of Agriculture. Kyoto University. Wood Science and Technology Series — Mem Coll Agric Kyoto Univ Wood Sci Technol Ser
Memoirs. College of Agriculture. National Taiwan University — Mem Coll Agric Natl Taiwan Univ
Memoirs. College of Agriculture. National Taiwan University/Kuo Li Taiwan Ta Hsueeh Nung Hsueeh Yuean Yen Chiu Pao K'an — Mem Coll Agric Natl Taiwan Univ
Memoirs. College of Engineering. Chubu University — Mem Coll Eng Chubu Univ
Memoirs. College of Engineering. Kyoto Imperial University — Mem Coll Eng Kyoto Imp Univ
Memoirs. College of Engineering. Kyushu Imperial University — Mem Coll Eng Kyushu Imp Univ
Memoirs. College of Medicine. National Taiwan University — Mem Coll Med Natl Taiwan Univ
Memoirs. College of Science and Engineering. Waseda University — Mem Coll Sci Eng Waseda Univ
Memoirs. College of Science. Kyoto Imperial University — Mem Coll Sci Kyoto Imp Univ
Memoirs. College of Science. Kyoto Imperial University. Series A — Mem Coll Sci Kyoto Imp Univ Ser A
Memoirs. College of Science. Kyoto Imperial University. Series B — Mem Coll Sci Kyoto Imp Univ Ser B
Memoirs. College of Science. University of Kyoto. Series A — Mem Coll Sci Univ Kyoto Ser A
Memoirs. College of Science. University of Kyoto. Series A. Mathematics — Mem Coll Sci Univ Kyoto Ser A Math
Memoirs. College of Science. University of Kyoto. Series B — MCKBA
Memoirs. College of Science. University of Kyoto. Series B [*Japan*] — Mem Coll Sci Univ Kyoto Ser B
Memoirs. College of Science. University of Kyoto. Series B. Geology and Biology — Mem Coll Sci Univ Kyoto Ser B Geol Biol
Memoirs. Connecticut Academy of Arts and Sciences — Mem Conn Acad Arts Sci
Memoirs. Connecticut Academy of Arts and Sciences — Mem Connecticut Acad Arts
Memoirs. Cornell University. Agricultural Experiment Station — Mem Cornell Univ Agric Exp Stn
Memoirs. Cornell University. Agricultural Experiment Station — Mem Cornell Univ Agric Exper Station
Memoirs. Defense Academy — Mem Def Acad
Memoirs. Defense Academy (Japan) — Mem Def Acad (Jap)
Memoirs. Defense Academy. Mathematics, Physics, Chemistry, and Engineering — Mem Def Acad Math Phys Chem Eng
Memoirs. Defense Academy. Mathematics, Physics, Chemistry, and Engineering [*Yokosuka*] — Mem Defense Acad
Memoirs. Defense Academy. Mathematics, Physics, Chemistry, and Engineering (Yokosuka, Japan) — Mem Def Acad Math Phys Chem Eng (Yokosuka Jpn)

Memoirs. Department of Agriculture in India. Bacteriological Series — Mem Dep Agric India Bacteriol Ser
Memoirs. Department of Agriculture in India. Botanical Series — Mem Dep Agric India Bot Ser
Memoirs. Department of Agriculture in India. Chemical Series — Mem Dep Agric India Chem Ser
Memoirs. Department of Agriculture in India. Entomological Series — Mem Dep Agric India Entomol Ser
Memoirs. Department of Archaeology in Pakistan — MDAP
Memoirs. Department of Engineering. Kyoto Imperial University — Mem Dep Eng Kyoto Imp Univ
Memoirs. Ecological Society of Australia — Mem Ecol Soc Aust
Memoirs. Egypt Exploration Society — MEES
Memoirs. Ehime University — Mem Ehime Univ
Memoirs. Ehime University. Natural Science. Series A — Mem Ehime Univ Natur Sci Ser A
Memoirs. Ehime University. Natural Science. Series B (Biology) — Mem Ehime Univ Nat Sci Ser B (Biol)
Memoirs. Ehime University. Natural Science. Series C — Mem Ehime Univ Nat Sci Ser C
Memoirs. Ehime University. Natural Science. Series D. Earth Science — Mem Ehime Univ Nat Sci Ser D
Memoirs. Ehime University. Section 2. Natural Science — Mem Ehime Univ Sect 2 Nat Sci
Memoirs. Ehime University. Section 2. Natural Science. Series C. Chemistry — Mem Ehime Univ Sect 2 Ser C
Memoirs. Ehime University. Section 3. Engineering [*Japan*] — Mem Ehime Univ Sect 3 Eng
Memoirs. Ehime University. Section 3. Engineering — Mem Ehime Univ Sect 3 Engrg
Memoirs. Ehime University. Section 6. Agriculture — Mem Ehime Univ Sect 6 Agr
Memoirs. Ehime University. Section 6 (Agriculture) — Mem Ehime Univ Sect 6 (Agric)
Memoirs. Entomological Society of Canada — Mem Ent S C
Memoirs. Entomological Society of Canada — Mem Ent Soc Can
Memoirs. Entomological Society of Canada — Mem Entomol Soc Can
Memoirs. Entomological Society of Quebec — Mem Entomol Soc Que
Memoirs. Entomological Society of Southern Africa — Mem Entomol Soc South Afr
Memoirs. Entomological Society of Southern Africa — Mem Entomol Soc Sthn Afr
Memoirs. Entomological Society of Washington — Mem Entomol Soc Wash
Memoirs et Publications. Societe des Sciences, des Arts, et des Lettres du Hainaut — Mem Pub Soc Sci Arts Lett Hainaut
Memoirs. Faculty of Agriculture. Hokkaido University — Mem Fac Agr Hokkaido U
Memoirs. Faculty of Agriculture. Hokkaido University — Mem Fac Agr Hokkaido Univ
Memoirs. Faculty of Agriculture. Hokkaido University — Mem Fac Agric Hokkaido Univ
Memoirs. Faculty of Agriculture. Kagawa University — Mem Fac Agr Kagawa Univ
Memoirs. Faculty of Agriculture. Kagawa University — Mem Fac Agric Kagawa Univ
Memoirs. Faculty of Agriculture. Kagoshima University — Mem Fac Agric Kagoshima Univ
Memoirs. Faculty of Agriculture. Kinki University — Mem Fac Agr Kinki Univ
Memoirs. Faculty of Agriculture. Kinki University — Mem Fac Agric Kinki Univ
Memoirs. Faculty of Agriculture. Kochi University — Mem Fac Agric Kochi Univ
Memoirs. Faculty of Agriculture. National Taiwan University/Kuo Li Tai Wan Ta Hsueeh Nung Hsueeh Yuean Yen Chiu Pao Kao — Mem Fac Agric Natl Taiwan Univ
Memoirs. Faculty of Agriculture. Niigata University — Mem Fac Agric Niigata Univ
Memoirs. Faculty of Agriculture. Taihoku Imperial University — Mem Fac Agric Taihoku Imp Univ
Memoirs. Faculty of Agriculture. University of Miyazaki — Mem Fac Agr Univ Miyazaki
Memoirs. Faculty of Agriculture. University of Miyazaki — Mem Fac Agric Univ Miyazaki
Memoirs. Faculty of Education. Akita University — Mem Fac Educ Akita Univ
Memoirs. Faculty of Education. Akita University. Natural Science — Mem Fac Educ Akita Univ Nat Sci
Memoirs. Faculty of Education. Kagawa University — Mem Fac Educ Kagawa Univ
Memoirs. Faculty of Education. Kumamoto University — Mem Fac Educ Kumamoto Univ
Memoirs. Faculty of Education. Kumamoto University. Natural Science — Mem Fac Educ Kumamoto Univ Nat Sci
Memoirs. Faculty of Education. Kumamoto University. Section 1 (Natural Science) — Mem Fac Ed Kumamoto Univ Sect 1
Memoirs. Faculty of Education. Kumamoto University. Section 1 (Natural Science) — Mem Fac Educ Kumamoto Univ Sect 1 (Nat Sci)
Memoirs. Faculty of Education. Mie University — Mem Fac Educ Mie Univ
Memoirs. Faculty of Education. Miyazaki University — Mem Fac Ed Miyazaki Univ
Memoirs. Faculty of Education. Niigata University — Mem Fac Educ Niigata Univ
Memoirs. Faculty of Education. Shiga University. Natural Science — Mem Fac Educ Shiga Univ Nat Sci
Memoirs. Faculty of Education. Shiga University. Natural Science and Pedagogic Science — Mem Fac Ed Shiga Univ Natur Sci Ped Sci
Memoirs. Faculty of Education. Shiga University. Natural Science and Pedagogic Science — Mem Fac Educ Shiga Univ Nat Sci Pedagog Sci
Memoirs. Faculty of Education. Toyama University — Mem Fac Educ Toyama Univ
Memoirs. Faculty of Education. Yamanashi University [*Japan*] — Mem Fac Educ Yamanashi Univ
Memoirs. Faculty of Engineering and Design. Kyoto Institute of Technology. Series of Science and Technology — Mem Fac Eng Des Kyoto Inst Technol Ser Sci Technol
Memoirs. Faculty of Engineering. Ehime University — Mem Fac Eng Ehime Univ
Memoirs. Faculty of Engineering. Fukui University [*Japan*] — Mem Fac Eng Fukui Univ
Memoirs. Faculty of Engineering. Hiroshima University — Mem Fac Eng Hiroshima Univ
Memoirs. Faculty of Engineering. Hiroshima University — Mem Fac Engrg Hiroshima Univ
Memoirs. Faculty of Engineering. Hiroshima University — MFEHA
Memoirs. Faculty of Engineering. Hokkaido Imperial University — Mem Fac Eng Hokkaido Imp Univ
Memoirs. Faculty of Engineering. Hokkaido University — MEHUA
Memoirs. Faculty of Engineering. Hokkaido University — Mem Fac Eng Hokkaido Univ
Memoirs. Faculty of Engineering. Hokkaido University (Sapporo, Japan) — Mem Fac Eng Hokkaido Univ (Sapporo Jpn)
Memoirs. Faculty of Engineering. Kagoshima University — Mem Fac Eng Kagoshima Univ
Memoirs. Faculty of Engineering. Kobe University — Mem Fac Eng Kobe Univ
Memoirs. Faculty of Engineering. Kobe University — MFEKA
Memoirs. Faculty of Engineering. Kumamoto University — MEKMA
Memoirs. Faculty of Engineering. Kumamoto University — Mem Fac Eng Kumamoto Univ
Memoirs. Faculty of Engineering. Kyoto University — MEKYA
Memoirs. Faculty of Engineering. Kyoto University — Mem Fac Eng Kyoto Univ
Memoirs. Faculty of Engineering. Kyoto University — Mem Fac Engng Kyoto Univ
Memoirs. Faculty of Engineering. Kyoto University — Mem Fac Engrg Kyoto Univ
Memoirs. Faculty of Engineering. Kyushu Imperial University — Mem Fac Eng Kyushu Imp Univ
Memoirs. Faculty of Engineering. Kyushu University — MEKSA
Memoirs. Faculty of Engineering. Kyushu University — Mem Fac Eng Kyushu Univ
Memoirs. Faculty of Engineering. Kyushu University — Mem Fac Engng Kyushu Univ
Memoirs. Faculty of Engineering. Miyazaki University — Mem Fac Eng Miyazaki Univ
Memoirs. Faculty of Engineering. Miyazaki University — Mem Fac Engrg Miyazaki Univ
Memoirs. Faculty of Engineering. Nagoya University — Mem Fac Eng Nagoya Univ
Memoirs. Faculty of Engineering. Nagoya University — Mem Fac Engng Nagoya Univ
Memoirs. Faculty of Engineering. Okayama University — Mem Fac Eng Okayama Univ
Memoirs. Faculty of Engineering. Osaka City University — Mem Fac Eng Osaka City Univ
Memoirs. Faculty of Engineering. Tamagawa University — Mem Fac Eng Tamagawa Univ
Memoirs. Faculty of Engineering. Tehran University — Mem Fac Eng Tehran Univ
Memoirs. Faculty of Engineering. Yamaguchi University [*Japan*] — Mem Fac Eng Yamaguchi Univ
Memoirs. Faculty of Fisheries. Hokkaido University — Mem Fac Fish Hokkaido Univ
Memoirs. Faculty of Fisheries. Kagoshima University — Mem Fac Fish Kagoshima Univ
Memoirs. Faculty of General Education. Hiroshima University — Mem Fac Gen Educ Hiroshima Univ
Memoirs. Faculty of General Education. Kumamoto University — Mem Fac Gen Educ Kumamoto Univ
Memoirs. Faculty of Industrial Arts. Kyoto Technical University. Science and Technology — Mem Fac Ind Arts Kyoto Tech Univ
Memoirs. Faculty of Industrial Arts. Kyoto Technical University. Science and Technology — Mem Fac Ind Arts Kyoto Tech Univ Sci and Technol
Memoirs. Faculty of Industrial Arts. Kyoto Technical University. Science and Technology — Mem Fac Indust Arts Kyoto Tech Univ Sci and Tech
Memoirs. Faculty of Industrial Arts. Kyoto Technical University. Science and Technology — Mem Kyoto Tech Univ Sci Tech
Memoirs. Faculty of Integrated Arts and Sciences. Hiroshima University — Mem Fac Intgr Arts Sci Hiroshima Univ
Memoirs. Faculty of Liberal Arts and Education. Akita University. Natural Science — Mem Fac Lib Arts Educ Akita Univ Nat Sci
Memoirs. Faculty of Liberal Arts and Education. Miyazaki University. Natural Science — Mem Fac Lib Arts Educ Miyazaki Univ Nat Sci
Memoirs. Faculty of Liberal Arts and Education. Part 2. Mathematics and Natural Sciences. Yamanashi University — Mem Fac Lib Arts Educ Part 2 Yamanashi Univ
Memoirs. Faculty of Liberal Arts and Education. Yamanashi University [*Japan*] — Mem Fac Liberal Arts Educ Yamanashi Univ
Memoirs. Faculty of Liberal Arts Education. Miyazaki University — Mem Fac Lib Arts Educ Miyazaki Univ
Memoirs. Faculty of Liberal Arts. Fukui University — Mem Fac Lib Arts Fukui Univ
Memoirs. Faculty of Literature and Science. Shimane University. Natural Sciences — Mem Fac Lit Sci Shimane Univ Nat Sci
Memoirs. Faculty of Literature and Science. Shimane University. Natural Sciences [*Matsue*] — Mem Fac Lit Sci Shimane Univ Natur Sci

Memoirs. Faculty of Medicine. National Taiwan University — Mem Fac Med Natl Taiwan Univ
Memoirs. Faculty of Science and Agriculture. Taihoku Imperial University — Mem Fac Sci Agric Taihoku Imp Univ
Memoirs. Faculty of Science and Agriculture. Taihoku Imperial University/ Rino-Gaku-Bu Kiyo — Mem Fac Sci Taihoku Imp Univ
Memoirs. Faculty of Science and Engineering. Waseda University — Mem Fac Sci Eng Waseda Univ
Memoirs. Faculty of Science. Kochi University. Series C. Chemistry — Mem Fac Sci Kochi Univ Ser C
Memoirs. Faculty of Science. Kochi University. Series D. Biology — Mem Fac Sci Kochi Univ Ser D Biol
Memoirs. Faculty of Science. Kyoto University. Series of Biology — Mem Fac Sci Kyoto Univ Ser Biol
Memoirs. Faculty of Science. Kyoto University. Series of Geology and Mineralogy — Mem Fac Sci Kyoto Univ Ser Geol Mineral
Memoirs. Faculty of Science. Kyoto University. Series of Physics, Astrophysics, Geophysics, and Chemistry — Mem Fac Sci Kyoto Univ Ser
Memoirs. Faculty of Science. Kyoto University. Series of Physics, Astrophysics, Geophysics, and Chemistry — Mem Fac Sci Kyoto Univ Ser Phys Astrophys Geophys Chem
Memoirs. Faculty of Science. Kyoto University. Series of Physics, Astrophysics, Geophysics, and Chemistry — MFKPA
Memoirs. Faculty of Science. Kyushu University — Mem Fac Sci Kyushu Univ
Memoirs. Faculty of Science. Kyushu University. Series A. Mathematics — Mem Fac Sci Kyushu Univ Ser A
Memoirs. Faculty of Science. Kyushu University. Series B — Mem Fac Sci Kyushu Univ B
Memoirs. Faculty of Science. Kyushu University. Series B. Physics — Mem Fac Sci Kyushu Univ Ser B
Memoirs. Faculty of Science. Kyushu University. Series C — Mem Fac Sci Kyushu Univ C
Memoirs. Faculty of Science. Kyushu University. Series C [*Japan*] — MFKCA
Memoirs. Faculty of Science. Kyushu University. Series C. Chemistry — Mem Fac Sci Kyushu Univ Ser C
Memoirs. Faculty of Science. Kyushu University. Series D. Geology — Mem Fac Sci Kyushu Univ Ser D
Memoirs. Faculty of Science. Kyushu University. Series D. Geology — Mem Fac Sci Kyushu Univ Ser D Geol
Memoirs. Faculty of Science. Kyushu University. Series D. Geology — MFKDA
Memoirs. Faculty of Science. Kyushu University. Series E. Biology — MEKEA
Memoirs. Faculty of Science. Kyushu University. Series E. Biology — Mem Fac Sci Kyushu Univ Ser E
Memoirs. Faculty of Science. Kyushu University. Series E. Biology — Mem Fac Sci Kyushu Univ Ser E Biol
Memoirs. Faculty of Technology. Kanazawa University — Mem Fac Technol Kanazawa Univ
Memoirs. Faculty of Technology. Tokyo Metropolitan University — Mem Fac Tech Tokyo Metropolitan Univ
Memoirs. Faculty of Technology. Tokyo Metropolitan University — Mem Fac Technol Tokyo Metrop Univ
Memoirs. Faculty of Technology. Tokyo Metropolitan University — MTTMA
Memoirs. Geological Society of America — Mem Geol Soc Amer
Memoirs. Geological Society of Japan — Mem Geol Soc Jpn
Memoirs. Geological Survey Department (Sudan) — Mem Geol Surv Dep (Sudan)
Memoirs. Geological Survey of Canada — Mem Geol Surv Can
Memoirs. Geological Survey of China. Series A — Mem Geol Surv China Ser A
Memoirs. Geological Survey of China. Series B — Mem Geol Surv China Ser B
Memoirs. Geological Survey of Great Britain — Mem Geol Surv Gt Br
Memoirs. Geological Survey of Great Britain. England and Wales Explanation Sheet — Mem Geol Surv GB Engl Wales Explan Sheet
Memoirs. Geological Survey of Great Britain (Scotland) — Mem Geol Surv GB (Scotl)
Memoirs. Geological Survey of Great Britain. Special Reports on the Mineral Resources of Great Britain — Mem Geol Surv GB Spec Rep Miner Resour GB
Memoirs. Geological Survey of India — Mem Geol Surv India
Memoirs. Geological Survey of New South Wales — Mem Geol Surv NSW
Memoirs. Geological Survey of New South Wales — Mem Geol Surv of NSW
Memoirs. Geological Survey of New South Wales. Department of Mines. Geology — Mem Geol Surv of NSW Geol
Memoirs. Geological Survey of New South Wales. Palaeontology — Mem Geol Surv NSW Palaeontol
Memoirs. Geological Survey of Papua New Guinea — Mem Geol Surv Papua New Guinea
Memoirs. Geological Survey of South Africa — Mem Geol Surv S Afr
Memoirs. Geological Survey of Victoria — Mem Geol Surv Vic
Memoirs. Geological Survey of Victoria — Mem Geol Surv Vict
Memoirs. Geological Survey of Western Australia — Mem Geol Surv West Aust
Memoirs. Gifu Technical College — Mem Gifu Tech Coll
Memoirs. Government Industrial Research Institute. Nagoya — Mem Gov Ind Res Inst Nagoya
Memoirs. Government Industrial Research Institute. Sikoku — Mem Gov Ind Res Inst Sikoku
Memoirs. Himeji Technical College — Mem Himeji Tech Coll
Memoirs. Hokkaido Automotive Junior College — Mem Hokkaido Automot Jr Coll
Memoirs. Hokkaido Institute of Technology — Mem Hokkaido Inst Technol
Memoirs. Hourglass Cruises — Mem Hourglass Cruises
Memoirs. Hyogo University of Agriculture — Mem Hyogo Univ Agric
Memoirs. Imperial Marine Observatory — Mem Imp Mar Observ
Memoirs. Imperial Mineralogical Society of St. Petersburg — Mem Imp Mineral Soc St Petersburg
Memoirs. Indian Botanical Society — Mem Indian Bot Soc
Memoirs. Indian Museum — Mem Indian Mus
Memoirs. Institute for Chemistry. Academy of Sciences. Ukrainian SSR — Mem Inst Chem Acad Sci Ukr SSR
Memoirs. Institute for Plant Protection. Belgrade — Mem Inst Plant Prot Belgrade
Memoirs. Institute of Chemical Technology. Academy of Sciences of the Ukrainian SSR — Mem Inst Chem Technol Acad Sci Ukr SSR
Memoirs. Institute of Chemistry. Ukrainian Academy of Sciences — Mem Inst Chem Ukr Acad Sci
Memoirs. Institute of High Speed Mechanics. Tohoku University [*Japan*] — Mem Inst High Speed Mech Tohoku Univ
Memoirs. Institute of Organic Chemistry and Technology. Academy of Sciences. Ukrainian SSR — Mem Inst Org Chem Technol Acad Sci Ukr SSR
Memoirs. Institute of Protein Research. Osaka University — Mem Inst Protein Res Osaka Univ
Memoirs. Institute of Sciences and Technology. Meiji University — Mem Inst Sci Technol Meiji Univ
Memoirs. Institute of Scientific and Industrial Research. Osaka University — Mem Inst Sci Ind Res Osaka Univ
Memoirs. Institute of Scientific and Industrial Research. Osaka University — MISIA
Memoirs. International Association of Hydrogeologists — Mem Int Assoc Hydrogeol
Memoirs. International Society of Sugar Cane Technologists — Mem Int Soc Sugar Cane Technol
Memoirs. Japan Meteorological Agency — Mem Jpn Meteorol Agency
Memoirs. Kagawa Agricultural College — Mem Kagawa Agric Coll
Memoirs. Kakioka Magnetic Observatory [*Japan*] — Mem Kakioka Magn Obs
Memoirs. Kanazawa Institute of Technology — Mem Kanazawa Inst Technol
Memoirs. Kanazawa Technical College — Mem Kanazawa Tech Coll
Memoirs. Kitami College of Technology — Mem Kitami Coll Technol
Memoirs. Kitami Institute of Technology — Mem Kitami Inst Tech
Memoirs. Kobe Marine Observatory — Mem Kobe Mar Observ
Memoirs. Kobe Marine Observatory (Kobe, Japan) — Mem Kobe Mar Obs (Kobe Jpn)
Memoirs. Konan University. Science Series — Mem Konan Univ Sci Ser
Memoirs. Konan University. Science Series — MKOUA
Memoirs. Kumamoto University. Faculty of General Education. Natural Sciences [*A publication*] — Mem Fac Gen Ed Kumamoto Univ Natur Sci
Memoirs. Kyushu Institute of Technology. Engineering — Mem Kyushu Inst Technol Eng
Memoirs. Literary and Philosophical Society of Manchester — Mem Lit Soc Manchester
Memoirs. Medical Society of London — Mem Med Soc London
Memoirs. Mineral Resources Division (Tanzania) — Mem Miner Resour Div (Tanzania)
Memoirs. Miyakonojo Technical College — Mem Miyakonojo Tech Coll
Memoirs. Muroran Institute of Technology — Mem Muroran Inst Tech
Memoirs. Muroran Institute of Technology [*Japan*] — Mem Muroran Inst Technol
Memoirs. Muroran Institute of Technology, Science, and Engineering — Mem Muroran Inst Technol Sci Eng
Memoirs. Mururan University of Engineering — Mem Mururan Univ Eng
Memoirs. Museum of Comparative Zoology at Harvard College — Mem Mus Comp Zool Harv Coll
Memoirs. Museum of Victoria — Mem Mus Victoria
Memoirs. Museum of Victoria — MMVIEB
Memoirs. Nagoya University. Faculty of Engineering — Mem Fac Eng Nagoya Univ
Memoirs. Nara University — Mem Nara Univ
Memoirs. Nasionale Museum Bloemfontein — Mem Nas Mus Bloemfontein
Memoirs. National Defense Academy — Mem Natl Def Acad
Memoirs. National Defense Academy. Mathematics, Physics, Chemistry, and Engineering [*Yokosuka*] — Mem Nat Defense Acad
Memoirs. National Institute of Polar Research. Series E. Biology and Medical Science — Mem Natl Inst Polar Res Ser E Biol Med Sci
Memoirs. National Institute of Polar Research. Special Issue (Japan) — Mem Natl Inst Polar Res Spec Issue (Jpn)
Memoirs. National Institute of Zoology and Botany. Academica Sinica. Botanical Series — Mem Natl Inst Zool Acad Sin Bot Ser
Memoirs. National Museum (Melbourne) — Mem Natn Mus (Melb)
Memoirs. National Museum of Victoria — Mem Nat Mus VIC
Memoirs. National Museum of Victoria — Mem Natl Mus Vict
Memoirs. National Museum of Victoria — Mem Natl Mus Victoria
Memoirs. National Museum of Victoria. Melbourne — Mem Natl Mus Victoria Melbourne
Memoirs. National Science Museum (Japan) — Mem Natl Sci Mus (Jpn)
Memoirs. National Science Museum (Tokyo) — Mem Natl Sci Mus (Tokyo)
Memoirs. New York. Agricultural Experiment Station (Ithaca) — Mem NY Agric Exp Stn (Ithaca)
Memoirs. New York Botanical Gardens — Mem NY Bot Gard
Memoirs. New York State Museum and Science Service — Mem NY State Mus Sci Serv
Memoirs. Niihama National College of Technology, Science, and Engineering — Mem Niihama Natl Coll Technol Sci Eng
Memoirs. Niihama Technical College [*Japan*] — Mem Niihama Tech Coll
Memoirs. Niihama Technical College. Natural Sciences — Mem Niihama Tech Coll Nat Sci
Memoirs. Niihama Technical College. Science and Engineering — Mem Niihama Tech Coll Sci Eng
Memoirs. Nova Scotia Department of Mines — Mem NS Dep Mines
Memoirs. Numazu College of Technology — Mem Numazu Coll Technol
Memoirs of Agriculture and Other Oeconomical Arts — Mem Agric Oecon Arts
Memoirs of Faculty of Engineering. Tokyo Metropolitan University — Mem Fac Eng Tokyo Metrop Univ
Memoirs of Gakugei Faculty. Akita University. Natural Science — Mem Gakugei Fac Akita Univ Nat Sci

Memoirs of Mineral Resources. Geological Survey of Szechuan — Mem Miner Resour Geol Surv Szechuan
Memoirs of Natural and Cultural Researches of the San-In Region — Mem Nat Cult Res San-In Reg
Memoirs of Natural Sciences. Museum. Brooklyn Institute of Arts and Sciences — Mem Nat Sci
Memoirs of Numerical Mathematics — Mem Numer Math
Memoirs of the College of Education. Akita University. Natural Science — Mem College Ed Akita Univ Natur Sci
Memoirs of the Faculty of Engineering and Design. Kyoto Institute of Technology. Series of Science and Technology — Mem Fac Engrg Design Kyoto Inst Tech Ser Sci Tech
Memoirs of the Institute of Science and Engineering. Ritsumeikan University — Mem Inst Sci Engrg Ritsumeikan Univ
Memoirs of the Research Institute of Science and Engineering Ritsumeikan University — Mem Res Inst Sci Engrg Ritsumeikan Univ
Memoirs. Osaka Institute of Technology. Series A. Science and Technology — Mem Osaka Inst Tech Ser A
Memoirs. Osaka Institute of Technology. Series A. Science and Technology — Mem Osaka Inst Technol Ser A Sci Technol
Memoirs. Osaka Kyoiku University. III. Natural Science and Applied Science — Mem Osaka Kyoiku Univ III Nat Sci Appl Sci
Memoirs. Osaka Kyoiku University. III. Natural Science and Applied Science — Mem Osaka Kyoiku Univ III Natur Sci Appl Sci
Memoirs. Osaka University of Liberal Arts and Education. B. Natural Science [*A publication*] — Mem Osaka Univ Lib Arts Educ B Natur Sci
Memoirs. Pacific Coast Entomological Society — Mem Pac Coast Entomol Soc
Memoirs. Palaeontology Series. Geological Survey (New South Wales) — Mem Palaeontol Ser Geol Surv (NSW)
Memoirs. Peabody Museum of Yale University — Mem Peabody Mus
Memoirs. Punjab Irrigation Research Institute — Mem Punjab Irrig Res Inst
Memoirs. Punjab Irrigation Research Laboratory — Mem Punjab Irrig Res Lab
Memoirs. Queensland Museum — Mem Qd Mus
Memoirs. Queensland Museum — Mem Queensl Mus
Memoirs. Queensland Museum — Mem Queensland Mus
Memoirs. Queensland Museum — Q Museum Memoirs
Memoirs. Raman Research Institute — Mem Raman Res Inst
Memoirs. Research Department. Toyo Bunko — Mem Res Depart Toyo Bunko
Memoirs. Research Department. Toyo Bunko — MRD
Memoirs. Research Department. Toyo Bunko — MRDTB
Memoirs. Research Department. Toyo Bunko — MTB
Memoirs. Research Institute for Food Science. Kyoto University — Mem Res Inst Food Sci Kyoto Univ
Memoirs. Research Institute of Acoustical Science. Osaka University — Mem Res Inst Acoust Sci Osaka Univ
Memoirs. Research Institute of Science and Engineering. Ritsumeikan University — Mem Res Inst Sci and Eng Ritsumeikan Univ
Memoirs. Research Institute of Science and Engineering. Ritsumeikan University [*Kyoto, Japan*] — Mem Res Inst Sci Eng Ritsumeikan Univ
Memoirs. Royal Asiatic Society of Bengal — Mem R Asiat Soc Bengal
Memoirs. Royal Astronomical Society — Mem R Astron Soc
Memoirs. Royal Astronomical Society — MRYAA
Memoirs. Royal Astronomical Society of London — Mem Astron Soc London
Memoirs. Royal Astronomical Society of London — Mem Roy Astron Soc Lond
Memoirs. Royal Society of South Australia — Mem Roy Soc South Australia
Memoirs. Ryojun College of Engineering — Mem Ryojun Coll Eng
Memoirs. Sagami Institute of Technology — Mem Sagami Inst Technol
Memoirs. School of Engineering. Okayama University — Mem Sch Eng Okayama Univ
Memoirs. School of Engineering. Okayama University — Mem School Engrg Okayama Univ
Memoirs. School of Science and Engineering. Waseda University — Mem Sch Sci and Eng Waseda Univ
Memoirs. School of Science and Engineering. Waseda University — Mem Sch Sci Eng Waseda Univ
Memoirs. School of Science and Engineering. Waseda University — Mem School Sci Eng Waseda Univ
Memoirs. School of Science and Engineering. Waseda University — Mem School Sci Engrg Waseda Univ
Memoirs. School of Science and Engineering. Waseda University — MSEWA
Memoirs. Science Department. University of Tokyo — Mem Sci Dept Univ Tokyo
Memoirs. Science Society of China/Chung Kuo K'o Hsueeh She Yen Chin Ts'ung K'an — Mem Sci Soc China
Memoirs. Seitoku Junior College of Nutrition — Mem Seitoku Jr Coll Nutr
Memoirs. Society for Endocrinology — Mem Soc Endocrinol
Memoirs. South Industrial Science Institute. Kagoshima University/Nanpo-Sango Kagaku Kenkyujo Hokoku. Kagoshima Daigaku — Mem S Industr Sci Inst Kagoshima Univ
Memoirs. Southern California Academy of Sciences — Mem South Calif Acad Sci
Memoirs. State Bureau of Mines and Mineral Resources (New Mexico) — Mem St Bur Mines Miner Resour (New Mex)
Memoirs. Suzuka College of Technology — Mem Suzuka Coll Technol
Memoirs. Tanaka Citrus Experiment Station/Tanaka Kankitsu Shiken-Jo. Mino-Mura, Fukuoka-Ken — Mem Tanaka Citrus Exp Sta
Memoirs. Technical Meeting of Corrosion Engineering Division. Society of Materials Science. Japan — Mem Tech Meet Corros Eng Div Soc Mater Sci Jpn
Memoirs. Tohoku Institute of Technology. Series 1. Science and Engineering — Mem Tohoku Inst Technol Ser 1
Memoirs. Tokyo Metropolitan College of Aeronautical Engineering — Mem Tokyo Metrop Coll Aeronaut Eng
Memoirs. Tokyo University of Agriculture — Mem Tokyo Univ Agr
Memoirs. Tokyo University of Agriculture — Mem Tokyo Univ Agric
Memoirs. Tomakomai Technical College — Mem Tomakomai Tech Coll
Memoirs. Torrey Botanical Club — Mem Torrey Bot Club
Memoirs. Tottori Agricultural College — Mem Tottori Agric Coll
Memoirs. University Laboratory of Physical Chemistry Related to Medicine and Public Health. Harvard University — Mem Univ Lab Phys Chem Med Public Health Har Univ
Memoirs. University of California — Mem Univ Calif
Memoirs. Wakayama National College of Technology — Mem Wakayama Natl Coll Technol
Memoirs. Wakayama Technical College — Mem Wakayama Tech Coll
Memorabilia Zoologica — Memorabilia Zool
Memoranda Societatis pro Fauna et Flora Fennica — Memo Soc Fauna Flora Fenn
Memoranda Societatis pro Fauna et Flora Fennica — MSFFF
Memorandum. Division of Chemical Engineering. Commonwealth Scientific and Industrial Research Organisation — Memo Div Chem Eng CSIRO
Memorandum. Division of Chemical Engineering. Commonwealth Scientific and Industrial Research Organisation — Memo Div Chem Engng CSIRO
Memorandum. Federal Department of Agricultural Research (Nigeria) — Memo Fed Dept Agr Res (Nigeria)
Memorandum. Indian Tea Association. Tocklai Experimental Station — Memo Indian Tea Assoc Tocklai Exp Stn
Memorandum. Meat Research Institute — Memo Meat Res Inst
Memorandum. Medical Research Council [*London*] — Memo Med Res Counc
Memorandum. Norges Landbrukshogskole Institutt foer Landbruksokonomi — Memo Nor Landbrukshogsk Inst Landbruksokom
Memorandum. Propellants, Explosives, and Rocket Motor Establishment (Westcott, England) — Mem Propellants Explos Rocket Mot Establ (Wescott Engl)
Memorandum. Royal Armament Research and Development Establishment (Great Britain) — Memo R Armament Res Dev Establ (GB)
Memorandum. Societe Royale de Liege — Mem Soc Roy Liege
Memorandum. University College of Wales. Department of Geography — Memo Univ Coll Wales Dept Geogr
Memoria. Academia de Geografia e Historia de Costa Rica (San Jose) — Mem Acad Geogr Hist S Jose
Memoria. Academia Nacional de Historia y Geografia (Mexico) — Mem Acad Nac Hist Geogr Mex
Memoria Antiquitatis Acta Musei Petrodavensis. Revista Muzeului Archeologic Piatra Neamt — Mem Antiq
Memoria Antiquitatis. Acta Musei Petrodavensis. Revista Muzeului Arheologic Piatra Neamt — Mem Ant
Memoria Anual. Museo Nacional de Historia Natural Bernardino Rivadavia — Mem Anual Mus Nac Hist Nat Bernardino Rivadavia
Memoria. Asociacion Latinoamericana de Produccion Animal — Mem Asoc Latinoam Prod Anim
Memoria. Conferencia Anual. Asociacion de Tecnicos Azucareros de Cuba — Mem Conf Anu Asoc Tec Azucar Cuba
Memoria. Conferencia Anual de la ATAC — Mem Conf Anu ATAC
Memoria. Congreso Internacional de la Lepra — Mem Congr Int Lepra
Memoria. Congreso Latinoamericano de Siderurgia — Mem Congr Latinoam Sider
Memoria. Congreso Medico Latino-Americano (Buenos Aires) — Mem Cong Med Latino-Am (Buenos Aires)
Memoria de Alfonso Hernandez Cata — MAHC
Memoria de El Colegio Nacional (Mexico) — Mem Col Nac Mex
Memoria. El Colegio Nacional — Col Nac Mem
Memoria General. Instituto Geologico y Minero de Espana — Mem Gen Inst Geol Min Esp
Memoria. Instituto de Quimica (Rio De Janeiro) — Mem Inst Quim (Rio De Janeiro)
Memoria. Instituto Geologico de Espana — Mem Inst Geol Esp
Memoria Jornadas Agronomicas — Mem Jornadas Agron
Memoria. Junta Directiva. Sociedad Nacional Agraria — Mem Junta Direct Soc Nac Agrar
Memoria. Laboratorio Nacional de Engenharia Civil (Portugal) — Mem Lab Nac Eng Civ (Port)
Memoria. Oficina de Estudios Especiales. Ministerio de Agricultura. Direccion de Agricultura y Pesca (Chile) — Mem Ofic Estud Espec Min Agr Dir Agr Pesca (Chile)
Memoria. Reunion Tecnica Nacional de Mania — Mem Reun Tec Nac Mania
Memoria. Seminario Latino-Americano de Irrigacion — Mem Semin Latino-Amer Irrig
Memoria. Sociedad de Ciencias Naturales (La Salle) — Mem Soc Ci Nat La Salle
Memoria. Sociedad de Ciencias Naturales (La Salle) — Mem Soc Cienc Nat (La Salle)
Memoria. Sociedad de Ciencias Naturales La Salle (Caracas) — Mem Soc Cien Nat La Salle Caracas
Memoria Tecnica. Congreso Latinoamericano de Siderurgia — Mem Tec Congr Latinoam Sider
Memoria Tecnica. ILAFA. Congreso Latinoamericano de Siderurgia — Mem Tec ILAFA Congr Latinoam Sider
Memoria. Universidad de Barcelona. Instituto de Arqueologia y Prehistoria — Mem Barcel A
Memorial de la Meteorologie Nationale — Mem Meteorol Natl
Memorial de la Meteorologie Nationale — Meml Meteorol Natl
Memorial de l'Artillerie Francaise — Mem Artillerie Fr
Memorial de l'Artillerie Francaise. Sciences et Techniques de l'Armement [*A publication*] — Mem Artillerie Fr Sci Tech Armement
Memorial de l'Artillerie Francaise. Sciences et Techniques de l'Armement — Meml Artillerie Fr Sci Tech Armement
Memorial des Poudres [*France*] — Mem Poudres
Memorial des Poudres — Meml Poudres
Memorial des Poudres — MPOUA
Memorial des Poudres et Salpetres — Meml Poudres Salpetres
Memorial des Services Chimiques de l'Etat — Mem Serv Chim Etat

Memorial des Services Chimiques de l'Etat — Meml Serv Chim Etat
Memorial du Service des Poudres — Meml Serv Poudres
Memorial du Service d'Exploitation Industrielle des Tabacs et des Allumettes. Serie B. Publications. Institut Experimental des Tabacs de Bergerac — Meml Serv Exploit Ind Tab Allumettes Ser B
Memorial Historico Espanol — Memorial Hist Esp
Memorial Historico Espanol — MHE
Memorial. Mision Arqueologica Espanola en Egypto — MMAE
Memorial University of Newfoundland. Occasional Papers in Biology — Memorial Univ Nowfoundland Occas Pap Biol
Memorial University of Newfoundland. Occasional Papers in Biology — MUNOPB
Memorias. Academia das Ciencias de Lisboa. Classe de Ciencias — ALMRB
Memorias. Academia das Ciencias de Lisboa. Classe de Ciencias — Mem Acad Cienc Lisb Cl Cienc
Memorias. Academia das Ciencias de Lisboa. Classe de Letras — MAC
Memorias. Academia das Ciencias de Lisboa. Classe de Letras — MACL
Memorias. Academia das Ciencias de Lisboa. Classe de Letras — MACLCL
Memorias. Academia das Ciencias de Lisboa. Classe de Letras — MACLL
Memorias. Academia de Ciencias de Zaragoza — Mem Acad Cienc Zaragoza
Memorias. Academia de Ciencias y Artes de Barcelona — Mem Acad Cienc Artes Barcelona
Memorias. Academia de la Historia — MAHi
Memorias. Academia Mexicana de Estudios Numismaticos — Mem Acad Mex Estud Num
Memorias. Academia Nacional de Historia y Geografia — Mem Acad Nac Hist
Memorias. Comision de Investigaciones Paleontologicas y Prehistoricas. Instituto Nacional de Ciencias Fisico-Naturales (Madrid) — Mems Comn Invest Paleont Prehist (Madr)
Memorias. Conferencia Internacional de Pesquisas em Cacau — Mem Conf Int Pesqui Cacau
Memorias. Congreso Ibero Latino Americano de Dermatologia — Mem Cong Ibero Lat Am Dermatol
Memorias. Congreso Internacional de Quimica Pura y Aplicada — Mem Congr Int Quim Pura Apl
Memorias. Congreso Mexicano de Anestesiologia — Mem Congr Mex Anestesiol
Memorias. Congreso Mundial de Cardiologia — Mem Congr Mund Cardiol
Memorias. Congreso Nacional de Medicina Veterinaria y Zootecnia — Mem Congr Nac Med Vet Zootec
Memorias. Consejo Oceanografico Ibero-Americano — Mem Cons Oceanogr Ibero Am
Memorias da Academia das Ciencias de Lisboa. Classe de Ciencias — Mem Acad Ci Lisboa Cl Ci
Memorias de Historia Antigua. Universidad de Oviedo — Mem Hist Ant
Memorias de Historia Natural, de Quimica, de Agricultura, Artes, e Medicina. Lidas na Academia Real das Ciencias de Lisboa — Mem Hist Nat Acad Real Ci Lisboa
Memorias de la Real Sociedad Espanola de Historia Natural — Mem Real Soc Esp Hist Nat
Memorias de los Museos Arqueologicos Provinciales — Mem MA
Memorias de los Museos Arqueologicos Provinciales — Mem MA Prov
Memorias de los Museos Arqueologicos Provinciales — Mem Mus Arq
Memorias de Matematica. Instituto Jorge Juan [*Madrid*] — Mem Mat Inst Jorge Juan
Memorias e Estudos. Museu Zoologico. Universidade de Coimbra — Mem Estud Mus Zool Univ Coimbra
Memorias e Estudos. Museu Zoologico. Universidade de Coimbra — Mems Estud Mus Zool Univ Coimbra
Memorias e Noticias. Museu e Laboratorio Mineralogico e Geologico. Universidade de Coimbra — Mem Not Publ Mus Lab Miner Geol Univ Coimbra
Memorias e Noticias. Museu e Laboratorio Mineralogico e Geologico. Universidade de Coimbra — Mem Notic Mus Miner Geol Univ Coimbra
Memorias e Noticias Publicacoes. Museu e Laboratorio Mineralogico e Geologico. Universidade de Coimbra — Mem Not Publ Mus Lab Mineral Geol Univ Coimbra
Memorias e Noticias Publicacoes. Museu e Laboratorio Mineralogico e Geologico. Universidade de Coimbra — MNUGD6
Memorias e Noticias Publicacoes. Museu e Laboratorio Mineralogico e Geologico. Universidade de Coimbra e Centro de Estudos Geologicos — PMUCAH
Memorias e Noticias. Universidade de Coimbra. Museu e Laboratorio Mineralogico e Geologico e Centro de Estudos Geologicas — Mem Not Univ Coimbra Mus Lab Mineral Geol Cent Estud Geol
Memorias Economicas. Academia Real das Sciencias de Lisboa — Mem Econ Acad Real Sci Lisboa
Memorias. Instituto Butantan — Mem Inst Butantan
Memorias. Instituto Butantan (Sao Paulo) — Mem Inst Butantan (Sao Paulo)
Memorias. Instituto de Biociencias. Universidade Federal de Pernambuco — Mem Inst Biocien Univ Fed Pernambuco
Memorias. Instituto de Investigacao Cientifica de Mocambique — Mem Inst Invest Ci Mocambique
Memorias. Instituto de Investigacao Cientifica de Mocambique. Serie A. Ciencias Biologicas — Mem Inst Invest Cient Mocambique Ser A Cienc Biol
Memorias. Instituto Espanol de Oceanografia — Mem Inst Esp Oceanogr
Memorias. Instituto Geologico y Minero de Espana — Mem Inst Geol Min Esp
Memorias. Instituto Oswaldo Cruz — IOC/M
Memorias. Instituto Oswaldo Cruz — Mem Inst Oswaldo Cruz
Memorias. Instituto Oswaldo Cruz — Mems Inst Oswaldo Cruz
Memorias. Instituto Oswaldo Cruz (Rio De Janeiro) — Mem Inst Oswaldo Cruz (Rio De J)
Memorias. Junta das Missoes Geograficas e de Investigacoes do Ultramar (Portugal) — Mem Junta Missoes Geogr Invest Ultramar (Port)
Memorias. Junta de Investigacoes Cientificas do Ultramar. Serie II — Mem Junta Invest Cient Ultramar Ser II
Memorias. Junta de Investigacoes do Ultramar — Mems Jta Invest Ultramar
Memorias. Junta de Investigacoes do Ultramar (Portugal) — Mem Junta Invest Ultramar (Port)
Memorias. Junta de Investigacoes do Ultramar. Serie II — Mem Junta Invest Ultramar Ser II
Memorias. Junta Superior de Excavaciones y Antiquedades — JSExc
Memorias. Junta Superior de Excavaciones y Antiquedades — Mem Exc
Memorias. Junta Superior de Excavaciones y Antiquedades — Mem Junta Exc
Memorias. Junta Superior de Excavaciones y Antiquedades — MJSExc
Memorias. Museo de Historia Natural "Javier Prado" — Mem Mus Hist Nat "Javier Prado"
Memorias. Museo de Parana — Mem Muc Parana
Memorias. Museos Arqueologicos Provinciales — Mem MAP
Memorias. Museos Arqueologicos Provinciales — Mem Mus A Provinc
Memorias. Museos Arqueologicos Provinciales — Mem Mus Arqu Provinciales
Memorias. Museos Arqueologicos Provinciales [*Madrid*] — MMAP
Memorias. Museu do Mar. Serie Zoologica — Mem Mus Mar Ser Zool
Memorias. Museu Dr. Alvaro De Castro — Mem Mus Dr Alvaro De Castro
Memorias. Real Academia de Ciencias Exactas, Fisicas, y Naturales de Madrid — Mem Acad Cienc Madrid
Memorias. Real Academia de Ciencias Exactas, Fisicas, y Naturales de Madrid — Mem R Acad Cienc Exactas Fis Nat Madrid
Memorias. Real Academia de Ciencias Exactas, Fisicas, y Naturales de Madrid. Serie de Ciencias Exactas — Mem R Acad Cienc Exactas Fis Nat Madrid Ser Cienc Exactas
Memorias. Real Academia de Ciencias Exactas, Fisicas, y Naturales de Madrid. Serie de Ciencias Exactas — Mem Real Acad Ci Exact Fis Natur Madrid
Memorias. Real Academia de Ciencias Exactas, Fisicas, y Naturales de Madrid. Serie de Ciencias Fisico-Quimicas — Mem R Acad Cienc Exactas Fis Nat Madrid Ser Cienc Fis-Quim
Memorias. Real Academia de Ciencias Exactas, Fisicas, y Naturales de Madrid. Serie de Ciencias Naturales — Mem R Acad Cienc Exactas Fis Nat Madr Ser Cienc Nat
Memorias. Real Academia de Ciencias Exactas, Fisicas, y Naturales de Madrid. Serie de Ciencias Naturales — Mem R Acad Cienc Exactas Fis Nat Madrid Ser Cienc Nat
Memorias. Real Academia de Ciencias y Artes de Barcelona — MACBAB
Memorias. Real Academia de Ciencias y Artes de Barcelona — Mem R Acad Cienc Artes Barc
Memorias. Real Academia de Ciencias y Artes de Barcelona — Mem Real Acad Ci Art Barcelona
Memorias. Real Academia de Ciencias y Artes de Barcelona — Mem Real Acad Ci Barcelona
Memorias. Real Academia de Ciencias y Artes de Barcelona — Mem Real Acad Cienc Artes Barcelona
Memorias. Real Academia de la Historia — Mem RAH
Memorias. Real Sociedad Economica Mallorquina de Amigos del Pais — Mem Real Soc Econ Mallorquina Amigos Pais
Memorias. Seminario Latino Americano de Quimica — Mem Semin Lat Am Quim
Memorias. Servicos Geologicos de Portugal — Mem Serv Geol Port
Memorias. Sociedad Cientifica "Antonio Alzate" — Mem Soc Cient "Antonio Alzate"
Memorias. Sociedad Cubana de Historia Natural "Felipe Poey" — Mem Soc Cubana Hist Nat "Felipe Poey"
Memorias. Sociedad Cubana de Historia Natural Felipe Poey (La Habana) — Mem Soc Cubana Hist Nat F Poey Hab
Memorias. Sociedad Iberica de Ciencias Naturales — Mem Soc Iber Ci Nat
Memorias. Sociedade Broteriana — Mem Soc Broteriana
Memorias Succintas. Kahal Kados [*Amsterdam*] — MS
Memorias. Tercer Seminario Latino Americano de Quimica — Mem Tercer Semin Lat Am Quim
Memorias y Comunicaciones. Instituto Geologico (Barcelona) — Mem Comun Inst Geol (Barcelona)
Memorias y Revista. Academia Nacional de Ciencias — Mem Rev Acad Nac Cienc
Memorias y Revista. Academia Nacional de Ciencias "Antonio Alzate" — Mem Rev Acad Nac Cienc "Antonio Alzate"
Memorias y Revista. Academia Nacional de Ciencias (Mexico) — Mem Rev Acad Nac Cien Mex
Memorias y Revista. Sociedad Cientifica "Antonio Alzate" — Mem Rev Soc Cient Antonio Alzate
Memorie. Accademia di Agricoltura, Scienze, e Lettere di Verona — Mem Accad Agric Sci Lett Verona
Memorie. Accademia delle Scienze di Torino. Classe di Scienze Fisiche, Matematiche, e Naturali — Mem Accad Sci Torino Cl Sci Fis Mat Nat
Memorie. Accademia delle Scienze di Torino. Classe di Scienze Fisiche, Matematiche, e Naturali [*Turin*] — Mem Accad Sci Torino Cl Sci Fis Mat Natur
Memorie. Accademia delle Scienze di Torino. Classe di Scienze Fisiche, Matematiche, e Naturali. Serie 4 [*Turin*] — Mem Accad Sci Torino Cl Sci Fis Mat Natur 4
Memorie. Accademia delle Scienze di Torino. Classe di Scienze Fisiche, Matematiche, e Naturali. Serie 4A — Mem Accad Sci Torino Cl Sci Fis Mat Nat Ser 4A
Memorie. Accademia delle Scienze. Istituto di Bologna — Atti Mem Bologna
Memorie. Accademia delle Scienze. Istituto di Bologna — Mem Acc Bologna
Memorie. Accademia delle Scienze. Istituto di Bologna — MIB
Memorie. Accademia delle Scienze. Istituto di Bologna. Classe di Scienze Fisiche — Mem Accad Sci Ist Bologna Cl Sci Fis
Memorie. Accademia delle Scienze, Lettere, ed Arti di Genova — Mem Accad Sci Genova
Memorie. Accademia di Archeologia, Lettere, e Belle Arti di Napoli — Mem Acc Nap
Memorie. Accademia di Archeologia, Lettere, e Belle Arti di Napoli — Mem Acc Napoli
Memorie. Accademia di Archeologia, Lettere, e Belle Arti di Napoli — Mem Nap

Memorie. Accademia di Archeologia, Lettere, e Belle Arti di Napoli — Mem Napoli
Memorie. Accademia di Scienze Mediche e Chirurgiche (Naples) — Mem Accad Sci Med Chir (Naples)
Memorie. Accademia Nazionale dei Lincei — Ac Naz Linc Mem
Memorie. Accademia Nazionale dei Lincei — Acc Naz Linc Mem
Memorie. Accademia Nazionale dei Lincei — MA Linc
Memorie. Accademia Nazionale dei Lincei — MANL
Memorie. Accademia Nazionale dei Lincei — Mem Acc Linc
Memorie. Accademia Nazionale dei Lincei — Mem Acc Naz Linc
Memorie. Accademia Nazionale dei Lincei — Mem AL
Memorie. Accademia Nazionale dei Lincei — Mem Linc
Memorie. Accademia Nazionale dei Lincei — Memorie Lincei
Memorie. Accademia Nazionale dei Lincei (Italia) — Mem Acc It
Memorie. Accademia Nazionale dei Lincei (Italia) — Mem Acc Linc d'Italia
Memorie. Accademia Patavina di Scienze, Lettere, ed Arti — Mem Accad Patav Sci Lett Arti
Memorie. Atti della Accademia Nazionale dei Lincei. Classe de Scienze Morali, Storiche, e Filologiche — Mem Acc Linc
Memorie. Classe di Scienze Morali, Storiche, e Filologiche. Accademia d'Italia (Roma) — MAIR
Memorie Classe di Scienze, Morali, Storiche, et Filologiche. Accademia Nazionale dei Lincei — Mem Cl Sci Morali Stor Filol Accad Naz Lincei
Memorie dell' Accademia Imperiale delle Scienze e Belle Arti di Genova — Mem Accad Imp Sci Genova
Memorie della Reale Accademia di Scienze, Lettere, e d' Arti di Modena — Mem Reale Accad Sci Modena
Memorie Descrittive della Carta Geologica d'Italia — Mem Descr Carta Geol Ital
Memorie di Biologia Marina e di Oceanografia — Mem Biol Mar Oceanogr
Memorie di Matematica e di Fisica. Societa Italiana delle Scienze Residente in Modena. Parte Contenente le Memorie di Fisica — Mem Mat Fis Soc Ital Sci Modena Pt Mem Fis
Memorie di Scienze Geologiche — Mem Sci Geol
Memorie Domenicane — M Dom
Memorie e Note. Istituto di Geologia Applicata. Universita di Napoli — Mem Note Ist Geol Appl Univ Napoli
Memorie e Rendiconti. Accademia di Scienze, Lettere, e Belle Arti degli Zelanti e dei Dafnici di Acireale — Mem Rend Accad Zel Acireale
Memorie e Rendiconti. Istituto delle Scienze di Bologna — Mem Rend Ist Sci Bologna
Memorie ed Atti. Centro di Studi per l'Ingegneria Agraria — Mem Atti Cent Studi Ing Agrar
Memorie Geopaleontologiche. Universita di Ferrara — Mem Geopaleontol Univ Ferrara
Memorie. Imperiale Reale Istituto Veneto di Scienze, Lettere, ed Arti — Mem Imp Reale Ist Veneto Sci
Memorie. Instituto di Corrispondenza Archeologica — MdI
Memorie. Instituto di Corrispondenza Archeologica — Mem Inst Cor Arch
Memorie. Instituto di Corrispondenza Archeologica — MI
Memorie. Istituti di Geologia e Mineralogia. Universita di Padova — Mem Ist Geol Mineral Univ Padova
Memorie. Istituti di Geologia e Mineralogia. Universita di Padova — MGMPA
Memorie. Istituto di Geologia e Paleontologia. Universita di Padova — Mem Ist Geol Paleontol Univ Padov
Memorie. Istituto Geologico. Universita di Padova — Mem Ist Geol Univ Padova
Memorie. Istituto Italiano di Idrobiologia — Mem Ist Ital Idrobiol
Memorie. Istituto Italiano di Idrobiologia Dottore Marco De Marchi [*Italy*] — Mem Ist Ital Idrobiol Dott Marco De Marchi
Memorie. Istituto Italiano di Idrobiologia Dottore Marco De Marchi — Mem Ist Ital Idrobiol Dott Marco Marchi
Memorie. Istituto Italiano di Idrobiologia Dottore Marco De Marchi — MIIMA
Memorie. Istituto Italiano di Idrobiologia Dottore Marco De Marchi (Pallanza, Italy) — Mem Ist Ital Idrobiol Dott Marco De Marchi (Pallanza Italy)
Memorie. Istituto Lombardo — MIL
Memorie. Istituto Lombardo Accademia di Scienze e Lettere. Classe di Scienze Matematiche e Naturali — Mem Ist Lombardo Accad Sci Lett Cl Sci Mat Natur
Memorie. Istituto Lombardo di Scienze e Lettere, Scienze, Morali e Storiche — Mem Ist Lomb Sc
Memorie. Istituto Lombardo di Scienze e Lettere, Scienze, Morali e Storiche — MIL
Memorie. Istituto Svizzero di Ricerche Forestali — Mem Ist Svizz Ric For
Memorie. Museo Civico di Storia Naturale di Verona — Mem Mus Civ Stor Nat Verona
Memorie. Museo Civico di Storia Naturale di Verona. IIA Serie. Sezione Scienze della Vita — Mem Mus Civ Stor Nat Verona IIA Ser Sez Sci Vita
Memorie. Museo di Storia Naturale della Venezia Tridentina — Mem Mus Stor Nat Venezia Tridentina
Memorie. Museo Tridentino di Scienze Naturali — Mem Mus Tridentino Sci Nat
Memorie. Pontificia Accademia dei Nuovi Lincei — MPANL
Memorie. Pontificia Accademia Romana di Archeologia — MPARA
Memorie. Reale Accademia delle Scienze di Torino — MAST
Memorie. Reale Accademia delle Scienze di Torino — MAT
Memorie. Reale Accademia delle Scienze. Istituto di Bologna. Classe di Scienze Fisiche — Mem R Accad Sci Ist Bologna Cl Sci Fis
Memorie. Reale Accademia delle Scienze. Istituto di Bologna. Classe di Scienze Fisiche — Mem Reale Accad Sci Ist Bologna Cl Sci Fis
Memorie. Reale Accademia di Archeologia, Lettere, e Belle Arti di Napoli — MAAN
Memorie. Reale Accademia di Scienze, Lettere, ed Arti di Padova — M Pad
Memorie. Reale Accademia di Scienze, Lettere, ed Arti (Modena) — Mem Accad Sci (Modena)
Memorie. Reale Accademia di Scienze, Lettere, ed Arti (Modena) — Mem R Accad Sci Lett Arti (Modena)
Memorie. Reale Accademia d'Italia. Classe di Scienze Fisiche, Matematiche, e Naturali — Mem R Accad Ital Cl Sci Fis Mat Nat
Memorie. Reale Accademia d'Italia. Classe di Scienze Fisiche, Matematiche, e Naturali. Biologia — Mem R Accad Ital Cl Sci Fis Mat Nat Biol
Memorie. Reale Accademia d'Italia. Classe di Scienze Fisiche, Matematiche, e Naturali. Chimica — Mem R Accad Ital Cl Sci Fis Mat Nat Chim
Memorie. Reale Accademia d'Italia. Classe di Scienze Fisiche, Matematiche, e Naturali. Fisica — Mem R Accad Ital Cl Sci Fis Mat Nat Fis
Memorie. Reale Accademia d'Italia. Classe di Scienze Fisiche, Matematiche, e Naturali. Ingegneria — Mem R Accad Ital Cl Sci Fis Mat Nat Ing
Memorie. Reale Accademia d'Italia. Classe di Scienze Fisiche, Matematiche, e Naturali. Matematica — Mem R Accad Ital Cl Sci Fis Mat Nat Mat
Memorie. Reale Accademia Nazionale dei Lincei — MRAL
Memorie. Reale Accademia Nazionale dei Lincei. Classe di Scienze Fisiche, Matematiche, e Naturali — Mem Accad Lincei
Memorie. Reale Accademia Nazionale dei Lincei. Classe di Scienze Fisiche, Matematiche, e Naturali — Mem R Accad Naz Lincei Cl Sci Fis Mat Nat
Memorie. Reale Comitato Talassagrafico Italiano — Mem Reale Comitato Talassogr Ital
Memorie. Royale Accademia delle Scienze di Torino. Classe di Scienze Morali, Storiche, e Filologiche — MASTM
Memorie. Societa Astronomica Italiana — Mem Soc Astron Ital
Memorie. Societa Astronomica Italiana. Nuova Serie — Mem Soc Astronom Ital NS
Memorie. Societa Entomologica Italiana — Mem Soc Entomol Ital
Memorie. Societa Entomologica Italiana — Memorie Soc Ent Ital
Memorie. Societa Geologica Italiana — Mem Soc Geol Ital
Memorie. Societa Italiana di Scienze Naturali e Museo Civico di Storia Naturale di Milano — Mem Soc Ital Sci Nat Mus Civ Stor Nat Milano
Memorie. Societa Toscana di Scienze Naturali Residente in Pisa — Mem Soc Toscana Sci Nat Pisa
Memorie Sopra la Fisica e Istoria Naturale di Diversi Valentuomini — Mem Fis Istoria Nat
Memorie Storiche Forogiuliesi — Mem Stor Forogiuliesi
Memorie Storiche Forogiuliesi — MSF
Memorie Storiche Forogiuliesi — MSForogiuliesi
Memorie Svizzere di Paleontologia — Mem Svizz Paleontol
Memorie Svizzere di Paleontologia — SPAAAX
Memorie Valdarnesi — Mem Vald
Memorie van Antwoord — MvA
Memorie van Antwoord aan de Eerste Kamer — MvA I
Memorie van Antwoord aan de Tweede Kamer — MvA II
Memorii. Institutul Geologie (Romania) — Mem Inst Geol (Rom)
Memoriile Comitetului Geologic (Romania) — Mem Com Geol (Rom)
Memoriile Institutului Geologic al Romaniei — Mem Inst Geol Rom
Memoriile Sectiilor Stiintifice. Academia Republicii Socialiste Romania — Mem Sect Stiint Acad Repub Soc Rom
Memoriile Sectiilor Stiintifice. Academia Republicii Socialiste Romania. Seria IV — Mem Sect Stiint Acad Repub Soc Romania Ser IV
Memoriile Sectiilor Stiintifice. Academia Romana. Seria IV — Mem Sect Stiint Acad Romana Ser IV
Memoriile Sectiunii Istorice. Academia Romana — An Ac Rov
Memoriile Sectiunii Istorice. Academia Romana — Anal Ac Rom
Memoriile Sectiunii Istorice. Academia Romana — Analele Acad Rom
Memoriile Sectiunii Stiintifice Academia Romana — Mem Sect Sti Acad Romane
Memory and Cognition — M & C
Memory and Cognition — Mem Cognit
Memory and Cognition — Mem Cognition
Memory and Cognition — MYCGA
Memory and Cognition — PMCO
Memphis and Mid-South Medical Journal — Memphis Mid-South Med J
Memphis Business Journal — Memphis Bs
Memphis Journal of the Medical Sciences — Memphis J Med Sc
Memphis Medical Journal — Memphis Med J
Memphis Medical Monthly — Memphis Med Mo
Memphis Medical Monthly — Memphis Med Month
Memphis Medical Monthly — Memphis Med Monthly
Memphis Medical Recorder — Memphis Med Rec
Memphis State University. Law Review — Mem St ULR
Memphis State University. Law Review — Memphis St U L Rev
Memphis State University. Law Review — Memphis State UL Rev
Memphis State University. Law Review — Memphis State Univ L Rev
Menabo di Letteratura — Menabo
Menarini Series on Immunopathology — Menarini Ser Immunopathol
Mendel Bulletin — Mendel Bull
Mendel Newsletter — Mendel Newsl
Mendel Newsletter — Mendel Newslett
Mendeleev Chemistry Journal — Mendel Chem J
Mendeleev Chemistry Journal — Mendeleev Chem J
Mendeleev Chemistry Journal (English Translation) — Mendeleev Chem J (Engl Transl)
Mendeleev Communications — Mendeleev Commun
Mendeleevskii S'ezd po Obshchei i Prikladnoi Khimii — Mendeleevsk Sezd Obshch Prikl Khim
Mendocino Review — Mendocino Rev
Menemui Matematik [*Kuala Lumpur*] — Menemui Mat
Menighedsbladet — Mngb
Menneske og Miljo — Menn o Mil
Mennonite — Menn
Mennonite Encyclopedia — ME
Mennonite Encyclopedia — Menn Enc
Mennonite Historical Bulletin — MHB
Mennonite Historical Series — Menn HS
Mennonite Life — Menn L
Mennonite Life — Menn Life
Mennonite Life — ML
Mennonite Quarterly Review — Menn Q R

Mennonite Quarterly Review — Mennonite Q R
Mennonite Quarterly Review — Mennonite Quart Rev
Mennonite Quarterly Review — MenQ
Mennonite Quarterly Review — MQR
Mennonite Research Journal — MRJ
Mennonitische Geschichtsblaetter — MGB
Mennonitische Geschichtsblaetter — Mennonit Gesch Bl
Mennonitische Rundschau — Menn R
Mennonitisches Lexikon — Menn Lex
Menologe de la Compagnie de Jesus — MCJ
Menomonie Review — Menomonie Rev
Menorah Journal — MenJ
Menorah Journal — Menorah J
Menorah Journal — Menorah Journ
Menorah Journal — MJ
Men's Antisexist Newsletter — MAN
Men's Association News — MAN
Mens en Maatschappij — Mens en Mij
Mens en Maatschappij — Mens Maatschap
Mens en Maatschappij — MM
Mens en Maatschappij. Tijdschrift voor Sociale Wetenschappen — MEM
Mens en Melodie — MeM
Mens en Melodie — Mens en Mel
Mens en Muziek — MeM
Mens en Onderneming — Mens Ond
Men's Fitness — Men's Fit
Men's Guide to Fashion — MGF
Men's Health — PMNH
Men's Wear — MWA
Men's, Women's, and Childrens' Footwear Fact File — Ftwr File
Mensaje — ME
Mensaje Boletin Informativo. Federacion Iberoamericana de Parques Zoologicos [*A publication*] — Mensaje Bol Inf Fed Iberoam Parques
Mensajero Agricola — Mensajero Agric
Mensajero del Corazon de Jesus — MCJ
Mensajero Forestal — Mensajero For
Mensajes. Institucion Hispanocubana de Cultura — MIHC
Mensario. Arquivo Nacional. Ministerio da Justica. Arquivo Nacional. Divisao de Publicacoes — MAN
Mensario das Casas do Povo — MCP
Mensch, Welt, Gott [*Freiburg*] — MWG
Mensch, Welt, Gott. Ergaenzungsband [*Freiburg, Switzerland*] — MWG E
Menschen der Kirche in Zeugnis und Urkunde — MKZU
Menschen Maatschappij — Mens Maat
Mensuario de Arte, Literatura, Historia, y Ciencia — MALHC
Mental and Physical Disability Law Reporter — Ment Phys Disabil Law Rep
Mental Disability Law Reporter — Men Dis LR
Mental Disability Law Reporter — Mental Disab L Rep
Mental Health — Ment Health
Mental Health and Society — Ment Health Soc
Mental Health Book Review Index — Ment Health Book Rev Index
Mental Health Book Review Index — MHBRI
Mental Health in Australia — Ment Health Aust
Mental Health in Australia — Mental Health in Aust
Mental Health Program Reports — Ment Health Program Rep
Mental Health Research Institute. University of Michigan. Annual Report — Ment Health Res Inst Univ Mich Annu Rep
Mental Health Statistical Note — Ment Health Stat Note
Mental Health Statistics — Ment Hlth Stat
Mental Hospitals — Ment Hosp
Mental Hospitals — MHOSA
Mental Hygiene — MEHYA
Mental Hygiene — Ment Hyg
Mental Hygiene — Mental Hyg
Mental Hygiene — MH
Mental Hygiene (Arlington, Virginia) — Ment Hyg (Arlington VA)
Mental Patients Liberation/Therapy — Mntl Pt
Mental Retardation — Men Retard
Mental Retardation — Ment Ret
Mental Retardation — Ment Retard
Mental Retardation — Mental Reta
Mental Retardation — MERTB
Mental Retardation — MNRTA
Mental Retardation Abstracts — Ment Retard Abstr
Mental Retardation Abstracts — Ment Retard Absts
Mental Retardation Abstracts — MRA
Mental Retardation and Developmental Disabilities — Ment Retard Dev Disabil
Mental Retardation and Developmental Disabilities — MRDDD8
Mental Retardation and Developmental Disabilities Abstracts — Ment Retard Abstr Dev Disab Abstr
Mental Retardation Bulletin — Ment Ret Bul
Mentalhygiejne — Menth
MEP: Multicultural Education Papers — MEP
MER (Marine Engineers Review) [*United States*] — MER
MER (Marine Engineers Review) — MER (Mar Eng Rev)
MER (Marine Engineers Review) — MMERD
Mer (Tokyo). Bulletin de la Societe Franco-Japonaise d'Oceanographie — Mer (Tokyo) Bull Soc Fr Jpn Oceanogr
MERADO [*Mechanical Engineering Research and Development Organisation*] **News** — MERADO N
Meran. Dokumentation der Vortraege. Internationaler Fortbildungskurs fuer Praktische und Wissenschaftliche Pharmazie — Meran Dok Vortr Int Fortbildungskurs Prakt Wiss Pharm
Mercer Dental Society. Newsletter — Mercer Dent Soc Newsl
Mercer Law Review — Mer
Mercer Law Review — Merc LR
Mercer Law Review — Mercer L Rev
Mercer Law Review — Mercer Law
Mercer Law Review — Mercer Law Rev
Mercersburg Review — Mercersb
Merchandising — Merch
Merchandising Monthly — Merch Mo
Merchandising Vision — Merchand Vision
Merchandising Week [*Later, Merchandising*] — Merch W
Mercian Geologist — Mercian Geol
Morck Agricultural Memo — Merck Agr Memo
Merck Report — Merck Rep
Merck, Sharp, and Dohme. Seminar Report — Merck Sharp Dohme Semin Rep
Merck-Symposium — Merck Symp
Mercure de France — MdF
Mercure de France — Merc France
Mercure de France — Mercure
Mercure de France — Mercure Fr
Mercure de France — MF
Mercure de France — MFr
Mercurio Peruano — MerP
Mercurio Peruano — MPer
Mercurio Peruano (Lima) — Mercur Peru Lima
Mercury [*Hobart*] — Merc
Mercury — MRCYA
Mercury — PMER
Mercury Reports (Newspaper) (Tasmania) — Merc (Newspr) (Tas)
Mercury Series. Archaeological Survey of Canada. Papers — Merc S Arch
Mercury Series. Ethnology Division. Papers — Merc S Ethn
Mercy Medicine — Mercy Med
Merentutkimuslaitoksen Julkaisu — Merentutkimuslaitoksen Julk
Meres es Automatika — Meres Autom
Meres es Automatika — Meres es Autom
Meresuegyi Koezlemenyek — Meresuegyi Koezl
Mergers and Acquisitions — MAC
Mergers and Acquisitions — Merg and Acq
Mergers and Acquisitions — Mergers
Mergers and Acquisitions — Mergers Acquis
Mergers and Acquisitions — Mergers & Acquis
Mergers and Acquisitions Almanac and Index — Merger & A I
Merian — Mer
Meridiens — Mer
Merino Breeders' Journal — Merino Breed J
MERIP [*Middle East Research and Information Project*] **Reports** — MERIP
MERIT [*Monitored Earth Rotation and Intercompared Techniques*] **Newsletter** — MERIT Newsl
Merkaz Volkani. Buletin (Bet Dagan, Israel) — Merkaz Volkani Bul (Bet Dagan Isr)
Merkblaetter der Bundesanstalt fuer Forst- und Holzwirtschaft — Merkbl Bundesanst Forst Holzwirtsch
Merkblaetter der Reichsinstitutes fuer Forst- und Holzwirtschaft — Merkbl Reichsinst Forst Holzwirtsch
Merkblaetter der Zentralinstitutes fuer Forst- und Holzwirtschaft — Merkbl Zentralinst Forst Holzwirtsch
Merkblaetter fuer den Aussenhandel — DMC
Merkblaetter ueber Angewandte Parasitenkunde und Schaedlingsbekaempfung — Merkbl Angew Parasitenkd Schaedlingsbekaempf
Merkblatt. Biologische Bundesanstalt fuer Land und Forstwirtschaft — Merkbl Biol Bundesanst Land Forstwirtsch
Merkblatt. Biologische Bundesanstalt fuer Land und Forstwirtschaft (Braunschweig) — Merkbl Biol Bundesanst Land Forstwirtsch (Braunschweig)
Merkblatt. Deutsche Landwirtschafts-Gesellschaft — Merkbl Deutsch Landwirtsch Ges
Merkblatt. Imker des Verbandes der Kleingaertner, Siedler, und Kleintierzuechter — Merkblatt Imker Verb Kleingaertner Siedler Kleintierz
Merkblatt. Verein der Zellstoff- und Papier-Chemiker und -Ingenieure — Merkbl Ver Zellst Chem
Merkur — M
Merkur — Merk
Merkur von Ungarn, oder Litterarzeitung fuer das Koenigreich Ungarn und Dessen Kronlaender — Merkur Ungarn
Merkwuerdige Abhandlungen Hollaendischer Aerzte — Merkwuerd Abh Holl Aerzte
Merlewood Research and Development Paper — Merlewood Res Dev Pap
Merlewood Research Station. Merlewood Research and Development Paper — Merlewood Res Stn Merlewood Res Dev Pap
Mernoekgeologiai Szemle — Mernoekgeol Sz
Meroitic Newsletter — Me Ne
Meroitic Newsletter — Meroitic Newsl
Mer-Outre-Mer — Mer O-Mer
Merova Technika — Merova Tech
Merrill Lynch Market Letter — Merrill ML
Merrill-Palmer Quarterly — Merrill-Palmer Q
Merrill-Palmer Quarterly — Merril-Pal
Mersey Quarterly — Mersey Quart
Mervyn Peake Review — MPR
Merzlotnye Issledovaniya — Merzlotnye Issled
MESA [*Mining Enforcement and Safety Administration*] **Magazine of Mining Health and Safety** [*United States*] — MESA Mag Min Health Saf
MESA [*Marine Ecosystems Analysis*] **New York. Bight Atlas Monograph** — MESA NY Bight Atlas Monogr
Mesa Redonda. Asociacion de Investigacion Tecnica de la Industria Papelera Espanola — Mesa Redonda Asoc Invest Tec Ind Papelera Esp
Mesaionike Bibliotheke — MB
Mescellanea Francescana di Storia, di Lettere, di Arti — MFS
Mesicni Prehled Meteorologickych Pozorovani — Mesic Prehl Met Pozor

Mesoamerica — MAG
Mesoamerica. Centro de Investigaciones Regionales de Mesoamerica — CIRMA/M
Mesoamerican Notes (Mexico) — Mesoam Notes Mex
Meson Resonances and Related Electromagnetic Phenomena. Proceedings. International Conference — Meson Reson Relat Electromagn Phenom Proc Int Conf
Mesopotamia [*Torino*] — Mes
Mesopotamia Agriculture — Mesopot Agric
Mesopotamia. Copenhagen Studies in Assyriology — Mes Cope St
Mesopotamia Journal of Agriculture — Mesopotamia J Agric
Mesopotamia Journal of Agriculture — MJAGDE
Mesopotamia. Rivista di Archeologia — Mesopo
Messager de l'Exarchat du Patriarche Russe en Europe Occidentale — MEPR
Messager de New York — MNY
Messager de Saint Benoit — MSB
Messager des Fideles — Mes Fid
Messager des Sciences et des Arts. Recueil Publie. Societe Royale des Beaux-Arts et des Lettres, et par Celle d'Agriculture et de Botanique de Gand — Messager Sci Arts Gand
Messager des Sciences Historiques de Belgique — Messager Sci Hist Belgique
Messager Evangelique de l'Eglise de la Confession d'Augsbourg — MEECA
Messager Technico-Economique — Messager Tech Econ
Messen, Pruefen, Automatisieren — Mess Pruefen Autom
Messen, Steuern, Regeln mit Automatisierungspraxis — Mess Steuern Regeln mit Automatisierungsprax
Messen und Pruefen — Mess Pruef
Messen und Pruefen — Mess und Pruef
Messen und Pruefen/Automatik — Mess Pruef Autom
Messen und Pruefen Vereinigt mit Automatik — Mess Pruef Ver Autom
Messenger — Mess
Messen-Steuern-Regeln — Mess-Steuern-Regeln
Messen-Steuern-Regeln — Mes-Steuern-Regeln
MessTec Spezial — MessTec Spez
Messtechnik im Korrosionschutz. Veranstaltung der Europaeischen Foederation Korrosion — Messtech Korrosionschutz Veranst Eur Foed Korros
Messtechnik, Regelunstechnik, Automatik [*Database*] — MRA
Messwerte — MSWFA
Mester — MR
Mestnaja Promyslennost' i Chudozestvennye Promysly — Mestn Promysl Chud Prom
Mesures — Mes
Mesures et Controle Industriel — Mes Controle Ind
Mesures, Regulation, Automatisme — Mes Reg Aut
Mesures, Regulation, Automatisme — Mes Regul Autom
Mesures, Regulation, Automatisme — Mes Regul Automat
Metaal en Kunststof — VSL
Metaal en Techniek — Metaal Tech
Metaal en Techniek. Vakblad voor de Metaalnijverheid — MAH
Metaalbewerking Werkplaatstechnisch Vakblad voor Nederland en Belgie — MBW
Metaalinstituut TNO [*Nederlands Centrale Organisatie voor Toegepast-Natuurwetenschappelijk Onderzoek*]. Circulaire — Metaalinst TNO Circ
Metaalinstituut TNO [*Nederlands Centrale Organisatie voor Toegepast-Natuurwetenschappelijk Onderzoek*]. Communications — Metaalinst TNO Commun
Metaalinstituut TNO [*Nederlands Centrale Organisatie voor Toegepast-Natuurwetenschappelijk Onderzoek*]. Publikatie — Metaalinst TNO Publ
Metabolic and Pediatric Ophthalmology — Metab Pediatr Ophthalmol
Metabolic Aspects of Cardiovascular Disease [*Elsevier Book Series*] — MACD
Metabolic Aspects of Cardiovascular Disease — Metab Aspects Cardiovasc Dis
Metabolic Biochemistry — Metab Biochem
Metabolic Bone Disease and Related Research — Metab Bone Dis Relat Res
Metabolic Eye Disease. Proceedings. International Symposium on Metabolic Eye Diseases — Metab Eye Dis Proc Int Symp
Metabolic Interconversion of Enzymes. International Symposium — Metab Interconvers Enzymes Int Symp
Metabolic Ophthalmology — Metab Ophthalmol
Metabolic Ophthalmology, Pediatric, and Systemic — Metab Ophthalmol Pediatr Syst
Metabolic Pathways [*Monograph*] — Metab Pathways
Metabolic, Pediatric, and Systemic Ophthalmology — Metab Pediatr Syst Ophthalmol
Metabolism and Disease [*Japan*] — Metab Dis
Metabolism and Enzymology of Nucleic Acids. Proceedings. International Symposium on Metalolism and Enzymology of Nucleic Acids — Metab Enzymol Nucleic Acids Proc Int Symp
Metabolism - Clinical and Experimental — Metab Clin Exp
Metabolism - Clinical and Experimental — Metabolism
Metabolism of the Nervous System. Proceedings. International Neurochemical Symposium — Metab Nerv Syst Proc Int Neurochem Symp
Metabolisme et Nutrition Azotes. Symposium International — Metab Nutr Azotes Symp Int
Metabolizm Azota u Sel'skokhozyaistvennykh Zhivotnykh, Doklady iz Simposiuma ob Azotistom Metabolizme Sel'skokhozyaistvennykh Zhivotnykh — Metab Azota Skh Zhivotn Dokl Simp
Metabolizm Miokarda. Materialy Sovetsko-Amerikanskogo Simpoziuma — Metab Miokarda Mater Sov Am Simp
Metal and Engineering — Met & Eng
Metal and Mineral Markets — Met Miner Mark
Metal Bulletin — MEL
Metal Bulletin — Met Bull
Metal Bulletin — Metal Bul
Metal Bulletin (London) — Met Bull London
Metal Bulletin Monthly — MBM
Metal Bulletin Monthly — MEQ
Metal Bulletin Monthly — Met Bull Mon
Metal Bulletin Monthly — Metal Bull Mon
Metal Bulletin Monthly — Metl Bul M
Metal Cleaning and Finishing — Met Clean Finish
Metal Construction — Met Const
Metal Construction — Met Constr
Metal Construction — Metal Cons
Metal Construction and British Welding Journal [*Later, Metal Construction*] — Met Constr Br Weld J
Metal Construction and British Welding Journal [*Later, Metal Construction*] — Metal Constr Br Weld J
Metal Fabricating News — Met Fabr News
Metal Fabricating News — MFN
Metal Finishers' Association of India. Transactions — Met Finish Assoc India Trans
Metal Finishing — Met Finish
Metal Finishing — Metal Fin
Metal Finishing — Metal Finish
Metal Finishing Abstracts — Met Finish Abstr
Metal Finishing Abstracts — Met Finishing Abstr
Metal Finishing Guidebook and Directory — Metal Fing
Metal Finishing Journal — Met Finish J
Metal Finishing Practice — Met Finish Pract
Metal Forming [*England*] — Met Form
Metal Forming — Metal Form
Metal Forming, Incorporating the Drop Forger — Met Form Drop Forger
Metal Industries (China) — Met Ind (China)
Metal Industries (Johannesburg) — Met Ind (Johannesburg)
Metal Industries (Kaohsing, Taiwan) — Met Ind Kaohsing Taiwan
Metal Industries Review — Met Ind Rev
Metal Industry — MEINA
Metal Industry — Metal Ind
Metal Industry (London) — Met Ind (London)
Metal Industry (London). Supplement — Met Ind London Suppl
Metal Ions in Biological Systems — Met Ions Biol Syst
Metal Ions in Biological Systems — Metal Ions Biol Syst
Metal Ions in Biology — Met Ions Biol
Metal Market Review — Met Mark Rev
Metal News (India) — Met News (India)
Metal Physics — Met Phys
Metal Physics. Lectures Delivered at the Institution of Metallurgists Refresher Course — Met Phys Lect Inst Metall Refresher Course
Metal Physics Seminar — Met Phys Semin
Metal Pi Complexes [*Elsevier Book Series*] — MPC
Metal Powder Industries Federation. MPIF Standard — Metal Powder Ind Fed Stand
Metal Powder Report — Met Powder Rep
Metal Products Manufacturing — Met Prod Manuf
Metal Progress — Met Prog
Metal Progress — Metal Prog
Metal Progress Databook — Met Prog Datab
Metal Properties Council. Publication — Met Prop Counc Publ
Metal Records and Electroplater — Met Rec Electroplat
Metal Science — Met Sci
Metal Science — Metal Sci
Metal Science — METSC
Metal Science and Heat Treatment — Met Sci and Heat Treat
Metal Science and Heat Treatment — Met Sci Heat Treat
Metal Science and Heat Treatment — Metal Sci H
Metal Science and Heat Treatment of Metals [*United States*] — Met Sci Heat Treat Met
Metal Science and Heat Treatment of Metals [*English Translation*] — MHTRA
Metal Science and Heat Treatment of Metals (English Translation) [*United States*] — Met Sci Heat Treat Met (Engl Transl)
Metal Science and Heat Treatment of Metals (USSR) — Met Sci Heat Treat Met (USSR)
Metal Science and Heat Treatment (USSR) — Met Sci Heat Treat (USSR)
Metal Science Journal [*Later, Metal Science*] — Met Sci J
Metal Science Journal [*Later, Metal Science*] — Metal Sci J
Metal Stamping — Met Stamp
Metal Stamping — Metal Stamp
Metal Statistics — Metal Stat
Metal Trades Journal — Metal Trades J
Metal Treating — Met Treat
Metal Treating — Metal Treat
Metal Treating (Rocky Mount, North Carolina) — Met Treat (Rocky Mount NC)
Metal Treatment and Drop Forging [*England*] — Met Treat Drop Forg
Metal Treatment and Drop Forging — MTDFA
Metal Treatment (London) — Met Treat (London)
Metal Working Press — Met Work Press
Metalectrovisie — MMQ
Metales No Ferreos — Met No Ferreos
Metall — Met
Metall. Internationale Zeitschrift fuer Technik und Wirtschaft — MWW
Metall und Chemie. Metallwoche — Met Chem Metallwoche
Metall und Erz — Metall u Erz
Metall und Erz — MetErz
Metall Woche — Met Woche
Metallgesellschaft AG [*Frankfurt/Main*]. Review of the Activities — Metallges Rev Activ
Metallgesellschaft. Mitteilungen aus dem Arbeitsbereich — Metallges Mitt Arbeitsbereich
Metallgesellschaft. Periodic Review — Metallges Period Rev
Metallgesellschaft. Review of the Activities — Metallges Rev Act

Metalli Leggeri e Loro Applicazioni — Met Leggeri Loro Appl
Metallic Bulletin (Loosdrecht, Netherlands) — Met Bull (Loosdrecht Netherlands)
Metallic Materials (Bratislava) — Met Mater (Bratislava)
Metallilaboratorio. Tiedonanto. Valtion Teknillinen Tutkimuskeskus — Metallilab Tied Valt Tek Tutkimuskeskus
Metallization. Performance and Reliability Issues for VLSI and ULSI — Met Perform Reliab Issues VLSI ULSI
Metallized Plastics. Fundamental and Applied Aspects — Met Plast
Metalloberflaeche-Angewandte Elektrochemie — Metalloberfl
Metalloberflaeche-Angewandte Elektrochemie — Metalloberflaeche-Angew Elektrochem
Metallofizika — Metallofiz
Metallofizika — MFIZA
Metallofizika. Akademiya Nauk Ukrainskoi SSR. Otdelenie Fiziki i Astronomii — Metallofizika Akad Nauk Ukr SSR Otd Fiz Astron
Metallogenicheskie i Geologicheskie Issledovaniya — Metallog Geol Issled
Metallogeniya Dokembriiskikh Shchitov i Drevnikh Podvizhnykh Zon. Doklady Vsesoyuznoi Ob'edinennoi Sessii po Zakonomernostyam Razmeshcheniya Poleznykh Iskopaemykh i Prognoznym Kartam — Metallog Dokembr Shchitov Drevnikh Podvizhnykh Zon Dokl Vses
Metallographic Review — Metallogr Rev
Metallographic Review — MTGRB
Metalloorganicheskaya Khimiya — Metalloorg Khim
Metallourgikes Ereunes — Metall Ereunes
Metallovedenie i Korroziya Metallov — Metalloved Korroz Met
Metallovedenie i Obrabotka Metallov — Metalloved Obrab Met
Metallovedenie i Prochnost Materialov — Metalloved Prochn Mater
Metallovedenie i Termicheskaja Obrabotka Metallov — M i TOM
Metallovedenie i Termicheskaya Obrabotka — Metalloved Term Obrab
Metallovedenie i Termicheskaya Obrabotka (Kalinin, USSR) — Metalloved Term Obrab (Kalinin USSR)
Metallovedenie i Termicheskaya Obrabotka Metallov — Metallov i Term Obrab Metal
Metallovedenie i Termicheskaya Obrabotka Metallov — Metalloved i Term Obrab Met
Metallovedenie i Termicheskaya Obrabotka Metallov — Metalloved Term Obrab Met
Metallovedenie i Termicheskaya Obrabotka (Moscow) — Metalloved Term Obrab (Moscow)
Metallovedenie. Sbornik Statei — Metalloved Sb Statei
Metall-Reinigung und Vorbehandlung — Met Reinig Vorbehandl
Metall-Reinigung und Vorbehandlung [*Germany*] — Metall-Reinig Vorbehandl
Metall-Reinigung, Vorbehandlung, Oberflaechentechnik, Formung — Met Reinig Vorbehandl Oberflaechentech Form
Metallreinigung Vorbehandlung, Oberflaechentechnik, Formung — Mr V
Metalltagung der DDR — Metalltag DDR
Metallurgia [*Redhill*] — Metallurg
Metallurgia and Metal Forming — MEMFA
Metallurgia and Metal Forming — Metall & Metal Form
Metallurgia and Metal Forming — Metall Met
Metallurgia and Metal Forming — Metall Met Form
Metallurgia Italiana — Met Ital
Metallurgia Italiana — Metall Ital
Metallurgical Abstracts — Met Abstr
Metallurgical Abstracts — Metall Abstr
Metallurgical and Chemical Engineering — Metall Chem Eng
Metallurgical Engineer — Metall Eng
Metallurgical Engineer (Bombay) — Metall Eng Bombay
Metallurgical Engineer. Indian Institute of Technology (Bombay) — Metall Eng IIT (Bombay)
Metallurgical Engineer. Indian Institute of Technology (Bombay) — MLEGB
Metallurgical Journal — Metall J
Metallurgical Journal. University of Strathclyde, Glasgow — Met J Univ Strathclyde Glasgow
Metallurgical Plant and Technology [*Germany*] — Metall Plant Technol
Metallurgical Reports. CRM [*Centre de Recherches Metallurgiques*] — Metall Rep CRM
Metallurgical Research (Athens) — Metall Res Athens
Metallurgical Review. MMIJ [*Mining and Metallurgical Institute of Japan*] — Metall Rev MMIJ
Metallurgical Reviews (Supplement to Metals and Materials) — Met Rev (Suppl Metals Mater)
Metallurgical Reviews (Supplement to Metals and Materials) — Metall Rev
Metallurgical Science and Technology — Metall Sci Technol
Metallurgical Slags and Fluxes. International Symposium. Proceedings — Metall Slags Fluxes Int Symp Proc
Metallurgical Society. American Institute of Mining, Metallurgical, and Petroleum Engineers. Conferences — Met Soc AIME Conf
Metallurgical Society. American Institute of Mining, Metallurgical, and Petroleum Engineers. Institute of Metals Division. Special Report — Met Soc AIME Inst Metals Div Spec Rep
Metallurgical Society. American Institute of Mining, Metallurgical, and Petroleum Engineers. TMS Papers — Met Soc AIME TMS Pap
Metallurgical Society. Conferences — Metall Soc Conf
Metallurgical Society. Conferences — MSCOA
Metallurgical Society. Conferences. Proceedings — Metall Soc Conf Proc
Metallurgical Society of AIME Proceedings — Metall Soc AIME Proc
Metallurgical Transactions — Met Trans
Metallurgical Transactions — Metall Trans
Metallurgical Transactions. A — Metall Trans A
Metallurgical Transactions. A. Physical Metallurgy and Materials Science — Metall T-A
Metallurgical Transactions. B — Metall Trans B
Metallurgical Transactions. B. Process Metallurgy — Metall T-B
Metallurgicheskaya i Gornorudnaya Promyshlennost — Metall Gornorudn Promst
Metallurgicheskaya i Gornorudnaya Promyshlennost — MGPNA
Metallurgicheskaya i Khimicheskaya Promyshlennost Kazakhstana — Metall Khim Prom Kaz
Metallurgicheskaya Teplotekhnika, Oborudovanie, Izmereniya, Kontrol i Avtomatizatsiya v Metallurgicheskom Proizvodstve — Metall Teplotekh Oborud Izmer Kontrol Avtom Metall Proizvod
Metallurgie — MTLGA
Metallurgie et la Construction Mecanique — Met Constr Mec
Metallurgie et la Construction Mecanique — Metall Constr Mec
Metallurgie Speciale (Paris) — Metall Spec (Paris)
Metallurgie und Giessereitechnik — Metall Giessereitech
Metallurgist — Metall
Metallurgist and Materials Technologist — Metall Mater Technol
Metallurgiya Chernykh Metallov — Metall Chern Met
Metallurgiya i Koksokhimiya — MEKOA
Metallurgiya i Koksokhimiya — Metall Koksokhim
Metallurgiya i Metallovedenie (Alma-Ata) — Metall Metalloved Alma Ata
Metallurgiya i Metallovedenie Chistykh Metallov — Metall Metalloved Chist Met
Metallurgiya i Metallovedenie Chistykh Metallov Moskovskij Inzhenerno-Fizicheskij Institut Sbornik Nauchnykh Rabot — Metall Metalloved Chist Met Sb Nauchn Rab
Metallurgiya SSSR — Metall SSSR
Metallurgy and Quality. Proceedings. Annual Conference — Metall Qual Proc Annu Conf
Metallurgy in Australasia. Proceedings. Annual Conference. Australian Institute of Metals — Metall Australas Proc Annu Conf Aust Inst Met
Metallurgy in Numismatics — Metall Numis
Metallurgy Note. Australia. Aeronautical Research Laboratories — Metall Note Aust Aeronaut Res Lab
Metallverarbeitung — MLVBA
Metallwaren-Industrie und Galvanotechnik — Metallwaren Ind Galvanotech
Metallwirtschaft, Metallwissenschaft, Metalltechnik — Metallwirtsch
Metallwirtschaft, Metallwissenschaft, Metalltechnik — Metallwirtsch Metallwiss Metalltech
Metallwirtschaft, Metallwissenschaft, Metalltechnik [*Germany*] — Metallwirtsch Wiss Tech
Metally Izvestiya Akademi Nauk SSSR — Met Izv Akad Nauk SSSR
Metaloznawstwo i Obrobka Cieplna — Metalozn Obrob Cieplna
Metals Abstracts — Met
Metals Abstracts — MetAb
Metals Abstracts Index — Metals Abstr Index
Metals Analysis and Outlook — Met Anal Outlook
Metals and Ceramics Information Center. Report — Met Ceram Inf Cent Rep
Metals and Materials — Met Mater
Metals and Materials — Metals Mater
Metals and Materials — Metals Mats
Metals and Materials (Metals Society) — Met Mater Met Soc
Metals and Materials (Seoul) — Met Mater Seoul
Metals and Minerals International — Metals Miner Int
Metals and Minerals Processing [*South Africa*] — Met Miner Process
Metals and Minerals Review [*India*] — Met Miner Rev
Metals and Minerals Review (Calcutta) — Met Miner Rev (Calcutta)
Metals and Technology (Japan) — Met Technol (Jpn)
Metals and Technology (Tokyo) — Met Technol (Tokyo)
Metals. Annual Conference. Australasian Institute of Metals — Met Annu Conf Australas Inst Met
Metals Australasia — Met Aust
Metals Australasia — Met Australas
Metals Australia [*Later, Metals Australasia*] — MAUSB
Metals Australia [*Later, Metals Australasia*] — Met Aust
Metals Australia [*Later, Metals Australasia*] — Metals Aust
Metals Crystallographic Data File [*Database*] — CRYSTMET
Metals Datafile [*Database*] — MDF
Metals Engineering Quarterly — Met Eng Q
Metals Engineering Quarterly — Metal Eng Q
Metals Engineering Quarterly — Metals Eng Quart
Metals for the Space Age. Plansee Proceedings. Papers Presented at the Plansee Seminar. De Re Metallica — Met Space Age Plansee Proc Pap Plansee Semin De Re Met
Metals Forum [*Australia*] — Met Forum
Metals Gazette — Met Gaz
Metals in Engineering [*Japan*] — Met Eng
Metals in Engineering (Tokyo) — Met Eng (Tokyo)
Metals in the Market Place. Metals Congress — Met Mark Place Met Congr
Metals Industry News — Metl Ind N
Metals. Japan Institute of Metals — Metals Jpn Inst Met
Metals, Materials, and Processes — Met Mater Processes
Metals Materials Manufacturing. Papers Presented. Annual Conference. Australasian Institute of Metals — Met Mater Manuf Pap Annu Conf Australas Inst Met
Metals/Materials Today — Met/Mater Today
Metals Review — Met Rev
Metals Society Book — Met Soc Book
Metals Society World — Met Soc World
Metals Society World — Metals Soc Wld
Metals Technology — Met Technol
Metals Technology — Metals Tech
Metals Technology. Institute of Metals (London) — Met Technol (London)
Metals Technology (New York) — Met Technol (NY)
Metals Week — Met Week
Metalurgia. ABM [*Associacao Brasileira de Metais*] — Met ABM
Metalurgia. ABM [*Associacao Brasileira de Metais*] — Metal ABM
Metalurgia i Odlewnictwo — Metal Odlew

Metalurgia Moderna — Metal Mod
Metalurgia Proszkow — Metal Proszkow
Metalurgia si Constructia de Masini — Metal Constr Mas
Metalurgia y Electricidad — Metal & Electr
Metalurgia y Electricidad — Metal Electr
Metalurgia y Electricidad (Madrid) — Met Electr (Madrid)
Metalurgija [*Sisak, Yugoslavia*] — METAB
Metalurgiya [*Sofia, Bulgaria*] — MTIAA
Metalworking — MTWOA
Metalworking Digest — MWD
Metalworking Economics — Metalwork Econ
Metalworking Interfaces — Metalwork Interfaces
Metalworking Management — Metalwork Manag
Metalworking Production — Metalwork Prod
Metalworking Production — Metalwrkg Prod
Metalworking Production — Metwork Prod
Metalworking Production — MHT
Metamedicine — METMD
Metano, Petrolio, e Nuove Energie — MENOA
Metano, Petrolio, e Nuove Energie — Metano Pet Nuove Energ
Metaphilosophy — Metaphilos
Metaux. Aciers Speciaux. Metaux et Alliages — Met Aciers Spec Met Alliages
Metaux and Corrosion — Met Corros
Metaux. Corrosion. Usure — Met Corros Usure
Metaux (Corrosion-Industries) — Met (Corros-Ind)
Metaux (Corrosion-Industries) — Metaux (Corros-Ind)
Metaux Deformation — Met Deform
Metaux Deformation — Metaux Deform
Metaux et Industries — Met Ind
Metaux et Machines — Met Mach
Metempirical UFO [*Unidentified Flying Object*] **Bulletin** — MUFOB
Meteor Forschungsergebnisse. Reihe A. Allgemeines, Physik, und Chemie des Meeres — Meteor Forschungsergeb Reihe A
Meteor Forschungsergebnisse. Reihe A/B. Allgemeines, Physik, und Chemie des Meeres. Maritime Meteorologie — Meteor Forschungsergeb Reihe AB
Meteor Forschungsergebnisse. Reihe B. Meteorologie und Aeronomie — Meteor Forschungsergen Reihe B
Meteor Forschungsergebnisse. Reihe C. Geologie und Geophysik — Meteor Forschungsergeb Reihe C
Meteor Forschungsergebnisse. Reihe D. Biologie — Meteor Forschungsergeb Reihe D Biol
Meteoric Stone and Meteoric Iron — Meteoric Stone Meteoric Iron
Meteoritica (English Translation) — Meteoritica (Engl Transl)
Meteoritical Society. Contributions — Meteorit Soc Contr
Meteoritics and Planetary Science — Meteorit Planet Sci
Meteoritika — MTTKA
Meteornoe Rasprostranenie Radiovoln — Meteornoe Rasprostr Radiovoln
Meteornoe Rasprostranenie Radiovoln — MRRVB
Meteorological Abstracts and Bibliography — Meteorol Abst and Biblio
Meteorological Abstracts and Bibliography — Meteorol Abst Bibliogr
Meteorological and Geoastrophysical Abstracts [*American Meteorological Society*] [*Bibliographic database*] — M & GA
Meteorological and Geoastrophysical Abstracts [*American Meteorological Society*] [*Bibliographic database*] — Met & GeoAb
Meteorological and Geoastrophysical Abstracts [*American Meteorological Society*] [*Bibliographic database*] — Met Geoastrophys Abstr
Meteorological and Geoastrophysical Abstracts [*American Meteorological Society*] [*Bibliographic database*] — Meteor & Geoastrophys Abstr
Meteorological and Geoastrophysical Abstracts [*American Meteorological Society*] [*Bibliographic database*] — Meteorol Geoastrophys Abstr
Meteorological and Geoastrophysical Abstracts [*American Meteorological Society*] [*Bibliographic database*] — MGA
Meteorological Bulletin — Meteorol Bull
Meteorological Magazine — Meteor Mag
Meteorological Magazine — Meteorol Mag
Meteorological Magazine — MM
Meteorological Magazine (London) — Met Mag (Lond)
Meteorological Monographs — Meteorol Monogr
Meteorological Study — Meteorol Stud
Meteorologicheskie Issledovaniya — Meteorol Issled
Meteorologicke Zpravy — Meteorol Zpr
Meteorologija, Klimatologija, i Gidrologija — Meteor Klimat Gidrol
Meteorologische Abhandlungen. Institut fuer Meteorologie und Geophysik. Freie Universitaet (Berlin) — Meteorol Abh Inst Meteorol Geophys Freie Univ (Berl)
Meteorologische Rundschau — Met Rdsch
Meteorologische Rundschau — Meteor Rund
Meteorologische Rundschau — Meteorol Rundsch
Meteorologische Zeitschrift — Meteorol Z
Meteorologische Zeitschrift — MZ
Meteorologischer Dienst der Deutschen Demokratischen Republik. Veroeffentlichungen — Meteorol Dienst DDR Veroeff
Meteorologiske Annaler — Met A
Meteorologiske Annaler — Met Ann
Meteorologiske Annaler — Meteorol Ann
Meteorologiya i Gidrologiya — Meteorol Gidrol
Meteorologiya i Gidrologiya — Meteorol Gidrolog
Meteorologiya i Gidrologiya — Meteorol i Gidrol
Meteorologiya i Gidrologiya. Informatsionnyi Byulleten — Meteor Gidrol Inf Byull
Meteorologiya i Gidrologiya Informatsionnyi Byulleten — Meteorol Gidrol Inf Byull
Meteorologiya i Gidrologiya Informatsionnyi Byulleten — MGITA2
Meteorology and Hydrology — MEHBA
Meteorology and Hydrology [*United States*] — Meteorol Hydrol
Method and Appraisal in the Physical Sciences — Method Appraisal Phys Sci
Methode de Mesure CRR (Centre de Recherches Routieres, Brussels) — Methode Mes CRR
Methoden und Verfahren der Mathematischen Physik — Methoden Verfahren Math Phys
Methodes et Pratiques de l'Ingenieur — Methodes Prat Ingen
Methodes Mathematiques de l'Informatique [*Paris*] — Methodes Math Inform
Methodes Mathematiques pour l'Ingenieur — Methodes Math Ingr
Methodes Physiques d'Analyse [*Revue de Groupement pour l'Avancement des Methodes Spectrographiques*] — Method Phys Anal
Methodes Physiques d'Analyse [*Revue de Groupement pour l'Avancement des Methodes Spectrographiques*] — Methodes Phys Anal
Methodicum Chimicum — Method Chim
Methodik der Information in der Medizin — Method Inf Med
Methodische Fortschritte im Medizinischen Laboratorium — Method Fortschr Med Lab
Methodist Federation for Social Service. Social Service Bulletin — Meth Feder Social Serv Social Serv Bul
Methodist History — MetH
Methodist History — MethH
Methodist History — MH
Methodist Hospital of Dallas. Medical Staff. Bulletin — Methodist Hosp Dallas Med Staff Bull
Methodist Magazine — Meth M
Methodist Magazine — Meth Mag
Methodist Periodical Index — Meth Per Ind
Methodist Periodical Index — Methodist Period Index
Methodist Periodical Index — MPI
Methodist Quarterly — Meth Q
Methodist Quarterly Review — Meth Q R
Methodist Quarterly Review — MQR
Methodist Recorder — Meth Rec
Methodist Review — Meth R
Methodist Review — MR
Methodological Developments in Biochemistry — Methodol Dev Biochem
Methodological Surveys — Methodol Surv
Methodological Surveys in Biochemistry — Methodol Surv Biochem
Methodological Surveys in Biochemistry — MSBIDK
Methodological Surveys in Biochemistry and Analysis — Methodol Surv Biochem Anal
Methodological Surveys. Sub-series B. Biochemistry — Methodol Surv Sub Ser B
Methodology and Science — Method Sci
Methodology and Science — Methodol Sci
Methods and Achievements in Experimental Pathology — Methods Achiev Exp Pathol
Methods and Applications of Analysis — Methods Appl Anal
Methods and Findings in Experimental and Clinical Pharmacology — Methods Find Exp Clin Pharmacol
Methods and Mechanisms for Producing Ions from Large Molecules — Methods Mech Prod Ions Large Mol
Methods and Phenomena [*Elsevier Book Series*] — MP
Methods and Phenomena. Their Applications in Science and Technology — Methods Phenom Their Appl Sci Technol
Methods and Principles in Medicinal Chemistry — Methods Princ Med Chem
Methods for the Examination of Waters and Associated Materials — Methods Exam Waters Assoc Mater
Methods in Cancer Research — Meth Cancer Res
Methods in Cancer Research — Methods Cancer Res
Methods in Carbohydrate Chemistry — Methods Carbohydr Chem
Methods in Cell Biology — Methods Cell Biol
Methods in Cell Physiology — Methods Cell Physiol
Methods in Chromatography — Methods Chromatogr
Methods in Clinical Pharmacology — Methods Clin Pharmacol
Methods in Computational Chemistry — Methods Comput Chem
Methods in Computational Physics — MCOPB
Methods in Computational Physics. Advances in Research and Applications — Methods Comput Phys
Methods in Diabetes Research — Methods Diabetes Res
Methods in Enzymology — MENZA
Methods in Enzymology — Methods Enzymol
Methods in Free Radical Chemistry — Methods Free Radical Chem
Methods in Geochemistry and Geophysics [*Elsevier Book Series*] — MGG
Methods in Geomathematics — Meth Geomath
Methods in Geomathematics [*Elsevier Book Series*] — MG
Methods in Hematology — Methods Hematol
Methods in Hormone Research — Methods Horm Res
Methods in Immunology and Immunochemistry — Methods Immunol Immunochem
Methods in Investigative and Diagnostic Endocrinology — Methods Invest Diagn Endocrinol
Methods in Investigative and Diagnostic Endocrinology [*Elsevier Book Series*] — MIDE
Methods in Laboratory Medicine — Methods Lab Med
Methods in Medical Research — Methods Med Res
Methods in Medical Research — MMRSA
Methods in Membrane Biology — MEMBBM
Methods in Membrane Biology — Meth Membrane Biol
Methods in Membrane Biology — Methods Membr Biol
Methods in Microbiology — Methods Microbiol
Methods in Molecular Biology — Meth Mol Biol
Methods in Molecular Biology — Methods Mol Biol
Methods in Mycoplasmology — Methods Mycoplasmol
Methods in Neurosciences — Methods Neurosci
Methods in Organic Synthesis — MOS
Methods in Pharmacology — Methods Pharmacol

Methods in Physiology Series — Methods Physiol Ser
Methods in Psychobiology — Methods Psychobiol
Methods in Stereochemical Analysis — Methods Stereochem Anal
Methods in Subnuclear Physics — Methods Subnucl Phys
Methods in Virology — Meth Virol
Methods in Virology — Methods Virol
Methods of Animal Experimentation — Methods Anim Exp
Methods of Biochemical Analysis — MBANA
Methods of Biochemical Analysis — Meth Biochem Analysis
Methods of Biochemical Analysis — Methods Biochem Anal
Methods of Cell Separation — Methods Cell Sep
Methods of Elemento-Organic Chemistry [*Elsevier Book Series*] — MEOC
Methods of Experimental Physics — MEEPA
Methods of Experimental Physics — Methods Exp Phys
Methods of Experimental Physics — Methods Experiment Phys
Methods of Forensic Science — Methods Forensic Sci
Methods of Functional Analysis and Topology — Methods Funct Anal Topology
Methods of Hormone Radioimmunoassay [*monograph*] — Methods Horm Radioimmunoassay
Methods of Information in Medicine — Met Inf Med
Methods of Information in Medicine — Meth Inf Med
Methods of Information in Medicine — Methods Inf Med
Methods of Information in Medicine (Supplement) — Methods Inf Med (Suppl)
Methods of Modern Biometrics — Methods Mod Biom
Methods of Modern Mathematical Physics — Methods Mod Math Phys
Methods of Neurochemistry — Methods Neurochem
Methods of Operations Research — Methods Oper Res
Methods of Surface Characterization — Methods Surf Charact
Metis — METI
Metis Newsletter. Metis Association of the Northwest Territories [*Canada*] — ME
Metodi Analitici per le Acque — Metodi Anal Acque
Metodicheskie Materialy i Nauchnye Soobshcheniya — Metod Mater Nauchn Soobshch
Metodicheskie Materialy. Institut Mineralogii. Geokhimii i Kristallokhimii Redkikh Elementov. Akademiya Nauk SSSR — Metod Mater Inst Mineral Geokhim Kristallokhim Redk Elem Aka
Metodicheskie Ukazaniya po Geologicheskoi S'emke Masshtaba 1:50,000 — Metod Ukazaniya Geol S'emke Masshtaba 1:50000
Metodicke Prirucky Experimentalni Botaniky — Metod Prirucky Exp Bot
Metodika i Tekhnika Razvedki — Metod Tekh Razved
Metodika Prepodavaniya Inostrannykh Yazykov v Vuze — Metod Prepod Inostr Yazykov Vuze
Metodika Prepodavaniya Khimii — Metod Prepod Khim
Metodiky pro Zavadeni Vysledku Vyzkumu do Praxe — Metod Zavad Vysled Vyzk Praxe
Metodiky pro Zavadeni Vysledku Vyzkumu do Praxe — Metod Zavadeni Vysledku Vyzk Praxe
Metodiky pro Zavadeni Vysledku Vyzkumu do Zemedelske Praxe — Metod Zavadeni Vysledku Vyzk Zemed Praxe
Metodologia delle Scienze e Filosofia del Linguaggio — MSFL
Metodologiceskie Problemy Nauki — Metodol Probl Nauki
Metodologiceskie Voprosy Nauki — Metod Vopr Nauki
Metodologicheskie i Sotsial'nye Problemy Tekhniki i Tekhnicheskikh Nauk — Metodol Sots Probl Tekh Tekh Nauk
Metody a Pochody Chemicke Technologie — Metody Pochody Chem Technol
Metody Analiza i Kontrolya Proizvodstva v Khimicheskoi Promyshlennosti — Metody Anal Kontrolya Proizvod Khim Promsti
Metody Analiza Khimicheskikh Reaktivov i Preparatov — Metody Anal Khim Reakt Prep
Metody Analiza Organicheskikh Soedinenii Nefti Ikh Smesei i Proizvodnykh [*Former USSR*] [*A publication*] — Metody Anal Org Soedin Neft Ikh Smesei Proizvodnykh
Metody Analiza Organicheskikh Soedinenii Nefti Ikh Smesei i Proizvodnykh — Metody Anal Org Soedin Nefti Ikh Smesei Proizvodnykh
Metody Analiza Redkometal'nykh Mineralov Rud i Gornykh Porod — Metody Anal Redkomet Miner Rud Gorn Porod
Metody Analiza Veshchestv Osoboi Chistoty i Monokristallov — Metody Anal Veshchestv Osoboi Chist Monokrist
Metody Diskretnogo Analiza — Metody Diskret Anal
Metody Diskretnogo Analiza [*Novosibirsk*] — Metody Diskret Analiz
Metody Eksperimental'noi Botaniki — Metody Eksp Bot
Metody i Pribory Avtomaticheskogo Nerazrushayushchego Kontrolya — Metody Prib Avtom Nerazrushayushchego Kontrolya
Metody i Pribory dlya Analiza Sostava Veshchestva — Metody Prib Anal Sostava Veshchestva
Metody i Problemy Ekotoksikologicheskogo Modelirovaniya i Prognozirovaniya. Materialy Vsesoyuznogo Rabochego Soveshchaniya po Mezhdunarodnoi Programme YUNESKO Chelovek i Biosfera — Metody Probl Ekotoksikol Model Prognozirovaniya Mater Vses
Metody i Protsessy Khimicheskoi Tekhnologii — Metody Protsessy Khim Tekhnol
Metody i Sredstva Issledovaniya Materialov i Konstruktsii. Rabotayushchikh pod Vozdeistviem Radiatsii — Metody Sredstva Issled Mater Konstr Rab Vozdeistv Radiats
Metody Ispytanii Detalei Mashin i Priborov — Metody Ispyt Detalei Mash Prib
Metody Issledovaniya Katalizatorov i Kataliticheskikh Reaktsii [*Former USSR*] — Metody Issled Katal Katal Reakts
Metody Issledovaniya Katalizatorov i Kataliticheskikh Reaktsii — MIKKA
Metody Issledovaniya v Vinodelii — Metody Issled Vinodel
Metody Izucheniya Veshchestvennogo Sostava i Ikh Primenenie — Metody Izuch Veshchestv Sostava i Ikh Primen
Metody Khimicheskogo Analiza Mineral'nogo Syr'ya — Metody Khim Anal Miner Syr'ya
Metody Kompleksnogo Izucheniya Fotosinteza — Metody Kompleksn Izuch Fotosint
Metody Lyuminestsentnogo Analiza. Materialy Soveshchaniya po Lyuminestsentsii — Metody Lyumin Anal Mater Soveshch
Metody Opredeleniya Absolyutnogo Vozrasta Geologicheskikh Obrazovanii — Metody Opred Absol Vozrasta Geol Obraz
Metody Opredeleniya i Issledovaniya Sostoyaniya Gazov v Metallakh. Doklady na Vsesoyuznom Simpoziume po Metodam Analiza Gazov v Metallakh — Metody Opred Issled Sostoyaniya Gazov Met Dokl Vses Simp
Metody Opredeleniya i Issledovaniya Sostoyaniya Gazov v Metallakh. Vsesoyuznaya Konferentsiya — Metody Opred Issled Sostoyaniya Gazov Met Vses Konf
Metody Opredeleniya Pestitsidov v Vode — Metody Opred Pestits Vode
Metody Paleogeograficheskikh Issledovanii — Metody Paleogeogr Issled
Metody Polucheniya Khimicheskikh Reaktivov i Preparatov — Metody Poluch Khim Reak Prep
Metody Razvedochnoi Geofiziki — Metody Razved Geofiz
Metody Razvedochnoi Geofiziki — MRZGA
Metody Rudnoi Geofiziki — Metody Rudn Geofiz
Metody Vycislenii — Metody Vycisl
Metokika a Technika Informaci — Met Tech Inf
Metric Bulletin — Metric Bul
Metric Information — Metric Info
Metroeconomica — Met
Metroeconomica — Metroecon
Metrologia — Metrol
Metrologia Aplicata — Metrol Apl
Metrologicheskie i Tekhnologicheskie Issledovaniya Kachestva Poverkhnosti — Metrol Tekhnol Issled Kach Poverkhn
Metrologicorum Scriptorum Reliquiae — Metrol Script
Metrologicorum Scriptorum Reliquiae — MS
Metrologicorum Scriptorum Reliquiae — Script Metr
Metrologiya i Poverochnoe Delo — Metrol Poverochn Delo
Metrology and Inspection — Metrol Insp
Metron. International Review of Statistics — Metron Int Rev Statist
Metronidazole. Proceedings. International Symposium on Metronidazole — Metronidazole Proc Int Symp Metronidazole
Metronome — Metro
Metropolis — Metr
Metropolitan — Metrop
Metropolitan Chamber of Commerce and Industry. Chamber News — CWS
Metropolitan Detroit Science Review — Metrop Detroit Sci Rev
Metropolitan Home — GMEH
Metropolitan Life Insurance Company. Statistical Bulletin — Met Life Stat Bull
Metropolitan Life Insurance Company. Statistical Bulletin — Metropolitan Life Stat Bul
Metropolitan Life Insurance Company. Statistical Bulletin — Metropolitan Life Statis Bul
Metropolitan Life Insurance Company. Statistical Bulletin — MLI
Metropolitan Magazine [*New York*] — MET M
Metropolitan Magazine — Metropol M
Metropolitan Museum. Journal — Met Mus J
Metropolitan Museum. Journal — Metr Mus J
Metropolitan Museum Journal — MMAJ
Metropolitan Museum of Art. Bulletin [*New York*] — Bull Metrop Mus Art
Metropolitan Museum of Art. Bulletin — Met Mus Bul
Metropolitan Museum of Art. Bulletin — Met Mus Bull
Metropolitan Museum of Art. Bulletin — Metrop Mus
Metropolitan Museum of Art Bulletin — MMAB
Metropolitan Museum Studies — Met Mus Stud
Metropolitan Museum Studies — Metr Mus Stud
Metropolitan Museum Studies — Metr Mus Studies
Metropolitan Museum Studies — MM St
Metropolitan Museum. Studies — MMS
Metropolitan Toronto Board of Trade. Journal — Metropolitan Toronto Bd Trade J
Metropolitan Toronto Business Journal — BJM
Metropolitan Toronto Business Journal — Metropolitan Toronto Bus J
Metropolitan-Vickers Gazette — Metrop Vickers Gaz
Metrovisie — MYK
Metsanduse Teadusliku Uurimise Laboratoorium. Metsanduslikud Uurimused — Metsanduse Tead Uurim Lab Metsandusl Uurim
Metsanduslikud Uurimused — Metsanduslik Uurim
Metsantutkimuslaitoksen Julkaisuja — Metsantutkimuslaitoksen Julk
Metsataloudellinen Aikakauslehti — Metsatal Aikakausl
Metsataloudellinen Aikakauslehti — Metsataloud Aikak
Metsatieteellisen Koelaitoken Julkaisuja — Metsatieteellisen Koelaitoken Julk
Metsatieteellisen Tutkimuslaitoksen Julkaisuja — Metsatieteellisen Tutkimuslaitoksen Julk
Metsniereba da Tekhnika — Metsniereba Tekh
Metallurgija i Toplivo — Metall Topl
Metting Index — MInd
METU [*Middle East Technical University*] **Faculty of Architecture. Occasional Paper Series** — METU Faculty of Archre Occasional Paper Series
Meubel. Weekblad voor de Meubelindustrie, Meubelhandel, Woninginrichting, en Toeleveringsbedrijven — VMI
Meubelecho — MNO
Meunerie Francaise — Meun Fr
Mex-Am Review — MRV
Mexican Art and Life (Mexico) — Mex Art Life Mex
Mexican Financial Report — Mex Fin Rep
Mexican Folkways — Mex Folkways
Mexican Mining Journal — Mex M J
Mexican Mining Journal — Mex Min J
Mexican-American Review [*Later, Mex-Am Review*] — Mex Am R

Mexican-American Review [*Later, Mex-Am Review*] — Mexicn Rev
Mexico Agricola — Mex Agr
Mexico. Anales del Instituto de Biologia — Mexico Anales Inst Biologia
Mexico. Comision de Fomento Minero. Boletin — Mex Com Fom Min Bol
Mexico. Comision de Fomento Minero. Boletin — Mexico Com Fomento Min Bol
Mexico. Comite Directivo para la Investigacion de los Recursos Minerales. Boletin — Mex Com Dir Invest Recur Miner Bol
Mexico. Consejo de Recursos Naturales No Renovables. Boletin — Mex Cons Recur Nat No Renov Bol
Mexico. Consejo de Recursos Naturales No Renovables. Boletin. Publicaciones — Mexico Consejo Rec Naturales No Renovables Bol Pub
Mexico. Consejo de Recursos Naturales No Renovables. Publicacion — Mex Cons Recur Nat No Renov Publ
Mexico. Consejo de Recursos Naturales No Renovables. Seminario Interno Anual sobre Exploracion Geologico-Minera. Memoria — Mex Cons Rec Nat No Ren Sem Int Anu Expl Geol Min Mem
Mexico en el Arte (Mexico) — Mex En Arte Mex
Mexico. Escuela Nacional de Ciencias Biologicas. Anales — Mexico Escuela Nac Cienc Biol Anales
Mexico Farmaceutico. Defensor de la Farmacia Mexicana — Mex Farm
Mexico Forestal — Mex For
Mexico Forestal. Sociedad Forestal Mexicana — Mexico Forest
Mexico. Instituto Geologico — Mex I G
Mexico. Instituto Nacional para la Investigacion de Recursos Minerales. Boletin — Mex Inst Nac Invest Recur Miner Bol
Mexico. Instituto Nacional para la Investigacion de Recursos Minerales. Boletin — Mexico Inst Nac Inv Rec Minerales Bol
Mexico. Ministerio de Fomento. Anales — Mex Min Fomento An
Mexico Quarterly Review — MQR
Mexico. Secretaria de Agricultura y Ganaderia. Oficina de Estudios Especiales. Folleto de Divulgacion — Mex Secr Agric Ganad Of Estud Espec Foll Divul
Mexico. Secretaria de Agricultura y Ganaderia. Oficina de Estudios Especiales. Folleto Miscelaneo — Mex Secr Agric Ganad Of Estud Espec Foll Misc
Mexico. Secretaria de Agricultura y Ganaderia. Oficina de Estudios Especiales. Folleto Tecnico — Mex Secr Agric Ganad Of Estud Espec Foll Tec
Mexico. Secretaria de Fomento. Boletin — Mex Sec Fomento Bol
Mexico. Universidad Nacional Autonoma. Instituto de Geografia. Boletin — Mexico Univ Nac Autonoma Inst Geografia Bol
Mexico. Universidad Nacional Autonoma. Instituto de Geologia. Boletin — Mexico Univ Nac Autonoma Inst Geologia Bol
Mexico. Universidad Nacional Autonoma. Instituto de Geologia. Paleontologia Mexicana — Mex Univ Nac Auton Inst Geol Paleontol Mex
Mexico. Universidad Nacional Autonoma. Instituto de Geologia. Revista — Mex Univ Nac Auton Inst Geol Rev
Mexico. Universidad Nacional Autonoma. Instituto de Geologia. Serie Divulgacion — Mex Univ Nac Auton Inst Geol Ser Divulg
Mexico y Sus Bosques — Mex Bosques
Meyers Enzyklopaedisches Lexikon — MEL
Meyers Lexikon — Mey Lex
Meyler and Peck's Drug-Induced Diseases — Meyler Pecks Drug Induced Dis
Meyler's Side Effects of Drugs — Meyler's Side Eff Drugs
Meyniana — MEYNA
Mezdunarodnaja Zizn — Mezdun Zizn
Mezdunarodni Otnosenija — Mezd Otnosenija
Mezdunarodnyj Ezegodnik. Politika i Ekonomika — Mezdun Ezeg Polit Ekon
Mezei Gazdak Baratja — Mezei Gazd Baratja
Mezhdunarodnaya Konferentsiya po Fizike Tyazhelykh Ionov — Mezhdunar Konf Fiz Tyazh Ionov
Mezhdunarodnaya Konferentsiya po Fizike Vysokikh Energii — Mezhdunar Konf Fiz Vys Energ
Mezhdunarodnaya Konferentsiya po Koordinatsionnoi Khimii. Tezisy Dokladov — Mezhdunar Konf Koord Khim Tezisy Dokl
Mezhdunarodnaya Konferentsiya po Merzlotovedeniyu — Mezhdunar Konf Merzlotoved
Mezhdunarodnaya Konferentsiya po Merzlotovedeniyu. Materialy — Mezhdunar Konf Merzlotoved Mater
Mezhdunarodnaya Konferentsiya po Meteorologii Karpat. Trudy — Mezhdunar Konf Meteorol Karpat Tr
Mezhdunarodnaya Konferentsiya po MGD [*Magnetogidrodinamika*]**-Preobrazovaniyu Energii** — Mezhdunar Konf MGD Preobraz Energ
Mezhdunarodnaya Konferentsiya po Optike Rentgenovskikh Luchei i Mikroanalizu — Mezhdunar Konf Op Rentgenovskikh Luchei Mikroanal
Mezhdunarodnaya Konferentsiya po Poroshkovoi Metallurgii — Mezhdunar Konf Poroshk Metall
Mezhdunarodnaya Konferentsiya po Primeneniyu Sinteticheskikh Almazov v Promyshlennosti — Mezhdunar Konf Primen Sint Almazov Promsti
Mezhdunarodnaya Konferentsiya po Radiatsionnoi Fizike Poluprovodnikov i Rodstvennykh Materialov — Mezhdunar Konf Radiats Fiz Poluprovodn Rodstvennykh Mater
Mezhdunarodnaya Konferentsiya po Teorii Plazmy — Mezhdunar Konf Teor Plazmy
Mezhdunarodnaya Konferentsiya po Titanu — Mezhdunar Konf Titanu
Mezhdunarodnaya Konferentsiya po Tuberkulezu. Trudy — Mezhdunar Konf Tuberk Tr
Mezhdunarodnaya Kongress po Astronavtike Doklady — Mezhdunar Kongr Astronavt Dokl
Mezhdunarodnaya Mineralogicheskaya Assotsiatsiya S'ezd — Mezhdunar Mineral Assots Sezd
Mezhdunarodnaya Shkola Biologicheskogo Monitoringa — Mezhdunar Shk Biol Monit
Mezhdunarodnaya Shkola Molodykh Uchenykh po Fizike Vysokikh Energii. Materialy — Mezhdunar Shk Molodykh Uch Fiz Vys Energ Mater
Mezhdunarodnaya Shkola OIYaI-TsERN po Fizike. Trudy — Mezhdunar Shk OIYaI TsERN Fiz Tr
Mezhdunarodnaya Shkola po Kogerentnoi Optike i Gologrfii-Varna — Mezhdunar Shk Kogerentnoi Opt Gologr Varna
Mezhdunarodnaya Shkola po Kogerentnoi Optike i Golografii-Varna — Mezhdunar Skh Kogerentnoi Opt Gologr Varna
Mezhdunarodnaya Shkola po Neitronnoi Fizike — Mezhdunar Shk Neitr Fiz
Mezhdunarodnaya Shkola po Protsessam Perenosa v Nepodvizhnykh i Psevdoozhizhennykh Zernistykh Sloyakh. Materialy — Mezhdunar Shk Protsessam Perenosa Nepodvizhnykh
Mezhdunarodnaya Shkola po Voprosam Ispol'zovaniya EVM v Yadernykh Issledovaniyakh — Mezhdunar Shk Vopr Ispol EVM Yad Issled
Mezhdunarodnaya Shkola Seminar Lazernaya Diagnostika Plazmy — Mezhdunar Shk Semin Lazernaya Diagn Plazmy
Mezhdunarodnaya Shkola Seminar Matematicheskie Modeli, Analiticheskie i Chislennye Metody v Teorii Perenosa — Mezhdunar Shk Semin Mat Modeli Anal Chislennn Metody Teor
Mezhdunarodnaya Shkola Seminar Metody Lazernoi Diagnostiki Odnofaznykh i Mnogofaznykh Techenii — Mezhdunar Shk Semin Metody Lazernoi Diagn Odnofaznykh
Mezhdunarodnaya Shkola Seminar Teplo i Massoobmen v Khimicheski Reagiruyushchikh Sistemakh — Mezhdunar Shk Semin Teplo Massoobmen Khim Reagiruyushchikh
Mezhdunarodnaya Shkola Spetsialistov po Rostu Kristallov — Mezhdunar Shk Spets Rostu Krist
Mezhdunarodnaya Shkola Stran-Chlenov SEV Svarka Poroshkovoi Provolokoi — Mezhdunar Shk Stran Chlenov SEV Svarka Poroshk Provolokoi
Mezhdunarodno Nauchno Suveshtanie po Kheterozisa — Mezhdunar Nauch Suvesh Kheterozisa
Mezhdunarodno Selskostopansko Spisanie — Mezhdunar Selskostop Spis
Mezhdunarodnoe Simpozium Kompozity — Mezhdunar Simp Kompoz
Mezhdunarodnoi Soveshchanie po Problemam Kvantovoi Teorii Polya — Mezhdunar Soveshch Probl Kvantovoi Teor Polya
Mezhdunarodnyi Agropromyshlennyi Zhurnal — Mezhdunar Agroprom Zh
Mezhdunarodnyi Entomologicheskii Kongress. Trudy — Mezhdunar Entomol Kongr Tr
Mezhdunarodnyi Gazovyi Kongress — Mezhdunar Gazov Kongr
Mezhdunarodnyi Geokhimicheskii Kongress. Doklady — Mezhdunar Geokhim Kongr Dokl
Mezhdunarodnyi Geologicheskii Kongress — Mezhdunar Geol Kongr
Mezhdunarodnyi Kollokvium. Mekhanicheskaya Ustalost Metallov — Mezhdunar Kollok Mekh Ustalost Met
Mezhdunarodnyi Kollokvium po Tonkim Magnitnym Plenkam — Mezhdunar Kollok Tonkim Magn Plenkam
Mezhdunarodnyi Konferentsiya po Amorfnym Zhidkum Poluprovodnikam — Mezhdunar Konf Amorfnym Zhidk Poluprovodn
Mezhdunarodnyi Kongress Antropologicheskikh i Etnograficheskikh Nauk. Trudy — Mezhdunar Kongr Antropol Etnogr Nauk Tr
Mezhdunarodnyi Kongress Gerontologov — Mezhdunar Kongr Gerontol
Mezhdunarodnyi Kongress Koloristov — Mezhdunar Kongr Koloristov
Mezhdunarodnyi Kongress Liteishchikov. Doklady — Mezhdunar Kongr Liteishchikov Dokl
Mezhdunarodnyi Kongress Mineralnym Udobreniyam. Doklady Sovetskikh Uchastnikov Kongressa — Mezhdunar Kongr Miner Udobr Dokl Sov Uchastnikov Kongr
Mezhdunarodnyi Kongress po Efirnym Maslam. Materialy — Mezhdunar Kongr Efirnym Maslam Mat
Mezhdunarodnyi Kongress po Katalizu — Mezhdunar Kongr Katal
Mezhdunarodnyi Kongress po Khimii Tsementa — Mezhdunar Kongr Khim Tsem
Mezhdunarodnyi Kongress po Lugovodstvu — Mezhdunar Kongr Lugovod
Mezhdunarodnyi Kongress po Mineralnym Udobreniyam. Doklady na Plenarnykh Zasedaniyakh — Mezhdunar Kongr Miner Udobr Dokl Plenarnykh Zased
Mezhdunarodnyi Kongress po Obogashcheniyu Poleznykh Iskopaemykh. Sbornik — Mezhdunar Kongr Obogashch Polezn Isko Sb
Mezhdunarodnyi Kongress po Obogashcheniyu Poleznykh Iskopaemykh. Trudy — Mezhdunar Kongr Obogashch Polezn Isko Tr
Mezhdunarodnyi Kongress po Obogashcheniyu Uglei — Mezhdunar Kongr Obogashch Uglei
Mezhdunarodnyi Kongress po Organicheskoi Geokhimii — Mezhdunar Kongr Org Geokhim
Mezhdunarodnyi Kongress po Poverkhnostno-Aktivnym Veshchestvam — Mezhdunar Kongr Poverkhn Akt Veshchestvam
Mezhdunarodnyi Kongress po Termicheskoi Obrabotke Materialov — Mezhdunar Kongr Term Obrab Mater
Mezhdunarodnyi Kongress po Zashchite Rastenii — Mezhdunar Kongr Zashch Rast
Mezhdunarodnyi Kongress po Zashchite Rastenii. Doklady — Mezhdunar Kongr Zashch Rast Dokl
Mezhdunarodnyi Kongress Pochvovedov. Problemy Pochvovedeniya — Mezhdunar Kongr Pochvovedov Probl Pochvoved
Mezhdunarodnyi Sel'skokhoziaistvennyi Zhurnal — Mezhdunar Sel-Khoz Zh
Mezhdunarodnyi Sel'skokhozyaistvennyi Zhurnal — Mezhdunar Sel'skokhoz Zh
Mezhdunarodnyi Sel'skokhozyaistvennyi Zhurnal — Mezhdunar S-Kh Zh
Mezhdunarodnyi Seminar po Problemam Fiziki Vysokikh Energii i Kvantovoi Teorii Polya — Mezhdunar Semin Probl Fiz Vys Energ Kvantovoi Teor Polya
Mezhdunarodnyi Seminar po Problemam Fiziki Vysokikh Energii. Obzornye Doklady — Mezhdunar Semin Probl Fiz Vys Energ Obz Dokl
Mezhdunarodnyi S'ezd po Infektsionnoi Patologii. Soobshcheniya — Mezhdunar Sezd Infekts Patol Soobshch
Mezhdunarodnyi Simpozium IFAK po Avtomaticheskomu Upravleniyu v Prostanstve — Mezhdunar Simp IFAK Avtom Upr Prostanstve

Mezhdunarodnyi Simpozium Meteorologicheskie Aspekty Radioaktivnogo Zagryazneniya Atmosfery. Trudy — Mezhdunar Simp Meteorol Aspekty Radioakt Zagryaz Atmos Tr
Mezhdunarodnyi Simpozium Metody Prikladnoi Geokhimii — Mezhdunar Simp Metody Prikl Geokhim
Mezhdunarodnyi Simpozium po Bor'be s Serois Gnil'yu Vinograda — Mezhdunar Simp Borbe Seroi Gnilyu Vinograda
Mezhdunarodnyi Simpozium po Boru — Mezhdunar Simp Boru
Mezhdunarodnyi Simpozium po Elektronnoi Strukture Perekhodnykh Metallov. Ikh Splavov i Intermetallicheskikh Soedinenii. Materialy — Mezhdunar Simp Elektron Strukt Perekhodnykh Met Ikh Splavov
Mezhdunarodnyi Simpozium po Fizike Luny i Planet — Mezhdunar Simp Fiz Luny Planet
Mezhdunarodnyi Simpozium po Fizike Vysokikh Energii i Elementarnykh Chastits — Mezhdunar Simp Fiz Vys Energ Elem Chastits
Mezhdunarodnyi Simpozium po Fotograficheskoi Zhelatine. Tezisy Dokladov — Mezhdunar Simp Fotogr Zhelatine Tezisy Dokl
Mezhdunarodnyi Simpozium po Geterogennomu Katalizu Trudy — Mezhdunar Simp Geterog Katal Tr
Mezhdunarodnyi Simpozium po Immunologii Reproduktsii — Mezhdunar Simp Immunol Reprod
Mezhdunarodnyi Simpozium po Izbrannym Problemam Statisticheskoi Mekhaniki. Trudy — Mezhdunar Simp Izbr Probl Stat Mekh Tr
Mezhdunarodnyi Simpozium po Khimicheskim Voloknam — Mezhdunar Simp Khim Voloknam
Mezhdunarodnyi Simpozium po Kompozitsionnym Metallicheskim Materialam — Mezhdunar Simp Kompoz Met Mater
Mezhdunarodnyi Simpozium po Kosmicheskoi Meteorologii — Mezhdunar Simp Kosm Meteorol
Mezhdunarodnyi Simpozium po Nauchno-Tekhnicheskim Problemam Kombikormovoi Promyshlennosti — Mezhdunar Simp Nauchno Tekh Probl Kombikormovoi Promsti
Mezhdunarodnyi Simpozium po Svyazi mezhdu Gomogennym i Geterogennym Katalizom — Mezhdunar Simp Svyazi Gomogennym Geterog Katal
Mezhdunarodnyi Simpozium po Yadernoi Elektronike. Trudy — Mezhdunar Simp Yad Elektron Tr
Mezhdunarodnyi Simpozium po Zharoprochnym Metallicheskim Materialam — Mezhdunar Simp Zharoprochn Met Mater
Mezhdunarodnyi Simpozium po Zimnemu Betonirovaniyu. Doklady — Mezhdunar Simp Zimnemu Betonirovaniyu Dokl
Mezhdunarodnyi Simpozium Polikondensatsii — Mezhdunar Simp Polikondens
Mezhdunarodnyi Simpozium Stran-Chlenov SEV — Mezhdunar Simp Stran Chlenov SEV
Mezhduvedomstvennyi Geofizicheskikh Komitet [*Former USSR*] — Mezhduved Geofiz Kom
Mezhmolekulyarnoe Vzaimodeistvie i Konformatsii Molekul. Tezisy Dokladov Vsesoyuznogo Simpoziuma — Mezhmol Vzaimodeistvie Konform Mole Tezisy Dokl Vses Simp
Mezhneironnaya Peredacha v Vegetativnoi Nervnoi Sisteme. Trudy Vsesoyuznogo Simpoziuma po Voprosam Obshchei Fiziologii Nervnoi Sistemy — Mezhneironnaya Peredacha Veg Nervn Sist Tr Vses Simp Vopr
Mezhvedomstvennoe Soveshchanie po Probleme Metamorfogennogo Rudoobrazovaniya — Mezhved Soveshch Probl Metamorfog Rudoobraz
Mezhvedomstvennyi Geofizicheskii Komitet pri Prezidiume Akademii Nauk Ukrainskoi SSR Informatsionnyi Byulleten — Mezhved Geofiz Kom Prezidiume Akad Nauk Ukr SSR Inf Byull
Mezhvedomstvennyi Sbornik. Leningradskii Gidrometeorologicheskii Institut — Mezhved Sb Lenengr Gidrometeorol Inst
Mezhvedomstvennyi Tematicheskii Sbornik. Moskovskii Energeticheskii Institut — Mezhved Temat Sb Mosk Energ Inst
Mezhvuzovskaya Gistologicheskaya Konferentsiya po Probleme. Reaktivnost i Plastichnost Epiteliya i Soedinietlnoi Tkani v Normalnykh Eksperimentalny Patologicheskikh Usloviyakh — Mezhvuz Gistol Konf Probl Reakt Plast Epiteliya Soedin Tkani
Mezhvuzovskaya Konferentsiya po Voprosam Ispareniya, Goreniya, i Gazovoi Dinamiki Dispersnykh Sistem. Materialy — Mezhvuz Konf Vopr Ispareniya Goreniya Gazov Din Dispersnykh
Mezhvuzovskaya Nauchnaya Konferentsiya Kaunasskogo Meditsinskogo Instituta — Mezhvuz Nauchn Konf Kaunas Med Inst
Mezhvuzovskii Sbornik Nauchnykh i Metodicheskikh Trudov. Yaroslavskii Gosudarstvennyi Pedagogicheskii Institut Imeni K. D. Ushinskogo — Mezhvuz Sb Nauchn Metod Tr Yarosl Gos Pedagog Inst
Mezhvuzovskii Sbornik Nauchnykh Trudov Erevanskii Politekhnicheskii Institut Imeni K. Marksa. Seriya 17. Radiotekhnika, Elektronika — Mezhvuz Sb Nauchn Tr Erevan Politekh Inst Im K Marksa Ser 17
Mezhvuzovskii Sbornik Nauchnykh Trudov Erevanskii Politekhnicheskii Institut Imeni K. Marksa. Seriya 18. Gornoe Delo i Metallurgiya — Mezhvuz Sb Nauchn Tr Erevan Politekh Inst Im K Marksa Ser 18
Mezhvuzovskii Sbornik Nauchnykh Trudov Erevanskii Politekhnicheskii Institut Imeni K. Marksa. Seriya 19. Khimicheskaya Tekhnologiya — Mezhvuz Sb Nauchn Tr Erevan Politekh Inst Im K Marksa Ser 19
Mezhvuzovskii Sbornik Nauchnykh Trudov. Erevanskii Politekhnicheskii Institut. Seriya 19. Khimicheskaya Tekhnologiya — Mezhvuz Sb Nauchn Tr Erevan Politekh Inst Ser 19
Mezhvuzovskii Sbornik Nauchnykh Trudov Leningradskii Tekhnologicheskii Institut Imeni Lensoveta. Mashiny i Tekhnologiya Pererabotki Polimerov — Mezhvuz Sb Nauchn Tr Leningr Tekhnol Inst Im Lensoveta Mash
Mezhvuzovskii Sbornik Nauchnykh Trudov. Permskii Politekhnicheskii Institut — Mezhvuzovskii Sbornik Nauchn Tr Permsk Politekh Inst
Mezhvuzovskii Sbornik Nauchnykh Trudov Yaroslavskii Gosudarstvennyi Pedagogicheskii Institut Imeni K. D. Ushinskogo — Mezhvuz Sb Nauchn Tr Yarosl Gos Pedagog Inst
Mezhvuzovskii Sbornik Trudov Biologicheskoi Kafedry Kirgizskogo Universiteta Seriya Botanicheskaya — Mezhvuz Sb Tr Biol Kafedry Kirg Univ Ser Bot
Mezhvuzovskii Sbornik. Uralskii Politekhnicheskii Institut Imeni S. M. Kirova i Magnitogorskii Gorno-Metallurgicheskii Institut Imeni G. I. Nosova — Mezhvuz Sb Ural Politekh Inst Im S M Kirova Magnitogorsk
Mezhvuzovskii Tematicheskii Sbornik Leningradskii Inzhenerno Stroitel'nyi Institut — Mezhvuz Temat Sb Leningr Inzh Stroit Inst
Mezhvuzovskii Tematicheskii Sbornik Nauchnykh Trudov Leningradskii Inzhenerno Stroitel'nyi Institut — Mezhvuz Temat Sb Nauchn Tr Leningr Inzh Stroit Inst
Mezhvuzovskii Tematicheskii Sbornik Trudov Leningradskii Inzhenerno Stroitel'nyi Institut — Mezhvuz Temat Sb Tr Leningr Inzh Stroit Inst
Mezhvuzovskii Tematicheskii Sbornik. Tyumenskii Gosudarstvennyi Universitet i Tyumenskii Industrial'nyi Institut — Mezhvuz Temat Sb Tr Tyumen Gos Univ Tyumen Ind Inst
Mezhvuzovskii Tematicheskii Sbornik-Yaroslavskii Gosudarstvennyi Universitet — Mezhvuz Temat Sb Yarosl Gos Univ
Mezhvuzovskii Tematicheskii Sbornik-Yaroslavskii Gosudarstvennyi Universitet — Mezhvuzovskii Tematicheskii Sb-Yaroslavskii Gos Univ
Mezinarodni Vztahy — Mezin Vztahy
Mezoegazdasagi Gepesitesi Tanulmanyok A. Mezoegazdasag Gepkiserleti Intezet — Mezogazd Gepesitesi Tanulmanyok Mezogazd Gepkiserl Intez
Mezoegazdasagi Kiserletuegyi Koezpont Evkoenyve — Mezoegazd Kiserl Koezp Evk
Mezoegazdasagi Kutatasok — Mezoegazd Kut
Mezoegazdasagi Kutatasok — Mezoegazd Kutat
Mezoegazdasagi Kutatasok — Mezoegazd Kutatas
Mezoegazdasagi Technika — Mezogazd Tech
Mezoegazdasagi Tudomanyos Koezlemenyek — Mezogazd Tud Kozl
Mezoegazdasagi Vilagirodalom — Mezogazd Vilagirod
Mezoegazdasagi Vilagirodalom — Mezogazd Vilagirodalom
Mezogazdasag es Ipar — Mezogazd Ip
Mezsaimniecibas Problemu Instituta Raksti — Mezsaimn Probl Inst Raksti
Mezzogiorno d'Europa — Mezzogiorn
Mezzogiorno d'Europa. Quarterly Review — Mezzogiorno d'Europa Q R
MF. Cooperative Extension Service. Kansas State University. Manhattan — MF Coop Ext Serv Kans State Univ Manhattan
MF. Society of Manufacturing Engineers — MF Soc Manuf Eng
MFA Bulletin. Museum of Fine Arts [*Boston*] — MFA Bull
MFM. Moderne Fototechnik — MFM Mod Fototech
MF-MP. Milchforschung-Milchpraxis — MF MP Milchforsch Milchprax
MGA Bulletin. Mushroom Growers' Association — MGA Bull
MGCN. Main Group Chemistry News — MGCN Main Group Chem News
MGD Teoriya Energetika Tekhnologiya — MGD Teor Energ Tekhnol
MGG. Molecular and General Genetics — MGG
MGG. Molecular and General Genetics — MGG Mol Gen Genet
MHD. International Conference on Electrical Power Generation — MHD Int Conf Electr Power Gener
MHD. International Conference on Magnetohydrodynamic Electrical Power Generation — MHD Int Conf Magnetohydrodyn Electr Power Gener
Miami Geological Society. Annual Field Trip (Guidebook) — Miami Geol Soc Annu Field Trip (Guideb)
Miami Herald — Miami Heral
Miami International Conference on Alternative Energy Sources — Miami Int Conf Altern Energy Sources
Miami Medicine — Miami Med
Miami Review — Miami Revw
Miami University. School of Marine and Atmospheric Science. Annual Report — Miami Univ Sch Marine Atmos Sci Annu Rep
Miami Winter Symposium — Miami Winter Symp
Miasnaia Industriia SSSR — Miasn Ind SSSR
MIB. Mineral Industries Bulletin [*United States*] — MIB Miner Ind Bull
MIC. Modeling, Identification, and Control [*Norway*] — MIC Model Identif Control
Michigan Academician — MACDA
Michigan Academician — MicA
Michigan Academician — Mich Acad
Michigan Academician — MichA
Michigan Academy of Science, Arts, and Letters. Papers — Mich Acad Sci Papers
Michigan Academy of Science. Report. Annual Report — Mich Ac Sc Rp An Rp
Michigan Administrative Code — Mich Admin Code
Michigan Agricultural College. Experiment Station. Quarterly Bulletin — Mich Agric Coll Exp Stn Q Bull
Michigan. Agricultural Experiment Station. Annual Report — Mich Agric Exp Stn Annu Rep
Michigan Agricultural Experiment Station. Elementary Science Bulletin — Michigan Agric Exp Sta Element Sci Bull
Michigan Agricultural Experiment Station. Folder — Michigan Agric Exp Sta Folder
Michigan. Agricultural Experiment Station. Memoir — Mich Agric Exp Stn Mem
Michigan. Agricultural Experiment Station. Publications — Mich Ag Exp
Michigan. Agricultural Experiment Station. Quarterly Bulletin — Mich Agric Exp Stn Q Bull
Michigan Agricultural Experiment Station. Research Bulletin — Michigan Agric Exp Sta Res Bull
Michigan. Agricultural Experiment Station. Special Bulletin — Mich Agric Exp Stn Spec Bull
Michigan Agricultural Experiment Station. Special Bulletin — Michigan Agric Exp Sta Special Bull
Michigan. Agricultural Experiment Station. Technical Bulletin — Mich Agric Exp Stn Tech Bull
Michigan Alumni Quarterly Review — MAQR
Michigan Alumni Quarterly Review — Mich Alumni Quar Rev
Michigan Appeals Reports — Mich App
Michigan Audubon Newsletter — Mich Audubon Newsl
Michigan Bar Journal — Mich BJ
Michigan Botanist — Mich Bot

Michigan Business — Michigan Bu
Michigan Business Education Association Today — MBEA Today
Michigan Business Papers — Mich Bus Pap
Michigan Business Reports — Mich Bus Rep
Michigan Business Review — Mich Bus R
Michigan Business Studies — Mich Bus Stud
Michigan Compiled Laws — Mich Comp Laws
Michigan Compiled Laws, Annotated (West) — Mich Comp Laws Ann (West)
Michigan Corporate Finance and Business Law Journal — Mich Corp Finance and Bus LJ
Michigan CPA [*Certified Public Accountant*] — MPA
Michigan Dental Association. Journal — Mich Dent Assoc J
Michigan. Department of Conservation. Game Division Report — Mich Dep Conserv Game Div Rep
Michigan. Department of Conservation. Geological Survey Division. Annual Statistical Summary — Mich Dep Conserv Geol Surv Div Annu Stat Summ
Michigan Department of Conservation. Geological Survey Division. Progress Report — Mich Dep Conserv Geol Surv Div Prog Rep
Michigan Department of Conservation. Geological Survey Division. Publication — Mich Dep Conserv Geol Surv Div Publ
Michigan. Department of Conservation. Geological Survey Division. Water Investigation — Mich Dep Conserv Geol Surv Div Water Invest
Michigan Department of Natural Resources. Geological Survey Division. Miscellany — Mich Dep Nat Resour Geol Surv Div Misc
Michigan Dry Bean Digest — Mich Dry Bean Dig
Michigan Economy — Mich Econ
Michigan Education Journal — Mich Ed J
Michigan Energy — Mich Energy
Michigan Entomologist — Mich Ent
Michigan Entomologist — Mich Entomol
Michigan Farm Economics. Michigan State University. Cooperative Extension Service — Mich Farm Econ
Michigan Feminist Studies — Mich Fem Stud
Michigan Geological and Biological Survey Publication. Biological Series — Michigan Geol Biol Surv Publ Biol Ser
Michigan. Geological Survey. Annual Statistical Summary — Michigan Geol Survey Ann Statistical Summ
Michigan. Geological Survey. Bulletin — Mich Geol Surv Bull
Michigan. Geological Survey. Circular — Mich Geol Surv Circ
Michigan Geological Survey Division. Annual Statistical Summary — Mich Geol Surv Div Annu Stat Summ
Michigan. Geological Survey Division. Bulletin — Mich Geol Surv Div Bull
Michigan. Geological Survey Division. Miscellany — MGSMC
Michigan. Geological Survey Division. Miscellany — Mich Geol Surv Div Misc
Michigan. Geological Survey Division. Progress Report — Mich Geol Surv Div Prog Rep
Michigan. Geological Survey Division. Publication — Mich Geol Surv Div Publ
Michigan Geological Survey Division. Report of Investigation — Mich Geol Surv Div Rep Invest
Michigan. Geological Survey Division. Water Investigation — Mich Geol Surv Div Water Invest
Michigan. Geological Survey. Michigan State Board of Geological Survey. Report — Mich G S Rp
Michigan. Geological Survey. Report of Investigation — Mich Geol Surv Rep Invest
Michigan. Geological Survey. Report of Investigation — Michigan Geol Survey Rept Inv
Michigan. Geological Survey. Water Investigation — Michigan Geol Survey Water Inv
Michigan Germanic Studies — MGS
Michigan Governmental Studies — Mich Gov Stud
Michigan Historical Commission. Collections — Mich His Col
Michigan History — MicH
Michigan History — Mich Hist
Michigan History Magazine — MH
Michigan History Magazine — MHM
Michigan History Magazine — Mich His M
Michigan History Magazine — Mich Hist M
Michigan History Magazine — MichH
Michigan Hospitals — Mich Hosp
Michigan International Business Studies — Mich Int Bus Stud
Michigan Investor — Mich Inv
Michigan Jewish History — MJH
Michigan Law Review — IMIL
Michigan Law Review — Mi L
Michigan Law Review — Mich L Rev
Michigan Law Review — Mich Law R
Michigan Law Review — Mich Law Rev
Michigan Law Review — Mich LR
Michigan Law Review — Michigan Law Rev
Michigan Legislative Service — Mich Legis Serv
Michigan Librarian — Mich Libn
Michigan Librarian — Mich Librn
Michigan Library News — Mich Lib News
Michigan Manufacturer and Financial Record — Mich Manuf Fin Rec
Michigan Mathematical Journal — MCMJ
Michigan Mathematical Journal — Mich Math J
Michigan Medical Society. Journal — Mich Med Soc J
Michigan Medicine — Mich Med
Michigan Medicine — Michigan Med
Michigan Miner — Mich Miner
Michigan Molecular Institute Press. Symposium Series — Mich Mol Inst Press Symp Ser
Michigan Municipal Review — Mich Munic R
Michigan Music Educator — Mic
Michigan Music Educator — Mich Mus Educ
Michigan Natural Resources Magazine — Mich Nat Resour Mag
Michigan Nurse — Mich Nurse
Michigan Nurse Newsletter — Mich Nurse Newsl
Michigan Papyri — Mich Papy
Michigan Papyri — P Mich
Michigan Pioneer and Historical Society Collections — Mich Hist Soc Coll
Michigan Quarterly Review — Mich Q Rev
Michigan Quarterly Review — Mich Quart Rev
Michigan Quarterly Review — MichQR
Michigan Quarterly Review — MQR
Michigan Quarterly Review — PMQR
Michigan Register — Mich Reg
Michigan Reports — Mich
Michigan Researcher — Mich Res
Michigan Romance Studies — MRS
Michigan Science in Action. Michigan Agricultural Experiment Station — Mich Sci Action Mich Agric Exp Stn
Michigan State Bar Journal — MBJ
Michigan State Bar Journal — Mich S B J
Michigan State Bar Journal — Mich St BJ
Michigan State College of Agricultural and Applied Science. Agricultural Experiment Station. Quarterly Bulletin — Mich State Coll Agric Appl Sci Agric Exp Stn Q Bull
Michigan State College of Agricultural and Applied Science. Agricultural Experiment Station. Special Bulletin — Mich State Coll Agric Appl Sci Agric Exp Stn Spec Bull
Michigan. State College of Agricultural and Applied Science. Agricultural Experiment Station. Technical Bulletin — Mich State Coll Agric Appl Sci Agric Exp Stn Tech Bull
Michigan State College Veterinarian — Mich State Coll Vet
Michigan State Dental Association. Journal — Mich State Dent Assoc J
Michigan State Dental Society. Bulletin — Mich State Dent Soc Bull
Michigan State Dental Society. Journal — Mich State Dent Soc J
Michigan State Economic Record — Mich State Econ Rec
Michigan State University. Agricultural Experiment Station. Annual Report — Mich State Univ Agric Exp Stn Annu Rep
Michigan. State University. Agricultural Experiment Station. Memoir — Mich State Univ Agric Exp Stn Mem
Michigan. State University. Agricultural Experiment Station. Quarterly Bulletin — Mich State Univ Agric Exp Stn Q Bull
Michigan. State University. Agricultural Experiment Station. Special Bulletin — Mich State Univ Agric Exp Stn Spec Bull
Michigan. State University. Agricultural Experiment Station. Technical Bulletin — Mich State Univ Agric Exp Stn Tech Bull
Michigan State University. Latin American Studies Center. Occasional Papers — Mich State Univ Lat Am Stud Cent Occ Pap
Michigan Statistical Abstract — Mich Stat Abstr
Michigan Statutes, Annotated (Callaghan) — Mich Stat Ann (Callaghan)
Michigan Technological University. Ford Forestry Center. Research Notes — Mich Technol Univ Ford For Cent Res Notes
Michigan University. Engineering Research Institute. Engineering Research Bulletin — Mich Univ Eng Res Inst Eng Res Bull
Michigan University. Institute of Science and Technology. Report — Mich Univ Inst Sci Technol Rep
Michigan University. Museum of Paleontology. Contributions — Michigan Univ Mus Paleontology Contr
Michigan University. Museum of Zoology. Occasional Papers — Mich Univ Mus Zool Oc P
Michigan University. Museum of Zoology. Occasional Papers — Michigan Univ Mus Zoology Occasional Paper
Michigan Water Resources Commission. Report — Mich Water Res Comm Rept
Michigan Yearbook of International Legal Studies — Mich YB Int'l Legal Stud
Michoacan, Mexico. Comision Forestal. Boletin. Serie Tecnica — Michoacan Mex Com For Bol Ser Tec
Micmac News — MIMN
Micologia Italiana — Micol Ital
Micro Decision — Micro Decis
Micro Marketworld — Micro Mktw
Micro Proceedings. Annual Workshop on Microprogramming — Micro Proc Annu Workshop Microprogram
Micro Publisher — Micro Pub
Micro Systems — Micro Syst
Micro - The 6502/6809 Journal — Micro-6502/6809 J
Microbeam Analysis (Deerfield Beach, Florida) — Microbeam Anal Deerfield Beach Fla
Microbeam Analysis. Proceedings. Annual Conference. Microbeam Analysis Society — Microbeam Anal
Microbeam Analysis Society. Annual Conference. Proceedings — Microbeam Anal Soc Annu Conf Proc
Microbial and Comparative Genomics — Microb Comp Genomics
Microbial Culture Information Service [*Database*] — MiCIS
Microbial Drug Resistance — Microb Drug Resist
Microbial Drug Resistance (Larchmont, New York) — Microb Drug Resist Larchmont NY
Microbial Ecology — MCBEB
Microbial Ecology — Microb Ecol
Microbial Ecology of the Phylloplane. Papers Read at the International Symposium on the Microbiology of Leaf Surfaces — Microb Ecol Phylloplane Pap Int Symp Microbiol Leaf Surf
Microbial Genetics Bulletin — Microb Genet Bull
Microbial Geochemistry — Microb Geochem
Microbial Growth on C1 Compounds. Proceedings. International Symposium — Microb Growth C1 Compounds Proc Int Symp
Microbial Pathogenesis — Microb Pathog

Microbiologia Espanola — Microbiol Esp
Microbiologia, Parazitologia, Epidemiologia — Microbiol Parazitol Epidemiol
Microbiologia, Parazitologia, Epidemiologia (Bucharest) — Microbiol Parazitol Epidemiol (Buchar)
Microbiological Abstracts — Microbiol Abstr
Microbiological Research — Microbiol Res
Microbiological Reviews — Microbiol Rev
Microbiological Sciences — Microbiol Sci
Microbiologie, Aliments, Nutrition — Microbiol Aliments Nutr
Microbiology — Microbiolog
Microbiology and Immunology [*Japan*] — Microbiol Immunol
Microbiology and Immunology — MIIMD
Microbiology (English Translation of Mikrobiologiya) — Microbiology (Engl Transl Mikrobiologiya)
Microbiology in Civil Engineering. Proceedings. Federation of European Microbiological Societies Symposium — Microbiol Civ Eng Proc Fed Eur Microbiol Soc Symp
Microbiology of Fish and Meat Curing Brines. Proceedings. International Symposium on Food Microbiology — Microbiol Fish Meat Curing Brines Proc Int Symp
Microbiology Series — Microbiol Ser
Microbiology Series — Microbiol Series
Microbios Letters — Microbios L
Microbios Letters — Microbios Lett
MICROBIOS LETTERS — MICROBIOS LETT
Microcard Theological Studies — MTS
Microchemical Journal — Microchem J
Microchemical Journal. Symposium Series — Microchem J Symp Ser
Microcirculation, Endothelium, and Lymphatics — Microcirc Endothelium Lymphatics
Microcirculation (New York) — Microcirculation (NY)
Microcomposites and Nanophase Materials. Proceedings. Symposium — Microcompos Nanophase Mater Proc Symp
Microcomputer Digest — Microcomp Dig
Microcomputer Index — Microcomput Index
Microcomputer Printout — Microcomput Printout
Microcomputers in Human Resource Management [*Database*] — MHRM
Microcomputing — Microcompu
Microecology and Therapy — Microecol Ther
Microelectronic Engineering — Microelectron Eng
Microelectronics and Reliability — Microel Rel
Microelectronics and Reliability — Microelectron and Reliab
Microelectronics and Reliability — Microelectron Reliab
Microelectronics and Signal Processing — Microelectron Signal Process
Microelectronics. English Translation — Microelectronics Engl Transl
Microelectronics International — Microelectron Int
Microelectronics Journal — Microelectron J
Microfiche Foundation. Newsletter — Microfiche Fdn Newsl
Microfilm Abstracts — MA
Microfilm Abstracts — MfAb
Microfilm Abstracts — Microfilm Abstr
Microform Market Place — MMP
Microform Publication. Geological Society of America — Microform Publ Geol Soc Am
Microform Review — MFRVA
Microform Review — Microform R
Microform Review — Microform Rev
Microform Review — MR
Micrographics Newsletter — Microgr Newsl
Microgravity Science and Technology — Microgravity Sci Technol
Microlepidoptera Palaearctica — Microlepid Palearct
Microlithography World — Microlithogr World
Microlog Fiche Service from Micromedia — MLF
Micron — MICOB
Micron and Microscopica Acta — Micron Microsc Acta
Micronesian Reporter — Micronesian Rep
Micronesica. Journal of the College of Guam — Micronesica J Coll Guam
Micronesica. Journal of the University of Guam — Micronesica J Univ Guam
Microorganisms and Fermentation — Microorg Ferment
Microorganisms and Industry — Microorg Ind
Microorganisms and Infectious Diseases — Microorg Infect Dis
Micropaleontology — Micropaleon
Micropaleontology. Special Publication — Micropaleontolog Spec Publ
Microprobe Analysis — Microprobe Anal
Microprocessing and Microprogramming — Micro
Microprocessing and Microprogramming — Microprocess and Microprogram
Microprocessing and Microprogramming — Microprocess Microprogram
Microprocessor Software Quarterly — Microprocess Software Q
Microprocessors and Microsystems — Microprocess and Microsyst
Microprocessors and Microsystems — Microprocessors Microsysts
Microprocessors at Work — Microprocess Work
Microscope — Microsc
Microscope and Crystal Front — MCRFA
Microscope and Crystal Front [*England*] — Microsc Cryst Front
Microscope and Entomological Monthly — Microsc Entomol Mon
Microscope and Entomological Monthly — Microscope Entomol Monthly
Microscopia Electronica y Biologia Celular — Microsc Electron Biol Cel
Microscopic Aspects of Adhesion and Lubrication. Proceedings. International Meeting. Society de Chimie Physique — Microsc Aspects Adhes Lubr Proc Int Meet Soc Chim Phys
Microscopica Acta — Microsc Act
Microscopica Acta — Microsc Acta
Microscopica Acta. Supplement — Microsc Acta Suppl
Microscopical Society of Canada. Bulletin — Microsc Soc Can Bull
Microscopical Society of Canada. Proceedings — Micros Soc Can Proc
Microscopy Handbooks — Microsc Handb
Microscopy. Journal of the Quekett Microscopical Club — Microsc J Quekett Microsc Club
Microscopy of Oxidation. Proceedings. International Conference — Microsc Oxid Proc Int Conf
Microscopy Research and Technique — Microsc Res Tech
Microscopy Symposium. Proceedings — Micros Symp Proc
Microsomal Particles and Protein Synthesis. Papers Presented at the Symposium — Microsomal Part Protein Synth Pap Symp
Microsomes, Drug Oxidations, and Chemical Carcinogenesis. International Symposium on Microsomes and Drug Oxidations — Microsomes Drug Oxid Chem Carcinog Int Symp Microsomes Drug
Microstructural Science — Microstruct Sci
Microstructural Science [*Elsevier Book Series*] — MS
Microstructural Science — MSSCD
Microsymposium on Macromolecules Polyvinyl Chloride — Microsymp Macromol Polyvinyl Chloride
Microsystems — Microsystm
Microtecnic — Microtec
Microvascular Research — Microvasc R
Microvascular Research — Microvasc Res
Microwave and Optical Technology Letters — Microw Opt Technol Lett
Microwave Energy Applications Newsletter — Microwave Energy Appl Newsl
Microwave Journal — Micro Jrl
Microwave Journal — Microwave J
Microwave Research Institute Symposia Series. Polytechnic Institute of Brooklyn — Microwave Res Inst Symp Ser Polytech Inst Brooklyn
Microwave Research Instutute Symposia Series. Polytechnic Institute of New York — Microwave Res Inst Symp Ser Polytech Inst NY
Microwave Systems News — Microw Syst News
Microwave Systems News — Microwave Syst News
Microwave Systems News — MSN
Microwaves, Optics, and Acoustics — Microwaves Opt Acoust
Microwaves, Optics, and Antennas — Microwaves Opt Antennas
Micul Atlas Lingvistic al Graiurilor Istoromine — MALGI
Mid-America: An Historical Review — M-A
Mid-America. An Historical Review — MAH
Mid-America: An Historical Review — MAHR
Mid-America: An Historical Review — MidA
Mid-America: An Historical Review — Mid-Am
Mid-America: An Historical Review — Mid-Am Hist
Mid-America Oil and Gas Reporter — Mid-Am Oil Gas Rep
Mid-America Spectroscopy Symposium. Proceedings — Mid-Am Spectrosc Symp Proc
Mid-American Outlook — Mid Am Outlk
Mid-American Review of Sociology — Mid Amer Rev Sociol
Mid-Atlantic Industrial Waste Conference — Mid-Atl Ind Waste Conf
Mid-Atlantic Industrial Waste Conference. Proceedings [*United States*] — Mid-Atl Ind Waste Conf Proc
Mid-Atlantic Industrial Waste Conference. Proceedings — MIWPD
Mid-Atlantic Journal of Business — JBZ
MIDC (Metals Industry Development Centre) Bulletin [*Taiwan*] — MIDC Bull
Midcon Conference Record — Midcon Conf Rec
Mid-Continent — Mid-Cont
Midcontinent American Studies. Journal — MASJ
Midcontinent American Studies. Journal — Midcontinent Am Studies Jour
Mid-Continent Banker — Mid Cont Bk
Mid-Continent Lepidoptera Series — Mid-Cont Lepid Ser
Middenstand — MDD
Middle American Research Records (New Orleans) — Mid Am Res Rec New Orleans
Middle East — Middle E
Middle East — Middle Eas
Middle East — MidEast
Middle East — MIL
Middle East. Abstracts and Index — Middle East Abstr Index
Middle East and African Economist — Mid East E
Middle East and African Economist — MIE
Middle East Annual Review — Mid East Ann Rev
Middle East Annual Review — Mid East Annu R
Middle East Architectural Design — Middle East Archtl Design
Middle East Bulletin — MEB
Middle East Business Weekly — Middle East Bus Wkly
Middle East Computing — Middle East Comp
Middle East Dentistry and Oral Health — Middle East Dent Oral Health
Middle East Economic Digest [*London*] — MEED
Middle East Economic Digest — MIA
Middle East Economic Digest — Middle East Econ Dig
Middle East Economic Handbook — ME Eco Hbk
Middle East Economic Papers — MEEP
Middle East Economic Survey — MHE
Middle East Economist [*Cairo*] — MEE
Middle East Electricity — Mid East Elect
Middle East Electronics — Middle East Electron
Middle East Executive Reports — MEE
Middle East Executive Reports — Middle E Executive Rep
Middle East Executive Reports — Middle East Exec Repts
Middle East Executive Reports — MIR
Middle East Financial Directory — Mid East Fin Dir
Middle East Focus — MEFo
Middle East Forum — MEF
Middle East Forum — Mid East Forum
Middle East Journal — GMEJ
Middle East Journal — MDJ
Middle East Journal — MEJ

Middle East Journal — Mid E J
Middle East Journal — Mid East J
Middle East Journal — Middle E J
Middle East Journal — Middle East J
Middle East Journal — MidE
Middle East Journal of Anaesthesiology — Mid East J Anaesthesiol
Middle East Journal of Anaesthesiology — Middle East J Anaesthesiol
Middle East Librarians' Association Notes — MELA Notes
Middle East Medical Assembly. Proceedings — Middle East Med Assem Proc
Middle East Observer — MFG
Middle East Opinion — MEO
Middle East Outreach Coordinators' Newsletter — MEOC News
Middle East Record — MER
Middle East Research and Information Project Reports — MERIP Reports
Middle East Review — Mid East R
Middle East Review — Middle East R
Middle East Review — MiER
Middle East Series [*Elsevier Book Series*] — ME
Middle East Studies Association Bulletin — MESA Bull
Middle East Technical University. Journal of Pure and Applied Sciences — METU J Pure Appl Sci
Middle East Technical University. Journal of Pure and Applied Sciences — Middle East Tech Univ J Pure Appl Sci
Middle East Technical University. Studies in Development — METU Studies Develop
Middle East Technical University. Studies in Development — Stud Develop
Middle East Transport — MST
Middle Eastern Affairs — MEA
Middle Eastern Monographs — MEM
Middle Eastern Monographs — Middle E Mg
Middle Eastern Studies — MES
Middle Eastern Studies — Mid E Stud
Middle Eastern Studies — Mid E Studies
Middle Eastern Studies — Mid East Stud
Middle Eastern Studies — Middle E St
Middle Eastern Studies — PMEA
Middle English Dictionary — MED
Middle States Association of Colleges and Secondary Schools. Proceedings — Middle States Assn Col & Sec Sch Proc
Middle States Council for the Social Studies. Proceedings — Middle States Council for Social Studies Proc
Middle Way. Buddhist Society — MW
Middlebury [*Vermont*] **Historical Society. Papers and Proceedings** — Middlebury Hist Soc Papers and Pr
Mideast File [*Database*] — MEF
Mideast Markets — MMK
Mid-Hudson Language Studies — MHLS
Midland Bank Review — MID
Midland Bank Review — Midland Bank R
Midland Bank Review — Midland Bank Rev
Midland Druggist and Pharmaceutical Review — Midl Drug Pharm Rev
Midland History — Midland Hist
Midland Macromolecular Monographs — Midl Macromol Monogr
Midland Medical and Surgical Reporter. And Topographical and Statistical Journal — Midl Med Surg Reporter Topogr Statist J
Midland Medical Review — Midl Med Rev
Midland Monthly — Midland
Midland Naturalist — Midl Naturalist
Midland Schools — Midland Sch
Midnight Sun. Igloolik — MS
Mid-South Folklore — Mid-S F
Mid-South Neuroscience Development Group Publication — Mid South Neurosci Dev Group Publ
Mid-South Quarterly Business Review — Mid-South Q Bus R
Midstream — Mid
Midstream — Midm
Midwest Conference on Endocrinology and Metabolism — Midwest Conf Endocrinol Metab
Midwest Conference on the Thyroid and Endocrinology — Midwest Conf Throid Endocrinol
Midwest Engineer — Midwest Eng
Midwest English Review — MER
Midwest Folklore — MF
Midwest Folklore — Midwest Folk
Midwest Folklore — MWFL
Midwest Folklore (Indiana University) — MF(I)
Midwest Journal — Midwest J
Midwest Journal — MJ
Midwest Journal of Philosophy — Midwest J Phil
Midwest Journal of Political Science — Midw Jour Pol Sci
Midwest Journal of Political Science — MJPS
Midwest Monographs — MidM
Midwest Museums Conference. American Association of Museums. Quarterly — Midwest Mus Conf Am Assoc Mus Q
Midwest Quarterly — MidQ
Midwest Quarterly — Midw Q
Midwest Quarterly — Midw Quar
Midwest Quarterly — Midwest Q
Midwest Quarterly — MQ
Midwest Quarterly — MWQ
Midwest Quarterly — PMIQ
Midwest Review — MidR
Midwest Review of Public Administration — Midwest R Publ Adm
Midwest Studies in Philosophy — Midw Stud P
Midwest Studies in Philosophy — Midwest Stud Phil
Mid-western Banker — Mid West Bank
Mid-Western Banker — Mid-West Bnk
Midwestern Dentist — Midwest Dent
Midwestern Journal of Language and Folklore — MJLF
Midwestern Miscellany — M Misc
Midwife and Health Visitor [*Later, Midwife, Health Visitor, and Community Nurse*] — Midwife Health Visit
Midwife, Health Visitor, and Community Nurse — Midwife Health Visit Community Nurse
Midwives Chronicle — Midwives Chron
Mie Igaku — MIIGA
Mie Medical Journal — Mie Med J
Mie Medical Journal. Supplement — Mie Med J Suppl
Mie Medical Science [*Japan*] — Mie Med Sci
Mie University. Faculty of Bioresources. Bulletin — Mie Univ Fac Bioresour Bull
Miel de France — Miel Fr
Miesiecznik Koscielny — MK
Miesiecznik Literacki — MLit
Migne Series. Graeca — MG
Migraine Symposium — Migraine Symp
Migration Today — Migr Today
Migrations dans le Monde — Migr dans le Monde
Migrations Internationales — Migr Int
Mikologiya i Fitopatologiya — Mikol Fitopat
Mikologiya i Fitopatologiya — Mikol Fitopatol
Mikrasiatika Chronika — M Khr
Mikrasiatiki Chronika — MCh
Mikrobielle Umwelt und Antimikrobielle Massnahmen — Mikrob Umwelt Antimikrob Massnahmen
Mikrobiologicheskaya Promyshlennost Referativnyi Sbornik — Mikrobiol Prom Ref Sb
Mikrobiologicheskie Protsessy v Pochvakh Moldavii — Mikrobiol Protsessy Pochvakh Mold
Mikrobiologicheskii Sbornik — Mikrobiol Sb
Mikrobiologicheskii Sintez — Mikrobiol Sint
Mikrobiologicheskii Sintez Sbornik Informatsii Materialov — Mikrobiol Sint Sb Inf Mater
Mikrobiologichnyi Zhurnal — Mikrobiol Zh
Mikrobiologicnyj Zurnal/Journal de Microbiologie — Mikrobiol Zurn
Mikrobiologiya — Mikrobiol
Mikrobiologiya dlya Narodnogo Gospodarstva i Meditsini. Materiali Zizdu Ukrainskogo Mikrobiologichnogo Tovaristva — Mikrobiol Nar Gospod Med Mater Zizdu Ukr Mikrobiol Tov
Mikrobiologiya i Proizvodstvo. Doklady Dolozhennye na Konferentsii Mikrobiologov Litovskoi SSR — Mikrobiol Proizvod Dokl Konf Mikrobiol Lit SSR
Mikrobiolohichnyi Zhurnal — Mikrobiol Z
Mikrobiolohichnyi Zhurnal (Kiev) — Mikrobiol Zh (Kiev)
Mikrobiyoloji Bulteni — MIBUB
Mikrobiyoloji Bulteni — Mikrobiyol Bul
Mikrobiyoloji Bulteni. Supplement — Mikrobiyol Bul Suppl
Mikrochemie Vereinigt mit Mikrochimica Acta — Mikrochem Ver Mikrochim Acta
Mikrochimica Acta — Mikroch Act
Mikrochimica Acta — Mikrochim Acta
Mikrochimica Acta. Supplement — Mikrochim Acta Suppl
Mikrochimica Acta. Supplement — MKASA
Mikrochimica et Ichnoanalytica Acta — Mikrochim Ichnoanal Acta
MikroComputer-Praxis — MikroComp Praxis
Mikrocomputer-Zeitschrift — Mikro Comp
Mikroehlektronika — Mikroehlektron
Mikroelektronik. Kongress des Internationalen Elektronik-Arbeitskreises. Vortraege — Mikroelektron Kongr Int Elektron Arbeitskreises Vortr
Mikroelektronika Akademiya Nauk SSSR [*Former USSR*] — Mikroelektronika Akad Nauk SSSR
Mikroelektronika Izdatelstvo Sovetskoe Radio — Mikroelektronika Izd Sov Radio
Mikroelementy v Meditsine [*Ukrainian SSR*] — Mikroelem Med
Mikroelementy v Meditsine — MKEMA
Mikroelementy v Mineralakh — Mikroelem Miner
Mikroelementy v Pochvakh Sovetskogo Soyuza — Mikroelem Pochvakh Sov Soyuza
Mikroelementy v Produktivnost' Rastenii — Mikroelem Prod Rast
Mikroelementy v Rastenievodstve. Trudy Instituta Biologii. Akademiya Nauk Latviiskoi SSR — Mikroelem Rastenievod Tr Inst Biol Akad Nauk Latv SSR
Mikroelementy v Selskom Khozyaistve. Doklady Respublikanskogo Soveshchaniya — Mikroelem Selsk Khoz Dokl Resp Soveshch
Mikroelementy v Selskom Khozyaistve i Meditsine — Mikroelem Sel'sk Khoz Med
Mikroelementy v Selskom Khozyaistve i Meditsine. Doklady Vsesoyuznogo Soveshchaniya po Mikroelementam — Mikroelem Selsk Khoz Med Dokl Vses Soveshch
Mikroelementy v Selskom Khozyaistve i Meditsine. Materialy Vsesoyuznogo Soveshchaniya po Voprosam Primeneniya Mikroelementov v Selskom Khozyaistve Meditsine — Mikroelem Selsk Khoz Med Mater Vses Soveshch
Mikroelementy v Selskom Khozyaistve i Meditsine Respublikanskii Mezhvedomstvennyi Sbornik (Kiev) — Mikroelem Sel Khoz Med Resp Mezhved Sb (Kiev)
Mikroelementy v Selskom Khozyaistve i Meditsine. Trudy Vsesoyuznogo Soveshchaniya po Mikroelementam — Mikroelem Selsk Khoz Med Tr Vses Soveshch
Mikroelementy v Sibiri — Mikroelem Sib
Mikroelementy v Sibiri Informatsionnyi Byulleten — Mikroelem Sib Inf Byull
Mikroelementy v SSSR. Naucnyj Sovet po Probleme Biologiceskaja rol' Mikroelementov v Zizni Rastenij, Zivotnyh i Celoveka — Mikroelem SSSR
Mikroelementy v Vostochnoi Sibiri i na Dal'nem Vostoke — Mikroelem Vost Sib Dal'nem Vostoke

Mikroelementy v Zhivotnovodstve i Rastenievodstve — Mikroelem Zhivotnovod Rastenievod
Mikroelementy v Zhizni Rastenii i Zhivotnykh. Trudy Konferentsii po Mikroelementam — Mikroelem Zhizni Rast Zhivotn Tr Konf
Mikrogeometriya i Ekspluatatsionnye Svoistva Mashin — Mikrogeom Ekspl Svoistva Mash
Mikro-Klein Computer — Mikro-Klein Comput
Mikrooekologie und Therapie — Mikrooekol Ther
Mikroorganizmy i Rasteniya — Mikroorg i Rast
Mikroorganizmy i Rasteniya. Trudy Instituta Mikrobiologii Akademii Nauk Latviiskoi SSR — Mikroorg Rast Trudy Inst Mikrobiol Akad Nauk Latvii SSR
Mikroorganizmy v Selskom Khozyaistve. Trudy Mezhvuzovskoi Nauchnoi Konferentsii — Mikroorg Selsk Khoz Tr Mezhvuz Nauchn Konf
Mikroprovod i Pribory Soprotivleniya — Mikroprovod Prib Sopr
Mikroskopie fuer Naturfreunde — Mikroskop Naturfr
Mikroweilen and Military Electronics — Mikrowelin
Mikrowellen Magazin — Mikrowellen Mag
Mikrozirkulation in Forschung und Klinik — Mikrozirk Forsch Klin
Milan. Seminario Matematico e Fisico. Rendiconti — Milan Semin Mat Fis Rend
Milbank Memorial Fund. Annual Report — Milbank Mem Fund Annu Rep
Milbank Memorial Fund. Quarterly — Milb Mem Fund Q
Milbank Memorial Fund. Quarterly — Milbank Mem
Milbank Memorial Fund. Quarterly — Milbank Mem Fund Q
Milbank Memorial Fund. Quarterly — Milbank Memor Fund Quart
Milbank Memorial Fund. Quarterly Bulletin — Milbank Mem Fund Q Bull
Milbank Memorial Fund. Quarterly. Health and Society — Milbank Meml Fund Q Health Soc
Milbank Memorial Fund. Quarterly. Health and Society — MMFQ
Milbank Quarterly — Milbank Q
Milch Praxis und Rindermast — Milch Prax Rindermast
Milch- und Butter-Industrie — Milch Butter Ind
Milchforschung-Milchpraxis — Milchforsch-Milchprax
Milchwirtschaftliche Berichte aus dem Bundesanstalten Wolfpassing und Rotholz — Milchwirtsch Ber Bundesanst Wolfpassing Rotholz
Milchwirtschaftliche Forschungen — Milchwirtsch Forsch
Milchwirtschaftliche Zeitung — Milchwirtsch Ztg
Milchwirtschaftliche Zeitung fuer den Alpen-, Sudeten- und Donauraum — Milchwirtsch Ztg Alpen Sudeten Donauraum
Milchwirtschaftliches Zentralblatt — Milchwirtsch Zentralbl
Milchwissenschaft — Milchwiss
Milchwissenschaft. Milk Science International — Milchwissenschaft Milk Sci Int
Milchwissenschaftliche Berichte — Milchwiss Ber
Milchwissenschaftliche Berichte — Miwi Ber
Milch-Zeitung — Milch Ztg
Miles International Symposium Series — Miles Int Symp Ser
Milestones in Connecticut Agricultural and Home Economics — Milestones Conn Agr Home Econ
Milieudefensie — MDY
Milieuhygiene — MYH
Militaergeschichte — Mil
Militaergeschichte — Militaergesch
Militaer-Musikerzeitung — Milit Musikerztg
Militaer-Musikerzeitung — MM Zt
Militaerpolitik Dokumentation — Militaerpol Dok
Militaerpsykologiska Institutet — MPI
Militaerregierungsgesetz — MRG
Militaerregierungsverordnung — MRVO
Militaert Tidsskrift — Mil T
Militaert Tidsskrift — Militaert T
Militaertechnik — MILTA
Militair Keuringsreglement — MKR
Militair Rechtelijk Tijdschrift — Mil R Ts
Militair Rechtelijk Tijdschrift — MRT
Militaire Spectator — M Sp
Military Affairs — MA
Military Affairs — Mil Aff
Military Affairs — Mil Affairs
Military Affairs — MilA
Military Affairs — Milit Aff
Military Airbase — Ml Airbase
Military Airports — Ml Airport
Military Balance — Ml Balance
Military Chaplains' Review — Mil Chapl Rev
Military Electronics — Mil Electron
Military Electronics/Countermeasures — Mil Electron/Countermeas
Military Engineer — Mil Eng
Military Engineer — Ml Eng
Military Fiber Optics News — Mil Fib Opt N
Military History Journal — Mil Hist J
Military History of Texas and the Southwest — Milit Hist Tex Southwest
Military History Quarterly — MHQ
Military Intelligence — Ml Intel
Military Law Reporter — Mil L Rep
Military Law Review — Mil L Rev
Military Law Review — Mil LR
Military Law Review — Milit LR
Military Law Review — Military Law R
Military Law Review — Milt Law R
Military Market Annual — Military M
Military Medical and Pharmaceutical Review (Belgrade) — Mil Med Pharm Rev (Belgrade)
Military Medicine — Mil Med
Military Medicine — Milit Med
Military Medicine — MMEDA
Military Review — Mil Rev
Military Review — Milit Rev
Military Review — Military R
Military Review — Ml Rev
Military Review (Kansas) — MRK
Military Science and Technology — Mil Sci Tech
Military Surgeon — Mil Surg
Military Surgeon — Mil Surgeon
Military Technology — ML Tech
Milk and Dairy Research. Report — Milk Dairy Res Rep
Milk Board Journal — Milk Board J
Milk Dealer — Milk Dlr
Milk Industry — Milk Ind
Milk Industry Foundation. Convention Proceedings. Laboratory Section — Milk Ind Found Conv Proc Lab Sect
Milk Industry Foundation. Convention Proceedings. Milk Supplies Section — Milk Ind Found Conv Proc Milk Supplies Sect
Milk Industry Foundation. Convention Proceedings. Plant Section — Milk Ind Found Conv Proc Plant Sect
Milk Inspector — Milk Insp
Milk Intolerances and Rejection. Symposium of Gastroenterology and Nutrition on Milk Intolerances — Milk Intolerances Rejection Symp Gastroenterol Nutr Milk
Milk Plant Monthly — Milk Plant Mo
Milk Plant Monthly — Milk Plant Mon
Milk Producer — Milk Prod
Milk Products Journal — Milk Prod J
Milk Sanitarian — Milk Sanit
Milk Science International — Milk Sci Int
Milk Trade Gazette — Milk Trade Gaz
Milkweed Chronicle — Milkweed Chron
Mill and Factory — Mill Fact
Mill News Letter — Mill News Lett
Mill Newsletter — Mill News
Mill Newsletter — MillN
Milla Wa-Milla — MWM
Millenaire Monastique du Mont Saint-Michel — MMMSM
Millgate Monthly — Millgate Mo
Milling and Baking News — Milling
Milling Feed and Fertiliser — Milling Feed Fert
Milling Feed and Fertilizer — FET
Milling Feed and Fertilizer — Milling F & F
Miloticky Hospodar. Milotice nad Becvou — Miloticky Hospod
Milton and the Romantics — M & R
Milton Centre of Japan. News — MCJ News
Milton Keynes Journal of Archaeology and History — Milton Keynes J Archaeol Hist
Milton Newsletter — Milton N
Milton Quarterly — Milton Q
Milton Quarterly — MQ
Milton Studies — Milton S
Milton Studies — Milton Stud
Milton Studies — MStud
Miltronics — Miltron
Milupa AG. Wissenschaftliche Abteilung. Wissenschaftliche Information — Milupa AG Wiss Abt Wiss Inf
Milupa Med. Wissenschaftliche Abteilung. Wissenschaftliche Information — Milupa Med Wiss Abt Wiss Inf
Milwaukee Bar Association. Gavel — Gavel
Milwaukee Bar Association. Gavel — Milw BAG
Milwaukee Journal — Milwau Jl
Milwaukee Public Museum. Contributions in Biology and Geology — Milw Public Mus Contrib Biol Geol
Milwaukee Public Museum. Occasional Papers. Natural History — Milw Public Mus Occas Pap Nat Hist
Milwaukee Public Museum. Publications in Biology and Geology — Milw Public Mus Publ Biol Geol
Milwaukee Public Museum. Special Publications in Biology and Geology — Milw Public Mus Spec Publ Biol Geol
Mimbar Ulama [*Jakarta*] — Mim Ulama
Mimeo AS. Indiana Agricultural Experiment Station — Mimeo AS Indiana Agr Exp Sta
Mimeo AY. Indiana Agricultural Experiment Station — Mimeo AY Indiana Agr Exp Sta
Mimeo. Co-Operative Extension Service. Purdue University — Mimeo Co-Op Ext Serv Purdue Univ
Mimeo EC. Purdue University. Cooperative Extension Service — Mimeo EC Purdue Univ Coop Ext Serv
Mimeo ID. Purdue University. Department of Agricultural Extension — Mimeo ID Purdue Univ Dept Agr Ext
Mimeo Report. Department of Agricultural Economics. Florida Agricultural Experiment Stations — Mimeo Rep Fla Dep Agric Econ
Mimeo Report. Department of Soils. Agricultural Experiment Station. University of Florida — Mimeo Rep Dep Soils Agric Exp Stn Univ Fl
Mimeo Report. Florida Everglades Experiment Station — Mimeo Rep Fla Everglades Exp Sta
Mimeograph Bulletin A-E. Ohio State University. Department of Agricultural Economics and Rural Sociology — Mimeogr Bull A-E Ohio State Univ Dept Agr Econ Rural Sociol
Mimeograph Circular. Oklahoma Agricultural Experiment Station — Mimeogr Circ Okla Agric Exp Stn
Mimeograph Circular. University of Rhode Island. Extension Service in Agriculture and Home Economics — Mimeogr Circ Univ RI Ext Serv Agr Home Econ
Mimeograph Circular. Wyoming Agricultural Experiment Station — Mimeo Circ Wyo Agric Exp Stn

Mimeograph Circular. Wyoming Agricultural Experiment Station — Mimeogr Circ Wyo Agr Exp Sta
Mimeograph Series. Arkansas Agricultural Experiment Station — Mimeogr Ser Ark Agr Exp Sta
Mimeograph Series. Arkansas Agricultural Experiment Station — Mimeogr Ser Ark Agric Exp Stn
Mimeograph Series. Arkansas. Agricultural Experiment Station — Mimeogr Ser Arkansas Agric Exp Stn
Mimeograph Series. Georgia Agricultural Experiment Station — Mimeogr Ser GA Agr Exp Sta
Mimeograph Series. Georgia Agricultural Experiment Station — Mimeogr Ser GA Agric Exp Stn
Mimeograph Series. Southwest Missouri State University. State Fruit Experiment Station — Mimeogr Ser Southwest Mo State Univ State Fruit Exp Stn
Mimeograph Series. University of Arkansas. Agricultural Experiment Station — Mimeogr Ser Univ Arkansas Agric Exp Stn
Mimeograph Series. Utah Agricultural Experiment Station — Mimeogr Ser Utah Agr Exp Sta
Mimeographed Circular. Research Council of Alberta — Mimeogr Circ Res Counc Alberta
Mimeographed Circular Service. Nova Scotia Department of Agriculture and Marketing — Mimeo Circ NS Dep Agric
Mimeographed Publication. Hawaii University. Department of Horticulture — Mimeogr Publ Hawaii Univ Dept Hort
Mimeographed Publications. Commonwealth Bureau of Pastures and Field Crops — Mimeogr Publ Commonwealth Bur Pastures Field Crops
Mimeographed Publications. Commonwealth Bureau of Pastures and Field Crops — Mimeogrd Publ Commonw Bur Past Fld Crops
Mimeographed Report. Cambridge University. School of Agriculture. Farm Economics Branch — Mimeogr Rep Cambridge Univ Sch Agr Farm Econ Br
Minamata Disease — Minamata Dis
Minas Gerais, Brazil. Instituto Agronomicao. Circular — Minas Gerais Braz Inst Agron Circ
Minas Gerais. Suplemento Literario — MGSL
Mind — Mi
Mind — PMND
Mind and Medicine Monographs — Mind Med Monogr
Mind as a Tissue. Proceedings of a Conference — Mind Tissue Proc Conf
Mind Your Own Business — Mind Your Own Bus
Mindenee Gyuejtemeny — Mind Gyuejt
Mindener Jahrbuch — MJB
Mine and Quarry — MQRYA
Mine and Quarry Engineering — Min Qua Engng
Mine and Quarry Engineering — Mine & Quarry Eng
Mine and Quarry Mechanisation — Mine Quarry Mech
Mine Data Sheets to Accompany Metallogenic Map 1:250,000 [*Sydney*] — Mine Data Sheets Metallog Map 1:250000
Mine Development Monthly — Mine Dev Mon
Mine Drainage. Proceedings. International Mine Drainage Symposium — Mine Drain Proc Int Mine Drain Symp
Mine Injuries and Worktime Quarterly — Mine Inj Worktime Q
Mine, Petrol, si Gaze [*Romania*] — Mine Pet Gaze
Mine, Petrol, si Gaze (Bucharest) — Mine Pet & Gaze (Bucharest)
Mine, Petrol, si Gaze (Bucharest) — Mine Pet Gaze (Bucharest)
Mine Safety and Health [*United States*] — Mine Saf Health
Mine Safety and Health Reporter. Bureau of National Affairs — Mine Safety & Health Rep BNA
Mine Subsidence Control. Proceedings. Bureau of Mines Technology Transfer Seminar — Mine Subsidence Control Proc Bur Mines Technol Transfer Semin
Mine Ventilation — Mine Vent
Mineracao e Metalurgia (Rio de Janeiro) — Miner Metalur Rio
Mineracao, Metalurgia [*Brazil*] — Min Metal
Mineracao, Metalurgia — Miner Metal
Mineracao, Metalurgia, Geologia — Min Metal Geol
Mineral and Electrolyte Metabolism [*Switzerland*] — Miner Electrolyte Metab
Mineral and Energy Resources [*United States*] — Miner Energy Resour
Mineral Assessment Report. Institute of Geological Sciences — Miner Assess Rep Inst Geol Sci
Mineral Bioprocessing. Proceedings. Conference — Miner Bioprocess Proc Conf
Mineral Brief. British Geological Survey — Miner Brief Br Geol Surv
Mineral Bulletin [*Canada*] — Miner Bull
Mineral Bulletin. Energy, Mines, and Resources Canada — Miner Bull Energy Mines Resour Can
Mineral Commodity Profiles — Miner Commod Profiles
Mineral Commodity Profiles. Aluminum — MCP Alum
Mineral Commodity Profiles. Chromium — MCP Chrom
Mineral Commodity Profiles. Clays — MCP Clays
Mineral Commodity Profiles. Cobalt — MCP Cobalt
Mineral Commodity Profiles. Columbium — MCP Columb
Mineral Commodity Profiles. Copper — MCP Copper
Mineral Commodity Profiles. Iron and Steel — MCP Iron
Mineral Commodity Profiles. Iron Ore — MCP Iron O
Mineral Commodity Profiles. Lead — MCP Lead
Mineral Commodity Profiles. Manganese — MCP Mang
Mineral Commodity Profiles. Nickel — MCP Nickel
Mineral Commodity Profiles. Platinum Group Metals — MCP Plat
Mineral Commodity Profiles. Potash — MCP Potash
Mineral Commodity Profiles. Silicon — MCP Silicn
Mineral Commodity Profiles. Silver — MCP Silver
Mineral Commodity Profiles. Soda Ash, Sodium Carbonate, and Sodium Sulfate — MCP Soda A
Mineral Commodity Profiles. Tantalum — MCP Tantlm
Mineral Commodity Profiles. Titanium — MCP Titanm
Mineral Commodity Profiles. US Bureau of Mines — MCP
Mineral Commodity Profiles. Vanadium — MCP Vandm
Mineral Commodity Profiles. Zinc — MCP Zinc
Mineral Deposit Inventory Database — MDI
Mineral Deposits — Miner Deposits
Mineral Deposits Circular. Ontario Geological Survey — Miner Deposits Circ Ontario Geol Surv
Mineral Deposits of the Alps and of the Alpine Epoch in Europe. Proceedings. International Symposium on Mineral Deposits of the Alps — Miner Deposits Alps Alp Epoch Eur Proc Int Symp
Mineral Dossier. Mineral Resources Consultative Committee — Miner Dossier Miner Resour Consult Comm
Mineral Dressing Notes — Miner Dressing Notes
Mineral Economics Series (Indiana Geological Survey) — Miner Econ Ser (Indiana Geol Surv)
Mineral Facts and Problems. Preprint. Aluminum — MFP Alum
Mineral Facts and Problems. Preprint. Antimony — MFP Antim
Mineral Facts and Problems. Preprint. Arsenic — MFP Arsenc
Mineral Facts and Problems. Preprint. Asbestos — MFP Asbsts
Mineral Facts and Problems. Preprint. Barite — MFP Barite
Mineral Facts and Problems. Preprint. Beryllium — MFP Beryl
Mineral Facts and Problems. Preprint. Bismuth — MFP Bis
Mineral Facts and Problems. Preprint. Boron — MFP Boron
Mineral Facts and Problems. Preprint. Bromine — MFP Bromin
Mineral Facts and Problems. Preprint. Cadmium — MFP Cadm
Mineral Facts and Problems. Preprint. Clays — MFP Clays
Mineral Facts and Problems. Preprint. Columbium — MFP Columb
Mineral Facts and Problems. Preprint. Copper — MFP Copper
Mineral Facts and Problems. Preprint. Crushed Stone — MFP C Stone
Mineral Facts and Problems. Preprint. Diamond - Industrial — MFP Diamnd
Mineral Facts and Problems. Preprint. Dimension Stone — MFP Dime S
Mineral Facts and Problems. Preprint. Feldspar — MFP Feldsp
Mineral Facts and Problems. Preprint. Gallium — MFP Gallm
Mineral Facts and Problems. Preprint. Garnet — MFP Garnet
Mineral Facts and Problems. Preprint. Germanium — MFP Germnu
Mineral Facts and Problems. Preprint. Gold — MFP Gold
Mineral Facts and Problems. Preprint. Gypsum — MFP Gypsum
Mineral Facts and Problems. Preprint. Indium — MFP Indium
Mineral Facts and Problems. Preprint. Iodine — MFP Iodine
Mineral Facts and Problems. Preprint. Iron Ore — MFP Iron O
Mineral Facts and Problems. Preprint. Lead — MFP Lead
Mineral Facts and Problems. Preprint. Magnesium — MFP Magn
Mineral Facts and Problems. Preprint. Manganese — MFP Mang
Mineral Facts and Problems. Preprint. Mica — MFP Mica
Mineral Facts and Problems. Preprint. Molybdenum — MFP Moly
Mineral Facts and Problems. Preprint. Peat — MFP Peat
Mineral Facts and Problems. Preprint. Perlite — MFP Perlit
Mineral Facts and Problems. Preprint. Quartz — MFP Quartz
Mineral Facts and Problems. Preprint. Rubidium — MFP Rubid
Mineral Facts and Problems. Preprint. Salt — MFP Salt
Mineral Facts and Problems. Preprint. Sand and Gravel — MFP Sand
Mineral Facts and Problems. Preprint. Selenium — MFP Sel
Mineral Facts and Problems. Preprint. Silicon — MFP Silicn
Mineral Facts and Problems. Preprint. Silver — MFP Silver
Mineral Facts and Problems. Preprint. Soda Ash and Sodium Sulfate — MFP Soda A
Mineral Facts and Problems. Preprint. Strontium — MFP Stront
Mineral Facts and Problems. Preprint. Sulfur — MFP Sulfur
Mineral Facts and Problems. Preprint. Tellurium — MFP Tellur
Mineral Facts and Problems. Preprint. Thorium — MFP Thorm
Mineral Facts and Problems. Preprint. Tin — MFP Tin
Mineral Facts and Problems. Preprint. Titanium — MFP Titanm
Mineral Facts and Problems. Preprint. Tungsten — MFP Tungst
Mineral Facts and Problems. Preprint. Vanadium — MFP Vandm
Mineral Facts and Problems. Preprint. Vermiculite — MFP Vermic
Mineral Facts and Problems. Preprint. Zinc — MFP Zinc
Mineral Facts and Problems. Preprint. Zirconium and Hafnium — MFP Zirc
Mineral Facts and Problems. Preprints — MFP Prepnt
Mineral Fertilizers and Insectofungicides — Miner Fert Insectofungi
Mineral Industries [*United States*] — Miner Ind
Mineral Industries Bulletin — Miner Ind Bull
Mineral Industries Bulletin. Colorado School of Mines — CSMIA
Mineral Industries Bulletin. Colorado School of Mines — Miner Ind Bull Colo Sch Mines
Mineral Industries Journal — Miner Ind J
Mineral Industries Journal — Mineral Industries Jour
Mineral Industries Research Laboratory. University of Alaska. Report — Miner Ind Res Lab Univ Alaska Rep
Mineral Industries (University Park, Pennsylvania) — Miner Ind (University Park PA)
Mineral Industry Location System [*Database*] — MILS
Mineral Industry (New York) — Miner Ind (NY)
Mineral Industry of New South Wales — Miner Ind NSW
Mineral Industry Quarterly — Min Ind Q
Mineral Industry Quarterly. South Australia — Miner Ind Q South Aust
Mineral Industry Research Laboratory Report. University of Alaska — Miner Ind Res Lab Rep Univ Alaska
Mineral Industry Surveys. Abrasive Materials — MIS Abr
Mineral Industry Surveys. Advance Data on Peat — MIS Peat
Mineral Industry Surveys. Aluminum — Miner Ind Surv Alum
Mineral Industry Surveys. Aluminum — MIS Alum
Mineral Industry Surveys. Aluminum and Bauxite — Miner Ind Surv Alum Baux
Mineral Industry Surveys. Antimony — Miner Ind Surv Antimony
Mineral Industry Surveys. Antimony — MIS Antim
Mineral Industry Surveys. Asbestos — MIS Asbsts
Mineral Industry Surveys. Asphalt — MIS Asphlt

Mineral Industry Surveys. Barite — MIS Barite
Mineral Industry Surveys. Bauxite — Miner Ind Surv Bauxite
Mineral Industry Surveys. Bauxite — MIS Baux
Mineral Industry Surveys. Bauxite — MIS Bauxit
Mineral Industry Surveys. Beryllium — MIS Beryl
Mineral Industry Surveys. Bismuth — Miner Ind Surv Bismuth
Mineral Industry Surveys. Bismuth — MIS Bis
Mineral Industry Surveys. Block and Film Mica — MIS B Mica
Mineral Industry Surveys. Boron. Annual Advance Summary — MIS Boron
Mineral Industry Surveys. Bromine — MIS Bromin
Mineral Industry Surveys. Cadmium — Miner Ind Surv Cadmium
Mineral Industry Surveys. Cadmium — MIS Cadm
Mineral Industry Surveys. Calcium and Calcium Compounds — MIS Calcm
Mineral Industry Surveys. Carbon Black — Miner Ind Surv Carbon Black
Mineral Industry Surveys. Cement — Miner Ind Surv Cem
Mineral Industry Surveys. Cement — MIS Cement
Mineral Industry Surveys. Cesium and Rubidium — MIS Cesium
Mineral Industry Surveys. Chromium — Miner Ind Surv Chromium
Mineral Industry Surveys. Chromium — MIS Chrom
Mineral Industry Surveys. Clays — MIS Clays
Mineral Industry Surveys. Cobalt — Miner Ind Surv Cobalt
Mineral Industry Surveys. Cobalt — MIS Cobalt
Mineral Industry Surveys. Coke and Coal Chemicals — Miner Ind Surv Coke Coal Chem
Mineral Industry Surveys. Columbium and Tantalum — MIS Columb
Mineral Industry Surveys. Copper — MIS Copper
Mineral Industry Surveys. Copper in the United States — Miner Ind Surv Copper US
Mineral Industry Surveys. Copper Industry — Miner Ind Surv Copper Ind
Mineral Industry Surveys. Copper Industry — MIS Cl
Mineral Industry Surveys. Copper Production — Miner Ind Surv Copper Prod
Mineral Industry Surveys. Copper Sulfate — Miner Ind Surv Copper Sulfate
Mineral Industry Surveys. Copper Sulfate — MIS Cs
Mineral Industry Surveys. Corundum — MIS Corund
Mineral Industry Surveys. Diamond - Industrial — MIS Diamnd
Mineral Industry Surveys. Diatomite — MIS Diato
Mineral Industry Surveys. Dimension Stone in 1982 — MIS Dime S
Mineral Industry Surveys. Explosives — Miner Ind Surv Explos
Mineral Industry Surveys. Explosives — MIS Explsv
Mineral Industry Surveys. Feldspar and Related Minerals — MIS Feldsp
Mineral Industry Surveys. Ferroalloys — MIS Ferro
Mineral Industry Surveys. Ferrosilicon — Miner Ind Surv Ferrosilicon
Mineral Industry Surveys. Ferrosilicon — MIS Ferros
Mineral Industry Surveys. Ferrous Metals Supply and Demand Data — MIS F Mtls
Mineral Industry Surveys. Fluorspar — Miner Ind Surv Fluorspar
Mineral Industry Surveys. Fluorspar in 1975 — MIS Fluor
Mineral Industry Surveys. Fuel Oils by Sulfur Content — Miner Ind Surv Fuel Oils Sulfur Content
Mineral Industry Surveys. Gallium — MIS Gallm
Mineral Industry Surveys. Garnet — MIS Garnet
Mineral Industry Surveys. Gem Stones — MIS Gem St
Mineral Industry Surveys. Gem Stones. Annual Advance Summary — MIS Gem
Mineral Industry Surveys. Gold and Silver — Miner Ind Surv Gold Silver
Mineral Industry Surveys. Gold and Silver — MIS Gold
Mineral Industry Surveys. Graphite — MIS Grapht
Mineral Industry Surveys. Gypsum — Miner Ind Surv Gypsum
Mineral Industry Surveys. Gypsum — MIS Gypsum
Mineral Industry Surveys. Gypsum Mines and Calcining Plants — MIS Gyp Mn
Mineral Industry Surveys. Iodine. Annual Advance Summary — MIS Iodine
Mineral Industry Surveys. Iron and Steel — MIS Iron
Mineral Industry Surveys. Iron and Steel Scrap — Miner Ind Surv Iron Steel Scrap
Mineral Industry Surveys. Iron and Steel Scrap — MIS I & S
Mineral Industry Surveys. Iron Ore — Miner Ind Surv Iron Ore
Mineral Industry Surveys. Iron Ore — MIS Iron O
Mineral Industry Surveys. Iron Oxide Pigments — MIS Ir Ox
Mineral Industry Surveys. Kyanite and Related Minerals — MIS Kyan
Mineral Industry Surveys. Lead Industry — Miner Ind Surv Lead Ind
Mineral Industry Surveys. Lead Industry — MIS Lead
Mineral Industry Surveys. Lead Production — Miner Ind Surv Lead Prod
Mineral Industry Surveys. Lead Production — MIS Lead P
Mineral Industry Surveys. Lime — Miner Ind Surv Lime
Mineral Industry Surveys. Lime — MIS Lime
Mineral Industry Surveys. Lithium — MIS Lith
Mineral Industry Surveys. Magnesium — Miner Ind Surv Magnesium
Mineral Industry Surveys. Magnesium and Magnesium Compounds — MIS Magn
Mineral Industry Surveys. Manganese — Miner Ind Surv Manganese
Mineral Industry Surveys. Manganese — MIS Mang
Mineral Industry Surveys. Mercury — Miner Ind Surv Mercury
Mineral Industry Surveys. Mercury — MIS Mercry
Mineral Industry Surveys. Mercury — MIS Mercury
Mineral Industry Surveys. Mica — MIS Mica
Mineral Industry Surveys. Molybdenum — Miner Ind Surv Molybdenum
Mineral Industry Surveys. Molybdenum — MIS Moly
Mineral Industry Surveys. Natural Gas — Miner Ind Surv Nat Gas
Mineral Industry Surveys. Natural Gas Liquids — Miner Ind Surv Nat Gas Liq
Mineral Industry Surveys. Natural Graphite — MIS Graph
Mineral Industry Surveys. Nickel — Miner Ind Surv Nickel
Mineral Industry Surveys. Nickel — MIS Nickel
Mineral Industry Surveys. Nitrogen — MIS Nitro
Mineral Industry Surveys. Nonferrous Metals — MIS Nonfer
Mineral Industry Surveys. PAD Districts Supply/Demand — Miner Ind Surv PAD Dist Supply/Demand
Mineral Industry Surveys. Peat Producers in the United States in 1980 — MIS Peat P
Mineral Industry Surveys. Perlite — MIS Perlit
Mineral Industry Surveys. Petroleum Statement — Miner Ind Surv Pet Statement
Mineral Industry Surveys. Phosphate Rock — Miner Ind Surv Phosphate Rock
Mineral Industry Surveys. Phosphate Rock — MIS Phos R
Mineral Industry Surveys. Platinum — Miner Ind Surv Platinum
Mineral Industry Surveys. Platinum — MIS Plat
Mineral Industry Surveys. Potash. Annual Advance Summary — MIS Potash
Mineral Industry Surveys. Primary Magnesium — MIS P Magn
Mineral Industry Surveys. Pumice and Volcanic Cinder — MIS Pumice
Mineral Industry Surveys. Quarterly — MIS Qtly
Mineral Industry Surveys. Quartz Crystals — MIS Quartz
Mineral Industry Surveys. Raw Nonfuel Mineral Production — MIS Nonfl M
Mineral Industry Surveys. Rhenium — MIS Rhenm
Mineral Industry Surveys. Salt — MIS Salt
Mineral Industry Surveys. Sand and Gravel — MIS Sand
Mineral Industry Surveys. Selenium — Miner Ind Surv Selenium
Mineral Industry Surveys. Selenium — MIS Sel
Mineral Industry Surveys. Silicon — Miner Ind Surv Silicon
Mineral Industry Surveys. Silicon — MIS Silicn
Mineral Industry Surveys. Slag, Iron, and Steel — MIS Slag
Mineral Industry Surveys. Sodium Compounds — Miner Ind Surv Sodium Compd
Mineral Industry Surveys. Sodium Compounds — MIS Sodium
Mineral Industry Surveys. Sodium Compounds Annual — MIS Sod C
Mineral Industry Surveys. Stone — MIS Stone
Mineral Industry Surveys. Strontium — MIS Stront
Mineral Industry Surveys. Sulfur — Miner Ind Surv Sulfur
Mineral Industry Surveys. Sulfur — MIS Sulfur
Mineral Industry Surveys. Talc, Soapstone, and Pyrophyllite — MIS Talc
Mineral Industry Surveys. Tin — Miner Ind Surv Tin
Mineral Industry Surveys. Tin — MIS Tin
Mineral Industry Surveys. Tin Industry — Miner Ind Surv Tin Ind
Mineral Industry Surveys. Titanium — Miner Ind Surv Titanium
Mineral Industry Surveys. Titanium — MIS Titanm
Mineral Industry Surveys. Tungsten — Miner Ind Surv Tungsten
Mineral Industry Surveys. Tungsten — MIS Tungst
Mineral Industry Surveys. Uranium — MIS Uranm
Mineral Industry Surveys. Vanadium — Miner Ind Surv Vanadium
Mineral Industry Surveys. Vanadium — MIS Van
Mineral Industry Surveys. Vanadium — MIS Vandm
Mineral Industry Surveys. Vermiculite — MIS Vermic
Mineral Industry Surveys. Weekly Coal Report — Miner Ind Surv Wkly Coal Rep
Mineral Industry Surveys. Zinc Industry — Miner Ind Surv Zinc Ind
Mineral Industry Surveys. Zinc Industry — MIS Zinc
Mineral Industry Surveys. Zinc Oxide — Miner Ind Surv Zinc Oxide
Mineral Industry Surveys. Zinc Oxide — MIS Zinc O
Mineral Industry Surveys. Zinc Production — Miner Ind Surv Zinc Prod
Mineral Industry Surveys. Zinc Production — MIS Zinc P
Mineral Industry Surveys. Zirconium and Hafnium — Miner Ind Surv Zirconium Hafnium
Mineral Industry Surveys. Zirconium and Hafnium — MIS Zirc
Mineral Magazine and Journal. Mineralogical Society — Miner Mag
Mineral Perspectives. United States Bureau of Mines — Miner Perspect US Bur Mines
Mineral Planning — Miner Plann
Mineral Planning — Mineral Plann
Mineral Policy Background Paper. Mineral Resources Branch (Ontario) — Miner Policy Background Pap Miner Resour Branch (Ontario)
Mineral PriceWatch — Miner PriceWatch
Mineral Processing and Extractive Metallurgy Review — Mineral Process Extr Metall Rev
Mineral Processing and Technology Review — Miner Process Technol Rev
Mineral Processing Design — Miner Process Des
Mineral Processing Information Note. Warren Spring Laboratory — Miner Process Inf Note Warren Spring Lab
Mineral Processing. International Mineral Processing Congress. Proceedings — Miner Process Int Miner Process Congr Proc
Mineral Processing. Proceedings. International Congress — Miner Process Proc Int Cong
Mineral Processing Technology [*Database*] — MINPROC
Mineral Products Abstracts — Miner Prod Abstr
Mineral Reconnaissance Programme Report. British Geological Survey — Miner Reconnaissance Programme Rep Br Geol Surv
Mineral Reconnaissance Programme Report. Institute of Geological Sciences — Miner Reconnaissance Programme Rep Inst Geol Sci
Mineral Report. Canada. Mineral Resources Branch — Miner Rep Can Miner Resour Branch
Mineral Research and Exploration Institute of Turkey. Bulletin — Miner Res Explor Inst Turk Bull
Mineral Research (Nagpur) — Miner Res (Nagpur)
Mineral Resource Circular (University of Texas at Austin. Bureau of Economic Geology) — Miner Resour Circ (Univ Tex Austin Bur Econ Geol)
Mineral Resource Report. Pennsylvania Topographic and Geologic Survey — Miner Resour Rep PA Topogr Geol Surv
Mineral Resources and Mining Industry of Cyprus. Bulletin — Miner Resour Min Ind Cyprus Bull
Mineral Resources Bulletin. Directorate General of Mineral Resources (Saudi Arabia) — Miner Resour Bull (Saudi Arabia)
Mineral Resources Bulletin (Geological Survey of Western Australia) — Miner Resour Bull (Geol Surv West Aust)
Mineral Resources Bulletin. Louisiana Geological Survey — Miner Resour Bull LA Geol Surv
Mineral Resources Bulletin. Louisiana Geological Survey — Miner Resour Bull Louisiana Geol Surv

Mineral Resources Bulletin. Saudi Arabia. Directorate General of Mineral Resources — Miner Resour Bull Saudi Arabia Dir Gen Miner Resour
Mineral Resources Consultative Committee. Mineral Dossier (Great Britain) — Miner Resour Consult Comm Miner Dossier (GB)
Mineral Resources Data System [*Database*] — MRDS
Mineral Resources. Geology and Geophysics. Bureau of 1:250,000 Geological Series — Miner Resour Geol Geophys Bur 1:250000 Geol Ser
Mineral Resources Institute. Technical Report Series — MRI Technical Report Series
Mineral Resources Pamphlet. Geological Survey Department. British Guiana — Miner Resour Pam Geol Surv Dep Br Guiana
Mineral Resources Pamphlet. Geological Survey of Guyana — Miner Resour Pam Geol Surv Guyana
Mineral Resources Report. Botswana Geological Survey Department — Miner Resour Rep Botswana Geol Surv Dep
Mineral Resources Report. Bureau of Mineral Resources. Geology and Geophysics — Miner Resour Rep
Mineral Resources Report. Commonwealth Geological Liaison Office — Miner Resour Rep Commonw Geol Liaison Off
Mineral Resources Report. Geological Survey Department (Botswana) — Miner Resour Rep Geol Surv Dep (Botswana)
Mineral Resources Report. Idaho. Bureau of Mines and Geology — Miner Resour Rep Idaho Bur Mines Geol
Mineral Resources Report. New Mexico Bureau of Mines and Mineral Resources — Miner Resour Rep NM Bur Mines Miner
Mineral Resources Report of Investigation. Saudi Arabia Directorate General of Mineral Resources — Miner Resour Rep Invest Saudi Arabia Dir Gen Miner Resour
Mineral Resources Report. Virginia Division of Mineral Resources — Miner Resour Rep Va Div Miner Resour
Mineral Resources Research. Directorate General of Mineral Resources (Saudi Arabia) — Miner Resour Res Dir Gen Miner Resour (Saudi Arabia)
Mineral Resources Review. Department of Mines. South Australia — Miner Resour Rev
Mineral Resources Review. Department of Mines. South Australia — Miner Resour Rev Dep Mines S Aust
Mineral Resources Review. Department of Mines. South Australia — Miner Resour Rev South Aust Dep Mines
Mineral Resources Review. South Australia Department of Mines and Energy — Miner Resour Rev South Aust Dep Mines Energy
Mineral Resources Section. Educational Series (North Carolina) — Miner Resour Sect Educ Ser (NC)
Mineral Resources Series. Division of Geology (South Carolina) — Miner Resour Ser Div Geol (SC)
Mineral Resources Series. Rhodesia Geological Survey — Miner Resour Ser Rhod Geol Surv
Mineral Resources Series. South Carolina. Division of Geology — Miner Resour Ser SC Div Geol
Mineral Resources Series. West Virginia Geological and Economic Survey — Miner Resour Ser WV Geol Econ Surv
Mineral Resources Survey (New Hampshire Division of Economic Development) — Miner Resour Surv (NH Div Econ Dev)
Mineral Trade Notes — Miner Trade Notes
Mineral Trade Notes — Mineral T N
Mineral Waste Utilization Symposium. Proceedings — Miner Waste Util Symp Proc
Mineral Wealth (Athens) — Miner Wealth (Athens)
Mineral Wealth. Gujarat Directorate of Geology and Mining — Miner Wealth Gujarat Dir Geol Min
Mineral Wealth (India) — Miner Wealth (India)
Mineralia Slovaca — Miner Slovaca
Mineralia Slovaca — Mineral Slovaca
Mineralia Slovaca — MSLOB
Mineralia Slovaca. Monografia — Miner Slovaca Monogr
Mineralische Duengemittel und Insektofungicide — Miner Duengem Insektofungic
Mineralische Rohstoffe — Miner Rohst
Mineralische Rohstoffe und Nichteisenmetalle — Miner Rohst Nichteisenmet
Mineralium Deposita — Min Deposit
Mineralium Deposita — Miner Deposita
Mineral'noe Syr'e — Miner Syr'e
Mineral'noe Syr'e i Ego Pererabotka — Miner Syr'e Ego Pererab
Mineral'noe Syr'e i Tsvetnye Metally — Miner Syr'e Tsvetn Met
Mineral'noe Syr'e. Vsesoyuznyi Institut Mineral'nogo Syr'ya — Miner Syr'e Vses Inst Miner Syr'ya
Mineral'noe Syr'e. Vsesoyuznyi Nauchno-Issledovatel'skii Institut Mineral'nogo Syr'ya — Miner Syr'e Vses Nauchno Issled Inst Miner Syr'ya
Mineral'nye Udobreniya i Insektofungisidy — Miner Udobr Insektofungis
Mineraloel — MIOEA
Mineraloel — MNRLD
Mineraloel-Technik — Min Techn
Mineralogia Polonica — Mineral Pol
Mineralogica et Petrographica Acta — Mineral Petrogr Acta
Mineralogica et Petrographica Acta — Mineralog et Petrog Acta
Mineralogical Abstracts — Mineral Abstr
Mineralogical Abstracts — Mineralog Abstr
Mineralogical Association of Canada. Short Course Handbook — Mineral Assoc Can Short Course Handb
Mineralogical Journal (Tokyo) — Mineral J (Tokyo)
Mineralogical Journal (Tokyo) — MJTOA
Mineralogical Magazine — Mineral Mag
Mineralogical Magazine — Mineralog Mag
Mineralogical Magazine — Mineralogical Mag
Mineralogical Magazine and Journal. Mineralogical Society — Mi M
Mineralogical Magazine and Journal. Mineralogical Society. Supplement — Mineral Mag Suppl
Mineralogical Magazine and Journal of the Mineralogical Society [*1876-1968*] [*England*] — MIASA
Mineralogical Magazine and Journal of the Mineralogical Society (1876-1968) [*England*] — Mineral Mag J Mineral Soc (1876-1968)
Mineralogical Record — GMIR
Mineralogical Record — Miner Rec
Mineralogical Record — Mineral Rec
Mineralogical Society. Bulletin — Mineral Soc Bull
Mineralogical Society Monograph — Mineral Soc Monogr
Mineralogical Society of America. Short Course Notes — Mineral Soc Am Short Course Notes
Mineralogical Society of America. Special Paper — Mineral Soc Am Spec Pap
Mineralogical Society of America. Special Paper — Mineralog Soc America Spec Paper
Mineralogical Society of Japan. Special Paper — Mineral Soc Jpn Spec Pap
Mineralogical Society of Utah. Bulletin — Mineralog Soc Utah Bull
Mineralogicheskie Issledovaniya — Mineral Issled
Mineralogicheskie Kriterii Svyazi Kislogo Magnatizma s Rudnoi Mineralizatsiei. Materialy Sezda MMA — Mineral Kriter Svyazi Kislogo Magnat Rudn Miner Mater Sezda
Mineralogicheskii Sbornik (Baku) — Mineral Sb (Baku)
Mineralogicheskii Sbornik (Lvov) — Mineral Sb (Lvov)
Mineralogicheskii Sbornik (Sverdlovsk) — Mineral Sb (Sverdlovsk)
Mineralogicheskiy Sbornik (L'vovskiy Gosudarstvennyy Universitet) — Mineral Sb (L'vov Gos Univ)
Mineralogicheskiy Zhurnal — Mineral Zh
Mineralogische und Petrographische Mitteilungen — Mineral Petrogr Mitt
Mineralogische und Petrographische Mitteilungen Tschermaks [*Austria*] — Mineral Petrogr Mitt Tschermaks
Mineralogisches Mitteilungsblatt. Landesmuseum Joanneum — Mineral Mitteilungsbl Landesmus Joanneum
Mineralogiya i Geokhimiya — MIGKA
Mineralogiya i Geokhimiya [*Former USSR*] — Mineral Geokhim
Mineralogiya i Petrografiya Urala — Mineral Petrogr Urala
Mineralogiya Osadochnykh Obrazovanii — Mineral Osad Obraz
Mineralogiya Tadzhikistana — Mineral Tadzh
Mineralogy and Petrology — Mineral Petrol
Minerals and Energy Bulletin [*Australia*] — Miner Energy Bull
Minerals and Materials — Miner Mater
Minerals and Materials: A Monthly Survey — Min & Mtrl
Minerals and Metallurgical Processing — Miner Metall Process
Minerals and Metals Review — Min Met Rev
Minerals and Metals Review — Miner Met Rev
Minerals and Mineral Development — Min Min Dev
Minerals and Rocks — Miner Rocks
Minerals and the Environment — MIENDE
Minerals and the Environment — Miner Environ
Minerals Availability System [*Database*] — MASNC
Minerals Dressing Journal — Miner Dress J
Minerals Engineering — Miner Eng
Minerals Engineering Society Technical Magazine — Miner Eng Soc Tech Mag
Minerals News Service. Bureau of Mines (Philippines) — Miner News Serv (Philipp)
Minerals Processing — Miner Process
Minerals Research in Commonwealth Scientific and Industrial Research Organisation — Miner Res CSIRO
Minerals Research in Commonwealth Scientific and Industrial Research Organisation — Minerals Res CSIRO
Minerals Research in Commonwealth Scientific and Industrial Research Organisation (Australia) — Miner Res CSIRO (Aust)
Minerals Science and Engineering — Miner Sci Eng
Minerals Science and Engineering (Johannesburg) — Miner Sci Eng (Johannesburg)
Minerals Yearbook [*United States*] — Miner Yearb
Minerals Yearbook — MYEAA
Minerals Yearbook. Preprint. Abrasive Materials — MYP A M
Minerals Yearbook. Preprint. Aluminum — MYP Alum
Minerals Yearbook. Preprint. Antimony — MYP Antim
Minerals Yearbook. Preprint. Area Reports. Individual States — MYP State
Minerals Yearbook. Preprint. Asbestos — MYP Asbsts
Minerals Yearbook. Preprint. Barite — MYP Barite
Minerals Yearbook. Preprint. Bauxite — MYP Bauxit
Minerals Yearbook. Preprint. Beryllium — MYP Beryl
Minerals Yearbook. Preprint. Bismuth — MYP Bis
Minerals Yearbook. Preprint. Boron — MYP Boron
Minerals Yearbook. Preprint. Bromine — MYP Bromin
Minerals Yearbook. Preprint. Cadmium — MYP Cadm
Minerals Yearbook. Preprint. Calcium and Calcium Compounds — MYP Calcm
Minerals Yearbook. Preprint. Cement — MYP Cement
Minerals Yearbook. Preprint. Chromium — MYP Chrom
Minerals Yearbook. Preprint. Clays — MYP Clays
Minerals Yearbook. Preprint. Cobalt — MYP Cobalt
Minerals Yearbook. Preprint. Columbium and Tantalum — MYP Columb
Minerals Yearbook. Preprint. Copper — MYP Copper
Minerals Yearbook. Preprint. Crushed Stone — MYP C Stone
Minerals Yearbook. Preprint. Diatomite — MYP Diato
Minerals Yearbook. Preprint. Dimension Stone — MYP Dime S
Minerals Yearbook. Preprint. Feldspar, Nepheline, Syenite, and Aplite — MYP Felsp
Minerals Yearbook. Preprint. Ferroalloys — MYP Ferro
Minerals Yearbook. Preprint. Fluorspar — MYP Fluor
Minerals Yearbook. Preprint. Gallium — MYP Gallm
Minerals Yearbook. Preprint. Gem Stones — MYP Gem St

Minerals Yearbook. Preprint. Gold — MYP Gold
Minerals Yearbook. Preprint. Graphite — MYP Grapht
Minerals Yearbook. Preprint. Gypsum — MYP Gypsum
Minerals Yearbook. Preprint. Helium — MYP Helium
Minerals Yearbook. Preprint. Iodine — MYP Iodine
Minerals Yearbook. Preprint. Iron and Steel — MYP Iron
Minerals Yearbook. Preprint. Iron and Steel Scrap — MYP I & S S
Minerals Yearbook. Preprint. Iron and Steel Slag — MYP Iron S S
Minerals Yearbook. Preprint. Iron Ore — MYP Iron O
Minerals Yearbook. Preprint. Iron Oxide Pigments — MYP Ir Ox
Minerals Yearbook. Preprint. Kyanite and Related Materials — MYP Kyan
Minerals Yearbook. Preprint. Lead — MYP Lead
Minerals Yearbook. Preprint. Lime — MYP Lime
Minerals Yearbook. Preprint. Lithium — MYP Lith
Minerals Yearbook. Preprint. Magnesium Compounds — MYP Magn C
Minerals Yearbook. Preprint. Mercury — MYP Mercry
Minerals Yearbook. Preprint. Mica — MYP Mica
Minerals Yearbook. Preprint. Minerals in the World Economy — MYP Wld Min
Minerals Yearbook. Preprint. Mining and Quarrying Trends in the Metal and Nonmetal Industries — MYP Mining
Minerals Yearbook. Preprint. Minor Nonmetals — MYP M N Mtl
Minerals Yearbook. Preprint. Molybdenum — MYP Moly
Minerals Yearbook. Preprint. Nitrogen — MYP Nitro
Minerals Yearbook. Preprint. Nonfuel Minerals Survey Methods — MYP Nonfl M
Minerals Yearbook. Preprint. Other Metals — MYP O Mtl
Minerals Yearbook. Preprint. Other Nonmetals — MYP O Nmtl
Minerals Yearbook. Preprint. Peat — MYP Peat
Minerals Yearbook. Preprint. Phosphate Rock — MYP Phos R
Minerals Yearbook. Preprint. Platinum - Group Metals — MYP Platnm
Minerals Yearbook. Preprint. Potash — MYP Potash
Minerals Yearbook. Preprint. Products — MYP Prod
Minerals Yearbook. Preprint. Pumice and Pumicite — MYP Pumice
Minerals Yearbook. Preprint. Pumice and Volcanic Cinder — MYP Pumic
Minerals Yearbook. Preprint. Review of the Mineral Industry — MYP Rev
Minerals Yearbook. Preprint. Rhenium — MYP Rhenm
Minerals Yearbook. Preprint. Salt — MYP Salt
Minerals Yearbook. Preprint. Sand and Gravel — MYP Sand
Minerals Yearbook. Preprint. Silver — MYP Silver
Minerals Yearbook. Preprint. Slag - Iron and Steel — MYP Slag
Minerals Yearbook. Preprint. Sodium and Sodium Compounds — MYP Sodium
Minerals Yearbook. Preprint. Statistical Summary — MYP Stat S
Minerals Yearbook. Preprint. Stone — MYP Stone
Minerals Yearbook. Preprint. Sulfur and Pyrites — MYP Sulfur
Minerals Yearbook. Preprint. Talc, Soapstone, and Pyrophyllite — MYP Talc
Minerals Yearbook. Preprint. Territorial Mineral Industry of Puerto Rico, Virgin Islands, and Pacific Islands — MYP Terr
Minerals Yearbook. Preprint. Thorium — MYP Thorm
Minerals Yearbook. Preprint. Tin — MYP Tin
Minerals Yearbook. Preprint. Titanium — MYP Titanm
Minerals Yearbook. Preprint. Tungsten — MYP Tungst
Minerals Yearbook. Preprint. Vanadium — MYP Vandm
Minerals Yearbook. Preprint. Vermiculite — MYP Vermic
Minerals Yearbook. Preprint. Zinc — MYP Zinc
Minerals Yearbook. Preprint. Zirconium and Hafnium — MYP Zirc
Minerals Yearbook. Volume 1. Metals and Minerals — Miner Yrbk
Minerals Yearbook. Volume 2. Area Reports, Domestic — Miner YB 2
Minerals Yearbook. Volume 3. Area Reports, International — Miner YB 3
Mineralwasser-Fabrikant — Mineralwasser Fabr
Mineralwasser-Fabrikant und Brunnen-Haendler — Mineralwasser Fabr Brunnen Haendler
Mineraux et Fossiles — Miner Fossiles
Mineraux et Fossiles. Guide du Collectionneur — Miner Fossiles Guide Collect
Mineria Boliviana — Min Boliv
Mineria Boliviana (La Paz) — Miner Boliviana La Paz
Mineria en Cuba — Min Cuba
Mineria y Metalurgia — Min Metal
Mineria y Metalurgia (Madrid) — Min Metal (Madrid)
Mineria y Metalurgia (Madrid) — Mineria Metal (Madrid)
Mineria y Metalurgia (Mexico City) — Min Metal (Mexico City)
Mineria y Metalurgia (Mexico City) — Mineria Met (Mexico City)
Mineria y Metalurgia, Plasticos y Electricidad — Min Metal Plast Electr
Minero Mexicano — Min Mex
Minerva — Min
Minerva — Mnva
Minerva Aerospaziale — Minerva Aerosp
Minerva Anestesiologica — Minerva Anestesiol
Minerva Bioepistemologica — Minerva Bioepistemol
Minerva Biologica — Minerva Biol
Minerva Cardioangiologica — Minerva Cardioangiol
Minerva Chirurgica — Minerva Chir
Minerva Dermatologica [*Italy*] — Minerva Dermatol
Minerva Dietologica — Minerva Diet
Minerva Dietologica [*Later, Minerva Dietologica e Gastroenterologica*] — Minerva Dietol
Minerva Dietologica e Gastroenterologica — Minerva Dietol Gastroenterol
Minerva Ecologia, Idroclimatologica, Fisiconucleare — Minerva Ecol Idroclimatol Fis Nucl
Minerva Ecologica, Idroclimatologica, Fisicosanitaria — MEIFD
Minerva Ecologica, Idroclimatologica, Fisicosanitaria — Minerva Ecol Idroclimatol Fis Sanit
Minerva Ecologica, Idroclimatologica, Fisicosanitaria — Minerva Ecol Idroclimatol Fisicosanit
Minerva Endocrinologica — Minerva Endocrinol
Minerva Farmaceutica — Minerva Farm
Minerva Fisiconucleare — Minerva Fisiconucl
Minerva Fisiconucleare. Giornale di Fisica, Sanitaria, e Protezione Contro le Radiazioni — Minerva Fisiconucl G Fis Sanit Prot Radiaz
Minerva Fisioterapica — Minerva Fisioter
Minerva Fisioterapica e Radiobiologica — Minerva Fisioter Radiobiol
Minerva Gastroenterologica — Minerva Gastroenterol
Minerva Ginecologica — Minerva Ginecol
Minerva Handbuecher — Min Hdb
Minerva Idroclimatologica [*Italy*] — Minerva Idroclimatol
Minerva Medica — MIMEA
Minerva Medica — Minerva Med
Minerva Medica. Europa Medica — Minerva Med Eur Med
Minerva Medica Guiliana — Minerva Med Guiliana
Minerva Medica. Rassegna Ipnosi e Medicina Psicosomatica — Minerva Med Rass Ipnosi Med Psicosom
Minerva Medica (Roma) — Minerva Med (Roma)
Minerva Medica Siciliana — Minerva Med Sicil
Minerva Medica. Supplement. Minerva Fisioterapica — Minerva Med Suppl Minerva Fisioter
Minerva Medica. Supplemento — MIMSA
Minerva Medica. Supplemento [*Italy*] — Minerva Med Suppl
Minerva Medica. Supplemento. Minerva Medica Siciliana — Minerva Med Suppl Minerva Med Sicil
Minerva Medicolegale — Minerva Medicoleg
Minerva Nefrologica — Minerva Nefrol
Minerva Neurochirurgica — Min Neurochir
Minerva Neurochirurgica — Minerva Neurochir
Minerva Nipiologica — Minerva Nipiol
Minerva Nucleare [*Italy*] — Minerva Nucl
Minerva Nucleare — MINUA
Minerva Nucleare. Journal of Nuclear Biology and Medicine — Minerva Nucl J Nucl Biol Med
Minerva Oftalmologica [*Italy*] — Minerva Oftalmol
Minerva Ortopedica — Minerva Ortop
Minerva Otorinolaringologica — Minerva ORL
Minerva Otorinolaringologica — Minerva Otorinolaringol
Minerva Otorinolaringologica — MIOTA
Minerva Pediatrica — Min Pediat
Minerva Pediatrica — Minerva Ped
Minerva Pediatrica — Minerva Pediatr
Minerva Pediatrica — MIPEA
Minerva Pneumologica — Minerva Pneumol
Minerva Psichiatrica — Minerva Psichiatr
Minerva Psichiatrica e Psicologica [*Later, Minerva Psichiatrica*] — Minerva Psichiatr Psicol
Minerva Radiologica — Minerva Radiol
Minerva Radiologica. Fisioterapica e Radio-Biologica [*Italy*] — Minerva Radiol Fisioter Radio-Biol
Minerva Stomatologica — Minerva Stomatol
Minerva Urologica — Minerva Urol
Minerva Urologica e Nefrologica — Minerva Urol Nefrol
Mines and Minerals (Nagpur, India) — Mines Miner (Nagpur India)
Mines and Minerals (Scranton, Pennsylvania) — Mines Miner (Scranton PA)
Mines and Prospects Map Series. Idaho Bureau of Mines and Geology — Mines Prospects Map Ser Idaho Bur Mines Geol
Mines Annual Report. Department of Mines. Western Australia — Mines Annu Rep Dep Mines West Aust
Mines Branch Monograph — Mines Branch Monogr
Mines Branch Research Report — Mines Branch Res Rep
Mines Branch Technical Bulletin — Mines Branch Tech Bull
Mines Department. Victoria Groundwater Investigation Program Report — Mines Dep Victoria Groundwater Invest Program Rep
Mines et Geologie — Mines Geol
Mines et Metallurgie — Mines Met
Mines et Metallurgie — Mines Metall
Mines, Geologie et Energie — Mines Geol Energ
Mines, Geologie, et Energie (Royaume du Maroc) — Mines Geol Energie (Maroc)
Mines Magazine — Mines Mag
Mines Year-End Review. Bureau of Mines and Geo-Sciences (Philippines) — Mines Year-End Rev Bur Mines (Philipp)
Minfacts. Ministry of Natural Resources (Ontario) — Minfacts Minist Nat Resour (Ontario)
Ming Studies — Ming Stud
Mingay's Electrical Weekly — Mingays Electrical W
Minia. Orgao do Instituto Minhoto de Estudos Regionais — MOIMER
Miniature Camera Magazine — Miniature Camera Mag
Miniature Camera World — Miniature Camera World
Minicam Photography — Minicam Photogr
Minicomputer and Computations in Chemistry. Report on the Workshop — Minicomput Comput Chem Rep Workshop
Minicomputer Applications Analyzer — Mini Applic
Minicomputer Review — Minicomput Rev
Minimally Invasive Neurosurgery — Minim Invasive Neurosurg
Mini-Micro Bulletin — Minimicro Bull
Mini-Micro Software — Mini Soft
Mini-Micro Systems — Mini Sys
Mini-Micro Systems — Mini-Micro
Mini-Micro Systems — Mini-Micro Syst
Mini-Micro Systems Special Peripherals Digest. Fall, 1983 — Mini Micro S
Mining Activity Digest — Min Act Dig
Mining and Chemical Engineering Review [*Australia*] — Min Chem Eng Rev
Mining and Chemical Engineering Review — Min Chem Engng Rev
Mining and Chemical Engineering Review — Mining & Chem Eng R
Mining and Chemical Engineering Review (Australia) — MCER(A)
Mining and Coking of Coal. Proceedings of the Conference — Min Coking Coal Proc Conf

Mining and Electrical Record — Min Electr Rec
Mining and Engineering (Harare) — Min Eng (Harare)
Mining and Engineering Record — Min Eng Rec
Mining and Engineering Review — Min Eng Rev
Mining and Engineering World — Min Eng World
Mining and Geological Journal — Min & Geol J
Mining and Geological Journal — Min Geol J
Mining and Industrial Magazine [*Manila*] — MIM
Mining and Industrial Magazine of Southern Africa — Min Ind Mag South Afr
Mining and Industrial Record — Min Ind Rec
Mining and Metallurgical Engineering — Min Metall Eng
Mining and Metallurgical Society of America. Bulletin — M Met Soc Am B
Mining and Metallurgical Society of America. Bulletin — Min Metall Soc America Bull
Mining and Metallurgy — Min & Met
Mining and Metallurgy — Min Metall
Mining and Metallurgy. Quarterly — Min Metall Q
Mining and Metallurgy. Quarterly — Mining Met Quart
Mining and Metallurgy. Quarterly [*English Translation*] — MMQUB
Mining and Metallurgy (Taipei) — Min Metal (Taipei)
Mining and Minerals Engineering — Min Miner Eng
Mining and Minerals Engineering — Min Miner Engng
Mining and Minerals Engineering — Mining Miner Eng
Mining and Oil Review — MOR
Mining and Safety — Min Saf
Mining and Scientific Press — M Sc Press
Mining and Scientific Press — Min Sci Press
Mining Annual Review — MAR
Mining Annual Review [*England*] — Min Annu Rev
Mining Annual Review — Mining Rev
Mining Bulletin — Min B
Mining Congress Journal — Min Cong J
Mining Congress Journal — Min Congr J
Mining Congress Journal — Mining Congr J
Mining Department Magazine. University of Nottingham — Min Dep Mag Univ Nottingham
Mining, Electrical, and Mechanical Engineer [*England*] — Min Electr Mech Eng
Mining, Electrical, and Mechanical Engineer — Mining Elec Mech Eng
Mining Engineer — Min Engr
Mining Engineer (London) — Min Eng (Lond)
Mining Engineer (London) — Mining Eng (London)
Mining Engineering — Min Eng
Mining Engineering — Min Engng
Mining Engineering and Electrical Record — Min Eng Electr Rec
Mining Engineering (Colorado) — Min Eng (Colorado)
Mining Engineering (Littleton, Colorado) — Min Eng (Littleton Colo)
Mining Engineering (New York) — Min Eng (NY)
Mining Engineering (New York) — Mining Eng (NY)
Mining Equipment International — Min Equip Int
Mining Geology [*Japan*] — Min Geol
Mining Geology and the Base Metals. A Symposium — Min Geol Base Met Symp
Mining Geology (Society of Mining Geologists of Japan) Journal — Min Geol (Soc Min Geol Jap)
Mining Geology [*Society of Mining Geologists of Japan*] **Special Issue (Tokyo)** — Min Geol Spec Issue (Tokyo)
Mining Herald and Colliery Engineer — Min Her Colliery Eng
Mining in Canada — Min Can
Mining in Zimbabwe — Min Zimbabwe
Mining Industry in Quebec — Min Ind Quebec
Mining Industry Technology [*Taiwan*] — Min Ind Technol
Mining Journal — Min J
Mining Journal — Mining Jrl
Mining Journal — MJ
Mining Journal — MNJ
Mining Journal (London) — Min J (Lond)
Mining Journal (London) — Min J (London)
Mining Magazine — MIM
Mining Magazine — Min Mag
Mining Magazine — Mining Mag
Mining Magazine — Mining Mg
Mining Magazine — MM
Mining Mirror — Min Mirror
Mining Monthly — Min Mon
Mining Newsletter — Min Newsletter
Mining Record — Min Record
Mining Reporter — M Reporter
Mining Research and Exploration Institute of Turkey. Bulletin — Min Res Explor Inst Turk Bull
Mining Research. Proceedings — Min Res Proc
Mining Review — Min R
Mining Review — Min Rev
Mining Review — Mining R
Mining Review — MIRV
Mining Review (Adelaide). South Australia Department of Mines — Min Rev (Adelaide)
Mining Science — M Science
Mining Science — Min Sci
Mining Society of Nova Scotia. Journal — M Soc NS J
Mining Survey [*Johannesburg*] — Min Surv
Mining Survey (Johannesburg) — Min Surv (Johannesb)
Mining Technology — Min Technol
Mining Technology — Mining Technol
Mining Technology Abstracts [*Database*] — MINTEC
Mining Technology (New York) — Min Technol NY
Mining Technology (Taipei) — Min Technol (Taipei)
Mining Week [*South Africa*] — Min Week
Mining World — M World
Mining World — Min World
Mining Year Book [*United States*] — Min Year Book
Mining Yearbook (Denver) — Min Yearb (Denver)
Minister van Justitie — MJ
Ministere de la France d'Outre Mer. Direction de l'Agriculture de l'Elevage et des Forets. Bulletin Scientifique — Minist Fr Outre Mer Dir Agric Elev For Bull Sci
Ministere de la Sante Publique (France). Rapport SCPRI — Minist Sante Publique (Fr) Rapp SCPRI
Ministere de l'Agriculture et de l'Alimentation de l'Ontario. Bulletin (Edition Francaise) — Minist Agric Aliment Ont Bull (Ed Fr)
Ministere de l'Energie et des Ressources. Etude Speciale ES (Quebec) — Minist Energ Ressour Etude Spec ES (Que)
Ministere de l'Industrie et du Commerce du Quebec. Rapport Annuel — Minist Ind Commer Que Rapp Annu
Ministerio das Obras Publicas. Laboratorio Nacional de Engenharia Civil (Portugal). Memoria — Minist Obras Publicas Lab Nac Eng Civ Port Mem
Ministerio de Agricultura. Instituto Colombiano Agropecuario. Programa Nacional de Entomologia — Minist Agric Inst Colomb Agropecu Programa Nac Entomol
Ministerio de Cultura y Educacion. Fundacion Miguel Lillo. Miscelanea — Minist Cult Educ Fund Miguel Lillo Misc
Ministerio de Educacao e Cultura — MEC
Ministerio de Fomento y Obras Publicas (Peru). Instituto Nacional de Investigacion y Fomento Mineros. Boletin — Minist Fom Obras Publicas Peru Inst Nac Invest Fom Min Bol
Ministerio de Ganaderia y Agricultura. Centro de Investigaciones Agricolas "Alberto Boerger." Boletim Tecnico — Minist Ganad Agric Cent Invest Agric Alberto Boerger Bol Tec
Ministerio de Salud Publica. Hospital Psiquiatrico de la Habana. Boletin de Psicologia — Minist Salud Publica Hosp Psiquiatr Habana Bol Psicol
Ministerio do Trabalho. Industria e Comercio. Instituto Nacional de Tecnologia. Publicacoes (Rio de Janeiro) — Minist Trab Ind Comer Inst Nac Tecnol Publ Rio de Janeiro
Ministero degli Affari Esteri. Monografie e Rapporto Coloniale — MAE
Ministero della Marina Mercantile. Memoria — Minist Mar Merc Mem
Minister's Letter. Letter to Indian People on Current Issues. Minister of Indian Affairs and Northern Development — MILT
Ministerstvo Oborony Narodowej — MON
Ministerstvo Prosvescenija RSFSR Kuibysevskii Gosudarstvennyi Pedagogiceskii Institut Imeni V. V. Kuibyseva Ucenyi Zapiski [*Kuybyshev*] — Kuibysev Gos Ped Inst Ucen Zap
Ministerstvo Prosvescenija RSFSR Tjumenskii Gosudarstvennyi Pedagogiceskii Institut. Ucenye Zapiski — Tjumen Gos Ped Inst Ucen Zap
Ministerstvo Prosvescenija RSSR Matematika v Skole — Mat v Skole
Ministerstvo Sel'skogo Khozyaistva Uzbekskoi SSR. Glavnoe Upravlenie Sel'skokhozyaistvennoi Nauki. Trudy — Minist Selsk Khoz Uzb SSR Gl Upr Skh Nauki Tr
Ministerstvo Vyssego i Srednigo Obrazovanija UzSSR Trudy Samarkandskogo Gosuda rstvennogo Universiteta Imeni A. Navoi Novaja Serija — Trudy Samarkand Gos Univ NS
Ministerstvo Vyssego Obrazovanija SSSR Voronezskii Gosudarstvennyi Universitet Trudy Seminara po Funkcional'nomu Analizu — Voronez Gos Univ Trudy Sem Funkcional Anal
Ministerstvo Vysshego i Srednego Spetsial'nogo Obrazovaniya Azerbaidzhanskoi SSR. Uchenye Zapiski. Seriya Biologicheskikh Nauk — Minist Vyssh Sredn Spets Obraz Az SSR Uch Zap Ser Biol Nauk
Ministery Studies — Min St
Ministry for Conservation. Victoria. Environmental Studies Series — Minist Conserv Victoria Environ Stud Ser
Ministry of Agriculture and Natural Resources. Central Agricultural Station. Research Report (Guyana) — Minist Agric Nat Resour Cent Agric Stn Res Rep (Guyana)
Ministry of Agriculture and Rural Development. Department of Botany. Publication (Tehran) — Minist Agric Rural Dev Dep Bot Publ (Tehran)
Ministry of Agriculture, Fisheries, and Food. Bulletin (Great Britain) — Minist Agric Fish Food Bull GB
Ministry of Agriculture, Fisheries, and Food. Publication RVG (United Kingdom) — Minist Agric Fish Food Publ RVG (UK)
Ministry of Agriculture, Fisheries, and Food. Reference Book (Great Britain) — Minist Agric Fish Food Ref Book GB
Ministry of Agriculture, Fisheries, and Food. Technical Bulletin — Minist Agric Fish Food Tech Bull
Ministry of Energy, Mines, and Petroleum Resources. Paper (British Columbia) — Minist Energy Mines Pet Resour Pap BC
Ministry Studies — Min St
Miniwatt Digest — Miniwatt Dig
Miniwatt Technical Bulletin — Miniwatt Tech Bull
Minji Saiban Geppo — Minsai Geppo
Minneapolis District Dental Journal — Minneap Dist Dent J
Minneapolis Institute of Arts. Bulletin — Minn Inst Arts Bul
Minneapolis Institute of Arts. Bulletin — Minn Inst Bul
Minneapolis Institute of Arts. Bulletin — Minneapolis Inst Bul
Minneapolis-St. Paul City Business — Minn St P B
Minnesota Academy of Natural Sciences. Bulletin — Minn Ac N Sc B
Minnesota Academy of Science. Journal — Minn Acad Sci J
Minnesota Academy of Science. Proceedings — Minn Acad Sci Proc
Minnesota Agricultural Economist — Minn Agric Economist
Minnesota Agricultural Economist. Minnesota Extension Service. University of Minnesota — Minn Agric Econ Minn Ext Serv Univ Minn
Minnesota. Agricultural Experiment Station. Bulletin — Minn Agric Exp Stn Bull

Minnesota. Agricultural Experiment Station. Miscellaneous Report — Minn Agric Exp Stn Misc Rep
Minnesota Agricultural Experiment Station. Miscellaneous Report — Minnesota Agric Exp Sta Misc Rep
Minnesota. Agricultural Experiment Station. Publications — Minn Ag Exp
Minnesota. Agricultural Experiment Station. Station Bulletin — Minn Agric Exp Stn Stn Bull
Minnesota. Agricultural Experiment Station. Technical Bulletin — Minn Agric Exp Stn Tech Bull
Minnesota Agricultural Experiment Station. Technical Bulletin — Minnesota Agric Exp Sta Techn Bull
Minnesota Beekeeper — Minn Beekpr
Minnesota Business Journal — Minn Bs Jl
Minnesota Cities — Minn Cities
Minnesota. Department of Agriculture. Annual Feed Bulletin — Minn Dep Agric Annu Feed Bull
Minnesota. Department of Conservation. Division of Game and Fish. Section on Research and Planning. Investigational Report — Minn Dep Conserv Div Game Fish Sect Res Plann Invest Rep
Minnesota. Department of Conservation. Division of Waters. Bulletin — Minn Dep Conserv Div Waters Bull
Minnesota. Department of Conservation. Division of Waters. Bulletin. Technical Paper — Minn Dept Conserv Div Waters Bull Tech Paper
Minnesota. Department of Conservation. Technical Bulletin — Minn Dep Conserv Tech Bull
Minnesota. Department of Natural Resources. Division of Fish and Wildlife. Section of Wildlife. Wildlife Research Quarterly — Minn Dep Nat Resour Div Fish Wildl Sect Wildl Wildl Res Q
Minnesota. Department of Natural Resources. Division of Game and Fish. Section of Technical Services. Investigational Report — Minn Dep Nat Resour Div Game Fish Sect Tech Serv Invest Rep
Minnesota. Department of Natural Resources. Game Research Project. Quarterly Progress Report — Minn Dep Nat Resour Game Res Proj Q Prog Rep
Minnesota. Department of Natural Resources. Section of Fisheries. Investigational Report — Minn Dep Nat Resour Sect Fish Invest Rep
Minnesota. Division of Waters. Bulletin — Minn Div Waters Bull
Minnesota. Division of Waters, Soils, and Minerals. Bulletin — Minn Div Waters Soils Miner Bull
Minnesota Farm and Home Science — Minn Farm & Home Sci
Minnesota Farm and Home Science — Minn Farm Home Sci
Minnesota Farm and Home Science. Entomology Fact Sheet — Minn Fm Home Fact Sh Ent
Minnesota Fish and Game Investigations. Fish Series — Minn Fish Game Invest Fish Ser
Minnesota Fisheries Investigations — Minn Fish Invest
Minnesota Forestry Notes — Minn For Notes
Minnesota Forestry Research Notes — Minn For Res Notes
Minnesota Forestry Research Notes — Minn Forestry Res Note
Minnesota. Geological and Natural History Survey — Minn G S
Minnesota. Geological Survey. Bulletin — Minn Geol Surv Bull
Minnesota Geological Survey. Information Circular — Minn Geol Surv Inf Circ
Minnesota. Geological Survey. Miscellaneous Map — Minnesota Geol Survey Misc Map
Minnesota. Geological Survey. Report of Investigations — Minn Geol Surv Rep Invest
Minnesota. Geological Survey. Report of Investigations — Minnesota Geol Survey Rept Inv
Minnesota. Geological Survey. Special Publication Series — Minn Geol Surv Spec Publ Ser
Minnesota. Geological Survey. Special Publication Series — Minnesota Geol Survey Spec Pub Ser
Minnesota Historical Society. Collections — Minn His S
Minnesota Historical Society. Educational Bulletin — Minn Hist Soc Educ Bull
Minnesota History — MH
Minnesota History — MinH
Minnesota History — Minn H
Minnesota History — Minn His
Minnesota History — Minn Hist
Minnesota History — Minn History
Minnesota History — MnH
Minnesota History. Bulletin — Minn His B
Minnesota History. Bulletin — Minn Hist B
Minnesota History Bulletin — Minn Hist Bul
Minnesota Horticulturist — Minn Hort
Minnesota Horticulturist — Minn Hortic
Minnesota Journal of Education — Minn J Ed
Minnesota Journal of Education — Minn J of Ed
Minnesota Journal of Science — Minn J Sci
Minnesota Journal of Science — Minn Jour Sci
Minnesota Language Review — Minn L R
Minnesota Law Review — Minn L Rev
Minnesota Law Review — Minn Law R
Minnesota Law Review — Minn LR
Minnesota Law Review — Minnesota L Rev
Minnesota Law Review — MN LR
Minnesota Libraries — Minn Lib
Minnesota Libraries — Minn Libr
Minnesota Medicine — Minn Med
Minnesota Medicine — Minnesota Med
Minnesota Messenia Expedition — MME
Minnesota Mining Directory — Minnesota Min Dir
Minnesota Municipalities — Minn Munic
Minnesota Nursing Accent — Minn Nurs Accent
Minnesota Nutrition Conference. Proceedings — Minn Nutr Conf Proc
Minnesota. Office of Iron Range Resources and Rehabilitation. Report of Inventory — Minn Off Iron Range Resour Rehabil Rep Inventory
Minnesota Optometrist — Minn Optom
Minnesota Pharmacist — Minn Pharm
Minnesota Plant Studies — Minnesota Pl Stud
Minnesota Report. University of Minnesota. Agricultural Experiment Station — Minn Rep Univ Minn Agric Exp Stn
Minnesota Reports — Minn
Minnesota Review — Mi R
Minnesota Review — Minn Rev
Minnesota Review — MinnR
Minnesota Review — MR
Minnesota Review — UMMR
Minnesota Rules — Minn R
Minnesota School of Mines. Experiment Station. Bulletin — Minn Sch Mines Exp Sta B
Minnesota Science — Minn Sci
Minnesota Science. Agricultural Experiment Station. University of Minnesota — Minn Sci Agric Exp Stn Univ Minn
Minnesota Science. Minnesota Agricultural Experiment Station — Minn Sci Minn Agric Exp Stn
Minnesota Session Law Service (West) — Minn Sess Law Serv (West)
Minnesota Star and Tribune — Minn Star
Minnesota State Florists' Bulletin — Minn State Florists Bull
Minnesota State Register — Minn Reg
Minnesota Statutes — Minn Stat
Minnesota Statutes, Annotated (West) — Minn Stat Ann (West)
Minnesota Studies in the Biological Sciences — Minnesota Stud Biol Sci
Minnesota Studies in the Philosophy of Science — Minn Stud Phil Sci
Minnesota Studies in the Philosophy of Science — Minnesota Stud Philos Sci
Minnesota Symposia on Child Psychology — Minn Symp Child Psychol
Minnesota Union List of Serials — MULS
Minnesota. University. Agricultural Experiment Station. Technical Bulletin — Minn Univ Agric Exp Stn Tech Bull
Minnesota University. Agricultural Extension Service. Extension Bulletin — Minn Univ Agric Ext Serv Ext Bull
Minnesota University. Agricultural Extension Service. Extension Folder — Minn Univ Agric Ext Serv Ext Folder
Minnesota University. Department of Soil Science. Soil Series — Soil Ser Dep Soil Sci Minnesota Univ
Minnesota University. Engineering Experiment Station. Bulletin — Minn Univ Eng Exp Stn Bull
Minnesota University. Engineering Experiment Station. Technical Paper — Minn Univ Eng Exp Stn Tech Pap
Minnesota University. Mining Symposium — Minn Univ Min Symp
Minnesota University. Quarterly Bulletin — Minn Univ Q B
Minnesota University. St. Anthony Falls Hydraulic Laboratory. Project Report — Minn Univ St Anthony Falls Hydraul Lab Proj Rep
Minnesota University. St. Anthony Falls Hydraulic Laboratory. Technical Paper [*A publication*] — Minn Univ St Anthony Falls Hydraul Lab Tech Pap
Minnesota University. Water Resources Research Center. Bulletin — Minn Univ Water Resour Res Cent Bull
Minoan and Mycenaean Art — MMA
Minoan-Mycenaean Religion and its Survival in Greek Religion — MMR
Minoeseg es Megbizhatosag [*Hungary*] — Minoes Megbizh
Minor Planet Circulars/Minor Planets and Comets — Minor Planet Circ
Minority Voices — MV
Minskii Gosudarstvennyi Meditsinskii Institut Sbornik Nauchnykh Rabot — Minsk Gos Med Inst Sb Nauchn Rab
Mintec. Mining Technology Abstracts — Mintec Min Technol Abstr
MINTEK [*Council for Mineral Technology*] **Research Digest** — MINTEK Res Dig
Minufiya Journal of Agricultural Research — Minufiya J Agric Res
Minutes and Proceedings. Institution of Civil Engineers — Minutes Proc Inst Civ Eng
Minutes. Annual Meeting. National Plant Board — Minutes Annu Meet Natl Plant Board
Minutes. International Symposium on Cyclodextrins — Minutes Int Symp Cyclodextrins
Minutes. Meeting. Pennsylvania Electric Association. Engineering Section — Minutes Meet PA Electr Assoc Eng Sect
Minutes of Proceedings. Institution of Civil Engineers — MPICE
Minutes. Seminar in Ukrainian Studies — Minutes
Minzoku Eisei — MEISA
Minzokugaku-Kenkyu [*Japanese Journal of Ethnology*] — Minzokugaku
Minzokugaku-Kenkyu [*Japanese Journal of Ethnology*] — MK
Miracle Science and Fantasy Stories — Mir
Mircen Journal of Applied Microbiology and Biotechnology — Mircen J Appl Microbiol Biotechnol
MIRINZ [*Meat Industry Research Institute. New Zealand*] **Report** — MIRINZ Rep
MIRL (Mineral Industry Research Laboratory) Report. University of Alaska — MIRL Rep Univ Alaska
Mirovaja Ekonomika i Mezdunarodnye Otnosenija — Mir Ek Mezd Otnos
Mirovaja Ekonomika i Mezdunarodnye Otnosenija — Mir Ekon Mezdun Otnos
Mirovaya Ekonomikai i Mezhdunarodnye Otnosheniya [*Former USSR*] — Mirovaya Ekon Mezhdunar Otnosheniya
Mirovoe Khoziaistvo i Mirovaia Politika — MKIMP
Mirovoe Rybolovstvo — Mir Rybolovstvo
Misaki Marine Biological Institute. Kyoto University. Special Report — Misaki Mar Biol Inst Kyoto Univ Spec Rep
Misaki Marine Biological Station. Contributions — Misaki Mar Biol Sta Contr
Miscelanea Comillas — MCom
Miscelanea Comillas — Misc Com
Miscelanea Comillas. Universidad Pontificia de Comillas — Misc Comillas
Miscelanea de Estudios Arabes y Hebraicos — MEAH
Miscelanea de Estudios Arabes y Hebraicos [*Granada*] — MESTARABH

Miscelanea de Estudios Dedicados a Fernando Ortiz por Sus Discipulos — MEFO
Miscelanea de Estudos a Memoria de Claudio Basto — MEMCB
Miscelanea de Etnologia e Arqueologia — MEA
Miscelanea. Fundacion Miguel Lillo — Misc Fund Miguel Lillo
Miscelanea Matematica — Miscelanea Mat
Miscelanea. Universidad Nacional de Tucuman. Facultad de Agronomia — Misc Univ Nac Tucuman Fac Agron
Miscelanea. Universidad Nacional de Tucuman. Facultad de Agronomia y Zootecnia — Misc Univ Nac Tucuman Fac Agron Zootech
Miscelanea Zoologica — Misc Zool
Miscelaneas Forestales. Administracion Nacional de Bosques — Misc Forest
Miscelaneas Forestales. Administracion Nacional de Bosques (Buenos Aires, Argentina) — Misc For Adm Nac Bosques (Argent)
Miscellanea — Misc
Miscellanea Agostiniana [*Rome*] — MiscAgost
Miscellanea Barcinonensia — MB
Miscellanea Barcinonensia — MiscBarc
Miscellanea Bavarica Monacensia — Misc Bav Mon
Miscellanea Bavarica Monacensia — Misc Mon
Miscellanea Biblica Edita a Pontificio Instituto Biblico ad Celebrandum Annum XXV ex quo Conditum est Institutum [*Rome*] — MiscBibl
Miscellanea Bryologica et Lichenologica — Misc Bryol Lichenol
Miscellanea Byzantina Monacensia — Misc Byz Mon
Miscellanea Cassinese — M Cass
Miscellanea Classico-Medievale — MCM
Miscellanea Curiosa Sive Ephemeridum Medico-Physicarum Germanicarum Academiae Imperialis Leopoldinae Naturae Curiosorum — Misc Cur Ephem Med Phys German Acad Imp Leop Nat Cur
Miscellanea di Storia e Cultura Ecclesiastica — MSCE
Miscellanea di Storia Italiana — MSI
Miscellanea di Storia Ligure — Misc Stor Lig
Miscellanea di Storia Ligure — MSL
Miscellanea di Studi di Letteratura Cristiana Antica — Misc St L Crist Ant
Miscellanea di Studi di Letteratura Cristiana Antica — MSLC
Miscellanea di Studi Letteratura Cristiana Antica — MSLCA
Miscellanea Francescana — MF
Miscellanea Francescana — MFr
Miscellanea Francescana — Mis Fra
Miscellanea Francescana — Misc Fr
Miscellanea Francescana — Misc Franc
Miscellanea Giovanni Mercati [*Vatican City*] — MGM
Miscellanea Graeca — MIGRA
Miscellanea Graeca — Misc Graec
Miscellanea Greca e Romana — MGR
Miscellanea Historiae Pontificiae — MHP
Miscellanea Laurentiana — Misc Lau
Miscellanea Lubecensia — Misc Lub
Miscellanea Mediaevalia — Misc Med
Miscellanea Mediaevalia — MM
Miscellanea Musicologica — Misc Mus
Miscellanea Musicologica — Misc Musicol
Miscellanea Musicologica — MMA
Miscellanea Musicologica — MMC
Miscellanea Numismatica — MN
Miscellanea Orientalia — MO
Miscellanea Phonetica — MisP
Miscellanea Storica della Valdelsa — Ms Val
Miscellanea Storica della Valdelsa — MSV
Miscellanea Wilbouriana. Brooklyn Museum — MW
Miscellanea Zoologica — MZOODG
Miscellanea Zoologica Hungarica — Misc Zool Hung
Miscellanea Zoologica Hungarica — MZOHDT
Miscellaneous Bulletin. Division of Marketing and Economics. Department of Agriculture. New South Wales — Misc Bull Div Market Econ Dep Agric NSW
Miscellaneous Bulletin Series. Economic Services Branch. Department of Primary Industries — Misc Bull Ser Econ Serv Branch Dep Primary Ind
Miscellaneous Bulletins. Council of Agricultural Research (India) — Misc Bull Coun Agric Res (India)
Miscellaneous Circular. United States Department of Agriculture — Misc Circ USDA
Miscellaneous Extension Publication. North Carolina University. Extension Service — Misc Ext Publ NC Univ Ext Serv
Miscellaneous Information. Tokyo University Forests — Misc Inf Tokyo Univ For
Miscellaneous Information. Tokyo University Forests/Ehshurin. Tokyo Daigaku Nogakubu Enshurin — Misc Inform Tokyo Univ Forests
Miscellaneous Investigation. Applied Scientific Research Corporation of Thailand — Misc Invest Appl Sci Res Corp Thailand
Miscellaneous Man — MM
Miscellaneous Paper. Geological Society (London) — Misc Pap Geol Soc (London)
Miscellaneous Paper. Ontario Division of Mines — Misc Pap Ont Div Mines
Miscellaneous Paper. Ontario Geological Survey — Misc Pap Ont Geol Surv
Miscellaneous Paper. Oregon Department of Geology and Mineral Industries — Misc Pap Oreg Dep Geol Miner Ind
Miscellaneous Paper. Oregon State College. Agricultural Experiment Station — Misc Pap Oreg State Coll Agr Exp Sta
Miscellaneous Paper. Pacific Southwest Forest and Range Experiment Station. US Forest Service — Misc Pap Pac Southwest Forest Range Exp Sta US Forest Serv
Miscellaneous Paper. United States Army Engineers. Waterways Experiment Station — Misc Pap US Army Eng Waterw Exp Stn
Miscellaneous Papers. Experimental Forest. National Taiwan University — Misc Pap Exp For Taiwan Univ
Miscellaneous Papers. Gronlands Geologiske Undersogelse — Misc Pap Gronl Geol Unders
Miscellaneous Papers. Horticultural Institute. Taihoku Imperial University/ Taihoku Teikoku Daigaku Rinogakubu Engeigaku Kiyoshitsu Zappo — Misc Pap Hort Inst Taihoku Imp Univ
Miscellaneous Papers. Landbouwhogeschool Wageningen — Misc Pap Landbouwhogesch Wageningen
Miscellaneous Publication. Agricultural Experiment Station. Oklahoma State University — Misc Publ Agric Exp Stn Okla State Univ
Miscellaneous Publication. Australian Entomological Society — Misc Publ Aust Ent Soc
Miscellaneous Publication. Australian Entomological Society — Misc Publ Aust Entomol Soc
Miscellaneous Publication. Bureau of Standards — Misc Publ Bur Stand
Miscellaneous Publication. Hawaii University. Cooperative Extension Service — Misc Publ Hawaii Univ Coop Ext Serv
Miscellaneous Publication. Hokkaido National Agricultural Experimentation Station — Misc Publ Hokkaido Natl Agric Exp Stn
Miscellaneous Publication. Horticultural Research Station/Rinji Hokoku — Misc Publ Hort Res Sta
Miscellaneous Publication. Land Resources Division. Directorate of Overseas Surveys — Misc Publ Land Resour Div Dir Overseas Surv
Miscellaneous Publication MP. Texas Agricultural Experiment Station — Misc Publ MP Tex Agric Exp Stn
Miscellaneous Publication. National Bureau of Standards — Misc Publ Natl Bur Stand
Miscellaneous Publication. National Institute of Agricultural Sciences (Japan). Series B. Soils and Fertilizers — Misc Publ Natl Inst Agric Sci Jpn Ser B
Miscellaneous Publication. National Institute of Agricultural Sciences. Series D. Physiology and Genetics — Misc Publ Natl Inst Agric Sci Ser D Physiol Genet
Miscellaneous Publication. Oklahoma State University. Agricultural Experiment Station — Misc Publ Okla State Univ Agr Exp Sta
Miscellaneous Publication. United States Department of Agriculture — Misc Pub US Dep Agric
Miscellaneous Publication. United States Department of Agriculture — Misc Publ US Dep Agric
Miscellaneous Publication. United States Department of Agriculture — Misc Publ USDA
Miscellaneous Publication. University of Kentucky. Cooperative Extension Service. Agriculture and Home Economics. HE — Misc Publ Univ KY Co-Op Ext Serv Agr Home Econ HE
Miscellaneous Publication. University of Maine. Agricultural Experiment Station — Misc Publ Univ Maine Agric Exp Stn
Miscellaneous Publication. University of Maryland. Agricultural Experiment Station — Misc Publ Univ MD Agr Exp Sta
Miscellaneous Publication. University of North Carolina. State College of Agriculture and Engineering. Department of Agricultural Economics — Misc Publ Univ NC State Coll Agr Eng Dept Agr Econ
Miscellaneous Publication. Washington State University. College of Agriculture. Extension Service — Misc Publ Wash State Univ Coll Agr Ext Serv
Miscellaneous Publication. West Virginia University. Agricultural and Forestry Experiment Station — Misc Publ W Va Univ Agric For Exp Stn
Miscellaneous Publication. West Virginia University. College of Agriculture. Agricultural Extension Service — Misc Publ W Va Univ Coll Agr Agr Ext Serv
Miscellaneous Publications. Department of Natural Sciences. Los Angeles County Museum — Misc Publ Dept Nat Sci Los Angeles County Mus
Miscellaneous Publications. Entomological Society of America — Misc Publ Entomol Soc Am
Miscellaneous Publications. Entomological Society of America — Misc Publs Ent Soc Am
Miscellaneous Publications. Forests Department. Western Australia — Misc Publs Forest Dep West Aust
Miscellaneous Publications. Genetics Society of Canada — Misc Publ Genet Soc Can
Miscellaneous Publications. Geological Survey of India — Misc Publ Geol Surv India
Miscellaneous Publications. International Tin Research and Development Council — Misc Publ Int Tin Res Dev Counc
Miscellaneous Publications. Museum of Zoology. University of Michigan — Misc Publ Mus Zool Univ Mich
Miscellaneous Publications. Museum of Zoology. University of Michigan — Misc Publs Mus Zool Univ Mich
Miscellaneous Publications. Nursery and Market Garden Industries Development Society. Experimental and Research Station — Misc Publ Nursery Mark Gard Ind Dev Soc Exp Res Stn
Miscellaneous Publications. South Carolina Extension Service — Misc Publ S Carol Ext Serv
Miscellaneous Publications. Texas Agricultural Experiment Station — Misc Publ Tex Agr Exp Sta
Miscellaneous Publications. United States Department of Agriculture — Misc Publs US Dep Agric
Miscellaneous Publications. United States Department of Agriculture. Soil Conservation Service — Misc Publs US Dep Agric Soil Conserv Serv
Miscellaneous Publications. University of Maine — Misc Publs Univ ME
Miscellaneous Report. Agricultural Experiment Station. University of Minnesota — Misc Rep Agric Exp Stn Univ Minn
Miscellaneous Report (Arusha). Tropical Pesticides Research Institute — Misc Rep (Arusha) Trop Pestic Res Inst
Miscellaneous Report. Laboratory of the Government Chemist (Great Britain) — Misc Rep Lab Gov Chem (GB)
Miscellaneous Report. Life Sciences and Agriculture Experiment Station. University of Maine — Misc Rep Life Sci Agric Exp Stn Univ Maine

Miscellaneous Report. Maine Agricultural Experiment Station — Misc Rep Maine Agr Exp Sta
Miscellaneous Report. Minnesota Agricultural Experiment Station — Misc Rep Minn Agric Exp Stn
Miscellaneous Report. Nebraska Agricultural Experiment Station — Misc Rep Nebr Agr Exp Sta
Miscellaneous Report. Ohio Division of Geological Survey — Misc Rep Ohio Div Geol Surv
Miscellaneous Report. Saskatchewan Energy and Mines — Misc Rep Saskatchewan Energy Mines
Miscellaneous Report. University of Maine Agricultural Experiment Station — Misc Rep Univ Maine Agric Exp Stn
Miscellaneous Report. University of Minnesota. Agricultural Experiment Station — Misc Rep Univ Minn Agr Exp Sta
Miscellaneous Report. University of Minnesota. Agricultural Experiment Station — Misc Rep Univ Minn Agric Exp Stn
Miscellaneous Reports. Phytopathological Laboratory. Faculty of Science and Agriculture. Taihoku Imperial University — Misc Rep Phytopathol Lab Fac Sci Taihoku Imp Univ
Miscellaneous Reports. Research Institute for Natural Resources (Tokyo) — Misc Rep Res Inst Nat Resourc (Tokyo)
Miscellaneous Reports. Yamashina Institute for Ornithology — Misc Rep Yamashina Inst Ornithol
Miscellaneous Reports. Yamashina Institute for Ornithology and Zoology — MRYIBO
Miscellaneous Reports. Yamashina's Institute for Ornithology and Zoology — Misc Rep Yamashina's Inst Ornithol Zool
Miscellaneous Series. North Dakota Geological Survey — Misc Ser ND Geol Surv
Miscellaneous Series. North Dakota Geological Survey — NDGXA
Miscellaneous Special Publication. Fisheries and Marine Service (Canada) — Misc Spec Publ Fish Mar Serv Can
Miscellaneous Special Publication. Fisheries Research Board of Canada — Misc Spec Publ Fish Res Board Can
Miscellanies Arqueologiques sobre Mataro i el Maresme — Misc A Mataro
Miscellanies. Jewish Historical Society of England — MJHSE
Miscellany. Geological Survey Division. Michigan — Misc Geol Surv Div Mich
Miscellany. Michigan. Geological Survey — Misc Mich Geol Surv
Miscellen aus der Neuesten Auslaendischen Literatur — Misc Neuesten Ausl Lit
Mises a Jour Cardiologiques — Mises Jour Cardiol
Mises a Jour Scientifiques [*France*] — Mises Jour Sci
Mises a Jour Scientifiques — MJSFA
Mises au Point de Chimie Analytique, Organique, Pharmaceutique, et Bromatologique — Mises Point Chim Anal Org Pharm Bromatol
Mises au Point de Chimie Analytique, Pure, et Appliquee et d'Analyse Bromatologique — Mises Point Chim Anal Pure Appl Anal Bromatol
Misiones Extranjeras — Mis Ex
Misiones Franciscanos — MF
Missale Romanum — Miss Rom
Missale Romanum — MR
Misset's Pakblad — MIS
Missie Integraal — Miss Int
Missiewerk — Miss W
Missiles and Rockets — Miss & Roc
Missili — MSSLA
Missinipe Achimowin. Churchill River Information — MSPA
Missinipe Achimowin. Interim Report Supplement — MSPAIRS
Missiology — M
Missiology — Mi
Missiology — Miss
Missiology — Missio
Missiology — MY
Mission Archeologique au Soudan — MAS
Mission Archeologique de Mari — MAM
Mission Bulletin — MB
Mission Bulletin — Miss B
Mission de Ras Shamra — MRS
Mission de Ras Shamra — RS
Mission Journal — Mission Jnl
Mission Pelliot en Asie Centrale — MPAC
Missionalia Hispanica — MH
Missionalia Hispanica — MHA
Missionalia Hispanica — MissHisp
Missionalia Hispanica [*Madrid*] — Mission Hisp
Missionalia Hispanica. CSIC (Consejo Superior de Investigaciones Cientificas) — Missionalia Hisp
Missionary Bulletin. Tokyo — Miss BT
Missionary Herald — MH
Missionary Review — Mission Rev
Missionary Review — Missionary R
Missionary Review of the World — Mis R
Missionary Review of the World — Miss Rev Wld
Missionary Review of the World — MRW
Missione Archeologica Italiana in Siria — MAIS
Missionerskoe Obozrienie — MO
Missioni Cattoliche — Miss Catt
Missionierende Gemeinde — Miss Gem
Missions Catholiques (Lyons) — MCL
Missions Catholiques (Milan) — MCM
Missions Catholiques (Paris) — MCP
Missionsblatt der Bruedergemeinde — MBBG
Missionsnachrichten der Ostindischen Missionsanstalt zu Halle — MNOIM
Missionstidning — Miss Tid
Missionswissenschaft und Religionswissenschaft — Missionswiss Religionswiss
Missionswissenschaft und Religionswissenschaft — MR
Missionswissenschaftliche Abhandlungen und Texte — MWAT
Missionswissenschaftliche Forschungen (Leipzig) — MWFL
Mississippi Academy of Sciences. Journal — Miss Acad Sci J
Mississippi Academy of Sciences. Journal — Miss Acad Sci Jour
Mississippi. Agricultural and Forestry Experiment Station. Annual Report — Miss Agric For Exp Stn Annu Rep
Mississippi. Agricultural and Forestry Experiment Station. Bulletin — BMASDI
Mississippi. Agricultural and Forestry Experiment Station. Bulletin — Miss Agric For Exp Stn Bull
Mississippi. Agricultural and Forestry Experiment Station. Information Sheet [*A publication*] — IMASDR
Mississippi. Agricultural and Forestry Experiment Station. Research Report — Miss Agric For Exp Stn Res Rep
Mississippi. Agricultural and Forestry Experiment Station. Technical Bulletin — Miss Agric For Exp Stn Tech Bull
Mississippi. Agricultural and Forestry Experiment Station. Technical Bulletin — TBMSDT
Mississippi Agricultural College. Technical Bulletin — Mississippi Agric Coll Techn Bull
Mississippi. Agricultural Experiment Station. Annual Report — Miss Agric Exp Stn Annu Rep
Mississippi. Agricultural Experiment Station. Bulletin — Miss Agr Exp Sta B
Mississippi. Agricultural Experiment Station. Bulletin — Miss Agric Exp Stn Bull
Mississippi. Agricultural Experiment Station. Circular — Miss Agric Exp Stn Circ
Mississippi Agricultural Experiment Station. Mississippi Agricultural and Mechanical College. Bulletin — Mississippi Agric Exp Sta Bull
Mississippi. Agricultural Experiment Station. Publications — Miss Ag Exp
Mississippi. Agricultural Experiment Station. Technical Bulletin — Miss Agric Exp Stn Tech Bull
Mississippi. Board of Water Commissioners. Bulletin — Miss Board Water Comm Bull
Mississippi Board of Water Commissioners. County Report — Miss Board Water Comm Cty Rep
Mississippi Business Education Association. Journal — MBEA J
Mississippi Business Journal — Miss Bus Jnl
Mississippi Business Journal — Mississipi
Mississippi Business Review — Miss Bus R
Mississippi Code Annotated — Miss Code Ann
Mississippi College. Law Review — Miss CL Rev
Mississippi College. Law Review — Miss Col LR
Mississippi Dental Association. Journal — Miss Dent Assoc J
Mississippi Farm Research. Mississippi Agricultural Experiment Station — Miss Farm Res
Mississippi Farm Research. Mississippi Agricultural Experiment Station — Mississippi Farm Res
Mississippi Folklore Register — MissFR
Mississippi. Geological, Economic, and Topographical Survey. Bulletin — Miss Geol Surv Bull
Mississippi. Geological, Economic, and Topographical Survey. Bulletin — Mississippi Geol Econ and Topog Survey Bull
Mississippi. Geological, Economic, and Topographical Survey. Information Series MGS — Miss Geol Econ Topogr Surv Inf Ser MGS
Mississippi. Geological Survey. Bulletin — Miss G S B
Mississippi Geology — Miss Geol
Mississippi Historical Society Publications — Miss H Soc P
Mississippi Historical Society. Publications — Miss His S
Mississippi Historical Society. Publications — Miss Hist Soc Publ
Mississippi Law Journal — Miss L J
Mississippi Law Journal — Miss Law J
Mississippi Law Journal — MLJ
Mississippi Law Journal — MS LJ
Mississippi Library News — Miss Lib News
Mississippi Medical Monthly. Mississippi State Medical Association and Its Component Societies — Mississippi Med Monthly
Mississippi Medical Record — Miss Med Rec
Mississippi Medical Record — Mississippi Med Rec
Mississippi Music Educator — MIS
Mississippi Quarterly — Miss Quart
Mississippi Quarterly — MissQ
Mississippi Quarterly — PMSQ
Mississippi Rag — Miss Rag
Mississippi Reports — Miss
Mississippi Review — Miss R
Mississippi RN — Miss RN
Mississippi State College. Agricultural Experiment Station. Annual Report — Miss State Coll Agric Exp Stn Annu Rep
Mississippi State College. Agricultural Experiment Station. Circular — Miss State Coll Agric Exp Stn Circ
Mississippi State Geological Survey. Bulletin — Miss State Geol Surv Bull
Mississippi State Geological Survey. Bulletin. Circular — Miss State Geol Survey Bull Circ
Mississippi State University. Agricultural Experiment Station. Annual Report — Miss State Univ Agric Exp Stn Annu Rep
Mississippi State University. Agricultural Experiment Station. Technical Bulletin — Miss State Univ Agr Expt Sta Tech Bull
Mississippi Valley Historial Review — Mississippi Valley Hist Rev
Mississippi Valley Historical Association. Proceedings — Miss V His As
Mississippi Valley Historical Association. Proceedings — Miss Val Hist Assn Proc
Mississippi Valley Historical Review — Miss V His R
Mississippi Valley Historical Review — Miss Val Hist R
Mississippi Valley Historical Review — Missi Valley Hist Rev
Mississippi Valley Historical Review — MVHR
Mississippi Valley Historical Review. A Journal of American History — Miss Val Hist Rev

Mississippi Valley Journal of Business and Economics — Mississippi Val J Busin Econ
Mississippi Valley Medical Journal — Miss V Med J
Mississippi Valley Medical Journal — Miss Val Med J
Mississippi Water Resources Conference. Proceedings — Miss Water Resour Conf Proc
Mississippi-Alabama Sea Grant Consortium. MASGP — MASMDP
Mississippi's Business — Mississippi's Bus
Missouri Academy of Science. Bulletin. Supplement — Mo Acad Sci Bull Suppl
Missouri Academy of Science. Occasional Paper — MO Acad Sci Occas Pap
Missouri Agricultural College. Agricultural Experiment Station. Circular — Missouri Agric Exp Sta Circ
Missouri Agricultural College. Agricultural Experiment Station. Circular of Information — Missouri Agric Exp Sta Circ Inform
Missouri Agricultural College. Agricultural Experiment Station. Special Report — Missouri Agric Exp Sta Special Rep
Missouri. Agricultural Experiment Station. Bulletin — MO Agric Exp Stn Bull
Missouri. Agricultural Experiment Station. Publications — MO Ag Exp
Missouri. Agricultural Experiment Station. Research Bulletin — MO Agric Exp Stn Res Bull
Missouri. Agricultural Experiment Station. Special Report — MO Agric Exp Stn Spec Rep
Missouri Appeal Reports — MO App
Missouri Architect — Missouri Arch
Missouri Bar. Journal — MO B J
Missouri Bar. Journal — MO Bar J
Missouri Botanical Garden. Annals — Missouri Bot Garden Annals
Missouri Botanical Garden. Annals — MO Bot Gard Ann
Missouri Botanical Garden. Bulletin — MO Bot Gard Bull
Missouri Bureau of Geology and Mines — MO B G
Missouri. Bureau of Geology and Mines. Reports — Mo Bur Geol Mines Rep
Missouri Code of State Regulations — MO Code Regs
Missouri Conservationist — MO Conserv
Missouri Dental Journal — MO Dent J
Missouri. Department of Conservation. Terrestrial Series — MO Dep Conserv Terr Ser
Missouri. Division of Geological Survey and Water Resources. Reports — Mo Div Geol Surv Water Resour Rep
Missouri Division of Geology and Land Survey. Report of Investigations — MO Div Geol Land Surv Rep Invest
Missouri English Bulletin — MEB
Missouri. Geological Survey and Water Resources. Educational Series — Missouri Geol Survey and Water Resources Educ Ser
Missouri. Geological Survey and Water Resources. Information Circular — Missouri Geol Survey and Water Resources Inf Circ
Missouri. Geological Survey and Water Resources. Information Circular — MO Geol Surv Water Resour Inf Circ
Missouri. Geological Survey and Water Resources. Information Circular — MO Geol Surv Water Resour Inform Circ
Missouri. Geological Survey and Water Resources. Miscellaneous Publication — MO Geol Surv Water Resour Misc Publ
Missouri. Geological Survey and Water Resources. Report — Missouri Geol Survey and Water Resources Report
Missouri. Geological Survey and Water Resources. Report — MO Geol Surv Water Resour Rep
Missouri. Geological Survey and Water Resources. Report of Investigations — Missouri Geol Survey and Water Resources Rept Inv
Missouri. Geological Survey and Water Resources. Report of Investigations — MO Geol Surv Water Resour Rep Invest
Missouri. Geological Survey and Water Resources. Special Publication — Missouri Geol Survey and Water Resources Spec Pub
Missouri. Geological Survey and Water Resources. Special Publication — MO Geol Surv Water Resour Spec Publ
Missouri. Geological Survey and Water Resources. Water Resources Report — MO Geol Surv Water Resour Water Resour Rep
Missouri. Geological Survey. Missouri Bureau of Geology and Mines — MO G S MO Bur G Mines
Missouri. Geological Survey. Report of Investigations — MO Geol Surv Rep Invest
Missouri Health Report — MO Hlth Rep
Missouri Historical Review — MHR
Missouri Historical Review — MisH
Missouri Historical Review — Missouri Hist R
Missouri Historical Review — MO His R
Missouri Historical Review — MO Hist Rev
Missouri Historical Society. Bulletin — MHSB
Missouri Historical Society. Bulletin — MO Hist Soc Bull
Missouri Historical Society. Collections — MO His Col
Missouri Journal of Mathematical Sciences — Missouri J Math Sci
Missouri Journal of Research in Music Education — MJR
Missouri Journal of Research in Music Education — MO J Res Mus Ed
Missouri Law Review — Missouri Law R
Missouri Law Review — MO L
Missouri Law Review — MO L Rev
Missouri Law Review — MO LR
Missouri Legislative Service — MO Legis Serv
Missouri Library Association. Newsletter — MO Lib Assn Newsl
Missouri Library Association. Quarterly — MLA Q
Missouri Library Association. Quarterly — MO Lib Assn Q
Missouri Library Association. Quarterly — MO Libr Ass Q
Missouri Medical Association. Journal — Missouri Med Assn J
Missouri Medicine — Miss Med
Missouri Medicine — MO Med
Missouri Nurse — MO Nurse
Missouri Register — MO Reg
Missouri Reports — MO
Missouri Review — Miss R
Missouri Revised Statutes — MO Rev Stat
Missouri School Music Magazine — MI
Missouri School of Mines and Metallurgy. Bulletin. General Series — MO Sch Mines Metall Bull Gen Ser
Missouri School of Mines and Metallurgy. Bulletin. Technical Series — MO Sch Mines Metall Bull Tech Ser
Missouri Speleology — MO Speleology
Missouri State Agricultural College. Bulletin — Missouri State Agric Coll Bull
Missouri State Board of Agriculture. Publications — MO Ag Bd
Missouri Tax Review — Missouri Tax Rev
Missouri University. Agricultural Experiment Station. Research Bulletin — Mo Univ Agric Exp Stn Res Bull
Missouri University. College of Agriculture. Agricultural Experiment Station. Bulletin — Mo Univ Coll Agric Agric Exp Stn Bull
Missouri. University. College of Agriculture. Agricultural Experiment Station. Special Report — MO Univ Coll Agric Agric Exp Stn Spec Rep
Missouri University. Engineering Experiment Station. Engineering Reprint Series — MO Univ Eng Exp Stn Eng Repr Ser
Missouri. University. Engineering Experiment Station. Engineering Series Bulletin — MO Univ Eng Exp Stn Eng Ser Bull
Missouri University. School of Mines and Metallurgy. Bulletin. General Series — MO Univ Sch Mines Metall Bull Gen Ser
Missouri Water and Sewerage Conference. Journal — Mo Water Sewerage Conf J
Misstofvereniging van Suid-Afrika Joernaal — Misstofvereniging S Afr J
MIT [*Massachusetts Institute of Technology*] **Hydrodynamics Laboratory. Technical Report** — MIT Hydrodyn Lab Tech Rep
MIT (Massachusetts Institute of Technology) Press. Research Monograph — MIT (Mass Inst Technol) Press Res Monogr
MIT (Massachusetts Institute of Technology) Studies in American Politics and Public Policy — MIT (Mass Inst Technol) Stud Am Polit Public Policy
MIT (Mindanao Institute of Technology) Research Journal — MIT Res J
MIT [*Massachusetts Institute of Technology*] **Press Energy Laboratory Series** — MIT Press Energy Lab Ser
MIT [*Massachusetts Institute of Technology*] **Press. Research Monograph** — MIT Press Res Monogr
MIT Press Series in Artificial Intelligence — MIT Press Ser Artificial Intelligence
MIT [*Massachusetts Institute of Technology*] **Press. Series in Computer Science** — MIT Press Ser Comput Sci
MIT Press Series in Computer Systems — MIT Press Ser Comput Syst
MIT Press Series in Logic Programming — MIT Press Ser Logic Program
MIT Press Series in Scientific Computation — MIT Press Ser Sci Comput
MIT [*Massachusetts Institute of Technology*] **Press. Series in Signal Processing. Optimization and Control** — MIT Press Ser Signal Process Optim Control
MIT Press Series in the Foundations of Computing — MIT Press Ser Found Comput
MIT [*Massachusetts Institute of Technology*] **Studies in American Politics and Public Policy** — MSAPD2
Mita Journal of Economics — Mita J Econ
Mitbestimmung — Mitb
Mitbestimmungsgespraech — Mitb Gespr
Mitchurin Bewegung — Mitchurin Beweg
Mitochondria. Structure and Function. Federation of European Biochemical Societies Meeting — Mitochondria Struct Funct Fed Eur Biochem Soc Meet
Mitokhondrii, Biokhimiya i Morfologiya, Materialy Simpoziuma Struktura i Funktsii Mitokhondrii — Mitokhondrii Biokhim Morfol Mater Simp
Mitre Corporation. Technical Report MTR — Mitre Corp Tech Rep MTR
Mitre Technical Report — Mitre Tech Rep
Mitropolia Ardealului — Mitr Art
Mitropolia Banatului — Mitr Ban
Mitropolia Olteniei — MitrOlt
Mitropolia Olteniei — Mitrop Olteniei
Mitsubishi Bank Review — MTR
Mitsubishi Chemical Research and Development Review — Mitsubishi Chem Res Dev Rev
Mitsubishi Denki Giho — MIDGA
Mitsubishi Denki Laboratory Reports — Mitsubishi Denki Lab Rep
Mitsubishi Denki Technical Review — Mitsubishi Denki Tech Rev
Mitsubishi Electric Advance — Mitsubishi Electr Adv
Mitsubishi Electric Engineer — Mitsubishi Electr Eng
Mitsubishi Heavy Industries. Mitsubishi Technical Bulletin — Mitsubishi Heavy Ind Mitsubishi Tech Bull
Mitsubishi Heavy Industries Technical Review — Mitsubishi Heavy Ind Tech Rev
Mitsubishi Heavy Industries Technical Review — Mitsubishi Tech Rev
Mitsubishi Kasei R & D Review — Mitsubishi Kasei R D Rev
Mitsubishi Plastics Technology [*Japan*] — Mitsubishi Plast Technol
Mitsubishi Steel Manufacturing Technical Review — Mitsubishi Steel Manuf Tech Rev
Mitsubishi Technical Bulletin — Mitsubishi Tech Bull
Mitsui Technical Review — Mitsui Tech Rev
Mitsui Zosen Technical Review — Mitsui Zosen Tech Rev
Mitteilung der Farbstoffkommission. Deutsche Forschungsgemeinschaft — Mitt Farbstoffkomm Dtsch Forschungsgem
Mitteilung. Deutsche Forschungsanstalt fuer Luft- und Raumfahrt — Mitt Dtsch Forschungsanst Luft Raumfahrt
Mitteilung. Deutsche Forschungsgemeinschaft, Kommission zur Erforschung der Luftverunreinigung — Mitt Dtsch Forschungsgem Komm Erforsch Luftverunreinig
Mitteilung. Deutsche Forschungsgemeinschaft. Kommission zur Pruefung Fremder Stoffe bei Lebensmitteln — Mitt Dtsch Forschungsgem Komm Pruef Fremder Stoff Lebensm

Mitteilung. Deutsche Forschungsgemeinschaft, Kommission zur Pruefung von Rueckstaenden in Lebensmitteln — Mitt Dtsch Forschungsgem Komm Pruef Rueckstaenden Lebensm
Mitteilung. Kommission zur Erforschung der Luftverunreinigung. Deutsche Forschungsgemeinschaft — Mitt Komm Erforsch Luftverunreinig Dtsch Forschungsgem
Mitteilung. Kommission zur Pruefung Fremder Stoffe bei Lebensmitteln, Deutsche Forschungsgemeinschaft — Mitt Komm Pruef Fremder Stoffe Lebensm Dtsch Forschungsgem
Mitteilung. Kommission zur Pruefung von Rueckstaenden in Lebensmitteln. Deutsche Forschungsgemeinschaft — Mitt Komm Pruef Rueckstaenden Lebensm Dtsch Forschungsgem
Mitteilunged der Bberliner Gesellschaft fuer Anthropologie, Ethnologie, und Urgeschichte — Mitt Berliner Ges Anthropol Ethnol u Urgesch
Mitteilungen (Agen) — Mitt (Agen)
Mitteilungen. Agrarwissenschaftliche Fakultaet zu Mosonmagyarovar (Ungarn) — Mitt Agrarwiss Fak Mosonmagyarovar (Ung)
Mitteilungen. Agrarwissenschaftliche Hochschule zu Mosonmagyarovar (Ungarn) — Mitt Agrarwiss Hochsch Mosonmagyarovar (Ung)
Mitteilungen. Akademie der Wissenschaften der UdSSR — Mitt Akad Wiss UdSSR
Mitteilungen. Alpenlaendischer Geologische Verein — Mitt Alpenl Geol Ver
Mitteilungen. Altertumskommission fuer Westphalen — MAKW
Mitteilungen. Altorientalische Gesellschaft — MAG
Mitteilungen. Altorientalische Gesellschaft [*Leipzig*] — MAoG
Mitteilungen. Anthropologische Gesellschaft in Wien — M Anthr G Wien
Mitteilungen. Anthropologische Gesellschaft in Wien — M Anthrop Ges Wien
Mitteilungen. Anthropologische Gesellschaft in Wien — MAG Wien
Mitteilungen. Anthropologische Gesellschaft in Wien — MAGW
Mitteilungen. Anthropologische Gesellschaft in Wien — Mitt Anthrop Ges W
Mitteilungen. Anthropologische Gesellschaft in Wien — Mitt Anthropol Ges Wien
Mitteilungen. Antiquarische Gesellschaft in Zurich — MAGZ
Mitteilungen. Arbeitsgemeinschaft fuer Floristik in Schleswig-Holstein und Hamburg — MAFSA9
Mitteilungen. Arbeitsgemeinschaft fuer Floristik in Schleswig-Holstein und Hamburg — Mitt Arbeitsgem Florist Schleswig-Holstein Hamb
Mitteilungen. Arbeitsgemeinschaft fuer Floristik in Schleswig-Holstein und Hamburg — Mitt Arbeitsgem Florist Schleswig-Holstein Hamburg
Mitteilungen. Arbeitsgemeinschaft fuer Rheinische Musikgeschichte — Mitt Rheinische Mg
Mitteilungen. Arbeitsgemeinschaft Geobotanik in Schleswig-Holstein und Hamburg — Mitt Arbeitsgem Geobot Schleswig-Holstein Hamburg
Mitteilungen. Arbeitsgemeinschaft zur Floristischen Kartierung Bayerns — Mitt Arbeitsgem Florist Kartierung Bayerns
Mitteilungen. Archaeologisches Institut der Ungarischen Akademie der Wissenschaften — MA Inst Ung Ak
Mitteilungen. Archaeologisches Institut der Ungarischen Akademie der Wissenschaften — Mitt Archaeol Inst Ung Akad Wiss
Mitteilungen. Astronomische Gesellschaft — Mitt Astr Ges
Mitteilungen. Astronomische Gesellschaft [*German Federal Republic*] — Mitt Astron Ges
Mitteilungen aus dem Arbeitsbereich. Metallgesellschaft AG — Mitt Arbeitsbereich Metallges AG
Mitteilungen aus dem Arbeitsbereich. Metallgesellschaft AG — MTGSA
Mitteilungen aus dem Ausschuss fuer Pulvermetallurgie — Mitt Ausschuss Pulvermetall
Mitteilungen aus dem Botanischen Garten St. Gallen — Mitt Bot Gart St Gallen
Mitteilungen aus dem Botanischen Garten und Museum Berlin-Dahlem — Mitt Bot Gart Berlin Dahlem
Mitteilungen aus dem Gebiete der Lebensmitteluntersuchung und Hygiene — Mitt Geb Lebensmittelunters Hyg
Mitteilungen aus dem Gebiete der Lebensmitteluntersuchung und Hygiene — Mitt LMU
Mitteilungen aus dem Gebiete der Lebensmitteluntersuchung und Hygiene. Travaux de Chimie Alimentaire et d'Hygiene — Mitt Geb Lebensmittelunters Hyg Trav Chim Aliment Hyg
Mitteilungen aus dem Gebiete der Statistik — MS
Mitteilungen aus dem Gebiete des Wasserbaues und der Grundbauforschung — Mitt Wasserbau
Mitteilungen aus dem Institut fuer Allgemeine Botanik [*Hamburg*] — MIAHDA
Mitteilungen aus dem Institut fuer Allgemeine Botanik (Hamburg) — Mitt Inst Allg Bot (Hamb)
Mitteilungen aus dem Institut fuer Allgemeine Botanik (Hamburg) — Mitt Inst Allgemeine Bot (Hamb)
Mitteilungen aus dem Institut fuer Angewandte Mathematik — Mitt Inst Angew Math
Mitteilungen aus dem Institut fuer Raumforschung [*Bonn*] — Mitt Inst Raumforsch
Mitteilungen aus dem Institut fuer Systematische Botanik und Pflanzengeographie der Martin-Luther-Universitaet Halle-Wittenberg — Mitt Inst Syst Bot Martin Luther Univ Halle Wittenberg
Mitteilungen aus dem Institut fuer Textiltechnik — Mitt Inst Text Tech
Mitteilungen aus dem Koeniglich Mineralogisch-Geologischen und Praehistorischen Museum zu Dresden — Mitt Koenigl Mineral Geol Mus Dresden
Mitteilungen aus dem Markscheidewesen — M Msch W
Mitteilungen aus dem Markscheidewesen [*Germany*] — Mitt Markscheidewes
Mitteilungen aus dem Max-Planck-Institut fuer Aeronomie — Mitt Max Planck Inst Aeron
Mitteilungen aus dem Max-Planck-Institut fuer Eisenforschung — Mitt Max Planck Inst Eisenforsch
Mitteilungen aus dem Museum fuer Voelkerkunde Hamburg — Mitt Mus fuer Voelkerkunde Hamburg
Mitteilungen aus dem Museum fuer Voelkerkunde in Hamburg — MMVKH
Mitteilungen aus dem Museum fuer Voelkerkunde Leipzig — Mitt Mus fuer Voelkerkunde Leipzig
Mitteilungen aus dem Technisch-Mikroskopischen Laboratorium der Technischen Hochschule in Wien — Mitt Techn Mikroskop Lab TH Wien
Mitteilungen aus dem Zoologischen Museum der Universitaet Kiel — Mitt Zool Mus Univ Kiel
Mitteilungen aus den Botanischen Staatsinstituten in Hamburg — Mitt Bot Staatsinst Hamburg
Mitteilungen aus den Deutschen Schutzgebieten — Mitt Aus D Deutschen Schutzgeb
Mitteilungen aus den Gebieten der Naturwissenschaft und Technik — Mitt Geb Naturwiss Tech
Mitteilungen aus den Grenzgebieten der Medizin und Chirurgie — Mitt Grenzgeb Med Chir
Mitteilungen aus den Grenzgebieten der Medizin und Chirurgie — Mitt Grenzgeb Med u Chir
Mitteilungen aus den Koeniglichen Technischen Versuchsanstalten zu Berlin — Mitt K Tech Versuchsanst Berlin
Mitteilungen aus den Laboratorien der Preussischen Geologischen Landesanstalt — Mitt Lab Preuss Geol Landesanst
Mitteilungen aus den Laboratorien des Geologischen Dienstes. Berlin — Mitt Lab Geol Dienstes Berlin
Mitteilungen aus der Aegyptischen Sammlung — MAeS
Mitteilungen aus der Arbeitsmarkt -und Berufsforschung — Mitt Arbeitsmarkt U Berufsforsch
Mitteilungen aus der Baltischen Geschichte — Mitt Balt Gesch
Mitteilungen aus der Biologischen Reichsanstalt fuer Land- und Forstwirtschaft. Berlin-Dahlem — Mitt Biol Reichsanst Land Forstwirtsch Berlin Dahlem
Mitteilungen aus der Biologischen Zentralanstalt fuer Land- und Forstwirtschaft, Berlin-Dahlem — Mitt Biol Zentralanst Land Forstwirtsch Berlin Dahlem
Mitteilungen aus der Botanischen Staatssammlung Muenchen — Mitt Bot Staatssamml Muenchen
Mitteilungen aus der Chirurgischen Klinik zu Tuebingen — Mitt Chir Klin Tuebingen
Mitteilungen aus der Dachpappen-Industrie — Mitt Dachpappen Ind
Mitteilungen aus der Freiburger Papyrussammlung — P Freib
Mitteilungen aus der Historischen Literatur — MHL
Mitteilungen aus der Koeniglichen Landesanstalt fuer Wasserhygiene zu Berlin-Dahlen — Mitt K Landesanst Wasserhyg Berlin Dahlem
Mitteilungen aus der Koeniglichen Pruefungsanstalt fuer Wasserversorgung und Abwaesserbeseitigung zu Berlin — Mitt K Pruefungsanst Wasserversorg Abwaesserbeseit Berlin
Mitteilungen aus der Koeniglichen Pruefungsanstalt fuer Wasserversorgung und Abwaesserbeseitigung zu Berlin — Mitt Pruefgsanst Wasserversorg Berl
Mitteilungen aus der Landesanstalt fuer Wasserhygiene zu Berlin-Dahlem — Mitt Landesanst Wasserhyg Berlin Dahlem
Mitteilungen aus der Livlandischen Geschichte — MLG
Mitteilungen aus der Medicinischen Facultaet der Kaiserlich-Japanischen Universitaet/Teikoku Daigaku Ika Kiyo — Mitt Med Fac Kaiserl Jap Univ
Mitteilungen aus der Medizinischen Akademie zu Keijo — Mitt Med Akad Keijo
Mitteilungen aus der Medizinischen Akademie zu Kioto — Mitt Med Akad Kioto
Mitteilungen aus der Medizinischen Fakultaet der Kaiserlichen Japanischen Universitaet zu Tokio — Mitt Med Fak Tok
Mitteilungen aus der Naturwissenschaftlichen Gesellschaft Isis in Bautzen — Mitt Naturwiss Ges Isis Bautzen
Mitteilungen aus der Papyrussammlung der Giessener Universitaetsbibliothek — MPSG
Mitteilungen aus der Papyrus-Sammlung der Oesterreichischen Nationalbibliothek. Papyrus Erzherzog Rainer — P Rain
Mitteilungen aus der Rechtspflege im Gebiete des Ehemaligen Kurfuerstentums Hessen — KurhessMitt
Mitteilungen aus der Studienabteilung des Oekumenischen Rates der Kirchen — MSOeRK
Mitteilungen aus der Universitaetsbibliothek Dortmund — Mitt Universitaetsbibl Dortmund
Mitteilungen aus der Wuerzburger Papyrussammlung — P Wuerzb
Mitteilungen aus Justus Perthes' Geographischer Anstalt — MJPGA
Mitteilungen. Badische Geologische Landesanstalt — Mitt Bad Geol Landesanst
Mitteilungen. Bayerische Landesanstalt fuer Tierzucht in Grub bei Muenchen — Mitt Bayer Landesanst Tier Grub Muenchen
Mitteilungen. Bayerische Landesanstalt fuer Tierzucht in Grub bei Muenchen — Mitt Bayer Landesanst Tierz Grub
Mitteilungen. Bayerische Staatssammlung fuer Palaeontologie und Historische Geologie — Mitt Bayer Staatssamml Palaeontol Hist Geol
Mitteilungen. Berliner Gesellschaft fuer Anthropologie, Ethnologie, und Urgeschichte — M Berl Ges Anthrop
Mitteilungen. Berliner Gesellschaft fuer Anthropologie, Ethnologie, und Urgeschichte — Mitt Berl Ges Anthropol
Mitteilungen. Berner Kunstmuseum — MBK
Mitteilungen. Biologische Bundesanstalt fuer Land- und Forstwirtschaft — Mitt Biol Bund Anst Ld- u Forstw
Mitteilungen. Biologische Bundesanstalt fuer Land- und Forstwirtschaft — Mitt Biol Bundesanst Land- u Forstw
Mitteilungen. Biologische Bundesanstalt fuer Land- und Forstwirtschaft (Berlin-Dahlem) — Mitt Biol Bundesanst Land-Forstwirt (Berlin-Dahlem)
Mitteilungen. Biologische Bundesanstalt fuer Land- und Forstwirtschaft (Berlin-Dahlem) — Mitt Biol Bundesanst Land-Forstwirtsch (Berl-Dahlem)
Mitteilungen. Botanische Staatssammlung Muenchen — Mitt Bot Muenchen
Mitteilungen. Botanische Staatssammlung Muenchen — Mitt Bot Staatssamml Muench
Mitteilungen. Botanischer Garten und Museum Berlin-Dahlem — Mitt Bot Gart Mus Berl-Dahlem
Mitteilungen. Brennstoffinstitut (Freiberg) — Mitt Brennstoffinst (Freiberg)

Mitteilungen. Bundesforschungsanstalt fuer Forst- und Holzwirtschaft — Mitt B Fors
Mitteilungen. Bundesforschungsanstalt fuer Forst- und Holzwirtschaft — Mitt Bundesforschanst Forst- u Holzw
Mitteilungen. Bundesforschungsanstalt fuer Forst- und Holzwirtschaft — Mitt Bundesforschungsanst Forst Holzwirtsch
Mitteilungen. Bundesforschungsanstalt fuer Forst- und Holzwirtschaft (Reinbek bei Hamburg) — Mitt Bundesforsch (Reinbek Hamburg)
Mitteilungen. Bundesstelle fuer Aussenhandelsinformation — MHL
Mitteilungen. Chemisches Forschungsinstitut der Wirtschaft Oesterreichs — Mitt Chem Forschungsinst Wirtsch Oesterr
Mitteilungen der Aargauischen Naturforschenden Gesellschaft — Mitt Aarg Nat Ges
Mitteilungen der Aargauischen Naturforschenden Gesellschaft — Mitt Aargau Natfd Ges
Mitteilungen der Abteilung fuer Bergbau, Geologie und Palaeontologie des Landesmuseums Joanneum — Mitt Abt Bergbau Geol Palaeontol Landesmus Joanneum
Mitteilungen der Abteilung fuer Mineralogie am Landesmuseum Joanneum — Mitt Abt Mineral Landesmus Joanneum
Mitteilungen der Afrikanische Gesellschaft in Deutschland — MAGD
Mitteilungen der Altertums Kommission fuer Westfalen — Mitt Alt Komm Westfalen
Mitteilungen der Altertums Kommission fuer Westfalen — Mitt Alter Kom Westfalen
Mitteilungen der Anthropologischen Gesellschaft in Wien — Mitt Anthr Ges
Mitteilungen der Antiquarischen Gesellschaft in Zurich — Mitt Ant Gesell
Mitteilungen der Antiquarischen Gesellschaft in Zurich — Mitt Zurich
Mitteilungen der Athener Akademie Sitzung — Mitt Athener Akad Sitz
Mitteilungen der Auslandhochschule an der Universitaet Berlin — MAHS
Mitteilungen der Badischen Geologischen Landesanstalt — Mitt Bad Geol Ldsanst
Mitteilungen der Basler Afrika Bibliographien — Mitt der Basler Afrika Bibliographien
Mitteilungen der Basler Botanischen Gesellschaft — Mitt Basl Bot Ges
Mitteilungen der Bayerischen Botanischen Gesellschaft zur Erforschung der Heimischen Flora — Mitt Bayer Bot Ges
Mitteilungen der Bayerischen Numismatischen Gesellschaft — MBNG
Mitteilungen der Berliner Gesellschaft fuer Anthropologie, Ethnologie, und Urgeschichte — MGAEU
Mitteilungen der Biologischen Reichsanstalt — MBRA
Mitteilungen der Centralkommission zur Erforschung der Denkmale — MCC
Mitteilungen der Deutschen Gesellschaft fuer Natur- und Voelkerkunde Ostasiens — Mitt Deutsch Ges Natur Voelkerk Ostasiens
Mitteilungen der Deutschen Gesellschaft fuer Volkskunde — MDGV
Mitteilungen der Deutschen Gesellschaft zur Bekaempfung der Geschlechtskrankheiten — Mitt Dt Ges Bekaempfg Geschlechtkrkht
Mitteilungen der Deutschen Gesellschft fuer Natur- und Voelkerkunde Ostasiens — MDGNO
Mitteilungen der Deutschen Gesellschft fuer Natur- und Voelkerkunde Ostasiens. Supplement — MDGNOS
Mitteilungen der Deutschen Landwirtschafts-Gesellschaft — MDLG
Mitteilungen der Deutschen Malakozoologischen Gesellschaft — DMGMAF
Mitteilungen der Deutschen Malakozoologischen Gesellschaft — Mitt Dtsch Malakozool Ges
Mitteilungen der Deutschen Orient Gesellschaft zu Berlin — MDOrG
Mitteilungen der Deutschen Orient Gesellschaft zu Berlin — Mitt Or Ges
Mitteilungen der Deutschen Orient-Gesellschaft — Mitt DOG
Mitteilungen der Deutschen Orient-Gesellschaft — Mitt Dt Orientges
Mitteilungen der Deutschen Orient-Gesellschaft zu Berlin — Mitt Dt Orient Ges
Mitteilungen der Deutschen Pharmazeutischen Gesellschaft und der Pharmazeutischen Gesellschaft der DDR — Mitt Dtsch Pharm Ges Pharm Ges DDR
Mitteilungen der Deutscher Schutzgebiet — MDS
Mitteilungen der Erdbebenkommission der Akademie der Wissenschaften in Wien — MEKAW
Mitteilungen der Floristisch-Soziologischen Arbeitsgemeinschaft in Niedersachsen — Mitt Florist Soziol Arbeitsgem Niedersachsen
Mitteilungen der Forschungsgesellschaft Blechverarbeitung — Mitt Forschungsges Blechverarb
Mitteilungen der Forstlichen Forschungsanstalt Schwedens — Mitt Forstl Forschungsanst Schwed
Mitteilungen der Forsttechnischen Akademie — Mitt Forsttech Akad
Mitteilungen der Fraenkischen Geographischen Gesellschaft — Mitt Fr Geogr Ges
Mitteilungen der Geographischen Gesellschaft fuer Thueringen zu Jena — Mitt Geogr Ges Thueringen Jena
Mitteilungen der Geographischen Gesellschaft in Hamburg — MGGH
Mitteilungen der Geographischen Gesellschaft in Muenchen — MGGM
Mitteilungen der Geographischen Gesellschaft in Muenchen — Mitt Geogr Ges Muench
Mitteilungen der Geographischen Gesellschaft und des Naturhistorischen Museums in Luebeck — Mitt Geogr Ges Naturhist Mus Luebeck
Mitteilungen der Gesellschaft fuer Angewandte Mathematik und Mechanik — Mitt Ges Angew Math Mech
Mitteilungen der Gesellschaft fuer Erdkunde zu Berlin — MGEB
Mitteilungen der Gesellschaft fuer Erdkunde zu Leipzig — Mitt Ges Erdk L
Mitteilungen der Gesellschaft fuer Historische Kostuem- und Waffenkunde — Mitt Ges Hist Kostuem U Waffenkde
Mitteilungen der Gesellschaft fuer Salzburger Landeskunde — MGSL
Mitteilungen der Gesellschaft Schweizerischer Landwirte — MGSchL
Mitteilungen der Gesellschaft Schweizerischer Landwirte — Mitt Ges Schweiz Ldwirte
Mitteilungen der Gesellschaft Teilhard de Chardin fuer den Deutschen Sprachraum — MGTC
Mitteilungen der Gesellschaft zur Foerderung der Forschung an der Eidgenoessischen Technischen Hochschule — GFF Mitt
Mitteilungen der Gruppe Deutscher Kolonialwirtschaftlicher Unternehmungen — Mitt Gruppe Dtsch Kolonialwirtsch Unternehm
Mitteilungen der Hermann-Goering-Akademie der Deutschen Forstwissenschaft — Mitt Hermann Goering Akad Deutsch Forstwiss
Mitteilungen der Hoeheren Bundeslehr- und Versuchsanstalten fuer Wein-, Obst-, und Gartenbau [*Klosterneuberg*] — Mitt Hoh Bundeslehr- u VersAnst Wein- Obst- u Gartenb
Mitteilungen der Hoeheren Bundeslehr- und Versuchsanstalten fuer Wein-, Obst-, und Gartenbau [*Klosterneuburg*]. Serie A. Rebe und Wein — MKARAH
Mitteilungen der Hoeheren Bundeslehr- und Versuchsanstalten fuer Wein- und Obstbau [*Klosterneuburg*]. Serie B. Obst und Garten — MKBOAD
Mitteilungen der Internationalen Bodenkundlichen Gesellschaft — Mitt Int Bodenkd Ges
Mitteilungen der Internationalen Kriminalistischen Vereinigung — Mitt Intern Kriminal Vereing
Mitteilungen der Internationalen Vereinigung fuer Samenkontrolle — Mitt Int Ver Samenkontrolle
Mitteilungen der K. K. Geographische Gesellschaft in Wien — MKKG
Mitteilungen der Kautschuk-Stiftung. Delft — Mitt Kautsch Stift Delft
Mitteilungen der Landwirtschaftlichen Institute der Koeniglichen Universitaet Breslau — Mitt Landw Inst Koenigl Univ Breslau
Mitteilungen der Landwirtschaftlichen Versuchsstellen Ungarns. B. Tierzucht — Mitt Landwirtsch Versuchsstellen Ung B
Mitteilungen der Litauischen Literarischen Gesellschaft — Mitt Litau Lit Ges
Mitteilungen der Mathematischen Gesellschaft der Deutschen Demokratischen Republik — Mitt Math Ges Deut Demokr Republ
Mitteilungen der Medizinischen Gesellschaft zu Chiba — Mitt Med Ges Chiba
Mitteilungen der Medizinischen Gesellschaft zu Nagoya — Mitt Med Ges Nagoya
Mitteilungen der Naturforschenden Gesellschaft in Solothurn — Mitt Naturf Ges Solothurn
Mitteilungen der Naturforschenden Gesellschaft Schaffhausen — Mitt Naturf Ges Schaffhausen
Mitteilungen der Niederlaendischen Ahnengemeinschaft. Hamburg — Mitt Niederl Ahnengemeinschaft
Mitteilungen der Nikolai-Hauptsternwarte Pulkowo — Mitt Nikolai Hauptsternwarte Pulkowo
Mitteilungen der Numismatischen Gesellschaft in Wien — Mitt Numismat Ges Wien
Mitteilungen der Oberhessischen Geschichtsverein — MitG
Mitteilungen der Obstbauversuchsanstalt — Mitt ObstbVersAnst
Mitteilungen der Oesterreichische Arbeitgemeinschaft fuer Ur- und Fruehgeschichte — M Oe Ur Frueh Gesch
Mitteilungen der Oesterreichischen Arbeitsgemeinschaft fuer Ur- und Fruehgeschichte — Mitt Oest Arbeitsg
Mitteilungen der Oesterreichischen Geographischen Gesellschaft — Mitt Oest Geogr Ges
Mitteilungen der Oesterreichischen Geographischen Gesellschaft — Mitt Oesterr Geogr Ges
Mitteilungen der Oesterreichischen Geologischen Gesellschaft — Mitt Osterreich Geol Ges
Mitteilungen der Oesterreichischen Gesellschaft fuer Muenz- und Medaillenkunde — MOeGMMK
Mitteilungen der Oesterreichischen Mykologischen Gesellschaft — Mitt Oesterr Mykol Ges
Mitteilungen der Oesterreichischen Numismatischen Gesellschaft — M Oe Num Ges
Mitteilungen der Oesterreichischen Numismatischen Gesellschaft — Mitt d Numismat Ges in Wien
Mitteilungen der Oesterreichischen Numismatischen Gesellschaft — Mitt Oesterr Numismat Ges
Mitteilungen der Oesterreichischen Numismatischen Gesellschaft — MO Num Ges
Mitteilungen der Oesterreichischen Numismatischen Gesellschaft — MOENG
Mitteilungen der Physikalisch-Technischen Reichsanstalt — Mitt Physik Techn Reichsanst
Mitteilungen der Pollichia — Mitt Pollichia
Mitteilungen der Praehistorischen Kommission der Kaiserlichen Akademie der Wissenschaften — Mitt Praeh Kom
Mitteilungen der Praehistorischen Kommission der Oesterreichischen Akademie der Wissenschaften — MPK
Mitteilungen der Praehistorischen Kommission der Oesterreichischen Akademie der Wissenschaften (Wien) — M Pr Hist Kom (Wien)
Mitteilungen der Raabe-Gesellschaft — Mitt RG
Mitteilungen der Raabe-Gesellschaft — MRG
Mitteilungen der Reichsstelle fuer Bodenforschung. Zweigstelle Freiburg — Mitt Reichsstelle Bodenforsch Zweigstelle Freiburg
Mitteilungen der Schlesischen Gesellschaft fuer Volkskunde — Mitt Schles Ges Volksk
Mitteilungen der Schlesischen Gesellschaft fuer Volkskunde — MSGVK
Mitteilungen der Schweizerischen Anstalt fuer das Forstliche Versuchswesen — MSAFV
Mitteilungen der Schweizerischen Kakteen-Gesellschaft — Mitt Schweiz Kakteen Ges
Mitteilungen der Technischen Hochschule. Budapest — Mitt Tech Hochsch Budapest
Mitteilungen der Technischen Universitaet fuer Schwerindustrie (Miskolc, Hungary) (Foreign Language Edition) — Mitt Tech Univ Schwerind Miskolc Hung Foreign Lang Ed
Mitteilungen der Thurgauischen Naturforschenden Gesellschaft — Mitt Thurg Natf Ges
Mitteilungen der Thurgauischen Naturforschenden Gesellschaft — Mitt Thurgau Natforsch Ges

Mitteilungen der Thurgauischen Naturforschenden Gesellschaft — MTNG
Mitteilungen der Tieraerztlichen Fakultaet der Staatsuniversitaet Gent — Mitt Tieraerztl Fak Staatsuniv Gent
Mitteilungen der Universitaet zu Brasov. Serie C — Mitt Univ Brasov Ser C
Mitteilungen der Vereinigungen von Freunden der Astronomie und Kosmischen Physik — VAP
Mitteilungen der Vereinigung der Grosskraftwerksbetreiber — Mitt Ver Grosskraftwerksbetr
Mitteilungen der Versuchsanstalt fuer das Gaerungsgewerbe und des Institutes fuer Angewandte Mikrobiologie — Mitt Versuchsanst Gaerungsgewerbe Inst Angew Mikrobiol
Mitteilungen der Versuchsstation fuer das Gaerungsgewerbe sowie des Institutes fuer Angewandte Mikrobiologie — Mitt Versuchsstat Gaerungsgewerbe Inst Angew Mikrobiol
Mitteilungen der VGB [*Vereinigung der Grosskraftwerksbetreiber*] — Mitt VGB
Mitteilungen der Vorderasiatischen Gesellschaft — MVAG
Mitteilungen der Wiener Katholischen Akademie — MWKA
Mitteilungen der Wuerttembergischen Forstlichen Versuchsanstalt — Mitt Wuerttemberg Forstl Versuchsanst
Mitteilungen der Zentralstelle fuer Deutsche Personen- und Familiengeschichte — Mitt Ztrstelle Dt Persongesch
Mitteilungen des Altertumvereins fuer Zwickau und Umgebung — Mitt Altertver Zwickau
Mitteilungen des Badischen Botanischen Vereins — Mitt Bad Bot Vereins
Mitteilungen des Badischen Landesvereins fuer Naturkunde und Naturschutz EV (Freiburg Im Breisgau) — Mitt Bad Landesver Naturkd Naturschutz (Freib Br)
Mitteilungen des Bundesdenkmalamtes — Mitt B
Mitteilungen des Bundesdenkmalamtes — Mitt Bundesdenk
Mitteilungen des Chemischen Forschungsinstitutes der Industrie Oesterreichs — Mitt Chem Forschungsinst Ind Oesterr
Mitteilungen des Chemischen Forschungs-Instituts der Industrie — Mitt Chem Forsch Inst Ind
Mitteilungen des Chemisch-Technischen Instituts der Technischen Hochschule Karlsruhe — Mitt Chem Tech Inst Tech Hochsch Karlsruhe
Mitteilungen des Copernicus-Vereins fuer Wissenschaft und Kunst zu Thorn — M Copern V
Mitteilungen des Copernicus-Vereins fuer Wissenschaft und Kunst zu Thorn — Mitt Copernikusver Thorn
Mitteilungen des Deutschen Archaeologen-Verbandes — MDA Verb
Mitteilungen des Deutschen Archaeologischen Instituts — MAI
Mitteilungen des Deutschen Archaeologischen Instituts — MI
Mitteilungen des Deutschen Archaeologischen Instituts — Mitt
Mitteilungen des Deutschen Archaeologischen Instituts — Mitt DAI
Mitteilungen des Deutschen Archaeologischen Instituts. Abteilung Kairo — DAWAK
Mitteilungen des Deutschen Archaeologischen Instituts. Abteilung Kairo — MAIK
Mitteilungen des Deutschen Archaeologischen Instituts. Abteilung Kairo — MDIAA
Mitteilungen des Deutschen Archaeologischen Instituts. Abteilung Kairo — MDIAK
Mitteilungen des Deutschen Archaeologischen Instituts. Athenische Abteilung — A M Erg H
Mitteilungen des Deutschen Archaeologischen Instituts. Athenische Abteilung — MIA
Mitteilungen des Deutschen Archaeologischen Instituts. Athenische Abteilung — Mitt Deut Arch Instzu Athen
Mitteilungen des Deutschen Archaeologischen Instituts. Athenische Abteilung — Mitth d Arch Instzu Athen
Mitteilungen des Deutschen Archaeologischen Instituts. Roemische Abteilung — DAWRA
Mitteilungen des Deutschen Archaeologischen Instituts. Roemische Abteilung — MDAI Rom Abt
Mitteilungen des Deutschen Archaeologischen Instituts. Roemische Abteilung — MDAIR
Mitteilungen des Deutschen Archaeologischen Instituts. Roemische Abteilung — MIR
Mitteilungen des Deutschen Archaeologischen Instituts. Roemische Abteilung — Mitt Dt Archaeol Inst Roem Abt
Mitteilungen des Deutschen Archaeologischen Instituts. Roemische Abteilung — RM
Mitteilungen des Deutschen Archaeologischen Instituts. Roemische Abteilung — Rom Mitteilungen
Mitteilungen des Deutschen Archaeologischen Instituts. Roemische Abteilung. Ergaenzungsheft — MDAI RE
Mitteilungen des Deutschen Boehmerwaldbundes — Mitt Deutsch Boehmerwaldbundes
Mitteilungen des Deutschen Germanisten-Verbandes — Mitt Dt Germ Verb
Mitteilungen des Deutschen Germanisten-Verbandes — Mitt Germ Verb
Mitteilungen des Deutschen Instituts fuer Aegyptische Altertumskunde in Kairo — MDIAeA
Mitteilungen des Deutschen Weinbauverbandes — Mitt Dt Weinbauverbd
Mitteilungen des Forschungsinstituts fuer Luftfahrtmaterialpruefung. Moscow — Mitt Forschungsinst Luftfahrtmaterialpruefung Moscow
Mitteilungen des Freiberger Altertumsvereins — M Freiberger Altert V
Mitteilungen des Germanischen Nationalmuseums (Nuernberg) — Mitt Germ Nationalmus Nuernbg
Mitteilungen des Grabmann-Instituts — MGI
Mitteilungen des Historischen Vereins der Dioezese Fulda — MHVDF
Mitteilungen des Historischen Vereins der Pfalz — M Hist Ver Pfalz
Mitteilungen des Historischen Vereins der Pfalz — MHVP
Mitteilungen des Historischen Vereins der Pfalz — Mitt Hist Ver Pfalz
Mitteilungen des Historischen Vereins des Kantons Schwyz — MHVS
Mitteilungen des Historischen Vereins fuer Osnabrueck — Mitt Hist Ver Osnabr
Mitteilungen des Historischen Vereins fuer Steiermark — MHVS
Mitteilungen des Institut fuer Oesterreisches Geschichtsforschung in Wien — Mitteil d Inst f Oesterr Geschichtsforschung in Wien
Mitteilungen des Institutes fuer Chemie- und Kaelteausruestungen der VVB Chemie- und Klimaanlagen. Ausgabe A — Mitt Inst Chem Kaelteausruest VVB Chem Klimaanlagen Ausg A
Mitteilungen des Institutes fuer Forstwissenschaften. Budapest — Mitt Inst Forstwiss Budapest
Mitteilungen des Instituts fuer Allgemeine und Anorganische Chemie. Bulgarische Akademie der Wissenschaften — Mitt Inst Allg Anorg Chem Bulg Akad Wiss
Mitteilungen des Instituts fuer Handelsforschung an der Universitaet Koeln — Mitt Inst Handelsforsch Univ Koeln
Mitteilungen des Instituts fuer Oesterreichische Geschichtsforschung — MIOe
Mitteilungen des Instituts fuer Oesterreichische Geschichtsforschung — Mitl
Mitteilungen des Instituts fuer Oesterreichische Geschichtsforschung — Mitt Inst Oesterr Gesch Forsch
Mitteilungen des Instituts fuer Oesterreichische Geschichtsforschung. Ergaenzungsband — MIOeG E
Mitteilungen des Instituts fuer Orientforschung — MIO
Mitteilungen des Instituts fuer Orientforschung — Mitt Inst Or F
Mitteilungen des Instituts fuer Orientforschung — Mitt Inst Orient F
Mitteilungen des Instituts fuer Wasserbau und Wasserwirtschaft der Rheinisch-Wesfaelischen Technishen Hochschule Aachen — Mitt Inst Wasserbau Wasserwirtsch Rheinisch Westfael Tech Hoch
Mitteilungen des Internationalen Entomologischen Vereins EV (Frankfurt) — Mitt Int Entomol Ver EV (Frankf)
Mitteilungen des Jahrbuches der Koeniglichen Ungarischen Geologischen Anstalt — Mitt Jahrb K Ung Geol Anst
Mitteilungen des Kunsthistorischen Instituts Florenz — MKhIF
Mitteilungen des Kunsthistorischen Instituts in Florenz — M Ku Hist Florenz
Mitteilungen des Kunsthistorischen Instituts in Florenz — Mitt Kunst
Mitteilungen des Landesvereines fuer Saechsischen Heimatschutz — Mitt Ldsver Saechs Heimatsch
Mitteilungen des Landesvereines fuer Saechsischen Heimatschutz — MLSaeH
Mitteilungen des Landwirtschaftlichen Instituts der Hochschule fuer Bodenkultur — MLIHB
Mitteilungen des Landwirtschaftlichen Instituts der Hochschule fuer Bodenkultur — MLIHfB
Mitteilungen des Materialpruefungsamtes — Mitt Materialpruefgsamt
Mitteilungen des Medizinischen Literatur-Dienstes — MLD
Mitteilungen des Musealvereins fuer Krain — Mitt Musealvereins Krain
Mitteilungen des Museums fuer Bergbau, Geologie und Technik am Landesmuseum Joanneum. Graz — Mitt Mus Bergbau Geol Tech Landesmus Joanneum Graz
Mitteilungen des Museumsvereins "Lauriacum" [*Enns*] — M Lauriacum
Mitteilungen des Museumsvereins "Lauriacum" [*Enns*] — M Mus Lauriacum
Mitteilungen des Museumsvereins. Lauriacum — MMV Laur
Mitteilungen des Naturwissenschaftlichen Vereines in Aschaffenburg — Mitt Naturwiss Vereins Aschaffenburg
Mitteilungen des Naturwissenschaftlichen Vereins der Universitaet Wien — Mitt Naturwiss Vereins Univ Wien
Mitteilungen des Naturwissenschaftlichen Vereins fuer die Steiermark — Mitt Natwiss Ver Steierm
Mitteilungen des Nordfriesischen Vereins fuer Heimatkunde — Mitt Nordfries Ver Heimatkde
Mitteilungen des Normenausschusses der Deutschen Industrie — MNDI
Mitteilungen des Oberhessischen Geschichtsvereins — MOG
Mitteilungen des Oberhessischen Geschichtsvereins — MOhGV
Mitteilungen des Oberoesterreichischen Landesarchivs — Mitt Oberoesterr Landesarch
Mitteilungen des Oesterreichischen Instituts fuer Geschichtsforschung. Ergaengsband — MOeIG E
Mitteilungen des Oesterreichischen Staatsarchivs — Mitt Oesterr Staatsarch
Mitteilungen des Oesterreichischen Staatsarchivs. Ergaenzungband — MOeSA E
Mitteilungen des Pfaelzischen Vereins fuer Naturkunde Pollichia — Mitt Pfaelz Vereins Naturk Pollichia
Mitteilungen des Pharmazeutischen Forschungs-Institutes — Mitt Pharm Forsch Inst
Mitteilungen des Reichsbunds Deutscher Technik — MRBDT
Mitteilungen des Reichsbunds Deutscher Techniker — Mitt Reichsbd Dt Techn
Mitteilungen des Reichsverbandes der Deutschen Industrie — IntMitt
Mitteilungen des Rumaenischen Instituts an der Universitaet Wien — MRIW
Mitteilungen des Saarpfaelzischen Vereins fuer Naturkunde und Naturschutz Pollichia mit dem Sitz in Bad Duerkheim — Mitt Saarpfaelz Vereins Naturk Pollichia Bad Duerkheim
Mitteilungen des Seminars fuer Orientalische Sprachen — Mitt D Sem F Orient Sp
Mitteilungen des Seminars fuer Orientalische Sprachen. Afrikanische Studien — MSOSAfr
Mitteilungen des Seminars fuer Orientalische Sprachen an der Friedrich-Wilhelms-Universitaet zu Berlin — MSOS
Mitteilungen des Seminars fuer Orientalische Sprachen. Westasiatische Studien — Mitt Semin Or Spr Westas St
Mitteilungen des Sonderforschungsbereichs 79 fuer Wasserforschung im Kuestenbereich der Technischen Universitaet Hannover — Mitt Sonderforschungsbereichs 79 Wasserforsch Kuestenbereich
Mitteilungen des Staatlichen Technischen Versuchsamtes — MTVA
Mitteilungen des Statistischen Landesamts des Koenigreichs Boehmen — MStLAB
Mitteilungen des Ungarischen Forschungsinstitutes fuer Bergbau — Mitt Ung Forschungsinst Bergbau
Mitteilungen des Ungarischen Verbands fuer Materialpruefung — Mitt Ung Verb Materialpruef

Mitteilungen des Ungarischen Zentralinstituts fuer die Entwicklung des Bergbaus — Mitt Ung Zentralinst Entwickl Bergbaus
Mitteilungen des Universitaetsbundes Marburg — MUBM
Mitteilungen des Verbandes der Vereine fuer Volkskunde — MVVV
Mitteilungen des Verbandes Deutscher Musikkritiker — MVDM
Mitteilungen des Verbandes Deutscher Vereine fuer Volkskunde — Mitt Vbd Dt Ver Volkskde
Mitteilungen des Verbandes Deutscher Vereine fuer Volkskunde — MVDVV
Mitteilungen des Vereins der Freunde Carnuntums — MVFC
Mitteilungen des Vereins der Freunde des Humanistischen Gymnasiums — Mitt Ver Frde Human Gymn
Mitteilungen des Vereins Deutscher Emailfachleute und des Deutschen EMAIL-Zentrums — Mitt Ver Dtsch Emailfachleute Dtsch EMAIL Zent
Mitteilungen des Vereins fuer Anhaltische Geschichte und Altertumskunde — VAG
Mitteilungen des Vereins fuer Chemnitzer Geschichte — Mitt Ver Chemnitz Gesch
Mitteilungen des Vereins fuer Erdkunde Leipzig — M V E Leipzig
Mitteilungen des Vereins fuer Erdkunde Leipzig — MVEL
Mitteilungen des Vereins fuer Forstliche Standortskartierung — Mitt Vereins Forstl Standortskart
Mitteilungen des Vereins fuer Forstliche Standortskunde und Forstpflanzenzuechtung — Mitt Vereins Forstl Standortsk
Mitteilungen des Vereins fuer Geschichte der Stadt Meissen — MVGM
Mitteilungen des Vereins fuer Geschichte der Stadt Nuernberg — Mitt Ver Gesch Nbg
Mitteilungen des Vereins fuer Geschichte der Stadt Nuernberg — Mitt Ver Gesch Stadt Nuernberg
Mitteilungen des Vereins fuer Geschichte der Stadt Nuernberg — Mitt VGN
Mitteilungen des Vereins fuer Geschichte der Stadt Nuernberg — MVGN
Mitteilungen des Vereins fuer Geschichte der Stadt Wien — Mitt Ver Gesch Wien
Mitteilungen des Vereins fuer Geschichte und Altertumskunde (Von Kahla und Roda) — Mitt Ver Gesch Kahla
Mitteilungen des Vereins fuer Geschichte und Landeskunde zu Bad Homburg vor der Hoehe — MVGBH
Mitteilungen des Vereins fuer Heimatkunde in Landkreis Birkenfeld — MVHB
Mitteilungen des Vereins fuer Heimatschutz, Innsbruck — MVHSchl
Mitteilungen des Vereins fuer Luebecker Geschichte — Mitt Ver Luebeck Gesch
Mitteilungen des Vereins zur Verbreiterung Naturwissenschaftlicher Kenntnis Noerdlich der Elbe — Mitt Ver Verbreiterg Natwiss Kenntn
Mitteilungen des Wirtschaftswissenschaftlichen Instituts der Gewerkschaften [*A publication*] — Mitt WWI
Mitteilungen des Zoologischen Museums. Berlin — MZoMB
Mitteilungen des Zoologischen Museums. Hamburg — Mitt Zool Mus Hambg
Mitteilungen. Deutsche Dendrologische Gesellschaft — Mitt Dtsch Dendrol Ges
Mitteilungen. Deutsche Entomologische Gesellschaft — Mitt Dt Ent Ges
Mitteilungen. Deutsche Entomologische Gesellschaft — Mitt Dtsch Entomol Ges
Mitteilungen. Deutsche Forschungsgesellschaft fuer Blechverarbeitung und Oberflaechenbehandlung — Mitt Dtsch Forschungsges Blechverarb Oberflaechenbehandl
Mitteilungen. Deutsche Gesellschaft fuer Holzforschung — Mitt Dtsch Ges Holzforsch
Mitteilungen. Deutsche Gesellschaft fuer Musik des Orients — Mitt Deutschen Ges M Orients
Mitteilungen. Deutsche Gesellschaft fuer Musik des Orients — Mitt Dtsche Ges Musik Orients
Mitteilungen. Deutsche Gesellschaft fuer Natur- und Voelkerkunde Ostasiens — MDGNVO
Mitteilungen. Deutsche Landwirtschafts Gesellschaft — Mitt Deut Landwirt Ges
Mitteilungen. Deutsche Landwirtschafts Gesellschaft — Mitt DLG
Mitteilungen. Deutsche Landwirtschafts Gesellschaft — Mitt Dt Landw Ges
Mitteilungen. Deutsche Landwirtschafts Gesellschaft — Mitt Dtsch Landwirtsch Ges
Mitteilungen. Deutsche Landwirtschafts Gesellschaft (Frankfurt/Main) — Mitt Dt LandsGes (Frankfurt/Main)
Mitteilungen. Deutsche Orient-Gesellschaft zu Berlin — MDO
Mitteilungen. Deutsche Orient-Gesellschaft zu Berlin — MDOG
Mitteilungen. Deutsche Pharmazeutische Gesellschaft — Mitt Dt Pharm Ges
Mitteilungen. Deutsche Pharmazeutische Gesellschaft — Mitt Dtsch Pharm Ges
Mitteilungen. Deutsche Shakespeare-Gesellschaft — MDtShG
Mitteilungen. Deutschen Archaeologischen Instituts. Roemische Abteilung — Mitt D Arch Inst
Mitteilungen. Deutsches Archaeologische Institut — MDAI
Mitteilungen. Deutsches Archaeologische Institut — MDI
Mitteilungen. Deutsches Archaeologische Institut. Abteilung Athens — Ath Mitt
Mitteilungen. Deutsches Archaeologische Institut. Abteilung Athens — MDAIA
Mitteilungen. Deutsches Archaeologische Institut. Abteilung Istanbul — Ist Mitt
Mitteilungen. Deutsches Archaeologische Institut. Abteilung Kairo — MDAIK
Mitteilungen. Deutsches Archaeologische Institut. Abteilung Kairo — MiDAIK
Mitteilungen. Deutsches Archaeologische Institut. Abteilung Kairo — Mitt Dtsch Archaeol Inst Abt Kairo
Mitteilungen. Deutsches Archaeologische Institut. Abteilung Madrid — Madr Mitt
Mitteilungen. Deutsches Archaeologische Institut. Abteilung Madrid — MDAIM
Mitteilungen. Deutsches Archaeologische Institut. Abteilung Rome — MDAIR
Mitteilungen. Deutsches Archaeologische Institut. Abteilung Rome — Roem Mitt
Mitteilungen. Deutsches Archaeologische Institut. Athenische Abteilung — DAI Athens
Mitteilungen. Deutsches Forschungsinstitut fuer Textilindustrie in Dresden — Mitt Dtsch Forschungsinst Textilind Dresden
Mitteilungen. Deutsches Institut fuer Aegyptische Altertumskunde [*Kairo*] — MDIA
Mitteilungen. Deutsches Institut fuer Aegyptische Altertumskunde (Kairo) — MDIK
Mitteilungen. Deutsches Institut fuer Aegyptische Altertumskunde (Kairo) — Mitt (Kairo)
Mitteilungen. Deutsch-Israelitischer Gemeindebund — MDIGB
Mitteilungen. Direktorium der Oesterreichischen National Bank — Mitt Direktor Osterr Nat Bank
Mitteilungen. E. T. A. Hoffman-Gesellschaft — MHG
Mitteilungen. Eisenhuettenmaennisches Institut der Technischen Hochschule (Aachen) — Mitt Eisenhuettenmaenn Inst Tech Hochsch (Aachen)
Mitteilungen. Entomologische Gesellschaft (Basel) — Mitt Ent Ges (Basel)
Mitteilungen. Entomologische Gesellschaft (Basel) — Mitt Entomol Ges (Basel)
Mitteilungen. Entomologische Gesellschaft in der Bundesrepublik Deutschland [*A publication*] — Mitt Entomol Ges BRD
Mitteilungen. Floristisch-Soziologische Arbeitsgemeinschaft — Mitt Flor Soz Arb
Mitteilungen. Floristisch-Soziologische Arbeitsgemeinschaft — Mitt Florist-Soziol Arbeitsgem
Mitteilungen. Forschungsanstalten von Gutehoffnungshuette-Konzerns — Mitt Forschungsanst Gutehoffnungshuette Konzerns
Mitteilungen. Forschungsinstitut der Vereinigten Stahlwerke Aktiengesellschaft (Dortmund) — Mitt Forschungsinst Ver Stahlwerke Ag (Dortmund)
Mitteilungen. Forschungsinstituts fuer Pflanzenzuechtung und Pflanzenbau in Sopronhorpacs — Mitt Forschungsinst Pflanzenzuecht Pflanzenbau Sopronhorpacs
Mitteilungen. Forschungslaboratorien der AGFA-Gevaert AG (Leverkusen-Muenchen) — Mitt Forschungslab AGFA Gevaert AG (Leverkusen Muenchen)
Mitteilungen. Forschungslaboratorium AGFA (Leverkusen) — Mitt Forschungslab AGFA (Leverkusen)
Mitteilungen. Forstliche Bundes-Versuchsanstalt — Mitt Forstl VersAnst
Mitteilungen. Forstliche Bundes-Versuchsanstalt (Mariabrunn) — MFBMA
Mitteilungen. Forstliche Bundes-Versuchsanstalt (Mariabrunn) — Mitt Forstl Bundes-Versuchsanst (Mariabrunn)
Mitteilungen. Forstliche Bundes-Versuchsanstalt (Mariabrunn) [*Austria*] — Mitt Forstl Bundesversuchsanstalt (Mariabrunn)
Mitteilungen. Forstliche Bundes-Versuchsanstalt (Wien) — Mitt Forstl Bundes-Versuchsanst (Wien)
Mitteilungen fuer den Landbau — Mitt Landbau
Mitteilungen fuer den Landbau. Agricultural Bulletin — Mitt Landbau Agric Bull
Mitteilungen fuer die Landwirtschaft — Mitt Landwirtsch
Mitteilungen fuer die Landwirtschaft (Berlin) — Mitt Landw (Berl)
Mitteilungen fuer die Mitglieder des Technischen Ueberwachungs-Vereins (Bayern) — Mitt Mitglieder Tech Ueberwach-Ver (Bayern)
Mitteilungen fuer die Schweizerische Landwirtschaft — Mitt Schw LW
Mitteilungen fuer die Schweizerische Landwirtschaft — Mitt Schweiz Landw
Mitteilungen fuer die Schweizerische Landwirtschaft — Mitt Schweiz Landwirt
Mitteilungen fuer die Schweizerische Landwirtschaft — Mitt Schweiz Landwirtsch
Mitteilungen fuer Juedischen Volkskunde — MJVK
Mitteilungen fuer Kinderaerzte — Mitt Kinderaerz
Mitteilungen fuer Kunst und Kunstgewerbe — Mitt Kunst Kunstgew
Mitteilungen fuer Namenkunde — Mitt Na Kde
Mitteilungen fuer Namenskunde [*Aachen*] — MFN
Mitteilungen fuer Naturkunde und Vorgeschichte aus dem Museum fuer Kulturgeschichte und dem Naturwissenschaftlichen Arbeitskreis — Mitt Naturk Vorgesch Mus Kulturgesch Naturwiss Arbeitskreis
Mitteilungen. Geodaetische Institut der Technischen Universitaet Graz — Mitt Geodaet Inst Tech Univ Graz
Mitteilungen. Geographische Gesellschaft in Hamburg — Mitt Geogr Ges Hamb
Mitteilungen. Geographische Gesellschaft in Muenchen — Mitt Geogr Ges Muenchen
Mitteilungen. Geographische Gesellschaft in Wien — MGGW
Mitteilungen. Geologische Gesellschaft in Wien — Mitt Geol Ges Wien
Mitteilungen. Geologisches Institut der Eidgenoessischen Technischen Hochschule und der Universitaet Zuerich — Mitt Geol Inst Eidg Tech Hochsch Univ Zurich
Mitteilungen. Geologisches Staatsinstitut in Hamburg — Mitt Geol Staatsinst Hamb
Mitteilungen. Geologisch-Palaeontologische Institut. Universitaet Hamburg — Mitt Geol Palaeontol Inst Univ Hamburg
Mitteilungen. Germanisches Nationalmuseum — MGNM
Mitteilungen. Gesamtarchiv der Deutschen Juden — MGA
Mitteilungen. Gesamtarchiv der Deutschen Juden — MGADJ
Mitteilungen. Gesellschaft der Geologie- und Bergbaustudenten in Oesterreich — Mitt Ges Geol Bergbaustud Oesterr
Mitteilungen. Gesellschaft der Geologie- und Bergbaustudenten in Wien — Mitt Ges Geol Bergbaustud Wien
Mitteilungen. Gesellschaft fuer Juedische Familienforschung [*Berlin*] — MGJF
Mitteilungen. Gesellschaft fuer Juedische Familienforschung [*Berlin*] — MGJFF
Mitteilungen. Gesellschaft fuer Juedische Volkskunde — MGJV
Mitteilungen. Gesellschaft fuer Juedische Volkskunde — MJV
Mitteilungen. Gesellschaft fuer Natur- und Voelkerkunde Ostasiens — MGNVO
Mitteilungen. Gesellschaft fuer Salzburger Landeskunde — M Ges Salzb
Mitteilungen. Gesellschaft fuer Salzburger Landeskunde — MGSLK
Mitteilungen. Gesellschaft zur Erforschung Judischer Kunstdenkmaeler — MGEK
Mitteilungen. Grossforschungszentrum Chemieanlagen — Mitt Grossforschungszentrum Chemieanlagen
Mitteilungen. Hamburgische Staatskrankenanstalten — Mitt Hamb Staatskrankenanst
Mitteilungen. Hamburgisches Zoologische Museum und Institut — Mitt Hamb Zool Mus Inst
Mitteilungen. Hans-Pfitzner-Gesellschaft — Mitt Hans Pfitzner Ges

Mitteilungen. Hessische Landesforstverwaltung — Mitt Hess Landesforstverw
Mitteilungen. Industrie- Forschungszentrum Chemieanlagen — Mitt Ind Forschungszent Chemieanlagen
Mitteilungen. Institut fuer Aerodynamik an der Eidgenoessischen Technischen Hochschule in Zuerich — Mitt Inst Aerodyn
Mitteilungen. Institut fuer Auslandsbeziehungen [*Stuttgart*] — MIA
Mitteilungen. Institut fuer Auslandsbeziehungen — MIAB
Mitteilungen. Institut fuer Baustatik. Eidgenoessische Technische Hochschule in Zuerich — Mitt Inst Baustatik
Mitteilungen. Institut fuer Bautechnik — Mitt Inst Bautech
Mitteilungen. Institut fuer Geschichtsforschung und Archivwissenschaft in Wien — MIGFW
Mitteilungen. Institut fuer Grundbau und Bodenmechanik. Eidgenoessische Technische Hochschule (Zurich) — Mitt Inst Grundbau Bodenmech Eidg Tech Hochsch (Zurich)
Mitteilungen. Institut fuer Handelsforschung. Universitaet zu Koeln — MFH
Mitteilungen. Institut fuer Hydraulik und Gewaesserkunde. Technische Hochschule [*Muenchen*] — Mitt Inst Hydraul Gewaesserkd
Mitteilungen. Institut fuer Oesterreichische Geschichtsforschung — MI Oe G
Mitteilungen. Institut fuer Oesterreichische Geschichtsforschung — MIOG
Mitteilungen. Institut fuer Oesterreichische Geschichtsforschung — MIOGF
Mitteilungen. Institut fuer Orientforschung — MI Or
Mitteilungen. Institut fuer Orientforschung. Deutsche Akademie der Wissenschaften zu Berlin — MIOF
Mitteilungen. Institut fuer Orientforschung. Deutsche Akademie der Wissenschaften zu Berlin — Mitt Inst Orientforsch Dtsch Akad Wiss Berl
Mitteilungen. Institut fuer Textiltechnologie der Chemiefasern Rudolstadt — Mitt Inst Textiltechnol Chemiefasern Rudolstadt
Mitteilungen. Institut fuer Thermische Turbomaschinen. Eidgenoessische Technische Hochschule [*Zuerich*] — Mitt Inst Therm Turbomasch
Mitteilungen. Institute fuer Allgemeine und Anorganische Chemie und Organische Chemie. Bulgarische Akademie der Wissenschaften — Mitt Inst Allg Anorg Chem Org Chem Bulg Akad Wiss
Mitteilungen. Institutes fuer Orientforschung — Mitt Inst Orientforsch
Mitteilungen. Instituto Colombo-Aleman de Investigaciones Cientificas "Punta De Betin" — Mitt Inst Colombo-Aleman Invest Cient "Punta De Betin"
Mitteilungen. Instituts fuer Wasserwirtschaft und Bauwesen. Bulgarische Akademie der Wissenschaften — Mitt Inst Wasserwirtsch Bauwes Bulg Akad Wiss
Mitteilungen. Internationale Moor- und Torf-Gesellschaft — Mitt Int Moor-Torf-Ges
Mitteilungen. Internationale Stiftung Mozarteum — ISM
Mitteilungen. Internationale Stiftung Mozarteum — Mitt Int Stiftung Mozarteum
Mitteilungen. Internationale Stiftung Mozarteum — MM
Mitteilungen. Internationale Vereinigung fuer Saatgutpruefung — Mitt Int Ver Saatgutpruef
Mitteilungen. Internationale Vereinigung fuer Saatgutpruefung — Mitt Int Ver Saatgutpruefung
Mitteilungen. Internationale Vereinigung fuer Theoretische und Angewandte Limnologie — Mitt Int Ver Theor Angew Limnol
Mitteilungen. Kaiserliche Anstalt fuer Land- und Forstwirtschaft — Mitt K Anst Land-u Forstw
Mitteilungen. Kaiser-Wilhelm-Institut fuer Eisenforschung zu Duesseldorf — Mitt Kaiser Wilhelm Inst Eisenforsch Duesseldorf
Mitteilungen. Kali-Forschungs-Anstalt — Mitt Kali Forsch Anst
Mitteilungen. Klasse der Mathematik, der Naturwissenschaften und der Medizin. Tschechische Akademie der Wissenschaften und Kuenste — Mitt Kl Math Naturwiss Med Tschech Akad Wiss Kuenste
Mitteilungen (Klosterneuburg) — Mitt (Klosterneuburg)
Mitteilungen Klosterneuburg. Rebe und Wein, Obstbau und Fruechteverwertung — Mitt Klosterneuburg Rebe Wein Obs Fruecht
Mitteilungen (Klosterneuburg). Serie A. Rebe und Wein — Mitt Klosterneuburg Ser A
Mitteilungen. Kohle- und Eisenforschung GmbH — Mitt Kohle Eisenforsch GmbH
Mitteilungen. Kraftwerksanlagenbau (DDR) — Mitt Kraftwerksanlagenbau (DDR)
Mitteilungen. Kunsthistorisches Institut. Florence — Flor Mitt
Mitteilungen. Kunsthistorisches Institut. Florence — M Kultist Florenz
Mitteilungen. Kunsthistorisches Institut. Florence — MKIF
Mitteilungen. Laboratorien der Preussischen Geologischen Landesanstalt — Mitt Lab Preuss Geol Landesanst
Mitteilungen. Laboratorien des Geologischen Dienstes (DDR) — Mitt Lab Geol Dienstes (DDR)
Mitteilungen. Landesanstalt fuer Tierzucht in Grub — Mitt Landesanst Tierz Grub
Mitteilungen. Landwirtschaftliche Versuchsstellen (Ungarn). A. Pflanzenbau — Mitt Landwirtsch Versuchsstellen (Ung) A
Mitteilungen. Landwirtschaftliche Versuchsstellen (Ungarn). C. Gartenbau — Mitt Landwirtsch Versuchsstellen (Ung) C
Mitteilungen. Materialpruefungsanstalt. Technische Hochschule (Darmstadt) — Mitt Materialpruefungsanst Tech Hochsch (Darmstadt)
Mitteilungen. Mathematische Gesellschaft (Deutsche Demokratische Republik) — Mitt Math Ges (DDR)
Mitteilungen. Mathematische Gesellschaft (Hamburg) — Mitt Math Gesellsch (Hamburg)
Mitteilungen. Mathematisches Seminar (Giessen) — Mitt Math Sem (Giessen)
Mitteilungen. Max Reger Institut — Mitt Max Reger Inst
Mitteilungen. Max Reger Institut [*Bonn*] — Reger
Mitteilungen. Max-Planck-Gesellschaft — Mitt Max-Planck-Ges
Mitteilungen. Max-Planck-Gesellschaft zur Foerderung der Wissenschaften — Mitt Max-Planck-Ges Foerd Wiss
Mitteilungen. Max-Planck-Institut fuer Aeronomie — Mitt MPI Aeron
Mitteilungen. Max-Planck-Institut fuer Stroemungsforschung und der Aerodynamischen Versuchsanstalt — Mitt Max-Planck-Inst Stroemungsforsch Aerodyn Versuchsanst
Mitteilungen. Max-Planck-Institut fuer Stroemungsforschung und der Aerodynamischen Versuchsanstalt — Mitt MPI Stroemungsforsch Aerodyn Versuchsanst
Mitteilungen. Medizinische Gesellschaft zu Tokyo — Mitt Med Ges Tokyo
Mitteilungen. Medizinische Gesellschaft zu Tokyo — Mitt Med Gesellsch Tokyo
Mitteilungen. Muenchener Entomologische Gesellschaft — Mitt Muench Ent Ges
Mitteilungen. Muenchener Entomologische Gesellschaft — Mitt Muench Entomol Ges
Mitteilungen. Museum fuer Voelkerkunde in Hamburg — Mitt Mus Voelkerk Hamburg
Mitteilungen. Museum fuer Voelkerkunde zu Leipzig — Mitt Mus Voelkerk Leipzig
Mitteilungen. Naturforschende Gesellschaft in Bern — Mitt Naturforsch Ges Bern
Mitteilungen. Naturforschende Gesellschaft in Bern — MNGBA
Mitteilungen. Naturwissenschaftliche Gesellschaft in Winterthur — Mitt Naturwiss Ges Winterthur
Mitteilungen. Naturwissenschaftlicher Verein fuer Steiermark — Mitt Naturwiss Ver Steiermark
Mitteilungen. Naturwissenschaftliches Museum der Stadt Aschaffenburg — Mitt Naturwiss Mus Stadt Aschaffenburg
Mitteilungen. Nordfriesischer Verein fuer Heimatkunde — M Nfr VH
Mitteilungen. Numismatische Gesellschaft — Mitt Num Ges
Mitteilungen. Obst und Garten — Mitt Obst Gart
Mitteilungen Obst und Garten — Mitt Obst Garten
Mitteilungen. Obstbauversuchsring des Alten Landes — Mitt Obstbauversuchsring Alten Landes
Mitteilungen. Obstbauversuchsring des Alten Landes — Mitt ObstbVersuchsr Alten Landes
Mitteilungen. Oesterreichische Bodenkundliche Gesellschaft — Mitt Ost Bodenk Ges
Mitteilungen. Oesterreichische Geographische Gesellschaft — Mitt O Geog
Mitteilungen. Oesterreichische Geologische Gesellschaft — Mitt Oesterr Geol Ges
Mitteilungen. Oesterreichische Gesellschaft fuer Anthropologie, Ethnologie, und Praehistorie — MOGA
Mitteilungen. Oesterreichische Gesellschaft fuer Holzforschung — Mitt Oesterr Ges Holzforsch
Mitteilungen. Oesterreichische Gesellschaft fuer Musikwissenschaft — Mitt Oesterreich Ges Mw
Mitteilungen. Oesterreichische Mineralogische Gesellschaft — Mitt Oesterr Mineral Ges
Mitteilungen. Oesterreichische Numismatische Gesellschaft — MONG
Mitteilungen. Oesterreichische Sanitaetsverwaltung — MOSVA
Mitteilungen. Oesterreichische Sanitaetsverwaltung (Vienna) — Mitt Oesterr Sanitaetsverwalt (Vienna)
Mitteilungen. Oesterreichischer Verein fuer Bibliothekwesen — MOVB
Mitteilungen. Oesterreichischer Verein fuer Bibliothekwesen — MOVBW
Mitteilungen. Oesterreichisches Institut fuer Geschichtsforschung — MIOeG
Mitteilungen. Oesterreichisches Institut fuer Geschichtsforschung — Mitt IOeG
Mitteilungen. Oesterreichisches Institut fuer Geschichtsforschung — MOEIG
Mitteilungen. Oesterreichisches Institut fuer Geschichtsforschung — MOIG
Mitteilungen. Oesterreichisches Institut fuer Geschichtsforschung — MOIGF
Mitteilungen. Oesterreichisches Staatsarchiv — MOSA
Mitteilungen. Pollichia des Pfaelzischen Vereins fuer Naturkunde und Naturschutz — Mitt Pollichia Pfaelz Ver Naturkd Naturschutz
Mitteilungen. Praehistorische Kommission. Akademie der Wissenschaften [*Vienna*] — Mitt Praeh Kom
Mitteilungen. Praehistorische Kommission. Akademie der Wissenschaften. Wien — Mitt Praehis Komm Wien
Mitteilungen. Rebe und Wein — Mitt Rebe Wein
Mitteilungen. Rebe und Wein, Obstbau und Fruechteverwertung — Mitt Rebe Wein Obstbau Fruechteverwert
Mitteilungen. Reichsamt Bodenforschung. Zweigstelle Wien — Mitt Reichsamts Bodenforsch Zweigstelle Wien
Mitteilungen. Rheinisch-Westfaelisches Institut fuer Wirtschaftsforschung — MQG
Mitteilungen. Schlesische Gesellschaft fuer Volkskunde — MSGV
Mitteilungen. Schweizerische Anstalt fuer das Forstliche Versuchswesen — Mitt Schweiz Anst Forstl Versuchsw
Mitteilungen. Schweizerische Anstalt fuer das Forstliche Versuchswesen — Mitt Schweiz Anst Forstl Versuchswes
Mitteilungen. Schweizerische Anstalt fuer das Forstliche Versuchswesen — Mitt SFV
Mitteilungen. Schweizerische Entomologische Gesellschaft — Mitt Schweiz Ent Ges
Mitteilungen. Schweizerische Entomologische Gesellschaft — Mitt Schweiz Entomol Ges
Mitteilungen. Schweizerische Entomologische Gesellschaft. Bulletin de la Societe Entomologique Suisse — Mitt Schweiz Entomol Ges Bull Soc Entomol Suisse
Mitteilungen. Schweizerische Gesellschaft der Freunde Ostasiatischer Kultur — MSGFOK
Mitteilungen. Schweizerische Zentralanstalt fuer das Forstliche Versuchswesen — Mitt Schweiz Zentralanst Forstl Versuchswes
Mitteilungen. Schweizerischer Apotheker-Verein — Mitt Schweiz Apoth Ver
Mitteilungen. Schweizerischer Fleckviehzuchtverband — Mitt Schweiz Fleckviehzuchtverb
Mitteilungen. Seminar fuer Orientalische Sprachen zu Berlin — MSOS
Mitteilungen. Septuaginta Unternehmen [*Berlin/Goettingen*] — MSU
Mitteilungen. Sonzino-Gesellschaft — MSG
Mitteilungen. Staatliches Heimat und Schlossmuseum Burgk/Saale — Mitt Staatl Heimat Schlossmus Burgk/Saale
Mitteilungen. Staatsforstverwaltung Bayern — Mitt Stforstverw Bayerns
Mitteilungen. Staatsinstitut fuer Allgemeine Botanik (Hamburg) — Mitt Staatsinst Allg Bot (Hamb)

Mitteilungen. Staatsinstitut fuer Allgemeine Botanik (Hamburg) — Mitt Staatsinst Allg Bot (Hamburg)
Mitteilungen. Stadtarchiv von Koeln — MSK
Mitteilungen. Technische Universitaet Carolo-Wilhelmina [*Germany*] — Mitt Tech Univ Carolo-Wilheimina
Mitteilungen. Technische Universitaet Carolo-Wilhelmina zu Braunschweig — Mitt Tech Univ Braunschweig
Mitteilungen. Technischen Universitaet Carolo-Wilhelmina zu Braunschweig — Mitt Tech Univ Carolo Wilhelmina Braunschweig
Mitteilungen. Technischen Universitaet fuer Schwerindustrie (Miskolc, Hungary) — Mitt Tech Univ Schwerind Miskolc Hung
Mitteilungen. Textilforschungs-Anstalt Krefeld — Mitt Textilforsch Anst Krefeld
Mitteilungen. Tieraerztliche Fakultaet der Reichsuniversitaet Gent — Mitt Tieraerztl Fak Reichsuniv Gent
Mitteilungen. Tieraerztliche Praxis im Preussischen Staate — Mitt Tieraerztl Praxis Preuss Staate
Mitteilungen ueber Allgemeine Pathologie und Pathologische Anatomie — Mitt Allg Pathol Pathol Anat
Mitteilungen ueber Forschung und Konstruktion in Stahlbau — Mitt Forsch Konstr Stahlbau
Mitteilungen ueber Forschungsarbeiten auf dem Gebiete des Ingenieur-Wesens — Mitt Forscharb Ing Wesens
Mitteilungen ueber Gegenstaende des Artillerie- und Geniewesens — Mitt Gegenstde Artillw
Mitteilungen ueber Naturdenkmalpflege in der Provinz Grenzmark Posen-Westpreussen — Mitt Naturdenkmalpflege Prov Grenzmark Posen Westpreussen
Mitteilungen ueber Textil-Industrie — Mitt Text Ind
Mitteilungen und Forschungsbeitraege. Cusanus-Gesellschaft — MFCG
Mitteilungen und Forschungsbeitraege. Cusanus-Gesellschaft — MFCusanusG
Mitteilungen und Forschungsbeitraege der Cusanus Gesellschaft — Mitt Forschungsbeitr Cusanus Ges
Mitteilungen und Nachrichten. Deutscher Palaestina-Verein — MDPV
Mitteilungen und Nachrichten. Deutscher Palaestina-Verein — MNDPV
Mitteilungen und Nachrichten fuer die Evangelische Kirche Russlands — Mitt Nachrr Evgl Kirche Russld
Mitteilungen. Universitaetsbund Marburg — Mitt Univ Bund
Mitteilungen. Verband Ehemaliger Breslauer und Schlesier in Israel [*Tel Aviv*] — MVBI
Mitteilungen. Verein der Freunde des Humanistischen Gymnasiums — MVHG
Mitteilungen. Verein Deutscher Emailfachleute [*Germany*] — Mitt Ver Dtsch Emailfachl
Mitteilungen. Verein Deutscher Emailfachleute — Mitt Ver Dtsch Emailfachleute
Mitteilungen. Verein fuer Forstliche Standortskunde und Forstpflanzenzuechtung — Mitt Ver Forstl Standortskunde ForstpflZucht
Mitteilungen. Verein fuer Geschichte der Deutschen in Boehmen — MVGDB
Mitteilungen. Verein fuer Geschichte der Stadt Nuernberg — MVGSN
Mitteilungen. Verein fuer Geschichte und Altertumskunde in Frankfurt-Am-Main — MVGAFr
Mitteilungen. Verein fuer Geschichte von Ost- und West Preussen — MVGOW
Mitteilungen. Verein fuer Kunst und Altertum in Ulm und Oberschwaben Ulm — MVKAUO
Mitteilungen. Verein fuer Nassauische Altertumskunde und Geschichts-Forschung — MVNAG
Mitteilungen. Verein Klassischer Philologen in Wien — MVPhW
Mitteilungen. Verein zur Abwehr des Antisemitismus — MVZADA
Mitteilungen. Vereinigte Metallwerke Ranshofen-Berndorf — Mitt Ver Metallwerke Ranshofen Berndorf
Mitteilungen. Vereinigung der Grosskesselbesitzer — Mitt Ver Grosskesselbesitzer
Mitteilungen. Vereinigung der Grosskesselbesitzer — MVGKA
Mitteilungen. Vereinigung der Grosskesselbetreiber — Mitt Ver Grosskesselbetr
Mitteilungen. Vereinigung Oesterreichischer Bibliothek — Mitt VOB
Mitteilungen. Versuchsanstalt fuer Wasserbau, Hydrologie, und Glaziologie — Mitt Vers Wasserbau Hydrol Glaziologie
Mitteilungen. Versuchsergebnissen der Bundesanstalt fuer Pflanzenbau und Samenpruefung in Wien — Mitt Versuchsergeb Bundesanst Pflanzenbau Samenpruf Wien
Mitteilungen. Versuchsstation fuer das Gaerungsgewerbe in Wien — Mitt Versuchsstn Gaerungsgewerbe Wein
Mitteilungen. Versuchsstation fuer das Gaerungsgewerbe in Wien (Austria) — MVGGA
Mitteilungen. VGB [*Technische Vereinigung der Grosskraftwerksbetreiber*] — MVGKB
Mitteilungen. VGB (Technische Vereinigung der Grosskraftwerksbetreiber) [*German Federal Republic*] — Mitt VGB (Tech Ver Grosskraftwerksbetr)
Mitteilungen. Vorderasiatisch-Aegyptische Gesellschaft — MVAeG
Mitteilungen. Vorderasiatisch-Aegyptische Gesellschaft — MVAG
Mitteilungen. Vorderasiatisch-Aegyptischen Gesellschaft — Mitt Vorderas Ges
Mitteilungen. Vorderasiatisch-Aegyptischen Gesellschaft — MVG
Mitteilungen. Wissenschaftlichen Bibliothekswesen der Deutschen Demokratischen Republik — Mitt DDR
Mitteilungen. Zentralinstitut fuer Schweisstechnik der Deutschen Demokratischen Republik — Mitt Zentralinst Schweisstech DDR
Mitteilungen. Zoologisches Museum in Berlin — Mitt Zool Mus Berl
Mitteilungen zur Geschichte der Medizin der Naturwissenschaften und Technik — Mitt Gesch Med Naturwiss Tech
Mitteilungen zur Geschichte der Medizin und der Naturwissenschaft — MMN
Mitteilungen zur Geschichte der Medizin und der Naturwissenschaften — Mitt Gesch Med Naturwiss
Mitteilungen zur Geschichte der Medizin und Naturwissenschaften — MGMNw
Mitteilungen zur Juedischen Volkskunde — MJV
Mitteilungen zur Vaterlaendische Geschichte — MVG
Mitteilungen zur Vaterlaendischen Geschichte. Historischer Verein in St. Gallen — Mitt Vaterl Gesch St Gall
Mitteilungsblaetter fuer den Jungen Gerberei-Techniker — Mitteilungsbl Jungen Gerberei Tech
Mitteilungsblaetter Strahlungsmessgeraete [*Germany*] — Mitteilungsbl Strahlungsmessgeraete
Mitteilungsblatt. Abteilung fuer Mineralogie am Landesmuseum Joanneum [*Austria*] — Mitteilungsbl Abt Mineral Landesmus Joanneum
Mitteilungsblatt. Allgemeiner Deutsche Neuphilologenverband — MADNV
Mitteilungsblatt. Bundesanstalt fuer Fleischforschung — MBFLD
Mitteilungsblatt. Bundesanstalt fuer Fleischforschung — Mitteilungsbl Bundesanst Fleischforsch
Mitteilungsblatt. Chemische Gesellschaft der Deutschen Demokratischen Republik — MittBl Chem Ges DDR
Mitteilungsblatt. Chemische Gesellschaft der Deutschen Demokratischen Republik [*Germany*] — Mitteilungsbl Chem Ges DDR
Mitteilungsblatt. Chemische Gesellschaft der Deutschen Demokratischen Republik. Beiheft — Mitteilungsbl Chem Ges Dtsch Demokr Repub Beih
Mitteilungsblatt der Berliner Zahnaerzte — Mitt Bl Ber Zahn Ae
Mitteilungsblatt der Bundesanstalt fuer Wasserbau (Federal Republic of Germany) — Mitteilungsbl Bundesanst Wasserbau (Fed Repub Ger)
Mitteilungsblatt der Deutschen Arbeitsgemeinschaft fuer Paradentose-Forschung — Mitt Bl Dt Gem Parad Fschg
Mitteilungsblatt der Gesellschaft fuer Voelkerkunde — MGVK
Mitteilungsblatt der Keramikfreunde der Schweiz — MKS
Mitteilungsblatt der Oesterreichischen Orchideengesellschaft — Mitteilungsbl Oesterr Orchideenges
Mitteilungsblatt der Vereins Deutscher Ingenieure in der Britischen Zone — Mitteilungsbl Ver Dtsch Ing Br Zone
Mitteilungsblatt. Deutsche Gesellschaft fuer Sonnenenergie [*Germany*] — Mitteilungsbl Dtsch Ges Sonnenenergie
Mitteilungsblatt. Deutsche Keramische Gesellschaft — Mitteilungsbl Dtsch Keram Ges
Mitteilungsblatt. Deutscher Verein fuer Vermessungswesen — Mitt Bl DVW
Mitteilungsblatt. Fraunhofer-Gesellschaft zur Foerderung der Angewandten Forschung EV — Mitteilungsbl Fraunhofer-Ges
Mitteilungsblatt. Fraunhofer-Gesellschaft zur Foerderung der Angewandten Forschung EV — Mitteilungsbl Fraunhofer-Ges Foerd Angew Forsch
Mitteilungsblatt fuer die Amtliche Materialpruefung in Niedersachsen — Mitteilungsbl Amtl Materialpruef Niedersachsen
Mitteilungsblatt fuer Mathematische Statistik — Mitt Bl Math Stat
Mitteilungsblatt fuer Mathematische Statistik und Ihre Anwendungsgebiete — MM St
Mitteilungsblatt. GDCh [*Gesellschaft Deutscher Chemiker*] **Fachgruppe Lebensmittelchemie und Gerichtliche Chemie** — Mitteilungsbl GDCh Fachgruppe Lebensmittelchem Gerichtl Chem
Mitteilungsblatt. Gesellschaft Deutscher Chemiker. Fachgruppe Analytische Chemie — Mitteilungsbl Ges Dtsch Chem Fachgruppe Anal Chem
Mitteilungsblatt. Gesellschaft fuer Bayerische Musikgeschichte — Mitt Ges Bayerische Mg
Mitteilungsblatt. Gesellschaft fuer Vor-und Fruehgeschichte — Mbl V Frueh Gesch
Mitteilungsblatt. Irgun Olej Merkas Europa [*Tel-Aviv*] — MB
Mitteilungsblatt. Irgun Olej Merkas Europa — MDIOME
Mitteilungsblatt. Josef-Haas-Gesellschaft — Mitt Josef Haas Ges
Mitteilungsblatt. Schweizerische Musikforschende Gesellschaft — Mitt Schweiz Mf Ges
Mitteilungsblatt. Vereinigung Schweizerischer Angestelltenverbaende — VSA
Mitteilungsblatt. Zentrale Sozialistische Arbeitsgemeinschaft — Mitt Zentr Soz Arbeitsgemeinsch
Mitteilung-Steiermarkisches Landesmuseum (Graz). Museum fuer Bergbau, Geologie, und Technik — Mitt Steiermarkisches Landesmus (Graz) Mus Bergbau Geol Tec
Mitteldeutsche Blaetter fuer Volkskunde — MDBVK
Mitteldeutsche Forschungen — MDF
Mitteldeutsche Studien — MSt
Mitteldeutsches Jahrbuch — MdJb
Mittellateinische Studien und Texte — MLST
Mittellateinische Studien und Texte — MST
Mittellateinisches Jahrbuch — Mit J
Mittellateinisches Jahrbuch — Mittellat Jb
Mittellateinisches Jahrbuch — MJ
Mittellateinisches Jahrbuch — MlatJb
Mittellateinisches Woerterbuch — MLW
Mittelrheinische Geschichtsblaetter — MRGB
Mitternachstbuecher — Mitternb
Mittheilungen aus dem Gebiete der Landwirthschaft — Mitth Landw
Mittheilungen aus dem Gebiete der Medizin, Chirurgie, und Pharmacie — Mitth Med
Mittheilungen aus dem Gebiete der Theoretischen Erdkunde — Mitth Theor Erdk
Mittheilungen aus dem Gesammtgebiete der Botanik — Mitth Gesammtgeb Bot
Mittheilungen aus dem Naturwissenschaftlichen Vereine von Neu-Vorpommern und Ruegen — Mitth Naturwiss Vereine Neu Vorpommern
Mittheilungen aus den Verhandlungen der Gesellschaft Naturforschender Freunde zu Berlin — Mitt Vhdlgg Ges Natfd Frde Berlin
Mittheilungen aus den Verhandlungen der Gesellschaft Naturforschender Freunde zu Berlin — Mitth Verh Ges Naturf Freunde Berlin
Mittheilungen aus den Verhandlungen der Naturwissenschaftlichen Gesellschaft in Hamburg — Mitth Verh Naturwiss Ges Hamburg
Mittheilungen aus Justus Perthes' Geographischer Anstalt ueber Wichtige Neue Erforschungen auf dem Gesammtgebiete der Geographie. Ergaenzungsband — Mitth Justus Perthes Geogr Anst Ergaenzungsband
Mittheilungen der Historischen und Atiquarischen Gesellschaft zu Basel — MHAGB
Mittheilungen der Philomatischen Gesellschaft in Elsass-Lothringen — Mitth Philom Ges Elsass Lothringen

Mittheilungen des Naturwissenschaftlichen Vereins zu Freiberg in Sachsen — Mitth Naturwiss Vereins Freiberg
Mittheilungen des Thurgauischen Naturforschenden Vereins ueber Seine Thaetigkeit — Mitth Thurgauischen Naturf Vereins Thaetigk
Mittheilungen ueber Flora. Gesellschaft fuer Botanik und Gartenbau in Dresden — Mitth Flora Ges Bot Dresden
Mittheilungen und Nachrichten. Deutscher Palaestina-Verein — MuNDPV
Mittilungen der Provinzialstelle fuer Naturdenkmalpflege Hannover — Mitt Provinzialstelle Naturdenkmalpflege Hannover
Mix. Ijzerwaren, Doe het Zelf — MYZ
Mixed Valency Systems. Applications in Chemistry, Physics, and Biology — Mixed Valency Syst Appl Chem Phys Biol
Mixing in Polymer Processing — Mixing Polym Process
Mixing of Particulate Solids. European Symposium — Mixing Part Solids Eur Symp
Mixing. Proceedings. European Conference — Mixing Proc Eur Conf
Miyagi Prefectural Institute of Public Health. Annual Report — Miyagi Prefect Inst Public Health. Annu Rep
Miyazaki Daigaku Nogakubu. Kenkyu Hokoku — MDNKA
Mizrah He-Hadas — Miz Had
Mjasnaja Industrija SSSR — Mjasn Ind
MKR [*Mitteldeutscher Kulturrat*] **Schriften** — MKR Schriften
MLA [*Modern Language Association of America*] **International Bibliography of Books and Articles on the Modern Languages and Literature** [*Database*] — MLA
MLA [*Modern Language Association*] **International Bibliography of Books and Articles on the Modern Languages and Literatures** — MLA Int Bibliogr Books Artic Mod Lang Lit
MLA (Music Library Association) List Online — MLA-L
MLA (Music Library Association) Northern California Chapter Newsletter — MLANCCN
Mladezka Misl — Mlad Misl
Mladinska Revija — MIR
Mladost — MI
Mlekarske Listy — Mlek Listy
MLM (Mound Facility) — MLM (Mound Facil)
MLN [*Minnesota League for Nursing*] **Bulletin** — MLN Bull
Mlody Technik [*Poland*] — Mlody Tech
MLS: Marketing Library Services — MLS
Mlynarske Listy — Mlyn L
Mlynarz Polski — Mlyn Pol
Mlynsko-Pekarensky Prumysl a Technika Skladovani Obili — Mlyn Pek Prum Tech Skladovani Obili
Mlynsko-Pekarensky Prumysl a Technika Skladovani Obili — Mlynsko-Pekar Prum Tech Sklad Obili
MM [*Metall und Maschinenindustrie*] **Industriejournal** — MM Industriej
MM. Minoeseg es Megbizhatosag — MM Minoes Megbizh
MM. Qualitaet und Zuverlaessigkeit. Sonderausgabe — MM Qual Zuverlaessigk Sonderausg
MMER Report. Department of Mechanical Engineering. Monash University — MMER Rep Dep Mech Eng Monash Univ
MMJ. Maryland Medical Journal — MMJ MD Med J
MMR. Minerals and Metals Review [*India*] — MMR Miner Met Rev
MMS Asia/Pacific Market Analysis [*Database*] — APMA
MMS Currency Market Analysis [*Database*] — CMA
MMS Debt Market Analysis [*Database*] — DMA
MMS Equity Market Analysis [*Database*] — EMA
MMS Gilt Market Analysis [*Database*] — GMA
MMW. Muenchener Medizinische Wochenschrift — MMW Muench Med Wochenschr
MMWR [*Morbidity and Mortality Weekly Report*] **- CDC Surveillance Summaries** [*Center for Disease Control*] — MMWR CDC Surveill Summ
MMWR. Morbidity and Mortality Weekly Report — MMWR Morb Mortal Wkly Rep
MMWR [*Morbidity and Mortality Weekly Report*] **Surveillance Summaries** — MMWR Surveill Summ
Mnemosyne — M
Mnemosyne — Mn
Mnemosyne. Bibliotheca Classica Batava — Mnem
Mnemosyne. Bibliotheca Classica Batava — Mnemos
Mnemosyne. Bibliotheca Classica Batava — Mnemosyne
Mnemosyne. Bibliotheca Classica Batava — PMNE
MNI. Microcomputer News International — MNI Microcomput News Int
MNU. Mathematische und Naturwissenschaftliche Unterricht — MNU Math Naturwiss Unterr
Mobelkultur. Fachzeitschrift fuer die Mobelwirtschaft — MKK
Mobelmarkt. Fachzeitschrift fuer die Mobelwirtschaft — MOM
Mobil Country Journal — Mobil Country J
Mobil Review — Mobil Rev
Mobile Particulate Systems — Mobile Part Syst
Mobile Phone News — Mobil Ph N
Mobile Satellite Reports [*Telecommunications service*] — MSR
Mobilization and Reassembly of Genetic Information — Mobilization Reassem Genet Inf
Mocambique Missao de Combate as Tripanossomiases. Annual Report — Mocambique Missao Combate Tripanossomiases Annu Rep
Mocambique. Provincia. Direccao dos Servicos de Geologia e Minas. Memorias e Communicacoes. Boletim — Mocambique Prov Dir Serv Geol Minas Mem Commun Bol
Mocambique. Provincia. Servicos de Industria e Geologia. Serie de Geologia e Minas. Memorias e Communicacoes. Boletim — Mocambique Prov Serv Ind Geol Ser Geol Minas Mem Commun Bol
Moccasin Telegraph — Moccasin Tel
Moccasin Telegraph — MOCT
Moccasin Telegraph. Fort Chipewyan — MT
Mode of Action of Anti-Parasitic Drugs — Mode Action Anti Parasit Drugs
Mode Selective Chemistry. Proceedings. Jerusalem Symposium on Quantum Chemistry and Biochemistry — Mode Sel Chem Proc Jerusalem Symp Quantum Chem Biochem
Model Airplane News — IMAI
Model Engineer — Model Eng
Model Railroader — IMRA
Modeles Linguistiques — M Ling
Modeling and Simulation. Proceedings. Annual Pittsburgh Conference — Model Simul Proc Annu Pittsburgh Conf
Modeling Identification and Control — MIC
Modeling Identification and Control — MIDCD
Modeling Identification and Control [*Norway*] — Model Identif Control
Modeling of Casting, Welding, and Advanced Solidification Processes V. Proceedings. International Conference on Modeling of Casting and Welding Processes — Model Cast Weld Adv Solidif Processes V Proc Int Conf
Modelirovanie i Optimizatsiya Khimicheskikh Protsessov — Model Optim Khim Protsessov
Modelirovanie Khimicheskikh Reaktorov. Trudy Vsesoyuznoi Konferentsii po Khimicheskim Reaktoram — Model Khim Reakt Tr Vses Konf Khim Reakt
Modelirovanie v Biologii i Meditsine Respublikanskii Mezhvedomstvennyi Sbornik — Model Biol Med Resp Mezhved Sb
Modelisation. Analyse. Simulation. Commande — Model Anal Simul Commande
Modelling and Control of Biotechnical Processes. Proceedings. IFAC Workshop — Modell Control Biotech Processes Proc IFAC Workshop
Modelling and Control of Biotechnological Processes. Proceedings. IFAC Symposium — Modell Control Biotechnol Processes Proc IFAC Symp
Modelling in Ecotoxicology — Modell Ecotoxicol
Modelling in Environmental Chemistry — Modell Environ Chem
Modelling of Environmental Effects on Electrical and General Engineering Equipment. Summary. International Symposium — Modell Environ Eff Electr Gen Eng Equip Summ Int Symp
Modelling the Effect of Climate on Electrical and Mechanical Engineering Equipment. International Symposium — Modell Eff Clim Electr Mech Eng Equip Int Symp
Models Laboratory Reports. Department of Architectural Science. University of Sydney — Models Lab Rep Dep Archit Sci Syd Univ
Modern Age — MA
Modern Age — Mod A
Modern Age — Mod Age
Modern Age — PMOA
Modern Aging Research — Mod Aging Res
Modern Agriculture (Athens) — Mod Agric Athens
Modern Analytical and Computational Methods in Science and Mathematics [*Elsevier Book Series*] — MCMSM
Modern and Classical Language Bulletin — MCLB
Modern Approaches in Geophysics — Modern Approaches Geophys
Modern Approaches to Chemical Reaction Searching. Proceedings. Conference — Mod Approaches Chem React Searching Proc Conf
Modern Arts News — Mod Arts News
Modern Asia — MNI
Modern Asian Studies — MAS
Modern Asian Studies — MoA
Modern Asian Studies [*London*] — Mod As Stud
Modern Asian Studies — Mod Asian S
Modern Asian Studies — Mod Asian Stud
Modern Asian Studies — PMOS
Modern Aspects of Electrochemistry — MAECA
Modern Aspects of Electrochemistry — Mod Aspects Electrochem
Modern Aspects of Neurosurgery — Mod Aspects Neurosurg
Modern Aspects of Particle Physics. Collection of Lectures. Spring School of Theoretical and Experimental Physics — Mod Aspects Part Phys Collect Lect Spring Sch Theor Exp Phys
Modern Aspects of the Vitreous State — Mod Aspects Vitreous State
Modern Aspects Series of Chemistry — Mod Aspects Ser Chem
Modern Athlete and Coach — Mod Ath and Coach
Modern Athlete and Coach — Mod Athl Coach
Modern Austrian Literature — MAL
Modern Austrian Literature — Mod Aust L
Modern Austrian Literature — Mod Austrian Lit
Modern Beekeeping — Mod Beekeep
Modern Biology — Mod Biol
Modern Boating — Mod B
Modern Boating and Seacraft — Modern Boating
Modern Brewer — Mod Brew
Modern Brewery Age — Mod Brew Age
Modern Brewery Age. Magazine Section — Mod Brew M
Modern British Literature — MBL
Modern Business Law — Mod Bus Law
Modern Camera Magazine — Mod Camera Mag
Modern Casting and American Foundryman — Mod Cast Am Foundryman
Modern Castings — Mod Cast
Modern Cell Biology — Mod Cell Biol
Modern Chemical Industry — Mod Chem Ind
Modern Chemistry [*Japan*] — Mod Chem
Modern China — Mod China
Modern China — PMOC
Modern China Studies — Mod China Stud
Modern Chinese Literature Newsletter [*Berkeley*] — Mod Chin Lit Newsl
Modern Chlor-Alkali Technology — Mod Chlor Alkali Technol
Modern Chlor-Alkali Technology. Papers Presented at the International Chlorine Symposium — Mod Chlor Alkali Technol Pap Int Chlorine Symp
Modern Churchman — MCM
Modern Churchman — Mod Ch
Modern Churchman — ModChm
Modern Clinics [*Japan*] — Mod Clin

Modern Concepts and Practices of Fiber Refining. Proceedings. Annual Pulp and Paper Conference — Mod Concepts Pract Fiber Refin Proc Annu Pulp Pap Conf
Modern Concepts in Penicillium and Aspergillus Classification — Mod Concepts Penicillium Aspergillus Classif
Modern Concepts in Psychiatric Surgery. Proceedings. World Congress of Psychiatric Surgery — Mod Concepts Psychiatr Surg Proc World Congr
Modern Concepts of Cardiovascular Disease — Mod C Cardi
Modern Concepts of Cardiovascular Disease — Mod Concepts Cardiovasc Dis
Modern Concrete — Mod Concr
Modern Dairy — Mod Dairy
Modern Data — Mod Data
Modern Development in Powder Metallurgy — Mod Dev Powder Metall
Modern Developments in Shock Tube Research. Proceedings. International Shock Tube Symposium — Mod Dev Shock Tube Res Proc Int Shock Tube Symp
Modern Drama — MD
Modern Drama — Mod Drama
Modern Drama — ModD
Modern Drama — ModDr
Modern Drama — PMOD
Modern Drug Encyclopedia and Therapeutic Index. Supplement — Mod Drug Encycl Ther Index Suppl
Modern Drugs — Mod Drugs
Modern Drummer — MD
Modern Drummer — MDr
Modern Drummer — Modern Drum
Modern East Asian Studies — Mod East Asian Stud
Modern Education — Mod Ed
Modern Encyclopedia of Religions in Russia and the Soviet Union — MERRSU
Modern Encyclopedia of Russian and Soviet Literature — MERSL
Modern Engineer — Mod Eng
Modern English Journal — Mod Engl Jnl
Modern European Philosophy — Modern European Philos
Modern Farmer — Mod Farmer
Modern Farming — Mod Farming
Modern Farming in Central Africa — Mod Farming Cent Afr
Modern Fiction Studies — GMOF
Modern Fiction Studies — MFS
Modern Fiction Studies — Mod Fict St
Modern Fiction Studies — Mod Fict Stud
Modern Geology — Mod Geol
Modern German Authors. Texts and Contexts — MGATC
Modern Healthcare — MHC
Modern Healthcare — Mod Health
Modern Healthcare — Mod Healthcare
Modern Hebrew Literature — MHL
Modern Hebrew Literature — Mod Heb Lit
Modern Hospital — Mod Hosp
Modern Hospital — MOHOA
Modern Humanities Research Association — MHRA
Modern Humanities Research Association. Bulletin — MHRA Bull
Modern Humanities Research Association. Dissertation Series — MHRADS
Modern India and the West. A study of the Interaction of their Civilizations [*monograph*] — MIW
Modern Industrial Energy [*United States*] — Mod Ind Energy
Modern Industrial Energy — MOIED
Modern Industry — Mod Ind
Modern Instrumental Methods of Elemental Analysis of Petroleum Products and Lubricants — Mod Instrum Methods Elem Anal Pet Prod Lubr
Modern International Drama — MIDr
Modern International Drama — Mod Int Dr
Modern Judaism — Mo J
Modern Judaism — Mod Jud
Modern Judaism — Mod Judaism
Modern Kemi — Mod Kemi
Modern Knitting Management — Mod Knit
Modern Language Abstracts — MLA
Modern Language Abstracts — Mod Lang Abstr
Modern Language Association of America. International Bibliography — MLA Int Bibl
Modern Language Association of America. Publications — Mod Lang Assn Pub
Modern Language Forum — MLF
Modern Language Forum — Mod Lang For
Modern Language Forum — Mod Lang Forum
Modern Language Journal — GMOL
Modern Language Journal — ML
Modern Language Journal — MLJ
Modern Language Journal — Mod Lang J
Modern Language Journal — MOLJA
Modern Language Notes — MLN
Modern Language Notes — Mod Lan
Modern Language Notes — Mod Lang N
Modern Language Notes — Mod Lang Notes
Modern Language Quarterly — MLQ
Modern Language Quarterly — Mod Lang Q
Modern Language Quarterly — Mod Lang Quarterly
Modern Language Quarterly — Mod Lang Quartl
Modern Language Quarterly — PLAQ
Modern Language Review — IMOL
Modern Language Review — MLJ
Modern Language Review — MLR
Modern Language Review — Mod Lang R
Modern Language Review — Mod Lang Rev
Modern Language Studies — MLS
Modern Language Studies — Mod Lang St
Modern Languages — M Lang
Modern Languages — ML
Modern Languages — Mod Lang
Modern Languages in Scotland — Mod Lang Scot
Modern Law and Society — Mod Law Soc
Modern Law Review — MLR
Modern Law Review — Mod L Rev
Modern Law Review — Mod Law R
Modern Law Review — Mod Law Rev
Modern Law Review — Mod LR
Modern Law Review — Modern L Rev
Modern Law Review — Modern LR
Modern Librarian — Mod Libn
Modern Lithography — Mod Lithography
Modern Liturgy — ML
Modern Liturgy — Mod Lit
Modern Liturgy — Modern Lit
Modern Machine Shop — MMASA
Modern Machine Shop — Mod Mach Shop
Modern Manufacturing — Mod Mfg
Modern Materials — Mod Mater
Modern Materials. Advances in Development and Applications — MMADA
Modern Materials. Advances in Development and Applications — Mod Mater Adv Dev Appl
Modern Materials Handling — Mod Mat H
Modern Materials Handling — Mod Mater Handl
Modern Maturity — GMOM
Modern Medical Laboratory — Mod Med Lab
Modern Medicine — Mod Med
Modern Medicine (Chicago) — Mod Med (Chicago)
Modern Medicine (Cleveland, Ohio) — Mod Med Cleveland Ohio
Modern Medicine (Japan) — Mod Med (Jpn)
Modern Medicine (Minneapolis) — Mod Med (Minneapolis)
Modern Medicine of Asia — Mod Med Asia
Modern Medicine. The Newsmagazine of Medicine (Minneapolis) — Modern Med Minneapolis
Modern Metal Finishing — Mod Met Finish
Modern Metals — Mod Met
Modern Metals — Mod Metals
Modern Methods in Pharmacology — Mod Methods Pharmacol
Modern Methods in Protein and Nucleic Acid Research. Review Articles — Mod Methods Protein Nucleic Acid Res
Modern Methods of Igneous Petrology. Understanding Magmatic Processes — Mod Methods Igneous Petrol Understanding Magmat Processes
Modern Methods of Plant Analysis — Mod Methods Plant Anal
Modern Methods of Plant Analysis. New Series — Mod Method Plant Anal New Ser
Modern Miller — Mod Miller
Modern Miller and Bakers News — Mod Miller Bakers News
Modern Mining — Mod Min
Modern Motor — Mod M
Modern Motor — Mod Motor
Modern Music — MM
Modern Music — Mod Mus
Modern Music — Mod Music
Modern NMR Techniques and Their Application in Chemistry — Mod NMR Tech Their Appl Chem
Modern Nursing Home — Mod Nurs Home
Modern Nutrition — Mod Nutr
Modern Occasions — Modern O
Modern Office — MOM
Modern Office and Data Equipment — Mode
Modern Office and Data Management — Mod Off and Data Manage
Modern Office Procedures — Mod Off
Modern Office Procedures — Mod Off Proc
Modern Office Procedures — Mod Off Proced
Modern Office Procedures — Mod Off Procedures
Modern Office Procedures — MOP
Modern Office Technology — Mod Off
Modern Office Technology — MOP
Modern Packaging — Mod Packag
Modern Packaging — Mod Pkg
Modern Packaging — MP
Modern Packaging Encyclopedia — Mod Packag Encycl
Modern Packaging Encyclopedia and Buyer's Guide Issue — Mod Pkg En
Modern Packaging Encyclopedia Issue — Mod Packag Encycl Issue
Modern Paint and Coatings — Mod Paint
Modern Paint and Coatings — Mod Paint Coat
Modern Paint and Coatings — PVP
Modern Pathology — Mod Pathol
Modern Perspectives in Psychiatry — Mod Perspect Psychiatry
Modern Pharmacology — Mod Pharm
Modern Pharmacology — Mod Pharmacol
Modern Pharmacology-Toxicology — Mod Pharmacol Toxicol
Modern Philology — M Phil
Modern Philology — Mod Phil
Modern Philology — Mod Philol
Modern Philology — Modern Phil
Modern Philology — MP
Modern Philology — MPh
Modern Philology — PMOP
Modern Photography — GMOP
Modern Photography — M Photo
Modern Photography — Mod Phot

Modern Photography — Mod Photogr
Modern Physics Letters A. Particles and Fields, Gravitation, Cosmology, Nuclear Physics — Mod Phys Lett A
Modern Physics Letters. A. Particles and Fields, Gravitation, Cosmology, Nuclear Physics — Modern Phys Lett A
Modern Physics Letters B. Condensed Matter Physics, Statistical Physics and Applied Physics — Mod Phys Lett B
Modern Physics Letters. B. Condensed Matter Physics, Statistical Physics, Applied Physics — Modern Phys Lett B
Modern Physics Monograph Series — Mod Phys Monogr Ser
Modern Phytochemical Methods — Mod Phytochem Methods
Modern Plastics — Mod Plas
Modern Plastics — Mod Plast
Modern Plastics — Mod Plastics
Modern Plastics International — Mod Plast Int
Modern Plastics International — Mod Plst Int
Modern Plastics International — Modern Plastics Int
Modern Plastics International — MOP
Modern Poetry Studies — Mod Poet St
Modern Poetry Studies — Mod Poetry Stud
Modern Poetry Studies — Modern P S
Modern Poetry Studies — MPS
Modern Powder Diffraction — Mod Powder Diffr
Modern Power and Engineering — Mod Power and Eng
Modern Power and Engineering — Mod Power Eng
Modern Power Systems — EHB
Modern Power Systems — Mod Power Syst
Modern Practice of Gas Chromatography — Mod Pract Gas Chromatogr
Modern Problems in Ophthalmology — Mod Prob Ophth
Modern Problems in Ophthalmology — Mod Probl Ophthalmol
Modern Problems in Ophthalmology — MPOTB
Modern Problems in Paediatrics — Mod Probl Paediatr
Modern Problems in Solid State Physics [*Elsevier Book Series*] — MPSSP
Modern Problems of Pharmacopsychiatry — Mod Probl Pharmacopsychiatry
Modern Problems of Surface Physics. International School on Condensed Matter Physics. Lectures — Mod Probl Surf Phys Int Sch Condens Matter Phys Lect
Modern Problems of the Activity and Structure of the Central Nervous System — Mod Probl Act Struct Cent Nerv Syst
Modern Psychoanalysis — Mod Psychoanal
Modern Quarterly — Mod Q
Modern Quarterly — MQ
Modern Quarterly Miscellany — Mod Quart Misc
Modern Quarterly Research in Southeast Asia [*Rotterdam*] — Mod Quart Res SE A
Modern Railroads — Mod Rr
Modern Railways — Mod Railw
Modern Railways — Modern Railw
Modern Refrigeration — Mod Refrig
Modern Refrigeration and Air Conditioning — Mod Refrig Air Cond
Modern Refrigeration and Air Control News — Mod Refrig Air Control News
Modern Review — Mod R
Modern Review — ModRev
Modern Review — MoR
Modern Review — MR
Modern Review (Calcutta) — Mod R (Calcutta)
Modern Schoolman — Mod Sch
Modern Schoolman — Mod Schoolm
Modern Schoolman — Mod Schoolman
Modern Schoolman — MSch
Modern Schoolman — MSM
Modern Science and Vedic Science — Modern Sci Vedic Sci
Modern Scot — MS
Modern Solid State Physics. Simon Fraser University. Lectures — Mod Solid State Phys Simon Fraser Univ Lect
Modern Studies Association Yearbook — Mod Stud Assoc Yearb
Modern Sugar Planter — Mod Sugar Plant
Modern Synthetic Methods. Conference Paper. International Seminar on Modern Synthetic Methods — Mod Synth Methods
Modern Teacher — Mod Teach
Modern Teaching — Mod Teach
Modern Technics in Surgery. Abdominal Surgery — Mod Tech Surg Abdom Surg
Modern Technics in Surgery. Cardiac-Thoracic Surgery — Mod Tech Surg Card Thor Surg
Modern Technics in Surgery. Plastic Surgery — Mod Tech Surg Plastic Surg
Modern Techniques in Computational Chemistry. MOTECC-90 — Mod Tech Comput Chem MOTECC 90
Modern Textile Business — Mod Tex B
Modern Textiles — Mod Text
Modern Textiles — Mod Textil
Modern Textiles Magazine — Mod Text
Modern Textiles Magazine — Mod Text Mag
Modern Theology — PMOT
Modern Theoretical Chemistry — Mod Theor Chem
Modern Tire Dealer — M Tire Dealr
Modern Tire Dealer — Mod Tire Dealer
Modern Tire Dealer — Tire Dealr
Modern Tramway — Mod Tramway
Modern Treatment — Mod Treat
Modern Trends in Anaesthesia — Mod Trends Anaesth
Modern Trends in Cardiology — Mod Trends Cardiol
Modern Trends in Cybernetics and Systems. Proceedings. International Congress of Cybernetics and Systems — Mod Trends Cyber Syst Proc Int Congr
Modern Trends in Dermatology — Mod Trends Dermatol
Modern Trends in Dermatology — MTDYA
Modern Trends in Drug Dependence and Alcoholism — Mod Trends Drug Depend Alcohol
Modern Trends in Endocrinology — Mod Trends Endocrinol
Modern Trends in Forensic Medicine — Mod Trends Forensic Med
Modern Trends in Gastroenterology — Mod Trends Gastroenterol
Modern Trends in Human Leukemia 2. Biological, Immunological, Therapeutical, and Virological Aspects — Mod Trends Hum Leuk 2
Modern Trends in Human Leukemia 4. Newest Results in Clinical and Biological Research Including Pediatric Oncology. Wiselde Joint Meeting on Pediatric Oncology — Mod Trends Hum Leuk 4 Wiselde Jt Meet Pediatr Oncol
Modern Trends in Human Reproductive Physiology — Mod Trends Hum Reprod Physiol
Modern Trends in Immunology — Mod Trends Immunol
Modern Trends in Medical Virology — Mod Trends Med Virol
Modern Trends in Neurology — Mod Trends Neurol
Modern Trends in Oncology — Mod Trends Oncol
Modern Trends in Orthopaedics — Mod Trends Orthop
Modern Trends in Pharmacology and Therapeutics — Mod Trends Pharmacol Ther
Modern Trends in Plastic Surgery — Mod Trends Plast Surg
Modern Trends in Psychosomatic Medicine — Mod Trends Psychosom Med
Modern Trends in Radiotherapy — Mod Trends Radiother
Modern Trends in Rheumatology — Mod Trends Rheumatol
Modern Trends in Surgery — Mod Trends Surg
Modern Trends in Toxicology — Mod Trends Toxicol
Modern Trends Series. Psychosomatic Medicine — Mod Trends Ser Psychosom Med
Modern Utilization of Infrared Technology — Mod Util Infrared Technol
Modern Utilization of Infrared Technology. Civilian and Military — Mod Util Infrared Technol Civ Mil
Modern Utopia — Mo Utopia
Modern Veterinary Practice — Mod Vet Pract
Modern Vocational Trends. Career Monographs — Modern Vocational Trends Career Mon
Modern World — Mod World
Modern Ytbehandling — Mod Ytbehandling
Moderna Sprak — MS
Moderna Sprak — MSpr
Moderna Sprak — MSprak
Moderne Arzneimittel-Therapie — Mod Arzneim Ther
Moderne Holzverarbeitung — Mod Holzverarb
Moderne Lehrtexte. Wirtschaftswissenschaften [*Cologne*] — Moderne Lehrtexte Wirtschaftwiss
Moderne Mathematik in Elementarer Darstellung — Moderne Math Elem Darstellung
Moderne Medizin — Mod Med
Moderne Predigt-Bibliothek — MPB
Moderne Probleme der Paediatrie [*Switzerland*] — Mod Probl Paediatr
Moderne Probleme der Paediatrie — MPPAA
Moderne Probleme der Pharmakopsychiatrie — Mod Probl Pharmakopsychiatr
Moderne Roentgen-Fotografie — Mod Roentgen-Fotogr
Moderne Sprachen — Mod Sp
Moderne Unfallverhuetung — Mod Unfallverhuet
Moderne Unfallverhuetung — MUNFA
Moderne Welt — Mod Welt
Modernist Studies — Mod Stud
Modernist Studies. Literature and Culture, 1920-1940 — Mod St Lit
Modernist Studies. Literature and Culture, 1920-1940 — MSLC
Modersmalslararnas Forening. Arsskrift — MLF
Modersmalslararnas Forening. Arsskrift — MLFA
Modification of the Information Content of Plant Cells. Proceedings. John Innes Symposium — Modif Inf Content Plant Cells Proc John Innes Symp
Modifikatsiya Polimernykh Materialov [*Latvian SSR*] — Modif Polim Mater
Modifikatsiya Polimernykh Materialov — MPLMB
Modilianum — Mod
Modoqua. Series II — Madoqua Ser II
Modszertani Kozlemenyek. Magyar Allami Foldtani Intezet — Modszertani Kozl Mag All Foldt Intez
Modular Instruction in Statistics — Modular I St
Modulated Structure Materials — Modulated Struct Mater
Modulation and Mediation of Cancer by Vitamins. Proceedings. International Conference on the Modulation and Mediation of Cancer by Vitam — Modulation Mediation Cancer Vitam Proc Int Conf
Modulation of Cellular Interactions by Vitamin A and Derivatives (Retinoids) — Modulation Cell Interact Vitam A Deriv Retinoids
Modulators of Experimental Carcinogenesis. Proceedings. Symposium — Modulators Exp Carcinog Proc Symp
Modules in Applied Mathematics — Modules Appl Math
Moeglinsche Annalen der Landwirthschaft — Moeglinsche Ann Landw
Moessbauer Effect Methodology — Moessbauer Eff Methodol
Moessbauer Effect Methodology. Proceedings of the Symposium — MEMPB
Moessbauer Effect Methodology. Proceedings of the Symposium — Moessbauer Eff Methodol Proc Symp
Moessbauer Effect. Proceedings. International Conference on the Moessbauer Effect — Moessbauer Eff Proc Int Conf
Moessbauer Effect Reference and Data Journal — MERJD
Moessbauer Spectroscopy — Moessbauer Spectrosc
Moffatt New Testament Commentary — MNTC
Moines et Monasteres — MeM
Moir's Australian Investments — Moirs Aust Investments
Mois Chimique et Electrochimique — Mois Chim Electrochim
Mois Economique et Financier — Mois Econ et Fin
Mois Economique et Financier — SBU

Mois Minier et Metallurgique — Mois Minier Metall
Mois Scientifique et Industriel — Mois Sci Ind
Mois Suisse — Ms
Moisture and Fertility. American Potash Institute — Moist Fert
Moisture and Frost-Related Soil Properties — Moisture Frost Relat Soil Prop
Mojave Revegetation Notes — Mojave Reveg Notes
Mokslas ir Technika — Mokslas Tech
Mokslo Darbai. Vilniaus Valstybinis Pedagoginis Institutas — Mokslo Darb Vilniaus Valstybinis Pedagog Inst
Mokuzai Gakkai Shi/Journal. Japan Wood Research Society — Mokuzai Gakkai Shi/J Jap Wood Res Soc
Mokuzai Gakkaishi — Mokuzai Gak
Molecular and Biochemical Parasitology — Mol Biochem Parasitol
Molecular and Cell Biology of Human Diseases Series — Mol Cell Biol Hum Dis Ser
Molecular and Cellular Biochemistry — Mol C Bioch
Molecular and Cellular Biochemistry — Mol Cell Biochem
Molecular and Cellular Biology — MCB
Molecular and Cellular Biology — Mol Cell Biol
Molecular and Cellular Endocrinology — Mol C Endoc
Molecular and Cellular Endocrinology — Mol Cell Endocr
Molecular and Cellular Endocrinology — Mol Cell Endocrinol
Molecular and Cellular Neurosciences — Mol Cell Neurosci
Molecular and Cellular Probes — Mol Cell Probes
Molecular and Chemical Neuropathology — Mol Chem Ne
Molecular and Chemical Neuropathology — Mol Chem Neuropathol
Molecular and General Genetics — Mol G Genet
Molecular and General Genetics — Mol Gen Genet
Molecular Aspects of Cell Regulation [*Elsevier Book Series*] — MACR
Molecular Aspects of Cellular Regulation — Mol Aspects Cell Regul
Molecular Aspects of Medicine — Mol Aspects Med
Molecular Aspects of Monooxygenases and Bioactivation of Toxic Compounds — Mol Aspects Monooxygenases Bioact Toxic Compd
Molecular Basis of Bacterial Metabolism — Mol Basis Bact Metab
Molecular Basis of Microbial Pathogenicity. Report of the Molecular Basis of the Ineffective Process, Berlin, 1979 — Mol Basis Microb Pathog
Molecular Beam Epitaxy. Proceedings. International Symposium — Mol Beam Epitaxy Proc Int Symp
Molecular Biology — Mol Biol
Molecular Biology — Molec Biol
Molecular Biology; an International Series of Monographs and Textbooks — Mol Biol Int Ser Monogr Textb
Molecular Biology and Evolution — Mol Biol Evol
Molecular Biology and Medicine — MBM
Molecular Biology and Medicine — Mol Biol & Med
Molecular Biology and Medicine — Mol Biol Med
Molecular Biology, Biochemistry, and Biophysics — Mol Biol Biochem Biophys
Molecular Biology. English Translation of Molekulyarnaya Biologiya (Moscow) — Mol Biol Engl Transl Mol Biol (Mosc)
Molecular Biology in Tumour Research. Annual Meeting. Arbeitsgemeinschaft fuer Gen-Diagnostik — Mol Biol Tumour Res Annu Meet Arbeitsgem Gen Diagn
Molecular Biology of Atherosclerosis. Proceedings. Steenbock Symposium — Mol Biol Atheroscler Proc Steenbock Symp
Molecular Biology of Cyanobacteria — Mol Biol Cyanobacteria
Molecular Biology of Diabetes — Mol Biol Diabetes
Molecular Biology of Erythropoiesis — Mol Biol Erythropoiesis
Molecular Biology of Free Radical Scavenging Systems — Mol Biol Free Radical Scavenging Syst
Molecular Biology of Plant Development — Mol Biol Plant Dev
Molecular Biology of the Cell — Mol Biol Cell
Molecular Biology of the Mammalian Genetic Apparatus — Mol Biol Mamm Gene Appar
Molecular Biology. Proceedings. International Conference — Mol Biol Proc Int Conf
Molecular Biology Reports — Mol Biol Rep
Molecular Biology Reports — Mol Biol Rp
Molecular Biotechnology — Mol Biotechnol
Molecular Brain Research — Mol Brain Res
Molecular Breeding — Mol Breed
Molecular Carcinogenesis — Mol Carcino
Molecular Carcinogenesis — Mol Carcinog
Molecular Complexes — Mol Complexes
Molecular Crystals — MOCRA
Molecular Crystals — Mol Cryst
Molecular Crystals and Liquid Crystals — Mol Cryst and Liq Cryst
Molecular Crystals and Liquid Crystals — Mol Cryst Liq Cryst
Molecular Crystals and Liquid Crystals — Molec Cryst
Molecular Crystals and Liquid Crystals Incorporating Nonlinear Optics — Mol Cryst Liq Cryst Incorporating Nonlinear Opt
Molecular Crystals and Liquid Crystals. Letters — Mol Cryst and Liq Cryst Lett
Molecular Crystals and Liquid Crystals. Letters — Mol Cryst Liq Cryst Lett
Molecular Crystals and Liquid Crystals. Letters Section — Mol Cryst Liq Cryst Lett Sect
Molecular Crystals and Liquid Crystals Science and Technology. Section C. Molecular Materials — Mol Cryst Liq Cryst Sci Technol Sect C
Molecular Crystals and Liquid Crystals. Supplement Series — Mol Cryst and Liq Cryst Suppl Ser
Molecular Cytogenetics. Proceedings. Annual Biology Division Research Conference — Mol Cytogenet Proc Annu Biol Div Res Conf
Molecular Design of Electrode Surfaces — Mol Des Electrode Surf
Molecular Diabetology — Mol Diabetol
Molecular Diversity — Mol Diversity
Molecular Ecology — Mol Ecol
Molecular Endocrinology [*Elsevier Book Series*] — MOE
Molecular Endocrinology — Mol Endocrinol
Molecular Engineering — Mol Eng
Molecular Genetic Medicine — Mol Genet Med
Molecular Genetics in Developmental Neurobiology. Taniguchi Symposium on Brain Sciences — Mol Genet Dev Neurobiol Taniguchi Symp Brain Sci
Molecular Genetics, Microbiology, and Virology [*Former USSR*] — MGMV
Molecular Human Reproduction — Mol Hum Reprod
Molecular Immunology — Mol Immunol
Molecular Insect Science. Proceedings. International Symposium on Molecular Insect Science — Mol Insect Sci Proc Int Symp
Molecular Interactions — Mol Interact
Molecular Marine Biology and Biotechnology — Mol Mar Biol Biotechnol
Molecular Materials — Mol Mater
Molecular Mechanisms of Immune Regulation — Mol Mech Immune Regul
Molecular Mechanisms of Insecticide Resistance — Mol Mech Insectic Resist
Molecular Mechanisms of Transport. Proceedings. Bari Meeting on Bioenergetics. International Symposium — Mol Mech Transp Proc Bari Meet Bioenerg Int Symp
Molecular Medicine — Mol Med
Molecular Medicine (Cambridge, Massachusetts) — Mol Med Cambridge Mass
Molecular Medicine Today — Mol Med Today
Molecular Membrane Biology — Mol Membr Biol
Molecular Microbiology — Mol Microbiol
Molecular Neurobiology — Mol Neurobiol
Molecular Neuropharmacology — Mol Neuropharmacol
Molecular Neuroscience. Expression of Neural Genes. Proceedings. Galveston Neuroscience Symposium — Mol Neurosci Proc Galveston Neurosci Symp
Molecular Pharmacology — Mol Pharmacol
Molecular Pharmacology — Molec Pharm
Molecular Pharmacology of Receptors — Mol Pharmacol Recept
Molecular Photochemistry — Mol Photoch
Molecular Photochemistry — Mol Photochem
Molecular Phylogenetics and Evolution — Mol Phylogenet Evol
Molecular Physics — Mol Phys
Molecular Physics — Molec Phys
Molecular Physics — Molecular Phys
Molecular Physics Reports — Mol Phys Rep
Molecular Physiology — Mol Physiol
Molecular Plant-Microbe Interactions — Mol Plant Microbe Interact
Molecular Plant-Microbe Interactions. MPMI — Mol Plant Microb Interact MPMI
Molecular Psychiatry — Mol Psychiatry
Molecular Reproduction and Development — Mol Reprod Dev
Molecular Simulation — Mol Simul
Molecular Spectroscopy — Mol Spectros
Molecular Spectroscopy, Electronic Structure, and Intramolecular Interactions — Mol Spectrosc Electron Struct Intramol Interact
Molecular Spectroscopy. Modern Research — Mol Spectrosc Mod Res
Molecular Spectroscopy. Proceedings. Conference — Mol Spectrosc Proc Conf
Molecular Structure and Energetics — Mol Struct Energ
Molecular Structure by Diffraction Methods — Mol Struct Diffr Methods
Molecular Structures and Dimensions — Mol Struct Dimens
Molecular Structures and Dimensions. Series A — Mol Struct Dimensions Ser A
Molecular Techniques in Taxonomy — Mol Tech Taxon
Molecular Toxicology — Mol Toxicol
Molecular Vision [*Electronic Publication*] — Mol Vision
Molecules and Cells — Mol Cells
Molekularbiologie, Biochemie, und Biophysik — Molekularbiol Biochem Biophys
Molekulyarna Meditsina (Sofia) — Mol Med Sofia
Molekulyarnaya Biologiya — Mol Biol
Molekulyarnaya Biologiya. Itogi Nauki i Tekhniki — Mol Biol Itogi Nauki Tekh
Molekulyarnaya Biologiya (Kiev) — Mol Biol (Kiev)
Molekulyarnaya Biologiya (Moscow) — Mol Biol (Mosc)
Molekulyarnaya Fizika i Biofizika Vodnykh Sistem — Mol Fiz Biofiz Vod Sis
Molekulyarnaya Fizika i Biofizika Vodnykh Sistem — Mol Fiz Biofiz Vodn Sist
Molekulyarnaya Genetika i Biofizika — Mol Genet Biofiz
Molekulyarnaya Genetika, Mikrobiologiya, i Virusologiya — Mol Genet Mikrobiol Virusol
Molekulyarnaya Spektroskopiya — Mol Spektrosk
Molekulyarnye Mekhanizmy Geneticheskikh Protsessov. Trudy — Mol Mekh Genet Protsessov Tr
Molenaar Weekblad voor de Graanverwerkende Industrie en Veevoederindustrie [*A publication*] — MOL
Molini d'Italia — Molini Ital
Molkerei- und Kaeserei- Zeitung — Molk Kaeserei Ztg
Molkerei-Zeitung (Berlin) — Molk Ztg (Berlin)
Molkerei-Zeitung (Hildesheim, Germany) — Molk Ztg (Hildesheim Ger)
Molkerei-Zeitung Welt der Milch [*Germany*] — Molk Ztg Welt Milch
Molkerei-Zeitung Welt der Milch — MZWMA
Molochnaya Promyshlennost — Molochn Prom-St
Molochnoe i Myasnoe Skotovodstvo (Kiev) — Molochno Myasn Skotovod (Kiev)
Molochnoe i Myasnoe Skotovodstvo (Moscow) — Molochn Myasn Skotovod (Moscow)
Molochnoe i Myasnoe Zhivotnovodstvo — Moloch Myas Zhivotnovod
Molochnoe i Myasnoe Zhivotnovodstvo — Molochn Myasn Zhivotnovod
Molochno-Maslodel'naya Promyshlennost — Molochno Masloden Promst
Molodaia Gvardiia. Ezhemesiachnyi Literaturno-Khudozhestvennyi i Obshchestvenn-Politicheskii Zhurnal — MGv
Molodaya Gvardiya [*Moscow*] — MG
Molodoi Nauchnyi Rabotnik. Estestvennye Nauki — Molodoi Nauchn Rab Estestv Nauki
Molten Metal — Molten Met
Molten Salt Chemistry and Technology — Molten Salt Chem Technol
Molybdenum Mosaic — MMOSD
Molysulfide Newsletter [*United States*] — Molysulfide Newslett
Momenti e Problemi della Storia del Pensiero — Momenti Probl Storia Pensiero

Monaco. Musee d'Anthropologie Prehistorique. Bulletin — Monaco Mus Anthropol Prehist Bull
Monaldi Archives for Chest Disease — Monaldi Arch Chest Dis
Monash University. Chemical Engineering Department. Report — Monash Univ Chem Eng Dep Rep
Monash University. Gazette — Monash Univ Gaz
Monash University. Law Review — Mon L R
Monash University. Law Review — Mon L Rev
Monash University. Law Review — Monash LR
Monash University. Law Review — Monash UL Rev
Monash University. Law Review — Monash Univ L Rev
Monastere de Phoebammon dans la Thebaide — M Ph T
Monastic Studies — Mon S
Monastic Studies — Mon Stud
Monastic Studies — MSt
Monasticon Anglicanum — Mon Angl
Monat — Mo
Monathliche Fruechte einer Gelehrten Gesellschaft in Ungern — Monathl Fruechte Gel Ges Ungern
Monatliche Correspondenz zur Befoerderung der Erd- und Himmelskunde — MC
Monatliche Correspondenz zur Befoerderung der Erd und Himmelskunde [*East Germany*] — Mon Corresp Befoerd Erd Himmelskunde
Monatliche Mittheilungen aus dem Gesammtgebiete der Naturwissenschaften — Monatl Mitth Gesammtgeb Naturwiss
Monatsbericht. Berliner Akademie der Wissenschaft — MbBAW
Monatsberichte der Deutschen Akademie der Wissenschaften zu Berlin — DAWBM
Monatsberichte der Deutschen Akademie der Wissenschaften zu Berlin — MDAW
Monatsberichte der Deutschen Akademie der Wissenschaften zu Berlin — Monatsb Berl
Monatsberichte der Koenigliche Preussischen Akademie der Wissenschaften — MPAW
Monatsberichte der Preussischen Akademie der Wissenschaften zu Berlin — Berl Ber
Monatsberichte der Preussischen Akademie der Wissenschaften zu Berlin — Berl MB
Monatsberichte der Preussischen Akademie der Wissenschaften zu Berlin — MPA
Monatsberichte. Deutsche Akademie der Wissenschaften zu Berlin — Monatsber Deut Akad Wiss Berlin
Monatsberichte. Deutsche Akademie der Wissenschaften zu Berlin — Monatsber Dtsch Akad Wiss Berl
Monatsberichte. Deutsche Bundesbank — Monatsber Dtschen Bundesbank
Monatsberichte fuer Internationale Altersforschung und Altersbekaempfung — Monatsber Int Altersforsch Altersbekaempf
Monatsberichte. Oesterreichisches Institut fuer Wirtschaftsforschung — Monatsber Oesterr Inst Wirtsch-Forsch
Monatsberichte ueber die Verhandlungen der Gesellschaft fuer Erdkunde zu Berlin — Monatsber Verh Ges Erdk Berlin
Monatsblaetter der Historischen Gesellschaft fuer die Provinz Posen — Mbll Hist Ges Posen
Monatsblaetter des Berliner Bezirksvereins Deutscher Ingenieure — MblBBDI
Monatsblaetter fuer den Evangelischen Religionsunterricht — MERU
Monatsblaetter fuer den Katholischen Religionsunterricht an den Hoeheren Lehranstalten — MblKRU
Monatsblaetter fuer Freiheitliche Wirtschaftspolitik — Mbl Freiheitliche Wirtschaftspol
Monatsblaetter fuer Freiheitliche Wirtschafts-Politik — Monatsblaett Freiheitliche Wirtsch Polit
Monatsblaetter fuer Freiheitliche Wirtschaftspolitik — Wirt Pol
Monatsblaetter fuer Innere Mission — MIM
Monatsblaetter fuer Innere Zeitgeschichte — MIZG
Monatsblaetter. Gesellschaft fuer Pommersche Geschichte und Altertumskunde — MGPGA
Monatsblatt der Norddeutschen Missions-Gesellschaft — MNDMG
Monatsblatt der Vereinigung der Evangelisch-Lutherischen Innerhalb der Preussischen Landeskirche — MVEL
Monats-Blatt des Landwirthschaftlichen Vereins fuer den Oberdonau-Kreis im Koenigreiche Bayern — Monats Blatt Landw Vereins Oberdonau Kreis Koenigr Bayern
Monatsblatt des Vereins fuer Landeskunde von Niederoesterreich und Wien — MVLNOe
Monats-Bulletin des Schweizerischen Vereins von Gas- und Wasserfachmaennern — Mon Bull Schweiz Ver Gas Wasserfachmaennern
Monatschefte fuer Auswaertige Politik — Monatsh Ausw Politik
Monatschefte fuer Evangelische Kirchengeschichte des Rheinlandes — Mh Evang Kirchengesch Rheinl
Monatschefte fuer Praktische Dermatologie — Monatsh Prakt Dermatol
Monatschrift fuer Pastoraltheologie — Mschr Pastoraltheol
Monatshefte — MO
Monatshefte — MoH
Monatshefte; a Journal Devoted to the Study of German Language and Literature [*A publication*] — Monat
Monatshefte der Comenius-Gesellschaft — MCG
Monatshefte der Kunstwissenschaftlichen Literatur — MKWL
Monatshefte fuer Chemie — Monats Chem
Monatshefte fuer Chemie — Monatsh Chem
Monatshefte fuer Chemie und Verwandte Teile Anderer Wissenschaften — Mh Chem
Monatshefte fuer Chemie und Verwandte Teile Anderer Wissenschaften — Monatsh Chem Verw Teile Anderer Wiss
Monatshefte fuer Christliche Politik und Kultur — MhChrPK
Monatshefte fuer Christliche Politik und Kultur — Mhh Christl Polit
Monatshefte fuer den Naturwissenschaftlichen Unterricht Aller Schulgattungen und Natur und Schule — Monatsh Naturwiss Unterr Aller Schulgattungen Natur Sch
Monatshefte fuer der Montanistischen Hochschule in Leoben — Monatsh Montan Hochsch Leoben
Monatshefte fuer Deutschen Unterricht — MDU
Monatshefte fuer Deutschen Unterricht — MFDU
Monatshefte fuer Deutschen Unterricht — Monat f Deut Unt
Monatshefte fuer Deutschen Unterricht. Deutsche Sprache und Literatur — Monatshefte
Monatshefte fuer Evangelische Kirchengeschichte des Rheinlandes — MEKGR
Monatshefte fuer Katholische Kirchenmusik — MKKM
Monatshefte fuer Kunstwissenschaft — Mhh Kunstwiss
Monatshefte fuer Kunstwissenschaft — MKW
Monatshefte fuer Mathematik — Monats Math
Monatshefte fuer Mathematik [*Vienna*] — Monatsh Math
Monatshefte fuer Mathematik und Physik — MhMPh
Monatshefte fuer Mathematik und Physik [*Austria*] — Monatsh Math Phys
Monatshefte fuer Musikgeschichte — M Mg
Monatshefte fuer Musikgeschichte — MfM
Monatshefte fuer Praktische Dermatologie — Mhh Prakt Dermatol
Monatshefte fuer Praktische Dermatologie — Monatsh Prakt Dermat
Monatshefte fuer Praktische Tierheilkunde — Monatsh Prakt Tierh
Monatshefte fuer Rheinische Kirchengeschichte — MHRKg
Monatshefte fuer Rheinische Kirchengeschichte — MRKG
Monatshefte fuer Seide und Kunstseide — Monatsh Seide Kunstseide
Monatshefte fuer Seide und Kunstseide. Zellwolle — Monatsh Seide Kunstseide Zellwolle
Monatshefte fuer Tierheilkunde — Mh Tierheilk
Monatshefte fuer Tierheilkunde — Monatsh Tierheilkd
Monatshefte fuer Veterinaermedizin — Mh VetMed
Monatshefte fuer Veterinaermedizin — Monatsh Vet
Monatshefte fuer Veterinaermedizin — Monatsh Veterinaermed
Monatshefte fuer Veterinaermedizin — Monatsh Veterinarmed
Monatskurse fuer die Aerztliche Fortbildung — Mk Aerztl Fortb
Monatskurse fuer die Aerztliche Fortbildung — Monatskurse Aerztl Fortbild
Monatsschrift — Moschr
Monatsschrift der Deutschen Kakteen-Gesellschaft — Monatsschr Deutsch Kakteen Ges
Monatsschrift des Rationalisierungs — Rationalisierung
Monatsschrift Deutscher Zahnarzte der Freie Zahnarzt — Monatsschr Dtsch Zahnarzte Freie Zahnarzt
Monatsschrift fuer Brauerei — Monatsschr Brau
Monatsschrift fuer Brauerei — Monatsschr Brauerei
Monatsschrift fuer Brauerei — MONBA
Monatsschrift fuer Brauwissenschaft — Monatschr Brauwiss
Monatsschrift fuer Christliche Politik und Kultur — Mschr Christl Polit
Monatsschrift fuer Christliche Sozialreform — MCSR
Monatsschrift fuer das Deutsche Geistesleben — MDG
Monatsschrift fuer Deutsches Recht — MDERD
Monatsschrift fuer Deutsches Recht — Monatsschr Dtsch Recht
Monatsschrift fuer die Geschichte und Wissenschaft des Judentums — MGJ
Monatsschrift fuer die Geschichte und Wissenschaft des Judentums — MGWJ
Monatsschrift fuer die Reformierte Schweiz — MSRS
Monatsschrift fuer Geburtshilfe und Gynaekologie — Monatschr Geburtsh u Gynak
Monatsschrift fuer Geburtshilfe und Gynaekologie — Monatsschr Geburshilfe Gynaekol
Monatsschrift fuer Geschichte und Wissenschaft des Judentums — Ms Gesch Jud
Monatsschrift fuer Gottesdienst und Kirchliche Kunst [*Goettingen*] — MGkK
Monatsschrift fuer Hoehere Schulen — MHS
Monatsschrift fuer Hoehere Schulen — MHSch
Monatsschrift fuer Hoehere Schulen — Ms Hoeh Sch
Monatsschrift fuer Innere Mission — MIM
Monatsschrift fuer Kinderheilkunde — MfKh
Monatsschrift fuer Kinderheilkunde — MOKIA
Monatsschrift fuer Kinderheilkunde — Monats Kind
Monatsschrift fuer Kinderheilkunde — Monatsschr Kinderheilkd
Monatsschrift fuer Kirchliche Praxis — MKP
Monatsschrift fuer Krebsbekaempfung — Monatsschr Krebsbekaempf
Monatsschrift fuer Literatur und Wissenschaft des Judentums — Mschr Lit Wiss Judent
Monatsschrift fuer Lungenkrankheiten und Tuberkulosebekaempfung — Monatschr Lungenkrankh Tuberkulosebekaempf
Monatsschrift fuer Lungenkrankheiten und Tuberkulose-Bekaempfung — Monatsschr Lungenkr Tuberk-Bekaempf
Monatsschrift fuer Medicin, Augenheilkunde, und Chirurgie — Monatsschr Med
Monatsschrift fuer Naturwissenschaftlichen Unterricht — MNU
Monatsschrift fuer Obst- und Weinbau — Monatsschr Obst Weinbau
Monatsschrift fuer Ohrenheilkunde sowie fuer Kehlkopf-, Nasen-, Rachenkrankheiten — Monatsschr Ohrenheilkd Kehlkopf Nasen Rachenkrankh
Monatsschrift fuer Ohrenheilkunde und Laryngo-Rhinologie — MOLAA
Monatsschrift fuer Ohrenheilkunde und Laryngo-Rhinologie — Monatsschr Ohrenheilkd Laryngo-Rhinol
Monatsschrift fuer Ornithologie und Vivarienkunde. Ausgabe B. Aquarien und Terrarien [*Germany*] — Monatschr Ornithol Vivarienkd Ausg B
Monatsschrift fuer Ornithologie und Vivarienkunde. Ausgabe B. Aquarien und Terrarien — Monatsschr Ornithol Vivarienkd Ausg B Aquarien Terrarien
Monatsschrift fuer Pastoraltheologie [*Goettingen*] — MPTh
Monatsschrift fuer Pomologie und Praktischen Obstbau — Monatsschr Pomol Prakt Obstbau
Monatsschrift fuer Praktische Tierheilkunde — M Pr T
Monatsschrift fuer Praktische Tierheilkunde — MPrTh
Monatsschrift fuer Psychiatrie und Neurologie — M Ps N

Monatsschrift fuer Psychiatrie und Neurologie — Monatschr Psychiat u Neurol
Monatsschrift fuer Psychiatrie und Neurologie — Monatsschr Psychiatr Neurol
Monatsschrift fuer Textil-Industrie — Monatsschr Text Ind
Monatsschrift fuer Textil-Industrie. Beilage — Monatsschr Text Ind Beil
Monatsschrift fuer Theologie und Kirche — MTK
Monatsschrift fuer Unfallheilkunde — Monats Unfa
Monatsschrift fuer Unfallheilkunde — Monatsschr Unfallheilkd
Monatsschrift fuer Unfallheilkunde. Versicherungs-, Versorgungs-, und Verkehrsmedizin — Monatsschr Unfallheikd Versicher-Versorg Verkehrsmed
Monatsschrift fuer Unfallheilkunde. Versicherungs-, Versorgungs-, und Verkehrsmedizin — Monatsschr Unfallheilkd Versicher Versorg Verkehrsmed
Monatsschrift Wiener Tieraerztliche — Mschr Wien Tieraerztl
Monatsschriften der Comenius-Gesellschaft — Mschrr Comeniusges
Mond Nickel Bulletin — Mond Nickel Bull
Monda Lingvo-Problemo — Monda Ling-Prob
Monde — M
Monde — MND
Monde Alpin et Rhodanien — Monde Alpin Rhod
Monde Apicole — Monde Apic
Monde Colonial Illustre — Monde Colon Illus
Monde de la Bible — MoB
Monde de l'Education — M Ed
Monde de l'Education — Monde de l'Educ
Monde Dentaire — Monde Dent
Monde Dental — Monde Dent
Monde des Plantes — Monde Plant
Monde des Plantes. Revue Mensuelle de Botanique. Organe. Academie Internationale de Geographie Botanique — Monde Pl
Monde et les Mineraux — Monde Miner
Monde Francais — Monde Fr
Monde Francais — MonF
Monde Hebdomadaire — MH
Monde Juif — MJ
Monde Medical (Paris) — Monde Med (Paris)
Monde Moderne — Monde Mod
Monde Musulman Contemporain. Initiations — MMCI
Monde Non-Chretien — MNC
Monde Nouveau-Paru — MNP
Monde Oriental — M Or
Monde Oriental — MO
Monde Slave — M Sl
Monde Slave — MS
Monde Textile (Ghent) — Monde Text (Ghent)
Mondes Asiatiques — Mondes Asiat
Mondes en Developpement [*Paris*] — Mondes Dev
Mondes en Developpement — Mondes en Develop
Mondes et Cultures — Mondes et Cult
Mondes et Development — Mondes et Dev
Mondo Agricolo — Mondo Agric
Mondo Classico — M Cl
Mondo Classico — MC
Mondo Classico — Mondo Class
Mondo Economico — Mondo Econ
Mondo Finanziario — Mondo Fin
Mondo Odontostomatologico — Mondo Odontostomatol
Mondo Ortodontico — Mondo Ortod
Mondo Sotterraneo. Circolo Speleologico e Idrologico Friulano. Pubblicazione. Nuova Serie — Mondo Sotterraneo Pubbl Nuova Ser
Mondo Tessile — Mondo Tess
Moneda y Credito — Moneda y Cred
Moneta e Credito — Moneta e Cred
Moneta Imperii Byzantini — MIB
Monetaria. Centro de Estudios Monetarios Latinoamericanos [*Mexico*] — CEMLA/M
Monetary Times — Mon Times
Money — Mo
Money — MON
[*The*] **Money Advocate** — TMA
Money Manager Profile Diskettes — MMPD
Money Market Rates [*Database*] — MRATE
Mongolia Society. Bulletin — BMS
Mongolia Society. Bulletin — MSB
Mongolian Studies — Mong Stud
Mongolian Studies. Journal of the Mongolia Society — MSB
[*The*] **Monist** — Mon
Moniteur Africain — Monit Afr
Moniteur Belge — Mon B
Moniteur Belge — Monit
Moniteur Belge — Monit Belge
Moniteur Bibliographique. Bulletin Officiel des Imprimes Publies en Pologne [*A publication*] — MBOP
Moniteur Congolais — Mon
Moniteur de la Ceramique et de la Verrerie et Journal du Ceramiste et de Chaufournier Reunis — Monit Ceram Verrerie J Ceram Chaufournier Reunis
Moniteur de la Maille — Monit Maille
Moniteur de la Papeterie Belge — Monit Papet Belge
Moniteur de la Papeterie Francaise — Monit Papet Fr
Moniteur de la Peinture — Monit Peint
Moniteur de la Photographie — Monit Photogr
Moniteur de la Teinture des Apprets et de l'Impression des Tissus — Monit Tein Apprets Impress Tissus
Moniteur des Hopitaux — Monit Hop
Moniteur des Produits Chimiques — Monit Prod Chim
Moniteur des Travaux Publics et du Batiment [*France*] — Monit Trav Publics Batim
Moniteur d'Hygiene et de Salubrite Publique — Monit Hyg Salubr Publique
Moniteur du Commerce International — MOI
Moniteur du Commerce International — Moniteur Commer Internat
Moniteur du Notariat et de l'Enregistrement. Journal de Legislation et de Jurisprudence — Mon Not
Moniteur du Petrole Roumain — Monit Pet Roum
Moniteur Professionnel de l'Electricite et Electronique [*France*] — Monit Prof Electr Electron
Moniteur Professionnel de l'Electricite et Electronique — MPEEA
Moniteur Scientifique du Docteur Quesneville — Monit Sci Doct Quesneville
Monitor de la Educacion Comun — MEC
Monitor de la Farmacia y de la Terapeutica — Monit Farm Ter
Monitor Ecclesiasticus — ME
Monitor Polski — Monit Pol
Monitor. Proceedings. Institution of Radio and Electronics Engineers (Australia) — Monitor Proc Inst Radio Electron Eng (Aust)
Monitore e Rapporti Coloniali — Mon E Rap Col
Monitore Ostetrico-Ginecologico — Monit Ostet-Ginecol
Monitore Ostetrico-Ginecologico di Endocrinologia e del Metabolismo — Monit Ostet-Ginecol Endocrinol Metab
Monitore Tecnico — Monit Tec
Monitore Zoologico Italiano [*Italian Journal of Zoology*] — Monit Zool Ital
Monitore Zoologico Italiano/Italian Journal of Zoology. New Series — Monit Zool Ital/Ital J Zool New Ser
Monitore Zoologico Italiano/Italian Journal of Zoology. New Series. Supplement — Monit Zool Ital/Ital J Zool New Ser Suppl
Monitore Zoologico Italiano [*Italian Journal of Zoology*]. Monografia — Monit Zool Ital Monogr
Monitore Zoologico Italiano [*Italian Journal of Zoology*]. Monografia — Monitore Zool Ital Monogr
Monitore Zoologico Italiano [*Italian Journal of Zoology*]. Supplemento — Monit Zool Ital Suppl
Monitore Zoologico Italiano [*Italian Journal of Zoology*]. Supplemento — MZISA
Monitoring and Assessment Research Centre. Report — Monit Assess Res Cent Rep
Monitorul Petrolului Roman — Monit Pet Roman
Mon-Khmer Studies — MKS
Monmouth County Medical Society. Newsletter — Monmouth County Med Soc Newsletter
Monmouth Historian — Monmouth Hist
Monmouth Review — Monmouth Rev
Monmouthshire Antiquary — Monmouth Ant
Monmouthshire Antiquary — Monmouthshire Antiq
Monmouthshire Antiquary. Proceedings. Monmouthshire and Caerleon Antiquarian Society — Monmouthshire Ant
Monnaies Grecques — Monn Gr
Monografia das Festas do S. Joao em Portugal — MFSJP
Monografia. Divisao de Geologia e Mineralogia (Brazil) — Monogr Div Geol Mineral (Braz)
Monografia. Politechnika Krakowska Imeni Tadeusza Kosciuszki — Monogr Politech Krakow Im Tadeusza Kosciuszki
Monografia. Programa Regional de Desarrollo Cientifico y Tecnologico. Serie de Biologia — Monogr Programa Reg Desarrollo Cient Tecnol Ser Biol
Monografia. Programa Regional de Desarrollo Cientifico y Tecnologico. Serie de Fisica — Monogr Programa Reg Desarrollo Cient Tecnol Ser Fis
Monografia. Programa Regional de Desarrollo Cientifico y Tecnologico. Serie de Quimica — Monogr Programa Reg Desarrollo Cient Tecnol Ser Quim
Monografias. Comision de Investigaciones Cientificas de la Provincia de Buenos Aires — Monogr Com Invest Cient Prov Buenos Aires
Monografias da Sociedade Paranaense de Matematica — Monograf Soc Paran Mat
Monografias da Sociedade Paranaense de Matematica — Monograf Soc Paranaense Mat
Monografias de la Academia de Ciencias Exactas, Fisicas, Quimicas, y Naturales de Zaragoza — Monogr Acad Ci Exact Fis Quim Nat Zaragoza
Monografias de Matematica [*Rio De Janeiro*] — Monograf Math
Monografias de Matematicas Pura e Aplicada [*Campinas*] — Monograf Mat Pura Apl
Monografias del Instituto de Estudios Geograficos — Monogr Inst Estud Geogr
Monografias. INIA [*Instituto Nacional de Investigaciones Agrarias*] — Monogr INIA
Monografias. Instituto Butantan (Sao Paulo) — Monogr Inst Butantan (Sao Paulo)
Monografias. Instituto de Matematicas [*Mexico City*] — Monograf Inst Mat
Monografias. Instituto Eduardo Torroja de la Construccion y del Cemento — Mongrafias Inst Eduardo Torroja Constr Cem
Monografias. Instituto Eduardo Torroja de la Construccion y del Cemento — Monogr Inst Eduardo Torroja Constr Cem
Monografias. Instituto Oswaldo Cruz (Rio De Janeiro) — Monogr Inst Oswaldo Cruz (Rio De J)
Monografie Archivii Orientalniho — MAO
Monografie Biochemiczne — Monogr Biochem
Monografie de il Lavoro Neuropsichiatrico — Monogr Lav Neuropsichiatr
Monografie di Archeologia Libica — MAL
Monografie di Genetica Agraria — MGAGES
Monografie di Genetica Agraria — Monogr Genet Agrar
Monografie di Storia Bresciana — MS Bres
Monografie Fauny Polski — Monogr Fauny Pol
Monografie Matematyczne — Monogr Mat
Monografie Matematyczne — Monograf Mat
Monografie Orientalniho Ustavu — MOU
Monografie Parazytologiczne — Monogr Parazytol
Monografie Psychologiczne — Monograf Psych
Monografie. Ustav pro Vyzkum a Vyuziti Paliv — Monogr UVP
Monografie. Ustav pro Vyzkum a Vyuziti Paliv (Bechovice, Czechoslovakia) — Monogr Ustav Vyzk Vyuziti Paliv (Bechovice Czech)
Monografieen over Vlaamse Letterkunde — MVL

Monografieen van de Nederlandse Entomologische Vereniging — Monogr Ned Entomol Ver
Monografies de la Seccio de Ciencies — Monograf Sec Cien
Monografii Srpska Akademija Nauka — Monogr Srpska Akad Nauka
Monografii Volzskoj Biologiceskoj Stancii/Monographien der Biologischen Wolga-Station — Monogr Volzsk Biol Stancii
Monograph. American Fisheries Society — Monogr Am Fish Soc
Monograph. American Oil Chemists' Society — Monogr Am Oil Chem Soc
Monograph. American Phytopathological Society — Monogr Amer Phytopathol Soc
Monograph and Report Series. Institute of Metals (London) — Monogr Rep Ser Inst Met (London)
Monograph. Asiatic Society of Bombay — MAS Bo
Monograph. British Crop Protection Council — Monogr Br Crop Prot Counc
Monograph. British Crop Protection Council — Monograph Br Crop Prot Counc
Monograph. British Plant Growth Regulator Group — Monogr Br Plant Growth Regul Group
Monograph. California Policy Seminar — Monogr Calif Policy Semin
Monograph. Directorate of Geology and Mining. Uttar Pradesh — Monogr Dir Geol Min Uttar Pradesh
Monograph. European Brewery Convention — Monogr Eur Brew Conv
Monograph. Geological Survey of Alabama — Monogr Geol Surv Alabama
Monograph. Hunter Valley Research Foundation — Monogr Hunter Valley Res Fdn
Monograph. Hunter Valley Research Foundation — Monogr Hunter Valley Res Found
Monograph. Institute for Research in Psychology and Relgion — MIRPR
Monograph. Kansas Agricultural Experiment Station — Monogr Kans Agric Exp Stn
Monograph. Koebenhavns Universitet. H. C. Oersted Institutet. Fysisk Laboratorium — Monogr Koebenhavns Univ H C Oersted Inst Fys Lab
Monograph. Melbourne and Metropolitan Board of Works — Melb Metro Board Works Monograph
Monograph. Mineralogical Society — Monogr Mineral Soc
Monograph MS. Cement Research Institute of India — Monogr MS Cem Res Inst India
Monograph. National Bureau of Standards (United States) — Monogr Natl Bur Stand (US)
Monograph. Royal Society of New South Wales — Monogr R Soc NSW
Monograph Series. American Association of Cereal Chemists — Monogr Ser Am Assoc Cereal Chem
Monograph Series. Australasian Institute of Mining and Metallurgy — Monogr Ser Australas Inst Min Metall
Monograph Series. Calvin Theological Seminary — MSCTS
Monograph Series. European Organization for Research on Treatment of Cancer — Monogr Ser Eur Organ Res Treat Cancer
Monograph Series in World Affairs. University of Denver — Mg S Wld
Monograph Series. Institute of Botany. Academia Sinica — Monogr Ser Inst Bot Acad Sin
Monograph Series. International Brain Research Organization — Monogr Ser Int Brain Res Organ
Monograph Series. International Council for Computer Communications [*Elsevier Book Series*] — MICCC
Monograph Series on Languages and Linguistics. Georgetown University — MSLL
Monograph Series on Mineral Deposits — Monogr Ser Miner Deposits
Monograph Series on Soviet Union — Monograph Ser Soviet Union
Monograph Series. Research Institute of Applied Electricity. Hokkaido University — Monogr Ser Res Inst Appl Electr Hokkaido Univ
Monograph Series. Society for New Testament Studies — MSSNTS
Monograph Series. Society for Old Testament Studies — MSSOTS
Monograph Series. Textile Institute (Manchester, UK) — Monogr Ser Text Inst (Manchester UK)
Monograph Series. Utah State University — Monograph Ser Utah St Univ
Monograph Series. Weed Science Society of America — Monogr Ser Weed Sci Soc Am
Monograph. Society for Analytical Chemistry — Monogr Soc Anal Chem
Monograph. Society of Chemical Industry (London) — Monogr Soc Chem Ind (London)
Monograph. Steel Castings Research and Trade Association — Monogr Steel Cast Res Trade Assoc
Monograph. T. Kosciuszko Technical University of Cracow — Monogr T Kosciuszko Tech Univ Cracow
Monographiae Biologicae — Monogr Biol
Monographiae Biologicae — Monographiae Biol
Monographiae Botanicae — Monogr Bot
Monographic Series. Natural Sciences Bulletin. College of Science. Sun Yatsen University/Kuo Li Chung Shan Ta Hsueeh Tzu Jan K'o Hsueeh K'o — Monogr Ser Nat Sci Bull Coll Sci Sun Yatsen Univ
Monographie Annuelle. Societe Francaise de Biologie Clinique — Monogr Annu Soc Fr Biol Clin
Monographie. BIPM [*Bureau International des Poids et Mesures*] — Monogr BIPM
Monographie de Physiologie Causale — Monogr Physiol Causale
Monographien. Gesamtgebiete der Neurologie und Psychiatrie — Monogr Gesamtgeb Neurol Psychiatr
Monographien. Gesamtgebiete der Psychiatrie — Monogr Gesamtgeb Psychiatr
Monographien. Gesamtgebiete der Psychiatrie. Psychiatry Series (Berlin) — Monogr Gesamtgeb Psychiatr (Berlin)
Monographien zur Angewandten Entomologie — Monogr Angew Entomol
Monographien zur Deutschen Kulturgeschichte — MDKG
Monographien zur Modernen Mathematik — Monograph Modernen Math
Monographien zur Philosophischen Forschung — MPF
Monographien zur Wissenschaftstheorie und Grundlagenforschung — Monograph Wissenschaftstheorie Grundlagenforsch
Monographies. Centre d'Actualisation Scientifique et Technique de l'INSA [*Institut National des Sciences Appliquees*] — Monogr Cent Actual Sci Tech INSA
Monographies de l'Enseignement Mathematique [*Geneva*] — Monograph Enseign Math
Monographies de Linguistique Mathematique — Monograph Linguist Math
Monographies de Mathematique — Monograph Math
Monographies de Physiologie Vegetale — Monogr Physiol Veg
Monographies de Radiologie — Monogr Radiol
Monographies des Annales de Radiologie — Monogr Ann Radiol
Monographies en Archeologie et Histoire Classique — MAHC
Monographies Francaises de Psychologie — MFPSA
Monographies Gregoriennes — M Gr
Monographies. Groupe d'Etude de la Main — Monogr Groupe Etude Main
Monographies Medicales et Scientifiques — Monogr Med Sci
Monographies Reine Elisabeth [*Brussels*] — MRE
Monographies Scientifiques de la Maison Franco-Japonaise — Monograph Sci Maison Franco-Japon
Monographies Techniques sur l'Utilisation des Aciers Speciaux — Monogr Tech Util Aciers Spec
Monographs. Academy of Natural Sciences of Philadelphia — Monogr Acad Nat Sci Phila
Monographs, Advanced Texts, and Surveys in Pure and Applied Mathematics — Monographs Adv Texts Surveys Pure Appl Math
Monographs. American Association on Mental Deficiency — Monogr Am Assoc Ment Defic
Monographs. American Association on Mental Retardation — Monogr Am Assoc Ment Retard
Monographs. American College of Nutrition — Monogr Am Coll Nutr
Monographs. American Ethnological Society — MAES
Monographs. American Jewish Archives — MAJA
Monographs. American Society of Agronomy — Monogr Am Soc Agron
Monographs and Memoranda. National Research Institute for Machine Design (Bechovice, Czechoslovakia) — Monogr Memo Natl Res Inst Mach Des (Bechovice Czech)
Monographs and Studies in Mathematics — Monographs Stud Math
Monographs and Surveys in Water Resource Engineering — Monographs Surveys Water Res Engrg
Monographs and Textbooks in Material Science — Monogr Textb Mater Sci
Monographs and Textbooks in Physical Science — Monographs Textbooks Phys Sci
Monographs and Textbooks in Physical Science. Lecture Notes — Monogr Textbooks Phys Sci Lecture Notes
Monographs and Textbooks in Physical Science. Lecture Notes — Monographs Textbooks Phys Sci Lecture Notes
Monographs and Textbooks in Pure and Applied Mathematics — Monogr Textbooks Pure Appl Math
Monographs and Textbooks in Pure and Applied Mathematics — Monographs Textbooks Pure Appl Math
Monographs and Textbooks on Mechanics of Solids and Fluids. Mechanics Analysis — Monogr Textb Mech Solids Fluids Mech Anal
Monographs and Textbooks on Mechanics of Solids and Fluids. Mechanics Analysis — Monographs Textbooks Mech Solids Fluids Mech Anal
Monographs and Textbooks on Mechanics of Solids and Fluids. Mechanics of Continua — Monographs Textbooks Mech Solids Fluids Mech Continua
Monographs and Textbooks on Mechanics of Solids and Fluids. Mechanics of Dynamical Systems — Monographs Textbooks Mech Solids Fluids Mech Dynam Systems
Monographs and Textbooks on Mechanics of Solids and Fluids. Mechanics of Elastic Stability — Monogr Textb Mech Solids Fluids Mech Elast Stab
Monographs and Textbooks on Mechanics of Solids and Fluids. Mechanics of Fluids and Transport Processes — Monographs Textbooks Mech Solids Fluids Mech Fluids Transport
Monographs and Textbooks on Mechanics of Solids and Fluids. Mechanics of Genesis and Method — Monographs Textbooks Mech Solids Fluids Mech Genesis Method
Monographs and Textbooks on Mechanics of Solids and Fluids. Mechanics of Plastic Solids — Monographs Textbooks Mech Solids Fluids Mech Plastic Solids
Monographs and Textbooks on Mechanics of Solids and Fluids. Mechanics of Surface Structures — Monogr Textb Mech Solids Fluids Mech Surf Struct
Monographs and Texts in Physics and Astronomy — Monogr Texts Phys Astron
Monographs. Andrews University — MAU
Monographs. Archiv Orientalni — MArOr
Monographs by the Bibliographic Society — Monographs by the Bibliogr Soc
Monographs. Carolina Population Center — Mg C Pop Cr
Monographs. Evangelical Theological Society — METS
Monographs for Teachers — Monogr Teach
Monographs. Giovanni Lorenzini Foundation — Monogr Giovanni Lorenzini Found
Monographs in Allergy — Monogr Allergy
Monographs in Anaesthesiology [*Elsevier Book Series*] — MA
Monographs in Anaesthesiology — Monogr Anaesthesiol
Monographs in Analysis — Monogr Anal
Monographs in Applied Toxicology — Monogr Appl Toxicol
Monographs in Church History — MCH
Monographs in Clinical Cytology — Monogr Clin Cytol
Monographs in Computer Science — Monogr Comput Sci
Monographs in Contemporary Mathematics — Monogr Contemp Math
Monographs in Developmental Biology — Monogr Dev Biol
Monographs in Developmental Pediatrics — Monogr Dev Pediatr
Monographs in Epidemiology and Biostatistics — MEBIEP
Monographs in Epidemiology and Biostatistics — Monogr Epidemiol Biostat
Monographs in Fetal Physiology [*Elsevier Book Series*] — MFP
Monographs in Fetal Physiology — Monogr Fetal Physiol

Monographs in Geometry and Topology — Monogr Geom Topology
Monographs in Harmonic Analysis — Monogr Harmon Anal
Monographs in History and Culture — Monogr Hist Cult
Monographs in Human Genetics — Monogr Hum Genet
Monographs in Materials and Society — Monogr Mater Soc
Monographs in Modern Chemistry — Monogr Mod Chem
Monographs in Neural Sciences — Monogr Neural Sci
Monographs in Ophthalmology — Monogr Ophthalmol
Monographs in Ophthalmology — MPTHDI
Monographs in Oral Science — Monogr Oral Sci
Monographs in Paediatrics — Mon Paediat
Monographs in Paediatrics — Monogr Paediatr
Monographs in Pathology — IAPMA
Monographs in Pathology — Monogr Pathol
Monographs in Pharmacology and Physiology — Monogr Pharmacol Physiol
Monographs in Population Biology — Monogr Popul Biol
Monographs in Population Biology — Monographs Population Biol
Monographs in Population Biology — MPOBA
Monographs in Primatology — Monogr Primatol
Monographs in Psychobiology and Disease [*Elsevier Book Series*] — MPD
Monographs in Semiconductor Physics — Monogr Semicond Phys
Monographs in the Economics of Development — Monogr Econ Dev
Monographs in the Surgical Sciences — Monogr Surg Sc
Monographs in the Surgical Sciences [*United States*] — Monogr Surg Sci
Monographs in Virology — Monogr Virol
Monographs in Visual Communication — Monogr Vis Commun
Monographs. National Cancer Institute — Monogr Natl Cancer Inst
Monographs of Marine Mollusca — MMMOEI
Monographs of Marine Mollusca — Monogr Mar Mollusca
Monographs of Psychiatria Fennica — Monogr Psychiatr Fenn
Monographs on Archaeology and Fine Arts — MAFA
Monographs on Atherosclerosis — Monogr Atheroscler
Monographs on Clinical Neurology and Neurosurgery — Monogr Clin Neurol Neurosurg
Monographs on Drugs — Monogr Drugs
Monographs on Endocrinology — Monogr Endocrinol
Monographs on Mediterranean Antiquity — MMA
Monographs on Neoplastic Disease at Various Sites [*Scotland*] — Monogr Neoplast Dis Various Sites
Monographs on Nuclear Medicine and Biology — Monogr Nucl Med Biol
Monographs on Nuclear Medicine and Biology Series — Monogr Nucl Med Biol Ser
Monographs on Numerical Analysis — Monogr Numer Anal
Monographs on Oceanographic Methodology — Monogr Oceanogr Methodol
Monographs on Plastics — Monogr Plast
Monographs on Social Anthropology — Mg Soc Anth
Monographs on Social Anthropology — MSA
Monographs on Statistics and Applied Probability — Monographs Statist Appl Probab
Monographs on Tea Production in Ceylon — Monogr Tea Prod Ceylon
Monographs on the Ancient Near East — MANE
Monographs on the Physics and Chemistry of Materials — Monographs Phys Chem Mater
Monographs on Theoretical and Applied Genetics — Monogr Theor Appl Genet
Monographs. Percy Fitzpatrick Institute of African Ornithology — Monogr Percy Fitzpatrick Inst Afr Ornithol
Monographs. Physiological Society — Monogr Physiol Soc
Monographs. Physiological Society of Philadelphia — Monogr Physiol Soc Phila
Monographs. Physiological Society of Philadelphia — Monogr Physiol Soc Philadelphia
Monographs. Psychiatric Clinic. Helsinki University Central Hospital — Monogr Psychiatr Clin Helsinki Univ Cent Hosp
Monographs. Quekett Microscopical Club — Monogr Quekett Microsc Club
Monographs. Rutgers Center of Alcohol Studies — Monogr Rutgers Cent Alcohol Stud
Monographs Series. Royal Asiatic Society of Bengal — MSASB
Monographs. Society for Research in Child Development — Mon S Res C
Monographs. Society for Research in Child Development — Monogr Soc Res Child Dev
Monographs. Society for Research in Child Development — MSCDA
Monographs. Studies in Entomology — Monogr Stud Entomol
Monographs. Western Foundation of Vertebrate Zoology — Monogr West Found Vertebr Zool
Monokristally i Tekhnika — Monokrist Tekh
Monokristally. Stsintillyatory i Organicheskie Lyuminofory — Monokrist Stsintill Org Lyuminofory
Monoufeia Journal of Agricultural Research — Monoufeia J Agric Res
Monsanto Research Corporation. Mound Facility. Report MLM — Monsanto Res Corp Mound Facil Rep MLM
Monsanto Research Corporation. Mound Laboratory. Report MLM — Monsanto Res Corp Mound Lab Rep MLM
Monsanto Research Corporation. Mound Laboratory. Research and Development Report — Monsanto Res Corp Mound Lab Res Dev Rep
Monsanto Review — Monsanto R
Monsanto Technical Review — Monsanto Tech Rev
Montajes e Instalaciones — Mont Instal
Montalban (Venezuela) — MNV
Montana Academy of Sciences. Proceedings — Mont Acad Sci Proc
Montana Academy of Sciences. Proceedings — Montana Acad Sci Proc
Montana Agresearch. Montana Agricultural Experiment Station. Montana University — Mont Agresearch Mont Agric Exp Stn Mont Univ
Montana. Agricultural Experiment Station. Bulletin — BMAEA7
Montana. Agricultural Experiment Station. Bulletin — Mont Agric Exp Stn Bull
Montana. Agricultural Experiment Station. Circular — Mont Agric Exp Stn Circ
Montana. Agricultural Experiment Station. Publications — Mont Ag Exp
Montana. Association of Language Teachers. Bulletin — MALT Bulletin
Montana. Bureau of Mines and Geology. Bulletin — MBGBA
Montana. Bureau of Mines and Geology. Bulletin — Mont Bur Mines Geol Bull
Montana. Bureau of Mines and Geology. Bulletin — Montana Bur Mines and Geology Bull
Montana. Bureau of Mines and Geology. Memoir — Mont Bur Mines Geol Mem
Montana. Bureau of Mines and Geology. Miscellaneous Contributions — Mont Bur Mines Geol Misc Contrib
Montana. Bureau of Mines and Geology. Special Publication — MBGSA
Montana. Bureau of Mines and Geology. Special Publication — Mont Bur Mines Geol Spec Publ
Montana. Bureau of Mines and Geology. Special Publication — Montana Bur Mines and Geology Spec Pub
Montana Business Quarterly — MBQ
Montana Business Quarterly — Mont Bus Q
Montana Code Annotated — Mont Code Ann
Montana College of Agriculture and Mechanic Arts. Agricultural Experiment Station. Circular — Montana Agric Exp Sta Circ
Montana Education — Mont Ed
Montana. Fish and Game Department. Technical Bulletin — Mont Fish Game Dep Tech Bull
Montana. Forest and Conservation Experiment Station. Bulletin — MFCBAC
Montana. Forest and Conservation Experiment Station. Bulletin — Mont For Conserv Exp Stn Bull
Montana. Forest and Conservation Experiment Station. Lubrecht Series — Mont For Conserv Exp Stn Lubrecht Ser
Montana. Forest and Conservation Experiment Station. Note — MFCNAE
Montana. Forest and Conservation Experiment Station. Note — Mont For Conserv Exp Stn Note
Montana. Forest and Conservation Experiment Station. Research Note — MFENAO
Montana. Forest and Conservation Experiment Station. Research Note — Mont For Conserv Exp Stn Res Note
Montana. Forest and Conservation Experiment Station. Special Publication — MFCSAT
Montana. Forest and Conservation Experiment Station. Special Publication — Mont For Conserv Exp Stn Spec Publ
Montana. Forest and Conservation Experiment Station. Study Report — Mont For Conserv Exp Stn Study Rep
Montana. Forest and Conservation Experiment Station. Study Report — SRMSDS
Montana Forest Industry News — Mont Forest Ind News
Montana Geological Society. Annual Field Conference. Guidebook — MGAGB
Montana Geological Society. Annual Field Conference. Guidebook — Mont Geol Soc Annu Field Conf Guideb
Montana Gothic — Mont G
Montana Historical Society. Contributions — Mont His S
Montana Law Review — Mon L Rev
Montana Law Review — Mont L Rev
Montana Law Review — Mont Law Re
Montana Law Review — Mont LR
Montana Law Review — Montana L Rev
Montana Law Review — MR
Montana Libraries — Montana Lib
Montana Library Quarterly — Montana Lib Q
Montana Reports — Mont
Montana Rural Electric News — Mont Rural Electr News
Montana State College. Agricultural Experiment Station. Bulletin — Mont State Coll Agric Exp Stn Bull
Montana State College. Agricultural Experiment Station. Miscellaneous Publication — Montana Agric Exp Sta Misc Publ
Montana State College. Agricultural Experiment Station. Special Report — Montana Agric Exp Sta Special Rep
Montana State College. Engineering Experiment Station. Bulletin — Mont State Coll Eng Exp Stn Bull
Montana State University. Cooperative Extension Service. Bulletin — Bull Coop Ext Serv Montana State Univ
Montana: The Magazine of Western History — MMH
Montana: The Magazine of Western History — Mont
Montana: The Magazine of Western History — Mont Mag Hist
Montana University. Bulletin — Mont Univ B
Montana University Joint Water Resources Research Center. MWRRC Report — Mont Univ Jt Water Resour Res Cent MWRRC Rep
Montana Water Resources Research Center. MWRRC Report — Mont Water Resour Res Cent MWRRC Rep
Montana Wool Grower — Mont Wool Grow
Montana Wool Grower — MWOGA2
Montanaro d'Italia - Monti e Boschi — MIMBD
Montanaro d'Italia - Monti e Boschi [*Italy*] — Montanaro Ital-Monti Boschi
Montanistische Rundschau. Supplement — Montan Rundsch Suppl
Montan-Rundschau [*Austria*] — Montan-Rundsch
Montan-Zeitung [*Austria*] — Montan-Ztg
Montazhnye i Spetsial'nye Raboty v Stroitel'stve — Montazhn Spet Rab Stroit
Montazhnye Raboty v Stroitel'stve — Montazhn Rab Stroit
Monte Carlo Methods and Applications — Monte Carlo Methods Appl
Monte Carmelo — M Carm
Monte Carmelo — MC
Monte Carmelo — MCar
Montecatini Edison. S.p.A. Istituto de Ricerche Agrarie. Contributi — Montecatini Edison SpA Ist Ric Agrar Contrib
Montech Conferences — Montech Conf
Montefiore Memorial Lecture — Mont ML
Montemora — Montr
Montfort. Vierteljahresschrift fuer Geschichte und Gegenwartskunde Vorarlbergs — Montfort

Montgomery County Law Reporter — Mont Co L Rep
Montgomery County Law Reporter — Mont Co LR
Montgomery County Law Reporter — Montg
Montgomery County Law Reporter — Montg Co
Montgomery County Law Reporter — Mont'g Co L Rep
Montgomery County Law Reporter — Montg Co L Rep'r
Montgomery County Law Reporter — Montg Co Law Rep'r
Montgomery County Law Reporter — Montg Co LR
Montgomery County Law Reporter — Mont'g L Rep
Montgomery County Law Reporter (Pennsylvania) — Montg Co LR (PA)
Montgomery County Law Reporter (Pennsylvania) — Montg (PA)
Montgomeryshire Collections — Montgomeryshire Collect
Montguide MT. Agriculture. Montana State University. Cooperative Extension Service — Montguide MT Agric Mont State Univ Coop Ext Serv
Montguide MT. Human Resource Development. Montana State University. Cooperative Extension Service — Montguide MT Hum Resour Dev Mont State Univ Coop Ext Serv
Month (London) — ML
Monthly Abstract Bulletin — Abstr Bull
Monthly Abstract of Statistics (New Zealand) — Stat Ab (NZ)
Monthly American Journal of Geology and Natural Science — Monthly Am J G
Monthly Analytical Bulletin. Inter-African Bureau for Soils — Mon Analyt Bull Inter-Afr Bur Soils
Monthly Archives. Medical Sciences — Monthly Arch Med Sci
Monthly Australian Demographic Review — Mo Aust Dem R
Monthly Bibliography of Medical Reviews — BMR
Monthly Bulletin. American Bakers Association — Mon Bull Am Bakers Assoc
Monthly Bulletin. Asiatic Society (Calcutta) — MBAS (Calcutta)
Monthly Bulletin. Canadian Institute of Mining and Metallurgy — Mon Bull Can Inst Min Metall
Monthly Bulletin. Canadian Mining Institute — Mon Bull Can Min Inst
Monthly Bulletin. Central Bank of Jordan — BCBJ
Monthly Bulletin. Coffee Board of Kenya — Mon Bull Coffee Board Kenya
Monthly Bulletin. Department of Agriculture (California) — Mon Bull Dep Agric (Calif)
Monthly Bulletin. Di Cyan and Brown — Mon Bull Di Cyan Brown
Monthly Bulletin. Emergency Public Health Laboratory Service [*Great Britain*] — Mon Bull Emerg Public Health Lab Serv
Monthly Bulletin for the Ceramic Industry — Mon Bull Ceram Ind
Monthly Bulletin. International Association of Refrigeration — Mon Bull Int Assoc Refrig
Monthly Bulletin. International Railway Congress Association — MBRWA
Monthly Bulletin. International Railway Congress Association — Mon Bull Int Railw Congr Assoc
Monthly Bulletin. International Railway Congress Association. Cybernetics and Electronics of the Railways — Mon Bull Int Ry Congr Ass Cybern Electron Ry
Monthly Bulletin. International Railway Congress Association (English Edition) — Mon Bull Int Railw Congr Assoc (Engl Ed)
Monthly Bulletin. Ministry of Health and the Emergency Public Health Laboratory Service — Mon Bull Minist Health Emerg Public Health Lab Serv
Monthly Bulletin. Ministry of Health and the Public Health Laboratory — Mon Bull Minist Health Public Health Lab
Monthly Bulletin. Ministry of Health and the Public Health Laboratory Service [*England*] — Mon Bull Minist Health Public Health Lab Serv
Monthly Bulletin. Ministry of Mines and Hydrocarbons (Caracas) — Mon Bull Minst Mines Hydrocarbons (Caracas)
Monthly Bulletin of Agricultural Intelligence and Plant Disease — Mon Bull Agric Intell Plant Dis
Monthly Bulletin of Agricultural Science and Practice — Mon Bull Agric Sci Pract
Monthly Bulletin of Construction Indices (Building and Civil Engineering) — Mthly Bull Constr Indices (Bldg Civil Engng)
Monthly Bulletin of Information on Refrigeration — Mon Bull Inf Refrig
Monthly Bulletin of Statistics — BSO
Monthly Bulletin of Statistics [*Israel*] — MBS
Monthly Bulletin of Statistics. United Nations — UN Mo Bul
Monthly Business Review — Month Bus Rev
Monthly Catalog of United States Government Publications — Mon Cat US Gov Publ
Monthly Catalog of United States Government Publications — Mon Cat US Gov Publications
Monthly Catalog of United States Government Publications — Monthly Cat US Govt Pub
Monthly Catalog of United States Government Publications — Monthly Catalog US Govt Publ
Monthly Checklist of State Publications [*United States*] — Mon Checkl State Publ
Monthly Circular. Baltic and International Maritime Conference — BIMC
Monthly Climatic Data for the World — MCDW
Monthly Coal Bulletin — Monthly Coal Bull
Monthly Criterion — MC
Monthly Critical Gazette — Monthly Crit Gaz
Monthly Crop Report — Monthly Crop Rep
Monthly Digest of Transport News — Mthly Dig Transp News
Monthly Economic Letter [*United States*] — Mon Econ Lett
Monthly Economic Survey. Taiwan — Taiw Svy
Monthly Energy Review — M Engy Rev
Monthly Energy Review [*Database*] — MER
Monthly Energy Review — MERDD
Monthly Energy Review — MET
Monthly Energy Review — Mon Energy Rev
Monthly Film Bulletin — M F B
Monthly Film Bulletin [*London*] — Monthly F Bull
Monthly Health Bulletin — Mon Health Bull
Monthly Illustrator — Mo Illust
Monthly Index of Medical Specialities — MIMS
Monthly Journal. Institute of Industrial Science. University of Tokyo — Mon J Inst Ind Sci Univ Tokyo
Monthly Journal of Medical Science — Mo J Med Sci
Monthly Journal of Psychiatry and Neurology — Mon J Psychiatry Neurol
Monthly Labor Review — M Lab R
Monthly Labor Review — M Labor R
Monthly Labor Review — MLR
Monthly Labor Review — Mo Lab Rev
Monthly Labor Review — Mo Labor R
Monthly Labor Review — Mo Labor Rev
Monthly Labor Review — Mo l br R
Monthly Labor Review — Mon Lab Re
Monthly Labor Review — Mon Labor Rev
Monthly Labor Review — Month Lab Rev
Monthly Labor Review — Monthly Labor R
Monthly Labor Review — Monthly Labor Rev
Monthly Labor Review — Mthly Lab R
Monthly Labor Review — MYL
Monthly Law Reporter — Mo Law Rep
Monthly Letter EMG — ML
Monthly List of Publications — MLP
Monthly List of Publications of South Australian Interest Received in the State Library of South Australia — MLPSA
Monthly Magazine — Monthly Mag
Monthly Magazine. Muslim World League — MMWL
Monthly Memorandum. Paint Research Station (Taddington) — Mon Memor Paint Res Stn (Taddington)
Monthly Microscopical Journal — Mo Micro J
Monthly Musical Record — MMR
Monthly Musical Record — Mo Mus Rec
Monthly Musical Record — Monthly Mus Rec
Monthly Notes. Astronomical Society of Southern Africa — Mon Not Astron Soc S Afr
Monthly Notes. Astronomical Society of Southern Africa — Mon Notes Astron Soc South Afr
Monthly Notes. Australian School of Pacific Administration — Mo Notes
Monthly Notices of Papers. Royal Society of Tasmania — Mon Not Pap R Soc Tasmania
Monthly Notices. Royal Astronomical Society — M Not R Ast
Monthly Notices. Royal Astronomical Society — MNRAA
Monthly Notices. Royal Astronomical Society [*England*] — Mon Not R Astron Soc
Monthly Notices. Royal Astronomical Society — Mon Not Roy Astron Soc
Monthly Notices. Royal Astronomical Society — Monthly Notices Roy Astronom Soc
Monthly Periodical Index — Mon Period Index
Monthly Petroleum Statement — Mon Pet Statement
Monthly Public Opinion Surveys — Mthly Publ Opin Surv
Monthly Record of Dental Science. Practice and Miscellany — Mon Rec Dent Sci Pract Misc
Monthly Religious Magazine — Mo Rel M
Monthly Report. Canadian Mineral Industry — Mon Rep Can Miner Ind
Monthly Report. Civil Engineering Research Institute of Hokkaido. Development Bureau [*Japan*] — Mon Rep Civ Eng Res Inst Hokkaido Dev Bur
Monthly Report. Deutsche Bundesbank — Deutsche Bundesbank
Monthly Report. Japan Perfumery and Flavouring Association — Mon Rep Jpn Perfum Flavour Assoc
Monthly Retail Trade. Current Business Report — MRL
Monthly Review — IMRE
Monthly Review — Mo R
Monthly Review — Mo Rev
Monthly Review — Mo Review
Monthly Review — Mon Rev
Monthly Review — Monthly R
Monthly Review — Monthly Rev
Monthly Review — MR
Monthly Review — MRev
Monthly Review — MRW
Monthly Review — Mthly R
Monthly Review. American Electroplaters' Society — Mon Rev Am Electroplat Soc
Monthly Review (Bangkok) — Bangkok R
Monthly Review. Federal Reserve Bank of Kansas City — Mon Rev Fed Reserve Bank Kans City
Monthly Review. Korea Exchange Bank — Korea Exchange Bank Mo R
Monthly Review of Dental Surgery — Monthly Rev Dental Surg
Monthly Review of Psychiatry and Neurology — Mon Rev Psychiatry Neurol
Monthly Science News — MSN
Monthly Statistical Bulletin (Greece) — Greek Stat
Monthly Statistical Review [*England*] — Monthly Statist Rev
Monthly Stethoscope and Medical Reporter — Mo Stethoscope Med Rep
Monthly Summary of Australian Conditions — Mo Summary Aust Cond
Monthly Tax Features — Mo Tax Features
Monthly Technical Review — Mon Tech Rev
Monthly Trade and Shipping Review — Mo Trade & Shipping R
Monthly Transactions. American Institute of Electrical Engineers — Mon Trans Am Inst Electr Eng
Monthly Vital Statistics Report [*US*] — Mon Vital Stat Rep
Monthly Vital Statistics Report [*United States*] — Monthly Vital Stat Rep
Monthly Vital Statistics Report. Advance Report of Final Mortality Statistics. 1981 [*US*] — Vital S MS
Monthly Vital Statistics Report. Advance Report of Final Natality Statistics. 1981 [*US*] — Vital St N
Monthly Vital Statistics Report. Annual Summary of Births, Deaths, Marriages, and Divorces. 1983 [*US*] — Vital St A

Monthly Vital Statistics Report. Births, Marriages, Divorces, and Deaths [*US*] — Vital Stat
Monthly Vital Statistics Report. Health Interview Survey [*US*] — Vital S HI
Monthly Vital Statistics Report. Health Statistics [*US*] — Vital S HS
Monthly Vital Statistics Report. Hospital Discharge Survey Data [*US*] — Vital S HD
Monthly Weather Review — M Weath Rev
Monthly Weather Review — M Weather R
Monthly Weather Review — Mon Weath Rev
Monthly Weather Review — Mon Weather Rev
Monthly Weather Review — Monthly Weather Rev
Monthly Wholesale Trade — MWR
Montpellier Medical — MOMEA
Montpellier Medical — Montpel Med
Montpellier Medical [*France*] — Montpellier Med
Montreal General Hospital. News — MGH News
Montreal Medical Journal — Montreal Med J
Montreal Pharmaceutical Journal — Montreal Pharm J
Montreal Universite. Service de Biogeographie. Bulletin — Montreal Univ Service Biogeographie Bull
Montreal Working Papers in Linguistics — MWPL
Montroll Memorial Lecture Series in Mathematical Physics — Montroll Memorial Lecture Ser Math Phys
Monumenta Aegyptiaca [*Brussels*] — MonAeg
Monumenta Archaeologica [*Los Angeles*] — MA
Monumenta Archaeologica (Novi Sad) — Mon A (Novi Sad)
Monumenta Archaeologica (Prague) — MA
Monumenta Archaeologica (Prague) — Mon A (Prague)
Monumenta Archaeologica (Prague) — Mon Arch
Monumenta Artis Romanae — MAR
Monumenta Asiae Minoris Antiqua [*Manchester*] — MAMA
Monumenta Asiae Minoris Antiqua — Mon As Min Ant
Monumenta Biblica et Ecclesiastica — MBE
Monumenta Boica — MB
Monumenta Boica — Mon Boica
Monumenta Christiana — MC
Monumenta Christiana. Geschriften uit de Middeleuwen — MCM
Monumenta Christiana. Geschriften van de Kerkvaders — MCK
Monumenta Christiana Selecta — MCS
Monumenta Conciliorum Generalium Saecli Decimiquinti — MCG
Monumenta Ecclesiae Liturgica — ME Li
Monumenta Epigraphica Christiana — MEC
Monumenta Germaniae Historica — MGH
Monumenta Germaniae Historica. Auctores Antiquissimi — MGHAA
Monumenta Germaniae Historica. Briefe der Deutschen Kaiserzeit — MGHB
Monumenta Germaniae Historica. Constitutiones — MGH Const
Monumenta Germaniae Historica. Diplomata Regnum Germaniae ex Stirpe Karolinorum — MGH DRG
Monumenta Germaniae Historica. Libelli de Lite — MGH LL
Monumenta Germaniae Historica. Scriptores. Auctores Antiquissimi — Mon Germ Hist Auct Ant
Monumenta Germaniae Historica. Scriptores Rerum Germanicarum — MGH SRG
Monumenta Germaniae Paedagogica — MGP
Monumenta Hispaniae Sacra — MHS
Monumenta Hispaniae Sacra. Serie Liturgica — MHS L
Monumenta Hispaniae Sacra. Subsidia — MHS S
Monumenta Hispaniae Vaticana — MHV
Monumenta Historica Ordinis Minorum Capuccinorum — HMOMC
Monumenta Historica Societatis Jesu — MHSJ
Monumenta Hungariae Historica. Irok — MHH I
Monumenta Hungariae Historica. Okmanytarak — MHH O
Monumenta Hungariae Judaica — MHJ
Monumenta Iuris Canonici — MIC
Monumenta Iuris Canonici. Corpus Glossatorum — MIC G
Monumenta Iuris Canonici. Subsidia — MIC S
Monumenta Linguae Ibericae — MLI
Monumenta Linguarum Asiae Maioris — MLAM
Monumenta Linguarum Hispanicarum — MLH
Monumenta Liturgiae Polychoralis. Ordinarium Missae cum Tribus Choris — MLP OT
Monumenta Missionum Societatis Jesu — MMSJ
Monumenta Monodica Medii Aevi — MMMA
Monumenta Musicae Belgicae — MMB
Monumenta Musicae Byzantinae — MGR
Monumenta Musicae Byzantinae — MMB
Monumenta Nipponica — MN
Monumenta Nipponica — MNip
Monumenta Nipponica — Mon Nipp
Monumenta Nipponica — MonN
Monumenta Nipponica — Monum Nippon
Monumenta Nipponica — Monumenta Nip
Monumenta Nipponica Monographs — MNM
Monumenta Ordinis Fratrum Praedicatorum Historica — MOFPH
Monumenta Poloniae Vaticana — MPV
Monumenta Polyphoniae Italicae — M P It
Monumenta Polyphoniae Liturgicae Sanctae Ecclesiae Romanae — MPL
Monumenta Sacra et Profana — MSP
Monumenta Serica — Mon Ser
Monumenta Serica — MS
Monumenta Serica — MSer
Monumenta Serica. Monograph Series — M Ser M
Monumenta Servorum Sanctae Mariae — MSSM
Monumenta Spectantia Historiam Slavorum Meridionalium — MHSM
Monumenta Vaticana Historiam Regni Hungariae Illustrantia — MVHRH
Monumenta Veteris Liturgiae Ambrosianae — MVLA
Monumenta Zollerana — Mon Zoll
Monumenti Annali e Bullettini Pubblicati. Instituto di Correspondenza Archaeologica — Mon
Monumenti Annali e Bullettini Pubblicati. Instituto di Correspondenza Archaeologica — Mon Ann Bull
Monumenti Annali e Bullettini Pubblicati. Instituto di Correspondenza Archaeologica — Mon Ann d Inst
Monumenti Annali e Bullettini Pubblicati. Instituto di Correspondenza Archaeologica — Mon dell'Inst
Monumenti Annali e Bullettini Pubblicati. Instituto di Correspondenza Archaeologica — Mon Inst
Monumenti Annali e Bullettini Pubblicati. Instituto di Correspondenza Archaeologica — Mond Inst
Monumenti Annali e Bullettini Pubblicati. Instituto di Correspondenza Archaeologica — Mondl
Monumenti Antichi — M Ant
Monumenti Antichi — Mon Ant
Monumenti Antichi. Accademia Nazionale dei Lincei — MAL
Monumenti Antichi. Accademia Nazionale dei Lincei — Mon Ant Linc
Monumenti Antichi. Accademia Nazionale dei Lincei — Mon Ant Lincei
Monumenti Antichi. Accademia Nazionale dei Lincei — Mon Linc
Monumenti Antichi. Accademia Nazionale dei Lincei — Mon Lincei
Monumenti Antichi. Accademia Nazionale dei Lincei — MondL
Monumenti Antichi Pubblicati dell'Accademia dei Lincei — MonAL
Monumenti Antichi. Reale Accademia Nazionale dei Lincei — MAAL
Monumenti d'Arte Antica — Mon Arte Ant
Monumenti della Pittura Antica Scoperti in Italia — Mon Pitt
Monumenti della Pittura Antica Scoperti in Italia — MPASI
Monumenti dell'Antichita Cristiana — MAC
Monumenti di Antichi Cristiana — MACr
Monumenti Etruschi — M Etr
Monumenti Etruschi — Mon Etr
Monumenti Inediti a Illustrazione della Storia degli Antichi Popoli Italiani — Mon In
Monumenti Inediti. Pubblicati dell'Instituto di Correspondenza Archeologica — Mon
Monumenti Inediti. Pubblicati dell'Instituto di Correspondenza Archeologica — Mon dell'Inst
Monumenti Inediti. Pubblicati dell'Instituto di Correspondenza Archeologica — Mond Inst
Monumenti Inediti Pubblicati dell'Istituto di Corrispondenza Archeologica — Mon Ist
Monumenti Inediti. Pubblicati. Instituto di Correspondenza Archeologica — Mon In
Monumenti Inediti. Pubblicati. Instituto di Correspondenza Archeologica — Mond I
Monumenti Vaticani di Archeologia e d'Arte — MVAA
Monumentorum ad Historiam Concilii Tridentini — MHCT
Monuments de l'Art Byzantin — MA Byz
Monuments de l'Art Byzantin — MABy
Monuments et Memoires Publies. Academie des Inscriptions et Belles-Lettres — MMPAIBL
Monuments et Memoires Publies par l'Academie des Inscriptions et Belles-Lettres — MM
Monuments et Memoires Publies par l'Academie des Inscriptions et Belles-Lettres — MMAI
Monuments et Memoires Publies par l'Academie des Inscriptions et Belles-Lettres — MMAIBL
Monuments et Memoires Publies par l'Academie des Inscriptions et Belles-Lettres. Fondation Piot — Mon Piot
Monuments Grecs. Association des Etudes Grecques — M Grecs
Monuments Grecs. Association des Etudes Grecques — Mon Gr
Monuments Historiques de la France — MHF
Monuments Illustrating New Comedy — MNC
Monuments Illustrating Old and Middle Comedy — MMC
Monuments Illustrating Tragedy and Satyr Plays — MTS
Monumentum. International Council of Monuments and Sites — MONU
Moody Monthly — MM
Moody Monthly — Moody M
Moody Street Irregulars — MSI
Moody's Bond Information Database Service — BIDS
Moody's Investors Service — Moody's Inv Serv
Moody's Magazine — Moody
Moon and the Planets — MOPLD
Moons and Lion Tailes — Moons L T
Moorgate and Wall Street — Moorg Wal S
Moorgate and Wall Street — Moorgate Wall St
Mora Ferenc Muzeum Evkoenyve — MFME
Mora Ferenc Muzeum Evkoenyve — Mora Ferenc Muz Ev
Moral Education — Moral Ed
Moravian Historical Society. Transactions — MHS
Moravian Missions — Morav Miss
Moravian Music Foundation. Bulletin — Moravian Mus
Moravian Music Journal — Moravian Mus
Moravian Music Journal — MorMJ
Moravian Theological Seminary. Bulletin — Morav Th S Bul
Moravske Numismaticke Zpravy — Morav Num Zpr
Moravske Numismaticke Zpravy — Moravske Num Zpravy
Morbidity and Mortality Weekly Report [*Information service or system*] — MMWR
Morbidity and Mortality Weekly Report — Morbid Mortal Weekly Rep
Morbidity and Mortality Weekly Report. United States Department of Health, Education, and Welfare — Morbidity Mortality Wkly Rep US Dep Hlth Educ Welf

Mordovskii Gosudarstvennyi Universitet. Uchenye Zapiski — Mord Gos Univ Uch Zap
More Books — MB
Moreana — Mor
Morfogenez i Regeneratsiya — Morfog Regener
Morfologia Normala si Patologica [*Bucharest*] — MNPAAS
Morfologia Normala si Patologica — Morfol Norm Patol
Morfologia Normala si Patologica — Morfol Norm si Pat
Morfologia Normala si Patologica (Bucharest) — Morfol Norm Patol (Buchar)
Morfologicheskie Osnovy Mikrotsirkulyatsii (Moscow) — Morfol Osn Mikrotsirk (Moscow)
Morfologiya Cheloveka i Zhivotnykh. Antropologiya — Morfol Chel Zhivotn Antropol
Morfologiya Cheloveka i Zhivotnykh. Embriologiya — Morfol Chel Zhivotn Embriol
Morfologiya Reaktivnykh Izmenenii Perifericheskoi Nervnoi Sistemy v Usloviyakh Eksperimenta — Morfol Reakt Izmen Perifer Nervn Sist Usloviyakh Eksp
Morgagni — MRGGAT
Morgan Guaranty Survey — Morgan Gty
Morgan Kaufmann Series in Data Management Systems — Morgan Kaufmann Ser Data Management Systems
Morgantown Energy Research Center. Special Publication. MERC/SP. United States Department of Energy — Morgantown Energy Res Cent Spec Publ MERC SP US Dep Energy
Morgantown Energy Technology Center. Report DOE/METC. United States Department of Energy — Morgantown Energy Technol Cent Rep DOE METC US Dep Energy
Morgenland [*Leipzig*] — Morgenl
Morioka Tabako Shikenjo Hokoku — Morioka Tab Shikenjo Hokoku
Morioka Tabako Shikenjo Hokoku — MTSHB5
Morning Watch — Morn Watch
Morocco. Service Geologique. Notes et Memoires — Morocco Serv Geol Notes Mem
Morovoe Khoziastvo i Morovaia Politica — MKMP
Morphologia Medica — Morphol Med
Morphologiai es Igazsagugyi Orvosi Szemle — Morphol Igazsagugyi Orv Sz
Morphologie et Embryologie [*Romania*] — Morphol Embryol
Morphologie et Embryologie (Bucurest) — Morphol Embryol (Bucur)
Morphologisches Jahrbuch — Morph Jb
Morphologisches Jahrbuch — Morphol Jahrb
Morphologisches Jahrbuch — Morphol Jb
Morphology of Polymers. Proceedings. Europhysics Conference on Macromolecular Physics — Morphol Polym Proc Europhys Conf Macromol Phys
Morris Arboretum. Bulletin — MARBAI
Morris Arboretum. Bulletin — Morris Arbor Bull
Morski Instytut Rybacki. Prace. Seria A. Oceanografia i Biologia Rybacka — Morski Inst Rybacki Pr Ser A
Morskie Gidrofizicheskie Issledovaniya — MGFIB
Morskie Gidrofizicheskie Issledovaniya — Morsk Gidrofiz Issled
Morskoe Sudostroenie — Morsk Sudostr
Morskoi Flot — MORFA
Morskoi Flot — Morsk Fl
Morskoi Flot — Morsk Flot
Morskoi Sbornik — Morsk Sb
Mortgage Banker — Mort Banker
Mortgage Banker — Mortg Bnkr
Mortgage Banking — MOB
Mortgage Banking — Mort Banking
Mortgage Banking — Mortg Bank
Morton Arboretum Quarterly — Morton Arbor Q
Mosaic — PMSA
Mosaic. A Journal for the Interdisciplinary Study of Literature — PMSC
Mosaic. Journal of Molybdenum Metallurgy — Mosaic J Molybdenum Metall
Mosaic Museum — Museum
Mosaici Antichi in Italia — Mos Ant It
Mosaics of Hagia Sophia at Istanbul — MHSI
Moscosoa — MOSCEQ
Moscosoa. Contribuciones Cientificas. Jardin Botanico Nacional Dr. Rafael M. Moscosoa — Moscosoa Contrib Cient Jard Bot Nac Dr Rafael M Moscosoa
Moscow Narodny Bank. Quarterly Review — Moscow Narodny Bank Q R
Moscow News — MN
Moscow University. Biological Sciences Bulletin — Mosc Univ Biol Sci Bull
Moscow University. Biological Sciences Bulletin — MUBBDD
Moscow University. Biological Sciences Bulletin (English Translation) — Moscow Univ Biol Sci Bull (Engl Transl)
Moscow University. Biological Sciences Bulletin (English Translation of Vestnik. Moskovskogo Universiteta. Biologiya) — Mosc Univ Biol Sci Bull (Engl Transl Vestn Mosk Univ Biol)
Moscow University. Bulletin. Series 3. Physics and Astronomy — Moscow Univ Bull Ser 3
Moscow University. Chemistry Bulletin — Mosc Univ Chem Bull
Moscow University. Chemistry Bulletin. English Translation — Moscow Univ Chem Bull Engl Transl
Moscow University. Computational Mathematics and Cybernetics — Mosc Univ Comput Math Cybern
Moscow University. Computational Mathematics and Cybernetics — Moscow Univ Comput Math and Cybern
Moscow University Computational Mathematics and Cybernetics — Moscow Univ Comput Math Cybernet
Moscow University. Geology Bulletin — Mosc Univ Geol Bull
Moscow University. Geology Bulletin (English Translation) — Moscow Univ Geol Bull (Engl Transl)
Moscow University. Mathematics Bulletin — Mosc Univ Math Bull
Moscow University. Mathematics Bulletin — Moscow Univ Math Bull
Moscow University. Mathematics Bulletin (English Translation) — Moscow Univ Math Bull (Engl Transl)
Moscow University. Mechanics Bulletin — Mosc Univ Mech Bull
Moscow University. Mechanics Bulletin [*English Translation of Vestnik Moskovskogo Universiteta. Mekhanika*] — Moscow Univ Mech Bull
Moscow University. Mechanics Bulletin (English Translation of Vestnik Moskovskogo Universiteta. Mekhanika) — Moscow Univ Mech Bull (Engl Transl)
Moscow University. Physics Bulletin — Mosc Univ Phys Bull
Moscow University. Physics Bulletin — Moscow Univ Phys Bull
Moscow University. Physics Bulletin. English Translation — Moscow Univ Phys Bull Engl Transl
Moscow University. Soil Science Bulletin — Mosc Univ Soil Sci Bull
Moscow University. Soil Science Bulletin — MUSBDU
Moscow University. Soil Science Bulletin (English Translation) — Moscow Univ Soil Sci Bull (Engl Transl)
Mosher Periodical Index — Mosher Period Index
Moskovskaya Nauchnaya Konferentsiya po Osnovnym Problemam Gigieny Truda — Mosk Nauchn Konf Osnovn Probl Gig Tr
Moskovskaya Sel'skokhozyaistvennaya Akademiya Imeni K. A. Timiryazeva. Doklady TSKhA — Mosk Skh Akad Im K A Timiryazeva Dokl TSKhA
Moskovskaya Sel'skokhozyaistvennaya Akademiya Imeni K. A. Timiryazeva. Sbornik Nauchnykh Trudov — Mosk Skh Akad Im K A Timiryazeva Sb Nauchn Tr
Moskovskaya Veterinarnaya Akademiya Imeni K. I. Skryabina. Sbornik Nauchnykh Trudov — Mosk Vet Akad Im K I Skryabina Sb Nauchn Tr
Moskovskaya Veterinarnaya Akademiya. Trudy — Mosk Vet Akad Tr
Moskovskii Aviatsionnyi Institut Imeni Sergo Ordzhonikidze. Tematicheskii Sbornik Nauchnykh Trudov — Mosk Aviats Inst Im Sergo Ordzhonikidze Temat Sb Nauchn Tr
Moskovskii Aviatsionnyi Institut Imeni Sergo Ordzhonikidze. Trudy — Mosk Aviats Inst Im Sergo Ordzhonikidze Tr
Moskovskii Energeticheskii Institut. Mezhvedomstvennyi Tematicheskii Sbornik — Mosk Energ Inst Mezhved Temat Sb
Moskovskii Fiziko-Tekhnicheskii Institut. Trudy MFTI. Seriya Radiotekhnika i Elektronika — Mosk Fiz Tekh Inst Tr MFTI Ser Radiotekh Elektron
Moskovskii Fiziko-Tekhnicheskii Institut. Trudy. Seriya "Obshchaya i Molekulyarnaya Fizika" — Mosk Fiz Tekh Inst Tr Ser Obshch Mol Fiz
Moskovskii Gidromeliorativnyi Institut. Nauchnye Zapiski — Mosk Gidromelior Inst Nauchn Zap
Moskovskii Gosudarstvennyi Pedagogiceskii Institut Imeni V. I. Lenina. Ucenye Zapiski — Moskov Gos Ped Inst Ucen Zap
Moskovskii Gosudarstvennyi Pedagogicheskii Institut. Uchenye Zapiski — Mosk Gos Pedagog Inst Uch Zap
Moskovskii Gosudarstvennyi Universitet Imeni M. V. Lomonosova. Soobscenija Gosudarstvennogo Astronomiceskogo Instituta Imeni P. K. Sternberga — Moskov Gos Univ Soobsc Gos Astronom Inst Sternberg
Moskovskii Gosudarstvennyi Universitet Imeni M. V. Lomonosova. Soobshcheniya Gosudarstvennogo Astronomicheskogo Instituta Imeni P. K. Sternberga — Moskov Gos Univ Soobshch Gos Astronom Inst Sternberga
Moskovskii Gosudarstvennyi Universitet Imeni M. V. Lomonosova. Trudy Gosudarstvennogo Astronomiceskogo Instituta Imeni P. K. Sternberga — Moskov Gos Univ Trudy Gos Astronom Inst Sternberg
Moskovskii Gosudarstvennyi Universitet imeni M. V. Lomonosova. Uchenye Zapiski — Mosk Gos Univ im M V Lomonosova Uch Zap
Moskovskii Gosudarstvennyi Universitet. Mehaniko-Matematiceskii Fakul'tet. Kafedra Teorii Funkcii i Funkcional'nogo Analiza. Trudy — Trudy Kaf Teorii Funkcii i Funkcional Anal Moskov Gos Univ
Moskovskii Gosudarstvennyi Universitet. Mehaniko-Matematiceskii Fakul'tet. Matematiceskii Voprosy Upravlenija Proizvodstvom — Mat Voprosy Upravlen Proizvodstvom
Moskovskii Gosudarstvennyi Zaocnyi Pedagogiceskii Institut. Sbornik Naucnyh Trudov — Moskov Gos Zaocn Ped Inst Sb Naucn Trudov
Moskovskii Institut Elektronnogo Mashinostroeniya. Trudy — Mosk Inst Elektron Mashinostr Tr
Moskovskii Institut Elektronnogo Masinostroenija. Trudy MIEM — Moskov Inst Elektron Masinostroenija-Trudy MIEM
Moskovskii Institut Inzenerov Zeleznodoroznogo Transporta. Trudy — Moskov Inst Inz Zeleznodoroz Transporta Trudy
Moskovskii Institut Inzhenerov Zheleznodorozhnogo Transporta. Trudy — Mosk Inst Inzh Zheleznodorozhn Transp Tr
Moskovskii Institut Khimicheskogo Mashinostroeniya. Trudy — Mosk Inst Khim Mashinostr Tr
Moskovskii Institut Narodnogo Khozyaistva. Sverdlovskii Filial. Sbornik Nauchnykh Trudov — Mosk Inst Nar Khoz Sverdl Fil Sb Nauchn Tr
Moskovskii Institut Neftekhimicheskoi i Gazovoi Promyshlennosti Imeni I. M. Gubkina. Trudy — Mosk Inst Neftekhim Gazov Promsti Im I M Gubkina Tr
Moskovskii Institut Stali i Splavov. Nauchnye Trudy — Mosk Inst Stali Splavov Nauchn Tr
Moskovskii Institut Stali i Splavov. Sbornik — Mosk Inst Stali Splavov Sb
Moskovskii Institut Stali. Sbornik — Mosk Inst Stali Sb
Moskovskii Institut Tonkoi Khimicheskoi Tekhnologii Imeni M. V. Lomonosova. Trudy Instituta — Mosk Inst Tonkoi Khim Tekhnol Im M V Lomonosova Tr Inst
Moskovskii Institut Tonkoi Khimicheskoi Tekhnologii. Trudy — Mosk Inst Tonkoi Khim Tekhnol Tr
Moskovskii Inzenerno-Stroitelskii Institut Imeni V. V. Kuibyseva. Sbornik Trudov — Moskov Inz-Stroitel Inst Sb Trudov
Moskovskii Inzhenerno-Stroitel'nyi Institut Imeni V. V. Kuibysheva. Sbornik Trudov — Mosk Inzh Stroit Inst Im V V Kuibysheva Sb Tr
Moskovskii Khimiko-Teckhnologicheskii Institut Imeni D. I. Mendeleeva. Trudy — Mosk Khim Tekhnol Inst Im D I Mendeleeva Tr
Moskovskii Kolkhoznik — MOKOAI
Moskovskii Kolkhoznik — Mosk Kolkhozn

Moskovskii Lesotehniceskii Institut. Naucnye Trudy — Moskov Lesotehn Inst Naucn Trudy
Moskovskii Lesotekhnicheskii Institut. Nauchnye Trudy — Mosk Lesotekh Inst Nauchn Tr
Moskovskii Nauchno-Issledovatel'skii Institut Gigieny Imeni F. F. Erismana. Sbornik Nauchnykh Trudov — Mosk Nauchno Issled Inst Gig Im F F Erismana Sb Nauchn Tr
Moskovskii Nauchno-Issledovatel'skii Institut Gigieny. Uchenye Zapiski — Mosk Nauchno Issled Inst Gig Uch Zap
Moskovskii Nauchno-Issledovatel'skii Institut Psikhiatrii. Trudy — Mosk Nauchno Issled Inst Psikhiatr Tr
Moskovskii Neftyanoi Institut. Trudy — Mosk Neft Inst Tr
Moskovskii Oblastnoi Pedagogiceskii Institut. Ucenye Zapiski — Moskov Oblast Ped Inst Ucen Zap
Moskovskii Oblastnoi Pedagogicheskii Institut Imeni N. K. Krupskoi. Uchenye Zapiski — Mosk Obl Pedagog Inst Im N K Krupskoi Uch Zap
Moskovskii Ordena Lenina Aviacionnyi Institut Imeni Sergo Ordzonikidze. Trudy [*A publication*] — Moskov Aviacion Inst Ordzonikidze Trudy
Moskovskii Ordena Trudovogo Krasnogo Znameni Inzenerno-Stroitel'nyi Institut Imeni V. V. Kuibyseva Sbornik Trudov — Inz-Stroitel Inst Kuibysev Sb Trudov
Moskovskii Tekhnologicheskii Institut Legkoi Promyshlennosti. Nauchnye Trudy — Mosk Tekhnol Inst Legk Promsti Nauchn Tr
Moskovskii Universitet. Sbornik Rabot Vychislitelnogo Tsentra Moskovskogo Universiteta. Vychislitel'nye Metody i Programmirovanie — Vychisl Metody i Programmirovanie
Moskovskii Universitet. Zoologicheskii Muzei. Sbornik Trudov — Mosk Univ Zool Muz Sb Tr
Moskovskii Zaochnyi Poligraficheskii Institut. Nauchnye Trudy — Mosk Zaochn Poligr Inst Nauchn Tr
Moskovskij Archeologiceskij Institut — MAI
Moskovskij Kraeved — MK
Moskovskij Letopisnyj Svod Konca — MLS
Moskovskiy Universitet. Vestnik. Seriya 6. Biologiya. Pochvovedeniye — Mosk Univ Vestn Ser 6 Biol Pochvoved
Moskovskiy Universitet. Vestnik. Seriya Geografii — Mosk Univ Vestn Ser Geogr
Moskovskoe Vysshee Tekhnicheskoi Uchilishche Imeni N. E. Baumana. Sbornik — Mosk Vyssh Tekh Uchil Im N E Baumana Sb
Moskovskoe Vysshee Tekhnicheskoi Uchilishche Imeni N. E. Baumana. Sbornik Trudov — Mosk Vyssh Tekh Uchil Im N E Baumana Sb Tr
Moskovskoe Vysshee Tekhnicheskoi Uchilishche Imeni N. E. Baumana. Trudy — Mosk Vyssh Tekh Uchil Im N E Baumana Tr
Moskovskoye Obshchestvo Ispytateley Prirody. Byulleten. Otdel Geologicheskiy — Mosk O-Vo Ispyt Prir Byull Otd Geol
Moskva — Mo
Moslem World — Moslem W
Moslem World — MW
Moslemische Revue — Mosl R
Mosonmagyarovari Agrartudomanyi Foiskola Kozlemenyei — Mosonmagy Agrartud Foisk Kozl
Mosonmagyarovari Agrartudomanyi Foiskola Kozlemenyei — Mosonmagyarovari Agrartud Foiskola Kozl
Mosonmagyarovari Mezogazdasagtudomanyi Kar Kozlemenyei — Mosonmagyarovari Mezogazdasagtud Kar Kozl
Mosquito Control Research. Annual Report — Mosq Control Res Annu Rep
Mosquito News — Mosq News
Mosquito News — MOSQAU
Mosquito News — Mosquito Ne
Mosquito Systematics — Mosq Syst
Mosquito Systematics — MSQSAK
Mosquito Systematics News Letter — Mosq Syst News Lett
Mosquito Systematics News Letter — MSYNAB
Most Thrilling Science Ever Told — MTS
Mostra dell'Arte e della Civilta Etrusca — Mostra
Mostra dell'Arte e della Civilta Etrusca — Mostra Etr
Mostra Internazionale delle Conserve e Relativi Imballaggi. Congressi — Mostra Int Conserve Relativi Imballaggi Congr
Mostra Internazionale delle Conserve ed Imballaggi. Congressi — Mostra Int Conserve Imballaggi Congr
Mostra Internazionale delle Industrie per le Conserve Alimentari. Congressi — Mostra Int Ind Conserve Aliment Congr
Mosvodokanalniiproekt. Trudy — Mosvodokanalniiproekt Tr
MOT. Schriftenreihe der Medizinisch-Orthopaedischen Technik — MOT Schriftenr Med Orthop Tech
Mother Earth News — GMTE
Mother Earth News — Moth Earth
Mother Jones — GMOJ
Mother Jones — MOJOD
Mother Jones — Moth Jones
Mother Jones — Mother J
Moths of America, North of Mexico — Moths Am North Mex
Motility of the Digestive Tract. Proceedings. International Symposium on Gastrointestinal Motility — Motil Dig Tract Proc Int Symp Gastrointest Motil
Motion Picture Technical Bulletin — Motion Pict Tech Bull
Motivation and Emotion — MOEMDJ
Motivation and Emotion — Motiv Emotion
Motor Accidents Cases — MAC
Motor Boat — Mot Boat
Motor Boat and Yachting — Mot Boat Yacht
Motor Boating — Mot Boating
Motor Boating — Motor B
Motor Boating and Sailing — GMBS
Motor Boating and Sailing — Motor B & S
Motor Business — Motor Bus
Motor Business — MOU
Motor Cycle — Mot Cycle
Motor Cycle News — MCN
Motor Manual — Motor M
Motor Report International — MotorIntnl
Motor Service (Chicago) — Motor Serv (Chicago)
Motor Ship — Mot Ship
Motor Skills. Theory into Practice — Mot Sk
Motor Trade Journal — Motor Trade J
Motor Trader — Mot Trader
Motor Transport — Motor Transp
Motor Trend — GMOT
Motor Trend — Motor T
Motor Vehicle Reports — MVR
Motorisation Agricole — Motoris Agr
Motorola Technical Developments — Motorola Tech Dev
Motorola Technical Disclosure Bulletin — Motorola Tech Disclosure Bull
Motortechnische Zeitschrift — Motortech Z
Motortechnische Zeitschrift [*Stuttgart*] — MTZ
Moudjahik — MJ
Mound Facility. Report MLM — Mound Facil Rep MLM
Mound Laboratory. Report MLM — Mound Lab Rep MLM
Mount Sinai Journal of Medicine — MSJMAZ
Mount Sinai Journal of Medicine — Mt Sinai J
Mount Sinai Journal of Medicine — Mt Sinai J Med
Mountain Geologist — Mountain Geol
Mountain Geologist — Mt Geol
Mountain Life and Work — MLW
Mountain Life and Work — Mntn Life
Mountain Life and Work — Motn Life
Mountain Plains Library Association. Quarterly — Mount Plains Libr Q
Mountain Plains Library Association. Quarterly — Mt Plains Lib Assn Q
Mountain Research and Development — MRED
Mountain Research and Development — Mt Res Dev
Mountain Review — Mount Rev
Mountain Safety Research Newsletter — MSRN
Mountain States Banker — Mtn St Bank
Mountain States Mineral Age — Mt States Miner Age
Mountain States Mining Age — Mt States Min Age
Mountaineer Grower — Mt Grow
Mouseion. International Museum Office — Mous
Mouseion. Rivista di Scienze Classiche — Mous
Mouth of the Dragon — Mouth
Mouvement Geographique — MG
Mouvement Social — MouS
Mouvement Social — Mouv Soc
Mouvement Social — Mouvement Soc
Mouvement Sociologique — MS
Mouvement Syndical Mondial — Mouvement Synd Mond
MOV [*Marine-Offizier-Vereinigung*] **Nachrichten** — MOV Nachr
Movement Disorders — Mov Disord
Movie Maker — Mov M
Movietone News — Movietone
Movietone News — Movietone N
Movietone News — Mtone News
Movimento Operaio — MO
Movimento Operaio — Mov Operaio
Movimento Operaio e Socialista — Mov Operaio Soc
Moving Image — Mov Im
Movoznavstvo — Mov
Moyen Age — MA
Moyen Francais — M Fra
Mozambique. Direccao dos Servicos de Geologia e Minas. Memorias e Communicacoes. Boletim — Mozambique Dir Serv Geol Minas Mem Commun Bol
Mozambique. Servicos de Geologia e Minas. Serie de Geologia e Minas. Memorias e Communicacoes. Boletim — Mozambique Serv Geol Minas Ser Geol Minas Mem Commun Bol
Mozambique. Servicos de Industria, Minas, e Geologia. Serie de Geologia e Minas. Memorias e Communicacoes. Boletim — Mozambique Serv Ind Minas Geol Ser Geol Minas Mem Commun Bol
Mozart-Jahrbuch — Moz Jb
Mozart-Jahrbuch — MozartJb
Mozart-Jahrbuch — MozJ
Mozoegazdasagi Kiserletugyi Kozpont Evkonyve — Mozoegazd Kiserletugyi Kozp Evk
MP. Maryland Agricultural Experiment Station — MP MD Agric Exp Stn
MP - University of Arkansas. Cooperative Extension Service — MP Arkansas Univ Coop Ext
MP. University of Arkansas. Cooperative Extension Service — MP Univ Arkansas Coop Ext Serv
MP. University of Missouri. Extension Division — MP Univ Mo Ext Div
MP. University of Nebraska. Agricultural Experiment Station — MP Univ Nebr Agric Exp Stn
MP. Vermont Agricultural Experiment Station — MP Vt Agric Exp Stn
MPG (Max-Planck-Gesellschaft) Spiegel. Aktuelle Informationen [*Germany*] — MPG (Max-Planck-Ges) Spiegel Aktuel Inf
MPG. News. Maine Potato Growers, Inc. — MPG News
MPG [*Max-Planck-Gesellschaft*] **Presseinformation** — MPG Presseinf
MPG [*Max-Planck-Gesellschaft*] **Spiegel. Aktuelle Informationen** — MPG Spiegel Aktuelle Inf
MPI [*McKee-Pedersen Instruments*] **Applications Notes** — MPI Appl Notes
MPI (McKee-Pedersen Instruments) Applications Notes — MPI (McKee Pedersen Instrum) Appl Notes
MPLS-St. Paul Magazine — IMPL
MPR. Metal Powder Report — MPR Met Powder Rep

MPT. Metallurgical Plant and Technology — MPT Metall Plant Technol
MR. Mississippi Agricultural Experiment Station — MR Miss Agr Exp Sta
MRC . Laboratory Animals Centre. Symposia [*Medical Research Council*] [*Great Britain*] — MASYDR
MRC . Laboratory Animals Centre Symposium [*Medical Research Council*] [*Great Britain*] — MRC Lab Anim Cent Symp
MRC (Medical Research Council) (Great Britain). Laboratory Animals Centre. Symposia — MRC (Med Res Counc) (GB) Lab Anim Cent Symp
MRC [*Medical Research Council. Great Britain*] **Memorandum** — MRC Memo
MRC [*Media Research Council*] **Review** — MRC Rev
MRC [*Medical Research Council. Great Britain*] **War Memorandum** — MRC War Memo
MRL [*Materials Research Laboratories*] **Bulletin of Research and Development** — MRL Bull Res Dev
MRS [*Materials Research Society*] **Bulletin** — MRS Bull
MRS Internet Journal of Nitride Semiconductor Research — MRS Internet J Nitride Semicond Res
Ms. — GMIZ
Ms Magazine — Ms
Ms Magazine — MsM
MS. Manuscript [*Los Angeles*] — MS
MSAC [*Mountain State Agricultural College*] **Research Journal** — MSAC Res J
MSDC (Medical Society of the District of Columbia) News — MSDC News
MSN. Microwave Systems News — MSN Microwave Syst News
MSR. Messen, Steuern, Regeln — MSR Mess Steuern Regeln
MSRT [*Michigan Society for Respiratory Therapy*] **Journal** — MSRT J
MST (Microsystem Technology) News Poland — MST News Pol
MSU [*Michigan State University*] **Business Topics** — MSU
MSU [*Michigan State University*] **Business Topics** — MSU Bus To
MSU [*Michigan State University*] **Business Topics** — MSU Bus Top
MSU [*Michigan State University*] **Business Topics** — MSU Bus Topics
MSU (Michigan State University) Business Topics — MSU (Mich State Univ) Bus Topics
MSV. Zeitschrift fuer Metall- und Schmuckwaren-Fabrikation sowie Verchromung — MSV Z Met Schmuckwaren Fabr Verchrom
MTA [*Motor Traders Association of New South Wales*] **Official Journal** — MTAJ
M-Tijdschrift. Werktuigkunde — M Tijdschr Werktuigkunde
MTM. Journal of Methods Time Measurement — MTY
MTP [*Medical & Technical Publishing Co.*] **International Review of Science. Biochemistry** — MTP Int Rev Sci Biochem
MTP [*Medical and Technical Publishing Company*] **International Review of Science. Physiology** — MTP Int Rev Sci Physiol
MTP [*Medical & Technical Publishing Co.*] **International Review of Science. Series One. Physiology** — MIRSDQ
MTP (Medical and Technical Publishing Company) International Review of Science. Series One. Physiology — MTP (Med Tech Publ Co) Int Rev Sci Ser One Physiol
MTZ. Motortechnische Zeitschrift — MTZ Motortech Z
Muegyetemi Kozlemenyek (Budapest) — Muegy Kozl (Budapest)
Muehle — MUEHA
Muehle und Mischfuttertechnik — Muehle Mischfuttertech
Muehle und Mischfuttertechnik — Muhle Mischfuttertech
Muehlenzeitung — MUHLA2
Muehlhauser Geschichtsblaetter — MGbl
Muell und Abfall. Beihefte — Muell Abfall Beih
Mueller. Fragmenta Historicorum Graecorum — FHG
Muellerei — MULRA6
Muelleria — MAJBAC
Muemlekvedelem — Mueved
Muemlekvedelem — Muved
Muenchen Allgemeine Zeitung — MAZ
Muenchen-Augsburger Abendzeitung — Muenchen Augsb Abendztg
Muenchener Aegyptologische Studien — MAe St
Muenchener Aegyptologische Studien [*Berlin*] — MAS
Muenchener Archiv fuer Philologie des Mittelalters und der Renaissance — MAPMA
Muenchener Beitraege zur Abwasser-, Fischerei-, und Flussbiologie — MABFAI
Muenchener Beitraege zur Abwasser-, Fischerei-, und Flussbiologie — Muench Beit Abwasser-Fisch- Flussbiol
Muenchener Beitraege zur Abwasser-, Fischerei-, und Flussbiologie [*West Germany*] — Muench Beitr Abwasser Fisch Flussbiol
Muenchener Beitraege zur Abwasser-, Fischerei-, und Flussbiologie — Muenchner Beitr Abwasser Fisch Flussbiol
Muenchener Beitraege zur Kunstgeschichte — MBKG
Muenchener Beitraege zur Mediaevistik und Renaissance-Forschung — MBM
Muenchener Beitraege zur Mediavistik und Renaissance-Forschung — MBMRF
Muenchener Beitraege zur Papyrusforschung — MBP
Muenchener Beitraege zur Papyrusforschung and Antiken Rechtsgeschichte — MBPF
Muenchener Beitraege zur Papyrusforschung und Antiken Rechtsgeschichte — MPR
Muenchener Beitraege zur Romanischen und Englischen Philologie — Muench Beitr
Muenchener Geographische Abhandlungen — Muench Geogr Abh
Muenchener Germanistische Beitraege — MGB
Muenchener Indologische Studien — MIS
Muenchener Jahrbuch der Bildenden Kunst — MJB
Muenchener Jahrbuch der Bildenden Kunst — MJBK
Muenchener Jahrbuch der Bildenden Kunst — Muench Jahr Bild Kunst
Muenchener Juedische Nachrichten — MJN
Muenchener Katholische Kirchenzeitung fuer das Erzbistum Muenchen und Freising — MKKZ
Muenchener Klebstoff- und Veredelungs-Seminar — Muench Klebst Veredel Semin
Muenchener Medizinische Wochenschrift — MMW
Muenchener Medizinische Wochenschrift — MMWOA
Muenchener Medizinische Wochenschrift — MMWOAU
Muenchener Medizinische Wochenschrift — Muench Med Wochenschr
Muenchener Medizinische Wochenschrift — Muench Med Wschr
Muenchener Medizinische Wochenschrift — Muenchen Med Wchnschr
Muenchener Medizinische Wochenschrift — Muenchener Med Wochens
Muenchener Museum — MM
Muenchener Neueste Nachrichten — MNN
Muenchener Papiere zur Linguistik — MPL
Muenchener Studien zur Historischen Theologie — MSH Th
Muenchener Studien zur Sprachwissenschaft — MSS
Muenchener Studien zur Sprachwissenschaft — MSZS
Muenchener Studien zur Sprachwissenschaft — Muench St Spr Wiss
Muenchener Studien zur Sprachwissenschaft. Beiheft — MSS B
Muenchener Texte und Untersuchungen zur Deutschen Literatur des Mittelalters — MTU
Muenchener Texte und Untersuchungen zur Deutschen Literatur des Mittelalters — MTUDLM
Muenchener Theologische Studien — MThS
Muenchener Theologische Studien. Historische Abteilung — M Th SH
Muenchener Theologische Studien. Historische Abteilung. Ergaenzungsband — M Th SHE
Muenchener Theologische Studien. Kanonistische Abteilung — M Th SK
Muenchener Theologische Studien. Systematische Abteilung — M Th SS
Muenchener Theologische Zeitschrift — M Th Z
Muenchener Theologische Zeitschrift — MTZ
Muenchener Theologische Zeitschrift — Muenchener Theol Z
Muenchener Theologische Zeitschrift [*Munich*] — MunchThZ
Muenchener Tieraerztliche Wochenschrift — Muench Tieraerztl Wochenschr
Muenchner Beitraege zur Papyrusforschung und Antiken Rechtsgeschichte — MBPR
Muenchner Beitraege zur Papyrusforschung und Antiken Rechtsgeschichte — Muench Beitr
Muenchner Beitraege zur Papyrusforschung und Antiken Rechtsgeschichte — Muench Beitr z Pap
Muenchner Beitraege zur Papyrusforschung und Antiken Rechtsgeschichte — Munch Beitr z Pap
Muenchner Jahrbuch der Bildenden Kunst — Mu Jb
Muenchner Jahrbuch der Bildenden Kunst — Mue Jb
Muenchner Jahrbuch der Bildenden Kunst — Muench Jarhb Bild K
Muenchner Jahrbuch der Bildenden Kunst — Muenchner Jahrb
Muenchner Jahrbuch der Bildenden Kunst — Muenchner Jb Bild Kunst
Muenchner Jahrbuch der Bildenden Kunst — Munchner Jahrb
Muenchner Museum fuer Philologie des Mittelalters und der Renaissance — MM
Muenchner Philosophische Forschungen — Mue PF
Muenchner Symposion fuer Experimentelle Orthopaedie — Muench Symp Exp Orthop
Muenchner Theologische Zeitschrift — Mue TZ
Muenster [*Muenchen*] — Muen
Muensterische Beitraege zur Geschichtsforschung — MBGF
Muensterische Beitraege zur Theologie — MB Th
Muensterisches Pastoralblatt — MP Bl
Muenstersche Beitraege zur Deutschen Literatur — MBDL
Muenstersche Beitraege zur Vor- und Fruehgeschichte — MBVF
Muenstersche Forschungen zur Geologie und Palaeontologie — Muenster Forsch Geol Palaeontol
Muenstersche Forschungen zur Geologie und Palaeontologie — Muenstersche Forsch Geol Palaeontol
Muenstersche Mittelalter-Schriften — MMS
Muenstersche Numismatische Zeitung — Muenstersche N Z
Muenzen und Medaillen — Mu M
Muenzen und Medaillen — Muenz Med
Muenzen und Medaillen — Munc M
Muenzen- und Medaillensammler Berichte aus allen Gebieten der Geld-, Muenzen-, und Medaillenkunde — Berichte
Muenzen- und Medaillensammler Berichte aus allen Gebieten der Geld-, Muenzen-, und Medaillenkunde — MMB
Mueszaki Koezlemenyek. Lang Gepgyar Mueszaki es Gazdasagi Tajekoztatoja [*Hungary*] — Muesz Koezl Lang Gepgyar Muesz Gazd Tajek
Mueszaki Tervezes — Mueszaki Terv
Mueszaki Tudomany [*Hungary*] — Muesz Tud
Mueszeruegyi es Merestechnikai Koezlemenyek [*Hungary*] — Mueszeruegyi Merestech Koezl
Mueveszettoerteneti Ertesitoe — Muves Ertes
Muhendis Mektebi Mecmuasi — Muhendis Mektebi Mecm
Muirhead Library of Philosophy — ML Ph
Muirhead Library of Philosophy — Muirh Lib P
Muirhead Technique — Muirhead Tech
MUJWRRC [*Montana University Joint Water Resources Research Center*] **Report** — MUJWRRC Rep
Mukogawa Joshi Daigaku Kiyo. Shizenkagakuhen — MJDSA
Mukogawa Joshi Daigaku Kiyo. Yakugaku Hen — MDKHD
Mukomol'e i Elevatorno-Skladskoe Khozyaistvo — Mukomole Elevat Skladskoe Khoz
Mukomol'no Elevatornaya i Kombikormovaya Promyshlennost — Mukomolno Elevat Kombikormovaya Promst
Mukomol'no-Elevatornaya Promyshlennost' — Mukomol' -Elevator Prom
Mukomol'no-Elevatornaya Promyshlennost' — Mukomolno Elevat Promst
Mulino — Mu
Mullard Technical Communications — Mullard Tech Commun
Multi Media Reviews Index — Multi Media Rev Index
Multicultural Education — Multicult Ed
Multicultural Education Abstracts — Multicult Educ Abstr
Multicultural Education Journal — Multicult Ed J

Multiculturalism — Multicult
Multidimensional Systems and Signal Processing — Multidimens Systems Signal Process
Multidisciplinary Research — MRINCS
Multidisciplinary Research — Multidiscip Res
Multidisciplinary Research — Multidisciplinary Res
Multilayer Ceramic Devices — Multilayer Ceram Devices
Multi-Media Reviews Index — MMRI
Multinational Business — MLS
Multinational Business — MQU
Multinational Business — Multinational Bus
Multinational Monitor — Mult Mon
Multinational Monitor — Multinatl
Multinational Monitor — Multinatl Monit
Multinational Services — MUS
Multiparticle Dynamics. International Symposium — Multipart Dyn Int Symp
Multiphase Science and Technology — Multiphase Sci Technol
Multiple Sclerosis — Mult Scler
Multiple Sclerosis Abstracts — Multi Scler Abstr
Multiple Sclerosis Indicative Abstracts — Multiple Sclerosis Indicative Abstr
Multipurpose Utilization of Mineral Resources — Multipurp Util Miner Resour
Multivariate Behavioral Research — MBR
Multivariate Behavioral Research — Multiv Be R
Multivariate Behavioral Research — Multivar Behav Res
Multivariate Behavioral Research — MVBRAV
Multivariate Behavioral Research Monograph — MBRMAO
Multivariate Behavioral Research Monograph — Multivar Behav Res Monogr
Multivariate Experimental Clinical Research — MCREDA
Munca Sanitara — Munca Sanit
Mundaiz — MZ
Mundo Apicola — Mundo Apic
Mundo Electronico — MUELC
Mundo Electronico — Mundo Electron
Mundo Hispanico — MH
Mundo Hispanico — MHis
Mundo Hispanico — MHisp
Mundo Medico — MUMEEA
Mundo Medico — Mundo Med
Mundo Nuevo — Mnu
Mundo Social — MS
Mundo Textil Argentino — Mundo Text Argent
Mundus Artium — MArt
Mundus Artium — Mund
Mundus Artium — Mundus Art
Mundus Artium — MundusA
Munger Africana Library Notes — Munger Africana Lib Notes
Munger Africana Library Notes — Munger Africana Libr Notes
Munibe. Sociedad de Ciencias Naturales Aranzadi [*San Sebastian*] — Munibe
Munich Symposia on Microbiology — Munich Symp Microbiol
Munich Symposium on Biology of Connective Tissue — Munich Symp Biol Connect Tissue
Municipal Administration and Engineering — Munic Adm Eng
Municipal Affairs — Munic Aff
Municipal and County Engineering — Munic & Co Eng
Municipal and County Engineering — Munic Cty Eng
Municipal and Industrial Waste. Annual Madison Waste Conference — Munic Ind Waste Annu Madison Waste Conf
Municipal and Planning Law Reports — MPLR
Municipal and Planning Law Reports — Mun Plan L Rep
Municipal and Public Services Journal — Munic and Public Services J
Municipal and Road Board Gazette — Munic & Road Board Gaz
Municipal and Road Board Gazette — Munic & Road Board Gazette
Municipal Association Reports — MAR
Municipal Attorney — Mun Att'y
Municipal Building Management — Munic Bldg Mgmt
Municipal Engineer — Munic Eng
Municipal Engineer — Munic Engr
Municipal Engineering — Munic Engng
Municipal Engineering in Australia — Munic Eng Aust
Municipal Engineering in Australia — Munic Eng in Aust
Municipal Engineering (Indianapolis) — Munic Eng (Indianapolis)
Municipal Engineering (London) — Munic Eng (London)
Municipal Engineers Journal — Munic Eng J
Municipal Finance Journal — MFJ
Municipal Finance Journal — Muni Fin J
Municipal Information — Munic Info
Municipal Journal — MJ
Municipal Journal — Munic J
Municipal Journal and Engineer — Munic J Eng
Municipal Journal and Public Works — Munic J Public Works
Municipal Law Court Decisions — Mun L Ct Dec
Municipal Management Directory — Munic Manage Dir
Municipal Mirror and Queensland Shire Record — Munic Mirror
Municipal News — Munic News
Municipal News and Water Works — Munic News Water Works
Municipal Ordinance Review — Mun Ord Rev
Municipal Registered Bond Interest Record [*Database*] — MRBIR
Municipal Review — Munic Rev
Municipal Sanitation — Munic Sanit
Municipal Sewage Treatment Plant Sludge Management — Munic Sewage Treat Plant Sludge Manage
Municipal Utilities — Munic Util
Municipal Utilities Magazine — Munic Util Mag
Munkavedelem. Munka-es Uezemegeszseguegy — Munkaved Munka Uezemeue
Munsey's Magazine — Munsey
Munsey's Magazine — Munseys M
Munshi Indological Felicitation Volume. Bharatiya Vidya — MIF
Munzautomat Mainz — MVH
Muon Catalyzed Fusion — Muon Catal Fusion
Murex Review — Murex Rev
Murmanskaya Olenevodcheskaya Opytnaya Stantsiya. Sbornik Nauchnykh Rabot — Murm Olenevodcheskaya Opytn Stn Sb Nauchn Rab
Muromskii Gosudarstvennyi Pedagogiceskii Institut. Ucenye Zapiski — Muromsk Gos Ped Inst Ucen Zap
Muroran Kogyo Daigaku Kenkyu Hokoku — MKDKA
Murray River and Tributaries - Current Awareness Bulletin — MRATCAB
Murray Valley Annual — Murray VA
Murray's Magazine — Murray
Murray's Reports [*New South Wales*] — Mur
Murray's Reports [*New South Wales*] — Murr
Murrelet — MRLTAP
Murrelet — MURT
Musart — MUUJA
Muscle & Fitness — Mus & Fit
Muscle and Nerve. Supplement — Muscle Nerve Suppl
Muscle Biology — MSLBA
Muscle Biology — Muscle Biol
Muscular Development — Mus Dev
Muscular Dystrophy Abstracts — Muscular Dystrophy Abstr
Muse des Saitenspiels — MdS
Musee Belge — MB
Musee Belge — MusB
Musee Belge. Revue de Philologie Classique — Mus Belg
Musee Belge. Revue de Philologie Classique — Mus Belge
Musee Botanique de Leide — Mus Bot Leide
Musee de Rethelois et du Porcien — MRP
Musee Guimet. Annales. Bibliotheque de Vulgarisation — Mus Guimet Ann Bibl Vulg
Musee Guimet. Annales. Bibliotheque de Vulgarisation — Musee Guimet Annales Bibl de Vulg
Musee Guimet. Annales. Bibliotheque d'Etudes — Mus Guimet Ann Bibl Etudes
Musee Guimet. Annales. Bibliotheque d'Etudes — Musee Guimet Annales Bibl d'Etud
Musee Heude. Notes de Botanique Chinoise — Mus Heude Notes Bot Chin
Musee Imperial Ottoman [*Istanbul*] — MIO
Musee National de l'Homme. Centre Canadien d'Etudes sur la Culture Traditionnelle — Musee Nat Homme Centre Canad Et Culture Trad
Musee National de l'Homme. Publications d'Archeologie — Mus Nat Homme Public Archeol
Musee National de l'Homme. Publications d'Ethnologie — Mus Nat Homme Publ Ethnol
Musee Neuchatelois. Recueil d'Histoire Nationale et d'Archeologie — Musee Neuchat
Musee Neuchatelois. Recueil d'Histoire Nationale et d'Archeologie Neuchatel — M Neuchatel
Musee Royal de l'Afrique Centrale [*Tervuren, Belgique*]. Annales. Serie in Octavo. Sciences Zoologiques — MRAZBN
Musee Royal de l'Afrique Centrale. Departement de Geologie et de Mineralogie. Rapport Annuel — Mus Roy Afr Cent Dep Geol Mineral Rap Ann
Musee Royal de l'Afrique Centrale [*Tervuren, Belgique*]. Rapport Annuel. Departement de Geologie et de Mineralogie — MRGRAS
Musee Royal de l'Afrique Centrale. Tervuren. Belgique. Annales, Serie in 8. Sciences Geologiques — Mus R Afr Cent Tervuren Belg Ann Ser 8 Sci Geol
Musee Royal de l'Afrique Centrale (Tervuren, Belgique). Annales. Serie in Octavo. Sciences Geologiques — Mus R Afr Cent (Tervuren Belg) Ann Ser Octavo Sci Geol
Musee Royal de l'Afrique Centrale (Tervuren, Belgique). Annales. Serie in Octavo. Sciences Zoologiques — Mus R Afr Cent (Tervuren Belg) Ann Ser Octavo Sci Zool
Musee Royal de l'Afrique Centrale (Tervuren, Belgique). Documentation Zoologique — Mus R Afr Cent (Tervuren Belg) Do Zool
Musee Royal de l'Afrique Centrale (Tervuren, Belgique). Documentation Zoologique — Mus R Afr Cent (Tervuren Belg) Doc Zool
Musee Royal de l'Afrique Centrale (Tervuren, Belgique). Rapport Annuel du Departement de Geologie et de Mineralogie — Mus R Afr Centr (Tervuren Belg) Rapp Annu Dep Geol Mineral
Musee Royal d'Histoire Naturelle de Belgique. Bulletin — Mus R d'Hist Nat Belgique B
Musee Teyler. Archives — Mus Teyler Archiv
Museen in Koeln. Bulletin — Mus Koeln
Musees de France — BMF
Musees de France — MdF
Musees de France — MdFr
Musees de France — Mus Fr
Musees de Geneve — M Geneve
Musees de Geneve — Mus Geneve
Musees et Collections Archeologiques de l'Algerie et de la Tunisie — MCAT
Musees et Collections Archeologiques de l'Algerie et de la Tunisie — Mus et Coll Al Tun
Musees et Collections Archeologiques de l'Algerie et de la Tunisie — Mus et Coll Alg Tun
Musees Suisses — MusS
Musei e Gallerie d'Italia — MGI
Musei e Gallerie d'Italia — Mus Gal It
Museion. Revue d'Etudes Orientales — MREO
Musejni Zpravy Prazskeho Kraje — Mus Zpravy Prazskeho Kraje
Museo Canario — M Can
Museo Civico di Storia Naturale di Trieste. Atti — Mus Civ Stor Nat Trieste Atti
Museo Civico di Storia Naturale di Verona. Memorie. Fuori Serie — MMFSBQ

Museo Civico di Storia Naturale di Verona. Memorie. Fuori Serie — Mus Civ Stor Nat Verona Mem Fuori Ser
Museo Civico di Storia Naturale Giacomo Doria. Annali — Mus Civ Stor Nat Giacomo Doria Ann
Museo de Pontevedra — M Pont
Museo de Pontevedra — MP
Museo de Pontevedra — Mus Pontevedra
Museo del Hombre Dominicano — MHD
Museo di Antropologia ed Etnografia — Mus Antropol Etnogr
Museo di Storia Naturale della Venezia Tridentina. Studi Trentini di Scienze Naturali [*Italy*] — Mus Stor Nat Ven Tridentia Studi Trentini Sci Nat
Museo "Felipe Poey." Academia de Ciencias de Cuba. Trabajos de Divulgacion [*A publication*] — ACMTBW
Museo "Felipe Poey." Academia de Ciencias de Cuba. Trabajos de Divulgacion [*A publication*] — Mus Felipe Poey Acad Cienc Cuba Trab Divulg
Museo Historico (Quito) — Mus Hist Quito
Museo Italiano di Antichita Classica — Mus It
Museo Nacional de Historia Natural. Boletin [*Santiago*] — BMHNAZ
Museo Nacional de Historia Natural. Boletin (Santiago) — Mus Nac Hist Nat Bol (Santiago)
Museo Nacional de Historia Natural. Boletin (Santiago De Chile) — Mus Nac Hist Nat Bol (Santiago De Chile)
Museo Nacional de Historia Natural de Buenos Aires. Anales — Mus Nac Hist Natur Buenos Aires An
Museo Nacional de Historia Natural de Buenos Aires. Anales — Museo Nac de Hist Nat de Buenos Aires Anales
Museo Nacional de Historia Natural. Noticiario Mensual [*Santiago, Chile*] — MNNMBL
Museo Nacional de Historia Natural. Noticiario Mensual (Santiago) [*Chile*] — Mus Nac Hist Nat Not Mens (Santiago)
Museo Nacional de Historia Natural. Noticiario Mensual (Santiago) [*Chile*] — Mus Nac Hist Nat Notic Mens (Santiago)
Museo Nacional de Historia Natural. Publicacion Ocasional [*Santiago, Chile*] — POMNDR
Museo Nacional de Historia Natural (Santiago De Chile). Publicacion Ocasional — Mus Nac Hist Nat (Santiago De Chile) Publ Ocas
Museo Nacional de Mexico. Anales — Mus Nac Mex An
Museo Regionale di Scienze Naturali. Bollettino — BMRNEL
Museo Regionale di Scienze Naturali. Bollettino — Mus Reg Sci Nat Boll
Museo Tridentino di Scienze Naturali. Memorie — Mus Tridentino Sci Nat Mem
Museon. Revue d'Etudes Orientales — M
Museon. Revue d'Etudes Orientales — Mus
Museu Nacional. Publicacoes Avulsas — Mus Nac Pubs Avulas
Museu Paraense Emilio Goeldi. Boletim. Geologia — Mus Para Emilio Goeldi Bol Geol
Museu Paraense Emilio Goeldi. Publicacoes Avulsas — Mus Par E Goeldi Pub Avulsas
Museu Paraense Emilio Goeldi. Publicacoes Avulsas — Mus Para Emilio Goeldi Publ Avulsas
Museum. A Quarterly Review Published by UNESCO — Museum UNESCO
Museum Africum — Mus Afr
Museum Applied Science Center for Archaeology. Journal — MASCA Journal
Museum Applied Science Center for Archaeology. Pamphlet — MASCAP
Museum Applied Science Center for Archaeology. Report — MASCAR
Museum Applied Science Center for Archaeology Research Papers in Science and Archaelogy — Mus Appl Sci Cent Archaeol Res Pap Sci Archaeol
Museum Bulletin — Mus Bull
Museum Bulletin. New York State Museum — Mus Bull NY State Mus
Museum Bulletin. Staten Island Institute of Arts and Science — Mus Bull Staten Island Inst Arts
Museum Criticum — MCr
Museum Criticum — Mus Crit
Museum der Altertumswissenschaft — Mus Alt
Museum der Naturgeschichte Helvetiens — Mus Naturgesch Helv
Museum d'Histoire Naturelle de Lyon. Archives — Museum d'Hist Nat de Lyon Archives
Museum d'Histoire Naturelle de Lyon. Nouvelles Archives — Mus Hist Nat Lyon Nouv Arch
Museum d'Histoire Naturelle de Lyon. Nouvelles Archives. Supplement — Mus Hist Nat Lyon Nouv Arch Suppl
Museum d'Histoire Naturelle de Marseille. Bulletin — Mus Hist Nat Mars Bull
Museum d'Histoire Naturelle Grigore Antipa. Travaux — Mus Hist Nat Grigore Antipa Trav
Museum Francisceum Annales — MFA
Museum fuer Kulturgeschichte. Abhandlungen und Berichte fuer Naturkunde und Vorgeschichte — Mus Kulturgesch Abh Ber Naturk Vorgesch
Museum fuer Naturkunde und Heimatkunde zu Magdeburg. Abhandlungen und Berichte — Mus Natur Heimatk Magdeburg Abh Ber
Museum fuer Religionswissenschaft in Ihrem Ganzen Umfange — MRW
Museum fuer Topographische Vaterlandskunde des Oesterreichischen Kaiserstaates — Mus Topogr Vaterlandsk Oesterr Kaiserstaates
Museum Ha'aretz Bulletin [*Tel Aviv*] — MHB
Museum Ha'aretz Bulletin [*Tel Aviv*] — Mus Ha'aretz Bull
Museum Haaretz. Bulletin — Muz Haaretz Bull
Museum Ha'aretz [*Tel-Aviv*] **Yearbook** — Mus Haaretz
Museum Haganum Historico-Philologico-Theologicum — MHHPT
Museum Helveticum — MH
Museum Helveticum — Mus Helv
Museum Helveticum — Mus Helvet
Museum Helveticum. Revue Suisse pour l'Etude de l'Antiquite Classique — MH
Museum Historico-Philologico-Theologicum — MHPT
Museum Journal — MJ
Museum Journal — Museum J
Museum Journal. University Museum. University of Pennsylvania — JUMP
Museum Journal. University Museum. University of Pennsylvania — Ms J
Museum Lessianum — ML
Museum Lessianum. Section Historique — ML H
Museum Lessianum. Section Philosophique — ML P
Museum. Maanblad voor Philologie en Geschiedenis — MPh
Museum. Maanblad voor Philologie en Geschiedenis — Mus
Museum. Maandblad voor Philologie en Geschiedenis — M
Museum Memoir [*Salisbury*] — MUMED9
Museum Memoir (Salisbury) — Mus Mem (Salisbury)
Museum National d'Histoire Naturelle. Bulletin — Mus Natl Hist Nat Bull
Museum National d'Histoire Naturelle. Bulletin — Mus Natl Histoire Nat Bull
Museum National d'Histoire Naturelle. Bulletin du Laboratoire Maritime de Dinard — Mus Natl Hist Nat Bull Lab Marit Dinard
Museum National d'Histoire Naturelle. Bulletin. Section B. Botanique, Biologie et Ecologie Vegetales, Phytochimie — Mus Natl Hist Nat Bull Sect B Bot Biol Ecol Veg Phytochim
Museum National d'Histoire Naturelle. Memoires. Serie A. Zoologie (Paris) — Mus Natl Hist Nat Mem Ser A (Paris)
Museum National d'Histoire Naturelle. Memoires. Serie C (Paris) — Mus Natnl Hist Nat (Paris) Mem Ser C
Museum National d'Histoire Naturelle. Memoires. Serie C. Sciences de la Terre (Paris) — Mus Natl Hist Nat (Paris) Mem Ser C
Museum National d'Histoire Naturelle. Notulae Systematicae — Mus Natl Hist Nat Not Syst
Museum National d'Histoire Naturelle. Notulae Systematicae — NOSYAV
Museum National d'Histoire Naturelle. (Paris). Bulletin. — Mus Natl Hist Nat Paris Bull
Museum Nationale Hungaricum. Annales Historico-Naturales — Mus Natl Hung Ann Hist-Nat
Museum News — MN
Museum News — Mus N
Museum Notes. American Numismatic Society — MN
Museum Notes. American Numismatic Society — MNANS
Museum Notes. American Numismatic Society — Mus Not
Museum Notes. American Numismatic Society — Mus Not Am Num Soc
Museum Notes and News. Idaho State College — Mus Notes News Idaho State Coll
Museum of Applied Arts and Sciences. Sydney. Researches on Essential Oils of the Australian Flora — Mus Appl Arts Sci Sydney Res Essent Oils Aust Flora
Museum of Classical Antiquites — Mus Clas Ant
Museum of Comparative Zoology [*Harvard University*]. Annual Report — MCZAAZ
Museum of Comparative Zoology (Harvard University). Annual Report — Mus Comp Zool (Harv Univ) Annu Rep
Museum of Comparative Zoology [*Harvard University*]. Memoirs — Mus Comp Zool Mem
Museum of Fine Arts. Bulletin — Bull Mus Fi A
Museum of Foreign Literature [*Littell's*] — Mus
Museum of Northern Arizona and Research Center (Flagstaff). Annual Report — Mus North Ariz Res Cent (Flagstaff) Annu Rep
Museum of Northern Arizona. Bulletin — Mus North Ariz Bull
Museum of Paleontology. Papers on Paleontology — Mus Paleontol Pap Paleontol
Museum of Paleontology. Papers on Paleontology — PPUMD3
Museum Philologum Londiniense — MPhL
Museum Rusticum et Commerciale (London) — Mus Rusticum Commerciale London
Museum Rusticum et Commerciale oder Auserlesene Schriften, den Ackerbau, die Handlung, die Kuenste und Manufacturen Betreffend (Leipzig) — Mus Rusticum Commerciale Leipzig
Museum Studies — Museum Stud
Museum Studies. Art Institute of Chicago — Mus Stud
Museum Studies Journal — Mus Stud Jnl
Museum Tusculanum — MT
Museum Tusculanum [*Kobenhavn*] — Mus Tusc
Museum voor Midden-Afrika. Annalen. Reeks in Octavo. Geologische Wetenschappen — Mus Midden-Afr Ann Reeks in 8O Geol Wet
Museums Australia — Mus Australia
Museums Journal — Mus J
Museums Journal — Museums Jnl
Museumskunde — Museumskde
Mushroom Journal — Mushroom J
Mushroom Science — Mushroom Sci
Music Academy. Journal — Mus Academy Jl
Music America — Music Am
Music. American Guild of Organists — MAUOA
Music Analysis — Mus Analysis
Music and Artists — Mus & Artists
Music and Dance — Mus & Dance
Music and Letters — M & L
Music and Letters — ML
Music and Letters — MLetters
Music and Letters — MuL
Music and Letters — Mus and Let
Music and Letters — Mus & Lett
Music and Letters — Mus Lett
Music and Letters — Music Lett
Music and Letters — MusL
Music and Letters — PMUS
Music and Liturgy — Mus Lit
Music and Man — Music Man
Music and Musicians — MaM
Music and Musicians — MM
Music and Musicians — MUMUA
Music and Musicians — Mus & Mus

Music and the Teacher — Music Teach
Music Article Guide — Music Artic Guide
Music at Home — Mus at Home
Music at Yale — MaY
Music Clubs Magazine — MCM
Music Clubs Magazine — MUMEB
Music Clubs Magazine — Mus Clubs Mag
Music Dealer — Mus Dealer
Music Educators Journal — M Ed J
Music Educators Journal — M Educators J
Music Educators Journal — MEDJA
Music Educators Journal — MEJ
Music Educators Journal — MuEJ
Music Educators Journal — Mus Ed J
Music Educators Journal — Mus Educ J
Music Educators Journal — Music Ed Jnl
Music Educators Journal — Music Educ
Music Forum — M Forum
Music Forum — Mus Forum
Music in Britain — MB
Music in Education — Mus in Ed
Music in Education — Music in Ed
Music in Education — MUSKA
Music in Higher Education — Mus High Educ
Music in New Zealand — Mus New Zealand
Music Index — MuI
Music Index — Mus I
Music Index — Music Ind
Music Index — MusicI
Music Industry — Mus Industry
Music Industry Directory — Mus Ind Dir
Music Journal — MJ
Music Journal — MuJ
Music Journal — Mus J
Music Journal — Mus Jl
Music Journal — Music J
Music Library Association. Newsletter — MLAN
Music Library Association. Notes — MLAN
Music Library Association. Notes — Mus Lib Assn Notes
Music Library Association. Notes — Music Lib Assn Notes
Music Library Association. Notes — Music Libr Ass Notes
Music Magazine — MM
Music Magazine — Mus Mag
Music Maker — Mus Mak
Music Ministry — MUM
Music Ministry — Mus Min
Music News — Mus News
Music News from Prague — MNfP
Music News from Prague — Mus News Prague
Music Now — MUS
Music of the West Magazine — Mus West
Music Parade — Mus Parade
Music Perception — MPer
Music Perception — Mus Perc
Music Reference Services Quarterly — Mus Ref Serv
Music Research Forum — MRF
Music Review — MR
Music Review — Mus R
Music Review — Mus Rev
Music Review — Music R
Music Review — Music Rev
Music Review — PMUR
Music Scene — M Scene
Music Scene — Mus Scene
Music (Schools of Music Association) — Music (SMA)
Music Supervisors Journal — Mus Superv J
Music Survey — MS
Music Survey — Mus Survey
Music Teacher — MUTSA
Music Teacher and Piano Student — Mus Tcr
Music Teachers National Association. Proceedings — Mus Teach Nat Assn Proc
Music Theory Spectrum — MT
Music Theory Spectrum — Mus Theory Spectrum
Music Therapy — Mus Therapy
Music Therapy Perspectives — MTP
Music Today Newsletter — Mus Today Nl
Music Trade Review — Mus Trade Rev
Music Trades — MTr
Music Trades — Mus Trades
Music Trades — MUSHA
Music Trades — Music Trad
Music und Musicians — MuM
Music USA. Review of the Music Industry and Amateur Music Participation — Mus USA
Music Weekly Magazine [*British*] — MW
Musica — M
Musica — Mu
Musica Antiqua — MuA
Musica Disciplina — M Disciplina
Musica Disciplina — MD
Musica Disciplina — Mus Disc
Musica Disciplina — Music Disci
Musica Disciplina. Renaissance News — Mus Disc RN
Musica Divina — Mus Div
Musica d'Oggi — MO
Musica d'Oggi. Rassegna di Vita e di Cultura Musicale — Mus d'Oggi
Musica d'Oggi. Rassegna di Vita e di Cultura Musicale — Mus Oggi
Musica Jazz — Mus Jazz
Musica Judaica — MJ
Musica Judaica — MJudaica
Musica Judaica — Mus Judaica
Musica Medii Aevi — M Medii Aevi
Musica Minima — M Minima
Musica Sacra — M Sacra
Musica Sacra — MS
Musica Sacra [*Brugge*] — MS N
Musica Sacra [*Regensburg*] — MSD
Musica Sacra — Mus Sacra
Musica Sacro-Hispana — MSH
Musica Schallplatte — M Schallplatte
Musica Schallplatte. Zeitschrift fuer Schallplattenfreunde — Mus Schall
Musica Universita — Mus Univ
Musica Viva Billetin — MVB
Musica y Arte — MArte
Musicae Sacrae Ministerium — M Sacrae Ministerium
Musical America — GMUS
Musical America — MA
Musical America — Mus Am
Musical Analysis — Mus Anal
Musical Antiquary — MA
Musical Association Proceedings — Mus Assoc Proc
Musical Courier — Mus Cour
Musical Denmark — Mus Denmark
Musical Events — Mus Events
Musical Leader — Mus Leader
Musical Newsletter — MUN
Musical Newsletter — Mus News
Musical Observer — Mus Observer
Musical Opinion — M Opinion
Musical Opinion — MO
Musical Opinion — Mus Op
Musical Quarterly — MQ
Musical Quarterly — Mus Q
Musical Quarterly — Mus Qu
Musical Quarterly — Music Quart
Musical Quarterly — PMUQ
Musical Quarterly. New York — MQNY
Musical Times — M Times
Musical Times — MT
Musical Times — Mus T
Musical Times — Mus Times
Musical Times — Music Time
Musical Times and Singing-Class Circular — Musical Times
MusiCanada — MuC
Musicanada [*English Edition*] — Muscan
Musichandel — MH
Musici Scriptores Graeci — MSG
Musici Scriptores Graeci — Mus Gr
Musician — Mus
Musician, Player, and Listener — MPL
Musician, Player, and Listener — Mus P & L
Musicologica Slovaca — Mus Slovaca
Musicologica Slovaca — Musicol Slovaca
Musicology — M
Musicology — Musicol
Musik des Ostens — M Ostens
Musik fuer Alle — MfA
Musik in der Schule — M Sc
Musik in der Schule — Mus in Schule
Musik in Geschichte und Gegenwart — MGG
Musik International - Instrumentenbau-Zeitschrift — Mus Int
Musik. Monatsschrift — Mk
Musik und Altar — M Altar
Musik und Altar — Mus Al
Musik und Bildung — M Bildung
Musik und Bildung — MuB
Musik und Bildung — Mus u Bild
Musik und Forskning — M Forskning
Musik und Gesellschaft — M Ges
Musik und Gesellschaft — MuG
Musik und Gesellschaft — Mus u Ges
Musik und Gottesdienst — MGD
Musik und Gottesdienst — MGottesdienst
Musik und Gottesdienst — Mus u Gottesd
Musik und Kirche — M Kirche
Musik und Kirche — MuK
Musik und Kirche — Mus u Kir
Musikalische Jugend — MJugend
Musikalisches Wochenblatt — MWBl
Musikantengilde — MG
Musikblaetter des Anbruch — Musikbll Anbruch
Musikbuehne — Mbuehne
Musikerziehung — M Erz
Musikerziehung — ME
Musikerziehung — Mkg
Musikforschung — MF
Musikforschung — Musikforsch
Musikindustrie — MI
Musikinstrument — MuI
Musikkmagasinet Ballade — Musikk Mag Ballade

Musikpaedagogische Blaetter — MP Bl
Musikpsychologie — Mus Psych
Musikrevy — Mr
Musiktheorie — MTH
Musiktherapeutische Umschau — Mus Thera Um
Musiktherapie — Mtherapie
Musil Studien — Musil S
Musique en Jeu — M Jeu
Musique en Jeu — Mus Jeu
Musique en Pologne — MPologne
Musique et Liturgie — MeL
Musique et Liturgie — Mus et Lit
Musk-Ox — MUOX
Musk-Ox — MUOXD
Muslim Association for the Advancement of Science. Proceedings — Muslim Assoc Adv Sci Proc
Muslim Courier — Musl Cour
Muslim Digest — Musl Dig
Muslim News International — MNI
Muslim Review — MsR
Muslim Review — Musl R
Muslim Scientist — Muslim Sci
Muslim World — Muslim W
Muslim World — Muslim Wld
Muslim World — Muslim Wrld
Muslim World — MuslW
Muslim World — MW
Muslim World — PMUW
Muslim World (Karachi) — MWK
Muslim World Series — MWS
Muslims of the Soviet East — MSE
Muszaki Elet — Musz Elet
Muszaki Tervezes — MUTED
Muszaki Tudomany — Musz Tud
Muszerugyi es Merestechnikai Kozlemenyek [*Hungary*] — Muszerugyi Merestech Kozl
Mutagens and Their Toxicities — Mutagens Their Toxic
Mutagens and Toxicology (Tokyo) — Mutagens Toxicol (Tokyo)
Mutation Research — Mutat Res
Mutation Research. DNA Repair — Mutat Res DNA Repair
Mutation Research. DNA Repair Reports — Mutat Res DNA Repair Rep
Mutation Research. DNAging. Genetic Instability and Aging — Mutat Res DNAging Genet Instab
Mutation Research. Environmental Mutagenesis and Related Subjects Including Methodology — Mutat Res Environ Mutagen Relat
Mutation Research. Fundamental and Molecular Mechanisms of Mutagenesis — Mutat Res Fundam Mol Mech Mutagen
Mutation Research; Genetic Toxicology Testing — Mutat Res Genet Toxicol Test
Mutation Research. International Journal on Mutagenesis, Chromosome Breakage, and Related Subjects — Mutat Res Int J Mutagen Chromosome Breakage Relat Subj
Mutation Research Letters — MRL
Mutation Research. Reviews in Genetic Toxicology — Mutat Res Rev Genet Toxicol
Mutation Research. Section on Environmental Mutagenesis and Related Subjects — MUREAV
Mutation Research. Section on Environmental Mutagenesis and Related Subjects — Mutat Res Sect Environ Mutagen
Mutation Research Section on Environmental Mutagenesis and Related Subjects — Mutat Res Sect Environ Mutagen Relat Subj
Mutation Research. Section on Environmental Mutagenesis and Related Subjects — Mutat Res Sect Environ Mutagenesis Relat Subj
Mutech Chemical Engineering Journal — Mutech Chem Eng J
Mutisia. Acta Botanica Colombiana — Mutisia Acta Bot Colomb
Muttersprache — MS
Muttersprache — MSp
Muttersprache — Mut
Muttersprache. Zeitschrift zur Pflege und Erforschung der Deutschen Sprache — Mu
Mutual Funds Guide. Commerce Clearing House — Mut Funds Guide CCH
Muveszettorteneti Ertesito — Mueves Ertes
Muveszettorteneti Ertesito — Muevtort Ert
Muzei i Pametnizi na Kulturata — Muz Pam Kul
Muzei i Pametnizi na Kulturata — Muz Pam Kult
Muzej Istocne Bosne u Tuzli — MIBT
Muzejni a Vlastivedna Prace — Muz Vlastivedna Prace
Muzeon — Muz
Muzeul de Istorie al Municipiului Bucuresti — Muz Istor Munic Bucur
Muzeul de Stiintele Naturii Bacau Studii si Comunicari — Muz Stiint Naturii Bacau Stud Comun
Muzeul din Pitesti. Studii si Comunicari. Istorie-Stiintele Naturii — Muz Pitesti
Muzeul National — Muz Nat
Muzeum Archeologiczne. Krakow. Materialy Archeologiczne — Muz Arch Krakow Mat Arch
Muzeum es Konyvtari Ertesito — MK Ert
Muzeum es Konyvtari Ertesito — MKE
Muziek & Wetenschap — Muz & Wetenschap
Muzikal'naja Zizn — M Zizn
Muzikal'niy Sovremennik — M S
Muzikoloski Zbornik — Muzikol Zbornik
Muzikoloski Zbornik - Musicological Annual — Muz Zbornik
Muzikoloski Zbornik - Musicological Annual — MZ
Muzykal'naya Akademiya — Muz Akademiya
Muzykal'naya Fol'kloristika — Muz F
Muzzio Scienze — Muzzio Sci
MVC (Miljoevardscentrum) Report — MVC Rep
MVP [*Max-Von-Pettenkofer-Institut*] **Berichte** — MVP Ber
MVSA (Fertilizer Society of South Africa) Joernaal (Afrikanns) — MVSA J
MWRRC [*Montana Water Resources Research Center*] **Report** — MWRRC Rep
Myakkangaku — MIAKB
Myasnaya i Molochnaya Promyshlennost SSSR — Myasn Molochn Promst SSSR
Myasnaya Industriya SSSR — Myasn Ind SSSR
Myasnoe Khozyaistvo SSSR — Myasn Khoz SSSR
Mycenae Tablets — MT
Mycenaeae Graecitatis Lexicon — MG Lex
Mycenaeae Graecitatis Lexicon — MGL
Mycenaean Greek Vocabulary — MGV
Mycenaean Pottery — MP
Mycologia — Mycol
Mycologia Helvetica — Mycol Helv
Mycologia Helvetica — MYHEED
Mycologia Memoir — Mycol Mem
Mycological Abstracts — Mycol Abstr
Mycological Journal of Nagao Institute — Mycol J Nagao Inst
Mycological Papers. Commonwealth Mycological Institute — Mycol Pap Commonw Mycol Inst
Mycological Research — Mycol Res
Mycological Society of America. Year Book — Mycol Soc Amer Year Book
Mycologisches Zentralblatt — Mycol Zcntralbl
Mycology Series — Mycol Ser
Mycopathologia — Mycopatholo
Mycopathologia et Mycologia Applicata — Mycopath Mycol Appl
Mycopathologia et Mycologia Applicata — Mycopathol Mycol Appl
Mycopathologia et Mycologia Applicata. Supplementum — Mycopathol Mycol Appl Suppl
Mycopathologia et Mycologia Applicata. Supplementum Iconographia Mycologica — Mycopathol Mycol Appl Suppl Iconogr Mycol
Mykenische Vasen — MV
Mykologicky Sbornik — Mykol Sb
Mykologicky Zpravodaj — Mykol Zprav
Mykologische Untersuchungen — Mykol Untersuch
Mykologisches Zentralblatt — Mykol Zentbl
Mykrobiolchichniyi Zhurnal — Mykrobiol Zh
Myonj-Ji University. Journal of Natural Science — Myonj-Ji Univ J Nat Sci
Myotis Mitteilungsblatt fuer Fledermauskundler — Myotis Mitteilungsbl Fledermauskundler
Mysl Karaimska — MK
Mysore Agricultural Journal — Mysore Agr J
Mysore Agricultural Journal — Mysore Agric J
Mysore. Department of Mines and Geology. Bulletin — Mysore Dep Mines Geol Bull
Mysore. Department of Mines and Geology. Geological Studies — Mysore Dep Mines Geol Geol Stud
Mysore Economic Review — Mysore Econ R
Mysore Journal of Agricultural Sciences — MJASA
Mysore Journal of Agricultural Sciences — Mysore J Agric Sci
Mysore Orientalist — Mysore Or
Mysore University. Half Yearly Journal. Series A. Arts — HYJMUA
Mystere Chretien — My C
Mysterious Traveler Mystery Reader — MYT
Mysterium Salutis — My Sal
Mystery and Detection Annual — MDAC
[*The*] **Mystery Readers Newsletter** — TMNP
[*The*] **Mystery Readers Newsletter** — TMRN
Mythes et Religions — MR
Mythic Society. Quarterly Journal — MS
Mythographi Graeci — Myth Gr
Mythographi Graeci — Myth Graec
Mythologies in the Ancient World — MAW
Mythologische Bibliothek — Myth Bibl
Mythology of All Races — MAR
Mythos Papers — MythosP

N

Na Okika O Hawaii/Hawaii Orchid Journal — Na Okika O Hawaii Hawaii Orchid J
Na Stroikakh Rossii — Na Stroikakh Ross
NAACP [*National Association for the Advancement of Colored People*] **Newsletter** — NAACP Newsl
Naamkunde — Nku
Naamloze Vennootschap — NV
Naamloze Vennootschap — NVE
NAAS [*National Agricultural Advisory Service*] **Quarterly Review** [*England*] — NAAS Q Rev
NAAS [*National Agricultural Advisory Service*] **Quarterly Review** [*England*] — NAAS Quart Rev
Nabozenska Revue Cirkve Ceskoslovenske — NRCC
NABTE [*National Association for Business Teacher Education*] **Review** — NABTE Rev
NABW [*National Association of Bank Women*] **Journal** — NBW
NAC [*National Agriculture Chemicals Association*] **News and Pesticide Review** [*United States*] — NAC News Pestic Rev
NACA [*US National Advisory Committee for Aeronautics*] **Technical Memorandum** — NACA Tech Memo
NACA (US National Advisory Committee for Aeronautics) Reports — NACA Rep
Nach Gottes Wort Reformiert — NGWR
Nachbarn — Nachb
Nachricht von dem Fortgange der Naturforschenden Gesellschaft zu Jena — Nachr Fortgange Naturf Ges Jena
Nachrichten. Akademie der Wissenschaften der UdSSR — Nachr Akad Wiss UdSSR
Nachrichten. Akademie der Wissenschaften in Goettingen — Nachr Ak Goett
Nachrichten. Akademie der Wissenschaften zu Goettingen — Goett Nach
Nachrichten. Akademie der Wissenschaften zu Goettingen — Gott Nachr
Nachrichten. Akademie der Wissenschaften zu Goettingen — Nachr Akad Wiss Goettingen
Nachrichten. Akademie der Wissenschaften zu Goettingen — Nachr Ges Wiss Goett
Nachrichten. Akademie der Wissenschaften zu Goettingen — Nachr Goettingen
Nachrichten. Akademie der Wissenschaften zu Goettingen — NAG
Nachrichten. Akademie der Wissenschaften zu Goettingen — NAkG
Nachrichten. Akademie der Wissenschaften zu Goettingen — NAWGott
Nachrichten. Akademie der Wissenschaften zu Goettingen. II. Mathematisch-Physikalische Klasse — Nachr Akad Wiss Goettingen Math-Phys Kl II
Nachrichten. Akademie der Wissenschaften zu Goettingen. Philologisch-Historische Klasse — Nachr Akad Wiss Goett Philologisch-Hist Kl
Nachrichten. Akademie der Wissenschaften zu Goettingen. Philologisch-Historische Klasse — NAWG
Nachrichten aus Chemie, Technik, und Laboratorium [*Formerly, Nachrichten aus Chemie und Technik*] — Nachr Chem Tech Lab
Nachrichten aus Chemie, Technik, und Laboratorium — Nachr Chem Tech Laborat
Nachrichten aus Chemie und Technik [*Later, Nachrichten aus Chemie, Technik, und Laboratorium*] — Nachr Chem Tech
Nachrichten aus der Aerztlichen Mission — Nachr Aerztl Miss
Nachrichten aus der Ostafrikanischen Mission — NOAM
Nachrichten aus Niedersachsens Urgeschichte — Nachr Niedersachs Urgesch
Nachrichten aus Niedersachsens Urgeschichte — NNSU
Nachrichten der Akademie der Wissenschaften der UkrSSR — Nachr Akad Wiss UkrSSR
Nachrichten der Akademie der Wissenschaften in Goettingen. Philologisch-Historische Klasse — Nachr Akad Wiss Goettingen Philol Hist Klasse
Nachrichten der Arbeitsgemeinschaft fuer das Gesundheitswesen — Nachr Arb Gem Ges Wes
Nachrichten der Deutschen Gesellschaft fuer Natur- und Voelkerkunde Ostasiens — NDGNO
Nachrichten der Elektroindustrie — Nachr Elektroind
Nachrichten der Georg-August-Universitaet — NGAU
Nachrichten der Gesellschaft der Wissenschaften in Goettingen — NGWG
Nachrichten der Gesellschaft der Wissenschaften in Goettingen. Philologisch-Historische Klasse — NGWG PH
Nachrichten der Gesellschaft fuer Natur und Voelkerkunde Ostasiens — Nachr Ges N Vk Ostas
Nachrichten der Giessener Hochschulgesellschaft — Nachr Giessen
Nachrichten der Giessener Hochschulgesellschaft — Nachr Giessener Hochschulges
Nachrichten der Giessener Hochschulgesellschaft — NGH
Nachrichten der Koeniglichen Gesellschaft der Wissenschaften zu Goettingen [*A publication*] — Nachr Kgl Ges WG
Nachrichten der Koeniglichen Gesellschaft der Wissenschaften zu Goettingen — Nachrr Ges Wiss Goettg
Nachrichten der Koeniglichen Gesellschaft der Wissenschaften zu Goettingen [*A publication*] — NKGWG
Nachrichten der Luther-Akademie — NLA
Nachrichten der Lutherakademie in der DDR — NLADDR
Nachrichten der Telefonbau und Normalzeit — Nachr Telefonbau & Normalzeit
Nachrichten der Tropischen Medizin (Tiflis) — Nachr Trop Med (Tiflis)
Nachrichten des Reichsversicherungsamts — Nachr RVA
Nachrichten des Schweizerischen Burgenvereins — NSB
Nachrichten. Deutsche Geologische Gesellschaft — Nachr Dtsch Geol Ges
Nachrichten. Deutsche Gesellschaft fuer Islamkunde — NDGI
Nachrichten. Forschungszentrum Karlsruhe — Nachr Forschungszent Karlsruhe
Nachrichten fuer Aussenhandel — Aushandel
Nachrichten fuer Aussenhandel — NFA
Nachrichten fuer Dokumentation — N f D
Nachrichten fuer Dokumentation — Nachr Dok
Nachrichten fuer Dokumentation — Nachr Dokum
Nachrichten fuer Dokumentation — Nachr fuer Dok
Nachrichten fuer Dokumentation. Zeitschrift fuer Information und Dokumentation — NAN
Nachrichten fuer Wissenschaftliche Bibliotheken — NfWB
Nachrichten. Gesellschaft der Wissenschaften (Goettingen) — NGW (Goett)
Nachrichten. Gesellschaft der Wissenschaften zu Goettingen — Goett Nachr
Nachrichten. Gesellschaft der Wissenschaften zu Goettingen — NGG
Nachrichten. Gesellschaft der Wissenschaften zu Goettingen — NGGW
Nachrichten. Gesellschaft der Wissenschaften zu Goettingen — NGWGott
Nachrichten. Gesellschaft der Wissenschaften zu Goettingen. Mathematisch-Physikalische Klasse — Nachr Ges Wiss Goettingen Math Phys Kl
Nachrichten. Gesellschaft der Wissenschaften zu Goettingen. Mathematisch-Physikalische Klasse. Fachgruppe 1. Mathematik — Nachr Ges Wiss Goetting Math Phys Kl Fachgruppe 1
Nachrichten. Gesellschaft der Wissenschaften zu Goettingen. Mathematisch-Physikalische Klasse. Fachgruppe 2. Physik, Astronomie, Geophysik, Technik [*West Germany*] — Nachr Ges Wiss Goettingen Math-Phys Kl Fachgruppe 2
Nachrichten. Gesellschaft der Wissenschaften zu Goettingen. Mathematisch-Physikalische Klasse. Fachgruppe 2. Physik, Astronomie, Geophysik, Technik — NWGPA
Nachrichten. Gesellschaft der Wissenschaften zu Goettingen. Mathematisch-Physikalische Klasse. Fachgruppe 3. Chemie, Einschliesslich Physikalische Chemie — Nachr Ges Wiss Goettingen Math Phys Kl Fachgruppe 3
Nachrichten. Gesellschaft der Wissenschaften zu Goettingen. Mathematisch-Physikalische Klasse. Fachgruppe 4. Geologie und Mineralogie — Nachr Ges Wiss Goettingen Math Phys Kl Fachgruppe 4
Nachrichten. Gesellschaft der Wissenschaften zu Goettingen. Mathematisch-Physikalische Klasse. Fachgruppe 6. Biologie — Nachr Ges Wiss Goettingen Math Phys Kl Fachgruppe 6
Nachrichten. Gesellschaft der Wissenschaften zu Goettingen. Philologisch-Historische Klasse — NGWG
Nachrichten. Gesellschaft fuer Natur- und Voelkerkunde Ostasiens — NGNVO
Nachrichten Mensch-Umwelt — Nachr Mensch Umwelt
Nachrichten Metallindustrie — Nachr Metallind
Nachrichten. Naturwissenschaftliches Museum der Stadt (Aschaffenburg) — Nachr Naturw Mus (Aschaffenb)
Nachrichten. Naturwissenschaftliches Museum der Stadt (Aschaffenburg) — Nachr Naturwiss Mus Stadt (Aschaffenburg)
Nachrichten/Nouvelles/Notizie — Nachr/Nouv/Notiz
Nachrichten Transportrationalisierung — NTR
Nachrichten ueber Venerologie und Dermatologie (Moscow) — Nachr Venerol Dermatol Moscow
Nachrichten. Vereinigung Schweizerischer Bibliothekare — Nachr Verein Schweizer Bibl
Nachrichten von den Neuesten Theologischen Buechern und Schriften — NNTB
Nachrichten von der Gesellschaft der Wissenschaften zu Goettingen. Geschaeftliche Mitteilungen — Nachr Ges Wiss Goettingen Geschaeftliche Mitt
Nachrichten von der Gesellschaft der Wissenschaften zu Goettingen. Jahresbericht — Nachr Ges Wiss Goettingen Jahresber
Nachrichten von der Koeniglichen Gesellschaft der Wissenschaften zu Goettingen. Geschaeftliche Mitteilungen — Nachr Koenigl Ges Wiss Goettingen Geschaeftl Mitt

Nachrichten von der Koeniglichen Gesellschaft der Wissenschaften zu Goettingen. Mathematisch-Physikalische Klasse — Nachr K Ges Wiss Goettingen Math Phys Kl
Nachrichten von der Koeniglichen Gesellschaft der Wissenschaften zu Goettingen. Mathematisch-Physikalische Klasse — Nachr Koenigl Ges Wiss Goettingen Math Phys Kl
Nachrichten von Gelehrten Sachen. Herausgegeben von der Akademie zu Erfurt — Nachr Gel Sachen
Nachrichtenblatt — Nachrbl
Nachrichtenblatt der Bayerischen Entomologen — Nachr Bl Bay Ent
Nachrichtenblatt der Bayerischen Entomologen — NachrBl Bayer Ent
Nachrichtenblatt der Deutschen Gesellschaft fuer Geschichte der Medizin, Naturwissenschaft und Technik — Nachrichtenbl Deutsch Ges Gesch Med
Nachrichtenblatt der Deutschen Kakteengesellschaft — Nachrichtenbl Deutsch Kakteenges
Nachrichtenblatt des Deutschen Pflanzenschutzdienstes (Braunschweig) — Nachrichtenbl Dtsch Pflanzenschutzdienst (Braunschw)
Nachrichtenblatt. Deutsche Gesellschaft fuer Geschichte der Medizin. Naturwissenschaft und Technik — Nachrichtenbl Dtsch Ges Gesch Med Naturwiss Tech
Nachrichtenblatt. Deutschen Pflanzenschutzdienst (Berlin) — NachrBl Dt PflSchutzdienst (Berlin)
Nachrichtenblatt. Deutschen Pflanzenschutzdienst (Berlin) — Nachrbl Dtsch Pflschdienst (Berlin)
Nachrichtenblatt. Deutschen Pflanzenschutzdienst (Berlin) — Nachrichtenbl Dtsch Pflanzenschutzdienst (Berlin)
Nachrichtenblatt. Deutschen Pflanzenschutzdienst (Braunschweig) — Nachrbl Dtsch Pflschdienst (Braunschweig)
Nachrichtenblatt. Deutschen Pflanzenschutzdienst (Braunschweig) — Nachrichtenbl Dtsch Pflanzenschutzdienstes (Braunschweig)
Nachrichtenblatt. Deutschen Pflanzenschutzdienst (Stuttgart) — Nachrbl Dt Pflschutzdienst (Stuttg)
Nachrichtenblatt. Deutschen Pflanzenschutzdienst (Stuttgart) — NachrBl Dt PflSchutzdienst (Stuttgart)
Nachrichtenblatt. Deutschen Pflanzenschutzdienst (Stuttgart) — Nachrichtenbl Deut Pflanzenschutzdienst (Stuttgarl)
Nachrichtenblatt. Deutscher Pflanzenschutzdienst (Berlin) — Nachrbl Dt Pflschutzdienst (Berl)
Nachrichtenblatt. Deutscher Pflanzenschutzdienst (Berlin) — Nachrichtenbl Deut Pflanzenschutzdienst (Berlin)
Nachrichtenblatt. Deutscher Verein vom Heiligen Lande — NB
Nachrichtenblatt fuer das Goldschmiede-, Juwelier-, und Graveur-Handwerk — Nachrichtenbl Goldschmiede Juwelier Graveur Handwerk
Nachrichtenblatt fuer das Optiker-Handwerk — Nachrichtenbl Opt Handwerk
Nachrichtenblatt fuer das Photographen Handwerk — Nachrichtenbl Photogr Handwerk
Nachrichtenblatt fuer das Schleswig-Holsteinische Schulwesen — N Bl Sch H Sch W
Nachrichtenblatt fuer den Pflanzenschutzdienst in der DDR — NachrBl PflSchutzdienst DDR
Nachrichtenblatt fuer den Pflanzenschutzdienst in der DDR — Nachrichtenbl Pflanzenschutz DDR
Nachrichtenblatt fuer den Pflanzenschutzdienst in der DDR — Nachrichtenbl Pflanzenschutzdienst DDR
Nachrichtenblatt fuer Deutsche Vorzeit — NdtV
Nachrichtenblatt fuer Deutsche Vorzeit — NfDV
Nachrichtenblatt fuer Deutsche Vorzeit (Giessen) — Nachr (Giessen)
Nachrichtendienst der Pressestelle der Evangelischen Kirche der Rheinprovinz — NPEKR
Nachrichtendienst des Deutschen Vereins fuer Oeffentliche und Private Fuersorge — Nachrrdienst Dt Ver Oefftl Fuers
Nachrichtendienst. Deutscher Verein fuer Oeffentliche und Private Fuersorge [*A publication*] — NDV
Nachrichten-Elektronik — Nachr Elektron
Nachrichten-Elektronik und Telematik — Nach Elktr
Nachrichten-Elektronik und Telematik — Nachr Elektron and Telematik
Nachrichtentechnik-Elektronik — Nach Elek
Nachrichtentechnik-Elektronik — Nachrichtentech Elektronik
Nachrichtentechnik-Elektronik — Nachrichtentech-Elektron
Nachrichtentechnik-Elektronik — NTELA
Nachrichtentechnische Fachberichte [*Germany*] — Nachrichtentech Fachber
Nachrichtentechnische Fachberichte. Beihefte der Nachrichtentechnische Zeitschrift — Nachrichtentech Fachber Beih NTZ
Nachrichtentechnische Gesellschaft. Fachberichte — Nachrichtentech Ges Fachber
Nachrichtentechnische Zeitschrift — Nach Zeit
Nachrichtentechnische Zeitschrift — Nachr Z
Nachrichtentechnische Zeitschrift — Nachrtech Z
Nachrichtentechnische Zeitschrift — NTZ
Nachrichtentechnische Zeitung — Nachrichtentech Z
Nacion — Nac
Nacional (Caracas) — NacC
Nacional (Venezuela) — NLV
NACLA (North American Congress of Latin America) Report on the Americas — NACLA
NACLA's [*North American Congress on Latin America*] **Latin America and Empire Report** — Latin Am and Empire Rept
NACTA Journal. National Association of Colleges and Teachers of Agriculture — NACTA J Natl Assoc Coll Teach Agric
NACWPI [*National Association of College Wind and Percussion Instructors*] **Journal** — NACWPI
Nada — N
NADA. Native Affairs Department Annual. Rhodesia Ministry of Internal Affairs — Native Affairs Dep A
Nadeznost i Kontrol'kacestva — Nadezn i Kontrol'kacestva
NADL [*National Association of Dental Laboratories*] **Journal** — NADL J
Naehrung. Chemie, Biochemie, Mikrobiologie, Technologie — Naehr
Naeringsforskning. Supplement — Naeringsforskning Suppl
Nagasaki Daigaku Suisan-Gakubu Kenkyu Hokoku — NADKA
Nagasaki Igakkai Zasshi — Nag Ig Zass
Nagasaki Igakkai Zasshi — NAGZA
Nagasaki Igakkai Zasshi. Supplement [*Japan*] — Nagasaki Igakkai Zasshi Suppl
Nagasaki Medical Journal — Nagasaki Med J
Nagoya Daigaku Bungakubu Kenkyu Ronshu [*Journal of the Faculty of Literature. Nagoya University*] — NagoKR
Nagoya Daigaku Kankyo Igaku Kenkyusho Nenpo — NDKIA
Nagoya Gakuin University Review. Humanities. Natural Science — Nagoya Gakuin Univ Rev Humanit Nat Sci
Nagoya Igaku — NAIGA
Nagoya Journal of Medical Science — Nag J Med Sci
Nagoya Journal of Medical Science — Nagoya J Med Sci
Nagoya Kogyo Daigaku Gakuho — NADGA
Nagoya Mathematical Journal — Nag Math J
Nagoya Mathematical Journal — Nagoya Math J
Nagoya Medical Journal — Nagoya Med J
Nagoya Shiritsu Daigaku Yakugakubu Kenkyu Nempo — NSDYA
Nagoya University. Department of Earth Sciences. Collected Papers on Earth Sciences — Nagoya Univ Dep Earth Sci Collect Pap Earth Sci
Nagoya University. Institute of Plasma Physics. Annual Review — Nagoya Univ Inst Plasma Phys Annu Rev
Nagoya University. Institute of Plasma Physics. Report IPPJ-AM — Nagoya Univ Inst Plasma Phys Rep IPPJ AM
Nagoya University. Journal of Earth Sciences — Nagoya Univ Jour Earth Sci
Nagpur Agricultural College. Magazine — Nagpur Agric Coll Mag
Nagpur College of Agriculture Magazine — Nagpur Coll Agric Mag
Nagpur University. Journal — Nagpur Univ J
Nagpur University. Journal — NAUJA
Nagpur University Journal — NUJ
Nagra Bulletin — Nagra Bull
Nagra Informiert — Nagra Inf
Nahost und Mittelostverein eV. Rundschreiben — NMD
Nahrung und Ernaehrung — Nahr Ernaehr
Nahrungsmittel-Industrie — Nahrungsm Ind
NAIG [*Nippon Atomic Industry Group*] **Annual Review** — NAIG AR
Naika Hokan — Naika Hok
Naikai-Ku Suisan Kenkyusho Kenkyu Hokoku — NKSHB
Nainen Kikan — NNKKB
Nairobi Journal of Medicine — Nairobi J Med
Names — NA
Names in South Carolina — NSC
Namibia News — Namibia N
Namm och Bygd — NB
Namm och Bygd — NoB
Namn och Bygd — NoB
Namn og Bygd — NB
Nankai Lectures on Mathematical Physics — Nankai Lectures Math Phys
Nankai Series in Pure, Applied Mathematics and Theoretical Physics — Nankai Ser Pure Appl Math Theoret Phys
Nankai Social and Economic Quarterly — NSEQ
Nankai University. Research Laboratory of Applied Chemistry. Reports — Nankai Univ Res Lab Appl Chem Rep
Nankyoku Shiryo [*Antarctic Record*] [*Japan*] — NSHIA
Nanostructured Materials — Nanostruct Mater
Nansei Regional Fisheries Research Laboratory. Bulletin [*Japan*] — Nansei Reg Fish Res Lab Bull
Nanta Mathematica — Nanta Math
Nanyang Quarterly — Nanyang Q
Nanyang University. Journal. Part III. Natural Sciences — Nanyang Univ J Part III
NAPEHE [*National Association for Physical Education in Higher Education*] **Proceedings** — NAPEHE Proc
Naples. Stazione Zoologica. Pubblicazioni — Naples Sta Zool Pubbl
Napoli Nobilissima — Nap Nobil
Napravlennyi Sintez Tverdykh Veshchestv — Napravlennyi Sint Tverd Veshchestv
Napredno Pcelarstvo — Napred Pcel
NAPT [*National Association of Physical Therapists*] **Journal** — NAPT J
Nara Gakugei Daigaku Kiyo — NAGDA
Nara Kogyo Koto Senmon Gakko Kenkyu Kiyo — NKKOB
NARAS [*National Academy of Recording Arts and Sciences*] **Institute Journal** — NARAS Inst Jnl
Narisi z Istorii Prirodoznavstva i Tekhniki [*Former USSR*] — Narisi Istor Prirodozn Tekh
Narisi z Istorii Prirodoznavstva i Tekhniki — Narisi Istor Prirodoznav i Tekhn
Narisi z Istorii Tekhniki i Prirodoznavstva — Narisi Istor Tekh Prirodozn
Narodna Kultura [*Sofia*] — NK
Narodna Tvorcist' ta Etnografija — Nar Tvor ta Etnogr
Narodna Tvorcist' ta Etnografija — NTE
Narodna Umjetnost — NUm
Narodni Muzeum. Casopis. Oddil Prirodovedny (Prague) — Nar Muz (Prague) Cas Oddil Prirodoved
Narodni Sumar — Nar Sumar
Narodno Stvaralastvo. Folklor — NStv
Narodno Zdravlje — Nar Zdrav
Narodno Zdravlje [*Yugoslavia*] — Nar Zdravlje
Narodnoe Khozyaistvo Sovetskoi Latvii — Nar Khoz Sov Latv
Narodnoe Khozyaistvo Uzbekistana — Nar Khoz Uzb
Narodnoe Khozyaistvo Uzbekistana — Narod Khoz Uzbek
Narodnoe Obrazovanie [*Moscow*] — NO
Narodnyj Komissariat Elektrostancij i Elektropromyslennosti — NKEP

Narodopisne Aktuality — NAk
Narodopisny Sbornik Ceskoslovansky (Prag) — Prag Narodop Sborn Ceskoslov
Narodopisny Vestnik Ceskoslovensky — NVC
Narody Azii i Afriki — NAA
Narody Azii i Afriki [*Moskva*] — Nar Azii i Afriki
Narody Azii i Afriki — Narod Azii Afriki
Narody Azii i Afriki [*Moscow*] — Narody AA
Narody Azii i Afriki — Narody Azii Afr
Naropa Magazine — Naropa Mag
Narragansett Historical Register — Narrag Hist Reg
Narragansett Historical Register — Narrag Reg
Narragansett Marine Laboratory. Collected Reprints. Graduate School of Oceanography. University of Rhode Island — Narragansett Mar Lab Collect Repr
Narrative Accomplishment Reporting System [*Database*] — NARS
Nas Jezik — NJ
Nas Jezik — NJe
Nas Sovremennik — N Sov
NASA [*National Aeronautics and Space Administration*] **Conference Publication** [*A publication*] — NASA Conf Publ
NASA [*National Aeronautics and Space Administration*] **Contractor Report** — NASA Contract Rep
NASA [*National Aeronautics and Space Administration*] **Contractor Report. CR** — NSCRA
NASA [*National Aeronautics and Space Administration*] **Directory of Numerical D atabases** — DND
NASA [*National Aeronautics and Space Administration*] **Memorandum** — NASA Memo
Nasa Rec [*Paris*] — NaR
NASA [*National Aeronautics and Space Administration*] **Reference Publication** — NASA Ref Publ
NASA [*National Aeronautics and Space Administration*] **Report to Educators** — NASA Rep Ed
NASA [*National Aeronautics and Space Administration*] **Republication** — NASA Republ
NASA [*National Aeronautics and Space Administration*] **Research and Technology Objectives and Plans Summary** [*Database*] — RTOPS
NASA [*US National Aeronautics and Space Administration*] **Special Publication SP** — NASA Spec Publ SP
NASA [*National Aeronautics and Space Administration*] **Special Publications** — NASA Spec Publ
NASA [*National Aeronautics and Space Administration*] **Special Publications** — NSSPA
NASA [*National Aeronautics and Space Administration*] **Technical Briefs** — NASA Tech Brief
NASA [*National Aeronautics and Space Administration*] **Technical Briefs** — NASA Tech Briefs
NASA [*National Aeronautics and Space Administration*] **Technical Memorandum** — NASA Tech Memo
NASA [*National Aeronautics and Space Administration*] **Technical Memorandum** — NATMA
NASA [*National Aeronautics and Space Administration*] **Technical Note** — NASA Tech Note
NASA [*National Aeronautics and Space Administration*] **Technical Note** — NASCA
NASA [*National Aeronautics and Space Administration*] **Technical Paper** — NASA Tech Pap
NASA [*National Aeronautics and Space Administration*] **Technical Report** — NASA Tech Rep
NASA [*National Aeronautics and Space Administration*] **Technical Translation** — NASA Tech Transl
NASA (US National Aeronautics and Space Administration) Technical Publications Announcements — NASA Tech Publ Announce
Nasa Zena — NZ
NASD [*National Association of Securities Dealers*] **Newsletter** — NASD Newsl
Nase Rec [*Prague*] — NR
Nase Veda — NV
Nashriyye(H)-Ye Daneshkade(H)-Ye Adabiyyat va Olum-E Ensani-Ye Tabriz — NDAT
Nashville Journal of Medicine and Surgery — Nashville J Med Surg
Nashville Monthly Record of Medical and Physical Science — Nashville Monthly Rec Med Phys Sci
Nasionale Instituut vir Metallurgie. Republiek van Suid-Afrika. Verslag — Nas Inst Metall Repub S Afr Versl
Nasionale Museum Bloemfontein Jaarverslag — Nas Mus Bloemfontein Jaarversl
Nasionale Versnellersentrum Nuus — Nas Versnellersentrum Nuus
Nasionale Versnellersentrum Nuus — NVS Nuus
NASPA [*National Association of Student Personnel Administrators*] **Journal** — NASPA J
NASPSPA [*North American Society for Psychology of Sport and Physical Activity*] **Newsletter** — NASPSPA Newsl
Nassau County Medical Center Proceedings — Nassau Cty Med Cent Proc
Nassau Lawyer — Nassau L
Nassau Review — NaRev
Nassau Review — NR
Nassauische Annalen — NAN
Nassauische Annalen — Nass Ann
Nassauische Annalen — Nassau Ann
Nassauische Annalen. Verein fuer Nassauische Altertumskunde und Geschictsforschung — NA
Nassauische Heimatblaetter — Nass Heim
Nassauische Heimatblaetter — NHBl
Nassauischer Verein fuer Naturkunde. Jahrbuecher — Nassauischer Ver Naturk Jb
NASSP [*National Association Secondary School Principals*] **Bulletin** — INSP
NASSP [*National Association of Secondary School Principals*] **Bulletin** — NASSP Bull
Nastava Jezika i Knjizevnosti u Srednoj Skoli — NJK
Nastavni Vjesnik — NV
NASW [*National Association of Social Workers*] **News** — NASW N
Nasza Ksiegarnia — NK
Nasza Przeszlosc — NP
Nasza Przeszlose — Nas Prz
Natal Institute of Engineers. Journal — Natal Inst Eng J
Natal Museum. Annals — Natal Mus Ann
Natal University. Law Review — Nat UL Rev
Natal University. Law Review — Natal UL Rev
Natal University. Law Review — Natal Univ Law Rev
Natal University Science — Natal Univ Sci
Nathaniel Hawthorne Journal — NHJ
Nation — GTNA
Nation — N
Nation — Na
Nation — Nat
Nation and Athenaeum — N & A
Nation and Athenaeum — NA
Nation and Athenaeum — Nation and Ath
Nation and Athenaeum — Nation Athen
Nation and Athenaeum (London) — Nation (Lond)
Nation Economic Survey [*Kenya*] — Nat Econ Surv
Nation Review — Nat R
Nation Review — Nat Rev
Nation Review — Nation Rev
Nation Review — NR
Nation und Staat — Nation U Staat
Nationaal Instituut voor de Steenkolennijverheid. Bulletin Technique. Houille et Derives — Natl Inst Steenkolennijverheid Bull Tech Houille Deriv
Nationaal Lucht- en Ruimtevaartlaboratorium. Rapport — Natl Lucht Ruimtevaartlab Rapp
Nationaal Lucht- en Ruimtevaartlaboratorium. Verslagen en Verhandelingen — Nat Lucht-Ruimtevaartlab Verslagen en Verhandel
Nationaal Lucht- en Ruimtevaartlaboratorium. Verslagen en Verhandelingen — Natl Lucht Ruimtevaartlab Versl Verh
National Academy of Medical Sciences (India). Annals — Natl Acad Med Sci (India) Ann
National Academy of Science and Letters [*India*] — Natl Acad Sci Lett
National Academy of Science and Technology. Republic of the Philippines. Transactions — Natl Acad Sci Technol Repub Philipp Trans
National Academy of Science Letters — Nat Acad Sci Lett
National Academy of Science. Letters (India) — Natl Acad Sci Lett (India)
National Academy of Sciences. Advisory Center on Toxicology. Report NAS/ACT (United States) — Natl Acad Sci Advis Cent Toxicol Rep NAS ACT US
National Academy of Sciences. Biographical Memoirs — Nat Acad Sci Biog Mem
National Academy of Sciences. Biographical Memoirs. Proceedings — Natl Acad Sci Biog Mem Proc
National Academy of Sciences. Committee on Polar Research. Report of United States Antarctic Research Activities. Report to SCAR [*Scientific Committee on Antarctic Research*] — Natl Acad Sci Comm Polar Res Rep US Antarc Res Act Rep SCAR
National Academy of Sciences (India). Annual Number — Natl Acad Sci (India) Annu Number
National Academy of Sciences - National Research Council. Division of Chemistry and Chemical Technology. Annual Report — NAS-NRC D Chem Chem Technol Annu Rep
National Academy of Sciences - National Research Council. Division of Chemistry and Chemical Technology. Annual Report — NAS-NRC Div Chem Chem Technol Annu Rep
National Academy of Sciences - National Research Council. Nuclear Sciences Series. Report — NAS-NRC Nucl Sci Ser Rep
National Academy of Sciences - National Research Council. Publication — NAS-NRC Publ
National Academy of Sciences - National Research Council. Publication [*United States*] — NASRA
National Academy of Sciences - National Research Council. Publication — Nat Acad Sci Nat Res Counc Publ
National Academy of Sciences - National Research Council. Publication — Natl Acad Sci Natl Research Council Pub
National Academy of Sciences of the United States of America. Biographical Memoirs — Natl Acad Sci USA Biogr Mem
National Academy of Sciences. Proceedings — Nat Acad Sci Proc
National Academy of Sciences. Proceedings — Natl Acad Sci Proc
National Academy of Sciences. Publication — Natl Acad Sci Pub
National Accelator Centre. News [*South Africa*] — Natl Accel Cent News
National Advisory Committee for Aeronautics. Annual Report — Natl Advis Comm Aeronaut Annu Rep
National Advisory Committee for Aeronautics. Reports — Natl Advis Comm Aeronaut Rep
National Advisory Committee for Aeronautics. Technical Memorandum — Natl Advis Comm Aeronaut Tech Memo
National Advisory Committee for Aeronautics. Technical Notes — Natl Advis Comm Aeronaut Tech Notes
National Advisory Committee for Aeronautics. Technical Report — Natl Advis Comm Aeronaut Tech Rep
National Advisory Committee on Research in the Geological Sciences — Natl Advisory Comm Research Geol Sci
National Aeronautical Establishment. Mechanical Engineering Report MS (Canada) — Natl Aeronaut Establ Mech Eng Rep MS (Can)
National Aeronautics and Space Administration — Natl Aeronaut Space Adm

National Aerospace Electronics Conference. Proceedings [*United States*] — Natl Aerosp Electron Conf Proc
National Aerospace Laboratory. Miscellaneous Publication NLR MP (Netherlands) — Natl Aerosp Lab Misc Publ NLR MP (Neth)
National Aerospace Laboratory. Netherlands. Report NLR TR — Natl Aerosp Lab Neth Rep NLR TR
National Agricultural Advisory Service. Advisory Papers [*England*] — NAAS Advis Pap
National Agricultural Advisory Service. Progress Report [*England*] — NAAS Prog Rep
National Agricultural Economic Research Inventory — NAERI
National Agricultural Society of Ceylon. Journal — Natl Agric Soc Ceylon J
National Air and Space Museum. Research Report — Nat Air Space Mus Res Rep
National Air Pollution Control Administration (United States). Publication. AP Series — Natl Air Pollut Control Adm (US) Publ AP Ser
National Air Pollution Control Administration (United States). Publication. APTD [*Air Pollution Technical Data*] **Series** — Natl Air Pollut Control Adm (US) Publ APTD Ser
National Air Pollution Symposium. Proceedings — Natl Air Pollut Symp Proc
National and American Miller — Natl Am Miller
National and English Review — NER
National and Provincial Parks Association. Newsletter — NPPA
National Art Education Association. Research Monograph — Nat Art Educ Assn Res Monogr
National Art Education Association. Yearbook — Nat Art Ed Assn Yrbk
National Arthritis News — Nat Arthritis N
National Assessment of Educational Progress [*Database*] — NAEP
National Association for the Prevention and Study of Tuberculosis. Bulletin — Nat Assn Prev Study Tuberc Bul
National Association for Women Deans, Administrators, and Counselors. Journal — NAWDAC Journal
National Association of Accountants. Bulletin — NAA Bul
National Association of College Wind and Percussion Instructors. Journal — NAC
National Association of Corrosion Engineers. Conference — Natl Assoc Corros Eng Conf
National Association of Corrosion Engineers. International Corrosion Conference Series — Natl Assoc Corros Eng Int Corros Conf Ser
National Association of Corrosion Engineers International Symposium — Natl Assoc Corros Eng Int Symp
National Association of Deans of Women. Journal — Nat Assn Deans Women J
National Association of Educational Broadcasters. Journal — NAEBJ
National Association of Historians of Islamic Art. Newsletter — NAHIA News
National Association of Inspectors and Educational Advisers. Journal — Nat Assoc of Inspectors and Ednl Advisers J
National Association of Language Laboratory Directors. Journal — NALLDJ
National Association of Margarine Manufacturers. Bulletin — Natl Assoc Margarine Manuf Bull
National Association of Referees in Bankruptcy. Journal — Ref J
National Association of Schools of Music. Proceedings — NASM
National Association of Secondary-School Principals. Bulletin — NASSP-B
National Association of Secondary-School Principals. Bulletin — Nat Assn Sec-Sch Prin Bul
National Association of Secondary-School Principals. Bulletin — Natl Assn Sec-Schl Princ
National Association of State Universities. Transactions and Proceedings — Nat Assn State Univs Trans & Proc
National Association of Student Councils. Yearbook — Nat Assn Stud Council Yrbk
National Association of Teachers of Singing. Bulletin — NAT
National Association of Teachers of Singing. Bulletin — NATS
National Association of Teachers of Singing. Bulletin — NATS Bull
National Association of Teachers of Singing. Journal — NATSJ
National Astronomical Bulletin [*Japan*] — Nat Astron Bull
National Automated Accounting Research System [*Database*] — NARS
National Bank. Monthly Summary [*Melbourne*] — NBA
National Bank Monthly Summary [*Australia*] — NBS
National Bank. Monthly Summary (Australia) — Nat Bk (Aus)
National Bank of Australasia. Monthly Summary of Australian Conditions — Nat Bank Austsia M Summ
National Bank of Belgium. Report — Nat B Belg
National Bank of Egypt. Economic Bulletin — Nat Bank Egypt Econ Bul
National Bank of Egypt. Economic Bulletin — NBE
National Bank of Ethiopia. Quarterly Bulletin. New Series — MRX
National Bank of Ethiopia. Quarterly Bulletin. New Series — Nat Bank Ethiopia Q Bul ns
National Bank of Greece. Bulletin — Greece Bk
National Bank of Pakistan. Monthly Economic Letter — NRD
National Bank of Yugoslavia. Quarterly Bulletin — Nat Bank Yugoslavia Q Bul
National Bank of Yugoslavia. Quarterly Bulletin — QUF
National Banking Review — Nat Banking R
National Bar Bulletin — Nat Bar Bull
National Bar Examination Digest — Nat Bar Exam Dig
National Bee Keepers Digest — Nat Bee Krs Dig
National Bibliography of Indian Literature — NBIL
National Biomedical Sciences Instrumentation Symposium. Proceedings — Natl Biomed Sci Instrum Symp Proc
National Bituminous Concrete Association. Quality Improvement Program. Publication — Natl Bitum Concr Assoc Qual Improv Program Publ
National Bituminous Concrete Association. Quality Improvement Program. Publication QIP — Natl Bitum Concr Assoc Qual Improv Program Publ QIP
National Black Law Journal — INBL
National Black Nurses Association. Newsletter — NBNA Newsl
National Board Examiner [*United States*] — Natl Board Examiner
National Board of Fire Underwriters. Research Report — Natl Board Fire Underwrit Res Rep
National Board of Fire Underwriters. Technical Survey — Natl Board Fire Underwrit Tech Surv
National Botanic Gardens (Lucknow). Annual Report — Natl Bot Gard (Lucknow) Annu Rep
National Botanical Research Institute. Lucknow. Bulletin — Nat Bot Res Inst Lucknow Bull
National Bottlers' Gazette — Nat Bottlers' Gaz
National Bottlers' Gazette — Natl Bottlers Gaz
National Budget for Finland — Fin Budget
National Budget of Norway — Norway Bud
National Builder — Nat Bldr
National Builder — Nat Builder
National Builder — Natn Bldr
National Building Studies. Research Paper — Natl Build Stud Res Pap
National Buildings Organisation. Journal — Nat Bldgs Organisation Jnl
National Bureau of Economic Research. General Studies — NBER Gen S
National Bureau of Economic Research. Occasional Papers — NBER Oc P
National Bureau of Standards. Annual Report (United States) — Natl Bur Stand Annu Rep (US)
National Bureau of Standards. Applied Mathematics Series — Nat Bur Stand Appl Math Ser
National Bureau of Standards. Building Science Series — BSSNB
National Bureau of Standards. Building Science Series — Nat Bur Stand Bldg Sci Ser
National Bureau of Standards. Building Science Series [*United States*] — NBS Build Sci Ser
National Bureau of Standards. Handbook — Nat Bur Stand Handb
National Bureau of Standards. Miscellaneous Publications — Nat Bur Stand Misc Pubs
National Bureau of Standards. Monographs — Nat Bur Stand Monogr
National Bureau of Standards. Monographs — NBS Monogr
National Bureau of Standards. Monographs — NBSMA
National Bureau of Standards. Special Publication — Nat Bur Stand Spec Publ
National Bureau of Standards. Special Publication — NBS Spec Publ
National Bureau of Standards. Special Publication [*United States*] — XNBSA
National Bureau of Standards. Technical News Bulletin — Nat Bur Stand Tech News Bull
National Bureau of Standards. Technical News Bulletin — Nat Bur Standards TNB
National Bureau of Standards. Technical News Bulletin — NBS Tech News Bull
National Bureau of Standards. Technical Note — Nat Bur Stand Tech Note
National Bureau of Standards (United States). Building Science Series — Natl Bur Stand US Build Sci Ser
National Bureau of Standards (United States). Circular — Natl Bur Stand (US) Circ
National Bureau of Standards (United States). Handbook — Natl Bur Stand (US) Handb
National Bureau of Standards (United States). Journal of Research — Natl Bur Stand (US) J Res
National Bureau of Standards (United States). Miscellaneous Publication — Natl Bur Stand (US) Misc Publ
National Bureau of Standards (United States). Monograph — Natl Bur Stand (US) Monogr
National Bureau of Standards (United States). Special Publication — Natl Bur Stand (US) Spec Publ
National Bureau of Standards (United States). Technical News Bulletin — Natl Bur Stand (US) Tech News Bull
National Bureau of Standards (United States). Technical Note — Natl Bur Stand (US) Tech Note
National Burn Information Exchange [*Database*] — NBIE
National Business Education Association. Quarterly — Nat Bsns Ed Q
National Business Education Association. Yearbook — Nat Bsns Ed Yrbk
National Business Education Association. Yearbook — Nat Bus Educ Yrbk
National Business Education Association. Yearbook — Natl Bus Educ Yrbk
National Business Education Association. Yearbook — NBEA Y
National Business Review [*New Zealand*] — NBR
National Business Woman — Nat Bsns Woman
National Business Woman — Natl Bus Woman
National Butter and Cheese Journal — Nat Butter & Cheese J
National Butter and Cheese Journal — Natl Butter Cheese J
National Butter Journal — Nat Butter J
National Butter Journal — Natl Butter J
National Cactus and Succulent Journal — Natl Cact Succ J
National Cactus and Succulent Journal — Natl Cactus Succulent J
National Cancer Conference. Proceedings — Natl Cancer Conf Proc
National Cancer Institute. Carcinogenesis Technical Report Series (United States) — Natl Cancer Inst Carcinog Tech Rep Ser (US)
National Cancer Institute. Journal — Nat Cancer Inst J
National Cancer Institute. Journal — Natl Cancer Inst J
National Cancer Institute. Monographs — Nat Can I M
National Cancer Institute. Monographs — Nat Cancer Inst Monogr
National Cancer Institute. Monographs — Natl Cancer Inst Monogr
National Cancer Institute. Monographs [*United States*] — NCIMA
National Cancer Institute. Research Report — Natl Cancer Inst Res Rep
National Canners' Association. Circulars — Natl Canners Assoc Circ
National Canners' Association. Research Laboratory. Bulletin — Natl Canners' Assoc Res Lab Bull
National Canners' Association. Research Laboratory. Circular [*United States*] — Natl Canners' Assoc Res Lab Circ
National Catalysis Symposium. Proceedings — Natl Catal Symp Proc
National Catholic Educational Association. Bulletin — Nat Cath Ed Assn Bul
National Catholic Educational Association. Proceedings — Nat Cath Ed Assn Proc

National Catholic Reporter — INCR
National Catholic Reporter — Nat Cath Rep
National Catholic Reporter — NCR
National Center for Atmospheric Research. Quarterly — NCAR Q
National Center for Health Education. Newsletter — NCHE
National Central Library. Occasional Newsletter — NCL Occ Newsl
National Central University. Bulletin of Geophysics (Taiwan) — Natl Cent Univ Bull Geophys Taiwan
National Central University Science Reports. Series B. Biological Sciences — Natl Cent Univ Sci Rep Ser B
National Centre for Scientific Research of Vietnam. Proceedings — Natl Cent Sci Res Vietnam Proc
National Cheese Journal — Nat Cheese J
National Cheese Journal [*United States*] — Natl Cheese J
National Chemical and Petroleum Instrumentation Symposium — Natl Chem Pet Instrum Symp
National Chemical Engineering Conference — Natl Chem Eng Conf
National Chiao Tung University. Journal — J Nat Chiao Tung Univ
National Child Labor Committee. Proceedings — Nat Child Labor Com Proc
National Christian Council. Review [*Mysore City*] — Nat Christ Coun R
National Christian Council Review — NCCR
National Civic Review — Nat Civ Rev
National Civic Review — Nat Civic R
National Civic Review — Nat Civic Rev
National Civic Review — Natl Civic Rev
National Civic Review — NCR
National Clay Products and Quarrying — Natl Clay Prod Quarrying
National Cleaner and Dyer [*United States*] — Natl Cleaner Dyer
National Clearinghouse for Poison Control Centers. Bulletin — Natl Clgh Poison Control Cent Bull
National Coal Resources Data System [*Database*] — NCRDS
National Coffee Drinking Survey — Nat Coffee
National Collection of Yeast Cultures Catalogue [*Database*] — NCYC CAT
National Commission on Libraries and Information Science — NCLIS
National Commission on Teacher Education and Professional Standards. Official Report — Nat Comm Teach Ed & Prof Stand Off Rep
National Companies and Securities Commission. Manual — NCSC Manual
National Computational Physics Conference — Natl Comput Phys Conf
National Computer Conference [*United States*] — Natl Comput Conf
National Computer Conference Proceedings — Nat Comp Conf Proc
National Computer Conference. Proceedings — NCC Proc
National Computer Index [*Database*] — NCI
National Conference about Hazardous Waste Management. Proceedings — Natl Conf Hazard Waste Manage Proc
National Conference for Good City Government. Proceedings — Conf City Govt
National Conference for Good City Government. Proceedings — Nat Conf City Govt
National Conference for Individual Onsite Wastewater Systems. Proceedings — Natl Conf Individ Onsite Wastewater Syst Proc
National Conference. Instrumentation for the Iron and Steel Industry — Natl Conf Instrum Iron Steel Ind
National Conference of Charities and Correction. Proceedings — Conf Char and Correc
National Conference of Social Work. Proceedings — Nat Conf Soc Work
National Conference of Social Work. Proceedings — Nat Conf Social Work Proc
National Conference on Acceptable Sludge Disposal Techniques. Proceedings — Natl Conf Acceptable Sludge Disposal Tech Proc
National Conference on Atomic Spectroscopy. Invited Papers — Natl Conf At Spectrosc Invited Pap
National Conference on City Planning. Proceedings — Conf City Planning
National Conference on Complete WateReuse. Proceedings — Natl Conf Complete WateReuse Proc
National Conference on Control of Hazardous Material Spills — Natl Conf Control Hazard Mater Spills
National Conference on Dental Public Relations [*US*] — Natl Conf Dent Public Relat
National Conference on Earth Science. Papers (Alberta University) — Natl Conf Earth Sci Pap (Alberta Univ)
National Conference on Electron Probe Analysis. Proceedings — Natl Conf Electron Probe Anal Proc
National Conference on Energy and the Environment — Natl Conf Energy Environ
National Conference on Environmental Effects on Aircraft and Propulsion Systems — Natl Conf Environ Eff Aircr Propul Syst
National Conference on Fluid Power — Natl Conf Fluid Power
National Conference on I.C. Engines and Combustion — Natl Conf IC Engines Combust
National Conference on IC [*Internal Combustion*] **Engines and Combustion. Proceed ings** — Natl Conf IC Engines Combust Proc
National Conference on Metallurgical Science and Technology — Natl Conf Metall Sci Technol
National Conference on Sludge Management Disposal and Utilization — Natl Conf Sludge Manage Disposal Util
National Conference on the Administration of Research. Proceedings — Natl Conf Adm Res Proc
National Conference on Thermal Spray. Conference Proceedings — Natl Conf Therm Spray Conf Proc
National Conference on Wheat Utilization Research. Report — Natl Conf Wheat Util Res Rep
National Conference Publication. Institution of Engineers of Australia — Nat Conf Publ Inst Eng Aust
National Conference Publications. Institution of Engineers of Australia — Nat Conf Publs Instn Engrs Aust
National Conference Publications. Institution of Engineers of Australia — Natl Conf Publ Inst Eng Aust
National Congress. Italian Headache Association. Papers — Natl Congr Ital Headache Assoc Pap
National Congress of Oncology. Reports — Natl Congr Oncol Rep
National Congress on Theoretical and Applied Mechanics. Proceedings — Natl Congr Theor Appl Mech Proc
National Contract Management Journal — NCM
National Convention on Combustion and Environment — Natl Conv Combust Environ
National Cooperative Highway Research Program. Report — Natl Coop Highw Res Program Rep
National Cooperative Highway Research Program. Report — NCHRP Prog Rep
National Cooperative Highway Research Program. Report — NCHRP Rep
National Cooperative Highway Research Program. Synthesis of Highway Practice [*A publication*] — Natl Coop Highw Res Program Synth Highw Pract
National Cooperative Highway Research Program. Synthesis of Highway Practice [*A publication*] — NCHRP Synthesis Highw Prac
National Corn Handbook — Natl Corn Handb
National Corporation Reporter — Nat Corp Rep
National Council for Research and Development. Report NCRD (Israel) — Natl Counc Res Dev Rep NCRD (Isr)
National Council for the Social Studies. Bulletin — NCSS B
National Council for the Social Studies. Readings — NCSS Read
National Council for the Social Studies. Research Bulletin — NCSS Res B
National Council for the Social Studies. Yearbook — Nat Council Social Stud Yrbk
National Council for the Social Studies. Yearbook — Natl Council Social Stud Yrbk
National Council for the Social Studies. Yearbook — NCSS Yearb
National Council of Churches of Christ in the USA. Information Service — Inf Serv
National Council of Teachers of Mathematics. Yearbook — Nat Council Teach Math Yrbk
National Council of Teachers of Mathematics. Yearbook — Natl Council Teach Math Yrbk
National Council of the Paper Industry for Air and Stream Improvement. Atmospheric Pollution Technical Bulletin — NCASI Atm Poll Tech Bull
National Council of the Paper Industry for Air and Stream Improvement. Monthly Bulletin — NCASI Monthly Bull
National Council of the Paper Industry for Air and Stream Improvement. Regulatory Review — NCASI Regul Rev
National Council of the Paper Industry for Air and Stream Improvement. Technical Bulletin — NCASI Tech Bull
National Council of the Paper Industry for Air and Stream Improvement. Technical Bulletin. Atmospheric Quality Improvement. Technical Bulletin — NCASI Tech Bull Atmos Qual Improv Tech Bull
National Council of the Paper Industry for Air and Stream Improvement. Technical Review — NCASI Tech Rev
National Council on Family Relations. Newsletter — NCFR
National Council on Radiation Protection and Measurements. Annual Meeting — Natl Counc Radiat Prot Meas Annu Meet
National Council on Radiation Protection and Measurements. Reports — NCRP Rep
National Council on Radiation Protection and Measurements (U.S.). Report — Natl Counc Radiat Prot Meas US Rep
National Council Outlook — Nat Council O
National Council Outlook — Natn Coun Outlook
National Council Outlook — NCO
National Council. Paper Industry for Air and Stream Improvement. Special Report — Natl Counc Pap Ind Air Stream Improv Spec Rep
National Credit Union Administration. Quarterly — NCUA Q
National Criminal Justice Reference Service [*Database*] — NCJRS
National Cycling — Natl Cycling
National Cyclopaedia of American Biography — NCAB
National Dairy Research Institute (Karnal). Annual Report — Natl Dairy Res Inst (Karnal) Annu Rep
National Defense — Natl Def
National Defense Medical Journal (Tokyo) — Natl Def Med J (Tokyo)
National Dental Association. Journal [*US*] — Natl Dent Assoc J
National Dental Health Conference [*US*] — Natl Dent Health Conf
National Development — Nat Development
National Development [*Australia*] — Natl Dev
National Development Quarterly — Nat Dev Q
National Directory of Newsletters and Reporting Services — NDNRS
National Directory of State Agencies [*United States*] — NDSA
National Disease and Therapeutic Index — NDTI
National District Heating Association. Official Proceedings — Natl Dist Heat Assoc Off Proc
National Drug Abuse Conference. Proceedings — Natl Drug Abuse Conf Proc
National Druggist — Natl Drug
National Eclectic Medical Quarterly — Natl Eclectic Med Q
National Economic Development Office. Construction Forecasts [*British*] — NEDO Frcst
National Economic Projections Series [*Database*] — NEPS
National Education — Natl Educ
National Education Association. Addresses and Proceedings — Nat Ed Assn Proc
National Education Association. Journal — Nat Educ Assn J
National Education Association. Journal — NEA J
National Education Association. Proceedings and Addresses — Nat Educ Assn Proc
National Education Association. Research Bulletin — Nat Ed Assn Res Bul
National Education Association. Research Bulletin — NEA Res Bul
National Education Association. Research Division. Reports — NEA Res Div Rept
National Electric Light Association. Bulletin — Natl Electr Light Assoc Bull

National Electric Light Association. Bulletin — NELA Bul
National Electrical Manufacturers Association. Standards Publication — Nat Elec Mfr Ass Stand Publ
National Electronics Review — Natl Electron Rev
National Elementary Principal — Nat El Prin
National Elementary Principal — Natl El Prin
National Emergency Equipment Locator System [*Database*] — NEELS
National Emissions Data System [*Database*] — NEDS
National Energy Accounts [*Database*] — NEA
National Energy Information Center Electronic Publication System [*Database*] — EIA/EPUB
National Energy Software [*Database*] — NEW
National Engineer — Nat Eng
National Engineer — Natl Eng
National Engineering Information Service [*Database*] — NEIS
National Engineering Laboratory. Report — Nat Eng Lab Rep
National Engineering Laboratory. Report (Great Britain) — Natl Eng Lab Rep (GB)
National Engineering Laboratory. Reports — NEL Reports
National Environmental Data Referral Service [*Database*] — NEDRES
National Event Clearinghouse Database — NECH
National Fabric Alternatives Forum. Proceedings — Natl Fabric Altern Forum Proc
National Fall Conference. American Society for Nondestructive Testing — Natl Fall Conf Am Soc Nondestr Test
National Farm and Garden Magazine — Natl Farm Gard Mag
National Farm Chemurgic Council. Bulletin — Natl Farm Chemurg Counc Bull
National Farm Chemurgic Council. Chemurgic Papers — Natl Farm Chemurg Counc Chemurg Pap
National Farmers' Union. Annual Conference — Nat Fmrs Un Annu Conf
National Fertilizer Development Center. Bulletin Y (United States) — Natl Fert Dev Cent Bull Y (US)
National Fertilizer Review — Natl Fert Rev
National Fire Codes [*United States*] — Natl Fire Codes
National Fire Protection Association. Quarterly — Natl Fire Prot Assoc Q
National Fisherman — Natl Fisherman
National Flute Association Newsletter — NFAN
National Food Engineering Conference Proceedings — Natl Food Eng Conf Proc
National Food Review — Natl Food Rev
National Food Review NFR. US Department of Agriculture. Economic Research Service — Natl Food Rev NFR US Dep Agric Econ Res Serv
National Forum — Nat F
National Forum — Nat Forum
National Forum on Hospital and Health Affairs [*US*] — Natl Forum Hosp Health Aff
National Forum. Phi Kappa Phi Journal — NAF
National Foundation for Cancer Research. Cancer Research Association Symposia — Natl Found Cancer Res Cancer Res Assoc Symp
National Foundation. March of Dimes. Birth Defects Original Article Series — Nat Found March Dimes Birth Defects Orig Artic Ser
National Foundation. March of Dimes. Birth Defects Original Article Series — Natl Found March Dimes Birth Defects Orig Artic Ser
National Fuels and Lubricants Meeting — Natl Fuels Lubr Mtg
National Gallery of Art. Report — Nat Gal Rep
National Gallery of South Australia. Bulletin — Nat Gall SA Bull
National Gallery of South Australia. Bulletin — So Aus Bul
National Gallery of Victoria. Annual Bulletin — Nat Gall VIC A Bull
National Gas Bulletin — NAGBA
National Gas Bulletin — Nat Gas Bul
National Gas Bulletin — Nat Gas Bull
National Gas Bulletin — Natl Gas Bull
National Gas Bulletin (Melbourne) — Natl Gas Bull (Melbourne)
National Gas Turbine Establishment. Report (United Kingdom) — Natl Gas Turbine Establ Rep (UK)
National Genealogical Society. Quarterly — NGSQ
National Geographic — GNAG
National Geographic Journal of India — NGJI
National Geographic Magazine — Nat Geog
National Geographic Magazine — Nat Geog M
National Geographic Magazine — Natl Geogr Mag
National Geographic Magazine — Natl Geographic Mag
National Geographic Magazine — Natn Geogr Mag
National Geographic Magazine — NGgM
National Geographic Magazine — NGM
National Geographic Magazine. National Geographic Society — NGS/NGM
National Geographic Magazine (Washington, DC) — Nat Geogr Mag Wash
National Geographic Research — NAGR
National Geographic Research — Nat Geog R
National Geographic Research — Natl Geogr Res
National Geographic Research — NGREEG
National Geographic Society. National Geographic Monographs — Nat Geog Soc Nat Geog Mon
National Geographic Society. Research Reports — Natl Geogr Soc Res Rep
National Geographic World — GNGW
National Geographic World — Nat Geog World
National Geographic World — World
National Geographical Journal of India [*Varanasi*] — Nat Geog J Ind
National Geological Survey of China. General Statement Mining Industry — Natl Geol Surv China Gen Statement Min Ind
National Geological Survey of China. Memoirs. Series C — Natl Geol Surv China Mem Ser C
National Geological Survey of China. Special Report — Natl Geol Surv China Spec Rep
National Geophysical Research Institute (Hyderabad, India). Bulletin — Natl Geophys Res Inst (Hyderabad India) Bull
National Glass Budget — Natl Glass
National Glass Budget [*United States*] — Natl Glass Budget
National Ground Water Quality Symposium. Proceedings — Natl Ground Water Qual Symp Proc
National Guardian — Natn Guardian
National Guild of Catholic Psychiatrists. Bulletin — Guild C Psych
National Health and Medical Research Council (Canberra). Medical Research — Natl Health Med Res Counc (Canberra) Med Res
National Health and Medical Research Council (Canberra). Medical Research Projects — Natl Health Med Res Counc (Canberra) Med Res Proj
National Health and Medical Research Council (Canberra). Report — Natl Health Med Res Counc (Canberra) Rep
National Health and Medical Research Council [*Canberra*]. Medical Research — NHMDAP
National Health Insurance Joint Committee. Medical Research Committee (Great Britain). Special Report Series — Natl Health Insur Jt Comm Med Res Comm (GB) Spec Rep Ser
National Health Insurance Reports [*United States*] — Natl Health Insur Rep
National Health Services Information Bulletin — Nat Health Serv Inf Bul
National Heat Transfer Conference — Natl Heat Transfer Conf
National Heat Transfer Conference. Preprints of AIChE [*American Institute of Chemical Engineers*] **Papers** — Natl Heat Transfer Conf Prepr AIChE Pap
National Herbarium of New South Wales. Contributions — Nat Herb NSW Contrib
National Horticultural Magazine — Nat Hort M
National Horticultural Magazine — Natl Hortic Mag
National Hospital — Nat Hosp
National Hospital — Nat Hospital
National Hospital Health Care — Natl Hosp Health Care
National Hydrology Research Institute. Paper — NHRI Paper
National Incinerator Conference. Proceedings — Natl Incinerator Conf Proc
National Income and Product Accounts [*Database*] — NIPA
National Indian Brotherhood. Newsletter — NIBN
National Industrial Research Institute. Annual Report — Natl Ind Res Inst Annu Rep
National Industrial Research Institute (Seoul). Review — Natl Ind Res Inst (Seoul) Rev
National Institute Economic Review — Nat Inst Econ R
National Institute Economic Review — Nat Inst Econ Rev
National Institute Economic Review — Natl Eco
National Institute Economic Review — Natl I Eco
National Institute Economic Review — Natl Inst Econ R
National Institute Economic Review — Natl Inst Econ Rev
National Institute Economic Review — NER
National Institute Economic Review [*London*] — NIQ
National Institute for Architectural Education. Bulletin — Nat Inst Arch Ed Bul
National Institute for Educational Research. Bulletin [*Tokyo*] — Nat Inst Educ Res B
National Institute for Environmental Studies. Japan. Report of Special Research — Natl Inst Environ Stud Jpn Rep Spec Res
National Institute for Metallurgy. Republic of South Africa. Report — Natl Inst Metall Repub S Afr Rep
National Institute for Research in Dairying. Biennial Reviews (United Kingdom) — Natl Inst Res Dairy Bienn Rev UK
National Institute for Research in Dairying. Report (England) — Natl Inst Res Dairy Rep (Engl)
National Institute for Research in Dairying. Technical Bulletin (United Kingdom) — Natl Inst Res Dairy Tech Bull (UK)
National Institute for Research in Nuclear Science (Great Britain). Report — Natl Inst Res Nucl Sci (GB) Rep
National Institute for Water Supply (Netherlands). Quarterly Report — Natl Inst Water Supply (Neth) Q Rep
National Institute of Agricultural Botany (Cambridge). Report and Accounts [*A publication*] — Natl Inst Agric Bot (Camb) Rep Acc
National Institute of Animal Health. Quarterly — Nat I Anim
National Institute of Animal Health. Quarterly — Natl Inst Anim Health Q
National Institute of Animal Health. Quarterly [*Yatabe*] — NIAHAI
National Institute of Animal Health. Quarterly (Yatabe) — Natl Inst Anim Health Q (Yatabe)
National Institute of Genetics (Mishima). Annual Report — Natl Inst Genet (Mishima) Annu Rep
National Institute of Geology and Mining. Bandung. Indonesia. Bulletin — Natl Inst Geol Min Bandung Indones Bull
National Institute of Health. Bulletin. United States Public Health Service — National Inst Health Bull US Pub Health Serv
National Institute of Mental Health and Neuro Sciences. Journal — NIMHANS Journal
National Institute of Mental Health. Publications — NIMH
National Institute of Nutrition. Annual Report — Natl Inst Nutr Annu Rep
National Institute of Occupational Safety and Health. Publications — NIOSH
National Institute of Polar Research. Memoirs. Series A. Aeronomy — NIPRMAA
National Institute of Polar Research. Memoirs. Series B. Meteorology — NIPRMBMT
National Institute of Polar Research. Memoirs. Series C. Earth Sciences — Natl Inst Polar Res Mem Ser C Earth Sci
National Institute of Polar Research. Memoirs. Series C. Earth Sciences — NIPRMCES
National Institute of Polar Research. Memoirs. Series E. Biology and Medical Science — NIPRMEB
National Institute of Polar Research. Memoirs. Series F. Logistics — NIPRMFL
National Institute of Polar Research. Memoirs. Special Issue — Natl Inst Polar Res Mem Spec Issue
National Institute of Polar Research. Memoirs. Special Issue — NIPRM
National Institute of Polar Research. Memoirs. Special Issue — NIPRMS

National Institute of Polar Research. Memoirs. Special Issue (Japan) — Natl Inst Polar Res Mem Spec Issue (Jpn)
National Institute of Polar Research. Special Map Series — NIPRSMS
National Institute of Polar Research Symposium on Antarctic Meteorites — Natl Inst Polar Res Symp Antarct Meteorites
National Institute of Polar Research (Tokyo). Antarctic Geological Map Series — Natl Inst Polar Res (Tokyo) Antarct Geol Map Ser
National Institute of Public Health Annals (Norway) — Natl Inst Public Health Ann (Norw)
National Institute of Radiological Sciences. Report. NIRS-M (Japan) — Natl Inst Radiol Sci Rep NIRS M Jpn
National Institute of Sciences of India. Transactions — Natl Inst Sci India Trans
National Institute of Social Sciences. Proceedings — Nat Inst Soc Sci
National Institute of Standards and Technology. Journal of Research — Natl Inst Stand Technol J Res
National Institute on Alcohol Abuse and Alcoholism. Research Monograph — Natl Inst Alcohol Abuse Alcohol Res Monogr
National Institute on Drug Abuse. Research Monograph — NIDA Res Monogr
National Institute on Drug Abuse. Research Monograph Series — Natl Inst Drug Abuse Res Monogr Ser
National Institutes of Health. Consensus Development Conference. Summaries [*US*] — Natl Inst Health Consensus Dev Conf Summ
National Institutes of Health Publication (United States) — Natl Inst Health Publ US
National Institutes of Health. Publications — NIH
National Institution for the Promotion of Science. Bulletin of the Proceedings. Proceedings. New Series — Nat Inst B Pr Pr N S
National Intelligence Daily [*Central Intelligence Agency*] — NID
National Interest — Nat Interest
National Jewish Monthly — Natn Jewish Mon
National Jewish Monthly — NJM
National Joint Committee on Fertilizer Application. Proceedings of the Annual Meeting — Natl Jt Comm Fert Appl Proc Annu Meet
National Journal — Nat J
National Journal [*United States*] — Natl J
National Journal of Criminal Defense — Nat J Crim Def
National Journal of Criminal Defense — Nat J Criminal Defense
National Journal of Criminal Defense — Natl J Crim Def
National Laboratory for High Energy Physics. Report KEK (Japan) — Natl Lab High Energy Phys KEK (Jpn)
National Lampoon — Nat Lamp
National Law Journal — INLJ
National Law Journal — Nat'l LJ
National Lawyers Guild. Practitioner — Nat'l Law Guild Prac
National League for Nursing. Publications — NLN Publ
National Legislative Network [*US*] [*Database*] — LEGISNET
National Lending Library. Translations Bulletin — NLL Transl Bull
National Liberation Movement in India and Bal Gangadhar — NLM
National Library of Medicine. Current Catalog — NLMC
National Library of Medicine. News — NLM News
National Library of Medicine. Technical Bulletin — NLM Tech Bull
National Library of Wales. Journal — Nat Libr Wales J
National Library of Wales. Journal — Natl Libr Wales J
National Library of Wales. Journal — NLW Journ
National Library of Wales. Journal — NLWJ
National Lime Association. Azbe Award — Natl Lime Assoc Azbe Award
National Lime Association. Bulletin — Nat Lime Ass Bull
National Literary Society Journal — Nat Lit Soc J
National Lithographer — Nat Lith
National Lithographer — Natl Lithogr
National LP-Gas Association Times [*United States*] — NLPGA Times
National Lucht- en Ruimtevaartlaboratorium — Nat Lucht Ruimtevaartlab
National Lucht- en Ruimtevaartlaboratorium. Miscellaneous Publication NLR MP (Netherlands) — Natl Lucht Ruimtevaartlab Misc Publ NLR MP Neth
National Lucht- en Ruimtevaartlaboratorium. Rapport NLR TR [*Netherlands*] — Natl Lucht Ruimtevaartlab Rapp NLR TR
National Luchtvaartlaboratorium. Miscellaneous Publication NLR MP (Netherlands) — Natl Luchtvaartlab Misc Publ NLR MP Neth
National Magazine — Nat M
National Magazine — Nat Mag
National Magazine — Natl M
National Magazine (Boston) — Nat'l M (Bost)
National Mapping Bulletin — Nat Map Bull
National Marine Fisheries Service (US). Circular — Natl Mar Fish Serv (US) Circ
National Marine Fisheries Service (US). Special Scientific Report-Fisheries — Natl Mar Fish Serv (US) Spec Sci Rep Fish
National Marketing Report — Natl Market Rep
National Master Specification [*Canada*] [*Database*] — NMS
National Mastitis Council. Annual Meeting — Natl Mastitis Counc Annu Meet
National Materials Advisory Board. Publication NMAB — Natl Mater Advis Board Publ NMAB
National Measurement Laboratory. Technical Paper (Australia) — Natl Meas Lab Tech Pap (Aust)
National Medical Association. Journal — Nat Med Assn J
National Medical Care Utilization and Expenditure Survey [*United States*] — Natl Med Care Utilization and Expenditure Survey
National Medical Journal of China (Beijing) — Natl Med J China (Beijing)
National Medical Journal of India — Natl Med J India
National Meeting. American Chemical Society. Division of Environmental Chemistry — Natl Meet Am Chem Soc Div Environ Chem
National Meeting. APhA Academy of Pharmaceutical Sciences — Natl Meet APhA Acad Pharm Sci
National Meeting on Biophysics and Medical Engineering in Finland. Proceedings — Natl Meet Biophys Med Eng Finl Proc
National Meeting. South African Institution of Chemical Engineers. Papers and Programme — Natl Meet S Afr Inst Chem Eng Pap Programme
National Metallurgical Laboratory. Jamshedpur, India. Technical Journal — Natl Metall Lab Jamshedpur India Tech J
National Microfilm Association. Journal — NMA Journal
National Miller [*United States*] — Natl Miller
National Miller and American Miller — Natl Miller Am Miller
National Municipal Review — Nat Mun Rev
National Municipal Review — Nat Munic R
National Municipal Review — Nat Munic Rev
National Municipal Review — Nat'l Mun Rev
National Municipal Review — Natn Munic Rev
National Museum Bloemfontein. Annual Report — Natl Mus Bloemfontein Annu Rep
National Museum Bloemfontein. Researches Memoir — Natl Mus Bloemfontein Res Mem
National Museum of Canada. Bulletin — Natl Mus Can Bull
National Museum of Canada Bulletin — Natl Mus Canada Bull
National Museum of Canada. Natural History Papers — Natl Mus Can Nat Hist Pap
National Museum of Korea. Art Magazine [*Republic of Korea*] — Natl Mus Korea Art Mag
National Museum of Man. Mercury Series. Canadian Centre for Folk Culture Studies. Papers — NMCCFCS
National Museum of Natural Sciences (Ottawa). Publications in Biological Oceanography — Natl Mus Nat Sci (Ottawa) Publ Biol Oceanogr
National Museum of Natural Sciences (Ottawa). Publications in Botany — Natl Mus Nat Sci (Ottawa) Publ Bot
National Museum of Natural Sciences (Ottawa). Publications in Natural Sciences — Natl Mus Nat Sci (Ottawa) Publ Nat Sci
National Museum of Natural Sciences (Ottawa). Publications in Palaeontology [*A publication*] — Natl Mus Nat Sci (Ottawa) Publ Palaeontol
National Museum of Natural Sciences (Ottawa). Publications in Zoology — Natl Mus Nat Sci (Ottawa) Publ Zool
National Museum of Natural Sciences [*Ottawa*]. Publications in Natural Sciences — PNSCEI
National Museum of New Zealand. Miscellaneous Series — Natl Mus NZ Misc Ser
National Museum of New Zealand. Records — Natl Mus NZ Rec
National Museum of Southern Rhodesia. Occasional Papers. Series B. Natural Sciences — Natl Mus South Rhod Occas Pap Ser B
National Museum of Victoria. Memoirs — Nat Mus VIC Mem
National Museum of Victoria. Memoirs — Natl Mus Victoria Mem
National Museum of Wales. Annual Report — Nat Mus Wales Ann Rep
National Museums of Canada. Mercury Series. Archaeological Survey of Canada. Papers — NMCMASC
National Museums of Canada. Mercury Series. Directorate Paper — NMCMSDP
National Museums of Canada. Mercury Series. Ethnology Division. Papers — NMCMED
National Museums of Canada. National Museum of Man. Mercury Series. Canadian Ethnology Service. Papers — NMCMCES
National Museums of Canada. Publications in Archaeology — NMCPA
National Museums of Canada. Publications in Biological Oceanography — NMCPBO
National Museums of Canada. Publications in Botany — NMCPB
National Museums of Canada. Publications in Ethnology — NMCPE
National Museums of Canada. Publications in Folk Culture — NMCPFC
National Museums of Canada. Publications in Natural Sciences — NMCPNS
National Museums of Canada. Publications in Zoology — NMCPZ
National Music Council. Bulletin — Nat Mus Council Bul
National Music Council. Bulletin — NM
National Music Council. Bulletin — NMC Bul
National Newspaper Index — Natl Newsp Index
National Nosocomial Infections Study — Natl Nosocomial Infect Study
National Nuclear Data Center. Report BNL-NCS (United States) — Natl Nucl Data Cent Rep BNL NCS US
National Nuclear Energy Series. Manhattan Project Technical Section. Division 1. Electromagnetic Separation Project — Natl Nucl Energy Ser Manhattan Proj Tech Sect Div 1
National Nuclear Energy Series. Manhattan Project Technical Section. Division 2. Gaseous Diffusion Project — Natl Nucl Energy Ser Manhattan Proj Tech Sect Div 2
National Nuclear Energy Series. Manhattan Project Technical Section. Division 3. [*Special Separations Project*] — Natl Nucl Energy Ser Manhattan Proj Tech Sect Div 3
National Nuclear Energy Series. Manhattan Project Technical Section. Division 4. Plutonium Project — Natl Nucl Energy Ser Manhattan Proj Tech Sect Div 4
National Nuclear Energy Series. Manhattan Project Technical Section. Division 6. University of Rochester Project — Natl Nucl Energy Ser Manhattan Proj Tech Sect Div 6
National Nuclear Energy Series. Manhattan Project Technical Section. Division 8. Manhattan Project — Natl Nucl Energy Ser Manhattan Proj Tech Sect Div 8
National Nuclear Energy Series. Manhattan Project Technical Section. Division 9. Thermal Diffusion Project — Natl Nucl Energy Ser Manhattan Proj Tech Sect Div 9
National Nuclear Instrumentation Conference. Proceedings — Natl Nucl Instrum Conf Proc
National Observer — Natl Observer
National Observer — NO
National Oceanic and Atmospheric Administration (United States). Circular — Natl Oceanic Atmos Adm (US) Circ
National Oceanic and Atmospheric Administration (United States). Fishery Bulletin — Natl Oceanic Atmos Adm (US) Fish Bull

National Oceanic and Atmospheric Administration (United States). Special Scientific Report. Fisheries — Natl Oceanic Atmos Adm (US) Spec Sci Rep Fish
National Oceanic and Atmospheric Administration (US) Technical Report. National Marine Fisheries Service Circular — Natl Oceanic Atmos Adm (US) Tech Rep Natl Mar Fish Serv Circ
National Older Workers Information System [*US*] [*Database*] — NOWIS
National Online Manpower Information System [*UK*] [*Database*] — NOMIS
National Online Regulatory Access [*US*] [*Database*] — NORA
National Open Hearth and Basic Oxygen Steel Conference. Proceedings — Natl Open Hearth Basic Oxygen Steel Conf Proc
National Paint Bulletin — Natl Paint Bull
National Paint, Varnish, and Lacquer Association. Abstract Review — Natl Paint Varn Lacquer Assoc Abstr Rev
National Paint, Varnish, and Lacquer Association. Scientific Section. Circulars — Natl Paint Varn Lacquer Assoc Sci Sect Circ
National Painters Magazine — Natl Painters Mag
National Palace Museum. Bulletin [*Taipai*] — Nat Pal Mus B
National Palace Museum Quarterly — Natl Palace Mus Q
National Parent-Teacher — Nat Parent-Teach
National Parks — GNAP
National Parks — NP
National Parks and Conservation Magazine [*Later, National Parks Magazine*] — Nat Parks & Con Mag
National Parks and Conservation Magazine [*Later, National Parks Magazine*] — Natl Parks Conserv Mag
National Parks and Conservation Magazine [*Later, National Parks Magazine*] — NPCM
National Parks Magazine [*Formerly, National Parks and Conservation Magazine*] — Nat Parks
National Parks Magazine [*Formerly, National Parks and Conservation Magazine*] — Natl Parks
National Parks Magazine [*Formerly, National Parks and Conservation Magazine*] — Natl Parks Mag
National Pecan Association. Report. Proceedings. Annual Convention — Natl Pecan Assoc Rep Proc Annu Conv
National Pecan Growers Association. Report. Proceedings. Annual Convention — Natl Pecan Grow Assoc Rep Proc Annu Conv
National Pesticide Information Retrieval System [*US*] [*Database*] — NPIRS
National Petroleum Bibliography — Natl Petroleum Bibliography
National Petroleum News — Nat Pet N
National Petroleum News [*United States*] — Natl Pet News
National Petroleum News — Natn Petrol News
National Petroleum News — NP News
National Petroleum News — NPN
National Petroleum Refiners Association. Papers — Natl Pet Refiners Assoc Pap
National Petroleum Refiners Association. Technical Papers — Nat Petrol Refiners Ass Tech Papers
National Petroleum Refiners Association. Technical Papers — Natl Pet Refin Assoc Tech Pap
National Petroleum Refiners Association. Technical Publication [*United States*] — Natl Pet Refin Assoc Tech Publ
National Petroleum Refiners Association. Technical Publication — Natl Pet Refiners Assoc Tech Publ
National Physical Laboratory. Division of Chemical Standards. NPL Report Chem (United Kingdom) — Natl Phys Lab Div Chem Stand NPL Rep Chem (UK)
National Physical Laboratory. Division of Materials Applications. NPL Report DMA (United Kingdom) — Natl Phys Lab Div Mater Appl NPL Rep DMA UK
National Physical Laboratory. Division of Materials Metrology. NPL Report DMM(A) (United Kingdom) — Natl Phys Lab Div Mater Metrol NPL Rep DMMA UK
National Physical Laboratory. Division of Quantum Metrology. NPL Report QU (United Kingdom) — Natl Phys Lab Div Quantum Metrol NPL Rep QU (UK)
National Physical Laboratory (Great Britain). Department of Scientific and Industrial Research. Notes on Applied Science — Nat Phys Lab (Gt Brit) Notes Appl Sci
National Physical Laboratory (India). Technical Bulletin — Natl Phys Lab India Tech Bull
National Physical Laboratory. Notes on Applied Science (United Kingdom) — Natl Phys Lab Notes Appl Sci (UK)
National Physical Laboratory. Reports [*United Kingdom*] — Natl Phys Lab Rep
National Physical Laboratory (U.K.). Collected Researches — Natl Phys Lab UK Collect Res
National Physical Laboratory (United Kingdom). Collected Researches — Nat Phys Lab UK Collect Res
National Physical Laboratory (United Kingdom). Division of Chemical Standards. Report — Natl Phys Lab (UK) Div Chem Stand Rep
National Physical Laboratory (United Kingdom). Proceedings of a Symposium — Natl Phys Lab (UK) Proc Symp
National Physical Laboratory (United Kingdom). Report — Natl Phys Lab (UK) Rep
National Physical Laboratory (United Kingdom). Report. CMMT(A) — Natl Phys Lab UK Rep CMMTA
National Physical Laboratory (United Kingdom). Symposium — Natl Phys Lab (UK) Symp
National Poultry Improvement Plan. Report. United States Department of Agriculture. Science and Education Administration — Nat Poult Impr Plan Rep US Dept Agric Sci Educ Admin
National Probation and Parole Association. Yearbook — Nat Probation Assn Yrbk
National Productivity Review — NLP
National Productivity Review — NPR
National Provisioner — Natl Prov
National Provisioner — Natl Provis
National Public Accountant — Nat Public Accountant
National Public Accountant — NPA
National Public Employment Reporter. Labor Relations Press — Natl Pub Empl Rep Lab Rel Press
National Purchasing Review — Nat Pur Rev
National Quantum Electronics Conference — Natl Quantum Electron Conf
National Quarterly Review — Nat Q
National Quarterly Review — Nat Q R
National Quarterly Review — Nat Q Rev
National Racquetball — Nat Racq
National Racquetball [*United States*] — Natl Racq
National Radiological Protection Board. Report NRPB-IE (United Kingdom) — Natl Radiol Prot Board Rep NRPB IE UK
National Radiological Protection Board. Report NRPB-R (United Kingdom) — Natl Radiol Prot Board Rep NRPB R UK
National Ready Mixed Concrete Association. Publication — Natl Ready Mixed Concr Assoc Publ
National Real Estate Investor — Nat Real Estate Invest
National Real Estate Investor — Nat Real Estate Investor
National Real Estate Investor — Natl Real Estate Investor
National Real Estate Investor — NRE
National Reporter [*Canada*] [*Database*] — NR
National Reporter System [*Canada*] [*Database*] — NRS
National Reprographic Centre for Documentation. Bulletin — NRCD Bull
National Republic — Nat Rep
National Research Center for Disaster Prevention. Report — Natl Res Cent Disaster Prev Rep
National Research Council. Advisory Center on Toxicology. Report NAS/ACT (United States) — Natl Res Counc Advis Cent Toxicol Rep NAS ACT (US)
National Research Council. Annual Report. Chairman. Division of Biology and Agriculture — Natl Res Council Annual Rep Chairm Div Biol
National Research Council. Building Research Advisory Board. Technical Report [*A publication*] — Nat Res Counc Bldg Res Adv Bd Tech Rep
National Research Council. Building Research Advisory Board. Technical Report [*A publication*] — Natl Res Counc Build Res Advis Board Tech Rep
National Research Council. Building Research Note — NRCBRN
National Research Council Canada. Marine Analytical Chemistry Standards Program. Report — Natl Res Counc Can Mar Anal Chem Stand Program Rep
National Research Council Canada. Report NRCC — Natl Res Counc Can Rep NRCC
National Research Council. Chemical-Biological Coordination Center. Review (United States) — Natl Res Counc Chem Biol Coord Cent Rev (US)
National Research Council. Committee of Problems of Drug Dependence. Proceedings. Annual Scientific Meeting (United States) — Nat Res Counc Comm Probl Drug Depend Proc Annu Sci Meet (US)
National Research Council. Committee on Problems of Drug Dependence. Proceedings. Annual Scientific Meeting (United States) — Natl Res Counc Comm Probl Drug Depend Proc Annu Sci Meet US
National Research Council. Conference on Electrical Insulation. Annual Report — Nat Res Counc Conf Elec Insul Annu Rep
National Research Council. Current Issues and Studies (United States) — Natl Res Counc Curr Issues Stud (US)
National Research Council. Issues and Studies (United States) — Natl Res Counc Issues Stud (US)
National Research Council of Canada. Aeronautical Report — Nat Res Counc Can Aeronaut Rep
National Research Council of Canada. Aeronautical Report — Natl Res Counc Can Aeronaut Rep
National Research Council of Canada. Annual Report — Nat Res Counc Can Annu Rep
National Research Council of Canada. Annual Report — Natl Res Counc Can Annu Rep
National Research Council of Canada. Associate Committee on Ecological Reserves. Newsletter — NRCE
National Research Council of Canada. Associate Committee on Geodesy and Geophysics. Proceedings of Hydrology Symposium — Nat Res Counc Can Ass Comm Geod Geophys Proc Hydrol Symp
National Research Council of Canada. Associate Committee on Geotechnical Research. Technical Memorandum — Nat Res Counc Can Ass Comm Geotech Res Tech Memo
National Research Council of Canada. Associate Committee on Geotechnical Research. Technical Memorandum — NRCAGTM
National Research Council of Canada. Associate Committee on Scientific Criteria for Environmental Quality. Publication — Natl Res Counc Can Assoc Comm Sci Criter Environ Qual Publ
National Research Council of Canada. Associate Committee on Scientific Criteria for Environmental Quality. Publication — NRCEBF
National Research Council of Canada. Bulletin — Natl Res Counc Can Bull
National Research Council of Canada. Division of Building Research. Bibliography — Nat Res Counc Can Div Bldg Res Bibliogr
National Research Council of Canada. Division of Building Research. Canadian Building Digest — Natl Res Counc Can Div Build Res Can Build Dig
National Research Council of Canada. Division of Building Research. DBR Paper — Natl Res Counc Can Div Build Res DBR Pap
National Research Council of Canada. Division of Building Research. DBR Paper — NRCDBP
National Research Council of Canada. Division of Building Research. Fire Study — Natl Res Counc Can Div Build Res Fire Study
National Research Council of Canada. Division of Building Research. Research Paper — NRCBRRP
National Research Council of Canada. Division of Building Research. Technical Paper — Natl Res Counc Can Div Build Res Tech Pap
National Research Council of Canada. Division of Building Research. Technical Paper — NRCBRTP

National Research Council of Canada. Division of Building Research. Technical Report — Natl Res Counc Can Div Build Res Tech Rep
National Research Council of Canada. Division of Mechanical Engineering. Energy — Natl Res Counc Can Div Mech Eng Energy
National Research Council of Canada. Division of Mechanical Engineering. Energy Newsletter — Natl Res Counc Can Div Mech Eng Energy Newsl
National Research Council of Canada. Division of Mechanical Engineering. General Newsletter — Nat Res Council Can Div Mech Engng Gen
National Research Council of Canada. Division of Mechanical Engineering. General Newsletter — Natl Res Counc Can Div Mech Gen Newsl
National Research Council of Canada. Division of Mechanical Engineering. Laboratory Technical Report — Natl Res Counc Can Div Mech Eng Lab Tech Rep
National Research Council of Canada. Division of Mechanical Engineering. Mechanical Engineering Report — Nat Res Counc Can Div Mech Eng Mech Eng Rep
National Research Council of Canada. Division of Mechanical Engineering. Mechanical Engineering Report — Natl Res Counc Can Div Mech Eng Mech Eng Rep
National Research Council of Canada. Division of Mechanical Engineering. Mechanical Engineering Report MS — Natl Res Counc Can Div Mech Eng Mech Eng Rep MS
National Research Council of Canada. Division of Mechanical Engineering. Mechanical Engineering Report. Series MP — Natl Res Counc Can Div Mech Eng Mech Eng Rep MP
National Research Council of Canada. Division of Mechanical Engineering. Quarterly Bulletin — Natl Res Counc Can Div Mech Eng Q Bull
National Research Council of Canada. Division of Mechanical Engineering. Transportation Newsletter — NRCMET
National Research Council of Canada. Environmental Secretariat. Publication — Natl Res Counc Can Environ Secr Publ
National Research Council of Canada. Mechanical Engineering Report. ME — Nat Res Counc Can Mech Eng Rep ME
National Research Council of Canada. Mechanical Engineering Report. Series MP — Natl Res Counc Can Mech Eng Rep MP
National Research Council of Canada. Report — Natl Res Counc Can Rep
National Research Council of Canada. Technical Translation — Natl Res Counc Can Tech Transl
National Research Council of Canada. Technical Translation — NRCCTT
National Research Council of Canada. Unsteady Aerodynamics Laboratory. Laboratory Technical Report — Nat Res Counc Can Unsteady Aerodyn Lab Lab Tech Rep
National Research Council of Canada. Unsteady Aerodynamics Laboratory. Laboratory Technical Report — Natl Res Counc Can Unsteady Aerodyn Lab Lab Tech Rep
National Research Council of Thailand. Journal — Natl Res Counc Thailand J
National Research Council of the Philippines. Bulletin — Natl Res Counc Philipp Bull
National Research Council. Philippines. Research Bulletin — Natl Res Counc Philipp Res Bull
National Research Council Publications. National Academy of Sciences — Natl Res Council Publ
National Research Council. Research News — NRC Res News
National Research Council. Review — Natl Res Counc Rev
National Research Council. Transportation Research Board. Special Report — Natl Res Counc Transp Res Board Spec Rep
National Research Council. Transportation Research Board. Transportation Research Record — Natl Res Counc Transp Res Board Transp Res Rec
National Research Council (US). Bulletin — Natl Res Counc US Bull
National Research Institute for Occupational Diseases. South African Medical Research Council. Annual Report — Natl Res Inst Occup Dis S Afr Med Res Counc Annu Rep
National Research Institute for Pollution and Resources. Japan. Report — Natl Res Inst Pollut Resour Jpn Rep
National Research Program. Agricultural Research Service — Natn Res Progm Agric Res Serv
National Resources Database — NRDB
National Review — GNAR
National Review — Nat R
National Review — Nat Rev
National Review — Natl Rev
National Review — Natn Rev
National Review — NR
National Review (London) — NLR
National Rural Letter Carrier — Natl Rural Letter Carrier
National Safety — Natl Saf
National Safety Congress. Occupational Health Nursing Section. Transactions — Natl Saf Congr Trans
National Safety News — Nat Saf News
National Safety News — Nat Safety News
National Safety News — Natl Saf News
National Safety News [*United States*] — Natl Sfty News
National SAMPE [*Society for the Advancement of Material and Process Engineering*] **Symposium and Exhibition. Proceedings** — Natl SAMPE Symp Exhib Proc
National SAMPE [*Society for the Advancement of Material and Process Engineering*] **Technical Conference** — Natl SAMPE Tech Conf
National Sand and Gravel Association. NSGA Circular — Nat Sand Gravel Ass NSGA Circ
National Sand and Gravel Association. NSGA Circular — Natl Sand Gravel Assoc NSGA Circ
National Savings and Loan League. Journal — Nat Savings and Loan League J
National Schedule of Rates — Nat Schedule Rates
National School Orchestra Association. Bulletin — NSO
National School Orchestra Association. Bulletin — NSOA
National Science and Technology Authority Technology Journal — Natl Sci Technol Auth Technol J
National Science and Technology Authority Technology Journal — NSTA Technol J
National Science Council. Monthly [*Taiwan*] — Natl Sci Counc Mon
National Science Council Monthly (Taipei) — Natl Sci Counc Mon (Taipei)
National Science Council. Proceedings. Part 2. Biological, Medical, and Agricultural Sciences (Taiwan) — Natl Sci Counc Proc Part 2 (Taiwan)
National Science Council. Republic of China. Proceedings. Part A. Applied Sciences — Natl Sci Counc Repub China Proc Part A Appl Sci
National Science Council. Republic of China. Proceedings. Part A. Physical Science and Engineering — Natl Sci Counc Repub China Proc Part A Phys Sci Eng
National Science Council. Republic of China. Proceedings. Part B. Basic Science — Natl Sci Counc Repub China Proc Part B Basic Sci
National Science Council. Republic of China. Proceedings. Part B. Life Sciences — Natl Sci Counc Repub China Proc Part B Life Sci
National Science Council. Special Publication — NSC Special Publication
National Science Council (Taipei). Proceedings. Part 1. Natural and Mathematical Sciences — Natl Sci Counc (Taipei) Proc Part 1 Nat Math Sci
National Science Development Board. Technology Journal (Philippines) — Natl Sci Dev Board Technol J Philipp
National Science Foundation. Annual Report — Natl Sci Found Annu Rep
National Science Foundation. Civil and Environmental Engineering. Report NSF/CEE (United States) — Natl Sci Found Civ Environ Eng Rep NSF CEE (US)
National Science Foundation. NSF — Natl Sci Found NSF
National Science Foundation. Publication NSF (United States) — Natl Sci Found NSF US
National Science Foundation. Research Applied to National Needs. Report NSF/RA (US) — Natl Sci Found Res Appl Natl Needs Rep NSF/RA (US)
National Science Foundation. Science Resources Studies Highlights — NSF SRS
National Science Foundation. Scientific Manpower Bulletin — Natl Sci Found Sci Manpower Bull
National Science Museum. Bulletin. Series C. Geology (Tokyo) — Natl Sci Mus Bull Ser C Geol Tokyo
National Science Museum. Bulletin. Series C. Geology (Tokyo) — Natl Sci Mus Bull Ser C (Tokyo)
National Science Museum (Tokyo). Bulletin. Series C. Geology and Paleontology — Natl Sci Mus (Tokyo) Bull Ser C Geol Paleontol
National Science Museum (Tokyo). Memoirs — Natl Sci Mus (Tokyo) Mem
National Sculpture Review — Nat Sculp R
National Sculpture Review — Nat Sculpt
National Sculpture Review — NSR
National Security Record — Nat Sec R
National Seed Symposium — Natl Seed Symp
National Seedsman — Nat Seedsman
National Seminar on Immobilized Enzyme Engineering. Proceedings — Natl Semin Immobilized Enzyme Eng Proc
National Shade Tree Conference. Proceedings — Natl Shade Tree Conf Proc
National Shorthand Reporter — NSR
National Socialist Bulletin — NSB
National Society for Clean Air. Annual Conference. Proceedings — Natl Soc Clean Air Annu Conf Proc
National Society for Clean Air. Annual Conference. Proceedings [*England*] — NSCAA
National Society for Medical Research. Bulletin [*United States*] — Nat Soc Med Res Bull
National Society for the Study of Education. Yearbook — Nat Soc Study Ed Yrbk
National Society for the Study of Education. Yearbook — Natl Soc Stud Educ Yrbk
National Solar Energy Convention. Proceedings — Natl Sol Energy Conv Proc
National Speleological Society. Bulletin — Natl Speleol Soc Bull
National Speleological Society. Bulletin — NSS Bulletin
National Speleological Society. Occasional Paper — Natl Speleol Soc Occasional Paper
National Spinal Cord Injury Statistical Center Database [*US*] — NSCISC
National Standard Reference Data Series. National Bureau of Standards — Natl Stand Ref Data Ser Natl Bur Stand
National Standard Reference Data Series. United States National Bureau of Standards — Natl Stand Ref Data Ser US Natl Bur Stand
National Standard Reference Data Series. United States National Bureau of Standards — NSRDA
National Standard Reference Data Series. US National Bureau of Standards — Natl Stand Ref Data Ser NBS
National Standard Reference Data System. Lawrence Berkeley Laboratory. University of California — Natl Stand Ref Data Syst LBL
National State of the Art Symposium. American Chemical Society — Natl State of the Art Symp Am Chem Soc
National Stockman and Farmer — Nat Stock & F
National Strength and Conditioning Association. Journal — NSCA J
National Swedish Building Research. Document [*Statens Institut foer Byggnadsforskning*] — Natl Swed Build Res Doc
National Symphony Program Notes — Natl Sym
National Symposium on Aquifer Restoration and Ground Water Monitoring — Natl Symp Aquifer Restor Ground Water Monit
National Symposium on Atomic Energy. Japan — Natl Symp At Energy Jpn
National Symposium on Developments in Irradiation Testing Technology. Papers — Natl Symp Dev Irradiat Test Technol Pap
National Symposium on Fiber Frontiers — Natl Symp Fiber Front
National Symposium on Hydrology — Natn Symp Hydrol
National Symposium on Industrial Isotope Radiography. Proceedings — Natl Symp Ind Isot Radiogr Proc

National Symposium on Refrigeration and Air Conditioning — Natl Symp Refrig Air Cond
National Symposium on Technical Use of Radioisotopes — Natl Symp Tech Use Radioisot
National Symposium on the Biology and Management of the Centrarchid Basses — Natl Symp Biol Manage Centrarchid Basses
National Tax Journal — Nat Tax J
National Tax Journal [*United States*] — Natl Tax J
National Tax Journal — NTJ
National Technical Association. Journal — Natl Tech Assoc J
National Technical Conference. Book of Papers. AATCC [*American Association of Textile Chemists and Colorists*] — Natl Tech Conf Book Pap AATCC
National Technical Information Service Search [*United States*] — Natl Tech Inf Serv Search
National Technical Report [*Matsushita Electric Industrial Co., Osaka*] — Nat Tech Rep
National Technical Report — Natl Tech Rep
National Technical Report. Matsushita Electric Industrial Co. — Natl Tech Rep Matsushita Electr Ind Co
National Technical Report (Matsushita Electric Industrial Co., Osaka) — Natl Tech Rep (Matsushita Electr Ind C Osaka)
National Theater File [*Database*] — NTF
National Times — Nat T
National Times — Nat Times
National Times — Natn Times
National Times — NLTSD
National Times — NT
National Times (Australia) — NTA
National Times Magazine — Nat T Mag
National Toxicology Program. Technical Report Series — Natl Toxicol Program Tech Rep Ser
National Toxicology Program Toxicity Report Series — Natl Toxicol Program Tox Rep Ser
National Trade Union of Coopers [*British*] — NTUC
National Trade Union of Wood Working Machinists [*British*] — NTUWWM
National Trade Union of Woodcutting Machinists [*British*] — NTUWM
National Tree News. National Arborist Association — Natl Tree News
National Trust — Nat Trust
National Trust Bulletin — Nat Trust Bul
National Trust of Australia. Bulletin — Nat Trust Aust Bull
National Trust Studies — Nat Trust Studies
National Tuberculosis Association. Bulletin — Nat Tuberc Assn Bul
National Tuberculosis Association. Transactions — Nat Tuberc Assn Trans
National Underwriter — Nat Underw
National Underwriter (Fire and Casualty Insurance Edition) — Nat Underw (Fire Ed)
National Underwriter (Life and Health Insurance Edition) — Nat Underw (Life)
National Underwriter (Life and Health Insurance Edition) — Nat Underw (Life Ed)
National Underwriter (Life and Health Insurance Edition) — Natl Underwrit (Life Health)
National Underwriter (Life and Health Insurance Edition) — Natl Underwrit (Life Health Insur Ed)
National Underwriter (Life and Health Insurance Edition) — NUH
National Underwriter (Life and Health Insurance Edition) — NULH
National Underwriter (Property and Casualty Insurance Edition) — Nat Underw (Prop Ed)
National Underwriter (Property and Casualty Insurance Edition) — Nat Underw (Property Ed)
National Underwriter (Property and Casualty Insurance Edition) — NUP
National Underwriter (Property and Casualty Insurance Edition) — NUPC
National Union Catalogue — NUC
National Union Catalogue — UC
National Union Catalogue of Audio-Visual Materials — NUCAV
National Union Catalogue of Library Materials for the Handicapped — NUC:H
National Union Catalogue of Monographs — NUCOM
National Union Catalogue of Music — NUCOMUSIC
National Union Catalogue of Serials — NUCOS
National University of Peiping. College of Agriculture. Research Bulletin — Natl Univ Peiping Coll Agric Res Bull
National Vacuum Symposium. Transactions — Natl Vac Symp Trans
National Vegetable Research Station. Annual Report (Wellsbourne) — Natl Veg Res Stn Annu Rep (Wellsbourne)
National Vitamin Foundation. Annual Report — Natl Vitam Found Annu Rep
National Vitamin Foundation. Annual Report — Natl Vitamin Found Annu Rep
National Vitamin Foundation. Annual Report — NVFAAB
National Vitamin Foundation. Nutrition Monograph Series — Natl Vitam Found Nutr Monogr Ser
National Vitamin Foundation. Nutrition Symposium Series [*United States*] — Natl Vitam Found Nutr Symp Ser
National Waste News [*United States*] — Natl Waste News
National Water Data Storage and Retrieval System [*Database*] — WATSTORE
National Water Supply Improvement Association. Annual Conference. Technical Proceedings — Natl Water Supply Improv Assoc Annu Conf Tech Proc
National Water Supply Improvement Association Journal — Natl Water Supply Improv Assoc J
National Weeds Conference of South Africa. Proceedings — Natl Weeds Conf S Afr Proc
National Westminster Bank. Quarterly Review — Nat W Bank
National Westminster Bank. Quarterly Review — Nat West Bank Q Rev
National Westminster Bank. Quarterly Review — Nat Westminster Bank Q R
National Westminster Bank Quarterly Review — Nat Westminster Bank Quart R
National Westminster Bank. Quarterly Review [*England*] — Natl Westminster Bank Q Rev
National Westminster Bank. Quarterly Review — WEB
National Wetlands Newsletter — Nat Wetlands Newsletter
National Wildlife — GNAW
National Wildlife — Nat Wildlife
National Wildlife — Natl Wildl
National Wool Grower — Natl Wool Grow
Nationalbibliothek — NB
Nationale Genossenschaft fuer die Lagerung Radioaktiver Abfaelle Informiert — Natl Genoss Lagerung Radioakt Abfaelle Inf
Nationale Pharmaceutische Dagen. Verslagen. Internationaal Symposium over de Controle van de Pharmaceutische Specialiteiten — Natl Pharm Dagen Versl Int Symp Controle Pharm Spec
Nationale Wirtschaft — Nation Wirtsch
Nationalities Papers — Nat P
Nationalmuseets Arbeidsmark — Nat A
Nationalmuseets Arbejdsmark — Nationalmus Arbejdsmark
Nationalmuseets Arbejdsmark (Kobenhavn) — Arbejdsmark (Kob)
Nationalmusei Skriftserie. Analecta Reginensia — NSAR
Nationalokonomisk Tidsskrift — Nat -Okon Tss
Nationalokonomisk Tidsskrift — Natok T
Nationalsozialistische Monatshefte — NSM
Nationalzeitung — N
Nationalzeitung und Soldatenzeitung — NZSZ
Nation's Agriculture — Nat Agr
Nation's Agriculture — Nation's Ag
Nation's Agriculture — Nation's Agric
Nation's Business — NAB
Nation's Business — Nation's Bus
Nation's Business — Natns Bus
Nation's Business (Washington, DC) — NBW
Nation's Cities — Nat Cities
Nation's Cities Weekly — INCW
Nations Nouvelles — Nations Nouv
Nation's Restaurant News — Natns Restr
Nation's Schools — Nat Sch
Nation's Schools — Nation's Sch
Native Affairs Department. Annual — NADA
Native Americans — Nat Am
Native Art Studies Association of Canada. Newsletter — NAST
Native Canadian — NACN
Native Counselling Services of Alberta. Newsletter — NCSA
Native Library Advocate [*Ottawa, Canada*] — NALA
Native News and BIA [*Bureau of Indian Affairs*] **Bulletin** — NNBB
Native Press — NP
Native School Bulletin — Native Sch Bul
Native Self-Sufficiency — Natv Self
Native Women's Association of Canada. Newsletter — NWAC
Native Women's Association of the NWT [*Northwest Territories, Canada*]. **Newsletter** — NWAN
NATNews. National Association of Theatre Nurses — NATNews
NATO Advanced Science Institute Series F. Computer and Systems Sciences — NATO Adv Sci Inst Ser F Comput Systems Sci
NATO Advanced Science Institutes Series. Series A. Life Sciences — NATO Adv Sci Inst Ser Ser A
NATO Advanced Science Institutes Series. Series G. Ecological Sciences — NATO Adv Sci Inst Ser G Ecolog Sci
NATO Advanced Science Institutes Series. Series G. Ecological Sciences — NATO Adv Sci Inst Ser Ser G
NATO Advanced Study Institute — NATO Adv Study Inst
NATO Advanced Study Institute Series D. Behavioural and Social Sciences — NATO Adv Study Inst Ser D Behav Soc Sci
NATO Advanced Study Institute Series. Series A. Life Sciences — NATO Adv Study Inst Ser Ser A
NATO [*North Atlantic Treaty Organization*] **Advanced Study Institutes. Series B. Physics** — NATO Adv Study Inst Ser B
NATO [*North Atlantic Treaty Organization*] **Advanced Study Institutes. Series B. Physics** — NATO Adv Study Inst Ser B Physics
NATO [*North Atlantic Treaty Organization*] **Advanced Study Institutes. Series C. Mathematical and Physical Sciences** — NATO Adv Study Inst Ser C
NATO [*North Atlantic Treaty Organization*] **Advanced Study Institutes. Series D. Behavioural and Social Sciences** — NATO Adv Study Inst Ser D
NATO [*North Atlantic Treaty Organization*] **Advanced Study Institutes. Series E. Applied Sciences** — NATO Adv Study Inst Ser E
NATO [*North Atlantic Treaty Organization*] **Advanced Study Institutes Series. Series A. Life Sciences** — NASSDK
NATO [*North Atlantic Treaty Organization*] **Advanced Study Institutes Series. Series A. Life Sciences** — NATO Adv Study Inst Ser Ser A Life Sci
NATO [*North Atlantic Treaty Organization*] **Advanced Study Institutes Series. Series E. Applied Science** — NASEDC
NATO [*North Atlantic Treaty Organization*] **Advanced Study Institutes Series. Series E. Applied Science** — NATO Adv Study Inst Ser Ser E Appl Sci
NATO [*North Atlantic Treaty Organization*] **and the Warsaw Pact Force Comparisons** — NATO War P
NATO [*North Atlantic Treaty Organization*] **ASI (Advanced Science Institutes) Series. Series A. Life Sciences** — NATO ASI (Adv Sci Inst) Ser Ser A Life Sci
NATO [*North Atlantic Treaty Organization*] **ASI (Advanced Science Institutes) Series. Series E. Applied Sciences** — NATO ASI (Adv Sci Inst) Ser Ser E Appl Sci
NATO [*North Atlantic Treaty Organization*] **ASI (Advanced Science Institutes) Series. Series G. Ecological Sciences** — NATO ASI (Adv Sci Inst) Ser Ser G Ecol Sci
NATO ASI Series 1. Disarmament Technologies — NATO ASI Ser 1
NATO [*North Atlantic Treaty Organization*] **ASI Series A. Life Sciences** [*Advanced Science Institutes*] — NATO ASI Ser Ser A
NATO ASI Series. Series 3. High Technology — NATO ASI Ser Ser 3

NATO [*North Atlantic Treaty Organization*] **ASI Series. Series A. Life Sciences** [*Advanced Science Institutes*] — NALSDJ
NATO ASI Series. Series B. Physics — NATO ASI Ser Ser B
NATO ASI Series. Series C. Mathematical and Physical Sciences — NATO ASI Ser Ser C
NATO [*North Atlantic Treaty Organization*] **ASI Series. Series E. Applied Sciences** [*Advanced Science Institutes*] — NAESDI
NATO ASI Series. Series E. Applied Sciences — NATO ASI Ser Ser E
NATO [*North Atlantic Treaty Organization*] **ASI Series. Series G. Ecological Sciences** [*Advanced Science Institutes*] — NASGEJ
NATO ASI Series. Series H. Cell Biology — NATO ASI Ser Ser H Cell Biol
NATO ASI Series. Series I. Global Environmental Change — NATO ASI Ser Ser I
NATO/CCMS [*North Atlantic Treaty Organization/Committee on the Challenges of Modern Society*] **Air Pollution** — NATO/CCMS Air Pollut
NATO Challenges of Modern Society — NATO Challenges Mod Soc
NATO [*North Atlantic Treaty Organization*]/Committee on the Challenges of Modern Society. Air Pollution — NATO Comm Challenges Mod Soc Air Pollut
NATO [*North Atlantic Treaty Organization*] **Conference Series 4. Marine Sciences** — NATO Conf Ser 4
NATO Conference Series. 6. Materials Science — NATO Conf Ser 6
NATO Conference Series II. Systems Science — NATO Conf Ser II Systems Sci
NATO Conference Series IV. Marine Sciences — NATO Conf Ser IV
NATO [*North Atlantic Treaty Organization*] **Review** — NFF
NATO's [*North Atlantic Treaty Organization*] **Fifteen Nations** — NATO's Fift Nations
NATO's Sixteen Nations. North Atlantic Treaty Organization — NATO 16
NATS [*National Association of Teachers of Singing*] **Bulletin** — NATS Bul
Natsionalen Kongres po Teoretichna i Prilozhna Mekhanika. Dokladi — Nats Kongr Teor Prilozh Mekh Dokl
Natsional'na Akademiya Nauk Ukraini. Institut Matematiki. Preprint — Nats Akad Nauk Ukrain Inst Mat Preprint
Natsionalna Konferentsiya po Salmonelite i Salmonelozite — Nats Konf Salmonelite Salmonelozite
Natsionalna Konferentsiya po Vodopodgotovka, Voden Rezhim i Koroziya v TETs i AETs. Sbornik Dokladi — Nats Konf Vodopodgot Voden Rezhim Koroz TETs AETs Sb Dokl
Natsional'naya Akademiya Nauk Armenii. Izvestiya. Matematika — Izv Nats Akad Nauk Armenii Mat
Natsional'naya Konferentsiya po Atomnoi Spektroskopii. Doklady — Nats Konf At Spektrosk Dokl
Natturufraedingurinn — NTFDA
Natuerliche und Kuenstliche Alterung von Kunststoffen. Donaulaendergespraech — Nat Kuenstliche Alterung Kunstst Donaulaendergespraech
Natur Jutlandica — Nat Jutlandica
Natur og Museum (Arhus) — Natur Mus (Arhus)
Natur und Heimat — Nat Heimat
Natur und Land — Nat Land
Natur und Landschaft — Nat Landschaft
Natur und Landschaft — Natur Landsch
Natur und Landschaft — NL
Natur und Mensch / La Nature et l'Homme / La Natura e l'Uomo — Natur Mensch
Natur und Mensch (Nuernberg) — Nat Mensch (Nuernb)
Natur und Museum — Nat Mus
Natur und Museum — Natur u Mus
Natur und Museum (Frankfurt) — Natur Mus (Frankf)
Natur und Museum. Senckenbergische Naturforschende Gesellschaft — Nat Mus Senckenb Naturforsch Ges
Natur und Offenbarung — Nu O
Natur und Technik — Nat Tech
Natur und Technik. Schweizerische Zeitschrift fuer Naturwissenschaften (Zurich) — Natur Techn Zurich
Natur und Technik (Vienna) — Natur Techn Vienna
Natur und Technik (Zurich) — Nat Tech Zurich
Natur und Volk — Nat Volk
Natur und Volk — Natur u Volk
Natur und Volk (Frankfurt) — Nat Volk (Frankf)
Natura Jutlandica — Nat Jutl
Natura Mosana — NAMOA9
Natura Mosana — Nat Mosana
Natura Mosana. Supplement B. Botanique — Nat Mosana Suppl B Bot
Natura Mosana. Supplement CD. Zoologie — Nat Mosana Suppl CD Zool
Natura (Plovdiv, Bulgaria) — NTURB
Natura. Seria Biologie — Nat Biol
Natura. Seria Biologie — Natura Biol
Natural and Applied Science Bulletin — Nat Appl Sci Bull
Natural and Synthetic Gas (Energy Data Report) — Nat Synth Gas Energy Data Rep
Natural Areas Journal — Nat Areas J
Natural Environment Research Council. Institute of Geological Sciences. Overseas Memoir — Nat Environ Res Counc Inst Geol Sci Overseas Mem
Natural Environment Research Council. Institute of Geological Sciences. Report (United Kingdom) — Nat Environ Res Counc Inst Geol Sci Rep (UK)
Natural Environment Research Council. Institute of Terrestrial Ecology. Annual Report — Nat Environ Res Counc Inst Terr Ecol Annu Rep
Natural Environment Research Council. News Journal — Nat Environ Res Counc News J
Natural Environment Research Council. Publications Series D (U.K.) — Nat Environ Res Counc Publ Ser D UK
Natural Food and Farming — Natural Food Fmg
Natural Gardening — Natural Gard
Natural Gas — Nat Gas
Natural Gas and Gasoline Journal — Nat Gas Gasoline J
Natural Gas Annual, 1983 — Nat Gas A
Natural Gas Association of America. Proceedings — Nat Gas As Am Pr
Natural Gas Chemical Industry — Nat Gas Chem Ind
Natural Gas (Cincinnati) — Nat Gas Cincinnati
Natural Gas (Energy Data Report) — Nat Gas (Energy Data Rep)
Natural Gas for Industry — Natural Gas Ind
Natural Gas/Fuel Forecast. Series A. Geographic [*United States*] — Nat Gas/Fuel Forecast Ser A
Natural Gas/Fuel Forecast. Series B. Industrial [*United States*] — Nat Gas/Fuel Forecast Ser B
Natural Gas Industry — Nat Gas Ind
Natural Gas Liquids — Nat Gas Liq
Natural Gas Magazine — Nat Gas Mag
Natural Gas Market through 1990 — N Gas M 1990
Natural Gas Monthly Report (Energy Data Report) — Nat Gas Mon Rep Energy Data Rep
Natural Gas Processors Association. Proceedings. Annual Convention. Technical Papers — Nat Gas Process Assoc Proc Annu Conv Tech Pap
Natural Gas Research and Technology. Proceedings. Conference — Nat Gas Res Technol Proc Conf
Natural Health Bulletin — Nat Hlth Bul
Natural History — GNAH
Natural History — Nat Hist
Natural History — Natur Hist
Natural History — Natural Hi
Natural History — NH
Natural History. American Museum of Natural History — AMNH/NH
Natural History Bulletin. Siam Society — Nat Hist Bull Siam Soc
Natural History Guides. Boston Society of Natural History — Nat Hist Guides Boston Soc Nat Hist
Natural History Magazine — Nat Hist Mag
Natural History Magazine. British Museum. Natural History — Nat Hist Mag
Natural History Miscellanae (Chicago) — Nat Hist Misc (Chic)
Natural History Museum of Los Angeles County. Contributions in Science — Nat Hist Mus Los Ang Cty Contrib Sci
Natural History Museum of Los Angeles County. Science Bulletin — Nat Hist Mus Los Ang Cty Sci Bull
Natural History Museum of Los Angeles County. Science Bulletin — Nat Hist Mus Los Angeles Cty Sci Bull
Natural History Museum of Los Angeles County. Science Series — Nat Hist Mus Los Ang Cty Sci Ser
Natural History (New York) — Nat Hist (NY)
Natural History of Rennell Island, British Solomon Islands — Nat Hist Rennell Isl Br Solomon Isl
Natural History of the National Parks of Hungary — Nat Hist Natl Parks Hung
Natural History Review — N H Rv
Natural History Review. A Quarterly Journal of Biological Science — Nat Hist Rev
Natural History Society of New Brunswick. Bulletin — N H Soc NB B
Natural Immunity — Nat Immun
Natural Immunity and Cell Growth Regulation — Nat Immun Cell Growth Regul
Natural Law Forum — Nat LF
Natural Law Forum — Natural L F
Natural Philosopher — Nat Philos
Natural Product Letters — Nat Prod Lett
Natural Product Reports — Nat Prod Rep
Natural Product Reports — NPRRDF
Natural Product Reports. A Journal of Current Developments in Bio-Organic Chemistry — Nat Prod Rep J Curr Dev Bio Org Chem
Natural Product Sciences — Nat Prod Sci
Natural Product Update — NPU
Natural Products R and D — Nat Prod RD
Natural Protectants and Natural Toxicants in Food — Nat Prot Nat Toxicants Food
Natural Radiation Environment. International Symposium on the Natural Radiation Evironment — Nat Radiat Environ Int Symp
Natural Resource Modeling — Natur Resource Modeling
Natural Resources and Earth Sciences. Abstract Newsletter — Nat Resour Earth Sci
Natural Resources and the Environment Series — Nat Resour Environ Ser
Natural Resources Forum — Nat Resour Forum
Natural Resources Forum — Nat Resources Forum
Natural Resources Forum — Natur Resources Forum
Natural Resources Forum — NRFOD
Natural Resources Forum Library — Nat Resour Forum Libr
Natural Resources Journal — Nat Res J
Natural Resources Journal — Nat Resour J
Natural Resources Journal — Nat Resources J
Natural Resources Journal — Nat Resources Jour
Natural Resources Journal — Natur Res J
Natural Resources Journal — Natur Resources J
Natural Resources Journal — Natural Resources J
Natural Resources Journal — Natural Resources Jnl
Natural Resources Journal — NRJ
Natural Resources Law — Nat Res Law
Natural Resources Law Newsletter — Nat Resources L Newsl
Natural Resources Lawyer — Nat Res Lawyer
Natural Resources Lawyer — Nat Resour Lawyer
Natural Resources Lawyer — Nat Resources Law
Natural Resources Lawyer — Natur Res L
Natural Resources Lawyer — Natur Resou
Natural Resources Lawyer — Natural Resources Law
Natural Resources Lawyer — Natural Resources Lawy
Natural Resources Research (Paris) — Nat Resour Res (Paris)
Natural Rubber Background — Nat Rubber Background

Natural Rubber News — Nat Rubb News
Natural Rubber News — Nat Rubber
Natural Rubber Technology — N R Technol
Natural Rubber Technology — Nat Rubber Technol
Natural Science — Nat Sci
Natural Science and Museum/Shizen Kagaku no Hakubutsukan — Nat Sci Mus
Natural Science Association of Staten Island. Proceedings — Nat Sc As Staten Island Pr
Natural Science Bulletin. University of Amoy — Nat Sci Bull Univ Amoy
Natural Science Journal of Xiangtan University — Nat Sci J Xiangtan Univ
Natural Science Journal of Xiangtan University — Natur Sci J Xiangtan Univ
Natural Science Report. Ochanomizu University — Nat Sci Rep Ochanomizu Univ
Natural Science Report. Ochanomizu University — Natur Sci Rep Ochanomizu Univ
Natural Science Research. Natural Science Institute. Chosun University — Nat Sci Res Nat Sci Inst Chosun Univ
Natural Sciences — Nat Sci
Natural Sciences Journal of Harbin Normal University — Natur Sci J Harbin Normal Univ
Natural Sciences Journal of Hunan Normal University — Nat Sci J Hunan Norm Univ
Natural Toxins — Nat Toxins
Natural Toxins. Proceedings. International Symposium on Animal, Plant, and Microbial Toxins — Nat Toxins Proc Int Symp Anim Plant Microb Toxins
Naturaleza y Gracia — Nat Grac
Naturalia — Na
Naturalia [*Lisbon*] — NTULA3
Naturalia Hispanica — Nat Hisp
Naturalia Hispanica — Nat Hispan
Naturalia Monspeliensia — Nat Monspel
Naturalia Monspeliensia. Revue de Botanique Generale et Mediterraneenne — Nat Monspel Rev Bot Gen Mediterr
Naturalia Monspeliensia. Serie Botanique — Nat Monspel Ser Bot
Naturalia Monspeliensia. Serie Botanique — Nat Monspeliensia Ser Bot
Naturalia Monspeliensia. Serie Botanique — Naturalia Monspel Ser Bot
Naturalia Monspeliensia. Serie Botanique — NMBQAA
Naturalist — Nat
Naturalista Siciliano — Nat Sicil
Naturalista Siciliano — NTSIAI
Naturaliste Canadien — Naturaliste Can
Naturaliste Canadien (Quebec) — Nat Can (Quebec)
Naturaliste Canadien (Quebec). Revue d'Ecologie et de Systematique — Nat Can Que
Naturaliste Malgache — Nat Malgache
Naturalistes Belges — Nat Belg
Naturalistes Belges — Natur Belges
Nature — GNAA
Nature — N
Nature [*London*] — Na
Nature — NATRA
Nature — NATUA
Nature and Culture — Nat Cult
Nature and Insects (Tokyo) — Nat Insects Tokyo
Nature and Life in Southeast Asia — Nat Life Southeast Asia
Nature and Life in Southeast Asia — Nature and Life SE Asia
Nature and Plants (Tokyo) — Nat Plants (Tokyo)
Nature and Resources [*France*] — NAREB
Nature and Resources — Nat Resour
Nature and Science Education Review — Nature and Sci Ed R
Nature and System — Natur Syst
Nature and System — Nature Syst
Nature Biotechnology — Nat Biotechnol
Nature Canada — INAC
Nature Canada — Nat Can
Nature Canada — Nat Canada
Nature Canada — NTCNB
Nature Canada (Ottawa) — Nat Can (Ottawa)
Nature Conservancy Council. Research Reports Digest — NCC Res Rep Dig
Nature Conservancy News [*United States*] — Nat Conserv News
Nature Conservation Branch. Transvaal Bulletin — Nat Conserv Branch Transvaal Bull
Nature Genetics — Nat Genet
Nature in Cambridgeshire — Nat Cambridgeshire
Nature in Cambridgeshire — Nat Cambs
Nature in East Africa. The Bulletin. East Africa Natural History Society — Nat E Africa
Nature in Wales — Nat Wales
Nature Journal — Natur J
Nature (London). New Biology — Nature (London) New Biol
Nature (London). Physical Science — Nature (London) Phys Sci
Nature Magazine — Nat Mag
Nature Magazine — Nature Mag
Nature Malaysiana — Nat Malays
Nature Medicine — Nat Med
Nature Medicine (New York) — Nat Med NY
Nature: New Biology — Nat New Biol
Nature: New Biology — Nature New Biol
Nature: New Biology — NNBYA
Nature Notes from the Grand Canyon — Nat Notes Grand Canyon
Nature of Life. Nobel Conference — Nat Life Nobel Conf
Nature: Physical Science — Nature: Phys Sci
Nature: Physical Science — NPS
Nature. Physical Universe. Nobel Conference — Nat Phys Universe Nobel Conf
Nature. Science Annual — Nat Sci Ann
Nature. Science Progress — Nat Sci Prog
Nature Structural Biology — Nat Struct Biol
Nature Study — Nat Study
Nature Study — Natur Study
Nature Vivante — Nat Vivante
Naturegraph Ocean Guide Books — Naturegp Ocean Guide Books
Naturegraph Ocean Guide Books — Naturegr Ocean Guide Books
Naturens Verden — Nat V
Naturens Verden — Nat Verden
Naturens Verden — Naturens Verd
Naturforschende Gesellschaft in Bamberg. Bericht — Naturf Ges Bamberg Ber
Naturforschende Gesellschaft in Basel. Verhandlungen — Naturf Gesell Basel Verh
Naturforschende Gesellschaft in Basel. Verhandlungen — Naturforsch Ges Basel Verh
Naturforschende Gesellschaft in Bern. Mitteilungen. Neue Folge — Naturf Gesell Bern Mitt Neue Folge
Naturforschende Gesellschaft in Zuerich. Vierteljahresschrift — Naturf Gesell Zurich Vierteljahrsschr
Naturforschende Gesellschaft in Zuerich. Vierteljahrsschrift — Naturforsch Ges Zuerich Vierteljahrsschr
Naturforschende Gesellschaft zu Freiburg im Breisgau. Berichte — Naturforsch Ges Freib im Breisgau Ber
Naturforschung und Medizin in Deutschland — NF Med Dt
Naturhistorische Gesellschaft Nuernberg. Jahresbericht — Naturhist Ges Nuernberg Jahresber
Naturhistorische Gesellschaft zu Hannover. Bericht — Naturhist Ges Hannover Ber
Naturhistorischer Verein der Preussischen Rheinlande und Westphalens. Verhandlungen — Naturh Ver Preus Rheinl Verh
Naturhistorischer Verein der Preussischen Rheinlande. Verhandlungen (Niederrheinische Gesellschaft fuer Naturund Heilkunde in Bonn). Sitzungsberichte — Naturh Ver Preus Rheinl Verh (Niederrhein Ges Bonn) Szb
Naturhistorisches Museum (Bern). Jahrbuch — Naturhist Mus (Bern) Jahrb
Naturhistorisches Museum der Stadt Bern. Jahrbuch — Naturhist Mus Stadt Bern Jahrb
Naturhistorisches Museum in Wien. Annalen — Naturhist Mus Wien Ann
Naturhistorisches Museum in Wien. Veroeffentlichungen. Neue Folge — Naturhist Mus Wien Veroeff Neue Folge
Naturhistorisch-Medicinischer Verein zu Heidelberg. Verhandlungen — Naturh-Med Ver Heidelberg Verh
Naturhistorisk Tidende — Nath T
Naturkundliches Jahrbuch der Stadt Linz — Naturk Jb Stadt Linz
Naturschutz und Landschaftspflege in Niedersachsen. Beiheft — Naturschutz Landschaftspflege Niedersachsen Beih
Naturschutz- und Naturparke — Natursch Naturp
Naturschutzarbeit in Berlin und Brandenburg. Beiheft — Naturschutzarbeit Berlin Brandenburg Beih
Naturschutzarbeit und Naturkundliche Heimatforschung in den Bezirken Rostock-Schwerin-Neubrandenburg — Naturschutzarbeit Naturk Heimatf Bez Rostock
Naturwissenschaft und Medizin — Naturwiss Med
Naturwissenschaft und Medizin — Naturwissenschaft Med
Naturwissenschaft und Medizin — NM
Naturwissenschaft und Theologie — NWT
Naturwissenschaften — Naturwiss
Naturwissenschaften — Naturwissen
Naturwissenschaften — Nw
Naturwissenschaften im Unterricht Chemie — Naturwiss Unterr Chem
Naturwissenschaften im Unterricht. Physik/Chemie/Biologie — Naturwiss Unterr Phys Chem Biol
Naturwissenschaften im Unterricht (Teil) Physik/Chemie [*Germany*] — Naturwiss Unterr Phys/Chem
Naturwissenschaftliche Abhandlungen — Naturw Abh
Naturwissenschaftliche Abhandlungen (Tuebingen) — Naturwiss Abh Tuebingen
Naturwissenschaftliche Abhandlungen (Wilhelm Haidinger, Editor) — Haidingers Abh
Naturwissenschaftliche Fakultaet Muenich Universitaet. Inaugural-Dissertation [*A publication*] — Naturwiss Fak Muenich Univ Inaug-Diss
Naturwissenschaftliche Gesellschaft Isis in Meissen. Mitteilungen aus den Sitzungen — Naturwiss Ges Isis Meissen Mitt Sitzungen
Naturwissenschaftliche Monatshefte fuer den Biologischen, Chemischen, Geographischen, und Geologischen Unterricht — Naturwiss Monatsh Biol Chem Geogr Geol Unterr
Naturwissenschaftliche Rundschau — Naturw Rdsch
Naturwissenschaftliche Rundschau — Naturwiss Rdsch
Naturwissenschaftliche Rundschau — Naturwiss Rundsch
Naturwissenschaftliche Rundschau — NR
Naturwissenschaftliche Rundschau (Stuttgart) — Naturw Rdsch (Stuttg)
Naturwissenschaftliche Rundschau (Stuttgart) — Naturwiss Rundschau Stuttgart
Naturwissenschaftliche Umschau der Chemiker-Zeitung — Naturwiss Umsch Chem Ztg
Naturwissenschaftliche Wochenschrift — Naturw Wchnschr
Naturwissenschaftliche Wochenschrift — Naturw Wochens
Naturwissenschaftliche Wochenschrift — Naturw Wochensch
Naturwissenschaftliche Wochenschrift — Naturwiss Wochenschr
Naturwissenschaftliche Wochenschrift — Natwiss Wschr
Naturwissenschaftliche Zeitschrift fuer Forst- und Landwirtschaft — Naturw Z Forst u Landw
Naturwissenschaftliche Zeitschrift fuer Forst- und Landwirtschaft — Naturwiss Z Forst Landwirtsch
Naturwissenschaftliche Zeitschrift fuer Forst- und Landwirtschaft — NZFL
Naturwissenschaftliche Zeitschrift fuer Land- und Forstwirtschaft — Naturw Z Land-u Forstw
Naturwissenschaftliche Zeitschrift fuer Land- und Forstwirtschaft — NatZLF

Naturwissenschaftliche Zeitschrift Lotos — Naturwiss Z Lotos
Naturwissenschaftlicher Anzeiger der Allgemeinen Schweizerischen Gesellschaft fuer die Gesammten Naturwissenschaften — Naturwiss Anz Allg Schweiz Ges Gesammten Naturwiss
Naturwissenschaftlicher Verein (Darmstadt). Bericht — Naturwiss Verein (Darmst) Ber
Naturwissenschaftlicher Verein fuer Neuvorpommern und Ruegen in Greifswald. Mitteilungen — Naturw Ver Neuvorpommern und Ruegen in Greifswald Mitt
Naturwissenschaftlicher Verein fuer Schleswig-Holstein. Schriften — Naturwiss Ver Schleswig-Holstein Schr
Naturwissenschaftlicher Verein fuer Steiermark. Mitteilungen — Naturw Ver Steiermark Mitt
Naturwissenschaftlicher Verein (Halle). Jahresberichte — Naturw Ver (Halle) Jber
Naturwissenschaftlicher Verein zu Bremen. Abhandlungen — Naturwiss Ver Bremen Abh
Natuur- en Geneeskundig Archief voor Nederlandsch-Indiee — Natuur Geneesk Arch Ned Indiee
Natuur- en Konstkabinet — Natuur Konstkab
Natuur en Landschap Tijdschrift van de Contact Commissie voor Natuur- en Landschapsebescherming — Nat Landschap
Natuur en Mensch — Nat Mensch
Natuur en Milieu — NLS
Natuur en Techniek — Nat Tech
Natuur en Techniek (Beek, Netherlands) — Nat Tech Beek Neth
Natuur en Technik (Maastricht, Netherlands) — Nat Tech (Maastricht Neth)
Natuurhistorisch Maandblad — Natuurh Maandbl
Natuurhistorisch Maandblad — Natuurhist Maandbl
Natuurkundig Tijdschrift voor Nederlandsch-Indie — Natuurk Tijdschr Ned-Indie
Natuurkundige Verhandelingen. Koninglijke Maatschappy der Wetenschappen te Haarlem — Natuurk Verh Kon Maatsch Wetensch Haarlem
Natuurkundige Verhandelingen van de Maatschappy der Wetenschappen te Haarlem — Natuurk Verh Maatsch Wetensch Haarlem
Natuurkundige Voordrachten — Natuurkd Voordr
Natuursteen — NAS
Natuurwetenschappelijk Tijdschrift — Natuurwet Tijdschr
Natuurwetenschappelijk Tijdschrift (Ghent) — NATGA
Natuurwetenschappelijk Tijdschrift voor Nederlandsch-Indie — Natuurwet Tijdschr Ned Indie
Natuurwetenschappelijk Tijdschrift voor Nederlandsch-Indiee — Natuurw Tijdschr Ned Indiee
Natuurwetenschappelijke Studiekring voor Suriname en de Nederlandse Antillen. Uitgaven — Natuurwet Studiekring Suriname Ned Antillen Uitg
Natuurwetenschappelijke Werkgroep Nederlandse Antillen Uitgaven — Natuurwet Werkgroep Nederlandse Antillen Uitgaven
Nauchnaya Apparatura — Nauchn Appar
Nauchnaya Informatsiya. Belorusskii Tekhnologicheskii Institut — Nauchn Inf Beloruss Tekhnol Inst
Nauchnaya Konferentsiya Geologov Litvy. Materialy — Nauchn Konf Geol Litvy Mater
Nauchnaya Konferentsiya Molodykh Uchenykh-Morfologov Moskvy — Nauchn Konf Molodykh Uch Morfol Moskvy
Nauchnaya Konferentsiya Moskovskogo Otdeleniya Vsesoyuznogo Mineralogicheskogo Obshchestva — Nauchn Konf Mosk Otd Vses Mineral Ova
Nauchnaya Konferentsiya po Izucheniyu Vnutrennikh Vodoemov Pribaltiki — Nauchn Konf Izuch Vnutr Vodoemov Pribaltiki
Nauchnaya Konferentsiya po Yadernoi Meteorologii (Obninsk) — Nauch Konf Yadern Meteor (Obninsk)
Nauchnaya Konferentsiya Selen v Biologii — Nauchn Konf Selen Biol
Nauchnaya Sessiya po Khimii i Tekhnologii Organicheskikh Soedinenii Sery i Sernistykh Neftei. Plenarnye Doklady — Nauchn Sess Khim Tekhnol Org Soedin Sery Sernistykh Neftei P
Nauchni Byulleten Vsesoyuznogo Nauchno Issledovatel'skogo Instituta po Khlopku — Nauchn Byull Vses Nauchno Issled Inst Khlopku
Nauchni Trudove. Institut po Konservna Promishlenost. Plovdiv — Nauchni Tr Inst Konservna Promst Plovdiv
Nauchni Trudove. Institut po Mlechna Promishlenost (Vidin, Bulgaria) — Nauchni Tr Inst Mlechna Promst (Vidin Bulg)
Nauchni Trudove. Institut po Rastitelni Masla, Protein, i Mieshti Sredstva-Sofiya — Nauchni Tr Inst Rastit Masla Protein Mieshti Sredstva Sofiya
Nauchni Trudove. Institut za Spetsializatsiya i Usuvurshenstvuvane na Lekarite — Nauchni Tr Inst Spets Usuvursh Lek
Nauchni Trudove. Instituta za Pochveni Izsledvaniya — Nauchni Tr Inst Pochv Izsled
Nauchni Trudove. Ministerstvo na Zemedelieto i Gorite — Nauchni Trud Minist Zemed Gorite
Nauchni Trudove na Dobrudzhanskiya Selskostopanski Nauchnoizsledovatelski Institut — Nauch Tr Dobrudzhan Selskostop Nauchnoizsled Inst
Nauchni Trudove na Visshiya Meditsinski Institut — NTVMA
Nauchni Trudove na Visshiya Meditsinski Institut (Sofia) — Nauchni Tr Vissh Med Inst (Sofia)
Nauchni Trudove na Visshiya Meditsinski Institut (Varna) — Nauchni Tr Vissh Med Inst (Varna)
Nauchni Trudove. Nauchnoizsledovatelski Institut po Konservna Promishlenost (Plovdiv) — Nauchni Tr Nauchnoizsled Inst Konservna Promst (Plovdiv)
Nauchni Trudove. Nauchnoizsledovatelski Institut po Radiobiologiya i Radiatsionna Khigiena — Nauchni Tr Nauchnoizsled Inst Radiobiol Radiats Khig
Nauchni Trudove. Nauchnoizsledovatelski Institut po Ribarstvo i Ribna Promishlenost. Varna — Nauchni Tr Nauchnoizsled Inst Ribar Ribna Promst Varna
Nauchni Trudove. Nauchnoizsledovatelski Institut po Vinarska i Pivovarna Promishlenost — NNVPA
Nauchni Trudove. Nauchnoizsledovatelski Institut po Vinarska i Pivovarna Promishlenost (Sofia) — Nauchni Tr Nauchnoizsled Inst Vinar Pivovar Promst (Sofia)
Nauchni Trudove. Nauchnoizsledovatelski Institut za Durzhaven Kontrol na Lekarstvenite Sredstva — Nauchni Tr Nauchnoizsled Inst Durzh Kontrol Lek Sredstva
Nauchni Trudove. Nauchnoizsledovatelskiya Institut po Pediatriya — Nauchni Tr Nauchnoizsled Inst Pediatr
Nauchni Trudove. Nauchnoizsledovatelskiya Instituta po Okhrana na Truda i Profesionalnite Zabolyavaniya — Nauchni Tr Nauchnoizsled Inst Okhr Tr Prof Zabol
Nauchni Trudove. Plovdivski Universitet — Nauchni Tr Plovdivski Univ
Nauchni Trudove. Plovdivski Universitet. Matematika, Fizika, Khimiya, Biologiya [*Bulgaria*] — Nauchni Tr Plovdivski Univ Mat Fiz Khim Biol
Nauchni Trudove. Plovdivski Universitet. Matematika, Fizika, Khimiya, Biologiya — NTPUB
Nauchni Trudove po Transportna Meditsina — Nauchni Tr Transp Med
Nauchni Trudove. Selskostopanska Akademiya Georgi Dimitrov. Agronomicheski Fakultet — Nauchni Tr Selskostop Akad Georgi Dimitrov Agron Fak
Nauchni Trudove. Selskostopanska Akademiya "Georgi Dimitrov" (Sofia) Seriya. Rastenievudstvo — Nauchni Tr Selskostop Akad (Sofia) Ser Rastenievud
Nauchni Trudove. Seriia Gorsko Stopanstvo — Nauchni Trudove Ser Gorsko Stop
Nauchni Trudove. Tsentralniya Nauchnoizsledovatelski Institut po Tekhnologiya na Mashinostroineto — Nauchni Tr Tsentr Nauchnoizsled Inst Tekhnol Mashinostr
Nauchni Trudove. Vissh Institut po Khranitelna i Vkusova Promishlenost (Plovdiv) — Nauchni Tr Vissh Inst Khranit Vkusova Promst (Plovdiv)
Nauchni Trudove. Vissh Lesotekhnicheski Institut — Nauchni Trud Vissh Lesotekh Inst
Nauchni Trudove. Vissh Lesotekhnicheski Institut (Sofia) [*Bulgaria*] — Nauchni Tr Vissh Lesotekh Inst (Sofia)
Nauchni Trudove. Vissh Lesotekhnicheski Institut (Sofia) — NVLSA
Nauchni Trudove. Vissh Lesotekhnicheski Institut (Sofia). Seriya Gorsko Stopanstvo — Nauchni Tr Vissh Lesotekh Inst (Sofia) Ser Gorsko Stop
Nauchni Trudove. Vissh Lesotekhnicheski Institut (Sofia). Seriya Mekhanichna Tekhnologiya na Durvesinata [*Bulgaria*] — Nauchni Tr Vissh Lesotekh Inst (Sofia) Ser Mekh Tekhnol Durv
Nauchni Trudove. Vissh Lesotekhnicheski Institut (Sofia). Seriya Mekhanichna Tekhnologiya na Durvesinata (Bulgaria) — NTMLB
Nauchni Trudove. Vissh Lesotekhnicheski Institut (Sofia). Seriya Ozelenyavane [*A publication*] — Nauchni Tr Vissh Lesotekh Inst (Sofia) Ser Ozelenyavane
Nauchni Trudove. Vissh Pedagogicheski Institut (Plovdiv). Matematika, Fizika, Khimiya, Biologiya — Nauchni Tr Vissh Pedagog Inst (Plovdiv) Mat Fiz Khim Biol
Nauchni Trudove. Vissh Selskostopanski Institut "Georgi Dimitrov." Agronomicheski Fakultet — Nauch Tr Vissh Selskostop Inst "Georgi Dimitrov" Agron Fak
Nauchni Trudove. Vissh Selskostopanski Institut "Georgi Dimitrov" (Sofia). Agronomicheski Fakultet — Nauchni Tr Vissh Selskostop Inst (Sofia) Agron Fak
Nauchni Trudove. Vissh Selskostopanski Institut "Georgi Dimitrov" (Sofia). Zootekhnicheski Fakultet — Nauch Tr Vissh Selskostop Inst "Georgi Dimitrov" Zootekh Fak
Nauchni Trudove. Vissh Selskostopanski Institut "Georgi Dimitrov" (Sofia). Zootekhnicheski Fakultet — Nauchni Tr Vissh Selskostop Inst (Sofia) Zootekh Fak
Nauchni Trudove. Vissh Selskostopanski Institut (Sofia). Agronomicheski Fakultet. Seriya Rastenievydstvo — Nauchni Tr Vissh Selskostop Inst Sofia Agron Fak Rastenievyd
Nauchni Trudove. Vissh Selskostopanski Institut "Vasil Kolarov" — Nauch Tr Vissh Selskostop Inst "Vasil Kolarov"
Nauchni Trudove. Vissh Selskostopanski Institut "Vasil Kolarov" — Nauchni Trud Vissh Selskostop Inst "Vasil Kolarov"
Nauchni Trudove. Vissh Selskostopanski Institut "Vasil Kolarov" (Plovdiv) — Nauchni Tr Vissh Selskostop Inst (Plovdiv)
Nauchni Trudove. Vissh Selskostopanski Institut Vasil Kolarov. Plovdiv — Nauchni Tr Vissh Selskostop Inst Vasil Kolarov Plovdiv
Nauchni Trudove. Vissh Veterinarnomeditsinski Institut Prof. Dr G. Pavlov — Nauchni Tr Vissh Veterinarnomed Inst Prof Dr G Pavlov
Nauchni Trudove. Vissh Veterinarnomeditsinski Institut "Prof. Dr. G. Pavlov" (Sofia) — Nauchni Tr Vissh Veterinarnomed Inst (Sofia)
Nauchno Agronomicheskii Zhurnal — Nauchno Agron Zh
Nauchno-Informatsionnyi Byulleten Nauchno-Issledovatel'skogo Otdeleniya Kievskogo Industrial'nogo Instituta — Nauchno Inf Byull Nauchno Issled Otd Kiev Ind Inst
Nauchno-Informatsionnyi Byulleten Tsentral'nogo Nauchno-Issledovatel'skogo Aptechnogo Instituta — Nauchno Inf Byull Tsentr Nauchno Issled Aptechn Inst
Nauchno-Issledovatel'skaya Laboratoriya Geologii Zarubezhnykh Stran Trudy — Nauchno-Issled Lab Geol Zarubezh Stran Tr
Nauchno-Issledovatel'skie Raboty po Otrasli Bumagi i Tsellyulozy — Nauchno Issled Rab Otrasli Bum Tsellyul
Nauchno-Issledovatel'skie Raboty Vsesoyuznogog Nauchno-Issledovatel'skogo Instituta Torfyanoi Promyshlennosti — Nauchno-Issled Rab Vses Nauchno Issled Inst Torf Promsti
Nauchno-Issledovatel'skie Trudy Ivanovskii Tekstil'nye Institut — Nauchno-Issled Tr Ivanov Tekst Inst

Nauchno-Issledovatel'skie Trudy Kalininskii Nauchno-Issledovatel'skii Institut Tekstil'noi Promyshlennosti — Nauchno-Issled Tr Kalinin Nauchno-Issled Inst Tekst Promsti
Nauchno-Issledovatel'skie Trudy Latviiskii Nauchno-Issledovatel'skii Institut Legkoi Promyshlennosti — Nauchno-Issled Tr Latv Nauchno-Issled Inst Legk Promsti
Nauchno-Issledovatel'skie Trudy Litovskii Nauchno-Issledovatel'skii Institut Tekstil'noi Promyshlennosti — Nauchno-Issled Tr Litov Nauchno-Issled Inst Tekst Promsti
Nauchno-Issledovatel'skie Trudy Moskovskii Tekstil'nyi Institut — Nauchno-Issled Tr Mosk Tekst Inst
Nauchno-Issledovatel'skie Trudy. Nauchno-Issledovatel'skii Institut Sherstyanoi Promyshlennosti — Nauchno Issled Tr Nauchno Issled Inst Sherst Promsti
Nauchno-Issledovatel'skie Trudy Tsentral'nogo Nauchno-Issledovatel'skogo Instituta Kozhevenno-Obuvnoi Promyshlennosti — NITTA
Nauchno-Issledovatel'skie Trudy Tsentral'nyi Institut Nauchno-Tekhnicheskoi Informatsii Legkoi Promyshlennosti — Nauchno-Issled Tr Tsentr Inst Nauchno-Tekh Inf Legk Promsti
Nauchno-Issledovatel'skie Trudy Tsentral'nyi Nauchno-Issledovatel'skii Institut Sherstyanoi Promyshlennosti — Nauchno-Issled Tr Tsentr Nauchno-Issled Inst Sherst Promsti
Nauchno-Issledovatel'skie Trudy. Ukrainskii Nauchno-Issledovatel'skii Institut Kozhevenno-Obuvnoi Promyshlennosti — Nauchno Issled Tr Ukr Nauchno Issled Inst Kozh Obuvn Promsti
Nauchno-Issledovatel'skie Trudy Vsesoyuznyi Nauchno-Issledovatel'skii Institut Mekhovoi Promyshlennosti — Nauchno-Issled Tr Vses Nauchno-Issled Inst Mekhovoi Promsti
Nauchno-Issledovatel'skie Trudy. Vsesoyuznyi Nauchno-Issledovatel'skii Institut Shveinoi Promyshlennosti — Nauchno Issled Tr Vses Nauchno Issled Inst Shveinoi Promsti
Nauchno-Issledovatel'skii Gornorazvedochnyi Institut NIGRIZoloto. Trudy — Nauchno Issled Gornorazved Inst NIGRIZoloto Tr
Nauchno-Issledovatel'skii Institut Biologii i Biofiziki pri Tomskom Gosudarstvennom Universitete. Trudy — Nauchno Issled Inst Biol Biofiz Tomsk Gos Univ Tr
Nauchno-Issledovatel'skii Institut Elektronno-Ionnoi Tekhnologii. Trudy (Tbilisi) — Nauchno Issled Inst Elektron Ionnoi Tekhnol Tr Tbilisi
Nauchno-Issledovatel'skii Institut Epidemiologii i Mikrobiologii Trudy (Sofia) — Nauchno-Issled Inst Epidemio Mikrobiol Tr (Sofia)
Nauchno-Issledovatel'skii Institut Gigieny Truda i Profzabolevanii imeni N. I. Makhviladze. Sbornik Trudov — Nauchno Issled Inst Gig Tr Profzabol im NI Makhviladze Sb Tr
Nauchno-Issledovatel'skii Institut Kartofel'nogo Khozyaistva. Trudy — Nauchno Issled Inst Kartofel Khoz Tr
Nauchno-Issledovatel'skii Institut Kurortologii i Fizioterapii imeni I.G. Koniashvili. Trudy — Nauchno Issled Inst Kurortol Fizioter im IG Koniashvili Tr
Nauchno-Issledovatel'skii Institut Monomerov dlya Sinteticheskogo Kauchuka. Sbornik Nauchnykh Trudov — Nauchno Issled Inst Monomerov Sint Kauch Sb Nauchn Tr
Nauchno-Issledovatel'skii Institut Onkologii. Trudy (Tbilisi) — Nauchno Issled Inst Onkol Tr (Tbilisi)
Nauchno-Issledovatel'skii Institut Osnovanii i Podzemnykh Sooruzhenii. Sbornik — Nauchno Issled Inst Osn Podzemn Sooruzh Sb
Nauchno-Issledovatel'skii Institut Pchelovodstva. Trudy — Nauchno Issled Inst Pchelovod Tr
Nauchno-Issledovatel'skii Institut Pochvovedeniya i Agrokhimii. Trudy (Yerevan) — Nauchno Issled Inst Pochvoved Agrokhim Tr (Yerevan)
Nauchno-Issledovatel'skii Institut Prikladnoi Matematiki i Mekhaniki pri Tomskom Gosudarstvennom Universitete. Trudy — Nauchno Issled Inst Prikl Mat Mekh Tomsk Gos Univ Tr
Nauchno-Issledovatel'skii Institut Promyshlennogo Stroitel'stva. Trudy Instituta — Nauchno Issled Inst Prom Stroit Tr Inst
Nauchno-Issledovatel'skii Institut Rentgenologii, Radiologii i Onkologii. Trudy — Nauchno Issled Inst Rentgenol Radiol Onkol Tr
Nauchno-Issledovatel'skii Institut Sanitarii i Gigieny imeni G.M. Natadze. Sbor nik Trudov — Nauchno Issled Inst Sanit Gig im GM Natadze Sb Tr
Nauchno-Issledovatel'skii Institut Sinteticheskikh Spirtov i Organicheskikh Produktov. Trudy — Nauchno Issled Inst Sint Spirtov Org Prod Tr
Nauchno-Issledovatel'skii Institut Stroitel'noi Fiziki. Trudy — Nauchno Issled Inst Stroit Fiz Tr
Nauchno-Issledovatel'skii Institut Stroitel'stva i Arkhitektury. Trudy (Yerevan) — Nauchno Issled Inst Stroit Arkhit Tr Yerevan
Nauchno-Issledovatel'skii Institut Tekhniko-Ekonomicheskikh Issledovanii. Sbornik Trudov — Nauchno Issled Inst Tekh Ekon Issled Sb Tr
Nauchno-Issledovatel'skii Institut Zashchity Rastenii. Trudy (Tbilisi) — Nauchno Issled Inst Zashch Rast Tr (Tbilisi)
Nauchno-Issledovatel'skii Institut Zemledeliya, Echmiadzin. Armenian SSR. Sbornik Nauchnykh Trudov — Nauchno Issled Inst Zemled Echmiadzin Arm SSR Sb Nauchn Tr
Nauchno-Issledovatel'skii Kozhno-Venerologicheskii Institut. Sbornik Nauchnykh Trudov (Minsk) — Nauchno Issled Kozhno Venerol Inst Sb Nauchn Tr (Minsk)
Nauchno-Issledovatel'skii Kozhno-Venerologicheskii Institut. Sbornik Trudov (Tbilisi) — Nauchno Issled Kozhno Venerol Inst Sb Tr Tbilisi
Nauchno-Issledovatel'skii Tekhnokhimicheskii Institut Bytovogo Obsluzhivaniya. Trudy — Nauchno Issled Tekhnokhim Inst Bytovogo Obsluzhivaniya Tr
Nauchno-Issledovatel'skii Trudy Ukrainskii Nauchno-Issledovatel'skii Institut Kozhevenno-Obuvnoi Promyshlennosti — NUKOA
Nauchno-Issledovatel'skiy Institut Geologii Arktiki Trudy — Nauchno Issled Inst Geol Arktiki Tr
Nauchnoizsledovatelski i Proektno-Konstruktorski Institut po Tsvetna Metalurgiya(Plovdiv). Godishnik — Nauchnoizsled Proektno Konstr Inst Tsvetna Metal Plovdiv God
Nauchnoizsledovatelski Institut po Epidemiologiya i Mikrobiologiya. Trudove [*A publication*] — Nauchnoizsled Inst Epidemiol Mikrobiol Tr
Nauchnoizsledovatelski Institut po Konservna Promishlenost. Plovdiv. Nauchni Trudove — Nauchnoizsled Inst Konservna Promst Plovdiv Nauchni Tr
Nauchnoizsledovatelski Institut po Okeanografiya i Ribno Stopanstvo. Varna. Izvestiya — Nauchnoizsled Inst Okeanogr Ribno Stop Varna Izv
Nauchnoizsledovatelski Institut po Okhrana na Truda i Profesionalnite Zabolyavaniya. Trudove — Nauchnoizsled Inst Okhr Tr Prof Zabol Tr
Nauchnoizsledovatelski Institut po Radiobiologiya i Radiatsionna Khigiena. Nauchni Trudove — Nauchnoizsled Inst Radiobiol Radiats Khig Nauchni Tr
Nauchnoizsledovatelski Institut po Stroitelni Materiali Trudove (Sofia) — Nauchnoizsled Inst Stroit Mater Tr (Sofia)
Nauchnoizsledovatelski Institut po Tsvetna Metalurgiya (Plovdiv). Godishnik — Nauchnoizsled Inst Tsvetna Metal (Plovdiv) God
Nauchnoizsledovatelski Khimiko-Farmatsevtichen Institut. Trudove — Nauchnoizsled Khim Farm Inst Tr
Nauchnoizsledovatelski Trudove na Instituta po Tekstilna Promishlenost (Sofia) — Nauchnoizsled Tr Inst Tekst Promost (Sofia)
Nauchno-Metodicheska Konferentsiya po Problemite na Prepodavane vuv VUZ — Nauchno Metod Konf Probl Prepod VUZ
Nauchno-Prakticheskaya Informatsiya. Tsentral'nyi Aptechnyi Nauchno-Issledovatel'skii Institut — Nauchno-Prakt Inf Tsentr Aptechn Nauchno-Issled Inst
Nauchno-Technicheskii Sbornik. Gosudarstvennoe Izdatel'stvo Literatury v Oblasti Atomnoi Nauki i Tekhniki — Nauchno Tekh Sb Gos Izd Lit Obl At Nauki Tekh
Nauchno-Tekhnicheska Konferentsiya po Zavaryavane v Stroitelstvoto i Montazha. Dokladi — Nauchno Tekh Konf Zavaryavane Stroit Montazha Dokl
Nauchno-Tekhnicheska Konferentsiya Stuklo i Fina Keramika — Nauchno Tekh Konf Stuklo Fina Keram
Nauchno-Tekhnicheskaya Informatsiya — Nauchno-Tekh Inf
Nauchno-Tekhnicheskaya Informatsiya — Nauch-Tekh Inf
Nauchno-Tekhnicheskaya Informatsiya. Gosudarstvennyi Nauchno-Tekhnicheskii Komitet Soveta Ministrov Estonskoi SSR — Nauchno Tekh Inf Gos Nauchno Tekh Kom Sov Minist Est SSR
Nauchno-Tekhnicheskaya Informatsiya Litovskii Nauchno-Issledovatel'skii Veterinarnyi Institut — Nauchno-Tekh Inf Litov Nauchno-Issled Vet Inst
Nauchno-Tekhnicheska Informatsiya po Tsellyulozno-Bumazhnoi. Gidroliznoi i Lesokhimicheskoi Promyshlennosti — Nauchno Tekh Inf Tsellyul Bum Gidroliz Lesokhim Promsti
Nauchno-Tekhnicheskaya Informatsiya. Seriya 1. Organizatsiya i Metodika Informatsionnoi Raboty — Nau Tekh Inf Ser 1
Nauchno-Tekhnicheskaya Informatsiya. Seriya 1. Organizatsiya i Metodika Informatsionnoi Raboty — Nauchno-Tekh Inf Ser 1
Nauchno-Tekhnicheskaya Informatsiya. Seriya 1. Organizatsiya i Metodika Informatsionnye Raboty — Nau-T Inf 1
Nauchno-Tekhnicheskaya Informatsiya. Seriya 2. Informatsionnye Protessy i Sistemy — Nau-T Inf 2
Nauchno-Tekhnicheskaya Informatsiya. Seriya 2. Informatsionnye Protsessy i Sistemy — Nauchno-Tekh Inf Ser 2
Nauchno-Tekhnicheskaya Informatsiya (Sofia) — Nauchno-Tekh Inf (Sofia)
Nauchno-Tekhnicheskaya Informatsiya. Tsentral'nyi Institut Nauchno-Tekhnicheskoi Informatsii Bumazhnoi i Drevoobrabatyvayushchei Promyshlennosti, Tsellyulozno-Baumazhnaya, Gidroliznaya i Lesokhimicheskaya Promyshlennost — NIGLA
Nauchno-Tekhnicheskaya Konferentsiya po Ispol'zovaniyu Ioniziruyushchikh Izluchenii v Narodnom Khozyaistve. Doklady — Nauchno Tekh Konf Ispolz Ioniz Izluch Nar Khoz Dokl
Nauchno-Tekhnicheskaya Konferentsiya. Raschet, Konstruirovanie i Primenenie Radiatsionnykh Trub v Promyshlennosti — Nauchno Tekh Konf Raschet Konstr Primen Radiats Trub Promsti
Nauchno-Tekhnicheskaya Konferentsiya Steklo i Tonkaya Keramika — Nauchno Tekh Konf Steklo Tonkaya Keram
Nauchno-Tekhnicheskie Obshchestva SSSR [*Former USSR*] — Nauchno-Tekh Ova SSSR
Nauchno-Tekhnicheskie Problemy Goreniya i Vzryva — Nauchno-Tekh Probl Goreniya Vzryva
Nauchno-Tekhnicheskii Biulleten. Vsesoiuznyi Nauchno-Issledovatel'skii Institut Mekhanizatsii Sel'skogo Khoziaistva — Nauchno Tekh Biul Vses Nauchno Issled Inst Mekh Sel'sk Khoz
Nauchno-Tekhnicheskii Byulleten Nauchno-Issledovatel'skii Institut Teploenergeticheskogo Priborostroeniya — Nauchno-Tekh Byull Nauchno-Issled Inst Teploenerg Priborostr
Nauchno-Tekhnicheskii Byulleten Nauchno-Issledovatel'skogo Instituta Mekhanizatsii Rybnoi Promyshlennosti — Nauchno-Tekh Byull Nauchno-Issled Inst Mekh Rybn Promsti
Nauchno-Tekhnicheskii Byulleten' po Agronomicheskoi Fizike — Nauchno-Tekh Byull Agron Fiz
Nauchno-Tekhnicheskii Byulleten. Sibirskii Nauchno-Issledovatel'skii Institut Khimizatsii Sel'skogo Khozyaistva — Nauchno Tekh Byull Sib Nauchno Issled Inst Khim Selsk Khoz
Nauchno-Tekhnicheskii Byulleten SoyuzNIKhl — Nauchno Tekh Byull SoyuzNIKhl
Nauchno-Tekhnicheskii Byulleten' Tsentral'noi Geneticheskoi Laboratorii — Nauchno-Tekh Byull Tsentr Genet Lab
Nauchno-Tekhnicheskii Byulleten' Vsesoyuznogo Selektsionno-Geneticheskogo Instituta — Nauchno-Tekh Byull Vses Sel-Genet Inst
Nauchno-Tekhnicheskii Byulleten. Vsesoyuznyi Nauchno-Issledovatel'skii Institut Khlopkovodstva — Nauchno-Tekh Byull Vses Nauchno-Issled Inst Khlopkovod
Nauchno-Tekhnicheskii Informatsionnyi Byulleten Leningradskogo Politekhnicheskogo Instituta [*Former USSR*] — Nauchno-Tekh Inf Byull Leningr Politekh Inst

Nauchno-Tekhnicheskii Informatsionnyi Byulleten Nauchnogo Instituta po Udobreniyam i Insektofungitsidam — Nauchno-Tekh Inf Byull Nauchn Inst Udobr Insektofungits
Nauchno-Tekhnicheskii Obzor. Seriya. Geologiya i Razvedka Gazovykh i Gazokondensatnykh Mestorozhdenii — Nauchno Tekh Obz Ser Geol Razved Gazov Gazokondens Mestorozh
Nauchno-Tekhnicheskii Obzor. Seriya. Geologiya, Razvedka Gazovykh, i Bazokondensatnykh Mestorozhdenii — Nauchno-Tekh Obz Ser Geol Razved Gaz Gazokondens Mestorozhd
Nauchno-Tekhnicheskii Obzor. Seriya. Pererabotka Gaza i Gazovogo Kondensata — Nauchno-Tekh Obz Ser Pererab Gaza Gazov Kondens
Nauchno-Tekhnicheskii Obzor. Seriya. Transport i Khranenie Gaza — Nauchno Tekh Obz Ser Transp Khranenie Gaza
Nauchno-Tekhnicheskii Progress i Profilakticheskaya Meditsina. Materialy Nauchnoi Konferentsii Klinicheskikh Kafedr — Nauchno Tekh Prog Profil Med Mater Nauchn Konf Klin Kafedr
Nauchno-Tekhnicheskii Referativnyi Sbornik. Drozhzhevaya Promyshlennost — Nauchno Tekh Ref Sb Drozhzhevaya Promst
Nauchno-Tekhnicheskii Referativnyi Sbornik. Maslo-Zhirovaya Promyshlennost — Nauchno Tekh Ref Sb Maslo Zhir Promst
Nauchno-Tekhnicheskii Referativnyi Sbornik. Sakharnaya Promyshlennost — Nauchno Tekh Ref Sb Sakh Promst
Nauchno-Tekhnicheskii Referativnyi Sbornik. Seriya. Avtomatizatsiya Khimicheskikh Proizvodstv — Nauchno Tekh Ref Sb Ser Avtom Khim Proizvod
Nauchno-Tekhnicheskii Referativnyi Sbornik. Seriya Fosfornaya Promyshlennost — Nauchno Tekh Ref Sb Ser Fosfornaya Promst
Nauchno-Tekhnicheskii Referativnyi Sbornik. Seriya. Kaliinaya Promyshlennost — Nauchno Tekh Ref Sb Ser Kaliinaya Promst
Nauchno-Tekhnicheskii Referativnyi Sbornik. Seriya. Khimiya i Tekhnologiya Lyuminoforov i Chistykh Neoganicheskikh Materialov — Nauchno Tekh Ref Sb Ser Khim Tekhnol Lyuminoforov Neorg Mater
Nauchno-Tekhnicheskii Referativnyi Sbornik. Seriya. Kislorodnaya Promyshlennost — Nauchno Tekh Ref Sb Ser Kislorodn Promst
Nauchno-Tekhnicheskii Referativnyi Sbornik. Seriya. Proizvodstvo i Pererabotka Plastmass i Sinteticheskikh Smol — Nauchno Tekh Ref Sb Ser Proizvod Pererab Plastmass Sint Smol
Nauchno-Tekhnicheskii Referativnyi Sbornik. Seriya. Promyshlennost Khimicheskikh Volokon — Nauchno Tekh Ref Sb Ser Promst Khim Volokon
Nauchno-Tekhnicheskii Referativnyi Sbornik. Seriya. Promyshlennost Tovarov Bytovoi Khimii — Nauchno Tekh Ref Sb Ser Promst Tovarov Bytovoi Khim
Nauchno-Tekhnicheskii Referativnyi Sbornik. Seriya. Reaktivy i Osobo Chistye Veshchestva — Nauchno Tekh Ref Sb Ser Reakt Osobo Chist Veshchestva
Nauchno-Tekhnicheskii Referativnyi Sbornik. Spirtovaya i Likero-Vodochnaya Promyshlennost — Nauchno Tekh Ref Sb Spirt Likero Vodochn Promst
Nauchno-Tekhnicheskii Sbornik po Dobyche Nefti — Nauchno-Tekh Sb Dobyche Nefti
Nauchno-Tekhnicheskii Sbornik po Geologii, Razrabotke, Transportu, i Ispol'zovaniyu Prirodnogo Gaza — Nauchno-Tekh Sb Geol Razrab Transp Ispolz Prir Gaza
Nauchno-Tekhnicheskoe Ob'edinenie GruzNIIstrom Sbornik Trudov — Nauchno Tekh Obedin GruzNIIstrom Sb Tr
Nauchno-Tematicheskii Sbornik. Ufimskii Neftyanoi Institut — Nauchno-Temat Sb Ufim Neft Inst
Nauchnye Byulleten Leningradskogo Gosudarstvennogo Universiteta — Nauchn Byull Leningr Gos Univ
Nauchnye Doklady. Rossiiskaya Akademiya Nauk. Ural'skoe Otdelenie. Komi Nauchnyi Tsentr — Nauchn Dokl Ross Akad Nauk Ural Otd Komi Nauchn Tsentr
Nauchnye Doklady Vysshei Shkoly Biologicheskie Nauki — Nauch Dokl Vysshei Shkoly Biol Nauk
Nauchnye Doklady Vysshei Shkoly Biologicheskie Nauki — Nauchn Dokl Vyssh Shk Biol Nauki
Nauchnye Doklady Vysshei Shkoly Elektromekhanika i Avtomatika — Nauchn Dokl Vyssh Shk Elektromekh Avtom
Nauchnye Doklady Vysshei Shkoly Energetika — Nauchn Dokl Vyssh Shk Energ
Nauchnye Doklady Vysshei Shkoly Filologicheskie Nauki [*Moscow*] — NDFN
Nauchnye Doklady Vysshei Shkoly Fiziko-Matematicheskie Nauki — Nauchn Dokl Vyssh Shk Fiz Mat Nauki
Nauchnye Doklady Vysshei Shkoly Geologo-Geograficheskie Nauki — Nauchn Dokl Vyssh Shk Geol Geogr Nauki
Nauchnye Doklady Vysshei Shkoly Gornoe Delo — Nauchn Dokl Vyssh Shk Gorn Delo
Nauchnye Doklady Vysshei Shkoly Khimiya i Khimicheskaya Tekhnologiya [*Former USSR*] — Nauchn Dokl Vyssh Shk Khim Khim Tekhnol
Nauchnye Doklady Vysshei Shkoly Lesoinzhenernoe Delo — Nauchn Dokl Vyssh Shk Lesoinzh Delo
Nauchnye Doklady Vysshei Shkoly Mashinostroenie i Priborostroenie — Nauchn Dokl Vyssh Shk Mashinostr Priborostr
Nauchnye Doklady Vysshei Shkoly Metallurgiya — Nauchn Dokl Vyssh Shk Metall
Nauchnye Doklady Vysshei Shkoly Radiotekhnika i Elektronika — Nauchn Dokl Vyssh Shk Radiotekh Elektron
Nauchnye Doklady Vysshei Shkoly Stroitel'stvo — Nauchn Dokl Vyssh Shk Stroit
Nauchnye Ezhegodnik Chernovitskogo Universiteta Biologicheskii Fakul'tet Chernovtsy — Nauchn Ezheg Chernovits Univ Biol Fak Chernovtsy
Nauchnye i Prikladnye Problemy Energetiki — Nauchn Prikl Probl Energ
Nauchnye Issledovaniva v Klinikakh I V Laboratoriyakh — Nauchn Issled Klin Lab
Nauchnye Osnovy i Prakticheskoe Ispol'zovanie Tipomorfizma Mineralov. Materialy S'ezda MMA — Nauchn Osn Prakt Ispolz Tipomorfizma Miner Mater Sezda MMA
Nauchnye Osnovy Materialovedeniya. Doklady Prochitannye na Sessii Nauchnye Osnovy Materialovedeniya — Nauchn Osn Materialoved Dokl Sess
Nauchnye Osnovy Okhrany Prirody — Nauchn Osn Okhr Prir
Nauchnye Osnovy Tekhnologii Obrabotki Vody — Nauchn Osn Tekhnol Obrab Vody
Nauchnye Raboty Institutov Okhrany Truda Vsesoyuznogo Tsentral'nogo Soveta Professional'nykh Soyuzov — Nauchn Rab Inst Okhr Tr Vses Tsentr Sov Prof Soyuz
Nauchnye Raboty Institutov Okhrany Truda Vsesoyuznogo Tsentral'nogo Soveta Professional'nykh Soyuzov — Nauchn Rab Inst Okhr Tr Vses Tsentr Sov Prof Soyuzov
Nauchnye Raboty Institutov Okhrany Truda VTsSPS [*Vsesoiuznyi Tsentral'nyi Sovet Professional'nykh Soiuzov*] — Nauchn Rab Inst Okhr Tr VTsSPS
Nauchnye Raboty Studentov Khimiko-Tekhnologicheskogo Fakul'teta. Novocherkasskii Politekhnicheskii Institut — Nauchn Rab Stud Khim Tekhnol Fak Novocherk Politekh Inst
Nauchnye Raboty Studentov. Moskovskaya Veterinarnaya Akademiya — Nauchn Rab Stud Mosk Vet Akad
Nauchnye Raboty Studentov Moskovskogo Farmatsevticheskogo Instituta — Nauchn Rab Stud Mosk Farm Inst
Nauchnye Raboty Studentov Moskovskogo Gornogo Instituta — Nauchn Rab Stud Mosk Gorn Inst
Nauchnye Raboty Studentov Moskovskogo Meditsinskogo Stomatologicheskogo Instituta — Nauchn Rab Stud Mosk Med Stomatol Inst
Nauchnye Raboty Studentov Novocherkasskii Politekhnicheskii Institut — Nauchn Rab Stud Novocherk Politekh Inst
Nauchnye Raboty Studentov Sverdlovskii Gornyi Institut — Nauchn Rab Stud Sverdl Gorn Inst
Nauchnye Raboty Studentov. Sverdlovskii Gornyi Institut imeni V. V. Vakhrusheva — Nauchn Rab Stud Sverdl Gorn Inst im V V Vakhrusheva
Nauchnye Raboty Vrachei Mordovskoi SSSR — Nauchn Rab Vrach Mord SSSR
Nauchnye Soobshcheniya. Akademiya Nauk SSSR. Sibirskoe Otdelenie. Yakutskii Filial — Nauchn Soobshch Akad Nauk SSSR Sib Otd Yakutsk Fil
Nauchnye Soobshcheniya Armyanskii Nauchno-Issledovatel'skii Institut Stroitel'nykh Materialov i Sooruzhenii — Nauchn Soobshch Arm Nauchno Issled Inst Stroit Mater Sooruzh
Nauchnye Soobshcheniya Gosudarstvennyi Vsesoyuznyi Nauchno-Issledovatel'skii Institut Tsementnoi Promyshlennosti [*Former USSR*] — Nauchn Soobshch Gos Vses Nauchno Issled Inst Tsem Prom-Sti
Nauchnye Soobshcheniya Institut Fiziologii Imeni I. P. Pavlova — Nauch Soobshch Inst Fiziol Pavlov
Nauchnye Soobshcheniya Institut Gornogo Dela Imeni A. A. Skochinskogo [*Former USSR*] — Nauchn Soobshch Inst Gorn Dela Im A A Skochinskogo
Nauchnye Soobshcheniya Institut Gornogo Dela (Moscow) — Nauchn Soobshch Inst Gorn Dela (Moscow)
Nauchnye Soobshcheniya Instituta Fiziologii Akademii Nauk SSSR — Nauchn Soobshch Inst Fiziol Akad Nauk SSSR
Nauchnye Soobshcheniya Instituta Geologii i Geografii. Akademiya Nauk Litovskoi SSR — Nauchn Soobshch Inst Geol Geogr Akad Nauk Lit SSR
Nauchnye Soobshcheniya Vsesoyuznyi Nauchno-Issledovatel'skii Institut Tsementnoi Promyshlennosti — Nauchn Soobshch Vses Nauchno Issled Inst Tsem Promsti
Nauchnye Soobshcheniya. Yakutskii Filial Akademiya Nauk SSSR — Nauchn Soobshch Yakutsk Fil Akad Nauk SSSR
Nauchnye Trudy — Nauch Trudy
Nauchnye Trudy Akademii Kommunal'nogo Khozyaistva — Nauchn Tr Akad Kommunal'n Khoz
Nauchnye Trudy. Akademiya Kommunal'nogo Khozyaistva imeni K. D. Pamfilova — Nauchn Tr Akad Kommunaln Khoz im K D Pamfilova
Nauchnye Trudy Altaiskogo Nauchno-Issledovatel'skogo Instituta Sel'skogo Khozyaistva — Nauch Trudy Altaisk Nauchno-Issled Inst Sel Khoz
Nauchnye Trudy. Arkhangel'skii Lesotekhnicheskii Institut — Nauchn Tr Arkhang Lesotekh Inst
Nauchnye Trudy Aspirantov i Ordinatorov Pervogo Moskovskogo Meditsinskogo Instituta — Nauchn Tr Aspir Ordinatorov Pervogo Mosk Med Inst
Nauchnye Trudy Aspirantov Odesskii Sel'skokhozyaistvennyi Institut — Nauchn Tr Aspir Odess Skh Inst
Nauchnye Trudy Aspirantov. Tashkentskii Gosudarstvennyi Universitet — Nauchn Tr Aspir Tashk Gos Univ
Nauchnye Trudy Bashkirskogo Gosudarstvennogo Meditsinskogo Instituta — Nauchn Tr Bashk Gos Med Inst
Nauchnye Trudy Bashkirskogo Meditsinskogo Instituta — Nauchn Tr Bashk Med Inst
Nauchnye Trudy. Belorusskii Institut Inzhenerov Zheleznodorozhnogo Transporta — Nauchn Tr Beloruss Inst Inzh Zheleznodorozhn Transp
Nauchnye Trudy. Belorusskii Institut Zhivotnovodstva — Nauchn Tr Beloruss Inst Zhivotnovod
Nauchnye Trudy. Belorusskii Nauchno-Issledovatel'skii Institut Zhivotnovodstva — Nauchn Tr Beloruss Nauchno Issled Inst Zhivotnovod
Nauchnye Trudy. Bukharestskii Sel'skokhozyaistvennyi Institut imeni N. Belchesku. Bukharest. Seriya. Agronomiya — Nauchn Tr Bukharestskii Skh Inst Bukharest Ser Agron
Nauchnye Trudy Bukharskii Gosudarstvennyi Pedagogicheskii Institut — Nauchn Tr Bukhar Gos Pedagog Inst
Nauchnye Trudy Bykovskoi Bakhchevoi Opytnai Stantsii — Nauchn Tr Bykovskoi Bakhchevoi Opytn Stn
Nauchnye Trudy Chelyabinskoi Oblastnoi Klinicheskoi Bol'nitsy — Nauchn Tr Chelyab Obl Klin Bol'n
Nauchnye Trudy Dnepropetrovskii Metallorgicheskii Institut — Nauchn Tr Dnepropetr Metall Inst
Nauchnye Trudy Donskoi Zonal'nyi Nauchno-Issledovatel'skii Institut Sel'skogo Khozyaistva — Nauchn Tr Donskoi Zon Nauchno Issled Inst Sel'sk Khoz
Nauchnye Trudy Erevanskii Gosudarstvennyi Universitet Seriya Geologicheskikh Nauk — Nauchn Tr Erevan Gos Univ Ser Geol Nauk
Nauchnye Trudy Erevanskii Gosudarstvennyi Universitet Seriya Khimicheskikh Nauk — Nauchn Tr Erevan Gos Univ Ser Khim Nauk

Nauchnye Trudy Erevanskogo Politekhnicheskogo Instituta — Nauchn Tr Erevan Politekh Inst
Nauchnye Trudy Giredmeta — Nauchn Tr Giredmeta
Nauchnye Trudy Gosudarstvennyi Nauchno-Issledovatel'skii i Proektnyi Institut Redkometallicheskoi Promyshlennosti [*Former USSR*] — Nauchn Tr Gos Nauchno-Issled Proektn Inst Redkomet Prom-Sti
Nauchnye Trudy Gosudarstvennyi Nauchno-Issledovatel'skii i Proektnyi Institut Redkometallicheskoi Promyshlennosti — NTGNA
Nauchnye Trudy. Gosudarstvennyi Nauchno-Issledovatel'skii Institut Tsvetnykh Metallov — Nauchn Tr Gos Nauchno Issled Inst Tsvetn Met
Nauchnye Trudy. Gosudarstvennyi Nikitskii Botanicheskii Sad — Nauchn Tr Gos Nikitsk Bot Sad
Nauchnye Trudy. Gruzinskii Politekhnicheskii Institut imeni V. I. Lenina — Nauchn Tr Gruz Politekh Inst im V I Lenina
Nauchnye Trudy Gruzinskii Sel'skokhozyaistvennyi Institut — Nauchn Tr Gruz Skh Inst
Nauchnye Trudy Industrial'no-Pedagogicheskogo Instituta — NTIPI
Nauchnye Trudy Institut Chernoi Metallurgii (Dnepropetrovsk) — Nauchn Tr Inst Chern Metall (Dnepropetrovsk)
Nauchnye Trudy Institut Fiziologii Rastenii i Agrokhimii. Akademiya Nauk Ukrainskoi SSR — Nauchn Tr Inst Fiziol Rast Agrokhim Akad Nauk Ukr SSR
Nauchnye Trudy. Institut Mekhaniki. Moskovskii Gosudarstvennyi Universitet — Nauchn Tr Inst Mekh Mosk Gos Univ
Nauchnye Trudy Instituta Avtomatiki [*Ukrainian SSR*] — Nauchn Tr Inst Avtom
Nauchnye Trudy Instituta Avtomatiki — NTIAA
Nauchnye Trudy Instituta Entomologii i Fitopatologii — Nauchn Tr Inst Entomol Fitopatol
Nauchnye Trudy Instituta Entomologii i Fitopatologii Akademii Nauk Ukrainskoi SSR — Nauchn Tr Inst Entomol Fitopatol Akad Nauk Ukr SSR
Nauchnye Trudy Instituta Giprotsvetmetobrabotka — Nauchn Tr Inst Giprotsvetmetobrabotka
Nauchnye Trudy Instituta Mineral'nykh Resursov (Ukrainian SSR) — Nauchn Tr Inst Mineral Resur (Ukrainian SSR)
Nauchnye Trudy Instituta Pochvennykh Issledovaniya — Nauchn Tr Inst Pochv Issled
Nauchnye Trudy. Instituta Sibtsvetmetniiproekt — Nauchn Tr Inst Sibtsvetmetniiproekt
Nauchnye Trudy Irkutskii Gosudarstvennyi Meditsinskii Institut — Nauchn Tr Irkutsk Gos Med Inst
Nauchnye Trudy Irkutskii Gosudarstvennyi Nauchno-Issledovatel'skii Institut Redkikh i Tsvetnykh Metallov — Nauchn Tr Irkutsk Gos Nauchno Issled Inst Redk Tsvetn Met
Nauchnye Trudy Irkutskii Gosudarstvennyi Nauchno-Issledovatel'skii Institut Redkikh Metallov — Nauchn Tr Irkutsk Gos Nauchno Issled Inst Redk Met
Nauchnye Trudy Irkutskii Meditsinskii Institut — Nauchn Tr Irkutsk Med Inst
Nauchnye Trudy. Irkutskii Nauchno-Issledovatel'skii Institut Epidemiologii i Mikrobiologii — Nauchn Tr Irkutsk Nauchno Issled Inst Epidemiol Mikrobiol
Nauchnye Trudy Irkutskogo Politekhnicheskogo Instituta — Nauchn Tr Irkutsk Politekh Inst
Nauchnye Trudy. Kalmytskii Nauchno-Issledovatel'skii Institut Myasnogo Skotovodstva — Nauchn Tr Kalmytskii Nauchno Issled Inst Myasn Skotovod
Nauchnye Trudy Kamenets Podol'skii Sel'skokhozyaistvennyi Institut — Nauchn Tr Kamenets Podol'sk Skh Inst
Nauchnye Trudy Karagandinskii Filial Instituta Obogashcheniya Tverdykh Goryuchikh Iskopaemykh [*Former USSR*] — Nauchn Tr Karagand Fil Inst Obogashch Tverd Goryuch Iskop
Nauchnye Trudy Karagandinskii Nauchno-Issledovatel'skii Ugol'nyi Institut — Nauchn Tr Karagand Nauchno Issled Ugol'n Inst
Nauchnye Trudy. Karshinskii Gosudarstvennyi Pedagogicheskii Institut — Nauchn Tr Karsh Gos Pedagog Inst
Nauchnye Trudy. Kazakhskii Sel'skokhozyaistvennyi Institut — Nauchn Tr Kaz Skh Inst
Nauchnye Trudy. Kazanskogo Gosudarstvennogo Veterinarnogo Instituta imeni N. E. Baumana — Nauchn Tr Kazan Gos Vet Inst im N E Baumana
Nauchnye Trudy Kazanskogo Meditsinskogo Instituta — Nauchn Tr Kazan Med Inst
Nauchnye Trudy Khar'kovskii Gornyi Institut — Nauchn Tr Khark Gorn Inst
Nauchnye Trudy Khar'kovskii Institut Inzhenerov Kommunal'nogo Stroitel'stva — Nauchn Tr Khar'k Inst Inzh Kommunal'n Stroit
Nauchnye Trudy. Khar'kovskogo Instituta Inzhenerov Zheleznodorozhnogo Transporta — Nauchn Tr Khark Inst Inzh Zheleznodorozhn Transp
Nauchnye Trudy Khar'kovskogo Sel'skokhozyaistvennogo Instituta — Nauchn Tr Khar'k S-Kh Inst
Nauchnye Trudy Kirgizskogo Meditsinskogo Instituta — Nauchn Tr Kirg Med Inst
Nauchnye Trudy Konferentsii. Posvyashchennoi 100-letiyu so Dnya Rozhdeniya V. I. Lenina. Astrakhanskii Tekhnicheskii Institut Rybnoi Promyshlennosti i Khozyaistva. Astrakhan — Nauchn Tr Konf Astrakh Tekh Inst Rybn Promsti Khoz
Nauchnye Trudy Krasnodarskogo Gosudarstvennogo Pedagogicheskogo Instituta — Nauchn Tr Krasnodar God Pedagog Inst
Nauchnye Trudy Krasnodarskogo Nauchno-Issledovatel'skogo Instituta Sel'skogo Khozyaistva — Nauchn Tr Krasnodar Nauchno Issled Inst Sel'sk Khoz
Nauchnye Trudy Krasnodarskogo Pedagogicheskogo Instituta — NTK
Nauchnye Trudy. Krasnodarskogo Politekhnicheskogo Instituta — Nauchn Tr Krasnodar Politekh Inst
Nauchnye Trudy Krasnodarskoi Nauchno-Issledovat'skoi Veterinarnoi Stantsii — Nauchn Tr Krasnodar Nauchno Issled Vet Stn
Nauchnye Trudy Krymskii Gosudarstvennyi Meditsinskii Institut — Nauchn Tr Krym Gos Med Inst
Nauchnye Trudy Kubanskii Gosudarstvennyi Universitet — Nauchn Tr Kuban Gos Univ
Nauchnye Trudy Kubanskogo Gosudarstvennogo Meditsinskogo Instituta — Nauchn Tr Kuban Gos Med Inst
Nauchnye Trudy Kuibyshevskii Gosudarstvennyi Pedagogicheskii Institut Imeni V. V. Kuibysheva — Nauch Trudy Kuibyshevskii Gos Ped Inst
Nauchnye Trudy. Kuibyshevskii Gosudarstvennyi Pedagogicheskii Institut imeni V. V. Kuibysheva — Nauchn Tr Kuibyshev Gos Pedagog Inst im V V Kuibysheva
Nauchnye Trudy Kuibyshevskii Gosudarstvennyi Pedagogicheskii Institut Zhivotnye Povolzh'ya — Nauch Trudy Kuibyshev Gos Pedagog Inst Zhivot Povolzh'ya
Nauchnye Trudy Kurganskogo Sel'skokhozyaistvennogo Instituta — Nauchn Tr Kurgan S-Kh Inst
Nauchnye Trudy Kurskii Politekhnicheskii Institut [*Former USSR*] — Nauchn Tr Kursk Politekh Inst
Nauchnye Trudy Kurskii Politekhnicheskii Institut — NTKPB
Nauchnye Trudy Kurskij Gosudarstvennyj Pedagogicheskij Institut — Nauchn Tr Kursk Gos Pedagog Inst
Nauchnye Trudy Kurskogo Sel'skokhozyaistvennogo Instituta — Nauchn Tr Kursk Selkh Inst
Nauchnye Trudy Kurskoi Gosudarstvennoi Sel'skokhozyaistvennoi Opytnoi Stantsii — Nauchn Tr Kursk Gos Skh Optn Stn
Nauchnye Trudy Kurskoi Gosudarstvennoi Sel'skokhozyaistvennoi Opytnoi Stantsii — Nauchn Tr Kursk Gos Skh Opytn Stn
Nauchnye Trudy. KuzNIIUgleobogashcheniya — Nauchn Tr KuzNIIUgleobogashcheniya
Nauchnye Trudy Leningradskaya Lesotekhnicheskaya Akademiya Imeni S. M. Kirova — NATLA
Nauchnye Trudy. Leningradskaya Lesotekhnicheskaya Akademiya imeni S. M. Kirova — Nauchn Tr Leningr Lesotekh Akad im S M Kirova
Nauchnye Trudy Leningradskii Gornyi Institut Novye Issledovaniya v Khimii, Metallurgii, i Obogashchenii — Nauchn Tr Leningr Gorn Inst Nov Issled Khim Metall Obogashch
Nauchnye Trudy Leningradskii Institut Tochnoi Mekhaniki i Optiki — Nauchn Tr Leningr Inst Tochn Mekh Opt
Nauchnye Trudy Leningradskii Inzhenerno-Stroitel'nyi Institut — Nauchn Tr Leningr Inzh Stroit Inst
Nauchnye Trudy Leningradskii Nauchno-Issledovatel'skii Institut Perelivaniya Krovi — Nauchn Tr Leningr Nauchno Issled Inst Pereliv Krovi
Nauchnye Trudy Leningradskogo Gosudarstvennogo Instituta Usovershenstvovaniya Vrachei — Nauchn Tr Leningr Gos Inst Usoversh Vrachei
Nauchnye Trudy Leningradskogo Gosudarstvennogo Instituta Usovershenstvovaniya Vrachei imeni S. M. Kirova — Nauchn Tr Leningr Gos Inst Usoversh Vrachei im S M Kirova
Nauchnye Trudy Leningradskogo Instituta Usovershenstvovaniya Vrachei Imeni S. M. Kirova — Nauchn Tr Leningr Inst Usoversh Vrachei Im S M Kirova
Nauchnye Trudy Leningradskogo Sel'skokhozyaistvennogo Instituta — Nauchn Tr Leningr Skh Inst
Nauchnye Trudy Leningradskogo Tekhnologicheskogo Instituta Imeni Lensoveta — Nauchn Tr Leningr Tekhnol Inst Im Lensoveta
Nauchnye Trudy Leningradskoi Lesotekhnicheskoi Akademii — Nauchn Tr Leningr Lesotekh Akad
Nauchnye Trudy Lesokhozyaistevennogo Fakul'teka Ukrainskoi Sel'skokhozyaistvennoi Akademii — Nauchn Tr Lesokhoz Fak Ukr Skh Akad
Nauchnye Trudy Litovskoi Sel'skokhozyaistvennoi Akademii — Nauchn Tr Litov S-Kh Akad
Nauchnye Trudy L'vovskii Zooveterinarnyi Institut — Nauchn Tr L'vov Zoovet Inst
Nauchnye Trudy L'vovskogo Lesotekhnicheskogo Instituta — Nauchn Tr L'vov Lesotekh Inst
Nauchnye Trudy. Magnitogorskii Gornometallurgicheskii Institut — Nauchn Tr Magnitogorsk Gornometall Inst
Nauchnye Trudy Melitopol'skoi Opytnoi Stantsii Sadovodstva — Nauchn Tr Melitop Opytn Stn Sadovod
Nauchnye Trudy Melitopol'skoi Opytnoi Stantsii Sadovodstva — Nauchn Tr Melitopol'skoi Opytn Stn Sadovod
Nauchnye Trudy. Moskovskii Institut Narodnogo Khozyaistva — Nauchn Tr Mosk Inst Nar Khoz
Nauchnye Trudy Moskovskii Institut Radioelektroniki i Gornoi Elektromekhaniki — Nauchn Tr Mosk Inst Radioelektron Gorn Elektromekh
Nauchnye Trudy. Moskovskii Institut Stali i Splavov — Nauchn Tr Mosk Inst Stali Splavov
Nauchnye Trudy Moskovskii Poligraficheskii Institut — Nauchn Tr Mosk Poligr Inst
Nauchnye Trudy. Moskovskii Zaochnyi Poligraficheskii Institut — Nauchn Tr Mosk Zaochn Poligr Inst
Nauchnye Trudy Moskovskogo Gornogo Instituta [*Former USSR*] — Nauchn Tr Mosk Gorn Inst
Nauchnye Trudy Moskovskogo Inzhenerno-Ekonomicheskogo Instituta [*Former USSR*] — Nauchn Tr Mosk Inzh Ekon Inst
Nauchnye Trudy Moskovskogo Inzhenerno-Ekonomicheskogo Instituta — NMEIA
Nauchnye Trudy Moskovskogo Lesotekhnicheskogo Instituta — Nauchn Tr Mosk Lesotekh Inst
Nauchnye Trudy Moskovskogo Nauchno-Issledovatel'skogo Instituta Vaktsin i Syvorotok — Nauchn Tr Mosk Nauchno-Issled Inst Vaktsin Syvorot
Nauchnye Trudy Moskovskogo Nauchno-Issledovatel'skogo Instituta Vaktsin i Syvorotok — Naucn Tr Mosk Nauchno-Issled Inst Vaktsin Syvorotok
Nauchnye Trudy Moskovskogo Tekhnologicheskogo Instituta Legkoi Promyshlennosti — Nauchn Tr Mosk Tekhnol Inst Legk Promsti
Nauchnye Trudy Moskovskogo Tekhnologicheskogo Instituta Legkoi Promyshlennosti — NTMTA
Nauchnye Trudy Moskovskoi Gorodskoi Kliniceskoi Bol'nitsy N 52 — Nauchn Tr Mosk Gor Klin Bol'n N 52
Nauchnye Trudy Nauchno-Issledovatel'skii Gornometallurgicheskii Institut [*Yerevan*] — NGMSA

Nauchnye Trudy Nauchno-Issledovatelskii Gornometallurgicheskii Institut (Yerevan) — Nauchn Tr Nauchno Issled Gornometall Inst (Yerevan)
Nauchnye Trudy Nauchno-Issledovatel'skii Institut Kartofel'nogo Khoziaistva — Nauchn Tr Nauchno-Issled Inst Kartofel'n Khoz
Nauchnye Trudy. Nauchno-Issledovatel'skii Institut Konservnoi Promyshlennosti. Plovdiv — Nauchn Tr Nauchno Issled Inst Konservn Promsti Plovdiv
Nauchnye Trudy. Nauchno-Issledovatel'skii Institut Materi i Rebenka — Nauchn Tr Nauchno Issled Inst Materi Rebenka
Nauchnye Trudy Nauchno-Issledovatel'skii Institut Pchelovodstva — Nauch Trudy Nauchno-Issled Inst Pchel
Nauchnye Trudy Nauchno-Issledovatel'skii Institut Pushnogo Zverovodstva i Krolikovodstva — Nauchn Tr Nauchno-Issled Inst Pushnogo Zverovod Krolikovod
Nauchnye Trudy Nauchno-Issledovatel'skii Institut Radiologii i Radiatsionnoi Gigieny [*Bulgaria*] — Nauchn Tr Nauchno-Issled Inst Radiol Radiats Gig
Nauchnye Trudy Nauchno-Issledovatel'skii Institut Sel'skogo Khozyaistva Yugo-Vostoka — Nauchn Tr Nauchno Issled Inst Sel'sk Khoz Yugo Vostoka
Nauchnye Trudy Nauchno-Issledovatel'skogo Instituta Gornogo Sadovodstva i Tsvetovodstva — Nauchn Tr Nauchno-Issled Inst Gorn Sadovod Tsvetovod
Nauchnye Trudy Nauchno-Issledovatel'skogo Instituta po Pediatrii — Nauchn Tr Nauchno-Issled Inst Pediatr
Nauchnye Trudy Nauchno-Issledovatel'skogo Instituta Rastenievodstva v G. Pieshtyany — Nauchn Tr Nauchno Issled Inst Rastenievod Pieshtyany
Nauchnye Trudy Nauchno-Issledovatel'skogo Instituta Sel'skokhozyaistva Yugo-Vostoka — Nauchn Tr Nauchno-Issled Inst S-Kh Yugo-Vost
Nauchnye Trudy Nauchno-Issledovatel'skogo Veterinarnogo Instituta (Minsk) — Nauchn Tr Nauchno Issled Vet Inst (Minsk)
Nauchnye Trudy. Nizhnedneprovskoi Nauchno-Issledovatel'skoi Stantsii po Obleseniyu Peskov i Vinogradarstvu na Peskakh — Nauchn Tr Nizhnednepr Nauchno Issled Stn Obleseniyu Peskov V
Nauchnye Trudy. Novocherkasskogo Politekhnicheskogo Instituta imeni Sergo Ordzhonikidze — Nauchn Tr Novocherk Politekh Inst im Sergo Ordzhonikidze
Nauchnye Trudy Novosibirskogo Meditsinskogo Instituta — Nauchn Tr Novosib Med Inst
Nauchnye Trudy Novosibirskoi Nauchno-Issledovatel'skoi Veterinarnoi Stantsii — Nauchn Tr Novosib Nauchno Issled Vet Stn
Nauchnye Trudy Obninskii Otdel Geograficheskogo Obshchestva SSSR — Nauchn Tr Obninskii Otd Geogr Ova SSSR
Nauchnye Trudy. Odesskii Gosudarstvennyi Meditsinskii Institut — Nauchn Tr Odess Gos Med Inst
Nauchnye Trudy. Omskii Gosudarstvennyi Meditsinskii Institut imeni M. I. Kalinina — Nauchn Tr Omsk Gos Med Inst im M I Kalinina
Nauchnye Trudy. Omskii Institut Inzhenerov Zheleznodorozhnogo Transporta — Nauchn Tr Omsk Inst Inzh Zheleznodorozhn Transp
Nauchnye Trudy Omskii Meditsinskii Institut — Nauchn Tr Omsk Med Inst
Nauchnye Trudy Omskogo Sel'skokhozyaistvennogo Instituta — Nauchn Tr Omsk S-Kh Inst
Nauchnye Trudy Omskogo Veterinarnogo Instituta — Nauchn Tr Omsk Vet Inst
Nauchnye Trudy Orlovskaya Oblastnaya Sel'skokhozyaistvennaya Opytnaya Stantsiya — Nauchn Tr Orlov Ob Skh Opytn Stn
Nauchnye Trudy. Orlovskaya Oblastnaya Sel'skokhozyaistvennaya Opytnaya Stantsiya imeni P. I. Lisitsyna — Nauchn Tr Orlov Obl Skh Opytn Stn im P I Lisitsyna
Nauchnye Trudy. Permskii Gornyi Institut — Nauchn Tr Permsk Gorn Inst
Nauchnye Trudy. Permskii Gosudarstvennyi Farmatsevticheskii Institut — Nauchn Tr Permsk Gos Farm Inst
Nauchnye Trudy Permskii Nauchno Issledovatel'skii Ugol'nye Institut — Nauchn Tr Permsk Nauchno Issled Ugoln Inst
Nauchnye Trudy Permskii Politekhnicheskii Institut [*Former USSR*] — Nauchn Tr Permsk Politekh Inst
Nauchnye Trudy Permskii Politekhnicheskii Institut — NTPPA
Nauchnye Trudy Permskogo Farmatsevticheskogo Instituta — Nauchn Tr Permsk Farm Inst
Nauchnye Trudy Permskogo Meditsinskogo Instituta — Nauchn Tr Permsk Med Inst
Nauchnye Trudy po Obogashcheniyu i Briketirovaniyu Uglei [*Former USSR*] — Nauchn Tr Obogashch Briket Uglei
Nauchnye Trudy Poltavskii Nauchno-Issledovatel'skii Institut Svinovodstva — Nauch Tr Poltav Nauch-Issled Inst Svinovod
Nauchnye Trudy Poltavskii Sel'skokhozyaistvennyi Institut — Nauchn Tr Poltav Skh Inst
Nauchnye Trudy Primorskogo Sel'skokhozyaistvennogo Instituta — Nauchn Tr Primorsk S-Kh Inst
Nauchnye Trudy Ptitsevodstvo Nauchno-Issledovatel'skii Institut Ptitsevodstva [*A publication*] — Nauchn Tr Ptitsevod Nauchno-Issled Inst Ptitsevod
Nauchnye Trudy Rizhskii Nauchno-Issledovatel'skii Institut Travmatologii i Ortopedii — Nauchn Tr Rizh Nauchno Issled Inst Travmatol Ortop
Nauchnye Trudy Rostovskii-Na-Donu Inzhenerno-Stroitel'nyi Institut — Nauchn Tr Rostov Na Donu Inzh Stroit Inst
Nauchnye Trudy Ryazanskii Meditsinskii Institut — Nauchn Tr Ryazan Med Inst
Nauchnye Trudy. Ryazanskii Meditsinskii Institut imeni Akademika I. P. Pavlova — Nauchn Tr Ryazan Med Inst im Akad I P Pavlova
Nauchnye Trudy. Samarkandskii Kooperativnyi Institut Tsentrosoyuza imeni V. Kui bysheva — Nauchn Tr Samark Koop Inst Tsentrosoyuza im V V Kuibysheva
Nauchnye Trudy Samarkandskii Meditsinskii Institut Imeni Akademika I. P. Pavlova — NSMPA
Nauchnye Trudy Samarkandskii Sel'skokhozyaistvennyi Institut — Nauchn Tr Samark Skh Inst
Nauchnye Trudy Samarkandskogo Gosudarstvennogo Universiteta — Nauchn Tr Samark Gos Univ
Nauchnye Trudy Samarkandskogo Kooperativnogo Instituta Tsentrosoyuza — Nauchn Tr Samark Koop Inst Tsentrosoyuza
Nauchnye Trudy Samarkandskogo Meditsinskogo Instituta — Nauchn Tr Samark Med Inst
Nauchnye Trudy Samarkandskogo Universiteta — Nauchn Tr Samark Univ
Nauchnye Trudy Saratovskii Politekhnicheskii Institut — Nauchn Tr Sarat Politekh Inst
Nauchnye Trudy. Sel'skokhozyaistvennaya Akademiya. Sofia. Seriya. Rastenievodstvo — Nauchn Tr Skh Akad Sofia Ser Rastenievod
Nauchnye Trudy. Sel'skokhozyaistvennogo Instituta Armyanskoi SSR — Nauchn Tr Skh Inst Arm SSR
Nauchnye Trudy. Sel'skokhozyaistvennyi Institut. Sofia. Agronomicheskii Fakul'tet — Nauchn Tr Skh Inst Sofia Agron Fak
Nauchnye Trudy. Sel'skokhozyaistvennyi Institut (Sofia). Agronomicheskii Fakul'tet. Seriya Obshchee Zemledelie — Nauchn Tr S'kh Inst (Sofia) Agron Fak Ser Obshch Zemled
Nauchnye Trudy. Sel'skokhozyaistvennyi Institut. Sofia. Agronomicheskii Fakultet. Seriya Rastenievodstrvo — Nauchn Tr Skh Inst Sofia Agron Fak Ser Rastenievod
Nauchnye Trudy Severo-Zapadnogo Nauchno-Issledovatel'skogo Instituta Sel'skogo Khozyaistva — Nauchn Tr Sev-Zapadn Nauchno-Issled Inst Sel'sk Khoz
Nauchnye Trudy Severo-Zapadnyi Nauchno-Issledovatel'skii Institut Sel'skogo Khozyaistva — NSZKA
Nauchnye Trudy Sibirskii Gosudarstvennyi Nauchno-Issledovatel'skii i Proektnyi Institut Tsvetnoi Metallurgii [*Former USSR*] — Nauchn Tr Sib Gos Nauchno Issled Proekt Inst Tsvet Metall
Nauchnye Trudy Sibirskii Gosudarstvennyi Nauchno-Issledovatel'skii i Proektnyi Institut Tsvetnoi Metallurgii — Nauchn Tr Sib Gos Nauchno Issled Proektn Inst Tsvetn Metall
Nauchnye Trudy Sibirskii Nauchno Issledovatel'skii Institut Sel'skogo Khozyaistva — Nauchn Tr Sib Nauchno Issled Inst Selsk Khoz
Nauchnye Trudy. Stavropol'skii Gosudarstvennyi Pedagogicheskii Institut — Nauchn Tr Stavrop Gos Pedagog Inst
Nauchnye Trudy Stavropol'skogo Sel'Skokhozyaistvennogo Instituta — Nauch Trudy Stavropol Sek'Khoz Inst
Nauchnye Trudy Stavropol'skogo Sel'skokhozyaistvennogo Instituta — Nauchn Tr Stavrop S-Kh Inst
Nauchnye Trudy Studentov Gruzinskii Sel'skokhozyaistvennyi Institut — Nauchn Tr Stud Gruz Skh Inst
Nauchnye Trudy Studentov Gruzinskogo Sel'skokhozyaistvennogo Instituta — Nauchn Tr Stud Gruz Ssk Inst
Nauchnye Trudy Sverdlovskii Gosudarstvennyi Pedagogicheskii Institut — Nauchn Tr Sverdl Gos Pedagog Inst
Nauchnye Trudy Tashkentskii Gosudarstvennyi Universitet Imeni V. I. Lenina [*Former USSR*] — Nauchn Tr Tashk Gos Univ Im V I Lenina
Nauchnye Trudy Tashkentskii Gosudarstvennyi Universitet imeni V. I. Lenina — NTGLA
Nauchnye Trudy. Tashkentskii Politekhnicheskii Institut — Nauchn Tr Tashk Politekh Inst
Nauchnye Trudy Tashkentskogo Gosudarstvennogo Universiteta — Nauchn Tr Tashk Gos Univ
Nauchnye Trudy Tashkentskogo Tekstil'nogo Instituta — Nauchn Tr Tashk Tekst Inst
Nauchnye Trudy Tsentral'nogo Instituta Usovershenstovaniya Vrachei — Nauchn Tr Tsentr Inst Usoversh Vrachei
Nauchnye Trudy Tsentral'nyi Nauchno Issledovatel'skii Institut Mekhanicheskoi Obrabotki Drevesiny — Nauchn Tr Tsentr Nauchno Issled Inst Mekh Obrab Drev
Nauchnye Trudy. Tsentral'nyi Nauchno-Issledovatel'skii Institut Morskogo Flota — Nauchn Tr Tsentr Nauchno Issled Inst Morsk Flota
Nauchnye Trudy Tsentral'nyi Nauchno-Issledovatel'skii Institut Olovyannoi Promyshlennosti — Nauchn Tr Tsentr Nauchno-Issled Inst Olovyannoi Promsti
Nauchnye Trudy Tsentral'nyi Nauchno-Issledovatel'skii Institut Tsellyuloznoi i Bumazhnoi Promyshlennosti — Nauchn Tr Tsentr Nauchno Issled Inst Tsellyul Bum Promsti
Nauchnye Trudy Tul'skogo Gornogo Instituta — Nauchn Tr Tul Gorn Inst
Nauchnye Trudy Tulskogo Gosudarstvennogo Pedagogicheskogo Instituta — Nauchn Tr Tul Gos Pedagog Inst
Nauchnye Trudy. Tyumenskii Gosudarstvennyi Universitet — Nauchn Tr Tyumen Gos Univ
Nauchnye Trudy. Tyumenskii Industrial'nyi Institut — Nauchn Tr Tyumen Ind Inst
Nauchnye Trudy Tyumenskogo Sel'skokhozyaistvennogo Instituta — Nauchn Tr Tyumen Skh Inst
Nauchnye Trudy Uchenykh i Prakticheskikh Vrachei Uzbekistana — Nauchn Tr Uch Prakt Vrachei Uzb
Nauchnye Trudy Ukrainskaya Sel'skokhozyaistvennaya Akademiya — Nauchn Tr Ukr Skh Akad
Nauchnye Trudy Ukrainskii Instituta Eksperimental'noi Veterinarii — Nauchn Tr Ukr Inst Eksp Vet
Nauchnye Trudy Ukrainskii Nauchno-Issledovatel'skii Institut Eksperimental'noi Veterinarii — Nauchn Tr Ukr Nauchno Issled Inst Eksp Vet
Nauchnye Trudy Ukrainskii Nauchno-Issledovatel'skii Institut Fiziologii Rastenii — Nauchn Tr Ukr Nauchno Issled Inst Fiziol Rast
Nauchnye Trudy Ukrainskii Nauchno-Issledovatel'skii Institut Gigieny Truda i Profzabolevanii — Nauchn Tr Ukr Nauchno Issled Inst Gig Tr Profzabol
Nauchnye Trudy Ukrainskii Nauchno-Issledovatel'skii Institut Mekhanicheskoi Obrabotki Drevesiny — Nauchn Tr Ukr Nauchno Issled Inst Mekh Obrab Drev
Nauchnye Trudy Ukrainskii Nauchno-Issledovatel'skii Institut Pochvovedeniya — Nauchn Tr Ukr Nauchno Issled Inst Pochvoved
Nauchnye Trudy Ukrainskii Nauchno-Issledovatel'skii Institut Sadovodstva — Nauchn Tr Ukr Nauchno Issled Inst Sadovod
Nauchnye Trudy Ukrainskii Nauchno-Issledovatel'skii Institut Zashchity Rastenii — Nauchn Tr Ukr Nauchno Issled Inst Zashch Rast
Nauchnye Trudy. Ukrainskii Nauchno-Issledovatel'skii Uglekhimicheskii Institut — Nauchn Tr Ukr Nauchno Issled Uglekhim Inst

Nauchnye Trudy Ukrainskii Nauchno-Issledovatel'skogo. Instituta Lesnogo Khozyaistva i Agrolesomelioratsii — Nauchn Tr Ukr Nauchno Issled Inst Lesn Khoz Agrolesomelior
Nauchnye Trudy Ukrainskogo Instituta Gidrotekhniki i Melioratsii — Nauchn Tr Ukr Inst Gidrotekh Melior
Nauchnye Trudy Ukrainskogo Nauchno-Issledovatel'skogo Instituta Lesnogo Khozyaistva i Agrolesomelioratsii — Nauch Trudy Ukr Nauchno-Issled Inst Les Khoz Agrolesomelior
Nauchnye Trudy Ukrainskogo Nauchno-Issledovatel'skogo Instituta Pochvovedeniya — Nauch Trudy Ukr Nauchno-Issled Inst Pochv
Nauchnye Trudy Ukrainskogo Nauchno-Issledovatel'skogo Instituta Rastenievodstva Selestsii i Genetiki — Nauchn Tr Ukr Nauchno-Issled Inst Rastenievod Sel Genet
Nauchnye Trudy Ukrainskogo Nauchno-Issledovatel'skogo Instituta Ugleobogashcheniya — Nauchn Tr Ukr Nauchno Issled Inst Ugleobogashch
Nauchnye Trudy Ukrainskogo Nauchno-Issledovatel'skogo Instituta Vinogradarstva i Vinodeliya — Nauchn Tr Ukr Nauchno Issled Inst Vinograd Vinodel
Nauchnye Trudy Ukrainskoi Nauchno-Issledovatel'skoi Stantsii Vinogradarstva i Osvoeniya Peskov — Nauchn Tr Ukr Nauchno-Issled Stn Vinograd Osvo Peskov
Nauchnye Trudy Ukrainskoi Sel'Skokhozyaistvennoi Akademii — Nauch Trudy Ukr Sel'Khoz Akad
Nauchnye Trudy USKhA (Ukrains'ka Sil's'kohospodars'ka Akademiia) — Nauchn Tr USKhA
Nauchnye Trudy Uzbekskogo Sel'skokhozyaistvennogo Instituta — Nauchn Tr Uzb Skh Inst
Nauchnye Trudy UzNIVI — Nauchn Tr UzNIVI
Nauchnye Trudy Veselopodolyanskoi Opytno-Selektsionnoi Stantsii — Nauch Tr Veselopodol Opyt-Selek Sta
Nauchnye Trudy Voprosam Pererabotki i Kachestva Uglei — Nauchn Tr Vopr Pererab Kach Uglei
Nauchnye Trudy Voronezhskii Inzhenerno-Stroitel'nyi Institut — Nauchn Tr Voronezh Inzh Stroit Inst
Nauchnye Trudy Voronezhskii Sel'skokhozyaistvennyi — Nauch Trudy Voronezh Sel'Khoz Inst
Nauchnye Trudy Voronezhskogo Lesotekhnicheskogo Instituta — Nauchn Tr Voronezh Lesotekh Inst
Nauchnye Trudy. Vostochnyi Nauchno-Issledovatel'skii Uglekhimicheskii Institut — Nauchn Tr Vost Nauchno Issled Uglekhim Inst
Nauchnye Trudy Vrachei Magnitogorsk — Nauchn Tr Vrachei Magnitogorsk
Nauchnye Trudy. Vsesoyuznogo Nauchno-Issledovatel'skogo Instituta Gidrotekhniki i Melioratsii — Nauchn Tr Vses Nauchno Issled Inst Gidrotekh Melior
Nauchnye Trudy Vsesoyuznogo Nauchno-Issledovatel'skogo Instituta Sel'skokhozyaistvennogo Mashinostroeniya — Nauchn Tr Vses Nauchno Issled Inst Skh Mashinostr
Nauchnye Trudy Vsesoyuznogo Selektsionno Geneticheskogo Instituta — Nauchn Tr Vses Sel Genet Inst
Nauchnye Trudy. Vsesoyuznyi Nauchno-Issledovatel'skii Institut Asbestovoi Promyshlennosti — Nauchn Tr Vses Nauchno Issled Inst Asbestovoi Promsti
Nauchnye Trudy. Vsesoyuznyi Nauchno-Issledovatel'skii Institut Farmatsii — Nauchn Tr Vses Nauchno Issled Inst Farm
Nauchnye Trudy Vsesoyuznyi Nauchno-Issledovatel'skii Institut Podzemnoi Gazifikatsii Uglei — Nauchn Tr Vses Nauchno Issled Inst Podzemn Gazif Uglei
Nauchnye Trudy Vsesoyuznyi Nauchno-Issledovatel'skii Institut Sazhevoi Promyshlennosti — Nauchn Tr Vses Nauchno Issled Inst Sazhevoi Promsti
Nauchnye Trudy Vsesoyuznyi Nauchno-Issledovatel'skii Institut Zernobobovykh Kul'tur — Nauchn Tr Vses Nauchno Issled Inst Zernobobovykh Kult
Nauchnye Trudy Vsesoyuznyi Zaochnyi Mashinostroitel'nyi Institut [*Former USSR*] — Nauchn Tr Vses Zaochn Mashinostroit Inst
Nauchnye Trudy. Vysshii Institut Zootekhniki i Veterinarnoi Meditsiny. Zootekhnicheskii Fakul'tet-Stara Zagora — Nauchn Tr Vyssh Inst Zootekh Vet Med Zootekh Fak Stara Zagor
Nauchnye Trudy. Vysshii Lesotekhnicheskii Institut. Sofiya. Seriya Mekhanicheskaya Tekhnologiya Drevesiny — Nauchn Tr Vyssh Lesotekh Inst Sofiya Ser Mekh Tekhnol Drev
Nauchnye Trudy. Vysshii Lesotekhnicheskii Institut. Sofiya. Seriya Ozelenenie — Nauchn Tr Vyssh Lesotekh Inst Sofiya Ser Ozelenenie
Nauchnye Trudy. Vysshii Sel'skokhozyaistvennyi Institut. Sofia. Zootekhnicheskii Fakul'tet — Nauchn Tr Vyssh Skh Inst Sofia Zootekh Fak
Nauchnye Trudy. Vysshii Veterinarno-Meditsinskii Institut imeni Prof. D-ra G. Pavlova — Nauchn Tr Vyssh Vet Med Inst im Prof D ra G Pavlova
Nauchnye Trudy Vysshikh Uchebnykh Zavedenii Litovskoi SSR. Elektrotekhnika i Avtomatika — Nauchn Tr Vyssh Uchebn Zaved Lit SSR Elektrotekh Avtom
Nauchnye Trudy Vysshikh Uchebnykh Zavedenii Litovskoi SSR. Geografiya — Nauchn Tr Vyssh Uchebn Zaved Lit SSR Geogr
Nauchnye Trudy Vysshikh Uchebnykh Zavedenii Litovskoi SSR. Geografiya i Geologiya — Nauchn Tr Vyssh Uchebn Zaved Lit SSR Geogr Geol
Nauchnye Trudy. Vysshikh Uchebnykh Zavedenii Litovskoi SSR. Khimiya i Khimicheskaya Tekhnologiya — Nauchn Tr Vyssh Uchebn Zaved Lit SSR Khim Khim Tekhnol
Nauchnye Trudy. Vysshikh Uchebnykh Zavedenii Litovskoi SSR. Mekhanicheskaya Tekhnologiya — Nauchn Tr Vyssh Uchebn Zaved Lit SSR Mekh Tekhnol
Nauchnye Trudy Vysshikh Uchebnykh Zavedenii Litovskoi SSR. Mekhanika — Nauchn Tr Vyssh Uchebn Zaved Lit SSR Mekh
Nauchnye Trudy Vysshikh Uchebnykh Zavedenii Litovskoi SSR Ultrazvuk — Nauchn Tr Vyssh Uchebn Zaved Lit SSR Ultrazvuk
Nauchnye Trudy Vysshikh Uchebnykh Zavedenii Litovskoi SSR Vibrotekhnika — Nauchn Tr Vyssh Uchebn Zaved Lit SSR Vibrotekh
Nauchnye Trudy Vysshykh Uchebnykh Zavedenii Litovskoi SSR Biologiya — Nauchn Tr Vyssh Uchebn Zaved Lit SSR Biol
Nauchnye Trudy Vysshykh Uchebnykh Zavedenii Litovskoi SSR Meditsina (Vilnius) [*A publication*] — Nauchn Tr Vyssh Uchebn Zaved Lit SSR Med (Vilnius)
Nauchnye Trudy Zhitomirskii Sel'skokhozyaistvennyi Institut — Nauchn Tr Zhitomir Skh Inst
Nauchnye Trudy Zootekhnologicheskogo Fakulteta Zooveterinarnogo Instituta — Nauchn Tr Zootekhnol Fak Zoovet Inst
Nauchnye Trudy Zootekhnologicheskogo Instituta — Nauchn Tr Zootekhnologicheskogo Inst
Nauchnye Zapiske. Nezhinskii Gosudarstvennyi Pedagogicheskii Institut — Nauchn Zap Nezhin Gos Pedagog Inst
Nauchnye Zapiski Belotserkovskogo Sel'skokhozyaistvennogo Instituta — Nauchn Zap Belotserk Skh Inst
Nauchnye Zapiski Chernovitskii Gosudarstvennyi Meditsinskii Institut — Nauchn Zap Chernovits Gos Med Inst
Nauchnye Zapiski Dnepropetrovskogo Gosudarstvennogo Universiteta — Nauchn Zap Dnepropetr Gos Univ
Nauchnye Zapiski Dnepropetrovskogo Gosudarstvennogo Universiteta — Nauchnye Zap Dnepropetr Gos Univ
Nauchnye Zapiski Donetskogo Instituta Sovetskoi Torgovli — Nauchn Zap Donetsk Inst Sov Torg
Nauchnye Zapiski Fiziko-Matematicheskogo Fakul'teta. Odesskii Gosudarstvennyi Pedagogicheskii Institut — Nauchn Zap Fiz Mat Fak Odess Gos Pedagog Inst
Nauchnye Zapiski Gosudarstvennogo Eksperimentnogo Instituta Sakharnoi Promyshlennosti — Nauchn Zap Gos Eksp Inst Sakh Promsti
Nauchnye Zapiski Gosudarstvennyi Nauchno-Issledovatel'skii i Proektnyi Institut Ugol'noi Promyshlennosti [*Former USSR*] — Nauchn Zap Gos Nauchno-Issled Proektn Inst Ugol'n Prom-Sti
Nauchnye Zapiski Gosudarstvennyi Nauchno-Issledovatel'skii i Proektnyi Institut Ugol'noi Promyshlennosti — NZURA
Nauchnye Zapiski Kafedr Matematiki. Fiziki i Estestvoznaniya. Odesskii Gosudarstvennyi Pedagogicheskii Institut — Nauchn Zap Kafedr Mat Fiz Estestvozn Odess Gos Pedagog Inst
Nauchnye Zapiski Khar'kovskii Institut Mekhanizatsii i Elektrifikatsii Sel'skogo Khozyaistva — Nauchn Zap Khar'k Inst Mekh Elektrif Sel'sk Khoz
Nauchnye Zapiski Khar'kovskii Institut Mekhanizatsii Sel'skogo Khozyaistva — Nauchn Zap Khar'k Inst Mekh Sel'sk Khoz
Nauchnye Zapiski Khar'kovskii Institut Mekhanizatsii Sotsialisticheskogo Sel'skogo Khozyaistva — Nauchn Zap Khar'k Inst Mekh Sots Sel'sk Khoz
Nauchnye Zapiski Khar'kovskii Poligraficheskii Institut — Nauchn Zap Khar'k Poligr Inst
Nauchnye Zapiski Khar'kovskogo Aviatsionnogo Instituta — Nauchn Zap Khar'k Aviats Inst
Nauchnye Zapiski Khersonskogo Gosudarstvennogo Pedagogicheskogo Instituta — Nauchn Zap Kherson Gos Pedagog Inst
Nauchnye Zapiski Khersonskogo Sel'skokhozyaistvennogo Instituta Imeni A. D. Tsiurupy — Nauchn Zap Kherson Skh Inst Im A D Tsiurupy
Nauchnye Zapiski Luganskogo Sel'skokhozyaistvennogo Instituta — Nauchn Zap Lugansk Skh Inst
Nauchnye Zapiski L'vovskogo Politekhnicheskogo Instituta — Nauchn Zap Lvov Politekh Inst
Nauchnye Zapiski L'vovskogo Sel'skokhozyaistvennogo Instituta — Nauchn Zap L'vov Skh Inst
Nauchnye Zapiski L'vovskogo Torgovo Ekonomicheskogo Instituta — Nauchn Zap L'vov Torg Ekon Inst
Nauchnye Zapiski Moskovskii Gidromeliorativnyi Institut — Nauchn Zap Mosk Gidromelior Inst
Nauchnye Zapiski. Odesskii Gosudarstvennyi Pedagogicheskii Institut — Nauchn Zap Odess Gos Pedagog Inst
Nauchnye Zapiski Odesskii Politekhnicheskii Institut — Nauchn Zap Odess Politekh Inst
Nauchnye Zapiski po Dermatologii i Venerologii Vrachei Kubani — Nauchn Zap Dermatol Venerol Vrachei Kubani
Nauchnye Zapiski po Sakharnoi Promyshlennost Agronomicheskii Vypusk — Nauchn Zap Sakh Promsti Agron Vyp
Nauchnye Zapiski po Sakharnoi Promyshlennosti Tekhnologicheskii Vypusk — Nauchn Zap Sakh Promsti Tekhnol Vyp
Nauchnye Zapiski po Sakhnarnoi Promyshlennosti — Nauchn Zap Sakh Promsti
Nauchnye Zapiski Ukrainskii Poligraficheskii Institut — Nauchn Zap Ukr Poligr Inst
Nauchnye Zapiski Uzhgorodskogo Gosudarstvennogo Universiteta — Nauchn Zap Uzhgorod Gos Univ
Nauchnye Zapiski Voronezhskogo Lesokhimicheskogo Instituta — Nauchn Zap Voronezh Lesokhim Inst
Nauchnye Zapiski Voronezhskogo Lesotekhnicheskogo Instituta — Nauchn Zap Voronezh Lesotekh Inst
Nauchnye Zapiski Voronezhskogo Otdela Geograficheskogo Obshchestva SSSR — Nauchn Zap Voronezh Otd Geogr Ova SSSR
Nauchnye Zapiski Voronezhskogo Otdeleniya Vsesoyuznogo Botanicheskogo Obshchestva — Nauchn Zap Voronezh Otd Vses Bot Ova
Nauchnye Zapiski Voroshilovgradskogo Sel'skokhozyaistvennogo Instituta — Nauchn Zap Voroshilovgr Skh Inst
Nauchnye Zhurnal Politekhnicheskogo Instituta Tun-Tsei — Nauchn Zh Politekh Inst Tun Tsei
Nauchnyi Avtomotornyi Institut. Trudy — Nauchn Avtomot Inst Tr
Nauchnyi Ezhegodnik Chernovitskogo Universiteta — Nauchn Ezheg Chernovits Univ
Nauchnyi Ezhegodnik Odesskii Gosudarstvennyi Universitet Biologicheskii Fakul'tet — Nauchn Ezheg Odess Gos Univ Biol Fak
Nauchnyi Ezhegodnik Odesskii Gosudarstvennyi Universitet Khimicheskii Fakul'tet — Nauchn Ezheg Odess Gos Univ Khim Fak
Nauchnyi Ezhegodnik Odesskogo Universiteta — Nauchn Ezheg Odess Univ

Nauchnyi Seminar po Polucheniyu i Issledovaniyu Svoistv Soedinenii Redkozemel'nykh Metallov — Nauchn Semin Poluch Issled Svoistv Soedin Redkozem Met
Nauchnyi Spravochnik Agrarnogo Universiteta — Nauchn Sprav Agrar Univ
Nauchnyi Studencheskii Zhurnal. Geologicheskii Fakul'tet. Moskovskii Gosudarstvennyi Universitet — Nauchn Stud Zh Geol Fak Mosk Gos Univ
Nauchnyi Vestnik Universiteta Agrarnykh Nauk. Gedelle. Vengriya — Nauchn Vestn Univ Agrar Nauk Gedelle Vengriya
Nauchnyi Zhurnal. Severo-Zapadnogo Sel'skokhozyaistvennogo Instituta — Nauchn Zh Sev Zapadn Skh Inst
Naucnaja Organizacija Truda i Chozjajstvo — NOT i Ch
Naucni Sastanak Slavista u Vulove Dane — NSSVD
Naucni Trudove Vissh Lesotehniceski Institut (Serija Gorsko Stopanstvo) — Nauc Trud Lesoteh Inst (Ser Gorsko Stop)
Naucno-Issledovatel'skij — NI
Naucno-Tehnicki Pregled — Naucno-Teh Pregl
Naucnye Doklady Vyssej Skoly — NDVS
Naucnye Doklady Vyssej Skoly Filologiceskie Nauki — NDVS-F
Naucnye Doklady Vyssej Skoly Filosofskie Nauki — Nauc Dokl Vyss Skoly Filos Nauki
Naucnye Doklady Vyssej Skoly Naucnyj Kommunizma — Nauc Dokl Vyss Skoly Nauc Kommunizma
Naucnye Raboty is Oobscenija Akademii Nauk Uzbekskoj SSR, Otdelenie Obscestvennych Nauk — NRS
Naucnye Trudove Vissh Lesotehniceski Institut (Serija Mehanicna Tehnologija na Darvesinata) — Nauc Trud Lesoteh Inst (Ser Meh Tehn Darv)
Naucnye Trudy Kurskogo Pedagogiceskogo Instituta — Nauc Trudy Kursk Pedag Inst
Naucnye Trudy Leningradskaja Ordena Lenina Lesotehniceskja Akademija Imeni S. M. Kirova — Nauc Trudy Leningr Lesoteh Akad
Naucnye Trudy (Novosibirskij Gosudarstvennyj Pedagogiceskij Institut) — Nauc Trudy (Novosib Gos Pedag Inst)
Naucnye Trudy Novosibirskogo Pedagogiceskogo Instituta — Nauc Trudy Novosib Pedag Inst
Naucnye Trudy Saratovskogo Politehniceskogo Instituta — Nauc Trudy Saratov Politehn Inst
Naucnye Trudy Sverdlovskogo Pedagogiceskogo Instituta — Nauc Trudy Sverdlovsk Pedag Inst
Naucnye Trudy Sverdlovskogo Pedagogiceskogo Instituta. Sociologiceskogo Problemi — Nauc Trudy Sverdlovsk Pedag Inst Sociol Probl
Naucnye Trudy (Taskentskij Pedagogiceskij Institut) — Nauc Trudy (Taskent Pedag Inst)
Naucnye Trudy Taskentskogo Universiteta — Nauc Trudy Taskent Univ
Naucnye Trudy Tjumenskogo Universiteta — Nauc Trudy Tjumensk Univ
Naucnye Trudy Vyssyh Ucebnyh Zavedennij Litovskoj SSR — Nauc Trudy Vyss Uceb Zaved Litov SSR
Naucnye Upravlenie Obscestva — Nauc Upravl Obsc
Naucnye Zapyski Dnepropetrovskogo Gosudarstvennogo Universiteta — NZDnepU
Naucnye Zapyski Kievskogo Pedagogiceskogo Instytutu Inostrannych Jazykov — NZKievPIIn
Naucnyj Bjulletin Leningradskogo Gosud. Universiteta — Nauc Bjulletin Leningrad
Naucnyj Bjulletin Leningradskogo Universiteta — NBLU
Naucnyj Rabotnik — NR
Nauheimer Fortbildungs-Lehrgaenge — Nauheimer Fortbild-Lehrgaenge
NAUI (National Association of Underwater Instructors) News — NAUI News
Nauka i Peredovoi Opyt v Sel'skom Khozyaistve — Nauka Pered Opyt Sel'Khoz
Nauka i Peredovoi Opyt v Sel'skom Khozyaistve — Nauka Peredovoi Opyt Sel'sk Khoz
Nauka i Religija — Ni R
Nauka i Religija — NR
Nauka i Tekhnika (Leningrad) — Nauka Tekh (Leningrad)
Nauka i Tekhnika v Gorodskom Khozyaistve — Nauka Tekh Gor Khoz
Nauka i Zhizn' [*Moscow*] — NZhi
Nauka o Zemi. Seria Geologica — Nauka Zemi Ser Geol
Nauka Polska — Nauka Pol
Nauka Polska — NP
Nauka Proizvodstvu (Tiflis) — Nauka Proizvod (Tiflis)
Nauka Sel'skokhozyaistvennomu Proizvodstvu — Nauka Skh Proizvod
Nauka Sel'skomu Khozyaistvu — Nauka Selsk Khoz
Nauka Tehnika Bezbednost — Nauka Teh Bezb
Nauka Zhivotnovodstvu — Nauka Zhivotnovod
Nauki Techniczne. Mechanika (Czestochowa, Poland) — Nauki Tech Mech Czestochowa Pol
Naukove Tovaristvo imeni Shevchenka. Khemichno-Biologichna-Medichna Sektsiya. Proceedings — Nauk Tov im Shevchenka Khem Biol Med Sekts Proc
Naukovedenie i Informatika — Nauk & Inf
Naukovedenie i Informatika — Naukoved Inf
Naukovi Pratse Ukrayins'ka Sil's'kohospodars'ka Akademiya — Nauk Pr Ukr Sil'kohospod Akad
Naukovi Pratsi Aspirantiv Ukrains'ka Akademiya Sil's'kogospodars'kikh Nauk — Nauk Pr Aspir Ukr Akad Sil's'kogospod Nauk
Naukovi Pratsi Institut Entomologii ta Fitopatologii Akademii Nauk Ukrains'koi RSR — Nauk Pr Inst Entomol Fitopatol Akad Nauk Ukr RSR
Naukovi Pratsi Institutu Livarnogo Virobnitstva Akademiya Nauk Ukrains'koi RSR — Nauk Pr Inst Livarnogo Virobnitstva Akad Nauk Ukr RSR
Naukovi Pratsi Kamenets-Podol'skii Sil's'kogospodars'kii Institut — Nauk Pr Kamenets Podol'sk Sil's'kogospod Inst
Naukovi Pratsi. Kharkivs'kii Institut Inzheneriv Kommunal'nogo Budivnitstva — Nauk Pr Khark Inst Inzh Kommunaln Budiv
Naukovi Pratsi Kharkivs'kii Sil's'kogospodars'kii Institut — Nauk Pr Khark Sil's'kogospod Inst
Naukovi Pratsi L'vivs'kii Sil's'kogospodars'kii Institut — Nauk Pr L'viv Sil's'kogospod Inst
Naukovi Pratsi L'vivs'kii Zootekhnichno-Veterinarnii Institut — Nauk Pr L'viv Zootekh Vet Inst
Naukovi Pratsi L'vivs'kii Zooveterinarnii Institut — Nauk Pr L'viv Zoovet Inst
Naukovi Pratsi Nauchnye Trudy Derzhavna Sil's'kohospodars'ka Doslidna Stantsiya — Nauk Pr Nauchn Tr Derzh Sil's'kohospod Dosl Stn
Naukovi Pratsi Poltavs'kogo Sil's'kogospodars'skogo Institutu — Nauk Pr Poltav Sil's'kogospod Inst
Naukovi Pratsi. Sums'ka Derzhavna Sil's'kogospodars'ka Doslidna Stantsiya — Nauk Pr Sums'ka Derzh Sil's'kogospod Dosl Stn
Naukovi Pratsi Ukrains'kii Institut Eksperimental'noi Veterinarii — Nauk Pr Ukr Inst Eksp Vet
Naukovi Pratsi Ukrains'kii Naukovo-Doslidnii Institut Eksperimental'noi Veterinarii — Nauk Pr Ukr Nauk Dosl Inst Eksp Vet
Naukovi Pratsi Ukrains'kii Naukovo-Doslidnii Institut Fiziologii Roslin — Nauk Pr Ukr Nauk Dosl Inst Fiziol Rosl
Naukovi Pratsi Ukrains'kii Naukovo-Doslidnii Institut Sadivnitstva — Nauk Pr Ukr Nauk Dosl Inst Sadivn
Naukovi Pratsi Ukrains'kii Naukovo-Doslidnii Institut Zakhistu Roslin — Nauk Pr Ukr Nauk Dosl Inst Zakhistu Rosl
Naukovi Pratsi Ukrainskii Naukovo-Doslidnoi Institut Zemlerobstva — Nauk Pr Ukr Nauk Dosl Inst Zemlerob
Naukovi Pratsi Ukrayins'ka Sil's'kohospodars'ka Akademiya — Nauk Pratsi Ukr Sil-Hospod Akad
Naukovi Pratsi Veterinarnogo Fakul'tetu L'vivs'kii Zooveterinarnii Institut — Nauk Pr Vet Fak L'viv Zoovet Inst
Naukovi Pratsi Veterynarnoho Fakul'tetu Ukrayins'koyi Sil's'kohospodars'koyi Akademii — Nauk Pr Vet Fak Ukr Sil's'kohospod Akad
Naukovi Pratsi Volyns'ka Derzhavna Sil's'kohospodars'ka Doslidna Stantsiya — Nauk Pr Volyn Derzh Sil's'kohospod Doslid Sta
Naukovi Pratsi Zhitomirs'kogo Sil's'kogospodars'kogo Institutu — Nauk Pr Zhitomir Silskogospod Inst
Naukovi Pratsi Zhytomyrs'koho Sil's'kohospodars'koho Instytutu — Nauk Pr Zhytomyr Sil's'kohospod Inst
Naukovi Pratsi Zootekhnichnogo Fakul'tetu Kamenets-Podol'skii Sil's'kogospodars'kii Institut — Nauk Pr Zootekh Fak Kamenets Podol'sk Sil's'kogospod Inst
Naukovi Zapiski. Chernivets'kii Derzhavnii Universitet — Nauk Zap Chernivets Derzh Univ
Naukovi Zapiski Dnepropetrovs'kii Derzhavnii Universitet — Nauk Zap Dnepropetr Derzh Univ
Naukovi Zapiski Ivano-Frankivs'kii Derzhavnii Medichnii Institut — Nauk Zap Ivano Frankivs'kii Derzh Med Inst
Naukovi Zapiski Katerinoslavs'koi Naukovo-Doslidchoi Katedri Khemii — Nauk Zap Katerinosl Nauk Dosl Katedri Khem
Naukovi Zapiski Khersons'kogo Derzhavnogo Pedagogichnogo Instituta — Nauk Zap Kherson Derzh Pedagog Inst
Naukovi Zapiski Kiivs'kii Derzhavnii Universitet — Nauk Zap Kiiv Derzh Univ
Naukovi Zapiski Kiivs'kii Derzhavnii Universitet Pratsi Botanichnogo Sadu — Nauk Zap Kiiv Derzh Univ Pr Bot Sadu
Naukovi Zapiski Kiivs'kogo Veterinarnogo Institutu — Nauk Zap Kiiv Vet Inst
Naukovi Zapiski Krivoriz'kogo Derzhavnogo Pedagogichnogo Instituta — Nauk Zap Krivoriz Derzh Pedagog Inst
Naukovi Zapiski L'vivs'kii Derzhavnii Universitet Seriya Biologichna — Nauk Zap L'viv Derzh Univ Ser Biol
Naukovi Zapiski L'vivs'kii Derzhavnii Universitet Seriya Fiziko-Matematichna — Nauk Zap L'viv Derzh Univ Ser Fiz Mat
Naukovi Zapiski L'vivs'kii Derzhavnii Universitet Seriya Geologichna — Nauk Zap L'viv Derzh Univ Ser Geol
Naukovi Zapiski. L'vivs'kii Derzhavnii Universitet. Seriya Khimichna — Nauk Zap Lviv Derzh Univ Ser Khim
Naukovi Zapiski. L'vivs'kii Politekhnichnii Institut — Nauk Zap Lviv Politekh Inst
Naukovi Zapiski L'vivs'kogo Sil's'kogospodars'kogo Institutu — Nauk Zap Lviv Silskogospod Inst
Naukovi Zapiski L'vivs'kogo Torgovo-Ekonomichnogo Institutu — Nauk Zap L'viv Torg Ekon Inst
Naukovi Zapiski Nizhins'kii Derzhavnii Pedagogichnii Institut — Nauk Zap Nizhin Derzh Pedagog Inst
Naukovi Zapiski Odes'kii Derzhavnii Pedagogichnii Institut — Nauk Zap Odes Derzh Pedagog Inst
Naukovi Zapiski Odes'kii Politekhnichnii Institut — Nauk Zap Odes Politekh Inst
Naukovi Zapiski Odes'koi Biologichnoi Stantsii Akademiya Nauk Ukrains'koi RSR [*A publication*] — Nauk Zap Odes Biol Stn Akad Nauk Ukr RSR
Naukovi Zapiski Stanislavs'kii Derzhavnii Medichnii Institut — Nauk Zap Stanisl Derzh Med Inst
Naukovi Zapiski Sumskogo Derzhavnego Pedagogicheskogo Instituta — Nauk Zap Sumskogo Derzh Pedagog Inst
Naukovi Zapiski Ukrains'kii Poligrafichnii Institut — Nauk Zap Ukr Poligr Inst
Naukovi Zapiski Ukrains'kii Tekhnichno-Gospodars'kii Institut (Munich) — Nauk Zap Ukr Tekh Gospod Inst (Munich)
Naukovi Zapiski Ukrains'kogo Biokhemichnogo Instituta — Nauk Zap Ukr Biokhem Inst
Naukovi Zapiski Uzhgorods'kogo Derzhavnogo Universitetu — Nauk Zap Uzhgorod Derzh Univ
Naukovi Zapiski Zhitomirs'kogo Sil's'kogospodars'kogo Institutu — Nauk Zap Zhitomir Silskogospod Inst
Naukovi Zapyski Cerkas'koho Derzavnoho Pedahohicnoho Instytutu — NZCerPI
Naukovi Zapyski Cernivec'koho Derzavnoho Universyteta — NZCernU
Naukovi Zapyski Donec'koho Derzavnoho Pedahohicnoho Instytutu — NZDonPI
Naukovi Zapyski Drohobyc'koho Derzavnoho Pedahohicnoho Instytutu — NZDrohPI

Naukovi Zapyski Izmail's'koho Derzavnoho Pedahohicnoho Instytutu — NZIzmPI
Naukovi Zapyski Kam'jancja-Polil's'koho Derzavnoho Pedahohicnoho Instytutu — NZKamPI
Naukovi Zapyski Kyjivs'koho Derzavnoho Pedahohicnoho Instytutu — NZKyiPI
Naukovi Zapyski Zytomyrs'koho Derzavnoho Pedahohicnoho Instytutu — NZZytPI
Naukovi Zapysky Cherkas'koho Derzhavnoho Pedagogichnoho Instytutu — Nauk Zap Cherk Derzh Pedagog Inst
Naukovi Zapysky. Kyjivs'kyj Derzavnyj Universytet imeny T.G. Sevcenka. Bulletin Scientifique. Universite d'Etat de Kiev — Nauk Zap Kyjivsk Derzavn Univ Sevcenka
Naukovi Zapysky L'vivs'koho Derzhavnoho Pedagogichnoho Instytutu — Nauk Za L'viv Derzh Pedagog Inst
Naukovi Zapysky L'vivs'koho Derzhavnoho Pedagogichnoho Instytutu — Nauk Zap L'viv Derzh Pedagog Inst
Naukovi Zapysky Nizhyns'koho Derzhavnoho Pedagogichnoho Institutu — Nauk Zap Nizhyns'koho Derzh Pedagog Inst
Naukovi Zapysky Uzhorods'koho Derzhavnoho Universytetu — Nauk Zap Uzhorod Derzh Univ
Naukovii Shchorichnik. Kiivs'kii Derzhavnii Universitet Imeni T. G. Shevchenka — Nauk Shchorichnik Kiiv Derzh Univ Im T G Shevchenka
Naukovo Tovarystvo Imeni Sevcenka — NTS
Naukovo-Tekhnichnii Visnik — Nauk-Tekh Visn
Naukovyj Zbirnik Museju Ukranjinskoji Kultury v Sydnyku — NZMUKS
Naunyn Schmiedeberg's Archives of Pharmacology — Naunyn Schmied Arch Pharmacol
Naunyn-Schmiedebergs Archiv fuer Experimentelle Pathologie und Pharmakologie — Naunyn-Schmiedebergs Arch Exp Path Pharmak
Naunyn-Schmiedebergs Archiv fuer Experimentelle Pathologie und Pharmakologie — Naunyn-Schmiedebergs Arch Exp Pathol Pharmakol
Naunyn-Schmiedebergs Archiv fuer Pharmakologie [*Formerly, Naunyn-Schmiedebergs Archiv fuer Pharmakologie und Experimentelle Pathologie*] — Naunyn-Schmiedebergs Arch Pharmakol
Naunyn-Schmiedebergs Archiv fuer Pharmakologie und Experimentelle Pathologie [*Later, Naunyn-Schmiedebergs Archiv fuer Pharmakologie*] — Naunyn-Schmiedebergs Arch Pharmakol Exp Pathol
Naunyn-Schmiedeberg's Archives of Pharmacology — Naunyn-Schmiedebergs Arch Pharmacol
Naunyn-Schmiedeberg's Archives of Pharmacology — N-S Arch Ph
Nautical Magazine — Naut M
Nautical Magazine — NM
Nautilus [*Madrid*] — Naut
Navajo Reporter — Navajo Rptr
Navajo Tribal Code — Navajo Trib Code
Naval Abstracts — Nav Abstr
Naval Architect — Nav Archit
Naval Architect — NVARA
Naval Aviation News — Nav Av Nws
Naval Engineers' Journal — Nav Eng J
Naval Engineers' Journal — Naval Eng J
Naval Engineers' Journal — Navl Eng J
Naval Forces — Naval F
Naval Magazine — Nav M
Naval Magazine — NAVMAG
Naval Magazine — NM
Naval Magazine — NMAG
Naval Ordnance Laboratory Symposium on Ammonia Batteries — Nav Ordnance Lab Symp Ammonia Batteries
Naval Research Laboratory Memorandum Report (United States) — Nav Res Lab Memo Rep US
Naval Research Logistics — Naval Res Logist
Naval Research Logistics. Quarterly — Nav Res Log
Naval Research Logistics. Quarterly — Nav Res Logist Q
Naval Research Logistics. Quarterly — Nav Res Logistics Q
Naval Research Logistics. Quarterly — Naval Res Log Quart
Naval Research Logistics. Quarterly — Naval Res Logist Quart
Naval Research Logistics. Quarterly — NRLQ
Naval Research Reviews — Na Rs Rev
Naval Research Reviews — Nav Res Rev
Naval Research Reviews — RR
Naval Reservist — Nav Reserv
Naval Stores Review — Nav Stores Rev
Naval Stores Review — Naval Stores R
Naval Stores Review — Naval Stores Rev
Naval Training Bulletin — Nav Train Bull
Naval War College — N War Coll
Naval War College. Review — Nav War Col Rev
Naval War College. Review — Naval War College R
NAVAS [*Nederlandse Aannemersvereniging van Afbouwen Stukadoorswerken*] 77 — STP
Navigantium atque Itinerarium Bibliotheca [*London*] — NIB
Navigation — Navig
Navigation Interieure — Navig Int
Navitecnia y Comercio Maritimo — Navitecnia Comer Marit
Navorscher — Nav
Navorsinge van die Nasionale Museum (Bloemfontein) — Navors Nas Mus (Bloemfontein)
Navorsinge van die Nasionale Museum (Bloemfontein) — Navorsinge Nas Mus (Bloemfontein)
Navorsingsverslag. Wetenskaplike en Nywerheidnavorsingsraad (South Africa) — Navorsingsversl Wet Nywerheidnavorsingsraad (S Afr)
Navy International — Navy Intnl
Navy League Journal — Navy League J
Navy News and Undersea Technology — Navy News
Navy Records Society. Publications — Navy Rec Soc Publ
Navy Technology Transfer Fact Sheet — Navy Tech F S
NBFU [*National Board of Fire Underwriters*] **Research Report** — NBFU Res Rep
NBRI (National Building Research Council. South Africa) Special Report BOU — NBRI Spec Rep BOU
NBS (National Bureau of Standards) Handbook (United States) — NBS Handb US
NBS [*National Bureau of Standards*] **Technical Note (United States)** — NBS Tech Note (US)
NBS [*National Bureau of Standards*] **Update** — NBS
NC [*North Carolina*] **League for Nursing News** — NC League Nurs News
NCASI [*National Council of the Paper Industry for Air and Stream Improvement*] **Special Report** — NCASI Spec Rep
NCHS (National Center for Health Statistics) Advance Data — NCHS (Natl Cent Health Stat) Adv Data
NCI [*National Cancer Institute*] **Monographs** [*US*] — NCI Monogr
NCMC [*Nassau County Medical Center*] **Proceedings** — NCMC Proc
NCRD (National Council for Research and Development) Report (Israel) — NCRD Rep Isr
NCRR [*National Center for Resource Recovery*] **Bulletin** [*United States*] — NCRR Bull
NCSDHA [*Northern California State Dental Hygienists Association*] **Dental Hygienist** — NCSDHA Dent Hyg
NCW News (National Council of Women of New South Wales) — NCW News
NDE [*Nondestructive Evaluation*] **in the Nuclear Industry and Equipment/ Services Exposition. International Conference** — NDE Nucl Ind Int Conf
NDH-Rapport. Norland Distrikshogskole — NDHR
NDTI [*National Disease and Therapeutic Index*] **Review** [*United States*] — NDTI Rev
NDZ (Neue Deliwa-Zeitschrift) Neue Deliwa-Zeitschrift — NDZ Neue Deliwa Z
NE. Cooperative Extension Services of the Northeastern States — NE Coop Ext Serv Northeast States
Nea Helliniki Vivliothiki — NHV
Nea Hestia — N Hest
Nea Hestia — NeaH
Nea Poreia — NP
Nea Sion — NSi
NEA [*National Education Association*] **Today** — INEA
Neapolis — Neap
Near and Middle East Series — NMES
Near East [*London*] — NE
Near East and India — Near East
Near East and India — NEI
Near East Archaeological Society. Bulletin — NEASB
Neblette's Handbook of Photography and Reprography. Materials, Processes, and Systems — Neblettes Handb Photogr Reprogr
Nebraska Academy of Sciences and Affiliated Societies. Proceedings — Nebraska Acad Sci Proc
Nebraska Academy of Sciences and Affiliated Societies. Transactions — Nebr Acad Sci Affil Soc Trans
Nebraska Academy of Sciences. Publications. Proceedings — Nebr Ac Sc Pub Pr
Nebraska Academy of Sciences. Transactions — Nebr Acad Sci Trans
Nebraska Administrative Rules and Regulations — Neb Admin R & Regs
Nebraska. Agricultural Experiment Station. Annual Report — Neb Agric Exp Stn Annu Rep
Nebraska. Agricultural Experiment Station. Annual Report — Nebr Agric Exp Stn Annu Rep
Nebraska Agricultural Experiment Station. Annual Report — Nebraska Agric Exp Sta Annual Rep
Nebraska. Agricultural Experiment Station. Bulletin — Nebr Agric Exp Stn Bull
Nebraska. Agricultural Experiment Station. Circular — Neb Agric Exp Stn Circ
Nebraska. Agricultural Experiment Station. Circular — Nebr Agric Exp Stn Circ
Nebraska Agricultural Experiment Station Circular — Nebraska Agric Exp Sta Circ
Nebraska. Agricultural Experiment Station. Publications — Neb Ag Exp
Nebraska. Agricultural Experiment Station. Research Bulletin — Nebr Agric Exp Stn Res Bull
Nebraska Agricultural Experiment Station Research Bulletin — Nebraska Agric Exp Sta Res Bull
Nebraska Agricultural Experiment Station Wheat Abstracts — Nebraska Agric Exp Sta Wheat Abstr
Nebraska Bird Review — Nebr Bird Rev
Nebraska Conservation Bulletin — Nebr Conserv Bull
Nebraska Educational Journal — Neb Ed J
Nebraska Energy News — Nebr Energy News
Nebraska Experiment Station Quarterly — Nebr Exp Stn Q
Nebraska Farm Ranch Economics — Nebr Farm Ranch Econ
Nebraska Geological Survey. Bulletin — Nebr Geol Surv Bull
Nebraska Geological Survey. Paper — Nebraska Geol Survey Paper
Nebraska History — Neb His
Nebraska History — Neb Hist
Nebraska History — NebH
Nebraska History — NH
Nebraska History. Magazine — Neb His M
Nebraska Journal of Economics and Business — Neb J Econ and Bus
Nebraska Journal of Economics and Business — NJE
Nebraska Law Review — Nb L
Nebraska Law Review — Nb LR
Nebraska Law Review — Neb L Rev
Nebraska Law Review — Neb LR
Nebraska Law Review — Nebr L Rev
Nebraska Law Review — Nebraska L Rev
Nebraska Library Association. Quarterly — Neb Lib Assn Q
Nebraska Medical Journal — Nebr Med J

Nebraska Music Educator — NE
Nebraska Nurse — Nebr Nurse
Nebraska Reports — Neb
Nebraska State Bar Journal — Neb SBJ
Nebraska State Bar Journal — Neb St BJ
Nebraska State Bar Journal — Nebr BA
Nebraska State Board of Agriculture. Annual Report — Nebr St Bd Agr An Rp
Nebraska State Historical Society. Collections — Neb His S
Nebraska State Historical Society. Proceedings and Collections — Nebr St Hist Soc Pr
Nebraska State Medical Journal — Nebr St Med J
Nebraska State Medical Journal — Nebr State Med J
Nebraska State Museum. Bulletin — Nebr State Mus Bull
Nebraska Symposium on Motivation — Nebr Symp Motiv
Nebraska Tractor Test. Nebraska Agricultural Experiment Station — Nebr Tractor Test Nebr Agric Exp Stn
Nebraska. University. Agricultural Experiment Station. Annual Report — Nebr Univ Agric Exp Stn Annu Rep
Nebraska. University. Agricultural Experiment Station. Bulletin — Nebr Univ Agric Exp Stn Bull
Nebraska. University. Agricultural Extension Service. Extension Circular — Nebr Univ Agric Ext Serv Ext Circ
Nebraska. University. College of Agriculture and Home Economics. Extension Service. Extension Circular — Nebr Univ Coll Agric Home Econ Ext Serv Ext Circ
Nebraska. University. College of Agriculture and Home Economics. Quarterly — NAHQAO
Nebraska. University. College of Agriculture and Home Economics. Quarterly — Nebr Univ Coll Agric Home Econ Q
Nebraska. University. Engineering Experiment Station. Bulletin — Nebr Univ Eng Exp Stn Bull
Nebraska. University. State Museum. Bulletin — Nebraska Univ State Mus Bull
Nebraska. University. Studies — Nebr Univ Studies
Nebraska Water Survey Paper — Nebr Water Surv Pap
Nebraska Wheat Variety Estimate. Nebraska Grain Improvement Association — Nebr Wheat Variety Estimate Nebr Grain Impr Ass
Nebula Science Fiction — Neb
NEC [*Nippon Electric Company*] **Research and Development** — NEC Res and Dev
NEC [*Nippon Electric Company*] **Research and Development** — NEC Res Dev
NEC [*Nippon Electric Company*] **Review** — NEC Rev
Necrocorinthia — NC
Nederduitse Gereformeerde Teologiese Tydskrif [*Kaapstad*] — NedGerefTTs
Nederduitse Gereformeerde Teologiese Tydskrif — NGTT
Nederland Industriele Eigendom — Ned Ind Eigendom
Nederland Israel — NIL
Nederland Taiwan Nieuws — NTN
Nederland USSR Instituut. Maandberichten — BUI
Nederlands Archievenblad — NA
Nederlands Bosbouw Tijdschrift — NEBTA
Nederlands Bosbouw Tijdschrift — Ned Bosb Tijdschr
Nederlands Bosbouw Tijdschrift Orgaan voor Bosbouw en Landschapsbouw — NBT
Nederlands Bosbouwtijdschrift — Ned Bosbouwtijdschr
Nederlands College voor Belastingconsulenten. Nationale Associatie van Accountantsadministratieconsulenten, Nederlandse Vereniging van Boekhoudbureaux en Administratiekantoren. Mededelingenblad — MNC
Nederlands Economisch Persbureau en Adviesbureau [*NEPAB*]. Nieuwsbrief — NEQ
Nederlands Geologisch Mijnbouwkundig Genootschap [*Koninklijk*]. Verhandelingen [*A publication*] — Ned Geol Mijnbouwkd Genoot Verh
Nederlands Instituut voor Zuivelonderzoek. Rapporten — Ned Inst Zuivelonderz Rapp
Nederlands Instituut voor Zuivelonderzoek. Verslag — Ned Inst Zuivelonderz Versl
Nederlands Instituut voor Zuiverlonderzoek Nieuws — NIZO Nieuws
Nederlands Juristenblad — Ned Jbl
Nederlands Juristenblad — Ned Jurbl
Nederlands Juristenblad — NJB
Nederlands Kunsthistorisch Jaarboek — Nederlands Kunsthist Jaar
Nederlands Melk-en Zuiveltijdschrift — Ned Melk Zuiveltijdschr
Nederlands Militair Geneeskundig Tijdschrift — Ned Mil Geneeskd Tijdschr
Nederlands Militair Geneeskundig Tijdschrift — NMGTA
Nederland's Patriciaat — Ned Patr
Nederlands Scheepsstudiecentrum TNO. Report — Ned Scheepsstudiecent TNO Rep
Nederlands Tandartsenblad — Ned Tandartsenbl
Nederlands Theologisch Tidsskrift — NT Ts
Nederlands Theologisch Tijdschrift — Ne T T
Nederlands Theologisch Tijdschrift [*Wageningen*] — NedThT
Nederlands Theologisch Tijdschrift [*Wageningen*] — NedTT
Nederlands Theologisch Tijdschrift [*Wageningen*] — NedTTs
Nederlands Theologisch Tijdschrift — NThTs
Nederlands Theologisch Tijdschrift — NTT
Nederlands Theologisch Tijdschrift — NTTij
Nederlands Tijdschrift voor de Psychologie en Haar Grensgebieden — Ned Tijdschr Psychol
Nederlands Tijdschrift voor de Psychologie en Haar Grensgebieden — NTPGB
Nederlands Tijdschrift voor Geneeskunde — Ned T v Gen
Nederlands Tijdschrift voor Geneeskunde — Ned Tijdschr Geneeskd
Nederlands Tijdschrift voor Geneeskunde — NETJA
Nederlands Tijdschrift voor Gerontologie — Ned Tijdschr Gerontol
Nederlands Tijdschrift voor Internationaal Recht — Ned Tijd
Nederlands Tijdschrift voor Internationaal Recht — Ned Tijdschr
Nederlands Tijdschrift voor Klinische Chemie — Ned Tijdschr Klin Chem
Nederlands Tijdschrift voor Natuurkunde — Ned Tijdschr Natuurk
Nederlands Tijdschrift voor Natuurkunde — Ned Tijdschr Natuurkd
Nederlands Tijdschrift voor Natuurkunde — NTNKA
Nederlands Tijdschrift voor Natuurkunde. Series A — Ned Tijdschr Natuurk A
Nederlands Tijdschrift voor Natuurkunde. Series A — Ned Tijdschr Natuurkd A
Nederlands Tijdschrift voor Psychologie — NTP
Nederlands Tijdschrift voor Tandheelkunde — Ned Tijdschr Tandheelkd
Nederlands Tijdschrift voor Vacuumtechniek — NDVTB
Nederlands Tijdschrift voor Vacuumtechniek — Ned Tijdschr Vacuumtech
Nederlands Transport — TPO
Nederlands-Belgische Vereniging van Graanonderzoekers. Handelingen — Ned Belg Ver Graanonderz Handel
Nederlandsch Archief voor Genealogie en Heraldik — Nederl Arch Geneal Heraldik
Nederlandsch Archief voor Kerkelijke Geschiedenis — Ne AKG
Nederlandsch Archief voor Kerkgeschiedenis — NAK
Nederlandsch Archief voor Kerkgeschiedenis — NAKG
Nederlandsch Archief voor Kerkgeschiedenis — Ned AKG
Nederlandsch Archief voor Kerkgeschiedenis — Nederl Arch Kerkgesch
Nederlandsch Archievenblad — NAB
Nederlandsch Archievenblad — NedA
Nederlandsch Boschbouw-Tijdschrift — Ned Boschbouw Tijdschr
Nederlandsch Economisch Tijdschrift — NET
Nederlandsch Historisch Instituut te Rome. Mededeelingen — Nederlandsch Hist Inst Rome Med
Nederlandsch Kruidkundig Archief — Ned Kruidkd Arch
Nederlandsch Kruidkundig Archief. Verslagen en Mededeelingen der Nederlandsche Botanische Vereeniging — Ned Kruidk Arch
Nederlandsch Kunsthistorisch Jaarboek — NKHJ
Nederlandsch Kunsthistorisch Jaarboek — NKJ
Nederlandsch Lancet — Nederl Lancet
Nederlandsch Maandschrift voor Geneeskunde — Ned Maandschr Geneeskd
Nederlandsch Tijdschrift voor de Psychologie en Haar Grensgebieden — NTsPsych
Nederlandsch Tijdschrift voor Geneeskunde — Ned Ts Geneesk
Nederlandsch Tijdschrift voor Geneeskunde — NTG
Nederlandsch Tijdschrift voor Hygiene, Microbiologie, en Serologie — Ned Tijdschr Hyg Microbiol Serol
Nederlandsch Tijdschrift voor Hygiene, Microbiologie, en Serologie — NETHA
Nederlandsch Tijdschrift voor Verloskunde en Gynaecologie — Ned Tijdschr Verloskd Gynaecol
Nederlandsch Tijdschrift voor Verloskunde en Gynaecologie — Ned Ts Verlosk
Nederlandsch Tijdschrift voor Verloskunde en Gynaecologie — NTVGA
Nederlandsch Tijdschrift voor Volkskunde — NTVK
Nederlandsche Bank NV. Kwartaalbericht — NBR
Nederlandsche Bijdragen op het Gebied van Germaansche Philologie en Linguistiek — NBGPL
Nederlandsche Historiebladen — NH Bl
Nederlandsche Historiebladen — NHB
Nederlandsche Jaarboeken voor Rechts-Geleerdheid en Wetgeving — JRW
Nederlandsche Katholieke Stemmen — NKS
Nederlandsche Landbouwcooperatie — NLC
Nederlandsche Letter-Courant — Ned Lett Courant
Nederlandsche Mercuur — NM
Nederlandsche Spectator — NS
Nederlandsche Tuinbouwblad — Ned Tuinbouwbl
Nederlandsch-Indisch Rubber- en Thee-Tijdschrift — Ned Indisch Rubber Thee Tijdschr
Nederlandsch-Indische Bladen voor Diergeneeskunde — Nederl-Ind Blad Diergeneesk
Nederlandsch-Indische Geografische Mededeelingen — NIGM
Nederlands-Duitse Kamer van Koophandel. Mededelingen — NDF
Nederlandse Akademie van Wetenschappen, Afdeling Natuurkunde. Verhandelingen. Eerste Reeks — Ned Akad Wet Afd Natuurkd Verh Eerste Reeks
Nederlandse Akademie van Wetenschappen [*Koninklijke*]. Proceedings. Series B. Physical Sciences — Ned Akad Wet Proc Ser B
Nederlandse Centrale Organisatie voor Toegepast-Natuurwetenschapelijk Onderzoek. Commissie voor Hydrologisch Onderzoek. Verslagen en Mededelingen — Ned Cent Organ TNO Comm Hydrol Onderz Versl Meded
Nederlandse Chemische Industrie — BCI
Nederlandse Chemische Industrie — Ned Chem Ind
Nederlandse Dendrologische Vereniging. Jaarboek — Ned Dendrol Ver Jaarb
Nederlandse Energiehuishouding. Witkomsten van Maandtellingen en Kwartaaltellingen — NHE
Nederlandse Entomologische Vereniging. Jaarboek — Ned Entomol Ver Jaarb
Nederlandse Gemeente — Ned Gem
Nederlandse Gemeente — NEG
Nederlandse Gemeente — NG
Nederlandse Jurisprudentie — Ned Jpd
Nederlandse Jurisprudentie. Uitspraken in Burgerlijke en Strafzaken — NJP
Nederlandse Leeuw — NedL
Nederlandse Onderneming — NO
Nederlandse Oudheidkundige Bond. Bulletin — Nederlandse Oudheidkundige Bond Bull
Nederlandse Rubberindustrie — Ned Rubberind
Nederlandse Staatscourant — Ned Staatscourant
Nederlandse Staatscourant — Ned Stcrt
Nederlandse Staatscourant — NS
Nederlandse Staatscourant — Sc
Nederlandse Staatscourant — Stcrt
Nederlandse Staatscourant. Officiele Uitgaven van het Koninkrijk der Nederlanden — NSC
Nederlandse Vereniging voor Klinische Chemie. Tijdschrift — Ned Ver Klin Chem Tijdschr

Nederlands-Spaanse Kamer van Koophandel. Spaanse Aanvragen voor Handelskontakten met Nederland — NSZ
Needlework Bulletin for Teachers in Secondary Schools — Needlework Bul
NEERI [*National Electrical Engineering Research Institute*] **News** [*South Africa*] — NEERI N
Neerlandia Franciscana — N Franc
Neerlandia Franciskana — NF
Neerlands Volksleven — NV
Nef: Cahier Trimestriel — Nef
Neft i Khimiya — Neft Khim
Neft i Khimiya (Burgas, Bulgaria) — Neft Khim (Burgas Bulg)
Neft i Khimiya (Sofia) — Neft Khim Sofia
Neftegazovaya Geologiya i Geofizika — Neftegazov Geol Geofiz
Neftegazovaya Geologiya i Geofizika — Neftegazovaya Geol Geofiz
Neftena i Vuglishtna Geologiya [*Bulgaria*] — Neft Vuglishtna Geol
Neftepererabotka i Neftekhimiya — NEFNB
Neftepererabotka i Neftekhimiya (Kazan) — Neftepererab Neftekhim Kazan
Neftepererabotka i Neftekhimiya (Kiev) — Neftepererab Neftekhim (Kiev)
Neftepererabotka i Neftekhimiya (Moscow) — Neftepererab Neftekhim (Moscow)
Neftepererabotka, Neftekhimiya, i Slantsepererabotka — Neftepererab Neftekhim Slantsepererab
Neftepromyslovoe Delo — Neftepromysl Delo
Neftepromyslovoe Delo (Moscow) — Neftepromysl Delo (Moscow)
Neftepromyslovoye Delo Referativnyy Nauchno-Tekhnicheskiy Sbornik — Neftepromysl Delo Ref Nauchno-Tekh Sb
Neftyanaya i Gazovaya Promyshlennost' — Neft Gazov Prom-St'
Neftyanaya i Gazovaya Promyshlennost' — NGPSA
Neftyanaya i Gazovaya Promyshlennost Srednei Azii — Neft Gazov Promst Sredn Azii
Neftyanaya i Gazovaya Promyshlennost Srednei Azii — Neft Gazova Promst Sredn Azii
Neftyanaya Promyshlennost. Seriya Neftegazovaya Geologiya i Geofizika — Neft Promst Ser Neftegazov Geol Geofiz
Neftyanaya Promyshlennost. Seriya Neftepromyslovoe Delo — Neft Promst Ser Neftepromysl Delo
Neftyanaya Promyshlennost. Seriya Neftepromyslovoe Stroitel'stvo — Neft Promst Ser Neftepromysl Stroit
Neftyanaya Promyshlennost SSSR — Neft Promst SSSR
Neftyanoe i Slantsevoe Khozyaistvo — Neft Slants Khoz
Neftyanoe Khozyaistvo — Neft Khoz
Neftyanye Udobreniya i Stimulyatory. Materialy Vsesoyuznogo Soveshchaniya — Neft Udobr Stimul Mater Vses Soveshch
Negentien Nu — LNU
Negro American Literature Forum — NALF
Negro Digest — ND
Negro Digest — Negro D
Negro Educational Review — Neg Ed Rev
Negro Educational Review — Negro Ed R
Negro Educational Review — Negro Educ R
Negro History Bulletin — INHB
Negro History Bulletin — Neg His Bull
Negro History Bulletin — NegH
Negro History Bulletin — Negro H B
Negro History Bulletin — Negro His B
Negro History Bulletin — Negro Hist B
Negro History Bulletin — Negro Hist Bul
Negro History Bulletin — Negro Hist Bull
Negro History Bulletin — NHB
Nehezipari Mueszaki Egyetem Koezlemenyei — Nehezip Muesz Egy Koezl
Nehezipari Mueszaki Egyetem, Miskolc, Idegennyelvu Koezlemenyei — Nehezip Musz Egy Miskolc Idegennyelvu Kozl
Nehezipari Mueszaki Egyetem, Miskolc, Koezlemenyei — Nehezip Musz Egy Miskolc Kozl
Nehezipari Muszaki Egyetem Kozlemenyei. 1. Sorozat. Banyaszat — Nehezip Musz Egy Kozl 1 Sorozat
Nehezipari Muszaki Egyetem Kozlemenyei. 2. Sorozat. Kohaszat — Nehezip Musz Egy Kozl 2 Sorozat
Nehezipari Muszaki Egyetem Kozlemenyei. 3. Sorozat. Gepeszet — Nehezip Musz Egy Kozl 3 Sorozat
Nehezipari Muszaki Egyetem Sopron. Banyamernoki es Foldmeromernoki Karok Kozlemenyei — Nehezip Musz Egy Sopron Banyamern Foldmeromern Karok Kozl
Nehezvegyipari Kutato Intezet Kozlemenyei — Nehezvegyip Kut Intez Kozl
Nehorlavost Polymernych Materialov — Nehorlavost Polym Mater
NEI [*Northern Engineering Industries*] **Review** [*England*] — NEI Rev
NE-INF. US Department of Agriculture. Forest Service. Northeastern Forest Experiment Station — NE INF US Dep Agric For Serv Northeast For Exp Stn
Neirofiziologila — NEFZB
Neirokhimiya i Fiziologiya Sinapticheskikh Protsessov — Neirokhim Fiziol Sinapticheskikh Protsessov
Neitronno-Aktivatsionnyi Analiz i Ego Primenenie v Narodnom Khozyaistve — Neitr Akt Anal Ego Primen Nar Khoz
Nekotorye Aktual'nye Voprosy Biologii i Meditsiny — Nek Aktual Vopr Biol Med
Nekotorye Aktual'nye Voprosy Biologii i Meditsiny (Gorkiy) — Nek Aktual Vopr Biol Med Gorkiy
Nekotorye Filosofskie Problemy Gosudarstva i Prava — Nek Filos Probl Gos Prava
Nekotorye Problemy Biokibernetiki Primenenie Elektroniki v Biologii i Meditsine [*Ukrainian SSR*] — Nekot Probl Biokibern Primen Elektron Biol Med
Nekotorye Voposry Eksperimental'noi Fiziki [*Former USSR*] — Nek Vopr Eksp Fiz
Nekotorye Voprosy Fiziki Yadra. Elementarnykh Chastits i Yadernofizicheskikh Izmerenii — Nek Vopr Fiz Yadra Elem Chastits Yadernofiz Izmer
Nekotorye Voprosy Geologii Aziatskoi Chasti SSSR — Nek Vopr Geol Aziat Chasti SSSR
Nekotorye Voprosy Inzhenernoi Fiziki — Nek Vopr Inzh Fiz
Nekotorye Voprosy Sovremennoi Elektrokhimicheskoi Kinetiki — Nek Vopr Sovrem Elektrokhim Kinet
Nekotorye Voprosy Stroitel'stva Skvazhin v Oslozhnennykh Usloviyakh Uzbekistana — Nek Vopr Stroit Skvazhin Oslozhnennykh Usloviyakh Uzb
Nekotorye Voprosy Vseobshchei Istorii — NVVI
NELA [*New England Library Association*] **Newsletter** — NELA Newsl
Nelineinaya Optika. Trudy Vsesoyuznogo Simpoziuma po Nelineinoi Optike — Nelineinaya Opt Tr Vses Simp
Nelineinaya Teoriya Plastin i Obolochek — Nelineinaya Teor Plastin Obolochek
Nelineinye Volny. Samoorganizatsiya. Sbornik Sostavlen po Materialam Vsesoyuznoi Shkoly po Nelineinym Volnam — Nelineinye Volny Samoorgan Sb Mater Vses Shk
Nelson Loose-Leaf Medicine — Nelson Loose-Leaf Med
Nelson's Bible Commentary — NBC
Neman [*Moscow*] — Nem
Nematologia Brasileira — NEBRET
Nematologia Brasileira — Nematol Bras
Nematologia Mediterranea — Nematol Mediterr
Nematologica — Nematol
Nemetallicheskie Poleznye Iskopaemye — Nemet Polezn Iskop
Nemzetkozi Anaesthesiologus Kongresszus — Nemzetkozi Anaesthesiol Kongr
Nemzetkozi Meres- es Muszertechnikai Konferencia Kozlemenyei — Nemzetkozi Meres Muszertech Konf Kozl
Nemzetkozi Mezogazdasagi Szemle — Nemzetkozi Mezogazd Sz
Neng Yuan Chi Kan — NYCKA
Nenryo Kyokai-Shi — NENKA
Nenryo Oyobi Nensho — NEONA
Neo-Latin News [*Queens College*] — NLN
Neonatal Network — Neonatal Netw
Neonatal Network. Journal of Neonatal Nursing — Neonat Network
Neonatal Screening — Neonat Screening
Neophilologus — N
Neophilologus — Neo
Neophilologus — Neoph
Neophilologus — Neophil
Neophilologus — Neophilolog
Neophilologus — Np
Neophilologus — NPh
Neoplasma [*Bratislava*] — NEOLA4
Neorganicheskaya Khimiya. Itogi Nauki i Tekhniki — Neorg Khim Itogi Nauki Tekh
Neorganicheskie Ionoobmennye Materialy — Neorg Ionoobmen Mater
Neorganicheskie Lyuminofory Prikladnogo Naznacheniya — Neorg Lyuminofory Prikl Naznacheniya
Neorganicheskie Materialy [*Former USSR*] — Neorg Mater
Neorganicheskie Stekla, Pokrytiya, i Materialy — Neorg Stekla Pokrytiya Mater
Neos Hellenomnemon — NH
Neosan Avicola — Neosan Avic
Nepal Gazette — Nepal Gaz
Nepalese Journal of Agriculture — Nepalese J Agric
Nepali Mathematical Sciences Report — Nepali Math Sci Rep
Nepegeszseguegy — NEPEA
Nepegeszseguegy — Nepeg
Nephrologie in Klinik und Praxis — Nephrol Klin Prax
Nephrologisches Symposium. Vortraege — Nephrol Symp Vortr
Nephrology, Dialysis, Transplantation — Nephrol Dial Transplant
Nephrology Nurse — Nephro Nurse
Nephrology Nurse — Nephrol Nurse
Nephrology Reviews — Nephrol Rev
Neprajzi Ertesito — Nepr Ert
Neprajzi Ertesito — Nepr Ertes
Neprajzi Koezlemenyek — Nepr Koezl
NERC [*National Electronics Research Council*] **News Journal** — NENJA
NERC [*National Electronics Research Council*] **News Journal** [*England*] — NERC News J
NEREM [*Northeast Electronics Research and Engineering Meeting*] **Record** — NEREM Rec
NERIC [*Nuclear Engineering Research in Cambridge*] **Bulletin** — NERIC Bull
Nerudnye Stroitel'nye Materialy — Nerudn Stroit Mater
Nerve Membrane. Biochemistry and Function of Channel Proteins. Proceedings. Taniguchi International Symposium on Structure and Function of Biological Membrane — Nerve Membr Proc Taniguchi Int Symp
Nervenarzt — NERVA
Nervnaia Sistema — Nerv Sist
Nervnaia Sistema Leningradskii Gosudarstvennii Universitet Imeni A. A. Zhdanova Fiziologicheskii Institut — NSLFA
Nervnaya Sistema — Nervn Sist
Nervnaya Sistema Leningradskij Gosudarstvennyj Universitet Imeni A. A. Zhdanova Fiziologicheskij Institut — Nerv Sist Leningr Gos Univ Fiziol Inst
Nervous Child — Nerv Child
Nervous Inhibition. Proceedings. Friday Harbor Symposium — Nerv Inhib Proc Friday Harbor Symp
Nervous System and Electric Currents — Nerv Syst Electr Curr
NESDIS [*National Environmental Satellite Data and Information Service*] **Environmental Inventory** — NEINEI
NESDIS (National Environmental Satellite Data and Information Service) Environmental Inventory — NESDIS (Natl Environ Satell Data Inf Serv) Environ Inventory
Nesika — NESI
Nesovershenstva Kristallicheskogo Stroeniya i Martensitnye Prevrashcheniya — Nesoversh Krist Str Martensitnye Prevrashch
NESP [*National Environmental Studies Project*] **Newsletter** — NESP Newsl
NESP [*National Environmental Studies Project*] **Report** [*United States*] — NESP Rep

Nestel's Rosengarten — Nestels Rosengart
Nestle Foundation Publication Series — Nestle Found Publ Ser
Nestle Nutrition Workshop Series — Nestle Nutr Workshop Ser
Nestle Nutrition Workshop Series — NNWSDT
Nestle Research News — Nestle Res News
Nestor-Chronik — Nest Chr
Netherlands American Trade — NCN
Netherlands Application Patent Document — Neth Appl
Netherlands Energy Research Foundation. ECN [*Energieonderzoek Centrum Nederland*] **Report** — Neth Energy Res Found ECN Rep
Netherlands Fertilizer Technical Bulletin — Neth Fertil Tech Bull
Netherlands Fertilizer Technical Bulletin — NFTBEA
Netherlands. Geologische Dienst. Toelichting bij de Geologische Kaart van Nederland 1:50,000 — Neth Geol Dienst Toelichting Geol Kaart Ned 1:50,000
Netherlands. Geologische Stichting. Mededelingen. Nieuwe Serie — Neth Geol Sticht Meded Nieuwe Ser
Netherlands. Institute for Sea Research. Publication Series — Neth Inst Sea Res Publ Ser
Netherlands Institute for Sea Research. Publication Series — NSRPDU
Netherlands International Law Review — NIL Rev
Netherlands International Law Review — NILR
Netherlands International Law Review — NIR
Netherlands Journal of Agricultural Science — Neth J Agr Sci
Netherlands Journal of Agricultural Science — Neth J Agric Sci
Netherlands Journal of Agricultural Science — Netherlands J Agric Sci
Netherlands Journal of Internal Medicine — Neth J Intern Med
Netherlands Journal of Medicine — Neth J Med
Netherlands Journal of Medicine — NLJMA
Netherlands Journal of Nutrition — Neth J Nutr
Netherlands Journal of Plant Pathology — Neth J Plant Pathol
Netherlands Journal of Sea Research — Neth J Sea
Netherlands Journal of Sea Research — Neth J Sea Res
Netherlands Journal of Sea Research — NJSRB
Netherlands Journal of Sociology — NJS
Netherlands Journal of Surgery — Neth J Surg
Netherlands Journal of Surgery — NJSUD
Netherlands Journal of Veterinary Science — Neth J Vet Sci
Netherlands Journal of Zoology — Neth J Zool
Netherlands Milk and Dairy Journal — Neth Milk D
Netherlands Milk and Dairy Journal — Neth Milk Dairy J
Netherlands Milk and Dairy Journal — NMDJA
Netherlands Nitrogen Technical Bulletin — Neth Nitrogen Tech Bull
Netherlands Patent Document — Neth
Netherlands. Patent Document. Octrooi — Neth Pat Doc Octrooi
Netherlands. Patent Document. Terinzagelegging — Neth Pat Doc Terinzagelegging
Netherlands. Rijks Geologische Dienst. Jaarverslag — Neth Rijks Geol Dienst Jaarversl
Netherlands. Rijks Geologische Dienst. Mededelingen. Nieuwe Serie — Neth Rijks Geol Dienst Meded Nieuwe Ser
Netherlands. Stichting voor Bodemkartering. Bodemkundige Studies — Neth Sticht Bodemkartering Bodemkund Stud
Netherlands Trade and News Bulletin — NTD
Netherlands Trade Colonial Review — NTCR
Network Computing — Network Comp
Network Newsletter — Network Newsl
Network Science — Network Sci
Networking Journal — Networking Jnl
Neuburger Kollektaneenblatt — Koll Bl Neuburg
Neuburger Kollektaneenblatt — NK Bl
Neudeutsche Bauzeitung — Nd B Zt
Neudrucke Deutscher Literaturwerke — NDL
Neue Ackerbau-Zeitung der Ackerbau-Gesellschaft und der vier Bezirks-Comitien des Niederrheins — Neue Ackerbau Zeitung Ackerbau Ges Niederrheins
Neue Allgemeine Missionszeitschrift — NAMZ
Neue Analekten fuer Erd- und Himmels-Kunde — Neue Analekten Erd Himmels Kunde
Neue Annalen der Blumisterei fuer Gartenbesitzer, Kunstgaertner, Samenhaendler, und Blumenfreunde — Neue Ann Blumisterei Gartenbesitz
Neue Arzneimittel. Spezialitaeten und Geheimmittel — Neue Arzneim Spez Geheimm
Neue Arzneimittel und Spezialitaeten — Neue Arzneim Spez
Neue Aspekte der Trasylol-Therapie — Neue Aspekte Trasylol-Ther
Neue Badener Landeszeitung — NBL
Neue Beitraege von Alten und Neuen Theologischen Sachen — NBATS
Neue Beitraege zur Bausparmathematik — NBB
Neue Beitraege zur Geschichte des Deutschen Altertums — Neue Beitr Gesch Deutsch Altert
Neue Beitraege zur Geschichte des Deutschen Altertums — Neue Btr Gesch Dt Altert
Neue Beitraege zur Kenntniss von Afrika — Neue Beitr Kenntn Afrika
Neue Beitraege zur Literaturwissenschaft — NB Lwss
Neue Beitraege zur Literaturwissenschaft — NBL
Neue Bergbautechnik — NEBBA
Neue Bergbautechnik [*Wissenschaftliche Zeitschrift fuer Bergbau, Geowissenschaften und Aufbereitung*] — Neue Bergbautech
Neue Berliner Illustrierte — NBI
Neue Berlinische Monatsschrift — Neue Berlin Monatsschr
Neue Betriebswirtschaft — NBW
Neue Betriebswirtschaft — Neue Betriebswirtsch
Neue Beytraege zur Botanik — Neue Beytr Bot
Neue Deliwa-Zeitschrift — NEUDA
Neue Deliwa-Zeitschrift — Neue Deliwa-Z
Neue Deliwa-Zeitschrift zur Foerderung des Gas-, Wasser- und Elektrizitaetsfaches — Neue Deliwa Z Foerd Gas Wasser Elektrizitaetsfaches
Neue Denkschriften. Abhandlungen der Physikalisch-Medicinischen Societaet zu Erlangen — Neue Denkschr Phys Med Soc Erlangen
Neue Denkschriften der Allgemeinen Schweizerischen Gesellschaft fuer die Gesammten Naturwissenschaften. Noveaux Memoires de la Societe Helvetique des Sciences Naturelles — Neue Denkschr Allg Schweiz Ges Gesammten Naturwiss
Neue Denkschriften der Schweizerischen Naturforschenden Gesellschaft — NDSchNG
Neue Denkschriften der Schweizerischen Naturforschenden Gesellschaft — Neue Denkschr Schweiz Naturforsch Ges
Neue Denkschriften des Naturhistorischen Museums in Wien — Neue Denkschr Naturhist Mus Wien
Neue Deutsche Beamtenzeitung — NDBZ
Neue Deutsche Biographie — NDB
Neue Deutsche Forschung — NDF
Neue Deutsche Hefte — NDH
Neue Deutsche Literatur — NDL
Neue Deutsche Literatur — Neue Dt Lit
Neue Deutsche Papier-Zeitung — Neue Dtsch Pap Ztg
Neue Deutsche Presse — NDP
Neue Deutsche Rundschau — NDR
Neue Entomologische Nachrichten — NENAD3
Neue Entomologische Nachrichten — Neue Entomol Nachr
Neue Entwicklungspolitik — Neue Entwicklungspol
Neue Ephemeris fuer Semitische Epigraphik — N Eph Sem Ep
Neue Ephemeris fuer Semitische Epigraphik — N Ephem Sem Epigr
Neue Evangelische Kirchenzeitung — NEKZ
Neue Faserstoffe — Neue Faserst
Neue Folge des Jahrbuchs der Goethe Gesellschaft — NFJGG
Neue Forschung — N Forsch
Neue Forschungen — NF
Neue Freie Presse — NFP
Neue Geisteswissenschaftliche Studien — NGS
Neue Germanistik — NG
Neue Gesellschaft — N Ges
Neue Gesellschaft — Neue Ges
Neue Gesellschaft — Neue Gesellsch
Neue Gesellschaft — NG
Neue Giesserei. Technisch-Wissenschaftliche Beihefte. Metallkunde und Giessereiwesen — Neue Giesserei Tech Wiss Beih Metallkd Giessereiwes
Neue Hefte fuer Philosophie — Neue Hefte Phil
Neue Hefte zur Morphologie — Neue Hefte Morphol
Neue Heidelberger Jahrbuecher — Neue Heidelb Jahrb
Neue Heidelberger Jahrbuecher — NHJ
Neue Heidelberger Jahrbuecher — NHJB
Neue Herder Bibliothek — NHB
Neue Historische Abhandlungen der Baierischen Akademie der Wissenschaften — Neue Hist Abh Baier Akad Wiss
Neue Hungarian Quarterly — Neue Hung Quart
Neue Jahrbuecher fuer Antike und Deutsche Bildung — N Jahrb
Neue Jahrbuecher fuer Antike und Deutsche Bildung — N Jhb
Neue Jahrbuecher fuer Antike und Deutsche Bildung — Neue J
Neue Jahrbuecher fuer Antike und Deutsche Bildung — Neue Jahrb
Neue Jahrbuecher fuer Antike und Deutsche Bildung — NJAB
Neue Jahrbuecher fuer Antike und Deutsche Bildung — NJADB
Neue Jahrbuecher fuer Antike und Deutsche Bildung — NJb
Neue Jahrbuecher fuer das Klassische Altertum — N Jb
Neue Jahrbuecher fuer das Klassische Altertum — N Jb A
Neue Jahrbuecher fuer das Klassische Altertum — N Jb KA
Neue Jahrbuecher fuer das Klassische Altertum — NJA
Neue Jahrbuecher fuer das Klassische Altertum — NJKA
Neue Jahrbuecher fuer das Klassische Altertum — NJKIA
Neue Jahrbuecher fuer das Klassische Altertum, Geschichte, und Deutsche Literatur — NJKA
Neue Jahrbuecher fuer das Klassische Altertum, Geschichte, und Deutsche Literatur — NJKAGDL
Neue Jahrbuecher fuer Deutsche Theologie — NJD Th
Neue Jahrbuecher fuer Deutsche Wissenschaft — NJDW
Neue Jahrbuecher fuer Paedogogik — NJP
Neue Jahrbuecher fuer Philologie und Paedagogik — N Jb
Neue Jahrbuecher fuer Philologie und Paedagogik — NJ Ph P
Neue Jahrbuecher fuer Philologie und Paedagogik — NJbbPh
Neue Jahrbuecher fuer Philologie und Paedagogik — NJP
Neue Jahrbuecher fuer Philologie und Paedagogik — NJPP
Neue Jahrbuecher fuer Wissenschaft und Jugendbildung — N Jb WJ
Neue Jahrbuecher fuer Wissenschaft und Jugendbildung — Neue Jbb Wiss Jugendbildg
Neue Jahrbuecher fuer Wissenschaft und Jugendbildung — NJb
Neue Jahrbuecher fuer Wissenschaft und Jugendbildung — NjbWJB
Neue Jahrbuecher fuer Wissenschaft und Jugendbildung — NJW
Neue Jahrbuecher fuer Wissenschaft und Jugendbildung — NJWJ
Neue Jenaische Allgemeine Literaturzeitung — Neue Jenaische Allg Literaturzeitung
Neue Juedische Monatshefte — NJM
Neue Juedische Nachrichten — NJN
Neue Juristische Wochenschrift — Neue Jur Wschr
Neue Juristische Wochenschrift — Neue Jurist Wochenschr
Neue Juristische Wochenschrift — NJW
Neue Justiz [*German Democratic Republic*] — NJ
Neue Keilschriftliche Rechtsurkunden aus der el-Amarna-Zeit [*Koschaker*] — NKRA
Neue Kirche — NK
Neue Kirchliche Zeitschrift — NKZ

Neue Koelner Rechtwissenschaftliche Abhandlungen — NKRWA
Neue Lausizische Monatsschrift — Neue Lausiz Monatsschr
Neue Literarische Welt — NLW
Neue Literatur — NLit
Neue Mannigfaltigkeiten — Neue Mannigfaltigk
Neue Medizinische Versuche Nebst Bemerkungen, Welche von Einer Gesellschaft in Edinburgh Durchgesehen und Herausgegeben Werden. Aus dem Englischen Uebersetzt — Neue Med Versuche Bemerk Ges Edinburgh
Neue Medizinische Welt — Neue Med W
Neue Medizinische Welt — Neue Med Welt
Neue Merkur — NMerk
Neue Militaerische Blaetter — Neue Milit Bll
Neue Mitteilungen fuer die Landwirtschaft — Neue Mitt Landwirtsch
Neue Monatliche Beitraege zur Naturkunde (Schwerin) — Neue Monatl Beitr Naturk Schwerin
Neue Muenchener Beitraege zur Kunstgeschichte — NMBKG
Neue Muenchner Beitraege zur Geschichte der Medizin und Naturwissenschaften. Medizinhistorische Reihe — Neue Muench Beitr Gesch Med Medizinhist
Neue Muenchner Beitraege zur Geschichte der Medizin und Naturwissenschaften. Medizinhistorische Reihe — Neue Muench Beitr Gesch Med Naturwiss Medizinhist Reihe
Neue Muensterische Beitraege zur Geschichtsforschung — NMBGF
Neue Musik Zeitung — NMZ
Neue Musikzeitung — Neue Mz
Neue Nuernbergische Gelehrte Zeitung — Neue Nuernberg Gel Zeitung
Neue Oberdeutsche Allgemeine Litteraturzeitung — Neue Oberdeutsche Allg Litteraturzeitung
Neue Oesterreichische Biographie — NOeB
Neue Oesterreichische Zeitschrift fuer Kinderheilkunde — Neue Oest Z Kinderheilk
Neue Oesterreichische Zeitschrift fuer Kinderheilkunde — Neue Oesterr Z Kinderheilkd
Neue Ordnung — N Ord
Neue Ordnung in Kirche, Staat, Gesellschaft, Kultur — Neue Ordnung
Neue Orient — NO
Neue Orientalische und Exegetische Bibliothek — NOEB
Neue Philologische Untersuchungen — N Phil Unt
Neue Philologische Untersuchungen — NPhU
Neue Physik — Neue Phys
Neue Physikalische Blaetter — Neue Phys Bl
Neue Politische Literatur — Neue Pol Lit
Neue Politische Literatur — Neue Polit Lit
Neue Pommersche Provinzialblaetter — Neue Pommersche Provinzialbl
Neue Psychologische Studien — N Ps St
Neue Quartalschrift fuer Katholische Geistliche — NQKG
Neue Reformierte Kirchenzeitung — NRKZ
Neue Ruhr Zeitung — NRZ
Neue Rundschau — N Rd
Neue Rundschau — N Rund
Neue Rundschau — Neue Rdsch
Neue Rundschau — Neue Rund
Neue Rundschau — Neue Rundsch
Neue Rundschau — NR
Neue Rundschau — NRs
Neue Rundschau — NRu
Neue Rundschau (Berlin) — NRB
Neue Sammlung — NSammlung
Neue Sammlung Interessanter und Zwekmaessig Abgefasster Reisebeschreibungen fuer die Jugend — Neue Samml Interessanter Zwekmaessig Abgefasster Reisebeschre
Neue Sammlung. Physisch-Oekonomischer Schriften. Herausgegeben von der Oekonomischen Gesellschaft in Bern — Neue Samml Phys Oekon Schriften Oekon Ges Bern
Neue Sammlung Verschiedener Schriften der Groessten Gelehrten in Schweden — Neue Samml Schriften Groessten Gel Schweden
Neue Schleswig-Holsteinische Provinzialberichte — Neue Schleswig Holst Provinzialber
Neue Schriften der Naturforschenden Gesellschaft zu Halle — Neue Schriften Naturf Ges Halle
Neue Schweizer Rundschau — NSchwRundschau
Neue Schweizer Rundschau — NSR
Neue Schwiezer Biographie — NSB
Neue Studien zur Anglistik und Amerikanistik — NSAA
Neue Studien zur Geschichte der Theologie und der Kirche — NSTGThK
Neue Studien zur Geschichte der Theologie und Kirche — NSGTK
Neue Technik — Neue Tech
Neue Technik. Abteilung A. Automatik und Industrielle Elektronik [*Switzerland*] — Neue Tech A
Neue Technik. Abteilung A. Automatik und Industrielle Elektronik — NTKAA
Neue Technik. Abteilung B. Kerntechnik [*Switzerland*] — Neue Tech B
Neue Technik. Abteilung B. Kerntechnik — NTKBA
Neue Technik im Buero — Neue Tech Buero
Neue Theologische Annalen und Theologische Nachrichten — NTATN
Neue Theologische Bibliothek — N Th B
Neue Theologische Grundrisse — NTG
Neue Theologische Zeitschrift — NTZ
Neue Verpackung [*Germany*] — Neue Verpack
Neue Verpackung. Zeitschrift fuer die Gesamte Verpackungswirtschaft des Inlandes und Auslandes — NPU
Neue Versuche Nuetzlicher Sammlungen zu der Natur- und Kunst-Geschichte Sonderlich von Ober-Sachsen — Neue Versuche Nuetzl Samml Natur Kunst Gesch Ober Sachsen
Neue Weg — NW
Neue Welt — NW
Neue Wirtschaft — Neue Wirtsch
Neue Wissenschaftliche Bibliothek — Neue Wiss Bibl
Neue Zeitschrift fuer Arbeitsrecht — Neue Zs Arbeitsr
Neue Zeitschrift fuer Missionswissenschaft — Neue Z Fuer Missionswissenschaft
Neue Zeitschrift fuer Missionswissenschaft — Neue Z Miss Wiss
Neue Zeitschrift fuer Missionswissenschaft — NZM
Neue Zeitschrift fuer Missionswissenschaft — NZMiss
Neue Zeitschrift fuer Missionswissenschaft [*Beckenried, Switzerland*] — NZMissWiss
Neue Zeitschrift fuer Missionswissenschaft — NZMW
Neue Zeitschrift fuer Missionswissenschaft/Nouvelle Revue de Science Missionaire — Neue Z Mission
Neue Zeitschrift fuer Missionswissenschaft. Supplement — NZMS
Neue Zeitschrift fuer Musik — N Z Musik
Neue Zeitschrift fuer Musik — Neue ZFM
Neue Zeitschrift fuer Musik — NZ
Neue Zeitschrift fuer Musik — NZfM
Neue Zeitschrift fuer Musik — NZM
Neue Zeitschrift fuer Ruebenzucker-Industrie — Neue Z Ruebenzucker Ind
Neue Zeitschrift fuer Systematische Theologie — NZST
Neue Zeitschrift fuer Systematische Theologie — NZSTh
Neue Zeitschrift fuer Systematische Theologie und Religionsphilosophie — ZSTh
Neue Zeitschrift fuer Systematische Theologie und Religionsgeschichte — NZ Syst T
Neue Zeitschrift fuer Systematische Theologie und Religionsphilosophie — Neue Z Sys Th
Neue Zeitschrift fuer Systematische Theologie und Religionsphilosophie — NZ Sys Th
Neue Zeitschrift fuer Systematische Theologie und Religionsphilosophie — NZSThR
Neue Zeitschrift fuer Verwaltungsrecht — Neue Z Verwaltungsr
Neue Zeitschrift fuer Wehrrecht — NZ Wehrr
Neue Zeitschrift fuer Wehrrecht — NZW
Neue Zeitungen von Gelehrten Sachen — Neue Zeitungen Gel Sachen
Neue Zuericher Zeitung [*Switzerland*] — Neue Zuer Ztg
Neue Zuericher Zeitung — NZZ
Neue Zurcher Zeitung und Schweizerisches Handelsblatt — NZT
Neuendettelsauer Missionsblatt — NMB
Neuer Almanach Aller um Hamburg Liegenden Gaerten — Neuer Alman Aller Um Hamburg Liegenden Gaert
Neuer Nekrolog der Deutschen — NND
Neuere Entwicklungen der Stossspannungsmesstechnik 2. Vortraege des PTB-Seminars — Neuere Entwickl Stossspannungsmesstech 2 Vortr PTB Semin
Neuere Geschichte der Evangelischen Missionsanstalten zur Bekehrung der Heiden in Ostindien — NGEMA
Neuere Sammlung der Merkwuerdigsten Reisegeschichten — Neuere Samml Merkwuerd Reisegesch
Neuere Sprachen — Neu Spr
Neuere Sprachen — NeuS
Neuere Sprachen — NS
Neuere Sprachen — NSp
Neueren Sprachen. Zeitschrift fuer Forschung Unterricht und Kontaktstudium — NSZFU
Neueres Forstmagazin. Zweyte Abtheilung von neuen Aufsaetzen, die Forstsachen und dahin Einschlagende Huelfreiche Wissenschaften Betreffend auch von Aeltern, Mittlern und Neuern Buechern Welche Eigentlich das Forstwesen Behandeln — Neueres Forstmag Abth 2
Neuerwerbungen Stadtbuecherei Nuernberg — NSB
Neues Abendland — NAb
Neues Abendland — Neues Abendl
Neues Allgemeines Repertorium der Neuesten In- und Auslaendischen Literatur — Neues Allg Repert Neuesten In Ausl Lit
Neues Archiv der Gesellschaft fuer Aeltere Deutsche Geschichtskunde — NA
Neues Archiv der Gesellschaft fuer Aeltere Deutsche Geschichtskunde — NA f G
Neues Archiv der Gesellschaft fuer Aeltere Deutsche Geschichtskunde — NAAeDG
Neues Archiv der Gesellschaft fuer Aeltere Deutsche Geschichtskunde — NAG
Neues Archiv der Gesellschaft fuer Aeltere Deutsche Geschichtskunde — NAGADGK
Neues Archiv der Gesellschaft fuer Aeltere Deutsche Geschichtskunde — Neues Arch Ges Aeltere Dt Geschkde
Neues Archiv fer Saechsische Geschichte und Altertumskunde — NASG
Neues Archiv fuer die Geschichte der Stadt Heidelberg und der Kurpfalz — NAGSHKP
Neues Archiv fuer die Geschichte der Stadt Heidelberg und der Rheinischen Pfalz — NAGSHRP
Neues Archiv fuer Niedersachsen — NAN
Neues Archiv fuer Niedersachsen — Neues Arch Niedersachs
Neues Archiv fuer Saechsische Geschichte und Altertumskunde — ASGA
Neues Archiv fuer Saechsische Geschichte und Altertumskunde — NASGA
Neues Archiv fuer Saechsische Geschichte und Altertumskunde — NASGAK
Neues Archiv fuer Saechsische Geschichte und Altertumskunde — Neues Arch Saechs Gesch
Neues aus Alt-Villach — NAV
Neues Beethoven Jahrbuch — NB Jb
Neues Beginnen. Zeitschrift der Arbeiterwohlfahrt — NB
Neues Bergmaennisches Journal — Neues Bergmaenn J
Neues Berlinisches Wochenblatt zur Belehrung und Unterhaltung — Neues Berlin Wochenbl Belehr Unterhalt
Neues Berner Taschenbuch — NBT
Neues Chemisches Archiv — Neues Chem Arch

Neues Deutsches Magazin — Neues Deutsch Mag
Neues Deutschland — ND
Neues Forum — NF
Neues Hamburgisches Magazin, oder Fortsetzung Gesammleter Schriften, aus der Naturforschung, der Allgemeinen Stadt- und Land-Oekonomie, und den Angenehmen Wissenschaften Ueberhaupt — Neues Hamburg Mag
Neues Hochland — NHochland
Neues Jahrbuch fuer Geologie und Palaeontologie. Abhandlungen — NEJPA
Neues Jahrbuch fuer Geologie und Palaeontologie. Abhandlungen — Neues Jahrb Geol Palaeontol Abh
Neues Jahrbuch fuer Geologie und Palaeontologie. Abhandlungen — Neues Jahrbuch Geol Palaeontol Abhandl
Neues Jahrbuch fuer Geologie und Palaeontologie. Abhandlungen B — Neues Jahrb Geol Palaeontol Abh B
Neues Jahrbuch fuer Geologie und Palaeontologie. Abhandlungen. Monatshefte — Neues Jahrbuch Geologie u Palaeontologie Abh Monatsh
Neues Jahrbuch fuer Geologie und Palaeontologie. Monatshefte — Neues Jahrb Geol Palaeontol Monatsh
Neues Jahrbuch fuer Geologie und Palaeontologie. Monatshefte — Neues Jahrb Geologie u Palaeontologie Monatsh
Neues Jahrbuch fuer Geologie und Palaeontologie. Monatshefte — Neues Jahrbuch Geol Palaeontol Monatsh
Neues Jahrbuch fuer Mineralogie — N J f M
Neues Jahrbuch fuer Mineralogie — Neues Jb Mineralog
Neues Jahrbuch fuer Mineralogie. Abhandlungen — Neues Jahrb Mineral Abh
Neues Jahrbuch fuer Mineralogie. Abhandlungen — Neues Jahrb Mineralogie Abh
Neues Jahrbuch fuer Mineralogie. Abhandlungen — NJMIA
Neues Jahrbuch fuer Mineralogie. Abhandlungen. Monatshefte — Neues Jahrbuch Mineralogie Abh Monatsh
Neues Jahrbuch fuer Mineralogie, Geognosie, Geologie, und Petrefaktenkunde — Neues Jahrb Mineral Geognosie
Neues Jahrbuch fuer Mineralogie, Geologie, und Palaeontologie. Abhandlungen. Abteilung A. Mineralogie, Petrographie — Neues Jahrb Mineral Geol Palaeontol Abh Abt A
Neues Jahrbuch fuer Mineralogie, Geologie, und Palaeontologie. Abhandlungen. Abteilung B. Geologie, Palaeontologie — Neues Jahrb Mineral Geol Palaeontol Abh Abt B
Neues Jahrbuch fuer Mineralogie, Geologie und Palaeontologie. Abhandlungen. Abteilung B. Geologie und Palaeontologie — Neues Jahrb Mineral Geol Abh Abt B Geol Palaeontol
Neues Jahrbuch fuer Mineralogie, Geologie und Palaeontologie. Abteilung A — Neues Jahrb Mineral Geol Palaeontol Abt A
Neues Jahrbuch fuer Mineralogie, Geologie, und Palaeontologie. Beilage Band [*A publication*] — N Jb Beil Bd
Neues Jahrbuch fuer Mineralogie, Geologie und Palaeontologie. Beilageband. Abteilung B — Neues Jahrb Mineral Geol Palaeontol Beilageband Abt B
Neues Jahrbuch fuer Mineralogie, Geologie, und Palaeontologie. Monatshefte — Neues Jb Miner Geol Palaeont Mh
Neues Jahrbuch fuer Mineralogie, Geologie, und Palaeontologie. Monatshefte. Abteilung 1. Mineralogie, Gesteinskunde — Neues Jahrb Mineral Geol Palaeontol Monatsh Abt 1
Neues Jahrbuch fuer Mineralogie, Geologie, und Palaeontologie. Monatshefte. Abteilung 2. Geologie, Palaeontologie — Neues Jahrb Mineral Geol Palaeontol Monatsh Abt 2
Neues Jahrbuch fuer Mineralogie, Geologie, und Palaeontologie. Monatshefte. Abteilung B. Geologie, Palaeontologie — Neues Jahrb Mineral Geol Monatsh Abt B Geol Palaeontol
Neues Jahrbuch fuer Mineralogie, Geologie, und Palaeontologie. Referate — Neues Jahrb Mineral Geol Palaeontol Ref
Neues Jahrbuch fuer Mineralogie, Geologie und Palaeontologie. Referate. Abteilung B. Geologie, Palaeontologie — Neues Jahrb Mineral Geol Ref Abt B Geol Palaeontol
Neues Jahrbuch fuer Mineralogie. Monatshefte — Neues Jahrb Mineral Monatsh
Neues Jahrbuch fuer Mineralogie. Monatshefte — Neues Jahrb Mineralogie Monatsh
Neues Journal der Pharmacie — Neues J Pharm
Neues Journal der Pharmacie fuer Aerzte, Apotheker und Chemiker — Neues J Pharm Aerzte
Neues Journal der Pharmacie fuer Aerzte Apotheker und Chemiker (Leipzig) — N Jour Pharm (Leipzig)
Neues Journal der Physik — Neues J Phys
Neues Journal fuer die Botanik — Neues J Bot
Neues Korrespondenzblatt fuer die Hoeheren Schulen in Wuerttemberg — N Ko Bl H Sch
Neues Kritisches Journal der Theologischen Literatur — NKJTL
Neues Lausitzisches Magazin — Neues Lausitz Mag
Neues Lausitzisches Magazin — NLM
Neues Magazin fuer Aerzte — Neues Mag Aerzte
Neues Magazin fuer Hanauische Geschichte — N Mag Hanau
Neues Optiker Journal — Neues Optiker Jl
Neues Paedagogisches Lexikon — NPL
Neues Reich in Aegypten — NR
Neues Repertorium fuer die Theologische Literatur und Kirchliche Statistik — NRTL
Neues Schweizerisches Museum — Neues Schweiz Mus
Neues Testament fuer Menschen Unserer Zeit — NTMUZ
Neues Theologisches Journal — N Th J
Neues Trierisches Jahrbuch — NTJ
Neues und Nutzbares aus dem Gebiete der Haus- und Landwirthschaft — Neues Nutzbares Geb Haus Landw
Neues Vaterlaendisches Archiv, oder Beitraege zur Kenntnis des Koenigreichs Hannover — Neues Vaterld Arch
Neueste Auslaendische Zeitschriften — NAZ
Neueste Beitraege zur Kunde der Insel Madagaskar — Neueste Beitr Kunde Insel Madagaskar
Neueste Kirchenrechts-Sammlungen — NKRS
Neueste Nachrichten aus dem Morgenlande — NNM
Neueste Nachrichten aus dem Reiche Gottes — NNRG
Neueste Nordische Beytraege zur Physikalischen und Geographischen Erd- und Voelkerbeschreibung, Naturgeschichte und Oekonomie — Neueste Nord Beytr Phys Geogr Erd Voelkerbeschreib
Neueste Religionsgeschichte — NRG
Neueste Theologische Bibliothek — N Th Bi
Neuesten Entdeckungen in der Chemie — Neuesten Entdeckungen Chem
Neuestes Chemisches Archiv — Neuestes Chem Arch
Neuestes Garten-Jahrbuch, nach Le bon Jardinier — Neuestes Gart Jahrb
Neuestes Journal der Erfindungen, Theorien und Widersprueche in der Gesammten Medizin — Neuestes J Erfind Gesammten Med
Neuheiten der Technik — Neuheiten Tech
Neujahrsblaetter Herausgegeben von der Historischen Kommission fuer die Provinz Sachsen — Neujahrsbl Sachs
Neujahrsblatt. Gesellschaft zur Befoerderung des Guten und Gemeinnuetzingen — NGBG
Neujahrsblatt Herausgegeben von der Naturforschenden Gesellschaft in Zuerich — Neujahrsbl Naturforsch Ges Zuerich
Neujahrsblatt. Historischer Verein des Kantons St. Gallen — NHV St Gall
Neujahrsblatt. Historischer Verein des Kantons St. Gallen — NHVKSG
Neujahrsblatt. Naturforschende Gesellschaft in Zuerich — Neujahrsblatt Naturforsch Ges Zur
Neujahrsblatt. Naturforschende Gesellschaft in Zuerich — NNGZB
Neujahrsblatt. Naturforschende Gesellschaft in Zuerich — NNGZB2
Neujahrsblatt. Naturforschenden Gesellschaft in Zuerich — Neujahrsbl Naturforsch Ges Zuer
Neujahrsblatt. Zuercher Kunstgesellschaft — NZKG
Neukirchener Studienbuecher — NS
Neukirchner Studienbuecher — N St B
Neuland — NL
Neuland in der Theologie — NLT
Neumologia y Cirugia de Torax — Neumol Cir Torax
Neuphilologische Mitteilungen — N Mitt
Neuphilologische Mitteilungen — Neuphil Mit
Neuphilologische Mitteilungen — Neuphilol M
Neuphilologische Mitteilungen — Neuphilol Mitt
Neuphilologische Mitteilungen — NM
Neuphilologische Mitteilungen — NMi
Neuphilologische Mitteilungen — Nph Mitt
Neuphilologische Mitteilungen — NphM
Neuphilologische Mitteilungen — NPM
Neuphilologische Monatsschrift — N Mon
Neuphilologische Monatsschrift — NeuP
Neuphilologische Monatsschrift — NMo
Neuphilologische Monatsschrift — NPM
Neuphilologische Zeitschrift — NphZ
Neuphilologische Zeitschrift — NZ
Neupunische Inschriften — NP
Neural Computation — Neural Comput
Neural, Parallel, and Scientific Computations — Neural Parallel Sci Comput
Neural Regulatory Mechanisms during Aging. Proceedings. Philadelphia Symposium on Aging — Neural Regul Mech Aging Proc Philadelphia Symp Aging
Neurobehavioral Toxicology — Neurobehav Toxicol
Neurobehavioral Toxicology and Teratology — Neurobehav Toxicol Teratol
Neurobehavioral Toxicology and Teratology — NTOTD
Neurobiological Basis of Learning and Memory. Taniguchi Symposium of Brain Sciences — Neurobiol Basis Learn Mem Taniguchi Symp Brain Sci
Neurobiology [*Copenhagen*] — NBBMAN
Neurobiology, Biochemistry, and Morphology — Neurobiol Biochem Morphol
Neurobiology of Aging — Neurobiol Aging
Neurobiology of Chemical Transmission. Proceedings. Taniguchi Symposium of Brain Sciences — Neurobiol Chem Transm Proc Taniguchi Symp Brain Sci
Neurobiology of Cholinergic and Adrenergic Transmitters. Annual OHOLO Biological Conference on Neuroactive Compounds and Their Cell Receptors — Neurobiol Cholinergic Adrenergic Transm Annu OHOLO Biol Conf
Neurobiology of Disease — Neurobiol Dis
Neurobiology of Learning and Memory — Neurobiol Learn Mem
Neurobiology of the Control of Breathing. Nobel Conference. Karolinska Institute — Neurobiol Control Breathing Nobel Conf Karolinska Inst
Neurochemical Pathology — Neuroc Path
Neurochemical Pathology — Neurochem Pathol
Neurochemical Research — Neurochem Res
Neurochemistry International — NEUIDS
Neurochemistry International — Neurochem Int
Neurochirurgia — Neurochira
Neuro-Chirurgie — Neuro Chir
Neuro-Chirurgie — Neuro-Chire
Neuroendocrine Perspectives [*Elsevier Book Series*] — NEPEEQ
Neuroendocrine Perspectives — Neuroendocr Perspect
Neuroendocrine Perspectives [*Elsevier Book Series*] — NP
Neuroendocrinology — Neuroendocr
Neuroendocrinology Letters — Neuroendocrinol Lett
Neuroendocrinology Letters — NLETDU
Neuro-Endocrinology of Reproduction. Proceedings. Reinier de Graaf Symposium — Neuro Endocrinol Reprod Proc Reinier de Graaf Symp
Neurogastroenterology and Motility — Neurogastroenterol Motil
Neurohypophysis. International Conference on the Neurohypophysis — Neurohypophysis Int Conf
Neuroimaging Clinics of North America — Neuroimaging Clin N Am
Neurologia i Neurochirurgia Polska — Neurol Neurochir Pol

Neurologia Medico-Chirurgica — Neurol Med-Chir
Neurologia, Neurochirurgia, i Psychiatria Polska [*Poland*] — Neurol Neurochir Psychiatr Pol
Neurologia, Neurochirurgia, i Psychiatria Polska — NNPPA
Neurologia, Neurocirurgia, Psiquiatria — Neurol Neurocir Psiquiatr
Neurologia Psihiatria Neurochirurgia (Bucharest) — Neurol Psihiatr Neurochir (Buchar)
Neurologic Clinics — Neurol Clin
Neurological Research — Neurol Res
Neurological Surgery — Neurol Surg
Neurological Surgery (Tokyo) — Neurol Surg Tokyo
Neurologie et Psychiatrie (Bucharest) — Neurol Psychiatr (Bucharest)
Neurologie et Psychiatrie (Bucuresti) — Neurol Psychiatr (Bucur)
Neurologisches Centralblatt — Neurol Centralbl
Neurology — NEURA
Neurology and Neurobiology [*New York*] — NEUND9
Neurology and Neurobiology — Neurol Neurobiol
Neurology and Neurobiology (New York) — Neurol Neurobiol (NY)
Neurology India — Neurol India
Neurology, Physiology, and Infectious Diseases — Neurol Physiol Infect Dis
Neurology. Proceedings. World Congress of Neurology — Neurol Proc World Congr
Neurology. Series One. Neural Mechanisms of Movement — Neurol Ser One Neural Mech Mov
Neurology. Series One. Neural Mechanisms of Movement — SKSODV
Neuromuscular Development and Disease — Neuromuscular Dev Dis
Neuromuscular Diseases. Proceedings. International Congress on Neuromuscular Diseases — Neuromuscular Dis Proc Int Congr
Neuromuscular Disorders — Neuromuscul Disord
Neurooncology [*Elsevier Book Series*] — NO
Neuropaediatrie — NEPAB
Neuropaediatrie — Neuropadiat
Neuropathology and Applied Neurobiology — NANED
Neuropathology and Applied Neurobiology — Neurop Ap N
Neuropathology and Applied Neurobiology — Neuropathol Appl Neurobiol
Neuropatologia Polska — Neuropatol Pol
Neuropeptides and Brain Function — Neuropept Brain Funct
Neuropeptides and Psychiatric Disorders — Neuropept Psychiatr Disord
Neuropeptides. Basic and Clinical Aspects. Proceedings. Pfizer International Symposium — Neuropept Basic Clin Aspects Proc Pfizer Int Symp
Neuropharmacology — Neuropharm
Neurophysiologie Clinique — Neurophysiol Clin
Neurophysiology [*English translation of Neirofiziologiya*] — NPHYBI
Neurophysiology (English Translation of Neirofiziologiya) — Neurophysiology (Engl Transl Neirofiziologiya)
Neuropsichiatria Infantile — Neuropsichiatr Infant
Neuropsychiatrie de l'Enfance et de l'Adolescence — Neuropsychiatr Enfance Adolesc
Neuropsychiatry, Neuropsychology, and Behavioral Neurology — Neuropsychiatry Neuropsychol Behav Neurol
Neuropsychologia — Neuropsycho
Neuropsychologia — NUPSA
Neuropsychology Review — Neuropsychol Rev
Neuroptera International — Neuroptera Int
Neuroptera International — NINND2
Neuroradiology — Neuroradiol
Neuroscience and Behavioral Physiology — NBHPB
Neuroscience and Behavioral Physiology — Neurosci Behav Physiol
Neuroscience and Biobehavioral Reviews — Neurosci Biobehav Rev
Neuroscience Approached through Cell Culture [*Monograph*] — Neurosci Approached Cell Cult
Neuroscience Letters — NELED
Neuroscience Letters — Neurosci L
Neuroscience Letters — Neurosci Lett
Neuroscience Letters. Supplement — Neurosci Lett Suppl
Neuroscience Research — NERADN
Neuroscience Research Communications — Neurosc R C
Neuroscience Research Communications — Neurosci Res Commun
Neuroscience Research (Shannon, Ireland) — Neurosci Res (Shannon Irel)
Neuroscience Research. Supplement — Neurosci Res Suppl
Neuroscience Series — Neurosci Ser
Neuroscience Symposia — Neurosci Symp
Neuroscience Translations — Neurosci Transl
Neuroscience-Net — Neurosci Net
Neurosciences Research — Neurosci Res
Neurosciences Research — NSREA
Neurosciences Research (New York) — Neurosci Res NY
Neurosciences Research. Program Bulletin — Neurosci Res Program Bull
Neurosciences Research. Program Bulletin — NRPBA
Neurosciences Research. Symposium Summaries — Neurosci Res Symp Summ
Neurosciences. Study Program — Neurosci Study Program
Neurosecretion. International Symposium on Neurosecretion — Neurosecretion Int Symp
Neurosecretion. Molecules, Cells, Systems. Proceedings. International Symposium on Neurosecretion — Neurosecretion Proc Int Symp
Neurospora Newsletter — Neurospora Newsl
Neurosurgery Clinics of North America — Neurosurg Clin N Am
Neurosurgical Review — Neurosurg Rev
Neurotoxicology and Teratology — Neurotoxicol Teratol
Neurourology and Urodynamics — NEUREM
Neurourology and Urodynamics — Neurourol Urodyn
Neusprachliche Mitteilungen aus Wissenschaft und Praxis — NM
Neusprachliche Mitteilungen aus Wissenschaft und Praxis — NSM
Neusumerischen Gerichtsurkunden — NG
Neusumerischen Gerichtsurkunden — NGu
Neutestamentliche Abhandlungen — NA
Neutestamentliche Abhandlungen [*Muenster*] — NtA
Neutestamentliche Abhandlungen. Ergaenzungsband — NTA E
Neutestamentliche Forschungen — NTF
Neutestamentliche Zeitgeschichte — NTZG
Neutestementliche Apokryphen in Deutscher Uebersetzung — NT Apo
Neutrino 81. Proceedings. International Conference on Neutrino Physics and Astrophysics — Neutrino 81 Proc Int Conf Neutrino Phys Astrophys
Neutron Cross Sections and Technology. Proceedings. Conference — Neutron Cross Sect Technol Proc Conf
Neutron Data of Structural Materials for Fast Reactors. Proceedings. Specialists' Meeting — Neutron Data Struct Mater Fast React Proc Spec Meet
Neutron Induced Reactions. Proceedings. Europhysics Topical Conference — Neutron Induced React Proc Europhys Top Conf
Neutron Induced Reactions. Proceedings. International Symposium — Neutron Induced React Proc Int Symp
Neutron Physics and Nuclear Data in Science and Technology — Neutron Phys Nucl Data Sci Technol
Neutron Transmutation Doping Conference — Neutron Transmutat Doping Conf
Neutron Transmutation Doping in Semiconductors. Proceedings. International Conference on Transmutation Doping in Semiconductors — Neutron Transmutat Doping Semicond Proc
Neuva Narrativa Hispanoamericana — NNH
Neva — Ne
Nevada Administrative Code — Nev Admin Code
Nevada. Agricultural Experiment Station. B — Nev Agric Exp Stn B
Nevada. Agricultural Experiment Station. Bulletin — Nev Agric Exp Stn Bull
Nevada. Agricultural Experiment Station. Bulletin — Nevada Agric Exp Sta Bull
Nevada. Agricultural Experiment Station. Circular — Nev Agric Exp Stn Circ
Nevada Agricultural Experiment Station. Forage Grasses Circular — Nevada Agric Exp Sta Forage Grasses Circ
Nevada. Agricultural Experiment Station. Publications — Nev Ag Exp
Nevada. Agricultural Experiment Station. R — Nev Agric Exp Stn R
Nevada. Agricultural Experiment Station. Report T — Nev Agric Exp Stn Rep T
Nevada. Agricultural Experiment Station. Series B — Nev Agric Exp Stn Ser B
Nevada. Agricultural Experiment Station. T — Nev Agric Exp Stn T
Nevada. Agricultural Experiment Station. Technical Bulletin — Nev Agric Exp Stn Tech Bull
Nevada. Bureau of Mines and Geology. Bulletin — Nev Bur Mines Geol Bull
Nevada. Bureau of Mines and Geology. Report — Nev Bur Mines Geol Rep
Nevada. Bureau of Mines. Bulletin — Nev Bur Mines Bull
Nevada. Bureau of Mines. Map — Nevada Bur Mines Map
Nevada. Bureau of Mines. Report — Nev Bur Mines Rep
Nevada. Department of Conservation and Natural Resources. Water Resources Bulletin — Nev Dep Conserv Nat Resour Water Resour Bull
Nevada. Department of Conservation and Natural Resources. Water Resources Information Series — Nev Dep Conserv Nat Resour Water Resour Inf Ser
Nevada. Department of Conservation and Natural Resources. Water Resources Reconnaissance Series — Nev Dep Conserv Nat Resour Water Resour Reconnaissance Ser
Nevada. Division of Water Resources. Water Resources Bulletin — Nev Div Water Resour Water Resour Bull
Nevada. Division of Water Resources. Water Resources Reconnaissance Series — Nev Div Water Resour Water Resour Reconnaissance Ser
Nevada Highways and Parks — Nev Highways and Parks
Nevada Historical Society Quarterly — Nevada Hist Soc Quart
Nevada Historical Society Quarterly — NHSQ
Nevada Nurses' Association. Quarterly Newsletter — Nev Nurses Assoc Q Newslett
Nevada. Office of the State Engineer. Water Resources Bulletin — Nev Off State Eng Water Resour Bull
Nevada Reports — Nev
Nevada Review of Business and Economics — Nev R Bus and Econ
Nevada Revised Statutes — Nev Rev Stat
Nevada Revised Statutes, Annotated (Michie) — Nev Rev Stat Ann (Michie)
Nevada RNformation — Nev RNformation
Nevada. State Engineer. Water Resources Bulletin — Nev State Eng Water Resour Bull
Nevada. State Engineer's Office. Water Resources Bulletin — Nev State Engineer's Office Water Res Bull
Nevada State Museum. Anthropological Papers — Nev State Mus Anthropol Pap
Nevada. University. Agricultural Experiment Station. Bulletin — Nev Univ Agric Exp Stn Bull
Nevada University. Department of Geology and Mining. Bulletin — Nev Univ Dp G M B
Nevada University. Desert Research Institute. Center for Water Resources Research. Project Report — Nevada Univ Center Water Resources Research Proj Rept
Nevada. University. Desert Research Institute. Technical Report — Nevada Univ Desert Research Inst Tech Rept
Nevada. University. Max C. Fleischmann College of Agriculture. Agricultural Experiment Station. Technical Bulletin — Nev Univ Max C Fleischmann Coll Agric Agric Exp Stn Tech Bul
Nevada. University. Max C. Fleischmann College of Agriculture. Report T — Nev Univ Max C Fleischmann Coll Agric Rep T
Nevada University. Max C. Fleischmann College of Agriculture. Series B — Nev Univ Max C Fleischmann Coll Agric B
Nevada University. Max C. Fleischmann College of Agriculture. Series R — Nev Univ Max C Fleischmann Coll Agric R
Nevada Wildlife — Nev Wildl
Nevelestudomanyi Koezlemenyek — Nevelestud Kozlem
Nevrologiya i Psikhiatriya — Nevrol Psikhiatr
Nevrologiya, Psikhiatriya, i Nevrokhirurgiya [*Neurology, Psychiatry, and Neurosurgery*] — Nevrol Psikhiat Nevrokhir
Nevrologiya, Psikhiatriya, i Nevrokhirurgiya — Nevrol Psikhiatr Nevrokhir

Nevrologiya, Psikhiatriya, i Nevrokhirurgiya — NPNMA
Nevropatologiya i Psikhiatriya — Nevropatol Psikhiat
Nevropatologiya. Psikhiatriya i Psikhogigiena — Nevropatol Psikhiatr Psikhogig
New Adelphi — Adel
New Adelphi — NA
New African — AFK
New African — NA
New African — NAF
New African — New Afr
New African — New Africa
New African — NewA
New African Development — Afric Dev
New African Development — New Afr Dev
New Age — New
New Alchemy Quarterly — New Alchemy Q
New Alliance — NA
New America — New Am
New American and Canadian Poetry — New A C P
New American Mercury — New Am Mercury
New American Review [*Later, American Review*] — NAR
New Approaches in the Diagnosis and Management of Cardiovascular Disease. Conference on Cardiovascular Disease — New Approaches Diagn Manage Cardiovasc Dis Conf
New Aspects of Storage and Release Mechanisms of Catecholamines. Bayer-Symposium — New Aspects Storage Release Mech Catecholamines Bayer Symp
New Aspects of Subnuclear Physics. Proceedings. International School of Subnuclear Physics — New Aspects Subnucl Phys Proc Int Sch Subnucl Phys
New Aspects of Trasylol Therapy — New Aspects Trasylol Ther
New Australasian Post — New A'sian Post
New Australian Fruit Grower — New Austral Fruit Grower
New Bible Dictionary — NB Dict
New Biology — New Biol
New Blackfriars — N Bl
New Blackfriars — New Blckfrs
New Books and Periodicals — NWB
New Boston Review — NBR
New Botanist — New Bot
New Braunfelser Zeitung — NBZ
New Breed. Association of Metis and Non-Status Indians of Saskatchewan — NEBR
New Brunswick. Department of Lands and Mines. Annual Report — New Brunswick Dept Lands and Mines Ann Rept
New Brunswick. Department of Natural Resources. Mineral Resources Branch. Report of Investigation — NB Dep Nat Resour Miner Resour Branch Rep Invest
New Brunswick. Department of Natural Resources. Mineral Resources Branch. Topical Report — NB Dep Nat Resour Miner Resour Branch Top Rep
New Brunswick. Department of Natural Resources. Reprint — NB Dep Nat Resour Repr
New Brunswick Historical Society. Collections — NB His S
New Brunswick. Mineral Resources Branch. Information Circular — NB Miner Resour Branch Inf Circ
New Brunswick. Mineral Resources Branch. Report of Investigations — NB Miner Resour Branch Rep Invest
New Brunswick. Mineral Resources Branch. Topical Report — NB Miner Resour Branch Top Rep
New Brunswick. Mines Branch. Information Circular — NB Mines Branch Inf Circ
New Brunswick Museum. Monographic Series — NB Mus Monogr Ser
New Brunswick Reports [*Database*] — NBR
New Brunswick. Research and Productivity Council. Research Note — NB Res Prod Counc Res Note
New Building Projects — New Bldg Projects
New Caledonia. Bulletin Geologique — New Caledonia Bull Geol
New Cambodge — NC
New Cambridge Bibliography of English Literature — New Camb Bibliog Eng Lit
New Cambridge Modern History — NCMH
New Canadian Film — New Can F
New Catholic Encyclopedia — NCE
New Catholic World — NCathW
New Catholic World — NCW
New Celtic Review — New Celtic Rev
New Century — NCent
New Century Bible — N Ce B
New Century Review — New Cent Rev
New Chemical Engineering — New Chem Eng
New China Magazine — New China
New Choices for the Best Years [*Formerly 50 Plus*] — GFIF
New Christianity — N Chr
New Church Magazine — NCM
New Church Review — N Church R
New Church Review — New Church R
New Civil Engineer [*United Kingdom*] — New Civ Eng
New Civil Engineer — New Civ Engnr
New Civil Engineer — New Civ Engr
New Civil Engineer — New Civil Engr
New Clarendon Bible — NCB
New Clarendon Bible. New Testament — NCB NT
New Clarendon Bible. Old Testament — NCB OT
New Collage — New C
New Colophon — N Col
New Commonwealth — New Commonw
New Commonwealth. British Caribbean Supplement — New Commonw Br Car Suppl
New Community — New Commun
New Comprehensive Biochemistry [*Elsevier Book Series*] — NCB
New Comprehensive Biochemistry — New Compr Biochem
New Covenant — New Cov
New Criterion — NC
New Dentist — New Dent
New Designs for Youth Development — New Des Youth Dev
New Development on Agriculture. Hatachi Nogyo. Field Agriculture Society — New Developm Agric
New Developments and Applications of Optical Radiometry. Proceedings. International Conference — New Dev Appl Opt Radiom Proc Int Conf
New Developments in Biosciences — New Dev Biosci
New Developments in Pediatric Research. International Congress of Pediatrics — New Dev Pediatr Res Int Congr Pediatr
New Diamond Science and Technology. Proceedings. International Conference — New Diamond Sci Technol Proc Int Conf
New Dictionary of American Slang — NDAS
New Directions — ND
New Directions — New Direct
New Directions for Child Development — NDCDDI
New Directions for Child Development — New Dir Child Dev
New Directions for Community Colleges — New Dir Com
New Directions for Community Colleges — New Direct Com Coll
New Directions for Higher Education — New Dir Hig
New Directions for Higher Education — New Direct Higher Educ
New Directions for Institutional Research — New Direct Inst Res
New Directions for Mental Health Services — New Dir Ment Health Serv
New Directions for Women — NDFW
New Divinity — New Div
New Doctor — New Dr
New Dominion Monthly — New Dom
New Drugs and Clinic — New Drugs Clin
New Drugs and Clinical Remedies — New Drugs Clin Rem
New Drugs Annual. Cardiovascular Drugs — NDADD8
New Drugs Annual. Cardiovascular Drugs — New Drugs Annu Cardiovasc Drugs
New Eclectic — N Ecl
New Ecologist — NECG
New Ecologist [*United Kingdom*] — New Ecol
New Edinburgh Review — New Edinburgh Rev
New Education — New Educ
New Electrical West — New Electr West
New Electronics — New Electron
New Electronics — NWELA
New Engineer [*United States*] — New Eng
New England Advertising Week — New Eng Adv W
New England and Regional Allergy Proceedings — N Engl Reg Allergy Proc
New England Bioengineering Conference. Proceedings — N Engl Bioeng Conf Proc
New England Business — N Engl Bus
New England Business — NENBD
New England Business — NEW
New England Business — New Eng Bs
New England Business — New England Bus
New England Dairyman — N Engl Dairyman
New England Economic Indicators — New England Econ Indicators
New England Economic Review — N Engl Econ Rev
New England Economic Review — New England Econ R
New England Economic Review. Federal Reserve Bank of Boston — NEE
New England Engineer — N Engl Eng
New England Fruit Meetings. Proceedings. Annual Meeting. Massachusetts Fruit Growers' Association — N Engl Fruit Meet Proc Annu Meet Mass Fruit Grow Assoc
New England Galaxy — N Engl Galaxy
New England Historical and Genealogical Register — N E Reg
New England Historical and Genealogical Register — N Eng Hist Geneal Reg
New England Historical and Genealogical Register — NEHGR
New England Historical and Genealogical Register — New Eng Hist
New England Historical and Genealogical Register — New Eng Hist Geneal Reg
New England Historical and Genealogical Register and Antiquarian Journal — NEHGR
New England Journal of Business and Economics — NEB
New England Journal of Business and Economics — New England J Bus and Econ
New England Journal of Human Services — New Engl J Hum Serv
New England Journal of Human Services — New England J Human Services
New England Journal of Medicine — GNEM
New England Journal of Medicine — N Eng J Med
New England Journal of Medicine — N Engl J Med
New England Journal of Medicine — N England J Med
New England Journal of Medicine — Ne Engl J Med
New England Journal of Medicine — NEJM
New England Journal of Medicine — NEJMA
New England Journal of Medicine — NEJMAG
New England Journal of Medicine — New Engl J Med
New England Journal of Medicine — New England J Med
New England Journal of Medicine. Medical Progress Series — N Engl J Med Med Prog Ser
New England Journal of Numismatics — New Eng J Numis
New England Journal of Parapsychology — New Eng J Parapsych
New England Journal of Photographic History — New England Jl Photogr Hist
New England Journal of Prison Law — New Eng J Prison
New England Journal of Prison Law — New Eng J Prison L
New England Journal of Prison Law — New England J Prison L
New England Journal on Criminal and Civil Confinement — NEJ Crim and Civ Con

New England Journal on Criminal and Civil Confinement — New Eng J Crim & Civil Confinement
New England Law Review — N Eng L Rev
New England Law Review — N Eng LR
New England Law Review — N Engl L Rev
New England Law Review — New Eng L Rev
New England Law Review — New England L Rev
New England Magazine — N Eng Mag
New England Magazine — NEM
New England Magazine — New Eng M
New England Magazine — New Eng Mag
New England Magazine (New Series) — New Eng M ns
New England Medical Gazette — New Engld Med Gaz
New England Quarterly — NE Quar
New England Quarterly — NEQ
New England Quarterly — New Eng Q
New England Quarterly — New Engl Quart
New England Quarterly — New England Quart
New England Quarterly — NewE
New England Quarterly — PNEQ
New England Quarterly. An Historical Review of the New England Life and Letters — N Eng Q
New England Review — N Eng Rev
New England Review [*Later, New England Review and Bread Loaf Quarterly*] — NER
New England Review and Bread Loaf Quarterly — NER
New England Review and Bread Loaf Quarterly — PNER
New England Social Studies Bulletin — N Eng Soc Stud Bull
New England Society of Allergy Proceedings — N Engl Soc Allergy Proc
New England University. Bulletin — NE Univ Bul
New England Water Works Association. Journal — N E Water Works Assn J
New England Water Works Association. Journal — New England Water Works Assoc Jour
New England Weekly Survey — NEWS
New Englander — N Eng
New Englander — New Eng
New English Dictionary on Historical Principles — NED
New Entomologist — New Entomol
New Entomologist (Ueda) — New Ent (Ueda)
New Equipment News [*South Africa*] — New Equip News
New Era in Home and School — New Era
New Era Nursing Image International — New Era Nurs Image Int
New Fiction — New Fic
New Flavours. Proceedings. Moriond Workshop — New Flavours Proc Moriond Workshop
New Flora and Silva — New Fl Silva
New Floral/Shin Kaki — New Fl
New Food Industry [*Japan*] — New Food Ind
New Forests — New For
New Found Land — NFL
New Frontiers in Theology — NFT
New General Collection of Voyages and Travels. Attributed to Greene [*Monograph*] — GVT
New Generation Computing — NGC
New German Critique — New Ger Cr
New German Critique — New Germ
New German Critique — New Germ Crit
New German Critique — NGC
New German Studies — New Ger Stud
New German Studies — NGS
New Grove Dictionary of Jazz — New Grove Jazz
New Grove Dictionary of Music and Musicians — New Grove
New Grove Dictionary of Musical Instruments — New Grove Mus Inst
New Guard — NG
New Guinea Agricultural Gazette — New Guinea Agric Gaz
New Guinea and Australia, the Pacific, and South East Asia — New Guinea Austral Pacific SE Asia
New Guinea Periodicals Index — NGPI
New Guinea Research Bulletin — New Guinea Res B
New Guinea Research Bulletin — NG Research Bul
New Hampshire Agricultural Experiment Station. Circular — New Hampshire Agric Exp Sta Circ
New Hampshire Agricultural Experiment Station. Publications — NH Ag Exp
New Hampshire Agricultural Experiment Station. Research Mimeograph — New Hampshire Agric Exp Sta Res Mimeogr
New Hampshire Bar Journal — New Hamp BJ
New Hampshire Bar Journal — NHB J
New Hampshire Bar Journal — NHJ
New Hampshire Basic-Data Report. Ground-Water Series — NH Basic Data Rep Ground Water Ser
New Hampshire Business Review — NH Bsns Rv
New Hampshire Code of Administrative Rules — NH Code Admin R
New Hampshire Department of Resources and Economic Development. Bulletin — NH Dep Resour Econ Dev Bull
New Hampshire. Division of Economic Development. Bulletin — NH Div Econ Dev Bull
New Hampshire Division of Economic Development. Mineral Resources Survey — NH Div Econ Dev Miner Resour Surv
New Hampshire Historical Society. Proceedings — NH His S
New Hampshire Progress Report — NH Progr Rep
New Hampshire Progress Report. University of New Hampshire Agricultural Experiment Station — New Hampshire Progr Rep
New Hampshire Quarter Notes — NH
New Hampshire Reports — NH
New Hampshire Revised Statutes Annotated — NH Rev Stat Ann
New Hampshire Rulemaking Register — NH Rulemaking Reg
New Hampshire State Planning and Development Commission. Mineral Resources Survey — NH State Plan Devel Comm Mineral Res Survey
New Hampshire State Planning and Development Commission. Mineral Resources Survey — NH State Plann Dev Comm Miner Resour Surv
New Hampshire University. Engineering Experiment Station. Engineering Publicati on — NH Univ Eng Exp Stn Eng Publ
New Harbinger — New Harb
New Haven Symphony Orchestra. Program Notes — New Haven Sym
New Hebrides Anglo-French Condominium. Progress Report. Geological Survey — New Hebrides Anglo Fr Condominium Prog Rep Geol Surv
New Hebrides Condominium. Geological Survey. Report — New Hebrides Condominium Geol Surv Rep
New Hebrides. Geological Survey. Annual Report — New Hebrides Geol Surv Annu Rep
New Hebrides. Geological Survey. Report — New Hebrides Geol Surv Rep
New Horizons — New Hor
New Horizons — New Horiz
New Horizons (Baltimore) — New Horiz Baltimore
New Horizons in Cardiovascular Diseases — New Horiz Cardiovasc Dis
New Horizons in Catalysis. Proceedings. International Congress on Catalysis — New Horiz Catal Proc Int Congr Catal
New Horizons in Education — New Hor Educ
New Horizons in Education — New Horiz Educ
New Horizons in Education — New Horizons in Educ
New Horizons in Oncology — New Horiz Oncol
New Hungarian Exporter — HUE
New Hungarian Quarterly — New Hung Q
New Hungarian Quarterly — New Hungar Quart
New Hungarian Quarterly — New Hungarian Q
New Hungarian Quarterly — NHQ
New Ideas in Psychology — New Ideas Psychol
New Ideas in Psychology — NIP
New Image of Man in Medicine — New Image Man Med
New India Antiquary — NIA
New India Antiquary. Extra Series — NIA ES
New Information Systems and Services [*United States*] — New Inf Syst Serv
New International Clinics — New Int Clin
New International Commentary on the New Testament — NIC
New International Realities [*United States*] — New Int Realities
New International Realities — NIRED
New International Review — New Intl
New International Year Book — NIYB
New Internationalist [*England*] — New Int
New Internationalist — New Inter
New Internationalist — NI
New Internationalist — NINTD
New Ireland Review — New Ir Rev
New Istanbul Contribution to Clinical Science — New Istanbul Contrib Clin Sci
New Jersey Administrative Code — NJ Admin Code
New Jersey Administrative Reports — NJ Admin
New Jersey Agricultural College Experiment Station. Botany Department Report — New Jersey Agric Coll Exp Sta Bot Dep Rep
New Jersey Agricultural College Experiment Station. Mimeographed Circular — New Jersey Agric Coll Exp Sta Mimeogr Circ
New Jersey. Agricultural Experiment Station. Bulletin — NJ Agr Expt Sta Bull
New Jersey. Agricultural Experiment Station. Bulletin — NJ Agric Exp Stn Bull
New Jersey. Agricultural Experiment Station. Circular — NJ Agric Exp Stn Circ
New Jersey. Agricultural Experiment Station. Publications — NJ Ag Exp
New Jersey Agriculture — NJ Ag
New Jersey Agriculture — NJ Agr
New Jersey Agriculture — NJ Agric
New Jersey Banker — NJ Bank
New Jersey Beekeepers Association. News — New Jers Beekprs Ass News
New Jersey. Bureau of Geology and Topography. Bulletin — NJ Bur Geol Topogr Bull
New Jersey. Bureau of Geology and Topography. Bulletin — NJ Geol Topogr Bull
New Jersey Business — NJ Bus
New Jersey Business Education Association. Newsletter — NJBEA Newsletter
New Jersey Business Education Observer — Bus Ed Observer
New Jersey Ceramist — NJ Ceram
New Jersey. Department of Agriculture. Publications — NJ Ag Dept
New Jersey. Department of Conservation and Development. Annual Report — NJ Dp Conservation An Rp
New Jersey. Department of Conservation and Economic Development. Division of Water Policy and Supply. Special Report — NJ Dep Conserv Econ Dev Div Water Policy Supply Spec Rep
New Jersey. Department of Conservation and Economic Development. Geologic Report Series — NJ Dep Conserv Econ Develop Geol Rep Ser
New Jersey. Department of Environmental Protection. Division of Natural Resources. Bureau of Geology and Topography. Bulletin — NJ Dep Environ Prot Div Nat Resour Bur Geol Topogr Bull
New Jersey. Division of Water Policy and Supply. Special Report — NJ Div Water Policy Supply Spec Rep
New Jersey. Division of Water Policy and Supply. Water Resources Circular — NJ Div Water Policy Supply Water Resour Cir
New Jersey. Division of Water Resources. Special Report — NJ Div Water Resour Spec Rep
New Jersey. Division of Water Resources. Special Report — NJ Water Resour Spec Rep
New Jersey Equity Reports — NJ Eq
New Jersey. Geological Survey — NJ G S
New Jersey Historical Society. Collections — NJ His S Col
New Jersey Historical Society. Proceedings — NJ His S

New Jersey Historical Society. Proceedings — NJHistS
New Jersey Historical Society. Proceedings — NJHS
New Jersey Historical Society. Proceedings — NJHSP
New Jersey History — NewJ
New Jersey History — NJ Hist
New Jersey History — NJH
New Jersey Journal of Optometry — NJ Jnl Optom
New Jersey. Journal of Pharmacy — NJ J Pharm
New Jersey Labor Herald — NJ Lab Hld
New Jersey Law Journal — New Jersey LJ
New Jersey Law Journal — NJ Law J
New Jersey Law Journal — NJLJ
New Jersey Law Reports — NJL
New Jersey Lawyer — NJ Law
New Jersey Lawyer — NJ Lawy
New Jersey League for Nursing. News — NJ League Nurs News
New Jersey Libraries — NJ Lib
New Jersey Libraries — NJ Libr
New Jersey Medicine — NJ Med
New Jersey Miscellaneous Reports — NJ Misc
New Jersey Mosquito Extermination Association. Proceedings. Annual Meeting — NJ Mosq Exterm Assoc Proc Annu Meet
New Jersey Nurse — NJ Nurse
New Jersey Register — NJ Reg
New Jersey Reports — NJ
New Jersey Revised Statutes — NJ Rev Stat
New Jersey School Librarian — NJ Sch Libn
New Jersey Session Law Service (West) — NJ Sess Law Serv (West)
New Jersey State Horticultural Society. News — New Jers St Hort Soc News
New Jersey Statutes Annotated (West) — NJ Stat Ann (West)
New Jersey Success — NJ Success
New Jersey Superior Court Reports — NJ Super
New Jersey Tax Court Reports — NJ Tax
New Jersey Zinc Company. Research Bulletin — NJ Zinc Co Res Bull
New Journal of Agriculture and Forestry. College of Agriculture. Chinling University/Nung Lin Hsin Pao — New J Agric Forest Coll Agric Chinling Univ
New Journal of Chemistry — New J Chem
New Journal of Statistics and Operational Research — New J Stat & Oper Res
New Judaea [*London*] — NJ
New Korea — NK
New Laurel Review — NLauR
New Law Journal — New L J
New Law Journal — New Law J
New Law Journal — NL
New Leader — GTNE
New Leader — NewL
New Leader — NL
New Left Review — New Left
New Left Review — New Left R
New Left Review — New Left Rev
New Left Review — NLR
New Letters — New L
New Liberal Review — New Lib
New Library of Catholic Knowledge — NLCK
New Library World — New Lib W
New Library World — New Lib World
New Library World — New Libr Wld
New Literary History — New Lit His
New Literary History — New Lit Hist
New Literary History — NLH
New Literary History — PNLH
New Literature and Ideology — New Lit Ideol
New Literature on Automation — Lit Automat
New Literature on Automation — New Lit Autom
New Literature Review — N L Rev
New London Commentary — NLC
New London Commentary on the New Testament — NLC
New Look at Tumour Immunology — New Look Tumour Immunol
New Magazine Review — NMR
New Management — NMG
New Materials Japan — New Mater Jpn
New Mathematical Library — New Math Library
New Medical and Physical Journal. Annals of Medicine, Natural History, and Chemistry — New Med Phys J
New Medical Journal — New Med J
New Metals and Technics [*Japan*] — New Met Tech
New Methods in Drug Research — New Methods Drug Res
New Mexico Academy of Science. Bulletin — NM Acad Sci Bull
New Mexico. Agricultural Experiment Station. Bulletin — NM Agric Exp Stn Bull
New Mexico. Agricultural Experiment Station. Publications — NM Ag Exp
New Mexico. Agricultural Experiment Station. Research Report — NM Agric Exp Stn Res Rep
New Mexico Agricultural Experiment Station. Research Report. New Mexico State College — New Mexico Agric Exp Sta Res Rep
New Mexico Anthropologist — New Mexico Anthropol
New Mexico Anthropologist — NMA
New Mexico Anthropologist (Albuquerque, New Mexico) — New Mex Anthrop Albuquerque
New Mexico. Bureau of Mines and Mineral Resources. Bulletin — NM Bur Mines Miner Resour Bull
New Mexico. Bureau of Mines and Mineral Resources. Bulletin. New Mexico Institute of Mining and Technology — New Mexico Bur Mines and Mineral Resources Bull
New Mexico. Bureau of Mines and Mineral Resources. Circular — NM Bur Mines Miner Resour Cir
New Mexico. Bureau of Mines and Mineral Resources. Circular — NM Bur Mines Miner Resour Circ
New Mexico. Bureau of Mines and Mineral Resources. Circular. New Mexico Institute of Mining and Technology — New Mexico Bur Mines and Mineral Resources Circ
New Mexico. Bureau of Mines and Mineral Resources. Geologic Map. New Mexico Institute of Mining and Technology — New Mexico Bur Mines and Mineral Resources Geol Map
New Mexico. Bureau of Mines and Mineral Resources. Ground Water Report — NM Bur Mines Miner Resour Ground Water Rep
New Mexico. Bureau of Mines and Mineral Resources. Ground Water Report — NM Bur Mines Miner Rsour Ground Water Rep
New Mexico. Bureau of Mines and Mineral Resources. Hydrologic Report — NM Bur Mines Miner Resour Hydrol Rep
New Mexico. Bureau of Mines and Mineral Resources. Memoir — NM Bur Mines Miner Resour Mem
New Mexico Bureau of Mines and Mineral Resources. Memoir. New Mexico Institute of Mining and Technology — New Mexico Bur Mines and Mineral Resources Mem
New Mexico. Bureau of Mines and Mineral Resources. Mineral Resources Report [*A publication*] — NM Bur Mines Miner Resour Miner Resour Rep
New Mexico. Bureau of Mines and Mineral Resources. Progress Report — NM Bur Mines Miner Resour Prog Rep
New Mexico. Bureau of Mines and Mineral Resources. Target Exploration Report — NM Bur Mines Miner Resour Target Explor Rep
New Mexico Business — N Mex Bus
New Mexico Business Journal — N Mex Bs Jl
New Mexico Business Journal — NM Bus J
New Mexico Business Journal — NMBJD
New Mexico Dental Journal — NM Dent J
New Mexico. Department of Game and Fish. Bulletin — BNMFDC
New Mexico. Department of Game and Fish. Bulletin — NM Dep Game Fish Bull
New Mexico Extension News — N Mex Ext N
New Mexico Extension News — NM Ext News
New Mexico Extension News. New Mexico State University. Agricultural Extension Service — N Mex Ext News N Mex State Univ Agr Ext Serv
New Mexico Folklore Record — NMFR
New Mexico Geological Society. Annual Field Conference Guidebook — NM Geol Soc Annu Field Conf Guideb
New Mexico Geological Society. Field Conference Guidebook — NM Geol Soc Field Conf Guideb
New Mexico Geological Society. Guidebook of Annual Field Conference — NM Geol Soc Guideb Annu Field Conf
New Mexico Geological Society. Special Publication — New Mexico Geol Soc Spec Pub
New Mexico Geological Society. Special Publication — NM Geol Soc Spec Publ
New Mexico Geology — N Mex Geol
New Mexico Geology — New Mex Geol
New Mexico Geology — NM Geol
New Mexico Highlands University. Journal — NMHUJ
New Mexico Historical Quarterly — NMHQ
New Mexico Historical Review — New Mex Hist Rev
New Mexico Historical Review — New Mexico Hist Rev
New Mexico Historical Review — NM His R
New Mexico Historical Review — NMHR
New Mexico Journal of Science — New Mexico J Sci
New Mexico Journal of Science — NM J Sci
New Mexico Law Review — N Mex L Rev
New Mexico Law Review — New Mex L Rev
New Mexico Law Review — New Mexico L Rev
New Mexico Law Review — NML
New Mexico Law Review — NML Rev
New Mexico Law Review — NMLR
New Mexico Libraries — N Mex Lib
New Mexico Libraries. Newsletter — NM Lib Newsl
New Mexico Library Bulletin — New Mexico Libr Bull
New Mexico Miner — N Mex Miner
New Mexico Musician — NEM
New Mexico Nurse — NM Nurse
New Mexico Quarterly — NMQ
New Mexico Quarterly. Review — NMQR
New Mexico Reports — NM
New Mexico Review — NMR
New Mexico Solar Energy Association. Southwest Bulletin — NM Sol Energy Assoc Southwest Bull
New Mexico State Bureau of Mines and Mineral Resources. Annual Report — NM State Bur Mines Miner Resour Annu Rep
New Mexico State Bureau of Mines and Mineral Resources. Bulletin — N Mex Bur Mines Mineral Resources Bull
New Mexico State Bureau of Mines and Mineral Resources. Bulletin — NM State Bur Mines Miner Resour Bull
New Mexico State Bureau of Mines and Mineral Resources. Circular — NM State Bur Mines Miner Resour Circ
New Mexico State Bureau of Mines and Mineral Resources. Geologic Map — NM State Bur Mines Miner Resour Geol Map
New Mexico State Bureau of Mines and Mineral Resources. Memoir — N Mex Bur Mines Mineral Resources Mem
New Mexico State Bureau of Mines and Mineral Resources. Memoir — NM State Bur Mines Miner Resour Mem
New Mexico State Bureau of Mines and Mineral Resources. Mineral Resources Report — NM State Bur Mines Miner Resour Miner Resour Rep
New Mexico State Bureau of Mines and Mineral Resources. Target Exploration Report — NM State Bur Mines Miner Resour Target Explor Rep
New Mexico State Engineer. Basic Data Report — NM State Eng Basic Data Rep

New Mexico State Engineer. Technical Report — New Mexico State Engineer Tech Rept
New Mexico State Engineer. Technical Report — NM State Eng Tech Rep
New Mexico State Engineer's Office. Technical Report — N Mex State Engineer Office Tech Rept
New Mexico State Engineer's Office. Technical Report — NM State Eng Off Tech Rep
New Mexico State University. Agricultural Experiment Station. Bulletin — NM State Univ Agric Exp Stn Bull
New Mexico State University. Agricultural Experiment Station. Research Report — NM State Univ Agric Exp Stn Res Rep
New Mexico Statutes Annotated — NM Stat Ann
New Mexico University. Bulletin. Geological Series — N Mex Univ B G S
New Mexico University. Publications in Geology. Publications in Meteoritics — N Mex Univ Pubs Geology Pubs Meteoritics
New Mexico University. Publications in Meteoritics — New Mexico Univ Pubs Meteoritics
New Mexico Wildlife — NM Wildl
New Microbiologica — New Microbiol
New Middle East [*London*] — NME
New Monthly Magazine and Universal Register — New Monthly Mag
New Music Review — N Music R
New Music Review and Church Music Review — New Mus R
New Musical Express — NME
New Nation. Manitoba Native Newspaper — NENA
New Native People — NNAP
New Nigerian — NN
New Nippon Electric Technical Review — New Nippon Electr Tech Rev
New Nuclear Physics with Advanced Techniques — New Nucl Phys Adv Tech
New Options in Energy Technology. Papers. AIAA/EEI/IEEE Conference (Edison Electric Institute) — New Options Energy Technol Pap AIAA EEI IEEE Conf
New Orient [*Prague*] — NO
New Orient Bimonthly — NOB
New Orleans Academy of Ophthalmology. Transactions — New Orleans Acad Ophthalmol Trans
New Orleans Academy of Sciences. Papers — New Orleans Ac Sc Papers
New Orleans Business — N Orlean Bs
New Orleans City Business — N Orleans CB
New Orleans Geographical Society. Log — NOGS Log
New Orleans Journal of Medicine — New Orleans J Med
New Orleans Magazine — INOM
New Orleans Medical and Surgical Journal — N Orl M & S J
New Orleans Medical and Surgical Journal — N Orl Med and S J
New Orleans Medical and Surgical Journal — New Orl Med Surg J
New Orleans Medical and Surgical Journal — New Orleans Med Surg J
New Orleans Medical News and Hospital Gazette — New Orl Med News Hosp Gaz
New Orleans Music — New Orleans Mus
New Orleans Poetry Journal — NOP
New Orleans Port Record — New Orleans Port Rec
New Orleans Review — New O R
New Orleans Review — New Orl Rev
New Orleans Review — NOR
New Orleans Times-Picayune — NOTP
New Outlook [*Tel Aviv*] — NO
New Oxford Outlook — NO
New Palaeographical Society — New Pal Soc
New Palaeographical Society — NPS
New Palestine — NP
New Perfumers' Journal — New Perfum J
New Periodical Titles — NPT
New Periodicals Index — New Per Ind
New Periodicals Index — New Period Index
New Periodicals Index — NPI
New Perspectives in Clinical Microbiology — New Perspect Clin Microbiol
New Perspectives in Powder Metallurgy — New Perspect Powder Metall
New Perspectives in Weed Science — New Perspect Weed Sci
New Perspectives Quarterly — GNPQ
New Perspectives Quarterly — NPQ
New Pharmacologie Vistas in Anesthesia — New Pharmacol Vistas Anesth
New Phenomena in Subnuclear Physics. International School of Subnuclear Physics — New Phenom Subnucl Phys Int Sch
New Philosophy — NP
New Physics — New Phys
New Physics (Korean Physical Society) — New Phys (Korean Phys Soc)
New Physics. Supplement — New Phys Suppl
New Phytologist — New Phytol
New Political Science — New Pol Sci
New Political Science — New Polit
New Politics — New Polit
New Polymerization Reactions — New Polym React
New Princeton Review — N Princ
New Princeton Review — New Princ
New Products and Processes Highlights — NPD
New Products International — NIN
New Publications. American Mathematical Society — New Publ Am Math Soc
New Publications. Bureau of Mines [*Washington, DC*] — New Publ Bur Mines
New Quarterly Review — New Q
New Rambler — NRam
New Realities — New Real
New Records — NR
New Remedies and Therapy — New Rem Ther
New Renaissance — New Rena
New Renaissance — NRena
New Republic — GTNR
[*The*] **New Republic** — New R
[*The*] **New Republic** — New Rep
[*The*] **New Republic** — New Repub
New Republic — New Republ
[*The*] **New Republic** — NR
[*The*] **New Republic** — NRep
New Republic — NRp
[*The*] **New Republic** — TNR
New Research in Plant Anatomy — New Res Plant Anat
New Research Reports — New Res Rep
New Review — New R
New Review — New Rev
New River Review — New Riv R
New Salt Creek Reader — Salt C R
New Schaff-Herzog Encyclopedia of Religious Knowledge — NSHE
New Scholar — New S
New Scholar (California) — NSC
New Scholasticism — N Schol
New Scholasticism — New Schol
New Scholasticism — New Scholas
New Scholasticism — New Scholast
New Scholasticism — NS
New Scholasticism — NSch
New Schools Exchange. Newsletter — New Sch Ex
New Schools Exchange. Newsletter — New Schl
New Schools Exchange. Newsletter — Nw School
New Science Review — N Sci R
New Scientist — GNSC
New Scientist — N Scientist
New Scientist — Ne Sci
New Scientist — New Sci
New Scientist — New Scient
New Scientist — NS
New Scientist — NST
New Scientist — NWJ
New Scientist and Science Journal — New Sci Sci J
New Scientist and Science Journal — NSSJ
New Scientist and Science Journal — NSSJB
New Scientist (London) — New Sci (London)
New Serial Titles — NST
New Silver Technology — New Silver Technol
New Society — New Soc
New Society (London) — New Soc (London)
New South Wales Art Gallery Quarterly — NSW Art Gallery Q
New South Wales Bankruptcy Cases — BC
New South Wales Bankruptcy Cases — BC (NSW)
New South Wales Bankruptcy Cases — NSW Bkptcy Cas
New South Wales Bankruptcy Cases — NSWB
New South Wales Carpenters' Journal — NSW Carpenters J
New South Wales Contract Reporter and Prices Current List — NSW Contract Reporter
New South Wales Conveyancing Law and Practice [*Australia*] — ANC
New South Wales Conveyancing Reports — NSW Conv R
New South Wales Council for the Mentally Handicapped. Journal — NSWCMHJ
New South Wales Country Trader and Storekeeper — NSW Country Trader
New South Wales Court of Review Decisions — NSW CRD
New South Wales. Department of Agriculture. Annual Report — NSW Dep Agric Annu Rep
New South Wales. Department of Agriculture. Biological and Chemical Research Institute. Annual Plant Disease Survey — NSW Dep Agric Biol Chem Res Inst Annu Plant Dis Surv
New South Wales. Department of Agriculture. Bulletin S — NSW Dep Agric Bull S
New South Wales. Department of Agriculture. Chemistry Branch. Bulletin S — NSW Dep Agric Chem Branch
New South Wales. Department of Agriculture. Chemistry Branch. Bulletin S — NSW Dep Agric Chem Branch Bull S
New South Wales. Department of Agriculture. Division of Science Services. Entomology Branch. Annual Report — NSW Dep Agric Div Sci Serv Entomol Branch Annu Rep
New South Wales. Department of Agriculture. Division of Science Services. Entomology Branch. Insect Pest Leaflet — NSW Dep Agric Div Sci Serv Entomol Branch Insect Pest Leafl
New South Wales. Department of Agriculture. Division of Science Services. Entomology Branch. Insect Pest Survey. Annual Report — NWAIAH
New South Wales. Department of Agriculture. Plant Disease Survey — NSW Dep Agric Plant Dis Surv
New South Wales. Department of Agriculture. Report — NSW Dep Agric Rep
New South Wales. Department of Agriculture. Science Bulletin — NSW Dep Agric Sci Bull
New South Wales. Department of Agriculture. Technical Bulletin — NSW Dep Agric Tech Bull
New South Wales. Department of Agriculture. Technical Bulletin — Tech Bull Dep Agric NSW
New South Wales. Department of Mines. Chemical Laboratory Report — NSW Dep Mines Chem Lab Rep
New South Wales. Department of Mines. Chemical Laboratory. Report — NSW Dept Mines Chem Lab Rep
New South Wales. Department of Mines. Coalfields Branch. Technical Report — NSW Dep Mines Coalfields Branch Tech Rep
New South Wales. Department of Mines. Coalfields Branch. Technical Report CF [*A publication*] — NSW Dep Mines Tech Rep CF
New South Wales. Department of Mines. Geological Survey. Bulletin — NSW Dep Mines Geol Surv Bull

New South Wales. Department of Mines. Geological Survey. Mineral Industry of New South Wales — NSW Dep Mines Geol Surv Miner Ind NSW
New South Wales. Department of Mines. Geological Survey. Report — NSW Dep Mines Geol Surv Rep
New South Wales. Department of Mines. Memoirs of the Geological Survey of New South Wales. Geology — NSW Dep Mines Mem Geol Surv NSW Geol
New South Wales. Department of Mines. Memoirs of the Geological Survey of New South Wales. Palaeontology — NSW Dep Mines Mem Geol Surv NSW Palaeontol
New South Wales. Department of Mines. Technical Report — NSW Dep Mines Tech Rep
New South Wales. Federation of Infants and Nursery School Clubs. General Newsletter — NSW Fed INS Clubs Gen Newsletter
New South Wales Federation of Infants and Nursery School Clubs. News — NSW Fed INSC News
New South Wales. Forestry Commission. Division of Forest Management. Research Note — NSW For Comm Dir For Mgmt Res Note
New South Wales. Forestry Commission. Division of Wood Technology. Bulletin — NSW For Comm Div Wood Technol Bull
New South Wales. Forestry Commission. Division of Wood Technology. Leaflet — NSW For Comm Div Wood Technol Leafl
New South Wales. Forestry Commission. Division of Wood Technology. Pamphlet — NSW For Comm Div Wood Technol Pamph
New South Wales. Forestry Commission. Division of Wood Technology. Project Reports — NSW For Comm Div Wood Technol Proj Rep
New South Wales. Forestry Commission. Division of Wood Technology. Technical Notes — NSW For Comm Div Wood Technol Tech
New South Wales. Forestry Commission. Division of Wood Technology. Technical Notes — NSW For Comm Div Wood Technol Tech Notes
New South Wales. Forestry Commission. Division of Wood Technology. Technical Notes — Tech Notes NSW For Comm Div Wood Technol
New South Wales. Forestry Commission. Research Notes — NSW For Comm Res Note
New South Wales. Forestry Commission. Research Notes — Res Notes NSW For Comm
New South Wales Forestry Recorder — NSW For Rec
New South Wales Freemason — NSW Freemason
New South Wales. Geological Survey. 1:250,000 Geological Series — NSW Geol Surv 1:250 000 Geol Ser
New South Wales. Geological Survey. 4-Mile Geological Series — NSW Geol Surv 4-Mile Geol Ser
New South Wales. Geological Survey. Bulletin — NSW Geol Surv Bull
New South Wales. Geological Survey. Memoirs. Geology — Mem Geol Surv NSW Geol
New South Wales. Geological Survey. Memoirs. Geology — NSW Geol Surv Mem Geol
New South Wales. Geological Survey. Memoirs. Palaeontology — NSW Geol Surv Mem Palaeontol
New South Wales. Geological Survey. Mineral Industry of New South Wales — Geol Surv NSW Miner Ind NSW
New South Wales. Geological Survey. Mineral Industry of New South Wales — NSW Geol Surv Mineral Industry of NSW
New South Wales. Geological Survey. Mineral Resources — Miner Resour Geol Surv NSW
New South Wales. Geological Survey. Mineral Resources — NSW Geol Surv Min Res
New South Wales. Geological Survey. Mineral Resources — NSW Geol Surv Miner Resour
New South Wales. Geological Survey. Quarterly Notes — NSW Geol Surv Q Notes
New South Wales. Geological Survey. Records — NSW Geol Surv Rec
New South Wales. Geological Survey. Report — NSW Geol Surv Rep
New South Wales Government Gazette — NSWGG
New South Wales. Higher Education Board. Annual Report — NSW High Educ Bd Ann Rep
New South Wales Industrial Gazette — NSW Ind Gaz
New South Wales Industrial Gazette [*Australia*] — NSWIG
New South Wales Institute for Educational Research. Bulletin — NSW Inst Ed Res Bul
New South Wales Institute for Educational Research. Bulletin — NSWIER Bul
New South Wales Land and Valuation Court Reports — NSWLVR
New South Wales Law Reports — New So WL
New South Wales Law Reports — NSWLR
New South Wales Letters of Registration — NSWLR
New South Wales Library Bulletin — NSW Lib Bul
New South Wales Local Government Reports — LGR
New South Wales Magazine — New South Wales Mag
New South Wales. National Herbarium. Contributions — NSW Herb Contr
New South Wales. National Herbarium. Contributions. Flora Series — NSW Herb Contr Flora Ser
New South Wales Official Publications — NSWOP
New South Wales. Parliament. Parliamentary Debates — NSW Parl Parl Deb
New South Wales Parliamentary Debates — NSW Parl Deb
New South Wales Parliamentary Debates — NSWPD
New South Wales Philatelic Annual — NSW Philatelic Ann
New South Wales Police News — NSW Police News
New South Wales Potato — NSW Potato
New South Wales Presbyterian — NSW Presbyterian
New South Wales. Soil Conservation Service. Journal — New South Wales Soil Conserv Serv J
New South Wales. State Fisheries Cruise Report — NSW State Fish Cruise Rep
New South Wales State Reports — New So W St
New South Wales State Reports — NSW St R
New South Wales State Reports — NSWSR
New South Wales State Reports — SR
New South Wales Statistical Register — NSW Stat Reg
New South Wales Statistical Summary — NSW Statist Summ
New South Wales Timber Worker — NSW Timber Worker
New South Wales. Traffic Accident Research Unit. TARU Research Note — TARU Research Note
New South Wales University. School of Civil Engineering. UNICIV Report. Series R — NSW Univ Sch Civ Eng UNICIV Rep Ser R
New South Wales. Water Conservation and Irrigation Commission. Survey of Thirty New South Wales River Valleys. Report — NSW Wat Conserv Irrig Comm Surv Thirty NSW River Valleys Rep
New South Wales Weather Report — NSW Weath Rep
New South Wales Weekly Notes — New So WWN
New South Wales Weekly Notes — NSWWN
New South Wales Weekly Notes — Week No
New Southern Literary Messenger — New South Lit Mess
New Statesman — GNES
New Statesman — N St
New Statesman — New Statesm
New Statesman — New Stsm
New Statesman — NewS
New Statesman — NewSt
New Statesman — NS
New Statesman — NSM
New Statesman — NStat
New Statesman and Nation — New Stsm Natn
New Statesman and Nation — NS & N
New Statesman and Nation — NSMN
New Statesman and Nation — NSN
New Statesman and Nation — NStN
New Statesman and Society — GNES
New Statesman (England) — NSE
New Steelmaking Technology from the Bureau of Mines. Proceedings. Open Industry Briefing — New Steelmaking Technol Bur Mines Proc Open Ind Briefing
New Stories — NS
New Studies in the Philosophy of Religion — NSPR
New Syndromes. Part B. Annual Review of Birth Defects — New Syndr Part B Annu Rev Birth Defects
New Synthetic Methods — New Synth Methods
New Teacher — New Teach
New Technical Books — New Tech Books
New Technical Books — NTB
New Techniques — New Tech
New Techniques in Biophysics and Cell Biology — New Tech Biophys Cell Biol
New Techniques in Nutritional Research — New Tech Nutr Res
New Techniques. Section B. Nuclear Engineering — New Tech B
New Technology — New Technol
New Technology Education Series — New Technol Educ Ser
New Testament — N T
New Testament Abstracts — New Test Abstr
New Testament Abstracts — New Testam Abstr
New Testament Abstracts — NT Ab
New Testament Abstracts — NTA
New Testament Abstracts [*Weston, MA*] — NTAbstr
New Testament Studies — New Test St
New Testament Studies — New Test Stud
New Testament Studies — NTS
New Testament Studies — NTSt
New Testament Studies — NTStud
New Testament Studies — PNTS
New Testament Texts and Studies — NTTS
New Testament Texts and Studies — NTTSt
New Testament Tools and Studies — NTTS
New Testament Tools and Studies [*Leiden*] — NTTSt
New Theatre Magazine — NThM
New Theatre Magazine — NTM
New Theatre Quarterly — NTQ
New Theatre Quarterly — PNTQ
New Therapy of Ischemic Heart Disease. International Adalat Symposium — New Ther Ischemic Heart Dis Int Adalat Symp
New Times — NT
New Tombs at Dendra near Midea — NT
New Tombs at Dendra near Midea — NTD
New Towns Bulletin — New Towns Bull
New Trends in Atomic Physics — New Trends At Phys
New Trends in Chemistry Teaching — New Trends Chem Teach
New Trends in Coal Science — New Trends Coal Sci
New Trends in Theoretical and Experimental Nuclear Physics. Predeal International Summer School — New Trends Theor Exp Nucl Phys Predeal Int Summer Sch
New Universities. Quarterly — New Univ Q
New Universities. Quarterly — New Univ Quart
New University and New Education — New University
New Verse — NV
New Woman — GNWW
New Womens Times — New Times
New World Antiquity — New Wld Antiq
New World Antiquity (London) — New World Antiq London
New World Archaeological Record — New World A
New World Quarterly — New Wld Q
New World Review — New W R
New World Review — New Wld Rev
New World Review — New World R
New World Writing — NWW
New Worlds — NW

New Worlds (British) — NWB
New Worlds. Quarterly — NWQ
New Worlds Science Fiction — NWA
New Writers Group Bulletin — NWGB
New Writing — NW
New Writing from Zambia — NWZam
New York — GNYC
New York — NY
New York Academy of Sciences Annals — New York Acad Sci Ann
New York Academy of Sciences. Annals — NY Acad Sci Ann
New York Academy of Sciences. Transactions — New York Acad Sci Trans
New York Academy of Sciences. Transactions — NY Acad Sci Trans
New York Academy of Sciences. Transactions. Annals — NY Acad Sci Trans Ann
New York Affairs — NY Aff
New York. Agricultural Experiment Station (Geneva). Annual Report — NY Agric Exp Stn (Geneva) Annu Rep
New York. Agricultural Experiment Station (Geneva). Bulletin — NY Agric Exp Stn (Geneva) Bull
New York. Agricultural Experiment Station (Geneva, New York). Annual Report — NY Agric Exp Stn Geneva NY Annu Rep
New York. Agricultural Experiment Station (Geneva). Research Circular — NY Agric Exp Stn (Geneva) Res Circ
New York. Agricultural Experiment Station (Geneva). Technical Bulletin — NY Agric Exp Stn (Geneva) Tech Bull
New York. Agricultural Experiment Station (Ithaca). Bulletin — NY Agric Exp Stn (Ithaca) Bull
New York. Agricultural Experiment Station (Ithaca). Memoir — NY Agric Exp Stn (Ithaca) Mem
New York Applied Forestry Research Institute. AFRI Miscellaneous Report — NY Appl For Res Inst AFRI Misc Rep
New York Applied Forestry Research Institute. AFRI Research Note — NY Appl For Res Inst AFRI Res Note
New York Applied Forestry Research Institute. AFRI Research Report — NY Appl For Res Inst AFRI Res Rep
New York Arts Journal — NY Arts J
New York Board of Agriculture. Memoirs — NY Bd Agr Mem
New York Botanical Garden. Annual Report — NY Bot Gard Annu Rep
New York Botanical Garden. Bulletin — NY Bot Garden B
New York Botanical Garden. Memoirs — NY Bot Gard Mem
New York Certified Public Accountant — NY Cert Pub Acct
New York City Board of Education. Curriculum Bulletins — New York City Board Education Curriculum Bull
New York City Board of Education. Curriculum Bulletins — NYC Bd Ed Curric Bul
New York City Civil Court Act — City Civ Ct Act
New York City Criminal Court Act — City Crim Ct Act
New York City Department of Health. Weekly Bulletin — New York City Dept Health W Bul
New York City Municipal Reference and Research Center. Notes — Munic Ref & Res Center Notes
New York City Museum of Modern Art. Bulletin — Mus Mod Art Bul
New York City Public Library. Bulletin — NY Public Lib Bull
New York City Public Library. Municipal Reference Library. Notes — Munic Ref Lib Notes
New York Code of Criminal Procedure — Code Crim Proc
New York Commissioners of the State Reservation at Niagara. Annual Report — NY Comm St Res Niagara An Rp
New York Conservation Department. Water Resources Commission. Bulletin — New York Water Resources Comm Bull
New York Conservation Department. Water Resources Commission. Report of Investigation — New York Water Resources Comm Rept Inv
New York Consolidated Laws Service — NY Law Consol
New York County Lawyers Association. Bar Bulletin — Bar Bull (NY County Law A)
New York County Lawyers Association. Bar Bulletin — NY County B Bull
New York County Lawyers Association. Bar Bulletin — NY County Law Ass'n B Bull
New York Court of Claims Act — Ct Cl Act
New York Department of Agriculture and Markets. Annual Report — NY Dep Agric Mark Annu Rep
New York Department of Agriculture and Markets. Circular — NY Dep Agric Mark Circ
New York Department of Agriculture. Publications — NY Ag Dept
New York. Department of Environmental Conservation. Bulletin — NY Dep Environ Conserv Bull
New York. Department of Environmental Conservation. Division of Water Resources. Bulletin — NY Dep Environ Conserv Div Water Resour Bull
New York Evening Post — New York Eve Post
New York Evening Post — NYEP
New York Evening Post Literary Review — NYEPLR
New York Family Court Act — Fam Ct Act
New York Fish and Game Journal — NY Fish Game J
New York Folklore — NY Folkl
New York Folklore — NY Folklore
New York Folklore. Quarterly — NF
New York Folklore. Quarterly — NY Folk Q
New York Folklore. Quarterly — NYFQ
New York Geological Survey — NY G S
New York Herald Tribune — NYHT
New York Herald Tribune. Book Review — NY Herald Tribune Bk R
New York Herald Tribune Books — Books
New York Herald Tribune Books — HTB
New York Herald Tribune. Lively Arts Section — NY Her Trib Lively Arts
New York Herald Tribune. Weekly Book Review — NY Herald Tribune W Bk R
New York Herald Tribune. Weekly Book Review — NYHTB
New York Historical Society. Collections — NY Hist Soc Coll
New York Historical Society Quarterly — NewY
New York Historical Society. Quarterly — NY Hist Soc Q
New York Historical Society. Quarterly — NY Hist Soc Quar
New York Historical Society. Quarterly — NYHS
New York Historical Society. Quarterly — NYHSQ
New York Historical Society. Quarterly Bulletin — NYHSQB
New York History — New York Hist
New York History — NewYH
New York History — NY His
New York History — NY Hist
New York History — NYH
New York Horticultural Review — New York Hort Rev
New York Journal of Dentistry — NY J Dent
New York Journal of Mathematics — New York J Math
New York Journal of Medicine — N York J Med
New York Language Association. Bulletin — NYLAB
New York Law Forum — NY L F
New York Law Forum — NY Law Forum
New York Law Forum — NYF
New York Law Journal — LJ
New York Law Journal — NY Law J
New York Law Journal — NYLJ
New York Law Journal Digest Annotator — New York Law J Dig Annot
New York Law Review — NY Law R
New York Law Review — NY Law Rev
New York Law Review — NYL Rev
New York Law School. International Law Society. Journal — NY L Sch Intl L Socy J
New York Law School. Journal of International and Comparative Law — NY L Sch J Intl and Comp L
New York Law School. Journal of International and Comparative Law — NYJ Int'l & Comp L
New York Law School. Law Review — New York Law School Law R
New York Law School. Law Review — NY L S L Rev
New York Law School. Law Review — NY L Sch L Rev
New York Law School. Law Review — NYL School Rev
New York Law School. Law Review — NYLSLR
New York Library Association. Bulletin — NY Lib Assn Bul
New York Literary Forum — NY Lit For
New York Magazine — New York
New York Magazine — NY
New York Medical and Physical Journal — NY Med Phys J
New York Medical College and Flower Hospital Bulletin — NY Med Coll Flower Hosp Bull
New York Medical Journal — N York Med J
New York Medical Journal — N York Med Journ
New York Medical Journal — New York Med J
New York Medical Journal — NY Med J
New York Medical Journal and Obstetrical Review — NY Med J Obstet Rev
New York Medical Quarterly — NY Med Quart
New York Medical Times — New York Med Times
New York Medicine — NY Med
New York Microscopical Society. Journal — NY Micro Soc J
New York Mineralogical Club. Bulletin — NY Miner Club B
New York Miscellaneous Reports — Misc
New York Miscellaneous Reports. Second Series — Misc 2d
New York Newsday — NNEW
New York Observer — NYO
New York Philharmonic Program Notes — NY Phil
New York Post — NYP
New York Produce Review and American Creamery — NY Prod R
New York Produce Review and American Creamery — NY Prod Rev Am Creamery
New York Public Library. Branch Library Book News — NY Pub Lib Br Lib Bk News
New York Public Library. Bulletin — NYPL Bull
New York Public Library. New Technical Books — NY New Tech Bks
New York Quarterly — New Y Q
New York Quarterly — NYQ
New York Reports — NY
New York Reports [*New York*] — NYR
New York Reports. Second Series — NY 2d
New York Review of Books — GTRB
New York Review of Books — New Y R B
New York Review of Books — NY Rev Bks
New York Review of Books — NY Rev Book
New York Review of Books — NY Rev Books
New York Review of Books — NY Review
New York Review of Books — NYR
New York Review of Books — NYR Bks
New York Review of Books — NYR of Bk
New York Review of Books — NYRB
New York Sea Grant Law and Policy Journal — NY Sea Grant L and Pol'y J
New York Society for the Experimental Study of Education. Yearbook — NY Soc Exp Study Ed Yrbk
New York Staatszeitung — NYSZ
New York (State) Agricultural Experiment Station. Circular — New York Agric Exp Sta Circ
New York State Agricultural Experiment Station (Geneva). Annual Report — NY State Agric Exp Stn (Geneva) Annu Rep
New York State Agricultural Experiment Station (Geneva, New York). Bulletin — NY State Agric Exp Stn Geneva NY Bull

New York State Agricultural Experiment Station. Publications — NY State Ag Exp
New York State Agricultural Experiment Station. Seed Research Circular — NY State Agric Exp Stn Seed Res Circ
New York State Agricultural Experiment Station. Special Report — NY State Agric Exp Stn Spec Rep
New York State Agricultural Experiment Station. Special Report (Geneva) — NY State Agric Exp Stn Spec Rep Geneva
New York State Agricultural Society. Transactions — NY St Agr Soc Tr
New York State Association of Milk and Food Sanitarians. Annual Report — NY State Assoc Milk Food Sanit Annu Rep
New York State Association of Milk Sanitarians. Annual Report — NY State Assoc Milk Sanit Annu Rep
New York State Bar Journal — NY St BJ
New York State Bar Journal — NY State Bar J
New York State Bar Journal — NYSB J
New York State Cabinet of Natural History. Annual Report. Regents University — NY St Cab An Rp
New York State College of Ceramics. Ceramic Experiment Station. Bulletin — NY State Coll Ceramics Ceramic Expt Sta Bull
New York State College of Forestry. Syracuse University. Bulletin — NY State Coll For Syracuse Univ Bull
New York State Conservation Department. Biological Survey — NY State Conserv Dep Biol Surv
New York State Conservationist — NY State Conserv
New York State Dental Journal — NY State Dent J
New York State Department of Agriculture. Nature Study Bulletin — New York State Dep Agric Nat Stud Bull
New York State Department of Conservation. Water Resources Commission. Bulletin — NY State Dep Conserv Water Resour Comm Bull
New York State Department of Environmental Conservation. Basin Planning Report. Series ARB — NY State Dep Environ Conserv Basin Plann Rep ARB
New York State Department of Environmental Conservation. Basin Planning Report. Series ORB — NY State Dep Environ Conserv Basin Plann Rep ORB
New York State Department of Environmental Conservation. Bulletin — NY State Dep Environ Conserv Bull
New York State Department of Environmental Conservation. Environmental Quality Research and Development Unit. Technical Paper — NY State Dep Environ Conserv Environ Qual Res Dev Unit Tech P
New York State Department of Environmental Conservation. Technical Paper — NY State Dep Environ Conserv Tech Pap
New York State Department of Farms and Markets. Publications — NY Farms & Markets Dept
New York State Department of Health. Annual Report. Division of Laboratories and Research — NY State Dep Health Annu Rep Div Lab Res
New York State Department of Health. Division of Laboratories and Research. Annual Report — NY State Dep Health Div Lab Res Annu Rep
New York State Department of Health. Division of Laboratories and Research. Operations Data — NY State Dep Health Lab Res Oper Data
New York State Department of Labor. Division of Industrial Hygiene. Monthly Review — NY State Dep Labor Div Ind Hyg Mon Rev
New York State Department of Labor. Monthly Review. Division of Industrial Hygiene — NY State Dep Labor Mon Rev Div Ind Hyg
New York State Department of Transport. Research Report — NY Dep Transp Res Rep
New York State Education — NY State Ed
New York State Flower Growers. Bulletin — NY State Flower Growers Bull
New York State Flower Industries. Bulletin — NY State Flower Ind Bull
New York State Fruit Growers' Association. Proceedings — New York State Fruit Growers Assoc Proc
New York State Geologist. Annual Report — NY St G An Rp
New York State Historical Association. Proceedings — NY St His As
New York State Historical Association. Quarterly Journal — NY St His As Q J
New York State Historical Association. Quarterly Journal — NY St Hist Assn J
New York State Horticultural Society. Proceedings — NY State Horti Soc Proc
New York State Journal of Medicine — New York J Med
New York State Journal of Medicine — New York State J Med
New York State Journal of Medicine — NY J Med
New York State Journal of Medicine — NY St J Med
New York State Journal of Medicine — NY State J Med
New York State Museum — NY St Mus
New York State Museum and Science Service. Bulletin — NY State Mus Sci Serv Bull
New York State Museum and Science Service. Bulletin. Circular — NY State Mus and Sci Service Bull Circ
New York State Museum and Science Service. Circular — NY State Mus Sci Serv Circ
New York State Museum and Science Service. Educational Leaflet — NY State Mus Sci Serv Educ Leafl
New York State Museum and Science Service. Map and Chart Series — New York State Mus and Sci Service Map and Chart Ser
New York State Museum and Science Service. Map and Chart Series — NY State Mus Sci Serv Map Chart Ser
New York State Museum and Science Service. Memoir — New York State Mus and Sci Service Mem
New York State Museum and Science Service. Memoir — NY State Mus Sci Serv Mem
New York State Museum. Bulletin — NY State Mus Bull
New York State Museum Circular. Handbook — NY State Mus Circ Handb
New York State Museum. Map and Chart Series — NY State Mus Map Chart Ser
New York State Museum. Memoir — NY State Mus Mem
New York State Museum Memoirs — New York State Mus Mem
New York State Museum of Natural History. Annual Report — NY St Mus An Rp
New York State Nurse — NY State Nurse
New York State Register — NY St Reg
New York State Science Service. Report of Investigation — NY State Sci Service Rept Inv
New York State Science Service. University of the State of New York. Report of Investigation — NY State Sci Serv Univ State NY Report Invest
New York State University College of Forestry. Syracuse University. Technical Publication — NY State Coll For Syracuse Univ Tech Publ
New York State University College of Forestry. Syracuse University. Technical Publication — NY State Univ Coll For Syracuse Univ Tech Publ
New York State Water Power and Control Commission. Bulletin — NY Water Power Control Comm Bull
New York State Water Resources Commission. Basin Planning Report — NY State Water Resour Comm Basin Plann Rep
New York State Water Resources Commission. Basin Planning Report. Series ORB — NY State Water Resour Comm Basin Plann Rep ORB
New York State Water Resources Commission. Bulletin — NY Water Resour Comm Bull
New York Stock Exchange. Fact Book — NYSE Fact
New York Stock Exchange Guide. Commerce Clearing House — NYSE Guide CCH
New York Sun — NYS
New York Theatre Critics. Reviews — NY Theat Cr
New York Times — NY Times
New York Times — NYT
New York Times — NYTIA
New York Times Biographical File [*Database*] — NYTBIO
New York Times Biographical Service — NY Times Biog Service
New York Times Book Review — N York Times Book Revw
New York Times Book Review — New York Times Book Rev
New York Times Book Review — NY Times
New York Times Book Review — NY Times Bk R
New York Times Book Review — NY Times Book Rev
New York Times Book Review — NY Times R
New York Times Book Review — NYBR
New York Times Book Review — NYT
New York Times Book Review — NYTB
New York Times Book Review — NYTBR
New York Times Book Review — TBR
New York Times Literary Supplement — NYTLS
New York Times Magazine — New York Times Mag
New York Times Magazine — NY Times M
New York Times Magazine — NY Times Mag
New York Times Magazine — NYTM
New York Times Magazine — NYTMag
New York Times Magazine Section — NYTMS
New York Times. National Edition — NY Times N
[*The*] **New York Times (New York Edition)** — NY Times NY Ed
New York Uniform City Court Act — Uniform City Ct Act
New York Uniform District Court Act — Uniform Dist Ct Act
New York Uniform Justice Court Act — Uniform Just Ct Act
New York University. Conference on Labor — NYU Conf Lab
New York University. Education Quarterly — NYU Educ Q
New York University. Education Quarterly — NYUEQ
New York University. Institute on Federal Taxation — NYU Inst Fed Tax
New York University. Institute on Federal Taxation — NYU Inst Fed Taxation
New York University. Institute on Federal Taxation — NYU Inst on Fed Tax
New York University. Intramural Law Review — NYU Intra L Rev
New York University. Intramural Law Review — NYU Intramur L Rev
New York University. Journal of Dentistry — NY Univ J Dent
New York University. Journal of International Law and Politics — New York Univ J Internat Law and Politics
New York University. Journal of International Law and Politics — NY Univ J of Internat L and Polit
New York University. Journal of International Law and Politics — NYU J Int L & Pol
New York University. Journal of International Law and Politics — NYU J Int L & Politics
New York University. Journal of International Law and Politics — NYU J Int'l L & Pol
New York University. Journal of International Law and Politics — NYUJ Int'l Law & Pol
New York University. Law Quarterly Review — NYU Law Q Rev
New York University. Law Quarterly Review — NYUL Qu Rev
New York University. Law Quarterly Review — NYULQ Rev
New York University Law Review — INYL
New York University. Law Review — New York Univ Law R
New York University Law Review — New York Univ Law Rev
New York University. Law Review — NY Univ L Rev
New York University. Law Review — NYL
New York University. Law Review — NYU L Rev
New York University. Law Review — NYULR
New York University Medical Center News — NYU Med Cent N
New York University. Research Bulletin in Commercial Education — NY Univ Res B
New York University. Review of Law and Social Change — NYU Rev L & Soc
New York University. Review of Law and Social Change — NYU Rev L and Soc Ch
New York University. Review of Law and Social Change — NYU Rev L & Soc Change
New York University. Review of Law and Social Change — NYU Rev Law & Soc C
New York University. Slavic Papers — NYU Slav P
New York University. Studies in Comparative Literature — NYU Univ Stud Comp Lit
New York University Studies in Near Eastern Civilization — New York Univ Stud Near East Civiliz

New York Water Power and Control Commission. Bulletin — NY Water Power and Control Comm Bull
New York World — NYW
New York World Journal Tribune — NYWJT
New Yorker — GTNY
New Yorker — NY
[The] **New Yorker (New York)** — NYNY
New York's Food and Life Sciences Bulletin — NY Food Life Sci Bull
New York's Food and Life Sciences Quarterly — NY Fd Life Sci Q
New York's Food and Life Sciences Quarterly — NY Food Life Sci Q
New Zealand Agricultural Science — New Zealand Agric Sci
New Zealand Agricultural Science — NZ Agr Sci
New Zealand Agricultural Science — NZ Agric Sci
New Zealand Agriculturist — NZ Agricst
New Zealand Antarctic Record — NZ Antarct Rec
New Zealand Architect — New Zealand Archt
New Zealand Architect — NZ Arch
New Zealand Architect — NZ Archit
New Zealand Beekeeper — NZ Beekeep
New Zealand Beekeeper — NZ Beekpr
New Zealand Beekeepers' Journal — NZ Beekprs J
New Zealand Bird Banding Scheme. Annual Report — NZ Bird Banding Scheme Annu Rep
New Zealand Building Economist — NZ Bu Econ
New Zealand Building Inspector — NZ Bu Insp
New Zealand Business Conditions — NZ Bus Con
New Zealand Cartographic Journal — NZ Cartogr J
New Zealand Chiropractic Journal — NZ Chiro J
New Zealand Coal — NZ Coal
New Zealand Commerce — NZ Com
New Zealand Commerce — NZC
New Zealand Commercial Grower — NZ Com Grow
New Zealand Commercial Grower — NZ Commer Grow
New Zealand Concrete Construction — NZ Conc Constr
New Zealand Conference. Australasian Institute of Mining and Metallurgy — NZ Conf Australas Inst Min Metall
New Zealand Dental Journal — NZ Dent J
New Zealand. Department of Agriculture. Report — NZ Dep Agric Rep
New Zealand. Department of Health. Special Report Series — NZ Dep Health Spec Rep Ser
New Zealand. Department of Internal Affairs. Wildlife Publication — NZ Dep Intern Aff Wildl Publ
New Zealand. Department of Maori Affairs. Annual Report — NZ Dept Maori Aff Ann Rep
New Zealand. Department of Scientific and Industrial Research. Applied Biochemistry Division. Technical Report — NZ Dep Sci Ind Res Appl Biochem Div Tech Rep
New Zealand. Department of Scientific and Industrial Research. Bulletin — New Zeal Dep Sci Ind Res Bull
New Zealand. Department of Scientific and Industrial Research. Bulletin — NZ Dep Sci Ind Res Bull
New Zealand. Department of Scientific and Industrial Research. Chemistry Division. Report — NZ Dep Sci Ind Res Chem Div Rep
New Zealand. Department of Scientific and Industrial Research. Crop Research News — NZ Dep Sci Ind Res Crop Res News
New Zealand. Department of Scientific and Industrial Research. Discussion Paper — NZ Dep Sci Ind Res Discuss Pap
New Zealand. Department of Scientific and Industrial Research. Dominion Laboratory. Report DL — NZ Dep Sci Ind Res Dom Lab Rep DL
New Zealand. Department of Scientific and Industrial Research. Geological Survey. Paleontological Bulletin — NZ Dep Sci Ind Res Geol Surv Paleontol Bull
New Zealand. Department of Scientific and Industrial Research. Geophysics Division. Report — NZ Dep Sci Ind Res Geophys Div Rep
New Zealand. Department of Scientific and Industrial Research. Geophysics Division. Technical Note — NZ Dep Sci Ind Res Geophys Div Tech Note
New Zealand. Department of Scientific and Industrial Research. Industrial Processing Division. Report — NZ Dep Sci Ind Res Ind Process Div Rep
New Zealand. Department of Scientific and Industrial Research. Information Series — NZ Dep Sci Ind Res Inf Ser
New Zealand. Department of Scientific and Industrial Research. Report — NZ Dep Sci Ind Res Rep
New Zealand. Department of Statistics. Transport Statistics — NZ Dep Stat Transp Stat
New Zealand Director-General of Forests. Report — NZ Dir Gen For Rep
New Zealand Draughtsman — NZ Draughtsman
New Zealand Ecological Society. Proceedings — NZ Ecol Soc Proc
New Zealand Economic Papers — New Zealand Econ Pap
New Zealand Economic Papers — NZEP
New Zealand Economic Statistics — NZ Econ Stat
New Zealand Electrical Journal — NZ Electr J
New Zealand Electron — NZ Elect
New Zealand Electronics Review — NZ Elect Rev
New Zealand Electronics Review — NZ Electron Rev
New Zealand Electronics. Supplement to Electrical Industry — NZ Electronics
New Zealand Energy Journal — NZ Energ J
New Zealand Energy Journal — NZ Energy J
New Zealand Energy Research and Development Committee. Newsletter — NZ Energy Res Dev Comm Newsl
New Zealand. Energy Research and Development Committee. Report — NZ Energy Res Dev Comm Rep
New Zealand Engineering — NZ Eng
New Zealand Engineering — NZ Engng
New Zealand Engineering News — NZ Eng News
New Zealand Entomologist — NZ Ent
New Zealand Entomologist — NZ Entomol
New Zealand Environment — NZ Environ
New Zealand Family Physician — NZ Fam Phys
New Zealand Family Physician — NZ Fam Physician
New Zealand Farmer — NZ Farmer
New Zealand. Federation of Labour. Bulletin — NZ Fed Lab Bull
New Zealand Fertiliser Journal — NZ Fert
New Zealand Fertiliser Journal — NZ Fert J
New Zealand Financial Review — NZ Fin Rev
New Zealand Financial Review — NZ Financ Rev
New Zealand Fisheries. Research Division. Fisheries Research Bulletin — NZ Fish Res Div Fish Res Bull
New Zealand Foreign Affairs Review — NFV
New Zealand Foreign Affairs Review — NZ For Affairs R
New Zealand Foreign Affairs Review — NZ Foreign Aff Rev
New Zealand Forest Research Institute. Forest Service Mapping. Series 6 — NZ For Res Inst For Serv Mapp Ser 6
New Zealand. Forest Service. Forest Research Institute. FRI Symposium — NZ For Serv For Res Inst FRI Symp
New Zealand. Forest Service. Forest Research Institute. Technical Paper — NZ For Serv For Res Inst Tech Pap
New Zealand. Forest Service. Information Series — NZ For Serv Inf Ser
New Zealand. Forest Service. Report of the Director-General of Forests — NZ For Serv Rep Dir-Gen For
New Zealand. Forest Service. Report of the Forest Research Institute — NZ For Serv Rep For Res Inst
New Zealand. Forest Service. Research Leaflet — NZ For Serv Res Leafl
New Zealand. Forest Service. Technical Paper — NZ For Serv Tech Pap
New Zealand Forestry Research Notes — NZ For Res Notes
New Zealand Fruit and Product Journal — NZ Fruit and Prod
New Zealand Furniture — NZ Furn
New Zealand Gardener — NZ Gard
New Zealand Genealogist — NZ Geneal
New Zealand Genetical Society Newsletter — New Zealand Genet Soc Newslett
New Zealand Geochemical Group. Newsletter — NZ Geochem Group Newsl
New Zealand Geographer — NZ Geogr
New Zealand Geographer — NZGG-A
New Zealand. Geological Survey. Bulletin — New Zeal Geol Surv Bull
New Zealand. Geological Survey. Bulletin — NZ Geol Surv Bull
New Zealand. Geological Survey. Industrial Minerals and Rocks — NZ Geol Surv Ind Miner Rocks
New Zealand. Geological Survey. Miscellaneous Series. Map — NZ Geol Surv Misc Ser Map
New Zealand. Geological Survey. Report — NZ Geol Surv Rep
New Zealand Herald — NZ He
New Zealand Home and Building — NZ Home and Bu
New Zealand Home and Building — NZ Home and Build
New Zealand Hospital — NZ Hosp
New Zealand. Institute for Turf Culture. Greenkeeping Research Committee. Reporton Greenkeeping Research — NZ Inst Turf Cult Greenkeep Res Comm Rep Greenkeep Res
New Zealand Institution of Agricultural Science. Bulletin — NZ Agi Sci
New Zealand Institution of Engineers. Proceedings of Technical Groups — NZ Inst Eng Proc Tech Groups
New Zealand Institution of Engineers. Transactions — NZ Inst Eng Trans
New Zealand Interface — NZ Inter
New Zealand International Review — NZ Int Rev
New Zealand Jewish Chronicle — NZJC
New Zealand Journal of Adult Learning — NZ J Adult Learn
New Zealand Journal of Agricultural Research — NZ J Agr Re
New Zealand Journal of Agricultural Research — NZ J Agr Res
New Zealand Journal of Agricultural Research — NZ J Agric Res
New Zealand Journal of Agricultural Research — NZ Jl Agric Res
New Zealand Journal of Agriculture — J Ag New Zealand
New Zealand Journal of Agriculture — New Zealand J Agric
New Zealand Journal of Agriculture — NZ J Agr
New Zealand Journal of Agriculture — NZ J Agric
New Zealand Journal of Agriculture — NZ Jl Agric
New Zealand Journal of Archaeology — NZ J Archaeol
New Zealand Journal of Botany — New Zealand J Bot
New Zealand Journal of Botany — NZ J Bot
New Zealand Journal of Botany — NZ Jl Bot
New Zealand Journal of Business — NZ J Bus
New Zealand Journal of Business — NZ Jnl Bus
New Zealand Journal of Crop and Horticultural Science — NZ J Crop H
New Zealand Journal of Crop and Horticultural Science — NZ J Crop Hortic Sci
New Zealand Journal of Dairy Science and Technology — NZ J Dairy
New Zealand Journal of Dairy Science and Technology — NZ J Dairy Sci
New Zealand Journal of Dairy Science and Technology — NZ Jnl D Sci
New Zealand Journal of Dairy Science and Technology — NZJ Dairy Sci Technol
New Zealand Journal of Dairy Technology — NZ J Dairy Technol
New Zealand Journal of Ecology — NZ J Ecol
New Zealand Journal of Educational Studies — NZ J Educ
New Zealand Journal of Educational Studies — NZ J Educ Stud
New Zealand Journal of Experimental Agriculture — NA Jl Expl Agric
New Zealand Journal of Experimental Agriculture — NZ J Exp Agric
New Zealand Journal of Family Planning — NZ J Fam Plann
New Zealand Journal of Forestry — New Zealand J For
New Zealand Journal of Forestry — NZ J For
New Zealand Journal of Forestry Science — NZ J For Sci
New Zealand Journal of Forestry Science — NZFSA
New Zealand Journal of French Studies — NZ J Fr Stud
New Zealand Journal of Geography — NZ J Geogr
New Zealand Journal of Geology and Geophysics — New Zeal J Geol Geophys

New Zealand Journal of Geology and Geophysics — New Zealand Jour Geology and Geophysics
New Zealand Journal of Geology and Geophysics — NZ J Geol
New Zealand Journal of Geology and Geophysics — NZ J Geol Geophys
New Zealand Journal of Health, Physical Education, and Recreation — NZ J Phys Educ
New Zealand Journal of Health, Physical Education, and Recreation — NZJHPER
New Zealand Journal of History — NeZ
New Zealand Journal of History — NZ J Hist
New Zealand Journal of Industrial Relations — NZ J Ind Relat
New Zealand Journal of Industrial Relations — NZ J Ind Relations
New Zealand Journal of Marine and Freshwater Research — NZ J Mar Freshw Res
New Zealand Journal of Marine and Freshwater Research — NZ J Mar Freshwater Res
New Zealand Journal of Marine and Freshwater Research — NZ J Mar Res
New Zealand Journal of Mathematics — New Zealand J Math
New Zealand Journal of Medical Laboratory Technology — NZ J Med Lab Technol
New Zealand Journal of Physiotherapy — NZ J Physiother
New Zealand Journal of Physiotherapy — NZ J Physiotherapy
New Zealand Journal of Public Administration — New Zealand J Publ Adm
New Zealand Journal of Public Administration — NZ J Pub Admin
New Zealand Journal of Public Administration — NZ J Public Admin
New Zealand Journal of Public Administration — NZJ Publ Adm
New Zealand Journal of Science — NZ J Sci
New Zealand Journal of Science — NZ Jl Sci
New Zealand Journal of Science — NZJSAB
New Zealand Journal of Science and Technology — New Zealand J Sci Tech
New Zealand Journal of Science and Technology — NZ J Sci Technol
New Zealand Journal of Science and Technology — NZ Jl Sci Technol
New Zealand Journal of Science and Technology. Section A — NZ J Sci Technol Sect A
New Zealand Journal of Science and Technology. Section B — NZ J Sci Technol Sect B
New Zealand Journal of Science and Technology. Section B. General Research — NZTBA
New Zealand Journal of Science (Dunedin) — New Zealand J Sci Dunedin
New Zealand Journal of Sports Medicine — NZ J Sports Med
New Zealand Journal of Technology — NZ J Technol
New Zealand Journal of Zoology — NZ J Zool
New Zealand Journal of Zoology — NZ Jl Zool
New Zealand Law Journal — New Zeal LJ
New Zealand Law Journal — NZ L J
New Zealand Law Journal — NZ Law J
New Zealand Libraries — N Zealand Lib
New Zealand Libraries — NZ Lib
New Zealand Libraries — NZ Libr
New Zealand Lincoln College. Technical Publication — NZ Lincoln Coll Tech Publ
New Zealand Listener — NZ List
New Zealand Local Government — NZ Loc Govt
New Zealand Local Government — NZ Local Gov
New Zealand Marine Department. Fisheries Research Division. Bulletin. New Series — NZ Mar Dep Fish Res Div Bull New Ser
New Zealand Marine Department. Fisheries Technical Report — NZ Mar Dep Fish Tech Rep
New Zealand Marine Department. Report — NZ Mar Dep Rep
New Zealand Marine News — NZ Mar News
New Zealand Mathematical Society Newsletter — New Zealand Math Soc Newslett
New Zealand Mathematics Magazine — New Zealand Math Mag
New Zealand Meat Producer — NZ Meat Prod
New Zealand Medical Journal — New Zeal Med J
New Zealand Medical Journal — New Zealand MJ
New Zealand Medical Journal — NZ Med J
New Zealand Medical Journal — NZMJA
New Zealand Medical Journal. Supplement — NZ Med J Suppl
New Zealand Ministry of Agriculture and Fisheries. Fisheries Technical Report — NZ Minist Agric Fish Fish Tech Rep
New Zealand Ministry of Agriculture and Fisheries. Report on Fisheries — NZ Minist Agric Fish Rep Fish
New Zealand. Ministry of Energy. Annual Report — NZ Min Ener Ann Rep
New Zealand National Bibliography — NZNB
New Zealand. National Radiation Laboratory. Environmental Radioactivity. Annual Report — NZ Natl Radiat Lab Environ Radioact Annu Rep
New Zealand Natural Sciences — NZ Nat Sci
New Zealand. Nature Conservation Council. Newsletter — NZ Nat Conserv Counc Newsl
New Zealand News — NZ News
New Zealand News Review — NZ News Rev
New Zealand Numismatic Journal — NZ Num J
New Zealand Numismatic Journal — NZNJ
New Zealand Nursing Forum — NZ Nurs Forum
New Zealand Nursing Journal — NZ Nurs J
New Zealand Oceanographic Institute. Collected Reprints — NZ Oceanogr Inst Collect Repr
New Zealand Oceanographic Institute. Memoir — NZ Oceanogr Inst Mem
New Zealand Oceanographic Institute. Oceanographic Field Report — NZOI Oceanographic Field Report
New Zealand Operational Research — New Zealand Oper Res
New Zealand Operational Research — NZ Oper Res
New Zealand Operational Research — NZOR
New Zealand Painter and Decorator — NZ Paint
New Zealand Pharmacy — NZ Pharm
New Zealand Plants and Gardens — New Zealand Pl Gard
New Zealand Plumbers Journal — NZ Plumb
New Zealand Population Review — NZ Pop
New Zealand Potato Bulletin — NZ Pot
New Zealand Potter — NZ Potter
New Zealand Psychic Gazette — NZPG
New Zealand Psychologist — NZ Psychol
New Zealand Purchasing and Materials Management Journal — NZ Purch
New Zealand Railway Observer — NZ Railw Obs
New Zealand Real Estate — NZ Real
New Zealand School Dental Service. Gazette — NZ Sch Dent Ser Gaz
New Zealand Science Abstracts — NZ Sci Abstr
New Zealand Science of Materials Conference. Proceedings — NZ Sci Mater Conf Proc
New Zealand Science Review — New Zealand Sci Rev
New Zealand Science Review — NZ Sci Rev
New Zealand Science Teacher — NZ Sci Teach
New Zealand Shadows — NZ Shadows
New Zealand Shipping Gazette — NZ Ship
New Zealand Slavonic Journal — NZ Slav J
New Zealand Slavonic Journal — NZSJ
New Zealand Social Worker — New Zealand Soc Wker
New Zealand Society for Earthquake Engineering. Bulletin — NZ Soc Earthquake Eng Bull
New Zealand Society of Soil Science. Proceedings — NZ Soc Soil Sci Proc
New Zealand Society of Soil Science. Proceedings. Conference — NZ Soc Soil Sci Proc Conf
New Zealand. Soil Bureau. Bibliographic Report — NZ Soil Bur Bibliogr Rep
New Zealand. Soil Bureau. Bulletin — NZ Soil Bur Bull
New Zealand. Soil Bureau. Scientific Report — NZ Soil Bur Sci Rep
New Zealand Soil News — NZ Soil News
New Zealand. Soil Survey Report — NZ Soil Surv Rep
New Zealand Speech Therapists' Journal — NZ Speech Ther J
New Zealand Speech Therapists' Journal — NZ Speech Therapist J
New Zealand Speleological Bulletin — NZ Speleol Bull
New Zealand Summer School in Laser Physics — NZ Summer Sch Laser Phys
New Zealand Surveyor — NZ Surv
New Zealand Timber Journal — NZ Timb J
New Zealand Timber Journal and Wood Products Review — NZ Timber J Wood Prod Rev
New Zealand Timber Worker — NZ Timb
New Zealand Tobacco Growers Journal. Tobacco Growers Federation — New Zealand Tobacco Growers J
New Zealand Tourism — NZ Tour
New Zealand Tourism Research Newsletter — NZ Tour Res
New Zealand Universities Law Review — NZ U L Rev
New Zealand Universities Law Review — NZ Univ L Rev
New Zealand Universities Law Review — NZ Univ Law Rev
New Zealand Universities Law Review — NZ Univ LR
New Zealand Universities Law Review — NZ Univs Law R
New Zealand Universities Law Review — NZULR
New Zealand Valuer — NZ Val
New Zealand Veterinary Journal — NEZTA
New Zealand Veterinary Journal — NZ Vet J
New Zealand Weed and Pest Control Conference. Proceedings — NZ Weed Pest Control Conf Proc
New Zealand Wheat Review — NZ Wheat Rev
New Zealand Wings — NZ Wings
New Zealand Woman's Weekly — NZ Womans Wkly
New Zealand's Tobacco Growers' Journal — NZ Tob Grow J
Newark Engineering Notes — Newark Eng Notes
Newberry Library. Bulletin — Newberry Lib Bul
Newberry Library. Bulletin — NLB
Newberry Library. Center for the History of the American Indian. Bibliographical Series — NLCHAIBS
Newcastle and Hunter District Historical Society. Journal and Proceedings — J Proc Newcastle Hunter Dist Hist Soc
Newcastle Chamber of Commerce Journal — Newcastle Ch Comm J
Newcastle Chamber of Commerce Journal — Newcastle Chamber of Commerce J
Newcastle Morning Herald — NMH
Newcastle School of Arts. Journal — J Newcastle Sch Arts
Newcastle Teachers College. Bulletin — Newcastle Teach Coll Bul
Newcastle Teachers College. Bulletin — Newcastle Teach Coll Bull
New-Church Review — NCR
Newcomen Society for the Study of the History of Engineering and Technology. Transactions — Newcomen Soc Study Hist Eng Technol Trans
Newcomen Society. Transactions — Newcomen Soc Trans
Newelectronics — Newel
New-England Galaxy — Newe
Newer Metal Industry [*Japan*] — Newer Met Ind
Newer Methods of Nutritional Biochemistry — Newer Methods Nutr Biochem
Newer Methods of Nutritional Biochemistry with Applications and Interpretations — Newer Methods Nutr Biochem Appl Interpret
Newfoundland and Labrador. Department of Mines, Agriculture, and Resources. Mineral Resources Division. Bulletin — Newfoundland and Labrador Mineral Resources Div Bull
Newfoundland and Labrador. Mineral Development Division. Report — Newfoundland Labrador Miner Dev Div Rep
Newfoundland and Labrador. Mineral Resources Division. Information Circular — Newfoundland Labrador Miner Resour Div Inf Circ
Newfoundland and Labrador. Mineral Resources Division. Mineral Resources Report — Newfoundland Labrador Miner Resour Div Miner Resour Rep

Newfoundland and Labrador. Mines Branch. Mineral Resources Report — Newfoundland Labrador Mines Branch Miner Resour Rep
Newfoundland and Prince Edward Island Reports — N & PEIR
Newfoundland and Prince Edward Island Reports [*Database*] — NFL
Newfoundland and Prince Edward Island Reports — Nfld & PEIR
Newfoundland. Department of Mines and Energy. Mineral Development Division. Report of Activities — Newfoundland Dep Mines Energy Miner Dev Div Rep Act
Newfoundland. Department of Mines and Resources. Geological Survey. Information Circular — Newfoundland Dep Mines Resour Geol Surv Inf Circ
Newfoundland Geological Survey. Bulletin — Newfoundland Geol Surv Bull
Newfoundland. Geological Survey. Information Circular — Newfoundland Geol Surv Inf Circ
Newfoundland. Geological Survey. Information Circular. Report — Newfoundland Geol Survey Inf Circ Rept
Newfoundland. Geological Survey. Report — Newfoundland Geol Surv Rep
Newfoundland Journal of Geological Education — Newfoundland J Geol Educ
Newfoundland. Mines Branch. Mineral Resources Report — Newfoundland Mines Branch Miner Resour Rep
Newfoundland Quarterly — Nfld Q
Newfoundland Teachers' Association. Bulletin — NTA Bul
Newfoundland Teachers' Association. Journal — NTAJ
Newman-Studien — Newm St
Newport Natural History Society. Proceedings — Newport N H Soc Pr
News Agencies — NA
News. American Jewish Historical Society — NAJHS
News. American Thoracic Society — News Am Thorac Soc
News and Comments [*American Academy of Pediatrics*] — News Comment
News and Information. Geological Society of America — News Info GSA
News and Letters — Nws Lettr
News and Observer — News Obser
News and Pesticide Review. National Agricultural Chemicals Association — News Pestic Rev Nat Agr Chem Ass
News and Views. Ohio League for Nursing — News Views Ohio League Nurs
News Bulletin and Calendar. Worchester Art Museum — Worcester Museum News
News Bulletin. Indian Dental Association — News Bull Indian Dent Assoc
News Bulletin. Society of Vertebrate Paleontology — News Bull Soc Vertebr Paleontol
News. Central Research Institute of Electrical Power Industry [*Japan*] — New Cent Res Inst Electr Power Ind
News. Centro Internacional de Mejoramiento de Maiz y Trigo — News CIMMYT
News Chronicle — NC
News Edition. American Chemical Society — News Ed Am Chem Soc
News for Farmer Cooperatives — News Farmer Coop
News for Farmer Cooperatives — News Farmer Coops
News from Behind the Iron Curtain — NBIC
News from Iceland — NEIC
News from International Resource Development, Incorporated — IRD News
News from Nowhere — News
News from Venture Development Corporation — Ventr Dev
News from Xinhua News Agency [*China*] — News Xinhua News Agency
News in Engineering — News Eng
News in Physiological Sciences — News Physiol Sci
News Inuit. News Releases from Inuit Tapirisat of Canada — NEIN
News Journal — News Jrl
News/Journal. Saskatchewan Mathematics Teachers' Society — NJ SMTS
News. Lepidopterists' Society — News Lepid Soc
News Letter. Association of Official Seed Analysts — News Lett Assoc Off Seed Anal
News Letter. Bulb Society — News Lett Bulb Soc
News Letter. Florence Nightingale International Nurses Association — News Lett Florence Nightingale Int Nurs Assoc
News Letter. India Population Project UP — News Lett India Popul Proj UP
News Letter. International College of Dentists — News Lett Int Coll Dent
News Letter. International Union of Biological Sciences — News Lett Int Union Biol Sci
News Letter. Population Centre (Bangalore) — News Lett Popul Cent (Bangalore)
News Letter. Powder Metallurgy Association of India — News Lett Powder Metall Assoc India
News Media and the Law — News Media and L
News National — Nws Nat
News Notes. American Society of Photogrammetry — News Notes Am Soc Photogramm
News Notes of California Libraries — News Notes Calif Libr
News Notes of California Libraries — News Notes Calif Libs
News. Nova Scotia Library Association — News NSLA
News of Geothermal Energy Conversion Technology [*United States*] — News Geotherm Energy Convers Technol
News of Literature and Fashion. Journal of Manners and Society, the Drama, the Fine Arts, Literature, Science. — News Lit Fashion
News of Norway — NENO
News of the Day — NOD
News of the North — NN
News on Sunday — NOS
News Release — NR
News/Retrieval For Your Information [*Database*] — FYI
News Review — NRv
News/Sun - Sentinel — N/Sun Sent
News Weekly — News W
Newscast Region 4. American Iris Society — Newscast Reg 4 Amer Iris Soc
Newsday — NEWD
Newsfront International — Newsfront
Newsletter. American Academy of Health Administration — Newsl Am Acad Health Adm
Newsletter. American Academy of Implant Dentistry — Newsl Am Acad Implant Dent
Newsletter. American Association of Equine Practitioners — Newsl Am Assoc Equine Pract
Newsletter. American Dialect Society — NADS
Newsletter. American Magnolia Society — Newslett Amer Magnolia Soc
Newsletter. American Schools of Oriental Research — Newsletter ASOR
Newsletter. American Society for Reformation Research — Newsl Am Soc Ref Res
Newsletter. American Symphony Orchestra League, Inc. — Newslet
Newsletter. American Theological Library Association — NATLA
Newsletter Argentina — New Argent
Newsletter. Association for Asian Studies — NAAS
Newsletter. Association of British Columbia Drama Educators — Newsl Assoc Br Col Drama Educ
Newsletter. Association of Official Seed Analysis — Newslett Ass Offic Seed Anal
Newsletter. Association of Official Seed Analysts — Newslett Assoc Off Seed Analysts
Newsletter. Australian and New Zealand Society of Nuclear Medicine — Newsl Aust NZ Soc Nucl Med
Newsletter. Australian Association for the History and Philosophy of Science — Newslett Austrl Assoc Hist Phil Sci
Newsletter. Australian Institute of Aboriginal Studies — Newsl Aust Inst Aborig St
Newsletter. British Universities Film and Video Council — Newsl Br Univ Film Video Counc
Newsletter. Canadian Council for International Cooperation — Newsl Can Counc Int Coop
Newsletter. Canadian Pulp and Paper Association. Technical Section — Newsl Can Pulp Pap Assoc Tech Sec
Newsletter. Commission of the European Communities — Newsl Comm Eur Communit
Newsletter. Commonwealth Geological Liaison Office — Newsl Commw Geol Liaison Off
Newsletter. Commonwealth Science Council. Earth Sciences Programme — Newsl Commonw Sci Counc Earth Sci Programme
Newsletter. Congregational Christian Historical Society — NCCHS
Newsletter. Copyright Society of Australia — NCSA
Newsletter. Council of Europe. Documentation Centre for Education in Europe — Newsl Counc Eur Doc Ctre Educ Eur
Newsletter. Environmental Mutagen Society — NEMSB
Newsletter. Environmental Mutagen Society — Newsl Environ Mutagen Soc
Newsletter. Folklore Society of Greater Washington. Supplement — NFSGWS
Newsletter for Research in Mental Health and Behavioral Sciences — Nl Res Men Health & Behav Sc
Newsletter for Targumic and Cognate Studies [*Toronto*] — NTCS
Newsletter for Ugaritic Studies — Newsletter Ug
Newsletter. Fusion Energy Foundation — Newsl Fusion Energy Found
Newsletter. Fusion Energy Foundation — NFEFD
Newsletter. Geological Society (London) — Newsl Geol Soc (London)
Newsletter. Geological Society of New Zealand — Newsl Geol Soc NZ
Newsletter. Geological Society of New Zealand — Newslett Geol Soc New Zealand
Newsletter. Geological Society of Zambia — Newsl Geol Soc Zambia
Newsletter. Geoscience Information Society — Newsl Geosci Inf Soc
Newsletter. Government of Western Australia. Mining — Newsl Gov West Aus
Newsletter. Hawaiian Botanical Garden Foundation — Newslett Hawaiian Bot Gard Found
Newsletter. Huntington Society of Canada — Newsl Huntington Soc Can
Newsletter. Indian Society for Nuclear Techniques in Agriculture and Biology — Newsl Indian Soc Nucl Tech Agric Biol
Newsletter. Indonesian Mining Association — Newsl Indones Min Assoc
Newsletter. International College of Dentists. India Section — Newsl Int Coll Dent India Sect
Newsletter. International Geological Correlation Programme. Project 156. Phosphorites — Newsl Int Geol Correl Programme Proj 156 Phosphorites
Newsletter. International Geological Correlation Programme. Project 167 — Newsl-IGCP Proj 167
Newsletter. International Rice Commission — Newsl Int Rice Comm
Newsletter. International Rice Commission — Newslett Int Rice Comm
Newsletter. International Society of Bassists — Newsl Int Soc Bass
Newsletter. International Society of Radiographers and Radiological Technicians — Newsl Int Soc Radiogr Radiol Tech
Newsletter. International Trombone Association — Newsl Int Tromb Assoc
Newsletter. International Union of Biological Sciences — Newsl Int Union Biol Sci
Newsletter. Isotopic Generator Information Centre [*France*] — Newsl Isot Generator Inf Cent
Newsletter. Kafka Society of America — NKSA
Newsletter. Labour History Association — Newsl Lab Hist Assoc
Newsletter. Language Teachers Association — Newsl Lang Teach Assoc
Newsletter. League for International Food Education — Newsl League Int Fd Educ
Newsletter. Lute Society of America — NLSA
Newsletter. Marine Technology Society — Newsl Mar Technol Soc
Newsletter. Nathaniel Hawthorne Society — Newsl Nathaniel Hawthorne Soc
Newsletter. NEA [*National Education Association*] **Computer Program Library** [*United States*] — Newsl NEA Comput Program Libr
Newsletter. NEA [*Nuclear Energy Agency*] **Data Bank** — Newsl NEA Data Bank
Newsletter. New Zealand Archaeological Association — Newsl New Zealand Archaeol Assoc
Newsletter. New Zealand Archaeological Association — Newsl NZ Archaeol Assoc
Newsletter. New Zealand Geochemical Group — Newsl NZ Geochem Group

Newsletter. New Zealand Mapkeepers Circle — Newsl NZ Map Circle
Newsletter. Norfolk Botanical Garden Society — Newslett Norfolk Bot Gard Soc
Newsletter of Biomedical Safety and Standards — Newsl Biomed Saf Stand
Newsletter of the Cooperative Investigations in the Mediterranean — Newsl Coop Invest Mediterr
Newsletter of the Democratic Left — Demo Left
Newsletter of Tree Improvement and Introduction — Newslett Tree Impr Introd
Newsletter on Comparative Studies of Communism — Newsletter Comp Stud Communism
Newsletter on Intellectual Freedom — Newsl Intellectual Freedom
Newsletter on Intellectual Freedom — NIF
Newsletter on Stratigraphy — Newslett Stratigr
Newsletter on the Application of Nuclear Methods in Biology and Agriculture [*Netherlands*] — Newsl Appl Nucl Methods Biol Agric
News-Letter. Peak District Mines Historical Society — Newsl Peak Dist Mines Hist Soc
Newsletter. Plant Propagators Society — Newslett Pl Propag Soc
Newsletter. Portuguese Industrial Association — NPI
Newsletter. Program on Public Conceptions of Science [*Harvard University*] — Newslett Program Publ Conc Sci
Newsletter. R and D in Uranium Exploration Techniques — Newsl R & D Uranium Explor Tech
Newsletter. Somerset Mines Research Group — Newsl Somerset Mines Res Group
Newsletter Soziale Kognition — Newsl Soz Kognit
Newsletter. Springfield Dental Society — Newsl Springfield Dent Soc
Newsletter. Teaching Language through Literature — NTLTL
Newsletter. Tokyo Book Development Centre — Newsl Tokyo Bk Dev Cen
Newsletter. Washington State Energy Office — Newsletter WSEO
Newsletter. Wildlife Disease Association — Newsl Wildl Dis Assoc
Newsletter. Wisconsin League for Nursing — Newsl Wis League Nurs
Newsletters of the Interdivisional Commission on History of the IAGA — Newslett Interdiv Comm Hist IAGA
Newsletters on Stratigraphy — Newsl Stratigr
Newspapers in Australian Libraries — NAL
Newsweek — GNEW
Newsweek — Newswk
Newsweek — Nw
Newsweek — NWK
Nexos (Mexico) — NSM
Next Year Country — Next Year
Nezelezne Kovy. Technickoekonomicky Zpravodaj [*Czechoslovakia*] — Nezelezne Kovy Technickoekon Zpravodaj
NFAIS (National Federation of Abstracting and Information Services) Bulletin — NFAIS Bull
NFAIS [*National Federation of Abstracting and Indexing Services*] **Newsletter** [*United States*] — NFAIS Newsl
NFAIS [*National Federation of Abstracting and Indexing Services*] **Newsletter** — NFNLA
NFCR [*National Foundation for Cancer Research*] **Cancer Research Association Symposia** — NFCR Cancer Res Assoc Symp
NFIB [*National Federation of Independent Business*] **Quarterly Economic Report** — NFI
NGTE (National Gas Turbine Establishment) Report [*British*] — NGTE Rep
NGU [*Norges Geologiske Undersoekelse*] **Skrifter** — NGU Skr
NHK [*Nippon Hoso Kyokai*] **Laboratories Note** — NHK Lab Note
NHK (Nippon Hoso Kyokai) Technical Monograph — NHOKA
NHK (Nippoon Hoso Kyokai) Technical Report — NHK Tech Rep
NHK [*Nippon Hoso Kyokai*] **Technical Journal** — NHK Tech J
NHK [*Nippon Hoso Kyokai*] **Technical Monograph** — NHK Tech Monogr
NIAAA (National Institute on Alcohol Abuse and Alcoholism) Research Monograph — NIAAA Res Monogr
Niagara Frontier — NiF
Niagara Historical Society. Publications — Niagara Hist Soc Publ
Nicaragua Indigena. Instituto Indigenista Nacional (Managua) — Nica Indig Managua
Nicaragua Instituto de Investigaciones Sismicas. Boletin — Nicar Inst Invest Sism Bol
Nicaragua Medica — Nicar Med
Nicaragua Odontologica — Nicar Odontol
Nicaragua Servicio Geologico Nacional. Boletin — Nicaragua Servicio Geol Nac Bol
Nicaraguan Perspectives (California) — NPC
Nicarauac Revista Cultural — NRC
Nice Historique — Nice Hi
Nice Historique — Nice Hist
Nice Medical — Nice Med
Nichidai Igaku Zasshi — Nich Ig Zass
Nichidai Koko Kagaku — NKOKD
Nichidai Shigaku — NISHB
Nicholls State University. Professional Papers Series. Biology — Nicholls State Univ Prof Pap Ser Biol
Nickel Berichte — Nickel Ber
Nickel Bulletin — Nickel Bull
Nickel Metallurgy. Symposium. Proceedings — Nickel Metall Symp Proc
Nickel. Spurenelement-Symposium — Nickel Spurenelem Symp
Nickel Steel Topics — Nickel Steel Top
Nickel Topics — Nickel Top
Nicko's Fruit Journal — Nickos Fruit J
NIDA Research Monograph — MIDAD
Niederbayerische Monatsschrift — N Bay Ms
Niederdeutsche Beitraege zur Kunstgeschichte — NBK
Niederdeutsche Beitraege zur Kunstgeschichte — NDBKG
Niederdeutsche Mitteilungen — Nd Mitt
Niederdeutsche Mitteilungen — NdM
Niederdeutsche Mitteilungen — Niederdeu Mit
Niederdeutsche Mitteilungen — NM
Niederdeutsche Studien — NdS
Niederdeutsche Zeitschrift fuer Volkskunde — NZV
Niederdeutsche Zeitschrift fuer Volkskunde und Blaetter fuer Niedersaechsische Heimatpflege — Nd Z Vk
Niederdeutsches Jahrbuch — Nd Jb
Niederdeutsches Jahrbuch — Ndd Jb
Niederdeutsches Jahrbuch — NJ
Niederdeutsches Jahrbuch — NJb
Niederdeutsches Jahrbuch fuer Volkskunde — Nd Jb
Niederdeutsches Wort — NDW
Niederlausitzer Floristische Mitteilungen — Niederlausitzer Florist Mitt
Niederoesterreichesche Imker — Niederoest Imker
Niederrheinische Gesellschaft fuer Natur und Heilkunde zu Bonn. Sitzungsberichte — Niederrhein Ges Bonn Szb
Niederrheinisches Jahrbuch — Nd Rhein Jb
Niederrheinisches Jahrbuch — Niederrhein Jahrb
Niederrheinisches Taschenbuch fuer Liebhaber des Schoenen und Guten — Niederrhein Taschenb Liebhaber Schoenen Guten
Niedersachsischer Zeitschriftennachweis [*Database*] — NZN
Niedersaechsisches Jahrbuch fuer Landesgeschichte — Niedersaechs Jahrb Landesgesch
Niedersaechsiches Jahrbuch fuer Landesgeschichte — NSJL
Niedersaechsische Neue Zeitungen von Gelehrten Sachen — Niedersaechs Neue Zeitungen Gel Sachen
Niedersaechsische Rechtspflege — Nds Rpfl
Niedersaechsisches Gesetz- und Verordnungsblatt — Nds GV Bl
Niedersaechsisches Gesetz- und Verordnungsblatt — NGV Bl
Niedersaechsisches Jahrbuch — Niedersaechs Jb
Niedersaechsisches Jahrbuch — NSJB
Niedersaechsisches Jahrbuch fuer Landesgeschichte — Nied Jb LG
Niedersaechsisches Jahrbuch fuer Landesgeschichte — NSJ
Niedersaechsisches Jahrbuch fuer Landesgeschichte — NSJLG
Niedersaechsisches Jahrbuch. Hildesheim — NSJBH
Niedersaechsisches Ministerialblatt — Niedersaechs Ministerialbl
Niedersaechsisches Zahnarzteblatt — Niedersachs Zahnarztebl
Niels Bohr. Collected Works [*Elsevier Book Series*] — NB
Nielsen Station Index [*Database*] — NSI
Nielsen Television Index [*Database*] — NTI
Nielson Researcher — Nielson Rs
Nieman Reports — INIE
Niemeyers Zeitschrift fuer Internationales Recht — Niem Z
Niemeyers Zeitschrift fuer Internationales Recht — Niemeyers Zeits F Int Recht
Niemeyers Zeitschrift fuer Internationales Recht — NZIR
Nien San. Annals. University of Cantho — Nien San Ann Univ Cantho
Niere im Kreislauf. Internationales Symposion der Deutschen Gesellschaft fuer Fortschritte auf dem Gebiet der Inneren Medizin — Niere Kreislauf Int Symp Dtsch Ges Fortschr Geb Inn Med
Nieren- und Hochdruckkrankheiten — Nieren- Hochdruckkr
Nieren- und Hochdruckkrankheiten — NIHOD
Nietzsche Studien — NietzscheS
Nietzsche-Studien — NS
Nieuw Archief voor Kerkelijke Geschiedenis — Ni AKG
Nieuw Archief voor Wiskunde — Nieuw Arch Wisk
Nieuw Burgerlijk Wetboek — NBW
Nieuw Europa. Tijdschrift van de Europese Beweging in Nederland — NWA
Nieuw Israelitisch Weekblad — NIW
Nieuw Magazijn van Handelsrecht — N M v H
Nieuw Nederlandsch Biografisch Woordenboek — NNBW
Nieuw Theologisch Tijdschrift — NTT
Nieuw Tijdschrift voor Wiskunde — Nieuw Tijdschr Wisk
Nieuw Vlaams Tijdschrift — NVT
Nieuwe Drentsche Volksalmanak — N Drent Volksalm
Nieuwe Gids — NG
Nieuwe Gids Bibliotheek. Verzameling Oorspronkelijke Bijdragen Op Het Gebied Van Letteren, Kunst, Wetenschap, en Wijsbegeerte — Nieuwe Gids Biblioth
Nieuwe Linie — LII
Nieuwe Natuur- en Geneeskundige Bibliotheek — Nieuwe Natuur Geneesk Biblioth
Nieuwe Rotterdamsche Courant — NRC
Nieuwe Stem — NStem
Nieuwe Taalgids — NT
Nieuwe Taalgids. Tijdschrift voor Neerlandici — NTg
Nieuwe Theologisch Tijdschrift — NThT
Nieuwe Theologische Studien — NThS
Nieuwe Theologische Studien — NThSt
Nieuwe Theologische Studien — NTS
Nieuwe Vaderlandsche Letteroefeningen — Nieuwe Vaderl Letteroefen
Nieuwe Verhandelingen van het Bataafsch Genootschap der Proefondervindelijke Wijsbegeerte — Nieuwe Verh Bataafsch Genoot Proefonderv Wijsbegeerte
Nieuwe West-Indische Gids — Nieuwe WIG
Nieuwe West-Indische Gids — NWIG
Nieuwe West-Indische Gids — WGI
Nieuwe West-Indishe Gids — NWG
Nieuw-Guinea Studien — NGS
Nieuws uit Japan — IEJ
Nieuws uit Zweden — NWI
Niger Developpement — Niger Dev
Nigeria and the Classics — N & C
Nigeria and the Classics — NC
Nigeria. Annual Report. Federal Department of Agricultural Research — Niger Annu Rep Fed Dep Agric Res

Nigeria. Annual Report. Federal Department of Agricultural Research — Nigeria Annu Rep Fed Dep Agric Res
Nigeria. Annual Report. Geological Survey Department — Niger Annu Rep Geol Surv Dep
Nigeria. Bulletin on Foreign Affairs — Nigeria Bull Foreign Affairs
Nigeria Cocoa Research Institute. Annual Report — Nigeria Cocoa Res Inst Annu Rep
Nigeria. Department of Forest Research. Programme of Work — Niger Dep For Res Programme Work
Nigeria. Department of Forest Research. Programme of Work — Nigeria Dep For Res Programme Work
Nigeria. Department of Forest Research. Technical Note — Niger Dep For Res Tech Note
Nigeria. Department of Forest Research. Technical Note — Nigeria Dep For Res Tech Note
Nigeria Federal Department of Agricultural Research. Memorandum — Niger Fed Dep Agric Res Memor
Nigeria Federal Department of Agricultural Research. Memorandum — Nigeria Fed Dep Agric Res Memo
Nigeria Federal Department of Fisheries. Annual Report — Nigeria Fed Dep Fish Annu Rep
Nigeria Federal Department of Fisheries. Federal Fisheries. Occasional Paper [*A publication*] — Nigeria Fed Dep Fish Fed Fish Occas Pap
Nigeria Federal Department of Forest Research. Annual Report — Nigeria Fed Dep For Res Annu Rep
Nigeria Federal Department of Forest Research. Research Paper (Forest Series) — Nigeria Fed Dep For Res Res Pap (For Ser)
Nigeria Federal Department of Forest Research. Research Paper (Savanna Series) — Nigeria Fed Dep For Res Res Pap (Savanna Ser)
Nigeria. Federal Institute of Industrial Research. Research Report — Niger Fed Inst Ind Res Res Rep
Nigeria. Federal Institute of Industrial Research. Technical Memorandum — Niger Fed Inst Ind Res Tech Memo
Nigeria Federation. Annual Report. Geological Survey — Niger Fed Annu Rep Geol Surv
Nigeria Forestry Information Bulletin — Nigeria For Inf Bull
Nigeria Geological Survey Division. Annual Report — Niger Geol Surv Div Annu Rep
Nigeria. Geological Survey. Records — Niger Geol Surv Rec
Nigeria Magazine — Nig
Nigeria Magazine — Niger Mag
Nigeria Magazine — Nigeria Mag
Nigeria Magazine — NigM
Nigeria Newsletter — Nigeria Newsl
Nigeria Newsletter — NNL
Nigeria Savanna Forestry Research Station. Samaru Zaria Annual Report — Nigeria Savanna For Res Stn Samaru Zaria Annu Rep
Nigeria Savanna Forestry Research Station. Series Research Paper — Nigeria Savanna For Res Stn Ser Res Pap
Nigeria Trade Journal — Nigeria Trade J
Nigerian Agricultural Journal — Niger Agric J
Nigerian Agricultural Journal — Nigerian Agr J
Nigerian Agricultural Journal — Nigerian Agric J
Nigerian Bar Journal — Nigerian Bar J
Nigerian Behavioural Sciences Journal — Niger Behav Sci J
Nigerian Dental Journal — Niger Dent J
Nigerian Entomologists' Magazine — Niger Entomol Mag
Nigerian Entomologists' Magazine — Nigerian Entomol Mag
Nigerian Field — NF
Nigerian Field — Niger Field
Nigerian Field — Niger Fld
Nigerian Forestry Information. Bulletin — Niger For Inform Bull
Nigerian Geographical Journal — Nig Geogr J
Nigerian Geographical Journal — Niger Geogr J
Nigerian Geographical Journal — Nigeria Geogr J
Nigerian Geographical Journal — Nigerian Geogr J
Nigerian Institute for Oil Palm Research. Annual Report — Niger Inst Oil Palm Res Annu Rep
Nigerian Institute for Oil Palm Research. Annual Report — Nigerian Inst Oil Palm Res Annu Rep
Nigerian Institute of Social and Economic Research — NISER
Nigerian Journal of Animal Production — Niger J Anim Prod
Nigerian Journal of Biochemistry — Niger J Biochem
Nigerian Journal of Contemporary Law — Nig J Contemp L
Nigerian Journal of Contemporary Law — Nigerian J Contemporary Law
Nigerian Journal of Economic and Social Studies — Nigerian J Econ and Social Studies
Nigerian Journal of Economic and Social Studies — Nigerian J Econ Soc Stud
Nigerian Journal of Economic and Social Studies — NJE
Nigerian Journal of Economic and Social Studies — NJESS
Nigerian Journal of Entomology — Niger J Entomol
Nigerian Journal of Entomology — Nigerian J Entomol
Nigerian Journal of Forestry — Niger J For
Nigerian Journal of Forestry — Nigerian J For
Nigerian Journal of International Affairs — Nigerian J Int Affairs
Nigerian Journal of International Studies — Nigerian J Internat Studies
Nigerian Journal of Islam — Nigerian J Islam
Nigerian Journal of Islam — NiJ
Nigerian Journal of Natural Sciences — Niger J Nat Sci
Nigerian Journal of Nutritional Sciences — Niger J Nutr Sci
Nigerian Journal of Paediatrics — Nigerian J Paediatr
Nigerian Journal of Pharmacy — Niger J Pharm
Nigerian Journal of Plant Protection — Niger J Plant Prot
Nigerian Journal of Public Affairs — Nigerian J Public Affairs
Nigerian Journal of Science — Niger J Sci
Nigerian Journal of Science — Nigerian J Sci
Nigerian Law Journal — Nigerian Law J
Nigerian Law Journal — NLJ
Nigerian Libraries — Nigerian Lib
Nigerian Libraries — Nigerian Libr
Nigerian Libraries — Nigerian Librs
Nigerian Libraries — Nigerian Libs
Nigerian Medical Journal — Niger Med J
Nigerian Medical Journal — Nigerian Med J
Nigerian Nurse — Niger Nurse
Nigerian Stored Products Research Institute. Annual Report — Nigerian Stored Prod Res Inst Annu Rep
Night and Day — ND
Nigiqpaq Northwind News [*Barrow, Alaska*] — NNNE
NIH [*National Institutes of Health*] **Consensus Development. Conference Summary** [*A publication*] — NIH Consensus Dev Conf Summ
NIH [National Institute of Health] Consensus Statement — NIH Consens Statement
NIH [National Institute of Health] Guide for Grants and Contracts — NIH Guide Grants Contracts
NIHAE [*National Institute of Health Administration and Education*] **Bulletin** — NIHAE Bull
Nihon Bukkyo — NB
Nihon Chikusan Gakkai Ho/Japanese Journal of Zootechnical Science — Nihon Chikusan Gakkai Ho Jap J Zootech
Nihon Daigaku Nojuigakubu Gakujutsu Kenkyu Hokoku — NIPDA
Nihon Juishikai Zasshi/Journal. Japan Veterinary Medical Association — Nihon Juishikai Zasshi J Jap Vet Med Assoc
Nihon Oyo Dobutsu Konchu Gakkai Shi/Japanese Journal of Applied Entomology and Zoology — Nihon Oyo Dobutsu Konchu Gakkai Shi Jap J Appl Entomol Zool
Nihon Rekishi — NiR
Nihon Ringakukai Shi. Journal. Japanese Forestry Society — Nihon Ringakkai Shi J Jap For Soc
Nihon Sanshigaku Zasshi. Journal of Sericultural Science of Japan — Nihon Sanshigaku Zasshi J Seric Sci Jap
Nihon Seirigaku Zasshi/Journal. Physiological Society of Japan — Nihon Seirigaku Zasshi Jap
Nihon Senchu Kenkyukai Shi/Japanese Journal of Nematology — Nihon Senchu Kenkyukai Shi Jap J Nematol
Nihon Shokubutsu Byori Gakkaiho/Annals. Phytopathological Society of Japan — Nihon Shokubutsu Byori Gakkaiho Ann Phytopathol Soc Jap
Nihon University. Dental Journal [*Japan*] — Nihon Univ Dent J
Nihon University. Journal of Medicine — Nihon Univ J Med
Nihon University. Journal of Medicine — NUMDA
Nihon University Journal of Oral Science — Nihon Univ J Oral Sci
Nihon University. Journal of Radiation Medicine and Biology [*Japan*] — Nihon Univ J Radiat Med Biol
Nihon University. Medical Journal [*Japan*] — Nihon Univ Med J
Nihon University. Mishima College of Humanities and Sciences. Annual Report of the Researches — Nihon Univ Mishima Coll Humanit Sci Annu Rep Res
Nihon University. Mishima College of Humanities and Sciences. Annual Report of the Researches. Natural Sciences — Nihon Univ Mishima Coll Humanit Sci Annu Rep Res Nat Sci
Nihonkai Mathematical Journal — Nihonkai Math J
Niigata Agricultural Science — Niigata Agr Sci
Niigata Agricultural Science — Niigata Agric Sci
Niigata Agriculture and Forestry Research — Niigata Agric For Res
Niigata Dental Journal — Niigata Dent J
Niigata Medical Journal [*Japan*] — Niigata Med J
Niigata University. Science Reports. Series E (Geology and Mineralogy) — Niigata Univ Sci Rep Ser E
Niigata-Ken Kogai Kenkyusho Kenkyu Hokoku — NIKHD
Nijhoff International Philosophy Series — Nijhoff Internat Philos Ser
Nikkei Weekly — Nikkei Wkly
Nikko Materials — Nikko Mater
Nikolaevskii Korablestroitel'nyi Institut. Trudy — Nikolaev Korablestroit Inst Tr
Niles' Register — Niles Reg
NIM [*National Institute for Metallurgy*] **Research Digest** [*United States*] — NIM Res Dig
NIMO [*Nederlands Instituut voor Maatschappelijke Opbouw*] **Kroniek. Nieuwsbulletin** — VBA
Nineteenth Century — N Cent
Nineteenth Century — NC
Nineteenth Century — Nine Ct
Nineteenth Century — Ninet Cent
Nineteenth Century — Nineteenth Cent
Nineteenth Century and After — NC
Nineteenth Century and After — Nineteenth Cent After
Nineteenth Century Literary Criticism — NCLC
Nineteenth Century Music — NC
Nineteenth Century Music — Nine Cen Mus
Nineteenth Century Music — Nine Ct Mus
Nineteenth Century Review — NCR
Nineteenth Century Theatre Research — Nineteenth Cent Theat Res
Nineteenth-Century Fiction — NCF
Nineteenth-Century Fiction — Nine-Ct Fic
Nineteenth-Century French Studies — NCFS
Nineteenth-Century French Studies — Nine-Ct Fr
Nineteenth-Century Literature — PNCL
Nineteenth-Century Theatre Research — NCTR
Nineteenth-Century Theatre Research — Nine Ct The
NINF Informasjon. Norsk Institutt for Naeringsmiddelforskning — NINF Informasjon Nor Inst Naeringsmidforsk
Ninth District Quarterly — Ninth District Q

Ninth Plan for Economic and Social Development, 1984-1988 (France) — French Pln
NIOSH/OSHA Current Intelligence Bulletin — NIOSH/OSHA Current Intell Bull
NIOSH [*National Institute for Occupational Safety and Health*] **Survey** — NIOSH Surv
NIOSH [*National Institute for Occupational Safety and Health*] **Technical Information Center Database** — NIOSHTIC
NIOSH [*National Institute for Occupational Safety and Health*] **Technical Information** — NIOSH Tech Inf
NIPH [*National Institute of Public Health*] **Annals** — NIPH Ann
NIPH (National Institute of Public Health) Annals (Oslo) — NIPH (Natl Inst Public Health) Ann (Oslo)
Nippon Acta Radiologica [*Japan*] — Nippon Acta Radiol
Nippon Butsuri Gakkaishi — NBGSA
Nippon Chugoku Gakkaiho [*Bulletin of the Sinological Society of Japan*] — NCGH
Nippon Daicho Komonbyo Gakkai Zasshi — NDKGA
Nippon Dental College. Annual Publications — NDCAB
Nippon Dental College. Annual Publications — Nippon Dent Coll Annu Publ
Nippon Dojo Hiryogaku Zasshi/Journal of the Science of Soil and Manure [*Japan*] — Nippon Dojo Hiryogaku Zasshi J Sci Soil Manure
Nippon Electric Company Research and Development — Nippon Electr Co Res Dev
Nippon Facts — NIF
Nippon Genshiryoku Kenkyusho Kenkyu Hokoku — NIPEA
Nippon Genshiryoku Kenkyusho Nenpo — NGKNA
Nippon Genshiryokusen Kaihatsu Jigyodan Nenpo — NGKJB
Nippon Hoshasen Gijutsu Gakkai Zasshi — NIPHA
Nippon Hoshasen Kobunshi Kenkyu Kyokai Nempo — NHKNA
Nippon Igaku Hoshasen Gakkai Zasshi — NHGZA
Nippon Ika Daigaku Zasshi — NIDZA
Nippon Institute for Biological Science. Bulletin. Biological Research — NIBS Bull Biol Res
Nippon Jibi-Inko-Ka Gakkai Kaiho Kaiho — NJIGA
Nippon Jinzo Gakkaishi — NJGKA
Nippon Jozo Kyokai Zasshi — NIJKA
Nippon Junkanki Gakushi — NJUGA
Nippon Kagaku Kaishi — Nip Kag Kai
Nippon Kagaku Kaishi — NKAKB
Nippon Kagaku Kaishi/Journal. Chemical Society of Japan. Chemistry and Industrial Chemistry — Nippon Kagaku Kaishi J Chem Soc Jap Chem
Nippon Kagaku Seni Kenkyusho Koenshu — NKSKA
Nippon Kagaku Zasshi — NPKZA
Nippon Kenchiku Gakkai Ronbun Hokoku-shu — NKGRB
Nippon Kikai Gakkai Ronbunshu. A Hen — NKGAD
Nippon Kikai Gakkai Ronbunshu. B Hen — NKGBD
Nippon Kikai Gakkai Ronbunshu. C Hen — NKCHD
Nippon Kinzoku Gakkai Kaiho — NKZKA
Nippon Kinzoku Gakkaishi — NIKGA
Nippon Kogyo Kaishi — NIKKA
Nippon Kokan Technical Bulletin — Nippon Kokan Tech Bull
Nippon Kokan Technical Reports — Nippon Kokan Tech Rep
Nippon Kokan Technical Reports Overseas — Nippon Kokan Tech Rep Overseas
Nippon Kokan Technical Reports Overseas — NKTRA
Nippon Kokoka Gakkai Zasshi — NKOGA
Nippon Koshu Eisei Zasshi — NKEZA
Nippon Kyobu Geka Gakkai Zasshi — NKZAA
Nippon Kyobu Rinsho — NKYRA
Nippon Nogei Kagakukai-Shi/Journal. Agricultural Chemical Society of Japan — Nippon Nogei Kagakukai Shi J Agric Chem Soc Jap
Nippon Noyaku Gakkaishi/Journal of Pesticide Science — Nippon Noyaku Gakkaishi/J Pestic Sci
Nippon Onkyo Gakkaishi — NIOGA
Nippon Rinsho — NRINA
Nippon Rinsho Saibo Gakkai Zasshi — NRSZD
Nippon Sakumotsu Gakkai Kiji — NISAA
Nippon Sanka Fujinka Gakkai Chugoku Shikoku Godo Chihobukai Zasshi — NSFZD
Nippon Sanso Engineering Report — Nippon Sanso Eng Rep
Nippon Seikosho Giho — NSEGA
Nippon Seirigaku Zasshi — NISEA
Nippon Setchaku Kyokaishi — NSKSA
Nippon Shashin Gakkai Kaishi — NSGKA
Nippon Shika Ishikai Zasshi — NSHKA
Nippon Shokaki Geka Gakkai Zasshi — NSGZD
Nippon Shokakibyo Gakkai Zasshi — NIPAA
Nippon Shokubutsu Byori Gakkaiho — NSBGA
Nippon Sochi Gakkai Shi/Journal. Japanese Society of Grassland Science — Nippon Sochi Gakkai Shi J Jap Soc Grassl Sci
Nippon Soshikigaku Kiroku — NSKIA
Nippon Stainless Technical Report — Nippon Stainless Tech Rep
Nippon Steel Technical Report — Nippon Steel Tech Rep
Nippon Steel Technical Report (Japanese Edition) — Nippon Steel Tech Rep (Jpn Ed)
Nippon Steel Technical Report (Overseas) — Nippon Steel Tech Rep (Overseas)
Nippon Taishitsugaku Zasshi — NTAZA
Nippon Tungsten Review — Nippon Tungsten Rev
Nippon Yuketsu Gakkai Zasshi — NYGZA
Nippon-Orient-Gakkai-Geppo — Nippon-Orient
NIPRORUDA [*Nauchnoizsledovatelski i Proektantski Institut za Rudodobiv i Obogatyavane*] **Sbornik Nauchni Trudove. Seriya. Obogatyavanne** — NIPRORUDA Sb Nauchni Tr Ser Obogat
NIRSA. Journal of the National Intramural-Recreational Sports Association — NIRSA
Nishinihon Journal of Dermatology — Nishinihon J Dermatol
Nishinihon Journal of Urology — Nishinihon J Urol
NISK (Norsk Instituut foer Skogforskning) Rapport — NISK (Nor Inst Skogforsk) Rapp
Nissan Diesel Review [*Japan*] — Nissan Diesel Rev
Nissan Technical Review — Nissan Tech Rev
Nisseki Technical Review [*Japan*] — Nisseki Tech Rev
Nisshin Seiko Giho — NISGA
Nisshin Steel Technical Report — Nisshin Steel Tech Rep
NIST [*National Institute of Standards and Technology*] **Special Publication** — NIST Spec Publ
Nitrate. Wirkung auf Herz und Kreislauf. Nitrat-Symposion — Nitrate Wirkung Herz Kreislauf Nitrat Symp
Nitro Compounds. Recent Advances in Synthesis and Chemistry [*Monograph*] — Nitro Compd
Nitrogen Fixation Research Progress. Proceedings. International Symposium on Nitrogen Fixation — Nitrogen Fixation Res Prog Proc Int Symp
Nivel — NIV
Nizkotemperaturnoe i Vakuumnoe Materialovedenie [*Ukrainian SSR*] — Nizkotemp Vak Materialoved
NIZO [*Nederlands Instituut voor Zuivelonderzoek*] **Rapporten** — NIZO Rapp
NIZO [*Nederlands Instituut voor Zuivelonderzoek*] **Verslagen** — NIZO Versl
NJSNA [*New Jersey State Nurses Association*] **Newsletter** [*New Jersey Nurse*] [*Later,*] — NJSNA News
NJSNA [*New Jersey State Nurses Association*] **Newsletter** [*New Jersey Nurse*] [*Later,*] — NJSNA Newsl
NLGI [*National Lubricating Grease Institute*] **Spokesman** — NLGI Spokesman
NLL Review — NLL Rev
NLN (National League for Nursing) News — NLN News
NLRB [*National Labor Relations Board*] **Decisions. Commerce Clearing House** — NLRB Dec CCH
NM/MIRD [*Society of Nuclear Medicine. Medical Internal Radiation Dose Committee*] **Pamphlet** — NM MIRD Pam
NML [*National Metallurgical Laboratory*] **Technical Journal** — NML Tech J
NMR [*Nuclear Magnetic Resonance*] **Basic Principles and Progress** — NMR Basic Princ Prog
NMR in Biomedicine — NMR Biomed
NMV. Noticias Medico-Veterinarias — NMV Not Med Vet
NN [*Netherlands Nitrogen*] **Technical Bulletin** — NN Tech Bull
NNF. Nytt Meddelelser fra Norsk Numismatisk Forening — NNF Nytt
No More Cages — No Cages
NOAA [*National Oceanic and Atmospheric Administration*] **Technical Report. NMFS Circular** [*National Marine Fisheries Service*] — NOAA Tech Rep NMFS Circ
Noah's Ark Toy Library for Handicapped Children. Newsletter — Noah's Ark Toy Libr Handicapped Child Newsletter
Nobel Foundation Symposia — Nobel Found Symp
Nobel Symposium — Nobel Symp
Nobelinstitut. Meddelanden Kungliga Vetenskapsakademien — Nobelinst Medd K Vetenskapsakad
Noble Savage — NS
Noda Institute for Scientific Research. Report — Noda Inst Sci Res Rep
NoDEA. Nonlinear Differential Equations and Applications — NoDEA Nonlinear Differential Equations Appl
Noerdlinger Bienenzeitung — Noerdlinger Bienenztg
Noevenyegeszegyuegyi Evkoenyv/Yearbook. Official Phytosanitary Service/ Jahrbuch des Amtlichen Pflanzengesundheitsdienstes — Noevenyegesz Evk
Noevenytani Koezlemenyek — Noevenyt Koezlem
Noevenyved Tudomanyos Tanacskozas Koezlemenyei — Noevenyved Tud Tanacskozas Koezlem
Noevenyvedelmi Koezloeny — Noevenyved Koezl
Noevenyvedelmi Kutato Intezet Evkoenyve (Budapest) — Noevenyved Kutato Intez Evkoen (Budapest)
Nogaku Iho. Agricultural Bulletin of Saga University. Saga Daigaku. Nogaku-Bu — Nogaku Iho Agric Bull Saga Univ Nogaku-Bu
Nogaku Shuho. Journal of Agricultural Science (Setagoya) — Nogaku Shusho J Agric Sci (Setagoya)
Noguchi Kenkyusho Jiho — NOGUA
Nogyo Doboku Gakkai Ronbunshu — NDGKA
Nogyo Doboku Gakkai-Shi — NOGDA
Nogyo Doboku Shikenjo Giho, F. Sogo — NDSFB
Nogyo Doboku Shikenjo Hokoku — NDBSB
Nogyo Doboku Shikenjo Hokoku/Bulletin. National Research Institute of Agricultural Engineering — Nogyo Doboku Shikenjo Hokoku Bull Natl Res Inst Agric Eng
Nogyo Gijutsu/Journal of Agricultural Science — Nogyo Gijutsu J Agric
Nogyo Gijutsu Kenkyusho Hokoku. B. Dojo Hiryo — NGKBA
Nogyo Gijutsu Kenkyusho Hokoku. C. Byori Konchu — NGKCA
Nogyo Gijutsu Kenkyusho Hokoku. D. Seiri, Iden, Sakumotsu Ippan — NGKDA
Nogyo Kikai Gakkai Shi/Journal. Society of Agricultural Machinery [*Japan*] — Nogyo Kikai Gakkai Shi J Soc Agric Mach
Nogyo Oyobi Engei/Agriculture and Horticulture — Nogyo Oyobi Engei/Agric Hortic
Noise and Vibration Bulletin — Noise Vib Bull
Noise and Vibration Bulletin — NVB
Noise and Vibration Control — Noise Vib Control
Noise and Vibration Control Worldwide — Noise & Vib Control Worldwide
Noise and Vibration Control Worldwide — Noise Vibr Contr Worldwide
Noise Control — NOCOA
Noise Control and Vibration Reduction [*Later, Noise and Vibration Control Worldwide*] — Noise Control and Vib Reduct
Noise Control and Vibration Reduction [*Later, Noise and Vibration Control Worldwide*] — Noise Control Vibr Reduct
Noise Control Engineering — NCEGA
Noise Control Engineering — Noise Control Eng
Noise Control Engineering — Noise Control Engrg

Noise Control Engineering Journal — Noise Control Eng J
Noise Control, Shock, and Vibration — Noise Control Shock Vib
Noise Control, Vibration Isolation [*Later, Noise and Vibration Control Worldwide*] — Noise Control Vib
Noise Control, Vibration Isolation [*Later, Noise and Vibration Control Worldwide*] — Noise Control Vib Isol
Noise Pollution Publications Abstract — Noise Pollut Publ Abstr
Noise Regulation Reporter. Bureau of National Affairs — Noise Reg Rep BNA
Nomenclatura Chimica — Nomencl Chim
Nomenclature Guide — Nomencl Guide
Nomina Geographica Flandrica — NGF
Nomina Geographica Neerlandica — NGN
Nomisma. Untersuchungen auf dem Gebiete der Antiken Munskunde — Nom
Nomismatika Chronika — Nom Chron
Nomismatika Khronika — Nom Khron
Nomograficheskii Sbornik — Nomograficheskii Sb
NOMOS Verlagskatalog [*Database*] — NOVE
Nomos. Yearbook of the American Society of Political and Legal Philosophy [*A publication*] — Nomos
Noms des Hittites — NH
Noms Propres Sud-Semitiques — NPS
Noms Propres Sud-Semitiques — NPSS
Nonconventional Yeasts in Biotechnology. A Handbook — Nonconv Yeasts Biotechnol
Nonconvex Optimization and its Applications — Nonconvex Optim Appl
Non-Destructive Testing — Non-Dest Test
Non-Destructive Testing — Non-Destr T
Non-Destructive Testing — Non-Destr Test
Non-Destructive Testing (Australia) — Non-Destr Test (Aust)
Non-Destructive Testing (Chicago) — Nondestr Test (Chicago)
Non-Destructive Testing (Guilford, England) — Non-Destr Test (Guilford Eng)
Non-Destructive Testing International — NDT Int
Non-Destructive Testing International — Non-Destr Test Int
Non-Destructive Testing News — NDT News
Nondestructive Testing (Shanghai) — Nondestr Test (Shanghai)
Nonequilibrium Effects in Ion and Electron Transport. Proceedings. International Swarm Seminar — Nonequilib Eff Ion Electron Transp Proc Int Swarm Semin
Nonequilibrium Problems in the Physical Sciences and Biology — Nonequilib Probl Phys Sci Biol
Nonferrous Castings. Current Industrial Reports — Nonferrous Cast Curr Ind Rep
Nonferrous Metals (Beijing) — Nonferrous Met (Beijing)
Non-Ferrous Metals (China) — Non-Ferrous Met (China)
Non-Ferrous Metals (Moscow) — Non Ferrous Met (Moscow)
Nonferrous Metals Society of China. Transactions — Nonferrous Met Soc China Trans
Non-Foods Merchandising — NonFMerch
Non-Ionizing Radiation — NOIRB
Non-Ionizing Radiation — Non-Ioniz Radiat
Nonlinear Analysis — Nonlinear Anal
Nonlinear Analysis. Theory and Applications. Proceedings. International Summer School — Nonlinear Anal Theory Appl Proc Int Summer Sch
Nonlinear Analysis. Theory, Methods, and Applications — Nonlinear Anal Theory Methods and Appl
Nonlinear Coherent Structures in Physics and Biology. Proceedings. Interdisciplinary Workshop — Nonlinear Coherent Struct Phys Biol Proc Interdiscip Workshop
Nonlinear Dynamics and Quantum Phenomena in Optical Systems. Proceedings. International Workshop — Nonlinear Dyn Quantum Phenom Opt Syst Proc Int Workshop
Nonlinear Optics. Proceedings. Vavilov Conference — Nonlinear Opt Proc Vavilov Conf
Nonlinear Phenomena and Complex Systems — Nonlinear Phenom Complex Syst
Nonlinear Phenomena and Complex Systems — Nonlinear Phenom Complex Systems
Nonlinear Science. Theory and Application — Nonlinear Sci Theory Appl
Nonlinear Science Today — Nonlinear Sci Today
Nonlinear Studies — Nonlinear Stud
Nonlinear Time Series and Chaos — Nonlinear Time Ser Chaos
Nonlinear Times and Digest — Nonlinear Times Digest
Nonlinear Topics in the Mathematical Sciences — Nonlinear Topics Math Sci
Nonlinear Vibration Problems — Nonlinear Vibr Probl
Nonmetallic Meterials and Composites at Low Temperatures. Proceedings. ICMC[*International Cryogenic Materials Conference*] **Symposium** — Nonmet Mater Compos Low Temp Proc ICMC Symp
Nonmetallic Minerals Processing — Nonmet Miner Process
Non-Metallic Mines — Non Met Mines
Nonmunjip. Inha Technical Junior College — Nonmunjip Inha Tech Jr Coll
Nonpetroleum Vehicle Fuels Symposium — Nonpet Veh Fuels Symp
Nonprofit Executive — Nonpr Exec
Nonrenewable Resources — Nonrenewable Resour
Nonwoven Patents Digest — Nonwoven Pat Dig
Nonwovens Industry — Nonwovens Ind
Nonwovens Industry — Nonwovn In
Noodzaak — NDZKA
Noord Brabant — NBJ
Noord-Holland — NH
NORD [*National Organization for Rare Disorders*] **Services/Rare Disease Database** — RDB
Nord und Sued — Nord u Sued
Nord und Sued — NuS
Norddeutsche Allgemeine Zeitung — NAZ
Norddeutsche Familienkunde — Ndt F
Norddeutsche Farben Zeitung — Norddsch Farben Ztg
Norddeutsche Farben Zeitung — Norddtsch Farben Ztg
Norddeutsche Missionsgesellschaft — NDMG
Norddeutsches Jahrbuch fuer Muenzkunde und Verwandte Gebiete — Nordd J Mv G
Norddeutsches Protestantenblatt — NDPB
Nordelbingen — NE
Nordelbingische Studien — NES
Norden Industritidning — Norden Industritidn
Nordenskioeld-Samfundets Tidskrift — Nordenskioeld Samf T
Nordeuropaeisk Mejeri-Tidsskrift — Nordeuropaeisk Mejeri-Tidsskr
Nordfriesisches Jahrbuch — Nf J
Nordharger Jahrbuch. Museen der Stadt Halberstadt — NHJ
Nordia — Nord
Nordic Economic Outlook — NDH
Nordic High Temperature Symposium — Nord High Temp Symp
Nordic Hydrology — NOHY
Nordic Hydrology — Nord Hydrol
Nordic Hydrology — Nordic Hydrol
Nordic Journal of Botany — NJBO
Nordic Journal of Botany — Nord J Bot
Nordic Journal of Botany. Supplement — Nord J Bot Suppl
Nordic Journal of Computing — Nordic J Comput
Nordic Journal of Documentation — Nord J Doc
Nordic Journal of Linguistics — NJL
Nordic Journal of Philosophical Logic — Nordic J Philos Logic
Nordic Meeting on Medical and Biological Engineering — Nord Meet Med Biol Eng
Nordic Pulp and Paper Research Journal — Nord Pulp Pap Res J
Nordic Semiconductor Meeting — Nord Semicond Meet
Nordic Society for Cell Biology. Proceedings. Congress — Nord Soc Cell Biol Proc Congr
Nordic Sounds — NorS
Nordic Sounds — NS
Nordic Symposium on Computer Simulation in Physics, Chemistry, Biology, and Mathematics — Nord Symp Comput Simul Phys Chem Biol Math
Nordic Symposium on Computer Simulations in Natural Science — Nord Symp Comput Simul Nat Sci
Nordic Symposium on Sensory Properties of Foods — Nord Symp Sens Prop of Foods
Nordic Veterinary Congress. Proceedings — Nord Vet Congr Proc
Nordic World — Nord World
Nordik Energi Indeks [*Database*] — NEI
Nordische Blaetter fuer die Chemie — Nord Bl Chem
Nordische Studien — NSt
Nordisches Archiv fuer Natur- und Arzneywissenschaft — Nord Arch Natur Arzneywiss
Nordisk Administrativt Tidsskrift — N Adm T
Nordisk Administrativt Tidsskrift — Nord Adm T
Nordisk Administrativt Tidsskrift — Nord Adm Tss
Nordisk Astronomisk Tidsskrift — N Astr T
Nordisk Betong — Nord Betong
Nordisk Bitidskrift — Nord Bitidskr
Nordisk Datanytt Med Data — Nord Datanytt Data
Nordisk Filatelistik Tidsskrift — N Filat T
Nordisk Fotohistorisk Journal — Nord Fotohist Jl
Nordisk Hygienisk Tidskrift — Nord Hyg Tidskr
Nordisk Hygienisk Tidskrift. Supplementum — Nord Hyg Tidskr Suppl
Nordisk Jordbrugsforskning — N Jbt
Nordisk Jordbrugsforskning — NOJOA
Nordisk Jordbrugsforskning — Nord Jordbrforsk
Nordisk Jordbrugsforskning — Nord Jordbrugsforsk
Nordisk Jordbrugsforskning. Supplement — Nord Jordbrugsforsk Suppl
Nordisk Jordbrugsforskning. Supplement — Suppl Nord Jordbrforsk
Nordisk Jordbrugsforskning. Supplement. Nordiska Jordbruksforskares Foerening — Nord Jordbrugsforskn Suppl
Nordisk Jordburgsforskning — N JbF
Nordisk Konversations Leksikon — NKL
Nordisk Kultur — Nord Kul
Nordisk Landvaesens Og Landhuusholdnings Magasin et Maanedsskrivt — Nord Landvaes Landhuushold Mag
Nordisk Matematisk Tidskrift — Nordisk Mat Tidskr
Nordisk Matematisk Tidsskrift — Nord Mat Tidsskr
Nordisk Medicin — N Med
Nordisk Medicin — Nord Med
Nordisk Medicinhistorisk Aarsbok — Nord Medicinhist Arsb
Nordisk Medicinsk Tidskrift — Nord Med Tidskr
Nordisk Mejeri Tidsskrift — Nord Mejeri Tidsskr
Nordisk Mejeri-Tidsskrift — N MT
Nordisk Missions-Tidsskrift — N Miss
Nordisk Missions-Tidsskrift — NMT
Nordisk Musikkultur — Nord Mus
Nordisk Numismatisk Arsskrift — N Num A
Nordisk Numismatisk Arsskrift — NNA
Nordisk Numismatisk Unions Medlemsblad — N Num U M
Nordisk Numismatisk Unions Medlemsblad — NNUM
Nordisk Psykiatrisk Tidsskrift — Nord Psykiatr Tidsskr
Nordisk Psykologi — NOPSA
Nordisk Psykologi — Nord Psykol
Nordisk Teologisk Leksikon for Kirke og Skole — NTLe
Nordisk Teologisk Uppslagsbok for Kyrka och Skola — NTU
Nordisk Texter och Undersokningar — NTUn
Nordisk Tidskrift — NT
Nordisk Tidskrift foer Beteendeterapi — Nord Tidskr Beteendeterapi

Nordisk Tidskrift foer Bok- Och Biblioteksvaesen — Nord T Bok Och Bibilioteksvaes
Nordisk Tidskrift foer Bok- och Biblioteksvaesen — Nord Tid
Nordisk Tidskrift foer Bok- och Biblioteksvaesen — Nord Tidskr
Nordisk Tidskrift foer Bok- och Biblioteksvaesen — Nordisk Tid
Nordisk Tidskrift foer Bok- och Biblioteksvaesen — Nordisk Tids Bok & Bibl
Nordisk Tidskrift foer Bok- och Biblioteksvaesen — NTBB
Nordisk Tidskrift foer Bok- och Biblioteksvaesen — NTBBV
Nordisk Tidskrift foer Dovundervisningen — Nord Tidskr Dov
Nordisk Tidskrift foer Fotografi — Nord Tidskr Fotogr
Nordisk Tidskrift foer Medicoteknik — Nord Tidskr Medicotek
Nordisk Tidskrift foer Sprogvidenskap — NTSV
Nordisk Tidskrift foer Vetenskap, Konst, och Industri — Nord Tidskr f Vetensk
Nordisk Tidskrift foer Vetenskap, Konst, och Industri — NT
Nordisk Tidskrift foer Vetenskap, Konst, och Industri — NTsV
Nordisk Tidskrift for Vetenskap, Konst och Industri — NTV
Nordisk Tidskrift utg. av Letterstedtska Foereningen — Nord T
Nordisk Tidsskrift foer Filologi — Nord Tidskrift
Nordisk Tidsskrift foer Kriminalvidenskab — Nord Tidsskr Kriminalvidensk
Nordisk Tidsskrift foer Lervare- og Sten-Industri — Nord Tidsskr Lervare Sten Ind
Nordisk Tidsskrift foer Logopedi og Foniatri — Nord Tidsskr Logop Foniat
Nordisk Tidsskrift foer Strafferet — Nord Tidsskr Strafferet
Nordisk Tidsskrift foer Tale og Stemme — NTTS
Nordisk Tidsskrift foer Teknisk Okonomi — NTTO
Nordisk Tidsskrift for Aandsvageforsorg — NT Aa
Nordisk Tidsskrift for Bok- ock Biblioteksvaesen — NTB
Nordisk Tidsskrift for Filologi — Nord Tidsskr Filol
Nordisk Tidsskrift for Filologi — NTF
Nordisk Tidsskrift for Filologi — NTiFil
Nordisk Tidsskrift for International Ret — Nord T Internat Ret
Nordisk Tidsskrift for International Ret — Nord Tss Int Ret
Nordisk Tidsskrift for International Ret — NTiR
Nordisk Tidsskrift for Sprogvidenskab. Supplement — NRSVS
Nordisk Tidsskrift for Strafferet — Nord Tidsskr Straf
Nordisk Tidsskrift for Tale og Stemme — NT f Ta o St
Nordisk Utredningsserie — Nord Utredningsser
Nordisk Utredningsserie — NOUTD
Nordisk Veterinaermedicin — N Vet
Nordisk Veterinaermedicin — Nord Veterinaermed
Nordisk Veterinaermedicin — Nord Vetmed
Nordisk Veterinaermedicin. Supplementum — Nord Veterinaermed Suppl
Nordiska Institutet foer Faergforskning. Report — Nord Inst Faergforsk Rep
Nordiska Kemistmoetet. Beraettelse och Foeredrag — Nord Kemistmoetet Beraett Foeredr
Nordiska Kemistmoetet. Foerhandlingar och Foeredrag — Nord Kemistmoetet Foerh Foeredr
Nordiska Moetet i Biomedicinsk Teknik — Nord Moetet Biomed Tek
Nordiska Museets och Skansens Arsbok — NM
Nordiska Symposiet Livsmedels Sensoriska Egenskaper — Nord Symp Livsmedels Sens Egenskaper
Nordiska Texter och Undersokningar — NTU
Nordiske Domme i Sjofartsanliggender — ND Sjo
Nordiske Kemikermoede — Nord Kemikermoede
Nordiske Symposium om Harskning af Fedtstoffer, Foeredrag og Diskussioner — Nord Symp Harskning Fedtstoffer Foeredrag Diskuss
Nordiske Veterinaermoede. Beretning — Nord Veterinaermoede Beret
Nordiskt Medicinskt Arkiv — Nord Med Ark
Nordiskt Medicinskt Arkiv. Afdeling 2. Inre Medicin. Arkiv foer Inre Medicin — Nord Med Ark Afd 2
Nordiskt Medicinskt Arkiv. Afdeling 2. Inre Medicine. Arkiv foer Inre Medicin — Nord Med Ark Afd 2 Med
Nordpfalzer Geschichtsverein — NPfG
Nordwestdeutsche Imkerzeitung — Nordwestdt Imkerztg
Norelco Reporter — Norelco Rep
Norfolk Archaeology — Norfolk A
Norfolk Archaeology — Norfolk Arch
Norfolk Archaeology — Norfolk Archaeol
Norges Apotekerforenings Tidsskrift — Nor Apotekerforen Tidsskr
Norges Bank. Economic Bulletin — NOB
Norges Bank. Economic Bulletin — Norges Bank Econ Bul
Norges Bank. Skrifter Series — NOBKSS
Norges Fiskerier — Nor Fisk
Norges Geologiske Undersoekelse — NOGU
Norges Geologiske Undersoekelse — Nor Geol Unders
Norges Geologiske Undersoekelse. Bulletin — Nor Geol Unders Bull
Norges Geologiske Undersoekelse. Publikasjoner — Nor Geol Unders Publ
Norges Geologiske Undersoekelse. Publikasjoner — Norg Geol Unders Publ
Norges Geologiske Undersoekelse. Skrifter — Nor Geol Unders Skr
Norges Geotekniske Institut. Publikasjon [*Oslo*] — Norg Geotek Inst Publ
Norges Landbrukshogskole Foringsforsokene Beretning — Nor Landbrukshogsk Foringsforsok Beret
Norges Offisielle Statistikk — NOSTA
Norges Teknisk Naturvitenskapelige Forskningsrad. Metallurgisk Komite. Meddelelse — Nor Tek Naturvitensk Forskningsrad Metall Kom Medd
Norges Tekniske Vitenskapsakademi. Meddelelse — Nor Tek Vitenskapsakad Medd
Norges Utenrikshandel — NUT
Norges Vel — Nor Vel
Norinsho Kachiku Eisei Shikenjo Kenkyu Hokoku — BNIAA
Normal Instructor and Primary Plans — Norm Instr and Prim Plans
Normale und Pathologische Anatomie (Stuttgart) — Norm Pathol Anat (Stuttg)
Normalfrequenzen und Normalzeit der Frequenz-Technischen Zentralstelle der Berliner Post — Normalfrequenzen
Normalisatie — NOR
Normes et Reglements Informations Accessibles en Ligne [*Database*] — NORIANE
Noroil — NOROD
Noro-Psikiyatri Arsivi — Noro-Psikiyatri Ars
Norpic — NORP
Norrlands Skogsvardsforbunds Tidskrift (Stockholm) — Norrlands Skogsvforb Tidskr (Stockh)
Norseman — No
Norseman [*London*] — Nor
Norseman — NORS
Norsk Artillerie Tidskrift — Norsk Artill Tidskr
Norsk Bibliografisk Bibliotek — NBB
Norsk Biografisk Leksikon — NBL
Norsk Datatidende — Norsk Data
Norsk Entomologisk Tidsskrift — Nor Entomol Tidsskr
Norsk Entomologisk Tidsskrift — Norsk Ent Tidsskr
Norsk Entomologisk Tidsskrift — Norsk Entomol Tidsskr
Norsk Fag Foto — Nor Fag Foto
Norsk Farmaceutisk Tidsskrift — Nor Farm Tidsskr
Norsk Farmaceutisk Tidsskrift — Norsk Farm T
Norsk Fiskeritidende — Nor Fiskeritid
Norsk Fotografisk Tidsskrift — Nor Fotogr Tidsskr
Norsk Gartnerforenings Tidsskrift — Nor Gartnerforenings Tidsskr
Norsk Geografisk Tidsskrift — N Ggr T
Norsk Geografisk Tidsskrift — NGET
Norsk Geografisk Tidsskrift — Norsk Geog Tid
Norsk Geografisk Tidsskrift — Norsk Geogr Tidsskr
Norsk Geografisk Tidsskrift — Norsk Geogr Ts
Norsk Geologisk Tidsskrift — NOGT
Norsk Geologisk Tidsskrift — Nor Geol Tidsskr
Norsk Geologisk Tidsskrift — Norsk Geol
Norsk Geologisk Tidsskrift — Norsk Geol Tids
Norsk Geologisk Tidsskrift — Norsk Geol Tidsskr
Norsk Hagetidend — Norsk Hagetid
Norsk Havetidende. Udgivet of Selskabet Havedyrkningens Venner — Norsk Havetid
Norsk Institutt foer Vannforskning. Aarbok — Nor Inst Vannforsk Aarb
Norsk Institutt foer Vannforskning. Rapport — Nor Inst Vannforsk Rapp
Norsk Institutt for Tang- og Tareforskning. Report — Nor Inst Tang- Tareforsk Rep
Norsk Litteraer Aarbok — NLA
Norsk Lovtidend — Nor Lovtid
Norsk Lovtidend Avdeling I [*Norway*] — Nor Lovtid Avd I
Norsk Magasin foer Laegevidenskapen — Nor Mag Laegevidensk
Norsk Magazin — Norsk Mag
Norsk Magazin foer Laegevidenskaben — Norsk Mag Laegevidensk
Norsk Meteorologisk Arbok — Nor Met Arb
Norsk Musikerblad — Norsk Mus
Norsk Natur — Nor Nat
Norsk Olje Revy — Nor Olje Revy
Norsk Olje Revy — NORED
Norsk Pelsdyrblad — Nor Pelsdyrbl
Norsk Polarinstitutt. Aarbok — NOPA
Norsk Polarinstitutt. Aarbok — Nor Polarinst Aarb
Norsk Polarinstitutt. Aarbok — Nor Polarinst Aarbok
Norsk Polarinstitutt. Aarbok — Norsk Polarinst Aarbok
Norsk Polarinstitutt. Meddelelser — NOPM
Norsk Polarinstitutt. Meddelelser — Nor Polarinst Medd
Norsk Polarinstitutt. Polarhandbok — NOPH
Norsk Polarinstitutt. Polarhandbok — Nor Polarinst Polarhandb
Norsk Polarinstitutt. Skrifter — NOPS
Norsk Polarinstitutt. Skrifter — Nor Polarinst Skr
Norsk Skogbruk — Nor Skogbruk
Norsk Skogbruk — Norsk Skogbr
Norsk Skogindustri — Nor Skogind
Norsk Skogindustri — Norsk Skog
Norsk Skogindustri — Norskind
Norsk Skogindustri — NOSK
Norsk Skogindustri — NOSKA
Norsk Skogindustri — NS
Norsk Slektshistorisk Tidsskrift — NSHT
Norsk Tekstiltidende — Norsk Tekstiltid
Norsk Teologisk Tidsskrift — No TT
Norsk Teologisk Tidsskrift — Nor TT
Norsk Teologisk Tidsskrift [*Oslo*] — NorTTs
Norsk Teologisk Tidsskrift — NTT
Norsk Teologisk Tidsskrift — NTTid
Norsk Tidende foer det Industrielle Rettsvern. Del 1. Patenter — Nor Tid Ind Rettsvern Del 1
Norsk Tidsskrift foer Sprogvidenskap — NT Spr
Norsk Tidsskrift foer Sprogvidenskap — NTS
Norsk Tidsskrift for Misjon — NTM
Norsk Tidsskrift for Sjovesen — Norsk T Sjoves
Norsk Tidsskrift for Sprogvidenskap — Nor Tidsskr Sprogvidenskap
Norsk Tidsskrift vor Misjon — No TM
Norsk Veterinaertidsskrift — Nor Veterinaertidsskr
Norsk Veterinaer-Tidsskrift — Nor Vet-Tidsskr
Norsk Veterinaer-Tidsskrift — Norsk Vet Tid
Norsk Veterinaer-Tidsskrift — Norsk Vet-Tidsskr
Norsk Veterinaer-Tidsskrift — NOVDA
Norsk VVS [*Norsk Forening foer Varme-, Ventilasjon-, og Sanitaerteknikk*] [*Norway*] — Nor VVS
Norske Klassiker-Tekster — NKT
Norske Meteorologiske Institutt. Meteorologiske Annaler — NMIA
Norske Meteorologiske Institutt. Meteorologiske Annaler — NMIMA

Norske Myrselskap. Meddelelser — Nor Myrselsk Medd
Norske Skogforsoeksvesen. Meddelelser — Nor Skogforsoeksves Medd
Norske Tannlaegeforenings Tidende — Nor Tannlaegeforen Tid
Norske Turistforenings Arbok — N Tur A
Norske Veritas. Publication — Nor Veritas Publ
Norske Videnskabers Selskab. Museet. Miscellanea — Nor Vidensk Selsk Mus Misc
Norske Videnskabers Selskab. Skrifter — Nor Vidensk Selsk Skr
Norske Videnskaps-Akademi. Aarbok — NVA
Norske Videnskaps-Akademi i Oslo. Aarbok — Nor Vidensk-Akad Oslo Arbok
Norske Videnskaps-Akademi i Oslo. Hvalradets Skrifter — NVHS
Norske Videnskaps-Akademi i Oslo. Matematisk-Naturvidenskapelig Klasse. Skrifter — Norske Vid-Akad Oslo Mat-Natur Kl Skr
Norske Videnskaps-Akademi i Oslo. Matematisk-Naturvidenskapelig Klasse. Skrifter. Ny Serie — Nor Vidensk-Akad Oslo Mat Natur Kl N Ser
Norske Videnskaps-Akademi. Matematisk-Naturvidenskapelig Klasse. Avhandlinger — Norske Vidensk Akad Mat Naturvidensk Kl Avh
Norske Videnskaps-Akademi. Matematisk-Naturvidenskapelig Klasse. Skrifter — Nor Vidensk Akad Mat Naturvidensk Kl Skr
Norske Videnskaps-Akademi. Skrifter — Nor Vidensk-Akad Skr
Norsk-Hvalfangst-Tidende — Nor Hvalfangst Tid
Norsk-Hvalfangst-Tidende — Nor Hvalfanst Tid
Norte Agronomico — Norte Agron
Nortext News — NOTN
North — NORT
North American Anarchist — NA Anarch
North American Archaeologist — NA
North American Bird Bander — N Am Bird Bander
North American Conference on Powder Coating. Proceedings — North Am Conf Powder Coat Proc
North American Fauna — N Am Fauna
North American Fauna — North Amer Fauna
North American Flora — N Am Flora
North American Flora — North Am Flora
North American Flora. Series II — N Am Flora Ser II
North American Flora. Series II — North Am Flora Ser II
North American Forest Biology Workshop — North Am For Biol Workshop
North American Forest Biology Workshop. Proceedings — North Am For Biol Workshop Proc
North American Forest Soils Conference — North Am For Soils Conf
North American Gladiolus Council. Bulletin — North Am Gladiolus Counc Bull
North American Journal of Fisheries Management — N Am J Fish Manage
North American Journal of Fisheries Management — NAJMDP
North American Journal of Fisheries Management — North Am J Fish Manage
North American Journal of Numismatics — NAJN
North American Manufacturing Research Conference. Proceedings — North Am Manu Res Conf Proc
North American Mentor Magazine — North Am Mentor Mag
North American Metalworking Research Conference. Proceedings — North Am Metalwork Res Conf Proc
North American Mineral News — North Am Miner News
North American Pomona — North Am Pomona
North American Practitioner — North Am Pract
North American Review — N Am R
North American Review — N Am Rev
North American Review — NA
North American Review — NAmerR
North American Review — NAR
North American Review — No Am
North American Review — No Am R
North American Review — No Am Rev
North American Review — North Am R
North American Review — North Amer Revw
North American Review — Nth Am Rev
North American Review — PNAR
North American Stock Market [*Database*] — NASTOCK
North American Veterinarian — N Am Vet
North American Veterinarian — North Am Vet
North American Wildlife and Natural Resources Conference. Transactions — North Am Wildl Nat Resour Conf Trans
North Atlantic Treaty Organization. Committee on the Challenges of Modern Society. Technical Report CCMS — NATO Comm Challenges Mod Soc Tech Rep CCMS
North Atlantic Treaty Organization. Committee on the Challenges of Modern Society. Technical Report NATO/CCMS — NATO Comm Challenges Mod Soc Tech Rep NATO CCMS
North Australia Research Bulletin — N Aust Res Bull
North Australian Monthly — N Aust M
North Australian Monthly — NA Monthly
North Bengal University Review — North Bengal Univ Rev
North British Review — No Brit
North Carolina Administrative Code — NC Admin Code
North Carolina. Agricultural Experiment Station. Bulletin — NC Agric Exp Stn Bull
North Carolina Agricultural Experiment Station Bulletin — North Carolina Agric Exp Sta Bull
North Carolina Agricultural Experiment Station. Department of Agronomy. Research Report — North Carolina Agric Exp Sta Dept Agron Res Rep
North Carolina. Agricultural Experiment Station. Publications — NC Ag Exp
North Carolina Agricultural Experiment Station Special Bulletin — North Carolina Agric Exp Sta Special Bull
North Carolina Agricultural Experiment Station. Special Publication — North Carolina Agric Exp Sta Special Publ
North Carolina. Agricultural Experiment Station. Technical Bulletin — NC Agric Exp Stn Tech Bull
North Carolina. Agricultural Extension Service. Extension Circular — NC Agric Ext Serv Ext Circ
North Carolina. Agricultural Extension Service. Extension Folder — NC Agric Ext Serv Ext Folder
North Carolina. Agricultural Extension Service. Leaflet — NC Agric Ext Serv Leafl
North Carolina. Agricultural Research Service. Bulletin — BARSDJ
North Carolina. Agricultural Research Service. Bulletin — NC Agric Res Serv Bull
North Carolina. Agricultural Research Service. Technical Bulletin — NC Agric Res Serv Tech Bull
North Carolina. Agricultural Research Service. Technical Bulletin — TNCSDT
North Carolina Agricultural Statistics — NC Agr Statist
North Carolina Architect — NC Arch
North Carolina Bar Newsletter — NC Bar Newsl
North Carolina Cave Survey — NC Cave Surv
North Carolina Central Law Journal — N Car Central LJ
North Carolina Central Law Journal — NC Cent LJ
North Carolina Central Law Journal — NC Central L J
North Carolina Central Law Journal — North Carolina Cent LJ
North Carolina Christian Advocate — NCCA
North Carolina Court of Appeals Reports — NC App
North Carolina Dairy Extension Newsletter — NC Dairy Ext Newsl
North Carolina Dental Gazette — N Carol Dent Gaz
North Carolina Dental Journal — NC Dent J
North Carolina. Department of Conservation and Development. Division of Mineral Resources. Bulletin — NC Dep Conserv Dev Div Miner Resour Bull
North Carolina. Department of Conservation and Development. Division of Mineral Resources. Bulletin — NC Div Miner Resour Bull
North Carolina. Department of Conservation and Development. Division of Mineral Resources. Geologic Map Series — North Carolina Div Mineral Resources Geol Map Ser
North Carolina. Department of Conservation and Development. Division of Mineral Resources. Information Circular — NC Dep Conserv Dev Div Miner Resour Inf Circ
North Carolina. Department of Conservation and Development. Division of Mineral Resources. Information Circular — North Carolina Div Mineral Resources Inf Circ
North Carolina. Department of Conservation and Development. Division of Mineral Resources. Special Publication — North Carolina Div Mineral Resources Spec Pub
North Carolina. Department of Conservation and Development. Economic Paper — NC Dep Conserv Dev Econ Pap
North Carolina. Department of Human Resources. Annual Report — NC Dep Hum Res Ann Rep
North Carolina. Department of Natural and Economic Resources. Geology and Mineral Resources Section. Special Publication — NC Dep Nat Econ Resour Geol Miner Resour Sect Spec Publ
North Carolina. Department of Natural and Economic Resources. Groundwater Section. Report of Investigation — NC Dep Nat Econ Resour Groundwater Sect Rep Invest
North Carolina. Department of Natural and Economic Resources. Regional Geology Series — NC Dep Nat Econ Resour Reg Geol Ser
North Carolina. Department of Water and Air Resources. Division of Ground Water. Ground Water Bulletin — North Carolina Div Ground Water Ground Water Bull
North Carolina. Department of Water Resources. Division of Ground Water. Ground-Water Bulletin — NC Dep Water Resour Div Ground Water Ground Water Bull
North Carolina. Department of Water Resources. Division of Stream Sanitation and Hydrology. Bulletin — NC Div Water Resour Div Stream Sanit Hydrol Bull
North Carolina. Division of Earth Sciences. Geology and Mineral Resources Section. Bulletin — NC Div Earth Sci Geol Miner Resour Sect Bull
North Carolina. Division of Ground Water. Ground Water Bulletin — NC Div Ground Water Ground Water Bull
North Carolina. Division of Ground Water. Ground Water Circular — NC Div Ground Water Ground Water Circ
North Carolina. Division of Ground Water. Report of Investigations — NC Div Ground Water Rep Invest
North Carolina. Division of Mineral Resources. Information Circular — NC Div Miner Resour Inf Circ
North Carolina. Division of Resource Planning and Evaluation. Mineral Resources Section. Bulletin — NC Div Resour Plann Eval Miner Resour Sect Bull
North Carolina. Division of Resource Planning and Evaluation. Mineral Resources Section. Educational Series — NC Div Resour Plann Eval Miner Resour Sect Educ Ser
North Carolina. Division of Resource Planning and Evaluation. Mineral Resources Section. Regional Geology Series — NC Div Resour Plann Eval Miner Resour Sect Reg Geol Ser
North Carolina. Division of Resource Planning and Evaluation. Regional Geology Series — NC Div Resour Plann Eval Reg Geol Ser
North Carolina. Division of Water Resources and Engineering. Bulletin — NC Div Water Resour Eng Bull
North Carolina. Division of Water Resources, Inlets, and Coastal Waterways. Bulletin — NC Div Water Resour Inlets Coastal Waterw Bull
North Carolina Folklore — NC Folk
North Carolina Folklore — NCarF
North Carolina Folklore — NCF
North Carolina Folklore — No Ca Fo
North Carolina Geological Survey. Bulletin — NCGS B
North Carolina. Geological Survey Section. Bulletin — NC Geol Surv Sect Bull
North Carolina Historical Review — NC His R
North Carolina Historical Review — NC Hist R
North Carolina Historical Review — NC Hist Rev

North Carolina Historical Review — NCHR
North Carolina Historical Review — No Car Hist R
North Carolina Historical Review — No Car Hist Rev
North Carolina Historical Review — NoC
North Carolina Historical Review — Nth Caro Hist Rev
North Carolina Journal of International Law and Commercial Regulation — NCJ Int'l L and Com Reg
North Carolina Law Journal — No Car Law J
North Carolina Law Review — NC L Rev
North Carolina Law Review — NC Law R
North Carolina Law Review — NCL
North Carolina Law Review — NCLR
North Carolina Law Review — No Car Law R
North Carolina Law Review — No Car Law Rev
North Carolina Libraries — N Carolina Lib
North Carolina Libraries — NC Lib
North Carolina Libraries — North Carolina Lib
North Carolina Medical Journal — NC Med J
North Carolina Medical Journal — No Car Med J
North Carolina Medical Journal — North Car Med J
North Carolina. Mineral Resources Section. Educational Series — NC Miner Resour Sect Educ Ser
North Carolina. Mineral Resources Section. Regional Geology Series — NC Miner Resour Sect Reg Geol Ser
North Carolina Music Educator — NCE
North Carolina Pesticide Manual — NC Pestic Manual
North Carolina Reports — NC
North Carolina Review of Business and Economics — NCR Bus and Econ
North Carolina State Bar Newsletter — NC St B Newsl
North Carolina State Bar Quarterly — NC St BQ
North Carolina State Board of Health. Bulletin — No Car State Bd Health Bul
North Carolina State College. Agricultural Experiment Station. Bulletin — NC State Coll Agric Exp Stn Bull
North Carolina State College. Agricultural Experiment Station. Technical Bulletin — NC State Coll Agric Exp Stn Tech Bull
North Carolina State College. Department of Engineering Research. Bulletin — NC State Coll Dep Eng Res Bull
North Carolina State College. Department of Engineering Research. Bulletin — NC State Coll Dept Eng Research Bull
North Carolina State College of Agriculture and Engineering. Engineering Experiment Station. Bulletin — NC State Coll Agric Eng Eng Exp Stn Bull
North Carolina State College Record — NC State Coll Rec
North Carolina State College. School of Agriculture. Annual Report — NC State Coll Sch Agric Annu Rep
North Carolina State University at Raleigh. Agricultural Experiment Station. Technical Bulletin — NC State Univ Raleigh Agric Exp Stn Tech Bull
North Carolina State University. Department of Engineering. Research Bulletin — NC State Univ Dep Eng Res Bull
North Carolina State University. Engineering School Bulletin — NC State Univ Eng Sch Bull
North Carolina State University. Minerals Research Laboratory. Laboratory Notes — NC State Univ Miner Res Lab Lab Notes
North Carolina State University. Minerals Research Laboratory. Report — NC State Univ Miner Res Lab Rep
North Carolina State University. Raleigh. Agricultural Experiment Station. Bulletin — NC State Univ Raleigh Agric Exp Stn Bull
North Carolina State University. School of Agriculture and Life Sciences. Annual Report — NC State Univ Sch Agric Life Sci Annu Rep
North Carolina Studies in Romance Languages and Literatures — NCSRLL
North Carolina Visions — NC Visions
North Central Association. Quarterly — N Cen Assn Q
North Central Association. Quarterly — North Cent Assn Q
North Central Corn Breeding Research Committee. Minutes of Meeting — N Cent Corn Breed Res Comm Minutes Meet
North Central Journal of Agricultural Economics — N Cent J Agric Econ
North Central Region Extension Publication. Michigan State University. Cooperative Extension Service — North Cent Reg Ext Publ Mich State Univ Coop Ext Serv
North Central Regional Extension Publication — North Cent Reg Ext Publ
North Central Weed Control Conference. Proceedings — North Cent Weed Control Conf Proc
North Country Anvil — North Co
North Country Libraries — North Country Lib
North Dakota Academy of Science. Proceedings — N Dak Acad Sci Proc
North Dakota Academy of Science. Proceedings — ND Acad Sci Proc
North Dakota Academy of Science. Proceedings — North Dakota Acad Sci Proc
North Dakota Administrative Code — ND Admin Code
North Dakota Agricultural College. Experiment Station. Biennial Report — N Dak Agr Coll Exp Sta Bien Rep
North Dakota Agricultural Experiment Station. Bimonthly Bulletin — North Dakota Agric Exp Sta Bimonthly Bull
North Dakota. Agricultural Experiment Station. Bulletin — ND Agric Exp Stn Bull
North Dakota Agricultural Experiment Station Bulletin — North Dakota Agric Exp Sta Bull
North Dakota. Agricultural Experiment Station. Publications — ND Ag Exp
North Dakota Agricultural Experiment Station. Research Report — North Dakota Agric Exp Sta Res Rep
North Dakota Agricultural Experiment Station Special Bulletin — North Dakota Agric Exp Sta Special Bull
North Dakota Century Code — ND Cent Code
North Dakota Farm Research — N Dak Fm Res
North Dakota Farm Research — ND Farm Res
North Dakota Farm Research. Bimonthly Bulletin. North Dakota Agricultural College. Agricultural Experiment Station — N Dak Farm Res Bimon Bull
North Dakota Farm Research. North Dakota Agricultural Experiment Station — ND Farm Res ND Agric Exp Stn
North Dakota. Geological Survey. Biennial Report — N Dak G S Bien Rp
North Dakota. Geological Survey. Bulletin — N Dak Geol Surv Bull
North Dakota. Geological Survey. Bulletin — ND Geol Surv Bull
North Dakota. Geological Survey. Bulletin — North Dakota Geol Survey Bull
North Dakota. Geological Survey. Circular — N Dak Geol Surv Circ
North Dakota. Geological Survey. Circular — ND Geol Surv Circ
North Dakota. Geological Survey. Educational Series — ND Geol Surv Educ Ser
North Dakota Geological Survey. Ground-Water Studies — ND Geol Surv Ground Water Stud
North Dakota. Geological Survey. Miscellaneous Map — ND Geol Surv Misc Map
North Dakota. Geological Survey. Miscellaneous Map — North Dakota Geol Survey Misc Map
North Dakota. Geological Survey. Miscellaneous Series — N Dak Geol Surv Misc Ser
North Dakota. Geological Survey. Miscellaneous Series — ND Geol Surv Misc Ser
North Dakota. Geological Survey. Miscellaneous Series — North Dakota Geol Survey Misc Ser
North Dakota. Geological Survey. Report of Investigations — N Dak Geol Surv Rep Invest
North Dakota. Geological Survey. Report of Investigations — ND Geol Surv Rep Invest
North Dakota. Geological Survey. Report of Investigations — North Dakota Geol Survey Rept Inv
North Dakota Historical Quarterly — ND His Q
North Dakota Historical Quarterly — NDHQ
North Dakota Historical Quarterly — No Dak Hist Quar
North Dakota History — N Dak History
North Dakota History — ND Hist
North Dakota History — NDH
North Dakota History — NDHi
North Dakota History — No Dak Hist
North Dakota History — NoD
North Dakota Law Review — ND L Review
North Dakota Law Review — NDL Rev
North Dakota Law Review — NDLR
North Dakota Law Review — NDR
North Dakota Law Review — North Dakota L Rev
North Dakota Library Notes — N Dak Lib Notes
North Dakota Magazine — N Dak M
North Dakota Music Educator — ND
North Dakota Outdoors — N Dak Outdoors
North Dakota Quarterly — NDQ
North Dakota Quarterly — No Dak Quar
North Dakota Quarterly — NoDQ
North Dakota REC [*Rural Electric Cooperatives*] **Magazine** — ND REC Mag
North Dakota Reports — ND
North Dakota Research Foundation Bulletin — ND Res Found Bull
North Dakota Research Foundation Bulletin. Circular — N Dak Research Found Bull Circ
North Dakota Research Report. North Dakota Agricultural Experiment Station — ND Res Rep ND Agric Exp Stn
North Dakota State Historical Society. Collections — N Dak His S
North Dakota. State Laboratories Department. Bulletin — ND State Lab Dep Bull
North Dakota University. Quarterly Journal — ND Quar J
North East Asia Journal of Theology — NEAJT
North East Coast Institution of Engineers and Shipbuilders. Transactions — North East Coast Inst Eng Shipbuild Trans
North Eastern Reporter — NE
North Eastern Reporter. Second Series — N E 2d
North Ireland Ministry of Agriculture. Annual Report on Research and Technical Work — North Irel Minist Agric Annu Rep Res Tech Work
North Ireland Ministry of Agriculture. Record of Agricultural Research — North Irel Minist Agric Rec Agric Res
North Louisiana Historical Association Journal — NoH
North Medicine — North Med
North Munster Antiquarian Journal — N Munster Antiq J
North Munster Antiquarian Journal — Nth Munster Antiq J
North of 60. Environmental Studies [*Canada*] — N60ES
North of England Institute of Mining and Mechanical Engineering. Transactions — Nth England Inst Min Mech Eng Trans
North of Scotland College of Agriculture. Bulletin — North Scotl Coll Agric Bull
North Pacific Fur Seal Commission. Proceedings of the Annual Meeting — North Pac Fur Seal Comm Proc Annu Meet
North Queensland Conference. Australasian Institute of Mining and Metallurgy — North Queensl Conf Australas Inst Min Metall
North Queensland Naturalist — N QD Nat
North Queensland Naturalist — N Qld Nat
North Queensland Naturalist — N Queensl Nat
North Queensland Naturalist — N Queensland Naturalist
North Queensland Naturalist — North Queensl Nat
North Queensland Register — NQ Register
North Riding School Library. Guild Bulletin — N Riding Sch Libr Guild Bull
North Sea Observer — NSR
North Sea Oil Information Sheet — North Sea Oil Inf Sheet
North South (Ottawa, Canada) — NSO
North Staffordshire Field Club and Archaeological Society. Transactions and Annual Report. — NSFC
North Staffordshire Journal of Field Studies — N Staffordshire J Fld Stud
North Staffordshire Journal of Field Studies — North Stafford J Field Stud
North Staffordshire Journal of Field Studies — North Staffordshire J Field Stud
North Staffordshire Journal of Field Studies — NSJFS

North West Farmer, Rancher — NW Farm Ranch
North Western Branch Papers. Institution of Chemical Engineers — North West Branch Pap Inst Chem Eng
North Western Newsletter — North West Newsl
North Western Newsletter — NW Newsl
North Western Reporter — NW
Northampton Archaeology — Northamp A
Northamptonshire Archaeology — Northampt Arch
Northamptonshire Archaeology — Northamptonshire Archaeol
Northamptonshire Past and Present — Noa
Northeast Asia Journal of Theology — NE Asia J Th
Northeast Asia Journal of Theology — No East As J Theo
Northeast Bioengineering Conference. Proceedings — Northeast Bioeng Conf Proc
Northeast Dialog — NE Dialog
Northeast Electronics Research and Engineering Meeting Record — Northeast Electron Res Eng Meet Rec
Northeast Folklore — NEF
Northeast Folklore — NF
Northeast Folklore — NoEF
Northeast Gulf Science — Northeast Gulf Sci
Northeast Journal of Business and Economics — NEJ
Northeast Louisiana Business Review — NLB
Northeastern China People's University Journal. Natural Science — Northeast China Peoples Univ J Nat Sci
Northeastern Environmental Science — Northeast Environ Sci
Northeastern Forest Experiment Station. Forest Service Research Note NE (US) — Northeast For Exp Stn For Serv Res Note NE (US)
Northeastern Geology — Northeast Geol
Northeastern Industrial World — Northeastern Ind World
Northeastern Journal of Agricultural and Resource Economics — Northeast J Agric Resour Econ
Northeastern Mathematical Journal — Northeast Math J
Northeastern Regional Antipollution Conference — Northeast Reg Antipollut Conf
Northeastern Technical Committee on Utilization of Beech. Northeastern Forest Experiment Station. Beech Utilization Series — Northeast Tech Comm Util Beech Northeast For Exp Stn Beech
Northeastern Weed Control Conference. Proceedings — Northeast Weed Control Conf Proc
Northeastern Weed Science Society. Proceedings. Annual Meeting — Northeast Weed Sci Soc Proc Annu Meet
Northeastern Wood Utilization Council, Incorporated. Bulletin — Northeast Wood Util Counc Inc Bull
Northeastern Wood Utilization Council, Incorporated. Woodnotes — Northeast Wood Util Counc Inc Woodnotes
Northern Adventures — NOAD
Northern Affairs. Ontario Ministry of Northern Affairs — NOAF
Northern Apiarist — Nth Apiar
Northern Architect — Northern Archt
Northern California Foreign Language Newsletter — NCFLN
Northern California Monthly — N Calif Mon
Northern California Review of Business and Economics — North Calif Rev Bus Econ
Northern California Review of Business and Economics — Northern Cal R Bus and Econ
Northern Cavern and Mine Research Society. Occasional Publication — North Cavern Mine Res Soc Occas Publ
Northern Cordilleran — No Cordilleran
Northern Development, Incorporating Arctic Digest — NODE
Northern Division Report ND-R. United Kingdom Atomic Energy Authority — North Div Rep NDR UK At Energy Auth
Northern Electric Telesis — N Elec Telesis
Northern Engineer — NOEN
Northern Engineer (Fairbanks) — North Eng (Fairbanks)
Northern Forest Ranger College Annual — Nth Forest Ranger Coll A
Northern Forest Research Centre (Canada). Information Report NOR-X — North For Res Cent (Can) Inf Rep NORX
Northern Forestry / Hoppo Ringyo — N Forest
Northern Fur Trade — North Fur Trade
Northern Gardener — Nth Gdnr
Northern Health Research Bulletin — NHRB
Northern History — NH
Northern History — NoH
Northern History — North Hist
Northern History. A Review of the History of the North of England — Northern Hist
Northern Housing — NOHO
Northern Illinois University. Law Review — N Ill LR
Northern Illinois University. Law Review — N Ill UL Rev
Northern Ireland. Government. Ministry of Commerce. Memoirs. Geological Survey — North Irel Gov Minist Commer Mem Geol Surv
Northern Ireland. Horticultural Centre. Annual Report — North Ire Hort Cent Ann Rep
Northern Ireland Legal Quarterly — N Ir Legal Q
Northern Ireland Legal Quarterly — N Ir LQ
Northern Ireland Legal Quarterly — N Ire LQ
Northern Ireland Legal Quarterly — NILQ
Northern Ireland Legal Quarterly — No Ire L Q
Northern Ireland Legal Quarterly — North Ireland LQ
Northern Ireland Legal Quarterly — Nth Ir Leg Qtr
Northern Ireland Libraries — NI Libr
Northern Ireland Libraries — Northern Ireland Lib
Northern Ireland. Memoirs. Geological Survey — North Irel Mem Geol Surv
Northern Ireland. Ministry of Agriculture. Record of Agricultural Research — North Irel Minist Agric Rec Agricultural Res
Northern Ireland. Ministry of Agriculture. Research and Experimental Record — North Irel Minist Agric Res Exper Rec
Northern Ireland News Service [*Database*] — NINS
Northern Ireland Record of Agricultural Research — N Ireland Rec Agr Res
Northern Ireland Revised Statutes — N Ir Rev Stat
Northern Journal [*Atlin, British Columbia*] — NJ
Northern Journal [*Canada*] — NOJO
Northern Journal of Applied Forestry — NJAF
Northern Journal of Applied Forestry — North J Appl For
Northern Kentucky Law Review — N KY L Rev
Northern Kentucky Law Review — NKYLR
Northern Kentucky Law Review — North KY LR
Northern Kentucky Law Review — Northern KY Law R
Northern Lights — Northern L
Northern Lights. Diocese of Yukon — NOLI
Northern Logger — Nth Logger
Northern Logger and Timber Processer — North Log Timber Process
Northern Logger and Timber Processor — Northern Logger
Northern Miner — NM
Northern Miner — No Miner
Northern Miner — North Miner
Northern Miner — Nth Miner
Northern Miscellany — NM
Northern News Report — NR
Northern Nigeria. Regional Research Station. Technical Report — North Niger Reg Res Stn Tech Rep
Northern Nigeria. Regional Research Station. Technical Report — North Nigeria Reg Res Stn Tech Rep
Northern Nut Growers Association. Annual Report — North Nut Grow Assoc Annu Rep
Northern Offshore — North Offshore
Northern Offshore. Norwegian Journal of Oil and Gas — NJOG
Northern Offshore. Norwegian Journal of Oil and Gas — NOG
Northern Ohio Business Journal — N Ohio Bus
Northern Ontario Business — N Ontario B
Northern Ontario Business — NONT
Northern Perspectives. Canadian Arctic Resources Committee — NOPE
Northern Pipeline Agency News Releases and Communiques — NPAC
Northern Principal — Nor Prin
Northern Projects Journal. British Columbia Hydro — NPJO
Northern Raven — NORA
Northern Raven. New Series — NRVN
Northern Reporter. Capital Communications Ltd. — NRE
Northern Review — NoR
Northern Review — North R
Northern Rhodesia. Annual Bulletin. Department of Agriculture — North Rhod Annu Bull Dep Agric
Northern Rhodesia. Department of Geological Survey. Bulletin — North Rhod Dep Geol Surv Bull
Northern Rhodesia. Department of Geological Survey. Report — North Rhod Dep Geol Surv Rep
Northern Rhodesia. Geological Survey. Bulletin — North Rhod Geol Surv Bull
Northern Rhodesia. Geological Survey. Report — North Rhod Geol Surv Rep
Northern Rhodesia Government. Geological Survey Department. Economic Unit Report — North Rhod Gov Geol Surv Dep Econ Unit Rep
Northern Science Education News Service. Scavengers College, Alaska — NSEN
Northern Science Network Newsletter. UNESCO-MAB Northern Science Network Secretariat [*Edmonton*] — NSNN
Northern Scotland — North Scot
Northern Scotland — Northern Scot
Northern Social Science Review — North Soc Sci Rev
Northern Studies — North Stud
Northern Studies [*England*] — Northern Stud
Northern Territory Judgements — NTJ
Northern Territory Reports — NTR
Northern Times — NO
Northern Times [*Whitehorse, Canada*] — NT
Northern Women Talk [*Canada*] — NOWT
North-Holland Linguistic Series [*Elsevier Book Series*] — NHLS
North-Holland Mathematical Library [*Elsevier Book Series*] — NHML
North-Holland Mathematical Library — North-Holland Math Library
North-Holland Mathematics Studies [*Elsevier Book Series*] — NHMS
North-Holland Mathematics Studies [*Elsevier Book Series*] — North-Holland Math Stud
North-Holland Mathematics Studies — North-Holland Math Studies
North-Holland Medieval Translations [*Elsevier Book Series*] — NHMT
North-Holland Research Series in Early Detection and Prevention of Behaviour Disorders [*Elsevier Book Series*] — NRS
North-Holland Series in Applied Mathematics and Mechanics [*Elsevier Book Series*] — NHAM
North-Holland Series in Applied Mathematics and Mechanics [*Elsevier Book Series*] — North-Holland Ser Appl Math Mech
North-Holland Series in Applied Mathematics and Mechanics — North-Holland Ser in Appl Math and Mech
North-Holland Series in Crystal Growth [*Elsevier Book Series*] — NHCG
North-Holland Series in Crystal Growth — North Holland Ser Cryst Growth
North-Holland Series in General Systems Research — North Holland Ser Gen Systems Res
North-Holland Series in General Systems Research [*Elsevier Book Series*] — NSGSR
North-Holland Series in Probability and Applied Mathematics — North Holland Ser Probab Appl Math

North-Holland Series in Probability and Applied Mathematics [*Elsevier Book Series*] — PAMS
North-Holland Series in Statistics and Probability — North Holland Ser Statist Probab
North-Holland Series in Systems and Software Development [*Elsevier Book Series*] — NHSSD
North-Holland Series in Systems Science and Engineering — North Holland Ser System Sci Engrg
North-Holland Series in Systems Science and Engineering [*Elsevier Book Series*] — SSE
North-Holland Studies in Silver [*Elsevier Book Series*] — NHSS
North-Holland Studies in Theoretical Poetics [*Elsevier Book Series*] — STP
North-Holland Systems and Control Series [*Elsevier Book Series*] — NHSC
North-Holland Systems and Control Series [*Elsevier Book Series*] — North Holland Syst Control Ser
Northian Newsletter — NORL
Northland — NOLD
Northland Free Press [*Slave Lake, Alberta*] — NF
Northland News — NL
Northline Association of Canadian Universities for Northern Studies — NOTL
Northrop University. Law Journal of Aerospace, Energy, and the Environment [*A publication*] — Northrop ULJ Aero Energy and Envt
Northumberland County Historical Society. Proceedings — NCoHS
Northumberland County Historical Society. Proceedings — NCoHSP
Northward Journal — NORJ
Northwater. Institute of Water Resources. University of Alaska — NOWR
Northwest Agricultural Bulletin. National Northwest Agricultural College. Hsi Pei Nung Pao — Northw Agric Bull
Northwest Anthropological Research Notes — Northwest Anthropol Res Notes
Northwest Atlantic Fisheries Organization. Annual Report — Northwest Atl Fish Organ Annu Rep
Northwest Atlantic Fisheries Organization. Scientific Council. Studies — Northwest Atl Fish Organ Sci Counc Stud
Northwest Atlantic Fisheries Organization. Statistical Bulletin — Northwest Atl Fish Organ Stat Bull
Northwest China Journal of Agricultural Science — Northwest China J Agric Sci
Northwest Dentistry — Northwest Dent
Northwest Environmental Journal — Northwest Environ J
Northwest Explorer. Northwest Territorial Airways [*Yellowknife, NT*] — NWEX
Northwest Geology — Northwest Geol
Northwest Livestock Directory — Northwest Livestock Dir
Northwest Medicine — Northw Med
Northwest Medicine — Northwest Med
Northwest Missouri State College Studies — NMSCS
Northwest Missouri State College Studies — NwMSCS
Northwest Ohio Quarterly — NOQ
Northwest Ohio Quarterly — Northw Ohio Quar
Northwest Ohio Quarterly — Northwest Ohio Q
Northwest Ohio Quarterly — NW Ohio Q
Northwest Ohio Quarterly — NWOQ
Northwest Orchid Bulletin — Northw Orchid Bull
Northwest Passage — NW Pasage
Northwest Prospector. Northwest Miners and Developers Bulletin — NWPR
Northwest Pulp and Paper News — NW Paper News
Northwest Review — Nowest R
Northwest Review — NR
Northwest Review — NWR
Northwest Science — Northwest Sci
Northwest Science — NW Sci
Northwest Science. Official Publication. Northwest Scientific Association — Northwest Sci Off Publ Northwest Sci Assoc
Northwest Territories Reports — NWT
Northwest Territories Reports — NWT Rep
Northwest Territories Reports (Canada) — NW Terr (Can)
Northwest Wood Products Clinic. Proceedings — Northwest Wood Prod Clin Proc
Northwestern Endicott Report, 1986. Employment Trends for College Graduates in Business — Endicott 86
Northwestern Journal of International Law and Business — Northwest J Int'l L & Bus
Northwestern Journal of International Law and Business — Northwestern J Internat Law and Bus
Northwestern Journal of International Law and Business — Nw J Intl L and Bus
Northwestern Lancet — Northwest Lancet
Northwestern Lumberman — Northwest Lumberman
Northwestern Miller — Northwest Miller
Northwestern Miller and American Baker — Northwest Miller Am Baker
Northwestern University. Dental Research and Graduate Study Bulletin — Northwest Univ Dent Res Grad Study Bull
Northwestern University. Department of Geography. Studies in Geography — Northwestern Univ Dept Geography Studies Geography
Northwestern University. Law Review — North UL Rev
Northwestern University. Law Review — Northw L Rev
Northwestern University. Law Review — Northw U La
Northwestern University. Law Review — Northw Univ Law Rev
Northwestern University. Law Review — Northwestern UL Rev
Northwestern University. Law Review — Northwestern Univ L Rev
Northwestern University. Law Review — Northwestern Univ Law R
Northwestern University. Law Review — NUL
Northwestern University. Law Review — NULR
Northwestern University. Law Review — NW U L Rev
Northwestern University. Law Review — NW Univ Law R
Northwestern University. Law Review — NWL
Northwestern University. Law Review — NWULR
Northwestern University. Law Review. Supplement — Nw LS
Northwestern University. Studies in the Humanities — NUSH
Norton's Literary Letter — Norton
Norveg. Journal of Norwegian Ethnology — NORV
Norvegia Sacra — Norv Sac
Norvegica Pharmaceutica Acta — Norv Pharm Acta
Norway — NWAY
Norway. Geologiske Undersoekelse. Bulletin — Norway Geol Undersoekelse Bull
Norway. Patent Document — Norw Pat Doc
Norwegian [*Patent Document*] — Norw
Norwegian American Commerce — Norwegian
Norwegian Archaeological Review — NAR
Norwegian Archaeological Review — NOAR
Norwegian Archaeological Review — Nor Arch Rev
Norwegian Archaeological Review — Norw AR
Norwegian Archaeological Review — Norw Archaeol Rev
Norwegian Bankers Association. Financial Review — NJS
Norwegian Canners' Export Journal — Norw Canners Export J
Norwegian Commercial Banks. Financial Review — Norwegian Commer Banks Fin R
Norwegian Forestry — Norw For
Norwegian Geotechnical Institute. Publication — Norw Geotech Inst Publ
Norwegian Journal of Agricultural Sciences — Norw J Agric Sci
Norwegian Journal of Agricultural Sciences. Supplement — Norw J Agric Sci Suppl
Norwegian Journal of Botany — NOJB
Norwegian Journal of Botany — Norw J Bot
Norwegian Journal of Chemistry, Mining, and Metallurgy — Norw J Chem Min Metall
Norwegian Journal of Entomology — Norw J Entomol
Norwegian Journal of Forestry — Norw J For
Norwegian Journal of Linguistics — NJL
Norwegian Journal of Zoology — NOJZ
Norwegian Journal of Zoology — Norw J Zool
Norwegian Maritime Research — Norw Marit Res
Norwegian Oil Review — Norw Oil Rev
Norwegian Petroleum Directorate. Paper — Norw Petrol Dir Pap
Norwegian Shipping News — Norw Shipp News
Norwegian Shipping News [*Oslo*] — NSH
Norwegian Studies in English — NSE
Norwegian Trade Bulletin — Nor Tr Bul
Norwegian Whaling Gazette — Norw Whaling Gaz
Norwegian-American Studies — NAS
Norwegian-American Studies and Records — NASR
Norwegian-American Studies and Records — Norwegian-Am Stud and Rec
Nor'-West Farmer — Nor'-West F
Norwiny Literackie — NL
Nos Cahiers — Nos C
Nos Oiseaux. Bulletin de la Societe Romande pour l'Etude et la Protection des Oiseaux — Nos Oiseaux Bull Romande Etude Prot Oiseaux
Nosokomeiaka Chronika — Nosokom Chron
Nosokomeiaka Chronika — Nosokomeiaka Chron
Nossos Classicos — NCL
Nostro Tempo — NTemp
Not Man Apart — Not Man A
Nota Genitiva — NG
Nota Informativa. Instituto Nacional de Investigaciones Forestales (Mexico) — Nota Inf Inst Nac Invest Forest (Mex)
Nota sobre Investigaciones. Centro de Investigaciones Pesqueras (Bauta, Cuba) — Nota Invest Cent Invest Pesq (Bauta Cuba)
Nota Tecnica. Instituto Forestal (Santiago De Chile) — Nota Tec Inst For (Chile)
Nota Tecnica. Instituto Nacional de Investigaciones Forestales (Mexico) — Nota Tec Inst Nac Invest For (Mex)
Notarieel Nieuwsbode — NN
Notarieel Weekblad — Not W
Notarieel Weekblad — NW
Notas Agronomicas — Notas Agron
Notas Biologicas. Facultad de Ciencias Exactas, Fisicas, y Naturales. Universidad Nacional del Nordeste. Corrientes Zoologia — NBNZAK
Notas. Centro de Biologia Aquatica Tropical (Lisbon) — Notas Cent Biol Aquat Trop (Lisb)
Notas Cientificas. Serie M. Matematica — Notas Ci Ser M Mat
Notas Cientificas. Serie M. Matematica [*Lima*] — Notas Cient Ser M Mat
Notas de Algebra y Analisis [*Bahia Blanca*] — Notas Algebra Anal
Notas de Divulgacion del Instituto Municipal de Botanica (Buenos Aires) — Notas Divulg Inst Munic Bot (Buenos Aires)
Notas de Fisica — Notas Fis
Notas de Fisica. Centro Brasileiro de Pesquisas Fisicas — Notas Fis Cent Bras Pesqui Fis
Notas de Geometria y Topologia [*Bahia Blanca*] — Notas Geom Topol
Notas de la Sociedad de Matematica de Chile — Notas Soc Mat Chile
Notas de Logica Matematica — Notas Logica Mat
Notas de Matematica [*Amsterdam*] — Notas Mat
Notas de Matematica Discreta — Notas Mat Discreta
Notas de Matematica y Simposia — Notas Mat Simpos
Notas de Poblacion — Notas Pobl
Notas del Museo de La Plata. Geologia — Notas Mus La Plata Geol
Notas e Estudos. Instituto de Biologia Maritima (Lisbon) — Notas Estud Inst Biol Marit (Lisb)
Notas e Estudos. Secretaria de Estado das Pescas. Serie Recursos e Ambiente Aquatico — NESADS
Notas e Estudos. Secretaria de Estado das Pescas. Serie Recursos e Ambiente Aquatico — Notas Estud Secr Estado Pescas Ser Recur Ambiente Aquat
Notas e Estudos. Universidade do Rio Grande Do Sul. Escola de Geologia — Notas Estud Univ Rio Grande Sul Esc Geol

Notas. Instituto de Matematica e Estatistica da Universidade de Sao Paulo. Serie Matematica — Notas Inst Mat Estatist Univ Sao Paulo Ser Mat
Notas Mimeografadas. Centro de Biologia Aquatica Tropical (Lisbon) — Notas Mimeogr Cent Biol Aquat Trop (Lisb)
Notas. Museo de La Plata. Antropologia — Notas Mus La Plata Antropol
Notas. Museo de La Plata. Botanica — Notas Mus La Plata Bot
Notas. Museo de La Plata. Paleontologia — Notas Mus La Plata Paleontol
Notas. Museo de La Plata. Zoologia — Notas Mus La Plata Zool
Notas Preliminares del Museo de La Plata. Universidad Nacional de La Plata — Notas Prelim Mus La Plata
Notas Preliminares e Estudos. Divisao de Geologia e Mineralogia (Brazil) — Notas Prelim Estud Div Geol Mineral (Braz)
Notas Preliminares e Estudos. Servico Geologico e Mineralogico do Brazil — Notas Prelim Estud Serv Geol Mineral Braz
Notas Quirurgicas del Sanatorio Deschamps — Not Quir Sanat Desch
Notas Quirurgicas. Sanatorio Deschamps — Notas Quir Sanat Deschamps
Notas Silvicolas. Administracion Nacional de Bosques (Buenos Aires, Argentina) — Nota Silvic Adm Nac Bosques (Argent)
Notas Sobre Portugal. Exposicao Nacional do Rio de Janeiro — NPENRJ
Notas Tecnicas. Instituto de Pesquisas da Marinha (Rio De Janeiro) — Notas Tec Inst Pesqui Mar (Rio De J)
Notas Tecnicas. Instituto de Pesquisas da Marinha (Rio De Janeiro) — Notas Tec Inst Pesqui Mar (Rio De Janeiro)
Notas Tecnicas. Instituto Nacional de Investigaciones Forestales — Notas Tecn Inst Nac Invest Forest
Notas Tecnico Forestales. Escuela de Ingenieria Forestal. Universidad de Chile — Nota Tec For Esc Ingen For Univ Chile
Notas Tecnologicas Forestales — Notas Tecnol For
Notas Tecnologicas Forestales. Administracion Nacional de Bosques (Buenos Aires, Argentina) — Nota Tecnol For Adm Nac Bosques (Argent)
Notas Tecnologicas Forestales. Direccion de Investigaciones Forestales (Argentina) — Notas Tecnol For Dir Invest For (Argent)
Notas y Comunicaciones. Instituto Geologico y Minero de Espana — Notas Comun Inst Geol Espana
Notas y Comunicaciones. Instituto Geologico y Minero de Espana — Notas Comun Inst Geol Min Esp
Notas y Estudios de Filosofia — NEF
Notationes Biologicae — Not Biol
Notationes Biologicae — Notat Biol
Notatki Ornitologiczne — Notatki Ornitol
Notatki Plockie — NPlockie
Note CEA-N (France). Commissariat a l'Energie Atomique — Note CEA-N (Fr) Commis Energ At
Note d'Archivio per la Storia Musicale — NA
Note de Frutticultura — Note Fruttic
Note de Recherche. Mineral Exploration Research Institute. McGill University [*A publication*] — Note Rech Miner Explor Res Inst McGill Univ
Note de Recherches. Departement d'Exploitation et Utilisation des Bois. Universite Laval — Note Rech Dep Exploit Util Bois Univ Laval
Note di Matematica — Note Mat
Note d'Information Technique. Laboratoire Central des Ponts et Chaussees — Note Inf Tech Lab Cent Ponts Chaussees
Note du Service Oceanographique des Peches de l'Indochine — Note Serv Oceanogr Peches Indochine
Note e Riviste di Psichiatria — Note Riv Psichiat
Note e Riviste di Psichiatria — Note Riv Psichiatr
Note Economiche — Note Econ
Note ed Apunti Sperimentale di Entomologia Agraria — Note Apunti Sper Ent Agr
Note. Laboratorio di Biologia Marina e Pesca-Fano — Note Lab Biol Mar Pesca-Fano
Note Recensioni e Notizie — Note Recens & Not
Note Technique. Centre de Recherches Agronomiques de l'Etat (Gembloux) — Note Tech Cent Rech Agron Etat (Gembloux)
Note Technique. Centre Scientifique et Technique de l'Industrie Textile Belge — Note Tech Cent Sci Tech Ind Text Belge
Note Technique. Centre Technique Forestier Tropical (Nogent-Sur-Marne, France) — Note Tech Cent Tech For Trop (Nogent Sur Marne Fr)
Note Technique. Centre Technique Forestier Tropicale — Note Tech Centre Tech For Trop
Note Technique. Departement d'Exploitation et Utilisation des Bois. Universite Laval — Note Tech Dep Exploit Util Bois Univ Laval
Note Technique. Institut de Reboisement de Tunis — Note Tech Inst Rebois Tunis
Note Technique. Office National d'Etudes et de Recherches Aerospatiales (France) — Note Tech Off Nat Etud Rech Aerosp (Fr)
Notebook of Empirical Petrology — Noteb Empirical Petrol
Notebooks for Knossos — NB
Notes — No
Notes — PMUN
Notes Africaines — NA
Notes Africaines — NAfr
Notes Africaines — Not Af
Notes Africaines — Notes Afr
Notes. Agricultural Research Centre Herbarium (Egypt) — Notes Agric Res Cent Herb (Egypt)
Notes and Documents. United Nations Unit on Apartheid — Notes Docum UN Unit Apartheid
Notes and Memoirs. United Arab Republic. Hydrobiological Department — Notes Mem UAR Hydrobiol Dep
Notes and Queries — N & Q
Notes and Queries — NoQ
Notes and Queries — Notes & Quer
Notes and Queries — Notes Quer
Notes and Queries — NQ
Notes and Queries — PNNQ
Notes and Queries for Readers and Writers, Collectors, and Librarians — Notes Read
Notes and Queries for Readers and Writers, Collectors, and Librarians — NQRW
Notes and Queries. New Series — NQNS
Notes and Queries. Society of West Highland and Island Historical Research [*A publication*] — Notes Queries Soc West Highl Isl Hist Res
Notes and Records. Royal Society of London — Note Rec Roy Soc London
Notes and Records. Royal Society of London — Notes and Records Roy Soc London
Notes and Records. Royal Society of London — Notes Rec R
Notes and Records. Royal Society of London — Notes Rec R Soc Lond
Notes and Records. Royal Society of London — Notes Rec Roy London
Notes and Records. Royal Society of London — Notes Rec Roy Soc Lond
Notes and Records. Royal Society of London — Notes Rec Roy Soc London
Notes and Records. Royal Society of London — NotR
Notes and Records. Royal Society of London — R Soc NR
Notes and Reports in Computer Science and Applied Mathematics — Notes Rep Comput Sci Appl Math
Notes and Reports in Mathematics in Science and Engineering — Notes Rep Math Sci Engrg
Notes. Botanical School of Trinity College — Notes Bot School Trinity Coll
Notes. Botanical School of Trinity College (Dublin) — Notes Bot Sch Trinity Coll (Dublin)
Notes de Pastorale Liturgique — NP Li
Notes de Recherche. Fondation Universitaire Luxembourgeoise — Notes Rech Fond Univ Luxemb
Notes d'Entomologie Chinoise — Notes Ent Chin
Notes d'Information CEA [*Comissariat a l'Energie Atomique*] — Notes Inf CEA
Notes d'Information et Statistiques. Banque — Notes Inform Statist Banque
Notes d'Information et Statistiques. Banque Centrale des Etats de l'Afrique de l'Ouest — Notes Inform Statist Banque Centr Afr Ouest
Notes du Service Geologique du Maroc — Notes Serv Geol Maroc
Notes du Service Geologique (Tunisia) — Notes Serv Geol (Tunis)
Notes et Documents Publiee. Direction des Antiquites et Arts de Tunisie — N et D
Notes et Documents Voltaiques — NDV
Notes et Documents Voltaiques — Notes Doc Volt
Notes et Documents Voltaiques — Notes et Docum Voltaiques
Notes et Etudes Documentaires — Notes et Etud Docum
Notes et Etudes Documentaires — Notes Etud Doc
Notes et Etudes Documentaires — SXD
Notes et Etudes Documentaires. Serie Problemes d'Amerique Latine — Notes et Etud Docum Ser Problemes Am Latine
Notes et Memoires. Service Geologique du Maroc — Notes Mem Serv Geol Maroc
Notes et Memoires. Service Geologique (Morocco) — Notes Mem Serv Geol (Morocco)
Notes et Memoires. Service Geologique (Rabat) — Notes Mem Serv Geol (Rabat)
Notes et Memoires sur le Moyen-Orient — Notes et Mem Moyen-Orient
Notes et Memoires sur le Moyen-Orient — Notes Mem Moyen-Orient
Notes from Strybing Arboretum — Notes Strybing Arbor
Notes. Institut za Oceanografiju i Ribarstvo (Split) — Notes Inst Oceanogr Ribar (Split)
Notes Marocaines — Not Mar
Notes Marocaines — Notes Maroc
Notes. Office of Seed and Plant Introduction — Notes Off Seed Introd
Notes on Applied Science. National Physical Laboratory — Notes Appl Sci NPL
Notes on Applied Science. United Kingdom National Physical Laboratory — Notes Appl Sci UK Natl Phys Lab
Notes on Contemporary Literature — NCL
Notes on Contemporary Literature — NConL
Notes on Education and Research in African Music — Notes on Education Res in Afr Music
Notes on Higher Education — Notes on Higher Educ
Notes on Islam — N Isl
Notes on Linguistics — NLing
Notes on Mississippi Writers — NMW
Notes on Modern American Literature — NMAL
Notes on Neurology — Notes Neurol
Notes on Numerical Fluid Mechanics — Notes Numer Fluid Mech
Notes on Pure Mathematics — Notes on Pure Math
Notes on Pure Mathematics — Notes Pure Math
Notes on Soil Technique [*Australia Commonwealth Scientific and Industrial Research Organisation. Division of Soils*] — Notes Soil Tech
Notes on the Science of Building [*Australia Commonwealth Experimental Building Station*] — Notes on Sc Build
Notes on the Science of Building [*Australia Commonwealth Experimental Building Station*] — Notes on the Science of Bldg
Notes on the Science of Building [*Australia Commonwealth Experimental Building Station*] — Notes Sci Bldg
Notes on the Science of Building [*Australia Commonwealth Experimental Building Station*] — Notes Sci Build
Notes on the Science of Building [*Australia Commonwealth Experimental Building Station*] — NSB
Notes on Translation — NOT
Notes on University Education — Notes on Univ Ed
Notes on Water Pollution (Stevenage) — Notes Water Pollut (Stevenage)
Notes on Water Research — Notes Wat Res
Notes on Water Research — Notes Water Res
Notes. Royal Botanic Garden (Edinburgh) — Notes R Bot Gard (Edinb)
Notes. Royal Botanic Garden (Edinburgh) — Notes R Bot Gdn (Edinb)
Notes Techniques en Hydrologie — Notes Tech Hydrol

Notice des Travaux de l'Academie du Gard — Not Trav Acad Gard
Notice Papers - House of Representatives — NPHR
Notice Papers - Senate — NPS
Notice to Airmen — NOTAMS
Notices. American Mathematical Society — Not Am Math
Notices. American Mathematical Society — Notices Amer Math Soc
Notices d'Archeologie Armoricaine — NAA
Notices et Extraits des Manuscrits de la Bibliotheque du Roi — NEMBR
Notices et Extraits des Manuscrits de la Bibliotheque Nationale — NE
Notices et Memoires. Societe Archeologique de Constantine — NSAC
Notices et Texts des Papyrus Grecs du Musee du Louvre et de la Bibliotheque Imperiale — PParis
Noticia Geomorfologica — Notic Geomorfol
Noticiario Arqueologico Hispanico — NA Hisp
Noticiario Arqueologico Hispanico — NAH
Noticiario Arqueologico Hispanico — Not A Hisp
Noticiario Arqueologico Hispanico — Noticiario Arq Hisp
Noticiario Arqueologico Hispanico — Noticiario Arqu Hispanico
Noticiario Arqueologico Hispanico Prehistoria — Notic Arqueol Hispan Prehist
Noticiario das Actividades Sociais da Federacao Brasileira de Engenheiros — FBE Not
Noticiario Instituto Forestal — Noticiario Inst Forestal
Noticiario Mensual. Museo Nacional de Historia Natural — Not Mens Mus Nac Hist Nat
Noticiario Mensual. Museo Nacional de Historial Natural (Santiago) — Noticiario Mens Santiago
Noticias Agricolas — NA
Noticias Agricolas/Compania Shell de Venezuela. Servicio Shell Para El Agricultor — Not Agric
Noticias Agricolas. Fundacion Servicio para el Agricultor — Not Agric Fund Serv Agric
Noticias Agricolas. Servicio para el Agricultor — Not Agric Serv Agric
Noticias Agricolas. Servicio Shell para el Agricultor — NASABW
Noticias Agricolas. Servicio Shell para el Agricultor — Not Agric Serv Shell Agric
Noticias Agricolas. Servicio Shell para el Agricultor — Notic Agr Serv Shell Agr
Noticias Cristianas de Israel — N Cr I
Noticias Culturales — NC
Noticias de Galapagos — Not Galapagos
Noticias Farmaceuticas — Not Farm
Noticias Farmaceuticas (Coimbra) — Not Farm (Coimbra)
Noticias Medico-Veterinarias — Not Med Vet
Noticias Quimicas — Not Quim
Noticiero Bibliotecario Interamericano — Not Bibliot Interamer
Noticiero del Plastico — Plastico
Notiser ur Saellskapets Pro Fauna et Flora Fennica Foerhandlinger — Not Saellsk Fauna Fl Fenn Foerh
Notitiae Siciliensium Ecclesiarum — NSE
Notities over Europa — BBH
Notizblatt des Botanischen Gartens und Museums zu Berlin-Dahlem — Notizbl Bot Gart Berlin Dahlem
Notizblatt des Koeniglichen Botanischen Gartens und Museums zu Berlin — Notizbl Koenigl Bot Gart Berlin
Notizblatt des Vereins fuer Erdkunde, Darmstadt — NbIVED
Notizblatt. Hessisches Landesamt fuer Bodenforschung zu Wiesbaden — Notizbl Hess Landesamtes Bodenforsch Wiesb
Notizblatt. Hessisches Landesamtes fuer Bodenforschung zu Wiesbaden — Notizbl Hess Landesamt Bodenforsch Wiesbaden
Notiziario Archeologico del Ministero delle Colonie — NAMC
Notiziario Archeologico del Ministero delle Colonie — Not Arq Hisp
Notiziario Archeologico del Ministero delle Colonie — Notiz Arch
Notiziario Archeologico. Ministero delle Colonie — Not Arch
Notiziario. Camerale. Camera di Commercio. Industria e Agricoltura di Cuneo [*A publication*] — Notiz Cam Cam Commer Ind Agr Cuneo
Notiziario. Centro Italiano Smalti Porcellanati — Not Cent Ital Smalti Porcellanati
Notiziario Chimico-Industriale — Not Chim Ind
Notiziario. Comitato Nazionale per 'Energia Nucleare (Italy) — Not Com Naz Energ Nucl (Italy)
Notiziario. Comitato Nazionale per l'Energia Nucleare [*Commission on Nulcear Energy*] — Not CNEN
Notiziario. Comitato Nazionale per l'Energia Nucleare — Not Com Naz Energ Nucl
Notiziario Culturale Italiano — NCI
Notiziario de "La Ricerca Scientifica" — Not Ric Sci
Notiziario dell'Amministrazione Sanitaria — Not Ammin Sanit
Notiziario dell'Ecologia — Not Ecol
Notiziario dell'ENEA — Not ENEA
Notiziario Enologico ed Alimentare — Not Enol Aliment
Notiziario Farmaceutico — Notiz Farm
Notiziario Informativo. Centro Italiano Smalti Porcellanati — Not Inf Cent Ital Smalti Porcellanati
Notiziario. Istituto di Automatica. Universita di Roma — Not Ist Autom Univ Roma
Notiziario. Istituto Vaccinogeno Antitubercolare — Not Ist Vaccinogeno Antituberc
Notiziario. Museo Civico ed Associazione Archeologica di Allumiere — Not Allumiere
Notiziario. Societa Italiana di Biochimica Clinica — Not Soc Ital Biochim Clin
Notiziario. Societa Italiana di Fitosociologia — Not Soc Ital Fitosoc
Notiziario sulle Malattie delle Piante — Not Mal Piante
Notiziario sulle Malattie delle Piante — Notiz Mal Piante
Notiziario sulle Malattie delle Piante — Notiz Malatt Piante
Notizie dal Chiostro del Monastero Maggiore — Not Chiostro Mon Magg
Notizie degli Archivi di Stato — NAS
Notizie degli Scavi di Antichita — N Scav Ant
Notizie degli Scavi di Antichita — NdS
Notizie degli Scavi di Antichita — NDSA
Notizie degli Scavi di Antichita — Not Scavi
Notizie degli Scavi di Antichita — Notizie Scavi
Notizie degli Scavi di Antichita — NSA
Notizie degli Scavi di Antichita — NSc
Notizie di Mineralogia Siciliana e Calabrese — Not Mineral Sicil Calabrese
Notizie IRI [*Istituto per la Ricostruzione Industriale*] — Notiz IRI
Notizie Pontifice — Not Pont
Notre Catechese — N Cat
Notre Dame English Journal — NDEJ
Notre Dame English Journal — Notr Dame E
Notre Dame English Journal — Notre Dame Eng J
Notre Dame Estate Planning Institute. Proceedings — Notre Dame Est Plan Inst Proc
Notre Dame Institute on Charitable Giving. Foundations and Trusts — Notre Dame Inst on Char Giving Found and Tr
Notre Dame Journal — NDJ
Notre Dame Journal of Education — N Dame J Ed
Notre Dame Journal of Formal Logic — Notre Dame J Form Log
Notre Dame Journal of Formal Logic — Notre Dame J Formal Logic
Notre Dame Law Review — No D Law
Notre Dame Law Review — Notre Dame L Rev
Notre Dame Law Review — Notre Dame Law R
Notre Dame Lawyer — NDL
Notre Dame Lawyer — Notre Dame L
Notre Dame Lawyer — Notre Dame Law
Notre Dame Mathematical Lectures — Notre Dame Math Lectures
Notre Dame Science Quarterly [*United States*] — Notre Dame Sci Q
Notre Foi et Notre Vie — NFNV
Notre Langue et Notre Culture — Langue et Culture
Notstromversorgung mit Batterien. Technisches Symposium — Notstromversorg Batterien Tech Symp
Nottingham and Nottinghamshire Technical Information Service. News Bulletin — NANTIS News Bull
Nottingham French Studies — NFS
Nottingham French Studies — Nott Fr St
Nottingham Medieval Studies — NMS
Nottingham Medieval Studies — Nottingham Medieval Stud
Nottingham Renaissance and Modern Studies — NRMS
Nottingham University. Mining Department Magazine [*England*] — Nottingham Univ Min Dep Mag
Notulae Entomologicae — Not Entomol
Notulae Entomologicae — Notul Ent
Notulae Entomologicae — Notulae Entomol
Notulae Naturae. Academy of Natural Sciences of Philadelphia — Not Nat Acad Nat Sci Philadelphia
Notulae Naturae (Philadelphia) — Not Nat (Phila)
Notulae Odonatologicae — NOODDJ
Notulae Odonatologicae — Not Odonatol
Notulae Systematicae — Not Syst
Noutati in Mecanica Aplicata si in Constructia de Masini — Noutati Med Apl Constr Mas
Noutati in Stiinte ale Naturii si in Pedagogie — Noutati Stiinte Nat Pedagog
Nouveau Cours de Mathematiques — Nouveau Cours de Math
Nouveau Journal de Chimie — NJCHD
Nouveau Journal de Chimie — Nouv J Chim
Nouveau Journal de Medecine, Chirurgie, et Pharmacie (Paris) — N Jour Med Chir Pharm (Paris)
Nouveau Journal Helvetique, Ou Annales Litteraires et Politiques de l'Europe et Principalement de la Suisse — Nouv J Helv
Nouveautes Medicales — Nouv Med
Nouveaux Cahiers — NoC
Nouveaux Cahiers — Nouv Cah
Nouveaux Memoires. Academie Royale des Sciences et Belles-Lettres. Avec l'Histoire (Berlin) — Nouv Mem Acad Roy Sci Hist Berlin
Nouveaux Memoires de l'Academie Royale des Sciences et Belles-Lettres de Bruxelles — Nouv Mem Acad Roy Sci Bruxelles
Nouveaux Rythmes du Monde — Nouv Rythmes Monde
Nouvel Automatisme — Nouv Autom
Nouvel Automatisme — Nouvel Autom
Nouvel Economiste (Paris) — ENP
Nouvel Observateur — N O
Nouvel Officiel de l'Ameublement — OMM
Nouvelle Bibliotheque Classique — N Bibl Classique
Nouvelle Bibliotheque Classique — N Biblioth Classique
Nouvelle Bibliotheque Classique — Nouv Bibl Class
Nouvelle Bibliotheque des Auteurs Ecclesiastiques — NBAE
Nouvelle Bibliotheque Litteraire — N Bibl Litt
Nouvelle Bibliotheque Litteraire — N Biblioth Litt
Nouvelle Bibliotheque Scientifique — Nouvelle Bibl Sci
Nouvelle Biographie Generale — NBG
Nouvelle Chine — Nouv Chine
Nouvelle Clio [*Bruxelles*] — NC
Nouvelle Clio. Collection [*Paris*] — NcC
Nouvelle Critique — NC
Nouvelle Critique — Nouv Crit
Nouvelle Critique — Nouv Critique
Nouvelle Critique. Revue du Marxisme Militant — NCRMM
Nouvelle Encyclopedie Theologique — N Enc Th
Nouvelle Histoire de l'Eglise — NHE
Nouvelle Initiation Philosophique — NIP
Nouvelle Nouvelle Revue Francaise — NNRF
Nouvelle Presse Medicale — Nouv Presse
Nouvelle Presse Medicale — Nouv Presse Med

Nouvelle Releve — NREL
Nouvelle Revue — NoR
Nouvelle Revue — Nouv Rev
Nouvelle Revue Apologetique — NRA
Nouvelle Revue Canadienne — NRC
Nouvelle Revue Critique — Nouv Rev Crit
Nouvelle Revue Critique — NRC
Nouvelle Revue de Bretagne — NR Bret
Nouvelle Revue de Bretagne — NRB
Nouvelle Revue de Champagne et de Brie — N Rev de Champagne et de Brie
Nouvelle Revue de Droit International Prive — NRDIP
Nouvelle Revue de Hongrie — NRH
Nouvelle Revue de Medecine de Toulouse — Nouv Rev Med Toulouse
Nouvelle Revue de Medecine de Toulouse — NRMTDA
Nouvelle Revue de Medecine de Toulouse. Supplement — NMTSD7
Nouvelle Revue de Medecine de Toulouse. Supplement — Nouv Rev Med Toulouse Suppl
Nouvelle Revue de Psychanalyse — Nouv Rev Psychanal
Nouvelle Revue de Psychoanalyse — Nouv Rev Psychoanalyse
Nouvelle Revue de Science Missionaire — NRSM
Nouvelle Revue d'Entomologie — Nouv Rev Entomol
Nouvelle Revue des Deux Mondes — Nouv R Deux Mondes
Nouvelle Revue Des Deux Mondes — Nouv Revue Des Deux Mondes
Nouvelle Revue des Deux Mondes — RDM
Nouvelle Revue des Traditions Populaires — NRTP
Nouvelle Revue d'Italie — Nouv Rev d Italie
Nouvelle Revue d'Optique — Nouv R Opt
Nouvelle Revue d'Optique — Nouv Rev Opt
Nouvelle Revue d'Optique — NVROB
Nouvelle Revue d'Optique Appliquee — Nouv Rev Opt Appl
Nouvelle Revue du Droit — NRDroit
Nouvelle Revue du Son — Nouv Rev Son
Nouvelle Revue Francaise — Nouv R Francaise
Nouvelle Revue Francaise — Nouv Rev Fr
Nouvelle Revue Francaise [*French periodical; initials also used on books published by Gallimard*] — NRF
Nouvelle Revue Francaise d'Hematologie. Blood Cells — Nouv R F Hem
Nouvelle Revue Francaise d'Hematologie. Blood Cells — Nouv Rev Fr Hematol
Nouvelle Revue Francaise d'Hematologie. Blood Cells — Nouv Rev Fr Hematol Blood Cells
Nouvelle Revue Historique de Droit Francais et Etranger — Nouv Rev Hist Droit Fr
Nouvelle Revue Historique de Droit Francais et Etranger — NRHD
Nouvelle Revue Historique de Droit Francais et Etranger — NRHDF
Nouvelle Revue Historique de Droit Francais et Etranger — NRHDFE
Nouvelle Revue Internationale — Nouv R Int
Nouvelle Revue Internationale Centrale des Etats de l'Afrique de l'Ouest — Nouv R Int Centr Afr Ouest
Nouvelle Revue Pedagogique — NRP
Nouvelle Revue Socialiste — Nouv R Social
Nouvelle Revue Theologique — N Rev Th
Nouvelle Revue Theologique — Nouv Rev Theo
Nouvelle Revue Theologique — Nouv Rev Theol
Nouvelle Revue Theologique — NRT
Nouvelle Revue Theologique — NRTh
Nouvelle Serie Theologique — NS Th
Nouvelle Serie Theologique — NST
Nouvelles Annales des Voyages — Nouv Annales D Voyages
Nouvelles Annales des Voyages, de la Geographie, et de l'Histoire — Nouv Ann Voyages
Nouvelles Archives de l'Art Francais — NAAF
Nouvelles Archives des Missions Scientifiques — Nouv Arch
Nouvelles Archives des Missions Scientifiques et Litteraires — NAM
Nouvelles Archives des Missions Scientifiques et Litteraires — NAMS
Nouvelles Archives des Missions Scientifiques et Litteraires — Nouv Arch Miss
Nouvelles Archives des Missions Scientifiques et Litteraires — Nouv Arch Missions Sci Litt
Nouvelles Archives du Museum d'Histoire Naturelle — Nouv Arch Mus Hist Nat
Nouvelles Archives Hospitalieres — Nouv Arch Hosp
Nouvelles Archives Italiennes de Biologie — Nouv Arch Ital Biol
Nouvelles Bibliques — Nouv Bib
Nouvelles Caledoniennes — Nouv Caledoniennes
Nouvelles Chretiennes d'Israel — N Chret Isr
Nouvelles Chretiennes d'Israel [*Jerusalem*] — NChrIsr
Nouvelles Chretiennes d'Israel [*Jerusalem*] — NCI
Nouvelles de Grasse — Nouv Grasse
Nouvelles de Hollande — Nouv Hol
Nouvelles de Hongrie — Nouv Hongrie
Nouvelles de la Politique Agricole Commune — Nouv Polit Agric Commune
Nouvelles de la Republique des Lettres — Nouv Republ Lett
Nouvelles de la Republique des Lettres — NRL
Nouvelles de l'Aviculture — Nouv Avic
Nouvelles de l'Ecodeveloppement — Nouv Ecodevelop
Nouvelles Economiques de Suisse — BHB
Nouvelles Etudes Hongroises — Nouv Etud Hongroises
Nouvelles Juives Mondiales [*Paris*] — NJM
Nouvelles Litteraires — NL
Nouvelles Litteraires — Nlles Lit
Nouvelles Litteraires [*Paris*] — NouvLitt
Nouvelles Litteraires, Artistiques, et Scientifiques — N Litt
Nouvelles Litteraires, Artistiques, et Scientifiques — NL
Nouvelles Litteraires, Artistiques, et Scientifiques — NLAS
Nouvelles Litteraires, Artistiques, et Scientifiques — Nouv Litt
Nouvelles Litteraires, Artistiques, et Scientifiques — Nouv Litter
Nouvelles. Organisation Mondiale de la Sante — OMS Nouv
Nouvelles Religieuses — N Rel
Nouvelles Techniques — Nouv Tech
Nouvelles Techniques. A. Automatique et Electronique Industrielle — Nouv Tech A
Nouvelles Techniques. B. Genie Nucleaire — Nouv Tech B
Nouvelliste Suisse, Historique, Politique, Litteraire et Amusant — Nouvelliste Suisse
Nova Acta Eruditorum — NAE
Nova Acta Eruditorum — Nova Acta Erud
Nova Acta Eruditorum. Supplementum — NAE S
Nova Acta Historico-Ecclesiastica — NAHE
Nova Acta Leopoldina — NOALA
Nova Acta Leopoldina — Nova Acta Leopold
Nova Acta Leopoldina. Supplementum — Nova Acta Leopold Suppl
Nova Acta Regiae Societatis Scientiarum Upsaliensis — Nova Acta R Soc Sc Upsaliensis
Nova Acta Regiae Societatis Scientiarum Upsaliensis — Nova Acta Regiae Soc Sci Ups
Nova Acta Regiae Societatis Scientiarum Upsaliensis — Nova Acta Regiae Soc Sci Upsal
Nova Acta Regiae Societatis Scientiarum Upsaliensis. Seria C — Nova Acta Regiae Soc Sci Ups C
Nova Acta Regiae Societatis Scientiarum Upsaliensis. Seria C. Botany, General Geology, Physical Geography, Paleontology, and Zoology — Nova Acta Regiae Soc Sci Ups Ser C
Nova Alvorada — NAI
Nova Americana. Giulio Einaudi Editore — GEE/NA
Nova Bibliotheca Ecclesiastica Friburgensis — NBEF
Nova Bibliotheca Lubecensis — NB Lub
Nova et Vetera — N & V
Nova et Vetera — No Ve
Nova et Vetera — NV
Nova et Vetera [*Fribourg*] — NVet
Nova Guinea. Geology — Nova Guinea Geol
Nova Hedwigia — Nova Hedwig
Nova Hedwigia Zeitschrift fuer Kryptogamenkunde — Nova Hedwigia Z Kryptogamenkd
Nova Historia — Nova Hist
Nova Journal of Algebra and Geometry — Nova J Algebra Geom
Nova Journal of Mathematics, Game Theory, and Algebra — Nova J Math Game Theory Algebra
Nova Law Journal — Nova LJ
Nova Literaria Circuli Franconici Oder Fraenkische Gelehrten-Historie — Nova Lit Circuli Francon
Nova Misao — NMis
Nova Obzorija — NO
Nova Proizvodnja — Nova Proizv
Nova Proizvodnya — Nova Proizvod
Nova Revija — NR
Nova Scotia. Department of Lands and Forests. Annual Report — NS Dep Lands For Annu Rep
Nova Scotia. Department of Mines and Energy. Paper — NS Dep Mines Energy Pap
Nova Scotia Department of Mines and Energy. Report — NS Dep Mines Energy Rep
Nova Scotia. Department of Mines. Annual Report. Memoir — Nova Scotia Dept Mines Ann Rept Mem
Nova Scotia. Department of Mines. Annual Report on Mines — NS Dep Mines Annu Rep Mines
Nova Scotia. Department of Mines. Memoir — NS Dep Mines Mem
Nova Scotia. Department of Mines. Paper — NS Dep Mines Pap
Nova Scotia Department of Mines. Report — NS Dep Mines Rep
Nova Scotia. Department of Mines. Report — NS Dp Mines Rp
Nova Scotia Historical Review — Nova Scotia Hist Rev
Nova Scotia Historical Society. Collections — Nova Scotia Hist Soc Coll
Nova Scotia Historical Society. Collections — NS His S
Nova Scotia History — NS Hist
Nova Scotia Institute of Natural Science. Proceedings and Transactions — NS Inst N Sc Pr Tr
Nova Scotia Law News — NSL News
Nova Scotia Literary and Scientific Society. Transactions — NS Lit Sc Soc Tr
Nova Scotia Medical Bulletin — Nova Scotia Med Bull
Nova Scotia Medical Bulletin — NS Med Bull
Nova Scotia Province. Department of Mines. Annual Report — NS Prov Dep Mines Annu Rep
Nova Scotia Reports [*Information service or system*] — NS
Nova Scotia Reports [*Information service or system*] — NS Rep
Nova Scotia Reports [*Information service or system*] — NSR
Nova Scotia Reports. Second Series — NSR 2d
Nova Scotia School Boards Association. Newsletter — NS Sch Bd Assn N
Nova Scotia Technical College (Halifax). Department of Civil Engineering. Essays on Timber Structures — NS Tech Coll Dep Civ Eng Essays Timber Struct
Nova Scotia Tourism News — NSTN
Nova Scotian Institute of Science. Proceedings — Nova Scotian Inst Sci Proc
Nova Scotian Institute of Science. Proceedings — NS Inst Sci Proc
Nova Subsidia Diplomatica — NSD
Nova Technika — Nova Tech
Novae Patrum Bibliothecae — Nov P Bibl
Novae Patrum Bibliothecae — NPB
Novaja i Novejsaja Istorija — Nov Novejs Ist
Novaja Sovetskaja i Inostrannaja Literatura po Voprosam Ateizma i Religii — NSLVA
Novaya Tekhnika i Peredovoi Opyt v Stroitel'stve — Nov Tekh Peredovoi Opyt Stroit

Novaya Tekhnika Montazhnykh i Spetsial'nykh Rabot v Stroitel'stve — Nov Tekhn Montazh Spets Rabot Stroit
Novaya Tekhnika v Astronomii — Nov Tekh Astron
Nove u Virobnitstvi Budivel'nikh Materialiv — Nove Virobnitstvi Budiv Mater
Noveaux Memoires. Missions de la Compagnie de Jesus — NMM
Novedades Cientificas. Contribuciones Ocasionales del Museo de Historia Natural La Salle [*Caracas*]. Serie Botanica — NCMBBJ
Novedades Cientificas. Serie Zoologia — NCMZAM
Novedades Cientificas. Serie Zoologia — Noved Cient Ser Zool
Novedades Economicas — Noved Econ
Noveishaya Tektonika. Noveishie Otlozheniya i Chelovek — Noveishaya Tekton Noveishie Otlozh Chel
Noveishaya Tektonika. Noveishie Otlozheniya i Chelovek — Noveishaya Tektonika Noveishie Otlozh Chel
Novel. A Forum on Fiction — PNOV
Novel Biodegradable Microbial Polymers — Novel Biodegrad Microb Polym
Novels [*Roman law*] — Nov
Novels of Empire [*monograph*] — NE
November — N
Novenynemesitesi es Novenytermesztesi Kutato Intezet. Sopronhorpacs Koezlemenyei — Novenynemes Novenytermesz Kutato Intez Koezl Sopronhorpacs
Novenytermeles — NOVEA
Novenytermeles/Crop Production — Novenytermeles Crop Prod
Novenyvedelem Idoszeru Kerdesei — Novenyved Idoszeru Kerdesei
Novenyvedelmi Kutato Intezet Evkonyve — Novenyved Kut Intez Evk
Noverim — Nov
Novgorodskaja Pervaja Letopis' Starsego i Mladsego Izvodov — NPL
Novgorodskii Golovnoi Gosudarstvennyi Pedagogicheskii Institut. Ucenye Zapiski — Novgorod Golovn Gos Ped Inst Ucen Zap
Novgorodskii Golovnoi Gosudarstvennyi Pedagogicheskii Institut. Uchenye Zapiski — Novgorod Golovn Gos Pedagog Inst Uch Zap
Novi Commentarii Academiae Scientiarum Imperalis Petropolitanae — Nov Comm Acad Sci Imp Petrop
Novi Commentarii Academiae Scientiarum Instituti Bononiensis — Novi Comment Acad Sci Inst Bononiensis
Novi Commentarii Societatis Regiae Scientiarum Gottingensis — Novi Comment Soc Regiae Sci Gott
Novi Commentarii Societatis Scientiarum Gottingensis — NCSSG
Novi Problemi v Pediatriyata — Novi Probl Pediatr
Novi Svet — NS
Novi Zbornik Matematickih Problema — Novi Zb Mat Prob
Novices' Gleanings in Bee Culture — Novices Glean Bee Cult
Novices' Gleanings in Bee Culture — Novices Gleanings Bee Cult
Novinky v Poligrafichem Prumyslu — Novinky Poligr Prum
Novissimo Digesto Italiano — ND
Novitates Arthropodae — NOARDP
Novitates Arthropodae — Novit Arthropodae
Novitates Zoologicae — Novitates Zool
Novocherkasskii Politekhnicheskii Institut Imeni Sergo Ordzhonikidze Trudy — Novocherk Politekh Inst Im Sergo Ordzhonikidze Tr
Novoe v Mashinostroenii — Nov Mashinostr
Novoe v Nauke i Tekhnike Vitaminov — Nov Nauke Tekh Vitam
Novoe v Oblasti Ispytanii na Mikrotverdost. Materialy Soveshchaniya po Mikrotverdosti — Nov Obl Ispyt Mikrotverdost Mater Soveshch Mikrotverdosti
Novoe v Proizvodstve Khimicheskikh Istochnikov Toka [*Former USSR*] — Nov Proizvod Khim Istochnikov Toka
Novoe v Proizvodstve Stroitel'nykh Materialov — Nov Proizvod Stroit Mater
Novoe v Reologii Polimerov. Materialy Vsesoyuznogo Simpoziuma po Reologii — Nov Reol Polim Mater Vses Simp Reol
Novoe v Zhizni, Nauke, Tekhnike. Khimiya — Nov Zhizni Nauke Tekh Khim
Novoe v Zhizni, Nauke, Tekhnike. Seriya 9. Fizika, Astronomiya — Nov Zhizni Nauke Tekh Ser 9 Fiz Astron
Novoe v Zhizni, Nauke, Tekhnike. Seriya Biologiia — Nov Zhizni Nauke Tekh Biol
Novoe v Zhizni, Nauke, Tekhnike. Seriya Biologiia — Nov Zhizni Nauke Tekh Ser Biol
Novoe v Zhizni, Nauke, Tekhnike. Seriya Fizika [*Former USSR*] — Nov Zhizni Nauke Tekh Ser Fiz
Novoe v Zhizni, Nauke, Tekhnike. Seriya IX. Fizika, Matematika, Astronomiya [*Former USSR*] — Nov Zhizni Nauke Tekh Ser IX Fiz Mat Astron
Novoe v Zhizni, Nauke, Tekhnike. Seriya Khimiya — Nov Zhizni Nauke Tekh Ser Khim
Novoe v Zhizni, Nauke, Tekhnike. Seriya Kosmonavtika Astronomiya [*Former USSR*] — Nov Zhizni Nauke Tekh Ser Kosmonavt Astron
Novoe v Zhizni, Nauke, Tekhnike. Seriya Tekhnika [*Former USSR*] — Nov Zhizni Nauke Tekh Ser Tekh
Novorossiiskii Gosudarstvennyi Proektnyi Institut Tsementnoi Promyshlennosti. Sbornik Trudov — Novoross Gos Proektnyi Inst Tsem Promsti Sb Tr
Novos Taxa Entomologicos — Novos Taxa Ent
Novos Taxa Entomologicos — Novos Taxa Entomol
Novosibirskii Gosudarstvennyi Meditsinskii Institut. Nauchnye Trudy — Novosib Gos Med Inst Nauchn Tr
Novosibirskii Gosudarstvennyi Meditsinskii Institut. Trudy — Novosib Gos Med Inst Tr
Novosibirskii Gosudarstvennyi Pedagogiceskii Institut Naucnye Trudy — Novosibirsk Gos Ped Inst Naucn Trudy
Novosibirskii Institut Inzhenerov Geodezii, Aerofotos'emki, i Kartografii. Trudy — Novosib Inst Inzh Geod Aerofotos'emki Kartogr Tr
Novosibirskii Institut Inzhenerov Zheleznodorozhnogo Transporta. Trudy — Novosib Inst Inzh Zheleznodorozhn Transp Tr
Novosibirskii Sel'skokhozyaistvennyi Institut. Trudy — Novosib Skh Inst Tr
Novosti Meditsinskogo Priborostroeniya [*Former USSR*] — Nov Med Priborostr
Novosti Meditsinskoi Tekhniki — NMDTA
Novosti Meditsinskoi Tekhniki — Nov Med Tek
Novosti Meditsinskoi Tekhniki — Nov Med Tekh
Novosti Meditsiny — Nov Med
Novosti Neftepererabotki — Nov Neftepererab
Novosti Neftyanoi i Gazovoi Tekhniki Gazovoe Delo — Nov Neft Gazov Tekh Gazov Delo
Novosti Neftyanoi i Gazovoi Tekhniki. Geologiya — Nov Neft Gazov Tekh Geol
Novosti Neftyanoi i Gazovoi Tekhniki, Neftepererabotka, i Neftekhimiya — NNGNA
Novosti Neftyanoi i Gazovoi Tekhniki, Neftepererabotka, i Neftekhimiya [*Former USSR*] — Nov Neft Gazov Tekh Neftepererab Neftekhim
Novosti Neftyanoi i Gazovoi Tekhniki Neftepromyslovoe Delo — Nov Neft Gazov Tekh Neftepromysl Delo
Novosti Neftyanoi i Gazovoi Tekhniki Neftyanoe Oborudovanie i Sredstva Avtomatizatsii — Nov Neft Gaz Tekh Neft Oborudovanie Sredstva Avtom
Novosti Neftyanoi i Gazovoi Tekhniki Transport i Khranenie Nefti i Nefteproduktov — Nov Neft Gazov Tekh Transp Khranenie Nefti Nefteprod
Novosti Neftyanoi Tekhniki — Nov Neft Tekh
Novosti Neftyanoi Tekhniki. Geologiya — Nov Neft Tekh Geol
Novosti Neftyanoi Tekhniki Neftepererabotka — Nov Neft Tekh Neftepererab
Novosti Neftyanoi Tekhniki Neftepromyslovoe Delo — Nov Neft Tekh Neftepromysl Delo
Novosti Neftyanoi Tekhniki Stroitel'stvo i Montazh — Nov Neft Tekh Stroit Montazh
Novosti Pishchevoi Promyshlennosti — Nov Pishch Promsti
Novosti Sistematiki Nizshikh Rastenii — Nov Sist Nizshikh Rast
Novosti Tekhniki — NOTEA
Novosti Tekhniki [*Former USSR*] — Nov Tekh
Novosti Tekhniki Bureniya — Nov Tekh Buren
Novosti Tekhniki. Energetika — Nov Tekh Energ
Novosti Tekhniki. Gornorudnaya Promyshlennost — Nov Tekh Gornorudn Promst
Novosti Tekhniki. Mashinostroenie — Nov Tekh Mashinostr
Novosti Tekhniki. Metallurgiya — Nov Tekh Metall
Novosti Tekhniki Neftedobychi — Nov Tekh Neftedobychi
Novosti Tekhniki Stroiindustriya — Nov Tekh Stroiind
Novosti Termoyadernykh Issledovanii v SSSR Informatsionnyi Byulleten [*Former USSR*] — Nov Termoyad Issled SSSR Inf Byull
Novosti v Tselulozno-Khartienata Promishlenost — Nov Tselul Khartienata Prom
Novum Gebrauchsgraphik — Novum Gebrauchs
Novum Glossarium — NG
Novum Glossarium Mediae Latinitatis — NGML
Novum Testamentum — No Tes
Novum Testamentum — Nov T
Novum Testamentum — NovTest
Novum Testamentum — Novum Test
Novum Testamentum — NT
Novum Testamentum [*Leiden*] — NvT
Novum Testamentum. Supplements [*Leiden*] — NT Suppls
Novum Testamentum. Supplements [*Leiden*] — NTS
Novum Testamentum. Supplements [*Leiden*] — NTSuppl
Novy Orient. Casopis Orientalniho Ustava v Praze — N O
Novy Zivot — NoZ
Novye Dannye o Mineralakh — Nov Dannye Miner
Novye Dannye o Mineralakh (SSSR) — Nov Dannye Miner (SSSR)
Novye Dannye po Geologii Boksitov — Nov Dannye Geol Boksitov
Novye Dannye po Geologii i Poleznym Iskopaemym Zapadnoi Sibiri — Nov Dannye Geol Polezn Iskop Zapadn Sib
Novye Fizicheskie Metody Obrabotki Pishchevykh Produktov — Nov Fiz Metody Obrab Pishch Prod
Novye i Maloizvestnye Vidy Fauny Sibiri — Nov Maloizvestnye Vidy Fauny Sib
Novye Issledovaniya v Khimii, Metallurgii, i Ogobashchenii — Nov Issled Khim Metall Obogashch
Novye Issledovaniya v Metallurgii, Khimii, i Obogashchenii — Nov Issled Metall Khim Obogashch
Novye Issledovaniya v Pedagogicheskikh Naukakh — Nov Issled Pedagog Naukakh
Novye Issledovaniya v Psikhologii i Vozrastnoi Fiziologii — Nov Issled Psikhol Vozrastn Fiziol
Novye Lekarstvennye Rasteniya Sibiri Ikh Lechebnye Preparaty i Primenenie — Nov Lek Rast Sib Ikh Lech Prep Primen
Novye Lekarstvennye Sredstva — Nov Lek Sredstva
Novye Metody i Modifikatsii Biokhimicheskikh i Fiziologicheskikh Issledovanii v Zhivotnovodstve — Nov Met Modif Biokhim Fiziol Issled Zhivotnovod
Novye Metody Ispytanii Metallov — Nov Metody Ispyt Met
Novye Razrabotki Elementov Radiotekhnicheskikh Ustroistv — Nov Razrab Elem Radiotekh Ustroistv
Novye Sorbenty dlya Khromatografii — Nov Sorbenty Khromatogr
Novye Sorbenty dlya Molekulyarnoi Khromatografii — Nov Sorbenty Mol Khromatogr
Novye Vidy Kompleksnykh Udobrenii — Nov Vidy Kompleksn Udobr
Novyi Khirurgicheskii Arkhiv — Nov Khir Arkh
Novyj Mir — NoM
Novyj Mir — NovM
Novyj Zurnal — NovZ
Novyj Zurnal — NZ
Novyj Zurnal — NZu
Nowa Technika w Inzynierii Sanitarnej — Nowa Tech Inz Sanit
Nowe Drogi — ND
Nowe Ksiazki — NKs
Nowe Kultura — NK
Nowe Rolnictwo — Nowe Roln
Nowiny Lekarskie — Now Lek
Nowiny Literackie i Wydawnicze — NLiW
Nowiny Literackie i Wydawnicze — NLW

Nowosci Weterynarii — Nowosci Weter
NPL Report Chem (United Kingdom). National Physical Laboratory. Division of Chemical Standards — NPL Rep Chem (UK) Natl Phys Lab Div Chem Stand
NPL Report DMA. United Kingdom. National Physical Laboratory. Division of Materials Applications — NPL Rep DMA UK Nat Phys Lab Div Mater Appl
NPL Report DMM(A) (United Kingdom. National Pnysical Laboratory. Division of Materials Metrology) — NPL Rep DMMA UK Natl Phys Lab Div Mater Metrol
NPL Report IMS. United Kingdom. National Physical Laboratory. Division of Inorganic and Metallic Structure — NPL Rep IMS UK Natl Phys Lab Div Inorg Met Struct
NPL Report MOM (United Kingdom). National Physical Laboratory. Division of Mechanical and Optical Metrology — NPL Rep MOM (UK) Natl Phys Lab Div Mech Opt Metrol
NPL Report QU. United Kingdom. National Physical Laboratory. Division of Quantum Metrology — NPL Rep QU UK Natl Phys Lab Div Quantum Metrol
NPL [*National Physical Laboratory*] **Technical Bulletin** — NPL Tech Bull
NR [*Natural Rubber*] **Technical Bulletin** — NR Tech Bull
NRA [*National Restaurant Association*] **Washington Report** — NRA Report
NRC [*National Research Council of Canada*] **Bulletin** — NRC Bull
NRC (National Research Council of Canada) Bulletin — NRC (Natl Res Counc Can) Bull
NRC (National Research Council of Canada) Technical Translation — NRC (Natl Res Counc Can) Tech Transl
NRC [*Northern Regions Centre*] **Newsletter** [*Hokkaido, Japan*] — NRCN
NRC [*National Research Council of Canada*] **Review** — NRC Rev
NRC [*National Research Council, Canada*] **Technical Translation** — NRC Tech Transl
NRCC [*National Research Council of Canada*] **Bulletin** — NRCC Bull
NRCL. National Research Council Laboratories [*Ottawa*] — NRCLAZ
NRCL. National Research Council Laboratories (Ottawa) — NRCL Natl Res Counc Lab (Ottawa)
NRCP [*National Research Council of the Philippines*] **Research Bulletin** — NRCP Res Bull
NRI [*Nomura Research Institute*] **Symposia on Modern Biology** — NRI Symp Mod Biol
NRIM (National Research Institute for Metals) Special Report — NRIM Spec Rep
NRL [*US Naval Research Laboratory*] **Memorandum Report** — NRL Memo Rep
NRPRA [*Natural Rubber Producers' Research Association*] **Technical Bulletin** — NRPRA Tech Bull
NS/Northsouth. Canadian Journal of Latin American Studies — NSIN
NS. NorthSouth NordSud NorteSur NorteSul. Canadian Association of Latin American Studies. University of Ottawa — NS
NSC (National Science Council) Symposium Series (Taipei) — NSC (Natl Sci Counc) Symp Ser (Taipei)
NSC [*National Science Council*] **Review 1977-8** [*Taiwan*] — NSC Rev 1977-8
NSC [*National Science Council. Taiwan*] **Symposium Series** — NSC Symp Ser
NSC [*National Science Council*] **Symposium Series** [*Taipei*] — NSYSD6
NSCA (National Society for Clean Air) Year Book — NSCA (Natl Soc Clean Air) Year Book
NSCA [*National Society for Clean Air*] **Year Book** — NSCBDF
NSDB [*National Science Development Board, Philippines*] **Technology Journal** — NSDB Technol J
NSF [*Namnden foer Skoglig Flygbildteknik*] **Information** — NSF Inform
NSFI [*Norges Skipaforsknings Institutt*] **Nytt** — NSFNB
NSG [*Nippon Sheet Glass*] **Technical Report** — NSG Tech Rep
NSRDS [*National Standards Reference Data System*] **Reference Data Report** [*United States*] — NSRDS Ref Data Rep
NSS [*National Speleological Society*] **Bulletin** — NSS Bull
NSS (National Speleological Society) News — NSS (Natl Speleol Soc) News
NSS [*National Speleological Society*] **News** — NSSNAQ
NSSRP. University of Tsukuba. Nuclear and Solid State Research Project — NSSRP Univ Tsukuba Nucl Solid State Res Proj
NSTA [*National Science and Technology Authority, Philippines*] **Technology Journal** — NSTA Technol J
NSTF [*National Scholariship Trust Fund*] **Report** — NSTF Rep
Nsukka Studies in African Literature — NSAL
Nsukka Studies in African Literature — Nsukka Stud
NT. Neue Technik [*Switzerland*] — NT Neue Tech
NT. Notiziario Tecnico AMMA [*Associazione Metallurgici Meccanici Affini*] — NT Not Tec AMMA
NTA [*National Technical Association*] **Journal** — NTA J
NTA [*National Teachers' Association*] **Journal** [*Zimbabwe*] — NTA Jnl
NTG [*Nachrichtentechnische Gesellschaft*] **Fachberichte** — NTG Fachber
NTIAC [*Nondestructive Testing Information Analysis Center*] **Information Support System** [*Database*] — ISS
NTIS [*National Technical Information Service*] **Energy Tech Notes** [*United States*] — NTN
NTIS [*National Technical Information Service*] **Materials Science** — NTIS Mater Sci
NTIS [*National Technical Information Service*] **Trade Announcements** — NTIS Announc
NTM. Schriftenreihe fuer Geschichte der Naturwissenschaften, Technik, und Medizin — NTM
NTM. Schriftenreihe fuer Geschichte der Naturwissenschaften, Technik, und Medizin — NTM Schr Geschichte Natur Tech Medizin
NTM. Schriftenreihe fuer Geschichte der Naturwissenschaften, Technik, und Medizin — NTM Schr Geschichte Naturwiss Tech Medizin
NTM. Schriftenreihe fuer Geschichte der Naturwissenschaften, Technik, und Medizin — NTM Schriftenr Gesch Naturwiss Tech Med
NTM. Schriftenreihe fuer Geschichte der Naturwissenschaften, Technik, und Medizin — NTMSB
NTM. Zeitschrift fuer Geschichte der Naturwissenschaft, Technik, und Medizin — NTM Zeit
NTM. Zeitschrift fuer Geschichte der Naturwissenschaften, Technik, und Medizin — NTM Z Gesch Naturwiss Tech Med
NTR. Nisseki Technical Review — NTR Nisseki Tech Rev
NTT [*Nippon Telegraph and Telephone Corporation*] **Review** — NTT Rev
NTU [*National Taiwan University*] **Phytopathologist and Entomologist** — NTU Phytopathol Entomol
NTZ. Nachrichtentechnische Zeitschrift Archiv — NTZ Arch
NTZ. Nachrichtentechnische Zeitschrift/NTZ-Communications Journal — NTZ Nachr Z NTZ-Commun J
NTZ. Nachrichtentechnische Zeitschrift. Report — NTZ Rep
NTZ-Communications Journal — NTZ-Commun J
NU [*Natal University*] **Science** — NU Sci
Nuc Compact. Compact News in Nuclear Medicine [*Germany*] — Nuc Compact Compact News Nucl Med
Nucleair Geneeskundig Bulletin — Nucl Geneeskd Bull
Nuclear Active — Nucl Act
Nuclear Active — Nucl Active
Nuclear Active — NULAB
Nuclear and Chemical Waste Management — Nucl Chem Waste Manage
Nuclear and Particle Physics. Annual — Nucl Part Phys Annu
Nuclear and Radiochemistry — Nucl Radiochem
Nuclear Applications — NUAPA
Nuclear Applications — Nucl Appl
Nuclear Applications and Technology — NUATA
Nuclear Applications and Technology — Nucl Appl and Technol
Nuclear Applications and Technology — Nucl Appl Technol
Nuclear Canada/Canada Nucleaire — Nucl Can/Can Nucl
Nuclear Canada Yearbook — NCYBD
Nuclear Canada Yearbook — Nucl Can Yearb
Nuclear Criticality Information System [*Database*] — NCIS
Nuclear Data. Section A — NDSAA
Nuclear Data. Section A — Nucl Data A
Nuclear Data. Section A — Nucl Data Sect A
Nuclear Data. Section B — Nucl Data Sect B
Nuclear Data Sheets — NDTSB
Nuclear Data Sheets — Nucl Data Sheets
Nuclear Data Tables — Nucl Data Tables
Nuclear Data Tables. United States Atomic Energy Commission — Nucl Data Tables US AEC
Nuclear Development Corporation of South Africa. Report — Nucl Dev Corp S Afr Rep
Nuclear Electronics and Detection Technology — Nucl Electron Detect Technol
Nuclear Energy — Nuc Energy
Nuclear Energy — Nucl Energy
Nuclear Energy. British Nuclear Energy Society — Nucl Energy Br Nucl Energy Soc
Nuclear Energy Digest — Nucl Energy Dig
Nuclear Energy Information Center (Warsaw). Review Report — Nucl Energy Inf Cent (Warsaw) Rev Rep
Nuclear Energy Prospects to 2000 — Nuc En Pros
Nuclear Engineer — Nucl Engr
Nuclear Engineer. Institution of Nuclear Engineers — Nucl Eng
Nuclear Engineer. Institution of Nuclear Engineers [*England*] — Nucl Eng Inst Nucl Eng
Nuclear Engineering — NUENA
Nuclear Engineering Abstracts — Nucl Eng Abstr
Nuclear Engineering and Design — Nucl Eng and Des
Nuclear Engineering and Design — Nucl Eng Des
Nuclear Engineering and Design — Nucl Engng & Des
Nuclear Engineering and Design — Nuclear Engng Design
Nuclear Engineering and Design/Fusion — Nucl Eng Des Fusion
Nuclear Engineering Bulletin — Nucl Eng Bull
Nuclear Engineering (Heywood-Temple) — Nucl Eng (Heywood Temple)
Nuclear Engineering International — NEI
Nuclear Engineering International — NLE
Nuclear Engineering International — Nucl Eng In
Nuclear Engineering International — Nucl Eng Int
Nuclear Engineering International — Nucl Engng Int
Nuclear Engineering International — Nuclear Eng
Nuclear Engineering (Tokyo) — Nucl Eng (Tokyo)
Nuclear Europe — Nucl Eur
Nuclear Europe Worldscan — Nucl Eur Worldscan
Nuclear Fuel Cycle — Nucl Fuel Cycle
Nuclear Fuel Cycle. Revised Edition — Nucl Fuel Cycle Revis Ed
Nuclear Fusion — Nucl Fusion
Nuclear Fusion Research Report [*Japan*] — Nucl Fusion Res Rep
Nuclear Fusion. Special Publication — Nucl Fusion Spec Publ
Nuclear Fusion. Supplement — Nucl F Supplm
Nuclear Fusion. Supplement — Nucl Fusion Suppl
Nuclear Geophysics — Nucl Geophys
Nuclear Hematology — Nucl Hematol
Nuclear Hematology — NUHEA
Nuclear India — Nucl India
Nuclear Industry — Nucl Ind
Nuclear Information — Nucl Inf
Nuclear Instruments — Nucl Instrum
Nuclear Instruments and Methods [*Later, Nuclear Instruments and Methods in Physics Research*] — N Instr Meth
Nuclear Instruments and Methods [*Later, Nuclear Instruments and Methods in Physics Research*] — Nucl Instr
Nuclear Instruments and Methods [*Later, Nuclear Instruments and Methods in Physics Research*] — Nucl Instrum and Methods
Nuclear Instruments and Methods [*Later, Nuclear Instruments and Methods in Physics Research*] — Nucl Instrum Methods
Nuclear Instruments and Methods in Physics Research — NIMRD
Nuclear Instruments and Methods in Physics Research [*Netherlands*] — Nucl Instrum Methods Phys Res

Nuclear Instruments and Methods in Physics Research. Section A. Accelerators, Spectrometers, Detectors, and Associated Equipment — Nucl Instrum Methods Phys Res Sect A
Nuclear Instruments and Methods in Physics Research. Section B. Beam Interactions with Materials and Atoms — Nucl Instrum Methods Phys Res Sect B
Nuclear Issues — Nucl Issues
Nuclear Law Bulletin — Nucl Law Bull
Nuclear Law Bulletin — Nuclear Law Bul
Nuclear Law Bulletin. Supplement — Nucl Law Bull Suppl
Nuclear Magnetic Resonance — NMRNB
Nuclear Magnetic Resonance — Nucl Magn Reson
Nuclear Magnetic Resonance Literature System [*Database*] — NMRLIT
Nuclear Materials Management — NUMMB
Nuclear Materials Management. Journal of the Institute of Nuclear Materials Management — Nucl Mater Manage
Nuclear Medicine — NMIMAX
Nuclear Medicine — Nucl Med
Nuclear Medicine (Amsterdam) — Nucl Med (Amsterdam)
Nuclear Medicine and Biology — Nucl Med Biol
Nuclear Medicine Annual — NMANDX
Nuclear Medicine Annual — Nucl Med Annu
Nuclear Medicine Communications — NMC
Nuclear Medicine Communications — Nucl Med Commun
Nuclear Medicine. Endocrinology — Nucl Med Endocrinol
Nuclear Medicine. Quantitative Analysis in Imaging and Function. European Nuclear Medicine Congress — Nucl Med Eur Nucl Med Congr
Nuclear Medicine (Stuttgart) — Nucl Med (Stuttgart)
Nuclear Metallurgy — Nucl Metall
Nuclear Methods Monographs [*Elsevier Book Series*] — NMM
Nuclear Methods Monographs — Nucl Methods Monogr
Nuclear Models. Lectures Given at Summer Meeting of Nuclear Physicists — Nucl Models Lect Summer Meet Nucl Phys
Nuclear News — Nucl N
Nuclear News — Nucl News
Nuclear News (Colombo, Sri Lanka) — Nucl News (Colombo Sri Lanka)
Nuclear News (Hinsdale, Illinois) — Nucl News (Hinsdale Ill)
Nuclear News (La Grange Park, Illinois) — Nucl News (La Grange Park Ill)
Nuclear Newsletter from Switzerland — Nucl Newsl Switz
Nuclear Physics — Nucl Phys
Nuclear Physics. A — Nucl Phys A
Nuclear Physics. A — Nuclear Phys A
Nuclear Physics, a Series of Monographs and Texts in High-Energy and Low-Energy Nuclear Physics — Nucl Phys Ser Monogr Texts High Energy Low Energy Nucl Phys
Nuclear Physics and Solid State Physics (India) — Nucl Phys Solid State Phys (India)
Nuclear Physics and Solid State Physics Symposium. Proceedings — Nucl Phys Solid State Phys Symp Proc
Nuclear Physics. B — Nucl Phys B
Nuclear Physics. B — Nuclear Phys B
Nuclear Physics. B — NUPBB
Nuclear Physics. B. Field Theory and Statistical Systems — Nucl Phys B Field Theory and Stat Syst
Nuclear Physics. B. Particle Physics — Nucl Phys B Part Phys
Nuclear Physics B. Proceedings Supplement — Nuclear Phys B Proc Suppl
Nuclear Plant Safety — Nuc Pl Saf
Nuclear Power — Nucl Pow
Nuclear Power — Nucl Power
Nuclear Power Engineering — Nucl Power Eng
Nuclear Power (Tokyo) — Nucl Power Tokyo
Nuclear Processes and Oncogenes — Nucl Processes Oncog
Nuclear Processes in Geologic Settings. Proceedings. Conference — Nucl Processes Geol Settings Proc Conf
Nuclear Reactions — Nucl React
Nuclear Reactor Safety — Nucl Reactor Saf
Nuclear Reactor Safety Heat Transfer — Nucl React Saf Heat Transfer
Nuclear Reactor Theory. Proceedings. Symposium on Applied Mathematics — Nucl Reactor Theory Proc Symp Appl Math
Nuclear Reactors Built, Being Built, or Planned — Nucl React Built Being Built Planned
Nuclear Regulatory Commission. Report. NUREG/CP (United States) — Nucl Regul Comm Rep NUREG CP US
Nuclear Research — Nucl Res
Nuclear Research Center "Democritus" (Report) — Nucl Res Cent "Democritus" (Rep)
Nuclear Safety — NS
Nuclear Safety — Nucl Saf
Nuclear Safety — Nucl Safety
Nuclear Science — Nucl Sci
Nuclear Science Abstracts [*Later, INIS Atomindex*] [*Information service or system*] — NSA
Nuclear Science Abstracts [*Later, INIS Atomindex*] [*Information service or system*] — Nucl Sci Abstr
Nuclear Science Abstracts [*Later, INIS Atomindex*] [*Information service or system*] — Nuclear Sci Abstr
Nuclear Science Abstracts [*Later, INIS Atomindex*] [*Information service or system*] — Nuclear Science Abstr
Nuclear Science Abstracts [*Later, INIS Atomindex*] [*Information service or system*] — NucSciAb
Nuclear Science Abstracts of Japan — Nucl Sci Abstr Jpn
Nuclear Science and Applications — NSAPA
Nuclear Science and Applications [*Pakistan*] — Nucl Sci Appl
Nuclear Science and Applications (Dacca) — Nucl Sci Appl Dacca
Nuclear Science and Applications. Series A — Nucl Sci Appl Ser A
Nuclear Science and Applications. Series A. Biological Science [*Pakistan*] — NSAAB
Nuclear Science and Applications. Series B — Nucl Sci Appl Ser B
Nuclear Science and Applications. Series B. Physical Sciences — NUSBA
Nuclear Science and Engineering — Nucl Sci and Eng
Nuclear Science and Engineering — Nucl Sci En
Nuclear Science and Engineering — Nucl Sci Eng
Nuclear Science and Engineering — Nuclear Sci Engng
Nuclear Science and Technology — Nucl Sci Technol
Nuclear Science Application. Section A. Short Reviews, Research Papers, and Comments — Nucl Sci Appl Sect A Short Rev
Nuclear Science Applications. Section A — Nucl Sci Appl Sect A
Nuclear Science Applications. Section B — Nucl Sci Appl Sect B
Nuclear Science Information of Japan — Nucl Sci Inf Jpn
Nuclear Science Journal — Nucl Sci J
Nuclear Science Journal (Bandar Baru Bangi, Malaysia) — Nucl Sci J (Bandar Baru Bangi Malays)
Nuclear Science Journal (Bangi, Malaysia) — Nucl Sci J Bangi Malays
Nuclear Science Journal of Malaysia — Nucl Sci J Malays
Nuclear Science Journal (Taiwan) — Nucl Sci J (Taiwan)
Nuclear Science Research Conference Series — Nucl Sci Res Conf Ser
Nuclear Science Series — Nucl Sci Ser
Nuclear Science (Taiwan) — Nucl Sci (Taiwan)
Nuclear Shapes and Nuclear Structures at Low Excitation Energies — Nucl Shapes Nucl Struct Low Excitation Energ
Nuclear Ships [*Japan*] — Nucl Ships
Nuclear Societies of Israel. Transactions. Joint Annual Meeting — Nucl Soc Isr Trans Jt Annu Meet
Nuclear Structural Engineering — NSTEA
Nuclear Structural Engineering [*Netherlands*] — Nucl Struct Eng
Nuclear Structure References [*Database*] — NSR
Nuclear Structure Study with Neutrons. Proceedings. International Conference on Nuclear Structure Study with Neutrons — Nucl Struct Study Neutrons Proc Int Conf
Nuclear Study [*Japan*] — Nucl Study
Nuclear Technology — Nucl Tech
Nuclear Technology — Nucl Technol
Nuclear Technology/Fusion — NTF
Nuclear Technology/Fusion — NTFUD
Nuclear Technology/Fusion — Nucl Technol/Fusion
Nuclear Technology. Supplement — Nucl Technol Suppl
Nuclear Theory [*Elsevier Book Series*] — NT
Nuclear Track Detection — Nucl Track Detect
Nuclear Tracks — Nucl Tracks
Nuclear Tracks and Radiation Measurements — Nucl Tracks and Radiat Meas
Nuclear Tracks. Methods, Instruments, and Applications — Nucl Tracks Methods Instrum and Appl
Nuclear Waste News [*Database*] — NWN
Nuclear-Chicago Technical Bulletin — Nucl-Chicago Tech Bull
Nuclear-Hydrogen Energy and Technology — Nucl Hydrogen Energy Technol
Nuclear-Medizin — Nucl-Med
Nuclear-Medizin (Stuttgart) — Nucl-Med (Stuttgart)
Nuclear-Medizin. Supplementum — Nucl Med Suppl
Nuclear-Medizin. Supplementum (Stuttgart) — Nucl-Med Suppl (Stuttgart)
Nucleic Acids and Molecular Biology — Nucleic Acids Mol Biol
Nucleic Acids Research — NARHA
Nucleic Acids Research — Nucl Acid R
Nucleic Acids Research — Nucleic Acids Res
Nucleic Acids Research. Special Publication — Nucleic Acids Res Spec Publ
Nucleic Acids Research. Symposium Series — Nucleic Acids Res Symp Ser
Nucleic Acids Symposium Series — Nucleic Acids Symp Ser
Nucleonics Week — NW
Nucleosides and Nucleotides — NN
Nucleus — Nucl
Nucleus [*Paris*] — NUCSA
Nudos (Argentina) — NCA
Nuernberger Forschungen — Nbg Forsch
Nuernberger Urkundenbuch — NUB
Nuestra Arquitectura (Buenos Aires) — Nuestra Arquit BA
Nuestra Historia — Nuestra Hist
Nuestra Industria. Revista Tecnologica — Nuestra Ind Rev Tecnol
Nuestra Tierra. Paz y Progreso — Nuestra Tierra
Nuestro — NO
Nuestro Tiempo — NT
Nuestro Tiempo — NTiem
Nuestro Tiempo (Madrid) — NTM
Nuetzliche Bemerkungen Fuer Garten- und Blumenfreunde — Nuetzl Bemerk Garten Blumenfr
Nuetzliche Sammlungen — Nuetzl Samml
Nuetzliches und Unterhaltendes Berlinisches Wochenblatt fuer den Gebildeten Buerger und Denkenden Landmann — Nuetzl Unterhalt Berlin Wochenbl Buerger Landmann
Nueva Atenea [*Chile*] — NAtenea
Nueva Democracia — ND
Nueva Democracia (New York) — Nueva Dem NY
Nueva Enfermeria — Nueva Enferm
Nueva Era. Revista Interamericana de Educacion y Cultura (Quito) — Nueva Era Quito
Nueva Estafeta — NE
Nueva Estafeta — Nueva Estaf
Nueva Gaceta Cubana — NGC
Nueva Historia. Revista de Historia de Chile — NH
Nueva Politica — NP
Nueva Politica — Nueva Pol
Nueva Revista Cubana — NRC

Nueva Revista de Filologia Hispanica — NRFH
Nueva Revista de Filologia Hispanica — Nueva R Filol Hisp
Nueva Revista de Filologia Hispanica — Nueva Revta Filol Hispan
Nueva Revista de Filologia Hispanica (Mexico) — Nueva Rev Filol Hisp Mex
Nueva Revista del Pacifico — NRP
Nueva Revista del Rio de la Plata — NRRP
Nueva Sangre — NSa
Nueva Sociedad — NS
Nueva Sociedad — NSO
Nueva Sociedad — Nueva Soc
Nueva York Hispano — NYH
Nuevas Tendencias — Nuevas Tend
Nuevo Indice — NI
Nuevo Texto Critico — NTC
Nuevo Texto Critico (Stanford, California) — NTCS
Nuisances et Environnement — Nuisances Environ
Nuisances et Environnement — Nuisances et Environ
Nuklearmedizin. Fortschritte der Nuklearmedizin in Klinischer und Technologischer Sicht. Jahrestagung der Gesellschaft fuer Nuclearmedizin — Nuklearmed Jahrestag Ges Nuclearmed
Nuklearmedizin. Supplementum (Stuttgart) — Nuklearmedizin Suppl Stuttgart
Nuklearmedizinisches Symposion — Nuklearmed Symp
Nuklearna Energija — Nukl Energ
Nuklearni Institut Jozef Stefan. NIJS Porocilo — Nukl Inst Jozef Stefan NIJS Porocilo
Nukleinovye Kisloty. Trudy Konferentsii po Nukleinovym Kislotam — Nukleinovye Kisloty Tr Konf
Nukleonika — NUKKA
Nukleonika — Nukl
Nukleonika. Supplement [*Poland*] — Nukleonika Suppl
Numario Hispanico — N Hisp
Numario Hispanico — NH
Numario Hispanico — Num Hisp
Numario Hispanico. Revista de Investigacion y Hallazgos Monetarios — Numario Hisp
Numen Supplements — NS
Numen Supplements [*Leiden*] — NuSup
Numen Supplements. Altera Series — NSA
Numerical Algorithms — Numer Algorithms
Numerical Computer Methods — Numer Comput Methods
Numerical Control Society Proceedings. Annual Meeting and Technical Conference — Numer Control Soc Proc Annu Meet Tech Conf
Numerical Engineering — Numer Eng
Numerical Functional Analysis and Optimization — NFAOD
Numerical Functional Analysis and Optimization — Numer Funct Anal Optim
Numerical Functional Analysis and Optimization — Numer Funct Anal Optimiz
Numerical Heat Transfer — Numer Heat Transfer
Numerical Heat Transfer. Part A. Applications — Numer Heat Transf Part A Appl
Numerical Heat Transfer. Part B. Fundamentals — Numer Heat Transfer Part B
Numerical Linear Algebra with Applications — Numer Linear Algebra Appl
Numerical Mathematics. A Journal of Chinese Universities [*Nanjing*] — Numer Math J Chinese Univ
Numerical Mathematics and Scientific Computation — Numer Math Sci Comput
Numerical Methods for Partial Differential Equations — Numer Methods Partial Differential Equations
Numerical Methods for the Simulation of Multi-Phase and Complex Flow. Proceedings. Workshop — Numer Methods Simul Multi Phase Complex Flow Proc Workshop
Numerische Mathematik — Num Math
Numerische Mathematik — Numer Math
Numerische Mathematik fuer Ingenieure und Physiker — Numer Math Ingenieure Physiker
Numerische Mathematik fuer Ingenieure und Physiker (Berlin) — Numer Math Ingenieure Physiker (Berl)
Numerische Verfahren in Aktion — Numer Verfahren Aktion
Numisma: An Occasional Numismatic Magazine (Australia) — Numisma (Austral)
Numisma. Revista de la Sociedad Ibero-Americana de Estudios Numismaticos — Numisma Rev Soc IA
Numismatic Chronicle — NCh
Numismatic Chronicle [*London*] — NChn
Numismatic Chronicle [*London*] — NChr
Numismatic Chronicle — Nu C
Numismatic Chronicle — Num Chron
Numismatic Chronicle — Numismat Chron
Numismatic Chronicle and Journal — NC
Numismatic Chronicle and Journal [*London*] — Num Chron
Numismatic Chronicle and Journal. Numismatic Society — Num C
Numismatic Chronicle and Journal. Royal Numismatic Society — N Chr
Numismatic Chronicle and Journal. Royal Numismatic Society — N Cr
Numismatic Chronicle and Journal. Royal Numismatic Society — Num Chr
Numismatic Chronicle. Series 7 — Numis Chron 7 Ser
Numismatic Chronicle. Series 7 (England) — Numis Chron 7 Ser (Engl)
Numismatic Circular — NCirc
Numismatic Circular — NumCirc
Numismatic Circular [*England*] — Numis Circ
Numismatic Digest — Num Digest
Numismatic Gazette Quarterly — NGQ
Numismatic Journal — Num J
Numismatic Literature — NL
Numismatic Literature — Num Lit
Numismatic Messenger — NMessenger
Numismatic News Weekly — NN
Numismatic Notes and Monographs — NNM
Numismatic Notes and Monographs. American Numismatic Society — Amer Num Soc N Mon
Numismatic Report (Cyprus) — NR(Cyprus)
Numismatic Review — NR
Numismatic Review — NuR
Numismatic Review and Coin Galleries [*Fixed Price List*] — NRCG
Numismatic Scrapbook Magazine — NSM
Numismatic Society of India. Journal — NSI
Numismatic Studies — NS
Numismatic Studies. American Numismatic Society — Num St
Numismatica e Antichita Classiche — NAC
Numismatica e Antichita Classiche — Num Ant Cl
Numismatica e Antichita Classiche. Quaderni Ticinesi — Num Ant Cl
Numismatica et Sphragistica — NS
Numismatica i Epigrafica — NE
Numismatica Moravica — Num Moravica
Numismatica (Rome) — Numismatica (Rom)
Numismatica Stockholmiensia. Annual Reports and Acquisitions of the Royal Coin Cabinet. National Museum of Monetary History — Num Stockholm
Numismaticke Listy — NListy
Numismaticke Listy — Num Listy
Numismaticky Sbornik — NS
Numismaticky Sbornik — NSb
Numismaticky Sbornik — Num Sbor
Numismaticky Sbornik (Czechoslovakia) — NS(Czech)
Numismatics in Israel — Num Israel
Numismatik Literatur Osteuropas und das Balkans — NLOB
Numismatique et Change — Num Change
Numismatische Beitraege — Num Beitr
Numismatische Literatur Osteuropas und des Balkans — Numismat Lit Osteur U Balkan
Numismatische Literatur-Zeitung — NLZ
Numismatische Zeitschrift — Num Z
Numismatische Zeitschrift — Num Zeit
Numismatische Zeitschrift — Num Zeitr
Numismatische Zeitschrift — Num Ztschr
Numismatische Zeitschrift — NZ
Numismatische Zeitschrift (Wien) — Num Zeitr Wien
Numismatische Zeitschrift (Wien) — Numism Zs Wien
Numismatisches Literatur-Blatt — NLB
Numismatisches Literatur-Blatt — NumLB
Numismatisches Nachrichtenblatt — NN
Numismatisches Nachrichtenblatt — Num Nachr Bl
Numismatisches Nachrichtenblatt. Organ des Verbandes der Deutschen Muenzvereine — NNb
Numismatisch-Sphragistischer Anzeiger — NSA
Numismatiska Meddelanden — NM
Numismatist — Nu
Numismatist — Num
Numismatist — Numis
Numizmaticheskii Sbornik Materialy k Katalogu Numizmaticheskogo Sobraniia Gosudarstvennyi Istoricheskii Muzei (USSR) — NS (USSR)
Numizmaticke Vijesti — Num Vij
Numizmaticke Vijesti — NV
Numizmatika i Epigrafika — Num Epigr
Numizmatika i Epigrafika. Institut Arkheologii. Akademiia Nauk SSSR — Num Epigr IA
Numizmatika i Epigrafika. Institut Arkheologii. Akademiia Nauk SSSR — Numi Epig
Numizmatika i Sfragistika — NSf
Numizmatika i Sfragistika — Num Sfrag
Numizmatikai Koezloeny — NK
Numizmatikai Koezloeny — Num Koezl
Numizmatikai Kozloeny — NumK
Numizmatikai Kozlony — NKoeZ
Nummus. Boletim da Sociedade Portuguesa de Numismatica — NBSPN
Nunasi News — NUNE
Nunasi Report — NURE
Nunatext News — NUTN
Nunatsiaq News — NU
Nunavut Onipkaat. Kitikmeot Inuit Association — NUON
Nuncius. Annali di Storia della Scienza — Nuncius Ann Storia Sci
Nuntiaturbericht aus Deutschland — NBD
Nuntiaturberichte aus der Schweiz — NBS
Nuntius Radiologicus — Nunt Radiol
Nuntius Socalicii Neotestamentici Upsaliensis — NSNU
Nuova Agricoltura Lucana — Nuova Agr Lucana
Nuova Antologia — N Ant
Nuova Antologia — NA
Nuova Antologia — NAnt
Nuova Antologia — NuA
Nuova Antologia — Nuo Ant
Nuova Antologia — Nuova Ant
Nuova Antologia — Nuova Antol
Nuova Antologia di Lettere, Arti, e Scienze — Nuova Antol
Nuova Antologia di Scienze, Lettere, ed Arti — NA
Nuova Antologia di Scienze, Lettere, ed Arti — NAnt
Nuova Antologia di Scienze, Lettere, ed Arti — NAR
Nuova Biblioteca Italiana — N Bibl Ital
Nuova Bulletino di Archeologia Cristiana — N B Arch Christ
Nuova Bulletino di Archeologia Cristiana — N Bull Arch Christ
Nuova Bulletino di Archeologia Cristiana — Nuova Bull di Arch Cristiana
Nuova Chimica — Nuova Chim
Nuova Collezione d'Opuscoli Scientifici — Nuova Collez Opusc Sci
Nuova Corrente — NC

Nuova Critica. Studi e Rivista di Filosofia delle Scienze — Nuova Crit
Nuova Cultura — NCult
Nuova Economia — Nuova Econ
Nuova Italia — NI
Nuova Italia — NIt
Nuova Italia — Nuo Ital
Nuova Rivista di Diritto Commerciale, Diritto dell'Economia, Diritto Sociale — N Riv Dir Comm
Nuova Rivista di Varia Umanita — NRVU
Nuova Rivista Musicale Italiana — NRM
Nuova Rivista Musicale Italiana — NRMI
Nuova Rivista Musicale Italiana — Nuov Riv M
Nuova Rivista Musicale Italiana — Nuova Riv Mus Ital
Nuova Rivista Musicale Italiana — Nuova RM Italiana
Nuova Rivista Musicale Italiana — R Ital Mus
Nuova Rivista Musicale Italiana. Trimestrale di Cultura e Informazione Musicale — R Mus Ital
Nuova Rivista Olii Vegetali e Saponi — Nuova Riv Olii Veg Saponi
Nuova Rivista Storica — N Ri St
Nuova Rivista Storica — N Riv St
Nuova Rivista Storica — N Riv Stor
Nuova Rivista Storica — NRS
Nuova Rivista Storica — Nuo Riv Stor
Nuova Rivista Storica — Nuov Riv St
Nuova Rivista Storica — Nuova R Stor
Nuova Rivista Storica — Nuova Riv Stor
Nuova Rivista Storica — NV
Nuova Rivista Storica. Biblioteca — NRS B
Nuova Veterinaria — Nuova Vet
Nuova Veterinaria — Nuova Veterin
Nuove Dimensioni — NDim
Nuovi Allevamenti — Nuovi Allevam
Nuovi Annali dell'Agricoltura — Nuovi Ann Agric
Nuovi Annali delle Scienze Naturali (Bologna) — N Ann Sc Nat (Bologna)
Nuovi Annali d'Igiene e Microbiologia — Nuovi Ann Ig Microbiol
Nuovi Annali d'Igiene e Microbiologia — Nuovi Annali Ig Microbiol
Nuovi Annali. Istituto Chimico-Agrario Sperimentale di Gorizia. Serie 2 — Nuovi Ann Ist Chim-Agr Sper Gorizia Ser 2
Nuovi Argomenti — N Arg
Nuovi Argomenti — NA
Nuovi Argomenti — NAr
Nuovi Quaderni del Meridione — NQM
Nuovi Quaderni del Meridione — NuQ
Nuovi Saggi Della Cesareo-Regia Accademia di Scienze, Lettere, ed Arti di Padova — Nuovi Saggi Ces Regia Accad Sci Padova
Nuovi Studi Medievali — N Studi Med
Nuovi Studi Medievali — NS Med
Nuovi Studi. Stazione Chimico-Agraria Sperimentale di Udine — Nuovi Studi Sta Chim-Agr Sper Udine
Nuovo Archivio Italiano di Otologia, Rinologia, e Laringologia — Nuovo Arch Ital ORL
Nuovo Archivio Italiano di Otologia, Rinologia, e Laringologia — Nuovo Arch Ital Otol Rinol Laringol
Nuovo Archivio Veneto — NAV
Nuovo Bulletino di Archeologia Cristiana — NBAC
Nuovo Bulletino di Archeologia Cristiana — Nuov Bull
Nuovo Cimento — Nuovo Cim
Nuovo Cimento. A — Nuov Cim A
Nuovo Cimento. A — Nuovo Cim A
Nuovo Cimento. B — Nuov Cim B
Nuovo Cimento. B — Nuovo Cim B
Nuovo Cimento. C — Nuovo Cim C
Nuovo Cimento. C. Serie 1 — Nuovo Cimento C 1
Nuovo Cimento. D. Serie 1 — Nuovo Cimento D 1
Nuovo Cimento. Lettere [*Italy*] — Nuovo Cimento Lett
Nuovo Cimento. Sezione A — NCIAA
Nuovo Cimento. Sezione. A — Nuovo Cimento A
Nuovo Cimento. Sezione B — NCIBA
Nuovo Cimento. Sezione. B — Nuovo Cimento B
Nuovo Cimento. Societa Italiana di Fisica. C. Geophysics and Space Physics — Nuovo Cimento Soc Ital Fis C
Nuovo Cimento. Societa Italiana di Fisica. Sezione A — NIFAA
Nuovo Cimento. Societa Italiana di Fisica. Sezione A — Nuovo Cimento Soc Ital Fis A
Nuovo Cimento. Societa Italiana di Fisica. Sezione B — NIFBA
Nuovo Cimento. Societa Italiana di Fisica. Sezione B — Nuovo Cimento Soc Ital Fis B
Nuovo Cimento. Societa Italiana di Fisica. Sezione C — NIFCA
Nuovo Cimento. Supplemento — NUCUA
Nuovo Cimento. Supplemento [*Italy*] — Nuovo Cimento Suppl
Nuovo Didaskaleion — N Did
Nuovo Didaskaleion — ND
Nuovo Digesto Italiano — NDI
Nuovo Digesto Italiano — Nov D I
Nuovo Digesto Italiano — NuD
Nuovo Ercolani — N Ercolani
Nuovo Giornale Botanico Italiano — Nu G Bot Ital
Nuovo Giornale Botanico Italiano — Nuo G Bot Ital
Nuovo Giornale Botanico Italiano — Nuovo G Bot Ital
Nuovo Giornale Botanico Italiano — Nuovo Giorn Bot Ital
Nuovo Giornale Botanico Italiano e Bollettino. Societa Botanica Italiana — Nuovo G Bot Ital Boll Soc Bot Ital
Nuovo Giornale Botanico Italiano (Nuovo Serie) — Nuovo G Bot Ital (Nuovo Ser)
Nuovo Giornale Ligustico di Lettere, Scienze, ed Arti — Nuovo Giorn Ligustico Lett
Nuovo Magazzino Toscano — Nuovo Mag Tosc
NUREG/CR (US Nuclear Regulatory Commission) Report CR — NUREG/CR
Nurse Education Today — Nurse Educ Today
Nurse Educator — Nurse Educ
Nurse Educators Opportunities and Innovations — Nurse Educ Oppor Innov
Nurse in Israel — Nurse Isr
Nurse Inquirer — Nurse Inquir
Nurse Leadership — Nurs Leader
Nurse Practitioner — Nurse Pract
Nurse Practitioner — Nurse Practit
Nurse, the Patient, and the Law — Nurse Patient Law
Nursery and Kindergarten Teachers — NKT
Nursery Business — Nursery Bus
Nurseryman and Garden Center — Nurserym Gdn Cent
Nurse's Drug Alert — Drug Alert
Nursing — INUR
Nursing '78 — Nurs '78
Nursing '80/'81 — Nurs '80/'81
Nursing '82 — Nurs '82
Nursing '83/'84 — Nurs 83/84
Nursing '85/'86 — Nurs 85/86
Nursing Abstracts — Nurs Abstr
Nursing Administration. Quarterly — Nurs Adm Q
Nursing Administration. Quarterly — Nurs Admin Q
Nursing and Allied Health Index — Nurs Allied Health Index
Nursing and Health Care — Nurs Health Care
Nursing and Health Care — Nurs Hlth Care
Nursing Care — Nurs Care
Nursing Careers — Nurs Careers
Nursing Clinics of North America — Nurs Clin N Am
Nursing Clinics of North America — Nurs Clin North Am
Nursing Digest — Nurs Dig
Nursing Digest — Nurs Digest
Nursing Dimensions — Nurs Dime
Nursing Dimensions — Nurs Dimens
Nursing Economics — Nurs Econ
Nursing Education Monographs — Nurs Educ Monogr
Nursing Focus — Nurs Focus
Nursing Forum — Nurs Forum
Nursing Forum (Auckland) — Nurs Forum (Auckl)
Nursing History Review — Nurs Hist Rev
Nursing Homes — Nurs Homes
Nursing Journal — Nurs J
Nursing Journal of India — Nurs J India
Nursing Journal of Singapore — Nurs J Singapore
Nursing Journal (Santo Tomas, Manila) — Nurs J (S Toms)
Nursing Law and Ethics — Nurs Law Ethics
Nursing Leadership — Nurs Leadersh
Nursing Leadership — Nurs Leadership
Nursing Life — Nurs Life
Nursing (London) — Nursing (Lond)
Nursing Management — Nurs M
Nursing Management — Nurs Manage
Nursing Mirror — NMIRA
Nursing Mirror and Midwives Journal [*Later, Nursing Mirror*] — Nurs Mirror
Nursing (Montreal) — Nurs (Montreal)
Nursing Mothers' Association of Australia. Newsletter — NMAA Newsletter
Nursing News (Concord) — Nurs News (Concord)
Nursing News (Connecticut) — Nurs News (Conn)
Nursing News (Hartford) — Nurs News (Hartford)
Nursing News (Meriden) — Nurs News (Meriden)
Nursing News (New Hampshire) — Nurs News (New Hamp)
Nursing News (South Africa) — Nurs News (So Africa)
Nursing Outlook — NUOL
Nursing Outlook — Nurs Outlook
Nursing Papers — Nurs Pap
Nursing Papers — Nurs Papers
Nursing Practice — Nurs Pract
Nursing Pulse of New England — Nurs Pulse New Engl
Nursing (Quebec) — Nurs (Que)
Nursing Research — Nurs Res
Nursing Research — NURVA
Nursing Research Conference — Nurs Res Conf
Nursing Research Report — Nurs Res Rep
Nursing Science — Nurs Sci
Nursing Standard — Nurs Stand
Nursing Studies Index — Nurs Stud Index
Nursing Success Today — Nurs Success Today
Nursing Times — Nurs Times
Nursing Times — NUTIA
Nursing Update — Nurs Update
Nutida Musik — Nutida M
Nutida Musik — Nutida Mus
Nutricia Symposium — Nutr Symp
Nutricion Bromatologia Toxicologia — Nutr Bromatol Toxicol
Nutricion Clinica. Dietetica Hospitalaria — Nutr Clin
Nutricion Hospitalaria — Nutr Hosp
Nutrient Requirements of Dairy Cattle — Nutr Requir Dairy Cattle
Nutrient Requirements of Domestic Animals — Nutr Requir Domest Anim
Nutrient Requirements of Sheep — Nutr Requir Sheep
Nutrient Requirements of Swine — Nutr Requir Swine
Nutrio et Dieta. European Review of Nutrition and Dietetics — Nutr Dieta Eur Nutr Diet
Nutritio et Dieta — NUDIA
Nutritio et Dieta — Nutr Dieta

Nutritio et Dieta. Supplement — Nutr Dieta Suppl
Nutrition Abstracts — NutrAb
Nutrition Abstracts and Reviews [*Information service or system*] — NAR
Nutrition Abstracts and Reviews [*Information service or system*] — Nutr Abstr Rev
Nutrition Abstracts and Reviews. Series A. Human and Experimental — Nutr Abstr Rev Ser A Hum Exp
Nutrition Action — Nutr Action
Nutrition Action Health Letter — Nutr Action Health Lett
Nutrition and Behavior — NUBEDX
Nutrition and Behavior — Nutr Behav
Nutrition and Cancer — NUCAD
Nutrition and Cancer — Nutr Cancer
Nutrition and Clinical Nutrition — Nutr Clin Nutr
Nutrition and Dental Health — Nutr Dent Health
Nutrition and Food Science — Nutr Food Sci
Nutrition and Food Science. Present Knowledge and Utilization — Nutr Food Sci Pres Knowl Util
Nutrition and Health — Nutr Health
Nutrition and Health. A Journal of Preventive Medicine — NUAH
Nutrition and Metabolism — Nutr Metab
Nutrition and the Brain — Nutr Brain
Nutrition and the MD — Nutr and MD
Nutrition Clinics — Nutr Clin
Nutrition Clinique et Metabolisme — Nutr Clin Metab
Nutrition Conference for Feed Manufacturers — Nutr Conf Feed Manuf
Nutrition Forum — Nutr Forum
Nutrition Foundation, Incorporated. Report — Nutr Found Inc Rep
Nutrition in Health and Disease — NHDIDW
Nutrition in Health and Disease — Nutr Health Dis
Nutrition in Transition. Proceedings. Western Hemisphere Nutrition Congress — Nutr Transition Proc West Hemisphere Nutr Congr
Nutrition International — Nutr Int
Nutrition Monograph Series — Nutr Monogr Ser
Nutrition News — NUTN
Nutrition News — Nutr News
Nutrition Newsletter [*Canada*] — NUNW
Nutrition Notes — Nutr Notes
Nutrition of Protected Crops. Papers. Colloquium. Potassium Institute — Nutr Prot Crops Pap Colloq Potassium Inst
Nutrition Planning — Nutr Plann
Nutrition Problems — Nutr Probl
Nutrition. Proceedings. International Congress — Nutr Proc Int Congr
Nutrition Reports International — Nutr Rep In
Nutrition Reports International — Nutr Rep Int
Nutrition Research — Nutr Res
Nutrition Research Bulletin — Nutr Res Bull
Nutrition Research (Los Angeles) — Nutr Res Los Angeles
Nutrition Research (New York) — Nutr Res New York
Nutrition Research Reviews — Nutr Res Rev
Nutrition Reviews — INUT
Nutrition Reviews — Nutr R
Nutrition Reviews — Nutr Rev
Nutrition Reviews' Present Knowledge in Nutrition — Nutr Rev Present Knowl Nutr
Nutrition Sciences — Nutr Sci
Nutrition Sciences — NUTSDT
Nutrition Society of Australia. Proceedings — Nutr Soc Aust Proc
Nutrition Society of New Zealand. Proceedings — Nutr Soc NZ Proc
Nutrition Society Proceedings [*British*] — Nutr Soc Proc
Nutrition Today — Nutr Today
Nutrition Today — PNUT
Nutrition Update — Nutr Update
Nutrition Week — Nutr Week
Nutritional Deficiencies in Industrialized Countries. Symposium. Group of European Nutritionists — Nutr Defic Ind Countries Symp Group Eur Nutr
Nutritional Support Services — Nutr Support Serv
Nuvuk News — NUVN
NWSIA [*National Water Supply Improvement Association*] **Journal** — NWSIA J
NWSIA [*National Water Supply Improvement Association*] **Newsletter** — NWSIA Newsl
NWT [*Northwest Territories, Canada*] **Gazette. Part II** — NWTGII
NWT [*Northwest Territories, Canada*] **Gazette. Part III** — NWTG3
NWT [*Northwest Territories, Canada*] **Wildlife Notes** — NWTWN
NWT [*Northwest Territories, Canada*] **Wildlife Service. Completion Reports** — NWTWSCR
NWT [*Northwest Territories, Canada*] **Wildlife Service. Contact Reports** — NWTWSCT
NWT [*Northwest Territories, Canada*] **Wildlife Service. File Reports** — NWTWSFR
NWT [*Northwest Territories, Canada*] **Wildlife Service. Progress Reports** — NWTWSPR
Ny Journal Uti Hushallningen — Ny J Hush
Ny Kirkehistoriske Samlinger — NKHS
Ny Kyrklig Tidsskrift — NKT
Ny Kyrklig Tidsskrift [*Uppsala*] — NKyrKTs
Ny Svensk Tidskrift — NySvT
Ny Teknik — Ny Tek
Ny Teknik — NYTKB
Nya Argus — NyA
Nya Botaniska Notiser — Nya Bot Not
Nya Perspektiv — Nya Perspekt
Nyasaland Farmer and Forester — Nyasal Farmer For
Nyasaland Farmer and Forester — Nyasaland Farmer Forest
Nyasaland Journal — Nyasa J
Nyasaland Protectorate. Geological Survey Department. Memoir — Nyasal Geol Surv Dep Mem
Nydanske Studier. Almen Kommunikationsteori — NDSK
Nydanske Studier. Almen Kommunikationsteori — NyS
Nye Danske Magazine — NDM
Nye Oeconomiske Annaler — Nye Oecon Ann
Nye Samling af det Danske Videnskabernes Selskabs Skrifter — NSDVS
Nye Samling af det Kongelige Danske Videnskabers Selskabs Skrifter — Nye Saml Kongel Danske Vidensk Selsk Skr
Nyelv-Es Irodalomtudomanyi Koezlemenyek — NIK
Nyelv-Es Irodalomtudomanyi Koezlemenyek — NyIroK
Nyelvtudomanyi Dolgozatok. Eotvos Lorand Tudomanyegyetum — Nyelvtudomanyi Dolg Eotvos Lorand TudomEgy
Nyelvtudomanyi Ertekezesek — NyE
Nyelvtudomanyi Intezet Koezlemenyek — NyIK
Nyelvtudomanyi Koezlemenyek — NK
Nyelvtudomanyi Koezlemenyek — NyK
Nyeste Samling Af Det Kongelige Norske Videnskabers-Selskabs Skrifter — Nyeste Saml Kongel Norske Vidensk Selsk Skr
Nyiregyhazi Josa Andras Muzeum Evkonyve — JAME
Nyiregyhazi Josa Andras Muzeum Evkonyve — Nyiregyhazi ME
Nyiregyhazi Josa Andras Muzeum Evkonyve — NyJME
Nymphenburger Texte zur Wissenschaft — NTW
NYSERDA [*New York State Energy Research and Development Authority*] **Review** — NYSERDA Rev
NYSFI (New York State Flower Industries) Bulletin — NYSFI Bull
NYSSNTA [*New York State School Nurse-Teachers Association*] **Journal** — NYSSNTA J
Nysvenska Studier — NSS
Nysvenska Studier — NsvS
Nysvenska Studier — Nys S
Nyt Bibliothek for Laeger — Nyt Bibl Laeg
Nyt Bibliothek for Physik, Medicin, og Oeconomie — Nyt Biblioth Phys
Nyt Historisk Tidsskrift — NHT
Nytestamentliga Avhandlingar — NTLA
Nytt Magasin foer Botanikk (Oslo) — Nytt Mag Bot (Oslo)
Nytt Magasin foer Naturvidenskapene — Nytt Mag Naturvid
Nytt Magasin foer Naturvidenskapene — Nytt Mag Naturvidensk
Nytt Magasin foer Zoologi — NYMZ
Nytt Magasin foer Zoology (Oslo) — Nytt Mag Zool (Oslo)
NYU Engineering Research Review — NYU Eng Res Rev
NZ [*New Zealand*] **Concrete Construction** — NZ Concr Constr
NZ DSIR [*New Zealand Department of Scientific and Industrial Research*] **Informat ion Series** — NZ DSIR Inf Ser
NZ [*New Zealand*] **Engineering** — NZ Eng
NZAEI [*New Zealand Agricultural Engineering Institute*] **Newsletter** — NZAEI Newsl
NZIE (New Zealand Institution of Engineers) Transactions. Electrical/ Mechanical/Chemical Engineering Section — NZIE Trans Electr Mech Chem Eng Sect
NZIE [*New Zealand Institution of Engineers*] **Proceedings of Technical Groups** — NZIE Proc Tech Groups
NZOI [*New Zealand Oceanographic Institute*] **Miscellaneous Publications** — NZOI Misc Publ
NZOI [*New Zealand Oceanographic Institute*] **Oceanographic Summary** — NZOI Oceanogr Sum
NZOI [*New Zealand Oceanographic Institute*] **Records** — NZOI Rec
NZTCA [*New Zealand Teachers' Colleges Association*] **Journal** — NZTCA Jnl

O

O Arqueologo Portugues — A Port
O Biologico — Biol
O Comercio do Porto — OCP
O Correio Medico de Lisboa — Correio Med Lisb
O Criador Paulista. Publicacao Official da Secretaria da Agricultura, Commercio, e Obras Publicas. Estado de Sao Paulo — Criador Paul
O Estado de Sao Paulo. Suplemento Literario — ESPSL
O Genezise Kapitalizma v Stranakh Vostoka — GKSV
O Instituto — OI
O Nosso Lar — ONL
O Pantheon. Revista Quinzenal de Sciencias e Letras — OPRQSL
O Positivismo. Revista de Philosophia — OP
O Primeiro de Janeiro — OPJ
O Tempo e o Modo — TeM
O Tempo e o Modo — TMo
O Tripeiro — OT
Oak Report. A Quarterly Journal on Music and Musicians — Oak Rept
Oak Ridge Associated Universities. Institute for Energy Analysis. Report and Proceedings. ORAU/IEA — Oak Ridge Assoc Univ Inst Energy Anal Rep Proc ORAU/IEA
Oak Ridge National Laboratory Conference on Analytical Chemistry in Energy Technology — Oak Ridge Natl Lab Conf Anal Chem Energy Technol
Oak Ridge National Laboratory. Heavy Section Steel Technology Program. Technical Report — Oak Ridge Natl Lab Heavy Sect Steel Technol Program Tech Rep
Oak Ridge National Laboratory. Radiation Shielding Information Center. Report [*A publication*] — Oak Ridge Nat Lab Radiat Shielding Inf Cent Rep
Oak Ridge National Laboratory. Report — Oak Ridge Natl Lab Rep
Oak Ridge National Laboratory. Report. ORNL (United States) — Oak Ridge Natl Lab Rep ORNL US
Oak Ridge National Laboratory. Report. ORNL-TM (United States) — Oak Ridge Natl Lab Rep ORNL TM (US)
Oak Ridge National Laboratory. Review — Oak Ridge Natl Lab Rev
Oak Ridge National Laboratory. Review — ORNRA
Oak Ridge National Laboratory. Technical Report. ORNL/FE — Oak Ridge Natl Lab Tech Rep ORNL FE
Oak Ridge National Laboratory. TM — ORNL TM
Oak Ridge National Laboratory (United States). Physics Division. Annual Progress Report — Oak Ridge Natl Lab (US) Phys Div Annu Prog Rep
Oak Ridge Operations Office. Report ORO — Oak Ridge Oper Off Rep ORO
Oakland Business Monthly — Oaklnd Bsn
Oakland Tribune — Oakland Trib
OAPEC [*Organization of Arab Petroleum Exporting Countries*] **News Bulletin** — OAP
OAPEC [*Organization of Arab Petroleum Exporting Countries*] **News Bulletin** [*Kuwait*] — OAPEC News Bull
OAR (Oesterreichische Abwasser-Rundschau) International — OAR Int
Oat Science and Technology — Oat Sci Technol
Obdorne Vcelarske Preklady — Obd Vcelar Prekl
Obecna Chemicka Technologie — Obecna Chem Technol
Ob'edinennaya Konferentsiya Gigienostov, Organizatorov Zdravookhraneniya, Epidemiologov, Mikrobiologov, i Infektsionistov — Obedin Konf Gig Organ Zdravookhr Epidemiol Mikrobiol Infekts
Ob'edinennye Nauchnye Chteniya po Kosmonavtike — Obedin Nauchn Chteniya Kosmonavt
Ob'edinennyi Institut Yadernykh Issledovanii (Dubna, USSR). Preprint — Obedin Inst Yad Issled (Dubna USSR) Prepr
Oberbayerisches Archiv fuer Vaterlaendische Geschichte — O Bay A
Oberbayerisches Archiv fuer Vaterlaendische Geschichte — OA
Oberbayerisches Archiv fuer Vaterlaendische Geschichte — OAVG
Oberbayerisches Archiv fuer Vaterlaendische Geschichte — OBA
Oberdeutsche Allgemeine Litteraturzeitung — Oberdeutsche Allg Litteraturzeitung
Oberdeutsche Beytraege zur Naturlehre und Oekonomie — Oberdeutsche Beytr Naturl Oekon
Oberdeutsche Zeitschrift fuer Volkskunde — ODZVK
Oberflaeche Surface — Oberflaeche Surf
Oberflaeche Surface — OBSUA
Oberflaechentechnik/Metallpraxis [*Germany*] — Oberflaechentech/Metallprax
Oberflaechentechnik/Metallpraxis — OTMPA
Obergermanisch-Raetische Limes des Roemerreiches — ORL
Oberhessische Naturwissenschaftliche Zeitschrift — Oberhess Naturwiss Z
Oberlin College. Allen Memorial Art Museum. Bulletin — Oberlin Coll Mus Bull
Oberoesterreichische Heimatblaetter — Oberoest H Bl
Oberoesterreichische Heimatblaetter — OOEH
Oberoesterreichische Imker — Oberoest Imker
Oberoesterreichische Nachrichten — Ooe N
Oberpfaelzer Heimat — OH
Oberrheinische Geologische Abhandlungen — Oberrhein Geol Abh
Oberrheinische Geologische Abhandlungen — Oberrheinische Geol Abh
Oberrheinisches Pastoralblatt — Obrh Past Bl
Oberrheinisches Pastoralblatt — ORPB
Obesity and Bariatric Medicine — Obesity & Bariatric Med
Obesity Research — Obes Res
Obituary — Obit
Obituary Notices. Royal Society of London — R Soc Obit N
Objets et Monde — Obj Monde
Objets et Monde — OM
Obogashchenie, Briketirovanie, i Koksovanie Uglya — Obogashch Briket Koksovanie Uglya
Obogashchenie i Briketirovanie Uglei — Obogashch Briket Uglei
Obogashchenie i Briketirovanie Uglei [*Former USSR*] — Obogashchenie Briket Uglei
Obogashchenie i Briketirovanie Uglya — Obogashch Briket Uglya
Obogashchenie i Ispol'zovanie Uglya — Obogashch Ispolz Uglya
Obogashchenie Poleznykh Iskopaemykh — Obogashch Polezn Iskop
Obogashchenie Rud — Obogashch Rud
Obogashchenie Rud Chernykh Metallov — Obogashch Rud Chern Met
Obogashchenie Rud (Irkutsk) — Obogashch Rud (Irkutsk)
Obogashchenie Rud (Leningrad) — Obogashch Rud (Leningrad)
Obra — Ob
Obrabotka i Interpretatsiya Fizicheskikh Eksperimentov — Obrab Interpret Fiz Eksp
Obrabotka Metallov Davleniem (Moscow) — Obrab Met Davleniem Moscow
Obrabotka Metallov Davleniem (Rostov-On-Don) — Obrab Met Davleniem (Rostov-On-Don)
Obrabotka Metallov Davleniem v Mashinostroenii — Obrab Met Davleniem Mashinostr
Obrabotka Metallov Davleniem v Mashinostroenii [*Ukrainian SSR*] — Obrab Metal Davleniem Mashinostr
Obras de Teatro Estrenadas en Espana [*Database*] — TEAT
Obras Escohidas de Machado de Assis — OEMA
Obras Espuestas en Museos Espanoles [*Database*] — ARTE
Obrazcy Narodnoj Slovesnosti Mongolov — ONSM
Obrazcy Narodnoj Slovesnosti Mongol'skich Plemen — ONSMP
Obrazotvorce Mistectvo — OM
Obrobka Plastyczna — Obrob Plast
Obrobka Plastyczna — Obrobka Plast
Obscestvennye Nauki (Moskva) — Obsc Nauki Moskva
Obscestvennye Nauki v Uzbekistane — Obsc N Uzbek
Obscestvennye Nauki v Uzbekistane — Obsc Nauki v Uzbek
Observador Economico e Financiero (Rio de Janeiro) — Observ Econ Finan Rio
Observationes Botanicae et Descriptiones Plantarum Novarum Herbarii Van Heurckiani/Recueil d'Observations Botaniques et de Descriptions de Plantes Nouvelles — Observ Bot Descript Pl Nov Herb Van Heurckiani
Observationes Sobre la Fisica, Historia Natural, y Artes Utiles — Observ Fis
Observations sur la Physique, sur l'Histoire Naturelle, et sur les Arts — Obs sur Phys
Observations Sur La Physique, Sur l'Histoire Naturelle et Sur Les Arts — Observ Phys
Observatorio Astronomico de la Universidad Nacional de La Plata. Serie Astronomica — Obs Astronom Univ Nac La Plata Ser Astronom
Observer [*London*] — O
Observer [*United Kingdom*] — OB
Observer — Obs
Observer Design Brief — Observer Des Brief
Observer's Handbook. Royal Astronomical Society of Canada — Obs Handb Can
Obshcha i Sravnitelna Patologiya — Obshcha Sravn Patol
Obshchaya Ekologiya, Biotsenologiya, Gidrobiologiya — Obshch Ekol Biotsenol Gidrobiol
Obshchaya Energetika — Obshch Energ
Obshchaya i Prikladnaya Khimiya — Obshch Prikl Khim
Obshchee Mashinostroenie — Obshch Mashinostr
Obshchestvennoe Pitanie — Obshchestv Pitan
Obshchestvennye Nauki v Usbekistane — ONU
Obshchestvennye Nauki v Uzbekistane — Obshchest Nauk Uzbek
Obshchestvo Remeslennovo i Zemledel'cheskovo Truda — OZET
Obshchestvo Zemleistroistva Evreiskikh Trudiashchikhsia v SSSR — OZET
Obshchie Atomnyi, Yadernyi, i Spetsial'nyi Yadernyi Praktikumy — Obshch At Yad Spets Yad Prakt
Obshchie Problemy Fiziko-Khimicheskoi Biologii. Itogi Nauki i Tekhnik — Obshch Probl Fiz Khim Biol Itogi Nauki Tekh

Obshchie Problemy Mashinostroeniya, Trudy Moskovskoi Konferentsii Molodykh Uchenykh — Obshch Probl Mashinostr Tr Mosk Konf Molodykh Uch
Obshchie Voprosy Fiziologicheskikh Mekhanizmov, Analiz, i Modelirovanie Biologicheskikh Sistem. Trudy Mezhdunarodnogo Simpoziuma po Tekhnicheskim i Biologicheskim Problemam Upravleniya — Obshch Vopr Fiziol Mekh Tr Mezhdunar Simp Tekh Biol Probl Up
Obshchie Zakonomernosti Morfogeneza i Regeneratsii — Obshch Zakonomern Morfog Regener
Obshta i Sravnitelna Patologiia — Obshta Sravnitelna Patol
Obshta I Sravnitelna Patologiia — OSPADK
Obshta i Sravnitelna Patologiya — Obshta Sravn Patol
Obsidian — Obs
Obst- und Gemuese-Verwertungs Industrie — Obst Gemuese Verwert Ind
Obstetrica si Ginecologia — Obstet Ginecol
Obstetrica si Ginecologia (Bucharest) — Obstet Ginecol (Buchar)
Obstetrical and Gynecological Survey — Obst Gynec Surv
Obstetrical and Gynecological Survey — Obstet Gynec Surv
Obstetrical and Gynecological Survey — Obstet Gynecol Surv
Obstetrical and Gynecological Therapy [*Japan*] — Obstet Gynecol Ther
Obstetrical and Gynecological Therapy (Osaka) — Obstet Gynecol Ther (Osaka)
Obstetrical Journal of Great Britain and Ireland — Obst J Gr Brit
Obstetricia y Ginecologia Latino-Americanas — Obstet Ginecol Lat-Am
Obstetrics and Gynecology — OBGNA
Obstetrics and Gynecology — Obst Gynec
Obstetrics and Gynecology — Obstet Gyn
Obstetrics and Gynecology — Obstet Gynec
Obstetrics and Gynecology — Obstet Gynecol
Obstetrics and Gynecology (Amsterdam) — Obstet Gynecol Amsterdam
Obstetrics and Gynecology. Annual — Obstet Gynecol Annu
Obstetrics and Gynecology Clinics of North America — Obstet Gynecol Clin North Am
Obstetrics and Gynecology (Moscow) — Obstet Gynecol Moscow
Obstetrics and Gynecology (Tokyo) — Obstet Gynecol (Tokyo)
Obzor Botaniceskoj Dejatel'nosti v Rossii — Obzor Bot Dejateln Rossii
Obzor Praehistoricky — OP
Obzor Praehistoricky Revue Prehistorique — Obzor Prehist
Obzor Praehistoricky Revue Prehistorique — OP
Obzor Vengerskoi Lesovodstvennoi Nauki — Obz Veng Lesovod Nauki
Obzornaya Informatsiya. Okhrana i Zashchita Lesa — Obz Inf Okhr Zashch Lesa
Obzornaya Informatsiya, Poligraficheskaya Promyshlennost — Obz Inf Poligr Promst
Obzornik za Matematiko in Fiziko — Obz Mat Fiz
Obzornik za Matematiko in Fiziko — Obzornik Mat Fiz
Obzornykh Dokladov Vsesoyuznogo Soveshchaniya po Mikroelementam — Obz Dokl Vses Soveshch Mikroelem
Obzory po Atomnoi Energii — Obz At Energ
Obzory po Elektronnoi Tekhnike — Obz Elektron Tekh
Obzory po Otdel'nym Proizvodstvam Khimicheskoi Promyshlennosti — Obz Otd Proizvod Khim Promsti
Obzory po Vysokotemperaturnoi Sverkhprovodimosti — Obz Vysokotemp Sverkhprovodimosti
O'Casey Annual — OCA
Occasional Bulletin. Missionary Resarch Library — OBMRL
Occasional Bulletin of Missionary Research — OBMR
Occasional Bulletin of Missionary Research — OcBul
Occasional Bulletin of Missionary Research — Occ Bul Miss R
Occasional Communications. Utrecht University. Biohistorical Institute — Commun Biohist
Occasional Contributions. Library (University of Kentucky, Lexington) — Occas Contr Libr Univ Kentucky Lexington
Occasional Newsletter. Lindsay Club — Occas Newsl Lindsay Club
Occasional Notes. Hongkong Horticultural Society — Occas Notes Hongkong Hort Soc
Occasional Paper. British Museum — Occas Pap Br Mus
Occasional Paper. Bureau of Forestry (Manila, Philippines) — Occ Pap Bur For (Philippines)
Occasional Paper. Department of Biochemistry. Makerere University — Occas Pap Dep Biochem Makerere Univ
Occasional Paper. Department of Transport (Bureau of Transport Economics) — Occ Pap Bur Trans Eco
Occasional Paper. Environment Canada — Occas Pap Environ Can
Occasional Paper. Fairchild Tropical Garden — Occas Pap Fairchild Trop Gard
Occasional Paper. Geological Survey (New Hebrides) — Occas Pap Geol Surv (New Hebrides)
Occasional Paper. Jamaica. Geological Survey Department — Occas Pap Jam Geol Surv Dep
Occasional Paper. Laboratory. Government Chemist (Great Britain) — Occas Pap Lab Gov Chem GB
Occasional Paper. Makerere University. Department of Geography — Occas Pap Makerere Univ Dep Geogr
Occasional Paper. Mauritius Sugar Industry Research Institute — Occ Pap Maurit Sug Ind Res Inst
Occasional Paper. Mauritius Sugar Industry Research Institute — Occas Pap Mauritius Sugar Ind Res Inst
Occasional Paper. Missouri Academy of Science — Occas Pap Mo Acad Sci
Occasional Paper. Nanyang University. College of Graduate Studies. Institute of Natural Sciences — Occas Pap Nanyang Univ Coll Grad Stud Inst Nat Sci
Occasional Paper. National College of Agricultural Engineering — Occas Pap Natl Coll Agric Eng
Occasional Paper. Royal College of General Practitioners — Occas Pap R Coll Gen Pract
Occasional Paper. Tropical Science Center (San Jose, Costa Rica) — Occas Pap Trop Sci Cent (San Jose Costa Rica)
Occasional Paper. Vegetation Survey of Western Australia — Occ Pap Vegn Surv West Aust
Occasional Papers. American Society for Reformation Research — Occas Pap Am Soc Reform Res
Occasional Papers. Archibishops' Commission on Christian Doctrine — OPACCD
Occasional Papers. Bell Museum of Natural History. University of Minnesota — Occas Pap Bell Mus Nat Hist Univ Minn
Occasional Papers. Bernice Pauahi Bishop Museum — Occas Pap Bernice Pauahi Bishop Mus
Occasional Papers. Boston Society of Natural History — Occas Pap Boston Soc Nat Hist
Occasional Papers. British Columbia Provincial Museum — Occas Pap BC Prov Mus
Occasional Papers. Buffalo Society of Natural Sciences — Occas Pap Buffalo Soc Nat Sci
Occasional Papers. Buffalo Society of Natural Sciences — OPBSDH
Occasional Papers. C. C. Adams Center for Ecological Studies. Western Michigan University — Occas Pap C C Adams Cent Ecol Stud West Mich Univ
Occasional Papers. California Academy of Sciences — Occ Pap Calif Acad Sci
Occasional Papers. California Academy of Sciences — Occas Pap Calif Acad Sci
Occasional Papers. Centre for Developing-Area Studies — Oc P Dev-A
Occasional Papers. Christian Brethren Research Fellowship — OPCBRF
Occasional Papers. Department of Biology. University of Guyana — Occ Pap Dep Biol Univ Guyana
Occasional Papers. Department of Biology. University of Puget Sound — Occas Pap Dep Biol Univ Puget Sound
Occasional Papers. Division of Systematic Biology. Stanford University — Occas Pap Div Syst Biol Stanford Univ
Occasional Papers. Farlow Herbarium of Cryptogamic Botany. Harvard University — Occas Pap Farlow Herb Cryptogam Bot Harv Univ
Occasional Papers. Florida State Collection of Arthropods — Occas Pap Fla State Collect Arthropods
Occasional Papers. Geological Survey of Nigeria — Occ Pap Geol Surv Nig
Occasional Papers. Geological Survey of Uganda — Occ Pap Geol Surv Ug
Occasional Papers in Anthropology. Pennsylvania State University — Oc P Anth P
Occasional Papers in Economic and Social History — Oc P Econ H
Occasional Papers in Entomology (Sacramento) — Occas Pap Entomol (Sacramento)
Occasional Papers in Geography — Oc P Geog
Occasional Papers in Industrial Relations — Occas Pap Ind Rel
Occasional Papers in International Affairs — Oc P Int Af
Occasional Papers in Language, Literature, and Linguistics — OPLLL
Occasional Papers in Linguistics and Language Learning — OPLiLL
Occasional Papers in Modern Languages — OPML
Occasional Papers. Institution of Mining and Metallurgy — Occas Pap Inst Min Metall
Occasional Papers. Minnesota Museum of Natural History — Occas Pap Minn Mus Nat Hist
Occasional Papers. Museum of Natural History. University of Kansas — Occas Pap Mus Nat Hist Univ Kans
Occasional Papers. Museum of Natural History. University of Minnesota — Occas Pap Mus Nat Hist Univ Minnesota
Occasional Papers. Museum of Natural History. University of Puget Sound — Occas Pap Mus Nat Hist Univ Puget Sound
Occasional Papers. Museum of Victoria — Occas Pap Mus Victoria
Occasional Papers. Museum of Zoology. Louisiana State University — Occas Pap Mus Zool LA State Univ
Occasional Papers. Museum of Zoology. University of Michigan — Occas Pap Mus Zool Univ Mich
Occasional Papers. National Museum of Southern Rhodesia. Series B. Natural Sciences — Occas Pap Natl Mus South Rhod Ser B
Occasional Papers. National Museums and Monuments of Rhodesia. Series B. Natural Sciences — Occas Pap Natl Mus Monum Rhod Ser B Nat Sci
Occasional Papers. National Speleological Society — Occas Pap Natl Speleol Soc
Occasional Papers. Natural History Society of New Brunswick — Occas Pap Nat Hist Soc New Brunswick
Occasional Papers on Aging — Occas Pap Aging
Occasional Papers on Linguistics — OPLing
Occasional Papers on Mollusks. Museum of Comparative Zoology. Harvard University — Occas Pap Mollusks Mus Comp Zool Harv Univ
Occasional Papers on Technology. Pitt Rivers Museum. University of Oxford — Occas Pap Technol Pitt Rivers Mus Univ Oxford
Occasional Papers. Rancho Santa Ana Botanical Garden — Occas Pap Rancho Santa Ana Bot Gard
Occasional Papers. Royal Ontario Museum of Zoology — Occas Pap R Ont Mus Zool
Occasional Papers. Rural Development Committee — Oc P Rur De
Occasional Papers. San Diego Society of Natural History — Occas Pap San Diego Soc Nat Hist
Occasional Papers Series. Australian Water Resources Council — Occas Pap Ser Aust Water Resour Counc
Occasional Papers. Southern Forest Experiment Station. United States Forest Service — Occas Pap S Forest Exp Sta US Forest Serv
Occasional Papers. University of Arkansas Museum — Occas Pap Univ Arkansas Mus
Occasional Papers. University of Hawaii — Occas Pap Univ Hawaii
Occasional Papers. Vegetation Survey of Western Australia. Department of Agriculture — Occas Pap Veg Surv West Aust
Occasional Papers. World Fertility Survey — Occas Pap World Fertil Surv
Occasional Publication. British Society of Animal Production — Occas Publ Br Soc Anim Prod
Occasional Publication. Canadian Church Historical Society — OPCCHS

Occasional Publication. Rowett Research Institute — Occas Publ Rowett Res Inst
Occasional Publication. University of Alaska. Institute of Marine Science — Occas Publ Univ Alaska Inst Mar Sci
Occasional Publications. African and Afro-American Research Institute. University of Texas, Austin — OPARI
Occasional Publications. Australian Conservation Foundation — Occ Publs Aust Conserv Fdn
Occasional Publications. British Institute of Archaeology at Ankara [*A publication*] — OPBIA
Occasional Publications in Classical Studies — Occas Publ Cl St
Occasional Publications in Mathematics — Occasional Publ in Math
Occasional Publications. Institute of Health Administration. Georgia State University — Occas Publ Inst Health Adm GA State Univ
Occasional Publications on Scientific Horticulture — Occ Publ Sci Hort
Occasional Report. Virginia Division of Forestry. Department of Conservation and Economic Development — Occas Rep VA Div For Dep Conserv Econ Dev
Occasional Review — O Rev
Occasional Review — Occas Rev
Occasional Series. University of Manitoba. Department of Agricultural Economics and Farm Management — Occas Ser Univ Manitoba Dep Agric Econ Farm Manage
Occasional Symposium. British Grassland Society — Occas Symp Br Grassl Soc
Occidental — Occ
Occidental Entomologist — Occident Entomol
Occidente — Oc
Occidente — Occid
Occupational and Environmental Dermatoses — Occup Environ Dermatoses
Occupational and Environmental Medicine — Occup Environ Med
Occupational Dermatoses — Occup Dermatoses
Occupational Hazards — Occ Hazards
Occupational Hazards — Occup Hazards
Occupational Hazards — Occup Hzrd
Occupational Hazards — OHA
Occupational Health — Occup Health
Occupational Health — Occup Hlth
Occupational Health and Safety — Occ Health & Sfty
Occupational Health and Safety — Occup Health and Saf
Occupational Health and Safety — Occup Health Saf
Occupational Health and Safety — OHSAD
Occupational Health Bulletin (Ottawa) — Occup Health Bull (Ottawa)
Occupational Health in the Chemical Industry. Proceedings. International Congress on Occupational Health in the Chemical Industry — Occup Health Chem Ind Proc Int Congr
Occupational Health (London) — Occup Health (Lond)
Occupational Health Nursing — Occ Health Nurs
Occupational Health Nursing — Occup Health Nurs
Occupational Health Nursing — Occup Hlth Nurs
Occupational Health Nursing (New York) — Occup Health Nurs (NY)
Occupational Health Review — Occup Health Rev
Occupational Health Review — Occup Hlth Rev
Occupational Hygiene — Occup Hyg
Occupational Hygiene Monograph — Occup Hyg Monogr
Occupational Medicine — Occup Med
Occupational Medicine — OCMEA
Occupational Medicine (Oxford) — Occup Med Oxf
Occupational Medicine. State of the Art Reviews — Occup Med State of the Art Rev
Occupational Mental Health Notes — Occup Ment Health Notes
Occupational Outlook Quarterly — Occ Outlook Q
Occupational Outlook Quarterly — Occup Outl Q
Occupational Outlook Quarterly — Occupational Outlook Q
Occupational Outlook Quarterly — OOQ
Occupational Projections and Training. BLS Bulletin 2202. US Bureau of Labor Statistics — BLS 2202
Occupational Psychology — Occup Psych
Occupational Psychology — Occup Psychol
Occupational Safety and Health — Occup Saf Health
Occupational Safety and Health — Occup Saf Hlth
Occupational Safety and Health Abstracts — Occup Saf Health Abstr
Occupational Safety and Health Administration. Subscription Service. Volumes 1 and 4 — Occup Saf Hlth Admin Sub Service Vols 1 & 4
Occupational Safety and Health Cases. Bureau of National Affairs — OSH Cas BNA
Occupational Safety and Health Decisions. Commerce Clearing House — OSH Dec CCH
Occupational Safety and Health Reporter — OSHR
Occupational Safety and Health Reporter (Bureau of National Affairs) — OSH Rep (BNA)
Occupational Safety and Health Series. International Labour Office — Occup Saf Health Ser Int Labour Off
Occupational Therapy in Health Care — Occup Ther Health Care
Occupational Therapy in Mental Health — Occup Ther Ment Health
Occupational Therapy Journal of Research — Occup Ther J Res
Occupational Therapy Journal of Research — OTJR
Ocean and Shoreline Management — Ocean & Shoreline Manage
Ocean Development and International Law — Oc Dev and Int L
Ocean Development and International Law — Ocean Dev & Int L
Ocean Development and International Law — Ocean Dev I
Ocean Development and International Law — Ocean Devel & Int L
Ocean Development and International Law — Ocean Develop Int Law
Ocean Development and International Law — Ocean Development and Internat Law
Ocean Development and International Law Journal — Ocean Dev and Intl LJ
Ocean Drilling Program. Proceedings. Initial Report — Ocean Drill Program Proc Initial Rep
Ocean Drilling Program. Proceedings. Scientific Results — Ocean Drill Program Proc Sci Results
Ocean Energy. Annual Conference. Marine Technology Society — Ocean Energy Annu Conf Mar Technol Soc
Ocean Engineering — Ocean Eng
Ocean Engineering — Ocean Engng
Ocean Engineering. Information Series — Ocean Eng Inf Ser
Ocean Industry — Ocean Ind
Ocean Industry. Engineering, Construction, and Operations — OCI
Ocean Management — Ocean Manage
Ocean Management — Ocean Mgt
Ocean Management — OCM
Ocean Research [*Seoul*] — HAYOE7
Ocean Research (Seoul) — Ocean Res (Seoul)
Ocean Science and Engineering — Ocean Sci Eng
Ocean Science and Engineering — OSEND
Ocean Science News — OSN
Ocean State Business — Ocean St B
Ocean Thermal Energy Conversion Conference. Proceedings — Ocean Therm Energy Convers Conf Proc
Ocean Yearbook — Ocean Yearb
Oceania — Oc
Oceania — POCE
Oceania Monographs — Oc M
Oceanic Abstracts [*Information service or system*] — OA
Oceanic Abstracts — Ocean Abstr
Oceanic Abstracts — OceanAb
Oceanic Abstracts with Indexes — Ocean Abstr Indexes
Oceanic Linguistics — Ocean Ling
Oceanic Linguistics — OcL
Oceanic Linguistics — OL
Oceanic Linguistics. Special Publications — OLSP
Oceanographic Abstracts and Bibliography — Oceanogr Abstr Bibliogr
Oceanographic Research Institute (Durban). Investigational Report — Oceanogr Res Inst (Durban) Invest Rep
Oceanographical Cruise Report. Division of Fisheries and Oceanography. Commonwealth Scientific and Industrial Research Organisation — Oceanogrl Cruise Rep Div Fish Oceanogr CSIRO
Oceanographical Cruise Report. Institute of Marine Research (Djakarta) — Oceanogr Cruise Rep Inst Mar Res (Djakarta)
Oceanographical Magazine — Oceanogr Mag
Oceanographical Magazine — OCMAA
Oceanographical Magazine (Tokyo) — Oceanogr Mag (Tokyo)
Oceanographical Society of Japan. Journal — Oceanogr Soc Jap J
Oceanographical Station List. Division of Fisheries and Oceanography. Commonwealth Scientific and Industrial Research Organisation — Oceanogrl Stn List Div Fish Oceanogr CSIRO
Oceanographie Tropicale — Oceanogr Trop
Oceanography and Marine Biology — Oceanogr Mar Biol
Oceanography and Marine Biology: An Annual Review — Oceanogr Mar Biol Annu Rev
Oceanologia et Limnologia Sinica — Oceanol Limn Sin
Oceanologica Acta — OCACD
Oceanologica Acta — Oceanol Acta
Oceanologica et Limnologia Sinica — Oceanol Limnol Sin
Oceanological Researches — Oceanol Res
Oceanology — Oceanol
Oceanology International — Oceanol Int
Oceans — GOCE
Oceans Magazine — Oceans Mag
Oceans of Canada — OCOC
Oceanus — POCS
OCED Bericht-Deutsche Landwirtschafts-Gesellschaft Prufungsabteilung fuer Landmaschinen — OECD Ber Dtsch Landwirtsch Ges Prufungsabt Landmasch
Ocerki Mordovskich Dialektov — OMorD
Ocerki po Izuceniju Jakutskogo Kraja — Ocerki Izuc Jakutsk Kraja
Ochanomizu Medical Journal [*Japan*] — Ochanomizu Med J
Ochanomizu University Studies — OUS
Ocherki Fiziko-Khimicheskoi Petrologii — Ocherki Fiz-Khim Petrol
Ocherki Istorii Estestvoznaniya i Tekhniki — Ocherki Istor Estestvoznan Tekhn
Ocherki po Geologii Sovetskikh Karpat — Ocherki Geol Sov Karpat
Ocherki po Istorii Estestvoznaniya i Tekhniki — Ocherki Istor Estestvozn Tekh
Ochistka i Povtornoe Ispol'zovanie Stochnykh Vod na Urale — Ochistka Povtorn Ispol'z Stochnykh Vod Urale
Ochistka Vodnogo i Vozdushnogo Basseinov na Predpriyatiyakh Chernoi Metallurgii — Ochistka Vodn Vozdushn Basseinov Predpr Chern Metall
Ochrana Ovzdusi. Supplement to Vodni Hospodarstvi. Rada B — Ochr Ovzdusi
Ochrana Prirody — Ochr Prir
Ochrana Rostlin — Ochr Rostl
Ochrona Powietrza — Ochr Powietrza
Ochrona Pracy — Ochr Pr
Ochrona Przeciwpozarowa w Przemysle Chemicznym — Ochr Przeciwpozarowa Przem Chem
Ochrona Przed Korozja — Ochr Koroz
Ochrona Przed Korozja — Ochr Przed Koroz
Ochrona Przyrody — Ochr Przyr
Ochrona Roslin — Ochr Rosl
OCLC [*Online Computer Library Center*] **Online Union Catalog** [*Database*] — OLUC
Ocrotierea Naturii — Ocrot Nat
Ocrotirea Naturii — Ocrotirea Nat
Ocrotirea Naturii si a Mediului Inconjurator — Ocrotirea Nat Med Inconjurator

Octagon Papers — Octagon Pap
October — O
Octogon Mathematical Magazine — Octogon Math Mag
Ocular Immunology and Inflammation — Ocul Immunol Inflamm
Ocular Therapy. Complications and Management — Ocul Ther Complications Manage
Oculus — ONO
ODC [*Oahu Development Conference*] **Planning Reports** — ODC Plan Rep
Odense University Studies in English — OUSE
ODI (Overseas Development Institute). Review — ODI (Overseas Development Inst) R
Odjeljenje Tehnickih Nauka [*Sarajevo*] — Odjel Teh Nauka
Odontoestomatologia Portuguesa — Odonto Est Port
Odontoiatria — ODONA
Odontoiatria Pratica — Odontoiatr Prat
Odontoiatria. Revista Ibero-Americana de Medicina de la Boca — Odontoiatr Rev Iberoam Med Boca
Odontoiatrike Epitheoresis — Odontoiatr Epith
Odontologia Argentina — Odont Arg
Odontologia Atual — Odontol Atual
Odontologia Capixaba — Odontol Capixaba
Odontologia Chilena — Odontol Chil
Odontologia de America — Odont Am
Odontologia Dinamica — Odontol Din
Odontologia (Mexico) — Odontol (Mexico)
Odontologia Peruana — Odontol Peru
Odontologia Uruguaya — Odontol Urug
Odontological Bulletin — Odontol Bull
Odontologie — Odontol
Odontologie Conservatrice — Odontol Conserv
Odontologisches Monatsblatt — Odontol Mbl
Odontologisk Revy — Odontol Revy
Odontologisk Tidskrift — Odontol Tidskr
Odontologisk Tidskrift — Odontol Ts
Odontologiska Foreningens Tidskrift — Odontol Foren Tidskr
Odontologiska Samfundft i Finland Arsbok — Odontol Samf Finl Arsb
Odontologiya i Stomatologiya — Odontol Stomatol
Odontologo Moderno — Odontol Mod
Odontoprotesi — Odontopr
Odontostomatologia e Implantoprotesi — Odontostomatol Implantoprotesi
Odontostomatological Progress — Odontostomatol Prog
Odonto-Stomatologie Tropicale — Odonto-Stomatol Trop
Odontostomatologike Proodos — Odontostomatol Proodos
Odor Control Association. Journal — Odor Control Assoc J
Odor Research — Odor Res
Odrodzenie — Od
Odrodzenie i Reformacja w Polsce — OR
Odrodzenie i Reformacja w Polsce — ORP
O'Dwyer's Newsletter [*Jack*] — O Dwyer New
Odyssey — Ody
Odyssey Review — Odyssey
Oe VE. Oesterreichische Vorschriften fuer die Elektrotechnik — Oe VE
Oe Z E/Oesterreichische Zeitschrift fuer Elektrizitaetswirtschaft — Oe Z E Oesterr Z Elek
Oe Z E/Oesterreichische Zeitschrift fuer Elektrizitaetswirtschaft — OZE Oesterr Z Elektr
OECD [*Organization for Economic Cooperation and Development*] **Economic Outlook** — OEC
OECD [*Organization for Economic Cooperation and Development*] **Economic Outlook** — OECD Outlk
OECD [*Organization for Economic Cooperation and Development*] **Informatics Studies** — OECD Inform
OECD [*Organization for Economic Cooperation and Development*] **Newsletter to Booksellers** — OECD Newsl Booksellers
OECD [*Organization for Economic Cooperation and Development*] **Observer** — OECD Observer
OECD [*Organization for Economic Cooperation and Development*] **Observer** — OEO
OECD [*Organization for Economic Cooperation and Development*] **Observer** — OOB
Oecologia Plantarum — Oeco Planta
Oecologia Plantarum — Oecol Plant
Oeconomica Polona — Oecon Polon
Oeconomica Polona — Oecon Polona
Oeconomisch-Physikalische Abhandlungen — Oecon Phys Abh
Oeconomiske Annaler — Oecon Ann
Oecumenica [*Guetersloh*] — Oec
Oecumenica — Oecum
Oeffentliche Gesundheitsdienst — Oeff GD
Oeffentliche Gesundheitsdienst [*Germany*] — Oeff Gesundheitsdienst
Oeffentliche Gesundheitswesen — Oeff Gesundheitswes
Oeffentliche Gesundheitswesen — OEGWA
Oeffentliche Gesundheitswesen — Off Gesundheitswes
Oeffentliche Sicherheit — Oefftl Sicherht
Oeffentliche Verwaltung — Oe V
Oeffentliche Verwaltung [*Zeitschrift fuer Verwaltungsrecht und Verwaltungspolitik*] — Oeff Verw
Oeffentliche Verwaltung [*Zeitschrift fuer Verwaltungsrecht und Verwaltungspolitik*] — Oeff Verwalt
Oeffentliche Verwaltung — Oeffentl Verwalt
Oeffentliche Verwaltung und Datenverarbeitung — Oe VD
Oeffentlicher Anzeiger fuer das Vereinigte Wirtschaftsgebiet — Oeff Anz
Oefversigt af Finska Vetenskaps-Societetens Foerhandlingar — Oefvers Fin Vetensk Soc Foerh
Oefversigt af Foerhandlingar. Finska Vetenskaps-Societeten — Oefvers Foerh Finska Vetensk Soc
OEFZS (Oesterreichisches Forschungszentrum Seibersdorf) Berichte — OEFZS (Oesterr Forschungszent Seibersdorf) Ber
Oekologie/Umwelttechnik — Oekol Umwelttech
Oekonometrie und Unternehmensforschung — Oekonom Unternehmensforsch
Oekonomisch-Botanisches Garten-Journal — Oekon Bot Gart J
Oekonomische Neuigkeiten und Verhandlungen — Oekon Neuigk Verh
Oekonomische und Soziale Entwicklung Indiens. Sowietische Beitraege zur Indischen Geschichte — OSEI
Oekosystemanalyse und Umweltforschung — Oekosystemanal Umweltforsch
Oekumenische Beihefte zur Freiburger Zeitschrift fuer Philosophie und Theologie — OeBFZ Ph Th
Oekumenische Studien — Oek S
Oekumenische Studien — OS
Oel + Gasfeuerung — Oel Gasfeuer
Oel und Gas und Feuerungstechnik [*Germany*] — Oel & Gas Feuerungstech
Oel und Kohle — OEKOA
Oelfeuer Technik — Oelfeuer Tech
Oelhydraulik und Pneumatik — Oelhydraul Pneum
Oelhydraulik und Pneumatik — OP
Oel-und Fett-Industrie — Oel Fett Ind
OEP. Office Equipment and Products [*Japan*] — OEP
Oerlikon Schweissmitteilungen — Oerlikon Schweissmitt
Oester Imkerkalender — Oest Imkerkal
Oesterbotten: Aarsbok — OA
Oesterbottnisk Arsbok — Oesterbottnisk Arsb
Oesterreich in Amerikanischer Sicht. Das Oesterreichbild im Amerikanischen Schulunterricht — OAS
Oesterreich in Geschichte und Literatur — Oesterr Gesch Lit
Oesterreich in Geschichte und Literatur [*Wien*] — OGL
Oesterreich in Geschichte und Literatur — OsG
Oesterreich Nederland — DOK
Oesterreichische Abwasser Rundschau — Oesterr Abwasser Rundsch
Oesterreichische Abwasser Rundschau. OAR International — OARID
Oesterreichische Aerztezeitung — Oesterr Aerztezg
Oesterreichische Akademie der Wissenschaften — Oe AW
Oesterreichische Akademie der Wissenschaften. Erdwissenschaftliche Kommission Schriftenreihe — Oesterr Akad Wiss Erdwissenschaftliche Komm Schriftenr
Oesterreichische Akademie der Wissenschaften. Mathematisch-Naturwissenschaftliche Klasse. Anzeiger — Oesterr Akad Wiss Math Naturwiss Kl Anz
Oesterreichische Akademie der Wissenschaften. Mathematisch-Naturwissenschaftliche Klasse. Denkschriften — Oesterr Akad Wiss Math Naturwiss Kl Denkschr
Oesterreichische Akademie der Wissenschaften. Mathematisch-Naturwissenschaftliche Klasse. Denkschriften — Oesterreich Akad Wiss Math Naturwiss Kl Denkschr
Oesterreichische Akademie der Wissenschaften. Mathematisch-Naturwissenschaftliche Klasse. Denkschriften — Oesterreich Akad Wiss Math-Natur Kl Denkschr
Oesterreichische Akademie der Wissenschaften. Mathematisch-Naturwissenschaftliche Klasse. Sitzungsberichte [*Austria*] — Oesterr Akad Wiss Math Naturwiss Kl Sitzungsber
Oesterreichische Akademie der Wissenschaften. Mathematisch-Naturwissenschaftliche Klasse. Sitzungsberichte. Abteilung 1. Biologie, Mineralogie, Erdkunde und Verwandte Wissenschaften — Oesterr Akad Wiss Math Naturwiss Kl Sitzungsber Abt 1 Biol
Oesterreichische Akademie der Wissenschaften. Mathematisch-Naturwissenschaftliche Klasse. Sitzungsberichte. Abteilung 1. Biologie, Mineralogie, Erdkunde, und Verwandte Wissenschaften — Oesterr Akad Wiss Math-Naturwiss Kl Sitzungsber Abt 1
Oesterreichische Akademie der Wissenschaften. Mathematisch-Naturwissenschaftliche Klasse. Sitzungsberichte. Abteilung 2. Mathematik, Astronomie, Physik, Meteorologie, und Technik — Oesterr Akad Wiss Math-Naturwiss Kl Sitzungsber Abt 2
Oesterreichische Akademie der Wissenschaften. Mathematisch-Naturwissenschaftliche Klasse. Sitzungsberichte. Abteilung 2. Mathematik, Astronomie, Physik, Meteorologie, und Technik — Oesterreich Akad Wiss Math-Natur Kl S-B 2
Oesterreichische Akademie der Wissenschaften. Mathematisch-Naturwissenschaftliche Klasse. Sitzungsberichte. Abteilung 2. Mathematik, Astronomie, Physik, Meteorologie, und Technik [*Vienna*] — Oesterreich Akad Wiss Math-Natur Kl Sitzungsber 2
Oesterreichische Akademie der Wissenschaften. Mathematisch-Naturwissenschaftliche Klasse. Sitzungsberichte. Abteilung 2. Mathematik, Astronomie, Physik, Meteorologie, und Technik — Oesterreich Akad Wiss Math-Naturwiss Kl SB 2
Oesterreichische Akademie der Wissenschaften. Mathematisch-Naturwissenschaftliche Klasse. Sitzungsberichte. Abteilung 2A. Mathematik, Astronomie, Physik, Meteorologie, und Technik — Oesterr Akad Wiss Math Naturwiss Kl Sitzungsber Abt 2A
Oesterreichische Akademie der Wissenschaften. Mathematisch-Naturwissenschaftliche Klasse. Sitzungsberichte. Abteilung 2B. Chemie — Oesterr Akad Wiss Math Naturwiss Kl Sitzungsber Abt 2B
Oesterreichische Akademie der Wissenschaften. Philosophisch-Historische Klasse — Oesterr Akad Wiss Philos-Hist Kl
Oesterreichische Akademie der Wissenschaften. Philosophisch-Historische Klasse. Denkschriften (Wien) — Denkschriften (Wien)
Oesterreichische Akademie der Wissenschaften. Philosophisch-Historische Klasse. Sitzungsberichte — OAW PHKS
Oesterreichische Anwalts-Zeitung — Oester Anwaltsztg
Oesterreichische Apotheker Zeitung — Oesterr Apoth Ztg
Oesterreichische Bibliographie — OeB

Oesterreichische Blasmusik — Oesterreich Blasm
Oesterreichische Botanische Zeitschrift — Oe Bot Zs
Oesterreichische Botanische Zeitschrift — Oe BZ
Oesterreichische Botanische Zeitschrift — OeBotZ
Oesterreichische Botanische Zeitschrift — Oest Bot Z
Oesterreichische Botanische Zeitschrift — Oesterr Bot Z
Oesterreichische Botanische Zeitschrift — Osterr Bot Z
Oesterreichische Brauer-und Hopfenzeitung — Oesterr Brau Hopfenztg
Oesterreichische Chemie-Zeitschrift — Oesterr Chem-Z
Oesterreichische Chemiker-Zeitung — OCHZA
Oesterreichische Chemiker-Zeitung — Oe Ch Zg
Oesterreichische Chemiker-Zeitung — Oesterr Chem-Ztg
Oesterreichische Dentisten Zeitschrift — Osterr Dent Z
Oesterreichische Forstzeitung — Oesterr Forstzeitung
Oesterreichische Gastgewerbe und Hotel Zeitung — OGA
Oesterreichische Gelehrte Anzeigen (Vienna) — Oesterr Gel Anz Vienna
Oesterreichische Geographische Gesellschaft. Mitteilungen — Oesterreich Geogr Ges Mitt
Oesterreichische Gesellschaft fuer Statistik und Informatik. Mitteilungsblatt — Oest Ges Statis und Informatik Mitteilungsbl
Oesterreichische Glaserzeitung — Oesterr Glaserztg
Oesterreichische Hebammenzeitung — Osterr Hebammenztg
Oesterreichische Imker — Oest Imker
Oesterreichische Ingenieur und Architekten. Zeitschrift — Oesterr Ing & Archit Z
Oesterreichische Ingenieur Zeitschrift — Osterreichische Ing Z
Oesterreichische Ingenieur-Zeitschrift — Oesterr Ing-Z
Oesterreichische Jahrbuch fuer Soziologie — Oesterr Jb Soziol
Oesterreichische Krankenpflegezeitschrift — Oesterr Krankenpflegez
Oesterreichische Krankenpflegezeitschrift — Osterr Krankenpflegez
Oesterreichische Kunststoff-Rundschau — Oesterr Kunstst Rundsch
Oesterreichische Kunststoff-Zeitschrift [*Austria*] — Oesterr Kunstst-Z
Oesterreichische Landtechnik [*Austria*] — Oesterr Landtech
Oesterreichische Leder und Haeuterwirtschaft — Oesterr Leder Haeutewirtsch
Oesterreichische Leder-Zeitung — Oesterr Leder Ztg
Oesterreichische Milchwirtschaft — Oesterr Milchwirtsch
Oesterreichische Milchwirtschaftliche Zeitung — Oesterr Milchwirtsch Ztg
Oesterreichische Militaerische Zeitschrift — Oesterr Milit Z
Oesterreichische Mineralogische Gesellschaft. Mitteilungen — Oesterr Mineral Ges Mitt
Oesterreichische Mittelschule — OeMSch
Oesterreichische Mittelschule — Oester Mittelschule
Oesterreichische Molkerei Zeitung — Oesterr Molk Ztg
Oesterreichische Monatshefte — Oest Mhefte
Oesterreichische Monatshefte — Oesterr Mh
Oesterreichische Monatsschrift fuer Christliche Socialreform — OeMCSR
Oesterreichische Monatsschrift fuer den Orient — OMO
Oesterreichische Monatsschrift fuer Forstwesen — Oesterr Monatsschr Forstwesen
Oesterreichische Moorzeitschrift — Oesterr Moorz
Oesterreichische Musikzeitschrift — O Mz
Oesterreichische Musikzeitschrift — OcMZ
Oesterreichische Musikzeitschrift — OEMZ
Oesterreichische Musikzeitschrift — Oster Musik
Oesterreichische Osthefte — Oest Osthefte
Oesterreichische Osthefte — Oesterr Osth
Oesterreichische Osthefte — OOH
Oesterreichische Osthefte — OsO
Oesterreichische Osthefte — Osterr Osth
Oesterreichische Osthefte — OSTO
Oesterreichische Papier — Oesterr Papier
Oesterreichische Papier-Zeitung — Oesterr Pap Ztg
Oesterreichische Papier-Zeitung — Oesterr Papier-Ztg
Oesterreichische Schwesternzeitung [*Austria*] — Oesterr Schwesternztg
Oesterreichische Spirituosen Zeitung — Oesterr Spirit Ztg
Oesterreichische Studiengesellschaft fuer Atomenergie — Oesterr Studienges Atomenerg
Oesterreichische Studiengesellschaft fuer Atomenergie. Berichte — Oesterr Studienges Atomenerg Ber
Oesterreichische Studiengesellschaft fuer Atomenergie. SGAE — Oesterr Studienges Atomenerg SGAE
Oesterreichische Textil Zeitung. Zentralblatt fuer die Gesamte Textilwirtschaft — OTZ
Oesterreichische Textilzeitschrift — Oesterr Textilz
Oesterreichische Tieraerzt — Oesterr Tierarzt
Oesterreichische Tieraerzte-Zeitung — Oest T Ae Zt
Oesterreichische Tieraerzte-Zeitung — Oesterr Tierarzte Ztg
Oesterreichische Vierteljahresschrift fuer Forstwesen — Oesterr Vierteljahresschr Forstwes
Oesterreichische Vierteljahresschrift fuer Katholische Theologie — OeVKT
Oesterreichische Vierteljahresschrift fuer Wissenschaftliche Veterinaerkunde [*A publication*] — Oesterr Vrtljschr Wissensch Veterinaerk
Oesterreichische Vierteljahrschrift fuer Forstwesen — Oesterr Vierteljahrschr Forstwesen
Oesterreichische Volkswirt — Oest Volkswirt
Oesterreichische Volkswirt — OEV
Oesterreichische Volkswirt — OV
Oesterreichische Wasserwirtschaft — Oest Wasserw
Oesterreichische Wasserwirtschaft — Oesterr Wasserwirtsch
Oesterreichische Weidwerk — Oesterr Weidwerk
Oesterreichische Zahnaerzte-Zeitung — Oesterr Zahnaerzteztg
Oesterreichische Zahnprothetik — Oesterr Zahnprothet
Oesterreichische Zahntechniker — Oesterr Zahntechnik
Oesterreichische Zeitschrift fuer Aussenpolitik — Oest Z Aussenpol
Oesterreichische Zeitschrift fuer Aussenpolitik — Oesterr Z Aussenpolit
Oesterreichische Zeitschrift fuer Aussenpolitik — Osterr Z Aussenpolit
Oesterreichische Zeitschrift fuer Berg- und Huettenwesen — Oester Zs Bergw
Oesterreichische Zeitschrift fuer Berg- und Huettenwesen — Oesterr Z Berg Huettenwes
Oesterreichische Zeitschrift fuer Berg- und Huettenwesen — Oesterreichische Zs Berg- u Huettenw
Oesterreichische Zeitschrift fuer Bibliothekswesen — OeZB
Oesterreichische Zeitschrift fuer Denkmalpflege — OeZDP
Oesterreichische Zeitschrift fuer Elektrizitaetswirtschaft — Oe ZE
Oesterreichische Zeitschrift fuer Elektrizitaetswirtschaft — Oesterr Z Elektrizitaetswirtsch
Oesterreichische Zeitschrift fuer Erforschung und Bekaempfung der Krebskrankheit — Oesterr Z Erforsch Bekaempf Krebskr
Oesterreichische Zeitschrift fuer Erforschung und Bekaempfung der Krebskrankheit [*Austria*] — Oesterr Z Erforsch Bekaempf Krebskrankheit
Oesterreichische Zeitschrift fuer Erforschung und Bekaempfung der Krebskrankheit — OZEBA
Oesterreichische Zeitschrift fuer Kinderheilkunde — Oesterr Ztschr Kinderh
Oesterreichische Zeitschrift fuer Kinderheilkunde und Kinderfuersorge — Oest Zs Kinderhk
Oesterreichische Zeitschrift fuer Kinderheilkunde und Kinderfuersorge — Oesterr Z Kinderheilkd Kinderfuersorge
Oesterreichische Zeitschrift fuer Kunst und Denkmalpflege — Oe ZKD
Oesterreichische Zeitschrift fuer Kunst und Denkmalpflege — OZDP
Oesterreichische Zeitschrift fuer Kunst und Denkmalpflege — OZKDP
Oesterreichische Zeitschrift fuer Oeffentliches Recht — Oe Z f Oe R
Oesterreichische Zeitschrift fuer Oeffentliches Recht — Oe Z Oe R
Oesterreichische Zeitschrift fuer Oeffentliches Recht — Oe Z Oeff R
Oesterreichische Zeitschrift fuer Oeffentliches Recht — Oest Z Oe R
Oesterreichische Zeitschrift fuer Oeffentliches Recht — Oesterr Z Oeff Recht
Oesterreichische Zeitschrift fuer Oeffentliches Recht — Osterr Z Off Recht
Oesterreichische Zeitschrift fuer Onkologie — Oesterr Z Onkol
Oesterreichische Zeitschrift fuer Pilzkunde — Oesterr Z Pilzk
Oesterreichische Zeitschrift fuer Politikwissenschaft — Oest Z Politikwiss
Oesterreichische Zeitschrift fuer Politikwissenschaft — Oester Z Pol
Oesterreichische Zeitschrift fuer Politikwissenschaft — Oesterr Z Polit -Wiss
Oesterreichische Zeitschrift fuer Politikwissenschaft — Osterr Z Polit-Wiss
Oesterreichische Zeitschrift fuer Stomatologie — Oesterr Z Stomatol
Oesterreichische Zeitschrift fuer Vermessungswesen — Oest Zs Verm W
Oesterreichische Zeitschrift fuer Volkskunde — Oe ZV
Oesterreichische Zeitschrift fuer Volkskunde — Oest Zs Volkskd
Oesterreichische Zeitschrift fuer Volkskunde — Oesterr Z Volkskd
Oesterreichische Zeitschrift fuer Volkskunde — Oesterr Zeits Volksk
Oesterreichische Zeitschrift fuer Volkskunde — OeZKV
Oesterreichische Zeitschrift fuer Volkskunde — OZV
Oesterreichische Zeitschrift fuer Volkskunde. Buchreihe — OeZVKB
Oesterreichische Zeitschrift fuer Zahnheilkunde — Oest Zs Zahn Hlkd
Oesterreichische Zoologische Zeitschrift — Oest Zool Z
Oesterreichische Zoologische Zeitschrift — Oesterr Zool Z
Oesterreichisches Archiv fuer Geschichte, Erdbeschreibung, Staatenkunde, Kunst und Literatur — Oesterr Arch Gesch
Oesterreichisches Archiv fuer Kirchenrecht — OAKR
Oesterreichisches Archiv fuer Kirchenrecht — Oe A f KR
Oesterreichisches Archiv fuer Kirchenrecht — Oe A Kr
Oesterreichisches Archiv fuer Kirchenrecht — Oesterr Arch Kirchenrecht
Oesterreichisches Bank-Archiv — Oest Bank-Arch
Oesterreichisches Bank-Archiv. Zeitschrift fuer das Gesamte Bankwesen und Sparkassenwesen, Borsenwesen, und Kreditwesen — OAA
Oesterreichisches Biographisches Lexikon — Oe BL
Oesterreichisches Botanisches Wochenblatt. Gemeinnuetziges Organ fuer Botanik — Oesterr Bot Wochenbl
Oesterreichisches Forschungsinstitut fuer Sparkassenwesen Viertel Jahres-Schriftenreihe — Oest Forschungsinst Sparkassenwesen VJ-Schriftenreihe
Oesterreichisches Forschungsinstitut fuer Wirtschaft und Politik. Berichte und Informationen — Oest Forschinst Wirt und Pol Ber
Oesterreichisches Forschungszentrum Seibersdorf. Berichte OEFZS — Oesterr Forschungszent Seibersdorf Ber OEFZS
Oesterreichisches Ingenieur Archiv — Oesterr Ing Arch
Oesterreichisches Institut fuer Wirtschaft Forschung. Monatsberichte — MOK
Oesterreichisches Jahrbuch fuer Politik — Oesterr Jb Polit
Oesterreichisches Klerusblatt — OeKB
Oesterreichisches Patentblatt — Oesterr Patentbl
Oesterreichisches Seifenfachblatt — Oesterr Seifenfachbl
Oesterreichisches Tuberkulose-Fuersorgeblatt — Oester Tuberkfuersbl
Oesterreichisches Tuberkulose-Fuersorgeblatt — OeTbcFBl
Oesterreichisches Verwaltungsarchiv — Oesterr Verwalt Arch
Oesterreichisch-Ungarische Zeitschrift fuer Zuckerindustrie und Landwirtschaft — Oesterr Ung Z Zuckerind Landwirtsch
Oesterreichs Forst- und Holzwirtschaft — Oe FH
Oesterreichs Forst- und Holzwirtschaft — Oesterr Forst-Holzwirtsch
Oesterreichs Wollen- und Leinen-Industrie — Oesterr Wollen Leinen Ind
Oesterreich-Ungarische Zeitschrift fuer Zuckerindustrie und Landwirtschaft — Oester Ung Zs Zuckerind
Oesterreich-Ungarische Zeitschrift fuer Zuckerindustrie und Landwirtschaft — OUZZL
Oestliche Christentum — OeC
OeTV [*Oeffentliche Dienste. Transport und Verkehr*] **Magazin** — OeTV Mag
Oeuvres Afro-Asiatiques — OAA
Oeuvres et Critiques — O et C
Oeuvres et Critiques — OeC
Oeuvres et Critiques — Oeuvre Crit
Oversigt af Finska Vetenskaps-Societetens Foerhandlingar — Oevers Fin Vetensk Soc Foerh

OFCCP [*Office of Federal Contract Compliance Programs*] **Federal Contract Compliance Manual. Commerce Clearing House** — OFCCP Fed Cont Compl Man CCH
Off Our Backs — O O B
Off Road — IOFF
Offa Berichte und Mitteilungen des Museums Vorgeschichtlicher Altertuemer in Kiel — Offa Ber Mitt
Offene Briefe fuer Gartenbau, Land- und Forstwirtschaft — Offene Briefe Gartenbau
Offene Torc — OT
Offenlegungsschrift (Federal Republic of Germany) — Offenlegungsschrift Fed Repub Ger
Office — Off
Office Administration — Office Admin
Office Administration and Automation — ADM
Office Administration and Automation — Off Adm Autom
Office Administration and Automation — Office A & A
Office Administration and Automation — Office Adm & Automation
Office de la Recherche Scientifique et Technique d'Outre-Mer. Travaux et Documents de l'ORSTOM — Off Rech Sci Tech Outre-Mer Trav Doc ORSTOM
Office Education Association. Communique — OEA Communique
Office Equipment and Products — Office Eqp
Office Executive — Office Exec
Office for Scientific and Technical Information. Newsletter — OSTI Newsl
Office International de la Vigne et du Vin. Bulletin — Off Int Vigne Vin Bull
Office International des Epizooties. Bulletin — Off Int Epizoot Bull
Office International des Epizooties. Bulletin [*France*] — Office Int Epizoot Bull
Office Machine Guide — Off Mach Guide
Office Management — Off Manage
Office Management — Office Mgt
Office Methods and Machines — Off Meth Mach
Office National d'Etudes et de Recherches Aeronautiques. Diverse (France) — Off Natl Etud Rech Aeronaut Diverse Fr
Office National d'Etudes et de Recherches Aeronautiques. Note Technique — Off Nat Etud Rech Aeronaut Note Tech
Office National d'Etudes et de Recherches Aeronautiques. Publication — Off Nat Etud Rech Aeronaut Publ
Office National d'Etudes et de Recherches Aeronautiques. Rapport Technique (France) — Off Natl Etud Rech Aeronaut Rapp Tech (Fr)
Office National d'Etudes et de Recherches Aerospatiales (France). Note Technique — Off Nat Etud Rech Aerosp (Fr) Note Tech
Office National d'Etudes et de Recherches Aerospatiales (France). Publication — Off Natl Etud Rech Aerosp (Fr) Publ
Office National d'Etudes et de Recherches Aerospatiales (France). Publication — Office Nat Etud Rech Aerosp (Fr) Publ
Office National d'Etudes et de Recherches Aerospatiales (France). Tire a Part — Off Natl Etud Rech Aerosp (Fr) Tire Part
Office National d'Etudes et de Recherches Aerospatiales. Note Technique — ONERA Note Tech
Office National d'Etudes et de Recherches Aerospatiales. Publication — ONERA Publ
Office National d'Etudes et de Recherches Aerospatiales. Reports — Office Natl Etud Rech Aerosp Rep
Office of Air Programs Publication. APTD Series (United States) — Off Air Programs Publ APTD Ser US
Office of Air Programs (United States). Publication. AP Series — Off Air Programs (US) Publ AP Ser
Office of Arid Lands Studies. Bulletin — OALS Bulletin
Office of Aviation Medicine. Report [*Federal Aviation Administration*] — FAA
Office of Child Development. Publications — OCD
Office of Education. Publications — OE
Office of Naval Research (United States). Research Review — Off Nav Res (US) Res Rev
Office of Technical Services (US). AD — Off Tech Serv (US) AD
Office of Technical Services (US). PB Report — Off Tech Serv US PB Rep
Office on Smoking and Health Database — OSH
Office Systems — Office Sys
Office Systems — OFS
Office: Technology and People — Office Tech People
Office: Technology and People — OTC
Office World News — OWN
Official Airline Guide — OAG
Official American Horseman — Off Amer Horseman
Official Architecture and Planning — Off Archit Plann
Official Architecture and Planning — Office Archit Plann
Official Board Markets — Offic Board Markets
Official Catholic Directory — O Cath D
Official Code of Georgia, Annotated (Michie) — GA Code Ann (Michie)
Official Communications. International Society of Soil Sciences — Off Commun Int Soc Soil Sci
Official Compilation of Codes, Rules, and Regulations of the State of New York — NY Comp Codes R & Regs
Official Compilation of the Rules and Regulations of the State of Georgia — GA Comp R & Regs
Official Compilation Rules and Regulations of the State of Tennessee — Tenn Comp R & Regs
Official Congressional Directory — O Con D
Official Digest. Federation of Paint and Varnish Production Clubs — Off Dig Fed Paint Varn Prod Clubs
Official Digest. Federation of Societies for Paint Technology — Off Dig Fed Soc Paint Technol
Official Gazette — Off Gaz
Official Gazette. United States Patent and Trademark Office — Offic Gaz US
Official Gazette. United States Patent and Trademark Office — OG
Official Gazette. United States Patent and Trademark Office. Patents — Off Gaz US Pat Trademark Off Pat
Official Gazette. United States Patent and Trademark Office. Patents — Off Gaz US Pat Trademks Off Pat
Official Gazette. United States Patent and Trademark Office. Trademarks — Off Gaz US Pat Trademks Off Trademks
Official Gazette. United States Patent Office — Off Gaz Pat Off
Official Gazette. United States Patent Office — Off Gaz US Pat Off
Official Gazette. United States Patent Office — OG Pat Off
Official Gazette. United States Patent Office — Pat Off Gaz
Official Gazette. United States Patent Office — POC
Official Gazette. United States Patent Office. Patents — Off Gaz US Pat Off Pat
Official Guide of the Railways — OGR
Official Journal. Dental Association of South Africa — Off J Dent Assoc S Afr
Official Journal. Institute of Art Education — Off J Inst Art Educ
Official Journal. Japan Rheumatism Association — Off J Jpn Rheum Assoc
Official Journal. Japanese Society of Pediatric Neurology — Off J Jpn Soc Pediatr Neurol
Official Journal of the European Communities — Off J Eur Communities
Official Journal of the European Communities — OJ
Official Journal of the European Communities — OJ Eur Comm
Official Journal of the European Communities. Information and Notices. English Edition — Off J Eur Communities Inf Not
Official Journal of the European Communities. Legislation — Off J Eur Communities Legis
Official Journal (Patents) — Off J (Pat)
Official Journal (Patents) — Off Jl (Pat)
Official Journal (Patents) (Great Britain) — Offic J (Pat) (Gr Brit)
Official Journal (Patents) (United Kingdom) — Off J (Pat)(UK)
Official Journal. Research Institute of Medical Science of Korea — Off J Res Inst Med Sci Korea
Official Printing Ink Maker — Off Print Ink Maker
Official Proceedings. American Association of Feed Microscopists — Off Proc Amer Ass Feed Micros
Official Proceedings. Annual Conference. International District Heating Association — Off Proc Annu Conf Int Dist Heat Assoc
Official Proceedings. Annual Meeting. American Association of Feed Microscopists — Off Proc Annu Meet Am Assoc Feed Microsc
Official Proceedings. Annual Meeting. International District Heating Association — Off Proc Annu Meet Int Dist Heat Assoc
Official Proceedings. Annual Meeting. Livestock Conservation Institute — Off Proc Annu Meet Livest Conserv Inst
Official Proceedings. Annual Meeting. Master Boiler Makers' Association — Off Proc Annu Meet Master Boiler Makers Assoc
Official Proceedings. National District Heating Association — Off Proc Natl Dist Heat Assoc
Official Proceedings. National Ginseng Conference — Off Proc Natl Ginseng Conf
Official Publication. Association of American Fertilizer Control Officials — Off Publ Assoc Am Fert Control Off
Official Publication. Association of American Plant Food Control Officials — Off Publ Assoc Am Plant Food Control Off
Official Publications of Western Australia — OPWA
Official Records. World Health Organization — Off Rec WHO
Official Recreation Guide [*Database*] — ORG
Official Yearbook. Church of England — OYCE
Official Yearbook of New South Wales — Off Yrbk NSW
Official Yearbook of Queensland — Off Yrbk Queensland
Official Yearbook of the Commonwealth of Australia — Off Yrbk Cwealth Aust
Official Yearbook of Western Australia — Off Yrbk WA
Officiantbladet — Off
Officiel des Activites des Plastiques et du Caoutchouc — Off Act Plast Caoutch
Officiel des Matieres Plastiques — Off Metieres Plast
Officiel des Plastiques et du Caoutchouc — Off Plast Caout
Officiel des Plastiques et du Caoutchouc — Off Plast Caoutch
Offizielle Protokolle der Italienischen Grosschmiedetagung — Off Protok Ital Grosschmiedetag
Offshore Abstracts — Offshore Abstr
Offshore Canada. Supplement of Offshore Oil Weekly — OFCA
Offshore Engineer — OFEND
Offshore Engineer — OFF
Offshore Engineer — Off Eng
Offshore Engineer — Offshore Eng
Offshore Engineer — Offshore Engr
Offshore Engineer. Incorporating Northern Offshore — OFEN
Offshore Lease Data System [*Database*] — OLDS
Offshore Oil International [*Formerly, Offshore Oil Weekly*] — OF
Offshore Oil Weekly [*Later, Offshore Oil International*] — OW
Offshore Patrol — Off Patrol
Offshore Report — Offshore Rep
Offshore Research Focus — OFC
Offshore Research Focus — Offshore Res Focus
Offshore Resources — OFSR
Offshore Services — Offshore Serv
Offshore Services — OFSVA
Offshore Services and Technology — Offshore Serv Technol
Offshore Technology Conference. Proceedings — Offshore Technol Conf Proc
Offshore. The Journal of Ocean Business — OFS
Oftal'mologicheskii Zhurnal — Oftalmol Zh
Oftal'mologicheskii Zhurnal — OFZHA
Ogneupory — OGNPA
Ogneupory i Tekhnicheskaya Keramika — Ogneupory Tekh Keram
Ogolnopolski Sympozjon Termodynamika Warstwy Fluidalnej. Materialy — Ogolnopol Symp Termodyn Warstwy Fluid Mater

Ogolnopolskie Seminarium na temat Mieszanie. Skroty Zgloszonych Prac — Ogolnopol Semin Mieszanie Skroty Zgloszonych Pr
Ogolnopolskie Sympozjum Polimerow Siarkowych — Ogolnopol Symp Polim Siarkowych
Ohio Administrative Code — Ohio Admin Code
Ohio Agricultural Experiment Station Bulletin — Ohio Agric Exp Sta Bull
Ohio Agricultural Experiment Station. Forestry Circular — Ohio Agric Exp Sta Forest Circ
Ohio. Agricultural Experiment Station. Publications — Ohio Ag Exp
Ohio. Agricultural Experiment Station. Research Bulletin — Ohio Agric Exp Stn Res Bull
Ohio Agricultural Experiment Station Research Circular — Ohio Agric Exp Sta Res Circ
Ohio. Agricultural Experiment Station. Research Circular — Ohio Agric Exp Stn Res Circ
Ohio Agricultural Experiment Station. Service Bulletin — Ohio Agric Exp Sta Serv Bull
Ohio. Agricultural Experiment Station. Special Circular — Ohio Agric Exp Stn Spec Circ
Ohio. Agricultural Research and Development Center. Research Bulletin — Ohio Agric Res Dev Cent Res Bull
Ohio. Agricultural Research and Development Center. Research Circular — Ohio Agr Res Develop Cent Res Circ
Ohio. Agricultural Research and Development Center. Research Circular — Ohio Agric Res Dev Cent Res Circ
Ohio. Agricultural Research and Development Center. Research Summary — Ohio Agric Res Dev Cent Res Summ
Ohio. Agricultural Research and Development Center. Special Circular — Ohio Agric Res Dev Cent Spec Circ
Ohio Appellate Reports — Ohio App
Ohio Appellate Reports. Third Series — Ohio App 3d
Ohio Archaeological and Historical Quarterly — O Arch Q
Ohio Archaeological and Historical Quarterly — O Archaeol and H Qtly
Ohio Archaeological and Historical Quarterly — OAHQ
Ohio Archaeological and Historical Quarterly — Ohio Archaeol Hist Q
Ohio Archaeologist — Ohio Archael
Ohio Association of School Librarians. Bulletin — Ohio Assn Sch Libn Bull
Ohio Bar Reports — Ohio B
Ohio Biological Survey. Biological Notes — Ohio Biol Surv Biol Notes
Ohio Biological Survey. Bulletin — Ohio Biol Surv Bull
Ohio Biological Survey. Informative Circular — Ohio Biol Surv Inf Circ
Ohio Brass Hi-Tension News — OB Hi-Tension News
Ohio Business — Ohio Busn
Ohio Business Teacher — Ohio Bus Tchr
Ohio Circuit Court Decisions — Ohio CC Dec
Ohio Circuit Court Reports — Ohio CC
Ohio Circuit Decisions — Ohio Cir Dec
Ohio Conference on Sewage Treatment. Annual Report — Ohio Conf Sewage Treat Annu Rep
Ohio Conference on Water Purification. Annual Report — Ohio Conf Water Purif Annu Rep
Ohio CPA [*Certified Public Accountant*] **Journal** — OCP
Ohio Decisions — Ohio Dec
Ohio Decisions Reprint — Ohio Dec Reprint
Ohio Dental Journal — Ohio Dent J
Ohio. Department of Agriculture. Bulletins — Ohio Ag Dept
Ohio. Department of Natural Resources. Division of Geological Survey. Miscellaneous Report — Ohio Dep Nat Resour Div Geol Surv Misc Rep
Ohio. Department of Natural Resources. Division of Water. Ohio Water Plan Inventory Report — Ohio Dep Nat Resour Div Water Ohio Water Plan Inventory Rep
Ohio Department Reports — Ohio Dept
Ohio. Division of Geological Survey. Bulletin — Ohio Div Geol Surv Bull
Ohio. Division of Geological Survey. Information Circular. — Ohio Div Geol Surv Inf Circ
Ohio. Division of Geological Survey. Information Circular — Ohio Div Geol Surv Inform Circ
Ohio. Division of Geological Survey. Miscellaneous Report — Ohio Div Geol Surv Misc Rep
Ohio. Division of Geological Survey. Report of Investigations — Ohio Div Geol Surv Rep Invest
Ohio. Division of Water. Bulletin — Ohio Div Water Bull
Ohio. Division of Water. Information Circular — Ohio Div Water Inform Circ
Ohio. Division of Water. Ohio Water Plan Inventory. Report — Ohio Div Water Ohio Water Plan Invent Rep
Ohio. Division of Water. Ohio Water Plan Inventory. Report — Ohio Div Water Ohio Water Plan Inventory Rep
Ohio. Division of Water. Report on Ohio Water Table Survey — Ohio Div Water Rep Ohio Water Table Surv
Ohio. Division of Water. Technical Report — Ohio Div Water Tech Rep
Ohio Farm and Home Research — Ohio Farm Home Res
Ohio Farm and Home Research — Ohio Fm Home Res
Ohio Farmer — Ohio F
Ohio Fish and Wildlife Report — Ohio Fish Wildl Rep
Ohio Fish Monographs — Ohio Fish Monogr
Ohio Florist's Association. Bulletin — Ohio Florists Assoc Bull
Ohio Florists Association. Monthly Bulletin — Ohio Florists Assoc Monthly Bull
Ohio Game Monographs — Ohio Game Monogr
Ohio. Geological Survey. Bulletin — Ohio G S B
Ohio Government Reports — Ohio Govt
Ohio Herpetological Society. Special Publication — Ohio Herpetol Soc Spec Publ
Ohio Historical Quarterly — Ohio HQ
Ohio Historical Quarterly — OHQ
Ohio History — OH
Ohio History — OhH
Ohio History — Ohio Hist
Ohio History — OhioH
Ohio Journal of Religious Studies — Ohio J Rel St
Ohio Journal of Science — Oh J Sci
Ohio Journal of Science — Ohio J Sci
Ohio Journal of Science — Ohio Jour Sci
Ohio Law Bulletin — Ohio Law Bul
Ohio Legislative Bulletin (Anderson) — Ohio Legis Bull (Anderson)
Ohio Library Association. Bulletin — Ohio Lib Assn Bul
Ohio Library Association. Bulletin — Ohio Libr Ass Bull
Ohio Medical Journal — Ohio Med J
Ohio Mining Journal — Ohio M J
Ohio Miscellaneous — Ohio Misc
Ohio Monthly Record — Ohio Monthly Rec
Ohio Naturalist. Ohio State University — Ohio Nat
Ohio Nisi Prius Reports — Ohio NP
Ohio Northern University. Law Review — Oh NULR
Ohio Northern University. Law Review — Ohio N Univ Law R
Ohio Northern University. Law Review — Ohio North L Rev
Ohio Northern University. Law Review — Ohio North Univ L Rev
Ohio Northern University. Law Review — Ohio Northern UL Rev
Ohio Northern University. Law Review — Ohio NUL Rev
Ohio Northern University. Law Review — ONU LR
Ohio Nurses Review — Ohio Nurses Rev
Ohio Opinions — Ohio Op
Ohio Report — Ohio Rep
Ohio Report on Research and Development — Ohio Rep Res Dev
Ohio Report on Research and Development (Biology, Agriculture, Home Economics). Ohio Agricultural Experiment Station — Ohio Rep Res Develop
Ohio Report on Research and Development in Biology, Agriculture, and Home Economics — Ohio Rep Res Developm Biol
Ohio Reports — Ohio
Ohio Review — Ohio Rev
Ohio Review — OhioR
Ohio Review — OhR
Ohio Review — POHR
Ohio Revised Code Annotated (Anderson) — Ohio Rev Code Ann (Anderson)
Ohio Revised Code Annotated (Baldwin) — Ohio Rev Code Ann (Baldwin)
Ohio Schools — Ohio Sch
Ohio Sociologist — Ohio Sociol
Ohio State Academy of Science. Annual Report — Ohio St Ac Sc An Rp
Ohio State Academy of Science. Proceedings — Ohio St Ac Sc Pr
Ohio State Academy of Science. Special Papers — Ohio St Ac Sc Sp P
Ohio State Archaeological and Historical Quarterly — Ohio State Archaeol and Hist Quar
Ohio State Archaeological and Historical Quarterly — OSAHQ
Ohio State Bar Association. Report — O Bar
Ohio State Bar Association. Report — Ohio Bar
Ohio State Bar Association. Report — Ohio St BA Rep
Ohio State Law Journal — LJ
Ohio State Law Journal — Oh SLJ
Ohio State Law Journal — Oh St LJ
Ohio State Law Journal — Ohio S L J
Ohio State Law Journal — Ohio St Law
Ohio State Law Journal — Ohio St LJ
Ohio State Law Journal — Ohio State Law J
Ohio State Law Journal — Ohio State LJ
Ohio State Medical Journal — Ohio State Med J
Ohio State Reports — Ohio St
Ohio State University. Biosciences Colloquia — Ohio State Univ Biosci Colloq
Ohio State University. Bulletin — Ohio St Univ B
Ohio State University. College of Engineering. Bulletin — Ohio State Univ Coll Eng Bull
Ohio State University. College of Law. Law Forum Series — Ohio St Univ Coll Law Law For Ser
Ohio State University. Contributions in Language and Literature — OSUCLL
Ohio State University. Cooperative Extension Service — Ohio St Univ Coop Ext Serv
Ohio State University. Engineering Experiment Station. Bulletin — Ohio State Univ Eng Exp Sta Bull
Ohio State University. Engineering Experiment Station. Circular — Ohio State Univ Eng Exp Stn Circ
Ohio State University. Engineering Experiment Station. News — Ohio State Univ Eng Exp Stn News
Ohio State University. Institute of Polar Studies. Report — Ohio State Univ Inst Polar Stud Rep
Ohio State University. Institute of Polar Studies. Report — Ohio State Univ Inst Polar Studies Rept
Ohio State University Mathematical Research Institute. Publications — Ohio State Univ Math Res Inst Publ
Ohio State University Studies. Engineering Series. Circular — Ohio State Univ Stud Eng Ser Cir
Ohio State University Studies. Ohio Biological Survey Bulletin — Ohio State Univ Stud Ohio Biol Surv Bull
Ohio State University. Theatre Collection Bulletin — OSUTCB
Ohio Swine Research and Industry Report. Animal Science Series. Ohio Agricultural Research and Development Center — Ohio Swine Res Ind Rep Anim Sci Ser Ohio Agric Res Dev Cent
Ohio University Review — Oh Univ Rev
Ohio University Review — OUR
Ohio Water Plan Inventory Report — Ohio Water Plan Inventory Rep
Ohio Wesleyan University. Perkins Observatory. Contributions — Ohio Wesleyan Univ Perkins Obs Contrib
Ohioana Quarterly — OhioanaQ

Ohioana Quarterly — OQ
Ohu University Dental Journal — Ohu Univ Dent J
OIAZ (Oesterreichische Ingenier und Architekten Zeitschrift) — OIAZ (Oesterreichische In Archit Z)
Oikos — OIKO
Oikos. Supplementum — Oikos Suppl
Oil and Chemical Pollution — Oil Chem Pollut
Oil and Colour Chemists' Association (Australia). Proceedings and News — Oil Colour Chem Assoc (Aust) Proc News
Oil and Colour Chemists' Association. Journal — Oil Colour Chem Assoc J
Oil and Colour Chemists' Association. Journal — Oil Colour Chemist Assoc J
Oil and Colour Trades Journal — Oil Colour Trades J
Oil and Fat Industry — Oil Fat Ind
Oil and Fat Industry (Moscow) — Oil Fat Ind Moscow
Oil and Gas Bulletin — Oil Gas
Oil and Gas Compact Bulletin — Oil and Gas Compact Bull
Oil and Gas Compact Bulletin — Oil Gas Compact Bull
Oil and Gas Directory — Oil Gas Direct
Oil and Gas Geology — Oil Gas Geol
Oil and Gas Industry (Kiev) — Oil Gas Ind Kiev
Oil and Gas International [*England*] — Oil Gas Int
Oil and Gas Investor — OGI
Oil and Gas Journal — OAG
Oil and Gas Journal — OGJ
Oil and Gas Journal — Oil & Gas J
Oil and Gas Journal — Oil Gas J
Oil and Gas Journal — OLV
Oil and Gas Journal. Forecast/Review — O & G Jour
Oil and Gas Magazine (Hamburg) — Oil Gas Mag (Hamburg)
Oil and Gas Report — Oil Gas Rep
Oil and Gas Tax Quarterly — Oil & Gas Tax Q
Oil and Gas Tax Quarterly [*United States*] — Oil Gas Tax Q
Oil and Hazardous Materials Technical Assistance Data System [*Database*] — OHM-TADS
Oil and Natural Gas Commission. Bulletin — Oil Nat Gas Comm Bull
Oil and Petrochemical Pollution — Oil Petrochem Pollut
Oil and Resource Development Supplement. Fairbanks Daily News Miner — OR
Oil Bulletin [*Canada*] — Oil Bull
Oil Bulletin — OILBA
Oil Engineering and Finance — OIEFA
Oil Engineering and Finance [*England*] — Oil Eng Finance
Oil Engineering and Technology — Oil Eng Technol
Oil Field Engineering — Oil Field Eng
Oil Forum — OF
Oil, Gas, and Petrochem Equipment — Oil Gas Petrochem Equip
Oil Gas European Magazine — Oil Gas Eur Mag
Oil Gas European Magazine — Oil Gas Europ Mag
Oil Geophysical Prospecting — Oil Geophys Prospect
Oil in Canada — Oil Can
Oil Mill Gazetteer — Oil Mill Gazet
Oil, Paint, and Drug Reporter — Oil Paint Drug Rep
Oil Palm Research — Oil Palm Res
Oil Progress — Oil Prog
Oil Shale and Related Fuels — Oil Shale Relat Fuels
Oil Shale Symposium Proceedings — Oil Shale Symp Proc
Oil Spill Intelligence Report — Oil Spill Intell Rep
Oil Statistics (Paris) — Oil Stat (Paris)
Oil Technologist — Oil Technol
Oil Trade Journal — Oil Trade J
Oil Weekly — Oil Wkly
Oil Weekly — OILWA
Oils and Oilseeds Journal — Oils Oilseeds J
Oilsander. Suncor Incorporated Resources Group. Oil Sands Division — OILS
Oilweek — OLWE
Oily Press Lipid Library — Oily Press Lipid Lib
Oiseau et la Revue Francaise d'Ornithologie — Oiseau Rev Fr Ornithol
Oita Daigaku Gakugeigakubu Kenkyu Kiyo. Shizenkagaku — ODGKA
Oita Prefectural Forest Experiment Station. Report — Oita Prefect For Exp Stn Rep
Oita University. Faculty of Engineering. Reports — Rep Fac Engrg Oita Univ
Okajimas Folia Anatomica Japonica — Okajimas Folia Anat Jpn
Okayama Daigaku Hobungakubu Gakujutsu Kiyo — OYGK
Okayama Daigaku Onsen Kenkyusho Hokoku — ODOKA
Okayama Igakkai Zasshi. Supplement [*Japan*] — Okayama Igakkai Zasshi Suppl
Okayama Mathematical Lectures — Okayama Math Lectures
Okayama University. Institute for Thermal Spring Research. Papers — Okayama Univ Inst Therm Spring Res Pap
Okeanologicheskie Issledovaniya — Okeanol Issled
Okeanologiya — Okeanol
Okhota i Okhotnich'e Khozyaistvo — Okhota Okhot Khoz
Okhrana i Zashchita Lesa. Obzornaya Informatsiya — Okhr Zashch Lesa Obz Inf
Okhrana Okruzhayushchei Sredy i Ratsional'noe Ispol'zovanie Prirodnykh Resursov. Obzornaya Informatsiya — Okhr Okruzh Sredy Ratsion Ispolz Prir Resur Obz Inf
Okhrana Okruzhayushchei Sredy ot Zagryazneniya Promyshlennymi Vybrosami — Okhr Okruzh Sredy Zagryaz Prom Vybrosami
Okhrana Okruzhayushchei Sredy ot Zagryazneniya Promyshlennymi Vybrosami Tsellyulozno-Bumazhnaya Promyshlennost — Okhr Okruzh Sredy Zagryaz Prom Vybrosami TsBP
Okhrana Prirodnykh Vod Urala [*Former USSR*] — Okhr Prir Vod Urala
Okhrana Prirody — Okhr Prir
Okhrana Prirody Moldavii — Okhr Prir Mold
Okhrana Prirody na Dal'nem Vostoke — Okhr Prir Dal'nem Vostoke
Okhrana Prirody na Urale — Okhr Prir Urale
Okhrana Prirody Tsentral'no-Chernozemnoi Polosy — Okhr Prir Tsent-Chernozem Polosy
Okhrana Prirody Tsentral'no-Chernozemnoi Polosy — Okhr Prir Tsentr Chernozemn Polosy
Okhrana Truda — Okr Tr
Okhrana Truda i Tekhnika Bezopasnosti v Chernoi Metallurgii — Okhr Tr Tekh Bezop Chern Metall
Okhrana Zdorov'ya Detei i Podrostkov (Kiev) — Okhr Zdor Detei Podrostkov (Kiev)
Okhrana Zdorov'ya Detei i Podrostkov (Kiev) — Okhr Zdorovya Detei Podrostkov (Kiev)
Oki Technical Review — Oki Tech Rev
Oklahoma Academy of Science. Proceedings — Okla Acad Sci Proc
Oklahoma Academy of Science. Proceedings — Oklahoma Acad Sci Proc
Oklahoma Agricultural and Mechanical College. Botanical Studies — Oklahoma Agric Coll Bot Stud
Oklahoma Agricultural and Mechanical College. Division of Engineering. Publication — Okla Agric Mech Coll Div Eng Publ
Oklahoma. Agricultural Experiment Station. Annual Report — Okla Agric Exp Stn Annu Rep
Oklahoma Agricultural Experiment Station. Annual Report — Oklahoma Agric Exp Sta Annual Rep
Oklahoma. Agricultural Experiment Station. Bulletin — Okla Agric Exp Stn Bull
Oklahoma Agricultural Experiment Station Forage Crops Leaflet — Oklahoma Agric Exp Sta Forage Crops Leafl
Oklahoma. Agricultural Experiment Station. Mimeographed Circular — Okla Agric Exp Stn Mimeogr Circ
Oklahoma Agricultural Experiment Station. Mimeographed Circular — Oklahoma Agric Exp Sta Mimeogr Circ
Oklahoma. Agricultural Experiment Station. Miscellaneous Publication — Okla Agric Exp Stn M P
Oklahoma. Agricultural Experiment Station. Miscellaneous Publication — Okla Agric Exp Stn Misc Publ
Oklahoma. Agricultural Experiment Station. Processed Series — Okla Agric Exp Stn Process Ser
Oklahoma. Agricultural Experiment Station. Processed Series — Okla Agric Exp Stn Processed Ser
Oklahoma. Agricultural Experiment Station. Progress Report — Okla Agric Exp Stn Prog Rep
Oklahoma. Agricultural Experiment Station. Publications — Okla Ag Exp
Oklahoma. Agricultural Experiment Station. Research Report — Okla Agric Exp Stn Res Rep
Oklahoma. Agricultural Experiment Station. Research Report — Res Rep Oklahoma Agric Exp St
Oklahoma. Agricultural Experiment Station. Technical Bulletin — Okla Agric Exp Stn Tech Bull
Oklahoma Bar Association. Journal — Okla B Ass'n J
Oklahoma Bar Association. Journal — Okla BA J
Oklahoma Bar Journal — Okla BJ
Oklahoma Business — Okla Bsns
Oklahoma Business — Okla Bus
Oklahoma City University. Law Review — Okla City UL Rev
Oklahoma Criminal Reports — Okla Crim
Oklahoma Current Farm Economics — Okla Curr Farm Econ
Oklahoma. Department of Geology and Natural History. Biennial Report — Okla Dp G N H Bien Rp
Oklahoma. Department of Human Services. Annual Statistical Report — Okla Dep Hum Serv Ann Stat Rep
Oklahoma. Division of Water Resources. Bulletin — Okla Div Water Resour Bull
Oklahoma Engineering Experiment Station. Publication — Okla Eng Exp Stn Publ
Oklahoma Gazette — Okla Gaz
Oklahoma. Geological Survey — Okla G S
Oklahoma. Geological Survey. Bulletin — Okla Geol Surv Bull
Oklahoma. Geological Survey. Circular — Okla Geol Surv Circ
Oklahoma. Geological Survey. Guidebook — Oklahoma Geol Survey Guidebook
Oklahoma. Geological Survey. Map — Okla Geol Surv Map
Oklahoma. Geological Survey. Map — Oklahoma Geol Survey Map
Oklahoma. Geological Survey. Mineral Report — Okla Geol Surv Miner Rep
Oklahoma Geology Notes — Okla Geol Notes
Oklahoma Geology Notes — Okla Geology Notes
Oklahoma Geology Notes. Oklahoma Geological Survey — Oklahoma Geology Notes
Oklahoma Law Review — OK LR
Oklahoma Law Review — Okl LR
Oklahoma Law Review — Okla L Rev
Oklahoma Law Review — Okla Law R
Oklahoma Law Review — Okla LR
Oklahoma Law Review — Oklahoma L Rev
Oklahoma Law Review — OR
Oklahoma Librarian — Okla Libn
Oklahoma Librarian — Okla Librn
Oklahoma Medical News Journal — Okla Med Ne J
Oklahoma Nurse — Okla Nurse
Oklahoma. Planning and Resources Board. Division of Water Resources. Bulletin — Okla Plann Resour Board Div Water Resour Bull
Oklahoma Register — Okla Reg
Oklahoma Reports — Okla
Oklahoma School Music News — OK
Oklahoma Session Law Service (West) — Okla Sess Law Serv (West)
Oklahoma Session Laws — Okla Sess Laws
Oklahoma State Medical Association. Journal — Okla State Med Assoc J
Oklahoma State Medical Association. Journal — Oklahoma State Med Assoc J
Oklahoma State University. Cooperative Extension Service. Extension Facts — Ext Facts Coop Ext Serv Oklahoma State Univ

Oklahoma State University of Agriculture and Applied Science. Engineering Experiment Station. Publication — Okla State Univ Agric Appl Sci Eng Exp Stn Publ
Oklahoma State University. Research Bulletin — Okla Univ Research B
Oklahoma Statutes — Okla Stat
Oklahoma Statutes Annotated (West) — Okla Stat Ann (West)
Oklahoma. University. Information Science Series. Monograph — Oklahoma Univ Inf Sci Ser Mon
Oklahoma. Water Resources Board. Bulletin — Okla Water Res Board Bull
OKL-Arbeit-Oesterreichisches Kuratorium fuer Landtechnik — OKL Arb Osterreichisches Kuratorium Landtech
Okonomi og Politik — Okon og Polit
Okonomi og Politik — OoP
Oktjabr — O
Oktjabr — Okt
Okuruk — OKRK
Olaj, Szappan, Kozmetika — Olaj Szappan Kozmet
Old and New — O & N
Old and New Testament Student — ONTS
Old Cornwall — OC
Old Dominion Journal of Medicine and Surgery — Old Dominion J Med and S
Old English Newsletter — OEN
Old Farmer's Almanac — OFA
Old Fort News — OIF
Old Irish — OI
Old Kilkenny Review — Old Kilk Rev
Old Kilkenny Review — Old Kilkenny Rev
Old Northwest — ON
Old Northwest Genealogical Quarterly — Old Northw Geneal Q
Old Northwest Genealogical Quarterly — Old NW
Old Testament Abstracts — Old Test Abstr
Old Testament Abstracts — Old Testam Abstr
Old Testament Lectures — OT Lect
Old Testament Library — OTL
Old Testament Studies — OTSt
Old Time Music — OTM
Old Westbury Review — Old Westbury Rev
Oldelft Scientific Engineering Quarterly — Oldelft Sci Eng Q
Oldelft Scientific Engineering Quarterly — OSEQD
Oldenburger Jahrbuch — Ojb
Oldenburger Jahrbuch des Oldenburger Landesvereins fuer Geschichte, Natur- und Heimatkunde. Teil 2 — Oldenburger Jahrb Oldenburger Landesvereins Gesch Teil 2
Oldenburger Jahrbuch. Verein fuer Landesgeschichte und Altertumskunde — OJ
Oldenburgisches Landwirtschaftsblatt — Oldenburg Landwirtschaftsbl
Old-House Journal — Old House Jnl
Old-Time New England — Old-Time N
Old-Time New England — Old-Time N E
Old-Time New England — Old-Time N Eng
Oleagineux. Revue Internationale des Corps Gras — Oleagineux Rev Int Corps Gras
Oleodinamica Pneumatica — Oleodin Pneum
Olfaction and Taste. Proceedings of the International Symposium — Olfaction Taste Proc Int Symp
Olii, Grassi, Derivati — Oli Grassi Deriv
Olii Minerali. Grassi e Saponi. Colori e Vernici — Olii Miner Grassi Saponi Colori Vernici
Olii Minerali. Olii e Grassi. Colori e Vernici — Olii Miner Olii Grassi Colori Vernici
Olimpiadas [*Database*] — OLIM
Olissipo — O
Oltenia Romana — Olt R
Oltenia Romana — OR
Oltenia Studii si Comunicari Istorie — Oltenia
Oltner Neujahrsblaetter — ON
Olympia. Die Ergebnisse der von dem Deutschen Reich Veranstalten Ausgrabung — Ol Erg
Olympic Message — Oly Message
Olympic Review — Oly Rev
Olympic Review/Revue Olympique — Olym Rev
Olympische Forschungen — OF
Olympische Forschungen — Ol Forsch
Omaha World Herald — Omaha World
Ombudsman. Tijdschrift voor Klachtrecht Tegen Overheidsoptreden — OBU
Omega — OME
Omega — POMG
Omega Journal of Death and Dying — Omega J Death Dying
Omega - The International Journal of Management Science — Omega-Int J
Omega. The Journal of Death and Dying — OM
Omega. The Journal of Death and Dying — OMEG
OMMI [*Orszagos Mezogazdasagi Minosegvizsgalo Intezet*] **Kiadvanyai. Sorozat 1. Genetikus Talajterkepek** — OMMI Kiad Sorozat 1
OMMI (Orszagos Mezogazdasagi Minosegvizsgalo Intezet) Kiadvanyai. Sorozat 1. Genetikus Talajterkepek — OMMI (Orsz Mezogazd Minosegvizsgalo Intez) Kiad Sorozat 1
Omni — GOMN
Omnia Medica — Omnia Med
Omnia Medica et Therapeutica — Omnia Med Ther
Omnia Medica et Therapeutica. Archivio — Omnia Med Ther Arch
Omnia Medica. Supplemento — Omnia Med Suppl
Omnia Therapeutica — Omnia Ther
Omnibus Magazine — Omnibus Mag
Omron Technics — Omron Tech
Omskii Gosudarstvennyi Meditsinskii Institut imeni M. I. Kalinina. Nauchnye Trudy — Omsk Gos Med Inst im M I Kalinina Mauchn Tr
Omskii Institut Inzenerov Zeleznodoroznogo Transporta. Naucnye Trudy — Omsk Inst Inz Zeleznodoroz Transporta Naucn Trudy
Omskii Meditsinskii Institut imeni M. I. Kalinina. Nauchnye Trudy — Omsk Med Inst im M. I. Kalinina Nauchn Tr
Omskii Meditsinskii Zhurnal — Omsk Med Zhurnal
On Campus Review — ONCR
On Communications — OCM
On Site in Alberta — OSIA
On the Boiler — OTB
On the History of Statistics and Probability — Hist St Prob
On the Knossos Tablets — OKT
On the Knossos Tablets — OTKT
Oncodevelopmental Biology and Medicine — OBIMD
Oncodevelopmental Biology and Medicine [*Netherlands*] — Oncodev Biol Med
Oncogene Research — Oncog Res
Oncologia — Onc
Oncologia — ONCOA
Oncologia si Radiologia — Oncol Radiol
Oncology Abstracts — Oncol Abstr
Oncology Nursing Forum — Oncol Nurs Forum
Oncology Reports — Oncol Rep
Oncology Research — Oncol Res
Onde Electrique — Onde Elec
Onde Electrique — Onde Electr
Onde Electrique. Supplement [*France*] — Onde Electr Suppl
Onder Eigen Vaandel — OEV
Ondernemersvisie — KNM
Onderneming — NEW
Onderstepoort Journal of Veterinary Research — Onderst J V
Onderstepoort Journal of Veterinary Research — Onderstepoort J Vet Res
Onderstepoort Journal of Veterinary Science and Animal Industry — Onderstepoort J Vet Sci
Onderstepoort Journal of Veterinary Science and Animal Industry — Onderstepoort J Vet Sci Anim Ind
One Church — One Ch
One in Christ — O Chr
One in Christ — OiC
One Sky Report — OSKR
One-Sheet Answers. Cooperative Extension. University of California — OSA Coop Ext Univ Calif
ONGC [*Oil and Natural Gas Commission*] **Bulletin** [*India*] — ONGC Bull
Onken Kiyo — ONKIA
Onkologiya — ONKLA
On-Land Drilling News — On-Land Drill News
Online — ONL
Online ADL-Nachrichten — Online ADL-Nachr
Online Database Report — Online Data
Online Database Report — Online Database Rep
Online Review — OIF
Online Review — Online
Online Review — Online Rev
On-Line Review — On-Line Rv
Online-ADL Nachrichten — OANAD
Only Music — OM
ONO [*Organisatie voor Natuurwetenschappelijk Onderzoek*] **Mededeelingen** — ONO Meded
Onoma — On
Onomastica — On
Onomastica — Ono
Onomastica — Onom
Onomastica — Onomast
Onomastica Jugoslavica — On Jug
Onomastica Jugoslavica — OnomJug
Onomastica Sacra — Onomast Sacra
Onomastica Sacra — OS
Onomastica Slavogermanica — On SG
Onomastica Slavogermanica — Onomast Slavogerm
Onondaga Academy of Science. Proceedings — Onondaga Ac Sc Pr
Onondaga Historical Association. Science Series — Onondaga Hist As Sc S
Onore del Professore Angelo Celli nel 25o Anno di Insegnamento — Onore Angelo Celli 25o An Insegnamento
ONR [*Office of Naval Research*] **Technical Report** [*US*] — ONR Tech Rep
Ons Erfdeel — OnsE
Ons Geestelijk Erf — OGE
Ons Geestelijk Leven — OGL
Ons Hemecht — Hem
Ons Nuis Vakblad voor de Meubelhandel, Meubelmakerij, Meubelindustrie, Interieurarchitecteur, Behangerij, Stoffeerderij, en Detailhandel in Woningtextiel — WWM
Onsei Gakkai Kaiho [*Bulletin of the Phonetic Society of Japan*] — OGK
Onsen Kagaku — ONKAA
Onsen Kogakkaishi — ONKOB
Ontario Appeal Cases [*Database*] — OAC
Ontario Appeals Report — OAR
Ontario Bird Banding — Ont Bird Banding
Ontario Birds — Ont Birds
Ontario. Bureau of Mines. Annual Report — Ont Bur Mines An Rp
Ontario. Bureau of Mines. Bulletin — Ont Bur Mines B
Ontario Business — Ont Bus
Ontario College of Pharmacy. Bulletin — Ont Coll Pharm Bull
Ontario Dentist — Ont Dent
Ontario. Department of Agriculture and Food. Publication — Ont Dep Agric Food Publ
Ontario. Department of Agriculture. Publication — Ont Dep Agric Publ
Ontario. Department of Agriculture. Publication — Ontario Ag Dept

Ontario Department of Mines and Northern Affairs. Bulletin — Ont Dep Mines North Aff Bull
Ontario. Department of Mines and Northern Affairs. Geological Report — Ont Dep Mines North Aff Geol Rep
Ontario. Department of Mines and Northern Affairs. Industrial Mineral Report — Ont Dep Mines North Aff Ind Miner Rep
Ontario. Department of Mines and Northern Affairs. Miscellaneous Paper — Ont Dep Mines North Aff Misc Pap
Ontario. Department of Mines. Annual Report — Ont Dep Mines Annu Rep
Ontario. Department of Mines. Geological Circular — Ont Dep Mines Geol Circ
Ontario. Department of Mines. Geological Report — Ont Dep Mines Geol Rep
Ontario. Department of Mines. Geological Report — Ontario Dept Mines Geol Rept
Ontario. Department of Mines. Industrial Mineral Report — Ont Dep Mines Ind Miner Rep
Ontario. Department of Mines. Industrial Mineral Report — Ontario Dept Mines Indus Mineral Rept
Ontario. Department of Mines. Map — Ontario Dept Mines Map
Ontario. Department of Mines. Mineral Resources Circular — Ont Dep Mines Miner Resour Circ
Ontario. Department of Mines. Mineral Resources Circular — Ontario Dept Mines Mineral Resources Circ
Ontario. Department of Mines. Mines Inspection Branch. Bulletin — Ont Dep Mines Bull
Ontario. Department of Mines. Miscellaneous Paper — Ont Dep Mines Misc Pap
Ontario. Department of Mines. Miscellaneous Paper — Ontario Dept Mines Misc Paper
Ontario. Department of Mines. Preliminary Geochemical Map — Ontario Dept Mines Prelim Geochem Map
Ontario. Department of Mines. Preliminary Geological Map — Ontario Dept Mines Prelim Geol Map
Ontario. Department of Mines. Preliminary Map — Ontario Dept Mines Prelim Map
Ontario. Department of Mines. Report — Ont Dep Mines Rep
Ontario Digest — Ont Dig
Ontario. Division of Mines. Geological Report — Ont Div Mines Geol Rep
Ontario. Division of Mines. Geoscience Report — Ont Div Mines Geosci Rep
Ontario Division of Mines. Geoscience Study — Ont Div Mines Geosci Study
Ontario. Division of Mines. Industrial Mineral Report — Ont Div Mines Ind Miner Rep
Ontario. Division of Mines. Miscellaneous Paper — Ont Div Mines Misc Pap
Ontario. Division of Mines. Preliminary Map. Geological Series — Ont Div Mines Prelim Map Geol Ser
Ontario. Division of Mines. Preliminary Map. Geophysical Series — Ont Div Mines Prelim Map Geophys Ser
Ontario Education — Ont Ed
Ontario Education Resources Information System [*Database*] — ONTERIS
Ontario Field Biologist — Ont Field Biol
Ontario Field Biologist — Ont Fld Biol
Ontario Field Biologist. Toronto Field Biologists' Club — Ontario Field Biol
Ontario Fish and Wildlife Review — Ont Fish Wildl Rev
Ontario Forests — Ont For
Ontario Fuel Board. Annual Report — Ontario Fuel Board Ann Rept
Ontario Geography — Ont Geography
Ontario. Geological Survey. Miscellaneous Paper — Ont Geol Surv Misc Pap
Ontario Geological Survey. Report — Ont Geol Surv Rep
Ontario Geological Survey. Special Volume — Ont Geol Surv Spec Vol
Ontario Geological Survey. Study — Ont Geol Surv Study
Ontario Government Information [*Database*] — OGI
Ontario Historical Society. Papers and Records — Ont His S
Ontario Historical Society. Papers and Records — Ont Hist Soc Pap Rec
Ontario Historical Society. Papers and Records — Ontario Hist Soc Papers
Ontario History — OH
Ontario History — OnH
Ontario History — Ont Hist
Ontario. Horticulture Experiment Stations and Products Laboratory. Report — Ont Hortic Exp Stn Prod Lab Rep
Ontario Hydro-Research News — OHRNA
Ontario Hydro-Research News — Ont Hydro-Res News
Ontario Hydro-Research News. Review — Ont Hydro Res Rev
Ontario Hydro-Research Quarterly — Ont Hydro-Res Q
Ontario Indian — ONIN
Ontario Industrial Arts Association. Bulletin — Ont Ind Arts Bul
Ontario Industrial Waste Conference. Proceedings — Ont Ind Waste Conf Proc
Ontario Journal of Educational Research — Ont J Educ Res
Ontario Labour — Ont Lab
Ontario Lawyers Weekly — Ont Law W
Ontario Library Review — OLR
Ontario Library Review — Ont Lib R
Ontario Library Review — Ont Libr Rev
Ontario Mathematics Gazette — Ont Math G
Ontario Medical Review — Ont Med Rev
Ontario Medical Review — Ontario Med Rev
Ontario Medical Technologist — Ont Med Technol
Ontario Mineral Policy. Background Paper — Ontario Miner Policy Background Pap
Ontario. Ministry of Agriculture and Food. Publication — Ont Minist Agric Food Publ
Ontario. Ministry of Agriculture and Food. Publication — POMFE4
Ontario Ministry of Natural Resources. Ontario Geological Survey Study — Ont Minist Nat Resour Ont Geol Surv Stud
Ontario. Ministry of Northern Affairs. News Release — OMNAN
Ontario Ministry of the Environment. API Report — Ont Minist Environ API Rep
Ontario Ministry of the Environment. Research Report — Ont Minist Environ Res Rep
Ontario. Ministry of Transportation and Communications. Engineering Materials Office. Report EM — Ont Minist Transp Commun Eng Mater Off Rep EM
Ontario Native Experience — ONEX
Ontario Naturalist — ONNA
Ontario Petroleum Institute. Annual Conference. Proceedings [*Canada*] — Ont Pet Inst Annu Conf Proc
Ontario Research Council. Report — Ontario Research Council Rept
Ontario Review — Ontario R
Ontario Securities Commission Decisions [*Database*] — OSCD
Ontario Statistics — Ont Stat
Ontario Technologist — Ont Technol
Ontario Technologist — ONTED
Ontario Veterinary College. Report — Ont Vet Coll Rep
Ontogenesis of the Brain — ONBRDY
Ontogenesis of the Brain — Ontog Brain
Ontogenetic and Phylogenetic Mechanisms of Neuroimmunomodulation — Ontog Phylogenet Mech Neuroimmunomodulation
Ontogeneticheskoe Razvitie Zhivotnykh — Ontog Razvit Zhivotn
Onza, Tigra, y Leon. Revista para la Infancia Venezolana — OTLV
Onze Eeuw — OE
Onze Kongo — OK
Onze Pius-Almanak — OPA
Onze Pius-Almanak — PA
Onze Taal — OTA
Onze Taaltuin — OT
Onze Tijd — OT
Onze Tijd — Tijd
Ookpik — OOPK
Oologists' Record — Oologists' Rec
Oost en West — Oost W
Oostvlaamse Zanten — OostvlZanten
Oostvlaamse Zanten. Tijdschrift van de Koninklijke Bond der Oostvlaamse Volkskundigen — Oostvlaam Zanten
Opbouw — Opb
Opciones — OS
OPEC [*Organization of Petroleum Exporting Countries*] **Bulletin** — OAM
OPEC [*Organization of Petroleum Exporting Countries*] **Bulletin** — OPEC Bull
OPEC (Organization of Petroleum Exporting Countries) Bulletin — OPEC (Org Petroleum Exporting Countries) Bul
OPEC (Organization of Petroleum Exporting Countries) Papers — OPEC (Org Petroleum Exporting Countries) Pas
OPEC (Organization of Petroleum Exporting Countries) Review — OPEC (Org Petroleum Exporting Countries) R
OPEC [*Organization of Petroleum Exporting Countries*] **Review** — OPO
Open Court — OC
Open Court (Chicago) — OCC
Open Hearth and Basic Oxygen Steel Conference. Proceedings [*United States*] — Open Hearth Basic Oxygen Steel Conf Proc
Open Hearth Proceedings — Open Hearth Proc
Open Hearth Proceedings. Metallurgical Society of AIME [*American Institute of Mining, Metallurgical, and Petroleum Engineers*]. Iron and Steel Division — Open Hearth Proc AIME
Open Learning Systems News — Open Learn Sys News
Open Places — O P
Open Tech Program News — Open Tech Prog News
Open University Set Book — Open Univ Set Book
Open; Vaktijdschrift voor Bibliothecarissen, Literatuuronderzoekers, Bedrijfsarchivarissen, en Documentalisten — BIB
Openbaar Vervoer — SPT
Openbare Bibliotheek — Openbare Biblioth
Openbare Uitgaven — OUV
Open-File Report. Geological Survey of Northern Ireland — Open File Rep Geol Surv North Irel
Open-File Report. United States Geological Survey — Open-File Rep US Geol Surv
Oper und Konzert — OuK
Opera — OP
Opera and Concert — Opera
Opera Botanica — Opera Bot
Opera Canada — OC
Opera Canada — OpC
Opera Canada — Opera Can
Opera Collecta. Centrum voor Bosbiologisch Onderzoek. Bokrijk-Genk — Opera Collecta Cent Bosbiol Onderz Bokrijk-Genk
Opera Journal — OJ
Opera Journal — Opera J
Opera News — GOPN
Opera News — ON
Opera News — OP
Opera News — Op News
Opera News — Opera
Opera News — Opera N
Opera News — OpN
Opera Quarterly — Opera Q
Opera Quarterly — POPQ
Operating and Programming Systems Series — Oper Program Systems Ser
Operating and Programming Systems Series [*Elsevier Book Series*] — OPSS
Operating Section Proceedings. American Gas Association — Oper Sect Proc Am Gas Assoc
Operating Systems Review — Oper Syst Rev
Operational Research Quarterly — Op Res Q
Operational Research Quarterly — Oper Res Q
Operational Research Quarterly — Oper Res Quart
Operational Research Quarterly — Operat R Q

Operational Research Quarterly — Operat Res Q
Operational Research Quarterly — Operational Res Quart
Operational Research Quarterly — OR
Operational Research Society Journal — Op Res Soc J
Operations Research — Op Res
Operations Research — Oper Res
Operations Research — Operat Res
Operations Research — Operation Res
Operations Research — Opns Res
Operations Research — OPR
Operations Research — Ops Research
Operations Research — OR
Operations Research Letters — Oper Res Lett
Operations Research Letters — ORL
Operations Research Society of America. Transportation Science Section. Transportation Science — Transportation Sci
Operations Research Spektrum — OR Spektrum
Operations Research Verfahren — ORV
Operations Reseearch and Industrial Engineering — Oper Res Indust Engrg
Operative Dentistry — Oper Dent
Operative Miller — Oper Miller
Operator Theory. Advances and Applications — Oper Theory Adv Appl
Operator Theory. Advances and Applications — Operator Theory Adv Appl
Operator Theory. Advances and Applications — Operator Theory Advances and Appl
Opern Welt — OpW
Ophrys — Oph
Ophthalmic and Physiological Optics — Ophthalmic Physiol Opt
Ophthalmic and Physiological Optics — OPO
Ophthalmic Epidemiology — Ophthalmic Epidemiol
Ophthalmic Forum — Ophthal For
Ophthalmic Genetics — Ophthalmic Genet
Ophthalmic Literature — Ophthal Lit
Ophthalmic Literature — Ophthalmic Lit
Ophthalmic Nursing Forum — Ophthalmic Nurs Forum
Ophthalmic Optician — Ophthal Opt
Ophthalmic Paediatrics and Genetics — Ophthalmic Paediatr Genet
Ophthalmic Plastic and Reconstructive Surgery — Ophthal Plast Reconstr Surg
Ophthalmic Plastic and Reconstructive Surgery — Ophthalmic Plast Reconstr Surg
Ophthalmic Record — Ophth Rec
Ophthalmic Research — Ophthal Res
Ophthalmic Research — Ophthalmic Res
Ophthalmic Seminars — Ophthalmic Semin
Ophthalmic Seminars — OPSED
Ophthalmic Surgery — Ophthalmic Surg
Ophthalmic Surgery and Lasers — Ophthalmic Surg Lasers
Ophthalmic Toxicology — Ophthalmic Toxicol
Ophthalmologia Ibero-Americana — Ophthalmol Ibero Am
Ophthalmologica — Ophthalmola
Ophthalmologica. Supplement — Ophthalmologica Suppl
Ophthalmological Society of Australia. Transactions — Ophth Soc Aust Trans
Ophthalmology in the War Years — Ophthalmol War Years
Ophthalmology. Proceedings. International Congress — Ophthalmol Proc Int Congr
Ophthalmology Times — Ophthalmol Times
Opinions Rendered by the International Commission on Zoological Nomenclature — Opin Int Commn Zool Nom
Opis Patentowy Patentu Tymczasowego — Opis Pat Pat Tymczasowego
Opis Patentowy (Poland) — Opis Pat Pol
Opisanie Izobreteniya k Avtorskomu Svidetel'stvu — Opisanie Izobret Avtorskomu Svidet
Opisanie Izobreteniya k Patentu — Opisanie Izobret Pat
Opolskie Roczniki Ekonomiczne — Opolsk Roczn Ekon
Opolskie Towarzystwo Przyjaciol Nauk. Wydzial 5 Nauk Medycznych. Prace Medyczne — Opolskie Tow Przyj Nauk Wydz 5 Nauk Med Pr Med
Opportunities for Man-Made Fibres. Papers Presented. Shirley International Seminar — Oppor Man Made Fibres Pap Shirley Int Semin
Opportunities in Materials. Proceedings. Buhl International Conference on Materials — Oppor Mat Proc Buhl Int Conf Mater
Opportunity in Northern Canada — Oppor North Can
Opsucula Patrum — OP
Opteolektronika i Poluprovodnikovaya Tekhnika — Opteolektorn and Poluprovodn Tekh
Optica Acta — OPACA
Optica Acta — Opt Acta
Optica Applicata — Opt Appl
Optica Pura y Aplicada — Opt Pura Apl
Optica Pura y Aplicada — Opt Pura y Apl
Optical Alliance — Opt Alliance
Optical and Digital GaAs Technologies for Signal-Processing Applications — Opt Digital GaAs Technol Signal Process Appl
Optical and Electrical Properties of Polymers. Symposium — Opt Electr Prop Polym Symp
Optical and Quantum Electronics — Opt and Quantum Electron
Optical and Quantum Electronics — Opt Quant E
Optical and Quantum Electronics — Opt Quantum Electron
Optical Data Storage — Opt Data Storage
Optical Data Storage Technologies — Opt Data Storage Technol
Optical Developments — Opt Dev
Optical Engineering — Opt Eng
Optical Engineering — Opt Engin
Optical Engineering — Opt Engrg
Optical Fabrication and Testing — Opt Fabr Test
Optical Fiber Transmission — Opt Fiber Transm
Optical Fibers in Medicine — Opt Fibers Med
Optical Fibre Sensors. International Conference — Opt Fibre Sens Int Conf
Optical Information-Processing Systems and Architectures — Opt Inf Process Syst Archit
Optical/Laser Microlithography — Opt Laser Microlithogr
Optical Mass Data Storage. International Conference — Opt Mass Data Storage Int Conf
Optical Materials — Opt Mat
Optical Materials (Amsterdam) — Opt Mater Amsterdam
Optical Memory and Neural Networks — Opt Mem Neural Networks
Optical Methods for Time- and State-Resolved Chemistry — Opt Methods Time State Resolved Chem
Optical Microlithography — Opt Microlithog
Optical Review — Opt Rev
Optical Society. London. Transactions — Opt Soc London Trans
Optical Society of America. Journal — Opt Soc Am J
Optical Space Communication — Opt Space Commun
Optical Spectra — Op Spectra
Optical Spectra — Opt Spectra
Optical Surfaces Resistant to Severe Environments — Opt Surf Resist Severe Environ
Optical Technology for Microwave Applications — Opt Technol Microwave Appl
Optics and Laser Technology — Opt and Laser Technol
Optics and Laser Technology — Opt Laser Technol
Optics and Laser Technology. Special Supplement — Opt Laser Technol Spec Suppl
Optics and Lasers in Engineering — Opt and Lasers Eng
Optics and Spectroscopy — Opt and Spectrosc
Optics and Spectroscopy — Opt Spectry
Optics and Spectroscopy (English Translation of Optika i Spektroskopiya) [*Former USSR*] — Opt Spectrosc (Engl Transl)
Optics and Spectroscopy (USSR) — Opt Spectrosc (USSR)
Optics Communications — Opt Commun
Optics in Agriculture — Opt Agric
Optics Letters — Opt Lett
Optics News — Opt News
Optics of Excitons in Confined Systems. Proceedings. International Meeting — Opt Excitons Confined Syst Proc Int Meet
Optics Technology — Opt Technol
Optik. Zeitschrift fuer Licht- und Elektronenoptik — Optik
Optika i Spektroskopiya — Opt & Spektrosk
Optika i Spektroskopiya — Opt Spektro
Optika i Spektroskopiya — Opt Spektrosk
Optika i Spektroskopiya. Akademiya Nauk SSSR. Otdelenie Fiziko-Matematicheskikh Nauk [*Former USSR*] — Opt Spektrosk Akad Nauk SSSR Otd Fiz-Mat Nauk
Optika i Spektroskopiya. Akademiya Nauk SSSR. Otdelenie Fiziko-Matematicheskikh Nauk — OSFMA
Optiko-Mekhanicheskaya Promyshlennost' — Optikomekh Prom
Optiko-Mekhanicheskaya Promyshlennost' — Opt-Mekh Prom
Optiko-Mekhanicheskaya Promyshlennost' — Opt-Mekh Prom-St'
Optima [*Johannesburg*] — OPT
Optimal Control Applications and Methods — Optimal Control Appl Methods
Optimal'noe Planirovanie — Optimal Planirovanie
Optimizatsiya Metallurgicheskikh Protsessov — Optim Metall Protsessov
Optimum — OPT
Options Mediterraneennes — Options Mediterr
Optisch-Mechanische Industrie (Leningrad) — Opt Mech Ind Leningrad
Optoelectronic Devices and Applications — Optoelectron Devices Appl
Opto-Electronics — Opto-Electron
Optoelectronics. Devices and Technologies — Optoelectron Devices Technol
Opto-Electronique — Opt-Electron
Optoelektronika i Poluprovodnikovaya Tekhnika — Optoelektron Poluprovodn Tekh
Optoelektronika i Spektroskopiya — Optoelektron Spektrosk
Optogalvanic Spectroscopy. Proceedings. International Meeting — Optogalvanic Spectrosc Proc Int Meet
Optomechanics and Dimensional Stability — Optomech Dimens Stab
Optometric Monthly — Optomet M
Optometry and Vision Science — Optom Vis Sci
Optometry and Vision Science — Optom Vision Sci
Optometry Clinics — Optom Clin
Opus Dei — OD
Opus Musicum — OM
Opus Musicum — Opus M
Opus Musicum — Opus Mus
Opuscula Archaeologica — OA
Opuscula Archaeologica — Opus Arch
Opuscula Archaeologica. Radovi Arheoloskog Instituta — Op Arch
Opuscula Archaeologica. Radovi Arheoloskog Instituta — OpA
Opuscula Archaeologica. Radovi Arheoloskog Instituta — Opusc Arch
Opuscula Archaeologica. Radovi Arheoloskog Instituta — Opusc Archaeol
Opuscula Atheniensia — OA
Opuscula Atheniensia — OAth
Opuscula Atheniensia — Op Ath
Opuscula Atheniensia — Op Athen
Opuscula Atheniensia — Opus Ath
Opuscula Atheniensia. Skrifter Utgivna av Svenska Institutet i Athen - Acta Instituti Atheniensis Regni Sueciae — Opusc Athen
Opuscula Entomologica — Opusc Ent
Opuscula Entomologica — Opusc Entomol
Opuscula et Textus Historiam Ecclesiae. Serie Liturgica — OTHEL
Opuscula et Textus Historiam Ecclesiae. Serie Scholastica et Mystica — OTHES
Opuscula Instituti Historico-Ecclesiastici Lundensis — OIHEL

Opuscula Mathematica — Opscula Math
Opuscula Medica — Opusc Med
Opuscula Medica. Supplementum — Opusc Med Suppl
Opuscula Philologica — OPh
Opuscula Philologica — Opus Ph
Opuscula Philosophica — OPh
Opuscula Romana — Op R
Opuscula Romana — Op Rom
Opuscula Romana — Opus Rom
Opuscula Romana — OR
Opuscula Romana — ORom
Opuscula Zoologica (Budapest) — Opusc Zool (Bpest)
Opuscula Zoologica (Budapest) — Opusc Zool (Budap)
Opuscula Zoologica (Muenchen) — Opus Zool (Muenchen)
Opuscula Zoologica (Munich) — Opusc Zool (Munich)
Opusculi Scelti Sulle Scienze e Sulle Arti — Opusc Scelti Sci Arti
Opyt Izucheniya Regulyatsii Fiziologicheskikh Funktsii — Opyt Izuch Regul Fiziol Funkts
Opyt Primeneniya Radioaktivnykh Metodov pri Poiskakh i Razvedke Neradioaktivnykh Rud — Opyt Primen Radioakt Metodov Poiskakh Razved Neradioakt Rud
Opyt Raboty Peredovogo Sovkhoznogo Proizvodstva — Opyt Rab Peredovogo Sovkhoznogo Proizvod
Opytnaya Agronomiya — Opytn Agron
Opytnaya Paseka — Opyt Paseka
Opytnaya Rabota Pchelovodov — Opyt Rab Pchel
Opyty — Op
OR. Journal of the Operational Research Society — ORA
OR Tech: Official Publication of the Association of Operating Room Technicians — OR Tech
Oracle Series. National Museums of Canada and Department of Indian and Northern Affairs — OC
Oral Biology — Oral Biol
Oral Health — Or Hlth
Oral History — Oral H
Oral History — Oral Hist
Oral History Index — OHI
Oral History Review — POHY
Oral Hygiene — Oral Hyg
Oral Implantology — Oral Implantol
Oral Implantology — ORIMB
Oral Microbiology with Basic Microbiology and Immunology [*Monograph*] — Oral Microbiol Basic Microbiol Immunol
Oral Research Abstracts — Oral Res Abstr
Oral Sciences Reviews — Oral Sci Rev
Oral Surgery, Oral Medicine, and Oral Pathology — Or Surg
Oral Surgery, Oral Medicine, and Oral Pathology — Oral Surg
Oral Surgery, Oral Medicine, and Oral Pathology — Oral Surg O
Oral Surgery, Oral Medicine, and Oral Pathology — Oral Surg Oral Med Oral Pathol
Oral Surgery, Oral Medicine, and Oral Pathology — Oral Surgery
Oral Surgery, Oral Medicine, Oral Pathology, Oral Radiology and Endodontics — Oral Surg Oral Med Oral Pathol Oral Radiol Endod
Oral Surgery. Transactions. International Conference on Oral Surgery — Oral Surg Trans Int Conf
Oral Therapeutics and Pharmacology — Oral Ther Pharmacol
Orale Implantologie — Orale Implantol
Orange County Bar Association. Journal — Orange County BJ
Orange County Business — Orange County Bus
Orange County Business Journal — Orang C BJ
Orange County [*California*] **Dental Society. Bulletin** — Orange Cty Dent Soc Bull
Orange County Register — OC Register
Orange Judd Farmer — O Judd Farmer
Orange Judd Illinois Farmer — O Judd Ill F
Oranie Medicale — Or Med
Orate Fratres — OF
Oratorum Romanorum Fragmenta [*Paris*] — ORFr
Oratorum Romanorum Fragmenta Liberae rei Publicae — ORF
Orbis — O
Orbis — OR
Orbis — PORB
Orbis. A Journal of World Affairs — ORK
Orbis Catholicus (Barcelona) — Orb Cath B
Orbis Catholicus (Wien) — Orb Cath
Orbis Christianus — Orb Chr
Orbis. Foreign Policy Research Institute — FPRI/O
Orbis Litterarum — O Lit
Orbis Litterarum — OL
Orbis Litterarum — Orb Lit
Orbis Litterarum — Orb Litt
Orbis Litterarum — Orbis Lit
Orbis Musicae — Orbis Mus
Orbis Romanus — Orb Rom
Orbit Science Fiction — OSF
Orchardist — Orch
Orchardist of New Zealand — Orchard NZ
Orchardist of New Zealand — Orchardist NZ
Orchester — Orc
Orchestra News — ON
Orchid Biology — Orchid Biol
Orchid Digest — Orchid Dig
Orchid Journal — Orchid J
Orchidologia Zeylancia — Orchidol Zeylancia
Ord och Bild — OB
Ord och Bild — OoB
Ordbog over det Danske Sprog — ODS
Orden der Kirche — OK
Ordenskunde Beitraege zur Geschichte der Auszeichnungen — Ordenskunde
Ordering at Surfaces and Interfaces. Proceedings. NEC Symposium — Ordering Surf Interfaces Proc NEC Symp
Ordinance Department Document — Ord Dept Doc
Ordini e Congregazioni Religiose — OCR
Ordnance Survey of Jerusalem — OSJ
Ordnungswidrigkeitengesetz — OWG
Ordo Canonicus — Ordo Can
Ordre des Architectes du Quebec. Bulletin Technique — Ordre des Architectes du Quebec Bull Technique
Ore-Concentration Industry — Ore Conc Ind
Oregon Administrative Rules — OR Admin R
Oregon Administrative Rules Bulletin — OR Admin R Bull
Oregon. Agricultural Experiment Station. Bulletin — Oreg Agric Exp Stn Bull
Oregon. Agricultural Experiment Station. Circular — Oreg Agric Exp Stn Cir
Oregon Agricultural Experiment Station Circular — Oregon Agric Exp Sta Circ
Oregon. Agricultural Experiment Station. Circular Information — Oregon Agric Exp Sta Circ Inform
Oregon. Agricultural Experiment Station. Miscellaneous Paper — Oreg Agric Exp Stn Misc Pap
Oregon. Agricultural Experiment Station. Publications — Ore Ag Exp
Oregon. Agricultural Experiment Station. Special Report — Oreg Agric Exp Stn Spec Rep
Oregon. Agricultural Experiment Station. Station Bulletin — Oreg Agric Exp Stn Stn Bull
Oregon. Agricultural Experiment Station. Technical Bulletin — Oreg Agric Exp Stn Tech Bull
Oregon. Bureau of Mines and Geology. Mineral Resources of Oregon — Oreg Bur Mines Min Res Oreg
Oregon Business — Oregon Bsn
Oregon Business Information System [*Database*] — ORBIS
Oregon. Department of Geology and Mineral Industries. Bulletin — Oreg Dep Geol Miner Ind Bull
Oregon. Department of Geology and Mineral Industries. Bulletin — Oregon Dept Geology and Mineral Industries Bull
Oregon. Department of Geology and Mineral Industries. Geological Map Series [*A publication*] — Oregon Dept Geology and Mineral Industries Geol Map Ser
Oregon. Department of Geology and Mineral Industries. GMI Short Paper — Oreg Dep Geol Miner Ind GMI Short Pap
Oregon. Department of Geology and Mineral Industries. Miscellaneous Paper — Oreg Dep Geol Miner Ind Misc Pap
Oregon. Department of Geology and Mineral Industries. Miscellaneous Paper — Oreg Dep Geol Miner Ind Misc Paper
Oregon. Department of Geology and Mineral Industries. Oil and Gas Investigation — Oregon Dep Geol Mineral Ind Oil Gas Invest
Oregon. Fish Commission. Contributions — Oreg Fish Comm Contrib
Oregon. Fish Commission. Research Briefs — Oreg Fish Comm Res Briefs
Oregon Folklore Bulletin — OFB
Oregon Forest Products Laboratory. Bulletin — Oreg For Prod Lab Bull
Oregon. Forest Products Laboratory (Corvallis). Progress Report — Oreg For Prod Lab (Corvallis) Prog Rep
Oregon Forest Products Laboratory. Information Circular — Oreg For Prod Lab Inf Circ
Oregon Forest Products Laboratory. Research Leaflet — Oreg For Prod Lab Res Leafl
Oregon Forest Products Research Center. Bulletin — Oreg For Prod Res Cent Bull
Oregon Forest Products Research Center. Information Circular — Oreg For Prod Res Cent Inf Circ
Oregon. Forest Products Research Center. Progress Report — Oreg For Prod Res Cent Prog Rep
Oregon Geology — Oregon Geol
Oregon. Ground Water Report — Oreg Ground Water Rep
Oregon Historical Quarterly — OHQ
Oregon Historical Quarterly — Ore Hist Q
Oregon Historical Quarterly — Oreg Hist Q
Oregon Historical Quarterly — Oregon Hist Q
Oregon Historical Quarterly — OreHQ
Oregon Historical Quarterly — OrH
Oregon Historical Quarterly — OrHQ
Oregon Historical Society. Quarterly — Ore H Soc Quar
Oregon Historical Society. Quarterly — ORE HIS Q
Oregon Historical Society. Quarterly — Ore Hist Soc Q
Oregon Historical Society. Quarterly — Ore Hist Soc Quar
Oregon Insect Control Handbook — Oreg Insect Contr Handb
Oregon Law Review — OLR
Oregon Law Review — Or L Rev
Oregon Law Review — Or LR
Oregon Law Review — Ore L Rev
Oregon Law Review — Ore LR
Oregon Law Review — Oreg L Rev
Oregon Laws and Resolutions — OR Laws
Oregon Laws and Resolutions. Special Session — OR Laws Spec Sess
Oregon Mineralogist — Oreg Min
Oregon Music Educator — OR
Oregon Nurse — Oreg Nurs
Oregon Nurse — Oreg Nurse
Oregon Orchid Society Bulletin — Oregon Orchid Soc Bull
Oregon Ornamental and Nursery Digest. Oregon Agricultural College. Agricultural Experiment Station — Oregon Ornam Nursery Digest
Oregon Reports — OR
Oregon Reports. Court of Appeals — OR App
Oregon Revised Statutes — OR Rev Stat

Oregon State Agricultural College. Agricultural Experiment Station. Bulletin — Oreg State Agric Coll Agric Exp Stn Bull
Oregon State Agricultural College. Agricultural Experiment Station. Circular — Oreg State Agric Coll Agric Exp Stn Circ
Oregon State Agricultural College. Engineering Experiment Station — Oreg State Agric Coll Eng Exp Stn
Oregon State College. Agricultural Experiment Station. Bulletin — Oreg State Coll Agric Exp Stn Bull
Oregon State College. Agricultural Experiment Station. Circular — Oreg State Coll Agric Exp Stn Circ
Oregon State College. Engineering Experiment Station. Bulletin — Oreg State Coll Eng Exp Stn Bull
Oregon State College. Engineering Experiment Station. Circular — Oreg State Coll Eng Exp Stn Circ
Oregon State College. Engineering Experiment Station. Reprint — Oreg State Coll Eng Exp Stn Repr
Oregon State Dental Journal — Oreg State Dent J
Oregon State Engineer. Ground Water Report — Oreg State Eng Ground Water Rep
Oregon State Horticultural Society. Annual Report — Oreg State Hortic Soc Ann Rep
Oregon State Monographs. Studies in Bacteriology — Oreg State Monogr Stud Bacteriol
Oregon State Monographs. Studies in Botany — Oreg State Monogr Stud Bot
Oregon State Monographs. Studies in Botany — Oregon State Monogr Stud Bot
Oregon State Monographs. Studies in Entomology — Oreg State Monogr Stud Entomol
Oregon State Monographs. Studies in Geology — Oreg State Monogr Stud Geol
Oregon State Monographs. Studies in Political Science — Oreg State Monogr Stud Pol Sci
Oregon State Monographs. Studies in Zoology — Oreg State Monogr Stud Zool
Oregon State University. Agricultural Experiment Station. Station Bulletin — Oreg St Univ Agric Exp Stn Stn Bull
Oregon State University. Biology Colloquium — Oreg State Univ Biol Colloq
Oregon State University (Corvallis). Engineering Experiment Station. Circular [*A publication*] — Oreg State Univ Eng Exp Sta Circ
Oregon State University. Engineering Experiment Station. Circular — Oreg State Univ Eng Exp Stn Circ
Oregon State University. Forest Research Laboratory. Annual Report — Oreg State Univ For Res Lab Annu Rep
Oregon State University. Forest Research Laboratory. Bulletin — Oreg State Univ For Res Lab Bull
Oregon State University. Forest Research Laboratory. Progress Report — Oreg State Univ For Res Lab Prog Rep
Oregon State University. Forest Research Laboratory. Research Bulletin — Oreg State Univ For Res Lab Res Bull
Oregon State University. Forest Research Laboratory. Research Paper — Oreg State Univ For Res Lab Res Pap
Oregon State University. School of Agriculture. Symposium Series — Oreg State Univ Sch Agric Symp Ser
Oregon State University. School of Forestry. Forest Research Laboratory. Research Notes — Oreg State Univ Sch For For Res Lab Res Note
Oregon State University. Water Resources Research Institute. Seminar Proceedings. SEMIN WR — Oreg State Univ Water Resour Res Inst Semin Proc SEMIN WR
Oregon Tax Reports — OR Tax
Oregon's Agricultural Progress — Ore Agric Progr
Oregon's Agricultural Progress — Oreg Agr Progr
Oregon's Agricultural Progress. Oregon Agricultural Experiment Station — Oreg Agric Prog Oreg Agric Exp Stn
Orehovo-Zuevskii Pedagogiceskii Institut. Ucenye Zapiski Kafedry Matematiki — Orehovo-Zuev Ped Inst Ucen Zap Kaf Mat
Orenburgskii Gosudarstvennyi Pedagogiceskii Institut Imeni V. P. Ckalova. Ucenye Zapiski — Orenburg Gos Ped Inst Ucen Zap
Orenburgskii Gosudarstvennyi Pedagogicheskii Institut. Uchenye Zapiski — Orenb Gos Pedagog Inst Uch Zap
Ores and Metals — Ores Met
Ores in Sediments. International Sedimentological Congress — Ores Sediments Int Sedimentol Congr
Organ Biology — Organ Biol
Organ der Militaerwissenschaftlichen Vereine [*Vienna*] — Org Militwiss Vereine
Organ Directed Toxicities of Anticancer Drugs. Proceedings. International Symposium on Organ Directed Toxicities of Anticancer Drugs — Organ Directed Toxic Anticancer Drugs Proc Int Symp
Organ fuer die Fortschritte des Eisenbahnwesens — OFEW
Organ fuer die Fortschritte des Eisenbahnwesens — Organ Fortschr Eisenbahnwes
Organ Institute. Quarterly — Org Inst
Organ Institute. Quarterly — Org Inst Q
Organ of Unemployed, Relief, and Sustenance Workers — OURS
Organ Yearbook — Organ Yb
Organic Chemical Bulletin — Org Chem Bull
Organic Chemical Industry — Org Chem Ind
Organic Chemistry. A Series of Monographs — Org Chem
Organic Chemistry: A Series of Monographs — Org Chem Ser Monogr
Organic Chemistry (New York) — Org Chem (New York)
Organic Coatings and Applied Polymer Science Proceedings — Org Coatings Appl Polym Sci Proc
Organic Coatings and Plastics Chemistry — Org Coat Plast Chem
Organic Coatings. International Meeting of Physical Chemistry — Org Coat Int Meet Phys Chem
Organic Coatings. Science and Technology — Org Coat
Organic Compounds in Aquatic Environments. Rudolfs Research Conference — Org Compd Aquat Environ Rudolfs Res Conf
Organic Compounds of Sulphur, Selenium, and Tellurium — Org Compd Sulphu Selenium Tellurium
Organic Crystal Chemistry. Papers. Symposium on Organic Crystal Chemistry — Org Cryst Chem Pap Symp
Organic Farmer — Org Farmer
Organic Finishing — Org Finish
Organic Gardening — GROG
Organic Gardening — Org Gard
Organic Gardening — Organic Gard
Organic Gardening and Farming — OGF
Organic Gardening and Farming — Org Gard Farming
Organic Gardening and Farming — Org Gdng Fmg
Organic Gardening and Farming — Organic Gard & F
Organic Geochemistry [*England*] — Org Geochem
Organic Geochemistry — Organic Geochem
Organic Magnetic Resonance — OMR-Org Mag
Organic Magnetic Resonance — Org Magn Resonance
Organic Mass Spectrometry — Org Mass Sp
Organic Mass Spectrometry — Org Mass Spectrom
Organic Mass Spectrometry — Organ Mass Spectr
Organic Photochemical Syntheses — Org Photochem Synth
Organic Photochemistry — Org Photochem
Organic Preparations and Procedures — Org Prep Proced
Organic Preparations and Procedures International — OPPI
Organic Preparations and Procedures International — Org Prep Proced Int
Organic Reaction Mechanisms — Org React Mech
Organic Reactions — Org React
Organic Reactions — Organ React
Organic Reactivity — Org React
Organic Reactivity (English Translation) [*New York*] — Org React (Eng Transl)
Organic Reactivity (Tartu) — Org React (Tartu)
Organic Reactivity (USSR) — Org React (USSR)
Organic Semiconductors. Proceedings. Inter-Industry Conference — Org Semicond Proc Inter Ind Conf
Organic Sulfur Compounds — Org Sulfur Compd
Organic Syntheses — Org Synt
Organic Synthesis at High Pressures [*Monograph*] — Org Synth High Pressures
Organic Synthesis via Organometallics. Proceedings. Symposium — Org Synth Organomet Proc Symp
Organicheskie Poluprodukty i Krasiteli — Org Poluprod Krasiteli
Organicheskie Poluprovodniki — Org Poluprovodn
Organicheskii Kataliz — Org Katal
Organisation Europeenne de Recherches Spatiales. Contractor Report — Organ Eur Rech Spat Contract Rep
Organisation Europeenne et Mediterraneenne pour la Protection des Plantes. Bulletin — Organ Eur Mediterr Prot Plant Bull
Organisation Europeenne et Mediterraneenne pour la Protection des Plantes. Publications. Serie A — Organ Eur Mediterr Prot Plant Publ Ser A
Organisation Europeenne et Mediterraneenne pour la Protection des Plantes. Publications. Serie D — Organ Eur Mediterr Prot Plant Publ Ser D
Organisation Europeenne pour la Recherche Nucleaire. Rapport — Organ Eur Rech Nucl Rapp
Organisation Scientifique — Org Scientifique
Organist [*Winterthur*] — Org
Organists Review — Organists R
Organist's Review — OrgR
Organizacion de los Estados Americanos. Programa Regional de Desarrollo Cientifico y Tecnologico. Monografia. Seriede Quimica — Organ Estados Am Programa Reg Desarrollo Cient Tecnol Monogr
Organizacion de los Estados Americanos. Programa Regional de Desarrollo Cientifico y Tecnologico. Serie de Biologia. Monografia — OEBMAL
Organizacion Techint. Boletin Informativo — Org Techint Bol Informativo
Organization and Expression of the Mitochondrial Genome. Proceedings. International Bari Conference — Organ Expression Mitochondrial Genome Proc Int Bari Conf
Organization for Economic Cooperation and Development. Economic Surveys of Member Countries — OECD Svys
Organization for Industrial Research TNO. Central Technical Institute. Heat Technology Department. Paper — Organ Ind Res TNO Cent Tech Inst Heat Technol Dep Pap
Organization Gestosis. International Meeting — Organ Gestosis Int Meet
Organization of African Unity. Scientific and Technical Research Commission. Publication — Organ Afr Unity Sci Tech Res Comm Publ
Organization of American States. Annals — Organ Am States Ann
Organization Studies — Organ Stud
Organization Studies — ORS
Organizational Behavior and Human Decision Processes — Organ Behav Hum Decis Process
Organizational Behavior and Human Performance — OBP
Organizational Behavior and Human Performance — Org Behav and Hum Perform
Organizational Behavior and Human Performance — Organ Beh H
Organizational Behavior and Human Performance — Organ Behav Hum Perform
Organizational Behavior and Human Performance — Organ Behavior & Human Perf
Organizational Communication — Org Comm
Organizational Dynamics — ORD
Organizational Dynamics — Org Dyn
Organizational Dynamics — Org Dynamics
Organizational Dynamics — Organ Dyn
Organizational Dynamics — Organ Dynam
Organizational Science — Org Sci
Organized Assemblies in Chemical Analysis — Organ Assem Chem Anal

Organized Structures in Polymer Solutions and Gels. Prague IUPAC Microsymposium on Macromolecules — Organ Struct Polym Solutions Gels Microsymp Macromol
Organizer — Organzr
Organizm v Usloviyakh Giperbarii — Org Usloviyakh Giperbarii
Organo de Falange Espanola — FE
Organometallic Chemistry — Organomet Chem
Organometallic Chemistry Reviews — Organomet Chem Rev
Organometallic Chemistry Reviews. Annual Surveys. Silicon-Germanium-Tin-Lead — Organomet Chem Rev Ann Surv Silicon Germanium Tin Lead
Organometallic Chemistry Reviews. Annual Surveys. Silicon-Tin-Lead — Organomet Chem Rev Ann Surv Silicon Tin Lead
Organometallic Chemistry Reviews. Annual Surveys. Transition Metals in Organic Synthesis, Organic Reactions of Selected n-Complexes — Organomet Chem Rev Ann Surv
Organometallic Chemistry Reviews. Organosilicon Reviews — Organomet Chem Rev Organosilicon Rev
Organometallic Chemistry Reviews. Section A. Subject Reviews [*Netherlands*] — Organomet Chem Rev Sect A
Organometallic Chemistry Reviews. Section B. Annual Surveys — Organomet Chem Rev Sect B
Organometallic News — Organomet News
Organometallic Reactions — Organomet React
Organometallic Reactions and Syntheses — Organomet React Synth
Organometallics — ORGND
Organometallics in Chemical Synthesis — Organomet Chem Synth
Organophosphorus Chemistry — Organophosphorus Chem
Organum — O
Orgelkunst. Viermaandelijks Tijdschrift — Oregelkunst Vier T
ORGREB [*Organisation fuer Abnahme, Betriebsfuehrung, und Rationalisierung von Energieanlagen*]**-Institut fuer Kraftwerke. Informationen** [*German Democratic Republic*] — ORGREB-Inst Kraftwerke Inf
Orgue — Org
Oriens — Ors
Oriens Academicus — OA
Oriens Antiquus — OA
Oriens Antiquus — Or An
Oriens Antiquus [*Rome*] — OrAnt
Oriens Antiquus [*Budapest*] — OrAntBud
Oriens Antiquus (Budapest) — OA (Bud)
Oriens Christianus — O Chr
Oriens Christianus — OC
Oriens Christianus — Or Christ
Oriens Christianus — OrChr
Oriens Extremus — OE
Oriens Extremus — Or Ex
Orient — Or
Orient Ancien Illustre — OAI
Orient. Deutsche Zeitschrift fuer Politik und Wirtschaft des Orients — ORL
Orient. Report of the Society for Near Eastern Studies in Japan — ONESJ
Orient Review — OR
Orient Syrien [*Vernon, France*] — OrSyr
Orient Syrien — OS
Orient und Occident — OuO
Orient/West — OW
Orientacion Economica — Orientacion Econ
Orientacion Economica (Caracas) — Orient Econ Caracas
Oriental Art — OA
Oriental Art [*United Kingdom*] — Or Art
Oriental Art — Orient Art
Oriental Ceramic Society. Transactions — TOCS
Oriental Economist — OE
Oriental Economist — OEC
Oriental Economist — Or Ec
Oriental Economist — OrEcon
Oriental Economist — Orient Economist
Oriental Geographer — OG
Oriental Geographer — ORGG-A
Oriental Geographer — ORGGAH
Oriental Geographer — Orient Geogr
Oriental Geographer (Dacca) — Orient Geogr (Dacca)
Oriental Herald — OH
Oriental Herald and Journal of General Literature — OH
Oriental Insects — Orient Insects
Oriental Insects. Supplementum — Orient Insects Suppl
Oriental Institute. Communications — OIC
Oriental Institute. Publications [*The Oriental Institute of the University of Chicago*] — OIP
Oriental Institute. Reports — OIR
Oriental Institute. University of Chicago. Studies in Ancient Oriental Civilization — OIUC SAOC
Oriental Library Publications — OLP
Oriental Library Publications. Sanskrit Series — OLPS
Oriental Magazine, Review, and Register — OMRR
Oriental Notes and Studies — ONS
Oriental Numismatic Society. Newsletter — ONSN
Oriental Numismatic Society. Occasional Paper — ONSOP
Oriental Philosophy Half-Monthly Magazine — OPM
Oriental Religious Series — ORS
Oriental Repertory — Orient Repert
Oriental Reprints — Or Rep
Oriental Research Institute Publications — ORIP
Oriental Research Institute Publications. Sanskrit Series — ORIPS
Oriental Review and Literary Digest — ORLD
Oriental Society of Australia. Journal — Oriental Soc Aust J
Oriental Society. Transactions. Glasgow University — OSTGU
Oriental Studies. Cambridge, Massachusetts — Or St C
Oriental Studies. Columbia University — OSCU
Oriental Studies. Oxford — Or St O
Oriental Studies published in Commemoration of the Fortieth Anniversary of Paul Haupt as Director of the Oriental Seminary. Johns Hopkins Universit — OPH
Oriental Studies (Washington, DC) — Or St W
Oriental Thought — Or Th
Oriental Translation Fund Publications — OTFP
Orientalia Christiana Analecta — O Ch A
Orientalia Christiana Analecta — OC
Orientalia Christiana Analecta — OCA
Orientalia Christiana Analecta — OrChrA
Orientalia Christiana Periodica — O Ch P
Orientalia Christiana Periodica — OChrP
Orientalia Christiana Periodica — OCP
Orientalia Christiana Periodica — Or Chr P
Orientalia Christiana Periodica [*Rome*] — OrChrPer
Orientalia Christiana Periodica — Orient Chr Per
Orientalia Christiana Periodica — Orient Christ Period
Orientalia. Commentarii de Rebus Assyro-Babylonicis, Arabicis, Aegyptiacis [*Rome*] — Orient
Orientalia. Commentarii Periodici Pontificii Instituti Biblici — OCPPIB
Orientalia. Commentarii Periodici Pontificii Instituti Biblici — Or
Orientalia et Biblica Lovaniensia — OBL
Orientalia et Biblica Lovaniensia [*Louvain*] — OrBiblLov
Orientalia et Biblica Lovaniensia [*Louvain*] — OrBibLov
Orientalia Gandensia [*Ghent*] — OG
Orientalia Gandensia — OrGand
Orientalia Lovaniensia Analecta — OLA
Orientalia Lovaniensia Analecta — Or Lov
Orientalia Lovaniensia Analecta — Orient Lovan
Orientalia Lovaniensia Periodica — OLoP
Orientalia Lovaniensia Periodica — OLP
Orientalia Lovaniensia Periodica — Orient Lovan
Orientalia Lovaniensia Periodica — Orient Lovan Per
Orientalia Lovaniensia Periodica — Orient Lovan Period
Orientalia Lovaniensia Periodica — OrLovPer
Orientalia Neerlandica [*Leiden, 1948*] — ON
Orientalia. Nova Series — OrNS
Orientalia Rheno-Traiectina — ORT
Orientalia Suecana — Or S
Orientalia Suecana — Orient Suecana
Orientalia Suecana [*Uppsala*] — OrSuec
Orientalia Suecana [*Uppsala*] — OS
Orientalia Suecana — OSu
Orientalische Bibliographie — OB
Orientalische Bibliographie — Or Bibl
Orientalische Miszellen — OM
Orientalische und Exegetische Bibliothek — OEB
Orientalisches Archiv — OA
Orientalisches Archiv — OAr
Orientalisches Archiv — Or Arch
Orientalist — Or
Orientalistische Literaturzeitung — OLZ
Orientalistische Literaturzeitung — Or Lit
Orientalistische Literaturzeitung — Orient Lit Ztg
Orientalistische Literaturzeitung — Orientalistische Lz
Orientalistische Literaturzeitung — OrLz
Orientamenti Culturali — Orient Cult
Orientamenti Pedagogici [*Torino*] — OrP
Orientamenti Sociali — Or Soc
Orientamenti Sociali — Orientam Soc
Orientation Professionnelle/Vocational Guidance — Orient Prof/Voc Guid
Orientation Scolaire et Professionnelle — Orientat Sc
Orientation Scolaire et Professionnelle — Orientat Scol Profes
Oriente Agropecuario — Oriente Agropecu
Oriente Cristiano — Oriente Crist
Oriente Cristiano. Madrid — Or Cr
Oriente Europeo — Or Eu
Oriente Europeo — Oriente Eur
Oriente Moderno — OM
Oriente Moderno — OMo
Oriente Moderno — Oriente Mod
Oriente Moderno [*Rome*] — OrMod
Orientierung [*Zuerich*] — Orien
Orientis Graeci Inscriptiones Selectae — OGI
Orientis Graeci Inscriptiones Selectae — OGIS
Orientis Graeci Inscriptiones Selectae — Or Gr Inscr Sel
Orientis Graeci Inscriptiones Selectae — Or Gr IS
Orient-Occident — Or Occ
Origin and Evolution of Interplanetary Dust. Proceedings. Colloquium. International Astronomical Union — Origin Evol Interplanet Dust Proc Colloq Int Astron Union
Origin of Cosmic Rays. Proceedings. NATO Advanced Study Institute — Origin Cosmic Rays Proc NATO Adv Study Inst
Origin Technical Journal — Origin Tech J
Original Science Fiction Stories — OSFS
Origins of Human Cancer. A Comprehensive Review. Origins of Human Cancer Conference — Origins Hum Cancer Origins Hum Cancer Conf
Origins of Human Cancer. Book A-C — Origins Hum Cancer Book A C
Origins of Life — Orig Life
Origins of Life and Evolution of the Biosphere — Orig Life Evol Biosph

Orissa Education Magazine — Orissa Ed Mag
Orissa Historical Research Journal — OHRJ
Orissa Journal of Agricultural Research — Orissa J Agric Res
Orissa Veterinary Journal — Orissa Vet J
Orizont — Or
Orizzonti della Ortopedia Odierna e della Riabilitazione [*Italy*] — Orizz Ortop Odie Riabil
Orizzonti Professionali — Orizz Profess
Orkester Journalen — Ork J
Orkester Journalen — Orkester JL
ORL [*Oto-Rhino-Laryngology*] [*Basel*] — ORLJAH
ORL - Journal for Oto-Rhino-Laryngology and Its Borderlands — ORL
ORL - Journal for Oto-Rhino-Laryngology and Its Borderlands — ORL-J Oto R
ORL. Journal of Oto-Rhino-Laryngology and Its Related Specialties — ORL J Otorhinolaryngol Relat Spec
ORL. Oto-Rhino-Laryngology (Basel) — ORL Oto-Rhino-Laryngol (Basel)
Orlando Business Journal — Orlando Bu J
Orlando Sentinel — Orland Sen
Orleans Parish Medical Society. Proceedings — Orl Parish Med Soc Proc
Orlovskii Gosudarstvennyi Pedagogiceskii Institut. Ucenye Zapiski — Orlov Gos Ped Inst Ucen Zap
Ormancilik Arastirma Enstituesue Dergisi — Orm Arast Enst Derg
Ormancilik Arastirma Enstituesue Muhtelif Yayinlar Serisi — Orm Arast Enst Muht Yay
Ormancilik Arastirma Enstituesue Teknik Buelten — Orm Arast Enst Tek Buelt
Ormoni e Vitamine — Orm Vitam
Ornamentals Northwest. Cooperative Extension Service. Oregon State University — Ornamentals Northwest Coop Ext Serv Oreg State Univ
Ornamentals Northwest. Newsletter. Cooperative Extension Service. Oregon State University — Ornamentals Northwest Newsl Coop Ext Serv Oreg State Univ
Ornis Fennica — ORFE
Ornis Fennica — Ornis Fenn
Ornis Scandinavica — Ornis Scand
Ornis Scandinavica — ORSC
Ornithologie Applique — Ornithol Appl
Ornithologische Abhandlungen — Orn Abh
Ornithologische Abhandlungen — Ornithol Abh
Ornithologische Beobachter — Ornithol Beob
Ornithologische Berichte — Orn Ber
Ornithologische Berichte — Ornithol Ber
Ornithologische Mitteilungen — Orn Mitt
Ornithologische Mitteilungen — Ornithol Mitt
Ornithologische Monatsberichte — Ornithol Mberr
Ornithologische Monatsberichte — Ornithol Monatsber
Oroems Antiquus — OA
Orogenic Mafic and Ultramafic Association — Orog Mafic Ultramafic Assoc
Orpheus [*Catania*] — Orph
Orpheus. Revista pentru Cultura Clasica — Or
Orpheus. Revista pentru Cultura Clasica — Orph
Orpheus. Rivista di Umanita Classica e Cristiana — ORUCC
Orphicorum Fragmenta — OF
Orphicorum Fragmenta — Orph F
Orphicorum Fragmenta — Orph Frag
Orquidea [*Mexico City*] — OQDEAN
Orquidea [*Rio De Janeiro*] — ORQUA7
ORSA [*Operations Research Society of America*]/TIMS Bulletin [*The Institute of Management Sciences*] — ORSA/TIMS Bull
Orskii Gosudarstvennyi Pedagogiceskii Institut Imeni T. G. Sevcenko. Ucenye Zapiski — Orsk Gos Ped Inst Ucen Zap
Orszagos Husipari Kutato Intezet Kozlemenyei — Orsz Husipari Kut Intez Kozl
Orszagos Magyar Izraelita Kozmuvelodesi Egyesuelet — OMIKE
Orszagos Magyar Regezeti Tarsulat Evkonyve — OMRTE
Orszagos Magyar Regezeti Tarsulat Evkonyve — ORTE
Orszagos Magyar Szepmuveszeti Muzeum Evkonyve — O M Szep Muz Evk
Orszagos Magyar Zsido Segitoe Akcio — OMZSA
Orszagos Meteorologiai Intezet Hivatalos Kiadvanyai — Orsz Met Intez Hivat Kiad
Orszagos Mezogazdasagi Minosegvizsgalo Intezet Evkonyve — Orsz Mezogazd Minosegv Intez Evk
Orszagos Mezogazdasagi Minosegvizsgalo Intezet Evkonyve — Orszagos Mezoegazd Minoesegvizsgalo Intez Evkoen
Orszagos Mezogazdasagi Minosegvizsgalo Intezet Kiadvanyai. Sorozat 1. Genetikus Talajterkepek — Orsz Mezogazd Minosegvizsgalo Intez Kiad Sorozat 1
Orszagos Muszaki Konyvtar es Dokumentacios Kozpont. Modszertani Kiadvanyok — OMKDK Modsz Kiad
Orszagos Orvostoerteneti Koenyvtar Koezlemenyei — Orsz Orvost Koenyv Koezl
Orthodontics — Orthod
Orthodontie Francaise — Orthod Fr
Orthodox Alaska — ORLA
Orthodox Christian Library — OCL
Orthodox Life — Orth L
Orthodoxe Beitraege — Orth Beitr
Orthodoxe Rundschau — Orth Rd
Orthodoxe Stimme — Orth St
Orthodoxie Heute — OH
Orthodoxos Parateretes — Orth Par
Orthomolecular Psychiatry — Orthomol Ps
Orthomolecular Psychiatry. Treatment of Schizophrenia [*Monograph*] — Orthomol Psychiatry Treat Schizophr
Orthopaede [*Germany*] — ORHPB
Orthopaedic Lectures — Orthop Lect
Orthopaedic Review — Orthop Rev
Orthopaedic Surgery — SEGEA
Orthopaedic Transactions — Orthop Trans
Orthopaedic Transactions — ORTTDM
Orthopaedische Praxis — Orthop Prax
Orthopedic Clinics of North America — Orthop Clin North Am
Orthopedic Clinics of North America — Orthoped Cl
Orthopedic Nurses' Association. Journal — ONA J
Orthopedic Nursing — Orthop Nurs
Orthopedic Surgery [*Japan*] — Orthop Surg
Orthopedics and Traumatology [*Japan*] — Orthop Traumatol
Orthopedie Traumatologie — Orthop Traumatol
Orthotics and Prosthetics — Orthot Pros
Orthotics and Prosthetics — Orthotics Prosthet
Ortnamnssaellskapets i Uppsala Aarsskrift — OsUA
Ortnamnssaellskapets i Uppsala Aarsskrift — OUA
Ortodoksia. Orthodoxia [*Istanbul*] — Orth
Ortodoncia — Ortod
Ortodoncia Clinica — Ortod Clin
Ortodoxia [*Bucuresti*] — Ort
Ortopedia e Traumatologia dell'Apparato Motore — Ortop Traumatol Appar Mot
Ortopedia Maxilar — Ortop Maxilar
Ortopedija, Travmatologija, i Protezirovanie — Ortop Travm Protez
Ortopediya i Travmatologiya (Sofia) — Ortop Travmatol (Sofia)
Ortopediya Respublikanskii Mezhvedomstvennyi Sbornik — Ortop Resp Mezhved Sb
Ortopediya, Travmatologiya, i Protezirovaniye — Ortop Travmatol Prot
Ortopediya, Travmatologiya, i Protezirovaniye — Ortop Travmatol Protez
Ortskrankenkasse — Orts KK
Ortung und Navigation [*Germany*] — Ortung Navig
Orvos es Technika — Orv Tech
Orvosi Hetilap — ORHEA
Orvosi Hetilap — Orv Hetil
Orvosi Hetilap — Orv Hetilap
Orvosi Szemle — Orv Sz
Orvosi Szemle — Orv Szle
Orvosok Lapja — Orv Lap
Orvosok Lapja — Orv Lapja
Orvos-Termeszettudomanyi Ertesitoe — Orv Termeszettud Ertes
Orvostorteneti Koezlemeneyek. Communicationes de Historia Artis Medicinae — Orvostort Kozl
Orvostudomany Aktualis Problemai — Orvostud Aktual Probl
Orvostudomanyi Beszamolo — Orvostud Beszam
Oryx Journal. Fauna Preservation Society — Oryx
Oryx Journal. Fauna Preservation Society — Oryx J Fauna Preserv Soc
Oryx Science Bibliographies — Oryx Sci Bibliogr
Oryx Science Bibliographies — OSBIE9
Oryza. Journal of the Association of Rice Research Workers — Oryza J Assoc Rice Res Work
Os Acores — OA
Osaka City Institute of Public Health and Environmental Sciences. Annual Report — Osaka City Inst Public Health Environ Sci Annu Rep
Osaka City Medical Journal — Os Cy Med J
Osaka City Medical Journal — Osaka City Med J
Osaka City University. Economic Review — Osaka City U Econ R
Osaka Daigaku Igaku Zasshi — ODIZA
Osaka Economic Papers — OEP
Osaka Economic Papers — Osaka Econ Pap
Osaka Economic Papers — OsEP
Osaka Furitsu Kogyo Shoreikan Hokoku — OFKSA
Osaka Ikadaigaku Zasshi — Os Ikad Zass
Osaka Joshi Ikadaigaku Zasshi — Os Josh Ikad Zass
Osaka Journal of Mathematics — Osaka J Mat
Osaka Journal of Mathematics — Osaka J Math
Osaka Kogyo Daigaku Kiyo. Riko-Hen — OKDIA
Osaka Mathematical Journal — Os Math J
Osaka Museum of Natural History. Bulletin — Osaka Mus Nat Hist Bull
Osaka Prefecture. University. Bulletin. Series A. Engineering and Natural Sciences — Osaka Prefect Univ Bull Ser A Eng Nat Sci
Osaka Prefecture University (Saikai). Bulletin. Series D — BUOPD
Osaka University Dental School. Journal — Osaka Univ Dent Sch J
Osaka University. Journal of Geosciences — Osaka Univ J Geosci
Osar Jehude Sefarad — OJS
Osawatomie — Osawatom
OSD. Overseas Standards Digest — OSD
Osgoode Hall. Law Journal — OHLJ
Osgoode Hall. Law Journal — Os Hall LJ
Osgoode Hall. Law Journal — Osgoode Hall L J
Osgoode Hall Law School. Journal — Osgoode Hall LSJ
OSHA [*Occupational Safety and Health Administration*] **Compliance Guide. Commerce Clearing House** — OSHA Compl Guide CCH
Osiris — Os
Osjecki Zbornik. Muzej Slavonije — O Zb
Osjecki Zbornik. Muzej Slavonije — Osj Zbor
Osjecki Zbornik. Muzej Slavonije — Osjecki Zb
Osjecki Zbornik. Muzej Slavonije — OZ
Oslo Studies in English — OSE
Osmania Journal of English Studies — OJES
Osmania Journal of Social Sciences — Osmania J Social Sciences
Osnabruecker Mitteilungen — Osnabr Mitt
Osnabruecker Mitteilungen — Osnabrueck Mitt
Osnabruecker Mitteilungen. Verein fuer Geschichte und Landeskunde von Osnabrueck — OM
Osnabruecker Schriften zur Mathematik — Osnabrueck Schrift Math
Osnabruecker Schriften zur Mathematik. Reihe M. Mathematische Manuskripte — Osnabrueck Schrift Math Reihe M Math Manuskr

Osnabruecker Schriften zur Mathematik. Reihe V. Vorlesungsskripten — Osnabruek Schrift Math Reihe V Vorlesungsskr
Osnabruecker Studien zur Mathematik — Osnabrueck Stud Math
Osnovaniya, Fundamenty, i Mekhanika Gruntov [*Former USSR*] — Osn Fundam Mekh Gruntov
Osnovaniya i Fundamenty — Osn Fundam
Osnovnoi Organicheskii Sintez i Neftekhimiya — Osnovn Org Sint Neftekhim
Osnovnye Usloviya Effektivnogo Primeneniya Udobrenii — Osnovn Usloviya Eff Primen Udobr
Osnovy Metallurgii — Osn Metall
Osobennosti Razvitiya Ryb v Razlichnykh Estestvennykh i Eksperimental'nykh Usloviyakh — Osob Razvit Ryb Razlichnykh Estestv Eksp Usloviyakh
Ospedale Maggiore [*Italy*] — Osp Magg
Ospedale Maggiore — Osped Maggiore
Ospedale Maggiore di Novara — Osp Magg Novara
Ospedale Psichiatrico — Osp Psichiatr
Ospedale Psichiatrico — Osped Psichiat
Ospedali d'Italia - Chirurgia — Osp Ital Chir
Ospedali d'Italia - Chirurgia — Osped Ital Chir
Ospedali Italiani - Pediatria e Specialita Chirurgiche — OSIPAR
Ospedali Italiani Pediatria (e Specialita Chirurgiche) — Osp Ital Pediatr (Spec Chir)
OSR [*Organisation for Scientific Research in Indonesia*] **Bulletin** — OSR Bull
Osrodek Badawczo-Rozwojowy Elektroniki Prozniowej (Prace) — Osrodek Badaw Rozwojowy Elektron Prozniowej (Pr)
Osrodek Informacji o Energii Jadrowej. Review Report — Osrodek Inf Energ Jad Rev Rep
Osrodek Naukowo-Produkcyjny Materialow Polprzewodnikowych. Prace — Osr Nauk Prod Mater Polprzewodn Pr
Osservatore — Osserv
Osservatore Medico — Oss Med
Osservatore Politico Letterario — OPL
Osservatore Romano — OR
Osservatore Romano — ORom
Osservatore Romano [*Vatican City*] — OsRom
Osservatore Romano [*Vatican City*] — OssRom
Osservatore Romano (English) — O R (English)
Osservatore Tributario — Osserv Trib
Osservazioni e Memorie. Osservatorio Astrofisico di Arcetri — Oss & Mem Oss Astrofis Arcetri
OSSTF [*Ontario Secondary School Teachers' Federation*] **Forum** — OSSTF For
Ost und West — OuW
Ost und West — OW
Ostasiatische Studien — OasSt
Ostasiatische Zeitschrift — OZ
Ostasiatischer Lloyd — Ostas Lloyd
Ostatnie Wiadomosci — OW
Ostbairische Grenzmarken — Ob Gr
Ostbairische Grenzmarken — Ostb Grenzm
Ostbairische Grenzmarken. Institut fuer Ostbairische Heimatforschung — OG
Ostbayerische Grenzmarken — Ostbayer Grenzmarken
Ostdeutsche Familienkunde — Ostdt Familienkde
Ostdeutsche Monatshefte — O Mh
Ostdeutsche Monatshefte — ODM
Ostdeutsche Monatshefte — OM
Ostdeutsche Monatshefte — OstM
Ostdeutsche Wissenschaft — O Wi
Ostdeutsche Wissenschaft — Od Wiss
Ostdeutsche Wissenschaft — ODW
Ostdeutsche Wissenschaft — Ostdt Wiss
Ostdeutsche Wissenschaft — OW
Ostdeutscher Naturwart — OdNtw
Ostdeutscher Naturwart — Ostdeutsch Naturwart
Osteopathic Annals — Osteopath Ann
Osteopathic Hospital Leadership — Osteopath Hosp Leadership
Osteopathic Hospitals — OH
Osteopathic Medicine — OSMDAB
Osteopathic Medicine — Osteopath Med
Osteopathic Profession — Osteopath Prof
Osteopathic Quarterly — Osteop Q
Osteoporosis International — Osteoporos Int
Osteoporosis International — Osteoporosis Int
Osteoporosis. Proceedings. International Symposium — Osteoporosis Proc Int Symp
Osteuropa — O
Osteuropa — OE
Osteuropa — Osteur
Osteuropa Naturwissenschaft — Osteur Naturwiss
Osteuropa Wirtschaft — OEW
Osteuropa Wirtschaft — Osteur Wirt
Osteuropa Wirtschaft — Osteuropa Wirtsch
Osteuropa. Zeitschrift fuer Gegenwartsfragen des Ostens — OST
Osteuropa-Recht — Osteur Recht
Osteuropastudien der Hochschulen des Landes Hessen. Reihe I. Giessener Abhandlungen zur Agrar und Wirtschaftsforschung des Europaeischen Ostens — OHLHA9
Osteuropa-Wirtschaft — Osteur Wirtsch
Ost-Friesische Mannigfaltigkeiten — Ost Fries Mannigfaltigk
Ostjydsk Hjemstavnforenings Aarsskrift — Ostjydsk Hjemstavn
Ostkirchliche Studien — OKS
Ostkirchliche Studien — OS
Ostkirchliche Studien — Ost K St
Ostkirchliche Studien — Ostkirch St
Ostkirchliche Studien — Ostkirchl Stud
Ostmaerkische Milchwirtschaftliche Zeitung — Ostmaerk Milchwirtsch Ztg
Ostmaerkische Spirituosen-Zeitung — Ostmaerk Spirit Ztg
Ost-Probleme — OP
Ost-Probleme — Ost Probl
Ostraca Grecs de la Collection Charles-Edwin Wilbour au Musee de Brooklyn — O Wilb
Ostraca Grecs de la Collection Charles-Edwin Wilbour au Musee de Brooklyn — Ostr Wilbour
Ostraca Osloensia. Greek Ostraca in Norwegian Collections — O Oslo
Ostrava. Vysoka Skola Banska. Sbornik. Rada Hornicko-Geologicka — Ostrava Vys Ak Banska Sb Rada Hornicko-Geol
Ostrich. Supplement — Ostrich Suppl
Ostwalds Klassiker der Exakten Wissenschaften — Ostwalds Klassiker Exakt Wiss
OSU Current Report. Oklahoma State University. Cooperative Extension Service — OSU Curr Rep Okla State Univ Coop Ext Serv
OSU Extension Facts. Cooperative Extension Service. Oklahoma State University [*A publication*] — OSU Ext Facts Coop Ext Serv Okla State Univ
Osvedomitel'nyj Bjulleten' Komissii Ekspedicionnych Issledovanij Akademii Nauk SSSR — OB
Osvit — Os
Otago Acclimatisation Society. Annual Report — Otago Acclim Soc Annu Rep
Otago Law Review — Otago L Rev
Otago Law Review — Otago Law Rev
Otago Law Review — Otago LR
Otago Law Review — OTLR
Otago Museum of Zoology. Bulletin — Otago Mus Zool Bull
OTAN [*Organization of Tropical American Nematologists*] **Newsletter** — OTAN Newsl
Otbor i Peredaca Informacii. Akademija Nauk Ukrainskoi SSR. Fiziko-Mehaniceskii Institut — Otbor i Peredaca Informacii
Otbor i Peredacha Informatsii — Otbor i Peredacha Inf
Otbor i Peredacha Informatsii — Otbor Pereda Inf
Otcet O Dejatel'nosti Tiflisskago Botaniceskago Sada — Otcet Dejateln Tiflissk Bot Sada
Otcet O Dejatel'nosti Volzskoj Biologiceskoj Stancii/Bericht ueber die Thaetigkeit der Biologischen Wolga-Station — Otcet Dejateln Volzsk Biol Stancii
Otcet O Prisuzdenii Akademieju Nauk — Otcet Prisuzd Akad Nauk
Otcet Volzskoj Biologiceskoj Stancii Saratovskogo Obscestva Estestvoispytatelej I Ljubitelej Estestvoznanija/Compte-Rendu des Travaux des Vacances. Station Biologique du Volga. Organisee Par la Societe des Naturalistes a Saratow — Otcet Volzsk Biol Stancii Saratovsk Obsc Estestvoisp
Otcety Archeologiceskoj Komissii — OAK
Otchery Mezhdunarodnogo Obshchestva po Khimii Serna — Otchery Mezhdunar O-Va Khim Serna
Otchet Imperatorskoi Arkheologicheskoi Kommissii — OIAK
Otdel Viz i Registratsii — OVIR
Otdelenie Ekonomiceskoi Kivernetiki Ekonomiceskogo Fakul'teta Moskovogo Gosudarstvennogo Universiteta Imeni M. V. Lomonosova. Modelirovanie Ekonomiceskih Processov — Modelirovanie Ekonom Processov
Otdelochnaya Tekhnika — Otd Tekh
Otemon Economic Studies — Otemon Econ Stud
Other Scenes — Oth Sce
Other Side — OS
Other Woman — Othr Womn
Other Worlds — OW
Otkhody Promyshlennosti i Mineral'noe Syr'e v Proizvodstve Tekhnicheskikh i Stroitel'nykh Materialov — Otkhody Promsti Miner Syre Proizvod Tekh Stroit Mater
Otkrytija Russkich Zemleprochodcev i Poljarnych Morechodov XVII Veka na Severovostoke Azii — ORZIM
Otkrytiya, Izobreteniya, Promyshlennye Obraztsy, Tovarnye Znaki [*Bulletin for Inventions, Designs, and Trademarks*] — OIPOB
Otkrytiya, Izobreteniya, Promyshlennye Obraztsy, Tovarnye Znaki [*Bulletin for Inventions, Designs, and Trademarks*] [*Former USSR*] — Otkryt Izobret
Otkrytiya, Izobreteniya, Promyshlennye Obraztsy, Tovarnye Znaki [*Bulletin for Inventions, Designs, and Trademarks*] [*Former USSR*] — Otkrytiya Izobret Prom Obraztsy Tovarnye Znaki
Oto-Laringologia — Oto Laring
Otolaryngologia Polska — Otolaryngol Pol
Otolaryngologia Polska — OTPOA
Otolaryngologic Clinics of North America — Otolar Clin
Otolaryngologic Clinics of North America — Otolaryngol Clin N Am
Otolaryngologic Clinics of North America — Otolaryngol Clin North Am
Otolaryngology and Head and Neck Surgery — Otolaryngol Head Neck Surg
Otologia Fukuoka — Otol Fukuoka
Otologia Fukuoka Jibi To Rinsho — Otol Fukuoka Jibi To Rinsho
Otology Japan — Otol Jpn
Oto-Noro Oftalmoloji — Oto Noro Oftalmol
Otoplenie. Ventilyatsiya i Stroitel'naya Teplofizika — Otoplenie Vent Stroit Teplofiz
Oto-Rhino-Laryngology [*Tokyo*] — JITEBR
Oto-Rhino-Laryngology — Oto-Rhino-Laryngol
Oto-Rhino-Laryngology (Tokyo) — Oto-Rhino-Laryngol (Tokyo)
Oto-Rino-Laringologia [*Bucharest*] — OTRLAX
Oto-Rino-Laringologia Italiana — ORLIA
Oto-Rino-Laringologia Italiana — Oto-Rino-Laringol Ital
Oto-Rino-Laringologie si Oftalmologie — Oto-Rino-Laringol Oftalmol
Otsenka Mestorozhdenii pri Poiskakh i Razvedkakh — Otsenka Mestorozhd Poiskakh Razved
Ottawa Bulletin — Ottawa Bul
Ottawa Field Naturalists' Club. Transactions — Ottawa Field Nat Club Tr
Ottawa Field-Naturalists' Club Transactions — Ottawa Field Naturalists Club Trans

Ottawa Hispanica — O His
Ottawa Law Review — Ott LR
Ottawa Law Review — Ottawa L Rev
Ottawa Law Review — Ottawa Law R
Ottawa Law Review — Ottawa LR
Ottawa Literary and Scientific Society. Transactions — Ottawa Lit Sc Soc Tr
Ottawa Naturalist — Ottawa Nat
Ottawa Report. Canadian Wildlife Federation — OTRE
Ottawa Week — Ottawa W
Ottendorfer Memorial Series of Germanic Monographs — OMSGM
Ottisk iz Aapisok Voronezhskogo Sel'skokhozyaistvennogo Instituta — Ott Voronezh Sel-Khoz Inst
Otto Graf Journal. Annual Journal of Research and Testing of Materials — Otto Graf J
Otto-Graf-Institut (Stuttgart). Technische Hochschule. Schriftenreihe — Otto Graf Inst (Stuttgart) Tech Hochsch Schriftenr
Otto-Graf-Institut (Stuttgart). Technische Hochschule. Schriftenreihe — Otto-Graf-Inst (Stutt) Tech Hochsch Schriftenr
Oude Land van Loon — OLL
Oudheidkundig Jaarboek. Bulletijn Uitgegeven door den Nederlandschen Oudkundigen Bond — OJ
Oudheidkundig Jaarboek. Bulletijn Uitgegeven door den Nederlandschen Oudkundigen Bond — OJBNOB
Oudheidkundige Medede e Lingen uit het Rijksmuseum van Oudheden te Leiden — OMRM
Oudheidkundige Mededeelingen — OKMD
Oudheidkundige Mededeelingen — Oudh Med
Oudheidkundige Mededeelingen uit s'Rijksmuseum van Oudheden te Leiden — OM
Oudheidkundige Mededeelingen uit s'Rijksmuseum van Oudheden te Leiden — OM Leiden
Oudheidkundige Mededeelingen uit s'Rijksmuseum van Oudheden te Leiden — OMRL
Oudheidkundige Mededeelingen uit s'Rijksmuseum van Oudheden te Leiden — Oudh Meded
Oudheidkundige Mededeelingen uit s'Rjksmuseum van Oudheden te Leiden — OMML
Oudheidkundige Mededelingen uit het Rijksmuseum van Oudheden te Leiden — OML
Oudheidkundige Mededelingen uit het Rijksmuseum van Oudheden te Leiden — OMRO
Oudheidkundige Mededelingen uit het Rijksmuseum van Oudheden te Leiden — OMROL
Oudheidkundige Mededelingen uit het Rijksmuseum van Oudheden te Leiden — ORm
Oudheidkundige Mededelingen uit het Rijksmuseum van Oudheden te Leiden — Oudheidk Mededelingen
Oud-Holland — OH
Oudtestamentisch Werkgezelschap in Nederland — OWN
Oudtestamentische Studien [*Leiden*] — OS
Oudtestamentische Studien — OTS
Oudtestamentische Studien [*Leiden*] — OTSt
Oudtestamentische Studien [*Leiden*] — OudSt
Oudtestamentische Studien [*Leiden*] — OuS
Ouest Medical — Ouest Med
Oulun Yliopiston Ydintekniikkan Laitoksen Julkaisuja — Oulun Yliopiston Ydintek Laitoksen Julk
Our Family. Ilavut. Family Newspaper. Diocese of the Arctic — OFIV
Our Generation — Our Gener
Our Native Land — ONLA
Our Public Lands — OPL
Our Public Lands — OPLA
Our Quarterly Magazine — Our Q Mag
Our Sunday Visitor — OSV
Our Sunday Visitor Magazine — OSVM
Our World Weekly — Our World W
Ouro Preto. Escola de Minas. Revista — Ouro Preto Esc Minas Rev
Out of Bounds — OB
Out of This World — OTW
Out of This World Adventures — OTWA
Outdoor America — Outdoor Am
Outdoor Digest — Outdoor Dig
Outdoor Facts [*Fort Collins, CO*] — OUFADI
Outdoor Indiana — Outdoor Ind
Outdoor Life — GOUL
Outdoor Oklahoma — Outdoor Okla
Outdoor Recreation Action — ORA
Outdoor Recreation Action — Outd Rec Act
Outdoor Review — Outdoor Rev
Outer Continental Shelf. Environmental Assessment Program. Arctic Project Bulletin — OCSAPB
Outer Continental Shelf. Environmental Assessment Program. Arctic Project Special Bulletin [*United States*] — OCSAPSB
Outer Continental Shelf. Environmental Assessment Program. Bering Sea - Gulf of Alaska Newsletter — OCSB
Outlands — Out
OUT-LOOK — IOUT
Outlook — Ou
Outlook — Outl
Outlook and Bulletin. Southern Dental Society of New Jersey — Outlook Bull South Dent Soc NJ
Outlook (London) — OL
Outlook on Agriculture — Outl Agric
Outlook on Agriculture — Outlook Agr
Outlook on Agriculture — Outlook Agric
Outlook. Proceedings. Agricultural Outlook Conference. US Department of Agriculture — Outlook Proc Agric Outlook Conf US Dep Agric
Outlook. United Fresh Fruit and Vegetable Association — Outlook United Fresh Fruit Veg Assoc
Outokumpu News — Outok News
Outsider — Out
Outstanding Soviet Scientists — Outstanding Soviet Sci
Outstate Testing Circular. University of Nebraska. College of Agriculture and Home Economics. Agricultural Experiment Station — Outstate Test Circ Univ Nebr Coll Agr Home Econ Agr Exp Sta
Ouvrages sur la Culture Nord-Africaine — OCNA
Ouvroir Liturgique — OLit
Ovation — GOVA
Ovation — OV
Ovation — Ova
Ove Arup Partnership. Newsletter — Ove Arup Ptnrship Newsletter
Overheidsdocumentatie. Orgaan voor Documentatie en Administratieve Organisatie der Overheid — GDS
Overijssel Jaarboek voor Cultuur en Historie — OJCH
Overland Monthly — Ov
Overland Monthly — Overland
Overland Monthly. New Series — Overland NS
Oversea Education — Oversea Educ
Overseas Building Notes — Overseas Bldg Notes
Overseas Business Reports — BFX
Overseas Business Reports — OBR
Overseas Education — OE
Overseas Education — Oversea Ed
Overseas Geology and Mineral Resources [*Great Britain*] — Overseas Geol Miner Resour
Overseas Geology and Mineral Resources. Supplement Series. Bulletin Supplement — Overseas Geol Miner Resour Suppl Ser Bull Suppl
Overseas Memoir. Institute of Geological Sciences — Overseas Mem Inst Geol Sci
Overseas Memoir. Institute of Geological Sciences (Great Britain) — Overseas Mem Inst Geol Sci (GB)
Overseas Reports Announcements — ORA
Overseas Trade Descriptions. Export and Import Statistics — Overseas Trade Descrip Export & Import Stat
Overseas Trade Statistics of the United Kingdom — Overseas Trade Stat UK
Overseas Trading — OVT
Oversigt over det Kongelige Danske Videnskabernes Selskabs. Forhandlinger — Overs K Dan Vidensk Selsk Forh
Oversigt over det Kongelige Danske Videnskabernes Selskabs. Forhandlinger — Overs K Danske Vidensk Selsk Forh
Oversigt over det Kongelige Danske Videnskabernes Selskabs Forhandlinger — OVS
Oversigt Over Det Kongelige Danske Videnskabernes Selskabs Forhandlinger Og Dets Medlemmers Arbeider — Overs Kongel Danske Vidensk Selsk Forh Medlemmers Arbeider
Oversigt over Selskabets Virksomhed. Kongelige Danske Videnskabernes Selskab [*A publication*] — Overs K Dan Vidensk Selsk
Oversigt over Selskabets Virksomhed. Kongelige Danske Videnskabernes Selskab — Overs Selsk Virksomhed K Dan Vidensk Selsk
Overzicht Rechtspraak — Ov Rspr
Overzicht van de Economische Ontwikkeling — TYS
Ovocnicke Rozhledy — Ovocn Rozhl
Oxford Abstracts — OxAbs
Oxford and Cambridge Series — OCS
Oxford Applied Mathematics and Computing Science Series — Oxford Appl Math Comput Sci Ser
Oxford Bibliographical Society. Proceedings — OBSP
Oxford Bibliographical Society. Proceedings — Oxford Bibliog Soc Proc
Oxford Bibliographical Society. Publications — OBSP
Oxford Biology Readers — Oxford Biol Readers
Oxford Book of Greek Verse — OBGV
Oxford Bulletin of Economics and Statistics — ISO
Oxford Bulletin of Economics and Statistics — Ox B Econ S
Oxford Bulletin of Economics and Statistics — OXF
Oxford Bulletin of Economics and Statistics — Oxford B Econ Statis
Oxford/Carolina Biology Readers — Oxford/Carol Biol Readers
Oxford Classical and Philosophical Monographs — OCPM
Oxford Classical Dictionary — OCD
Oxford Classical Dictionary — Oxf Class Dict
Oxford Commentaries — Oxf Com
Oxford Dictionary of the Christian Church — ODCC
Oxford Early Christian Texts — OECT
Oxford Economic Papers — OEP
Oxford Economic Papers — OFE
Oxford Economic Papers — Ox Econ Pap
Oxford Economic Papers — Oxford Econ Pa
Oxford Economic Papers — Oxford Econ Pap
Oxford Economic Papers — Oxford Econ Pas
Oxford Editions of Cuneiform Texts — OECT
Oxford Energy Forum — Oxf Energy Forum
Oxford Engineering Science Series — Oxford Engrg Sci Ser
Oxford English Dictionary [*Monograph*] — OED
Oxford English Dictionary Supplement [*Monograph*] — OEDS
Oxford English Monographs — OEM
Oxford English Novels — OEN
Oxford English Studies — OES
Oxford English Texts — OET
Oxford German Studies — OGS
Oxford German Studies — Oxf Ger Stud
Oxford Historical Series — OHS

Oxford History of English Literature — OHEL
Oxford Journal of Legal Studies — Oxford J Legal Stud
Oxford Latin Dictionary [*Monograph*] — OLD
Oxford Latin Dictionary — Oxf Lat Dic
Oxford Lecture Series in Mathematics and its Applications — Oxford Lecture Ser Math Appl
Oxford Literary Review — OLR
Oxford Literary Review — Ox Lit Rev
Oxford Magazine — OM
Oxford Magazine — Oxf Mag
Oxford Mathematical Monographs — Oxford Math Monogr
Oxford Mathematical Monographs — Oxford Math Monographs
Oxford Medical School Gazette — Oxf Med Sch Gaz
Oxford Medieval Texts — OMT
Oxford Modern Languages and Literature Monographs — OMLLM
Oxford Outlook — OO
Oxford Pamphlet on World Affairs — OPWA
Oxford Pamphlets on World Affairs — Oxford Pamphl Wld Aff
Oxford Paperbacks — OPB
Oxford Physics Series — Oxf Phys Ser
Oxford Prize Essays — Ox Prize Ess
Oxford Psychology Series — Oxford Psych Ser
Oxford Readings in Philosophy — ORPh
Oxford Review — OR
Oxford Review — Oxf R
Oxford Review of Education — Oxford R Educ
Oxford Review of Education — Oxford Rev Educ
Oxford Reviews of Reproductive Biology — ORRBDQ
Oxford Reviews of Reproductive Biology — Oxf Rev Reprod Biol
Oxford Reviews of Reproductive Biology — Oxford Rev Reprod Biol
Oxford Science Publications — Oxford Sci Publ
Oxford Series on Optical Sciences — Oxford Ser Opt Sci
Oxford Slavonic Papers — OSLP
Oxford Slavonic Papers — OSP
Oxford Slavonic Papers — Oxf Slav Pap
Oxford Slavonic Papers — Oxford Slavonic Pa
Oxford Slavonic Papers — Oxford Slavonic Pap
Oxford Studies in Ancient Philosophy — Oxford Stud Ancient Phil
Oxford Studies in Probability — Oxford Stud Probab
Oxford Surveys in Evolutionary Biology — OSEBE3
Oxford Surveys in Evolutionary Biology — Oxf Surv Evol Biol
Oxford Surveys of Plant Molecular and Cell Biology — Oxf Surv Plant Mol Cell Biol
Oxford Surveys on Eukaryotic Genes — Oxf Surv Eukaryot Genes
Oxford Surveys on Eukaryotic Genes — Oxford Surv Eukaryotic Genes
Oxford Theological Monographs — OTM
Oxford University. Institute of Economics and Statistics. Bulletin — OIS
Oxford University. Pitt Rivers Museum. Occasional Papers on Technology — Oxf Univ Pitt Rivers Mus Occas Pap Technol
Oxfordshire Record Society — Oxfordshire Rec Soc
Oxford-Warburg Studies — OWS
Oxidation and Combustion Reviews — Oxid Combust Rev
Oxidation in Organic Chemistry. Part A — Oxid Org Chem Part A
Oxidation of Metals — Oxid Met
Oxidation Reviews and Abstracts — Oxid Rev Abstr
Oxidative Damage and Repair. Chemical, Biological, and Medical Aspects. International Society for Free Radical Research. Biennial Meeting — Oxid Damage Repair Int Soc Free Radical Res Bienn Meet
Oxoniensa — Ox
Oxoniensia — Oxon
Oxygen Transfer from Atmosphere to Tissues — Oxygen Transfer Atmos Tissues
Oxyrhynchus Papyri — Pap Ox
Oxyrhynchus Papyri — PapOxy
Oxyrhynchus Papyri — POxy
Oyo Butsuri — OYBSA
Ozbek Tili va Adabiet Masalalari — OTAM
OZE. Oesterreichische Zeitschrift fuer Elektrizitaetswirtschaft — OZE Oesterr Z fuer Elektrizitaetswirtsch
Ozean und Technik [*Germany*] — Ozean Tech
Ozone. Science and Engineering — Ozone Sci Eng

P

P/M in Aerospace and Defence Technologies Symposium — PM Aerosp Def Technol Symp
PA Journal [*Formerly, Physician's Associate*] — PA J
PAABS (Pan-American Association of Biochemical Societies) Symposium Series — PAABS Symp Ser
PAABS [*Pan-American Association of Biochemical Societies*] **Revista** [*United States*] — PAABS Rev
PAABS [*Pan-American Association of Biochemical Societies*] **Symposium** — PAABS Symp
Paar Sammukest Eesti Kirjanduse Uurimise Teed — PSEKUT
PACE [*Process and Control Engineering*] — PACE Process Control Eng
Pace Law Review — Pace L Rev
Pace Law Review — Pace LR
PACE. Pacing and Clinical Electrophysiology — PACE
PACE. Process and Chemical Engineering — PACE
PACE. Process and Chemical Engineering — PACE Process Chem Eng
Pachart History of Astronomy Series — Pachart Hist Astronom Ser
Pacht — P
Pacific Affairs — PA
Pacific Affairs — Pac A
Pacific Affairs — Pac Aff
Pacific Affairs — Pac Affairs
Pacific Affairs — Pacif Aff
Pacific Affairs — Pacific Aff
Pacific Affairs — PAF
Pacific Affairs — PPAF
Pacific Affairs. Current Awareness Bulletin — PACAB
Pacific Arts Newsletter — Pac Arts Newsl
Pacific Bird Observer — Pac Bird Obs
Pacific Builder and Engineer — Pac Builder Eng
Pacific Business — Pacific Bus
Pacific Business News — Pacif Bs N
Pacific Chemical and Metallurgical Industries — Pac Chem Metall Ind
Pacific Chemical Engineering Congress — Pac Chem Eng Congr
Pacific Chemical Engineering Congress. Proceedings [*United States*] — Pac Chem Eng Cong Proc
Pacific Coast Gas Association. Proceedings — Pac Coast Gas Assoc Proc
Pacific Coast Journal of Nursing — Pacif Coa J Nurs
Pacific Coast Medicine — Pac Coast Med
Pacific Coast Medicine — Pacific Coast Med
Pacific Coast Philology — PCP
Pacific Community [*Tokyo*] — Pac Com
Pacific Community — Pac Commun
Pacific Defence Reporter — Pac D Rep
Pacific Defence Reporter — Pac Def Report
Pacific Discovery — Pac Discov
Pacific Discovery — Pac Discovery
Pacific Discovery — Pacific Disc
Pacific Discovery — Pacific Discov
Pacific Fisherman — Pac Fisherman
Pacific Geology — Pac Geol
Pacific Historian — Pac Hist
Pacific Historian — PacH
Pacific Historical Review — Pac Hist R
Pacific Historical Review — Pac Hist Rev
Pacific Historical Review — PacHR
Pacific Historical Review — Pacif Hist R
Pacific Historical Review — Pacif Hist Rev
Pacific Historical Review — Pacific His R
Pacific Historical Review — Pacific Hist Rev
Pacific Historical Review — PHR
Pacific Historical Review — PPHR
Pacific History Review — Pac Hist Rev
Pacific Horticulture — Pac Hortic
Pacific Imperialism Notebook — Pacif Imp
Pacific Insects — Pac Insects
Pacific Insects — Pacif Insects
Pacific Insects Monograph — Pac Insects Mongr
Pacific Insects Monograph — Pac Insects Monogr
Pacific Islands Communication Journal — Pacific Islands Com J
Pacific Islands Communication Journal — PICJ
Pacific Islands Ecosystems [*Database*] — PIE
Pacific Islands Monthly — Pacific Islands M
Pacific Islands Monthly — PIM
Pacific Islands Year Book — Pacific Islands Yrbk
Pacific Journal of Mathematics — Pac J Math
Pacific Journal of Mathematics — Pacif J Math
Pacific Journal of Mathematics — Pacific J Math
Pacific Journal of Theology — PJT
Pacific Law Journal — Pac LJ
Pacific Law Journal — Pacific L J
Pacific Marine Fisheries Commission. Annual Report — Pac Mar Fish Comm Annu Rep
Pacific Marine Fisheries Commission. Bulletin — Pac Mar Fish Comm Bull
Pacific Marine Science Report — Pac Mar Sci Rep
Pacific Medical Journal — Pacific Med J
Pacific Medicine and Surgery — Pac Med Surg
Pacific Medicine and Surgery — Pacific Med Surg
Pacific Minerals Review — Pac Miner Rev
Pacific Monthly [*Portland, Oregon*] — Pac Mo
Pacific Neighbours — Pac Neighbours
Pacific Northwest Forest and Range Experiment Station. Research Note PNW — Pac Northwest For Range Exp Stn Res Note PNW
Pacific Northwest Forest and Range Experiment Station. Research Paper PNW — Pac Northwest For Range Exp Stn Res Pap PNW
Pacific Northwest Laboratory Annual Report to the DOE Assistant Secretary for Environment — Pac Northwest Lab Annu Rep DOE Assist Secr Environ
Pacific Northwest Laboratory. Technical Report PNL — Pac Northwest Lab Tech Rep PNL
Pacific Northwest Library Association. Quarterly — PNLA Q
Pacific Northwest Quarterly — Pac Northw
Pacific Northwest Quarterly — Pac Northwest Q
Pacific Northwest Quarterly — Pac NWQ
Pacific Northwest Quarterly — Pacific Northw Q
Pacific Northwest Quarterly — Pacific Northwest Quart
Pacific Northwest Quarterly — PacN
Pacific Northwest Quarterly — PacNQ
Pacific Northwest Quarterly — PNQ
Pacific Northwest Sea — Pac Northwest Sea
Pacific Northwesterner — Pac Northwest
Pacific Northwesterner — Pac Northwesterner
Pacific Ocean — Pac Ocean
Pacific Packers Report — Pac Pack Rep
Pacific Perspective — Pacific Perspect
Pacific Pharmacist — Pac Pharm
Pacific Philosophical Quarterly — Pac Phil Q
Pacific Philosophical Quarterly — Pac Phil Quart
Pacific Philosophical Quarterly — Pac Philos Q
Pacific Philosophical Quarterly — Pacific Phil Quart
Pacific Philosophical Quarterly — PPHQ
Pacific Plastics — Pac Plast
Pacific Pulp and Paper Industry — Pac Pulp Pap Ind
Pacific Quarterly — Pac Q
Pacific Quarterly (Moana): An International Review of Arts and Ideas — PQM
Pacific Reporter — P
Pacific Reporter. Second — P 2d
Pacific Research [*Formerly, Pacific Research and World Empire Telegram*] — Pac Res
Pacific Review of Ethnomusicology — Pacific R
Pacific Rocket Society. Bulletin — Pac Rocket Soc Bull
Pacific Rockets — Pac Rockets
Pacific Science — Pac Sci
Pacific Science — Pacif Sci
Pacific Science — Pacific Sci
Pacific Science Congress. Proceedings — Pac Sci Congr Proc
Pacific Science Congress. Record of Proceedings — Pac Sci Congr Rec Proc
Pacific Science Information. Bernice P. Bishop Museum — Pacific Sci Inform
Pacific Search [*United States*] — Pac Search
Pacific Sociological Review — Pac Soc R
Pacific Sociological Review — Pac Soc Rev
Pacific Sociological Review — Pac Sociol R
Pacific Sociological Review — Pacif Soc Rev
Pacific Sociological Review — Pacif Sociol Rev
Pacific Sociological Review — Pacific Sociol R
Pacific Sociological Review — PSR
Pacific Spectator — PacSp
Pacific Spectator — PS
Pacific Spectator — PSp
Pacific Studies — Pacific Stud
Pacific University Bulletin — PUB
Pacific Viewpoint [*New Zealand*] — Pac View
Pacific Viewpoint — Pac Viewp

Pacific Viewpoint — PCI
Pacific Viewpoint — PV
Pacific Wine Spirit Review — Pac Wine Spirit Rev
Pacing and Cardiac Electrophysiology Retrieval System [*Database*] — PACERS
Pacing and Clinical Electrophysiology — Pacing Clin Electrophysiol
Pack Report. Fachzeitschrift fuer Verpackungs Marketing und Verpackungs (Technik) — POR
Package Development — Package Dev
Package Development and Systems — Package Dev Syst
Package Engineering — Packago Eng
Package Engineering — Package Engng
Package Engineering — PCG
Package Engineering — Pkg Eng
Package Engineering Encyclopedia, Including Modern Packaging Encyclopedia — Pckg Eng En
Package Printing and Diecutting. Flexography, Gravure, Offset — Package Print Diecutting
Package Printing and Dyecutting — Pack Print and Dyecutting
Packaging — Pac
Packaging — Pack
Packaging — PAG
Packaging Abstracts — Packag Abstr
Packaging Abstracts — Pkg Abstr
Packaging Encyclopedia — Pack Encyc
Packaging Engineering — Pckgng Eng
Packaging Engineering — PE
Packaging (India) — Packag (India)
Packaging (India) — Pkg (India)
Packaging Institute. Special Report — Packag Inst Spec Rep
Packaging (London) — Pkg (London)
Packaging News — PAN
Packaging News — Pkg News
Packaging Review — Packa Rev
Packaging Review — Packag Rev
Packaging Review — PAV
Packaging Review — Pckgng Rev
Packaging Review (South Africa) — Packag Rev (S Afr)
Packaging Science and Technology Abstracts [*Database*] — PSTA
Packaging Technology — Pack Technol
Packaging Technology — PDF
Packaging Technology and Management — Pkg Technol
Packaging Technology and Science — Packag Technol Sci
Packaging Technology (Hillsdale, New Jersey) — Packag Technol (Hillsdale NJ)
Packaging Week — Pckgng Wek
Packaging with Plastics — Packag Plast
Packer, Processor — Packer Process
Packung und Transport in der Chemische Industrie — Packung
Packung und Transport in der Chemischen Industrie — PTC
Paderborner Schriften zur Paedagogik und Katechetik — PSPK
Padova e la Sua Provincia — PProv
Paedagogica Historica — Paedag Hist
Paedagogica Historica — Paedagog Hist
Paedagogica Historica — Paedagogica Hist
Paedagogik — Pae
Paedagogische Blaetter — PB
Paedagogische Forschungen — PF
Paedagogische Hochschule Karl Liebknecht Potsdam. Wissenschaftliche Zeitschrift — Paedagog Hochsch Karl Liebknecht Potsdam Wiss Z
Paedagogische Provinz — PPr
Paedagogische Rundschau — Paedagog Run
Paedagogische Rundschau — PaedR
Paedagogische Rundschau — PRu
Paedagogische Welt — PW
Paedagogischer Anzeiger fuer Russland — Paedag Anz Russld
Paedagogisches Lexikon — Paed Lex
Paedagogisches Lexikon. Herausgegeben von Hans-Hermann Groothoff — Paed LexG
Paedagogisches Magazin — Paedag Mag
Paedagogisches Zentralblatt — Paedag Zbl
Paedagogisk-Psykologisk Tidsskrift — Paed Psyk T
Paediatria Universitatis Tokyo — Paediatr Univ Tokyo
Paediatric Anaesthesia — Paediatr Anaesth
Paediatric and Perinatal Epidemiology — Paediatr Perinat Epidemiol
Paediatric Endocrinology — Paediatr Endocrinol
Paediatric Osteology. New Developments in Diagnostics and Therapy Proceedings of the International Workshop on Paediatric Osteology — Paediatr Osteology New Dev Diagn Ther Proc Int Workshop
Paediatrica Indonesiana — Paediatr Indones
Paediatrician — PDTNBH
Paediatrie und Grenzgebiete — Paediatr Grenzgeb
Paediatrie und Paedologie — Padiatr Pad
Paediatrie und Paedologie — Paediatr Paedol
Paediatrie und Paedologie (Supplementum) — Paediatr Paedol (Suppl)
Paediatrische Fortbildungskurse fuer die Praxis — Paediatr Fortbildungskurse Prax
Paedigogica Historica — PH
Paepstliche Dokumente — PD
Paepstliche Rundschreiben — Paepst Rdschr
PAFAI (Perfumes and Flavours Association of India) Journal — PAFAI J
PAFTE (Philippine Association for Teacher Education) Review — PAFTE Rev
PAGE (Philippine Association for Graduate Education) Journal — Page J
Pages Bleues Informatisees [*Database*] — PABLI
Paginas de Literatura y Ensayo — PLE
Pagine di Storia della Medicina — Pagine Stor Med
Pagine di Storia della Medicina — PSM
Pagine Istriane — PI
Pahasapa Quarterly — Pahasapa Q
Pahlavi Medical Journal — Pahlavi Med J
Paid My Dues — Paid Dues
Paideia — Pa
Paideia Studies in Philosophia Mathematica at Large — Paideia Stud Philos Math at Large
Paideia Studies in the Nature of Modern Mathematics — Paideia Studies in Nature of Modern Math
Paideuma [*Frankfurt*] — Paid
Paidologist — PAIDOL
Pain Francais — Pain Fr
Pain. Supplement — Pain Suppl
Paine, Webber, Jackson & Curtis, Inc. Research Notes — Paine Webb
Paint and Colour Record — Paint Colour Rec
Paint and Ink International — Paint Ink Int
Paint and Resin — Paint Res
Paint and Resin International — Paint Resin Int
Paint and Resin News — PMF
Paint and Varnish Production — P & V Prod
Paint and Varnish Production — Paint Varn Prod
Paint and Varnish Production Manager — Paint Varn Prod Manager
Paint Colour; Journal of the Master Painter of Australia — Paint Colour J Master Painter Aust
Paint, Colour, Oil, Varnish, Ink, Lacquer, Manufacture — Paint Colour Oil Varn Ink Lacquer Manuf
Paint Industry — Paint Ind
Paint Industry Magazine — Paint Ind Mag
Paint Journal — Paint J
Paint Journal of Australia and New Zealand — Paint J
Paint Journal of Australia and New Zealand — Paint J Aust NZ
Paint Manufacture [*England*] — Paint Manuf
Paint Manufacture and Resin News — Paint Manuf Resin News
Paint Manufacturers Association. United States. Technical Circulars. Educational Bureau. Scientific Section — Paint Manuf Assoc US Tech Circ Educ Bur Sci Sect
Paint Oil and Chemical Review — Paint Oil Chem Rev
Paint Oil and Colour Journal — Paint Oil Colour J
Paint Technology — Paint Technol
Paint, Varnish, Lacquer, Enamel, and Colour Manufacture — Paint Varn Lacquer Enamel Colour Manuf
Paintbrush — Paint
Painters and Allied Trades Journal — Painters J
Painters Magazine — Painters Mag
Paintindia. Annual — Paintindia Annu
Painting and Decorating — Paint Decor
Painting and Decorating Journal — Paint Dec J
Painting Technology (Tokyo) — Painting Technol (Tokyo)
Paints in Pakistan — Paints Pak
PAIS [*Public Affairs Information Service*] **Bulletin** — PAIS Bull
PAIS [*Public Affairs Information Service*] **Foreign Language Index** — PAIS Foreign Lang Index
Paix et Droit [*Paris*] — PD
Pajarita de Papel — PajP
Pakistan Academy of Sciences. Proceedings — Pak Acad Sci Proc
Pakistan Academy of Sciences. Transactions — Pak Acad Sci Trans
Pakistan Agriculture — Pak Agric
Pakistan and Gulf Economist — PKE
Pakistan Association for the Advancement of Science. Annual Report — Pak Assoc Adv Sci Annu Rep
Pakistan Association for the Advancement of Science. Scientific Monograph — Pak Assoc Adv Sci Sci Monogr
Pakistan. Atomic Energy Centre. Report — Pak At Energy Cent Rep
Pakistan Congress of Zoology. Proceedings — Pak Congr Zool Proc
Pakistan Cottons — Pak Cottons
Pakistan Council of Scientific and Industrial Research. Bulletin. Monograph [*A publication*] — Pak CSIR Bull Monogr
Pakistan Dental Review — Pak Dent Rev
Pakistan Development Review — Pak Dev R
Pakistan Development Review — Pak Dev Rev
Pakistan Development Review — Pak DR
Pakistan Development Review — Pakistan Develop R
Pakistan Development Review — PDB
Pakistan Development Review — PDR
Pakistan Development Review — PKDR-B
Pakistan Economic and Social Review — Pakistan Econ and Social R
Pakistan Economic Journal — PEJ
Pakistan Educational Review — Pak Ed Rev
Pakistan Engineer — Pak Eng
Pakistan Engineer — Pakistan Eng
Pakistan Geographical Review — Pak Geogr R
Pakistan Geographical Review — Pak Geogr Rev
Pakistan Geographical Review — PGR
Pakistan Geological Survey. Information Release — Pak Geol Surv Inf Release
Pakistan. Geological Survey. Interim Geological Report — Pak Geol Surv Interim Geol Rep
Pakistan Geological Survey. Records — Pak Geol Surv Rec
Pakistan Historical Society. Journal — JPHS
Pakistan Historical Society. Journal — PHS
Pakistan Historical Society. Memoir — PHSM
Pakistan History Conference. Proceedings — PPHC
Pakistan Horizon — PH
Pakistan Journal of Agricultural Research — Pak J Agri Res
Pakistan Journal of Agricultural Sciences — Pak J Agric Sci
Pakistan Journal of Agricultural Sciences — Pakist J Agric Sci

Pakistan Journal of Biochemistry — Pak J Biochem
Pakistan Journal of Biological and Agricultural Sciences — Pak J Biol Agric Sci
Pakistan Journal of Biological and Agricultural Sciences — Pakistan J Biol Agr Sci
Pakistan Journal of Botany — Pak J Bot
Pakistan Journal of Botany — Pakist J Bot
Pakistan Journal of Family Planning — Pak J Fam Plann
Pakistan Journal of Forestry — Pak J For
Pakistan Journal of Forestry — Pakistan J For
Pakistan Journal of Geriatrics — Pak J Geriatr
Pakistan Journal of Health — Pak J Health
Pakistan Journal of Hydrocarbon Research — Pak J Hydrocarb Res
Pakistan Journal of Medical Research — Pak J Med Res
Pakistan Journal of Medical Research — Pakistan J Med Res
Pakistan Journal of Nematology — Pak J Nematol
Pakistan Journal of Nematology — PJNEE5
Pakistan Journal of Pharmaceutical Sciences — Pak J Pharm Sci
Pakistan Journal of Pharmacology — Pak J Pharmacol
Pakistan Journal of Pharmacy — Pak J Pharm
Pakistan Journal of Psychology — PJOPA
Pakistan Journal of Science — Pak J Sci
Pakistan Journal of Science — Pakistan J Sci
Pakistan Journal of Scientific and Industrial Research — Pak J Sci and Ind Res
Pakistan Journal of Scientific and Industrial Research — Pak J Sci Ind Res
Pakistan Journal of Scientific and Industrial Research — Pakistan J Sci Ind Res
Pakistan Journal of Scientific Research — Pak J Sci Res
Pakistan Journal of Scientific Research — Pakist J Scient Res
Pakistan Journal of Scientific Research — Pakistan J Sci Res
Pakistan Journal of Scientific Research — PJSRA
Pakistan Journal of Soil Sciences — Pakistan J Soil Sci
Pakistan Journal of Statistics — Pakistan J Statist
Pakistan Journal of Surgery, Gynaecology, and Obstetrics — Pak J Surg Gyn Obst
Pakistan Journal of Surgery, Gynaecology, and Obstetrics — Pak J Surg Gynaecol Obstet
Pakistan Journal of Zoology — Pak J Zool
Pakistan Journal of Zoology — Pakist J Zool
Pakistan Labour Gazette — PLG
Pakistan Library Association. Quarterly Journal — Pak Libr Ass Q J
Pakistan Library Bulletin — Pakistan Lib Bull
Pakistan Library Review — Pak Libr Rev
Pakistan Library Review — Pakistan Lib R
Pakistan Management Review — Pak Manage Rev
Pakistan Medical Forum — Pak Med For
Pakistan Medical Forum — Pak Med Forum
Pakistan Medical Journal — Pak Med J
Pakistan Medical Review — Pak Med Rev
Pakistan Nursing and Health Review — Pak Nurs Health Rev
Pakistan Philosophical Congress. Proceedings — Pak Philos Congr Proc
Pakistan Philosophical Journal — Pakistan Phil J
Pakistan Philosophical Journal — PPJ
Pakistan Quarterly — PakQ
Pakistan Quarterly — PQ
Pakistan Review — PakR
Pakistan Review — PR
Pakistan Review of Agriculture — Pak Rev Agric
Pakistan Science Conference. Proceedings — Pak Sci Conf Proc
Pakistan Textile Journal — Pak Text J
Pakistan Veterinary Journal — Pak Vet J
Palabra y el Hombre — Palabra Hom
Palabra y el Hombre. Revista de la Universidad Veracruzana — PH
Palace of Minos — PM
Palace of Minos — PoM
Palace of Nestor at Pylos in Western Messenia — PN
Palacio — P
Palaentologia Indica — Palaeontol Indica
Palaeoecology of Africa and the Surrounding Islands — Palaeoecol Afr Surround Isl
Palaeogeography, Palaeoclimatology, Palaeoecology — Palaeogeo P
Palaeogeography, Palaeoclimatology, Palaeoecology — Palaeogeogr Palaeoclimatol Palaeoecol
Palaeographia Latina — PL
Palaeographical Society. Facsimiles of Manuscripts and Inscriptions — Pal Soc
Palaeohistoria. Acta et Communicationes Instituti Bio-Archaeologici Universitatis Groninganae — Palaeo
Palaeontographia Italia — Palaeontogr Ital
Palaeontographica — Pal
Palaeontographica — Palaeont
Palaeontographica. Abteilung A. Palaeozoologie-Stratigraphie — Palaeontogr Abt A
Palaeontographica. Abteilung A. Palaeozoologie-Stratigraphie — Palaeontogr Abt A Palaeozool-Stratigr
Palaeontographica. Abteilung B. Palaeophytologie — Palaeontogr Abt B
Palaeontographica. Abteilung B. Palaeophytologie — Palaeontogr Abt B Palaeophytol
Palaeontographica Americana — Palaeontogr Am
Palaeontographica Canadiana — Palaeontogr Can
Palaeontographical Society. Monographs — Palaeont Soc Mon
Palaeontographical Society. Monographs — Palaeontogr Soc Monogr
Palaeontographical Society. Monographs (London) — Palaeontogr Soc Monogr (Lond)
Palaeontologia Africana — Palaeontol Afr
Palaeontologia Jugoslavica — Palaeontol Jugosl
Palaeontologia Jugoslavica — Palaeontol Jugoslav
Palaeontologia Mexicana. Instituto de Geologia (Mexico) — Palaeontol Mex Inst Geol (Mex)
Palaeontologia Polonica — Palaeontol Pol
Palaeontologia Sinica. Series B — Palaeontol Sin Ser B
Palaeontologia Sinica. Series C — Palaeontol Sin Ser C
Palaeontologia Sinica. Series D — Palaeontol Sin Ser D
Palaeontological Society of Japan. Special Papers — Palaeontol Soc Jpn Spec Pap
Palaeontological Society of Japan. Transactions and Proceedings — Palaeont Soc Japan Trans and Proc
Palaeontological Society of Japan. Transactions and Proceedings. New Series [*A publication*] — Palaeontol Soc Japan Trans Proc NS
Palaeontologische Abhandlungen — Palaeontol Abh
Palaeontologische Abhandlungen (Dames und Kayser) — Palaeont Abh (Dames u Kayser)
Palaeontologische Zeitschrift — Palaeont Zeitschr
Palaeontologische Zeitschrift — Palaeont Zs
Palaeontologische Zeitschrift — Palaeontol Z
Palaeontology Papers. Geological Survey of Queensland — Palaeontol Pap Publ Geol Surv Queensl
Palaeontology, Stratigraphy, and Lithology — Palaeontol Stratigr Lithol
Palaeovertebrata. Memoire Extraordinaire — Palaeovertebrata. Mem Extraordinaire
Palaeovertebrata (Montpellier) — Palaeovertebr (Montp)
Palaestina Treuhandstelle zur Beratung Deutscher Juden — PALTREU
Palaestina Treuhandstelle zur Beratung Deutscher Juden — PATREU
Palaestinahefte des Deutschen Vereins vom Heiligen Lande — PDVHL
Palaestina-Jahrbuch — PalJ
Palaestina-Jahrbuch — PalJb
Palaestra — P
Palaestra Latina — Pal Lat
Palais Royal d'Ugarit — PRU
Palastinajahrbuch. Deutsches Evangelische Institut fuer Altertumswissenschaft des Heiligen Landes zu Jerusalem [*Berlin*] — PJ
Palastinajahrbuch. Deutsches Evangelische Institut fuer Altertumswissenschaft des Heiligen Landes zu Jerusalem [*Berlin*] — PJB
Paleis van Justitie. Nieuwsblad Gewijd aan Binnen- en Buitenlandse Rechtspleging — PvJ
Palenque Literario — PalL
Paleobiologie Continentale — Paleobiol Cont
Paleographie Musicale — Pal Mus
Paleographie Musicale — PM
Paleolimnology of Lake Biwa and the Japanese Pleistocene — Paleolimnol Lake Biwa Jpn Pleistocene
Paleonapryazhennost. Fizicheskie Osnovy i Metody Issledovaniya — Paleonapryazhennost Fiz Osn Metody Issled
Paleontologia Mexicana — Paleontol Mex
Paleontologia y Evolucion-Barcelona. Instituto Provincial de Paleontologia — Paleontol Evol-Barc Inst Prov Paleontol
Paleontological Bulletins — Pal B
Paleontological Journal — Paleontol J
Paleontological Journal (English Translation of Paleontologicheskii Zhurnal) — Paleontol J (Engl Transl Paleontol Zh)
Paleontological Research Laboratories. Special Investigation. Report — Paleont Research Lab Special Inv Rept
Paleontological Society. Memoir — Paleontol Soc Mem
Paleontologiceskij Sbornik. Lvov — Paleontol Sborn Lvov
Paleontologiceskij Sbornik. Moscow and Leningrad — Paleontol Sborn Moscow Leningrad
Paleontologicheskii Zhurnal — Paleontol Zh
Paleontologicheskiy Sbornik — Paleontol Sb
Paleontologiya Stratigrafiya i Litologiya — Paleontol Stratigr Litol
Paleontology Papers. Publications. Geological Survey of Queensland — Paleont Pap Publs Geol Suv QD
Paleopathological Newsletter — Paleopathol Newsl
Palestine — P
Palestine Affairs — PA
Palestine Board for Scientific and Industrial Research. Reports — Palest Board Sci Ind Res Rep
Palestine Citrograph — Palest Citrogr
Palestine Correspondence — PALCOR
Palestine Economist — Palest Econ
Palestine Exploration Fund Annual [*London*] — Pal EFA
Palestine Exploration Fund. Annual — PEFA
Palestine Exploration Fund. Memoirs — PEFM
Palestine Exploration Fund. Quarterly Statement — PEFQ
Palestine Exploration Fund. Quarterly Statement — PEFQSt
Palestine Exploration Fund. Quarterly Statement — PQS
Palestine Exploration Quarterly — Pal Ex Q
Palestine Exploration Quarterly [*London*] — Pal Expl Qu
Palestine Exploration Quarterly — PalEQ
Palestine Exploration Quarterly [*London*] — Palest Expl Quarterly
Palestine Exploration Quarterly — Palestine Explor Q
Palestine Exploration Quarterly — Palestine Explor Quart
Palestine Exploration Quarterly — PEQ
Palestine Exploration Quarterly (London) — PEQL
Palestine Gazette — PG
Palestine. Government. Board for Scientific and Industrial Research. Reports — Palest Gov Board Sci Ind Res Rep
Palestine Journal of Botany and Horticultural Science — Palest J Bot Hortic Sci
Palestine Journal of Botany. Jerusalem Series — Palest J Bot Jerus Ser
Palestine Journal of Botany. Jerusalem Series — Palest J Bot Jerusalem Ser
Palestine Journal of Botany. Rehovot Series — Palest J Bot Rehovot Ser
Palestine Law Reports — PLR
Palestine Pilgrims Text Society — PPTS

Palestine Post — PP
Palestine Tribune — Palest Trib
Palestinskii Sbornik — Pal Sbor
Palestinskii Sbornik — Pal Sborn
Palestinskii Sbornik [*Moscow/Leningrad*] — PalSb
Palestinskii Sbornik — PS
Palestinskii Sbornik — PSb
Palestra del Clero [*Rovigo, Italy*] — PalCl
Palestra Oftalmologica Panamericana — Palestra Oftalmol Panam
Pali Text Society — Pali Text Soc
Pali Text Society — PTS
Pali Text Society Translation Series — PTSTS
Palimpsest — P
Palimpsest — Pal
Pall Mall Magazine — Pall Mall M
Pall Mall Magazine — PMM
Palladio. Rivista di Storia dell'Architettura — Palladio
Palliative Medicine — Palliat Med
Palsgrave Dictionary — PALSGR
Palyavalasztasi Tanacsadas — Palyaval Tanacs
Palynological Bulletin — Palynol Bull
Pamatky a Priroda — Pamatky Prir
Pamatky Archaeologicke. Skupina Historicka — PAH
Pamatky Archaeologicke. Skupina Praveka — PAP
Pamatky Archeologicke — PA
Pamatky Archeologicke — Pam A
Pamatky Archeologicke — Pam Arch
Pamatky Archeologicke — Pamatky Arch
Pamatky Archeologicke — Pamatky Archeol
Pamatky - Priroda - Zivot — Pamatky Prir Zivot
Pam'iatniki Kul'tury. Novye Otkrytiia — PK
Pam'iatniki Turkmenistana — Pam Turkm
Pamietnik Akademii Umiejetnosci Krakowie — PAU
Pamietnik Akademii Umiejetnosci W Krakowie. Wydzial Matematiczne-Przyrodniczy — Pamietn Akad Umiejetn W Krakowie Wydz Mat Przyr
Pamietnik Biblioteki Kornickiej — PBK
Pamietnik Farmaceutyczny — Pamiet Farm
Pamietnik i Wiadomosci Farmaceutyczne — Pamiet Wiad Farm
Pamietnik Konferencji Naukowej Otolaryngologii Dzieciecej Zakopane — Pamiet Konf Nauk Otolaryngol Dzieciecej Zakopane
Pamietnik Literacki — Pamietnik L
Pamietnik Literacki — PamL
Pamietnik Literacki — PL
Pamietnik Pulawski — Pam Pulaw
Pamietnik Pulawski — Pam Pulawski
Pamietnik Pulawski — Pamiet Pulawski
Pamietnik Slowianski — Pa Slow
Pamietnik Slowianski — Pam Slow
Pamietnik Slowianski — PaS
Pamietnik Slowianski — PS
Pamietnik Slowianski Czasopismo Naukowe Posiecone Slowianoznawstwu — PamSL
Pamietnik Teatralny — PT
Pamietnik Zjazdu Otolaryngologow Polskich w Katowicach — Pamiet Zjazdu Otolaryngol Pol Katowicach
Pamietniki Zjazdow Polskiego Zwiazku Entomologicznego — PZE
Pamjatniki Russkogo Prava — PRP
Pamphlet. Amateur Entomologists' Society — Pamph Amat Ent Soc
Pamphlet Architecture — Pamphlet Archre
Pamphlet Bible Series — PBiS
Pamphlet. Department of Agriculture (Queensland) — Pamph Dep Agric (Qd)
Pamphlet. Department of Agriculture (Tanganyika Territory) — Pamph Dep Agric (Tanganyika)
Pamphlet. Department of Agriculture. Union of South Africa — Pamph Dep Agric Un S Afr
Pamphlet. Division of Scientific Publications. Volcani Center. Agricultural Research Organisation — Pamph Div Sci Publs Volcani Cent Agric Res Orgn
Pamphlet. Division of Wood Technology. Forestry Commission. New South Wales — Pam Div Wood Technol For Comm NSW
Pamphlet. Division of Wood Technology. Forestry Commission. New South Wales — Pamph Div Wood Technol For Comm NSW
Pamphlet. Forestry Research and Education Project. Forests Department (Khartoum, Sudan) — Pamphl For Res Educ Proj For Dep (Sudan)
Pamphlet. Idaho Bureau of Mines and Geology — Pamph Idaho Bur Mines Geol
Pamphlet. Iowa State University of Science and Technology. Cooperative Extension Service — Pam Iowa State Univ Sci Tech Coop Ext Serv
Pamphlet. Tea Research Institute of Ceylon — Pam Tea Res Inst Ceylon
Pamphlet. Vermont Agricultural Experiment Station — Pam Vt Agric Exp Stn
Pamphlet. Volcani Center (Bet Dagan, Israel) — Pam Volcani Cent Bet Dagan Isr
Pamphlet. Volcani Institute of Agricultural Research — Pamph Volcani Inst Agric Res
Pamphleteer — P
Pamphleteer — Pamph
Pamphlets. Anglo-Israel Association — PAIA
Pamphlets of Lewis Carroll — Pam Lewis Carroll
Pan American — PAm
Pan American Fisherman — Pan Am Fisherman
Pan American Health Organization. Official Document — Pan Am Health Organ Off Doc
Pan American Health Organization. Research in Progress — Pan Am Health Organ Res Prog
Pan American Health Organization. Scientific Publication — Pan Am Health Organ Sci Publ
Pan American Institute of Mining Engineering and Geology. United States Section. Technical Paper — Pan Am Inst Min Eng Geol US Sect Tech Pap
Pan American Magazine — Pan Am M
Pan American Magazine — Pan Am Mag
Pan American Magazine (Washington, DC) — Pan Am Mag Wash
Pan American Review — PanAR
Pan American Union. Boletin de Ciencia y Tecnologia — Pan Am Union Bol Ciencia y Tecnologia
Pan American Union. Bulletin — Pan Am Union Bul
Pan American Woman's Journal — Pan Am Womans J
Pan Indian Ocean Science Congress. Proceedings. Section D. Agricultural Sciences — Pan Indian Ocean Sci Congr Proc Sect D Agr Sci
Pan Pipes — PP
Pan Pipes of Sigma Alpha Iota — Pan Pipes
Pan. Studi dell'Istituto di Filologia Latina — PSIFL
Panache — Pan
Pan-African Journal — PAJ
Pan-African Journal — Pan Afr J
Pan-African Journal — Pan Afr Jnl
Pan-African Journal — PanA
Pan-Africanist — PanA
Panama This Month (Panama) — Panama Month Panama
Panama Universidad. Departamento de Geografia. Publicacion — Panama Univ Dept Geografia Pub
Pan-America (Tegucigalpa) — Pan Am Tegucigalpa
Pan-American Institute of Geography and History. Publication — Pan-Am Inst Geography and History Pub
Panamerican Mathematical Journal — Panamer Math J
Pan-American Medical Congress. Transactions — Pan Am Med Cong Trans
Panamericana Comercial (Washington, DC) — Panam Comer Wash
Pandectes Belges — Pand B
Pandectes Periodiques — Pand Per
Panhandle Geological Society. Stratigraphic Cross Section — Panhandle Geol Soc Strat Cross Sec
Panjab Geographical Review — Panjab Geogr Rev
Panjab University (Chandigarh). Centre of Advanced Study in Geology. Publication — Panjab Univ (Chandigarh) Cent Adv Stu Geol Publ
Panjab University. Research Bulletin (Arts) — PURBA
Panjabi Adabi Academy. Publication — PAAP
Panminerva Medica — Panminerva Med
Pannonhalmi Szemle — P Sz
Pannonhalmi Szemle — Pann Szle
Panorama — Pan
Panorama de la Musique et des Instruments — Panorama M Instruments
Panorama Democrate Chretien — Panorama Democr Chr
Panorama Economico (Chile). Segunda Epoca — Panorama Econ (Chile) 2a Epoca
Panorama Economico (Mexico) — Panorama Econ (Mexico)
Panoramas et Syntheses — Panor Synth
Panoramas et Syntheses — Panor Syntheses
Pan-Pacific Entomologist — Pan-Pac Ent
Pan-Pacific Entomologist — Pan-Pac Entomol
Pan-Pacific Entomologist — Pan-Pacif Ent
Panpipes of Sigma Alpha Iota — Panp
PANS. Pest Articles and News Summaries — PANS Pest Artic News Summ
PANS. Pest Articles and News Summaries. Section C. Weed Control — PANS Sect C Weed Control
Panstwo i Prawo — Pan i Prawo
Panstwo i Prawo — PP
Panstwowa Sluzba Geologiczna. Pantswowy Instytut. Geologiczny Biuletyn — Panstw Sluzba Geol Panstw Inst Geol Biul
Panstwowe Wydawnictwo Naukowe — PWN
Panstwowe Wydawnictwo Techniczne — PWT
Panstwowe Zaklady Wydawnictwo Szkolnych — PZWS
Panta Journal of Medicine — Panta J Med
Pantainos [*Alexandria*] — Pant
Pantheon [*Muenchen*] — Panth
Pantheon Babylonicum: Nomina Deorum — PB
Pantheon. Internationale Zeitschrift fuer Kunst — PIZK
Pantheon Litteraire — Pantheon Litt
Pantnagar Journal of Research — Pantnagar J Res
Panzer Annales — Panz Ann
Papeis Avulsos de Zoologia — Pap Avul Zool
Papeis Avulsos de Zoologia (Sao Paulo) — Pap Avulsos Zool (Sao Paulo)
Papeis Avulsos. Departmento de Zoologia (Sao Paulo) — Pap Avulsos Dep Zool (Sao Paulo)
Papeis Avulsos. Departmento de Zoologia. Secretaria de Agricultura Industria e Comercio (Sao Paulo) — Pap Avulsos Dep Zool Secr Agric Ind Comer (Sao Paulo)
Papeles de Arquelogia — PLAV
Papeles de la India — PDI
Papeles de Son Armadans — PSA
Paper. American Society of Agricultural Engineers — Pap Amer Soc Agr Eng
Paper. American Society of Agricultural Engineers — Pap ASAE
Paper and Board Abstracts — Pap Board Abstr
Paper and Board Abstracts — Paper & Board Abs
Paper and Board Abstracts — Pbd Abstr
Paper and Packaging Bulletin — Paper Bul
Paper and Packaging Bulletin — PAZ
Paper and Printing Digest — Pap Print Dig
Paper and Printing Technics — Pap Print Tech
Paper and Pulp Mill Catalogue/Engineering Handbook — Paper Pulp Mill Catalogue
Paper and Twine Journal — Paper Twine J

Paper. Architectural Science Unit. University of Queensland — Pap Archit Sci Unit Univ Queensl
Paper Chemistry — Pap Chem
Paper Coating Additives — Pap Coat Add
Paper. Commonwealth Forestry Conference — Pap Commonw For Conf
Paper Converting — Pap Converting
Paper. Egyptian Geological Survey — Pap Egypt Geol Surv
Paper. European Journal for the Pulp, Paper, and Board Industries — WPT
Paper. FAO [*Food and Agriculture Organization of the United Nations*]/IUFRO World Consultation on Forest Tree Breeding [*International Union of Forestry Research Organization*] — Pap FAO/IUFRO World Consult For Tree Breed
Paper, Film, and Foil Converter — Pap Film Foil Converter
Paper, Film, and Foil Converter — Paper Film Foil Conv
Paper, Film, and Foil Converter — PFE
Paper, Film, and Foil Converter — PFF Convrt
Paper, Film, and Foil Converter — PFF Convt
Paper Industry — Pap Ind
Paper Industry and Paper World — Pap Ind Pap World
Paper Industry and Paper World — PIPWA
Paper Industry (Moscow) — Pap Ind Moscow
Paper. Institute for Defense Analyses — Pap Inst Def Anal
Paper. International Conference on Fluid Sealing — Pap Int Conf Fluid Sealing
Paper Maker — Paper Mkr
Paper Maker — PM
Paper Maker and British Paper Trade Journal — Pap Maker Br Pap Trade J
Paper Maker and British Paper Trade Journal (London) — Pap Maker (London)
Paper Maker (Wilmington, Delaware) — Pap Maker (Wilmington Del)
Paper Makers and Merchants. Directory of All Nations — Paper Makers Merch Dir
Paper Makers' Association (Great Britain and Ireland). Proceedings of the Technical Section — Pap Makers Assoc (GB Irel) Proc Tech Sect
Paper Makers' Monthly Journal — Pap Makers Mon J
Paper Making and Paper Selling — Pap Making Pap Selling
Paper Making and Selling — Pap Making Selling
Paper Mill and Wood Pulp News — Pap Mill Wood Pulp News
Paper Mill News — Pap Mill News
Paper. Mineral Exploration Research Institute. McGill University — Pap Miner Explor Res Inst McGill Univ
Paper. Ministry of Energy, Mines, and Petroleum Resources (Province of British Columbia) — Pap Minist Energy Mines Pet Resour (Br Columbia)
Paper Money — PM
Paper. Nova Scotia Department of Mines — Pap Nova Scotia Dep Mines
Paper. Nova Scotia Department of Mines and Energy — Pap NS Dep Mines Energy
Paper. Oregon State University. Forest Research Laboratory — Pap Oreg State Univ For Res Lab
Paper. Province of Nova Scotia. Department of Mines — Pap Prov NS Dep Mines
Paper. SESA [*Society for Experimental Stress Analysis*] — Pap SESA
Paper Southern Africa — Pap Sthn Afr
Paper Synthetics Conference. Proceedings [*United States*] — Pap Synth Conf Proc
Paper. Technical Meeting. International Union for the Conservation of Nature and Natural Resources — Pap Tech Mtg Int Union Conserv Nature
Paper Technology [*England*] — Pap Technol
Paper Technology — Paper Technol
Paper Technology and Industry — Pap Technol
Paper Technology and Industry — Pap Technol Ind
Paper Technology and Industry — Paper Technol Ind
Paper Technology and Industry — PTIND
Paper Technology (Bury, United Kingdom) — Pap Technol Bury UK
Paper Technology (London) — Pap Technol London
Paper Trade Journal — Pa Tr J
Paper Trade Journal — Pa Trade J
Paper Trade Journal — Pap Trade J
Paper Trade Journal — Paper Jour
Paper Trade Journal — Paper Tr J
Paper Trade Journal — PAT
Paper Trade Review — Pap Trade Rev
Paper. United States Geological Survey. Water Supply — Pap US Geol Surv Wat Supply
Paper. University of Maine. Technology Experiment Station — Pap Univ Maine Technol Exp Stn
Paper. University of Missouri-Columbia. Department of Agricultural Economics — Pap Univ MO-Columbia Dep Agric Econ
Paper World — Pap World
Paper Year Book — Paper Yrb
Paperboard Packaging — Papbrd Pkg
Paperboard Packaging — Paperboard Packag
Paperboard Packaging — Paperboard Pkg
Paperboard Packaging — Pbd Pkg
Paperbound Books in Print — PBIP
Paperbound Books in Print — PBP
Paperi ja Puu — P j P
Paperi ja Puu — Pap ja Puu
Paperi ja Puu. A Painos — Pap Puu A Painos
Paperi ja Puu. A Painos — Pap Puu Painos
Paperi ja Puu. B Painos — Pap Puu B Painos
Paperi ja Puu - Papper och Tra — Pap Puu
Papermakers Conference. Proceedings — Papermakers Conf Proc
Papers. American Chemical Society. Division of Paint, Plastics, and Printing Ink — Pap Am Chem Soc Div Paint Plast Print Ink
Papers. American Musicological Society — PAMS
Papers. American School of Classical Studies [*Athens*] — PAS
Papers. American School of Classical Studies at Athens — Pap Am Sch Ath
Papers. American School of Classical Studies at Athens — Papers ASA
Papers. American School of Classical Studies at Athens — PAS Ath
Papers. American School of Classical Studies at Athens — PAS Cl St
Papers. American School of Classical Studies at Athens — PASA
Papers. American Society of Church History — Pap Am Soc Ch Hist
Papers. American Society of Church History — PASCH
Papers and Monographs. American Academy in Rome — PMAAR
Papers and Presentations-Proceedings. Digital Equipment Computer Users Society — Pap Presentations Proc Digital Equip Comput Users Soc
Papers and Proceedings. Hampshire Field Club and Archaeological Society — P Proc Hampshire Field Club
Papers and Proceedings. Royal Society of Tasmania — Pap Proc R Soc Tas
Papers and Proceedings. Royal Society of Tasmania — Pap Proc R Soc Tasm
Papers and Proceedings. Royal Society of Tasmania — Pap Proc R Soc Tasmania
Papers and Proceedings. Royal Society of Tasmania — Papers & Proc Roy Soc Tas
Papers and Proceedings. Royal Society of Tasmania — Papers and Proc Roy Soc Tasmania
Papers and Proceedings. Royal Society of Tasmania — Papers Proc Roy Soc Tasmania
Papers and Proceedings. Royal Society of Van Diemen's Land — Pap Proc Roy Soc Van Diemens Land
Papers and Proceedings. Tasmanian Historical Research Association — Papers & Proc Tas Hist Res Assn
Papers and Studies in Contrastive Linguistics — PSCL
Papers. Annual Conference. Textile Institute (Manchester, United Kingdom) — Pap Annu Conf Text Inst (Manchester UK)
Papers. Annual Meeting. Canadian Pest Management Society — Pap Annu Meet Can Pest Manage Soc
Papers. Bibliographical Society of America — Pap Bibl Soc Am
Papers. Bibliographical Society of America — Pap Bibliog
Papers. Bibliographical Society of America — Pap Biblog Soc Am
Papers. Bibliographical Society of America — Pap Bibliogr Soc Am
Papers. Bibliographical Society of America — Pap Bibliogr Soc Amer
Papers. Bibliographical Society of America — Papers Biblio Soc Am
Papers. Bibliographical Society of America — PBSA
Papers. Bibliographical Society of Canada — PBSC
Papers. Bibliographical Society. University of Virginia — PBSUV
Papers. British School at Rome — BSR
Papers. British School at Rome — BSR Papers
Papers. British School at Rome — BSRP
Papers. British School at Rome — Pap Brit Sch Rome
Papers. British School at Rome — Pap Brit School Rome
Papers. British School at Rome — Papers B S Rome
Papers. British School at Rome — Papers Br Sch Rome
Papers. British School at Rome — Papers Brit School Rome
Papers. British School at Rome — PBSR
Papers. Coal Utilization Symposium. Focus on SO_2 Emission Control — Pap Coal Util Symp Focus SO_2 Emiss Control
Papers. Congress of the Federation Internationale de la Precontrainte — Pap Congr Fed Int Precontrainte
Papers. Czechoslovak Soil Science Conference — Pap Czech Soil Sci Conf
Papers. Department of Agriculture. University of Queensland — Pap Dep Agric QD Univ
Papers. Department of Botany. McGill University — Pap Dep Bot McGill Univ
Papers. Department of Entomology. University of Queensland — Pap Dep Entomol Univ Queensl
Papers. Department of Geology. University of Queensland — Pap Dep Geol QD Univ
Papers. Department of Geology. University of Queensland — Pap Dep Geol Queensl Univ
Papers. Department of Geology. University of Queensland — Pap Dep Geol Univ QD
Papers. Department of Zoology. University of Queensland — Pap Dep Zool QD Univ
Papers. Eastbourne Natural History Society — Pap Eastbourne Nat Hist Soc
Papers. Estonian Theological Society in Exile — PETSE
Papers from the Convention. American Nurses' Association — Pap Conv Am Nurs Assoc
Papers from the Eranos Yearbooks — PEY
Papers. Geological Survey of Canada — Pap Geol Surv Can
Papers. Geological Survey of Egypt — Pap Geol Surv Egypt
Papers. Gifu University. School of Medicine [*Japan*] — Pap Gifu Univ Sch Med
Papers. Great Barrier Reef Committee — Pap Grt Barrier Reef Comm
Papers in Anthropology [*Oklahoma*] — Pap Anthro
Papers in Australian Linguistics — PAusL
Papers in Borneo Linguistics — Pap Borneo Ling
Papers in Borneo Linguistics — PBL
Papers in Education (Anstey College of Physical Education) — Papers in Ed (Anstey Coll)
Papers in International Studies. Africa Series. Ohio University — Pap Is Afr
Papers in International Studies. Africa Series. Ohio University — PSAS
Papers in International Studies. Southeast Asia Series. Ohio University — Pap Is Se A
Papers in International Studies. Southeast Asia Series. Ohio University — PSSEAS
Papers in Linguistics — Pap Ling
Papers in Linguistics — PIL
Papers in Linguistics — PL
Papers in Linguistics — PLing
Papers in Linguistics of Melanesia — PLM
Papers in Meteorology and Geophysics — Pap Met Geo
Papers in Meteorology and Geophysics — Pap Meteorol Geophys

Papers in Meteorology and Geophysics (Tokyo) — Pap Meteorol Geophys (Tokyo)
Papers in New Guinea Linguistics — PNGL
Papers in Philippine Linguistics — P Ph L
Papers in Philippine Linguistics. Pacific Linguistics. Series A [*Canberra*] — Pap Phil Ling
Papers in Romance — P Rom
Papers in Science Series — Pap Sci Ser
Papers in Slavonic Linguistics — Pap Slav Ling
Papers in South East Asian Linguistics — PSEAL
Papers in South East Asian Linguistics. Pacific Linguistics. Series A [*Canberra*] — Pap SE As Ling
Papers. Institute for Thermal Spring Research. Okayama University — Pap Inst Therm Spring Res Okayama Univ
Papers. Institute of Jewish Studies — PIJS
Papers. International Association of Agricultural Librarians and Documentalists. World Congress — Pap IAALD World Congr
Papers. International Conference on Liquefied Natural Gas — Pap Int Conf Liquefied Nat Gas
Papers. International Institute on the Prevention and Treatment of Alcoholism — Pap Int Inst Prev Treat Alcohol
Papers. International Institute on the Prevention and Treatment of Drug Dependence — Pap Int Inst Prev Treat Drug Depend
Papers. Kroeber Anthropological Society — Pap Kroeber Anthropol Soc
Papers. Laboratory of Tree-Ring Research. University of Arizona — Pap Lab Tree-Ring Res Univ Ariz
Papers. Meeting. American Chemical Society. Division of Organic Coatings and Plastics Chemistry — Pap Meet Am Chem Soc Div Org Coat Plast Chem
Papers. Michigan Academy of Science, Arts, and Letters — Pap Mich Acad
Papers. Michigan Academy of Science, Arts, and Letters — Pap Mich Acad Sci
Papers. Michigan Academy of Science, Arts, and Letters — Pap Mich Acad Sci Arts Lett
Papers. Midwest Modern Language Association — PMMLA
Papers. National Conference for Professional Nurses and Physicians [*US*] — Pap Natl Conf Prof Nurses Physicians
Papers. New Haven Colony Historical Society — Pap N Haven Col Hist Soc
Papers. Norwegian State Game Research Institute — Pap Norw State Game Res Inst
Papers of the Commission on Ceramical Sciences. Ceramics — Pap Comm Ceram Sci Ceram
Papers on Far Eastern History — Pap Far Eas
Papers on Far Eastern History [*Australia*] — Pap Far East Hist
Papers on Far Eastern History — Papers Far East Hist
Papers on Far Eastern History — PFEH
Papers on French Seventeenth Century Literature — PFSCL
Papers on General Topology and Applications. Summer Conference at Slippery Rock University — Pap Gen Topol Appl Summer Conf Slippery Rock Univ
Papers on Japan — PJa
Papers on Language and Literature — Pa Lang & Lit
Papers on Language and Literature — Pap Lang L
Papers on Language and Literature — Pap Lang Lit
Papers on Language and Literature — PLL
Papers on Language and Literature — PPLL
Papers on Plant Genetics — Pap Pl Genet
Papers on Poetics and Semiotics — PP & S
Papers. Ontario Industrial Waste Conference — Pap Ont Ind Waste Conf
Papers. Ou Testamentiese Werkgemeenskap in Suid-Afrika — OTWSAP
Papers. Peabody Museum of Archaeology and Ethnology. Harvard University — Pap Peabody Mus Archaeol Ethnol Harv Univ
Papers. Pedagogical Faculty in Ostrava — Pap Pedagog Fac Ostrava
Papers. Portland Cement Association Fellowship at the National Bureau of Standards — Pap Portland Cem Assoc Fellowship Natl Bur Stand
Papers Presented at the Annual Conference. Rural Electric Power Conference — Pap Presented Annu Conf Rural Electr Power Conf
Papers Presented at the Annual Convention. Western Canada Water and Sewage Conference — Pap Annu Conv West Can Water Sewage Conf
Papers Presented before the Symposium on Coal Management Techniques — Pap Symp Coal Manage Tech
Papers Presented before the Symposium on Coal Mine Drainage Research — Pap Symp Coal Mine Drainage Res
Papers Presented before the Symposium on Coal Preparation and Utilization [*A publication*] — Pap Symp Coal Prep Util
Papers Presented before the Symposium on Coal Preparation (Washington, DC) [*A publication*] — Pap Symp Coal Prep (Washington DC)
Papers Presented before the Symposium on Coal Utilization — Pap Symp Coal Util
Papers Presented before the Symposium on Management — Pap Symp Manage
Papers Presented before the Symposium on Surface Mining and Reclamation — Pap Symp Surf Min Reclam
Papers Presented before the Symposium on Underground Mining — Pap Symp Underground Min
Papers. Regional Meeting. Chicago Linguistics Society — PRMCLS
Papers. Research and Applied Technology Symposium on Mined-Land Reclamation — Pap Res Appl Technol Symp Mined Land Reclam
Papers. Research Conference. Meat Industry of New Zealand — Pap Res Conf Meat Ind NZ
Papers. Revista de Sociologia — Pap R Sociol
Papers. Ship Research Institute — PSRIA
Papers. Ship Research Institute (Tokyo) — Pap Ship Res Inst (Tokyo)
Papers. South Shields Archaeological and Historical Society — Pap S Shields Archaeol Hist Soc
Papers. Symposium on Mine and Preparation Plant Refuse Disposal — Pap Symp Mine Prep Plant Refuse Disposal
Papers. Symposium on Surface Coal Mining and Reclamation — Pap Symp Surf Coal Min Reclam
Papers. University of Queensland. Department of Geology — Pap Univ Queensland Dep Geol
Papers. Western Region Home Management Family Economics Educators. Annual Conference — Pap West Reg Home Manage Fam Econ Educ Annu Conf
Papeterie. Numero Special — Papeterie Numero Spec
Papier. Carton et Cellulose — Pap Carton Cellul
Papier (Darmstadt). Beilage — Papier (Darmstadt) Beil
Papier Geschichte — Papiergesch
Papier und Druck — Pap Druck
Papier und Druck — PD
Papier- und Kunststoffverarbeiter — Papierverarb
Papiere zur Textlinguistik [*Papers in Textlinguistics*] — PText
Papierfabrikant — PapF
Papierfabrikant - Wochenblatt fuer Papierfabrikation — Papierfabr Wochenbl Papierfabr
Papier-Zeitung — Pap Ztg
Papir a Celuloza — Pap Celul
Papir es Nyomdatechnika — Pap Nyomdatech
Papiri Milanesi — P Mil
Papiri. Universita degli Studi di Milano — PRUM
Papiri. Universita degli Studi di Milano — PUSM
Papiripar es Magyar Grafika — Papirip Magy Grafika
Papir-Journalen — Pap J
Papoli e Civilta dell'Italia Antica — PCIA
Papper och Trae — POT
Pappers och Traevarutidskrift foer Finland — Papp Traevarutidskr Finl
Papsturkunden in Portugal — PUP
Papsturkunden in Spanien — PUS
Papua and New Guinea Agricultural Gazette — Papua New Guinea Agric Gaz
Papua and New Guinea Agricultural Journal — Papua New Guin Agric J
Papua and New Guinea Agricultural Journal — Papua New Guinea Agr J
Papua and New Guinea Agricultural Journal — Papua New Guinea Agric J
Papua and New Guinea Journal of Education — Papua New Guinea J Ed
Papua and New Guinea Law Reports — P & NGLR
Papua and New Guinea Law Reports — Papua & NG
Papua and New Guinea Scientific Society. Transactions — Papua New Guinea Sci Soc Trans
Papua Annual Report — Papua Annual Rep
Papua New Guinea. Department of Agriculture, Stock, and Fisheries. Annual Report — Papua New Guinea Dep Agric Stock Fish Annu Rep
Papua New Guinea. Department of Agriculture, Stock, and Fisheries. Research Bulletin — Papua New Guinea Dep Agric Stock Fish Res Bull
Papua New Guinea. Geological Survey. Memoir — Papua New Guinea Geol Surv Mem
Papua New Guinea. Geological Survey. Report — Papua New Guinea Geol Surv Rep
Papua New Guinea. Institute of Medical Research. Monograph Series — Papua New Guinea Inst Med Res Monogr Ser
Papua New Guinea Journal of Agriculture, Forestry, and Fisheries — Papua New Guinea J Agric For Fish
Papua New Guinea Medical Journal — Papua New Guinea Med J
Papua New Guinea Medical Journal — PNG Med J
Papyri der Universitaetsbibliothek Erlangen — P Erl
Papyri from Karanis — Pap Karanis
Papyri Graecae Haunienses — P Haun
Papyri Graecae Magicae — Pap GM
Papyri Graecae Magicae — PGM
Papyri Graecae Magicae — PMag
Papyri Graeci Musei Antiquarii Publici Lugduni-Batavi — PGMAPLB
Papyri in the Princeton University Collections — P Princet
Papyri Michaelidae — P Michaelides
Papyri Osloenses — P Oslo
Papyri Russischer und Georgischer Sammlungen — P Russ Georg
Papyri Societatis Archaeologicae Atheniensis — P Athen
Papyri Societatis Archaeologicae Atheniensis — PSA Athen
Papyri Varsovienses — P Vars
Papyrologica — PAP
Papyrologica Bruxellensia — Pap Brux
Papyrologica Lugduno-Batava — Pap Lugd Bat
Papyrologica Lugduno-Batava — PLB
Papyrological Primer — Pap Primer
Papyrologische Texte und Abhandlungen — PTA
Papyrus Bouriant — P Bour
Papyrus Bouriant — P Bouriant
Papyrus Bouriant — PBN
Papyrus de Geneve — PGen
Papyrus de la Sorbonne — P Sorb
Papyrus de Philadelphie — P Philad
Papyrus de Theadelphie — P Thead
Papyrus Fouad I — P Fouad
Papyrus Graecus Holmensis — P Holm
Papyrus Grecs de la Bibliotheque Municipale de Gothenbourg — P Goth
Papyrus Grecs d'Epoque Byzantine — PGEB
Papyrus Grecs et Demotiques Recueillis en Egypte — PGDRE
Papyrus Grecs. Institut Papyrologique. Universite de Lille — P Lille
Papyrusfunde und Papyrusforschung — PP
Papyrusurkunden der Oeffentlichen Bibliothek der Universitaet zu Basel — P Basel
PAR [*Public Affairs Research*] **Legislative Bulletin** — PAR Legis Bul
PAR. Pseudo-Allergic Reactions — PAR Pseudo-Allerg React
PAR. Pseudo-Allergic Reactions. Involvement of Drugs and Chemicals — PAR Pseudo-Allerg React Involvement Drugs Chem

Parabola — PPAR
Paradosis — Par
Paradoxographoi. Scriptores Rerum Mirabilium Graeci — SRMG
Paradoxographorum Graecorum Reliquiae — PGR
Paragone — Par
Paraguay Industrial y Comercial (Asuncion) — Paraguay Indus Comer Asuncion
Paralipomena — P
Paralipomena — Par
Paralipomena — Para
Parallel Computing — Parallel Comput
Parallel Processing Letters — Parallel Process Lett
Paramagnitnyj Rezonans — Paramagn Rezon
Paramaribo-Suriname. Agricultural Experiment Station. Bulletin — Paramaribo-Suriname Agric Exp Stn Bull
Para-Medico — Para-Med
Paramedics International — Paramed Int
Parasite Immunology — Parasite Immunol
Parasite Immunology (Oxford) — Parasite Immunol (Oxf)
Parasitic Diseases — Parasit Dis
Parasitica — Parasit
Parasitologia Hungarica — Parasit Hung
Parasitologia Hungarica — Parasitol Hung
Parasitologische Schriftenreihe — Parasitol Schriftenr
Parasitology — Parasitol
Parasitology Research — Parasit Res
Parasitology Research — Parasitol Res
Parasitology Today — Parasitol Today
Paraula Cristiana — PC
Parazitologiceskii Sbornik — Parazit Sb
Parazitologicheskii Sbornik — Parazitol Sb
Parazity Zhivotnykh i Rastenii — Parazity Zhivotn Rast
Parbhani Agricultural College. Magazine — Parbhani Agric Coll Mag
Parent and Citizen — Parent & Cit
Parent Australia — Parent Aust
Parenteral Drug Association. Bulletin — Parenter Drug Assoc Bull
Parenteral Drug Association. Journal — Parenter Drug Assoc J
Parents — GPAR
Parents' Buletin — Parents Bull
Parents' Magazine — Par M
Parents' Magazine — Parents
Parents' Magazine and Better Family Living [*Later, Parents' Magazine*] — Par
Parents' Magazine and Better Family Living [*Later, Parents' Magazine*] — Parents' Mag
Parfuemerie und Kosmetik [*Germany*] — Parfuem Kosmet
Parfuemerie und Kosmetik. Internationale Zeitschrift fuer Wissenschaftliche und Technische Grundlagen der Parfuem- und Kosmetika Industrie — PKO
Parfumerie Moderne — Parfum Mod
Parfums, Cosmetiques, Actualites — Parfums Cosmet Actual
Parfums, Cosmetiques, Aromes — Parfums Cos
Parfums, Cosmetiques, Aromes — Parfums Cosmet Aromes
Parfums, Cosmetiques, Aromes. L'Unique Journal Francais de Son Secteur — OUB
Parfums, Cosmetiques, Savons — Parfum Cosmet Savons
Parfums, Cosmetiques, Savons — Parfums Cosmet Savons
Parfums, Cosmetiques, Savons de France — Parfums Cosmet Savons Fr
Parfums de France — Parfums Fr
Pariosse et Liturgie — Lar Li
Paris et Ile-De-France. Memoires — P & IF
Paris et Ile-De-France. Memoires — PIF
Paris Match — P M
Paris Medical — Par Med
Paris Medical — Paris Med
Paris Review — Paris Rev
Paris Review — ParisR
Paris Review — ParR
Paris Review — PPRE
Paris Review — PR
Paris. Universite. Laboratoire de Micropaleontologie. Travaux — Paris Univ Lab Micropaleontol Trav
Paris. Universite. Laboratoire de Paleontologie. Travaux — Paris Univ Lab Paleontol Trav
Pariser Verbandsuebereinkunft zum Schutze des Gewerblichen Eigentums — PV Ue
Paristwo i Prawo — Pari I Prawo
Park Administration — Park Adm
Park News — PANE
Park Practice Grist — Park Pract Grist
Park Practice Index — PPI
Park Practice Program. Design, Grist, Trends. Index — Park Pract Prog
Parkes Catalogue of Radio Sources [*Database*] — PKSCAT
Parkett — Pa
Parks and Recreation — IPNR
Parks and Recreation — P & R
Parks and Recreation — Parks and R
Parks and Recreation — Parks & Rec
Parks and Recreation — Pks & Rec
Parks and Recreation — PRKRA
Parks and Wilderness — PAWI
Parks and Wildlife — Parks & Wild
Parks and Wildlife — Parks Wildl
Parks Canada. Research Bulletin — PCRB
Parks. International Journal for Managers of National Parks, Historic Sites, and Other Protected Areas — PARK
Parks Library Pamphlets — PLP
Parkscan. Parks Canada — PASC
Parlament — Par
Parlament — Parl
Parlament Beilage aus Politik und Zeitgeschichte — Parlam Beil Polit Zeitgesch
Parliamentarian [*British*] — Parl
Parliamentary Affairs — PA
Parliamentary Affairs — Parl Aff
Parliamentary Affairs — Parliam Aff
Parliamentary Affairs — Parliamentary Aff
Parliamentary Affairs — Parlim Aff
Parliamentary Affairs — PPLF
Parliamentary Affairs — PrlA
Parliamentary Affairs. Journal. Hansard Society — Parl Aff J Hans Soc
Parliamentary Debates — Parl Deb
Parliamentary Debates — PD
Parliamentary Debates. House of Commons [*United Kingdom*] — Parl Deb HC
Parliamentary Debates. House of Lords [*United Kingdom*] — Parl Deb HL
Parliamentary Liaison Group for Alternative Energy Strategies. Bulletin — Parliam Liaison Group Altern Energy Strategies Bull
Parliamentary On-Line Information System [*Database*] — POLIS
Parliamentary Paper — PP
Parliamentary Paper (Commonwealth of Australia) — Parliament Pap (Commonw Aust)
Parliamentary Papers. East India [*London*] — PPEI
Parliamentary Papers. Foreign Office Command Paper [*London*] — CPFO
Parliamentary White Paper — PWP
Parnassus [*New York*] — Parn
Parnassus. Poetry in Review — PPOR
Parodontologia e Stomatologia Nuova — Parodontol Stomatol Nuova
Parodontologie and Academy Review — Parodontol Acad Rev
Paroi Arterielle-Arterial Wall — Par Arter
Parola del Passato — Par Pass
Parola del Passato — PP
Parola del Passato — PPa
Parola del Passato. Rivista di Studi Antichi — Par d Pass
Parola del Passato. Rivista di Studi Antichi [*Naples*] — Parola Passato
Parola del Popolo — PdP
Parole de l'Orient — Par Or
Parole d'Orient — PdO
Parole e le Idee — P & I
Parole e le Idee — PeI
Parole e le Idee — PId
Parole e Metodi — PeM
Parole et Mission — Par Miss
Parole et Mission — PM
Parole et Societe — Parole et Soc
Parool (Amsterdam) — PRA
Parques y Jardines — Parques Jard
Parramatta and District Historical Society. Journal and Proceedings — J Proc Parramatta Dist Hist Soc
PARS [*Performing Arts Referral Service*] **Information Quarterly** — PARS Info Q
Parsons Journal — Parsons J
Particle Accelerators — Part Accel
Particle and Particle Systems Characterization — Part Part Syst Charact
Particle Characterization — Part Charact
Particle Size Analysis — Part Size Anal
Particleboard and Medium Density Fibreboard. Annual Publication and Shipments — Particle B
Particleboard/Composite Materials Series — Particleboard/Compos Mater Ser
Particles and Nuclei — Par Nucl
Particles and Nuclei — Part and Nucl
Particles and Nuclei — Part Nucl
Particles on Surfaces. Detection, Adhesion, and Removal — Part Surf
Particulate Debris from Medical Implants. Mechanisms of Formation and Biological Consequences — Part Debris Med Implants
Particulate Science and Technology — Part Sci Technol
Partiinaya Zhizn — Part Z
Partiinaya Zhizn — PZ
Partijnaja Shisn — PS
Partisan Review — ParR
Partisan Review — Part R
Partisan Review — Partisan R
Partisan Review — Partisan Rev
Partisan Review — PPTR
Partisan Review — PR
Party Newspapers — Party
Paru — Pa
Pascal Newsletter — Pascal Newsl
Pasicrisie Luxembourgeoise — Pas L
Pasicrisie Luxembourgeoise — Pas Lux
Pasicrisie Luxembourgeoise — Pasc Lxb
PasKen (Pasuturu Kenkyusho) Journal — PasKen J
Passauer Monatsschrift — PassM
Passenger Transport — Passenger Transp
Passenger Transport Journal [*England*] — Passeng Transp J
Passive Solar Journal — PASJD
Passive Solar Journal — Passive Sol J
Past and Present — P & P
Past and Present — PaP
Past and Present — PasP
Past and Present — Past & Pres
Past and Present — Past Presen
Past and Present. A Journal of Historical Studies — PPNP
Past and Present. Studies in the History of Civilization — Past Pres

Pasteur Institute of Southern India (Coonoor). Annual Report of the Director and Scientific Report — Pasteur Inst South India (Coonoor) Annu Rep Dir Sci Rep
Pastor Bonus — Past B
Pastor Bonus — Pastor Bon
Pastor Bonus — PB
Pastoral Care and Counseling Abstracts — Past Care & Couns Abstr
Pastoral Care and Counseling Abstracts — Pastor Care Couns Abstr
Pastoral Care in Education — Pastor Care Educ
Pastoral Music — PA
Pastoral Music — Pas Mus
Pastoral Music — Past Mus
Pastoral Music Notebook — PAN
Pastoral Psychology — Past Psych
Pastoral Psychology Series — PPsS
Pastoral Review — Pastoral Rev
Pastoral Review and Graziers' Record — Past R
Pastoral Review and Graziers' Record — Past Rev
Pastoral Review and Graziers' Record — Pastoral Rev Graz Rec
Pastoralblaetter [*Stuttgart*] — PastBl
Pastoralblaetter — PBL
Pastoralblaetter fuer Homiletik, Katechetik, und Seelsorge — PBl
Pastoralblaetter fuer Predigt, Katechetik, und Kirchliche Unterweisung — Pbl
Pastoralblatt — Pastbl
Pastorales Forum fuer die Seelsorger im Erzbistum Muenchen-Freising — Past Forum
Pastoralist and Grazier — Pastoralist
Pastoraltheologie [*Goettingen*] — P Th
Patclass [*Database*] — PATC
Patent Abridgments Supplement. Australian Official Journal of Patents. Trade Marks and Designs — Pat Abr Suppl Aust Off J Pat Trade Marks Des
Patent and Trade Mark Review — Pat and TM Rev
Patent and Trade Mark Review — Pat & Tr Mk Rev
Patent Cooperation Treaty International Application — Pat Coop Treaty Int Appl
Patent Journal, Including Trade Marks and Designs — Pat J Incl Trade Marks Des
Patent Journal, Including Trade Marks, Designs, and Copyright in Cinematograph Films — Pat J Incl Trade Marks Des Copyright Cinematogr Films
Patent Law Annual — Pat L Ann
Patent Office Society. Journal — Pat Off Soc J
Patent Office Society. Journal — Patent Off Soc Jour
Patent Specification. Amended Specification (United Kingdom) — Pat Specif Amended Specif UK
Patent Specification (Australia) — Pat Specif (Aust)
Patent Specification (Petty) (Australia) — Pat Specif (Petty)(Aust)
Patent, Trademark, and Copyright Journal — Pat TM & Copy J
Patent, Trademark, and Copyright Journal — PTC J
Patentblatt — P Bl
Patentblatt — Pat Bl
Patentblatt — Patentbl
Patentblatt. Ausgabe A — Patentbl Ausg A
Patentblatt. Ausgabe B — Patentbl Ausg B
Patente de Introduccion (Spain) — Pat Introd Spain
Patente de Invencion (Spain) — Pat Invenc (Spain)
Patentjoernaal Insluitende Handels-Merke en Modelle — Patentj Insluitende Handels Merke Modelle
Patentjoernaal Insluitende Handelsmerke. Modelle en Outeursreg in Rolprente — Patentj Insluitende Handelsmerke Modelle Outeursreg Rolprent
Patentjoernaal (South Africa) — Patentjoernaal (S Afr)
Patents, Trademark, and Copyright Journal. Bureau of National Affairs — Pat Trademark & Copyright J BNA
Patentschrift. Ausschliessungspatent (German Democratic Republic) — Patentschr Ausschliessungspat Ger Democr Repub
Paternoster Church History — PCH
Pathobiology Annual — Pathobiol Annu
Pathobiology Annual — PBANB
Pathologia et Microbiologia — Path Microb
Pathologia et Microbiologia — Pathol Microbiol
Pathologia et Microbiologia. Additamentum — Pathol Microbiol Addit
Pathologia et Microbiologia. Supplementum [*Switzerland*] — Pathol Microbiol Suppl
Pathologia Europaea — Path Europ
Pathologia Europaea — Pathol Eur
Pathologia Europaea. Supplement — Pathol Eur Suppl
Pathologia Veterinaria — Pathol Vet
Pathological Society of Philadelphia. Proceedings — Pathol Soc Phila Proc
Pathologie et Biologie — PABIA
Pathologie et Biologie [*Paris*] — Path Biol
Pathologie et Biologie [*Paris*] — Pathol Biol
Pathologie et Biologie. La Semaine des Hopitaux — Pathol Biol Sem Hop
Pathologie et Biologie (Paris) — Pathol Biol (Paris)
Pathologie Generale — Pathol Gen
Pathology — Pathol
Pathology and Clinical Medicine (Tokyo) — Pathol Clin Med (Tokyo)
Pathology and Immunopathology Research — Pathol Immunopathol Res
Pathology Annual — Pathol Annu
Pathology. Research and Practice — Path Res Pract
Pathology. Research and Practice — Pathol Res Pract
Patient Accounts — Patient Acc
Patient Counselling and Health Education — Patient Couns Health Educ
Patient Education and Counseling — Patient Educ Couns
Patient Education Newsletter — Patient Educ Newsl
Patma-Banasirakan Handes. Istoriko-Filologicheskii Zhurnal — Patma-Banasirakan Handes Ist-Filol Zh
Patma-Banasirakan Handes. Istoriko-Filologicheskii Zhurnal — PBH
Patna Journal of Medicine — Patna J Med
Patna University. Journal — PU
Patogenez i Terapiya Dermatozov — Patog Ter Dermatozov
Patogenez i Terapiya Kozhnykh i Venericheskikh Zabolevanii — Patog Ter Kozhnykh Vener Zabol
Patologia Comparata della Tubercolosi — Patol Comp Tuberc
Patologia e Clinica Ostetrica e Ginecologica — Patol Clin Ostet Ginecol
Patologia Polska — Pat Pol
Patologia Polska — Patol Pol
Patologia Sperimentale — Patol Sper
Patologia Sperimentale e Chirurgia — Patol Sper Chir
Patologia-Mexico City — Patol-Mex
Patologiceskaya Fiziologiya i Eksperimental'naya Terapija — Pat Fiz Eksp Ter
Patologicheskaya Fiziologiya i Eksperimental'naya Terapiya — PAFEA
Patologicheskaya Fiziologiya i Eksperimental'naya Terapiya — Patol Fiziol Eksp Ter
Patres Ecclesiae Anglicanae — PEA
Patria. Revista Portuguesa de Cultura — Pa
Patriarchs and Prophets — PP
Patriotische Medicus — Patriot Med
Patristic and Byzantine Review — P and BR
Patristic Greek Lexicon — PGL
Patristic Studies — Pat St
Patristica Sorbonensia — Patrist Sorb
Patrologia Graeca — P Gr
Patrologia Graeca — PG
Patrologia Graeca (Migne) — Migne P G
Patrologia Latina — PL
Patrologia Latina (Migne) — Migne P L
Patrologia Orientalis — Patr Or
Patrologia Orientalis — PO
Patrologia Syriaca — PS
Patrologia Syriaca — PSyr
Patrologiae Cursus Completus. Series Graeca — MPG
Patrologiae Cursus Completus. Series Graeca — Pat Graec
Patrologiae Cursus Completus. Series Graeca — Patrol Gr
Patrologiae Cursus Completus. Series Latina — Patr Lat
Patrologiae Cursus Completus. Series Latina — PCCL
Patrologiae Cursus Completus. Series Latina — PL
Patrologiae Latinae Supplementum — PLS
Patronato de Biologia Animal. Revista — Patronato Biol Anim Rev
Patronato de Investigacion Cientifica y Tecnica "Juan De La Cierva." Memoria — Patronato Invest Cient Tec "Juan De La Cierva" Mem
Patronato de Investigacion Cientifica y Tecnica "Juan De La Cierva." Publicaciones Tecnicas — Patronato Invest Cient Tec "Juan De La Cierva" Publ Tec
Pattern Recognition — Patt Recog
Pattern Recognition — Pattern Recogn
Pattern Recognition — PTNRA8
Pattern Recognition Letters — Pattern Recognition Lett
Patterns of Myth — PoM
Patterns of Myth. Myth and Experience — PoMM
Patterns of Prejudice — PaP
Patterns of Religious Commitment — PRC
Paul Arendt's Monatsschrift fuer Kakteenkunde — Paul Arendts Monatsschr Kakteenk
Paul und Braunes Beitraege zur Geschichte der Deutschen Sprache und Literatur — Btr Gesch Dt Spr
Paulys Real-Encyclopaedie der Classischen Alterthumswissenschaft — PRE
Pauly-Wissowa. Realenzyklopaedie der Klassischen Altertumswissenschaft — Realenz Klass Altertswiss
Pauly-Wissowas Realencyclopaedie der Classischen Altertumswissenschaft — PRECA
Pavia Universita. Istituto Geologico. Atti — Pavia Univ Ist Geol Atti
Paving Conference. Proceedings — Paving Conf Proc
Pavlov Journal of Higher Nervous Activity — Pavlov J Higher Nerv Act
Pavlov Journal of Higher Nervous Activity [*English translation of Zhurnal Vysshei Nervnoi Deyatelnosti Imeni I. P. Pavlova*] — PJHNAW
Pavlovian Journal of Biological Science — Pav J Biol
Pavlovian Journal of Biological Science — Pavlov J Biol Sci
Pavlovian Journal of Biological Science — Pavlovian J Biol Sci
Pavlovian Journal of Biological Science — PJBSA
Pawathy Stare Literatury Ceske — PSLC
Pawlow-Zeitschrift fuer Hoehere Nerventaetigkeit — Pawl Zs Hoeh Nerv Taet
Pax Romana — Pax Rom
Paxton's Flower Garden — Paxtons Fl Gard
Pays d'Argentan — P Arg
Pays de Bourgogne — PB
Pays Gaumais. La Terre et les Hommes. Revue Regionale — Pays Gaumais
Pays Lorrain — Pays Lor
Pays Lorrain — PL
Paysans — Pays
Payton Lectures — Payt L
Pazmaveb — P
Pazmaveb [*Venezia*] — Pazm
PC Computing — GPCC
PC Digest Ratings Report — PCDRR
PC Magazine — IPCM
PC Week — IPCW
PC World — GPCW
PCEA [*Programa Cooperativo de Experimentacion Agropecuaria*] **Boletin Trimestral de Experimentacion Agropecuaria** — PCEA Bol Trimest Exp Agropecu

PCH: PhysicoChemical Hydrodynamics [*Physicochemical Hydrodynamics*] [*England*] [*Later,*] — PCH PhysicoChem Hydrodyn
Pchela Sofiya — Pchela Sof
Pchelovodnaya Zhizn' — Pchel Zhizn
Pchelovodnyi Mir — Pchel Mir
PCLA [*Polish Canadian Librarians Association*] **Newsletter** — PCLA Newsl
PCR (Polymerase Chain Reaction) in Neuroscience — PCR Neurosci
PCR (Polymerase Chain Reaction) Methods and Applications — PCR Methods Appl
PCSIR [*Pakistan Council of Scientific and Industrial Research*] **Bulletin/Monograph** — PCSIR Bull Monogr
PCT (Patent Cooperation Treaty) International Application — PCT Int Appl
PDA [Parental Drug Association] Journal of Pharmaceutical Science andTechnology — PDA J Pharm Sci Technol
PDM. Physicians' Drug Manual — PDMLA
Peabody Journal of Education — Peabody J E
Peabody Journal of Education — Peabody J Ed
Peabody Journal of Education — Peabody J Educ
Peabody Journal of Education — PJE
Peabody Museum of Natural History. Yale University. Bulletin — Peabody Mus Nat Hist Yale Univ Bull
Peabody Museum Papers — Peab Mus Pap
Peabody Museum Papers — PMP
Peace and the Sciences — Peace and Sci
Peace Country [*Grande Prairie, Alberta*] — PECO
Peace, Happiness, Prosperity for All — PHP
Peace Messenger. Diocese of Athabasca. Peace River — PMDA
Peace News — Peace Nws
Peace Newsletter — Peace
Peace/Non-Violence — Peace
Peace Research Abstracts — PeaceResAb
Peace Research Abstracts Journal — Peace Res Abstr J
Peace Research Abstracts Journal — PRAJ
Peace Research in Japan — Peace Res Ja
Peace Research Reviews — Peace Res Rev
Peace Science Society. International Papers — Peace Science Soc Internat Pas
Peaceful Nuclear Explosions. Proceedings of a Technical Committee — Peaceful Nucl Explos
Peacemaker — Peacemak
Peake [*A.S.*] **Memorial Lectures** — PML
Peake's Commentary on the Bible — PC
Peake's Commentary on the Bible — PCB
Peanut Journal and Nut World — Peanut J Nut World
Peanut Science — Peanut Sci
Pearce-Sellards Series. Texas Memorial Museum — Pearce-Sellards Ser Tex Mem Mus
Pearson's Magazine (New York) — Pearsons M NY
Peasant Studies Newsletter — Peasant Stud Newsl
Peasant Studies. University of Utah. Department of History — UU/PS
Peat Abstracts — Peat Abstr
Peat and Plant Yearbook — Peat Plant Yearb
Peat Industry — Peat Ind
Peat Industry. Proceedings. Symposium of Commission. International Peat Society — Peat Ind Proc Symp Comm Int Peat Soc
Pebble — Peb
Pecan Journal. Southeastern Pecan Growers Association — Pecan J
Pecan Quarterly — Pecan Q
Pecan South Including Pecan Quarterly — Pecan South Incl Pecan Q
Pecat' i Revoljucija — PiR
Peche Maritime — Peche Mar
Peche Maritime — Peche Marit
Pecsi Mueszaki Szemle [*Hungary*] — Pecsi Muesz Sz
Pedagogia — PA
Pedagogia — Ped
Pedagogiai Szemle — Pedag Szle
Pedagogical Institute in Gorki. Transactions — GGPI
Pedagogical Seminary — Ped Sem
Pedagogical Seminary — Pedagog Sem
Pedagogical Seminary and Journal of Genetic Psychology — PS
Pedagogicka Fakulta v Plzni. Sbornik. Chemie — Pedagog Fak Plzni Sb Chem
Pedagogicka Fakulta v Plzni. Sbornik. Serie Chemie — Pedagog Fak Plzni Sb Ser Chem
Pedagogicka Fakulta v Usti nad Labem. Sbornik. Rada Chemicka — Pedagog Fak Usti nad Labem Sb Rada Chem
Pedagogika i Psihologija — Pedag i Psihol
Pedagogika ir Psichologija — Ped Psich
Pedagogisk Tidskrift — Pd T
Pedagogisk Tidskrift — Pedag Tidskr
Pedagogiska Foereningen Tidskrift — PFT
Pedagogiska Meddelanden fran Skoloeverstyrelsen — Pedag Meddel
Pediatria [*Buenos Aires*] — PDTRDV
Pediatria [*Bucharest*] — PEDBA9
Pediatria. Archivio di Patologia e Clinica Pediatrica — Pediatria Arch
Pediatria Ecuatoriana — Ped Ecuat
Pediatria Espanola — Pediatr Esp
Pediatria in Calabria — Ped Cal
Pediatria Internazionale — Ped Int
Pediatria Internazionale — Pediatr Int
Pediatria Medica e Chirurgica — Pediatr Med Chir
Pediatria Moderna — Pediatr Mod
Pediatria Panamericana — Ped Panam
Pediatria Panamericana — Pediatr Panamericana
Pediatria Polska — Pediatr Pol
Pediatria Pratica — Pediatr Prat
Pediatric Allergy and Immunology — Pediatr Allergy Immunol
Pediatric and Adolescent Endocrinology — Pediatr Adolesc Endocrinol
Pediatric and Adolescent Gynecology — PAGYDY
Pediatric and Adolescent Gynecology — Pediatr Adolesc Gynecol
Pediatric Annals — PDANB
Pediatric Annals — Pediatr Ann
Pediatric Cardiology — PECAD4
Pediatric Cardiology — Pediatr Cardiol
Pediatric Clinics of North America — P Clin North America
Pediatric Clinics of North America — Ped Clin NA
Pediatric Clinics of North America — Pediat Clins N Am
Pediatric Clinics of North America — Pediatr Clin N Am
Pediatric Clinics of North America — Pediatr Clin North Am
Pediatric Continuing Education Courses for the Practitioner — Pediatr Contin Educ Courses Pract
Pediatric Continuing Education Courses for the Practitioner — PFPXA6
Pediatric Dentistry — Pediatr Dent
Pediatric Dermatology — Pediatr Dermatol
Pediatric Emergency Care — Pediatr Emerg Care
Pediatric Hematology and Oncology — Pediatr Hematol Oncol
Pediatric Infectious Disease — Pediat Inf
Pediatric Infectious Disease — Pediatr Infect Dis
Pediatric Infectious Disease Journal — Pediatr Infect Dis J
Pediatric Nephrology — Pediatr Nephrol
Pediatric Nephrology (Berlin) — Pediatr Nephrol Berlin
Pediatric Neurology — Pediatr Neurol
Pediatric Neuroscience — Pediatr Neurosci
Pediatric Neuroscience — PENEE4
Pediatric Neurosurgery — Pediatr Neurosurg
Pediatric News — Pediatr News
Pediatric Nurse Practitioner — Pediatr Nurse Pract
Pediatric Nursing — Pediat Nurs
Pediatric Nursing — Pediatr Nurs
Pediatric Pathology — Pediatr Pathol
Pediatric Pathology — PPATDQ
Pediatric Pathology and Laboratory Medicine — Pediatr Pathol Lab Med
Pediatric Pharmacology — Pediatr Pharmacol
Pediatric Pulmonology — Pediatr Pulmonol
Pediatric Pulmonology. Supplement — Pediatr Pulmonol Suppl
Pediatric Radiology — Pediatr Radiol
Pediatric Research — Pediat Res
Pediatric Research — Pediatr Res
Pediatric Review — Pediatr Rev
Pediatric Surgery International — Pediatr Surg Int
Pediatricke Listy — Pediatr Listy
Pediatrics — Pedia
Pediatrics Supplement — Pediatrics Suppl
Pediatrics Update — Pediatr Update
Pediatriia, Akusherstvo, i Ginekologiia — PDAGA
Pediatriia, Akusherstvo, i Ginekologiia — Ped Akus Ginek
Pediatriia, Akusherstvo, i Ginekologiia — Pediat Akush Ginek
Pediatriia, Akusherstvo, i Ginekologiia — Pediatr Akush Ginekol
Pediatriya [*Moscow*] — PEDTAT
Pedjatrja Polska — Pedjatr Pol
Pedoatrocoam — PEDIEY
Pedobiologia — Pedobiolog
Pedodontie Francaise — Pedod Fr
Pedology (Leningrad) — Pedology (Leningr)
Pedro Vitorino. In Memoriam — PVIM
Peel Valley Historical Society. Journal — Peel Valley Hist Soc J
Pegaso — Peg
Pegmatitovye Redkometal'nye Mestorozhdeniya — Pegmatitovye Redkomet Mestorozhd
Peine und Salzgitter Berichte — Peine Salzgitter Ber
Peintures, Pigments, Vernis — Peint Pigm Vernis
Peking Mining College Journal — Peking Min Coll J
Peking Natural History Bulletin — Peking Nat Hist Bull
Peking Review — Peking R
Peking Review — PR
Pelican Gospel Commentaries [*Harmondsworth*] — PGC
Pelican Guide to Modern Theology — PGMT
Pelican History of the Church — PHC
Peloponnesiaka — Pelop
Peltier's Decisions. Court of Appeal. Parish of Orleans — Pelt
PEM Process Engineering Magazine — PEM Process Eng Mag
Pembroke Magazine — Pembroke Mag
Pemmican Journal — PEMJ
PEN Hongrois — HPEN
Penelitian Laut di Indonesia [*Marine Research in Indonesia*] — Penelitian Indones
Penelitian Laut di Indonesia (Marine Research in Indonesia) — Penelitian Laut Indones (Mar Res Indones)
Penerbitan Teknik. Pusat Pengembangan Teknologi Mineral — Penerbitan Tek Pusat Pengembangan Teknol Miner
Penguin English Library — PEL
Penguin Parade — P
Pengumuman. Lembaga Penelitian Kehutanan — Pengum Lemb Penelit Kehutanan
Penjelidikan Laut di Indonesia — Penjelidikan Indones
Penn Club Internacional (London) — PIL
Penn Dental Journal — Penn Dent J
Penn Monthly — Penn Mo
Penn State Farmer — Penn State F
Penn State Mining Quarterly — Penn St M Q
Penn State Series in German Literature — PSSGL
Penn State Studies — Penn State Stud
Pennington Center Nutrition Series — Pennington Cent Nutr Ser

PennState Agriculture — PennState Agric
Pennsylvania Academy of Science. Journal — Pa Acad Sci J
Pennsylvania Academy of Science. Newsletter — Pennsylvania Acad Sci Newsletter
Pennsylvania Academy of Science. Proceedings — PA Acad Sci Proc
Pennsylvania Academy of Science. Proceedings — Pennsylvania Acad Sci Proc
Pennsylvania. Agricultural Experiment Station. Bulletin — PA Agric Exp Stn Bull
Pennsylvania. Agricultural Experiment Station. Progress Report — PA Agric Exp Stn Prog Rep
Pennsylvania. Agricultural Experiment Station. Publications — PA Ag Exp
Pennsylvania Archaeologist — PA Arch
Pennsylvania Archaeologist — PA Archaeol
Pennsylvania Bar Association. Quarterly — PA B Ass'n Q
Pennsylvania Bar Association. Quarterly — PA Bar Asso Q
Pennsylvania Bar Association. Quarterly — PABAQ
Pennsylvania Bar Association. Quarterly — Penn Ba Q
Pennsylvania Bar Association. Quarterly — Penn Bar Assc Q
Pennsylvania Bar Association. Report — Penn BAR
Pennsylvania Beekeeper — Penn Beekpr
Pennsylvania Bulletin — Pa Bull
Pennsylvania. Bureau of Topographic and Geologic Survey. Atlas — Pa Bur Topogr Geol Surv Atlas
Pennsylvania. Bureau of Topographic and Geologic Survey. Bulletin C [*County Report*] — PA Topogr Geol Surv Bull C
Pennsylvania. Bureau of Topographic and Geologic Survey. Bulletin G [*General Geology Report*] — PA Topogr Geol Surv Bull G
Pennsylvania. Bureau of Topographic and Geologic Survey. Geologic Atlas of Pennsylvania — PA Topogr Geol Surv Geol Atlas PA
Pennsylvania. Bureau of Topographic and Geologic Survey. Information Circular — PA Topogr Geol Surv Inform Circ
Pennsylvania. Bureau of Topographic and Geologic Survey. Mineral Resource Report — PA Bur Topogr Geol Surv Miner Resour Rep
Pennsylvania. Bureau of Topographic and Geologic Survey. Progress Report — PA Topogr Geol Surv Progr Rep
Pennsylvania. Bureau of Topographic and Geologic Survey. Special Bulletin — PA Topogr Geol Surv Spec Bull
Pennsylvania Business Education Association. Newsletter — PBEA Newsletter
Pennsylvania Business Survey — PA Bsns Survey
Pennsylvania Business Survey — Pennsylvania Bus Survey
Pennsylvania Code — Pa Code
Pennsylvania Commonwealth Court Reports — Pa Commw
Pennsylvania Consolidated Statutes — Pa Cons Stat
Pennsylvania Consolidated Statutes Annotated (Purdon) — Pa Cons Stat Ann (Purdon)
Pennsylvania Council of Teachers of English. Bulletin — PCTE Bull
Pennsylvania Council of Teachers of English. Bulletin — PCTE Bulletin
Pennsylvania Council of Teachers of English. Bulletin — PCTEB
Pennsylvania County Reports — Pa C
Pennsylvania Dental Journal — PA Dent J
Pennsylvania. Department of Agriculture. Annual Report — PA Dp Agr An Rp
Pennsylvania. Department of Environmental Resources. Water Resources Bulletin — PA Dep Environ Resour Water Resour Bull
Pennsylvania. Department of Forests and Waters. Water Resources Bulletin — PA Dep For Waters Water Resour Bull
Pennsylvania. Department of Internal Affairs. Monthly Bulletin — PA Dept Int Affairs Monthly Bull
Pennsylvania District and County Reports — Pa D & C
Pennsylvania District Reports — Pa D
Pennsylvania Dutchman — PD
Pennsylvania Electric Association. Annual Report — PA Electr Assoc Annu Rep
Pennsylvania Electric Association. Engineering Section. Minutes of the Meeting — PA Electr Assoc Eng Sect Minutes Meet
Pennsylvania Electric Association. Engineering Section. Transmission and Distribution Committee. Minutes — PA Elec Ass Eng Sect Transm Distrib
Pennsylvania Energy Extension Service. News — PA Energy Ext Serv News
Pennsylvania English — PE
Pennsylvania English — PEng
Pennsylvania Farm Economics — PA Farm Econ
Pennsylvania Folklife — PA F
Pennsylvania Folklife — PA Folklife
Pennsylvania Folklife — PennsF
Pennsylvania Folklife — PF
Pennsylvania Folklife — PFL
Pennsylvania Forests — PA For
Pennsylvania Fruit News — PA Fruit News
Pennsylvania General Assembly — PA Gen As
Pennsylvania. Geological Survey — PA G S
Pennsylvania. Geological Survey. Atlas — PA Geol Surv Atlas
Pennsylvania. Geological Survey. Atlas — Penn Geol Surv Atlas
Pennsylvania. Geological Survey. Bulletin — Penn Geol Surv Bull
Pennsylvania. Geological Survey. Bulletin — Pennsylvania Geol Survey Bull
Pennsylvania. Geological Survey. General Geology Report — PA Geol Surv Gen Geol Rep
Pennsylvania. Geological Survey. General Geology Report — Penn Geol Surv Gen Geol Rep
Pennsylvania. Geological Survey. Ground Water Report — Penn Geol Surv Ground Water Rep
Pennsylvania. Geological Survey. Information Circular — PA Geol Surv Inf Circ
Pennsylvania. Geological Survey. Information Circular — Penn Geol Surv Inform Circ
Pennsylvania. Geological Survey. Information Circular — Pennsylvania Geol Survey Inf Circ
Pennsylvania. Geological Survey. Mineral Resource Report — PA Geol Surv Miner Resour Rep
Pennsylvania. Geological Survey. Progress Report — PA Geol Surv Prog Rep
Pennsylvania. Geological Survey. Progress Report — Penn Geol Surv Progr Rep
Pennsylvania. Geological Survey. Progress Report — Pennsylvania Geol Survey Prog Rept
Pennsylvania. Geological Survey. Water Resource Report — PA Geol Surv Water Resour Rep
Pennsylvania Geology — PA Geol
Pennsylvania Geology — PAGYB
Pennsylvania Geology — Pennsylvania Geol
Pennsylvania German Folklore Society. Bulletin — PGFS
Pennsylvania German Folklore Society. Year Book — PA Ger Folk Soc Yr Bk
Pennsylvania German Society. Proceedings — Penn German Soc Proc
Pennsylvania German Society. Proceedings and Addresses — PGS
Pennsylvania German Society. Proceedings and Addresses — PGSP
Pennsylvania Historical Society. Memoirs — Pa Hist Soc Memoirs
Pennsylvania History — PA His
Pennsylvania History — PA Hist
Pennsylvania History — PenH
Pennsylvania History — Penn Hist
Pennsylvania History — PH
Pennsylvania Hospital Reports — Penn Hosp Rep
Pennsylvania Journal for Health, Physical Education, and Recreation — PSHP
Pennsylvania Law Finder — Pa Law Finder
Pennsylvania Law Journal-Reporter — PA LJ Rep
Pennsylvania Law Series — Pa Law Ser
Pennsylvania Lawyer — Penn Law
Pennsylvania Legislative Service (Purdon) — Pa Legis Serv (Purdon)
Pennsylvania Library Association. Bulletin — PA Lib Assn Bull
Pennsylvania Library Association. Bulletin — Penn Lib Assn Bull
Pennsylvania Magazine of History and Biography — PA M
Pennsylvania Magazine of History and Biography — Pa M Hist
Pennsylvania Magazine of History and Biography — PA Mag Hist
Pennsylvania Magazine of History and Biography — PA Mag Hist Biogr
Pennsylvania Magazine of History and Biography — PenM
Pennsylvania Magazine of History and Biography — Penn Mag H
Pennsylvania Magazine of History and Biography — Penn Mag Hist Biog
Pennsylvania Magazine of History and Biography — Pennsyl M
Pennsylvania Magazine of History and Biography — PMHB
Pennsylvania Medical Journal — PA Med J
Pennsylvania Medicine — PA Med
Pennsylvania Nurse — PA Nurse
Pennsylvania Nurse — Penn Nurse
Pennsylvania Psychiatric Quarterly — PA Psychiatr Q
Pennsylvania Researcher — Penn Res
Pennsylvania School Journal — PA Sch J
Pennsylvania School Journal — Pa School J
Pennsylvania. State College. Agricultural Experiment Station. Bulletin — Pa State Coll Agric Exp Stn Bull
Pennsylvania State College. Agricultural Experiment Station. Bulletin — Pennsylvania State Coll Agric Exp Sta Bull
Pennsylvania State College Agricultural Experiment Station. Bulletin of Information — Pennsylvania State Coll Agric Exp Sta Bull Inform
Pennsylvania State College. Annual Report — PA St Coll An Rp
Pennsylvania State College. Mineral Industries Experiment Station. Bulletin — PA State Coll Miner Ind Exp Stn Bull
Pennsylvania State College. Mineral Industries Experiment Station. Circular — PA State Coll Miner Ind Exp Stn Circ
Pennsylvania State College. Studies — PA State Coll Stud
Pennsylvania State College Studies — Pennsylvania State Coll Stud
Pennsylvania State Reports — Pa
Pennsylvania State University. College of Agriculture. Agricultural Experiment Station. Bulletin — Pa State Univ Coll Agric Agric Exp Stn Bull
Pennsylvania State University. College of Agriculture. Agricultural Experiment Station. Progress Report — PA State Univ Coll Agric Agric Exp Stn Prog Rep
Pennsylvania State University. College of Agriculture. Agricultural Extension Service. Special Circular — PA State Univ Coll Agric Ext Serv Spec Circ
Pennsylvania State University. College of Earth and Mineral Sciences. Experiment Station. Circular — PA State Univ Coll Earth Miner Sci Exp Stn Circ
Pennsylvania State University. College of Earth and Mineral Sciences. Special Publication — PA State Univ Coll Earth Miner Sci Spec Publ
Pennsylvania State University. College of Engineering. Engineering Proceedings — PA State Univ Coll Eng Eng Proc
Pennsylvania State University. College of Engineering. Engineering Research Bulletin — PA State Univ Coll Eng Eng Res Bull
Pennsylvania State University. Earth and Mineral Sciences Experiment Station. Circular — PA State Univ Earth Miner Sci Exp Stn Circ
Pennsylvania State University. Experiment Station. Bulletin — Penn State Univ Exp Sta Bull
Pennsylvania State University. Experiment Station. Circular — Penn State Univ Exp Sta Circ
Pennsylvania State University. Mineral Industries Experiment Station. Bulletin — PA State Univ Miner Ind Exp Stn Bull
Pennsylvania State University. Mineral Industries Experiment Station. Circular — PA State Univ Miner Ind Exp Stn Circ
Pennsylvania State University. Mineral Sciences Experiment Station. Special Publication — Pa State Univ Miner Sci Exp Stn Spec Publ
Pennsylvania State University. School of Forest Resources. Research Briefs — PA State Univ Sch For Resour Res Briefs
Pennsylvania State University. Studies — PA State Univ Stud
Pennsylvania State University-Abstracts of Doctoral Dissertations — PSU-ADA
Pennsylvania Stockman and Farmer — Penn Stock & F
Pennsylvania Superior Court Reports — Pa Super
Pennsylvania Topographic and Geologic Survey. Bulletin A. Atlas Series — PA Topogr Geol Surv Bull A

Pennsylvania Topographic and Geologic Survey. Bulletin M — PA Topogr Geol Surv Bull M
Pennsylvania Topographic and Geologic Survey. Bulletin W — PA Topogr Geol Surv Bull W
Pennsylvania Topographic and Geologic Survey Commission — PA Top G S Com
Pennsylvania. Topographic and Geologic Survey. County Report — Pa Topogr Geol Surv Cty Rep
Pennsylvania. Topographic and Geologic Survey. Ground Water Report — Pa Topogr Geol Surv Ground Water Rep
Pennsylvania Topographic and Geologic Survey. Mineral Resources Report — PA Topogr Geol Surv Miner Resour Rep
Pennsylvania. Topographic and Geologic Survey. Water Resource Report — Pa Topogr Geol Surv Water Resour Rep
Pennsylvania University. Laboratory Contributions — PA Univ Lab Contr
Pennsylvania University. Schoolmen's Week. Proceedings — PA Univ Schoolmen's Week Proc
Pennsylvania University. University Museum. Bulletin — PA Univ Mus Bul
Pennsylvania University. University Museum. Bulletin — Penn Univ Mus Bul
Pennsylvania-German — PA-Ger
Penny Illustrated Paper — PIP
Penny Magazine — Penny M
Penny Mechanic and the Chemist — Penny Mech Chem
Penny Power — Pen Pow
Penny Stock Performance Digest — PSPD
Penrose Annual — Penrose Ann
Pensamiento — P
Pensamiento [*Madrid*] — Pen
Pensamiento [*Madrid*] — Pens
Pensamiento Critico — PCr
Pensamiento Economico — Pensamiento Econ
Pensamiento Politico — PenP
Pensamiento Politico — Pensamiento Polit
Pensamiento Politico Mexicano — PPM
Pensamiento y Accion — Pensam y Accion
Pensamiento y Accion — PYA
Pensamiento y Accion (Colombia) — PAC
Pensee Catholique — Pen Cath
Pensee Francaise — PF
Pensee Nationale — Pensee Nat
Penseiro Critico — Pen Cri
Pensez Plastiques — Pensez Plast
Pensiero Critico — PC
Pensiero e Linguaggio in Operazioni/Thought and Language in Operations — PLO
Pensiero e Scuola — PS
Pensiero Medico — Pensiero Med
Pensiero Politico — Pens Polit
Pensiero Politico — Pensiero Polit
Pensiero Politico — PPol
Pension and Profit-Sharing Tax Journal — PPS
Pension Benefit Guaranty Corporation. Manual of Opinion Letters — PBGC Manual of Opinion Letters
Pension Briefings — Pension Br
Pension Facts — Pension Fc
Pension Fund Sponsors Ranked by Assets — Pension FA
Pension Plan Guide. Commerce Clearing House — Pens Plan Guide CCH
Pension World — Pen Wld
Pension World — Pension Wld
Pension World — PW
Pensions and Investment Age — Pensions Investm Age
Pensions and Investment Age — PIA
Pensions and Investment Age — PNI
Pensions and Investments [*Later, Pension & Investment Age*] — Pensions
Pensionsforsikringsanstaltens Tidsskrift — Pensf T
Pentax Photography — Pentax Photogr
Pentecostal Evangel — P Evang
Penzenskii Inzhenerno-Stroitel'nyi Institut. Sbornik Nauchnykh Rabot — Penz Inzh Stroit Inst Sb Nauchn Rab
Penzenskii Pedagogiceskii Institut Imeni V. G. Belinskogo. Ucenye Zapiski — Penz Ped Inst Ucen Zap
Penzenskii Politehniceskii Institut. Matematika i Mehanika. Ucenye Zapiski — Penz Politehn Inst Ucen Zap Mat Meh
Penzuegyi Szemle — Penzuegyi Szemle
Penzuegyi Szemle — Penzugyi Szle
People and Planning — People and Plann
People and Taxes — Peopl Tax
People (London) — PL
People, Plans, and the Peace. Peace River Planning Commission — PPPE
People Say. Bimonthly Newsletter [*Canada*] — PESY
People Weekly — GPEW
People Weekly — People
People Weekly — People Wkly
People's China — PC
People's Journal — Peop J
People's Republic of China. Patent Document — Peoples Repub China Pat Doc
People's World — Peo World
Peoria Medical Monthly — Peoria Med Month
Pepinieristes, Horticulteurs, Maraichers [*France*] — Pepinier Hortic Maraichers
Pepperdine Law Review — Pepp LR
Pepperdine Law Review — Pepperdine L Rev
Pepperdine Law Review — Pepperdine LR
Peptide Analysis Protocols — Pept Anal Protoc
Peptide and Protein Drug Delivery — Pept Protein Drug Delivery
Peptide and Protein Reviews — Pept Protein Rev
Peptide and Protein Reviews — PPRRD3
Peptide Pharmaceuticals [*Monograph*] — Pept Pharm
Peptide Research — Pept Res
Peptidergic Neuron. Proceedings. International Symposium on Neurosecretion — Peptidergic Neuron Proc Int Symp Neurosecretion
Peptides [*New York*] — PEPTDO
Peptides. Chemistry and Biology. Proceedings. American Peptide Symposium — Pept Chem Biol Proc Am Pept Symp
Peptides. Proceedings. European Symposium — Pept Proc Eur Symp
Peptides. Structure and Biological Function. Proceedings. American Peptide Symposium — Pept Struct Biol Funct Proc Am Pept Symp
Peptides. Synthesis, Structure, Function. Proceedings. American Peptide Symposium — Pept Synth Struct Funct Proc Am Pept Symp
Pequeno Universo — PU
Per lo Studio e l'Uso del Latino — SUL
Perception — PCTNB
Perception and Psychophysics — P and P
Perception and Psychophysics — PEPSB
Perception and Psychophysics — Perc Psych
Perception and Psychophysics — Percept Psychophys
Perception. Canadian Magazine of Social Comment — PCPT
Perceptual and Motor Skills — IPMS
Perceptual and Motor Skills — Perc Mot Sk
Perceptual and Motor Skills — Percept and Mot Sk
Perceptual and Motor Skills — Percept & Motor Skills
Perceptual and Motor Skills — Percept Mot Skills
Perceptual and Motor Skills — PMOSA
Perceptual and Motor Skills — PMS
Perceptual Cognitive Development — Percept Cogn Dev
Perceptual Cognitive Development — Percept Cognit Devel
Percussionist — PE
Percussionist — PRCMC
Percussive Notes — Perc Notes
Percussive Notes — PN
Percussive Notes. Research Edition — Perc Notes Res Ed
Peredneaziatskij Sbornik — PAS
Peredovoi Opyt v Stroitel'stve i Ekspluatatsii Shakht [*Former USSR*] — Peredovoi Opyt Stroit Eksp Shakht
Peredovoi Opyt v Stroitel'stve i Ekspluatatsii Shakht — Peredovoi Opyt Stroit Ekspl Shakht
Peredovoi Opyt v Stroitel'stve i Ekspluatatsii Shakht — POSEA
Pererabotka Gaza i Gazovogo Kondensata. Nauchno-Tekhnicheskii Obzor — Pererab Gaza Gazov Kondens Nauchno-Tekh Obz
Pererabotka Margantsevykh i Polimetallicheskikh Rud Gruzii — Pererab Margantsevykh Polimet Rud Gruz
Pererabotka Neftyanykh Gazov — Pererab Neft Gazov
Pererabotka Tverdogo Topliva [*Former USSR*] — Pererab Tverd Topl
Perfiles Educativos (Mexico) — PEM
Performance and Instruction — Performance Instr
Performance and Instruction Journal — Perform Instr J
Performance Evaluation — Perf Eval
Performance Evaluation — Performance Eval
Performance Evaluation Review — Perf Eval Rev
Performance Evaluation Review — Performance Eval Rev
Performance Monitoring for Geotechnical Construction. Symposium — Perform Monit Geotech Constr Symp
Performance of Protective Clothing. Symposium — Perform Prot Clothing Symp
Performance Practice Review — PPR
Performing Arts and Entertainment in Canada — IPAC
Performing Arts & Entertainment in Canada — Per Arts & Ent Can
Performing Arts in Canada — IPAC
Performing Arts in Canada — Perf Art C
Performing Arts in Canada — Perf Arts
Performing Arts in Canada — Perf Arts Can
Performing Arts Information Guide Series — PAIGS
Performing Arts Journal — Per AJ
Performing Arts Journal — Perf Art J
Performing Arts Journal — PPAJ
Performing Arts Resources — PAR
Performing Arts Review — PAR
Performing Arts Review — Per A R
Performing Arts Review — Perf Art R
Performing Arts Review — Perf Arts R
Performing Arts Review — Performing Arts Rev
Performing Right — Perf Right
Perftorirovannye Uglerody v Biologii i Meditsine [*monograph*] — Perftorirovannye Uglerody Biol Med
Perfumer and Flavorist — Perfum Flavor
Perfumer and Flavorist — Perfum Flavorist
Perfumer and Flavorist — Perfumer
Perfumer and Flavorist International — Perfum Flavor Int
Perfumer and Flavorist International — Perfum Flavorist Int
Perfumerie und Kosmetik — Perfum Kosmet
Perfumers' Journal — Perfum J
Perfumers' Journal and Essential Oil Recorder — Perfumers J
Perfumery and Essential Oil Record — Perfum Essent Oil Rec
Perfumery and Flavouring [*Japan*] — Perfum Flavour
Pergamenische Forschungen — PF
Pergamon General Psychology Series — Pergamon Gen Psychol Ser
Pergamon General Psychology Series — PGPSDZ
Pergamon International Library of Science, Technology, Engineering, and Social Studies — Pergamon Internat Library Sci Tech Engrg Social Stud
Pergamon International Series on Dance and Related Disciplines — Perg I S Da

Pergamon Series of Monographs in Laboratory Techniques — Pergamon Ser Monogr Lab Tech
Pergamon Series on Environmental Science — Pergamon Ser Environ Sci
Pergamon Texts in Inorganic Chemistry — Pergamon Texts Inorg Chem
Pericardial Diseases — Pericard Dis
Perinatal Medicine — Perinat Med
Perinatal Medicine. Clinical and Biochemical Aspects — Perinat Med Clin Biochem Aspects
Perinatal Medicine. European Congress — Perinat Med Eur Congr
Perinatal Medicine (Tokyo) — Perinat Med Tokyo
Perinatal Pharmacology and Therapeutics [*Monograph*] — Perinat Pharmacol Ther
Perinatal Thyroid Physiology and Disease — Perinat Thyroid Physiol Dis
Perinatology/Neonatology — Perinat Neonat
Perinatology-Neonatology Directory — Perinatol Neonatol Dir
Periodic Bulletin. International Sugar Confectionery Manufacturers' Association and International Office of Cocoa and Chocolate — Period Bull Int Sugar Confect Manuf Assoc Int Off Cocoa Choc
Periodica de Re Morali Canonica Liturgica — PMCL
Periodica de Re Morali Canonica Liturgica — PRMCL
Periodica Mathematica Hungarica — Period Math Hung
Periodica Mathematica Hungarica — Period Math Hungar
Periodica Polytechnica — Period Polytech
Periodica Polytechnica. Chemical Engineering — Per Poly CE
Periodica Polytechnica. Chemical Engineering — Period Polytech Chem Eng
Periodica Polytechnica. Chemisches Ingenieurwesen — Period Polytech Chem Ingenieurwes
Periodica Polytechnica. Civil Engineering [*Hungary*] — Period Polytech Civ Eng
Periodica Polytechnica. Civil Engineering — Period Polytech Civ Engng
Periodica Polytechnica. Electrical Engineering — Per Poly EE
Periodica Polytechnica. Electrical Engineering — Period Polytech Electr Eng
Periodica Polytechnica. Engineering — Period Polytech Eng
Periodica Polytechnica. Khimiya — Period Polytech Khim
Periodica Polytechnica. Maschinen- und Bauwesen — Period Polytech Masch Bauwes
Periodica Polytechnica. Mechanical Engineering — Per Poly ME
Periodica Polytechnica. Mechanical Engineering [*Hungary*] — Period Polytech Mech Eng
Periodica Polytechnica. Mechanical Engineering — Period Polytech Mech Engng
Periodica Polytechnica. Mechanical Engineering — PPMMB
Periodica Polytechnica. Stroitel'stvo — Period Polytech Stroit
Periodica Polytechnica. Transportation Engineering — Period Polytech Trans Engng
Periodical Accounts Relating to the Moravian Missions — PAMM
Periodical Guide for Computerists — Period Guide Comput
Periodical Guide for Computerists [*Database*] — PGFC
Periodical on Animal Production — Period Anim Prod
Periodically Speaking — Period Speaking
Periodically Speaking — PESPD
Periodico di Matematiche — Period Mat
Periodico di Matematiche. Serie V — Period Mat 5
Periodico di Mineralogia [*Italy*] — Period Mineral
Periodico. Sociedad Medico-Quirurgica de Cadiz — Period Soc Med Quir Cadiz
Periodico. Societa Storia Comense — PSC
Periodicum Biologorum — PDBIA
Periodicum Biologorum — Per Biol
Periodicum Biologorum — Period Biol
Periodicum Mathematico-Physicum et Astronomicum — Period Math Phys Astron
Periodieke Verzameling van Administratieve en Rechterlijke Beslissingen — Adm B
Periodieke Verzameling van Administratieve en Rechterlijke Beslissingen Betreffende het Openbaar Bestuur in Nederland — PV
Periodieke Verzameling van Administratieve en Rechterlijke Beslissingen Betreffende het Openbaar Bestuur in Nederland met Register Volgens Kaartsys — ARB
Periodiekenparade — SFK
Periodiske Meddelelser fra Demonstrationslokalet for Gas og Elektricitet — PMGoE
Periodontal Abstracts. Journal of the Western Society of Periodontology — Periodont Abstr
Periodontal Case Reports — Periodont Case Rep
Perioperative Nursing Quarterly — Periopr Nurs Q
Peripheral Arterial Chemoreceptors. Proceedings. International Symposium — Peripher Arterial Chemorecept Proc Int Symp
Peripheral Arterial Chemoreceptors. Proceedings. International Workshop — Peripher Arterial Chemorecept Proc Int Workshop
Peripheral Circulation. Proceedings. International Symposium on the Peripheral Circulation — Peripher Circ Proc Int Symp
Peritoneal Dialysis Bulletin — Periton Dia
Peritoneal Dialysis International — Perit Dial Int
Perkin-Elmer Instrument News for Science and Industry — Perkin Elmer Instrum News Sci Ind
Perkin-Elmer Technical News — Perkin-Elmer Tech News
Perkin-Elmer Thermal Analysis Application Study — Perkin Elmer Therm Anal Appl Study
Perkins Journal — Perk
Perkins Observatory Contributions — Perkins Obs Contrib
Perkins Observatory. Contributions. Series 2 — Perkins Obs Contrib Ser 2
Perkins School of Theology. Journal — Perkins J
Permanence of Organic Coatings. Symposium — Permanence Org Coat Symp
Permanency Report — Permanency Rep
Permanent Way — Perm Way
Permanent Way Institution. Journal — J Perm Way Instn
Permanente Foundation Medical Bulletin — Perm Found Med Bull
Permanente Foundation (Oakland, California) Medical Bulletin — Perm Found Oakland Calif Med Bull
Permbledhje Studimesh — Permbledhje Stud
Permbledhje Studimesh. Instituti i Kerkimeve Gjeologjike dhe Minerale — Permbledhje Stud Inst Kerkimeve Gjeol Miner
Permbledhje Studimesh. Instituti i Studimeve dhe Kerkimeve Industirale e Minerale — Permbledhje Stud Inst Stud Kerkimeve Ind Miner
Permskaya Gosudarstvennaya Sel'skokhozyaistvennaya Opytnaya Stantsiya. Sbornik Nauchnykh Trudov — Permsk Gos Skh Opytn Stn Sb Nauchn Tr
Permskaya Oblastnaya Nauchno-Tekhnicheskaya Konferentsiya po Spektroskopii — Permsk Obl Nauchno Tekh Konf Spektrosk
Permskii Gosudarstvennyi Farmatsevticheskii Institut. Nauchnye Trudy — Permsk Gos Farm Inst Nauchn Tr
Permskii Gosudarstvennyi Pedagogiceskii Institut. Ucenye Zapiski — Perm Gos Ped Inst Ucen Zap
Permskii Gosudarstvennyi Sel'skokhozyaistvennyi Institut. Trudy — Permsk Gos Skh Inst Tr
Permskii Gosudarstvennyi Universitet Imeni A. M. Gor'kogo. Ucenye Zapiski — Perm Gos Univ Ucen Zap
Permskii Nauchno-Issledovatel'skii Ugol'nyi Institut. Nauchnye Trudy — Permsk Nauchno Issled Ugoln Inst Nauchn Tr
Permskii Politehniceskii Institut. Sbornik Naucnyh Trudov — Perm Politehn Inst Sb Naucn Trudov
Permskii Sel'skokhozyaistvennyi Institut imeni Akademika D.N. Pryanishnikova. Trudy — Permsk Skh Inst im Akad DN Pryanishnikova Tr
Pernambuco Odontologica — Pernamb Odont
Pero Galego — PG
Peroxidases in Chemistry and Biology [*Monograph*] — Peroxidases Chem Biol
Persatuan Biokimia Malaysia. Proceedings. Malaysian Biochemical Society Conference — Persat Biokim Malays Proc Malays Biochem Soc Conf
Persian Gulf Administration Report — PGAR
Persian Gulf Political Residency Administration Reports — PGPRAR
Persica. Jaarboek van het Genootschap Nederland-Iran — PJGNI
Personal Communications — Pers Commun
Personal Computer World — Pers Comput World
Personal Computers Today — Per Comp T
Personal Computing — PSC
Personal Finance Law Quarterly Report — Pers Finance LQ
Personal Finance Law Quarterly Report — Pers Finance LQ Rep
Personal Injury Annual — Pers Inj Ann
Personal Injury Deskbook — Pers Inj Deskbook
Personal Management Abstracts — PerManAb
Personal. Mensch und Arbeit in Betrieb — MAZ
Personal Names from Cuneiform Inscriptions of Cappadocia — PNC
Personal Radio Exchange — PRE
Personal Report for the Executive — Pers Rep Exec
Personal Report for the Executive — PREXA
Personalist — Pers
Personalist — Person
Personality and Individual Differences — PEIDD9
Personality and Individual Differences — Pers Indiv
Personality and Individual Differences — Pers Individ Differ
Personality and Psychopathology — Pers Psychopathol
Personality and Social Psychology Bulletin — Personal & Soc Psychol Bull
Personality and Social Psychology Bulletin — PPSB
Personality Tests and Reviews — PTR
Personalvertretung — Pers V
Personalvertretungsgesetz — PVG
Personeelbeleid — PSB
Personenbefoerderungsgesetz — P Bef G
Personenvervoer — BVP
Personhistorisk Tidskrift — Personhist T
Personhistorisk Tidskrift — PHT
Personnel — PER
Personnel — Pers
Personnel Administration — Pers Adm
Personnel Administrator [*Database*] — PA
Personnel Administrator — PAD
Personnel Administrator — Pers Adm
Personnel Administrator — Pers Admin
Personnel Administrator — Psl Admr
Personnel and Guidance Journal — Pers Guid J
Personnel and Guidance Journal — Personnel & Guid J
Personnel and Guidance Journal — Personnel Guidance J
Personnel and Guidance Journal — PGD
Personnel and Guidance Journal — PGJ
Personnel and Guidance Journal — Psl & Guid J
Personnel and Training Abstracts — PTA
Personnel Executive — PE
Personnel Executive — Personnel Exec
Personnel Executive — Psl Exec
Personnel Journal — PEJ
Personnel Journal — PEJOA
Personnel Journal — Pers J
Personnel Journal — Pers Jrl
Personnel Journal — Personnel J
Personnel Journal — PJ
Personnel Journal — Psl J
Personnel Journal Index [*Database*] — PJI
Personnel Literature — Pers Lit
Personnel Management — JPM
Personnel Management — Pers Manage
Personnel Management — Pers Mgt
Personnel Management — Personnel Mgmt
Personnel Management — PSL

Personnel Management Abstracts — Pers Manage Abstr
Personnel Management Abstracts — Pers Mgmt Abstr
Personnel Management Abstracts — Person Manage Abstr
Personnel Management Abstracts — Personnel Mgt Abstracts
Personnel Management Abstracts — PMA
Personnel Management (London) — Personnel Manag (London)
Personnel Management. Prentice-Hall — Personnel Mgmt P-H
Personnel Practice Bulletin — Per Pract B
Personnel Practice Bulletin — Pers Prac Bul
Personnel Practice Bulletin — Pers Pract Bull
Personnel Practice Bulletin — Personn Pract Bull
Personnel Practice Bulletin — Personnel Practice B
Personnel Practice Bulletin — Personnel Practice Bul
Personnel Practice Bulletin — PPBUA
Personnel Practices Newsletter — Pers Pract Newsl
Personnel Psychology — Per Psy
Personnel Psychology — Pers Psych
Personnel Psychology — Pers Psychol
Personnel Psychology — Personnel Psych
Personnel Psychology — Personnel Psychol
Personnel Psychology — PPS
Personnel Psychology — PPSYA
Personnel Psychology — Psl Psy
Personnel Review — PRV
Personnel Review — Psl R
Persoon en Gemeenschap — PerG
Perspectiva Teologica — Persp Teol
Perspectivas de la Economia Mundial — PEM
Perspective — Per
Perspective — Perspec
Perspective (Karachi) — Perspective K
Perspective Report Series — Perspect Rep Ser
Perspectives — P
Perspectives — Per
Perspectives — Persp
Perspectives de Catholicite — Persp Cath
Perspectives de l'Economie Mondiale — PEM
Perspectives Euro-Africaines — Perspectives Euro-Afr
Perspectives in American History — PerH
Perspectives in American History — Pers Am Hist
Perspectives in American History — Perspect Am Hist
Perspectives in American History — Perspect Amer Hist
Perspectives in Asthma — Perspect Asthma
Perspectives in Biological Dynamics and Theoretical Medicine — Perspect Biol Dyn Theor Med
Perspectives in Biology and Medicine — PBMEA
Perspectives in Biology and Medicine — Persp Biol
Perspectives in Biology and Medicine — Perspec Biol & Med
Perspectives in Biology and Medicine — Perspect Biol Med
Perspectives in Biology and Medicine — Perspectives Biol Med
Perspectives in Biometrics — PEBIDN
Perspectives in Biometrics — Perspect Biom
Perspectives in Biotechnology — Perspect Biotechnol
Perspectives in Brain Research. Proceedings. International Summer School of Brain Research — Perspect Brain Res Proc Int Summer Sch
Perspectives in Cancer Research and Treatment — Perspect Cancer Res Treat
Perspectives in Cardiovascular Research — Perspect Cardiovasc Res
Perspectives in Clinical Pharmacology — Perspect Clin Pharmacol
Perspectives in Clinical Pharmacy — Perspect Clin Pharm
Perspectives in Coeliac Disease. Proceedings. Symposium on Coeliac Disease — Perspect Coeliac Dis Proc Symp
Perspectives in Computing — Perspect Comput
Perspectives in Computing — PIC
Perspectives in Cystic Fibrosis. Proceedings. International Cystic Fibrosis Congress — Perspect Cystic Fibrosis Proc Int Cystic Fibrosis Congr
Perspectives in Education — Perspect in Educ
Perspectives in Ethology — Perspect Ethol
Perspectives in Grassland Ecology — Perspect Grassl Ecol
Perspectives in Hemostasis. Selected Proceedings. Symposia — Perspect Hemostasis Sel Proc Symp
Perspectives in Human Reproduction — Perspect Hum Reprod
Perspectives in Industrial Psychology — Perspect Ind Psychol
Perspectives in Inherited Metabolic Diseases — Perspect Inherited Metab Dis
Perspectives in Mathematical Logic — Perspect Math Logic
Perspectives in Mathematics — Perspect Math
Perspectives in Medicine — Perspect Med
Perspectives in Membrane Biology. Mexican Society of Biochemistry Symposium — Perspect Membr Biol Mex Soc Biochem Symp
Perspectives in Membrane Biophysics — Perspect Membr Biophys
Perspectives in Nephrology and Hypertension — Perspect Nephrol Hypertens
Perspectives in Nephrology and Hypertension — PNHYD
Perspectives in Neuroendocrine Research — Perspect Neuroendocr Res
Perspectives in Ophthalmology — PEOPD7
Perspectives in Ophthalmology — Perspect Ophthalmol
Perspectives in Pediatric Pathology — Perspect Pediatr Pathol
Perspectives in Powder Metallurgy — Perspect Powder Metall
Perspectives in Probability and Statistics: in Honor of M. S. Bartlett — PPrStBrt
Perspectives in Psychiatric Care — Pers Psych C
Perspectives in Psychiatric Care — Perspect Psychiatr Care
Perspectives in Quantum Chemistry and Biochemistry — Perspect Quantum Chem Biochem
Perspectives in Religious Studies — Per Rel St
Perspectives in Religious Studies — PIRS
Perspectives in Religious Studies — PRS
Perspectives in Shock Research. Proceedings. Annual Conference on Shock — Perspect Shock Res Proc Annu Conf Shock
Perspectives in Structural Chemistry — Perspect Struct Chem
Perspectives in Supramolecular Chemistry — Perspect Supramol Chem
Perspectives in the Brain Sciences — Perspect Brain Sci
Perspectives in Vertebrate Science — Perspect Vertebr Sci
Perspectives in Vertebrate Science — PVSCD5
Perspectives in Virology — Perspect Virol
Perspectives Internationales — Perspect Int
Perspectives Latino-Americaines — Perspectives Latino-Am
Perspectives of Biophysical Ecology — Perspect Biophys Ecol
Perspectives of New Music — Pers New Mus
Perspectives of New Music — Persp N Mus
Perspectives of New Music — Perspectives New M
Perspectives of New Music — PNM
Perspectives of New Music — PNMUB
Perspectives of New Music — PPNM
Perspectives on Accreditation — Perspect Accredit
Perspectives on Contemporary Literature — PCL
Perspectives on Developmental Neurobiology — Perspect Dev Neurobiol
Perspectives on Education — Perspec Ed
Perspectives on Medicaid and Medicare Management — Perspect Medicaid Medicare Manage
Perspectives on Medicaid Management — Perspect Medicaid Manage
Perspectives on Science. Historical, Philosophical, Social — Perspect Sci
Perspectives Polonaises — Persp Pol
Perspectives Polonaises — Perspect Polon
Perspectives Psychiatriques — Perspect Psychiatr
Perspectives Socialistes — Persp Soc
Perspectives. The Civil Rights Quarterly — Perspectives Civ Rights Q
Perspectives USA — PUSA
Perspektiv — Pers
Perspektiven der Philosophie — Perspekt Phil
Perspektiven der Zukunft — PdZ
Perspektivy Zakladneho Vyskuma Dreva. Prace — Perspekt Zakl Vysk Dreva Pr
Peru Indigena — Peru Indig
Peru Indigena — PI
Peru. Instituto Nacional de Investigacion y Fomento Mineros. Serie Memorandum — Peru Inst Nac Invest Fom Min Ser Memo
Peru. Ministerio de Agricultura. Direccion General de Agricultura. Boletin — Peru Minist Agric Dir Gen Agric Bol
Peru. Ministerio de Agricultura. Direccion General de Investigaciones Agropecuarias. Boletin Tecnico — Peru Minist Agric Dir Gen Invest Agropecu Bol Tec
Peru. Ministerio de Agricultura. Servicio de Investigacion y Promocion Agraria. Boletin Tecnico — Peru Minist Agric Serv Invest Promoc Agrar Bol Tec
Peru. Ministerio de Energia y Minas. Servicio de Geologia y Mineria. Estudios Especiales — Peru Minist Energ Minas Serv Geol Min Estud Espec
Peru. Ministerio de Fomento y Obras Publicas. Direccion General de Mineria. Boletin — Peru Dir Gen Mineria Bol
Peru. Ministerio de Fomento y Obras Publicas. Instituto Nacional de Investigacion y Fomento Mineros. Boletin — Peru Minist Fom Obras Publicas Inst Nac Invest Fom Min Bol
Peru. Servicio de Geologia y Mineria. Boletin — Peru Serv Geol Min Bol
Peru. Servicio de Geologia y Mineria. Estudios Especiales — Peru Serv Geol Min Estud Espec
Peru. Servicio de Geologia y Mineria. Geodinamica e Ingenieria Geologica — Peru Serv Geol Min Geodinamica Ing Geol
Perugia Quadrennial International Conference on Cancer. Proceedings — Perugia Quadrenn Int Conf Cancer Proc
Peruvian Quarterly Report — PQR
Pervyi Global'nyi Eksperiment PIGAP (Programma Issledovaniya Global'nykh Atmosfernykh Protsessov) — Pervyi Globalnyi Eksp PIGAP
PESC Record. IEEE [*Institute of Electrical and Electronics Engineers*] **Power Electronics Specialists Conference** — PESC Rec IEEE Power Electron Spec Conf
Pesca y Marina — Pesca Mar
Pesca y Pesquisa — Pesca Pesqui
Peshawar. University. Department of Geology. Geological Bulletin — Peshawar Univ Dep Geol Geol Bull
Pesquisa Agropecuaria Brasileira — Pesqui Agropecu Bras
Pesquisa Agropecuaria Brasileira. Serie Agronomia — PAGAA
Pesquisa Agropecuaria Brasileira. Serie Agronomia — Pesqui Agropecu Bras Ser Agron
Pesquisa Agropecuaria Brasileira. Serie Agronomia — Pesqui Agropecuar Brasil Ser Agron
Pesquisa Agropecuaria Brasileira. Serie Veterinaria — PABVA
Pesquisa Agropecuaria Brasileira. Serie Veterinaria — Pesqui Agropecu Bras Ser Vet
Pesquisa Agropecuaria Brasileira. Serie Veterinaria — Pesqui Agropecuar Brasil Ser Vet
Pesquisa Agropecuaria Brasileira. Serie Zootecnia — Pesqui Agropecu Bras Ser Zootec
Pesquisa Agropecuaria Pernambucana — PAPEDJ
Pesquisa Agropecuaria Pernambucana — Pesqui Agropecu Pernambucana
Pesquisa Aplicada Latino Americana — Pesqui Apl Lat Am
Pesquisa e Planejamento Economico — Pesquisa e Planejamento Econ
Pesquisa Medica — Pesqui Med
Pesquisa Veterinaria Brasileira — Pesqui Vet Bras
Pesquisa Veterinaria Brasileira [*Brazilian Journal of Veterinary Research*] — PVBRDX
Pesquisas — Pesqu
Pesquisas Agropecuarias do Nordeste Recife — Pesqui Agropecu Nordeste Recife

Pesquisas Antropologia — Pesquisas Antropol
Pesquisas. Anuario do Instituto Anchietano de Pesquisas — IAP/P
Pesquisas Botanica — PQBOAK
Pesquisas Botanica (Porto Alegre) — Pesqui Bot (Porto Alegre)
Pesquisas Communications (Porto Alegre) — Pesqui Commun (Porto Alegre)
Pesquisas. Seccao B. Ciencias Naturais (Porto Alegre) — Pesqui Secc B Cienc Nat (Porto Alegre)
Pesquisas. Universidade Federal do Rio Grande do Sul. Instituto de Geociencias — Pesquisas Univ Fed Rio Grande Sul Inst Geocienc
Pesquisas Zoologia (Porto Alegre) — Pesqui Zool (Porto Alegre)
Pest Articles and News Summaries — Pest Artic News Summ
Pest Control — PCONA
Pest Control — Pest Contr
Pest Control — Pest Contro
Pest Control Circular — Pest Control Circ
Pest Control Literature Documentation [*Database*] — PESTDOC
Pest Infestation Control. Laboratory Report (London) — Pest Infest Control Lab Rep (Lond)
Pest Infestation Control. Laboratory Report (London) — Pest Infest Control (Lond)
Pest Infestation Research Report. Pest Infestation Laboratory. Agricultural Research Council — Pest Infest Res Rep Pest Infest Lab Agric Res Counc
Pest Leaflet. Pacific Forest Research Centre — Pest Leafl Pac For Res Cent
Pest Management Research Information System [*Database*] — PRIS
Pester Medicinisch-Chirurgische Presse — Pester Med Chir Presse
Pesticide and Technique — Pestic Tech
Pesticide and Toxic Chemical News — Pestic Toxic Chem News
Pesticide Biochemistry and Physiology — PCBPB
Pesticide Biochemistry and Physiology — Pest Bioch
Pesticide Biochemistry and Physiology — Pestic Biochem Physiol
Pesticide Chemistry. Proceedings. International IUPAC Congress of Pesticide Chemistry — Pestic Chem Proc Int IUPAC Congr Pestic Chem
Pesticide Formulations and Application Systems — Pestic Formulations Appl Syst
Pesticide Formulations and Application Systems. Conference — Pestic Formulations Appl Syst Conf
Pesticide Formulations and Application Systems. Symposium — Pestic Formulations Appl Syst Symp
Pesticide Progress — Pestic Progr
Pesticide Research Bulletin — Pestic Res Bull
Pesticide Research Report — Pestic Res Rep
Pesticide Research Report. Agriculture Canada — Pestic Res Rep Agric Can
Pesticide Science — Pest Sci
Pesticide Science — Pestic Sci
Pesticide Selectivity — Pestic Sel
Pesticide Tank Mix Applications. Conference — Pestic Tank Mix Appl Conf
Pesticides Abstracts and News Summary — Pestic Abstr
Pesticides Abstracts and News Summary. Section C. Herbicides — Pestic Abstr News Sum Sect C Herbic
Pesticides and Toxic Substances Monitoring Report — Pestic Toxic Subst Mon Rep
Pesticides Annual — Pesticide A
Pesticides. CIPAC [*Collaborative International Pesticides Analytical Council*] **Methods and Proceedings Series** — Pestic CIPAC Methods Proc Ser
Pesticides Documentation Bulletin — Pestic Doc Bull
Pesticides in Aquatic Environments — Pestic Aquat Environ
Pesticides Monitoring Journal — PEMJA
Pesticides Monitoring Journal — Pest Mon J
Pesticides Monitoring Journal — Pestic Monit J
Pesticides Monitoring Journal — PMOJ
Pestycydy w Swietle Toksykologii Srodowiska — Pestyc Swietle Toksykol Srodowiska
Peter De Ridder Press Publications — PDR
Petera Stuckas Latvijas Valsts Universitate Zinatniskie Raksti — LUZR
Petera Stuckas Latvijas Valsts Universitate Zinatniskie Raksti. Filologijas Zinatnes. A Serija (Riga) — LUR
Petera Stuckas Latvijas Valsts Universitates Botaniska Darza Raksti — Petera Stuckas Latv Valsts Univ Bot Darza Raksti
Peterborough Museum Society. Occasional Papers — Peterborough Mus Soc Occas Pap
Petermanns. A. Mitteilungen aus J. Perthes Geographischer Anstalt — Petermanns Mitt
Petermanns Geographische Mitteilungen — Pet Geogr Mitt
Petermanns Geographische Mitteilungen — Peterm Geog
Petermanns Geographische Mitteilungen — Petermanns Geog Mitt
Petermanns Geographische Mitteilungen — Petermanns Geogr Mitt
Petermanns Geographische Mitteilungen — PGgM
Petermanns Geographische Mitteilungen — PGM
Petermanns Geographische Mitteilungen — PM
Petermanns Geographische Mitteilungen. Ergaenzungshefte — PGM E
Petermanns Mitteilungen — Pet Mitt
Petermanns Mitteilungen — PM
Petermanns Mitteilungen aus Perthes' Geographischer Anstalt — PMPGA
Petermanns Mitteilungen. Ergaenzungsheft [*Gotha*] — Petermanns Mitt Erg
Peters Notes — Pet
Petersen's Photographic — GPPM
Petersen's Photographic Magazine — Pet P M
Petersen's Photographic Magazine — Peter Phot Mag
Petit Journal du Brasseur — Petit J Brass
Petite Revue des Deux Mondes de Geographie et d'Histoire — Pet Rev Deux Mond Geogr Hist
Petkim Dergisi — Petkim Derg
Petkim Petrokimya A.S. Arastirma Mudurlugu. Teknik Bulten — Petkim Petrokimya AS Arastirma Mudurlugu Tek Bul
Petro/Chem Engineer — PCHEA
Petro/Chem Engineer — Petro/Chem Eng
Petrochemical Equipment — Petrochem Equip
Petrochemical Technology (Beijing) — Petrochem Technol Beijing
Petrocorp Review — Pet Rev
Petrofi Irodalmi Muzeum Evkonyve — PIME
Petrografiya Tsentral'nogo Kazakhstana — Petrogr Tsentr Kaz
Petrografiya Vostochnoi Sibiri — Petrogr Vost Sib
Petrography Applied to Concrete and Concrete Aggregates — Petrogr Appl Concr Concr Aggregates
Petrokhimiya. Kriterii Rudonosnosti Magmaticheskikh Kompleksov — Petrokhim Kriter Rudonosn Magmat Kompleksov
Petrol si Gaze [*Romania*] — Pet & Gaze
Petrol si Gaze — Pet Gaze
Petrol si Gaze — PGAZA
Petrol si Gaze. Supliment [*Romania*] — Pet Gaze Supl
Petrole et Gaz (Budapest) — Pet Gaz (Budapest)
Petrole et Ses Derives — Pet Ses Deriv
Petrole et Techniques — Pet Tech
Petrole et Techniques — Petrol Tech
Petrole Informations — Pet Inf
Petrole Informations — Petrol Inform
Petroleo Interamericano — Pet Interam
Petroleo Interamericano — Pet Interamericano
Petroleo Internacional — Pet Int
Petroleo Internacional — Petrol Int
Petroleo Internacional — Petroleo
Petroleo Internacional (Great Neck, New York) — Pet Int Great Neck NY
Petroleo Internacional (Tulsa, Oklahoma) — Pet Int Tulsa Okla
Petroleo y Tecnologia — Petrol Tecnol
Petroleos Mexicanos Servicio de Informacion — Petroleos Mexicanos Servicio Inf
Petrole-Progres — Petr Prog
Petroleum Abstracts [*Also, an information service or system*] — PA
Petroleum Abstracts — PEABA
Petroleum Abstracts — Pet Abstr
Petroleum Abstracts — Pet Abstracts
Petroleum Abstracts — Petrol Abstr
Petroleum Abstracts [*Online*] — TULSA
Petroleum Age — Pet Age
Petroleum and Chemical Industry Conference. Record of Conference Papers [*United States*] — Pet Chem Ind Conf Rec Conf Pap
Petroleum and Chemical Industry Developments [*India*] — Pet Chem Ind Dev
Petroleum and Chemical Industry Developments. Annual — Pet Chem Ind Dev Annu
Petroleum and Coal — Pet Coal
Petroleum and Gas Processing — Pet Gas Process
Petroleum and Global Tectonics. Papers Presented at the Meeting. Princeton University Conference — Pet Global Tecton Pap Meet Princeton Univ Conf
Petroleum and Hydrocarbons — PEHYA
Petroleum and Hydrocarbons [*India*] — Pet Hydrocarbons
Petroleum and Microorganisms (Tokyo) — Pet Microorg (Tokyo)
Petroleum and Oil-Shale Industry — Pet Oil Shale Ind
Petroleum and Petrochemical International [*England*] — Pet Petrochem Int
Petroleum and Petrochemicals [*Japan*] — Pet Petrochem
Petroleum and Petrochemicals (Tokyo) [*Japan*] — Pet Petrochem (Tokyo)
Petroleum Chemistry — Pet Chem
Petroleum Chemistry USSR [*English Translation*] — PECHA
Petroleum Chemistry USSR — Pet Chem USSR
Petroleum Economist — IPK
Petroleum Economist — PEECD
Petroleum Economist — Pet Econ
Petroleum Economist — Petroleum
Petroleum Economist — PPSE
Petroleum Economy — Pet Econ
Petroleum/Energy Business News Index — Pet Energy Bus News Index
Petroleum Engineer — PE
Petroleum Engineer — Pet Eng
Petroleum Engineer — Petrol Eng
Petroleum Engineer (Dallas) — Pet Eng Dallas
Petroleum Engineer International — PEEID
Petroleum Engineer International — Pet Eng Int
Petroleum Engineer International — Petrol Eng Int
Petroleum Engineering (Los Angeles) — Pet Eng Los Angeles
Petroleum Equipment — Pet Equip
Petroleum Equipment and Services — Pet Equip Serv
Petroleum Exploration and Development — Pet Explor Dev
Petroleum Gazette — Pet Gaz
Petroleum Gazette — Petrol Gaz
Petroleum Gazette — Petroleum Gaz
Petroleum Geology [*English Translation*] — PEGEA
Petroleum Geology — Pet Geol
Petroleum Geology — Petrol Geol
Petroleum Geology (English Translation) — Pet Geol Engl Transl
Petroleum Geology of Taiwan — Pet Geol Taiwan
Petroleum Geology of Taiwan — PGTWA
Petroleum Independent — Pet Indep
Petroleum Independent — Petr Inde
Petroleum Independent — Petrol Independ
Petroleum Industry of the USSR — Pet Ind USSR
Petroleum Intelligence Weekly — PIW
Petroleum International (London) — Pet Int (London)
Petroleum Land Journal — Pet Land J
Petroleum Management — Pet Manage
Petroleum Marketing Monthly [*Database*] — PMM
Petroleum News [*Taiwan*] — Pet News

Petroleum News — Petrol News
Petroleum News. Asia's Energy Journal — PEN
Petroleum Newsletter — Pet Newsl
Petroleum Outlook — PEOUD
Petroleum Outlook — Pet Outlook
Petroleum Press Service [*England*] — Pet Press Serv
Petroleum Press Service — Pet Press Service
Petroleum Press Service — PRPSA
Petroleum Process Engineering — Pet Process Eng
Petroleum Processing — Pet Process
Petroleum Processing (Beijing) — Pet Process Beijing
Petroleum Refiner — Pet Refin
Petroleum Refiner — Pet Refiner
Petroleum Refiner — Petrol Ref
Petroleum Refining — Pet Refin
Petroleum Refining and Petrochemicals Literature Abstracts — Pet Refin Petrochem Lit Abstr
Petroleum Review — Pet Rev
Petroleum Review — PETRB
Petroleum Review — Petrol Rev
Petroleum Review — PR
Petroleum Situation — Petr Sit
Petroleum Situation — Petro Sit
Petroleum Society of CIM. Annual Technical Meeting — Pet Soc CIM Annu Tech Meet
Petroleum Statement. Energy Data Reports — Pet Statement Energy Data Rep
Petroleum Substitutes — Pet Substitutes
Petroleum Technical Review — Pet Tech Rev
Petroleum Technology — Pet Technol
Petroleum Technology — Petr Techn
Petroleum Technology — Petrol Technol
Petroleum Technology (London) — Pet Technol London
Petroleum Times — Pet Times
Petroleum Times — Petr Times
Petroleum Times — Petro Times
Petroleum Times — PETTA
Petroleum Times — PT
Petroleum Times — PTI
Petroleum Times Price Report — Petr Tm R
Petroleum Today — Pet Today
Petroleum Today — PTTDA
Petroleum Transactions. AIME (American Institute of Mining, Metallurgy, and Petroleum Engineering) — Am Inst Min Metal Pet Eng Pet Trans
Petroleum Transport Scheme for Assistance in Freight Emergencies — PETRASAFE
Petroleum und Oelschieferindustrie — Pet Oelschieferind
Petroleum Week — Pet W
Petroleum Week — Pet Week
Petroleum World [*London*] — Pet World
Petroleum World and Oil — Pet World Oil
Petroleum World and Oil Age — Pet World Oil Age
Petroleum World (London) — Pet World (London)
Petroleum World (Los Angeles) — Pet World (Los Angeles)
Petroleum-Industrie — Pet Ind
Petroleum-Industrie von Aserbaidshan — Pet Ind Aserb
Petroleum-Wirtschaft — Pet Wirtsch
Petrolieri d'Italia — Pet Ital
Petrolieri International — Petrolieri Int
Petrolieri International (Milan) — Pet Int Milan
Petrologie — PETRD
Petrotecnica — PETOA
Petrozavodskii Gosudarstvennyi Universitet. Ucenye Zapiski — Petrozavodsk Gos Univ Ucen Zap
Petrus Nonius — PN
Petty Sessions Review — Petty SR
Petty Sessions Review — PSR
Peuce. Studii si Communicari de Istorie si Arheologie — PSCIA
Peuples et Civilisations — PeC
Peuples Mediterraneens — PM
Peuples Mediterraneens/Mediterranean Peoples — Peuples Medit Medit Peoples
PF. Boletin Informativo de Patrimonio Forestal del Estado — P F Bol Inform Patrimonio Forest Estado
Pfaelzer Heimat — Pfaelz Heimat
Pfaelzer Heimat — Pfaelzer H
Pfaelzer Heimat — PfH
Pfaelzer Heimat — PFHEDE
Pfaelzer Museum und Pfaelzische Heimatkunde — PfM
Pfaelzische Gartenzeitung — Pfaelz Gartenzeitung
Pfaelzische Heimatblaetter — PfH
Pfaelzische Heimatkunde — PfHK
Pfaelzische Rundschau — Pfaelz Rdsch
Pfaelzisches Kirchenlexikon — PKL
Pfalzbaierisches Museum — Pfalzbaier Mus
Pfizer Medical Monographs — Pfizer Med Monogr
Pflanzenbau, Pflanzenschutz, Pflanzenzucht — PflBau PflSchutz PflZucht
Pflanzenphysiologische Untersuchungen — Pflanzenphysiol Untersuch
Pflanzenschutz, Wissenschaft, und Wirtschaft — Pflanzenschutz Wiss Wirtsch
Pflanzenschutzberichte — Pflanzenschutzber
Pflanzenschutz-Nachrichten — Pflanzenschutz-Nachr
Pflanzenschutz-Nachrichten (American Edition) — Pflanzenschutz-Nachr (Am Ed)
Pflanzenschutz-Nachrichten Bayer — Pflanzenschutz Nachr Bayer
Pflanzenschutz-Nachrichten Bayer — Pflanz-Nach Bayer
Pflanzenschutz-Nachrichten Bayer (German Edition) — Pflanzenschutz Nachr Bayer (Ger Ed)
Pfluegers Archiv. European Journal of Physiology — PFLAB
Pfluegers Archiv. European Journal of Physiology — Pflueg Arch
Pfluegers Archiv. European Journal of Physiology — Pfluegers Arch
Pfluegers Archiv. European Journal of Physiology — Pfluegers Arch Eur J Physiol
Pfluegers Archiv fuer die Gesamte Physiologie — Arch Ges Physiol
Pfluegers Archiv fuer die Gesamte Physiologie — Pfluegers Arch Ges Physiol
Pfluegers Archiv fuer die Gesamte Physiologie des Menschen und der Tiere — Pf A
Pfluegers Archiv fuer die Gesamte Physiologie des Menschen und der Tiere [*A publication*] — Pfluegers Archiv Gesamte Physiol Menschen Tiere
PFNA [*Pentecostal Fellowship of North America*] **News** — PFNA N
PGRSA (Plant Growth Regulator Society of America) Quarterly — PGRSA Q
PHAC. Pathologie Humaine et Animale Comparee — PHAC Pathol Hum Anim Comp
PHAC. Pathologie Humaine et Animale Comparee — PHACCK
Phaenomenologisch-Psychologische Forschungen — PPF
Phanerogamarum Monographiae — Phanerogamarum Monogr
Phanerogamarum Monographiae — PHMODF
Phantom — Pnm
Pharm Tech Japan — Pharm Tech Jpn
Pharma International — Pharma Int
Pharma International (English Edition) — Pharma Int Engl Ed
Pharma Japan — Pharma Jpn
Pharma Japan — PHR
Pharma Medica — Pharma Med
Pharma Technologie Journal — Pharma Technol J
Pharmaceutica Acta Helvetiae — PAHEA
Pharmaceutica Acta Helvetiae — Pharm Act H
Pharmaceutica Acta Helvetiae — Pharm Acta Helv
Pharmaceutical Abstracts — Pharm Abstr
Pharmaceutical and Cosmetics Review [*South Africa*] — Pharm Cosmet Rev
Pharmaceutical and Healthcare Industries News Database — PHIND
Pharmaceutical and Pharmacological Letters — Pharm Pharmacol Lett
Pharmaceutical Archives — Pharm Arch
Pharmaceutical Biotechnology — Pharm Biotechnol
Pharmaceutical Bulletin — Pharm Bull
Pharmaceutical Bulletin. Fukuoka University — Pharm Bull Fukuoka Univ
Pharmaceutical Bulletin. Nihon University — Pharm Bull Nihon Univ
Pharmaceutical Business News — Pharm Bus News
Pharmaceutical Chemistry Journal — PCJOAU
Pharmaceutical Chemistry Journal — Pharm Chem J
Pharmaceutical Chemistry Journal (English Translation of Khimiko-Farmatsevticheskii Zhurnal) — Pharm Chem J (Engl Transl Khim Farm Zh)
Pharmaceutical Chemistry Journal (USSR) — Pharm Chem J (USSR)
Pharmaceutical Development and Technology — Pharm Dev Technol
Pharmaceutical Era — Pharm Era
Pharmaceutical Historian (Great Britain) — Pharm Hist Gt Br
Pharmaceutical Industry of Yugoslavia — Pharm Ind Yugosl
Pharmaceutical Industry (Shanghai) — Pharm Ind (Shanghai)
Pharmaceutical Journal — Pharm J
Pharmaceutical Journal — PJ
Pharmaceutical Journal and Pharmacist — Pharm J Pharm
Pharmaceutical Journal and Transactions — Pharmaceutical J
Pharmaceutical Journal and Transactions. Pharmaceutical Society of Great Britain — Pharm J Trans
Pharmaceutical Journal (Dunedin, New Zealand) — Pharm J (Dunedin NZ)
Pharmaceutical Journal of New Zealand — Pharm J NZ
Pharmaceutical Library Bulletin — Pharm Libr Bull
Pharmaceutical Literature Documentation [*Database*] — RINGDOC
Pharmaceutical Manufacturers Association. Yearbook — Pharm Manuf Assoc Yearb
Pharmaceutical Medicine — Pharm Med
Pharmaceutical Medicine [*Hampshire*] — PHMDEH
Pharmaceutical Medicine (Hampshire) — Pharm Med (Hamps)
Pharmaceutical Medicine - the Future. International Meeting of Pharmaceutical Physicians — Pharm Med Future Int Meet Pharm Physicians
Pharmaceutical Monographs — Pharm Monogr
Pharmaceutical News — Pharm News
Pharmaceutical News Index — Pharm News Index
Pharmaceutical News Index [*Database*] — PNI
Pharmaceutical Record [*New York*] — PR
Pharmaceutical Research — Pharm Res
Pharmaceutical Review — Pharm Rev
Pharmaceutical Review (Tokyo) — Pharm Rev (Tokyo)
Pharmaceutical Science Communications — Pharm Sci Commun
Pharmaceutical Sciences — Pharm Sci
Pharmaceutical Society of Japan. Journal — Pharm Soc Jpn J
Pharmaceutical Society (Pilani). Journal — Pharm Soc (Pilani) J
Pharmaceutical Technology — Pharm Technol
Pharmaceutical Technology International — Pharm Technol Int
Pharmaceuticals and Cosmetics — Pharm Cosmet
Pharmaceuticals Monthly — Pharm Mon
Pharmaceutisch Tijdschrift van Vlaanderen — Pharm Tijdschr Vlaanderen
Pharmaceutisch Tijdschrift voor Nederlandsch-Indie — Pharm Tijdschr Ned Indie
Pharmaceutisch Weekblad — PHA
Pharmaceutisch Weekblad — Pharm Weekbl
Pharmaceutisch Weekblad — PHWEA
Pharmaceutisch Weekblad. Scientific Edition — Pharm Weekbl Sci
Pharmaceutische Rundschau (Berlin) — Pharm Rundsch (Berlin)
Pharmaceutische Tijdschrift voor Belgie — Pharm Tijdschr Belg
Pharmaceutische Zeitschrift fuer Russland — Pharm Z Russl
Pharmaceutisches Centralblatt — Pharm Centralbl

Pharmaceutisches Correspondenzblatt fuer Sueddeutschland Nebst Anzeigeblatt — Pharm Correspondenzbl Sueddeutschl
Pharmacia-JTPA — Pharm JTPA
Pharmacie Hospitaliere Francaise — Pharm Hosp Fr
Pharmacien Biologiste — Pharm Biol
Pharmacien Biologiste — PHBIA
Pharmacien d'Aquitaine — Pharm Aquitaine
Pharmacien de France — Pharm Fr
Pharmacien Rural — Pharm Rural
Pharmacie-Produits Pharmaceutiques — Pharm Prod Pharm
Pharmacochemistry Library — Pharmacochem Libr
Pharmacochemistry Library [*Elsevier Book Series*] — PhCL
Pharmacognosy and Phytochemistry. International Congress — Pharmacogn Phytochem Int Congr
Pharmacognosy Titles — Pharmacog Tit
Pharmacologia Clinica — Pharmacol Clin
Pharmacological and Biochemical Properties of Drug Substances — Pharmacol Biochem Prop Drug Subst
Pharmacological Basis of Therapeutics [*monograph*] — Pharmacol Basis Ther
Pharmacological Basis on Migraine Therapy. Papers. International Symposium — Pharmacol Basis Migraine Ther Pap Int Symp
Pharmacological Effect of Lipids — Pharmacol Eff Lipids
Pharmacological Research — Pharmac Res
Pharmacological Research — Pharmacol Res
Pharmacological Research Communications — Pharmacol R
Pharmacological Research Communications — Pharmacol Res Commun
Pharmacological Research Communications — PLRCA
Pharmacological Reviews — PAREA
Pharmacological Reviews — Pharm Rev
Pharmacological Reviews — Pharmacol Rev
Pharmacologist — Pharmacolog
Pharmacology — Pharmacol
Pharmacology — PHMGB
Pharmacology and the Skin — Pharmacol Skin
Pharmacology and Therapeutics — Pharmacol Ther
Pharmacology and Therapeutics in Dentistry — Pharmacol Ther Dent
Pharmacology and Therapeutics. Part A. Chemotherapy, Toxicology, and Metabolic Inhibitors — Pharmacol Ther Part A Chemother Toxicol Metab Inhibitors
Pharmacology and Therapeutics. Part B. General and Systematic Pharmacology — Pharmacol Ther (B)
Pharmacology and Therapeutics. Part B. General and Systematic Pharmacology — Pharmacol Ther Part B Gen Syst Pharmacol
Pharmacology and Therapeutics. Part C. Clinical Pharmacology and Therapeutics — Pharmacol Ther Part C
Pharmacology and Toxicology — Pharm Tox
Pharmacology and Toxicology (Amsterdam) — Pharmacol Toxicol (Amsterdam)
Pharmacology and Toxicology (Copenhagen) — Pharmacol Toxicol (Copenhagen)
Pharmacology and Toxicology (English Translation of Farmakologiya Toksikologiya) [*Moscow*] — Pharmacol Toxicol (Engl Transl)
Pharmacology and Toxicology (Mannheim) — Pharmacol Toxicol Mannheim
Pharmacology and Toxicology (USSR) — Pharmacol Toxicol (USSR)
Pharmacology, Biochemistry, and Behavior — PBBHA
Pharmacology, Biochemistry, and Behavior — Pharm Bio B
Pharmacology, Biochemistry, and Behavior — Pharmacol Biochem Behav
Pharmacology for Physicians — Pharmacol Physicians
Pharmacology in Medicine — Pharmacol Med
Pharmacology of Conditioning, Learning, and Retention. Proceedings. International Pharmacological Meeting — Pharmacol Cond Learn Retention Proc Int Pharmacol Meet
Pharmacology of Eating Disorders (Monograph). Theoretical and Clinical Developments — Pharmacol Eating Disord
Pharmacology of Sleep — Pharmacol Sleep
Pharmacy in History — Pharm Hist
Pharmacy International [*Netherlands*] — Pharm Int
Pharmacy International — PHIND
Pharmacy Management — Pharm Manage
Pharmacy Management Combined with the American Journal of Pharmacy — Pharm Manage Comb Am J Pharm
Pharmacy Pakistan — Pharm Pak
Pharmacy Reports (Beijing) — Pharm Rep (Beijing)
Pharmacy Times — Pharm Times
Pharmakeutikon Deltion. Epistemonike Ekdosis — Pharmakeutickon Delt Epistem Ekodosis
Pharmakopsychiatrie Neuro-Psychopharmakologie — Pharmakopsy
Pharmakopsychiatrie Neuro-Psychopharmakologie — Pharmakopsychiatr Neuro-Psychopharmakol
Pharmazeutische Berichte — Pharm Ber
Pharmazeutische Betrieb — Pharm Betr
Pharmazeutische Industrie — Pharm Ind
Pharmazeutische Industrie — PHINA
Pharmazeutische Industrie — PHR
Pharmazeutische Monatsblaetter — Pharm Monatsbl
Pharmazeutische Monatshefte — Pharm Monatsh
Pharmazeutische Post — Pharm Post
Pharmazeutische Post. Beilage — Pharm Post Beil
Pharmazeutische Praxis — Pharm Prax
Pharmazeutische Praxis — PHPXA
Pharmazeutische Presse — Pharm Presse
Pharmazeutische Presse. Beilage — Pharm Presse Beil
Pharmazeutische Presse. Wissenschaftlich-Praktische Hefte — Pharm Presse Wiss Prakt Hefte
Pharmazeutische Rundschau — Pharm Rundsch
Pharmazeutische Verfahrenstechnik Heute — Pharm Verfahrenstech Heute
Pharmazeutische Zeitung — Pharm Zeitung
Pharmazeutische Zeitung — Pharm Ztg
Pharmazeutische Zeitung — PHZIA
Pharmazeutische Zeitung (Berlin) — Pharm Ztg (Berl)
Pharmazeutische Zeitung Nachrichten — Pharm Ztg Nachr
Pharmazeutische Zeitung. Scientific Edition — Pharm Ztg Sci Ed
Pharmazeutische Zeitung. Vereinigt mit Apotheker-Zeitung [*Germany*] — Pharm Ztg Ver Apotheker-Ztg
Pharmazeutische Zeitung. Vereinigt mit Apotheker-Zeitung — PHZAA
Pharmazeutische Zentralhalle — Pharm Zentralhalle
Pharmazeutische Zentralhalle fuer Deutschland — Pharm Zentralhalle Dtl
Pharmazeutische Zentralhalle fuer Deutschland — Pharm Zentralhalle Dtschl
Pharmazeutisches Journal (Kiev) — Pharm J (Kiev)
Pharmazeutisch-Technische Assistenten Heute — Pharm Tech Assist Heute
Pharmazie — PHARA
Pharmazie. Beihefte — Pharmazie Beih
Pharmazie Heute — Pharm Heute
Pharmazie in Unserer Zeit — Pharm Unserer Zeit
Pharmazie und Pharmakologie (Moscow) — Pharm Pharmakol (Moscow)
PharmChem Newsletter (Menlo Park, California) — PharmChem Newsl (Menlo Park Calif)
Pharmeceutisch Weekblad voor Nederland — Pharm Weekbl Ned
Pharmkeutikon Deltion Epistemonike Ekdosis — Pharm Delt Epistem Ekdosis
Pharos of Alpha Omega Alpha Honor Medical Society — PAMSB
Pharos of Alpha Omega Alpha Honor Medical Society — Pharos
Phase Transition Phenomena [*Elsevier Book Series*] — PTP
Phase Transitions. Proceedings. Conference on Chemistry — Phase Transitions Proc Conf Chem
Phenomena in Ionized Gases. Contributed Papers. International Conference — Phenom Ioniz Gases Contrib Pap Int Conf
Phenomenology and Pedagogy — Phen & Ped
Phi Delta Kappan — GPDK
Phi Delta Kappan — PDK
Phi Delta Kappan — PHDK
Phi Delta Kappan — Phi D K
Phi Delta Kappan — Phi Del Kap
Phi Mu Alpha Sinfonian — Sin
Philadelphia Botanic Sentinel and Thomsonian Medical Revolutionist — Philadelphia Bot Sentinel Thomsonian Med Revolutionist
Philadelphia Business Journal — Phila Bs J
Philadelphia Free Press — Phl Freep
Philadelphia Geographical Society. Bulletin — Phila Geog Soc Bull
Philadelphia Inquirer — Phila Inqr
Philadelphia Inquirer — PI
Philadelphia Journal. Medical and Physical Sciences — Phila J Med Phys Sci
Philadelphia Journal of the Medical and Physical Sciences — Philadelphia J Med Phys Sci
Philadelphia Library Association. Bulletin — PLAB
Philadelphia Magazine — IPHL
Philadelphia Medical and Physical Journal — Phila Med Phys J
Philadelphia Medical Journal — Phila Med J
Philadelphia Medicine — Phila Med
Philadelphia Medicine — Philadelphia Med
Philadelphia Museum of Art. Bulletin — Phila Mus Bull
Philadelphia Orchestra. Program Notes — Phila Orch
Philadelphia Photographer — Phila Phot
Philanthropist — Philanthrop
Philatelen Pregled — Philat Pregl
Philatelic Bulletin — Phil Bull
Philatelic Bulletin — Philat Bul
Philately from Australia — Philat Aust
Philately from Australia — Philately from Aust
Philharmonic — Philhar
Philharmonic Post — Phil Post
Philip Morris Science Symposium. Proceedings — Philip Morris Sci Symp Proc
Philippiana Sacra [*Manila*] — PhilipSa
Philippine Abstracts — Philip Abstr
Philippine Agricultural Engineering Journal — Philipp Agric Eng J
Philippine Agricultural Review — Phil Ag R
Philippine Agricultural Review — Philipp Agric Rev
Philippine Agricultural Review — Philippine Ag R
Philippine Agricultural Situation — Philippine Agr Situation
Philippine Agriculturist — PHAGA
Philippine Agriculturist — Phil Ag
Philippine Agriculturist — Philipp Agric
Philippine Agriculturist — Philippine Agr
Philippine Atomic Bulletin — Philipp At Bull
Philippine Atomic Energy Commission. Annual Report — Philipp AEC Annu Rep
Philippine Atomic Energy Commission. Publications — Philipp AEC
Philippine Atomic Energy Commission. Reports — Philipp AEC Rep
Philippine Biochemical Society. Bulletin — Philipp Biochem Soc Bull
Philippine Business Review — Phil Bus R
Philippine Business Review — Philipp Bus Rev
Philippine Chinese Historical Association. Annals — PCHAA
Philippine Development — FAF
Philippine Development — Phil Dev
Philippine Economic Journal — PhEJ
Philippine Economic Journal — Philippine Econ J
Philippine Economy and Industrial Journal — Philippine Economy and Ind J
Philippine Economy Bulletin — PEB
Philippine Educational Forum — Phil Ed Forum
Philippine Educator — PE
Philippine Entomologist — Philipp Ent
Philippine Entomologist — Philipp Entomol
Philippine Farms and Gardens — Philipp Farms Gard

Philippine Farms and Gardens — Philippine Farm Gard
Philippine Forests — Philipp For
Philippine Geographical Journal — PGGJ-A
Philippine Geographical Journal — Phil Geog J
Philippine Geographical Journal — Philipp Geogr J
Philippine Geologist — Philipp Geol
Philippine Historical Review — PHR
Philippine Journal of Agriculture — Phil J Ag
Philippine Journal of Agriculture — Philipp J Agric
Philippine Journal of Anesthesiology — Philipp J Anesthesiol
Philippine Journal of Animal Industry — Philipp J Anim Ind
Philippine Journal of Animal Industry — PJAIA
Philippine Journal of Cancer — Philipp J Cancer
Philippine Journal of Cardiology — Philipp J Cardiol
Philippine Journal of Coconut Studies — Philipp J Coconut Stud
Philippine Journal of Crop Science — Philipp J Crop Sci
Philippine Journal of Education — Phil J Ed
Philippine Journal of Fisheries — Phil J Fish
Philippine Journal of Fisheries — Philipp J Fish
Philippine Journal of Food Science and Technology — Philipp J Food Sci Technol
Philippine Journal of Forestry — Philipp J For
Philippine Journal of Internal Medicine — Philipp J Intern Med
Philippine Journal of Language Teaching — PJLT
Philippine Journal of Linguistics — Phil J Ling
Philippine Journal of Linguistics — PJL
Philippine Journal of Nursing — Philipp J Nurs
Philippine Journal of Nursing — PJN
Philippine Journal of Nutrition — Philipp J Nutr
Philippine Journal of Nutrition — Philippine J Nutr
Philippine Journal of Nutrition — PJNu
Philippine Journal of Ophthalmology — Philipp J Ophthal
Philippine Journal of Ophthalmology — Philipp J Ophthalmol
Philippine Journal of Pediatrics — Philipp J Pediat
Philippine Journal of Pediatrics — Philipp J Pediatr
Philippine Journal of Pediatrics — PJP
Philippine Journal of Plant Industry — Philipp J Plant Ind
Philippine Journal of Plant Industry — Philippine J Plant Ind
Philippine Journal of Plant Industry — PJPI
Philippine Journal of Public Administration — Phil J Pub Admin
Philippine Journal of Public Administration — Philipp J Pub Admin
Philippine Journal of Public Administration — Philippine J Pub Adm
Philippine Journal of Public Administration — Philippine J Pub Admin
Philippine Journal of Public Administration — Philippine J Public Admin
Philippine Journal of Public Administration — PJPA
Philippine Journal of Science — Phil J Sci
Philippine Journal of Science — Philipp J Sci
Philippine Journal of Science — Philippine J Sci
Philippine Journal of Science — PHSCA
Philippine Journal of Science — PJS
Philippine Journal of Science. Section A. Chemical Sciences — Philipp J Sci Sect A
Philippine Journal of Science. Section B. Medical Sciences — Philipp J Sci Sect B
Philippine Journal of Science. Section C. Botany — Philipp J Sci Sect C
Philippine Journal of Science Teachers — Phil J Sci Teach
Philippine Journal of Surgery — Philipp J Surg
Philippine Journal of Surgery and Surgical Specialties — Philipp J Surg Surg Spec
Philippine Journal of Surgery, Obstetrics, and Gynecology — Philipp J Surg Obstet Gynecol
Philippine Journal of Surgical Specialties — PJSS
Philippine Journal of Tropical Medicine — Philipp J Trop Med
Philippine Journal of Veterinary and Animal Sciences — Philipp J Vet Anim Sci
Philippine Journal of Veterinary Medicine — Philipp J Vet Med
Philippine Journal of Vocational Education — Phil J Voc Ed
Philippine Junior Red Cross Magazine — PJRCM
Philippine Labor Review — Phil Lab R
Philippine Library Association. Bulletin — PLAB
Philippine Library Journal — PLJ
Philippine Lumberman — Philipp Lumberm
Philippine Manager — PM
Philippine Medical World — Philipp Med World
Philippine Medical World (1946-1951) — Philipp Med World (1946-1951)
Philippine Medical World (1952-1962) — Philipp Med World (1952-1962)
Philippine Medical-Dental Journal — Philipp Med Dent J
Philippine Metals — Philipp Met
Philippine Mining Journal — Philipp Min J
Philippine Mining Record — PMR
Philippine Normal College Language Study Center. Occasional Paper — Philipp Norm Coll Lang Stud Cent Occ Pap
Philippine Orchid Review — Philipp Orchid Rev
Philippine Phytopathology — Philipp Phytopathol
Philippine Planning Journal — Phil Plan J
Philippine Planning Journal — Philippine Planning J
Philippine Planning Journal — PPJ
Philippine Political Science Journal — Phil Pol Sci J
Philippine Population Journal — Philip Popul J
Philippine Population Journal — Philipp Popul J
Philippine Quarterly of Culture and Society — Phil Q Cult Soc
Philippine Quarterly of Culture and Society — Philipp Q Cult Soc
Philippine Quarterly of Culture and Society — Philipp Quart Cult Soc
Philippine Quarterly of Culture and Society — PQCS
Philippine Report — Philipp Rep
Philippine Review of Business and Economics — Phil R Bus Econ
Philippine Sacra — Phil Sacra
Philippine Science Index — Philipp Sci Index
Philippine Scientist — Philipp Sci
Philippine Social Science Review — PSSR
Philippine Social Sciences and Humanities Review — Phil Soc Sci Hum R
Philippine Social Sciences and Humanities Review — PSSHR
Philippine Sociological Review — Phil Sociol R
Philippine Sociological Review — Phili S Rev
Philippine Sociological Review — Philippine Sociol R
Philippine Sociological Review — PhSR
Philippine Sociological Review — PSR
Philippine Statistican — PSta
Philippine Studies — Phil Stud
Philippine Studies — Philippine Stud
Philippine Studies [*Manila*] — PhilipSt
Philippine Studies — PhiS
Philippine Studies — PS
Philippine Studies — PStu
Philippine Studies (Manila) — PSM
Philippine Sugar Institute. Quarterly — Philipp Sugar Inst Q
Philippine Sugar Institute Quarterly — Philipp Sugar Inst Quart
Philippine Textile Digest — Philipp Text Dig
Philippine Textile Information Digest — Philipp Text Inf Dig
Philippine Weed Science Bulletin — Philipp Weed Sci Bull
Philippines. Bureau of Agricultural Economics. Report — Philipp Bur Agric Econ Rep
Philippines. Bureau of Mines and Geo-Sciences. Report of Investigation — Philipp Bur Mines Geo Sci Rep Invest
Philippines. Bureau of Mines and Geo-Sciences. Report of Investigation — Philippines Bur Mines Geo-Sci Rep Invest
Philippines. Bureau of Mines. Information Circular — Philipp Bur Mines Inf Circ
Philippines. Bureau of Mines. Report of Investigations — Philipp Bur Mines Rep Invest
Philippines. Bureau of Mines. Special Projects Series. Publication — Philipp Bur Mines Spec Proj Ser Publ
Philippines. Department of Agriculture and Natural Resources. Bureau of Mines. Information Circular — Philipp Dep Agric Nat Resour Bur Mines Inf Circ
Philippines. Department of Agriculture and Natural Resources. Bureau of Mines. Report of Investigation — Philipp Dep Agric Nat Resour Bur Mines Rep Invest
Philippines. Department of Agriculture and Natural Resources. Bureau of Mines. Special Projects Series Publication — Philipp Dep Agric Nat Resour Bur Mines Spec Proj Ser Publ
Philippines. Department of Natural Resources. Bureau of Mines. Report of Investigation — Philipp Dep Nat Resour Bur Mines Rep Invest
Philippines. Forest Products Research and Industries Development Commission. FORPRIDE Digest — Philipp For Prod Res Ind Dev Comm FORPRIDE Dig
Philippines Nuclear Journal — Philipp Nucl J
Philippines Quarterly — P Qu
Philippines Quarterly — Phil Q
Philippines Rice and Corn Progress — Philippine Rice Corn Progr
Philippiniana Sacra — Philip Sac
Philippiniana Sacra — PSa
Philips Industrial Engineering Bulletin — Philips Ind Eng Bul
Philips Journal of Research — Philips J Res
Philips Journal of Research — PHJRD
Philips Music Herald — Philips
Philips Research Reports — Phil Res R
Philips Research Reports — Philips Res Rep
Philips Research Reports — PRREA
Philips Research Reports. Supplements — Philips Res Rep Suppl
Philips Research Reports. Supplements — PRSSA
Philips Serving Science and Industry — Philips Serv Sci Ind
Philips Technical Review — Phil Tech R
Philips Technical Review — Phil Techn Rev
Philips Technical Review — Philips Tech Rev
Philips Technical Review — PTREA
Philips Technisch Tijdschrift — Philips Tech Tijdschr
Philips Technische Rundschau — Phil Techn Rd
Philips Technische Rundschau — Philips Tech Rundsch
Philips Technische Rundschau [*Netherlands*] — Philips Tech Rundschau
Philips Technische Tijdschrift — PHTTA
Philips Telecommunication Review — Philips Telecommun Rev
Philips Welding Reporter — Philips Weld Rep
Phillippine Journal of Science — Phillip J Sci
Phillips' Paper Trade Directory of the World — Phillips Dir
Philobiblon — PhB
Philologia Classica — Phil Class
Philologia Orientalis — PhO
Philologiae Turcicae Fundamenta — Ph TF
Philologica — Pha
Philologica Pragensia — Ph Prag
Philologica Pragensia — PhP
Philologica Pragensia — PP
Philological Association of the Pacific Coast — PAPC
Philological Monographs. American Philological Association — APA
Philological Museum — Phil Mus
Philological Quarterly — Ph Q
Philological Quarterly — Phil Qy
Philological Quarterly — Philol Q
Philological Quarterly — Philol Quart
Philological Quarterly — PPQU
Philological Quarterly — PQ

Philological Society. Publications. Occasional Studies — PSPOS
Philological Society. Transactions — Phil Soc
Philological Society Transactions — Philol Soc Trans
Philological Society. Transactions — PST
Philological Transactions — Philol Trans
Philologike Kypros — PK
Philologike Protochronia — PhP
Philologische Studien — Ph Studien
Philologische Studien — Phil St
Philologische Studien — Phil Stud
Philologische Studien — PhS
Philologische Studien und Quellen — PSQ
Philologische Studien und Quellen — PSuQ
Philologische Untersuchungen — Phil Unters
Philologische Untersuchungen — PhU
Philologische Wochenschrift — Bp W
Philologische Wochenschrift [*Berlin*] — Ph Wschr
Philologische Wochenschrift — Phil Woch
Philologische Wochenschrift — Phil Wochenschr
Philologische Wochenschrift — PhW
Philologische Wochenschrift — PW
Philologische Wochenschrift (Berlin) — Berl Philol Woch
Philologischer Anzeiger als Ergaenzung des Philologus — PhA
Philologus. Supplement [*Wiesbaden*] — Ph S
Philologus. Zeitschrift fuer das Klassiche Altertum — Philol
Philologus. Zeitschrift fuer Klassische Altertum — P
Philologus. Zeitschrift fuer Klassische Altertum — Ph
Philologus. Zeitschrift fuer Klassische Altertum — Phil
Philologus. Zeitschrift fuer Klassische Altertum — Philologus ZKA
Philologus. Zeitschrift fuer Klassische Altertum — PZKA
Philologus. Zeitschrift fuer Klassische Philologie — PZKP
Philosopher's Index — Phil Ind
Philosopher's Index — Philos Index
Philosopher's Index — Philosl
Philosopher's Index — PI
Philosophes Medievaux — Ph Med
Philosophia Antiqua — Ph Ant
Philosophia Antiqua — PHA
Philosophia Antiqua — Phil Ant
Philosophia Antiqua — Philos Antiq
Philosophia Lovaniensis — Ph L
Philosophia Mathematica — Phil Math
Philosophia Mathematica — Philos Math
Philosophia. Mendoza — Phil M
Philosophia Naturalis — Ph N
Philosophia Naturalis — Ph Nat
Philosophia Naturalis — Phil Natur
Philosophia Naturalis — Philos Nat
Philosophia Naturalis — Philos Natur
Philosophia Naturalis — PHSNA
Philosophia Naturalis. Beiheft — Ph N B
Philosophia Patrum — Ph P
Philosophia Patrum — Phil Patr
Philosophia Patrum — PP
Philosophia Reformata — Ph Ref
Philosophia Reformata — Phil Reform
Philosophia Religionis — Ph Rel
Philosophic Exchange — Phil Exch
Philosophica (Valparaiso, Chile) — PAV
Philosophical and Historical Studies — PHS
Philosophical Books — Phil Books
Philosophical Books — Philos Book
Philosophical Collections. Royal Society of London — Philos Collect R Soc London
Philosophical Currents — Philos Curr
Philosophical Explorations — Philos Explor
Philosophical Forum — Phil Forum
Philosophical Forum — Philos Forum
Philosophical Forum. A Quarterly — Philos Forum Quart
Philosophical Forum (Boston) — Phil Forum (Boston)
Philosophical Inquiry — Phil Inq
Philosophical Investigators — Phil Invest
Philosophical Journal — Ph J
Philosophical Journal — Philos J
Philosophical Journal (Edinburgh) — Ph JE
Philosophical Journal. Transactions. Royal Philosophical Society of Glasgow — Phil J
Philosophical Linguistics — Phil Ling
Philosophical Magazine — Ph Mag
Philosophical Magazine — Phil Mag
Philosophical Magazine — Philos M
Philosophical Magazine — Philos Mag
Philosophical Magazine — PHMAA
Philosophical Magazine A. Physics of Condensed Matter, Defects, and Mechanical Properties — Philos Mag A
Philosophical Magazine B. Physics of Condensed Matter, Electronic, Optical, and Magnetic Properties — Philos Mag B
Philosophical Magazine Letters — Philos Mag Lett
Philosophical Magazine. Supplement — Philos Mag Suppl
Philosophical Papers — Phil Papers
Philosophical Papers — Philos Pap
Philosophical Phenomenological Review — Ph Rev
Philosophical Quarterly — GPHQ
Philosophical Quarterly — Phil Q
Philosophical Quarterly — Phil Quart
Philosophical Quarterly — Philos Quart
Philosophical Quarterly — PhilosQ
Philosophical Quarterly — PhQ
Philosophical Quarterly — PQ
Philosophical Review — Ph Rev
Philosophical Review — Phil R
Philosophical Review — Phil Rev
Philosophical Review — Philos R
Philosophical Review — Philos Rev
Philosophical Review — PhR
Philosophical Review — PPSR
Philosophical Review — PR
Philosophical Review — PRv
Philosophical Review (Taiwan) — Phil Rev (Taiwan)
Philosophical Society of Glasgow. Proceedings — Ph Soc Glasgow Pr
Philosophical Society of Washington. Bulletin — Ph Soc Wash B
Philosophical Studies — Phil Stud
Philosophical Studies — Philo Stds
Philosophical Studies — Philos Stud
Philosophical Studies [*Dordrecht*] — Philos Studies
Philosophical Studies — PhilS
Philosophical Studies — PhS
Philosophical Studies — PhSt
Philosophical Studies — PS
Philosophical Studies. American Catholic Philosophical Association — PSACPA
Philosophical Studies in Education — Phil Stud Educ
Philosophical Studies (Ireland) — Phil Stud (Ireland)
Philosophical Studies of Japan — PSJ
Philosophical Studies Series in Philosophy — Philos Stud Ser Philos
Philosophical Topics — Phil Topics
Philosophical Topics — Philos Top
Philosophical Transactions — Phil Trans
Philosophical Transactions Abridged (Hutton, Editor) — Philos Trans Abr Hutton
Philosophical Transactions. Giving Some Account of the Present Undertakings, Studies, and Labours of the Ingenious in Many Parts of the World — Philos Trans
Philosophical Transactions. Mathematical, Physical, and Engineering Sciences — Philos Trans Phys Eng Sci
Philosophical Transactions. Royal Society. London. Series A — Phil Trans Roy Soc Lond Ser A
Philosophical Transactions. Royal Society of London — Phil Trans R Soc
Philosophical Transactions. Royal Society of London — Phil Trans Roy Soc Lond
Philosophical Transactions. Royal Society of London — Philos Trans R Soc London
Philosophical Transactions. Royal Society of London. B. Biological Sciences — Philos Trans R Soc Lond B Biol Sci
Philosophical Transactions. Royal Society of London. Series A. Mathematical and Physical Sciences — Phi T Roy A
Philosophical Transactions. Royal Society of London. Series A. Mathematical and Physical Sciences — Phil Trans Roy Soc London Ser A Math Phys Sci
Philosophical Transactions. Royal Society of London. Series A. Mathematical and Physical Sciences — Phil Trans Royal Soc London Ser A
Philosophical Transactions. Royal Society of London. Series A. Mathematical and Physical Sciences — Philos Trans R Soc A
Philosophical Transactions. Royal Society of London. Series A. Mathematical and Physical Sciences — Philos Trans R Soc Lond A Math Phys Sci
Philosophical Transactions. Royal Society of London. Series A. Mathematical and Physical Sciences — Philos Trans R Soc Lond Ser A
Philosophical Transactions. Royal Society of London. Series A. Mathematical and Physical Sciences — Philos Trans R Soc London A
Philosophical Transactions. Royal Society of London. Series A. Mathematical and Physical Sciences — Philos Trans R Soc London Ser A
Philosophical Transactions. Royal Society of London. Series A. Mathematical and Physical Sciences — Philos Trans Roy Soc London Ser A
Philosophical Transactions. Royal Society of London. Series B. Biological Sciences — Phi T Roy B
Philosophical Transactions. Royal Society of London. Series B. Biological Sciences — Phil Trans Roy Soc Lond B
Philosophical Transactions. Royal Society of London. Series B. Biological Sciences — Philos Trans R Soc Lond Biol
Philosophical Transactions. Royal Society of London. Series B. Biological Sciences — Philos Trans R Soc Lond Ser A
Philosophical Transactions. Royal Society of London. Series B. Biological Sciences — Philos Trans R Soc London Ser B
Philosophie de l'Esprit — Ph Esp
Philosophie et Logique — Phil Log
Philosophie in Einzeldarstellungen — Ph E
Philosophie in Einzeldarstellungen. Ergaenzungsband — Ph E E
Philosophie und Geschichte — Ph G
Philosophie und Grenzwissenschaften — PGW
Philosophische Abhandlungen — P Abh
Philosophische Abhandlungen — PA
Philosophische Abhandlungen — Ph A
Philosophische Abhandlungen — Philos Abhandlungen
Philosophische Abhandlungen (Berlin) — Ph AB
Philosophische Arbeiten — Phil Arb
Philosophische Bibliothek [*Meiner*] — PhB
Philosophische Bibliothek [*Hamburg*] — Philos Bibliothek
Philosophische Blaetter der Kant-Gesellschaft — PhBlKG
Philosophische Forschungen — P Fsch
Philosophische Forschungen — PF
Philosophische Forschungen — Ph F
Philosophische Monatshefte — Ph M

Philosophische Monatshefte — PhilMh
Philosophische Perspektiven — Phil Perspekt
Philosophische Rundschau — Ph R
Philosophische Rundschau — Ph Rdschau
Philosophische Rundschau — Ph Ru
Philosophische Rundschau — Phil Rundsch
Philosophische Rundschau — Philos Rd
Philosophische Rundschau — Philos Rund
Philosophische Rundschau — PhilosRdschau
Philosophische Rundschau. Beiheft — Ph RB
Philosophischer Anzeiger — Philos Anz
Philosophischer Literaturanzeiger — Ph La
Philosophischer Literaturanzeiger — Ph Lit
Philosophischer Literaturanzeiger — PL
Philosophischer Literaturanzeiger — PLA
Philosophisches Jahrbuch — Ph
Philosophisches Jahrbuch — Ph Jb
Philosophisches Jahrbuch — Phil Jahr
Philosophisches Jahrbuch — Phil Jahrb
Philosophisches Jahrbuch — Philos Jahr
Philosophisches Jahrbuch — Philos Jb
Philosophisches Jahrbuch — PhJ
Philosophisches Jahrbuch — PJ
Philosophisches Jahrbuch der Goerres-Gesellschaft — Ph J
Philosophisches Jahrbuch der Goerres-Gesellschaft — PJGG
Philosophisches Jahrbuch. Goerres-Gesellschaft — Philos Jb Goerresges
Philosophy — P
Philosophy — Ph
Philosophy — Phi
Philosophy [*London*] — Phil
Philosophy — Philos
Philosophy — PPHY
Philosophy and History — Philos His
Philosophy and History. German Studies Section I — Philos Hist
Philosophy and Literature — P & L
Philosophy and Literature — Phil Lit
Philosophy and Literature — Philos Lit
Philosophy and Medicine — Philos Med
Philosophy and Phenomenological Research — Ph & Phen R
Philosophy and Phenomenological Research — Ph Res
Philosophy and Phenomenological Research — Phil Phenomenol Res
Philosophy and Phenomenological Research — Philos & Phenom Res
Philosophy and Phenomenological Research — Philos Phen
Philosophy and Phenomenological Research — Philos Phenomenol Res
Philosophy and Phenomenological Research — PPHRA
Philosophy and Phenomenological Research — PPR
Philosophy and Public Affairs — Phil Pub Affairs
Philosophy and Public Affairs — Philos & Pub Affairs
Philosophy and Public Affairs — Philos Pub
Philosophy and Public Affairs — Philos Publ Aff
Philosophy and Public Affairs — PPPA
Philosophy and Rhetoric — P & R
Philosophy and Rhetoric — Ph & Rh
Philosophy and Rhetoric — Phil Rhet
Philosophy and Rhetoric — Philos Rhet
Philosophy and Rhetoric — PhilR
Philosophy and Social Action — Phil Soc Act
Philosophy and Social Criticism — Phil Soc Cr
Philosophy and Social Criticism — Phil Soc Crit
Philosophy East and West — PE & W
Philosophy East and West — PEW
Philosophy East and West — Ph E W
Philosophy East and West — Phil East West
Philosophy East and West — Philos East & West
Philosophy East and West — Philos EW
Philosophy East and West — PPEW
Philosophy Forum — PF
Philosophy Forum — Philos Foru
Philosophy Forum — Philos Forum
Philosophy Forum (De Kalb) — Phil Forum (De Kalb)
Philosophy in Context — Phil Context
Philosophy in the Mid-Century — PMCe
Philosophy of Education Society of Great Britain. Proceedings — Philosophy of Ed Soc Proc
Philosophy of Frege — Philos Frege
Philosophy of Music Education Review — Philos Mus Ed
Philosophy of Religion Series — PRS
Philosophy of Science — Phil Sci
Philosophy of Science — Philos Sci
Philosophy of Science — PPOS
Philosophy of the Social Sciences — Phil Soc Sci
Philosophy of the Social Sciences — Philos S Sc
Philosophy of the Social Sciences — Philos Soc Sci
Philosophy Research Archives — Phil Res Arch
Philosophy/Social Theory/Sociology — Ph Soc
Philosophy Today — GPHL
Philosophy Today — Phil Today
Philosophy Today — Philos Tod
Philosophy Today — PhilT
Philsophical Transactions. Royal Society of London — Philos Transact Royal Soc
Phlebologie — PHLBA
Phoenix — Ph
Phoenix [*Leiden*] — Phoe
Phoenix. Bulletin Uitgegeven door het Vooraziatisch-Egyptisch Genootschap Ex Oriente Lux — Phoenix Ex Or Lux
Phoenix Business Journal — Phoenix BJ
Phoenix Business Journal — Phoenix Bus J
Phoenix (Korea) — PhoenixK
Phoenix Quarterly — Phoenix Q
Phoenix Quarterly — PHXQA
Phoenix Shocker — Phoe Sh
Phoenix: The Classical Association of Canada — PhoenixC
Phoenizisch-Punische Grammatik — PPG
Phonetica — PHNTA
Phonetica — Phon
Phonetica Pragensia — PhonPr
Phonon Scattering in Condensed Matter. Proceedings. International Conference — Phonon Scattering Condens Matter Proc Int Conf
Phonons. Proceedings. International Conference — Phonons Proc Int Conf
Phosphore et Agriculture [*France*] — Phosphore Agric
Phosphorus and Potassium — Phospho Potas
Phosphorus and Potassium — Phosphorus
Phosphorus and Potassium — POPOA
Phosphorus and Sulfur and the Related Elements — Phosphor Sulfur Relat Elem
Phosphorus and the Related Group V Elements — Phosphorus Relat Group V Elem
Phosphorus in Agriculture — Phosphorus Agric
Phosphorus, Sulfur, and Silicon and the Related Elements — Phosphorus Sulfur Silicon Relat Elem
Photo Art Monthly — Photo Art Mon
Photo Canada — Photo Can
Photo Chemical Machining - Photo Chemical Etching — Photo Chem Mach Photo Chem Etching
Photo Communique — Photo Comm
Photo Lab Management — Photo Lab Manag
Photo Marketing — Photo Mkt
Photo Methods for Industry — Photo Methods Ind
Photo Methods for Industry — PMI
Photo Technique — Phot Tech
Photo Technique — Photo Tech
Photobiochemistry and Photobiophysics — PHOPD
Photobiochemistry and Photobiophysics — Photobiochem and Photobiophys
Photobiochemistry and Photobiophysics — Photobiochem Photobiophys
Photobiological Techniques — Photobiol Tech
Photobiology Bulletin — Photobiol Bull
Photoblaetter — Photobl
Photochemical and Photobiological Reviews — Photochem Photobiol Rev
Photochemical and Photobiological Reviews — PPHRD
Photochemical Conversion and Storage of Solar Energy. International Conference on Photochemical Conversion and Storage of Solar Energy — Photochem Convers Storage Sol Energy Int Conf
Photochemistry and Photobiology — PHCBA
Photochemistry and Photobiology — Photochem P
Photochemistry and Photobiology — Photochem Photobiol
Photochemistry and Photophysics — Photochem Photophys
Photo-Cine-Review — Photo Cine Rev
Photo-Dermatology — Photodermatol
Photodermatology, Photoimmunology and Photomedicine — Photodermatol Photoimmunol Photomed
Photoelastic and Soil Mechanics Journal — Photoelastic Soil Mech J
Photoelastic Journal — Photoelastic J
Photoelectric Spectrometry Group Bulletin — Photoelectr Spectrom Group Bull
Photo-Engravers' Bulletin — Photo Engravers Bull
Photo-Era Magazine — Photo Era Mag
Photogeometric Pottery — PGP
Photogrammetria — Photogramma
Photogrammetria — PTGMA
Photogrammetric Engineering [*Later, Photogrammetric Engineering and Remote Sensing*] — Photogramm Eng
Photogrammetric Engineering [*Later, Photogrammetric Engineering and Remote Sensing*] — Photogrammetric Eng
Photogrammetric Engineering and Remote Sensing — Photogr E R
Photogrammetric Engineering and Remote Sensing — Photogram Eng Remote Sensing
Photogrammetric Engineering and Remote Sensing — Photogramm Eng and Remote Sensing
Photogrammetric Engineering and Remote Sensing — Photogramm Eng Remote Sensing
Photogrammetric Record — Photogramm Rec
Photographic Abstracts — PhAb
Photographic Abstracts — Phot Abstr
Photographic Abstracts — Photo Abstr
Photographic Abstracts — Photog Abstr
Photographic Abstracts — Photogr Abstr
Photographic Applications in Science, Technology, and Medicine — Phot Appl Sci Tech Med
Photographic Applications in Science, Technology, and Medicine — Phot Appln Sci
Photographic Applications in Science, Technology, and Medicine — Photogr Appl Sci Technol and Med
Photographic Applications in Science, Technology, and Medicine — Photogr Appl Sci Technol Med
Photographic Applications in Science, Technology, and Medicine — PTASB
Photographic Canadiana — Photogr Canadiana
Photographic Collector — Photogr Collector
Photographic Engineering — Photogr Eng
Photographic Industries (Tokyo) — Photogr Ind Tokyo
Photographic Journal — Phot J

Photographic Journal — Photogr J
Photographic Journal of America — Phot J Amer
Photographic Journal. Section A. Pictorial and General Photography — Photogr J Sect A
Photographic Journal. Section B. Scientific and Technical Photography — Photogr J Sect B
Photographic Literature — Photo Lit
Photographic Science and Engineering — Phot Sci En
Photographic Science and Engineering — Phot Sci Eng
Photographic Science and Engineering — Photogr Sci and Eng
Photographic Science and Engineering — Photogr Sci Eng
Photographic Science and Engineering — PS and E
Photographic Science and Engineering — PSENA
Photographic Science and Photochemistry — Photogr Sci Photochem
Photographic Science and Technique — Photogr Sci Tech
Photographic Science. Symposium — Photogr Sci Symp
Photographic Sensitivity — Photogr Sensitivity
Photographic Society of America. Journal — Photogr Soc Am J
Photographic Society of America. Journal — PSA Jl
Photographic Society of America. Journal — PSA Journal
Photographic Society of America. Journal. Section B. Photographic Science and Technique — Phot Sci Tech
Photographic Society of America. Journal. Section B. Photographic Science and Technique — Photogr Soc Am J Sect B
Photographic Society of America. Journal. Supplement — Photogr Soc Am J Suppl
Photographic Techniques in Scientific Research — Photogr Tech Sci Res
Photographie Corpusculaire. Comptes-Rendus du Colloque International — Photogr Corpusc CR Colloq Int
Photographie fuer Alle — Photogr Alle
Photographie und Forschung — Photogr Forsch
Photographie und Forschung — Photographie Forsch
Photographie und Wissenschaft — Photogr Wiss
Photographische Chronik — Photogr Chron
Photographische Chronik und Allgemeine Photographische Zeitung — Photogr Chron Allg Photogr Ztg
Photographische Einzelaufnahmen Antiker Skulpturen — PEAS
Photographische Industrie — Phot Industrie
Photographische Industrie — Photo Ind
Photographische Industrie — Photogr Ind
Photographische Korrespondenz — Phot Ko
Photographische Korrespondenz — Phot Korr
Photographische Korrespondenz — Photogr Korresp
Photographische Korrespondenz (Austria) — PHKOA
Photographische Rundschau und Mitteilungen — Photogr Rundsch Mitt
Photographische Welt — Photogr Welt
Photographisches Archiv — Phot Arch
Photography and Focus — P & F
Photography and Focus — Photogr Focus
Photography Index — Photogr Index
Photography Magazine — Photogr Mag
Photo-Industrie und -Handel — Photo Ind
Photo-Kino-Chemical Industry — Photo Kino Chem Ind
Photo-Magazin — Photo-Mag
Photomethods — Photomethd
Photo-Miniature — Photo Min
Photo-Miniature — Photo-M
Photon — Phot
Photon Correlation Techniques in Fluid Mechanics. Proceedings. International Conference — Photon Correl Tech Fluid Mech Proc Int Conf
Photon Photon Collisions. Proceedings. International Workshop on Photon Photon Collisions — Photon Photon Collisions Proc Int Workshop
Photon-Detectors. Proceedings. International Symposium. Technical Committee — Photon Detect Proc Int Symp Tech Comm
Photonic Measurements Photon-Detectors. Proceedings. International Symposium. Technical Committee — Photonic Meas Photon Detect Proc Int Symp Tech Comm
Photonics Applied to Nuclear Physics — Photonics Appl Nucl Phys
Photonics Science News — Photonics Sci News
Photonics Spectra — Photo Spec
Photophysiology — PHCTB
Photophysiology. Current Topics — Photophysiol Curr Top
Photoplay, Movies, and Video — Photoplay
Photo-Revue — Photo-Rev
Photoselective Chemistry — Photosel Chem
Photosensitive Materials — Photosensit Mater
Photosynthesis. Proceedings. International Congress on Photosynthesis — Photosynth Proc Int Congr
Photosynthesis Research — Photosynth Res
Photosynthetic Solar Energy Conversion — Photosynth Sol Energy Convers
Photosynthetica — Photosynthe
Photosynthetica — PHSYB
Photo-Technik und -Wirtschaft — Phot Tech Wirt
Photovoltaic Generators in Space. Proceedings. European Symposium — Photovoltaic Gener Space Proc Eur Symp
Photovoltaic Solar Energy Conference. Proceedings. International Conference — Photovoltaic Sol Energy Conf Proc Int Conf
Phronesis [*Assen*] — Phron
Phycologia — PYCOA
Phycological Newsletter. Phycological Society of America — Phycol Newslett
Phycological Research — Phycol Res
Phylon — Phy
Phylon — Phyl
Phylon — PN
Phylon. Atlanta University — AU/P
Physica A. Europhysics Journal — Phys A
Physica A. Theoretical and Statistical Physics — Physica A
Physica (Amsterdam) — PHYSA
Physica B + C — PHBCD
Physica B. Europhysics Journal. Low Temperature and Solid State Physics — Phys B
Physica B. Europhysics Journal. Low Temperature and Solid State Physics — Physica B
Physica C. Europhysics Journal. Atomic, Molecular, and Plasma Physics Optics — Phys C
Physica C. Europhysics Journal. Atomic, Molecular, and Plasma Physics Optics [*A publication*] — Physica C
Physica D. Nonlinear Phenomena — PDNPD
Physica D. Nonlinear Phenomena — Phys D
Physica Energiae Fortis et Physica Nuclearis [*People's Republic of China*] — Phys Energ Fortis Phys Nucl
Physica Energiae Fortis et Physica Nuclearis [*People's Republic of China*] — Phys Energi Fort Phys Nuclear
Physica Fennica — PHFEA
Physica Fennica — Phys Fenn
Physica Norvegica — PHNOA
Physica Norvegica — Phys Norv
Physica Norvegica — Phys Norveg
Physica Scripta — PHSTB
Physica Scripta — Phys Scr
Physica Scripta [*Stockholm*] — Phys Scripta
Physica Scripta. T — Phys Scr T
Physica Solariterrestris — Phys Solariterr
Physica Status Solidi — PHSSA
Physica Status Solidi — Phys Status Solidi
Physica Status Solidi. Sectio A. Applied Research — Phys St S-A
Physica Status Solidi. Sectio A. Applied Research — Phys Stat Sol A
Physica Status Solidi. Sectio A. Applied Research — Phys Status Solidi A
Physica Status Solidi. Sectio A. Applied Research — Physica Status Solidi A
Physica Status Solidi. Sectio A. Applied Research — PSSAB
Physica Status Solidi. Sectio B. Basic Research — Phys St S-B
Physica Status Solidi. Sectio B. Basic Research — Phys Stat Sol B
Physica Status Solidi. Sectio B. Basic Research — Phys Status Solidi B
Physica Status Solidi. Sectio B. Basic Research — Physica Status Solidi B
Physical Acoustics. Principles and Methods — Phys Acoust
Physical Activities Report — Phys Act Rep
Physical Activity and Coronary Heart Disease. Paavo Nurmi Symposium — Phys Act Coron Heart Dis Paavo Nurmi Symp
Physical and Chemical Sciences Research Report — Phys Chem Sci Res Rep
Physical and Mechanical Properties of Rocks — Phys Mech Prop Rocks
Physical and Occupational Therapy in Geriatrics — Phys Occup Ther Geriatr
Physical and Occupational Therapy in Pediatrics — Phys Occup Ther Pediatr
Physical Aspects of Microscopic Characterization of Materials. Proceedings. Pfefferkorn Conference — Phys Aspects Microsc Charact Mater Proc Pfefferkorn Conf
Physical Bioinorganic Chemistry Series — Phys Bioinorg Chem Ser
Physical, Chemical, and Earth Sciences Research Report — Phys Chem Earth Sci Res Rep
Physical Chemical Biology and Medicine — Phys Chem Biol Med
Physical Chemistry — Phys Chem
Physical Chemistry (New York) — Phys Chem (NY)
Physical Chemistry of Fast Reactions — Phys Chem Fast React
Physical Chemistry of Magmas — Phys Chem Magmas
Physical Chemistry of Organic Solvent Systems [*Monograph*] — Phys Chem Org Solvent Syst
Physical Chemistry (Peshawar, Pakistan) — Phys Chem (Peshawar Pak)
Physical Chemistry. Series of Monographs — Phys Chem Ser Monogr
Physical Education — Phys Educ
Physical Education Bulletin for Teachers in Secondary Schools — Phys Ed Bul
Physical Education Index — PEI
Physical Education Index — Phys Educ Index
Physical Education Journal — Phys Ed J
Physical Education Journal — Physical Educ J
Physical Education News — Phys Ed News
Physical Education Newsletter — Phys Educ Newsl
Physical Education Review — PE Rev
Physical Education/Sports Index — PESI
Physical Educator — P Educator
Physical Educator — Phys Ed
Physical Educator — Phys Educ
Physical Environment Report. Department of Architectural Science. University of Sydney — Phys Environ Rep Dep Archit Sci Syd Univ
Physical Fitness Newsletter — Phys Fit Newsl
Physical Fitness Research Digest — Phys Fit Res Dig
Physical Fitness/Sports Medicine — PFSM
Physical Hazards, Dust, and Vapours. Occupational Hygiene — Phys Hazards Dust Vap Occup Hyg
Physical Inorganic Chemistry [*Elsevier Book Series*] — PIC
Physical Mechanisms in Radiation Biology. Proceedings. Conference — Phys Mech Radiat Biol Proc Conf
Physical Metallurgy — Phys Metall
Physical Metallurgy of Beryllium. Conference — Phys Metall Beryllium Conf
Physical Methods in Chemical Analysis — Phys Methods Chem Anal
Physical Methods in Heterocyclic Chemistry — Phys Methods Heterocycl Chem
Physical Methods in Macromolecular Chemistry — Phys Methods Macromol Chem
Physical Methods in Modern Chemical Analysis [*Monograph*] — Phys Methods Mod Chem Anal
Physical Principles and Techniques of Protein Chemistry [*Monograph*] — Phys Princ Tech Protein Chem

Physical Properties of Polymers [*Monograph*] — Phys Prop Polym
Physical Property Data Service [*Database*] — PPDS
Physical Research — Phys Res
Physical Research Methods of Sedimentary Rocks and Minerals — Phys Res Methods Sediment Rocks Miner
Physical Review — PHRVA
Physical Review — Phys R
Physical Review — Phys Rev
Physical Review B. Solid State — Phys Rev B Solid State
Physical Review C. Nuclear Physics — Phys Rev C Nucl Phys
Physical Review E. Statistical Physics, Plasmas, Fluids, and Related Interdiscplinary Topics. Third Series — Phys Rev E 3
Physical Review. Letters — Phys Rev L
Physical Review. Letters — Phys Rev Lett
Physical Review. Letters — PRLTA
Physical Review. Section A. General Physics — Phys Rev A
Physical Review. Section A. General Physics — Phys Rev A Gen Phys
Physical Review. Section A. General Physics — Phys Rev Sect A
Physical Review. Section A. General Physics. Third Series — Phys Rev A 3
Physical Review. Section B. Condensed Matter — Phys Rev B Conden Matt
Physical Review. Section B. Condensed Matter — Phys Rev B Condens Matter
Physical Review. Section B. Condensed Matter — Phys Rev Sect B
Physical Review. Section B. Condensed Matter — PRBMD
Physical Review. Section B. Condensed Matter. Third Series — Phys Rev B 3
Physical Review. Section C. Nuclear Physics — Phys Rev C
Physical Review. Section C. Nuclear Physics. Third Series — Phys Rev C 3
Physical Review. Section D. Particles and Fields — Phys Rev D
Physical Review. Section D. Particles and Fields. Third Series — Phys Rev D 3
Physical Review. Supplement — Phys Rev Suppl
Physical Sciences Data [*Amsterdam*] — Phys Sci Data
Physical Sciences Data [*Elsevier Book Series*] — PSD
Physical Sciences Research Papers. United States. Air Force Cambridge Research Laboratories — Phys Sci Res Pap US Air Force Cambridge Res Lab
Physical Sciences. Some Recent Advances in France and the United States. Proceedings. Symposium on Basic Science in France and the United States — Phys Sci Some Recent Adv Fr US Proc Symp Basic Sci Fr US
Physical Society of London. Proceedings — Phys Soc Lond Proc
Physical Society. Year Book — Phys Soc Year Book
Physical Techniques in Biological Research — Phys Tech Biol Res
Physical Therapy — Phys Ther
Physical Therapy — Phys Therapy
Physical Therapy — PTHEA
Physical Therapy Review — Phys Therapy Rev
Physicalia Magazine — Phys Mag
Physicalische Zeitung — Phys Zeitung
Physica-Schriften zur Betriebswirtschaft — Physica Schrift Betriebswirtsch
Physici et Medici Graeci Minores — PMGM
Physician and Sports Medicine — Physician Sportsmed
Physician and Sportsmedicine — IPSM
Physician and Surgeon — Physician and Surg
Physician Assistant [*Later, Physician Assistant/Health Practitioner*] — Physician Assist
Physician Assistant/Health Practitioner — Physician Assist Health
Physician Assistant/Health Practitioner — Physician Assist Health Pract
Physician Communications Service [*Database*] — PHYCOM
Physician Computer Monthly — Physician Comput Monthly
Physician Executive — Physician Exec
Physician's Desk Reference [*Database*] — PDR
Physicians Drug Manual — PDM
Physicians' Drug Manual — Physicians Drug Man
Physician's Guide to Practical Gastroenterology — Physicians Guide Pract Gastroenterol
Physicians Management — Physicians Manage
Physico-Chemical Aspects of Soil and Related Materials — Phys Chem Aspects Soil Relat Mater
Physico-Chemical Behaviour of Atmospheric Pollutants. Proceedings. European Symposium — Phys Chem Behav Atmos Pollut Proc Eur Symp
Physico-Chemical Biology — Phys Chem Biol
Physico-Chemical Biology (Chiba) — Phys-Chem Biol (Chiba)
Physicochemical Hydrodynamics [*England*] — Physicochem Hydrodyn
Physics — PHYCA
Physics Abstracts [*Database*] — PA
Physics Abstracts — Phys Abstr
Physics and Applications — Phys Appl
Physics and Chemistry — Phys & Chem
Physics and Chemistry — Physics & Chem
Physics and Chemistry in Space — Phys Chem Space
Physics and Chemistry of Fission. Proceedings. IAEA [*International Atomic Energy Agency*] **Symposium. Physics and Chemistry of Fission** — Phys Chem Fission Proc IAEA Symp
Physics and Chemistry of Glasses — PCGLA
Physics and Chemistry of Glasses — Phys C Glas
Physics and Chemistry of Glasses — Phys Chem Glasses
Physics and Chemistry of Glasses. Section B. Journal. Society of Glass Technology — Phys and Chem Glasses
Physics and Chemistry of Liquids — PCLQA
Physics and Chemistry of Liquids — Phys and Chem Liq
Physics and Chemistry of Liquids — Phys Chem Liq
Physics and Chemistry of Materials with Layered Structures — Phys Chem Mater Layered Struct
Physics and Chemistry of Minerals — Phys and Chem Miner
Physics and Chemistry of Minerals — Phys Chem Miner
Physics and Chemistry of Solids — Phys Chem Solids
Physics and Chemistry of the Earth — Phys and Chem Earth
Physics and Chemistry of the Earth — Phys Chem Earth
Physics and Chemistry (Washington, D. C.) — Phys Chem (Washington DC)
Physics and Contemporary Needs. Proceedings. International Summer College — Phys Contemp Needs
Physics and Engineering Applications of Magnetism — Phys Eng Appl Magn
Physics and Materials Science of High Temperature Superconductors. II — Phys Mater Sci High Temp Supercond II
Physics and Medicine of the Atmosphere and Space. Proceedings. International Symposium — Phys Med Atmos Space Proc Int Symp
Physics and Nondestructive Testing. Proceedings. Symposium — Phys Nondestr Test Proc Symp
Physics and Simulation of Optoelectronic Devices — Phys Simul Optoelectron Devices
Physics and Technics of Semiconductors — Phys Tech Semicond
Physics at LEP (Large Electron-Positron) — Phys LEP
Physics Briefs [*Database*] — PB
Physics Briefs [*Germany*] — Phys Briefs
Physics Bulletin — PHSBB
Physics Bulletin — Phys Bull
Physics Bulletin (Baoding, People's Republic of China) — Phys Bull Baoding Peoples Repub China
Physics Bulletin (Peking) — Phys Bull (Peking)
Physics Data. Zentralstelle fuer Atomkernenergie-Dokumentation — Phys Data Zentralstelle Atomkernenerg Dok
Physics. Doklady — Phys Dokl
Physics Education — PHEDA
Physics Education — Phys Educ
Physics Education — Physics Ed
Physics Essays — Phys Essays
Physics, Geometry, and Topology — Phys Geom Topol
Physics in Canada — PHCAA
Physics in Canada — Phys Can
Physics in Collision. High-Energy ee/ep/pp Interactions — Phys Collision
Physics in Industry — Phys Ind
Physics in Medicine and Biology — PHMBA
Physics in Medicine and Biology — Phys Med and Biol
Physics in Medicine and Biology — Phys Med Bi
Physics in Medicine and Biology — Phys Med Biol
Physics in Medicine and Biology — Physics Med Biol
Physics in Technology — Phys Technol
Physics in Technology — PHYTB
Physics in the Steel Industry. Lehigh University — Phys Steel Ind Lehigh Univ
Physics Letters — PHLTA
Physics Letters [*Netherlands*] — Phys Lett
Physics Letters — Phys Letters
Physics Letters. Section A — Phys Lett A
Physics Letters. Section B — Phys Lett B
Physics Letters. Section C [*Netherlands*] — Phys Lett C
Physics News (Bombay) — Phys News Bombay
Physics News Bulletin. Indian Physics Association — Phys News
Physics Notes — Phys Notes
Physics of Atomic Nuclei — Phys Atomic Nuclei
Physics of Atoms and Molecules — Phys Atoms and Molecules
Physics of Chaos and Related Problems. Proceedings. Nobel Symposium — Phys Chaos Relat Probl Proc Nobel Symp
Physics of Condensed Matter — PCOMB
Physics of Condensed Matter — Phys Con Matt
Physics of Condensed Matter — Phys Condens Matter
Physics of Electronic and Atomic Collisions. International Conference — Phys Electron At Collisions Int Conf
Physics of Electronic and Atomic Collisions. Invited Papers. International Conference — Phys Electron At Collisions Invited Pap Int Conf
Physics of Elementary Particles and Atomic Nuclei — Phys Elem Part At Nucl
Physics of Failure in Electronics — Phys Failure Electron
Physics of Fluids — PFLDA
Physics of Fluids — Phys Fluids
Physics of Fluids A. Fluid Dynamics — Phys Flu A
Physics of Fluids. A. Fluid Dynamics — Phys Fluids A
Physics of Fluids B. Plasma Physics — Phys Flu B
Physics of Fluids B. Plasma Physics — Phys Fluids B
Physics of Fluids. Supplement — PFLSA
Physics of Fluids. Supplement — Phys Fluids Suppl
Physics of Ionized Gases — Phys Ioniz Gases
Physics of Magmatic Processes. Proceedings — Phys Magmat Processes Proc
Physics of Magnetic Materials. Proceedings. International Conference on Physics of Magnetic Materials — Phys Magn Mater Proc Int Conf
Physics of Metals — Phys Met
Physics of Metals and Metallography [*English Translation*] — PHMMA
Physics of Metals and Metallography — Phys Met Metallogr
Physics of Metals (USSR) — Phys Met (USSR)
Physics of Narrow Gap Semiconductors. Proceedings. International Conference — Phys Narrow Gap Semicond Proc Int Conf
Physics of Non-Thermal Radio Sources — Phys Non Therm Radio Sources
Physics of Particles and Nuclei — Phys Particles Nuclei
Physics of Plasmas — Phys Plasmas
Physics of Quantum Electronics — Phys Quantum Electron
Physics of Semiconducting Compounds. Proceedings. Conference on Physics of Semiconducting Compounds — Phys Semicond Compd Proc Conf
Physics of Semiconductor Devices. Proceedings. International Workshop — Phys Semicond Devices Proc Int Workshop
Physics of Semiconductors. International Conference — Phys Semicond Int Conf
Physics of Semiconductors. Invited and Contributed Papers. International Conference on the Physics of Semiconductors — Phys Semicond Invited Contrib Pap Int Conf

Physics of Semiconductors. Proceedings. International Conference — Phys Semicond Proc Int Conf
Physics of Sintering — PHSNB
Physics of Sintering [*Yugoslavia*] — Phys Sintering
Physics of Solar Prominences. Proceedings. International Astronomical Union Colloquium — Phys Sol Prominences Proc Int Astron Union Colloq
Physics of Solid Surfaces. Proceedings. Symposium on Surface Physics — Phys Solid Surf Proc Symp Surf Phys
Physics of Solids and Liquids — Phys Solids Liq
Physics of Strength and Plasticity — Phys Strength Plast
Physics of SuperLEAR. Proceedings. SuperLEAR Workshop — Phys SuperLEAR Proc SuperLEAR Workshop
Physics of the Earth and Planetary Interiors — PEPIA
Physics of the Earth and Planetary Interiors — Phys E Plan
Physics of the Earth and Planetary Interiors — Phys Earth and Planet Inter
Physics of the Earth and Planetary Interiors — Phys Earth Planet Inter
Physics of the Earth and Planetary Interiors — Phys Earth Planetary Interiors
Physics of the Solid Earth (English Edition) — Phys Solid Earth (Engl Ed)
Physics of Thin Films. Advances in Research and Development — Phys Thin Films
Physics Papers — Phys Pap
Physics Papers. Silesian University in Katowice [*Poland*] — Phys Pap Silesian Univ Katowice
Physics Reports. Kumamoto University — Phys Rep Kumamoto Univ
Physics Reports. Physics Letters. Section C — Phys Rep Phys Lett Sect C
Physics Reports. Reprints Book Series [*Elsevier Book Series*] — PRRB
Physics Reports. Review Section of Physics Letters. Section C [*Netherlands*] — Phys Rep
Physics Teacher — PHTEA
Physics Teacher — Phys Teach
Physics Teacher — Phys Teacher
Physics Teacher — Physics Teach
Physics Teacher — PPST
Physics Today — GPHT
Physics Today — PHTOA
Physics Today — Phys Today
Physics up to 200 TeV — Phys 200 TeV
Physics with Antiprotons at LEAR [*Low Energy Antiproton Ring*] **in the ACOL Era. Proceedings. LEAR Workshop** [*Antiproton Collector*] — Phys Antiprotons LEAR ACOL Era Proc LEAR Workshop
Physik Daten [*Physics Data*] — Phys Daten
Physik Daten/Physics Data — Phys Daten Phys Data
Physik der Halbleiteroberflaeche. Tagungsbericht der Arbeitstagung — Phys Halbleiteroberflaeche
Physik der Kondensierten Materie — Phys Kondens Mater
Physik der Kondensierten Materie — PKOMA
Physik. Grundlage der Technik. Plenarvortraege der Physikertagung — Phys Grundlage Tech Plenarvortr Physikertag
Physik in der Schule — Phys Schule
Physik in Regelmaessigen Berichten — Phys Regelm Ber
Physik in Unserer Zeit — PHUZA
Physik in Unserer Zeit — Phys Unserer Zeit
Physik Plenarvortraege der Physikertagung — Phys Plenarvortr Physikertag
Physik und Chemie — Phys Chem
Physik und Chemie (Vienna) — Phys Chem (Vienna)
Physik und Didaktik — Phys Didak
Physik und Didaktik — Phys Didakt
Physikalisch-Chemisches Centralblatt — Phys Chem Centralbl
Physikalisch-Diaetetische Therapie [*Germany*] — Phys-Diaet Ther
Physikalische Abhandlungen — Phys Abh
Physikalische Belustigungen — Phys Belust
Physikalische Belustigungen — Phys Belustigungen
Physikalische Berichte — Phys Ber
Physikalische Bibliothek. Rostock und Wismar — Phys Biblioth Rostock Wismar
Physikalische Blaetter — PHBLA
Physikalische Blaetter — Phys Bl
Physikalische Blaetter. Beilage — Phys Bl Beil
Physikalische Grundlagen der Medizin. Abhandlungen aus der Biophysik — Phys Grundlagen Med Abh Biophys
Physikalische und Medicinische Abhandlungen der Koeniglichen Akademie der Wissenschaften zu Berlin — Phys Med Abh Koenigl Acad Wiss Berlin
Physikalische Verhandlungen — Phys Verh
Physikalische Zeitschrift [*Germany*] — Phys Z
Physikalische Zeitschrift — Phys Zeit
Physikalische Zeitschrift — Phys Zschr
Physikalische Zeitschrift — Physikal Zs
Physikalische Zeitschrift. Beihefte — Phys Z Beih
Physikalische Zeitschrift der Sowjetunion — Phys Z Sowjetunion
Physikalisches Taschenbuch Fuer Freunde der Naturlehre und Kuenstler — Phys Taschenb Freunde Naturl Kuenstler
Physikalisch-Oekonomische Monaths- und Quartalschrifft — Phys Oekon Monaths Quartalschr
Physikalisch-Technische Bundesanstalt. Bericht APh — Phys Tech Bundesanst Ber APh
Physikalisch-Technische Bundesanstalt. Bericht ATWD — Phys Tech Bundesanst Ber ATWD
Physikalisch-Technische Bundesanstalt. Bericht Dos — Phys Tech Bundesanst Ber Dos
Physikalisch-Technische Bundesanstalt. Bericht ND — Phys Tech Bundesanst Ber ND
Physikalisch-Technische Bundesanstalt. Bericht Opt — Phys Tech Bundesanst Ber Opt
Physikalisch-Technische Bundesanstalt. Bericht PG — Phys Tech Bundesanst Ber PG
Physikalisch-Technische Bundesanstalt. Bericht Ra — Phys Tech Bundesanst Ber Ra
Physikalisch-Technische Bundesanstalt. Bericht SE — Phys Tech Bundesanst Ber SE
Physikertagung. Hauptvortraege der Jahrestagung des Verbandes Deutscher Physikalischer Gesellschaften — Physikertag Hauptvortr Jahrestag Verb Dtsch Phys Ges
Physikertagung, Plenarvortraege — Physikertag Plenarvortr
Physikertagung. Vorabdrucke der Kurzfassungen der Fachberichte — Physikertag Vorabdrucke Kurzfassungen Fachber
Physikunterricht — Physikunterr
Physiographiska Saelskapets Magazin — Physiogr Saelsk Mag
Physiologia Bohemoslovaca — Physiol Bohemoslov
Physiologia Bohemoslovaca — Physl Bohem
Physiologia Bohemoslovenica [*Later, Physiologia Bohemoslovaca*] — PHBOA
Physiologia Bohemoslovenica [*Later, Physiologia Bohemoslovaca*] — Phys Bohemoslov
Physiologia Comparata et Oecologia — Phys Comp
Physiologia Comparata et Oecologia — Physiologia Comp Oecol
Physiologia Plantarum — PHPLA
Physiologia Plantarum — Physiol Plant
Physiologia Plantarum — Physiologia Pl
Physiologia Plantarum — Physl Plant
Physiologia Plantarum. Supplementum — Physiol Plant Suppl
Physiological Abstracts — Physiol Abstr
Physiological and Molecular Plant Pathology — Physiol Mol Plant Pathol
Physiological and Molecular Plant Pathology — PMPPEZ
Physiological and Pathological Effects of Cytokines. Proceedings. International Workshop on Cytokines — Physiol Pathol Eff Cytokines Proc Int Workshop Cytokines
Physiological Chemistry and Physics — Phys Chem Phys
Physiological Chemistry and Physics [*Later, Physiological Chemistry and Physics and Medical NMR*] — Physiol Chem Phys
Physiological Chemistry and Physics [*Later, Physiological Chemistry and Physics and Medical NMR*] — Physl Chem
Physiological Chemistry and Physics [*Later, Physiological Chemistry and Physics and Medical NMR*] — PLCHB
Physiological Chemistry and Physics and Medical NMR — Physiol Chem Phys Med NMR
Physiological Entomology — Physiol Ent
Physiological Entomology — Physiol Entomol
Physiological Genetics — Physiol Genet
Physiological Measurement — Physiol Meas
Physiological Plant Pathology — Physiol Plant Pathol
Physiological Plant Pathology — Physl Pl P
Physiological Plant Pathology — PPPYBC
Physiological Properties of Plant Protoplasts [*monograph*] — Physiol Prop Plant Protoplasts
Physiological Psychology — Physiol Psychol
Physiological Psychology — Physl Psych
Physiological Psychology — PLPSA
Physiological Research — Physiol Res
Physiological Reviews — PHREA
Physiological Reviews — Phys Rev
Physiological Reviews — Physiol Rev
Physiological Reviews — PPRV
Physiological Society of Philadelphia. Monographs — Physiol Soc Philadelphia Monogr
Physiological Strategies for Gas Exchange and Metabolism — Physiol Strategies Gas Exch Metab
Physiological Zoology — Phys Zool
Physiological Zoology — Physiol Zool
Physiological Zoology — Physl Zool
Physiological Zoology — PHZOA
Physiologie des Menschen — Physiol Menschen
Physiologie et Pathologie Perinatales chez les Animaux de Ferme. Exposes presentes aux Journees du Grenier de Theix — Physiol Pathol Perinat Anim Ferme Exp Journ Grenier Theix
Physiologie Vegetale — Physiol Veg
Physiologie Vegetale — Physl Veget
Physiologie Vegetale — PHYVA
Physiologist — PYSOA
Physiologiste Russe — Physiol Russe
Physiology and Behavior — PHBHA
Physiology and Behavior — Physiol Behav
Physiology and Behavior — Physl Behav
Physiology and Behaviour of Marine Organisms. Proceedings. European Symposium on Marine Biology — Physiol Behav Mar Org Proc Eur Symp Mar Biol
Physiology and Biochemistry of Cultivated Plants — Physiol Biochem Cultiv Plants
Physiology and Biochemistry of Cultivated Plants (USSR) — Physiol Biochem Cult Plants (USSR)
Physiology and Ecology — Physiol Ecol
Physiology and Ecology (Japan) — Physiol Ecol (Jpn)
Physiology and Oecology — Physiol Oecol
Physiology and Pathophysiology of Plasma Protein Metabolism. Proceedings. International Symposium — Physiol Pathophysiol Plasma Protein Metab Proc Int Symp
Physiology and Pathophysiology of the Skin — Physiol Pathophysiol Skin
Physiology and Pharmacology for Physicians — Physiol Pharmacol Physicians
Physiology and Pharmacology of Adenosine Derivatives. Proceedings. Meeting — Physiol Pharmacol Adenosine Deriv Proc Meet
Physiology and Pharmacology of Epileptogenic Phenomena — Physiol Pharmacol Epileptogenic Phenom

Physiology and Pharmacology of the Microcirculation [*Monograph*] — Physiol Pharmacol Microcirc
Physiology Canada — Physiol Can
Physiology for Physicians — Physiol Physicians
Physiology of Digestion in the Ruminant. Papers Presented. International Symposium on the Physiology of Digestion in the Ruminant — Physiol Dig Ruminant Pap Int Symp
Physiology of Immunity [*monograph*] — Physiol Immun
Physiology of the Domestic Fowl. British Egg Marketing Board Symposium — Physiol Domest Fowl Br Egg Mark Board Symp
Physiology of the Intestinal Circulation [*Monograph*] — Physiol Intest Circ
Physiology of the Newborn Infant [*monograph*] — Physiol Newborn Infant
Physiology Teacher — PHTED
Physiology Teacher — Physiol Teach
Physiotherapy — PHSIA
Physiotherapy Canada — Physiother Can
Physiotherapy Practice — Physiother Pract
Physiotherapy Research Newsletter — Physiother Res Newsl
Physique Appliquee — Phys Appl
Physique Atomique et Moleculaire et Matiere Interstellaire. Ecole d'Ete de Physique Theorique — Phys At Mol Matiere Interstellaire Ec Ete Phys Theor
Physique des Semiconducteurs. Comptes Rendus. Congres International — Phys Semicond CR Congr Int
Physis — Phys
Physis. Rivista Internazionale di Storia della Scienza — Physis Riv Internaz Storia Sci
Physis. Rivista Internazionale di Storia della Scienza. Nuova Serie — Physis Riv Internaz Storia Sci NS
Physis. Rivista Internazionale di Storia della Scienze — PRIS
Physis. Seccion A: Oceanos y Sus Organismos — Physis Secc A Oceanos Org
Physis. Seccion A: Oceanos y Sus Organismos — Physis Secc A Oceanos Sus Org
Physis. Seccion B: Aguas Continentales y Sus Organismos — Physis Secc B Aguas Cont Org
Physis. Seccion B: Aguas Continentales y Sus Organismos — Physis Secc B Aguas Cont Sus Org
Physis. Seccion C: Continentes y Organismos Terrestres — Physis Secc C Cont Org Terr
Physis. Seccion C: los Continentes y los Organismos Terrestres — Physis Secc C Cont los Org Terr
Phytiatrie-Phytopharmacie — Phytiat Phytopharm
Phytiatrie-Phytopharmacie. Revue Francaise de Medicine et de Pharmacie des Vegetaux — Phytiatr-Phytopharm Rev Fr Med Pharm Veg
Phytochemical Analysis — Phytochem Anal
Phytochemical Effects of Environmental Compounds — Phytochem Eff Environ Compd
Phytochemical Society. Annual Proceedings — Phytochem Soc Annu Proc
Phytochemical Society of Europe. Proceedings — Phytochem Soc Eur Proc
Phytochemical Society of Europe. Symposia Series — Phytochem Soc Eur Symp Ser
Phytochemistry [*Oxford*] — Phytochem
Phytochemistry — PYTCA
Phytochemistry (Oxford) — Phytochemistr (Oxf)
Phytodepuration and Use of the Produced Biomasses. Proceedings. International Congress — Phytodepur Use Prod Biomasses Proc Int Congr
Phytoma. Defense des Cultures [*France*] — Phytoma Def Cult
Phytomorphology — PHYMA
Phytomorphology — Phytomorph
Phytomorphology — Phytomorphol
Phyton. Annales Rei Botanicae — Phyton Ann Rei Bot
Phyton. Annales Rei Botanicae (Austria) — Phyton (Aust)
Phyton (Buenos Aires) — PHYBA
Phyton. International Journal of Experimental Botany — Phyton Int J Exp Bot
Phyton. Revista Internacional de Botanica Experimental — Phyton Rev Int Bot Exp
Phytoparasitica. Israel Journal of Plant Protection Sciences — Phytoparasit Isr J Plant Prot Sci
Phytopathologia Mediterranea — Phytopathol Medit
Phytopathological Knowledge — Phytopathol Knowl
Phytopathologie Mediterranea — Phytopathol Mediterr
Phytopathologische Zeitschrift [*Journal of Phytopathology*] — Phytopath Z
Phytopathologische Zeitschrift [*Journal of Phytopathology*] — Phytopathol Z
Phytopathologische Zeitschrift [*Journal of Phytopathology*] — PHYZA
Phytopathologische Zeitschrift [*Journal of Phytopathology*] — PZ
Phytopathologische Zeitschrift/Journal of Phytopathology — Phytopathol ZJ Phytopathol
Phytopathology — Phyt
Phytopathology — PHYTA
Phytopathology — Phytopathol
Phytopathology News — Phytopathol News
Phytoprotection — Phytoprot
Phytotherapy Research — Phytother R
Phytotronic Newsletter — Phytotronic Newsl
Pi Mu Epsilon Journal — Pi Mu Epsilon J
Piagetian Theory and the Helping Professions — Piaget Theor Help Prof
Piano and Keyboard — PaK
Piano Guild Notes — PGN
Piano Quarterly — Piano Q
Piano Quarterly — Piano Quart
Piano Quarterly — PQ
Piano Teachers Journal — PITBB
Piano Technician — Piano Tech
Piano Technician's Journal — PTJ
Picardie Information — Picardie Inform
Piccole Storie Illustrate — PSI
Pick Resources Guide/International [*Database*] — PRG/I
Picker Clinical Scintillator — Picker Clin Scintil
Pickle Pak Science — Pickle Pak Sci
Picosecond Phenomena. Proceedings. International Conference on Picosecond Phenomena — Picosecond Phenom Proc Int Conf
Pictoral Dictionary of Ancient Athens — PDAA
Pictorial and Artifact Retrieval and Information System [*Database*] — PARIS
Pictorial Review — PictR
Pielegniarka i Polozna — Pieleg Polozna
Pienpuualan Toimikunnan Julkaisu — Pienpuu Toimikun Julk
Pietismus und Neuzeit. Ein Jahrbuch zur Geschichte des Neueren Protestantismus — Piet Neuzeit
Pig Iron — Pig
Pig News and Information — Pig News Inf
Pigment and Resin Technology — Pig Rsn Tech
Pigment and Resin Technology — Pigment Resin Tech
Pigment and Resin Technology — Pigment Resin Technol
Pigment Cell — Pigm Cell
Pigment Cell Biology. Proceedings. Conference on the Biology of Normal and Atypical Pigment Cell Growth — Pigm Cell Biol Proc Conf Biol Norm Atyp Pig Cell Growth
Pigment Cell Research — Pigment Cell Res
Pigments in Pathology — Pigm Pathol
PIK. Northern Magazine for Children [*Northwest Territory, Canada*] — PIKM
Pillnitzer Merkblaetter fuer Pflanzenschutz — Pillnitzer Merkbl Pflanzenschutz
Pilot. Fort Smith and Simpson [*Northwest Territory, Canada*] — PI
PIMA [*Paper Industry Management Association*] **Magazine** [*United States*] — PIMA Mag
PIMA [*Paper Industry Management Association*] **Yearbook** — PIMA Yrb
Pine Institute of America. Abstracts. Chemical Section — Pine Inst Am Abstr Chem Sect
Pine Institute of America. Technical Bulletin — Pine Inst Am Tech Bull
Pineal Function. Proceedings. Satellite Symposium. International Congress of Endocrinology — Pineal Funct Proc Satell Symp Int Congr Endocrinol
Pineal Research Reviews — Pineal Res Rev
Pineapple Quarterly — Pineapple Q
Pinepointer — PP
Pinkas Bractwa Pogrzebowego — PBP
Pinkas ha-Kehilot [*Encyclopedia of Jewish Communities*] — PK
Pinturas y Acabados Industriales — Pint Acabados Ind
Pinturas y Acabados Industriales. Seccion. Recubrimientos Metalicos — Pint Acabados Ind Secc Recubrimientos Met
Pinturas y Acabados Industriales. Seccion. Recubrimientos Organicos — Pint Acabados Ind Secc Recubrimientos Org
Pio Istituto di S. Spirito ed Ospedali Riuniti di Roma. Centro di Reumatologia. Bollettino — Pio Ist S Spirito Osp Riuniti Roma Cent Reumatol Boll
Pioneer [*Kumasi*] — PR
Pioneering Concepts in Modern Science — Pioneering Concepts Mod Sci
Pioneers' Association of South Australia. Publications — Pioneers' Assoc of SA Pubs
Pionerskaja Pravda — P Pr
Pipe Line Industry — Pipe Line Ind
Pipe Line Industry — PLINA
Pipeline and Gas Journal — P & G Jour
Pipeline and Gas Journal — Pipeline & Gas J
Pipeline and Gas Journal — Pipeline Gas J
Pipeline and Gas Journal — PLGJA
Pipeline and Gas Journal Buyer's Guide Issue Handbook — P & G Jour BG
Pipeline and Underground Utilities Construction — Pipeline Underground Util Constr
Pipeline Annual Directory and Equipment Guide — Pipe Line D
Pipeline Contractors Association of Canada — Pipeline Contractors Assoc Can
Pipeline Engineer — Pipeline Eng
Pipeline Engineer International — Pipeline Eng Int
Pipeline Engineering — Pipleine Eng
Pipeline Management, Operations, Engineering, and Gas Distribution News — Pipeline Manage Oper Eng Gas Distrib News
Pipeline. Report of the Northern Pipeline Agency — PIPE
Pipelines, Politics, and People. Capital Communications Ltd. — PPP
Pipes and Pipelines International — Pipes & Pipelines Int
Pipes and Pipelines International — Pipes Pipelines Int
Piping and Process Machinery (Tokyo) — Piping Process Mach (Tokyo)
Piping Engineering — Piping Eng
PIRA [*Printing Industry Research Association*] **Packaging Abstracts** — PIRA Packag Abstr
Pirprofen in the Treatment of Pain and Inflammation. Proceedings. International Symposium — Pirprofen Treat Pain Inflammation Proc Int Symp
Piscovye Knigi Obonezskoj Pjatiny — PKOP
Pishchevaya i Pererabatyvayushchaya Promyshlennost' — Pishch Pererabatyvayushchaya Promst
Pishchevaya Promyshlennost [*Kiev, 1965*] — PPMVA
Pishchevaya Promyshlennost Kazakhstana — Pishch Prom Kaz
Pishchevaya Promyshlennost Kazakhstana Mezhvedomstvennyi Respublikanskii Nauchno Tekhnicheskii Sbornik — Pishch Promst Kaz Mezhved Resp Nauchno Tekh Sb
Pishchevaya Promyshlennost (Kiev) — Pishch Prom Kiev
Pishchevaya Promyshlennost (Kiev, 1965) — Pishch Prom-St (Kiev 1965)
Pishchevaya Promyshlennost (Moscow) — Pishch Promst (Moscow)
Pishchevaya Promyshlennost Nauchno-Proizvodstvennyi Sbornik — Pishch Prom-St' Nauchno-Proizvod Sb
Pishchevaya Promyshlennost. Seriya 6. Maslo-Zhirovaya Promyshlennost. Obzornaya Informatsiya — Pishch Promst Ser 6 Obz Inf
Pishchevaya Promyshlennost. Seriya 12. Spirtavya i Likero-Vodochnaya Promyshlennost — PPPMD

Pishchevaya Promyshlennost. Seriya 20. Maslo-Zhirovaya Promyshlennost. Obzornaya Informatsiya — Pishch Promst Ser 20 Obz Inf
Pishchevaya Promyshlennost. Seriya. Vinodel'cheskaya Promyshlennost. Nauchno-Tekhnicheskii Referativnyi Sbornik — Pishch Promst Ser Nauchno Tekh Ref Sb
Pishchevaya Promyshlennost SSSR — Pishch Promst SSSR
Pishchevaya Tekhnologiya — Pishch Tekhnol
Pis'ma v Astronomicheskii Zhurnal — Pis'ma Astron Zh
Pis'ma v Astronomicheskii Zhurnal — Pis'ma v Astron Zh
Pis'ma v Zhurnal Eksperimental'noi i Teoreticheskoi Fiziki — Pis'ma v Zh Eksp i Teor Fiz
Pis'ma v Zhurnal Eksperimental'noi i Teoreticheskoi Fiziki — Pis'ma Zh Eksp Teor Fiz
Pis'ma v Zhurnal Eksperimental'noi i Teoreticheskoi Fiziki — Pisma Zh Eksper Teoret Fiz
Pis'ma v Zhurnal Tekhnicheskoi Fiziki — Pis'ma v Zh Tekh Fiz
Pis'ma v Zhurnal Tekhnicheskoi Fiziki — Pis'ma Zh Tekh Fiz
Pis'ma v Zhurnal Tekhnicheskoii Fiziki — PZTFD
Pis'ma v Zhurnal Tekhnicheskoi Fiziki — Pisma Zh Tekhn Fiz
Pis'mennye Pamiatniki Vostoka — Pism Pam Vostoka
Pismo Swiete Nowego Testamentu [*Posen*] — PSNT
Pismo Swiete Starego Testamentu — PSST
Pit and Quarry — PIQUA
Pit and Quarry — Pit & Quar
Pit and Quarry — Pit Quarry
Pitanie i Kormlenie Ryb. Mezhdunarodnyi Seminar — Pitan Korml Ryb Mezhdunar Semin
Pitanie i Obmen Veshchestv u Rastenii — Pitan Obmen Veshchestv Rast
Pitanie i Produktivnost Rastenii — Pitan Prod Rast
Pitanie i Udobrenie Rastenii — Pitanie Udobr Rast
Pitanie i Udobrenie Sel'skokhozyaistvennykh Rastenii v Moldavii — Pitan Udobr Skh Rast Mold
Pitanja Knjizevnosti a Jezika — PKJ
Pitanja Savremenog Knjizevnog Jezika — PSKJ
Pitannya Eksperimental'noi Botaniki — Pitannya Eksp Bot
Pitannya Fiziki Tverdogo Tila — Pitannya Fiz Tverd Tila
Pitannya Tekhnologii Obrobki Vodi Promislovogo ta Pitnogo Vodopostachannya — Pitannya Tekhnol Obrob Vodi Promisl Pitnogo Vodopostachannya
Pitch Pine Naturalist — Pitch Pine Nat
Pitch Pine Naturalist — PPNADY
Pitman Monographs and Surveys in Pure and Applied Mathematics — Pitman Monographs Surveys Pure Appl Math
Pitman Research Notes in Mathematics Series — Pitman Res Notes Math Ser
Pitt Press Series — PP
Pitt Rivers Museum. University of Oxford. Occasional Papers on Technology — Pitt Rivers Mus Univ Oxford Occas Pap Technol
Pittsburgh Business Review — Pittsbg Bs
Pittsburgh Business Review — Pittsburgh Bus R
Pittsburgh Business Times-Journal — Pittsb Bs T
Pittsburgh Press — Pittsbg P
Pittsburgh Schools — Pittsburgh Sch
Pittsburgh Symphony Orchestra. Program Notes — Pitt Sym
Pittsburgh University. Bulletin — Pittsburgh Univ Bull
Pittsburgh University. School of Education Journal — Pittsburgh Univ Sch Ed J
Pittsburgher Magazine — Pittsburgher Mag
Pitture e Vernici — Pitture Vern
Pitture e Vernici Europe — Pitture Vernici Eur
Pivnicne Sjajvo — PivS
Pivovarsky Casopis Kvas — Pivovar Cas Kvas
PKV [*Punjabrao Krishi Vidyapeeth*] **Research Journal** — PKV Res J
PKV [*Punjabrao Krishi Vidyapeeth*] **Research Journal** — PKVJA
PLA [*Pennsylvania Library Association*] **Bulletin** — PLA Bull
PLA [*Private Libraries Association*] **Quarterly** — PLAQ
Placenta. Supplement — Placenta Suppl
Placer Mining Times [*Whitehorse*] — PM
Plain Dealer — Pln Dealr
Plain Rapper — Plain Ra
Plains Anthropologist — Pl Anth
Plains Anthropologist — Plains Anthropol
Plains Aquatic Research Conference. Proceedings — PARC
Plainsong & Medieval Music — Plain/Medieval
Plaintiff's Advocate — Plf Adv
Plan — PLNN-A
Plan Canada — Plan Can
Plan Canada — PLCN-A
Plan East Africa — Plan E Afr
Plan og Bygg — PLBYD
Plan Quinquennal de Developpement Economique et Social, 1979-1983 (Niger) — Niger Pl Dev
Plan Quinquennal de Developpement Economique, Social, et Culturel, 1981-1986 (Cameroon) — Cameroon P
Plan. Zeitschrift fuer Planen, Bauen, und Umwelt — PLR
Plana — PLA
Planeacion Regional — Planeacion Reg
Planeacion y Programa. Organizacion y Metodo — PPOM
Planen und Bauen — PB
Planen-Pruefen-Investieren — PPI
Planen-Pruefen-Investieren. PPI [*Germany*] — Planen Pruef Investieren PPI
Planet Stories — PS
Planetary and Space Science — Planet and Space Sci
Planetary and Space Science — Planet Spac
Planetary and Space Science — Planet Space Sci
Planetary and Space Science — PLSSA
Planetary Association for Clean Energy. Newsletter [*Canada*] — Planet Assoc Clean Energy Newsl
Planification, Habitat, Information — Planif Habitat Inform
Planirovanie Eksperimenta. Doklady. Prochitannye na Vsesoyuznom Soveshchanii — Plan Eksp Dokl Vses Soveshch
Planned Innovation — PDI
Planned Innovation — Plan Inovtn
Planned Innovation [*England*] — Planned Innov
Planned Parenthood Review — Plann Parenthood Rev
Planned Parenthood Review — PPHR
Planner Journal. Royal Town Planning Institute — PJTP
Planner Newsletter. NWT [*Northwest Territories, Canada*] **Land Use Planning Commission** — PLAN
Planning — PLN
Planning and Administration — Plann Admin
Planning and Administration — Planning and Adm
Planning and Building Developments — Plann Build Dev
Planning and Development in the Netherlands — Planning Develop Netherl
Planning and Development in the Netherlands (Assen) — PDA
Planning and Public Policy — Plann Pub Pol
Planning and Transportation Abstracts — Plann Transp Abs
Planning Bulletin — Planning Bul
Planning Exchange [*Database*] — PLANEX
Planning for Higher Education — Plan Higher Educ
Planning History Bulletin — Planning History Bull
Planning News — Plann News
Planning Outlook — Plann Outlook
Planning Outlook — PNOU-A
Planning Pamphlets. National Planning Association — Plann Pam Nat Plann Ass
Planning Quarterly — Plan Q
Planning Review — Plan Rev
Planning Review — PLR
Planning the Uses and Management of Land — Plann Uses Manage Land
Planovane Hospodarstvi — Plan Hospod
Planovoe Chozjajstvo — P Ch
Planovoe Chozjajstvo — Plan Choz
Planovoe Hozjajstvo — Plan Hoz
Planovoe Khozyaistvo — PLAKA
Planovoe Khozyaistvo — Plan Khoz
Plansee Proceedings. Papers. Plansee Seminar. De Re Metallica — Plansee Proc Pap Plansee Semin De Re Met
Planseeberichte fuer Pulvermetallurgie — Planseeber Pulvermet
Planseeberichte fuer Pulvermetallurgie — Planseeberichte
Planseeberichte fuer Pulvermetallurgie (Austria) — PLPUA
Plant and Cell Physiology — PCPHA
Plant and Cell Physiology — Plant Cel P
Plant and Cell Physiology — Plant Cell Physiol
Plant and Cell Physiology — PLCPB
Plant and Cell Physiology (Kyoto) — Plant Cell Physiol (Kyoto)
Plant and Cell Physiology. Nihon Shokubutsu Seiri Gakkai. Japanese Society of Plant Physiologists — Pl Cell Physiol
Plant and Cell Physiology (Tokyo) — Plant Cell Physiol (Tokyo)
Plant and Engineering Applications — Plant & Eng Applications
Plant and Nature — Plant Nat
Plant and Power Services Engineer — Plant & Power Services Eng
Plant and Power Services Engineer — PPENA
Plant and Soil — Pl Soil
Plant and Soil — Plant Soil
Plant and Soil — PLSOA
Plant Bibliography — Plant Bibliogr
Plant Biochemical Journal — PBJOD
Plant Biochemical Journal — Pl Biochem J
Plant Biochemical Journal — Plant Biochem J
Plant Biochemistry and Physiology Symposium — Plant Biochem Physiol Symp
Plant Biochemistry (Tbilisi) — Plant Biochem Tbilisi
Plant Biology [*New York*] — PBIOEM
Plant Biology — Plant Biol
Plant Biology (New York) — Plant Biol (NY)
Plant Breeding — PLABED
Plant Breeding — Plant Breed
Plant Breeding Abstracts — Pl Breed Abstr
Plant Breeding Abstracts — Plant Breed Abstr
Plant Breeding, Acclimatization, and Seed Production — Plant Breed Acclim Seed Prod
Plant Breeding Reviews — PBREE3
Plant Breeding Reviews — Plant Breed Rev
Plant Breeding Symposium — Plant Breed Symp
Plant Breeding. Zeitschrift fuer Pflanzenzuchtung — Plant Breed Z Pflanzenzucht
Plant Cell — Pl Cell
Plant Cell — Plant C
Plant Cell and Environment — Plant Cell Environ
Plant Cell and Environment — PLCEDV
Plant Cell Reports — PCRPD8
Plant Cell Reports — Plant Cell Rep
Plant Cell Tissue and Organ Culture — Plant Cell Tissue Organ Cult
Plant Cell Tissue and Organ Culture — PTCEDJ
Plant Disease — Plant Dis
Plant Disease. An Advanced Treatise — Plant Dis Adv Treatise
Plant Disease Knowledge/Zhibing Zhishi (Chih P'ing Chih Shih) — Pl Dis Knowl
Plant Disease Leaflet. Department of Agriculture. Biological Branch (New South Wales) — Plant Dis Leafl Dept Agr Biol Br (NSW)
Plant Disease Reporter — PDR
Plant Disease Reporter — Plant Dis R

Plant Disease Reporter — Plant Dis Rep
Plant Disease Reporter — PLDRA
Plant Disease Reporter. Bureau of Plant Industry. US Department of Agriculture — Pl Dis Reporter
Plant Disease Reporter. Supplement — Plant Dis Rep Suppl
Plant Energy Management — Plant Energy Manage
Plant Engineer — Plant Eng
Plant Engineer (London) — Plant Eng (Lond)
Plant Engineer (Tokyo) — Plant Eng (Tokyo)
Plant Engineering — Plant Eng
Plant Engineering — Plant Engng
Plant Engineering — PLEGA
Plant Engineering — PLENA
Plant Engineering and Maintenance — Plant Engng & Maint
Plant Engineering and Technology. PET Japan. Chemical Week Supplement — J Chem PET
Plant Food Review — Plant Food Rev
Plant Foods for Human Nutrition — Plant Foods Hum Nutr
Plant Foods for Human Nutrition (Dordrecht, Netherlands) — Plant Foods Hum Nutr Dordrecht Neth
Plant Genetic Engineering — Plant Genet Eng
Plant Genetic Resources Newsletter — Plant Genet Resour Lett
Plant Growing — Plant Grow
Plant Growth Regulation — PGR
Plant Growth Regulation — Plant Growth Regul
Plant Growth Regulator Society of America. Proceedings — Plant Growth Regul Soc Am Proc
Plant Growth Regulator Society of America Quarterly — Plant Growth Regul Soc Am Q
Plant Growth Regulators in Agriculture — Plant Growth Regul Agric
Plant Growth Substances. Proceedings. International Conference on Plant Growth Substances — Plant Growth Subst Proc Int Conf
Plant Hire — PLHID
Plant Hormone Receptors — Plant Horm Recept
Plant Husbandry — Plant Husb
Plant Industry Digest (Manila) — Plant Ind Dig (Manila)
Plant Industry Series. Chinese-American Joint Commission on Rural Reconstruction — Plant Ind Ser Chin-Amer Joint Comm Rural Reconstr
Plant Industry Series. Joint Commission on Rural Reconstruction in China (United States and Republic of China) — Plant Ind Ser J Comm Rural Reconstr China (US Repub China)
Plant Information Bulletin — Plant Info Bul
Plant Journal — Plant J
Plant Journal for Cell and Molecular Biology — Plant J Cell Mol Biol
Plant Life. American Plant Life Society — Pl Life
Plant Lipid Biochemistry, Structure, and Utilization. Proceedings. International Symposium on Plant Lipids — Plant Lipid Biochem Struct Util Proc Int Symp Plant Lipids
Plant Maintenance — Plant Maint
Plant Maintenance and Engineering — Plant
Plant Maintenance and Import Substitution — Plant Maint Import Substitution
Plant Management and Engineering — Plant Manage Eng
Plant Management and Engineering — PLG
Plant Molecular Biology — Plant Mol Biol
Plant Molecular Biology — PMBIDB
Plant Nutrition. Proceedings. International Colloquium on Plant Analysis and Fertilizer Problems — Plant Nutr Proc Int Colloq Plant Anal Fert Probl
Plant Nutrition. Proceedings. International Plant Nutrition Colloquium — Plant Nutr Proc Int Plant Nutr Colloq
Plant Operating Management — Plant Oper Manage
Plant/Operations Progress — Plant Operations Prog
Plant/Operations Progress — POPPD
Plant Patent. United States Patent and Trademark Office — Plant Pat US Pat Trademark Off
Plant Pathology — Pl Path
Plant Pathology [*London*] — Plant Path
Plant Pathology — Plant Pathol
Plant Pathology Bulletin — Plant Pathol Bull
Plant Pathology (London) — Plant Pathol (Lond)
Plant Pathology Problems and Progress [*Monograph*] — Plant Pathol
Plant Physiology — Plant Physiol
Plant Physiology — Plant Physl
Plant Physiology — PLPHA
Plant Physiology [*English Translation*] — PPHYA
Plant Physiology and Biochemistry — Plant Physiol & Biochem
Plant Physiology and Biochemistry — PPHBD7
Plant Physiology and Biochemistry (New Delhi) — Plant Physiol Biochem New Delhi
Plant Physiology and Biochemistry (Paris) — Plant Physiol Biochem Paris
Plant Physiology (Bethesda) — Plant Physiol (Bethesda)
Plant Physiology Communications (Shanghai) — Plant Physiol Commun (Shanghai)
Plant Physiology (English Translation) — Plant Physiol Engl Transl
Plant Physiology (Lancaster) — Pl Physiol (Lancaster)
Plant Physiology (Moscow) — Plant Physiol (Moscow)
Plant Physiology. Supplement — Plant Physiol Suppl
Plant Physiology. Supplement — PPYSA
Plant Physiology (Washington) — Pl Physiol (Wash)
Plant Propagator — Plant Propagat
Plant Propagator. International Plant Propagators Society — Pl Propag
Plant Protection — Plant Prot
Plant Protection Abstracts — Plant Prot Abstr
Plant Protection (Belgrade) — Plant Prot Belgrade
Plant Protection (Budapest) — Plant Prot (Budapest)
Plant Protection Bulletin — Plant Prot Bull
Plant Protection Bulletin (Ankara) — Plant Prot Bull (Ankara)
Plant Protection Bulletin. FAO [*Food and Agriculture Organization*] **United Nations** — Plant Prot Bull FAO
Plant Protection Bulletin (Faridabad, India) — Plant Prot Bull Faridabad India
Plant Protection Bulletin (New Delhi) — Plant Prot Bull (New Delhi)
Plant Protection Bulletin (Rome) — Plant Prot Bull (Rome)
Plant Protection. Chih Wupao Hu Zhiwu Baohu (Peking) — Pl Protect Peking
Plant Protection for Human Welfare. International Congress of Plant Protection. Proceedings of Congress — Plant Prot Hum Welfare Int Congr Plant Prot Proc Congr
Plant Protection Overseas Review — Plant Prot Overseas Rev
Plant Protection Quarterly — Plant Prot Q
Plant Protection Quarterly — PPQUE8
Plant Protection (Sofia) — Plant Prot Sofia
Plant Protection (Tokyo) — Pl Prot (Tokyo)
Plant Protection (Tokyo) — Plant Prot Tokyo
Plant Research and Development — Plant Res Dev
Plant Science [*Shannon*] — PLSCE4
Plant Science Bulletin — Plant Sci Bull
Plant Science Letters — Plant Sci L
Plant Science Letters — Plant Sci Lett
Plant Science Letters — PTSLA
Plant Science (Limerick, Ireland) — Plant Sci (Limerick Irel)
Plant Science (Lucknow, India) — Plant Sci (Lucknow)
Plant Science (Lucknow, India) — Plant Sci (Lucknow India)
Plant Science Pamphlet. Plant Science Department. Agricultural Experiment Station. South Dakota State University — Plant Sci Pam Plant Sci Dep Agric Exp Stn SD State Univ
Plant Science (Shannon) — Plant Sci (Shannon)
Plant Science (Sofia) — Plant Sci (Sofia)
Plant Systematics and Evolution — Plant Sys E
Plant Systematics and Evolution — Plant Syst Evol
Plant Systematics and Evolution. Supplementum — Plant Syst Evol Suppl
Plant Tissue Culture Letters — Plant Tissue Cult Lett
Plant Tissue Culture. Proceedings. International Congress of Plant Tissue and Cell Culture — Plant Tissue Cult Proc Int Congr Plant Tissue Cell Cult
Plant Varieties and Seeds — Plant Var Seeds
Plant Varieties and Seeds Gazette — Pl Var Seeds Gaz
Plant World. A Monthly Journal of Popular Botany — Pl World
Planta — Pl
Planta — PLANA
Planta Medica — Plant Med
Planta Medica — Planta Med
Planta Medica — PLMEA
Planta Medica. Journal of Medicinal Plant Research — Plant Med J Med Plant Res
Plantas Cultivadas en la Republica Argentina. Instituto de Botanica Agricola (Buenos Aires) — Plant Cultiv Repub Argent Inst Bot Agric (B Aires)
Plantas Medicinales [*Database*] — PLAMED
Plantation Field Laboratory Mimeo Report. Florida University — Plant Field Lab Mimeo Rep Fla Univ
Plantation Society in the Americas — PSIA
Plantations, Recherche, Developpement — Plant Rech Dev
Planter and Sugar Manufacturer — Plant Sugar Manuf
Planter and Sugar Manufacturer — Planter
Planters' Bulletin. Rubber Research Institute of Malaya — Pl Bull
Planters' Bulletin. Rubber Research Institute of Malaya — Plrs' Bull Rubb Res Inst Malaya
Planters' Bulletin. Rubber Research Institute of Malaysia — Plant Bull Rubber Res Inst Malays
Planters' Bulletin. Rubber Research Institute of Malaysia — Planters' Bull
Planters' Chronicle — Plant Chron
Plantes Medicinales et Phytotherapie — Plant Med Phytother
Plant-Microbe Interactions — Plant Microbe Interact
Plants and Gardens — Plant Gard
Plants and Gardens — Plants Gard
Plants and Gardens — PLGAA
Plants and Gardens — Pls Gds
Plants and Gardens. Brooklyn Botanical Garden — Pl Gard
Plant-Soil Interactions at Low pH. Proceedings. International Symposium — Plant Soil Inter Low pH Proc Int Symp
Planwell — P'well
Plasir de France — Plasir Fr
Plasma Astrophysics. International School and Workshop — Plasma Astrophys Int Sch Workshop
Plasma Chemistry and Plasma Processing — PCPP
Plasma Chemistry and Plasma Processing — PCPPD
Plasma Chemistry and Plasma Processing — Plasma Chem
Plasma Chemistry and Plasma Processing — Plasma Chem Plasma Process
Plasma Devices and Operations — Plasma Devices Oper
Plasma Physics — Pl Physics
Plasma Physics — Plasma Phys
Plasma Physics — PLPHB
Plasma Physics, Accelerators, Thermonuclear Research — Plasma Phys Accel Thermonucl Res
Plasma Physics and Controlled Fusion — Plasma Phys Control Fusion
Plasma Physics and Controlled Fusion — Plasma Phys Controlled Fusion
Plasma Physics and Controlled Nuclear Fusion Research. Conference Proceedings — Plasma Phys Contr Nucl Fusion Res Conf Proc
Plasma Physics Index [*Germany*] — Plasma Phys Index
Plasma Physics Index — PPHID
Plasma Processing. Proceedings. Symposium — Plasma Process Proc Symp
Plasma Protein Turnover. Proceedings. Meeting. Plasma Protein Group — Plasma Protein Turnover Proc Meet Plasma Protein Group
Plasma Sources Science and Technology — Plasma Sources Sci Technol

Plasma Surface Engineering. Papers. International Conference on Plasma Surface Engineering — Plasma Surf Eng Pap Int Conf
Plasma Therapy — Plasma Ther
Plasma Therapy and Transfusion Technology — Plasma Ther Transfus Technol
Plasma-Based and Novel Accelerators. Proceedings. Workshop on Plasma-Based and Novel Accelerators. Nagoya — Plasma Based Novel Accel Proc Workshop
Plasmabericht. Universitaet Heidelberg. Institut fuer Angewandte Physik — Plasmabericht Univ Heidelberg Inst Angew Phys
Plasmas and Polymers — Plasmas Polym
Plast Panorama Scandinavia — Plast Panorama
Plast Panorama Scandinavia — Plast Panorama Scand
Plast. Rivista delle Materie Plastiche — Plast Matr
Plaste und Kautschuk — PK
Plaste und Kautschuk — Plaste Kaut
Plaste und Kautschuk — Plaste u Kaut
Plaste und Kautschuk — Plaste und Kautsch
Plaste und Kautschuk — PLKAA
PLASTEC [*Plastics Technical Evaluation Center*] **Note** — PLASTEC Note
PLASTEC [*Plastics Technical Evaluation Center*] **Report** — PLASTEC Rep
Plastic Abstracts — Plast Abstr
Plastic and Reconstructive Surgery — Plas R Surg
Plastic and Reconstructive Surgery — Plast Reconstr Surg
Plastic and Reconstructive Surgery — PRSUA
Plastic and Reconstructive Surgery and the Transplantation Bulletin — Plast Reconstr Surg Transplant Bull
Plastic Industry [*India*] — Plast Ind
Plastic Materials (Leningrad) — Plast Mater Leningrad
Plastic Optical Fibers — Plast Opt Fibers
Plastic Products — Plast Prod
Plastic Products — Plastic Prod
Plastic Surgical Nursing — Plast Surg Nurs
Plastica (Puerto Rico) — PPR
Plasticheskie Massy — Plas Massy
Plasticheskie Massy — Plast Massy
Plasticheskie Massy — PLMSA
Plastichnost i Obrabotka Metallov Davleniem — Plast Obrab Met Davleniem
Plasticita nella Scienza delle Costruzioni. Memorie Presentate al Symposium — Plast Sci Costr Mem Symp
Plasticity and Regeneration of the Nervous System — Plast Regener Nerv Syst
Plasticity of the Neuromuscular System — Plast Neuromuscular Syst
Plasticke Hmoty a Kaucuk — Plast Hmoty Kauc
Plasticos em Revista — Plast em Rev
Plasticos Modernos — Plast Mod
Plasticos Modernos Latinoamericanos — Plast Mod Latinoam
Plasticos Universales — Plast Univers
Plasticos y Resinas [*Mexico*] — Plast Resinas
Plasticos y Resinas — PLRSA
Plastics Age — Plast Age
Plastics and Molded Products — Plast Molded Prod
Plastics and Polymers — Plast and Polym
Plastics and Polymers — Plast Polym
Plastics and Polymers. Conference Supplement — Plast Polym Conf Suppl
Plastics and Resins — Plast Resins
Plastics and Rubber [*Later, Plastics and Rubber International*] — Plast and Rubber
Plastics and Rubber [*Later, Plastics and Rubber International*] — Plast Rubber
Plastics and Rubber (Budapest) — Plast Rubber (Budapest)
Plastics and Rubber Institute. Annual National Conference — Plast Rubber Inst Annu Natl Conf
Plastics and Rubber International — Plas Rub Int
Plastics and Rubber International — Plast and Rubber Int
Plastics and Rubber International — Plast Rubb Int
Plastics and Rubber International — Plast Rubber Int
Plastics and Rubber. Material and Applications — Plast Rubber Mater Appl
Plastics and Rubber News [*South Africa*] — Plast Rubb News
Plastics and Rubber News [*South Africa*] — Plast Rubber News
Plastics and Rubber News — PRUND
Plastics and Rubber. Processing — Plast Rubber Process
Plastics and Rubber Processing and Applications — Plast & Rubber Process & Appl
Plastics and Rubber Processing and Applications — Plast Rubb Process Appln
Plastics and Rubber Processing and Applications — Plast Rubber Proc Appl
Plastics and Rubber Processing and Applications — Plast Rubber Process
Plastics and Rubber Processing and Applications — Plast Rubber Process Appl
Plastics and Rubber Weekly — Plas Rubr
Plastics and Rubber Weekly — Plast Rub Wkly
Plastics and Rubber Weekly [*England*] — Plast Rubber Wkly
Plastics Bulletin (London) — Plast Bull (London)
Plastics Business — Plast Busin
Plastics Compounding — Plas Compd
Plastics Compounding — Plast Compd
Plastics Compounding — Plast Compounding
Plastics Compounding Redbook — Plas Com R
Plastics. Computer Aided Materials Selector [*Database*] — PLASCAMS
Plastics Correspondence — Plast Corresp
Plastics Design and Processing — PDPRA
Plastics Design and Processing — Plast Des Process
Plastics Design Forum — Plas Desgn
Plastics Digest — Plast Dig
Plastics Engineering — Plas Eng
Plastics Engineering — Plast Eng
Plastics Engineering — Plast Engng
Plastics Engineering — Plastics Engng
Plastics Engineering — PLEGB
Plastics in Australia — Plast Aust
Plastics in Australia — Plastics in Aust
Plastics in Australia. Supplement — Plast Aust Suppl
Plastics in Bearings. Conference. Papers — Plast Bear Conf Pap
Plastics in Building Construction — Plast Bldg Constr
Plastics in Building Construction — Plast Build Constr
Plastics in Furniture. National Technical Conference. Society of Plastics Engineers — Plast Furnit Natl Tech Conf Soc Plast Eng
Plastics in Retail Packaging Bulletin — Plast Retail Packag Bull
Plastics in Surface Transportation. National Technical Conference. Society of Plastics Engineers — Plast Surf Transp Natl Tech Conf Soc Plast Eng
Plastics in Telecommuncations. International Conference. Preprints — Plast Telecommun Int Conf Prepr
Plastics Industry Europe — Plas Ind Eur
Plastics Industry Europe. Special Report — Plas Ind ES
Plastics Industry (Hong Kong) — Plast Ind (Hong Kong)
Plastics Industry (New York) — Plast Ind (NY)
Plastics Industry News — Plas Ind N
Plastics Industry News — Plast Ind News
Plastics Industry News — Plastic IN
Plastics Industry News (Japan) — Plast Ind News (Jap)
Plastics Institute. Transactions — Plast Inst Trans
Plastics Institute. Transactions and Journal — Plast Inst Trans J
Plastics Institute. Transactions and Journal. Conference Supplement — Plast Inst Trans J Conf Suppl
Plastics Machinery and Equipment — Plast M & E
Plastics Materials in Medicine — Plast Mater Med
Plastics Materials Patents Newsletter — Plast Mat Pat Newsl
Plastics Materials (Tokyo) — Plast Mater (Tokyo)
Plastics News — Plast News
Plastics News (Australia) — Plast News (Aust)
Plastics News. Briefs — Plast News Briefs
Plastics Packaging — Plast Pack
Plastics, Paint, and Rubber — Plast Paint Rubber
Plastics Processing Patents Newsletter — Plast Proc Pat Newsl
Plastics Progress in India — Plast Prog India
Plastics, Rubber, and Composites Processing and Applications — Plast Rubber Compos Process Appl
Plastics, Rubbers, Textiles — Plas Rubbers Text
Plastics, Rubbers, Textiles — Plast Rubbers Text
Plastics (Solothurn, Switzerland) — Plast Solothurn Switz
Plastics (Southern Africa) — Plast (S Afr)
Plastics (Southern Africa) — Plast (S Africa)
Plastics (Southern Africa) — Plast (Sthn Afr)
Plastics (Southern Africa) — SAFD
Plastics Technical Evaluation Center. Note — Plast Tech Eval Cent Note
Plastics Technical Evaluation Center. Report — Plast Tech Eval Cent Rep
Plastics Technology — Plast Tech
Plastics Technology — Plast Technol
Plastics Technology — PLTEA
Plastics Today — Plast Today
Plastics Trends — Plast Trends
Plastics World — Plast World
Plastics World — PLAWA
Plastics World — PLZ
Plastiques et Industrie (Paris) — Plast Ind (Paris)
Plastiques Flash — Plast Flash
Plastiques Modernes et Elastomeres — Plast Mod Elast
Plastiques Modernes et Elastomeres — Plast Mod Elastomeres
Plastiques Modernes et Elastomeres — PMELA
Plastiques Renforces Fibres de Verre Textile — Plast Renf Fibres Verre Text
Plastische Massen — Plast Massen
Plastische Massen in Wissenschaft und Technik — Plast Massen Wiss Tech
Plastvaerlden — PLTVA
Plastverarbeiter — PLARA
Plasty a Kaucuk — Plast Kauc
Plateau — Pl
Plateau. Quarterly of the Museum of Northern Arizona — Plateau Q Mus North Ariz
Plating — PLATA
Plating and Surface Finishing — Plat and Surf Finish
Plating and Surface Finishing — Plat Surf Finish
Plating and Surface Finishing — Plating & Surface Finish
Plating in the Electronics Industry. Symposium — Plat Electron Ind
Platinum Metals Review — Platinum Met Rev
Platinum Metals Review — Platinum Metals Rev
Platinum Metals Review — PTMRA
Platoon School — Platoon Sch
Plato's Theory of Knowledge — PTK
Platte Valley Review — PVR
Platt's Oilgram News Service — PONSA
Playboy — GPLY
Playboy — Pb
Playboy — Playb
Players Chess News — PCN
Players Magazine — Players Mag
Playfulness, Revelry, Nonsense [*Quarterly Newsletter of Nurses for Laughter*] [*Title is derived from the pharmaceutical term PRN (Pro Re Nata)*] — PRN
[*The*] **Playgoer** — PLAY
Plenar- und Posterbeitraege. Tagung der Forschungsgemeinschaft Organische Festkoerper — Plenar Posterbeitr Tag Forschungsgem Org Festkoerper
Plenarvortraege der Physikertagungen — Plenarvortr Physikertag
Plenarvortraege. Internationaler Kongress fuer Reprographie und Information — Plenarvortr Int Kongr Reprogr Inf

Plenarvortraege und Kurzreferate der Tagung der Deutschen Arbeitsgemeinschaft fuer Akustik — Plenarvortr Kurzref Tag Dtsch Arbeitsgem Akust
Plenary and Invited Contributions. Australian Electrochemistry Conference — Plenary Invited Contrib Aust Electrochem Conf
Plenary and Main Lectures. International Symposium on Macromolecules — Plenary Main Lect Int Symp Macromol
Plenary and Main Section Lectures. International Congress of Pure and Applied Chemistry — Plenary Main Sect Lect Int Congr Pure Appl Chem
Plenary Lectures. International Congress of Pesticide Chemistry — Plenary Lect Int Congr Pestic Chem
Plenary Lectures. World Conference on Non-Destructive Testing — Plenary Lect World Conf Non Destr Test
Plenary Session. International Fair and Technical Meetings of Nuclear Industries — Plenary Sess Int Fair Tech Meet Nucl Ind
Plenary Session Lectures. Congress. World Federation of Hemophilia — Plenary Sess Lect Congr World Fed Hemophilia
Plenary Session Papers. International Congress of Soil Science — Plenary Sess Pap Int Congr Soil Sci
Plenochnye Polimernye Materialy i Ikh Primenenie. Marerialy Kratkosrochnogo Seminara — Plenochn Polim Mater Ikh Primen Mater Kratkosrochnogo Semin
PLF [*Projektgruppe fuer Laserforschung*] **Bericht** — PLF Ber
Plodoovoscnoe Hozjajstvo — Plodoovoscn Hoz
Plodoovoshchnoi Institut imeni I.V. Michurina. Trudy — Plodoovoshchn Inst IV Michurina Tr
Plodorodie Pochv Karelii. Akademiya Nauk SSSR. Karel'skii Filial — Plodorodie Pochv Karelii Akad Nauk SSSR Karel'sk Filial
Ploughshare — PS
Ploughshares — Ploughs
Ploughshares — PPLG
Plovdivski Universitet. Naucni Trudove — Plovdiv Univ Naucn Trud
Plovdivski Universitet Paisii Khilendarski. Nauchni Trudove. Matematika — Plovdiv Univ Paisii Khilendarski Nauchn Trud Mat
Plucne Bolesti i Tuberkuloza — Plucne Boles Tuberk
Plucne Bolesti i Tuberkuloza — Plucne Bolesti Tuberk
Pluimveehouderij — PUF
Plumbing and Heating Equipment News — Plumbing Heat Equip News
Plumbing and Heating Journal — PLHJA
Plumbing and Heating Journal — Plumb Heat J
Plumbing Engineer — PLEND
Plumbing Engineer — Plumbing Eng
Plumbing Engineer — Plumbing Engr
Plural — PE
Plural Societies [*The Hague*] — Plural Soc
Plural Societies — PluS
Plutonium-Dokumentation — PLUDA
Plutonium-Dokumentation [*Germany*] — Plutonium-Dok
Plymouth Mineral and Mining Club. Journal — Plymouth Miner Min Club J
Plyn — PVZTA
Plyn Voda a Zdravotni Technika — Plyn Voda Zdra Tech
Plywood and Plywood Products — Plyw and Plyw Prod
Plywood and Plywood Products — Plyw Plyw Prod
Plzen. Pedagogicka Fakulta. Sbornik. Chemie — Plzen Pedagog Fak Sb Chem
Plzensky Lekarsky Sbornik — PLLSA
Plzensky Lekarsky Sbornik — Plzen Lek Sb
Plzensky Lekarsky Sbornik. Supplementum — Plzen Lek Sb Suppl
PM. Iowa State University. Cooperative Extension Service — PM Iowa State Univ Coop Ext Serv
PM. Iowa State University of Science and Technology. Cooperative Extension Service — PM Iowa State Univ Sci Technol Coop Ext Serv
PM. Pharmacy Management — PM
PM (Pharmacy Management) — PM Pharm Manage
PMA [*Pharmaceutical Manufacturers Association*] **Newsletter** — PMA News
PMAI [*Powder Metallurgy Association of India*] **News Letter** — PMAI News Lett
PMLA. Publications of the Modern Language Association — GPML
PMS. Public Management Sources — PMS Public Manage Source
PMTF. Zhurnal Prikladnoi Mekhaniki Tekhnickeskio Fiziki — PMTF Zh Prikl Mekh Tekh Fiz
PN [*Poetry Nation*] **Review** — PNR
Pneumatic Digest and Druckluft Praxis — Pneum Dig & Druckluft Prax
Pneumatike Kypros — PKy
Pneumoftiziologie [*Bucharest*] — PNEUDZ
Pneumokoniosenavorsingseenheid Jaarverslag — Pneumokoniosenavorsingseenheid Jaarversl
Pneumokoniosenavorsingseenheid Jaarverslag Pochvoznanie Agrokhimiya i Rastitelna Zashtita — PKSVAG
Pneumologia Hungarica [*Hungary*] — Pneumolog Hung
Pneumologia i Ftiziatria — Pneumol Ftiziatr
Pneumonologia Hungarica — Pneumonol Hung
Pneumonologia i Alergologia Polska — Pneumonol Alergol Pol
Pneumonologia Polska — Pneumonol Pol
Pneumonologie/Pneumonology — Pneumol/Pneumol
Pneumonologie/Pneumonology — Pneumonol Pneumonol
Pneumonologie/Pneumonology — Pneumonol-P
PNM Update — PNMUD
PNW. Pacific Northwest Extension Publication. Oregon State University. Cooperative Extension Service — PNW Pac Northwest Ext Publ Oreg State Univ Coop Ext Serv
PNW-RN Research Note. US Department of Agriculture. Forest Service. Pacific Northwest Research Station — PNW RN Res Note US Dep Agric For Serv Pac Northwest Res Stn
Pochva i Urozhai. Latviiskii Nauchno-Issledovatel'skii Institut Zemledeliya — Poch Urozhai Latv Nauch-Issled Inst Zemled
Pochvenno-Biogeotsenologicheskie Issledovaniya v Priazov'e — Pochv Biogeotsenol Issled Priazove
Pochvenno-Geograficheskie i Landshaftno-Geokhimicheskie Issledovaniya v Zone BAM — Pochv Geogr Landshaftno Geokhim Issled Zone BAM
Pochvennye Issledovaniya i Primenenie Udobrenii — Pochv Issled Primen Udobr
Pochvennye Usloviya i Effektivnost Udobrenii — Pochv Usloviya Eff Udobr
Pochvovedenie — Pochvoved
Pochvovedenie i Agrokhimiya (Moscow) — Pochvoved Agrokhim (Moscow)
Pochvoznanie, Agrokhimiya i Ekologiya — Pochvozn Agrokhim Ekol
Pochvoznanie Agrokhimiya i Rastitelna Zashtita — PARZEP
Pochvoznanie Agrokhimiya i Rastitelna Zashtita — Pochvozn Agrokhim Rastit Zasht
Pochvoznanie i Agrokhimiya — Pochvozn Agrokhim
Pochvoznanie i Agrokhimiya — PVAGA
Pochvy Bashkirii i Puti Ratsional'nogo Ikh Ispol'zovaniya — PBIBA
Pochvy Baskhirii i Puti Ratsional'nogo Ikh Ispol'zovaniya [*Former USSR*] — Pochvy Baskh Puti Ratsion Ikh Ispol'z
Pochvy i Biologicheskaya Produktivnost — Pochvy Biol Prod
Pochvy Kaliningradskoi Oblasti — Pochvy Kaliningr Obl
Pochvy Yuzhnogo Urala i Povolzh'ya — Pochvy Yuzhn Urala Povolzhya
Pochvy Zapadnoi Sibiri i Povyshenie Ikh Biologicheskoi Aktivnosti — Pochvy Zapadn Sib Povysh Ikh Biol Akt
Pocket Picture Guides to Clinical Medicine — Pocket Pict Guides Clin Med
Pod Znamenem Marksizma — PZM
Podgotovka i Koksovanie Uglei — Podgot Koksovanie Uglei
Podgotovka i Pererabotka Gaza i Gazovogo Kondensata. Referativnyi Sbornik — Podgot Pererab Gaza Gazov Kondens
Podgotovka i Vosstanovlenie Rud — Podgot Vosstanov Rud
Podiplomski Seminar iz Matematike — Podiplomski Sem Mat
Podravska Revija — PR
Podreczniki Akademickie. Elektronika. Informatyka. Telekomunikacja — Podreczn Akad Elektron Inform Telekom
Podstawowe Nauki Techniczne. Monografia — Podstaw Nauki Tech Monogr
Podstawowe Problemy Wspolczesnej Techniki — Podstawowe Probl Wspolczesnej Tech
Podstawy Sterowania — Podst Sterow
Podstawy Teorii Wyladowan Elektrycznych w Gazach. Sympozium — Podstawy Teor Wyladowan Elektr Gazach Symp
Podzemnaya Gazifikatsiya Uglei [*Former USSR*] — Podzemn Gazif Uglei
Podzemnaya Gazifikatsiya Uglei (1934-35) — Podzemn Gazif Uglei (1934-35)
Podzemnaya Gazifikatsiya Uglei (1957-59) — Podzemn Gazif Uglei (1957-59)
Podzemnaya Razrabotka Moshchnykh Rudnykh Mestorozhdenii — Podzemn Razrab Moshchn Rudn Mestorozhd
Podzemnye Vody SSSR — Podzemn Vody SSSR
Poe Newsletter — PN
Poe Studies — Poe Stud
Poe Studies — PoeS
Poems on Affairs of State — POAS
Poesia de Venezuela — PV
Poesia e Critica — PC
Poesia e Critica — PeC
Poesia e Verita — PV
Poesia Espanola — PE
Poesia Espanola — PEsp
Poesia Hispanica — PHisp
Poesia Hispanica Moderna — PHM
Poesia Nuova — PN
Poesie — Po
Poesie Francaise — PF
Poesie und Wissenschaft — PuW
Poet and Critic — P & C
Poet and Critic — Poet Crit
Poet and Critic — PoetC
Poet Lore — PL
Poet Lore — Poet L
Poetae Latini Minores — PLM
Poetae Lyrici Graeci — PLG
Poetae Lyrici Graeci — Poet Lyr Gr
Poetae Melici Graeci — P Mel Gr
Poetae Melici Graeci — PMG
Poetae Melici Graeci — Poet Mel Gr
Poetalk Quarterly — Poetalk Quart
Poetarum Lesbiorum Fragmenta — LP
Poetarum Lesbiorum Fragmenta — PLF
Poetarum Philosophorum Fragmenta — PPF
Poetarum Romanorum Veterum Reliquiae — Poet Rom Vet
Poetarum Romanorum Veterum Reliquiae — PRVR
Poetic Drama — PD
Poetica — Poet
Poetics Today — Po T
Poetics Today — Poetics Tod
Poetik — Poe
Poetry — IPOE
Poetry — P
Poetry — Poet
Poetry and Drama Magazine — PDM
Poetry and the People — PP
Poetry Australia — PAus
Poetry Australia — Poetry Aust
Poetry Bag — PB
Poetry Book Magazine — PBM
Poetry Chapbook — PCB
Poetry Chapbook — Poe Chpbk
Poetry Dial — PDial
Poetry (London) — PL
Poetry Magazine — Poetry Mag
Poetry Nation Review — P N Review

Poetry New York — PNY
Poetry Northwest — PN
Poetry Northwest — Poetry NW
Poetry Now — Po Now
Poetry Palisade — Poe Pal
Poetry Quarterly — PQ
Poetry Review [*London*] — Poetry R
Poetry Review [*London*] — PoR
Poetry Review — PR
Poetry Wales — Poetry Wale
Poetry Wales — PoetW
Poetry Wales — PW
Poets in the South — Poets
Poeyana Instituto de Biologia. La Habana. Serie A — Poeyana Inst Biol La Habana Ser A
Poeyana Instituto de Biologia. La Habana. Serie B — Poeyana Inst Biol La Habana Ser B
Poeyana Instituto de Zoologia. Academia de Ciencias de Cuba — Poeyana Inst Zool Acad Cienc Cuba
Poggendorffs Annalen — Poggendorffs Ann
Pogledi — Pog
Pogranichnye Sloi v Slozhnykh Usloviyakh. Materialy Sibirskogo Teplofizicheskogo Seminara — Pogran Sloi Slozhnykh Usloviyakh Mater Sib Teplofiz Semin
Poimennye Pochvy Russkoi Ravniny — Poimennye Pochvy Russ Ravniny
Point Defects and Defect Interactions in Metals. Proceedings. Yamada Conference — Point Defects Defect Interact Met Proc Yamada Conf
Point Defects and Related Properties of Ceramics — Point Defects Relat Prop Ceram
Point Veterinaire — Point Vet
Points d'Appui pour l'Economie Rhone-Alpes — Points Appui Econ Rhone-Alpes
Points de Vente. Le Magazine des Magasins — PVC
Point-to-Point Communication [*Later, Communication and Broadcasting*] — Point Point Commun
Point-to-Point Telecommunications — Point Point Telecommun
Pokroky Matematiky, Fyziky, a Astronomie — PMFAA
Pokroky Matematiky, Fyziky, a Astronomie — Pokroky Mat Fyz Astron
Pokroky Praskove Metalurgie — Pokroky Praskove Metal
Pokroky Praskove Metalurgie VUPM [*Vyzkumny Ustav pro Praskovou Metalurgii*] — Pokroky Praskove Metal VUPM
Pokroky vo Vinohradnickom a Vinarskom Vyskume — Pokroky Vinohrad Vina-Vysk
Poland China World — Poland China
Poland. Instytut Geologiczny. Bibliografia Geologiczna Polski — Pol Inst Geol Bibliogr Geol Pol
Poland. Instytut Geologiczny. Biuletyn — Poland Inst Geol Biul
Poland. Instytut Meteorologii i Gospodarki Wodnej. Prace — Pol Inst Meteorol Gospod Wodnej Pr
Poland. Patent Document — Pol Pat Doc
Poland. Urzad Patentowy. Wiadomosci Urzedu Patentowego — Pol Urzad Pat Wiad Urzedu Pat
Polar Biology — POBI
Polar Biology — Polar Biol
Polar Gas News — PGNS
Polar Geography and Geology — POGE
Polar News. Japan Polar Research Association — PONE
Polar Notes — PONS
Polar Post. Polar Postal History Society of Great Britain — POPO
Polar Record — Polar Rec
Polar Record — POLRA
Polar Record — PORE
Polar Research — Polar Res
Polar Research — POREEQ
Polar Research — PORS
Polar Times — PT
Polarboken — POB
Polarforschung — PLFS
Polarforschung — POLFA
Polarographische Berichte — Polarogr Ber
Polemon — Pol
Polet — Po
Police Chief — IPCH
Police Journal — Pol J
Police Journal — Police J
Police Labor Review — Pol Lab Rev
Police Labor Review — Police Lab Rev
Police Magazine — Police Mag
Police Magazine (Syria) — Police Mag (Syria)
Police Research Bulletin — Pol Res Bull
Police Research Bulletin — Police Res Bull
Police Review — Police Rev
Police Science Abstracts — Police Sc Abs
Police Science Abstracts — Police Sci Abstr
Police Science Abstracts — PSA
Policlinico Infantile — Policlin Infant
Policlinico. Sezione Chirurgica — Policlinico Sez Chir
Policlinico. Sezione Medica — Policlinico Sez Med
Policlinico. Sezione Practica — Policlinico Sez Prat
Policy Analysis — Pol Anal
Policy Analysis [*Later, Journal of Policy Analysis and Management*] — Policy Anal
Policy Analysis and Information Systems — PASYD
Policy and Politics — Pol and Polit
Policy and Politics — Policy Pol
Policy and Politics — Policy Polit
Policy Options/Options Politiques — PLOP
Policy Papers Series — Pol Pap Ser
Policy Publication Review [*England*] — Policy Publ Rev
Policy Review — PIN
Policy Review — Pol R
Policy Review — Policy R
Policy Review — Policy Rev
Policy Review — PPOW
Policy Sciences — PLSCB
Policy Sciences — Pol Sci
Policy Sciences — Policy Sci
Policy Sciences Book Series [*Elsevier Book Series*] — PSBS
Policy Statement. Royal College of General Practitioners — Policy Statemont R Coll Gen Pract
Policy Studies — Policy Stud
Policy Studies Journal — Pol Stud J
Policy Studies Journal — Policy Stud J
Policy Studies Journal — Policy Studies J
Policy Studies Journal — PPSJ
Policy Studies Journal. Policy Studies Institute [*London*] — PST
Policy Studies Review — Policy Stud Rev
Policy Studies Review — Policy Studies R
Policy Studies Review — PSRWD
Policy Studies Review Annual — Pol Stud Rev Ann
Polifonia (Buenos Aires) — Polifon BA
Poligraficheskaya Promyshlennost. Obzornaya Informatsiya — Poligr Promst Obz Inf
Poligraficheskaya Promyshlennost. Referativnaya Informatsiya — Poligr Promst Ref Inf
Poligraficheskoe Proizvodstvo — Poligr Proizvod
Poligrafiya — PLGFA
Polimeri Sbornik ot Trudove na Nauchnoizsledovatelskiya Institut po Kauchukova i Plastmasova Promishlenost — Polim Sb Tr Nauchnoizsled Inst Kauch Plastmasova Promst
Polimeri Sbornik ot Trudove na Nauchnoizsledovatelskiya Institut po Prerabotkka na Plastmasi — Polim Sb Tr Nauchnoizsled Inst Prerabotka Plastmasi
Polimerim Vehomarim Plastiim — Polim Vehomarim Plast
Polimerines Medziagos ir Ju Tyrimas — Polim Medziagos Ju Tyrimas
Polimeriniu Medziagu Panaudojimas Liaudies Ukyje — Polim Medziagu Panaudojimas Liaudies Ukyje
Polimernye Materialy i Ikh Issledovanie — Polim Mater Ikh Issled
Polimernye Materialy i Ikh Primenenie — Polim Mater Ikh Primen
Polimernye Stroitel'nye Materialy — Polim Stroit Mater
Polimeros. Ciencia e Tecnologia — Polim Cienc Tecnol
Polimery — POLIA
Polimery Tworzywa [*Poland*] — Polim Tworzwa
Polimery Tworzywa — POTWA
Polimery Tworzywa Wielkoczasteczkowe — Polim Tworzywa Wielkoczasteczkowe
Polimery v Mashinostroenii [*Ukrainian SSR*] — Polim Mashinostr
Polimery w Medycynie — Polim Med
Polimery-Tworzywa Wielkoczasteczkowe [*Poland*] — Polim Tworz Wielk
Polimery-Tworzywa Wielkoczasteczkowe — Polim Tworz Wielkoczast
Poliomyelitis. Papers and Discussions Presented at the International Poliomyelitis Confernce — Polio Pap Discuss Int Polio Conf
Poliplasti e Materiali Rinforzati — Poliplasti Mater Rinf
Poliplasti e Plastici Rinforzati — Poliplasti Plast Rinf
Poliplasti e Plastici Rinforzati — PPRFA
Polish [*Patent Document*] — Pol
Polish Academy of Sciences. Bulletin. Biology — Pol Acad Sci Bull Biol
Polish Academy of Sciences. Bulletin. Chemistry — Pol Acad Sci Bull Chem
Polish Academy of Sciences. Bulletin. Earth Sciences — Pol Acad Sci Bull Earth Sci
Polish Academy of Sciences. Bulletin. Technical Sciences — Pol Acad Sci Bull Tech Sci
Polish Academy of Sciences. Institute of Ecology. Report on Scientific Activities — Pol Acad Sci Inst Ecol Rep Sci Act
Polish Academy of Sciences. Institute of Fundamental Technical Research. Nonlinear Vibration Problems — Pol Acad Sci Inst Fundam Tech Res Nonlinear Vib Probl
Polish Academy of Sciences. Institute of Fundamental Technical Research. Proceedings of Vibration Problems — Pol Acad Sci Inst Fundam Tech Res Proc Vib Probl
Polish Academy of Sciences. Institute of Geophysics. Publications. D. Physics of the Atmosphere — Pol Acad Sci Inst Geophys Publ D
Polish Academy of Sciences. Institute of Geophysics. Publications. Series D. Atmosphere Physics — Pol Acad Sci Inst Geophys Publ Ser D
Polish Academy of Sciences. Institute of Nuclear Research. Report — Pol Acad Sci Inst Nucl Res Rep
Polish Academy of Sciences. Institute of Philosophy and Sociology. Bulletin of the Section of Logic — Polish Acad Sci Inst Philos Sociol Bull Sect Logic
Polish Academy of Sciences. Institute of Physics. Reports — Pol Acad Sci Inst Phys Rep
Polish Academy of Sciences. Medical Section. Annals — Pol Acad Sci Med Sect Ann
Polish Academy of Sciences. Publications. Institute of Geophysics. D. Physics of the Atmosphere — Pol Acad Sci Publ Inst Geophys D
Polish Academy of Sciences. Review — Pol Acad Sci Rev
Polish Academy of Sciences. Transactions. Institute of Fluid Flow Machinery [*Warsaw*] — Polish Acad Sci Fluid Flow
Polish Agricultural and Forest Annual — Pol Agric For Annu
Polish Agricultural Annual. Series E. Plant Protection — Pol Agric Annu Ser E
Polish American Studies — PoA
Polish American Studies — Pol Am Stds
Polish American Studies — Polish Am Stud
Polish Ecological Bibliography — Pol Ecol Bibliogr

Polish Ecological Studies — Pol Ecol Stud
Polish Economic News — PEC
Polish Economic Survey — PES
Polish Ecumenical Review — PER
Polish Endocrinology — PENDA
Polish Endocrinology — Pol Endocrinol
Polish Endocrinology (English Translation of Endokrynologia Polska) — Pol Endocrinol (Engl Transl Endokrynol Pol)
Polish Engineering — Pol Eng
Polish Engineering Review — Pol Eng Rev
Polish Film — Polish F
Polish Folklore — PF
Polish Journal of Animal Science and Technology — Pol J Anim Sci Technol
Polish Journal of Animal Science and Technology — RNZOD8
Polish Journal of Applied Chemistry — Pol J Appl Chem
Polish Journal of Chemistry — Pol J Chem
Polish Journal of Chemistry — Polish J Chem
Polish Journal of Ecology — Pol J Ecol
Polish Journal of Immunology — Pol J Immunol
Polish Journal of Medicine and Pharmacy — Pol J Med Pharm
Polish Journal of Pathology — Pol J Pathol
Polish Journal of Pharmacology — Pol J Pharmacol
Polish Journal of Pharmacology and Pharmacy — Pol J Phar
Polish Journal of Pharmacology and Pharmacy — Pol J Pharmacol Pharm
Polish Journal of Pharmacology and Pharmacy — Polish J Pharmacol Pharmacy
Polish Journal of Soil Science — Pol J Soil Sci
Polish Literature/Litterature Polonaise — PLLP
Polish Machine Industry — Pol Mach Ind
Polish Machine Industry Offers — Pol Mach Ind Offers
Polish Maritime News — PMB
Polish Medical History and Science Bulletin — Pol Med Hist Sci Bull
Polish Medical Journal — Pol Med J
Polish Medical Journal — POMJA
Polish Medical Journal (English Translation of Polskie Archiwum Medycyny Wewnetrznej) — Pol Med J (Engl Transl Pol Arch Med Wewn)
Polish Medical Science and History Bulletin — PMHBA
Polish Medical Science and History Bulletin — Pol Med Sci Hist Bull
Polish Museum Geological Magazine — Pol Mus Geol Mag
Polish Music — PM
Polish Music — Polish Mus
Polish Perspectives — Pol Perspect
Polish Perspectives — Polish Perspect
Polish Perspectives — PolP
Polish Perspectives — PPD
Polish Psychological Bulletin — Pol Psych B
Polish Psychological Bulletin — POPDA
Polish Review — Pol Rev
Polish Review — Polish R
Polish Review — Polish Rev
Polish Review [*New York*] — PolR
Polish Review — PoR
Polish Review of Radiology and Nuclear Medicine — Pol Rev Radiol Nucl Med
Polish Review of Radiology and Nuclear Medicine (English Translation) — Pol Rev Radiol Nucl Med (Engl Transl)
Polish Science and Learning — Pol Sci Learning
Polish Sociological Bulletin — Pol Soc B
Polish Sociological Bulletin — Polish Sociol B
Polish Sociological Bulletin — POSB
Polish Technical Abstracts — Pol Tech Abstr
Polish Technical and Economic Abstracts — Pol Tech Econ Abstr
Polish Technical and Economic Abstracts — Polish Tech & Econ Abstr
Polish Technical Review — Pol Tech Rev
Polish Technological News — Pol Technol News
Polish Western Affairs — PoW
Politechnika Bialostocka. Zeszyty Naukowe. Matematyka, Fizyka, Chemia — Politech Bialostoca Zesz Nauk Mat Fiz Chim
Politechnika Czestochowska. Zeszyty Naukowe. Hutnictwo — Politech Czestochow Zesz Nauk Hutn
Politechnika Czestochowska. Zeszyty Naukowe. Nauki Techniczne. Seria Mechanika — Politech Czestochow Zesz Nauk Nauki Tech Ser Mech
Politechnika Krakowska imeni Tadeusza Kosciuszki. Monografia — Politech Krakow im Tadeusza Kosciuszki Monogr
Politechnika Krakowska, Zeszyt Naukowe, Inzynieria i Technologia Chemiczna — Politech Krakow Zesz Nauk Inz Technol Chem
Politechnika Krakowska. Zeszyty Naukowe. Chemia — Politech Krakow Zesz Nauk Chem
Politechnika Lodzka. Zeszyty Naukowe. Chemia Spozywcza — Politech Lodz Zesz Nauk Chem Spozyw
Politechnika Lodzka. Zeszyty Naukowe. Fizyka — Politech Lodz Zesz Nauk Fiz
Politechnika Lodzka. Zeszyty Naukowe. Inzynieria Chemiczna — Politech Lodz Zesz Nauk Inz Chem
Politechnika Lodzka. Zeszyty Naukowe. Technologia i Chemia Spozywcza — Politech Lodz Zesz Nauk Technol Chem Spozyw
Politechnika Lodzka. Zeszyty Naukowe. Wlokiennictwo — Politech Lodz Zesz Nauk Wlok
Politechnika Rzeszowska Imienia Ignacego Lukasiewicza. Rozprawy — Politech Rzeszowska Im Ignacego Lukasiewicza Rozpr
Politechnika Rzeszowska. Zeszyty Naukowe — Politech Rzeszowska Zesz Nauk
Politechnika Slaska imienia W. Pstrowskiego. Skrypty Uczelniane — Politech Slaska im W Pstrowskiego Skr Uczelniane
Politechnika Slaska. Zeszyty Naukowe. Hutnictwo — Politech Slaska Zesz Nauk Hutn
Politechnika Slaska. Zeszyty Naukowe. Mechanika — Politech Slaska Zesz Nauk Mech
Politechnika Szczecinska. Prace Naukowe — Politech Szczecin Pr Nauk
Politechnika Warszawska. Instytut Fizyki. Prace — Politech Warsz Inst Fiz Pr
Politechnika Warszawska. Prace Instytutu Inzynierii Chemicznej i Procesowej — Politech Warsz Pr Inst Inz Chem Procesowej
Politechnika Warszawska. Prace Instytutu Podstaw Konstrukcji Maszyn — Politech Warsz Pr Inst Podstaw Konstr Masz
Politechnika Warszawska. Prace Naukowe. Chemia — Politech Warsz Pr Nauk Chem
Politechnika Warszawska. Prace Naukowe. Mechanika — Politech Warsz Pr Nauk Mech
Politechnika Warszawska, Prace Naukowe. Mechanika — PWPMA
Politechnika Wroclawska. Instytut Budownictwa. Prace Naukowe — Politech Wroclaw Inst Budow Pr Nauk
Politechnika Wroclawska. Instytut Inzynierii Ochrony Srodowiska. Prace Naukowe — Politech Wroclaw Inst Inz Ochr Srodowiska Pr Nauk
Politechnika Wroclawska. Instytut Inzynierii Sanitarnej i Wodnej. Prace Naukowe — Politech Wroclaw Inst Inz Sanit Wodnej Pr Nauk
Politechnika Wroclawska. Instytut Ukladow ELektromaszynowych. Prace Naukowe — Politech Wroclaw Inst Ukladow Elektromasz Pr Nauk
Politechnika Wroclawskiej. Instytut Metrologii Elektrycznej. Prace Naukowe — Politech Wroclaw Inst Metrol Elektr Pr Nauk
Politechniki Wroclawskiej. Instytutu Matematyki. Prace Naukowe. Seria Studia i Materialy — Prace Nauk Inst Mat Politech Wroclaw Ser Stud i Materialy
Politechniki Wroclawskiej. Instytutu Matematyki. Prace Naukowe. Seria Studia i Materialy — Prace Nauk Inst Mat Politech Wroclaw Ser Stud Materialy
Politehnica University of Bucharest. Scientific Bulletin. Series A. Applied Mathematics and Physics — Politehn Univ Bucharest Sci Bull Ser A Appl Math Phys
Politehnica University of Bucharest. Scientific Bulletin. Series D. Mechanical Engineers — Politehn Univ Bucharest Sci Bull Ser D Mech Engrg
Politica (Caracas) — Polit Caracas
Politica de Mexico — PM
Politica de Venezuela — POL
Politica dei Trasporti — Pol Trasporti
Politica del Diritto — Pol Diritto
Politica del Diritto — Polit Dir
Politica ed Economia — Polit Econ
Politica ed Economia — Polit ed Econ
Politica Externa — Pol Ext
Politica (Havanna) — PoliticaH
Politica Internacional — PI
Politica Internacional — PolI
Politica Internacional. Instituto de Estudios Politicos — Pol Int
Politica Internacional (Madrid) — PIM
Politica Internazionale (Milano) — Polit Int Milano
Politica Internazionale (Roma) — Polit Int (Roma)
Politica (Venezuela) — POV
Politica y Espiritu — PYE
Political Affairs — Pol Affairs
Political Affairs — Polit Aff
Political Communication and Persuasion — Pol Communication and Persuasion
Political India [*Monograph*] — PI
Political Methodology — Pol Methodol
Political Methodology — Polit Methodol
Political Psychology — PoP
Political Quarterly — Pol Q
Political Quarterly — Pol Qtr
Political Quarterly — Pol Quar
Political Quarterly — Poli Q
Political Quarterly — Polit Q
Political Quarterly — Polit Quart
Political Quarterly — PoQ
Political Quarterly — PQTR
Political Quotations — PQ
Political Risk Letter [*Database*] — PRL
Political Science — Pol Sci
Political Science — Poli Sci
Political Science — Polit Sci
Political Science Annual — Polit Sci Ann
Political Science Discussion Papers — Polit Sci Disc Pap
Political Science Quarterly — GPSQ
Political Science Quarterly — Pol Sci Q
Political Science Quarterly — Pol Science Q
Political Science Quarterly — Poli Sci Q
Political Science Quarterly — Polit Sc Quartl
Political Science Quarterly — Polit Sci Q
Political Science Quarterly — Polit Sci Quart
Political Science Quarterly — PolSQ
Political Science Quarterly — PScQ
Political Science Quarterly — PSQ
Political Science Review [*Jaipur*] — Pol Sci R
Political Science Review — Polit Sci R
Political Science Review — PSR
Political Science Reviewer — Polit Sci R'er
Political Science (Wellington) — Polit Sci (Wellington)
Political Scientist — Polit Scientist
Political, Social, Economic Review — Polit Soc Econ Rev
Political Studies — Pol St
Political Studies — Pol Stud
Political Studies — Pol Studies
Political Studies [*Oxford*] — Polit Stud
Political Studies — PoS
Political Studies — PPSU
Political Studies — PS
Political Studies - London — Politic St
Political Studies (London) — PSL

Political Studies. Political Studies Association [*United Kingdom*] — PSA/PS
Political Theory — Pol Theory
Political Theory — Polit Theor
Political Theory — Polit Theory
Political Theory — PPTH
Politiceskoe Samoobrazovanie — Polit Samoobr
Politicka Ekonomie — Polit Ekon
Politicka Knihovna Ceskoslovenske Strany Lidove — PK
Politics — Pol
Politics and Letters — P & L
Politics and Society — PAS
Politics and Society — Pol & Soc
Politics and Society — Pol Soc
Politics and Society — Poli Societ
Politics and Society — Polit and Soc
Politics and Society — Polit Soc
Politics and Society — PPNS
Politics and Society in India — PSI
Politics and Society. Iowa State University — ISU/PS
Politics Today — Pol Today
Politics Today — Polit Today
Politie-Gids — PG
Politiek Economisch Weekblad — PEW
Politiek Perspectief — Polit Perspect
Politik und Zeitgeschichte — Polit u Zeitgesch
Politikai Foiskola Kozlemenyei — Polit Foisk Kozlem
Politikai Gazdasagtan Tanulmanyok — Polit Gazdasag Tanulmany
Politique Belge — Polit Belge
Politique d'Aujourd'hui — Polit Aujourd
Politique Etrangere — PE
Politique Etrangere — POI
Politique Etrangere — Pol Etr
Politique Etrangere [*Paris*] — Pol Etrang
Politique Etrangere — Pol Etrangere
Politique Etrangere — Polit Etr
Politique Etrangere — Polit Etrangere
Politique Internationale — Pol Internat
Politique Internationale — Polit Int
Politische Bildung — Pol Bildung
Politische Dokumentation — Pol Dokum
Politische Dokumente aus Kleinasien — PD
Politische Meinung — Pol Meinung
Politische Meinung — Polit Meinung
Politische Rundschau — Polit Rdsch
Politische Studien [*Muenchen*] — Pol Studien
Politische Studien [*Muenchen*] — Polit Stud
Politische Studien — PolST
Politische Vierteljahresschrift — Pol Vjschr
Politische Vierteljahresschrift — Polit Vjschr
Politische Vierteljahresschrift — PVS
Politische Vierteljahresschrift. Sonderheft — Polit Vjschr Sonderh
Politisches Jahrbuch der Schweizerischen Eidgenoessenschaft — PJ Schw E
Politisches Jahrbuch der Schweizerischen Eidgenossenschaft — PJSchE
Politisch-Religioese Texte aus der Sargonidenzeit — PRTS
Politiske Og Physiske Magazin — Polit Phys Mag
Polityka Spoleczna — Polit Spolecz
Polizei — Pol
Polizeiverordnung — Pol VO
Poljodjelska Znanstvena Smotra — Poljodjelska Znan Smotra
Poljoprivreda i Sumarstvo — Poljopr Sumar
Poljoprivreda i Sumarstvo — Poljopriv Sumar
Poljoprivredna Naucna Smotra — Poljopr Naucna Smotra
Poljoprivredna Znanstvena Smotra — Poljopr Znan Smotra
Poljoprivredna Znanstvena Smotra — Poljopr Znanst Smotra
Poljoprivredna Znanstvena Smotra — Poljopriv Znan Smotra
Poljoprivredni Pregled — Poljopriv Pregl
Pollack Mihaly Mueszaki Foeiskola Tudomanyos Koezlemenyei — Pollack Mihaly Muesz Foeisk Tud Koezl
Pollen Grain. United States Forest Service. Southeastern Area — Pollen Grain US For Serv Southeast Area
Pollen Physiology and Fertilization. Symposium — Pollen Physiol Fert Symp
Pollimo — POLLD
Pollution — PLUTA
Pollution Abstracts — PA
Pollution Abstracts — PolAb
Pollution Abstracts — Poll Abstr
Pollution Abstracts — Pollut Abstr
Pollution Abstracts with Indexes — Pollut Abstr Indexes
Pollution Atmospherique — Pollut Atmos
Pollution Control [*Japan*] — Pollut Control
Pollution Control in the Marine Industries. Proceedings. Annual International Conference — Pollut Control Mar Ind Proc Annu Int Conf
Pollution Control Technology for Oil and Gas Drilling and Production Operations — Pollut Control Technol Oil Gas Drill Prod Oper
Pollution Engineering — PMC
Pollution Engineering — Pollut Eng
Pollution Engineering and Technology — Pollut Eng Technol
Pollution. Environmental News Bulletin — PCB
Pollution Equipment News — Pollution
Pollution Monitor — Pollut Monitor
Pollution Prevention via Process and Product Modification — Pollut Prev Process Prod Modif
Pollution Report. United Kingdom. Central Directorate on Environmental Pollution — Pollut Rep UK Cent Dir Environ Pollut
Pollution Research — Pollut Res
Pollution Technology — Pollut Tech
Polnoe Sobranie Postanovlenii i Rasporiazhenii po Vedomstvu Pravoslavnogo Ispovedaniia — PSPR
Polnoe Sobranie Russkikh Letopisei — PSRL
Polnoe Sobranie Zakonov Rossisskoi Imperii — PSZ
Polnohospodarstvo — POLNA
Polnohospodarstvo — Polnohospod
Polnyi Pravoslavnyi Bogoslovskii Entsiklopedicheskii Slovar — PPBES
Pologne Contemporaine — Pologne Contemp
Pologne et les Affaires Occidentales — Pologne Aff Occid
Polonia Sacra — Pol Sac
Polonista (Lublin) — PolL
Polonystyka — P
Polonystyka — Pa
Polonystyka [*Warsaw*] — Pol
Polotitscheskoje Samoorbrasowanije — P Sa
Pol'ovnicky Zbornik — Pol'ovnicky Zb
Polska Akademia Nauk. Instytut Fizyki. Prace — Pol Akad Nauk Inst Fiz Pr
Polska Akademia Nauk. Instytut Geofizyki. Materialy i Prace — Pol Akad Nauk Inst Geofiz Mater Pr
Polska Akademia Nauk. Instytut Matematyczny. Zastosowania Matematyki — Zastos Mat
Polska Akademia Nauk. Instytut Podstawowych Problemow Techniki. Prace — Pol Akad Nauk Inst Podstawowych Probl Tech Pr
Polska Akademia Nauk. Instytut Podstawowych Problemow Techniki. Proceedings of Vibration Problems — Pol Akad Nauk Inst Podstawowych Probl Tech Proc Vib Probl
Polska Akademia Nauk. Komisja Biologii Nowotworow. Konferencja — Pol Akad Nauk Kom Biol Nowotworow Konf
Polska Akademia Nauk. Komisja Ceramiczna. Prace. Ceramika — Pol Akad Nauk Kom Ceram Pr Ceram
Polska Akademia Nauk. Komisja Ceramiczna. Prace. Serja Ceramika — Pol Akad Nauk Kom Ceram Pr Ser Ceram
Polska Akademia Nauk. Komisja Krystalografii. Biuletyn Informacyjny — Pol Akad Nauk Kom Krystalogr Biul Inf
Polska Akademia Nauk. Komitet Geologiczny. Acta Geologica Polonica — Pol Akad Nauk Kom Geol Acta Geol Pol
Polska Akademia Nauk. Komitet Jezykoznawstwa. Prace Jezykoznawcze — PANPJ
Polska Akademia Nauk. Metalurgia — Polska Akad Nauk Met
Polska Akademia Nauk. Muzeum Ziemi. Prace — Pol Akad Nauk Muz Ziemi Pr
Polska Akademia Nauk. Oddzial w Krakowie. Folia Quaternaria — Pol Akad Nauk Oddzial Krakowie Folia Quat
Polska Akademia Nauk. Oddzial w Krakowie. Komisja Nauk Geologicznych. Prace Geologicane — Pol Akad Nauk Oddzial Krakowie Kom Nauk Geol Pr Geol
Polska Akademia Nauk. Oddzial w Krakowie. Komisja Nauk Mineralogicznych. Prace Mineralogiczne — Pol Akad Nauk Oddzial Krakowie Kom Nauk Mineral Pr Mineral
Polska Akademia Nauk. Oddzial w Krakowie. Komisja Nauk Mineralogicznych. Prace Mineralogiczne — Pol Akad Nauk Oddzial Krakowie Nauk Mineral Pr Mineral
Polska Akademia Nauk. Oddzial w Krakowie. Nauka dla Wszystkich — Pol Akad Nauk Oddzial Krakowie Nauka Wszystkich
Polska Akademia Nauk. Oddzial w Krakowie. Prace Komisji Ceramicznej. Ceramika — Pol Akad Nauk Oddzial Krakowie Pr Kom Ceram Ceram
Polska Akademia Nauk. Oddzial w Krakowie. Prace Komisji Ceramicznej. Serja Ceramika — Pol Akad Nauk Oddzial Krakowie Pr Kom Ceram Ser Ceram
Polska Akademia Nauk. Oddzial w Krakowie. Prace Komisji Historycznoliterackiej — PANPKHL
Polska Akademia Nauk. Oddzial w Krakowie. Prace Komisji Metalurgiczno-Odlewniczej. Metalurgia — Pol Akad Nauk Oddzial Krakowie Pr Kom Metal Odlew Metal
Polska Akademia Nauk. Oddzial w Krakowie. Prace Komisji Metalurgiczno-Odlewniczej. Metalurgia — Pol Akad Nauk Oddzial Krakowie Pr Kom Metal-Odlew Metalurg
Polska Akademia Nauk. Oddzial w Krakowie. Prace Komisji Nauk Technicznych. Serja Ceramika — Pol Akad Nauk Oddzial Krakowie Pr Kom Nauk Tech Ser Ceram
Polska Akademia Nauk. Oddzial w Krakowie. Prace Komisji Nauk Technicznych. Serja Ceramika — Polska Akad Nauk Oddzial Krakowie Pr Kom Nauk Tech Ceram
Polska Akademia Nauk. Oddzial w Krakowie. Prace Komisji Slowianoznawstwa — PANPKS
Polska Akademia Nauk. Prace Instytutu Maszyn Przeplywowych — Pol Akad Nauk Pr Inst Masz Przeplyw
Polska Akademia Nauk. Prace Komisji Nauk Technicznych Metalurgia Fizyka Metali i Stopow — Pol Akad Nauk Pr Kom Nauk Tech Metal Fiz Met Stopow
Polska Akademia Nauk. Prace Komisji Nauk Technicznych. Serja Ceramika — Pol Akad Nauk Pr Kom Nauk Tech Ser Ceram
Polska Akademia Nauk. Rozprawy Wydzialu Nauk Medycznych — Pol Akad Nauk Rozpr Wydz Nauk Med
Polska Akademia Nauk. Zaklad Nauk Geologicznych. Studia Geologica Polonica — Pol Akad Nauk Zakl Nauk Geol Stud Geol Pol
Polska Akademia Nauk. Zaklad Ochrony Przyrody. Studia Naturae. Seria A. Wydawnictwa Naukowe — Pol Akad Nauk Zakl Ochr Przyr Stud Nat Ser A
Polska Akademia Nauk. Zeszyty Problemowe Nauki Polskiej — Pol Akad Nauk Zesz Probl Nauki Pol
Polska Akademia Umiejetnosci — PAU
Polska Akademia Umiejetnosci. Archivum Neophilologicum — PAU-AN
Polska Akademia Umiejetnosci. Materialy do Fizjografii Kraju — Pol Akad Umiejet Mater Fizjogr Kraju
Polska Akademia Umiejetnosci. Prace Komisji Nauk Farmaceutycznych — Pol Akad Umiejet Pr Kom Nauk Farm

Polska Akademia Umiejetnosci. Prace Muzeum Przyrodniczego — Pol Akad Umiejet Pr Muz Przyr
Polska Akademia Umiejetnosci. Prace Rolniczo-Lesne — Pol Akad Umiejet Pr Roln Lesne
Polska Akademia Umiejetnosci. Rozprawy Wydzialu Lekarskiego — Pol Akad Umiejet Rozpr Wydz Lek
Polska Akademia Umiejetnosci. Rozprawy Wydzialu Matematyczno-Przyrodniczego. Dzial A. Nauki Matematyczno-Fizyczne — Pol Akad Umiejet Rozpr Wydz Mat Przyr Dzial A
Polska Akademia Umiejetnosci. Rozprawy Wydzialu Matematyczno-Przyrodniczego. Dzial B. Nauki Biologiezne — Pol Akad Umiejet Rozpr Wydz Mat Przyr Dzial B
Polska Akademia Umiejetnosci. Wydawnictwa Slaskie. Prace Biologiczne — Pol Akad Umiejet Wydawn Slask Pr Biol
Polska Bibliografia Analityczna — PBA
Polska Bibliografia Analityczna. Mechanika — Polska Biblio Analit Mech
Polska Bibliografja Biblijna Adnotowana — PBRA
Polska Gazeta Lekarska — Polska Gaz Lekar
Polska Ludowa Akcja Niepodleglosci — PLAN
Polska Sztuka Ludowa — Pol Szt Lud
Polska Sztuka Ludowa — PSzL
Polski Biuletyn Orientalistyczny — PBO
Polski Instytut Wydawniczy — PIW
Polski Przeglad Chirurgiczny — Pol Przegl Chir
Polski Przeglad Radiologiczny — PPRAA
Polski Przeglad Radiologii i Medycyny Nuklearnej — Pol Przegl Radiol
Polski Przeglad Radiologii i Medycyny Nuklearnej — Pol Przegl Radiol Med Nukl
Polski Przeglad Radiologii i Medycyny Nuklearnej — PPMNA
Polski Rocznik Muzykologiczny — PRM
Polski Slownik Biograficzny — PSB
Polski Tygodnik Lekarski — Pol Tyg Lek
Polski Tygodnik Lekarski — POLEA
Polski Tygodnik Lekarski — Polski Tygod Lek
Polski Tygodnik Lekarski i Wiadomosci Lekarskie — Pol Tyg Lek Wiad Lek
Polskie Archiwum Hydrobiologii/Polish Archives of Hydrobiology — Pol Arch Hydrobiol
Polskie Archiwum Medycyny Wewnetrznej — Pol Arch Med Wewn
Polskie Archiwum Medycyny Wewnetrznej — Polskie Arch Med Wewnetrznej
Polskie Archiwum Weterynaryjne — Pol Arch Wet
Polskie Archiwum Weterynaryjne — Pol Arch Weter
Polskie Archiwum Weterynaryjne — Polskie Archwm Wet
Polskie Pismo Entomologiczne — Pol Pismo Entomol
Polskie Pismo Entomologiczne — Polskie Pismo Entomol
Polskie Pismo Entomologiczne. Seria B. Entomologia Stosowana — Pol Pismo Entomol Ser B
Polskie Pismo Entomologiczne. Seria B. Entomologia Stosowana — Pol Pismo Entomol Ser B Entomol Stosow
Polskie Pismo Entomologiczne. Seria B. Entomologia Stosowana — Polskie Pismo Entomol Ser B Entomol Stosow
Polskie Towarzystwo Entomologiczne. Klucze do Oznaczania Owadow Polski — Pol Tow Entomol Klucze Oznaczania Owadow Pol
Polskie Towarzystwo Entomologiczne. Klucze do Oznaczania Owadow Polski — Polskie Tow Ent Klucze Oznaczania Owadow Pol
Polskie Towarzystwo Geologiczne. Rocznik — Pol Tow Geol Rocz
Polskie Towarzystwo Gleboznawcze. Komisja Chemii Gleby. Prace Komisji Naukowych — Pol Tow Glebozn Kom Chem Gleby Pr Kom Nauk
Polskie Towarzystwo Gleboznawcze. Komisja Zyznosci i Odzywiania Roslin. Prace Komisji Naukowych — Pol Tow Glebozn Kom Zyznosci Odzywiania Rosl Pr Kom Nauk
Polskie Towarzystwo Mechaniki Teoretycznej i Stosowana — Mech Teoret Stos
Polskie Wydawnictwe Naukowe — PWN
Pol'skii Zhurnal Zootekhniki i Tekhnologii — Pol Zh Zootekh Tekhnol
Poltto- ja Voiteluainelaboratorio. Tiedonanto. Valtion Teknillinen Tutkimuskeskus — Poltto Voiteluainelab Tied Valt Tek Tutkimuskeskus
Poluchenie i Analiz Chistykh Veshchestv — Poluch Anal Chist Veshchestv
Poluchenie i Analiz Veshchestv Osoboi Chistoty. Doklady Vsesoyuznoi Konferentsii po Poluchenlyu i Analiyu veshchestv Osoboi Chistoty — Poluch Anal Veshchestv Osoboi Chist Dokl Vses Konf
Poluchenie i Issledovanie Svoistv Soedinenii RZM. Materialy Nauchnogo Seminara po Polucheniyu i Issledovaniyu Svoistv Soedinenii Redkozemel'nykh Metallov — Poluch Issled Svoistv Soedin RZM Mater Nauchn Semin
Poluchenie i Preimenenie Fermentov. Vitaminov i Aminokislot. Obzornaya Informatsiya — Poluch Primen Fermentov Vitam Aminokislt Obz Inf
Poluchenie i Svoistva Tonkikh Plenok [*Ukrainian SSR*] — Poluch Svoistva Tonkikh Plenok
Poluchenie Izdelii iz Zhidkikh Metallov s Uskorennoi Kristallizatsiei. Doklady na Nauchno-Tekhnicheskoi Konferentsii po Voprosam Proizvodstva Chugunnogo Lista i Otlivok iz Magnievogo Chuguna v Mekhanizirovannykh Kokilyakh — Poluch Izdelii Zhidk Met Uskor Krist Dokl Nauchno Tekh Konf
Poluchenie Lateksov i Modifikatsiya Ikh Svoistv. Trudy Vsesoyuznoi Lateksnoi Konferentsii — Poluch Lateksov Modif Ikh Svoistv Tr Vses Lateksnoi Konf
Poluchenie, Struktura, i Svoistva Sorbentov — Poluch Strukt Svoistva Sorbentov
Poluprovodniki i Ikh Primenenie v Elektrotekhnike — Poluprovodn Ikh Primen Elektrotekh
Poluprovodniki-Segnetoelektriki — Poluprovodn Segnetoelektr
Poluprovodnikovaya Elektronika — Poluprovodn Elektron
Poluprovodnikovaya Tekhnika i Mikroelektronika [*Ukrainian SSR*] — Poluprov Tekh Mikroelektron
Poluprovodnikovaya Tekhnika i Mikroelektronika — Poluprovodn Tekh i Mikroelektron
Poluprovodnikovye Pribory i Ikh Primenenie — Poluprovodn Prib Ikh Primen
Poluprovodnikovye Pribory i Ikh Primenenie — Poluprovodn Prib Primen
Poluprovodnikovye Pribory i Ikh Primenenie Sbornik Statei [*Former USSR*] — Poluprov Prib Ikh Primen Sb Statei
Poluprovodnikovye Pribory v Tekhnike Elektrosvyazi — Poluprovodn Prib Tekh Elektrosvyazi
Poly Law Review — Poly L Rev
POLY-AE/AM Report (Polytechnic Institute of New York. Department of Aerospace Engineering and Applied Mechanics) — POLY-AE/AM Rep (Polytech Inst NY Dep Aerosp Eng Appl Mech)
Polyamines in the Gastrointestinal Tract. Proceedings. Falk Symposium — Polyamines Gastrointest Tract Proc Falk Symp
Polyarnye Siyaniya [*Former USSR*] — Polyar Siyaniya
Polyarnye Siyaniya — POSID
Polyarnye Siyaniya i Svechenie Nochnogo Neba — Polyarn Siyaniya Svechenie Nochnogo Neba
Polybiblion. Partie Litteraire — PPB
Polybiblion. Partie Litteraire — PPL
Polygraphischer Betrieb — Polygr Betr
Polyhedron — PLYHD
Polyimides and Other High-Temperature Polymers. Proceedings. European Technical Symposium on Polyimides and High-Temperature Polymers — Polyimides Other High Temp Polym Proc Eur Tech Symp
Polymer Age — Polym Age
Polymer Analysis and Characterization. Proceedings. International Symposium on Polymer Analysis and Characterization — Polym Anal Charact Proc Int Symp
Polymer Application [*Japan*] — Polym Appl
Polymer Bulletin — POBUD
Polymer Bulletin — Polym Bull
Polymer Bulletin (Beijing) — Polym Bull (Beijing)
Polymer Bulletin (Berlin) — Polym Bull (Berlin)
Polymer Communications — Polym Commun
Polymer Compatibility and Incompatibility. Papers. Midland Macromolecular Meeting — Polym Compat Incompat Pap Midl Macromol Meet
Polymer Composites — Polym Compos
Polymer Composites — Polym Composites
Polymer Composites. Proceedings. Microsymposium on Macromolecules — Polym Compos Proc Microsymp Macromol
Polymer Compositions Stabilizers — Polym Compos Stab
Polymer Degradation and Stability — Polym Degradat Stabil
Polymer Engineering and Science — Polym Eng and Sci
Polymer Engineering and Science — Polym Eng S
Polymer Engineering and Science — Polym Eng Sci
Polymer Engineering and Science — Polym Engng Sci
Polymer Engineering and Science — Polymer Engng Science
Polymer Engineering News — Polym Engng News
Polymer Engineering Reviews — Polym Eng Rev
Polymer Engineering Reviews — Polym Engng Rev
Polymer International — Polym Int
Polymer Journal — Polym J
Polymer Journal — Polymer J
Polymer Journal (Japan) — Polym J (Jap)
Polymer Journal (Singapore) — Polym J Singapore
Polymer Journal (Tokyo) — Polym J (Tokyo)
Polymer Letters — Polym Lett
Polymer Materials [*Database*] — POLYMAT
Polymer Mechanics — Polym Mech
Polymer Mechanics (English Translation) — Polym Mech (Engl Transl)
Polymer Monographs — Polym Monogr
Polymer News — Polym News
Polymer Photochemistry — Polym Photochem
Polymer Preprints — Polym Preprints
Polymer Preprints. American Chemical Society. Division of Polymer Chemistry — Polym Prepr Am Chem Soc Div Polym Chem
Polymer Processing (Kyoto) — Polym Process (Kyoto)
Polymer Reaction Engineering — Polym React Eng
Polymer Report — Polym Rep
Polymer Reviews — Polym Rev
Polymer Science and Technology [*American Chemical Society*] [*Information service or system*] — Polym Sci Technol
Polymer Science and Technology [*American Chemical Society*] [*Information service or system*] — POST
Polymer Science and Technology (Comtex) — Polym Sci Technol Comtex
Polymer Science and Technology - Journals — POST-J
Polymer Science and Technology - Patents — POST-P
Polymer Science and Technology (Tehran) — Polym Sci Technol Tehran
Polymer Science Library [*Elsevier Book Series*] — PSL
Polymer Science. USSR [*English Translation of Vysokomolekulyarnye Soyedineniya. Series A*] — Polym Sci USSR
Polymer Symposia — Polym Symp
Polymer Testing — Polym Test
Polymer Theory Abstracts — Polym Theor Abst
Polymerase Chain Reaction Methods and Applications — Polymerase Chain React Methods Appl
Polymere in Medizin — Polym Med
Polymeric Materials Science and Engineering. Proceedings. ACS Division of Polymeric Materials Sciences and Engineering — Polym Mater Sci Eng
Polymer-Plastics Technology and Engineering — Polym-Plast
Polymer-Plastics Technology and Engineering — Polym-Plast Technol Eng
Polymer-Plastics Technology and Engineering — PPTEC
Polymers and Plastic Materials — Polym Plast Mater
Polymers as Colloid Systems — Polym Colloid Syst
Polymers for Advanced Technologies — Polym Adv Technol
Polymers for Microelectronics. Science and Technology. Proceedings. International Symposium — Polym Microelectron Proc Int Symp
Polymers in Biology and Medicine — Polym Biol Med

Polymers in Concrete. International Congress on Polymers in Concrete. Proceedings — Polym Concr Int Congr Proc
Polymers in Concrete. Proceedings. International Congress on Polymer Concretes — Polym Concr Proc Int Congr
Polymers in Medicine — Polym Med
Polymers in Solution [*Monograph*] — Polym Solution
Polymers in the Engineering Curriculum. Proceedings. Buhl International Conference on Materials — Polym Eng Curric Proc Buhl Int Conf Mater
Polymers, Paint, and Colour Journal — OIC
Polymers, Paint, and Colour Journal — Polym Paint Col J
Polymers, Paint, and Colour Journal — Polym Paint Colour J
Polymers, Paint, and Colour Journal — PPC Jrl
Polymers, Paint, Colour Journal. Supplement. Adhesives and Sealants — Polym Paint Colour J Suppl Adhes Sealants
Polymers with Specific Properties. New Aspects and Developments. Lectures. Macromolecular Symposium Japan-FRG — Polym Specific Prop Lect Macromol Symp Jpn FRG
Polymers with Unusual Properties. Proceedings. Northeast Regional Meeting. American Chemical Society — Polym Unusual Prop Proc Northeast Reg Meet Am Chem Soc
Polynesian Society Journal — Polyn Soc J
Polynuclear Aromatic Hydrocarbons. Chemistry, Characterization, and Carcinogenesis. International Symposium — Polynucl Aromat Hydrocarbons Chem Charact Carcinog Int Symp
Polynuclear Aromatic Hydrocarbons. Mechanisms, Methods, and Metabolism. Papers. International Symposium on Polynuclear Aromatic Hydrocarbons — Polynucl Aromat Hydrocarbons Pap Int Symp Pap
Polynuclear Aromatic Hydrocarbons Nomenclature Guide [*Monograph*] — Polynucl Aromat Hydrocarbons Nomencl Guide
Polyolefin and Plastics — Polyolefin Plast
Polysaccharides in Biology. Transactions of the Conference — Polysaccharides Biol Trans Conf
Polysar Progress — Polysar Prog
Polyscope. Automatik und Elektronik — Polyscope Autom und Elektron
Polyscope. Computer und Elektronik — Polyscope Comput und Elektron
Polytechnic Institute of Brooklyn. Microwave Research Institute. Symposia Series — Polytech Inst Brooklyn Microwave Res Inst Symp Ser
Polytechnic Institute of Bucharest. Scientific Bulletin. Chemistry and Materials Science — Polytech Inst Bucharest Sci Bull Chem Mater Sci
Polytechnic Institute of Bucharest. Scientific Bulletin. Chemistry and Materials Science — Polytech Inst Bucharest Sci Bull Chem Materials Sci
Polytechnic Institute of Bucharest. Scientific Bulletin. Electrical Engineering — Polytech Inst Bucharest Sci Bull Electr Engrg
Polytechnic Institute of New York. Department of Mechanical and Aerospace Engineering. Report POLY M/AE — PNYMD
Polytechnic Institute of New York. Microwave Research Institute. Symposia Series — Polytech Inst N Y Microwave Res Inst Symp Ser
Polytechnic Notes on Artificial Intelligence — Polytech Notes Artif Intell
Polytechnic Review — Polyt Rv
Polytechnique Exchange — Polytech Exch
Polytechnisch Tijdschrift — Pol Tijd
Polytechnisch Tijdschrift Bouwkune Wegen- en Waterbouw — Polytech Tijdschr Bouwk Wegen- & Waterbouw
Polytechnisch Tijdschrift. Editie A. Werktuigbouwkunde en Elektrotechniek — Polytech Tijdschr Ed A
Polytechnisch Tijdschrift. Editie B — Polytech Tijdschr Ed B
Polytechnisch Tijdschrift. Editie. Procestechniek — Polytech Tijdschr Ed Procestech
Polytechnisch Tijdschrift. Elektrotechniek. Elektronica — Polytech Tijdschr Elektrotech
Polytechnisch Tijdschrift. Elektrotechniek. Elektronica — Polytech Tijdschr Elektrotech Elektron
Polytechnisch Tijdschrift. Procestechniek — Polytech Tijdschr Procestech
Polytechnisch Tijdschrift. Werktuigbouw — Polytech Tijdschr Werktuigbouw
Polytechnisch Weekblad — Polytech Weekbl
Polytechnisches Journal — Polytech J
Polyteknisk Revy [*Norway*] — Polytek Revy
Polyteknisk Revy — PRVYD
Pomiary Automatyka Kontrola — Pomiary Autom Kontrola
Pomme de Terre Francaise — Pomme Terre Fr
Pommersche Bibliothek — Pommersche Biblioth
Pommersches Archiv der Wissenschaften und des Geschmaks — Pommersches Arch Wiss Geschmaks
Pommersfeldener Beitraege — Pommersfeldener Beitr
Pomological and Fruit Growing Society. Annual Report — Pomol Fruit Grow Soc Annu Rep
Pomologie Francaise — Pomol Fr
Pomologische Monatshefte — Pomol Monatsh
Pomona College Journal of Economic Botany, as Applied to Subtropical Horticulture — Pomona Coll J Econ Bot
Pomorania Antiqua — Pomor Ant
Pompebledon — Pompebl
Pompeianarum Antiquitatum Historia — PAH
Ponpu Kogaku — PPKGA
Ponte — P
Ponte — Pon
Ponte. Rivista Mensile di Politica e Letteratura — Ponte Riv M
Pontica. Studii si Materiale de Istorie, Arheologie, si Muzeografie [*Constanta*] — PSMIAM
Pontifical Institute of Mediaeval Studies. Studies and Texts — PIMSST
Pontifical Institute of Mediaeval Studies. Studies and Texts — PIMST
Pontifical Institute of Mediaeval Studies. Studies and Texts — PST
Pontificale Romanum — Pont Rom
Pontificia Academia Scientiarum. Acta — Pontif Acad Sci Acta
Pontificia Academia Scientiarum. Commentarii — Pontif Acad Sci Comment
Pontificia Academia Scientiarum. Scripta Varia — Pontif Acad Sci Scr Varia
Pontificia Accademia delle Scienze. Annuario — Pontif Acad Sci Annu
Pontificia Accademia Scientiarum. Acta — Pontif Accad Sci Acta
Pontificia Accademia Scientiarum. Commentationes — Pontif Accad Sci Commentat
Pontificia Accademia Scientiarum. Novi Lyncaei. Scientiarum Nuncius Radiophonicus — Pontif Accad Sci Novi Lyncaei Sci Nuncius Radiophonicus
Pontificia Universidad Catolica del Ecuador. Revista — Pontif Univ Catol Ecuador Rev
Pontificiae Academiae Scientiarum Scripta Varia — PASSV
Poole's Index to Periodical Literature — Pooles Index Period Lit
Poona Agricultural College Magazine — Poona Agr Col Mag
Poona Agricultural College Magazine — Poona Agric Coll Mag
Poona Orientalist — PO
Poona Orientalist — Po Or
Poona Orientalist — POr
Poona Sarvajanik Sabha. Quarterly Journal — PSS
Poona University and Deccan College Publications in Archaeology and History of Maharashtra — PUDCPAHM
Poona University Journal. Science and Technology — Poona Univ J Sci Technol
Pootaardappelwereld — PHK
Pop Shop Magazine — PS
[*The*] **Pope Speaks** — TPS
Popes Through History — PTH
Populaer Radio — Pop Rad
Populaer-Wissenschaftliche Monatsblaetter zur Belehrung ueber das Judentum — PWMBJ
Popular Astronomy — Pop Astron
Popular Astronomy — Pop Astronomy
Popular Bulletin. Colorado State University. Agricultural Experiment Station — Pop Bull Colo State Univ Agr Exp Sta
Popular Computing — Pop Comput
Popular Difference — Pop Diff
Popular Educator — Pop Educ
Popular Electronics — Pop Electr
Popular Foodservice — PF
Popular Gardening — Pop Gard
Popular Government — Pop Govt
Popular Government — Popular Govt
Popular Lectures in Mathematics — Pop Lect Math
Popular Magazine Review — Pop Mag Rev
Popular Magazine Review Online [*Database*] — PMRO
Popular Mechanics — GPOM
Popular Mechanics — PM
Popular Mechanics (Chicago) — PMC
Popular Mechanics Magazine — Pop Mech
Popular Mechanics Magazine — Pop Mech M
Popular Medicine (Tokyo) — Pop Med (Tokyo)
Popular Music — Pop Mus
Popular Music and Society — PMS
Popular Music and Society — Pop Mus & Soc
Popular Music and Society — Pop Music S
Popular Music and Society — Popular M Soc
Popular Music Periodicals Index — Pop Mus Per Ind
Popular Music Periodicals Index — Pop Music Period Index
Popular Periodical Index — Pop Per Ind
Popular Periodical Index — PPI
Popular Photography — GPOP
Popular Photography — Pop Phot
Popular Photography — Pop Photog
Popular Plastics — Pop Plast
Popular Plastics and Packaging — Pop Plast Packag
Popular Plastics Annual — Pop Plast Annu
Popular Science — GPOS
Popular Science — PS
Popular Science Monthly — Pop Sci
Popular Science Monthly — Pop Sci Mo
Popular Science Monthly — Pop Sci Mon
Popular Science (Peking) — Pop Sci (Peking)
Popular Science Review — Pop Sci R
Popular Science Review — Popular Sci Rev
Popular Technique pour Tous — Pop Tech Tous
Population — Pop
Population — Popul
Population and Development Review [*New York*] — Pop Dev R
Population and Development Review — Popul Dev Rev
Population and Development Review — Popul Develop R
Population and Development Review — PPDR
Population and Environment — PENVDK
Population and Environment — Popul Environ
Population and Pollution. Proceedings. Annual Symposium. Eugenics Society — Popul Pollut Proc Annu Symp Eugen Soc
Population Bulletin — GPOB
Population Bulletin — Pop B
Population Bulletin — Pop Bul
Population Bulletin — Popul Bull
Population Bulletin — Population Bul
Population Bulletin. United Nations — Population Bul UN
Population Bulletin. United Nations Economic Commission for Western Asia — Popul B UN Econ Com West Asia
Population Bulletin. United Nations Economic Commission for Western Asia — Popul Bull UN Econ Comm West Asia
Population Council. Annual Report — Popul Counc Annu Rep
Population Data Information Service — Popul Data Inf Serv
Population Education News — Popul Educ News

Population et Avenir — Popul et Avenir
Population et Famille — Popul et Famille
Population et Famille/Bevolking en Gezin — Popul et Famille/Bevolk en Gezin
Population et Societes — Popul et Societes
Population Exposures. Proceedings. Midyear Topical Symposium. Health Physics Society — Popul Exposures Proc Midyear Top Symp Health Phys Soc
Population Forum — Popul Forum
Population Geography — Popul Geogr
Population Index — Pop Ind
Population Index — Pop Index
Population Index — Popl
Population Index — Popul I
Population Index — Popul Ind
Population Index — Popul Index
Population. Institut National d'Etudes Demographiques — INED/P
Population Newsletter — Popul Newsl
Population (Paris) — PP
Population Policy Compendium — Popul Policy Compend
Population Reports. Series A. Oral Contraceptives — Popul Rep A
Population Reports. Series B [*United States*] — PREBD
Population Reports. Series B. Intrauterine Devices — Popul Rep B
Population Reports. Series C [*United States*] — PORCD
Population Reports. Series C. Sterilization. Female — Popul Rep C
Population Reports. Series D. Sterilization (Male) — Popul Rep D
Population Reports. Series E. Law and Policy — Popul Rep E
Population Reports. Series F. Pregnancy Termination — Popul Rep F
Population Reports. Series G. Prostaglandins — Popul Rep G
Population Reports. Series G. Prostaglandins — Popul Rep Ser G
Population Reports. Series H. Barrier Methods — Popul Rep H
Population Reports. Series I. Periodic Abstinence — Popul Rep I
Population Reports. Series J. Family Planning Programs — Popul Rep J
Population Reports. Series K. Injectables and Implants — Popul Rep K
Population Reports. Series L. Issues in World Health — Popul Rep L
Population Reports. Series M. Special Topics — Popul Rep M
Population Reports. Special Topics. Monographs — Popul Rep Spec Top Monogr
Population Research and Policy Review — Population Research and Policy R
Population Research Laboratory. University of Alberta. Department of Sociology. Alberta Series Report — PRLASR
Population Research Laboratory. University of Alberta. Department of Sociology. Western Canada Series Report — PRLWCSR
Population Review — Popul Rev
Population Review — Population R
Population Review — PoR
Population Review — PPUR-A
Population Studies [*London*] — Pop Stud
Population Studies — Popul Stud
Population Studies — Population Stud
Population Studies — POS
Population Studies — POST-A
Population Studies — PS
Population Studies (London) — Pop Stud (Lo)
Population Studies (New York) — Pop Stud (NY)
Population Today — GPOT
Population Today — Popul Today
Population Trends — Popul Trends
Populations Studies — Pop St
Poradnik Jezykowy — PJ
Poradnik Jezykowy — Por Jez
Poradnik Muzyczny — Poradnik M
Pork Industry Gazette — PIG
Pork Industry Gazette — Pork Ind Gaz
Porodoobrazuyushchie Mineraly. Materialy S'ezda MMA — Porodoobrazuyushchie Miner Mater Sezda MMA
Poroshkovaya Metallurgiya — Porosh Met
Poroshkovaya Metallurgiya — Poroshk Metall
Poroshkovaya Metallurgiya (Kiev) — Poroshk Metall (Kiev)
Poroshkovaya Metallurgiya (Kuibyshev) — Poroshk Metall (Kuibyshev)
Poroshkovaya Metallurgiya. Materialy Vsesoyuznoi Konferentsii po Poroshkovoi Metallurgii — Poroshk Metall Mater Vses Konf
Poroshkovaya Metallurgiya (Minsk) — Poroshk Metall Minsk
Porosimetry and Its Application — Porosim Its Appl
Porozimetrie a Jeji Pouziti — Porozim Jeji Pouziti
Port Import/Export Reporting Service [*Database*] — PIERS
Port Of Melbourne — Port Melb
Port Of Melbourne Quarterly — Port Melb Q
Port Of Melbourne Quarterly — Port Melbourne Quart
Port Of Melbourne Quarterly — Port Of Melb Q
Port Of Melbourne Quarterly — Port Of Melb Quart
Port Of Melbourne Quarterly — Port Of Melbourne Q
Port Of Melbourne Quarterly — Port Of Melbourne Quart
Port Of Sydney — Port Of Syd
Port Of Sydney — Port Syd
Port Of Sydney Journal — Port Of Sydney J
Port Phillip Gazette — Port Phillip Gaz
Port Phillip Gazette — Pt Phil Gaz
Porta Linguarum Orientalium — PLO
Porta Orientale — POr
Portfolio — Portfo
Portfolio (Dennie's) — Portfo (Den)
Portia Law Journal — Portia L J
Portland Cement Association. Advanced Engineering Bulletin — Portland Cem Ass Advanced Eng Bull
Portland Cement Association Fellowship at the National Bureau of Standards. Papers — Portland Cem Assoc Fellowship Natl Bur Stand Pap
Portland Cement Association. Journal of the PCA Research and Development Laboratories — Portland Cem Ass J PCA Res Develop Lab
Portland Cement Association. Research and Development Laboratories. Development Department. Bulletin D — Portland Cem Assoc Res Dev Lab Dev Dep Bull D
Portland Cement Association. Research and Development Laboratories. Journal — Portland Cem Assoc Res Dev Lab J
Portland Magazine — Portland Mag
Portland Review — Port R
Portland Roses and Flowers — Portland Roses Fl
Portland Scribe — P Scribe
Portland Society of Natural History. Proceedings — Portland Soc N H Pr
Porto Rico Health Review — PR Health Rev
Porto Rico Review of Public Health and Tropical Medicine — PR Rev Public Health Trop Med
Ports and Dredging — PORDB
Ports and Dredging and Oil Report — Ports Dredging Oil Rep
Portsmouth News [*United Kingdom*] — PN
Portucale [*Porto*] — Po
Portugal, Belgique, Luxembourg. Informations Economiques — PTG
Portugal em Africa — Port Afr
Portugal em Africa — Port em Afr
Portugal em Africa — Portugal em Afr
Portugal Ilustrado — PI
Portugal. Informative Review — Portugal Inf Rev
Portugal. Junta de Investigacoes Cientificas do Ultramar. Estudos, Ensaios, e Documentos — Port Junta Invest Cient Ultramar Estud Ensaios Doc
Portugal. Laboratorio Nacional de Engenharia Civil. Memoria — Port Lab Nac Eng Civ Mem
Portugal. Ministerio do Ultramar. Junta de Investigacoes do Ultramar. Anais — Port Minist Ultramar Junta Invest Ultramar An
Portugal. Ministerio do Ultramar. Junta de Investigacoes do Ultramar. Estudos, Ensaios, e Documentos — Port Minist Ultramar Junta Invest Ultramar Estud Ensaios Doc
Portugal. Ministerio do Ultramar. Junta de Investigacoes do Ultramar. Memorias. Serie Antropologica e Etnologica — Port Minist Ultramar Junta Invest Ultramar Mem Ser Antropol
Portugal. Ministerio do Ultramar. Junta de Investigacoes do Ultramar. Memorias. Serie Botanica — Port Minist Ultramar Junta Invest Ultramar Mem Ser Bot
Portugal. Ministerio do Ultramar. Junta de Investigacoes do Ultramar. Memorias. Serie Botanica — Port Minist Ultramar Junta Invest Ultramar Mem Ser Botanica
Portugal. Ministerio do Ultramar. Junta de Investigacoes do Ultramar. Memorias. Serie Geologica — Port Minist Ultramar Junta Invest Ultramar Mem Ser Geol
Portugal. Ministerio do Ultramar. Memorias da Junta de Investigacoes do Ultramar — Port Minist Ultramar Mem Junta Invest Ultramar
Portugal. Servico de Fomento Mineiro. Estudos, Notas, e Trabalhos — Port Serv Fom Min Estud Notas Trab
Portugal. Servicos Geologicos. Memoria — Port Serv Geol Mem
Portugale — Por
Portugale — Port
Portugalia — P
Portugaliae Acta Biologica — Portug Acta Biol
Portugaliae Acta Biologica. A. Morfologia, Fisiologia, Genetica, e Biologia Geral — Port Acta Biol A
Portugaliae Acta Biologica. Serie A — Port Acta Biol Ser A
Portugaliae Acta Biologica. Serie A — Portugaliae Acta Biol Ser A
Portugaliae Acta Biologica. Serie B — Port Acta Biol Ser B
Portugaliae Electrochimica Acta — Port Electrochim Acta
Portugaliae Mathematica — Portugal Math
Portugaliae Monumenta Historica — PMH
Portugaliae Physica — POPYA
Portugaliae Physica — Port Phy
Portugaliae Physica — Port Phys
Portugaliae Physica — Portugal Phys
Porzellan und Glas — PUG
Posebna Izdanja — Posebna Izdan
Posebna Izdanja Bioloski Institut N R Srbije Beograd — Posebna Izd Biol Inst N R Srb Beograd
Posebna Izdanja Geoloskog Glasnika (Sarajevo) — Posebna Izd Geol Glas (Sarajevo)
Positions Lutheriennes [*Paris*] — PosLuth
Positron and Positronium Chemistry. International Workshop — Positron Positronium Chem Int Workshop
Positron Annihilation. Proceedings. International Conference on Positron Annihilation — Positron Annihilation Proc Int Conf
Posselt's Textile Journal — Posselt's Text J
Possible Episomes in Eukaryotes. Proceedings. Lepetit Colloquium — Possible Episomes Eukaryotes Proc Lepetit Colloq
Post Accident Heat Removal Information Exchange Meeting — Post Accid Heat Removal Inf Exch Meet
Post Graduate Course. International Meeting of Anaesthesiology and Resuscitation — Post Grad Course Int Meet Anaesthesiol Resusc
Post Harvest Technology of Cassava — Post Harvest Technol Cassava
Post Magazine and Insurance Monitor — PM
Post Office Electrical Engineers. Journal — P O Elect Engrs J
Post Office Electrical Engineers. Journal — P O Electr Eng J
Post Office Electrical Engineers. Journal — Post O E E J
Post Office Electrical Engineers. Journal — Post Off Electr Eng J
Post Office (Great Britain). Research Department Report — Post Off (GB) Res Dep Rep
Post Office Historical Society. Transactions [*Queensland*] — Post Office Hist Soc Trans

Post Office Telecommunications Journal — P O Telecommun J
Post Office Telecommunications Journal — Post Off Telecommun J
Post Script — Post S
Post Script — Post Scr
Post Script — PS
Postal Bulletin. United States Postal Service — Postal Bull US Postal Serv
Postal Bulletin. Weekly — Postal Bull
Postal History Society Bulletin — Post Hist Soc Bull
Postal Life — POLI
Postal Supervisor — Postal Spvr
Postavy a Problemy — PP
Postcensal Survey of Scientists and Engineers. National Science Foundation. Report No. 84-330 [*United States*] — NSF Svy SE
Postdiplomski Seminar iz Fizike — Postdiplom Sem Fiz
Postdiplomski Seminar iz Matematike — Postdiplom Sem Mat
Poste e Telecommunicazioni — Poste Telecommun
Postepy Astronautyki — Postepy Astronaut
Postepy Astronomii — Postepy Astron
Postepy Astronomii — PYAIA
Postepy Biochemii — Post Bioch
Postepy Biochemii — Postepy Biochem
Postepy Biologii Komorki — Postepy Biol Komorki
Postepy Cybernetyki — Postepy Cybernet
Postepy Endokrynologii Okresu Rozwojowego. Konferencja Naukowa. Materialy Naukowe — Postepy Endokrynol Okresu Rozwoj Konf Nauk Mater Nauk
Postepy Fizjologii — Postepy Fizjol
Postepy Fizyki — Postepy Fiz
Postepy Fizyki Medycznej — Postepy Fiz Med
Postepy Ftyzjatrii i Pneumonologii — Postepy Ftyz Pneumon
Postepy Higieny i Medycyny Doswiadczalnej — Postepy Hig Med Dosw
Postepy Medycyny — Postepy Med
Postepy Mikrobiologii — Postepy Mikrobiol
Postepy Nauk Rolniczych — Postepy Nauk Roln
Postepy Nauki Rolniczej — Postepy Nauki Roln
Postepy Techniki Jadrowej — Postepy Techn Jadr
Postepy Techniki Jadrowej — PTCJB
Postepy Techniki Jadrowеki — Postepy Tech Jad
Postepy Technologii Maszyn i Urzadzen — Postepy Technol Masz Urzadz
Postepy Technologii Maszyn i Urzadzen — Postepy Technol Masz Urzadzen
Postepy Technologii Maszyn i Urzadzen — PTMUD
Postepy Wiedzy Medycznej — Postepy Wied Med
Postepy Wiedzy Medycznej — Postepy Wiedzy Med
Postepy Wiedzy Rolniczej — Postepy Wiedzy Roln
Postgraduate Bulletin — Postgraduate Bull
Postgraduate Courses in Pediatrics — Postgrad Courses Pediatr
Postgraduate Dental Handbook Series — Postgrad Dent Handb Ser
Postgraduate Medical Journal — Postg Med J
Postgraduate Medical Journal — Postgrad Med J
Postgraduate Medical Journal — Postgrad MJ
Postgraduate Medical Journal. Supplement — Postgrad Med J Suppl
Postgraduate Medicine — PGM
Postgraduate Medicine — POMDA
Postgraduate Medicine — Postgr Med
Postgraduate Medicine — Postgrad Med
Postgraduate Medicine Series — Postgrad Med Ser
Postgraduate Paediatrics Series — Postgrad Paediatr Ser
Postgraduate Paediatrics Series — PPSEE4
Postgraduate Radiology — PORADD
Postgraduate Radiology — Postgrad Radiol
Postilla Bohemica — PostB
Postmasters Advocate — Postmasters Adv
Post-Medieval Archaeology — Post-Medieval Arch
Post-Medieval Archaeology — Post-Medieval Archaeol
Post's Paper Mill Directory — Post Dir
Potash 1990. Feast or Famine — Potash 90
Potash and Tropical Agriculture — Potash Trop Agric
Potash Journal — Potash J
Potash Review — Potash Rev
Potassium and the Quality of Agricultural Products. Proceedings. Congress. International Potash Institute — Potassium Qual Agric Prod Proc Congr Int Potash Inst
Potassium et la Qualite des Produits Agricoles. Comptes Rendus du Colloque Regional. Institute International de la Potasse — Potassium Qual Prod Agric CR Colloq Reg Inst Int Potasse
Potassium Institute Limited. Colloquium Proceedings — Potassium Inst Ltd Colloq Proc
Potassium Potasio Kalium Symposium — Potassium Potasio Kalium Symp
Potassium. Symposium — Potassium Symp
Potassium Symposium. Papers — Potassium Symp Pap
Potato Abstracts — Potato Abstr
Potato Grower — Potato Grow
Potato Handbook — Potato Handb
Potato Journal — Potato J
Potato Magazine — Potato M
Potato Research — Potato Res
Potential Analysis — Potential Anal
Potential New Methods of Detection of Irradiated Food — Potential New Methods Detect Irradiat Food
Potfuzetek a Termeszettudomanyi Kozlonyhoz — Potfuzetek Termeszettud Kozl
Potomac Appalachian Trail Club. Bulletin — Potomac Appalachian Trail Club Bull
Potomac Law Review — Potomac L Rev
Potomac Review — Potomac R
Potomac Review — Potomac Rev
Potravinarska a Chladici Technika — Potravin Chladici Tech
Potravinarske Vedy — Potravin Vedy
Potsdamer Forschungen. Reihe B. Naturwissenschaftliche Reihe — Potsdamer Forsch Reihe B
Potter's American Monthly — Potter Am Mo
Pottery and Glass Record — Pottery Glass Rec
Pottery and Glass Trades Journal — Pottery Glass Trades J
Pottery Gazette and Glass Trade Review — Pottery Gaz Glass Trade Rev
Pottery in Australia — Pot Aust
Pottery in Australia — Pottery
Pottery in Australia — Pottery Aust
Pottery in Australia — Pottery in Aust
Pottery Notebooks for Knossos — PN
Pottery Notebooks for Knossos — PNB
Potvrda o Valjanosti Broj-Institut za Mehanizaciju Poljoprivrede — Potvrda Valjanosti Broj Inst Meh Poljopr
Poughkeepsie Society of Natural Science. Proceedings — Poughkeepsie Soc N Sc Pr
Poultry Abstracts — Poult Abstr
Poultry Adviser — Poult Advis
Poultry and Egg Situation. PES. United States Department of Agriculture. Economic Research Service — Poult Egg Situat PES US Dep Agric Econ Res Serv
Poultry and Livestock Comment — Poultry Livestock Comment
Poultry Bulletin — Poult Bull
Poultry Digest — POUDAY
Poultry Digest — Poult Dig
Poultry Digest — Poultry Dig
Poultry Forum — Poult
Poultry Health Symposium — Poult Health Symp
Poultry Industry — Poult Ind
Poultry Processing and Marketing — Poultry Process
Poultry Science — Poult Sci
Poultry Science — Poultry Sci
Poultry Trials Bulletin — Poult Trials Bull
Poultry Tribune — Poult Trib
Poultry World — Poult World
Pour la Science (Paris) (Edition Francaise de Scientific American) — Pour Sci (Paris)
Pour Nos Jardins. Bulletin. Societe d'Horticulture et des Jardins Populaires de France — Pour Nos Jard
Povedenie Materialov v Usloviyakh Vakuuma i Nizkikh Temperatur — Povedenie Mater Usloviyakh Vak Nizk Temp
Poverkhnostnye Yavleniya v Polimerakh — Poverkhn Yavleniya Polim
Poverkhnostnye Yavleniya v Zhidkostyakh i Zhidkikh Rastvorakh — Poverkhn Yavleniya Zhidk Zhidk Rastvorakh
Poverty and Human Resources — Pov Hum Resour
Poverty and Human Resources Abstracts — PHRA
Poverty and Human Resources Abstracts — Pov & Human Resour Abstr
Poverty and Human Resources Abstracts — Pov Hum Resour Abstr
Povest' Vremennych Let — PVL
Povoa de Varzim — PV
Povoa de Varzim. Boletim Cultural — PVBC
Povolzhskii Lesotekhnicheskii Institut Sbornik Trudov — Povolzh Lesotekh Inst Sb Tr
Povyshenie Effektivnosti Primeneniya Tsementnykh i Asfal'tovykh Betonov v Sibiri — Povysh Eff Primen Tsem Asfaltovykh Betonov Sib
Povyshenie Plodorodiya Pochv Nechernozemnoi Polosy — Povysh Plodorodiya Pochv Nechernozemn Polosy
Powder and Bulk Engineering — Powder Bulk Eng
Powder Coatings — PCOAD
Powder Coatings — Powder Coat
Powder Diffraction — Powder Diffr
Powder Engineering [*Former USSR*] — Powder Eng
Powder Handling and Processing — Powder Handl Process
Powder Industry Research — Powder Ind Res
Powder Metallurgy — Powd Metall
Powder Metallurgy — Powder Met
Powder Metallurgy — Powder Metall
Powder Metallurgy Bulletin — Powder Metall Bull
Powder Metallurgy in Defense Technology — Powder Metall Def Technol
Powder Metallurgy Industry — Powder Metall Ind
Powder Metallurgy International — Powder Metall Int
Powder Metallurgy International — PWMIB
Powder Science and Engineering — Powder Sci Eng
Powder Science and Technology in Japan — Powder Sci Technol Jpn
Powder Technology — Powd Tech
Powder Technology — Powder Technol
Powder Technology — PWTCA
Powder Technology (Lausanne) — Powder Technol (Lausanne)
Powder Technology Publication Series — Powder Technol Publ Ser
Powder Technology (Tokyo) — Powder Technol (Tokyo)
Power and Fuel Bulletin — Power Fuel Bull
Power and Plant Engineering in South Africa — Power Plant Eng S Afr
Power and Plant in Southern Africa — Power Plant S Afr
Power and Plant in Southern Africa — Power Plant South Afr
Power and Plant in Southern Africa — Power Plant Sthn Afr
Power and the Engineer (New York) — Power Eng N Y
Power and Works Engineering — Power & Works Engng
Power and Works Engineering — Power Works Eng
Power and Works Engineering — Pwr Wks Engng
Power Apparatus and Systems — Power Appar Syst
Power Electronics and Variable-Speed Drives. International Conference — Power Electron Var Speed Drives Int Conf
Power Engineer — POERD
Power Engineer (India) — Power Eng (India)

Power Engineering — Power Eng
Power Engineering (Barrington, Illinois) — Power Eng Barrington Ill
Power Engineering Journal. Academy of Sciences [*Former USSR*] — Power Eng J Acad Sci (USSR)
Power Engineering (New York, English Translation) — Power Eng (NY Eng Transl)
Power Farming — Power F
Power Farming — Pwr Fmg
Power Farming and Better Farming Digest (Australia) — PFBFA
Power Farming and Better Farming Digest in Australia and New Zealand [*Later, Power Farming*] — Power Farming Better Farming Dig Aust NZ
Power Farming in Australia — Power Farming Aust
Power Farming in Australia and New Zealand — Pwr Frmg
Power Farming in Australia and New Zealand — Pwr Frmg Aust NZ
Power Farming in Australia and New Zealand and Better Farming Digest — Pwr Fmg Aust NZ
Power Farming Magazine — Power Farming Mag
Power Farming Magazine — Pwr Fmg Mag
Power from Radioisotopes. Proceedings. International Symposium — Power Radioisot Proc Int Symp
Power Generation — Power Gener
Power Industry, Including Industrial Power and Industry Power — Power Ind
Power Industry Research — PIRED
Power Industry Research [*England*] — Power Ind Res
Power Line — POLID
Power News — Power N
Power Plant Engineering — Power Pl Eng
Power Plant Engineering — Power Plant Eng
Power Reactor and Nuclear Fuel Development Corporation. Tokai Works Semi-Annual Progress Report — Power React Nucl Fuel Dev Corp Tokai Works Semi Annu Prog Re
Power Reactor Technology — Power React Technol
Power Reactor Technology [*Japan*] — Power Reactor Technol
Power Reactor Technology and Reactor Fuel Processing — Power React Technol React Fuel Process
Power Reactor Technology and Reactor Fuel Processing [*United States*] — Power Reactor Technol Reactor Fuel Process
Power Reactor Technology (Tokyo) — Power Reactor Technol (Tokyo)
Power Sources Symposium. Proceedings [*United States*] — Power Sources Symp Proc
Power Transmission Design — Power Trans Des
Power Transmission Design — Power Transm Des
PowerConversion International — PowerConvers Int
Powloki Ochronne — Powloki Ochr
POWTECH. International Powder Technology and Bulk Solids Exhibition and Congress — POWTECH Int Powder Technol Bulk Solids Exhib Congr
Powys Newsletter — Powys N
Powys Review — P Rev
Powys Review — Powys Rev
Pozharnaya Okhrana — Pozharnaya Okhr
Poznan — Pn
Poznan Agricultural University. Annals — Poznan Agric Univ Ann
Poznan Studies — Poznan Stud
Poznan Studies in the Philosophy of the Sciences and the Humanities — Poznan Stud Philos Sci Humanities
Poznanskie Roczniki Medyczne — POMDD
Poznanskie Roczniki Medyczne [*Poland*] — Poznan Rocz Med
Poznanskie Studie Teologiczne — Pozn St Teol
Poznanskie Towarzystwo Przyjaciol Nauk — PTPN
Poznanskie Towarzystwo Przyjaciol Nauk. Komisja Biologiczna. Prace — Poznan Tow Przyj Nauk Kom Biol Pr
Poznanskie Towarzystwo Przyjaciol Nauk. Prace Komisji Biologicznej — Poznan Tow Przyj Nauk Pr Kom Biol
Poznanskie Towarzystwo Przyjaciol Nauk. Prace Komisji Farmaceutycznej — Poznan Tow Przyj Nauk Pr Kom Farm
Poznanskie Towarzystwo Przyjaciol Nauk. Prace Komisji Lekarskiej — Poznan Tow Przyj Nauk Pr Kom Lek
Poznanskie Towarzystwo Przyjaciol Nauk. Prace Komisji Matematyczno-Przyrodniczej — Poznan Tow Przyj Nauk Pr Kom Mat Przyr
Poznanskie Towarzystwo Przyjaciol Nauk. Prace Komisji Matematyczno-Przyrodniczej. Prace Chemiczne — Poznan Tow Przyj Nauk Pr Kom Mat Przyr Pr Chem
Poznanskie Towarzystwo Przyjaciol Nauk. Prace Komisji Matematyczno-Przyrodniczej. Seria A — Poznan Tow Przyj Nauk Pr Kom Mat Przyr Ser A
Poznanskie Towarzystwo Przyjaciol Nauk. Prace Komisji Matematyczno-Przyrodniczej. Seria B — Poznan Tow Przyj Nauk Pr Kom Mat Przyr Ser B
Poznanskie Towarzystwo Przyjaciol Nauk. Prace Komisji Medycyny Doswiadezalnej [*A publication*] — Poznan Tow Przyj Nauk Pr Kom Med Dosw
Poznanskie Towarzystwo Przyjaciol Nauk. Prace Komisji Nauk Podstawowych Stosowanych — Poznan Tow Przyj Nauk Pr Kom Nauk Podstawowych Stosow
Poznanskie Towarzystwo Przyjaciol Nauk. Prace Komisji Nauk Rolniczych i Komisji Nauk Lesnych — Poznan Tow Przyj Nauk Pr Kom Nauk Roln Kom Nauk Lesn
Poznanskie Towarzystwo Przyjaciol Nauk. Sprawozdania — Poznan Tow Przyj Nauk Spraw
Poznanskie Towarzystwo Przyjaciol Nauk. Wydzial Lekarski. Prace Komisji Farmaceutycznej — Poznan Tow Przyj Nauk Wydz Lek Pr Kom Farm
Poznanskie Towarzystwo Przyjaciol Nauk. Wydzial Lekarski. Prace Komisji Farmaceutycznej — PTPFA
Poznanskie Towarzystwo Przyjaciol Nauk. Wydzial Lekarski. Prace Komisji Medycyny Doswiadczalnej [*Poland*] — Poznan Tow Przyj Nauk Wydz Lek Pr Kom Med Doswi
Poznanskie Towarzystwo Przyjaciol Nauk. Wydzial Lekarski. Prace Komisji Medycyny Doswiadczalnej — PTPMA
Poznanskie Towarzystwo Przyjaciol Nauk. Wydzial Matematyczno-Przyrodniczy. Komisja Biologiczna Prace [*Poland*] — Poznan Tow Przyj Nauk Wydz Mat-Przyr Kom Biol Pr
Poznanskie Towarzystwo Przyjaciol Nauk. Wydzial Matematyczno-Przyrodniczy Prace Komisji Biologicznej — Poznan Tow Przyj Nauk Wydz Mat Przyr Pr Kom Biol
Poznanskie Towarzystwo Przyjaciol Nauk, Wydzial Matematyczno-Przyrodniczy Prace Komisji Biologicznej — PTPRAI
Poznanskie Towarzystwo Przyjaciol Nauk, Wydzial Matematyczno-Przyrodniczy Prace Komisji Matematyczno-Przyrodniczej — Poznan Tow Przyj Nauk Wydz Mat Przyr Pr Kom Mat Przyr
PPA. University of Kentucky. Cooperative Extension Service — PPA Univ KY Coop Ext Serv
PPCJ Polymers Paint Colour Journal — PPCJ Polym Paint Colour J
PPI. Planen, Pruefen, Investieren — PPI Planen Pruef Investieren
PPI. Pulp and Paper International — PPI Pulp Pap Int
PPL Series on Mankind and the Engineer — PPL Ser Mankind Eng
PPTA [*Post-Primary Teachers Association*] **Journal** — PPTA J
PR Magazin. Public Relations und Informationspolitik in Medien und Gesellschaft — PRM
PR Newswire [*Database*] — PRN
PR. Published Report. Australian Coal Industry Research Laboratories — PR Publ Rep Aust Coal Ind Res Lab
PR Revue. Schweizerische Zeitschrift fuer Public Relations — PVU
PR. Texas Agricultural Experiment Station — PR Tex Agric Exp Stn
PR. Texas Agricultural Experiment Station — PR Texas Agric Exp Stn
Prabuddha Bharata [*Calcutta*] — PB
Prabuddha Bharata — PBh
Prabuddha Bharata [*Calcutta*] — Pra Bhar
Praca i Zabezpieczenie Spoleczne — Praca Zabezp Spolecz
Prace 2. Sekcie Slovenskej Akademie Vied — Prace 2 Sekc Slov Akad Vied
Prace 2 Sekcieje Slovenskej Akademie Vied. Seria Biologicka — Pr 2 Sekc Slov Akad Vied Ser Biol
Prace a Studie. Vyskumny Ustav Vodneho Hospodarstva (Bratislava) — Pr Stud Vysk Ustav Vodn Hospod (Bratislava)
Prace a Studie Vysokej Skoly Dopravnej v Ziline. Seria Matematicko-Fyzikalna — Prace Stud Vysokej Skoly Doprav Ziline Ser Mat-Fyz
Prace a Studie Vysokej Skoly Dopravnej v Ziline. Seria Strojnicka — Pr Stud Vys Sk Dopravnej Ziline Ser Strojnicka
Prace a Studie Vysokej Skoly Dopravy a Spojov v Ziline. Seria Matematicko-Fyzikalna — Prace Stud Vysokej Skoly Doprav Spojov Ziline Ser Mat-Fyz
Prace a Studie. Vyzkumny Ustav Vodohospodarsky — Pr Stud Vyzk Ustav Vodohospod
Prace Archaeologiczne — Prace A
Prace Archeologiczne [*Cracow*] — Prac Arch
Prace Badawcze Instytutu Badawczego Lesnictwa — Pr Badaw Inst Badaw Lesn
Prace Biologiczne. Polska Akademia Umiejetnosci. Wydawnictwa Slaskie — Pr Biol Pol Akad Umiejet Wydawn Slask
Prace Botaniczne. Uniwersytet Jagiellonski — Pr Bot Uniw Jagiellon
Prace Brnenske Zakladny Ceskoslovenske Akademie Ved — Pr Brnenske Zakl Cesk Akad Ved
Prace Brnenske Zakladny Ceskoslovenske Akademie Ved — Prace Brnenske Zakl Ceskoslov Akad Ved
Prace Centralnege Instytutu Ochrony Pracy — Pr Cent Inst Ochr Pr
Prace Centralnego Laboratorium Gazownictwa. Seria B — Pr Cent Lab Gazownictwa Ser B
Prace Ceskoslovenskeho Vyzkumu Slevarenskeho — Pr Cesk Vyzk Slevarenskeho
Prace Chemiczne — Pr Chem
Prace Chemiczne. Prace Naukowe Uniwersytetu Slaskiego w Katowicach — Pr Chem Pr Nauk Uniw Slask Katowic
Prace CVUT v Praze — Pr CVUT Praze
Prace CVUT v Praze. 1. Stavebni — Pr CVUT Praze 1
Prace Dzialu Zywenia Roslin i Nawozenia — PDZRA
Prace Dzialu Zywenia Roslin i Nawozenia [*Poland*] — Pr Dzialu Zywenia Rosl Nawoz
Prace Farmaceutyczne — Pr Farm
Prace Filologiczne — PF
Prace Filologiczne — PFil
Prace Filologiczne — Pr Fil
Prace Fizyczne (Katowice) — Pr Fiz Katowice
Prace Fizyczne. Prace Naukowe Uniwersytetu Slaskiego w Katowicach — Pr Fiz Pr Nauk Uniw Slask Katowic
Prace Fizyczne. Prace Naukowe Uniwersytetu Slaskiego w Katowicach [*Poland*] — Pr Fiz Pr Nauk Uniw Slaskiego Katowic
Prace Geologiczno-Mineralogiczne. Acta Universitatis Wratislaviensis — Pr Geol-Mineral Acta Univ Wratislav
Prace Glownego Instytutu Gornictwa [*Poland*] — Pr Gl Inst Gorn
Prace Glownego Instytutu Gornictwa. Komunikat — Pr Gl Inst Gorn Komun
Prace Glownego Instytutu Lotnictwa — Pr Gl Inst Lotnictwa
Prace Glownego Instytutu Metalurgii. Gliwice, Poland — Pr Gl Inst Metal Gliwice Pol
Prace Glownego Instytutu Naftowego. Cracow — Pr Gl Inst Naft Cracow
Prace Glownego Instytutu Przemyslu Rolnego i Spozywczego — Pr Gl Inst Przem Rolnego Spozyw
Prace Historyczno-Kulturanie — PraH
Prace Historycznoliterackie — PrHlit
Prace i Materialy Etnograficzne — PME
Prace i Materialy Muzeum Archeologicznego i Etnograficznego w Lodzi — Prace Mat Lodz
Prace i Materialy Naukowe. Instytut Matki i Dziecka — Pr Mater Nauk Inst Matki Dziecka
Prace i Materialy Zootechniczne — Pr Mater Zootech

Prace i Studia Zakladu Badan Naukowych Gornoslaskiego Okregu Przemyslowego Polskiej Akademii Nauk [*Poland*] — Pr Stud Zakl Badan Nauk Gorn Okregu Przem Pol Akad Nauk
Prace i Studia Zakladu Badan Naukowych Gornoslaskiego Okregu Przemyslowego Polskiej Akademii Nauk — PSZBA
Prace Instytut Badawezy Lesnictwa — Prace Inst Bad Lesn
Prace Instytut Technologii Drewna — Pr Inst Technol Drewna
Prace Instytut Technologii Drewna — Prace Inst Tech Drewna
Prace Instytut Technologii Drewna — Prace Inst Technol Drewna
Prace Instytutow Hutniczych — PIHUA
Prace Instytutow Hutniczych — Pr Inst Hutn
Prace Instytutow i Laboratoriow Badawczych Przemyslu Spozywczego — Pr Inst Lab Badaw Przem Spozyw
Prace Instytutow Mechaniki — Pr Inst Mech
Prace Instytutu Badawczego Lesnictwa — Pr Inst Badaw Lesn
Prace Instytutu Celulozowo-Papierniczego — Pr Inst Celul Papier
Prace Instytutu Celulozowo-Papierniczego. Komunikat — Pr Inst Celul Papier Komun
Prace Instytutu Cybernetyki Stosowanej PAN [*Polska Akademia Nauk*] — Pr Inst Cybern PAN
Prace Instytutu Elektrotechniki — Pr Inst Elektrotech
Prace Instytutu Elektrotechniki (Warsaw) — Pr Inst Elektrotech (Warsaw)
Prace Instytutu Fizyki — Prace Inst Fiz
Prace Instytutu Fizyki Politechnica Warszawska — Pr Inst Fiz Politech Warsz
Prace Instytutu Fizyki. Polska Akademia Nauk — Pr Inst Fiz Pol Akad Nauk
Prace Instytutu Geologii — PRIGA
Prace Instytutu Gornictwa Naftowego i Gazownictwa — PGNGD
Prace Instytutu Gornictwa Naftowego i Gazownictwa (Krakow) — Pr Inst Gorn Naft Gazownictwa Krakow
Prace Instytutu Gospodarki Wodnej — PIGWA
Prace Instytutu Gospodarki Wodnej — Pr Inst Gospod Wodnej
Prace Instytutu. Instytut Techniki Budowlanej. Biuletyn Informacyjny — Pr Inst Inst Tech Budow Biul Inf
Prace Instytutu Inzynierii Chemicznej i Procesowej Politechniki Warszawskiej — Pr Inst Inz Chem Procesowej Politech Warsz
Prace Instytutu Inzynierii Chemicznej Politechniki Warszawskiej — Pr Inst Inz Chem Politech Warsz
Prace Instytutu Jedwabiu Naturalnego — Pr Inst Jedwabiu Nat
Prace Instytutu Lacznosci — Pr Inst Lacznosci
Prace Instytutu Lotnictwa — PILOA
Prace Instytutu Lotnictwa — Pr Inst Lotnictwa
Prace Instytutu Maszyn Matematycznych — Pr Inst Masz Mat
Prace Instytutu Maszyn Przeplywowych — Pr Inst Masz Przeplyw
Prace Instytutu Maszyn Przeplywowych — Prace Inst Maszyn Przeplywowych
Prace Instytutu Maszyn Przeplywowych. Polska Akademia Nauk [*Poland*] — Pr Inst Masz Przeplyw Pol Akad Nauk
Prace Instytutu Mechaniki Precyzyjnej [*Poland*] — Pr Inst Mech Precyz
Prace Instytutu Metali Niezelaznych — Pr Inst Met Niezelaz
Prace Instytutu Metalurgii. Gliwice (Poland) — Pr Inst Metal Gliwice (Pol)
Prace Instytutu Metalurgii Zelaza — Pr Inst Metal Zelaza
Prace Instytutu Metalurgii Zelaza imienia Stanislawa Staszica — Pr Inst Metal Zelaza im Stanislawa Staszica
Prace Instytutu Metalurgue — Pr Inst Met
Prace Instytutu Meteorologii i Gospodarki Wodnej — Pr Inst Meteorol Gospod Wodnej
Prace Instytutu Ministerstwa Hutnictwa (Poland) — Pr Inst Minist Hutn (Pol)
Prace Instytutu Naftowego (Krakow) [*Poland*] — Pr Inst Naft (Krakow)
Prace Instytutu Obrobki Skrawaniem [*Poland*] — Pr Inst Obrobki Skrawaniem
Prace Instytutu Odlewnictwa — Pr Inst Odlew
Prace Instytutu Odlewnictwa. Zeszyty Specjalne — Pr Inst Odlew Zesz Spec
Prace Instytutu Odlewnictwa. Zeszyty Specjalne [*Poland*] — Pr Inst Odlew Zesz Specjalne
Prace Instytutu Przemyslu Cukrowniczego — Pr Inst Przem Cukrow
Prace Instytutu Przemyslu Mieczarskiego — Pr Inst Przem Miecz
Prace Instytutu Przemyslu Organicznego — Pr Inst Przem Org
Prace Instytutu Przemyslu Skorzanego — Pr Inst Przem Skorzanego
Prace Instytutu Przemyslu Szkla i Ceramiki — Pr Inst Przem Szkla Ceram
Prace Instytutu Przemyslu Wlokien Lykowych — Pr Inst Przem Wlok Lykowych
Prace Instytutu Sadownictwa. Seria E. Materialy Zjazdow i Konferencji — Pr Inst Sadow Ser E Mater Zjazdow Konf
Prace Instytutu Sadownictwa. Skierniewice. Seria E. Materialy Zjazdow i Konferencji — Pr Inst Sadow Skierniewice Ser E
Prace Instytutu Sadownictwa w Skierniewicach — Pr Inst Sadow Skierniew
Prace Instytutu Sadownictwa w Skierniewicach — Pr Inst Sadow Skierniewicach
Prace Instytutu Sadownictwa w Skierniewicach. Seria A. Prace Doswiadczalne z Zakresu Sadownictiva — Pr Inst Sadow Skierniewicach Ser A
Prace Instytutu Sadownictwa w Skierniewicach. Seria A. Prace Doswiadczalne Z Zakresu Sadownictwa — Pr Inst Sadow Skierniewicach Ser A Pr Dosw Z Zakresu Sadow
Prace Instytutu Techniki Budowlanej. Seria 1. Materialy Budowlane i Ich Zastosowanie — Pr Inst Tech Budow Ser 1
Prace Instytutu Techniki Budowlanej. Seria 2. Konstrukeje Budowlane i Inzynierskie — Pr Inst Tech Budow Ser 2
Prace Instytutu Techniki Cieplnej [*Poland*] — Pr Inst Tech Ciepl
Prace Instytutu Technologii Elektronowej — Pr Inst Technol Elektron
Prace Instytutu Tele- i Radiotechnicznego — Pr Inst Tele- & Radiotech
Prace Instytutu Wlokiennictwa — Pr Inst Wlok
Prace Instytutu Wlokiennictwa (Lodz) — Pr Inst Wlok (Lodz)
Prace IPO [*Instytutu Przemyslu Organicznego*] — Pr IPO
Prace IPPT (Instytut Podstawowych Problemow Techniki) — Pr IPPT
Prace ITME [*Instytut Technologii Materialow Elektronicznych*] — Pr ITME
Prace Jezykoznawcze — PJK
Prace Jezykoznawcze Polskiej Akademii Nauk — PJez
Prace Komisji Biologicznej (Poznan) — Pr Kom Biol (Poznan)
Prace Komisji Biologicznej. Poznanskie Towarzystwo Przyjaciol Nauk [*Poland*] — Pr Kom Biol Poznan Tow Przyj Nauk
Prace Komisji Biologiznej. Poznanskie Towarzystwo Przyjaciol Nauk. Wydzial Matematiczno-Przyrodniczy — Prace Komis Biol
Prace Komisji Ceramicznej. Polskiej Akademii Nauk. Ceramica — PPKCB
Prace Komisji Ceramicznej. Polskiej Akademii Nauk. Ceramica — Pr Kom Ceram Pol Akad Nauk Ceram
Prace Komisji Farmaceutycznej. Poznanskie Towarzystwo Przyjaciol Nauk — Pr Kom Farm Poznan Tow Przyj Nauk
Prace Komisji Historii Medycyny i Nauk Przyrodniczych-Matematicznych — Prace Komis Hist Med Nauk Przyr Mat
Prace Komisji Jezykowej Polskiej Akademii Umiejetnosci. Travaux de la Commission Linguistique de l'Academie Polonaise des Sciences et des Lettres — TLAP
Prace Komisji Lekarskiej. Poznanskie Towarzystwo Przyjaciol Nauk — Pr Kom Lek Poznan Tow Przyj Nauk
Prace Komisji Matematyczno-Przyrodniczej. Poznanskie Towarzystwo Przyjaciol Nauk [*Poland*] — Pr Kom Mat-Przyr Poznan Tow Przyj Nauk
Prace Komisji Metalurgiczno-Odlewniczej. Metalurgia. Polska Akademia Nauk — Pr Kom Metal Odlew Metal Pol Akad Nauk
Prace Komisji Nauk Ceramicznych. Ceramika. Polska Akademia Nauk — Pr Kom Nauk Ceram Ceram Pol Akad Nauk
Prace Komisji Nauk Lekarskich (Bydgoszcz, Poland) — Pr Kom Nauk Lek Bydgoszcz Pol
Prace Komisji Nauk Rolniczych i Biologicznych (Bydgoszcz, Poland) — Pr Kom Nauk Roln Biol Bydgoszcz Pol
Prace Komisji Nauk Rolniczych i Komisji Nauk Lesnych. Poznanskiej Towarzystwo Przyjaciol — Pr Kom Nauk Roln Kom Nauk Lesn Poznan Tow Przyj Nauk
Prace Komisji Nauk Rolniczych i Lesnych. Poznanskie Towarzystwo Przyjaciol Nauk (Poznan) — Pr Kom Nauk Roln Lesn (Poznan)
Prace Komisji Nauk Technicznych. Polska Akademia Nauk. Serja Ceramika — Pr Kom Nauk Tech Pol Akad Nauk Ser Ceram
Prace Komisji Naukowych. Polskie Towarzystwo Gleboznawcze. Komisja Biologii Gleby — Pr Kom Nauk Pol Tow Glebozn Kom Biol Gleby
Prace Komisji Naukowych. Polskie Towarzystwo Gleboznawcze. Komisja Chemii Gleby — Pr Kom Nauk Pol Tow Glebozn Kom Chem Gleby
Prace Komisji Naukowych. Polskie Towarzystwo Gleboznawcze. Komisja Genezy, Klasyfikaeji, i Kartografii Gleb — Pr Kom Nauk Pol Tow Glebozn Kom Glenezy Klasyf Kartogr Gleb
Prace Komisji Orientalistycznej Polskiej Akademii Umiejetnosci. Travaux de la Commission Orientaliste de l'Academie Polonaise des Sciences et des Lettres — TOAP
Prace Komisji Technologii Drewna. Poznanskie Towarzystwo Przyjaciol Nauk — PKTDA
Prace Komisji Technologii Drewna. Poznanskie Towarzystwo Przyjaciol Nauk [*Poland*] — Pr Kom Technol Drewna Poznan Tow Przyj Nauk
Prace Komitetu Krystalografii. Polska Akademia Nauk. Instytut Niskich Temperatur i Badan Strukturalnych — Pr Kom Krystalogr Pol Akad Nauk Inst Nisk Temp Badan Strukt
Prace Konferencji Elektrochemicznej — Pr Konf Elektrochem
Prace. Krajskeho Musea v Hradci Kralove/Acta Musei Reginaehradicensis — Prace Krajsk Mus V Hradci Kralove
Prace Literackie — PrLit
Prace. Lodzkie Towarzystwo Naukowe. Wydzial IV. Nauk Lekarskich — Pr Lodz Tow Nauk IV
Prace Medyczne. Opolskie Towarzystwo Przyjaciol Nauk. Wydzial 5. Nauk Medycznych — Pr Med Opolskie Tow Przyj Nauk Wyd Nauk Med
Prace Mineralogiczne Polska Akademia Nauk — Pr Mineral Pol Akad Nauk
Prace Mineralogiczne. Polska Akademia Nauk. Oddzial w Krakowie. Komisja Nauk Mineralogicznych — Pr Mineral Pol Akad Nauk Oddzial Krakowie Kom Nauk Mineral
Prace Moravske Prirodovedecke Spolecnosti. Acta Societatis Scientiarum Naturalium Moraviae — Prace Morav Prir Spolecn
Prace Moravskoslezske Akademie Ved Prirodnich — Pr Moravskoslezske Akad Ved Prir
Prace Morski Instytut Rybacki w Gdyni — PMRGA
Prace Morski Instytut Rybacki w Gdyni [*Poland*] — Pr Morsk Inst Rybacki Gdyni
Prace Morskiego Instytutu Rybackiego. Seria A. Oceanografia i Biologia Rybacka — Pr Morsk Inst Rybackiego Ser A
Prace Morskiego Instytutu Rybackiego. Seria B. Technika Rybacka i Technologia Ryb — Pr Morsk Inst Rybackiego Ser B
Prace Muzeum Przyrodniczego/Acta Musei Historiae Naturalis — Prace Muz Przyr
Prace Muzeum Przyrodniczego. Polska Akademia Umiejetnosci — Pr Muz Przyr Pol Akad Umiejet
Prace Muzeum Ziemi — Pr Muz Ziemi
Prace Naukowe Akademii Ekonomicznej Imienia Oskara Langego we Wroclawiu. Chemia — Pr Nauk Akad Ekon Oskara Langego Wroclaw Chem
Prace Naukowe Akademii Ekonomicznej w Poznaniu — Prace Nauk Akad Ekon Poznan
Prace Naukowe Akademii Ekonomicznej we Wroclawiv — Prace Nauk Akad Ekon Wroclaw
Prace Naukowe Akademii Medycznej we Wroclawiu — Pr Nauk Akad Med Wroclawiu
Prace Naukowe Instytutu Budownictwa Politechniki Wroclawskiej — Pr Nauk Inst Budow Politech Wroclaw
Prace Naukowe Instytutu Chemii i Technologii Nafty i Wegla Politechniki Wroclawskiej [*Poland*] — Pr Nauk Inst Chem Technol Nafty Wegla Politech Wroclaw
Prace Naukowe Instytutu Chemii Organicznej i Fizycznej Politechniki Wroclawskiej — Pr Nauk Inst Chem Org Fiz Politech Wroclaw
Prace Naukowe Instytutu Chemii Organicznej i Fizycznej Politechniki Wroclawskiej. Seria. Konferencje — Pr Nauk Inst Chem Org Fiz Politech Wroclaw Ser K

Prace Naukowe Instytutu Chemii Organicznej i Fizycznej Politechniki Wroclawskiej. Seria Konferencje — Pr Nauk Inst Chem Org Fiz Politech Wroclaw Ser Konf
Prace Naukowe Instytutu Chemii Organicznej i Fizycznej Politechniki Wroclawskiej. Seria Studia i Materialy — Pr Nauk Inst Chem Org Fiz Politech Wroclaw Ser S
Prace Naukowe Instytutu Cybernetyki Technicznej Politechniki Wroclawskiej. Seria Konferencje — Pr Nauk Inst Cybern Tech Politech Wroclaw Ser K
Prace Naukowe Instytutu Cybernetyki Technicznej Politechniki Wroclawskiej. Seria Monografie — Pr Nauk Inst Cybern Tech Politech Wroclaw Ser M
Prace Naukowe Instytutu Cybernetyki Technicznej Politechniki Wroclawskiej. Seria Studia i Materialy — Pr Nauk Inst Cybern Tech Politech Wroclaw Ser S
Prace Naukowe Instytutu Energoelektryki Politechniki Wroclawskiej — PIEWD
Prace Naukowe Instytutu Energoelektryki Politechniki Wroclawskiej — Pr Nauk Inst Energoelektr Politech Wroclaw
Prace Naukowe Instytutu Fizyki Politechniki Wroclawskiej — PIFWD
Prace Naukowe Instytutu Fizyki Politechniki Wroclawskiej — Pr Nauk Inst Fiz Politech Wroclaw
Prace Naukowe Instytutu Fizyki Politechniki Wroclawskiej. Seria Monografie — Pr Nauk Inst Fiz Politech Wroclaw Ser M
Prace Naukowe Instytutu Fizyki Politechniki Wroclawskiej. Seria Monografie — Pr Nauk Inst Fiz Politech Wroclaw Ser Monogr
Prace Naukowe Instytutu Fizyki Politechniki Wroclawskiej. Seria Studia i Materialy — Pr Nauk Inst Fiz Politech Wroclaw Ser S
Prace Naukowe Instytutu Fizyki Technicznej Politechniki Wroclawskiej — Pr Nauk Inst Fiz Tech Politech Wroclaw
Prace Naukowe Instytutu Geotechniki Politechniki Wroclawskiej [*Poland*] — Pr Nauk Inst Geotech Politech Wroclaw
Prace Naukowe Instytutu Gornictwa Politechniki Wroclawskiej [*Poland*] — Pr Nauk Inst Gorn Politech Wroclaw
Prace Naukowe Instytutu Gornictwa Politechniki Wroclawskiej — Pr Nauk Inst Gorn Wroclaw
Prace Naukowe Instytutu Inzynierii Chemicznej i Urzadzen Cieplnych Politechniki Wroclawskiej [*Poland*] — Pr Nauk Inst Inz Chem Urzadzen Cieplnych Politech Wroclaw
Prace Naukowe Instytutu Inzynierii Chemicznej i Urzadzen Cieplnych Politechniki Wroclawskiej. Seria. Monografie — Pr Nauk Inst Inz Chem Urzadz Ciepl Politech Wroclaw Ser M
Prace Naukowe Instytutu Inzynierii Ladowej Politechniki Wroclawskiej — Pr Nauk Inst Inz Ladowej Politech Wroclaw
Prace Naukowe Instytutu Inzynierii Ochrony Srodowiska Politechniki Wroclawskiej — PNIIA
Prace Naukowe Instytutu Inzynierii Ochrony Srodowiska Politechniki Wroclawskiej — Pr Nauk Inst Inz Ochr Sr Politech Wroclaw
Prace Naukowe Instytutu Inzynierii Ochrony Srodowiska Politechniki Wroclawskiej [*Poland*] — Pr Nauk Inst Inz Ochr Srodowiska Politech Wroclaw
Prace Naukowe Instytutu Inzynierii Sanitarnej i Wodnej Politechniki Wroclawskiej — Pr Nauk Inst Inz Sanit Wodnej Politech Wroclaw
Prace Naukowe Instytutu Matematyki Politechniki Wroclawskiej. Seria Monografie — Pr Nauk Inst Mat Politech Wroclaw Ser M
Prace Naukowe Instytutu Matematyki Politechniki Wroclawskiej. Seria Monografie — Prace Nauk Inst Mat Politech Wroclaw Ser Monograf
Prace Naukowe Instytutu Matematyki Politechniki Wroclawskiej. Seria Studia i Materialy — Pr Nauk Inst Mat Politech Wroclaw Ser S
Prace Naukowe Instytutu Materialoznawstwa i Mechaniki Technicznej Politechniki Wroclawskiej. Seria. Monografie — Pr Nauk Inst Materialozn Mech Tech Politech Wroclaw Ser M
Prace Naukowe Instytutu Materialoznawstwa i Mechaniki Technicznej Politechniki Wroclawskiej. Seria. Studia i Materialy — Pr Nauk Inst Materialozn Mech Tech Politech Wroclaw Ser S
Prace Naukowe Instytutu Materialoznawstwa i Technicznej Politechniki Wroclawskiej — Pr Nauk Inst Materialozn Mech Tech Politech Wroclaw
Prace Naukowe Instytutu Metrologii Elektrycznej Politechniki Wroclawskiej — Pr Nauk Inst Metrol Elektr Politech Wroclaw
Prace Naukowe Instytutu Metrologii Elektrycznej Politechniki Wroclawskiej. Seria. Konferencje — Pr Nauk Inst Metrol Elektr Politech Wroclaw Ser K
Prace Naukowe Instytutu Metrologii Elektrycznej Politechniki Wroclawskiej. Seria Konferencje — Pr Nauk Inst Metrol Elektr Politech Wroclaw Ser Konf
Prace Naukowe Instytutu Metrologii Elektrycznej Politechniki Wroclawskiej. Seria. Monografie — Pr Nauk Inst Metrol Elektr Politech Wroclaw Ser M
Prace Naukowe Instytutu Metrologii Elektrycznej Politechniki Wroclawskiej. Seria. Studia i Materialy — Pr Nauk Inst Metrol Elektr Politech Wroclaw Ser S
Prace Naukowe Instytutu Ochrony Roslin — Pr Nauk Inst Ochr Rosl
Prace Naukowe Instytutu Ochrony Roslin — Prace Nauk Inst Ochr Rosl
Prace Naukowe Instytutu Ochrony Roslin (Warszawa) — Pr Nauk Inst Ochr Rosl (Warsz)
Prace Naukowe Instytutu Przemyslu Organicznego (Warsaw) — Pr Nauk Inst Przem Org (Warsaw)
Prace Naukowe Instytutu Techniki Cieplnej i Mechaniki Plynow Politechniki Wroclawskiej — Pr Nauk Inst Tech Ciepl Mech Plynow Politech Wroclaw
Prace Naukowe Instytutu Techniki Cieplnej i Mechaniki Plynow Politechniki Wroclawskiej. Seria. Monografie — Pr Nauk Inst Tech Ciepl Mech Plynow Politech Wroclaw Ser M
Prace Naukowe Instytutu Techniki Cieplnej i Mechaniki Plynow Politechniki Wroclawskiej. Seria. Studia i Materialy — Pr Nauk Inst Tech Ciepl Mech Plynow Politech Wroclaw Ser S
Prace Naukowe Instytutu Technologii Elektronowej Politechniki Wroclawskiej — Pr Nauk Inst Technol Elektron Politech Wroclaw
Prace Naukowe Instytutu Technologii Elektronowej Politechniki Wroclawskiej. Seria Monografie — Pr Nauk Inst Technol Elektron Politech Wroclaw Ser Monogr
Prace Naukowe Instytutu Technologii Elektronowej Politechniki Wroclawskiej. Seria. Studia i Materialy — Pr Nauk Inst Technol Elektron Politech Wroclaw Ser S
Prace Naukowe Instytutu Technologii Nieorganicznej i Nawozow Mineralnych Politechniki Wroclawskiej — Pr Nauk Inst Technol Nieorg Nawozow Miner Politech Wroclaw
Prace Naukowe Instytutu Technologii Organicznej i Tworzyw Sztucznych Politechniki Wroclawskiej — Pr Nauk Inst Technol Org Tworzyw Sztucznych Politech Wroclaw
Prace Naukowe Instytutu Technologii Organicznej i Tworzyw Sztucznych Politechniki Wroclawskiej. Seria. Studia i Materialy — Pr Nauk Inst Technol Org Tworz Sztucz Politech Wroclaw Ser S
Prace Naukowe Instytutu Telekomunikacji i Akustyki Politechniki Wroclawskiej. Seria. Konferencje — Pr Nauk Inst Telekomun Akust Politech Wroclaw Ser K
Prace Naukowe Instytutu Telekomunikacji i Akustyki Politechniki Wroclawskiej. Seria. Monografie — Pr Nauk Inst Telekomun Akust Politech Wroclaw Ser M
Prace Naukowe Instytutu Telekomunikacji i Akustyki Politechniki Wroclawskiej. Seria. Studia i Materialy — Pr Nauk Inst Telekomun Akust Politech Wroclaw Ser S
Prace Naukowe Instytutu Ukladow Elektromaszynowych Politechniki Wroclawskiej — Pr Nauk Inst Ukladow Elektromasz Politech Wroclaw
Prace Naukowe Instytutu Ukladow Elektromaszynowych Politechniki Wroclawskiej. Seria. Studia i Materialy — Pr Nauk Inst Ukladow Elektromasz Politech Wroclaw Ser S
Prace Naukowe. Politechnika Warszawska. Chemia — Pr Nauk Politech Warsz Chem
Prace Naukowe Politechnika Warszawska Elektronika — Pr Nauk Politech Warsz Elektron
Prace Naukowe Politechniki Szczecinskiej — PNPSD
Prace Naukowe Politechniki Szczecinskiej [*Poland*] — Pr Nauk Politech Szczecin
Prace Naukowe Politechniki Wroclawskiej. Prace Naukowe Instytutu Budownictwa — Pr Nauk Politech Wroclaw Pr Nauk Inst Budow
Prace Naukowe Politechniki Wroclawskiej. Seria Konferencje — Pr Nauk Politech Wroclaw Ser Konf
Prace Naukowe Politechniki Wroclawskiej. Seria Monografie — Pr Nauk Politech Wroclaw Ser Monogr
Prace Naukowe Politechniki Wroclawskiej. Seria Studia i Materialy — Pr Nauk Politech Wroclaw Ser Stud Mater
Prace Naukowe Politechniki Wroclawskiej. Seria Wspolpraca — Pr Nauk Politech Wroclaw Ser Wspolpraca
Prace Naukowe Uniwersytetu Slaskiego — PNUS
Prace Naukowe Uniwersytetu Slaskiego w Katowicach — Pr Nauk Uniw Slask Katowicach
Prace Naukowe Uniwersytetu Slaskiego w Katowicach — Prace Nauk Uniw Slask Katowic
Prace Naukowe Uniwersytetu Slaskiego w Katowicach. Prace Fizyczne — Pr Nauk Uniw Slask Katowic Pr Fiz
Prace Naukowe Wyzszej Szkoly Ekonomicznej we Wroclawiu — Pr Nauk Wyzsz Szk Ekon Wroclawiu
Prace Naukowo-Badawcze Instytutu Maszyn Matematycznych — Prace Nauk Bad Inst Masz Mat
Prace ONPMP [*Osrodek Naukowo-Produkcyjny Materialow Polprzewodnikowych*] — Pr ONPMP
Prace Osrodek Naukowo-Produkcyjny Materialow Polprzewodnikowych — Pr Osr Nauk Prod Mater Polprzewodn
Prace Osrodka Badawczo-Rozwojowego Elektroniki Prozniowej — Pr Osr Badaw-Rozwoj Elektron Prozniowej
Prace Osrodka Badawczo-Rozwojowego Elektroniki Prozniowej — Pr Osrodka Badaw Rozwojowego Elektron Prozniowej
Prace Osrodka Badawczo-Rozwojowego Przetwornikow Obrazu — Pr Osr Badaw Rozwoj Przetwornikow Obrazu
Prace Osrodka Badawczo-Rozwojowego Przetwornikow Obrazu — Pr Osrodka Badawczo-Rozwojowego Przetwornikow Obrazu
Prace Osrodka Badawczo-Rozwojowego Techniki Telewizyjnej — Pr Osr Badaw Rozwoj Tech Telew
Prace Panstwowego Instytutu Geologicznego — Pr Panstw Inst Geol
Prace PIT [*Przemyslowego Instytutu Telekomunikacji*] — Pr PIT
Prace Polonistyczne [*Warsaw*] — PP
Prace Polonistyczne [*Warsaw*] — PraPol
Prace Polonistyczne [*Warsaw*] — PrPol
Prace Polonistyczne (Lodz) — PPL
Prace Polonistyczne (Wroclaw) — PPW
Prace Przemyslowego Instytutu Elektroniki — Pr Przem Inst Elektron
Prace Przemyslowego Instytutu Elektroniki (Warsaw) — Pr Przem Inst Elektron (Warsaw)
Prace Przemyslowego Instytutu Telekomunikacji — Pr Przem Inst Telekomun
Prace Rady Naukowo-Technicznej Huty Imienia Lenina — Pr Rady Nauk-Tech Huty Lenina
Prace Rolniczo-Lesne. Polska Akademia Umiejetnosci — Pr Roln Lesne Pol Akad Umiejet
Prace Statneho Geologickeho Ustavu (Bratislava) — Pr Statneho Geol Ustavu (Bratisl)
Prace Statneho Geologickeho Ustavu (Bratislava) — Pr Statneho Geol Ustavu (Bratislava)
Prace Ustavu Geologickeho Inzenyrstvu — Pr Ustavu Geol Inz
Prace Ustavu pro Naftovy Vyzkum — Pr Ustavu Naft Vyzk
Prace Ustavu pro Vyzkum a Vyuziti Paliv — Pr Ustavu Vyzk Vyuziti Paliv
Prace Ustavu pro Vyzkum Paliv [*Czechoslovakia*] — Pr Ustavu Vyzk Paliv
Prace Vyzkumneho Ustavu CS Naftovych Dolu — Pr Vyzk Ustavu CS Naft Dolu
Prace Vyzkumneho Ustavu Geologickeho Inzenyrstvi — Pr Vyzk Ustavu Geol Inz
Prace Vyzkumneho Ustavu Lesneho Hospodarstvi a Myslivosti — Prace Vyzkum Ust Lesn Hosp Mysl
Prace Vyzkumneho Ustavu Lesneho Hospodarstvi a Myslivosti (Strnady) — Pr Vyzk Ustavu Lesn Hospod Myslivosti (Strnady)
Prace Wroclawskiego Towarzystwa Naukowego — TSW

Prace Wroclawskiego Towarzystwa Naukowego. A — PWTN-A
Prace Wroclawskiego Towarzystwa Naukowego. Seria A — Prace Wroclaw Towarz Nauk Ser A
Prace Wroclawskiego Towarzystwa Naukowego. Seria B — Pr Wroclaw Tow Nauk Ser B
Prace Wydzialu 4. Nauk Lekarskich. Lodzkie Towarzystwo Naukowe — Pr Wydz 4 Nauk Lek Lod Tow Nauk
Prace Wydzialu Nauk Przyrodniczych. Bydgoskie Towarzystwo Naukowe. Seria A — Pr Wydz Nauk Przyr Bydgoskie Tow Nauk Ser A
Prace Wydzialu Nauk Tcohnicznych. Bydgoskie Towarzystwo Naukowe. Seria A. Technologia Chemiczna — Pr Wydz Nauk Tech Bydgoskie Tow Nauk Ser A
Prace Wydzialu Nauk Technicznych. Bydgoskie Towarzystwo Naukowe. Seria C. Elektronika, Elektrotechnika — Pr Wydz Nauk Tech Bydgoskie Tow Nauk Ser C
Prace Wydzialu Nauk Technicznych. Bydogoskie Towarzystwo Naukowe. Seria B — Pr Wydz Nauk Tech Bydgoskie Tow Nauk Ser B
Prace Wydzialu Techniki (Katowice) — Pr Wydz Tech (Katowice)
Prace z Biologii Molekularnej (Uniwersytet Jagiellonski) — Pr Biol Mol Uniw Jagiellon
Prace z Nauk Spolecznych (Katowice) — Pr Nauk Spolecznych Katowice
Prace z Zakresu Lesnictwa [*Poland*] — Pr Zakresu Lesn
Prace z Zakresu Lesnictwa — PZLSA
Prace z Zakresu Nauk Rolniczych — Pr Zakresu Nauk Roln
Prace z Zakresu Nauk Rolniczych i Lesnych (Poznan) — Prace Zakr Nauk Roln Lesn (Poznan)
Prace z Zakresu Towaroznawstwa i Chemii — Pr Zakresu Towarozn Chem
Prace. Zakladu Dendrologii i Pomologii w Korniku/Publications. Institute of Dendrology and Pomology — Prace Zakladu Dendrol W Korniku
Prace Zoologiczne. Uniwersytet Jagiellonski — Pr Zool Uniw Jagiellon
Prace-Poznanskie Towarzystwo Przyjaciol Nauk. Wydzial Nauk Rolniczych i Lesnych — Pr Poznan Tow Przyj Nauk Wydz Nauk Roln Lesn
Praci Biologo-Gruntovogo Fakul'tetu — Praci Biol Gruntov Fak
Praci Odes'kogo Derzavnogo Universytetu imeny I. I. Mecnikova/Trudy Odesskogo Gosudarstvennogo Universiteta imeni I. I. Mecnikova — Praci Odesk Derzavn Univ Mecnikova
Praci Odes'koho Derzavnoho Universytetu — PODU
Pracovni Lekarstvi — Prac Lek
Pracovni Lekarstvi — PRLEA
Practica Otologica (Kyoto) — Pract Otol (Kyoto)
Practica Oto-Rhino-Laryngologica — PORLA
Practica Oto-Rhinolaryngologica — Pract Otorhinolaryng
Practica Oto-Rhino-Laryngologica — Pract Oto-Rhino-Laryngol
Practical Accountant — Prac Acc
Practical Accountant — Prac Accnt
Practical Accountant — Pract Account
Practical Accountant — PTA
Practical Anthropology — Prac Anth
Practical Anthropology — Pract Anthrop
Practical Applications of Biochemistry to the Economies of Developing Countries. Proceedings. FAOB (Federation of Asian and Oceanian Biochemists) Symposium — Pract Appl Biochem Econ Dev Countries Proc FAOB Symp
Practical Approach to Patents, Trademarks, and Copyrights — PAPTC
Practical Approach to Patents, Trademarks, and Copyrights — Prac Appr Pat TM and Copyright
Practical Aspects of Industrial Compaction — Pract Aspects Ind Compaction
Practical Biotechnology — Pract Biotechnol
Practical Brewer (Monograph) — Pract Brew
Practical Colloid Chemistry — Pract Colloid Chem
Practical Computing — Pract Comput
Practical Computing — Practical Comput
Practical Electronics — Pract Electron
Practical Electronics — Pract Electronics
Practical Energy — Pract Energy
Practical Energy — PRAED
Practical Engineer (Chicago) — Pract Eng (Chicago)
Practical Engineering (London) — Pract Eng (London)
Practical Farmer — Prac F
Practical Forecast for Home Economics — Prac Forecast
Practical Gastroenterology — Pract Gastroenterol
Practical Genetics — Pract Genet
Practical Holography — Pract Hologr
Practical Home Economics — Prac Home Econ
Practical Homeowner — PH
Practical Homeowner — Pract Homeowner
Practical Horticulture/Jissai Engei — Pract Hort
Practical Householder [*England*] — Pract House
Practical Investor — Pract Invest
Practical Lawyer — Prac Law
Practical Lawyer — Prac Lawyer
Practical Magazine — Pract M
Practical Metallography — Pract Metallogr
Practical Metallography. Special Issues — Pract Metallogr Spec Issues
Practical Methods in Electron Microscopy — Pract Methods Electron Microsc
Practical Motorist — Pract Mot
Practical Neurochemistry — Pract Neurochem
Practical Papers for the Bible Translator — Pract Paps for the Bible Translator
Practical Parenting — Pract Parent
Practical Pharmacy (Tokyo) — Pract Pharm (Tokyo)
Practical Plastics — Pract Plast
Practical Plastics in Australia and New Zealand — Pract Plast Aust NZ
Practical Power Farming — Pract Power Farming
Practical Solar — Pract Solar
Practical Spectroscopy — Pract Spectrosc
Practical Spectroscopy Series — Pract Spectrosc Ser
Practical Surface Technology [*Japan*] — Pract Surf Technol
Practical Welder — Prac Wel
Practical Welder — Pract Welder
Practical Wireless — Pract Wireless
Practical Woodworking [*England*] — Pract Woodworking
Practice Digest — Pract Dig
Practice of Anaesthesia [*Monograph*] — Pract Anaesth
Practice of Medicine (Philadelphia) — Pract Med (Phila)
Practising Administrator — Pract Adm
Practising Manager — PTM
Practitioner — Pr
Practitioner — PRACA
Practitioner — Practition
Pracy Instytuta Movaznaustva Akademii Nauk Belaruskaj SSR — PIMBel
Praedica Verbum — Pr V
Praehistorische Blaetter — Praehist Bl
Praehistorische Blaetter — Prahist Bl
Praehistorische Bronzefunde — PBF
Praehistorische Zeitschrift — Praeh Z
Praehistorische Zeitschrift — Praehist Z
Praehistorische Zeitschrift — Praehist Zft
Praehistorische Zeitschrift — PrZ
Praehistorische Zeitschrift — PZ
Prae-Italic Dialects of Italy — PID
Praeparative Pharmazie — Praep Pharmazie
Praesteforeningens Blad — Pr Bl
Prag. Beiblaetter zu Ost und West — Prag Beibl Ost West
Prager Deutsche Studien — Prag Dt St
Prager Juristische Vierteljahrsschrift — P Jur Vj
Prager Medizinische Wochenschrift — Prager Med Wochenschr
Prager Tieraerztliches Archiv — PGTAA
Pragmateiai tes Akademias Athenon — PAA
Pragmatics and Beyond — P and B
Pragmatics and Beyond Companion Series — Pragmatics & Beyond Companion Ser
Pragmatics Microficke — Prag Micro
Prague Bulletin of Mathematical Linguistics — PBML
Prague Bulletin of Mathematical Linguistics — Prague Bull Math Linguist
Prague International Symposium of Child Neurology — Prague Int Symp Child Neurol
Prague IUPAC (International Union of Pure and Applied Chemistry) Microsymposium on Macromolecules — Prague IUPAC Microsymp Macromol
Prague Studies in English — PSE
Prague Studies in Mathematical Linguistics — Prague Stud Math Linguist
Prague Studies in Mathematical Linguistics — PSML
Prairie Forum. Journal. Canadian Plains Research Centre — PRFO
Prairie Garden — Prairie Gard
Prairie Institute of Environmental Health. Report PIEH — Prairie Inst Environ Health PIEH
Prairie Naturalist — Prairie Nat
Prairie Overcomer — PO
Prairie Primer — Pr Primer
Prairie School Review — Prairie Sch R
Prairie Schooner — P Sch
Prairie Schooner — PPSC
Prairie Schooner — Pra S
Prairie Schooner — Prairie Sch
Prairie Schooner — Prairie Schoon
Prairie Schooner — PrS
Prairie Schooner — PS
Prakla-Seismos Report [*Germany*] — Prakla-Seismos Rep
Prakla-Seismos Report — PSRPD
Prakruti Utkal University Journal of Science — Prakruti Utkal Univ J Sci
Prakticheskaia Veterinariia (Moskva) — Prakt Vet (Moskva)
Prakticheskaya Gazovaya Khromatografiya. Materialy Seminara. Minsk Oc — Prakt Gazov Khromatogr Mater Semin
Prakticheskaya Veterinariya — Prakt Vet
Prakticheskie Zadachi Genetiki v Sel'skom Khozyaistve — Prakt Zadachi Genet Selsk Khoz
Prakticke Zubni Lekarstvi — Prakt Zubn Lek
Prakticky Lekar — Prakt Lek
Praktijkgids — PRK
Praktika. Hellenic Hydrobiological Institute — Prakt Hell Hydrobiol Inst
Praktika Khimicheskogo Mutageneza. Sbornik Trudov Vsesoyuznogo Soveshchaniya po Khimicheskomu Mutagenezu. Institut Khimicheskoi Fiziki. Mo — Prakt Khim Mutagen Sb Tr Vses Soveshch
Praktika Panelleniou Chemikou Synedriou — Prakt Panelleniou Chem Synedriou
Praktika Sudebnopsikhiatricheskoi Ekspertizy — Prakt Sudebnopsikhiatr Ekspert
Praktika Teplovoi Mikroskopii — Prakt Tepl Mikrosk
Praktika tes Akademias Athenon — PAA
Praktika tes Akademias Athenon — PAATA
Praktika tes Akademias Athenon — Prak Ak Ath
Praktika tes Akademias Athenon — Prakt
Praktika tes Akademias Athenon — Prakt Ak Ath
Praktika tes Akademias Athenon — Prakt Akad
Praktika tes Akademias Athenon — Prakt Akad Athenon
Praktika tes Akademias Athenon — Pratika Athen
Praktika tes en Athenais Archaiologikes Hetaireias — PAAH
Praktika tes en Athenais Archaiologikes Hetaireias — Prak Athen Arch het
Praktika tes en Athenais Arkhaiologikes Hetairias — Praktika
Praktikum po Yadernoi Fizike — Prakt Yad Fiz
Praktisch Theologisches Handbuch — P Th H
Praktische Allergiediagnostik. 2. Neubearbeitete und Erweiterte Auflage — Prakt Allergiediagn 2 Neubearb Erweiterte Aufl

Praktische Anaesthesie, Wiederbelebung, und Intensivtherapie — Prakt Anaesth
Praktische Anwendung des Enzymimmunoassays in Klinischer Chemie und Serologie — Prakt Anwend Enzymimmunoassays Klin Chem Serol
Praktische Arzt — Prakt Arzt
Praktische Betriebswirt — PB
Praktische Blaetter fuer Pflanzenbau und Pflanzenschutz — Prakt Bl Pflanzenbau Pflanzenschutz
Praktische Blaetter fuer Pflanzenbau und Pflanzenschutz — Prakt Blaett Pflanzenbau Pflanzenschutz
Praktische Chemie — Prakt Chem
Praktische Desinfektor — Prakt Desinfekt
Praktische Energiekunde — Prakt Energiek
Praktische Enzymologie. Grundlagen, Gesichertes und Grenzen. Konferenz der Gesellschaft fuer Biologische Chemie — Prakt Enzymol Konf Ges Biol Chem
Praktische Landtechnik — Prakt Landtech
Praktische Metallographie — Prakt Metallogr
Praktische Metallographie. Sonderbaende — Prakt Metallogr Sonderb
Praktische Psychologie — PrPs
Praktische Schadlingsbekampfer — Prakt Schadlingsbekampf
Praktische Schaedlingsbekaempfer [*Braunschweig*] — Pr Schae B
Praktische Tieraerzt — Prakt Tier
Praktische Tieraerzt [*German Federal Republic*] — Prakt Tierarzt
Praktische Tuberkulose Blaetter — Prakt Tuberk Bl
Praktischer Wegweiser fuer Bienenzuechter — Prakt Wegw Bienenz
Praktisches Bibellexikon — PBL
Praktisch-Theologische Handbibliothek. Sonderband — P Th HB S
Pramana — PRAMC
Prasa Polska — PP
Pratica del Medico — Pratica Med
Pratique de la Medicine Infantile — Prat Med Infant
Pratique de Laboratoire (Moscow) — Prat Lab Moscow
Pratique des Industries Mecanique — Prat Ind Mec
Pratique du Soudage — Prat Soudage
Pratique Medicale — Prat Med
Pratique Veterinaire Equine — Prat Vet Equine
Pratsa Navukovaga Tavarystva pa Vyvuchen'nyu Belarusi — Pr Navuk Tav Vyvuch Belarusi
Pratsi Belaruskaga Dzyarzhaunaga Universiteta — Pr Belarus Dzyarzh Univ
Pratsi Botanichnogo Sadu Kiivs'kii Derzhavnii Universitet — Pr Bot Sadu Kiiv Derzh Univ
Pratsi i Materiali Pershogo Kharkivs'kogo Derzhavnogo Medichnogo Institutu — Pr Mater Pershogo Khark Derzh Med Inst
Pratsi Institut Geologii Korisnikh Kopalin Akademiya Nauk Ukrains'koi — Pr Inst Geol Korisnikh Kopalin Akad Nauk Ukr
Pratsi Institutu Gidrobiologii Akademiya Nauk Ukrains'koi RSR — Pr Inst Gidrobiol Akad Nauk Ukr RSR
Pratsi Institutu Zoologii Akademiya Nauk Ukrains'koi RSR — Pratsi Inst Zool Akad Nauk Ukr RSR
Pratsi Molodikh Uchenikh Ukrains'ka Akademiya Sil's'kogospodars'kikh Nauk — Pr Molodikh Uch Ukr Akad Sil's'kogospod Nauk
Pratsi Odes'kogo Derzhavnogo Universitetu. Prirodnichi Nauki — Pr Odes Derzh Univ Prir Nauki
Pratsi Odeskogo Derzhavnogo Universitetu. Seriya Biologichnikh Nauk — Pratsi Odes Derzh Univ Ser Biol Nauk
Pratsi Odes'kogo Derzhavnogo Universitetu. Seriya Fizichnikh Nauk — Pr Odes Derzh Univ Ser Fiz Nauk
Pratsi Odes'kogo Derzhavnogo Universitetu. Seriya Khimichnikh Nauk — Pr Odes Derzh Univ Ser Khim Nauk
Pratsi Odes'kogo Derzhavnogo Universitetu. Zbirnik Biologichnogo Fakul'tetu — Pr Odes Derzh Univ Zb Biol Fak
Pratsi Odes'Kogo Derzhavnogo Universitetu. Zbirnik Khimichnogo Fakul'tetu — Pr Odes Derzh Univ Zb Khim Fak
Pratsi Odes'kogo Derzhavnogo Universitetu. Zbirnik Robit Disertantiv Aspirantiv — Pr Odes Derzh Univ Zb Rob Disertantiv
Pratsi Odes'kogo Derzhavnogo Universitetu. Zbirnik Students'kokh Robit — Pr Odes Derzh Univ Zb Stud Rob
Pratsi Odes'kogo Gidrometeorologichnogo Institutu — Pr Odes Gidrometeorol Inst
Pratsi Odes'kogo Sil's'kogospodars'kogo Institutu — Pr Odes Silskogospod Inst
Pratsi Ukrains'kogo Institutu Eksperimental'noi Farmatsii — Pr Ukr Inst Eksp Farm
Pratsi Ukrains'kogo Naukovo-Doslidnogo Institutu Torfovoi Promislovosti — Pr Ukr Nauk Dosl Inst Torf Promsti
Pratsi Ukrains'kogo Naukovo-Doslidnogo Institutu Zernovogo Gospodarstva — Pr Ukr Nauk Dosl Inst Zernovogo Gospod
Pratsi Vinnits'kogo Derzhavnogo Medichnogo Institutu — Pr Vinnits'k Derzh Med Inst
Pratsy Gory Goretskaga Navukov aga Tavarystva — Pr Gory Goretskaga Navuk Tav
Pravda — PRAVA
Pravda Ukrainy — Pr U
Pravda Vostoka — PRVOA
Pravne-Historicke Studie — PraHS
Pravoslavna Misao — Prav Mis
Pravoslavnaia Boggoslovskaia Entsiklopediia — PBE
Pravoslavnaja Mysl' — Prav Mysl
Pravoslavnaja Mysl' (Praha) — Prav Mysl P
Pravoslavnaja Rus — Prav Rus
Pravoslav'nija Bukovyna — PB
Pravoslavnoe Obozrenie — PO
Pravoslavny Theologicky Sbornik — PTSb
Pravoslavnyi Palestinskii Sbornik — PPS
Pravoslavnyi Sobesiednik — PS
Pravoslavnyj Palestinskij Sbornik — PPSb
Prawda Wostoka — Pr W
Prawo Kanoniczne — PK
Prawo Kanoniczne — Pra Kan
Praxis — PRAXA
Praxis der Kinderpsychologie und Kinderpsychiatrie — PKIKA
Praxis der Kinderpsychologie und Kinderpsychiatrie — Prax Kinder
Praxis der Kinderpsychologie und Kinderpsychiatrie — Prax Kinderpsychol Kinderpsychiatr
Praxis der Kinderpsychologie und Kinderpsychiatrie. Beiheft — Prax Kinderpsychol Kinderpsychiatr Beih
Praxis der Mathematik — Praxis Math
Praxis der Naturwissenschaften — Prax Naturw
Praxis der Naturwissenschaften. Chemie — Prax Naturwiss Chem
Praxis der Naturwissenschaften. Physik — Prax Naturwiss Phy
Praxis der Naturwissenschaften. Physik im Unterricht der Schulen — Prax Naturwiss Phys Unterr Sch
Praxis der Naturwissenschaften. Teil 3. Chemie — Pr Naturwiss Teil 3
Praxis der Naturwissenschaften. Teil 3. Chemie [*Germany*] — Prax Naturwiss Teil 3
Praxis der Pneumologie — Prax Pneumol
Praxis der Psychotherapie — Prax Psychother
Praxis der Psychotherapie — PRPYA
Praxis der Psychotherapie und Psychosomatik — Prax Psychother Psychosom
Praxis der Sicherheitstechnik — Prax Sicherheitstech
Praxis des Neusprachlichen Unterrichts — Praxis
Praxis des Reichsgerichts (Bolze, Editor) — BolzePr
Praxis International — Praxis Int
Praxis Schriftenreihe Physik — Prax Schriftenr Phys
Praxis und Forschung — Prax Forsch
Praxis und Klinik der Pneumologie — Prax Klin Pneumol
Praxis Veterinaria — Prax Vet
Praxis-Kurier — PK
Praxis-Schriftenreihe. Abteilung Physik — Prax Schriftenreihe Abt Phys
Prazosin. Evaluation of a New Anti-Hypertensive Agent. Proceedings. Symposium — Prazosin Eval New Anti Hypertens Agent Proc Symp
Prazske Hospodarske Noviny — Prazske Hospod Noviny
Prazsky Sbornik Historicky — Prazsky Sbor Hist
Preacher's Commentaries — Prea Com
Preacher's Handbook — Pr Hdb
Precambrian Research — Precamb Res
Precambrian Research — Precambrian Res
Precambrian Trough Structures of the Baikal-Amur Region and Their Metallogeny — Precambrian Trough Struct Baikal Amur Reg Their Metallog
Precancerous Lesions of the Gastrointestinal Tract. Proceedings. International Symposium on Precancerous Lesions of the Gastrointestinal Tract — Precancerous Lesions Gastrointest Tract Proc Int Symp
Precast Concrete — Precast Concr
Precious Metals — Precious Met
Precious Metals Performance Digest — Precious Met Perform Dig
Precious Metals. Proceedings. International Precious Metals Institute Conference — Precious Met Proc Int Precious Met Inst Conf
Precis Analytique des Travaux. Academie des Sciences, Belles-Lettres, et Arts de Rouen — Precis Analytique Trav Acad Sci Rouen
Precision Engineering — Precis Eng
Precision Engineering — Precis Engng
Precision Instrument Design — Precis Instrum Des
Precision Metal — Precis Met
Precision Metal Molding — Precis Met Molding
Precision Surface Metrology — Precis Surf Metrol
Pre-Columbian Metallurgy of South America. Conference — Pre Columbian Metall South Am Conf
Preconcentration and Drying of Food Materials. Thijssen Memorial Symposium. Proceedings. International Symposium — Preconc Drying Food Mater Thijssen Meml Symp Proc Int Symp
Predeal International School — Predeal Int Sch
Predeal International Summer School — Predeal Int Summer Sch
Predel no Dopustimye Kontsentratsii Atmosfernykh Zagryaznenii — Predel no Dopustimye Konts Atmos Zagryaz
Predicador Evangelico — Pr Ev
Predicasts. Glass and Advanced Fibers Industry Study 163 — Predi 163
Predicasts. Industrial Packaging Paper Trends P-55 — Predi P55
Predicasts. Recreational Vehicles Industry Study 161 — Predi 161
Predicasts Special Study — Predi
Predicasts. Water Treatment Chemicals Industry Study 165 — Predi 165
Predicasts. World Housing Industry Study 168 — Predi 168
Predicasts. World Rubber and Tire Markets Industry Study 162 — Predi 162
Predictability, Stability, and Chaos in N-Body Dynamical Systems — Predict Stab Chaos N Body Dyn Syst
Predicting Dependence Liability of Stimulant and Depressant Drugs. Proceedings. Conference — Predict Depend Liability Stimul Depressant Drugs Proc Conf
Predicting Photosynthesis for Ecosystem Models [*Monograph*] — Predict Photosynth Ecosyst Models
Predicting Plastics Performance. Division Technical Conference. Society of Plastics Engineers — Predict Plast Perform Div Tech Conf Soc Plast Eng
Prediction of Chronic Toxicity from Short Term Studies. Proceedings. Meeting — Predict Chronic Toxic Short Term Stud Proc Meet
Prediger und Katechet — Pr Kat
Predigt der Kirche — PdK
Pregled Naucnotehnickih Radova i Informacija. Zavod za Tehnologiiu Drveta — Pregled Naucnoteh Rad Inform Zavod Tehn Drveta
Pregled Problema Mentalno Retardiranih Osoba — Pregl Probl Ment Retard Osoba
Prehistoire — Preh

Prehistoire Ariegeoise — Prehist Arieg
Prehistoire et Speleologie Ariegeoises — Prehist Speleol Ariegeoises
Prehistoric Art Archaeology — Prehist Art Arch
Prehistoric Macedonia — P Mac
Prehistoric Macedonia — PM
Prehistoric Macedonia — Pr Mac
Prehistoric Thessaly — PT
Prehistoric Tombs at Knossos — PTK
Prohl'ad Lesnickej. Drevarskej. Celulozovej a Papierenskej Literatury — Prehlad Lesnickej Lit
Prehled Lesnicke a Myslivecke Literatury — Prehl Lesn Mysliv Lit
Prehled Zahranicni Zemedelske Literatury — Prehl Zahr Zemed Lit
Prehled Zemedelske Literatury — Prehl Zemed Lit
Prehled Zemedelske Literatury Zahranicni i Domaci — Prehl Zemed Lit Zahr Domaci
Prehrambena Industrija — Prehrambena Ind
Prehrambeno Tehnoloska Revija — Prehrambeno Tehnol Rev
Prehrambeno-Tehnoloska i Biotehnoloska Revija — Prehrambeno Tehnol Biotehnol Rev
Preisschriften, Gekroent und Herausgegeben von der Fuerstlich Jablonowski'schen Gesellschaft zu Leipzig — Preisschr Fuerstl Jablonowskischen Ges Leipzig
Preistoria Alpina [*Museo Tridentino di Scienze Naturali*] — Preist Alp
Preliminary Determination of Epicenters [*National Oceanic and Atmospheric Administration*] — PDE
Preliminary Determination of Epicenters [*National Oceanic and Atmospheric Administration*] — PRDE
Preliminary Report. Department of Natural Resources. Province of Quebec — Prelim Rep Dep Nat Resour Prov Que
Preliminary Report. Direction Generale des Mines (Quebec) — Prelim Rep Dir Gen Mines (Queb)
Preliminary Report. Geological Survey. Wyoming — Prelim Rep Geol Surv Wyo
Preliminary Report. Rehovot. National and University Institute of Agriculture — Prelim Rep Rehovot Nat Univ Inst Agr
Preliminary Report. Volcani Center (Bet Dagan, Israel) — Prelim Rep Volcani Cent (Bet Dagan Isr)
Preliminary Report. Volcani Institute of Agricultural Research — Prelim Rep Volcani Inst Agric Res
Preliminary Reports. International Symposium on Testing In Situ of Concrete Structures — Prelim Rep Int Symp Test In Situ Concr Struct
Preliminary Reports. Memoranda and Technical Notes. Materials Research Council Summer Conference — Prelim Rep Memo Tech Notes Mater Res Counc Summer Conf
Premiere — IPRE
Premiers Travaux de la Societe Libre d'Agriculture et d'Economie Interieure du Departement du Bas-Rhin, Seante a Strasbourg — Prem Trav Soc Libre Agric Dep Bas Rhin Strasbourg
Premium/Incentive Business — Pr Incntv
Premium/Incentive Business — Premium/Incentive Bus
Prenatal Diagnosis — Prenat Diagn
Prenatal Diagnosis — Prenatal Diagn
Prensa Literaria — PLit
Prensa Medica Argentina — Prensa Med Argent
Prensa Medica Mexicana — PMMEA
Prensa Medica Mexicana — Prensa Med Mex
Prentice Hall Information and System Sciences Series — Prentice Hall Inform System Sci Ser
Prentice Hall Information Network [*Database*] — PHINet
Prentice Hall International Series in Acoustics, Speech, and Signal Processing — Prentice Hall Internat Ser Acoust Speech Signal Process
Prentice Hall International Series in Computer Science — Prentice Hall Internat Ser Comput Sci
Prentice Hall International Series in Industrial and Systems Engineering — Prentice Hall Internat Ser Indust Systems Engrg
Prentice-Hall International Series in Systems and Control Engineering — Prentice Hall Internat Ser Syst Control Engin
Prentice-Hall Series in Computational Mathematics — Prentice Hall Ser Comput Math
Prentice-Hall Signal Processing Series — Prentice Hall Signal Process Ser
Preoceedings. Meeting. International Committee of Electrochemical Thermodynamics and Kinetics — Proc Meet Int Comm Electrochem Thermodyn Kinet
Preparation and Bio-Medical Application of Labeled Molecules. Proceedings. Symposium — Prep Bio Med Appl Labeled Mol Proc Symp
Preparation and Characterization of Materials. Proceedings. Indo-U.S. Workshop — Prep Charact Mater Proc Indo US Workshop
Preparation and Properties of Solid State Materials — Prep Prop Solid State Mat
Preparation of Catalysis. Proceedings. International Symposium — Prep Catal Proc Int Symp
Preparations for Rapid Diagnosis — Prep Rapid Diagn
Preparative Biochemistry — PRBCB
Preparative Biochemistry — Prep Bioch
Preparative Biochemistry — Prep Biochem
Preparative Biochemistry and Biotechnology — Prep Biochem Biotechnol
Preparative Chromatography — Prep Chromatogr
Preparative Inorganic Reactions — Prep Inorg React
Prepared Foods — Prep Foods
Prepared Foods New Food Products Directory — Prep Food D
Prepodavanie Istorii v Shkole — PIS
Preprint. Akademiya Nauk Ukrainskoi SSR Institut Elektrodinamiki — PNUED
Preprint. American Wood Preservers' Association — Prepr Amer Wood Pres Ass
Preprint. Daresbury Laboratory — Prepr Daresbury Lab
Preprint. Daresbury Laboratory. DL/P — Prepr Daresbury Lab DL P
Preprint. Institut Prikladnoi Matematiki Akademii Nauk SSSR — PIPSD
Preprint. Institution of Engineers of Australia. Conference — Preprint Inst Eng Aust Conf
Preprint. Joint Institute for Nuclear Research. Dubna, USSR — Prepr Jt Inst Nucl Res Dubna USSR
Preprint Ob'edinennogo Instituta Yadernykh Issledovanii. OIYal [*Joint Institute of Nuclear Research*] — Prepr Obedin Inst Yad Issled OIYal
Preprint. Powder Metallurgy Group Meeting — Prepr Powder Metall Group Meet
Preprint. Rubber Technology Conference — Prepr Rubber Technol Conf
Preprint Series. Institute of Mathematics. University of Oslo — MPSOA
Preprint Series. Institute of Mathematics. University of Oslo [*Norway*] — Prepr Ser Inst Math Univ Oclo
Preprint Series. University of Oslo. Institute of Mathematics — Prepr Ser
Preprint. Universitatea din Timisoara. Facultatea de Stiinte ale Naturii — Prepr Univ Timisoara Fac Stiinte Nat
Pre-Printed Papers. Annual Industrial Water and Waste Conference — Pre Printed Pap Annu Ind Water Waste Conf
Preprints. American Chemical Society. Division of Fuel Chemistry — Prepr Am Chem Soc Div Fuel Chem
Preprints. American Chemical Society. Division of Petroleum Chemistry — Prepr Am Chem Soc Div Pet Chem
Preprints. American Chemical Society. Division of Petroleum Chemistry — Prepr Div Pet Chem Am Chem Soc
Preprints. American Society of Lubrication Engineers — Prepr Am Soc Lubr Eng
Preprints. Annual Scientific Meeting. Aerospace Medical Association — Prepr Annu Sci Meet Aerosp Med Assoc
Preprints. Australian Mineral Industry. Annual Review — Prepr Aust Miner Ind Annu Rev
Preprints. Conference on Atmospheric Environment of Aerospace Systems and Applied Meteorology — Prepr Conf Atmos Environ Aerosp Syst Appl Meteorol
Preprints. Eastern Gas Shales Symposium — Prepr East Gas Shales Symp
Preprints. European Congress on Biotechnology — Prepr Eur Congr Biotechnol
Preprints from Conference. Australasian Corrosion Association — Prepr Conf Australas Corros Assoc
Preprints. Invited Talks and Contributed Papers. Symposium on Solvent Extracti on of Metals — Prepr Invited Talks Contrib Pap Symp Solvent Extr Met
Preprints. Joint Conference on Applications of Air Pollution Meteorology — Prepr Jt Conf Appl Air Pollut Meteorol
Preprints of AIChE [*American Institute of Chemical Engineers*] **Papers. National Heat Transfer Conference** — Prepr AIChE Pap Natl Heat Transfer Conf
Preprints of Papers. American Chemical Society. Division of Fuel Chemistry — Prepr Pap Am Chem Soc Div Fuel
Preprints of Papers. Annual Meeting. Canadian Pulp and Paper Association. Technical Section — Prepr Pap Annu Meet Can Pulp Pap Assoc Techn Sect
Preprints of Papers. Environmental Engineering Conference — Prepr Pap Environ Eng Conf
Preprints of Papers. International Mineral Processing Congress — Prepr Pap Int Miner Process Congr
Preprints of Papers. Oilseed Processing Clinic — Prepr Pap Oilseed Process Clin
Preprints of Papers Presented at National Meeting. Division of Environmental Chemistry. American Chemical Society — ACEPC
Preprints of Papers Presented at National Meeting. Division of Environmental Chemistry. American Chemical Society — Prepr Pap Natl Meet Div Environ Chem Am Chem Soc
Preprints of Papers Presented at National Meeting. Division of Water, Air, and Waste Chemistry. American Chemical Society — Prepr Pap Natl Meet Div Water Air Waste Chem Am Chem Soc
Preprints of Papers presented at the ACS National Meeting. American Chemical Society. Division of Environmental Chemistry — Prepr Pap ACS Natl Meet Am Chem Soc Div Environ Chem
Preprints of Papers Presented before Symposium on Coal Mine Drainage Research — Prepr Pap Symp Coal Mine Drain Res
Preprints of Papers Read. International Symposium on Free Radicals — Prepr Pap Int Symp Free Radicals
Preprints of Short Contributions. Bratislava IUPAC (International Union of Pure and Applied Chemistry) sponsored International Conference on Modified Polymers — Prepr Short Contrib Bratislava IUPAC Int Conf Modif Polym
Preprints. Scientific Papers. International Federation of Societies of Cosmetic Chemists Congress — Prepr Sci Pap Int Fed Soc Cosmet Chem Congr
Preprints. Scientific Program. Aerospace Medical Association — Prepr Sci Program Aerosp Med Assoc
Preprints. Symposium on Atmospheric Turbulence, Diffusion, and Air Quality — Prepr Symp Atmos Turbul Diffus Air Qual
Preprinty. Mezhdunarodnyi Simpozium po Khimicheskim Voloknam — Prepr Mezhdunar Simp Khim Voloknam
Prepublication de l'Institut de Recherche Mathematique Avancee — Prepubl Inst Rech Math Av
Prepublications du Laboratoire de Geometrie et Analyse — Prepubl Lab Grom Anal
Pre-Raphaelite Brotherhood — PRB
Pre-Raphaelite Review — PRR
Presbyterian — Pres
Presbyterian and Reformed Review — Presb & Ref R
Presbyterian and Reformed Review — PRR
Presbyterian Historical Society. Journal — Pres His S
Presbyterian Historical Society. Journal — Pres His SJ
Presbyterian Historical Society. Journal — Presb Hist Soc J
Presbyterian Journal — Pres J
Presbyterian Life — Pres Life
Presbyterian Medical Mission Fund — PMMF
Presbyterian Quarterly Review — Presb Q

Presbyterian Quarterly Review — Prsb Q
Presbyterian Register — Pres Reg
Presbyterian Review — Presb R
Presbyterian World — Pres W
Presbyterian-St. Luke's Hospital. Medical Bulletin — Presbyt-St. Luke's Hosp Med Bull
Presbyterian-St. Luke's Hospital. Research Report — Presbyt-St. Luke's Hosp Res Rep
Pre-School Years — Pre-Sch Years
Prescription Proprietaries Guide — PP Guide
Presence — PREEB
Presence Africaine — PA
Presence Africaine — Pr Afr
Presence Africaine — PreA
Presence Africaine — PresAfr
Presence Africaine — Presence Afr
Presence Chretienne — PC
Presence Francophone — PFr
Presencia de la Poesia Cuencana (Cuenca, Ecuador) — Presen Poesia Cuencana Cuenca
Presencia Ecumenica (Venezuela) — PEV
Present and Future of the Forms Industry — Forms Ind
Present Concepts in Internal Medicine — Present Concepts Intern Med
Present Status and Aims of Quantum Electrodynamics. Proceedings. Symposium — Present Status Aims Quantum Electrodyn Proc Symp
Presenza del Carmelo — Pres Carm
Preservacao de Madeiras — Preserv Madeiras
Preservacao de Madeiras. Boletim Tecnico — Preserv Madeiras Bol Tec
Preservation and Transplantation of Normal Tissues. Ciba Foundation Symposium — Preserv Transplant Norm Tissues Ciba Found Symp
Preservation of Documents and Papers — Preserv Doc Pap
Preservation of Food by Ionizing Radiation [*monograph*] — Preserv Food Ioniz Radiat
Preservation of Paper and Textiles of Historic and Artistic Value. Symposium — Preserv Pap Text Hist Artistic Value Symp
Preserved Context Index System [*Database*] — PRECIS
Presidency College. Physiological Institute Journal — Pres Coll Physiol Inst J
Presidential Documents — PD
Presidential Studies Quarterly — PPSQ
Presidential Studies Quarterly — Pres Stud Q
Presidential Studies Quarterly — Pres Studies Q
Presidential Studies Quarterly — Presid Stud Quart
Presocratic Philosophers — PP
Press [*Christchurch, New Zealand*] — Pr
Press Bulletin. Moscow Narodny Bank Ltd. — Moscow Nar
Press Clippings of Greenland — PCOG
Press Extracts on Greenland — PEGR
Press Independent — PR
Press Releases [*United Kingdom*] — PR
Press Summary — PRS
Presse Actualite — Presse Actual
Presse Medicale — PM
Presse Medicale — Pr Med
Presse Medicale — Presse Med
Presse Medicale — PRMEA
Presse Medicale Belge — Presse Med Belge
Presse Thermale et Climatique — Presse Therm Clim
Presse Thermale et Climatique — PTCLA
Pressedienst. Bundesministerium fuer Bildung und Wissenschaft — Pressedienst Bundesminist Bild Wiss
Pressedienst fuer das Bauspar — PBS
Pressemitteilung Nordrhein-Westfalen — PMNWA
Pressemitteilung Nordrhein-Westfalen — Pressemitt Nordrh-Westfalen
Presses Universitaires de France — PUF
Presse-Umschau — Presse-Umsch
Pressluft Industrie — Pressluft Ind
Pressure Engineering [*Japan*] — Pressure Eng
Pressure Vessel Technology — Pressure Vessel Technol
Pressure Vessel Technology. Papers Presented at the International Conference on Pressure Vessel Technology — Pressure Vessel Technol Pap Int Conf
Pressure Vessels and Piping Computer Program Evaluation and Qualification — Pressure Vessels Piping Comput Program Eval Qualif
Prestel Directory and Magazine — Prestel D
Prestige de la Photographie — Prestige de la Photogr
Presynaptic Receptors. Proceedings. Satellite Symposium — Presynaptic Recept Proc Satell Symp
Pre-Term Labour. Proceedings. Study Group. Royal College of Obstetricians and Gynaecologists — Pre Term Labour Proc Study Group R Coll Obstet Gynaecol
Pretoria Oriental Series — POS
Pretoria Theological Studies — P Th St
Pretre et Apotre — PeA
Pretreatment in Chemical Water and Wastewater Treatment. Proceedings. Gothenburg Symposium — Pretreat Chem Water Wastewater Treat Proc Gothenburg Symp
Preussiche Jahrbuecher — Pr Jb
Preussiche Jahrbuecher — Preuss Jb
Preussische Akademie der Wissenschaften. Sitzungsbericht — Preuss Sitzb
Preussische Jahrbuecher — PJ
Preussische Jahrbuecher — PJb
Preussische Jahrbuecher — Preuss Jahrb
Preussische Jahrbuecher — Preuss Jbb
Preussische Jahrbuecher — PrJ
Preussische Jahrbuecher — PrJbb
Preussische Kirchenzeitung — Pr KZ
Preussische Provinzialblaetter — Preuss Provinzialbl
Preussischer Gesamtkatalog — PGK
Preussisches Justizministerialblatt — Preuss Justizministbl
Preussisches Pfarrarchiv — PPA
Preventability of Perinatal Injury. Proceedings. Symposium — Prev Perinat Inj Proc Symp
Prevention — GPRE
Prevention — Pr
Prevention des Accidents. Controles Techniques. Hygiene et Maladies Professionelles — Prev Accid Controles Tech Hyg Mal Prof
Prevention des Accidents, Controles Techniques, Hygiene, et Maladies Professionnelles — PACT
Prevention in Human Services — Prev Hum Serv
Prevention in Psychiatry. International Meeting — Prev Psychiatry Int Meet
Prevention of Fracture. Conference of the Australian Fracture Group — Prev Fract Conf Aust Fract Group
Prevention of Hereditary Large Bowel Cancer. Proceedings. Conference — Prev Hered Large Bowel Cancer Proc Conf
Prevention of Mental Handicap. A World View — Prev Ment Handicap
Prevention of Occupational Cancer [*Monograph*] — Prev Occup Cancer
Prevention Resources — PRER
Preventive Law Reporter — Prev L Rep
Preventive Medicine — Prev Med
Preventive Medicine — PVTMA
Preventive Veterinary Medicine — Prev Vet M
Preventive Veterinary Medicine — Prev Vet Med
Prevenzione e Assistenza Dentale — Prev Assist Dent
Prevenzione Stomatologica — Prev Stomatol
Previdenza Sociale — Previd Soc
Previdenza Sociale — Previdenza Soc
Previews of Heat and Mass Transfer — PHMTD
Prevision Social (Santiago) — Prev Soc Santiago
Prevrashcheniya v Splavakh i Vzaimodeistvie Faz — Prevrashch Splavakh Vzaimodeistvie Faz
Priblizennye Metody Resenija Differencial nyh Uravnenii — Pribliz Metod Resen Differencial Uravnen
Priborostroenie i Avtomaticheskii Kontrol — Priborostr Avtom Kontrol
Pribory i Metody Analiza Izluchenii — Prib Metody Anal Izluch
Pribory i Metody Izmereniya Magnitnykh Polei. Materialy Nauchno-Tekhnicheskoi Konferentsii — Prib Metody Izmer Magn Polei Mater Nauchno Tekh Konf
Pribory i Sistemy Avtomatiki — Prib Sist Avtom
Pribory i Sistemy Avtomatiki — Pribory i Sistemy Avtomat
Pribory i Sistemy Avtomatiki — PSAVA
Pribory i Sistemy Upravleniya — Prib i Sist Upr
Pribory i Sistemy Upravleniya — Prib Sist Upr
Pribory i Sistemy Upravleniya — PRSUB
Pribory i Sistemy Upravleniya — PSUPB
Pribory i Tekhnika Eksperimenta — Prib i Tekh Eksp
Pribory i Tekhnika Eksperimenta — Prib Tekhn
Pribory i Tekhnika Eksperimenta — PRTEA
Pribory i Ustroistva Sredstv Avtomatiki i Telemekhaniki — Prib Ustroistva Sredstv Avtom Telemekh
Price Index Numbers for Current Cost Accounting [*Database*] — PINCCA
Price Waterhouse Review — P W Rev
Price Waterhouse Review — Price Waterhouse R
Price Waterhouse Review — Price Waterhouse Rev
Pride Institute. Journal of Long Term Home Health Care — Pride Inst J Long Term Home Health Care
Priestley Lectures — Priestley Lect
Prikladna Mekhanika — Prikl Mekh
Prikladnaja Geometrija i Inzenernaja Grafika — Prikl Geom i Inzener Grafika
Prikladnaja Matematika i Programmirovanie — Prikl Mat i Programmirovanie
Prikladnaya Biokhimiya i Mikrobiologiya — Prikl Biokhim Mikrobiol
Prikladnaya Fizika Tverdogo Tela — Prikl Fiz Tverd Tela
Prikladnaya Geofizika — Prikl Geofiz
Prikladnaya Geofizika — Prikladnaya Geofiz
Prikladnaya Geokhimiya i Mineralogiya — Prikl Geokhim Mineral
Prikladnaya Khimiya v Mashinostroenii — Prikl Khim Mashinostr
Prikladnaya Matematika i Mekhanika — PMAMA
Prikladnaya Matematika i Mekhanika — Prikl Mat
Prikladnaya Matematika i Mekhanika — Prikl Mat i Mekh
Prikladnaya Matematika i Mekhanika — Prikl Mat Mekh
Prikladnaya Mekhanika — PKMKA
Prikladnaya Mekhanika i Tekhnicheskaya Fizika — Prikl Mekh Tekh Fiz
Prikladnaya Mekhanika v Priborostroenii — Prikl Mekh Priborostr
Prikladnaya Reologiya — Prikl Reol
Prikladnaya Spektroskopiya — Prikl Spektrosk
Prikladnaya Spektroskopiya. Materialy Soveshchaniya po Spektroskopii — Prikl Spektrosk Mater Soveshch
Prikladnaya Yadernaya Fizika — Prikl Yad Fiz
Prikladnaya Yadernaya Spektroskopiya — Prikl Yad Spektrosk
Prikladnye Issledovaniya po Dinamike Vysokotemperaturnogo Gaza — Prikl Issled Din Vysokotemp Gaza
Prikladnye Problemy Pryamogo Preobrazovaniya Energii — Prikl Probl Pryamogo Preobraz Energ
Prikladnye Voprosy Fiziki — Prikl Vopr Fiz
Prikladnye Voprosy Fiziki Goreniya — Prikl Vopr Fiz Goreniya
Prikladnye Voprosy Teplomassoobmena — Prikl Vopr Teplomassoobmena
Prikladnye Zadachi Matematicheskoi Fiziki — Prikl Zadachi Mat Fiz
Prikladnye Zadachi Teorii Perenosa — Prikl Zadachi Teor Perenosa
Prilozhenie k Sborniku Nauchnykh Rabot Meditsinskogo Fakul'teta Karlova Universiteta v Gradtse Kralove — Prilozh Sb Nauchn Rab Med Fak Karlova Univ Gradtse Kralove

Prilozhna Mikrobiologiya — Prilozh Mikrobiol
Prilozi. Makedonska Akademija na Naukite i Umetnostite. Oddelenie za Prirodo-Matematicki Nauki — Prilozi Maked Akad Nauk Umet Odd Prir Mat Nauki
Prilozi Povijesti Umjetnosti u Malmaciju — PPUM
Prilozi Proucavanju Jezika — PPJ
Prilozi Proucavanju Jezika — PrilPJ
Prilozi za Knjizevnost, Jezik, Istoriju, i Folklor — PrilKJIF
Prilozi za Knjizevnost, Jezik, Istoriju, i Folklor — Prilozi
Prilozi za Orijentalnu Filologiju — POF
Primaer-Packmittel — Primaer Packm
Primary and Tertiary Structure of Nucleic Acids and Cancer Research — Primary Tertiary Struct Nucleic Acids Cancer Res
Primary Cardiology — Primary Cardiol
Primary Care — PRCAD
Primary Care Physician's Guide to Practical Gastroenterology — Primary Care Physicians Guide Pract Gastroenterol
Primary Education — Prim Educ
Primary Education — Primary Educ
Primary Education - Popular Educator — Prim Ed-Pop Ed
Primary Journal — Primary J
Primary Mathematics — Primary Maths
Primary Productivity of the Biosphere — Primary Prod Biosphere
Primary Radioactive Minerals — Primary Radioact Miner
Primary Science Bulletin — Primary Sci Bull
Primary Sensory Neuron — Primary Sens Neuron
Primate Behavior — Primate Behav
Primates in Medicine — Primates Med
Primatologia — Primatolog
Primenenie Aktivatsionnogo Analiza v Biologii i Meditsine — Primen Akt Anal Biol Med
Primenenie Antibiotikov v Rastenievodstve. Trudy Vsesoyuznoi Konferentsii po Izucheniyu i Primeneniyu Antibiotikov v Rastenievodstve — Primen Antibiot Rastenievod Tr Vses Konf
Primenenie Antibiotikov v Zhivotnovodstve. Materialy Soveshchaniya — Primen Antibiot Zhivotnovod Mater Soveshch
Primenenie Dobavok v Proizvodstve Keramicheskikh Stroitel'nykh Materialov — Primen Dobavok Proizvod Keram Stroit Mater
Primenenie Lazerov v Atomnoi. Molekulyarnoi i Yadernoi Fizike. Trudy Vsesoyuznoi Shkoly — Primen Lazerov At Mol Yad Fiz Tr Vses Shk
Primenenie Matematicheskikh Metodov v Biologii — Primen Mat Metodov Biol
Primenenie Matematiki v Ekonomike — Primenen Mat Ekonom
Primenenie Mikroelementov Sel'skom Khozyaistve Akademiya Nauk Ukrainskoi SSR [*A publication*] — Primen Mikroelem Sel-Khoz Akad Nauk UkrSSR
Primenenie Mikroelementov v Sel'skom Khozyaistve i Meditsine. Trudy Vsesoyuznogo Soveshchaniya po Mikroelementam — Primen Mikroelem Selsk Khoz Med Tr Vses Soveshch
Primenenie Polimernykh Materialov v Narodnom Khozyaistve — Primen Polim Mater Nar Khoz
Primenenie Radioaktivnykh Izotopov v Metallurgii — Primen Radioakt Izot Metall
Primenenie Teorii Verojatnostei i Matematiceskoi Statistiki — Primenen Teor Verojatnost i Mat Statist
Primenenie Tsifrovykh i Analogovykh Vychislitel'nykh Mashin v Yadernoi Fizike i Tekhnike — Primen Tsifrovykh Analogovykh Vychisl Mash Yad Fiz Tekh
Primenenie Ul'traakustiki k Issledovaniyu Veshchestva — Primen Ul'traakust Issled Veshchestva
Primenenie Ul'trazvuka v Promyshlennosti. Doklady. Prochitannye na Konferentsii — Primen Ultrazvuka Promsti Dokl Konf
Primenenie Vakuuma v Metallurgii. Trudy Soveshchaniya po Primeneniyu Vakuuma v Metallurgi — Primen Vak Metall Tr Soveshch
Primer Acto [*Madrid*] — PrA
Primeros Puestos del Deporte Espanol [*Database*] — DESP
Primitive Man — Pr Man
Primjena Savremenih Metoda u Ispitivanju Celika. Kokokvij — Primjena Savrem Metoda Ispit Celika Kolok
Primordial Nucleosynthesis and Evolution of Early Universe. Proceedings. International Conference — Primordial Nucleosynth Evol Early Universe Proc Int Conf
Primorskii Sel'skokhozyaistvennyi Institut. Trudy — Primorsk Skh Inst Tr
Princess Takamatsu Cancer Research Fund. Proceedings. International Symposium — Princess Takamatsu Cancer Res Fund Proc Int Symp
Princess Takamatsu Symposia — Princess Takamatsu Symp
Princeton College. Bulletin — Princeton Coll B
Princeton Conference on Cerebral Vascular Diseases [*Later, Princeton Conference on Cerebrovascular Diseases*] — Princeton Conf Cereb Vasc Dis
Princeton Conference on Cerebrovascular Diseases — Princeton Conf Cerebrovasc Dis
Princeton Encyclopedia of Classical Sites — PECS
Princeton Landmarks in Mathematics — Princeton Landmarks Math
Princeton Landmarks in Physics — Princeton Landmarks Phys
Princeton Mathematical Series — Princeton Math Ser
Princeton Monographs in Art and Archaeology — PMAA
Princeton Oriental Series — Pr O S
Princeton Oriental Studies — POSt
Princeton Oriental Studies. Social Science — POStS
Princeton Oriental Texts — POT
Princeton Review — Princ
Princeton Review — Princeton R
Princeton Review (New Series) — Princ NS
Princeton Science Library — Princeton Sci Lib
Princeton Seminary Bulletin — Prince S B
Princeton Seminary Bulletin — PrincSB
Princeton Seminary Bulletin [*Princeton, NJ*] — PrincSemB
Princeton Seminary Bulletin — PSB
Princeton Seminary Pamphlets — PSP
Princeton Series in Computer Science — Princeton Ser Comput Sci
Princeton Series in Physics — Princeton Ser Phys
Princeton Studies in English — PSE
Princeton Studies in Mathematical Economics — Princeton Stud Math Econom
Princeton Studies in the History of Religions — PSHR
Princeton Theological Review — Princ Theol R
Princeton Theological Review — PrThR
Princeton Theological Review — PThR
Princeton Theological Review — PTR
Princeton University. Bulletin — Princ Univ Bull
Princeton University. Library. Chronicle — PLC
Princeton University. Library. Chronicle — Princeton Univ Lib Chron
Princeton University Library Chronicle — PriU
Princeton University. Library. Chronicle — PULC
Princeton University. Museum of Historic Art. Record — Princeton Mus Rec
Principal Food. Rice — Princ Food Rice
Principals in Council — Princ in Counc
Principe de Viana — Pr de V
Principe de Viana — Princ Viana
Principe de Viana — PV
Principia Cardiologica — Principia Cardiol
Principles and Practice of the Pediatric Surgical Specialities — Princ Pract Pediatr Surg Spec
Principles and Techniques of Human Research and Therapeutics — Princ Tech Hum Res Ther
Principles, Mechanisms, and Biological Consequences of Induction — Princ Mech Biol Consequences Induct
Principles of Cattle Production. Proceedings. Easter School — Princ Cattle Prod Proc Easter Sch
Principles of Computer Science Series — Principles Comput Sci Ser
Principles of Desalination — Princ Desalin
Principles of Food Science. Part 1. Food Chemistry — Princ Food Sci Part 1 Food Chem
Principles of Pathobiology [*monograph*] — Princ Pathobiol
Principles of Tribology — Princ Tribol
Principles on Tetanus. Proceedings. International Conference on Tetanus — Princ Tetanus Proc Int Conf
Principos Activos [*Database*] — PACTIV
Prindle, Weber, and Schmidt Series in Advanced Mathematics — Prindle Weber Schmidt Ser Adv Math
Prindle, Weber, and Schmidt Series in Mathematics — Prindle Weber Schmidt Ser Math
Print Collector's Newsletter — PCN
Print Collector's Quarterly — Print Coll Q
Print Review — Print R
Print Review — Print Rev
Printed Papers. Institution of Post Office Electrical Engineers — Pap Inst Post Off Electr Eng
Printed Salesmanship — Print Sales
Printed Salesmanship — Print Salesmanship
Printed Salesmanship — Ptd Salesmanship
Printers' Ink — PI
Printers' Ink — Ptr Ink
Printers' Ink Monthly — Ptr Ink Mo
Printing Abstracts — Print Abstr
Printing Abstracts — Printing Abs
Printing Abstracts — Printing Abstr
Printing and Bookbinding Trade Review — Print Bookbind Trade Rev
Printing and Graphic Arts — PaGa
Printing and Graphic Arts — PGA
Printing and Graphic Arts — Print Graph Arts
Printing and Publishing — Print & Pub
Printing and Publishing — Printing and Pub
Printing Art [*Massachusetts*] — Print Art
Printing Art — Ptg Art
Printing Art Quarterly — Print Art Q
Printing Equipment Engineer — Print Equip Eng
Printing Impressions — Printing
Printing Impressions — Printing Impr
Printing Magazine — Print Mag
Printing Magazine National Lithographer — Print Mag Natl Lithogr
Printing Management — Print Manag
Printing Management with Printing Magazine — Print Manage Print Mag
Printing Production — Print Prod
Printing Technology — Print Technol
Printing Trades Journal — Print Trades J
Printing Trades Journal — Printing Trades J
Printing World — CVI
Printout Annual — Printout Ann
Printsipy i Metody Mineragenicheskogo Analiza — Prints Metody Mineragenicheskogo Anal
Priroda [*Moscow*] — PRIRA
Priroda i Socialisticeskoe Hozjajstvo — Prir Socialist Hoz
Priroda i Znanie — Prir Znanie
Priroda Ivanovskoi Oblasti — Prir Ivanov Obl
Priroda (Moscow) — Prir (Moscow)
Priroda Organicheskogo Veshchestva Sovremennykh i Iskopaemykh Osadkov. Doklady Vsesoyuznogo Seminara — Prir Org Veshchestva Sovrem Iskop Osadkov Dokl Vses Semin
Priroda (Sofia) — Prir (Sofia)
Priroda (Sofia, Bulgaria) — PRIRB
Priroda Tatranskeho Narodneho Parku — Prir Tatransk Nar Parku

Prirodno-Matematicka Fakultet na Univerzitetot Kiril i Metodij (Skopje). Godisen Zbornik — Prirod-Mat Fak Univ Kiril i Metodij (Skopje) Godisen Zb
Prirodno-Matematicka Fakultet na Univerzitetot Kiril i Metodij (Skopje). Godisen Zbornik — Prirod-Mat Fak Univ Kiril Metodij (Skopje) Godisen Zb
Prirodno-Matematicka Fakultet na Univerzitetot Kiril i Metodij (Skopje). Godisen Zbornik. Biologija — Prir-Mat Fak Univ Kiril Metodij (Skopje) God Zb Biol
Prirodno-Matematicka Fakultet na Univerzitetot Kiril i Metodij (Skopje). Godisen Zbornik. Sekcja A. Matematika, Fizika, i Hemija — Prir Mat Fak Univ Kiril Metodij (Skopje) God Zb Sek A
Prirodnye i Trudot ye Resursy Levoberezhnoi Ukrainy i Ikh Ispolzovanie — Prir Tr Resur Levoberezhnoi Ukr Ikh Ispolz
Prirodnye Mineral'nye Sorbenty. Trudy Soveshchaniya — Prir Miner Sorbenty Tr Soveshch
Prirodnye Sorbenty Povolzh'ya — Prir Sorbenty Povolzhya
Prirodnye Usloviya Zapadnoi Sibiri — Prir Usloviya Zapadn Sib
Prirodnyi Gaz Sibiri — Prir Gaz Sib
Prirodonaucen Muzej Skopje Posebno Izdanie — Prirodonauc Muz Skopje Posebno Izd
Prirodoslovna Istrazivanja Acta Biologica — Prirodosl Istraz Acta Biol
Prirodoslovna Istrazivanja Acta Geologica — Prirodosl Istraz Acta Geol
Prirodoslovna Istrazivanja Kraljevine Jugoslavije — Prir Istraz Kral Jugoslavije
Prirodoslovne Razprave — Prir Razpr
Prirodovedecka Edice — Prir Edice
Prirodovedecka Fakulta Univerzita J. E. Purkyne v Brne. Folia. Biologia — Prirodoved Fak Univ J E Purkyne Brne Folia Biol
Prirodovedne Prace Slovenskych Muzei. Acta Rerum Naturalium Museorum Slovenicorum — Prir Prace Slov Muz
Prirodovedne Prace Ustavu Ceskoslovenske Akademie Ved v Brne — Prirodoved Pr Ustavu Cesk Akad Ved Brne
Prirodovedny Casopis Slezsky — Prirodoved Cas Slezsky
Prisadki i Smazochnym Maslam — Prisadki Smaz Maslam
Prisadki k Maslam. Trudy Vsesoyuznogo Nauchno-Tekhnicheskogo Soveshchaniya — Prisadki Maslam Tr Vses Nauchno Tekh Soveshch
Priscae Latinitatis Monumenta Epigraphica — Prisc Lat Mon Epigr
Prism International — Prism Int
Prisma. Revista de Filosofia, Ciencia e Arte — PRFCA
Prisoner Rehabilitation on Discharge — PROD
Prisoners — Prsnrs
Prisoners Journal — Pris Jrnl
Prispevky k Problematice Rudneho Hornictvi — Prispevky Probl Rudn Horn
Privacy Journal — PJ
Privacy Report — Privacy Rept
Private Acts of the State of Tennessee — Tenn Priv Acts
Private Label — PL
Private Label — Prvt Label
Private Library — PL
Private Library — Priv Lib
Private Library — Priv Libr
Private Practice — Private Pract
Privatization Review — Priv Rev
Privy Council. Law Reports [*United Kingdom*] — LR PC
Prize Essays and Transactions. Highland and Agricultural Society of Scotland — Prize Essays Trans Highl Agric Soc Scotland
Prize Essays and Transactions. Highland Society of Scotland — Prize Essays Trans Highl Soc Scotland
Pro Alesia — PAL
Pro Alesia. Revue Trimestrielle des Fouilles d'Alise et des Questions Relative a Alesia — PA
Pro Arte — PA
Pro Austria Romana — PAR
Pro Canada — PROC
Pro Familia Informationen — Pro Fam Inf
Pro Medico — Pro Med
Pro Metal — Pro Met
Pro Mundi Vita Bulletin — Pro Mundi Vita
Pro Mundi Vita Dossiers. Africa — Pro Mundi A
Pro Mundi Vita Dossiers. Africa — Pro Mundi Vita Africa Dossier
Pro Mundi Vita Dossiers. Asia and Australasia — Pro Mundi Vita Asia-Australasia Dossier
Pro Mundi Vita Dossiers. Europe/North America — Pro Mundi Vita Europe N Am Dossier
Pro Musica — PRO
Pro Natura — Pro Nat
Pro Nervia — PN
Probability and its Applications — Probab Appl
Probability and Mathematical Statistics — Probab Math Stat
Probability and Mathematical Statistics — Probab Math Statist
Probability and Stochastics Series — Probab Stochastics Ser
Probability in the Engineering and Informational Sciences — Probab Engrg Inform Sci
Probability: Pure and Applied — Probab Pure Appl
Probability Theory and Related Fields — Probab Theory Related Fields
Probability Winter School. Proceedings of the Fourth Winter School on Probability — Pr Winter
Probate and Property — Prob and Prop
Probate Lawyer — Prob Law
Probe — Pr
Probe Post — PRPT
Problem Books in Mathematics — Problem Books in Math
Problemas Agricolas e Industriales de Mexico — Prob Agric Ind Mex
Problemas Agricolas e Industriales de Mexico — Probl Agr Indus Mex
Problemas Agricolas e Industriales de Mexico — Probl Agric Ind Mex
Problemas Brasileiros — Problemas Bras
Problemas del Desarrollo — PDD
Problemas del Desarrollo — Probl Desarr
Probleme Agricole [*Romania*] — PRAGA
Probleme Agricole — Probl Agric
Probleme Agricole (Bucharest) — Probl Agr (Bucharest)
Probleme de Agrofitotehnie Teoretica si Aplicata — Probl Agrofitoteh Teor Apl
Probleme de Automatizare — Probleme de Automat
Probleme de Documentare si Informare — Probl Doc Inf
Probleme de Informare si Documentare — Probl Inf & Doc
Probleme de Informare si Documentare — Probl Inf Docum
Probleme de Informare si Documentare (English Issue) — Probl Inf Doc Engl Issue
Probleme de Lingvistica Genarala — PLG
Probleme de Morfopatologie — Probl Morfopatol
Probleme de Muzeografie — Probl Muz
Probleme de Patologie Comparata — Probl Patol Comp
Probleme de Protectia Plantelor — Probl Prot Plant
Probleme de Protectia Plantelor — Probleme Prot Plantelor
Probleme de Terapeutica — Probl Ter
Probleme der Aegyptologie — PAe
Probleme der Aegyptologie [*Leiden*] — PrAeg
Probleme der Dichtung — PD
Probleme der Dichtung — PdD
Probleme der Entwicklungslaender — Probl Entwicklungslaender
Probleme der Ernaehrungs- und Lebensmittelwissenschaft — Probl Ernaehr Lebensmittelwiss
Probleme der Festkoerperelektronik — Probl Festkoerperelektron
Probleme der Fetalen Endokrinologie — Probl Fetalen Endokrinol
Probleme der Informatik in Medizin und Biologie. Wissenschaftliches Kolloquium zur Organisation der Informationsverarbeitung — Probl Inf Med Biol Wiss Kolloq Organ Informationsverarb
Probleme der Intravenoesen Anaesthesie. Bericht ueber das Bremer Neuroleptanalgesie-Symposion. Teil 1 — Probl Intravenoesen Anaesth Ber Bremer Neuroleptanalg Symp 1
Probleme der Kosmichen Physik — PRKPA
Probleme der Kosmichen Physik [*Germany*] — Probl Kosm Phys
Probleme der Modernen Chemischen Technologie — Probl Mod Chem Technol
Probleme der Perinatalen Medizin — Probl Perinat Med
Probleme der Tierzucht — Probl Tierz
Probleme Economice (Bucharest) — Probl Econ (Bucharest)
Probleme Phlebologischer Therapie. Internationaler Kongress fuer Phlebologie — Probl Phlebol Ther Int Kongr Phlebol
Probleme Zootehnice si Veterinare — Probl Zooteh Vet
Problemes Actuels de Biochimie Appliquee — Probl Actuels Biochim Appl
Problemes Actuels de Biochimie Generale — Probl Actuels Biochim Gen
Problemes Actuels de Paediatrie — Probl Actuels Paediatr
Problemes Actuels de Pharmacopsychiatrie — Probl Actuels Pharmacopsychiatr
Problemes Actuels de Phoniatrie et Logopedie — Probl Actuels Phoniatr Logop
Problemes Actuels de Psychotherapie — Probl Actuels Psychotherap
Problemes Actuels d'Endocrinologie et de Nutrition — Probl Actuels Endocrinol Nutr
Problemes Actuels d'Ophtalmologie — PAOTA
Problemes Actuels d'Ophthalmologie — Probl Actuels Ophthal
Problemes Actuels d'Oto-Rhino-Laryngologie — PAORB
Problemes Actuels d'Oto-Rhino-Laryngologie — Prob Actuels ORL
Problemes d'Afrique Centrale — Probl Afr Centr
Problemes de Biologie et de Medecine — Probl Biol Med
Problemes de Farine — Probl Farine
Problemes de la Pensee Chretienne — PPC
Problemes de l'Enterprise Agricole — Probl Entrep Agric
Problemes de l'Europe — Problemes Eur
Problemes d'Oncologie (Kharkov) — Probl Oncol Kharkov
Problemes Economiques — Probl Ec
Problemes Economiques. Selection de Textes Francais et Etrangers — PBE
Problemes et Controverses — Probl Controv
Problemes Politiques et Sociaux — Probl Polit Soc
Problemes Pratiques d'Endocrinologie — Probl Prat Endocrinol
Problemes Sociaux Zairois — Probl Soc Zair
Problemes Sociaux Zairois — Probl Soc Zairois
Problemes Sociaux Zairoises — Probl Soc Zairoises
Problemes Sovietiques — Probl Soviet
Problemi Attuali di Scienza e di Cultura — Probl Attuali Sci Cult
Problemi del Socialismo (Milano) — Probl Social (Milano)
Problemi della Pedagogia — PPeda
Problemi della Pedagogia — Probl Ped
Problemi della Sicurezza Sociale — Probl Sicur Soc
Problemi della Sicurezza Sociale — Problemi Sicurezza Soc
Problemi dell'Azoto in Agricoltura — Probl Azoto Agric
Problemi di Gestione — Probl Gestione
Problemi di Ulisse — PU
Problemi e Ricerche di Storia Antica — PRSA
Problemi na Biologiyata (Sofia) — Probl Biol Sofia
Problemi na Farmakologiyata — Probl Farmakol
Problemi na Farmakologiyata i Farmatsiyata — Probl Farmakol Farm
Problemi na Khigienata — Prob Khig
Problemi na Khigienata — Probl Khig
Problemi na Khraneneto — Probl Khraneneto
Problemi na Nevrologiyata, Psikhiatriyata, i Nevrokhirurgiyata — Probl Nevrol Psikhiatr Nevrokhir
Problemi na Nuklearnata Meditsina, Radiobiologiyata i Radiatsionnata Khigiena — Probl Nukl Med Radiobiol Radiat
Problemi na Onkologiyata (Sofia) — Probl Onkol (Sofia)
Problemi na Pnevmologiyata i Ftiziatriyata — Probl Pnevmol Ftiziatr
Problemi na Rentgenologiyata i Radiobiologiyata — Probl Rentgenol Radiobiol
Problemi na Stomatologiyata — Probl Stomatol

Problemi na Tehniceskata Kibernetika [*Problems of Engineering Cybernetics*] — Problemi Tehn Kibernet
Problemi na Tekhnicheskata Kibernetika i Robotika [*Problems of Engineering Cybernetics and Robotics*] — Problemi Tekhn Kibernet Robot
Problemi na V-Treshtnata Meditsina — Probl V-Tr Med
Problemi na Vutreshnata Meditsina — Probl Vutr Med
Problemi na Zaraznite i Parazitnite Bolesti — Probl Zaraznite Parazit Bolesti
Problems Actuels de Dermatologie — Probl Actuels Dermatol
Problems Actuels d'Otorhinolaryngologie — Probl Actuels Otorhinolaryngol
Problems and Wonders of Chiral Molecules — Probl Wonders Chiral Mol
Problems in Biology — Probl Biol
Problems in Biology (Oxford) — Probl Biol (Oxford)
Problems in Geometry in the Key Word Index [*Moscow*] — Problems in Geometry
Problems in Liver Diseases — Probl Liver Dis
Problems in Perinatology. Proceedings of Asia Oceania Congress of Perinatology — Probl Perinatol Proc Asia Oceania Congr Perinatol
Problems in Private International Law [*Elsevier Book Series*] — PPIL
Problems of Aging. Transactions. Conference — Probl Aging Trans Conf
Problems of Biocybernetics and Biomedical Engineering — Probl Biocybern Biomed Eng
Problems of Communism — GPRC
Problems of Communism — PC
Problems of Communism — PoC
Problems of Communism — PrCo
Problems of Communism — Prob Com
Problems of Communism — Prob Commun
Problems of Communism — Probl Commu
Problems of Communism — Probl Communism
Problems of Communism — PROC
Problems of Communism — PRQ
Problems of Communism. United States Information Agency — USIA/PC
Problems of Control and Information Theory — Probl Control and Inf Theory
Problems of Control and Information Theory — Probl Control Inf Theor
Problems of Control and Information Theory (English Translation of the Papers in Russian) — Probl Control and Inf Theory (Engl Transl Pap Rus)
Problems of Control and Information Theory. Problemy Upravlenija i Teorii Informacii [*Budapest*] — Problems Control Inform Theory/Problemy Upravlen Teor Inform
Problems of Cryolithology — Probl Cryolithol
Problems of Cybernetics — Probl Cybern
Problems of Cybernetics (English Translation) — Probl Cybern (Engl Transl)
Problems of Cybernetics (USSR) — Probl Cybern (USSR)
Problems of Desert Development — Probl Desert Dev
Problems of Desert Development (English Translation of Problemy Osvoeniya Pustyn) — Probl Desert Dev (Engl Transl Probl Osvoeniya Pustyn)
Problems of Drug Dependence — Probl Drug Depend
Problems of Drug Dependence. Proceedings. Annual Scientific Meeting. The Committee on Problems of Drug Dependence — Probl Drug Depend Proc Annu Sci Meet Comm Probl Drug Depend
Problems of Early Infancy. Transactions. Conference — Probl Early Infancy Trans Conf
Problems of Ecological Monitoring and Ecosystem Modelling — Probl Ecol Monit Ecosyst Modell
Problems of Ecology and Biocenology — Probl Ecol Biocenol
Problems of Economics — PE
Problems of Economics — Prob Econ
Problems of Economics — Probl Econ
Problems of Economics — Problems Econ
Problems of Economics. A Journal of Translations — PYB
Problems of Elementary Particle and Atomic Nucleus Physics — Probl Elem Part At Nucl Phys
Problems of Geochemistry and Cosmology — Probl Geochem Cosmol
Problems of Geology. Session. International Geological Congress — Probl Geol Sess Int Geol Congr
Problems of Hematology and Blood Transfusion — Probl Hematol Blood Transfus
Problems of Hematology and Blood Transfusion (USSR) — Probl Hematol Blood Transfus (USSR)
Problems of Human Reproduction — Probl Hum Reprod
Problems of Infectious and Parasitic Diseases — Probl Infect Parasit Dis
Problems of Influenza and Acute Respiratory Diseases — Probl Influenza Acute Respir Dis
Problems of Information Transmission — PRITA
Problems of Information Transmission — Probl Inf Transm
Problems of Information Transmission — Problems Inform Transmission
Problems of Information Transmission (English Translation) — Probl Inf Transm Engl Transl
Problems of Information Transmission (USSR) — Probl Inf Transm (USSR)
Problems of Low Temperature Physics and Thermodynamics — Probl Low Temp Phys Thermodyn
Problems of Modern Nuclear Physics. Proceedings. Problem Symposium on Nuclear Physics — Probl Mod Nucl Phys Proc Probl Symp Nucl Phys
Problems of Neurosurgery — Probl Neurosurg
Problems of Oncology (English Translation) — Probl Oncol (Engl Transl)
Problems of Oncology (English Translation of Voprosy Onkologii) — Probl Oncol (Engl Transl Vopr Onkol)
Problems of Oncology (Leningrad) — Probl Oncol Leningrad
Problems of Photosynthesis. Reports of All-Union Conference on Photosynthesis — Probl Photosynth Rep All Union Conf Photosynth
Problems of Physiological Optics — Probl Physiol Opt
Problems of Psychiatry and Neuropathology — Probl Psychiatry Neuropathol
Problems of Psychology (English Translation of Voprosy Psikhologii) — Probl Psychol (Engl Transl Vopr Psikhol)
Problems of Siberian Oil — Probl Sib Oil
Problems of Stellar Convection. Proceedings. Colloquium — Probl Stellar Convect Proc Colloq
Problems of the Arctic and the Antarctic — POAA
Problems of the Contemporary World — Probl Contemp World
Problems of the Evolution of Functions and Enzymochemistry of Excitation Processes — Probl Evol Funct Enzymochem Excitation Processes
Problems of the North — POTN
Problems of the North — Probl North
Problems of the Quaternary Geology of Siberia — Probl Quat Geol Sib
Problems of Theoretical Physics — Probl Theor Phys
Problems of Virology (English Translation of Voprosy Virusologii) — Probl Virol (Engl Transl Vopr Virusol)
Problems of World Nutrition. Proceedings. International Congress of Nutrition — Probl World Nutr Proc Int Congr Nutr
Problemy Agrofizyki — Probl Agrofiz
Problemy Analiticheskoi Khimii — Probl Anal Khim
Problemy Arkheologii i Etnografii — PAE
Problemy Arktiki i Antarktiki — Probl Ark Antark
Problemy Arktiki i Antarktiki — Probl Arkt Antarkt
Problemy Arktiki i Antarktiki — Probl Arktiki Antarkt
Problemy Arktiki i Antarktiki [*Former USSR*] — Probl Arktiki Antarktiki
Problemy Biologie Krajiny — Probl Biol Krajiny
Problemy Bioniki — Probl Bioniki
Problemy Bioniki Respublikanskii Mezhvedomstvennyi Nauchno-Tekhnicheskii Sbornik — Probl Bioniki Resp Mezhved Nauchno-Tekh Sb
Problemy Bor'by Protiv Burzuaznoj Ideologii — Probl Bor'by Protiv Burz Ideol
Problemy Botaniki — Probl Bot
Problemy Dal'nego Vostok — Probl Dal'nego Vost
Problemy Dialektiki — Probl Dialektiki
Problemy Ekologicheskogo Monitoringa i Modelirovaniya Ekosistem — Probl Ekol Monit Model Ekosist
Problemy Ekologii — Probl Ekol
Problemy Ekonomiczne (Krakow) — Probl Ekon Krakow
Problemy Ekonomiczne (Warszawa) — Probl Ekon (Warszawa)
Problemy Ekonomiki Morja — Probl Ekon Morja
Problemy Elektrokhimii i Korrozii Metallov — Probl Elektrokhim Korroz Met
Problemy Endokrinologii — Probl Endokrinol
Problemy Endokrinologii i Gormonoterapii — PEGTA
Problemy Endokrinologii i Gormonoterapii — Probl Endokr Gormonot
Problemy Endokrinologii i Gormonoterapii [*Later, Problemy Endokrinologii*] — Probl Endokrinol Gormonoter
Problemy Endokrinologii (Moskva) — Probl Endokrinol (Mosk)
Problemy Evolyutsii — Probl Evol
Problemy Filosofii i Naucnogo Kommunizma — Probl Filos Nauc Kommunizma
Problemy Fizicheskoi Khimii — Probl Fiz Khim
Problemy Fiziki Atmosfery — PFATA
Problemy Fiziki Atmosfery — Probl Fiz Atmos
Problemy Fiziki Elementarnykh Chastits i Atomnogo Yadra — Probl Fiz Elem Chastits At Yadra
Problemy Fiziki Soedinenii AIIBVI. Materialy Vsesoyuznogo Soveshchaniya — Probl Fiz Soedin AIIBVI Mater Vses Soveshch
Problemy Fiziko-Khimicheskoi Petrologii — Probl Fiz Khim Petrol
Problemy Fiziologicheskoj Optiki — Probl Fiziol Opt
Problemy Fiziologii Gipotalamusa — Probl Fiziol Gipotal
Problemy Fiziologii i Biokhimii Drevesnykh Rastenii. Tezisy Dokladov Vsesoyuznoi Konferentsii po Fiziologii i Biokhimii Drevesnykh Rastenii — Probl Fiziol Biokhim Drev Rast Tezisy Dokl Vses Konf
Problemy Fiziologii i Patologii Vysshei Nervnoi Deyatel'nosti — Probl Fiziol Patol Vyssh Nervn Deyat
Problemy Fonovogo Monitoringa Sostoyaniya Prirodnoi Sredy — Probl Fonovogo Monit Sostoyaniya Prir Sredy
Problemy Funktsional'noi Morfologii — Probl Funkts Morfol
Problemy Funktsionirovaniya Bol'shikh Ekonomicheskikh Sistem — Probl Funkts Bolshikh Ekon Sist
Problemy Gastroenterologii — Probl Gastroenterol
Problemy Gematologii i Perelivanija Krovi — Probl Gemat
Problemy Gematologii i Perelivaniya Krovi — PGPKA
Problemy Gematologii i Perelivaniya Krovi — Probl Gematol Pereliv Krovi
Problemy Geodinamiki Kavkaza. Doklady Prochitannye na Seminare po Geodinamike Kavkaza — Probl Geodin Kavk Dokl Semin
Problemy Geokhimii — Probl Geokhim
Problemy Geokhronologii i Geokhimii Izotopov — Probl Geokhronol Geokhim Izot
Problemy Geokhronologii i Izotopnoi Geologii — Probl Geokhronol Izot Geol
Problemy Geologii i Geografii Severo-Vostoka Evropeiskoi Chasti SSSR — Probl Geol Geogr Sev Vostoka Evr Chasti SSSR
Problemy Geologii i Metallogenii Kavkaza — Probl Geol Metallog Kavk
Problemy Geologii i Poleznykh Iskopaemykh na Sessii Mezhdunarodnogo Geologicheskogo Kongressa — Probl Geol Polezn Isk Sess Mezhdunar Geol Kongr
Problemy Geologii Karelii i Kol'skogo Poluostrova — Probl Geol Karelii Kolsk Poluostrova
Problemy Geologii Mineral'nykh Mestorozhdenii, Petrologii i Mineralogii — Probl Geol Miner Mestorozhd Petrol Mineral
Problemy Geologii na Sessii Mezhdunarodnogo Geologicheskogo Kongressa — Probl Geol Sess Mezhdunar Geol Kongr
Problemy Geologii Nefti [*Former USSR*] — Probl Geol Nefti
Problemy Geologii Tsentral'nogo Kazakhstana — Probl Geol Tsentr Kaz
Problemy Gidroenergetiki i Vodnogo Khozyaistva — Probl Gidroenerg Vod Khoz
Problemy Glubokikh Mikozov — Probl Glubokikh Mikozov
Problemy Gosudarstva i Prava — Probl Gos Prava
Problemy Grippa i Ostrykh Respiratornykh Zabolevanii — Probl Grippa Ostrykh Respir Zabol
Problemy Inzhenernoi Geologii Severnogo Kavkaza — Probl Inzh Geol Sev Kavk

Problemy Jadernoi Fiziki i Kosmiceskih Lucei — Problemy Jadern Fiz i Kosm Lucei
Problemy Kamennogo Lit'ya — Probl Kamen Litya
Problemy Khimicheskoi Kinetiki — Probl Khim Kinet
Problemy Kibernetiki — PK
Problemy Kibernetiki — Probl Kibern
Problemy Kibernetiki — Problemy Kibernet
Problemy Kinetiki i Kataliza — Probl Kinet Katal
Problemy Kontrolya i Zashchita Atmosfery ot Zagryazneniya — PKZZD
Problemy Kontrolya i Zashchita Atmosfery ot Zagryazneniya — Probl Kontrolya Zashch Atmos Zagryaz
Problemy Korrozii i Zashchity Metallov. Trudy Vsesoyuznogo Soveshchaniya po Korrozii i Zashchite Metallov — Probl Korroz Zashch Met Tr Vses Soveshch
Problemy Kosmicheskoi Biologii — Probl Kosm Biol
Problemy Kosmicheskoi Biologii Akademiya Nauk SSSR — Problemy Kosmich Biol Akad Nauk SSSR
Problemy Kosmicheskoj Fiziki — Probl Kosm Fiz
Problemy Kriolitologii — Probl Kriolitol
Problemy Kriolitologii — Probl Kriolitologii
Problemy Lekarskie — Probl Lek
Problemy Mashinostroeniya — PRMSD
Problemy Mashinostroeniya [*Ukrainian SSR*] — Probl Mashinostr
Problemy Mashinostroeniya i Nadezhnosti Mashin — Probl Mashinostr Nadezhnosti Mash
Problemy Matematiceskogo Analiza [*Leningrad*] — Problemy Matematiceskogo Analiza
Problemy Matematiceskogo Analiza Sloznyh Sistem — Problemy Mat Anal Sloz Sistem
Problemy Matematicheskoj Fiziki — Probl Mat Fiz
Problemy Meditsinskoi Enzimologii. Materialy. Dolozhennye na Vsesoyuznom Simpoziume po Meditsinskoi Enzimologii — Probl Med Enzimol Mater Vses Simp
Problemy Meditsinskoi Genetiki — Probl Med Genet
Problemy Meditsinskoi Khimii — Probl Med Khim
Problemy Meditsinskoi Radiologii — Probl Med Radiol
Problemy Medycyny Wieku Rozwojowego — Probl Med Wieku Rozwoj
Problemy Metallogenii i Rudogeneza — Probl Metallog Rudog
Problemy Metallovedeniya i Fiziki Metallov [*Former USSR*] — Probl Metalloved Fiz Met
Problemy Metallovedeniya i Fiziki Metallov. Institut Metallovedeniya i Fiziki Metallov — Probl Metalloved Fiz Met Inst Metalloved Fiz Met
Problemy Metallovedeniya i Termicheskoi Obrabotki — Probl Metalloved Term Obrab
Problemy Metodologii Istoriko-Filosofskogo Issledovanija — Probl Metodol Ist-Filos Issled
Problemy Mira i Sotsializma — Problemy Mira Sots
Problemy na Farmatsiyata — Probl Farm
Problemy na Tekhnicheskata Kibernetika — Probl Tekh Kibern
Problemy na Tekhnicheskata Kibernetika i Robotikata — Probl Tekh Kibern na Robotikata
Problemy Narodonaselenija i Trudovyh Resursov — Probl Narodonas Trud Resursov
Problemy Naucnogo Kommunizma (Leningrad) — Probl Nauc Kommunizma (Leningrad)
Problemy Naucnogo Kommunizma (Moskva) — Probl Nauc Kommunizma (Moskva)
Problemy Naucnogo Upravlenija Social'nymi Processami — Probl Nauc Uprav Soc Processami
Problemy Neftegazonosnosti Tadzhikistana — Probl Neftegazonosn Tadzh
Problemy Nefti i Gaza Tyumeni — Probl Nefti Gaza Tyumeni
Problemy Neirokhimii — Probl Neirokhim
Problemy Neirokhirurgii — Probl Neirokhir
Problemy Neirokhirurgii (1955-1963) — Probl Neirokhir (1955-1963)
Problemy Neirokhirurgii Respublikanskii Mezhvedomstvenhyi Sbornik — Probl Neirokhir Resp Mezhved Sb
Problemy Neirokibernetiki — Probl Neirokibern
Problemy Nevrologii Respublikanskii Mezhvedomstvennyi Sbornik — Probl Nevrol Resp Mezhved Sb
Problemy Obogashcheniya Tverdykh Goryuchikh Iskopaemykh — Probl Obogashch Tverd Goryuch Iskop
Problemy Obshchei i Molekulyarnoi Biologii — Probl Obshch Mol Biol
Problemy Okhrany i Ispol'zovaniya Vod — Probl Okhr Ispolz Vod
Problemy Okhrany Vod — Probl Okh Vod
Problemy Organizacji — Probl Organ
Problemy Ornitologii. Trudy Vsesoyuznoi Ornitologicheskoi Konferentsii — Probl Ornitol Tr Vses Ornitol Konf
Problemy Ortopedicheskoi Stomatologii — Probl Ortop Stomatol
Problemy Osadochnogo Rudoobrazovaniya — Probl Osad Rudoobraz
Problemy Osadochnoy Geologii Dokembriya — Probl Osad Geol Dokembr
Problemy Osobo Opasnykh Infektsii — Probl Osobo Opasnykh Infekts
Problemy Osvoeniya Pustyn — POSPB
Problemy Osvoeniya Pustyn — Probl Osvo Pustyn
Problemy Osvoeniya Pustyn — Probl Osvoeniya Pustyn
Problemy Parazitologii — Probl Parazitol
Problemy Parazitologii. Materialy Nauchnoi Konferentsii Parazitologov Ukrainskoi SSR — Probl Parazitol Mater Nauchn Konf Parazitol Ukr SSR
Problemy Parazitologii. Trudy Nauchnoi Konferentsii Parazitologov Ukrainskoi SSR — Probl Parazitol Tr Nauchn Konf Parazitol Ukr SSR
Problemy Parazitologii v Pribaltike. Materialy Nauchno-Koordinatsionnoi Konferentsii po Problemam Parazitologii v Pribaltiiskikh Respublikakh — Probl Parazitol Pribaltike Mater Nauchno Koord Konf
Problemy Parenteral'nogo Pitaniya. Materialy Soveshchaniya po Parenteral'nomu Pitaniyu — Probl Parenter Pitan Mater Soveshch
Problemy Pediatrii — Probl Pediatr
Problemy Peredachi Informatsii — Probl Pereda Inf
Problemy Peredachi Informatsii — Probl Peredachi Inf
Problemy Peredachi Informatsii — Problemy Pered Inf
Problemy Pererabotki Vysokosernistykh Neftei. Materialy Otraslevoi Konferentsii po Pererabotke Vysokosernistykh Neftei — Probl Pererab Vysokosernistykh Neftei Mater Otrasl Konf
Problemy Poles'ya — Probl Polesya
Problemy Prawa Karnego (Katowice) — Probl Prawa Karnego (Katowice)
Problemy Prikladnoi Geokhimii. Materialy Mezhdunarodnogo Simpoziuma Metody Prikladnoi Geokhimii — Probl Prikl Geokhim Mater Mezhdunar Simp Metody Prikl Geokhim
Problemy Prochnosti — Probl Prochn
Problemy Prochnosti v Mashinostroenii — PPMMA
Problemy Prochnosti v Mashinostroenii [*Former USSR*] — Probl Proch Mashinostr
Problemy Prochnosti v Mashinostroenii — Probl Prochn Mashinostr
Problemy Projectowa — Probl Proj
Problemy Projektowe Hutnictwa i Przemyslu Maszynowego — PPHPB
Problemy Razrabotki Poleznykh Iskopaemykh — Probl Razrab Polezn Iskop
Problemy Razvitiya Metallurgicheskoi Promyshlennosti — Probl Razvit Metall Promsti
Problemy Rudnichnoi Aerologii — Probl Rudn Aerol
Problemy Sel'skogo Khozyaistva Priamur'ya — Probl Selsk Khoz Priamurya
Problemy Severa — Probl Ser
Problemy Severa — Probl Sev
Problemy Severnogo Khozyaistva — Probl Sev Khoz
Problemy Severnogo Rastenievodstva — Probl Sev Rastenievod
Problemy Social'nogo Prognozirovanija — Probl Soc Prognoz
Problemy Social'noj Aktivnosti — Probl Soc Aktivnosti
Problemy Sotsialnoi Gigieny i Istoriia Meditsiny — Probl Sotsialnoi Gig Istor Med
Problemy Sovetskogo Gosudarstva i Prava — Probl Sov Gos Prava
Problemy Sovetskoi Geologii [*Former USSR*] — Probl Sov Geol
Problemy Sovremennmoi Teorii Elementarnykh Chastits — Probl Sovrem Teor Elem Chastits
Problemy Sovremennoi Analiticheskoi Khimii — Probl Sovrem Anal Khim
Problemy Sovremennoi Khimicheskoi Tekhnologii — Probl Sovrem Khim Tekhnol
Problemy Sovremennoi Khimii Koordinatsionnykh Soedinenii [*Former USSR*] — Probl Sovrem Khim Koord Soedin
Problemy Sovremennoi Yadernoi Fiziki. Sbornik Dokladov na Problemnom Simpoziume po Fizike Yadra — Probl Sovrem Yad Fiz Sb Dokl Probl Simp Fiz Yadra
Problemy Sovremennoj Khimii Koordinatsionnykh Soedinenij Leningradskij Gosudarstvennyj Universitet — Probl Sovrem Khim Koord Soedin Leningr Gos Univ
Problemy Spetsial'noi Elektrometallurgii — Probl Spets Elektrometall
Problemy Stratigrafii Rannego Dokembriya Srednei Sibiri — Probl Stratigr Rannego Dokembr Sredn Sib
Problemy Techniki w Medycynie — Probl Tech Med
Problemy Tekhnicheskoi Elektrodinamiki — Probl Tekh Elektrodin
Problemy Teorii Gravitacii i Elementarnyh Castic — Problemy Teor Gravitacii i Element Castic
Problemy Teorii Gravitatsii i Elementarnykh Chastits [*Former USSR*] — Probl Teor Gravitatsii Elem Chastits
Problemy Teorii Plazmy. Trudy Mezhdunarodnoi Konferentsii po Teorii Plazmy — Probl Teor Plazmy Tr Mezhdunar Konf
Problemy Teploenergetiki i Prikladnoi Teplofiziki [*Former USSR*] — Probl Teploenerg Prikl Teplofiz
Problemy Terapeuticheskoi Stomatologii — Probl Ter Stomatol
Problemy Tovarovedeniya Pishchevykh Produktov i Obshchestvennogo Pitaniya — Probl Tovaroved Pishch Prod Obshchestv Pitan
Problemy Treniya i Iznashivaniya — Probl Treniya Iznashivaniya
Problemy Tuberkuleza — Probl Tub
Problemy Tuberkuleza — Probl Tuberk
Problemy Tuberkuleza — PRTUA
Problemy Vazhneishikh Infektsionnykh Zabolevanii — Probl Vazhneishikh Infekts Zabol
Problemy Venerologii i Dermatologii (Minsk) — Probl Venerol Dermatol (Minsk)
Problemy Veterinarnoi Immunologii — Probl Vet Immunol
Problemy Vostokovedeniia — Prob Vostok
Problemy Vostokovedenija — PV
Problemy Yadernoi Fiziki i Kosmicheskikh Luchei — PIFLD
Problemy Yadernoi Fiziki i Kosmicheskikh Luchei — Problemy Yadern Fiz i Kosm Luchei
Problemy Yadernoi Geofiziki — Probl Yad Geofiz
Problemy Yadernoj Fiziki i Kosmicheskikh Luchej — Probl Yad Fiz Kosm Luchej
Problemy Zhivotnovodstva — Probl Zhivotnovod
Procedimiento. Conferencia Internacional de Pesquisas en Cacao — Procedimiento Conf Int Pesqui Cacao
Procedure. National Microfilm Association — Proc NMFA
Proceeding. Society of Soil and Plant Diagnosticians — Proc Soc Soil Diagn
Proceedings. 31st Annual Blueberry Open House — Proc 31 A Blueberry Open House
Proceedings. 1980 British Crop Protection Conference. Weeds — Proc Br Crop Prot Conf
Proceedings. Academy of Management — Proc Acad Man
Proceedings. Academy of Natural Sciences of Philadelphia — P Ac Nat S
Proceedings. Academy of Natural Sciences of Philadelphia — Proc Acad Nat Sci Phil
Proceedings. Academy of Natural Sciences of Philadelphia — Proc Acad Nat Sci Phila
Proceedings. Academy of Natural Sciences of Philadelphia — Proc Acad Nat Sci Philadelphia
Proceedings. Academy of Natural Sciences of Philadelphia — Proc Acad Natur Sci Phil

Proceedings. Academy of Political Science — P Ac Poli S
Proceedings. Academy of Political Science — Proc Acad Pol Sci
Proceedings. Academy of Political Science — Proc Acad Polit Sci
Proceedings. Academy of Political Science (USA) — Pro Acad Pol Sci (USA)
Proceedings. Academy of Science. North Dakota — Proc Acad Sci ND
Proceedings. Academy of Science. USSR. Section. Biochemistry — Proc Acad Sci USSR Sect Biochem
Proceedings. Academy of Sciences. Georgian SSR. Biological Series — Proc Acad Sci Georgian SSR Biol Ser
Proceedings. Academy of Sciences of Amsterdam — Proc Acad Sci Amsterdam
Proceedings. Academy of Sciences of Georgia. Biological Series — Proc Acad Sci Georgia Biol Ser
Proceedings. Academy of Sciences of the Armenian SSR — Proc Acad Sci Armenian SSR
Proceedings. Academy of Sciences of the Georgian SSR. Biological Series — IGSBDO
Proceedings. Academy of Sciences of the USSR. Geochemistry Section — Proc Acad Sci USSR Geochem Sect
Proceedings. Academy of Sciences of the USSR. Section Agrochemistry — Proc Acad Sci USSR Sect Agrochem
Proceedings. Academy of Sciences of the USSR. Section Applied Physics — Proc Acad Sci USSR Sect Appl Phys
Proceedings. Academy of Sciences. Turkmen SSR. Series of Biological Sciences — Proc Acad Sci Turkmen SSR Ser Biol Sci
Proceedings. Academy of Sciences. Turkmen SSR. Series of Physico-Technical, Chemical, and Geological Sciences — Proc Acad Sci Turk SSR Ser Phys Tech Chem Geol Sci
Proceedings. Academy of Sciences. Turkmenistan. Series of Biological Sciences — Proc Acad Sci Turkm Ser Biol Sci
Proceedings. Academy of Sciences. United Provinces of Agra and Oudh India — Proc Acad Sci United Prov Agra Oudh India
Proceedings. Academy of Sciences. USSR. Botanical Sciences Section — Proc Acad Sci USSR Bot Sci Sect
Proceedings. Academy of Sciences. USSR. Chemical Technology Section — Proc Acad Sci USSR Chem Technol Sect
Proceedings. Academy of Sciences. USSR. Chemistry Section — Proc Acad Sci USSR Chem Sect
Proceedings. Academy of Sciences. USSR. Geological Sciences Sections — Proc Acad Sci USSR Geol Sci Sect
Proceedings. Advanced Summer Study Institute — Proc Adv Summer Study Inst
Proceedings. Advanced Technology Conference — Proc Adv Technol Conf
Proceedings. AEC Air Cleaning Conference — Proc AEC Air Clean Conf
Proceedings. African Classical Association — PACA
Proceedings. African Classical Association — Proc Afr Classical Assoc
Proceedings. African Classical Associations — Proc Afr Cl Ass
Proceedings. African Weed Control Conference — Proc Afr Weed Control Conf
Proceedings. Agassiz Institute (Sacramento, CA) — Proc Agassiz Inst Sacramento
Proceedings. Agricultural Experiment Station (Palestine) — Proc Agric Exp Stn (Palest)
Proceedings. Agricultural Outlook Conference — Proc Agr Outlook Conf
Proceedings. Agricultural Pesticide Society — Proc Agric Pestic Soc
Proceedings. Agricultural Pesticide Technical Society — Proc Agr Pestic Tech Soc
Proceedings. Agricultural Pesticide Technical Society — Proc Agric Pestic Tech Soc
Proceedings. Agricultural Society of Trinidad and Tobago — Proc Agric Soc Trin Tob
Proceedings. Agricultural Society (Trinidad and Tobago) — Proc Agric Soc (Trinidad Tobago)
Proceedings. Agronomy Society of New Zealand — Proc Agron Soc NZ
Proceedings. Air and Waste Management Association. Annual Meeting — Proc Air Waste Manage Assoc Annu Meet
Proceedings. Air Pollution Control Association — Proc Air Pollut Contr Ass
Proceedings. Air Pollution Control Association — Proc Air Pollut Control Assoc
Proceedings. Alaska Science Conference — Proc Alaska Sci Conf
Proceedings. Alaskan Science Conference — Proc Alaskan Sci Conf
Proceedings. Alberta Sulphur Gas Research Workshop — Proc Alberta Sulphur Gas Res Workshop
Proceedings. Alfred Benzon Symposium — Proc Alfred Benzon Symp
Proceedings. All Pakistan Science Conference — Proc All Pak Sci Conf
Proceedings. All-Union Conference on Radiation Chemistry — Proc All Union Conf Radiat Chem
Proceedings. All-Union Neurochemical Conference — Proc All Union Neurochem Conf
Proceedings. Alumni Association (Malaya) — Proc Alumni Assoc (Malaya)
Proceedings. American Academy and Institute of Arts and Letters — P Am Ac Ins
Proceedings. American Academy for Jewish Research — PAAJR
Proceedings. American Academy for Jewish Research — Proc Amer Acad Jew Res
Proceedings. American Academy of Arts and Sciences — P Amer Ac
Proceedings. American Academy of Arts and Sciences — PAAAS
Proceedings. American Academy of Arts and Sciences — Proc Am Acad
Proceedings. American Academy of Arts and Sciences — Proc Am Acad Arts Sci
Proceedings. American Academy of Arts and Sciences — Proc Amer Ac Arts
Proceedings. American Academy of Arts and Sciences — Proc Amer Acad Arts Sci
Proceedings. American Academy of Arts and Sciences — ProcAmAcAS
Proceedings. American Antiquarian Society — P Am Antiq
Proceedings. American Antiquarian Society — PAAS
Proceedings. American Antiquarian Society — Proc Am Ant Soc
Proceedings. American Antiquarian Society — Proc Am Antiq Soc
Proceedings. American Association for Cancer Research — P Am Ass Ca
Proceedings. American Association for Cancer Research — Proc Am Ass Can Res
Proceedings. American Association for Cancer Research — Proc Am Assoc Cancer Res
Proceedings. American Association for Cancer Research and American Society of Clinical Oncology — PAAOD8
Proceedings. American Association for Cancer Research and American Society of Clinical Oncology — Proc Am Assoc Cancer Res Am Soc Clin Oncol
Proceedings. American Association for Cancer Research. Annual Meeting — PAMREA
Proceedings. American Association for Cancer Research. Annual Meeting — Proc Am Assoc Cancer Res Annu Meet
Proceedings. American Association for the Advancement of Science — ProcAAAS
Proceedings. American Association of Economic Entomologists. North Central States Branch — Proc Am Assoc Econ Entomol North Cent States Branch
Proceedings. American Association of State Highway Officials — Proc Am Assoc State Highw Off
Proceedings. American Association of State Highway Officials — Proc Amer Ass State Highw Offic
Proceedings. American Catholic Philosophical Association — P Am Cath P
Proceedings. American Catholic Philosophical Association — PACPA
Proceedings. American Catholic Philosophical Association — PACPhA
Proceedings. American Catholic Philosophical Association — Proc Amer Cath Phil Assoc
Proceedings. American Catholic Philosophical Association — Proc Cath Phil Ass
Proceedings. American Chemical Society Symposium on Analytical Calorimetry — Proc Am Chem Soc Symp Anal Calorim
Proceedings. American Concrete Institute — Proc Am Concr Inst
Proceedings. American Congress on Surveying and Mapping — Proc Am Congr Surv Mapp
Proceedings. American Cotton Congress — Proc Am Cotton Congr
Proceedings. American Cranberry Growers' Association — Proc Am Cranberry Grow Assoc
Proceedings. American Cranberry Growers' Association — Proc Am Cranberry Growers' Ass
Proceedings. American Diabetes Association — Proc Am Diabetes Assoc
Proceedings. American Documentation Institute — Proc Am Doc Inst
Proceedings. American Drug Manufacturers Association. Annual Meeting — Proc Am Drug Manuf Assoc Annu Meet
Proceedings. American Ethnological Society — Proc Amer Ethnol Soc
Proceedings. American Feed Manufacturers Association. Nutrition Council — Proc Am Feed Manuf Assoc Nutr Counc
Proceedings. American Gas Institute — Pro Am Gas Inst
Proceedings. American Gas Institute — Proc Am Gas Inst
Proceedings. American Horticultural Congress — Proc Am Hortic Congr
Proceedings. American Institute of Electrical Engineers — Proc Am Inst Electr Eng
Proceedings. American Mathematical Society — P Am Math S
Proceedings. American Mathematical Society — PAMS
Proceedings. American Mathematical Society — PAMYA
Proceedings. American Mathematical Society — Proc Am Math Soc
Proceedings. American Mathematical Society — Proc Amer Math Soc
Proceedings. American Microscopical Society — Proc Amer Microscop Soc
Proceedings. American Oriental Society — PAOS
Proceedings. American Oriental Society [*Baltimore, MD*] — ProAOS
Proceedings. American Peanut Research and Education Association — Proc Am Peanut Res Educ Assoc
Proceedings. American Peanut Research and Education Society — Proc Am Peanut Res Educ Soc
Proceedings. American Peony Society — Proc Amer Peony Soc
Proceedings. American Peptide Symposium — Proc Am Pept Symp
Proceedings. American Petroleum Institute. Division of Refining — Proc Am Pet Inst Div Refining
Proceedings. American Petroleum Institute. Refining Department — Proc Am Pet Inst Refin Dep
Proceedings. American Petroleum Institute. Section 1 — Proc Am Pet Inst Sect 1
Proceedings. American Petroleum Institute. Section 2. Marketing — Proc Am Pet Inst Sect 2
Proceedings. American Petroleum Institute. Section 3. Refining — Proc Am Pet Inst Sect 3
Proceedings. American Petroleum Institute. Section 3. Refining — Proc Am Pet Inst Sect 3 Refining
Proceedings. American Petroleum Institute. Section 4. Production — Proc Am Pet Inst Sect 4
Proceedings. American Petroleum Institute. Section 5. Transportation — Proc Am Pet Inst Sect 5
Proceedings. American Petroleum Institute. Section 6. Interdivisional — Proc Am Pet Inst Sect 6
Proceedings. American Petroleum Institute. Section 8. Science and Technology [*A publication*] — Proc Am Pet Inst Sect 8
Proceedings. American Pharmaceutical Manufacturers' Association. Annual Meeting — Proc Am Pharm Manuf Assoc Annu Meet
Proceedings. American Pharmaceutical Manufacturers' Association. Midyear Eastern Section Meeting — Proc Am Pharm Manuf Assoc Midyear East Sect Meet
Proceedings. American Philological Association — PAPA
Proceedings. American Philological Association — PrAPhA
Proceedings. American Philological Association — Proc Phil As
Proceedings. American Philosophical Society — APS/P
Proceedings. American Philosophical Society — P Am Phil S
Proceedings. American Philosophical Society — PAPhilosS

Proceedings. American Philosophical Society — PAPhS
Proceedings. American Philosophical Society — PAPS
Proceedings. American Philosophical Society — ProA
Proceedings. American Philosophical Society — Proc Am Phil Soc
Proceedings. American Philosophical Society — Proc Am Philos Soc
Proceedings. American Philosophical Society — Proc Amer Phil Soc
Proceedings. American Philosophical Society — Proc Amer Philos Soc
Proceedings. American Philosophical Society — Proc Amer Philosophical Soc
Proceedings. American Philosophical Society — Proc Phil Soc
Proceedings. American Philosophical Society (Philadelphia) — PAPSP
Proceedings. American Phytopathological Society — Proc Am Phytopathol Soc
Proceedings. American Power Conference — Proc Am Power Conf
Proceedings. American Power Conference — Proc Amer Power Conf
Proceedings. American Railway Engineering Association — Proc Am Railw Eng Assoc
Proceedings. American Scientific Congress — Proc Am Sci Congr
Proceedings. American Seed Trade Association — Proc Amer Seed Trade Assoc
Proceedings. American Society for Horticultural Science — Proc Am Soc Hort Sci
Proceedings. American Society for Horticultural Science — Proc Am Soc Hortic Sci
Proceedings. American Society for Horticultural Science — Proc Amer Soc Hort Sci
Proceedings. American Society for Horticultural Science. Tropical Region — Proc Am Soc Hortic Sci Trop Reg
Proceedings. American Society for Information Science — P Am S Info
Proceedings. American Society for Information Science — Proc Am Soc Inf Sci
Proceedings. American Society for Testing and Materials — Proc Am Soc Test & Mater
Proceedings. American Society for Testing and Materials — Proc Amer Soc Testing Materials
Proceedings. American Society for Testing and Materials — Proc ASTM
Proceedings. American Society of Animal Production. Western Section — Proc Amer Soc Anim Pro W Sect
Proceedings. American Society of Animal Science. Western Section — Proc Amer Soc Anim Sci W Sect
Proceedings. American Society of Bakery Engineers — Proc Amer Soc Bakery Eng
Proceedings. American Society of Brewing Chemists — Proc Am Soc Brew Chem
Proceedings. American Society of Brewing Chemists — Proc Amer Soc Brew Chem
Proceedings. American Society of Civil Engineers — Proc Am Soc Civ Eng
Proceedings. American Society of Civil Engineers. Transportation Engineering Journal — Proc Am Soc Civ Eng Transp Eng J
Proceedings. American Society of Clinical Oncology. Annual Meeting — PMAODO
Proceedings. American Society of Clinical Oncology. Annual Meeting — Proc Am Soc Clin Oncol Annu Meet
Proceedings. American Society of Enologists — Proc Am Soc Enol
Proceedings. American Society of International Law — ASIL Proc
Proceedings. American Society of Sugar Beet — Proc Am Soc Sugar Beet
Proceedings. American Society of Therapeutic Radiologists' Annual Meeting — Proc Am Soc Ther Radiol Annu Meet
Proceedings. American Society of University Composers — PR
Proceedings. American Society of University Composers — Proc Amer Soc U Composers
Proceedings. American Soybean Association — Proc Amer Soybean Assoc
Proceedings. American Veterinary Medical Association — Proc Am Vet Med Ass
Proceedings. American Veterinary Medical Association — Proc Am Vet Med Assoc
Proceedings. American Water Works Association — Proc Am Water Works Assoc
Proceedings. American Water Works Association Annual Conference — Proc Am Water Works Assoc Annu Conf
Proceedings. American Welding Society — Proc Am Weld Soc
Proceedings. American Wood-Preservers' Association — Proc Am Wood-Preserv Assoc
Proceedings. American Wood-Preservers' Association — Proc Amer Wood-Preserv Ass
Proceedings. Analytical Division. Chemical Society — PADSD
Proceedings. Analytical Division. Chemical Society — Proc Anal Div Chem Soc
Proceedings and Abstracts. Society of Biological Chemists (Bangalore) — Proc Abstr Soc Biol Chem (Bangalore)
Proceedings and Addresses. American Philosophical Association — Proc Amer Phil Ass
Proceedings and Addresses. Pennsylvania-German Society — Proc PA Ger Soc
Proceedings and Discussions. International Plastics Congress — Proc Discuss Int Plast Congr
Proceedings and Information. Committee for Hydrological Research, CHO-TNO [*Toegepast Natuurwetenschappelijk Onderzoek. Commissie Voor Hydrologisch Onderzoek*] — Proc Inf Comm Hydrol Res CHO TNO
Proceedings and Minutes. Annual Meeting of the Agricultural Research Institute — Proc Minutes Ann Meet Agric Res Inst
Proceedings and News. Australian Oil and Colour Chemists Association — Proc News Aust Oil Colour Chem Assoc
Proceedings and News. Australian Oil and Colour Chemists Association — Proc News Aust Oil Colour Chemists Assoc
Proceedings and Papers. Annual Conference. California Mosquito and Vector Control Association — Proc Pap Annu Conf Calif Mosq Vector Control Assoc
Proceedings and Papers. Annual Conference. California Mosquito Control Association — Proc Pap Annu Conf Calif Mosq Control Assoc
Proceedings and Papers. Graphic Arts Conference — Proc Pap Graphic Arts Conf
Proceedings and Papers. International Union for the Conservation of Nature and Natural Resources — Proc Pap Int Union Conserv Nature Nat Resour
Proceedings and Report. Ashmolean Natural History Society of Oxfordshire — Proc Rep Ashmolean Nat Hist Soc Oxfordshire
Proceedings and Reports. Belfast Natural History and Philosophical Society — Proc Rep Belfast Nat Hist Philos Soc
Proceedings and Reports. Southern Seedmen's Association — Proc Rep S Seedmen's Ass
Proceedings and Technical Papers. General Fisheries Council for the Mediterranean — Proc Tech Pap Gen Fish Counc Mediterr
Proceedings and Transactions. All India Oriental Conference — PAIOC
Proceedings and Transactions. All-India Oriental Conferences — PTAIOC
Proceedings and Transactions. British Entomological and Natural History Society — Proc Trans Br Entomol Nat Hist Soc
Proceedings and Transactions. Croydon Natural History and Scientific Society — Proc Trans Croydon Natur Hist Sci Soc
Proceedings and Transactions. Liverpool Biological Society — Proc and Tr Liverpool Biol Soc
Proceedings and Transactions. Liverpool Biological Society — Proc Trans Liverp Biol Soc
Proceedings and Transactions. Nova Scotian Institute of Science — Proc Trans Nova Scotian Inst Sci
Proceedings and Transactions. Nova Scotian Institute of Science — Proc Trans NS Inst Sci
Proceedings and Transactions of Texas Academy of Science — Proc Trans Tex Acad Sci
Proceedings and Transactions. Rhodesia Scientific Association — Proc and Trans Rhod Sci Assoc
Proceedings and Transactions. Rhodesia Scientific Association — Proc Trans Rhod Sci Assoc
Proceedings and Transactions. Royal Society of Canada — Proc Trans R Soc Can
Proceedings and Transactions. Royal Society of Canada — Proc Trans Roy Soc Canada
Proceedings and Transactions. Royal Society of Canada — PTRSC
Proceedings. Animal Care Panel — Proc Anim Care Panel
Proceedings. Animal Sciences. Indian Academy of Sciences — Proc Anim Sci Indian Acad Sci
Proceedings. Anniversary Conference. SPI Reinforced Plastics/Composites Division — Proc Anniv Conf SPI Reinf Plast Compos Div
Proceedings. Anniversary Technical Conference. SPI Reinforced Plastics Division — Proc Anniv Tech Conf SPI Reinf Plast Div
Proceedings. Annual A. N. Richards Symposium — Proc Annu A N Richards Symp
Proceedings. Annual AIChE [*American Institute of Chemical Engineers*] **Southwestern Ohio Conference on Energy and the Environment** — Proc Annu AIChE Southwest Ohio Conf Energy Environ
Proceedings. Annual Air Pollution Control Conference — Proc Annu Air Pollut Control Conf
Proceedings. Annual Alberta Soil Science Workshop — Proc Annu Alberta Soil Sci Workshop
Proceedings. Annual Allerton Conference on Circuit and System Theory [*Later, Proceedings. Annual Allerton Conference on Communication, Control, and Computing*] — Proc Annu Allerton Conf Circuit Syst Theory
Proceedings. Annual Allerton Conference on Communication, Control, and Computing — PCCCD
Proceedings. Annual Allerton Conference on Communication, Control, and Computing [*Annual Allerton Conference on Circuit and System Theory*] [*United States*] [*Formerly,*] — Proc Annu Allerton Conf Commun Control Comput
Proceedings. Annual American Water Resources Conference — Proc Annu Am Water Resour Conf
Proceedings. Annual Appalachian Underground Corrosion Short Course — Proc Annu Appalachian Underground Corros Short Course
Proceedings. Annual Arkansas Water Works and Pollution Control Conference and Short School — Proc Annu Arkansas Water Works Pollut Control Conf Short Sch
Proceedings. Annual ASME Symposium. New Mexico Section — Proc Annu ASME Symp NM Sect
Proceedings. Annual Battery Conference on Applications and Advances — Proc Annu Battery Conf Appl Adv
Proceedings. Annual Battery Research and Development Conference — Proc Annu Battery Res Dev Conf
Proceedings. Annual Biochemical Engineering Symposium [*United States*] — Proc Annu Biochem Eng Symp
Proceedings. Annual Biology Colloquium — Proc A Biol Colloq
Proceedings. Annual Biology Colloquium (Oregon State University) — Proc Annu Biol Colloq (Oreg State Univ)
Proceedings. Annual Biomedical Sciences Instrumentation Symposium — Proc Annu Biomed Sci Instrum Symp
Proceedings. Annual Blueberry Open House — Proc Annu Blueberry Open House
Proceedings. Annual California Weed Conference — Proc Annu Calif Weed Conf
Proceedings. Annual Clinical Spinal Cord Injury Conference — Proc Annu Cli Spinal Cord Inj Conf
Proceedings. Annual Conference. Agronomy Society of New Zealand — Proc Annu Conf Agron Soc NZ
Proceedings. Annual Conference. American Water Works Association — Proc Annu Conf Am Water Works Assoc
Proceedings. Annual Conference and International Symposium. North American Lake Management Society — Proc Annu Conf Int Symp N Am Lake Manage Soc
Proceedings. Annual Conference and International Symposium of the North American Lake Management Society — PAISER
Proceedings. Annual Conference. Association for Computing Machinery — Proc Annu Conf Assoc Comput Mach

Proceedings. Annual Conference. Australasian Institute of Metals — Proc Annu Conf Australas Inst Met
Proceedings. Annual Conference. British Columbia Water and Waste Association — Proc Annu Conf BC Water Waste Assoc
Proceedings. Annual Conference. Canadian Nuclear Association — Proc Annu Conf Can Nucl Assoc
Proceedings. Annual Conference. Canadian Society for the Study of Education and Cooperating Associations — Proc Annu Conf Can Soc Stud Educ Coop Assoc
Proceedings. Annual Conference. Maryland-Delaware Water and Sewage Association — Proc Annu Conf MD Del Water Sewage Assoc
Proceedings. Annual Conference. Microbeam Analysis Society — Proc Annu Conf Microbeam Anal Soc
Proceedings. Annual Conference. Nigerian Society for Animal Production Symposium on Drought — Proc Annu Conf Niger Soc Anim Prod
Proceedings. Annual Conference. Nutrition Society of New Zealand — Proc Annu Conf Nutr Soc NZ
Proceedings. Annual Conference of Alcoholism — Proc Annu Conf Alcohol
Proceedings. Annual Conference of Canadian Technical Asphalt Association — Proc Annu Conf Can Tech Asphalt Assoc
Proceedings. Annual Conference of Manitoba Agronomists — Proc Annu Conf Manitoba Agron
Proceedings. Annual Conference on Activated Sludge Process Control — Proc Annu Conf Act Sludge Process Control
Proceedings. Annual Conference on Automatic Control in the Petroleum and Chemical Industries — Proc Annu Conf Autom Control Pet Chem Ind
Proceedings. Annual Conference on Biological Sonar and Diving Mammals — Proc Annu Conf Biol Sonar Diving Mamm
Proceedings. Annual Conference on Biological Sonar and Diving Mammals — Proc Annu Conf Biol Sonar Diving Mammals
Proceedings. Annual Conference on Effects of Lithium Doping on Silicon Solar Cells — Proc Annu Conf Eff Lithium Doping Silicon Sol Cells
Proceedings. Annual Conference on Energy Conversion and Storage — Proc Annu Conf Energy Convers Storage
Proceedings. Annual Conference on Engineering in Medicine and Biology — Proc Annu Conf Eng Med Biol
Proceedings. Annual Conference on Environmental Chemicals. Human and Animal Health — Proc Annu Conf Environ Chem Hum Anim Health
Proceedings. Annual Conference on Environmental Toxicology — Proc Annu Conf Environ Toxicol
Proceedings. Annual Conference on High Energy Nuclear Physics — Proc Ann Conf High En Nucl Phys
Proceedings. Annual Conference on Industrial Applications of X-Ray Analysis [*A publication*] — Proc Annu Conf Ind Appl X Ray Anal
Proceedings. Annual Conference on Rehabilitation Engineering — Proc Ann Conf Rehab Eng
Proceedings. Annual Conference on Research in Medical Education — Proc Annu Conf Res Med Educ
Proceedings. Annual Conference on Restoration of Coastal Vegetation in Florida — PACFDP
Proceedings. Annual Conference on Restoration of Coastal Vegetation in Florida — Proc Annu Conf Restor Coastal Veg Fla
Proceedings. Annual Conference on the Administration of Research — Proc Annu Conf Adm Res
Proceedings. Annual Conference on the Kidney — Proc Annu Conf Kidney
Proceedings. Annual Conference. Reinforced Plastics/Composites Institute. Society of the Plastics Industry — Proc Annu Conf Reinf Plast Compos Inst Soc Plast Ind
Proceedings. Annual Conference. Society of Vacuum Coaters — Proc Annu Conf Soc Vac Coaters
Proceedings. Annual Conference. Southeastern Association of Fish and Wildlife Agencies — Proc Annu Conf Southeast Assoc Fish Wildl Agencies
Proceedings. Annual Conference. Southeastern Association of Fish and Wildlife Agencies — PSFADF
Proceedings. Annual Conference. Southeastern Association of Game and Fish Commissioners — Proc Annu Conf Southeast Assoc Game Fish Comm
Proceedings. Annual Conference. Steel Castings Research and Trade Association — Proc Annu Conf Steel Cast Res Trade Assoc
Proceedings. Annual Conference. Steel Castings Research and Trade Association. Steel Foundry Practice — Proc Annu Conf Steel Cast Res Trade Assoc St Found Prac
Proceedings. Annual Conference. Texas Pecan Growers Association — Proc Annu Conf Tex Pecan Grow Assoc
Proceedings. Annual Conference. United States Public Health Service with the State and Territorial Health Officers — Proc Annu Conf US Public Health Serv State Territ Health Off
Proceedings. Annual Congress. South African Sugar Technologists Association — Proc Annu Congr S Afr Sugar Technol Assoc
Proceedings. Annual Connector Symposium — Proc Annu Connector Symp
Proceedings. Annual Convention. American Association of Equine Practitioners — Proc Annu Conv Am Assoc Equine Pract
Proceedings. Annual Convention. American Cranberry Growers' Association — Proc A Conv Am Cranberry Growers' Ass
Proceedings. Annual Convention. American Railway Engineering Association — Proc Annu Conv Am Railw Eng Assoc
Proceedings. Annual Convention and Journal. Oil Technologists' Association — Proc Annu Conv J Oil Technol Assoc
Proceedings. Annual Convention and Scientific Program. Society of Biological Psychiatry — Proc Annu Conv Sci Program Soc Biol Psychiatry
Proceedings. Annual Convention Association. American Pesticide Control Officials — Proc Annu Conv Assoc Am Pestic Control Off
Proceedings. Annual Convention. Flavoring Extract Manufacturers' Association of the United States — Proc Annu Conv Flavoring Ext Manuf Assoc US
Proceedings. Annual Convention. Gas Processors Association. Meeting Papers — Proc Annu Conv Gas Process Assoc Meet Pap
Proceedings. Annual Convention. Gas Processors Association. Technical Papers — Proc Annu Conv Gas Process Assoc Tech Pap
Proceedings. Annual Convention. Georgia-Florida Pecan Growers Association — Proc Annu Conv Ga Fla Pecan Grow Assoc
Proceedings. Annual Convention. Indonesian Petroleum Association — Proc Annu Conv Indones Pet Assoc
Proceedings. Annual Convention. Magnesium Association — Proc Annu Conv Magnesium Assoc
Proceedings. Annual Convention. Milk Industry Foundation — Proc Annu Conv Milk Ind Found
Proceedings. Annual Convention. Milk Industry Foundation. Laboratory Section — Proc Annu Conv Milk Ind Found Lab Sect
Proceedings. Annual Convention. Milk Industry Foundation. Plant Section — Proc Annu Conv Milk Ind Found Plant Sect
Proceedings. Annual Convention. National Fertilizer Association — Proc Annu Conv Natl Fert Assoc
Proceedings. Annual Convention. Natural Gas Processors Association. Technical Papers [*United States*] — Proc Annu Conv Nat Gas Process Assoc Tech Pap
Proceedings. Annual Convention. Natural Gas Processors Association. Technical Papers — Proc Annu Conv Natur Gas Process Ass Tech Pap
Proceedings. Annual Convention. Natural Gasoline Association of America. Technical Papers — Proc Annu Conv Nat Gasoline Assoc Am Tech Pap
Proceedings. Annual Convention. Oil Technologists Association — Proc Annu Conv Oil Technol Assoc
Proceedings. Annual Convention. Philippine Sugar Association — Proc Annu Conv Philipp Sugar Assoc
Proceedings. Annual Convention. Society of Leather Trades Chemists — Proc Annu Conv Soc Leather Trades Chem
Proceedings. Annual Convention. Southeastern Pecan Growers Association — Proc Annu Conv Southeast Pecan Grow Assoc
Proceedings. Annual Convention. Sugar Technologists' Association of India — Proc Annu Conv Sugar Technol Assoc India
Proceedings. Annual Convention. Western Canada Water and Sewage Conference (1960-1975) — Proc Annu Conv West Can Water Sewage Conf
Proceedings. Annual Convention. Western Canada Water and Wastewater Association — Proc Annu Conv West Can Water Wastewater Assoc
Proceedings. Annual Eastern Theoretical Physics Conference — Proc Annu East Theor Phys Conf
Proceedings. Annual Education Symposium. Instrument Society of America — Proc Annu Educ Symp Instrum Soc Am
Proceedings. Annual Electron Microscopy Colloquium — Proc Annu Electron Microsc Colloq
Proceedings. Annual Engineering Geology and Soils Engineering Symposium — Proc Annu Eng Geol Soils Eng Symp
Proceedings. Annual Engineering Geology Symposium — Proc Annu Eng Geol Symp
Proceedings. Annual Environmental and Water Resources Engineering Conference [*A publication*] — Proc Annu Environ Water Resour Eng Conf
Proceedings. Annual Fall Meeting. California Natural Gasoline Association — Proc Annu Fall Meet Calif Nat Gasoline Assoc
Proceedings. Annual Fall Meeting Sponsored by the American Physiological Society — Proc Annu Fall Meet Am Physiol Soc
Proceedings. Annual Fall Meeting. Western Gas Processors and Oil Refiners Association — Proc Annu Fall Meet West Gas Process Oil Refin Assoc
Proceedings. Annual Fall Meeting. Western Gas Processors and Oil Refiners Association — Proc Annu Fall Meet West Gas Process Oil Refiners Assoc
Proceedings. Annual Forest Vegetation Management Conference — Proc Annu For Veg Manage Conf
Proceedings. Annual Forestry Symposium. Louisiana State University. School of Forestry and Wildlife Management — Proc For Symp LA Sch For
Proceedings. Annual Frequency Control Symposium — Proc Annu Freq Control Symp
Proceedings. Annual Fuels from Biomass Symposium — Proc Annu Fuels Biomass Symp
Proceedings. Annual Gas Chromatography Institute — Proc Annu Gas Chromatogr Inst
Proceedings. Annual Gasification Projects Contractors Meeting — Proc Annu Gasif Proj Contract Meet
Proceedings. Annual General Meeting. International Institute of Synthetic Rubber Producers — Proc Annu Gen Meet Int Inst Synth Rubber Prod
Proceedings. Annual Glass Symposium — Proc Annu Glass Symp
Proceedings. Annual Hardwood Symposium. Hardwood Research Council — Proc Annu Hardwood Symp Hardwood Res Counc
Proceedings. Annual Highway Geology Symposium — Proc Annu Highw Geol Symp
Proceedings. Annual Holm Conference on Electrical Contacts — Proc Annu Holm Conf Electr Contacts
Proceedings. Annual Holm Seminar on Electrical Contacts — Proc Annu Holm Semin Electr Contacts
Proceedings. Annual Industrial Air Pollution Control Conference — Proc Annu Ind Air Pollut Control Conf
Proceedings. Annual Industrial Fabrics Association International Convention — Proc Annu Ind Fabr Assoc Int Conv
Proceedings. Annual Industrial Pollution Conference [*United States*] — Proc Annu Ind Pollut Conf
Proceedings. Annual Instrument Society of America Chemical and Petroleum Industries Division Symposium — Proc Annu Instrum Soc Am Chem Pet Ind Div Symp
Proceedings. Annual Instrumentation Conference — Proc Annu Instrum Conf
Proceedings. Annual International Conference. Canadian Nuclear Association — Proc Annu Int Conf Can Nucl Assoc

Proceedings. Annual International Conference of Plasma Chemistry and Technology — Proc Annu Int Conf Plasma Chem Technol
Proceedings. Annual International Conference on Fault-Tolerant Computing — Proc Annu Int Conf Fault Tolerant Comput
Proceedings. Annual International Conference on High Energy Physics — Proc Annu Int Conf High Energy Phys
Proceedings. Annual International Conference on Pollution Control in the Marine Industries — Proc Annu Int Conf Pollut Control Mar Ind
Proceedings. Annual International Game Fish Research Conference — Proc Annu Int Game Fish Res Conf
Proceedings. Annual ISA Analysis Division Symposium — Proc Annu ISA Anal Div Symp
Proceedings. Annual ISA Analysis Instrumentation Symposium — Proc Annu ISA Anal Instrum Symp
Proceedings. Annual Leucocyte Culture Conference — Proc Annu Leucocyte Cult Conf
Proceedings. Annual Maine Biomedical Symposium — Proc Annu Maine Biomed Symp
Proceedings. Annual Management Conference. American Dental Association — Proc Annu Manage Conf Am Dent Assoc
Proceedings. Annual Marine Coatings Conference — Proc Annu Mar Coat Conf
Proceedings. Annual Meat Science Institute — Proc Annu Meat Sci Inst
Proceedings. Annual Meeting. AFMA Nutrition Council — Proc Annu Meet AFMA Nutr Counc
Proceedings. Annual Meeting. Agricultural Research Institute — Proc Annu Meet Agric Res Inst
Proceedings. Annual Meeting. Air Pollution Control Association — Proc Annu Meet Air Pollut Control Assoc
Proceedings. Annual Meeting. American Association for the Study of Goiter — Proc Annu Meet Am Assoc Study Goiter
Proceedings. Annual Meeting. American Association of Feed Microscopists — Proc Annu Meet Am Assoc Feed Microsc
Proceedings. Annual Meeting. American Association of Swine Practitioners — Proc Annu Meet Am Assoc Swine Pract
Proceedings. Annual Meeting. American Association of Veterinary Laboratory Diagnosticians — Proc Annu Meet Am Assoc Vet Lab Diagn
Proceedings. Annual Meeting. American Carnation Society — Proc Annual Meeting Amer Carnation Soc
Proceedings. Annual Meeting. American College of Nutrition — Proc Annu Meet Am Coll Nutr
Proceedings. Annual Meeting. American College of Psychiatrists — Proc Annu Meet Am Coll Psychiatr
Proceedings. Annual Meeting. American Petroleum Institute — Proc Annu Meet Am Pet Inst
Proceedings. Annual Meeting. American Psychopathological Association — Proc Annu Meet Am Psychopathol Assoc
Proceedings. Annual Meeting. American Section. International Solar Energy Society — Proc Annu Meet Am Sect Int Sol Energy Soc
Proceedings. Annual Meeting. American Society for Horticultural Science. Caribbean Region — Proc Annu Meet Amer Soc Hort Sci Caribbean Reg
Proceedings. Annual Meeting. American Society for Horticulture Science. Tropical Region — Proc Annu Meet Am Soc Hortic Sci Trop Reg
Proceedings. Annual Meeting. American Society for Information Science — Proc Annu Meet Am Soc Inf Sci
Proceedings. Annual Meeting. American Society of Animal Production — Proc Am Soc Anim Prod
Proceedings. Annual Meeting. American Society of Animal Science. Western Section — Proc Annu Meet Am Soc Anim Sci West Sect
Proceedings. Annual Meeting. American Society of Bakery Engineers — Proc Annu Meet Am Soc Bak Eng
Proceedings. Annual Meeting. American Society of Bakery Engineers — Proc Annu Meet Am Soc Bakery Eng
Proceedings. Annual Meeting. American Society of International Law — Proc Annu Meeting Amer Soc Int Law
Proceedings. Annual Meeting. American Society of Plant Physiologists at the University of Maryland — Proc A Meet Pl Physiol Univ MD
Proceedings. Annual Meeting. American Solar Energy Society, Inc. — Proc Annu Meet Am Sol Energy Soc Inc
Proceedings. Annual Meeting. American Soybean Association — Proc Annu Meet Am Soybean Assoc
Proceedings. Annual Meeting. American Veterinary Medical Association — Proc Annu Meet Am Vet Med Assoc
Proceedings. Annual Meeting. American Wood-Preservers' Association — Proc Annu Meet Am Wood Preserv Assoc
Proceedings. Annual Meeting and Continuing Education Lectures — Proc Annu Meet Contin Educ Lect
Proceedings. Annual Meeting and Convention. National Microfilm Association — Proc Annu Meet Conv Natl Microfilm Assoc
Proceedings. Annual Meeting. Arkansas State Horticultural Society — Proc Annu Meet Arkansas State Hortic Soc
Proceedings. Annual Meeting. Canada Grains Council — Proc Annu Meet Can Grains Counc
Proceedings. Annual Meeting. Canadian Nuclear Association — Proc Annu Meet Can Nucl Assoc
Proceedings. Annual Meeting. Canadian Society for Biomechanics — Proc Annu Meet Can Soc Biomech
Proceedings. Annual Meeting. Canadian Society of Agronomy — Proc Annu Meet Can Soc Agron
Proceedings. Annual Meeting. Caribbean Food Crops Society — Proc Annual Meeting Caribbean Food Crops Soc
Proceedings. Annual Meeting. Catholic Theological Society of America — PCTSA
Proceedings. Annual Meeting. Chemical Specialties Manufacturers Association — Proc Annu Meet Chem Spec Manuf Assoc
Proceedings. Annual Meeting. Compressed Gas Association — Proc Annu Meet Compressed Gas Assoc
Proceedings. Annual Meeting. Connecticut Pomological Society — Proc Annu Meet Conn Pomol Soc
Proceedings. Annual Meeting. Council on Fertilizer Application — Proc A Meet Coun Fertil Applic
Proceedings. Annual Meeting. Electron Beam Symposium — Proc Annu Meet Electron Beam Symp
Proceedings. Annual Meeting. Electron Microscopy Society of America — Proc Annu Meet Electron Microsc Soc Am
Proceedings. Annual Meeting. European Academy of Allergology and Clinical Immunology — Proc Annu Meet Eur Acad Allergol Clin Immunol
Proceedings. Annual Meeting. Fertilizer Industry Round Table — Proc Annu Meet Fert Ind Round Table
Proceedings. Annual Meeting. Florida State Horticultural Society — Proc Annu Meet Fla State Hortic Soc
Proceedings. Annual Meeting. Hawaiian Sugar Planters Association — Proc Annu Meet Hawaii Sugar Plant Assoc
Proceedings. Annual Meeting. Hawaiian Sugar Technologists — Proc Annu Meet Hawaii Sugar Technol
Proceedings. Annual Meeting. Industrial Hygiene Foundation of America — Proc Annu Meet Ind Hyg Found Am
Proceedings. Annual Meeting. Institute of Environmental Sciences — Proc Annu Meet Inst Environ Sci
Proceedings. Annual Meeting. Institute of Nuclear Materials Management — Proc Annu Meet Inst Nucl Mater Manage
Proceedings. Annual Meeting. International Commission on Glass — Proc Annu Meet Int Comm Glass
Proceedings. Annual Meeting. International Magnesium Association — Proc Annu Meet Int Magnesium Assoc
Proceedings. Annual Meeting. International Society of Petroleum Industry Biologists — Proc Annu Meet Int Soc Pet Ind Biol
Proceedings. Annual Meeting. Japan Endocrinological Society — Proc Annu Meet Jpn Endocrinol Soc
Proceedings. Annual Meeting. Japanese Association for Anaerobic Infection Research — Proc Annu Meet Jpn Assoc Anaerobic Infect Res
Proceedings. Annual Meeting. Japanese Neurochemical Society — Proc Annu Meet Jpn Neurochem Soc
Proceedings. Annual Meeting. Japanese Society for Medical Mycology — Proc Annu Meet Jpn Soc Med Mycol
Proceedings. Annual Meeting. Lightwood Research Conference — Proc Annu Meet Lightwood Res Conf
Proceedings. Annual Meeting. Massachusetts Fruit Growers' Association — Proc Annu Meet Mass Fruit Grow Assoc
Proceedings. Annual Meeting. Medical Section. American Council of Life Insurance — Proc Annu Meet Med Sect Am Counc Life Insur
Proceedings. Annual Meeting. Medical Section. American Life Convention — Proc Annu Meet Med Sect Am Life Conv
Proceedings. Annual Meeting. Medical Section. American Life Insurance Association — Proc Annu Meet Med Sect Am Life Insur Assoc
Proceedings. Annual Meeting. Metal Powder Association — Proc Annu Meet Met Powder Assoc
Proceedings. Annual Meeting. Microscopical Society of Canada — Proc Annu Meet Microsc Soc Can
Proceedings. Annual Meeting. Minnesota Section. AIME — Proc Annu Meet Minn Sect AIME
Proceedings. Annual Meeting. National Academy of Clinical Biochemistry — Proc Annu Meet Natl Acad Clin Biochem
Proceedings. Annual Meeting. National Association of Corrosion Engineers — Proc Annu Meet Nat Assoc Corros Eng
Proceedings. Annual Meeting. National Association of Wheat Growers — Proc Annu Meet Nat Ass Wheat Growers
Proceedings. Annual Meeting. National Council on Radiation Protection and Measurements [*United States*] — Proc Annu Meet Natl Counc Radiat Prot Meas
Proceedings. Annual Meeting. National Joint Committee on Fertilizer Application — Proc Annu Meet Natl Jt Comm Fert Appl
Proceedings. Annual Meeting. National Research Council. Agricultural Research Institute — Proc Annu Meet Nat Res Counc Agr Res Inst
Proceedings. Annual Meeting. New Jersey Mosquito Control Association — Proc Annu Meet NJ Mosq Control Assoc
Proceedings. Annual Meeting. New Jersey Mosquito Extermination Association — Proc Annu Meet NJ
Proceedings. Annual Meeting. New Jersey Mosquito Extermination Association — Proc Annu Meet NJ Mosq Exterm Assoc
Proceedings. Annual Meeting. New York State Horticultural Society — Proc Annu Meet NY State Hort Soc
Proceedings. Annual Meeting. North Central Weed Control Conference — Proc Annu Meet N Cent Weed Contr Conf
Proceedings. Annual Meeting. North Central Weed Control Conference — Proc Annu Meet North Cent Weed Control Conf
Proceedings. Annual Meeting. Northeastern Weed Science Society — Proc Annu Meet Northeast Weed Sci Soc
Proceedings. Annual Meeting of Biochemistry (Hungary) — Proc Annu Meet Biochem (Hung)
Proceedings. Annual Meeting of Sugar Industry Technicians — Proc A Meeting Sugar Ind Technicians
Proceedings. Annual Meeting. Ohio State Horticultural Society — Proc Annu Meet Ohio State Hortic Soc
Proceedings. Annual Meeting on Upper Atmosphere Studies by Optical Methods — Proc Annu Meet Upper Atmos Stud Opt Methods
Proceedings. Annual Meeting. Pacific Coast Fertility Society — Proc Annu Meet Pac Coast Fertil Soc
Proceedings. Annual Meeting. Plant Growth Regulator Society of America — Proc Annu Meet Plant Growth Regul Soc Am

Proceedings. Annual Meeting. Society for the Promotion of Agricultural Science — Proc Annu Meet Soc Promot Agric Sci
Proceedings. Annual Meeting. Society of Engineering Science — Proc Annu Meet Soc Eng Sci
Proceedings. Annual Meeting. Soil Conservation Society of America — Proc Annu Meet Soil Conserv Soc Am
Proceedings. Annual Meeting. Southern Weed Conference — Proc Annu Meet South Weed Conf
Proceedings. Annual Meeting. Southwestern Petroleum Short Course — Proc Annu Meet Southwest Pet Short Course
Proceedings. Annual Meeting. United States Animal Health Association — Proc Annu Meet US Anim Health Assoc
Proceedings. Annual Meeting. Utah Mosquito Abatement Association — Proc Annu Meet Utah Mosq Abatement Assoc
Proceedings. Annual Meeting. Western Division. American Dairy Science Association — Proc Annu Meet West Div Am Dairy Sci Assoc
Proceedings. Annual Meeting. Western Farm Economics Association — Proc Annu Meet W Farm Econ Ass
Proceedings. Annual Meeting. Western Section. American Society of Animal Science — Proc Annu Meet West Sect Am Soc Anim Sci
Proceedings. Annual Meeting. Western Society for French History — PAMWS
Proceedings. Annual Meeting. Western Society for French History — Proc Annu Meet West Soc Fr Hist
Proceedings. Annual Meeting. World Mariculture Society — Proc Annu Meet World Maric Soc
Proceedings. Annual Meetings. American Society of Zoologists — Proc Annu Meet Am Soc Zool
Proceedings. Annual Meetings. International Shade Tree Conference — Proc Int Shade Tree Conf
Proceedings. Annual Meetings. Society for the Promotion of Agricultural Science — Proc Annual Meetings Soc Promot Agric Sci
Proceedings. Annual Mid-America Spectroscopy Symposium — Proc Annu Mid-Am Spectrosc Symp
Proceedings. Annual Midwest Fertilizer Conference — Proc Annu Midwest Fert Conf
Proceedings. Annual Mississippi Water Resources Conference — Proc Annu Miss Water Resour Conf
Proceedings. Annual National Dairy and Food Engineering Conference — Proc Annu Nat Dairy Food Eng Conf
Proceedings. Annual National Dairy Engineering Conference — Proc Annu Nat Dairy Eng Conf
Proceedings. Annual National Dairy Engineering Conference — Proc Annu Natl Dairy Eng Conf
Proceedings. Annual New York State Health Department Birth Defects Symposium — Proc Annu NY State Health Dep Birth Defects Symp
Proceedings. Annual Northeastern Regional Antipollution Conference — Proc Annu Northeast Reg Antipollut Conf
Proceedings. Annual Northwest Wood Products Clinic — Proc Annu Northwest Wood Prod Clin
Proceedings. Annual NSF [*National Science Foundation*] **Trace Contaminants Conference** — Proc Annu NSF Trace Contam Conf
Proceedings. Annual Offshore Technology Conference — Proc Annu Offshore Technol Conf
Proceedings. Annual Pacific Northwest Industrial Waste Conference — Proc Annu Pac Northwest Ind Waste Conf
Proceedings. Annual Pfizer Research Conference — Proc Annu Pfizer Res Conf
Proceedings. Annual Pittsburgh Conference on Modeling and Simulation — Proc Annu Pittsburgh Conf Model Simul
Proceedings. Annual Power Sources Conference — Proc Annu Power Sources Conf
Proceedings. Annual Program Review/Workshop. Virginia Tech Center for Adhesion Science — Proc Annu Program Rev Workshop Va Tech Cent Adhes Sci
Proceedings. Annual Pulp and Paper Conference — Proc Annu Pulp Paper Conf
Proceedings. Annual Purdue Air Quality Conference — Proc Annu Purdue Air Qual Conf
Proceedings. Annual Reciprocal Meat Conference. American Meat Science Association — Proc Annu Recipro Meat Conf Am Meat Sci Assoc
Proceedings. Annual Reliability and Maintainability Symposium — P An Rel M
Proceedings. Annual Reliability and Maintainability Symposium — PRMSC
Proceedings. Annual Reliability and Maintainability Symposium — Proc Annu Reliab Maintain Symp
Proceedings. Annual Reliability and Maintainability Symposium — Proc Annu Reliab Maintainability Symp
Proceedings. Annual Research Conference. Pfizer Agricultural Research and Development Department — Proc Annu Res Conf Pfizer Agric Res Dev Dep
Proceedings. Annual Rochester Conference on High Energy Nuclear Physics — Proc Annu Rochester Conf High Energy Nucl Phys
Proceedings. Annual Rocky Mountain Bioengineering Symposium — Proc Annu Rocky Mount Bioeng Symp
Proceedings. Annual Rocky Mountain Bioengineering Symposium — Proc Annu Rocky Mt Bioeng Symp
Proceedings. Annual San Francisco Cancer Symposium — Proc Annu San Franc Cancer Symp
Proceedings. Annual Sausage and Processed Meats Short Course — Proc Annu Sausage Processed Meats Short Course
Proceedings. Annual Scanning Electron Microscope Symposium — Proc Annu Scanning Electron Microsc Symp
Proceedings. Annual Scientific Conference. East African Medical Research Council — Proc Annu Sci Conf East Afr Med Res Counc
Proceedings. Annual Scientific Meeting. Committee on Problems of Drug Dependence. United States National Research Council — Proc Annu Sci Meet Comm Probl Drug Depend US Nat Res Counc
Proceedings. Annual Senior Staff Conference. United States Agricultural Research Service — Proc Annu Senior Staff Conf USARS
Proceedings. Annual Session. Ceylon Association for the Advancement of Science — Proc Annu Sess Ceylon Assoc Adv Sci
Proceedings. Annual Session. Sri Lanka Association for the Advancement of Science — Proc Annu Sess Sri Lanka Assoc Adv Sci
Proceedings. Annual Southwestern Petroleum Short Course [*United States*] — Proc Annu Southwest Pet Short Course
Proceedings. Annual Southwestern Petroleum Short Course — PSPCD
Proceedings. Annual Student Conference — Proc Annu Stud Conf
Proceedings. Annual Symposium. American College of Cardiology — Proc Annu Symp Am Coll Cardiol
Proceedings. Annual Symposium. East African Academy — Proc Annu Symp East Afr Acad
Proceedings. Annual Symposium Energy Research and Development — Proc Annu Symp Energy Res Dev
Proceedings. Annual Symposium in Botany — Proc Annu Symp Bot
Proceedings. Annual Symposium. Incremental Motion Control Systems and Devices — Proc Annu Symp Incremental Motion Control Syst Devices
Proceedings. Annual Symposium of the Eugenics Society — Proc Annu Symp Eugen Soc
Proceedings. Annual Symposium on Computer Applications in Medical Care — Proc Annu Symp Comput Appl Med Care
Proceedings. Annual Symposium on Engineering Geology and Soils Engineering — Proc Annu Symp Eng Geol Soils Eng
Proceedings. Annual Symposium on Environmental Pollution — Proc Annu Symp Environ Pollut
Proceedings. Annual Symposium on Frequency Control — Proc Annu Symp Freq Control
Proceedings. Annual Symposium on Industrial Waste Control — Proc Annu Symp Ind Waste Control
Proceedings. Annual Symposium on Instrumentation for the Process Industries — Proc Annu Symp Instrum Process Ind
Proceedings. Annual Symposium on Reduction of Costs in Hand-Operated Glass Plants — Proc Annu Symp Reduct Costs Hand Oper Glass Plants
Proceedings. Annual Symposium on Spectroscopy — Proc Annu Symp Spectrosc
Proceedings. Annual Symposium on the Physiology and Pathology of Human Reproduction — Proc Annu Symp Physiol Pathol Hum Reprod
Proceedings. Annual Symposium on the Scientific Basis of Medicine — Proc Annu Symp Sci Basis Med
Proceedings. Annual Symposium. Society of Flight Test Engineers — PASED
Proceedings. Annual Symposium Trace Analysis and Detection in the Environment — Proc Annu Symp Trace Anal Detect Environ
Proceedings. Annual Tall Timbers Fire Ecology Conference — Proc Annu Tall Timbers Fire Ecol Conf
Proceedings. Annual Technical and Management Conference. Society of the Plastics Industry. Reinforced Plastics Division — Proc Annu Tech Manage Conf Soc Plast Ind Reinf Plast Div
Proceedings. Annual Technical Conference. Society of Vacuum Coaters — Proc Annu Tech Conf Soc Vac Coaters
Proceedings. Annual Technical Conference. SPI Reinforced Plastics Division — Proc Annu Tech Conf SPI Reinf Plast Div
Proceedings. Annual Technical Meeting and Exhibit. American Association for Contamination Control — Proc Annu Tech Meet Exhib Am Assoc Contam Control
Proceedings. Annual Technical Meeting. Institute of Environmental Sciences — Proc Annu Tech Meet Inst Environ Sci
Proceedings. Annual Technical Meeting. International Metallographic Society, Inc. — PIMTB
Proceedings. Annual Technical Meeting. International Metallographic Society, Inc. — Proc Annu Tech Meet Int Metallogr Soc Inc
Proceedings. Annual Technical Meeting. Technical Association. Graphic Arts — Proc Annu Tech Meet Tech Assoc Graphic Arts
Proceedings. Annual Texas Conference on the Utilization of Atomic Energy — Proc Annu Tex Conf Util At Energy
Proceedings. Annual Texas Nutrition Conference — Proc Annu Tex Nutr Conf
Proceedings. Annual Tri-Service Microwave Conference on the Biological Effects of Microwave Radiation — Proc Annu Tri Serv Microwave Conf Biol Eff Microwave Radiat
Proceedings. Annual Tropical and Subtropical Fisheries Technological Conference — Proc Annu Trop Subtrop Fish Technol Conf
Proceedings. Annual Tropical and Subtropical Fisheries Technological Conference of the Americas — Proc Annu Trop Subtrop Fish Technol Conf Am
Proceedings. Annual Tung Industry Convention — Proc Annu Tung Ind Conv
Proceedings. Annual UMR-DNR Conference on Energy — Proc Annu UMR DNR Conf Energy
Proceedings. Annual UMR-MEC [*University of Missouri at Rolla - Missouri Energy Council*] **Conference on Energy** — Proc Annu UMR-MEC Conf Energy
Proceedings. Annual Underground Coal Conversion Symposium — Proc Annu Underground Coal Convers Symp
Proceedings. Annual Washington State University Institute of Dairying — Proc Annu Wash State Univ Inst Dairy
Proceedings. Annual Water Works School at the University of Kansas — Proc Annu Water Works Sch Univ Kans
Proceedings. Annual West Texas Oil Lifting Short Course — Proc Annu West Tex Oil Lifting Short Course
Proceedings. Annual Western Weed Control Conference — Proc Annu West Weed Control Conf
Proceedings. Annual Workshop on Pesticide Residue Analysis. Western Canada — Proc Annu Workshop Pestic Residue Anal West Can
Proceedings. Annual Workshop. World Mariculture Society — Proc Annu Workshop World Maricult Soc
Proceedings. Annual World Conference on Magnesium — Proc Annu World Conf Magnesium

Proceedings. Annual WWEMA [*Water and Wastewater Equipment Manufacturers Association*] **Industrial Pollution Conference** [*United States*] — Proc Annu WWEMA Ind Pollut Conf
Proceedings. Anthropological Society of Bombay — Proc Anthropol Soc Bombay
Proceedings. APCA [*Air Pollution Control Association*] **Annual Meeting** — Proc APCA Annu Meet
Proceedings. Applied Superconductivity Conference — Proc Appl Supercond Conf
Proceedings. APREA [*American Peanut Research and Education Association*] — Proc APREA
Proceedings. APRES [*American Peanut Research and Education Society*] — PPESD9
Proceedings. APRES (American Peanut Research and Education Society) — Proc APRES (Am Peanut Res Educ Soc)
Proceedings. Arab Regional Conference on Sulphur and Its Usages in the Arab World — Proc Arab Reg Conf Sulphur Its Usages Arab World
Proceedings. Argenteuil Symposium — Proc Argenteuil Symp
Proceedings. Aristotelian Society — PAS
Proceedings. Aristotelian Society — Proc Aris Soc
Proceedings. Arkansas Academy of Science — Proc Ark Acad Sci
Proceedings. Arkansas Academy of Science — Proc Arkansas Acad Sci
Proceedings. Arkansas Nutrition Conference — Proc Arkansas Nutr Conf
Proceedings. Arkansas Water Works and Pollution Control Conference and Short School — Proc Arkansas Water Works Pollut Control Conf Short Sch
Proceedings. Arnold O. Beckman Conference in Clinical Chemistry — Proc Arnold O Beckman Conf Clin Chem
Proceedings. Artificial Reef Conference — Proc Artif Reef Conf
Proceedings ASA — Proc ASA
Proceedings. A.S.A. Symposium on Soybean Processing — Proc ASA Symp Soybean Process
Proceedings. ASHRAE [*American Society of Heating, Refrigerating, and Air-Conditioning Engineers*] **Semiannual Meeting** — Proc ASHRAE Semiannu Meet
Proceedings. Asian Congress of Fluid Mechanics — Proc Asian Congr Fluid Mech
Proceedings. Asian Congress of Obstetrics and Gynaecology — Proc Asian Congr Obstet Gynaecol
Proceedings. Asian/Pacific Congress on Antisepsis — Proc Asian Pac Congr Antisepsis
Proceedings. Asian Symposium on Medicinal Plants and Spices — Proc Asian Symp Med Plants Spices
Proceedings. Asian-Pacific Congress of Cardiology — Proc Asian-Pac Congr Cardiol
Proceedings. Asian-Pacific Weed Science Society Conference — Proc Asian Pac Weed Sci Soc Conf
Proceedings. Asia-Pacific Physics Conference — Proc Asia Pac Phys Conf
Proceedings. Asiatic Society (Bengal) — Proc Asiat Soc (Bengal)
Proceedings. Asiatic Society of Bengal — PASB
Proceedings. Asiatic Society of Bengal — PASBe
Proceedings. ASIS [*American Society for Information Science*] **Annual Meeting** — Proc ASIS Annu Meet
Proceedings. ASM Heat Treatment and Surface Engineering Conference in Europe — Proc ASM Heat Treat Surf Eng Conf Eur
Proceedings. Aso Symposium — Proc Aso Symp
Proceedings. Association for Plant Protection of Kyushu — Proc Ass Plant Prot Kyushu
Proceedings. Association for Plant Protection of Kyushu — Proc Assoc Plant Prot Kyushu
Proceedings. Association for Plant Protection of Shikoku — Proc Assoc Plant Prot Shikoku
Proceedings. Association for Research in Nervous and Mental Diseases — Proc Ass Res Nerv Ment Dis
Proceedings. Association of American Physicians — Proc Assoc Am Physicians
Proceedings. Association of Asphalt Paving Technologists — Proc Ass Asphalt Paving Technol
Proceedings. Association of Asphalt Paving Technologists — Proc Assoc Asphalt Paving Technol
Proceedings. Association of Asphalt Paving Technologists — PRPTA
Proceedings. Association of Asphalt Paving Technologists. Technical Sessions — Proc Assoc Asphalt Paving Technol Tech Sess
Proceedings. Association of Clinical Biochemists — Proc Assoc Clin Biochem
Proceedings. Association of Economic Biologists — Proc Ass Econ Biol
Proceedings. Association of Economic Biologists. Coimbatore — Proc Assoc Econ Biol Coimbatore
Proceedings. Association of Military Surgeons of the US — Proc Assoc Military Surgeons US
Proceedings. Association of Official Seed Analysts — Proc Ass Offic Seed Anal
Proceedings. Association of Official Seed Analysts — Proc Assoc Off Seed Anal
Proceedings. Association of Official Seed Analysts (North America) — Proc Assoc Off Seed Anal (North Am)
Proceedings. Association of Plant Protection of Hokuriku — Proc Ass Plant Prot Hokuriku
Proceedings. Association of Southern Agricultural Workers — Proc Ass S Agr Workers
Proceedings. Association of Southern Agricultural Workers — Proc Ass Sth Agric Wkrs
Proceedings. Association of Southern Agricultural Workers — Proc Assoc South Agric Work
Proceedings. Association of Sugar Technologists — Proc Assoc Sugar Technol
Proceedings. Astronomical Society of Australia — AAUPB
Proceedings. Astronomical Society of Australia — Proc Astr Soc Aust
Proceedings. Astronomical Society of Australia — Proc Astron Soc Aust
Proceedings. Atlantic Workshop — Proc Atl Workshop
Proceedings. Australasian Association for the History, Philosophy, and Social Studies of Science — Proc AAHPSSS
Proceedings. Australasian Conference on Grassland Invertebrate Ecology — Proc Australas Conf Grassland Invertebr Ecol
Proceedings. Australasian Conference on Radiation Biology — Proc Australas Conf Radiat Biol
Proceedings. Australasian Conference on Radiobiology — Proc Australas Conf Radiobiol
Proceedings. Australasian Corrosion Association Conference — Proc Australas Corros Assoc Conf
Proceedings. Australasian Institute of Mining and Metallurgy — Proc Aust Inst Min Metall
Proceedings. Australasian Institute of Mining and Metallurgy — Proc Australas Inst Min Metall
Proceedings. Australasian Institute of Mining Engineers — Proc Australas Inst Min Eng
Proceedings. Australasian Poultry Science Convention — Proc Australasian Poultry Sci Conv
Proceedings. Australian Association of Clinical Biochemists — Proc Aust Ass Clin Biochem
Proceedings. Australian Association of Neurologists — Proc Aust Assoc Neurol
Proceedings. Australian Biochemical Society — ABIPB
Proceedings. Australian Biochemical Society — P Aust Bioc
Proceedings. Australian Biochemical Society — Proc Aust Biochem Soc
Proceedings. Australian Computer Conference — Proc Aust Comput Conf
Proceedings. Australian Conference on Electrochemistry — Proc Aust Conf Electrochem
Proceedings. Australian Goethe Society — PAGS
Proceedings. Australian Grasslands Conference — Proc Aust Grasslds Conf
Proceedings. Australian Institute of Mining Engineers — Proc Aust Inst Min Eng
Proceedings. Australian Physiological and Pharmacological Society — Proc Aust Physiol Pharmacol Soc
Proceedings. Australian Pulp and Paper Industry Technical Association — Proc Aust Pulp Pap Ind Tech Assoc
Proceedings. Australian Society for Medical Research — PASMB
Proceedings. Australian Society for Medical Research — Proc Aust Soc Med Res
Proceedings. Australian Society of Animal Production — PAANA
Proceedings. Australian Society of Animal Production — Proc Aust Soc Anim Prod
Proceedings. Australian Society of Sugar Cane Technologists — PAUTDL
Proceedings. Australian Society of Sugar Cane Technologists — Proc Aust Soc Sugar Cane Technol
Proceedings. Australian Thermodynamics Conference — Proc Aust Thermodyn Conf
Proceedings. Australian Veterinary Association. New South Wales Division — NSW Vet Proc
Proceedings. Australian Weed Conference — Proc Aust Weed Conf
Proceedings. Austrian-Italian-Yugoslav Chemical Engineering Conference — Proc Austrian Ital Yugosl Chem Eng Conf
Proceedings. Automobile Division. Institution of Mechanical Engineers — Proc Automob Div Inst Mech Eng
Proceedings. Aviation Materials Research Institute. Moscow — Proc Aviat Mater Res Inst Moscow
Proceedings. AWWA [*American Water Works Association*] **Annual Conference** — Proc AWWA Annu Conf
Proceedings. AWWA [*American Water Works Association*] **Water Quality Technology Conference** — Proc AWWA Water Qual Technol Conf
Proceedings. Bakish Materials Corporation Publication — Proc Bakish Mater Corp Publ
Proceedings. Balaton Symposium on Particle Physics — Proc Balaton Symp Part Phys
Proceedings. Banff Summer Institute on Particles and Fields — Proc Banff Summer Inst Part Fields
Proceedings. Bangkok Symposium on Acid Sulphate Soils. International Symposium on Acid Sulphate Soils — Proc Bangkok Symp Acid Sulphate Soils Int Symp
Proceedings. Bath Natural History and Antiquarian Field Club — Bath FCP
Proceedings. Bath Natural History and Antiquarian Field Club — Proc Bath Nat Hist Field Club
Proceedings. Battle Conference on Anglo-Norman Studies — P Bat Conf
Proceedings. Belfast Natural History and Philosophical Society — Proc Belfast Nat Hist Philos Soc
Proceedings. Belgian Congress of Anesthesiology — Proc Belg Congr Anesthesiol
Proceedings. Beltwide Cotton Production Conference — Proc Beltwide Cotton Prod Conf
Proceedings. Beltwide Cotton Production Research Conferences — Proc Beltwide Cotton Prod Res Conf
Proceedings. Berkeley International Materials Conference — Proc Berkeley Int Mater Conf
Proceedings. Berkeley Symposium on Mathematical Statistics and Probability — Proc Berkeley Symp Math Stat Probab
Proceedings. Berwickshire Naturalists Club — Proc Bewickwhire Nat Club
Proceedings. Biannual International Estuarine Research Conference — Proc Biannu Int Estuarine Res Conf
Proceedings. Biennial Conference. Institute for Briquetting and Agglomeration — Proc Bienn Conf Inst Briquet Agglom
Proceedings. Biennial Conference. International Briqueting Association — Proc Bienn Conf Int Briquet Assoc
Proceedings. Biennial Conference on Ground Water — Proc Bienn Conf Ground Water
Proceedings. Biennial Cornell Electrical Engineering Conference — Proc Bienn Cornell Electr Eng Conf
Proceedings. Biennial Gas Dynamics Symposium — Proc Bienn Gas Dyn Symp

Proceedings. Biennial International Estuarine Research Conference — Proc Bienn Int Estuarine Res Conf
Proceedings. Biennial Plains Aquatic Research Conference — Proc Bienn Plains Aquat Res Conf
Proceedings. Biennial Symposium on Cryogenic Instrumentation — Proc Bienn Symp Cryog Instrum
Proceedings. Biennial Symposium on Turbulence in Liquids — Proc Bienn Symp Turbul Liq
Proceedings. Biennial Western Conference on Anesthesiology — Proc Bienn West Conf Anesthesiol
Proceedings. Bihar Academy of Agricultural Sciences — PBASA
Proceedings. Bihar Academy of Agricultural Sciences — Proc Bihar Acad Agr Sci
Proceedings. Bihar Academy of Agricultural Sciences — Proc Bihar Acad Agric Sci
Proceedings. Bioenergy R and D Seminar — PBSED
Proceedings. Biological Society of Washington — PBSWA
Proceedings. Biological Society of Washington — Proc Biol Soc Wash
Proceedings. Biomass Thermochemical Conversion Contractor's Meeting — Proc Biomass Thermochem Convers Contract Meet
Proceedings. Bird Control Seminar — Proc Bird Control Semin
Proceedings. Birmingham Natural History and Microscopical Society — Proc Birmingham Nat Hist Soc
Proceedings. Bolton Landing Conference — Proc Bolton Landing Conf
Proceedings. Bombay Geographical Society — PBGS
Proceedings. Bostonian Society — Proc Bos Soc
Proceedings. Botanical Society of London — Proc Bot Soc London
Proceedings. Botanical Society of the British Isles — Proc Bot Soc Br Isles
Proceedings. Brasov International School — Proc Brasov Int Sch
Proceedings. Brighton Crop Protection Conference. Pests and Diseases — Proc Brighton Crop Prot Conf Pests Dis
Proceedings. Bristol and Gloucestershire Archaeological Society — BGAS
Proceedings. Bristol Naturalists Society — Proc Bristol Nat Soc
Proceedings. British Academy — PBA
Proceedings. British Academy — Proc Br Acad
Proceedings. British Academy — Proc Brit Ac
Proceedings. British Academy — Proc Brit Acad
Proceedings. British Academy — Proceed of the Brit Acad
Proceedings. British Academy. Supplement Paper — PBSA SPap
Proceedings. British Acoustical Society — Proc Br Acoust Soc
Proceedings. British Association for Japanese Studies — Proc British Asso Ja Stud
Proceedings. British Association for Refrigeration — Proc Br Assoc Refrig
Proceedings. British Ceramic Society — PBRCA
Proceedings. British Ceramic Society — Proc Br Ceram Soc
Proceedings. British Ceramic Society — Proc Brit Ceram Soc
Proceedings. British Crop Protection Conference. Pests and Diseases — Proc Br Crop Prot Conf Pests Dis
Proceedings. British Crop Protection Conference. Weeds — Proc Br Crop Prot Conf Weeds
Proceedings. British Insecticide and Fungicide Conference — Proc Br Insectic Fungic Conf
Proceedings. British Insecticide and Fungicide Conference — Proc Brit Insectic Fungic Conf
Proceedings. British Nuclear Energy Society European Conference — Proc Br Nucl Energy Soc Eur Conf
Proceedings. British Paedodontic Society — Proc Br Paedod Soc
Proceedings. British Pest Control Conference — Proc Br Pest Control Conf
Proceedings. British Society of Animal Production — Proc Br Soc Anim Prod
Proceedings. British Sulphur Corporation's International Conference on Fertilizer Technology — Proc Br Sulphur Corp Int Conf Fert Technol
Proceedings. British Weed Control Conference — Proc Br Weed Control Conf
Proceedings. British Weed Control Conference — Proc Brit Weed Contr Conf
Proceedings. British West Indies Sugar Technologists Conference — Proc Br West Indies Sugar Technol Conf
Proceedings. Brown University Symposium on the Biology of Skin — Proc Brown Univ Symp Biol Skin
Proceedings. Buffalo-Milan Symposium on Molecular Pharmacology — Proc Buffalo Milan Symp Mol Pharmacol
Proceedings. Buhl International Conference on Materials — Proc Buhl Int Conf Mater
Proceedings. C. C. Furnas Memorial Conference — Proc C C Furnas Meml Conf
Proceedings C. Indian Academy of Sciences — Proc C Indian Acad Sci
Proceedings. California Academy of Natural Sciences — Proc Calif Acad Nat Sci
Proceedings. California Academy of Sciences — Proc Calif Acad Sci
Proceedings. California Annual Weed Conference — Proc Calif Ann Weed Conf
Proceedings. California Conference on Fire Toxicity — Proc Calif Conf Fire Toxic
Proceedings. California Conference on Product Flammability — Proc Calif Conf Prod Flammability
Proceedings. California Conference on Rubber-Toughened Plastics — Proc Calif Conf Rubber Toughened Plast
Proceedings. California Linguistics Association Conference — PCLAC
Proceedings. California Weed Conference — Proc Calif Weed Conf
Proceedings. California Zoological Club — Proc Calif Zool Club
Proceedings. Cambridge Antiquarian Society — PCAS
Proceedings. Cambridge Antiquarian Society — Proc Cambr
Proceedings. Cambridge Antiquarian Society — Proc Cambridge Ant Soc
Proceedings. Cambridge Antiquarian Society — Proc Cambridge Antiq Soc
Proceedings. Cambridge Philological Society — P Camb Ph S
Proceedings. Cambridge Philological Society — PCPhS
Proceedings. Cambridge Philological Society — PCPS
Proceedings. Cambridge Philological Society — Proc Cambr Phil Soc
Proceedings. Cambridge Philological Society — Proc Cambridge Phil Soc
Proceedings. Cambridge Philosophical Society [*England*] — PCPSA
Proceedings. Cambridge Philosophical Society — Proc Camb Philos Soc
Proceedings. Cambridge Philosophical Society — Proc Cambridge Philos Soc
Proceedings. Cambridge Philosophical Society. Mathematical and Physical Sciences — Proc Camb Phil Soc Math Phys Sci
Proceedings. Canadian Cancer Research Conference — Proc Can Cancer Res Conf
Proceedings. Canadian Centennial Wheat Symposium — Proc Can Centen Wheat Symp
Proceedings. Canadian Conference on Nondestructive Testing — Proc Can Conf Nondestr Test
Proceedings. Canadian Conference on Research in the Rheumatic Diseases — Proc Can Conf Res Rheum Dis
Proceedings. Canadian Federation of Biological Societies — Proc Can Fed Biol Soc
Proceedings. Canadian Institute — PCI
Proceedings. Canadian National Power Alcohol Conference — Proc Can Natl Power Alcohol Conf
Proceedings. Canadian National Weed Committee. Eastern Section — Proc Can Nat Weed Comm E Sect
Proceedings. Canadian National Weed Committee. Western Section — Proc Can Nat Weed Comm W Sect
Proceedings. Canadian Nuclear Association Annual International Conference — Proc Can Nucl Assoc Annu Int Conf
Proceedings. Canadian Otolaryngological Society — Proc Canad Oto Soc
Proceedings. Canadian Phytopathological Society — Proc Can Phytopathol Soc
Proceedings. Canadian Phytopathological Society — Proc Canad Phytopathol Soc
Proceedings. Canadian Rock Mechanics Symposium — PCRSB
Proceedings. Canadian Rock Mechanics Symposium — Proc Can Rock Mech Symp
Proceedings. Canadian Society of Forensic Science — Proc Can Soc Forensic Sci
Proceedings. Canadian Society of Plant Physiologists — Proc Can Soc Pl Physiol
Proceedings. Canadian Symposium on Nonwovens and Disposables — Proc Can Symp Nonwovens Disposables
Proceedings. Canadian Symposium on Water Pollution Research — Proc Can Symp Water Pollut Res
Proceedings. Canadian Wood Chemistry Symposium — Proc Can Wood Chem Symp
Proceedings. Cardiff Medical Society — Proc Cardiff Med Soc
Proceedings. Caribbean Region. American Society for Horticultural Science — Proc Caribb Reg Am Soc Hort Sci
Proceedings. CAS-CERN Accelerator School. Advanced Accelerator Physics Course — Proc CAS CERN Accel Sch Adv Accel Phys Course
Proceedings. Catholic Theological Society of America — Proc Cath
Proceedings. Catholic Theological Society of America — ProcCTSA
Proceedings. Cell Wall Meeting — Proc Cell Wall Meet
Proceedings. Cellulose Conference — Proc Cellul Conf
Proceedings. Central Asian Society — PCAS
Proceedings. CERN Accelerator School Advanced Accelerator Physics Course — Proc CERN Accel Sch Adv Accel Phys Course
Proceedings. CERN [*Conseil Europeen pour la Recherche Nucleaire*] **School of Computing** — Pro CERN Sch Comput
Proceedings. Ceylon Branch. Royal Asiatic Society — Proc Ceylon Branch Asiat Soc
Proceedings. Chemical Engineering Group. Society of Chemical Industry. London — Proc Chem Eng Group Soc Chem Ind London
Proceedings. Chemical Society — P Ch S
Proceedings. Chemical Society — Proc Chem Soc
Proceedings. Chemical Society (London) — Proc Chem Soc (London)
Proceedings. Chester Society of Natural Science, Literature, and Art — Proc Chester Soc Nat Sci
Proceedings. Chicago Congress. Meteorological Section — PCC
Proceedings. Chinese Academy of Medical Sciences and the Peking Union Medical College — Proc Chin Acad Med Sci Peking Union Med Coll
Proceedings. Chinese Physiological Society. Chengtu Branch — Proc Chin Physiol Soc Chengtu Branch
Proceedings. Chromates Symposium — Proc Chromates Symp
Proceedings. Classical Association — P Cl A
Proceedings. Classical Association — PCA
Proceedings. Classical Association of Scotland — PCAS
Proceedings. Cleveland Institution of Engineers — Proc Cleveland Inst Eng
Proceedings. Clinical Dialysis and Transplant Forum — Proc Clin Dial Transplant Forum
Proceedings. Clinical Research Centre Symposium — Proc Clin Res Cent Symp
Proceedings. Coal Briquetting Conference — Proc Coal Briquet Conf
Proceedings. Coal Mining Institute of America — Proc Coal Mining Inst Amer
Proceedings. Coal Testing Conference — Proc Coal Test Conf
Proceedings. College of Medicine. University of the Philippines — Proc Coll Med Univ Philipp
Proceedings. College of Natural Sciences [*Seoul*] — CKTNDR
Proceedings. College of Natural Sciences. Section 2. Physics, Astronomy. Seoul National University — Proc Coll Nat Sci Sect 2 Seoul Nat Univ
Proceedings. College of Natural Sciences. Section 3. Chemistry. Seoul National University — Proc Coll Nat Sci Sect 3 Seoul Nat Univ
Proceedings. College of Natural Sciences. Section 4. Biological Sciences. Seoul National University — Proc Coll Nat Sci Sect 4 Biol Sci Seoul Natl Univ
Proceedings. College of Natural Sciences. Section 4. Life Sciences. Seoul National University — Proc Coll Nat Sci Sect 4 Life Sci Seoul Natl Univ
Proceedings. College of Natural Sciences. Section 4. Life Sciences. Seoul National University — Proc Coll Nat Sci Sect 4 Seoul Nat Univ
Proceedings. College of Natural Sciences. Section 5. Geology, Meteorology, and Oceanography. Seoul National University — Proc Coll Nat Sci Sect 5 Seoul Nat Univ

Proceedings. College of Natural Sciences (Seoul) — Proc Coll Nat Sci (Seoul)
Proceedings. College of Natural Sciences. Seoul National University — Proc Coll Nat Sci Seoul Natl Univ
Proceedings. College of Radiologists of Australia — Proc Coll Radiol Aust
Proceedings. College Park Colloquium on Chemical Evolution — Proc College Park Colloq Chem Evol
Proceedings. College Theology Society — ProcCTS
Proceedings. College Theology Society — ProCTS
Proceedings. Colloquium. Johnson Research Foundation. University of Pennsylvania — Proc Colloq Johnson Res Found Univ Pa
Proceedings. Colloquium of the International Potash Institute — Proc Colloq Int Potash Inst
Proceedings. Colloquium on Thin Films — Proc Colloq Thin Films
Proceedings. Colloquium Spectroscopicum Internationale — Proc Colloq Spectrosc Int
Proceedings. Colorado Scientific Society — Proc Colorado Sci Soc
Proceedings. Columbia River Basalt Symposium — Proc Columbia River Basalt Symp
Proceedings. Commission International Technique de Sucrerie — Proc Comm Int Tech Sucr
Proceedings. Commonwealth Mining and Metallurgical Congress — Proc Commonw Min Metall Congr
Proceedings. Comparative Literature Symposium — P Comp Lit
Proceedings. Comparative Literature Symposium — PCLS
Proceedings. Computer Science and Statistics — P Cmp Sc St
Proceedings. Conference. European Dialysis and Transplant Association — Proc Conf Eur Dial Transplant Assoc
Proceedings. Conference. German Biochemical Society — Proc Conf Ger Biochem Soc
Proceedings. Conference in Physics — Proc Conf Phys
Proceedings. Conference. Institute of Information Scientists — Proc Conf Inst Inf Sci
Proceedings. Conference (International) on Solid State Devices — Proc Conf (Int) Solid State Devices
Proceedings. Conference. International Organization of Citrus Virologists — Proc Conf Int Organ Citrus Virol
Proceedings. Conference. Ion Plating and Allied Techniques — Proc Conf Ion Plat Allied Tech
Proceedings. Conference. National Association of Corrosion Engineers — Proc Conf Natl Assoc Corros Eng
Proceedings. Conference. New Zealand Grassland Association — Proc Conf NZ Grassl Assoc
Proceedings. Conference of Charles University Medical Faculty — Proc Conf Charles Univ Med Fac
Proceedings. Conference of Engineering in Medicine and Biology — Proc Conf Eng Med Biol
Proceedings. Conference of Experimental Medicine and Surgery in Primates — Proc Conf Exp Med Surg Primates
Proceedings. Conference of Fruit Growers. Dominion of Canada — Proc Conf Fruit Growers Domin Canada
Proceedings. Conference of the Australian Road Research Board — Proc Conf Aust Road Res Board
Proceedings. Conference on Accelerator Targets Designed for the Production of Neutrons — Proc Conf Accel Targets Des Prod Neutrons
Proceedings. Conference on Application of Small Accelerators — Proc Conf Appl Small Accel
Proceedings. Conference on Applied Physical Chemistry — Proc Conf Appl Phys Chem
Proceedings. Conference on Chemical Vapor Deposition. International Conference — Proc Conf Chem Vap Deposition Int Conf
Proceedings. Conference on Cutaneous Toxicity — Proc Conf Cutaneous Toxic
Proceedings. Conference on Dimensioning and Strength Calculations — Proc Conf Dimens Strength Calc
Proceedings. Conference on Environmental Toxicology — Proc Conf Environ Toxicol
Proceedings. Conference on Fluid Machinery — Proc Conf Fluid Mach
Proceedings. Conference on Glass Problems — Proc Conf Glass Probl
Proceedings. Conference on Great Lakes Research — Proc Conf Great Lakes Res
Proceedings. Conference on Hot Laboratories and Equipment — Proc Conf Hot Lab Equip
Proceedings. Conference on Industrial Energy Conservation Technology — Proc Conf Ind Energy Conserv Technol
Proceedings. Conference on Industrial Waste. Pacific Northwest — Proc Conf Ind Waste Pac Northwest
Proceedings. Conference on Materials Engineering — Proc Conf Mater Eng
Proceedings. Conference on Microcirculatory Physiology and Pathology — Proc Conf Microcirc Physiol Pathol
Proceedings. Conference on Middle East Agriculture. Middle East Supply Centre Agricultural Report [*Cairo*] — MEAD
Proceedings. Conference on Natural Gas Research and Technology — Proc Conf Nat Gas Res Technol
Proceedings. Conference on Nuclear Processes in Geologic Settings — Proc Conf Nucl Processes Geol Settings
Proceedings. Conference on Radioisotopes — Proc Conf Radioisot
Proceedings. Conference on Rare Earth Research — Proc Conf Rare Earth Res
Proceedings. Conference on Reactions between Complex Nuclei — Proc Conf React Complex Nucl
Proceedings. Conference on Remote Systems Technology — CRSTB
Proceedings. Conference on Remote Systems Technology — Proc Conf Remote Syst Technol
Proceedings. Conference on Solid State Devices — Proc Conf Solid State Devices
Proceedings. Conference on the Application of Physical Sciences to Food Research, Processing, and Preservation — Proc Conf Appl Phys Sci Food Res Process Preserv
Proceedings. Conference on the Climatic Impact Assessment Program — Proc Conf Clim Impact Assess Program
Proceedings. Conference on the Design of Experiments in Army Research Development and Testing — Proc Conf Des Exp Army Res Dev Test
Proceedings. Conference on the Exploding Wire Phenomenon — Proc Conf Exploding Wire Phenom
Proceedings. Conference on the Silicate Industry — Proc Conf Silic Ind
Proceedings. Conference on Toxicology — Proc Conf Toxicol
Proceedings. Conference on Vacuum Microbalance Techniques — Proc Conf Vac Microbalance Tech
Proceedings. Conference. Reinforced Plastics/Composites Division. Society of the Plastics Industry — Proc Conf Reinf Plast Compos Div Soc Plast Ind
Proceedings. Conferences on Carbon — Proc Conf Carbon
Proceedings. Congenital Anomalies. Research Association. Annual Report — Proc Congenital Anomalies Res Assoc Annu Rep
Proceedings. Congres Annuel. Corporation des Ingenieurs Forestiers (Quebec) [*A publication*] — Proc Congr Ann Corp Ingen For (Quebec)
Proceedings. Congreso Nacional de Quimica — Proc Congr Nac Quim
Proceedings. Congress Ampere — Proc Congr Ampere
Proceedings. Congress. Asian and Pacific Society of Hematology — Proc Congr Asian Pac Soc Hematol
Proceedings. Congress. Council of Mining and Metallurgical Institutions — Proc Congr Counc Min Metall Inst
Proceedings. Congress. European Brewery Convention — Proc Congr Eur Brew Conv
Proceedings. Congress. European Organization for Research on Fluorine and Dental Caries Prevention — Proc Congr Eur Organ Res Fluorine Dent Caries Prev
Proceedings. Congress. European Society for Comparative Physiology and Biochemistry — Proc Congr Eur Soc Comp Physiol Biochem
Proceedings. Congress. European Society of Parenteral and Enteral Nutrition — Proc Congr Eur Soc Parenter Enteral Nutr
Proceedings. Congress. Grassland Society of Southern Africa — Proc Congr Grassl Soc South Afr
Proceedings. Congress. Hungarian Pharmacological Society — Proc Congr Hung Pharmacol Soc
Proceedings. Congress. Hungarian Society of Endocrinology and Metabolism — Proc Congr Hung Soc Endocrinol Metab
Proceedings. Congress. International Radiation Protection Society — Proc Congr Int Radiat Prot Soc
Proceedings. Congress. International Society for Rock Mechanics — Proc Congr Int Soc Rock Mech
Proceedings. Congress. International Society of Hematology — Proc Congr Int Soc Hematol
Proceedings. Congress. Mediterranean Phytopathological Union — Proc Congr Mediterr Phytopathol Union
Proceedings. Congress of Obesity — Proc Congr Obes
Proceedings. Congress of Obstetrics and Gynaecology — Proc Congr Obstet Gynaecol
Proceedings. Congress of Orientalists — PCO
Proceedings. Congress of Pharmaceutical Sciences — Proc Congr Pharm Sci
Proceedings. Congress of the European Society of Haematology — Proc Congr Eur Soc Haematol
Proceedings. Congress of the Federation Internationale de la Precontrainte — Proc Congr Fed Int Precontrainte
Proceedings. Congress of the Hungarian Association of Microbiologists — Proc Congr Hung Assoc Microbiol
Proceedings. Congress of the International Association for the Scientific Study of Mental Deficiency — Proc Congr Int Assoc Sci Study Ment Defic
Proceedings. Congress of the International Commission for Optics — Proc Congr Int Comm Opt
Proceedings. Congress of the International Potash Institute — Proc Congr Int Potash Inst
Proceedings. Congress of the International Society of Blood Transfusion — PIBTAD
Proceedings. Congress of the International Society of Blood Transfusion — Proc Congr Int Soc Blood Transf
Proceedings. Congress of the International Society of Blood Transfusion — Proc Congr Int Soc Blood Transfus
Proceedings. Congress of the International Society of Sugar Cane Technologists — Proc Congr Int Soc Sugar Cane Technol
Proceedings. Congress of the International Union of Forest Research Organizations — Proc Congr Int Union For Res Organ
Proceedings. Congress of the Japan Society for Cancer Therapy — Proc Congr Jpn Soc Cancer Ther
Proceedings. Congress of the Mediterranean Phytopathological Union — Proc Cong Mediterr Phytopathol Union
Proceedings. Congress of the South African Genetic Society — Proc Congr S Afr Genet Soc
Proceedings. Congress of the South African Sugar Technologists' Association [*A publication*] — Proc Congr S Afr Sug Technol Ass
Proceedings. Congress on the Leather Industry — Proc Congr Leather Ind
Proceedings. Connecticut Academy of Arts and Sciences — PCAAS
Proceedings. Connecticut Pomological Society — Proc Conn Pomol Soc
Proceedings. Consortium for Revolutionary Europe — ProC
Proceedings. Convention. Institute of Brewing. Australia and New Zealand Section — Proc Conv Inst Brew Aust NZ Sect
Proceedings. Convention. International Association of Fish and Wildlife Agencies — Proc Conv Int Assoc Fish Wildl Agencies
Proceedings. Cornell Agricultural Waste Management Conference — Proc Cornell Agric Waste Manage Conf

Proceedings. Cornell Nutrition Conference for Feed Manufacturers — Proc Cornell Nutr Conf Feed Manuf
Proceedings. Cornell Nutrition Conference for Feed Manufacturers — Proc Cornell Nutr Conf Feed Mfr
Proceedings. Cosmic-Ray Research Laboratory. Nagoya University — Proc Cosmic-Ray Res Lab Nagoya Univ
Proceedings. Cotteswold Naturalists' Field Club — Proc Cotteswold Natur Fld Club
Proceedings. Cotton Dust Research Conference. Beltwide Cotton Production Research Conferences — Proc Cotton Dust Res Conf Beltwide Cotton Prod Res Conf
Proceedings. Cotton Research Congress — Proc Cotton Res Congr
Proceedings. Council of Economics. American Institute of Mining, Metallurgical, and Petroleum Engineers — Proc Counc Econ AIME
Proceedings. Course. International School of Intermediate Energy Nuclear Physics — Proc Course Int Sch Intermed Energy Nucl Phys
Proceedings. Course on Developmental Neurobiology — Proc Course Dev Neurobiol
Proceedings. Coventry District Natural History and Scientific Society — Proc Coventry Dist Natur Hist Sci Soc
Proceedings. Crayford Manor House Historical and Archaeological Society — Proc Crayford Manor House Hist Archaeol Soc
Proceedings. Crop Science. Chugoku Branch of the Crop Science Society — Proc Crop Sci Chugoku Br Crop Sci Soc
Proceedings. Crop Science Society of Japan — Proc Crop Sci Soc Jap
Proceedings. Crop Science Society of Japan — Proc Crop Sci Soc Jpn
Proceedings. Crop Science Society of Japan / Nihon Sakumotsu Gakkai Kiji — Proc Crop Sci Soc Japan
Proceedings. Croydon Natural History Science Society — Proc Croydon Nat Hist Sci Soc
Proceedings. Cryogenic Engineering Conference — Proc Cryog Eng Conf
Proceedings. Cumberland Geological Society — Proc Cumberland Geol Soc
Proceedings. Cybernetic Sciences Symposium — Proc Cybern Sci Symp
Proceedings. Davenport Academy of Natural Sciences — Proc Davenport Acad Nat Sci
Proceedings. Department of Horticulture and Plant Health. Massey University [*A publication*] — Proc Dep Hortic Plant Health Massey Univ
Proceedings. Deutsch-Deutsches Symposium Umweltforschung in der DDR — Proc Dtsch Dtsch Symp Umweltforsch DDR
Proceedings. Developmental Immunology Workshop — Proc Dev Immunol Workshop
Proceedings. Devon Archaeological Exploration Society — DAES
Proceedings. Devon Archaeological Exploration Society — Proc Devon Arch Expl Soc
Proceedings. Devon Archaeological Society — Proc Devon Arch Soc
Proceedings. Devon Archaeological Society — Proc Devon Archaeol Soc
Proceedings. Distillers Feed Conference — Proc Distill Feed Conf
Proceedings. Distillers Feed Research Council Conference — Proc Distill Feed Res Counc Conf
Proceedings. Divers' Gas Purity Symposium — Proc Divers' Gas Purity Symp
Proceedings. Division of Refining. American Petroleum Institute — Proc Div Refin Am Pet Inst
Proceedings. Divisional Conference. European Physical Society. Nuclear Physics Division — Proc Div Conf Eur Phys Soc Nucl Phys Div
Proceedings. DOE (Department of Energy) Nuclear Airborne Waste Management and Air cleaning Conference (US) — Proc DOE Nucl Airborne Wast Manage Air Clean Conf
Proceedings. Dorset Natural History and Archaeological Society — PDANHS
Proceedings. Dorset Natural History and Archaeological Society — Proc Dorset Nat Hist Archaeol Soc
Proceedings. Dorset Natural History and Archaeological Society — Proc Dorset Natur Hist Arch Soc
Proceedings. Dorset Natural History and Archaeological Society — Proc Dorset Natur Hist Archaeol Soc
Proceedings. Dudley and Midland Geological and Scientific Society and Field Club — Proc Dudley Midl Geol Soc
Proceedings. East African Academy — Proc East Afr Acad
Proceedings. East African Weed Science Conference — Proc East Afr Weed Sci Conf
Proceedings. Easter School in Agricultural Science. University of Nottingham — PEANA
Proceedings. Easter School in Agricultural Science. University of Nottingham [*England*] — Proc Easter Sch Agric Sci Univ Nottingham
Proceedings. Eastern Theoretical Physics Conference — Proc East Theor Phys Conf
Proceedings. Ecological Society of Australia — Proc Ecol Soc Aust
Proceedings. Edinburgh Mathematical Society — P Edin Math
Proceedings. Edinburgh Mathematical Society — Proc Edinburgh Math Soc
Proceedings. Edinburgh Mathematical Society. Edinburgh Mathematical Notes — Proc Edinburgh Math Soc Edinburgh Math Notes
Proceedings. Edinburgh Mathematical Society. Series 2 — Proc Edinburgh Math Soc 2
Proceedings. EGAS Conference. European Group for Atomic Spectroscopy — Proc EGAS Conf Eur Group At Spectrosc
Proceedings. Egyptian Academy of Sciences — Proc Egypt Acad Sci
Proceedings. Eighth British Weed Control Conference — Proc Eighth Br Weed Control Conf
Proceedings. Electric Furnace Conference — Proc Electr Furn Conf
Proceedings. Electrical/Electronics Insulation Conference — Proc Elctr Electron Insul Conf
Proceedings. Electrochemical Society — PESOD
Proceedings. Electron Microscopy Society of America — Proc Electron Microsc Soc Am
Proceedings. Electron Microscopy Society of Southern Africa — Proc Electron Microsc Soc South Afr
Proceedings. Electronic Components Conference — Proc Electron Compon Conf
Proceedings. Electronic Components Conference — Proc Electron Components Conf
Proceedings. Electronic Components Symposium — Proc Electron Compon Symp
Proceedings. Empire Mining and Metallurgical Congress — Proc Emp Min Metall Congr
Proceedings. Endocrine Society of Australia — Proc Endoc Soc Aust
Proceedings. Endocrine Society of Australia — Proc Endocr Soc Aust
Proceedings. Energy Resource Conference — Proc Energy Resour Conf
Proceedings. Energy Symposium — Proc Energy Symp
Proceedings. Engineering Foundation Conference — Proc Eng Found Conf
Proceedings. Engineering Foundation Conference on Fundamentals of Adsorption — Proc Eng Found Conf Fundam Adsorpt
Proceedings. Engineering Society of Hong Kong — Proc Eng Soc Hong Kong
Proceedings. Engineers' Society of Western Pennsylvania — Proc Eng Soc West PA
Proceedings. Entomological Society of America. North Central Branch — Proc Entomol Soc Amer N Cent Br
Proceedings. Entomological Society of British Columbia — Proc Ent Soc Br Columb
Proceedings. Entomological Society of British Columbia — Proc Entomol Soc BC
Proceedings. Entomological Society of British Columbia — Proc Entomol Soc Brit Columbia
Proceedings. Entomological Society of Manitoba — Proc Ent Soc Manitoba
Proceedings. Entomological Society of Manitoba — Proc Entomol Soc Manit
Proceedings. Entomological Society of Manitoba — Proc Entomol Soc Manitoba
Proceedings. Entomological Society of Ontario — P Ent S Ont
Proceedings. Entomological Society of Ontario — Proc Ent Soc Ont
Proceedings. Entomological Society of Ontario — Proc Entomol Soc Ont
Proceedings. Entomological Society of Ontario — Proc Entomol Soc Ontario
Proceedings. Entomological Society of Washington — P Ent S Was
Proceedings. Entomological Society of Washington — Proc Ent Soc Wash
Proceedings. Entomological Society of Washington — Proc Entomol Soc Wash
Proceedings. Entomological Society of Washington, DC — Proc Entomol Soc Wash DC
Proceedings. Environmental Engineering and Science Conference — Proc Environ Eng Sci Conf
Proceedings. Environmental Symposium — Proc Environ Symp
Proceedings. ERDA [*Office of Exploratory Research and Problem Assessment*] **Air Cleaning Conference** — Proc ERDA Air Clean Conf
Proceedings. Essex Institute — Proc Essex Inst
Proceedings. Estonian Academy of Sciences. Physics. Mathematics — Proc Estonian Acad Sci Phys Math
Proceedings. European and Mediterranean Cereal Rusts Conference — Proc Eur Mediterr Cereal Rusts Conf
Proceedings. European Biophysics Congress — Proc Eur Biophys Cong
Proceedings. European Conference on Chemical Vapor Deposition — Proc Eur Conf Chem Vap Deposition
Proceedings. European Conference on Computational Physics — Proc Eur Conf Comput Phys
Proceedings. European Conference on Controlled Fusion and Plasma Physics — Proc Eur Conf Controlled Fusion Plasma Phys
Proceedings. European Conference on Mixing — Proc Eur Conf Mixing
Proceedings. European Conference on Particle Physics — Proc Eur Conf Part Phys
Proceedings. European Conference on Prenatal Diagnosis of Genetic Disorders — Proc Eur Conf Prenatal Diagn Genet Disord
Proceedings. European Conference on Surface Science — Proc Eur Conf Surf Sci
Proceedings. European Congress of Allergology and Clinical Immunology — Proc Eur Congr Allergol Clin Immunol
Proceedings. European Congress of Biopharmaceutics and Pharmacokinetics — Proc Eur Congr Biopharm Pharmacokinet
Proceedings. European Congress on Biotechnology — Proc Eur Congr Biotechnol
Proceedings. European Dialysis and Transplant Association — Proc Eur Dial Transplant Assoc
Proceedings. European Dialysis and Transplant Association - European Renal Association — Proc Eur Dial Transplant Assoc Eur Renal Assoc
Proceedings. European Electric Propulsion Conference — Proc Eur Electr Propul Conf
Proceedings. European Great Projects International Seminar — Proc Eur Great Proj Int Semin
Proceedings. European Immunology Meeting — Proc Eur Immunol Meet
Proceedings. European Marine Biology Symposium — Proc Eur Mar Biol Symp
Proceedings. European Meeting of Radioisotope Producers — Proc Eur Meet Radioisot Prod
Proceedings. European Meeting on Bacterial Transformation and Transfection — Proc Eur Meet Bact Transform Transfection
Proceedings. European Offshore Petroleum Conference and Exhibition — PEOED
Proceedings. European Peptide Symposium — Proc Eur Pept Symp
Proceedings. European Prosthodontic Association — Proc Eur Prosthodontic Assoc
Proceedings. European Regional Meeting in Astronomy — Proc Eur Reg Meet Astron
Proceedings. European Regional Technical Conference. Plastics and Processing — Proc Eur Reg Tech Conf Plast Process
Proceedings. European Society for Artificial Organs. Annual Meeting — Proc Eur Soc Artif Organs Annu Meet
Proceedings. European Society for Neurochemistry. Meeting of the ESN — Proc Eur Soc Neurochem Meet ESN
Proceedings. European Society of Drug Toxicity [*Elsevier Book Series*] — PDT

Proceedings. European Society of Toxicology — PESTD
Proceedings. European Society of Toxicology — Proc Eur Soc Toxicol
Proceedings. European Sterility Congress — Proc Eur Steril Cong
Proceedings. European Symposium on Bone and Tooth — Proc Eur Symp Bone Tooth
Proceedings. European Symposium on Calcified Tissues — Proc Eur Symp Calcif Tissues
Proceedings. European Symposium on Live Sciences Research in Space — Proc Eur Symp Life Sci Res Space
Proceedings. European Symposium on Marine Biology — Proc Eur Symp Mar Biol
Proceedings. European Symposium on Nucleon Anti-Nucleon Interactions — Proc Eur Symp Nucleon Anti Nucleon Interact
Proceedings. European Symposium on Polymer Spectroscopy — Proc Eur Symp Polym Spectrosc
Proceedings. European Symposium on Radiopharmacology — Proc Eur Symp Radiopharmacol
Proceedings. European Symposium on Thermal Analysis — Proc Eur Symp Therm Anal
Proceedings. Faculty of Agriculture. Kyushu Tokai University — KDNKDR
Proceedings. Faculty of Agriculture. Kyushu Tokai University — Proc Fac Agric Kyushu Tokai Univ
Proceedings. Faculty of Engineering. Keiogijuku University — Proc Fac Eng Keiogijuku Univ
Proceedings. Faculty of Engineering. Kyushu University — Proc Fac Eng Kyushu Univ
Proceedings. Faculty of Engineering of Tokai University (Japan Edition) — Proc Fac Eng Tokai Univ (Jpn Ed)
Proceedings. Faculty of Engineering. Tokai University [*Japan*] — Proc Fac Eng Tokai Univ
Proceedings. Faculty of Science. Tokai University [*Japan*] — Proc Fac Sci Tokai Univ
Proceedings. Faculty of Science. Tokai University — TUFPB
Proceedings. Falk Symposium — Proc Falk Symp
Proceedings. Fall Meeting. Materials and Equipment and Whitewares Divisions. American Ceramic Society — Proc Fall Meet Mater Equip Whitewares Div Am Ceram Soc
Proceedings. Far Western Philosophy of Education Society — Phil Educ Proc
Proceedings. Farm Seed Conference — Proc Farm Seed Conf
Proceedings. FEBS [*Federation of European Biochemical Societies*] — Proc FEBS Congr
Proceedings. FEBS [*Federation of European Biochemical Societies*] **Meeting** — Proc FEBS Meet
Proceedings. Federal Conference on the Great Lakes (US) — Proc Fed Conf Great Lakes
Proceedings. Federal Science Congress — Proc Fed Sci Congr
Proceedings. Federation of American Societies for Experimental Biology — Fed Proc
Proceedings. Fertiliser Association of India. Tech Series — Proc Fert Assoc India Tech Ser
Proceedings. Fertiliser Institute (Delhi) — Proc Fert Inst Delhi
Proceedings. [*The*] **Fertiliser Society of London** — Proc Fert Soc Lond
Proceedings. Fertilizer Industry Round Table — Proc Fert Ind Round Table
Proceedings. Fertilizer Society — Proc Fertil Soc
Proceedings. Fifth World Congress of Jewish Studies [*1969*] — PWCJS
Proceedings. Finnish Academy of Science and Letters — Proc Finn Acad Sci Lett
Proceedings. Finnish Dental Society of Washington — Proc Finn Dent Soc
Proceedings. Finnish-Swedish Seminar on the Gulf of Bothnia — Proc Finn Swed Semin Gulf Bothnia
Proceedings. Finnish-US Joint Symposium on Occupational Safety and Healty with Swedish Participation — Proc Finn US Jt Symp Occup Saf Health Swed Participation
Proceedings. First Livestock by Ocean Conference — Proc First Livest Ocean Conf
Proceedings. First Victorian Weed Conference — Proc 1st Vic Weed Conf
Proceedings. Flash Radiography Symposium Presented at the National Fall Conference, American Society for Nondestructive Testing — Proc Flash Radiogr Symp Natl Fall Conf Am Soc Nondestr Test
Proceedings. Florida Academy of Sciences — Proc Fla Acad Sci
Proceedings. Florida Anti-Mosquito Association — Proc Fla Anti-Mosq
Proceedings. Florida Lychee Growers Association — Proc Fla Lychee Grow Ass
Proceedings. Florida State Horticultural Society — Proc Fla St Hort Soc
Proceedings. Florida State Horticultural Society — Proc Fla State Hort Soc
Proceedings. Florida State Horticultural Society — Proc Fla State Hortic Soc
Proceedings. Florida Turf Association — Proc Florida Turf Assoc
Proceedings. FOC. Fiber Optics and Communications — Proc FOC Fiber Opt Commun
Proceedings. Food Conference. Institute of Food Technologists — Proc Food Conf Inst Food Technol
Proceedings. Forage and Grassland Conference — Proc Forage Grassl Conf
Proceedings. Forest Microclimate Symposium. Canada Department of Fisheries and Forestry — Proc For Microclim Symp Can Dep Fish For
Proceedings. Forest Products Research Society — Proc For Prod Res Soc
Proceedings. Forest Products Research Society National Meeting — Proc Forest Prod Res Soc Natl Meeting
Proceedings. Forest Products Symposium — Proc For Prod Symp
Proceedings. Forum on Fundamental Surgical Problems. Clinical Congress of the American College of Surgeons — Proc Forum Fundam Surg Probl Clin Congr Am Coll Surg
Proceedings. Forum on Geology of Industrial Minerals — Proc Forum Geol Ind Miner
Proceedings. Foundation for Orthodontic Research — Proc Found Orthod Res
Proceedings. (Fourth) New Zealand Geographical Conference — Proc (Fourth) NZ Geogr Conf
Proceedings. FPLC [*Fast Protein, Polypeptide, and Polynucleotide Liquid Chromatography*] **Symposium** — Proc FPLC Symp
Proceedings. FRI Symposium. Forest Research Institute. New Zealand Forest Service — Proc FRI Symp For Res Inst NZ For Serv
Proceedings. Frontiers in Education Conference — Proc Front Educ Conf
Proceedings. Frontiers of Power Technology Conference — Proc Front Power Technol Conf
Proceedings. Fujihara Memorial Faculty of Engineering. Keio University — Proc Fujihara Mem Fac Eng Keio Univ
Proceedings. Fujihara Memorial Faculty of Engineering. Keio University (Tokyo) — Proc Fujihara Mem Fac Eng Keio Univ (Tokyo)
Proceedings. Fusion/Fission Energy Systems Review Meeting — Proc Fusion Fission Energy Syst Rev Meet
Proceedings. Gas Conditioning Conference [*United States*] — Proc Gas Cond Conf
Proceedings. Gastech — Proc Gastech
Proceedings. Gemmological Association of Great Britain — Proc Gemmol Assoc GB
Proceedings. General Meeting. European Grassland Federation — Proc Gen Meet Eur Grassl Fed
Proceedings. General Meeting. European Society of Animal Cell Technology — Proc Gen Meet Eur Soc Anim Cell Technol
Proceedings. General Meeting of the Society for Industrial Microbiology — Proc Gen Meet Soc Ind Microbiol
Proceedings. Genetics Society of Canada — Proc Genet Soc Can
Proceedings. Geoinstitut — Proc Geoinst
Proceedings. Geological Association — Proc Geol Ass
Proceedings. Geological Association of Canada — Proc Geol Ass Can
Proceedings. Geological Association of Canada — Proc Geol Assoc Can
Proceedings. Geological Society of China [*Taipei*] — Proc Geol Soc China
Proceedings. Geological Society of London — Proc Geol Soc Lond
Proceedings. Geological Society of South Africa — Proc Geol Soc S Afr
Proceedings. Geologists' Association — Proc Geol Assoc
Proceedings. Geologists' Association (England) — PGAEA
Proceedings. Geologists' Association of London — Proc Geol Assoc London
Proceedings. Geophysical Society of Tulsa — Proc Geophys Soc Tulsa
Proceedings. Geopressured Geothermal Eenrgy Conference — Proc Geopressured Geotherm Energy Conf
Proceedings. Georgia Nutrition Conference for the Feed Industry — Proc Ga Nutr Conf Feed Ind
Proceedings. Geoscience Information Society — Proc Geosci Inf Soc
Proceedings. Geoscience Information Society — Proc Geosci Inform Soc
Proceedings. German Society of Neurosurgery — Proc Ger Soc Neurosurg
Proceedings. German Solar Energy Forum — Proc Ger Sol Energy Forum
Proceedings. Ghana Academy of Arts and Sciences — Proc Ghana Acad Arts Sci
Proceedings. Grass Breeders Work Planning Conference — Proc Grass Breeders Work Plann Conf
Proceedings. Grassland Society of Southern Africa — Proc Grassl Soc South Afr
Proceedings. Great Plains Agricultural Council — Proc Great Plains Agric Counc
Proceedings. Great Plains Agricultural Council — Proc Great Plains Agric Council
Proceedings. Great Plains Agriculture Conference — Proc Great Plains Agr Conf
Proceedings. Gulf and Caribbean Fisheries Institute — Proc Gulf Caribb Fish Inst
Proceedings. Hampshire Field Club and Archaeological Society — Proc Hamp Soc
Proceedings. Hampshire Field Club and Archaeological Society — Proc Hampshire Field Club
Proceedings. Hampshire Field Club and Archaeological Society — Proc Hampshire Fld Club Archaeol Soc
Proceedings. Hawaii International Conference on System Science — Proc Hawaii Int Conf Syst Sci
Proceedings. Hawaii Topical Conference in Particle Physics — Proc Hawaii Top Conf Part Phys
Proceedings. Hawaiian Academy of Science — Proc Hawaii Acad Sci
Proceedings. Hawaiian Academy of Science — Proc Hawaiian Acad Sci
Proceedings. Hawaiian Entomological Society — P Hawaii En
Proceedings. Hawaiian Entomological Society — PHESA
Proceedings. Hawaiian Entomological Society — Proc Hawaii Ent Soc
Proceedings. Hawaiian Entomological Society — Proc Hawaii Entomol Soc
Proceedings. Health Physics Society. Annual Meeting — Proc Health Phys Soc Annu Meet
Proceedings. Health Policy Forum — Proc Health Policy Forum
Proceedings. Heat Transfer and Fluid Mechanics Institute — Proc Heat Transfer Fluid Mech Inst
Proceedings. Hellenic School on Elementary Partical Physics — Proc Hell Sch Elem Part Phys
Proceedings. Helminthological Society of Washington — P Helm Soc
Proceedings. Helminthological Society of Washington — PHSWA
Proceedings. Helminthological Society of Washington — Proc Helminth Soc Wash
Proceedings. Helminthological Society of Washington — Proc Helminthol Soc Wash
Proceedings. Helminthological Society (Washington, DC) — Proc Helminthol Soc (Wash DC)
Proceedings. High Lysine Corn Conference — Proc High Lysine Corn Conf
Proceedings. High-Temperature Liquid-Metal Heat Transfer Technology Meeting — Proc High Temp Liq Met Heat Transfer Technol Meet
Proceedings. Hokkaido Symposium of Plant Breeding and Crop Science Society — Proc Hokkaido Symp Plant Breed Crop Sci Soc
Proceedings. Hokuriku Branch of Crop Science Society (Japan) — Proc Hokuriku Br Crop Sci Soc (Jap)
Proceedings. Horticultural Society of London — Proc Hortic Soc London

Proceedings. Horticultural Society of Northern Illinois — Proc Hort Soc N Illinois
Proceedings. Hoshi College of Pharmacy — HYDKAK
Proceedings. Hoshi College of Pharmacy — Proc Hoshi Coll Pharm
Proceedings. Hot Laboratories and Equipment Conference — Proc Hot Lab Equip Conf
Proceedings. Huguenot Society of London — PHSL
Proceedings. Huguenot Society of London — Proc Huguenot Soc Lond
Proceedings. Huguenot Society of London — Proc Huguenot Soc London
Proceedings. Hungarian Annual Meeting for Biochemistry — Proc Hung Annu Meet Biochem
Proceedings. Hungarian Bioflavonoid Symposium — Proc Hung Bioflavonoid Symp
Proceedings. Hungarian Textile Conference — Proc Hung Text Conf
Proceedings. Hydrology Symposium — Proc Hydrol Symp
Proceedings. IAEA [*Internationa Atomic Energy Agency*] **Symposium on the Physics and Chemistry of Fission** — Proc IAEA Symp Phys Chem Fission
Proceedings. ICMR [*International Center for Medical Research, Kobe University*] **Seminar** — Proc ICMR Semin
Proceedings. IEEE Computer Society's International Computer Software and Applications Conference — PSICD
Proceedings. IEEE Conference on Decision and Control — Proc IEEE Conf Decis Control
Proceedings. IEEE Conference on Decision and Control Including the Symposium on Adaptive Processes — Proc IEEE Conf Decis Control Incl Symp Adapt Processes
Proceedings. IEEE International Symposium on Circuits and Systems — Proc IEEE Int Symp Circuits Syst
Proceedings. IEEE Micro Electro Mechanical Systems — Proc IEEE Micro Electro Mech Syst
Proceedings. IEEE [*Institute of Electrical and Electronics Engineers*] **Minicourse on Inertial Confinement Fusion** — Proc IEEE Minicourse Inertial Confinement Fusion
Proceedings. IFAC [*International Federation of Automatic Control*] **World Congress** — Proc IFAC World Congr
Proceedings. Illinois Mining Institute — Proc Ill Min Inst
Proceedings. Illinois Mining Institute — Proc Ill Mining Inst
Proceedings. Imperial Academy of Japan — Proc Imp Acad Japan
Proceedings. Imperial Academy (Tokyo) — Proc Imp Acad (Tokyo)
Proceedings. Imperial Cancer Research Fund Symposium — Proc Imp Cancer Res Fund Symp
Proceedings in English. International Conference on Clean Steel — Proc Engl Int Conf Clean Steel
Proceedings in Nonlinear Science — Proc Nonlinear Sci
Proceedings. Indian Academy of Sciences — Proc Indian Acad Sci
Proceedings. Indian Academy of Sciences. Animal Sciences — Proc Indian Acad Sci Anim Sci
Proceedings. Indian Academy of Sciences. Chemical Sciences — Proc Indian Acad Sci Chem Sci
Proceedings. Indian Academy of Sciences. Earth and Planetary Sciences — Proc Indian Acad Sci Earth and Planet Sci
Proceedings. Indian Academy of Sciences. Earth and Planetary Sciences — Proc Indian Acad Sci Earth Planet
Proceedings. Indian Academy of Sciences. Earth and Planetary Sciences — Proc Indian Acad Sci Earth Planet Sci
Proceedings. Indian Academy of Sciences. Earth and Planetary Sciences — Proc Indian Acad Sci Earth Planetary Sci
Proceedings. Indian Academy of Sciences. Engineering Sciences — Proc Indian Acad Sci Eng Sci
Proceedings. Indian Academy of Sciences. Mathematical Sciences — Proc Indian Acad Sci Math Sci
Proceedings. Indian Academy of Sciences. Plant Sciences — Proc Indian Acad Sci Plant Sci
Proceedings. Indian Academy of Sciences. Section A — P I A Sci A
Proceedings. Indian Academy of Sciences. Section A — Proc Indian Acad Sci A
Proceedings. Indian Academy of Sciences. Section A — Proc Indian Acad Sci Sect A
Proceedings. Indian Academy of Sciences. Section A. Chemical Sciences — Proc Indian Acad Sci Sect A Chem Sci
Proceedings. Indian Academy of Sciences. Section A. Mathematical Sciences — Proc Indian Acad Sci Sect A Math Sci
Proceedings. Indian Academy of Sciences. Section B — P I A Sci B
Proceedings. Indian Academy of Sciences. Section B — Proc Indian Acad Sci B
Proceedings. Indian Academy of Sciences. Section B — Proc Indian Acad Sci Sect B
Proceedings. Indian Academy of Sciences. Section C. Engineering Sciences [*India*] — Proc Indian Acad Sci Sect C
Proceedings. Indian Academy of Sciences. Series Animal Sciences — PIAND
Proceedings. Indian Academy of Sciences. Series Chemical Sciences — PIAAD
Proceedings. Indian Academy of Sciences. Series Earth and Planetary Sciences — PIESD
Proceedings. Indian Academy of Sciences. Series Engineering Sciences — PRISD
Proceedings. Indian Academy of Sciences. Series Mathematical Sciences — PIAMD
Proceedings. Indian Academy of Sciences. Series Plant Sciences — PIPLD
Proceedings. Indian Association for Cultivation of Sciences — Proc Indian Assoc Cultiv Sci
Proceedings. Indian Historical Record Commission — PIHRC
Proceedings. Indian Historical Records Commission — IHRC
Proceedings. Indian National Science Academy. Part A — Proc Indian Natl Sci Acad Part A
Proceedings. Indian National Science Academy. Part A. Physical Sciences — Proc Indian Nat Sci Acad Part A
Proceedings. Indian National Science Academy. Part A. Physical Sciences — Proc Indian Natl Sci Acad A
Proceedings. Indian National Science Academy. Part A. Physical Sciences — Proc Indian Natl Sci Acad Part A Phys Sci
Proceedings. Indian National Science Academy. Part B. Biological Sciences — PIBSB
Proceedings. Indian National Science Academy. Part B. Biological Sciences — Proc Indian Natl Sci Acad Part B
Proceedings. Indian National Science Academy. Part B. Biological Sciences — Proc Indian Natl Sci Acad Part B Biol Sci
Proceedings. Indian Roads Congress — Proc Indian Roads Congr
Proceedings. Indian Science Congress — Proc Indian Sci Congr
Proceedings. Indiana Academy of Science — PIACA
Proceedings. Indiana Academy of Science — Proc Indiana Acad Sci
Proceedings. Indiana Academy of Sciences — Proc Ind Acad Sci
Proceedings. Indo-German Seminar — Proc Indo Ger Semin
Proceedings. Indo-Pacific Fisheries Council — Proc Indo Pac Fish Counc
Proceedings. Industrial Foundation of America — Proc Ind Hyg Found Am
Proceedings. Industrial Minerals International Congress — Proc Ind Miner Int Congr
Proceedings. Industrial Waste Conference — Proc Ind Waste Conf
Proceedings. Industrial Waste Conference. Purdue University — Proc Ind Waste Conf Purdue Univ
Proceedings. Industrial Waste Utilization Conference — Proc Ind Waste Util Conf
Proceedings. Industrial Water and Waste Conference — Proc Ind Water Waste Conf
Proceedings. Institut Teknologi Bandung [*Indonesia*] — Proc Inst Teknol Bandung
Proceedings. Institut Teknologi Bandung. Supplement — PITKA
Proceedings. Institut Teknologi Bandung. Supplement [*Indonesia*] — Proc Inst Teknol Bandung Suppl
Proceedings. Institute for Scientific Research in the Food Industry. USSR — Proc Inst Sci Res Food Ind USSR
Proceedings. Institute of British Foundrymen — Proc Inst Br Foundrymen
Proceedings. Institute of Chemistry of Great Britain and Ireland — Proc Inst Chem GB Irel
Proceedings. Institute of Electrical and Electronics Engineers — P IEEE
Proceedings. Institute of Electrical and Electronics Engineers — Proc IEEE
Proceedings. Institute of Electrical and Electronics Engineers — Proceedings of the IEEE
Proceedings. Institute of Environmental Sciences — IESPA
Proceedings. Institute of Environmental Sciences — Proc Inst Environ Sci
Proceedings. Institute of Fisheries (Varna) — Proc Inst Fish Varna
Proceedings. Institute of Food Science and Technology — Proc Inst Fd Sci Technol
Proceedings. Institute of Food Science and Technology of the United Kingdom — Proc Inst Food Sci Technol UK
Proceedings. Institute of Food Technologists — Proc Inst Food Technol
Proceedings. Institute of Mechanical Engineers. Automobile Division — Proc Inst Mech Eng Automob Div
Proceedings. Institute of Mechanical Engineers. Part 3 — Proc Inst Mech Eng Part 3
Proceedings. Institute of Medicine of Chicago — PMICA
Proceedings. Institute of Medicine of Chicago — Proc Inst Med Chic
Proceedings. Institute of Medicine of Chicago — Proc Inst Med Chicago
Proceedings. Institute of Medicine of Chicago — Proc Institute Med Chicago
Proceedings. Institute of Natural Sciences. Nihon University — Proc Inst Nat Sci Nihon Univ
Proceedings. Institute of Neurological Sciences Symposium in Neurobiology — Proc Inst Neurol Sci Symp Neurobiol
Proceedings. Institute of Oceanography and Fisheries. Bulgarian Academy of Sciences — Proc Inst Oceanogr Fish Bulg Acad Sci
Proceedings. Institute of Refrigeration — Proc Inst Refrig
Proceedings. Institute of Sewage Purification — Proc Inst Sewage Purif
Proceedings. Institute of Statistical Mathematics — Proc Inst Statist Math
Proceedings. Institute of Vitreous Enamellers — Proc Inst Vitreous Enamellers
Proceedings. Institution of Automobile Engineers (London) — Proc Inst Automob Eng (London)
Proceedings. Institution of Chemists (Calcutta) — Proc Inst Chem (Calcutta)
Proceedings. Institution of Civil Engineers [*London*] — Proc Inst Civ Eng
Proceedings. Institution of Civil Engineers — Proc Instn CE
Proceedings. Institution of Civil Engineers — Proc Instn Civ Engrs
Proceedings. Institution of Civil Engineers (London). Supplement — Proc Inst Civ Eng (London) Suppl
Proceedings. Institution of Civil Engineers. Part 1. Design and Construction — P I Civ E 1
Proceedings. Institution of Civil Engineers. Part 1. Design and Construction — Proc Inst Civ Eng Part 1
Proceedings. Institution of Civil Engineers. Part 1. Design and Construction — Proc Inst Civ Eng Part 1 Des
Proceedings. Institution of Civil Engineers. Part 2. Research and Theory — P I Civ E 2
Proceedings. Institution of Civil Engineers. Part 2. Research and Theory [*United Kingdom*] — Proc Inst Civ Eng Part 2
Proceedings. Institution of Civil Engineers. Part 2. Research and Theory — Proc Inst Civ Eng Part 2 Res
Proceedings. Institution of Civil Engineers. Parts 1 and 2 — Proc ICE
Proceedings. Institution of Civil Engineers. Parts 1 and 2 — Proc Instn Civ Engrs 1 2
Proceedings. Institution of Electrical Engineers — PIEEA
Proceedings. Institution of Electrical Engineers — Proc Inst Elec Engrs
Proceedings. Institution of Electrical Engineers — Proc Inst Elect
Proceedings. Institution of Electrical Engineers — Proc Inst Electr Eng
Proceedings. Institution of Electrical Engineers — Proc Instn Elect Engrs
Proceedings. Institution of Electrical Engineers. H — Proc IEE H
Proceedings. Institution of Electrical Engineers. I — Proc IEE I

Proceedings. Institution of Electrical Engineers (London) — P IEE (Lond)
Proceedings. Institution of Electrical Engineers (London) — Proc Inst Elec Eng (London)
Proceedings. Institution of Electrical Engineers (London) — Proc Inst Electr Eng (London)
Proceedings. Institution of Electrical Engineers. Part 1. General — Proc Inst Electr Eng Part 1
Proceedings. Institution of Electrical Engineers. Part 2. Power Engineering — Proc Inst Electr Eng Part 2
Proceedings. Institution of Electrical Engineers. Part 3. Radio and Communication Engineering — Proc Inst Electr Eng Part 3
Proceedings. Institution of Electrical Engineers. Part 4. Monographs — Proc Inst Electr Eng Part 4
Proceedings. Institution of Electrical Engineers. Part A. Power Engineering — Proc Inst Electr Eng Part A
Proceedings. Institution of Electrical Engineers. Part A. Supplement — Proc Inst Electr Eng Part A Suppl
Proceedings. Institution of Electrical Engineers. Part B. Electric Power Applications — Proc Inst Elec Eng Pt B Elec Power Appl
Proceedings. Institution of Electrical Engineers. Part B. Electronic and Communication Engineering Including Radio Engineering — Proc Inst Electr Eng Part B
Proceedings. Institution of Electrical Engineers. Part B. Supplement — Proc Inst Electr Eng Part B Suppl
Proceedings. Institution of Electrical Engineers. Part C. Generation-Transmission-Distribution — Proc Inst Elec Eng Pt C Generation Transmission Distribution
Proceedings. Institution of Electrical Engineers. Part C. Monographs — Proc Inst Electr Eng Part C
Proceedings. Institution of Electrical Engineers. Part E. Computers and Digital Techniques — Proc Inst Elec Eng Pt E Computers Digital Tech
Proceedings. Institution of Electrical Engineers. Part F. Communications, Radar, and Signal Processing — Proc Inst Elec Eng Pt F Commun Radar Signal Process
Proceedings. Institution of Electrical Engineers. Part G. Electronics Circuits and Systems — Proc Inst Elec Eng Pt G Electron Circuits Syst
Proceedings. Institution of Electrical Engineers. Part H. Microwaves, Optics, and Antennas — Proc Inst Elec Eng Pt H Microwaves Opt Antennas
Proceedings. Institution of Electrical Engineers. Special Issue — Proc Inst Electr Eng Spec Issue
Proceedings. Institution of Mechanical Engineers — Proc Inst Mech Eng
Proceedings. Institution of Mechanical Engineers — Proc Inst Mech Engrs
Proceedings. Institution of Mechanical Engineers — Proc Instn Mech Engrs
Proceedings. Institution of Mechanical Engineers. Auto Division — Proc Auto Div Instn Mech Engrs
Proceedings. Institution of Mechanical Engineers (London) — Proc Inst Mech Eng (London)
Proceedings. Institution of Mechanical Engineers. Part A. Power and Process Engineering — Proc Inst Mech Eng Part A
Proceedings. Institution of Mechanical Engineers. Part A. Power and Process Engineering — Proc Inst Mech Eng Part A Power
Proceedings. Institution of Mechanical Engineers. Part B. Management and Engineering Manufacture — Proc Inst Mech Eng Part B
Proceedings. Institution of Mechanical Engineers. Part B. Management and Engineering Manufacture — Proc Inst Mech Eng Part B Manage
Proceedings. Institution of Mechanical Engineers. Part B. Management and Engineering Manufacture — Proc Instn Mech Engrs Pt B Mgmt Engng Mf
Proceedings. Institution of Mechanical Engineers. Part C. Mechanical Engineering Science — Proc Inst Mech Eng Part C
Proceedings. Institution of Mechanical Engineers. Part C. Mechanical Engineering Science — Proc Instn Mech Engrs Pt C Mech Engng Sci
Proceedings. Institution of Mechanical Engineers. Part D. Transport Engineering — Proc Instn Mech Engrs Pt D Transp Engng
Proceedings. Institution of Mechanical Engineers. Part H. Journal of Engineering in Medicine — Proc Inst Mech Eng H
Proceedings. Institution of Radio and Electronics Engineers of Australia — Proc Inst Radio Electron Eng Aust
Proceedings. Institution of Radio and Electronics Engineers of Australia — Proc Instn Radio Electron Engrs Aust
Proceedings. Institution of Radio Engineers of Australia — Proc Instn Radio Engrs Aust
Proceedings. Institution of Railway Signal Engineers — Proc Inst Railw Signal Eng
Proceedings. Institution of the Rubber Industry — Proc Inst Rubber Ind
Proceedings. Instrument Society of America — Proc Instrum Soc Am
Proceedings. Instrument Society of America — Proc ISA
Proceedings. Inter-African Soils Conference — Proc Inter Afr Soils Conf
Proceedings. Inter-America Symposium on Space Research — Proc Inter Am Symp Space Res
Proceedings. Inter-American Symposium on Hemoglobins — Proc Inter Am Symp Hemoglobins
Proceedings. International Academy of Oral Pathology — Proc Int Acad Oral Pathol
Proceedings. International Aluminum-Lithium Conference — Proc Int Alum Lithium Conf
Proceedings. International Ash Utilization Symposium and Exposition — Proc Inst Ash Util Symp Expo
Proceedings. International Asparagus-Symposium — Proc Int Asparagus Symp
Proceedings. International Association for Testing Materials — Proc Int Assoc Test Mater
Proceedings. International Association of Milk Dealers — Proc Int Assoc Milk Dealers
Proceedings. International Association of Theoretical and Applied Limnology [*A publication*] — Proc Int Assoc Theor Appl Limnol
Proceedings. International Association of Veterinary Food Hygienists — Proc Int Assoc Vet Food Hyg
Proceedings. International Astronautical Congress — IACPA
Proceedings. International Astronautical Congress — Proc Int Astronaut Congr
Proceedings. International Astronomical Union Colloquium — Proc Int Astron Union Colloq
Proceedings. International Bari Conference on the Genetic Function of Mitochondrial DNA [*Deoxynbonucleic Acid*] — Proc Int Bari Conf Genet Funct Mitochondrial DNA
Proceedings. International Barley Genetics Symposium — Proc Int Barley Genet Symp
Proceedings. International Bedding Plant Conference — Proc Int Bedding Plant Conf
Proceedings. International Betatron Symposium — Proc Int Betatron Symp
Proceedings. International Bioclimatological Congress — Proc Int Bioclimatol Congr
Proceedings. International Biodegradation Symposium — Proc Int Biodegrad Symp
Proceedings. International Biotechnology Symposium — Proc Int Biotechnol Symp
Proceedings. International Botanical Congress — Proc Int Bot Congr
Proceedings. International Brick-Masonry Conference — Proc Int Brick Masonry Conf
Proceedings. International Briquetting Association. Biennial Conference — Proc Int Briquet Assoc Bienn Conf
Proceedings. International Cement Seminar — Proc Int Cem Semin
Proceedings. International Clean Air Conference — Proc Int Clean Air Conf
Proceedings. International Clean Air Congress — Proc Int Clean Air Congr
Proceedings. International Coal Exploration Symposium — Proc Int Coal Explor Symp
Proceedings. International Coal Testing Conference — Proc Int Coal Test Conf
Proceedings. International Cocoa Research Conference — Proc Int Cocoa Res Conf
Proceedings. International Coelenterate Conference — Proc Int Coelenterate Conf
Proceedings. International Coeliac Symposium — Proc Int Coeliac Symp
Proceedings. International Colloquium. CNRS (Centre National de la Recherche Scientifique) — Proc Int Colloq CNRS
Proceedings. International Colloquium of Spectroscopy — Proc Int Colloq Spectrosc
Proceedings. International Colloquium on Group Theoretical Methods in Physics — Proc Int Colloq Group Theor Methods Phys
Proceedings. International Colloquium on Invertebrate Pathology — PIPYDX
Proceedings. International Colloquium on Invertebrate Pathology — Proc Int Colloq Invertebr Pathol
Proceedings. International Colloquium on Oxygen Isotopes — Proc Int Colloq Oxygen Isot
Proceedings. International Colloquium on Physical and Chemical Information Transfer in Regulation and Aging — Proc Int Colloq Phys Chem Inf Transfer Regul Reprod Aging
Proceedings. International Colloquium on Plant Analysis and Fertilizer Problems — Proc Int Colloq Plant Anal Fert Probl
Proceedings. International Colloquium on Renal Lithiasis — Proc Int Colloq Renal Lithiasis
Proceedings. International Colloquium on Soil Zoology — Proc Int Colloq Soil Zool
Proceedings. International Commission on Glass — Proc Int Comm Glass
Proceedings. International Conference. Center for High Energy Forming — Proc Int Conf Cent High Energy Form
Proceedings. International Conference From Theoretical Physics to Biology — Proc Int Conf From Theor Phys Biol
Proceedings. International Conference in Organic Coatings Science and Technology. Technomic Publication — Proc Int Conf Org Coat Sci Technol Technomic Publ
Proceedings. International Conference in Particle Technology — Proc Int Conf Part Technol
Proceedings. International Conference of ESNA (European Society of Nuclear Methods in Agriculture) Working Group on Waste Irradiation — Proc Int Conf ESNA Work Group Waste Irradiat
Proceedings. International Conference of the International Association on Water Pollution Research — Proc Int Conf Int Assoc Water Pollut Res
Proceedings. International Conference on Aluminum and Health — Proc Int Conf Alum Health
Proceedings. International Conference on Aluminum Weldments — Proc Int Conf Alum Weldments
Proceedings. International Conference on Amorphous and Liquid Semiconductors — Proc Int Conf Amorphous Liq Semicond
Proceedings. International Conference on Aquaculture Nutrition — Proc Int Conf Aquacult Nutr
Proceedings. International Conference on Aquaculture Nutrition. Biochemical and Physiological Approaches to Shellfish Nutrition — Proc Int Conf Aquacult Nutr Biochem Physiol Approaches Shell
Proceedings. International Conference on Atmospheric Electricity — Proc Int Conf Atmos Electr
Proceedings. International Conference on Atomic Collisions in Solids — Proc Int Conf At Collisions Solids
Proceedings. International Conference on Atomic Masses and Fundamental Constants — Proc Int Conf At Masses Fundam Constants
Proceedings. International Conference on Atomic Physics — Proc Int Conf At Phys
Proceedings. International Conference on Beam-Foil Spectroscopy — Proc Int Conf Beam Foil Spectrosc
Proceedings. International Conference on Biochemical Problems of Lipids — Proc Int Conf Biochem Probl Lipids

Proceedings. International Conference on Cement Microscopy — Proc Int Conf Cem Microsc
Proceedings. International Conference on Chemical Vapor Deposition — Proc Int Conf Chem Vap Deposition
Proceedings. International Conference on Chitin/Chitosan — Proc Int Conf Chitin Chitosan
Proceedings. International Conference on Cloud Physics — Proc Int Conf Cloud Phys
Proceedings. International Conference on Clustering Phenomena in Nuclei — Proc Int Conf Clustering Phenom Nucl
Proceedings. International Conference on Comparative Virology — Proc Int Conf Comp Virol
Proceedings. International Conference on Conduction and Breakdown in Dielectric Liquids — Proc Int Conf Conduct Breakdown Dielectr Liq
Proceedings. International Conference on Continuum Models of Discrete Systems — Proc Int Conf Continuum Models Discrete Syst
Proceedings. International Conference on Cosmic Rays — Proc Int Conf Cosmic Rays
Proceedings. International Conference on Crystalline Electric Field and Structural Effects in F-Electron Systems — Proc Int Conf Cryst Electr Field Struct Eff F-Electron Syst
Proceedings. International Conference on Cybernetics and Society — PCCSD
Proceedings. International Conference on Cybernetics and Society — Proc Int Conf Cybern Soc
Proceedings. International Conference on Differentiation — Proc Int Conf Differ
Proceedings. International Conference on Effect of Hydrogen on Behavior of Materials — Proc Int Conf Eff Hydrogen Behav Mater
Proceedings. International Conference on Electrical and Electronic Materials — Proc Int Conf Electr Electron Mater
Proceedings. International Conference on Electrodeposition — Proc Int Conf Electrodeposition
Proceedings. International Conference on Electrodeposition and Metal Finishing — Proc Int Conf Electrodeposition Met Finish
Proceedings. International Conference on Electron Microscopy — Proc Int Conf Electron Microsc
Proceedings. International Conference on Electrostatic Precipitation — Proc Int Conf Electrost Precip
Proceedings. International Conference on Environmental Degradation of Engineering Materials — Proc Int Conf Environ Degrad Eng Mater
Proceedings. International Conference on Environmental Mutagens — Proc Int Conf Environ Mutagens
Proceedings. International Conference on Erosion by Liquid and Solid Impact — Proc Int Conf Erosion Liq Solid Impact
Proceedings. International Conference on Erythropoiesis — Proc Int Conf Erythropoiesis
Proceedings. International Conference on Fast Neutron Physics — Proc Int Conf Fast Neutron Phys
Proceedings. International Conference on Fatigue of Metals — Proc Int Conf Fatigue Met
Proceedings. International Conference on Finite Elements in Flow Problems — Proc Int Conf Finite Elem Flow Probl
Proceedings. International Conference on Fire Safety — Proc Int Conf Fire Saf
Proceedings. International Conference on Fixed-Film Biological Processes — Proc Int Conf Fixed Film Biol Processes
Proceedings. International Conference on Fluid Sealing — Proc Int Conf Fluid Sealing
Proceedings. International Conference on Fluidization — Proc Int Conf Fluid
Proceedings. International Conference on Fluidized Bed Combustion — Proc Int Conf Fluid Bed Combust
Proceedings. International Conference on Genetic Engineering — Proc Int Conf Genet Eng
Proceedings. International Conference on Hadron Spectroscopy — Proc Int Conf Hadron Spectrosc
Proceedings. International Conference on Heat Treatment of Materials — Proc Int Conf Heat Treat Mater
Proceedings. International Conference on Heavy Ion Physics — Proc Int Conf Heavy Ion Phys
Proceedings. International Conference on High Energy Collisions — Proc Int Conf High Energy Collisions
Proceedings. International Conference on High Energy Physics — Proc Int Conf High Energy Phys
Proceedings. International Conference on High Energy Rate Fabrication — Proc Int Conf High Energy Rate Fabr
Proceedings. International Conference on High-Energy Accelerators — Proc Int Conf High Energy Accel
Proceedings. International Conference on Hot Dip Galvanizing — Proc Int Conf Hot Dip Galvanizing
Proceedings. International Conference on Immunopharmacology — Proc Int Conf Immunopharmacol
Proceedings. International Conference on Indoor Air Quality and Climate — Proc Int Conf Indoor Air Qual Clim
Proceedings. International Conference on Infrared Physics — Proc Int Conf Infrared Phys
Proceedings. International Conference on Ion Beam Modification of Materials — Proc Int Conf Ion Beam Modif Mater
Proceedings. International Conference on Ion Implantation in Semiconductors and Other Materials — Proc Int Conf Ion Implant Semicond Other Mater
Proceedings. International Conference on Ion Plating and Allied Techniques — Proc Int Conf Ion Plat Allied Tech
Proceedings. International Conference on Ion Sources — Proc Int Conf Ion Sources
Proceedings. International Conference on Land for Waste Management — Proc Int Conf Land Waste Manage
Proceedings. International Conference on Lasers — Proc Int Conf Lasers
Proceedings. International Conference on Leukemia-Lymphoma — Proc Int Conf Leuk Lymphoma
Proceedings. International Conference on Light Scattering in Solids — Proc Int Conf Light Scattering Solids
Proceedings. International Conference on Liquid Atomization and Spray Systems — Proc Int Conf Liq Atomization Spray Syst
Proceedings. International Conference on Liquid Metal Technology in Energy Production — Proc Int Conf Liq Met Technol Energy Prod
Proceedings. International Conference on Localized Excitations in Solids — Proc Int Conf Localized Excitations Solids
Proceedings. International Conference on Low Temperature Physics and Chemistry — Proc Int Conf Low Temp Phys Chem
Proceedings. International Conference on Mechanical Behavior of Materials — Proc Int Conf Mech Behav Mater
Proceedings. International Conference on Mechanisms in Bioenergetics — Proc Int Conf Mech Bioenerg
Proceedings. International Conference on Medical Electronics — Proc Int Conf Med Electron
Proceedings. International Conference on Megagauss Magnetic Field Generation and Related Topics — Proc Int Conf Megagauss Magn Field Gener Relat Top
Proceedings. International Conference on Methods of Preparing and Storing Labelled Compounds — Proc Int Conf Methods Prep Storing Labelled Comp
Proceedings. International Conference on Modification of Surface Properties of Metals by Ion Implantation — Proc Int Conf Modif Surf Prop Met Ion Implant
Proceedings. International Conference on Moessbauer Spectroscopy — Proc Int Conf Moessbauer Spectrosc
Proceedings. International Conference on Neuropsychology of Learning Disorders — Proc Int Conf Neuropsychol Learn Disord
Proceedings. International Conference on New Frontiers for Hazardous Waste Management — Proc Int Conf New Front Hazard Waste Manage
Proceedings. International Conference on Noise Control Engineering — PICED
Proceedings. International Conference on Noise Control Engineering — Proc Int Conf Noise Control Eng
Proceedings. International Conference on Nuclear Data for Reactors — Proc Int Conf Nucl Data React
Proceedings. International Conference on Nuclear Methods in Environmental and Energy Research — Proc Int Conf Nucl Methods Environ Energy Res
Proceedings. International Conference on Nuclear Photography and Solid State Track Detectors — Proc Int Conf Nucl Photogr Solid State Track Detect
Proceedings. International Conference on Nuclear Physics — Proc Int Conf Nucl Phys
Proceedings. International Conference on Nuclear Power and Its Fuel Cycle — Proc Int Conf Nucl Power Its Fuel Cycle
Proceedings. International Conference on Nuclear Structure — Proc Int Conf Nucl Struct
Proceedings. International Conference on Nuclei Far from Stability — Proc Int Conf Nucl Far Stab
Proceedings. International Conference on Numerical Methods in Fluid Mechanics — Proc Int Conf Numer Methods Fluid Mech
Proceedings. International Conference on Nutrition, Dietetics, and Sport — Proc Int Conf Nutr Diet Sport
Proceedings. International Conference on Permafrost — Proc Int Conf Permafrost
Proceedings. International Conference on Pervaporation Processes in the Chemical Industry — Proc Int Conf Pervaporation Processes Chem Ind
Proceedings. International Conference on Phase Transformations in Ferrous Alloys — Proc Int Conf Phase Transform Ferrous Alloys
Proceedings. International Conference on Phenomena in Ionized Gases — Proc Int Conf Phenom Ioniz Gases
Proceedings. International Conference on Phonon Scattering in Condensed Matter — Proc Int Conf Phonon Scattering Condens Matter
Proceedings. International Conference on Photonuclear Reactions and Applications — Proc Int Conf Photonucl React Appl
Proceedings. International Conference on Plant Growth Regulation — Proc Int Conf Plant Growth Regulat
Proceedings. International Conference on Plant Pathogenic Bacteria — Proc Int Conf Plant Pathog Bact
Proceedings. International Conference on Plutonium — Proc Int Conf Plutonium
Proceedings. International Conference on Positron Annihilation — Proc Int Conf Positron Annihilation
Proceedings. International Conference on Radiation Biology and Cancer — Proc Int Conf Radiat Biol Cancer
Proceedings. International Conference on Radiocarbon Dating — Proc Int Conf Radiocarbon Dating
Proceedings. International Conference on Raman Spectroscopy — Proc Int Conf Raman Spectrosc
Proceedings. International Conference on Rapidly Quenched Metals — Proc Int Conf Rapidly Quenched Met
Proceedings. International Conference on Reactor Shielding — Proc Int Conf React Shielding
Proceedings. International Conference on Robot Vision and Sensory Controls — Proc Int Conf Rob Vision Sens Controls
Proceedings. International Conference on Scientific Aspects of Mushroom Growing — Proc Int Conf Sci Aspects Mushroom Grow
Proceedings. International Conference on Silicon Carbide — Proc Int Conf Silicon Carbide
Proceedings. International Conference on Simulation Methods in Nuclear Engineering — Proc Int Conf Simul Methods Nucl Eng
Proceedings. International Conference on Soil Mechanics and Foundation Engineering — Proc Int Conf Soil Mech Found Eng
Proceedings. International Conference on Solid Phase Methods in Protein Sequence Analysis — Proc Int Conf Solid Phase Methods Protein Sequence Anal

Proceedings. International Conference on Solid Surfaces — Proc Int Conf Solid Surf
Proceedings. International Conference on Spectroscopy — Proc Int Conf Spectrosc
Proceedings. International Conference on Spectroscopy at Radiofrequencies — Proc Int Conf Spectrosc Radiofreq
Proceedings. International Conference on Stable Isotopes in Chemistry, Biology, and Medicine — Proc Int Conf Stable Isot Chem Biol Med
Proceedings. International Conference on Statistical Properties of Nuclei — Proc Int Conf Stat Prop Nucl
Proceedings. International Conference on Superconducting Quantum Devices — Proc Int Conf Supercond Quantum Devices
Proceedings. International Conference on Synthetic Fibrinolytic-Thrombolytic Agents — Proc Int Conf Synth Fibrinolytic Thrombolytic Agents
Proceedings. International Conference on Ternary and Multinary Compounds — Proc Int Conf Ternary Multinary Compd
Proceedings. International Conference on Texture — Proc Int Conf Texture
Proceedings. International Conference on Textures of Materials — Proc Int Conf Textures Mater
Proceedings. International Conference on the Application of Charge-Coupled Devices — Proc Int Conf Appl Charge Coupled Devices
Proceedings. International Conference on the Automation of Cancer Cytology and Cell Image Analysis — Proc Int Conf Autom Cancer Cytol Cell Image Anal
Proceedings. International Conference on the Biochemistry of Lipids — Proc Int Conf Biochem Lipids
Proceedings. International Conference on the Chemistry and Uses of Molybdenum — Proc Int Conf Chem Uses Molybdenum
Proceedings. International Conference on the Compaction and Consolidation of Particulate Matter — Proc Int Conf Compaction Consol Part Matter
Proceedings. International Conference on the Effects of Corynebacterium Parvum in Experimental and Clinical Oncology — Proc Int Conf Eff Corynebacterium Parvum Exp Clin Oncol
Proceedings. International Conference on the Electronic Structure of the Actinides — Proc Int Conf Electron Struct Actinides
Proceedings. International Conference on the Fundamentals of Tribology — Proc Int Conf Fundam Tribol
Proceedings. International Conference on the Hydraulic Transport of Solids in Pipes — Proc Int Conf Hydraul Transp Solids Pipes
Proceedings. International Conference on the Insulin Treatment in Psychiatry — Proc Int Conf Insulin Treat Psychiatry
Proceedings. International Conference on the Internal and External Protection of Pipes — Proc Int Conf Intern External Prot Pipes
Proceedings. International Conference on the Ionosphere — Proc Int Conf Ionos
Proceedings. International Conference on the Metallurgy, Welding, and Qualification of Microalloyed (HSLA) Steel Weldments — Proc Int Conf Metall Weld Qualif Microalloyed HSLA Steel Weld
Proceedings. International Conference on the Moessbauer Effect — Proc Int Conf Moessbauer Eff
Proceedings. International Conference on the Mycoses — Proc Int Conf Mycoses
Proceedings. International Conference on the Mycoses. Superficial, Cutaneous, and Subcutaneous Infections — Proc Int Conf Mycoses Superficial Cutaneous Subcutaneous Inf
Proceedings. International Conference on the Peaceful Uses of Atomic Energy — Proc Int Conf Peaceful Uses At Energy
Proceedings. International Conference on the Peaceful Uses of Atomic Energy — Proc Int Conf Peaceful Uses Atomic Energy
Proceedings. International Conference on the Photochemical Conversion and Storage of Solar Energy — Proc Int Conf Photochem Convers Storage Sol Energy
Proceedings. International Conference on the Physics of Electronic and Atomic Collisions — Proc Int Conf Phys Electron At Collisions
Proceedings. International Conference on the Physics of Semiconductors — Proc Int Conf Phys Semicond
Proceedings. International Conference on the Physics of Solids at High Pressures — Proc Int Conf Phys Solids High Pressures
Proceedings. International Conference on the Problems of Quantum Field Theory — Proc Int Conf Probl Quantum Field Theory
Proceedings. International Conference on the Properties of Water and Steam — Proc Int Conf Prop Water Steam
Proceedings. International Conference on the Role of Formaldehyde in Biological Systems — Proc Int Conf Role Formaldehyde Biol Syst
Proceedings. International Conference on the Strength of Metals and Alloys — Proc Int Conf Strength Met Alloys
Proceedings. International Conference on Theoretical Physics and Biology — Proc Int Conf Theor Phys Biol
Proceedings. International Conference on Thermal Analysis — Proc Int Conf Therm Anal
Proceedings. International Conference on Thermoelectric Energy Conversion — Proc Int Conf Thermoelectr Energy Convers
Proceedings. International Conference on Titanium — Proc Int Conf Titanium
Proceedings. International Conference on Toxic Dinoflagellate Blooms — Proc Int Conf Toxic Dinoflagellate Blooms
Proceedings. International Conference on Trichinellosis — Proc Int Conf Trichinellosis
Proceedings. International Conference on Vacuum Metallurgy — Proc Int Conf Vac Metall
Proceedings. International Conference on Vacuum Metallurgy and Electroslag Remelting Processes — Proc Int Conf Vac Metall Electroslag Remelting Processes
Proceedings. International Conference on Valence Instabilities — Proc Int Conf Valence Instab
Proceedings. International Conference on Waste Disposal in the Marine Environment — Proc Int Conf Waste Disposal Mar Environ
Proceedings. International Conference on Wildlife Disease — Proc Int Conf Wildl Dis
Proceedings. International Congress for Hygiene and Preventive Medicine — Proc Int Congr Hyg Prev Med
Proceedings. International Congress for Microbiological Standardization — Proc Int Congr Microbiol Stand
Proceedings. International Congress for Stereology — Proc Int Congr Stereol
Proceedings. International Congress for Virology — Proc Int Congr Virol
Proceedings. International Congress. International Association of Hydrogeologists — Proc Int Congr Int Assoc Hydrogeol
Proceedings. International Congress. International Commission for Optics — Proc Int Congr Int Comm Opt
Proceedings. International Congress. International Federation of Automatic Control — Proc Int Congr Int Fed Autom Control
Proceedings. International Congress. International Radiation Protection Association — Proc Int Congr Int Radiat Prot Assoc
Proceedings. International Congress. International Union for the Study of Social Insects — Proc Int Congr Int Union Study Soc Insects
Proceedings. International Congress of Acarology — Proc Int Congr Acarol
Proceedings. International Congress of Allergology — Proc Int Congr Allergol
Proceedings. International Congress of Americanists — PICAM
Proceedings. International Congress of Biochemistry — Proc Int Congr Biochem
Proceedings. International Congress of Chemotherapy — Proc Int Congr Chemother
Proceedings. International Congress of Cybernetics and Systems — Proc Int Congr Cybern Syst
Proceedings. International Congress of Entomology — Proc Int Congr Ent
Proceedings. International Congress of Entomology — Proc Int Congr Entomol
Proceedings. International Congress of Essential Oils, Fragrances, and Flavours — Proc Int Congr Essent Oils Fragrances Flavours
Proceedings. International Congress of Exfoliative Cytology — Proc Int Congr Exfoliative Cytol
Proceedings. International Congress of Food Science and Technology — Proc Int Congr Food Sci Technol
Proceedings. International Congress of Gastroenterology — Proc Int Congr Gastroenterol
Proceedings. International Congress of Genetics — Proc Int Congr Genet
Proceedings. International Congress of Human Genetics — Proc Int Congr Hum Genet
Proceedings. International Congress of Immunology — Proc Int Congr Immunol
Proceedings. International Congress of Immunology. Satellite Workshop — Proc Int Congr Immunol Satell Workshop
Proceedings. International Congress of Internal Medicine — Proc Int Congr Intern Med
Proceedings. International Congress of Linguists — PICL
Proceedings. International Congress of Nephrology — Proc Int Congr Nephrol
Proceedings. International Congress of Neuro-Genetics and Neuro-Ophthalmology — Proc Int Congr Neuro Genet Neuro Ophthalmol
Proceedings. International Congress of Neuropathology — Proc Int Congr Neuropathol
Proceedings. International Congress of Neuro-Pharmacology — Proc Int Congr Neuro Pharmacol
Proceedings. International Congress of Neuro-Psychopharmacology — Proc Int Congr Neuro Psychopharmacol
Proceedings. International Congress of Nutrition (Hamburg) — Proc Int Congr Nutr (Hamburg)
Proceedings. International Congress of Orientalists — PICO
Proceedings. International Congress of Parasitology — Proc Int Congr Parasitol
Proceedings. International Congress of Pharmaceutical Sciences — Proc Int Congr Pharm Sci
Proceedings. International Congress of Pharmaceutical Sciences of FIP [*International Pharmaceutical Federation*] — Proc Int Congr Pharm Sci FIP
Proceedings. International Congress of Philosophy — PICP
Proceedings. International Congress of Phonetic Sciences — PICPS
Proceedings. International Congress of Photography — Proc Int Cong Phot
Proceedings. International Congress of Physical Medicine — Proc Int Congr Phys Med
Proceedings. International Congress of Plant Sciences — Proc Int Congr Plant Sci
Proceedings. International Congress of Plant Tissue and Cell Culture — Proc Int Congr Plant Tissue Cell Cult
Proceedings. International Congress of Primatology — Proc Int Congr Primatol
Proceedings. International Congress of Psychotherapy — Proc Int Congr Psychother
Proceedings. International Congress of Pure and Applied Chemistry — Proc Int Congr Pure Appl Chem
Proceedings. International Congress of Radiation Protection — Proc Int Congr Radiat Prot
Proceedings. International Congress of Radiation Research — Proc Int Congr Radiat Res
Proceedings. International Congress of Refrigeration — Proc Int Congr Refrig
Proceedings. International Congress of Rural Medicine — Proc Int Congr Rural Med
Proceedings. International Congress of Surface Activity — Proc Int Congr Surf Act
Proceedings. International Congress of the History of Medicine — Proc Int Congr Hist Med
Proceedings. International Congress of the History of Science — Proc Int Congr Hist Sci
Proceedings. International Congress of Zoology — Proc Int Congr Zool
Proceedings. International Congress on Air Pollution — Proc Int Congr Air Pollut
Proceedings. International Congress on Animal Reproduction — Proc Int Congr Anim Reprod
Proceedings. International Congress on Animal Reproduction and Artificial Insemination — Proc Int Congr Anim Reprod Artif Insemin

Proceedings. International Congress on Aviation and Space Medicine — Proc Int Congr Aviat Space Med
Proceedings. International Congress on Bioelectrochemistry and Bioenergetics — Proc Int Congr Bioelectrochem Bioenerg
Proceedings. International Congress on Catalysis — Proc Int Congr Catal
Proceedings. International Congress on Clinical Chemistry — Proc Int Congr Clin Chem
Proceedings. International Congress on Comparative Physiology — Proc Int Congr Comp Physiol
Proceedings. International Congress on Crop Protection — Proc Int Congr Crop Prot
Proceedings. International Congress on Deterioration and Conservation of Stone — Proc Int Congr Deterior Conserv Stone
Proceedings. International Congress on Diamonds in Industry — Proc Int Congr Diamonds Ind
Proceedings. International Congress on Gerontology — Proc Int Congr Geront
Proceedings. International Congress on Gerontology — Proc Int Congr Gerontol
Proceedings. International Congress on Hair Research — Proc Int Congr Hair Res
Proceedings. International Congress on Heat Treatment of Materials — Proc Int Congr Heat Treat Mater
Proceedings. International Congress on High Speed Photography — Proc Int Congr High Speed Photogr
Proceedings. International Congress on High Speed Photography and Photonics — Proc Int Congr High Speed Photogr Photonics
Proceedings. International Congress on Hormonal Steroids — Proc Int Congr Horm Steroids
Proceedings. International Congress on Lightweight Concrete — Proc Int Congr Lightweight Concr
Proceedings. International Congress on Marine Corrosion and Fouling — Proc Int Congr Mar Corros Fouling
Proceedings. International Congress on Medicinal Plant Research — Proc Int Congr Med Plant Res
Proceedings. International Congress on Mental Retardation — Proc Int Congr Ment Retard
Proceedings. International Congress on Muscle Diseases — Proc Int Congr Muscle Dis
Proceedings. International Congress on Mushroom Science — Proc Int Congr Mushroom Sci
Proceedings. International Congress on Neurotoxicology — Proc Int Congr Neurotoxicol
Proceedings. International Congress on Obesity — Proc Int Congr Obes
Proceedings. International Congress on Organic Geochemistry — Proc Int Congr Org Geochem
Proceedings. International Congress on Pathological Physiology — Proc Int Congr Pathol Physiol
Proceedings. International Congress on Pharmacology — Proc Int Congr Pharmacol
Proceedings. International Congress on Photobiology — Proc Int Congr Photobiol
Proceedings. International Congress on Photosynthesis Research — Proc Int Congr Photosynth Res
Proceedings. International Congress on Polymers in Concrete — Proc Int Congr Polym Concr
Proceedings. International Congress on Protozoology — Proc Int Congr Protozool
Proceedings. International Congress on Quantum Electronics — Proc Int Congr Quantum Electron
Proceedings. International Congress on Research in Burns — Proc Int Congr Res Burns
Proceedings. International Congress on Rheology — Proc Int Congr Rheol
Proceedings. International Congress on Rock Mechanics — Proc Int Congr Rock Mech
Proceedings. International Congress on Soilless Culture — Proc Int Congr Soilless Cult
Proceedings. International Congress on Surface Active Substances — Proc Int Congr Surf Act Subst
Proceedings. International Congress on the Menopause — Proc Int Congr Menopause
Proceedings. International Congress PRO AQUA — Proc Int Congr PRO AQUA
Proceedings. International Congress. Transplantation Society — Proc Int Congr Transplant Soc
Proceedings. International Convention on Automation and Instrumentation — Proc Int Conv Autom Instrum
Proceedings. International Convocation on Immunology — Proc Int Convoc Immunol
Proceedings. International Coral Reef Symposium — Proc Int Coral Reef Symp
Proceedings. International Course on Peritoneal Dialysis — Proc Int Course Peritoneal Dial
Proceedings. International Cystic Fibrosis Congress — Proc Int Cystic Fibrosis Congr
Proceedings. International District Heating Association — IDHOA
Proceedings. International District Heating Association — Proc Int Dist Heat Assoc
Proceedings. International Electrodeposition Conference — Proc Int Electrodeposition Conf
Proceedings. International Electron Beam Processing Seminar — Proc Int Electron Beam Process Semin
Proceedings. International EMIS [*Electromagnetic Isotope Separation*] **Conference on Low Energy Ion Accelerators and Mass Separators** — Proc Int EMIS Conf Low Energy Ion Accel Mass Sep
Proceedings. International Estuarine Research Conference — Proc Int Estuarine Res Conf
Proceedings. International Europhysics Conference on High Energy Physics — Proc Int Europhys Conf High Energy Phys
Proceedings. International Federation for Modern Languages and Literatures — PIFMLL
Proceedings. International Fermentation Symposium — Proc Int Ferment Symp
Proceedings. International Fungal Spore Symposium — Proc Int Fungal Spore Symp
Proceedings. International Gas Research Conference — Proc Int Gas Res Conf
Proceedings. International Geochemical Exploration Symposium — Proc Int Geochem Explor Symp
Proceedings. International Grassland Congress — Proc Int Grassland Congr
Proceedings. International Green Crop Drying Congress — Proc Int Green Crop Drying Congr
Proceedings. International Gstaad Symposium — Proc Int Gstaad Symp
Proceedings. International Heat Pipe Conference — Proc Int Heat Pipe Conf
Proceedings. International Heat Transfer Conference — Proc Int Heat Trans Conf
Proceedings. International Heavy Oil Symposium — Proc Int Heavy Oil Symp
Proceedings. International Horticultural Congress — Proc Int Hort Congr
Proceedings. International Horticultural Congress — Proc Int Hortic Congr
Proceedings. International Immunobiological Symposium — Proc Int Immunobiol Symp
Proceedings. International Instrumentation Symposium — Proc Int Instrum Symp
Proceedings. International Iron and Steel Congress — Proc Int Iron Steel Congr
Proceedings. International ISA [*Instrument Society of America*] **Biomedical Sciences Instrumentation Symposium** — Proc Int ISA Biomed Sci Instrum Symp
Proceedings. International ISA [*Instrument Society of America*] **Iron and Steel Instrumentation Symposium** — Proc Int ISA Iron Steel Instrum Symp
Proceedings. International IUPAC [*International Union of Pure and Applied Chemistry*] **Congress of Pesticide Chemistry** — Proc Int IUPAC Congr Pestic Chem
Proceedings. International Kilmer Memorial Conference on the Sterilization of Medical Products — Proc Int Kilmer Meml Conf Steril Med Prod
Proceedings. International Kimberlite Conference — Proc Int Kimberlite Conf
Proceedings. International Kupffer Cell Symposium — Proc Int Kupffer Cell Symp
Proceedings. International Leucocyte Conference — Proc Int Leucocyte Conf
Proceedings. International Leucocyte Culture Conference — Proc Int Leucocyte Cult Conf
Proceedings. International Liver Conference with Special Reference to Africa — Proc Int Liver Conf Spec Ref Afr
Proceedings. International Lymphokine Workshop — Proc Int Lymphokine Workshop
Proceedings. International Materials Symposium — Proc Int Mater Symp
Proceedings. International Meeting and International Exhibition on Sealing Technology — Proc Int Meet Int Exhib Sealing Technol
Proceedings. International Meeting of Biological Standardization — Proc Int Meet Biol Stand
Proceedings. International Meeting of Neurobiologists — Proc Int Meet Neurobiol
Proceedings. International Meeting on Ferroelectricity — Proc Int Meet Ferroelectr
Proceedings. International Meeting on Future Trends in Inflammation — Proc Int Meet Future Trends Inflammation
Proceedings. International Meeting on Inflammation — Proc Int Meet Inflammation
Proceedings. International Meeting on Modern Ceramics Technologies — Proc Int Meet Mod Ceram Technol
Proceedings. International Meeting on Organic Geochemistry — Proc Int Meet Org Geochem
Proceedings. International Microchemical Symposium — Proc Int Microchem Symp
Proceedings. International Microelectronics Symposium — Proc Int Microelectron Symp
Proceedings. International Microscopy Symposium — Proc Int Microsc Symp
Proceedings. International Mine Drainage Symposium — Proc Int Mine Drain Symp
Proceedings. International Mine Water Congress. International Mine Water Association — Proc Int Mine Water Congr Int Mine Water Assoc
Proceedings. International Minisymposium on Neonatal Diarrhea — Proc Int Minisymp Neonat Diarrhea
Proceedings. International Narcotic Research Conference — Proc Int Narc Res Conf
Proceedings. International Neem Conference — Proc Int Neem Conf
Proceedings. International Neuropathological Symposium — Proc Int Neuropathol Symp
Proceedings. International Ornithological Congress — Proc Int Ornithol Congr
Proceedings. International Particleboard/Composite Materials Symposium — Proc Int Particleboard Compos Mater Symp
Proceedings. International Peat Congress — Proc Int Peat Congr
Proceedings. International Pharmacological Meeting — Proc Int Pharmacol Meet
Proceedings. International Photobiological Congress — Proc Int Photobiol Congr
Proceedings. International Plant Propagators' Society — Proc Int Pl Propag Soc
Proceedings. International Polarographic Congress — Proc Int Polarogr Congr
Proceedings. International Powder Metallurgy Conference — Proc Int Powder Metall Conf
Proceedings. International Power Sources Symposium (London) — Proc Int Power Sources Symp (London)
Proceedings. International Precious Metals Institute Conference — Proc Int Precious Met Inst Conf
Proceedings. International Propulsion Symposium — Proc Int Propul Symp
Proceedings. International Pyrotechnics Seminar — Proc Int Pyrotech Semin
Proceedings. International Rapeseed Conference — Proc Int Rapeseed Conf

Proceedings. International Reindeer/Caribou Symposium — Proc Int Reindeer Caribou Symp
Proceedings. International Rheological Congress — Proc Int Rheol Congr
Proceedings. International Rubber Conference — Proc Int Rubber Conf
Proceedings. International School of Elementary Particle Physics — Proc Int Sch Elem Part Phys
Proceedings. International School of Physics "Enrico Fermi" — Proc Int Sch Phys Enrico Fermi
Proceedings. International School of Physics "Enrico Fermi" — Proc Internat School of Phys Enrico Fermi
Proceedings. International School on Condensed Matter Physics — Proc Int Sch Condens Matter Phys
Proceedings. International School on Excited States of Transition Elements — Proc Int Sch Excited States Transition Elem
Proceedings. International School on Mass Spectrometry — Proc Int Sch Mass Spectrom
Proceedings. International School on Symmetry and Structural Properties of Condensed Matter — Proc Int Sch Symmetry Struct Prop Condens Matter
Proceedings. International Scientific Congress on the Cultivation of Edible Fungi — Proc Int Sci Congr Cultiv Edible Fungi
Proceedings. International Seaweed Symposium — Proc Int Seaweed Symp
Proceedings. International Seed Testing Association — Proc Int Seed Test Ass
Proceedings. International Seed Testing Association — Proc Int Seed Test Assoc
Proceedings. International Seed Testing Association — Proc Int Seed Testing Assoc
Proceedings. International Seminar on High Energy Physics and Quantum Field Theory — Proc Int Semin High Energy Phys Quantum Field Theory
Proceedings. International Seminar on Magnetism — Proc Int Semin Magn
Proceedings. International Seminar on Non-Destructive Examination in Relation to Structural Integrity — Proc Int Semin Non Destr Exam Relat Struct Integr
Proceedings. International Seminar on Sampling and Assaying of Precious Metals — Proc Int Semin Sampling Assaying Precious Met
Proceedings. International Shock Tube Symposium — Proc Int Shock Tube Symp
Proceedings. International Society of Citriculture — Proc Int Soc Citric
Proceedings. International Society of Soil Science — Proc Int Soc Soil Sci
Proceedings. International Society of Soil Science. Supplement — Proc Int Soc Soil Sci Suppl
Proceedings. International Society of Sugar Cane Technologists — Proc Int Soc Sugar Cane Technol
Proceedings. International Spent Fuel Storage Technology Symposium/Workshop — Proc Int Spent Fuel Storage Technol Symp Workshop
Proceedings. International Spore Conference — Proc Int Spore Conf
Proceedings. International Steel Foundry Congress — Proc Int Steel Foundry Congr
Proceedings. International Summer Meeting of Nuclear Physicists on Nuclear Structure — Proc Int Summer Meet Nucl Phys Nucl Struct
Proceedings. International Summer School on Crystallographic Computing — Proc Int Summer Sch Crystallogr Computing
Proceedings. International Summer School on the Accurate Determination of Neutron Intensities and Structure Factors — Proc Int Summer Sch Accurate Determ Neutron Intensities Struc
Proceedings. International Symposium. British Photobiology Society — Proc Int Symp Br Photobiol Soc
Proceedings. International Symposium. Canadian Society for Immunology — Proc Int Symp Can Soc Immunol
Proceedings. International Symposium devoted to Tests on Bitumens and Bituminous Materials — Proc Int Symp Tests Bitumens Bitum Mater
Proceedings. International Symposium for Cellular Chemistry — Proc Int Symp Cell Chem
Proceedings. International Symposium for the History of Arabic Science — Proc Int Symp Hist Arabic Sci
Proceedings. International Symposium Geodesy and Physics of the Earth — Proc Int Symp Geod Phys Earth
Proceedings. International Symposium. International Committee for Studies of Bauxites, Oxides, and Hydroxides — Proc Int Symp Int Comm Stud Bauxites Oxides Hydroxides
Proceedings. International Symposium. Large Chemical Plants — Proc Int Symp Large Chem Plants
Proceedings. International Symposium Neuroontogeneticum — Proc Int Symp Neuroontog
Proceedings. International Symposium of Mass Spectrometry in Biochemistry and Medicine — Proc Int Symp Mass Spectrom Biochem Med
Proceedings. International Symposium of the Institute for Biomedical Research. American Medical Association Education and Research Foundation — Proc Int Symp Inst Biomed Res Am Med Assoc Educ Res Found
Proceedings. International Symposium of the Princess Takamatsu Cancer Research Fund — Proc Int Symp Princess Takamatsu Cancer Res Fund
Proceedings. International Symposium on Advanced Materials for ULSI — Proc Int Symp Adv Mater ULSI
Proceedings. International Symposium on Advances in Chromatography — Proc Int Symp Adv Chromatog
Proceedings. International Symposium on Advances in Gas Chromatography — Proc Int Symp Adv Gas Chromatogr
Proceedings. International Symposium on Advances in Refractories for the Metallurgical Industries — Proc Int Symp Adv Refract Metall Ind
Proceedings. International Symposium on Agglomeration — Proc Int Symp Agglom
Proceedings. International Symposium on Alcohol Fuel Technology. Methanol and Ethanol — Proc Int Symp Alcohol Fuel Technol Methanol Ethanol
Proceedings. International Symposium on Anaerobic Digestion — Proc Int Symp Anaerobic Dig
Proceedings. International Symposium on Analytical Pyrolysis — Proc Int Symp Anal Pyrolysis
Proceedings. International Symposium on Animal, Plant, and Microbial Toxins — Proc Int Symp Anim Plant Microb Toxins
Proceedings. International Symposium on Antarctic Geology — Proc Int Symp Antarct Geol
Proceedings. International Symposium on Antidepressant Drugs — Proc Int Symp Antidepressant Drugs
Proceedings. International Symposium on Aquatic Weeds — Proc Int Symp Aquat Weeds
Proceedings. International Symposium on Aroma Research — Proc Int Symp Aroma Res
Proceedings. International Symposium on Atomic, Molecular, and Solid-State Theory and Quantum Biology — Proc Int Symp At Mol Solid State Theory Quantum Biol
Proceedings. International Symposium on Automotive Technology and Automation — PISAD
Proceedings. International Symposium on Automotive Technology and Automation — Proc Int Symp Automot Technol Autom
Proceedings. International Symposium on Basic Environmental Problems of Man in Space — Proc Int Symp Basic Environ Probl Man Space
Proceedings. International Symposium on Batteries — Proc Int Symp Batteries
Proceedings. International Symposium on Beneficiation and Agglomeration — Proc Int Symp Benefic Agglom
Proceedings. International Symposium on Benzodiazepines — Proc Int Symp Benzodiazepines
Proceedings. International Symposium on Biocybernetics — Proc Int Symp Biocybern
Proceedings. International Symposium on Brain-Endocrine Interaction — Proc Int Symp Brain Endocr Interact
Proceedings. International Symposium on Bronchitis — Proc Int Symp Bronchitis
Proceedings. International Symposium on Calcium-Binding Proteins and Calcium Function in Health and Disease — Proc Int Symp Calcium Binding Proteins Calcium Funct Health D
Proceedings. International Symposium on Cancer Therapy by Hyperthermia and Radiation — Proc Int Symp Cancer Ther Hyperthermia Radiat
Proceedings. International Symposium on Capillary Chromatography — Proc Int Symp Capillary Chromatogr
Proceedings. International Symposium on Catecholamines and Stress — Proc Int Symp Catecholamines Stress
Proceedings. International Symposium on Cellular Aspects of Transplantation — Proc Int Symp Cell Aspects Transplant
Proceedings. International Symposium on Chemical and Biological Aspects of Pyridoxal Catalysis — Proc Int Symp Chem Biol Aspects Pyridoxal Catal
Proceedings. International Symposium on Clinical Immunosuppression — Proc Int Symp Clin Immunosuppr
Proceedings. International Symposium on Coal Slurry Fuels Preparation and Utilization — Proc Int Symp Coal Slurry Fuels Prep Util
Proceedings. International Symposium on Coal-Oil Mixture Combustion — Proc Int Symp Coal Oil Mixture Combust
Proceedings. International Symposium on Comparative Biology of Reproduction — Proc Int Symp Comp Biol Reprod
Proceedings. International Symposium on Comparative Research on Leukemia and Related Diseases — Proc Int Symp Comp Res Leuk Relat Dis
Proceedings. International Symposium on Condensation and Evaporation of Solids — Proc Int Symp Condens Evaporation Solids
Proceedings. International Symposium on Condition and Meat Quality of Pigs — Proc Int Symp Cond Meat Qual Pigs
Proceedings. International Symposium on Coral Reefs — Proc Int Symp Coral Reefs
Proceedings. International Symposium on Curare and Curare-Like Agents — Proc Int Symp Curare Curare Like Agents
Proceedings. International Symposium on Detection and Prevention of Cancer — Proc Int Symp Detect Prev Cancer
Proceedings. International Symposium on Diamond and Diamond-Like Films — Proc Int Symp Diamond Diamond Like Films
Proceedings. International Symposium on Discharges and Electrical Insulation in Vacuum — Proc Int Symp Discharges Electr Insul Vac
Proceedings. International Symposium on Dynamics of Ionized Gases — Proc Int Symp Dyn Ioniz Gases
Proceedings. International Symposium on Electrets — Proc Int Symp Electrets
Proceedings. International Symposium on Electric Contact Phenomena — Proc Int Symp Electr Contact Phenom
Proceedings. International Symposium on Electrochemistry in Mineral and Metal Processing III — Proc Int Symp Electrochem Miner Met Process III
Proceedings. International Symposium on Electron and Photon Interactions at High Energies — Proc Int Symp Electron Photon Interact High Energ
Proceedings. International Symposium on Electroslag Remelting Processes — Proc Int Symp Electroslag Remelting Processes
Proceedings. International Symposium on Endemic Nephropathy — Proc Int Symp Endem Nephropathy
Proceedings. International Symposium on Enzyme Chemistry — Proc Int Symp Enzyme Chem
Proceedings. International Symposium on Essential Oils — Proc Int Symp Essent Oils
Proceedings. International Symposium on Ethanol from Biomass — Proc Int Symp Ethanol Biomass
Proceedings. International Symposium on Exoelectron Emission and Applications — Proc Int Symp Exoelectron Emiss Appl
Proceedings. International Symposium on Experimental Models and Pathophysiology of Acute Renal Failure — Proc Int Symp Exp Models Pathophysiol Acute Renal Failure

Proceedings. International Symposium on Fertilization in Higher Plants — Proc Int Symp Fert Higher Plants
Proceedings. International Symposium on Flammability and Fire Retardants — Proc Int Symp Flammability Fire Retard
Proceedings. International Symposium on Flow Visualization — Proc Int Symp Flow Visualization
Proceedings. International Symposium on Fluidization — Proc Int Symp Fluid
Proceedings. International Symposium on Food Irradiation — Proc Int Symp Food Irradiation
Proceedings. International Symposium on Food Microbiology — Proc Int Symp Food Microbiol
Proceedings. International Symposium on Food Preservation by Irradiation — Proc Int Symp Food Preserv Irradiat
Proceedings. International Symposium on Food Protection — Proc Int Symp Food Prot
Proceedings. International Symposium on Fresh Water from the Sea — Proc Int Symp Fresh Water Sea
Proceedings. International Symposium on Gastrointestinal Motility — Proc Int Symp Gastrointest Motil
Proceedings. International Symposium on Geographical Nephrology — Proc Int Symp Geogr Nephrol
Proceedings. International Symposium on Geology and Geochemistry of Manganese — Proc Int Symp Geol Geochem Manganese
Proceedings. International Symposium on Germfree Research — Proc Int Symp Germfree Res
Proceedings. International Symposium on Glass Capillary Chromatography — Proc Int Symp Glass Capillary Chromatogr
Proceedings. International Symposium on Gnotobiology — Proc Int Symp Gnotobiol
Proceedings. International Symposium on Hormonal Receptors in Digestive Tract Physiology — Proc Int Symp Horm Recept Dig Tract Physiol
Proceedings. International Symposium on Industrial Uses of Selenium and Tellurium — Proc Int Symp Ind Uses Selenium Tellurium
Proceedings. International Symposium on Instrumental High Performance Thin-Layer Chromatography — Proc Int Symp Instrum High Perform Thin Layer Chromatogr
Proceedings. International Symposium on Isoelectric Focusing and Isotachophoresis — Proc Int Symp Isoelectr Focusing Isotachophoresis
Proceedings. International Symposium on Isotope Separation — Proc Int Symp Isot Sep
Proceedings. International Symposium on Lepton and Photon Interactions at High Energies — Proc Int Symp Lepton Photon Interact High Energ
Proceedings. International Symposium on Livestock Wastes — Proc Int Symp Livest Wastes
Proceedings. International Symposium on Medical Mycology — Proc Int Symp Med Mycol
Proceedings. International Symposium on Medicinal Chemistry. Main Lectures — Proc Int Symp Med Chem Main Lect
Proceedings. International Symposium on Metabolic Eye Diseases — Proc Int Symp Metab Eye Dis
Proceedings. International Symposium on Microsomes and Drug Oxidations — Proc Int Symp Microsomes Drug Oxid
Proceedings. International Symposium on Multiparticle Dynamics — Proc Int Symp Multipart Dyn
Proceedings. International Symposium on Multiple-Valued Logic — Proc Int Symp Mult Valued Logic
Proceedings. International Symposium on Neonatal Diarrhea — Proc Int Symp Neonat Diarrhea
Proceedings. International Symposium on Neurosecretion — Proc Int Symp Neurosecretion
Proceedings. International Symposium on Neutron Capture Gamma Ray Spectroscopy and Related Topics — Proc Int Symp Neutron Capture Gamma Ray Spectrosc Relat Top
Proceedings. International Symposium on Neutron Capture Therapy — Proc Int Symp Neutron Capture Ther
Proceedings. International Symposium on Nuclear Medicine — Proc Int Symp Nucl Med
Proceedings. International Symposium on Nuclear Quadrupole Resonance Spectroscopy — Proc Int Symp Nucl Quadrupole Reson Spectrosc
Proceedings. International Symposium on Nucleon-Antinucleon Interactions — Proc Int Symp Nucleon Antinucleon Interact
Proceedings. International Symposium on Olfaction and Taste — Proc Int Symp Olfaction Taste
Proceedings. International Symposium on Organic Selenium and Tellurium Compounds — Proc Int Symp Org Selenium Tellurium Compd
Proceedings. International Symposium on Osteoporosis — Proc Int Symp Osteoporosis
Proceedings. International Symposium on Packaging and Transportation of Radioactive Materials — Proc Int Symp Packag Transp Radioact Mater
Proceedings. International Symposium on Parasitic Weeds — Proc Int Symp Parasit Weeds
Proceedings. International Symposium on Phosphogypsum — Proc Int Symp Phosphogypsum
Proceedings. International Symposium on Physics of Ice — Proc Int Symp Phys Ice
Proceedings. International Symposium on Plant Pathology — Proc Int Symp Plant Pathol
Proceedings. International Symposium on Pollination — Proc Int Symp Poll
Proceedings. International Symposium on Protection against Chemical Warfare Agents — Proc Int Symp Prot Chem War Agents
Proceedings. International Symposium on Psoriasis — Proc Int Symp Psoriasis
Proceedings. International Symposium on Quantum Biology and Quantum Pharmacology — Proc Int Symp Quantum Biol Quantum Pharmacol
Proceedings. International Symposium on Radioimmunology — Proc Int Symp Radioimmunol
Proceedings. International Symposium on Radionuclides in Nephrology — Proc Int Symp Radionuclides Nephrol
Proceedings. International Symposium on Radiopharmaceuticals — Proc Int Symp Radiopharm
Proceedings. International Symposium on Recent Advances in Tumor Immunology — Proc Int Symp Recent Adv Tumor Immunol
Proceedings. International Symposium on Remote Sensing of Environment — Proc Int Symp Remote Sens Environ
Proceedings. International Symposium on Remote Sensing of Environment — Proc Int Symp Remote Sensing Environ
Proceedings. International Symposium on Rickettsiae and Rickettsial Diseases — Proc Int Symp Rickettsiae Rickettsial Dis
Proceedings. International Symposium on Ruminant Physiology — Proc Int Symp Ruminant Physiol
Proceedings. International Symposium on Silicon Molecular Beam Epitaxy — Proc Int Symp Silicon Mol Beam Epitaxy
Proceedings. International Symposium on Silicon-on-Insulator Technology and Devices — Proc Int Symp Silicon On Insul Technol Devices
Proceedings. International Symposium on Space Technology and Science — Proc Int Symp Space Technol Sci
Proceedings. International Symposium on Steel Product-Process Integration — Proc Int Symp Steel Prod Process Integr
Proceedings. International Symposium on Streptococci and Streptococcal Diseases — Proc Int Symp Streptococci Streptococcal Dis
Proceedings. International Symposium on Stress and Alcohol Use — Proc Int Symp Stress Alcohol Use
Proceedings. International Symposium on Sub-Tropical and Tropical Horticulture — Proc Int Symp Sub Trop Trop Hortic
Proceedings. International Symposium on Synthetic Fibrinolytic Agents — Proc Int Symp Synth Fibrinolytic Agents
Proceedings. International Symposium on the Baboon and Its Use as an Experimental Animal — Proc Int Symp Baboon Its Use Exp Anim
Proceedings. International Symposium on the Biochemistry of Parasites and Host-Parasite Relationships — Proc Int Symp Biochem Parasites Host Parasite Relat
Proceedings. International Symposium on the Biology and Chemistry of Basement Membranes — Proc Int Symp Biol Chem Basement Membr
Proceedings. International Symposium on the Cerebral Sphingolipidoses — Proc Int Symp Cereb Sphingolipidoses
Proceedings. International Symposium on the Chemistry of Cement — Proc Int Symp Chem Cem
Proceedings. International Symposium on the Control and Effects of Inclusions and Residuals in Steels — Proc Int Symp Control Eff Inclusions Residuals Steels
Proceedings. International Symposium on the Extractive Metallurgy of Aluminum — Proc Int Symp Extr Metall Alum
Proceedings. International Symposium on the Interaction of Fast Neutrons with Nuclei. Neutron Generators and Application — Proc Int Symp Interact Fast Neutrons Nucl Neutron Gener Appl
Proceedings. International Symposium on the Mineral Deposits of the Alps — Proc Int Symp Miner Deposits Alps
Proceedings. International Symposium on the Physics and Medicine of the Atmosphere and Space — Proc Int Symp Phys Med Atmos Space
Proceedings. International Symposium on the Reactivity of Solids — Proc Int Symp React Solids
Proceedings. International Symposium on the Safe Use of Solvents — Proc Int Symp Safe Use Solvents
Proceedings. International Symposium on the Skin Senses — Proc Int Symp Skin Senses
Proceedings. International Symposium on Water Desalination — Proc Int Symp Water Desalin
Proceedings. International Symposium on Water-Rock Interaction — Proc Int Symp Water Rock Interact
Proceedings. International Symposium on Wine and Health — Proc Int Symp Wine Health
Proceedings. International Symposium on Yeasts — Proc Int Symp Yeasts
Proceedings. International Symposium. Radiological Protection. Advances in Theory and Practice — Proc Int Symp Radiol Prot Adv Theory Pract
Proceedings. International Symposium. Technical Committee on Photonic Measurements (Photon-Detectors). International Measurement Confederation — Proc Int Symp Tech Comm Photonic Meas Photon Detect Int Meas
Proceedings. International Tailing Symposium — Proc Int Tailing Symp
Proceedings. International Technical Conference. American Production and Inventory Control Society — Proc Int Tech Conf APICS
Proceedings. International Technical Meeting on Air Pollution Modeling and Its Application — Proc Int Tech Meet Air Pollut Model Its Appl
Proceedings. International Titanium Casting Seminar — Proc Int Titanium Cast Semin
Proceedings. International Topical Conference on High Power Electron and Ion Beam Research and Technology — Proc Int Top Conf High Power Electron Ion Beam Res Technol
Proceedings. International Topical Meeting on Reactor Thermal Hydraulics — Proc Int Top Meet React Therm Hydraul
Proceedings. International Transplutonium Element Symposium — Proc Int Transplutonium Elem Symp
Proceedings. International Tungsten Symposium — Proc Int Tungsten Symp
Proceedings. International Union of Biochemistry/International Union of Biological Sciences International Symposium — Proc Int Union Biochem Int Union Biol Sci Int Symp
Proceedings. International Union of Biological Sciences. Series B — Proc Int Union Biol Sci Ser B
Proceedings. International Union of Forest Research Organizations — Proc Int Union Forest Res Organ

Proceedings. International Union of Physiological Sciences. International Congress — Proc Int Union Physiol Sci Int Congr
Proceedings. International Vacuum Congress — Proc Int Vac Congr
Proceedings. International Velsicol Symposium — Proc Int Velsicol Symp
Proceedings. International Veterinary Congress — Proc Int Vet Congr
Proceedings. International Waste Conference — PIWCA
Proceedings. International Water Conference. Engineers' Society of Western Pennsylvania — Proc Int Water Conf Eng Soc West Pa
Proceedings. International Water Quality Symposium — Proc Int Water Qual Symp
Proceedings. International Wheat Genetics Symposium — Proc Int Wheat Genet Symp
Proceedings. International Wheat Surplus Utilization Conference — Proc Int Wheat Surplus Util Conf
Proceedings. International Winter Meeting on Fundamental Physics — Proc Int Winter Meet Fundam Phys
Proceedings. International Wire and Cable Symposium — PIWSD
Proceedings. International Wire and Cable Symposium — Proc Int Wire Cable Symp
Proceedings. International Working-Meeting on Soil Micromorphology — Proc Int Work Meet Soil Micromorphol
Proceedings. International Workshop on Basic Properties and Clinical Applications of Transfer Factor — Proc Int Workshop Basic Prop Clin Appl Transfer Factor
Proceedings. International Workshop on Dynamic Aspects of Cerebral Edema — Proc Int Workshop Dyn Aspects Cereb Edema
Proceedings. International Workshop on Laser Velocimetry — Proc Int Workshop Laser Velocimetry
Proceedings. International Workshop on Nude Mice — Proc Int Workshop Nude Mice
Proceedings. International Workshop on Personal Computers and Databases in Occupational Health — Proc Int Workshop Pers Comput Databases Occup Health
Proceedings. International Workshop on Rare Earth-Cobalt Permanent Magnets and Their Applications — Proc Int Workshop Rare Earth-Cobalt Perm Magnets Their Appl
Proceedings. International Zeolite Conference — Proc Int Zeolite Conf
Proceedings. Inter-Naval Corrosion Conference — Proc Inter Nav Corros Conf
Proceedings. Interscience Conference on Antimicrobial Agents and Chemotherapy — Proc Intersci Conf Antimicrob Agents Chemother
Proceedings. Intersociety Energy Conversion Engineering Conference — Proc Intersoc Energy Conver Eng Conf
Proceedings. Intersociety Energy Conversion Engineering Conference — Proc Intersoc Energy Convers Eng Conf
Proceedings. Interuniversity Faculty Work Conference — Proc Interuniv Fac Work Conf
Proceedings. Intra-Science Research Foundation Symposium — Proc Intra Sci Res Found Symp
Proceedings. Inuyama Symposium — Proc Inuyama Symp
Proceedings. Iowa Academy of Science — Proc Iowa Acad Sci
Proceedings. IPCR (Institute of Physical and Chemical Research) Symposium on Intestinal Flora — Proc IPCR Intest Flora
Proceedings. IPI [*International Potash Institute*] **Congress** — Proc IPI Congr
Proceedings. Iran Society — PIS
Proceedings. Iranian Congress of Chemical Engineering — Proc Iran Congr Chem Eng
Proceedings. Iraqi Scientific Societies — Proc Iraqi Sci Soc
Proceedings. IRE [*Institute of Radio Engineers*] [*United States*] — Proc IRE
Proceedings. Irish Academy — PIA
Proceedings. Ironmaking Conference — Proc Ironmaking Conf
Proceedings. Irwin Strasburger Memorial Seminar on Immunology — Proc Irwin Strasburger Meml Semin Immunol
Proceedings. IS and T Symposium on Electronic and Ionic Properties of Silver Halides — Proc IST Symp Electron Ionic Prop Silver Halides
Proceedings. ISA International Conference and Exhibit — Proc ISA Int Conf Exhib
Proceedings. Isle of Man Natural History and Antiquarian Society — Proc Isle Man Natur Hist Antiq Soc
Proceedings. Isle of Wight Natural History and Archaeological Society — Proc Isle Wight Natur Hist Archaeol Soc
Proceedings. Israel Academy of Sciences and Humanities [*Jerusalem*] — PIASH
Proceedings. Israel Academy of Sciences and Humanities [*Jerusalem*] — PrisrAcSci&Hum
Proceedings. Israel Academy of Sciences and Humanities — Proc Israel Acad Sci Hum
Proceedings. Israel Academy of Sciences and Humanities. Section of Sciences — Proc Isr Acad Sci Humanit Sect Sci
Proceedings. Israel Conference on Theoretical and Applied Mechanics — Proc Isr Conf Theor Appl Mech
Proceedings. ISSOL [*International Society for the Study of Origins of Life*] **Meeting** — Proc ISSOL Meet
Proceedings. Italian Meeting on Heavy Forgings — Proc Ital Meet Heavy Forg
Proceedings. IUB/IUBS [*International Union of Biochemistry/International Union of Biological Sciences*] **International Symposium** — Proc IUB IUBS Int Symp
Proceedings. IUPAC (International Union of Pure and Applied Chemistry) Macromolecular Symposium — Proc IUPAC Macromol Symp
Proceedings. IUPAC [*International Union of Pure and Applied Chemistry*] **Symposium on Photochemistry** — Proc IPUAC Symp Photochem
Proceedings. Japan Academy — P Jap Acad
Proceedings. Japan Academy — PJACA
Proceedings. Japan Academy — Proc Jap Acad
Proceedings. Japan Academy — Proc Japan Acad
Proceedings. Japan Academy — Proc Jpn Acad
Proceedings. Japan Academy. Series A. Mathematical Sciences — Proc Japan Acad Ser A Math Sci
Proceedings. Japan Academy. Series A. Mathematical Sciences — Proc Jpn Acad Ser A
Proceedings. Japan Academy. Series B. Physical and Biological Sciences — Proc Japan Acad Ser B Phys Biol Sci
Proceedings. Japan Academy. Series B. Physical and Biological Sciences — Proc Jpn Acad Ser B
Proceedings. Japan Academy. Series B. Physical and Biological Sciences — Proc Jpn Acad Ser B Phys Biol Sci
Proceedings. Japan Atomic Industrial Forum, Incorporated — Proc Jpn At Ind Forum Inc
Proceedings. Japan Cement Engineering Association — Proc Jpn Cem Eng Assoc
Proceedings. Japan Conference on Radioisotopes — JCRDA
Proceedings. Japan Conference on Radioisotopes — Proc Jpn Conf Radioisot
Proceedings. Japan Congress on Materials Research — Proc Jpn Congr Mater Res
Proceedings. Japan National Congress for Applied Mechanics — Proc Jpn Natl Congr Appl Mech
Proceedings. Japan National Symposium on Strength, Fracture, and Fatigue — Proc Jpn Natl Symp Strength Fract Fatigue
Proceedings. Japan Society of Civil Engineers — JSCPB
Proceedings. Japan Society of Civil Engineers — Proc Jap Soc Civ Eng
Proceedings. Japan Society of Civil Engineers — Proc Jpn Soc Civ Eng
Proceedings. Japan Society of Clinical Biochemistry and Metabolism — Proc Jpn Soc Clin Biochem Metab
Proceedings. Japan Society of RES — Proc Jpn Soc RES
Proceedings. Japan Society of the Reticuloendothelial System — Proc Jpn Soc Reticuloendothel Syst
Proceedings. Japan Symposium on Thermophysical Properties — Proc Jpn Symp Thermophys Prop
Proceedings. Japanese Association for the Advancement of Science/Nihon Gakujutsu Kyokai Hokoku — Proc Jap Assoc Advancem Sci
Proceedings. Japanese Congress for Testing Materials — Proc Jpn Congr Test Mater
Proceedings. Japanese Pharmacology Society — Proc Jpn Pharmacol Soc
Proceedings. Japanese Society for Medical Mass Spectrometry — Proc Jpn Soc Med Mass Spectrom
Proceedings. Japanese Society of Antimicrobials for Animals — Proc Jpn Soc Antimicrob Anim
Proceedings. Japanese Society of Forensic Medicine — Proc Jpn Soc Forensic Med
Proceedings. Japanese Society of Internal Medicine — Proc Jpn Soc Intern Med
Proceedings. Japanese Symposium on Plasma Chemistry — Proc Jpn Symp Plasma Chem
Proceedings. Japanese-American Seminar on Prospects in Organotransition-Metal Chemistry — Proc Jpn Am Semin Prospects Organotransition Met Chem
Proceedings. Japan-US Conference on Composite Materials — Proc J US Conf Compos Mater
Proceedings. Japan-US Conference on Composite Materials — Proc Jpn US Conf Compos Mater
Proceedings. Jewish Palestine Exploration Society — ProcJPES
Proceedings. John Innes Symposium — Proc John Innes Symp
Proceedings. John Jacob Abel Symposium on Drug Development — Proc John Jacob Abel Symp Drug Dev
Proceedings. Joint Conference on Cholera (United States-Japan Cooperative Medical Science Program) — Proc Jt Conf Cholera US Jpn Coop Med Sci Program
Proceedings. Joint Conference. US-Japan Cooperative Medical Science Program. C holera Panel — Proc Jt Conf US Jpn Coop Med Sci Program Cholera Panel
Proceedings. Joint Convention of All India Sugar Technologists — Proc Jt Conv All India Sugar Technol
Proceedings. Jubilee Scientific Meeting. Higher Medical Institute-Varna — Proc Jubilee Sci Meet High Med Inst Varna
Proceedings. Kansai Plant Protection Society — Proc Kansai Plant Prot Soc
Proceedings. Kanto-Tosan Plant Protection Society — Proc Kanto-Tosan Plant Prot Soc
Proceedings. Kentucky Coal Refuse Disposal and Utilization Seminar — Proc Ky Coal Refuse Disposal Util Semin
Proceedings. Kimbrough Urological Seminar — Proc Kimbrough Urol Semin
Proceedings. Kinki Symposium of Crop Science and Plant Breeding Society — Proc Kinki Symp Crop Sci Plant Breed Soc
Proceedings. Koninklijke Akademie van Wetenschappen te Amsterdam — Proc K Akad Wet Amsterdam
Proceedings. Koninklijke Nederlandse Akademie van Wetenschappen — Proc K Ned Akad Wet
Proceedings. Koninklijke Nederlandse Akademie van Wetenschappen — Proc Ned Akad Wet
Proceedings. Koninklijke Nederlandse Akademie van Wetenschappen. Series A. Mathematical Sciences — P Kon Ned A
Proceedings. Koninklijke Nederlandse Akademie van Wetenschappen. Series A. Mathematical Sciences — Proc K Ned Akad Wet Ser A
Proceedings. Koninklijke Nederlandse Akademie van Wetenschappen. Series B. Palaeontology, Geology, Physics, and Chemistry [*Later, Proceedings. Koninklijke Nederlandse Akademie van Wetenschappen. Series B. Palaeontology, Geology, Physics, Chemistry, Anthropology*] — Proc K Ned Akad Wet Ser B Palaeontol Geol Phys Chem
Proceedings. Koninklijke Nederlandse Akademie van Wetenschappen. Series B. Palaeontology, Geology, Physics, Chemistry, Anthropology — Proc K Ned Akad Wet Ser B Palaeontol Geol Phys Chem Anthropo
Proceedings. Koninklijke Nederlandse Akademie van Wetenschappen. Series B. Physical Sciences — KNWBA
Proceedings. Koninklijke Nederlandse Akademie van Wetenschappen. Series B. Physical Sciences — P Kon Ned B

Proceedings. Koninklijke Nederlandse Akademie van Wetenschappen. Series B. Physical Sciences — Proc K Ned Akad Wet B
Proceedings. Koninklijke Nederlandse Akademie van Wetenschappen. Series B. Physical Sciences — Proc K Ned Akad Wet Ser B
Proceedings. Koninklijke Nederlandse Akademie van Wetenschappen. Series B. Physical Sciences — Proc K Ned Akad Wet Ser B Phys Sci
Proceedings. Koninklijke Nederlandse Akademie van Wetenschappen. Series B. Physical Sciences — Proc K Ned Wet Ser B Phys
Proceedings. Koninklijke Nederlandse Akademie van Wetenschappen. Series C. Biological and Medical Sciences — P Kon Ned C
Proceedings. Koninklijke Nederlandse Akademie van Wetenschappen. Series C. Biological and Medical Sciences — Proc K Ned Akad Wet Ser C
Proceedings. Koninklijke Nederlandse Akademie van Wetenschappen. Series C. Biological and Medical Sciences — Proc K Ned Akad Wet Ser C Biol Med Sci
Proceedings. Koninklijke Nederlandische Akademie von Wetenschappen — PKNAW
Proceedings. L. Farkas Memorial Symposium — Proc L Farkas Mem Symp
Proceedings. Lake Superior Mining Institute — Proc Lake Superior Min Inst
Proceedings. Latin International Biochemical Meeting — Proc Latin Int Biochem Meet
Proceedings. Latvian Academy of Sciences. Part B — Proc Latv Acad Sci Part B
Proceedings. Laurance Reid Gas Conditioning Conference — Proc Laurance Reid Gas Cond Conf
Proceedings. Laurentian Hormone Conference — Proc Laurentian Horm Conf
Proceedings. Leatherhead and District Local History Society — Proc Leatherhead Dist Local Hist Soc
Proceedings. Lectin Meeting — Proc Lectin Meet
Proceedings. Leeds Philosophical and Literary Society — PLPLS
Proceedings. Leeds Philosophical and Literary Society — PLPS
Proceedings. Leeds Philosophical and Literary Society — Proc Leeds Philos & Lit Soc
Proceedings. Leeds Philosophical and Literary Society. Literary and Historical Section — PLPLS-LHS
Proceedings. Leeds Philosophical and Literary Society. Literary and Historical Section — Proc Leeds Phil Lit Soc Lit Hist Sect
Proceedings. Leeds Philosophical and Literary Society. Literary and Historical Section — Proc Leeds Philos Lit Soc Lit Hist Sect
Proceedings. Leeds Philosophical and Literary Society. Scientific Section — PLPLS-SS
Proceedings. Leeds Philosophical and Literary Society. Scientific Section — Proc Leeds Phil Lit Soc Sci Sect
Proceedings. Leeds Philosophical and Literary Society. Scientific Section — Proc Leeds Philos Lit Soc Sci Sect
Proceedings. Leeds-Lyon Symposium on Tribology — Proc Leeds Lyon Symp Tribol
Proceedings. Lenin Academy of Agricultural Sciences. USSR — Proc Lenin Acad Agric Sci USSR
Proceedings. Leningrad Society of Anatomists, Histologists, and Embryologists — Proc Leningrad Soc Anat Histol Embryol
Proceedings. Lepetit Colloquium — Proc Lepetit Colloq
Proceedings. Leucocyte Culture Conference — Proc Leucocyte Cult Conf
Proceedings. Leukemia Marker Conference — Proc Leuk Marker Conf
Proceedings. L.H. Gray Conference — Proc L H Gray Conf
Proceedings. Lincoln College. Farmer's Conference — Proc Lincoln Coll Farmers Conf
Proceedings. Linguistic Circle of Manitoba and North Dakota — PLCM & ND
Proceedings. Linnaean Society (London) — PLSL
Proceedings. Linnean Society of London — Proc Linn Soc Lond
Proceedings. Linnean Society of London — Proc Linn Soc London
Proceedings. Linnean Society of New South Wales — Linnean Soc NSW Proc
Proceedings. Linnean Society of New South Wales — Proc Linn Soc NSW
Proceedings. Linnean Society of New South Wales — Proc Linnean Soc NS Wales
Proceedings. Linnean Society of New South Wales — Proc Linnean Soc NSW
Proceedings. Linnean Society of New York — Proc Linn Soc NY
Proceedings. Liquid Crystal Conference. Socialist Countries — Proc Liq Cryst Conf Soc Countries
Proceedings. Literary and Philosophical Society of Liverpool — PLPSL
Proceedings. Liverpool Botanical Society — Proc Liverpool Bot Soc
Proceedings. Liverpool Geological Society — Proc Liverpool Geol Soc
Proceedings. London Classical Society — PLCS
Proceedings. London International Carbon and Graphite Conference — Proc London Int Carbon Graphite Conf
Proceedings. London Mathematical Society — P Lond Math
Proceedings. London Mathematical Society — Proc London Math Soc
Proceedings. London Mathematical Society. Third Series — Proc London Math Soc 3
Proceedings. Louisiana Academy of Sciences — Proc LA Acad Sci
Proceedings. Louisiana Association of Agronomists — Proc LA Ass Agron
Proceedings. Louisiana State Horticultural Society — Proc Louisiana State Hort Soc
Proceedings. Lunar and Planetary Science Conference — Proc Lunar Planet Sci Conf
Proceedings. Lunar Science Conference [*United States*] — Proc Lunar Sci Conf
Proceedings. Lund International Conference on Elementary Particles — Proc Lund Int Conf Elem Part
Proceedings. Luxembourg Conference on the Psychobiology of Aging — Proc Luxemb Conf Psychobiol Aging
Proceedings. Machinery Dynamics Seminar — Proc Mach Dyn Semin
Proceedings. Malacological Society of London — PMS
Proceedings. Malacological Society of London — Proc Malacol Soc London
Proceedings. Malaysian Biochemical Society Conference — Proc Malays Biochem Soc Conf
Proceedings. Manchester Literary and Philosophical Society — Proc Manchester Lit Soc
Proceedings. Marine Safety Council. United States Coast Guard — Proc Mar Safety Council USCG
Proceedings. Market Milk Conference — Proc Mark Milk Conf
Proceedings. Maryland Nutrition Conference for Feed Manufacturers — Proc MD Nutr Conf Feed Manuf
Proceedings. Maryland-Delaware Water and Pollution Control Association — Proc MD Del Water Pollut Control Assoc
Proceedings. Massachusetts Historical Society — PMHS
Proceedings. Massachusetts Historical Society — Proc Mass Hist Soc
Proceedings. Massachusetts Historical Society — Proc Massachusetts Hist Soc
Proceedings. Master Brewers Association of America — Proc Master Brew Assoc Am
Proceedings. Mathematical and Physical Society (Egypt) — Proc Math Phys Soc (Egypt)
Proceedings. Mayo Clinic Staff Meeting — Proc Mayo Clin Staff Meet
Proceedings. Measurement and Monitoring of Non-Criteria (Toxic) Contaminants in Air — Proc Meas Monit Non Criter Toxic Contam Air
Proceedings. Meat Industry Research Conference — Proc Meat Ind Res Conf
Proceedings. Meat Processing Conference — Proc Meat Process Conf
Proceedings. Medico-Legal Society of Victoria — Proc Medico-Legal Soc Vict
Proceedings. Meeting. Federation of European Biochemical Societies — Proc Meet Fed Eur Biochem Soc
Proceedings. Meeting. International Conference on Biological Membranes — Proc Meet Int Conf Biol Membr
Proceedings. Meeting. International Foundation for Biochemical Endocrinology — Proc Meet Int Found Biochem Endocrinol
Proceedings. Meeting. International Society for Artificial Organs — Proc Meet Int Soc Artif Organs
Proceedings. Meeting. International Society of Hypertension — Proc Meet Int Soc Hypertens
Proceedings. Meeting. International Study Group for Steroid Hormones — Proc Meet Int Study Group Steroid Horm
Proceedings. Meeting of British West Indies Sugar Technologies — Proc Meet Br West Ind Sugar Technol
Proceedings. Meeting of Section. International Union of Forest Research Organizations — Proc Mtg Sect Int Union For Res Organ
Proceedings. Meeting of the Animal Husbandry Wing. Board of Agriculture and Animal Husbandry in India — Proc Meet Anim Husb Wing Board Agric Anim Husb India
Proceedings. Meeting of the Committee on Forest Tree Breeding in Canada — Proc Mtg Comm For Tree Breeding Can
Proceedings. Meeting of the Japanese Society for Medical Mass Spectrometry [*A publication*] — Proc Meet Jpn Soc Med Mass Spectrom
Proceedings. Meeting of West Indies Sugar Technologists — Proc Meet West Indies Sugar Technol
Proceedings. Meeting on Adrenergic Mechanisms — Proc Meet Adrenergic Mech
Proceedings. Meeting on Mycotoxins in Animal Disease — Proc Meet Mycotoxins Anim Dis
Proceedings. Meeting on Nuclear Analytical Methods — Proc Meet Nucl Anal Methods
Proceedings. Meeting. P and S Biomedical Sciences Symposia — Proc Meet P S Biomed Sci Symp
Proceedings. Meeting. Textile Information Users Council — Proc Meet Text Inf Users Counc
Proceedings. Membrane Technology Conference — Proc Membr Technol Conf
Proceedings. Memorial Lecture Meeting on the Anniversary of the Foundation of National Research Institute for Metals — Proc Mem Lect Meet Anniv Found Natl Res Inst Met
Proceedings. Metallurgical Society. Canadian Institute of Mining and Metallurgy — Proc Metall Soc Can Inst Min Metall
Proceedings. Mexican Urethane Symposium — Proc Mex Urethane Symp
Proceedings. Microbiological Research Group. Hungarian Academy of Science — Proc Microbiol Res Group Hung Acad Sci
Proceedings. Microscopical Society of Canada — PMSCD
Proceedings. Microscopical Society of Canada — Proc Microsc Soc Can
Proceedings. Mid-America Spectroscopy Symposium — Proc Mid Am Spectrosc Symp
Proceedings. Mid-Atlantic Industrial Waste Conference [*United States*] — Proc Mid-Atl Ind Waste Conf
Proceedings. Middle East Congress on Osteoporosis — Proc Middle East Congr Osteoporosis
Proceedings. Midwest Conference on Fluid Mechanics — Proc Midwest Conf Fluid Mech
Proceedings. Midwest Conference on the Thyroid — Proc Midwest Conf Thyroid
Proceedings. Midwestern Conference on Solid Mechanics — Proc Midwest Conf Solid Mech
Proceedings. Midwestern Fertilizer Conference — Proc Midwest Fert Conf
Proceedings. Mid-Year Meeting. American Petroleum Institute — Proc Mid Year Meet Am Pet Inst
Proceedings. Mid-Year Meeting. Chemical Specialties Manufacturers Association — Proc Mid Year Meet Chem Spec Manuf Assoc
Proceedings. Midyear Topical Symposium. Health Physics Society — Proc Midyear Top Symp Health Phys Soc
Proceedings. Mine Medical Officers Association — Proc Mine Med Off Assoc
Proceedings. Mine Medical Officers Association of South Africa — Proc Mine Med Off Assoc SA
Proceedings. Mineral Conference — Proc Miner Conf
Proceedings. Mineral Waste Utilization Symposium — Proc Miner Waste Util Symp
Proceedings. Miniconference on Coincidence Reactions with Electromagnetic Probes — Proc Miniconf Coincidence React Electromagn Probes
Proceedings. Minnesota Academy of Sciences — Proc Minn Acad Sci

Proceedings. Minnesota Nutrition Conference — Proc Minn Nutr Conf
Proceedings. Mississippi Water Resources Conference — Proc Miss Water Resour Conf
Proceedings. Montana Academy of Sciences — Proc Mont Acad Sci
Proceedings. Montana Livestock Nutrition Conference — Proc Mont Livest Nutr Conf
Proceedings. Montana Nutrition Conference — Proc Mont Nutr Conf
Proceedings. Montpellier Symposium — Proc Montpellier Symp
Proceedings. Munich Symposium on Biology of Connective Tissue — Proc Munich Symp Biol Connect Tissue
Proceedings. Muslim Association for the Advancement of Science — Proc Muslim Assoc Adv Sci
Proceedings. Mycological Symposium. Polish Dermatological Society — Proc Mycol Symp Pol Dermatol Soc
Proceedings. Nagano Prefectural Agricultural Experiment Station — Proc Nagano Pref Agr Exp Sta
Proceedings. Nagano Prefectural Agricultural Experiment Station/ Nagano-Ken Nogyo Shikenjo Shuho — Proc Nagano Prefect Agric Exp Sta
Proceedings. Nairobi Scientific and Philosophical Society — Proc Nairobi Sci Soc
Proceedings. Nassau County Medical Center — Proc Nassau Cty Med Cent
Proceedings. National Academy of Science — Proc Nat Acad Sc
Proceedings. National Academy of Sciences — PNAS
Proceedings. National Academy of Sciences — PNASc
Proceedings. National Academy of Sciences — Proc NA Sci
Proceedings. National Academy of Sciences [*United States of America*] — Proc Nat Acad Sci
Proceedings. National Academy of Sciences [*United States of America*] — Proc Natl Acad Sci
Proceedings. National Academy of Sciences [*Washington, D.C.*] — Proc Natn Acad Sci
Proceedings. National Academy of Sciences (India) — Proc Natl Acad Sci (India)
Proceedings. National Academy of Sciences (India) — Proc Natn Acad Sci (India)
Proceedings. National Academy of Sciences (India). Section A — PAIAA
Proceedings. National Academy of Sciences (India). Section A — Proc Nat Acad Sci (India) Sect A
Proceedings. National Academy of Sciences (India). Section A. Physical Sciences — P NAS (Ind) A
Proceedings. National Academy of Sciences (India). Section A. Physical Sciences — Proc Natl Acad Sci (India) Sect A
Proceedings. National Academy of Sciences (India). Section A. Physical Sciences — Proc Natl Acad Sci (India) Sect A Phys Sci
Proceedings. National Academy of Sciences (India). Section B. Biological Sciences — P NAS (Ind) B
Proceedings. National Academy of Sciences (India). Section B. Biological Sciences — Proc Nat Acad Sci (India) Sect B
Proceedings. National Academy of Sciences (India). Section B. Biological Sciences — Proc Natl Acad Sci (India) Sect B
Proceedings. National Academy of Sciences (India). Section B. Biological Sciences — Proc Natl Acad Sci (India) Sect B Biol Sci
Proceedings. National Academy of Sciences (United States of America) — P NAS (US)
Proceedings. National Academy of Sciences (United States of America) — Proc Nat Acad Sci (USA)
Proceedings. National Academy of Sciences (United States of America) — Proc Natl Acad Sci (USA)
Proceedings. National Academy of Sciences (United States of America) — Proc Natn Acad Sci (USA)
Proceedings. National Academy of Sciences (United States of America). Biological Sciences — Proc Nat Acad Sci (USA) Biol Sci
Proceedings. National Academy of Sciences (United States of America). Physical Sciences — Proc Nat Acad Sci (USA) Phys Sci
Proceedings. National Academy. United States of America — Proc Natl Acad USA
Proceedings. National Agricultural Plastics Congress — Proc Natl Agric Plast Congr
Proceedings. National Air Pollution Symposium — Proc Natl Air Pollut Symp
Proceedings. National Asphalt Conference — Proc Natl Asphalt Conf
Proceedings. National Association for Physical Education in Higher Education — Proceedings NAPEHE
Proceedings. National Association of Wheat Growers — Proc Nat Ass Wheat Growers
Proceedings. National Biomedical Sciences Instrumentation Symposium — Proc Natl Biomed Sci Instrum Symp
Proceedings. National Cancer Conference [*United States*] — PNCCA
Proceedings. National Cancer Conference — Proc Natl Cancer Conf
Proceedings. National Chemical Engineering Conference — Proc Natl Chem Eng Conf
Proceedings. National Computational Physics Conference — Proc Natl Comput Phys Conf
Proceedings. National Conference. Australian Institute of Agricultural Science — Proc Nat Conf AIAS
Proceedings. National Conference for Individual Onsite Wastewater Systems — Proc Natl Conf Individ Onsite Wastewater Syst
Proceedings. National Conference on Aerosols — Proc Natl Conf Aerosols
Proceedings. National Conference on Control of Hazardous Material Spills — Proc Natl Conf Control Hazard Mater Spills
Proceedings. National Conference on Electron Probe Analysis — Proc Natl Conf Electron Probe Anal
Proceedings. National Conference on Environmental Effects on Aircraft and Propulsion Systems — Proc Natl Conf Environ Eff Aircr Propul Syst
Proceedings. National Conference on Fluid Power [*United States*] — Proc Natl Conf Fluid Power
Proceedings. National Conference on Fluid Power. Annual Meeting — Proc Nat Conf Fluid Power Annu Meet
Proceedings. National Conference on Fluid Power. Annual Meeting — Proc Natl Conf Fluid Power Annu Meet
Proceedings National Conference on Hazardous Wastes and Hazardous Materials — Proc Natl Conf Hazard Wastes Hazard Mater
Proceedings. National Conference on Health Education Goals — PNCH
Proceedings. National Conference on IC Engines and Combustion — Proc Natl Conf IC Engines Combust
Proceedings. National Conference on Methadone Treatment — Proc Natl Conf Methadone Treat
Proceedings. National Conference on Municipal Sludge Management — Proc Natl Conf Munic Sludge Manage
Proceedings. National Conference on Power Transmission — PNCTD
Proceedings. National Conference on Sludge Management Disposal and Utilization — Proc Natl Conf Sludge Manage Disposal Util
Proceedings. National Conference on the Administration of Research — Proc Natl Conf Adm Res
Proceedings. National Congress. Czechoslovak Physiological Society — Proc Natl Congr Czech Physiol Soc
Proceedings. National Convention for the Study of Information and Documentation [*Japan*] — Proc Natl Conv Study Inf Doc
Proceedings. National Council on Radiation Protection and Measurements — Proc Natl Counc Radiat Prot Meas
Proceedings. National Council on Science Development (Republic of China) — Proc Natl Counc Sci Dev (Repub China)
Proceedings. National District Heating Association — Proc Natl Dist Heat Assoc
Proceedings. National Drainage Symposium — Proc Natl Drain Symp
Proceedings. National Electronics Conference — PNEC
Proceedings. National Electronics Conference [*United States*] — PNECA
Proceedings. National Electronics Conference — Proc Nat Electron Conf
Proceedings. National Electronics Conference — Proc Natl Electron Conf
Proceedings. National Entomological Society (United States of America) — Proc Natn Ent Soc (USA)
Proceedings. National Fertilizer Association — Proc Natl Fert Assoc
Proceedings. National Food Engineering Conference — Proc Nat Food Eng Conf
Proceedings. National Food Engineering Conference — Proc Natl Food Eng Conf
Proceedings. National Forum on Mercury in Fish — Proc Natl Forum Mercury Fish
Proceedings. National Ginseng Conference — Proc Natl Ginseng Conf
Proceedings. National Heat and Mass Transfer Conference — Proc Natl Heat Mass Transfer Conf
Proceedings. National Incinerator Conference — Proc Natl Incinerator Conf
Proceedings. National Institute of Sciences (India) — Proc Natl Inst Sci (India)
Proceedings. National Institute of Sciences (India) — Proc Natn Inst Sci (India)
Proceedings. National Institute of Sciences (India). Part A. Physical Sciences — PIIAA
Proceedings. National Institute of Sciences (India). Part A. Physical Sciences — Proc Natl Inst Sci (India) A
Proceedings. National Institute of Sciences (India). Part A. Physical Sciences — Proc Natl Inst Sci (India) Part A
Proceedings. National Institute of Sciences (India). Part A. Physical Sciences — Proc Natl Inst Sci (India) Part A Phys Sci
Proceedings. National Institute of Sciences (India). Part A. Supplement — Proc Natl Inst Sci (India) Part A Suppl
Proceedings. National Institute of Sciences (India). Part B. Biological Sciences — Proc Natl Inst Sci (India) Part B
Proceedings. National Institute of Sciences (India). Part B. Biological Sciences — Proc Natl Inst Sci (India) Part B Biol Sci
Proceedings. National Instrument Society of America. Chemical and Petroleum Instrumentation Symposium — Proc Natl Instrum Soc Am Chem Pet Instrum Symp
Proceedings. National Intramural Recreational Sports Association — Proceedings NIRSA
Proceedings. National Meeting. Forest Products Research Society — Proc Natl Meet For Prod Res Soc
Proceedings. National Meeting. Institute of Environmental Sciences — Proc Natl Meet Inst Environ Sci
Proceedings. National Meeting on Biophysics and Biotechnology in Finland — Proc Natl Meet Biophys Biotechnol Finl
Proceedings. National Meeting on Biophysics and Medical Engineering in Finland — Proc Natl Meet Biophys Med Eng Finl
Proceedings. National Meeting. South African Institution of Chemical Engineers — Proc Natl Meet S Afr Inst Chem Eng
Proceedings. National Open Hearth and Basic Oxygen Steel Conference — Proc Natl Open Hearth Basic Oxygen Steel Conf
Proceedings. National Pecan Association (US) — Proc Natl Pecan Assoc US
Proceedings. National Pollution Control Conference (US) — Proc Natl Pollut Control Conf (US)
Proceedings. National SAMPE (Society for the Advancement of Material and Process Engineering) Symposium — Proc Natl SAMPE Symp
Proceedings. National Science Council — Proc Natl Sci Counc
Proceedings. National Science Council (Republic of China) — Proc Natl Sci Counc (Repub China)
Proceedings. National Science Council (Republic of China). Part A. Applied Sciences — Proc Natl Sci Counc (Repub China) Part A Appl Sci
Proceedings. National Science Council (Republic of China). Part A. Physical Science and Engineering — Proc Natl Sci Counc (Repub China) Part A Phys Sci Eng
Proceedings. National Science Council (Republic of China). Part B. Basic Science — Proc Natl Sci Counc (Repub China) Part B Basic Sci
Proceedings. National Science Council. Republic of China. Part B. Life Sciences — Proc Natl Sci Counc Repub China B

Proceedings. National Science Council (Republic of China). Part B. Life Sciences — Proc Natl Sci Counc (Repub China) Part B Life Sci
Proceedings. National Seminar on Immobilized Enzyme Engineering — Proc Natl Semin Immobilized Enzyme Eng
Proceedings. National Shade Tree Conference — Proc Natl Shade Tree Conf
Proceedings. National Shellfisheries Association [*United States*] — PNSFA
Proceedings. National Shellfisheries Association — Proc Natl Shellfish Assoc
Proceedings. National Silo Association — Proc Nat Silo Ass
Proceedings. National Smoke Abatement Society — Proc Natl Smoke Abatement Soc
Proceedings. National Society for Clean Air — Proc Natl Soc Clean Air
Proceedings. National Symposia — PDIS
Proceedings. National Symposium on Aquifer Restoration and Ground Water Monitoring — Proc Natl Symp Aquifer Restor Ground Water Monit
Proceedings. National Symposium on Assessment of Environmental Pollution — Proc Natl Symp Assess Environ Pollut
Proceedings. National Symposium on Catalysis — Proc Natl Symp Catal
Proceedings. National Symposium on Desalination — Proc Natl Symp Desalin
Proceedings. National Symposium on Radioecology — Proc Natl Symp Radioecol
Proceedings. National Symposium on Thermal Pollution — Proc Natl Symp Therm Pollut
Proceedings. National Telecommunications Conference — Proc Natl Telecommun Conf
Proceedings. National Telemetering Conference — Proc Nat Telemetering Conf
Proceedings. National Topical Meeting on Nuclear Process Heat Applications — Proc Natl Top Meet Nucl Process Heat Appl
Proceedings. National Weeds Conference of South Africa — Proc Natl Weeds Conf S Afr
Proceedings. NATO [*North Atlantic Treaty Organization*] **Advanced Study Institute of Mass Spectrometry on Theory, Design, and Application** — Proc NATO Adv Study Inst Mass Spectrom Theory Des Appl
Proceedings. NATO Advanced Study Institute on Feldspars — Proc NATO Adv Study Inst Feldspars
Proceedings. Natural Gas Processors Association — Proc Natur Gas Processors Ass
Proceedings. Natural Gas Processors Association. Annual Convention — Proc Nat Gas Processors Assoc Annu Conv
Proceedings. Natural Gas Processors Association. Technical Papers — Proc Nat Gas Process Assoc Tech Pap
Proceedings. Natural History Society of Wisconsin — Proc Nat Hist Soc Wisconsin
Proceedings. Near East - South Africa Irrigation Practices Seminar — Proc Near E S Afr Irrig Pract Semin
Proceedings. Nebraska Academy of Sciences — Proc Nebr Acad Sci
Proceedings. Nebraska Academy of Sciences and Affiliated Societies — Proc Nebr Acad Sci Affil Soc
Proceedings. New England Bioengineering Conference — Proc N Engl Bioeng Conf
Proceedings. New England (Northeast) Bioengineering Conference — Proc N Engl Northeast Bioeng Conf
Proceedings. New Hampshire Academy of Science — Proc NH Acad Sci
Proceedings. New Jersey Historical Society — PNJHS
Proceedings. New Jersey Historical Society — Proc NJ Hist Soc
Proceedings. New Jersey Mosquito Control Association — Proc NJ Mosq Control Assoc
Proceedings. New Jersey Mosquito Control Association. Supplement — Proc NJ Mosq Control Assoc Suppl
Proceedings. New Jersey Mosquito Extermination Association — Proc NJ Mosq Exterm Assoc
Proceedings. New Mexico-West Texas Philosophical Society — Proc N Mex W Tex Phil Soc
Proceedings. New York State Historical Association — Proc NY St Hist Assn
Proceedings. New York State Horticultural Society — Proc NY St Hort Soc
Proceedings. New Zealand Ecological Society — Proc NZ Ecol Soc
Proceedings. New Zealand Grassland Association — Proc NZ Grassl Assoc
Proceedings. New Zealand Grassland Association — Proc NZ Grassld Ass
Proceedings. New Zealand Grassland Association. Conference — Proc NZ Grassl Assoc Conf
Proceedings. New Zealand Grasslands Association — Proc New Zealand Grasslands Assoc
Proceedings. New Zealand Institute of Agricultural Science — Proc NZ Inst Agr Sci
Proceedings. New Zealand Seminar on Trace Elements and Health — Proc NZ Semin Trace Elem Health
Proceedings. New Zealand Society of Animal Production — Proc NZ Soc Anim Proc
Proceedings. New Zealand Weed and Pest Control Conference — Proc NZ Weed & Pest Control Conf
Proceedings. New Zealand Weed and Pest Control Conference — Proc NZ Weed Conf
Proceedings. New Zealand Weed and Pest Control Conference — Proc NZ Weed Pest Contr Conf
Proceedings. New Zealand Weed Control Conference — Proc NZ Weed Control Conf
Proceedings. Ninth International Grassland Congress — Proc Ninth Int Grassld Congr
Proceedings. No. R and D. Fertilizer Association of India — Proc No RD Fert Assoc India
Proceedings. Nobel Symposium — Proc Nobel Symp
Proceedings. Nordic Aroma Symposium — Proc Nord Aroma Symp
Proceedings. Nordic Meeting on Medical and Biological Engineering — Proc Nord Meet Med Biol Eng
Proceedings. North American Conference on Powder Coating — Proc North Am Conf Powder Coat
Proceedings. North American Forest Soils Conference — Proc North Am For Soils Conf
Proceedings. North American Metalworking Research Conference — Proc North Am Metalwork Res Conf
Proceedings. North American Society for Sport History — Proc NASSH
Proceedings. North Central Branch. American Association of Economic Entomologists — Proc N Cent Brch Am Ass Econ Ent
Proceedings. North Central Branch. Entomological Society of America — Proc N Cent Brch Ent Soc Am
Proceedings. North Central Branch. Entomological Society of America — Proc North Cent Branch Entomol Soc Am
Proceedings. North Central Tree Improvement Conference — Proc North Cent Tree Improv Conf
Proceedings. North Central Weed Control Conference — Proc North Cent Weed Control Conf
Proceedings. North Dakota Academy of Science — Proc N Dak Acad Sci
Proceedings. North Dakota Academy of Science — Proc ND Acad Sci
Proceedings. North Dakota Academy of Science — Proc North Dakota Acad Sci
Proceedings. North of England Soils Discussion Group — Proc N Engl Soils Discuss Grp
Proceedings. Northeastern Forest Tree Improvement Conference — Proc Ntheast For Tree Impr Conf
Proceedings. Northeastern Weed Control Conference — Proc Northeast Weed Contr Conf
Proceedings. Northeastern Weed Control Conference — Proc Northeast Weed Control Conf
Proceedings. Northeastern Weed Science Society — Proc Northeast Weed Sci Soc
Proceedings. Northwest Conference of Structural Engineers — Proc Northwest Conf Struct Eng
Proceedings. Northwest Wood Products Clinic — Proc Northwest Wood Prod Clin
Proceedings. Nova Scotian Institute of Science — Proc NS Inst Sci
Proceedings. Nuclear and Radiation Chemistry Symposium — Proc Nucl Radiat Chem Symp
Proceedings. Nuclear Engineering and Science Conference — Proc Nucl Eng Sci Conf
Proceedings. Nuclear Physics and Solid State Physics Symposium — PPSSA
Proceedings. Nuclear Physics and Solid State Physics Symposium [*India*] — Proc Nucl Phys Solid State Phys Symp
Proceedings. Nursing Theory Conference — Proc Nurs Theory Conf
Proceedings. Nut Growers Society of Oregon, Washington, and British Columbia — Proc Nut Grow Soc Oreg Wash BC
Proceedings. Nutrition Conference for Feed Manufacturers — Proc Nucl Conf Feed Manuf
Proceedings. Nutrition Council. American Feed Manufacturers Association — Proc Nutr Counc Am Feed Manuf Assoc
Proceedings. Nutrition Society — P Nutr Soc
Proceedings. Nutrition Society — Proc Nutr Soc
Proceedings. Nutrition Society of Australia — Proc Nutr Soc Aust
Proceedings. Nutrition Society of Australia. Annual Conference — Proc Nutr Soc Aust Annu Conf
Proceedings. Nutrition Society of Southern Africa — Proc Nutr Soc South Afr
Proceedings. NWWA-EPA [*National Water Well Association - Environmental Protection Agency*] **National Ground Water Quality Symposium** [*US*] — Proc NWWA EPA Natl Ground Water Qual Symp
Proceedings. Ocean Drilling Program. Initial Reports — Proc Ocean Drill Program Init Rep
Proceedings. Ocean Drilling Program. Scientific Results — Proc Ocean Drill Program Sci Results
Proceedings. Ocean Energy Conference — Proc Ocean Energy Conf
Proceedings. Ocean Thermal Energy Conversion Conference — Proc Ocean Therm Energy Convers Conf
Proceedings of A. Razmadze Mathematical Institute. Georgian Academy of Sciences — Proc A Razmadze Math Inst
Proceedings of Applied Bacteriology — Proc Appl Bacteriol
Proceedings of Bauxite Symposium — Proc Bauxite Symp
Proceedings of Einstein Foundation International — Proc Einstein Found Internat
Proceedings of Hydrotransport — Proc Hydrotransp
Proceedings of Lasers in Dermatology and Tissue Welding — Proc Lasers Dermatol Tissue Weld
Proceedings of MoBBEL (Molekularbiologische und Biotechnologische Entwicklungsliga) — Proc MoBBEL
Proceedings of Ophthalmic Technologies — Proc Ophthalmic Technol
Proceedings of Pakistan Congress of Zoology — Proc Pak Congr Zool
Proceedings of Technical Groups. New Zealand Institution of Engineers — Proc Tech Groups NZ Inst Eng
Proceedings of the Academy of Sciences of Turkmenistan — Proc Acad Sci Turkm
Proceedings of the Beijing International Symposium on Pyrotechnics and Explosives — Proc Beijing Int Symp Pyrotech Explos
Proceedings of the Bioengineering Conference — Proc Bioeng Conf
Proceedings of the Centre for Mathematical Analysis. Australian National University — Proc Centre Math Anal Austral Nat Univ
Proceedings of the Conference on Robotics and Remote Systems — Proc Conf Rob Remote Syst
Proceedings of the Convention. Institute of Brewing (Australia and New Zealand Section) — IBAZA
Proceedings of the Estonian Academy of Sciences. Engineering — Proc Est Acad Sci Eng
Proceedings of the GRI (Gas Research Institute) Sulfur Recovery Conference — Proc GRI Sulfur Recovery Conf
Proceedings of the IEEE International Frequency Control Symposium — Proc IEEE Int Freq Control Symp

Proceedings of the International Centre for Heat and Mass Transfer — Proc Int Cent Heat Mass Transfer
Proceedings of the International Electronics Packaging Conference — Proc Int Electron Packag Conf
Proceedings of the International Symposium on Controlled Release of Bioactive Materials — Proc Int Symp Controlled Release Bioact Mater
Proceedings of the International Symposium on Natural Antioxidants. Molecular Mechanisms and Health Effects — Proc Int Symp Nat Antioxid Mol Mech Health Eff
Proceedings of the International Symposium on Power Semiconductor Devices and ICs — Proc Int Symp Power Semicond Devices ICs
Proceedings of the International Symposium on Weak and Electromagnetic Interactions in Nuclei — Proc Int Symp Weak Electromagn Interact Nucl
Proceedings of the International Workshop on Physics with Recoil Separators and Detector Arrays — Proc Int Workshop Phys Recoil Sep Detect Arrays
Proceedings of the Koninklijke Nederlandse Akademie van Wetenschappen. Series A. Mathematical Sciences — Proc K Ned Akad Wet Ser A Math Sci
Proceedings of the Lebedev Physics Institute. Academy of Sciences of Russia — Proc Lebedev Phys Inst Acad Sci Russia
Proceedings of the Mathematical Society — Proc Math Soc
Proceedings of the Mexican School of Particles and Fields — Proc Mex Sch Part Fields
Proceedings of the Modern Language Association — PMLA
Proceedings of the Pakistan Academy of Sciences — Proc Pakistan Acad Sci
Proceedings of the Power Sources Conference — Proc Power Sources Conf
Proceedings of the School of Science of Tokai University — Proc School Sci Tokai Univ
Proceedings of the SEM (Society for Experimental Mechanics) Conference on Experimental Mechanics — Proc SEM Conf Exp Mech
Proceedings of the SEM (Society for Experimental Mechanics) Spring Conference on Experimental Mechanics — Proc SEM Spring Conf Exp Mech
Proceedings of the Sony Research Forum — Proc Sony Res Forum
Proceedings of the SPI (Society of the Plastics Industry) Annual Technical/Marketing Conference — Proc SPI Annu Tech Mark Conf
Proceedings of the US/Mexico Symposium on Atomic and Molecular Physics — Proc US Mex Symp At Mol Phys
Proceedings of the Workshop on Wendelstein 7-X and Helias Reactors — Proc Workshop Wendelstein 7 X Helias React
Proceedings of Vibration Problems — Proc Vib Probl
Proceedings of Vibration Problems [*Poland*] — PVBPA
Proceedings. Ohio Academy of Science — Proc Ohio Acad Sci
Proceedings. Ohio State Horticultural Society — Proc Ohio State Hort Soc
Proceedings. Ohio State Horticultural Society — Proc Ohio State Hortic Soc
Proceedings. Oil Recovery Conference. Texas Petroleum Research Committee — Proc Oil Recovery Conf Tex Petrol Res Comm
Proceedings. Oil Shale Symposium — Proc Oil Shale Symp
Proceedings. Oklahoma Academy of Science — Proc Okla Acad Sci
Proceedings on the Study of the Fauna and Flora of the USSR. Section of Botany — Proc Study Fauna Flora USSR Sect Bot
Proceedings. Ontario Industrial Waste Conference — Proc Ont Ind Waste Conf
Proceedings. Opening Session and Plenary Session Symposium. International Congress of Plant Protection — Proc Opening Sess Plenary Sess Symp Int Congr Plant Prot
Proceedings. Oregon Academy of Science — Proc Oreg Acad Sci
Proceedings. Oregon Academy of Science — Proc Oregon Acad Sci
Proceedings. Oregon Weed Conference — Proc Oreg Weed Conf
Proceedings. Organ Institute of New South Wales — Proc Organ Inst NSW
Proceedings. Organic Coatings Symposium — Proc Org Coat Symp
Proceedings. Osaka Prefectural Institute of Public Health. Edition of Environmental Health — Proc Osaka Prefect Inst Public Health Ed Environ Health
Proceedings. Osaka Prefectural Institute of Public Health. Edition of Environmental Hygiene — Proc Osaka Prefect Inst Public Health Ed Environ Hyg
Proceedings. Osaka Prefecture Institute of Public Health. Edition of Food Sanitation — Proc Osaka Prefect Inst Public Health Ed Food Sanit
Proceedings. Osaka Prefecture Institute of Public Health. Edition of Industrial Health — Proc Osaka Prefect Inst Public Health Ed Ind Health
Proceedings. Osaka Prefecture Institute of Public Health. Edition of Mental Health — OKHED4
Proceedings. Osaka Prefecture Institute of Public Health. Edition of Mental Health — Proc Osaka Prefect Inst Public Health Ed Ment Health
Proceedings. Osaka Prefecture Institute of Public Health. Edition of Pharmaceutical Affairs — OFKYDA
Proceedings. Osaka Prefecture Institute of Public Health. Edition of Pharmaceutical Affairs — Proc Osaka Prefect Inst Public Health Ed Pharm Aff
Proceedings. Osaka Prefecture Institute of Public Health. Edition of Public Health — OKEHDW
Proceedings. Osaka Prefecture Institute of Public Health. Edition of Public Health — Proc Osaka Prefect Inst Public Health Ed Public Health
Proceedings. Osaka Public Health Institute [*Japan*] — Proc Osaka Public Health Inst
Proceedings. Oxford Bibliographical Society — POBS
Proceedings. P. N. Lebedev Physics Institute — Proc PN Lebedev Phys Inst
Proceedings. P. N. Lebedev Physics Institute. Academy of Sciences of the USSR — Proc PN Lebedev Phys Inst Acad Sci USSR
Proceedings. P. P. Shirshov Institute of Oceanology. Academy of Sciences. USSR — Proc PP Shirshov Inst Oceanol Acad Sci USSR
Proceedings. Pacific Basin Conference — Proc Pac Basin Conf
Proceedings. Pacific Basin Conference on Nuclear Power Development and the Fuel Cycle — Proc Pac Basin Conf Nucl Power Dev Fuel Cycle
Proceedings. Pacific Chemical Engineering Congress — Proc Pac Chem Eng Congr
Proceedings. Pacific Coast Council on Latin American Studies — PCCLAS/P
Proceedings. Pacific Coast Gas Association, Inc. [*California*] — Proc Pac Coast Gas Ass
Proceedings. Pacific International Summer School in Physics — Proc Pac Int Summer Sch Phys
Proceedings. Pacific Northwest Conference on Foreign Languages — PPNCFL
Proceedings. Pacific Northwest Fertilizer Conference — Proc Pac Northwest Fert Conf
Proceedings. Pacific Northwest Industrial Waste Conference — Proc Pac Northwest Ind Waste Conf
Proceedings. Pacific Science Congress — Proc Pac Sci Congr
Proceedings. Pakistan Academy of Sciences — Proc Pak Acad Sci
Proceedings. Pakistan Science Conference — Proc Pak Sci Conf
Proceedings. Pakistan Science Conference — Proc Pakist Sci Conf
Proceedings. Pakistan Statistical Association — Proc Pakistan Statist Assoc
Proceedings. Pan Indian Ocean Science Congress — Proc Pan Indian Ocean Sci Congr
Proceedings. Pan-American Congress of Endocrinology — Proc Pan Am Congr Endocrinol
Proceedings. Panamerican Congress of Rheumatology — Proc Panam Congr Rheumatol
Proceedings. Panel on Moessbauer Spectroscopy and Its Applications — Proc Panel Moessbauer Spectrosc Its Appl
Proceedings. Panel on Neutron Standard Reference Data — Proc Panel Neutron Stand Ref Data
Proceedings. Panel on Radon in Uranium Mining — Proc Panel Radon Uranium Min
Proceedings. Panel on Reactor Burn-up Physics — Proc Panel React Burn up Phys
Proceedings. Panel on the Practical Applications of the Peaceful Uses of Nuclear Explosions — Proc Panel Pract Appl Peaceful Uses Nucl Explos
Proceedings. Panel on the Use of Nuclear Techniques in Studies of Mineral Metabolism and Disease in Domestic Animals — Proc Panel Use Nucl Tech Stud Miner Metab Dis Domestic Anim
Proceedings. Panel on the Use of Tracer Techniques for Plant Breeding — Proc Panel Use Tracer Tech Plant Breed
Proceedings. Panel on Uranium Exploration Geology — Proc Panel Uranium Explor Geol
Proceedings. Pan-Pacific Science Congress — Proc Pan Pac Sci Congr
Proceedings. Paper Synthetics Conference — Proc Pap Synth Conf
Proceedings. Pathological Society of Philadelphia — Proc Path Soc Phila
Proceedings. Patristic, Mediaeval, and Renaissance Conference — PMR
Proceedings. Paving Conference — Proc Paving Conf
Proceedings. Pennsylvania Academy of Science — Proc PA Acad Sci
Proceedings. Pennsylvania Academy of Science — Proc Penn Acad Sci
Proceedings. Peoria Academy of Science — Proc Peoria Acad Sci
Proceedings. Perthshire Society of Natural Science — Proc Perthshire Soc Nat Sci
Proceedings. Perugia Quadrennial International Conference on Cancer — Proc Perugia Quadrenn Int Conf Cancer
Proceedings. Pfefferkorn Conference — Proc Pfefferkorn Conf
Proceedings. Pfizer Annual Research Conference — Proc Pfizer Annu Res Conf
Proceedings. Pharmaceutical Society of Egypt — Proc Pharm Soc Egypt
Proceedings. Pharmaceutical Society of Egypt. Scientific Edition — Proc Pharm Soc Egypt Sci Ed
Proceedings. Philadelphia Symposia on Ocular and Visual Development — Proc Philadelphia Symp Ocul Visual Dev
Proceedings. Philippine Sugar Association — Proc Philipp Sugar Assoc
Proceedings. Philological Society (London) — PPSL
Proceedings. Philosophy of Education Society of Australasia — Proc Phil Educ Soc Austl
Proceedings. Philosophy of Education Society of Great Britain — Proc Phil Educ Soc GB
Proceedings. Physical Society. London. General Physics — Proc Phys Soc London Gen Phys
Proceedings. Physical Society. London. Solid State Physics — Proc Phys Soc London Solid State Phys
Proceedings. Physical Society of Edinburgh — Proc Phys Soc Edinb
Proceedings. Physical Society of Japan — Proc Phys Soc Jpn
Proceedings. Physical Society of London — Pr Phys Soc L
Proceedings. Physical Society of London — Proc Phys Soc Lond
Proceedings. Physical Society of London — Proc Phys Soc London
Proceedings. Physical Society of London. Section A — Proc Phys Soc London Sect A
Proceedings. Physical Society of London. Section B — Proc Phys Soc London Sect B
Proceedings. Physico-Mathematical Society of Japan — Proc Phys Math Soc Jpn
Proceedings. Physics Seminar in Trondheim [*Norway*] — Proc Phys Semin Trondheim
Proceedings. Physics Society — Proc Phys Soc
Proceedings. Physiological Society (London) — Proc Physiol Soc London
Proceedings. Phytochemical Society — Proc Phytochem Soc
Proceedings. Phytochemical Society of Europe — Proc Phytochem Soc Eur
Proceedings. Phytochemical Society Symposium — Proc Phytochem Soc Symp
Proceedings. Pineapple Technologists' Society — Proc Pineapple Technol Soc
Proceedings. Pittsburgh Sanitary Engineering Conference — Proc Pittsburgh Sanit Eng Conf
Proceedings. Plant Growth Regulator Society of America — Proc Plant Growth Regul Soc Am
Proceedings. Plant Growth Regulator Working Group — Proc Plant Growth Regul Work Group
Proceedings. Plant Propagators' Society [*United States*] — Proc Plant Propagators' Soc
Proceedings. Plenary Sessions. International Congress of Biochemistry — Proc Plenary Sess Int Congr Biochem

Proceedings. Plenary Sessions. World Congress on Chemical Engineering — Proc Plenary Sess World Congr Chem Eng
Proceedings. PMR Conference. Annual Publication of the International Patristic, Mediaeval, and Renaissance Conference — PPMRC
Proceedings. Polish Conference on Ultrasonics — Proc Pol Conf Ultrason
Proceedings. Porcelain Enamel Institute. Technical Forum — Proc Porcelain Enamel Inst Tech Forum
Proceedings. Post Accident Heat Removal Information Exchange Meeting — Proc Post Accid Heat Removal Inf Exch Meet
Proceedings. Potato Association of America — Proc Potato Assoc Amer
Proceedings. Poultry Science Symposium — Proc Poult Sci Symp
Proceedings. Power Plant Dynamics. Control and Testing Symposium — Proc Power Plant Dyn Control Test Symp
Proceedings. Power Sources Symposium — Proc Power Sources Symp
Proceedings. Prehistoric Society — P Prehist S
Proceedings. Prehistoric Society — PPS
Proceedings. Prehistoric Society — Pr Preh Soc
Proceedings. Prehistoric Society — Prehist Soc Proc
Proceedings. Prehistoric Society — Proc Pr Hist Soc
Proceedings. Prehistoric Society — Proc Prehist Soc
Proceedings. Prehistoric Society — Proc PS
Proceedings. Prehistoric Society of East Anglia — Proc of Preh Soc
Proceedings. Prehistoric Society of East Anglia — Proc Pr Soc
Proceedings. Prehistoric Society of East Anglia — Proc PS
Proceedings. Process Technology Conference — Proc Process Technol Conf
Proceedings. Processing Instructors' Meeting — Proc Process Inst Meet
Proceedings. Product Liability Prevention Conference — Proc Prod Liability Prev Conf
Proceedings. Public Health Engineering Conference [*Loughborough University of Technology*] — Proc Public Health Eng Conf
Proceedings. Public Works Congress — Proc Public Works Congr
Proceedings. Publication. Rochester International Conference on Environmental Toxicity — Proc Publ Rochester Int Conf Environ Tox
Proceedings. Pyroteknikdagen — Proc Pyroteknikdagen
Proceedings. Quadrennial Conference on Cancer — Proc Quadrenn Conf Cancer
Proceedings. Quadrennial IAGOD [*International Association on the Genesis of Ore Deposits*] **Symposium** — Proc Quadrenn IAGOD Symp
Proceedings. Quadrennial International Ozone Symposium — Proc Quadrenn Int Ozone Symp
Proceedings. Queensland Society of Sugar Cane Technologists — Proc QD Soc Sug Cane Technol
Proceedings. Queensland Society of Sugar Cane Technologists — Proc Queensl Soc Sugar Cane Technol
Proceedings. Radio Club of America — Proc Radio Club Am
Proceedings. Radioisotope Conference — Proc Radioisot Conf
Proceedings. Radioisotope Society of the Philippines — Proc Radioisot Soc Philipp
Proceedings. Rajasthan Academy of Sciences — Proc Rajasthan Acad Sci
Proceedings. Rare Earth Research Conference — Proc Rare Earth Res Conf
Proceedings. Refining Department. American Petroleum Institute — Proc Refin Dep Am Pet Inst
Proceedings. Regge Cut Conference — Proc Regge Cut Conf
Proceedings. Regional Conference for Africa — Proc Reg Conf Afr
Proceedings. Regional Conference. International Potash Institute — Proc Reg Conf Int Potash Inst
Proceedings. Regional Conference on Electron-Microscopy in Asia and Oceania — Proc Reg Conf Electron Micros Asia Oceania
Proceedings. Regional Meeting on Modern Trends in Chemotherapy of Tuberculosis and Symposium on Rifampicin — Proc Reg Meet Mod Trends Chemother Tuber Symp Rifampicin
Proceedings. Relay Conference — Proc Relay Conf
Proceedings. Reliability and Maintainability Conference — Proc Reliab Maint Conf
Proceedings. Reliability and Maintainability Conference — RLMPB
Proceedings. Remote Systems Technology Division of the American Nuclear Society — Proc Remote Syst Technol Div ANS
Proceedings. Rencontre de Moriond — Proc Rencontre Moriond
Proceedings. Research Conference Sponsored by the Council on Research. American Meat Institute. University of Chicago — Proc Res Conf Counc Res Am Meat Inst Univ Chicago
Proceedings. Research Conference Sponsored by the Research Council of the American Meat Institute Foundation. University of Chicago — Proc Res Conf Res Counc Am Meat Inst Found Univ Chicago
Proceedings. Research Coordination Meeting. Seed Protein Improvement Programme — Proc Res Coord Meet Seed Protein Improv Programme
Proceedings. Research Institute for Nuclear Medicine and Biology — PRNBA
Proceedings. Research Institute for Nuclear Medicine and Biology — Proc Res Inst Nucl Med Biol
Proceedings. Research Institute for Nuclear Medicine and Biology. Hiroshima — Proc Res Inst Nucl Med Biol Hiroshima
Proceedings. Research Institute for Nuclear Medicine and Biology. Hiroshima University [*Japan*] — Proc Res Inst Nucl Med Biol Hiroshima Univ
Proceedings. Research Institute of Atmospherics. Nagoya University — PATUA
Proceedings. Research Institute of Atmospherics. Nagoya University — Proc Res Inst Atmos Nagoya Univ
Proceedings. Research Institute of Fisheries and Oceanography — Proc Res Inst Fish Oceanogr
Proceedings. Research Institute of Oceanography and Fisheries (Varna) — Proc Res Inst Oceanogr Fish (Varna)
Proceedings. Research Institute of Pomology [*Skierniewice, Poland*]. Series E. Conferences and Symposia — PISEAJ
Proceedings. Research Institute of Pomology (Skierniewice, Poland). Series E. Conferences and Symposia — Proc Inst Pomol (Skierniewice Pol) Ser E Conf Symp
Proceedings. Research Institute of Pomology (Skierniewice, Poland). Series E. Conferences and Symposia — Proc Res Inst Pomol (Skierniewice Pol) Ser E Conf Symp
Proceedings. Research Society of Japan Sugar Refineries' Technologists — Proc Res Soc Jap Sugar Refin Technol
Proceedings. Research Society of Japan Sugar Refineries' Technologists — Proc Res Soc Jpn Sugar Refineries' Technol
Proceedings. Rhone-Poulence Round Table Conference — Proc Rhone Poulence Round Table Conf
Proceedings. Rio Grande Valley Horticultural Institute — Proc Rio Grande Val Hortic Inst
Proceedings. Rio Grande Valley Horticultural Society — Proc Rio Grande Valley Hort Soc
Proceedings. Risoe International Symposium on Metallurgy and Materials Science — Proc Risoe Int Symp Metall Mater Sci
Proceedings. Robert A. Welch Foundation. Conferences on Chemical Research — Proc Robert A Welch Found Conf Chem Res
Proceedings. Rochester Academy of Science — Proc Rochester Acad Sci
Proceedings. Rochester Conference on Coherence and Quantum Optics — Proc Rochester Conf Coherence Quantum Opt
Proceedings. Rochester Conference on Meson Physics — Proc Rochester Conf Meson Phys
Proceedings. Rocky Mountain Coal Mining Institute — Proc Rocky Mt Coal Min Inst
Proceedings. Royal Academy of Sciences of Amsterdam — Proc R Acad Sci Amsterdam
Proceedings. Royal Anthropological Institute — Proc Roy Anthropol Inst
Proceedings. Royal Anthropological Institute of Great Britain and Ireland — Proc Roy Anthropol Inst Gr Brit Ir
Proceedings. Royal Australian Chemical Institute — PAUCA
Proceedings. Royal Australian Chemical Institute — Proc R Aust Chem Inst
Proceedings. Royal Australian Chemical Institute — Proc Roy Aust Chem Inst
Proceedings. Royal Australian Chemical Institute — Proc Royal Aust Chem Inst
Proceedings. Royal Canadian Institute — Proc R Can Inst
Proceedings. Royal Canadian Institute — Proc Roy Canad Inst
Proceedings. Royal Colonial Institute — PRCI
Proceedings. Royal Entomological Society — Proc R Ent Soc
Proceedings. Royal Entomological Society of London — Proc Roy Entomol Soc Lond
Proceedings. Royal Entomological Society of London. A — Proc R Ent Soc Lond A
Proceedings. Royal Entomological Society of London. Series A — Proc Roy Entomol Soc London Ser A
Proceedings. Royal Entomological Society of London. Series A. General Entomology — Proc R Entomol Soc Lond Ser A Gen Entomol
Proceedings. Royal Entomological Society of London. Series B. Taxonomy — Proc R Entomol Soc Lond Ser B Taxon
Proceedings. Royal Entomological Society of London. Series C. Journal of Meetings — Proc Roy Entomol Soc Lond C
Proceedings. Royal Geographical Society — PGS
Proceedings. Royal Geographical Society — PRGS
Proceedings. Royal Geographical Society — Proc RGS
Proceedings. Royal Geographical Society of Australasia. South Australian Branch — Proc R Geog Soc Aust S Aust Br
Proceedings. Royal Geographical Society of Australasia. South Australian Branch — Proc R Geogr Soc Australas S Aust Br
Proceedings. Royal Geographical Society of Australasia. South Australian Branch — Proc R Geogr Soc Australas South Aust Branch
Proceedings. Royal Geographical Society of Australia. South Australian Branch — Proc Roy Geog Soc Austral
Proceedings. Royal Horticulture Society — Proc R Hortic Soc
Proceedings. Royal Institution of Great Britain — PIGBA
Proceedings. Royal Institution of Great Britain — Proc R Inst GB
Proceedings. Royal Institution of Great Britain — Proc R Instn Gt Br
Proceedings. Royal Institution of Great Britain — Proc Roy Inst
Proceedings. Royal Institution of Great Britain — Proc Roy Inst Gr Brit
Proceedings. Royal Irish Academy — PIA
Proceedings. Royal Irish Academy — PRIA
Proceedings. Royal Irish Academy — Proc R Ir Acad
Proceedings. Royal Irish Academy — Proc Roy Irish Acad
Proceedings. Royal Irish Academy — Proc Royal Irish Acad
Proceedings. Royal Irish Academy. Section A. Mathematical and Physical Sciences — PRIAA
Proceedings. Royal Irish Academy. Section A. Mathematical and Physical Sciences — Proc R Ir Acad Sect A
Proceedings. Royal Irish Academy. Section A. Mathematical, Astronomical, and Physical Science — P R Ir Ac A
Proceedings. Royal Irish Academy. Section A. Mathematical, Astronomical, and Physical Science — Proc R Ir Acad A
Proceedings. Royal Irish Academy. Section A. Mathematical, Astronomical, and Physical Science — Proc R Irish Acad Sect A
Proceedings. Royal Irish Academy. Section A. Mathematical, Astronomical, and Physical Science — Proc Roy Irish Acad Sect A
Proceedings. Royal Irish Academy. Section B. Biological, Geological, and Chemical Science — P R Ir Ac B
Proceedings. Royal Irish Academy. Section B. Biological, Geological, and Chemical Science — PRIBA
Proceedings. Royal Irish Academy. Section B. Biological, Geological, and Chemical Science — PRIBAN
Proceedings. Royal Irish Academy. Section B. Biological, Geological, and Chemical Science — Proc R Ir Acad Sect B
Proceedings. Royal Irish Academy. Section B. Biological, Geological, and Chemical Science — Proc R Ir Acad Sect B Biol Geol Chem Sci
Proceedings. Royal Irish Academy. Section B. Biological, Geological, and Chemical Science — Proc R Irish Acad Sect B

Proceedings. Royal Irish Academy. Section C. Archaeology, Celtic Studies, History, Linguistics, Literature — P R Ir Ac C
Proceedings. Royal Irish Academy. Section C. Archaeology, Celtic Studies, History, Linguistics, Literature — Proc Irish Ac Section C
Proceedings. Royal Irish Academy. Series B and C — Proc Roy Ir Acad B C
Proceedings. Royal Microscopical Society — PRMSB
Proceedings. Royal Microscopical Society [*England*] — Proc R Microsc Soc
Proceedings. Royal Microscopical Society — Proc Roy Microsc Soc
Proceedings. Royal Musical Association — P Roy Music
Proceedings. Royal Musical Association — PMA
Proceedings. Royal Musical Association — PRMA
Proceedings. Royal Musical Association — Proc Royal M Assoc
Proceedings. Royal Numismatic Society — Proc RNS
Proceedings. Royal Philosophical Society of Glasgow — Proc R Philos Soc Glasgow
Proceedings. Royal Philosophical Society of Glasgow — Proc Roy Philos Soc Glasgow
Proceedings. Royal Philosophical Society of Glasgow — Proceed R Philos Soc of Glasgow
Proceedings. Royal Physical Society of Edinburgh — Proc R Phys Soc Edinb
Proceedings. Royal Physical Society of Edinburgh — Proc Roy Phys Soc Edinb
Proceedings. Royal Physiograph Society at Lund — Proc R Physiogr Soc Lund
Proceedings. Royal Society — Pr Roy Soc
Proceedings. Royal Society — Proc R Soc
Proceedings. Royal Society — Proc Roy Soc
Proceedings. Royal Society — Roy Soc Proc
Proceedings. Royal Society. London. Series A. Physical Sciences — Proc Roy Soc Lond A
Proceedings. Royal Society. London. Series B — Proc Roy Soc Lond B
Proceedings. Royal Society. London. Series B. Biological Sciences — Proc R Soc Lond Ser B Biol Sci
Proceedings. Royal Society of Canada — Proc R Soc Can
Proceedings. Royal Society of Canada — Proc Roy Soc Can
Proceedings. Royal Society of Canada — Proc Roy Soc Canada
Proceedings. Royal Society of Canada — Proc Royal Soc Canad
Proceedings. Royal Society of Canada — Proc Soc Can
Proceedings. Royal Society of Canada. Fourth Series — Proc Roy Soc Canada 4
Proceedings. Royal Society of Edinburgh — Proc R Soc Edinburgh
Proceedings. Royal Society of Edinburgh — Proc Roy Soc Edinb
Proceedings. Royal Society of Edinburgh — Proc Roy Soc Edinburgh
Proceedings. Royal Society of Edinburgh — Proc Royal Soc Edinb
Proceedings. Royal Society of Edinburgh — PRSE
Proceedings. Royal Society of Edinburgh. Section A. Mathematical and Physical Sciences — P RS Edin A
Proceedings. Royal Society of Edinburgh. Section A. Mathematical and Physical Sciences [*Later, Proceedings. Royal Society of Edinburgh. Mathematics*] — Proc R Soc Edinb Sect A
Proceedings. Royal Society of Edinburgh. Section A. Mathematical and Physical Sciences [*Later, Proceedings. Royal Society of Edinburgh. Mathematics*] — Proc R Soc Edinb Sect A Math Phys Sci
Proceedings. Royal Society of Edinburgh. Section A. Mathematical and Physical Sciences — Proc R Soc Edinburgh Sect A
Proceedings. Royal Society of Edinburgh. Section A. Mathematical and Physical Sciences — Proc R Soc Edinburgh Sect A Math Phys Sci
Proceedings. Royal Society of Edinburgh. Section A. Mathematical and Physical Sciences — Proc Roy Soc Edinburgh Sect A
Proceedings. Royal Society of Edinburgh. Section A. Mathematics — Proc R Soc Edinburgh Sect A Math
Proceedings. Royal Society of Edinburgh. Section B. Biological Sciences — PREBA3
Proceedings. Royal Society of Edinburgh. Section B. Biological Sciences — Proc R Soc Edinb Sect B
Proceedings. Royal Society of Edinburgh. Section B. Biological Sciences — Proc R Soc Edinburgh B
Proceedings. Royal Society of Edinburgh. Section B. Biological Sciences — Proc R Soc Edinburgh Biol Sci
Proceedings. Royal Society of Edinburgh. Section B. Biological Sciences — Proc Roy Soc Edinb B
Proceedings. Royal Society of Edinburgh. Section B. Biology — Proc R Soc Edinb Biol
Proceedings. Royal Society of Edinburgh. Section B. Biology — Proc R Soc Edinb Sect B
Proceedings. Royal Society of Edinburgh. Section B. Biology — Proc R Soc Edinb Sect B Biol
Proceedings. Royal Society of Edinburgh. Section B. Natural Environment — P RS Edin B
Proceedings. Royal Society of Edinburgh. Section B. Natural Environment — Proc R Soc Edinb Nat Environ
Proceedings. Royal Society of Edinburgh. Section B. Natural Environment — Proc R Soc Edinb Sect B Nat Environ
Proceedings. Royal Society of Edinburgh. Section B. Natural Environment — Proc R Soc Edinburgh Sect B Nat Environ
Proceedings. Royal Society of London — Proc R Soc London
Proceedings. Royal Society of London — Proc Roy Soc London
Proceedings. Royal Society of London — Proc Soc Lond
Proceedings. Royal Society of London. Series A — Proc Royal Soc London Series A
Proceedings. Royal Society of London. Series A. Mathematical and Physical Sciences — P Roy Soc A
Proceedings. Royal Society of London. Series A. Mathematical and Physical Sciences — Proc R Soc A
Proceedings. Royal Society of London. Series A. Mathematical and Physical Sciences — Proc R Soc London A
Proceedings. Royal Society of London. Series A. Mathematical and Physical Sciences — Proc R Soc London Ser A
Proceedings. Royal Society of London. Series A. Mathematical and Physical Sciences — Proc Roy Soc London Ser A
Proceedings. Royal Society of London. Series A. Mathematical and Physical Sciences — Proc Royal Soc London Ser A
Proceedings. Royal Society of London. Series B. Biological Sciences — P Roy Soc B
Proceedings. Royal Society of London. Series B. Biological Sciences — Proc R Soc B
Proceedings. Royal Society of London. Series B. Biological Sciences — Proc R Soc Lond
Proceedings. Royal Society of London. Series B. Biological Sciences — Proc R Soc Lond B Biol Sci
Proceedings. Royal Society of London. Series B. Biological Sciences — Proc R Soc Lond Biol
Proceedings. Royal Society of London. Series B. Biological Sciences — Proc Roy Soc B
Proceedings. Royal Society of London. Series B. Biological Sciences — Proc Roy Soc London S B
Proceedings. Royal Society of Medicine — P Roy S Med
Proceedings. Royal Society of Medicine — Pr RS Med
Proceedings. Royal Society of Medicine — Proc R Soc Med
Proceedings. Royal Society of Medicine — Proc Roy Soc Med
Proceedings. Royal Society of Medicine — Proc Soc Med
Proceedings. Royal Society of Medicine — PRSM
Proceedings. Royal Society of Medicine — PRSMA
Proceedings. Royal Society of Medicine. Supplement [*England*] — Proc R Soc Med Suppl
Proceedings. Royal Society of New Zealand — Proc R Soc NZ
Proceedings. Royal Society of Queensland — Proc R Soc QD
Proceedings. Royal Society of Queensland — Proc R Soc Queensl
Proceedings. Royal Society of Victoria — Proc R Soc Vict
Proceedings. Royal Society of Victoria — Proc R Soc Victoria
Proceedings. Royal Society of Victoria — Proc Soc Vict
Proceedings. Royal Society. Series A — Proc Roy Soc Ser A
Proceedings. Royal Society. Series B. Biological Sciences — Proc Royal Soc Ser B
Proceedings. Royal Zoological Society of New South Wales — Proc R Zool Soc NSW
Proceedings. RRIM [*Rubber Research Institute of Malaysia*] **Planters' Conference** — Proc RRIM Plant Conf
Proceedings. Ruakura Farmers' Conference — Proc Ruakura Farmers Conf
Proceedings. Ruakura Farmers' Conference Week — Proc Ruakura Farmers Conf Week
Proceedings. Rubber Research Institute of Malaysia Planters' Conference — Proc Rubber Res Inst Malays Plant Conf
Proceedings. Rudolf Virchow Medical Society in the City of New York — Proc Rudolf Virchow Med Soc City NY
Proceedings. Rudolph Virchow Medical Society of New York — Proc Rudolph Virchow Med Soc NY
Proceedings. Russian Academy of Sciences. Series Biological — Proc Russ Acad Sci Ser Biol
Proceedings. Sagamore Army Materials Research Conference — Proc Sagamore Army Mater Res Conf
Proceedings. San Diego Biomedical Engineering Symposium — Proc San Diego Biomed Eng Symp
Proceedings. San Diego Biomedical Symposium — Proc San Diego Biomed Symp
Proceedings. Santa Fe Meeting. Annual Meeting. Division of Particles and Fields. American Physical Society — Proc St Fe Meet Annu Meet Div Part Fields Am Phys Soc
Proceedings. Satellite Symposium. International Congress of Pharmacology — Proc Satell Symp Int Congr Pharmacol
Proceedings. Scandinavian Congress of Cardiology — Proc Scand Congr Cardiol
Proceedings. Scandinavian Congress of Neurology — Proc Scand Congr Neurol
Proceedings. Scandinavian Corrosion Congress — Proc Scand Corros Congr
Proceedings. Scandinavian Symposium on Surface Activity — Proc Scand Symp Surf Act
Proceedings. Scandinavian Transplantation Meeting — Proc Scand Transplant Meet
Proceedings. Science Association of Nigeria — Proc Sci Assoc Nigeria
Proceedings. Science Institution. Kinki University — Proc Sci Inst Kinki Univ
Proceedings. Scientific Association of Trinidad — Proc Sci Assoc Trinidad
Proceedings. Scientific Institute for Vitamin Research. Moscow — Proc Sci Inst Vitam Res Moscow
Proceedings. Scientific Section of the Toilet Goods Association — Proc Sci Sect Toilet Goods Assoc
Proceedings. Scientific Society of London — Proc Sci Soc London
Proceedings. Scottish Universities Summer School in Physics — Proc Scott Univ Summer Sch Phys
Proceedings. Scotts Turfgrass Research Conference — Proc Scotts Turfgrass Res Conf
Proceedings. Sea Grant Conference — Proc Sea Grant Conf
Proceedings. Second International Symposium on Veterinary Epidemiology and Economics — Proc Sec Int Symp Vet Epidemiol Econ
Proceedings. Second Malaysian Soil Conference (Kuala Lumpur) — Proc Second Malays Soil Conf (Kuala Lumpur)
Proceedings. Section of Sciences. Israel Academy of Sciences and Humanities — Proc Sect Sci Is Acad Sci Humanit
Proceedings. Section of Sciences. Koninklijke Nederlandse Akademie van Wetenschappen — Proc Sect Sci K Ned Akad Wet
Proceedings. Seed Protein Conference — Proc Seed Protein Conf

Proceedings. Semiannual Meeting. AFMA [*American Feed Manufacturers Association*] **Nutrition Council** — Proc Semiann Meet AFMA Nutr Counc
Proceedings. Seminar Electromagnetic Interactions of Nuclei at Low and Medium Energies — Proc Semin Electromagn Interact Nucl Low Medium Energ
Proceedings. Seminar on Biomass Energy for City, Farm, and Industry — Proc Semin Biomass Energy City Farm Ind
Proceedings. Seminar on Computational Methods in Quantum Chemistry — Proc Semin Comput Methods Quantum Chem
Proceedings. Seminar on Electrochemistry — Proc Semin Electrochem
Proceedings. Seminar on Nuclear Data — Proc Semin Nucl Data
Proceedings. Seminar on Nuclear Power — Proc Semin Nucl Power
Proceedings. Seminar on Pesticides and Environment — Proc Semin Pestic Environ
Proceedings. Seminar on Surface Physics — Proc Semin Surf Phys
Proceedings Series. American Water Resources Association — Proc Ser Am Water Resour Assoc
Proceedings. Serono Clinical Colloquia on Reproduction — PCCRD7
Proceedings. Serono Clinical Colloquia on Reproduction — Proc Serono Clin Colloq Reprod
Proceedings. Serono Symposia — Proc Serono Symp
Proceedings. Shevchenko Scientific Society. Philological Section — PSSS
Proceedings. Shevchenko Scientific Society. Philological Section — PSSSP
Proceedings. Shevchenko Scientific Society. Section of Chemistry, Biology, and Medicine — Proc Shevchenko Sci Soc Sect Chem Biol Med
Proceedings. Shikoku Branch of Crop Science Society (Japan) — Proc Shikoku Br Crop Sci Soc (Jap)
Proceedings. SID [*Society for Information Display*] — Proc SID
Proceedings. Sigatoka Workshop — Proc Sigatoka Workshop
Proceedings. Sigrid Juselius Foundation Symposium — Proc Sigrid Juselius Found Symp
Proceedings. Sigrid Juselius Symposium — Proc Sigrid Juselius Symp
Proceedings. Silviculture Conference — Proc Silvic Conf
Proceedings. Society for Analytical Chemistry — Proc Soc Anal Chem
Proceedings. Society for Analytical Chemistry Conference — Proc Soc Anal Chem Conf
Proceedings. Society for Applied Bacteriology — Proc Soc Appl Bact
Proceedings. Society for Applied Bacteriology — Proc Soc Appl Bacteriol
Proceedings. Society for Experimental Biology and Medicine — P Soc Exp M
Proceedings. Society for Experimental Biology and Medicine — Pr Soc Exp Biol Med
Proceedings. Society for Experimental Biology and Medicine — Proc Soc Exp Biol Med
Proceedings. Society for Experimental Biology and Medicine — Proc Soc Exper Biol Med
Proceedings. Society for Experimental Biology and Medicine — PSEBA
Proceedings. Society for Experimental Biology and Medicine (New York) — Proc Soc Exp Biol (NY)
Proceedings. Society for Experimental Stress Analysis — Proc SESA
Proceedings. Society for Experimental Stress Analysis — Proc Soc Exp Stress Anal
Proceedings. Society for Experimental Stress Analysis — Proc Soc Exp Stress Analysis
Proceedings. Society for Horticultural Science — Proc Soc Hortic Sci
Proceedings. Society for Industrial Microbiology — Proc Soc Ind Microbiol
Proceedings. Society for Information Display — Proc Soc Inf Disp
Proceedings. Society for Psychical Research — Proc Soc Psych Res
Proceedings. Society for Psychical Research — Psy R
Proceedings. Society for the Promotion of Agricultural Science — Proc Soc Promot Agric Sci
Proceedings. Society for the Study of Fertility — Proc Soc Study Fertil
Proceedings. Society for the Study of Industrial Medicine — Proc Soc Study Ind Med
Proceedings. Society for Water Treatment and Examination — Pro Soc Water Treat Exam
Proceedings. Society for Water Treatment and Examination — Proc Soc Water Treat Exam
Proceedings. Society of Agricultural Bacteriologists — Proc Soc Agric Bacteriol
Proceedings. Society of American Foresters — Proc Soc Am For
Proceedings. Society of American Foresters National Convention — Proc Soc Am For Natl Conv
Proceedings. Society of Antiquaries of London — Proc Soc Antiqu London
Proceedings. Society of Antiquaries of London — PSA
Proceedings. Society of Antiquaries of London — PSAL
Proceedings. Society of Antiquaries of London — PSL
Proceedings. Society of Antiquaries of New Castle-upon-Tyne — Proc NewC
Proceedings. Society of Antiquaries of New Castle-upon-Tyne — PSAN
Proceedings. Society of Antiquaries of New Castle-upon-Tyne — PSN
Proceedings. Society of Antiquaries of Scotland — Proc SA Scot
Proceedings. Society of Antiquaries of Scotland — Proc Soc Antiq Scot
Proceedings. Society of Antiquaries of Scotland — Proc Soc Antiq Scotland
Proceedings. Society of Antiquaries of Scotland — Proceeds Scotl
Proceedings. Society of Antiquaries of Scotland — PSAS
Proceedings. Society of Biblical Archaeology — Proceedings SBA
Proceedings. Society of Biblical Archaeology — PSBA
Proceedings. Society of Biblical Archaeology — PSBH
Proceedings. Society of Biological Chemists — Proc Soc Biol Chem
Proceedings. Society of Biological Chemists of India — Proc Soc Biol Chem India
Proceedings. Society of Chemical Industry. Chemical Engineering Group — Proc Soc Chem Ind Chem Eng Group
Proceedings. Society of Chemical Industry (Victoria) — Proc Soc Chem Ind (Victoria)
Proceedings. Society of Petroleum Engineers. American Institute of Mining, Metallurgical, and Petroleum Engineers. Symposium on Formation Damage Control — Proc SPE Symp Form Damage Control
Proceedings. Society of Petroleum Engineers. American Institute of Mining, Metallurgical, and Petroleum Engineers. Symposium on Improved Oil Recovery — Proc SPE Symp Improv Oil Recovery
Proceedings. Society of Photo-Optical Instrumentation Engineers — Proc Soc Photo Opt Instrum Eng
Proceedings. Society of Photo-Optical Instrumentation Engineers — SPIEC
Proceedings. Society of Protozoologists — Proc Soc Protozool
Proceedings. Society of Relay Engineers — Proc Soc Relay Eng
Proceedings. Society of the Plastics Industry in Canada — Proc Soc Plast Ind Can
Proceedings. Soil and Crop Science Society of Florida — Proc Soil Crop Sci Soc Fla
Proceedings. Soil Science Society of America — Proc Soil Sci Soc Am
Proceedings. Soil Science Society of America — Proc Soil Sci Soc Amer
Proceedings. Soil Science Society of America — Proc SSSA
Proceedings. Soil Science Society of Florida — Proc Soil Sci Soc Fla
Proceedings. Solvay Conference on Physics — Proc Solvay Conf Phys
Proceedings. Somerset Archaeology and Natural History Society — Proc Somerset Arch Natur Hist Soc
Proceedings. SOS [*Science of Survival*]. International Congress of Food Science and Technology — Proc SOS Int Congr Food Sci Technol
Proceedings. South African Society of Animal Production — Proc S Afr Soc Anim Prod
Proceedings. South African Sugar Technologists' Association — Proc S Afr Sugar Technol Assoc
Proceedings. South African Sugar Technologists Association. Annual Congress — Proc S Afr Sugar Technol Assoc Annu Congr
Proceedings. South Carolina Historical Association — Proc SC Hist Assn
Proceedings. South Carolina Historical Society — ProS
Proceedings. South Dakota Academy of Science — Proc S Dak Acad Sci
Proceedings. South Dakota Academy of Science — Proc SD Acad Sci
Proceedings. South Dakota Academy of Sciences — Proc South Dakota Acad Sci
Proceedings. South London Entomological and Natural History Society — Proc South Lond Entom and Nat Hist Soc
Proceedings. South Staffordshire Institute of Iron and Steel Works Managers — Proc South Staffs Inst Iron Steel Works Managers
Proceedings. South Wales Institute of Engineers — Proc S Wales Inst Eng
Proceedings. South Wales Institute of Engineers — Proc South Wales Inst Eng
Proceedings. South Wales Institute of Engineers — PSWEA
Proceedings. Southeast Asian Regional Seminar on Tropical Medicine and Public Health — Proc Southeast Asian Reg Semin Trop Med Public Health
Proceedings. Southeastcon Region 3 (Three) Conference [*United States*] — Proc Southeastcon Reg 3 (Three) Conf
Proceedings. Southeastern Conference on Theoretical and Applied Mechanics — Proc Southeast Conf Theor Appl Mech
Proceedings. Southeastern Pecan Growers Association [*US*] — Proc Southeast Pecan Grow Assoc
Proceedings. Southeastern Seminar on Thermal Sciences — Proc Southeast Semin Therm Sci
Proceedings. Southern African Electron Microscopy Society-Verrigtings — Proc South Afr Electron Microsc Soc Verrigtings
Proceedings. Southern Conference on Corrections — P S Conf Co
Proceedings. Southern Conference on Forest Tree Improvement — Proc South Conf For Tree Improv
Proceedings. Southern Conference on Forest Tree Improvement — Proc Sth Conf For Tree Impr
Proceedings. Southern Forest Tree Improvement Conference — Proc South For Tree Improv Conf
Proceedings. Southern Municipal and Industrial Waste Conference — Proc South Munic Ind Waste Conf
Proceedings. Southern Pasture and Forage Crop Improvement Conference — PPFCDY
Proceedings. Southern Pasture and Forage Crop Improvement Conference — Proc South Pasture Forage Crop Imp Conf
Proceedings. Southern Pasture and Forage Crop Improvement Conference — Proc South Pasture Forage Crop Improv Conf
Proceedings. Southern States Association of Commissioners of Agriculture and Other Agricultural Workers — Proc South States Assoc Comm Agric Other Agric Work
Proceedings. Southern Water Resources and Pollution Control Conference — Proc South Water Resour Pollut Control Conf
Proceedings. Southern Weed Conference — Proc South Weed Conf
Proceedings. Southern Weed Control Conference — Proc Sth Weed Control Conf
Proceedings. Southern Weed Science Society — Proc South Weed Sci Soc
Proceedings. Southern Weed Science Society — Proc Sth Weed Sci Soc
Proceedings. Southwestern Agricultural Trade Farm Policy Conference — Proc Southwest Agr Trade Farm Policy Conf
Proceedings. Space Congress. Technology for the New Horizon — Proc Space Congr
Proceedings. Specialty Conference. Control Technology for Agricultural Air Pollutants — Proc Spec Conf Control Technol Agric Air Pollut
Proceedings. Specialty Conference on Cold-Formed Steel Structures — Proc Spec Conf Cold Formed Steel Struct
Proceedings. Specialty Conference. State-of-the-Art of Odor Control Technology — Proc Spec Conf State of the Art Odor Control Tech
Proceedings. SPI [*Society of the Plastics Industry*] **Annual Structural Foam Conference** — Proc SPI Annu Struct Foam Conf
Proceedings. SPI [*Society of the Plastic Industry*] **Annual Technical Conference** — Proc SPI Annu Tech Conf
Proceedings. SPI [*Society of the Plastic Industry*] **Annual Technical Conference. Urethane Division** — Proc SPI Annu Tech Conf Urethane Div
Proceedings. SPI [*Society of the Plastic Industry*] **Annual Urethane Division Technical Conference** — Proc SPI Annu Urethane Div Tech Conf

Proceedings. SPI [*Society of the Plastic Industry*] **International Technical/Marketing Conference** — Proc SPI Int Tech Mark Conf
Proceedings. SPI (Society of the Plastic Industry) Annual Technical/Marketing Conference — Proc SPI Annu Tech Mark Conf
Proceedings. SPI [*Society of the Plastics Industry*] **Structural Foam Conference** — Proc SPI Struct Foam Conf
Proceedings. Spring Systematics Symposium — Proc Spring Syst Symp
Proceedings. Sprinkler Irrigation Association. Technical Conference — Proc Sprinkler Irrig Assoc Tech Conf
Proceedings. Staff Meeting. Mayo Clinic — Proc Staff Meet Mayo Clin
Proceedings. Staff Meeting of the Mayo Clinic — PSMMAF
Proceedings. Staff Meetings of the Mayo Clinic — Proc Mayo Clin
Proceedings. Staff Meetings of the Mayo Clinic — Proc Staff Meetings Mayo Clin
Proceedings. Staffordshire Iron and Steel Institute — Proc Staffs Iron Steel Inst
Proceedings. State College of Washington. Institute of Dairying — Proc State Coll Wash Inst Dairy
Proceedings. State Horticultural Association of Pennsylvania — Proc State Horti Assoc PA
Proceedings. State Secretaries Management Conference. American Dental Association — Proc State Secr Manage Conf Am Dent Assoc
Proceedings. Staten Island Institute of Arts and Sciences — Proc Staten Island Inst Arts
Proceedings. State-of-the-Art of Odor Control Technology Specialty Conference — Proc State of the Art Odor Control Technol Spec Conf
Proceedings. Statusseminar der PBWU zum Forschungsschwerpunkt Waldschaeden — Proc Statussemin PBWU Forschungsschwerpunkt Waldschaeden
Proceedings. Steel Treating Research Society — Proc Steel Treat Res Soc
Proceedings. Steelmaking Conference — Proc Steelmaking Conf
Proceedings. Steenbock Symposium — Proc Steenbock Symp
Proceedings. Steklov Institute of Mathematics — Proc Steklov Inst Math
Proceedings. Streams Workshop — Proc Stream Workshop
Proceedings. Suffolk Institute of Archaeology — P Suffolk I Arch
Proceedings. Suffolk Institute of Archaeology — Proc Suff Inst A
Proceedings. Suffolk Institute of Archaeology — Proc Suffolk Inst Arch
Proceedings. Suffolk Institute of Archaeology and History — Proc Suffolk Inst Archaeol Hist
Proceedings. Sugar Beet Research Association — Proc Sugar Beet Res Assoc
Proceedings. Sugar Processing Research Conference — Proc Sugar Process Res Conf
Proceedings. Sugar Processing Research Conference — PSPCE4
Proceedings. Sugar Technologists Association of India — Proc Sugar Technol Assoc India
Proceedings. Summer Colloquium on Electronic Transition Lasers — Proc Summer Colloq Electron Transition Lasers
Proceedings. Summer Computer Simulation Conference — Proc Summer Comput Simul Conf
Proceedings. Summer Conference on Spectroscopy and Its Application — Proc Summer Conf Spectrosc Its Appl
Proceedings. Summer Institute on Particle Physics — Proc Summer Inst Part Phys
Proceedings. Summer School on Elementary Particle Physics — Proc Summer Sch Elem Part Phys
Proceedings. Symposia in Applied Mathematics — Proc Symp Appl Math
Proceedings. Symposia in Applied Mathematics — Proc Sympos Appl Math
Proceedings. Symposia in Pure Mathematics — Proc Sympos Pure Math
Proceedings. Symposia on Arctic Biology and Medicine — Proc Symp Arct Biol Med
Proceedings. Symposia on the Fracture Mechanics of Ceramics — Proc Symp Fract Mech Ceram
Proceedings. Symposium. Baltic Marine Biologists — Proc Symp Balt Mar Biol
Proceedings. Symposium by the Biology Department. Brookhaven National Laboratory — Proc Symp Biol Dep Brookhaven Natl Lab
Proceedings. Symposium. East African Academy — Proc Symp East Afr Acad
Proceedings. Symposium. Educational Foundation. American Society of Plastic and Reconstructive Surgeons — Proc Symp Educ Found Am Soc Plast Reconstr Surg
Proceedings. Symposium. Engineering Aspects of Magnetohydrodynamics — Proc Symp Eng Aspects Magnetohydrodyn
Proceedings. Symposium. Gesellschaft fuer Nephrologie — Proc Symp Ges Nephrol
Proceedings. Symposium. International Astronomical Union — Proc Symp Int Astron Union
Proceedings. Symposium. International Society for Corneal Research — Proc Symp Int Soc Corneal Res
Proceedings. Symposium. Northwest Scientific Association Annual Meeting — Proc Symp Northwest Sci Assoc Annu Meet
Proceedings. Symposium of Pests and Pesticides — Proc Symp Pests Pestic
Proceedings. Symposium of the Society for the Study of Inborn Errors of Metabolism — PSSMDE
Proceedings. Symposium on Algology — Proc Symp Algol
Proceedings. Symposium on Andean and Antarctic Volcanology Problems — Proc Symp Andean Antarct Volcanol Probl
Proceedings. Symposium on Antarctic Meteorites — Proc Symp Antarct Meteorites
Proceedings. Symposium on Chemical Data. Royal Australian Chemical Institute [*A publication*] — Proc Symp Chem Data Append R Aust Chem Inst
Proceedings. Symposium on Chemical Physiology and Pathology — Proc Symp Chem Physiol Pathol
Proceedings. Symposium on Coeliac Disease — Proc Symp Coeliac Dis
Proceedings. Symposium on Comparative Biology of Reproduction — Proc Symp Comp Biol Reprod
Proceedings. Symposium on Coordinated Observations of the Ionosphere and the Magnetosphere in the Polar Regions — Proc Symp Coord Obs Ionos Magnetos Polar Reg
Proceedings. Symposium on Cosmic Rays, Astrophysics, Geophysics, and Elementary Partide Physics — Proc Symp Cosmic Rays Astrophys Geophys Elem Part Phys
Proceedings. Symposium on Cosmic Rays, Elementary Particle Physics, and Astrophysics — Proc Symp Cosmic Rays Elem Part Phys Astrophys
Proceedings. Symposium on Detonation — Proc Symp Detonation
Proceedings. Symposium on Electrochemical Engineering and Small Scale Electrolytic Processing — Proc Symp Electrochem Eng Small Scale Electrolytic Process
Proceedings. Symposium on Electron and Ion Beam Science and Technology. International Conference — Proc Symp Electron Ion Beam Sci Technol Int Conf
Proceedings. Symposium on Electron Beam Technology — Proc Symp Electron Beam Technol
Proceedings. Symposium on Engineering Problems of Fusion Research — Proc Symp Eng Probl Fusion Res
Proceedings. Symposium on Explosives and Pyrotechnics — Proc Symp Explos Pyrotech
Proceedings. Symposium on Fast Reactions. Chemistry and Measurements — Proc Symp Fast React Chem Meas
Proceedings. Symposium on Fertility of Indian Soils — Proc Symp Fertil Indian Soils
Proceedings. Symposium on Flue Gas Desulfurization — Proc Symp Flue Gas Desulfurization
Proceedings. Symposium on Fusion Technology — Proc Symp Fusion Technol
Proceedings. Symposium on Hadron Spectroscopy — Proc Symp Hadron Spectrosc
Proceedings. Symposium on Hazardous Chemicals Handling and Disposal — Proc Symp Hazard Chem Handl Disposal
Proceedings. Symposium on High Temperature Lamp Chemistry — Proc Symp High Temp Lamp Chem
Proceedings. Symposium on High Temperature Metal Halide Chemistry — Proc Symp High Temp Met Halide Chem
Proceedings. Symposium on Hydrogen Storage Materials, Batteries, and Electrochemistry — Proc Symp Hydrogen Storage Mater Batteries Electrochem
Proceedings. Symposium on Industrial Crystallization — Proc Symp Ind Cryst
Proceedings. Symposium on Industrial Waste Control — Proc Symp Ind Waste Control
Proceedings. Symposium on Ion Sources and Ion Application Technology — Proc Symp Ion Sources Ion Appl Technol
Proceedings. Symposium on Ion Sources and Ion-Assisted Technology — Proc Symp Ion Sources Ion Assisted Technol
Proceedings. Symposium on Irradiation Facilities for Research Reactors — Proc Symp Irradiat Facil Res React
Proceedings. Symposium on Isotopes in Plant Nutrition and Physiology (Vienna, Austria) — Proc Symp Isotop Plant Nutr Physiol (Vienna Austria)
Proceedings. Symposium on Liquid and Solid Helium Three — Proc Symp Liq Solid Helium Three
Proceedings. Symposium on Materials Science Research — Proc Symp Mater Sci Res
Proceedings. Symposium on Mechanical Behavior of Materials — Proc Symp Mech Behav Mater
Proceedings. Symposium on Medicated Feeds — Proc Symp Med Feeds
Proceedings. Symposium on Microdosimetry — Proc Symp Microdosim
Proceedings. Symposium on Molecular Biology — Proc Symp Mol Biol
Proceedings. Symposium on Naval Structural Mechanics — Proc Symp Nav Struct Mech
Proceedings. Symposium on Neutron Dosimetry — Proc Symp Neutron Dosim
Proceedings. Symposium on Neutron Dosimetry in Biology and Medicine — Proc Symp Neutron Dosim Biol Med
Proceedings. Symposium on Neutron Inelastic Scattering — Proc Symp Neutron Inelastic Scattering
Proceedings. Symposium on Neutron Monitoring for Radiological Protection — Proc Symp Neutron Monit Radiol Prot
Proceedings. Symposium on Non-Silver Photographic Processes — Proc Symp Non Silver Photogr Processes
Proceedings. Symposium on Packaging of Electronic Devices — Proc Symp Packag Electron Devices
Proceedings. Symposium on Particleboard — Proc Symp Particleboard
Proceedings. Symposium on Perspectives in Industrial Microbiology — Proc Symp Perspect Ind Microbiol
Proceedings. Symposium on Photographic Processing — Proc Symp Photogr Process
Proceedings. Symposium on Photographic Sensitivity — Proc Symp Photogr Sensitivity
Proceedings. Symposium on Physics and Nondestructive Testing — Proc Symp Phys Nondestr Test
Proceedings. Symposium on Plasma Processing — Proc Symp Plasma Process
Proceedings. Symposium on Practice in the Treatment of Low- and Intermediate-Level Radioactive Wastes — Proc Symp Pract Treat Low Intermed Level Radioact Wastes
Proceedings. Symposium on Productivity in Research — Proc Symp Prod Res
Proceedings. Symposium on Quantum Statistics and Many-Body Problems — Proc Symp Quantum Stat Many Body Probl
Proceedings. Symposium on Radiation-Induced Cancer — Proc Symp Radiat Induced Cancer
Proceedings. Symposium on Reliability in Electronics — Proc Symp Reliab Electron
Proceedings. Symposium on Rock Mechanics — Proc Symp Rock Mech
Proceedings. Symposium on Space Nuclear Power Systems — Proc Symp Space Nucl Power Syst
Proceedings. Symposium on Special Ceramics — Proc Symp Spec Ceram
Proceedings. Symposium on Special Ceramics held by the British Ceramic Research Association — Proc Symp Spec Ceram Br Ceram Res Assoc

Proceedings. Symposium on Statistics and Related Topics. Carleton University — P Sy St Carletn
Proceedings. Symposium on Structure-Solubility Relationships in Polymers — Proc Symp Struct Solubility Relat Polym
Proceedings. Symposium on Textile Flammability — Proc Symp Text Flammability
Proceedings. Symposium on the Biology of Skin — Proc Symp Biol Skin
Proceedings. Symposium on the Chemical Composition of Tobacco and Tobacco Smoke — Proc Symp Chem Compos Tob Tob Smoke
Proceedings. Symposium on the Chemistry and Biochemistry of Prostanoids — Proc Symp Chem Biochem Prostanoids
Proceedings. Symposium on the Development of Iron Chelators for Clinical Use — Proc Symp Dev Iron Chelators Clin Use
Proceedings. Symposium on the Effects of Ionizing Radiation on Seeds and Their Significance for Crop Improvement — Proc Symp Effects Ionizing Radiat Seed Signific Crop Impr
Proceedings. Symposium on the Geology of Rocky Mountain Coal — Proc Symp Geol Rocky Mt Coal
Proceedings. Symposium on the Safety of Nuclear Ships — Proc Symp Saf Nucl Ships
Proceedings. Symposium on the Use of Isotopes and Radiation in Soil Organic-Matter Studies — Proc Symp Use Isot Radiat Soil Org Matter Stud
Proceedings. Symposium on the Use of Isotopes in Weed Research [*Vienna, Austria*] — Proc Symp Use Isotop Weed Res
Proceedings. Symposium on the Use of Radioisotopes in Soil-Plant Nutrition Studies — Proc Symp Use Radioisotop Soil Plant Nutr Stud
Proceedings. Symposium on Thermophysical Properties — Proc Symp Thermophys Prop
Proceedings. Symposium on Toxicity of Metals [*Pittsburgh*] — Proc Symp Toxic Met
Proceedings. Symposium on Turbulence in Liquids — Proc Symp Turbul Liq
Proceedings. Symposium on Underwater Physiology — Proc Symp Underwater Physiol
Proceedings. Symposium on Upper Mantle Project — Proc Symp Upper Mantle Proj
Proceedings. Symposium on Veterinary Pharmacology and Therapeutics — Proc Symp Vet Pharmacol Ther
Proceedings. Symposium on Wakan-Yaku — Proc Symp Wakan Yaku
Proceedings. Symposium on Waste Management — Proc Symp Waste Manage
Proceedings. Symposium on Wastewater Treatment — Proc Symp Wastewater Treat
Proceedings. Symposium on Yamato Meteorites — Proc Symp Yamato Meteorites
Proceedings. Symposium. Parkinson's Disease Information and Research Center — Proc Symp Parkinsons Dis Inf Res Cent
Proceedings. Symposium. Society for the Study of Inborn Errors of Metabolism — Proc Symp Soc Study Inborn Errors Metab
Proceedings. Synthetic Pipeline Gas Symposium — Proc Synth Pipeline Gas Symp
Proceedings. Systems Symposium — Proc Syst Symp
Proceedings. TAGA [*Technical Association of the Graphic Arts*] — Proc TAGA
Proceedings. Tall Timbers Conference on Ecological Animal Control by Habitat Management — Proc Tall Timbers Conf Ecol Anim Control Habitat Manage
Proceedings. Tall Timbers Fire Ecology Conference — Proc Tall Timbers Fire Ecol Conf
Proceedings. Tbilisi Symposium on Cerebral Circulation — Proc Tbilisi Symp Cereb Circ
Proceedings. Tbilisi University — Proc Tbilisi Univ
Proceedings. Technical Association. Pulp and Paper Industry — Proc Tech Assoc Pulp Pap Ind
Proceedings. Technical Conference. American Railway Engineering Association — Proc Tech Conf Am Railway Eng Assoc
Proceedings. Technical Conference. Society of Vacuum Coaters — Proc Tech Conf Soc Vac Coaters
Proceedings. Technical Meeting. International Union for Conservation of Nature and Natural Resources — Proc Tech Mtg Int Union Conserv Nature
Proceedings. Technical Meeting. Society of Engineering Science — Proc Tech Meet Soc Eng Sci
Proceedings. Technical Meeting. Technical Association. Graphic Arts — Proc Tech Meet Tech Assoc Graphic Arts
Proceedings. Technical Meeting. West Coast Section. Air Pollution Control Association — Proc Tech Meet West Coast Sect Air Pollut Control Assoc
Proceedings. Technical Program. Annual International Electronics Packaging Conference — Proc Tech Program Annu Int Electron Packag Conf
Proceedings. Technical Program. Electro-Optics/Laser Conference and Exposition — Proc Tech Program Electro Opt Laser Conf Expo
Proceedings. Technical Program. Electro-Optics/Laser Conference and Exposition — Proc Tech Program Electro-Opt Laser Conf Exp
Proceedings. Technical Program. International Microelectronics Conference — Proc Tech Program Int Microelectron Conf
Proceedings. Technical Program. International Powder and Bulk Solids Handling and Processing — Proc Tech Program Int Powder Bulk Solids Handl Process
Proceedings. Technical Program. National Electronic Packaging and Production Conference — Proc Tech Program Natl Electron Packag Prod Conf
Proceedings. Technical Section. British Paper and Board Makers' Association — Proc Tech Sect Br Pap Board Makers Assoc
Proceedings. Technical Seminar on Chemical Spills — Proc Tech Semin Chem Spills
Proceedings. Technical Session on Cane Sugar Refining Research — Proc Tech Sess Cane Sugar Refin Res
Proceedings. Technical Session on Cane Sugar Refining Research — PTREDQ
Proceedings. Technical Sessions. Annual Convention. American Electroplaters' Society — Proc Am Electroplat Soc
Proceedings. Technical Sessions. Annual Convention. American Electroplaters' Society — Proc Tech Sess Annu Conv Amer Electroplat Soc
Proceedings. Technical Sessions on Bone Char — Proc Tech Sess Bone Char
Proceedings. Technological Conference. South India Textile Research Association — Proc Technol Conf
Proceedings. Tenovus Workshop — Proc Tenovus Workshop
Proceedings. Texas A & M Annual Symposium on Instrumentation for the Process Indtries — Proc Tex AM Annu Symp Instrum Process Ind
Proceedings. Texas Conference on Computing Systems — Proc Tex Conf Comput Syst
Proceedings. Texas Nutrition Conference — Proc Tex Nutr Conf
Proceedings. Texas Water and Sewage Works Short School — Proc Tex Water Sewage Works Short Sch
Proceedings. Texas Water Utilities Short School — Proc Tex Water Util Short Sch
Proceedings. Texas Water Works and Sewerage Short School — Proc Tex Water Works Sewerage Short Sch
Proceedings. Thermal Power Conference — Proc Therm Power Conf
Proceedings. Third International Conference on the Peaceful Uses of Atomic Energy — Proc 3rd Int Conf Peaceful Uses Atom Energy
Proceedings. Third National Peanut Research Conference — Proc III Natn Peanut Res Conf
Proceedings. Tihany Symposium on Radiation Chemistry — Proc Tihany Symp Radiat Chem
Proceedings. Tobacco and Health Conference — Proc Tob Health Conf
Proceedings. Tokyo International Symposium on Free Electron Lasers — Proc Tokyo Int Symp Free Electron Lasers
Proceedings. Topical Conference on RF Heating in Plasma and Workshop on Antennas and Couples — Proc Top Conf RF Heating Plasma
Proceedings. Topical Conference on RF Plasma Heating — Proc Top Conf RF Plasma heat
Proceedings. Topical Meeting on the Technology of Controlled Nuclear Fusion — Proc Top Meet Technol Controlled Nucl Fusion
Proceedings. Tree Wardens, Arborists, and Utilities Conference — Proc Tree Wardens Arborists Util Conf
Proceedings. Triangle Seminar — Proc Triangle Semin
Proceedings. Tropical Region ASHS [*American Society for Horticultural Science*] — Proc Trop Reg ASHS
Proceedings (Trudy). P. N. Lebedev Physics Institute — Proc Lebedev Phys Inst
Proceedings (Trudy). P. N. Lebedev Physics Institute — Proc Tr PN Lebedev Phys Inst
Proceedings (Trudy). P. N. Lebedev Physics Institute — Proc (Trudy) P N Lebedev Phys Inst
Proceedings. Trudy. P.N. Lebedev Physics Institute. Academy of Sciences of the USSR. (English Translation) — Proc Tr PN Lebedev Phys Inst Acad Sci USSR Engl Transl
Proceedings. Tuberculosis Research Council — Proc Tub Res Coun
Proceedings. Tucson Comet Conference — Proc Tucson Comet Conf
Proceedings. Turbomachinery Symposium — Proc Turbomachinery Symp
Proceedings. Turfgrass Sprinkler Irrigation Conference — Proc Turfgrass Sprinkler Irrig Conf
Proceedings. Ultrasonics Symposium — Proc Ultrason Symp
Proceedings. Underground Coal Conversion Symposium — Proc Underground Coal Convers Symp
Proceedings. UNESCO Conference on Radioisotopes in Scientific Research — Proc UNESCO Conf Radioisot Sci Res
Proceedings. UNESCO International Conference on Radioisotopes in Scientific Research — Proc UNESCO Int Conf Radioisot Sci Res
Proceedings. Union of American Hebrew Congregations — PUAHC
Proceedings. Unitarian Historical Society — PUHS
Proceedings. United Nations International Conference on the Peaceful Uses of Atomic Energy — Proc UN Int Conf Peaceful Uses At Energy
Proceedings. United Nations Symposium on the Development and Use of Geothermal Resources — Proc UN Symp Dev Use Geotherm Resour
Proceedings. United States Gulf Coast Geopressured-Geothermal Energy Conference — Proc US Gulf Coast Geopressured Geotherm Energy Conf
Proceedings. United States National Museum — Proc US Nat Mus
Proceedings. United States National Museum — Proc US Natl Mus
Proceedings. United States Naval Institute — Proceedngs
Proceedings. United States Veterinary Medical Association — Proc US Vet Med Assoc
Proceedings. United States-Japan Conference on Marine Microbiology — Proc US Jpn Conf Mar Microbiol
Proceedings. United States-Japan Conference on Toxic Micro-Organisms. Micotoxins, Botulism — Proc US Jpn Conf Toxic Micro Org
Proceedings. United States-Japan Cooperative Science Program — Proc US Jpn Coop Sci Program
Proceedings. United States-Japan Seminar on Basic Science of Ceramics — Proc US Jpn Semin Basic Sci Ceram
Proceedings. University of Bristol Spelaeological Society — Proc Univ Bristol Spelaeol Soc
Proceedings. University of Durham. Philosophical Society — Proc Univ Durham Phil Soc
Proceedings. University of Durham Philosophical Society. Series A. Science — Proc Univ Durham Philos Soc Ser A
Proceedings. University of Durham Philosophical Society. Series B. Arts — Proc Univ Durham Philos Soc Ser B
Proceedings. University of Kentucky. Tobacco and Health Research Institute. Conference Report — Proc Univ Ky Tob Health Res Inst Conf Rep
Proceedings. University of Maryland. Nutrition Conference for Feed Manufacturers — Proc Univ MD Nutr Conf Feed Mfr
Proceedings. University of Missouri. Annual Conference on Trace Substances in Environmental Health — Proc Univ MO Annu Conf Trace Subst Environ Health

Proceedings. University of Newcastle-Upon-Tyne Philosophical Society — Proc Univ Newcastle Upon Tyne Philos Soc
Proceedings. University of Nottingham Easter School in Agricultural Science — Proc Univ Nottingham Easter Sch Agric Sci
Proceedings. University of Nottingham Nutrition Conference for Feed Manufacturers — Proc Univ Nottingham Nutr Conf Feed Manuf
Proceedings. University of Otago Medical School — P U Otago M
Proceedings. University of Otago Medical School — Proc Univ Otago Med Sch
Proceedings. US Department of Energy Technical Contractors' Conference on Peat — Proc US Dep Energy Tech Contract Conf Peat
Proceedings. US DOE [*Department of Energy*] **Photovoltaics Technology Development and Applications Program Review** — Proc US DOE Photovoltaics Technol Dev Appl Program Rev
Proceedings. US Nuclear Regulatory Commission Water Reactor Safety Information Meeting — Proc US Nucl Regul Comm Water Reactor Saf Inf Meet
Proceedings. USAID [*United States Agency for International Development*]. Ghana Agriculture Conference — Proc USAID Ghana Agr Conf
Proceedings. USA-USSR Symposium on Fracture of Composite Materials — Proc USA USSR Symp Fract Compos Mater
Proceedings. User and Fabric Filtration Equipment — Proc User Fabr Filtr Equip
Proceedings. US-Japan Workshop on Advanced Plasma Modeling — Proc US Jpn Workshop Adv Plasma Model
Proceedings. Ussher Society — Proc Ussher Soc
Proceedings. USSR Academy of Sciences. Biological Series — Proc USSR Acad Sci Biol Ser
Proceedings. Utah Academy of Sciences, Arts, and Letters — Proc Utah Acad Sci
Proceedings. Utah Academy of Sciences, Arts, and Letters — Proc Utah Acad Sci Arts Lett
Proceedings. Utah Academy of Sciences, Arts, and Letters — PUASAL
Proceedings. V. V. Kuibyshev State University of Tomsk — Proc VV Kuibyshev State Univ Tomsk
Proceedings. Vertebrate Pest Conference — Proc Vertebr Pest Conf
Proceedings. Veterans Administration Spinal Cord Injury Conference — Proc Veterans Adm Spinal Cord Inj Conf
Proceedings. Veterans Administration Spinal Cord Injury Conference — PVSCA
Proceedings. Victorian Weeds Science Society — Proc VIC Weeds Conf
Proceedings. Virchow-Pirquet Medical Society — Proc Virchow-Pirquet Med Soc
Proceedings. Virgil Society — Proc Virgil Soc
Proceedings. Virgil Society — PVS
Proceedings. Virginia Turfgrass Conference and Trade Show — Proc Va Turfgrass Conf Trade Show
Proceedings. Viticultural Science Symposium — Proc Vitic Sci Symp
Proceedings Volume. Bakish Materials Corporation. Publication — Proc Vol Bakish Mater Corp Publ
Proceedings Volume. Electrochemical Society — Proc Vol Electrochem Soc
Proceedings Volume. Geological Society of America — Proc Vol Geol Soc Am
Proceedings Volume. International Conference on Mississippi Valley Type Lead-Zinc Deposits — Proc Vol Int Conf Miss Val Type Lead Zinc Deposits
Proceedings. Warsaw Symposium on Elementary Particle Physics — Proc Warsaw Symp Elem Part Phys
Proceedings. Washington Animal Nutrition Conference — Proc Wash Anim Nutr Conf
Proceedings. Washington State Entomological Society — Proc Wash St Ent Soc
Proceedings. Washington State Entomological Society — Proc Wash State Entomol Soc
Proceedings. Washington State Horticultural Association — Proc Wash St Hort Ass
Proceedings. Washington State Horticultural Association — Proc Wash State Hort Assoc
Proceedings. Washington State Horticultural Association — Proc Wash State Hortic Assoc
Proceedings. Washington State Horticultural Association — Wash State Hortic Assoc Proc
Proceedings. Washington State University International Particleboard/ Composite Materials Series — Proc Wash State Univ Int Particleboard/ Compos Mater Ser
Proceedings. Washington State University. International Symposium on Particleboard — Proc Wash State Univ Int Symp Part
Proceedings. Washington State University International Symposium on Particleboard — Proc Wash State Univ Int Symp Particleboard
Proceedings. Washington State University Symposium on Particleboard — Proc Wash State Univ Symp Particleboard
Proceedings. Water Economics Research Institute (Warsaw) — Proc Water Econ Res Inst (Warsaw)
Proceedings. Water Quality Conference — Proc Water Qual Conf
Proceedings. Water Quality Technology Conference — Proc Water Qual Technol Conf
Proceedings. Water Reuse Symposium — Proc Water Reuse Symp
Proceedings. Water-Borne and Higher-Solids Coatings Symposium — Proc Water Borne Higher Solids Coat Symp
Proceedings. Weed Society of New South Wales — Proc Weed Soc NSW
Proceedings. Weekly Seminar in Neurology — Proc Wkly Semin Neurol
Proceedings. Wesley Historical Society — PWHS
Proceedings. West African International Cacao Research Conference — Proc West Afr Int Cacao Res Conf
Proceedings. West Virginia Academy of Science — Proc W Va Acad Sci
Proceedings. West Virginia Academy of Science — Proc West Virginia Acad Sci
Proceedings. Western Canadian Weed Control Conference — Proc West Can Weed Control Conf
Proceedings. Western Chapter. International Shade Tree Conference — Proc West Chapter Int Shade Tree Conf
Proceedings. Western Europe Conference on Photosynthesis — Proc West Eur Conf Photosyn
Proceedings. Western Forestry Conference. Western Forestry and Conservation Association — Proc West For Conserv Ass
Proceedings. Western Foundation of Vertebrate Zoology — Proc West Found Vertebr Zool
Proceedings. Western Hemisphere Nutrition Congress — Proc West Hemisphere Nutr Congr
Proceedings. Western Pharmacology Society — P West Ph S
Proceedings. Western Pharmacology Society — Proc West Pharmacol Soc
Proceedings. Western Poultry Disease Conference — Proc West Poult Dis Conf
Proceedings. Western Poultry Disease Conference and Poultry Health Symposia [*United States*] — Proc West Poult Dis Conf Poult Health Symp
Proceedings. Western Poultry Disease Conference and Poultry Health Symposia — Proc West Poult Dis Conf Poult Heath Symp
Proceedings. Western Section. American Society of Animal Science — Proc West Sect Am Soc Anim Sci
Proceedings. Western Snow Conference — Proc West Snow Conf
Proceedings. Western Society for French History — Proc West Soc French Hist
Proceedings. Western Society of Weed Science — Proc West Soc Weed Sci
Proceedings. Western States Corrosion Seminar — Proc West States Corros Semin
Proceedings. Wind Energy R and D Contractor Meeting — Proc Wind Energy RD Contract Meet
Proceedings. Wisconsin State Historical Society — Proc Wis Hist Soc
Proceedings. Wood Pole Institute. Colorado State University — Proc Wood Pole Inst Colo State Univ
Proceedings. Wood Products Clinic — Proc Wood Prod Clin
Proceedings. Working Meeting on Radiation Interaction — Proc Work Meet Radiat Interact
Proceedings. Workshop on Coal Pillar Mechanics and Design — Proc Workshop Coal Pillar Mech Des
Proceedings. Workshop on Folyl and Antifolyl Polyglutamates — Proc Workshop Folyl Antifolyl Polyglutamates
Proceedings. Workshop on Photon Radiation from Quarks — Proc Workshop Photon Radiat Quarks
Proceedings. Workshop on Short Pulse High Current Cathodes — Proc Workshop Short Pulse High Curr Cathodes
Proceedings. Workshop on Vitamin D — Proc Workshop Vitam D
Proceedings. World Conference in Industrial Tribology — Proc World Conf Ind Tribol
Proceedings. World Conference on Clinical Pharmacology and Therapeutics — Proc World Conf Clin Pharmacol Ther
Proceedings. World Congress for Milk Utilization — Proc World Congr Milk Util
Proceedings. World Congress for the Lay Apostolate — PWCLA
Proceedings. World Congress. New Compounds in Biological and Chemical Warfare. Toxicological Evaluation — Proc World Congr New Compd Biol Chem Warf Toxicol Eval
Proceedings. World Congress of Agricultural Research — Proc World Congr Agr Res
Proceedings. World Congress of Biological Psychiatry — Proc World Congr Biol Psychiatry
Proceedings. World Congress of Gastroenterology — Proc World Congr Gastroenterol
Proceedings. World Congress of Jewish Studies [*Jerusalem*] — PrWCJewSt
Proceedings. World Congress on Fertility and Sterility — Proc World Congr Fertil Steril
Proceedings. World Congress on Metal Finishing — Proc World Congr Met Finish
Proceedings. World Congress on Pain — Proc World Congr Pain
Proceedings. World Congress on Psychiatry — Proc World Congr Psychiatry
Proceedings. World Forestry Congress — Proc Wld For Congr
Proceedings. World Forestry Congress — Proc World For Congr
Proceedings. World Mariculture Society — Proc World Maric Soc
Proceedings. World Muslim Conference — PWMC
Proceedings. World Orchid Conference — Proc Wld Orchid Conf
Proceedings. World Petroleum Congress — Proc World Pet Congr
Proceedings. World Poultry Congress — Proc World Poultry Congr
Proceedings. World Tobacco Scientific Congress — Proc World Tob Sci Congr
Proceedings. WVU [*West Virginia University*] **Conference on Coal Mine Electrotechnology** — Proc WVU Conf Coal Mine Electrotechnol
Proceedings. Yale Mineralogical Society — Proc Yale Mineral Soc
Proceedings. Yamada Conference on Free Radicals — Proc Yamada Conf Free Radicals
Proceedings. Yorkshire Geological Society [*England*] — Proc Yorks Geol Soc
Proceedings. Yorkshire Geological Society — Proc Yorkshire Geol Soc
Proceedings. Zoological Society — Proc Zool Soc
Proceedings. Zoological Society — PZS
Proceedings. Zoological Society (Calcutta) — Proc Zool Soc (Calcutta)
Proceedings. Zoological Society of London — Proc Zool Soc Lond
Procellaria — Proc
Proces Verbaux et Memoires de l'Academie des Sciences, Belles-Lettres, et Arts. Besancon — Proces Verbaux Mem Acad Sci Besancon
Proceso (Mexico) — POM
Process and Chemical Engineering — Process Chem Eng
Process Architecture — Process Archre
Process Automation — P Automtn
Process Automation — Process Autom
Process Biochemistry — PRBCA
Process Biochemistry — Process Bio
Process Biochemistry — Process Biochem
Process Biochemistry (Barking, UK) — Process Biochem Barking UK
Process Control and Automation — Process Control Autom
Process Design and Development — Process Des Dev
Process Economics International — Process Econ Int
Process Engineering — Process Eng
Process Engineering — Process Engng

Process Engineering (Coburg, Federal Republic of Germany) — Process Eng (Coburg Fed Repub Ger)
Process Engineering Magazine — Process Eng Mag
Process Engineering. Plant and Control — Process Eng Plant and Control
Process Engravers Monthly — Process Engravers Mon
Process Industries Canada — Proc I Cda
Process Industries Canada — Process Ind Can
Process Industries Canada Magazine — Process Ind Can Mag
Process Instrumentation — Process Instrum
Process Metallurgy [*Elsevier Book Series*] — PM
Process Metallurgy — Process Metall
Process Safety and Environmental Protection — Process Saf Environ Prot
Process Studies — Proc St
Process Studies — Process St
Process Studies — Process Stud
Process Studies — PS
Process Technology International — Process Technol Int
Process Technology Proceedings — Process Technol Proc
Processed Prepared Food — FPK
Processed Prepared Food — Proc Food
Processed Series. Oklahoma. Agricultural Experiment Station — Processed Ser Okla Agric Exp Stn
Processed Series. Oklahoma State University. Agricultural Experimental Station — Process Ser Okla State Univ Agr Exp Sta
Processing [*England*] — PCSNA
Processing [*Johannesburg*] — PROCD
Processing and Fabrication of Advanced Materials for High Temperature Applications. Proceedings. Symposium — Process Fabr Adv Mater High Temp Appl Proc Symp
Processing Fruits. Science and Technology — Process Fruits Sci Technol
Processing of Advanced Materials — Process Adv Mater
Proces-Verbaux. Academie des Sciences (Ukraine) — PV Acad Sci (Ukr)
Proces-Verbaux des Seances. Comite International des Poids et Mesures — P-V Seances Com Int Poids Mes
Proces-Verbaux des Seances. Societe des Lettres, Sciences, et Arts de l'Aveyron — PV Aveyron
Proces-Verbaux des Seances. Societe des Sciences Physiques et Naturelles de Bordeaux [*France*] — Proces-Verb Seances Soc Sci Phys Nat Bordeaux
Proces-Verbaux des Seances. Societe des Sciences Physiques et Naturelles de Bordeaux — P-V Seances Soc Sci Phys Nat Bord
Proces-Verbaux des Seances. Societe des Sciences Physiques et Naturelles de Bordeaux — P-V Seances Soc Sci Phys Nat Bordeaux
Proces-Verbaux et Rapports de la Reunion Technique. Union Internationale pour la Protection de la Nature — PV Rapp Reun Tech Union Int Prot Nat
Proces-Verbaux. Societe Linneenne de Bordeaux — P V Soc Linn Bordeaux
Proche-Orient Chretien — P-O Chr
Proche-Orient Chretien — POC
Proche-Orient Chretien [*Jerusalem*] — PrOrChr
Prochnost i Deformatsiya Materialov v Neravnomernykh Fizicheskikh Polyakh — Prochn Deform Mater Neravnomernykh Fiz Polyakh
Prochnost i Dinamika Aviatsionnykh Dvigatelei [*Former USSR*] — Prochnost Din Aviats Dvigatelei
Prochnost Metallov pri Tsiklicheskikh Nagruzkakh. Materialy Soveshchaniya po Ustalosti Metallov — Prochn Met Tsikl Nagruzkakh Mater Soveshch Ustalosti Met
Prodotti Alimentari. Chimica e Tecnologia — Prod Aliment
Prodotto Chimico and Aerosol Selezione — Prod Chim Aerosol Sel
Producao Mineral Servico de Fomento da Producao Mineral. Avulso — Prod Miner Serv Fom Prod Miner Avulso
Producao Mineral Servico de Fomento da Producao Mineral. Boletim — Prod Miner Serv Fom Prod Miner Bol
Produccion Animal — Produccion Anim
Produccion Rural Argentina — Prod Rur Argent
Produce Marketing — Prod Marketing
Producer Price Indexes [*Database*] — PPI
Producer Prices and Price Indexes [*later, Producer Price Indexes*]. Supplement to Data for 1983. US Bureau of Labor Statistics — BLS PPIA
Producers Guild of America. Journal — Prod G Am J
Producers Monthly [*United States*] — Prod Mon
Producers' Review — Prod Rev
Producers' Review — Producers R
Producers' Review — Producers' Rev
Product Engineering [*New York*] — PRENA
Product Engineering — Prod Eng
Product Engineering — Product Eng
Product Finishing [*London*] — PRFIA
Product Finishing [*Cincinnati*] — Prod Finish
Product Finishing (Cincinnati) — Prod Finish (Cinci)
Product Finishing (London) — Prod Finish (Lond)
Product Improvement Program — PIP
Product Liability International — Prod Liab Int
Product Liability International — Prod Liability Int
Product Liability Reporter. Commerce Clearing House — Prod Liab Rep CCH
Product Marketing — Prod Market
Product Marketing — Prod Mkt
Product Marketing — Prod Mktg
Product R & D — Prod R & D
Product Research and Development — Product Res Dev
Product Research and Development R & D — Prod Res Dev R & D
Product Safety and Liability Reporter. Bureau of National Affairs — Prod Safety & Liab Rep BNA
Producteur Agricole Francais — Prod Agric Fr
Productia Vegetala. Cereale si Plante Tehnice — Prod Veg Cereale Plante Teh
Productia Vegetala. Mecanizarea Agriculturii — Prod Veg Mec Agric
Production — PRD
Production and Analysis of Polarized X Rays — Prod Anal Polariz X Rays
Production and Application of Microbial Enzymatic Preparations — Prod Appl Microb Enzym Prep
Production and Inventory Management — PIMGA
Production and Inventory Management — Prod and Inventory Manage
Production and Inventory Management — Prod Invent Manage
Production and Neutralization of Negative Ions and Beams. International Symposium — Prod Neutralization Negat Ions Beams Int Symp
Production and Productivity Bulletin. National Coal Board. Mining Department [*A publication*] — Prod Prod Bull Natl Coal Board Min Dep
Production and Technique (Osaka) [*Japan*] — Prod Tech (Osaka)
Production and Technique (Suita) [*Japan*] — Prod Tech (Suita)
Production Ecology of Ants and Termites [*monograph*] — Prod Ecol Ants Termites
Production Engineer [*London*] — PDENA
Production Engineer [*London*] — Prod Engr
Production Engineer — Prodn Engnr
Production Engineer (London) — Prod Eng (Lond)
Production Engineering — PEG
Production Engineering — Prod Engng
Production Engineering — Production
Production Engineering (Cleveland) — Prod Eng (Cleveland)
Production et Gestion — Product et Gestion
Production Journal — Prodn J
Production Laitiere Moderne — Prod Lait Mod
Production Management — Prod Manage
Production of Aggregates in Great Britain — Prod Aggregates GB
Production Publication. Association of Official Seed Certifying Agencies — Prod Publ Assoc Off Seed Certifying Agencies
Production Publication. International Crop Improvement Association — Prod Publ Int Crop Impr Ass
Production, Refining, Fabrication, and Recycling of Light Metals. Proceedings. International Symposium — Prod Refin Fabr Recycl Light Met Proc Int Symp
Production Research Report — Prod Res Rep
Production Research Report. United States Department of Agriculture — Prod Res Rep US Dep Agric
Production Research Report. United States Department of Agriculture. Science and Education Administration — Prod Res Rep US Dep Agric Sci Educ Adm
Production Research Report. US Department of Agriculture. Agricultural Research Service — Prod Res Rep US Dep Agric Agric Res Serv
Production with Safety — Prod with Safety
Production Yearbook FAO [*Food and Agriculture Organization*] — Prod Yb FAO
Productivity and Performance — Prod Perf
Productivity and Technology — Prod Technol
Productivity Improvement Bulletin — Prod Improve Bull
Productivity Insights — Prod Insights
Productivity Measures for Selected Industries, 1954-80. BLS Bulletin 2128. US Bureau of Labor Statistics — BLS 2128
Productivity Measures for Selected Industries, 1954-83. BLS Bulletin 2224. US Bureau of Labor Statistics — BLS 2224
Productivity Measures for Selected Industries, 1958-84. BLS Bulletin 2256. US Bureau of Labor Statistics — BLS 2256
Products Finishing (Cincinnati) — PRFCA
Products Finishing (Cincinnati) — Prod Finish (Cincinnati)
Products, Projects, and Trends in Building — Prod Proj Trends Bldg
Produits et Problemes Pharmaceutiques — PPRPA
Produits et Problemes Pharmaceutiques — Prod Probl Pharm
Produits et Problemes Pharmaceutiques — Produits Pharm
Produits Pharmaceutiques [*France*] — Prod Pharm
Produktion — Prod
Produktivnost — PKVOA
Produktnieuws voor Kantoor en Bedrijf. Investeringsinformatie voor Managers — PRO
Produzione Animale — Prod Anim
Proefstation voor de Akker- en Weidebouw, Wageningen, Gestencilde Verslagen van Interprovinciale Proeven — Proefstn Akker Weidebouw Wageningen Gestencilde Versl Interp
Proefstation voor de Akkerbouw en de Groenteteelt in de Volle Grond. Verslagen van Interprovinciale Proeven — Proefstn Akkerbouw Groenteteelt Volle Grond Versl Interprov P
Proefstation voor de Akkerbouw Lelystad. Verslagen van Interprovinciale Proeven — Proefstn Akkerbouw Lelystad Versl Interprov Proeven
Proefstation voor de Akkerbouw (Wageningen). Verslagen van Interprovinciale Proeven — Proefstn Akkerbouw (Wageningen) Versl Interprov Proeven
Proefstation voor de Groenteteelt in de Vollegrond in Nederland. Mededeling — Proefstn Groenteteelt Vollegrond Ned Meded
Proefstation voor de Java-Suikerindustrie. Mededeelingen — Proefstn Java Suikerind Meded
Proefstation voor Rubber. Mededeeling — Proefstn Rubber Meded
Proefstation voor Vorstenlandsche Tabak. Mededeelingen — Proefstn Vorstenl Tab Meded
Proektnyi i Nauchno-Issledovatel'skii Institut "Ural'skii Promstroiniiproekt." Trudy — Proektn Nauchno-Issled Inst Ural Promstroiniiproekt Tr
Proektnyi i Nauchno-Issledovatel'skii Institut Gipronikel. Trudy — Proektn Nauchno Issled Inst Gipronikel Tr
Profession Medicale — Profession Med
Professional Administration — PA
Professional Administration — Prof Admin
Professional Builder — Prof Build
Professional Builder and Apartment Business — Prof Build Apartm Bus
Professional Builder and Apartment Business — Prof Builder & Apt Bus
Professional Builder and Apartment Business — Prof Builder/Apt Bus
Professional Camera — Prof Camera
Professional Casting Report — PCR

Professional Computing — Prof Comput
Professional Contributions. Colorado School of Mines — PCCOA
Professional Development Week — Prof Dev W
Professional Engineer [*Washington, DC*] — PENRB
Professional Engineer — Pro Engr
Professional Engineer — Professional Eng
Professional Engineer (Pretoria) — Prof Eng (Pretoria)
Professional Engineer (Washington, DC) — Prof Eng (Wash DC)
Professional Flashes — Prof Flashes
Professional Garden — Profess Gard
Professional Geographer — PfGg
Professional Geographer — PFGGA
Professional Geographer — PPGE
Professional Geographer — Prof Geog
Professional Geographer — Prof Geogr
Professional Geologist — Prof Geologist
Professional Horticulture — Prof Hortic
Professional Investor Report [*Database*] — PIR
Professional Liability Reporter — Pro LR
Professional Marketing Report — Prof Mark Rep
Professional Medical Assistant — Prof Med Assist
Professional Monitor — Prof Mon
Professional Nurse — Prof Nurse
Professional Nursing Home — PRNHA
Professional Nursing Home — Prof Nurs Home
Professional Nutritionist — Prof Nutr
Professional Officers' Association Chronicle — POA Chronicle
Professional Papers. Deputy Ministry for Mineral Resources (Saudi Arabia) — Prof Pap Deputy Minist Miner Resour (Saudi Arabia)
Professional Papers Series. Florida Department of Natural Resources. Marine Research Laboratory — Prof Pap Ser Fla Dep Nat Resour Mar Res Lab
Professional Papers Series. Florida State Board of Conservation. Marine Laboratory — Profess Pap Ser Florida State Board Conservation Mar Lab
Professional Papers. United States Geological Survey — Prof Pap Geol Surv
Professional Papers. United States Geological Survey — Prof Pap US Geol Surv
Professional Photographer — Prof Photogr
Professional Practice Management — Prof Prac Man
Professional Practice Management — Prof Pract Man
Professional Printer — Prof Print
Professional Psychology — Prof Psycho
Professional Regulation News — Prof Regulation N
Professional Report — PRO
Professional Report — Prof Rpt
Professional Safety — Prof Saf
Professional Safety — Prof Safety
Professional Sanitation Management — Prof Sanit Manage
Professional'nye Bolezni Pylevoi Etiologii — Prof Bolezni Pylevoi Etiol
Professioni Infermieristiche — Prof Inferm
Professions and Occupations Sourcebook — POS
Professions et Entreprises — Professions et Entr
Profil Litteraire de la France — Prof Lit Fr
Profilaktika i Lechenie Tuberkuleza — Profil Lech Tuberk
Profilaktika Osobo Opasnykh Infektsii — Profil Osobo Opasnykh Infekts
Profile Index. Micromedia Ltd. — PFI
Profile of Medical Practice — Profile Med Pract
Profiles — Profile
Profiles in Hospital Marketing — Profiles Hosp Mark
Profiles of Genius Series — Profiles Genius Ser
Profils de l'Economie Nord-Pas-De-Calais — Profils Econ Nord-Pas-De-Calais
Profit-Building Strategies — Prft Bldg St
Prognosen-Trends-Entwicklungen [*Database*] — PROGNO
Program Aid. United States Department of Agriculture — Program Aid US Dep Agric
Program. American Dairy Science Association. Annual Meeting and Branch Abstracts — Program Am Dairy Sci Assoc Annu Meet Branch Abstr
Program and Abstracts. American Society of Parasitologists. Annual Meeting — Program Abstr Am Soc Parasitol Annu Meet
Program: Automated Library and Information Systems — PALSD
Program. Automated Library and Information Systems [*England*] — Program Autom Libr Inf Syst
Program Manager — PGM
Program Manager — Pro Managr
Program. News of Computers in Libraries — Program News Comput Libr
Program Notes. Association of University Programs in Health Administration — Program Notes Assoc Univ Programs Health Adm
Program/Proceedings. National Horsemen's Seminar — Program/Proc Natl Horsemen's Semin
Program Review. Forest Products Laboratory (Ottawa) — Progr Rev For Prod Lab (Ottawa)
Program Review. Forest Products Laboratory (Vancouver) [*British Columbia, Canada*] — Progr Rev For Prod Lab (Vancouver)
Programa Cooperativo Centroamericano para el Mejoramiento del Maiz — Progr Coop Centroamer Mejor Maiz
Programa Cooperativo de Experimentacion Agropecuaria. United States and Peru. Boletim Trimestral de Experimentacion Agropecuaria — Programa Coop Exp Agropecu US Peru Bol Trimest Exp Agropecu
Programa Regional de Desarrollo Cientifico y Tecnologico. Monografia. Serie de Quimica — Programa Reg Desarrollo Cient Tecnol Monogr Ser Quim
Programa Regional de Desarrollo Cientifico y Tecnologico. Serie de Fisica — Programa Reg Desarrollo Cient Tecnol Ser Fis
Programma di Matematica, Fisica, Elettronica — Program Mat Fis Elettron
Programma i Tezisy Dokladov Soveshchaniya po Yadernoi Spektroskopii i Strukture Atomnogo Yadra — Programma Tezis Dokl Soveshch Yad Spektrosk Strukt At Yadra
Programme — PR
Programme and Papers. Rubber Conference — Programme Pap Rubber Conf
Programme Officiel. Journee Interregionale de Recolte Mechanique du Mais-Grain — Progr Offic Journee Interreg Recolte Mec Mais-Grain
Programmed Instruction and Educational Technology — Prog Instr & Ed Tech
Programmed Instruction Bulletin — Prog Instr Bul
Programmed Learning and Educational Technology — Prog Learn
Programmed Learning and Educational Technology — Progr Learn Educ Technol
Programmed Learning and Educational Technology — Program Learn and Educ Technol
Programmed Learning and Educational Technology — Programmed Learning
Programminformationssystem Sozialwissenschaften [*Database*] — PROFIS
Programming and Computer Software — Program and Comput Software
Programming and Computer Software — Programming and Comput Software
Programming Languages Series [*Elsevier Book Series*] — PL
Programming Languages Series — Programming Lang Ser
Programmirovanie. Akademija Nauk SSSR — Programmirovan
Progres Agricole de France — Prog Agri Fr
Progres Agricole et Viticole — PAGVA
Progres Agricole et Viticole [*France*] — Prog Agric Vitic
Progres Agricole et Viticole — Progr Agr Vitic
Progres dans la Chimie des Substances Organiques Naturelles — Prog Chim Subst Org Nat
Progres dans la Science et la Technique du Froid. Comptes Rendus. Congres International du Froid — Prog Sci Tech Froid CR Congr Int Froid
Progres dans les Recherches sur le Cancer — Prog Rech Cancer
Progres de la Recherche Experimentale des Tumeurs — Prog Rech Exp Tumeurs
Progres de l'Exploration de la Tuberculose — Prog Explor Tuberc
Progres des Recherches Pharmaceutiques — Prog Rech Pharm
Progres en Andrologie — Prog Androl
Progres en Medecine Psychosomatique — Prog Med Psychosom
Progres en Neonatologie — Prog Neonatol
Progres en Obstetrique et Gynecologie — Prog Obstet Gynecol
Progres en Ophtalmologie — Prog Ophtalmol
Progres en Oto-Rhino-Laryngologie — Prog Oto-Rhino-Laryngol
Progres en Virologie Medicale — Prog Virol Med
Progres Medical — Prog Med
Progres Medical (Paris) — Progr Med (Paris)
Progres Medical (Paris) — Progres Med (Paris)
Progres Odonto-Stomatologique — Prog Odontostomatol
Progres Scientifique [*France*] — Prog Sci
Progres Scientifique — Progres Scientif
Progres Scientifique — PSNTA
Progres Social — Prog Soc
Progres Social — Progr Soc
Progres Social. Troisieme Serie — Progres Soc 3e Ser
Progres Technique — Prog Tech
Progres Technique — Progres Techn
Progres Technique — PRTCD
Progres Veterinaire — Progres Vet
Progresele Stiintei — Progr Stiintei
Progresele Stiintei — PRSTB
Progreso Medico (Habana) — Progreso Med (Habana)
Progresos de Pediatria y Puericultura — Prog Pediatr Pueric
Progresos de Terapeutica Clinica — Progr Ter Clin
Progresos en Psicofarmacologia — Prog Psicofarmacol
Progress and Topics in Cytogenetics — Prog Top Cytogenet
Progress Bulletin. Alberta University Extension Department — Progr Bull Alberta Univ Ext Dept
Progress in Aeronautical Science — Prog Aeronaut Sci
Progress in Aerospace Sciences — Prog Aerosp Sci
Progress in AIDS Pathology — Prog AIDS Pathol
Progress in Allergy — Prog Allerg
Progress in Allergy — Prog Allergy
Progress in Allergy — Progr Allergy
Progress in Anaesthesiology. Proceedings. World Congress of Anaesthesiologists — Prog Anaesthesiol Proc World Congr Anaesthesiol
Progress in Analytical Atomic Spectroscopy — Prog Anal At Spectrosc
Progress in Analytical Chemistry — Prog Anal Chem
Progress in Analytical Spectroscopy — Prog Anal Spectros
Progress in Analytical Ultracentrifugation — Prog Anal Ultracentrifugation
Progress in Anatomy — PANTDK
Progress in Anatomy — Prog Anat
Progress in Anesthesiology — PRANDM
Progress in Anesthesiology — Prog Anesthesiol
Progress in Anesthetic Mechanism — Prog Anesth Mech
Progress in Animal Biometeorology — Prog Anim Biometeorol
Progress in Antimicrobial and Anticancer Chemotherapy. Proceedings. International Congress of Chemotherapy — Prog Antimicrob Anticancer Chemother Proc Int Congr Chemother
Progress in Applied Materials Research — Prog Appl Mater Res
Progress in Applied Microcirculation — MFKLDH
Progress in Applied Microcirculation — Prog Appl Microcirc
Progress in Astronautics and Aeronautics — Prog Astronaut Aeronaut
Progress in Astronautics and Rocketry — Prog Astronaut Rocketry
Progress in Atomic Medicine — PAMDA
Progress in Atomic Medicine — Prog At Med
Progress in Batteries and Battery Materials — Prog Batteries Battery Mater
Progress in Batteries and Solar Cells — Prog Batteries Sol Cell
Progress in Behavior Modification — PBMOE8
Progress in Behavior Modification — Prog Behav Modif
Progress in Biochemical Pharmacology — Prog Biochem Pharmacol
Progress in Biochemistry and Biophysics [*People's Republic of China*] — Prog Biochem Biophys

Progress in Biocybernetics — Prog Biocybern
Progress in Biomass Conversion — Prog Biomass Convers
Progress in Biomedical Engineering — Prog Biomed Eng
Progress in Biomedical Polymers. Proceedings. American Chemical Society Symposium — Prog Biomed Polym Proc Am Chem Soc Symp
Progress in Biometeorology — Prog Biometeorol
Progress in Biometeorology. Division A. Progress in Human Biometeorology [*Netherlands*] — Prog Biometeorol Div A
Progress in Biometeorology. Division B. Progress in Animal Biometeorology — Prog Biometeorol Div B
Progress in Bioorganic Chemistry — Prog Bioorg Chem
Progress in Biophysics and Biophysical Chemistry — Prog Biophys Biophys Chem
Progress in Biophysics and Biophysical Chemistry — Progr Biophys Biophys Chem
Progress in Biophysics and Molecular Biology — Prog Biophys and Mol Biol
Progress in Biophysics and Molecular Biology — Prog Biophys Mol Biol
Progress in Biotechnology — Prog Biotechnol
Progress in Boron Chemistry — Prog Boron Chem
Progress in Botany — Prog Bot
Progress in Botany-Fortschritt der Botanik — Prog Bot Fortschr Bot
Progress in Brain Research [*Elsevier Book Series*] — PBR
Progress in Brain Research — Prog Brain Res
Progress in Calorimetry and Thermal Analysis — Prog Calorim Therm Anal
Progress in Cancer Research and Therapy — Prog Cancer Res Ther
Progress in Cardiology — Prog Cardiol
Progress in Cardiovascular Diseases — PCVDA
Progress in Cardiovascular Diseases — Prog Cardiovasc Dis
Progress in Cardiovascular Diseases — Progr Card
Progress in Cardiovascular Diseases — Progr Cardiovas Dis
Progress in Cardiovascular Nursing — Prog Cardiovasc Nurs
Progress in Catalysis. Proceedings. Canadian Symposium on Catalysis — Prog Catal Proc Can Symp Catal
Progress in Catecholamine Research. Part A. Basic Aspects and Peripheral Mechanisms. Proceedings. International Catecholamine Symposium — Prog Catecholamine Res Part A Proc Int Catecholamine Symp
Progress in Catecholamine Research. Part B. Central Aspects. Proceedings. International Catecholamine Symposium — Prog Catecholamine Res Part B Proc Int Catecholamine Symp
Progress in Catecholamine Research. Part C. Clinical Aspects. Proceedings. International Catecholamine Symposium — Prog Catecholamine Res Part C Proc Int Catecholamine Symp
Progress in Cell Cycle Research — Prog Cell Cycle Res
Progress in Ceramic Science — Prog Ceram Sci
Progress in Chemical Fibrinolysis and Thrombolysis — Prog Chem Fibrinolysis Thrombolysis
Progress in Chemical Toxicology — Prog Chem Toxicol
Progress in Chemistry (Moscow) — Prog Chem Moscow
Progress in Clay Science — Prog Clay Sci
Progress in Clinical and Biological Research [*Elsevier Book Series*] — PCBR
Progress in Clinical and Biological Research — PCBRD
Progress in Clinical and Biological Research — Prog Clin Biol Res
Progress in Clinical Biochemistry and Medicine — PCBMEM
Progress in Clinical Biochemistry and Medicine — Prog Clin Biochem Med
Progress in Clinical Cancer — Prog Clin Cancer
Progress in Clinical Cancer — Progr Clin Cancer
Progress in Clinical Immunology — PCIYA
Progress in Clinical Immunology — Prog Clin Immunol
Progress in Clinical Medicine [*Monograph*] — Prog Clin Med
Progress in Clinical Neurophysiology — Prog Clin Neurophysiol
Progress in Clinical Parasitology — Prog Clin Parasitol
Progress in Clinical Pathology — Prog Clin Pathol
Progress in Clinical Pharmacology — Prog Clin Pharmacol
Progress in Clinical Pharmacy — Prog Clin Pharm
Progress in Colloid and Polymer Science — PCPSD
Progress in Colloid and Polymer Science — Prog Coll & Polym Sci
Progress in Colloid and Polymer Science — Prog Colloid Polym Sci
Progress in Combustion Science and Technology — Prog Combus Sci Technol
Progress in Computer Science and Applied Logic — Prog Comput Sci Appl Logic
Progress in Conception Control — Prog Concept Control
Progress in Contraceptive Delivery Systems — Prog Contracept Delivery Syst
Progress in Control Engineering — Progr Contr Eng
Progress in Cosmic Ray Physics — Prog Cosmic Ray Phys
Progress in Critical Care Medicine — Prog Crit Care Med
Progress in Cryogenics — Prog Cryog
Progress in Crystal Growth and Characterization — Prog Cryst Growth Charact
Progress in Crystal Physics — Prog Cryst Phys
Progress in Dielectrics — Prog Dielectr
Progress in Drug Metabolism — Prog Drug Metab
Progress in Drug Research — Prog Drug Res
Progress in Ecology — Prog Ecol
Progress in Education — Prog Educ
Progress in Electromagnetics Research — Prog Electromagn Res
Progress in Elementary Particle and Cosmic Ray Physics — Prog Elem Part Cosmic Ray Phys
Progress in Endocrine Research and Therapy — Prog Endocr Res Ther
Progress in Energy and Combustion Science — Prog Energy Combust Sci
Progress in Experimental Personality and Psychopathology Research — Prog Exp Pers Psychopathol Res
Progress in Experimental Personality Research — Prog Exp Pers Res
Progress in Experimental Tumor Research — Prog Ex Tum
Progress in Experimental Tumor Research — Prog Exp Tumor Res
Progress in Extractive Metallurgy — Prog Extr Metall
Progress in Filtration and Separation [*Elsevier Book Series*] — PFS
Progress in Filtration and Separation — Prog Filtr Sep
Progress in Fire Retardancy Series — Prog Fire Retard Ser
Progress in Flavour Research. Proceedings. Weurman Flavour Research Symposium — Prog Flavour Res Proc Weurman Flavour Res Symp
Progress in Food and Nutrition Science — Prog Food Nutr Sci
Progress in Gastroenterology — Prog Gastroenterol
Progress in Geography — Prog Geogr
Progress in Growth Factor Research — Prog Growth Factor Res
Progress in Gynecology — Prog Gynecol
Progress in Hazardous Chemicals Handling and Disposal. Proceedings. Symposium on Hazardous Chemicals Handling and Disposal — Prog Hazard Chem Handl Disposal Proc Symp
Progress in Heat and Mass Transfer — Prog Heat Mass Transf
Progress in Heat and Mass Transfer — Prog Heat Mass Transfer
Progress in Hematology — Prog Hematol
Progress in Hematology — Progr Hemat
Progress in Hemostasis and Thrombosis — PGHTA
Progress in Hemostasis and Thrombosis — Prog Hemost Thromb
Progress in Hemostasis and Thrombosis — Prog Hemostasis Thromb
Progress in Hepato-Pharmacology — Prog Hepato Pharmacol
Progress in High Polymers — Prog High Polym
Progress in High Temperature Physics and Chemistry — Prog High Temp Phys Chem
Progress in High-Temperature Superconducting Transistors and Other Devices — Prog High Temp Supercond Transistors Other Devices
Progress in Histochemistry and Cytochemistry — PHCCA
Progress in Histochemistry and Cytochemistry — Prog Histochem Cytochem
Progress in Hodgkin's Disease — Prog Hodgkins Dis
Progress in Hormone Biochemistry and Pharmacology — Prog Horm Biochem Pharmacol
Progress in HPLC [*High-Performance Liquid Chromatography*] — Prog HPLC
Progress in Human Biometeorology — Prog Hum Biometeorol
Progress in Human Geography — PHG
Progress in Human Geography — Prog Human Geogr
Progress in Human Geography. International Review of Current Research — Progr Hum Geogr
Progress in Human Nutrition — Prog Hum Nutr
Progress in Immunobiological Standardization — PILSA
Progress in Immunobiological Standardization — Prog Immunobiol Stand
Progress in Immunology. International Congress of Immunology — Prog Immunol Int Congr Immunol
Progress in Industrial Gas Chromatography. Proceedings. Annual Gas Chromatography Institute — Prog Ind Gas Chromatogr Proc Annu Gas Chromatogr Inst
Progress in Industrial Microbiology [*Elsevier Book Series*] — PIM
Progress in Industrial Microbiology — PIMRA
Progress in Industrial Microbiology — Prog Ind Microbiol
Progress in Industrial Microbiology — Progr Indust Microbiol
Progress in Infrared Spectroscopy — Prog Infrared Spectrosc
Progress in Inorganic Chemistry — PIOCA
Progress in Inorganic Chemistry — Prog Inorg Chem
Progress in Learning Disabilities — Prog Learn Disabil
Progress in Leukocyte Biology — Prog Leukocyte Biol
Progress in Lipid Research — Prog Lipid Res
Progress in Liver Diseases — PLVDA
Progress in Liver Diseases — Prog Liver Dis
Progress in Low Temperature Physics [*Elsevier Book Series*] — PLT
Progress in Low Temperature Physics — PLTPA
Progress in Low Temperature Physics — Prog Low Temp Phys
Progress in Materials Science — PRMSA
Progress in Materials Science — Prog Mat Sc
Progress in Materials Science — Prog Mater Sci
Progress in Materials Science — Progr Mater Sci
Progress in Mathematical Social Sciences [*Elsevier Book Series*] — PMSS
Progress in Mathematics — Progress in Math
Progress in Medical Genetics — PMOGA
Progress in Medical Genetics — Prog Med Ge
Progress in Medical Genetics — Prog Med Genet
Progress in Medical Parasitology in Japan — Prog Med Parasitol Jpn
Progress in Medical Ultrasound [*Elsevier Book Series*] — PMU
Progress in Medical Virology — PMVIA
Progress in Medical Virology — Prog Med Vi
Progress in Medical Virology — Prog Med Virol
Progress in Medical Virology — Progr Med Virol
Progress in Medicinal Chemistry [*Elsevier Book Series*] — PMC
Progress in Medicinal Chemistry — PMDCA
Progress in Medicinal Chemistry — Prog Med Chem
Progress in Medicine (Tokyo) — Prog Med (Tokyo)
Progress in Metal Physics — Prog Met Phys
Progress in Migraine Research — Prog Migraine Res
Progress in Molecular and Subcellular Biology — Prog Mol Subcell Biol
Progress in Mutation Research [*Elsevier Book Series*] — PMR
Progress in Mutation Research — Prog Mutat Res
Progress in Natural Science — Prog Nat Sci
Progress in Neurobiology — Prog Neurobiol
Progress in Neurobiology (New York) — Prog Neurobiol (NY)
Progress in Neurobiology (Oxford) — Prog Neurobiol (Oxf)
Progress in Neurological Surgery — Prog Neurol Surg
Progress in Neurology and Psychiatry — PNPSA
Progress in Neurology and Psychiatry — Prog Neurol Psychiatry
Progress in Neurology and Psychiatry — Progr Neurol Psychiat
Progress in Neuropathology — Prog Neuropathol
Progress in Neuro-Psychopharmacology — Prog Neuro-Psychopharmacol
Progress in Neuro-Psychopharmacology and Biological Psychiatry — Prog Neuro-Psychopharmacol & Biol Psychiatry

Progress in Neuropsychopharmacology and Biological Psychiatry — Prog Neuropsychopharmacol Biol Psychiatry
Progress in Neutron Capture Therapy for Cancer. Proceedings. International Symposium on Neutron Capture Therapy for Cancer — Prog Neutron Capture Ther Cancer Proc Int Symp
Progress in Non-Destructive Testing — Prog Non Destr Test
Progress in Nonlinear Differential Equations and their Applications — Progr Nonlinear Differential Equations Appl
Progress in Nuclear Energy — PNEND
Progress in Nuclear Energy [*England*] — Prog Nucl Energy
Progress in Nuclear Energy. Analytical Chemistry — Prog Nucl Energy Anal Chem
Progress in Nuclear Energy. New Series — Prog Nucl Energy New Ser
Progress in Nuclear Energy. Series 1. Physics and Mathematics — Prog Nucl Energy Ser 1
Progress in Nuclear Energy. Series 1. Physics and Mathematics — Progr Nucl Energy Ser 1 Phys Math
Progress in Nuclear Energy. Series 2. Reactors — Prog Nucl Energy Ser 2
Progress in Nuclear Energy. Series 2. Reactors — Progr Nucl Energy Ser 2 Reactors
Progress in Nuclear Energy. Series 3. Process Chemistry — PNPRA
Progress in Nuclear Energy. Series 3. Process Chemistry — Prog Nucl Energy Ser 3
Progress in Nuclear Energy. Series 3. Process Chemistry — Progr Nucl Energy Ser 3 Process Chem
Progress in Nuclear Energy. Series 4 — PNTEA
Progress in Nuclear Energy. Series 4. Technology and Engineering — Progr Nucl Energy Ser 4 Technol Eng
Progress in Nuclear Energy. Series 4. Technology, Engineering, and Safety — Prog Nucl Energy Ser 4
Progress in Nuclear Energy. Series 5. Metallurgy and Fuels — Prog Nucl Energy Ser 5
Progress in Nuclear Energy. Series 5. Metallurgy and Fuels — Progr Nucl Energy Ser 5 Met Fuels
Progress in Nuclear Energy. Series 6 [*England*] — Prog Nucl Energy Ser 6
Progress in Nuclear Energy. Series 6. Biological Sciences — Progr Nucl Energy Ser 6
Progress in Nuclear Energy. Series 7. Medical Sciences — Prog Nucl Energy Ser 7
Progress in Nuclear Energy. Series 7. Medical Sciences — Prog Nucl Energy Ser 7 Med Sci
Progress in Nuclear Energy. Series 8. Economics — Progr Nucl Energy Ser 8 Econ
Progress in Nuclear Energy. Series 8. The Economics of Nuclear Power Including Administration and Law — Prog Nucl Energy Ser 8
Progress in Nuclear Energy. Series 9 — PEACA
Progress in Nuclear Energy. Series 9 [*England*] — Prog Nucl Energy Ser 9
Progress in Nuclear Energy. Series 10 — PELAA
Progress in Nuclear Energy. Series 10. Law and Administration — Prog Nucl Energy Ser 10
Progress in Nuclear Energy. Series 10. Law and Administration — Progr Nucl Energy Ser 10 Law Admin
Progress in Nuclear Energy. Series 11. Plasma Physics and Thermonuclear Research — Prog Nucl Energy Ser 11
Progress in Nuclear Energy. Series 11. Plasma Physics and Thermonuclear Research — Progr Nucl Energy Ser 11 Plasma Phys Thermonucl Res
Progress in Nuclear Energy. Series 12 — PEHPA
Progress in Nuclear Energy. Series 12. Health Physics — Prog Nucl Energy Ser 12
Progress in Nuclear Magnetic Resonance Spectroscopy — PNMRA
Progress in Nuclear Magnetic Resonance Spectroscopy — Prog Nucl Magn Reson Spectrosc
Progress in Nuclear Medicine — PGNMA
Progress in Nuclear Medicine — Prog Nucl Med
Progress in Nuclear Physics — PNUPA
Progress in Nuclear Physics — Prog Nucl Phys
Progress in Nuclear Techniques and Instrumentation [*Netherlands*] — Prog Nucl Tech Instrum
Progress in Nucleic Acid Research — Prog Nucleic Acid Res
Progress in Nucleic Acid Research — Progr Nucl Acid Res
Progress in Nucleic Acid Research and Molecular Biology — PNMBA
Progress in Nucleic Acid Research and Molecular Biology — Prog Nucleic Acid Res Mol Biol
Progress in Oceanography — Prog Oceanogr
Progress in Ophthalmology and Otolaryngology — Prog Ophthalmol Otolaryngol
Progress in Opioid Research. Proceedings. International Narcotics Research Conference — Prog Opioid Res Proc Int Narc Res Conf
Progress in Optics — Prog Opt
Progress in Organic Chemistry — Prog Org Chem
Progress in Organic Coatings — POGCA
Progress in Organic Coatings — Prog Org Coat
Progress in Organic Coatings — Prog Org Coatings
Progress in Organic Coatings — Progress Organic Coatings
Progress in Paper Recycling — Progr Pap Recycl
Progress in Particle and Nuclear Physics — PPNPD
Progress in Particle and Nuclear Physics [*England*] — Prog Part Nucl Phys
Progress in Particle and Nuclear Physics — Progr Particle and Nuclear Phys
Progress in Particle and Nuclear Physics — Progress in Particle and Nuclear Phys
Progress in Passive Solar Energy Systems — Prog Pass Sol Energy Syst
Progress in Pathology — Prog Pathol
Progress in Pathophysiology. Proceedings. International Congress on Pathological Physiology — Prog Pathophysiol Proc Int Congr
Progress in Pediatric Hematology/Oncology — Prog Pediatr Hematol/Oncol
Progress in Pediatric Radiology — PPERB
Progress in Pediatric Radiology [*Switzerland*] — Prog Pediatr Radiol
Progress in Pediatric Surgery — Prog Pediatr Surg
Progress in Peptide Research. Proceedings. American Peptide Symposium — Prog Pept Res Proc Am Pept Symp
Progress in Pesticide Biochemistry — Prog Pestic Biochem
Progress in Pesticide Biochemistry and Toxicology — Prog Pestic Biochem Toxicol
Progress in Pharmaceutical and Biomedical Analysis — Prog Pharm Biomed Anal
Progress in Pharmacology — Prog Pharmacol
Progress in Pharmacology and Clinical Pharmacology — Prog Pharmacol Clin Pharmacol
Progress in Photography — Prog Photogr
Progress in Photosynthesis Research. Proceedings. International Congress of Photosynthesis Research — Prog Photosynth Res Proc Int Congr
Progress in Phycological Research — Prog Phycol Res
Progress in Physical Geography — Prog Phys Geogr
Progress in Physical Organic Chemistry — Prog Phys Org Chem
Progress in Physical Sciences (Moscow) — Prog Phys Sci (Moscow)
Progress in Physical Therapy — Prog Phys Ther
Progress in Physics — Progr Phys
Progress in Physics — Progress in Phys
Progress in Physics. Astrophysics. A Reprint Series — Prog Phys Astrophys Repr Ser
Progress in Physiological Psychology — Prog Physiol Psychol
Progress in Physiological Psychology — Progr Physiol Psych
Progress in Physiological Sciences (Beijing) — Prog Physiol Sci Beijing
Progress in Physiological Sciences (English Translation of Uspekhi Fiziologicheskikh Nauk) — Prog Physiol Sci (Engl Transl Usp Fiziol Nauk)
Progress in Physiological Sciences (USSR) — Prog Physiol Sci (USSR)
Progress in Physiology — Prog Physiol
Progress in Phytochemistry — Prog Phytochem
Progress in Phytochemistry — Progress Phytochem
Progress in Planning — Prog Plann
Progress in Polymer Processing — Prog Polym Process
Progress in Polymer Science — Prog Polym Sci
Progress in Polymer Science — Progr Polymer Sci
Progress in Polymer Science — PRPSB
Progress in Powder Metallurgy — PPWMA
Progress in Powder Metallurgy — Prog Powder Metall
Progress in Powder Metallurgy — Progr Powder Met
Progress in Probability — Progr Probab
Progress in Probability and Statistics — Progr Prob Statist
Progress in Protein-Lipid Interactions — Prog Protein Lipid Interact
Progress in Protozoology. Proceedings. International Congress on Protozoology — Prog Protozool Proc Int Congr Protozool
Progress in Psychiatric Drug Treatment — Prog Psychiatr Drug Treat
Progress in Psychiatry — Prog Psychiatry
Progress in Psychobiology and Physiological Psychology — Prog Psychobiol Physiol Psychol
Progress in Pure and Applied Discrete Mathematics — Progr Pure Appl Discrete Math
Progress in Quantum Electronics — PQUEA
Progress in Quantum Electronics — Prog Quantum Electron
Progress in Radiation Protection — Prog Radiat Prot
Progress in Radiation Therapy — Prog Radiat Ther
Progress in Radiation Therapy — PRTHA
Progress in Radiology. Symposia and Invited Papers. International Congress of Radiology — Prog Radiol Symp Invited Pap Int Congr Radiol
Progress in Radiopharmacology — Prog Radiopharmacol
Progress in Radiopharmacology [*Elsevier Book Series*] — PRP
Progress in Radiopharmacy — Prog Radiopharm
Progress in Reaction Kinetics — PRKNA
Progress in Reaction Kinetics — Prog React Kinet
Progress in Refrigeration Science and Technology. Proceedings. International Congress of Refrigeration — Prog Refrig Sci Technol Proc Int Congr Refrig
Progress in Reproductive Biology — Prog Reprod Biol
Progress in Reproductive Biology and Medicine — Prog Reprod Biol Med
Progress in Research and Clinical Applications of Corticosteroids. Proceedings. Annual Clinical Symposium — Prog Res Clin Appl Corticosteroids Proc Annu Clin Symp
Progress in Research in Emphysema and Chronic Bronchitis — Prog Res Emphysema Chronic Bronchitis
Progress in Respiration Research — Prog Respir Res
Progress in Retinal Research — Prog Retinal Res
Progress in Rural Extension and Community Development — Prog Rural Ext Commun Dev
Progress in Science (Amoy) — Prog Sci (Amoy)
Progress in Science and Engineering of Composites. Proceedings. International Conference on Composite Materials — Prog Sci Eng Compos Proc Int Conf Compos Mater
Progress in Scientific Computing — Progr Sci Comput
Progress in Semiconductors — Prog Semicond
Progress in Sensory Physiology — Prog Sens Physiol
Progress in Separation and Purification — Prog Sep Purif
Progress in Separation and Purification — PSEPB
Progress in Sexology. Selected Papers. Proceedings. International Congress of Sexology — Prog Sex Sel Pap Proc Int Congr
Progress in Soil Science (Nanjing, People's Republic of China) — Prog Soil Sci (Nanjing Peoples Repub China)
Progress in Soil Zoology. Proceedings. International Colloquium on Soil Zoology — Prog Soil Zool Proc Int Colloq
Progress in Solar Energy — Prog Sol Energy
Progress in Solid State Chemistry [*England*] — Prog Solid State Chem
Progress in Solid State Chemistry — PSSTA

Progress in Standardization — Prog Stand
Progress in Steel Construction Work. Steel Congress — Prog Steel Constr Work Steel Congr
Progress in Steel Processing. Steel Congress — Prog Steel Process Steel Congr
Progress in Stereochemistry — Prog Stereochem
Progress in Stereochemistry — PRSTA
Progress in Surface and Membrane Science — Prog Surf Membr Sci
Progress in Surface Science — Prog Surf Sci
Progress in Surface Science — PSSFB
Progress in Surgery — Prog Surg
Progress in Surgery — Progr Surg
Progress in Surgery — PSURA
Progress in Systems and Control Theory — Progr Systems Control Theory
Progress in Technology [*United States*] — Prog Technol
Progress in the Astronautical Sciences — Prog Astronaut Sci
Progress in the Biological Sciences in Relation to Dermatology — Prog Biol Sci Relat Dermatol
Progress in the Chemistry of Fats and Other Lipids — Prog Chem Fats
Progress in the Chemistry of Fats and Other Lipids — Prog Chem Fats Other Lipids
Progress in the Science and Technology of the Rare Earths — Prog Sci Technol Rare Earths
Progress in the Science and Technology of the Rare Earths — PSRAA
Progress in Theoretical Biology — Prog Theor Biol
Progress in Theoretical Computer Science — Progr Theoret Comput Sci
Progress in Theoretical Organic Chemistry — Prog Theor Org Chem
Progress in Theoretical Organic Chemistry [*Elsevier Book Series*] — PTOC
Progress in Thin-Layer Chromatography and Related Methods — Prog Thin-Layer Chromatogr Relat Methods
Progress in Underwater Science — Prog Underwater Sci
Progress in Vacuum Microbalance Techniques — Prog Vac Microbalance Tech
Progress in Veterinary Microbiology and Immunology — Prog Vet Microbiol Immunol
Progress in Water Technology — Prog Water Technol
Progress in Zoology — Prog Zool
Progress Notes. Walter Reed Army Medical Center — Prog Notes Walter Reed Army Med Cent
Progress of Allergology in Japan — Prog Allergol Jpn
Progress of Analytical Chemistry in the Iron and Steel Industry — Prog Anal Chem Iron Steel Ind
Progress of Education in the United States of America — Prog Educ USA
Progress of Education (Poona) [*India*] — Prog Educ (Poona)
Progress of Mathematics (Allahabad) — Progr Math (Allahabad)
Progress of Mathematics (Varanasi) — Progr Math Varanasi
Progress of Medieval and Renaissance Studies in the United States and Canada — PMRS
Progress of Physical Sciences — Progr Phys Sci
Progress of Physics [*Germany*] — Prog Phys
Progress of Physics (Berlin) — Prog Phys Berlin
Progress of Rubber Technology — Progr Rubber Technol
Progress of Science in India — Prog Sci Ind
Progress of Theoretical Physics — Prog T Phys
Progress of Theoretical Physics — Prog Theor Phys
Progress of Theoretical Physics — Progr Theoret Phys
Progress of Theoretical Physics (Kyoto) — PTPKA
Progress of Theoretical Physics. Supplement — Prog Theor Phys Suppl
Progress of Theoretical Physics. Supplement — Progr Theoret Phys Suppl
Progress Report. Agricultural Experiment Station. University of Idaho — Prog Rep Agric Exp Stn Univ Idaho
Progress Report. Alabama Agricultural Experiment Station — Prog Rep Ala Agric Exp Stn
Progress Report. Arizona Experiment Station — Prog Rep Ariz Exp Stn
Progress Report. Cereal Breeding Laboratory — Progr Rep Cereal Breed Lab
Progress Report. Clovers and Special Legumes Research — Prog Rep Clovers Spec Purpose Legumes Res
Progress Report. Clovers and Special Purpose Legumes Research. University of Wisconsin. Department of Agronomy — Prog Rep Clovers Spec Purpose Legumes Res Univ Wis Dep Agron
Progress Report. Colorado Experiment Station — Prog Rep Colo Exp Stn
Progress Report. Colorado State University. Agricultural Experiment Station — Progr Rep Colo State Univ Agr Exp Sta
Progress Report. Connecticut Agricultural Experiment Station — Progr Rep Conn Agr Exp Sta
Progress Report. Dominion Apiarist. Canadian Department of Agriculture — Prog Rep Dom Apiarist Canad Dep Agric
Progress Report. General Review of the World Coal Industry — Prog Rep Gen Rev World Coal Ind
Progress Report. Geological Survey Department. Swaziland — Prog Rep Geol Surv Dep Swaziland
Progress Report. Idaho Agricultural Research — Progr Rep Idaho Agr Res
Progress Report. Kentucky Agricultural Experiment Station — Prog Rep KY Agric Exp Stn
Progress Report. Kentucky Agricultural Experiment Station — Progr Rep KY Agr Exp Sta
Progress Report. Ministry of Agriculture, Fisheries, and Food. Experimental Husbandry Farms and Experimental Horticulture Stations — Prog Rep Minist Agric Fish Fd Exp Husb Fms Exp Hort Stns
Progress Report. New Mexico Bureau of Mines and Mineral Resources — Prog Rep NM Bur Mines Miner Resour
Progress Report. Nuclear Energy Research in Japan — Prog Rep Nucl Energy Res Jpn
Progress Report. Pennsylvania Agricultural Experiment Station — Prog Rep PA Agric Exp Stn
Progress Report. Pennsylvania State University. Agricultural Experiment Station — Prog Rep Pa State Univ Agric Exp Stn
Progress Report. Pennsylvania State University. Agricultural Experiment Station — Progr Rep PA Agric Exp Sta
Progress Report. Pennsylvania State University. Agricultural Experiment Station — Progr Rep PA State Univ Agr Exp Sta
Progress Report. Pennsylvania. Topographic and Geologic Survey — Prog Rep Pa Topogr Geol Surv
Progress Report Series. Agricultural Experiment Station. Auburn University (Alabama) — Prog Rep Ser Agric Exp Stn Auburn Univ (Ala)
Progress Report Series. Alabama Agricultural Experiment Station — Progr Rep Ser Ala Agr Exp Sta
Progress Report Series. Alabama. Agricultural Experiment Station (Auburn, Alabama) — Prog Rep Ser Ala Agric Exp Stn Auburn Ala
Progress Report. Texas Agricultural Experiment Station — Prog Rep Texas Agric Exp Stn
Progress Report. Texas Agricultural Experiment Station — Progr Rep Tex Agr Exp Sta
Progress Report. Tohoku Agricultural Experiment Station — Progr Rep Tohoku Agr Exp Sta
Progress Report. University of California. Water Resources Center — Prog Rep Univ Calif Water Resour Cent
Progress Report. University of Nebraska. College of Agriculture. Department of Agricultural Economics — Progr Rep Univ Nebr Coll Agr Dept Agr Econ
Progress Report. Washington. Department of Fisheries — Prog Rep Wash Dep Fish
Progress Reports. Experiment Stations (Tanzania) — Prog Rep Exp Stns (Tanzania)
Progress thru Research — Prog Res
Progressi in Biochimica — Prog Biochim
Progressi nelle Industrie Tintorie e Tessili — Prog Ind Tintorie Tess
Progressive — GTPR
Progressive — PRGVB
Progressive — Prog
Progressive — Progressv
Progressive Age — Prog Age
Progressive Agriculture in Arizona — PAAZA
Progressive Agriculture in Arizona — Prog Agric Ariz
Progressive Agriculture in Arizona — Progr Agr Ariz
Progressive Agriculture in Arizona — Progve Agric Ariz
Progressive Architecture — PGRAA
Progressive Architecture — Prog Arch
Progressive Architecture — Prog Archit
Progressive Architecture — Progres Arch
Progressive Architecture — Progressive Archit
Progressive Architecture — Progressive Archre
Progressive Builder — Prog Build
Progressive Education — Prog Educ
Progressive Education — Progres Ed
Progressive Farmer — Prog Farmer
Progressive Farmer and Farm Woman — Prog F
Progressive Farmer for the West — Prog Farmer West
Progressive Farming — Prog Farming
Progressive Farming — Progve Fmg
Progressive Farming/Farmer — Prog Farming/Farmer
Progressive Fish-Culturist — PFC
Progressive Fish-Culturist — PFCUA
Progressive Fish-Culturist — Prog Fish-C
Progressive Fish-Culturist — Prog Fish-Cult
Progressive Forensics — Progr For
Progressive Grocer — PGO
Progressive Grocer — Pgr
Progressive Grocer — Prog Groc
Progressive Grocer — Prog Grocer
Progressive Horticulture [*India*] — Prog Hort
Progressive Horticulture — Prog Hortic
Progressive Nurse — Prog Nurse
Progressive Perfumery and Cosmetics — Prog Perfum Cosmet
Progressive Plastics — Prog Plast
Progressive Plastics — Progr Plast
Progressivnaya Tekhnologiya Mashinostroeniya — Prog Tekhnol Mashinostr
Progressivt Lantbruk — Prog Lantbruk
Progresso Agricolo — Prog Agric
Progresso Agricolo — Progr Agr
Progresso. Driemaandelijks Tijdschrift van de Nederlands Italiaanse Kamer van Koophandel — PRG
Progresso Fotografico — Progresso Fotogr
Progresso Fotografico (Barcelona) — Prog Fotogr (Barcelona)
Progresso Fotografico (Milan) — Prog Fotogr (Milan)
Progresso Medico (Rome) — Prog Med (Rome)
Progresso Terapeutico — Prog Ter
Progresso Veterinario — Prog Vet
Progressus Medicinae (Istanbul) — Prog Med (Istanbul)
Progressus Rei Botanicae/Fortschritte der Botanik/Progres de la Botanique/Progress of Botany — Progr Rei Bot
Prohemio — Pr
Proiskhozhdenie Shchelochnykh Porod. Trudy Vsesoyuznogo Petrograficheskogo Soveshchaniya — Proiskhozhd Shchelochnykh Porod Tr Vses Petrogr Soveshch
Proizvodstvennoe Obucenie — Proizv Obuc
Proizvodstvennye Stochnye Vody — Proizvod Stochnye Vody
Proizvodstvennyi i Nauchno-Issledovatel'skii Institut po Inzhenernym Izyskaniyam v Stroitel'stve Trudy — Proizvod Nauchno-Issled Inst Inzh Izyskaniyam Stroit Tr
Proizvodstvo Chuguna — Proizvod Chuguna
Proizvodstvo Chuguna i Stali — Proizvod Chuguna Stali
Proizvodstvo Elektrostali — Proizvod Elektrostali

Proizvodstvo Ferrosplavov — Proizvod Ferrosplavov
Proizvodstvo i Ispol'zovanie Elastomerov. Nauchno-Tekhnicheskie Dostizheniya i Peredovoi Opyt — Proizvod Ispolz Elastomerov
Proizvodstvo i Issledovanie Stalei i Splavov — Proizvod Issled Stalei Splavov
Proizvodstvo i Obrabotka Stali i Splavov — Proizvod Obrab Stali Splavov
Proizvodstvo i Pererabotka Plastmass i Sinteticheskikh Smol — Proizvod Pererab Plastmass Sint Smol
Proizvodstvo i Primenenie Mikrobnykh Fermentnykh Preparatov — Proizvod Primen Mikrobn Fermentn Prep
Proizvodstvo Koksa — Proizvod Koksa
Proizvodstvo Krupnykh Mashin — Proizvod Krupnykh Mash
Proizvodstvo Lista — Proizvod Lista
Proizvodstvo Ogneuporov — Proizvod Ogneuporov
Proizvodstvo Shin Rezinotekhnicheskikh i Asbestotekhnicheskikh Izdelii — Proizv Shin RTI i ATI
Proizvodstvo Smazochnykh Materialov — Proizvod Smaz Mater
Proizvodstvo Spetsial'nykh Ogneuporov — Proizvod Spets Ogneuporov
Proizvodstvo Svarnykh i Besshovnykh Trub — Proizvod Svarnykh Besshovnykh Trub
Proizvodstvo Tekhnicheskogo i Stroitel'nogo Stekla — Proizvod Tekh Stroit Stekla
Proizvodstvo Tolstolistovoi Stali — Proizvod Tolstolistovoi Stali
Proizvodstvo Trub — Proizvod Trub
Proizvodstvo Vysokokachestvennogo Prokata — Proizvod Vysokokach Prokata
Project for Historical Biobibliography — Project Hist Biobibliog
Project. International Union for Conservation of Nature. World Wildlife Fund. Joint Project Operations — Project IUCN/Wld Wildl Fund
Project Management Journal — PMJ
Project North Journal — PRNJ
Project North Newsletter — PRNN
Projections of Education Statistics to 1988-89 — Educatn 89
Projections of Education Statistics to 1992-93 — Educ Stat
Projekt Angewandte Oekologie — Proj Angew Oekol
Projektgruppe fuer Laserforschung. Bericht. PLF — Projektgruppe Laserforsch Ber PLF
Projektrapport. Grafiska Forskningslaboratoriet — Projektrapp Grafiska Forskningslab
Projet. Civilisation, Travail, Economie [*France*] — Proj Civ Trav Econ
Projeto RADAMBRASIL [*Radar da Amazonia, Brasil*]. Levantamento de Recursos Naturais — Proj RADAMBRAS Levantamento Recursos Nat
Prolactin. Basic and Clinical Correlates. Proceedings. International Congress on Prolactin — Prolactin Proc Int Congr
Prometheus — Pr
Prometheus. Revista Quadrimestrale di Studi Classici — Prometheus
Prometheus. Rivista Quadrimestrale di Studi Classici — Prom Riv Quad Studi Class
Promet-Meteorologische Fortbildung [*Germany*] — Promet-Meteorol Fortbild
Promoclim A. Actualites, Equipement, Technique [*France*] — Promoclim A Actual Equip Tech
Promoclim B. Bulletin du Genie Climatique — PBBCD
Promoclim E. Etudes Thermiques et Aerauliques — PEEAD
Promoclim E. Etudes Thermiques et Aerauliques — Promoclim E
Promoclim. Industries Thermiques et Aerauliques — Promoclim Ind Therm Aerauliques
Promoting Health — PROH
Promoting Health — Promot Health
Promotion — Prom
Promotion Dentaire — Promot Dent
Promotion et Education — Promot Educ
Promotions Marketing and Advertising Data — PROMADATA
Promozione Sociale — Promozione Soc
Promyshlennaya Aerodinamika [*Former USSR*] — Prom Aerod
Promyshlennaya Energetika — PREGA
Promyshlennaya Energetika — Prom Energ
Promyshlennaya i Sanitarnaya Ochistka Gazov — Prom Sanit Ochistka Gazov
Promyshlennaya Teplotekhnika [*Ukrainian SSR*] — Prom Teplotekh
Promyshlennoe Stroitel'stvo — PMSTA
Promyshlennoe Stroitel'stvo — Prom Stroit
Promyshlennoe Stroitel'stvo i Inzhenernye Sooruzheniya — Prom Stroit Inzh Sooruzh
Promyshlenno-Ekonomicheskii Byulleten Sovet Narodnogo Khozyaistva Ivanovskogo Ekonomicheskogo Administrativnogo Raiona — Prom Ekon Byull Sov Nar Khoz Ivanov Ekon Adm Raiona
Promyshlennost Armenii — PAKBA
Promyshlennost Armenii — Promst Arm
Promyshlennost Armenii Sovet Narodnogo Khozyajstva Armyanskoj SSR Tekhniko-Ekonomicheskij Byulleten — Prom-St Arm Sov Nar Khoz Arm SSR Tekh-Ekon Byull
Promyshlennost Belorussii — PBELB
Promyshlennost Belorussii — Promst Beloruss
Promyshlennost Khimicheskikh Reaktivov i Osobo Chistykh Veshchestv — PKCVA
Promyshlennost Khimicheskikh Reaktivov i Osobo Chistykh Veshchestv — Promst Khim Reakt Osobo Chist Veshchestv
Promyshlennost Khimicheskikh Reaktivov i Osobo Chistykh Veshchestv [*Former USSR*] — Prom-St Khim Reaktivov Osobo Chist Veshchestv
Promyshlennost Lubyanykh Volokon — Promst Lub Volokon
Promyshlennost Organicheskoi Khimii [*Former USSR*] — Prom-St Org Khim
Promyshlennost Sinteticheskogo Kauchuka — Prom Sint Kauch
Promyshlennost Sinteticheskogo Kauchuka — Promst Sint Kauch
Promyshlennost Sinteticheskogo Kauchuka — PSKAD
Promyshlennost Stroitel'nykh Materialov — Promst Stroit Mater
Promyshlennost Stroitel'nykh Materialov. Seriya 5. Keramicheskaya Promyshlennost — Promst Stroit Mater Ser 5
Promyshlennost, Stroitel'stvo i Arkhitektura Armenii — Promst Stroit Arkhit Arm
Promyshlennost Tovarov Bytovoi Khimii — Promst Tovarov Bytovoi Khim
Promyshlennye Zagryazneniya Vodoemov — Prom Zagryaz Vodoemov
Promyslennyj Organiceskij Sintez — Prom Org Sint
Propane Canada — Propane Can
Propellants and Explosives — PREXD
Propellants and Explosives — Propellants Explos
Propellants, Explosives, and Rocket Motor Establishment. Memorandum — Propellants Explos Rocket Mot Establ Memo
Propellents, Explosives, and Pyrotechnics — Prop & Ex
Property — Prop
Property Monthly Review — PMR
Property Monthly Review — Property Mthly Rev
Property Services Agency Information on Construction and Architecture [*Database*] — PICA
Property Tax Journal — Property Tax J
Property Tax Journal — PTJ
Prophezei [*Zuerich*] — Proph
Prophylaxie Sanitaire et Morale — Proph Sanit Mor
Prophylaxie Sanitaire et Morale — Prophyl Sanit Morale
Propiedad Industrial y Artistica — PIA
Proposte Sociali — Proposte Soc
Propriete Agricole — Propr Agric
Propylaeen Kunstgeschichte — PKG
Propylaeen-Weltgeschichte — PWG
Propylaen Kunstgeschichte — Prop Kg
Prose — Pe
Prose Studies — PSt
Prose Studies 1800-1900 — PS
Prosecutor. Journal of the National District Attorneys Association — Pros J Natl Dist Att'y A
PROSI [*Public Relations Office of the Sugar Industry*] **Bulletin Mensuel** — ACZ
PROSI [*Public Relations Office of the Sugar Industry*] **Bulletin Mensuel** [*Port Louis*] — PRO Bull Men
Prosopographia Attica — PA
Prosopographia Attica — Prosop Att
Prosopographia Imperii Romani — PIR
Prosopographia Imperii Romani — Prosop Imp Rom
Prosopographia Militiarum Equestrium quae Fuerunt ab Augusto ad Gallienum — PME
Prosopographia Militiarum Equestrium quae Fuerunt ab Augusto ad Gallienum — Pros Mil Eq
Prosopographia Ptolemaica — Pros Ptol
Prosopography of the Later Roman Empire — PLRE
Prospect Western Australia — Prospect West Aust
Prospective Review — Prosp R
Prospects Business News Survey — PBNS
Prospects for Antisense Nucleic Acid Therapy of Cancer and AIDS — Prospects Antisense Nucleic Acid Ther Cancer AIDS
Prospetti — Pros
Prospettiva. Rivista d'Arte Antica e Moderna — Prospettiva
Prospettive dell'Industria Italiana — Prosp Ind Ital
Prospettive Meridionali — Prospett Merid
Prospezioni Archeologiche — Prosp Arch
Prospezioni Archeologiche — Prospezioni Arch
Prospezioni. Bollettino di Informazioni Scientifiche — PBIS
Prostaglandins — PRGLB
Prostaglandins — Prostagland
Prostaglandins and Medicine — Prostaglandins Med
Prostaglandins and Related Lipids — Prostaglandins Relat Lipids
Prostaglandins and Therapeutics — Prostaglandins Ther
Prostaglandins in the Cardiovascular System — Prostaglandins Cardiovasc Syst
Prostaglandins Leukotrienes and Essential Fatty Acids — Prostaglandins Leukot Essent Fatty Acids
Prostaglandins, Leukotrienes, and Medicine — Prostaglandins Leukotrienes Med
Prostaglandins Research Studies Series — Prostaglandins Res Stud Ser
Prostaglandins Series — Prostaglandins Ser
Prostate Supplement — Prostate Suppl
Proster in Cas — PrC
Prosthetics and Orthotics International — Prosthet and Orthotics Int
Prosthetics and Orthotics International — Prosthet Orthot Int
Prostor [*Moscow*] — Pr
Protease Inhibitors. Proceedings. International Conference on Fibrinolysis — Protease Inhib Proc Int Conf Fibrinolysis
Proteccion de Plantas (Havana) — Prot Plant (Havana)
Protecting Steel with Zinc Dust Paints. Papers. Seminar — Prot Steel Zinc Dust Paints Pap Semin
Protectio Vitae — Prot Vitae
Protection [*London*] — PCTCA
Protection Aerienne — Prot Aer
Protection Civile et Securite Industrielle — PCSIB
Protection Civile et Securite Industrielle — Prot Civ Secur Ind
Protection Ecology — Prot Ecol
Protection of Metals — Prot Met
Protection of Metals — Prot Metals
Protection of Metals [*English Translation*] — PTNMA
Protection of Metals (Translation of Zashchita Metallov) — Prot Met Transl of Zashch Met
Protection of Metals (Union of Soviet Socialist Republics) — Prot Met (USSR)
Protection Report R8-PR — Prot Rep R8 PR
Protective Coatings on Metals [*English Translation*] — PRCMC
Protective Coatings on Metals — Prot Coat Met
Protective Coatings on Metals (English Translation) — Prot Coat Met Engl Transl
Protein Abnormalities — Protein Abnorm
Protein Engineering — Protein Eng

Protein Expression and Purification — Protein Expr Purif
Protein Expression and Purification — Protein Expression Purif
Protein Nucleic Acid Enzyme — Protein Nucl Acid Enzyme
Protein Science — Protein Sci
Protein Sequences and Data Analysis — Protein Sequences Data Anal
Protein Structure — Protein Struct
Protein Structure, Prediction, and Design — Protein Struct Predict Des
Protein Syntheses: A Series of Advances — Protein Synth Ser Adv
Protein Synthesis — Protein Synth
Protein Targeting. Proceedings. John Innes Symposium — Protein Targeting Proc John Innes Symp
Protein Traffic in Eukaryotic Cells. Selected Reviews — Protein Traffic Eukaryotic Cells
Proteins of Iron Metabolism. Proceedings. International Meeting — Proteins Iron Metab Proc Int Meet
Proteins. Structure, Function, and Genetics — Proteins Struct Funct Genet
Proteinuria. Symposium of Nephrology — Proteinuria Symp Nephrol
Protesista Dental — Protes Dent
Protestanisk Tidende — Prot T
Protestans Szemle — Prot Sz
Protestant [*Berlin*] — Prot
Protestant Episcopal Church. Historical Magazine — Prot Epis His M
Protestant World — PW
Protestantenblatt [*Berlin*] — Pr Bl
Protestantesimo — Prot
Protestantesimo — Protest
Protestantische Kirchenzeitung — PKZ
Protestantische Kirchenzeitung fuer das Evangelische Deutschland — PKZ
Protestantische Monatsblaetter fuer Innere Zeitgeschichte — PMIZG
Protestantische Monatshefte — PrM
Protestantische Monatshefte — Protest Mhh
Protestantische Realencyklopaedie — PRE
Protestantische Studien — Prot St
Protestantische Texte — PT
Protetyka Stomatologiczna — Protet Stomatol
Prothetik und Werkstoffkunde — Proth Werkst Kd
Protides of the Biological Fluids. Proceedings of the Colloquium — PBFPA
Protides of the Biological Fluids. Proceedings of the Colloquium [*Belgium*] — Protides Biol Fluids Proc Colloq
Protides of the Biological Fluids. Proceedings of the Colloquium (Bruges) [*A publication*] — Protides Biol Fluids Proc Colloq (Bruges)
Protocols in Human Molecular Genetics — Protoc Hum Mol Genet
Protokolle zur Fischereitechnik — Protok Fischereitech
Protokoly Obscego Sobranija Akademii Nauk — Protok OS
Protokoly Obscestva Estestvoispytatelej i Vracej pri Imperatorskom Tomskom Universitete — Protok Obsc Estestvoisp Imp Tomsk Univ
Protokoly Obscestva Ispytatelej Prirody pri Imperatorskom Har'kovskom Universitete — Protok Obsc Isp Prir Imp Harkovsk Univ
Protokoly Obshchestva Estestvoispytatelei pri Imperatorskom Yur'evskom Universitete — Protok Ova Estestvoispyt Imp Yurev Univ
Protokoly Zasedanij Obscestva Estestvoispytatelej Pri Imperatorskom Kazanskom Universitete — Protok Zased Obsc Estestvoisp Imp Kazansk Univ
Protokoly Zasedanij Soveta Imperatorskago Moskovskago Universiteta — Protok Zased Soveta Imp Moscovsk Univ
Protokorinthische Vasenmalerei — PKV
Protokorinthische Vasenmalerei — PV
Proto-Oncogenes in Cell Development — Proto Oncog Cell Dev
Protoplasma [*Austria*] — PROTA
Protoplasma Supplementum — Protoplasma Suppl
Protoplasma-Monographien — Protoplasma Monogr
Protsessy i Apparaty dlya Razdeleniya Zhidkikh i Gazovykh Smesei — Protsessy Appar Razdeleniya Zhidk Gazov Smesei
Protsessy i Apparaty Khimicheskoi Tekhnologii — Protsessy Appar Khim Tekhnol
Protsessy v Khromatograficheskikh Kolonakh — Protsessy Khromatogr Kolonkakh
Prouchvaniya vurkhu Mikroelementite i Mikrotorovete v Bulgariya — Prouchvaniya Mikroelem Mikrotorovete Bulg
Proust Research Association. Newsletter — PRAN
Provebruksmelding-Norges Landbruksokonomiske Institutt — Provebruksmeld Nor Landbruksokonomiske Inst
Provence Historique — PH
Provence Historique — Prov Hist
Provence Historique — Provence Hist
Provence Universite. Annales. Geologie Mediterraneenne — Provence Univ Ann Geol Mediterr
Provence Universite. Laboratoire de Paleontologie Humaine et de Prehistoire. Etudes Quaternaires. Memoire — Provence Univ Lab Paleontol Hum Prehist Etud Quat Mem
Providence Hospital of Detroit. Medical Bulletin — Providence Hosp Detroit Med Bull
Providence Hospital (Southfield, Michigan). Medical Bulletin — Providence Hosp (Southfield Mich) Med Bull
Providence Journal — Providnc J
Providence Journal-Bulletin — PROV
Providence Journal-Bulletin — Providen JB
Providence Sunday Journal — Providen SJ
Province de Liege-Tourisme — Prov Liege Tour
Province du Maine — PM
Province du Maine — PMaine
Province of Newfoundland. Mineral Development Division. Report — Prov Newfoundland Miner Dev Div Rep
Provincia — Prov
Provincia. Bulletin de la Societe d'Histoire et d'Archeologie de Marseille et de la Provence — BSHAP
Provincia de Buenos Aires. Comision de Investigaciones Cientificas. Informes — Prov Buenos Aires Com Invest Cient Inf
Provincia de Buenos Aires. Comision de Investigaciones Cientificas. Memoria [*A publication*] — Prov Buenos Aires Com Invest Cient Mem
Provincia de Buenos Airos. Comision de Investigaciones Cientificas. Monografias — Prov Buenos Aires Com Invest Cient Monogr
Provincia de Sao Pedro [*Brazil*] — PSP
Provincia de Sao Pedro (Porto Alegre) — Prov S Pedro P Alegre
Provincia di Lucca — PdL
Provincia di Lucca — Prov Lucca
Provinciaal Blad — Prov Bl
Provincial — Prov
Provincial Bank of Canada. Economic Review — Provincial Bank Can Econ R
Provincial Economies — Prov Econ
Provincial Inheritance and Gift Tax Reporter. Commerce Clearing House — Prov Inher & Gift Tax Rep CCH
Provincial Judges Journal — PJJ
Provincial Judges Journal — Prov Judges J
Provincial Kaohsiung Teachers College Chemistry Department. Journal — Prov Kaohsiung Teach Coll Chem Dep J
Provinzial-Blaetter fuer Volkskunde — ProvBlVk
Proyeccion (Espana) — PNE
Proyecto de Desarrollo Pesquero. Publicacion — Proyecto Desarrollo Pesq Publ
Proyecto Principal de Educacion UNESCO-America Latina (La Habana; Santiago, Chile) — Proy Prin Educ UNESCO Hav Santiago
PRT. Plastics, Rubbers, Textiles — PRT Plast Rubbers Text
PRT Polymer Age — PRT Polym Age
Prudhoe Bay Journal — PJ
Pruefenden Gesellschaft zu Halle Herausgegebene Schriften — Pruefenden Ges Halle Schriften
Prumysl Potravin — PPOTA
Prumysl Potravin — Prum Potravin
Prumysl Potravin. Priloha — Prum Potravin Priloha
Pryamoe Poluchenie Zheleza i Poroshkovaya Metallurgiya — Pryamoe Poluch Zheleza Poroshk Metall
Przeglad Antropologiczny — Przegl Antrop
Przeglad Antropologiczny — Przegl Antropol
Przeglad Archeologiczny — P Arch
Przeglad Archeologiczny — PA
Przeglad Archeologiczny — Prz Arch
Przeglad Archeologiczny — Przeg Arch
Przeglad Archeologiczny — Przegl A
Przeglad Archeologiczny — Przeglad Arch
Przeglad Bibliograficzny Chemii — Przegl Bibliogr Chem
Przeglad Biblioteczny — PB
Przeglad Biblioteczny — Przegl Bibl
Przeglad Biblioteczny — Przeglad Bibliot
Przeglad Biuletynow Instytutu Maszyn Przeplywowych Polskiej Akademii Nauk w Gdansku — Przegl Biul Inst Masz Przeplyw Pol Akad Nauk Gdansku
Przeglad Budowlany — Przegl Budow
Przeglad Budowlany [*Poland*] — PZBUA
Przeglad Dermatologiczny — Przegl Dermatol
Przeglad Dermatologii i Wenerologii — Przegl Derm Wener
Przeglad Dermatologii i Wenerologii — Przegl Dermatol Wenerol
Przeglad Dokumentacyjny Ceramiki Szlachetnej i Szkla — Przegl Dok Ceram Szlachetnej Szkla
Przeglad Dokumentacyjny Chemii — Przegl Dokum Chem
Przeglad Dokumentacyjny Nafty — Przegl Dok Nafty
Przeglad Dokumentacyjny Ochrony Prace — Przegl Dok Ochr Pr
Przeglad Dokumentacyjny Papiernictwa — Przegl Dok Papier
Przeglad Doswiadczalnictwa Rolniczego — Przegl Dosw Roln
Przeglad Elektroniki [*Poland*] — PRELA
Przeglad Elektroniki — Prz Elektr
Przeglad Elektroniki — Przegl Elektr
Przeglad Elektroniki — Przegl Elektron
Przeglad Elektrotechniczny — Przegl Elektrotech
Przeglad Elektrotechniczny — PZELA
Przeglad Epidemiologiczny — PREPA
Przeglad Epidemiologiczny — Przegl Epidemiol
Przeglad Filozoficzny — PFil
Przeglad Filozoficzny — Prz Fil
Przeglad Geofizyczny — PRGEA
Przeglad Geofizyczny — Przegl Geofiz
Przeglad Geograficzny — PG
Przeglad Geograficzny — Przegl Geogr
Przeglad Geograficzny — Przeglad Geog
Przeglad Geograficzny — Przeglad Geogr
Przeglad Geograficzny/Polish Geographical Review — Przegl Geogr Pol Geogr Rev
Przeglad Geologiczny — Przegl Geol
Przeglad Geologiczny — PRZGA
Przeglad Gorniczo Hutniczy — Przegl Gorn Hutn
Przeglad Gorniczy — Przegl Gorn
Przeglad Historyczny — PH
Przeglad Historyczny — Prz Hi
Przeglad Historyczny — Prz Hist
Przeglad Historyczny — Przegl Hist
Przeglad Historyczny — Przeglad Hist
Przeglad Hodowlany — Przegl Hodowlany
Przeglad Humanistyczny — PHum
Przeglad Humanistyczny — PrzH
Przeglad Klasyczny — PK
Przeglad Klasyczny — PrzKl
Przeglad Komunikacyjny — Przegl Kom
Przeglad Komunikacyjny — Przegl Komunik

Przeglad Koscielny — PK
Przeglad Kulturalny — PK
Przeglad Kulturalny — PrzK
Przeglad Lekarski — PRLKA
Przeglad Lekarski — Przegl Lek
Przeglad Mechaniczny — Przegl Mech
Przeglad Mechaniczny — Przeglad Mech
Przeglad Mechaniczny — PZMEA
Przeglad Meteorologiczny i Hydrologiczny — Przegl Met Hydrol
Przeglad Mleczarski — Przegl Mlecz
Przeglad Morski — Przegl Morski
Przeglad Naukowej Literatury Zootechnicznej — Przegl Nauk Lit Zootech
Przeglad Naukowo Techniczny. Akademia Gorniczo Hutnicza w Krakowie. Seria G. Gornictwo — Przegl Nauk Tech Akad Gorn Hutn Krakowie Ser G
Przeglad Naukowo Techniczny. Akademia Gorniczo Hutnicza w Krakowie. Seria H. Hutnictwo — Przegl Nauk Tech Akad Gorn Hutn Krakowie Ser H
Przeglad Odlewnictwa — Przegl Odlew
Przeglad Organizacji — Przegl Organ
Przeglad Orientalistyczny — PO
Przeglad Orientalistyczny — POr
Przeglad Orientalistyczny — Pr Or
Przeglad Orientalistyczny [*Cracow/Warsaw*] — PrzOr
Przeglad Papierniczy — Przegl Papiern
Przeglad Papierniczy — Przeglad Papier
Przeglad Papierniczy. Dodatek. Przeglad Dokumentacyjny Papiernictwa — Przegl Papier Dodatek
Przeglad Pismiennictwa Zagadnien Informacji — PPZI
Przeglad Polski — PPol
Przeglad Polskiego Pismiennictwa Technicznego — Przegl Pol Pism Tech
Przeglad Powszechny — PP
Przeglad Powszechny — PPow
Przeglad Przemyslu Olejowego — Przegl Przem Olejowego
Przeglad Psychologiczny — PRZPB
Przeglad Skorzany — Przegl Skorzany
Przeglad Socjologiczny — Przegl Socjol
Przeglad Socjologiczny — PrzS
Przeglad Socjologiczny — PSoc
Przeglad Spawalnictwa — Przegl Spawalnictwa
Przeglad Statystyczny — Prz Stat
Przeglad Statystyczny — Przegd St
Przeglad Statystyczny — Przegl Stat
Przeglad Statystyczny — Przeglad Statyst
Przeglad Telekomunikacyjny — Przegl Telekomun
Przeglad Teologiczny — PT
Przeglad Ubezpieczen Spolecznych — PUS
Przeglad Ustawodawstwa Gospodarczego — PUG
Przeglad Wlokienniczy — Przegl Wlok
Przeglad Wlokienniczy — Przeglad Wlok
Przeglad Wojsk Ladowych [*Poland*] — Przegl Wojsk Ladowych
Przeglad Wspotczesny — PWsp
Przeglad Zachodni — PDZI
Przeglad Zachodni — Przegl Zachod
Przeglad Zachodni — PrzZ
Przeglad Zachodni — PZ
Przeglad Zagadnien Socjalnych — PZS
Przeglad Zbozowo Mlynarski — Przegl Zboz Mlyn
Przeglad Zbozowo Mlynarski — Przegl Zbozowo Mlyn
Przeglad Zologiczny — Przegl Zool
Przejscia Fazowe i Zjawiska Krytyczne. Wyklady z Wiosennego Sympozjum — Przejscia Fazowe Zjawiska Kryt
Przekazy/Opinie — Przekazy
Przemysl Chemiczny — Przem Chem
Przemysl Chemiczny — Przemy Chem
Przemysl Chemiczny — Przemysl Chem
Przemysl Drzewny — PD
Przemysl Drzewny — Przem Drzew
Przemysl Drzewny — Przem Drzewny
Przemysl Fermentacyjny — Przem Ferment
Przemysl Fermentacyjny i Owocowo-Warzywny — Przem Ferment Owocowo Warzywny
Przemysl Fermentacyjny i Rolny — Przem Ferment Rolny
Przemysl Naftowy — Przem Naft
Przemysl Rolny i Spozywczy — Przem Roln Spozyw
Przemysl Spozywczy — Przem Spozyw
Przemysl Spozywczy — Przem Spozywczy
Przemysl Wlokienniczy — Przem Wlok
Przewodnik Naukowy i Literacki — PNL
Przyroda Polski Zachodniej — Przyr Polski Zachodn
PS. Przeglad Spawalnictwa — PS Przegl Spawal
PSA Journal — IPSA
PSA [*Photographic Society of America*] **Journal** — PSA J
PSA [*Photographic Society of America*] **Journal. Section B. Photographic Science and Technique** — PSA J Sect B
PSA [*Photographic Society of America*] **Journal. Supplement** — PSA J Suppl
Pseudepigrapha Veteris Testamenti Graecae — PsVTGr
Pseudepigrapha Veteris Testamenti Graece — PVTG
PSI [*Paul Scherrer Institut*] **Bericht** — PSI Ber
Psihijatrija Danas — Psihijatr Danas
PSIR [*Pakistan Council of Scientific and Industrial Research*] **Bulletin Monograph** — PSIR Bull Monogr
Pskovskii Gosudarstvennyi Pedagogicheskii Institut. Uchenye Zapiski — Pskov Gos Pedagog Inst Uch Zap
Pskovskii Pedagogicheskii Institut. Fiziko-Matematiceskii Fakul'tet. Ucenye Zapiski — Pskov Ped Inst Fiz-Mat Fak Ucen Zap
Pskovskij Oblastnoj Slovar's Istoriceskimi Dannymi — POS
Psoriasis. Proceedings. International Symposium — Psoriasis Proc Int Symp
PSR [*Pacific School of Religion*] **Bulletin** — BPSR
PSRS Augstakas Izglitibas Ministrija. Petera Stuckas Latvijas Valsts Universitate. Zinatniskie Raksti — Latvijas Valsts Univ Zinatn Raksti
Psyche — Ps
Psyche — PSYSA
Psychedelic Review — Psychedelic Rev
Psychendocrinology — PSYCD
Psychiatria Clinica — Psychiat Cl
Psychiatria Clinica — Psychiatr Clin
Psychiatria Clinica (Basel) — Psychiatr Clin (Basel)
Psychiatria et Neurologia — Psychiatr Neurol
Psychiatria et Neurologia Japonica — Psychiatr Neurol Jpn
Psychiatria Fennica — Psychiatr Fenn
Psychiatria Fennica Monografiasarja — MPFEE8
Psychiatria Fennica. Monografiasarja — Psychiatr Fenn Monogr
Psychiatria, Neurologia, Neurochirurgia — Psychiatr Neurol Neurochir
Psychiatria, Neurologia, Neurochirurgia — PYNNA
Psychiatria Polska — PSPOB
Psychiatria Polska — Psychiatr Pol
Psychiatric Annals — PSNEB
Psychiatric Annals — Psychiatr Ann
Psychiatric Annals — Psychiatr Annals
Psychiatric Clinics of North America — Psychiatr Clin North Am
Psychiatric Communications — PSCOB
Psychiatric Communications — Psychiatr Commun
Psychiatric Developments — Psychiatr Dev
Psychiatric Forum — Psychiat Fo
Psychiatric Forum — Psychiatr Forum
Psychiatric Genetics — Psychiatr Genet
Psychiatric Hospital — Psychiatr Hosp
Psychiatric Journal. University of Ottawa — Psychiatr J Univ Ottawa
Psychiatric Medicine — PSMDEQ
Psychiatric Medicine — Psychiatr Med
Psychiatric News — Psychiatr News
Psychiatric Nursing Forum — Psychiatr Nurs Forum
Psychiatric Opinion — Psychiat Opin
Psychiatric Opinion — Psychiatr Opinion
Psychiatric Quarterly — PQ
Psychiatric Quarterly — PSQUA
Psychiatric Quarterly — Psychiat Q
Psychiatric Quarterly — Psychiatr Q
Psychiatric Quarterly (New York) — Psychiatr Q (NY)
Psychiatric Quarterly. Supplement — PSQSA
Psychiatric Quarterly. Supplement — Psychiatr Q Suppl
Psychiatric Research Reports — Psychiatr Res Rep
Psychiatric Research Reports. American Psychiatric Association — Psychiatr Res Rep Am Psychiatr Assoc
Psychiatric Services — Psychiatr Serv
Psychiatrie de l'Enfant — Psychiatr Enfant
Psychiatrie, Neurologie, und Medizinische Psychologie — PNMPA
Psychiatrie, Neurologie, und Medizinische Psychologie — Psychiatr Neurol Med Psychol
Psychiatrie, Neurologie, und Medizinische Psychologie (Leipzig) — Psychiatr Neurol Med Psychol (Leipz)
Psychiatrie Sociale — Psychiatr Soc
Psychiatrisch Neurologische Wochenschrift — Psychiatr Neurol Wochenschr
Psychiatrische Praxis — Psychiatr Prax
Psychiatrische Wochenschrift — Psychiatr Wochenschr
Psychiatrisch-Neurologische Wochenschrift — PsNW
Psychiatrisch-Neurologische Wochenschrift — Psychiatr Neurol Wschr
Psychiatry — PPSY
Psychiatry — PSYCA
Psychiatry — Psychiat
Psychiatry and Clinical Neurosciences — Psychiatry Clin Neurosci
Psychiatry Digest — Psychiat Digest
Psychiatry Digest — Psychiatry Dig
Psychiatry in Medicine — Psychiat Me
Psychiatry in Medicine — Psychiatry Med
Psychiatry in Practice — Psych Pract
Psychiatry Research — Psychiatry Res
Psychiatry Series (Berlin) — Psychiatry Ser (Berlin)
Psychic Dependence. Definition, Assessment in Animals and Man. Theoretical and Clinical Implications. Bayer-Symposium — Psych Depend Bayer Symp
Psychic News — PN
Psychical Review — Psychic R
Psychoanalysis and Contemporary Science — PCOSD2
Psychoanalysis and Contemporary Science — Psychoanal Contemp Sci
Psychoanalysis and Contemporary Thought — PCTHDS
Psychoanalysis and Contemporary Thought — Psychoanal Contemp Thought
Psychoanalysis and the Psychoanalytic Review — P & PR
Psychoanalytic Quarterly — PsaQ
Psychoanalytic Quarterly — PSQAA
Psychoanalytic Quarterly — Psychoan Q
Psychoanalytic Quarterly — Psychoanal Q
Psychoanalytic Quarterly — Psychoanal Quart
Psychoanalytic Review — PR
Psychoanalytic Review — PsaR
Psychoanalytic Review — PsR
Psychoanalytic Review — PSREA
Psychoanalytic Review — Psychoan Re
Psychoanalytic Review — Psychoanal R
Psychoanalytic Review — Psychoanal Rev
Psychoanalytic Review — PsyR
Psychoanalytic Study of Society — PYSSB

Psychoanalytic Study of the Child — Psychoanal Stud Child
Psychoanalytic Study of the Child — Psychoanal Study Child
Psychoanalytic Study of the Child — PYACA
Psychoanalytic Study of the Child. Monograph Series — Psychoanal Study Child Monogr Ser
Psychobiology and Psychopathology [*Elsevier Book Series*] — PAP
Psychobiology and Psychopathology — Psychobiol Psychopathol
Psychocultural Review — Psychocultural R
Psychocultural Review — Psycul R
Psychohistory Review — Psychohist Rev
Psychologia Africana — Psychol Afr
Psychologia Africana — Psychol Africana
Psychologia Africana — PYAFB
Psychologia: An International Journal of Psychology in the Orient — PLYGA
Psychologia Universalis — PU
Psychologia Wychowawcza — PSWYA
Psychologica Belgica — Psychol Bel
Psychologica Belgica — Psychol Belg
Psychological Abstracts — PA
Psychological Abstracts — PsyAb
Psychological Abstracts — Psychol Abstr
Psychological Abstracts — Psychol Absts
Psychological Bulletin — GPSB
Psychological Bulletin — PB
Psychological Bulletin — Ps Bull
Psychological Bulletin — PsB
Psychological Bulletin — PSBUA
Psychological Bulletin — Psy B
Psychological Bulletin — Psych Bull
Psychological Bulletin — Psychol B
Psychological Bulletin — Psychol Bul
Psychological Bulletin — Psychol Bull
Psychological Clinic — Psychol Clinic
Psychological Issues — PI
Psychological Issues — Psychol Iss
Psychological Issues — Psychol Issues
Psychological Issues. Monographs — Psychol Issues Monogr
Psychological Medicine — PSMDC
Psychological Medicine — Psychol Med
Psychological Medicine. Monograph Supplement — Psychol Med Monogr Suppl
Psychological Monographs — Psychol Monogr
Psychological Monographs. General and Applied — Psychol Monogr Gen Appl
Psychological Monographs. General and Applied — PYMOA
Psychological Readers' Guide — PRG
Psychological Reader's Guide — Psychol Read Guide
Psychological Record — Psychol Rec
Psychological Record — PSYR
Psychological Record — PYRCA
Psychological Report — Ps Rep
Psychological Report. Monograph Supplement — Ps Rep M
Psychological Reports — IPSR
Psychological Reports — Psychol Rep
Psychological Reports — PYRTA
Psychological Research — PSRED
Psychological Research — Psychol Res
Psychological Review — GPSR
Psychological Review — PR
Psychological Review — Ps Rev
Psychological Review — PsR
Psychological Review — PSRVA
Psychological Review — Psychol R
Psychological Review — Psychol Rev
Psychological Studies — PsS
Psychological Studies [*Mysore*] — Psych Stud
Psychological Studies — Psychol Stu
Psychologie Africana. Monograph and Supplement — Psychol Afr Monogr Suppl
Psychologie Canadienne — Psychol Can
Psychologie Francaise — Psychol Fr
Psychologie Heute — PSHED
Psychologie in Erziehung und Unterricht — Psychol Erz
Psychologie Medicale — Psychol Med
Psychologie. Schweizerische Zeitschrift fuer Psychologie und Ihre Anwendungen — PSSZAG
Psychologie; Schweizerische Zeitschrift fuer Psychologie und Ihre Anwendungen [*A publication*] — Psychol Schweiz Z Psychol Anwendungen
Psychologische Beitraege — Psychol Be
Psychologische Beitraege — Psychol Beitr
Psychologische Beitraege fuer alle Gebiete der Psychologie — Ps B
Psychologische Forschung — PF
Psychologische Forschung — PsF
Psychologische Forschung — Psychol Forsch
Psychologische Praxis — Psych Prax
Psychologische Praxis — Psychol Prax
Psychologische Rundschau — PsR
Psychologische Rundschau — Psy Rund
Psychologische Rundschau — Psychol Rundsch
Psychologische Studien — Psychol St
Psychology — PYCHB
Psychology and Aging — Psychol Aging
Psychology and Social Theory — Psych Soc
Psychology in the Schools — Psychol in the Schs
Psychology in the Schools — Psychol Sch
Psychology in the Schools — PYSCB
Psychology of Learning and Motivation — Psychol Learn & Motiv
Psychology of Music — PSMUD
Psychology of Music — Psych of Music
Psychology of Music — Psychology M
Psychology of Women Quarterly — PPWQ
Psychology of Women Quarterly — Psychol Women Q
Psychology of Women Quarterly — Psychol Women Quart
Psychology of Women Quarterly — PWOQD
Psychology Teaching — Psych Teaching
Psychology Today — GPSY
Psychology Today — PSTOA
Psychology Today — Psy T
Psychology Today — Psych Today
Psychology Today — Psychol Tod
Psychology Today — Psychol Today
Psychology Today — PT
Psychometrika — Psychometri
Psychometrika. Monograph Supplement — Psychometrika Monogr Suppl
Psychomusicology — Psy
Psycho-Mycological Studies — Psycho Mycol Stud
Psychonomic Science — Psychon Sci
Psychonomic Science — PsyS
Psychonomic Science. Section on Animal and Physiological Psychology — Psychon Sci Sect Anim Physiol Psychol
Psychonomic Science. Section on Human Experimental Psychology — Psychon Sci Sect Hum Exp Psychol
Psychopathologie Africaine — Ps Af
Psychopathologie Africaine — Psychop Afr
Psychopathologie Africaine — Psychopathol Afr
Psychopathologie de l'Expression. Supplement de l'Encephale — Psychopathol Expression Suppl Encephale
Psychopathology and Pictorial Expression — Psychopathol Pict Expression
Psychopharmacologia — Psychopharm
Psychopharmacologie. Supplement de l'Encephale — Psychopharmacol Suppl Encephale
Psychopharmacology — PSCHO
Psychopharmacology Abstracts — PSA
Psychopharmacology Abstracts — Psychopharmacol Abstr
Psychopharmacology Bulletin — PSBU
Psychopharmacology Bulletin — PSYBB
Psychopharmacology Bulletin — Psychopharmacol Bull
Psychopharmacology Communications — Psychoph C
Psychopharmacology Communications — Psychopharmacol Commun
Psychopharmacology Frontiers. Proceedings. Psychopharmacology Symposium — Psychopharmacol Front Proc Psychopharmacol Symp
Psychopharmacology Series — PSPHDI
Psychopharmacology Series — Psychopharmacol Ser
Psychopharmacology Series (Dekker) — Psychopharmacol Ser (Dekker)
Psychopharmacology Service Center. Bulletin — Psychopharmacol Serv Cent Bull
Psychopharmacology. Supplementum — PSSUE5
Psychopharmacology. Supplementum — Psychopharmacol Suppl
Psychopharmacology. Supplementum — Psychopharmacology Suppl
Psychophysiology — PSPHA
Psychophysiology — Psychophysl
Psychophysiology (Baltimore) — PYPYB
Psychosocial Process. Issues in Child Mental Health — Psychosoc Proc Iss Child Ment Health
Psychosocial Rehabilitation Journal — Psychosoc Rehabil J
Psychosocial Rehabilitation Journal — Psychosocial Rehabil J
Psychosomatic Medicine — PSMEA
Psychosomatic Medicine — Psychos Med
Psychosomatic Medicine — Psychosom Med
Psychosomatics — Psychosomat
Psychotherapie, Psychosomatik, Medizinische Psychologie — Psychother Psychosom Med Psychol
Psychotherapie und Medizinische Psychologie — PSMSC
Psychotherapie und Medizinische Psychologie — Psychoth MP
Psychotherapie und Medizinische Psychologie — Psychother Med Psychol
Psychotherapy and Psychosomatics — PSPSB
Psychotherapy and Psychosomatics — Psychoth Ps
Psychotherapy and Psychosomatics — Psychother Psychosom
Psychotherapy (New York) — Psychotherapy (NY)
Psychotherapy Newsletter — Psychother Newsl
Psychotherapy Patient — PSPAEW
Psychotherapy Patient — Psychother Patient
Psychotherapy: Theory, Research, and Practice — Psychoth/TR
Psychotherapy: Theory, Research, and Practice — Psychother Theory Res Pract
Psykologien og Erhvervslivet — Psyk o Erhv
Pszczelnicze Zeszyty Naukowe — Pszczel Zesz Nauk
Pszczelnicze Zeszyty Naukowe — Pszczelnicze Zesz Nauk
PT [*Polytechnisch Tijdschrift*]-Procestechniek — PT Procestech
PTA [*Pharmazeutisch-Technische Assistenten*] **in der Apotheke** — PTA Apoth
PTA [*Pharmazeutisch-Technische Assistenten*] **in der Praktischen Pharmazie. Beilage** — PTA Prakt Pharm Beil
PTA [*Pharmazeutisch-Technische Assistenten*] **in der Praktischen Pharmazie. Fachzeitschrift fuer Pharmazeutisch-Technische Assistenten** — PTA Prakt Pharm
PTA [*Parent-Teacher Association*] **Magazine** — PTA Mag
PTB [*Physikalisch-Technische Bundesanstalt*]-Bericht. Abteilung Allgemeine Technisch-Wissenschaftliche Dienste — PTB Ber Abt Allg Tech Wiss Dienste
PTB [*Physikalisch-Technische Bundesanstalt*]-Bericht. Abteilung Atomphysik — PTB Ber Abt Atomphys
PTB [*Physikalisch-Technische Bundesanstalt*]-Bericht. Abteilung Elektrizitaet — PTB Ber Abt Elektr
PTB [*Physikalisch-Technische Bundesanstalt*]-Bericht. Abteilung Mechanik — PTB Ber Abt Mech

PTB [*Physikalisch-Technische Bundesanstalt*]-Bericht. Abteilung Optik — PTB Ber Abt Opt
PTB [*Physikalisch-Technische Bundesanstalt*]-Bericht. Abteilung Sicherstellung und Endlagerung Radioaktiver Abfaelle — PTB Ber Abt Sicherstellung Endlagerung Radioakt Abfaelle
PTB [*Physikalisch-Technische Bundesanstalt*]-Bericht. Abteilung Waerme — PTB Ber Abt Waerme
PTB [*Physikalisch-Technische Bundesanstalt*]-Bericht. Dosimetrie — PTB Ber Dosim
PTB [*Physikalisch-Technische Bundesanstalt*]-Bericht. Forschungs- und Messreaktor Braunschweig — PTB Ber Forsch Messreaktor Braunschweig
PTB [*Physikalisch-Technische Bundesanstalt*]-Bericht. Neutronendosimetrie — PTB Ber Neutronendosimetrie
PTB [*Physikalisch-Technische Bundesanstalt*]-Bericht. Physikalische Grundlagen — PTB Ber Phys Grundlagen
PTB [*Physikalisch-Technische Bundesanstalt*]-Bericht. Radioaktivitaet — PTB Ber Radioakt
PTB [*Physikalisch-Technische Bundesanstalt*] **Mitteilungen. Amts- und Mitteilungsblatt der Physikalisch- Technische Bundesanstalt** [*Braunschweig-Berlin*] — PTB Mitt
PTB [*Physikalisch-Technische Bundesanstalt*] **Mitteilungen. Forschen und Pruefen** — PTB Mitt Forsch Pruefen
Pteridine Chemistry. Proceedings. International Symposium — Pteridine Chem Proc Int Symp
Pterodactyl — Ptero
Ptolemaeische Koenigsurkunden — PKroll
PTRC. Planning and Transport Research and Computation — PTRC
PTS [*Predicasts*] **Aerospace/Defense Markets and Technology** [*Database*] — A/DM & T
PTS [*Predicasts*] **Annual Reports Abstracts** [*Database*] — ARA
PTS [*Predicasts*] **Marketing and Advertising Reference Service** [*Database*] — MARS
PTS [*Predicasts*] **Regional Business News** [*Database*] — RBN
PTT [*Schweizerische Post Telephon und Telegraphenbetrieben*] **Technische Mitteilungen** — PTT Tech Mitt
PTTI [*Postal, Telegraph, and Telephone International*] **Studies** — PTTI Stud
Ptujski Zbornik — Ptuj Zbor
Pubblicazione. Centro Studi Capuccini Lombardi — PCSCL
Pubblicazione. Istituto Chimico Agrario Sperimentale di Gorizia. Nuovi Annali — Pubbl Ist Chim Agrar Sper Gorizia Nuovi Ann
Pubblicazione. Istituto di Geologia, Paleontologia, e Geografica Fisica. Universita di Milano. Serie G — Pubbl Ist Geol Paleontol Geogr Fis Univ Milano Ser G
Pubblicazione. Istituto di Geologia. Universita di Milano. Serie G — Pubbl Ist Geol Univ Milano Ser G
Pubblicazione. Istituto Geofisico (Trieste) — Pubbl Ist Geofis (Trieste)
Pubblicazione. Istituto Italo-Latino Americano — Pubbl Ist Italo Lat Am
Pubblicazione. Istituto Sperimentale Talassografico (Trieste) — Pubbl Ist Sper Talassogr (Trieste)
Pubblicazione. Serie III — Pubbl Ser III
Pubblicazione. Stazione Sperimentale di Granicoltura per la Sicilia-Catania — Pubbl Stn Sper Granic Sicil Catania
Pubblicazione. Universita degli Studi di Trieste. Facolta di Economia e Commercio. Istituto di Merceologia — Pubbl Univ Studi Trieste Fac Econ Commer Ist Merceol
Pubblicazioni a Cura del Centro Superiore di Logica e Scienze Comparate — Pubbl Centro Sup Logica Sci Comparate
Pubblicazioni (Bergamo) Stazione Sperimentale di Maiscoltura — Pubbl (Bergamo) Sta Sper Maiscoltura
Pubblicazioni. Centro di Sperimentazione Agricola e Forestale — Pubbl Cent Sper Agric For
Pubblicazioni. Centro di Sperimentazione Agricola e Forestale — Pubbl Centro Sperim Agric
Pubblicazioni. Centro di Sperimentazione Agricola e Forestale. Ente Nazionale per la Cellulosa e per la Carta — Pubbl Centro Sper Agr Forest ENCC
Pubblicazioni. Centro di Sperimentazione Agricola e Forestale (Rome) — Pubbl Cent Sper Agric For (Rome)
Pubblicazioni. Centro di Studi per la Citogenetica Vegetale. Consiglio Nazionale delle Ricerche — Publ Cent Stud Citogenet Veg CNR
Pubblicazioni. Centro di Studi per la Citogenetica Vegetale. Consiglio Nazionale delle Ricerche — PUCVA6
Pubblicazioni. Centro di Studio per la Citogenetica Vegetale. Consiglio Nazionale della Ricerche — Pubbl Cent Stud Citogenet Veg CNR
Pubblicazioni Chimiche, Biologiche, e Mediche. Istituto "Carlo Erba" per Ricerche Terapeutiche — Pubbl Chim Biol Med Ist "Carlo Erba" Ric Ter
Pubblicazioni. Commissione Italiana per la Geofisica — Pubbl Comm Ital Geofis
Pubblicazioni del Centro Talassografico Tirreno — Pubbl Centro Talassogr Tirreno
Pubblicazioni della Facolta di Lettere e Filosofia dell'Universita di Milano — Pubbl Fac Lett Filos Univ Milano
Pubblicazioni della Stazione Zoologica di Napoli. Section II. History and Philosophy of the Life Sciences — Pubbl Stn Zool Napoli II
Pubblicazioni dell'Universita di Ferrara — Pubbl Univ Ferrara
Pubblicazioni di Verifiche — Pub Verifiche
Pubblicazioni. Ente Nazionale per la Cellulosa e per la Carta — Pubbl Ente Naz Cellulosa Carta
Pubblicazioni. Facolta di Lettere e Filosofia. Universita di Torino — PFLFT
Pubblicazioni. Facolta di Scienze e d'Ingegneria. Universita di Trieste. Serie A — Pubbl Fac Sci Ing Univ Trieste Ser A
Pubblicazioni. Facolta di Scienze e d'Ingegneria. Universita di Trieste. Serie B — Pubbl Fac Sci Ing Univ Trieste Ser B
Pubblicazioni. Faculta di Lettres e Filosofia. Universita di Torino — PFLUT
Pubblicazioni. Istituto di Geologia e Mineralogia. Universita di Ferrara — Pubbl Ist Geol Mineral Univ Ferrara
Pubblicazioni. Istituto di Matematica Applicata. Facolta di Ingegneria. Universita degli Studi di Roma — Pubbl Ist Mat Appl Fac Ingegneria Univ Stud Roma
Pubblicazioni. Istituto di Storia della Filosofia — PISF
Pubblicazioni. Istituto per le Applicazioni del Calcolo. Consiglio Nazionale delle Ricerche — Pubbl IAC
Pubblicazioni. Istituto Sperimentale per la Selvicoltura (Arezzo, Italy) — Pubbl Ist Sper Selv (Arezzo)
Pubblicazioni. Osservatorio Geofisico di Trieste — Pubbl Oss Geofis Trieste
Pubblicazioni. Pontificio Ateneo Salesiano — PPAS
Pubblicazioni. Provincia Patavina dei Fratri Minori Conventuali — PPPFMC
Pubblicazioni. Reale Universita degli Studi di Firenze. Facolta di Scienze Matematiche, Fisiche, e Naturali — Pubbl R Univ Studi Firenze Fac Sci Mat Fis Nat
Pubblicazioni. Scuola di Studi Storico-Religiosi — PSSSR
Pubblicazioni. Seminario de Semitistica. Istituto Orientale di Napoli — PSS
Pubblicazioni. Societa Italiana per la Ricerca dei Papiri Greci e Latini in Egitto [*Florence*] — PSI
Pubblicazioni. Stazione Zoologica di Napoli — Pubbl Staz Zool Napoli
Pubblicazioni. Stazione Zoologica di Napoli — Pubbl Stn Zool Napoli
Pubblicazioni. Studium Biblicum Franciscanum — PSBF
Pubblicazioni. Studium Biblicum Franciscanum. Collectio Major — PSBF Ma
Pubblicazioni. Studium Biblicum Franciscanum. Collectio Minor — PSBF Mi
Pubblicazioni. Universita Cattolica del Sacro Cuore — PUC
Pubblicazioni. Universita Cattolica del Sacro Cuore — PUCSC
Pubblicazioni. Universita Cattolica del Sacro Cuore — PUSC
Pubblicazioni. Universita degli Studi di Firenze. Facolta di Scienze Matematiche, Fisiche, e Naturali — Pubbl Univ Studi Firenze Fac Sci Mat Fis Nat
Pubblicazioni. Universita degli Studi di Perugia. Facolta di Medicina Veterinaria — Pubbl Univ Stud Perugia Fac Med Vet
Pubbliccazioni. Istituto di Studi Filosofici — PIStF
Public Acts of the State of Tennessee — Tenn Pub Acts
Public Administration — PA
Public Administration — PLF
Public Administration — PPAD
Public Administration — PUA
Public Administration — Pub Adm
Public Administration — Pub Admin
Public Administration — PubA
Public Administration — Publ Adm
Public Administration — Public Adm
Public Administration — Public Admin
Public Administration Abstracts and Index of Articles — Pub Admin Abstr
Public Administration Abstracts and Index of Articles (India) — Public Adm Abstr Index Artic (India)
Public Administration and Development — PAT
Public Administration and Development — Public Admin and Development
Public Administration Bulletin — Public Adm Bull
Public Administration Bulletin — Public Admin Bull
Public Administration Journal (Kathmandu) — Public Admin J (Kathmandu)
Public Administration (London) — Publ Adm London
Public Administration Quarterly — PAQ
Public Administration Review — PAR
Public Administration Review — Pub Ad Rev
Public Administration Review — Pub Adm R
Public Administration Review — Pub Adm Rev
Public Administration Review — Publ Adm R
Public Administration Review — Publ Adm Re
Public Administration Review — Public Adm R
Public Administration Review — Public Adm Rev
Public Administration Review — Public Admin R
Public Administration Survey — Pub Admin Survey
Public Administration Survey — Public Admin Survey
Public Affairs — Publ Aff
Public Affairs Bulletin — PAB
Public Affairs Bulletin — Publ Aff B
Public Affairs Information Service [*Bibliographic database*] — PAIS
Public Affairs Information Service Bulletin — Public Aff Inf Serv Bull
Public Affairs Report — Public Aff Rep
Public Affairs Report — Public Affairs Rept
Public Analysts Association. Journal [*England*] — Public Anal Assoc J
Public and Local Acts of the Legislature of the State of Michigan — Mich Pub Acts
Public Archives of Canada. Report — Pub Archives Can Report
Public Budgeting and Finance — PBF
Public Budgeting and Finance — Public Budgeting and Fin
Public Business (Detroit) — Pub Business Detroit
Public Choice — Publ Choice
Public Cleansing — Publ Cleans
Public Cleansing Technical Report — Public Clean Tech Rep
Public Contract Law Journal — Pub Cont LJ
Public Contract Law Journal — Pub Contract L J
Public Contract Law Journal — Publ Contr LJ
Public Contract Newsletter — Pub Cont Newsl
Public Domain Software on File. IBM [*International Business Machines*] [*Database*] — PDSOF IBM
Public Employee — Pub Emp
Public Employee Bargaining. Commerce Clearing House — Pub Employee Bargaining CCH
Public Finance — PF
Public Finance — Publ Finan
Public Finance — Publ Finance
Public Finance — Public Fin
Public Finance and Accountancy — PFA

Public Finance and Accountancy — Public Fin Account
Public Finance (Berlin) — Public Fin (Berlin)
Public Finance. International Quarterly Journal — OPF
Public Finance Quarterly — PFQ
Public Finance Quarterly — Publ Fin Q
Public Finance Quarterly — Publ Finance Quart
Public Finance Quarterly — Public Fin Q
Public Garden. Journal. American Association of Botanical Gardens and Arboreta — Public Gard J Am Assoc Bot Gard Arbor
Public General Acts and Church Assembly Measure — PGA
Public Health — Publ Hlth
Public Health Bulletin — Pub Health Bul
Public Health Congress. Proceedings, Addresses, and Discussions — Pub Health Cong Proc Add Disc
Public Health Engineer — Pub Hlth Eng
Public Health Engineer [*England*] — Public Health Eng
Public Health Engineer — Public Hlth Engr
Public Health Engineering Abstracts — Public Health Eng Abstr
Public Health Engineering Conference. Proceedings — Public Health Eng Conf Proc
Public Health in Europe — Public Health Eur
Public Health Journal — Public Health J
Public Health Journal (Peking) — Public Health J (Peking)
Public Health Laboratory — Publ Health Lab
Public Health Laboratory [*United States*] — Public Health Lab
Public Health Monograph — Public Health Monogr
Public Health Monographs — Pub Health Monogr
Public Health News — Publ Hlth Ne
Public Health Nurse — Pub Health Nurse
Public Health Nursing — Pub Health Nurs
Public Health Nursing — Public Health Nurs
Public Health Papers — Public Health Pap
Public Health Reports — PHRE
Public Health Reports — PPHL
Public Health Reports — Pub Health Rep
Public Health Reports — Pub Health Rept
Public Health Reports — Pub Health Rpts
Public Health Reports — Publ Hea Re
Public Health Reports — Public Health Rep
Public Health Reports. United States Public Health Service — Pub Health Rep US Pub Health Serv
Public Health Reports. United States Surgeon-General. Public Health and Marine Hospital Service — Pub Health Rep US Pub Health and Mar Hosp Serv
Public Health Reports (Washington, DC) — Publ Hlth Rep (Wash)
Public Health Reviews — PHRV
Public Health Reviews — Publ Heal R
Public Health Reviews — Public Health Rev
Public Health Reviews — Public Health Revs
Public Health Service. Publications — PHS
Public Health. Social Medicine and Hygiene — Public Health Soc Med Hyg
Public Health Society. Bulletin [*Kuala Lumpur*] — Pub Health Soc B
Public Health: The Journal of the Society of Community Medicine — Publ Heal
Public Information Bulletin [*Australian Taxation Office*] — PIB
Public Information Circular. Geological Survey of Wyoming — Public Inf Circ Geol Surv Wy
Public Information Circular. Iowa Geological Survey — IGPIA
Public Information Circular. Iowa Geological Survey — Public Inf Circ Iowa Geol Surv
Public Interest — PBI
Public Interest — PIN
Public Interest — Pub Interest
Public Interest — Publ Int
Public Interest — Publ Inter
Public Interest — Publ Interest
Public Interest — PUI
Public International Law — Pub Intl L
Public Land and Resources Law Digest — Pub Land & Res L Dig
Public Land and Resources Law Digest [*United States*] — Public Land Resour Law Dig
Public Law — Pub L
Public Law — Publ L
Public Law Forum — Pub Law For
Public Law (London) — Publ Law (London)
Public Laws of Rhode Island and Providence Plantations — RI Pub Laws
Public Ledger — PUL
Public Libraries — Pub Lib
Public Libraries — Public Lib
Public Libraries Division. Reporter — PLD
Public Library Abstracts — Pub Lib Abst
Public Library of New South Wales. Staff News — PLNSW Staff News
Public Library Opinion — Pub Lib Op
Public Library Reporters — Pub Lib Rep
Public Library Trustee — Pub Lib Trustee
Public Lighting — Publ Ltg
Public Lighting — Public Light
Public Management — PBM
Public Management — PM
Public Management — Pub Manag
Public Management — Pub Mgt
Public Management — Public Mgt
Public Management Sources — Public Manage Source
Public Opinion — PON
Public Opinion — Pub Opin
Public Opinion — Pub Opinion
Public Opinion — Public Opin
Public Opinion Location Library [*Database*] — POLL
Public Opinion Quarterly — POQ
Public Opinion Quarterly — Pub Op Q
Public Opinion Quarterly — Pub Opinion Q
Public Opinion Quarterly — Pub Opn Q
Public Opinion Quarterly — Publ Opin Q
Public Opinion Quarterly — Public Opin Q
Public Opinion Quarterly — Public Opinion Q
Public Personnel Management — PPM
Public Personnel Management — Pub Pers Mgt
Public Personnel Management — Publ Pers M
Public Personnel Management — Publ Personnel Manag
Public Personnel Management — Public Pers Manage
Public Policy — Pub Pol
Public Policy — Publ Pol
Public Policy — Publ Policy
Public Productivity Review — PPR
Public Productivity Review — Public Prod Rev
Public Relations Journal — PRJ
Public Relations Journal — Pub Rel J
Public Relations Journal — Publ Rel J
Public Relations Journal — Public Rel
Public Relations Journal — Public Relat J
Public Relations Quarterly — Pub Rel Q
Public Relations Quarterly — Public Relat Q
Public Relations Quarterly — PUQ
Public Relations Review — PRR
Public Relations Review — Pub Rel Rv
Public Relations Review — Public Relat Rev
Public Relations Review — Public Relations R
Public Roads — PR
Public Roads — Pub Roads
Public Roads — Publ Roads
Public School Magazine — PSM
Public Sector [*New Zealand*] — Pub Sector
Public Sector. Health Care Risk Management — Public Sector Health Care Risk Manage
Public Sector. New Zealand Institute of Public Administration — Public Sect
Public Service Action — Public Serv Action
Public Service and Local Government — PSLG
Public Service Journal of Victoria — Pub Service J Vic
Public Service Management — Pub Serv Management
Public Technology News — Pub Technol N
Public Telecommunications Review — Public TC Review
Public Utilities Fortnightly — PU Fort
Public Utilities Fortnightly — Pub Util
Public Utilities Fortnightly — Pub Util Fort
Public Utilities Fortnightly — Pub Util Fortnightly
Public Utilities Fortnightly — Public Util Fortn
Public Utilities Fortnightly — PUF
Public Utilities Reports [*Database*] — PUR
Public Water Supply Engineers Conference. Proceedings — Public Water Supply Eng Conf Proc
Public Welfare — GPWE
Public Welfare — Pub Wel
Public Welfare — Publ Welfar
Public Welfare — Publ Welfare
Public Welfare — Public Welf
Public Works — Publ Wks
Public Works and Local Government Engineering — Publ Wks Local Govt Engng
Public Works and Local Government Engineering — Public Works Local Gov Eng
Public Works and Services — Public Works Ser
Public Works and Services (Sydney) — Public Work (Syd)
Public Works Congress. Proceedings — Public Works Congr Proc
Public Works Engineers' Yearbook — Public Works Eng Yearb
Public Works Review [*Japan*] — Public Works Rev
Public Works, Roads, and Transport — Public Works Roads Transp
Publicacao. Academia de Ciencias. Estado de Sao Paulo — Publ Acad Cienc Estado Sao Paulo
Publicacao. Academia de Ciencias. Estado de Sao Paulo — Publ ACIESP
Publicacao Avulsa FZB. Fundacao Zoobotanica do Rio Grande Do Sul — Publ Avulsa FZB Fund Zoobot Rio Grande Sul
Publicacao Avulsa. Universidade Federal de Pernambuco. Escola de Quimica. Departamento de Tecnologia — Publ Avulsa Univ Fed Pernambuco Esc Quim Dep Tecnol
Publicacao de Pedido de Privilegio (Brazil) — Publ Pedido Privilegio (Braz)
Publicacao Especial. Instituto Oceanografico (San Paulo) — Publ Espec Inst Oceanogr (San Paulo)
Publicacao Especial. Universidade do Rio Grande Do Sul. Escola de Geologia — Publ Espec Univ Rio Grande Sul Esc Geol
Publicacao. Instituto de Energia Atomica — Publ IEA
Publicacao. Instituto de Energia Atomica (Sao Paulo) — Publ Inst Energ At (Sao Paulo)
Publicacao. Instituto de Pesquisas da Marinha — Publ Inst Pesqui Mar
Publicacao. Instituto de Pesquisas da Marinha (Rio De Janeiro) — Publ Inst Pesqui Mar Rio De Janeiro
Publicacao. Instituto de Pesquisas Energeticas e Nucleares — Publ Inst Pesqui Energ Nucl
Publicacao. Instituto de Pesquisas Tecnologicas (Estado de Sao Paulo) — Publ Inst Pesqui Tecnol (Estado Sao Paulo)
Publicacao. Instituto de Zootecnia (Rio De Janeiro) — Publ Inst Zootec (Rio De J)

Publicacao. Instituto Florestal — Publ Inst Florestal
Publicacao IPEN [*Instituto de Pesquisas Energeticas e Nucleares*] — Publ IPEN
Publicacao. IPRNR (Instituto de Pesquisas de Recursos Naturais Renovaveis) — Publ IPRNR (Inst Pesqui Recur Nat Renovaveis)
Publicacao IPT [*Instituto de Pesquisas Tecnologicas*] — Publ IPT
Publicacao. Servico de Piscicultura. Serie I-C — Publ Serv Piscic Ser I-C
Publicacao. Sociedade Brasileira de Nematologia — Pub Soc Bras Nematol
Publicacao. Sociedade Brasileira de Nematologia — Publ Soc Bras Nematol
Publicacion. Centro de Investigaciones Tecnologicas (Pando, Uruguay) — Publ Cent Invest Tecnol (Pando Urug)
Publicacion. Centro de Quimicos Industriales (Buenos Aires) — Publ Cent Quim Ind (Buenos Aires)
Publicacion. Consejo de Recursos Minerales — Publ Cons Recursos Miner
Publicacion. Consejo de Recursos Naturales No Renovables (Mexico) — Publ Cons Recur Nat No Renov (Mex)
Publicacion de la Catedra Lastanosa. Instituto de Estudios Oscenses — Publ Catedra Lastanosa Inst Est Oscenses
Publicacion. Direccion General de Geologia y Minas. Republica del Ecuador — Publ Dir Gen Geol Minas Repub Ecuador
Publicacion. Direccion General del Inventario Nacional Forestal (Coyoacan, Mexico) — Publ Dir Gen Invent Nac For (Mex)
Publicacion Especial. Instituto Nacional de Investigaciones Forestal (Mexico) — Publ Espec Inst Nac Invest Forest (Mex)
Publicacion Especial. Instituto Nacional de Investigaciones Forestales [*Mexico*] — IIFPAC
Publicacion. Estacion Experimental Agricola de Tucuman — Publ Estac Exp Agric Tucuman
Publicacion INCAR [*Instituto Nacional del Carbon y Sus Derivados "Francisco Pintado Fe"*] — Publ INCAR
Publicacion. Instituto Antartico Argentino (Buenos Aires) — Publ Inst Antart Argent (B Aires)
Publicacion. Instituto de Fisica. Universidad Nacional de Tucuman — Publ Inst Fis Univ Nac Tucuman
Publicacion. Instituto de Nutricion de Centro America y Panama — Publ INCAP
Publicacion. Instituto de Nutricion de Centro America y Panama — Publ Inst Nutr Cent Am Panama
Publicacion. Instituto de Suelos y Agrotecnia — Publn Inst Suelos Agrotec
Publicacion. Instituto de Suflos y Agrotecnia (Buenos Aires) — Publ Inst Suflos Agrotec (B Aires)
Publicacion. Instituto Geografico Agustin Codazzi (Bogota) — Publ Inst Geogr (Bogota)
Publicacion. Instituto Italo-Latinoamericano — Publ Inst Italo Latinoam
Publicacion. Instituto Mexicano de Recursos Naturales Renovables — Publ Inst Mex Recursos Nat Renov
Publicacion. Instituto Nacional de Tecnologia Agropecuaria (Buenos Aires) — Publn Inst Nac Tec Agropec (B Aires)
Publicacion. Instituto Nacional del Carbon y Sus Derivados "Francisco Pintado Fe" — Publ Inst Nac Carbon Sus Deriv "Francisco Pintado Fe"
Publicacion. Servicio de Plagas Forestales (Madrid) — Publ Serv Plagas For (Madrid)
Publicacion sobre Energia — Energia
Publicacion sobre Energia — Publ Energ
Publicacion Tecnica. Instituto de Botanica — Publ Tecn Inst Bot
Publicacion Tecnica. Instituto de Fitotecnia. Buenos Aires — Publ Tecn Inst Fitotecn Buenos Aires
Publicacion Tecnica. Instituto de Patologia Vegetal (Buenos Aires) — Publ Tec Inst Patol Veg (B Aires)
Publicacion Trimestral. Universidad Pontificia Bolivariana — Publ Trimest Univ Pontif Bolivar
Publicacion. Universidad Nacional de Tucuman. Facultad de Agronomia y Zootecnia — Publ Univ Nac Tucuman Fac Agron Zootec
Publicacion. Universidad Nacional de Tucuman. Instituto de Fisica — Publ Univ Nac Tucuman Inst Fis
Publicacion. Universidad Nacional de Tucuman. Instituto de Ingenieria Quimica — Publ Univ Nac Tucuman Inst Ing Quim
Publicaciones Biologicas. Direccion General de la Investigacion Cientifica UANL (Universidad Autonoma de Nuevo Leon) — Publ Biol Dir Gen Invest Cient UANL (Univ Auton Nuevo Leon)
Publicaciones Biologicas. Instituto de Investigaciones Cientificas UANL [*Universidad Autonoma de Nuevo Leon*] — PBICAG
Publicaciones Biologicas. Instituto de Investigaciones Cientificas UANL (Universidad Autonoma de Nuevo Leon) — Publ Biol Inst Invest Cient UANL (Univ Auton Nuevo Leon)
Publicaciones. Centro de Estudios Entomologicos. Universidad de Chile — Publ Cent Estud Entomol Univ Chile
Publicaciones. Centro de Investigaciones Tisiologicas — Publ Cent Invest Tisiol
Publicaciones. Centro Pirenaico de Biologia Experimental — Centro Pirenaico Biolog Exp
Publicaciones Ceramicas — Pubs Ceramicas
Publicaciones. Chile Universidad. Centro de Estudios Entomologicos — Publ Chile Univ Cent Estud Entomol
Publicaciones Cientificas (Alter) — Publ Cient (Alter)
Publicaciones Cientificas. Universidad Austral de Chile (Facultad de Ingenieria Forestal) — Publ Cient Univ Austral Chile (Fac Ingen For)
Publicaciones. Comision Nacional de Energia Atomica (Argentina). Miscelanea — Publ Com Nac Energ At (Argent) Misc
Publicaciones. Comision Nacional de Energia Atomica (Argentina). Serie Fisica — Publ Com Nac Energ At (Argent) Ser Fis
Publicaciones. Comision Nacional de Energia Atomica (Argentina). Serie Geologia — Publ Com Nac Energ At (Argent) Ser Geol
Publicaciones. Comision Nacional de Energia Atomica (Argentina). Serie Informe — Publ Com Nac Energ At (Argent) Ser Inf
Publicaciones. Comision Nacional de Energia Atomica (Argentina). Serie Matematica — Publ Com Nac Energ At (Argent) Ser Mat
Publicaciones. Comision Nacional de Energia Atomica (Argentina). Serie Quimica — Publ Com Nac Energ At (Argent) Ser Quim
Publicaciones de Biologia. Universidad de Navarra. Serie Zoologica — PBUZDC
Publicaciones de Biologia. Universidad de Navarra. Serie Zoologica — Publ Biol Univ Navarra Ser Zool
Publicaciones de la Catedra de Historia de la Medicina. Univerisdad de Buenos Aires — Publ Catedra Hist Med
Publicaciones de Medicina Experimental. Universidad de Chile — Publ Med Exp Univ Chile
Publicaciones del Departamento de Algebra y Fundamentos. Universidad de Murcia — Publ Dep Algebra Fund Univ Murcia
Publicaciones del Departamento de Geometria y Topologia — Publ Dep Geom Topol
Publicaciones del Departamento de Matematicas. Universidad de Extremadura — Publ Dep Mat Univ Extremadura
Publicaciones del Seminario Matematico Garcia de Galdeano. Serie II — Publ Sem Mat Garcia de Galdeano Ser II
Publicaciones. Departamento de Agricultura de Costa Rica — Publicaciones Dept Agric Costa Rica
Publicaciones. Departamento de Cristalografia y Mineralogia. Consejo Superior de Investigaciones Cientificas (Spain) — Publ Dep Cristalogr Miner CSIC (Spain)
Publicaciones. Departamento de Cristalografia y Mineralogia (Madrid) — Publ Dep Cristalogr Mineral (Madrid)
Publicaciones. Departamento de Cristalografia y Mineralogia. Universidad de Barcelona — Publ Dep Cristalogr Mineral Univ Barcelona
Publicaciones. Departamento de Zoologia [*Barcelona*] — PDZBDD
Publicaciones. Departamento de Zoologia (Barcelona) — Publ Dep Zool (Barc)
Publicaciones Especiales. Instituto Espanol de Oceanografia — Publ Espec Inst Esp Oceanogr
Publicaciones Especiales. Servicio Nacional del Trigo. Ministerio de Agricultura (Madrid) — Publ Espec Serv Nac Trigo Min Agr (Madrid)
Publicaciones. Facultad de Ciencias Fisicomatematicas. Universidad Nacional de La Plata — Publ Fac Cienc Fisicomat Univ Nac La Plata
Publicaciones. Facultad de Ciencias Fisicomatematicas. Universidad Nacional de La Plata. Serie 2. Revista — Publ Fac Cienc Fisicomat Univ Nac La Plata Ser 2
Publicaciones Geologicas Especiales del Ingeominas — Publ Geol Espec Ingeominas
Publicaciones Geologicas. ICAITI [*Instituto Centroamericano de Investigacion y Tecnologia Industrial*] — Publ Geol ICAITI
Publicaciones Geologicas. Instituto Centroamericano de Investigacion y Tecnologia Industrial — Publ Geol Inst Centroam Invest Tecnol Ind
Publicaciones. Institucion Tello Tellez de Meneses — Publ Inst TT Meneses
Publicaciones. Instituto de Biologia Aplicada (Barcelona) — Publ Inst Biol Apl (Barc)
Publicaciones. Instituto de Biologia Aplicada (Barcelona) — Publ Inst Biol Apl (Barcelona)
Publicaciones. Instituto de Edafologia e Hidrologia. Universidad Nacional del Sur (Bahia Blanca) — Publ Inst Edafol Hidrol Univ Nac Sur (Bahia Blanca)
Publicaciones. Instituto de Filologia. Anejo de Sphinx — PIFAS
Publicaciones. Instituto de Fisica "Alonso De Santa Cruz" — Publ Inst Fis "Alonso De St Cruz"
Publicaciones. Instituto de Geologia del Universidade de Chile — Publ Inst Geol Univ Chile
Publicaciones. Instituto de Investigaciones Geologicas. Diputacion de Barcelona — Publ Inst Invest Geol Diputacion Barcelona
Publicaciones. Instituto de Investigaciones Geologicas. Diputacion Provincial de Barcelona — Publ Inst Invest Geol Diputacion Prov Barcelona
Publicaciones. Instituto de Investigaciones Microquimicas. Universidad Nacional del Litoral (Rosario, Argentina) — Publ Inst Invest Microquim Univ Nac Litoral (Rosario Argent)
Publicaciones. Instituto de Optica Daza de Valdes de Madrid — Publ Inst Opt Madrid
Publicaciones. Instituto de Quimica Fisica "Antonio Gregorio Rocasolano" — Publ Inst Quim Fis Antonio Gregorio Rocasolano
Publicaciones. Instituto de Quimica Fisica "Rocasolano" — Publ Inst Quim Fis Rocasolano
Publicaciones. Instituto Geologico (Barcelona) — Publ Inst Geol (Barcelona)
Publicaciones. Instituto Geologico Topografico — Publ Inst Geol Topogr
Publicaciones. Instituto Nacional de la Nutricion (Argentina). Publicaciones Cientificas — Publ Inst Nac Nutr (Argent) Publ Cient
Publicaciones. Instituto Tecnico de la Construccion y del Cemento — Publ Inst Tec Constr Cem
Publicaciones. Instituto Tecnologico y de Estudios Superiores de Monterrey. Serie Ciencias Biologicas — Publ Inst Tecnol Estud Super Monterrey Ser Cienc Biol
Publicaciones Internas del Postgrado — Publ Intern Postgrado
Publicaciones. Laboratorio de Medicina Experimental. Clinica Medica del Prof. E. Prado-Tagle. Hospital Clinica San Vicente. Universidad de Chile — Publ Lab Med Exp Clin Med E Prado Tagle Univ Chile
Publicaciones Matematicas del Uruguay — Publ Mat Urug
Publicaciones. Ministerio de Agricultura. Serie. Premios Nacionales de Investigacion Agraria — Publ Min Agr Ser Premios Nac Invest Agr
Publicaciones Miscelaneas Agricolas. Universidad de Chile. Facultad de Agronomia — Publ Misc Agric Univ Chile Fac Agron
Publicaciones Miscelaneas. Estacion Experimental Agricola de Tucuman — Publ Misc Estac Exp Agr Tucuman
Publicaciones Miscelaneas. Ministerio de Agricultura y Ganaderia. Republica de Argentina — Publnes Misc Minist Agric Ganad Repub Argent
Publicaciones. Museo de Historia Natural Javier Prado (Lima) — Publ Mus Hist Nat J Prado Lima
Publicaciones. Museo de Historia Natural "Javier Prado." Series A. Zoologia — Publ Mus Hist Nat "Javier Prado" Ser A Zool

Publicaciones. Museo de Historia Natural "Javier Prado." Series B. Botanica — Publ Mus Hist Nat "Javier Prado" Ser B Bot
Publicaciones. Museo de Historia Natural "Javier Prado." Series C. Geologia — Publ Mus Hist Nat Javier Prado Ser C Geol
Publicaciones Ocasionales. Museo de Ciencias Naturales (Caracas). Zoologia — Publ Ocas Mus Cienc Nat (Caracas) Zool
Publicaciones. Real Academia de Farmacia de Barcelona. Serie A. Anuarios, Memorias, y Discursos Inaugurales de Curso — Publ R Acad Farm Barcelona Ser A
Publicaciones. Real Academia de Farmacia de Barcelona. Serie B. Revista — Publ R Acad Farm Barcelona Ser B
Publicaciones. Real Academia de Farmacia de Barcelona. Serie C. Discurso de Ingreso — Publ R Acad Farm Barcelona Ser C
Publicaciones. Seminario de Arqueologia y Numismatica Aragonesa — Publ Semin Arqueol Numism Aragonesa
Publicaciones. Seminario Matematico Garcia De Galdeano — Publ Sem Mat Garcia De Galdeano
Publicaciones. Seminario Metropolitano — PSM
Publicaciones Tecnicas. Estacion Experimental Agropecuaria de Manfredi (Argentina) — Publ Tec Estac Exp Agropecuar Manfredi (Argentina)
Publicaciones Tecnicas. Estacion Experimental Agropecuaria. INTA [*Instituto Nacional de Tecnologia Agropecuaria*] **(Pergamino)** — Publ Tec Estac Exp Agropecuar INTA (Pergamino)
Publicaciones Tecnicas. Patronato de Investigacion Cientifica y Tecnica "Juan De La Cierva" — Publ Tec Patronato Invest Cient Tec "Juan De La Cierva"
Publicaciones. Universidad Autonoma de Santo Domingo — Publ Univ Auton St Domingo
Publicaciones. Universidad de Costa Rica. Serie Ciencias Naturales — Publ Univ Costa Rica Ser Cienc Nat
Publicaciones. Universidad de Sevilla. Serie Ciencias — Publ Univ Sevilla Ser Cienc
Publicaciones. Universidad de Sevilla. Serie Medicina — Publ Univ Sevilla Ser Med
Publicaciones. Universidad Nacional del Litoral. Instituto de Fisiografia y Geologia — Publ Univ Nac Litoral Inst Fisiogr Geol
Publicacions de la Seccio de Mathematiques — Publ Sec Mat
Publicacions Matematiques — Publ Mat
Publicacoes Avulsas. Centro de Pesquisas Aggeu Megalhaes (Recife, Brazil) [*A publication*] — Publ Avulsas Cent Pesqui Aggeu Magalhaes (Recife Braz)
Publicacoes Avulsas. Instituto Aggeu Magalhaes (Recife, Brazil) — Publ Avulsas Inst Aggeu Magalhaes (Recife Braz)
Publicacoes Avulsas. Museu Nacional (Rio De Janeiro) — Publ Avulsas Mus Nac (Rio De J)
Publicacoes Avulsas. Museu Paranaense — Publcoes Avuls Mus Parana
Publicacoes Avulsas. Revista Brasileira de Malariologia — Publ Avuls Rev Bras Malariol
Publicacoes. Centro de Estudos Leprologicos — Publ Cent Estud Leprol
Publicacoes Culturais. Companhia de Diamantes de Angola — Publ Cult Cia Diamantes Angola
Publicacoes Culturais. Companhia de Diamantes de Angola — Publcoes Cult Co Diam Angola
Publicacoes de Fisica Matematica — Publ Fis Mat
Publicacoes. Direccao Geral dos Servicos Florestais e Aqueicolas — Publcoes Dir Ger Servs Flor Aquic
Publicacoes. Direccao Geral dos Servicos Florestais e Aqueicolas (Lisbon, Portugal) — Publ Serv Flor Aqueic (Portugal)
Publicacoes do Departamento de Matematica — Publ Dep Mat
Publicacoes do Instituto de Botanica Dr. Goncalo Sampaio — Publ Inst Bot Dr Goncalo Sampaio
Publicacoes Farmaceuticas (Sao Paulo) — Publ Farm (Sao Paulo)
Publicacoes. Instituto de Botanica "Dr. Goncalo Sampaio." Faculdade de Ciencias. Universidade do Porto — Publ Inst Bot "Dr Goncalo Sampaio" Fac Cienc Univ Porto
Publicacoes. Instituto de Zoologia "Dr. Augusto Nobreda." Faculdade de Ciencias. Universidade do Porto — Publ Inst Zool "Dr Augusto Nobre" Fac Cienc Porto
Publicacoes. Instituto Nacional de Pesquisas da Amazonia. Serie Quimica — Publ Inst Nac Pesqui Amazonia Ser Quim
Publicacoes. Junta Nacional dos Produtos Pecuarios. Serie A. Serie Cientifica e de Investigacao — Publ Junta Nac Prod Pecu Ser A Ser Cient Invest
Publicacoes Medicas — Publ Med
Publicacoes. Museu e Laboratorio Mineralogico e Geologico. Faculdade de Ciencias do Porto — Publ Mus Lab Mineral Geol Fac Cienc Porto
Publicacoes. Museu e Laboratorio Mineralogico e Geologico. Universidade de Coimbra — Publ Mus Lab Mineral Geol Univ Coimbra
Publicacoes. Museu e Laboratorio Mineralogico e Geologico. Universidade de Coimbra e Centro de Estudos Geologicos — Publ Mus Lab Mineral Geol Univ Coimbra Cent Estud Geol
Publicacoes Pharmaceuticas — Publ Pharm
Publicacoes. Servicos de Agricultura. Servicos de Veterinaria (Lourenco Marques, Mozambique) — Publ Serv Agric (Mozambique)
Publicatieblad — PB
Publicatieblad van de Europese Gemeenschappen — Pb
Publicatieblad van de Europese Gemeenschappen — Pb EG
Publicatieblad van de Europese Gemeenschappen — Pbl
Publicatieblad van de Europese Gemeenschappen — PEG
Publicatieblad van de Europese Gemeenschappen — Publ Eur Gem
Publicatieblad van de Nederlandse Antillen — PB
Publicaties. Koninklijk Meteorologisch Instituut van Belgie. Serie A — Publ K Meteorol Inst Belg Ser A
Publicaties. Koninklijk Meteorologisch Instituut van Belgie. Serie B — Publ K Meteorol Inst Belg Ser B
Publicaties. Natuurhistorisch Genootschap in Limburg — Publ Natuurhist Genoot Limburg
Publicatiile Muzeului Judatului Hunedoara — Publ Muz Judatului Hunedoara
Publication AEEE. School of Agricultural Economics and Extension Education. University of Guelph — Publ AEEE Sch Agric Econ Ext Educ Univ Guelph
Publication. Agricultural Extension Service. North Carolina State University — Publ Agric Ext Serv N Carol St Univ
Publication. Agricultural Research Service. United States Department of Agriculture — Publ Agric Res Serv US Dep Agric
Publication. Agriculture (Canada) — Publ Agric (Can)
Publication. Alberta Department of Agriculture — Publ Alberta Dept Agr
Publication. American Association for the Advancement of Science — PAAAS
Publication. American Association for the Advancement of Science — Publ Am Assoc Adv Scl
Publication. American Association for the Advancement of Science — Publ Amer Ass Advan Sci
Publication. American Concrete Institute — Publ Am Concr Inst
Publication. American Institute of Biological Sciences — Publ Am Inst Biol Sci
Publication. American Institute of the History of Pharmacy — Publ Am Inst Hist Pharm
Publication. American Jewish Historical Society — PAJHS
Publication. American Petroleum Institute — Publ Am Pet Inst
Publication. American University of Beirut. Faculty of Agricultural Sciences — Publ Am Univ Beirut Fac Agric Sci
Publication. American University of Beirut. Faculty of Agricultural Sciences — Publ Amer Univ Beirut Fac Agr Sci
Publication. Association Foret-Cellulose — Publ Ass For-Cell
Publication. Association pour l'Etude de la Paleontologie et de la Stratigraphie Houilleres — Publ Assoc Etude Paleontol Stratigr Houilleres
Publication. Beaverlodge Research Station — Publ Beaverlodge Res Stn
Publication. British Columbia Department of Agriculture — Publ Brit Columbia Dept Agr
Publication. California Department of Agriculture — Publ Calif Dep Agric
Publication. California State Water Resources Control Board — Publ Calif State Water Resour Control Board
Publication. Canada Department of Agriculture — Publ Can Dep Agric
Publication. Canada Department of Agriculture — Publ Can Dept Agr
Publication. Canada Department of Agriculture — Publ Canada Dep Agric
Publication. Canada Department of Forestry — Publ Canada Dep For
Publication. Canadian Forestry Service — Publ Can For Serv
Publication. Carnegie Institution of Washington — Publ Carnegie Inst Washington
Publication. Centre de Recherches Zootechniques. Universite de Louvain — Publ Cent Rech Zootech Univ Louvain
Publication. Centre d'Etude pour l'Utilisation des Sciures de Bois — Publ Cent Etude Util Sciures de Bois
Publication. Centre National de Documentation Pedagogique — PCNDP
Publication. Centre National de Geologie Houillere — Publ Cent Natl Geol Houillere
Publication. Centre of Advanced Study in Geology (Chandigarh, India) — Publ Cent Adv Study Geol (Chandigarh India)
Publication. Centre Technique Forestier Tropical — Publ Centre Tech For Trop
Publication. Centre Technique Forestier Tropical (Nogent-Sur-Marne, France) — Publ Cent Tech For Trop (Nogent-Sur-Marne Fr)
Publication. Coffee Brewing Institute — Publ Coffee Brew Inst
Publication. Conference Geologique des Caraibes — Publ Conf Geol Caraibes
Publication. Cooperative Extension Service. Louisiana State University and Agricultural and Mechanical College — Publ Coop Ext Serv La State Univ Agric Mech Coll
Publication. Cooperative Extension Service. Mississippi State University — Publ Coop Ext Serv Miss State Univ
Publication. Cooperative Extension Service. University of Arizona. College of Agriculture — Publ Coop Ext Serv Univ Ariz Coll Agric
Publication. Cooperative Extension Service. Washington State University — Publ Coop Ext Serv Wash St Univ
Publication. Cooperative Extension. University of California — Publ Co-Op Ext Univ Calif
Publication de l'Institut de Recherche Mathematique Avancee — Publ Inst Rech Math Av
Publication. Department of Agriculture (Ottawa, Canada) — Publ Dep Agric (Can)
Publication. Department of Engineering Physics. Research School of Physical Sciences. Australian National University — Publ Dep Eng Phys Res Sch Phys Sci Aust Natl Univ
Publication. Department of History. Muslim University (Aligarh) — PDHMUA
Publication des Laboratoires d'Ecole Normale Superieure — Publ Lab Ecole Norm Super
Publication des Seminaires de Mathematiques — Publ Sem Math
Publication Diverse Speciale. Service des Peches et des Sciences de la Mer (Canada) — Publ Diverse Spec Serv Peches Sci Mer (Can)
Publication E. Purdue University. Cooperative Extension Service — Publ E Purdue Univ Coop Ext Serv
Publication EE. University of Toronto. Institute for Environmental Studies — Publ EE Univ Toronto Inst Environ Stud
Publication. Engineering Experiment Station. State University of Agriculture and Applied Science (Oklahoma) — Publ Eng Exp St State Univ Agric Appl Sci (Okla)
Publication. European Association for Animal Production — Publ Eur Assoc Ani Prod
Publication. FAO [*Food and Agriculture Organization of the United Nations*]/ECE Joint Committee on Forest Working Techniques and Training Forest Workers [*Economic Commission for Europe*] — Publ FAO/ECE Jt Comm Working Tech
Publication. Fertilizer Society of South Africa — Publ Fert Soc S Afr
Publication. Foreign Agricultural Service. United States Department of Agriculture — Publ Foreign Agric Serv US Dep Agric
Publication. Forest Research Branch. Canada Department of Forestry — Publ Forest Res Brch Canada Dep For

Publication. Forestry Commission of New South Wales — Publ For Commn NSW
Publication. Forestry Service. Department of Fisheries and Forestry (Ottawa, Canada) — Publ For Serv (Can)
Publication Fund Series. Rochester Historical Society — Pub Roch Hist Soc
Publication. Geological Survey of Queensland — Publ Geol Surv Queensl
Publication. Geology Department and the Extension Service. University of Western Australia — Publ Geol Dep Ext Serv Univ West Aust
Publication. Geology Department. Victoria University of Wellington — Publ Geol Dep Victoria Univ Wellington
Publication. Great Lakes Research Division. University of Michigan — Publ Great Lakes Res Div Univ Mich
Publication. Groupement pour l'Avancement des Methodes Spectrographiques — Publ Group Av Methodes Spectrogr
Publication. Groups for the Advancement of Psychiatry — Publ Group Adv Psychiatry
Publication. Hannah Institute for the History of Medicine — Publ Hannah Inst Hist Med
Publication. ID Cooperative Extension Service. Purdue University — Publ ID Coop Ext Serv Purdue Univ
Publication. Institut de Recherches Agronomiques du Liban. Serie Scientifique — Publ Inst Rech Agron Liban Ser Sci
Publication. Institut de Recherches Agronomiques du Liban. Serie Technique — Publ Inst Rech Agron Liban Ser Tech
Publication. Institut de Recherches Entomologiques et Phytopathologiques (Teheran) — Publ Inst Rech Entomol Phytopathol (Teheran)
Publication. Institute of Geophysics. Polish Academy of Sciences — Publ Inst Geophys Pol Acad Sci
Publication. Institute of Social Anthropology — PISA
Publication. International Association of Scientific Hydrology. Symposium (Budapest) — Publ Int Ass Scient Hydrol Symp (Budapest)
Publication. International Institute for Land Reclamation and Improvement — Publ Int Inst Land Reclam Improv
Publication. International Tin Research Institute — Publ Int Tin Res Inst
Publication IOM [*Institute of Medicine*]. National Academy of Sciences. Institute of Medicine — Publ IOM Natl Acad Sci Inst Med
Publication. Japan Medical Research Foundation — Publ Jpn Med Res Found
Publication. Laboratoire de Biochimie de la Nutrition. Universite Catholique de Louvain. Faculte des Sciences Agronomiques — Publ Lab Biochim Nutr Univ Cathol Louvain Fac Sci Agron
Publication. Laboratorio Central de Ensayo de Materiales de Construccion (Madrid) — Publ Lab Cent Ensayo Mater Constr (Madrid)
Publication. Land Capability Survey of Trinidad and Tobago — Publ Ld Capability Surv Trinidad & Tobago
Publication. Maitland Club — PMC
Publication. Manitoba Beekeepers' Association — Publ Manitoba Beekprs Ass
Publication. Manitoba Department of Mines and Natural Resources. Mines Branch — Publ Manit Dep Mines Nat Resour Mines Branch
Publication. Manitoba. Department of Mines, Resources, and Environmental Management. Mines Branch — Publ Manit Dep Mines Resour Environ Manage Mines Branch
Publication. Marie Moors Cabot Foundation for Botanical Research — Publ Maria Moors Cabot Found Bot Res
Publication. Mathematics Research Center. United States Army. University of Wisconsin — Publ Math Res Cent US Army Univ Wis
Publication. Mathematics Research Center. University of Wisconsin — Publ Math Res Cent Univ Wis
Publication. Mathematics Research Center. University of Wisconsin-Madison — Publ Math Res Cent Univ Wis Madison
Publication. Mid-South Neuroscience Development Group — Publ Mid South Neurosci Dev Group
Publication. Mineral Resources Division (Winnipeg) — Publ Miner Resour Div (Winnipeg)
Publication. Ministry of Agriculture (Canada) — Publ Minist Agric (Can)
Publication. Mississippi State University. Agricultural Extension Service — Publ Miss State Univ Agr Ext Serv
Publication. National Academy of Sciences. National Research Council — Publ Nat Acad Sci Nat Res Counc
Publication. National Academy of Sciences. National Research Council (Washington) — Publ Natn Acad Sci Natn Res Coun (Wash)
Publication. NMAB. National Materials Advisory Board (US) — Publ NMAB Natl Mater Advis Board (US)
Publication. OECD [*Organization for Economic Cooperation and Development*] **(Paris)** — Publ OECD (Paris)
Publication of Technical Papers and Proceedings. Annual Meeting of Sugar Industry Technologists, Incorporated — Publ Tech Pap Proc Annu Meet Sugar Ind Technol Inc
Publication. Office National d'Etudes et de Recherches Aerospatiales (France) — Publ Off Natl Etud Rech Aerosp (Fr)
Publication. Oklahoma State University. Agricultural Information Service — Publ Okla State Univ Agr Inform Serv
Publication. Ontario Department of Agriculture and Food — Publ Ont Dep Agric
Publication. Pacific Northwest Cooperative Extension Service — Publ Pacif Nth-West Co-Op Ext Serv
Publication. Pakistan Philosophic Congress — PPPC
Publication. Purdue University. School of Civil Engineering — Publ Purdue Univ Sch Civ Eng
Publication. Rapeseed Association of Canada — Publ Rapeseed Assoc Can
Publication. Research Institute. Aabo Akademi Foundation — Publ Res Inst Aabo Akad Found
Publication. Royal College of Physicians of Edinburgh — Publ R Coll Physicians Edinburgh
Publication. Royal Tropical Institute. Amsterdam — Publ R Trop Inst Amsterdam
Publication. Scientific, Technical, and Research Commission. Organization of African Unity — Publ Sci Tech Res Comm Organ Afr Unity
Publication Series. European Federation of Chemical Engineering — Publ Ser Eur Fed Chem Eng
Publication. Shirley Institute — Publ Shirley Inst
Publication. Smithsonian Institution — Publ Smithson Inst
Publication. Societe Calviniste de France — PSCF
Publication. Societe Geologique du Nord — Publ Soc Geol Nord
Publication. Soil Bureau. Department of Scientific and Industrial Research (New Zealand) — Publ Soil Bur (NZ)
Publication. Southern Illinois University. School of Agriculture — Publ S Ill Univ Sch Agr
Publication SP. American Concrete Institute — Publ SP Am Concr Inst
Publication. Stations Federales d'Essais Agricoles (Lausanne) — Publ Stn Fed Essais Agric (Lausanne)
Publication. Systematics Association — Publ Systematics Ass
Publication. Technical Research Centre of Finland. Materials and Processing Technology — Publ Tech Res Cen Finl Mater Process Technol
Publication. Texas Forest Service. [*A*] **Part of the Texas A & M University System** — Publ Tex For Serv Part Tex A&M Univ Syst
Publication. Transactions. Conference Geologique des Caraibes — Publ Trans Conf Geol Caraibes
Publication Trimestrielle. Institut Belge pour l'Amelioration de la Betterave — Publ Trimest Inst Belge Amelior Betterave
Publication. United States Agricultural Research Service — Publ US Agric Res Serv
Publication. United States Agricultural Research Service. Eastern Regional Research Center — Publ US Agric Res Serv East Reg Res Cent
Publication. United States International Trade Commission — Publ US Int Trade Commn
Publication. University of Alaska. Cooperative Extension Service — Publ Univ Alaska Coop Ext Serv
Publication. University of California. Agricultural Extension Service — Publ Univ Calif Agric Ext Serv
Publication. University of Florida. Institute of Food and Agricultural Sciences — Publ Univ Fl Inst Food Agric Sci
Publication. University of Massachusetts. Water Resources Research Center — Publ Univ Mass Water Resour Res Cent
Publication. University of Texas. Bureau of Economic Geology — Publ Univ Tex Bur Econ Geol
Publication. University of Toronto. Department of Civil Engineering — Publ Univ Toronto Dep Civ Eng
Publication. University of Toronto. Institute for Environmental Studies — Publ Univ Toronto Inst Environ Stud
Publication. University of Wisconsin. Cooperative Extension Service — Publ Univ Wis Coop Ext Serv
Publication. University of Wisconsin Extension — Publ Univ Wis Ext
Publication. Utah Geological Association — Publ Utah Geol Assoc
Publication. Utah Geological Association — UGAPB
Publication. Virginia Cooperative Extension Service — Publ Va Coop Ext Serv
Publication. Virginia Division of Mineral Resources — Publ Va Div Miner Resour
Publication. Virginia Division of Mineral Resources — Publ Virginia Div Miner Resour
Publication. W. J. Barrow Research Laboratory — Publ W J Barrow Res Lab
Publication. West Texas Geological Society — Publ West Tex Geol Soc
Publication. West Virginia University. Engineering Experiment Station — Publ W Va Univ Eng Exp Stn
Publicationen. Kaiserlich Osmanische Museen [*Constantinople*] — PKOM
Publicationes Academiae Horti- et Viticulturae — Publ Acad Horti Vitic
Publicationes Mathematicae. Universitatis Debreceniensis — Publ Math Debrecen
Publicationes Universitatis Horticulturae — Publ Univ Hortic
Publications. Abertay Historical Society — PAHS
Publications. Akkeshi Marine Biological Station — Publ Akkeshi Mar Biol Sta
Publications. Allan Hancock Pacific Expeditions — Publ Allan Hancock Pacific Exped
Publications. Allegheny Observatory. University of Pittsburgh — Publ Allegheny Obs Univ Pittsburgh
Publications. Amakusa Marine Biological Laboratory. Kyushu University — Publ Amakusa Mar Biol Lab Kyushu Univ
Publications. American Association for the Advancement of Science — Publ Amer Assoc Advancem Sci
Publications. American Church History Seminar — PACHS
Publications. American Dialect Society — PADS
Publications. American Economic Association — PAEA
Publications. American Economic Association — Publs Am Econ Ass
Publications. American Folklore Society — PAFS
Publications. American Folklore Society — Publs Am Folk Soc
Publications. American Jewish Archives — PAJA
Publications. American Jewish Historical Society — Publ Amer Jew Hist Soc
Publications. American Society for Archeoogical Research in Asia Minor — PASA
Publications. American Statistical Association — Pub Am Stat Assn
Publications. ANARE [*Australian National Antarctic Research Expeditions*] **Data Reports Series** — Publ ANARE Data Rep Ser
Publications. ANARE [*Australian National Antarctic Research Expeditions*] **Data Reports Series** — Publs ANARE Data Rep Ser
Publications. ANARE [*Australian National Antarctic Research Expeditions*] **Interim Reports Series** — Publs ANARE Interim Rep Ser
Publications. ANARE [*Australian National Antarctic Research Expeditions*] **Scientific Reports Series** — Publs ANARE Sci Rep Ser
Publications. Arkansas Philological Association — PAPA
Publications. Association des Ingenieurs. Faculte Polytechnique de Mons — Publ Assoc Ing Fac Polytech Mons
Publications. Astronomical Society of Australia — Publ Astron Soc Aust
Publications. Astronomical Society of Japan — Pub Ast S J
Publications. Astronomical Society of Japan — Publ Astron Soc Jpn

Publications. Astronomical Society of the Pacific — Pub Ast S P
Publications. Astronomical Society of the Pacific — Publ Astron Soc Pac
Publications. Astronomical Society of the Pacific — Publ Astron Soc Pacific
Publications. Atkins Institution — Publ Atkins Inst
Publications. Australasian Institute of Mining and Metallurgy — Publ Australas Inst Min Metall
Publications. Australian Society of Soil Science — Publs Aust Soc Soil Sci
Publications. Australian Society of Soil Science — Publs Aust Soc Soil Science
Publications. Babylonian Section. University Museum. University of Pennsylvania [*Philadelphia*] — PBS
Publications. Baptist Historical Society — PBHS
Publications. Bibliographical Society of America — PBSA
Publications. British Columbia Ministry of Agriculture — Publ BC Minist Agric
Publications. British Columbia Ministry of Agriculture and Food — Publ BC Minist Agric Food
Publications. British School of Archeology in Egypt — PBSAE
Publications. British Society of Franciscan Studies — PBSFS
Publications. British Society of Franciscan Studies. Extra Series — PBSFSE
Publications. Bureau de Recherches Geologiques, Geophysiques, et Minieres (France) — Publ Bur Rech Geol Geophys Minieres (Fr)
Publications. Bureau d'Etudes Geologiques et Minieres Coloniales (Paris) — Publ Bur Etud Geol Minieres Colon (Paris)
Publications. Bureau of American Ethnology — PBAE
Publications. Cairo University Herbarium — Publ Cairo Univ Herb
Publications. Camden Society — PCS
Publications. Carnegie Institution of Washington — Publ Carnegie Inst Wash
Publications. Catholic Anthropological Conference — PCAC
Publications. Catholic Record Society. Annual Report — PCRS AR
Publications. Center for Medieval and Renaissance Studies. UCLA [*University of California at Los Angeles*] — Publ Center Medieval Ren Stud UCLA
Publications. Center for the Study of Comparative Folklore and Mythology — PCSCF
Publications. Centre de Recherches d'Histoire et de Philologie — PCRHP
Publications. Centre de Recherches d'Histoire et de Philologie. Hautes Etudes du Monde Grecoromain — PCRHP Gr
Publications. Centre de Recherches d'Histoire et de Philologie. Hautes Etudes Medievales et Modernes — PCRHPM
Publications. Centre de Recherches d'Histoire et de Philologie. Hautes Etudes Numismatiques — PCRHPN
Publications. Centre de Recherches d'Histoire et de Philologie. Histoire et Civilisation du Livre — PCRHP H
Publications. Centre de Recherches en Mathematiques Pures — Publ Centre Rech Math Pures
Publications. Centre de Recherches en Mathematiques Pures. Serie 1 — Publ Centre Rech Math Pures 1
Publications. Centre de Recherches en Mathematiques Pures. Serie 3 — Publ Centre Rech Math Pures Ser 3
Publications. Centre National pour l'Exploitation des Oceans. Actes de Colloques — PCNCDH
Publications. Centre National pour l'Exploitation des Oceans. Actes de Colloques — Publ Cent Natl Exploit Oceans Actes Colloq
Publications. Centre National pour l'Exploitation des Oceans. Rapports Scientifiques et Techniques — PCNFDQ
Publications. Centre National pour l'Exploitation des Oceans. Rapports Scientifiques et Techniques — Publ Cent Natl Exploit Oceans Rapp Sci Tech
Publications. Centre National pour l'Exploitation des Oceans. Resultats des Campagnes a la Mer — PCNMDD
Publications. Centre National pour l'Exploitation des Oceans. Resultats des Campagnes a la Mer — Publ Cent Natl Exploit Oceans Result Campagnes Mer
Publications. Centre National pour l'Exploitation des Oceans. Serie. Rapport Scientifique et Technique (France) — Publ Cent Natl Exploit Oceans Ser Rapp Sci Tech (Fr)
Publications. Church Historical Society — PCHS
Publications. Church Historical Society. Sources — PCHSS
Publications. Clark Library Professorship. University of California at Los Angeles — Publ Clark
Publications. CMMI [*Council of Mining and Metallurgical Institutions*] **Congress** — Publ CMMI Congr
Publications. Colonial Society of Massachusetts — Pub Col Soc Mass
Publications. Colonial Society of Massachusetts — Publ Colonial Soc Massach
Publications. Co-Operative Extension Service. University of Massachusetts. College of Agriculture — Publs Co-Op Ext Univ Mass Coll Agric
Publications de la Societe de l'Histoire de l'Orient Latin — Publ de la Soc Hist de l Orient Latin
Publications de la Societe d'Histoire du Theatre. Revue de la Societe d'Histoire du Theatre — Revue d'Histoire du Theatre
Publications de l'Ecole des Languages Orientales Vivantes — PELOV
Publications de l'Ecole des Langues Orientales Vivantes — Publ De L Ecole D Lang Orient Viv
Publications de l'Ecole Francaise d'Extreme-Orient — PEFEO
Publications de l'Institut d'Art et d'Archeologie de l'Universite de Paris — PIAUP
Publications de l'Institut de Recherche de Mathematiques de Rennes — Publ Inst Rech Math Rennes
Publications de l'Universite de Rouen — Publ Univ Rouen
Publications de Scriptorium — PSc
Publications. Departement de Mathematiques. Faculte des Sciences de Lyon — Publ Dep Math Lyon
Publications. Department of Agriculture (Alberta) — Publs Dep Agric (Alberta)
Publications. Department of Agriculture and Conservation (Manitoba) — Publ Dept Agr Conserv (Manitoba)
Publications. Department of Agriculture (Canada) — Publ Dept Agr (Can)
Publications. Department of Agriculture (Canada) — Publs Dep Agric (Can)
Publications des Sciences Forestieres — Publ Sci For
Publications. Diaspora Research Institute — PDRI
Publications Diverses. Museum National d'Histoire Naturelle — Publ Diverses Mus Natl Hist Nat
Publications. Dominion Astrophysical Observatory — Pub Dom Ast
Publications. Dominion Astrophysical Observatory [*Victoria, British Columbia*] [*A publication*] — Publ Dom Astrophys Obs
Publications. Dominion Astrophysical Observatory (Victoria, British Columbia) [*A publication*] — Publ Dom Astrophys Obs (Victoria BC)
Publications. Dominion Observatory (Ottawa) — ODOPA
Publications. Dominion Observatory (Ottawa) — Publ Dom Obs (Ottawa)
Publications du Centre de Recherches en Mathematiques Pures. Serie IV — Publ Centre Rech Math Pures Ser IV
Publications du Departement de Mathematiques. Nouvelle Serie — Pub Dep Math Nouvelle Ser
Publications du Departement de Mathematiques. Nouvelle Serie. D — Publ Dep Math Nouvelle Ser D
Publications. Earth Physics Branch (Canada) — Publ Earth Phys Branch (Can)
Publications. Earth Physics Branch. Department of Energy, Mines, and Resources — Publ Earth Phys Branch Dep Energy Mines & Resour
Publications Econometriques — Publ Econometriques
Publications. Egyptian Department. University Museum. University of Pennsylvania — PED
Publications. Elisabethville. Universite de l'Etat — Publ Elisabethville Univ Etat
Publications. Empire Marketing Board — Publs Mktg Bd
Publications. English Goethe Society — PEGS
Publications. Faculte d'Agronomie. Universite de Teheran — Publ Fac Agron Univ Teheran
Publications. Faculte de Droit et d'Economie d'Amiens — Publ Fac Dr Econ Amiens
Publications. Faculte de Droit et des Sciences Politiques et Sociales d'Amiens — Publ Fac Dr Sci Polit Soc Amiens
Publications. Faculte de l'Agriculture. Universite d'Ankara — Publ Fac Agric Univ Ankara
Publications. Faculte de Theologie. Universite Lovanium — PFTUL
Publications. Faculte d'Electrotechnique. Universite a Belgrade. Serie Mathematiques et Physique — Publ Fac Electrotech Univ Belgrade Ser Math Phys
Publications. Faculte des Lettres et Sciences Humaines d'Alger — PFLA
Publications. Faculte des Lettres et Sciences Humaines de Paris — PFLSH
Publications. Faculte des Lettres. Universite de Strasbourg — PFLUS
Publications. Faculte des Sciences. Universite a Brno — Publ Fac Sci Univ Brno
Publications. Faculte des Sciences. Universite de Clermont. Geologie et Mineralogie — Publ Fac Sci Univ Clermont Geol Mineral
Publications. Faculte des Sciences. Universite J. E. Purkyne (Brno) — Publ Fac Sci Univ J E Purkyne (Brno)
Publications. Faculte des Sciences. Universite Masaryk — Publ Fac Sci Univ Masaryk
Publications. Faculty of Agricultural Sciences. American University (Beirut) [*A publication*] — Publ Fac Agr Sci Amer Univ (Beirut)
Publications. Far Eastern Regional Institute for Scientific Research. Vladivostok — Publ Far East Reg Inst Sci Res Vladivostok
Publications. Far Eastern State University (Vladivostok) — Publ Far East State Univ (Vladivostok)
Publications. Field Columbian Museum. Botanical Series — Publ Field Columbian Mus Bot Ser
Publications. Finnish State Agricultural Research Board — Publ Finn State Agric Res Board
Publications. Forest Research Institute in Finland — Publ For Res Inst Finl
Publications. Foundation Agathon de Potter — Publ Fond Agathon de Potter
Publications. Foundation for Scientific Research in Surinam and the Netherlands Antilles — Publ Found Sci Res Surinam Neth Antilles
Publications. Geological Survey of Queensland — Publs Geol Surv QD
Publications. Geological Survey of Queensland. Palaeontological Papers — Publs Geol Surv QD Palaeont Pap
Publications. GRA [*Groupement Francais pour le Developpement des Recherches Aeronautiques*] **Rapport Technique** — Publ GRA Rapp Tech
Publications. Great Lakes Research Division. University of Michigan. Institute of Science and Technology — Publ Great Lakes Res Div Univ Michigan Inst Sci
Publications. Gulf Coast Research Laboratory. Museum — Publ Gulf Coast Res Lab Mus
Publications. Haewundae Marine Laboratory. Pusan Fisheries College — Publ Haewundae Mar Lab Pusan Fish Coll
Publications. Hartley Botanical Laboratories — Publ Hartley Bot Lab
Publications. Hebrew University (Jerusalem) — Publ Heb Univ (Jerusalem)
Publications. Henry Bradshaw Society — PHBS
Publications. Historical Society of the Church in Wales — PHSCW
Publications. Hungarian Central Institute for the Development of Mining — Publ Hung Cent Inst Dev Min
Publications. Hungarian Mining Research Institute — HRIPA
Publications. Hungarian Mining Research Institute — Publ Hung Min Res Inst
Publications. Hungarian Research Institute for Mining — Publ Hung Res Inst Mining
Publications. Illinois Institute of Technology — Publ Ill Inst Technol
Publications in Botany — Publ Bot
Publications in Botany. University of California, Berkeley — Publ Bot Univ Calif Berkeley
Publications in Classical Philology — PCP
Publications in East Asiatic Philology — PEAP
Publications in Egyptian Archaeology — PEAr
Publications in Ethnology — Publ Ethnol
Publications in Geological Sciences. University of California — Publ Geol Sci Univ Calif
Publications in Mediaeval Studies — PMS
Publications in Operations Research Series [*Elsevier Book Series*] — PORS
Publications in Operations Research Series — Publ Oper Res Ser

Publications in Semitic Philology. University of California — PSPUC
Publications in Zoology — Publ Zoo
Publications. Indian Tea Association. Scientific Department — Publ Indian Tea Assoc Sci Dept
Publications. Indiana Department of Conservation — Publs Indiana Dep Conserv
Publications INED [*Institut National d'Etudes Demographiques*] — Publ INED
Publications. Institut Belge pour l'Amelioration de la Betterave — Publ Inst Belge Amelior Betterave
Publications. Institut Central de Developpement Minier de Hongrie — Publ Inst Cent Dev Min Hong
Publications. Institut de Botanique de l'Universite de Geneve — Publ Inst Bot Univ Geneve
Publications. Institut de Civilisation Indienne — PICI
Publications. Institut de Mathematiques. Universite de Strasbourg — Publ Inst Math Univ Strasbourg
Publications. Institut de Recherche et d'Histoire des Textes — PIRHT
Publications. Institut de Recherches de la Siderurgie. Serie A — Publ Inst Rech Sider Ser A
Publications. Institut de Recherches de la Siderurgie [*Saint-Germain-En-Laye*]. **Serie A** — Publ Inst Rech Siderurg Ser A
Publications. Institut de Recherches de la Siderurgie. Serie B — Publ Inst Rech Sider Ser B
Publications. Institut de Recherches Minieres de Hongrie — Publ Inst Rech Min Hong
Publications. Institut de Statistique. Universite de Paris — Publ Inst Statist Univ Paris
Publications. Institut d'Etudes et de Recherches Minieres de Turquie — Publ Inst Etud Rech Min Turq
Publications. Institut d'Etudes Medievales — PIEM
Publications. Institut d'Etudes Medievales d'Ottawa — PIEMO
Publications. Institut d'Etudes Orientales d'Alger — PIEOA
Publications. Institut d'Etudes Orientales de la Bibliotheque Patriarcale d'Alexandrie — PIEO
Publications. Institut et Musee Voltaire — Publ Inst Musee Voltaire
Publications. Institut Francais d'Archeologie Orientale. Bibliotheque d'Etudes Coptes — PIFAO BEC
Publications. Institut Francais d'Archeologie Orientale du Caire — PIFAO
Publications. Institut Francais du Petrole. Collection Colloques et Seminaires [*France*] — Publ Inst Fr Pet Collect Colloq Semin
Publications. Institut Francaise d'Indologie — PIFI
Publications. Institut Historique et Archeologique Neerlandais de Stamboul [*Leiden*] — PIHANS
Publications. Institut Mathematique. Nouvelle Serie (Belgrade) — Publ Inst Math (Belgrade)
Publications. Institut Mathematique. Universite de Nancago [*Paris*] — Publ Inst Math Univ Nancago
Publications. Institut National pour l'Etude Agronomique du Congo — Publ Inst Nat Etude Agron Congo
Publications. Institut National pour l'Etude Agronomique du Congo Belge. Serie Scientifique — Publ Inst Natl Etude Agron Congo Belge Ser Sci
Publications. Institut National pour l'Etude Agronomique du Congo (INEAC). Serie Scientifique — Publ Inst Nat Etude Agron Congo (INEAC) Serie Scientifique
Publications. Institut National pour l'Etude Agronomique du Congo. Serie Scientifique — Publ Inst Natl Etude Agron Congo Ser Sci
Publications. Institut National pour l'Etude Agronomique du Congo. Serie Scientifique — Publs Inst Natn Etude Agron Congo Ser Sci
Publications. Institut National pour l'Etude Agronomique du Congo. Serie Technique — Publ Inst Natl Etude Agron Congo Ser Tech
Publications. Institut of French Studies — Publ Inst French Studies
Publications. Institut Orientaliste de Louvain — PIOL
Publications. Institut Royal Meteorologique de Belgique. Serie A — PMBAA
Publications. Institut Royal Meteorologique de Belgique. Serie A. Format in-4 — Publ Inst R Meteorol Belg A
Publications. Institut Royal Meteorologique de Belgique. Serie A. Format in-4 — Publ Inst R Meteorol Belg Ser A
Publications. Institut Royal Meteorologique de Belgique. Serie B — Publ Inst R Meteorol Belg Ser B
Publications. Institut Royal Meteorologique de Belgique. Serie B. Format in-8 — Publ Inst R Meteorol Belg B
Publications. Institut Slave d'Upsal — PISU
Publications. Institute for Soil and Rock Mechanics. University of Fridericiana (Karlsruhe) — Publ Inst Soil Rock Mech Univ Fridericiana (Karlsruhe)
Publications. Institute of Foundation Engineering, Soil Mechanics, Rock Mechanics, and Waterways Construction — Publ Inst Found Engng Soil Mech Rock Mech Waterways Constr
Publications. Institute of Geophysics. Polish Academy of Sciences D. Physics of the Atmosphere — Publ Inst Geophys Pol Acad Sci D
Publications. Institute of Geophysics. Polish Academy of Sciences. Series A. Physics of the Earth Interior — Publ Inst Geophys Pol Acad Sci Ser A
Publications. Institute of Geophysics. Polish Academy of Sciences. Series B. Seismology — Publ Inst Geophys Pol Acad Sci Ser B
Publications. Institute of Geophysics. Polish Academy of Sciences. Series C. Earth Magnetism — Publ Inst Geophys Pol Acad Sci Ser C
Publications. Institute of Geophysics. Polish Academy of Sciences. Series D. Atmosphere Physics — Publ Inst Geophys Ser D Pol Acad Sci
Publications. Institute of Geophysics. Polish Academy of Sciences. Series E. Ionosphere Physics — Publ Inst Geophys Pol Acad Sci Ser E
Publications. Institute of Geophysics. Polish Academy of Sciences. Series F. Planetary Geodesy — Publ Inst Geophys Pol Acad Sci Ser F
Publications. Institute of Marine Science. University of Texas — Publ Inst Mar Sci Univ Tex
Publications. Institute of Marine Science. University of Texas — Publ Inst Mar Sci Univ Texas
Publications. Institute of Marine Sciences. National Fisheries. University of Busan — Publ Inst Mar Sci Nat Fish Univ Busan
Publications. Institute of Marine Sciences. National Fisheries University of Busan — Publ Inst Mar Sci Natl Fish Univ Busan
Publications. Institutes of Mineralogy, Paleontology, and Quaternary Geology. University of Lund — Publ Inst Mineral Paleontol Quat Geol Univ Lund
Publications. Irish Church Missions — PICM
Publications. Istanbul University Observatory — Publ Istanbul Univ Obs
Publications. Iwata Institute of Plant Biochemistry — Publ Iwata Inst Pl Biochem
Publications. Jefferson Medical College Hospital — Publ Jefferson Med Coll Hosp
Publications. Jews' College [*London*] — PJC
Publications. Korean National Astronomical Observatory [*Republic of Korea*] — Publ Korean Natl Astron Obs
Publications. Kyoto University. Research Institute for Mathematical Sciences [*A publication*] — Publ Res Inst Math Sci
Publications. Laboratoire de Photoelasticite. Ecole Polytechnique Federale (Zurich) — Publ Lab Photoelasticite Ecole Polytech Fed (Zurich)
Publications. Laboratories of the Jefferson Medical College Hospital — Publ Lab Jefferson Med Coll Hosp
Publications. Laboratory of Physiological Chemistry. University of Amsterdam — Publ Lab Physiol Chem Univ Amsterdam
Publications. Linguistic Circle of New York — PLCNY
Publications. London Record Society — PLRS
Publications. Manitoba Department of Agriculture — Publs Manitoba Dep Agric
Publications. Maria Moors Cabot Foundation for Botanical Research — Publs Maria Moors Cabot Fdn Bot Res
Publications. Marine Biological Station (Al Ghardaqa, Red Sea) — Publ Mar Biol Stn (Al Ghardaqa)
Publications. Marine Biological Station (Al Ghardaqa, Red Sea) — Publ Mar Biol Stn (Ghardaqa Red Sea)
Publications. Marine Biological Station. Ghardaga, Red Sea. Faculty of Science. Fouad I University — Publ Mar Biol Sta Ghardaga
Publications. Marine Biological Station of Stalin — Publ Mar Biol Stn Stalin
Publications. Marine Laboratory. Pusan Fisheries College [*South Korea*] — Publ Mar Lab Pusan Fish Coll
Publications. Marsh Botanical Garden. Yale University — Publ Marsh Bot Gard
Publications. Mathematical Research Institute (Istanbul) — Publ Math Res Inst (Istanbul)
Publications. Mathematical Society of Japan — Publ Math Soc Japan
Publications. Mathematics Research Center. University of Wisconsin — Publ Math Res Center Univ Wisconsin
Publications Mathematiques de la Faculte des Sciences de Besancon — Publ Math Fac Sci Besancon
Publications Mathematiques de l'Universite Paris 7 (Denis Diderot) — Publ Math Univ Paris 7 Denis Diderot
Publications Mathematiques d'Orsay 80 — Publ Math Orsay 80
Publications Mathematiques d'Orsay 81 — Publ Math Orsay 81
Publications Mathematiques d'Orsay 82 — Publ Math Orsay 82
Publications Mathematiques. Universite de Bordeaux — Publ Math Univ Bordeaux
Publications Mathematiques. Universite de Paris. VII — Publ Math Univ Paris VII
Publications Mathematiques. Universite Pierre et Marie Curie — Publ Math Univ Pierre et Marie Curie
Publications. Maya Society — Publ Maya Soc
Publications. McGill University. Series 2. Botany — Publ McGill Univ Ser 2 Bot
Publications. Mediaeval Academy — PMA
Publications. Meteorology Department. University of Melbourne — Publs Met Dep Melb Univ
Publications. Metropolitan Museum of Art. Egyptian Expedition — METEE
Publications. Metropolitan Museum of Art. Egyptian Expedition [*New York*] — PMMA
Publications. Michigan Academy of Science, Arts, and Letters — PMASAL
Publications. Michigan State University Museum. Biological Series — Publ Mich State Univ Mus Biol Ser
Publications. Mineral Research and Exploration Institute of Turkey — Publ Miner Res Explor Inst Turk
Publications. Mississippi Philological Association — POMPA
Publications. Missouri Philological Association — PMPA
Publications. Modern Language Association of America [*Database*] — PMLA
Publications. Modern Language Association of America — PMLAAm
Publications. Modern Language Association of America — PMLAss
Publications. Modern Language Association of America — Publ Mod Lang Ass
Publications. Modern Language Association of America — Publs Mod Language Ass Amer
Publications. Modern Language Association of America — Pubs Mod Lang Ass Am
Publications. Modern Languages Association of America — Publ Mod Lang Assoc
Publications. Museum. Michigan State University. Biological Series — Publ Mus Mich State Univ Biol Ser
Publications. Museum National d'Histoire Naturelle — Publs Mus Natn Hist Nat
Publications. Museum of Natural History. University of Kansas — Publ Mus Nat Hist Univ Kansas
Publications. Nantucket Maria Mitchell Association — Publ Nantucket Maria Mitchell Assoc
Publications. Netherlands Institute of Archaeology and Arabic Studies [*Cairo*] — PNI
Publications. Observatoire Astronomique. Universite de Belgrade — Publ Obs Astr Univ Belgr
Publications. Observatory. University of Michigan — Publ Obs Univ Mich
Publications of Forestry Science — Publ For Sci
Publications of Technical and Scientific Papers. Technical University (Brno). A — Publ Tech Sci Pap Tech Univ (Brno) A

Publications of Technical and Scientific Papers. Technical University. Brno. B — Publ Tech Sci Pap Tech Univ Brno B
Publications of the Faculty of Electrical Engineering. Series. Automatic Control — Publ Fac Electr Engrg Ser Automat Control
Publications of the HoChiMinh City Mathematical Society — Publ HoChiMinh City Math Soc
Publications of the Institute for Applied Mathematics — Publ Inst Appl Math
Publications of the Newton Institute — Publ Newton Inst
Publications. Ontario Fisheries Research Laboratory — Publ Ont Fish Res Lab
Publications. Oriental Translation Fund — POTF
Publications. Osaka Museum of Natural History — Publs Osaka Mus Nat Hist
Publications. Palaeontological Institution. University of Uppsala. Special Volume — Publ Palaeontol Inst Univ Upps Spec Vol
Publications. Palestine Section. Museum. University of Pennsylvania — PPSP
Publications. Pennsylvania German Society — PPGS
Publications. Pennsylvania-Yale Expedition to Egypt — PPYEE
Publications. Petroleum Search Subsidy Acts. Bureau of Mineral Resources, Geology, and Geophysics [*Australia*] — Publs Petrol Search Subsidy Acts
Publications. Petroleum Search Subsidy Acts. Bureau of Mineral Resources, Geology, and Geophysics [*Australia*] — Pubs Petrol Search Subsidy Acts
Publications. Philological Society — PPS
Publications. Philological Society — Publ Phil Soc
Publications. Prehistoric Society — Publ Prehist Soc
Publications. Presbyterian Historical Society — PPHS
Publications. Princeton University Archaeological Expeditions to Syria — PAES
Publications. Princeton University Archaeological Expeditions to Syria in 1904-5 and 1909 — PPUAES
Publications. Puget Sound Biological Station. University of Washington — Publ Puget Sound Biol St Univ Wash
Publications. Puget Sound Marine Station. University of Washington — Publ Puget Sound Mar Stn Univ Wash
Publications. Ramanujan Institute — Publ Ramanujan Inst
Publications Relatives au Congo Belge et aux Regions Voisines — Publ Relat Congo Belg Reg Voisines
Publications. Research Center in Anthropology, Folklore, and Linguistics — PRCAFL
Publications. Research Institute for Mathematical Sciences. Series A [*Japan*] — PBMAA
Publications. Research Institute for Mathematical Sciences. Series A [*Japan*] [*A publication*] — Publ Res Inst Math Sci Ser A
Publications. Research Institute for Mathematical Sciences. Series B [*Japan*] [*A publication*] — Publ Res Inst Math Sci Ser B
Publications. Research Scientists' Christian Fellowship — PRSCF
Publications Review — Publ Rev
Publications Review. Management and Technology and Policy — Publ Rev Manage Technol Policy
Publications Romanes et Francaises — PRF
Publications Romanes et Francaises — Publ Rom Fr
Publications. Royal Observatory (Edinburgh) — Publ R Obs (Edinburgh)
Publications. School of Sacred Sciences — PSSS
Publications Scientifiques. Association Internationale des Botanistes — Publ Sci Assoc Int Bot
Publications Scientifiques et Techniques. Direction des Industries Aeronautiques (France) — Publ Sci Tech Dir Ind Aeronaut (Fr)
Publications Scientifiques et Techniques. Direction des Industries Aeronautiques (France). Bulletin. Services Techniques — Publ Sci Tech Dir Ind Aeronaut (Fr) Bull Serv Tech
Publications Scientifiques et Techniques. Direction des Industries Aeronautiques (France). Notes Techniques — Publ Sci Tech Dir Ind Aeronaut (Fr) Notes Tech
Publications Scientifiques et Techniques. Ministere de l'Air [*France*] — Publ Sci Tech Min Air
Publications Scientifiques et Techniques. Ministere de l'Air. Bulletins des Services Techniques [*France*] — Publ Sci Tech Min Air Bull Serv Tech
Publications Scientifiques et Techniques. Ministere de l'Air (France) — Publ Sci Tech Minist Air (Fr)
Publications Scientifiques et Techniques. Ministere de l'Air (France). Bulletin des Services Techniques — Publ Sci Tech Minist Air (Fr) Bull Serv Tech
Publications Scientifiques et Techniques. Ministere de l'Air [*France*]. Notes Techniques — Publ Sci Tech Min Air Notes Tech
Publications Scientifiques et Techniques. Secretariat d'Etat a l'Aviation (France) — Publ Sci Tech Secr Etat Aviat (Fr)
Publications Scientifiques et Techniques. Secretariat d'Etat a l'Aviation (France). Bulletin des Services Techniques — Publ Sci Tech Secr Etat Aviat (Fr) Bull Serv Tech
Publications Scientifiques et Techniques. Secretariat d'Etat a l'Aviation (France). Notes Techniques — Publ Sci Tech Secr Etat Aviat (Fr) Notes Tech
Publications Scientifiques Forestieres et du Bois — Publ Sci For Bois
Publications Scientifiques. Universite d'Alger. Serie B. Sciences Physiques — Publ Sci Univ Alger Ser B
Publications Scientifiques. Universite d'Alger. Serie B. Sciences Physiques — Publ Scient Univ Alger Ser B
Publications Scientifiques. Universite Forestiere et du Bois — Publ Sci Univ For Bois
Publications. Section Historique. Institut Grand-Ducal de Luxembourg — PSHIGDL
Publications. Section Historique. Institut Grand-Ducal de Luxembourg — PSHIL
Publications. Section Historique. Institut Grand-Ducal de Luxembourg — Pub Hist Inst Luxembourg
Publications. Section Historique. Institut Royal Grandducal de Luxembourg — Pl Lux
Publications. Seminaire de Geometrie. Universite de Neuchatel. Serie 2 — Publ Sem Geom Univ Neuchatel Ser 2
Publications. Seminaire de Geometrie. Universite de Neuchatel. Serie 3 — Publ Sem Geom Univ Neuchatel Ser 3
Publications. Serie A. Institut Royal Meteorologique de Belgique — Publ Ser A Inst R Meteorol Belg
Publications. Serie B. Institut Royal Meteorologique de Belgique — Publ Ser B Inst R Meteorol Belg
Publications. Service de la Carte Geologique (Algerie). Bulletin — Publ Serv Carte Geol (Alger) Bull
Publications. Service de la Carte Geologique (Luxembourg) — Publ Serv Carte Geol (Luxemb)
Publications. Service des Antiquites du Maroc — PSAM
Publications. Service des Antiquites du Maroc — PUAES
Publications. Service Geologique de l'Algerie. Bulletin — Publ Serv Geol Alger Bull
Publications. Service Geologique de Luxembourg — Publ Serv Geol Luxemb
Publications. Service Geologique de Luxembourg. Bulletin — Publ Serv Geol Luxemb Bull
Publications. Service Meteorologique de Madagascar — Publ Serv Met Madag
Publications. Seto Marine Biological Laboratory — Publ Seto Mar Biol Lab
Publications. Seto Marine Biological Laboratory. Special Publication Series — Publ Seto Mar Biol Lab Spec Publ Ser
Publications. Societe d'Archeologie Copte — PSAC
Publications. Societe d'Archeologie Copte. Textes et Documents — PSAC TD
Publications. Societe d'Archeologie Copte. Textes et Documents — PSACT
Publications. Societe de l'Histoire de France — PSHF
Publications. Societe d'Histoire de l'Eglise d'Alsace — PSHEA
Publications. Societe d'Histoire de l'Eglise d'Alsace. Sources — PSHEAS
Publications. Societe Egyptologique a l'Universite d'Etat de Leningrad — PSEL
Publications. Societe Francaise de Musicologie — PSFM
Publications. Societe Historique et Archeologique a Maestrich — PSHM
Publications. Societe Historique et Archeologique dans le Duche de Limbourg — PSHADL
Publications. Societe Historique et Archeologique dans le Duche de Limbourg — PSHAL
Publications. Societe Historique et Archeologique dans le Duche de Limbourg — PSHL
Publications. Societe pour la Recherche et la Conservation des Monuments Historiques dans le Grand Duche de Luxembourg — PSMHL
Publications. Societe Savante d'Alsace et des Regions de l'Est — Publ Soc Savante Alsace Reg Est
Publications. Soeren Kierkegaard Selskabet — PSKS
Publications. South African Institute for Medical Research — Publ S Afr Inst Med Res
Publications. St. Antony's College — PStAC
Publications. State Institute for Technical Research — Publ State Inst Tech Res
Publications. State Institute of Agricultural Chemistry (Finland) — Publ State Inst Agric Chem (Finl)
Publications. Stations Federales d'Essais Agricoles (Lausanne) — Publ Sta Fed Essais Agr (Lausanne)
Publications. Surtees Society — PSS
Publications. Sussex Record Society — PSRS
Publications. Systematics Association — Publ Syst Assoc
Publications. Tallinn Institute of Technology. Series A — Publ Tallinn Inst Technol Ser A
Publications. Technical Research Centre of Finland — Publ Tech Res Cent Finl
Publications. Technical Research Centre of Finland. Electrical and Nuclear Technology — Publ Tech Res Cent Finl Electr Nucl Technol
Publications. Technical University for Heavy Industry (Miskolc, Hungary) — Publ Tech Univ Heavy Ind (Miskolc Hung)
Publications. Technical University for Heavy Industry (Miskolc, Hungary). Foreign Language Edition — Publ Tech Univ Heavy Ind (Miskolc Hung) Foreign Lang Ed
Publications. Technical University for Heavy Industry (Miskolc). Series B. Metallurgy [*Hungary*] — Publ Tech Univ Heavy Ind (Miskolc) Ser B Metall
Publications. Technical University for Heavy Industry. Series A. Mining (Miskolc, Hungary) — Publ Tech Univ Heavy Ind Ser A (Miskolc Hung)
Publications. Technical University for Heavy Industry. Series B. Metallurgy (Miskolc, Hungary) — Publ Tech Univ Heavy Ind Ser B (Miskolc Hung)
Publications. Technical University of Estonia at Tallinn. Series A — Publ Tech Univ Est Tallinn Ser A
Publications Techniques des Charbonnages de France. Bulletin d'Informations Techniques — Publ Tech Charbon Fr Bull Inf Tech
Publications Techniques des Charbonnages de France. Documents Techniques — Publ Tech Charbon Fr Doc Tech
Publications Techniques des Charbonnages de France. Informations Techniques [*A publication*] — Publ Tech Charbon Fr Inf Tech
Publications Techniques. Institut Belge pour l'Amelioration de la Betterave — Publ Tech Inst Belge Amelior Betterave
Publications Techniques. Institut Belge pour l'Amelioration de la Betterave Tirlemont — Publ Tech Inst Belge Amelior Betterave Tirlemont
Publications. Texas Folklore Society — PTFS
Publications. Thoresby Society — Publ Thoresby Soc
Publications. Unites d'Enseignement et de Recherche de Mathematiques Pures et Appliquees. Institut de Recherche de Mathematiques Avancees — Publ UER Math Pures Appl IRMA
Publications Universitaires Europeennes [*Frankfurt Am Main*] — Publ Univ Europ
Publications Universitaires Europeennes. Serie 8. Chimie. Division A. Pharmacie — Publ Univ Eur Ser 8 Chim Div A
Publications Universitaires Europeennes. Serie 8. Chimie. Division B. Biochimie — Publ Univ Eur Ser 8 Chim Div B
Publications Universitaires Europeennes. Serie V. Sciences Economiques — Publ Univ Europeennes Ser V Sci Econom
Publications. Universite de Grenoble — PUG
Publications. Universite de l'Etat a Elisabethville — PUEE

Publications. Universite de Toulouse-Le Mirail. Serie A. — Publ Univ Toulouse-Le Mirail Ser A
Publications. Universite d'Etat a l'Extreme-Orient — Publ Univ Etat Extreme Orient
Publications. Universite Laval — Publ Univ Laval
Publications. Universite Officielle du Congo a Elisabethville — Publ Univ Off Congo Elisabethville
Publications. Universite Officielle du Congo a Lubumbashi — Publ Univ Off Congo Lubumbashi
Publications. University Museum. Babylonian Section. University of Pennsylvania — UMBS
Publications. University of California. Languages and Literature [*A publication*] — PUCalLL
Publications. University of Innsbruck — Publ Univ Innsbruck
Publications. University of Joensuu. Series B [*Finland*] — Publ Univ Joensuu Ser B
Publications. University of Joensuu. Series B-I — Publ Univ Joensuu Ser B-I
Publications. University of Joensuu. Series B-II — Publ Univ Joensuu Ser B-II
Publications. University of Kuopio. Community Health Series. Original Reports — Publ Univ Kuopio Community Health Ser Orig Rep
Publications. University of Manchester — PUM
Publications. University of Manchester. Economic History Series — PUMEH
Publications. University of Manchester. English Series — PUME
Publications. University of Manchester. French Series — PUMF
Publications. University of Manchester. Germanic Series — PUMG
Publications. University of Manchester. Historical Series — PUMH
Publications. University of Manchester. School of Education — PUMSE
Publications. University of Manchester. Theological Series — PUMT
Publications. University of Pennsylvania — Publ Univers Pennsylv
Publications. University of Pennsylvania — UnivPennPub
Publications. University of Technical Sciences. Budapest — Publ Univ Tech Sci Budapest
Publications. University of Wyoming — Publ Univ Wyo
Publications. University of Zululand. Series 3. Specialized Publications — Publ Univ Zululand Ser 3
Publications. Victoria University of Manchester — PVUM
Publications. Victoria University of Manchester. Historical Series — PVUMH
Publications. Wagner Free Institute of Science of Philadelphia — Publ Wagner Free Inst Sci Philadelphia
Publications. Water and Environment Research Institute — Publ Water Environ Res Inst
Publications. Water Research Institute — Publ Water Res Inst
Publication-Technion. Israel Institute of Technology. Agricultural Engineering Faculty — Publ Technion Israel Inst Technol Agric Eng Fac
Publicatiunile Asociatiei Excursionistilor Romani. Sectiunea Stiintific — Publ Asoc Excurs Romani Sect Sti
Publicatiunile Institutului Botanic Din Bucuresti — Publ Inst Bot Bucuresti
Publicatiunile Societatii Naturalistilor din Romania — Publ Soc Nat Romania
Publikace. Statni Ustav Geofysikalni — Publ SUG
Publikacije Elektrotehnickog Fakulteta. Serija Elektroenergetika — Publ Elektroteh Fak Ser Elektroenerg
Publikacije Elektrotehnickog Fakulteta. Serija Elektronika Telekomunikacije. Automatika — Publ Elektroteh Fak Ser Elektron Telekommun Autom
Publikacije Elektrotehnickog Fakulteta. Serija Matematika i Fizika — Publ Elektroteh Fak Ser Mat & Fiz
Publikacije Elektrotehnickog Fakulteta Univerziteta u Beogradu. Serija Matematika i Fizika — PEUBA
Publikacije Elektrotehnickog Fakulteta Univerziteta u Beogradu. Serija Matematika i Fizika — Publ Elektrote Fak Univ Beogradu Ser Mat Fiz
Publikacije Elektrotehnickog Fakulteta Univerziteta u Beogradu. Serija Matematika i Fizika — Publ Elektroteh Fak Univ Beogr Ser Mat Fiz
Publikacije Tehnickog Fakulteta u Sarajevu — Publ Tehn Fak u Sarajevu
Publikasi Chusus (Indonesia). Direktorat Geologi — Publ Chusus (Indones) Dir Geol
Publikasi Teknik. Direktorat Geologi. Seri Geologi Ekonomi (Indonesia) — Publ Tek Dir Geol Seri Geol Ekon (Indones)
Publikasies. Universiteit van Pretoria — Publ Univ Pretoria
Publikasies. Universiteit van Zoeloeland. Reeks 3. Vakpublikasies — Publ Univ Zoeloeland Reeks 3
Publikasjoner. Institutt for Kirkehistorie — PIKH
Publikasjoner. Norske Institutt foer Kosmisk Fysikk — Publ Nor Inst Kosm Fys
Publikatie. Belgisch Instituut tot Verbetering van de Biet — Publ Belg Inst Verbetering Biet
Publikatie. Metaalinstituut TNO [*Nederlands Centrale Organisatie voor Toegepast-Natuurwetenschappelijk Onderzoek*] — Publ Metaalinst TNO
Publikatieblad van de Europese Gemeenschappen. Handelingen van het Europese Parlement — PKH
Publikatieblad van de Europese Gemeenschappen. Supplement — PKS
Publikation B. Chalmers Tekniska Hoegskola — Publ B Chalmers Tek Hoegsk
Publikation. Chalmers Tekniska Hoegskola. Goeteborg. Institutionen foer Vattenfoersoerjnings- och Avloppsteknik — Publ Chalmers Tek Hoegsk Goeteborg Inst Vattenfoersoerjnings
Publikation der Agraroekonomischen Fakultaet der Landwirtschaftlichen Universitaet — Publ Agraroekon Fak Landwirtsch Univ
Publikation. Nordforsk, Miljoevardssekretariatet — Publ Nordforsk Miljoevardssekr
Publikation. Statens Levnedsmiddelinstitut (Denmark) — Publ Statens Levnedsmiddelinst (Den)
Publikation. Svenska Institutet foer Konserveringsforskning — Publ Sven Inst Konserveringsforsk
Publikationen Aelteerer Musik — PaeM
Publikationen Aelterer Praktischer und Theoretischer Musik-Werke — PGfM
Publikationen aus den Preussischen Staatsarchiven — PPSA
Publikationen der Gesellschaft fuer Rheinische Geschichtskunde — PGRGK
Publikationen des Henri-Poincare-Archivs — Publ Henri Poincare Arch
Publikationen des Institutes der Elektroindustrie (Sofia) — Publ Inst Elektroind (Sofia)
Publikationen des Oesterreichischen Historischen Instituts in Rom — POeHIR
Publikationen Herausgegeben von der Stiftung Vulkaninstitut Immanuel Friedlaender — Publ Stift Vulkaninst Immanuel Friedlaender
Publikationen Herausgegeben von der Stiftung Vulkaninstitut Immanuel Friedlaender — Publ Vulkaninst Immanuel Friedlaender
Publikationen zu Wissenschaftlichen Filmen. Sektion Technische Wissenschaften. Naturwissenschaften — Publ Wiss Filmen Sekt Tech Wiss Naturwiss
Publikationen zu Wissenschaftlichen Filmen. Sektion Technische Wissenschaften. Naturwissenschaften — PWFND
Publikationsreihe Fortschritte im Strahlenschutz — Publikationsr Fortschr Strahlenschutz
Publikationsserie B. Chalmers Tekniska Hoegskola — Publikationsser B Chalmers Tek Hoegsk
Publikatsii Tartuskoi Astrofizicheskoi Observatorii [*Estonian SSR*] — Publ Tartu Astrofiz Obs
Publikatsiya Dushanbinskogo Instituta Epidemiologii i Gigieny — Publ Dushanb Inst Epidemiol Gig
Published Reports. Australian Coal Industry Research Laboratories — Publ Rep Aust Coal Ind Res Lab
Publisher — Pub
Publishers' Circular and Booksellers' Record — Pub Circ
Publishers' International ISBN [*International Standard Book Number*] **Directory** — PIID
Publishers Weekly — GPUB
Publishers' Weekly — Pub W
Publishers' Weekly — Publ W
Publishers' Weekly — Publ Wkly
Publishers' Weekly — Publishers
Publishers' Weekly — PW
Publishing, Entertainment, Advertising, and Allied Fields Law Quarterly — PEAL
Publishing, Entertainment, Advertising, and Allied Fields Law Quarterly — PEALQ
Publishing, Entertainment, Advertising, and Allied Fields Law Quarterly — Pub Ent Adv LQ
Publishing, Entertainment, Advertising, and Allied Fields Law Quarterly — Publ Ent Adv A
Publishing History — Publ Hist
Publishing Information Bulletin — PIB
Publishing News — PN
Publishing Trade — PTR
Publius — PBLSA
Publius. Journal of Federalism — Publius J F
PUDOC [*Centre for Agricultural Publishing and Documentation*] **Annual Report** — PUDOC Annu Rep
PUDOC (Centrum voor Landbouwpublikaties en Landbouwdocumentatie) Literatuuroverzicht — PUDOC (Cent Landbouwpubl Landbouwdoc) Literatuuroverz
Pueblo y Cultura — PyC
Pueblos — PLAA
Puerto Rico Agricultural Experiment Station. Annual Report — Puerto Rico Agric Exp Sta Annual Rep
Puerto Rico. Agricultural Experiment Station. Bulletin — PR Agric Exp Stn Bull
Puerto Rico Agricultural Experiment Station. Report — Puerto Rico Agric Exp Sta Rep
Puerto Rico. Agricultural Experiment Station. Rio Piedras. Bulletin — PR Agric Exp Stn Rio Piedras Bull
Puerto Rico. Agricultural Experiment Station. Technical Paper — PR Agric Exp Stn Tech Pap
Puerto Rico Business Review — Puerto Rico Bus R
Puerto Rico Commonwealth. Water Resources Bulletin — PR Commonw Water Resour Bull
Puerto Rico. Department of Health. Bulletin — PR Dep Health Bull
Puerto Rico. Department of Industrial Research. Bulletin — Puerto Rico Dept Indus Research Bull
Puerto Rico Health Bulletin — PR Health Bull
Puerto Rico Health Sciences Journal — PR Health Sci J
Puerto Rico Journal of Public Health and Tropical Medicine — PR J Public Health Trop Med
Puerto Rico Journal of Public Health and Tropical Medicine — Puerto Rico J Publ Hlth
Puerto Rico Laws Annotated — PR Laws Ann
Puerto Rico Libre — Puer Rico
Puerto Rico Reports — PRR
Puerto Rico Sugar Manual — PR Sugar Man
Puerto Rico University. Agricultural Experiment Station. Technical Paper — Puerto Rico Univ Agr Expt Sta Tech Paper
Puerto Rico. Water Resources Authority. Water Resources Bulletin — Puerto Rico Water Resources Authority Water Resources Bull
Puerto Rico. Water Resources Bulletin — PR Water Resour Bull
Puerto Rico y Su Enferma — PR Enferm
Puget Sound Business Journal — Puget Snd
Puget Sound Marine Station Publications — Puget Sound Mar Sta Publ
Puglia Chirurgica — Puglia Chir
Pullacher Philosophische Forschungen — PPhF
Pulmonary Hypertension. Proceedings. International Symposium on Pulmonary Circulation — Pulm Hypertens Proc Int Symp
Pulmonary Macrophage and Epithelial Cells. Proceedings. Annual Hanford Biology Symposium — Pulm Macrophage Epithelial Cells Proc Annu Hanford Biol Symp
Pulmonary Pharmacology — Pulm Pharm
Pulmonary Pharmacology — Pulm Pharmacol

Pulmonary Surfactant. Biochemical, Functional, Regulatory, and Clinical Concepts — Pulm Surfactant Biochem Funct Regul Clin Concepts
Pulp and Paper — Pulp & Pa
Pulp and Paper — Pulp Pap
Pulp and Paper — PUP
Pulp and Paper — PUV
Pulp and Paper (Canada) — Pulp and Pap (Can)
Pulp and Paper (Canada) — Pulp Pap (Can)
Pulp and Paper Engineering — Pulp & Pap Eng
Pulp and Paper Europo — Pulp Pap Eur
Pulp and Paper Industry — Pulp Pap Ind
Pulp and Paper Industry Corrosion Problems. International Seminar on Pulp and Paper Industry Corrosion Problems — Pulp Pap Ind Corros Probl Int Semin
Pulp and Paper Industry Corrosion Problems. Proceedings. International Symposium on Corrosion in the Pulp and Paper Industry — Pulp Pap Ind Corros Probl Proc Int Symp Corros Pulp Pap Ind
Pulp and Paper International — PPI
Pulp and Paper International — PPP
Pulp and Paper International — Pulp Pap Int
Pulp and Paper International Annual Review — P & P Intnl
Pulp and Paper Journal — P & P Jrl
Pulp and Paper Magazine of Canada [*Later, Pulp and Paper (Canada)*] — PPM
Pulp and Paper Magazine of Canada [*Later, Pulp and Paper (Canada)*] — Pulp & Pa Can
Pulp and Paper Magazine of Canada — Pulp Pap Mag Can
Pulp and Paper Magazine of Canada [*Later, Pulp and Paper (Canada)*] — Pulp Paper Mag Can
Pulp and Paper Manual of Canada — Pulp Paper Manual Can
Pulp and Paper Quarterly Statistics — P & P Qtly
Pulp and Paper (Sofia) — Pulp Pap (Sofia)
Pulp, Paper, and Board — Pulp Pap & Board
Pulping Conference. Proceedings — Pulping Conf Proc
Pulpudeva. Semaines Philippopolitaines de l'Histoire et de la Culture Thrace — Pulpudeva
Pulpwood Annual [*United States*] — Pulpwood Annu
Pulpwood Production and Sawmill Logging — Pulpwood Prodn
Pulse. Montana State Nurses Association — Pulse
Pump Engineering (Tokyo) — Pump Eng (Tokyo)
Pumpen und Verdichter Information — Pumpen & Verdichter Inf
Pumps and Their Applications [*England*] — Pumps Their Appl
Pumps-Pompes-Pumpen [*England*] — Pumps
Punch — GPUN
Punime Matematike — Punime Mat
Punjab Fruit Journal — Punjab Fruit J
Punjab Historical Society. Journal — JPHS
Punjab Horticultural Journal — Punjab Hortic J
Punjab Irrigation Research Institute. Annual Report — Punjab Irrig Res Inst Annu Rep
Punjab Irrigation Research Institute. Memoirs — Punjab Irrig Res Inst Mem
Punjab Irrigation Research Institute. Research Publication — Punjab Irrig Res Inst Res Publ
Punjab Irrigation Research Laboratory. Memoirs — Punjab Irrig Res Lab Mem
Punjab Medical Journal — Punj Med J
Punjab Medical Journal — Punjab Med J
Punjab University Botanical Publication — Punjab Univ Bot Publ
Punjab University. Journal of Mathematics (Lahore) — Punjab Univ J Math (Lahore)
Punjabrao Krishi Vidyapeeth. College of Agriculture (Nagpur). Magazine — Punjabrao Krishi Vidyapeeth Coll Agric (Nagpur) Mag
Punjabrao Krishi Vidyapeeth. Research Journal — Punjabrao Krishi Vidyapeeth Res J
Punta Europa — PE
Punto de Partida — PdP
Punto de Vista — PDV
Purasuchikku Materiaru — PURMA
Purchas His Pilgrimes, containing a history of the world in sea voyages and lande travels by Englishmen and others. Samuel Purchas [*Monograph*] — PuP
Purchasing — PUH
Purchasing — PUR
Purchasing Administration — Purch Adm
Purchasing Professional — Purch Prof
Purchasing (South Africa) — Purch (S Afr)
Purchasing World — PRW
Purchasing World — Purchasing
Purdon's Pennsylvania Statutes Annotated — Pa Stat Ann
Purdue Agricultural Economics Report. Purdue University. Cooperative Extension Service — Purdue Agric Econ Rep Purdue Univ Coop Ext Serv
Purdue Agriculturist — Purdue Ag
Purdue Air Quality Conference. Proceedings — Purdue Air Qual Conf Proc
Purdue Industrial Waste Conference. Proceedings — Purdue Ind Waste Conf Proc
Purdue University. Agricultural Experiment Station. Circular — Purdue Univ Agric Exp Stn Circ
Purdue University. Agricultural Experiment Station. Extension Bulletin — Purdue Univ Agric Exp Stn Ext Bull
Purdue University. Agricultural Experiment Station. Extension Leaflet — Purdue Univ Agric Exp Stn Ext Leafl
Purdue University. Agricultural Experiment Station. Inspection Report — Purdue Univ Agric Exp Stn Insp Rep
Purdue University. Agricultural Experiment Station. Research Bulletin — Purdue Univ Agric Exp Stn Res Bull
Purdue University. Agricultural Experiment Station. Research Progress Report — Purdue Univ Agric Exp Stn Res Prog Rep
Purdue University. Agricultural Experiment Station. Station Bulletin — Purdue Univ Agric Exp Stn Stn Bull
Purdue University. Agricultural Experiment Station. Station Circular — Purdue Univ Agric Exp Stn Res Stn Circ
Purdue University. Agricultural Extension Service. Extension Bulletin — Purdue Univ Agric Ext Serv Ext Bull
Purdue University. Agricultural Extension Service. Extension Leaflet — Purdue Univ Agric Ext Serv Ext Leaflet
Purdue University. Department of Agricultural Extension. Mimeo AY — Purdue Univ Dept Agr Ext Mimeo AY
Purdue University. Engineering Bulletin. Engineering Extension Series — Purdue Univ Eng Bull Eng Ext Ser
Purdue University. Engineering Bulletin. Extension Series — Purdue Univ Eng Bull Ext Ser
Purdue University. Engineering Experiment Station. Research Bulletin — Purdue Univ Eng Exp Sta Res Bull
Purdue University. Engineering Extension Series — Purdue Univ Eng Ext Ser
Purdue University. Extension Publications — Purdue Univ Ext Publ
Purdue University. Indiana Agricultural Experiment Station. Publications — Ind Ag Exp
Purdue University. Monographs in Romance Languages — PUMRL
Purdue University. School of Aeronautics, Astronautics, and Engineering Sciences. Research Project — Purdue Univ Sch Aeronaut Astronaut Eng Sci Res Proj
Purdue University. School of Civil Engineering. Publication CE-MAT — Purdue Univ Sch Civ Eng Publ CE-MAT
Purdue University. Water Resources Research Center. Technical Report — Purdue Univ Water Resour Res Cent Tech Rep
Purdue University. Water Resources Research Center. Technical Report — Purdue Univ Water Resources Research Center Tech Rept
Pure and Applied Chemistry — Pur A Chem
Pure and Applied Chemistry — Pure and Appl Chem
Pure and Applied Chemistry — Pure Appl Chem
Pure and Applied Cryogenics — Pure Appl Cryog
Pure and Applied Geophysics — Pur A Geoph
Pure and Applied Geophysics — Pure and Appl Geophys
Pure and Applied Geophysics — Pure Appl Geophys
Pure and Applied Mathematics — Pure and Appl Math
Pure and Applied Mathematics — Pure Appl Math
Pure and Applied Optics — Pure Appl Opt
Pure and Applied Physics — Pure Appl Phys
Pure Chemicals Daiichi — Pure Chem Daiichi
Pure Mathematics Manuscript — Pure Math Manuscript
Pure Products — Pure Prod
Puresutoresuto Konkurito — PUKOD
Pusat Penelitian dan Pengembangan Geologi. Bulletin — Pusat Penelitian Pengembangan Geol Bull
Pusat Pengembangan Teknologi Mineral. Buletin — Pusat Pengembangan Teknol Miner Bul
Pusat Pengembangan Teknologi Mineral. Penerbitan Teknik — Pusat Pengembangan Teknol Miner Penerbitan Tek
Pusat Penyelidikan Getah Malaysia. Jurnal Sains — Pusat Penyelidikan Getah Malays J Sains
Push from the Bush — PB
Puskin i Ego Sovremenniki — PiS
Pustyni SSSR i ih Osvoenie — Pustyni SSSR Ih Osvoenie
Puteoli. Studi di Storia Antica — PSSA
Puti Povysheniya Intensivnosti i Produktivnosti Fotosinteza — Puti Povysh Intensivn Prod Fotosint
Puti Povysheniya Intensivnosti i Produktivnosti Fotosinteza Respublikanskii Mezhvedomstvennyi Sbornik — Puti Povysh Intensivn Prod Fotosint Resp Mezhved Sb
Puti Povysheniya Urozhainosti Polevykh Kul'tur — Puti Povysh Urozhainosti Polevykh Kult
Puti Sinteza i Izyskaniya Protivoopukholevykh Preparatov — Puti Sint Izyskaniya Protivoopukholevykh Prep
Putnam's Magazine — Putnams M
Putnam's Monthly Magazine — Putnam
Puzzles on the Electroweak Scale. Proceedings. International Warsaw Meeting on Elementary Particle Physics — Puzzles Electroweak Scale Proc Int Warsaw Meet Elem Part Phys
PW. Maandblad voor Personeelswerk en Arbeidsverhoudingen — PUM
PWA. Report fuer Mitarbeiter und Freunde der Papierwerke "Waldhof-Aschaffenburg" — PWA Rep
Pyelonephritis. Hahnenklee-Symposion — Pyelonephritis Hahnenklee Symp
Pynchon Notes — PNotes
Pyridine and Its Derivatives — Pyridine Its Deriv
Pytannia Klasychnoi Filologii — PKF
Pytannia Klasychnoi Filologii — PKFil
Pytannja Slov'jans'koho Movoznavstva — PSM
Pytannja Tekstolohiji — PT
Pytannja Ukrajins'koho Movoznavstva — PUM

Q

QACC [*Queensland Automobile Chamber of Commerce*] **Motor Trader** — QACC Mot Trader
Qadmonijot/Qadmoniot. Quarterly for the Antiquities of Eretz-Israel and Biblical Land — Qad
Qantas Empire Airways — Qantas E Air
Qatar University. Science Bulletin — Qatar Univ Sci Bull
Qatar University Science Journal — Qatar Univ Sci J
Qazaq Tili Tarychi Men Dyalektology Jasinin Moseleleri — QTDM
QCOA: Journal of the Queensland Council on the Ageing — QCOA
QHTA [*Queensland History Teachers Association*] **Bulletin** — QHTA Bull
QIER [*Queensland Institute for Educational Research*] **Journal** — QIER J
QIMA. Institute of Municipal Administration, Queensland Division — QIMA
QIP Report. National Asphalt Pavement Association — QIP Rep Natl Asphalt Pavement Assoc
Qirjat Sefer — QS
QMW (Queen Mary and Westfield College) Maths Notes — QMW Maths Notes
QR [*Quality and Reliability*] **Journal** — QRJOD
QR Journal. Indian Association for Quality and Reliability — QR J
QSAR [*Quantitative Structure-Activity Relationships*] **in Drug Design and Toxicology. Proceedings. European Symposium on Quantitative Structure-Activity Relationships** — QSAR Drug Des Toxicol Proc Eur Symp Quan Struct Act Relat
Quaderni. Associazione Ligure di Archeologia e Storia Navale — Q Assoc Lig Arch Stor Nav
Quaderni Catanesi di Studi Classici e Medievali — QC
Quaderni Catanesi di Studi Classici e Medievali — Quad Cat
Quaderni. Centro di Studi Lunesi — Quad St Lun
Quaderni. Centro di Studi sulla Deportazione e l'Internamento — QCS
Quaderni Dannunziani — QD
Quaderni d'Archeologia Reggiana — Quad A Reggio
Quaderni de Clinica Ostetrica e Ginecologica — Quad Clin Ostet Ginecol
Quaderni de la Ricerca Scientifica — Quad Ric Sci
Quaderni de la Ricerca Scientifica — Quad Ricerca Sci
Quaderni dei Padri Benedettini di San Giorgio Maggiore — QPB
Quaderni del Consiglio Nazionale delle Richerche. Gruppo Nazionale di Fisica Matematica — Quad Cons Naz Ricerche Gruppo Naz Fis Mat
Quaderni del Frutticoltore — Quad Fruttic
Quaderni del Giornale di Fisica [*Italy*] — Quad G Fis
Quaderni del Vittoriale — Q Vit
Quaderni della Coagulazione — Quad Coagulazione
Quaderni della Coagulazione e Argomenti Connessi — Quad Coagulazione Argomenti Connessi
Quaderni della Critica — Q Crit
Quaderni della Critica — QC
Quaderni della Nutrizione — Quad Nutr
Quaderni della Nutrizione (Bologna) — Quad Nutr (Bologna)
Quaderni della Rassegna Musicale — Q Rass Mus
Quaderni della Rassegna Musicale — Quaderni della Ra M
Quaderni dell'Economia (Sarda) — Quad Econ (Sarda)
Quaderni dell'Ingegnere Chimico Italiano — Ing Chim It
Quaderni dell'Ingegnere Chimico Italiano — Quad Ing Chim Ital
Quaderni dell'Istituto di Filologia Greca — Quad Ist Fil Gr
Quaderni dell'Umanesimo — QU
Quaderni dell'Unione Matematica Italiana — Quad Unione Mat Italiana
Quaderni di Acta Neurologica — Quad Acta Neurol
Quaderni di Anatomia Pratica — Quad Anat Prat
Quaderni di Archeologia della Libia — QAL
Quaderni di Archeologia della Libia — Quad A Libia
Quaderni di Archeologia della Libia — Quad Arch Libia
Quaderni di Archeologia Reggiana — QAR
Quaderni di Azione Sociale — Quad Azione Soc
Quaderni di Bilychnis — Q Bil
Quaderni di Chimica. Consiglio Nazionale delle Ricerche (Italy) — Quad Chim CNR (Italy)
Quaderni di Civilta Cinese — Civ C
Quaderni di Clinica Ostetrica e Ginecologica — Quad Clin Ostet
Quaderni di Criminologia Clinica — Quad Criminol Clin
Quaderni di Cultura Contemporanea — QCC
Quaderni di Cultura e Storia Sociale — QCSS
Quaderni di Filologia Classica — QFC
Quaderni di Filologia Germanica. Facolta di Lettere e Filosofia. Universita di Bologna — QFG
Quaderni di Fitoterapia — Quad Fitoter
Quaderni di Formazione — Quad Formaz
Quaderni di Geofisica Applicata — Quad Geofis Appl
Quaderni di Laboratorio di Spettrometria di Massa — Quad Lab Spettrom Massa
Quaderni di Lingue e Letterature — QLL
Quaderni di Merceologia — Quad Merceol
Quaderni di Merceologia. Istituto di Merceologia. Universita Bari — Quad Merceol Ist Merceol Univ Bari
Quaderni di Radiologia — QRADA
Quaderni di Radiologia — Quad Radiol
Quaderni di Ricerca e Progettazione — Quad Ric Progettazione
Quaderni di Roma — Quad Roma
Quaderni di Semantica — QSem
Quaderni di Semitistica [*Florence*] — QS
Quaderni di Sociologia — Quad Sociol
Quaderni di Storia — QdS
Quaderni di Storia — QS
Quaderni di Storia — Quad Stor
Quaderni di Storia and Critica della Scienza — Quad Storia Crit Sci
Quaderni di Storia della Scienza e della Medicina. Universita degli Studi di Ferrara — Quad Storia Sci Med Univ Studi Ferrara
Quaderni di Storia dell'Economia Politica — Quad Stor Econ Polit
Quaderni di Studi e Notizie. Societa Generale Italiana Edison de Elettricita — Quad Studi Not Soc Gen Ital Edison Elettr
Quaderni di Studi Etruschi — QSEt
Quaderni di Studi Etruschi. Richerche Peistoriche in Etruria — QSEtP
Quaderni di Studi Romani — Q St Ro
Quaderni di Tecniche e Sintesi Speciali Organiche — Quad Tec Sint Spec Org
Quaderni di Urologia — Quad Urol
Quaderni d'Italianistica — QI
Quaderni Emiliani — Quad Emiliani
Quaderni Esegetici — QE
Quaderni Ibero-Americani — QI
Quaderni Ibero-Americani — QIA
Quaderni Ibero-Americani — Quad Ibero Am
Quaderni. Istituto Botanico. Universita Laboratorio Crittogamico (Pavia) [*A publication*] — Quad Ist Bot Univ Lab Crittogam (Pavia)
Quaderni. Istituto di Filologia Latina. Universita di Padova — QIFL
Quaderni. Istituto di Glottologia [*Bologna*] — QIG
Quaderni. Istituto di Glottologia (Bologna) — QIGB
Quaderni. Istituto di Lingue e Litteratura Classiche — QILCL
Quaderni. Istituto di Ricerca sulle Acque — Quad Ist Ric Acque
Quaderni. Istituto di Ricerca sulle Acque. Appendice. Metodi Analitici per le Acque — Quad Ist Ric Acque Append Metodi Anal Acque
Quaderni. Istituto di Storia dell'Architettura — QISA
Quaderni. Istituto di Topografia Antica — Quad Ist Top
Quaderni. Istituto di Topografia Antica. Universita di Roma — Quad Top Ant
Quaderni Italiani di Buenos Aires — QIBA
Quaderni Italiani di Psichiatria — Quad Ital Psichiatr
Quaderni Linguistici — QL
Quaderni Modenesi — Quad Mod
Quaderni. Museo Archeologico F. Ribezzo di Brindisi — QMAB
Quaderni per la Storia. Universita di Padova — Quad Stor Univ Padova
Quaderni Pignone — Quad Pignone
Quaderni Portoghesi — QP
Quaderni Sardi di Economia — Quad Sardi Econ
Quaderni Scientifici Loescher — Quad Sci Loescher
Quaderni Sclavo di Diagnostica Clinica e di Laboratorio — Quad Sclavo Diagn
Quaderni Sclavo di Diagnostica Clinica e di Laboratorio — Quad Sclavo Diagn Clin Lab
Quaderni. Serie III — Quad Ser III
Quaderni. Sezione Perugina. Societa Italiana di Biologia Sperimentale — Quad Sez Perugina Soc Ital Biol Sper
Quaderni Storici — Quad Stor
Quaderni Ticinesi. Numismatica e Antichita Classiche — Num Ant Clas
Quaderni Ticinesi. Numismatica e Antichita Classiche — Q Tic Num Ant Clas
Quaderni Triestini per il Lessico della Lirica Corale Greca — QTLCG
Quaderni Triestini sul Teatro Antico — QTTA
Quaderni Urbinati di Cultura Classica — Quad Urb C
Quaderni Urbinati di Cultura Classica — Quad Urbin
Quaderni Urbinati di Cultura Classica — QUCC
Quaderno. Ente Nazionale Sementi Elette — Quad Ente Naz Semen Elette
Quaderno. Fondazione Politecnica per il Mezzogiorno d'Italia — Quad Fond Politec Mezzogiorno Ital
Quaderns d'Estadistica. Sistemes. Informatica i Investigacio Operativa — QUESTIIO
Quadrangle Report. Connecticut. State Geological and Natural History Survey — Quadrangle Rep Conn State Geol Nat Hist Surv
Quadrangle Series 1:50,000. Geological Survey of Japan — Quadrangle Ser 1:50000 Geol Surv Jap

Quadrennial Meeting. International Association for the Study of the Liver — Quadrenn Meet Int Assoc Study Liver
Quadrivium — Q
Quadrivium — Quad
Quaestiones Entomologicae — Quaest Ent
Quaestiones Entomologicae — Quaest Entomol
Quaestiones Geobiologicae — Quaest Geobiol
Quaestiones Informaticae — Quaest Inf
Quaestiones Mathematicae — Quaestiones Math
Quai d'Orsay Archives — QOA
Quaker History — QH
Quaker History — QuakerH
Qualitaet und Zuverlaessigkeit — Qual und Zuverlassigkeit
Qualitaet und Zuverlaessigkeit — Qual Zuverlaessigk
Qualitaet von Kernkraftwerken aus Amerikanischer und Deutscher Sicht. Internationale Tagung — Qual Kernkraftwerken Am Dtsch Sicht Int Tag
Qualitas Plantarum et Materiae Vegetabiles — Qual Pl Mater Veg
Qualitas Plantarum et Materiae Vegetabiles [*Later, Qualitas Plantarum/Plant Foods for Human Nutrition*] — Qual Plant Mater Veg
Qualitas Plantarum/Plant Foods for Human Nutrition — Qual Plant
Qualitas Plantarum/Plant Foods for Human Nutrition — Qual Plant Plant Foods Hum Nutr
Qualitas Plantarum/Plant Foods for Human Nutrition — Qualitas Pl Pl Fds Human Nutr
Qualite. Revue Pratique de Controle Industriel — Qual Rev Prat Controle Ind
Qualite. Revue Pratique de Controle Industriel — Qualite Rev Prat Controle Ind
Quality — QUA
Quality and Quantity — Qual Quant
Quality and Reliability Journal [*India*] — Qual Reliab J
Quality Assurance — Qual Assur
Quality Assurance — QUASD
Quality Circles Journal — QCJ
Quality Control and Applied Statistics — Qual Contr Appl Stat
Quality Control and Applied Statistics — Qual Control Appl Stat
Quality Control in Clinical Chemistry. Transactions. International Symposium — Qual Control Clin Chem Trans Int Symp
Quality Control in Remedial Site Investigation. Hazardous and Industrial Solid Waste Testing — Qual Control Rem Site Invest Hazard Ind Solid Waste Test
Quality Control of Medicines. Proceedings. International Congress of Pharmaceutical Sciences — Qual Control Med Proc Int Congr Pharm Sci
Quality Control Reports: the Gold Sheet — QCR
Quality Engineer — Qual Eng
Quality Evaluation — Qual Eval
Quality of Foods and Beverages. Chemistry and Technology. Proceedings. Symposium. International Flavor Conference — Qual Foods Beverages Chem Technol Proc Symp Int Flavor Conf
Quality of Groundwater. Proceedings. International Symposium — Qual Groundwater Proc Int Symp
Quality of Life Research — Qual Life Res
Quality of Poultry Meat. Proceedings. European Symposium on Poultry Meat Quality — Qual Poult Meat Proc Eur Symp
Quality of Sheffield and South Yorkshire — Quality
Quality of Worklife Database — QWLD
Quality Progress — QPR
Quality Progress — Qual Prog
Quality Progress — Quality Prog
Quality Publication. Malting Barley Improvement Association — Qual Publ Malting Barley Improv Assoc
Quality Review Bulletin — QRB
Quality Today — Qual Today
Quantas Empire Airways — Qantas
Quantitative Applications in the Social Sciences — Quantitative Appl in the Social Sciences
Quantitative Approaches to Drug Design — Quant Approaches Drug Des
Quantitative Aspects of Risk Assessment in Chemical Carcinogenesis. Symposium — Quant Aspects Risk Assess Chem Carcinog Symp
Quantitative Description of Metal Extraction Processes — Quant Descr Met Extr Processes
Quantitative Linguistics — QLing
Quantitative Mass Spectrometry in Life Sciences. Proceedings. International Symposium — Quant Mass Spectrom Life Sci
Quantitative Methoden der Unternehmungsplanung — Quantitative Meth Unternehmungsplanung
Quantitative Sociology — Quan Sociol
Quantitative Structure-Activity Relationships — QSAR
Quantitative Structure-Activity Relationships — Quant Struct Act Relat
Quantity Surveyor — Quantity Surv
Quantity Surveyor Weekly — QS Wkly
Quantum and Semiclassical Optics — Quantum Semiclass Optics
Quantum and Semiclassical Optics. Journal of the European Optical Society. Part B — Quantum Semiclassical Opt B
Quantum Biology Symposium. International Journal of Quantum Chemistry — Quantum Biol Symp Int J Quantum Chem
Quantum Chaos and Statistical Nuclear Physics. Proceedings — Quantum Chaos Stat Nucl Phys Proc
Quantum Chemistry Symposia — Quant Chem Symp
Quantum Chemistry Symposia — Quantum Chem Symp
Quantum Electronics — QE
Quantum Electronics and Electro-Optics. Proceedings. National Quantum Electronics Conference — Quantum Electron Electro Opt Proc Nat Quantum Electron Conf
Quantum Electronics and Plasma Physics. Italian Conference — Quantum Electron Plasma Phys Ital Conf
Quantum Electronics (New York) — Quantum Electron (New York)
Quantum Electronics. Proceedings. International Congress — Quantum Electron Proc Int Congr
Quantum Mechanics of Fundamental Systems — Quantum Mech Fundam Syst
Quantum Optics. Journal of the European Optical Society. Part B — Quantum Opt
Quantum Optics. Proceedings. International Symposium — Quantum Opt Proc Int Symp
Quantum Statistical Mechanics in the Natural Sciences — Quantum Stat Mech Nat Sci
Quantum Statistics and the Many-Body Problem. Proceedings. Symposium on Quantum Statistics and Many-Body Problems — Quantum Stat Many Body Probl Proc Symp
Quarber Merkur — QME
Quark-Gluon Structure of Hadrons and Nuclei. Proceedings. International Workshop — Quark Gluon Struct Hadrons Nucl Proc Int Workshop
Quarks and Nuclear Structure. Proceedings. Klaus Erkelenz Symposium — Quarks Nucl Struct Proc Klaus Erkelenz Symp
Quarks, Mesons, and Isobars in Nuclei. Proceedings. Topical School — Quarks Mesons Isobars Nucl Proc Top Sch
Quarries and Mines Other than Coal. Health and Safety — Quarries Mines Coal Health Saf
Quarry and Mining News — Quarry Min News
Quarry and Surveyors' Contractors' Journal — Quarry Aurv Contract J
Quarry Management — Quarry Mgmt
Quarry Management and Products [*Later, Quarry Management*] — QMGPA
Quarry Management and Products [*Later, Quarry Management*] — Quarry Manage Prod
Quarry Management and Products [*Later, Quarry Management*] — Quarry Mgmt Products
Quarry, Mine, and Pit — QMP
Quartalblaetter des Historischen Vereins fuer das Grossherzogtum Hessen — Hess Quart Bl
Quartalschrift [*Milwaukee, Wisconsin*] — Qschr
Quartalschrift fuer Katholische Geistliche — QKG
Quarter Horse Digest — Quarter Horse Dig
Quarterly. American Primrose Society — Quart Amer Primrose Soc
Quarterly. Art Institute of Chicago — QAIC
Quarterly Bibliography of Computers and Data Processing — Q Bibliogr Comput Data Process
Quarterly Bibliography of Computers and Data Processing — QBCDP
Quarterly Bibliography of Computers and Data Processing — QBib
Quarterly Bottling Supplement — Q Bottling Suppl
Quarterly Bulletin — Qu Bull
Quarterly Bulletin. Alpine Garden Society — Q Bull Alp Gdn Soc
Quarterly Bulletin. American Rhododendron Society — Q Bull Am Rhodod Soc
Quarterly Bulletin. American Rhododendron Society — Quart Bull Amer Rhododendron Soc
Quarterly Bulletin. Association of Food and Drug Officials — Q Bull Assoc Food Drug Off
Quarterly Bulletin. Association of Food and Drug Officials of the United States [*Later, Quarterly Bulletin. Association of Food and Drug Officials*] — Q Bull Assoc Food Drug Off US
Quarterly Bulletin. Association of Food and Drug Officials of the United States [*Later, Quarterly Bulletin. Association of Food and Drug Officials*] — Quart Bul Ass Food Drug Offic US
Quarterly Bulletin. Association of Food and Drug Officials (United States) — Q Bull Ass Fd Drug Off (US)
Quarterly Bulletin. Faculty of Science. Tehran University — Q Bull Fac Sci Tehran Univ
Quarterly Bulletin. Faculty of Science. Tehran University — TUSQA
Quarterly Bulletin. Faculty of Science. University of Tehran — Q Bull Fac Sci Univ Tehran
Quarterly Bulletin. Geo-Heat Utilization Center [*United States*] — Q Bull Geo-Heat Util Cent
Quarterly Bulletin. Health Organisation. League of Nations — Q Bull Health Organ League Nations
Quarterly Bulletin. Indiana University. Medical Center — Q Bull Indiana Univ Med Cent
Quarterly Bulletin. International Association of Agricultural Librarians and Documentalists — Q Bull IAALD
Quarterly Bulletin. International Association of Agricultural Librarians and Documentalists — Q Bull Int Ass Agric Libr
Quarterly Bulletin. International Association of Agricultural Librarians and Documentalists — Q Bull Int Assoc Agric Libr & Doc
Quarterly Bulletin. International Association of Agricultural Librarians and Documentalists — Quart Bull Int Ass Agric Libr Docum
Quarterly Bulletin. International Association of Agricultural Librarians and Documentalists/Bulletin Trimestriel (Association Internationale des Bibliothecaires et Documentalistes Agricoles) — Q Bull Int Assoc Agric Libr Doc Bull Trimest Assoc Int Bibl
Quarterly Bulletin. Michigan State University. Agricultural Experiment Station — Q Bull Mich St Univ Agric Exp Stn
Quarterly Bulletin. Michigan State University. Agricultural Experiment Station — Quart Bull Mich Agric Exp Sta
Quarterly Bulletin. Michigan State University. Agricultural Experiment Station — Quart Bull Mich State Univ Agr Exp Sta
Quarterly Bulletin. Monetary Authority of Singapore — Q Bull Mon Auth Sing
Quarterly Bulletin. National Chrysanthemum Society — Quart Bull Natl Chrysanthemum Soc
Quarterly Bulletin. National Research Council of Canada. Division of Mechanical Engineering — Q Bull Natl Res Counc Can Div Mech Eng
Quarterly Bulletin. Northwestern University. Medical School — Q Bull Northwest Univ Med Sch
Quarterly Bulletin. Northwestern University. Medical School — Q Bull NWest Univ Med Sch

Quarterly Bulletin. Northwestern University Medical School — Quart Bull Northwestern Univ M School
Quarterly Bulletin of Chinese Bibliography — QBCB
Quarterly Bulletin of Science Education. K'o Hsueeh Chiao Hsueeh Chi K'an. Szechuan Provincial Science Education Institute — Quart Bull Sci Educ
Quarterly Bulletin of Statistics for Asia and the Pacific — Asia Pac Q
Quarterly Bulletin of Statistics for Asia and the Pacific — Quart Bull Stat Asia Pac
Quarterly Bulletin of Steel Statistics for Europe — Steel Stat Q
Quarterly Bulletin of the South African Library — QBSAL
Quarterly Bulletin. Sea View Hospital — Q Bull Sea View Hosp
Quarterly Bulletin. South African Library — Q Bull S Afr Libr
Quarterly Bulletin. South African Library — QuaB
Quarterly Bulletin. South African National Gallery — Q Bull S Afr Natl Gall
Quarterly. Charleston Museum — Quart Charleston Mus
Quarterly Check-List of Biblical Studies — QCBS
Quarterly Check-List of Biblical Studies — QCLBS
Quarterly Checklist of Classical Studies — QCLCS
Quarterly Checklist of Medievalia — QCLM
Quarterly Check-List of Renaissance Studies — QCLRS
Quarterly. Chicago Medical School — Q Chicago Med Sch
Quarterly Circular. Rubber Research Institute of Ceylon — Q Circ Rubber Res Inst Ceylon
Quarterly Coal Report — Q Coal Rpt
Quarterly. Colorado School of Mines — Q Colo Sch Mines
Quarterly. Colorado School of Mines — Q Colorado Sch Mines
Quarterly. Colorado School of Mines — QCSMA
Quarterly. Colorado School of Mines — Quart Colo Sch Mines
Quarterly Cumulative Index Medicus — Q Cum Index Med
Quarterly Dental Review — Q Dent Rev
Quarterly. Department of Antiquities in Palestine — DAP
Quarterly. Department of Antiquities in Palestine [*Jerusalem*] — QDA
Quarterly. Department of Antiquities in Palestine — QDA Pal
Quarterly. Department of Antiquities in Palestine [*Jerusalem*] — QDAP
Quarterly. Department of Antiquities in Palestine — Qu Ant Pal
Quarterly. Department of Antiquities of Jordan — QDAJ
Quarterly Economic Commentary — Q Econ Comment
Quarterly Economic Review [*Seoul*] — Q Econ R
Quarterly Economic Review — QER
Quarterly Economic Review of Algeria — Q Econ Rev Algeria
Quarterly Economic Review of Chile — Q Econ Rev Chile
Quarterly Economic Review of Egypt — Q Econ Rev Egypt
Quarterly Economic Review of Iran — Q Econ Rev Iran
Quarterly Economic Review of the United Kingdom — Q Economic Rev of UK
Quarterly Economic Review of Yugoslavia — Q Econ Rev Yugoslavia
Quarterly Economic Review. Oil in Western Europe — Q Econ Rev Oil West Eur
Quarterly Energy Review. Africa — Quart En Rev Afr
Quarterly Energy Review. Far East and Australia — Quart En Rev Aust
Quarterly Energy Review. Middle East — Quart En Rev Mid East
Quarterly Energy Review. North America — Quart En Rev NA
Quarterly Energy Review. Western Europe — Quart En Rev West Eur
Quarterly English Journal. Technical Association of Refractories. Japan — Q Engl J Tech Assoc Refract Jpn
Quarterly Financial Report [*Database*] — QFR
Quarterly Financial Report for Manufacturing, Mining, and Trade Companies [*Information service or system*] — QFR
Quarterly Fuel and Energy Summary [*United States*] — Q Fuel Energy Summ
Quarterly Geological Notes [*Australia*] — Q Geol Notes
Quarterly Illustrator — Q Illust
Quarterly Index — QI
Quarterly. Israel Institute of Metals — Q Isr Inst Metals
Quarterly Jewish Review — QJewR
Quarterly Journal. Chemical Society. London — Q J Chem Soc London
Quarterly Journal. Department of Antiquities in Palestine — QDAP
Quarterly Journal. Florida Academy of Sciences — Q J Fla Acad Sci
Quarterly Journal. Geological, Mining, and Metallurgical Society (India) — Q J Geol Min Metall Soc (India)
Quarterly Journal. Geological Society — Q J Geol Soc
Quarterly Journal. Geological Society — QJGS
Quarterly Journal. Geological Society of London — Q J Geol Soc Lond
Quarterly Journal. Geological Society of London — Q J Geol Soc London
Quarterly Journal. Illinois State Agricultural Society — Quart J Illinois State Agric Soc
Quarterly Journal. Indian Chemical Society — Q J Indian Chem Soc
Quarterly Journal. Indian Institute of Science — Q J Indian Inst Sci
Quarterly Journal. Indian Institute of Science — Quart J Indian Inst Sci
Quarterly Journal. Indian Teas Association. Scientific Department — Quart J Indian Tea Assoc Sci Dept
Quarterly Journal. Indonesian Atomic Energy Agency — Q J Indones At Energy Agency
Quarterly Journal. Japan Welding Society — Q J Jpn Weld Soc
Quarterly Journal. Library of Congress — Q J Lib Con
Quarterly Journal. Library of Congress — QJ
Quarterly Journal. Library of Congress — QJLC
Quarterly Journal. Library of Congress — Quart J Libr Congress
Quarterly Journal. Liverpool University Institute of Commercial Research in the Tropics — Q J Liverpool Univer Inst Commer Res Trop
Quarterly Journal. Local Self-Government Institute [*Bombay*] — Q J Local Self Govt Inst
Quarterly Journal. Local Self-Government Institute [*Bombay*] — QJLSGI
Quarterly Journal. Local Self-Government Institute [*Bombay*] — QJLSI
Quarterly Journal. Meteorological Society — QJMS
Quarterly Journal. Microscopical Society of Victoria — Quart J Microscop Soc Victoria
Quarterly Journal. Mythic Society — QJMS
Quarterly Journal. Mythic Society [*Bangalore*] — QMS
Quarterly Journal of Administration — QJ Adm
Quarterly Journal of Administration — Quart J Adm
Quarterly Journal of Agricultural Economy — QJ Agric Econ
Quarterly Journal of Agricultural Economy — Quart J Agr Econ
Quarterly Journal of Business and Economics — QJBE
Quarterly Journal of Chinese Forestry (Taipei) — Quart J Chin For (Taipei)
Quarterly Journal of Comparative Legislation — Q J Comp Legis
Quarterly Journal of Crude Drug Research — Q J Crude Drug Res
Quarterly Journal of Crude Drug Research — Quart J Crude Drug Res
Quarterly Journal of Current Acquisitions — QJCA
Quarterly Journal of Current Acquisitions. Library of Congress — Quart J Curr Acquisitions
Quarterly Journal of Current Acquisitions. Library of Congress (Washington, DC) — Quart Jour Cur Acq Wash
Quarterly Journal of Economics — Q J Econ
Quarterly Journal of Economics — QJE
Quarterly Journal of Economics — Quar Jour Econ
Quarterly Journal of Economics — Quart J Econ
Quarterly Journal of Economics — Quart J Econom
Quarterly Journal of Economics — Quartl Journ Econ
Quarterly Journal of Engineering Geology — QJ Eng Geol
Quarterly Journal of Experimental Physiology — Quart J Exp Physiol
Quarterly Journal of Experimental Physiology and Cognate Medical Sciences — Q J Exp Physiol
Quarterly Journal of Experimental Physiology and Cognate Medical Sciences — Q J Exp Physiol Cogn Med Sci
Quarterly Journal of Experimental Psychology — Q J Exp Psy
Quarterly Journal of Experimental Psychology — Q J Exp Psychol
Quarterly Journal of Experimental Psychology — QJEPs
Quarterly Journal of Experimental Psychology — QJXPA
Quarterly Journal of Experimental Psychology — Quart J Exp Psychol
Quarterly Journal of Experimental Psychology. A. Human Experimental Psychology — QJ Exp Psychol A
Quarterly Journal of Experimental Psychology. A. Human Experimental Psychology — QJ Exp Psychol A Hum Exp Psychol
Quarterly Journal of Experimental Psychology. B. Comparative and Physiological Psychology — Q J Exp Psychol B
Quarterly Journal of Experimental Psychology. B. Comparative and Physiological Psychology — QJ Exp Psychol B Comp Physiol Psychol
Quarterly Journal of Forestry — Q J For
Quarterly Journal of Forestry — Q J Forestry
Quarterly Journal of Forestry — Qtr J Forestry
Quarterly Journal of Forestry — Quart J For
Quarterly Journal of Forestry — Quart J Forest
Quarterly Journal of International Agriculture — QJ Int Agric
Quarterly Journal of Literature, Science, and the Arts — Q J Lit Sci Arts
Quarterly Journal of Mathematics — Q J Math
Quarterly Journal of Mathematics. Oxford. Second Series — Quart J Math Oxford Ser 2
Quarterly Journal of Mechanics and Applied Mathematics — Q J Mech Ap
Quarterly Journal of Mechanics and Applied Mathematics — QJ Mech and Appl Math
Quarterly Journal of Mechanics and Applied Mathematics — QJ Mech Appl Math
Quarterly Journal of Mechanics and Applied Mathematics — Quart J Mech Appl Math
Quarterly Journal of Mechanics and Applied Mathematics — Quart J Mech Appld Math
Quarterly Journal of Medicine — Q J Med
Quarterly Journal of Medicine — Quart J Med
Quarterly Journal of Microscopical Science — Q J Micro Sc
Quarterly Journal of Microscopical Science — Q J Microsc Sci
Quarterly Journal of Microscopical Science — Q Jl Microsc Sci
Quarterly Journal of Microscopical Science — Quart J Micr Sc
Quarterly Journal of Microscopical Science — Quart J Microsc Sci
Quarterly Journal of Music Teaching — Quarterly J of Mus Teaching
Quarterly Journal of Nuclear Medicine — QJ Nucl Med
Quarterly Journal of Pharmacy and Allied Sciences — QJ Pharm Allied Sci
Quarterly Journal of Pharmacy and Pharmacology — Q J Pharm Pharmacol
Quarterly Journal of Political and Social Science — QJPSS
Quarterly Journal of Psychological Medicine — Q J Psychol Med
Quarterly Journal of Public Speaking — Q J Pub Speak
Quarterly Journal of Science — Q J Sc
Quarterly Journal of Science and the Arts — Q J Sci Arts
Quarterly Journal of Science, Literature, and the Arts — Q J Sc
Quarterly Journal of Science, Literature, and the Arts — QJ Sci Lit Arts
Quarterly Journal of Science, Literature, and the Arts — Quart J Sci Lit Arts
Quarterly Journal of Seismology — QJ Seismol
Quarterly Journal of Social Affairs — Quart J Soc Aff
Quarterly Journal of Speech — GQJS
Quarterly Journal of Speech — Q J Speech
Quarterly Journal of Speech — Q Jnl Speech
Quarterly Journal of Speech — QJS
Quarterly Journal of Speech — QJSp
Quarterly Journal of Speech — QJSPA
Quarterly Journal of Speech — QuaJ
Quarterly Journal of Studies on Alcohol — Q J Stud Al
Quarterly Journal of Studies on Alcohol — Q J Stud Alcohol
Quarterly Journal of Studies on Alcohol. Part A — Q J Stud Alcohol Part A
Quarterly Journal of Studies on Alcohol. Supplement — QJ Stud Alcohol Suppl
Quarterly Journal of Surgical Sciences — QJ Surg Sci
Quarterly Journal of the History of Science and Technology — Q J Hist Sci Technol

Quarterly Journal of Veterinary Science in India and Army Animal Management — Quart J Vet Sc India
Quarterly Journal. Pakistan Library Association [*Karachi*] — Q J Pakistan Lib Assn
Quarterly Journal. Royal Astronomical Society — Q J R Astro
Quarterly Journal. Royal Astronomical Society — QJR Astron Soc
Quarterly Journal. Royal Astronomical Society — QJRAA
Quarterly Journal. Royal Astronomical Society — Quart J Roy Astron Soc
Quarterly Journal. Royal Meteorological Society — Q J R Meteo
Quarterly Journal. Royal Meteorological Society — Q J R Meteorol Soc
Quarterly Journal. Royal Meteorological Society — Q Jl R Met Soc
Quarterly Journal. Royal Meteorological Society — QJR Met Soc
Quarterly Journal. Royal Meteorological Society — QJRMA
Quarterly Journal. Royal Meteorological Society — Quart J Roy Meteorol Soc
Quarterly Journal. Royal Netherlands Society for Agricultural Science — Q J R Neth Soc Agric Sci
Quarterly Journal. Rubber Research Institute of Ceylon — Q J Rubber Res Inst Ceylon
Quarterly Journal. Rubber Research Institute of Ceylon [*later, Sri Lanka*] — Q Jl Rubb Res Inst Ceylon
Quarterly Journal. Rubber Research Institute of Sri Lanka [*formerly, Ceylon*] [*A publication*] — Q J Rubber Res Inst Sri Lanka
Quarterly Journal. Taiwan Museum — Quart J Taiwan Mus
Quarterly Journal. Taiwan Museum (Taipei) — Q J Taiwan Mus (Taipei)
Quarterly Journal. University of North Dakota — QJ
Quarterly Medical Review — Q Med Rev
Quarterly National Accounts Bulletin — Q Nat Acc Bull
Quarterly. National Dental Association [*US*] — Q Natl Dent Assoc
Quarterly. National Dental Association — Quart Nat Dent Ass
Quarterly. National Fire Protection Association — Q Natl Fire Prot Assoc
Quarterly. Nebraska Agricultural Experiment Station — Quart Nebr Agr Exp Sta
Quarterly News Bulletin. Geological Society of South Africa — Q News Bull Geol Soc S Afr
Quarterly News Letter [*Book Club of California*] — QNL
Quarterly News Letter. Forest Research Institute and Colleges (Dehra Dun) — Quart Newsl (Dehra Dun)
Quarterly Newsletter. Rhodesia Nurses Association — Q Newsl Rhod Nurses Assoc
Quarterly Notes on Christianity and Chinese Religion — QNCCR
Quarterly of Applied Mathematics — Q Ap Math
Quarterly of Applied Mathematics — Q App Math
Quarterly of Applied Mathematics — Q Appl Math
Quarterly of Applied Mathematics — QAMAA
Quarterly of Applied Mathematics — Quart Appl Math
Quarterly of Applied Mathematics — Quarterly Appl Math
Quarterly of Canadian Studies — Q Can Studies
Quarterly of Film, Radio, and Television — Q Film Radio TV
Quarterly of Film, Radio, and Television — QFRT
Quarterly of Film, Radio, and Television — Quarterly of F R TV
Quarterly of Jewish Studies. Jewish Chronicle — QJewSt
Quarterly of Magnetic Resonance in Biology and Medicine — Q Magn Reson Biol Med
Quarterly Oil Statistics [*France*] — Q Oil Stat
Quarterly Pediatric Bulletin — Q Pediatr Bull
Quarterly. Philippine Sugar Institute — Q Philipp Sugar Inst
Quarterly. Philippine Sugar Institute — Quart Philippine Sugar Inst
Quarterly Population Bulletin (New Zealand) — Q Population Bul NZ
Quarterly Poultry Bulletin — Q Poul Bull
Quarterly Poultry Bulletin — Q Poult Bull
Quarterly Predictions of National Income and Expenditure [*New Zealand*] — Q Predict
Quarterly Publications. American Statistical Association — Q Publ Am Stat Assoc
Quarterly Record. Royal Botanical Society of London — Quart Rec Roy Bot Soc London
Quarterly Register. Organ. Alliance of Reformed Churches — RARC
Quarterly Report — Quart Rep
Quarterly Report. Railway Technical Research Institute — QRTIA
Quarterly Report. Railway Technical Research Institute [*Tokyo*] — Quart Rep Ry Tech Res Inst
Quarterly Report. Railway Technical Research Institute (Tokyo) — Q Rep Railw Tech Res Inst (Tokyo)
Quarterly Report. University of the West Indies. School of Agriculture — Q Rep Univ W Indies Sch Agric
Quarterly Reports on Sulfur Chemistry — Q Rep Sulfur Chem
Quarterly Research Report. Southeast Asian Fisheries Development Center. Aquaculture Department — Q Res Rep Southeast Asian Fish Dev Cent Aquacult Dep
Quarterly Review — Q Rev
Quarterly Review — QR
Quarterly Review — Quar
Quarterly Review — QuaR
Quarterly Review — Quar Rev
Quarterly Review [*Manila*] — QuaRe
Quarterly Review — Quart
Quarterly Review — Quart R
Quarterly Review — Quart Rev
Quarterly Review. American Electroplaters' Society — Q Rev Am Electroplat Soc
Quarterly Review. Central Bank of Ireland — Quart R Centr Bank Ireland
Quarterly Review. District of Columbia Nurses Association — Q Rev DC Nurses Assoc
Quarterly Review. Drilling Statistics for the United States — Q Rev Drill Stat US
Quarterly Review. Evangelical Lutheran Church — Q Rev Evan Luth Ch
Quarterly Review. Evangelical Lutheran Church — RELC
Quarterly Review. Guernsey Society — Quart Rev Guernsey Soc
Quarterly Review NAAS [*National Agriculture Advisory Service, London*] — Q Rev NAAS
Quarterly Review of Agricultural Economics — Q R Agric Econ
Quarterly Review of Agricultural Economics — Q Rev Ag Economics
Quarterly Review of Agricultural Economics — Q Rev Agric Econ
Quarterly Review of Agricultural Economics — QR Ag Econ
Quarterly Review of Agricultural Economics — Quart R Agric
Quarterly Review of Agricultural Economics — Quart R Agric Econ
Quarterly Review of Agricultural Economics — Quart Rev Agr Econ
Quarterly Review of Agricultural Economics — Quart Rev Agric Econ
Quarterly Review of Allergy and Applied Immunology — Q Rev Allergy Appl Immunol
Quarterly Review of Allergy and Applied Immunology — Quart Rev Allergy
Quarterly Review of Australian Education — Q Rev Aust Ed
Quarterly Review of Australian Education — QR Aust Educ
Quarterly Review of Biology — PQRB
Quarterly Review of Biology — Q R Biol
Quarterly Review of Biology — Q Rev Biol
Quarterly Review of Biology — QRB
Quarterly Review of Biology — QRBIA
Quarterly Review of Biology — Quar R Biol
Quarterly Review of Biology — Quart Rev Biol
Quarterly Review of Biophysics — Q R Biophys
Quarterly Review of Economics and Business — EAB
Quarterly Review of Economics and Business — ECB
Quarterly Review of Economics and Business — Q R Econ & Bus
Quarterly Review of Economics and Business — Q R Econ Bu
Quarterly Review of Economics and Business — Q Rev Econ Bus
Quarterly Review of Economics and Business — QRE
Quarterly Review of Economics and Business — QREB
Quarterly Review of Economics and Business — QREBA
Quarterly Review of Economics and Business — Quart R Econ Busin
Quarterly Review of Film and Video — PQRF
Quarterly Review of Film Studies — Q R Film S
Quarterly Review of Film Studies — Q Rev F Studies
Quarterly Review of Film Studies — Q Rev Film
Quarterly Review of Film Studies — Q Review of F Studies
Quarterly Review of Higher Education among Negroes — Q R Higher Ed Among Negroes
Quarterly Review of Higher Education among Negroes — QR Higher Ed Negroes
Quarterly Review of Historical Studies — Q R Hist Stud
Quarterly Review of Historical Studies — Q Rev Hist S
Quarterly Review of Historical Studies — QRHS
Quarterly Review of Historical Studies — QuaRH
Quarterly Review of Internal Medicine and Dermatology — Q Rev Intern Med Dermatol
Quarterly Review of Literature — IQRL
Quarterly Review of Literature — Q Rev Lit
Quarterly Review of Literature — QR of Lit
Quarterly Review of Literature — QRL
Quarterly Review of Marketing — QRM
Quarterly Review of Medicine — Q Rev Med
Quarterly Review of Obstetrics and Gynecology — Q Rev Obstet Gynecol
Quarterly Review of Pediatrics — Q Rev Pediatr
Quarterly Review of Surgery — Q Rev Surg
Quarterly Review of Surgery and Surgical Specialities — Q Rev Surg Surg Spec
Quarterly Review of Surgery. Obstetrics and Gynecology — Q Rev Surg Obstet Gynecol
Quarterly Review of the Harefuah — Q Rev Harefuah
Quarterly Review of the Rural Economy — Q R Rural Economy
Quarterly Review of Urology — Q Rev Urol
Quarterly Review of Urology — QRU
Quarterly Review on Environment [*Japan*] — Q Rev Environ
Quarterly Review (Seattle) — (Seattle) Q
Quarterly Review. The Soil Association — Q Rev Soil Assoc
Quarterly Reviews. Chemical Society — Q Rev Chem Soc
Quarterly Reviews. Chemical Society — Quart R
Quarterly Reviews. Chemical Society — Quart Rev
Quarterly Reviews. Chemical Society — Quart Rev Chem Soc
Quarterly Reviews. Chemical Society — Quart Revs
Quarterly Reviews. Chemical Society — QUREA
Quarterly Reviews. Chemical Society (London) — Q Rev Chem Soc (Lond)
Quarterly Reviews of Biophysics — Q Rev Bioph
Quarterly Reviews of Biophysics — Q Rev Biophys
Quarterly Reviews of Biophysics — QURBA
Quarterly Reviews on Drug Metabolism and Drug Interactions — Q Rev Drug Metab Drug Interact
Quarterly Statement — QST
Quarterly Statement. Palestine Exploration Fund — Quartl Statement Palest Expl Fund
Quarterly Statements. Palestine Exploration Fund — QST
Quarterly Summary and Meteorological Readings. Royal Botanic Society of London — Quart Summary Meteorol Readings Roy Bot Soc London
Quarterly Supplement. Board of Trade Journal — Quart Suppl Board Trade J
Quarterly Transactions. American Institute of Electrical Engineers — Q Trans Am Inst Electr Eng
Quarterly Transactions. Royal Institution of Naval Architects [*London*] — Trans R Instn Naval Archit
Quarterly Transactions. Society of Automotive Engineers — Quart Trans Soc Autom Eng
Quarterly. University of Nebraska. College of Agriculture and Home Economics. Agricultural Experiment Station — Quart Univ Nebr Coll Agr Home Econ Agr Exp Sta
Quarterly West — Q W

Quartermaster Food and Container Institute for the Armed Forces. Activities Report — Quartermaster Food Container Inst Armed Forces Act Rep
Quartet — Qt
Quatember [*Kassel*] — Quat
Quaternary Geology and Environment of China — Quat Geol Environ China
Quaternary Research — QR
Quaternary Research [*New York*] — QRESA
Quaternary Research — Quatern Res
Quaternary Research — Quaternary Res
Quaternary Research (Japan Association of Quaternary Research) — Quat Res (Jap Assoc Quat Res)
Quaternary Research (New York) — Quat Res (NY)
Quaternary Research (Tokyo) — Quat Res (Tokyo)
Quaternary Science Reviews — Quat Sci R
Quaternary Science Reviews — Quat Sci Rev
Quatro Ventos — QV
Que Sais Je — QSJ
Que Sais-je. Le Point des Connaissances Humaines — Que Sais Je
Quebec Appeal Cases [*Database*] — QAC
Quebec. Conseil de la Recherche et du Developpement Forestiers. Rapport — Que Cons Rech Dev For Rapp
Quebec. Conseil de la Recherche et du Developpement Forestiers. Rapport Annuel — Que Cons Rech Dev For Rapp Annu
Quebec. Department of Colonization, Mines, and Fisheries. Mines Branch. Report on Mining Operations — Que Dp Col Mines Br Rp
Quebec. Department of Industry and Commerce. Annual Report — Que Dep Ind Commer Annu Rep
Quebec. Department of Lands and Forest Research Service. Research Paper — Que Dep Lands For Res Serv Res Pap
Quebec. Department of Natural Resources. Geological Report — Que Dep Natur Resour Geol Rep
Quebec. Department of Natural Resources. Preliminary Report — Que Dep Natur Resour Prelim Rep
Quebec. Department of Natural Resources. Preliminary Report — Quebec Dept Nat Resources Prelim Rept
Quebec. Department of Natural Resources. Special Paper — Quebec Dept Nat Resources Spec Paper
Quebec. Department of Trade and Commerce. Geographical Service. Publication [*A publication*] — Quebec Dept Trade and Commerce Geog Service Pub
Quebec. Direction de la Geologie. Travaux sur le Terrain — Que Dir Geol Trav Terrain
Quebec Historical Society. Transactions — Quebec Hist Soc Trans
Quebec Laitier — Qu Lait
Quebec. Litteraire — QLit
Quebec. Ministere de la Chasse et des Pecheries. Contributions — Que Minist Chasse Pech Contrib
Quebec. Ministere de l'Agriculture, des Pecheries, et de l'Alimentation. Direction de la Recherche Scientifique et Technique. Cahier d'Information — Que Minist Agric Pech Aliment Dir Rech Sci Tech Cah Inf
Quebec. Ministere de l'Agriculture, des Pecheries, et de l'Alimentation. Direction General des Peches Maritimes. Cahier d'Information — Que Minist Agric Pech Aliment Dir Gen Pech Marit Cah Inf
Quebec. Ministere de l'Energie et des Ressources. Etude Speciale ES — Que Minist Energ Ressour Etude Spec ES
Quebec. Ministere de l'Energie et des Ressources. Rapport Geologique — Que Minist Energ Ressour Rapp Geol
Quebec. Ministere de l'Energie et des Ressources. Service de la Recherche Forestiere. Memoire — Que Minist Energ Ressour Serv Rech For Mem
Quebec. Ministere de l'Energie et des Ressources. Service de la Recherche Forestiere. Note — Que Minist Energ Ressour Serv Rech For Note
Quebec. Ministere de l'Energie et des Ressources. Service de la Recherche. Memoire — Que Minist Energ Ressour Serv Rech Mem
Quebec. Ministere de l'Industrie et du Commerce. Direction de la Recherches Cahiers d'Information — Que Minist Ind Commer Dir Rech Cah Inf
Quebec. Ministere de l'Industrie et du Commerce. Rapport sur les Pecheries — Que Minist Ind Commer Rapp Pech
Quebec. Ministere de l'Industrie et du Commerce. Service de Biologie. Rapport Annuel — Que Minist Ind Commer Serv Biol Rapp Annu
Quebec. Ministere de l'Industrie et du Commerce. Service de la Recherche. Cahiers d'Information — Qu Minist Ind Commer Serv Rech Cah Inf
Quebec. Ministere des Richesses Naturelles. Etude Speciale — Que Minist Richesses Nat Etude Spec
Quebec. Ministere des Richesses Naturelles. Etude Speciale ES — Que Minist Richesses Nat Etude Spec ES
Quebec. Ministere des Terres et Forets. Service de la Recherche. Memoire — Qu Minist Terres For Serv Rech Mem
Quebec. Ministere des Terres et Forets. Service de la Recherche. Memoire — Que Minist Terres For Serv Rech Mem
Quebec. Ministere des Terres et Forets. Service de la Recherche. Note — Qu Minist Terres For Serv Rech Note
Quebec. Ministere des Terres et Forets. Service de la Recherche. Note — Que Minist Terres For Serv Rech Note
Quebec (Province). Bureau of Mines. Preliminary Report — Que (Prov) Bur Mines Prelim Rep
Quebec (Province). Department of Mines. General Report. Minister of Mines — Qu (Prov) Dep Mines Gen Rep Minist Mines
Quebec (Province). Department of Mines. General Report of the Minister of Mines — Que (Prov) Dep Mines Gen Rep Minist Mines
Quebec (Province). Department of Mines. Preliminary Report — Qu (Prov) Dep Mines Prelim Rep
Quebec (Province). Department of Mines. Preliminary Report — Que Prov Dep Mines Prelim Rep
Quebec (Province). Department of Natural Resources. Geological Report — Que Prov Dep Nat Resour Geol Rep
Quebec (Province). Department of Natural Resources. Preliminary Report — Que (Prov) Dep Nat Resour Prelim Rep
Quebec (Province). Department of Natural Resources. Special Paper — Qu (Prov) Dep Nat Resour Spec Pap
Quebec (Province). Ministere des Richesses Naturelles. Rapport Geologique — Que Prov Minist Richesses Nat Rapp Geol
Quebec (Province). Ministere des Richesses Naturelles. Rapport Preliminaire — Que (Prov) Minist Richesses Nat Rapp Prelim
Quebec Science — Que Sci
Quebec. Service de la Faune. Bulletin — Qu Serv Faune Bull
Quebec. Service de la Faune. Bulletin — Que Serv Faune Bull
Quebec. Service de la Faune. Rapport — Qu Serv Faune Rapp
Quebec. Service de la Faune. Rapport — Que Serv Faune Rapp
Quebec Society for the Protection of Plants. Report — Que Soc Prot Plants Rep
Quebec [*City*]. Universite Laval. Faculte de Droit. Cahiers de Droit — Cahiers Droit
Queen's Law Journal — Q LJ
Queen's Law Journal — Queen's L J
Queen's Nursing Journal — Queen's Nurs J
Queen's Papers in Pure and Applied Mathematics — Queen's Papers in Pure and Appl Math
Queen's Quarterly — Q
Queen's Quarterly — QQ
Queen's Quarterly — Queen Q
Queen's Quarterly — Queen's Q
Queen's Quarterly — Queen's Quart
Queen's Quarterly — QueQ
Queen's Quarterly — QuQu
Queen's University. Thermal and Fluid Science Group. Report — Queens Univ Therm Fluid Sci Group Rep
Queensland Agricultural Journal — Q Ag J
Queensland Agricultural Journal — Qd Ag J
Queensland Agricultural Journal — Qd Agric J
Queensland Agricultural Journal — Queensl Agric J
Queensland Agricultural Journal — Queensland Ag J
Queensland Agricultural Journal — Queensland Agr J
Queensland Bar News — Q Bar News
Queensland Botanical Bulletin — Queensland Bot Bull
Queensland Building Yearbook — Q Building Yrbk
Queensland. Bureau of Sugar Experiment Stations. Technical Communication — Bur Sug Exp Sta Tech Commun
Queensland. Bureau of Sugar Experiment Stations. Technical Communication — Bur Sug Exp Stat Tech Commun
Queensland. Bureau of Sugar Experiment Stations. Technical Communication — Qd Bur Sug Exp Stat Tech Commun
Queensland. Bureau of Sugar Experiment Stations. Technical Communication — Qd Bur Sug Exp Stn Tech Commun
Queensland Chamber of Manufacturers. Yearbook — Qd Chamber Manufacturers Yb
Queensland Conveyancing Library — QCL
Queensland Co-Operator — Q Coop
Queensland Countrywoman — Q Countrywoman
Queensland Criminal Reports — QCR
Queensland Crown Lands Law Reports — QCLLR
Queensland Dental Journal — Qd Dent J
Queensland Dental Journal — Queensl Dent J
Queensland Dental Magazine — Qd Dent Mag
Queensland Dental Magazine — Queensland Dent Mag
Queensland. Department of Agriculture and Stock. Annual Report — Queensl Dep Agric Stock
Queensland Department of Agriculture and Stock. Division of Plant Industry. Bulletin — Queensland Dept Agric Div Pl Industr Bull
Queensland. Department of Forestry. Advisory Leaflet — Qd For Dep Adv Leafl
Queensland. Department of Forestry. Pamphlet — Qd For Dep Pamph
Queensland. Department of Forestry. Research Note — QFRNAV
Queensland. Department of Forestry. Research Paper — RPDQDK
Queensland Department of Harbours and Marine. Fisheries Notes — Dep Harbours Mar Queensl Fish Notes
Queensland. Department of Harbours and Marine. Fisheries Notes — Fish Notes
Queensland. Department of Harbours and Marine. Fisheries Notes — QFINBL
Queensland. Department of Mines. Geological Survey of Queensland. Publication — Queensl Dep Mines Geol Surv Queensl Publ
Queensland. Department of Mines. Geological Survey of Queensland. Report — Queensl Dep Mines Geol Surv Queensl Rep
Queensland. Department of Primary Industries. Agricultural Chemistry Branch. Technical Report — Queensl Dep Primary Ind Agric Chem Branch Tech Rep
Queensland. Department of Primary Industries. Division of Animal Industry. Bulletin — Queensl Dep Primary Ind Div Anim Ind Bull
Queensland. Department of Primary Industries. Division of Dairying. Bulletin — Queensl Dep Primary Ind Div Dairy Bull
Queensland. Department of Primary Industries. Division of Plant Industry. Bulletin — Queensl Dep Primary Ind Div Plant Ind Bull
Queensland. Department of Primary Industries. Information Series — Queensl Dep Primary Ind Inf Ser
Queensland. Department of Public Lands. Bureau of Investigation. Technical Bulletin — Qd Bur Invest Tech Bull
Queensland Digger — Q Digger
Queensland Electrical Contractor — Q Elec Contractor
Queensland. Fisheries Service. Research Bulletin — Queensl Fish Serv Res Bull
Queensland. Fisheries Service. Technical Report — Queensl Fish Serv Tech Rep
Queensland Forest Bulletin — Qd Forest Bull
Queensland Fruit and Vegetable News — Q Fruit & Veg News
Queensland Geographical Journal — Q Geog J
Queensland Geographical Journal — Qd Geogr J

Queensland Geographical Journal — Qld Geog J
Queensland Geographical Journal — Queensl Geogr J
Queensland. Geological Survey. 1:250,000 Geological Series — Qd Geol Surv 1:250 000 Geol Ser
Queensland. Geological Survey. 1:250,000 Geological Series — Queensl Geol Surv 1:250000 Geol Ser
Queensland. Geological Survey. Publication — Queensl Geol Surv Publ
Queensland. Geological Survey. Report — Qd Geol Surv Rep
Queensland. Geological Survey. Report — Queensl Geol Surv Rep
Queensland Geology — Queensl Geol
Queensland Government Gazette — QGG
Queensland Government Industrial Gazette — Q Gov Indus Gaz
Queensland Government Industrial Gazette — QGIG
Queensland Government Industrial Gazette — Qld Govt Indust Gaz
Queensland Government Mining Journal — Q Govt Min J
Queensland Government Mining Journal — Qd Govt Min J
Queensland Government Mining Journal — QGMJA
Queensland Government Mining Journal — Queensl Gov Min J
Queensland Government Mining Journal — Queensland Gov Min J
Queensland Government Mining Journal — Queensland Govt Min Jour
Queensland Government. Public Relations Bureau. News Bulletin — Q Govt PRB News Bul
Queensland Government Publications — QGP
Queensland Graingrower — Q Graingrower
Queensland Heritage — Qd Heritage
Queensland Heritage — QH
Queensland Heritage — Qld Heritage
Queensland Heritage — Queensl Herit
Queensland Historical Review — QHR
Queensland Historical Review — Queensland Hist R
Queensland Industry — Q Ind
Queensland Industry — Q Industry
Queensland Journal of Agricultural and Animal Sciences — Qd J Agric Anim Sci
Queensland Journal of Agricultural and Animal Sciences — QJAAA
Queensland Journal of Agricultural and Animal Sciences — Queensl J Agric & Anim Sci
Queensland Journal of Agricultural and Animal Sciences — Queensl J Agric Anim Sci
Queensland Journal of Agricultural and Animal Sciences — Queensland J Agr Anim Sci
Queensland Journal of Agricultural Science [*Later, Queensland Journal of Agricultural and Animal Sciences*] — Qd J Agric Sci
Queensland Journal of Agricultural Science [*Later, Queensland Journal of Agricultural and Animal Sciences*] — Queensl J Agric Sci
Queensland Journal of Agricultural Science [*Later, Queensland Journal of Agricultural and Animal Sciences*] — Queensland J Ag Sci
Queensland Justice of the Peace (Magisterial Cases) — QJP (Mag Cas)
Queensland Justice of the Peace. Reports — QJPR
Queensland Land Court Reports — QLCR
Queensland Land Court Reports — Queensland Land Court Rep
Queensland Law Journal — QLJ
Queensland Law Journal and Reports — Queens LJ
Queensland Law Journal and Reports — Queensl LJ & R
Queensland Law Journal (Australia) — Queensl LJ (Austr)
Queensland Law Journal (Notes of Cases) — QLJ (NC)
Queensland Law Reporter — QLR
Queensland Law Reporter Case Note — Q Case Note
Queensland Law Reports — QLR
Queensland Law Reports — Queensl LR
Queensland Law Reports (Beor) — Beor
Queensland Law Reports (Beor) — QLR (Beor)
Queensland Law Reports (Beor) — Queens LR
Queensland Law Society. Journal — Q Law Soc J
Queensland Law Society. Journal — QLSJ
Queensland Law Society. Journal — Queensl L Soc'y J
Queensland Law Society. Journal — Queensland L Soc'y J
Queensland Lawyer [*Australia*] — Qd L
Queensland Lawyer — QL
Queensland Liberal — Q Liberal
Queensland Master Plumber — Q Master Plumber
Queensland Museum. Memoirs — Qld Mus Mem
Queensland Naturalist — Qd Nat
Queensland Naturalist — Qld Nat
Queensland Naturalist — Queensl Nat
Queensland Nurse — Qld Nurs
Queensland Nurses Journal — Queensl Nurses J
Queensland Nurses Journal — QUNJA
Queensland Papers in Economic Policy — Queensland Pap in Econ Policy
Queensland Parliamentary Debates — Qld Parl Deb
Queensland Parliamentary Debates — QPD
Queensland Parliamentary Papers — QPP
Queensland Planning Law Reports — QPLR
Queensland Police Journal — Q Police J
Queensland Practice Reports — QPR
Queensland Producer — Qd Prod
Queensland Reports — Qd R
Queensland Reports — Queensl
Queensland Science Teacher — Qld Sci Teach
Queensland Society of Sugar Cane Technologists. Proceedings — Proc QD Soc Sug Cane Tech
Queensland Society of Sugar Cane Technologists. Proceedings — Proc Queens Soc Sugar Cane Technol
Queensland Society of Sugar Cane Technologists. Proceedings — Proc Queensl Soc Sug Cane Technol
Queensland Society of Sugar Cane Technologists. Proceedings — Queensl Soc Sugar Cane Technol Proc
Queensland Studies in German Language and Literature — QSGLL
Queensland. Supreme Court. Reports — QSCR
Queensland. Supreme Court. Reports — Queensl S Ct R
Queensland. Supreme Court. Reports — SCR (Q)
Queensland. Supreme Court. Reports (Australia) — Queensl SC (Austr)
Queensland Surveyor — Qd Surv
Queensland Teachers' Journal — Q Teachers J
Queensland Teachers' Journal — Qld Teach J
Queensland University. Department of Civil Engineering. Bulletin — Queensl Univ Dep Civ Eng Bull
Queensland University. Department of Geology. Papers — Queensl Univ Dep Geol Pap
Queensland University. Gazette — QU Gazette
Queensland University. Law Journal — QULJ
Queensland Veterinary Proceedings — Qd Vet Proc
Queensland Veterinary Proceedings (Australian Veterinary Association, Queensland Division) — Queensl Vet Proc
Queensland's Health — Q Health
Queensland's Health — Qld Health
Quellen der Religionsgeschichte — QRG
Quellen des Deutschen Evangelischen Kirchenrechts — QDEKR
Quellen und Abhandlungen zur Geschichte der Abtei und der Dioezese Fulda — QAGAF
Quellen und Abhandlungen zur Geschichte des Schweizerischen Protestantismus — QAGSP
Quellen und Abhandlungen zur Mittelrheinischen Kirchengeschichte — Q Abh Mittelrh Kg
Quellen und Abhandlungen zur Mittelrheinischen Kirchengeschichte — QA Mrh K
Quellen und Abhandlungen zur Mittelrheinischen Kirchengeschichte — QMRKG
Quellen und Abhandlungen zur Schweizerischen Reformationsgeschichte — QASRG
Quellen und Darstellungen zur Geschichte der Burschenschaft und der Deutschen Einheitsbewegung — Qu Darst Gesch Burschensch
Quellen und Eroerterungen zur Bayerischen Geschichte — QEBG
Quellen und Forschungen aus dem Gebiet der Geschichte — QFG
Quellen und Forschungen aus dem Gebiet der Geschichte — QFGG
Quellen und Forschungen aus Italienischen Archiven und Bibliotheken — QF
Quellen und Forschungen aus Italienischen Archiven und Bibliotheken — QFAB
Quellen und Forschungen aus Italienischen Archiven und Bibliotheken — QFI
Quellen und Forschungen aus Italienischen Archiven und Bibliotheken — QFIAB
Quellen und Forschungen zur Bayerischen Kirchengeschichte — QFBKG
Quellen und Forschungen zur Geschichte der Juden in Deutsch-Oesterreich — QGJDOe
Quellen und Forschungen zur Geschichte der Stadt Muenster — QFGSM
Quellen und Forschungen zur Geschichte des Bistums und Hochstiftes Wuerzburg — QFGBW
Quellen und Forschungen zur Geschichte des Dominikanerordens in Deutschland — QGDOD
Quellen und Forschungen zur Geschichte, Literatur, und Sprache Oesterreichs — QFGLOe
Quellen und Forschungen zur Natur und Geschichte des Kreises Wiedenbrueck — QFNKW
Quellen und Forschungen zur Reformationsgeschichte — QFRG
Quellen und Forschungen zur Sprach- und Kulturgeschichte der Germanischen Voelker — QF
Quellen und Forschungen zur Sprach- und Kulturgeschichte der Germanischen Voelker — QFSK
Quellen und Forschungen zur Sprach- und Kulturgeschichte der Germanischen Voelker — Qu Forschgg Sprach Gesch Germ Voelker
Quellen und Forschungen zur Westfaelischen Geschichte — QFWG
Quellen und Schriften zu Philipp Matthaus Hahn — Quellen Schriften P M Hahn
Quellen und Studien ueber die Geschichte der Arabischen Mathematik — Quellen Stud Gesch Arabischen Math
Quellen und Studien zur Geschichte der Helvetischen Kirche — QSGHK
Quellen und Studien zur Geschichte der Mathematik — QGM
Quellen und Studien zur Geschichte der Mathematik — QGMath
Quellen und Studien zur Geschichte der Mathematik, Astronomie, und Physik — QSG Math
Quellen und Studien zur Geschichte der Mathematik, Astronomie, und Physik — Quell Stud Gesch Nat
Quellen und Studien zur Geschichte der Naturwissenschaften und der Medizin — QGN
Quellen und Studien zur Geschichte der Naturwissenschaften und der Medizin — QSGNM
Quellen und Studien zur Geschichte der Philosophie — QSGP
Quellen und Studien zur Geschichte und Kultur des Altertums und des Mittelalters — QSt
Quellen und Studien zur Musikgeschichte von der Antike bis in die Gegenwart — Quellen Stud Musikgesch Antike Gegenwart
Quellen und Studien zur Philosophie — QSP
Quellen und Studien zur Philosophie — Quellen Stud Philos
Quellen und Studien zur Verfassungsgeschichte des Deutschen Reichs im Mittelalter und Neuzeit — QVGDR
Quellen und Untersuchungen zur Konfessionskunde der Orthodoxie — QUKO
Quellen zum Christlichen Verstaendnis der Liebe — QCVL
Quellen zur Geschichte der Juden in Deutschland — QGJD
Quellen zur Geschichte der Taeufer — QGT
Quellen zur Geschichte der Wiedertaeufer — QGWT

Quellen zur Geschichte des Humanismus und der Reformation in Facsimile-Ausgaben — QGHR
Quellen zur Geschichte des Roemischkanonischen Prozesses im Mittelalter — QGRKP
Quellen zur Neueren Geschichte — QNG
Quellen zur Schweizer Geschichte — QSG
Quellen zur Schweizer Geschichte. Akten — QSGA
Quellen zur Schweizer Geschichte. Briefe und Denkwuerdigkeiten — QSGB
Quellen zur Schweizer Geschichte. Chroniken — QSGC
Quellen zur Schweizer Geschichte. Handbuecher — QSGH
Quellen zur Schweizerischen Reformationsgeschichte — QSRG
Quellen-Handbuch der Systematischen Theologie — QHST
Quellenhefte zum Religionsunterricht. Quellen zur Geschichte der Ausserchristlichen Religionen — QRUR
Quellenhefte zur Kirchengeschichte — QHKG
Quellenhefte zur Ostdeutschen und Osteuropaeischen Kirchengeschichte — QODKG
Quellenhefte zur Ostdeutschen und Osteuropaeischen Kirchengeschichte — Qu H Ostdt Osteur Kirchengesch
Quellensammlung fuer das Geltende Kirchenrecht — QGKR
Quellensammlung zur Kirchlichen Rechtsgeschichte — QKRG
Quellensammlung zur Kirchlichen Rechtsgeschichte und zum Kirchenrecht — QKRGK
Quellensammlung zur Kulturgeschichte — QSKG
Quellenschriften zur Geschichte des Protestantismus — QGP
Quellenverzeichnis der Justizverwaltungsvorschriften des Landes Nordrhein-Westfalen — QVJVVNW
Query File. Commonwealth Bureau of Horticulture and Plantation Crops — Query File Commonw Bur Hortic Plant Crops
Quest — Q
Questioni di Storia Contemporanea — Quest Stor Contemp
Questioni Disputate — QDI
Questions Actuelles du Socialisme — Quest Act Soc
Questions Actuelles du Socialisme — Quest Act Socialisme
Questions Diplomatiques et Coloniales — QDC
Questions Diplomatiques et Coloniales — Quest Dip
Questions Diplomatiques et Coloniales — Quest Diplom Colon
Questions d'Israel — QI
Questions for Christians — Qu Chr
Questions Liturgiques et Paroissiales — QLP
Questions of Forestry — Quest For
Questions of Quaternary Geology — Quest Quat Geol
Questo e Alto — QeA
Quetico-Superior Wilderness Research Center. Annual Report — Quetico-Super Wilderness Res Cent Annu Rep
Quetico-Superior Wilderness Research Center. Technical Note — Quetico-Super Wilderness Res Cent Tech Note
Queueing Systems. Theory and Applications — Queueing Systems Theory Appl
Quick Bibliography Series. US Department of Agriculture. National Agricultural Library (US) — Quick Bibliogr Ser US Dep Agric Natl Agric Libr US
Quick Frozen Foods — Qk Froz Fd
Quicksilver Times — Qckslv
Quill — IQLL
Quill and Quire — Q and Q
Quill and Quire — Quill & Q
QUILL: Queensland Inter-Library Liaison — QUILL
Quilter's Newsletter Magazine — QNM
Quimera — QA
Quimica Analitica — Quim Anal
Quimica Analitica (Barcelona) — Quim Anal Barcelona
Quimica Clinica — Quim Clin
Quimica e Industria [*Madrid*] — QUIBA
Quimica e Industria — Quim Ind
Quimica e Industria (Barcelona) — Quim Ind (Barcelona)
Quimica e Industria (Bogota) — Quim Ind (Bogota)
Quimica e Industria (Madrid) — Quim Ind (Madrid)
Quimica e Industria (Sao Paulo) — Quim Ind (Sao Paulo)
Quimica Industrial (Montevideo) — Quim Ind (Montevideo)
Quimica Nova — Quim Nova
Quimica y Farmica — Quim Farm
Quinquennial Congres International de la Recherche Textile Lainiere — Quinquenn Congr Int Rech Text Lainiere
Quintessence International — QUIJA
Quintessence International — Quintessence Int
Quintessence International Dental Digest — Quintessence Int Dent Dig
Quintessence of Dental Technology — Quintessence Dent Technol
Quintessencia de Protese de Laboratorio — Quintessencia Protese Lab
Quintessenz der Zahntechnik — Quintessenz Zahntech
Quintessenz Journal — Quintessenz J
Quintessenz Journal — QUSZA
Quinzaine — Q
Quinzaine Litteraire — QL
Quinzaine Litteraire — Quinz Lit
Quixote — Quix
Quo Vadis — QV
Quodlibet [*Newsletter of the Southeastern Region*] — QUODD

R

R and D Magazine — R D Mag
R and D [*Research and Development*] **Management** — R and D Manage
R and D [*Research and Development*] **Management** — R & D Mangt
R and D [*Research and Development*] **Management** — RDMAA
R and D. Research and Development (Cahners) — R D Res Dev Cahners
R & D. Research and Development (Kobe Steel Limited) — RD Res Dev (Kobe Steel Ltd)
R and D (Research and Development) Management — RED
R & D Review of Toyota RD Center — RD Rev Toyota RD Cent
R & E Research and Exposition in Mathematics — R & E Res Exp Math
R/D. Research/Development — R/D Res/Develop
Raad van Advies voor het Wetenschapsbeleid. Informatiebank. Tweekbericht — RAW
Raad van Beroep. Sociale Verzekering — R v B S V
Raad van Commissarissen — RvC
Rabbinical Council Record [*New York*] — RCR
Rabbinische Texte — RT
Rabobank — RFB
Rabochii Metallurg (Moscow) — Rab Metall (Moscow)
Rabochii Neftyanik — Rab Neft
Rabocij Klass i Sovremennyj Mir — Rabocij Klass Sovrem Mir
Raboty Azovsko-Chernomorskoi Nauchnoi Rybokhozyaistvennoi Stantsii — Rab Azovsko-Chernomorsk Nauchn Rybokhoz Stn
Raboty Donetskii Nauchno-Issledovatel'skii Ugol'nyi Institut — Rab Donetsk Nauchno Issled Ugoln Inst
Raboty i Issledovaniya. Institut Meteorologii i Gidrologii. Chast 2. Gidrologiya — Rab Issled Inst Meteorol Gidrol Chast 2
Raboty Molodykh Uchenykh Vsesoyuznaya Akademiya Sel'skokhozyaistvennykh Nauk — Rab Molodykh Uch Vses Akad Skh Nauk
Raboty Okskoj Biologiceskoj Stancii v Gorode Murome. Arbeiten der Biologischen Oka-Station — Raboty Oksk Biol Stancii Gorode Murome
Raboty po Fizike Tverdogo Tela — Rab Fiz Tverd Tela
Raboty po Khimii Rastvorov i Kompleksnykh Soedinenii — Rab Khim Rastvorov Kompleksn Soedin
Raboty Tyan-Shan'skoi Fiziko-Geograficheskoi Stantsii. Akademiya Nauk Kirgizskoi SSR — Rab Tyan Shan'skoi Fiz Geogr Stn Akad Nauk Kirg SSR
Raboty Tyan-Shan'skoi Fiziko-Geograficheskoi Stantsii. Akademiya Nauk Kirgizskoi SSR — Rab Tyan-Shan Fiz-Geogr Sta
Raboty Volzskoj Biologiceskoj Stancii. Arbeiten (aus) der Biologischen Wolga-Station. Travaux. Station Biologique a Volga — Raboty Volzsk Biol Stancii
Raccoglitore Medico Fano Forli — Raccoglitore Med Forli
Raccolta di Memorie. Turin. Universita. Facolta di Scienze Agrarie — Raccolta Mem Turin Univ Fac Sci Agr
Raccolta d'Opuscoli Scientifici e Filologici — Racc Opuscoli Sci Filol
Raccolta Fisico-Chimica Italiana — Racc Fis-Chim Ital
Raccolta Sistematica del Diritto Federale [*Switzerland*] — RS
Raccolta Ufficiale delle Leggi, Decreti, e Regolamente della Confederazione Svizzera — RU
Raccolta Ufficiale delle Leggi e dei Decreti della Repubblica Italiana — Rac Uff
Raccolta Ufficiale delle Sentenze e Ordinanze delle Corte Costituzionale — Rac Uff Corte Cost
Race — R
Race — RAC
Race and Class — Race
Race and Class — Race Clas
Race and Class — RC
Race Hygiene [*Japan*] — Race Hyg
Race Relations Law Reporter — Race Rela L R
Race Relations Law Survey — Race Rela L Sur
Raceduen — Rac
Rackham Journal of the Arts and Humanities — Ra JAH
Rackham Literary Studies — R L St
Rad Hrvatske Akademije Znanosti i Umjetnosti — Rad Hrvatske Akad Znan Umjet
Rad Jugoslavenske Akademije — Rad Jugoslav Akad
Rad Jugoslavenski Akademija Znanosti i Umjetnosti — Rad
Rad Kongresa Folklorista Jugoslavije — RKFJ
Rad Vojvodanskich Muzeja — Rad Voj Muz
Rada Narodowa — RN
Rada Pomocy Zydom — RPZ
Rada Zydowska — RZ
RADAR. Repertoire Analytique d'Articles de Revues du Quebec — Rep Anal Artic Rev Que
Radex Rundschau — Radex Rundsch
Radex Rundschau — Radex Runsch
Radex Rundschau (Austria) — RAXRA
Radiata Pine Technical Bulletin (Radiata Pine Association of Australia) — Radiata Pine Tech Bull
Radiation and Cellular Response. Report. John Lawrence Interdisciplinary Symposium on the Physical and Biomedical Sciences — Radiat Cell Response Rep John Lawrence Interdiscip Symp Phys
Radiation and Environmental Biophysics — Radiat and Environ Biophys
Radiation and Environmental Biophysics — Radiat Env
Radiation and Environmental Biophysics — Radiat Environ Biophys
Radiation Biology [*England*] — Radiat Biol
Radiation Botany — RABOA
Radiation Botany — Radiat Bot
Radiation Center of Osaka Prefecture. Technical Report — Radiat Cent Osaka Prefect Tech Rep
Radiation Chemistry of Aqueous Systems. Proceedings of the L. Farkas Memorial Symposium — Radiat Chem Aqueous Syst Proc L Farkas Mem Symp
Radiation Chemistry (Sapporo) — Radiat Chem Sapporo
Radiation Data and Reports — Radiat Data Rep
Radiation Detectors and Their Uses. Proceedings. Workshop on Radiation Detectors and Their Uses — Radiat Detect Their Uses Proc Workshop
Radiation Effects — Radiat Eff
Radiation Effects — Radiat Effects
Radiation Effects — RAEFB
Radiation Effects Express — Radiat Eff Express
Radiation Effects Information Center Report — Radiat Eff Inf Cent Rep
Radiation Effects. Letters Section — Radiat Eff Lett
Radiation Effects. Letters Section — Radiat Eff Lett Sect
Radiation Medicine — Radiat Med
Radiation Oncology Investigations — Radiat Oncol Investig
Radiation Physics and Chemistry — Radiat Phys and Chem
Radiation Physics and Chemistry — Radiat Phys Chem
Radiation Protection [*Republic of Korea*] — Radiat Prot
Radiation Protection Dosimetry — Radiat Prot Dosim
Radiation Protection Dosimetry — RPD
Radiation Protection. ICRP [*International Commission on Radiological Protection*] **Publication** — Radiat Prot ICRP Publ
Radiation Protection in Australia — Radiat Prot Aust
Radiation Protection Management — Radiat Prot Manage
Radiation Protection (Seoul) — Radiat Prot (Seoul)
Radiation Protection (Taiyuan, People's Republic of China) — Radiat Prot (Taiyuan People's Repub China)
Radiation Report — Radiat Rep
Radiation Research — Radiat Res
Radiation Research — RAREA
Radiation Research on Polymers [*Japan*] — Radiat Res Polym
Radiation Research. Proceedings. International Congress of Radiation Research — Radiat Res Proc Int Congr
Radiation Research Reviews — Radiat Res Rev
Radiation Research Reviews — RRREA
Radiation Research. Supplement — Radiat Res Suppl
Radiation Research. Supplement — RARSA
Radiation Shielding Information Center. Report — Radiat Shielding Inf Cent Rep
Radiative Recombination in Semiconductors. International Conference on the Physics of Semiconductors — Radiat Recomb Semicond Int Conf Phys Semicond
Radiatsionnaia Biologiia, Radioecologiia — Radiats Biol Radioecol
Radiatsionnaya Bezopasnost' i Zashchita AEhS. Sbornik Statej — Radiats Bezop Zashch AEhS
Radiatsionnaya Biologiya — Radiats Biol
Radiatsionnaya Fizika — Radiats Fiz
Radiatsionnaya Fizika. Akademiya Nauk Latviiskoi SSR. Institut Fiziki [*Latvian SSR*] — Radiats Fiz Akad Nauk Latv SSR Inst Fiz
Radiatsionnaya Fizika. Akademiya Nauk Latviiskoi SSR. Institut Fiziki — RAFIA
Radiatsionnaya Fizika Nemetallicheskikh Kristallov — Radiats Fiz Nemet Krist
Radiatsionnaya Fizika Tverdogo Tela i Radiatsionnoe Materialovedenie — Radiats Fiz Tverd Tela Radiats Materialoved
Radiatsionnaya Gigiena [*Former USSR*] — Radiats Gig
Radiatsionnaya Tekhnika — Radiats Tekh
Radiatsionno-Khimicheskaya Tekhnologiya — Radiats Khim Tekhnol
Radiatsionnye Defekty v Metallakh. Materialy Vsesoyuznogo Soveshchaniya — Radiats Defekty Met Mater Vses Soveshch
Radiatsionnye Effekty v Metallakh i Splavakh. Materialy Vsesoyuznogo Soveshchaniya — Radiats Eff Met Splavakh Mater Vses Soveshch
Radiatsionnye Issledovaniya — Radiats Issled
Radiazioni di Alta Energia — Radiaz Alta Energ
Radiazioni e Radioisotopi — Radiaz Radioisot

Radiazioni e Radioisotopi — RDRIA
Radical America — Rad Am
Radical America — Rad Amer
Radical America — Radical Am
Radical Community Medicine — Radical Commun Med
Radical Education Dossier — Radical Educ Dossier
Radical Education Dossier — RED
Radical History Review — Rad Hist
Radical History Review — Radical His
Radical Humanist — Rad Humanist
Radical Humanist — RH
Radical Philosopher's Newsjournal — Rad Phil News
Radical Philosophy — Rad Phil
Radical Philosophy — Radic Phil
Radical Religion — Rad Rel
Radical Religion — Rad Relig
Radical Science — Radic Sci
Radical Science Journal — Rad Scien
Radical Science Journal — Radic Sci J
Radical Scotland — Radical Scot
Radical Teacher — Rad
Radical Teacher — Rad Teach
Radio and Electronic Engineer — Radio and Electron Eng
Radio and Electronic Engineer — Radio & Electronic Eng
Radio and Electronic Engineer — Radio El En
Radio and Electronic Engineer — Radio Electron Eng
Radio and Electronic Engineer — RDEEA
Radio and Electronic Engineer (London) — Radio Electron Eng (London)
Radio and Electronics Constructor — Radio & Electron Constructor
Radio and Electronics World — Radio and Electron World
Radio and Electronics World — Radio Electron Wld
Radio and Television News — Radio & TV N
Radio (BBC Monitoring) — R
Radio Communication — Radio Commun
Radio Electrical Weekly — Radio Elec W
Radio Electronica [*Netherlands*] — Radio Electron
Radio Electronics and Communications Systems — Radio Electron Commun Syst
Radio Elektronica — Radio Elektron
Radio Elektronik Schau — Radio Elektron Schau
Radio Elektronik Schau — RELSA
Radio Engineering — Radio Eng
Radio Engineering and Electronic Physics — Radio Eng and Electron Phys
Radio Engineering and Electronic Physics — Radio Eng Electron Phys
Radio Engineering and Electronic Physics — Radio Engrg Electron Phys
Radio Engineering and Electronic Physics [*English Translation*] — RENPA
Radio Engineering and Electronic Physics. English Translation — Radio Eng Electron Phys Engl Transl
Radio Engineering and Electronic Physics (USSR) — Radio Eng Electron (USSR)
Radio Engineering and Electronics. English Translation — Radio Eng Electron Engl Transl
Radio Engineering (London) — Rad Eng (London)
Radio Engineering (USSR) — Radio Eng (USSR)
Radio es TV Szemle — Radio es TV Szle
Radio Fernsehen Elektronik — Radio Fernsehen Elektron
Radio Fernsehen Elektronik — RFELB
Radio Free Europe — RFE
Radio Free Europe. Research Bulletin — RFERB
Radio Free Jazz — RFJ
Radio Frequency Power in Plasmas — Radio Freq Power Plasmas
Radio Industria — Radio Ind
Radio Industria — RAINB
Radio- ja Elektroniikkalaboratoriot. Teknillinen Korkeakoulu. Kertomus — Radio Elektroniikkalab Tek Korkeakoulu Kertomus
Radio Laboratory. Technical University of Helsinki. Internal Report — Radio Lab Tech Univ Helsinki Intern Rep
Radio Liberty — RL
Radio Liberty Research Bulletin — RLRB
Radio Mentor Electronic — Radio Mentor Electron
Radio Mentor Electronic — Radio Mntr
Radio Mentor Electronic — RMELB
Radio News — Radio N
Radio Regulation. Pike and Fischer — Rad Reg P & F
Radio Science — Radio Sci
Radio Science — RAS
Radio Science — RASCA
Radio Service Bulletin — Radio Serv Bul
Radio Television — Radio Telev
Radio, Television, and Hobbies — Radio Tel & Hobbies
Radio, Television, and Hobbies — Radio TVH
Radio - Television International Review — Radio Telev Int Rev
Radio Times [*United Kingdom*] — Radio T
Radio Times — RT
Radio-Active Magazine — RAM
Radioactive Waste Disposal. Research Series. Institute of Geological Sciences — Radioact Waste Disposal Res Ser Inst Geol Sci
Radioactive Waste Management — Radioact Waste Manage
Radioactive Waste Management — RWAMD
Radioactive Waste Management and the Nuclear Fuel Cycle — Radioact Waste Manage and Nucl Fuel Cycle
Radioactive Waste Management and the Nuclear Fuel Cycle — Radioact Waste Manage Nucl Fuel Cycle
Radioactive Waste Management (Oak Ridge, Tennessee) — Radioact Waste Manage (Oak Ridge Tenn)
Radioactive Waste Technology — Radioact Waste Technol
Radioactivity in the Sea [*Austria*] — Radioact Sea
Radioactivity Survey Data in Japan — Radioact Surv Data Jap
Radioaktive Isotope in Klinik und Forschung — Radioakt Isot Klin Forsch
Radioaktivita a Zivotne Prostredie — Radioaktiv Zivotn Prostr
Radiobiologia, Radioterapia, e Fisica Medica — Radiobiol Radioter Fis Med
Radiobiologia, Radioterapia, e Fisica Medica — RRFIA
Radiobiologia si Biologia Moleculara — RABMA
Radiobiologia si Biologia Moleculara [*Romania*] — Radiobiol Biol Mol
Radiobiologia-Radiotherapia — Radiobiol-Radiother
Radiobiologia-Radiotherapia — RDBGA
Radiobiologia-Radiotherapia (Berlin) — Radiobiol-Radiother (Berl)
Radiobiologia-Radiotherapia (Berlin) — Radiobiol-Radiother (Berlin)
Radiobiologica Latina [*Italy*] — Radiobiol Lat
Radiobiologiya — Radiobiol
Radiobiologiya — RADOA
Radiobiologiya Informatsionnyi Byulleten' — Radiobiol Inf Byull
Radiobiology [*English Translation*] — RADBA
Radiobiology. A Portion of the Proceedings. All-Union Scientific and Technical Conference on the Application of Radioactive Isotopes — Radiobiol Proc All Union Sci Tech Conf Appl Radioact Isot
Radiobiology. Proceedings. Australasian Conference on Radiobiology — Radiobiol Proc Australas Conf
Radiocarbon — RACAA
Radiochemical and Radioanalytical Letters — Radioch Rad
Radiochemical and Radioanalytical Letters — Radiochem and Radioanal Lett
Radiochemical and Radioanalytical Letters — Radiochem Radioanal Lett
Radiochemical and Radioanalytical Letters — RRALA
Radiochimica Acta — RAACA
Radiochimica Acta — Radioch Act
Radiochimica Acta — Radiochim Acta
Radiochuvstvitel'nost i Mutabil'nost Rastenii — Radiochuvstvitelnost Mutabilnost Rast
Radioekologiya Vodnykh Organizmov — Radioekol Vodn Org
Radio-Electronics — GRAD
Radio-Electronics — Radio Elec
Radio-Electronics — Radio-Electr
Radio-Electronics — Radio-Electron
Radioelectronics and Communication Systems — Radioelectron and Commun Syst
Radioelectronics and Communications Systems. English Translation — Radioelectron Commun Syst Engl Transl
Radiographer — Radiogr
Radiographer — RDGRA
Radiographer (East Melbourne, Australia) — Radiographer East Melbourne Aust
Radiography — RADIA
Radiography Today — Radiogr Today
Radioindustria Elettronica-Televisione — Radioind Elettron-Telev
Radioisotopes [*Tokyo*] — RAISA
Radioisotopes (Tokyo) — Radioisot (Tokyo)
Radioisotopy (Praha) — Radioisot (Praha)
Radiokhimiya — RADKA
Radiologe — RDLGB
Radiologia [*Madrid*] — RBSEBR
Radiologia [*Bucharest*] — ROORD3
Radiologia Austriaca — Radiol Austriaca
Radiologia Brasileira — Radiol Bras
Radiologia Clinica — Rad Clinica
Radiologia Clinica — Radiol Clin
Radiologia Clinica (Basel) — Radiol Clin (Basel)
Radiologia Clinica et Biologica — Radiol Clin Biol
Radiologia Clinica et Biologica — RCBOA
Radiologia Diagnostica — Rad Diagn
Radiologia Diagnostica — Radiol Diagn
Radiologia Diagnostica — RDGNA
Radiologia Diagnostica (Berlin) — Radiol Diagn (Berlin)
Radiologia Hungarica — Radiol Hung
Radiologia Iugoslavica (Ljubljana) — Radiol Iugosl (Ljubljana)
Radiologia Medica — Radiol Med
Radiologia Medica — RAMEA
Radiologia Medica (Torino) — Radiol Med (Torino)
Radiologia Pratica [*Italy*] — Radiol Prat
Radiologiai Kozlemenyek — Radiol Kozl
Radiologic Clinics of North America — Rad Clin NA
Radiologic Clinics of North America — Radiol Clin N Am
Radiologic Clinics of North America — Radiol Clin North Am
Radiologic Clinics of North America — Radiol Clin North America
Radiologic Clinics of North America — RCNAA
Radiologic Technology — Radiol Technol
Radiologic Technology — RATIB
Radiologica Clinica et Biologica — Radiol Clin
Radiological Health Data — Radiol Health Data
Radiological Health Data and Reports — Radiol Health Data Rep
Radiological Health Data and Reports — RHDRA
Radiological Protection Bulletin — Radiol Prot Bull
Radiological Protection Bulletin — Radiological Protect Bull
Radiological Review and Mississippi Valley Medical Journal — Radiol Rev Miss Val Med J
Radiology — RADLA
Radiology and Imaging Letter — RIL
Radiology and Oncology — Radiol Oncol
Radiology Management — Radiol Manage
Radiology of Cancer. Selected Papers. International Congress of Radiology — Radiol Cancer Sel Pap Int Congr Radiol

Radiology. Proceedings of the Congress of the European Association of Radiology — Radiol Proc Congr Eur Assoc Radiol
Radiometer News — Radiom News
Radiometer Polarographics — Radiom Polarogr
Radiophysics and Quantum Electronics — Radiophys & Quantum Electron
Radiophysics and Quantum Electronics — Radiophys Quantum Electron
Radiophysics and Quantum Electronics [*English Translation*] — RPQEA
Radiophysics and Quantum Electronics. English Translation — Radiophys Quantum Electron Engl Transl
Radiophysiologie et Radiotherapie — Radiophysiol Radiother
Radioprotection — RAPRB
Radiotehnika (Kharkov) — Radiotehn (Kharkov)
Radiotekhnicheskoe Proizvodstvo — Radiotekh Proizvod
Radiotekhnika — Radiotekh
Radiotekhnika [*Moscow*] — RATEA
Radiotekhnika i Elektronika — Radiotek El
Radiotekhnika i Elektronika — Radiotekh Elektron
Radiotekhnika i Elektronika — Radiotekh i Elektron
Radiotekhnika i Elektronika — RAELA
Radiotekhnika i Elektronika. Akademiya Nauk SSSR — Radiotekhn i Elektron
Radiotekhnika i Elektronika (Moscow) — Radiotekh Elektron (Moscow)
Radiotekhnika (Kharkov) — RTKHA
Radioterapia, Radiobiologia, e Fisica Medica — Radioter Radiobiol Fis Med
Radiotherapy and Oncology — Radiother Oncol
Radiotherapy and Oncology — RAONDT
Radiotherapy Oncology — Radioth Onc
Radio-TV-Electronic [*Later, RTE. Radio-TV-Electronic*] — Radio-TV-Electron
Radio-TV-Electronic Service [*RTE. Radio-TV-Electronic*] [*Switzerland*] [*Later,*] — Radio-TV-Electron Serv
Radio-TV-Electronic Service [*Later, RTE. Radio-TV-Electronic*] — RTESB
Radjans'ke Literaturoznavstvo. Naukovo-Teoretycnyj Zurnal — R Lz
Radostna Zeme — RZ
Radovi. Akademija Nauka i Umjetnosti Bosne i Hercegovine. Odjeljenje Prirodnih i Matematickih Nauka — Rad Akad Nauka Umjet Bosne Hercegovine Od Prir Met Nauka
Radovi (Filozofski Fakultet-Zadar) — RZ
Radovi - Geoinstitut — Rad Geoinst
Radovi Imunoloskog Zavoda (Zagreb) — Rad Imunol Zavoda (Zagreb)
Radovi Institut za Sumarska Istrazivanja. Sumarskog Fakulteta. Sveucilista u Zagrebu — Rad Inst Sum Istraz
Radovi Instituta Jugoslavenske Akademije Znanosti i Umjetnosti u Zadru — JAZU
Radovi Instituta Jugoslavenske Akademije Znanosti i Umjetnosti u Zadru — RIJAZ
Radovi Instituta Jugoslavenske Akademije Znanosti i Umjetnosti u Zadru — RIJAZUZ
Radovi Instituta za Geolosko-Rudarska Istrazivanja i Ispitivanja Nuklearnih i Drugih Mineralnih Sirovina [*Yugoslavia*] — Rad Inst Geol-Rud Istraz Ispit Nukl Drugih Miner Sirovina
Radovi Instituta za Geolosko-Rudarska Istrazivanja i Ispitivanja Nuklearnih i Drugih Mineralnih Sirovina — RIGIB
Radovi Instituta za Proucavanje i Suzbijanje Alkoholizma i Drugih Narkomanija u Zagrebu — Rad Inst Prouc Suzbijanje Alkohol Drugih Narkomanija Zagrebu
Radovi Instituta za Proucavanje i Suzbijanje Alkoholizma i Drugih Narkomanija u Zagrebu — Rad Inst Proucavanje Suzbijanje Alkohol Drugih Narkomanija
Radovi Instituta za Proucavanje i Suzbijanje Alkoholizma i Drugih Narkomanija u Zagrebu — RIADAG
Radovi Jugoslavenske Akademije Znanosti i Umjetnosti — Rad Jugosl Akad Znan Umjet
Radovi Jugoslavenske Akademije Znanosti i Umjetnosti — Rad Jugoslav Akad Znan Umjet
Radovi Jugoslavenske Akademije Znanosti i Umjetnosti — RadJA
Radovi Jugoslavenske Akademije Znanosti i Umjetnosti. Odjel za Prirodne Nauke — Rad Jugoslav Akad Znan Umjet Odjel Prir Nauke
Radovi Matematicki — Rad Mat
Radovi Medicinskogo Fakulteta. Rijeka — Rad Med Fak Rijeka
Radovi Medicinskogo Fakulteta u Zagrebu — Rad Med Fak Zagrebu
Radovi Medicinskogo Fakulteta u Zagrebu — RMFZA
Radovi. Odsjek za Povijest Filozofski Fakultet. Universita Zagreb — Rad OPFFZ
Radovi Poljoprivrednog Fakulteta Univerziteta u Sarajevu — Rad Poljopriv Fak Univ Saraj
Radovi Poljoprivrednog Fakulteta Univerziteta u Sarajevu — Rad Poljopriv Fak Univ Sarajevu
Radovi Poljoprivrednog Fakulteta Univerziteta u Sarajevu — RPFUB
Radovi Sarajevo Univerzitet. Poljoprivredni Fakultet — Rad Sarajevo Univ Poljopr Fak
Radovi Slavenskog Instituta — RSII
Radovi Staroslavenskog Instituta — RSSLI
Radovi Staroslovenskog Instituta — RSSI
Radovi Sumarski Fakultet i Institut za Sumarstvo — Rad Sum Fak i Inst Sum
Radovi Sumarskog Fakulteta i Instituta za Sumarstvo u Sarajevo — Rad Sumar Fak Inst Sumar Sarajevo
Radovi Zavoda za Fiziku — Rad Zavoda Fiz
Radovi Zavoda za Slavensku Filologiju — RadZSF
Radovi Zavoda za Slavensku Filologiju — RZSF
RadTech Report — RadTech Rep
Raduga [*Moscow*] — Ra
Radyans'ke Literaturoznavstvo [*Kiev*] — RadL
Ragioni Critiche. Rivista di Studi Linguistici e Letterari — RCrit
Ragioni Narrative — RNar
Raguaglio Librario — RagL
Rahnema-Ye Ketab — RaKet
Raiffeisen-Rundschau — Raiffeisen-Rundsch
Rail Engineering International — Rail Eng Int
Rail International — Rail Int
Rail Transportation Proceedings — Rail Transport Proc
Railroad Gazette — Railroad Gaz
Railroad Research Bulletin — Railroad Res Bul
Railroad Research Information Service [*Database*] — RRIS
Railway — R
Railway — Rly
Railway Age — IRAA
Railway Age [*New York*] — RAAGA
Railway Age — Railw Age
Railway Age — RME
Railway Age — Rwy Age
Railway Age — Ry Age
Railway Age Gazette — Railw Age Gaz
Railway and Engineering Review — Railw Eng Rev
Railway Clerk Interchange — Rail Clerk
Railway Development News — Railw Dev News
Railway Engineer [*Later, Railway Engineer International*] — Rail Eng
Railway Engineer [*Later, Railway Engineer International*] — Railw Eng
Railway Engineer [*Later, Railway Engineer International*] — Railw Engr
Railway Engineer International — Railw Eng Int
Railway Engineering and Maintenance — Railw Eng Maint
Railway Engineering Journal [*Incorporated in Railway Engineer International*] — Railw Eng J
Railway Engineering Journal [*Incorporated in Railway Engineer International*] — Rly Engng
Railway Gazette [*Railway Gazette International*] [*England*] [*Later,*] — Railw Gaz
Railway Gazette [*Later, Railway Gazette International*] — RGZTA
Railway Gazette [*Later, Railway Gazette International*] — Rly Gaz
Railway Gazette International — Railw Gaz Int
Railway Gazette International — Ry Gaz Int
Railway Locomotives and Cars — Railw Locomot Cars
Railway Locomotives and Cars — RLCAA
Railway Locomotives and Cars — Ry Loco & Cars
Railway Magazine — Rail M
Railway Magazine — Rly Mag
Railway Maintenance Engineer — Railw Maint Eng
Railway Management Review — Railw Manage Rev
Railway Mechanical and Electrical Engineer — Ry Mech & Elec Eng
Railway Mechanical Engineer [*United States*] — Railw Mech Eng
Railway Mechanical Engineer — RWMEB
Railway Mechanical Engineer — Ry Mech Eng
Railway Quarterly — Railw Q
Railway Research and Engineering News — Railw Res Eng N
Railway Review — Railw Rev
Railway Review — Railway R
Railway Review — Ry R
Railway Signalling and Communications [*United States*] — Railw Signal Commun
Railway Surgical Journal — Ry Surg J
Railway Systems Control — Rail Syst Contr
Railway Systems Control — Railw Syst Control
Railway Systems Control — RSC
Railway Systems Control — RSYCA
Railway Track and Structures — Railw Track Struct
Railway Track and Structures — RTSTA
Railway Track and Structures — Ry Track Struct
Railway Transportation — Railway Trans
Railways in Australia — Railways in Aust
Railways Southern Africa — Railw South Afr
Railways Union Gazette — Railways Union Gaz
Raina Gadagramata — R Gad
Raina un Aspazijas Gadagramata — RAG
RAIRO [*Revue Francaise d'Automatique, d'Informatique, et de Recherche Operationnelle*] **Analyse Numerique** — RAIRO Anal Num
RAIRO [*Revue Francaise d'Automatique, d'Informatique, et de Recherche Operationnelle*] **Analyse Numerique** — RAIRO Anal Numer
RAIRO [*Revue Francaise d'Automatique, d'Informatique, et de Recherche Operationnelle*] **Analyse Numerique/Numerical Analysis** — RAIRO Anal Numer Numer Anal
RAIRO [*Revue Francaise d'Automatique, d'Informatique, et de Recherche Operationnelle*] **Automatique** — RAIRO Automat
RAIRO [*Revue Francaise d'Automatique, d'Informatique, et de Recherche Operationnelle*] **Automatique/Systems Analysis and Control** — RAIRO Autom Syst Anal Control
RAIRO [*Revue Francaise d'Automatique, d'Informatique, et de Recherche Operationnelle*] **Automatique/Systems Analysis and Control** — RAIRO Autom/Syst Anal et Control
RAIRO [*Revue Francaise d'Automatique, d'Informatique, et de Recherche Operationnelle*] **Informatique** — RAIRO Inform
RAIRO [*Revue Francaise d'Automatique, d'Informatique, et de Recherche Operationnelle*] **Informatique** — RAIRO Informat
RAIRO [*Revue Francaise d'Automatique, d'Informatique, et de Recherche Operationnelle*] **Informatique/Computer Science** — RAIRO Inf/Comput Sci
RAIRO [*Revue Francaise d'Automatique, d'Informatique, et de Recherche Operationnelle*] **Informatique Theorique** — RAIRO Informat Theor
RAIRO [*Revue Francaise d'Automatique, d'Informatique, et de Recherche Operationnelle*] **Informatique Theorique/Theoretical Informatics** — RAIRO Inf Theor Theor Inf
RAIRO [*Revue Francaise d'Automatique, d'Informatique, et de Recherche Operationnelle*] **Informatique Theorique/Theoretical Informatics** — RAIRO Inform Theor
RAIRO [*Revue Francaise d'Automatique, d'Informatique, et de Recherche Operationnelle*] **Recherche Operationnelle/Operations Research** — RAIRO Operations Research

RAIRO [*Revue Francaise d'Automatique, d'Informatique, et de Recherche Operationelle*] **Recherche Operationnelle/Operations Research** — RAIRO Rech Oper Oper Res
RAIRO. Revue Franciase d'Automatique d'Informatique et de Recherche Operationalle. Analyse Numerique — RAIRO Rev Fr Autom Inf Rech Oper
RAJ [*Rhodesia Agricultural Journal*] **Technical Bulletin** — RAJ Tech Bull
Rajasthan Agriculturist — Rajasthan Agric
Rajasthan Journal of Agricultural Sciences — Rajasthan J Agric Sci
Rajasthan Medical Journal — Rajasthan Med J
Rajasthan University. Studies. Arts [*Jaipur*] — RU
Rajasthan University. Studies in English — RUSEng
Rajasthan University. Studies in Statistics. Science Series — Rajasthan Univ Stud Statist
Rajasthan University. Studies in Statistics. Science Series — Rajasthan Univ Studies Statist
RAK. Reichstoffe, Aromen, Kosmetica — RAK Reichst Aromen Kosmet
Rakennusteknikka — RKTEA
Raketentechnik und Raumfahrtforschung — Raketentech Raumfahrtforsch
Rakstı. Latvijas PSR Zinatnu Akademija. Valodas und Literaturas Instituta — RVLI
Rakstu Krajums — RKr
Rakstu Krajums. Daugavpils Pedagogiskais Instituts — Rakstu Krajums Daugavpils Pedagog Inst
Rakuno Kagaku No Kenkyu — RKNKA
Raleigh Lecture on History — RLH
Raleigh News and Observer — RN and O
RAM. Research in Applied Mathematics — RAM Res Appl Math
Raman Effect — Raman Eff
Raman Research Institute. Memoirs — Raman Res Inst Mem
Ramarkrishna Mission Institute of Culture [*Calcutta*]. Bulletin — BRMIC
Ramparts Magazine — Ramp
Ramparts Magazine — Ramp Mag
Ranch Magazine — Ranch Mag
Ranchi University. Journal of Agricultural Research — Ranchi Univ J Agric Res
Ranchi University. Mathematical Journal — Ranchi Univ Math J
Rancho Mexicano — Rancho Mex
Rancho Santa Ana Botanic Garden. Monographs. Botanical Series — Rancho Santa Ana Bot Gard Monogr Bot Ser
Rand Corporation. Papers — Rand Corp Pap
Rand Corporation. Report — Rand Corp Rep
Rand Corporation. Report R — Rand Corp Rep R
Rand Journal of Economics — Rand J Econom
Rand Research Review — Rand Revw
Random and Computational Dynamics — Random Comput Dynam
Random House/Birkhaeuser Mathematics Series — Random House Birkhaeuser Math Ser
Random Materials and Processes — Random Mater Process
Random Operators and Stochastic Equations — Random Oper Stochastic Equations
RANF [*Royal Australian Nursing Federation*] **Review** — RANF Rev
Range Improvement Notes. United States Forest Service. Intermountain Region — Range Improv Notes US For Serv Intermt Reg
Range Improvement Studies. California Department of Conservation. Division of Forestry — Range Improv Studies Calif Dep Conserv Div For
Range Improvement Studies. California Division of Forestry — Range Impr Stud Calif Div For
Range Science Department Series. Colorado State University — Range Sci Dep Ser Colo State Univ
Range Science Series. Colorado State University. Range Science Department — Range Sci Ser Colo State Univ Range Sci Dep
Rangifer. Nordisk Organ foer Reinforskning — RAN
Rannsoknastofnun Fiskidnadarins Arsskyrsla — Rannsoknastofnun Fiskidnadarins Arsskyrs
RAOU [*Royal Australasian Ornithologists Union*] **Newsletter** — RAOU Newsl
Rapeseed Association of Canada. Publication — Rapeseed Assoc Can Publ
Rapid Access Tariff Expediting Service [*Database*] — RATES
Rapid Communications in Mass Spectrometry — Rapid Commun Mass Spectrom
Rapidly Quenched Metals. Proceedings. International Conference — Rapidly Quenched Met Proc Int Conf
RAPIJ: Royal Australian Planning Institute. Journal — R Aust Plann Inst J
Raport. Instytut Fizyki i Techniki Jadrowej AGH [*Akademia Gorniczo-Hutnicza*] [*A publication*] — Rap Inst Fiz Tech Jad AGH
Raport. Instytut Fizyki Jadrowej (Krakow) — Rap Inst Fiz Jad Krakow
Raport. Instytut Techniki Jadrowej AGH [*Akademia Gorniczo-Hutnicza*] — Rap Inst Tech Jad AGH
Rapport — Rapp
Rapport a l'Industrie Canadien sur les Sciences Halieutiques et Aquatiques — CRFSDL
Rapport a l'Industrie Canadien sur les Sciences Halieutiques et Aquatiques — Rapp Ind Can Sci Halieutiques Aquat
Rapport. Activite du Bureau Voltaique de le Geologie et des Mines — Rapp Act Bur Voltaique Geol Mines
Rapport Annuel. AFOCEL (Association Foret-Cellulose) — Rapp Annu AFOCEL (Assoc For Cellul)
Rapport Annuel de l'Institut Geologique de Hongrie — Rapp Annu Inst Geol Hong
Rapport Annuel. Federation des Chambres Syndicales des Minerais et des Metaux Non Ferreux — Rapp Annu Fed Chambres Synd Miner Met Non Ferreux
Rapport Annuel. Institut des Recherches Agronomiques de l'Etat a Sofia — Rapp Annu Inst Rech Agron Etat Sofia
Rapport Annuel. Service Geologique (Malagasy) — Rapp Annu Serv Geol (Malagasy)
Rapport Annuel. Station Agronomique de l'Etat a Sofia — Rapp Annu Stn Agron Etat Sofia
Rapport. BIPM [*Bureau International des Poids et Mesures*] — Rapp BIPM
Rapport. Bureau de la Nutrition Animale et de l'Elevage — Rap Bur Nutr Anim Elev
Rapport CEA-R. France Commissariat a l'Energie Atomique — Rapp CEA R Fr Commis Energ At
Rapport. Chalmers Tekniska Hoegskola. Institutionen foer Vattenfoersoerjnings- och Avloppsteknik — Rapp Chalmers Tek Hoegsk Inst Vattenfoersoerjnings Avloppstek
Rapport. Commissariat a l'Energie Atomique [*France*] — Rapp Commissar Energie Atom
Rapport. Commission Internationale pour la Mer Mediterranee [*France*] — Rapp Comm Int Mer Mediter
Rapport. Congres International. Federation Internationale des Societes d'Ingenieurs des Techniques de l'Automobile — Rapp Congr Int Fed Int Soc Ing Tech Automob
Rapport. Conseil de l'Experimentation et des Recherches Agronomiques. Inspection Generale de l'Agriculture (Algeria) — Rapp Cons Exp Rech Agron Insp Gen Agric (Algeria)
Rapport d'Activite. Service Geologique (Madagascar) — Rapp Act Serv Geol (Madagascar)
Rapport d'Activite. Service Geologique (Malagasy) — Rapp Act Serv Geol (Malagasy)
Rapport d'Activite. Station d'Amelioration des Plants Maraicheres — Rapp Act Stn Amelior Plant Maraicheres
Rapport d'Activites. Institut de Phonetique — RAIP
Rapport de Conjoncture — Rapport Conjonct
Rapport de Recherche. Centre Regional d'Etudes Nucleaires de Kinshasa — Rapp Rech Cent Reg Etud Nucl Kinshasa
Rapport de Recherche. Laboratoire Central des Ponts et Chaussees — Rapp Rech Lab Cent Ponts Chaussees
Rapport de Recherche. Laboratoires des Ponts et Chaussees — Rapp Rech Lab Ponts Chaussees
Rapport de Recherche LPC [*Laboratoire Central des Ponts et Chaussees*] — Rapp Rech LPC
Rapport de Recherche sur les Pesticides — Rapp Rech Pestic
Rapport d'Information LAU-X. Centre de Recherches Forestieres des Laurentides — Rapp Inf LAU X Cent Rech For Laurentides
Rapport d'Information LAU-X. Laurentian Forest Research Centre — Rapp Inf LAU X Laurentian For Res Cent
Rapport du Comite Consultatif pour la Definition du Metre au Comite International des Poids et Mesures — Rapp Com Consult Definition Metre Com Int Poids Mes
Rapport Final. Conference Technique. OCEAC [*Organisation de Coordination pour la Lutte Contre les Endemies en Afrique Centrale*] — Rapp Final Conf Tech OCEAC
Rapport fra Nordiske Fettharskningssymposium — Rapp Nord Fettharskningssymp
Rapport fra Nordiske Korrosjonsmoete — Rapp Nord Korrosjonsmoete
Rapport Geologique. Ministere de l'Energie et des Ressources (Quebec) — Rapp Geol Minist Energie Ressour (Quebec)
Rapport Geologique. Quebec, Ministere de l'Energie et des Ressources — Rapp Geol Que Minist Energ Ressour
Rapport. Gronlands Geologiske Undersogelse — Rapp Gronl Geol Unders
Rapport. Institut National pour l'Etude Agronomique du Congo (INEAC) — Rap Inst Nat Etude Agron Congo (INEAC)
Rapport. Instituut voor Bodemvruchtbaarheid — Rapp Inst Bodemvruchtbaar
Rapport. Instituut voor Bodemvruchtbaarheid — Rapp Inst Bodemvruchtbaarheid
Rapport. Instituut voor Gezondheidstechniek TNO — Rapp Inst Gezondheidstech TNO
Rapport Interieur d'une Etude Effectuee au Laboratoire J. Dedek Raffinerie Tirlemontoise — Rapp Inter Etude Lab J Dedek Raffinerie Tirlemontoise
Rapport. Korrosionsinstitutet — Rapp Korrosionsinst
Rapport. Laboratoire des Produits Forestiers de l'Est (Canada) — Rapp Lab Prod For Est (Can)
Rapport. Office International des Epizooties — Rapp Off Int Epizoot
Rapport Preliminaire. Ministere des Richesses Naturelles (Quebec) — Rapp Prelim Minist Richesses Nat (Que)
Rapport. Proefstation voor de Groenteteelt in de Vollegrond in Nederland [*A publication*] — Rapp Proefstn Groenteteelt Vollegrond Ned
Rapport. Station Biologique du St. Laurent a Trois Pistoles — Rapp Stat Biol St Laurent Trois Pistoles
Rapport Statistique Canadien sur l'Hydrographie et les Sciences Oceaniques — CDHSDZ
Rapport Statistique Canadien sur l'Hydrographie et les Sciences Oceaniques — Rapp Stat Can Hydrogr Sci Oceaniques
Rapport sur le Fonctionnement Technique. Institut Pasteur de Dakar — Rapp Fonct Tech Inst Pasteur Dakar
Rapport sur les Analyses Physico-Chimiques de l'Eau du Rhin — Rapp Anal Phys Chim Eau Rhin
Rapport. Svenska Institutet foer Konserveringsforskning — Rapp Sven Inst Konserveringsforsk
Rapport. Svenska Livsmedelsinstitutet — Rapp Sven Livsmedel-Sinstitutet
Rapport. Sveriges Lantbruksuniversitet. Institutionen foer Vaextodling — Rapp Sver Lantbruksuniv Inst Vaextodling
Rapport Technique Canadien des Sciences Halieutiques et Aquatiques — CTRSDR
Rapport Technique Canadien des Sciences Halieutiques et Aquatiques — Rapp Tech Can Sci Halieutiques et Aquat
Rapport Technique de Foresterie. Service Canadien des Forets — Rapp Tech For Serv Can For
Rapport Technique. Laboratoire de Recherches et de Controle Du Caoutchouc — Rapp Tech Lab Rech Controle Caoutch
Rapport Technique. Nagra — Rapp Tech Nagra
Rapport Technique. Office National d'Etudes et de Recherches Aeronautiques (France) — Rapp Tech Off Natl Etud Rech Aeronaut (Fr)

Rapport. Universitetet i Oslo. Fysisk Institutt — Rapp Univ i Oslo Fys Inst
Rapporten van het Nederlands Instituut voor Zuivelonderzoek — Rapp Ned Inst Zuivelonderz
Rapporter fraan Laboratoriet foer Klinisk Stressforskning. Karolinska Institutet — Rapp Lab Klin Stressforsk Karolinska Inst
Rapporter. Institutionen for Virkeslara. Skogshogskolan — Rapp Instn Virkeslara Skogshogsk
Rapporter och Meddelanden. Sveriges Geologiska Undersoekning — Rapp Medd Sver Geol Unders
Rapporter och Uppsatser. Avdelningen foer Skogsekologi. Skogshogskolan — Rapp Uppsats Avd Skogsekol Skogshogsk
Rapporter och Uppsatser. Institutionen foer Skoglig Matematisk Statistik. Skogshogskolan — Rapp Uppsats Instn Skoglig Mat Statist Skogshogsk
Rapporter och Uppsatser. Institutionen foer Skogsforyngring. Skogshogskolan [*A publication*] — Rapp Uppsats Instn Skogsforyngr Skogshogsk
Rapporter och Uppsatser. Institutionen foer Skogsgenetik. Skogshogskolan — Rapp Uppsats Instn Skogsgenet Skogshogsk
Rapporter och Uppsatser. Institutionen foer Skogsproduktion. Skogshogskolan [*A publication*] — Rapp Uppsats Instn Skogsprod Skogshogsk
Rapporter och Uppsatser. Institutionen foer Skogstaxering. Skogshogskolan — Rapp Uppsats Instn Skogstax Skogshogsk
Rapporter och Uppsatser. Institutionen foer Skogsteknik. Skogshogskolan — Rapp Uppsats Instn Skogstek Skogshogsk
Rapporter. Svenska Forskningsinstitutet foer Cement och Betong vid Tekniska Hoegskolan i Stockholm — Rapp Sven Forskningsinst Cem Betong Tek Hoegsk Stockholm
Rapporti al Congresso Internazionale del Petrolio — Rapp Congr Int Pet
Rapporti e Studi. Commissione di Studio dei Provvedimenti per la Conservazione e Difesa della Laguna e della Citta di Venezia — Rapp Studi Comm Stud Provvedimenti Conserv Dif
Rapporti ISTISAN [*Istituto Superiore di Sanita*] — Rapp ISTISAN
Rapporti Tecnici. Istituto de Ricerca sulle Acque — Rapp Tec Ist Ric Acque
Rapporto Interno. Instituto di Ricerca sulle Acque — Rapp Interno Ist Ric Acque
Rapports. Association Internationale de Chimie Cerealiere — Rapp Assoc Int Chim Cerealiere
Rapports. Commission Scientifique et Technique. Federation Internationale des Producteurs de Jus de Fruits — Rapp Comm Sci Tech Fed Int Prod Jus Fruits
Rapports. Congres International d'Hygiene et de Medecine Preventive — Rapp Congr Int Hyg Med Prev
Rapports de l'Assemblee Generale. Centre International des Engrais Chimiques — Rapp Assem Gen Cent Int Engrais Chim
Rapports des Fouilles — RF
Rapports et Discussions. Conseil de Chimie. Institut International de Chimie Solvay — Rapp Discuss Cons Chim Inst Int Chim Solvay
Rapports et Discussions sur les Isotopes. Institut International de Chimie Solvay. Conseil de Chimie — Rapp Discuss Isot Inst Int Chim Solvay Cons Chim
Rapports et Proces-Verbaux des Reunions — Rapp Proc Verb
Rapports et Proces-Verbaux des Reunions. Commission Internationale pour l'Exploration Scientifique de la Mer Mediterranee [*Monaco*] — CIRPB7
Rapports et Proces-Verbaux des Reunions. Commission Internationale pour l'Exploration Scientifique de la Mer Mediterranee (Monaco) — Rapp PV Reun Comm Int Explor Sci Mer Mediterr (Monaco)
Rapports et Proces-Verbaux des Reunions. Conseil International pour l'Exploration de la Mer — Rapp P-V Reun Cons Int Explor Mer
Rapports et Proces-Verbaux des Reunions. Conseil International pour l'Exploration de la Mer — RIEMA
Rapports Generaux des Travaux. Societe Philomatique de Paris — Rapp Gen Trav Soc Philom Paris
Rapports Scientifiques et Techniques. CNEXO [*Centre National pour l'Exploitation des Oceans*] **(France)** — Rapp Sci Tech CNEXO (Fr)
Rapports sur les Hydrates de Carbone (Glucides). Conference. Union Internationale de Chimie. Comptes Rendus — Rapp Hydrates Carbone Glucides Conf Union Int Chim CR
Rapports Techniques. Centre Belge d'Etude de la Corrosion — Rapp Tech Cent Belge Etude Corros
RAPRA [*Rubber and Plastics Research Association*] **Abstract** — RAPRA Abst
RAPRA [*Rubber and Plastics Research Association*] **Abstracts** — RAPRA Abstr
RAPRA [*Rubber and Plastics Research Association*] **Members Journal** [*England*] — RAPRA Members J
Raptor Research — Raptor Res
Rare Books and Manuscripts Librarianship — RBML
Rare Earth Research Conference — Rare Earth Res Conf
Rare Earths in Modern Science and Technology — Rare Earths Mod Sci Technol
Rare Metals (Tokyo) — Rare Met Tokyo
Rare Nuclear Processes. Proceedings. Europhysics Conference on Nuclear Physics — Rare Nucl Processes Proc Europhys Conf Nucl Phys
Rarefied Gas Dynamics — Rarefied Gas Dyn
Rarefied Gas Dynamics. Proceedings of the International Symposium — Rarefied Gas Dyn Proc Int Symp
Raritan — PRAR
RAS. Rohr-Armatur-Sanitaer-Heizung — RASHA
RAS. Rohr-Armatur-Sanitaer-Heizung Informationsblatt fuer den Fachhandel und das Sanitaerfach und Heizungsfach — ROA
Raschet i Konstruirovanie Neftezavodskogo Oborudovaniya — Raschet Konstr Neftezavod Oborud
Raschet i Konstruirovanie Neftezavodskogo Oborudovaniya — Raschet Konstr Neftezvod Oborudovaniya
Raschet. Konstruirovanie i Issledovanie Oborudovaniya Proizvodstva Istochnikov Toka — Raschet Konstr Issled Oborud Proizvod Istochnikov Toka
Raschet, Konstruirovanie, i Primenenie Radiatsionnykh Trub v Promyshlennosti. Materialy Nauchno-Tekhnicheskoi Konferentsii — Raschet Konstr Prim Radiats Trub Prom Mater Nauch Tekh Konf
Raschety na Prochnost — Raschety Prochn
Rasegna Indo-Greco-Italica — Rass Indo Greco Ital
Rasprave i Gradja za Povijest Nauka — Raspr Gradja Povij Nauka
Rassegna — Ra
Rassegna Abruzzese di Storia ed Arte — RASA
Rassegna. Archivi di Stato — RAS
Rassegna Bibliografica della Letteratura Italiana — RBLI
Rassegna Chimica — RACHA
Rassegna Chimica — Rass Chim
Rassegna Clinico-Scientifica — Rass Clin Sci
Rassegna Clinico-Scientifica. Istituto Biochimico Italiano — Rass Clin Sci Ist Biochim Ital
Rassegna Critica della Letteratura Italiana — Rass Crit d Lett Ital
Rassegna Critica della Letteratura Italiana — RCLI
Rassegna d'Arte Antica e Moderna — Rassd'A
Rassegna dei Lavori Pubblici — Rass Lav Pubbl
Rassegna del Lavoro — Rass del Lav
Rassegna del Lazio. Rivista Mensile. Provincia di Roma — Rass Lazio
Rassegna della Letteratura Italiana — RAS
Rassegna della Letteratura Italiana — Rass Let It
Rassegna della Letteratura Italiana — RLeIt
Rassegna della Letteratura Italiana — RLI
Rassegna della Proprieta Industriale, Letteraria, e Artistica — Rass Propr Ind Lett Art
Rassegna dell'Agricoltura Italiana — Rass Agr Ital
Rassegna dell'Arte Antica e Moderna — Rass dell Arte Ant e Mod
Rassegna di Asetica e Mistica S. Caterina da Siena — RAMC
Rassegna di Clinica Terapia e Scienze Affini — Rass Clin Ter Sci Affini
Rassegna di Coltura — RCol
Rassegna di Coltura — RColt
Rassegna di Cultura — RassCult
Rassegna di Cultura e Vita Scolastica — RCVS
Rassegna di Cultura Militare — Rass Cult Mil
Rassegna di Dermatologia e di Sifilografia — Rass Dermatol Sifilogr
Rassegna di Diritto Ecclesiastico — RDE
Rassegna di Diritto Pubblico — Rass Pubbl
Rassegna di Filosofia — RasF
Rassegna di Filosofia — RassFilos
Rassegna di Filosofia (Roma) — RFR
Rassegna di Fisiopatologia Clinica e Terapeutica — Rass Fisiopat Clin Ter
Rassegna di Fisiopatologia Clinica e Terapeutica — Rass Fisiopatol Clin Ter
Rassegna di Fisiopatologia Clinica e Terapeutica — RFCTA
Rassegna di Letteratura Tomistica — RLT
Rassegna di Medicina Applicata al Lavoro Industriale — Rass Med Appl Lav Ind
Rassegna di Medicina del Traffico — Rass Med Traf
Rassegna di Medicina Industriale — Rass Med Ind
Rassegna di Medicina Industriale e di Igiene del Lavoro — Rass Med Ind Ig Lav
Rassegna di Medicina Industriale e di Igiene del Lavoro — RMIIA
Rassegna di Medicina Sperimentale — Rass Med Sper
Rassegna di Medicina Sperimentale. Supplemento — Rass Med Sper Suppl
Rassegna di Neurologia Vegetativa — Rass Neurol Veg
Rassegna di Neuropsichiatria e Scienze Affini — Rass Neuropsich
Rassegna di Neuropsichiatria e Scienze Affini — Rass Neuropsichiatr Sci Affini
Rassegna di Patologia dell'Apparato Respiratorio — Rass Patol Appar Respir
Rassegna di Politica Internazionale — RPI
Rassegna di Psicologia Generale e Clinica — Rass Psicol Gen Clin
Rassegna di Scienze Filosofiche — RSF
Rassegna di Scienze Filosofiche — RSFil
Rassegna di Servizio Sociale — Rass Serv Soc
Rassegna di Statistiche del Lavoro — Rass Statis Lav
Rassegna di Studi Etiopici — Rass Studi Etiop
Rassegna di Studi Etiopici [*Rome*] — RaStEt
Rassegna di Studi Etiopici — RSE
Rassegna di Studi Etiopici — RSEt
Rassegna di Studi Francesi — Rass di Studi Francesi
Rassegna di Studi Francesi — RSF
Rassegna di Studi Psichiatrici — Rass Studi Psichiatr
Rassegna di Terapia e Patologia Clinica — Rass Ter Patol Clin
Rassegna di Urologia e Nefrologia — Rass Urol Nefrol
Rassegna di Urologia e Nefrologia — RSUNAC
Rassegna d'Informazioni. Istituto di Studi Romani — RISR
Rassegna d'Italia — Rass d Italia
Rassegna d'Italia — Rass d'It
Rassegna Economica — Rass Ec
Rassegna Economica — Rass Econ
Rassegna Economica. Camera di Commercio, Industria, e Agricoltura di Alessandria — Rass Econ Cam Commer Ind Agr Alessandria
Rassegna Economica dell'Africa Italiana — Rass Econ Afr Ital
Rassegna Economica delle Colonie — Rass Econ Colon
Rassegna Economica (Napoli) — Rass Econ (Napoli)
Rassegna ed Archivio di Chirurgia — Rass Arch Chir
Rassegna Frignanese — RFrign
Rassegna Gallaratese di Storia e d'Arte — RGSA
Rassegna Giuliana di Medicina — Rass Giuliana Med
Rassegna Giuridica Sarda — Rass Giur Sard
Rassegna Gregoriana — RGr
Rassegna Gregoriana per Gli Studi Liturgici e Pel Canto Sacro — RGSL
Rassegna Iberistica — R Iber
Rassegna Indo-Greco-Italica — Rass IGI
Rassegna Internazionale di Clinica e Terapia — Rass Int Clin
Rassegna Internazionale di Clinica e Terapia — Rass Int Clin Ter
Rassegna Internazionale di Stomatologia Pratica — Rass Int Stomatol Prat
Rassegna Internazionale Elettronica e Nucleare. Atti del Congresso Scientifico. Sezione Nucleare — Rass Int Elettron Nucl Atti Congr Sci Sez Nucl
Rassegna Italiana — RasI

Rassegna Italiana — RI
Rassegna Italiana di Chirurgia e Medicina — Rass Ital Chir Med
Rassegna Italiana di Gastro-Enterologia — Rass Ital Gastro-Enterol
Rassegna Italiana di Gastro-Enterologia. Supplemento — Rass Ital Gastro-Enterol Suppl
Rassegna Italiana di Lingue e Letteratura Classiche — RLC
Rassegna Italiana di Lingue e Letterature Classiche — Rass Ital Ling Lett Cl
Rassegna Italiana di Lingue e Letterature Classiche — Rassegna Ital
Rassegna Italiana di Linguistica Applicata — RILA
Rassegna Italiana di Politica e di Cultura — RIPC
Rassegna Italiana di Sociologia — Rass Ital Soc
Rassegna Italiana di Sociologia — Rass Ital Sociol
Rassegna Italiana di Sociologia — Rassegna Ital Sociol
Rassegna Italiana di Sociologia — RIS
Rassegna Italiana d'Ottalmologia — Rass Ital Ottalmol
Rassegna Lucchese — RLu
Rassegna Lucchese — RLuc
Rassegna Medica — Rass Med
Rassegna Medica - Convivium Sanitatis — Rass Med Convivium Sanit
Rassegna Medica e Culturale — Rass Med Cult
Rassegna Medica Sarda — Rass Med Sarda
Rassegna Medica Sarda. Supplemento — Rass Med Sarda Suppl
Rassegna Mensile di Clinica, di Patologia, di Terapia, e di Vita Professionale del Medico Condotto e del Medico Pratico — Rass Mens Clin Patol Ter Vita Prof Med Condotto Med Prat
Rassegna Mensile di Israel [*Rome*] — RaMIsr
Rassegna Mensile di Israel — Ras Isr
Rassegna Mensile di Israel — Rass Mens Israel
Rassegna Mensile di Israel — RMI
Rassegna Mensile di Israel — RMIs
Rassegna Mineraria e Metallurgica Italiana — Rass Min Metall Ital
Rassegna Mineraria, Metallurgia, e Chimica — Rass Min Metall Chim
Rassegna Monetaria — R Mon
Rassegna Monetaria — R Monet
Rassegna Monetaria — Rass Mon
Rassegna Monetaria — RM
Rassegna Monetaria — RN
Rassegna Musicale — Ra M
Rassegna Musicale — Rass Mus
Rassegna Musicale — RM
Rassegna Musicale Curci — Rass Mus Curci
Rassegna Musicale Curci — Rassegna M Curci
Rassegna Musicale Curci Anno — RMCA
Rassegna Nazionale — Rass Nazion
Rassegna Nazionale — RNaz
Rassegna Numismatica — RNum
Rassegna Odontotecnica — Rass Odontotec
Rassegna Penitenziaria e Criminologica — Rass Penitenziaria Crim
Rassegna Pugliese — RPu
Rassegna Sindacale. Quaderni — Rass Sind Quad
Rassegna Sovietica — RSov
Rassegna Storica del Risorgimento — RaS
Rassegna Storica del Risorgimento — Rass Stor R
Rassegna Storica del Risorgimento — Rass Stor Risorg
Rassegna Storica del Risorgimento — RSR
Rassegna Storica del Risorgimento — RSRis
Rassegna Storica Salernitana — Rass Stor Salern
Rassegna Storica Salernitana — Rassegna St Salern
Rassegna Storica Salernitana — RSS
Rassegna Storica Salernitana — RSSal
Rassegna Storica Toscana — Rass Stor Toscana
Rassegna Trimestrale di Odontoiatria — Rass Trimest Odontoiatr
Rassegna Trimestrale di Odontoiatria — RTODA
Rassegna Volterrana — RV
Rasseyanie Energii pri Kolebaniyakh Mekhanicheskikh Sistem. Materialy Nauchnogo Soveshchaniya — Rasseyan Energ Kolebaniyakh Mekh Sist Mater Nauchn Soveshch
Rasshirennye Tezisy Dokladov na Vsesoyuznoi Konferentsii po Teoreticheskim Voprosam Adsorbtsii — Rasshir Tezisy Dokl Vses Konf Teor Vopr Adsorbts
Rastenievadni Nauki — Rasteniev Nauki
Rasteniev'dni Nauki — Rasteniev'd Nauki
Rastenievudni Nauki — Rast Nauki
Rastenievudni Nauki — Rastenievud Nauk
Rastenievudni Nauki — Rastenievud Nauki
Rasteniya i Promyshlennaya Sreda — Rast Prom Sreda
Rastitelna Zashchita — Rast Zashch
Rastitelna Zashtita [*Plant Protection*] — Rastit Zasht
Rastitelna Zashtita/Plant Protection — Rastit Zasht Plant Prot
Rastitel'nost Krainego Severa i Ee Osvoenie — Rastit Krainego Sev Ee Osvoenie
Rastitel'nost Krainego Severa SSSR i Ee Osvoenie — Rastit Krainego Sev SSSR Ee Osvoenie
Rastitel'nost Latviiskoi SSR — Rastit Latv SSR
Rastitel'nost' SSSR. Vegetatio URSS — Rastiteln SSSR
Rastitel'nye Belki — Rastit Belki
Rastitel'nye Resursy — Rast Resursy
Rastitel'nye Resursy — Rastit Resur
Rastitel'nye Resursy — RRESA
Rat News Letter — Rat News Lett
Rating Appeals [*United Kingdom*] — RA
Rational Drug Therapy — Ration Drug Ther
Rational Drug Therapy — RDGTA
Rationalisierung [*Munich*] — RTNLB
Rationality of Drug Development. Proceedings. International Meeting of Medical Advisers in the Pharmaceutical Industry — Ration Drug Dev Proc Int Meet Med Advis Pharm Ind
Rauch Guide to the United States Paint Industry Data — Rauch Pnt
Raumfahrtforschung — RMFFA
Raumforschung und Raumordnung — Raumforsch und Raumordnung
Raumforschung und Raumordnung — Raumforsch u-Ordnung
Raumforschung und Raumordnung — RFRO
Raumforschung und Raumordnung — RFRR-A
Raumordnung, Stadtebau, Wohnungswesen, Bauwesen [*Database*] — RSWB
Raven — RV
Raven Press Series on Molecular and Cellular Biology — Raven Press Ser Mol Cell Biol
Ravensberger Blaetter fuer Geschichts-, Volks-, und Heimatkunde — Rav Bl
Raw Material — Raw Mater
Raw Materials Report [*Sweden*] — Raw Mater Rep
Raw Materials Survey. Resource Report — Raw Materials Survey Res Rept
Ray Society Publications — Ray Soc Pub
Raymond W. Brink Selected Mathematical Papers — Raymond W Brink Selected Math Papers
Rayon and Melliand Textile Monthly — Rayon Melliand Text Mon
Rayon and Synthetic Textiles — Rayon
Rayon and Synthetic Textiles — Rayon Synth Text
Rayon and Synthetic Yarn Journal — Rayon Synth Yarn J
Rayon and the Rayon Journal — Rayon Rayon J
Rayon Journal — Rayon J
Rayon Journal and Cellulose Fibers — Rayon J Cellul Fibers
Rayon Record — Rayon Rec
Rayon Revue — Rayon Rev
Rayon Textile Monthly — Rayon Text Mon
Rayonne et Fibres Synthetiques — Rayonne Fibres Synth
Rayonnements Ionisants — Rayonnem Ionis
Rayonnements Ionisants — RITMB
Rayonnements Ionisants. Techniques de Mesures et de Protection — Rayonnem Ionis Tech Mes Prot
Raziskave in Studije-Kmetijski Institut Slovenije — Raziskave Stud Kmetijski Inst Slov
Razon y Fabula — RF
Razon y Fabula — RyFa
Razon y Fabula — RyFab
Razon y Fe — R Fe
Razon y Fe [*Madrid*] — RazFe
Razon y Fe — RF
Razon y Fe — RyF
Razon y Fe (Madrid) — RFM
Razon y Fe. Revista Hispano-Americana de Cultura — Razon y Fe
Razprave Matematicno-Pri-Rodoslovnega Razreda Akademije Znanosti in Umetnosti v Ljubljani — Razpr Mat Prir Razr Akad Znan v Ljubljani
Razprave Razreda za Filoloske in Literarne vede Slovenske Akademije Znanoste in Umetnosti — Raz SAZU
Razprave. Slovenska Akademija Znanosti i Umetnosti — Razprave SAZU
Razprave. Slovenska Akademija Znanosti in Umetnosti. IV — Razpr Slov Akad Znan Umet IV
Razprave. Slovenska Akademija Znanosti in Umetnosti. Razred za Matematicne, Fizikalne, in Tehnicne Vede. Serija A. Matematicne, Fizikalne, in Kemicne Vede — Razpr Slov Akad Znan Umet Razred Mat Fiz Teh Vede Ser A
Razrabotka i Ehksplutatsiya Gazovykh i Gazokondensatnykh Mestorozhdenij — Razrab Ehkspl Gazov Gazokondens Mestorozhd
Razrabotka Mestorozhdenii Poleznykh Iskopaemykh — RMPIA
Razrabotka Mestorozhdenii Poleznykh Iskopaemykh (Kiev) — Razrab Mestorozhd Polezn Iskop (Kiev)
Razrabotka Mestorozhdenii Poleznykh Iskopaemykh (Tiflis) — Razrab Mestorozhd Polezn Iskop (Tiflis)
Razrabotka Neftyanykh i Gazovykh Mestorozhdenii — Razrab Neft Gazov Mestorozhd
Razrabotka Rudnykh Mestorozhdenii — RARMB
Razrabotka Rudnykh Mestorozhdenii [*Ukrainian SSR*] — Razrab Rudn Mestorozhd
Razred za Matematicne, Fizikalne in Tehnicne Vede Dela [*Ljubliana*] — Razred Mat Fiz Teh Vede Dela
Razvedka i Okhrana Nedr — Razved i Okhr Nedr
Razvedka i Okhrana Nedr — Razved Okhr Nedr
Razvedka i Okhrana Nedr — RZONA
Razvedka i Razrabotka Neftyanykh i Gazovykh Mestorozhdenii — Razved Razrab Neft Gazov Mestorozhd
Razvedka i Razrabotka Neftyanykh i Gazovykh Mestorozhdenii — RRNGA
Razvedka Nedr [*Former USSR*] — Razved Nedr
Razvedka Nedr — RZNDA
Razvedochnaya Geofizika — RAGEA
Razvedochnaya Geofizika — Razved Geofiz
Razvedochnaya Geofizika (Leningrad) — Razved Geofiz (Leningrad)
Razvedochnaya i Promyslovaya Geofizika — Razved Promysl Geofiz
Razvitie Proizvodstva Kovkogo Chuguna. Trudy Vsesoyuznoi Konferentsii po Teorii i Praktike Proizvodstva Otlivok iz Kovkogo Chuguna — Razvit Proizvod Kovkogo Chuguna Tr Vses Konf
RBE. Revista Brasileira de Engenharia — RBE Rev Bras Eng
RBM. Revue Europeenne de Biotechnologie Medicale — RBM Rev Eur Biotechnol Med
RCA [*Radio Corporation of America*] **Engineer** — RCA Eng
RCA [*Radio Corporation of America*] **Engineer** — RCAEB
RCA [*Radio Corporation of America*] **Review** — RCA R
RCA [*Radio Corporation of America*] **Review** — RCA Rev
RCA [*Radio Corporation of America*] **Review** — RCARC
RCA [*Radio Corporation of America*] **Technical Notes** — RCA Tech Not

RCA [*Radio Corporation of America*] **Technical Notes** — RCA Tech Notes
RCI. Riscaldamento, Condizionamento, Idrosanitaria — RCI Riscaldamento Cond Idrosanit
RCI (Riscaldamento, Refrigerazione, Condizionamento, Idrosanitaria) — RCI Riscaldamento Refrig Cond Idrosanit
RCL [*Ricegrowers' Cooperative Ltd.*] **Magazine** — RCL Mag
RCMP [*Royal Canadian Mounted Police*] **Quarterly** — RCMP
RCN [*Reactor Centrum Nederland*] **Bulletin** — RCN Bull
Re Artes Liberales — ReAL
Re: Arts and Letters — REAL
REA [*Rural Electrification Administration*] **Bulletin** — REA Bull
REA (Rural Electrification Administration) Bulletin (United States) — REA (Rural Electr Adm) Bull (US)
Reaction Kinetics [*Later, Gas Kinetics and Energy Transfer*] — React Kinet
Reaction Kinetics and Catalysis Letters — React Kin C
Reaction Kinetics and Catalysis Letters — React Kinet Catal Lett
Reaction Kinetics and Catalysis Letters — RKCLA
Reaction Kinetics in Heterogeneous Chemical Systems. Proceedings. International Meeting. Societe de Chimie Physique — React Kinet Heterog Chem Syst Proc Int Meet Soc Chim Phys
Reaction Mechanisms in Organic Chemistry [*Elsevier Book Series*] — RMOC
Reaction Research Society. News — React Res Soc News
Reaction Research Society. Report — React Res Soc Rep
Reactive and Functional Polymers — React Funct Polym
Reactive Intermediates — React Intermed
Reactive Intermediates — RINTDU
Reactive Intermediates (Plenum) — React Intermed (Plenum)
Reactive Intermediates (Wiley) — React Intermed Wiley
Reactive Polymers [*The Netherlands*] — React Polym
Reactive Polymers, Ion Exchangers. Sorbents — React Polym Ion Exch Sorbents
Reactivity and Structure Concepts in Organic Chemistry — React Struct Concepts Org Chem
Reactivity and Structure Concepts in Organic Chemistry — RSCCDS
Reactivity of Solids. International Symposium on Reactivity of Solids — React Solids Int Symp
Reactivity of Solids. Proceedings. International Symposium on the Reactivity of Solids — React Solids Proc Int Symp
Reactor and Fuel-Processing Technology — React Fuel-Process Technol
Reactor Centrum Nederland. Mededeling — RCN Meded
Reactor Centrum Nederland. Report — RCN Rep
Reactor Centrum Nederland. Report — React Cent Ned Rep
Reactor Centrum Nederland-Mededeling — React Cent Ned Meded
Reactor Fuel Processing — React Fuel Process
Reactor Fuel Processing — Reactor Fuel Process
Reactor Fuel Processing — RFPRA
Reactor Materials — Reactor Mater
Reactor Materials — RRMTA
Reactor Research Centre, Kalpakkam. Report RRC — React Res Cent Kalpakkam Rep RRC
Reactor Science and Technology — React Sci Technol
Reactor Technology — React Technol
Reactor Technology — RETNA
REACTS. Proceedings. Regional Educators Annual Chemistry Teaching Symposium — REACTS Proc Reg Educ Annu Chem Teach Symp
Reader Magazine — Reader
Readers Advisory Service — RAS
Reader's Digest — GRDI
Reader's Digest — RDIGA
Reader's Digest — Read Dig
Reader's Digest — Read Digest
Reader's Digest — Readers D
Reader's Digest — Reader's Dig
Reader's Digest (Canadian English Edition) — IRDC
Readers' Guide Abstracts — RGA
Readers' Guide to Periodical Literature — Read Guide Period Lit
Readers' Guide to Periodical Literature — RG
Reading Abstracts — Read Abstr
Reading Disability Digest — Read Disabil Dig
Reading Education — Read Educ
Reading Education — Reading Educ
Reading Geographer — Read Geog
Reading Improvement — Read Improv
Reading Manitoba — Read Man
Reading Material for the Blind and Physically Handicapped [*Database*] — BLND
Reading Medieval Studies — RMSt
Reading Psychology — R Psych
Reading Psychology — Read Psychol
Reading Psychology — RRPSDW
Reading Research Quarterly — Read Res Q
Reading Teacher — GRTE
Reading Teacher — Read Teach
Reading Teacher — RT
Reading Test and Reviews — RTR
Reading Time — Read Time
Reading Today International — Read Today Int
Reading University. Geological Reports — Reading Univ Geol Rep
Reading World — Read World
Reading-Canada-Lecture — RCL
Readings in Glass History — Read Glass Hist
Readings in Literary Criticism — RLitC
Readings in Mathematics — Read Math
Reaktivy i Osobo Chistye Veshchestva — Reakt Osobo Chist Veshchestva
Reaktor Bulletin — Reakt Bull
Reaktortagung (Fachvortraege) [*Germany*] — Reaktortag (Fachvortr)
Reaktsii i Metody Issledovaniya Organicheskikh Soedinenii [*Former USSR*] — Reakts Metody Issled Org Soedin
Reaktsionnaya Sposobnost' i Mekhanizmy Reaktsii Organicheskikh Soedinenii — Reakts Sposobn Mekh Reakts Org Soedin
Reaktsionnaya Sposobnost' Koordinatsionnykh Soedinenii — Reakts Sposobn Koord Soedin
Reaktsionnaya Sposobnost' Organicheskikh Soedinenij — Reakts Sposobn Org Soedin
Reaktsionnaya Sposobnost' Organicheskikh Soedinenij. Tartuskij Gosudarstvennyj Universitet — Reakts Sposobnost' Org Soedin Tartu Gos Univ
Real Academia de Ciencias Exactas, Fisicas, y Naturales de Madrid. Memorias — R Acad Cienc Exactas Fis Nat Madrid Mem
Real Academia de Ciencias Exactas, Fisicas, y Naturales de Madrid. Memorias. Serie de Ciencias Exactas — R Acad Cienc Exactas Fis Nat Madrid Mem Ser Cienc Exactas
Real Academia de Ciencias Exactas, Fisicas, y Naturales de Madrid. Memorias. Serie de Ciencias Naturales — R Acad Cienc Exactas Fis Nat Madrid Mem Ser Cienc Nat
Real Academia de Ciencias Exactas, Fisicas, y Naturales de Madrid. Revista [*A publication*] — Rev Real Acad Cienc Exact Fis Natur Madrid
Real Academia de Ciencias Medicas, Fisicas, y Naturales de la Habana. Anales — R Ac Cienc Habana An
Real Academia de Ciencias Medicas, Fisicas y Naturales de la Habana. Anales — R Acad De Cienc Med Fis Y Nat De La Habana Anales
Real Academia de Ciencias y Artes de Barcelona. Memorias — R Acad Cienc y Artes Barcelona Mem
Real Academia de Farmacia de Barcelona. Discurso de Ingreso — R Acad Farm Barcelona Discurso Ingreso
Real Academia de Farmacia de Barcelona. Discursos de Recepcion — R Acad Farm Barcelona Discursos Recepcion
Real Academia de Farmacia de Barcelona. Publicaciones. Serie A. Anuarios, Memorias, y Discursos Inaugurales de Curso — R Acad Farm Barcelona Publ Ser A
Real Academia de Farmacia de Barcelona. Sesion Inaugural — R Acad Farm Barcelona Ses Inaug
Real Academia de la Historia. Boletin — RAHBol
Real Academia Espanola. Boletin — Acad Esp Bol
Real Academia Espanola. Boletin — RAE
Real Academia Galega de Ciencis. Revista — R Acad Galega Cienc Rev
Real Analysis Exchange — Real Anal Exchange
Real Encyclopaedie der Classischen Altertumswissenschaft — RA
Real Encyclopaedie der Classischen Altertumswissenschaft [*Pauly*] — Real Enc
Real Encyclopaedie der Classischen Altertumswissenschaft [*Pauly*] — RECA
Real Estate and Stock Journal — Real Estate & Stock J
Real Estate Appraiser and Analyst — Real Estate Appraiser & Anal
Real Estate Bulletin — Real Estate Bull
Real Estate Investing Letter [*Database*] — REIL
Real Estate Investment Digest — Real Estate Invest Dig
Real Estate Journal — Real Estate J
Real Estate Law Journal — R Est LJ
Real Estate Law Journal — Real Est L
Real Estate Law Journal — Real Est LJ
Real Estate Law Journal — Real Estate L J
Real Estate Law Journal — REL
Real Estate Listing Service [*Database*] — RELS
Real Estate Newsletter — REN
Real Estate Quarterly — Real Estate Quart
Real Estate Review — Real Est Re
Real Estate Review — Real Est Rev
Real Estate Review — Real Estate R
Real Estate Review — Real Estate Rev
Real Estate Review — RER
Real Estate Today — IRTO
Real Estate Today — RESTD
Real Gardening — Real Gard
Real Property Practice — RPP
Real Property, Probate, and Trust Journal — R Prop Prob and Tr J
Real Property, Probate, and Trust Journal — Real Prop P
Real Property, Probate, and Trust Journal — Real Prop Prob and Tr J
Real Property, Probate, and Trust Journal — Real Prop Probate & Trust J
Real Property, Probate, and Trust Journal — RPP
Real Property Reports — Real Prop Rep
Real Property Reports — RPR
Real Sociedad Espanola de Fisica y Quimica. Reunion Bienal — R Soc Esp Fis Quim Reun Bienal
REAL. The Yearbook of Research in English and American Literature — REALB
Real Time Signal Processing — Real Time Signal Process
Reale Accademia dei Lincei. Atti. Notizie degli Scavi — RAL Scav
Reale Accademia di Medicina di Torino. Giornale — R Accad Di Med Di Torino Giorn
Reale Accademia di Scienze, Lettere, ed Arti in Modena. Memorie — R Accad Sci Lett Arti Modena Mem
Reale Comitato Geologico d'Italia. Bolletino — R Comitato G Italia B
Reale Istituto Veneto di Scienze, Lettere, ed Arti. Memorie — R Istituto Veneto Memorie
Reale Istituto Veneto di Scienze, Lettere, ed Arti. Memorie — Real Ist Veneto Mem
Real-Encyclopaedie der Gesammten Heilkunde Medicinisch-Chirurgisches Handwoerterbuch fuer Praktische Aerzte — Real-Encycl Ges Heilk
Real-Encyclopaedie der Klassischen Altertumswissenschaft — RE
Realencyclopaedie fuer Protestantische Theologie und Kirche — PRE
Real-Encyklopaedie der Christlichen Altertuemer — RE Chr A
Realidad — Re

Realidad Economica — Realidad Econ
Realismo Lirico — RLir
Realist Writer — Real Wr
Realites — R
Realites Secretes — RS
Reallexikon der Aegyptischen Religionsgeschichte — RAeRG
Reallexikon der Aegyptischen Religionsgeschichte — Reallexikon
Reallexikon der Assyriologie — R Lex Assyr
Reallexikon der Assyriologie — RLA
Reallexikon der Byzantinischen Kunst — RBK
Reallexikon der Byzantinistik — R Byz
Reallexikon der Byzantinistik — RB
Reallexikon der Deutschen Literaturgeschichte — RDL
Reallexikon der Germanischen Altertumskunde — RGA
Reallexikon der Indo-Germanischen Altertumskunde — RIA
Reallexikon der Vorgeschichte — Real Vorg
Reallexikon der Vorgeschichte — RLV
Reallexikon fuer Antike und Christentum — R Ant Christ
Reallexikon fuer Antike und Christentum — RAC
Reallexikon fuer Antike und Christentum — RACh
Reallexikon fuer Antike und Christentum — Reallex fur Ant und Christ
Reallexikon fuer Antike und Christentum — RLAC
Realta del Mezzogiorno — Realta Mezzogiorno
Realta del Mezzogiorno. Mensile di Politica, Economia, Cultura — Real M
Realta Economica — Real Econ
Realta Economica — Realta Econ
Realta Nuova — RealN
Realta Nuova — RN
Reanimation et Medecine d'Urgence — Reanim Med Urgence
Reanimation et Organes Artificiels — Reanim Organes Artif
Reason — PREA
Recent Achievements in Restorative Neurology — RARNEB
Recent Achievements in Restorative Neurology — Recent Achiev Restor Neurol
Recent Achievements in Restorative Neurology — Recent Achiev Restorative Neurol
Recent Advances and New Syndromes — Recent Adv New Syndr
Recent Advances as a Core Curriculum Course — Recent Adv Core Curric Course
Recent Advances in Acarology. Proceedings. International Congress of Acarology — Recent Adv Acarol Proc Int Congr
Recent Advances in Adaptive and Sensory Materials and Their Applications — Recent Adv Adapt Sens Mater Their Appl
Recent Advances in Aerospace Medicine — Recent Adv Aerosp Med
Recent Advances in Anaesthesia and Analgesia — Recent Adv Anaesth Analg
Recent Advances in Animal Nutrition — RAANES
Recent Advances in Animal Nutrition — Recent Adv Anim Nutr
Recent Advances in Aquatic Mycology — Recent Adv Aquat Mycol
Recent Advances in Basic Microcirculatory Research. European Conference on Microcirculation — Recent Adv Basic Microcirc Res Eur Conf
Recent Advances in Behcet's Disease — Recent Adv Behcets Dis
Recent Advances in Biological Membrane Studies — Recent Adv Biol Membr Stud
Recent Advances in Biological Nitrogen Fixation — Recent Adv Biol Nitrogen Fixation
Recent Advances in Biological Psychiatry — Recent Adv Biol Psychiatry
Recent Advances in Biotechnology — Recent Adv Biotechnol
Recent Advances in Blood Coagulation — Recent Adv Blood Coagulation
Recent Advances in Blood Group Biochemistry — Recent Adv Blood Group Biochem
Recent Advances in Botany — Recent Advanc Bot
Recent Advances in Buffalo Research and Development — Recent Adv Buffalo Res Dev
Recent Advances in Cancer Research. Cell Biology, Molecular Biology, and Tumor Virology — Recent Adv Cancer Res Cell Biol Mol Biol Tumor Virol
Recent Advances in Cancer Treatment — Recent Adv Cancer Treat
Recent Advances in Capillary Gas Chromatography — Recent Adv Capillary Gas Chromatogr
Recent Advances in Cardiac Arrhythmias — Recent Adv Card Arrhythmias
Recent Advances in Chemical Information — Recent Adv Chem Inf
Recent Advances in Clinical Biochemistry — Recent Adv Clin Biochem
Recent Advances in Clinical Nuclear Medicine — Recent Adv Clin Nucl Med
Recent Advances in Clinical Nutrition — Recent Adv Clin Nutr
Recent Advances in Clinical Pathology — Recent Adv Clin Pathol
Recent Advances in Clinical Pharmacology — Recent Adv Clin Pharmacol
Recent Advances in Clinical Therapeutics — Recent Adv Clin Ther
Recent Advances in Community Medicine — RCOMD6
Recent Advances in Community Medicine — Recent Adv Community Med
Recent Advances in Drug Delivery Systems — Recent Adv Drug Delivery Syst
Recent Advances in Drug Research — Recent Adv Drug Res
Recent Advances in Endocrinology and Metabolism — Recent Adv Endocrinol Metab
Recent Advances in Engineering Science — Recent Adv Eng Sci
Recent Advances in Food Irradiation — Recent Adv Food Irradiat
Recent Advances in Food Science — Recent Adv Food Sci
Recent Advances in Gastroenterology — Recent Adv Gastroenterol
Recent Advances in Geriatric Medicine — Recent Adv Geriatr Med
Recent Advances in Germfree Research. Proceedings. International Symposium on Gnotobiology — Recent Adv Germfree Res Proc Int Symp Gnotobiol
Recent Advances in Glaucoma. Proceedings. International Symposium on Glaucoma — Recent Adv Glaucoma Proc Int Symp Glaucoma
Recent Advances in Gut Hormone Research — Recent Adv Gut Horm Res
Recent Advances in Haematology — Recent Adv Haematol
Recent Advances in Human Biology — Recent Adv Hum Biol
Recent Advances in Infection — Recent Adv Infect
Recent Advances in Invertebrate Physiology — Recent Advanc Invert Physiol
Recent Advances in Liquid Crystalline Polymers — Recent Adv Liq Cryst Polym
Recent Advances in Mechanistic and Synthetic Aspects of Polymerization — Recent Adv Mech Synth Aspects Polym
Recent Advances in Medicine — Recent Adv Med
Recent Advances in Microcirculatory Research — Recent Adv Microcirc Res
Recent Advances in Mucosal Immunity — Recent Adv Mucosal Immun
Recent Advances in Mucosal Immunology. Part A. Cellular Interactions — Recent Adv Mucosal Immunol Part A
Recent Advances in Myology. Proceedings. International Congress on Muscle Diseases — Recent Adv Myology Proc Int Congr Muscle Dis
Recent Advances in Nervous System Toxicology — Recent Adv Nerv Syst Toxicol
Recent Advances in Non-Linear Computational Mechanics — Recent Adv Non Linear Comput Mech
Recent Advances in Nuclear Medicine — Recent Adv Nucl Med
Recent Advances in Nuclear Structure. Lectures. Predeal International School — Recent Adv Nucl Struct Lect Predeal Int Sch
Recent Advances in Numerical Methods in Fluids — Recent Adv Numer Methods Fluids
Recent Advances in Nursing — Recent Adv Nurs
Recent Advances in Obesity and Diabetes Research — Recent Adv Obes Diabetes Res
Recent Advances in Obesity Research — Recent Adv Obes Res
Recent Advances in Obesity Research — Recent Adv Obesity Res
Recent Advances in Occupational Health — Recent Adv Occ Hlth
Recent Advances in Pediatric Nephrology — Recent Adv Pediatr Nephrol
Recent Advances in Pharmacology and Therapeutics — Recent Adv Pharmacol Ther
Recent Advances in Physiology — Recent Adv Physiol
Recent Advances in Phytochemistry — Recent Adv Phytochem
Recent Advances in Plant Nutrition. Proceedings. Colloquium on Plant Analysis and Fertilizer Problems — Recent Adv Plant Nutr Proc Colloq Plant Anal Fert Probl
Recent Advances in Polymer Blends, Grafts, and Blocks — Recent Adv Polym Blends Grafts Blocks
Recent Advances in Renal Disease — Recent Adv Renal Dis
Recent Advances in RES [*Reticuloendothelial System*] **Research** — Recent Adv RES Res
Recent Advances in Research of Nervous System — Recent Adv Res Nerv Syst
Recent Advances in Science and Technology of Materials — Recent Adv Sci Technol Mater
Recent Advances in Semiconductors. Theory and Technology — Recent Adv Semicond Theory Technol
Recent Advances in Studies on Cardiac Structure and Metabolism — RCSMC
Recent Advances in Studies on Cardiac Structure and Metabolism — Recent Adv Stud Card Struct Metab
Recent Advances in the Biochemistry of Cereals — Recent Adv Biochem Cereals
Recent Advances in the Biochemistry of Fruits and Vegetables — Recent Adv Biochem Fruits Veg
Recent Advances in the Chemistry and Biochemistry of Plant Lipids — Recent Adv Chem Biochem Plant Lipids
Recent Advances in the Chemistry of Insect Control — Recent Adv Chem Insect Control
Recent Advances in the Chronobiology of Allergy and Immunology. Proceedings — Recent Adv Chronobiol Allergy Immunol Proc
Recent Advances in the Diagnosis and Treatment of Pituitary Tumors — Recent Adv Diagn Treat Pituitary Tumors
Recent Advances in the Treatment of Depression — Recent Adv Treat Depression
Recent Advances in the Uses of Light in Physics, Chemistry, Engineering, and Medicine — Recent Adv Uses Light Phys Chem Eng Med
Recent Advances in Tuberculosis Research — Recent Adv Tuber Res
Recent Advances in Urology — Recent Adv Urol
Recent Advances in Weed Research — Recent Adv Weed Res
Recent Advances of Avian Endocrinology — Recent Adv Avian Endocrinol
Recent Advances on Pain. Pathophysiology and Clinical Aspects — Recent Adv Pain Pathophysiol Clin Aspects
Recent Developments in Alcoholism — Recent Dev Alcohol
Recent Developments in Cardiac Muscle Pharmacology — Recent Dev Card Muscle Pharmacol
Recent Developments in Cardiovascular Drugs — Recent Dev Cardiovasc Drugs
Recent Developments in Chromatography and Electrophoresis — Recent Dev Chromatogr Electrophor
Recent Developments in International Banking and Finance — RDIBF
Recent Developments in Ion Exchange 2. Proceedings. International Conference on Ion Exchange Processes — Recent Dev Ion Exch 2 Proc Int Conf Ion Exch Processes
Recent Developments in Laboratory Identification Techniques — Recent Dev Lab Identif Tech
Recent Developments in Mass Spectrometry in Biochemistry, Medicine, and Environmental Research — Recent Dev Mass Spectrom Biochem Med Environ Res
Recent Developments in Pipeline Welding — Recent Dev Pipeline Weld
Recent Developments in the Chemistry of Natural Carbon Compounds — Recent Dev Chem Nat Carbon Compd
Recent Developments in the History of Chemistry — Recent Dev Hist Chem
Recent Developments in the Pharmacology of Inflammatory Mediators — Recent Dev Pharmacol Inflammatory Mediators
Recent Developments in the Technology of Surfactants — Recent Dev Technol Surfactants
Recent Developments of Neurobiology in Hungary — Recent Dev Neurobiol Hung
Recent Economic Developments [*Jerusalem*] — RES

Recent Literature on Hazardous Environments in Industry — Recent Lit Hazard Environ Ind
Recent Medicine (Osaka) — Recent Med Osaka
Recent Progress in Hormone Research — Recent Prog Horm Res
Recent Progress in Hormone Research — Recent Progr Hormone Res
Recent Progress in Hormone Research — RPHRA
Recent Progress in Many-Body Theories — Recent Prog Many Body Theor
Recent Progress in Microbiology — Recent Prog Microbiol
Recent Progress in Microbiology — Recent Progr Microbiol
Recent Progress in Neurological Surgery — Recent Prog Neurol Surg
Recent Progress in Obstetrics and Gynaecology — Recent Prog Obstet Gynaecol
Recent Progress in Pediatric Endocrinology — Recent Prog Pediatr Endocrinol
Recent Progress in Photobiology — Recent Prog Photobiol
Recent Progress in Psychiatry — Recent Prog Psychiatry
Recent Progress in Surface Science — Recent Prog Surf Sci
Recent Progress in the Chemical Synthesis of Antibiotics — Recent Prog Chem Synth Antibiot
Recent Progress of Natural Sciences in Japan — Recent Prog Nat Sci Jap
Recent Progress of Natural Sciences in Japan — Recent Progr Natur Sci Japan
Recent Progress on Kinins — Recent Prog Kinins
Recent Publications on Governmental Problems [*United States*] — Recent Publ Gov Probl
Recent Publications on Governmental Problems — Recent Pubns Governmental Problems
Recent Publications on Governmental Problems — RPGPA
Recent Research in Climatology — Recent Res Climatol
Recent Research in Molecular Beams — Recent Res Mol Beams
Recent Research on Carnitine — Recent Res Carnitine
Recent Research on Cast Iron — Recent Res Cast Iron
Recent Research on Mechanical Behavior of Solids — Recent Res Mech Behav Solids
Recent Research on Scleroderris Canker of Conifers — Recent Res Scleroderris Canker Conifers
Recent Researches in Geology — Recent Res Geol
Recent Results in Cancer Research — Recent Results Cancer Res
Recent Results in Cancer Research — RRCRB
Recent Results in Peptide, Hormone, and Androgenic Steroid Research. Proceedings. Congress. Hungarian Society of Endocrinology and Metabolism — Recent Results Pept Horm Androg Steroid Res Proc Congr Hung
Recent Results of Cancer Treatment in Japan — Recent Results Cancer Treat Jpn
Recent Studies of Hypothalamic Function — Recent Stud Hypothal Funct
Recent Trends in Clinical Pharmacology. National Clinical Pharmacology Conference — Recent Trends Clin Pharmacol Natl Clin Pharmacol Conf
Recent Trends in Clinical Pharmacology. National Meeting on Clinical Pharmacology — Recent Trends Clin Pharmacol Natl Meet Clin Pharmacol
Recent Trends in Diabetes Research — Recent Trends Diabetes Res
Recenti Progressi in Medicina — Recenti Prog Med
Recenti Progressi in Medicina — RPMDA
Recenti Progressi in Medicina (Roma) — Recent Prog Med (Roma)
Recentia Medica — Recent Med
Recently Published Articles. American Historical Association — Recent Publ Artic
Recents Progres en Cryotechnique — Recents Prog Cryotech
Recents Progres en Genie des Procedes — Recents Prog Genie Procedes
Receptor Biochemistry — Recept Biochem
Receptor Biochemistry and Methodology — Recept Biochem Methodol
Receptor Purification — Recept Purif
Receptors. A Comprehensive Treatise — Recept Compr Treatise
Receptors and Hormone Action — Recept Horm Action
Receptors and Ligands in Intercellular Communication — Recept Ligands Intercell Commun
Receptors and Recognition. Series B — Recept Recognit Ser B
Receptors, Antibodies, and Disease — Recept Antibodies Dis
Receptors in Pharmacology — Recept Pharmacol
Rechentechnik-Datenverarbeitung — RDV
Rechentechnik-Datenverarbeitung — Rechentech Datenverarb
Rechentechnik-Datenverarbeitung — RTDVA
Recherche — RCHE
Recherche — Rech
Recherche Aeronautique — Rech Aeronaut
Recherche Aerospatiale — REARA
Recherche Aerospatiale — Rech Aerosp
Recherche Aerospatiale — Rech Aerospat
Recherche Agronomique en Suisse — Rech Agron Suisse
Recherche dans la Clinique et le Laboratoire — Rech Clin Lab
Recherche Europeenne en Toxicologie — Rech Eur Toxicol
Recherche Graphique — Rech Graphique
Recherche Graphique. Communications — Rech Graphique Commun
Recherche Sociale (Paris) — Rech Soc (Paris)
Recherche Sociale (Paris) — Recherche Soc (Paris)
Recherche Spatiale — Rech Spat
Recherche Spatiale — Rech Spatiale
Recherche Spatiale — RSPTA
Recherche Technique — RCTCA
Recherche Technique — Rech Tech
Recherches Africaines — Rech Afr
Recherches Agronomiques — Rech Agron
Recherches Agronomiques (Quebec) — Rech Agron (Quebec)
Recherches Amerindiennes — Rech Amerind
Recherches Amerindiennes au Quebec. Bulletin d'Information — RAAQ
Recherches Anglaises et Americaines — RANAM
Recherches Archeologiques. Institut d'Archeologie. Universite de Cracovie — Rech A Crac
Recherches Augustiniennes — RecAug
Recherches Augustiniennes — Rech Aug
Recherches Augustiniennes — RechA
Recherches Bibliques — RB
Recherches Bibliques — RBl
Recherches Bibliques. Journees du Colloque Biblique de Louvain — RechBib
Recherches Bibliques. Journees du Colloque Biblique de Louvain — RechBibl
Recherches Chirurgicales Europeennes — Rech Chir Eur
Recherches d'Archeologie, de Philologie,et d'Histoire [*Cairo*] — RAPH
Recherches de Papyrologie — Rech de Pap
Recherches de Papyrologie — RecPap
Recherches de Philologie et de Linguistique [*Louvain*] — RecPhL
Recherches de Philosophie — Rech Phil
Recherches de Science Religieuse — R Sc Relig
Recherches de Science Religieuse — RchScR
Recherches de Science Religieuse — Rec Sci Rel
Recherches de Science Religieuse — Rech Sc Relig
Recherches de Science Religieuse — Rech Sci Rel
Recherches de Science Religieuse — Rech Sci Relig
Recherches de Science Religieuse — Recher Sc Rel
Recherches de Science Religieuse — RechScR
Recherches de Science Religieuse — RechSR
Recherches de Science Religieuse — RecSR
Recherches de Science Religieuse — ReSR
Recherches de Science Religieuse — RSR
Recherches de Theologie Ancienne et Medievale — R Th A
Recherches de Theologie Ancienne et Medievale — RechTh
Recherches de Theologie Ancienne et Medievale — RecTh
Recherches de Theologie Ancienne et Medievale — RTAM
Recherches de Theologie Ancienne et Medievale — RThAM
Recherches d'Hydrobiologie Continentale — Rech Hydrobiol Cont
Recherches Economiques de Louvain — BSE
Recherches Economiques de Louvain — Rech Econ Louvain
Recherches Economiques et Sociales — Rech Econ Soc
Recherches en Mathematiques Appliquees — Rech Math Appl
Recherches et Debats du Centre Catholique des Intellectuels Francais — RDCCIF
Recherches et Etudes Camerounaises — Rech et Cam
Recherches et Etudes Comparatistes Ibero-Francaises de la Sorbonne Nouvelle — RECIFS
Recherches et Inventions — Rech Invent
Recherches et Travaux — R & T
Recherches et Travaux. Universite Catholique de l'Ouest — RTUCO
Recherches Geologiques en Afrique — Rech Geol Afr
Recherches Germaniques — RG
Recherches Germaniques — RGer
Recherches Interdisciplinaires — Rech Interdisciplinaires
Recherches Internationales a la Lumiere du Marxism — Rech Int
Recherches Internationales a la Lumiere du Marxisme — Rech Internat Marxisme
Recherches Oecumeniques — Rech Oe
Recherches Philosophiques — RecPh
Recherches Publiees sous la Direction de l'Institut de Lettres Orientales de Beyrouth — RILOB
Recherches. Societe Anonyme des Etablissments Roure Bertrand Fils et Justin Dupont — Rech Soc Anonyme Etabl Roure Bertrand Fils Justin Dupont
Recherches Sociographiques — Rech Sociogr
Recherches Sociographiques — Rech Sociographiques
Recherches Sociologiques — Rech Sociol
Recherches Sovietiques — Rech Soviet
Recherches sur la Musique Francaise Classique — R M F C
Recherches sur la Musique Francaise Classique — Recherches
Recherches sur la Philosophie et le Langage — Rech Philos Lang
Recherches sur le Sol — Rech Sol
Recherches sur le XVIIeme Siecle — Rech Dix Sept Siecle
Recherches sur les Produits de la Foret — Rech Prod Foret
Recherches Theatrales — RT
Recherches Theologiques — Rech Th
Recherches Veterinaires — RCVTB
Recherches Veterinaires — Rech Vet
Recherches Veterinaires (Paris) — Rech Vet (Paris)
Rechnergestuetzte Analytik und Labordatensysteme. Aachener Seminar — Rechnergestuetzte Anal Labordatensyst Aachener Semin
Rechnoi Transport — Rechn Transp
Rechnungswesen, Datentechnik, Organisation — RDO
Recht der Elektrizitaetswirtschaft [*Germany*] — Recht Elektrizitaetswirtsch
Recht der Internationalen Wirtschaft Aussenwirtschaftsdienst des Betriebsberaters — AWD
Recht der Internationaler Wirtschaft — Recht Int Wirtsch
Recht der Landwirtschaft — R d L
Recht der Landwirtschaft — Recht Landwirtsch
Recht der Landwirtschaft — RELAA
Recht, Staat, Wirtschaft — R St Wi
Recht und Staat in Geschichte und Gegenwart — RSGG
Recht und Steuern im Gas- und Wasserfach [*Germany*] — Recht Steuern Gas-Wasserfach
Rechtsarchiv der Wirtschaft — R d W
Rechtsgeleerd Bijblad — R Bb
Rechtsgeleerd Bijblad — RB
Rechtsgeleerd Magazijn — RM
Rechtsgeleerd Magazijn Themis — Rg Mag Th
Rechtsgeleerd Magazijn Themis — RM Th
Rechtsgeleerd Magazijn Themis — RM Themis

Rechtsgeleerd Magazijn Themis — Themis
Rechtsgeleerd Magazijn Themis (Zwolle) — Themis (Zwolle)
Rechtsgeleerde Adviezen — RA
Rechtsgeleerde Bijdragen en Bijblad — RB en B
Rechtsinformation. Berichte und Dokumente zum Auslaendischen Wirtschafts- und Steuerrecht — ROT
Rechtskundig Blad voor het Notairs-Ambt — R B v N
Rechtskundig Tijdschrift — RTijd
Rechtskundig Tijdschrift voor Belgie — Rechtsk T Belg
Rechtskundig Tijdschrift voor Belgie — Rechtsk Tijdschr v Belg
Rechtskundig Tijdschrift voor Belgie — Rk Ts B
Rechtskundig Tijdschrift voor Belgie — RT
Rechtskundig Tijdschrift voor Belgie — RTB
Rechtskundig Weekblad — R Week
Rechtskundig Weekblad — Rechtsk Weekbl
Rechtskundig Weekblad — Rk Wkbl
Rechtskundig Weekblad — RW
Rechtskundige Adviseur — RA
Rechtsprechung der Oberlandesgerichte auf dem Gebiete des Zivilrechts — OLGE
Rechtsprechung der Oberlandesgerichte auf dem Gebiete des Zivilrechts — Rechtsprechg Oberldsger Zivilr
Rechtsstrijd — R
Rechtsstrijd — RS
Rechtswissenschaftliche Experten und Gutachter [*Database*] — REX
Recipe Periodical Index — Recipe Period Index
Reclamation and Revegetation Research — Reclam & Reveg Res
Reclamation and Revegetation Research — Reclam Reveg Res
Reclamation and Revegetation Research — RRRED
Reclamation Era — Reclam Era
Reclamation Era — RERA
Reclamation Era — RERAA
Reclamation Review — Reclam Rev
Reclamation Review — RECR
Recombinant DNA Technical Bulletin — Recomb DNA Tech Bull
Recombinant DNA Technical Bulletin. Supplement — Recomb DNA Tech Bull Suppl
Recommended Nutrient Allowances for Domestic Animals — Recomm Nutr Allowances Domest Anim
Reconciliation Quarterly — Reconciliation Quart
Reconstruction Surgery and Traumatology — Recons Surg
Reconstruction Surgery and Traumatology — Reconstr Surg Traumatol
Reconstruction Surgery and Traumatology — Recontr Surg Traumatol
Reconstruction Surgery and Traumatology — RSUTA
Recontre Assyriologique Internationale. Compte Rendu — RencAssyrInt
Recontre Oecumenique — Ren Oe
Record — Rec
Record and Tape Buyer's Guide — RTBG
Record. Art Museum. Princeton University — Rec Art Mus
Record. Asilomar Conference on Circuits, Systems, and Computers — Rec Asilomar Conf Circuits Syst Comput
Record. Association of the Bar of the City of New York — Rec Ass'n Bar City of NY
Record. Association of the Bar of the City of New York — Record
Record. Association of the Bar of the City of New York — Record of NYCBA
Record. Broward County Medical Association [*Florida*] — Record Broward County Med Assoc
Record Changer — Rec Changer
Record Collector — Rec Coll
Record. IEEE International Electromagnetic Compatibility Symposium — Rec IEEE Int Electromagn Compat Symp
Record Mirror — RM
Record of Agricultural Research — Rec Agric Res
Record of Agricultural Research (Belfast) — Rec Agric Res (Belfast)
Record of Agricultural Research. Ministry of Agriculture (Northern Ireland) [*A publication*] — Rec Agric Res Minist Agric (Nth Ire)
Record of Agricultural Research (Northern Ireland) — Rec Agr Res (N Ireland)
Record of Chemical Progress — RCPRA
Record of Chemical Progress — Rec Chem Prog
Record of Electrical and Communication Engineering Conversation. Tohoku University [*Japan*] — Rec Electr Commun Eng Conversat Tohoku Univ
Record of Proceedings. Annual Meeting. American Society of Animal Production — Rec Proc Am Soc Anim Prod
Record of Research. Annual Report. East African Agriculture and Forestry Research Organisation — Rec Res Annu Rep East Afr Agric For Res Organ
Record of the Annual Convention. British Wood Preserving Association — Rec Annu Conv Br Wood Preserv Assoc
Record of the Annual Convention. British Wood Preserving Association — Rec Conv Brit Wood Pres Ass
Record of the Arab World [*Beirut*] — RAW
Record. Regional College of Education [*Mysore, India*] — Rec
Record Research — Rec Res
Record Research — RR
Record Review — Rec R
Record Review — RR
Record. Scottish Church History Society — RSCHS
Record. Symposium on Electron, Ion, and Laser Beam Technology — Rec Symp Electron Ion Laser Beam Technol
Record. United States Department of State — Rec US Dep State
Recorded Sound — Rec Sound
Recorded Sound — RecS
Recorder — Rec
Recorder and Music — Recorder and Mus
Recorder and Music Magazine — Recorder & Mus Mag
Recorder and Music Magazine — Recorder M Magazine
Recorder. Columbia Medical Society of Richland County [*South Carolina*] — Recorder Columbia Med Soc
Recorder Magazine — Recorder Mag
Records. Agricultural Research Station. Rehovot — Rec Agric Res Stn Rehovot
Records. American Catholic Historical Society of Philadelphia — RACathHS
Records. American Catholic Historical Society of Philadelphia — RACHS
Records. American Catholic Historical Society of Philadelphia — RACHSP
Records. American Catholic Historical Society of Philadelphia — Rec Am Cath Hist Soc
Records. American Catholic Historical Society of Philadelphia — RecA
Records and Recording — ReR
Records and Recording — RR
Records. Auckland Institute and Museum [*New Zealand*] — Rec Ak Inst Mus
Records. Auckland Institute and Museum — Rec Auckl Inst Mus
Records. Auckland Institute and Museum — Rec Auckland Inst
Records. Auckland Institute and Museum — Rec Auckland Inst Mus
Records. Australian Academy of Science — AUSRA
Records. Australian Academy of Science — Rec Aust Acad Sci
Records. Australian Academy of Science — Rec Austral Acad Sci
Records. Australian Museum — Rec Aust Mus
Records. Australian Museum — Rec Aust Museum
Records. Australian Museum. Supplement — RAMSEZ
Records. Australian Museum. Supplement — Rec Aust Mus Suppl
Records. Botanical Survey of India — RBSI
Records. Botanical Survey of India — Rec Bot Surv India
Records. Canterbury Museum [*Christchurch, New Zealand*] — Rec Canterbury Mus
Records. Columbia Historical Society of Washington, D.C. — RecC
Records. Dominion Museum (Wellington, New Zealand) — Rec Dom Mus (Wellington)
Records. Geological Survey Department. Northern Rhodesia — Rec Geol Surv Dep North Rhod
Records. Geological Survey of British Guiana — Rec Geol Surv Br Guiana
Records. Geological Survey of Guyana — Rec Geol Surv Guyana
Records. Geological Survey of India — Rec Geol Surv India
Records. Geological Survey of India — RGSI
Records. Geological Survey of India — RGSIA
Records. Geological Survey of Malawi — Rec Geol Surv Malawi
Records. Geological Survey of New South Wales — Rec Geol Surv New South Wales
Records. Geological Survey of New South Wales — Rec Geol Surv NSW
Records. Geological Survey of New South Wales — RGSWA
Records. Geological Survey of Nigeria — Rec Geol Surv Niger
Records. Geological Survey of Pakistan — Rec Geol Surv Pak
Records. Geological Survey of Tanganyika — Rec Geol Surv Tanganyika
Records. Geological Survey (Zambia) — Rec Geol Surv (Zambia)
Records. Hungarian Agricultural Experiment Stations. A. Plant Production — Rec Hung Agric Exp Stn A
Records. Hungarian Agricultural Experiment Stations. B. Animal Breeding — Rec Hung Agric Exp Stn B
Records. Hungarian Agricultural Experiment Stations. C. Horticulture — Rec Hung Agric Exp Stn C
Records in Review — Rec Rev
Records. Indian Museum — Rec Indian Mus
Records. Indian Museum (Calcutta) — Rec Indian Mus (Calcutta)
Records. Intersociety Energy Conversion Engineering Conference — Rec Intersoc Energy Convers Eng Conf
Records Management Quarterly — RMGQA
Records Management Quarterly — RMQ
Records. Medical Research Laboratories (Nairobi) — Rec Med Res Lab Nairobi
Records of Buckinghamshire — Bucks Records
Records of Buckinghamshire — Rec Buckinghamshire
Records of Buckinghamshire — Records Buck
Records of Civilization — RoC
Records of Early English Drama. Newsletter — REEDN
Records of General Science — Rec Gen Sci
Records of Huntingdonshire — Rec Huntingdonshire
Records of Observations. Scripps Institution of Oceanography — Rec Obs Scripps Inst Oceanogr
Records of Oceanographic Work in Japan — Rec Oceanogr Work Japan
Records of Oceanographic Works in Japan — Rec Oceanogr Works Jpn
Records of Oceanographic Works in Japan — ROWJ
Records of Oceanographic Works in Japan — ROWJA
Records of Oceanographic Works in Japan. Special Number — Rec Oceanogr Works Jpn Sp Number
Records of Researches. Faculty of Agriculture. University of Tokyo — Rec Res Fac Agric Univ Tokyo
Records of Researches. Faculty of Agriculture. University of Tokyo [*A publication*] — Recd Res Fac Agr Univ Tokyo
Records of the Malaria Survey of India — Rec Malar Surv India
Records of the Past — Rec Past
Records. Papua New Guinea Museum — Rec Papua New Guinea Mus
Records. Queen Victoria Museum — Rec Q Vict Mus
Records. Queen Victoria Museum — Rec Queen Vic Mus
Records. Queen Victoria Museum — Rec Queen Vict Mus
Records. Queen Victoria Museum — Rec Queen Victoria Mus
Records. Queen Victoria Museum — Records Queen Museum
Records. Queen Victoria Museum of Launceston — Rec Queen Victoria Mus Launceston
Records. Scottish Church History Society — Rec Scott Church Hist Soc
Records. South Australian Museum — Rec S Aust Mus
Records. South Australian Museum — Rec South Aust Mus
Records. South Australian Museum — Records SA Museum
Records. South Australian Museum (Adelaide) — Rec S Aust Mus (Adelaide)
Records. South Australian Museum (Adelaide) — Rec South Aust Mus (Adelaide)

Records. Western Australian Museum — Rec West Aust Mus
Records. Western Australian Museum — REMUDY
Records. Western Australian Museum. Supplement — Rec West Aust Mus Suppl
Records. Western Australian Museum. Supplement — RESUDU
Records. Zoological Survey of India — Rec Zool Surv India
Records. Zoological Survey of Pakistan — Rec Zool Surv Pak
Recovering Literature — Rec L
Recovery Engineering News — Rec Eng N
Recovery Engineering News — Recovery Eng News
Recovery of Pulping Chemicals — Recovery Pulping Chem
Recrea Plus — RCP
Recreatie — NVV
Recreatie-Documentatie. Literatuuroverzicht Inzake Dagrecreatie, Verblijfsrecreatie, en Toerisme — RDT
Recreatievoorzieningen. Maandblad voor Recreatie, Milieu, en Landschap — RCV
Recreation Information Management System [*Database*] — RIM
Recreation Management Handbook — Rec Man Handb
Recreational and Educational Computing — REC
Recreational Mathematics — Rec Math
Recreational Vehicle Business — RV Bsns
Recreational Vehicle Dealer — RV Dealer
Recreations in Agriculture, Natural History, Arts, and Miscellaneous Literature — Recreations Agric
Recreations in Mathematics — Rec Math
Recreative Science — Recr Sci
Recrystallization and Grain Growth of Multi-Phase and Particle Containing Materials. Proceedings. Risoe International Symposium on Metallurgy and Materials Science — Recryst Grain Growth Multi Phase Part Containing Mater Proc
Recueil Annuel de Jurisprudence Belge — R An Jpd B
Recueil Annuel de Jurisprudence Belge — RAJB
Recueil d'Archeologie Orientale — RAO
Recueil d'Archeologie Orientale — Rec Arch Orient
Recueil de Jurisprudence. Cour Superieure [*Quebec, Canada*] — CS
Recueil de Jurisprudence des Tribunaux de Charleroi — Rec Trib Charl
Recueil de Jurisprudence des Tribunaux de l'Arrondissement de Nivelles — Rec Jur T A Ni
Recueil de Jurisprudence des Tribunaux de l'Arrondissement de Nivelles — TANi
Recueil de Jurisprudence du Droit Administratif et du Conseil d'Etat — JDA
Recueil de Jurisprudence du Droit Administratif et du Conseil d'Etat — Rec Jur Dr Adm
Recueil de la Jurisprudence de la Cour de Justice des Communautes Europeennes — Rec Jur CJCE
Recueil de la Jurisprudence de la Propriete et du Batiment — Rec Bat
Recueil de la Legislation Generale en Vigueur en Belgique — Rec Legisl Gen
Recueil de Medecine Veterinaire — Rec Med Vet
Recueil de Medecine Veterinaire — Recl Med Vet
Recueil de Medecine Veterinaire. Ecole d'Alfort — Rec Med Vet Ecole Alfort
Recueil de Medecine Veterinaire. Ecole d'Alfort — Recl Med Vet Ec Alfort
Recueil de Medecine Veterinaire Exotique — Rec Med Vet Exot
Recueil de Memoires de Medecine, de Chirurgie, et de Pharmacie Militaires — Recueil Mem Med
Recueil de Memoires et Travaux. Societe d'Histoire du Droit et des Institutionsde Anciens Pays de Droit Ecrit — RMTHD
Recueil de Travaux. Conference d'Histoire et de Philologie — RTCHP
Recueil de Travaux de l'Institut Superieur de Medecine I. P. Pavlov — Recl Trav Inst Super Med IP Pavlov
Recueil de Travaux de Sciences Medicales au Congo Belge — Rec Trav Sci Med
Recueil de Travaux. Faculte des Lettres. Universite de Neuchatel — RTFL
Recueil de Travaux. Institut de Recherches sur la Structure de la Matiere (Belgrade) — Recl Trav Inst Rech Struct Matiere (Belgrade)
Recueil de Travaux Publie par l'Universite d'Uppsala — Recl Trav Univ Uppsala
Recueil de Travaux Relatifs a la Philologie et a l'Archeologie Egyptiennes et Assyriennes — Recueil de Travaux
Recueil de Travaux Relatifs a la Philologie et a l'Archeologie Egyptiennes et Assyriennes — RTPE
Recueil de Travaux Relatifs a l'Archeologie et a la Philologie — Recueil Trav Archeol
Recueil des Actes de la Seance Publique de l'Academie Imperiale des Sciences de St. Petersbourg — Recueil Actes Seance Publique Acad Imp Sci St Petersbourg
Recueil des Actes de la Seance Solennelle. Academie Imperiale des Sciences de St. Petersbourg — Recueil Actes Seance Solennelle Acad Imp Sci St Petersbourg
Recueil des Anciennes Coutumes de Belgique — Rec Anc Cout Belg
Recueil des Arrets et Avis du Conseil d'Etat — R Ar Av C Et
Recueil des Arrets et Avis du Conseil d'Etat — RAA
Recueil des Arrets et Avis du Conseil d'Etat — RAACE
Recueil des Brevets d'Invention — Recl Brev Invent
Recueil des Circulaires, Instructions, et Autres Actes. Ministere de la Justice — R Circ Min Just
Recueil des Cours. Academie de Droit International — Recueil
Recueil des Cours. Academie de Droit International de La Haye — RCADI
Recueil des Cours. Academie de Droit International de La Haye — RdC
Recueil des Decisions de la Commission Europeenne de Droits de l'Homme — Rec CEDH
Recueil des Historiens des Croisades — RHC
Recueil des Historiens des Gaules et de la France — RHGL
Recueil des Inscriptions en Lineaire A — RILA
Recueil des Inscriptions Juridiques Grecques — IJG
Recueil des Inscriptions Juridiques Grecques — Inscr Jurid
Recueil des Inscriptions Juridiques Grecques — RIJG
Recueil des Inscriptions Libyques — RIL
Recueil des Memoires de Medecine, de Chirurgie, et de Pharmacie Militaires — Rec Mem Med Mil
Recueil des Memoires et Actes. Societe des Sciences et Arts du Departement du Mont-Tonnerre. Seant a Mayence — Recueil Mem Actes Soc Sci Dep Mont Tonnerre
Recueil des Memoires et Observations sur l'Hygiene et la Medecine Veterinaires Militaires — Rec Mem et Obs Hyg et Med Vet Mil
Recueil des Notices et Memoires. Societe Archeologique de Constantine — RSAC
Recueil des Notices et Memoires. Societe Archeologiques, Historique, et Geographique du Departement de Constantine — Rec Constantine
Recueil des Notices et Memoires. Societe Archeologiques, Historique, et Geographique du Departement de Constantine — RSAC
Recueil des Observations de Medecine des Hopitaux Militaires — Rec Obs Med Hop Mil
Recueil des Pieces Lues Dans Les Seances Publiques et Particulieres, de l'Academie Royale de Nismes — Recueil Pieces Seances Acad Roy Nismes
Recueil des Prix Remportes sur les Questions Proposees Par l'Academie de Bruxelles — Recueil Prix Remportes Quest Prop Acad Bruxelles
Recueil des Publications. Societe Havraise d'Etudes Diverses — RPSHED
Recueil des Travaux Botaniques Neerlandais [*Netherlands*] — Rec Trav Bot Neerl
Recueil des Travaux Botaniques Neerlandais — Recl Trav Bot Neerl
Recueil des Travaux Botaniques Neerlandais — RTBNA
Recueil des Travaux. Centre Interfacultaire du Travail. Universite de Liege — Rec Trav Cent Int Trav Liege
Recueil des Travaux. Centre Oceanologique de Bretagne — Recl Trav Cent Oceanol Bretagne
Recueil des Travaux Chimiques des Pays-Bas — Rec Tr Chim
Recueil des Travaux Chimiques des Pays-Bas — Rec Trav Chim
Recueil des Travaux Chimiques des Pays-Bas — Rec Trav Chim Pays-Bas
Recueil des Travaux Chimiques des Pays-Bas — Recl Trav Chim Pays Bas
Recueil des Travaux Chimiques des Pays-Bas — RTCPA
Recueil des Travaux Chimiques des Pays-Bas et de la Belgique — Recl Trav Chim Pays-Bas Belg
Recueil des Travaux de Recherches. Faculte Agronomique. Universite de Belgrade — Recl Trav Rech Fac Agron Univ Belgrade
Recueil des Travaux des Laboratoires de Botanique, Geologie, et Zoologie. Faculte des Sciences. Universite de Montpellier. Serie Botanique — Recueil Trav Lab Bot Fac Sci Univ Montpellier Ser Bot
Recueil des Travaux. Institut Biologique (Beograd) — Recl Trav Inst Biol (Beogr)
Recueil des Travaux. Institut d'Ecologie et de Biogeographie. Academie Serbe des Sciences — Recl Trav Inst Ecol Biogeogr Acad Serbe Sci
Recueil des Travaux. Institut National d'Hygiene — Rec Trav Inst Nat Hyg
Recueil des Travaux. Laboratoire de Physiologie Vegetale. Faculte des Sciences de Bordeaux — Rec Trav Lab Physiol Veg Fac Sci Bordeaux
Recueil des Travaux Relatifs a la Philologie et a l'Archeologie Egyptiennes et Assyriennes — Rec Trav
Recueil des Travaux Relatifs a la Philologie et a l'Archeologie Egyptiennes et Assyriennes — RT
Recueil des Travaux Relatifs a la Philologie et a l'Archeologie Egyptiennes et Assyriennes [*Paris*] — RTRPAEA
Recueil des Travaux Relatifs a la Philologie et a l'Archeologie Egyptiennes et Assyriennes [*Paris*] — RTRPhAEA
Recueil des Travaux. Societe des Sciences, d l'IAgriculture, et des Arts de Lille — Recueil Trav Soc Sci Lille
Recueil des Travaux. Station Marine d'Endoume. Faculte des Sciences de Marseille — Recl Trav Stn Mar Endoume Fac Sci Mars
Recueil des Travaux. Station Marine d'Endoume-Marseille. Fascicule Hors Serie. Supplement — Recl Trav Stn Mar Endoume Marseille Fasc Hors Ser Suppl
Recueil des Travaux. Station Marine d'Endoume-Marseille. Fascicule Hors Serie. Supplement — Recl Trav Stn Mar Endoume-Mars Fasc Hors Ser Suppl
Recueil d'Etudes Orthodoxes — REO
Recueil d'Etudes Theologiques et Dogmatiques — RETD
Recueil d'Inscriptions Grecques — RIG
Recueil d'Ophtalmologie — Recueil Ophtalmol
Recueil. Faculte de Theologie Protestante (Geneve) — RFTPG
Recueil General de l'Enregistrement et du Notariat — Rec Gen
Recueil General de l'Enregistrement et du Notariat — Rec Gen Enr et Not
Recueil General des Bas-Reliefs de la Gaule Romaine — RGBR
Recueil General des Monnaies Grecques d'Asie Mineure — Rec
Recueil General des Monnaies Grecques d'Asie Mineure — RG
Recueil General des Mosaiques de la Gaule — RGMG
Recueil. Institut Botanique. Universite Libre de Bruxelles — Recueil Inst Bot
Recueil. Journal. Royal Netherlands Chemical Society — Recl J R Neth Chem Soc
Recueil Officiel des Lois et Ordonnances de la Confederation Suisse — RO
Recueil. Societe de Geographie — RSG
Recueil. Societe de Prehistoire et d'Archeologie de Tebessa — RSAT
Recueil. Societe Jean Bodin — Rec Soc J Bodin
Recueil. Societe Jean Bodin pour l'Histoire Comparative des Institutions — Rec Soc J Bodin
Recueil. Societe Jean Bodin pour l'Histoire Comparative des Institutions — RS Bodin
Recueil Systematique du Droit Federal [*Switzerland*] — RS
Recueil Tablettes Chaldeennes — RTC
Recueil Travaux. Institut Geologique Jovan Zujovic — Recl Trav Inst Geol Jovan Zujovic
Recueils de Jurisprudence. Cour d'Appel [*Quebec, Canada*] — CA
Recueils. Societe Jean Bodin — RSJB
Recueils.Societe Jean Bodin pour l'Histoire Comparative des Institutions — Recu Soc Jean Bodin Hist Comp Institutions
Recurrence — Rec

Recursos Hidraulicos — Recur Hidraul
Recursos Hidraulicos [*Mexico*] — Recursos Hidraul
Recursos Hidraulicos — REHID
Recursos Minerales — Recursos Min
Recusant History — RE H
Recusant History — RecH
Recycling [*Den Haag*] — REI
Recycling [*Dusseldorf*] — SHT
Recycling and Waste Disposal — Recycl Waste Disposal
Recycling and Waste Disposal — Recycling Waste Disposal
Recycling of Metals and Engineered Materials. International Symposium — Recycl Met Eng Mater Int Symp
Recycling Weltkongress. Konferenz-Niederschriften — Recycl Weltkongr Konf Niederschr
Recycling World Congress. Congress Proceedings — Recycl World Congr Congr Proc
Red Cell. Proceedings. International Conference on Red Cell Metabolism and Function — Red Cell Proc Int Conf
Red Cross Magazine — Red Cross M
Red Documental [*Database*] — REDO
Red Menace — Red Menac
Red River Valley Historical Review — RedR
Redbook — GRED
Redbook — REDBA
Rede CONSISDATA [*Consultoria, Sistemas, e Processamento de Dados Ltda.*] **de Servicos Integrados** [*Database*] — RCCSI
Red-Figured Vases of Apulia — RVA
Red-Figured Vases of Apulia — RVAP
Redia Giornale di Zoologia — Redia G Zool
Redkie Elementy — Redk Elem
Redkie Metally — Redk Met
Redkie Metally i Splavy. Trudy Vsesoyuznogo Soveshchaniya po Splavam Redkikh Metallov — Redk Met Splavy Tr Vses Soveshch
Redogorelse. Forskningsstiftelsen Skogsarbeten — Redog ForsknStift Skogsarb
Reed's Marine and Equipment News and Marine Digest — Reed's Mar Equip News Mar Dig
Reeducation Orthophonique — Reeduc Orthophon
Reef Point Gardens Bulletin — Reef Point Gard Bull
Reeves Journal — Reeves J
Reeves Journal — REJOD
REFA [*Reichsausschuss fuer Arbeitsstudien*] **Nachrichten** — REFA Nachr
REFA [*Reichsausschuss fuer Arbeitsstudien*] **Nachrichten** — REFNA
Referat Zhurnal Fotokinotekhnika — Referat Zh Fotokinotekh
Referate aus dem Gebiet der Chemischen Industrie — Ref Chem Ind
Referate und Zusammenfassung. Internationale Kongress ueber Kinderkrankheiten — Ref Zusammenfassung Int Kongr Kinderkrankh
Referateblatt zur Raumentwicklung — Referatebl zur Raumentwicklung
Referateblatt zur Raumordnung — Referatebl zur Raumordnung
Referate-Zeitschrift Plutonium-Dokumentation — Ref Z Plutonium Dok
Referati Dopovidei pro Naukovo-Doslidnu Robotu Aspirantiv. Ukrains'ka Akademiya Sil's'kogospodars'kikh Nauk — Ref Dopov Nauk Dosl Rob Aspir Ukr Akad Sil's'kogospod Nauk
Referati. Jugoslovanski Simpozij za Hmeljarstvo — Ref Jugosl Simp Hmeljarstvo
Referati Savetovanja. Savez Geoloskih Drustava SFR Jugoslavije — Ref Savetovanja Savez Geol Drus SFR Jugosl
Referativnaya Informatsiya. Avtomatizatsiya Khimicheskikh Proizvodstv — Ref Inf Avtom Khim Proizvod
Referativnaya Informatsiya. Lesokhimiya i Podsochka — Ref Inf Lesokhim Podsochka
Referativnaya Informatsiya. Poligraficheskaya Promyshlennost — Ref Inf Poligr Promst
Referativnaya Informatsiya. Seriya. Keramicheskaya Promyshlennost — Ref Inf Ser Keram Promst
Referativnyi Sbornik. Azotnaya Promyshlennost — Ref Sb Azotn Promst
Referativnyi Sbornik. Ekonomika Promyshlennosti. D. Primenenie Matematiceskih Metodov v Ekonomiceskih Issledovanijah i Planirovanii — R Sb Ekonom Promysl D
Referativnyi Sbornik. Fosfornaya Promyshlennost — Ref Sb Fosfornaya Promst
Referativnyi Sbornik. Khimiya i Tekhnologiya Izotopov i Mechenykh Soedinenii — Ref Sb Khim Tekhnol Izot Mechenykh Soedin
Referativnyi Sbornik. Metody Analiza i Kontrolya Kachestva Produktsii v Khimicheskoi Promyshlennosti — Ref Sb Metody Anal Kontrolya Kach Prod Khim Promsti
Referativnyi Sbornik. Proizvodstvo i Pererabotka Plastmass i Sinteticheskikh Smol — Ref Sb Proizvod Pererab Plastmass Sint Smol
Referativnyi Zhurnal — Ref Z
Referativnyi Zhurnal — Ref Zh
Referativnyi Zhurnal — Referat Z
Referativnyi Zhurnal. Astronomiya — Ref Zh Astron
Referativnyi Zhurnal. Astronomiya. Geodeziya — Ref Zh Astron Geod
Referativnyi Zhurnal. Avtomatika. Telemehanika i Vycislitelnaja Tehnika — R Z Avtomat Telemeh i Vycisl Tehn
Referativnyi Zhurnal. Biologicheskaya Khimiya — Ref Zh Biol Khim
Referativnyi Zhurnal. Biologiya — Ref Zh Biol
Referativnyi Zhurnal. Biologiya — Referat Zh Biol
Referativnyi Zhurnal. Biologiya — RZBLA
Referativnyi Zhurnal. Elektrosvyaz — Ref Zh Elek
Referativnyi Zhurnal. Farmakologiya. Khimioterapeuticheskie Sredstva. Toksikologiya — Ref Zh Faramakol Khimioter Sredstva Toksikol
Referativnyi Zhurnal. Fizika — R Z Fiz
Referativnyi Zhurnal. Fizika — Ref Z Fizika
Referativnyi Zhurnal. Fizika — Ref Zh Fiz
Referativnyi Zhurnal. Fizika — RZFZA
Referativnyi Zhurnal. Fiziko-Khimicheskaya Biologiya i Biotekhnologiya — Ref Zh Fiz-Khim Biol Biotekhnol
Referativnyi Zhurnal. Fotokinotekhnika — Ref Zh Fotokinotekh
Referativnyi Zhurnal. Geodeziya — Ref Zh Geod
Referativnyi Zhurnal. Geodeziya i Aeros'emka — Ref Zh Geod Aerosemka
Referativnyi Zhurnal. Geofizika — Ref Zh Geof
Referativnyi Zhurnal. Geofizika — Ref Zh Geofiz
Referativnyi Zhurnal. Geologiya — Ref Zh Geol
Referativnyi Zhurnal. Geologiya i Geografiya — Ref Zh Geol Geogr
Referativnyi Zhurnal. Informatika — Ref Zh Inf
Referativnyi Zhurnal. Informatika — RZ
Referativnyi Zhurnal. Informatika — RZInformat
Referativnyi Zhurnal. Izmeritel'naya Tekhnika — Ref Zh Izmer Tekh
Referativnyi Zhurnal. Khimicheskoe i Kholodil'noe Mashinostroenie — Ref Zh Khim Kholod Mashinostr
Referativnyi Zhurnal. Khimicheskoe Mashinostroenie — Ref Zh Khim Mashinostr
Referativnyi Zhurnal. Khimicheskoe. Neftepererabatyuayushchee i Polimerjnoe Mashinostroenie — Re Zh Khim Neftepererab Polim Mashinostr
Referativnyi Zhurnal. Khimiya — Ref Zh Khim
Referativnyi Zhurnal. Khimiya. Biologicheskaya Khimiya — Ref Zh Khim Biol Khim
Referativnyi Zhurnal. Kibernetika — RZKibernet
Referativnyi Zhurnal. Korroziya — Ref Zh Korroz
Referativnyi Zhurnal. Korroziya i Zashchita ot Korrozii — Ref Zh Korroz Zashch Korroz
Referativnyi Zhurnal. Legkaya Promyshlennost — Ref Zh Legk Promst
Referativnyi Zhurnal. Lesovedenie i Lesovodstvo — Ref Zh Lesoved Lesovod
Referativnyi Zhurnal. Matematika — Ref Z Math
Referativnyi Zhurnal. Matematika — RZMat
Referativnyi Zhurnal. Mehanika — RZMeh
Referativnyi Zhurnal. Mekhanika — Ref Zh Mekh
Referativnyi Zhurnal. Mekhanika. Akademiya Nauk SSSR. Institut Nauchnoi Informatsii — RZhMekh
Referativnyi Zhurnal. Metallurgiya [*Former USSR*] — Ref Zh Metall
Referativnyi Zhurnal. Metallurgiya — RZMTA
Referativnyi Zhurnal. Metrologiya i Izmeritel'naya Tekhnika — Ref Zh Metrol Izmer Tekh
Referativnyi Zhurnal. Nasosostroenie i Kompressorostroenie — Ref Zh Nasosostr Kompressorostr
Referativnyi Zhurnal. Nasosostroenie i Kompressorostroenie. Kholodil'noe Mashinostroenie — Ref Zh Nasosostr Kompressorostr Kholod Mashinostr
Referativnyi Zhurnal. Nauchnaya i Teckhnicheskaya Informatsiya — Ref Zh Nauchn Tekh Inf
Referativnyi Zhurnal. Oborudovanie i Tekhnologiya — Ref Zh Oborud Tekhnol
Referativnyi Zhurnal. Obshchie Voprosy Patologii. Onkologiya — Ref Zh Obshch Vop Patol Onkol
Referativnyi Zhurnal. Okhrana Prirody i Vosproizvodstvo Prirodnykh Resursov [*Former USSR*] — Ref Zh Okhr Prir Vosproizvod Prir Resur
Referativnyi Zhurnal. Pochvovedenie i Agrokhimiya — Ref Zh Pochvoved Agrokhim
Referativnyi Zhurnal. Radiatsionnaya Biologiya [*Former USSR*] — Ref Zh Radiats Biol
Referativnyi Zhurnal. Rastenievodstvo — Ref Zh Rastenievod
Referativnyi Zhurnal. Tekhnologiya i Oborudovanie Bumago-Delatel'nogo i Poligraficheskogo Proizvodstva — Ref Zh Tekhnol Oborud Bum Delatelnogo Poligr Proizvod
Referativnyi Zhurnal. Tekhnologiya i Oborudovanie Tsellyulozno-Bumazhnogo i Poligraficheskogo Proizvodstva — Ref Zh Tekhnol Oborud Tsellyul Bum Poligr Proizvod
Referativnyi Zhurnal. Tekhnologiya Mashinostroeniya — Ref Zh Tekhnol Mashinostr
Referativnyi Zhurnal. Teploenergetika — Ref Zh Teploenerg
Referativnyi Zhurnal. Toksikologiya — Ref Zh Toksikol
Referativnyi Zhurnal. Veterinariya — Ref Zh Vet
Referativnyi Zhurnal. Yadernye Reaktory — Ref Zh Yad Reakt
Referativnyi Zhurnal. Zhivotnovodstvo i Veterinariya — Ref Zh Zhivotnovod Vet
Referativnyi Zhurnal. Zhivotnovodstvo i Veterinariya — Referat Zh Zhivot Vet
Referativnyj Zurnal. Biologija — Ref Zurn Biol
Referatkartei der Silikatliteratur — Referatkartei Silikatlit
Referaty Dokladov i Soobshchenii. Mendeleevskii S'ezd po Obshchei i Prikladnoi Khimii — Ref Dokl Soobshch Mendeleevsk Sezd Obshch Prikl Khim
Referaty Dokladov Moskovskaya Sel'skokhozyaistvennaya Akademiya Imeni K. A. Timiryazeva — Ref Dok Mosk Skh Akad
Referaty Dokladov o Nauchno-Issledovatel'skoi Rabote Aspirantov. Ukrainskaya Sel'skokhozyaistvennaya Akademiya — Ref Dokl Nauchno-Issled Rab Aspir Ukr Skh Akad
Referaty i Komunikaty zgloszone na Zjazd Naukowy na temat. Nieorganiczne Zwiazki Fosforowe — Ref Komun Zjazd Nauk Nieorg Zwiazki Fosforowe
Referaty Nauchno-Issledovatel'skikh Rabot Instituta Biologii. Akademiya Nauk Belorusskoi SSR — Ref Nauchno Issled Rab Inst Biol Akad Nauk B SSR
Referaty Nauchnykh Rabot Instituta Biologii Morya. Dal'nevostochnyi Filial. Akademiya Nauk SSSR — Ref Nauchn Rab Inst Biol Morya Dalnevost Fil Akad Nauk SSSR
Referaty Nauchnykh Soobshchenii - Vsesoyuznyi Biokhimicheskii S'ezd — Ref Nauchn Soobshch Vses Biokhim Sezd
Referaty Trudov Ivanovskogo Khimiko-Tekhnologicheskogo Instituta — Ref Tr Ivanov Khim Tekhnol Inst
Referee Magazine — Ref Mag
Reference Book of Corporate Management [*Database*] — RBCM
Reference Book Review Index — RBRI
Reference Book Review Index — Ref Book Rev Index
Reference Books Bulletin — RBB
Reference Librarian — Ref Libr
Reference Librarian — REFL
Reference Quarterly — RQ
Reference Services Review — Ref Serv R
Reference Services Review — Ref Serv Rev

Reference Services Review — RSR
Reference Shelf — Ref Shelf
Reference Shelf — RS
Reference Sources — Ref Source
References to Scientific Literature on Fire — Ref Sc Lit Fire
Refiner and Natural Gasoline Manufacturer — Refin Nat Gasoline Manuf
Refiner and Natural Gasoline Manufacturer — Refiner Nat Gasoline Manuf
Refiner and Natural Gasoline Manufacturer — RNGMA
Refining Engineer — Refin Eng
Reflets de l'Economie Franc-Comtoise — Reflets Econ Franc-Comtoise
Reflets et Perspectives de la Vie Economique — Refl Persp Vie Ec
Reflets et Perspectives de la Vie Economique — Reflets et Perspectives
Reflets et Perspectives de la Vie Economique — Reflets Perspect Vie Econ
Reflets et Perspectives de la Vie Economique — RFK
Reforestation Monthly — Refor Mon
Reform Zeitung [*Berlin*] — RefZtg
Reforma Medica — Ref Med
Reformacja w Polsce — Ref Pol
Reformacja w Polsce — RWP
Reformacni Sbornik — Ref Sb
Reformatio — Ref
Reformation Essays and Studies — Ref ES
Reformationsgeschichtliche Studien — Reformatgesch St
Reformationsgeschichtliche Studien und Texte — RGST
Reformatus Egyhaz — Ref Egy
Reformatus Egyhaz [*Budapest*] — RefEgyhaz
Reforme — Re
Reforme — Ref
Reformed and Presbyterian World — Ref Pres W
Reformed and Presbyterian World — RPW
Reformed Church of America — RCAm
Reformed Church Review — Ref Ch R
Reformed Journal — Ref J
Reformed Journal — RJ
Reformed Liturgy and Music — Ref Lit Music
Reformed Quarterly Review — Ref Q
Reformed Review — Ref R
Reformed Review — RR
Reformed Review (Holland, MI) — Ref RH
Reformed Review (Philadelphia) — Ref R Ph
Reformed Theological Review — R Th R
Reformed Theological Review — Ref Th R
Reformed Theological Review — Ref Theol R
Reformed Theological Review [*Australia*] — RefTR
Reformed Theological Review — RTR
Reformed World — Ref W
Reformed World — RW
Reformierte Kirchenzeitung — RKZ
Reformierte Schweiz — Ref Schw
Reformistas Antiquos Espanoles — RAEsp
Refractories [*English Translation*] — REFRA
Refractories. Current Industrial Reports — Refractories Curr Ind Rep
Refractories Institute. Technical Bulletin — Refract Inst Tech Bull
Refractories Journal — Refract J
Refractories Journal — Refractor J
Refractory Materials — Refract Mater
Refractory Metals. Extraction, Processing, and Applications. Proceedings. Symposium at the Annual Meeting. Minerals, Metals, and Materials Society — Refract Met Proc Symp Annu Meet Miner Met Mater Soc
Refrigerating Engineering — REENA
Refrigerating Engineering — Refrig Eng
Refrigerating World — Refrig W
Refrigeration — Refrig
Refrigeration, Air Conditioning, and Heat Recovery — Refrig Air Condit Heat Recovery
Refrigeration and Air Conditioning — Refrig Air
Refrigeration and Air Conditioning — Refrig Air Condit
Refrigeration and Cold Storage — Refrig Cold Storage
Refrigeration Annual — Refrig A
Refrigeration Annual — Refrig Ann
Refrigeration Annual — Refrig Annual
Refrigeration, Cold Storage, and Air-Conditioning — Refrig Cold Stor
Refrigeration, Cold Storage, and Air-Conditioning — Refrig Cold Storage Air Cond
Refrigeration Industry — Refrig Ind
Refrigeration Journal — Refrig J
Refrigeration Journal — Refrigeration J
Refrigeration Journal, Incorporating Air Conditioning and Heating — Refrig Air Cond & Heat
Refrigeration Science and Technology — Refrig Sci Technol
Refuah Veterinarith — Refu Vet
Refuah Veterinarith — RVETA5
Regan Report on Nursing Law — Regan Rep Nurs Law
Regardie's Magazine — REG
Regelungstechnik — Regelungstech
Regelungstechnik — RLSTA
Regelungstechnik — Rt
Regelungstechnik. RT [*Germany*] — Regelungstech RT
Regelungstechnik. RT — RERTD
Regelungstechnik und Prozess-Datenverarbeitung — Regelungstech Prozess Datenverarb
Regelungstechnik und Prozess-Datenverarbeitung — Regelungstech Prozess-Datenverarb
Regelungstechnik und Prozess-Datenverarbeitung — Regelungstech Prozess-Datenverarbeitung
Regelungstechnik und Prozess-Datenverarbeitung — Regelungstech und Prozess-Datenverarb
Regelungstechnik und Prozess-Datenverarbeitung — RPZDA
Regelungstechnische Praxis — Regelungstech Prax
Regelungstechnische Praxis und Prozess-Rechentechnik — Regelungstech Prax Prozess-Rechentech
Regelungstechnische Praxis und Prozess-Rechentechnik — Regelungstech Prax und Prozess-Rechentech
Regensbergs Roemische Reihe — RRR
Regensburger Beitrage zur Deutschen Sprach- und Literaturwissenschaft — RBSL
Regensburger Jahrbuch fuer Aerztliche Fortbildung — Reg Jb Aerztl Fortbild
Regensburger Mathematische Schriften — Regensburger Math Schriften
Regensburger Naturwissenschaften — Regensb Naturwiss
Regensburger Neues Testament — RNT
Regensburger Universitaets-Zeitung — Regensb Univ-Ztg
Regents Renaissance Drama Series — RRDS
Regents Restoration Drama Series — R Rest DS
Regesta Chartarum Italiae — RCI
Regesta Episcoporum Constantiensium — REConst
Regesta Historico-Diplomatica Ordinis S. Mariae Theutonicorum — ROSMT
Regesta Historico-Diplomatica Ordinis S. Mariae Theutonicorum. Index Tabularii Ordinis — ROSMTT
Regesta Historico-Diplomatica Ordinis S. Mariae Theutonicorum. Regesta Privilegiorum — ROSMTR
Regesta Imperii — RI
Regesta Imperii. Die Regesten der Karolinger — RIK
Regesta Imperii. Die Regesten des Kaiserreiches — RIKR
Regesta Pontificum Romanorum. Germania Pontificia — RPRGP
Regesta Pontificum Romanorum. Italia Pontificia — RPRIP
Regesten der Bischoefe von Strassburg — RBSt
Regesten der Erzbischoefe von Koeln im Mittelalter — Reg Erzb Koeln
Regesten der Erzbischoefe von Koeln im Mittelalter — REK
Regesten der Erzbischoefe von Mainz — REBM
Regesten van de Aanwinsten van het Institut voor Vergelijkend Literatuuronderzoek aan de Rijksuniversiteit te Utrecht — RIVL
Regestum Clementis Papae V — RCPQ
Regeszeti Dolgozatok az Eoetvoes Lorand Tudomanyegyetem Regeszeti Lutezeteboel — Reg Dolg
Regeszeti Dologozatok as Eotvos Lorand Tudomanyegyetem Regeszeti Interetebol — RDELTRI
Regeszeti Dologozatok as Eotvos Lorand Tudomanyegyetem Regeszeti Interetebol — Reg Dol Eot Lor Tudo Reg Int
Regeszeti Dologozatok as Eotvos Lorand Tudomanyegyetem Regeszeti Interetebol — Reg Dolg Eoetvoes
Regeszeti Fuezetek — Reg Fuez
Regeszeti Fuzetek. Magyar Nemzeti Muzeum — Reg Fuz
Regeszeti Fuzetek. Magyar Nemzeti Muzeum — RF
Regeszeti Tanulmanyok — Reg Tan
Regeszeti Tanulmanyok — Regeszeti Tan
Reggae Report — Reggae Rept
Regia Societas Scientiarum Upsaliensis. Nova Acta — Reg Soc Sci Upsal Nova Acta
Regia Societas Scientiarum Upsaliensis. Nova Acta — Regia Soc Sci Upsal Nova Acta
Regia Stazione Chimico-Agraria Sperimentale di Roma. Pubblicazione — Regia Stn Chim Agrar Sper Roma Pubbl
Regia Stazione Sperimentale per la Seta. Bollettino Ufficiale (Italy) — Regia Stn Sper Seta Boll Uffic (Italy)
Regio Istituto Superiore Navale (Napoli). Annali — Regio Ist Super Nav (Napoli) Ann
Regio Istituto Universitario Navale (Napoli). Annali — Regio Ist Univ Nav (Napoli) Ann
Regional Anaesthesia — Reg Anaesth
Regional and Urban Economics [*Netherlands*] — Reg Urban Econ
Regional and Urban Economics Operational Methods — Region Urb Econ
Regional Antipollution Conference — Reg Antipollut Conf
Regional Catalogue of Earthquakes — Reg Cat Earthquakes
Regional Conference Series in Applied Mathematics — Reg Conf Ser Appl Math
Regional Development Journal — Region Develop J
Regional Development Journal — Regional Development J
Regional Development News [*New Zealand*] — Reg Dev
Regional Economic Information System [*Database*] — REIS
Regional Economic Projections Series [*Database*] — REPS
Regional Geology Series. North Carolina Division of Resource Planning and Evaluation. Mineral Resources Section — Reg Geol Ser NC Div Resour Plann Eval Miner Resour Sect
Regional Geology Series. North Carolina Mineral Resources Section — Reg Geol Ser NC Miner Resour Sect
Regional Immunology — Reg Immunol
Regional Journal of Energy, Heat, and Mass Transfer [*India*] — Reg J Energy Heat Mass Transfer
Regional Language Studies [*Newfoundland*] — RLS
Regional Meeting. American Filtration Society — Reg Meet Amer Filtr Soc
Regional Report. New Hebrides Geological Survey — Reg Rep New Hebrides Geol Surv
Regional Science and Urban Economics — REG
Regional Science and Urban Economics — Reg Urb Econ
Regional Science and Urban Economics — Region Sci Urb Econ
Regional Science and Urban Economics — Regional Science and Urban Econ
Regional Science and Urban Economics [*Netherlands*] — RSU
Regional Science and Urban Economics — RSUED
Regional Science Association. Papers and Proceedings — RSAP
Regional Studies — Reg Stud
Regional Studies — Region Stud

Regional Studies [*Oxford*] — Regional Stud
Regional Studies — REGS-A
Regional Studies Association. Newsletter — Reg Stud Assoc Newsl
Regional Technical Conference. Society of Plastics Engineers — Reg Tech Conf Soc Plast Eng
Regional Technical Meetings. American Iron and Steel Institute — Reg Tech Meet Am Iron Steel Inst
Regional-Anaesthesie (Berlin) — Reg Anaesth (Berlin)
Regionalism and the Female Imagination — RFI
Regionalna Geologia Zapadnych Karpat — Reg Geol Zapadn Karpat
Regional'naya Geologiya Nekotorykh Raionov SSSR — Reg Geol Nek Raionov SSSR
Regional'naya Geologiya Srednei Azii — Reg Geol Sredn Azii
Regional'naya i Geneticheskaya Mineralogiya — Reg Genet Mineral
Register. Kentucky Historical Society — Regist KY Hist Soc
Register. Kentucky Historical Society — Register of Kentucky Hist Soc
Register. Kentucky Historical Society — RegK
Register. Kentucky Historical Society — RKHS
Registered Nurse — RN
Registro Trimestre o Coleccion de Memorias de Historia, Literatura, Ciencias y Artes — Reg Trimestre
Registros Sonoros [*Database*] — BNRS
Registry of Toxic Effects of Chemical Substances [*Database*] — RTECS
Reglement Dienstvoorwaarden — RDV
Regnum Dei — Reg Dei
Regnum Vegetabile — Regnum Veg
Regue des Sciences Religieuses [*Strasbourg/Paris*] — RevScR
Regulacion y Mando Automatico — Regul y Mando Autom
Regulae Benedicti Studia — RBS
Regulation — RGO
Regulations of British Columbia [*Database*] — RBC
Regulations of Connecticut State Agencies — Conn Agencies Regs
Regulatory Action Network — Regulatory Action Net
Regulatory Bulletin. Kentucky Agricultural Experiment Station — Regul Bull KY Agr Exp Sta
Regulatory Bulletin. Kentucky Agricultural Experiment Station — Regul Bull Ky Agric Exp Stn
Regulatory Bulletin. University of Kentucky. College of Agriculture. Agricultural Experiment Station — Regul Bull Univ KY Coll Agric Agric Exp Stn
Regulatory Gut Peptides in Paediatric Gastroenterology and Nutrition. Annual Meeting. GPGE — Regul Gut Pept Paediatr Gastroenterol Nutr Annu Meet GPGE
Regulatory Peptides — Regul Pept
Regulatory Peptides — RP
Regulatory Peptides. Supplement — Regul Pept Suppl
Regulatory Toxicology and Pharmacology — Regul Tox P
Regulatory Toxicology and Pharmacology — Regul Toxicol Pharmacol
Regulatory Toxicology and Pharmacology. RTP — Regul Toxicol Pharmacol RTP
Rehabilitacia Supplementum (Bratislava) — Rehabil Suppl (Bratisl)
Rehabilitation — Rehab
Rehabilitation — RHBNA
Rehabilitation Counseling Bulletin — Rehab Couns
Rehabilitation in Australia — Rehabil Aust
Rehabilitation in South Africa — Rehabil S Afr
Rehabilitation in South Africa — Rehabil SA
Rehabilitation Literature — Rehab Lit
Rehabilitation Literature — Rehabil Lit
Rehabilitation Literature — RELIA
Rehabilitation Nursing — Rehabil Nurs
Rehabilitation Psychology — Rehabil Psychol
Rehabilitation Record — Rehabil Rec
Rehabilitation Record — RHRCA
Rei Cretariae Romanae Fautorum Acta — RCRF
Rei Cretariae Romanae Fautorum Acta — Rei Cret Rom Faut Acta
REIC (Radiation Effects Information Center) Report — REIC (Radiat Eff Inf Cent) Rep
Reichdenkmale Deutscher Musik — RD
Reichhold-Albert-Nachrichten — Reichhold-Albert-Nachr
Reichministerialblatt — RM Bl
Reichsarbeitsblatt — Reichsarbeitsbl
Reichsberichte fuer Physik — Reichsber Phys
[Entscheidungen des] Reichsgerichts in Strafsachen — RGSt
Reichstoff Industrie und Kosmetik — Reichstoff Ind Kosmet
Reichsverwaltungsblatt — Reichsverwalt Bl
Reidel Texts in the Mathematical Sciences — Reidel Texts Math Sci
Reihe Automatisierungstechnik — Reihe Automatisierungstech
Reihe Germanistische Linguistik — RGL
Reihe Hanser Literature-Kommentare — RHLK
Reihe Informatik — Reihe Informat
Reihe Mathematik — Reihe Math
Rein et Foie. Maladies de la Nutrition [*France*] — Rein Foie Mal Nutr
Rein et Foie. Maladies de la Nutrition — RFMNB
Reinare en Espana — RenE
Reinare en Espana — ReS
Reindeer Herders Newsletter. Institute of Arctic Biology. University of Alaska — RHNL
Reine und Angewandte Geophysik — Reine Angew Geophys
Reine und Angewandte Metallkunde in Einzeldarstellungen — RAMED
Reine und Angewandte Metallkunde in Einzeldarstellungen — Reine Angew Metallkd Einzeldarst
Reinforced Plastics — Reinf Plast
Reinforced Plastics — RPLAA
Reinforced Plastics and Composites World — Reinf Plast Compos World
Reinforced Plastics (Boston) — Reinf Plast (Boston)
Reinforced Plastics Composites. BPF (British Plastics Federation) Business Conference — Reinf Plast Compos BPF Bus Conf
Reinforced Plastics (London) — Reinf Plast (London)
Reinsurance — Re
Reintegro (Puerto Rico) — RPR
Reiss-Davis Clinic. Bulletin — Reiss-Davis Clin Bull
Rekishi Chiri — RC
Rekishigaku Kenkyu. Journal. Historical Science Society — RK
Rekomendatsii po Voprosam Pozharnoi Profilaktiki — Rekom Vopr Pozharnoi Profil
Rekreaksie. Vakblad voor Recreatie Ondernemers — ORE
Relaciones. Colegio de Michoacan — CM/RE
Relaciones Internacionales — Relac Int
Relaciones. Sociedad Argentina de Antropologia — SAA/R
Relais Statistiques de l'Economie Picarde — Relais
Relais Statistiques de l'Economie Picarde — Relais Econ Picarde
Relata Technica — Relata Tech
Relata Technica di Chimica e Biologia Applicata — Relata Tech Chim Biol Appl
Relationes Annuae. Instituti Geologica Regii Hungarici — Relat Annu Inst Geol Regii Hung
Relationes Annuae. Instituti Geologici Publicii Hungarici — Relat Annu Inst Geol Publ Hung
Relationes Annuae. Instituti Geologici Publicii Hungarici — Relat Annu Inst Geol Publicii Hung
Relations Industrielles — Rel Ind
Relations Industrielles — Relat Ind
Relations Industrielles — Relat Industr
Relations Industrielles (Quebec) — Relations Inds (Quebec)
Relations Internationales — Relat Int
Relations Internationales (Geneve) — Relat Int (Geneve)
Relations Internationales/International Relations — Internat Relations
Relativistic Aspects of Nuclear Physics — Relativ Aspects Nucl Phys
Relativity — Relat
Relatoria. DNOCS [*Departamento Nacional de Obras Contra as Secas*] — Relat DNOCS
Relatorio. Aquario Vasco de Gama — Relat Aquar Vasco De Gama
Relatorio Cientifico. Escola Superior de Agricultura Luiz de Queiroz. Departamento e Instituto de Genetica — Relat Cient Esc Super Agric Luiz Queiroz Dep Inst Genet
Relaxation in Polymers — Relax Polym
Relay Engineer — Relay Eng
Relazione Accademica. Accademia Degli Zelanti di Aci-Reale di Scienze, Lettere, ed Arti — Relaz Accad Accad Zelanti Aci Reale Sci
Relazione Clinico Scientifiche — Relaz Clin Sci
Relazione. Commissione Direttiva. Istituto Zootecnico Laziale (Roma) — Relazione Comm Dirett Ist Zootec Laziale (Roma)
Relazione Internationale (Milan) — RIM
Relazione sull'Attivita della Stazione Sperimentale di Praticoltura di Lodi — Relaz Attiv Stn Sper Pratic Lodi
Relazione sull'Attivita della Stazione Sperimentale di Praticoltura di Lodi — Relaz Attivita Stn Sper Pratic Lodi
Relazioni Sociali — Relaz Soc
RELC [*Regional English Language Centre*] **Journal** [*Singapore*] — RELC
RELC (Regional English Language Centre) Journal — RELC J
Relevance Logic Newsletter — Relev Log News
Relevance Logic Newsletter — Relevance Logic Newslett
Relgioese Stimmen der Voelker — RSV
Relgion, Wissenschaft, Kultur — RWK
Relgionsgeschichtliches Lesebuch — RGL
Relgionswissenschaftliche Bibliothek — RWB
Reliability Engineering — Reliab Eng
Reliability Engineering — Reliability Eng
Reliability of Offshore Operations. Proceedings. International Workshop — Reliab Offshore Oper Proc Int Workshop
Reliable Poultry Journal — Reliable P J
Religioese Quellenschriften — RQS
Religioese Schriftenreihe — Rel Schr
Religion — PREL
Religion — Rel
Religion and Literature — R and L
Religion and Public Order — RPO
Religion and Reason — RaR
Religion and Society — Rel Soc
Religion and Society — Relig Soc
Religion et Societes — ReS
Religion in Communist Dominated Areas [*Monograph*] — RCDA
Religion in Communist Lands — RCL
Religion in Communist Lands — Rel Comm Lands
Religion in Education (London) — Rel Ed L
Religion in Geschichte und Gegenwart — RGG
Religion in Life — Rel Life
Religion in Life — Relig in Life
Religion in Life — RIL
Religion in Life — RL
Religion in Southern Africa — Rel So Africa
Religion in Southern Africa — Relig Sthn Afr
Religion Index One — Rel Ind One
Religion Index One. Periodicals — Relig Index One Period
Religion Indexes — RI
Religion och Bibel [*Uppsala*] — RelB
Religion och Bibel [*Uppsala*] — RelBib
Religion och Bibel — RoB
Religion och Kultur — RK
Religion Teacher's Journal — Relig T J
Religion und Geisteskultur — RG

Religion und Kultus der Roemer — RK
Religion und Kultus der Roemer — RKR
Religion und Kultus der Roemer — RUKR
Religion y Cultura — R & C
Religion y Cultura — Rel Cult
Religion y Cultura — RyC
Religionen der Menschheit — RM
Religioni dell'Umanita — RU
Religioni e Civitia — R & C
Religions de l'Europe Ancienne — R Eur A
Religions (London) — Rel L
Religionsgeschichtliche Texte — RGT
Religionsgeschichtliche Versuche und Vorarbeiten — Rel
Religionsgeschichtliche Versuche und Vorarbeiten — Rel Veru Vorarb
Religionsgeschichtliche Versuche und Vorarbeiten — RGVV
Religionsgeschichtliche Versuche und Vorarbeiten — RVV
Religionsgeschichtliche Volksbuecher — RV
Religionspaedagogische Zeitfragen — RPZ
Religionswissenschaft der Gegenwart in Selbstdarstellungen — RWGS
Religionswissenschaftliche Studien — RWS
Religionswissenschaftliches Woerterbuch — RWW
Religious and Theological Abstracts — Rel & Theol Abstr
Religious and Theological Abstracts — RelAb
Religious and Theological Abstracts — Relig Theol Abstr
Religious and Theological Abstracts [*Myerstown, PA*] — RelTAbstr
Religious and Theological Abstracts — RTA
Religious and Theological Abstracts — RThAbstr
Religious Books and Serials in Print — RBSP
Religious Broadcasting — RB
Religious Cabinet — Rel Cab
Religious Education — R Ed
Religious Education — RE
Religious Education — Rel Ed
Religious Education — Relig Ed
Religious Education — Relig Educ
Religious Encyclopedia — Rel Enc
Religious Humanism — Relig Hum
Religious Humanism — RH
Religious Leaders of America — RLA
Religious Periodicals Index — RelPerl
Religious Periodicals Index — RPI
Religious Studies — PRSU
Religious Studies — Rel St
Religious Studies [*London*] — Rel Stud
Religious Studies — Relig Stud
Religious Studies — RelS
Religious Studies — RS
Religious Studies Review — Rel St R
Religious Studies Review — Rel St Rev
Religious Theatre — RT
Religious Traditions — Rel Trad
Reliquary and Illustrated Archaeologist — Reliquary Il Archaeol
Remarques Africaines — Remarques Afr
Remedes des Corps et des Ames — Rem Corps Ames
Remedes-Actualites — Rem Actual
Remedial Education — Rem Educ
Remedial Education — Remedial Ed
Remedial Education — Remedial Educ
Remington Review — Rem R
Remote Sensing — Sensing
Remote Sensing Association of Australia. Bulletin — Bull Rem Sens Soc Aust
Remote Sensing of Earth Resources — Remote Sensing Earth Resour
Remote Sensing of Earth Resources and Environment — Remote Sens Earth Resour Environ
Remote Sensing of Environment — Remote Sens Environ
Remote Sensing of Environment — Remote Sensing Environ
Remote Sensing of Environment — RSEEA
Remote Sensing On-Line Retrieval System [*Database*] — RESORS
Remote Sensing Yearbook — Remote Sensing Yearb
Renaissance — Ren
Renaissance and Modern Studies — ReMS
Renaissance and Modern Studies — Ren Mod St
Renaissance and Modern Studies — Ren Mod Stud
Renaissance and Modern Studies — Ren MS
Renaissance and Modern Studies — Renaiss Mod Stud
Renaissance and Modern Studies — RMS
Renaissance and Reformation — RAR
Renaissance and Reformation — Ren & R
Renaissance and Reformation — Ren & Ref
Renaissance and Reformation — Renaiss Ref
Renaissance and Reformation — Renaiss Reform
Renaissance and Renascences in Western Literature — RRWL
Renaissance Bulletin — Ren B
Renaissance Drama — RD
Renaissance Drama — Renaiss Dr
Renaissance Drama — RenD
Renaissance Editions. San Fernando Valley State College — RESFV
Renaissance Monographs — Ren M
Renaissance News — Ren News
Renaissance News — Renais News
Renaissance News — RenN
Renaissance News — RN
Renaissance Papers — RenP
Renaissance Papers — RP
Renaissance Quarterly — PRNQ
Renaissance Quarterly — Renaiss Q
Renaissance Quarterly — Renaiss Quart
Renaissance Quarterly — Renaissance Q
Renaissance Quarterly — RenQ
Renaissance Quarterly — RQ
Renaissance Text Series — RTS
Renaissance und Philosophie — RuP
Renal Function — Ren Funct
Renal Function. Transactions. Conference — Renal Funct Trans Conf
Renal Physiology — Renal Physiol
Renal Physiology and Biochemistry — Ren Physiol Biochem
Renal Physiology and Biochemistry — Renal Physiol Biochem
Renascence — PRNC
Renascence — Ren
Renascence — Rena
Rencontre Assyriologique Internationale — RAI
Rencontre Biologique — Rencontre Biol
Rencontre. Chretiens et Juifs — R Ch J
Rencontre de Moriond. Compte Rendu — Rencontre Moriond CR
Rencontre de Moriond. Proceedings — Rencontre Moriond Proc
Rencontres Biblique — RenBib
Rencontres Caraibes en Lutte Biologique — Rencontres Caraibes Lutte Biol
Rencontres Internationales de Chimie Therapeutique — Rencontres Int Chim Ther
Renda sobre o Congresso da Sociedade Europeia de Hematologia — Renda Congr Soc Eur Hematol
Rendel Harris Papyri of Woodbrooke College. Birmingham — P Harr
Rendezvous — Rend
Rendiconti [*Bologna*] — Rend
Rendiconti. Accademia delle Scienze. Istituto di Bologna — RAIB
Rendiconti. Accademia di Archeologia, Lettere, e Belle Arti [*Napoli*] — RAA
Rendiconti. Accademia di Archeologia, Lettere, e Belle Arti di Napoli — AAN
Rendiconti. Accademia di Archeologia, Lettere, e Belle Arti di Napoli — Atti Acc Nap
Rendiconti. Accademia di Archeologia, Lettere, e Belle Arti di Napoli — Atti Acc Napoli
Rendiconti. Accademia di Archeologia, Lettere, e Belle Arti di Napoli — Rd Nap
Rendiconti. Accademia di Archeologia, Lettere, e Belle Arti di Napoli — Ren Accad Napoli
Rendiconti. Accademia di Archeologia, Lettere, e Belle Arti di Napoli — Rend Acc Arch Nap
Rendiconti. Accademia di Archeologia, Lettere, e Belle Arti (Napoli) — RAAN
Rendiconti. Accademia di Archeologia, Lettere, e Belle Arti (Napoli) — RAN
Rendiconti. Accademia di Archeologia, Lettere, e Belle Arti (Napoli) — Rend Acc (Napoli)
Rendiconti. Accademia di Scienze Fisiche, Matematiche, e Naturali. Societa Reale di Napoli — Rend Accad Sci Fis Mat Nat Soc R Napoli
Rendiconti. Accademia Nazionale dei 40 (Quaranta) — Rend Accad Naz 40 (Quaranta)
Rendiconti. Accademia Nazionale dei Lincei — Ac Naz Linc Ren
Rendiconti. Accademia Nazionale dei Lincei — Acc Naz Linc
Rendiconti. Accademia Nazionale dei Lincei — RAL
Rendiconti. Accademia Nazionale dei Lincei — Rd Linc
Rendiconti. Accademia Nazionale dei Lincei — Rend Acc Linc
Rendiconti. Accademia Nazionale dei Lincei — Rend Accad Lincei
Rendiconti. Accademia Nazionale dei Lincei — Rend Accad Naz Lincei
Rendiconti. Accademia Nazionale dei Lincei — Rendic Acc d'Italia
Rendiconti. Accademia Nazionale dei Lincei — Rendic Acc Lincei
Rendiconti. Accademia Nazionale dei Lincei — Rendiconti Accad Lincei
Rendiconti. Accademia Nazionale dei Lincei. Classe di Scienze Morali. Storiche e Filologiche — Rc Accad Lincei Cl di Sci Mor Stor Fil
Rendiconti. Accademia Nazionale dei XL — Rend Accad Naz XL
Rendiconti. Accademia Nazionale delle Scienze detta dei XL. Serie V. Memorie di Matematica e Applicazioni. Parte I — Rend Accad Naz Sci XL Mem Mat Appl 5
Rendiconti. Accademia Nazionale delle Scienze detta dei XL. Serie V. Memorie di Matematica. Parte I — Rend Accad Naz Sci XL Mem Mat 5
Rendiconti. Accademia Nazionale Italiana di Entomologia — Rend Accad Naz Ital Entomol
Rendiconti. Associazione Mineraria Sarda — Rend Assoc Min Sarda
Rendiconti. Circolo Matematico di Palermo — Rend Circ Mat Palermo
Rendiconti. Circolo Matematico di Palermo. Serie II — Rend Circ Mat Palermo 2
Rendiconti. Classe di Scienze Morali e Storiche. Accademia dei Lincei — RAL
Rendiconti. Classe di Scienze Morali e Storiche. Accademia dei Lincei — RALinc
Rendiconti. Classe di Scienze Morali e Storiche. Accademia dei Lincei — RALincei
Rendiconti. Classe di Scienze Morali e Storiche. Accademia dei Lincei — RALRend
Rendiconti. Classe di Scienze Morali e Storiche. Accademia d'Italia — RAI
Rendiconti del Circolo Matematico di Palermo. Serie II. Supplemento — Rend Circ Mat Palermo 2 Suppl
Rendiconti del Seminario Matematico di Messina. Serie II — Rend Sem Mat Messina Ser II
Rendiconti della Accademia Nazionale delle Scienze della dei XL. Memorie di Scienze Fisiche e Naturali. Serie V — Rend Accad Nat Sci XL Mem Sci Fis Natur 5
Rendiconti della Reale Accademia dei Lincei — Rendic Accad Linc
Rendiconti della Reale Accademia dei Lincei — Rendic R Acc Linc
Rendiconti delle Sedute della Accademia Nazionale dei Lincei. Classe di Scienze Fisiche, Matematiche, e Naturali — Rend Sedute Accad Naz Lincei Cl Sci Fis Mat Nat
Rendiconti di Gastro-Enterologia — Rend Gastro
Rendiconti di Matematica — Rend Mat
Rendiconti di Matematica — RNMTA

Rendiconti di Matematica. Serie VI — Rend Mat 6
Rendiconti di Matematica. Serie VII — Rend Mat 7
Rendiconti e Atti. Accademia di Scienze Mediche e Chirurgiche — Rend Atti Accad Sci Med Chir
Rendiconti e Atti. Accademia Nazionale dei Lincei — Rc Atti Accad Naz Lincei
Rendiconti. Istituti Scientifici. Universita di Camerino — Rend Ist Sci Univ Camerino
Rendiconti. Istituto di Matematica. Universita di Trieste — Rend Ist Mat Univ Trieste
Rendiconti. Istituto di Matematica. Universita di Trieste — Rend Istit Mat Univ Trieste
Rendiconti. Istituto di Sanita Pubblica — Rend Ist Sanita Pubblica
Rendiconti. Istituto Lombardo. Accademia di Scienze e Lettere — Rend Ist Lomb
Rendiconti. Istituto Lombardo. Accademia di Scienze e Lettere. Parte Generale e Atti Ufficiali — Rend Ist Lomb Accad Sci Lett Parte Gen Atti Uffic
Rendiconti. Istituto Lombardo. Accademia di Scienze e Lettere. Parte Generale e Atti Ufficiali — Rend Ist Lomb Sci Lett Parte Gen Atti Uffic
Rendiconti. Istituto Lombardo. Accademia di Scienze e Lettere. Sezione A. Scienze Matematiche, Fisiche, Chimiche, e Geologiche — Rend Ist Lomb Accad Sci Lett A Sci Mat Fis Chim Geol
Rendiconti. Istituto Lombardo. Accademia di Scienze e Lettere. Sezione A. Scienze Matematiche, Fisiche, e Geologiche [*Italy*] — Rend Ist Lomb Accad Sci Lett A
Rendiconti. Istituto Lombardo. Accademia di Scienze e Lettere. Sezione B. Scienze Biologiche e Mediche [*Italy*] — Rend Ist Lomb Accad Sci Lett B
Rendiconti. Istituto Lombardo. Accademia di Scienze e Lettere. Sezione B. Scienze Biologiche e Mediche — RLMBA
Rendiconti. Istituto Lombardo. Classe di Lettere, Scienze Morali, e Storiche — RILSL
Rendiconti. Istituto Lombardo di Scienze e Lettere — R Ist Lomb
Rendiconti. Istituto Lombardo di Scienze e Lettere — Rc Ist Lomb Sci Lett
Rendiconti. Istituto Lombardo di Scienze e Lettere — Rend Ist Lomb Sci
Rendiconti. Istituto Lombardo di Scienze e Lettere — Rend Ist Lomb Sci Lett
Rendiconti. Istituto Lombardo di Scienze e Lettere — RIL
Rendiconti. Istituto Lombardo di Scienze e Lettere. Classe di Lettere e Scienze Morali e Politiche — Rend R Ist Lomb Sci Lett
Rendiconti. Istituto Lombardo di Scienze e Lettere. Classe di Lettere e Scienze Morali e Politiche — RIL di Scienze e Lettere
Rendiconti. Istituto Lombardo di Scienze e Lettere. Classe di Lettere e Scienze Morali e Politiche — RILLM
Rendiconti. Istituto Lombardo di Scienze e Lettere. Classe di Lettere e Scienze Morali e Storiche — RILL
Rendiconti. Istituto Lombardo di Scienze e Lettere. Classe di Scienze Matematiche e Naturali — Rend Ist Lomb Sci Lett Cl Sci Mat Nat
Rendiconti. Istituto Lombardo di Scienze e Lettere. Parte Generale e Atti Ufficiali — Rend Ist Lomb Sci Lett Parte Gen Atti Uff
Rendiconti. Istituto Lombardo di Scienze e Lettere. Parte Generale e Atti Ufficiali — RILPG
Rendiconti. Istituto Lombardo di Scienze e Lettere. Sezione A. Scienze Matematiche, Fisiche, Chimiche, e Geologiche — Rend Ist Lomb Sci Lett A
Rendiconti. Istituto Lombardo di Scienze e Lettere. Sezione A. Scienze Matematiche, Fisiche, Chimiche, e Geologiche — Rend Ist Lomb Sci Lett A Sci Mat Fis Chim Geol
Rendiconti. Istituto Superiore di Sanita — Rc Ist Sup Sanita
Rendiconti. Istituto Superiore di Sanita — Rend Ist Super Sanita
Rendiconti. Istituto Superiore di Sanita. English Edition — Rend Ist Super Sanita Engl Ed
Rendiconti. Istituto Superiore di Sanita. Italian Edition — Rend Ist Super Sanita Ital Ed
Rendiconti. Pontificia Accademia di Archeologia — RPAA
Rendiconti. Pontificia Accademia Romana di Archeologia — Rend Pont
Rendiconti. Pontificia Accademia Romana di Archeologia — Rend Pont Acc
Rendiconti. Pontificia Accademia Romana di Archologia — RPARA
Rendiconti. Reale Accademia dei Lincei — Rend Linc
Rendiconti. Reale Accademia di Archeologia, Lettere, ed Arti (Naples) [*A publication*] — Rend (Nap)
Rendiconti. Reale Accademia d'Italia — RAIT
Rendiconti. Reale Accademia Nazionale dei Lincei — RANL
Rendiconti. Reale Accademia Nazionale dei Lincei — Rend R Accad Naz Lincei
Rendiconti. Reale Accademia Nazionale dei Lincei — RRAL
Rendiconti. Reale Istituto Lombardo di Scienze e Lettere — Rend R Ist Lomb Sci Lett
Rendiconti. Reale Istituto Lombardo di Scienze e Lettere [*Milan*] — RRIL
Rendiconti. Reale Istituto Lombardo di Scienze e Lettere. Classe di Scienze Matematiche e Naturali — Rend R Ist Lomb Sci Lett Cl Sci Mat Nat
Rendiconti. Reale Istituto Lombardo di Scienze e Lettere. Parte Generale e Atti Ufficiali — Rend R Ist Lomb Sci Lett Parte Gen Atti Uffic
Rendiconti. Riunione Annuale. Associazione Elettrotecnica ed Elettronica Italiana — Rend Riun Annu Assoc Elettrotec Elettron Ital
Rendiconti. Riunione Annuale. Associazione Elettrotecnica Italiana [*Italy*] — Rend Riun Annu Assoc Elettrotec Ital
Rendiconti. Riunione Annuale. Associazione Elettrotecnica Italiana — Rend Riunione Assoc Elettrotec Ital
Rendiconti. Riunione Annuale. Associazione Elettrotecnica Italiana — RRAEA
Rendiconti Romani di Gastroenterologia [*Italy*] — Rend Rom Gastroenterol
Rendiconti Romani di Gastroenterologia — RRGAB
Rendiconti. Scuola Internazionale di Fisica "Enrico Fermi" — Rend Sc Int Fis Enrico Fermi
Rendiconti. Scuola Internazionale di Fisica "Enrico Fermi" — Rend Sc Int Fis Fermi
Rendiconti. Scuola Internazionale di Fisica "Enrico Fermi" [*Italy*] — Rend Scu Int Fis Enrico Fermi
Rendiconti. Scuola Internazionale di Fisica "Enrico Fermi" — RSFFA
Rendiconti. Seminario della Facolta di Scienze. Universita di Cagliari — Rend Sem Fac Sci Univ Cagliari
Rendiconti. Seminario della Facolta di Scienze. Universita di Cagliari — Rend Semin Fac Sci Univ Cagliari
Rendiconti. Seminario della Facolta di Scienze. Universita di Cagliari — RSFSA
Rendiconti. Seminario Matematico di Brescia — Rend Sem Mat Brescia
Rendiconti. Seminario Matematico e Fisico di Milano — Rend Sem Mat Fis Milano
Rendiconti. Seminario Matematico e Fisico di Milano — Rend Semin Mat Fis Milano
Rendiconti. Seminario Matematico e Fisico di Milano — RSMFA
Rendiconti. Seminario Matematico gia Conferenze di Fisica e di Matematica. Universita e Politecnico di Torino — Rend Sem Mat Univ Politec Torino
Rendiconti. Seminario Matematico. Universita di Padova — Rend Sem Mat Univ Padova
Rendiconti. Seminario Matematico. Universita e Politecnico di Torino — Rend Sem Mat Univ e Politec Torino
Rendiconti. Societa Chimica Italiana — Rend Soc Chim Ital
Rendiconti. Societa Italiana delle Scienze detta Accademia dei XL — Rend Soc Ital Sci Accad XL
Rendiconti. Societa Italiana di Mineralogia e Petrologia — Rend Soc Ital Mineral Petrol
Rendiconti. Societa Italiana di Mineralogia e Petrologia — SIMPA
Rendiconti. Societa Mineralogica Italiana — Rend Soc Mineral Ital
Rendiconto. Accademia della Scienze. Istituto di Bologna — RABo
Rendiconto. Accademia della Scienze. Istituto di Bologna — RIB
Rendiconto. Accademia delle Scienze Fisiche e Matematiche (Napoli) — Rend Accad Sci Fis Mat (Napoli)
Rendiconto. Accademia delle Scienze Fisiche e Matematiche (Napoli) — Rendic Accad Sc Fis e Mat (Napoli)
Rendiconto. Accademia delle Scienze. Istituto di Bologna — RABol
Rendiconto. Accademia delle Scienze. Istituto di Bologna — RASIB
Rendiconto. Reale Accademia delle Scienze. Istituto di Bologna — Rendic R Accad Sc Ist Bologna
Renewable Energy Bulletin — REBUD
Renewable Energy Bulletin [*England*] — Renew Energy Bull
Renewable Energy Index [*Database*] — REI
Renewable Sources of Energy — RSE
Renewal — Renew
Renseignements Agricoles. Bulletin Periodique du Ministere de l'Agriculture et des Domaines (Bulgaria) — Renseign Agric Bull Period (Bulg)
Rensselaer Polytechnic Institute. Engineering and Science Series — Rensselaer Polytech Inst Eng Sci Ser
Rental Equipment Register — Rent Equip
Rental Product News — Rental
Rentgenografiya Mineral'nogo Syr'ya — Rentgenogr Miner Syr'ya
Rentgenologiya i Radiologiya — RENRA
Rentgenologiya i Radiologiya — Rentgenol Radiol
Rep — R
Repatriation Department. Medical Research Bulletin [*Australia*] — Med Res Bull Repat Dept
Reperes-Economie du Languedoc-Roussillon — Reperes-Econ Languedoc-Roussillon
Repertoire Analytique d'Articles de Revues de Quebec [*Database*] — RADAR
Repertoire Analytique de Litterature Francaise [*Bordeaux*] — RALF
Repertoire Analytique de Litterature Francaise [*Bordeaux*] — Repertoire Anal Litt Francaise
Repertoire Bibliographique de la Philosophie — RBP
Repertoire Bibliographique de la Philosophie — Rep Bibl Phil
Repertoire Bibliographique de la Philosophie — Rep Bibliogr Philos
Repertoire Bibliographique de la Philosophie — RepBibPhil
Repertoire Bibliographique des Institutions Chretiennes — RBIC
Repertoire Bibliographique des Institutions Chretiennes — Rep Bibliogr Inst Chret
Repertoire Bibliographique des Institutions Chretiennes [*Database*] — RIC
Repertoire Biomed — Rep Biomed
Repertoire Canadien sur l'Education [*See also CEI*] — RCE
Repertoire Chronologique d'Epigraphie Arabe — RCEA
Repertoire d'Art et d'Archeologie — RAA
Repertoire de la Statuaire Grecque et Romaine — RSGR
Repertoire de Peintures Grecques et Romaines — RP
Repertoire de Peintures Grecques et Romaines — RPGR
Repertoire de Pharmacie — Repert Pharm
Repertoire de Prehistoire et d'Archeologie de la Suisse — Rep PAS
Repertoire de Prehistoire et d'Archeologie de la Suisse — RPAS
Repertoire de Reliefs Grecs et Romains — Rep Rel
Repertoire de Reliefs Grecs et Romains — RR
Repertoire de Reliefs Grecs et Romains — RRGR
Repertoire d'Epigraphie Meroitique — REM
Repertoire d'Epigraphie Semitique [*Paris*] — RES
Repertoire des Banques de Donnees en Conversationnel [*Database*] — REBK
Repertoire des Vases Peints Grecs et Etrusques — Rep Vases
Repertoire Fiscal — REF
Repertoire Fiscal — Rep F
Repertoire Fiscal — Rep Fisc
Repertoire General des Sciences Religieuses — RGSR
Repertoire International de la Litterature de l'Art [*RILA*] — Rep Int Litt Art
Repertoire International de la Litterature de l'Art [*International Repertory of the Literature of Art*] [*Information service or system*] — RILA
Repertoire International des Sources Musicales — RISM
Repertoire Medical Pratique. Serie Biologie — Repert Med Prat Ser Biol
Repertoire Pratique du Droit Belge — Rep Prat
Repertoire Pratique du Droit Belge — Rep Prat Dr B
Repertorio Americano — Ra
Repertorio Americano — RAm

Repertorio Americano — RAmer
Repertorio Americano — RepAm
Repertorio Americano (San Jose, Costa Rica) — Reper Am S Jose
Repertorio Chmico Italiano — Rep Chim Ital
Repertorio di Agricoltura Pratica e di Economica Domestica — Repert Agric Prat Econ Domest
Repertorio Historico — RH
Repertorio Latinoamericano — RLA
Repertorio Latinoamericano — RLati
Repertorio Medico-Farmaceutico y de Ciencias Auxiliares — Repert Med Farm Ci Auxiliares
Repertorium Biblicum Medii Aevi — RBMA
Repertorium der Photographie — Repertorium der Phot
Repertorium des Neuesten und Wissenswuerdigsten aus der Gesammten Naturkunde — Repert Neuesten Wissenswuerd Gesammten Naturk
Repertorium Fontium Historiae Medii Aevi — RFHMA
Repertorium fuer Biblische und Morgenlaendische Litteratur [*Leipzig*] — RBML
Repertorium fuer Kunstwissenschaft — Rep Kunst W
Repertorium fuer Kunstwissenschaft — RepKw
Repertorium fuer Kunstwissenschaft — RKW
Repertorium Plantarum Succulentarum — Repert Plant Succulentarum
Repertorium Specierum Novarum Regni Vegatabilis. Centralblatt fuer Sammlung und Veroeffentlichung von Einzeldiagnosen Neuer Pflanzen — Repert Spec Nov Regni Veg
Repertorium Specierum Novarum Regni Vegetabilis. Sonderbeiheft A — Repert Spec Nov Regni Veg Sonderbeih A
Repertorium Specierum Novarum Regni Vegetabilis. Sonderbeiheft B — Repert Spec Nov Regni Veg Sonderbeih B
Repertorium Specierum Novarum Regni Vegetabilis. Sonderbeiheft D — Repert Spec Nov Regni Veg Sonderbeih D
Reponses Chretiennes aux Hommes de Notre Temps — RCHNT
Report. Activities of the Danish Atomic Energy Commission — Rep Activ Dan Atom Energy Commn
Report. Activities. Research Institute for Water Resources. Budapest — Rep Act Res Inst Water Resour Budapest
Report. Administration of the Persian Gulf Residency [*Aden*] — RAPGR
Report. Administration of the Persian Gulf Residency and Muscat Political Agency [*Aden*] — RAPA
Report. Advisory Council of Scientific and Industrial Research of Alberta — Rep Advis CSIR Alberta
Report. Aeronautical Research Institute — Rep Aeronaut Res Inst
Report. Aeronautical Research Institute. University of Tokyo — Rep Aeronaut Res Inst Univ Tokyo
Report AFL. University of Cincinnati. Department of Aerospace Engineering — Rep AFL Univ Cincinnati Dep Aerosp Eng
Report. Agricultural and Horticultural Research Station. University of Bristol — Rep Agric Hort Res Stn Univ Bristol
Report. Agricultural Department (Hong Kong) — Rep Agric Dept Hong Kong
Report. Agricultural Research Council. Radiobiological Laboratory — Rep Agric Res Coun Radiobiol Lab
Report. Agronomy Branch. Department of Agriculture and Fisheries. South Australia — Rep Agron Branch Dep Agric South Aust
Report. Aichi Institute of Public Health [*Japan*] — Rep Aichi Inst Public Health
Report. Aichi Prefectural Institute of Public Health — Rep Aichi Prefect Inst Public Health
Report. Akita Prefecture. Institute of Public Health [*Japan*] — Rep Akita Prefect Inst Public Health
Report. Alaska Division of Mines and Geology — Rep Alaska Div Mines Geol
Report. Alaska Division of Mines and Minerals — Rep Alaska Div Mines Miner
Report. Alberta Research Council — Rep Alberta Res Counc
Report. Alfalfa Improvement Conference — Rep Alfalfa Improv Conf
Report. Alfred P. Sloan Foundation — Rep Alfred Sloan Found
Report. American Museum of Natural History — Rep Am Mus Nat Hist
Report. Analytical Chemistry Unit. Institute of Geological Sciences — Rep Anal Chem Unit Inst Geol Sci
Report and Accounts. National Coal Board [*British*] — Rep Acc Natl Coal Board
Report and Proceedings. ORAU/IEA (Oak Ridge Associated Universities. Institute for Energy Analysis) — Rep Proc ORAU IEA (Oak Ridge Assoc Univ Inst Energy Anal)
Report and Reprints of Scientific Papers. Saranac Laboratory for the Study of Tuberculosis — Rep Repr Sci Pap Saranac Lab Study Tuberc
Report and Transactions. Cardiff Naturalists' Society — Rep Trans Cardiff Naturalists Soc
Report and Transactions (Devonshire) — Rep Trans (Devonshire)
Report and Transactions. Societe Guernesiaise — Rep Trans Soc Guernesiaise
Report. Animal Breeding Research Organisation — Rep Anim Breed Res Organ
Report. Animal Research Division. Department of Agriculture (New Zealand) — Rep Anim Res Div (NZ)
Report. Annual Conference. Ontario Department of Agriculture. Extension Branch — Rep Annu Conf Ontario Dept Agr Ext Br
Report. Annual Date Growers Institute — Rep Annu Date Grow Inst
Report. Annual General Meeting. Scottish Society for Research in Plant Breeding — Rep Annu Gen Meet Scott Soc Res Plant Breed
Report. Annual Meeting. Washington State Horticultural Association — Rep Annu Meet Wash State Hortic Assoc
Report. Applied Geophysics Unit. Institute of Geological Sciences — Rep Appl Geophys Unit Inst Geol Sci
Report. Architectural Science Unit. University of Queensland — Rep Archit Sci Unit Univ Queensl
Report. Arizona Agricultural Experiment Station — Rep Ariz Agr Exp Sta
Report. Arizona Agricultural Experiment Station — Rep Ariz Agric Exp Stn
Report. Arkansas Agricultural Experiment Station — Rep Ark Agric Exp Stn
Report. Army Research and Testing Laboratory [*South Korea*] — Rep Army Res Test Lab
Report. Association of Occupational Therapists — Rep Ass Occup Ther
Report. Australia Commonwealth Scientific and Industrial Research Organisation. Division of Textile Industry — Rep Aust CSIRO Div Text Ind
Report. Australia Defence Standards Laboratories — Rep Aust Def Stand Lab
Report. Australia. Materials Research Laboratory — Rep Aust Mater Res Lab
Report. Australian and New Zealand Association for the Advancement of Science — Rep Aust NZ Assoc Adv Sci
Report. Australian Atomic Energy Commission — Rep Aust At Energy Comm
Report. Australian Government Analytical Laboratories — Rep Aust Gov Anal Lab
Report. Australian Numismatic Society — RANS
Report. Australian Road Research Board — Rep Aust Road Res Board
Report BC-X. Canadian Forestry Service. Pacific Forest Research Centre — Rep BC-X Can For Serv Pac For Res Cent
Report. BISRA [*British Iron and Steel Research Association*] — Rep BISRA
Report. Botanical and Forestry Department Hong Kong — Rep Bot Dept Hong Kong
Report. Botanical Society. British Isles — Rep Bot Soc Brit Isles
Report. Botanical Survey of India — Rep Bot Surv Ind
Report. Botanical Survey of India — Rep Bot Surv India
Report. British and Foreign Bible Society — RBFBS
Report. British Association for the Advancement of Science — RBAAS
Report. British Association for the Advancement of Science — Rep Brit Ass Adv Sc
Report. British Association for the Advancement of Science — Rep Brit Assoc Adv Sci
Report. British Beekeepers Association — Rep Br Beekprs Ass
Report. British Bryological Society — Rep Brit Bryol Soc
Report. British Electrical and Allied Industries Research Association — Rep Brit El All Ind Res Ass
Report. British Empire Cancer Campaign — Rep Brit Canc Camp
Report. British Museum. Natural History — Rep Brit Mus Natur Hist
Report. [*Australia*] **Bureau of Mineral Resources. Geology and Geophysics** — Rep Bur Miner Resour Geol Geophys
Report. Bureau of Mineral Resources, Geology, and Geophysics (Australia) — Rep Bur Miner Resour Geol Geophys (Aust)
Report. Bureau of Mines and Mineral Resources. Geology and Geophysics Microform — Rep Bur Mines Miner Resour Geol Geophys Microform
Report BWRA [*British Welding Research Association*] — Rep BWRA
Report. California Water Resources Center — Rep Calif Water Resour Cent
Report. California Water Resources Center. University of California — Rep Calif Water Resour Cent Univ Calif
Report. Canadian Catholic Historical Association — RCCHA
Report. Canadian Seed Growers' Association — Rep Canad Seed Growers Assoc
Report. Canterbury Agricultural College — Rep Cant Agric Coll
Report. Cape Cod Cranberry Growers' Association — Rep Cape Cod Cranberry Growers Assoc
Report. Castings Research Laboratory — Rep Cast Res Lab
Report. Castings Research Laboratory. Waseda University — Rep Cast Res Lab Waseda Univ
Report CC-X. Chemical Control Research Institute — Rep CC-X Chem Control Res Inst
Report CE. Technion-Israel Institute of Technology. Department of Chemical Engineering — Rep CE Technion-Isr Inst Technol Dep Chem Eng
Report. Center of Advanced Instrumental Analysis. Kyushu University — Rep Cent Adv Instrum Anal Kyushu Univ
Report. CENTO [*Central Treaty Organization*] **Scientific Programme** — Rep CENTO Sci Programme
Report. Central Inspection Institute of Weights and Measures. Tokyo — Rep Cent Insp Inst Weights Meas Tokyo
Report. Central Research Institute. Electric Power Industry Agricultural Laboratory — Rep Cent Res Inst Electr Power Indust Agric Lab
Report. Central Research Institute. Electric Power Industry Technical Laboratory — Rep Cent Res Inst Electr Power Ind Tech Lab
Report. Ceskoslovenska Akademia Ved. Ustav Jaderne Fyziky — Rep Cesk Akad Ved Ustav Jad Fyz
Report CG-D. United States Coast Guard. Office of Research and Development — Rep CG D US Coast Guard Off Res Dev
Report. Chemical Branch. Mines Department (Western Australia) — Rep Chem Branch Mines Dep (West Aust)
Report. Chemical Engineering Department. Monash University — Rep Chem Eng Dep Monash Univ
Report. Chemical Fiber Research Institute. Kyoto University — Rep Chem Fiber Res Inst Kyoto Univ
Report. Chemical Laboratory (Western Australia) — Rep Chem Lab (West Aust)
Report. Chiba Institute of Technology — Rep Chiba Inst Technol
Report. Chiba Institute of Technology. Scientific Series — Rep Chiba Inst Technol Sci Ser
Report. Clemson University. Water Resources Research Institute — Rep Clemson Univ Water Resour Res Inst
Report CLM-R - UKAEA [*United Kingdom Atomic Energy Authority*] **Research Group. Culham Laboratory** — Rep CLM R UKAEA Res Group Culham Lab
Report CLM-R. United Kingdom Atomic Energy Authority. Culham Laboratory — Rep CLM R UKAEA Culham Lab
Report CLM-R. United Kingdom Atomic Energy Authority. Research Group. Culham Laboratory — Rep CLM R UK At Energy Auth Res Group Culham Lab
Report. Cocoa Research Institute (Tafo, Ghana) — Rep Cocoa Res Inst (Tafo Ghana)
Report. College of Engineering. Hosei University — Rep Coll Eng Hosei Univ
Report. Commission on Accreditation of Rehabilitation Facilities — Rep Comm Accredit Rehabil Facil
Report. Commissioner of Agriculture — Rep Commiss Agric
Report. Commonwealth Conference on Plant Pathology — Rep Commonw Conf Plant Pathol

Report. Commonwealth Entomological Conference — Rep Commonwealth Entomol Conf
Report. Commonwealth Mycological Conference — Rep Commonw Mycol Conf
Report. Commonwealth Mycological Conference — Rep Commonwealth Mycol Conf
Report. Commonwealth Scientific and Industrial Research Organisation. Division of Fisheries and Oceanography (Australia) — Rep CSIRO Div Fish Oceanogr (Aust)
Report. Commonwealth Scientific and Industrial Research Organisation. Division of Mineral Engineering (Australia) — Rep CSIRO Div Miner Eng (Aust)
Report. Commonwealth Scientific and Industrial Research Organisation. Solar Energy Studies — Rep CSIRO Sol Energy Stud
Report. Commonwealth Scientific and Industrial Research Organization. Division of Textile Industry (Australia) — Rep CSIRO Div Text Ind (Aust)
Report. Computer Centre. University of Tokyo — Rep Comput Cent Univ Tokyo
Report. Computer Centre. University of Tokyo — Rep Comput Centre Univ Tokyo
Report. CONCAWE [*Conservation of Clean Air and Water, Europe*] — Rep CONCAWE
Report. Concrete and Silicate Laboratory. Technical Research Centre of Finland — Rep Concr Silic Lab Tech Res Cent Finl
Report. Conference on the Role of Wheat in the World's Food Supply — Rep Conf Role Wheat World Food Supply
Report. Congress. European Orthodontic Society — Rep Congr Eur Orthod Soc
Report. Congress of the European Association for Research on Plant Breeding — Rep Congr Eur Ass Res Plant Breed
Report. Cooperative Research in Kinki-Chugoku Region — Rep Coop Res Kinki Chugoku Reg
Report. Coordinating Research Council, Incorporated — Rep Coord Res Counc Inc
Report. Council for Mineral Technology (Randburg, South Africa) — Rep Counc Miner Technol (Randburg S Afr)
Report. CSIRO [*Commonwealth Scientific and Industrial Research Organisation*] **Marine Laboratories** — Rep CSIRO Mar Lab
Report. Culham Laboratory. United Kingdom Atomic Energy Authority — Rep Culham Lab UK At Energy Auth
Report. Curators. Botanical Exchange Club. British Isles — Rep Curators Bot Exch Club Brit Isles
Report. Danish Biological Station to the Ministry of Agriculture and Fisheries — Rep Danish Biol Sta Minist Agric
Report. Deir-Alla Research Station [*Jordan*] — Rep Deir-Alla Res Sta
Report. Department of Agricultural Economics. University of Nebraska. Agricultural Experiment Station — Rep Dep Agric Econ Univ Nebr Agric Exp Stn
Report. Department of Agriculture (British East Africa) — Rep Dept Agric (Brit East Africa)
Report. Department of Agriculture of New South Wales — Rep Dep Agric NSW
Report. Department of Antiquities of Cyprus — RDAC
Report. Department of Antiquities of Cyprus — Rep Dept Antiquities Cyprus
Report. Department of Chemical Engineering. Monash University — Rep Dep Chem Eng Monash Univ
Report. Department of Fisheries and Fauna. Western Australia — Rep Dep Fish Fauna West Aust
Report. Department of Fisheries and Wildlife. Western Australia — Rep Dep Fish Wildl West Aust
Report. Department of Mines and Energy. Government of Newfoundland and Labrador — Rep Dep Mines Energy Gov Newfoundland Labrador
Report. Department of Mines (Nova Scotia) — Rep Dep Mines (NSc)
Report. Department of Mines. Western Australia — Rep Dep Mines West Aust
Report. Department of Physics. University of Oulu — Rep Dep Phys Univ Oulu
Report des Staatlichen Amtes fuer Atomsicherheit und Strahlenschutz der DDR — Rep Staatl Amtes Atomsicherh Strahlenschutz DDR
Report. Director of Government Chemical Laboratories (Western Australia) — Rep Dir Gov Chem Lab (West Aust)
Report. Director of Mines (Tasmania) — Rep Dir Mines (Tasmania)
Report. Director of Veterinary Services and Animal Industry. Department of Agriculture (Union of South Africa) — Rep Director Vet Serv Dept Agric (Union South Africa)
Report. Director of Veterinary Services and Animal Industry (Onderstepoort) [*A publication*] — Rep Dir Vet Serv Anim Ind (Onderstepoort)
Report. Division for Nutrition and Food Research TNO — Rep Div Nutr Food Res TNO
Report. Division of Building Research. Commonwealth Scientific and Industrial Research Organisation — Rep Div Bldg Res CSIRO
Report. Division of Building Research. Commonwealth Scientific and Industrial Research Organisation — Rep Div Build Res CSIRO
Report. Division of Chemical Engineering. Commonwealth Scientific and Industrial Research Organisation — Rep Div Chem Eng CSIRO
Report. Division of Chemical Engineering. Commonwealth Scientific and Industrial Research Organisation — Rep Div Chem Engng CSIRO
Report. Division of Fisheries and Oceanography. Commonwealth Scientific and Industrial Research Organisation — Rep Div Fish Oceanogr CSIRO
Report. Division of Horticultural Research. Commonwealth Scientific and Industrial Research Organisation — Rep Div Hort Res CSIRO
Report. Division of Mechanical Engineering. Commonwealth Scientific and Industrial Research Organisation — Rep Div Mech Engng CSIRO
Report. Division of Mineralogy. Commonwealth Scientific and Industrial Research Organisation — Rep Div Miner CSIRO
Report. Division of Mineralogy. Minerals Research Laboratory. Commonwealth Scientific and Industrial Research Organisation — Rep Miner Res Lab CSIRO
Report. Division of Textile Industry. Commonwealth Scientific and Industrial Research Organisation — Rep Div Text Ind CSIRO
Report. Division of Water and Land Development. Hawaii — Rep Div Water Land Dev Hawaii
Report DL. New Zealand Department of Scientific and Industrial Research. Dominion Laboratory — Rep DL NZ Dep Sci Ind Res Dom Lab
Report. Dove Marine Laboratory of Kings College. Durham University — Rep Dove Mar Lab
Report. East Malling Research Station (Maidstone, England) — Rep East Malling Res Stn (Maidstone Engl)
Report. Eastern Forest Products Laboratory (Canada) — Rep East For Prod Lab (Can)
Report ED. Engineering Section. Commonwealth Scientific and Industrial Research Organisation — Rep ED Eng Sect CSIRO
Report. Ehime Prefectural Research Institute for Environmental Science — Rep Ehime Prefect Res Inst Environ Sci
Report EM. Ontario Ministry of Transportation and Communications. Engineering Materials Office — Rep EM Ont Minist Transp Commun Eng Mater Off
Report. Engineering Institute. Faculty of Engineering. Tokyo University [*Japan*] — Rep Eng Inst Fac Eng Tokyo Univ
Report. Engineering Research Laboratory. Obayashi-Gumi Limited [*Japan*] — Rep Eng Res Lab Obayashi-Gumi Ltd
Report. Entomological Society of Ontario — Rep Ent Soc Ont
Report. Environment Science Institute. Mie Prefecture — Rep Environ Sci Inst Mie Prefect
Report. Environmental Protection Service. Series EPS-3 (Canada) — Rep Environ Prot Serv Ser EPS 3 (Can)
Report. Environmental Protection Service. Series EPS-4 (Canada) — Rep Environ Prot Serv Ser EPS 4 (Can)
Report. Environmental Radiation Surveillance. Washington Department of Social and Health Services — Rep Environ Radiat Surveill Wash Dep Soc Health Serv
Report. Environmental Research Organization. Chiba University — Rep Environ Res Organ Chiba Univ
Report. Environmental Science Institute. Kinki University — Rep Environ Sci Inst Kinki Univ
Report. Environmental Science Institute of Hyogo Prefecture — Rep Environ Sci Inst Hyogo Prefect
Report. Environmental Science Research Center of Shiga Prefecture — Rep Environ Sci Res Cent Shiga Prefect
Report. Environmental Science Research Institute. Kinki University — Rep Environ Sci Res Inst Kinki Univ
Report EPS. Canada. Environmental Protection Service. Solid Waste Management Branch — Rep EPS Can Environ Prot Serv Solid Waste Manage Branch
Report ERP/PMRL. Physical Metallurgy Research Laboratories (Canada) — Rep ERP/PMRL Phys Metall Res Lab (Can)
Report. Experimental and Research Station. Nursery and Market Garden Industries Development Society, Ltd. (Cheshunt) — Rep Exp Res Stn (Cheshunt)
Report. Faculty of Agriculture. Shizuoka University/Shizuoka Daigaku Nogakubu Kenkyu Hokoku — Rep Fac Agric Shizuoka Univ
Report. Faculty of Fisheries. Prefectural University of Mie — Rep Fac Fish Prefect Univ Mie
Report. FAO [*Food and Agriculture Organization of the United Nations*]/IAEA Technical Meeting (Brunswick-Volkenrode) [*International Atomic Energy Agency*] — Rep FAO/IAEA Tech Meet (Brunswick-Volkenrode)
Report. Federal Railroad Administration [*United States*] — Rep Fed Railroad Adm
Report. Fermentation Research Institute — Rep Ferment Res Inst
Report. Fermentation Research Institute (Chiba) — Rep Ferment Res Inst (Chiba)
Report. Fermentation Research Institute (Tsukuba-Gun, Japan) — Rep Ferment Res Inst (Tsukuba-Gun Jpn)
Report. Fermentation Research Institute (Yatabe) — Rep Ferment Res Inst (Yatabe)
Report. Fermented Foods Experimental Station. Kagawa Prefecture — Rep Fermented Foods Exp Stn Kagawa Prefect
Report. Finnish Academy of Science and Letters. Sodankyla Geophysical Observatory — Rep Finn Acad Sci Lett Sodankyla Geophys Obs
Report. Fire Research Institute of Japan — Rep Fire Res Inst Jpn
Report. Fishery Board of Sweden. Institute of Marine Research — Rep Fish Board Swed Inst Mar Res
Report. Fishery Research Laboratory. Kyushu University — Rep Fish Res Lab Kyushu Univ
Report. Florida Agricultural Experiment Station — Rep Fla Agric Exp Stn
Report FM. University of California, Berkeley — Rep FM Univ Calif Berkeley
Report. Food Industrial Experiment Station. Hiroshima Prefecture — Rep Food Ind Exp Stn Hiroshima Prefect
Report. Food Research Institute. Niigata Prefecture — Rep Food Res Inst Niigata Prefect
Report. Food Research Institute (Tokyo) — Rep Fd Res Inst (Tokyo)
Report. Food Research Institute (Tokyo) — Rep Food Res Inst (Tokyo)
Report. Food Research Institute. Yamanashi Prefecture — Rep Food Res Inst Yamanashi Prefect
Report for the Year. Egypt Exploration Society — Rep Eg Expl Soc
Report. Forest Department (Tanganyika Territory) — Rep Forest Dep (Tanganyika)
Report. Forest Experiment Station. Bureau of Plant Industry. Government of Formosa/Ringyo Shiken-Jo Hokoku. Shokusan-Kyoku — Rep Forest Exp Sta Bur Pl Industr Gov Formosa
Report. Forest Products Research Institute (Bogor, Indonesia) — Rep For Prod Res Inst (Bogor Indones)
Report. Forest Products Research Institute/Ringyo Shidojo Kenkyu Hokoku — Rep Forest Prod Res Inst

Report. Forest Resources Reconnaissance Survey of Malaya — Rep For Resour Reconn Surv Malaya
Report FPM-X. Forest Pest Management Institute — Rep FPM-X For Pest Manage Inst
Report. Freedom from Hunger Campaign. FAO [*Food and Agriculture Organization of the United Nations*] — Rep Freedom Hunger Campaign
Report from Europe — Rep Europe
Report from South Africa — RSA
Report. Fuel Research Institute — Rep Fuel Res Inst
Report. Fukushima Prefectural Institute of Public Health — Rep Fukushima Prefect Inst Public Health
Report. Fukushima Prefectural Public Health Institute [*Japan*] — Rep Fukushima Prefect Public Health Inst
Report. Fukushima Sericultural Experimental Station — Rep Fukushima Seric Exp Stn
Report. Fysisk Laboratorium I. Danmarks Tekniske Hoejskole (Lyngby) — Rep Fys Lab I Tek Hoejsk (Lyngby)
Report. General Fisheries Council for the Mediterranean — Rep Gen Fish Counc Mediterr
Report. Geodetic Institute (Denmark) — Rep Geod Inst (Den)
Report. Geological and Mining Survey of Iran — Rep Geol Min Surv Iran
Report. Geological Survey and Mines Department (Uganda) — Rep Geol Surv Mines Dep (Uganda)
Report. Geological Survey Department. British Guiana — Rep Geol Surv Dep Br Guiana
Report. Geological Survey Department (Guyana) — Rep Geol Surv Dep (Guyana)
Report. Geological Survey Department (Zambia) — Rep Geol Surv Dep (Zambia)
Report. Geological Survey of East Malaysia — Rep Geol Surv East Malays
Report. Geological Survey of Greenland — Rep Geol Surv Greenl
Report. Geological Survey of Hokkaido [*Japan*] — Rep Geol Surv Hokkaido
Report. Geological Survey of Iran — Rep Geol Surv Iran
Report. Geological Survey of Japan — Rep Geol Surv Jpn
Report. Geological Survey of Kenya — Rep Geol Surv Kenya
Report. Geological Survey of Malaysia — Rep Geol Surv Malays
Report. Geological Survey of New South Wales — Rep Geol Surv NSW
Report. Geological Survey of New Zealand — Rep Geol Surv NZ
Report. Geological Survey of Papua, New Guinea — Rep Geol Surv Papua New Guinea
Report. Geological Survey of Queensland — Rep Geol Surv Qd
Report. Geological Survey of Queensland — Rep Geol Surv Queensl
Report. Geological Survey of Tasmania — Rep Geol Surv Tasm
Report. Geological Survey of the Borneo Region, Malaysia — Rep Geol Surv Borneo Reg Malays
Report. Geological Survey of Uganda — Rep Geol Surv Uganda
Report. Geological Survey of Victoria — Rep Geol Surv Vic
Report. Geological Survey of Victoria — Rep Geol Surv Vict
Report. Geological Survey of Western Australia — Rep Geol Surv West Aust
Report. Geological Survey of Zambia — Rep Geol Surv Zambia
Report. Georgia Forest Research Council — Rep GA For Res Coun
Report. Ghana Geological Survey — Rep Ghana Geol Surv
Report. Gifu Pefectural Institute of Public Health — Rep Gifu Prefect Inst Public Health
Report. Glass Research Institute. Tohoku University — Rep Glass Res Inst Tohoku Univ
Report. Glasshouse Crops Research Institute — Rep Glasshouse Crops Res Inst
Report. Government Chemical Laboratories (Western Australia) — Rep Gov Chem Lab (West Aust)
Report. Government Forest Experiment Station — Rep Gov For Exp Stn
Report. Government Forest Experiment Station/Ringyo Shiken Syuho — Rep Gov Forest Exp Sta
Report. Government Institute for Veterinary Research (Fusan, Chosen) — Rep Govt Inst Vet Research (Fusan Chosen)
Report. Government Mechanical Laboratory. Tokyo — Rep Gov Mech Lab Tokyo
Report. Government Mechanical Laboratory (Tokyo) — Rep Govt Mech Lab (Tokyo)
Report. Government Mineralogist, Analyst, and Chemist (Western Australia) — Rep Gov Mineral Anal Chem (West Aust)
Report. Government Sugar Experiment Station (Tainan, Formosa) — Rep Gov Sugar Exp Stn (Tainan Formosa)
Report. Government Sugar Experiment Station/Taiwan Sotokufu Togyo Shikenjo Hokoku — Rep Gov Sugar Exp Sta
Report. Great Britain Agricultural Research Council — Rep Gr Brit Agr Res Counc
Report. Great Britain Colonial Pesticides Research Unit. CPRU/Porton — Rep Gr Brit Colon Pestic Res Unit CPRU/Porton
Report. Great Britain Tropical Pesticides Research Unit. TPRU/Porton — Rep Gt Brit Trop Pestic Res Unit TPRU/Porton
Report. Group for the Advancement of Psychiatry — Rep Group Adv Psychiatry
Report. Hawaii. Division of Water and Land Development — Rep Hawaii Div Water Land Dev
Report. Helsinki University of Technology. Radio Laboratory — Rep Helsinki Univ Technol Radio Lab
Report. Henry Phipps Institute for the Study, Treatment, and Prevention of Tuberculosis — Rep H Phipps Inst Tuberc
Report. Hokkaido Branch. Government Forest Experiment Station/Ringyo Shikenjo Hokkaido Shijo Gyomu Hokoku — Rep Hokkaido Branch Gov Forest Exp Sta
Report. Hokkaido Forest Products Research Institute [*Japan*] — Rep Hokkaido For Prod Res Inst
Report. Hokkaido Forest Products Research Institute (Asahikawa, Hokkaido) — Rep For Prod Res Inst (Hokkaido)
Report. Hokkaido Institute of Public Health — Rep Hokkaido Inst Public Health
Report. Hokkaido National Agricultural Experiment Station — Rep Hokkaido Nat Agr Exp Sta
Report. Hokkaido National Agricultural Experiment Station — Rep Hokkaido Natn Agric Exp Stn
Report. Hokkaido Prefectural Agricultural Experiment Station — Rep Hokkaido Pref Agr Exp Sta
Report. Hokkaido Prefectural Agricultural Experiment Stations — Rep Hokkaido Prefect Agric Exp Stn
Report. Hokkaido Research Institute for Environmental Pollution — Rep Hokkaido Res Inst Environ Pollut
Report. Honourable Company's Botanic Gardens. Calcutta Royal Botanic Garden — Rep Hon Companys Bot Gard Calcutta
Report. Horace Lamb Institute of Oceanography — Rep Horace Lamb Inst Oceanogr
Report. Horticultural Experiment Station and Products Laboratory (Vineland Station) [*Ontario*] — Rep Hort Exp Stn Prod Lab (Vineland)
Report. Horticultural Experiment Station (Ontario) — Rep Hort Exp Sta (Ontario)
Report. Hungarian Academy of Sciences. Central Research Institute for Physics. Koezponti Fizikai Kutato Intezet — Rep Hung Acad Sci Cent Res Inst Phys
Report. Hybrid Corn Industry. Research Conference — Rep Hybrid Corn Ind Res Conf
Report. Hygiene Laboratory of Shiga Prefecture — Rep Hyg Lab Shiga Prefect
Report. Hyogo Prefectural Forest Experiment Station — Rep Hyogo Prefect For Exp Stn
Report. Hyogo Prefectural Institute of Environmental Science — Rep Hyogo Prefect Inst Environ Sci
Report ICTIS/ER [*IEA Coal Research Technical Information Service/Executive Review*] **IEA Coal Research** [*International Energy Agency*] — Rep ICTIS/ER IEA Coal Res
Report ICTIS/TR [*IEA Coal Research Technical Information Service/Technical Report*]. IEA Coal Research [*International Energy Agency*] — Rep ICTIS/TR IEA Coal Res
Report. Illinois Beekeeping Association — Rep Ill Beekeep Ass
Report. Imperial Bureau of Fisheries. Scientific Investigation — Rep Imp Bur Fish Sci Invest
Report. Imperial Council of Agricultural Research — Rep Imp Coun Agric Res
Report. Imperial Mycological Conference — Rep Imp Mycol Conf
Report. India Ministry of Rural Development — Rep India Min Rur Dev
Report. Indian Council of Agricultural Research — Rep Ind Coun Agric Res
Report. Industrial Education Research Center. Chungnam National University [*Republic of Korea*] — Rep Ind Educ Res Cent Chungnam Natl Univ
Report. Industrial Health Research Board — Rep Ind Hlth Res Bo
Report. Industrial Research Institute. Kumamoto Prefecture — Rep Ind Res Inst Kumamoto Prefect
Report. Industrial Research Institute of Ishikawa — Rep Ind Res Inst Ishikawa
Report. Industrial Research Institute of Kanagawa Prefecture — Rep Ind Res Inst Kanagawa Prefect
Report. Information Center. Joint Institute for Laboratory Astrophysics — Rep Inf Cent Jt Inst Lab Astrophys
Report. Institute for Land and Water Management Research — Rep Inst Ld Wat Mgmt Res
Report. Institute for Systems Design and Optimization. Kansas State University — KISDA
Report. Institute for Systems Design and Optimization. Kansas State University — Rep Inst Syst Des Optim Kans State Univ
Report. Institute for Wine and Food Technology. Yamanashi Prefecture — Rep Inst Wine Food Technol Yamanashi Prefect
Report. Institute of Agricultural Research (Korea) — Rep Inst Agr Res (Korea)
Report. Institute of Animal Physiology — Rep Inst Anim Physiol
Report. Institute of Basic Medical Sciences — Rep Inst Bas Med Sci
Report. Institute of Clinical Research and Experimental Medicine. Middlesex Hospital Medical School — Rep Inst Clin Res Exp Med
Report. Institute of Fishery Biology. Ministry of Economic Affairs. National Taiwan University — Rep Inst Fish Biol Minist Econ Aff Natl Taiwan Univ
Report. Institute of Freshwater Research (Drottningholm) — Rep Inst Freshwater Res (Drottningholm)
Report. Institute of Geological Sciences — IGREB
Report. Institute of Geological Sciences — Rep Inst Geol Sci
Report. Institute of Geological Sciences (United Kingdom) — Rep Inst Geol Sci (UK)
Report. Institute of Industrial Science. University of Tokyo — Rep Inst Ind Sci Univ Tokyo
Report. Institute of Industrial Science. University of Tokyo — RIISA
Report. Institute of Industrial Technology. Yeung Nam University — Rep Inst Ind Technol Yeung Nam
Report. Institute of Industrial Technology. Yeung Nam University — Rep Inst Ind Technol Yeung Nam Univ
Report. Institute of Marine Research. Fishery Board of Sweden — Rep Inst Mar Res Fish Board Swed
Report. Institute of Medical and Veterinary Science (South Australia) — Rep Inst Med Vet Sci (SA)
Report. Institute of Mining Research. University of Rhodesia — Rep Inst Min Res Univ Rhod
Report. Institute of Mining Research. University of Zimbabwe — Rep Inst Min Res Univ Zimbabwe
Report. Institute of Natural Products. Yeungnam University — Rep Inst Nat Prod Yeungnam Univ
Report. Institute of Nuclear Physics (Krakow) — Rep Inst Nucl Phys (Krakow)
Report. Institute of Science and Technology [*Republic of Korea*] — Rep Inst Sci Technol
Report. Institute of Science and Technology. Sung Kyun Kwan University — Rep Inst Sci Technol Sung Kyun Kwan Univ
Report. Institute of Science and Technology. Tokyo University — Rep Inst Sci Technol Tokyo Univ
Report. Institute of Scientific Research (Manchoukuo)/Tairiku Kagakuin Kenkyu Hokoku — Rep Inst Sci Res Manchoukuo

Report. Institute of Social Medicine — Rep Inst Soc Med
Report. Institute of Space and Astronautical Science (Tokyo) — Rep Inst Space Astronaut Sci (Tokyo)
Report. Institute of Theoretical Astrophysics. University of Oslo — Rep Inst Theor Astrophys Univ Oslo
Report. International Council of Scientific Unions — Rep Int Counc Scient Un
Report. International Horticultural Congress — Rep Int Hortic Congr
Report. International Pacific Halibut Commission — Rep Int Pac Halibut Comm
Report. International Whaling Commission — Rep Int Whaling Comm
Report. International Whaling Commission. Special Issue — Rep Int Whaling Comm Spec Issue
Report. International Workshop. International Histocompatibility Conference — Rep Int Workshop Int Histocompat Conf
Report. Iowa State Horticultural Society — Rep Iowa St Hort Soc
Report. Iowa State University. Engineering Research Institute — Rep Iowa State Univ Eng Res Inst
Report. Japan Institute of Baking — Rep Jpn Inst Baking
Report. Japan Spinners' Inspecting Foundation — Rep Jpn Spinners Insp Found
Report. Japanese Botanical Garden Association/Nippon Shokubutsuen Kyokwai Kaiho — Rep Jap Bot Gard Assoc
Report. Joint Institute for Laboratory Astrophysics — Rep Jt Inst Lab Astrophys
Report. Kagawa Prefectural Institute of Public Health — Rep Kagawa Prefect Inst Public Health
Report. Kagawa Prefectural Research Center for Environmental Pollution Control — Rep Kagawa Prefect Res Cent Environ Pollut Control
Report. Kagawa-Ken Shoyu Experiment Station — Rep Kagawa Ken Shoyu Exp Stn
Report. Kagoshima Prefectural Institute of Environmental Pollution and Public Health — Rep Kagoshima Prefect Inst Environ Pollut Public Health
Report. Kagoshima Prefectural Institute of Public Health — Rep Kagoshima Prefect Inst Public Health
Report. Kanagawa-Ken Agricultural Experiment Station. Kanawaga-Kenritsu Noji Shiken-Jo Moji Shiken Seiseki — Rep Kanagawa Ken Agric Exp Sta
Report. Kansas Agricultural Experiment Station — Rep Kansas Agric Exper Station
Report. Kansas State Board of Agriculture — Rep Kans State Board Agr
Report. Kansas State University. Center for Energy Studies — Rep Kans State Univ Cent Energy Stud
Report. Kansas State University. Institute for Systems Design and Optimization — Rep Kans State Univ Inst Syst Des Optim
Report. Kansas Water and Sewage Works Association — Rep Kans Water Sewage Works Assoc
Report. Kentucky Agricultural Experiment Station. University of Kentucky — Rep KY Agric Exp Stat
Report. Kenya. Mines and Geological Department — Rep Kenya Mines Geol Dep
Report. Kumamoto Prefecture Sericulture Experiment Station — Rep Kumamoto Prefect Seric Exp Stn
Report. Kyoto College of Pharmacy — Rep Kyoto Coll Pharm
Report. Kyoto University Forest/Kyoto Daigaku Nogakubu Enshurin Iho — Rep Kyoto Univ Forest
Report. Kyushu Branch. Crop Science Society of Japan — Rep Kyushu Br Crop Sci Soc Jap
Report. Labrador Inuit Association — LIAR
Report. Lawrence Livermore Laboratory. University of California [*Livermore*] — Rep Lawrence Livermore Lab
Report. Liberal Arts and Science Faculty. Shizuoka University — Rep Lib Arts Sci Fac Shizuoka Univ
Report. Liverpool Medical Institution — Rep Liv Med Inst
Report. Long Ashton Research Station. University of Bristol — Rep Long Ashton Res Stn
Report. Marine Analytical Chemistry Standards Program. National Research Council (Canada) — Rep Mar Anal Chem Stand Program Natl Res Counc (Can)
Report. Marine Pollution Laboratory — Rep Mar Pollut Lab
Report. Maryland Agricultural Society — Rep MD Agr Soc
Report. Maryland Beekeepers' Association — Rep MD Beekprs Ass
Report. Maryland State Horticultural Society — Rep Maryland State Hort Soc
Report. Mauritius Sugar Industry Research Institute — Rep Maurit Sug Ind Res Inst
Report. Mechanical Development Committee. Forestry Commission (London) — Rep Mech Developm Comm For Comm (Lond)
Report. Mechanical Engineering Laboratory (Tokyo) — Rep Mech Eng Lab (Tokyo)
Report. Mechanical Laboratory. Tokyo — Rep Mech Lab Tokyo
Report. Medical and Health Department (Mauritius) — Rep Med and Health Dept (Mauritius)
Report. Medical Research Society for Mining and Smelting Industries — Rep Med Res Soc Min Smelting Ind
Report. Meeting. Association for the Advancement of Science (Australia) — Rep AAS (Austral)
Report. Meeting. Australian and New Zealand Association for the Advancement of Science — Rep Meet Aust NZ Assoc Adv Sci
Report. Meeting. British Association for the Advancement of Science — RBAASc
Report. Melbourne and Metropolitan Board of Works — Rep Melb Metrop Board Works
Report. Michigan Department of Conservation. Game Division — Rep Mich Dept Conserv Game Div
Report. Mineral Development Division. Department of Mines (Newfoundland) — Rep Miner Dev Div (Newfoundland)
Report. Mineral Industry Research Laboratory. University of Alaska — Rep Miner Ind Res Lab Univ Alaska
Report. Minerals Bureau. Department of Mines (South Africa) — Rep Miner Bur (S Afr)
Report. MINTEK [*Council for Mineral Technology*] — Rep MINTEK
Report. Mississippi Agricultural Experiment Station — Rep Miss Agr Exp Sta
Report. Montana University Joint Water Resources Research Center — Rep Mont Univ Jt Water Resour Res Cent
Report. Montrose Natural History and Antiquarian Society — Rep Montrose Nat Hist Soc
Report MRL. North Carolina State University. Minerals Research Laboratory — Rep MRL NC State Univ Miner Res Lab
Report MRP/MSL. Canada Centre for Mineral Energy Technology. Minerals Research Program/Mineral Sciences Laboratories — Rep MRP MSL Can Cent Miner Energy Technol Miner Res Program
Report MRP/PMRL (Physical Metallurgy Research Laboratories). Canada — Rep MRP PMRL (Phys Metall Res Lab) Can
Report. Nankai Regional Fisheries Research Laboratory — Rep Nankai Reg Fish Res Lab
Report. National Food Research Institute — Rep Natl Food Res Inst
Report. National Food Research Institute (Japan) — Rep Natn Fd Res Inst (Jap)
Report. National Food Research Institute (Tokyo) — Rep Natl Food Res Inst (Tokyo)
Report. National Gas Turbine Establishment. United Kingdom — Rep Natl Gas Turbine Establ UK
Report. National Industrial Research Institute (Korea) — Rep Natl Ind Res Inst (Korea)
Report. National Industrial Standards Research Institute (Korea) — Rep Natl Ind Stand Res Inst (Korea)
Report. National Institute for Metallurgy — Rep Natl Inst Metall
Report. National Institute for Metallurgy (South Africa) — Rep Natl Inst Metall (S Afr)
Report. National Institute for Metallurgy (South Africa) — Rep Natn Inst Metall (S Afr)
Report. National Institute for Veterinary Research (Pusan, South Korea) — Rep Natl Inst Vet Res (Pusan South Korea)
Report. National Institute of Genetics (Misima) — Rep Natn Inst Genet (Misima)
Report. National Institute of Health (Republic of Korea) — Rep Natl Inst Health (Repub Korea)
Report. National Institute of Nutrition — Rep Nat Inst Nutr
Report. National Radiological Protection Board — Rep Natl Radiol Prot Board
Report. National Research Council Canada. Marine Analytical Chemistry Standards Program — Rep Natl Res Counc Can Mar Anal Chem Stand Program
Report. National Research Institute for Metals [*Tokyo*] — Rep Natl Res Inst Met
Report. National Research Institute for Pollution and Resources (Japan) — Rep Nat Res Inst Pollut Resour (Jpn)
Report. National Research Institute for Pollution and Resources (Kawaguchi, Japan) — Rep Natl Res Inst Pollut Resour (Kawaguchi Jpn)
Report. National Research Laboratory of Metrology — Rep Natl Res Lab Metrol
Report. National Swedish Environment Protection Board — Rep Natl Swed Environ Prot Board
Report. National Water Resources Council. Republic of the Philippines — Rep Natl Water Resour Counc Repub Philipp
Report. Nederlands Scheepsstudiecentrum TNO — Rep Ned Scheepsstudiecent TNO
Report. Nevada Bureau of Mines — Rep Nev Bur Mines
Report. Nevada Bureau of Mines and Geology — Rep Nev Bur Mines Geol
Report. Nevada Bureau of Mines and Geology — Rep Nevada Bur Mines Geol
Report. New England Association of Chemistry Teachers — Rep N Engl Assoc Chem Teach
Report. New Hebrides Geological Survey — Rep New Hebrides Geol Surv
Report. New Jersey State Agricultural Experiment Station — Rep NJ St Agric Exp Stat
Report. New York State Veterinary College at Cornell University — Rep NY State Vet Coll Cornell Univ
Report. New Zealand. Department of Scientific and Industrial Research. Chemistry Division — Rep NZ Dep Sci Ind Res Chem Div
Report. New Zealand. Department of Scientific and Industrial Research. Dominion Laboratory — Rep NZ Dep Sci Ind Res Dom Lab
Report. New Zealand Energy Research and Development Committee — Rep NZ Energy Res Dev Comm
Report. New Zealand Geological Survey — Rep NZ Geol Surv
Report. New Zealand Geological Survey — Rep NZGS
Report. New Zealand Science Congress — Rep NZ Sci Cong
Report. Newfoundland. Mineral Development Division — Rep Newfoundland Miner Dev Div
Report. Niigata Agricultural Experiment Station — Rep Niigata Agric Exp Stn
Report. Niigata Food Research Institute — Rep Niigata Food Res Inst
Report NIM [*National Institute of Metallurgy, South Africa*] — Rep NIM
Report. Noda Institute for Scientific Research — Rep Noda Inst Sci Res
Report. Nordic PAH [*Polycyclic Aromatic Hydrocarbons*] **Project** — Rep Nord PAH Proj
Report. Northeastern Corn Improvement Conference — Rep Northeast Corn Impr Conf
Report. Nottingham University. School of Agriculture — Rep Nottingham Univ Sch Agr
Report. Nova Scotia Department of Mines — Rep NS Dep Mines
Report. Nova Scotia Department of Mines and Energy — Rep Nova Scotia Dep Mines Energy
Report of Environmental Science. Mie University — Rep Environ Sci Mie Univ
Report of Field Activities. Mineral Resources Division (Manitoba) — Rep Field Act Miner Resour Div (Manitoba)
Report of Geological and Mineral Exploration [*South Korea*] — Rep Geol Min Explor
Report of Geological and Mineral Exploration (Seoul) — Rep Geol Miner Explor (Seoul)
Report of Geophysical and Geochemical Exploration. Geological Survey of Korea — Rep Geophys Geochem Explor Geol Surv Korea

Report of Hokkaido Institute of Environmental Sciences — Rep Hokkaido Inst Environ Sci
Report of Inventory. Minnesota Office of Iron Range Resources and Rehabilitation — Rep Inventory Minn Off Iron Range Resour Rehabil
Report of Investigation. Geological Survey of Finland — Rep Invest Geol Surv Finl
Report of Investigation. Illinois State Water Survey — Rep Invest Ill State Water Surv
Report of Investigation. Michigan Geological Survey Division — Rep Invest Mich Geol Surv Div
Report of Investigation. New Brunswick. Mineral Resources Branch — Rep Invest N B Miner Resour Branch
Report of Investigation. Philippines. Bureau of Mines — Rep Invest Philipp Bur Mines
Report of Investigation. Philippines Bureau of Mines and Geo-Sciences — Rep Invest Philipp Bur Mines Geo Sci
Report of Investigation. State Water Survey of Illinois — Rep Invest State Water Surv Ill
Report of Investigations. Bureau of Economic Geology (Texas) — Rep Invest Bur Econ Geol (Texas)
Report of Investigations. Bureau of Mines of the Philippines — Rep Invest Bur Mines Philipp
Report of Investigations. Connecticut State Geological and Natural History Survey — Rep Invest Conn State Geol Nat Hist Surv
Report of Investigations. Delaware. Geological Survey — Rep Invest Del Geol Surv
Report of Investigations. Delaware Geological Survey — Rep Invest Delaware Geol Surv
Report of Investigations. Division of Mineral Resources (Virginia) — Rep Invest Div Miner Resour (VA)
Report of Investigations. Florida Bureau of Geology — Rep Invest Fla Bur Geol
Report of Investigations. Geological Survey Division of Michigan — Rep Invest Geol Surv Div Mich
Report of Investigations. Geological Survey of Missouri — Rep Invest Geol Surv MO
Report of Investigations. Geological Survey of South Australia — Rep Invest Geol Surv S Aust
Report of Investigations. Geological Survey of South Australia — Rep Invest Geol Surv South Aust
Report of Investigations. Geological Survey of Wyoming — Rep Invest Geol Surv Wyo
Report of Investigations. Geological Survey of Wyoming — Rep Invest Geol Surv Wyoming
Report of Investigations. Government Chemical Laboratories. Western Australia — Rep Invest Gov Chem Labs West Aust
Report of Investigations. Government Chemical Laboratories. Western Australia — Rep Invest WA Govt Chem Labs
Report of Investigations. Illinois State Geological Survey — ILGIA
Report of Investigations. Illinois State Geological Survey — Rep Invest Ill State Geol Surv
Report of Investigations. Iowa Geological Survey — Rep Invest Iowa Geol Surv
Report of Investigations. Kentucky. Geological Survey — Rep Invest Ky Geol Surv
Report of Investigations. Maryland Geological Survey — Rep Invest Md Geol Surv
Report of Investigations. Minnesota Geological Survey — Rep Invest Minnesota Geol Surv
Report of Investigations. Missouri Division of Geology and Land Survey — Rep Invest Mo Div Geol Land Surv
Report of Investigations. Missouri Geological Survey — Rep Invest Mo Geol Surv
Report of Investigations. Missouri Geological Survey and Water Resources — Rep Invest Mo Geol Surv Water Resources
Report of Investigations. North Carolina Division of Ground Water — Rep Invest NC Div Ground Water
Report of Investigations. North Dakota Geological Survey — Rep Invest ND Geol Surv
Report of Investigations. Ohio Division of Geological Survey — Rep Invest Ohio Div Geol Surv
Report of Investigations. South Australia Geological Survey — Rep Invest South Aust Geol Surv
Report of Investigations. South Australia Geological Survey — Rep Invest South Australia Geol Surv
Report of Investigations. South Dakota Geological Survey — Rep Invest SD Geol Surv
Report of Investigations. South Dakota Geological Survey — SDGRA
Report of Investigations. Tennessee Division of Geology — Rep Invest Tenn Div Geol
Report of Investigations. United States Bureau of Mines — Rep Invest US Bur Mines
Report of Investigations. United States Bureau of Mines — XBMIA
Report of Investigations. University of Texas at Austin. Bureau of Economic Geology — Rep Invest Univ Tex Austin Bur Econ Geol
Report of Investigations. University of Texas at Austin. Bureau of Economic Geology — TUGRA
Report of Investigations. Virginia Division of Mineral Resources — Rep Invest Va Div Miner Resour
Report of Investigations. Washington Division of Mines and Geology — Report of Invest Wash Div Mines Geol
Report of Investigations. West Virginia Geological and Economic Survey — Rep Invest W Va Geol Econ Surv
Report of Investigations. Western Australia. Government Chemical Laboratories — Rep Invest West Aust Gov Chem Lab
Report of Ionosphere and Space Research in Japan — Rep Ion Spa
Report of Ionosphere and Space Research in Japan — Rep Ionos & Space Res Jap
Report of Ionosphere and Space Research in Japan — Rep Ionos and Space Res Jpn
Report of Ionosphere and Space Research in Japan — RISRA
Report of Ionosphere Research in Japan [*Later, Report of Ionosphere and Space Research in Japan*] — Rep Ionos Res Jpn
Report of Iowa State Apiarist — Rep IA St Apiar
Report of Naval Research Laboratory Progress — Rep Nav Res Lab Prog
Report of Naval Research Laboratory Progress [*United States*] — RNRLA
Report of NRL [*Naval Research Laboratory*] **Progress** — Rep NRL Prog
Report of Proceedings. Annual Conference. International Iron and Steel Institute — Rep Proc Annu Conf Int Iron Steel Inst
Report of Proceedings. Annual Convention. American Electroplaters' Society — Rep Proc Annu Conv Am Electroplat Soc
Report of Proceedings. British Society of Animal Production — Rep Proc Br Soc Anim Prod
Report of Proceedings. International Association of Ice Cream Manufacturers [*A publication*] — Rep Proc Int Assoc Ice Cream Manuf
Report of Progress. Indiana. Geological Survey — Rep Prog Indiana Geol Surv
Report of Progress. Kansas Agricultural Experiment Station — Rep Progr Kans Agr Exp Sta
Report of Progress. Kansas Agricultural Experiment Station — Rep Progr Kansas Agric Exp Stn
Report of Progress. Kansas Agricultural Experiment Station. Kansas State College of Agriculture and Applied Science — Rep Prog Kans Agric Exp Stn Kans State Coll Agric Appl Sci
Report of Projects. Louisiana Agricultural Experiment Station. Department of Agronomy — Rep Proj LA Agr Exp Sta Dept Agron
Report of Projects. Louisiana Agricultural Experiment Station. Department of Agronomy — Rep Proj La Agric Exp Stn Dep Agron
Report of Rain-Making in Japan — Rep Rain Making Jpn
Report of Research. Worcester Foundation for Experimental Biology — Rep Res Worcester Found Exp Biol
Report of Research. Worcester Foundation for Experimental Biology — RRWBDG
Report of Researches. Nippon Institute of Technology — Rep Res Nippon Inst Technol
Report of Special Research. National Institute for Environmental Studies (Japan) — Rep Spec Res Natl Inst Environ Stud (Jpn)
Report of Symposium. Brookhaven National Laboratory. Biology Department — Rep Symp Brookhaven Natl Lab Biol Dep
Report of the Chief. United States Forest Service — Rep Chief US Forest Serv
Report of the Cooperative Research in Chugoku Region — Rep Coop Res Chugoku Reg
Report of the Session. General Fisheries Council for the Mediterranean — Rep Sess Gen Fish Counc Mediterr
Report of the Social Research on the City of Futu — Rep Soc Res City Futu
Report of the Studies on Upland Farming in Kawatabi Farm. Tohoku University — Rep Stud Upland Farming Kawatabi Farm Tohoku Univ
Report of the Year. Dublin University College. Agricultural Department — Rep Yr Dublin Univ Coll Agr Dept
Report. Ohara Institute of Agricultural Biology — Rep Ohara Inst Agr Biol
Report. Ohara Institute of Agricultural Biology — Rep Ohara Inst Agric Biol
Report on Animal Health Services in Great Britain — Rep Anim Hlth Serv G Br
Report on British Palaeobotany and Palynology — Rep Br Palaeobot & Palynol
Report on Cacao Research. Imperial College of Tropical Agriculture (St. Augustine, Trinidad) — Rep Cacao Res Imp Coll Trop Agric (St Augustine Trinidad)
Report on Cacao Research. Regional Research Centre of the British Caribbean — Rep Cacao Res Reg Cent Br Caribb
Report on Canada, 1985 — Canada Rpt
Report on Crop Research in Lesotho — Rep Crop Res Lesotho
Report on Forest Research — Rep For Res
Report on Geoscience and Mineral Resources [*Republic of Korea*] — Rep Geosci Miner Resour
Report on Geoscience and Mineral Resources. Korea Institute of Energy and Resources — Rep Geosci Miner Resour Korea Inst Energy Resour
Report on Geoscience and Mineral Resources. Korea Research Institute of Geoscience and Mineral Resources — Rep Geosci Miner Resour Korea Res Inst Geosci Miner Resour
Report on Greenkeeping Research. New Zealand Institute for Turf Culture. Greenkeeping Research Committee — Rep Greenkeep Res NZ Inst Turf Cult Greenkeep Res Comm
Report on Medical and Health Work in the Sudan — Rep Med and Health Work Sudan
Report on Statistical Applications Research — Rept Statist Appl Res
Report on Technology. Iwate University [*Japan*] — Rep Technol Iwate Univ
Report on the Fermentation Industries — Rep Ferment Ind
Report on the Natal Botanic Gardens and Colonial Herbarium — Rep Natal Bot Gard Colon Herb
Report on the ORT Activities [*Paris/Geneva*] — ROA
Report on the Progress of Chemistry — Rep Progr Chem
Report on the Results of the Bacteriological, Chemical, and Biological Examination of the London Waters — Rep Results Bacteriol Chem Biol Exam London Waters
Report on the Working of the Museum Department for the Year. Malta Department of Information — Rep Malta
Report on World Affairs — Rep World Aff
Report. Ontario Department of Agriculture — Rep Ont Dep Agric
Report. Ontario Geological Survey — Rep Ont Geol Surv
Report. Ontario Geological Survey — Rep Ontario Geol Surv
Report. Ontario Ministry of the Environment — Rep Ont Minist Environ
Report. Ontario Veterinary College — Rep Ont Vet Coll
Report. Oregon Agricultural Experiment Station — Rep Oreg Agric Exp Stat

Report. Oregon State University. Forest Research Laboratory — Rep Ore For Res Lab
Report. Oregon Wheat Commission — Rep Oreg Wheat Comm
Report. Oriental Canning Institute — Rep Orient Cann Inst
Report ORO [*Oak Ridge Operations Office*] **US Department of Energy** — Rep ORO US Dep Energy
Report. Osaka City Institute of Hygiene — Rep Osaka City Inst Hyg
Report. Osaka City Institute of Public Health and Environmental Sciences — Rep Osaka City Inst Public Health Environ Sci
Report. Osaka Industrial Research Institute — Rep Osaka Ind Res Inst
Report. Osaka Industrial Technical Research Institute — Rep Ind Tech Res Inst
Report. Osaka Municipal Hygienic Laboratory — Rep Osaka Munic Hyg Lab
Report. Osaka Municipal Institute for Domestic Science — Rep Osaka Munic Inst Domest Sci
Report. Overseas Division. Institute of Geological Sciences — Rep Overseas Div Inst Geol Sci
Report. Planning Conference on the Strategy for Virus Management in Potatoes. II — Rep Plann Conf Strategy Virus Manage Potato II
Report. Plant Breeding Station of University College (Aberystwyth, Wales) — Rep Pl Breed Sta Univ Coll Aberystwyth
Report. President. National Research Council. Canada — Rep Pres Nat Res Counc Can
Report. Proceedings. American Historical Society — RPAHS
Report. Proceedings. Annual Convention. National Pecan Association — Rep Proc Annu Conv Natl Pecan Assoc
Report. Proceedings. Association of Shellfish Commissioners — Rep Proc Assoc Shellfish Comm
Report. Proceedings. National Association of Ice Cream Manufacturers — Rep Proc Natl Assoc Ice Cream Manuf
Report. Proceedings. Northern Nut Growers Association — Rep Proc N Nut Growers Assoc
Report. Proceedings. Western Canadian Society for Horticulture — Rep Proc W Canad Soc Hort
Report. Province of Nova Scotia Department of Mines — Rep Prov NS Dep Mines
Report. Province of Nova Scotia Department of Mines and Energy — Rep Prov NS Dep Mines Energy
Report. Public Health Commissioner, India — Rep Publ Hlth Comm Ind
Report. Punjab Irrigation Research Institute — Rep Punjab Irrig Res Inst
Report. Quebec Society for the Protection of Plants — Rep Que Soc Prot Plants
Report. Quebec Society for the Protection of Plants — Rep Quebec Soc Prot Plant
Report. Quebec Society for the Protection of Plants — Rep Quebec Soc Protect Pl
Report. Queensland Geological Survey — Rep Queensland Geol Surv
Report. Reactor Centrum (Nederlandse) — Rep React Cent (Ned)
Report. Redogorelse. Forskningsstiftelsen Skogsarbeten — Rep Forsknstift Skogsarb
Report. Reelfoot Lake Biological Station. Tennessee Academy of Science — Rep Reelfoot Lake Biol Stn Tenn Acad Sci
Report. Regional Research Centre of the British Caribbean. Imperial College of Tropical Agriculture (Trinidad) — Rep Reg Res Cent ICTA (Trinidad)
Report. Research Center. Association of American Railroads — Rep Res Cent Assoc Am Railroads
Report. Research Center of Ion Beam Technology. Hosei University — Rep Res Cent Ion Beam Technol Hosei Univ
Report. Research Center of Ion Beam Technology. Hosei University. Supplement — Rep Res Cent Ion Beam Technol Hosei Univ Suppl
Report. Research Committee. North Central Weed Control Conference — Rep Res Comm North Cent Weed Control Conf
Report. Research Council of Alberta — Rep Res Counc Alberta
Report. Research Department. Kyushu Electric Power Company, Incorporated [*Japan*] — Rep Res Dept Kyushu Electr Power Co Inc
Report. Research Institute for Applied Mechanics (Kyushu University) — RMKUA
Report. Research Institute of Brewing — Rep Res Inst Brew
Report. Research Institute of Dental Materials. Tokyo Medical and Dental University — Rep Res Inst Dent Mater Tokyo Med Dent Univ
Report. Research Institute of Natural Resources. Mining College. Akita University — Rep Res Inst Nat Resour Min Coll Akita Univ
Report. Research Institute of Natural Sciences [*Republic of Korea*] — Rep Res Inst Nat Sci
Report. Research Institute of Science and Technology. Nihon University — Rep Res Inst Sci Technol Nihon Univ
Report. Research Institute of Science and Technology. Nihon University — RRITA
Report. Research Institute of Technology. Nihon University — Rep Res Inst Technol Nihon Univ
Report. Research Institute of Underground Resources. Mining College. Akita University [*Japan*] — Rep Res Inst Underground Resour Min Coll Akita Univ
Report. Research Laboratories of Kirin Brewery Company — Rep Res Lab Kirin Brew Co
Report. Research Laboratories of Kirin Brewery Company Limited [*Japan*] — Rep Res Lab Kirin Brewery Co Ltd
Report. Research Laboratories of Kirin Brewery Company Limited — RLKBAD
Report. Research Laboratory. Asahi Glass Company Limited — Rep Res Lab Asahi Glass Co Ltd
Report. Research Laboratory. Imperial Iron Works (Japan) — Rep Res Lab Imp Iron Works (Jpn)
Report. Research Laboratory. Nippon Seitetsu. Yawata Steel Works — Rep Res Lab Nippon Seitetsu Yawata Steel Works
Report. Research Laboratory of Engineering Materials. Tokyo Institute of Technology — Rep Res Lab Eng Mater Tokyo Inst Technol
Report. Research Laboratory of Engineering Materials. Tokyo Institute of Technology — RRLTD
Report. Research Laboratory. Tohoku Electric Power Company Limited [*Japan*] — Rep Res Lab Tohoku Electr Power Co Ltd
Report. Research Progress at the Illinois Agricultural Experiment Station — Rep Res Progr Ill Agr Exp Sta
Report. Research Project for Diseases of Ornamental Plants (Victorian Plant Research Institute) — Rep Res Proj Dis Ornam Pl
Report. Resource Research Institute (Kawaguchi) [*Japan*] — Rep Resour Res Inst (Kawaguchi)
Report. Road Research Laboratory. Ministry of Transport — Rep Rd Res Lab Minist Transp
Report. Rockefeller Foundation — Rep Rock Found
Report. Ross Conference on Medical Research — Rep Ross Conf Med Res
Report. Ross Conference on Obstetric Research — Rep Ross Conf Obstet Res
Report. Ross Conference on Pediatric Research — Rep Ross Conf Pediatr Res
Report. Ross Pediatric Research Conference — Rep Ross Pediatr Res Conf
Report. Rothamsted Experimental Station — Rep Rothamsted Exp Sta
Report. Rothamsted Experimental Station — Rep Rothamsted Exp Stn
Report. Rowett Institute — Rep Rowett Inst
Report. Royal Society of Van Diemen's Land — Rep Roy Soc Van Diemens Land
Report. Royal Swedish Academy of Agriculture. Scientific Section — Rep R Swed Acad Agric Sci Sect
Report RRL. Great Britain Department of Scientific and Industrial Research. Road Research Laboratory — Rep RRL GB Dep Sci Ind Res Road Res Lab
Report. Rugby School Natural History Society — Rep Rugby School Nat Hist Soc
Report. Sado Marine Biological Station. Niigata University — NRFHE8
Report. Sado Marine Biological Station. Niigata University — Rep Sado Mar Biol Stn Niigata Univ
Report. Safety in Mines Research Establishment (Great Britain) — Rep Saf Mines Res Establ (GB)
Report. Saitama Institute of Environmental Pollution — Rep Saitama Inst Environ Pollut
Report. Saitama Prefectural Brewery Institute — Rep Saitama Prefect Brew Inst
Report. Saskatchewan Department of Mineral Resources — Rep Sask Dep Miner Resour
Report. Saskatchewan Department of Mineral Resources — SMRRA
Report. Saskatchewan Energy and Mines — Rep Saskatchewan Energy Mines
Report. Saskatchewan Research Council — Rep Sask Res Counc
Report. Saskatchewan Research Council. Geology Division — Rep Sask Res Counc Geol Div
Report SCAT [*Sewage Collection and Treatment*] — Rep SCAT
Report. School of Agriculture. University of Nottingham — Rep Sch Agric Univ Nottingham
Report. Science and Industry Forum. Australian Academy of Science — Rep Sci Ind Forum
Report. Science and Industry Forum. Australian Academy of Science — Rep Sci Indust Forum
Report. Science and Industry Forum. Australian Academy of Science — Rep Sci Indust Forum Aust Acad Sci
Report. Scottish Beekeepers Association — Rep Scott Beekprs Ass
Report. Secretary of Agriculture — Rep Secr Agric
Report. Selskapet for Industriell og Teknisk Forskning ved Norges Tekniske Hoegskole — Rep Selsk Ind Tek Forsk Nor Tek Hoegsk
Report. Sendai Municipal Institute of Public Health — Rep Sendai Munic Inst Public Health
Report. Sendai Public Health Center — Rep Sendai Public Health Cent
Report Series. Arkansas Agricultural Experiment Station — Rep Ser Ark Agr Exp Sta
Report Series. Arkansas Agricultural Experiment Station — Rep Ser Ark Agric Exp Stn
Report Series. Arkansas Agricultural Experiment Station — Rep Ser Arkansas Agric Exp Stn
Report Series. Geological Survey of Ireland — Rep Ser Geol Surv Irel
Report Series in Chemistry. University of Oulu — Rep Ser Chem Univ Oulu
Report Series in Physics. University of Helsinki — Rep Ser Phys Univ Helsinki
Report Series in Theoretical Physics — Rep Ser Theoret Phys
Report Series. Inland Waters Branch (Canada) — Rep Ser Inland Waters Branch (Can)
Report Series. Inland Waters Directorate (Canada) — Rep Ser Inland Waters Dir (Can)
Report Series. University of Oslo. Department of Physics — Rep Ser Univ Oslo Dep Phys
Report Series. University of Oslo. Institute of Physics — Rep Ser Univ Inst Phys
Report. Shiga Prefectural Institute of Public Health — Rep Shiga Prefect Inst Public Health
Report. Shiga Prefectural Institute of Public Health and Environmental Science — Rep Shiga Prefect Inst Public Health Environ Sci
Report. Shikoku Engineering Association — Rep Shikoku Eng Assoc
Report. Shimane Prefectural Institute of Public Health and Environmental Science — Rep Shimane Prefect Inst Public Health Environ Sci
Report. Ship Research Institute (Tokyo) — Rep Ship Res Inst (Tokyo)
Report. Shizuoka Citrus Experiment Station/Shizuoka-Ken Kankitsu Shikenjo Hokoku — Rep Shizuoka Citrus Exp Sta
Report SIPRE [*Snow, Ice, and Permafrost Research Establishment*] — Rep SIPRE
Report. Sixth Conference. International Association on Quaternary Research — Rep (Sixth) Conf Int Ass Quatern Res
Report. Smithsonian Institution — Rep Smithson Instn
Report. Society for Nautical Research — Rep Soc Naut Res
Report. Solar Energy Studies. Commonwealth Scientific and Industrial Research Organisation — Rep Sol Energy Stud CSIRO
Report. South African Association for the Advancement of Science — Rep S Afr Ass Adv Sci
Report. South African Association for the Advancement of Science — Rep S Afr Assoc Adv Sci

Report. South African Association for the Advancement of Science — Rep SA Ass Adv Sci
Report. South African Institute for Medical Research — Rep S Afr Inst Med Res
Report. South Carolina Water Resources Commission — Rep SC Water Resour Comm
Report. Southern Conference on Gerontology — Rep South Conf Geront
Report. Southern Corn Improvement Conference — Rep South Corn Impr Conf
Report. Special Research Project. National Institute for Environmental Studies (Japan) — Rep Spec Res Proj Natl Inst Environ Stud (Jpn)
Report. Staatliche Zentrale fuer Strahlenschutz der DDR — Rep Staat Zent Strahlenschutz DDR
Report. Stanford University. John A. Blume Earthquake Engineering Center — Rep Stanford Univ John A Blume Earthquake Eng Cent
Report. State Board of Health of Iowa — Rep State Bd Health Iowa
Report. State Energy Commission of Western Australia — Rep State Energy Comm WA
Report. Stichting CONCAWE [*Conservation of Clean Air and Water, Europe*] — Rep Sticht CONCAWE
Report. Stiftelsen Svensk Skeppsforskning — Rep Stiftelsen Sven Skeppsforsk
Report. Sugar Experimental Station (Taiwan) — Rep Sugar Exp Sta (Taiwan)
Report. Suginami Ward Institute of Public Health Research — Rep Suginami Ward Inst Public Health Res
Report. Supervising Surgeon-General. Marine Hospital (Washington) — Rpt Superv Surg Gen Mar Hosp Wash
Report. Surgeon General. United States Navy — Rep Surg Gen US Navy
Report. Surgeon-General. United States Army — Rep Surg-Gen US Army
Report. Survey of Thirty-Two New South Wales River Valleys — Rep Surv Thirty-Two NSW River Valleys
Report. Swedish Academy of Engineering Sciences in Finland — Rep Swed Acad Eng Sci Finl
Report. Swedish Univeristy of Agricultural Sciences. Department of Radioecology — Rep Swed Univ Agric Sci Dep Radioecol
Report. Swedish University of Agricultural Sciences. Department of Agricultural Engineering — Rep Swed Univ Agric Sci Dep Agric Eng
Report. Swedish University of Agricultural Sciences. Department of Farm Buildings — Rep Swed Univ Agric Sci Dep Farm Build
Report. Swedish University of Agricultural Sciences. Department of Forest Products — Rep Swed Univ Agric Sci Dep For Prod
Report. Swedish University of Agricultural Sciences. Department of Plant Husbandry — Rep Swed Univ Agric Sci Dep Plant Husb
Report. Swedish University of Agricultural Sciences. Department of Radiobiology — Rep Swed Univ Agric Sci Dep Radiobiol
Report. Swedish Wood Preservation Institute — Rep Swed Wood Preserv Inst
Report. Taiwan Sugar Experiment Station — Rep Taiwan Sugar Exp Stn
Report. Taiwan Sugar Research Institute — Rep Taiwan Sugar Res Inst
Report. Technical College. Hosei University (Tokyo) — Rep Tech Coll Hosei Univ (Tokyo)
Report. Technical Research Centre of Finland. Biotechnical Laboratory — Rep Tech Res Cent Finl Biotech Lab
Report. Technical Research Centre of Finland. Food Research Laboratory — Rep Tech Res Cent Finl Food Res Lab
Report. Technical Research Centre of Finland. Fuel Lubricant Research Laboratory — Rep Tech Res Cent Finl Fuel Lubr Res Lab
Report. Technical Research Centre of Finland. Metals Laboratory — Rep Tech Res Cent Finl Met Lab
Report. Technical Research Centre of Finland. Reactor Laboratory — Rep Tech Res Cent Finl React Lab
Report. Technical Research Institute. Ohbayashi Corporation — Rep Tech Res Inst Ohbayashi Corp
Report. Tennessee Agricultural Experiment Station — Rep Tenn Agric Exp Stat
Report. Texas Agricultural Experiment Station — Rep Tex Agric Exp Stn
Report. Texas Department of Water Resources — Rep Tex Dep Water Resour
Report. Texas Water Development Board — Rep Tex Water Dev Board
Report. Texas Water Development Board — TWDRA
Report TKK-V. Helsinki University of Technology. Institution of Process Metallurgy — Rep TKKV Helsinki Univ Technol Inst Process Metall
Report TKK-V-B. Helsinki University of Technology. Laboratory of Materials Processing and Powder Metallurgy — Rep TKKVB Helsinki Univ Technol Lab Mater Process Powder Met
Report. TNO. Division for Nutrition and Food Research TNO — Report TNO Div Nutr Food Res TNO
Report to the Evolution Committee. Royal Society of London — Rep Evol Comm Roy Soc Lond
Report. Tobacco Research Institute. Taiwan Tobacco and Wine Monopoly Bureau — Rep Tob Res Inst Taiwan Tob Wine Monop Bur
Report. Tochigi Prefectural Hygienic Institute — Rep Tochigi Prefect Hyg Inst
Report. Tohoku Branch. Crop Science Society of Japan — Rep Tohoku Br Crop Sci Soc Jap
Report. Tokai Branch. Crop Science Society of Japan — Rep Tokai Br Crop Sci Soc Jap
Report. Tokushima Agricultural Experiment Station — Rep Tokushima Agr Exp Sta
Report. Tokushima Food Research Institute — Rep Tokushima Food Res Inst
Report. Tokushima Prefectural Industrial Research Institute — Rep Tokushima Prefect Ind Res Inst
Report. Tokyo Industrial Research Institute — Rep Tokyo Industr Res Inst
Report. Tokyo Metropolitan Industrial Technic Institute — Rep Tokyo Metrop Ind Tech Inst
Report. Tokyo University. Fisheries — Rep Tokyo Univ Fish
Report. Tokyo-to Laboratories for Medical Sciences — Rep Tokyo-to Lab Med Sci
Report. Toyoda Physical and Chemical Research Institute — Rep Toyoda Phys Chem Res Inst
Report. Training Institute for Engineering Teachers. Kyoto University [*Japan*] — Rep Train Inst Eng Teach Kyoto Univ
Report. Transportation Technical Research Institute (Tokyo) — Rep Transp Tech Res Inst (Tokyo)
Report. United States Department of Agriculture Forest Service. Northern Region. State and Private Forestry — Rep US Dep Agric For Serv North Reg State Priv For
Report. University of Alaska. Institute of Marine Science — Rep Univ Alaska Inst Mar Sci
Report. University of California, Berkeley. Sanitary Engineering Research Laboratory — Rep Univ Calif Berkeley Sanit Eng Res Lab
Report. University of California, Davis. California Water Resources Center — Rep Univ Calif Davis Calif Water Resour Cent
Report. University of California. Water Resources Center. Universitywide — Rep Univ Calif Water Resour Cent Universitywide
Report. University of Copenhagen. Physics Laboratory — Rep Univ Copenhagen Phys Lab
Report. University of Leeds. Centre for Computer Studies — Rep Univ Leeds Cent Comput Stud
Report. University of Leeds. Department of Computer Studies — Rep Univ Leeds Dep Comput Stud
Report. University of Melbourne. Department of Electrical Engineering — Rep Univ Melbourne Dep Electr Eng
Report. University of Natal. Wattle Research Institute — Rep Univ Natal Wattle Res Inst
Report. University of New South Wales. Water Research Laboratory — Rep Univ NSW Water Res Lab
Report. University of Oslo. Department of Physics — Rep Univ Oslo Dep Phys
Report. University of Oulu. Department of Physics — Rep Univ Oulu Dep Phys
Report. University of Oxford. Department of Engineering Science — Rep Univ Oxford Dep Eng Sci
Report. University of Rhodesia. Institute of Mining Research — Rep Univ Rhod Inst Min Res
Report. University of Tokyo. Institute of Space and Aeronautical Science — Rep Univ Tokyo Inst Space Aeronaut Sci
Report. University of Waikato. Antarctic Research Unit — Rep Univ Waikato Antarct Res Unit
Report. University of Wisconsin. Engineering Experiment Station — Rep Univ Wis Eng Exp Stn
Report. University of Zimbabwe. Institute of Mining Research — Rep Univ Zimbabwe Inst Min Res
Report. US Department of Agriculture. Forest Pest Management. Methods Application Group — Rep US Dep Agric For Pest Manage Methods Appl Group
Report. US Department of Agriculture. Forest Service. Cooperative Forestry and Pest Management. Northern Region — Rep US Dep Agric For Serv Coop For Pest Manage North Reg
Report. Vermont Wood Products Conference — Rep VT Wood Prod Conf
Report. Veterinary Laboratory. Institute of Agriculture (South Korea) — Rep Vet Lab Inst Agric (South Korea)
Report. Victoria University of Wellington. Chemistry Department — Rep Victoria Univ Wellington Chem Dep
Report. Waite Agricultural Research Institute — Rep Waite Agric Res Inst
Report. Washington State Highway Department. Research Program — Rep Wash State Highw Dep Res Program
Report. Water Research Foundation of Australia — Rep Wat Res Fdn
Report. Water Research Foundation of Australia — Rep Wat Res Fdn Aust
Report. Water Research Foundation of Australia — Rep Water Res Found Aust
Report. Water Research Foundation of Australia Limited — Rep Water Res Found Aust Ltd
Report. Water Research Laboratory. University of New South Wales — Rep Wat Res Lab NSW Univ
Report. Water Research Laboratory. University of New South Wales — Rep Water Res Lab NSW Univ
Report. Water Resources Research Institute. University of North Carolina — Rep Water Resour Res Inst Univ NC
Report. Water Resources Survey. Tasmania — Rep Water Resour Surv
Report. Watt Committee on Energy — Rep Watt Comm Energy
Report. Wellcome Research Laboratories — Rep Wellcome Res Lab
Report. Wellcome Research Laboratories — Rep Wellcome Research Lab
Report. Wellcome Research Laboratories at the Gordon Memorial College — Rep Wellcome Res Lab
Report. Wellcome Tropical Research Laboratories — Rep Wellcome Trop Research Lab
Report. Welsh Plant Breeding Station — Rep Welsh Pl Breed Stn
Report. Welsh Plant Breeding Station (Aberystwyth, Wales) — Rep Welsh Plant Breed Stn (Aberystwyth Wales)
Report. Welsh Soils Discussion Group — Rep Welsh Soils Discuss Grp
Report. West of Scotland Agricultural College. Economics Department — Rep W Scot Agr Coll Econ Dept
Report. West Virginia Geological Survey — Rep W Va Geol Surv
Report. Wheat Quality Conference — Rep Wheat Qual Conf
Report. Wood Saccharification Discussion Committee — Rep Wood Saccharif Discuss Comm
Report. Wool Research Organisation of New Zealand — Rep Wool Res Organ NZ
Report. World Congress on Agricultural Research — Rep World Congr Agr Res
Report WS. Undersea Medical Society — Rep WS Undersea Med Soc
Report. Wye Agricultural College — Rep Wye Agric Coll
Report. Wye College. Department of Hop Research — Rep Wye Coll Dep Hop Res
Report. Yamagata Prefectural Institute of Public Health — Rep Yamagata Prefect Inst Public Health
Report. Yamanashi Industrial Technology Center — Rep Yamanashi Ind Technol Cent
Report. Yamanouchi Central Research Laboratories — Rep Yamanouchi Cent Res Lab

Report. Yeungnam University. Institute of Industrial Technology — Rep Yeungnam Univ Inst Ind Technol
Report. Yeungnam University. Institute of Natural Products — Rep Yeungnam Univ Inst Nat Prod
Reporte de Investigacion del Instituto de Matematica. Cibernetica y Computacion — Rep Investigacion Inst Mat Cibernet Comput
Reporter. Australian Institute of Criminology. Quarterly — Reporter Aust Inst of Crim Qrtly
Reporter Canadien — Rep Can
Reporter. Delaware Nurses Association — Rep Del Nurses Assoc
Reporter Dispatch — Reportr D
Reporter. Muscular Dystrophy Association of Canada — Rep Musc Dyst Assoc Can
Reporter on Human Reproduction and the Law — Human Reproduction & L Rep
Reporting Classroom Research — Rep Class Research
Reportorio Anual de Legislacion [*Mexico*] — Reportorio
Reportorium Novum — Rep Nov
Reports. Academy of Science (Lemberg, Poland) — Rep Acad Sci (Lemberg Pol)
Reports. Academy of Sciences of the Ukrainian SSR — Rep Acad Sci Ukr SSR
Reports. Academy of Sciences. Ukrainian SSR (English Translation of Dopovidi Akademii Nauk Ukrains'koi RSR) — Rep Acad Sci Ukr SSR (Engl Transl Dopov Akad Nauk Ukr RSR)
Reports. Aeromedical Laboratory — Rep Aeromed Lab
Reports. Agricultural College of Sweden. Series A — Rep Agric Coll Swed Ser A
Reports. Agricultural College of Sweden. Series B — Rep Agric Coll Swed Ser B
Reports. American Universities Field Staff — Rep Am Univ Field Staff
Reports and Accounts. National Institute of Agricultural Botany — Rep Accounts Natl Inst Agric Bot
Reports and Dissertations. Agricultural College of Sweden. Department of Plant Husbandry — Rep Diss Agric Coll Swed Dep Plant Husb
Reports and Papers. Northamptonshire Antiquarian Society — Rep Pap Northamptonshire Antiq Soc
Reports and Proceedings. Belfast Natural History and Philosophical Society — Rep Proc Belfast Nat Hist Philos Soc
Reports and Studies. GESAMP (Joint Group of Experts on the Scientific Aspects of Marine Pollution) — Rep Stud GESAMP
Reports and Transactions. Devonshire Association for the Advancement of Science, Literature, and Art — Rep Trans Devonshire Ass
Reports and Transactions. East Kent Scientific and Natural History Society — Rep Trans E Kent Sci Soc
Reports. Annual Conference. Hawaiian Sugar Technologists — Rep Annu Conf Hawaii Sugar Technol
Reports. Asahi Glass Foundation — Rep Asahi Glass Found
Reports. Asahi Glass Foundation for Industrial Technology — Rep Asahi Glass Found Ind Technol
Reports. Association of American Geologists and Naturalists — Rep Assoc Amer Geol
Reports. Association of Hawaiian Sugar Technologists — Rep Assoc Hawaii Sugar Technol
Reports. Association of Trimeresurus Research. Kagoshima University — Rep Assoc Trimeresurus Res Kagoshima Univ
Reports. Australian Academy of Science — Rep Aust Acad Sci
Reports. Biochemical Research Foundation. Franklin Institute — Rep Biochem Res Found Franklin Inst
Reports. Botanical Institute. University of Aarhus — Rep Bot Inst Univ Aarhus
Reports. British Association for the Advancement of Science — Rep Brit Assoc Advancem Sci
Reports. Central Customs Laboratory (Japan) — Rep Cent Customs Lab (Jpn)
Reports. Central Institute of Metals (Leningrad) — Rep Cent Inst Met (Leningrad)
Reports. Central Research Institute for Chemistry. Hungarian Academy of Sciences — Rep Cent Res Inst Chem Hung Acad Sci
Reports. Central Research Institute for Physics (Budapest) — Rep Cent Res Inst Phys (Budapest)
Reports. Central Research Laboratory. Nippon Suisan Company — Rep Cent Res Lab Nippon Suisan Co
Reports. Chemical Laboratory. American Medical Association — Rep Chem Lab Am Med Assoc
Reports. Chiba Prefectural Industrial Research Institute — Rep Chiba Prefect Ind Res Inst
Reports. Construction Engineering Research Institute Foundation (Kobe) [*Japan*] — Rep Constr Eng Res Inst Found (Kobe)
Reports. Department of Nuclear Technics. University of Oulu (Finland) — Rep Dep Nucl Tech Univ Oulu (Finl)
Reports. Deputy Keeper. Public Records in Ireland — Rep DK Pub Rec Ir
Reports. Dudley Observatory — Rep Dudley Obs
Reports. Environmental Science and Technology Laboratory. Nippon Bunri University — Rep Environ Sci Tech Lab Nippon Bunri Univ
Reports. Environmental Science and Technology Laboratory. Nippon Bunri University — Rep Environ Sci Technol Lab Nippon Bunri Univ
Reports. Environmental Science and Technology Laboratory. Oita Institute of Technology — Rep Environ Sci Technol Lab Oita Inst Technol
Reports. Faculty for Animal Husbandry. Hungarian University of Agricultural Science (Godollo) — Rep Fac Anim Husb Hung Univ Agric Sci (Godollo)
Reports. Faculty of Agriculture. Shizuoka University — Rep Fac Agr Shizuoka Univ
Reports. Faculty of Engineering. Himeji Institute of Technology — Rep Fac Eng Himeji Inst Technol
Reports. Faculty of Engineering. Kanagawa University — Rep Fac Eng Kanagawa Univ
Reports. Faculty of Engineering. Kinki University in Kyushu. Science and Technology Section — Rep Fac Eng Kinki Univ Kyushu Sci Technol Sect
Reports. Faculty of Engineering. Nagasaki University — Rep Fac Eng Nagasaki Univ
Reports. Faculty of Engineering. Shizuoka University — Rep Fac Eng Shizuoka Univ
Reports. Faculty of Engineering. Tottori University — Rep Fac Eng Tottori Univ
Reports. Faculty of Engineering. Yamanashi University — Rep Fac Eng Yamanashi Univ
Reports. Faculty of Science and Engineering. Saga University. Mathematics — Rep Fac Sci Engrg Saga Univ Math
Reports. Faculty of Science and Technology. Meijyo University — Rep Fac Sci Technol Meijyo Univ
Reports. Faculty of Science. Kagoshima University — Rep Fac Sci Kagoshima Univ
Reports. Faculty of Science. Kagoshima University. Earth Sciences and Biology — Rep Fac Sci Kagoshima Univ (Earth Sci Biol)
Reports. Faculty of Science. Kagoshima University. Mathematics, Physics, and Chemistry — Rep Fac Sci Kagoshima Univ Math Phys Chem
Reports. Faculty of Science. Shizuoka University — Rep Fac Sci Shizuoka Univ
Reports. Faculty of Science. Shizuoka University — SDFRA
Reports. Faculty of Technology. Kanagawa University — Rep Fac Technol Kanagawa Univ
Reports. Far Eastern State University (Vladivostok) — Rep Far East State Univ (Vladivostok)
Reports. Fire Technology Laboratory. Technical Research Centre of Finland — Rep Fire Technol Lab Tech Res Cent Finl
Reports. Fishery Board of Sweden. Series Hydrography — Rep Fish Board Swed Ser Hydrogr
Reports. Forestry and Game Management Research Institute — Rep For Game Manage Res Inst
Reports. Geophysical Research Station. Kyoto University — Rep Geophys Res Stn Kyoto Univ
Reports. Government Chemical Industrial Research Institute (Tokyo) — Rep Gov Chem Ind Res Inst (Tokyo)
Reports. Government Industrial Development Laboratory (Hokkaido) — Rep Gov Ind Dev Lab (Hokkaido)
Reports. Government Industrial Research Institute (Kyushu) [*Japan*] — Rep Gov Ind Res Inst (Kyushu)
Reports. Government Industrial Research Institute (Nagoya) — Rep Gov Ind Res Inst (Nagoya)
Reports. Government Industrial Research Institute (Osaka) — Rep Gov Ind Res Inst (Osaka)
Reports. Government Industrial Research Institute (Shikoku) — Rep Gov Ind Res Inst (Shikoku)
Reports. Government Industrial Research Institute (Tohoku) — Rep Gov Ind Res Inst (Tohoku)
Reports. Hawaiian Sugar Technologists — Rep Hawaii Sugar Technol
Reports. Health and Social Subjects (London) — Rep Health Soc Subj (Lond)
Reports. Himeji Institute of Technology — Rep Himeji Inst Technol
Reports. Himeji Technical College — Rep Himeji Tech Coll
Reports. Hokkaido Fish Hatchery — Rep Hokkaido Fish Hatchery
Reports. Hokkaido Industrial Research Institute — Rep Hokkaido Ind Res Inst
Reports. Hungarian Agricultural Experiment Station — Rep Hung Agric Exp Stn
Reports. Hungarian Biological Station at Tihany — Rep Hung Biol Stn Tihany
Reports. Imperial Fuel Research Institute (Japan) — Rep Imp Fuel Res Inst (Jpn)
Reports. Industrial Research Center. Shiga Prefecture — Rep Ind Res Cent Shiga Prefect
Reports. Industrial Research Institute. Aichi Prefectural Government — Rep Ind Res Inst Aichi Prefect Gov
Reports. Industrial Research Institute. Hyogo Prefecture — Rep Ind Res Inst Hyogo Prefect
Reports. Industrial Research Institute of Nagano and Technology Development Center of Nagano — Rep Ind Res Inst Nagano Technol Dev Cent Nagano
Reports. Industrial Research Institute. Osaka Prefecture [*Japan*] — Rep Ind Res Inst Osaka Prefect
Reports. Institute for Agricultural Research. Tohoku University — Rep Inst Agric Res Tohoku Univ
Reports. Institute for Chemical Research. Kyoto University — Rep Inst Chem Res Kyoto Univ
Reports. Institute for Medical and Dental Engineering. Tokyo Medical and Dental University — Rep Inst Med Dent Eng Tokyo Med Dent Univ
Reports. Institute for Optical Research (Tokyo) — Rep Inst Opt Res (Tokyo)
Reports. Institute for Science of Labour (Tokyo) — Rep Inst Sci Labour (Tokyo)
Reports. Institute of Applied Microbiology. University of Tokyo — Rep Inst Appl Microbiol Univ Tokyo
Reports. Institute of High Speed Mechanics. Tohoku University — Rep Inst High Speed Mech Tohoku Univ
Reports. Institute of High Speed Mechanics. Tohoku University — Reports Inst High Speed Mech Tohoku Univ
Reports. Institute of Japanese Chemical Fibers. Kyoto University — Rep Inst Jpn Chem Fibers Kyoto Univ
Reports. Institute of Metals (Leningrad) — Rep Inst Met (Leningrad)
Reports. Institute of Physical and Chemical Research — Rep Inst Phys Chem Res
Reports. Institute of Physical and Chemical Research (Japan) — Rep Inst Phys Chem Res (Jpn)
Reports. Institute of Physical Chemistry. Academy of Sciences. Ukrainian SSR — Rep Inst Phys Chem Acad Sci Ukr SSR
Reports. Institute of Physics. Warsaw Technical University — Rep Inst Phys Warsaw Tech Univ
Reports. Institute of the Pulp and Paper Industry. Shizuoka Prefecture — Rep Inst Pulp Pap Ind Shizuoka Prefect
Reports. International Association of Cereal Chemistry — Rep Int Assoc Cereal Chem
Reports. International Conference on Ironmaking — Rep Int Conf Ironmaking
Reports. Japan Marine Products Company. Research Laboratory — Rep Jpn Mar Prod Co Res Lab
Reports. Kennan Industrial Research Institute of Tochigi Prefecture — Rep Kennan Ind Res Inst Tochigi Prefect
Reports. Kevo Subarctic Research Station — Rep Kevo Subarct Res Stn

Reports. Kihara Institute for Biological Research [*Japan*] — Rep Kihara Inst Biol Res
Reports. Kochi University. Natural Science — Rep Kochi Univ Nat Sci
Reports. Kyoto University Forests — Rep Kyoto Univ For
Reports. Kyushu University Forests — Rep Kyushu Univ For
Reports. Laboratory for Clinical Stress Research. Karolinska Institute — Rep Lab Clin Stress Res Karolinska Inst
Reports. Laboratory of Soils and Fertilizers. Faculty of Agriculture. Okayama University — Rep Lab Soils Fert Fac Agric Okayama Univ
Reports. Liberal Arts and Science Faculty. Shizuoka University. Natural Science — Rep Lib Arts Sci Fac Shizuoka Univ Nat Sci
Reports. Liberal Arts and Science Faculty. Shizuoka University. Natural Science [*Japan*] — Rep Liberal Arts Sci Fac Shizuoka Univ Nat Sci
Reports. Liberal Arts and Science Faculty. Shizuoka University. Natural Science — RFSHA
Reports. Liberal Arts Faculty. Shizuoka University. Natural Science — Rep Lib Arts Fac Shizuoka Univ Nat Sci
Reports. Liberal Arts Faculty. Shizuoka University. Series B. Natural Science/ Shizuoka Daigaku Bunruigakubu Kenkyu Hokuku. B. Shizen Kagaku — Rep Liberal Arts Fac Shizuoka Univ Ser B Nat Sci
Reports. Local Government Board (London) — Rep Local Govt Bd (London)
Reports. Marine Biological Laboratory — Rep Mar Biol Lab
Reports. Nagano Prefectural Industrial Research Institute — Rep Nagano Prefect Ind Res Inst
Reports. National Museum of Victoria — Rep Natl Mus Victoria
Reports. National Museum of Victoria — RNMVDW
Reports. National Research Institute of Police Science — Rep Nat Res Inst Police Sci
Reports. National Research Institute of Police Science (Japan). Research on Forensic Science — Rep Natl Res Inst Police Sci (Jpn) Res Forensic Sci
Reports. National Research Institute of Police Science. Research on Traffic Safety and Regulation — Rep Nat Res Inst Police Sci Res Traffic Saf Regul
Reports. Natto Research Center — Rep Natto Res Cent
Reports. Natural History Society of Northumberland, Durham, and Newcastle-upon-Tyne — Rep Nat Hist Soc Northunberland
Reports. Netherlands-Indian Civil Medical Service — Rep Neth Indian Civ Med Serv
Reports. Norwegian Forest Research Institute — Rep Norw For Res Inst
Reports of Basic Sciences. Chungnam National University — Rep Basic Sci Chungnam Nat Univ
Reports of Czechoslovak Foundry Research — Rep Czech Foundry Res
Reports of Family Law — Rep Fam L
Reports of Family Law — RFL
Reports of Family Law. Second Series — RFL 2d
Reports of Interest to Lawyers [*Database*] — ROITL
Reports of Patent, Design, and Trade Mark Cases [*United Kingdom*] — RPD & TM
Reports of Research. Kagawa-Ken Meizen Junior College — Rep Res Kagawa-Ken Meizen Jr Coll
Reports of Research. Matsuyama Shinonome Junior College — Rep Res Matsuyama Shinonome Jr Coll
Reports of St. Bartholomew's Hospital — Rep St Bartholomews Hosp
Reports of Statistical Application Research. Union of Japanese Scientists and Engineers — Rep Stat Appl Res UJSE
Reports of Statistical Application Research. Union of Japanese Scientists and Engineers — Rep Stat Appl Res Union Jpn Sci Eng
Reports of Statistical Application Research. Union of Japanese Scientists and Engineers — Rep Statist Appl Res Un Japan Sci Engrs
Reports of Studies. Tokyo College of Domestic Science — Rep Stud Tokyo Coll Domest Sci
Reports of Tax Cases [*United Kingdom*] — TC
Reports of the Science of Living — Rep Sci Living
Reports of the Working Committees. Northeast Conference — RWCNEC
Reports of the Working Committees. Northeast Conference on the Teaching of Foreign Languages — RNCT
Reports on Earth Science. College of General Education. Kyushu University — Rep Earth Sci Coll Gen Educ Kyushu Univ
Reports on Earth Science. Department of General Education. Kyushu University — Rep Earth Sci Dep Gen Educ Kyushu Univ
Reports on Mathematical Logic — Rep Math Log
Reports on Mathematical Logic [*Warsaw/Krakow*] — Rep Math Logic
Reports on Mathematical Physics — Rep Math Phys
Reports on Mathematical Physics — Rep Mathematical Phys
Reports on Mathematical Physics — RMHPB
Reports on Medical Research Problems of the Japan Anti-Tuberculosis Association — Rep Med Res Probl Jpn Anti-Tuberc Assoc
Reports on Norwegian Fishery and Marine Investigation. Reports on Technological Research — Rep Norw Fish Mar Invest Rep Technol Res
Reports on Philosophy — Rep Phil
Reports on Polar Research. Berichte zur Polarforschung — REPR
Reports on Population-Family Planning — Rep Popul-Fam Plann
Reports on Progress in Physics — Rep Pr Ph
Reports on Progress in Physics — Rep Pr Phys
Reports on Progress in Physics — Rep Prog Phys
Reports on Progress in Physics — Rep Progr Phys
Reports on Progress in Physics — Rept Progr Phys
Reports on Progress in Physics — RPPHA
Reports on Progress in Polymer Physics (Japan) — Rep Prog Polym Phys (Jpn)
Reports on Progress in Polymer Physics (Japan) — Rept Progr Polymer Phys (Japan)
Reports on Progress in Polymer Physics (Japan) — RPPJA
Reports on Public Health and Medical Subjects (London) — Rep Public Health Med Subj (Lond)
Reports on Researches by Grantees. Ministry of Education (Japan) — Rep Res Grantees Minist Educ (Jpn)
Reports on Rheumatic Diseases — Rep Rheum Dis
Reports on Rheumatic Diseases — RRHDAC
Reports on Rheumatic Diseases. Series 2. Practical Problems — Rep Rheum Dis Ser 2 Pract Probl
Reports on Rheumatic Diseases. Series 2. Topical Reviews — Rep Rheum Dis Ser 2 Top Rev
Reports on Technological Research Concerning Norwegian Fish Industry — Rep Technol Res Norw Fish Ind
Reports on Telephone Engineering — Rep Teleph Eng
Reports on the Progress of Applied Chemistry — Rep Prog Appl Chem
Reports on the Progress of Applied Chemistry — Rep Progr Appl Chem
Reports on the Progress of Applied Chemistry — Rept Progr Appl
Reports on the Progress of Applied Chemistry — RPACA
Reports on the World Fertility Survey — Rep World Fertil Surv
Reports on the World Fertility Survey — RWFSDH
Reports. Ontario Department of Mines — Rep Ont Dep Mines
Reports. Osaka Prefectural Industrial Research Institute [*Japan*] — Rep Osaka Prefect Ind Res Inst
Reports. Prefectural Industrial Research Institute (Shizuoka) [*Japan*] — Rep Prefect Ind Res Inst (Shizuoka)
Reports. Radiation Chemistry Research Institute. Tokyo University — Rep Radiat Chem Res Inst Tokyo Univ
Reports. Research Committee. Society of Antiquaries of London — RSAL
Reports. Research Institute for Applied Mechanics — Rep Res Inst Appl Mech
Reports. Research Institute for Applied Mechanics. Kyushu University — Rep Res Inst Appl Mech Kyushu Univ
Reports. Research Institute for Applied Mechanics. Kyushu University — Reports Res Inst Appl Mech Kyushu Univ
Reports. Research Institute for Strength and Fracture of Materials — Rep Res Inst Strength and Fract Mater
Reports. Research Institute for Strength and Fracture of Materials. Tohoku University — Rep Res Inst Strength Fract Mater Tohoku Univ
Reports. Research Institute for Strength and Fracture of Materials. Tohoku University — TDSKB
Reports. Research Institute for Strength and Fracture of Materials. Tohoku University (Sendai) [*Japan*] — Rep Res Inst Strength Fracture Mater Tohoku Univ (Sendai)
Reports. Research Institute. Gunze Silk Manufacturing Co. Ltd. — Rep Res Inst Gunze Silk Manuf Co Ltd
Reports. Research Institute of Basic Sciences. Chungnam National University — Rep Res Inst Basic Sci Chungnam Nat Univ
Reports. Research Institute of Ceramics. Tokyo Institute of Technology — Rep Res Inst Ceram Tokyo Inst Technol
Reports. Research Institute of Chemical Spectroscopy. Chungnam National University — Rep Res Inst Chem Spectrosc Chungnam Natl Univ
Reports. Research Institute of Electrical Communication. Tohoku University — Rep Res Inst Electr Commun Tohoku Univ
Reports. Research Institute of Electrical Communication. Tohoku University — RRETA
Reports. Research Institute of Industrial Safety [*Japan*] — Rep Res Inst Ind Saf
Reports. Research Institute of Industrial Science. Kyushu University — Rep Res Inst Ind Sci Kyushu Univ
Reports. Research Institute of Natural Sciences. Chungnam National University — Rep Res Inst Nat Sci Chungnam Natl Univ
Reports. Research Institute of Physics and Chemistry. Chungnam National University — Rep Res Inst Phys Chem Chungnam Natl Univ
Reports. Research Institute of Science and Industry. Kyushu University [*Japan*] — Rep Res Inst Sci Ind Kyushu Univ
Reports. Research Laboratory for Surface Science. Okayama University — Rep Res Lab Surf Sci Okayama Univ
Reports. Research Laboratory. Nippon Suisan Co. — Rep Res Lab Nippon Suisan Co
Reports. Research Laboratory of Hydrothermal Chemistry (Kochi, Japan) — Rep Res Lab Hydrotherm Chem (Kochi Jpn)
Reports. Research Laboratory of Shimizu Construction Company Limited [*Japan*] [*A publication*] — Rep Res Lab Shimizu Constr Co Ltd
Reports. Research Laboratory. Snow Brand Milk Products Company — Rep Res Lab Snow Brand Milk Prod Co
Reports. Researches. Mishimagakuen Women's Junior and Senior College — Rep Res Mishimagakuen Women's Jr Sr Coll
Reports. Royal Agricultural College of Sweden. Series A — Rep R Agric Coll Swed Ser A
Reports. Ryojun College of Engineering — Rep Ryojun Coll Eng
Reports. Scientific Research Institute — Rep Sci Res Inst
Reports. Scientific Research Institute. Tokyo — Rep Sci Res Inst Tokyo
Reports. Scientific Session. Japan Dental Association — Rep Sci Sess Jpn Dent Assoc
Reports. Sea Fisheries Institute. Series B. Fishing Technique and Fishery Technology (Gdynia, Poland) — Rep Sea Fish Inst Ser B (Gdynia Pol)
Reports. Shinshu-Miso Research Institute — Rep Shinshu-Miso Res Inst
Reports. Shizuoka Industrial Technology Center — Rep Shizuoka Ind Technol Cent
Reports. Shizuoka Prefectural Hamamatsu Textile Industrial Research Institute — Rep Shizuoka Prefect Hamamatsu Text Ind Res Inst
Reports. Shizuoka Prefectural Industrial Research Institute — Rep Shizuoka Prefect Ind Res Inst
Reports. Shizuoka Prefectural Industrial Technology Center — Rep Shizuoka Prefect Ind Technol Cent
Reports. Silk Science Research Institute [*Japan*] — Rep Silk Sci Res Inst
Reports. Society for the History of German in Maryland — Rep Soc Hist Germ Maryld
Reports. State Biological Survey of Kansas — Rep State Biol Surv Kans
Reports. State Biological Survey of Kansas — RSBKDD
Reports. State Board of Health of California — Rep Bd Health Calif
Reports. State Board of Health of Ohio — Rep Bd Health Ohio

Reports. Steno Memorial Hospital and the Nordisk Insulinlaboratorium — Rep Steno Mem Hosp Nord Insulinlab
Reports. Swedish Deep-Sea Expedition, 1947-1948 — Rep Swed Deep Sea Exped 1947-1948
Reports. Swedish Weed Conference — Rep Swed Weed Conf
Reports. Technical Research Institute. Taisei Corporation — Rep Tech Res Inst Taisei Corp
Reports. Textile Research Institute. Saitama Prefecture — Rep Text Res Inst Saitama Prefect
Reports. Tokoname Ceramic Research Institute. Aichi Prefectural Government — Rep Tokoname Ceram Res Inst Aichi Prefect Gov
Reports. Tokyo Imperial Industrial Research Institute Laboratory — Rep Tokyo Imp Ind Res Inst Lab
Reports. Tokyo Industrial Research Institute Laboratory — Rep Tokyo Ind Res Inst Lab
Reports. Tokyo Industrial Testing Laboratory — Rep Tokyo Ind Test Lab
Reports. Tokyo Metropolitan Industrial Research Institute — Rep Tokyo Metrop Ind Res Inst
Reports. Tokyo Metropolitan Research Laboratory of Public Health — Rep Tokyo Metrop Res Lab Public Health
Reports. Tottori Mycological Institute — Rep Tottori Mycol Inst
Reports. Toyo Junior College of Food Technology and Toyo Institute of Food Technology — Rep Toyo Jr Coll Food Technol Toyo Inst Food Technol
Reports. Tuberculosis Research Institute. Kyoto University — Rep Tuberc Res Inst Kyoto Univ
Reports. University of Electro-Communications — Rep Univ Electro-Comm
Reports. University of Electro-Communications — Rep Univ Electro-Commun
Reports. USA Marine Biological Institute. Kochi University — Rep USA Mar Biol Inst Kochi Univ
Reports. USA Marine Biological Institute. Kochi University — RUMUDA
Reports. USA Marine Biological Station — Rep USA Mar Biol Stn
Reports. V. I. Lenin All-Union Academy of Agricultural Sciences — Rep V I Lenin All Union Acad Agric Sci
Reports. White Sea Biological Station. State University of Moscow — Rep White Sea Biol Stn State Univ Moscow
Repositorio de Trabalhos do LNIV-Portugal. Laboratorio Nacional de Investigacao Veterinaria — Repos Trab LNIV Port Lab Nac Inves Vet
Representation and Mind — Represent Mind
Representative Research in Social Psychology — Repr Res SP
Reprint. Bee Research Association — Repr BRA
Reprint Bulletin. Book Reviews — Repr Bull Bk R
Reprint Bulletin. Book Reviews — Reprint Bull Bk R
Reprint Bulletin. Book Reviews — Rp B Bk R
Reprint. Division of Forest Products (Melbourne, Australia) — Repr For Prod (Aust)
Reprint. Engineering Experiment Station. Oregon State College — Repr Eng Exp Stn Oreg State Coll
Reprint. Kansas State University. Kansas Engineering Experiment Station — Repr Kans State Univ Kans Eng Exp Stn
Reprint. New Zealand Forest Service — Repr NZ For Serv
Reprint of the Statutes of New Zealand — RS
Reprint. Wisconsin Engineering Experiment Station — Repr Wis Eng Exp Stn
Reprints from the Bulletin of the American Mathematical Society — Repr Bull Amer Math Soc
Repro en Druk — DRW
Reprocessing Newsletter — Reprocess Newsl
Reproduccion — Reproduccio
Reproduccion Campechano (Campeche, Mexico) — Reproduc Campech Campeche
Reproduction and Contraception — Reprod Contracept
Reproduction Engineering — Reproduction Eng
Reproduction Fertility and Development — Reprod Fert
Reproduction, Fertility, and Development — Reprod Fertil Dev
Reproduction, Growth, and Development — Reprod Growth Dev
Reproduction, Nutrition, Developpement — Reprod Nutr Dev
Reproduction Paper News. Bulletin — Reprodn Paper News Bull
Reproductions Review — Reprod Rev
Reproductions Review and Methods — Reprodn Rev
Reproductive and Perinatal Medicine — Reprod Perinat Med
Reproductive Immunology — Reprod Immunol
Reproductive Physiology of Fish — Reprod Physiol Fish
Reproductive Toxicology — Reprod Tox
Reproductive Toxicology — Reprod Toxicol
Reproduktie — DOR
Reprographics — REPGA
Reprographics Quarterly — Reprogr Q
Reprographics Quarterly — Reprographics Q
Reprography Newsletter — Reprography Newsl
Reptertorium Germanicum — Rep Germ
Repubblica Italiana Ministero dell'Agricoltura e delle Foreste Collana Verde — Repubb Ital Minist Agri For Collana Verde
Republic [*Quezon City*] — Re
Republic — Repub
Republic of South Africa. Atomic Energy Board. Report PEL — Repub S Afr At Energy Board Rep PEL
Republic of South Africa. Atomic Energy Board. Report PER — Repub S Afr At Energy Board Rep PER
Republic of South Africa. Department of Agricultural Technical Services. Bulletin — Repub S Afr Dep Agric Tech Serv Bull
Republic of South Africa. Department of Agricultural Technical Services. Entomology Memoirs — Repub S Afr Dep Agric Tech Serv Entomol Mem
Republic of South Africa. Department of Agricultural Technical Services. Science Bulletin — Repub S Afr Dep Agric Tech Serv Sci Bull
Republic of South Africa. Department of Agricultural Technical Services. Technical Communication — Repub S Afr Dep Agric Tech Serv Tech Commun
Republic of South Africa. Department of Mines. Geological Survey. Explanation of Sheets — Repub S Afr Dep Mines Geol Surv Explan Sheets
Republic of South Africa. Department of Mines. Geological Survey. Memoir — Repub S Afr Dep Mines Geol Surv Mem
Republic of South Africa. Geological Survey. Handbook — Repub S Afr Geol Surv Handb
Republic of South Africa. Geological Survey. Memoir — Repub S Afr Geol Surv Mem
Republic of the Philippines. Department of Agriculture and Natural Resources. Bureau of Mines. Information Circular — Repub Philipp Dep Agric Nat Resour Bur Mines Inf Circ
Republic of the Philippines. Department of Agriculture and Natural Resources. Bureau of Mines. Report of Investigation — Repub Philipp Dep Agric Nat Resour Bur Mines Rep Invest
Republica de Argentina. Ministerio de Agricultura y Ganaderia. Publicacion Miscelanea — Argent Repub Minist Agric Ganad Publ
Republica de Argentina. Ministerio de Agricultura y Ganaderia. Publicacion Tecnia — Argent Repub Minist Agric Ganad Publ Tec
Republica de Argentina. Subsecretaria de Mineria. Serie Argentina — Argent Repub Subsecr Min Ser Argent
Republica de Colombia. Ministerio de Minas y Petroleos. Boletin de Minas — Colomb Repub Minist Minas Pet Bol Minas
Republica de Colombia. Ministerio de Minas y Petroleos. Boletin Nacional de Minas — Colomb Repub Minist Minas Pet Bol Nac Minas
Republica de Panama. Administracion de Recursos Minerales. Mapa — Panama Admin Recursos Minerales Mapa
Republica de Venezuela. Boletin. Academia de Ciencias Fisicas, Matematicas, y Naturales — Repub Venezuela Bol Acad Ci Fis Mat Natur
Republica de Venezuela. Boletin. Academia de Ciencias Fisicas, Matematicas, y Naturales — Repub Venezuela Bol Acad Cienc Fis Mat Natur
Republica Populara Romina. Comitetul Geologic. Studii Tehnice si Economice — Repub Pop Rom Com Geol Stud Teh Econ
Republica Socialista Romania. Comitetul Geologic. Studii Tehnice si Economice — Repub Soc Rom Com Geol Stud Teh Econ
Republicki Zavod za Zastitu Prirode i Prirodnjacki Muzej u Titogradu. Glasnik — Repub Zavod Zast Prir Prir Muz Titogradu Glas
Republiek van Suid-Afrika. Departement van Mynwese. Geologiese Opname. Annale van die Geologiese Opname — Repub S Afr Dep Mynwese Geol Opname Ann Geol Opname
Republiek van Suid-Afrika. Departement van Mynwese. Geologiese Opname. Handbook — Repub S Afr Dep Mynwese Geol Opname Handb
Republiek van Suid-Afrika. Departement van Mynwese. Geologiese Opname. Toeligting van Blaaie — Repub S Afr Dep Mynwese Geol Opname Toeligting Blaaie
Republiek van Suid-Afrika. Geologiese Opname. Bulletin — Repub S Afr Geol Opname Bull
Republiek van Suid-Afrika. Geologiese Opname. Handboek — Repub S Afr Geol Opname Handb
Republika [*Zagreb*] — R
Republika [*Zagreb*] — Rep
Republique de Cote d'Ivoire. Direction des Mines et de la Geologie. Bulletin — Repub Cote Ivoire Dir Mines Geol Bull
Republique Federale du Cameroun. Bulletin. Direction des Mines et de la Geologie — Repub Fed Cameroun Bull Dir Mines Geol
Republique Francaise — RF
Republique Malagasy. Annales Geologiques de Madagascar — Repub Malagasy Ann Geol Madagascar
Republique Malagasy. Documentation du Bureau Geologique — Repub Malagasy Doc Bur Geol
Republique Malgache. Documentation du Bureau Geologique — Repub Malgache Doc Bur Geol
Republique Malgache. Rapport Annuel du Service Geologique — Repub Malgache Rapp Annu Serv Geol
Republique Rwandaise. Bulletin du Service Geologique — Repub Rwandaise Bull Serv Geol
RERA: Official Monthly Journal. Radio and Electrical Retailers' Association of New South Wales — RERA
Rerum Britannicarum Medii Aevi Scriptores — RBMAS
Rerum Ecclesiasticarum Documenta — RED
Rerum Italicarum Scriptores ab Anno Aerae Christianae 500 ad 1500 — RIS
Rerum Naturalium Scriptores Graeci Minores — Rer Nat Scr Graec Min
RES. Journal of the Reticuloendothelial Society — RES J Reticuloendothel Soc
RES. Journal of the Reticuloendothelial Society — RESJA
Res Judicatae — Res Jud
Res Mechanica — Res Mech
Res Mechanica Letters — Res Mech Lett
Res Publica — Res Publ
Res Publica Litterarum — RPLit
Res Publica Litterarum. Studies in the Classical Tradition — RP Lit
Rescue Archaeology in Hampshire — Rescue Archaeol Hampshire
Research [*European Economic Community*] [*Luxembourg*] — Euro Abstr Sec 1
Research Abstracts [*University Microfilms International*] — RA
Research Abstracts and Newsletter — Res Abstrs Newsl
Research Abstracts and Reclassification Notice. National Advisory Committee for Aeronautics (United States) — Res Abstr Reclassif Not Nat Advis Comm Aeronaut (US)
Research/Accelerators — Res/Accel
Research Activities. Faculty of Science and Engineering of Tokyo Denki University — Res Act Fac Sci Engrg Tokyo Denki Univ
Research Activity. Forests Commission (Victoria, Australia) — Res Act For Comm (Victoria Aust)

Research Advances in Alcohol and Drug Problems — Res Adv Alcohol Drug Probl
Research and Applied Technology Symposium on Mined-Land Reclamation. Papers [*A publication*] — Res Appl Technol Symp Mined-Land Reclam Pap
Research and Clinical Forums — Res Clin Forums
Research and Clinical Studies in Headache — Res Clin Stud Headache
Research and Design — Res Des
Research and Development — Res & Dev
Research and Development Associates for Military Food and Packaging Systems. Activities Report — Res Dev Assoc Mil Food Packag Syst Act Rep
Research and Development Associates for Military Food and Packaging Systems. Activities Report. R and D Associates — Res Dev Assoc Mil Food Packag Syst Act Rep R & D Assoc
Research and Development Bulletin. Portland Cement Association — Res Dev Bull Portland Cem Assoc
Research and Development Contracts Monthly — R & D Con Mn
Research and Development for Industry — Res Dev Ind
Research and Development in Agriculture — Res Dev Agric
Research and Development in Mexico — RDM
Research and Development in Non-Mechanical Electrical Power Sources — Res Dev Non Mech Electr Power Sources
Research and Development Laboratories. Portland Cement Association. Research Department Bulletin — Res Dev Lab Portland Cem Assoc Res Dep Bull
Research and Development Paper. Forestry Commission (Great Britain) — Res Dev Pap For Comm (GB)
Research and Development Paper. Forestry Commission (London) — Res Developm Pap For Comm (Lond)
Research and Development Paper. United Kingdom Forestry Commission — Res Dev Pap UK For Comm
Research and Development Report. Monsanto Research Corp. Mound Laboratory — Res Dev Rep Monsanto Res Corp Mound Lab
Research and Development Report. United States Department of the Interior. Office of Coal Research — Res Dev Rep US Dep Inter Off Coal Res
Research and Development Report. United States Office of Coal Research — Res Dev Rep US Off Coal Res
Research and Development Report. United States Office of Coal Research — XCRDA
Research and Development Reports. British Library — Res Dev Rep Br Libr
Research and Development Review. Mitsubishi Chemical — Res Dev Rev Mitsubishi Chem
Research and Development Review. Mitsubishi Kasei Corporation — Res Dev Rev Mitsubishi Kasei Corp
Research and Development Technical Report ECOM. United States Army Electronics Command — Res Dev Tech Rep ECOM US Army Electron Command
Research and Development Technical Report. United States Army Electronics Command — Res Dev Tech Rep US Army Electron Command
Research and Experimental Record. Ministry of Agriculture. Northern Ireland — Res Exp Rec Minist Agric North Irel
Research and Experimental Record. Ministry of Agriculture (Northern Ireland) — Res Exp Rec Minist Agric (Nth Ire)
Research and Exposition in Mathematics — Res Exp Math
Research and Farming [*North Carolina Agricultural Research Service*] — REFAA4
Research and Farming [*North Carolina Agricultural Experiment Station*] — Res & Farm
Research and Farming [*North Carolina Agricultural Experiment Station*] — Res Farming
Research and Farming (North Carolina Agricultural Experiment Station) — Res Farming (NC Agric Exp Stn)
Research and Farming. North Carolina Agricultural Research Service — Res Farming NC Agric Res Serv
Research and Industry — Res Ind
Research and Industry — Res Indus
Research and Industry — RSIDA
Research and Industry (New Delhi) — Res Ind (New Delhi)
Research and Intelligence News — Res Intell News
Research and Invention — Res & Invt
Research and Lecture Notes in Mathematics — Res Lecture Notes Math
Research and Lecture Notes in Mathematics. Complex Analysis and Geometry — Res Lecture Notes Math Complex Anal Geom
Research and Practice in Forensic Medicine — Res Pract Forensic Med
Research and Productivity Council. New Brunswick. Research Note. — Res Prod Coun NB Res Note
Research and Progress — Res Prog
Research and Progress — ResP
Research and Statistics Note. Health Care Financing Administration. Office of Policy, Planning, and Research — Res Stat Note Health Care Financ Adm Off Policy Plann Res
Research and Statistics Note. Social Security Administration. Office of Research and Statistics — Res Stat Note
Research and the Retarded — RSRPB
Research Annual. Nihon Nosan Kogyo — Res Annu Nihon Nosan Kogyo
Research Applied in Industry — Res Appl Ind
Research Applied in Industry — Res Appl Industr
Research Applied to National Needs. Report. NSF/RA [*National Science Foundation/Research Applied*] **(United States)** — Res Appl Natl Needs Rep NSF/RA (US)
Research Association of British Paint, Colour, and Varnish Manufacturers. Bulletin — Res Assoc Br Paint Colour Varn Manuf Bull
Research Branch Report. Canada Department of Agriculture — Res Brch Rep Can Dep Agric
Research Briefs — Res Briefs
Research Briefs. Fish Commission of Oregon — Res Briefs Fish Comm Oreg
Research Briefs. School of Forest Resources. Pennsylvania State University — Res Briefs Sch For Resour PA St Univ
Research Bulletin. Agricultural and Home Economics Experiment Station (Iowa) — Res Bull Agric Home Econ Exp Stn (Iowa)
Research Bulletin. Agricultural and Home Economics Experiment Station. Iowa State College — Res Bull Agr Home Econ Exp Sta Iowa State Coll
Research Bulletin. Agricultural Experiment Station. College of Agriculture. University of Wisconsin — Res Bull Agric Exp Stn Univ Wis
Research Bulletin. Agricultural Experiment Station (Iowa) — Res Bull Agric Exp Stn (Iowa)
Research Bulletin. Agricultural Experiment Station. Kung-chu-ling, Manchoukuo/Man Chu Kuo Litsi Kung Chu Ling. Noji Shikenjo Kenkyu Jiho — Res Bull Agric Exp Sta Kung Chu Ling Manchoukuo
Research Bulletin. Agricultural Experiment Station. South Manchuria Railway Company — Rep Bull Agr Exp Sta S Manchuria Ry Co
Research Bulletin. Agricultural Experiment Station. University of Idaho — Res Bull Agric Exp Stn Univ Idaho
Research Bulletin. Agricultural Experiment Station. University of Nebraska — Res Bull Agric Exp Stn Univ Nebr
Research Bulletin. Agricultural Experiment Stations (Georgia) — Res Bull Agric Exp Stn (Ga)
Research Bulletin. Aichi-Ken Agricultural Research Center — Res Bull Aichi-Ken Agric Res Cent
Research Bulletin. Aichi-Ken Agricultural Research Center. Series A. Food Crop — Res Bull Aichi-Ken Agric Res Cent Ser A
Research Bulletin. Aichi-Ken Agricultural Research Center. Series B. Horticulture — Res Bull Aichi-Ken Agric Res Cent Ser B
Research Bulletin. Aichi-Ken Agricultural Research Center. Series B. Horticulture [*Japan*] — Res Bull Aichi-Ken Agric Res Cent Ser B Hortic
Research Bulletin. Aichi-Ken Agricultural Research Center. Series C. Poultry — Res Bull Aichi-Ken Agric Res Cent Ser C
Research Bulletin. Aichi-Ken Agricultural Research Center. Series D. Sericulture — Res Bull Aichi-Ken Agric Res Cent Ser D
Research Bulletin. Aichi-Ken Agricultural Research Center. Series E. Animal Industry — Res Bull Aichi-Ken Agric Res Cent Ser E
Research Bulletin. BCSIR [*(Bangladesh Council of Scientific and Industrial Research*]) Laboratories (Chittagong) — Res Bull BCSIR Lab (Chittagong)
Research Bulletin. Birla Archaeological and Cultural Research Institute — Res Bull Birla Archaeol Cult Res Inst
Research Bulletin. Bunda College of Agriculture. University of Malawi — Res Bull Bunda Coll Agric Univ Malawi
Research Bulletin. Cement Research Institue of India — Res Bull Cem Res Inst India
Research Bulletin. Central Education Research Institute — Res Bul CERI
Research Bulletin. Centre for Arabic Documentation (Ibadan) — Res Bull Cent Arabic Documn Univ Ibadan
Research Bulletin. Centre of Arabic Documentation — Research B
Research Bulletin. Centre of Arabic Documentation. University of Ibadan — Res Bull Centre Arabic Doc Ibadan
Research Bulletin. Centro Internacional de Mejoramiento de Maiz y Trigo — Res Bull CIMMYT
Research Bulletin. College Experiment Forests. Hokkaido University — Res Bull Exp For Hokkaido Univ
Research Bulletin. College of General Education. Nagoya University. Natural Sciences and Psychology — Res Bull Coll Gen Educ Nagoya Univ Nat Sci Psychol
Research Bulletin. Colorado Greenhouse Growers Association — Res Bull Colo Greenhouse Grow Assoc
Research Bulletin. East Panjab University — Res Bull East Panjab Univ
Research Bulletin. Egyptian Sugar and Distillation Company. Sugar-Cane Department — Res Bull Egypt Sugar Distill Co Sugar Cane Dep
Research Bulletin. Electric Power Development Company Limited [*Japan*] — Res Bull Electr Power Dev Co Ltd
Research Bulletin. Faculty of Agriculture. Ain Shams University — Res Bull Fac Agric Ain Shams Univ
Research Bulletin. Faculty of Agriculture. Gifu University — Res Bull Fac Agr Gifu Univ
Research Bulletin. Faculty of Agriculture. Gifu University — Res Bull Fac Agric Gifu Univ
Research Bulletin. Faculty of Agriculture. Gifu-Ken Prefectural University — Res Bull Fac Agric Gifu-Ken Prefect Univ
Research Bulletin. Faculty of Education. Oita University — Res Bull Fac Ed Oita Univ
Research Bulletin. Faculty of Education. Oita University. Natural Science — Res Bull Fac Educ Oita Univ Nat Sci
Research Bulletin. Faculty of Liberal Arts. Oita University — Res Bull Fac Lib Arts Oita Univ
Research Bulletin. Forest Experiment Station/Ryukyu Seifu, Keizai-Kyoku Ringyo Shikenjo/Ryukyu Government. Economics Department. Forest Experiment Station — Res Bull Forest Exp Sta
Research Bulletin. Forest Research Laboratory. Oregon State University — Res Bull For Res Lab Oreg State Univ
Research Bulletin. Gangweon National University — Res Bull Gangweon Natl Univ
Research Bulletin. Geological and Mineralogical Institute. Tokyo University of Education — Res Bull Geol Mineral Inst Tokyo Univ Educ
Research Bulletin. Georgia Agricultural Experiment Stations — Res Bull Ga Agric Exp Stn
Research Bulletin. Gifu Imperial College of Agriculture — Res Bull Gifu Imp Coll Agr
Research Bulletin. Gifu Imperial College of Agriculture — Res Bull Gifu Imp Coll Agric
Research Bulletin. Gifu University. Faculty of Agriculture — Res Bull Gifu Univ Fac Agric

Research Bulletin. Government Printing Bureau [*Japan*] — Res Bull Gov Print Bur
Research Bulletin. Hawaii Agricultural Experiment Station — Res Bull Hawaii Agric Exp Stn
Research Bulletin. Hiroshima Institute of Technology — Res Bull Hiroshima Inst Technol
Research Bulletin. Hokkaido National Agricultural Experiment Station — Res Bull Hokkaido Nat Agr Exp Sta
Research Bulletin. Hokkaido National Agricultural Experiment Station — Res Bull Hokkaido Natl Agric Exp Stn
Research Bulletin. Hokkaido National Agricultural Experiment Station — Res Bull Hokkaido Natn Agric Exp Stn
Research Bulletin. Idaho Agricultural Experiment Station — Res Bull Idaho Agric Exp Stn
Research Bulletin. Iida Women's Junior College — Res Bull Iida Women's Jr Coll
Research Bulletin. Indiana Agricultural Experiment Station — Res Bull Indiana Agr Exp Sta
Research Bulletin. International Center for the Improvement of Maize and Wheat — Res Bull Int Cent Impr Maize Wheat
Research Bulletin. Iowa Agricultural and Home Economics Experiment Station — Res Bull Iowa Agric Home Econ Exp Stn
Research Bulletin. Iowa Agricultural Experiment Station — Res Bull Iowa Agric Exp Stn
Research Bulletin. Iowa State University Agricultural and Home Economics Experiment Station — Res Bull Iowa St Univ Agric Home Econ Exp Stn
Research Bulletin. Iowa State University of Science and Technology. Agriculture and Home Economics Experiment Station — Res Bull Iowa State Univ Sci Technol Agric Home Econ Exp Stn
Research Bulletin. Kangweon National University [*Republic of Korea*] — Res Bull Kangweon Natl Univ
Research Bulletin. Korean Society of Animal Science — Res Bull Korean Soc Anim Sci
Research Bulletin. Marathwada Agricultural University — RBMUDD
Research Bulletin. Marathwada Agricultural University — Res Bull Marathwada Agric Univ
Research Bulletin. Massachusetts Agricultural Experiment Station — Res Bull Mass Agric Exp Stn
Research Bulletin. Matsumoto Dental College. General Education — Res Bull Matsumoto Dent Coll Gen Educ
Research Bulletin. Meguro Parasitological Museum — Res Bull Meguro Parasitol Mus
Research Bulletin. Meisei University — Res Bull Meisei Univ
Research Bulletin. Meisei University. Physical Sciences and Engineering — Res Bull Meisei Univ Phys Sci Eng
Research Bulletin. Missouri Agricultural Experiment Station — Res Bull Missouri Agric Exp Stn
Research Bulletin. Missouri Agricultural Experiment Station — Res Bull MO Agric Exp Sta
Research Bulletin. Missouri Agricultural Experiment Station — Res Bull Mo Agric Exp Stn
Research Bulletin. National Historic Parks and Site Branch — Res Bull Nat Hist Parks Site Branch
Research Bulletin. National Institute for Educational Research — Res Bul NIER
Research Bulletin. Nebraska Agricultural Experiment Station — Res Bull Neb Agric Exp Stn
Research Bulletin. Nebraska Agricultural Experiment Station — Res Bull Nebr Agric Exp Stn
Research Bulletin. New Jersey Zinc Company — Res Bull NJ Zinc Co
Research Bulletin. Obihiro University. Series I — Res Bull Obihiro Univ Ser I
Research Bulletin. Obihiro Zootechnical University. Series I — Res Bull Obihiro Zootech Univ
Research Bulletin. Obihiro Zootechnical University. Series I — Res Bull Obihiro Zootech Univ Ser I
Research Bulletin of Plant Protection Service (Japan) / Shokubutso Bolkisho Chosa Kenkyu Hokoku — Res Bull Pl Protect Serv Japan
Research Bulletin of the Iwate Industrial Research Institute — Res Bull Iwate Ind Res Inst
Research Bulletin of the University Forests. Tokyo University of Agriculture and Technology — Res Bull Univ For Tokyo Univ Agric Technol
Research Bulletin. Ohio Agricultural Research and Development Center — Res Bull Ohio Agric Res Dev Cent
Research Bulletin. Ohio Agricultural Research and Development Center — Res Bull Ohio Agric Res Dev Center
Research Bulletin. Ohio Agricultural Research and Development Center — Res Bull Ohio Agric Res Developm Cent
Research Bulletin. Oita Research Station for Agricultural Utilization of Hotspring — Res Bull Oita Res Stn Agric Util Hotspring
Research Bulletin. Oregon State University. Forest Research Laboratory — Res Bull Ore For Res Lab
Research Bulletin. Pakistan Council of Scientific and Industrial Research Laboratories (Rajshahi) — Res Bull Pak CSIR Lab (Rajshahi)
Research Bulletin. Panjab University — Res Bull Panjab Univ
Research Bulletin. Panjab University. New Series — Res Bull Panjab Univ NS
Research Bulletin. Panjab University. Science — Res Bull Panjab Univ Sci
Research Bulletin. PCSIR [*Pakistan Council of Scientific and Industrial Research*] **Laboratories** — Res Bull PCSIR Lab
Research Bulletin. PCSIR [*Pakistan Council of Scientific and Industrial Research*] **Laboratories (Rajshahi)** — Res Bull PCSIR Lab (Rajshahi)
Research Bulletin. Perusahaan Negara Bio Farma — Res Bull Perusahaan Negara Bio Farma
Research Bulletin. Plant Protection Service (Japan) — Res Bull Plant Prot Serv (Jap)
Research Bulletin. Plant Protection Service (Japan) — Res Bull Plant Prot Serv (Jpn)
Research Bulletin. PN [*Perusahaan Negara*] **Bio Farma** — Res Bull PN Bio Farma
Research Bulletin. Printing Bureau. Ministry of Finance — Res Bull Print Bur Minist Finance
Research Bulletin. Printing Bureau. Ministry of Finance (Tokyo) — Res Bull Printing Bur (Tokyo)
Research Bulletin. Purdue University. Agricultural Experiment Station — Res Bull Purdue Univ Agr Exp Sta
Research Bulletin. Purdue University. Agricultural Experiment Station — Res Bull Purdue Univ Agric Exp Stn
Research Bulletin. Regional Engineering College (Warangal) — Res Bull Reg Eng Coll (Warangal)
Research Bulletin. Research Institute of Comparative Education and Culture — Res Bul RICEC
Research Bulletin. Saitama Agricultural Experiment Station — Res Bull Saitama Agr Exp Sta
Research Bulletin. State University of Oklahoma — Res Bull State Univ Oklahoma
Research Bulletin. Sugar-Cane Department. Egyptian Sugar and Distillation Company — Res Bull Sugar-Cane Dep Egypt Sugar Distill Co
Research Bulletin. Tokushima Bunri University — Res Bull Tokushima Bunri Univ
Research Bulletin. Toyama Prefectural College of Technology — Res Bull Toyama Prefect Coll Technol
Research Bulletin. University Farm. Hokkaido University — Res Bull Univ Farm Hokkaido Univ
Research Bulletin. University of Calcutta — Res Bull Univ Calcutta
Research Bulletin. University of Georgia. College of Agriculture Experiment Stations — Res Bull Univ Ga Coll Agric Exp Stn
Research Bulletin. University of Georgia. Experiment Stations — Res Bull Univ GA Exp Stn
Research Bulletin. University of Idaho. Agricultural Experiment Station — Res Bull Univ Idaho Agric Exp Stn
Research Bulletin. University of Missouri. College of Agriculture. Experiment Station — Res Bull Univ MO Coll Agr Exp Sta
Research Bulletin. University of Nebraska. College of Agriculture and Home Economics. Agricultural Experiment Station — Res Bull Univ Nebr Coll Agr Home Econ Agr Exp Sta
Research Bulletin. University of Nebraska-Lincoln. Agricultural Experiment Station — Res Bull Univ Nebr Lincoln Agric Exp Stn
Research Bulletin. University of Wisconsin-Madison. College of Agricultural and Life Sciences. Research Division — Res Bull Univ Wis Madison Coll Agric Life Sci Res Div
Research Bulletin. University of Wisconsin-Madison. Research Division. College of Agricultural and Life Sciences — Res Bull Univ Wis Madison Res Div Coll Agric Life Sci
Research Bulletin. Washington State University. Agricultural Research Center — Res Bull Wash State Univ Agric Res Cent
Research Bulletin. West of Scotland Agricultural College — Res Bull West Scotl Agric Coll
Research Bulletin. West of Scotland College of Agriculture — Res Bull W Scotl Coll Agric
Research Bulletin. Wisconsin Agricultural Experiment Station — Res Bull Wis Agr Exp Sta
Research Bulletin. Wisconsin Agricultural Experiment Station — Res Bull Wis Agric Exp Stn
Research Bulletins. College Experiment Forests. Hokkaido University — Res Bull Coll Exp For Hokkaido Univ
Research Bulletins. College Experiment Forests. Hokkaido University — Res Bull Coll Expt Forest Hokkaido Univ
Research Center of Ion Beam Technology. Hosei University. Report. Supplement — Res Cent Ion Beam Technol Hosei Univ Rep Suppl
Research Chronicle. Royal Musical Association — Res Chron
Research Circular. Ohio Agricultural Experiment Station — Res Circ Ohio Agric Exp Stn
Research Circular. Ohio Agricultural Research and Development Center — Res Circ Ohio Agr Res Develop Cent
Research Circular. Ohio Agricultural Research and Development Center — Res Circ Ohio Agric Res Dev Cent
Research Circular. Washington State University. Agricultural Research Center — Res Circ Wash State Univ Agric Res Cent
Research Communications in Alcohol and Substances of Abuse — Res Commun Alcohol Subst Abuse
Research Communications in Biological Psychology and Psychiatry — Res Commun Biol Psychol Psychiatr
Research Communications in Chemical Pathology and Pharmacology — RCOCB
Research Communications in Chemical Pathology and Pharmacology — Res Comm C P
Research Communications in Chemical Pathology and Pharmacology — Res Commun Chem Pathol Pharmacol
Research Communications in Chemical Pathology and Pharmacology — Res Communs Chem Path Pharmac
Research Communications in Molecular Pathology and Pharmacology — Res Commun Mol Pathol Pharmacol
Research Communications in Pharmacology and Toxicology — Res Commun Pharmacol Toxicol
Research Communications in Psychology, Psychiatry, and Behavior — RCPBO
Research Communications in Psychology, Psychiatry, and Behavior — Res Commun Psychol Psychiatry Behav
Research Communications in Substances of Abuse — RCSADO
Research Communications in Substances of Abuse — Res Commun Subst Abuse
Research Communications. Institute for Fermentation (Osaka) — Res Commun Inst Ferment (Osaka)
Research Constructs on Peaceful Uses of Nuclear Energy [*Japan*] — Res Constructs Peaceful Uses Nucl Energy

Research Correspondence — Res Corresp
Research Council. National Academy of Sciences. Reports [*US*] — Nat Res Counc Nat Acad Sci Rep
Research Council of Alberta. Bulletin — Res Counc Alberta Bull
Research Council of Alberta. Bulletin — Research Council Alberta Bull
Research Council of Alberta (Canada). Information Series — Res Counc Alberta (Can) Inform Ser
Research Council of Alberta. Economic Geology Report — Res Counc Alberta Econ Geol Rep
Research Council of Alberta. Geological Division. Bulletin — Res Counc Alberta Geol Div Bull
Research Council of Alberta. Geological Division. Memoir — Res Counc Alberta Geol Div Mem
Research Council of Alberta. Geological Division. Report — Res Counc Alberta Geol Div Rep
Research Council of Alberta. Information Series — Res Counc Alberta Inf Ser
Research Council of Alberta. Mimeographed Circular — Res Counc Alberta Mimeogr Circ
Research Council of Alberta. Mimeographed Series — Res Counc Alberta Mimeogr Ser
Research Council of Alberta. Report — Res Counc Alberta Rep
Research Council of Alberta. Report — Research Council Alberta Rept
Research Council of Israel. Annual Report — Res Counc Isr Annu Rep
Research Department Report. Post Office Research Centre (United Kingdom) — Res Dep Rep Post Off Res Cent (UK)
Research/Development — REDEA
Research/Development — Res Dev
Research/Development — Res/Develop
Research, Development, and Acquisition — RD & A
Research Disclosure — Res Discl
Research Disclosure — Res Disclosure
Research Division Bulletin. Virginia Polytechnic Institute and State University — Res Div Bull Va Polytech Inst State Univ
Research Division Report. Virginia Polytechnic Institute and State University — Res Div Rep Va Polytech Inst State Univ
Research Engineer — Res Eng
Research Establishment Risoe. Report. Risoe-M (Denmark) — Res Establ Risoe Rep Risoe-M (Den)
Research Establishment Risoe. Risoe Report (Denmark) — Res Establ Risoe Risoe Rep (Den)
Research Extension Series. Hawaii Institute of Tropical Agriculture and Human Resources — Res Ext Ser Hawaii Inst Trop Agric Hum Resour
Research Film — Res Film
Research Film — Research F
Research Findings on Smoking of Abused Substances — Res Find Smok Abused Subst
Research for Coatings — Res Coat
Research for Farmers — Res Farmers
Research Frontiers in Fertility Regulation — Res Front Fertil Regul
Research Futures — Res Futures
Research Guide to Australian Politics [*A*] — ARGAP
Research in African Literatures — PRAL
Research in African Literatures — RAL
Research in African Literatures — Res Afr Lit
Research in African Literatures — Res Afr Literatures
Research in African Literatures — Res Afric Lit
Research in African Literatures — Res African Lit
Research in Business Economics and Public Policy — Res Bus Econ Pub Pol
Research in Clinic and Laboratory — Res Clin L
Research in Clinic and Laboratory — Res Clin Lab
Research in Developmental Disabilities — Res Dev Disabil
Research in Domestic and International Agribusiness Management — Res Domest Int Agribusiness Manage
Research in Economic Anthropology — Res Econ Anthropol
Research in Economic History — Res Econ Hist
Research in Education [*England*] — Res Educ
Research in Education — Research in Ed
Research in Experimental Economics — Res Exp Econ
Research in Experimental Medicine — Res Exp Med
Research in Experimental Medicine (Berlin) — Res Exp Med (Berlin)
Research in Finance — RIF
Research in Fisheries. Annual Report. College of Fisheries. University of Washington — Res Fish Annu Rep Coll Fish Univ Wash
Research in Fisheries. Annual Report. School of Fisheries. University of Washington — Res Fish Annu Rep Sch Fish Univ Wash
Research in Fisheries. Annual Report. School of Fisheries. University of Washington — UWRFAY
Research in Fisheries (Seattle) — Res Fish (Seattle)
Research in Food Science — Res Food Sci
Research in Food Science and Nutrition — Res Food Sci Nutr
Research in Health Economics — Res Health Econ
Research in Higher Education — Res Higher Educ
Research in Immunochemistry and Immunobiology — Res Immunochem Immunobiol
Research in Immunology — Res Immunol
Research in Law and Economics — Res L & Econ
Research in Law and Sociology — Res L and Soc
Research in Law, Deviance, and Social Control — Res L Deviance and Soc Control
Research in Librarianship — Res Libnship
Research in Librarianship — Res Librarianship
Research in Life Sciences — Res Life Sci
Research in Life Sciences — RLSCA
Research in Marketing — RIM
Research in Mathematics — Res Math
Research in Microbiology — Res Microb
Research in Microbiology — Res Microbiol
Research in Molecular Biology — Res Mol Biol
Research in Norwegian Agriculture — Res Norw Agric
Research in Nursing and Health — Res Nurs Health
Research in Nursing and Health — Res Nurs Hlth
Research in Ocean Engineering. University Sources and Resources — RIOE
Research in Parapsychology — Res Parapsychol
Research in Phenomenology — PRPH
Research in Phenomenology — Res Phenomenol
Research in Philosophy and Technology — Res Phil Technol
Research in Photobiology. Proceedings. International Congress on Photobiology — Res Photobiol Proc Int Congr
Research in Political Economy — Res Polit Econ
Research in Prostaglandins — Res Prostaglandins
Research in Reproduction — Res Reprod
Research in Review — Res R
Research in Review. Florida State University. Bulletin — Res Rev Florida State Univ Bull
Research in Rural Sociology and Development — Res Rural Sociol Dev
Research in Sociology of Knowledge — Res Sociol Knowl
Research in Sociology of Knowledge, Sciences, and Art — Res Sociol Knowl Sci Art
Research in Surface Forces. Reports Presented. Conference — Res Surf Forces Rep Conf
Research in Text Theory/Untersuchungen zur Text-Theorie — RTT
Research in the Life Sciences. Maine Life Sciences and Agriculture Experiment Station — Res Life Sci Maine Life Sci Agric Exp Stn
Research in the Psychology of Music — RSPMB
Research in the Sociology of Health Care — RSHC
Research in the Teaching of English — Res Teach Engl
Research in Veterinary Science [*United Kingdom*] — Res Vet Sci
Research in Veterinary Science — RVTSA
Research in Virology — Res Virol
Research Institute for Applied Mechanics. Kyushu University. Reports — Res Inst Appl Mech Kyushu Univ Report
Research Institute for the Education of Exceptional Children — RIEEC
Research Institute Nedri As (Hveragerdi, Iceland). Bulletin — RINAB
Research Institute Nedri As (Hveragerdi, Iceland). Report — Res Inst Nedri As (Hveragerdi Icel) Rep
Research Institute of Applied Electricity. Hokkaido University. Monograph Series — Res Inst Appl Electr Hokkaido Univ Monogr Ser
Research Institute of Fundamental Information Science. Research Report — Res Inst Fund Information Sci Res Rep
Research Institute of Industrial Technology. Chungnam National University. Report — Res Inst Ind Technol Chungnam Natl Univ Rep
Research Institute of Industrial Technology. Chungnam University — Res Inst Ind Technol Chungnam Univ
Research Institute of Physics. Annual Report (Sweden) — Res Inst Phys Annu Rep (Swed)
Research Institute. Sumatra Planters Association. Bulletin — Res Inst Sumatra Plant Assoc Bull
Research Institute. Sumatra Planters Association. Communications. Rubber Series — Res Inst Sumatra Plant Assoc Commun Rubber Ser
Research into Higher Education. Abstracts — Res High Educ Abstr
Research into Higher Education. Abstracts — RHEA
Research Journal — Res J
Research Journal. Aleppo University. Basic Sciences Series — Res J Aleppo Univ Basic Sci Ser
Research Journal. Directorate General of Higher Education. Indonesia — Res J Dir Gen Higher Educ Indones
Research Journal. Directorate of Higher Education (Indonesia) — Res J Dir Higher Educ (Indones)
Research Journal. Faculty of Agriculture. Andalas University — Res J Fac Agric Andalas Univ
Research Journal. Faculty of Science. Kashmir University — Res J Fac Sci Kashmir Univ
Research Journal. Hindi Science Academy — Res J Hindi Sci Acad
Research Journal. Kanpur Agricultural College — Res J Kanpur Agr Coll
Research Journal. Mahatma Phule Agricultural University — Res J Mahatma Phule Agric Univ
Research Journal of Agriculture and Animal Sciences (Karnal, India) — Res J Agric Anim Sci (Karnal India)
Research Journal of Living Science — Res J Living Sci
Research Journal of Philosophy and Social Sciences [*Meerut Cantt, India*] — Res J Philo Soc Sci
Research Journal of Physical Education — Res J Phys Educ
Research Journal of Physical Education — TAKEAZ
Research Journal of Sciences — Res J Sci
Research Journal. Science. Devi Ahilya Vishwavidyalaya. Indore — Res J Sci Devi Ahilya Vishwavidyalaya Indore
Research Journal: Science. University of Indore — Res J Sci Univ Indore
Research Journal. University of Wyoming. Agricultural Experiment Station — Res J Univ Wyo Agric Exp Stn
Research Journal. Water Pollution Control Federation — Res J Water
Research Journal. Water Pollution Control Federation — Res J Water Pollut Control Fed
Research Journal. Western Mindanao State University. University Research Center — Res J West Mindanao State Univ Univ Res Cent
Research Laboratories. General Motors Corporation. Research Publication — Res Lab Gen Mot Corp Res Publ
Research Laboratories. Portland Cement Association. Bulletin — Res Lab Portland Cem Assoc Bull

Research Laboratory of Communication Science. University of Electro-Communications. Annual Report — Res Lab Commun Sci Univ Electro-Commun Annu Rep
Research Laboratory of Engineering Materials. Tokyo Institute of Technology. Report — Res Lab Eng Mater Tokyo Inst Technol Rep
Research Laboratory Precision Machinery and Electronics — Res Lab Precis Mach Electron
Research Laboratory Record — Res Lab Rec
Research Leaflet. Forest Research Institute. New Zealand Forest Service — Res Leafl For Res Inst NZ For Serv
Research Leaflet. New Zealand Forest Research Institute — Res Leafl New Zealand Forest Res Inst
Research Leaflet. Oregon Forest Products Laboratory — Res Leafl Oreg For Prod Lab
Research Leaflet. Savanna Forestry Research Station — Res Leafl Sav For Res Sta
Research Letters on Atmospheric Electricity — Res Lett Atmos Electr
Research Management — REM
Research Management — Res Manag
Research Management — Res Management
Research Management — Res Mgt
Research Management — Research Mgt
Research Management — RESMA
Research Management. The International Journal of Research Management — RMF
Research McGill — Res McGill
Research - Measurement - Approval — Res Meas Approv
Research Memorandum. International Institute for Applied Systems Analysis — Res Memo Int Inst Appl Syst Anal
Research Memorandum. International Institute for Applied Systems Analysis — Res Memor Int Inst Appl Syst Anal
Research Methods in Neurochemistry — Res Meth Neurochem
Research Methods in Neurochemistry — Res Methods Neurochem
Research Methods in Neurochemistry — RMNUBP
Research Monograph. National Institute on Alcohol Abuse and Alcoholism — Res Monogr Natl Inst Alcohol Abuse Alcohol
Research Monograph Series. National Institute on Drug Abuse (United States) — Res Monogr Ser Natl Inst Drug Abuse (US)
Research Monograph. Texas A and M University. Texas Agricultural Experiment Station — Res Monogr Tex A & M Univ Tex Agric Exp Stn
Research Monographs in Cell and Tissue Physiology — Res Monogr Cell Tissue Physiol
Research Monographs in Cell and Tissue Physiology [*Elsevier Book Series*] — RMCT
Research Monographs in Immunology — Res Monogr Immunol
Research Monographs in Immunology [*Elsevier Book Series*] — RMI
Research Monographs in Immunology [*Elsevier Book Series*] — RMIMDC
Research News — RNWSD
Research News. Office of Research Administration. University of Michigan (Ann Arbor) — Res News Off Res Adm Univ Mich (Ann Arbor)
Research Note. Bureau of Forestry (Philippines) — Res Note Bur For (Philippines)
Research Note. Colorado State University. College of Forestry and Natural Resources — Res Note Colo Coll For Nat Resour
Research Note. Division of Forest Research (Zambia) — Res Note Div For Res (Zambia)
Research Note. Faculty of Forestry. University of British Columbia — Res Note Fac For Univ BC
Research Note. Ford Forestry Center — Res Not Ford For Cent
Research Note. Forest Management Research. Oregon State University. Forest Research Laboratory — Res Note For Mgmt Res Ore For Res Lab
Research Note. Forestry Commission of New South Wales — Res Note For Comm NSW
Research Note FPL. Forest Products Laboratory [*United States*] — Res Note FPL For Prod Lab
Research Note FPL. Forest Products Laboratory [*United States*] — XALNA
Research Note FPL. US Department of Agriculture. Forest Service. Forest Products Laboratory — Res Note FPL US Dep Agric For Serv For Prod Lab
Research Note INT. US Department of Agriculture. Forest Service. Intermountain Research Station — Res Note Int US Dep Agric For Serv Intermt Res Stn
Research Note NC. US Forest Service — Res Note NC US For Serv
Research Note NE. US Department of Agriculture. Forest Service — Res Note NE US Dep Agric For Serv
Research Note NE-RN. US Department of Agriculture. Forest Service. Northeastern Forest Experiment Station — Res Note NE RN US Dep Agric For Serv Northeast For Exp Stn
Research Note. New Brunswick Research and Productivity Council — Res Note NB Res Prod Counc
Research Note. North Central Forest Experiment Station. US Department of Agriculture — Res Note N Cent Forest Exp Stn US Dep Agric
Research Note. Pacific Southwest Forest and Range Experiment Station. US Department of Agriculture — Res Note Pacif SW For Exp Stn
Research Note. Province of British Columbia. Ministry of Forests — Res Note Prov BC Minist For
Research Note. Research and Productivity Council (New Brunswick) — Res Note Res Prod Counc (NB)
Research Note RM. US Department of Agriculture. Forest Service. Rocky Mountain Forest and Range Experiment Station — Res Note RM US Dep Agric For Serv Rocky Mt For Range Exp Stn
Research Note SE. US Department of Agriculture. Forest Service. Southeastern Forest Experiment Station — Res Note SE US Dep Agric For Serv Southeast For Exp Stn
Research Note SO. US Department of Agriculture. Forest Service. Southern Forest Experiment Station — Res Note SO US Dep Agric For Serv South For Exp Stn
Research Note. Texas Forest Service — Res Note Tex For Serv
Research Note. University of Texas at Austin. Bureau of Economic Geology — Res Note Univ Tex Austin Bur Econ Geol
Research Notes and Memoranda of Applied Geometry for Prevenient Natural Philosophy [*Tokyo*] — RAAG Res Notes
Research Notes and Memoranda of Applied Geometry in Post-RAAG [*Research Association of Applied Geometry*] — Res Notes Memoranda Appl Geom Post-RAAG
Research Notes. British Columbia Forest Service — Res Note BC For Serv
Research Notes. Department of Linguistics and Nigerian Languages — Res Notes Dep Linguistics
Research Notes (Ibadan) — RNI
Research Notes in Artificial Intelligence — Res Notes Artif Intell
Research Notes in Mathematics — Res Notes in Math
Research Notes in Theoretical Computer Science — Res Notes Theoret Comput Sci
Research Notes. Oregon State University. School of Forestry. Forest Research Laboratory — Res Note Oreg State Univ Sch For For Res Lab
Research Notes. Queensland Department of Forestry — Res Notes Qd Dep For
Research Notes. Queensland Forest Service — Res Note Qd For Serv
Research Notes. University of British Columbia. Forest Club — Res Note UBC For Club
Research of Engineering. Jeonbug National University [*Republic of Korea*] — Res Eng Jeonbug Natl Univ
Research of Engineering. Research Institute of Industrial Technology. Jeonbug National University [*Republic of Korea*] — Res Eng Res Inst Ind Technol Jeonbug Natl Univ
Research on Aging — PRAG
Research on Aging — Res Aging
Research on Chemical Intermediates — Res Chem In
Research on Chemical Intermediates — Res Chem Intermed
Research on Drug Actions and Interactions — Res Drug Actions Interact
Research on Environmental Disruption toward Interdisciplinary Cooperation [*Japan*] — Res Environ Disruption Interdiscip Coop
Research on Norway — RENO
Research on Steroids — Res Steroids
Research on Steroids [*Elsevier Book Series*] — RS
Research Opportunities in Renaissance Drama — RORD
Research Outlook — Res Outlook
Research Outlook — RSOLB
Research Pamphlet (Division of Forest Research, Zambia) — Res Pam (Div For Res Zambia)
Research Pamphlet. Forest Research Institute (Kepong) — Res Pam For Res Inst (Kepong)
Research Pamphlet. Forest Research Institute (Malaya) — Res Pamphl For Res Inst (Malaya)
Research Paper. Department of Forestry (Queensland) — Res Pap Dep For (Qd)
Research Paper. Department of Forestry (Queensland) — Res Pap Dep For (Queensl)
Research Paper. Faculty of Forestry. University of British Columbia — Res Pap Fac For Univ BC
Research Paper. Forest Research Laboratory. Oregon State University — Res Pap For Res Lab Oreg State Univ
Research Paper (Forest Series). Federal Department of Forest Research (Nigeria) — Res Pap (Forest Ser) Fed Dep Forest Res (Niger)
Research Paper. Forests Department (Western Australia) — Res Pap For Dep (West Aust)
Research Paper. Forests Department (Western Australia) — Res Pap Forests Dep (West Aust)
Research Paper FPL. Forest Products Laboratory (US) — Res Pap FPL For Prod Lab (US)
Research Paper FPL. US Department of Agriculture. Forest Service. Forest Products Laboratory — Res Pap FPL US Dep Agric For Serv For Prod Lab
Research Paper. Georgia Forest Research Council — Res Pap GA For Res Coun
Research Paper. Horace Lamb Centre for Oceanographical Research. Flinders University [*South Australia*] — Res Pap Horace Lamb Centre Oceanogrl Res
Research Paper. Horace Lamb Centre for Oceanographical Research. Flinders University [*South Australia*] — Res Paper Horace Lamb Centre Oceanogr Res
Research Paper INT. US Department of Agriculture. Forest Service. Intermountain Research Station — Res Pap INT US Dep Agric For Serv Intermt Res Stn
Research Paper. National Building Studies — Res Pap Natl Build Stud
Research Paper NC. US Department of Agriculture. Forest Service. North Central Forest Experiment Station — Res Pap NC US Dep Agric For Serv North Cent For Exp Stn
Research Paper NE. US Department of Agriculture. Forest Service. Northeastern Forest Experiment Station — Res Pap NE US Dep Agric For Serv Northeast For Exp Stn
Research Paper. Oregon State University. Forest Research Lab — Res Pap Oreg State Univ For Res Lab
Research Paper. Oregon State University. Forest Research Laboratory — Res Pap Ore For Res Lab
Research Paper PNW (Pacific Northwest Forest and Range Experiment Station) — Res Pap PNW (Pac Northwest For Range Exp Stn)
Research Paper PNW. US Department of Agriculture. Forest Service. Pacific Northwest Research Station — Res Pap PNW US Dep Agric For Serv Pac Northwest Res Stn
Research Paper PNW [*Pacific Northwest Forest and Range Experiment Station*]. **US Forest Service** — Res Pap PNW US For Serv
Research Paper. Resources for the Future — Res Pap Resour Future

Research Paper RM. US Department of Agriculture. Forest Service. Rocky Mountain Forest and Range Experiment Station — Res Pap RM US Dep Agric For Serv Rocky Mt For Range Exp Stn
Research Paper. Savanna Forestry Research Station — Res Pap Sav For Res Sta
Research Paper. School of Forest Resources. Pennsylvania State University — Res Pap Sch For Resour PA St Univ
Research Paper Series. International Rice Research Institute — Res Pap Ser Int Rice Res Inst
Research Paper SO. US Department of Agriculture. Forest Service. Southern Forest Experiment Station — Res Pap SO US Dep Agric For Serv South For Exp Stn
Research Paper. Tobacco Research Council — Res Pap Tob Res Counc
Research Paper. United States Forest Service. Lake States Forest Experiment Station — Res Pap US Forest Serv Lake St Forest Exp Stn
Research Paper (Western Australia). Forests Department — Res Pap (West Aust) For Dep
Research Papers. Helsinki University of Technology — Res Pap Helsinki Univ Technol
Research Papers in Geography. University of Newcastle — Res Pap Geogr Univ Newcastle
Research Papers in Physical Education — Res Pap Phys Educ
Research Perspectives — Res Perspect
Research Policy [*Netherlands*] — REPYB
Research Policy — Res Pol
Research Policy. A Journal Devoted to Research Policy, Research Management, and Planning — RNI
Research Previews — Res Preview
Research Program of the USSR. New York Series — RPUSSR
Research Program Report. Washington State Highway Department — Res Program Rep Wash State Highw Dep
Research Progress at the Illinois Agricultural Experiment Station — Res Prog Ill Agric Exp Stn
Research Progress. Graphic Arts Technical Foundation — Res Prog Graphic Arts Tech Found
Research Progress in Organic-Biological and Medicinal Chemistry — Res Prog Org-Biol Med Chem
Research Progress. Lithographic Technical Foundation — Res Prog Lithogr Tech Found
Research Progress Report. Indiana. Agricultural Experiment Station — Res Prog Rep Indiana Agric Exp Stn
Research Progress Report. Indiana Agricultural Experiment Station — Res Progr Rep Indiana Agr Exp Sta
Research Progress Report. Purdue University. Agricultural Experiment Station [*Indiana*] — Res Prog Rep Purdue Univ Agric Exp Stn
Research Progress Report. Purdue University. Agricultural Experiment Station [*Indiana*] — Res Progr Rep Purdue Agric Exp Sta
Research Progress Report. Purdue University. Agricultural Experiment Station [*Indiana*] — Res Progr Rep Purdue Univ Agr Exp Sta
Research Progress Report. Tokai-Kinki National Agricultural Experiment Station — Res Prog Rep Tokai-Kinki Natn Agric Exp Stn
Research Progress Report. Tokai-Kinki National Agricultural Experiment Station — Res Progr Rep Tokai-Kinki Nat Agr Exp Sta
Research Progress Report. Tokai-Kinki National Agricultural Experiment Station/Norin-Sho Tokai Kinki Nogyo Shikenjo Kenkyu Sokuho — Res Progr Rep Tokai Kinki Natl Agric Exp Sta
Research Progress Report. United Kingdom Atomic Energy Research Establishment. Health Physics and Medical Division — Res Prog Rep UK At Energy Res Establ Health Phys Med Div
Research Progress Report. Western Society of Weed Science — Res Prog Rep West Soc Weed Sci
Research Progress Report. Western Weed Control Conference — Res Progr Rep West Weed Control Conf
Research Project Report. Graphic Arts Technical Foundation — Res Proj Rep Graphic Arts Tech Found
Research Project Series. Department of Agriculture (Victoria) — Res Proj Ser Dep Agric Victoria
Research Publication. General Motors Corporation. Research Laboratories — GMRLA
Research Publication. General Motors Corporation. Research Laboratories — Res Publ Gen Mot Corp Res Lab
Research Publication. Kansas Agricultural Experiment Station — Res Publ Kan Agric Exp Stn
Research Publication. Punjab Irrigation Research Institute — Res Publ Punjab Irrig Res Inst
Research Publications Association for Research in Nervous and Mental Disease — Res Publ Assoc Res Nerv Ment Dis
Research Publications. Illinois Institute of Technology — Res Publ Ill Inst Technol
Research Publications of the Institute for the History of Arabic Science — Res Publ Inst Hist Arabic Sci
Research Quarterly — Res Q
Research Quarterly — Res Quart
Research Quarterly. American Alliance for Health, Physical Education, and Recreation — Res Q Am Alliance Health Phys Educ Recreat
Research Quarterly. American Association for Health, Physical Education, and Recreation — Res Q (AAHPER)
Research Quarterly. American Association for Health, Physical Education, and Recreation — Res Q Am Assoc Health Phys Educ Recreat
Research Quarterly. American Association for Health, Physical Education, and Recreation — Res Q Am Assoc Health Phys Educ Recreation
Research Quarterly. American Association for Health, Physical Education, and Recreation — RQAHA
Research Quarterly for Exercise and Sport — Res Q Exerc Sport
Research Quarterly for Exercise and Sport — Res Q Exercise Sport
Research Quarterly. Ontario Hydro — Res Q Ont Hydro
Research Reactors. Proceedings. United Nations International Conference. Peaceful Uses of Atomic Energy — Res React Proc UN Int Conf Peaceful Uses At Energy
Research Record. Malawi Forest Research Institute — Res Rec Malawi For Res Inst
Research Relating to Children — Res Relat Child
Research Report. Agricultural Experiment Station. Michigan State University — Res Rep Agric Exp Stn Mich St Univ
Research Report. Agricultural Experiment Station. University of Wisconsin — Res Rep Agric Exp Stn Univ Wisc
Research Report. Agricultural Experiment Station. Utah State University — Res Rep Agric Exp Stn Utah St Univ
Research Report. Atomic Energy Control Board — Res Rep At Energy Control Board
Research Report. Biomass Conversion Program — Res Rep Biomass Convers Program
Research Report C/RR. Timber Research and Development Association. High Wycombe, England — Res Rep CRR Timber Res Dev Assoc High Wycombe Engl
Research Report. Canada Department of Agriculture. National Weed Committee. Western Section — Res Rep Can Dept Agr Nat Weed Comm West Sect
Research Report. Center for Highway Research. University of Texas at Austin — Res Rep Cent Highw Res Univ Tex Austin
Research Report. College of Engineering. Busan National University — Res Rep Coll Eng Busan Natl Univ
Research Report. Connecticut. Storrs Agricultural Research Station — Res Rep Conn Storrs Agric Res Stn
Research Report. Council for British Archaeology — Res Rep Counc Br Archaeol
Research Report. Czechoslovak Academy of Sciences. Institute of Plasma Physics — Res Rep Czech Acad Sci Inst Plasma Phys
Research Report. Department of Agricultural Economics and Agri-Business. Louisiana State University and Agricultural Experiment Station — Res Rep DAE LA St Univ Agric Exp Stn
Research Report. Department of Crop Science. North Carolina State University. Agricultural Experiment Station — Res Rep Dep Crop Sci NC State Univ
Research Report. Department of Electrical Engineering. University of Melbourne — Res Rep Dep Electl Engng Melb Univ
Research Report. Department of Electrical Engineering. University of Melbourne — Res Rep Dep Electr Eng Melb Univ
Research Report. Division of Applied Organic Chemistry. Commonwealth Scientific and Industrial Research Organisation — Res Rep Div Appl Org Chem CSIRO
Research Report. Eastern Section. National Weed Committee of Canada — Res Rep East Sect Nat Weed Comm Can
Research Report. Electronics General Research Institute [*Japan*] — Res Rep Electron Gen Res Inst
Research Report. Experiment Station. College of Agriculture. University of Wisconsin — Res Rep Coll Agric Univ Wis
Research Report. Faculty of Engineering. Gifu University — Res Rep Fac Eng Gifu Univ
Research Report. Faculty of Engineering. Niigata University — Res Rep Fac Eng Niigata Univ
Research Report. Federal Institute of Industrial Research (Lagos, Nigeria) — Res Rep Inst Industr Res (Nigeria)
Research Report. Fish and Wildlife Service (United States) — Res Rep Fish Wildl Serv (US)
Research Report. Flinders Institute of Atmospheric and Marine Sciences. Flinders University — Res Rep Flinders Inst Atmos Mar Sci
Research Report. Florida Agricultural Experiment Station — Res Rep Fla Agric Exp Stn
Research Report. Food Industry Research and Development Institute (Taiwan) — Res Rep Food Ind Res Dev Inst (Taiwan)
Research Report. Forest Products Utilization Laboratory. Mississippi State University — Res Rep For Prod Util Lab Miss St Univ
Research Report. Fukuoka Agricultural Experiment Station — Res Rep Fukuoka Agr Exp Sta
Research Report. Fukuoka Agricultural Experiment Station — Res Rep Fukuoka Agric Exp Stn
Research Report. Georgia Agricultural Experiment Station — Res Rep GA Agr Exp Sta
Research Report. Hawaii Agricultural Experiment Station — Res Rep Hawaii Agric Exp Stn
Research Report. Helsinki University of Technology. Laboratory of Physics — Res Rep Helsinki Univ Technol Lab Phys
Research Report. Hokkaido National Agricultural Experiment Station — Res Rep Hokkaido Natl Agric Exp Stn
Research Report. Hunter Valley Research Foundation — Res Rep Hunter Valley Res Fdn
Research Report. Hunter Valley Research Foundation — Res Rep Hunter Valley Res Found
Research Report. Hyogo Agricultural College / Hyogo Nogyo Tanki Daigaku Kenkyu Shuroku — Res Rep Hyogo Agric Coll
Research Report. Institute of Forest Genetics — Res Rep Inst For Genet
Research Report. Institute of Forest Genetics (Suwon). Imop Sihomjang — Res Rep Inst For Genet (Suwon) Imop Sihomjang
Research Report. Institute of Forest Genetics (Suwon, Korea) — Res Rep Inst For Genet (Korea)
Research Report. Institute of Plasma Physics. Nagoya University — Res Rep Inst Plasma Phys Nagoya Univ
Research Report. International Food Policy Research Institute — Res Rep Int Food Policy Res Inst

Research Report IPPCZ. Czechoslovak Academy of Sciences. Institute of Plasma Physics — Res Rep IPPCZ Czech Acad Sci Inst Plasma Phys
Research Report. Kitakyushu Technical College — Res Rep Kitakyushu Tech Coll
Research Report. Laboratory of Nuclear Science. Tohoku University — Res Rep Lab Nucl Sci Tohoku Univ
Research Report. Laboratory of Nuclear Science. Tohoku University. Supplement [*Japan*] — Res Rep Lab Nucl Sci Tohoku Univ Suppl
Research Report. MAFES [*Mississippi Agricultural and Forestry Experiment Station*] — Res Rep MAFES
Research Report. Michigan State University. Agricultural Experiment Station — Res Rep Mich State Univ Agric Exp Stn
Research Report. Michigan State University. Agricultural Experiment Station. East Lansing — Res Rep Mich State Univ Agric Exp Stn East Lansing
Research Report. Mississippi Agricultural and Forestry Experiment Station — Res Rep Miss Agric For Exp Stn
Research Report. Miyakonojo National College of Technology — Res Rep Miyakonojo Natl Coll Technol
Research Report. Miyakonojo Technical College — Res Rep Miyakonojo Tech Coll
Research Report. Montana Agricultural Experiment Station — Res Rep Mont Agric Exp Stn
Research Report. Nagano State Laboratory of Food Technology — Res Rep Nagano State Lab Food Technol
Research Report. Nagano Technical College [*Japan*] — Res Rep Nagano Tech Coll
Research Report. Nagoya University. Institute of Plasma Physics — Res Rep Nagoya Univ Inst Plasma Phys
Research Report. National Institute for Environmental Studies. Japan — Res Rep Natl Inst Environ Stud Jpn
Research Report. National Institute of Nutrition [*Japan*] — Res Rep Natl Inst Nutr
Research Report. National Research Institute for Metals (Japan) — Res Rep Natl Res Inst Met J
Research Report. New Hampshire Agricultural Experiment Station — Res Rep NH Agric Exp Stn
Research Report. New Mexico Agricultural Experiment Station — Res Rep N Mex Agr Exp Sta
Research Report. New Mexico Agricultural Experiment Station — Res Rep New Mex Agric Exp Stn
Research Report. New Mexico. Agricultural Experiment Station — Res Rep NM Agric Exp Stn
Research Report. Nigeria. Federal Institute of Industrial Research — Res Rep Niger Fed Inst Ind Res
Research Report. Norfolk Agricultural Experiment Station — Res Rep Norfolk Agr Exp Sta
Research Report. North Carolina Agricultural Experiment Station. Department of Crop Science — Res Rep NC Agr Exp Sta Dept Crop Sci
Research Report. North Carolina Agricultural Experiment Station. Department of Field Crops — Res Rep NC Agr Exp Sta Dept Field Crops
Research Report. North Carolina State University. Department of Crop Science — Res Rep NC State Univ Dep Crop Sci
Research Report. North Central Weed Control Conference — Res Rep N Cent Weed Contr Conf
Research Report. North Central Weed Control Conference — Res Rep North Cent Weed Control Conf
Research Report. North Central Weed Control Conference — Res Rep Nth Cent Weed Control Conf
Research Report. North Dakota Agricultural Experiment Station — Res Rep N Dak Agr Exp Sta
Research Report. Oregon State University. Forest Research Laboratory — Res Rep Ore St Univ Forest Res Lab
Research Report. Osaka Municipal Institute for Domestic Science — Res Rep Osaka Munic Inst Domest Sci
Research Report P. Agricultural Experiment Station. Oklahoma State University [*A publication*] — Res Rep P Agric Exp Stn Okla State Univ
Research Report P. Oklahoma Agricultural Experiment Station — Res Rep P Okla Agric Exp Stn
Research Report. Pollution Control Branch (Toronto) — Res Rep Pollut Control Branch Toronto
Research Report. Research Institute of Industrial Safety — Res Rep Res Inst Ind Saf
Research Report. Research Program for the Abatement of Municipal Pollution under Provisions of the Canada-Ontario Agreement on Great Lakes Water Quality — Res Rep Res Program Abatement Munic Pollut Provis Can Ont Ag
Research Report. School of Civil Engineering. University of Sydney — Res Rep Sch Civ Engng Syd Univ
Research Report Series. Alabama Agricultural Experiment Station. Auburn University — Res Rep Ser Ala Agric Exp Stn Auburn Univ
Research Report. Storrs Agricultural Experiment Station — Res Rep Storrs Agric Exp Stn
Research Report. Taiwan Sugar Experiment Station — Res Rep Taiwan Sugar Exp Stn
Research Report. Timber Development Association (London) — Res Rep Timber Dev Assoc (London)
Research Report. Timber Research and Development Association — Res Rep Timb Res Developm Ass
Research Report. United States Army Material Command. Cold Regions Research and Engineering Laboratory — Res Rep US Army Mater Command Cold Reg Res Engng Lab
Research Report. United States Bureau of Sport Fisheries and Wildlife — Res Rep US Bur Sport Fish Wildl
Research Report. United States Fish and Wildlife Service — Res Rep US Fish Wildl Serv
Research Report. University of Arkansas. Engineering Experiment Station — Res Rep Univ Arkansas Eng Exp Stn
Research Report. University of Florida. School of Forest Resources and Conservation — Res Rep Univ Fla Sch For Resour Conserv
Research Report. University of Florida. School of Forestry — Res Rep Fla Sch For
Research Report. University of Georgia. College of Agriculture. Experiment Stations — Res Rep Univ GA Coll Agric Exp Stn
Research Report. University of Illinois at Urbana-Champaign. Water Resources Center — Res Rep Univ Ill Urbana Champaign Water Resour Cent
Research Report. University of Melbourne. Department of Electrical Engineering — Res Rep Univ Melbourne Dep Electr Eng
Research Report. University of Texas at Austin. Center for Highway Research — Res Rep Univ Tex Austin Cent Highw Res
Research Report. University of Wisconsin. College of Agricultural and Life Sciences. Research Division — Res Rep Univ Wis Coll Agric Life Sci Res Div
Research Report. University of Wisconsin. Engineering Experiment Station — Res Rep Univ Wis Eng Exp Stn
Research Report. US Army Engineers. Waterways Experiment Station — Res Rep US Army Eng Waterw Exp Stn
Research Report. Vermont Agricultural Experiment Station — Res Rep Vt Agric Exp Stn
Research Report. Virginia Agricultural Experiment Station — Res Rep VA Agr Exp Sta
Research Report. Western Section. National Weed Committee of Canada — Res Rep West Sect Nat Weed Comm Can
Research Report. Western Section. Weed Committee (Canada) — Res Rep West Sect Weed Comm Can
Research Report. Winnipeg, Manitoba Research Station — Res Rep Winnipeg Manitoba Res Sta
Research Report. Wisconsin Agricultural Experiment Station — Res Rep Wis Agr Exp Sta
Research Reporter — Res Rep
Research Reports. Akita National College of Technology — Res Rep Akita Natl Coll Technol
Research Reports. Akita Technical College — Res Rep Akita Tech Coll
Research Reports. Anan College of Technology — Res Rep Anan Coll Technol
Research Reports. Anan Technical College — Res Rep Anan Tech College
Research Reports. Ariake National College of Technology — Res Rep Ariake Natl Coll Technol
Research Reports. Ashikaga Institute of Technology — Res Rep Ashikaga Inst Technol
Research Reports. Automatic Control Laboratory. Faculty of Engineering. Nagoya University — Res Rep Autom Control Lab Fac Eng Nagoya Univ
Research Reports. Biotechnical Faculty. University of Edvard Kardelj (Ljubljana). Veterinary Issue — Res Rep Biotech Fac Univ Edvard Kardelj (Ljublj) Vet Issue
Research Reports. Biotechnical Faculty. University of Ljubljana. Agricultural Issue — Res Rep Biotech Fac Univ Ljublj Agric Issue
Research Reports. College of Agriculture and Veterinary Medicine. Nihon University [*Japan*] — Res Rep Coll Agric Vet Med Nihon Univ
Research Reports. College of Agriculture. Korea University — Res Rep Coll Agric Korea Univ
Research Reports. Faculty of Biotechnics. University of Ljubljana. Veterinary Issue — Res Rep Fac Biotech Univ Ljublj Vet Issue
Research Reports. Faculty of Engineering. Kagoshima University [*Japan*] — Res Rep Fac Eng Kagoshima Univ
Research Reports. Faculty of Engineering. Kinki University — Res Rep Fac Eng Kinki Univ
Research Reports. Faculty of Engineering. Meiji University — Res Rep Fac Eng Meiji Univ
Research Reports. Faculty of Engineering. Meiji University — Res Reports Fac Engng Meiji Univ
Research Reports. Faculty of Engineering. Mie University — Res Rep Fac Eng Mie Univ
Research Reports. Faculty of Engineering. Nagoya University — Res Rep Fac Eng Nagoya Univ
Research Reports. Faculty of Engineering. Tokyo Denki University — Res Rep Fac Eng Tokyo Denki Univ
Research Reports. Faculty of Engineering. Tokyo Denki University — Res Rep Fac Engrg Tokyo Denki Univ
Research Reports. Faculty of Engineering. Toyo University — Res Rep Fac Eng Toyo Univ
Research Reports. Faculty of Science and Technology. Meijyo University — Res Rep Fac Sci and Technol Meijyo Univ
Research Reports. Faculty of Textiles and Sericulture. Shinshu University — Res Rep Fac Text Seric Shinshu Univ
Research Reports. Fish Commission of Oregon — Res Rep Fish Comm Oreg
Research Reports. Forest Research Institute — Res Rep For Res Inst
Research Reports. Fuel Research Institute (Japan) — Res Rep Fuel Res Inst (Jpn)
Research Reports. Fukui Technical College. Natural Science and Engineering [*Japan*] — Res Rep Fukui Tech Coll Nat Sci Eng
Research Reports. Fukushima Technical College — Res Rep Fukushima Tech Coll
Research Reports. General Education Course. Faculty of Engineering. Toyo University — Res Rep Gen Educ Course Fac Eng Toyo Univ
Research Reports. Hakodate Technical College — Res Rep Hakodate Tech Coll
Research Reports. Hanyang Research Institute of Industrial Sciences — Res Rep Hanyang Res Inst Ind Sci
Research Reports. Ibaraki Technical College — Res Rep Ibaraki Tech Coll
Research Reports. Ikutoku Technical University. Part B. Science and Technology — Res Rep Ikutoku Tech Univ Part B
Research Reports in Physics — Res Rep Phys

Research Reports. Institute of Information Science and Technology. Tokyo Denki University — Res Rep Inst Inf Sci and Technol Tokyo Denki Univ
Research Reports. Kagoshima Technical College — Res Rep Kagoshima Tech Coll
Research Reports. Kasetsart University — Res Rep Kasetsart Univ
Research Reports. Kochi University. Agricultural Science — Res Rep Kochi Univ Agric Sci
Research Reports. Kochi University/Kochi Daigaku Gakujutsu Kenkyu Hokoku — Res Rep Kochi Univ
Research Reports. Kogakuin University [*Japan*] — Res Rep Kogakuin Univ
Research Reports. Kurume Technical College — Res Rep Kurume Tech Coll
Research Reports. Kushiro Technical College — Res Rep Kushiro Tech College
Research Reports. Maizuru College of Technology — Res Rep Maizuru Coll Technol
Research Reports. Maizuru Technical College — Res Rep Maizuru Tech Coll
Research Reports. Matsue College of Technology, Natural Science, and Engineering — Res Rep Matsue Coll Technol Nat Sci Eng
Research Reports. Matsue Technical College — Res Rep Matsue Tech Coll
Research Reports. Miyagi National College of Technology — Res Rep Miyagi Natl Coll Technol
Research Reports. Miyagi Technical College — Res Rep Miyagi Tech College
Research Reports. Nagaoka College of Technology — Res Rep Nagaoka Coll Technol
Research Reports. Nagaoka Technical College — Res Rep Nagaoka Tech Coll
Research Reports. Nagoya Industrial Science Research Institute [*Japan*] — Res Rep Nagoya Ind Sci Res Inst
Research Reports. Nara National College of Technology — Res Rep Nara Natl Coll Technol
Research Reports. Nara Technical College [*Japan*] — Res Rep Nara Tech Coll
Research Reports. National Geographic Society — Res Rep Natl Geogr Soc
Research Reports. National Science Council. Mathematics Research Center — Res Rep Nat Sci Council Math Res Center
Research Reports. Numazu Technical College — Res Rep Numazu Tech Coll
Research Reports of Nagaoka College of Technology — Res Rep Nagaoka College Tech
Research Reports of Suzuka University of Medical Science and Technology — Res Rep Suzuka Univ Med Sci Technol
Research Reports. Office of Rural Development. Agricultural Engineering, Farm Management, and Sericulture (Suweon) — Res Rep Off Rural Dev Agric Eng Farm Manage & Seric (Suweon)
Research Reports. Office of Rural Development. Crop (Suwon, South Korea) — Res Rep Off Rural Dev Crop (Suwon)
Research Reports. Office of Rural Development. Horticulture and Agricultural Engineering (Korea Republic) — Res Rep Off Rural Dev Hortic Agric Eng (Korea Repub)
Research Reports. Office of Rural Development. Horticulture (Suwon, South Korea) — Res Rep Off Rural Dev Hortic (Suwon)
Research Reports. Office of Rural Development. Livestock and Veterinary (Suweon) — Res Rep Off Rural Dev Livest & Vet (Suweon)
Research Reports. Office of Rural Development. Livestock (Korea Republic) — Res Rep Off Rural Dev Livest (Korea Republic)
Research Reports. Office of Rural Development. Livestock, Sericulture (Suwon, South Korea) — Res Rep Off Rural Dev Livest Seric (Suwon)
Research Reports. Office of Rural Development. Livestock (Suwon, South Korea) — Res Rep Off Rural Dev Livest (Suwon)
Research Reports. Office of Rural Development. Ministry of Agriculture and Forestry (Suwon, South Korea) — Res Rep Office Rur Dev Minist Agric For (Korea)
Research Reports. Office of Rural Development. Plant Environment (Suwon, South Korea) — Res Rep Off Rural Dev Plant Environ (Suwon)
Research Reports. Office of Rural Development. Sericulture-Veterinary (Suwon, South Korea) — Res Rep Off Rural Dev Seric-Vet (Suwon)
Research Reports. Office of Rural Development (Suwon, Korea) — Res Rep Off Rural Dev Suwon Korea
Research Reports. Office of Rural Development (Suwon, South Korea) — Res Rep Off Rural Dev (Suwon)
Research Reports. Office of Rural Development (Suwon, South Korea). Livestock — Res Rep Off Rural Dev (Suwon) Livestock
Research Reports. Office of Rural Development. Veterinary and Sericulture (Korea Republic) — Res Rep Off Rural Dev Vet Seric (Korea Republic)
Research Reports. Office of Rural Development. Veterinary (Suwon, South Korea) — Res Rep Off Rural Dev Vet (Suwon)
Research Reports. Oyama National College of Technology — Res Rep Oyama Natl Coll Technol
Research Reports. Oyama Technical College — Res Rep Oyama Tech Coll
Research Reports. Raw Silk Testing — Res Rep Raw Silk Test
Research Reports. Republic of Korea Ministry of Agriculture and Forestry. Office of Rural Development — Res Rep Korea Min Agr Forest Office Rural Develop
Research Reports. Research Laboratory. Gunze Silk Manufacturing Company, Limited — Res Rep Res Lab Gunze Silk Manuf Co Ltd
Research Reports. Rural Development Administration — Res Rep Rural Dev Adm
Research Reports. Rural Development Administration (Suweon) — Res Rep Rural Dev Adm (Suweon)
Research Reports. Sasebo College of Technology — Res Rep Sasebo Coll Technol
Research Reports. Sasebo Technical College — Res Rep Sasebo Tech Coll
Research Reports. Shibaura Institute of Technology [*Japan*] — Res Rep Shibaura Inst Technol
Research Reports. Silk Conditioning Houses — Res Rep Silk Cond Houses
Research Reports. Technical Research Centre of Finland — Res Rep Tech Res Cent Finl
Research Reports. Tokyo Denki University — Res Rep Tokyo Denki Univ
Research Reports. Tokyo Electrical Engineering College — Res Rep Tokyo Electr Eng Coll
Research Reports. Tokyo Electrical Engineering College — Res Rep Tokyo Electr Engrg College
Research Reports. Tokyo Electrical Engineering College — Res Rep Tokyo Electrical Engrg College
Research Reports. Tokyo National Technical College — Res Rep Tokyo Natl Tech Coll
Research Reports. Toyama National College of Technology — Res Rep Toyama Natl Coll Technol
Research Reports. Tsuruoka Technical College — Res Rep Tsuruoka Tech Coll
Research Reports. Veterinary Issue — Res Rep Vet Issue
Research Reports. Yonago Technical College — Res Rep Yonago Tech Coll
Research Results Data Base — RRDB
Research Results Digest — Res Results Dig
Research Review — ResRev
Research Review. Australia. Commonwealth Scientific and Industrial Research Organization. Division of Chemical Technology — Res Rev Aust CSIRO Div Chem Technol
Research Review. Canada Research Station. (Agassiz, British Columbia) — Res Rev Can Res Stn (Agassiz BC)
Research Review. Chung-Buk National University — Res Rev Chung-Buk Natl Univ
Research Review. Commonwealth Bureau of Horticulture and Plantation Crops — Res Rev Bur Hort Plantat Crops
Research Review. Division of Chemical Technology. Commonwealth Scientific and Industrial Research Organisation — Res Rev Div Chem Technol CSIRO
Research Review. Institute of African Studies — Research R
Research Review. Institute of African Studies. University of Ghana — Res Rev Inst Afr Stud
Research Review. Kyungpook University — Res Rev Kyungpook Univ
Research Review (Office of Aerospace Research) — Res Rev (Off Aerosp Res)
Research Reviews in Biochemistry — Res Rev Biochem
Research Reviews in Immunology — Res Rev Immunol
Research Reviews in Medicine — Res Rev Med
Research Reviews in Neuroscience — Res Rev Neurosci
Research Reviews in Pharmacology — Res Rev Pharmacol
Research Series. Fowlers Gap Arid Zone Research Station. University of New England — Res Ser Fowlers Gap Arid Zone Res Stn
Research Series ICAR. Indian Council of Agricultural Research — Res Ser ICAR
Research Series in Applied Geography. University of New England — Res Ser Appl Geogr New Engl Univ
Research Service Bibliographies — Res Bib
Research Service Bibliographies. State Library of Victoria — VSL Bibs
Research Studies — Res Stud
Research Studies [*Pullman*] — RS
Research Studies — RSt
Research Studies. State College of Washington — Res Stud State Coll Wash
Research Studies. State College of Washington [*Pullman*] — RSSCW
Research Studies. State University of Washington — Res Stud State Univ Wash
Research Studies. Udaipur University. College of Agriculture — Res Stud Udaipur Univ Coll Agr
Research Studies. Washington State University [*Pullman*] — Res Stud Wash State Univ
Research Studies. Washington State University [*Pullman*] — RSWSU
Research Studies. Washington State University (Pullman, Washington) — Research Stud Pullman
Research Summary. Ohio Agricultural Research and Development Center — Res Sum Ohio Agr Res Develop Cent
Research Techniques and Instrumentation — Res Tech Instrum
Research Technology Management — Res Technol Man
Research Today — Res Today
Research Topics in Physiology — Res Top Physiol
Research Topics in Physiology — Res Topics Physiol
Research Trends — Res Trends
Research Trends in Physics — Res Trends Phys
Research Volumes. Surrey Archaeological Society — Res Vol Surrey Archaeol Soc
Research Working Papers. Instituto Eduardo Torroja de la Construccion y del Cemento — Res Work Pap Inst Eduardo Torroja Constr Cem
Research Works. Georgian Beekeeping Research Station (Tbilisi) — Res Wks Georgian Beekeep Res Stn (Tbilisi)
Research Works of the Graduate School. Dong-A University — Res Works Grad Sch Dong A Univ
Researcher [*Samar*] — Res
Researches. Electrotechnical Laboratory [*Japan*] — Res Electrotech Lab
Researches. Electrotechnical Laboratory (Tokyo) — Res Electrotech Lab (Tokyo)
Researches in the Social Sciences on Japan. East Asian Institute. Columbia University — RSSJ
Researches. National Museum (Bloemfontein) — Res Natl Mus (Bloemfontein)
Researches on Essential Oils of the Australian Flora — Res Essent Oils Aust Flora
Researches on Essential Oils of the Australian Flora — Res Esst Oils Aust Flora
Researches on Population Ecology — Res Popul Ecol
Researches on Population Ecology (Kyoto) — Res Popul Ecol (Kyoto)
Researches on Population Ecology. Kyoto University — Researches Popul Ecol Kyoto Univ
Researches on Population Ecology. Society of Population Ecology — Res Populat Ecol
Reseau Documentaire en Sciences Humaines de la Sante [*Database*] — RESHUS
Reseaux — RESE
Resena de Literatura, Arte, y Espectaculo — RLAE
Resenha Clinico-Cientifica — Resen Clin Cient

Reserve Bank Bulletin [*New Zealand*] — Res Bk
Reserve Bank of Australia. Statistical Bulletin — Reserve Bank Australia Statis Bul
Reserve Bank of Australia. Statistical Bulletin — SSB
Reserve Bank of India. Bulletin — RBD
Reserve Bank of India. Bulletin [*Bombay*] — RBIB
Reserve Bank of India. Bulletin — Reserve Bank India B
Reserve Bank of Malawi. Financial and Economic Review — RMH
Reserve Bank of New Zealand. Bulletin — Res Bk NZ
Reserve Bank of New Zealand. Bulletin — Reserve Bank NZ Bul
Reserve Bank of New Zealand. Bulletin — RNZ
Reserved and Equity Judgements [*New South Wales*] — Res & Eq J
Reserved and Equity Judgements [*New South Wales*] — Res & Eq Jud
Reserved and Equity Judgements [*New South Wales*] — Res & Eq Judgm
Resident and Staff Physician — Resid Staff Physician
Residential Group Care and Treatment — Resid Group Care & Treat
Residential Group Care and Treatment — RGCT
Residential Interiors — Res Int
Residual Effects of Abused Drugs on Behavior — Residual Eff Abused Drugs Behav
Residual Gases in Electron Tubes. Proceedings. International Conference — Residual Gases Electron Tubes Proc Int Conf
Residuals and Trace Elements in Iron and Steel. International Conference — Residuals Trace Elem Iron Steel Int Conf
Residue Reviews — Residue Rev
Residue Reviews — RREVA
Residues and Effluents. Processing and Environmental Considerations. Proceedings. International Symposium — Residues Effluents Process Environ Consid Proc Int Symp
Resin Review — Resin Rev
Resin Review (Philadelphia) — Resin Rev (Philadelphia)
Resin Review (Richmond, England) — Resin Rev (Richmond Engl)
Resistencia (Serie de Economia e Gestao) — Resistencia (Ser Econ e Gestao)
Resoconti. Associazione Mineraria Sarda — Resoconti Assoc Min Sarda
Resoconti delle Riunioni dell'Associazione Mineraria Sarda — Resoconti Riun Assoc MIn Sarda
Resoconti delle Sedute dell'Associazione Mineraria Sarda — Resoconti Sedute Assoc Min Sarda
Resonans — RSO
Resource and Environmental Biotechnology — Resour Environ Biotechnol
Resource Atlas. University of Nebraska-Lincoln. Conservation and Survey Divsion — Resour Atlas Univ Nebr Lincoln Conserv Surv Div
Resource Bulletin FPL. US Department of Agriculture. Forest Service. Forest Products Laboratory — Resour Bull FPL US Dep Agric For Serv For Prod Lab
Resource Bulletin RM. US Department of Agriculture. Rocky Mountain Forest and Range Experiment Station — Resour Bull RM US Dep Agric Rocky Mt For Range Exp Stn
Resource Bulletin SE. US Department of Agriculture. Forest Service. Southeastern Forest Experiment Station — Resour Bull SE US Dep Agric For Serv Southeast For Exp Stn
Resource Development. Incorporating Northern Development and Oceanic Industries — REDV
Resource Development Report. Alabama Cooperative Extension Service. Auburn University — Resour Dev Rep Ala Coop Ext Serv Auburn Univ
Resource Management and Optimization — Resour Manage and Optimiz
Resource Management and Optimization [*United States*] — Resour Manage Optim
Resource Management and Optimization — Resour Manage Optimization
Resource Management Series. West Virginia University. College of Agriculture and Forestry. Agricultural Experiment Station. Division of Resource Management — Resour Manage Ser W Va Univ Coll Agric For Agric Exp Stn
Resource Organizations and Meetings for Educators [*Database*] — ROME
Resource Publications in Geography — Res Publ Geogr
Resource Recovery and Conservation [*Netherlands*] — Resour Recovery Conserv
Resource Recovery and Conservation — RRCOD
Resource Recovery and Energy Review — Resour Recovery Energy Rev
Resource Recovery and Energy Review — RRERD
Resource Recovery Update — Resrce Recv
Resource Report. Cooperative Extension. University of Wisconsin — Resour Rep Coop Ext Univ Wis
Resource Sharing and Library Networks — Resour Sharing and Libr Networks
Resource Technology — RSTN
Resources — RESUB
Resources and Conservation — RCOND
Resources and Conservation — Resour Conserv
Resources and Conservation [*Netherlands*] — Resources Conserv
Resources and Energy — REE
Resources and Energy — RESND
Resources and Energy — Resour and Energy
Resources and Energy [*Netherlands*] — Resour Energy
Resources Bulletin. Man and Resources Conference Program — RESO
Resources, Conservation, and Recycling — Resour Conserv Recycl
Resources for American Literary Study — RALS
Resources for American Literary Study — Resour Am L
Resources for Biomedical Research and Education — Resour Biomed Res Educ
Resources for Book Publishers [*United States*] — Resour Book Publ
Resources for the Future Research Paper — Res Future Res Pap
Resources Group Review. Suncor, Inc. — REGR
Resources in Computer Education [*Database*] — RICE
Resources in Education — RESEB
Resources in Education — ResEduc
Resources in Education — Resour Educ
Resources in Vocational Education — Res Voc Educ
Resources in Vocational Education [*Database*] — RIVE
Resources Industry — Resour Ind
Resources of the Biosphere (USSR) — Resour Biosphere (USSR)
Resources Policy — Resour Policy
Resources Policy — Resources Pol
Resources Policy — RGL
Respiration and Circulation — Respir Circ
Respiration Physiology — Resp Physl
Respiration Physiology — Respir Physiol
Respiration Research — Respir Res
Respiration. Supplement [*Switzerland*] — Respiration Suppl
Respiratory Care — RC
Respiratory Care — Resp C
Respiratory Care — Resp Care
Respiratory Care — Respir Care
Respiratory Medicine — Resp Med
Respiratory Medicine — Respir Med
Respiratory Technology — Resp Technol
Respiratory Technology — Respir Technol
Respiratory Therapy — Resp Ther
Respiratory Therapy — Respir Ther
Responsabilita del Sapere — RdS
Response — Re
Respublica Literaria — Res Lit
Respublikanskaya Konferentsiya Elektrokhimikov Litovskoi SSR — Resp Konf Elektrokhim Lit SSR
Respublikanskaya Konferentsiya Fiziologov i Biokhimikov — Resp Konf Fiziol Biokhim
Respublikanskaya Konferentsiya po Analiticheskoi Khimii. Tezisy Dokladov — Resp Konf Anal Khim Tezisy Dokl
Respublikanskaya Nauchno-Proizvodstvennaya Konferentsiya po Zashchite Rastenii v Kazakhstane — Resp Nauchno Proizvod Konf Zashch Rast Kaz
Respublikanskaya Nauchno-Tekhnicheskaya Konferentsiya Molodykh Uchenykh po Pererabotke Nefti i Neftekhimii — Resp Nauchno Tekh Konf Molodykh Uch Pererab Nefti Neftekhim
Respublikanskaya Nauchno-Tekhnicheskaya Konferentsiya Povyshenie Effektivnosti Proizvodstva I Uluchsheniya Kachestva Elektroferrosplavov — Resp Nauchno Tekh Konf Povysh Eff Proizvod Uluchsheniya Kach
Respublikanskaya Shkola-Seminar Spektroskopiya Molekul i Kristallov — Resp Shk Semin Spektrosk Mol Krist
Respublikanskii Sbornik Nauchnykh Trudov. Yaroslavskii Gosudarstvennyi Pedagogicheskii Institut imeni K.D. Ushinskogo — Resp Sb Nauchn Tr Yarosl Gos Pedagog Inst im KD Ushinskogo
Respublikanskoe Soveshchanie po Neorganicheskoi Khimii — Resp Soveshch Neorg Khim
Ressurection (Toulouse) — Res T
Restaurant Business — Restau Bus
Restaurant Business — Restaurant Bus
Restaurant Business — Restaurnt B
Restaurant Business and Economic Research — Restaur Bus
Restaurant Hospitality — Restrnt H
Restaurant Hospitality — RH
Restaurant Management — Restaurant Manage
Restaurant Management — Restr Mgt
Restaurant Reporter — Restr Rep
Restaurants and Institutions — R & I
Restaurants and Institutions — Rest Inst
Restaurants and Institutions — Restau & Inst
Restaurants and Institutions — Restaurants Inst
Resto del Carlino — RdC
Restoration and Eighteenth Century Theatre Research — RECTR
Restoration and Eighteenth Century Theatre Research — Restor Eigh
Restoration and Eighteenth Century Theatre Research — RTR
Restoration Quarterly — Rest Q
Restoration Quarterly — Restoration Q
Restoration Quarterly — RQ
Restorative Dentistry — Restorative Dent
Restorative Neurology and Neuroscience — Restor Neurol Neurosci
Resultados Expediciones Cientificas — Result Exped Cient
Resultados Expediciones Cientificas del Buque Oceanografico "Cornide de Saavedra" — Result Exped Cient Buque Oceanogr "Cornide de Saavedra"
Resultate der Mathematik — Resultate Math
Resultaten van de Conjunctuurenquete bij het Bedrijfsleven in de Gemeenschap — REB
Resultats Statistiques du Poitou-Charentes — Resultats
Results and Perspectives in Particle Physics. Recontres de Physique de la Vallee d'Aoste — Results Perspect Part Phys Recontres Phys Vallee Aoste
Results and Problems in Cell Differentiation — Results Probl Cell Differ
Results in Mathematics — Results Math
Results of Research. Agricultural Experiment Station. University of Kentucky — Results Res Agric Exp Stn Univ Ky
Results of Research. Annual Report. University of Kentucky. Agricultural Experiment Station — Results Res Annu Rep Univ KY Agr Exp Sta
Results of the Norwegian Scientific Expedition to Tristan Da Cunha 1937-1938 — Results Norw Sci Exped Tristan Da Cunha 1937-1938
Resume des Communications. Societe de Microscopie du Canada — Resume Commun Microsc Can
Resume des Memoires, Envoyes, au Concours Ouvert Par la Societe Vaudoise des Sciences Naturelles — Resume Mem Soc Vaud Sci Nat
Resumen Bimestral de Arte y Cultura — RBAC
Resumenes de Investigacion. INP-CIP [*Instituto Nacional de la Pesca-Centro de Investigaciones Pesqueras*] — Resumenes Invest INP-CIP
Resumes des Communications. Conference Internationale sur la Physique et la Chimie des Mineraux d'Amiante — Resumes Commun Conf Int Phys Chim Miner Amiante

Resumes des Conferences et Communications. Symposium International sur les Jets Moleculaires — Resumes Conf Commun Symp Int Jets Mol
Resumos Indicativos da Industria de Petroleo — Resumos Indicativos Ind Pet
Resumos Indicativos do Petroleo — Res Indicat Petrol
Resumptio Genetica — Resumptio Genet
Resurrection — Res
Resursy Biosfery — Resur Biosfery
Retail and Distribution Management — RDM
Retail and Distribution Management — Retail Dist Mgmt
Retail Business — RB
Retail Business. A Monthly Journal Concerned with Consumer Goods Markets, Marketing and Management, and Distribution in the United Kingdom — RTH
Retail Control — REC
Retail News — Ret News
Retail Newsletter — RNL
Retail Packaging — Retail Packag
Retail Packaging — Retail Pkg
Retail/Services Labor Report — Ret Serv Lab Rep
Retailer of Queensland — Retailer of Q
Retailing in Tennessee — Retail Tenn
Reticuloendothelial Society. Journal — Reticuloendothel Soc J
Reticuloendothelial Structure and Function. Proceedings. International Symposium — Reticuloendothel Struct Funct Proc Int Symp
Retina Foundation. Institute of Biological and Medical Sciences. Monographs and Conferences — Retina Found Inst Biol Med Sci Monogr Conf
Retirement Living — Ret Liv
Retrospective Machine Readable Cataloging [*Database*] — REMARC
Retrospective Review — Retros
RETS [*Research Engineering Technical Services*] **Digest** — RETS Dig
Reumatismo — REUMA
Reumatismo. Supplement — Reumatismo Suppl
Reuniao Anual. Sociedade Brasileira de Genetica — Reun A Soc Bras Genet
Reuniao da Cultura do Arroz. Anais — Reun Cult Arroz An
Reuniao de Trabalho sobre Fisica de Energias Intermediarias — Reun Trab Fis Energ Intermed
Reuniao de Trabalho sobre Fisica Nuclear no Brasil. Anais — Reun Trab Fis Nucl Bras An
Reunioes em Matematica Aplicada e Computacao Cientifica — Reun Mat Apl Comput Cient
Reunion Annuelle des Sciences de la Terre (Programme et Resumes) — Reun Annu Sci Terre (Programme Resumes)
Reunion de Sociedad Argentina de Pathologia Regional del Norte — Reunion Soc Argent Pathol Regional N
Reunion del Grupo de Trabajo del Cuaternario — Reun Grupo Trab Cuat
Reunion. Grupo Espanol de Trabajo del Cuaternario — Reun Grupo Esp Trab Cuat
Reunion Latinoamericana de Fitotecnia. Actas — Reun Latinoamer Fitotec Actas
Reunion Latinoamericana de Produccion Animal — Reunion Latinoam Prod Anim
Reunion Nacional el Cuaternario en Mediós Semiaridos — Reun Nac Cuat Medios Semiaridos
Reunion sobre Produccion Marina y Explotacion Pesquera — Reun Prod Mar Explot Pesq
Reunion sobre Productividad y Pesquerias. Actas — Reun Prod Pesq Actas
Re-Union ut Omnes Unum Sint — RUOUS
Reuse/Recycle — REURD
Revealing Antiquity — Reveal Antiq
Revenue Canada. Customs and Excise Institutions List [*Database*] — INST
Revenue Laws of Ptolemy Philadelphus — P Ptol
Revenue Laws of Ptolemy Philadelphus — P Rev
Revenue Laws of Ptolemy Philadelphus — P Rev Laws
Revidierte Berner Uebereinkunft — RB Ue
Review — Rev
Review. American Society for Metals — Rev Am Soc Met
Review. Amersham Corporation — Rev Amersham Corp
Review and Expositor — R EX
Review and Expositor — R Exp
Review and Expositor — RE
Review and Expositor — Rev and Expositor
Review and Expositor — RevExp
Review and Expositor — RvEx
Review and Perspective — Rev Perspect
Review. Architectural Science Unit. University of Queensland — Rev Archit Sci Unit Univ Queensl
Review. Bank of London and South America — Rev Bank London South Am
Review. Bank of New South Wales — Rev Bank NSW
Review. Bulgarian Geological Society — Rev Bulg Geol Soc
Review Bulletin. Calcutta Mathematical Society — Rev Bull Calcutta Math Soc
Review. Electrical Communication Laboratory [*Tokyo*] — Rev El Comm
Review. Electrical Communication Laboratory — Rev Electr Commun Lab
Review. Electrical Communication Laboratory (Tokyo) — Rev Elec Commun Lab (Tokyo)
Review. Electrical Communication Laboratory (Tokyo) — Rev Electr Commun Lab (Tokyo)
Review. Faculty of Agriculture. Ege University — Rev Fac Agric Ege Univ
Review. Faculty of Science. University of Istanbul. Series C [*Istanbul Universitesi fen Fakultesi Mecmuasi. Serie C*] — Rev Fac Sci Univ Istanbul Ser C
Review. Federation of American Health Systems — Rev Fed Am Health Syst
Review. Federation of American Hospitals — R Fed Am Hosp
Review. Federation of American Hospitals — Rev Fed Am Hosp
Review. Fernand Braudel Center for the Study of Economies, Historical Systems, and Civilizations — R Fernand Braudel Center
Review Fiction and Poetry — RFP
Review for Religious — R Rel
Review for Religious — Rev Relig
Review for Religious — RR
Review for Religious (St. Mary's) — RRStM
Review. General Association of Turkish Chemists. Section B — Rev Gen Assoc Turk Chem Sect B
Review. Institute of Nuclear Power Operations — Review Inst Nucl Power Oper
Review. International Biological Programme — Rev Int Biol Prog
Review. International Commission of Jurists — ICJ Rev
Review. International Commission of Jurists — R Int Commiss Jurists
Review. International Commission of Jurists — Rev Int Commission of Jurists
Review. International Commission of Jurists — Rev Int'l Comm Jurists
Review. International Statistical Institute — RISI
Review Journal of Philosophy and Social Science — Rev J Phil Soc Sci
Review. Kobe University of Mercantile Marine. Part 2 [*Japan*] — Rev Kobe Univ Merc Mar Part 2
Review. Kobe University of Mercantile Marine. Part 2. Maritime Studies, and Science and Engineering — Rev Kobe Univ Merc Mar Part 2 Marit Stud Sci Eng
Review. National Research Council of Canada — Rev Nat Res Counc Can
Review. Oak Ridge National Laboratory (United States) — Rev Oak Ridge Natl Lab (US)
Review of Activities. Metallgesellschaft — Rev Act Metallges
Review of Activities. Metallgesellschaft AG — Rev Act Metallges AG
Review of African Political Economy — Afri Econ
Review of African Political Economy — R Afr Polit Econ
Review of African Political Economy — R African Pol Economy
Review of African Political Economy — Rev Afr Polit Economy
Review of Agricultural Economics. Hokkaido University — Rev Agric Econ Hokkaido Univ
Review of Agricultural Economics of Malaysia — R Agr Econ Mal
Review of Agricultural Research — Rev Agric Res
Review of Allergy and Applied Immunology — Rev Allergy
Review of Allergy and Applied Immunology — Rev Allergy Appl Immunol
Review of Allied Health Education — RAHE
Review of Applied Entomology — Rev Appl Ent
Review of Applied Entomology. Series B. Medical and Veterinary — Rev Appl Entomol Ser B
Review of Applied Mycology — Rev Appl Mycol
Review of Atomic Industries [*Japan*] — Rev At Ind
Review of Biological Research in Aging — Rev Biol Res Aging
Review of Black Political Economy — Black Pol Econ
Review of Black Political Economy — PRBP
Review of Black Political Economy — R Black Pol Econ
Review of Black Political Economy — R Black Pol Economy
Review of Black Political Economy — Rev Bl Pol
Review of Books and Religion — R Bk Rel
Review of Business — ROB
Review of Business and Economic Research — R Bus & Econ Res
Review of Business and Economic Research — R Bus and Econ Research
Review of Business and Economic Research — RBE
Review of Business and Economic Research — RBER
Review of Business and Economic Research — Rev Bus Econ Res
Review of Business. St. John's University — R Bus St John's Univ
Review of Clinical Pharmacology and Pharmacokinetics — Rev Clin Pharmacol Pharmacokinet
Review of Clinical Pharmacology and Pharmacokinetics. International Edition — Rev Clin Pharmacol Pharmacokinet Ind Ed
Review of Compagnie Generale d'Electricite [*France*] — Rev Cie Gen Electr
Review of Compagnie Generale d'Electricite — RGNEB
Review of Contemporary Fiction — PRCF
Review of Contemporary Fiction — RCF
Review of Contemporary Law — RCL
Review of Contemporary Law — Rev Cont L
Review of Contemporary Sociology — R Contemp Sociol
Review of Current Activities in Technical Education — R Current Activities Tech Ed
Review of Current Activities in Technical Education — Rev Current Activities Tech Ed
Review of Current Literature Relating to the Paint, Colour, Varnish, and Allied Industries — Rev Curr Lit Paint Colour Varn Allied Ind
Review of Czechoslovak Medicine — Rev Czech Med
Review of Dentistry for Children — Rev Dent Child
Review of Eastern Medical Sciences — Rev East Med Sci
Review of Economic Conditions [*Ankara*] — TUH
Review of Economic Statistics — Rev Econ Stat
Review of Economic Studies — R E Stud
Review of Economic Studies — R Econ Stud
Review of Economic Studies — Rev Econ S
Review of Economic Studies — Rev Econ Stud
Review of Economic Studies — Rev Econom Stud
Review of Economic Studies — RST
Review of Economic Studies [*Edinburgh*] — RVC
Review of Economics and Statistics — R Econ Stat
Review of Economics and Statistics — R Econ Statist
Review of Economics and Statistics — R Econ Statistics
Review of Economics and Statistics — RES
Review of Economics and Statistics — RESTAT
Review of Economics and Statistics — Rev Econ St
Review of Economics and Statistics — Rev Econ Stat
Review of Economics and Statistics — Rev Econ Statist
Review of Economics and Statistics — Rev Econom Statist
Review of Economics and Statistics — ROE
Review of Education — R Educ
Review of Educational Research — GRER

Review of Educational Research — R Ed Res
Review of Educational Research — R Educ Res
Review of Educational Research — RER
Review of Educational Research — Rev Educ Re
Review of Educational Research — Rev Educ Res
Review of Educational Research — Rev Educational Res
Review of English Literature — R Engl Lit
Review of English Literature — REL
Review of English Literature — Rev Eng Lit
Review of English Studies — PRES
Review of English Studies — R Eng Stud
Review of English Studies — R Engl Stud
Review of English Studies — REngS
Review of English Studies — RES
Review of English Studies — RESt
Review of English Studies — Rev Engl St
Review of English Studies — Rev Engl Stu
Review of English Studies — Rev Engl Stud
Review of English Studies. New Series — R Eng Stud NS
Review of English Studies. New Series — RESNS
Review of Ethnology — R Ethnol
Review of Ethnology — RE
Review of Ethnology — Review Ethnol
Review of Existential Psychology and Psychiatry — R Exist Psych Psych
Review of Existential Psychology and Psychiatry — Rev Exist Psych Psychiat
Review of Existential Psychology and Psychiatry — Rev Exist Psychol Psychiat
Review of Financial Studies — RFS
Review of Futures Markets — RFM
Review of Gastroenterology — Rev Gastroenterol
Review of General Meeting. Technical Session. Cement Association of Japan — Rev Gen Meet Tech Sess Cem Assoc Jpn
Review of Geology and the Connected Sciences — Rev Geol Connected Sci
Review of Ghana Law — R Ghana Law
Review of Ghana Law — Rev Ghana Law
Review of Ghana Law — Rev of Ghana L
Review of Ghana Law — RGL
Review of Hanazono College — R Hanazono Coll
Review of High Pressure Science and Technology — Rev High Pressure Sci Technol
Review of Historical Publications Relating to Canada — RHPC
Review of Income and Wealth — R Income Wealth
Review of Income and Wealth — Rev Income Wealth
Review of Income and Wealth — RIW
Review of Indonesian and Malayan Affairs [*Australia*] — R Indo Mal Aff
Review of Indonesian and Malayan Affairs — R Indones Malay Aff
Review of Indonesian and Malayan Affairs — R Indones Malayan Aff
Review of Indonesian and Malayan Affairs — Rev Indon & Malayan Affairs
Review of Indonesian and Malayan Affairs — RevIMA
Review of Infectious Diseases — Rev Infect Dis
Review of International Affairs — R Internat Affairs
Review of International Affairs — RIAf
Review of International Affairs. Politics, Economics, Law, Science, Culture — RIB
Review of International Broadcasting — RIB
Review of International Cooperation — R Int Coop
Review of International Cooperation — Rev Int Coop
Review of International Cooperation — RIC
Review of Iranian Political Economy and History — RIPEH
Review of Laser Engineering [*Japan*] — Rev Laser Eng
Review of Litigation — Rev Litigation
Review of Marketing and Agricultural Economics — R Marketing & Ag Econ
Review of Marketing and Agricultural Economics — R Marketing and Agric Econ
Review of Marketing and Agricultural Economics — R Mkting Agric Econ
Review of Marketing and Agricultural Economics — Rev Mark Agric Econ
Review of Marketing and Agricultural Economics — Rev Market Agric Econ
Review of Marketing and Agricultural Economics — Rev Market & Ag Econ
Review of Marketing and Agricultural Economics — Rev Marketing Agr Econ
Review of Marketing and Agricultural Economics (Sydney) — Rev Market Agric Econ (Sydney)
Review of Marketing and Agricultural Economics (Sydney) — Rev Mktg Agric Econ (Sydney)
Review of Medical and Veterinary Mycology — Rev Med Vet Mycol
Review of Medical Pharmacology — Rev Med Pharmacol
Review of Metal Literature — Rev Met Lit
Review of Metal Literature [*American Society for Metals*] — RML
Review of Metals Technology — Rev Met Technol
Review of Metaphysics — PRMP
Review of Metaphysics — R Met
Review of Metaphysics — R Meta
Review of Metaphysics — R Metaphys
Review of Metaphysics — Rev Metaph
Review of Metaphysics — Rev Metaphy
Review of Metaphysics — RM
Review of National Literatures — Rev Nat Lit
Review of National Literatures — RNL
Review of Nations [*Geneva*] — RN
Review of New Energy Technology — Rev New Energ Technol
Review of Palaeobotany and Palynology — R Palaeobot & Palynol
Review of Palaeobotany and Palynology — Rev Palae P
Review of Palaeobotany and Palynology — Rev Palaeobot Palynol
Review of Palaeobotany and Palynology — Rev Palaeobot Palynology
Review of Petroleum Technology — Rev Petrol Technol
Review of Philosophy and Religion — RPR
Review of Physical Chemistry of Japan — Rev Ph Ch J
Review of Physical Chemistry of Japan — Rev Phys Chem Jpn
Review of Physics in Technology [*United Kingdom*] — Rev Phys Technol
Review of Plant Pathology — Rev Plant Path
Review of Plant Pathology — Rev Plant Pathol
Review of Plant Protection Research — Rev Plant Prot Res
Review of Polarography — Rev Polarogr
Review of Polarography (Japan) — Rev Polarogr (Jpn)
Review of Politics — PRPO
Review of Politics — R Pol
Review of Politics — R Polit
Review of Politics — R Politics
Review of Politics — ReP
Review of Politics — Rev Pol
Review of Politics — Rev Polit
Review of Politics — RP
Review of Progress in Coloration and Related Topics — Rev Prog Color Relat Top
Review of Progress in Quantitative Nondestructive Evaluation — Rev Prog Quant Nondestr Eval
Review of Psychology of Music — RVPMB
Review of Public Data Use — R Public Data Use
Review of Public Data Use — Rev Pub Dat
Review of Public Data Use — Rev Pub Data Use
Review of Public Data Use — RPD
Review of Public Personnel Administration — RPP
Review of Quantitative Finance and Accounting — RQFA
Review of Radical Political Economics — IRRP
Review of Radical Political Economics — Polit Eco
Review of Radical Political Economics — R Rad Pol Econ
Review of Radical Political Economics — R Radic Polit Econ
Review of Radical Political Economics — R Radical Pol Econ
Review of Radical Political Economics — Rev Radic Polit Econ
Review of Radical Political Economics — Rev Radical Polit Econ
Review of Regional Economics and Business — R Regional Econ and Bus
Review of Regional Economics and Business — REB
Review of Regional Economics and Business — RRE
Review of Religion — R of Religion
Review of Religion — RoR
Review of Religion — RR
Review of Religion — RRel
Review of Religions (Rabwah) — RRR
Review of Religious Research — R Rel Res
Review of Religious Research — R Relig Res
Review of Religious Research — Rev Rel Res
Review of Religious Research — RRR
Review of Research in Visual Arts Education — Rev Res Vis Arts Educ
Review of Reviews — R of R'=s
Review of Reviews — R Rs
Review of Reviews [*London*] — RR
Review of Reviews [*United States*] — RRA
Review of Reviews. Australasian Edition — Rev Revs Australas Ed
Review of Scientific Instruments — R Sci Instr
Review of Scientific Instruments — Rev Sci Ins
Review of Scientific Instruments — Rev Sci Instr
Review of Scientific Instruments — Rev Sci Instrum
Review of Scientific Instruments — RSI
Review of Scottish Culture — ROSC
Review of Securities Regulation — Rev Sec Reg
Review of Social Economy — R Soc Econ
Review of Social Economy — R Social Economy
Review of Social Economy — Rev Soc Ec
Review of Social Economy — Rev Soc Econ
Review of Social Economy — RSE
Review of Social Theory — R Soc Theory
Review of Socialist Law — Rev Soc L
Review of Southeast Asian Studies [*Singapore*] — R Se As Stud
Review of Soviet Medical Sciences — Rev Sov Med Sci
Review of Soviet Medicine — Rev Sov Med
Review of Sport and Leisure — Rev Sport Leisure
Review of Surgery — Rev Surg
Review of Taxation of Individuals — R Taxation Individuals
Review of Taxation of Individuals — Rev Tax Indiv
Review of Taxation of Individuals — RTI
Review of Textile Progress — Rev Text Progr
Review of Textile Progress — Rev Textile Progr
Review of the Churches — RC
Review of the Economic Conditions in Italy — BEI
Review of the Economic Conditions in Italy — R Econ Condit Italy
Review of the Economic Conditions in Italy — R Econ Conditions Italy
Review of the Economic Conditions in Italy — Rev Econ Co
Review of the Economic Situation of Mexico — Econ Mex
Review of the Economic Situation of Mexico — ESE
Review of the Economy and Employment — Rev Economy Emplyment
Review of the Marketing and Agricultural Economy — R Mark Agric Econ
Review of the River Plate — R River Plate
Review of the River Plate — Rev River Plate
Review of the River Plate — River Plat
Review of the River Plate — RPL
Review of Theology and Philosophy — RofThPh
Review of World Economics — RWE
Review on the Deformation Behavior of Materials — RDBMD
Review. Polish Academy of Sciences — Rev Pol Acad Sci
Review. Polish Academy of Sciences — RPAS
Review. Radio Research Laboratories — Rev Radio Res Lab
Review. Radiochemical Centre (Amersham, England) — Rev Radiochem Cent (Amersham Eng)

Review Report Information Center. Polish Atomic Energy Commission — Rev Rep Inf Cent Pol AEC
Review Series. International Atomic Energy Agency — Rev Ser IAEA
Review. Tussock Grasslands and Mountain Lands Institute — Rev Tussock Grassl Mt Lands Inst
Review. Warren Spring Laboratory (United Kingdom) — Rev Warren Spring Lab (UK)
Reviews. Argonne National Laboratory (United States) — Rev Argonne Natl Lab US
Reviews for Physicians [*Elsevier Book Series*] — RFP
Reviews from College on Plasma Physics — Rev Coll Plasma Phys
Reviews. Immunopharmacology Symposium — Rev Immunopharmacol Symp
Reviews in American History — GRAH
Reviews in American History — R Am Hist
Reviews in American History — RAH
Reviews in American History — Rev Am Hist
Reviews in American History — Rev Amer Hist
Reviews in Analytical Chemistry — RACYA
Reviews in Analytical Chemistry — Rev Anal Chem
Reviews in Anthropology — R Anthrop
Reviews in Anthropology — RA
Reviews in Aquatic Sciences — R Aquat Sci
Reviews in Aquatic Sciences — Rev Aquat Sci
Reviews in Biochemical Toxicology [*Elsevier Book Series*] — RBT
Reviews in Biochemical Toxicology — Rev Biochem Toxicol
Reviews in Cancer Epidemiology [*Elsevier Book Series*] — RCE
Reviews in Chemical Engineering — Rev Chem En
Reviews in Chemical Engineering — Rev Chem Eng
Reviews in Clinical and Basic Pharmacology — RCBPEJ
Reviews in Clinical and Basic Pharmacology — Rev Clin Basic Pharm
Reviews in Clinical and Basic Pharmacology — Rev Clin Basic Pharmacol
Reviews in Computational Chemistry — Rev Comput Chem
Reviews in Engineering Geology [*United States*] — Rev Eng Geol
Reviews in Environmental Toxicology — RETXEB
Reviews in Environmental Toxicology — Rev Environ Toxicol
Reviews in Food Science and Technology — Rev Food Sci Technol
Reviews in Food Sciences and Technology (Mysore) — Rev Food Sci Technol (Mysore)
Reviews in Food Technology (Mysore) — Rev Food Technol (Mysore)
Reviews in Inorganic Chemistry — Rev Inorg Chem
Reviews in Inorganic Chemistry — RICHD
Reviews in Leukemia and Lymphoma [*Elsevier Book Series*] — RLL
Reviews in Macromolecular Chemistry — Rev Macromol Chem
Reviews in Mathematical Physics — Rev Math Phys
Reviews in Medical Virology — Rev Med Virol
Reviews in Mineralogy — Rev Mineral
Reviews in Mineralogy — RMIND
Reviews in Perinatal Medicine — Rev Perinat Med
Reviews in Polymer Technology — Rev Polym Technol
Reviews in Pure and Applied Pharmacological Sciences — Rev Pure Appl Pharmacol Sci
Reviews in Pure and Applied Pharmacological Sciences — RPASDB
Reviews of Data on Science Resources [*United States*] — Rev Data Sci Resour
Reviews of Data on Science Resources. National Sciences Foundation — Rev Data Sci Resour Natl Sci Found
Reviews of Environmental Contamination and Toxicology — Rev Environ Contam Toxicol
Reviews of Geophysics [*Later, Reviews of Geophysics and Space Physics*] — Rev Geophys
Reviews of Geophysics [*Later, Reviews of Geophysics and Space Physics*] — Rev Geophysics
Reviews of Geophysics [*Later, Reviews of Geophysics and Space Physics*] — RVGPA
Reviews of Geophysics and Space Physics — Rev Geophys
Reviews of Geophysics and Space Physics — Rev Geophys and Space Phys
Reviews of Geophysics and Space Physics — Rev Geophys Space Phys
Reviews of Geophysics and Space Physics — Revs Geophys Space Phys
Reviews of Infrared and Millimeter Waves — Rev Infrared Millimeter Waves
Reviews of Modern Physics — Rev M Phys
Reviews of Modern Physics — Rev Mod Phys
Reviews of Modern Physics — Rev Modern Phys
Reviews of Modern Physics — Rs Mod Physics
Reviews of Modern Physics Monographs — Rev Mod Phy Monogr
Reviews of Neuroscience — Rev Neurosci
Reviews of Oculomotor Research — Rev Oculomot Res
Reviews of Petroleum Technology — RPTEA
Reviews of Petroleum Technology (London) — Rev Pet Technol (London)
Reviews of Physiology, Biochemistry, and Experimental Pharmacology — Rev Physiol Biochem Exp Pharmacol
Reviews of Physiology, Biochemistry, and Pharmacology — Rev Phys B
Reviews of Physiology, Biochemistry, and Pharmacology — Rev Physiol Biochem Pharmacol
Reviews of Plasma Physics — Rev Plasma Phys
Reviews of Plasma Physics [*English Translation*] — RPLPA
Reviews of Pure and Applied Chemistry — Rev Pure Appl Chem
Reviews of Reproduction — Rev Reprod
Reviews of Research and Practice. Institute for Research into Mental and Multiple Handicap [*Elsevier Book Series*] — RRP
Reviews of Solid State Science — Rev Solid State Sci
Reviews of Weed Science — Rev Weed Sci
Reviews on Analytical Chemistry. Euroanalysis — Rev Anal Chem Euroanal
Reviews on Coatings and Corrosion — Rev Coat Corros
Reviews on Coatings and Corrosion — RVCCB
Reviews on Drug Metabolism and Drug Interactions — Rev Drug Metabol Drug Interact
Reviews on Endocrine-Related Cancer — Rev Endocr Relat Cancer
Reviews on Endocrine-Related Cancer. Supplement — Rev Endocr Relat Cancer Suppl
Reviews on Environmental Health — Rev Environ Health
Reviews on Environmental Health — REVHA
Reviews on Heteroatom Chemistry — Rev Heteroat Chem
Reviews on High-Temperature Materials — Rev High-Temp Mater
Reviews on High-Temperature Materials — RHTMA
Reviews on Immunoassay Technology — Rev Immunoassay Technol
Reviews on Powder Metallurgy and Physical Ceramics — Rev Powder Metall Phys Ceram
Reviews on Reactive Species in Chemical Reactions — Rev React Species Chem React
Reviews on Silicon, Germanium, Tin, and Lead Compounds — Rev Silicon Germanium Tin Lead Compd
Reviews on the Deformation Behavior of Materials — Rev Deform Behav Mater
Revija za Sociologiju — R Sociol
Revised Code of Washington — Wash Rev Code
Revised Code of Washington Annotated — Wash Rev Code Ann
Revised Ordinances of the Northwest Territories — NWT Rev Ord
Revised Regulations of Prince Edward Island [*Canada*] — PEI Rev Regs
Revised Regulations of Quebec — Que Rev Regs
Revised Statues of Canada [*Database*] — RSC
Revised Statutes of Alberta — Alta Rev Stat
Revised Statutes of British Columbia — BC Rev Stat
Revised Statutes of Nebraska — Neb Rev Stat
Revised Statutes of Quebec — Que Rev Stat
Revision Historica (Tucuman, Argentina) — Revision Hist Tucuman
Revision og Regnskabsvaesen — RoR
Revisions-Ingenieur und Gewerbe-Anwalt (Berlin) — Rev Ingenieur Berlin
Revisor Politico y Literario — RPL
Revist Litteraria. Periodico de Litteratura, Philosophia, Viagem, Eciencias e Bellas Artes — Revista Litt
Revista. ABIA/SAPRO [*Associacao Brasileira das Industrias da Alimentacao/Setor de Alimentos Calorico-Proteicos*] — Rev ABIA/SAPRO
Revista. Academia Colombiana de Ciencias Exactas Fisicas y Naturales — Rev Acad Colomb Cienc Exactas Fis Nat
Revista. Academia Colombiana de Ciencias Exactas, Fisicas, y Naturales — Rev Acad Colombiana Cienc Exact Fis Natur
Revista. Academia Colombiana de Ciencias Exactas, Fisicas, y Naturales (Bogota) — Rev Acad Col Cien Exact Fis Nat Bogota
Revista. Academia Colombiana de Historia Ecclesiastica — RACHE
Revista. Academia Costarricense de Historia (San Jose, Costa Rica) — Rev Acad Costarricense Hist S Jose
Revista. Academia de Ciencias Exactas, Fisico-Quimicas, y Naturales de Madrid — Rev Acad Cienc Exactas Fis Quim Nat Madrid
Revista. Academia de Ciencias Exactas, Fisico-Quimicas, y Naturales de Zaragoza — RACZA
Revista. Academia de Ciencias Exactas, Fisico-Quimicas, y Naturales de Zaragoza — Rev Acad Ci Zaragoza
Revista. Academia de Ciencias Exactas, Fisico-Quimicas, y Naturales de Zaragoza — Rev Acad Cienc Exactas Fis-Quim Nat Zaragoza
Revista. Academia de Ciencias Exactas, Fisico-Quimicas, y Naturales de Zaragoza. Serie 2 — Rev Acad Cienc Zaragoza 2
Revista. Academia de Ciencias (Zaragoza) — Rev Acad Cienc (Zaragoza)
Revista. Academia de Geographia and Historia de Costa Rica (San Jose) — Rev Acad Geogr Hist S Jose
Revista. Academia Galega de Ciencias — Rev Acad Galega Cienc
Revista. Academias de Letras — RAL
Revista Acoriana — RAc
Revista. Administracion Nacional del Agua (Argentina) — Rev Adm Nac Agua (Argent)
Revista Agricola (Bogota) — Rev Agric (Bogota)
Revista Agricola (Chicago) — Rev Agricola (Chicago)
Revista Agricola (Guatemala City) — Revista Agric Guatemala City
Revista Agricola (Mocambique) — Rev Agr (Mocambique)
Revista Agricola (San Jacinto, Mexico) — Rev Agric (San Jacinto Mex)
Revista Agricola (Sao Paulo) — Revista Agric Sao Paulo
Revista Agricolo-Veterinaria (Olinda) — Revista Agric Veterin Olinda
Revista Agronomica — Rev Agron
Revista Agronomica del Noroeste Argentino — Rev Agron Noroeste Argent
Revista Agronomica del Noroeste Argentino — Revta Agron NE Argent
Revista Agronomica (Lisbon) — Rev Agron (Lisb)
Revista Agronomica/Sociedade de Sciencias Agronomicas de Portugal (Lisbon) — Revista Agron Lisbon
Revista Agropecuaria — Revista Agropecu
Revista Alergia Mexico — Rev Alerg Mex
Revista Americana de Buenos Aires — RABA
Revista. AMRIGS [*Associacao Medica do Rio Grande Do Sul*] — Rev AMRIGS
Revista Analitica de Educacion (Paris) — Rev Anal Educ Paris
Revista ANDI [*Asociacion Nacional de Industriales*] — R ANDI
Revista Antioquena de Economia — RAE
Revista. Archivo Historico del Cuzco (Cuzco, Peru) — Rev Arch Hist Cuzco
Revista. Archivo Nacional (Bogota) — Rev Arch Nac Bogota
Revista. Archivo Nacional (Lima) — Rev Arch Nac Lima
Revista. Archivo y Biblioteca Nacionales (Tegucigalpa) — Rev Arch Bibl Nac Tegucigalpa
Revista. Archivos Nacionales de Costa Rica — RANCR
Revista Argentina de Agronomia — Rev Argent Agron
Revista Argentina de Alergia — Rev Argent Alerg
Revista Argentina de Alergia — Rev Argent Alergia
Revista Argentina de Anestesia y Analgesia — Rev Argent Anest
Revista Argentina de Anestesiologia — Rev Argent Anestesiol
Revista Argentina de Angiologia — Rev Argent Angiol
Revista Argentina de Cancerologia — Rev Argent Cancerol

Revista Argentina de Cardiologia — Rev Argent Cardiol
Revista Argentina de Cirugia — Rev Argent Cir
Revista Argentina de Derecho Internacional (Buenos Aires) — Rev Arg Der Intern BA
Revista Argentina de Dermatologia — Rev Argent Dermatol
Revista Argentina de Endocrinologia y Metabolismo — Rev Argent Endocrinol Metab
Revista Argentina de Implantologia Estomatologica — Rev Argent Implantol Estomatol
Revista Argentina de Microbiologia — Rev Argent Microbiol
Revista Argentina de Neurologia, Psiquiatria, y Medicina Legal — Rev Argent Neurol
Revista Argentina de Neurologia, Psiquiatria, y Medicina Legal — Rev Argent Neurol Psiquiat y Med Leg
Revista Argentina de Psicologia — Rev Arg Psicol
Revista Argentina de Puericultura y Neonatologia — Rev Argent Pueric Neonatol
Revista Argentina de Quimica e Industrias — Rev Argent Quim Ind
Revista Argentina de Radiologia — Rev Argent Radiol
Revista Argentina de Relaciones Internacionales — R Argent Relac Int
Revista Argentina de Reumatologia — Rev Argent Reum
Revista Argentina de Reumatologia — Rev Argent Reumatol
Revista Argentina de Tuberculosis, Enfermedades, Pulmonares, y Salud Publica — Rev Argent Tuberc Enferm Pulm Salud Publica
Revista Argentina de Tuberculosis y Enfermedades Pulmonares — Rev Argent Tuberc Enferm Pulm
Revista Argentina de Urologia y Nefrologia — Rev Argent Urol Nefrol
Revista Argentino-Norteamericana de Ciencias Medicas — Rev Argent Norteam Cienc Med
Revista Arhivelor — Rev Arh
Revista Arhivelor — Rev Arhiv
Revista. Asociacion Argentina Criadores de Cerdos — Rev Asoc Argent Criad Cerdos
Revista. Asociacion Argentina de Dietologia — Rev Asoc Argent Dietol
Revista. Asociacion Argentina de los Quimicos y Tecnicos de la Industria del Cuero — Rev Asoc Argent Quim Tec Ind Cuero
Revista. Asociacion Argentina de Microbiologia — Rev Asoc Argent Microbiol
Revista. Asociacion Argentina de Mineralogia, Petrologia, y Sedimentologia — Rev Asoc Argent Mineral Petrol Sedimentol
Revista. Asociacion Argentina de Nutricion y Dietologia — Rev Asoc Argent Nutr Dietol
Revista. Asociacion Bioquimica Argentina — Rev Asoc Bioquim Argent
Revista. Asociacion de Ciencias Naturales del Litoral — Rev Asoc Cienc Nat Litoral
Revista. Asociacion de Escribanos del Uruguay — RAEU
Revista. Asociacion de Ingenieros Agronomos — Rev Asoc Ing Agron
Revista. Asociacion de Profesionales. Hospital Nacional de Odontologia — Rev Asoc Prof Hosp Nac Odontol
Revista. Asociacion Dental Mexicana — Rev Asoc Dent Mex
Revista. Asociacion Farmaceutica Mexicana — Rev Asoc Farm Mex
Revista. Asociacion Geologica Argentina — Rev Asoc Geol Argent
Revista. Asociacion Medica Argentina — Rev Asoc Med Argent
Revista. Asociacion Medica Argentina — Revista Asoc Med Argent
Revista. Asociacion Medica de Cuenca — Rev Asoc Med Cuen
Revista. Asociacion Medica Mexicana — Rev Asoc Med Mex
Revista. Asociacion Mexicana de Enfermeras — Rev Asoc Mex Enferm
Revista. Asociacion Odontologica Argentina — Rev Asoc Odontol Argent
Revista. Asociacion Odontologica de Costa Rica — Rev Asoc Odontol Costa Rica
Revista. Asociacion Rural del Uruguay — Rev Asoc Rural Urug
Revista. Asociacion Rural del Uruguay — Rev Asoc Rural Uruguay
Revista. Associacao Medica Brasileira — Rev Assoc Med Bras
Revista. Associacao Medica de Minas Gerais — Rev Assoc Med Minas Gerais
Revista. Associacao Medica do Rio Grande Do Sul — Rev Assoc Med Rio Grande Do Sul
Revista. Associacao Paulista de Cirurgioes Dentistas — Rev Assoc Paul Cir Dent
Revista. Associacao Paulista de Cirurgioes Dentistas Regional de Aracatuba — Rev Assoc Paul Cir Dent Reg Aracatuba
Revista. Associacao Paulista de Medicina — Rev Assoc Paul Med
Revista Astronomica — Rev Astron
Revista Asturiana de Ciencias Medicas — Rev Asturiana Cien Med
Revista. Ateneo de la Catedra de Tecnica de Operatoria Dental — Rev Ateneo Catedra Tec Oper Dent
Revista Augustiniana de Espiritualidad — RAE
Revista Azucarera — Rev Azucar
Revista Bancaria — R Bancaria
Revista Bancaria Brasileira — R Bancaria Bras
Revista. Banco de la Republica — R Banco Republ
Revista. Banco de la Republica (Bogota) — Rev Banco Repub Bogota
Revista (Barcelona) — RevB
Revista. Bibilioteca Nacional Jose Marti (Cuba) — RBNC
Revista Biblica — ReB
Revista Biblica — Rev Bib
Revista Biblica con Seccion Liturgica [*Buenos Aires*] — RBArg
Revista Biblica. Villa Calbada [*Argentina*] — RBCalb
Revista Bibliografica Cubana — RBibC
Revista Bibliografica Cubana (La Habana) — Rev Bibliogr Cubana Hav
Revista Bibliografica Jose Marti — RBJM
Revista Bibliografica y Documental — R Bibliogr Doc
Revista Bibliografica y Documental [*Madrid*] — RBD
Revista. Biblioteca, Archivo, y Museo del Ayuntamiento de Madrid — RBAM
Revista. Biblioteca, Archivo, y Museo del Ayuntamiento de Madrid — RBAMM
Revista. Biblioteca, Archivo, y Museo del Ayuntamiento de Madrid — RevBAM
Revista. Biblioteca Nacional (Buenos Aires) — Rev Bibl Nac BA
Revista. Biblioteca Nacional de Cuba — R Bibl Nac (Cuba)
Revista. Biblioteca Nacional de Cuba — RBNC
Revista. Biblioteca Nacional de Cuba — RBNH
Revista. Biblioteca Nacional (Guatemala) — Rev Bibl Nac Guat
Revista. Biblioteca Nacional Jose Marti — RBNJM
Revista. Biblioteca Nacional Jose Marti — RevN
Revista. Biblioteca Nacional (La Habana) — Rev Bibl Nac Hav
Revista. Biblioteca Nacional (San Salvador) — Rev Bibl Nac S Salvador
Revista Bibliotecilor [*Bucharest*] — RB
Revista Bibliotecilor [*Bucharest*] — Rev Bib
Revista Bimestre Cubana — RBC
Revista Bimestre Cubana. Sociedad Economica de Amigos del Pais (La Habana) — Rev Bimes Cubana Hav
Revista Bolivariana. Sociedad Bolivariana de Colombia (Bogota) — Rev Bolivar Bogota
Revista Boliviana de Quimica — Rev Boliv Quim
Revista. Bolsa de Cereales — Rev Bolsa Cereal
Revista. Bolsa de Comercio de Rosario — R Bolsa Comer Rosario
Revista. Bolsa de Comercio de Rosario — Rev Bolsa Comer Rosario
Revista Brasileira Cardiovascular — Rev Bras Cardiovasc
Revista Brasileira de Analises Clinicas — RBACB
Revista Brasileira de Analises Clinicas — Rev Bras Anal Clin
Revista Brasileira de Anestesiologia — Rev Bras Anestesiol
Revista Brasileira de Armazenamento — Rev Bras Armazenamento
Revista Brasileira de Biologia — Rev Bras Biol
Revista Brasileira de Biologia — Revta Bras Biol
Revista Brasileira de Botanica — Rev Bras Bot
Revista Brasileira de Cancerologia — Rev Bras Cancerol
Revista Brasileira de Chimica (Sao Paulo) — Rev Bras Chim (Sao Paulo)
Revista Brasileira de Ciencia do Solo — Rev Bras Cienc Solo
Revista Brasileira de Ciencias Sociais. Faculdade de Ciencias Economicas. Universidade Federal do Minas Gerais (Belo Horizonte, Brazil) — Rev Bras Cien Soc Belo Horizonte
Revista Brasileira de Cirurgia — Rev Bras Cir
Revista Brasileira de Cirurgia — Rev Bras Cirurg
Revista Brasileira de Clinica e Terapeutica — Rev Bras Clin Ter
Revista Brasileira de Deficiencia Mental — Rev Bras Defic Ment
Revista Brasileira de Economia — R Bras Ec
Revista Brasileira de Economia — R Bras Econ
Revista Brasileira de Economia — R Brasil Econ
Revista Brasileira de Economia — Rev Bra Ec
Revista Brasileira de Economia. Fundacao Getulia Vargas. Instituto Brasileiro de Economia — IBE/RBE
Revista Brasileira de Economia. Organo do Instituto Brasileiro de Economia (Rio de Janeiro) — Rev Bras Econ Rio
Revista Brasileira de Enfermagem — Rev Bras Enferm
Revista Brasileira de Engenharia — Rev Bras Eng
Revista Brasileira de Engenharia. Caderno de Engenharia Quimica — Rev Bras Eng Cad Eng Quim
Revista Brasileira de Engenharia Quimica — Rev Bras Eng Quim
Revista Brasileira de Entomologia — Rev Bras Ent
Revista Brasileira de Entomologia — Rev Bras Entomol
Revista Brasileira de Entomologia — Revta Bras Ent
Revista Brasileira de Estatistica — R Bras Estatistica
Revista Brasileira de Estatistica — R Brasil Estatist
Revista Brasileira de Estatistica — Rev Bras Estat
Revista Brasileira de Estatistica. Ministerio do Planejamento e Coordenacao Geral. Instituto Brasileiro de Geografia e Estatistica — IBGE/RBE
Revista Brasileira de Estudos Pedagogicos. Instituto Nacional de Estudos Pedagogicos (Rio de Janeiro) — Rev Bras Estud Pedag Rio
Revista Brasileira de Estudos Politicos — R Bras Estud Pol
Revista Brasileira de Estudos Politicos — R Brasil Estud Polit
Revista Brasileira de Estudos Politicos (Belo Horizonte, Brazil) — Rev Bras Estud Pol Belo Horizonte
Revista Brasileira de Farmacia — Rev Bras Farm
Revista Brasileira de Farmacognosia — Rev Bras Farmacogn
Revista Brasileira de Filologia — RBFl
Revista Brasileira de Filologia — RBFilol
Revista Brasileira de Filosofia — RBdeF
Revista Brasileira de Filosofia — RBF
Revista Brasileira de Filosofia. Instituto Brasileiro de Filosofia (Sao Paulo) — Rev Bras Filos S Paulo
Revista Brasileira de Fisica — RBFSA
Revista Brasileira de Fisica — Rev Bras Fis
Revista Brasileira de Fisiologia Vegetal — Rev Bras Fisiol Veg
Revista Brasileira de Folclore — RBF
Revista Brasileira de Folclore (Rio de Janeiro) — Rev Bras Folk Rio
Revista Brasileira de Fruticultura — Rev Bras Frutic
Revista Brasileira de Gastroenterologia — Rev Bras Gastroenterol
Revista Brasileira de Genetica — Rev Bras Genet
Revista Brasileira de Geociencias — RBGCA
Revista Brasileira de Geociencias — Rev Bras Geocienc
Revista Brasileira de Geografia — R Brasil Geogr
Revista Brasileira de Geografia — Rev Bras Geogr
Revista Brasileira de Geografia — Rev Brasil Geogr
Revista Brasileira de Geografia. Conselho Nacional de Geografia. Instituto Brasileiro de Geografia e Estatistica — IBGE/R
Revista Brasileira de Geografia/Conselho Nacional de Geografia. Instituto Brasileiro de Geografia e Estatistica — Revista Brasil Geogr
Revista Brasileira de Ginecologia e Obstetricia — Rev Bras Ginecol Obstet
Revista Brasileira de Leprologia — Rev Bras Leprol
Revista Brasileira de Lingua e Literatura — RBLL
Revista Brasileira de Linguistica — RBL
Revista Brasileira de Malariologia e Doencas Tropicais — Rev Bras Malariol Doencas Trop

Revista Brasileira de Malariologia e Doencas Tropicais — Revta Brasil Mala Do Trop
Revista Brasileira de Malariologia e Doencas Tropicais. Publicacoes Avulsas [*A publication*] — Rev Bras Malariol Doencas Trop Publ Avulsas
Revista Brasileira de Mandioca — Rev Bras Mandioca
Revista Brasileira de Medicina — Rev Bras Med
Revista Brasileira de Mercado de Capitais — R Bras Mercado Capitais
Revista Brasileira de Mercado de Capitais. Instituto Brasileiro de Mercado de Capitais — RMBC
Revista Brasileira de Musica — R Brasileira
Revista Brasileira de Odontologia — Rev Bras Odont
Revista Brasileira de Odontologia — Rev Bras Odontol
Revista Brasileira de Oftalmologia — Rev Bras Oftalmol
Revista Brasileira de Patologia Clinica — Rev Bras Patol Clin
Revista Brasileira de Pesquisas Medicas e Biologicas — Rev Bras Pesqui Med Biol
Revista Brasileira de Pesquisas Medicas e Biologicas — Revta Bras Pesquisas Med Biol
Revista Brasileira de Politica Internacional — R Bras Pol Internac
Revista Brasileira de Politica Internacional — R Brasil Polit Int
Revista Brasileira de Politica Internacional — Revta Brasil Polit Int
Revista Brasileira de Politica Internacional. Instituto Brasileiro de Relacoes Internacionais — IBRI/R
Revista Brasileira de Politica Internacional (Rio de Janeiro) — Rev Bras Pol Intern Rio
Revista Brasileira de Psiquiatria — Rev Bras Psiquiatr
Revista Brasileira de Quimica — Rev Brasil Quim
Revista Brasileira de Quimica. Ciencia and Industria — Rev Bras Quim
Revista Brasileira de Quimica (Sao Paulo) — RBQSA
Revista Brasileira de Quimica (Sao Paulo) — Rev Bras Quim (Sao Paulo)
Revista Brasileira de Reproducao Animal — Rev Bras Reprod Anim
Revista Brasileira de Reumatologia — Rev Bras Reum
Revista Brasileira de Reumatologia — Rev Bras Reumatol
Revista Brasileira de Tecnologia — RBTNA
Revista Brasileira de Tecnologia — Rev Bras Tecnol
Revista Brasileira de Tuberculose e Doencas Toracicas — Rev Bras Tuberc Doencas Torac
Revista Brasileira de Zoologia — Rev Bras Zool
Revista Brasileira dos Municipios. Conselho Nacional de Estatistica. Organo da Associacao Brasileira dos Municipios (Rio de Janeiro) — Rev Bras Munici Rio
Revista Brasileira (Rio De Janeiro) — RBRJ
Revista Brasileira (Rio de Janeiro) — Rev Bras Rio
Revista Brasiliense — RBr
Revista Brasiliense (Sao Paulo) — Rev Bras S Paulo
Revista Brazileira de Estudios Politicos — RBEP
Revista Cafetalera [*Spain*] — RCAFA
Revista Cafetalera (Guatemala) — Rev Cafetalera (Guatem)
Revista Cafetera de Colombia — Rev Cafetera Colomb
Revista Cafetera de Colombia. Federacion Nacional de Cafeteros (Bogota) — Rev Cafe Col Bogota
Revista. Caja de Jubilaciones y Pensiones de la Industria y Comercio (Montevideo) — Rev Caja Jubil Pension Monte
Revista Calasancia — RCal
Revista Camoniana [*Sao Paulo*] — RCam
Revista Camoniana [*Sao Paulo*] — RevC
Revista Canadiense de Estudios Hispanicos — RCEH
Revista Canaria de Estudios Ingleses — RCEI
Revista Cartografica. Instituto Panamericano de Geografia e Historia (Buenos Aires) — Rev Cart BA
Revista CASL (Centro Academico Sarmento Leite) — Rev CASL
Revista Catalana de Teologia — RCT
Revista Catarinense de Odontologie — Rev Catarinense Odontol
Revista Catolica (Chile) — RCC
Revista Catolica de las Cuestiones Sociales — RCCS
Revista CENIC [*Centro Nacional de Investigaciones Cientificas*]. **Ciencias Biologicas** — Rev CENIC Cienc Biol
Revista CENIC [*Centro Nacional de Investigaciones Cientificas*]. **Ciencias Fisicas** [*Cuba*] — RCCFB
Revista CENIC [*Centro Nacional de Investigaciones Cientificas*]. **Ciencias Fisicas** [*Cuba*] — Rev CENIC Cienc Fis
Revista. Centro Academico Sarmento Leite — Rev Cent Acad Sarmento Leite
Revista. Centro Cientifico Luis Pasteur — Rev Cent Cient Luis Pasteur
Revista. Centro de Ciencias Biomedicas. Universidade Federal de Santa Maria — Rev Cent Cienc Biomed Univ Fed Santa Maria
Revista. Centro de Ciencias da Saude — Rev Cent Cienc Saude
Revista. Centro de Ciencias da Saude. Universidade Federal de Santa Maria — Rev Cent Cienc Saude Univ Fed St Maria
Revista. Centro de Ciencias Rurais — Rev Cent Cienc Rurais
Revista. Centro de Ciencias Rurais. Universidade Federal de Santa Maria — Rev Cent Cienc Rurais Univ Fed St Maria
Revista. Centro de Cultura Scientifica (Pelotas, Brazil) — Rev Cent Cult Sci (Pelotas Braz)
Revista. Centro de Estudiantes de Agronomia y Veterinaria. Universidad de Buenos Aires — Rev Centro Estud Agronom y Vet Univ Buenos Aires
Revista. Centro de Estudiantes de Medicina Veterinaria — Rev Centr Estud Med Vet
Revista. Centro de Estudiantes del Doctorado en Ciencias Naturales — Revista Centro Estud Doct Ci Nat
Revista. Centro de Estudios Educativos — Rev Cent Ed
Revista. Centro de Estudios Extemoenos — RCEE
Revista. Centro de Estudos Historico-Militares del Peru — R Centro Est Hist Milit
Revista. Centro de Estudos de Cabo Verde. Serie de Ciencias Biologicas — Rev Cent Estud Cabo Verde Ser Cienc Biol
Revista. Centro de Ingenieros. Provincia de Buenos Aires — Rev Cent Ing Prov Buenos Aires
Revista. Centro Nacional de Patologia Animal — Rev Cent Nac Patol Anim
Revista Centroamericana de Economia — R Centroam Econ
Revista Centroamericana de Economia. Universidad Nacional Autonoma de Honduras. Programa de Postgrado Centroamericano en Economia y Planificacion — UNAH/RCE
Revista Centroamericana de Nutricion y Ciencias de Alimentos — Rev Centroam Nutr Cienc Aliment
Revista Ceres — Rev Ceres
Revista Chapingo — Rev Chapingo
Revista Chicano-Riquena — RC-R
Revista Chicano-Riquena — Rev Chicano-Riquena
Revista Chilena de Anestesia — Rev Chil Anest
Revista Chilena de Derecho — RCD
Revista Chilena de Educacion Fisica. Instituto de Educacion Fisica y Tenica. Universidad de Chile (Santiago) — Rev Chil Educ Fisic Santiago
Revista Chilena de Entomologia — Rev Chil Entomol
Revista Chilena de Entomologia — Revta Chil Ent
Revista Chilena de Higiene y Medicina Preventiva — Rev Chil Hig Med Prev
Revista Chilena de Historia Natural — Rev Chil Hist Nat
Revista Chilena de Historia Natural — Revista Chilena Hist Nat
Revista Chilena de Historia y Geografia — R Chil Hist Geogr
Revista Chilena de Historia y Geografia — R Chile Hist Geogr
Revista Chilena de Historia y Geografia — R Chilena De Hist Y Geog
Revista Chilena de Historia y Geografia — RCHG
Revista Chilena de Historia y Geografia. Sociedad Chilena de Historia y Geografia [*Santiago*] — SCHG/R
Revista Chilena de Historia y Geografia. Sociedad Chilena de Historia y Geografia (Santiago) — Rev Chil Hist Geogr Santiago
Revista Chilena de Ingenieria — RCINA
Revista Chilena de Ingenieria — Rev Chil Ing
Revista Chilena de Ingenieria — Rev Chilena Ing
Revista Chilena de Literatura — RChL
Revista Chilena de Literatura — RCL
Revista Chilena de Obstetricia y Ginecologia — RCOBA
Revista Chilena de Obstetricia y Ginecologia — Rev Chil Obstet Ginecol
Revista Chilena de Ortopedia y Traumatologia — Rev Chil Ortop Traum
Revista Chilena de Pediatria — RCPEA
Revista Chilena de Pediatria — Rev Chil Pediatr
Revista Chilena de Tecnologia Medica — Rev Chil Tecnol Med
Revista Chilena de Urologia — Rev Chil Urol
Revista Cientifica. CASL [*Centro Academico Sarmento Leite*] — Rev Cient CASL
Revista Cientifica. Centro de Investigaciones Cientificas — Rev Cient Cent Invest Cient
Revista Cientifica de Investigaciones del Museo de Historia Natural de San Rafael (Mendoza) — Rev Cient Invest Mus Hist Nat San Rafael (Mendoza)
Revista Cientifica/Instituto Cientifico Argentina (Buenos Aires) — Revista Ci Buenos Aires
Revista Cientifica. Universidad Autonoma Tomas Frias — Rev Cient Univ Auton Tomas Frias
Revista Cientifica. Universidad Boliviana Tomas Frias — Rev Cient Univ Boliv Tomas Frias
Revista Cientifica y Literaria de Mexico — Revista Ci Lit Mexico
Revista. Circulo Argentino de Odontologia — Rev Circ Argent Odontol
Revista. Circulo de Engenharia Militar [*Brazil*] — Rev Circ Eng Mil
Revista. Circulo Odontologico del Sur — Rev Circ Odontol Sur
Revista Citobiologica — Rev Citobiol
Revista Civilizacao Brasileira [*Rio De Janeiro*] — RCivB
Revista Clasica — Rev Clasica
Revista Clinica — Rev Clin
Revista Clinica de Sao Paulo — Rev Clin Sao Paulo
Revista Clinica Espanola [*Spain*] — Rev Clin Esp
Revista Clinica Espanola. Europa Medica — Rev Clin Esp Eur Med
Revista Clinica. Instituto Maternal (Lisbon) — Rev Clin Inst Matern (Lisb)
Revista. Colegio de Abogados de Buenos Aires — RCABA
Revista. Colegio de Abogados de Puerto Rico — RCA
Revista. Colegio de Abogados de Puerto Rico — Rev C Abo PR
Revista. Colegio de Abogados del Distrito Federal (Caracas) — Rev Col Abogad Caracas
Revista. Colegio de Abogados Francisco Echeverria Garcia (San Jose, Costa Rica) — Rev Col Abogad S Jose
Revista. Colegio de Abogados (La Habana) — Rev Col Abogad Hav
Revista. Colegio de Abogados (Rosario, Argentina) — Rev Col Abogad Rosario
Revista. Colegio de Boyaca (Tunja, Colombia) — Rev Col Boyaca Tunja
Revista. Colegio de Ingenieros de Venezuela — Rev Col Ing Venez
Revista. Colegio de Ingenieros de Venezuela (Caracas) — Rev Col Ing Caracas
Revista. Colegio de Quimicos de Puerto Rico — Rev Col Quim PR
Revista. Colegio de Quimicos e Ingenieros Quimicos de Costa Rica — Rev Col Quim Ing Quim Costa Rica
Revista. Colegio Estomatologico de Guatemala — Rev Col Estomatol Guatem
Revista. Colegio Mayor de Nuestra Senora del Rosario (Bogota) — Rev Col Mayor Nues Sra Rosario Bogota
Revista. Colegio Medico de Guatemala — Rev Col Med Guatem
Revista. Colegio Nacional de Enfermeras — Rev Col Nac Enferm
Revista. Colegio Nacional Vicente Rocafuerte (Guayaquil) — Rev Col Nac V Rocafuerte Guayaquil
Revista Colombiana de Antropologia — RCA
Revista Colombiana de Antropologia — RCDA
Revista Colombiana de Antropologia (Bogota) — Rev Col Antrop Bogota
Revista Colombiana de Ciencias Quimico-Farmaceuticas — RCQFAQ
Revista Colombiana de Ciencias Quimico-Farmaceuticas — Rev Colomb Cienc Quimico-Farm
Revista Colombiana de Entomologia — RCENDR
Revista Colombiana de Entomologia — Rev Colomb Entomol

Revista Colombiana de Fisica — Rev Colomb Fis
Revista Colombiana de Folclor — RCF
Revista Colombiana de Folclor — Revista CF
Revista Colombiana de Folklore (Bogota) — Rev Col Folk Bogota
Revista Colombiana de Matematicas — Rev Colombiana Mat
Revista Colombiana de Obstetricia y Ginecologia — Rev Colomb Obstet Ginecol
Revista Colombiana de Pediatria y Puericultura — Rev Colomb Pediatr Pueric
Revista Colombiana de Quimica — Rev Colomb Quim
Revista Colombiana Estadistica — Rev Colombiana Estadist
Revista Columbiana de Ciencias Quimico-Farmaceuticas — Rev Columb Cienc Quim Farm
Revista COMALFI [*Sociedad Colombiana de Control de Malezas y Fisiologia Vegetal*] — Rev COMALFI
Revista. Confederacion Medica Panamericana — Rev Confed Med Panam
Revista. Consejo de Rectores. Universidades Chilenas — RCRUA
Revista. Consejo de Rectores. Universidades Chilenas — Rev Cons Rectores Univ Chilenas
Revista Conservadora del Pensamiento Centroamericano (Managua) — Rev Conserv Pens Centroam Managua
Revista. Consorcio de Centros Agricolas de Manabi — Rev Consor Cent Agr Manabi
Revista Constructiilor si a Materialelor de Constructii — Rev Constr Mater Constr
Revista Contemporanea — RC
Revista Costarricense de Ciencias Medicas — RCCMEF
Revista Costarricense de Ciencias Medicas — Rev Costarric Cienc Med
Revista. CREA (Asociacion Argentina de Consorcios Regionales de Experimentacion Agricola) — Rev CREA (Asoc Argent Consorcios Reg Exp Agric)
Revista Cristiana — Rev Cr
Revista Critica de Derecho Inmobiliario Moderno — RCDIM
Revista Critica de Historia y Literatura Espanolas — RHLE
Revista Cubana — RC
Revista Cubana — RCub
Revista Cubana — Rev Cubana
Revista Cubana — RevC
Revista Cubana — RevCu
Revista Cubana de Cardiologia — Rev Cubana Cardiol
Revista Cubana de Ciencia Agricola — Rev Cubana Cienc Agric
Revista Cubana de Ciencia Avicola — Rev Cubana Cienc Avic
Revista Cubana de Ciencias Veterinarias — Rev Cub Cienc Vet
Revista Cubana de Ciencias Veterinarias — Rev Cubana Cienc Vet
Revista Cubana de Cirugia — Rev Cubana Cir
Revista Cubana de Derecho — Rev Cubana Der
Revista Cubana de Enfermeria — Rev Cubana Enferm
Revista Cubana de Estomatologia — Rev Cubana Estomatol
Revista Cubana de Farmacia — Rev Cubana Farm
Revista Cubana de Filosofia — RCF
Revista Cubana de Fisica — RECFD
Revista Cubana de Fisica — Rev Cubana Fis
Revista Cubana de Higiene y Epidemiologia — Rev Cuba Hig Epidemiol
Revista Cubana de Higiene y Epidemiologia — Rev Cubana Hig Epidemiol
Revista Cubana de Investigaciones Biomedicas — Rev Cubana Invest Biomed
Revista Cubana de Investigaciones Pesqueras — RCIPDJ
Revista Cubana de Investigaciones Pesqueras — Rev Cubana Invest Pesq
Revista Cubana de Laboratorio Clinico — Rev Cubana Lab Clin
Revista Cubana de Medicina — Rev Cubana Med
Revista Cubana de Medicina Tropical — Rev Cubana Med Trop
Revista Cubana de Obstetricia y Ginecologia — RCOGB
Revista Cubana de Oftalmologia — Rev Cubana Oftal
Revista Cubana de Pediatria — Rev Cubana Pediatr
Revista Cubana de Quimica — Rev Cubana Quim
Revista Cubana de Reproduccion Animal — RCRADJ
Revista Cubana de Reproduccion Animal — Rev Cubana Reprod Anim
Revista da Academia Brasileira de Letras (Rio de Janeiro) — Rev Acad Bras Letr Rio
Revista da Academia de Letras da Bahia (Salvador, Brazil) — Rev Acad Letr Bahia Salvador
Revista da Academia Paulista de Letras (Sao Paulo) — Rev Acad Paulista Letr S Paulo
Revista da AMB (Associacao Medica Brasiliera) — Rev AMB
Revista da AMMG (Associacao Medica de Minas Gerais) — Rev AMMG
Revista da Escola de Belas Artes de Pernambuco (Recife, Brazil) — Rev Escola Belas Art Pernam Recife
Revista da Faculdade de Agronomia e Veterinaria da Universidade do Rio Grande do Sul — Revista Fac Agron Univ Rio Grande Do Sul
Revista da Faculdade de Ciencias — RFC
Revista da Faculdade de Ciencias, Universidade de Lisboa. Ser. 2. C. Ciencias Naturais — Revista Fac Ci Univ Lisboa Ser 2 C Ci Nat
Revista da Faculdade de Direito. Universidade de Sao Paulo — Rev Fac Direit S Paulo
Revista da Flora Medicinal — Rev Flora Med
Revista da Fundacao Servicos de Saude Publica (Brazil) — Rev Fund Serv Saude Publica (Braz)
Revista da Imagem — REIMD
Revista da Imagem — Rev Imagem
Revista da Madeira (Sao Paulo) — Rev Madeira (Sao Paulo)
Revista da Universidade Catolica de Sao Paulo — Rev Univ Cato S Paulo
Revista das Academias de Letras (Rio de Janeiro) — Rev Acad Letr Rio
Revista de Academia de Ciencias Exactas, Fisico-Quimicas y Naturales de Zaragoza — Revista Acad Ci Exact Zaragoza
Revista de Actualidad Estomatologica Espanola — Rev Actual Estomatol Esp
Revista de Administracao de Empresas — R Adm Empresas
Revista de Administracao de Empresas — R Admin Empresas
Revista de Administracao Municipal (Rio De Janeiro) — R Adm Municip (Rio De Janeiro)
Revista de Administracao Municipal. Rio de Janeiro — Rev Admin Munici Rio
Revista de Administracao Publica (Rio De Janeiro) — R Adm Publ (Rio De Janeiro)
Revista de Administracao. Universidade de Sao Paulo — Rev Admin S Paulo
Revista de Administracion Publica — R Admin Publica
Revista de Administracion Publica — RAP
Revista de Administracion Publica. Instituto de la Superintendencia de Administracion Publica (Buenos Aires) — Rev Admin Publ BA
Revista de Administracion Publica (Madrid) — R Adm Publ (Madrid)
Revista de Administracion Publica (Madrid) — Rev Admin Publ Madrid
Revista de Administracion Publica (Mexico) — Rev Admin Publ Mex
Revista de Aeronautica — Rev Aeronaut
Revista de Agricultura [*Brazil*] — Rev Agri
Revista de Agricultura — Rev Agricultura
Revista de Agricultura (Ciudad Trujillo) — Rev Agric (Ciudad Trujillo)
Revista de Agricultura (Cuba) — R Ag (Cuba)
Revista de Agricultura (Cuba) — R de Ag (Cuba)
Revista de Agricultura Cubana — Revista Agric Cub
Revista de Agricultura de Puerto Rico — Revista Agric Puerto Rico
Revista de Agricultura (Habana) — Revta Agric (Habana)
Revista de Agricultura (Havana) — Rev Agric (Havana)
Revista de Agricultura. Industria y Comercio de Puerto Rico — Rev Agric Ind Comer PR
Revista de Agricultura (Piracicaba) — Rev Agr (Piracicaba)
Revista de Agricultura (Piracicaba) — Rev Agric (Piracicaba)
Revista de Agricultura (Piracicaba) — Revista Agric Piracicaba
Revista de Agricultura (Piracicaba) — Revta Agric (Piracicaba)
Revista de Agricultura (Piracicaba) (Estado de Sao Paulo) — Rev Agric (Piracicaba) (S Paulo)
Revista de Agricultura (Puerto Rico) — Rev Agric (PR)
Revista de Agricultura (Recife) — Rev Agric (Recife)
Revista de Agricultura (Santiago) — Revista Agric Santiago
Revista de Agricultura (Santo Domingo) — Rev Agric St Domingo
Revista de Agricultura (Sao Paulo) — Rev Agric (Sao Paulo)
Revista de Agricultura Tropical/Review of Tropical Agriculture (Mexico City) — Revista Agric Trop Mexico City
Revista de Agricultura/Universidad Autonoma Simon Bolivar. Escuela Superior de Agronomia (Cochabamba) — Revista Agric Cochabamba
Revista de Agricultura y Comercio/Panama. Ministerio de Agricultura y Comercio — Revista Agric Comercio Panama
Revista de Agricultura y Ganaderia (Buenos Aires) — Revista Agric Ganad Buenos Aires
Revista de Agricultura y Ganaderia. Departamento de Agricultura (La Habana) — Rev Agr Ganad Hav
Revista de Agricultura y Ganaderia Nicaraguense/Liberia Moderna — Revista Agric Ganad Nicarag
Revista de Agricultura y Ganaderia/Paraguay. Ministerio de Agricultura — Revista Agric Ganad Asuncion Minist Agric
Revista de Agroquimica y Tecnologia de Alimentos — Rev Agroquim Tecnol Aliment
Revista de Agroquimica y Tecnologia de Alimentos/Instituto de Quimica — Revista Agroquim Tecnol Aliment
Revista de America — RdAm
Revista de America — RevAm
Revista de Analiza Numerica si Teoria Aproximatiei — Rev Anal Numer Teoria Aproximatiei
Revista de Antropologia [*Sao Paulo*] — RA
Revista de Antropologia. Casa de la Cultura Ecuatoriana, Nucleo del Azuay [*Cuenca*] — CCE/RA
Revista de Antropologia (Sao Paulo) — R Antropol (Sao Paulo)
Revista de Antropologia (Sao Paulo) — Rev Antropol (Sao Paulo)
Revista de Antropologia. Universidad de Sao Paulo. Faculdade de Filosofia, Letras, e Ciencias Humanas e Associacao de Antropologia — USP/RA
Revista de Antropologia. Universidade de Sao Paulo — Rev Antrop S Paulo
Revista de Archivos, Bibliotecas, y Museos — R Arch Bibl Mus
Revista de Archivos, Bibliotecas, y Museos — RABM
Revista de Archivos, Bibliotecas, y Museos — Rev Arch Bibl Mus
Revista de Archivos, Bibliotecas, y Museos — RevA
Revista de Archivos, Bibliotecas, y Museos — Revista ABM
Revista de Arqueologia — RArq
Revista de Arqueologia — RArqueol
Revista de Arqueologia y Etnologia. Junta Nacional de Arqueologia (La Habana) — Rev Arqueol Etnol Hav
Revista de Atualidade Indigena — Rev Atual Indig
Revista de Automatica — Rev Autom
Revista de Bellas Artes — RBA
Revista de Bibliografia Nacional [*Madrid*] — RBN
Revista de Bibliografia Nacional [*Madrid*] — RevBN
Revista de Biblioteconomia de Brasilia — R Biblio Brasilia
Revista de Biblioteconomia de Brasilia — RBBRD
Revista de Biologia — Revta Biol
Revista de Biologia del Uruguay — Rev Biol Urug
Revista de Biologia Forestal y Limnologia — Rev Biol For Limnol
Revista de Biologia (Lisbon) — Rev Biol (Lisb)
Revista de Biologia (Lisbon) — Rev Biol Lisbon
Revista de Biologia Marina — Rev Biol Mar
Revista de Biologia Oral — Rev Biol Oral
Revista de Biologia Tropical — Rev Biol Trop
Revista de Biologia Tropical — Revta Biol Trop
Revista de Biologia Tropical/Universidad Nacional — Revista Biol Trop
Revista de Biologia. Universidad de Oviedo — Rev Biol Univ Oviedo
Revista de Biologia y Medicina Nuclear — Rev Biol Med Nucl
Revista de Caballeria — Revista Caball

Revista de Catalunya — RCat
Revista de Chimica e Pharmacia Militar — Rev Chim Pharm Mil
Revista de Chimica Industrial — Rev Chim Ind
Revista de Chimie — Rev Chim
Revista de Chimie (Bucharest) — Rev Chim (Bucharest)
Revista de Chimie (Bucharest). Supliment — Rev Chim Bucharest Supl
Revista de Chirurgie, Oncologie, ORL, Radiologie, Oftalmologie, Stomatologie. Seria Stomatologie — RCOSDO
Revista de Chirurgie, Oncologie, Radiologie, ORL, Oftalmologie, Stomatologie [*A publication*] — Rev Chir Oncol Radiol ORL Oftalmol Stomatol
Revista de Chirurgie, Oncologie, Radiologie, ORL, Oftalmologie, Stomatologie. Oncologia — Rev Chir Oncol Radiol ORL Oftalmol Stomatol Oncol
Revista de Chirurgie, Oncologie, Radiologie, ORL, Oftalmologie, Stomatologie. Radiologia — Rev Chir Oncol Radiol ORL Oftalmol Stomatol Radiol
Revista de Chirurgie, Oncologie, Radiologie, ORL, Oftalmologie, Stomatologie. Seria Chirurgie — Rev Chir Oncol Radiol ORL Oftalmol Stomatol Ser Chir
Revista de Chirurgie, Oncologie, Radiologie, ORL, Oftalmologie, Stomatologie. Seria Oncologie — Rev Chir Oncol Radiol ORL Oftalmol Stomatol Ser Oncol
Revista de Chirurgie, Oncologie, Radiologie, ORL, Oftalmologie, Stomatologie. Seria Radiologie — Rev Chir Oncol Radiol ORL Oftalmol Stomatol Ser Radiol
Revista de Chirurgie, Oncologie, Radiologie, ORL, Oftalmologie, Stomatologie. Seria Stomatologie — Rev Chir Oncol Radiol ORL Oftalmol Stomatol Ser Stomatol
Revista de Chirurgie. Stomatologie — Rev Chir
Revista de Ciencia Aplicada — RCAPA
Revista de Ciencia Aplicada — Rev Cienc Apl
Revista de Ciencia de la Educacion — RCE
Revista de Ciencia Politica — R Cienc Polit
Revista de Ciencia Politica — R Ciencia Pol
Revista de Ciencia Politica — RCP
Revista de Ciencias [*Lima*] — Rev Cienc
Revista de Ciencias Agrarias — RCAPDD
Revista de Ciencias Agrarias — Rev Cienc Agrar
Revista de Ciencias Agronomicas — Rev Cienc Agron
Revista de Ciencias Agronomicas. Serie A — Rev Cienc Agron Ser A
Revista de Ciencias Agronomicas. Serie B — Rev Cienc Agron Ser B
Revista de Ciencias Aplicadas (Madrid) — Rev Cienc Apl (Madrid)
Revista de Ciencias Biologicas [*Belem*] — RCIBDB
Revista de Ciencias Biologicas — Rev Ci Biol
Revista de Ciencias Biologicas — Rev Cienc Biol
Revista de Ciencias Biologicas (Belem) — Rev Cienc Biol (Belem)
Revista de Ciencias Biologicas (Havana) — Rev Cienc Biol (Havana)
Revista de Ciencias Biologicas. Serie A (Lourenco Marques) — Rev Cienc Biol Ser A (Lourenco Marques)
Revista de Ciencias Biologicas. Serie B — Rev Cienc Biol Ser B
Revista de Ciencias Biologicas. Serie B (Lourenco Marques) — Rev Cienc Biol Ser B (Lourenco Marques)
Revista de Ciencias Biomedicas — Rev Cienc Biomed
Revista de Ciencias Economicas — R Cienc Ec
Revista de Ciencias Economicas — R Ciencias Econs
Revista de Ciencias Economicas — Rev Cien Econ
Revista de Ciencias Economicas (Buenos Aires) — Rev Cien Econ BA
Revista de Ciencias Farmaceuticas — RCIFDN
Revista de Ciencias Farmaceuticas — Rev Cienc Farm
Revista de Ciencias Farmaceuticas (Araraquara, Brazil) — Rev Cienc Farm (Araraquara Braz)
Revista de Ciencias Farmaceuticas (Sao Paulo) — Rev Cienc Farm Sao Paulo
Revista de Ciencias i Letras — Revista Ci Letras
Revista de Ciencias Juridicas — R Ciencias Juridicas
Revista de Ciencias Juridicas — RCJ
Revista de Ciencias Juridicas (San Jose, Costa Rica) — Rev Cien Jur S Jose
Revista de Ciencias Juridicas y Sociales — RCJS
Revista de Ciencias Juridicas y Sociales (Santa Fe, Argentina) — Rev Cien Jur Soc Sante Fe
Revista de Ciencias Juridico-Sociales (San Jose, Costa Rica) — Rev Cien Jur Soc S Jose
Revista de Ciencias (Lima) — Rev Ci (Lima)
Revista de Ciencias (Lima) — Rev Cien Lima
Revista de Ciencias Matematicas. Universidade de Lourenco Marques — Rev Ci Mat Univ Lourenco Marques
Revista de Ciencias Matematicas. Universidade de Lourenco Marques — Rev Cienc Mat Univ Lourenco Marques
Revista de Ciencias Matematicas. Universidade de Lourenco Marques. Serie A — Rev Ci Mat Univ Lourenco Marques Ser A
Revista de Ciencias Medicas (Havana) — Rev Cienc Med (Havana)
Revista de Ciencias Medicas. Serie A (Lourenco Marques) — Rev Cienc Med (Lourenco Marques)
Revista de Ciencias Medicas. Serie A (Lourenco Marques) — Rev Cienc Med Ser A (Lourenco Marques)
Revista de Ciencias Medicas. Serie B (Lourenco Marques) — Rev Cienc Med Ser B (Lourenco Marques)
Revista de Ciencias Penales (Santiago) — Rev Cien Penal Santiago
Revista de Ciencias Psicologicas y Neurologicas (Lima) — Rev Cienc Psicol Neurol (Lima)
Revista de Ciencias Quimicas — RCQUD
Revista de Ciencias Quimicas — Rev Cienc Quim
Revista de Ciencias Sociales — PCS
Revista de Ciencias Sociales — RCS
Revista de Ciencias Sociales — RDCS
Revista de Ciencias Sociales — Revta Cienc Social
Revista de Ciencias Sociales (Ceara) — R Cienc Soc (Ceara)
Revista de Ciencias Sociales (Costa Rica) — R Ciencias Socs (Costa Rica)
Revista de Ciencias Sociales (Fortaleza) — R Cienc Soc Fortaleza
Revista de Ciencias Sociales (Puerto Rico) — R Cienc Soc (Puerto Rico)
Revista de Ciencias Sociales (Puerto Rico) — R Ciencias Socs (Puerto Rico)
Revista de Ciencias Sociales (Rio Piedras) — Rev Cien Soc Rio Piedras
Revista de Ciencias Sociales. Universidad de Costa Rica — UCR/RCS
Revista de Ciencias Sociales. Universidad de Puerto Rico. Colegio de Ciencias Sociales — UPR/RCS
Revista de Ciencias. Universidad de Oviedo — Rev Cienc Univ Oviedo
Revista de Ciencias. Universidad Nacional Mayor de San Marcos — Rev Cienc Univ Nac Mayor San Marcos
Revista de Ciencias Veterinarias — Rev Cien Vet
Revista de Ciencias Veterinarias — Rev Cienc Vet
Revista de Ciencias Veterinarias (Lisbon) — Rev Cienc Vet Lisbon
Revista de Cirugia — Rev Cir
Revista de Cirugia — Rev Cirug
Revista de Cirugia del Uruguay — Rev Cir Urug
Revista de Cirugia (Mexico) — Rev Cir (Mex)
Revista de Clinica Medica — Rev Clin Med
Revista de Comunicaciones (Buenos Aires) — Rev Comunic BA
Revista de Coroziune [*Romania*] — Rev Coroz
Revista de Coroziune — RVCZA
Revista de Correos y Telegrafos (Buenos Aires) — Rev Correos Telegr BA
Revista de Corrosao e Proteccao de Materiais — Rev Corros Prot Mater
Revista de Cresterea Animalelor — Rev Cresterea Anim
Revista de Critica Literaria Latinoamericana — RCLL
Revista de Critica Literaria Latinoamericana — Rev Crit L
Revista de Cuba — RdC
Revista de Cultura Biblica [*Rio De Janeiro/Sao Paulo, Brazil*] — RCB
Revista de Cultura Biblica [*Rio De Janeiro/Sao Paulo, Brazil*] — RCuBib
Revista de Cultura Brasilena — RCB
Revista de Cultura Brasilena — Rev Cult Bras
Revista de Cultura (Rio de Janeiro) — Rev Cult Rio
Revista de Cultura Teologica — RCT
Revista de Cultura Teologica [*Sao Paulo, Brazil*] — RCuTeol
Revista de Derecho (Concepcion) — R Der (Concepcion)
Revista de Derecho de Costa Rica — RDCR
Revista de Derecho Espanol y Americano — RDEA
Revista de Derecho Espanol y Americano (Madrid) — Rev Der Espanol Am Madrid
Revista de Derecho Financiero y de Hacienda Publica — R Derecho Financiero Hacienda Pbl
Revista de Derecho Inmobiliario (Madrid) — RDIM
Revista de Derecho Internacional (La Habana) — Rev Der Intern Hav
Revista de Derecho Internacional y Ciencias Diplomaticas — R Der Int Cienc Diplom
Revista de Derecho Internacional y Ciencias Diplomaticas — RDICP
Revista de Derecho Internacional y Ciencias Diplomaticas — Rev de Derecho Internac y Cienc Diplom
Revista de Derecho Internacional y Ciencias Diplomaticas (Rosario, Argentina) — Rev Der Intern Cien Diplom Rosario
Revista de Derecho (La Paz, Bolivia) — Rev Der La Paz
Revista de Derecho Mercantil — R Derecho Mercantil
Revista de Derecho (Montevideo) — Rev Der Juris Admin Monte
Revista de Derecho Penal (Buenos Aires) — Rev Der Penal BA
Revista de Derecho Privado — R Derecho Privado
Revista de Derecho Publico. Universidad de Chile. Escuela de Derecho — Rev de Derecho Publ
Revista de Derecho Puertorriqueno — PCI
Revista de Derecho Puertorriqueno — RDP
Revista de Derecho Puertorriqueno — Rev D P
Revista de Derecho Puertorriqueno — Rev DPR
Revista de Derecho Puertorriqueno — Rev PR
Revista de Derecho (Quito) — Rev Der Quito
Revista de Derecho Social Ecuatoriano (Quito) — Rev Der Soc Ecuat Quito
Revista de Derecho y Ciencias Politicas — RDCP
Revista de Derecho y Ciencias Politicas — RevD
Revista de Derecho y Ciencias Politicas (Lima) — Rev Der Cien Pol Lima
Revista de Derecho y Ciencias Politicas. Organo de la Facultad de Derecho. Universidad Nacional Mayor de San Marcos — Rev de Derecho y Cienc Polit
Revista de Derecho y Ciencias Politicas. Universidad de San Marcos — R Der Cienc Polit
Revista de Derecho y Ciencias Sociales (Quito) — Rev Der Cien Soc Quito
Revista de Derecho y Legislacion (Caracas) — Rev Der Legis Caracas
Revista de Derechos Humanos — R Derechos Humanos
Revista de Diagnostico Biologico — Rev Diagn Biol
Revista de Dialectologia y Tradiciones Populares — R Dialect & Tradic Popul
Revista de Dialectologia y Tradiciones Populares — RD
Revista de Dialectologia y Tradiciones Populares — RDPT
Revista de Dialectologia y Tradiciones Populares — RDTP
Revista de Dialectologia y Tradiciones Populares — RDyTP
Revista de Dialectologia y Tradiciones Populares CSIC (Consejo Superior de Investigaciones Cientificas) — R Dialectol Trad Popul
Revista de Direito Administrativo — R Dir Adm
Revista de Direito Administrativo (Coimbra) — Rev de Direito Adm (Coimbra)
Revista de Direito Administrativo (Rio De Janeiro) — Rev de Direito Adm (Rio De Janeiro)
Revista de Direito Publico e Ciencia Politica (Rio de Janeiro) — Rev Direit Publ Cien Pol Rio
Revista de Economia. Banco de la Provincia de Cordoba — BPC/RE
Revista de Economia Continental (Mexico) — Rev Econ Cont Mex
Revista de Economia (Cordoba) — R Econ (Cordoba)
Revista de Economia (Cordoba) — Rev Econ Cordoba
Revista de Economia de El Salvador — Rev Econ S Salvador
Revista de Economia Latinoamericana — R Econ Latinoam
Revista de Economia Latinoamericana — R Econ Latinoamer
Revista de Economia Latinoamericana (Caracas) — Rev Econ Latinoam Caracas
Revista de Economia (Mexico) — Rev Econ Mex
Revista de Economia Politica (Madrid) — R Econ Pol (Madrid)

Revista de Economia Politica (Madrid) — R Econ Polit (Madrid)
Revista de Economia Politica (Sao Paulo) — R Econ Pol (Sao Paulo)
Revista de Economia y Estadistica — R Econ Estadist
Revista de Economia y Estadistica — R Econ y Estadistica
Revista de Economia y Estadistica — REE
Revista de Economia y Estadistica (Cordoba, Argentina) — Rev Econ Estad Cordoba
Revista de Economia y Estadistica. Universidad Nacional de Cordoba. Facultad de Ciencias Economicas — UNC/REE
Revista de Educacao (Rio de Janeiro) — Rev Educ Publ Rio
Revista de Educacion — Rev Ed
Revista de Educacion — RevE
Revista de Educacion (Asuncion) — Rev Educ Asuncion
Revista de Educacion (Ciudad Trujillo, Santo Domingo) — Rev Educ C Trujillo S Domingo
Revista de Educacion (Guatemala) — RevEG
Revista de Educacion (La Plata, Argentina) — Rev Educ La Plata
Revista de Educacion (Madrid) — R Educ (Madrid)
Revista de Educacion (Madrid) — REM
Revista de Educacion. Ministerio de Educacion Nacional. Desde Marzo-Abril de 1952 Sustituye a la Revista Nacional de Educacion — R Educacion
Revista de Educacion (Santiago) — Rev Educ Santiago
Revista de Energia Atomica — Rev Energ At
Revista de Enfermagem (Lisboa) — Rev Enferm (Lisboa)
Revista de Engenharia do Estado da Guanabara (Rio de Janeiro) — Rev Engen Rio
Revista de Engenharia Mackenzie — Rev Eng Mackenzie
Revista de Entomologia de Mocambique — Rev Entomol Mocambique
Revista de Entomologia de Mocambique. Suplemento — Rev Entomol Mocambique Supl
Revista de Entomologia (Rio De Janeiro) — Rev Entomol (Rio De J)
Revista de Entomologia (Rio De Janeiro) — Revta Ent (Rio De J)
Revista de Espana — REsp
Revista de Especialidades — Rev Espec
Revista de Espiritualidad — RDE
Revista de Espiritualidad — REspir
Revista de Estadistica y Geografia — Rev Estad Geogr
Revista de Estudios Agro Sociales — REAS
Revista de Estudios Agro-Sociales — R Estud Agro-Soc
Revista de Estudios Agro-Sociales. Instituto de Estudios Agro-Sociales — IEAS/R
Revista de Estudios Agro-Sociales. Instituto de Estudios Agro-Sociales. Ministerio de Agricultura — R Est Agrosociales
Revista de Estudios Clasicos — REC
Revista de Estudios de la Vida Local — R Est Vida Local
Revista de Estudios de la Vida Local — R Estud Vida Loc
Revista de Estudios de la Vida Local — R Estud Vida Local
Revista de Estudios de Teatro (Buenos Aires) — Rev Estud Teatro BA
Revista de Estudios Extremenos — REE
Revista de Estudios Extremenos — Rev Estud Extremenos
Revista de Estudios Extremenos. Publicacion. Institucion de Servicios Culturales de la Diputacion Provincial de Badajoz — R Est Extremenos
Revista de Estudios Extremenos. Revista Historica, Literaria, y Artistica — Rev de Est Extremenos
Revista de Estudios Franceses (Madrid) — REFM
Revista de Estudios Franciscanos — REF
Revista de Estudios Hispanicos — REH
Revista de Estudios Hispanicos — Rev Est His
Revista de Estudios Hispanicos (Rio Piedras, Puerto Rico) — REH-PR
Revista de Estudios Historico-Juridicos — REHJ
Revista de Estudios Internacionales — RDEH
Revista de Estudios Juridicos, Politicos, y Sociales (Sucre, Bolivia) — Rev Estud Jur Pol Soc Sucre
Revista de Estudios Musicales. Departamento de Musicologia. Universidad Nacional de Cuyo — REMC
Revista de Estudios Musicales (Mendoza, Argentina) — Rev Estud Music Mendoza
Revista de Estudios Penales. Universidad de Valladolid — R Est Penales
Revista de Estudios Penitenciarios — R Estud Penitenciarios
Revista de Estudios Politicos — R Estud Pol
Revista de Estudios Politicos — R Estud Polit
Revista de Estudios Politicos — REP
Revista de Estudios Politicos — REPS
Revista de Estudios Politicos — Rev Pol
Revista de Estudios Politicos (Madrid) — Rev Estud Pol Madrid
Revista de Estudios Politicos. Suplemento de Politica Social — R Est Pol
Revista de Estudios Sindicales — R Estud Sindic
Revista de Estudios Sociales — R Estud Soc
Revista de Estudios Universitarios — REU
Revista de Estudios Yucatecos (Merida, Yucatan) — Rev Estud Yucat Merida
Revista de Estudos Gerais Universitarios de Mocambique. Serie 3. Ciencias Medicas — Rev Estud Gerais Univ Mocambique Ser 3 Cienc Med
Revista de Estudos Historicos. Boletim. Instituto de Estudos Historicos da Faculdade de Letras do Porto — REH
Revista de Estudos Livres [*Lisboa*] — REL
Revista de Etnografia — RdEt
Revista de Etnografie si Folclor — R Etnografie Folclor
Revista de Etnografie si Folclor — REF
Revista de Etnologia e de Glotologia — REG
Revista de Extension Agraria — Rev Exp Agrar
Revista de Farmacia e Bioquimica — Rev Farm Bioquim
Revista de Farmacia e Bioquimica (Belo Horizonte, Brazil) — Rev Farm Bioquim Belo Horizonte Braz
Revista de Farmacia e Bioquimica da Amazonia — Rev Farm Bioquim Amazonia
Revista de Farmacia e Bioquimica. Universidade de Sao Paulo — Rev Farm Bioquim Univ Sao Paulo
Revista de Farmacia e Bioquimica. Universidade de Sao Paulo (Brazil) — RFBUB
Revista de Farmacia e Odontologia — Rev Farm Odontol
Revista de Farmacia y Bioquimica (Lima) — Rev Farm Bioquim (Lima)
Revista de Farmacia y Quimica — Rev Farm Quim
Revista de Farmacologia Clinica y Experimental — Rev Farmacol Clin Exp
Revista de Filologia e Historia (Sao Paulo) — RFHSP
Revista de Filologia Espanola — R Filol Esp
Revista de Filologia Espanola — Revista Filol Esp
Revista de Filologia Espanola — RFE
Revista de Filologia Espanola. Anejos — RFEA
Revista de Filologia Espanola. CSIC (Consejo Superior de Investigaciones Cientificas) — R Filol Espan
Revista de Filologia Espanola. Publicaciones — RFEP
Revista de Filologia Hispanica — RFH
Revista de Filologia Portuguesa — RFP
Revista de Filologie — RF
Revista de Filologie (Cernauti) — RF (Cern)
Revista de Filologie Romanica si Germanica [*Bucarest*] — FRG
Revista de Filologie Romanica si Germanica [*Bucarest*] — RFRG
Revista de Filosofia — R Fil
Revista de Filosofia — RFi
Revista de Filosofia (Argentina) — Rev Filosof (Argentina)
Revista de Filosofia. Escuela Nacional Preparatoria (Mexico) — Rev Filos Mex
Revista de Filosofia (Espana) — RFE
Revista de Filosofia (Madrid) — RFM
Revista de Filosofia (Mexico) — Rev Filosof (Mexico)
Revista de Filosofia (Spain) — Rev Filosof (Spain)
Revista de Filosofia. Universidad de Costa Rica — Rev Filosof Costa Rica
Revista de Filosofia. Universidad de Costa Rica — RFCR
Revista de Filosofia. Universidad de Costa Rica — RFUCR
Revista de Filosofia. Universidad de Costa Rica (San Jose, Costa Rica) — Rev Filos S Jose
Revista de Filozofie — R Filoz
Revista de Filozofie — Rev Filoz
Revista de Filozofie — RF
Revista de Financas Publicas — R Fins Publicas
Revista de Financas Publicas (Rio de Janeiro) — Rev Finan Publ Rio
Revista de Fisica — Rev Fis
Revista de Fisica — RFISA
Revista de Fisica, Quimica, e Engenharia — Rev Fis Quim Eng
Revista de Fisica, Quimica, e Engenharia. Serie A — Rev Fis Quim Eng Ser A
Revista de Fizica si Chimie — Rev Fiz Chim
Revista de Fizica si Chimie. Seria A — Rev Fiz Chim Ser A
Revista de Fizica si Chimie. Seria B — Rev Fiz Chim Ser B
Revista de Fiziologie Normala si Patologica — Rev Fiziol Norm Patol
Revista de Folclor — RFolc
Revista de Folklore (Colombia) — RFC
Revista de Folklore. Organo de la Comision Nacional de Folklore (Colombia) — RFCC
Revista de Fomento (Caracas) — Rev Fomen Caracas
Revista de Fomento Social — R Fom Soc
Revista de Fomento Social — R Fomento Soc
Revista de Fomento/Venezuela. Ministerio del Fomento — Revista Fomento
Revista de Gastroenterologia de Mexico — Rev Gastroenterol Mex
Revista de Gastroenterologia del Peru — Rev Gastroenterol Peru
Revista de Geodesia (La Plata) — Rev Geodesia La Plata
Revista de Geofisica — Rev Geofis
Revista de Geografia — RDG
Revista de Geografia (Chile) — RGC
Revista de Geografic Commercial (Madrid) — RGCM
Revista de Geologia — Rev Geologia
Revista de Geologia y Minas. Ecuador. Direccion General de Geologia y Minas — Rev Geol Minas Ecuador Dir Gen Geol Minas
Revista de Gerona — Rev Ger
Revista de Ginecologia e d'Obstetricia — Rev Ginecol Obstet
Revista de Guatemala — RevG
Revista de Guatemala (Guatemala) — Rev Guat Guat
Revista de Guimaraes — R de G
Revista de Guimaraes — R de Guimaraes
Revista de Guimaraes — R Guimar
Revista de Guimaraes — R Guimaraes
Revista de Guimaraes — Rev Guim
Revista de Guimaraes — Rev Guimaraes
Revista de Guimaraes — Revista Guimaraes
Revista de Guimaraes — RG
Revista de Guimaraes — RGuim
Revista de Gynecologia e d'Obstetricia — Rev Gynecol Obstet
Revista de Hacienda — R Hacienda
Revista de Hacienda (Caracas) — Rev Hac Caracas
Revista de Hacienda (Lima) — Rev Hac Lima
Revista de Hacienda (Mexico) — Rev Hac Mex
Revista de Hidrocarburos y Minas — Rev Hidrocarburos Minas
Revista de Higiene y Medicina Escolares — Rev Hig Med Esc
Revista de Higiene y Sanidad Pecuarias — Rev Hig y San Pecuarias
Revista de Higiene y Sanidad Veterinaria (Madrid) — Rev Hig y San Vet (Madrid)
Revista de Historia — R Hist
Revista de Historia — RdH
Revista de Historia [*Lisbon*] — RevH
Revista de Historia [*Sao Paulo*] — RevHist
Revista de Historia — RH
Revista de Historia — RHCR

Revista de Historia Americana y Argentina (Mendoza, Argentina) — Rev Hist Am Arg
Revista de Historia (Buenos Aires) — Rev Hist BA
Revista de Historia Canaria — Rev Hist Canaria
Revista de Historia (Caracas) — Rev Hist Caracas
Revista de Historia de America — R Hist Am
Revista de Historia de America — R Hist America
Revista de Historia de America — Rev Hist Am
Revista de Historia de America — RevH
Revista de Historia de America — Revta Hist Am
Revista de Historia de America — RHA
Revista de Historia de America. Instituto Panamericano de Geografia e Historia. Comision de Historia — PAIGH/H
Revista de Historia de America (Mexico) — Rev Hist Am Mex
Revista de Historia de las Ideas. Instituto Panamericano de Geografia e Historia — IPGH/RHI
Revista de Historia de las Ideas (Quito) — Rev Hist Idea Quito
Revista de Historia de Puerto Rico — RHPR
Revista de Historia Economica — RHE
Revista de Historia. La Laguna de Tenerife — RevHL
Revista de Historia. La Laguna de Tenerife — RHL
Revista de Historia (Lisbon) — RevHL
Revista de Historia Literaria de Portugal — RHLP
Revista de Historia (Mendoza) — Rev Hist Mendoza
Revista de Historia Militar — Rev Hist Mil
Revista de Historia (Pasto, Colombia) — Rev Hist Pasto
Revista de Historia (San Juan, Argentina) — Rev Hist S Juan
Revista de Historia (Sao Paulo) — R Hist Sao Paulo
Revista de Historia (Sao Paulo) — Rev Hist S Paulo
Revista de Historia (Sao Paulo) — RevHS
Revista de Historia (Sao Paulo) — RHSP
Revista de Historia. Universidad de La Laguna — RHUL
Revista de Historia (Venezuela) — RHV
Revista de Horticultura si Viticultura [*Romania*] — Rev Hort Viticult
Revista de Horticultura si Viticultura — Rev Hortic Vitic
Revista de Horticultura si Viticultura — Revta Hort Vitic
Revista de Humanidades (Cordoba, Argentina) — Rev Human Cordoba
Revista de Ideas Esteticas — RdeIE
Revista de Ideas Esteticas — RevIE
Revista de Ideas Esteticas — RIE
Revista de Ideas Esteticas. CSIC (Consejo Superior de Investigaciones Cientificas) — R Ideas Estet
Revista de Igiena, Bacteriologie, Virusologie, Parazitologie, Epidemiologie, Pneumoftiziologie. Igiena — Rev Ig Bacteriol Virusol Parazitol Epidemiol Pneumoftiziol I
Revista de Igiena Sociala — Rev Ig Soc
Revista de Imigracao e Colonizacao (Rio de Janeiro) — Rev Imigr Coloniz Rio
Revista de Indias — RDI
Revista de Indias — RevI
Revista de Indias — Revta Indias
Revista de Indias. Instituto Gonzalo Fernandez de Oviedo y Consejo Superior de Investigaciones Cientificas — IGFO/RI
Revista de Indias (Madrid) — Rev Indias Madrid
Revista de Industria Agricola — Rev Ind Agr
Revista de Industria Animal — Rev Ind Anim
Revista de Informacao Legislativa — R Info Legis
Revista de Informacao Legislativa — Rev Inf Legis
Revista de Informacao Legislativa (Brasilia) — Rev Inform Legis Brasilia
Revista de Informacion Municipal (Buenos Aires) — Rev Inform Munici BA
Revista de Informatica y Automatica — Rev Inf & Autom
Revista de Informatica y Automatica — Rev Inform Automat
Revista de Ingenieria (Buenos Aires) — Rev Ing (Buenos Aires)
Revista de Ingenieria Industrial — Rev Ing Ind
Revista de Ingenieria (Montevideo) — Rev Ing (Montevideo)
Revista de Ingenieria Quimica — Rev Ing Quim
Revista de Instituciones Europeas — R Instit Europ
Revista de Integracion — RDLI
Revista de Investigacion — Rev Invest
Revista de Investigacion Clinica — Rev Inv Cli
Revista de Investigacion Clinica — Rev Invest Clin
Revista de Investigacion en Salud Publica — Rev Invest Salud Publica
Revista de Investigacion en Salud Publica — Revista Invest Salud Publica
Revista de Investigacion. Universidad de Guadalajara (Mexico) — Rev Invest Univ Guadalajara (Mex)
Revista de Investigacion y Desarrollo Pesquero — Rev Invest Desarrollo Pesq
Revista de Investigaciones Agricolas — Rev Invest Agr
Revista de Investigaciones Agricolas — Rev Invest Agric
Revista de Investigaciones Agricolas — Revista Invest Agric
Revista de Investigaciones Agropecuarias (Buenos Aires) — Revta Invest Agropec (B Aires)
Revista de Investigaciones Agropecuarias. Serie — Rev Invest Agropec Ser
Revista de Investigaciones Agropecuarias. Serie 1. Biologia y Produccion Animal — Rev Invest Agropecu Ser 1
Revista de Investigaciones Agropecuarias. Serie 1. Biologia y Produccion Animal — Rev Invest Agropecu Ser 1 Biol Prod Anim
Revista de Investigaciones Agropecuarias. Serie 2. Biologia y Produccion Vegetal — Rev Invest Agropecu Ser 2 Biol Prod Veg
Revista de Investigaciones Agropecuarias. Serie 2. Biologia y Produccion Vegetal — Rev Invest Agropecuar Ser 2
Revista de Investigaciones Agropecuarias. Serie 3. Clima y Suelo — Rev Invest Agropecu Ser 3
Revista de Investigaciones Agropecuarias. Serie 3. Clima y Suelo — Rev Invest Agropecu Ser 3 Clima Suelo
Revista de Investigaciones Agropecuarias. Serie 4. Patologia Animal — Rev Invest Agropecu Ser 4
Revista de Investigaciones Agropecuarias. Serie 4. Patologia Animal — Rev Invest Agropecu Ser 4 Patol Anim
Revista de Investigaciones Agropecuarias. Serie 4. Patologia Animal — RQPAA
Revista de Investigaciones Agropecuarias. Serie 5. Patologia Vegetal — Rev Invest Agropecu Ser 5 Patol Veg
Revista de Investigaciones Agropecuarias. Serie 5. Patologia Vegetal — Rev Invest Agropecuar Ser 5
Revista de Investigaciones Agropecuarias. Serie 6. Economia y Administracion Rural — Rev Invest Agropecu Ser 6
Revista de Investigaciones Forestales — Rev Invest For
Revista de Investigaciones Forestales/Argentina. Administracion Nacional de Bosques — Revista Invest Forest
Revista de Investigaciones Ganaderas — Rev Invest Ganad
Revista de Investigaciones. Instituto Nacional de la Pesca — Rev Invest Inst Nac Pesca
Revista de Investigaciones Juridicas — RIJ
Revista de Investigaciones Marinas — Rev Invest Mar
Revista de Istorie — Rev Ist
Revista de Istorie — RI
Revista de Istorie — RIst
Revista de Istorie si Theori Literara — RITL
Revista de Jurisprudencia do Tribunal Federal de Recursos [*Brazil*] — RTFR
Revista de Jurisprudencia do Tribunal Superior do Trabalho [*Brazil*] — RTST
Revista de la Academia Canaria de Ciencias — Rev Acad Canaria Cienc
Revista de la Cepal — RDC
Revista de la Economia Politica — REP
Revista de la Educacion Superior — RDES
Revista de la Facultad de Ingenieria. Universidad Central de Venezuela — Rev Fac Ing Univ Cent Venez
Revista de la Habana — RevH
Revista de La Habana (La Habana) — Rev Habana Hav
Revista de la Industria Textil — Rev Ind Text
Revista de la Integracion — R Integr
Revista de la Integracion — R Integracion
Revista de la Integracion y el Desarrollo de Centroamerica — R Integracion y Desarrollo Centroam
Revista de la Policlinica (Caracas) — Rev Policlin (Caracas)
Revista de la Policlinica Caracas — Revta Policl Cara
Revista de la Sanidad de las Fuerzas Policiales — Rev Sanid Fuerzas Policiales
Revista de la Sanidad de las Fuerzas Policiales del Peru — RSFPA
Revista de la Sanidad de Policia — Rev Sanid Polic
Revista de la Sanidad Militar (Argentina) — Rev Sanid Mil (Argent)
Revista de la Sanidad Militar (Buenos Aires) — Rev San Mil (Buenos Aires)
Revista de la Sociedad Espanola de Bioquimica Clinica y Patologia Molecular — Rev Soc Esp Bioquim Clin Patol Mol
Revista de la Sociedad Espanola de Quimica Clinica — Rev Soc Esp Quim Clin
Revista de la Sociedad Mexicana de Historia Natural — Revista Soc Mex Hist Nat
Revista de la UNESCO — RDU
Revista de la Union Industrial — R Union Ind
Revista de la Universidad. Universidad Nacional Autonoma de Honduras [*Tegucigalpa*] — HUN/RU
Revista de las Espanas — RdE
Revista de las Fuerzas Armadas de Venezuela — Rev Fuerzas Armadas Venez
Revista de las Indias — R Ind
Revista de las Indias — R Indias
Revista de las Indias — RdeInd
Revista de las Indias — Rev Indias
Revista de las Indias — RI
Revista de las Indias — RIn
Revista de las Indias — RLI
Revista de las Indias (Bogota) — Rev Indias Bogota
Revista de las Indias (Madrid) — RIndM
Revista de Leprologia de Sao Paulo — Rev Leprol Sao Paulo
Revista de Leprologia, Dermatologia, y Sifilografia — Rev Leprol Dermatol Sifilogr
Revista de Letras — R Let
Revista de Letras — RdL
Revista de Letras — RevL
Revista de Letras — RL
Revista de Letras (Assis) — RevLA
Revista de Letras. Faculdade de Filosofia, Ciencias, e Letras (Assis) — RLA
Revista de Letras. Serie Literatura — RdLet
Revista de Linguistica Teorica y Aplicada — RLTA
Revista de Literatura — Rev Lit
Revista de Literatura — RL
Revista de Literatura — RLit
Revista de Literatura Argentina e Iberoamericana (Mendoza, Argentina) — Rev Lit Arg Iberoam Mendoza
Revista de Literatura. CSIC (Consejo Superior de Investigaciones Cientificas) — R Literatura
Revista de Literatura Cubana — RDLC
Revista de Literatura (Madrid) — Rev Lit Madrid
Revista de Literaturas Modernas — RLM
Revista de los Archivos Nacionales (San Jose, Costa Rica) — Rev Arch Nac S Jose
Revista de los Progresos de las Ciencias Exactas, Fisicas, y Naturales — Revista Progr Ci Exact
Revista de Marina (Callao, Peru) — Rev Marina Callao
Revista de Matematica e Estatistica — Rev Mat Estatist
Revista de Matematicas Aplicadas — Rev Mat Apl
Revista de Medicina — Rev Med
Revista de Medicina. ATM [*Associacao da Turma Medica*] — Rev Med ATM

Revista de Medicina da PUCRS [*Pontificia Universidade Catolica do Rio Grande do Sul*] — Rev Med PUCRS
Revista de Medicina del Estudio General de Navarro — Rev Med Estud Gen Navarro
Revista de Medicina do Rio Grande Do Sul — Rev Med Rio Grande Do Sul
Revista de Medicina e Cirurgia de Sao Paulo — Rev Med Cir Sao Paulo
Revista de Medicina Experimental — Rev Med Exp
Revista de Medicina Experimental (Lima) — Rev Med Exp (Lima)
Revista de Medicina. Hospital Ernesto Dornelles — Rev Med Hosp Ernesto Dornelles
Revista de Medicina Interna, Neurologie, Psihiatrie, Neurochirurgie, Dermato-Venerologie — Rev Med Interna Neurol Psihiatr Neurochir Dermato-Venerol
Revista de Medicina Interna, Neurologie, Psihiatrie, Neurochirurgie, Dermato-Venerologie. Neurologie, Psihiatrie, Neurochirurgie — Rev Med Interna Neurol Psihiatr
Revista de Medicina Interna, Neurologie, Psihiatrie, Neurochirurgie, Dermato-Venerologie. Seria Dermato-Venerologia — RMIDDJ
Revista de Medicina Interna, Neurologie, Psihiatrie, Neurochirurgie, Dermato-Venerologie. Seria Medicina Interna — Rev Med Interna Med Interna
Revista de Medicina Interna, Neurologie, Psihiatrie, Neurochirurgie, Dermato-Venerologie. Seria Medicina Interna — RMIIDY
Revista de Medicina Interna, Neurologie, Psihiatrie, Neurochirurgie, Dermato-Venerologie. Seria Neurologia, Psihiatrie, Neurochirurgie — RMEIDE
Revista de Medicina Legal — R Medicina Legal
Revista de Medicina Legal de Colombia — Rev Med Leg Colomb
Revista de Medicina Militar — Rev Med Mil
Revista de Medicina Militar (Oporto) — Revista Med Militar Oporto
Revista de Medicina (Rosario) — Rev de Med (Rosario)
Revista de Medicina (Sao Paulo) — Rev de Med (S Paulo)
Revista de Medicina (Sao Paulo) — Rev Med (Sao Paulo)
Revista de Medicina Tropical — Rev Med Trop
Revista de Medicina. Universidad de Navarra — Rev Med Univ Navarra
Revista de Medicina. Universidad de Navarra — RMUNA
Revista de Medicina. Universidade Federal do Ceara — Rev Med Univ Fed Ceara
Revista de Medicina (Valparaiso) — Rev Med (Valparaiso)
Revista de Medicina Veterinaria — Rev Med Vet
Revista de Medicina Veterinaria (Bogota) — Rev Med Vet (Bogota)
Revista de Medicina Veterinaria (Buenos Aires) — Rev Med Vet (B Aires)
Revista de Medicina Veterinaria. Escuela de Montevideo — Rev Med Vet Escuela Montevideo
Revista de Medicina Veterinaria (Montevideo) — Rev Med Vet (Montev)
Revista de Medicina Veterinaria (Santiago) — Rev Med Vet (Santiago)
Revista de Medicina Veterinaria (Sao Paulo) — Rev Med Vet (Sao Paulo)
Revista de Medicina Veterinaria y Parasitologia — Rev Med Vet Parasit
Revista de Medicina Veterinaria y Parasitologia (Caracas) — Revta Med Vet Parasit (Caracas)
Revista de Medicina Veterinaria y Parasitologia (Maracay) — Rev Med Vet Parasitol (Maracay)
Revista de Medicina y Alimentacion — Rev Med Aliment
Revista de Medicina y Ciencias Afines — Rev Med Cienc Afines
Revista de Medicina y Cirugia (Caracas) — Rev Med y Cirug (Caracas)
Revista de Medicina y Cirugia de La Habana — Rev Med Cir Habana
Revista de Medicina y Cirugia de La Habana — Rev Med y Cirug Habana
Revista de Medicina-Interna, Neurologie, Psihiatrie, Neurochirurgie, Dermato-Venerologie. Seria Medicina Interna — Rev Med Interna Neurol Psihiatr Neurochir Dermato
Revista de Menorca — R Menorca
Revista de Metalurgia — Rev Metal
Revista de Metalurgia (Madrid) — Rev Met (Madrid)
Revista de Metalurgia (Madrid) — Rev Metal (Madrid)
Revista de Microbiologia — Rev Microbiol
Revista de Microscopia Electronica — Rev Micr El
Revista de Minas — Rev Minas
Revista de Minas e Hidrocarburos — Rev Minas Hidrocarburos
Revista de Neurologia — Rev Neurol
Revista de Neurologia Clinica (Madrid) — Rev Neurol Clin (Madrid)
Revista de Neuro-Psiquiatria — Rev Neuro-Psiquiatr
Revista de Nutricion Animal — Rev Nutr Anim
Revista de Obras Publicas — Rev Obras Pub
Revista de Obras Publicas — Rev Obras Publicas
Revista de Obras Sanitarias de la Nacion (Argentina) — Rev Obras Sanit Nac (Argent)
Revista de Obras Sanitarias de la Nacion (Buenos Aires) — Rev Obras Sanit Nac (B Aires)
Revista de Obstetricia y Ginecologia de Venezuela — Rev Obstet Ginecol Venez
Revista de Occidente — Rev Oc
Revista de Occidente — Rev Occidente
Revista de Occidente — RevsO
Revista de Occidente — RO
Revista de Occidente — ROc
Revista de Odontologia da UNESP (Universidade Estadual Paulista) — Rev Odontol UNESP (Univ Estadual Paul)
Revista de Odontologia. Universidade Federal de Santa Catarina — Rev Odontol St Catarina
Revista de Ortopedia y Traumatologia Latinoamericana — Rev Ortop Traumatol Latinoam
Revista de Oto-Neuro-Oftalmologica y de Cirugia Neurologica Sud-Americana — Rev Oto-Neuro-Oftalmol Cir Neurol Sud-Am
Revista de Otorrinolaringologia — Rev Orl
Revista de Otorrinolaringologia — Rev Otorrinolaringol
Revista de Pedagogia — Rev Pedag
Revista de Pediatrie, Obstetrica, si Ginecologie — Rev Pediatr Obstet Ginecol
Revista de Pediatrie, Obstetrica, si Ginecologie. Pediatria — Rev Pediatr Obstet Ginecol Pediatr
Revista de Pediatrie, Obstetrica, si Ginecologie. Seria Obstetrica si Ginecologie — Rev Pediatr Obstet Ginecol Ser Obstet Ginecol
Revista de Pediatrie, Obstetrica, si Ginecologie. Seria Pediatria — Rev Pediatr Obstet Ginecol Ser Pediatr
Revista de Planeacion y Desarrollo — R Planeacion y Desarrollo
Revista de Planeacion y Desarrollo — Rev Planeacion Desarrollo
Revista de Planeacion y Desarrollo (Bogota) — R Plan Desarr (Bogota)
Revista de Plasticos (Madrid) — Rev Plast (Madrid)
Revista de Plasticos Modernos — Rev Plast Mod
Revista de Politica Internacional — R Pol Internac
Revista de Politica Internacional — Rev Polit Int
Revista de Politica Internacional (Madrid) — R Polit Int (Madrid)
Revista de Politica Social — R Pol Soc
Revista de Politica Social — R Polit Soc
Revista de Politica Social — RPS
Revista de Portugal — RP
Revista de Preistorie si Antichitati Nationale — RPAN
Revista de Prevencion de Readaptacion Social — RMPR
Revista de Psicoanalisis — REPSA
Revista de Psicologia — Rev Psicol
Revista de Psicologia General Aplicada — RPGA
Revista de Psicologia General y Aplicada — R Psicol Gen Apl
Revista de Psicologia General y Aplicada — Rev Psicol Gen Apl
Revista de Psicologia Normal e Patologica — Revta Psicol Norm Patol
Revista de Psihologie — Rev Psihol
Revista de Psiquiatria — Rev Psiquiatr
Revista de Psiquiatria Dinamica — Rev Psiquiat Dinam
Revista de Psiquiatria y Psicologia Medica de Europeo y America Latina — Rev Psiquiat Psicol Med
Revista de Quimica e Farmacia (Rio De Janeiro) — Rev Quim Farm (Rio De Janeiro)
Revista de Quimica e Ingenieria Quimica — Rev Quim Ing Quim
Revista de Quimica Industrial (Buenos Aires) — Rev Quim Ind (Buenos Aires)
Revista de Quimica Industrial (Rio De Janeiro) — Rev Quim Ind (Rio De Janeiro)
Revista de Quimica Industrial (Rio de Janeiro) — Rev Quim Indus Rio
Revista de Quimica Industrial (Rio De Janeiro) — RQIRA
Revista de Quimica Pura e Aplicada — Rev Quim Pura Apl
Revista de Quimica Textil — Rev Quim Text
Revista de Quimica y Farmacia (Tegucigalpa) — Rev Quim Farm (Tegucigalpa)
Revista de Salud Animal — Rev Salud Anim
Revista de Sanidad de Aeronautica — Rev Sanid Aeronaut
Revista de Sanidad e Higiene Publica — Rev Sanid Hig Publica
Revista de Sanidad e Higiene Publica (Madrid) — Rev Sanid Hig Publica (Madr)
Revista de Sanidad Militar Argentina — Rev Sanid Mil Arg
Revista de Sanidad y Asistencia Social. Ministerio de Sanidad y Asistencia Social (Caracas) — Rev Sanid Asist Soc Caracas
Revista de Santa Fe y Bogota — RSFB
Revista de Saude Publica — Rev Saude Publica
Revista de Sciencias Naturais e Sociais — RSNS
Revista de Servicio Social (San Juan, Puerto Rico) — Rev Serv Soc S Juan
Revista de Sifilografia, Leprologia, y Dermatologia — Rev Sifilogr Leprol Dermatol
Revista de Soldadura — Rev Soldadura
Revista de Statistica (Bucuresti) — R Statist (Bucuresti)
Revista de Teatro — RdT
Revista de Teatro (Rio de Janeiro) — Rev Teatro Rio
Revista de Tecnologia Educativa — RTE
Revista de Tecnologia Medica — Rev Tecnol Med
Revista de Telecomunicacion — Rev Telecom
Revista de Telecomunicacion (Madrid) — Rev Telecomun (Madrid)
Revista de Temas Militares — Rev Temas Mil
Revista de Tisiologia y Neumonologia — Rev Tisiol Neumonol
Revista de Toxicologia — Rev Toxicol
Revista de Trabajo — Rev Trab
Revista de Trabajo (Madrid) — R Trab (Madrid)
Revista de Trabajo. Ministerio de Trabajo — R Trabajo
Revista de Trabajo (San Salvador) — Rev Trab S Salvador
Revista de Tradiciones Populares (Madrid) — RTPM
Revista de Urologia (Caracas) — Rev Urol (Caracas)
Revista de Veterinaria Militar — Rev Vet Milit
Revista de Veterinaria y Zootecnia (Manizales) — Rev Vet Zootec (Manizales)
Revista de Zootechnic si Medicina Veterinara — RZMVA
Revista de Zootehnie si Medicina Veterinara — Rev Zooteh Med Vet
Revista degli Studi Orientali [*Rome*] — R Stud Or
Revista del Alteneo Paraguayo — Rev Alteneo Paraguayo
Revista del Archivo, Biblioteca, y Museo del Ayuntamiento de Madrid — R Arch Bibl Mus Ayunt
Revista del Archivo Central — RevtA
Revista del Cafe — Revista Cafe
Revista del Caucho — Rev d Caucho
Revista del Centro de Quimicos Industriales. Buenos Aires — Rev Cent Quim Ind Buenos Aires
Revista del Centro Nacional de Agricultura — Revista Centro Nac Agric
Revista del Circulo Odontologico de Cordoba — Rev Circ Odontol Cordoba
Revista del Consejo Oceanografico Ibero-Americana — Revista Cons Oceanogr Ibero Amer
Revista del Foro (Lima) — Rev Foro Lima
Revista del Frio — Rev Frio
Revista del Instituto Nacional de Investigacion de las Ciencias Naturales Anexo al Museo Argentino de Ciencias Naturales Bernardino Rivadavia. Ciencias Botanicas — Revista Inst Nac Invest Ci Nat Ci Bot
Revista del Instituto Nacional de Medicina Legal de Colombia — Rev Inst Nac Med Leg Colomb

Revista del Maestro (Guatemala) — Rev Maestro Guat
Revista del Mexico Agrario — R Mex Agr
Revista del Ministerio de Justicia — RMJ
Revista del Museo de La Plata. Seccion Botanica — Revista Mus La Plata Secc Bot
Revista del Notariado (Argentina) — RNA
Revista del Nucleo del Azuay de la Casa de la Cultura Ecuatoriana (Cuenca) — Rev Nucl Azuay Casa Cult Ecuat Cuenca
Revista del Nucleo Guayas. Casa de la Cultura Ecuatoriana (Guayaquil) — Rev Nucl Guayas Casa Cult Ecuat Guayaquil
Revista del Pacifico — RdPac
Revista del Pacifico — RevP
Revista del Patronato de Biologia Animal — Rev Patronato Biol Anim
Revista del Pensamiento Centroamericano. Consejo Superior de la Empresa Privada [*COSEP*] — RPC
Revista del Petroleo (Bogota) — Rev Petrol Bogota
Revista del Trabajo (Caracas) — Rev Trab Caracas
Revista del Viernes Medico — Rev Viernes Med
Revista delle Colonie Italiane — RCI
Revista Dental de Chile — Rev Dent Chil
Revista Dental (San Salvador) — Rev Dent (San Salv)
Revista Dental (Santo Domingo) — Rev Dent (St Domingo)
Revista. Departamento de Quimica. Universidad Nacional de Colombia — Rev Dep Quim Univ Nac Colomb
Revista di Ciencias Naturales de Madrid — Revista Ci Nat Madrid
Revista di Filologia e di Isturzione Classica — Rev Filol Istr Cl
Revista di Letterature Moderne e Comparate — RLM
Revista di Politica Economica. Terza Serie — R Pol Econ Terza Ser
Revista Diplomatica — R Diplomatica
Revista. Direccion General de Geologia y Minas (Ecuador) — Rev Dir Gen Geol Minas (Ecuador)
Revista do Arquivo Municipal (Sao Paulo) — RAMSP
Revista do Arquivo Municipal (Sao Paulo) — Rev Arquiv Munici S Paulo
Revista do Brasil — R Do Brasil
Revista do Cafe Portugues — Rev Cafe Port
Revista do Centro de Estudos Demograficos — RCED
Revista do Centro de Letras (Curitiba, Brazil) — Rev Cent Letr Curitiba
Revista do Circulo de Estudos Bandeirantes — RCEB
Revista do Instituto Brasil-Estados Unidos (Rio de Janeiro) — Rev Inst Bras Estad Unidos Rio
Revista do Instituto de Antibioticos/Universidade de Recife — Revista Inst Antibiot
Revista do Instituto do Ceara (Fortaleza, Brazil) — Rev Inst Ceara Fortaleza
Revista do IRB [*Instituto de Resseguros do Brasil*] **Ministerio da Industria e Comercio (Rio de Janeiro)** — Rev Irb Rio
Revista do Livro — RdL
Revista do Livro — Rev Livro
Revista do Livro (Rio) — RevLR
Revista do Museu Paulista (Sao Paulo) — Rev Mus Paulista S Paulo
Revista do Patrimonio Historico e Artistico Nacional (Rio de Janeiro) — Rev Patrim Hist Artist Nac Rio
Revista do Servico Publico (Rio de Janeiro) — Rev Serv Publ Rio
Revista do Supremo Tribunal [*Brazil*] — RST
Revista Dominicana de Cultura — RDC
Revista Dominicana de Cultura (Ciudad Trujillo) — Rev Dom Cult C Trujillo
Revista Dominicana de Filosofia — RDF
Revista Dominicana di Cultura — R Dom Cult
Revista dos Criadores — Rev Criad
Revista dos Criadores — Rev Criadores
Revista dos Mercados — R Mercados
Revista dos Tribunais [*Brazil*] — RT
Revista Doyma de Inmunologia — Rev Doyma Inmunol
Revista Eclesiastica — RE
Revista Eclesiastica Argentina — REArg
Revista Eclesiastica Brasileira — REB
Revista Eclesiastica Brasileira — REBras
Revista Eclesiastica Brasileira (Petropolis, Brazil) — Rev Ecles Bras Petropolis
Revista Economica do Nordeste — R Econ Nordeste
Revista Economica do Nordeste. Banco do Nordeste do Brasil. Departamento de Estudos Economicos do Nordeste — BNB/REN
Revista Economica Interamericana — REI
Revista Ecuatoriana de Educacion (Quito) — Rev Ecuat Educ Quito
Revista Ecuatoriana de Entomologia y Parasitologia — Rev Ecuat Ent Parasit
Revista Ecuatoriana de Entomologia y Parasitologia — Rev Ecuat Entomol Parasitol
Revista Ecuatoriana de Higiene y Medicina Tropical — Rev Ecuat Hig Med
Revista Ecuatoriana de Higiene y Medicina Tropical — Rev Ecuat Hig Med Trop
Revista Ecuatoriana de Medicina y Ciencias Biologicas — Rev Ecuat Med Cienc Biol
Revista Ecuatoriana de Pediatria — Rev Ecuat Pediatr
Revista Electricidade — REELB
Revista Electricidade [*Portugal*] — Rev Electr
Revista Electrotecnica — Rev Electrotec
Revista Electrotecnica — RVELA
Revista Electrotecnica (Buenos Aires) — Rev Electrotec (Buenos Aires)
Revista Empresas Publicas de Medellin [*Columbia*] — Rev Empresas Publicas Medellin
Revista Enfermagem em Novas Dimensoes — Rev Enferm Nov Dimens
Revista. Escola de Agronomia e Veterinaria da Universidade do Rio Grande Do Sul (Porto Alegre) — Rev Esc Agron Vet Univ Rio Grande Do Sul (Porto Alegre)
Revista. Escola de Agronomia e Veterinaria. Universidade Federal do Parana — Rev Esc Agron Vet Univ Fed Parana
Revista. Escola de Enfermagem. Universidade de Sao Paulo — Rev Esc Enferm USP
Revista. Escola de Minas [*Brazil*] — REMOA
Revista. Escola de Minas — Rev Esc Minas
Revista. Escuela de Contabilidad, Economia, y Administracion. Instituto Tecnologico y de Estudios Superiores (Monterrey, Mexico) — Rev Escuela Contab Econ Adm Monterrey
Revista. Escuela de Defensa Nacional — R Escuela Def Nac
Revista. Escuela de Estudios Penitenciarios — REEP
Revista. Escuela de Estudios Penitenciarios. Publicacion Oficial de la Direccion General de Prisiones — R Esc Est Penitenciarios
Revista. Escuela de Odontologia. Universidad Nacional de Tucuman. Faculdad de Medicina — Rev Esc Odontol Tucuman
Revista. Escuela Militar (Chorillos, Peru) — Rev Escuela Militar Chorillos
Revista Espanola de Ambos Mundos — REAM
Revista Espanola de Anestesiologia — Rev Esp Anest
Revista Espanola de Anestesiologia — Rev Esp Anestesiol
Revista Espanola de Anestesiologia y Reanimacion — Rev Esp Anestesiol Reanim
Revista Espanola de Antropologia Americana — REAA
Revista Espanola de Antropologia Americana — Rev Esp Antropol Amer
Revista Espanola de Biologia — Revista Esp Biol
Revista Espanola de Cardiologia — Rev Esp Cardiol
Revista Espanola de Ciencia y Tecnologia de Alimentos — Rev Esp Cienc Tecnol Aliment
Revista Espanola de Derecho Canonico — R Espan Derecho Canonico
Revista Espanola de Derecho Canonico — RE Der Can
Revista Espanola de Derecho Canonico — REDC
Revista Espanola de Derecho Canonico — Rev Esp de Derecho Canonico
Revista Espanola de Derecho Canonico — Rev Esp Der Can
Revista Espanola de Derecho Canonico (Salamanca) — REDCS
Revista Espanola de Derecho Internacional — R Esp Der Int
Revista Espanola de Derecho Internacional — R Espan Derecho Int
Revista Espanola de Derecho Internacional — Rev Esp de Derecho Internac
Revista Espanola de Derecho Militar — Rev Esp de Derecho Mil
Revista Espanola de Documentacion Cientifica — Rev Esp Doc Cient
Revista Espanola de Electronica — Rev Esp Electron
Revista Espanola de Endodoncia — Rev Esp Endodoncia
Revista Espanola de Estomatologia — Rev Esp Estomatol
Revista Espanola de Fisiologia — Rev Esp Fis
Revista Espanola de Fisiologia — Rev Esp Fisiol
Revista Espanola de Fisiologia — Rev Espan Fisiol
Revista Espanola de Fisiologia — Revta Esp Fisiol
Revista Espanola de Fisiologia. Supplement — Rev Esp Fisiol Suppl
Revista Espanola de la Opinion Publica — R Esp Opin Publ
Revista Espanola de la Opinion Publica — R Esp Opinion Publica
Revista Espanola de las Enfermedades del Aparato Digestivo — Rev Esp Enferm Apar Dig
Revista Espanola de las Enfermedades del Aparato Digestivo y de la Nutricion — Rev Esp Enferm Apar Dig Nutr
Revista Espanola de Linguistica — RELing
Revista Espanola de Linguistica — REspL
Revista Espanola de Literatura, Historia, y Arte — RELHA
Revista Espanola de Medicina y Cirugia de Guerra — Rev Esp Med Cirug Guerra
Revista Espanola de Micropaleontologia — Rev Esp Micropaleontol
Revista Espanola de Micropaleontologia — Rev Espanola Micropaleontologia
Revista Espanola de Micropaleontologia — RTEMB5
Revista Espanola de Obstetricia y Ginecologia — Rev Esp Obstet Ginecol
Revista Espanola de Obstetricia y Ginecologia. Suplemento — Rev Esp Obstet Ginecol Supl
Revista Espanola de Oncologia — Rev Esp Oncol
Revista Espanola de Oto-Neuro-Oftalmologia y Neurocirugia — Rev Esp Oto Neu Oft
Revista Espanola de Oto-Neuro-Oftalmologia y Neurocirugia — Rev Esp Oto-Neuro-Oftalmol Neurocir
Revista Espanola de Paradoncia — Rev Esp Parad
Revista Espanola de Pedagogia — REPed
Revista Espanola de Pedagogia. CSIC (Consejo Superior de Investigaciones Cientificas) — R Espan Pedag
Revista Espanola de Pedagogia (Madrid) — REPM
Revista Espanola de Pediatria — Rev Esp Pediatr
Revista Espanola de Reumatismo y Enfermedades Osteoarticulares — Rev Esp Reum Enferm Osteoartic
Revista Espanola de Seguros — R Espan Seguros
Revista Espanola de Teologia [*Madrid*] — REspT
Revista Espanola de Teologia [*Madrid*] — RET
Revista Espanola de Teologia — Rev ET
Revista Espanola de Teologia. CSIC (Consejo Superior de Investigaciones Cientificas) — R Espan Teol
Revista Espanola de Tuberculosis — Rev Esp Tuberc
Revista Espanola de Tuberculosis y Archivos Nacionales de Enfermedades del Torax — Rev Esp Tuber Arch Nac Enferm Torax
Revista Espanola do Lecheria — Rev Esp Lech
Revista Europa de Farmacia de Hospital — Rev Eur Farm Hosp
Revista. Faculdade de Agronomia e Veterinaria. Universidade do Rio Grande Do Sul — Rev Fac Agron Vet Univ Rio Grande Do Sul
Revista. Faculdade de Agronomia e Veterinaria. Universidade do Rio Grande Do Sul — Rev Fac Agron Vet Univ Rio Grande Sul
Revista. Faculdade de Agronomia. Universidade Federal do Rio Grande Do Sul — Rev Fac Agron Univ Fed Rio Grande Sul
Revista. Faculdade de Ciencias Farmaceuticas [*Araraquara*] — RFCFDE
Revista. Faculdade de Ciencias Farmaceuticas (Araraquara) — Rev Fac Cienc Farm (Araraquara)
Revista. Faculdade de Ciencias Medicas. Universidade Catolica do Parana — Rev Fac Cienc Med Univ Catol Parana

Revista. Faculdade de Ciencias. Universidade de Coimbra — Rev Fac Cienc Univ Coimbra
Revista. Faculdade de Ciencias. Universidade de Lisboa. 2a Serie A. Ciencias Matematicas [*Portugal*] — Rev Fac Cienc 2a Ser A Cienc Mat
Revista. Faculdade de Ciencias. Universidade de Lisboa. Serie B. Ciencias Fisico-Quimicas — Rev Fac Cienc Univ Lisboa B
Revista. Faculdade de Ciencias. Universidade de Lisboa. Serie B. Ciencias Fisico-Quimicas — Rev Fac Cienc Univ Lisboa Ser B
Revista. Faculdade de Ciencias. Universidade de Lisboa. Serie C. Ciencias Naturais — Rev Fac Cienc Univ Lisb Ser C Cienc Nat
Revista. Faculdade de Ciencias. Universidade de Lisboa. Serie C. Ciencias Naturais — Rev Fac Cienc Univ Lisboa Ser C
Revista. Faculdade de Engenharia. Universidade do Porto — Rev Fac Eng Univ Porto
Revista. Faculdade de Farmacia de Santa Maria. Universidade do Rio Grande do Sul — Rev Fac Farm St Maria Univ Rio Grande Sul
Revista. Faculdade de Farmacia e Bioquimica. Universidade de Sao Paulo — Rev Fac Farm Bioquim Univ Sao Paulo
Revista. Faculdade de Farmacia e Bioquimica. Universidade de Sao Paulo — Revta Fac Farm Bioquim S Paulo
Revista. Faculdade de Farmacia e Bioquimica. Universidade Federal de Santa Maria — Rev Fac Farm Bioquim Univ Fed St Maria
Revista. Faculdade de Farmacia e Odontologia de Araraquara — Rev Fac Farm Odontol Araraquara
Revista. Faculdade de Filosofia e Letras. Universidade do Parana — RFFLUP
Revista. Faculdade de Letras. Serie de Historia. Universidade do Porto — R Porto
Revista. Faculdade de Letras. Universidade de Lisboa — RFL
Revista. Faculdade de Letras. Universidade de Lisboa — RFLL
Revista. Faculdade de Letras. Universidade de Lisboa — RFLUL
Revista. Faculdade de Letras. Universidade de Porto — RUP
Revista. Faculdade de Medicina. Universidade Federal de Santa Maria — Rev Fac Med Univ Fed Santa Maria
Revista. Faculdade de Medicina. Universidade Federal do Ceara — Rev Fac Med Univ Fed Ceara
Revista. Faculdade de Medicina Veterinaria e Zootecnia. Universidade de Sao Paulo — Rev Fac Med Vet Zootec Univ Sao Paulo
Revista. Faculdade de Medicina Veterinaria. Universidade de Sao Paulo — Rev Fac Med Vet Univ Sao Paulo
Revista. Faculdade de Odontologia de Aracatuba — Rev Fac Odontol Aracatuba
Revista. Faculdade de Odontologia de Araraquara — Rev Fac Odontol Araraquara
Revista. Faculdade de Odontologia de Araraquara — RFOFD6
Revista. Faculdade de Odontologia de Pernambuco — Rev Fac Odontol Pernambuco
Revista. Faculdade de Odontologia de Port Alegre — Rev Fac Odontol Port Alegre
Revista. Faculdade de Odontologia de Ribeirao Preto — Rev Fac Odontol Ribeirao Preto
Revista. Faculdade de Odontologia de Sao Jose Dos Campos — Rev Fac Odontol Sao Jose Dos Campos
Revista. Faculdade de Odontologia (Porto Alegre) — Rev Fac Odontol (P Alegre)
Revista. Faculdade de Odontologia. Universidade de Sao Paulo — Rev Fac Odontol Sao Paulo
Revista. Faculdade de Odontologia. Universidade de Sao Paulo — Rev Fac Odontol Univ Sao Paulo
Revista. Faculdade de Odontologia. Universidade Federal da Bahia — Rev Fac Odontol Univ Fed Bahia
Revista. Facultad de Agronomia — RFA
Revista. Facultad de Agronomia Alcance (Maracay) — Rev Fac Agron Alcance (Maracay)
Revista. Facultad de Agronomia (Maracay) — Rev Fac Agron (Maracay)
Revista. Facultad de Agronomia. Universidad Central de Venezuela — Rev Fac Agron Univ Cent Venez
Revista. Facultad de Agronomia. Universidad Central de Venezuela — Rev Fac Agron Univ Cent Venezuela
Revista. Facultad de Agronomia. Universidad Central de Venezuela — Revta Fac Agron Univ Cent Venez
Revista. Facultad de Agronomia. Universidad de la Republica (Montevideo) — Rev Fac Agron Monte
Revista. Facultad de Agronomia. Universidad de la Republica (Montevideo) — Rev Fac Agron Univ Repub (Montevideo)
Revista. Facultad de Agronomia. Universidad de la Republica (Uruguay) — Revta Fac Agron Univ Repub (Urug)
Revista. Facultad de Agronomia. Universidad Nacional de La Plata — Rev Fac Agron Univ Nac La Plata
Revista. Facultad de Agronomia. Universidad Nacional de La Plata — Revista Fac Agron Univ Nac La Plata
Revista. Facultad de Agronomia. Universidad Nacional de La Plata — RFAPA
Revista. Facultad de Agronomia. Universidad Nacional de La Plata (La Plata, Argentina) — Rev Fac Agron La Plata
Revista. Facultad de Agronomia y Veterinaria (Buenos Aires) — Rev Fac Agron Vet (Buenos Aires)
Revista. Facultad de Agronomia y Veterinaria. Universidad de Buenos Aires — Rev Fac Agron Vet Univ B Aires
Revista. Facultad de Agronomia y Veterinaria. Universidad de Buenos Aires — Rev Fac Agron Vet Univ Buenos Aires
Revista. Facultad de Agronomia y Veterinaria. Universidad de Buenos Aires — Revta Fac Agron Vet Univ B Aires
Revista. Facultad de Agronomia y Veterinaria. Universidad Nacional de La Plata — Revta Fac Agron Univ Nac La Plata
Revista. Facultad de Agronomia (Zulia, Venezuela). Universidad — Rev Fac Agron (Zulia Venez) Univ
Revista. Facultad de Arquitectura. Universidad de la Republica (Montevideo) — Rev Fac Arquit Monte
Revista. Facultad de Ciencias Agrarias. Ministerio de Educacion. Universidad Nacional de Cuyo (Mendoza) [*Argentina*] — Rev Fac Agrar Minist Educ Univ Nac Cuyo (Mendoza)
Revista. Facultad de Ciencias Agrarias. Ministerio de Educacion. Universidad Nacional de Cuyo (Mendoza) — Rev Fac Cienc Agrar Minist Educ Univ Nac Cuyo (Mendoza)
Revista. Facultad de Ciencias Agrarias. Universidad Nacional de Cuyo — Rev Fac Cienc Agr Univ Nac Cuyo
Revista. Facultad de Ciencias Agrarias. Universidad Nacional do Cuyo [*A publication*] — Rev Fac Cienc Agrar Univ Nac Cuyo
Revista. Facultad de Ciencias Agrarias. Universidad Nacional de Cuyo — Revta Fac Cienc Agrar Univ Nac Cuyo
Revista. Facultad de Ciencias Agrarias. Universidad Nacional de Cuyo — RFACA
Revista. Facultad de Ciencias Economicas, Comerciales, y Politicas. Universidad Nacional del Litoral (Rosario, Argentina) — Rev Fac Cien Econ Comer Pol Rosario
Revista. Facultad de Ciencias Economicas. Universidad de Cordoba (Cordoba, Argentina) — Rev Fac Cien Econ Cordoba
Revista. Facultad de Ciencias Economicas. Universidad Mayor de San Marcos (Lima) — Rev Fac Cien Econ Lima
Revista. Facultad de Ciencias Economicas. Universidad Mayor de San Simon (Cochabamba, Bolivia) — Rev Fac Cien Econ Cochabamba
Revista. Facultad de Ciencias Economicas. Universidad Nacional de Buenos Aires — Rev Fac Cien Econ BA
Revista. Facultad de Ciencias Economicas y Comerciales — R Fac Cienc Ec Com
Revista. Facultad de Ciencias Economicas y Comerciales. Universidad Mayor de San Marcos (Lima) — Rev Fac Cien Econ Comer Lima
Revista. Facultad de Ciencias Economicas y de Administracion. Universidad de la Republica (Montevideo) — Rev Fac Cien Econ Admin Monte
Revista. Facultad de Ciencias Exactas, Fisicas, y Naturales (Cordoba, Argentina) — Rev Fac Cien Exact Fis Nat Cordoba
Revista. Facultad de Ciencias Exactas y Naturales y Agrimensura. Universidad Nacional del Nordeste — Rev Fac Cienc Exactas Nat Agrimensura Univ Nac Nordeste
Revista. Facultad de Ciencias Juridicas Politicas — RFCJP
Revista. Facultad de Ciencias Juridicas y Sociales. Universidad de San Carlos (Guatemala) — Rev Fac Cien Jur Soc Guat
Revista. Facultad de Ciencias Medicas de Buenos Aires — Rev Fac Cienc Med Buenos Aires
Revista. Facultad de Ciencias Medicas de Cordoba — Rev Fac Cienc Med Cordoba
Revista. Facultad de Ciencias Medicas. Universidad Central del Ecuador — Rev Fac Cienc Med Univ Cent Ecuador
Revista. Facultad de Ciencias Medicas. Universidad Nacional de Cordoba — Rev Fac Cien Med Univ Nac Cordoba
Revista. Facultad de Ciencias Medicas. Universidad Nacional de Cordoba — Rev Fac Cienc Med Univ Nac Cordoba
Revista. Facultad de Ciencias Medicas. Universidad Nacional de Cuyo — Rev Fac Cienc Med Univ Nac Cuyo
Revista. Facultad de Ciencias Medicas. Universidad Nacional de Rosario — Rev Fac Cienc Med Univ Nac Rosario
Revista. Facultad de Ciencias Medicas. Universidad Nacional del Litoral Rosario — RCMLAO
Revista. Facultad de Ciencias Medicas. Universidad Nacional del Litoral Rosario — Rev Fac Cienc Med Univ Nac Litoral Rosario
Revista. Facultad de Ciencias Naturales de Salta. Universidad Nacional de Tucuman — Rev Fac Cienc Nat Salta Univ Nac Tucuman
Revista. Facultad de Ciencias Quimicas. Universidad Nacional de La Plata — Rev Fac Cienc Quim Univ Nac La Plata
Revista. Facultad de Ciencias. Universidad de Oviedo — Rev Fac Cienc Univ Oviedo
Revista. Facultad de Ciencias Veterinarias — Rev Fac Cienc Vet
Revista. Facultad de Ciencias Veterinarias — RFCVET
Revista. Facultad de Ciencias Veterinarias de La Plata — Rev Fac Cienc Vet La Plata
Revista. Facultad de Derecho (Caracas) — R Fac Der (Caracas)
Revista. Facultad de Derecho de Caracas — RFDC
Revista. Facultad de Derecho de Mexico — R Fac Der Mexico
Revista. Facultad de Derecho de Mexico — Rev de la Fac de Derecho de Mex
Revista. Facultad de Derecho de Mexico — RFDM
Revista. Facultad de Derecho. Universidad Central de Venezuela (Caracas) — Rev Fac Der Caracas
Revista. Facultad de Derecho. Universidad del Zulia (Maracaibo) — Rev Fac Der Maracaibo
Revista. Facultad de Derecho. Universidad Nacional Autonoma de Mexico — Rev Fac Der Mex
Revista. Facultad de Derecho y Ciencias Sociales. Universidad de la Republica (Montevideo) — Rev Fac Der Cien Soc Monte
Revista. Facultad de Educacion. Universidad Catolica del Peru (Lima) — Rev Fac Educ Univ Catol Lima
Revista. Facultad de Farmacia. Universidad Central de Venezuela — Rev Fac Farm Univ Cent Venez
Revista. Facultad de Farmacia. Universidad de Los Andes — Rev Fac Farm Univ Los Andes
Revista. Facultad de Farmacia y Bioquimica. Universidad Central del Ecuador — Rev Fac Farm Bioquim Univ Cent Ecuador
Revista. Facultad de Farmacia y Bioquimica. Universidad Nacional Mayor de San Marcos — Rev Fac Farm Bioquim Univ Nac Mayor San Marcos
Revista. Facultad de Farmacia y Bioquimica. Universidad Nacional Mayor de San Marcos (Lima) — Rev Fac Farm Bioquim Univ Nac Mayor San Marcos (Lima)
Revista. Facultad de Filosofia y Humanidades — RFFH
Revista. Facultad de Filosofia y Letras — RFFL

Revista. Facultad de Humanidades y Ciencias — RFHC
Revista. Facultad de Humanidades y Ciencias. Universidad de la Republica (Montevideo) — Rev Fac Human Cien Monte
Revista. Facultad de Humanidades y Ciencias. Universidad de la Republica, Montevideo — Rev Fac Humanid Cienc Univ Repub Montevideo
Revista. Facultad de Ingenieria Agronomica. Universidad Central de Venezuela — Rev Fac Ing Agron Univ Cent Venez
Revista. Facultad de Ingenieria Quimica. Universidad Nacional del Litoral [*Argentina*] — Rev Fac Ing Quim Univ Nac Litoral
Revista. Facultad de Letras [*Veracruz, Mexico*] — RFL
Revista. Facultad de Letras y Ciencias. Universidad de la Habana — RFLC
Revista. Facultad de Medicina (Maracaibo) — Rev Fac Med (Maracaibo)
Revista. Facultad de Medicina (Mexico) — Rev Fac Med (Mex)
Revista. Facultad de Medicina (Mexico City) — Rev Fac Med (Mexico City)
Revista. Facultad de Medicina (Tucuman) — Rev Fac Med (Tucuman)
Revista. Facultad de Medicina UNAM [*Universidad Nacional Autonoma de Mexico*] — Rev Fac Med UNAM
Revista. Facultad de Medicina. Universidad Nacional de Colombia (Bogota) — Rev Fac Med Univ Nac Colomb (Bogota)
Revista. Facultad de Medicina Veterinaria. Universidad Nacional Mayor de San Marcos — Rev Fac Med Vet Univ Nac Mayor San Marcos
Revista. Facultad de Medicina Veterinaria y de Zootecnia. Universidad Nacional de Colombia — Rev Fac Med Vet Zootec Univ Nac Colomb
Revista. Facultad de Medicina, Veterinaria, y Zootecnia (Bogota) — Rev Fac Med Vet Zootec (Bogota)
Revista. Facultad de Medicina, Veterinaria, y Zootecnia. Universidad de San Carlos — Rev Fac Med Vet Zootec Univ San Carlos
Revista. Facultad de Medicina, Veterinaria, y Zootecnia. Universidad Nacional de Colombia — Rev Fac Med Vet Zoot Univ Nac Colomb
Revista. Facultad de Odontologia. Universidad Nacional de Tucuman — Rev Fac Odontol Tucuman
Revista. Facultad de Quimica Industrial y Agricola. Universidad Nacional del Litoral — Rev Fac Quim Ind Agric Univ Nac Litoral
Revista. Facultad de Quimica. Universidad Nacional Mayor de San Marcos — Rev Fac Quim Univ Nac Mayor San Marcos
Revista. Facultad de Quimica y Farmacia. Universidad Central del Ecuador — Rev Fac Quim Farm Univ Cent Ecuador
Revista. Facultad Nacional de Agronomia (Medellin) — Rev Fac Nac Agron (Medellin)
Revista. Facultad Nacional de Agronomia (Medellin, Colombia) — Rev Fac Nac Agron (Medellin Colomb)
Revista. Facultad Nacional de Agronomia. Medellin Universidad de Antioquia — Revista Fac Nac Agron Medellin Univ Antioquia
Revista. Facultad Nacional de Agronomia. Universidad de Antioquia — Rev Fac Nac Agron Univ Antioquia
Revista. Facultad Nacional de Agronomia. Universidad Nacional (Colombia) — Rev Fac Nac Agron Univ Nac (Colombia)
Revista. Facultade de Farmacia e Odontologia de Ribeirao Preto — Rev Fac Farm Odontol Ribeirao Preto
Revista. Facultade de Odontologia. Universidad Nacional de Colombia — Rev Fac Odontol Univ Nac Colomb
Revista. Facultdade de Ciencias Farmaceuticas. Universidade Estadual Paulista Julio de Mesquita Filho — Rev Fac Cienc Farm Univ Estadual Paul Julio de Mesquita Filh
Revista Farmaceutica/Associacion Farmaceutica y Bioquimica Argentina — Revista Farm
Revista Farmaceutica (Buenos Aires) — Rev Farm (B Aires)
Revista Farmaceutica da Bahia — Rev Farm Bahia
Revista Farmaceutica de Cuba — Rev Farm Cuba
Revista Farmaceutica de Puerto Rico — Rev Farm PR
Revista Farmaceutica Peruana — Rev Farm Peru
Revista Farmaciei (Bucharest) — Rev Farm (Bucharest)
Revista. Federacion de Doctores en Ciencias y en Filosofia y Letras — RFD
Revista. Federacion de Doctors en Ciencias y en Filosofia y Letras (Havana) — Rev Fed Doct Cienc Filos Let (Havana)
Revista. Federacion de Estudiantes de Venezuela — RFEV
Revista. Federacion Odontologica Colombiana — Rev Fed Odontol Colomb
Revista. Federacion Odontologica Ecuatoriana — Rev Fed Odontol Ecuat
Revista Filipina de Medicina y Farmacia — Rev Filip Med Farm
Revista Financiera. Bursatil y Minera — Rev Financ Bursatil Min
Revista Floresta — Revta Floresta
Revista Forense [*Brazil*] — RF
Revista Forestal Argentina — Rev Fort Argent
Revista Forestal Chilena — Revista Forest Chilena
Revista Forestal del Peru — Rev For Peru
Revista Forestal Venezolana — Rev For Venez
Revista Forestal Venezolana — Rev Forest Venezolana
Revista. Fundacao Servicos de Saude Publica [*Brazil*] — Rev Fund SESP
Revista. Fundacao Servicos de Saude Publica (Brazil) — Rev Fund SESP (Braz)
Revista Gaucha de Enfermagem — Rev Gaucha Enferm
Revista Gaucha de Odontologia — Rev Gaucha Odontol
Revista Genealogica Latina (Sao Paulo) — Rev Geneal Lat S Paulo
Revista General de Derecho — R Gener Derecho
Revista General de Legislacion y Jurisprudencia — R Gener Legisl Jurisp
Revista General de Marina — R Gener Marina
Revista General de Marina — Rev Gen Mar
Revista General. Universidad Nacional Pedro Henriquez Urena — AULA
Revista Geografica — R Geog
Revista Geografica — Rev Geog
Revista Geografica — RG
Revista Geografica Americana — R Geogr Am
Revista Geografica Americana — Revta Geogr Am
Revista Geografica Americana (Buenos Aires) — Rev Geogr Am BA
Revista Geografica de America Central — RGAC
Revista Geografica de Chile Terra Australis (Santiago) — Rev Geogr Chile Santiago
Revista Geografica Espanola — R Geogr Espan
Revista Geografica/Instituto de Investigacion Etnologica (Barranquilla) — Rev Geogr Barranquilla
Revista Geografica. Instituto Geografico Militar del Ecuador. Departamento Geografico — IGME/RG
Revista Geografica Italiana — RGI
Revista Geografica (La Habana) — Rev Geogr Hav
Revista Geografica (Merida, Venezuela) — Rev Geogr Merida
Revista Geografica [Instituto Panamericano de Geografia i Historia] (Mexico City) — Revista Geogr Mexico City
Revista Geografica (Rio De Janeiro) — R Geogr (Rio De Janeiro)
Revista Geografica (Rio de Janeiro) — Rev Geogr Rio
Revista Geografica. Universidad de Los Andes — ULA/RG
Revista Geograhica Americana — RGA
Revista Geologica de Chile — Rev Geol Chile
Revista Germanistilor Romani — RGR
Revista Goiana de Medicina — Rev Goiana Med
Revista Gospodariilor Agricole de Stat (Bucharest) — Rev Gospod Agr Stat (Bucharest)
Revista Guatemalteca de Estomatologia — Rev Guatem Estomatol
Revista Habanera — RHab
Revista Hispanica Moderna — R Hispan Mod
Revista Hispanica Moderna — Rev Hisp Mod
Revista Hispanica Moderna — Rev Hispan
Revista Hispanica Moderna — RHiM
Revista Hispanica Moderna — RHM
Revista Historica Critica y Bibliografica de la Literatura Cubana — RHCB
Revista Historica (Lima) — Rev Hist Lima
Revista Historica (Montevideo) — Rev Hist Monte
Revista Historica. Publicacion del Museo Historico Nacional — R Hist
Revista Historica-Critica de la Literatura Centro-Americana — RLC
Revista Historico. Critica de Literatura Centroamericana — Rev Hist Crit Lit Centroam
Revista. Hospital das Clinicas. Faculdade de Medicina. Universidade de Sao Paulo — Rev Hosp Clin Fac Med Univ Sao Paulo
Revista. Hospital das Clinicas. Faculdade de Medicina. Universidade de Sao Paulo — Rev Hosp Clin Sao Paulo
Revista. Hospital das Clinicas. Faculdade de Medicina. Universidade de Sao Paulo — RHCFA
Revista. Hospital das Clinicas. Faculdade de Medicina. Universidade de Sao Paulo. Suplemento — Rev Hosp Clin Fac Med Univ Sao Paulo Supl
Revista. Hospital de Ninos (Buenos Aires) — Rev Hosp Ninos (B Aires)
Revista. Hospital de San Juan de Dios [*Bogota*] — Rev Hosp S Juan
Revista. Hospital de San Juan de Dios (Bogota) — Rev Hosp San Juan De Dios (Bogota)
Revista. Hospital del Nino (Lima) — Rev Hosp Nino (Lima)
Revista. Hospital Psiquiatrico de la Habana — Rev Hosp Psiquiatr Habana
Revista Iberica de Endocrinologia — Rev Iber Endocr
Revista Iberica de Endocrinologia — Rev Iber Endocrinol
Revista Iberica de Micologia — Rev Iber Micol
Revista Iberica de Parasitologia — Rev Iber Parasitol
Revista Iberoamericana — Rev Iberoam
Revista Iberoamericana — RevIb
Revista Iberoamericana — RI
Revista Iberoamericana — RIA
Revista Iberoamericana de Bibliografia — RIB
Revista Iberoamericana de Corrosion y Proteccion — Rev Iberoam Corros Prot
Revista Iberoamericana de Educacion Quimica — Rev Iberoam Educ Quim
Revista Iberoamericana de Educacion Quimica — RIDEQ
Revista Iberoamericana de Literatura — RIL
Revista Iberoamericana de Literatura (Montevideo) — Rev Iberoam Lit Monte
Revista Ibero-Americana de Ortodoncia — Rev Iberoam Ortod
Revista Iberoamericana de Seguridad Social — R Iberoam Seguridad Soc
Revista Iberoamericana de Seguridad Social — R Iberoamer Segur Soc
Revista Iberoamericana de Seguridad Social — Rev Iberoam Segur Soc
Revista IBPT [*Instituto de Biologia e Pesquisas Tecnologicas*]. **Curitiba** — Rev IBPT Curitiba
Revista. IBYS [*Instituto de Biologia y Sueroterapia*] — Rev IBYS
Revista ICA [*Instituto Colombiano Agropecuario*] — Rev ICA
Revista. ICIDCA [*Instituto Cubano de Investigaciones de los Derivados de la Cana de Azucar*] — Rev ICIDCA
Revista. IDIEM [*Instituto de Investigaciones de Engoyes de Materiales*] — Rev IDIEM
Revista. Igiena, Bacteriologie, Virusologie, Parazitologie, Epidemiologie, Pneumoftiziologie — Rev Ig
Revista. Igiena, Bacteriologie, Virusologie, Parazitologie, Epidemiologie, Pneumoftiziologie — Rev Ig Bacteriol Virusol Parazitol Epidemiol Pneumoftiziol
Revista. IMESC (Instituto de Medicina Social e de Criminologia de Sao Paulo) — Rev IMESC (Inst Med Soc Criminol Sao Paulo)
Revista Industrial de Sao Paulo — Rev Ind S Paulo
Revista Industrial y Agricola de Tucuman (Tucuman, Argentina) — Rev Indus Agri Tucuman
Revista Industrial y Agricola (Tucuman) — Rev Ind Agric (Tucuman)
Revista Industrial y Agricola (Tucuman) — Rev Industr Agric (Tucuman)
Revista Industrial y Agricola (Tucuman) — Revta Ind Agric (Tucuman)
Revista Industrial y Fabril [*France*] — Rev Ind Fabril
Revista Industrial y Fabril — RIFAA
Revista Industriei Alimentare. Produse Animale — Rev Ind Aliment Prod Anim
Revista Industriei Alimentare. Produse Vegetale — Rev Ind Aliment Prod Veg
Revista Ingenieria Hidraulica en Mexico — Rev Ing Hidraul Mex
Revista. Instituto Adolfo Lutz — Rev Inst Adolfo Lutz
Revista. Instituto Agricola Catalan de San Isidro — Rev Inst Agr Catalan San Isidro

Revista. Instituto Agricola Catalan de San Isidro/Servicio Sindical de Alta Cultura Agricola — Revista Inst Agric Catalan San Isidro
Revista. Instituto Americano de Arte (Cuzco, Peru) — Rev Inst Am Arte Cuzco
Revista. Instituto Bacteriologica. Buenos Aires — Rev Inst Bacteriol Buenos Aires
Revista. Instituto Bacteriologico. Departamento Nacional de Higiene (Argentina) — Rev Inst Bacteriol Dep Nac Hig (Argent)
Revista. Instituto Bacteriologico Dr. Carlos G. Malbran — Rev Inst Bacteriol Dr Carlos G Malbran
Revista. Instituto Bacteriologico Malbran — Rev Inst Bacteriol Malbran
Revista. Instituto Centroamericano de Investigacion y Tecnologia Industrial — Rev Inst Centroam Invest Tecnol Ind
Revista. Instituto Colombiano Agropecuario — Rev Inst Colomb Agropecu
Revista. Instituto de Antibioticos. Universidade do Recife — Rev Inst Antibiot Univ Recife
Revista. Instituto de Antibioticos. Universidade Federal de Pernambuco — Rev Inst Antibiot Univ Fed Pernambuco
Revista. Instituto de Antibioticos. Universidade Federal de Pernambuco (Recife) — Rev Inst Antibiot (Recife)
Revista. Instituto de Antropologia. (Cordoba, Argentina) — Rev Inst Antrop Cordoba
Revista. Instituto de Antropologia. Universidad de Cordoba — R Inst Antropol Cordoba
Revista. Instituto de Antropologia. Universidad Nacional de Cordoba — Rev Inst Antropol Univ Cordoba
Revista. Instituto de Antropologia. Universidad Nacional de Tucuman (Tucuman, Argentina) — Rev Inst Antrop Tucuman
Revista. Instituto de Biologia e Pesquisas Tecnologicas. Curitiba — Rev Inst Biol Pesquis Tecnol Curitiba
Revista. Instituto de Ciencias Sociales — Inst Ciencias Socs R
Revista. Instituto de Ciencias Sociales — R Inst Cienc Soc
Revista. Instituto de Cultura Puertorriquena — ICP/R
Revista. Instituto de Cultura Puertorriquena — RICP
Revista. Instituto de Cultura Puertorriquena (San Juan, Puerto Rico) — Rev Inst Cult Puertorriq S Juan
Revista. Instituto de Defensa del Cafe — Revista Inst Defensa Cafe
Revista. Instituto de Defensa del Cafe de Costa Rica (San Jose, Costa Rica) — Rev Inst Defensa Cafe S Jose
Revista. Instituto de Derecho del Trabajo y de Investigaciones Sociales (Quito) — Rev Inst Der Trab Invest Soc Quito
Revista. Instituto de Estudios Alicantinos — R Alicante
Revista. Instituto de Estudios Islamicos — R Inst Est Islam
Revista. Instituto de Estudios Islamicos — Rev Inst Est Isl
Revista. Instituto de Estudios Islamicos — RIEI
Revista. Instituto de Estudios Superiores (Montevideo) — Rev Inst Estud Super Monte
Revista. Instituto de Estudos Brasileiros — RIEB
Revista. Instituto de Etnologia — Revta Inst Etnol
Revista. Instituto de Geologia. Universidad Nacional Autonoma de Mexico — Rev Inst Geol Univ Nac Auton Mex
Revista. Instituto de Geologia y Mineria. Universidad Nacional de Tucuman — Rev Inst Geol Min Univ Nac Tucuman
Revista. Instituto de Historia de Derecho Ricardo Levene — RevtI
Revista. Instituto de Historia del Derecho — IHRL
Revista. Instituto de Historia del Derecho. Universidad Nacional de Buenos Aires — Rev Inst Hist Der BA
Revista. Instituto de Investigaciones Economicas (Rosario, Argentina) — Rev Inst Invest Econ Rosario
Revista. Instituto de Investigaciones Historicas. Universidad Tomas Frias (Potosi, Bolivia) — Rev Inst Invest Hist Univ T Frias Potosi
Revista. Instituto de Investigaciones Medicas — Rev Inst Invest Med
Revista. Instituto de Investigaciones Tecnologicas (Bogota) — Rev Inst Invest Tecnol (Bogota)
Revista. Instituto de Laticinios Candido Tostes — Rev Inst Laticinios Candido Tostes
Revista. Instituto de Medicina Tropical de Sao Paulo — Rev Inst Med Trop Sao Paulo
Revista. Instituto de Medicina Tropical de Sao Paulo — RMTSA
Revista. Instituto de Salubridad y Enfermedades Tropicales — Rev Inst Salubr Enferm Trop
Revista. Instituto de Salubridad y Enfermedades Tropicales. Mexico City — Rev Inst Salubr Enferm Trop Mexico City
Revista. Instituto de Sociologia. Boliviana (Sucre) — Rev Inst Sociol Boliv Sucre
Revista. Instituto Egipcio de Estudios Islamicos — R Inst Egip Est Islam
Revista. Instituto Etnologico Nacional — RIEtnN
Revista. Instituto Etnologico Nacional (Bogota) — Rev Inst Etnol Nac Bogota
Revista. Instituto Geografico e Geologico (Sao Paulo) — Rev Inst Geogr Geol (Sao Paulo)
Revista. Instituto Historico e Geografico Brasileiro — Rev Inst Hist Geogr Bras
Revista. Instituto Historico e Geografico de Sao Paulo — Rev Inst Hist Geogr S Paulo
Revista. Instituto Historico e Geografico de Sao Paulo — RIHGSP
Revista. Instituto Historico e Geografico de Sergipe (Aracaju, Brazil) — Rev Inst Hist Geogr Aracaju
Revista. Instituto Malbran — Rev Inst Malbran
Revista. Instituto Medico-Legal do Estado da Guanabara — Rev Inst Med Leg Estado Guanabara
Revista. Instituto Mexicano del Petroleo — Rev Inst Mex Pet
Revista. Instituto Mexicano del Petroleo — Rev Inst Mex Petrol
Revista. Instituto Municipal de Botanica (Buenos Aires) — Rev Inst Munic Bot (B Aires)
Revista. Instituto Nacional de Cancerologia (Mexico) — Rev Inst Nacl Cancerol (Mex)
Revista. Instituto Nacional de Geologia y Mineria (Argentina) — Rev Inst Nac Geol Min (Argent)
Revista. Instituto Nacional de Higiene — Rev Inst Nac Hig
Revista. Instituto Nacional de Investigacion de las Ciencias Naturales Anexo. Museo Argentino de Ciencias Naturales Bernardino Rivadavia. Ciencias Geologicas — Revista Inst Nac Invest Ci Nat Ci Geol
Revista. Instituto Nacional de la Tradicion — RINT
Revista. Instituto Nacional de la Tradicion (Buenos Aires) — Rev Inst Nac Tradicion BA
Revista. Instituto Nacional de Medicina Legal de Colombia — Rev Inst Nac Med Leg Colombia
Revista. Instituto Nacional del Cafe — Revista Inst Nac Cafe
Revista. Instituto Nacional General Francisco Menendez (San Salvador) — Rev Inst Nac Gen Frco Menendez S Salvador
Revista. Instituto Pedagogico Nacional (Caracas) — Rev Inst Pedag Nac Caracas
Revista. Instituto Peruano de Investigaciones Genealogicas — R Inst Peruano Investigaciones Genealogicas
Revista. Instituto Tenico Administrativo del Trabajo (Mexico) — Rev Inst Tec Admin Trab Mex
Revista Insulana. Instituto Cultural de Ponta Delgada — RI
Revista Integracion. Temas de Matematicas — Rev Integr Temas Mat
Revista Interamericana de Bibliografia — R Interam Bibl
Revista Interamericana de Bibliografia — R Interam Bibliog
Revista Interamericana de Bibliografia [*Inter-American Review of Bibliography*] — Rev Inter B
Revista Interamericana de Bibliografia — RIAB
Revista Interamericana de Bibliografia. Organization of American States — RIB
Revista Interamericana de Bibliografia/Pan American Union — Revista Interamer Bibliogr
Revista Interamericana de Ciencias Sociales — R Interam Cienc Soc
Revista Interamericana de Ciencias Sociales — Rev Interamer Cienc Soc
Revista Interamericana de Educacion (Bogota) — Rev Interam Educ Bogota
Revista Interamericana de Planificacion — R Interamer Planif
Revista Interamericana de Psicologia — Revta Interam Psicologia
Revista Interamericana de Psicologia — RIP
Revista Interamericana de Radiologia — Rev Interam Radiol
Revista Interamericana de Sociologia — R Interam Sociol
Revista Interamericana do Ministerio Publico (Sao Paulo) — Rev Interam Min Publ S Paulo
Revista Interamericana Review — RIR
Revista Internacional de Contaminacion Ambiental — Rev Int Contam Ambiental
Revista Internacional de Estudios Vascos — RIEV
Revista Internacional de Metodos Numericos para Calculo y Diseno en Ingenieria — Rev Internac Metod Numer Calc Disen Ingr
Revista Internacional de Sociologia — R Internac Sociol
Revista Internacional de Sociologia — RIS
Revista Internacional de Sociologia — RISO
Revista Internacional de Sociologia. CSIC (Consejo Superior de Investigaciones Cientificas) — R Int Sociologia
Revista Internacional de Sociologia (Madrid) — R Int Sociol (Madrid)
Revista Internacional del Trabajo — Rev Intern Trab
Revista International de Agricultura — Rev Int Agric
Revista International de Sociologia. Instituto Balmes de Sociologia — RISB
Revista Internazionale dei Trasporti — R Internaz Econ Trasporti
Revista Internazionale di Scienze Economiche e Commerciali — Rev Int Sc
Revista Ion — Rev Ion
Revista. Istituto d'Archeologia e Storia dell'Arte — RIASA
Revista Istorica Romana — R Ist Rom
Revista Istorica Romana — RIR
Revista. Jardin Botanico Nacional — Rev Jard Bot Nac
Revista Javeriana — R Javer
Revista Javeriana — RJ
Revista Javeriana — RJav
Revista Javeriana (Bogota) — Rev Javer Bogota
Revista. Junta de Estudios Historicos (Mendoza, Argentina) — Rev Junt Estud Hist Mendoza
Revista. Junta de Historia y Letras (La Rioja, Argentina) — Rev Junt Hist Letr La Rioja
Revista Juridica — Rev Jur
Revista Juridica Argentina (Buenos Aires) — Rev Jur Arg BA
Revista Juridica (Cochabamba, Bolivia) — Rev Jur Cochabamba
Revista Juridica de Buenos Aires — Rev Jur BA
Revista Juridica de Cataluna — R Juridica Cataluna
Revista Juridica del Peru — Rev Jur del Peru
Revista Juridica Dominicana (Ciudad, Trujillo) — Rev Jur Dom C Trujillo
Revista Juridica Latinoamericana — RJL
Revista Juridica (Rio Piedras, Puerto Rico) — Rev Jur Rio Piedras
Revista Juridica (Tucuman, Argentina) — Rev Jur Tucuman
Revista Juridica. Universidad de Puerto Rico — Rev Jur de la Univ de Puerto Rico
Revista Juridica. Universidad de Puerto Rico — Rev Jur UPR
Revista Juridica. Universidad Interamericana — RJUI
Revista Juridica. Universidad Interamericana de Puerto Rico — Rev Jur U Inter PR
Revista Kuba de Medicina Tropical y Parasitologia — Rev Kuba Med Trop Parasitol
Revista. Laboratorio de Fonetica Experimental — RLFE
Revista Latino Americana de Filosofia — RLAF
Revista Latinoamericana de Anatomia Patologica — Rev Latinoam Anat Patol
Revista Latinoamericana de Ciencias Agricolas — Rev Latinoam Cienc Agric
Revista Latinoamericana de Ciencias Agricolas — RLCAD
Revista Latinoamericana de Cirugia Plastica — RLCP
Revista Latinoamericana de Cirurgia Plastica — Rev Latinoam Cir Plast
Revista Latinoamericana de Educacion (Educadores) — RLE
Revista Latinoamericana de Estudios Educativos — R Latinoamer Estud Educ

Revista Latinoamericana de Estudios Urbano Regionales — R Latinoam Estud Urbano Reg
Revista Latinoamericana de Filosofia — Rev Latin de Filosof
Revista Latinoamericana de Filosofia — RLF
Revista Latinoamericana de Historia Economica y Social — HISLA
Revista Latinoamericana de Ingenieria Quimica y Quimica Aplicada — Rev Latinoam Ing Quim Quim Apl
Revista Latinoamericana de Microbiologia — Rev Latam Microbiol
Revista Latinoamericana de Microbiologia — Rev Latinoam Microbiol
Revista Latinoamericana de Microbiologia. Suplemento — Rev Latinoam Microbiol Supl
Revista Latinoamericana de Microbiologia y Parasitologia [*Later, Revista Latinoamericana de Microbiologia*] — Rev Latinoam Microbiol Parasitol
Revista Latinoamericana de Microbiologia y Parasitologia [*Later, Revista Latinoamericana de Microbiologia*] — RLMPA
Revista Latinoamericana de Patologia — Rev Latam Patol
Revista Latinoamericana de Patologia — Rev Latinoam Patol
Revista Latinoamericana de Psicologia — R Latinoamer Psicol
Revista Latinoamericana de Psicologia — Rev Latam P
Revista Latinoamericana de Psicologia — Rev Latinoam Psicol
Revista Latinoamericana de Psicologia — RLP
Revista Latinoamericana de Psiquiatria — Rev Lat Am Psiquiat
Revista Latinoamericana de Quimica — Rev Latinoam Quim
Revista Latinoamericana de Quimica — RLAQA
Revista Latinoamericana de Siderurgia — Rev Latinoam Sider
Revista Latinoamericana de Sociologia — R Latinoamer Sociol
Revista Latinoamericana de Sociologia — RLS
Revista Latinoamericana de Sociologia (Instituto Di Tella, Buenos Aires) — Rev Latinoam Sociol BA
Revista Liturgica Argentina — RLA
Revista Lusitana — RL
Revista Lyceum (La Habana) — Rev Lyceum Hav
Revista (Madrid) — RevM
Revista Matematica de la Universidad Complutense de Madrid — Rev Mat Univ Complut Madrid
Revista Matematica Dominicana — Rev Mat Dominicana
Revista Matematica Hispano-Americana — Rev Mat Hisp-Amer
Revista Matematica Hispano-Americana. Serie 4 — Rev Mat Hisp-Amer 4
Revista Matematica Iberoamericana — Rev Mat Iberoamericana
Revista Medica — Rev Med
Revista Medica Brasileira — Rev Med Bras
Revista Medica Cubana — Rev Med Cubana
Revista Medica Cubana — RMC
Revista Medica da Aeronautica — Rev Med Aero
Revista Medica da Aeronautica — Rev Med Aeronaut
Revista Medica de Angola — Rev Med Angola
Revista Medica de Bahia — Rev Med Bahia
Revista Medica de Bogota — Rev Med Bogota
Revista Medica de Chile — Rev Med Chi
Revista Medica de Chile — Rev Med Chil
Revista Medica de Chile — Rev Med Chile
Revista Medica de Cordoba — Rev Med Cordoba
Revista Medica de Costa Rica — Rev Med Costa Rica
Revista Medica de Galicia — Rev Med Galicia
Revista Medica de Juiz de Fora — Rev Med Juiz de Fora
Revista Medica de Mocambique — Rev Med Mocambique
Revista Medica de Mocambique — RMDMDL
Revista Medica de Panama — Rev Med Panama
Revista Medica de Sao Paulo — Rev Med de S Paulo
Revista Medica de Sevilla — Rev Med Sevilla
Revista Medica de Yucatan — Rev Med Yucatan
Revista Medica del Paraguay — Rev Med Parag
Revista Medica del Rosario — Rev Med d Rosario
Revista Medica del Rosario — Rev Med Rosario
Revista Medica del Uruguay — Rev Med Uruguay
Revista Medica del Uruguay — Revista Med Uruguay
Revista Medica do Estado da Guanabara — Rev Med Estado Guanabara
Revista Medica do Estado do Rio De Janeiro — Rev Med Estado Rio De J
Revista Medica Hondurena — Rev Med Hondur
Revista Medica. Hospital Central del Empleado (Lima) — Rev Med Hosp Cent Empl (Lima)
Revista Medica. Hospital Colonia — Rev Med Hosp Colon
Revista Medica. Hospital Colonia (Mexico) — Rev Med Hosp Colon (Mex)
Revista Medica. Hospital dos Servidores do Estado — Rev Med Hosp Servidores Estado
Revista Medica. Hospital dos Servidores do Estado — Rev Med HSE
Revista Medica. Hospital Espanol — Rev Med Hosp Esp
Revista Medica. Hospital General (Mexico) — Rev Med Hosp Gen (Mex)
Revista Medica. Hospital General (Mexico City) — Rev Med Hosp Gen (Mexico City)
Revista Medica. Hospital Obrero — Rev Med Hosp Obrero
Revista Medica. Instituto de Previdencia dos Servidores do Estado de Minas Gerais — Rev Med Inst Previdencia Serv Estado Minas Gerais
Revista Medica. Instituto de Previdencia dos Servidores do Estado de Minas Gerais — Rev Med Inst Previdencia Servidores Estado Minas Gerais
Revista Medica. Instituto Mexicano del Seguro Social — Rev Med Inst Mex Seguro Soc
Revista Medica Latino-Americana — Revista Med Latino Amer
Revista Medica Veracruzana — Rev Med Veracruz
Revista Medicala — Rev Med
Revista Medicala (Tirgu-Mures) [*Romania*] — Rev Med (Tirgu-Mures)
Revista Medico-Chirurgicala — Rev Med Chir
Revista Medico-Chirurgicala. Societatii de Medici si Naturalisti din Iasi — Rev Med-Chir Soc Med Nat din Iasi
Revista Medico-Chirurgicala. Societatii de Medici si Naturalisti din Iasi — Rev Med-Chir Soc Med Nat Iasi
Revista Medico-Cirurgica do Brasil — Rev Med Cirurg Brasil
Revista Medico-Quirurgica. Asociacion Medica del Hospital Rivadavia — RMARDL
Revista Medico-Quirurgica. Asociacion Medica. Hospital Rivadavia — Rev Med Quir Asoc Med Hosp Rivadavia
Revista Medico-Quirurgica (Buenos Aires) — Rev Med-Quir (Buenos Aires)
Revista Medico-Quirurgica de Patologia Femenina — Rev Med Quir Patol Femenina
Revista Medico-Quirurgica Teguelgalpa — Rev Med Quir Teguelgalpa
Revista Mensual. Asociacion Rural del Uruguay — Rev Mens Asoc Rural Urug
Revista Mensual de Medicina e Cirugia — Rev Mens Med Cirug
Revista Meteorologica — Rev Meteorol
Revista Mexicana de Anestesiologia — Rev Mex Anestesiol
Revista Mexicana de Astronomia y Astrofisica — Rev Mex Astron Astrof
Revista Mexicana de Astronomia y Astrofisica — Rev Mex Astron Astrofis
Revista Mexicana de Astronomia y Astrofisica — Rev Mex Astron y Astrofis
Revista Mexicana de Astronomia y Astrofisica — Rev Mexicana Astronom Astrofis
Revista Mexicana de Astronomia y Astrofisica — RMAAD
Revista Mexicana de Astronomia y Astrofisica. Serie de Conferencias — Rev Mex Astron Astrofis Ser Conf
Revista Mexicana de Ciencias Farmaceuticas — Rev Mex Cienc Farm
Revista Mexicana de Ciencias Medicas y Biologicas — Rev Mex Cienc Med Biol
Revista Mexicana de Ciencias Politicas y Sociales — R Mex Ciencias Pols y Socs
Revista Mexicana de Ciencias Politicas y Sociales — RMCPS
Revista Mexicana de Cirugia, Ginecologia, y Cancer — Rev Mex Cir Ginecol Cancer
Revista Mexicana de Cirugia, Ginecologia, y Cancer — Rev Mex Cirug Ginec Canc
Revista Mexicana de Electricidad — Rev Mex Electr
Revista Mexicana de Estudios Antropologicos (Mexico) — Rev Mex Estud Antrop Mex
Revista Mexicana de Estudios Antropologicos y Historicos — RMEA
Revista Mexicana de Fisica — Rev Mex Fis
Revista Mexicana de Fisica — Rev Mexicana Fis
Revista Mexicana de Fisica. Suplemento de Ensenanza — Rev Mex Fis Supl Ensenanza
Revista Mexicana de Fisica. Suplemento de Ensenanza — RMFEB
Revista Mexicana de Fisica. Suplemento de Fisica Aplicada — Rev Mex Fis Supl Fis Apl
Revista Mexicana de Fisica. Suplemento de Fisica Aplicada — RMSFA
Revista Mexicana de Fisica. Suplemento del Reactor — Rev Mex Fis Supl Reactor
Revista Mexicana de Fisica. Suplemento del Reactor — RMFSA
Revista Mexicana de Fitopatologia — Rev Mex Fitopatol
Revista Mexicana de Fitopatologia — RMFIEK
Revista Mexicana de Geografia — Revta Mex Geogr
Revista Mexicana de Geografia (Mexico) — Rev Mex Geogr Mex
Revista Mexicana de Ingenieria y Arquitectura (Mexico) — Rev Mex Ing Arquitec Mex
Revista Mexicana de la Construccion — Rev Mex Constr
Revista Mexicana de Laboratorio Clinico — Rev Mex Lab Clin
Revista Mexicana de Literatura — RML
Revista Mexicana de Pediatria — Rev Mex Pediatr
Revista Mexicana de Psiquiatria, Neurologia, y Medicina Legal — Rev Mex Psiquiat Neurol Med Leg
Revista Mexicana de Radiologia — Rev Mex Radiol
Revista Mexicana de Sociologia — R Mexic Sociol
Revista Mexicana de Sociologia — Rev Mex Soc
Revista Mexicana de Sociologia — Rev Mex Sociol
Revista Mexicana de Sociologia — RMS
Revista Mexicana de Sociologia — RMSoc
Revista Mexicana de Sociologia (Mexico) — Rev Mex Sociol Mex
Revista Mexicana de Sociologia. Universidad Nacional Autonoma de Mexico. Instituto de Investigaciones Sociales — UNAM/RMS
Revista Mexicana de Tuberculosis y Aparto Respiratorio — Rev Mex Tuberc Apar Respir
Revista Mexicana de Tuberculosis y Enfermedades del Aparato Respiratorio — Rev Mex Tuber Enferm Apar Respir
Revista Mexicana de Urologia — Rev Mex Urol
Revista Mexicana del Trabajo — R Mexic Trab
Revista Mexicana del Trabajo (Mexico) — Rev Mex Trab Mex
Revista Mexicana del Trabajo. Secretaria del Trabajo y Prevision Social — MSTPS/R
Revista Mexicana. Periodico Cientifico y Literario — Revista Mex
Revista Militar — Rev Mil
Revista Militar de Medicina Veterinaria — Rev Mil Med Vet
Revista Militar de Remonta e Veterinaria — Rev Mil Remonta Vet
Revista Militar de Veterinaria — Rev Mil Vet
Revista Militar de Veterinaria (Rio De Janeiro) — Rev Mil Vet (Rio De Janeiro)
Revista Mineira de Engenharia — Rev Min Eng
Revista Minelor — Rev Minelor
Revista Minelor (Bucharest) — Rev Minelor (Bucharest)
Revista Minera (Buenos Aires) — Rev Minera BA
Revista Minera, Geologia, y Mineralogia — Rev Min Geol Mineral
Revista Minera, Geologia, y Mineralogia — Rev Minera Geol Mineral
Revista Minera, Geologia, y Mineralogia (Buenos Aires) — Rev Minera Geol Mineral BA
Revista Minera y Petrolera — Rev Minera y Petrolera
Revista Mineria — Rev Min
Revista. Ministerio de Agricultura — Revista Minist Agric
Revista. Ministerio de Justicia (Caracas) — Rev Min Jus Caracas

Revista. Ministerio de Justicia (Venezuela) — Minist Justicia R (Venezuela)
Revista Monserratena — R Mons
Revista Municipal de Costa Rica (San Jose, Costa Rica) — Rev Munici S Jose
Revista Municipal de Engenharia — Rev Munic Eng
Revista Municipal de Engenharia (Rio de Janeiro) — Rev Munici Engen Rio
Revista Municipal. [Camara Municipal de] Lisboa — RML
Revista. Museo Argentino de Ciencias Naturales Bernardino Rivadavia e Instituto Nacional de Investigacion de las Ciencias Naturales. Ciencias Botanicas — RABBAR
Revista. Museo Argentino de Ciencias Naturales Bernardino Rivadavia e Instituto Nacional de Investigacion de las Ciencias Naturales. Zoologia — RMAZDB
Revista. Museo Argentino de Ciencias Naturales Bernardino Rivadavia. Zoologia — Revta Mus Argent Cienc Nat Bernardina Rivadavia Zool
Revista. Museo de Historia Natural de Mendoza — Rev Mus Hist Nat Mendoza
Revista. Museo de La Plata — Rev Mus La Plata
Revista. Museo de La Plata. Seccion Antropologia — R Mus La Plata Antropol
Revista. Museo de La Plata. Seccion Antropologia — Rev Mus La Plata Secc Antropol
Revista. Museo de La Plata. Seccion Botanica — Rev Mus La Plata Secc Bot
Revista. Museo de La Plata. Seccion Geologia — Rev Mus La Plata Secc Geol
Revista. Museo de La Plata. Seccion Paleontologia — Rev Mus La Plata Secc Paleontol
Revista. Museo de La Plata. Seccion Zoologia — Rev Mus La Plata Secc Zool
Revista. Museo de La Plata. Universidad Nacional de La Plata. Facultad de Ciencias Naturales y Museo — UNLPM/R
Revista. Museo del Atlantico (Barranquilla, Colombia) — Rev Mus Atlantico Barranquilla
Revista. Museo e Instituto Arqueologico (Cuzco, Peru) — Rev Mus Inst Arqueol Cuzco
Revista. Museo Historico Nacional de Chile (Santiago) — Rev Mus Hist Nac Santiago
Revista. Museo Historico (Quito) — Rev Mus Hist Quito
Revista. Museo Julio de Castilhos e Arquivo Historico do Rio Grande do Sul (Porto Alegre, Brazil) — Rev Mus J Castilhos Arquiv Hist P Alegre
Revista. Museo Nacional — R Mus Nac
Revista. Museo Nacional — RMN
Revista. Museo Nacional — RMNac
Revista. Museo Nacional de Antropologia y Arqueologia (Lima) — Rev Mus Nac Antrop Arqueol Lima
Revista. Museo Nacional de la Cultura Peruana — PEMN/R
Revista. Museo Nacional (Lima) — Rev Mus Nac Lima
Revista. Museu Paulista — Revta Mus Paul
Revista. Museu Paulista — RMPaul
Revista Musical Chilena — R M Ch
Revista Musical Chilena — R Mus Chile
Revista Musical Chilena — Rev Mus Chilena
Revista Musical Chilena — Rev Music Chilena
Revista Musical Chilena — RM Chilena
Revista Musical Chilena — RMC
Revista Musical Chilena (Santiago) — Rev Music Chil Santiago
Revista Muzeelor — Rev Muz
Revista Muzeelor — RMM
Revista Muzeelor si Monumentelor — Rev Muz
Revista Muzeelor si Monumentelor — RMM
Revista Muzeelor si Monumentelor. Seria Monumente Istorice si Arta — Rev Muz M Mon
Revista Muzeelor si Monumentelor. Seria Muzee — Rev Muz M Muz
Revista Muzeelor si Monumentelor. Seria Muzee — Rev Muz Monum Muz
Revista Nacional de Agricultura — Rev Nac Agr
Revista Nacional de Agricultura (Bogota) — Rev Nac Agric (Bogota)
Revista Nacional de Arquitectura — R Nac Arquitectura
Revista Nacional de Cultura — RNC
Revista Nacional de Cultura (Argentina) — RNCA
Revista Nacional de Cultura (Caracas) — Rev Nac Cult Caracas
Revista Nacional de Cultura. Ministerio de Educacion Nacional — R Nac Cult
Revista Nacional de Hospitales — Rev Nac Hosp
Revista Nacional de Teatro — RNT
Revista Nacional (Montevideo) — Rev Nac Monte
Revista Nacional (Montevideo) — RNM
Revista Neurologica de Buenos Aires — Rev Neurol B Aires
Revista Neurologica de Buenos Aires — Rev Neurol Buenos Aires
Revista Nordestina de Biologia — Rev Nordestina Biol
Revista Nordestina de Biologia — RNOBDG
Revista Notarial — RN
Revista Numismatica Argentina — Rev Num Arg
Revista Ocrotirea Mediului Inconjurator Natura. Terra Natura — Rev Ocrotirea Mediului Inconjurator Nat Terr Nat
Revista Odonto-Estomatologica — Rev Odontoestomatol
Revista Odontologica. Circulo de Odontologos del Paraguay — Rev Odontol Circ Odontol Parag
Revista Odontologica (Cordoba) — Rev Odontol (Cordoba)
Revista Odontologica de Concepcion — Rev Odontol Concepcion
Revista Odontologica de Costa Rica — Rev Odontol Costa Rica
Revista Odontologica de Puerto Rico — Rev Odontol PR
Revista Odontologica de Puerto Rico (Santurce) — Rev Odontol PR (Santurce)
Revista Odontologica do Parana — Rev Odontol Parana
Revista Odontologica Ecuatoriana — Rev Odontol Ecuat
Revista Oficial. Federacion Medica del Ecuador — Rev Of Fed Med Ecuador
Revista Oto-Laringologica de Sao Paulo — Revista Oto Laringol Sao Paulo
Revista Padurilor — Rev Padurilor
Revista Padurilor — Revta Padur
Revista Padurilor. Silvicultura si Exploatarea Padurilor — Rev Padurilor Silvic Exploat Padurilor
Revista Padurilor-Industria Lemnului. Celuloza si Hirtie. Industria Lemnului [*A publication*] — Rev Padurilor Ind Lemnului Celul Hirtie Ind Lemnului
Revista Padurilor-Industria Lemnului. Celuloza si Hirtie. Seria Celuloza si Hirtie — RPLHD
Revista Padurilor-Industria Lemnului. Celuloza si Hirtie. Seria Industria Lemnului — RPLLD
Revista Padurilor-Industria Lemnului. Celuloza si Hirtie. Silvicultura si Exploatarea Padurilor — Rev Padurilor Ind Lemnului Celul Hirtie Silvic Exploatarea
Revista Padurilor-Industria Lemnului. Seria Industria Lemnului [*Hungary*] — Rev Padurilor-Ind Lemnului Ser Ind Lemnului
Revista Padurilor-Industria Lemnului. Seria Industria Lemnului — RISID
Revista Padurilor-Industria Lemnului. Seria Silvicultura si Exploatarea Padurilor — Rev Padurilor Ind Lemnului Ser Silvic Exploat Padurilor
Revista Padurilor-Industria Lemnului. Seria Silvicultura si Exploatarea Padurilor — Rev Padurilor-Ind Lemnului Ser Silvic Exploatarea Padurilor
Revista Pan-America — RPA
Revista Paraguaya de Sociologia — R Paraguaya Sociol
Revista Paraguaya de Sociologia — RPDS
Revista Paraguaya de Sociologia (Asuncion) — Rev Paraguaya Sociol Asuncion
Revista Paraguaya de Sociologia. Centro Paraguayo de Estudios Sociologicos — CPES/RPS
Revista Paulista de Endodontia — Rev Paul Endodontia
Revista Paulista de Enfermagem — Rev Paul Enferm
Revista Paulista de Medicina — Rev Paul Med
Revista Paulista de Medicina — Revista Paul Med
Revista Paulista de Tisiologia e do Torax — Rev Paul Tisiol Torax
Revista Penal y Penitenciaria (Buenos Aires) — Rev Penal Peniten BA
Revista Pentru Istorie, Arheologie, si Filologie — RIAF
Revista Pernambucana de Desenvolvimento — R Pernambucana Desenvolvimento
Revista Pernambucana de Direito Penal e Criminologia — Rev Pernam Dir Penal Crimin
Revista Pernambucana de Odontologia — Rev Pernambucana Odontol
Revista Peruana de Cultura (Lima) — Rev Peruana Cult Lima
Revista Peruana de Derecho Internacional — R Peruana Derecho Internac
Revista Peruana de Entomologia — Rev Peru Entomol
Revista Peruana de Entomologia Agricola — Rev Per Ent Agric
Revista Peruana de Entomologia Agricola — Rev Peru Entomol Agr
Revista Peruana de Entomologia Agricola — Rev Peru Entomol Agric
Revista Peruana de Entomologia Agricola — Revta Peru Ent Agric
Revista Peruana de Fisica — Rev Per Fis
Revista Peruana de Medicina Tropical — Rev Peru Med Trop
Revista Peruana de Salud Publica — Rev Peru Salud Publica
Revista Peruana de Tuberculosis y Enfermedades Respiratorias — Rev Per Tuberc
Revista Peruana de Tuberculosis y Enfermedades Respiratorias — Rev Peru Tuberc Enferm Respir
Revista Politecnica — Rev Politec
Revista Portugal. Serie A. A Lingua Portuguesa — ALP
Revista Portuguesa de Bioquimica Aplicada — Rev Port Bioquim Apl
Revista Portuguesa de Cardiologia — Rev Port Cardiol
Revista Portuguesa de Ciencias Veterinarias — Rev Port Cienc Vet
Revista Portuguesa de Estomatologia e Cirurgia Maxilofacial — Rev Port Estomat
Revista Portuguesa de Estomatologia e Cirurgia Maxilofacial — Rev Port Estomatol Cir Maxilofac
Revista Portuguesa de Farmacia — Rev Port Farm
Revista Portuguesa de Filologia — RPF
Revista Portuguesa de Filosofia — Rev Port Filosof
Revista Portuguesa de Filosofia — RevPF
Revista Portuguesa de Filosofia — RPFilos
Revista Portuguesa de Historia — R Portug Hist
Revista Portuguesa de Historia — RPH
Revista Portuguesa de Medicina — Rev Port Med
Revista Portuguesa de Medicina Militar — Rev Port Med Milit
Revista Portuguesa de Obstetricia, Ginecologia, e Cirurgia — Rev Port Obstet
Revista Portuguesa de Pediatria — Rev Port Pediatr
Revista Portuguesa de Pediatria e Puericultura — Rev Port Pediatr Pueric
Revista Portuguesa de Quimica — Rev Po Quim
Revista Portuguesa de Quimica — Rev Port Quim
Revista Portuguesa de Quimica (Lisbon) — Rev Port Quim (Lisbon)
Revista Portuguesa de Zoologia e Biologia Geral — Rev Port Zool Biol Geral
Revista Psiquiatrica Peruana — Rev Psiquiatr Peru
Revista Quimica — Rev Quim
Revista Quimico-Farmaceutica (Santiago) — Rev Quim Farm (Santiago)
Revista Quirurgica Espanola — Rev Quirurgica Esp
Revista. Real Academia de Ciencias Exactas, Fisicas, y Naturales de Madrid [*A publication*] — RCFNA
Revista. Real Academia de Ciencias Exactas, Fisicas, y Naturales de Madrid — Rev R Acad Cienc Exactas Fis Nat Madr
Revista. Real Academia de Ciencias Exactas, Fisicas, y Naturales de Madrid [*A publication*] — Rev Real Acad Ci Exact Fis Natur Madrid
Revista. Real Academia de Farmacia de Barcelona — Rev R Acad Farm Barcelona
Revista. Real Academia de Jurisprudencia y Legislacion — R Acad Jurispr Legisl
Revista. Real Academia Galega de Ciencias — Rev R Acad Galega Cienc
Revista/Review Interamericana — R/RIA
Revista/Review Interamericana — Rev/I
Revista/Review Interamericana — RInter
Revista/Review Interamericana — RRI
Revista "Roche" de Farmacia — Rev "Roche" Farm
Revista Romana de Petrol — Rev Rom Pet

Revista Salvadorena de Ciencias Sociales (San Salvador) — Rev Salvador Cien Soc S Salvador
Revista Sanitara Militara — Rev Sanit Mil
Revista Sanitara Militara — RVSMB
Revista Sanitaria Militar (Asuncion) — Rev Sanit Milit Asuncion
Revista. Sao Paulo Universidade. Faculdade de Medicina Veterinaria e Zootecnia — Rev Sao Paulo Braz Univ Fac Med Vet Zootec
Revista Saude — RESAD
Revista Saude — Rev Saude
Revista Scientifica — RS
Revista. Servicio Especial de Saude Publica — Rev Serv Espec Saude Publica
Revista. Servicio Especial de Saude Publica — Rev SESP
Revista. Servicio Nacional de Salud — Rev Serv Nac Salud
Revista. Servicio Nacional Minero Geologico (Argentina) — Rev Serv Nac Min Geol (Argent)
Revista Shell — Rev Shell
Revista Shell — RSh
Revista Shell — Shell
Revista Shorthorn — Rev Shorthorn
Revista Signos de Valparaiso — RSV
Revista Sindical de Estadistica — R Sind Estadist
Revista Sindical de Estadistica — R Sindical Estadistica
Revista Sindical de Estadistica — Rev Sind Estad
Revista sobre Relaciones Industriales y Laborales — RIL
Revista. Sociedad Amigos de la Arqueologia (Montevideo) — Rev Soc Amig Arqueol Monte
Revista. Sociedad Argentina de Biologia — Rev Soc Argent Biol
Revista. Sociedad Argentina de Biologia — RSABA
Revista. Sociedad Argentina de Neurologia y Psiquiatria — Rev Soc Argent Neurol y Psiquiat
Revista. Sociedad Bolivariana — RSB
Revista. Sociedad Bolivariana de Venezuela — RevS
Revista. Sociedad Bolivariana de Venezuela — RSBV
Revista. Sociedad Bolivariana de Venezuela (Caracas) — Rev Soc Bolivar Venez Caracas
Revista. Sociedad Boliviana de Historia Natural — Rev Soc Boliv Hist Nat
Revista. Sociedad Cientifica del Paraguay — Rev Soc Cient Parag
Revista. Sociedad Cientifica del Paraguay — SCPGB
Revista. Sociedad Colombiana de Endocrinologia — Rev Soc Colomb Endocrinol
Revista. Sociedad Colombiana de Ortodonicia — Rev Soc Colomb Ortod
Revista. Sociedad Cubana de Botanica — Rev Soc Cubana Bot
Revista. Sociedad Cubana de Ingenieros — Rev Soc Cubana Ing
Revista. Sociedad Cubana de la Historia de Medicina — Rev Soc Cub Hist Med
Revista. Sociedad de Geografia e Historia de Honduras (Tegucigalpa) — Rev Soc Geogr Hist Tegucigalpa
Revista. Sociedad de Medicina Interna — Rev Soc Med Int
Revista. Sociedad de Medicina Interna y Sociedad de Tisiologia — Rev Soc Med Int y Soc Tisiol
Revista. Sociedad de Medicina Veterinaria (Buenos Aires) — Rev Soc Med Vet (Buenos Aires)
Revista. Sociedad de Medicina Veterinaria de Chile — Rev Soc Med Vet Chile
Revista. Sociedad de Obstetricia y Ginecologia de Buenos Aires — Rev Soc Obstet Ginec
Revista. Sociedad de Pediatria — Rev Soc Pediat
Revista. Sociedad de Pediatria del Litoral — Rev Soc Pediatr Litoral
Revista. Sociedad Entomologica Argentina — Rev Soc Entomol Argent
Revista. Sociedad Geologica Argentina — Rev Soc Geol Argent
Revista. Sociedad Lunar Internacional — Rev Soc Lun Int
Revista. Sociedad Malacologica Carlos de la Torre — Rev Soc Malacol Carlos Torre
Revista. Sociedad Medica Argentina — Rev Soc Med Argent
Revista. Sociedad Mexicana de Higiene — Rev Soc Mex Hig
Revista. Sociedad Mexicana de Historia Natural — Rev Soc Mex Hist Nat
Revista. Sociedad Mexicana de Historia Natural — Rev Soc Mex Hist Natur
Revista. Sociedad Mexicana de Lepidopterologia. AC — Rev Soc Mex Lepid AC
Revista. Sociedad Mexicana de Lepidopterologia. AC — Rev Soc Mex Lepidopterol AC
Revista. Sociedad Peruana de Endocrinologia — Rev Soc Peru Endocrinol
Revista. Sociedad Quimica de Mexico — Rev Soc Quim Mex
Revista. Sociedad Quimica de Mexico — Revista Soc Quim Mexico
Revista. Sociedad Rural de Rosario — Rev Soc Rural Rosario
Revista. Sociedad Venezolana de Cardiologia — Rev Soc Venez Cardiol
Revista. Sociedad Venezolana de Historia de la Medicina — Rev Soc Venez Hist Med
Revista. Sociedad Venezolana de Quimica — Rev Soc Venez Quim
Revista. Sociedade Brasileira de Agronomia — Rev Soc Bras Agron
Revista. Sociedade Brasileira de Geografia — Revta Soc Brasil Geogr
Revista. Sociedade Brasileira de Medicina Tropical — Rev Soc Bras Med Trop
Revista. Sociedade Brasileira de Quimica — Rev Soc Bras Quim
Revista. Sociedade Brasileira de Zootecnia — Rev Soc Bras Zootec
Revista. Sociedade de Geografia do Rio de Janeiro — Revta Soc Geogr Rio Jan
Revista. Sociedade de Medicina e Cirurgia de Sao Jose Do Rio Preto — Rev Soc Med Cir Sao Jose Rio Preto
Revista. Sociedade dos Agronomos e Veterinarios do Para — Revista Soc Agron Para
Revista Stiintelor Veterinare — Revta Stiint Vet
Revista Stiintifica "V. Adamachi" — Rev Stiint "V Adamachi"
Revista Sudamericana de Botanica — Rev Sudam Bot
Revista Sud-Americana de Ciencias Medicas — Rev Sud-Am Cien Med
Revista Sud-Americana de Endocrinologia — Rev Sud-Am Endocrin
Revista Sud-Americana de Endocrinologia, Immunologia, y Quimioterapia — Rev Sud-Am Endocrinol Immunol Quimioter
Revista Sudamericana de Morfologia — Rev Sudam Morfol
Revista Sudamericana de Morfologia — Revista Sudamer Morfol
Revista Sur — Sur
Revista Syniatrica — Rev Syniatrica
Revista Tecnica — Rev Tec
Revista Tecnica. Colegio de Ingenieros Agronomos de Mexico — Rev Tec Col Ing Agron Mex
Revista Tecnica. Facultad de Ingenieria. Universidad del Zulia — Rev Tecn Fac Ingr Univ Zulia
Revista Tecnica. Instituto Nacional de Electronica — Rev Tec Inst Nac Electron
Revista Tecnica INTEVEP [*Instituto de Tecnologia Venezolana del Petroleo*] — Rev Tec INTEVEP
Revista Tecnica INTEVEP [*Instituto de Tecnologia Venezolana del Petroleo*] — RTEID
Revista Tecnica Sulzer [*Switzerland*] — Rev Tec Sulzer
Revista Tecnica Sulzer — RTSZA
Revista Tecnica Textil-Vestido — Rev Tec Text Vestido
Revista Tecnica. Yacimientos Petroliferos Fiscales Bolivianos — Rev Tec Yacimientos Pet Fiscales Boliv
Revista Tecnica. Zulia University — Rev Tec Zulia Univ
Revista Telegrafica Electronica — Rev Telegr Electron
Revista Teologica — RTel
Revista Theobroma — Rev Theobroma
Revista Transporturilor si Telecomunicatiilor [*Romania*] — Rev Transp Telecomun
Revista Transporturilor si Telecomunicatiilor — RTTLA
Revista Trimensal de Historia e Geografia/Jornal. Instituto Historico, Geografico, e Ethnografico do Brazil — Revista Trimensal Hist Geogr
Revista Trimestral de Jurisprudencia [*Brazil*] — RTJ
Revista Uniao Pharmaceutica (Sao Paulo) — Rev Uniao Pharm (Sao Paulo)
Revista. Union de Escritores y Artistas de Cuba — RUEAC
Revista. Union Industrial Argentina (Buenos Aires) — Rev Union Indus Arg BA
Revista. Union Matematica Argentina — Rev Un Mat Argentina
Revista. Union Matematica Argentina — Rev Union Mat Argent
Revista. Union Matematica Argentina y Asociacion Fisica Argentina — Rev Union Mat Argent Asoc Fis Argent
Revista. Union Matematica Argentina y Asociacion Fisica Argentina — RMAFA
Revista Universal Lisbonense — RUL
Revista. Universidad Autonoma Gabriel Rene Moreno — Revta Univ Auton G R Moreno
Revista. Universidad Autonoma Gabriel Rene Moreno (Santa Cruz de la Sierra, Bolivia) — Rev Univ G Rene Moreno Santa Cruz
Revista. Universidad Catolica del Peru — RUCP
Revista. Universidad Catolica del Peru (Lima) — Rev Univ Catol Lima
Revista. Universidad Catolica (Ecuador) — RUCE
Revista. Universidad Complutense de Madrid — RUCM
Revista Universidad de Antioquia — RUA
Revista. Universidad de Arequipa (Peru) — Rev Univ Arequipa
Revista. Universidad de Buenos Aires — R Univ Buenos Aires
Revista. Universidad de Buenos Aires — RUBA
Revista. Universidad de Buenos Aires (Buenos Aires) — Rev Univ BA
Revista. Universidad de Caldas (Manizales, Colombia) — Rev Univ Caldas Manizales
Revista. Universidad de Cordoba — RUC
Revista. Universidad de Costa Rica — Revista Univ Costa Rica
Revista. Universidad de Costa Rica — RUCR
Revista. Universidad de Costa Rica (San Jose, Costa Rica) — Rev Univ S Jose
Revista. Universidad de Guayaquil — RUG
Revista. Universidad de Guayaquil (Guayaquil, Ecuador) — Rev Univ Guayaquil Guayaquil
Revista. Universidad de La Plata — RULP
Revista. Universidad de La Plata — RUNP
Revista. Universidad de La Salle — RUL
Revista. Universidad de los Andes (Bogota) — Rev Univ Andes Bogota
Revista. Universidad de Los Andes (Bogota) — Rev Univ Los Andes (Bogota)
Revista. Universidad de Madrid — R Univ Madrid
Revista. Universidad de Madrid [*Spain*] — Rev Univ Madrid
Revista. Universidad de Madrid — RUM
Revista. Universidad de Madrid — RUMa
Revista. Universidad de Medellin — Rev UDEM
Revista. Universidad de Mexico — Rev Univ Mex
Revista. Universidad de Mexico — RUM
Revista. Universidad de Oviedo — R Univ Oviedo
Revista. Universidad de Oviedo — RUO
Revista. Universidad de Oviedo — RUOv
Revista. Universidad de Puebla — Rev Univ Puebla
Revista. Universidad de Sonora (Hermosillo, Mexico) — Rev Univ Sonora Hermosillo
Revista. Universidad de Yucatan — Rev Univ Yucatan
Revista. Universidad de Yucatan — RUY
Revista. Universidad de Yucatan — UY/R
Revista. Universidad de Zulia — RUZ
Revista. Universidad del Cauca — Rev Univ Cauca
Revista. Universidad del Cauca (Popayan, Colombia) — Rev Univ Cauca Popayan
Revista. Universidad del Norte (Chile) — Rev Univ Norte (Chile)
Revista. Universidad del Zulia — Rev Univ Zulia
Revista. Universidad del Zulia (Maracaibo) — Rev Univ Zulia (Maracaibo)
Revista. Universidad Externado de Colombia — UEC
Revista. Universidad Industrial de Santander — Rev Univ Ind Santander
Revista. Universidad Industrial de Santander — RUIS
Revista. Universidad Industrial de Santander — RUISA
Revista. Universidad Industrial de Santander (Bucaramanga, Colombia) — Rev Univ Indus Santander Bucaramanga
Revista. Universidad Industrial de Santander. Investigaciones — Rev Univ Ind Santander Invest

Revista. Universidad Industrial de Santander. Tecnologia — Rev Univ Ind Santander Tecnolo
Revista. Universidad (La Plata, Argentina) — Rev Univ La Plata
Revista. Universidad Nacional — RUN
Revista. Universidad Nacional de Cordoba — Rev Univ Nac Cordoba
Revista. Universidad Nacional de Cordoba — RUNC
Revista. Universidad Nacional de Cordoba (Cordoba, Argentina) — Rev Univ Cordoba
Revista. Universidad Nacional de San Agustin (Arequipa, Peru) — Rev Univ S Augustin Arequipa
Revista. Universidad Nacional de Tucuman. Serie A. Matematica y Fisica Teorica [*Argentina*] — Rev Univ Nac Tucuman Ser A
Revista. Universidad Nacional de Tucuman. Serie A. Matematica y Fisica Teorica — RUNAA
Revista. Universidad Nacional del Centro — RUNC
Revista. Universidad Nacional (Ecuador) — RUNE
Revista. Universidad (Puno, Peru) — Rev Univ Puno
Revista Universidad Social Catolica — RUSC
Revista. Universidad (Tegucigalpa) — Rev Univ Hond Tegucigalpa
Revista. Universidad (Tegucigalpa) — RUT
Revista. Universidade de Coimbra — Rev Univ Coimbra
Revista. Universidade de Coimbra — RUC
Revista. Universidade de Minas Gerais — RUMG
Revista. Universidade de Minas Gerais (Belo Horizonte, Brazil) — Rev Univ Minas Gerais Belo Horizonte
Revista. Universidade Federal do Para. Serie II — Rev Univ Fed Para Ser II
Revista Universitaria — R Universitaria
Revista Universitaria (Cuzco, Peru) — Rev Univ Cuzco
Revista Universitaria de Letras — RULet
Revista Universitaria (Guadalajara, Mexico) — Rev Univ Guadalajara
Revista Universitaria (Trujillo, Peru) — Rev Univ Trujillo
Revista Universitaria. Universidad Catolica de Chile — Revta Univ Univ Catol Chile
Revista Universitaria. Universidad Catolica de Chile — RU
Revista Universitaria. Universidad Catolica de Chile (Santiago) — Rev Univ Univ Catol Santiago
Revista Universitaria. Universidad Nacinal de Cuzco — RUC
Revista Universitaria. Universidad Nacional del Cuzco — Rev Univ Univ Nac Cuzco
Revista Universitati "Al. I. Cuza" si a Institutului Politehnic din Iasi — Rev Univ Al I Cuza Inst Politeh Iasi
Revista Universitatii "C. I. Parhon" si a Politehnicii Bucuresti. Seria Stiintelor Naturii — Rev Univ C I Parhon Politeh Bucuresti Ser Stiint Nat
Revista Uruguaya de Ciencias Sociales — R Uruguaya Ciencias Socs
Revista Uruguaya de Dermatologia y Sifilografia — Revista Uruguaya Dermatol Sifilogr
Revista Uruguaya de Estudios Internacionales — Rev Urug Est Internac
Revista Uruguaya de Geografia (Montevideo) — Rev Urug Georgr Monte
Revista Usem — Rev Usem
Revista Valenciana de Filologia — RVF
Revista Valenciana de Filologia. Instituto de Literatura y Estudios Filologicos. Institucion Alfonso el Magnanimo — R Valenciana Filol
Revista Venezolana de Cirugia — Rev Venez Cir
Revista Venezolana de Estudios Municipales — R Venezolana Estud Municipales
Revista Venezolana de Filosofia — Rev Ven Filosof
Revista Venezolana de Filosofia — RVF
Revista Venezolana de Folklore — R Venez Folk
Revista Venezolana de Folklore — R Venezolana Folklore
Revista Venezolana de Folklore — RVF
Revista Venezolana de Folklore — RVFO
Revista Venezolana de Sanidad y Asistencia Social — R Venezolana Sanidad y Asistencia Soc
Revista Venezolana de Sanidad y Asistencia Social — Rev Venez Sanid Asist Soc
Revista Venezolana de Urologia — Rev Venez Urol
Revista Veterinaria Venezolana — Rev Vet Venez
Revista Vinicola y de Agricultura — Revista Vinic Agric
Revista Ximenez de Quesada — XDQ
Revista YPF [*Yacimientos Petroliferos Fiscales*] **(Argentina)** — RYPFA
Revista Zooiatria — Rev Zooiatr
Revista Zootecnica (Buenos Aires) — Rev Zootec (B Aires)
Revista Zurita Saragosse — RZ
Revmatizm Respublikanskii Mezhvedomstvennyi Sbornik — Revm Resp Mezhved Sb
Revolucion y Cultura — Rev Cult
Revolucion y Cultura — RyC
Revolution Francaise — Rev Fr
Revolution Francaise — RFr
Revolutionary Action Power — RAP
Revolutionary World — Rev World
Revolutionary World — Revol Wld
Revolutionary World — Revol World
Revue — R
Revue A [*Revue Trimestrielle d'Automatique*] [*Belgium*] — Rev A
Revue Abolitionniste — R Abolit
Revue. Academie Arabe — RAA
Revue. Academie Arabe de Damas — RAAD
Revue. Academie Internationale du Tourisme — RAT
Revue Academique du Centre — RAC
Revue Administrative — R Adm
Revue Administrative (Paris) — R Admin (Paris)
Revue Africaine — RAf
Revue Africaine — RAfr
Revue Africaine — Rev Afr
Revue Africaine (Algiers) — RAA
Revue Africaine de Management — R Afr Manag
Revue Africaine de Management — Revue Afr Mgmt
Revue Africaine de Strategie — Rev Afr Strat
Revue Agricole de France — Rev Agr France
Revue Agricole de la Nouvelle-Caledonie et Dependances — Revue Agric Nouv Caled
Revue Agricole de l'Ile Maurice — Rev Agric Ile Maurice
Revue Agricole d'Haiti — Rev Agric Haiti
Revue Agricole d'Haiti (Port-au-Prince) — Rev Agrico Port Au Prince
Revue Agricole et Sucriere de l'Ile Maurice — RASMA
Revue Agricole et Sucriere de l'Ile Maurice — Rev Agric Sucr Ile Maurice
Revue Agrologique et Botanique du Kivu — Rev Agrol Bot Kivu
Revue Agronomique Canadienne — Rev Agron Can
Revue Algerienne des Lettres et des Sciences Humaines — RALSH
Revue Algerienne des Sciences Juridiques, Economiques, et Politiques — R Algerienne Sciences Juridiques Econs et Pols
Revue Algerienne des Sciences Juridiques, Economiques, et Politiques — Revue Algerienne Sci Juridiques Econ et Polit
Revue Algerienne du Travail — R Alger Trav
Revue Algerienne/Societe des Beaux-Arts — Rev Alger
Revue Algologique — Rev Algol
Revue Anglo-Americaine — RA
Revue Anglo-Americaine — RAA
Revue Anglo-Americaine — RAAm
Revue Anglo-Americaine — Rev Ang-Am
Revue Annuelle de Chimiotherapie et de Physiatrie du Cancer — Rev Annu Chimiother Physiatr Cancer
Revue Annuelle de Chimiotherapie et de Prophylaxie du Cancer — Rev Annu Chimiother Prophyl Cancer
Revue Annuelle de Physiatrie et de Prophylaxie du Cancer — Rev Annu Physiatr Prophyl Cancer
Revue Annuelle. Societe Odonto-Stomatologique du Nord-Est — Rev Annu Soc Odontostomatol Nordest
Revue Anthropologique — R Anth
Revue Anthropologique — R Anthr
Revue Anthropologique — Rev Anthr
Revue Anthropologique — Revue Anthr
Revue Anthropologique (Paris) — Rev Anthropol (Paris)
Revue Apologetique — RAp
Revue Arachnologique — Rev Arachnol
Revue Archeologique — R Ar
Revue Archeologique — R Arch
Revue Archeologique — R Archeol
Revue Archeologique — RA
Revue Archeologique — Rev A
Revue Archeologique — Rev Arch
Revue Archeologique — Rev Archeol
Revue Archeologique — Revue Archeol
Revue Archeologique. Centre Consacree aux Antiquites Nationales — RA C Ant Nat
Revue Archeologique de l'Est et du Centre-Est — RA Est
Revue Archeologique de l'Est et du Centre-Est — RAE
Revue Archeologique de l'Est et du Centre-Est — RAECE
Revue Archeologique de l'Est et du Centre-Est — Rev Arch ECE
Revue Archeologique de l'Est et du Centre-Est — Rev Arch Est et Centre Est
Revue Archeologique de l'Oise — RA Oise
Revue Archeologique de Narbonnaise — RA Narb
Revue Archeologique de Narbonnaise — RAN
Revue Archeologique de Narbonnaise — Rev Arch Narbonn
Revue Archeologique du Centre — Revue Arch Centre
Revue Archeologique du Centre de la France — RACF
Revue Archeologique Syrienne — RAS
Revue Archeologique Syrienne — RASyr
Revue Archeologique Syrienne — Revue Arch Syr
Revue. Archives Italiennes de Biologie — Rev Arch Ital Biol
Revue. Association Canadienne d'Education de Langue Francaise — R Assoc Canad Educ Langue Franc
Revue. Association des Juristes Democrates — Rev Assoc Jur Dem
Revue. Association des Psychiatres du Canada — Rev Assoc Psychiatres Can
Revue. Association Francaise des Techniciens du Petrole — Rev Assoc Fr Tech Pet
Revue. Association Nationale des Agronomes Haitiens — Rev Assoc Natl Agron Haitiens
Revue. Association pour la Prevention de la Pollution Atmospherique — Rev Assoc Prev Pollut Atmos
Revue. Association Technique de l'Industrie Papetiere — Rev Assoc Tech Ind Papet
Revue ATB [*Assistance Technique Belge*] **Metallurgie** [*Belgium*] — RAMTB
Revue ATIP [*Association Technique de l'Industrie Papetiere*] — Rev ATIP
Revue Augustinienne — RAug
Revue Bancaire Belge — RBB
Revue. Barreau de la Province de Quebec — Rev du B
Revue. Barreau de Quebec — Rev Barreau Que
Revue Belge — R Belge
Revue Belge d'Archeologie et d'Histoire de l'Art — R Belg Arch
Revue Belge d'Archeologie et d'Histoire de l'Art — R Belge Archeol
Revue Belge d'Archeologie et d'Histoire de l'Art — RBA
Revue Belge d'Archeologie et d'Histoire de l'Art — RBAHA
Revue Belge d'Archeologie et d'Histoire de l'Art — RBArch
Revue Belge d'Archeologie et d'Histoire de l'Art — Rev Belg Arch
Revue Belge d'Archeologie et d'Histoire de l'Art — Revue Belge Arch et Hist Art
Revue Belge d'Art et d'Archeologie — RBAA
Revue Belge de Droit International — R Belge Dr Int
Revue Belge de Droit International — R Belge Droit Internat
Revue Belge de Droit International — RBDI

Revue Belge de Droit International — Rev Belge de Droit Internat
Revue Belge de Droit International — Rev Belge Dr Int'l
Revue Belge de Droit Maritime — RBDM
Revue Belge de Medecine Dentaire — Rev Belge Med Dent
Revue Belge de Musicologie — R Belge Mus
Revue Belge de Musicologie — RBM
Revue Belge de Musicologie — RBMus
Revue Belge de Numismatique — RBN
Revue Belge de Numismatique — RNB
Revue Belge de Numismatique et de Sigillographie — R B Num
Revue Belge de Numismatique et de Sigillographie — R Belg Num
Revue Belge de Numismatique et de Sigillographie — RBNS
Revue Belge de Numismatique et de Sigillographie — Rev Belg Num
Revue Belge de Numismatique et de Sigillographie — Rev Belge de Num
Revue Belge de Pathologie et de Medecine Experimentale — RBPMA
Revue Belge de Pathologie et de Medecine Experimentale — Rev Belg Pathol Med Exp
Revue Belge de Pathologie et de Medecine Experimentale — Rev Belge Pathol Med Exp
Revue Belge de Philogogie et d'Histoire — RBelPhH
Revue Belge de Philologie et d'Histoire — R Belge Philol & Hist
Revue Belge de Philologie et d'Histoire — R Belgue Philol Hist
Revue Belge de Philologie et d'Histoire — RBPh
Revue Belge de Philologie et d'Histoire — RBPhil
Revue Belge de Philologie et d'Histoire — Rev B
Revue Belge de Philologie et d'Histoire — Rev Bel Ph
Revue Belge de Philologie et d'Histoire — Rev Belg Philol Hist
Revue Belge de Philologie et d'Histoire — Rev Belge
Revue Belge de Philologie et d'Histoire — Rev Belge de Phil et d'Hist
Revue Belge de Philologie et d'Histoire — Rev Belge de Philologie et d Hist
Revue Belge de Philologie et d'Histoire — Rev Belge Phil Hist
Revue Belge de Philologie et d'Histoire — Rev Belge Philol
Revue Belge de Philologie et d'Histoire — Rev Belge Philol Hist
Revue Belge de Philologie et d'Histoire — RevuB
Revue Belge de Philologie et d'Histoire — RPH
Revue Belge de Securite Sociale — R Belg Sec Soc
Revue Belge de Securite Sociale — R Belge Secur Soc
Revue Belge de Securite Sociale — R Belge Securite Soc
Revue Belge de Securite Sociale — RBSS
Revue Belge de Securite Sociale — Rev B Sec Soc
Revue Belge de Securite Sociale — Rev Sec Soc
Revue Belge de Statistique, d'Informatique, et de Recherche Operationnelle — RBSTARO
Revue Belge de Statistique, d'Informatique, et de Recherche Operationnelle — Rev Belge Stat Inf et Rech Oper
Revue Belge des Industries Verrieres — Rev Belge Ind Verrieres
Revue Belge des Industries Verrieres. Ceramiques et de l'Emaillerie — Rev Belge Ind Verrieres Ceram Emaill
Revue Belge des Matieres Plastiques — Rev Belge Matieres Plast
Revue Belge des Sciences Commerciales — RSCom
Revue Belge des Sciences Medicales — Rev Belge Sci Med
Revue Belge des Transports [*Belgium*] — Rev Belge Transp
Revue Belge des Transports — RVBTA
Revue Belge d'Histoire Contemporaine — Revue Belge Hist Contemporaine
Revue Belge d'Histoire Militaire — Rev Belge Hist Mil
Revue Belge d'Histoire Militaire — Rev Belge Hist Milit
Revue Belge d'Homoeopathie — Rev Belge Homoeopath
Revue Belge du Cinema — Rev Belge du C
Revue Benedictine — RB
Revue Benedictine — RBen
Revue Benedictine — Rev Ben
Revue Benedictine — Rev Bened
Revue Bibliographique Belge — RBB
Revue Bibliographique de Sinologie — RBS
Revue Bibliographique pour Servir de Complement aux Annales des Sciences Naturelles — Rev Bibliogr Complement Ann Sci Nat
Revue Biblique — R Bibl
Revue Biblique — R Bible
Revue Biblique — RB
Revue Biblique — RBi
Revue Biblique — RBib
Revue Biblique — ReB
Revue Biblique — Rev Bibl
Revue Biblique Internationale — RBI
Revue Bimestrielle d'Informations. Banque Marocaine du Commerce Exterieur — R Bimestr Inform Banque Maroc Com Ext
Revue Bleue — RBL
Revue Bleue Politique et Litteraire — Rev Bl Polit Lit
Revue Bossuet — RB
Revue Botanique. Recueil Mensuel — Rev Bot Recueil Mens
Revue Bretonne de Botanique Pure et Appliquee — Rev Bretonne Bot Pure Appl
Revue Brown Boveri — Rev Brown Boveri
Revue Brown Boveri et Cie — Rev Brown Boveri Cie
Revue Bryologique et Lichenologique — R Bryol & Lichenol
Revue Bryologique et Lichenologique — RBRLA
Revue Bryologique et Lichenologique — Rev Bryol Lichenol
Revue Byzantine — RB
Revue C. Genie Civil. Construction — Rev C Genie Civil Constr
Revue C. Tijdschrift Civiele Techniek. Genie Civil — Rev C Tijdschr Civ Tech Genie Civ
Revue Canadienne — R Canad
Revue Canadienne d'Anthropologie — Rev Can Anthropol
Revue Canadienne de Biochimie et Biologie Cellulaire — Rev Can Biochim Biol Cell
Revue Canadienne de Biologie — R Canad Biol
Revue Canadienne de Biologie — RCBIA
Revue Canadienne de Biologie — Rev Can Bio
Revue Canadienne de Biologie — Rev Can Biol
Revue Canadienne de Biologie — Rev Canad Biol
Revue Canadienne de Biologie — Revue Can Biol
Revue Canadienne de Biologie Experimentale — Rev Can Biol Exp
Revue Canadienne de Genie Electrique [*Canada*] — Rev Can Gen Electr
Revue Canadienne de Geographie — R Canad Geogr
Revue Canadienne de Geographie — Rev Canadienne Geographie
Revue Canadienne de Geotechnique — Rev Can Geotech
Revue Canadienne de la Science du Sol — Rev Can Sci Sol
Revue Canadienne de Medecine Comparee — Rev Can Med Comp
Revue Canadienne de Phytopathologie — Rev Can Phytopathol
Revue Canadienne de Phytotechnie — Rev Can Phytotechnie
Revue Canadienne de Psychologie — Rev Can Psychol
Revue Canadienne de Recherche Veterinaire — Rev Can Rech Vet
Revue Canadienne de Sante Publique — Rev Can Sante Publique
Revue Canadienne d'Economie Publique et Cooperative. Canadian Journal of Public and Cooperative Economy — Rev Can Econ Publique Coop Can J Public Coop Econ
Revue Canadienne des Etudes Africaines — R Canad Et Afr
Revue Canadienne des Etudes sur le Nationalisme — R Can Etud Nationalisme
Revue Canadienne des Sciences de l'Information — R Can Sciences Info
Revue Canadienne des Sciences du Comportement — Rev Can Sci Comport
Revue Canadienne des Sciences du Comportement — Rev Can Sci Comportement
Revue Canadienne d'Hygiene Publique — Rev Can Hyg Publique
Revue Canadienne-Americaine d'Etudes Slaves — R Canad-Amer Et Slaves
Revue Canonique — RCan
Revue Catholique — R Cath
Revue Catholique d'Alsace — RCA
Revue Catholique d'Alsace — RCAls
Revue Catholique de Normandie — RCN
Revue Catholique des Eglises — RCE
Revue Catholique des Institutions et de Droit — RCID
Revue Catholique d'Histoire, d'Archeologie et Litterature de Normandie — RCHN
Revue Catholique Sociale et Juridique — RCS
Revue Celfan/Celfan Review — Celfan R
Revue Celtique — R Celt
Revue Celtique — RC
Revue Celtique — RCel
Revue Celtique — Rev Celt
Revue. Centre d'Etudes Theoriques de la Detection et des Communications — Rev CETHEDEC
Revue. Centre d'Etudes Theoriques de la Detection et des Communications. Cahier [*Paris*] — Rev CETHEDEC Cahier
Revue. Centre Technique. Fonderie et de l'Association Technique de Fonderie — Rev Cent Tech Fonderie Assoc Tech Fonderie
Revue. Chambre de Commerce de Marseille — R Ch Comm Marseille
Revue. Chambre de Commerce Francaise au Canada — R Ch Com Franc Canada
Revue Charlemagne — RC
Revue Charlemagne — RCh
Revue Chimique (Zagreb) — Rev Chim Zagreb
Revue Chretienne — RChr
Revue Coloniale Internationale — RCI
Revue Commerce — R Commer
Revue Commerce — Rev Commer
Revue Commerciale — HON
Revue Commerciale - Handelsoverzicht. Chambre de Commerce Neerlandaise pour la Belgique et le Luxembourg — RC
Revue Communale — Rev Comm
Revue Communale de Belgique — R Com
Revue Communale de Belgique — R Com B
Revue Communale de Belgique — RC
Revue Congolaise — RCong
Revue Congolaise des Sciences Humaines — RCSH
Revue Contemporaine — R Contemp
Revue Critique — RC
Revue Critique — RCr
Revue Critique de Droit International Prive — R Crit Dr Int Prive
Revue Critique de Droit International Prive — RCDIP
Revue Critique de Droit International Prive — Rev Crit de Droit Internat Prive
Revue Critique de Jurisprudence Belge — R Crit Jpd B
Revue Critique de Jurisprudence Belge — RCJ
Revue Critique de Jurisprudence Belge — RCJB
Revue Critique de Jurisprudence Belge — Rev Crit de Jurispr Belge
Revue Critique de Jurisprudence Belge — Rev Crit Jur B
Revue Critique des Idees et des Livres — Rev Crit des Id et des Livr
Revue Critique des Idees et des Livres — Rev Crit des Id et des Livres
Revue Critique d'Histoire et de Litterature — RC
Revue Critique d'Histoire et de Litterature — RCHL
Revue Critique d'Histoire et de Litterature — RCr
Revue Critique d'Histoire et de Litterature — Rev Cr
Revue Cytobiologique — Rev Cytobiol
Revue d'Acoustique — Rev Acoust
Revue d'Acoustique — Rev d'Acoustique
Revue d'Acoustique — RVAHA
Revue d'Action Sociale — R Action Soc
Revue d'Algerie — R Alg
Revue d'Allemagne — R Allem
Revue d'Allemagne — R Allemagne
Revue d'Allemagne — RevA
Revue d'Allemagne — RevudA

Revue d'Alsace — RAls
Revue d'Analyse Numerique et de la Theorie de l'Approximation — Rev Anal Numer Theor Approx
Revue d'Analyse Numerique et de la Theorie de l'Approximation — Rev Anal Numer Theorie Approximation
Revue d'Anthropologie — R Anthr
Revue d'Anthropologie [*Paris*] — R D Anthropol
Revue d'Anthropologie — Rev Anthr
Revue d'Anthropologie — Rev d'Anthropol
Revue d'Anthropologie — Revue Anthr
Revue d'Archeologie Polonaise — RAP
Revue d'Archeometrie — R Archeom
Revue d'Art et d'Esthetique — RAE
Revue d'Ascetique et de Mystique — R Ascetique & Mystique
Revue d'Ascetique et de Mystique — RAM
Revue d'Ascetique et de Mystique [*Paris*] — RAsMyst
Revue d'Assyriologie — RA
Revue d'Assyriologie — RAssyr
Revue d'Assyriologie — Rev d Assyr
Revue d'Assyriologie et d'Archeologie Orientale — R Assyr
Revue d'Assyriologie et d'Archeologie Orientale — RA
Revue d'Assyriologie et d'Archeologie Orientale — RAA
Revue d'Assyriologie et d'Archeologie Orientale — RAAO
Revue d'Assyriologie et d'Archeologie Orientale — RAss
Revue d'Assyriologie et d'Archeologie Orientale — Rev Assyriol
Revue d'Assyriologie et d'Archeologie Orientale — Rev d'Assyr
Revue d'Assyriologie et d'Archeologie Orientale — Revue Assyriol
Revue d'Auvergne — R Au
Revue d'Auvergne — RAuv
Revue d'Auvergne — Rev Auvergne
Revue de 'Activite Scientifique — Rev Act Sci
Revue de Biologie. Academie de la Republique Populaire Roumaine — Rev Biol Acad Rep Pop Roumaine
Revue de Biologie (Bucharest) — Rev Biol (Buchar)
Revue de Bio-Mathematique — Rev Bio-Math
Revue de Botanique Appliquee et d'Agriculture Tropicale — Rev Bot Appl Agr Trop
Revue de Botanique Appliquee et d'Agriculture Tropicale — Rev Bot Appl Agric Trop
Revue de Botanique Appliquee et d'Agriculture Tropicale. Supplement — Rev Bot Appl Agric Trop Suppl
Revue de Boulogne — RBo
Revue de Chimie. Academie de la Republique Populaire Roumaine — RCHRA
Revue de Chimie. Academie de la Republique Populaire Roumaine [*Romania*] — Rev Chim Acad Repub Pop Roum
Revue de Chimie Minerale — Rev Chim Mi
Revue de Chimie Minerale [*France*] — Rev Chim Miner
Revue de Chirurgie Orthopedique et Reparatrice de l'Appareil Moteur — Rev Chir Or
Revue de Chirurgie Orthopedique et Reparatrice de l'Appareil Moteur — Rev Chir Orthop
Revue de Chirurgie Orthopedique et Reparatrice de l'Appareil Moteur — Rev Chir Orthop Reparatrice Appar Mot
Revue de Coree — R Coree
Revue de Cytologie et de Biologie Vegetales [*France*] — Rev Cytol Biol Veg
Revue de Cytologie et de Biologie Vegetales - La Botaniste — RCBBDA
Revue de Cytologie et de Biologie Vegetales -La Botaniste — Rev Cytol Biol Veg Bot
Revue de Cytologie et de Cytophysiologie Vegetales — Rev Cytol Cytophysiol Veg
Revue de Debrecen — Rev Debrecen
Revue de Defense Nationale [*France*] — Rev Def Natl
Revue de Defense Nationale — Rev Defense Nat
Revue de Doctrine et de Jurisprudence Coloniales et Financieres — R Col
Revue de Doctrine et de Jurisprudence Coloniales et Financieres — RDJC
Revue de Driot Prospectif — R Dr Prospect
Revue de Droit Belge — RDB
Revue de Droit Belge — RDBel
Revue de Droit Belge — Rev Dr Belge
Revue de Droit Canonique — R Droit Can
Revue de Droit Canonique — RDC
Revue de Droit Canonique — Rev de Droit Canonique
Revue de Droit Compare. Association Quebecoise pour l'Etude Comparative du Droit — RDC
Revue de Droit Contemporain — R Dr Cont
Revue de Droit Contemporain ou des Juristes Democrates — Rev Dr Contemp
Revue de Droit Familial — R Dr Fam
Revue de Droit Familial — RDF
Revue de Droit Familial — Rev Dr Fam
Revue de Droit Intellectuel — RDIntel
Revue de Droit Intellectuel "l'Ingenieur Conseil" — IC
Revue de Droit Intellectuel "l'Ingenieur Conseil" — RIC
Revue de Droit International — R Droit Int
Revue de Droit International de Sciences Diplomatiques et Politiques — R Dr Int Sci Dipl
Revue de Droit International de Sciences Diplomatiques et Politiques — R Droit Int Sci Dipl Pol
Revue de Droit International de Sciences Diplomatiques et Politiques — Rev de Dr Int'l de Sci Dip et Pol
Revue de Droit International de Sciences Diplomatiques et Politiques — Rev de Droit Internat de Sci Diplom
Revue de Droit International et de Droit Compare — R Dr Int Dr Comp
Revue de Droit International et de Droit Compare — RDI et Comp
Revue de Droit International et de Droit Compare — RDIC
Revue de Droit International et de Droit Compare — RDIDC
Revue de Droit International et de Droit Compare — Rev de Droit Compare
Revue de Droit International et de Droit Compare — Rev de Droit Internat et de Droit Compare
Revue de Droit International et de Droit Compare — Rev Dr Intern et Dr Comp
Revue de Droit International et de Legislation Comparee — R De Droit Int Et De Legis Comp
Revue de Droit International et de Legislation Comparee — RDI
Revue de Droit International et de Legislation Comparee — RDInt
Revue de Droit International et de Legislation Comparee — Rev Droit Intern Legisl Compar
Revue de Droit Minier — RDM
Revue de Droit Minier — RDMin
Revue de Droit Minier — Rev Dr Min
Revue de Droit Penal et de Criminologie — R Dr Pen Crim
Revue de Droit Penal et de Criminologie — RDP
Revue de Droit Penal et de Criminologie — RDPen
Revue de Droit Penal et de Criminologie — Rev de Droit Penal et de Criminologie
Revue de Droit Penal et de Criminologie — Rev Dr Pen
Revue de Droit Rural — R Dr Rur
Revue de Droit Social — R Dr Soc
Revue de Droit Social — R Droit Soc
Revue de Droit Social — Rev Dr Soc
Revue de Droit. Universite de Sherbrooke — R D U S
Revue de Droit. Universite de Sherbrooke — R de D
Revue de Droit. Universite de Sherbrooke — Rev de Droit
Revue de Droit. Universite de Sherbrooke — Rev Droit U Sher
Revue de Fonderie Moderne — Rev Fonderie Mod
Revue de France — RDF
Revue de France — RF
Revue de Gemmologie. Association Francaise de Gemmologie — Rev Gemmol AFG
Revue de Generale de Thermique — Rev Generale Thermique
Revue de Geneve — Rev Geneve
Revue de Geogaphie Alpine (Grenoble) — RGAG
Revue de Geograhie Marocaine — RGM
Revue de Geographie — RG
Revue de Geographie Alpine — R Geogr Alp
Revue de Geographie Alpine — R Geogr Alpine
Revue de Geographie Alpine — Rev Geogr Alpine
Revue de Geographie Alpine — Rev Geographie Alpine
Revue de Geographie Alpine [*France*] — RVGA-A
Revue de Geographie de Lyon — R Geogr Lyon
Revue de Geographie de Lyon — RGL
Revue de Geographie de Montreal — R de Geog de Mtl
Revue de Geographie de Montreal — Rev Geographie Montreal
Revue de Geographie du Maroc — R Geogr Maroc
Revue de Geographie du Maroc — Rev Geogr Maroc
Revue de Geographie du Maroc — Revue Geogr Maroc
Revue de Geographie Humaine et d'Ethnologie — RGeogrH
Revue de Geographie Physique et de Geologie Dynamique — Rev Geog Ph Geol Dyn
Revue de Geographie Physique et de Geologie Dynamique — Rev Geogr Phys Geol Dyn
Revue de Geographie Physique et de Geologie Dynamique — Rev Geogr Phys Geol Dynam
Revue de Geographie Physique et de Geologie Dynamique — Revue Geogr Phys Geol Dyn
Revue de Geographie Physique et de Geologie Dynamique — RGPGD
Revue de Geologie Dynamique et de Geographie Physique — Rev Geol Dyn Geogr Phys
Revue de Geologie Dynamique et de Geographie Physique [*France*] — Revue Geol Dyn Geogr Phys
Revue de Geologie Dynamique et de Geographie Physique — RGDPD
Revue de Geomorphologie Dynamique — Rev Geomorphol Dyn
Revue de Geriatrie — Rev Geriatr
Revue de Gerontologie d'Expression Francaise — Rev Gerontol Expression Fr
Revue de Gynaecologie et de Chirurgie Abdominale — Rev Gynae et Chir Abd
Revue de la Banque — R Banque
Revue de la Banque — RB
Revue de la Banque — RBA
Revue de la Banque [*Bruxelles*] — RBQ
Revue de la Banque — Rev Banque
Revue de la Brasserie et des Boissons — Rev Brass Boissons
Revue de la Conserve [*France*] — Rev Conserve
Revue de la Conserve. Alimentation Moderne — Rev Conserve Aliment Mod
Revue de la Conserve de France et de l'Union Francaise — Rev Conserve Fr Union Fr
Revue de la Conserve de France et d'Outre-Mer — Rev Conserve Fr Outre-Mer
Revue de la Cooperation Internationale — R Coop Int
Revue de la Defense Nationale — RDN
Revue de la Documentation — Rev Doc
Revue de la Formation Permanente — R Format Perm
Revue de la Franco-Ancienne — RFA
Revue de la Haute Auvergne — RH Auv
Revue de la Haute Auvergne. Societe des Sciences et Arts — Rev Haute Auvergne
Revue de la Mecanique — Rev M
Revue de la Mecanique — Rev Mecan
Revue de la Mediterranee — R Medit
Revue de la Mediterranee — R Mediterr
Revue de la Mediterranee — RdM
Revue de la Mediterranee — Rev Mediterranee
Revue de la Mediterranee — RM
Revue de la Mediterranee — RMed
Revue de la Navigation Fluviale Europeenne — R Navig Fluv Europ
Revue de la Navigation Fluviale Europeenne. Ports et Industries — NDR

Revue de la Pensee Francaise — R P Fr
Revue de la Pensee Francaise — RPF
Revue de la Pensee Juive — RPJ
Revue de la Protection [*France*] — Rev Prot
Revue de la Renaissance — RR
Revue de la Revolution — Rev Revolut
Revue de la Revolution — RRev
Revue de la Saintonge et de l'Aunis — R Saintonge
Revue de la Securite Sociale — R Secur Soc
Revue de la Societe de Biometrie Humaine — Revue Soc Biometrie Hum
Revue de la Soudure Autogene — Rev Soudure Autogene
Revue de la Soudure/Lastijdschrift — Rev Soudre Lastijdschrift
Revue de la Soudure/Lastijdschrift [*Brussels*] — Rev Soudure
Revue de la Soudure/Lastijdschrift — Rev Soudure/Lastijdschrift
Revue de la Suisse Catholique — Rev Suisse Cathol
Revue de l'Action Populaire [*Later, Projet*] — RAP
Revue de l'Administration et du Droit Administratif — Rev Adm
Revue de l'Administration et du Droit Administratif de la Belgique — R Adm
Revue de l'Administration et du Droit Administratif de la Belgique — RA
Revue de l'Administration et du Droit Administratif de la Belgique — RADA
Revue de l'Administration et du Droit Administratif de la Belgique — RDA
Revue de l'Administration et du Droit Administratif de la Belgique — Rev de l'Adm
Revue de l'Agriculture — R Agric
Revue de l'Agriculture — Rev Agr
Revue de l'Agriculture (Brussels) — Rev Agr (Brussels)
Revue de l'Agriculture (Brussels) — Rev Agric (Bruss)
Revue de l'Agriculture (Bruxelles) — Revue Agric (Brux)
Revue de l'Alcoolisme — Rev Alcool
Revue de l'Alimentation Animale — Rev Aliment Anim
Revue de l'Alliance Francaise — R All Fr
Revue de l'Aluminum — Rev Alum
Revue de l'Aluminum et de Ses Applications — RALAB
Revue de l'Aluminum et de Ses Applications [*France*] — Rev Alum Ses Appl
Revue de l'Ameublement — RAM
Revue de Langue et Litterature d'Oc — RLLO
Revue de Langue et Litterature Provencales — RLLP
Revue de Langue et Litterature Provencales — RLLProv
Revue de Languedoc — R Lang
Revue de l'Armee Belge — Rev Armee Belge
Revue de l'Art — RArt
Revue de l'Art — Rev Art
Revue de l'Art Ancien et Moderne — RAA
Revue de l'Art Ancien et Moderne — RAAM
Revue de l'Art Ancien et Moderne — Rev Art Anc
Revue de l'Art Chretien — R Art C
Revue de l'Art Chretien — R Art Chr
Revue de l'Art Chretien — RAC
Revue de l'Art Chretien — RevAC
Revue de l'Art Chretien. Supplement — R Art C S
Revue de l'Art Francais — RAFr
Revue de Laryngologie, Otologie, Rhinologie — Rev Laryngol Otol Rhinol
Revue de Laryngologie, Otologie, Rhinologie — RLORA
Revue de Laryngologie, Otologie, Rhinologie (Bordeaux) — Rev Laryngol Otol Rhinol (Bord)
Revue de Laryngologie, Otologie, Rhinologie. Supplement [*France*] — Rev Laryngol Otol Rhino Suppl
Revue de Laryngologie, Otologie, Rhinologie. Supplement — RLOSA
Revue de l'Assistance Publique et de la Prevoyance Sociale — RAP
Revue de l'Atherosclerose [*France*] — Rev Atheroscler
Revue de l'Atherosclerose — RVASA
Revue de l'Atherosclerose et des Arteriopathies Peripheriques — Rev Atheroscler Arteriopathies Peripher
Revue de l'Atherosclerose et des Arteriopathies Peripheriques — Rev Atheroscler Arteriopathies Peripheriques
Revue de l'AUPELF. Association des Universites Partiellement ou Entierement de Langue Francaise — Rev AUPELF
Revue de l'Avranchin — R Avr
Revue de l'Ecole d'Anthropologie de Paris — R De L Ecole D Anthropol De Paris
Revue de l'Economie du Centre-Est — R Econ Centre-Est
Revue de l'Economie Franc-Comtoise — R Econ Franc-Comtoise
Revue de l'Economie Meridionale — R Econ Merid
Revue de Legislation Ancienne et Moderne Francaise et Etrangere — RLAF
Revue de l'Egypte Ancienne [*Paris*] — REA
Revue de l'Egypte Ancienne — REgA
Revue de l'Electricite et de l'Electronique — Rev Electr Electron
Revue de l'Elevage. Betail et Basse Cour — Rev Elevage
Revue de l'Energie — R Energie
Revue de l'Energie — Rev Energ
Revue de l'Energie — Rev Energie
Revue de l'Energie [*Paris*] — RFA
Revue de l'Energie Primaire [*Belgium*] — Rev Energ Primaire
Revue de l'Enregistrement et des Domaines — RED
Revue de l'Enregistrement et des Douanes — Rev Enr
Revue de l'Enseignement des Langues Vivantes — RELV
Revue de l'Enseignement Philosophique — REPh
Revue de l'Enseignement Philosophique — Rev Ens Phil
Revue de l'Enseignement Superieur — R Ens Sup
Revue de l'Enseignement Superieur — RES
Revue de l'Enseignement Superieur — Rev Ens Sup
Revue de l'Est — R Est
Revue de l'Est — Rev Est
Revue de l'Extradition — Rev Extr
Revue de l'Extreme-Orient — REO
Revue de l'Histoire des Colonies — Rev Hist Col
Revue de l'Histoire des Colonies Francaises — R Hist D Col Fr
Revue de l'Histoire des Colonies Francaises — Rev Hist Colon Fr
Revue de l'Histoire des Colonies Francaises — RHCF
Revue de l'Histoire des Religions — R De L Hist D Relig
Revue de l'Histoire des Religions — R Hist Rel
Revue de l'Histoire des Religions — Rev Hist R
Revue de l'Histoire des Religions — Rev Hist Relig
Revue de l'Histoire des Religions — Rev Hist Religions
Revue de l'Histoire des Religions — RHR
Revue de l'Histoire Juive en Egypte — RHJE
Revue de l'Horticulture Belge et Etrangere — Rev Hort Belge Etrangere
Revue de l'Hygiene Professionnelle — Rev Hyg Prof
Revue de Lille — RL
Revue de l'Industrie Minerale — Rev Ind Miner
Revue de l'Industrie Minerale. Mines — Rev Ind Miner Mines
Revue de l'Infirmiere — Rev Infirm
Revue de l'Ingenierie (Montreal) — Rev Ing (Montreal)
Revue de Linguistique — RL
Revue de Linguistique — RLi
Revue de Linguistique — RLing
Revue de Linguistique et de Philologie Comparee — Rev Linguist Philol Compar
Revue de Linguistique et de Philologie Comparee — RLPC
Revue de Linguistique Romane — Rev Ling Rom
Revue de Linguistique Romane — RLiR
Revue de Linguistique Romane — RLR
Revue de l'Institut Catholique de Paris — RICP
Revue de l'Institut de Sociologie. Institut de Sociologie Solvay — RISS
Revue de l'Institut des Manuscrits Arabes — RIMA
Revue de l'Institut Napoleon — Revudl
Revue de l'Instruction Publique en Belgique — RIB
Revue de l'Instruction Publique en Belgique — RIPB
Revue de Litterature Comparee — R Litt Comp
Revue de Litterature Comparee — Rev de Lit Comp
Revue de Litterature Comparee — Rev Lit
Revue de Litterature Comparee — Rev Lit Comp
Revue de Litterature Comparee — Rev Litt Comp
Revue de Litterature Comparee — Revue Lit Comp
Revue de Litterature Comparee — RLC
Revue de Litterature, Histoire, Arts, et Sciences — RLHAS
Revue de l'Occident Musulman et de la Mediterranee — R Occid Musul Mediterr
Revue de l'Orient — RO
Revue de l'Orient Chretien — Rev de l'Or Chret
Revue de l'Orient Chretien — Rev O Chr
Revue de l'Orient Chretien — Rev Or Chr
Revue de l'Orient Chretien — RO Chr
Revue de l'Orient Chretien — ROC
Revue de l'Orient, de l'Algerie et des Colonies — R Or
Revue de l'Orient Latin — Rev Or Lat
Revue de l'Orient Latin — ROL
Revue de Louisiane/Louisiana Review — RLLR
Revue de Madagascar — R Mad
Revue de Mathematiques et de Physique — Rev Math Phys
Revue de Mathematiques Pures et Appliquees — Rev Math Pures Appl
Revue de Mecanique Appliquee — Rev Mec Appl
Revue de Medecine Aeronautique — RMDAB
Revue de Medecine Aeronautique et Spatiale [*Later, Medecine Aeronautique et Spatial - Medecine Subaquatique et Hyperbare*] — Rev Med Aeronaut Spat
Revue de Medecine Aeronautique et Spatiale - Medecine Subaquatique et Hyperbare — Rev Med Aeronaut Spat Med Subaquat Hyperbare
Revue de Medecine Aeronautique (Paris) [*Later, Medecine Aeronautique et Spatial - Medecine Subaquatique et Hyperbare*] — Rev Med Aeronaut (Paris)
Revue de Medecine de Limoges — Rev Med Limoges
Revue de Medecine de Toulouse — Rev Med Toulouse
Revue de Medecine de Toulouse. Supplement — Rev Med Toulouse Suppl
Revue de Medecine de Toulouse. Supplement — RTOSA
Revue de Medecine de Tours — Rev Med Tours
Revue de Medecine des Accidents et des Maladies Professionnelles — Rev Med Accid Mal Prof
Revue de Medecine des Accidents et des Maladies Professionnelles — Rev Med Accidents Mal Prof
Revue de Medecine des Accidents et des Maladies Professionnelles — ZUBEAQ
Revue de Medecine du Limousin — Rev Med Limousin
Revue de Medecine du Limousin — RMLMDR
Revue de Medecine du Travail [*France*] — Rev Med Trav
Revue de Medecine Interne — Rev Med Interne
Revue de Medecine Navale (Metropole et Outre-Mer) — Rev Med Nav
Revue de Medecine (Paris) — Rev Med (Paris)
Revue de Medecine Preventive — Rev Med Prev
Revue de Medecine Psychosomatique et de Psychologie Medicale [*France*] — Rev Med Psychosomat Psychol Med
Revue de Medecine Psychosomatique et de Psychologie Medicale — RMPPA
Revue de Medecine Veterinaire — Rev Med Vet
Revue de Medecine Veterinaire (Toulouse) — Rev Med Vet (Toulouse)
Revue de Medicine du Travail — RMTRD
Revue de Metallurgie [*Paris*] — Rev Metall
Revue de Metallurgie. Cahiers d'Informations Techniques — Rev Metall Cah Inf Tech
Revue de Metallurgie (Paris) — Rev Met (Paris)
Revue de Metallurgie (Paris) — Rev Metall (Paris)
Revue de Metallurgie (Paris) Part 1. Memoires — Rev Metall (Paris) Part 1
Revue de Metallurgie (Paris) Part 2. Extraits — Rev Metall (Paris) Part 2
Revue de Metaphysique et de Morale — R Metaph Mor
Revue de Metaphysique et de Morale — Rev Met Mor
Revue de Metaphysique et de Morale — Rev Metaph Mor

Revue de Metaphysique et de Morale — Rev Metaph Morale
Revue de Metaphysique et de Morale — Rev Metaphys Morale
Revue de Metaphysique et de Morale — RM
Revue de Metaphysique et de Morale — RMM
Revue de Metrologie Pratique et Legale — Rev Metrol Prat Leg
Revue de Microbiologie Appliquee a l'Agriculture, a l'Hygiene, a l'Industrie — Rev Microbiol Appl Agric Hyg Ind
Revue de Micropaleontologie — Rev Micropal
Revue de Micropaleontologie — Rev Micropaleontol
Revue de Morpho-Physiologie Humaine — Rev Morpho-Phys Hum
Revue de Musicologie [*Paris*] — R de MU
Revue de Musicologie — R de Mus
Revue de Musicologie — R MI
Revue de Musicologie — R Musicol
Revue de Musicologie [*Paris*] — RdM
Revue de Musicologie — Rev Music
Revue de Mycologie — Rev Mycol
Revue de Mycologie (Paris) — Rev Mycol (Paris)
Revue de Mycologie. Supplement Colonial (Paris) — Rev Mycol (Paris) Suppl Colon
Revue de Nematologie — Rev Nematol
Revue de Nematologie — RNEMDX
Revue de Neuropsychiatrie Infantile et d'Hygiene Mentale de l'Enfance — Rev Neurops
Revue de Neuropsychiatrie Infantile et d'Hygiene Mentale de l'Enfance — Rev Neuropsychiatr Infant
Revue de Neuropsychiatrie Infantile et d'Hygiene Mentale de l'Enfance — Rev Neuropsychiatr Infant Hyg Ment Enfance
Revue de Paleobiologie — Rev Paleobiol
Revue de Paris — R de Paris
Revue de Paris — R Par
Revue de Paris — RdP
Revue de Paris — Rev de Paris
Revue de Paris — Rev Paris
Revue de Paris — RevudP
Revue de Paris — RP
Revue de Paris — RPa
Revue de Pathologie Comparee — Rev Path Comp
Revue de Pathologie Comparee — Rev Pathol Comp
Revue de Pathologie Comparee — Revue Path Comp
Revue de Pathologie Comparee et de Medecine Experimentale [*France*] — Rev Pathol Comp Med Exp
Revue de Pathologie Comparee et Hygiene Generale — Rev Pathol Comp Hyg Gen
Revue de Pathologie Comparee et Hygiene Generale — Revue Path Comp Hyg Gen
Revue de Pathologie Generale et Comparee — Rev Pathol Gen Comp
Revue de Pathologie Generale et de Physiologie Clinique — Rev Path Gen Physiol Clin
Revue de Pathologie Generale et de Physiologie Clinique — Rev Pathol Gen Physiol Clin
Revue de Pathologie Generale et de Physiologie Clinique — Revue Path Gen Physiol Clin
Revue de Pathologie Vegetale et d'Entomologie Agricole — Rev Path Veg et Entom Agric
Revue de Pathologie Vegetale et d'Entomologie Agricole de France — Rev Pathol Veg Entomol Agr France
Revue de Pathologie Vegetale et d'Entomologie Agricole de France — Rev Pathol Veg Entomol Agric Fr
Revue de Pathologie Vegetale et d'Entomologie Agricole de France — Revue Path Veg Ent Agric Fr
Revue de Pau et du Bearn — Rev Pau Bearn
Revue de Pediatrie — Rev Pediatr
Revue de Pharmacologie et de Therapeutique Experimentale — Rev Pharmacol Ter Exp
Revue de Philologie — RPh
Revue de Philologie, de Litterature, et d'Histoire Anciennes — R d P
Revue de Philologie de Litterature et d'Histoire Anciennes — R Ph LHA
Revue de Philologie, de Litterature, et d'Histoire Anciennes — Rev Ph
Revue de Philologie, de Litterature, et d'Histoire Anciennes — Rev Phil
Revue de Philologie, de Litterature, et d'Histoire Anciennes — Rev Philol
Revue de Philologie, de Litterature et d'Histoire Anciennes — Rev Philol Litt Hist Ancien
Revue de Philologie, de Litterature, et d'Histoire Anciennes — RP
Revue de Philologie, de Litterature, et d'Histoire Anciennes — RPh
Revue de Philologie, de Litterature, et d'Histoire Anciennes — RphLH
Revue de Philologie, de Litterature, et d'Histoire Anciennes. Troisieme Serie — RPLHA
Revue de Philologie Francaise et de Litterature — RPFL
Revue de Philosophie — Rev Phil
Revue de Philosophie — Rev Philos
Revue de Philosophie — RPh
Revue de Philosophie — RPhil
Revue de Phonetique [*Paris*] — RP
Revue de Phonetique Appliquee — Rev Phonet Appl
Revue de Phonetique Appliquee [*Paris*] — RPA
Revue de Physiotherapie Chirurgicale et de Radiologie — Rev Physiother Chir Rad
Revue de Physique — Rev Phys
Revue de Physique. Academie de la Republique Populaire Roumaine [*Romania*] — Rev Phys Acad Repub Pop Roum
Revue de Physique. Academie de la Republique Populaire Roumaine — RPRRA
Revue de Physique Appliquee — Rev Phys Ap
Revue de Physique Appliquee — Rev Phys Appl
Revue de Physique Appliquee. Supplement — Rev Phys Appl Suppl
Revue de Physique Appliquee (Supplement to Journal de Physique) — Rev Phys Appl (Suppl J Phys)
Revue de Phytotherapie — Rev Phytother
Revue de Pneumologie Clinique — Rev Pneumol Clin
Revue de Politique Internationale — R Polit Int
Revue de Presse d'Economie Miniere — Rev Presse Econ Min
Revue de Psychiatrie. Universite d'Ottawa — Rev Psychiatr Univ Ottawa
Revue de Psychologie Appliquee — Rev Psy App
Revue de Psychologie Appliquee — Rev Psych Appl
Revue de Psychologie des Peuples — Rev Psychol Peuples
Revue de Psychologie des Peuples — RPsP
Revue de Qumran — R QUM
Revue de Qumran — RD Q
Revue de Qumran — RdQ
Revue de Qumran — RevQum
Revue de Qumran — RQ
Revue de Qumran — RQu
Revue de Savoie — RSav
Revue de Science Criminelle et de Droit Penal Compare — Rev Sc Crim
Revue de Science et de Legislation Financiere — R S Leg F
Revue de Science et de Legislation Financiere — Rev Sc Leg Fin
Revue de Science et de Legislation Financiere — RSLF
Revue de Science Financiere — R Sci Financ
Revue de Science Financiere — R Science Fin
Revue de Science Financiere — RSF
Revue de Securite Sociale — RSS
Revue de Statistique Appliquee — Rev Stat Ap
Revue de Statistique Appliquee — Rev Statist Appl
Revue de Stomatologie [*Later, Revue de Stomatologie et de Chirurgie Maxillo-Faciale*] — RESTA
Revue de Stomatologie — Rev de Stomat
Revue de Stomatologie [*Later, Revue de Stomatologie et de Chirurgie Maxillo-Faciale*] — Rev Stomat
Revue de Stomatologie [*Later, Revue de Stomatologie et de Chirurgie Maxillo-Faciale*] — Rev Stomatol
Revue de Stomatologie et de Chirurgie Maxillo-Faciale — Rev Stomatol Chir Maxillo-Fac
Revue de Sud-Est Asiatique — RSEA
Revue de Synthese — RdS
Revue de Synthese — Rev Syn
Revue de Synthese — Rev Synthese
Revue de Synthese — RS
Revue de Synthese — RSyn
Revue de Synthese Historique — RSH
Revue de Synthese Historique — RSynH
Revue de Theologie — R Th
Revue de Theologie et d'Action Evangelique — RTAE
Revue de Theologie et de Philosophie — Rev Th Philos
Revue de Theologie et de Philosophie — Rev Theol Phil
Revue de Theologie et de Philosophie — Rev Theol Philos
Revue de Theologie et de Philosophie — RTh
Revue de Theologie et de Philosophie — RThPh
Revue de Theologie et de Philosophie — RTP
Revue de Theologie et de Philosophie — RTPh
Revue de Theologie et de Philosophie — RTPhil
Revue de Theologie et de Questions Religieuses — RThQR
Revue de Therapeutique Medico-Chirurgicale — Rev Therap Med-Chir
Revue de Tourisme — R Tourisme
Revue de Tourisme [*Berne*] — RTO
Revue de Tuberculose — RETUA
Revue de Tuberculose — Rev Tuberc
Revue de Tuberculose et de Pneumologie [*Later, Revue Francaise des Maladies Respiratoires*] — Rev Tuberc Pneumol
Revue de Turcologie — RTur
Revue de Viticulture — Rev Vitic
Revue de Zoologie Africaine — Rev Zool Afr
Revue de Zoologie Africaine — Revue Zool Afr
Revue de Zoologie Agricole et Appliquee — Rev Zool Agric Appl
Revue de Zoologie Agricole et Appliquee — Revue Zool Agric Appl
Revue de Zoologie Agricole et de Pathologie Vegetale — Rev Zoo Agr
Revue de Zoologie Agricole et de Pathologie Vegetale — Rev Zool Agric Pathol Veg
Revue de Zoologie et de Botanique Africaines — Rev Zool Bot Afr
Revue de Zoologie et de Botanique Africaines — Rev Zool Bot Africaines
Revue de Zoologie et de Botanique Africaines — Revue Zool Bot Afr
Revue d'Ecologie et de Biologie du Sol — Rev Ecol Biol Sol
Revue d'Ecologie et de Biologie du Sol — Rev Ecol BS
Revue d'Ecologie; la Terre et la Vie — RETVE5
Revue d'Ecologie; la Terre et la Vie — Rev Ecol Terre Vie
Revue d'Economie et de Droit Immobilier — R Econ Dr Immob
Revue d'Economie et de Gestion — R Econ Gestion
Revue d'Economie Industrielle — R Econ Industr
Revue d'Economie Politique — REP
Revue d'Economie Politique — Rev Econ Polit
Revue d'Economie Politique (Paris) — R Econ Pol (Paris)
Revue d'Economie Politique (Paris) — R Econ Polit (Paris)
Revue d'Economie Regionale et Urbaine — R Econ Region Urb
Revue d'EEG et de Neurophysiologie Clinique de Langue Francaise — Rev EEG Neurophysiol Clin
Revue d'Egypte — RE
Revue d'Egyptologie — R Egypt
Revue d'Egyptologie [*Cairo*] — Rd'E
Revue d'Egyptologie — REg
Revue d'Egyptologie — Rev d'Egypt

Revue d'Egyptologie — Rev Eg
Revue d'Egyptologie — Rev Egypt
Revue d'Egyptologie. Cahiers Complementaires — RDEC
Revue d'Electricite et de Mecanique — Rev El Mecan
Revue d'Electricite et de Mecanique — Rev Electr & Mec
Revue d'Electricite et de Mecanique [*France*] — Rev Electr Mecan
Revue d'Electroencephalographie et de Neurophysiologie Clinique — RENCB
Revue d'Electroencephalographie et de Neurophysiologie Clinique — Rev Electroencephalogr Neurophysiol Clin
Revue d'Electrotechnique et d'Energetique — Rev Electrotech Energ
Revue d'Electrotechnique et d'Energetique. Serie A. Electrotechnique, Electroenergetique et Energetique Generale — Rev Electrotech Energ Ser A
Revue d'Electrotechnique et d'Energetique. Serie B. Thermoenergetique et Utilisation Energetique des Combustibles — Rev Electrotech Energ Ser B
Revue d'Elevage et de Medecine Veterinaire des Pays Tropicaux — Rev Elev Med Vet Pays Trop
Revue Dentaire Libanaise — Rev Dent Liban
Revue d'Entomologie du Quebec — REQUEL
Revue d'Entomologie du Quebec — Rev Entomol Que
Revue. Departement de la Manche — R Manche
Revue d'Epidemiologie et de Sante Publique — RESPD
Revue d'Epidemiologie et de Sante Publique — Rev Epidemiol Sante Publique
Revue d'Epidemiologie, Medecine Sociale, et Sante Publique [*Later, Revue d'Epidemiologie et de Sante Publique*] — Rev Epidem
Revue d'Epidemiologie, Medecine Sociale, et Sante Publique [*Later, Revue d'Epidemiologie et de Sante Publique*] — Rev Epidemiol Med Soc Sante Publique
Revue der Fortschritte der Naturwissenschaften in Theoretischer und Praktischer Beziehung — Rev Fortschr Naturwiss
Revue des Accidents du Travail — R Acc
Revue des Accidents du Travail — Rev Acc Tr
Revue des Accidents du Travail et de Droit Industriel et Social — RAT
Revue des Agriculteurs de France — R Ag France
Revue des Agriculteurs de France — Rev Agric Fr
Revue des Agriculteurs de France et l'Agriculture Pratique — Rev Agric Fr Agric Prat
Revue des Anciens Etudiants del'Institut Technique Roubaisien — Rev Anc Etud Inst Tech Roubaisien
Revue des Applications de l'Electricite — Rev Appl Elect
Revue des Archeologues et Historiens d'Art de Louvain — R Arch Hist Art Louvain
Revue des Archeologues et Historiens d'Art de Louvain — RA Art Louvain
Revue des Arts — R Arts
Revue des Arts — R des Arts
Revue des Arts — RA
Revue des Arts Asiatiques — R Arts As
Revue des Arts Asiatiques — RAA
Revue des Arts Asiatiques — RAAs
Revue des Arts. Musees de France — Rev Arts
Revue des Assurances et des Responsabilites — Rev Ass Resp
Revue des Auteurs et des Livres — RAut & L
Revue des Bibliotheques — RBibl
Revue des Bibliotheques — RBques
Revue des Bibliotheques — RdB
Revue des Bibliotheques — Rev Biblioth
Revue des Bibliotheques et des Archives de la Belgique — RBAB
Revue des Collectivites Locales — R Collect Loc
Revue des Combustibles Liquides — Rev Combust Liq
Revue des Communautes Religieusses — RCR
Revue des Corps de Sante des Armees — Rev Corps Sante Armees
Revue des Corps de Sante des Armees. Terre, Mer, Air — Rev Corps Sante Armees Terre Mer Air
Revue des Cours et Conferences — RCC
Revue des Cours et Conferences — Rev Cours Conf
Revue des Cours et Conferences — Rev des Cours et Conf
Revue des Cours Scientifiques de la France et de l'Etranger — Rev Cours Sci France Etranger
Revue des Deux Mondes — R d 2 Mds
Revue des Deux Mondes — R Deux Mondes
Revue des Deux Mondes — RdDM
Revue des Deux Mondes — RdDxM
Revue des Deux Mondes — RDM
Revue des Deux Mondes — Rev Deux Mondes
Revue des Droits de l'Homme — R Dr Homme
Revue des Droits de l'Homme — R Droits Homme
Revue des Droits de l'Homme. Droit International et Droit Compare — Rev des Droits de l'Homme
Revue des Eaux et Forets — Rev Eaux Forets
Revue des Ecoles de l'Alliance Israelite Universelle — REAIU
Revue des Etudes Anciennes — R Et Anc
Revue des Etudes Anciennes — REA
Revue des Etudes Anciennes — REAnc
Revue des Etudes Anciennes — Rev Et Anc
Revue des Etudes Armeniennes — R E Ar
Revue des Etudes Armeniennes — R Et Arm
Revue des Etudes Armeniennes — REA
Revue des Etudes Armeniennes — REArm
Revue des Etudes Armeniennes — REArmen
Revue des Etudes Armeniennes — Rev Et Armen
Revue des Etudes Armeniennes. Nouvelle Serie — REArmNS
Revue des Etudes Augustiniennes — R E Ag
Revue des Etudes Augustiniennes — REA
Revue des Etudes Augustiniennes — REAug
Revue des Etudes Augustiniennes — Rev Etud Augustin
Revue des Etudes Byzantines — EB
Revue des Etudes Byzantines — R Etud Byzantines
Revue des Etudes Byzantines — REB
Revue des Etudes Byzantines — REByz
Revue des Etudes Byzantines — Rev Et Byzant
Revue des Etudes Byzantines — Rev Etud Byz
Revue des Etudes Byzantines — Rev Etud Byzant
Revue des Etudes Byzantines — Rv Et Byz
Revue des Etudes Cooperatives — R Et Coop
Revue des Etudes Cooperatives — R Etud Coops
Revue des Etudes Cooperatives — Rev Etud Coop
Revue des Etudes Corses — RECorses
Revue des Etudes Ethnographiques et Sociologiques — R D Etudes Ethnog
Revue des Etudes Grecques — R Et Gr
Revue des Etudes Grecques — R Etud Grecques
Revue des Etudes Grecques — REG
Revue des Etudes Grecques — REGr
Revue des Etudes Grecques — Rev Et Gr
Revue des Etudes Grecques — Rev Et Grec
Revue des Etudes Grecques — Rev Etud Grec
Revue des Etudes Historiques — REH
Revue des Etudes Historiques — REH
Revue des Etudes Historiques — Rev des Et Histor
Revue des Etudes Historiques — Rev des Et Historiques
Revue des Etudes Historiques — Rev des Etudes Histor
Revue des Etudes Historiques — Rev des Etudes Historiques
Revue des Etudes Historiques — Rev Et Hist
Revue des Etudes Homeriques — REHom
Revue des Etudes Hongroises — REH
Revue des Etudes Hongroises — REHong
Revue des Etudes Indo-Europeennes — REI
Revue des Etudes Indo-Europeennes — REIE
Revue des Etudes Indo-Europeennes — Rev EIE
Revue des Etudes Indo-Europeennes — Rev Et Ind
Revue des Etudes Islamiques — R Etud Islamiques
Revue des Etudes Islamiques — R Islamique
Revue des Etudes Islamiques — RdE
Revue des Etudes Islamiques — REI
Revue des Etudes Islamiques — REIsl
Revue des Etudes Islamiques — REIslam
Revue des Etudes Islamiques — Rev Et Islam
Revue des Etudes Islamiques. Memoires — REIM
Revue des Etudes Italiennes — REI
Revue des Etudes Italiennes — REIt
Revue des Etudes Italiennes — Rev des Et It
Revue des Etudes Italiennes — Rev des Et Ital
Revue des Etudes Italiennes — Rev Etud It
Revue des Etudes Italiennes — Rev Etud Ital
Revue des Etudes Juives — R Etud Juives
Revue des Etudes Juives — REJ
Revue des Etudes Juives — REJuiv
Revue des Etudes Juives — Rev Et Juiv
Revue des Etudes Juives et Historia Judaica [*Paris*] — REJuivHJud
Revue des Etudes Juives et Historia Judaica — Rev Etud Juives
Revue des Etudes Latines — REL
Revue des Etudes Latines — RELat
Revue des Etudes Latines — Rev Et Lat
Revue des Etudes Napoleoniennes — REN
Revue des Etudes Neo-Helleniques — RENH
Revue des Etudes Rabelaisiennes — R Et Rab
Revue des Etudes Rabelaisiennes — RER
Revue des Etudes Roumaines — RE Roum
Revue des Etudes Roumaines — RER
Revue des Etudes Roumaines — RERo
Revue des Etudes Roumaines — Rev Et Roum
Revue des Etudes Roumaines — RevER
Revue des Etudes Semitiques — RES
Revue des Etudes Semitiques — RESem
Revue des Etudes Semitiques et Babyloniaca — RES
Revue des ETudes Semitiques et Babyloniaca — RESB
Revue des Etudes Slaves — RES
Revue des Etudes Slaves — RESL
Revue des Etudes Slaves — RESlaves
Revue des Etudes Slaves — Rev Et Slav
Revue des Etudes Slaves — Rev Etud Slav
Revue des Etudes Slaves — RSI
Revue des Etudes Sud-Est Europeenes — RevudS
Revue des Etudes Sud-Est Europeennes — R Et Sud-Est Europ
Revue des Etudes Sud-Est Europeennes — RESEE
Revue des Etudes Sud-Est Europeennes — Rev Et SE Eur
Revue des Etudes Sud-Est Europeennes — Rev Etud Sud Est Eur
Revue des Facultes Catholiques d'Angres — RFCA
Revue des Facultes Catholiques de l'Ouest — RFCO
Revue des Faillites, Concordats, et Liquidations — Rev Faill
Revue des Faillites, Concordats, et Liquidations — RF
Revue des Fermentations et des Industries Alimentaires — Rev Ferment Ind Aliment
Revue des Fermentations et des Industries Alimentaires — Revue Ferment Ind Aliment
Revue des Fermentations et des Industries Alimentaires — RFIAAQ
Revue des Fonds de Commerce — Rev F de C
Revue des Hautes Temperatures et des Refractaires — Rev Hautes Temp Refract
Revue des Hautes Temperatures et des Refractaires — RHTRB
Revue des Huissiers — Rev Huis

Revue des Infirmieres et Infirmiers Auxiliaires du Quebec — Rev Infirm Infirm Aux Que
Revue des Ingenieurs des Ecoles Nationales Superieures des Mines — Rev Ing
Revue des Jardins — Rev Jard
Revue des Jeunes — R Jeu
Revue des Justices de Paix — Rev J de P
Revue des Langues Modernes — RLM
Revue des Langues Romanes — R d LR
Revue des Langues Romanes — R Lang Rom
Revue des Langues Romanes — RdLR
Revue des Langues Romanes — Rev Lang R
Revue des Langues Romanes — RLaR
Revue des Langues Romanes — RLR
Revue des Langues Romanes — RLR
Revue des Langues Vivantes — Rev Lang Viv
Revue des Langues Vivantes — RLaV
Revue des Langues Vivantes — RLV
Revue des Langues Vivantes/Tijdschrift voor Levende Talen — Rev Lang V
Revue des Lettres Modernes — R Lett Mod
Revue des Lettres Modernes — Rev Lettr Mod
Revue des Lettres Modernes — RLM
Revue des Lettres Modernes — RLMod
Revue des Lois, Decrets, Traites de Commerce. Institut International du Commerce — RLIC
Revue des Maladies Respiratoires — Rev Mal Respir
Revue des Maladies Respiratoires — RMREEY
Revue des Marques de la Parfumerie et de la Savonnerie — Rev Marq Parfum Savonn
Revue des Marques des Parfums de France — Rev Marques Parfums Fr
Revue des Materiaux de Construction et de Travaux Publics — Rev Mater Constr Trav Publics
Revue des Materiaux de Construction et de Travaux Publics — RMC
Revue des Materiaux de Construction et de Travaux Publics. Edition B. Brique, Tuile, Ceramique — Rev Mater Constr Trav Publics Ed B
Revue des Nations — R Nations
Revue des Pays de l'Est — R Pays Est
Revue des Pays de l'Est — RPP
Revue des Produits Chimiques — Rev Prod Chim
Revue des Produits Chimiques et l'Actualite Scientifique Reunis — Rev Prod Chim Actual Sci Reunis
Revue des Questions Historiques — R Quest Hist
Revue des Questions Historiques — RdQH
Revue des Questions Historiques — Rev des Questions Histor
Revue des Questions Historiques — Rev Quest Hist
Revue des Questions Historiques — RQ
Revue des Questions Historiques — RQH
Revue des Questions Historiques — RQHist
Revue des Questions Scientifiques — Rev Quest Sci
Revue des Questions Scientifiques — Rev Questions Sci
Revue des Questions Scientifiques — Revue Quest Scient
Revue des Questions Scientifiques — RQS
Revue des Questions Scientifiques — RQSc
Revue des Religions (Paris) — RRP
Revue des Sciences de l'Eau — Rev Sci Eau
Revue des Sciences de l'Education — Rev Sci Ed
Revue des Sciences Ecclesiastiques — RSE
Revue des Sciences Ecclesiastiques et la Science Catholique Reunies — RSESC
Revue des Sciences Economiques — R Sc Eco
Revue des Sciences Economiques — R Sciences Econs
Revue des Sciences Economiques — RSE
Revue des Sciences Economiques — RSEc
Revue des Sciences Humaines — R Sc Hum
Revue des Sciences Humaines — R Sci Hum
Revue des Sciences Humaines — Rev Sci Hum
Revue des Sciences Humaines — RSH
Revue des Sciences Humaines — RSHum
Revue des Sciences Medicales — Rev Sci Med
Revue des Sciences Naturelles d'Auvergne — Rev Sci Nat Auvergne
Revue des Sciences Naturelles d'Auvergne — Rev Sci Natur Auvergne
Revue des Sciences Philosophiques et Theologiques — R Sci Ph Th
Revue des Sciences Philosophiques et Theologiques — R Sci Philos & Theol
Revue des Sciences Philosophiques et Theologiques — Rev Sc Phil Theol
Revue des Sciences Philosophiques et Theologiques — Rev Sci Ph
Revue des Sciences Philosophiques et Theologiques — Rev Sci Phil Theol
Revue des Sciences Philosophiques et Theologiques — RevScPhTh
Revue des Sciences Philosophiques et Theologiques [*Paris*] — RScPhilT
Revue des Sciences Philosophiques et Theologiques [*Paris*] — RscPhTh
Revue des Sciences Philosophiques et Theologiques — RSPh
Revue des Sciences Philosophiques et Theologiques — RSPhTh
Revue des Sciences Philosophiques et Theologiques — RSPT
Revue des Sciences Politiques — R D Sci Polit
Revue des Sciences Politiques — R Sci Pol
Revue des Sciences Politiques — RSP
Revue des Sciences Religieuses — R Sc Relig
Revue des Sciences Religieuses — R Sci Rel
Revue des Sciences Religieuses — Rev Sci Rel
Revue des Sciences Religieuses — Rev Sci Relig
Revue des Sciences Religieuses [*Strasbourg/Paris*] — RevScRel
Revue des Sciences Religieuses [*Strasbourg/Paris*] — RevSR
Revue des Sciences Religieuses — RScR
Revue des Sciences Religieuses — RScRel
Revue des Sciences Religieuses — RSRS
Revue des Sciences Religieuses. Universite de Strasbourg — RSR
Revue des Sciences Religieuses. Universite de Strasbourg — RSRel
Revue des Sciences Religieuses. Universite de Strasbourg — RSRUS
Revue des Sciences Sociales de la France de l'Est — R Sci Soc France Est
Revue des Societe Savantes de la France et de l'Etranger — Rev Soc Savantes France Etranger
Revue des Societes — R Soc
Revue des Societes — Rev Soc
Revue des Societes Savantes de Haute-Normandie — Rev Soc Savantes Haute Normandie
Revue des Societes Svantes de Haute Normandie — RSSHN
Revue des Tabacs Helleniques — Rev Tabacs Hellen
Revue des Telecommunications [*France*] — Rev Telecommun
Revue des Traditions Populaires — R D Trad Pop
Revue des Traditions Populaires — Rev Tradit Popul
Revue des Travaux. Academie des Sciences Morales et Politiques — R Trav Acad Sci Mor Polit
Revue des Travaux. Academie des Sciences Morales et Politiques — RTASM
Revue des Travaux. Academie des Sciences Morales et Politiques et Comptes-Rendus de ses Seances — Rev Trav Acad Sci Morales Polit
Revue des Travaux. Academie des Sciences Morales et Publiques — RevudT
Revue des Travaux. Institut des Peches Maritimes — Rev Trav Inst Peches Marit
Revue des Travaux. Institut des Peches Maritimes — RIPMA
Revue des Travaux. Institut Scientifique et Technique des Peches Maritimes — Rev Trav Inst Sci Tech Peches Marit
Revue des Troupes Coloniales — R D Troupes Col
Revue des Troupes Coloniales — Rev Troup Colon
Revue des Universites du Midi — RUM
Revue des Ventes et Transports — Rev V Tr
Revue d'Esthetique — R d'Esthetique
Revue d'Esthetique — R Esthet
Revue d'Esthetique — RDE
Revue d'Esthetique — RE
Revue d'Esthetique — Rev Esth
Revue d'Ethnographie — R D Ethnog
Revue d'Ethnographie — REth
Revue d'Ethnographie — Rev Ethn
Revue d'Ethnographie et de Sociologie — R D Ethnog Et De Sociol
Revue d'Ethnographie et des Traditions Populaires — R D Ethnog Et D Trad Pop
Revue d'Ethnographie (Paris) — REP
Revue d'Etudes Comparatives Est-Ouest — R Et Comp Est-Ouest
Revue d'Etudes Comparatives Est-Ouest — Rev Etud Comp Est Ouest
Revue d'Etudes Comparatives Est-Ouest — RPE
Revue d'Etudes Comparatives Est-Ouest. Economie, Planification, et Organisation — Revue Etud Comp Est Ouest
Revue d'Hematologie — Rev Hemat
Revue d'Hematologie — Rev Hematol
Revue d'Histoire Comparee — Rev Hist Comp
Revue d'Histoire Comparee — RHC
Revue d'Histoire Comparee — RHComp
Revue d'Histoire de [La Deuxieme] Guerre Mondiale — Revue Hist 2 Guerre Mondiale
Revue d'Histoire de la Deuxieme Guerre Mondiale — R Hist Deuxieme Geurre Mondiale
Revue d'Histoire de la Deuxieme Guerre Mondiale — Re Hist De
Revue d'Histoire de la Deuxieme Guerre Mondiale — Rev Hist Deux Guerre Mond
Revue d'Histoire de la Deuxieme Guerre Mondiale — RHDGM
Revue d'Histoire de la Medecine Hebraique — Rev Hist Med Hebr
Revue d'Histoire de la Medecine Hebraique — Rev Hist Med Hebraique
Revue d'Histoire de la Medecine Hebraique / Societe de la Medecine Hebraique — Rev Hist Med Hebraique
Revue d'Histoire de la Medicine Hebraique [*Paris*] — RHMH
Revue d'Histoire de la Pharmacie — Rev Hist Pharm
Revue d'Histoire de la Pharmacie — RevudHP
Revue d'Histoire de la Philosophie et d'Histoire Generale de la Civilisation — RHP
Revue d'Histoire de la Philosophie et d'Histoire Generale de la Civilisation — RHPH
Revue d'Histoire de la Philosophie et d'Histoire Generale de la Civilisation — RHPhC
Revue d'Histoire de la Spiritualite — R Hist Spiritualite
Revue d'Histoire de la Spiritualite — RH Spir
Revue d'Histoire de la Spiritualite — RHS
Revue d'Histoire de l'Amerique Francaise — R d'Hist
Revue d'Histoire de l'Amerique Francaise — Rev His A F
Revue d'Histoire de l'Amerique Francaise — Rev Hist Am
Revue d'Histoire de l'Amerique Francaise — Rev Hist Am Fr
Revue d'Histoire de l'Amerique Francaise — Rev Hist Amer Fr
Revue d'Histoire de l'Amerique Francaise — RevudHA
Revue d'Histoire de l'Amerique Francaise — RHAF
Revue d'Histoire de l'Eglise de France — RE Fr
Revue d'Histoire de l'Eglise de France — Rev d Hist de l Eglise de France
Revue d'Histoire de l'Eglise de France — Rev HE Fr
Revue d'Histoire de l'Eglise de France — RevudHF
Revue d'Histoire de l'Eglise de France — RHEF
Revue d'Histoire des Colonies — Rev Hist Colon
Revue d'Histoire des Doctrines Economiques — Rev Hist Doctr Econ
Revue d'Histoire des Doctrines Economiques et Sociales — RHDE
Revue d'Histoire des Mathematiques — Rev Histoire Math
Revue d'Histoire des Missions — R D Hist D Mis
Revue d'Histoire des Missions — RH Miss
Revue d'Histoire des Missions — RHMis
Revue d'Histoire des Religions — Rev Hist Rel
Revue d'Histoire des Religions — Rev Rel
Revue d'Histoire des Religions — RH Rel

Revue d'Histoire des Sciences — Rev Hist Sci
Revue d'Histoire des Sciences — Rev Histoire Sci
Revue d'Histoire des Sciences et de Leurs Applications — R Hist Sci & Ap
Revue d'Histoire des Sciences et de Leurs Applications — Rev Hist Sci Applic
Revue d'Histoire des Sciences et de Leurs Applications — Rev Hist Sci Leurs Appl
Revue d'Histoire des Sciences et de Leurs Applications — Rev Histoire Sci Appl
Revue d'Histoire des Sciences et de Leurs Applications — RHS
Revue d'Histoire des Sciences et de Leurs Applications — RHSA
Revue d'Histoire des Textes — Rev H Text
Revue d'Histoire des Textes — Rev Hist Textes
Revue d'Histoire des Textes — RHT
Revue d'Histoire des Textes — RHTe
Revue d'Histoire Diplomatique — R Hist Diplom
Revue d'Histoire Diplomatique — Rev d Hist Diplom
Revue d'Histoire Diplomatique — Rev Hist Di
Revue d'Histoire Diplomatique — Rev Hist Dipl
Revue d'Histoire Diplomatique — Rev Hist Diplomat
Revue d'Histoire Diplomatique — RHD
Revue d'Histoire Diplomatique — RHDip
Revue d'Histoire du Droit — Rev H Dr
Revue d'Histoire du Droit — Rev Hist Dr
Revue d'Histoire du Droit — Rev Hist Droit
Revue d'Histoire du Droit — RHD
Revue d'Histoire du Droit Francais et Etranger — Rev Hist Dr Fr et Etrang
Revue d'Histoire du Fascisme — R Hist Fascisme
Revue d'Histoire du Theatre — Rev Hist Th
Revue d'Histoire du Theatre — Revue Hist Theatre
Revue d'Histoire du Theatre — RHT
Revue d'Histoire Ecclesiastique — R Hist Eccl
Revue d'Histoire Ecclesiastique — Rev Eccl
Revue d'Histoire Ecclesiastique — Rev Hist Eccl
Revue d'Histoire Ecclesiastique — Rev Hist Eccles
Revue d'Histoire Ecclesiastique — RevudHE
Revue d'Histoire Ecclesiastique — RHE
Revue d'Histoire Eclesiastique — R Hist Eccles
Revue d'Histoire Economique et Sociale — Rev Hist Econ Soc
Revue d'Histoire Economique et Sociale — Rev Hist Econ Social
Revue d'Histoire Economique et Sociale — Revue Hist Econ et Soc
Revue d'Histoire Economique et Sociale — RHES
Revue d'Histoire et de Civilisation du Maghreb — R Hist Civ Maghreb
Revue d'Histoire et de Civilisation du Maghreb — Revue Hist et de Civilisation du Maghreb
Revue d'Histoire et de Civilisation du Maghreb — RHCM
Revue d'Histoire et de Litterature Religieuse — RHLR
Revue d'Histoire et de Littetature Religieuses — Rev D Hist Litt Relig
Revue d'Histoire et de Philosophie Religieuse — Rev H Philos
Revue d'Histoire et de Philosophie Religieuse — Rev Hist Philos Relig
Revue d'Histoire et de Philosophie Religieuse — RH Phil Rel
Revue d'Histoire et de Philosophie Religieuses — R Hist & Philos Rel
Revue d'Histoire et de Philosophie Religieuses — R Hist Ph Rel
Revue d'Histoire et de Philosophie Religieuses — Rev d Hist et de Philos Religieuses
Revue d'Histoire et de Philosophie Religieuses — Rev Hist Ph
Revue d'Histoire et de Philosophie Religieuses — RHPhR
Revue d'Histoire et de Philosophie Religieuses — RHPhRel
Revue d'Histoire et de Philosophie Religieuses — RHPR
Revue d'Histoire Franciscaine — RHF
Revue d'Histoire Litteraire (Bucharest) — RHLB
Revue d'Histoire Litteraire de la France — R Hist Litt France
Revue d'Histoire Litteraire de la France — Rev Hist L
Revue d'Histoire Litteraire de la France — Rev Hist Litt
Revue d'Histoire Litteraire de la France — Rev Hist Litt Fr
Revue d'Histoire Litteraire de la France — Rev Hist Litt France
Revue d'Histoire Litteraire de la France — Revue d Histoire Litteraire
Revue d'Histoire Litteraire de la France — RHL
Revue d'Histoire Litteraire de la France — RHLF
Revue d'Histoire Maghrebine — Rev Hist Maghrebine
Revue d'Histoire Moderne — Rev Hist Mod
Revue d'Histoire Moderne — RH Mo
Revue d'Histoire Moderne — RHM
Revue d'Histoire Moderne et Contemporaine — R Hist Mod & Contemp
Revue d'Histoire Moderne et Contemporaine — Rev d Histoire Mod et Cont
Revue d'Histoire Moderne et Contemporaine — Rev Hist M
Revue d'Histoire Moderne et Contemporaine — Rev Hist Mod Cont
Revue d'Histoire Moderne et Contemporaine — Rev Hist Mod Contemp
Revue d'Histoire Moderne et Contemporaine — RevudHM
Revue d'Histoire Moderne et Contemporaine — Revue Hist Mod et Contemporaine
Revue d'Histoire Moderne et Contemporaine — RHMC
Revue d'Histoire Naturelle Appliquee — Rev Hist Nat Appliq
Revue d'Histoire Vaudoise — RevudHV
Revue d'Hydraulique — Rev Hydraul
Revue d'Hydrobiologie Tropicale — Rev Hydrobiol Trop
Revue d'Hygiene — Rev Hyg
Revue d'Hygiene (Ankara) — Rev Hyg (Ankara)
Revue d'Hygiene du Travail — Rev Hyg Trav
Revue d'Hygiene et de Medecine Infantiles et Annales de la Polyclinique H. de Rothschild — Rev Hyg Med Infant Ann Polyclin H de Rothschild
Revue d'Hygiene et de Medecine Preventive — Rev Hyg et Med Prevent
Revue d'Hygiene et de Medecine Preventive — Rev Hyg Med Prev
Revue d'Hygiene et de Medecine Sociale — Rev Hyg Med Soc
Revue d'Hygiene et de Medecine Sociale — RHMSA
Revue d'Hygiene et de Police Sanitaire — RHPS
Revue d'Hygiene et Medecine Scolaire et Universitaire — Rev Hyg Med Sc Univ
Revue d'Immunologie — Rev Immunol
Revue d'Immunologie et de Therapie Antimicrobienne — Rev Immunol Ther Antimicrob
Revue d'Immunologie et de Therapie Antimicrobienne — RITAA
Revue d'Informatique Medicale — Rev Inf Med
Revue Diocesaine de Namur — RDNamur
Revue Diocesaine de Tournai — RDT
Revue Diocesaine de Tournai — RDTournai
Revue Diogene — Diog
Revue d'Odonto-Stomatologie — Rev Odonto Stomatol
Revue d'Odonto-Stomatologie — RODSB
Revue d'Odonto-Stomatologie (Bordeaux) — Rev Odonto-Stomatol (Bord)
Revue d'Odonto-Stomatologie du Midi de la France — Rev Odonto-Stomatol Midi Fr
Revue d'Odonto-Stomatologie (Paris) — Rev Odonto-Stomatol (Paris)
Revue d'Oka — Rev Oka
Revue d'Oka. Agronomie. Medicine. Veterinaire — Revue Oka
Revue d'Optique — Rev d'Optique
Revue d'Optique Theorique et Instrumentale — Rev Opt
Revue d'Optique Theorique et Instrumentale [*France*] — Rev Opt Theor Instrum
Revue d'Orthopedie Dento-Faciale — Rev Orthop Dento-Faciale
Revue d'Oto-Neuro-Ophtalmologie — Rev Oto-Neuro-Ophtalmol
Revue d'Oto-Neuro-Ophtalmologie — RONOA
Revue d'Oto-Neuro-Ophtalmologie (Paris) — Rev Oto-Neuro-Ophtalmol (Paris)
Revue Dromoise — Bull Drome
Revue Dromoise — Rev Drome
Revue du Barreau — R du B
Revue du Barreau — Rev Bar
Revue du Bas-Poitou — R Bas Poitou
Revue du Bois et de Ses Applications — RBAPA
Revue du Bois et de Ses Applications — RDB
Revue du Bois et de Ses Applications — Rev Bois Appl
Revue du Caire — R Caire
Revue du Chant Gregorien — RCG
Revue du Christianisme Social — RC Soc
Revue du Cinema — R Cin
Revue du Cinema/Image et Son — R Cin
Revue du Cinema/Image et Son. Ecran — Rev Cinema
Revue du Clerge Africain — R Cl Afr
Revue du Clerge Francais — RCF
Revue du Clerge Francais — RClFr
Revue du Comportement Animal — Revue Comp Anim
Revue du Corps de Sante Militaire — Rev Corps Sante Mil
Revue du Developpement International — R Developpement Internat
Revue du Droit Public et de la Science Politique en France et a l'Etranger — R Dr Publ Sci Polit
Revue du Droit Public et de la Science Politique en France et a l'Etranger — R Droit Public
Revue du Droit Public et de la Science Politique en France et a l'Etranger — Rev Droit Publ Sci Poli France Et Etranger
Revue du Droit Public et de la Science Politique en France et a l'Etranger — Rev Droit Public Sci Polit
Revue du Droit Public et de la Science Politique en France et a l'Etranger — Rev du Droit Publ et de la Sci Polit en France
Revue du Droit Social et des Tribunaux du Travail — RDS
Revue du Foie — Rev Foie
Revue du Louvre et des Musees de France — R du Louvre
Revue du Louvre et des Musees de France — R Louvre
Revue du Louvre et des Musees de France — Rev Louvre
Revue du Louvre et des Musees de France — RLMF
Revue du Marche Commun — R Marche Commun
Revue du Marche Commun — Rev du Marche Commun
Revue du Marche Commun — RMC
Revue du Monde, Ancien et Moderne — RMAM
Revue du Monde Catholique — RMC
Revue du Monde Latin — Rev Monde Lat
Revue du Monde Musulman — R Du Monde Musulm
Revue du Monde Musulman — R Mo Mu
Revue du Monde Musulman — RMM
Revue du Moyen-Age Latin — Rev du Moyen-Age Latin
Revue du Moyen-Age Latin — Rev Moyen A
Revue du Moyen-Age Latin [*Strasbourg*] — RMAL
Revue du Nickel — Rev Nickel
Revue du Nord — R Nord
Revue du Nord — RDN
Revue du Nord — Rev du Nord
Revue du Nord — Rev Nord
Revue du Nord — RevuduN
Revue du Nord — RN
Revue du Notariat — R du N
Revue du Notariat — R du Not
Revue du Notariat — Rev du Not
Revue du Notariat — Rev du Notariat
Revue du Notariat — Rev Not
Revue du Notariat — Rev Notariat
Revue du Pacifique. Etudes de Litterature Francaise — R Pac
Revue du Palais de la Decouverte [*France*] — Rev Palais Decouv
Revue du Palais de la Deouverte — RPDED
Revue du Paludisme et de Medecine Tropicale — Rev Palud Med Trop
Revue du Praticien — Rev Prat
Revue du Rhumatisme. English Edition — Rev Rhum Engl Ed
Revue du Rhumatisme et des Maladies Osteo-Articulaires — Rev Rhum
Revue du Rhumatisme et des Maladies Osteo-Articulaires — Rev Rhum Mal Osteo-Artic
Revue du Seizieme Siecle — R du XVIe S

Revue du Seizieme Siecle — Rev du Siezieme Siecle
Revue du Seizieme Siecle — RSS
Revue du SESDA [*Secretariat de Sante Dentaire de l'Afrique*] — Rev SESDA
Revue du Tarn — R Tarn
Revue du Trachome — Rev Trach
Revue du Travail — R Trav
Revue du Travail [*Brussels*] — R Travail Bruxelles
Revue du Travail — Rev Trav
Revue du Travail — RT
Revue du Travail (Bruxelles) — R Trav (Bruxelles)
Revue du Travail et du Bien-Etre Social — Rev Trav
Revue du Tresor — R Tres
Revue du Tresor — R Tresor
Revue du Ver a Soie — Rev Ver Soie
Revue du Vivarais — R Vivarais
Revue du Vivarais — Rev Vivarais
Revue E. Electricite, Electrotechnique Generale, Courants Forts, et Applications [*Belgium*] — Rev E
Revue E. Electricite, Electrotechnique Generale, Courants Forts, et Applications — Rev E Elec Electrotech Gen
Revue Ecclesiastique de Liege — REcL
Revue Ecclesiastique de Liege — REL
Revue Ecclesiastique de Liege [*Belgium*] — RELiege
Revue Ecclesiastique de Metz — REM
Revue. Ecole Nationale des Langues Orientales — RENLO
Revue Economique — Rev Econ
Revue Economique [*Paris*] — RVU
Revue Economique. Banque Nationale de Paris — R Econ Banque Nat Paris
Revue Economique du Sud-Ouest — R Econ Sud-Ouest
Revue Economique et Financiere Ivoirienne — R Econ et Fin
Revue Economique et Sociale — R Econ et Soc
Revue Economique et Sociale — R Econ Soc
Revue Economique et Sociale — Rev Econ Soc
Revue Economique et Sociale (Lausanne) — RVL
Revue Economique Francaise — R Econ Fr
Revue Economique Francaise — R Econ Franc
Revue Economique Francaise — Rev Econ Fr
Revue Economique Franco-Suisse — R Econ Franco-Suisse
Revue Economique Franco-Suisse — R Econ Fr-Suisse
Revue Economique Internationale — R Ec Int
Revue Economique Internationale — REI
Revue Economique (Paris) — R Econ (Paris)
Revue Egyptienne de Droit International — R Eg Dr Int
Revue Egyptienne de Droit International — R Egypt Dr Int
Revue Egyptienne de Droit International — REDI
Revue Egyptienne de Droit International — Rev Egypt de Droit Internat
Revue Egyptologique — RE
Revue Egyptologique — REg
Revue Egyptologique — Rev Egyptol
Revue Electrotechnique et Energetique. Academie de la Republique Populaire Roumaine [*Romania*] — Rev Electrotech Energ Acad Repub Pop Roum
Revue Encyclopedique — RE
Revue Entomologique — Rev Entomol
Revue Epigraphique — R Epi
Revue Epigraphique — REp
Revue Epigraphique — REpigr
Revue Epigraphique — Rev Ep
Revue Epigraphique — RevEpigr
Revue Europeenne de la Pomme de Terre — Rev Eur Pomme Terre
Revue Europeenne d'Endocrinologie — Rev Eur Endocrinol
Revue Europeenne des Elements Finis — Rev Europeenne Elem Finis
Revue Europeenne des Papiers Cartons-Complexes — Rev Europ Papiers Cartons Complexes
Revue Europeenne des Sciences Sociales. Cahiers Vilfredo Pareto — R Europ Sci Soc
Revue Europeenne d'Etudes Cliniques et Biologiques [*France*] — Rev Eur Etud Clin Biol
Revue Europeenne pour les Sciences Medicales et Pharmacologiques — Rev Eur Sci Med Pharmacol
Revue. Faculte de Langues, d'Histoire, et de Geographie. Universite d'Ankara — RFLHGA
Revue. Faculte de Medecine Veterinaire de Teheran — Rev Fac Med Vet Teheran
Revue. Faculte des Lettres. Universite de Teheran — RUT
Revue. Faculte des Sciences Economiques de l'Universite d'Istanbul — Rev Fac Sci Econ Univ Istanbul
Revue. Faculte des Sciences Forestieres. Universite d'Istanbul — Rev Fac Sci For Univ Istanbul
Revue. Faculte des Sciences. Universite d'Istanbul — Rev Fac Sci Univ Istanbul
Revue. Faculte des Sciences. Universite d'Istanbul. Serie A. Mathematiques Pures et Appliquees — Rev Fac Sci Univ Istanbul Ser A
Revue. Faculte des Sciences. Universite d'Istanbul. Serie B. Sciences Naturelles — Rev Fac Sci Univ Istanbul Ser B Sci Nat
Revue. Faculte des Sciences. Universite d'Istanbul. Serie C — Rev Fac Sci Univ Istanbul C
Revue. Faculte Veterinaire. Universite de Teheran — Rev Fac Vet Univ Teheran
Revue. Federation Francaise des Societes de Sciences Naturelles — Rev Fed Fr Soc Sci Nat
Revue Financiere — R Financ
Revue Fiscale — Rev F
Revue Fiscale — Rev Fisc
Revue Fiscale — RF
Revue Fiscale — RFI
Revue FITCE [*Federation des Ingenieurs des Telecommunications de la Communaute Europeenne*] — Rev FITCE
Revue Forestiere Francaise — R For Franc
Revue Forestiere Francaise — Rev For Franc
Revue Forestiere Francaise — Revue For Fr
Revue Forestiere Francaise (Nancy) — Rev For Fr (Nancy)
Revue Francais de l'Agriculture — Rev Franc Agr
Revue Francaise — RF
Revue Francaise — RFr
Revue Francaise d'Administration Publique — R Franc Adm Publ
Revue Francaise d'Administration Publique — Revue Fr d Adm Publique
Revue Francaise d'Allergie — Rev Fr Allerg
Revue Francaise d'Allergie — RFALA
Revue Francaise d'Allergologie [*Later, Revue Francaise d'Allergologie et d'Immunologie Clinique*] — Rev Fr Alle
Revue Francaise d'Allergologie — Rev Fr Allergol
Revue Francaise d'Allergologie [*Later, Revue Francaise d'Allergologie et d'Immunologie Clinique*] — Revue Fr Allergol
Revue Francaise d'Allergologie et d'Immunologie Clinique — Rev Fr Allergol Immunol Clin
Revue Francaise d'Allergologie et d'Immunologie Clinique — Revue Fr Allergol Immunol Clin
Revue Francaise d'Apiculture — Revue Fr Apic
Revue Francaise d'Astronautique [*France*] — Rev Fr Astronaut
Revue Francaise d'Automatique, d'Informatique, et de Recherche Operationelle. Analyse Numerique — Rev Fr Autom Inf Rech Oper Anal
Revue Francaise d'Automatique, d'Informatique, et de Recherche Operationnelle — Rev Fr Autom Inf Rech Oper
Revue Francaise d'Automatique, d'Informatique, et de Recherche Operationnelle. Serie Analyse Numerique — Rev Fr Aut Inf Rech Oper Anal Num
Revue Francaise d'Automatique, d'Informatique, et de Recherche Operationnelle. Serie Analyse Numerique — RFAND
Revue Francaise d'Automatique, d'Informatique, et de Recherche Operationnelle. Serie Automatique — RFAAD
Revue Francaise d'Automatique, d'Informatique, et de Recherche Operationnelle. Serie Bleue — Rev Francaise Automat Inform Rech Oper Ser Bleue
Revue Francaise d'Automatique, d'Informatique, et de Recherche Operationnelle. Serie Informatique Theorique — RSITD
Revue Francaise d'Automatique, d'Informatique, et de Recherche Operationnelle. Serie Jaune — Rev Francaise Automat Inform Rech Oper Ser Jaune
Revue Francaise d'Automatique, d'Informatique, et de Recherche Operationnelle. Serie Recherche Operationnelle — RSROD
Revue Francaise d'Automatique, d'Informatique, et de Recherche Operationnelle. Serie Rouge. Analyse Numerique — Rev Francaise Automat Inform Rech Oper Ser Rouge Anal Numer
Revue Francaise d'Automatique, d'Informatique, et de Recherche Operationnelle. Serie Verte — Rev Francaise Automat Inform Rech Oper Ser Verte
Revue Francaise de Communication — Rev Fr de C
Revue Francaise de Comptabilite — R Franc Comptab
Revue Francaise de Droit Aerien — R Franc Dr Aer
Revue Francaise de Droit Aerien — Rev Franc de Droit Aer
Revue Francaise de Geotechnique — Rev Fr Geotech
Revue Francaise de Gerontologie — Rev Fr Gerontol
Revue Francaise de Gerontologie — Revue Fr Geront
Revue Francaise de Gestion — R Fr Gestion
Revue Francaise de Gestion — R Franc Gestion
Revue Francaise de Gestion. Hommes et Techniques — HTQ
Revue Francaise de Gynecologie et d'Obstetrique — Rev F Gy Ob
Revue Francaise de Gynecologie et d'Obstetrique — Rev Fr Gynecol Obstet
Revue Francaise de la Sociologie — RevuFS
Revue Francaise de l'Electricite — Rev Fr Electr
Revue Francaise de l'Elite — R Fr El
Revue Francaise de l'Energie — R Fr Energ
Revue Francaise de l'Energie — R Franc En
Revue Francaise de l'Energie — Rev Fr Energ
Revue Francaise de l'Etranger et des Colonies — Rev Fr Etr Colon
Revue Francaise de l'Etranger et des Colonies — RFEC
Revue Francaise de Mecanique — Rev Fr Mec
Revue Francaise de Pedagogie — R Franc Pedag
Revue Francaise de Pedagogie — Rev Fr Pedagog
Revue Francaise de Pediatrie — Rev Fr Pediatr
Revue Francaise de Photographie — Rev Franc Phot
Revue Francaise de Photographie et de Cinematographie — Rev Fr Photogr Cinematogr
Revue Francaise de Psychanalyse — Rev Fr Psychanal
Revue Francaise de Psychoanalyse — R Franc Psych
Revue Francaise de Science Politique — R Fr Science Pol
Revue Francaise de Science Politique — R Franc Sci Polit
Revue Francaise de Science Politique — R Francaise Sci Pol
Revue Francaise de Science Politique — Rev Fr Sc P
Revue Francaise de Science Politique — Rev Fr Sci Polit
Revue Francaise de Science Politique — Rev Franc Sci Polit
Revue Francaise de Science Politique — Revue Fr Sci Polit
Revue Francaise de Science Politique — RevuFSP
Revue Francaise de Science Politique — RFSP
Revue Francaise de Sociologie — R Fr Sociol
Revue Francaise de Sociologie — R Franc Soc
Revue Francaise de Sociologie — R Franc Sociol
Revue Francaise de Sociologie — R Francaise Sociol
Revue Francaise de Sociologie — Rev Fr Soc
Revue Francaise de Sociologie — Rev Fr Sociol
Revue Francaise de Sociologie — Revue Fr Sociologie
Revue Francaise de Sociologie — RFS

Revue Francaise de Sociologie — RFSO-A
Revue Francaise de Traitement de l'Information — Rev Fr Trait Inf
Revue Francaise de Traitement de l'Information — RFTRA
Revue Francaise de Transfusion [*Later, Revue Francaise de Transfusion et Immuno-Hematologie*] — Rev Fr Tran
Revue Francaise de Transfusion [*Later, Revue Francaise de Transfusion et Immuno-Hematologie*] — Rev Fr Transfus
Revue Francaise de Transfusion — RFT
Revue Francaise de Transfusion et Immuno-Hematologie — Rev Fr Transfus Immuno-Hematol
Revue Francaise d'Endocrinologie — Rev Fr Endocrinol
Revue Francaise d'Endocrinologie Clinique, Nutrition, et Metabolisme — Rev Fr Endocrinol Clin Nutr Metab
Revue Francaise d'Entomologie — Rev Fr Entomol
Revue Francaise d'Entomologie. Nouvelle Serie — Rev Fr Entomol Nouv Ser
Revue Francaise des Affaires Sociales — R Fr Affaires Socs
Revue Francaise des Affaires Sociales — R Franc Aff Soc
Revue Francaise des Corps Gras — Rev Fr Corps Gras
Revue Francaise des Maladies Respiratoires — Rev Fr Mal Respir
Revue Francaise des Sciences de l'Eau — Rev Fr Sci Eau
Revue Francaise des Telecommunications — Rev Fr Tel
Revue Francaise des Telecommunications — TEX
Revue Francaise d'Etudes Americaines — R Franc Et Amer
Revue Francaise d'Etudes Americaines — RFEA
Revue Francaise d'Etudes Cliniques et Biologiques — Rev Fr Etud Clin Biol
Revue Francaise d'Etudes Cliniques et Biologiques — RFECA
Revue Francaise d'Etudes Politiques Africaines — R Fr Etud Pol Afr
Revue Francaise d'Etudes Politiques Africaines — R Franc Et Polit Afr
Revue Francaise d'Etudes Politiques Africaines — Revue Fr Etud Polit Afr
Revue Francaise d'Etudes Politiques Africaines — RevuFE
Revue Francaise d'Etudes Politiques Mediterraneennes — R Fr Etud Pol Mediterraneennes
Revue Francaise d'Etudes Politiques Mediterraneennes — R Franc Et Polit Medit
Revue Francaise d'Heraldique et de Sigillographie — Rev Franc Herald Sigillogr
Revue Francaise d'Histoire d'Outre Mer — Rev Fr Hist OM
Revue Francaise d'Histoire d'Outre Mer — Rev Fr Hist Outre Mer
Revue Francaise d'Histoire d'Outre-Mer — R Franc Hist O Mer
Revue Francaise d'Histoire d'Outre-Mer — R Franc Hist Outre-Mer
Revue Francaise d'Histoire d'Outre-Mer — R Francaise Hist Outre-Mer
Revue Francaise d'Histoire d'Outre-Mer — Rev Fr Hist
Revue Francaise d'Histoire d'Outre-Mer — Rev Franc Hist Outre-Mer
Revue Francaise d'Histoire d'Outre-Mer — Revue Fr Hist Outre Mer
Revue Francaise d'Histoire d'Outre-Mer — RFHOM
Revue Francaise d'Histoire du Livre — R Francaise Hist Livre
Revue Francaise d'Histoire du Livre — Rev Fr Hist Livre
Revue Francaise d'Histoire du Livre — RFHL
Revue Francaise d'Informatique et de Recherche Operationnelle — Rev Fr Inf and Rech Oper
Revue Francaise d'Informatique et de Recherche Operationnelle — RFIOA
Revue Francaise d'Odonto-Stomatologie — RFOSA
Revue Francaise d'Odonto-Stomatologie (Paris) — Rev Fr Odonto Stomatol (Paris)
Revue Francaise d'Oenologit — Rev Fr Oenol
Revue Francaise du Dommage Corporel — Rev Fr Dommage Corpor
Revue Francaise du Marketing — R Fr Marketing
Revue Francaise du Marketing — R Franc Mkting
Revue Francaise du Marketing — Rev Fr Mkt
Revue Francaise du Marketing — RFM
Revue fuer Anorganische Chemie (Paris) — Rev Anorg Chem Paris
Revue Gabonaise d'Etudes Politiques. Economiques et Juridiques — R Gabonaise Etud Pols Econs et Juridiques
Revue Generale — R Gen
Revue Generale — RG
Revue Generale Agronomique — Rev Gen Agron
Revue Generale Belge — R Gle B
Revue Generale Belge — RGB
Revue Generale Belge — RGBelge
Revue Generale de Botanique — Rev Gen Bot
Revue Generale de Botanique — Revue Gen Bot
Revue Generale de Chimie Pure et Appliquee — Rev Gen Chim Pure Appl
Revue Generale de Clinique et de Therapeutique — Rev Gen Clin et Therap
Revue Generale de Droit — R Gen
Revue Generale de Droit — Rev Gen de Droit
Revue Generale de Droit — Rev Gen Droit
Revue Generale de Droit — Rev Generale de Droit
Revue Generale de Droit — RGD
Revue Generale de Droit International Public — R Gen De Droit Int Pub
Revue Generale de Droit International Public — R Gen Dr Int Publ
Revue Generale de Droit International Public — Revue Gen de Droit Int Public
Revue Generale de l'Air et de l'Espace — R Gen Air Espace
Revue Generale de Lait — Rev Gen Lait
Revue Generale de l'Electricite — Electricte
Revue Generale de l'Electricite — Rev Gen Elec
Revue Generale de l'Electricite — Rev Gen Electr
Revue Generale de l'Industrie Textile — Rev Gen Ind Text
Revue Generale de Mecanique — Rev Gen Mec
Revue Generale de Mecanique. Electricite — Rev Gen Mec Electr
Revue Generale de Medecine Veterinaire (Toulouse) — Rev Gen Med Vet (Toulouse)
Revue Generale de Teinture, Impression, Blanchiment, Appret — Rev Gen Teint Impress Blanchiment Appret
Revue Generale de Thermique — Rev G Therm
Revue Generale de Thermique — Rev Gen Therm
Revue Generale de Thermique — RGTHA
Revue Generale de tous Textiles Chimiques — Rev Gen Text Chim
Revue Generale des Assurances et des Responsabilites — R Ass Resp
Revue Generale des Assurances et des Responsabilites — RAR
Revue Generale des Assurances et des Responsabilites — Rev Gen Ass et Resp
Revue Generale des Assurances et des Responsabilites — RGAR
Revue Generale des Assurances Terrestres — R Gen Assur Terr
Revue Generale des Assurances Terrestres — Rev Ass Terr
Revue Generale des Assurances Terrestres — Rev Gen Ass Terr
Revue Generale des Assurances Terrestres — Rev Gen Assur Terr
Revue Generale des Caoutchoucs et Plastiques — R Plastiq
Revue Generale des Caoutchoucs et Plastiques — Rev Gen Caoutch Plast
Revue Generale des Caoutchoucs et Plastiques. Edition Plastiques — Rev Gen Caoutch Plast Ed Plast
Revue Generale des Chemins de Fer — R Gen Chem de Fer
Revue Generale des Chemins de Fer — Rev Gen Chem Fer
Revue Generale des Chemins de Fer — Rev Gen Chemins de Fer
Revue Generale des Chemins de Fer — Rev Gen Chemins Fer
Revue Generale des Colloides — Rev Gen Colloides
Revue Generale des Colloides. Supplement — Rev Gen Colloides Suppl
Revue Generale des Matieres Colorantes du Blanchiment de la Teinture de l'Impression et des Apprets — Rev Gen Matieres Color Blanchiment Teint Impress Apprets
Revue Generale des Matieres Plastiques — Rev Gen Matieres Plast
Revue Generale des Matieres Plastiques. Supplement — Rev Gen Matieres Plast Suppl
Revue Generale des Sciences — Rev Gen Sci
Revue Generale des Sciences Appliquees — Rev Gen Sci Appl
Revue Generale des Sciences Pures et Appliquees — R Gen Sci
Revue Generale des Sciences Pures et Appliquees — R Gen Sci Pures et Ap
Revue Generale des Sciences Pures et Appliquees — Rev Gen Sc Pures et Appliq
Revue Generale des Sciences Pures et Appliquees — Rev Gen Sci Pures Appl
Revue Generale des Sciences Pures et Appliquees — Rv Gen Sciences
Revue Generale des Sciences Pures et Appliquees et Bulletin de la Societe Philomathique — Rev Gen Sci Pures Appl Bull Soc Philomath
Revue Generale des Sciences Pures et Appliquees et Bulletin de l'Association Francaise pour l'Avancement des Sciences — Rev Gen Sci Pures Appl Bull Assoc Fr Av Sci
Revue Generale des Techniques [*France*] — Rev Gen Tech
Revue Generale du Caoutchouc — Rev Gen Caoutch
Revue Generale du Caoutchouc/Institut Francais du Caoutchouc — Rev Gen Caoutchouc
Revue Generale du Froid — Rev Gen Froid
Revue Generale du Froid — RGEFA
Revue Generale du Gaz — Rev Gen Gaz
Revue Generale du Gaz [*Belgium*] — Revue Gen Gaz
Revue Generale Hebdomadaire de l'Industrie Nationale — Rev Gener Hebdom Industr Nation
Revue Generale. Lettres, Arts, et Science Humaines — Revue Generale Lettres Arts et Sci Hum
Revue Generale Nucleaire — Rev Gen Nucl
Revue Generale Nucleaire — RGNUD
Revue Geographique de l'Est — R Geogr Est
Revue Geographique de l'Est — RGE
Revue Geographique des Pyrenees et du Sud-Ouest — R Geogr Pyrenees
Revue Geographique des Pyrenees et du Sud-Ouest — Rev Geogr Pyrenees Sud-Ouest
Revue Geographique. Extrait de la Revue Maritime et Coloniale — Rev Geogr
Revue Germanique — Rev Germ
Revue Germanique — RG
Revue Gregorienne — R Gregor
Revue Gregorienne — RGr
Revue Guadeloupeenne — Rev Guad
Revue Hebdomadaire — R Hebd
Revue Hebdomadaire — RH
Revue Hebdomadaire — RHeb
Revue Hebdomadaire de Laryngologie, d'Otologie, et de Rhinologie — Rev Hebd Laryngol Otol Rhinol
Revue Hebdomadaire de l'Industrie Electrique et Electronique — Rev Ind Elec
Revue Hebdomadaire des Industries Chimiques — Rev Ind Chim
Revue Hellenique de Droit International — R Hell Dr Int
Revue Hellenique de Droit International — Rev Hell Dr Int
Revue Hellenique de Droit International — Rev Hellen de Droit Internat
Revue Hellenique de Droit International — Rev Hellenique de Dr Int'l
Revue Henri Maigret — Rev Maigret
Revue HF, Electronique, Telecommunications — Rev HF Electron Telecommun
Revue HF, Electronique, Telecommunications [*Brussels*] — RVUHA
Revue Hispanique — RH
Revue Hispanique — RHi
Revue Hispanique — RHisp
Revue Histoire Missions — RHM
Revue Historique — R Hist
Revue Historique — Rev Hist
Revue Historique — Rev Histor
Revue Historique — Revue Hist
Revue Historique — RevuH
Revue Historique — RH
Revue Historique — RH
Revue Historique — RHis
Revue Historique [*Paris*] — RHistorique
Revue Historique Ardennaise — R Hist Ard
Revue Historique Ardennaise — RH Ard
Revue Historique. Bulletins Critiques — R Hist Bul
Revue Historique (Constantinople) — RHC

Revue Historique de Bordeaux [et du Departement de la Gironde] — RevuHB
Revue Historique de Bordeaux et du Departement de la Gironde — Rev Hist Bordeaux Dep Gironde
Revue Historique de Bordeaux et du Departement de la Gironde — RH Bord
Revue Historique de Droit Francais et Etranger — R Hist Droit
Revue Historique de Droit Francais et Etranger — RD
Revue Historique de Droit Francais et Etranger — Rev Hist de Droit Fr et Etr
Revue Historique de Droit Francais et Etranger — Rev Hist Dr
Revue Historique de Droit Francais et Etranger — Rev Hist Droit Franc Etr
Revue Historique de Droit Francais et Etranger — RHD
Revue Historique de Droit Francais et Etranger — RHD Fr Etr
Revue Historique de Droit Francais et Etranger — RHDF
Revue Historique de Droit Francais et Etranger — RHDFE
Revue Historique de l'Armee — Rev Hist Armee
Revue Historique de l'Armee — RevuHA
Revue Historique de Toulouse — R Hist Toulouse
Revue Historique des Armees — Rev Hist Armees
Revue Historique du Sud-Est Europeen — RHSE
Revue Historique du Sud-Est Europeen — RHSEE
Revue Historique et Archeologique du Libournais — R Libourne
Revue Historique et Archeologique du Maine — R Maine
Revue Historique et Archeologique du Maine — Rev Hist et Archeol du Maine
Revue Historique. Memoires et Etudes — R Hist Mem
Revue Historique Nobiliaire — Rev Hist Nobil
Revue Historique Vaudoise — RHV
Revue Hittite et Asianique — R Hitt As
Revue Hittite et Asianique — RHAs
Revue Hittite et Asiatique — RHA
Revue Hongroise de Metallurgie — Rev Hong Metall
Revue Hongroise de Mines et Metallurgie. Mines — Rev Hong Mines Metall Mines
Revue Horticole — Rev Hort
Revue Horticole — Rev Hortic
Revue Horticole (Paris) — Rev Hortic (Paris)
Revue Horticole Suisse — Rev Hortic Suisse
Revue Hospitaliere de France — R Hospital France
Revue Indigene — R Indigene
Revue Indochinoise — RI
Revue Industrielle — Rev Ind
Revue Industrielle — Rev Industr
Revue Industrielle — RINDA
Revue. Institut Belge de Droit Compare — Rev Dr Comp
Revue. Institut de Sociologie — Inst Sociol R
Revue. Institut de Sociologie — R Ins Soc
Revue. Institut de Sociologie — R Inst Sociol
Revue. Institut de Sociologie — Rev I Soc
Revue. Institut de Sociologie — Rev Inst Sociol
Revue. Institut de Sociologie — Revue Inst Sociologie
Revue. Institut de Sociologie — RIS
Revue. Institut de Sociologie [*Solvay*] — RISoc
Revue. Institut de Sociologie (Solvay) — R Ins (Solv)
Revue. Institut de Sociologie. Universite Libre de Bruxelles — RISULB
Revue. Institut d'Hygiene des Mines — Rev Inst Hyg Mines
Revue. Institut d'Hygiene des Mines (Hasselt) — Rev Inst Hyg Mines (Hasselt)
Revue. Institut Francais du Petrole — Rev I F Pet
Revue. Institut Francais du Petrole — Rev Inst Fr Pet
Revue. Institut Francais du Petrole — Rev Inst Franc Petrol
Revue. Institut Francais du Petrole et Annales des Combustibles Liquides [*Later, Revue. Institut Francais du Petrole*] — Rev Inst Fr Pet
Revue. Institut Francais du Petrole et Annales des Combustibles Liquides [*Later, Revue. Institut Francais du Petrole*] — Rev Inst Fr Pet Ann Combust Liq
Revue. Institut Francais du Petrole et Annales des Combustibles Liquides [*Later, Revue. Institut Francais du Petrole*] — RIFPA
Revue. Institut Napoleon — Rev Inst Napoleon
Revue. Institut Pasteur de Lyon — IPLRB
Revue. Institut Pasteur de Lyon — Rev Inst Pasteur Lyon
Revue Institut Technique Roubaisien — Rev Inst Tech Roubaisien
Revue. Instituts de Recherches Scientifiques aupres du Ministere de l'Agriculture (Bulgaria) — Rev Inst Rech Sci Minist Agric Bulg
Revue International des Sciences — Rev Int Sci
Revue. International Organization for Ancient Languages Analysis by Computer — RELO
Revue. International Organization for Ancient Languages Analysis by Computer — RIOAL
Revue Internationale — RI
Revue Internationale d'Apiculture — Revue Int Apic
Revue Internationale de Botanique Appliquee et d'Agriculture Tropicale — Rev Int Bot Appl Agric Trop
Revue Internationale de Brasserie et de Malterie — Rev Int Brass Malt
Revue Internationale de Criminologie et de Police Technique — Rev Int Criminol Police Tech
Revue Internationale de Criminologie et de Police Technique — Rev Intern Crim et Pol Tech
Revue Internationale de Defense Sociale — Rev Intern Def Soc
Revue Internationale de Droit Compare — R Int Dr Comp
Revue Internationale de Droit Compare — Rev Intern Dr Comp
Revue Internationale de Droit Compare — Rev Internat de Droit Compare
Revue Internationale de Droit Compare — RIDC
Revue Internationale de Droit Compare. Continuation du Bulletin de la Societe de Legislation Comparee — Rev Internat de Droit Compare
Revue Internationale de Droit Penal — R Int Dr Penal
Revue Internationale de Droit Penal — Rev Intern Dr Pen
Revue Internationale de Droit Penal. Bulletin de l'Association Internationale de Droit Penal — Rev Internat de Droit Penal
Revue Internationale de la Chocolaterie — Rev Int Choc
Revue Internationale de la Concurrence — Rev Int Conc
Revue Internationale de la Croix Rouge — R Int Cr Rouge
Revue Internationale de la Croix Rouge — R Int Croix Rouge
Revue Internationale de la Documentation — Rev Int Doc
Revue Internationale de la Propriete Industrielle et Litteraire — RIPIA
Revue Internationale de la Securite Sociale — R Int Secur Soc
Revue Internationale de l'Enseignement — Rev Intern Enseign
Revue Internationale de l'Enseignement — RIE
Revue Internationale de Musique — Rev Int Mus
Revue Internationale de Pediatrie — Rev Int Pediatr
Revue Internationale de Pharmacie — Rev Int Pharm
Revue Internationale de Philosophie — Rev Int Ph
Revue Internationale de Philosophie — Rev Int Phil
Revue Internationale de Philosophie — Rev Int Philos
Revue Internationale de Philosophie — Rev Internat Philos
Revue Internationale de Philosophie — RIdeP
Revue Internationale de Philosophie — RIP
Revue Internationale de Philosophie — RIPh
Revue Internationale de Police Criminelle — R Int Pol Crim
Revue Internationale de Police Criminelle — Rev Intern Pol Crim
Revue Internationale de Psychologie Appliquee — Rev I Psych
Revue Internationale de Psychologie Appliquee — Rev Int Psy
Revue Internationale de Recherche Urbaine et Regionale — R Internat Rech Urbaine et Reg
Revue Internationale de Recherches en Readaptation — Rev Int Rech Readapt
Revue Internationale de Renseignements Agricoles — Rev Int Renseign Agric
Revue Internationale de Sociologie [*International Review of Sociology*] [*Rome*] — R Int Sociol
Revue Internationale de Sociologie (Paris) — RISP
Revue Internationale de Statistique — R Int Stat
Revue Internationale de Theologie — RiTh
Revue Internationale de Trachome et de Pathologie Oculaire Tropicale et Subtropicale et de Sante Publique — Rev Int Trach Pathol Ocul Trop Subtrop Sante Publique
Revue Internationale des Droits de l'Antiquite — R Int Droits Ant
Revue Internationale des Droits de l'Antiquite — R Int Droits Antiquite
Revue Internationale des Droits de l'Antiquite — Rev Intern Dr Ant
Revue Internationale des Droits de l'Antiquite — Rev Internat Droits Antiquite
Revue Internationale des Droits de l'Antiquite — RIDA
Revue Internationale des Etudes Balkaniques — REB
Revue Internationale des Etudes Balkaniques — RIEB
Revue Internationale des Falsifications — Rev Int Falsif
Revue Internationale des Falsifications et d'Analyse des Matieres Alimentaires — Rev Int Falsif Anal Matieres Aliment
Revue Internationale des Hautes Temperatures et des Refractaires — Rev In Haut
Revue Internationale des Hautes Temperatures et des Refractaires — Rev Int Hautes Temp et Refract
Revue Internationale des Hautes Temperatures et des Refractaires — Rev Int Hautes Temp Refract
Revue Internationale des Hautes Temperatures et des Refractaires — RIHTA
Revue Internationale des Industries Agricoles — Ind Agr
Revue Internationale des Industries Agricoles — Rev Int Ind Agric
Revue Internationale des Industries Minieres, Metallurgiques, Electrothermiques, et Electrochimiques — Rev Int Ind Min Metall Electrotherm Electrochim
Revue Internationale des Institutions Economiques et Sociales — RIES
Revue Internationale des Produits Coloniaux et du Materiel Colonial — Rev Int Prod Colon Mater Colon
Revue Internationale des Produits Tropicaux et du Materiel Tropical — Rev Int Prod Trop Mater Trop
Revue Internationale des Sciences Administratives — R Int Sci Adm
Revue Internationale des Sciences Administratives — Rev Intern Sc Adm
Revue Internationale des Sciences Administratives — Rev Internat Sci Adm
Revue Internationale des Sciences Administratives — RISA
Revue Internationale des Sciences Administratives — RSA
Revue Internationale des Sciences Sociales — R Int Sci Soc
Revue Internationale des Sciences Sociales — RISS
Revue Internationale des Services de Sante des Armees de Terre, de Mer, et de l'Air — Rev Int Serv Sante Armees
Revue Internationale des Services de Sante des Armees de Terre, de Mer, et de l'Air — Rev Int Serv Sante Armees Terre Mer Air
Revue Internationale des Services de Sante des Armees de Terre, de Mer, et de l'Air — RSSAA
Revue Internationale des Tabacs — Rev Int Tab
Revue Internationale d'Heliotechnique [*France*] — Rev Int Heliotech
Revue Internationale d'Hepatologie — Rev Int Hepatol
Revue Internationale d'Histoire de la Banque — R Internat Hist Banque
Revue Internationale d'Histoire de la Banque — Rev Int Hist Banque
Revue Internationale d'Histoire de la Psychiatrie — Rev Int Hist Psychiat
Revue Internationale d'Histoire Militaire — R Int Hist Milit
Revue Internationale d'Histoire Militaire — Rev Internat Hist Milit
Revue Internationale d'Histoire Politique et Constitutionnelle — Rev Internat Hist Polit Constitut
Revue Internationale d'Histoire Politique et Constitutionnelle — RIHPC
Revue Internationale d'Oceanographie Medicale — Rev Int Oceanogr Med
Revue Internationale d'Oceanographie Medicale — RVOMA
Revue Internationale d'Onomastique — R Onom
Revue Internationale d'Onomastique — Rev Internat Onomast
Revue Internationale d'Onomastique — RIO
Revue Internationale d'Onomastique — RIOno
Revue Internationale du Bois — Rev Int Bois
Revue Internationale du Bois et des Materieres Premieres Vegetales — Rev Int Bois Mater Premieres Veg
Revue Internationale du Bois et des Matieres Premieres et Produits Industriels d'Origine Vegetale — Rev Int Bois Matieres Premieres Prod Ind Origine Veg

Revue Internationale du Criminalistique — Rev Int Crim
Revue Internationale du Notariat — Rev Intern Not
Revue Internationale du Notariat — RIN
Revue Internationale du Socialisme — RIS
Revue Internationale du Soja — Rev Int Soja
Revue Internationale du Trachome — Rev Int Trach
Revue Internationale du Trachome et de Pathologie Oculaire Tropicale et Subtropicale — Rev Int Trach Pathol Ocul Trop Subtrop
Revue Internationale du Trachome et de Pathologie Oculaire Tropicale et Subtropicale et de Sante Publique — Rev Int Trach Pathol Oculaire Trop Subtrop Sante Publique
Revue Internationale du Travail — R Int Trav
Revue Internationale du Travail — Rev Intern Trav
Revue Internationale du Travail — RIT
Revue Internationale Pierre Teilhard de Chardin — RIPTC
Revue Iranienne des Relations Internationales — R Iran Relat Int
Revue Iranienne des Relations Internationales — R Iranienne Relations Internat
Revue Iranienne des Relations Internationales — Revue Iranienne des Relations Int
Revue. IRE [*Institut National des Radioelements*] — Rev IRE
Revue. IRE [*Institut National des Radioelements*] [*Belgium*] — RIRED
Revue Jeumont-Schneider — Rev Jeumont-Schneider
Revue Jeumont-Schneider — RJSCA
Revue Judiciaire Congolaise — R Jud C
Revue Juive de la Lorraine — RJL
Revue Juridique — R Jur
Revue Juridique — R Juridique
Revue Juridique de l'Afrique Centrale — R Jur Afr Cent
Revue Juridique de l'Afrique Centrale — RJAC
Revue Juridique de l'Environnement — R Jur Environ
Revue Juridique de Madagascar — Rev Juridique de Madagascar
Revue Juridique du Congo — RJC
Revue Juridique du Congo Belge — R Cong
Revue Juridique du Congo Belge — R Jur Cong B
Revue Juridique du Congo Belge — RCB
Revue Juridique du Congo Belge — Rev Jur Congo
Revue Juridique du Congo Belge — RJCB
Revue Juridique du Rwanda et du Burundi — RJRB
Revue Juridique et Economique du Sud-Ouest — RJE
Revue Juridique et Economique du Sud-Ouest. Serie Economique — R Juridique et Econ Sud-Ouest Ser Econ
Revue Juridique et Politique — R Juridique et Pol
Revue Juridique et Politique de l'Union Francaise — Rev Jur Polit Un Fr
Revue Juridique et Politique de l'Union Francaise — RJPUF
Revue Juridique et Politique. Independance et Cooperation — R Jur Polit
Revue Juridique et Politique, Independance et Cooperation — Revue Juridique et Polit Independance et Cooperation
Revue Juridique, Fiscale, et Financiere — Rev JFF
Revue Juridique, Fiscale, et Financiere — Rev Jur Fisc Fin
Revue Juridique, Fiscale, et Financiere — RFI
Revue Juridique, Fiscale, et Financiere — RJFF
Revue Juridique Politique et Economique du Maroc (Rabat) — Revue Juridique Polit et Econ du Maroc Rabat
Revue Juridique Themis — Rev Jur Themis
Revue Juridique Themis — RJT
Revue Juridique Themis — Themis
Revue l'Air Liquide — Rev Air Liq
Revue Liberale — Rev Liberale
Revue Liturgique et Benedictine — RLB
Revue Liturgique et Monastique — RLM
Revue Lyonnaise de Medecine — Rev Lyon Med
Revue M [*Belgium*] — Rev M
Revue M - Mecanique — Rev M Mec
Revue M - Mecanique [*Belgium*] — RMRMA
Revue Mabillon — RMab
Revue Maghrebine de Mathematiques — Rev Maghrebine Math
Revue Maritime — Rev Marit
Revue Maritime et Coloniale — RMC
Revue MBLE [*Manufacture Belge de Lampes et de Materiel*] [*Belgium*] — Rev MBLE
Revue MBLE [*Manufacture Belge de Lampes et de Materiel*] — RMLMA
Revue Mecanique Tijdschrift [*Belgium*] — Rev Mec Tijdsch
Revue Medicale de Bruxelles — Rev Med Brux
Revue Medicale de Bruxelles — Rev Med Bruxelles
Revue Medicale de Bruxelles. Nouvelle Serie — Rev Med Brux Nouv Ser
Revue Medicale de Bruxelles. Nouvelle Serie — RMBRDQ
Revue Medicale de Dijon — Rev Med Dijon
Revue Medicale de la Suisse Romande — Rev Med Suisse Romande
Revue Medicale de la Suisse Romande — RMSRA
Revue Medicale de l'Est — Rev Med Est
Revue Medicale de Liege — Rev Med Liege
Revue Medicale de Liege — Revue Med Liege
Revue Medicale de Liege. Supplement — Rev Med Liege Suppl
Revue Medicale de Liege. Supplement (Belgium) — RVDSB
Revue Medicale de Louvain — Rev Med Louvain
Revue Medicale de Nancy — Rev Med Nancy
Revue Medicale de Tours — Rev Med Tours
Revue Medicale de Tours — RMTOB3
Revue Medicale du Moyen-Orient — Rev Med Moyen-Orient
Revue Medicale et Veterinaire — Revue Med Vet
Revue Medicale Francaise — Rev Med Fr
Revue Medicale Francaise et Etrangere — R Med Fr Et Etrang
Revue Medicale (Hanoi) — Rev Med (Hanoi)
Revue Medicale Internationale de Photo, Cinema, Television — Rev Med Int Photo Cinema Telev
Revue Medicale Miniere — Rev Med Min
Revue Medicale Miniere — Rev Med Miniere
Revue Medicale Miniere — RMEMAN
Revue Medicale (Paris) — Rev Med Paris
Revue Medicale. Universite de Montreal — Rev Med Univ Montr
Revue Medico-Chirurgicale — Rev Med Chir
Revue Medico-Chirurgicale — RMCLB
Revue Medico-Chirurgicale des Maladies du Foie — Rev Med-Chir Mal Foie
Revue Medico-Chirurgicale des Maladies du Foie, de la Rate, et du Pancreas [*France*] — Rev Med-Chir Mal Foie Rate Pancreas
Revue Medico-Chirurgicale des Maladies du Foie, de la Rate, et du Pancreas — RMMFA
Revue Medico-Chirurgicale (Iasi) — Rev Med-Chir (Iasi)
Revue Mediterraneenne des Sciences Medicales — Rev Mediterr Sci Med
Revue Mensuelle de Blanchissage, du Blanchiment, et des Apprets — Rev Mens Blanchissage Blanchiment Apprets
Revue Mensuelle de l'Ecole d'Anthropologie de Paris — REAP
Revue Mensuelle de l'Oeuvre Nationale de l'Enfance — REnf
Revue Mensuelle de Pediatrie — Rev Mens Pediat
Revue Mensuelle des Maladies de l'Enfance — Rev Mens Mal Enf
Revue Mensuelle. Ecole d'Anthropologie de Paris — Rev Mens Ecole Anthropol
Revue Mensuelle Suisse d'Odontologie — Rev Mens Sui Odont
Revue Mensuelle Suisse d'Odonto-Stomatologie — Rev Mens Suisse Odonto-Stomatol
Revue Militaire Generale — Rev Milit Gen
Revue Militaire Suisse — Rev Milit Suisse
Revue Moderne — RMod
Revue Mondiale — RM
Revue. Musee d'Art et d'Archeologie — R Mus Art Archeol
Revue Musicale — R Mus
Revue Musicale — Rev Mus
Revue Musicale — Rev Musical
Revue Musicale — RM
Revue Musicale — RMu
Revue Musicale de Suisse Romande — R Mus de Suisse Romande
Revue Musicale de Suisse Romande — RM Suisse Romande
Revue Napoleonienne — RNap
Revue Nationale — R Nat
Revue Nationale — Rev Nat
Revue Neo-Scolastique de Philosophie — RNeosc
Revue Neo-Scolastique de Philosophie — RNP
Revue Neo-Scolastique de Philosophie — RNS
Revue Neo-Scolastique de Philosophie — RNSP
Revue Neurologique — RENEA
Revue Neurologique — Rev Neurol
Revue Neurologique (Paris) — Rev Neurol (Paris)
Revue Neuve — R Neuve
Revue Nouvelle — R Nlle
Revue Nouvelle — R Nouv
Revue Nouvelle [*Belgium*] — Rev Nouv
Revue Nouvelle [*Paris*] — RevN
Revue Nouvelle — RN
Revue Nouvelle — RNOUD
Revue Numismatique — Rev Numism
Revue Numismatique — RevNum
Revue Numismatique — Revue Num
Revue Numismatique — RN
Revue Numismatique — RNum
Revue Odonto-Implantologique — Rev Odontoimplantol
Revue Odonto-Stomatologique du Nord-Est — Rev Odontostomatol Nordest
Revue of Energie Atomique — Rev Energ At
Revue. Ordre de Premontre et de Ses Missions — ROPM
Revue. Organisation Internationale pour l'Etude des Langues Anciennes par Ordinateur — RELO
Revue Orientale — RO
Revue Orientale et Africaine — ROA
Revue Palladienne — R Pallad
Revue Palladienne — RPall
Revue Pedagogique — RPed
Revue Periodique de "La Physiophile." Societe d'Etudes des Sciences Naturelles et Historiques de Montceau-Les-Mines — R Montceau
Revue Petrolifere — Rev Petrolifere
Revue Pharmaceutique — Rev Pharm
Revue Pharmaceutique Libanaise — Rev Pharm Liban
Revue Philosophique — R Philos
Revue Philosophique — RP
Revue Philosophique — RPhs
Revue Philosophique de la France et de l'Etranger — R Ph
Revue Philosophique de la France et de l'Etranger — R Ph F E
Revue Philosophique de la France et de l'Etranger — R Phil
Revue Philosophique de la France et de l'Etranger — R Philos
Revue Philosophique de la France et de l'Etranger — Rev Phil Fr
Revue Philosophique de la France et de l'Etranger — Rev Phil Fr Etrang
Revue Philosophique de la France et de l'Etranger — Rev Philos Fr Etrang
Revue Philosophique de la France et de l'Etranger — RPFE
Revue Philosophique de Louvain — R Phil Louvain
Revue Philosophique de Louvain — Rev Phil Louvain
Revue Philosophique de Louvain — Rev Philos
Revue Philosophique de Louvain — Rev Philos Louv
Revue Philosophique de Louvain — RPhL
Revue Philosophique de Louvain — RPL
Revue Physiologique — Rev Physiol
Revue Politique — Rev Polit
Revue Politique et Litteraire — R Pol et Litt
Revue Politique et Litteraire — R Polit et Litt

Revue Politique et Litteraire — Rev Polit Litt
Revue Politique et Litteraire — RPL
Revue Politique et Litteraire. Revue Bleue — Rev Bleue
Revue Politique et Litteraire. Revue Bleue — Rev Polit et Litt Rev Bleue
Revue Politique et Litteraire. Revue Bleue — Revue Bleue
Revue Politique et Parlementaire — R Pol et Parlementaire
Revue Politique et Parlementaire — R Polit Parl
Revue Politique et Parlementaire — Rev Polit Parl
Revue Politique et Parlementaire — RevuP
Revue Politique et Parlementaire — RPP
Revue Politique et Parlementaire — RPPA
Revue Politique Internationale — RPI
Revue Polytechnique [*Switzerland*] — Rev Polytech
Revue Polytechnique — RVPTB
Revue Pour l'Etude des Calamites (Geneva) — Rev Etud Calamites Geneva
Revue Pratique d'Apologetique — RPA
Revue Pratique d'Apologetique — RPrat
Revue Pratique de Biologie Appliquee a la Clinique et a la Therapeutique — Rev Prat Biol Appl Clin Ther
Revue Pratique de Droit Commercial, Financier, et Fiscal — RPDC
Revue Pratique de Droit Social — R Prat Dr Soc
Revue Pratique de Droit Social — Rev Prat Dr Soc
Revue Pratique des Connaissances Medicales — Rev Prat Connaiss Med
Revue Pratique des Maladies des Pays Chands — Rev Prat Mal Pays Chands
Revue Pratique des Questions Commerciales et Economiques — R Com Ec
Revue Pratique des Questions Commerciales et Economiques — R Pratique Questions Commer et Econs
Revue Pratique des Questions Commerciales et Economiques — Rev Prat Quest Com et Econom
Revue Pratique des Societes Civiles et Commerciales — Rev Prat Soc
Revue Pratique des Societes Civiles et Commerciales — Rev Soc
Revue Pratique des Societes Civiles et Commerciales — RPS
Revue Pratique des Societes Civiles et Commerciales — RPSoc
Revue Pratique du Controle Industriel [*France*] — Rev Prat Controle Ind
Revue Pratique du Froid [*Later, Journal RPF*] — Rev Prat Froid
Revue Pratique du Froid [*Later, Journal RPF*] — RPRFA
Revue Pratique du Froid et du Conditionnement de l'Air [*Later, Journal RPF*] [*A publication*] — Rev Prat Froid Cond Air
Revue Pratique du Froid et du Conditionnement de l'Air [*Later, Journal RPF*] [*A publication*] — RPFCA
Revue Pratique du Notariat — Rev Prat Not
Revue Pratique du Notariat — RPN
Revue Pratique du Notariat Belge — Rev Not
Revue Pratique du Notariat Belge — RPNB
Revue Prehistorique — R Prehist
Revue Prehistorique — Rev Preh
Revue Prehistorique — Rev Prehist
Revue Protestante Belge — RPB
Revue Prumyslu a Obchodu [*Czechoslovakia*] — Rev Prum Obchodu
Revue Reformee — Rev Reform
Revue Reformee — RRef
Revue Romande d'Agriculture, de Viticulture, et d'Arboriculture — Rev Romande Agr Viticult Arboricult
Revue Romande d'Agriculture, de Viticulture, et d'Arboriculture — Rev Romande Agric Vitic Arboric
Revue Romande d'Agriculture, de Viticulture, et d'Arboriculture — Revue Romande Agric Vitic Arboric
Revue Romane — Rev Roman
Revue Romane — RevR
Revue Roumaine de Biochimie — Rev Ro Bioc
Revue Roumaine de Biochimie — Rev Roum Biochim
Revue Roumaine de Biochimie — Revue Roum Biochim
Revue Roumaine de Biologie — Rev Roum Biol
Revue Roumaine de Biologie. Serie Biologie Vegetale [*Romania*] — Rev Roum Biol Ser Biol Veg
Revue Roumaine de Biologie. Serie Biologie Vegetale — RRBVD
Revue Roumaine de Biologie. Serie Botanique — Rev Roum Biol Ser Bot
Revue Roumaine de Biologie. Serie Botanique — Revue Roum Biol Ser Bot
Revue Roumaine de Biologie. Serie Botanique — RRBBA
Revue Roumaine de Biologie. Serie de Biologie Animale — Rev Roum Biol Ser Biol Anim
Revue Roumaine de Biologie. Serie Zoologie — Rev Roum Biol Ser Zool
Revue Roumaine de Biologie. Serie Zoologie — RRBZA
Revue Roumaine de Chimie — Rev Ro Chim
Revue Roumaine de Chimie — Rev Roum Chim
Revue Roumaine de Chimie — RRCHA
Revue Roumaine de Geologie, Geophysique, et Geographie. Serie de Geographie — Rev Roum Geol Geophys Geogr Ser Geogr
Revue Roumaine de Geologie, Geophysique, et Geographie. Serie de Geographie [*Rumania*] — RRGA
Revue Roumaine de Geologie, Geophysique, et Geographie. Serie de Geologie — Rev Roum Geol Geophys Geogr Ser Geol
Revue Roumaine de Geologie, Geophysique, et Geographie. Serie de Geophysique — Rev Roum Geol Geophys Geogr Ser Geophys
Revue Roumaine de Linguistique — R Ling
Revue Roumaine de Linguistique — Rev Roumaine Linguist
Revue Roumaine de Linguistique — RL
Revue Roumaine de Linguistique — RRL
Revue Roumaine de Mathematiques Pures et Appliquees — Rev Roum Math Pures Appl
Revue Roumaine de Mathematiques Pures et Appliquees — Rev Roumaine Math Pures Appl
Revue Roumaine de Mathematiques Pures et Appliquees — RRMPB
Revue Roumaine de Medecine — Rev Roum Med
Revue Roumaine de Medecine. Endocrinologie — Rev Roum Med Endocrinol
Revue Roumaine de Medecine Interne [*Later, Revue Roumaine de Medecine. Medecine Interne*] — Rev Roum Med Interne
Revue Roumaine de Medecine Interne [*Later, Revue Roumaine de Medecine. Medecine Interne*] — RRMIA
Revue Roumaine de Medecine. Medecine Interne — Rev Roum Med Med Interne
Revue Roumaine de Medecine. Medecine Interne — RMMID
Revue Roumaine de Medecine. Neurologie et Psychiatrie — Rev Roum Med Neurol Psychiatr
Revue Roumaine de Medecine. Serie de Neurologie et Psychiatrie — Rev Roum Med Ser Neurol Psychiatr
Revue Roumaine de Medecine. Virologie — Rev Roum Med Virol
Revue Roumaine de Metallurgie — Rev Roum Metall
Revue Roumaine de Morphologie, d'Embryologie, et de Physiologie. Serie Morphologie et Embryologie — Rev Roum Morphol Embryol Physiol Morphol Embryol
Revue Roumaine de Morphologie, d'Embryologie, et de Physiologie. Serie Morphologie et Embryologie — RMEMD
Revue Roumaine de Morphologie, d'Embryologie, et de Physiologie. Serie Physiologie — Rev Roum Morphol Embryol Physiol Physiol
Revue Roumaine de Morphologie, d'Embryologie, et de Physiologie. Serie Physiologie — RMEPD
Revue Roumaine de Morphologie et d'Embryologie — Rev Roum Morphol Embryol
Revue Roumaine de Morphologie et du Physiologie — Rev Roum Morphol Physiol
Revue Roumaine de Neurologie [*Later, Revue Roumaine de Medecine. Serie Neurologie et Psychiatrie*] — Rev Roum Neurol
Revue Roumaine de Neurologie [*Later, Revue Roumaine de Medecine. Serie Neurologie et Psychiatrie*] — RRNUA
Revue Roumaine de Neurologie et de Psychiatrie [*Later, Revue Roumaine de Medecine. Serie Neurologie et Psychiatrie*] — Rev Roum Neurol Psychiatr
Revue Roumaine de Physiologie [*Later, Revue Roumaine de Morphologie, d'Embryologie, et de Physiologie*] — Rev Roum Physiol
Revue Roumaine de Physiologie — RRPHA
Revue Roumaine de Physique — Rev Ro Phys
Revue Roumaine de Physique — Rev Roum Phys
Revue Roumaine de Physique — Rev Roumaine Phys
Revue Roumaine de Physique — RRPQA
Revue Roumaine de Virologie — Rev Roum Virol
Revue Roumaine de Virologie — RRVRA
Revue Roumaine d'Embryologie — Rev Roum Embryol
Revue Roumaine d'Embryologie et de Cytologie. Serie d'Embryologie — RECYA
Revue Roumaine d'Embryologie et de Cytologie. Serie d'Embryologie — Rev Roum Embryol Cytol Ser Embryol
Revue Roumaine d'Endocrinologie — Rev Roum Endocrinol
Revue Roumaine d'Endocrinologie — RRENA
Revue Roumaine des Sciences Sociales — R Roum Sci Soc
Revue Roumaine des Sciences Sociales. Serie de Philosophie et de Logique — R Roum Sci Soc Ser Philos Logique
Revue Roumaine des Sciences Sociales. Serie de Philosophie et de Logique — Rev Roum Sci Soc Philos Logique
Revue Roumaine des Sciences Sociales. Serie de Sciences Economiques — R Roum Sci Soc Ser Sci Econ
Revue Roumaine des Sciences Sociales. Serie de Sciences Economiques — R Roumaine Sciences Socs Ser Sciences Econs
Revue Roumaine des Sciences Sociales. Serie de Sciences Juridiques — R Roum Sci Soc Ser Sci Jur
Revue Roumaine des Sciences Sociales. Serie de Sciences Juridiques — R Roumaine Sciences Socs Ser Sciences Juridiques
Revue Roumaine des Sciences Sociales. Serie de Sciences Juridiques — Rev Roumaine Sci Soc
Revue Roumaine des Sciences Sociales. Serie de Sociologie — R Roum Sci Soc Ser Sociol
Revue Roumaine des Sciences Techniques. Serie de Mecanique Appliquee [*Romania*] — Rev Roum Sci Tech Mec Appl
Revue Roumaine des Sciences Techniques. Serie de Mecanique Appliquee — Rev Roum Sci Tech Ser Mec Appl
Revue Roumaine des Sciences Techniques. Serie de Mecanique Appliquee — Rev Roumaine Sci Tech Ser Mec Appl
Revue Roumaine des Sciences Techniques. Serie de Mecanique Appliquee — RTMAA
Revue Roumaine des Sciences Techniques. Serie de Metallurgie — Rev Roum Sci Tech Ser Met
Revue Roumaine des Sciences Techniques. Serie de Metallurgie — RTMTA
Revue Roumaine des Sciences Techniques. Serie Electrotechnique et Energetique — Rev Roum Sci Tech Ser Electrotech Energ
Revue Roumaine des Sciences Techniques. Serie Electrotechnique et Energetique — Rev Roumaine Sci Tech Ser Electrotech Energet
Revue Roumaine des Sciences Techniques. Serie Electrotechnique et Energetique — RTEEA
Revue Roumaine d'Etudes Internationales — R Roum Et Int
Revue Roumaine d'Etudes Internationales — Revue Roumaine d Etud Int
Revue Roumaine d'Histoire — R Roum Hist
Revue Roumaine d'Histoire — R Roumaine Hist
Revue Roumaine d'Histoire — Rev Roum H
Revue Roumaine d'Histoire — Rev Roum Hist
Revue Roumaine d'Histoire — RevuR
Revue Roumaine d'Histoire — RRH
Revue Roumaine d'Histoire de l'Art — R Roumaine
Revue Roumaine d'Histoire de l'Art — R Roumaine Hist Art
Revue Roumaine d'Inframicrobiologie — Rev Roum Inframicrobiol
Revue Roumaine d'Inframicrobiologie — RRIMA
Revue. Royal Automobile Club de Belgique — Royal Auto
Revue Savoisienne — R Sav

Revue Scientifique — R Sci
Revue Scientifique — Rev Sci
Revue Scientifique — Rv Scient
Revue Scientifique du Bourbonnais et du Centre de la France — Rev Sci Bourbonnais Cent Fr
Revue Scientifique du Bourbonnais et du Centre de la France — Rev Sci Bourbonnais Centr France
Revue Scientifique et Industrielle (Breton, Editor) — Rev Sci Industr Breton
Revue Scientifique et Technique — Rev Sci Tech
Revue Scientifique et Technique OIE (Office International des Epizooties) — Rev Sci Tech OIE (Off Int Epizoot)
Revue Scientifique (Paris) — Rev Scient (Paris)
Revue Scolaire — R Scolaire
Revue Semitique d'Epigraphie et d'Histoire Ancienne — RSEHA
Revue Senegalaise de Droit — R Seneg Dr
Revue Senegalaise de Droit — Rev Senegalaise de Droit
Revue SNCASO [*Societe Nationale de Constructions Aeronautiques du Sud-Ouest*] — Rev SNCASO
Revue Sociale Catholique — RSC
Revue Socialiste — Rev Social
Revue Socialiste — Rev Socialiste
Revue Socialiste — RSoc
Revue. Societe de Biometre Humaine — Rev Soc Biom Hum
Revue. Societe des Etudes Historiques — REH
Revue. Societe des Etudes Historiques — RSEH
Revue. Societe d'Etudes et d'Expansion — R Soc Et Expans
Revue. Societe d'Etudes et d'Expansion — RSE
Revue. Societe d'Histoire du Theatre — Rev Soc Hist Theatre
Revue. Societe d'Histoire et de Geographie d'Haiti — Rev Soc Hist Geogr Haiti
Revue. Societe d'Histoire et Geographie d'Haiti (Port-au-Prince) — Rev Soc Hist Geogr Port Au Prince
Revue. Societe Haitienne d'Histoire, de Geographie, et de Geologie [*A publication*] — RSHG
Revue. Societe Haitienne d'Histoire, de Geographie, et de Geologie (Port-au-Prince) — Rev Soc Hait Hist Geogr Geol Port Au Prince
Revue. Societe Historique — RSH
Revue. Societe Royale Belge des Ingenieurs et des Industriels — Rev Soc R Belge Ing Ind
Revue. Societe Scientifique d'Hygiene Alimentaire et de l'Alimentation Rationnelle de l'Homme — Rev Soc Sci Hyg Aliment Aliment Ration Homme
Revue Statistique du Quebec — R Statis Quebec
Revue Stomato-Odontologique du Nord de la France — Rev Stomato-Odontol Nord Fr
Revue Stomato-Odontologique du Nord de la France — RSONA
Revue Suisse — RS
Revue Suisse d'Agriculture — Rev Suisse Agric
Revue Suisse d'Art et d'Archeologie — RSAA
Revue Suisse de Gynecologie et d'Obstetrique — Rev Suisse Gynecol Obstet
Revue Suisse de Gynecologie et d'Obstetrique. Supplementum — Rev Suisse Gynecol Obstet Suppl
Revue Suisse de la Tuberculose et de Pneumonologie — Rev Suisse Tuberc Pneum
Revue Suisse de Medecine des Sports — Rev Suisse Med Sport
Revue Suisse de Medecine des Sports — Rev Suisse Med Sports
Revue Suisse de Medecine. Praxis — Rev Suisse Med Prax
Revue Suisse de Numismatique — Rev Suis Num
Revue Suisse de Numismatique — Rev Suisse Num
Revue Suisse de Numismatique — RSN
Revue Suisse de Numismatique — SNR
Revue Suisse de Pathologie Generale et de Bacteriologie — Rev Suisse Pathol Gen Bact
Revue Suisse de Psychologie Pure et Appliquee — Rev Suisse Psychol Pure Appl
Revue Suisse de Viticulture et Arboriculture — Rev Suisse Vitic Arboric
Revue Suisse de Viticulture et Arboriculture. Horticulture — Rev Suisse Vitic Arboric Hortic
Revue Suisse de Zoologie — R Suisse Zool
Revue Suisse de Zoologie — Rev Suisse Zool
Revue Suisse de Zoologie — Revue Suisse Zool
Revue Suisse de Zoologie — RSZOA
Revue Suisse d'Hydrologie — Rev Suisse Hydrol
Revue Syndicale Suisse — R Synd Suisse
Revue Technique de l'Industrie Alimentaire — Rev Tech Ind Aliment
Revue Technique des Industries du Cuir — Rev Tech Ind Cuir
Revue Technique des Industries du Cuir — Rev Techn Ind Cuir
Revue Technique du Batiment et des Constructions Industrielles [*France*] — Rev Tech Batim Constr Ind
Revue Technique du Batiment et des Constructions Industrielles — RTBCA
Revue Technique Luxembourgeoise — Rev Tech Luxemb
Revue Technique Luxembourgeoise — RTLXA
Revue Technique Thomson - CSF — Rev Tech Thomson CSF
Revue Technique Thomson - CSF — RTTCB
Revue Teilhard de Chardin — Rev Teilhard de Chardin
Revue Textile (Paris) — Rev Text (Paris)
Revue Textile Tiba — Rev Text Tiba
Revue Textilis (Ghent) — Rev Text (Ghent)
Revue Theatrale — RT
Revue Theologique — RTh
Revue Theologique de Louvain — R Theol Louvain
Revue Theologique de Louvain — RThL
Revue Theologique de Louvain — RTL
Revue Theologique Francaise — RTF
Revue Theologique (Paris) — RThP
Revue Therapeutique — Rev Ther
Revue Therapeutique — Rev Therap
Revue Therapeutique et Bibliographie Medicale — Rev Therap Bibliogr Med
Revue Thomiste — Rev Thomiste
Revue Thomiste [*Brussels*] — RT
Revue Thomiste — RTh
Revue Thomiste — RThom
Revue Tiers-Monde — R Tiers-Monde
Revue Tiers-Monde — TMC
Revue Trimestrielle — RT
Revue Trimestrielle Canadienne — Rev Trimest Can
Revue Trimestrielle Canadienne — Rev Trimestrielle Canadienne
Revue Trimestrielle Canadienne — RTC
Revue Trimestrielle Canadienne — Rv Trim Can
Revue Trimestrielle. Centre Scientifique et Technique de la Construction [*Belgium*] — CSTC Trim
Revue Trimestrielle de Droit Civil — Rev Tr Dr Civ
Revue Trimestrielle de Droit Commercial — R Trim Dr Com
Revue Trimestrielle de Droit Europeen — R Trim Dr Europ
Revue Trimestrielle de Droit Europeen — R Trim Droit Eur
Revue Trimestrielle de Droit Europeen — Rev Trimestr de Droit Eur
Revue Trimestrielle de Droit Europeen — RTDE
Revue Trimestrielle de Droit Sanitaire et Social — R Trim Dr Sanit Soc
Revue Trimestrielle d'Etudes Linguistiques, Folkloriques, et Toponymiques (Luxembourg) — Revue Lux
Revue Trimestrielle d'Etudes Linguistiques, Folkloriques, et Toponymiques (Luxembourg) — RLux
Revue Tunisienne — R Tun
Revue Tunisienne — RT
Revue Tunisienne de Droit — Rev Tun Droit
Revue Tunisienne de Geographie — R Tunis Geogr
Revue Tunisienne de Sciences Sociales — R Tunis Sci Soc
Revue Tunisienne de Sciences Sociales — R Tunisienne Sciences Socs
Revue Tunisienne de Sciences Sociales — Rev Tunis Sci Soc
Revue Tunisienne de Sciences Sociales — Revue Tunisienne Sci Soc
Revue Tunisienne de Sciences Sociales — RTSS
Revue Tunisienne des Sciences Medicales — RT
Revue Tunisienne des Sciences Sociales — Rev Tun Sc Soc
Revue Turque d'Hygiene et de Biologie Experimentale — Rev Turq Hyg Biol Exp
Revue Turque d'Hygiene et de Biologie Experimentale — Rev Turque Hyg Biol Exp
Revue ueber die Fett- und Harz-Industrie — Rev Fett Harz Ind
Revue Universelle — RU
Revue Universelle — RUniv
Revue Universelle des Mines, de la Metallurgie, de la Mecanique, des Travaux Publics, des Sciences, et des Arts Appliques a l'Industrie — Rev Univers Mines Metall Mec
Revue Universelle des Mines, de la Metallurgie, de la Mecanique, des Travaux Publics, des Sciences, et des Arts Appliques a l'Industrie — RUMRA
Revue Universelle des Mines, de la Metallurgie des Travaux Publics, des Sciences et des Arts Appliques a l'Industries — Rev Univers Min Metall Trav Publ Sci Arts Appl Indus
Revue Universitaire — R Univ
Revue Universitaire — Rev Uni
Revue Universitaire — Rev Univ
Revue. Universite de Bruxelles — R Univ Bruxelles
Revue. Universite de Bruxelles — Rev Un B
Revue. Universite de Bruxelles — Rev Univ Brux
Revue. Universite de Bruxelles — Rev Univ Bruxelles
Revue. Universite de Bruxelles — RU Brux
Revue. Universite de Bruxelles — RUB
Revue. Universite de Bruxelles [*Brussels*] — RUBruxelles
Revue. Universite de Bruxelles — RUnBrux
Revue. Universite de Lyon — RUL
Revue. Universite de Sherbrooke — R de l'Univ de Sherbrooke
Revue. Universite d'Ottawa — R de l'Univ d'Ott
Revue. Universite d'Ottawa — R Univ Ottawa
Revue. Universite d'Ottawa — Rev Univ Ottawa
Revue. Universite d'Ottawa — RevudO
Revue. Universite d'Ottawa — RU Ottawa
Revue. Universite d'Ottawa — RUnOtt
Revue. Universite d'Ottawa — RUO
Revue. Universite d'Ottawa — RUOt
Revue. Universite du Burundi — R Univ Burundi
Revue. Universite du Burundi — Rev Univ Burundi
Revue. Universite Laval — R de l'Univ Laval
Revue. Universite Laval [*Quebec*] — RUL
Revue. Universite Laval — RUnLav
Revue. Universite Libre de Bruxelles — Rev ULB
Revue. Universite Nationale du Zaire. Campus de Lubumbashi. Serie B. Sciences — Rev Univ Natl Zaire Campus Lubumbashi Ser B
Revue Vervietoise d'Histoire Naturelle — Rev Vervietoise Hist Nat
Revue Veterinaire Canadienne — Rev Vet Can
Revue X [*Belgium*] — Rev X
Revue X [*Belgium*] — RVUXA
Revue Zairoise de Psychologie et de Pedagogie — Revue Zairoise Psychol Pedagogie
Revue Zairoise des Sciences Nucleaires [*Zaire*] — Rev Zair Sci Nucl
Revue Zairoise des Sciences Nucleaires — RZSND
Revues d'Anatomie et de Morphologie Experimentale — Rev Anat Morphol Exp
Revues des Allocations Familiales — Rev Alloc Fam
Revues Medicales Normandes — Rev Med Normandes
REWE Echo. Fachzeitschrift fuer Modernen Handel — RWE
Rexroth Informationen — Rexroth Inf
Reyon, Synthetica, Zellwolle — Reyon Synth Zellwolle
Reyon, Zellwolle, und Andere Chemie Fasern — Reyon Zellwolle Andere Chem Fasern

Reyrolle Parsons Review — Reyrolle Parsons Rev
Rezanie i Instrument — Rezanie Instrum
Rezpravy. Ceska Academie Ved. Filologicka — RCAVF
Rezpravy. Ceska Academie Ved. Pro Vedy Filosoficke, Pravni, a Historicke — RCAVFPH
Rezpravy. Ceska Academie Ved. Rada Spolecenskych Ved — RCAVRSV
Rezul'taty Issledovanyi po Mezhdunarodny Geofizicheskim Proektam [*Former USSR*] — Rezul't Issled Mezhdunar Geofiz Proektam
Rezul'taty Issledovanyi po Mezhdunarodny Geofizicheskim Proektam — RIGPA
RF [*Rockefeller Foundation*] **Illustrated** — RF Illus
RFM. Revue Francaise de Mecanique — RFM Rev Fr Mec
Rheinische Beitraege und Hilfsbuecher zur Germanischen Philologie und Volkskunde — RBHGPV
Rheinische Bienenzeitung — Rhein Bienenztg
Rheinische Blaetter — RhB
Rheinische Heimatblaetter — RHB
Rheinische Landesmuseum (Bonn) — Rhein Mus (Bonn)
Rheinische Mannigfaltigkeiten — Rhein Mannigfaltigk
Rheinische Merkur — RhM
Rheinische Musikblaetter — RhMBl
Rheinische Neujahrsblaetter — Rh N
Rheinische Vierteljahresblaetter — Rhein Vb
Rheinische Vierteljahresblaetter — RhV
Rheinische Vierteljahresblaetter — RhVJ
Rheinische Vierteljahresblaetter — RV
Rheinische Vierteljahresblaetter — RVB
Rheinische Vierteljahrsblaetter — Rhein Viert Jbl
Rheinische Vierteljahrsblaetter — Rhein Vjsbll
Rheinische Vorzeit in Wort und Bild — RhV
Rheinische Zeitschrift fuer Zivil- und Prozessrecht des In- und Auslandes — Rhein Z
Rheinische Zeitschrift fuer Zivil- und Prozessrecht des In- und Auslandes — RZZP
Rheinische Zeitschrift fuer Zivil- und Zivilprozessrecht — Rhein Zs Zivilr
Rheinisches Archiv — RA
Rheinisches Jahrbuch fuer Volkskunde — RhJbV
Rheinisches Jahrbuch fuer Volkskunde — RJV
Rheinisches Jahrbuch fuer Volkskunde — RJVK
Rheinisches Magazin zur Erweiterung der Naturkunde — Rhein Mag Erweit Naturk
Rheinisches Museum fuer Philologie — R Mf Ph
Rheinisches Museum fuer Philologie — Rh M Ph
Rheinisches Museum fuer Philologie — Rh Mus
Rheinisches Museum fuer Philologie — Rhein Museum Philol
Rheinisches Museum fuer Philologie — Rheinisch Museum Philol
Rheinisches Museum fuer Philologie — Rheinisches Mus Philol
Rheinisches Museum fuer Philologie — RhM
Rheinisches Museum fuer Philologie — RhMP
Rheinisches Museum fuer Philologie — RM
Rheinisches Museum fuer Philologie — RMP
Rheinisch-Westfaelische Akademie der Wissenschaften. Natur-, Ingenieur-, und Wirtschaftswissenschaften — Rheinisch Westfaelische Akad Wiss Natur Ingr Wirtschaftswiss
Rheinisch-Westfaelische Akademie der Wissenschaften Natur-, Ingenieur-, und Wirtschaftswissenschaften. Vortraege — Rheinisch-Westfael Akad Wiss Nat-Ing- Wirtschaftswiss Vort
Rheinisch-Westfaelische Akademie der Wissenschaften Natur-, Ingenieur-, und Wirtschaftswissenschaften. Vortraege — Rhein-Westfael Akad Wiss Vortr N
Rheinisch-Westfaelische Akademie der Wissenschaften Natur-, Ingenieur-, und Wirtschaftswissenschaften. Vortraege — RWAVA
Rheinisch-Westfaelische Zeitschrift fuer Volkskunde — Rheinisch Westfael Z Volkskd
Rheinisch-Westfaelische Zeitschrift fuer Volkskunde — RWZVK
Rheinisch-Westfaelisches Institut fuer Wirtschaftsforschung. Konjunkturberichte — KBR
Rheinisch-Westfaelisches Institut fuer Wirtschaftsforschung. Mitteilungen — Rhein Westfael Inst Wirtsch Forsch Mitt
Rhein-Neckar-Zeitung — RNZ
Rheinpreussen Notariat Zeitschrift [*Zeitschrift fuer das Notariat*] [*Herausgegeben von dem Verein fuer das Notariat in Rheinpreussen*] — Rhein Not Z
Rheinstahl Technik — Rheinstahl Tech
Rheinstahl Technik — RHTKA
Rheologica Acta — RHEAA
Rheologica Acta — Rheol Act
Rheologica Acta — Rheol Acta
Rheological Fundamentals of Polymer Processing — Rheol Fundam Polym Process
Rheological Memoirs — Rheol Mem
Rheology Abstracts — Rheol Abstr
Rheology and Texture in Food Quality — Rheol Texture Food Qual
Rheology Bulletin — Rheol Bull
Rheology Leaflet — Rheol Leafl
Rheology Series — Rheology Ser
Rhetores Graeci — Rh Gr
Rhetores Graeci — Rhet Gr
Rhetores Graeci — Rhet Graec
Rhetores Latini Minores — Rh Lat Min
Rhetores Latini Minores — Rhet Lat Min
Rhetoric Society. Quarterly — RSQ
Rheumatism [*England*] — RHUEA
Rheumatologia, Balneologia, Allergologia — Rheumatol Balneo Allergol
Rheumatology and Physical Medicine — Rheumatol Phys Med
Rheumatology and Rehabilitation — Rheumatol Rehabil
Rheumatology and Rehabilitation — RMRHB
Rheumatology International — Rheum Intl
Rheumatology International — Rheumatol Int
Rhinology — RNGYA
Rhinology. Supplement — Rhinol Suppl
Rhode Island. Agricultural Experiment Station. Bulletin — RI Agric Exp Stn Bull
Rhode Island. Agricultural Experiment Station. Publications — RI Ag Exp
Rhode Island. Agricultural Experiment Station. Research Quarterly Review — RI Agric Exp Stn Res Q Rev
Rhode Island Agriculture — Rhode Isl Agric
Rhode Island Agriculture — RI Ag
Rhode Island Agriculture — RI Agric
Rhode Island Agriculture. Rhode Island Agricultural Experiment Station — RI Agr
Rhode Island Bar Journal — RIBJ
Rhode Island Bureau of Industrial Statistics. Annual Report. Natural Resources Survey. Bulletin — RI Bur Industrial Statistics An Rp Nat Res S B
Rhode Island Dental Journal — RI Dent J
Rhode Island Development Council. Geological Bulletin — RI Dev Counc Geol Bull
Rhode Island Development Council. Geological Bulletin. Scientific Contribution — RI Devel Council Geol Bull Sci Contr
Rhode Island Foreign Language Gazette — Gazette
Rhode Island Graduate School of Oceanography. Occasional Publication — RI Grad Sch Oceanogr Occas Publ
Rhode Island Historical Society. Collections — RI His S
Rhode Island Historical Society. Collections — RI Hist Soc Coll
Rhode Island History — RhI
Rhode Island History — RI Hist
Rhode Island History — RIH
Rhode Island Jewish Historical Notes — RI Jew Hist Note
Rhode Island Jewish Historical Notes — RI Jewish Historical Notes
Rhode Island Jewish Historical Notes — RIJHN
Rhode Island Medical Journal — Rhode Island Med J
Rhode Island Medical Journal — RI Med J
Rhode Island Medical Journal — RIMJA
Rhode Island Medicine — RI Med
Rhode Island Music Educators Review — RI
Rhode Island. Port and Industrial Development Commission. Geological Bulletin. Scientific Contribution — RI Port Indus Devel Comm Geol Bull Sci Contr
Rhode Island Reports — RI
Rhode Island Resources — RI Resour
Rhode Island School of Design. Bulletin — RI Sch Des Bul
Rhode Island University. Agricultural Experiment Station. Bulletin — RI Univ Agric Exp Stn Bull
Rhode Island University. Division of Engineering. Research and Development Engineering Reprint — RI Univ Div Eng Res Dev Eng Repr
Rhode Island University. Division of Engineering. Research and Development Leaflet — RI Univ Div Eng Res Dev Leafl
Rhode Island University. Engineering Experiment Station. Bulletin — RI Univ Eng Exp Stn Bull
Rhode Island University. Engineering Experiment Station. Engineering Reprint — RI Univ Eng Exp Stn Eng Repr
Rhode Island University. Marine Technical Report — RI Univ Mar Tech Rep
Rhode Island. Water Resources Board. Hydrologic Bulletin — RI Water Resour Board Hydrol Bull
Rhode Island. Water Resources Center. Annual Report — RI Water Resour Cent Annu Rep
Rhode Island. Water Resources Coordinating Board. Geological Bulletin — RI Water Resour Coord Board Geol Bull
Rhode Island. Water Resources Coordinating Board. Geological Bulletin — RI Water Resour Coordinating Board Geol Bull
Rhode Island. Water Resources Coordinating Board. Geological Bulletin. Hydrologic Bulletin — RI Water Res Coordinating Board Geol Bull Hydrol Bull
Rhodes University. Department of Ichthyology. Ichthyological Bulletin — Rhodes Univ Dep Ichthyol Ichthyol Bull
Rhodes University. Department of Ichthyology. Occasional Paper — Rhodes Univ Dep Ichthyol Occas Pap
Rhodes University. J. L. B. Smith Institute of Ichthyology. Special Publication — Rhodes Univ J L B Smith Inst Ichthyol Spec Publ
Rhodesia Agricultural Journal — Rhod Agric J
Rhodesia Agricultural Journal — Rhodesia Ag J
Rhodesia Agricultural Journal — Rhodesia Agr J
Rhodesia Agricultural Journal — Rhodesia Agric J
Rhodesia Agricultural Journal. Technical Handbook — Rhod Agric J Tech Handb
Rhodesia and Nyasaland Law Journal — RNLJ
Rhodesia. Bulletin of Forestry Research — Rhod Bull For Res
Rhodesia. Chibero College of Agriculture. Annual Report — Rhod Chibero Coll Agric Annu Rep
Rhodesia Cotton Research Institute. Annual Report — Rhod Cotton Res Inst Annu Rep
Rhodesia. Division of Livestock and Pastures. Annual Report — Rhod Div Livest Pastures Annu Rep
Rhodesia. Esigodini Agricultural Institute. Annual Report — Rhod Esigodini Agric Inst Annu Rep
Rhodesia. Geological Survey. Bulletin — Rhod Geol Surv Bull
Rhodesia. Geological Survey. Mineral Resources Series — Rhod Geol Surv Miner Resour Ser
Rhodesia. Geological Survey. Short Report — Rhod Geol Surv Short Rep
Rhodesia Grasslands Research Station. Annual Report — Rhod Grassl Res Stn Annu Rep
Rhodesia Journal of Agricultural Research — Rhod J Agric Res
Rhodesia Law Journal — RLJ
Rhodesia. Lowveld Research Station. Annual Report — Rhod Lowveld Res Stn Annu Rep

Rhodesia. Ministry of Agriculture. Department of Research and Specialist Services. Seed Services. Annual Report — Rhod Minist Agric Dep Res Spec Serv Seed Serv Annu Rep
Rhodesia. Ministry of Agriculture. Gatooma Research Station. Annual Report — Rhod Minist Agric Gatooma Res Stn Annu Rep
Rhodesia. Ministry of Agriculture. Grasslands Research Station. Annual Report — Rhod Minist Agric Grassl Res Stn Annu Rep
Rhodesia. Salisbury Research Station. Annual Report — Rhod Salisbury Res Stn Annu Rep
Rhodesia Science News — Rhod Sci News
Rhodesia Scientific Association. Proceedings — Rhodes Sci Assn Proc
Rhodesia, Zambia, and Malawi Journal of Agricultural Research — Rhod Zambia Malawi J Agric Res
Rhodesia, Zambia, and Malawi Journal of Agricultural Research — Rhodesia Zambia Malawi J Agr Res
Rhodesian Agricultural Journal — Rhodesian Agric J
Rhodesian Bee News — Rhod Bee News
Rhodesian Beekeeping — Rhod Beekeeping
Rhodesian Engineer — Rhod Eng
Rhodesian Farmer — Rhod Fmr
Rhodesian History — Rhod Hist
Rhodesian History — Rhodesian Hist
Rhodesian Journal of Agricultural Research — Rhod Jl Agric Res
Rhodesian Journal of Agricultural Research — Rhodesian J Agr Res
Rhodesian Journal of Agricultural Research. Agricultural Research Council of Central Africa — Rhodesian J Agric Res
Rhodesian Journal of Economics — Rhodesian J Econ
Rhodesian Law Journal — Rhod Law J
Rhodesian Librarian — Rhod Librn
Rhodesian Mining Journal — Rhodesian Min Jour
Rhodesian Nurse — Rhod Nurse
Rhodesian Prehistory — Rhod Prehist
Rhodesian Tobacco — Rhod Tob
Rhodesian Tobacco Journal — Rhodesian Tob J
Rhodesian Tobacco Journal — Rhodesian Tobacco J
Rhodes-Livingstone Journal — Rhodes Liv J
Rhodes-Livingstone Journal — RLJ
Rhododendron Society Notes — Rhododendron Soc Notes
Rhodora — RHODA
Rhumatologie [*Paris*] — RHMTA
Rhumatologie — RHUMA
Rhythmes du Monde — Rhythmes Monde
RIA. Revue Economique et Technique de l'Industrie Alimentaire Europeenne — RIA Rev Econ Tech Ind Aliment Eur
Riazi. Journal of Karachi Mathematical Association — Riazi J Karachi Math Assoc
Riazi Souvenir. Karachi Mathematics Association — Karachi Math Assoc Riazi Souvenir
RIBA [*Royal Institute of British Architects*] **Journal** — RIBJD
Ribe Stifts Aarbog — Rb St Aa
RIC. Repertoire Bibliographique des Institutions Chretiennes — Bibliogr Repert Inst Chret
Rice and Sugar Journal — Rice Sugar J
Rice Institute Pamphlet — RI
Rice Institute Pamphlet — Rice Inst P
Rice Institute Pamphlet — Rice Inst Pam
Rice Institute Pamphlet — RIP
Rice Journal — Rice J
Rice Journal — RICJA
Rice University. Aero-Astronautic Report — Rice Univ Aero-Astronaut Rep
Rice University. Studies — Rice Univ Stud
Rice University. Studies — Rice Univ Studies
Rice University. Studies — RiceUS
Rice University. Studies — RUS
Ricerca e Documentazione Tessile — Ric Doc Tess
Ricerca in Clinica e in Laboratorio — RCLAD
Ricerca in Clinica e in Laboratorio — Ric Clin Lab
Ricerca Scientifica — Ric Sci
Ricerca Scientifica — Ricerca Scient
Ricerca Scientifica — RISCA
Ricerca Scientifica e Ricostruzione — Ric Sci Ricostr
Ricerca Scientifica ed il Progresso Tecnico — Ric Sci Prog Tec
Ricerca Scientifica. Parte 1. Rivista — Ric Sci Parte 1
Ricerca Scientifica. Parte 2. Rendiconti. Sezione A. Biologica — Ric Sci Parte 2 Sez A
Ricerca Scientifica. Parte 2. Rendiconti. Sezione B. Biologica — Ric Sci Parte 2 Sez B
Ricerca Scientifica. Quaderni — Ric Sci Quad
Ricerca Scientifica. Rendiconti — Ricerca Scient Rc
Ricerca Scientifica. Serie 2a. Parte II. Rendiconti. Sezione B. Biologica — Ric Sci Ser 2a Pt 2 Rendiconti Sez B Biol
Ricerca Scientifica. Serie Seconda. Parte II. Rendiconti. Sezione B. Biologica — Ric Sci Rend Sez B
Ricerca Scientifica. Supplemento — Ric Sci Suppl
Ricerche Bibliche e Religiose — RBR
Ricerche Bibliche e Religiose [*Milan*] — RicBibRel
Ricerche Demoscopiche — Ric Demos
Ricerche di Automatica — Ric Autom
Ricerche di Automatica — Ricerche Automat
Ricerche di Biologia della Selvaggina — Ric Biol Selvaggina
Ricerche di Matematica — RCMTA
Ricerche di Matematica — Ric Mat
Ricerche di Matematica — Ricerche Mat
Ricerche di Morfologia — Ric Morfol
Ricerche di Storia Religiosa — RicSRel
Ricerche di Storia Religiosa [*Rome*] — RicStRel
Ricerche di Storia Religiosa — RiSR
Ricerche di Termotecnica — RCERB
Ricerche di Termotecnica [*Italy*] — Ric Termotecnica
Ricerche di Zoologia Applicata alla Caccia — Ric Zool Appl Caccia
Ricerche di Zoologia Applicata alla Caccia. Supplemento — Ric Zool Appl Caccia Suppl
Ricerche e Lavori. Istituto Botanico. Univerista di Pisa — Ric Lav Ist Bot Univ Pisa
Ricerche e Studi di Medicina Sperimentale — Ric Studi Med Sper
Ricerche e Studi. Museo Provinciale Francesco Ribezzo (Brindisi) — Ric St (Brindisi)
Ricerche Economiche — Ric Econ
Ricerche Filosofiche — RicF
Ricerche Linguistiche — RicLing
Ricerche Linguistiche — RL
Ricerche Linguistiche — RLing
Ricerche Musicali — RicM
Ricerche Patristiche — Pic Patr
Ricerche Religiose — RicR
Ricerche Religiose — RicRel
Ricerche Religiose — RR
Ricerche Slavistiche — Ric Slavist
Ricerche Slavistiche — RicSL
Ricerche Slavistiche — RS
Ricerche Slavistiche — RSL
Ricerche Slavistiche — RSlav
Ricerche Spettroscopiche — Ric Spettrosc
Ricerche Spettroscopiche. Laboratorio Astrofisico della Specola Vaticana — Ric Spettros Lab Astrofis Specola
Richard Edens' History of Travayle [*Monograph*] — REHT
Richard Hakluyt's Principal Navigations and Voyages [*Monograph*] — HPN
Richerche Astronomiche — RIASB
Richerche Lingistiche — Ric Lg
Richerche Medievali — Ric Med
Richmond and Louisville Medical Journal — Richmond Louisville Med J
Richmond County History [*Georgia*] — Richmond Co Hist
Richmond County History — Richmond Cty Hist
Richmond Journal of Practice — Richmond J Pract
Richmond Times-Dispatch — Richmd T-D
Richters Annalen der Deutschen Geschichte — Richters Annalen
Richtlinien fuer das Strafverfahren — Ri St V
Rickia. Arquivos de Botanica do Estado de Sao Paulo. Serie Criptogamica — Rickia Arq Bot Estado Sao Paulo Ser Criptogam
Rickia. Arquivos de Botanica do Estado de Sao Paulo. Serie Criptogamica — Rickia Arq Bot Estado Sao Paulo Ser Criptogam Supl
Rickia. Suplemento — Rickia Supl
Rickmansworth Historian — Rickmansworth Hist
RICS [*Royal Institution of Chartered Surveyors*] **Abstracts and Review** — RICS Abs Rev
Riddell Memorial Lectures — RML
RIdIM (Repertoire Internationale d'Iconographie Musicale) Newsletter — RIdIMN
Ridotto — Rid
Riechstoffe, Aromen, Koerperpflegemittel [*Later, Riechstoffe, Aromen, Kosmetica*] [*A publication*] — Riechst Aromen Koerperpflegem
Riechstoffe, Aromen, Kosmetica — Riech Aromen Kosmet
Riechstoffe und Aromen — Riechst Aromen
Riforma Agraria — RFAGB
Riforma Agraria [*Italy*] — Riforma Agrar
Riforma Medica — Riforma Med
Rig — R
Rigas Medicinas Instituta Zinatnisko Rakstu Krajums — Rigas Med Inst Zinat Rakstu Krajums
Rigas Politehniskais Instituts. Zinatniskie Raksti — Rigas Politeh Inst Zinat Raksti
Rigasche Industrie Zeitung — Rigasche Ind Ztg
Right Review — RR
Rihaknonjip. Research Institute of Applied Science. Kon-Kuk University — INKYD
Rihaknonjip. Research Institute of Applied Science. Kon-Kuk University [*Republic Of Korea*] — Rihaknonjip Res Inst Appl Sci Kon-Kuk Univ
Riista- ja Kalataloudes Tutkimuslaitos Kalantutkimusosasto Tiedonantoja — Riista-Kalataloudes Tutkimuslaitos Kalantutkimusosasto Tied
Riistatieteellisia Julkaisuja — Riistatiet Julk
Riistatieteellisia Julkaisuja — Riistatiet Julkaisuja
Riistatieteellisia Julkaisuja. Finnish Game Research — RIJU
Rijecka Revija — RRev
Rijks Geologische Dienst. Mededelingen. Nieuwe Serie (Netherlands) — Rijks Geol Dienst Meded Nieuwe Ser (Neth)
Rijks Geschiedkundige Publicaties — RGP
Rijksdienst voor het Oudheidkundig Bodemonderzoek — ROB
Rijkseenheid — RE
Rijkslandbouwvoorlichtingsdienst — Landbouwvoorlichting
Rijksuniversiteit Utrecht. Jaarverslag Wetenschappelijk Deel — Rijksuniv Utrecht Jaarversl Wet Deel
Rijkswaterstaat Communications — Rijksw Commun
Rijkswaterstaat Communications — Rijkswaterstaat Commun
Rikagaku Kenkyusho Hokoku — RKKHA
Rikagaku Kenkyusho Iho — BPYCA
Rikagaku Kenkyusho Kenkyu Nempo — RGKNA
Rikuyo Nainen Kikan — RNKID
RILA [*Repertoire International de la Litterature de l'Art / International Repertory of the Literature of Art*] **News** — RILAN
Rilievi delle Urne Etrusche — Ril Urne Et

Rilievi delle Urne Etrusche — RUE
RILM [*Repertoire International de la Litterature Musicale*] **Abstracts** — RILM Abstr
RILM [*Repertoire International de la Litterature Musicale*] **Abstracts of Music Literature** [*City University of New York*] [*Database*] — RILM
RIM Monographs in Mathematics — RIM Monogr Math
Rimba Indonesia — Rimba Indones
Rimini Storia Arte e Cultura — Rimini Stor Art Cult
Rinascenza Medica — Rinascenza Med
Rinascenza Salentina — Rin S
Rinasciemento [*Firenze*] — Rinasc
Rinascimento — Rin
Rinascita — Rin
Rinascita. Biblioteca [*Firenze*] — Rin B
Rinascita (Firenze) — Rin F
Rinascita. Supplement [*Firenze*] — Rin S
Rindertuberkulose und Brucellose — Rindertuberk Brucell
Ring. International Ornithological Bulletin — Ring Int Ornithol Bull
Ringing and Migration — Ringing Migr
Rinsan Shikenjo Geppo — RSGPB
Rinsho Byori — RBYOA
Rinsho Ganka — RIGAA
Rinsho Hinyokika — RIHYA
Rinsho Hoshasen — RHOSA
Rinsho Kagaku — RIKAA
Rinsho Ketsueki — RIKEB
Rinsho Seijinbyo — RNSJA
Rinsho Shinkeigaku — RISHB
Rio De Janeiro — R
Rio Grande Do Sul. Departamento Producao Animal. Divisao de Zootecnia. Servico de Experimentacao Zootecnia. Boletim Tecnico — RSBTA3
Rio Grande Do Sul. Instituto de Pesquisas Zootecnicas. Boletim Tecnico — Rio Grande Do Sul Inst Pesqui Zootec Bol Tec
Rio Piedras — RP
Risicobank — Rb
Rising Up Angry — Rising Up
Risk Analysis — RIAND
Risk Analysis — Risk Anal
Risk. Book Series — Risk Bk Ser
Risk Management — Risk Manage
Risk Management — Risk Mgmt
Risk Management — Risk Mgt
Risk Management — RKM
Risk Management — RM
Risoe Information [*Denmark*] — Risoe Inf
Risoe National Laboratory. Report Risoe-M (Denmark) — Risoe Natl Lab Rep Risoe-M (Den)
Risoe National Laboratory. Report. Risoe-R — Risoe Natl Lab Rep Risoe R
Risoe Report — Riso Rep
Risoe Report. (Denmark) Research Establishment Risoe — Risoe Rep (Den) Res Establ Risoe
Risorgimento — Ris
Risorgimento — Risorgiment
Risorgimento Italiano — RI
Ritsumeikan Daigaku Rikogaku Kenkyusho Kiyo — RDRKB
Ritus Orientalium, Coptorum, Syrorum, et Armenorum in Administrandis Sacramentis — ROAS
Riunione Annuale della Associazione Elettrotecnica ed Elettronica Italiana. Rendiconti — Riun Annu Assoc Elettrot Elettron Ital Rend
River Basin Bulletin — Riv Bas Bull
River World — Riv World
Riverina Library Review — RLR
Rivers and Harbors — RIHAA
Riverside Quarterly — RQ
Riverside Studies in Literature — RSLit
Riviera Scientifique — Riviera Sci
Riviera Scientifique — RSCQAX
Rivista Abruzzese — RAbr
Rivista Aeronautica — Riv Aeronaut
Rivista Aeronautica — RVAEA
Rivista Aeronautica-Astronautica-Missilistica [*Italy*] — Riv Aeronaut-Astronaut-Missil
Rivista Aeronautica-Astronautica-Missilistica. Supplemento Tecnico — Riv Aeronaut Astronaut Missil Suppl Tec
Rivista Araldica — Riv Arald
Rivista Archeologia della Provincia e Diocesi di Como — Riv Arch Como
Rivista Archeologia. Provincia e Diocesi di Como — RAC
Rivista Archeologia. Provincia e Diocesi di Como — RAComo
Rivista Archeologica dell'Antica Provincia e Diocesi di Como — R A Como
Rivista Biblica [*Rome*] — RB
Rivista Biblica — Ri B
Rivista Biblica — Riv B
Rivista Biblica — Riv Bib
Rivista Biblica — RivBibl
Rivista Biblica Italiana [*Rome*] — RBI
Rivista Biblica Italiana [*Rome*] — RBibIT
Rivista Biblica Italiana [*Rome*] — RBilt
Rivista Bibliografica — RivB
Rivista. Biblioteche e Degli Archivi — RBA
Rivista Clasica — RCl
Rivista Clinica di Bologna — Riv Clin Bologna
Rivista Clinica. Universita di Napoli — Riv Clin Univ Napoli
Rivista Coloniale — Riv Col
Rivista Coloniale. Istituto Coloniale Italiano — RC
Rivista Cristiana — Riv Cr
Rivista Cristiana — Riv Crist
Rivista Critica delle Scienze Giuridiche e Sociali — RCSGS
Rivista Critica di Clinica Medica — RCCMA
Rivista Critica di Clinica Medica — Riv Crit Clin Med
Rivista Critica di Storia della Filosofia — RCSF
Rivista Critica di Storia della Filosofia — Riv Crit St
Rivista Critica di Storia della Filosofia — Riv Crit Stor Fil
Rivista Critica di Storia della Filosofia — Riv Crit Stor Filos
Rivista Critica di Storia della Filosofia — RSF
Rivista Critica di Storia della Filosofia. Pubblicazioni — RCSFP
Rivista d'Albania — RAlb
Rivista d'Albania — Riv Albania
Rivista d'Albania — Riv d'Alb
Rivista Dalmatica — RD
Rivista Dalmatica — RivDal
Rivista d'Arte — RArte
Rivista d'Arte — Riv A
Rivista d'Arte — Riv Arte
Rivista de Ascetica e Mistica — RAMi
Rivista de Odontoiatria degli Amici de Brugg — Riv Odontoiatr
Rivista de Odontostomatologia e Implantoprotesi — Riv Odontostomatol Implantoprotesi
Rivista degli Infortuni e delle Malattie Professionali — RIMPA
Rivista degli Infortuni e delle Malattie Professionali — Riv Infort Mal Prof
Rivista degli Ospedali — Riv Osp
Rivista degli Studi Orientali — R St O
Rivista degli Studi Orientali — RdSO
Rivista degli Studi Orientali — Riv SO
Rivista degli Studi Orientali — Riv St Or
Rivista degli Studi Orientali — Riv Stud Orient
Rivista degli Studi Orientali — RivStudOr
Rivista degli Studi Orientali — RS Or
Rivista degli Studi Orientali — RSO
Rivista dei Combustibili — RICOA
Rivista dei Combustibili — Riv Combust
Rivista dei Combustibili — Riv Combustibili
Rivista del Cinematografo — R Cinematografo
Rivista del Clero Italiano — RCI
Rivista del Colore-Verniciatura Industriale — Riv Colore Verniciatura Ind
Rivista del Diritto Commerciale e del Diritto Generale delle Obbligazioni [*A publication*] — Riv Comm
Rivista del Diritto Commerciale e del Diritto Generale delle Obbligazioni [*A publication*] — Riv Dir Comm
Rivista del Freddo — Riv Freddo
Rivista del Latte — Riv Latte
Rivista del Nuovo Cimento — Riv Nuovo Cim
Rivista del Nuovo Cimento — Riv Nuovo Cimento
Rivista del Nuovo Cimento. Serie 1 — Riv Nuovo Cimento Ser 1
Rivista del Nuovo Cimento. Serie 2 — Riv Nuovo Cimento 2
Rivista del Nuovo Cimento. Serie 3 — Riv Nuovo Cimento 3
Rivista del Nuovo Cimento. Societa Italiana di Fisica [*Italy*] — Riv Nuovo Cimento Soc Ital Fis
Rivista del Nuovo Cimento. Societa Italiana di Fisica — RNUCA
Rivista della Finanza Locale — Riv Fin Loc
Rivista della Guardia di Finanza — R Guardia Fin
Rivista della Guardia di Finanza — Riv Guard Fin
Rivista della Ortoflorofrutticoltura Italiana — Riv Ortoflorofruttic Ital
Rivista della Societa Italiana di Scienze dell'Alimentazione — Riv Soc Ital Sci Aliment
Rivista della Stazione Sperimentale del Vetro (Murano, Italy) — Riv Stn Sper Vetro (Murano Italy)
Rivista della Tripolitania — RTr
Rivista della Tubercolosi e delle Malattie dell'Apparato Respiratorio — Riv Tuberc Mal App Resp
Rivista della Tubercolosi e delle Malattie dell'Apparato Respiratorio — Riv Tuberc Mal Appar Respir
Rivista delle Biblioteche — Riv Bibliot
Rivista delle Biblioteche e degli Archivi — Riv Bibl
Rivista delle Biblioteche e degli Archivi — Riv d Bibl e d Arch
Rivista delle Biblioteche e degli Archivi — RivBA
Rivista delle Colonie — RC
Rivista delle Religioni — RivR
Rivista dell'Infermiere — Riv Inferm
Rivista dell'Informazione — Riv Inf
Rivista dell'Informazione/Information Review — Riv Inf
Rivista di Agricoltura — Riv Agric
Rivista di Agricoltura Subtropicale e Tropicale — Riv Agr Subtrop Trop
Rivista di Agricoltura Subtropicale e Tropicale — Riv Agric Subtrop Trop
Rivista di Agronomia — RAGOA
Rivista di Agronomia — Riv Agron
Rivista di Anatomia Patologica e di Oncologia — Riv Anat Patol Oncol
Rivista di Antropologia — Riv Ant
Rivista di Antropologia — Riv Antr
Rivista di Antropologia — Riv Antrop
Rivista di Antropologia — Riv Antropol
Rivista di Antropologia — Riv di Antr
Rivista di Archeologia — Rd A
Rivista di Archeologia Cristiana — RA Cr
Rivista di Archeologia Cristiana — RAC
Rivista di Archeologia Cristiana — RACrist
Rivista di Archeologia Cristiana [*Rome*] — RArchCr
Rivista di Archeologia Cristiana — Riv AC
Rivista di Archeologia Cristiana — Riv Arch Cr
Rivista di Archeologia Cristiana — Riv Arch Crist
Rivista di Archeologia Cristiana — Riv d Arch Cristiana
Rivista di Biologia — RBILA

Rivista di Biologia — Riv Biol
Rivista di Biologia — Rivista Biol
Rivista di Biologia Coloniale — Riv Biol Colon
Rivista di Biologia Generale — Rivista Biol Gen
Rivista di Biologia Normale e Patologica — Riv Biol Norm Patol
Rivista di Biologia (Perugia) — Riv Biol (Perugia)
Rivista di Chimica Scientifica e Industriale — Riv Chim Sci Ind
Rivista di Chirurgia (Como) — Riv Chir (Como)
Rivista di Chirurgia e Medicina — Riv Chir Med
Rivista di Chirurgia Pediatrica — Riv Chir Pediat
Rivista di Clinica Medica — Riv Clin Med
Rivista di Clinica Pediatrica — Riv Clin Pediat
Rivista di Clinica Pediatrica — Riv Clin Pediatr
Rivista di Clinica Tossicologia — Riv Clin Tossicol
Rivista di Coniglicoltura — Riv Coniglicolt
Rivista di Cultura Classica e Medievale — Riv Cult Class Mediev
Rivista di Cultura Classica e Medioevale — R Cul Cl Medioev
Rivista di Cultura Classica e Medioevale — R Cul Medioev
Rivista di Cultura Classica e Medioevale — RCCM
Rivista di Cultura Classica e Medioevale — Riv Cult Class Med
Rivista di Cultura Classica e Medioevale — Riv di Cultura Class e Med
Rivista di Cultura Marinara — Riv Cult Mar
Rivista di Difesa Sociale — Riv Dif Soc
Rivista di Diritto Agrario — Riv Dir Agr
Rivista di Diritto Civile — R D Civ
Rivista di Diritto Civile — Riv Civ
Rivista di Diritto Civile — Riv di Diritto Civile
Rivista di Diritto Civile — Riv Dir Civ
Rivista di Diritto e Procedura Civile — Riv Dir Proc Civ
Rivista di Diritto Ecclesiastico — RDEc
Rivista di Diritto Europeo — Riv Dir Europ
Rivista di Diritto Finanziaro e Scienza delle Finanze — Riv Dir Finanz
Rivista di Diritto Industriale — Riv Dir Ind
Rivista di Diritto Industriale — Riv Ind
Rivista di Diritto Internazionale — RDI
Rivista di Diritto Internazionale — RDIn
Rivista di Diritto Internazionale — Riv di Diritto Internaz
Rivista di Diritto Internazionale — Riv Dir Int
Rivista di Diritto Internazionale — Riv Dir Int'le
Rivista di Diritto Internazionale — Riv Int
Rivista di Diritto Sportivo — Riv Dir Sport
Rivista di Ecologia — Riv Ecol
Rivista di Economia Agraria — R Econ Agr
Rivista di Economia Agraria — RIEAA
Rivista di Economia Agraria — Riv Econ Agr
Rivista di Economia e Politica Industriale — R Econ e Pol Ind
Rivista di Emoterapia ed Immunoematologia — Riv Emoter Immunoematol
Rivista di Epigrafia Etrusca — REE
Rivista di Epigrafia Italica — REI
Rivista di Estetica — R Est
Rivista di Estetica — RdE
Rivista di Estetica — RdiE
Rivista di Estetica — Riv Est
Rivista di Etnografia — Riv Et
Rivista di Etnografia — Riv Etnogr
Rivista di Farmacologia e Terapia — Riv Farmacol Ter
Rivista di Filologia — RFil
Rivista di Filologia — RivFil
Rivista di Filologia Classica — RFC
Rivista di Filologia e di Istruzione Classica — RF
Rivista di Filologia e di Istruzione Classica — RFC
Rivista di Filologia e di Istruzione Classica — RFIC
Rivista di Filologia e di Istruzione Classica — Riv Fil
Rivista di Filologia e di Istruzione Classica — Riv Fil Class
Rivista di Filologia e di Istruzione Classica — Riv Filol Istruz Classica
Rivista di Filologia e di Istruzione Classica — RivFC
Rivista di Filologia e d'Istruzione Classica — R Fil Cl
Rivista di Filologia e d'Istruzione Classica — R Fil Ist Cl
Rivista di Filologia e d'Istruzione Classica — RFICl
Rivista di Filologia e d'Istruzione Classica — Riv Fil Cl
Rivista di Filologia e d'Istruzione Classica — Riv Filol
Rivista di Filosofia — RdF
Rivista di Filosofia — RdiF
Rivista di Filosofia — RF
Rivista di Filosofia — RFilos
Rivista di Filosofia — Riv Fil
Rivista di Filosofia — Riv Filos
Rivista di Filosofia — Riv Filosof
Rivista di Filosofia Neo-Scolastica — RFN
Rivista di Filosofia Neo-Scolastica — RFNS
Rivista di Filosofia Neo-Scolastica — Riv Filos Neo Scolast
Rivista di Filosofia Neo-Scolastica — Riv Filosof Neo-Scolas
Rivista di Filosofia (Torino) — RFT
Rivista di Fisica, Matematica, e Scienze Naturali — Riv Fis Mat Sci Nat
Rivista di Frutticoltura — Riv Frutti
Rivista di Frutticoltura — Riv Fruttic
Rivista di Frutticoltura e di Ortofloricoltura — RFORE9
Rivista di Frutticoltura e di Ortofloricoltura — Riv Fruttic Ortofloric
Rivista di Frutticultura — Rivista Fruttic
Rivista di Gastro-Enterologia — Riv Gastro Enterol
Rivista di Geofisica Applicata — Riv Geofis Appl
Rivista di Gerontologia e Geriatria — Riv Geront Geriat
Rivista di Gerontologia e Geriatria — Riv Gerontol Geriatr
Rivista di Idrobiologia — Riv Idrobiol
Rivista di Informatica — Riv Inf
Rivista di Ingegneria — Riv Ing
Rivista di Ingegneria Nucleare — RINUA
Rivista di Ingegneria Nucleare — Riv Ing Nucl
Rivista di Istochimica Normale e Patologica — RINPA
Rivista di Istochimica Normale e Patologica — Riv Istochim Norm Patol
Rivista di Letteratura Classiche — Riv Lett Class
Rivista di Letteratura Moderne — RiLM
Rivista di Letteratura Moderne — Riv Lett Mod
Rivista di Letterature Moderne e Comparate — Riv Let Mod
Rivista di Letterature Moderne e Comparate — RLM
Rivista di Letterature Moderne e Comparate — RLMC
Rivista di Letterature Moderne — Riv di LM
Rivista di Letterature Moderne — RLM
Rivista di Livorno — RLiv
Rivista di Matematica della Universita di Parma. Serie 5 — Riv Mat Univ Parma 5
Rivista di Matematica per le Scienze Economiche e Sociali — Riv Mat Sci Econom Social
Rivista di Matematica Pura ed Applicata — Riv Mat Pura Appl
Rivista di Matematica. Universita di Parma — Riv Mat Univ Parma
Rivista di Matematica. Universita di Parma. Serie 4 — Riv Mat Univ Parma 4
Rivista di Meccanica — Riv Mecc
Rivista di Meccanica — RVMCA
Rivista di Medicina Aeronautica e Spaziale — Riv Med Aer
Rivista di Medicina Aeronautica e Spaziale — Riv Med Aeronaut
Rivista di Medicina Aeronautica e Spaziale — Riv Med Aeronaut Spaz
Rivista di Medicina Aeronautica e Spaziale — RMDSA
Rivista di Medicina del Lavoro ed Igiene Industriale — Riv Med Lav Ig Ind
Rivista di Medicina Veterinaria e Zootecnica — Riv Med Vet Zootec
Rivista di Merceologia — Riv Merceol
Rivista di Meteorologia Aeronautica — Riv Meteo A
Rivista di Meteorologia Aeronautica — Riv Meteorol Aeronaut
Rivista di Meteorologia Aeronautica — RMTAA
Rivista di Mineralogia e Cristallografia Italiana — Riv Mineral Cristallogr Ital
Rivista di Neurobiologia — Riv Neurobiol
Rivista di Neurobiologia — RNBLA
Rivista di Neurologia — Riv Neurol
Rivista di Neuropsichiatria e Scienze Affini — Riv Neuropsichiatr Sci Affini
Rivista di Ostetricia e Ginecologia — Riv Ostet Ginecol
Rivista di Ostetricia e Ginecologia — ROGNA
Rivista di Ostetricia e Ginecologia (Florence) — Riv Ostet Ginecol (Flor)
Rivista di Ostetricia e Ginecologia Pratica — Riv Ostet Ginecol Prat
Rivista di Ostetricia e Ginecologia Pratica e di Medicina Perinatale — Riv Ostet Ginecol Prat Med Perinat
Rivista di Parassitologia — Riv Parassit
Rivista di Parassitologia — Riv Parassitol
Rivista di Parassitologia — RPSTA
Rivista di Patologia Clinica e Sperimentale — Riv Patol Clin Sper
Rivista di Patologia Clinica e Sperimentale — RPCSB
Rivista di Patologia e Clinica — Riv Patol Clin
Rivista di Patologia e Clinica della Tubercolosi — Riv Patol Clin Tuberc
Rivista di Patologia e Clinica della Tubercolosi e di Pneumologia — Riv Patol Clin Tuberc Pneumol
Rivista di Patologia Nervosa e Mentale — Riv Patol Nerv Ment
Rivista di Patologia Sperimentale — Riv Patol Sper
Rivista di Patologia Umana — Riv Patol Um
Rivista di Patologia Vegetale — Riv Patol Veg
Rivista di Pedagogia e Scienze Religiose — RPSR
Rivista di Politica Agraria — R Pol Agr
Rivista di Politica Agraria — Riv Polit Agr
Rivista di Politica Economica — Riv Polit Econ
Rivista di Politica Economica — RPE
Rivista di Radiologia — RIRAB
Rivista di Radiologia — Riv Radiol
Rivista di Radiologia e Fisica Medica — Rivista Radiol Fis Med
Rivista di Scienza e Tecnologia degli Alimenti e di Nutrizione Umana — Riv Sci Tecnol Aliment Nutr Umana
Rivista di Scienza e Tecnologia degli Alimenti e di Nutrizione Umana — Riv Sci Tecnol Alimenti Nutr Um
Rivista di Scienza e Tecnologia degli Alimenti e di Nutrizione Umana — RSTUD
Rivista di Scienze Preistoriche — R Sc Pr
Rivista di Scienze Preistoriche — R Sci Preistor
Rivista di Scienze Preistoriche — Riv Sc Pr
Rivista di Scienze Preistoriche — Riv Sci Preist
Rivista di Scienze Preistoriche — Riv Scienze Preist
Rivista di Scienze Preistoriche — RSP
Rivista di Scienze Storiche — RSS
Rivista di Servizio Sociale — R Servizio Soc
Rivista di Sintesi Litteraria — RSL
Rivista di Sociologia — Riv Sociol
Rivista di Storia Antica — R Stor Ant
Rivista di Storia Antica — Riv St Ant
Rivista di Storia Antica — Riv Stor Ant
Rivista di Storia Antica — Riv Stor Antica
Rivista di Storia Antica — RSA
Rivista di Storia Antica — RStA
Rivista di Storia Antica — RStAnt
Rivista di Storia, Arte Archeologia — RSAA
Rivista di Storia Contemporanea — R Storia Contemporanea
Rivista di Storia del Diritto Italiano — RSDI
Rivista di Storia della Chiesa in Italia — Riv Stor Chiesa Ital
Rivista di Storia della Chiesa in Italia — RSCI
Rivista di Storia della Filosofia — Riv Stor Fil
Rivista di Storia della Filosofia — RSF

Rivista di Storia della Medicina — Riv Stor Med
Rivista di Storia della Scienza — Riv Stor Sci
Rivista di Storia delle Scienze Mediche e Naturali — RSSMN
Rivista di Storia e Letteratura Religiosa — RSLR
Rivista di Storia Economica — RSE
Rivista di Studi Bizantini e Neoellenici — R St Biz Neoell
Rivista di Studi Bizantini e Neoellenici — RSB
Rivista di Studi Bizantini e Neoellenici — RSBN
Rivista di Studi Bizantini e Neoellenici — St Biz
Rivista di Studi Bizantini e Neoellenici — Stud Byz
Rivista di Studi Classici — Riv St Cl
Rivista di Studi Classici — Riv Studi Cl
Rivista di Studi Classici — RSC
Rivista di Studi Classici — RSCL
Rivista di Studi Crociani — Riv Stud Croci
Rivista di Studi Crociani — Riv Stud Crociani
Rivista di Studi Crociani — RSC
Rivista di Studi Europei — R Studi Eur
Rivista di Studi Fenici — R St Fen
Rivista di Studi Fenici — R Stud Fen
Rivista di Studi Fenici — Riv St Fen
Rivista di Studi Filosofici e Religiosi — RSFR
Rivista di Studi Liguri — R St Lig
Rivista di Studi Liguri — R Stud Liguri
Rivista di Studi Liguri — RE Lig
Rivista di Studi Liguri — Riv Lig
Rivista di Studi Liguri — Riv St Lig
Rivista di Studi Liguri — Riv Stu Lig
Rivista di Studi Liguri — Riv Stud Lig
Rivista di Studi Liguri — RSL
Rivista di Studi Liguri — RSLig
Rivista di Studi Marchigiani — R St March
Rivista di Studi Orientali — Riv Stud Or
Rivista di Studi Politici Internazionali — Riv Studi Polit Int
Rivista di Studi Politici Internazionali — Riv Studi Polit Internaz
Rivista di Studi Politici Internazionali — Riv Studi Politici Int
Rivista di Studi Politici Internazionali — RSPI
Rivista di Studi Pompeiani — R St Pomp
Rivista di Studi Pompeiani — RS Pomp
Rivista di Studi Pompeiani — RSP
Rivista di Studi Religiosi — RSR
Rivista di Studi Teatrali — RST
Rivista di Suinicoltura — Riv Suinicolt
Rivista di Teologia Morale — RTM
Rivista di Tossicologia Sperimentale e Clinica — Riv Tossicol Sper Clin
Rivista di Veterinaria — Riv Vet
Rivista di Vita Spirituale — RVS
Rivista di Viticoltura e di Enologia — Riv Vitic Enol
Rivista di Viticoltura e di Enologia — RVENA
Rivista di Zootecnia — RZOOA
Rivista di Zootecnia e Veterinaria — Riv Zootec
Rivista di Zootecnia e Veterinaria — Riv Zootec Vet
Rivista d'Igiene e Sanita Pubblica — Riv Ig e San Pubb
Rivista d'Italia — RI
Rivista d'Italia — Riv d It
Rivista Europea per le Scienze Mediche e Farmacologiche — RESFDJ
Rivista Europea per le Scienze Mediche e Farmacologiche — Riv Eur Sci Med Farmacol
Rivista Filosofica (Pavia) — RFP
Rivista Fitosanitaria — Riv Fitosanit
Rivista Fotografica Italiana — Riv Fotogr Ital
Rivista Generale Italiana di Chirurgia — RGIRAG
Rivista Generale Italiana di Chirurgia — Riv Gen Ital Chir
Rivista Geografica Italiana — Riv Geogr Ital
Rivista Geografica Italiana. Societa di Studi Geografici e Coloniali — SSG/RGI
Rivista Indo-Greco-Italica [di Filologia, Lingua, Antichita] — Riv Indo Greco Ital
Rivista Indo-Greco-Italica di Filologia [*Lingua, Antichita*] — RIGI
Rivista Indo-Greco-Italica di Filologia [*Lingua, Antichita*] — Riv Indo Greco It
Rivista Indo-Greco-Italica di Filologia, Lingua, Antichita — RIGI
Rivista Indo-Greco-Italico — RIGI
Rivista Indo-Greco-Italico di Filologia, Lingua, Antichita — RivIGI
Rivista Ingauna e Intemelia — R Ing Intem
Rivista Ingauna e Intemelia N.S. — Riv Inguana
Rivista Ingauna et Intemelia N.S. — Ingauna et Intemelia NS
Rivista Ingauna et Intemelia N.S. — Riv Ing
Rivista Inguana et Intemelia — RII
Rivista Inguana et Intemelia — Riv Ing Int
Rivista Internazionale di Agricoltura — Riv Int Agric
Rivista Internazionale di Agricoltura — Rivista Int Agric
Rivista Internazionale di Filosofia del Diritto — RIFD
Rivista Internazionale di Filosofia del Diritto — Riv Int Filosof Diritto
Rivista Internazionale di Filosofia del Diritto — Riv Intern di Filos del Diritto
Rivista Internazionale di Filosofia del Diritto — Riv Internaz di Filos del Diritto
Rivista Internazionale di Filosofia Politica e Sociale e di Diritto Comparato — Riv Int Filos Polit Soc Dir Comp
Rivista Internazionale di Musica Sacra — RIMS
Rivista Internazionale di Musica Sacra — RIntMS
Rivista Internazionale di Scienze Economiche e Commerciali — R Internaz Scienze Econ e Commer
Rivista Internazionale di Scienze Economiche e Commerciali — RISE
Rivista Internazionale di Scienze Economiche e Commerciali — Riv Int Ec
Rivista Internazionale di Scienze Economiche e Commerciali — Riv Int Sci Econ Com
Rivista Internazionale di Scienze Economiche e Commerciali — Riv Intern Sci Ec Comm
Rivista Internazionale di Scienze Sociali — R Internaz Scienze Soc
Rivista Internazionale di Scienze Sociali — Riv Int Sci Soc
Rivista Internazionale di Scienze Sociali — Riv Intern Sci Soc
Rivista Internazionale di Scienze Sociali — Riv Internaz Sci Soc
Rivista Internazionale di Scienze Sociali e Discipline Ausiliari — RISS
Rivista Israelitica — RI
Rivista. Istituto Nazionale d'Archeologia e Storia dell'Arte — RIA
Rivista. Istituto Nazionale d'Archeologia e Storia dell'Arte — RINA
Rivista. Istituto Nazionale d'Archeologia e Storia dell'Arte — RINASA
Rivista. Istituto Nazionale d'Archeologia e Storia dell'Arte — Riv Ist
Rivista. Istituto Nazionale d'Archeologia e Storia dell'Arte — Riv Ist Arch e St Arte
Rivista. Istituto Sieroterapico Italiano — Riv Ist Sieroter Ital
Rivista. Istituto Vaccinogeno e Consorzi Provinciali Antitubercolari — Riv Ist Vaccinogeno Consorzi Prov Antituberc
Rivista Italiana de Metano — Riv Ital Metano
Rivista Italiana degli Odontotecnici — Riv Ital Odontotec
Rivista Italiana del Drama — RID
Rivista Italiana del Dramma — Riv Ital del Dramma
Rivista Italiana del Petrolio — Riv Ital Pet
Rivista Italiana del Teatro — RIT
Rivista Italiana del Tracoma e di Patologia Oculare, Virale, ed Esotica — Riv Ital Trac Patol Ocul Virale Esotica
Rivista Italiana della Saldatura — RISAA
Rivista Italiana della Saldatura — Riv Ital Saldatura
Rivista Italiana delle Essenze — Riv Ital Essenze
Rivista Italiana delle Essenze dei Profumi e delle Piante Officinali — Riv Ital Essenze Profumi Piante Off
Rivista Italiana delle Essenze dei Profumi e delle Piante Officinali Aromi Saponi Cosmetici — Riv Ital Essenze Profumi Piante Off Aromi Saponi Cosmet
Rivista Italiana delle Essenze dei Profumi e delle Piante Officinali Aromi Saponi Cosmetici — Riv Ital Essenze Profumi Piante Offic Aromi Saponi Cosmet
Rivista Italiana delle Essenze dei Profumi e delle Piante Officinali Aromi Saponi Cosmetici Aerosol — RIPOAM
Rivista Italiana delle Essenze dei Profumi e delle Piante Officinali Olii Vegetali Saponi — Riv Ital Essenze Profumi Piante Offic Olii Veg Saponi
Rivista Italiana delle Essenze e Profumi — Riv Ital Essenze Profumi
Rivista Italiana delle Sostanze Grasse — Riv Ital Sost Grasse
Rivista Italiana delle Sostanze Grasse — Riv Ital Sostanze Grasse
Rivista Italiana delle Sostanze Grasse. Supplemento — Riv Ital Sostanze Grasse Suppl
Rivista Italiana di Amministrazione dell'Economia e Sociologia Industriale [*A publication*] — Riv Ital Amm Ec
Rivista Italiana di Dialettologia — RID
Rivista Italiana di Diritto del Lavoro — R Ital Diritto Lav
Rivista Italiana di Diritto e Procedura Penale — Riv Ital Dir Proc Pen
Rivista Italiana di Diritto Sociale — Riv Ital Dir Soc
Rivista Italiana di Drammaturgia. Trimestrale dell'Istituto del Dramma Italiano — RIDD
Rivista Italiana di Economia. Demografia e Statistica — R Ital Econ Demografia e Statis
Rivista Italiana di Geofisica [*Italy*] — Riv Ital Geofis
Rivista Italiana di Geofisica e Scienze Affini — Riv Ital Ge
Rivista Italiana di Geotecnica — Riv Ital Geotec
Rivista Italiana di Ginecologia — Riv Ital Ginecol
Rivista Italiana di Letteratura Dialettale — RILD
Rivista Italiana di Musicologia — R Ital Mus
Rivista Italiana di Musicologia — R Italiana Musicol
Rivista Italiana di Musicologia — RIdM
Rivista Italiana di Musicologia — RIM
Rivista Italiana di Numismatica — RIN
Rivista Italiana di Numismatica e Scienze Affini — R I Num
Rivista Italiana di Numismatica e Scienze Affini — R It Num
Rivista Italiana di Numismatica e Scienze Affini — RIN
Rivista Italiana di Numismatica e Scienze Affini — Riv It Num
Rivista Italiana di Numismatica e Scienze Affini — Riv Ital Num
Rivista Italiana di Numismatica e Scienze Affini — Riv Num
Rivista Italiana di Nutrizione Parenterale ed Enterale — RINEEK
Rivista Italiana di Nutrizione Parenterale ed Enterale — Riv Ital Nutr Parenter Enterale
Rivista Italiana di Ornitologia — Riv Ital Ornitol
Rivista Italiana di Ortopedia e Traumatologia [*Italian Review of Orthopaedics and Traumatology*] — RIOTE2
Rivista Italiana di Ortopedia e Traumatologia — Riv Ital Ortop Traumatol
Rivista Italiana di Paleontologia e Stratigrafia — Riv Ital Paleontol Stratigr
Rivista Italiana di Paleontologia e Stratigrafia — Riv Italiana Paleontologia e Stratigrafia
Rivista Italiana di Radiologia Clinica — Riv Ital Radiol Clin
Rivista Italiana di Scienza degli Alimenti — Riv Ital Sci Alimenti
Rivista Italiana di Scienza Politica — Riv Ital Sci Polit
Rivista Italiana di Scienze Giuridiche — RISG
Rivista Italiana di Sociologia — RIS
Rivista Italiana di Stomatologia — RISTA
Rivista Italiana di Stomatologia — Riv Ital Stomatol
Rivista Italiana di Stomatologia / Associazione Medici Dentisti Italiani. Venice — Rivista Ital Stomatol Venice
Rivista Italiana di Stomatologia. Rome — Rivista Ital Stomatol Rome
Rivista Italiana d'Igiene — RIIGA
Rivista Italiana d'Igiene — Riv Ital Ig
Rivista Italiana per la Scienze Giuridiche — RI Sc G
Rivista Italiana per la Scienze Giuridiche — Riv Ital per la Sc Giur
Rivista Italiana per le Scienze Giuridiche — Riv It Scienze Giur
Rivista Italiana per le Scienze Giuridiche — Riv Ital Sci Giur
Rivista Lasalliana — RiL

Rivista Letteraria — RL
Rivista Letteraria. Licei Classico, Scientifico, Artistico, e Istituto Magistrale — RivL
Rivista Liturgica — Riv Li
Rivista Liturgica — Riv Liturg
Rivista l'Ospedale Psichiatrico — Riv Osp Psichiatr
Rivista Malariologia — Riv Malariol
Rivista Marittima — Riv Maritt
Rivista Mensile di Israel — RMI
Rivista Mensile Svizzera di Odontologia e Stomatologia — Riv Mens Svizz Odontol Stomatol
Rivista Militare Italiana — Riv Milit It
Rivista Mineralogica Italiana — Riv Mineral Ital
Rivista Mineraria Siciliana — Riv Min Sicil
Rivista Mineraria Siciliana [*Italy*] — Riv Mineraria Sicil
Rivista Mineraria Siciliana — RMSCA
Rivista Mineraria Ungarica — Riv Min Ung
Rivista Musicale Italiana — R Mus Ital
Rivista Musicale Italiana — Riv Mus Ital
Rivista Musicale Italiana — Riv Mus Italiana
Rivista Musicale Italiana — RMI
Rivista Ospedaliera Roma — Riv Osp Roma
Rivista Oto-Neuro-Oftalmologica — Riv Oto-Neuro-Oftalmol
Rivista Oto-Neuro-Oftalmologica — RVOOA
Rivista Oto-Neuro-Oftalmologica e Radio-Neuro-Chirurgica — Riv Oto-Neuro-Oftalmol Radio-Neuro-Chir
Rivista Patologia dell'Apparato Respiratorio — Riv Patol Appar Respir
Rivista Pedagogica — Riv Pedag
Rivista Pedagogica — RivPed
Rivista Pediatricia Siciliana — Riv Pediatr Sicil
Rivista Periodica del Lavori. Accademia di Scienze, Lettere, ed Arti di Padova — Riv Per Lav Accad Sc Lett ed Arti Padova
Rivista. Periodico Nautico (Trieste) — Riv Per Naut Triest
Rivista Portuguesa de Filosofia. Supplement Bibliografico — RPFB
Rivista. Reale Istituto d'Archeologia e Storia dell'Arte — Riv Ist Arch
Rivista Romana — Riv Rom
Rivista Rosminiana — RRo
Rivista Rosminiana di Filosofia e di Cultura — Riv Rosmin Filos Cult
Rivista Rosminiana di Filosofia e di Cultura — RRFC
Rivista Sanitaria Siciliana — Rivista Sanit Sicil
Rivista Siciliana della Tubercolosi — Riv Sicil Tuberc
Rivista Siciliana della Tubercolosi e delle Malattie Respiratorie — Riv Sicil Tuberc Mal Respir
Rivista. Societa Toscana di Orticultura — Rivista Soc Tosc Ortic
Rivista Sperimentale di Freniatria e Medicina Legale delle Alienazioni Mentali — Riv Sper Freniatr Med Leg Alienazioni Ment
Rivista Sperimentale di Freniatria e Medicina Legale delle Alienazioni Mentali — RSFMA
Rivista Storica Benedettina — RSB
Rivista Storica del Socialismo — Riv Stor Socialismo
Rivista Storica dell'Antichita — R Stor Ant
Rivista Storica dell'Antichita — Riv Stor Ant
Rivista Storica dell'Antichita — Riv Stor dell Antichita
Rivista Storica Italiana — R Stor Italiana
Rivista Storica Italiana — RiS
Rivista Storica Italiana — Riv Stor
Rivista Storica Italiana — Riv Stor It
Rivista Storica Italiana — Riv Stor Ital
Rivista Storica Italiana — RSI
Rivista Storica Italiana — RSIt
Rivista Storica Ticinese — RST
Rivista Storico-Critica delle Scienze Mediche e Naturali — RSM
Rivista Storico-Critica delle Scienze Teologiche — RSCST
Rivista Storico-Critica delle Scienze Teologiche — RStCr
Rivista Svizzera della Tubercolosi e della Pneumonologia — Riv Svizz Tuberc Pneumonol
Rivista Svizzera delle Birrerie — Riv Svizz Birr
Rivista Svizzera di Apicoltura — Riv Svizz Apic
Rivista Svizzera di Medicina dello Sport — Riv Svizz Med Sport
Rivista Tecnica d'Elettricita — Riv Tec Elettr
Rivista Tecnica delle Ferrovie Italiane — Riv Tec Ferrovie Ital
Rivista Tecnica Selenia (English Edition) — Riv Tec Selenia (Engl Ed)
Rivista Tecnica Svizzera — Riv Tec Svizz
Rivista Tessile — Riv Tess
Rivista Tessile Aracne — Riv Tess Aracne
Rivista Tessile-Textilia — Riv Tess Text
Rivista Trimestrale di Diritto Pubblico — Riv Trim Dir Pubbl
Rivista Trimestrale di Diritto Pubblico — Riv Trimest di Diritto Pubbl
Rivista Trimestrale di Studi Filosofici e Religiosi — RTSFR
Rivista Ungherese de Metallurgia — Riv Ung Metall
Rivista Veneta di Scienze Mediche — Riv Veneta Sc Med
Rivoluzione Industriale — Rivol Ind
Rivoluzione Industriale [*Italy*] — Rivoluzione Ind
RIVON [*Rijksinstituut voor Veldbiologische Onderzoek ten Behoeve van het Natuurbehoud*] **Jaarverslag** — MRVNAN
RIVON (Rijksinstituut voor Veldbiologische Onderzoek ten Behoeve van het Natuurbehoud) Jaarverslag — RIVON (Rijksinst Veldbiol Onderz Natuurbehd) Jaarversl
Riyad University. Faculty of Science. Bulletin — Riyad Univ Fac Sci Bull
Riyad University. Faculty of Science. Journal — J Fac Sci Riyad Univ
Riyad University. Faculty of Science. Journal — Riyad Univ Fac Sci J
Riz et Riziculture — Riz Rizi
Riz et Riziculture et Cultures Vivieres Tropicales — Riz Rizic Cult Vivieres Trop
Riz et Riziculture et Cultures Vivrieres Tropicales — Riz Rizicult Cult Vivr Trop
Rizhskii Meditsinskii Institut. Sbornik Nauchnykh Rabot — Rizh Med Inst Sb Nauchn Rab
Rizskii Institut Inzenerov Grazdanskoi Aviacii Imeni Leninskogo Komsomola — Rizsk Inst Inz Grazdan Aviacii
Rizskii Politehniceskii Institut. Voprosy Dinamiki i Procnosti — Voprosy Dinamiki i Procnosti
Rjazanskii Gosudarstvennyi Pedagogiceskii Institut. Ucenye Zapiski — Rjazansk Gos Ped Inst Ucen Zap
RKhT. Radiatsionno-Khimicheskaya Tekhnologiya — RKhT Radiats Khim Tekhnol
RLG [*Research Libraries Group, Inc.*] **Research-in-Progress Database** — RIPD
RM. Revista Medica do Estado da Guanabara — RM Rev Med Estado Guanabara
RMA [*Rubber Manufacturers Association*] **Industry Rubber Report** — RMA Rubber
RMA [*Royal Musical Association*] **Research Chronicle** — RMA Res Chron
RMA [*Royal Musical Association*] **Research Chronicle** — RMA Research Chron
RMA. Research Notes in Applied Mathematics — RMA Res Notes Appl Math
RMA [*Rubber Manufacturers Association*] **Tire and Innertube Statistical Report** — RMA Tire
RN Idaho — RN ID
RN Magazine — RN Mag
RN. Registered Nurse — RN Regist Nurse
RNA. Revista de Nutricion Animal — RNA Rev Nutr Anim
RNABC (Registered Nurses Association of British Columbia) News — RNABC News
RNAO (Registered Nurses Association of Ontario) News — RNAO News
Road Abstracts — Road Abstr
Road and Track — GRNT
Road and Track — R & T
Road Apple Review — Road A R
Road Note. Road Research Laboratory (United Kingdom) — Road Note Road Res Lab (UK)
Road Research Bulletin — Road Res Bull
Road Research Laboratory (United Kingdom). RRL Report — Road Res Lab (UK) RRL Rep
Road Research Monographs — Road Res Monogr
Road Research Notes — Road Res Notes
Road Research Papers — Road Res Pap
Road Research Technical Papers — Road Res Techn Pap
Road Safety — Road Saf
Road Tar — ROTAA
Road Transporter of Australia — Road Transp Aust
Road Transporter of Australia — Road Transp of Aust
Roads and Bridges — Roads & Bridges
Roads and Construction — Roads & Constr
Roads and Construction — Roads Construct
Roads and Engineering Construction — Rds Eng Constr
Roads and Engineering Construction — Roads & Eng Constr
Roads and Road Construction — Rds Rd Constn
Roads and Road Construction — Roads Road Constr
Roads and Streets — Roads St
Roads and Streets — ROSTA
Robert A. Taft Sanitary Engineering Center. Technical Report — Robert A Taft Sanit Eng Cent Tech Rep
Robert A. Taft Water Research Center. Report — Robert A Taft Water Res Cent Rep
Robert A. Welch Foundation. Conferences on Chemical Research. Proceedings — Robert A Welch Found Conf Chem Res Proc
Robert A. Welch Foundation. Research Bulletin — Robert A Welch Found Res Bull
Robert Morris Associates. Bulletin — Robert Morris Associates Bull
Robinson Jeffers Newsletter — RJN
Robot Experimenter — Robot Exp
Robot Experimenter. Supplement — Rob Exp Suppl
Robotic Patents Newsletter — Robotic Pat Newsl
Robotics Abstracts [*Database*] — Robot Abstr
Robotics Age — ROB
Robotics Age — Robot Age
Robotics Engineering — Robot Eng
Robotics Today — Robotics T
Robotics World — Robot Wld
Robotron Technical Communications — Robotron Tech Commun
Robotron Technische Mitteilungen — Robotron Tech Mitt
Rocas y Minerales — Rocas Miner
Rocenka Slovanskeho Ustavu — RSU
Rocenka Slovanskeho Ustavu v Praze — RSIU
Rocenka Vlastivedne Spolecnosti Jihoceske v Ceskych Budejovicich — Rocenka Vlastiv Spolec Jihoceske V Ceskych Budejovicich
Roche Image of Medicine and Research — Roche Image Med Res
Roche Medical Image and Commentary — Roche Med Image Comment
Rochester Academy of Science. Proceedings — Rochester Acad Sci Proc
Rochester Conference on Coherence and Quantum Optics. Proceedings — Rochester Conf Coherence Quantum Opt Proc
Rochester Conference on Data Acquisition and Processing in Biology and Medicine. Proceedings — Rochester Conf Data Acquis Processing Biol Med Proc
Rochester Conference on Toxicity — Rochester Conf Toxic
Rochester Diocesan Chronicle — RDC
Rochester Historical Society. Publication Fund Series — Rochester Hist Soc Publ Fund Ser
Rochester History — RH
Rochester History — RocH
Rochester History — Rochester Hist
Rochester International Conference on Environmental Toxicity — Rochester Int Conf Environ Toxic

Rochester Patriot — Roch Patr
Rochester Philharmonic Orchestra. Program Notes — Roch Phil
Rock Analysis Storage System [*Database*] — RASS
Rock and Mineral Analysis — Rock Miner Anal
Rock & Rap Confidential — R&R
Rock Australia Magazine — RAM
Rock Chemical Database — PETROCH
Rock Magnetism and Paleogeophysics — Rock Magn Paleogeophys
Rock Mechanics — RMFMA
Rock Mechanics — Rock Mech
Rock Mechanics and Engineering Geology — Rock Mech Eng Geol
Rock Mechanics/Felsmechanik/Mecanique des Roches — Rock Mech Felsmech Mec Roches
Rock Mechanics. The American Northwest. Congress Expedition Guide — Rock Mech Am Northwest Congr Exped Guide
Rock Oil Industry — Rock Oil Ind
Rock Products — Rock Prod
Rock Products — ROPRA
Rockefeller Institute Review — Rockefeller Inst Rev
Rocket News Letter — Rocket News Lett
Rocket News Letter and Journal of Space Flight — Rocket News Lett J Space Flight
Rocket Propulsion Technology — Rocket Propul Technol
Rocket Stories — RKS
Rock-Forming Minerals. Proceedings. General Meeting of IMA [*International Mineralogical Association*] — Rock Form Miner Proc Gen Meet IMA
Rocks and Minerals — Rocks Miner
Rocky Mountain Association of Geologists — Rocky Mt Assoc Geol
Rocky Mountain Association of Geologists. Field Conference — RMGCA
Rocky Mountain Bioengineering Symposium. Proceedings — Rocky Mt Bioeng Symp Proc
Rocky Mountain Business Journal — Rocky Mt B
Rocky Mountain Journal of Mathematics — RMJMA
Rocky Mountain Journal of Mathematics — Rocky Mountain J Math
Rocky Mountain Journal of Mathematics — Rocky Mt J Math
Rocky Mountain Law Review [*Later, University of Colorado. Law Review*] — RMLR
Rocky Mountain Law Review [*Later, University of Colorado. Law Review*] — RMR
Rocky Mountain Law Review [*Later, University of Colorado. Law Review*] — Rocky Mt L Rev
Rocky Mountain Law Review [*Later, University of Colorado. Law Review*] — Rocky Mtn L Rev
Rocky Mountain Medical Journal — RMMJA
Rocky Mountain Medical Journal — Rocky Mount Med J
Rocky Mountain Medical Journal — Rocky Mountain MJ
Rocky Mountain Medical Journal — Rocky Mt Med J
Rocky Mountain Medical Journal — Rocky Mtn Med J
Rocky Mountain Mineral Law Institute. Annual Institute. Proceedings — Rocky Mt Miner Law Inst Annu Inst Proc
Rocky Mountain Mineral Law Institute. Proceedings — Rocky Mt Min L Inst
Rocky Mountain Mineral Law Institute. Proceedings — Rocky Mt Min L Inst Proc
Rocky Mountain Mineral Law Newsletter — RMMND
Rocky Mountain Oil Reporter — Rocky Mtn Oil Reporter
Rocky Mountain Review — RMR
Rocky Mountain Review of Language and Literature — RMR
Rocky Mountain Review of Language and Literature — Rocky Mt R
Rocky Mountain Social Science Journal — RMSSJ
Rocky Mountain Social Science Journal — Rocky Mt So
Rocky Mountain Social Science Journal — Rocky Mt Soc Sci J
Rocky Mountain Social Science Journal — Rocky Mtn Soc Sci J
Rocky Mountain Social Science Journal — RocM
Rocky Mountain Spectroscopy Conference. Program and Abstracts — Rocky Mt Spectrosc Conf Program Abstr
Rocla Pipes Limited. Technical Journal — Rocla Pipes Ltd Tech J
Rocznik Bialostocki — Rocz Bial
Rocznik Bialostocki — Rocz Bialostocki
Rocznik Bibliotek Narodowe — Roczn Bibliot Narodowe
Rocznik Biblioteki Gdanskiej Pan — RBGd
Rocznik Biblioteki Pan w Krakowie — RBKr
Rocznik Historii Czasopismiennictwa Polskiego — RHCS
Rocznik Jeleniogorski — Rocz Jeleniogorski
Rocznik Komisji Historycznoliterackiej Pan — RKHLit
Rocznik Krakowski — Rocz Krakowski
Rocznik Lubelski — RLub
Rocznik Muzeum Etnograficznego w Krakowie — Rocz Muz Etnogr
Rocznik Muzeum Narodowego w Warszawie — Rocz Muz Narod Warszawie
Rocznik Muzeum Narodowego w Warszawie — Rocz Muz Warsz
Rocznik Muzeum Swietokrzyskiego — Rocz Muz Swiet
Rocznik Muzeum w Toruniu — Rocz Muz Toruniu
Rocznik Naukowe Zootechniki. Polish Journal of Animal Science and Technology — Rocz Nauk Zootech Pol J Anim Sci Technol
Rocznik Naukowo-Dydaktyczny — RND
Rocznik Naukowo-Dydaktyczny. Prace Matematyczne — Rocznik Nauk Dydakt Prace Mat
Rocznik Orientalistyczny — RO
Rocznik Orientalistyczny — Roc Or
Rocznik Orientalistyczny [*Warszawa*] — RocO
Rocznik Orientalistyczny [*Warsaw*] — RoczOr
Rocznik Orjentalistyczny — Rocz Orjent
Rocznik Polskiego Towarzystwa — RPTOW
Rocznik Polskiego Towarzystwa Geologicznego — Rocz Pol Tow Geol
Rocznik Polskiego Towarzystwa Geologicznego — RPTGA
Rocznik Pomorskiej Akademii Medycznej Imienia Generala Karola Swierczewskiego w Szczecinie [*Poland*] — Rocz Pomor Akad Med Szczecinie
Rocznik Pomorskiej Akademii Medycznej Imienia Generala Karola Swierczewskiego w Szczecinie — RPMKA
Rocznik Sekcji Dendrologicznej Polskiego Towarzystwa Botanicznego — Rocz Sekc Dendrol Pol Tow Bot
Rocznik Sekcji Dendrologicznej Polskiego Towarzystwa Botanicznego — Roczn Dendrol Polsk Tow Bot
Rocznik Slawistyczny — RoczSl
Rocznik Slawistyczny — RoSlaw
Rocznik Slawistyczny — RS
Rocznik Slawistyczny — RSl
Rocznik Statystyczny Powiatu Tarnow — Rocz Stat Pow Tar
Rocznik Statystyczny Powiatu Zotow — Rocz Stat Pow Zot
Rocznik Teologiczny Slyska Opolskiego — RTSO
Rocznik Torunski — RTor
Rocznik Wojskowego Instytutu Higieny i Epidemiologii [*Poland*] — Rocz Wojsk Inst Hig Epidemiol
Rocznik Wolnej Mysli — RWM
Rocznik Wroclawski — Rocz Wroclaw
Rocznik Wyzszej Szkoly Rolniczej Poznaniu — Roczn Wyz Szk Roln Poznan
Roczniki Akademii Medycznej Imienia Juliana Marchlewskiego w Bialymstoku — RJMBA
Roczniki Akademii Medycznej Imienia Juliana Marchlewskiego w Bialymstoku — Rocz Akad Med Bialymstoku
Roczniki Akademii Medycznej Imienia Juliana Marchlewskiego w Bialymstoku — Rocz Akad Med Juliana Marchlewskiego Bialymstoku
Roczniki Akademii Medycznej Imienia Juliana Marchlewskiego w Bialymstoku. Suplement — RMJSA
Roczniki Akademii Medycznej Imienia Juliana Marchlewskiego w Bialymstoku. Suplement — Rocz Akad Med Bialymstoku Supl
Roczniki Akademii Medycznej Imienia Juliana Marchlewskiego w Bialymstoku. Suplement — Rocz Akad Med Im Juliana Marchlewskiego Bialymstoku Supl
Roczniki Akademii Medycznej Imienia Juliana Marchlewskiego w Bialymstoku. Suplement — Rocz Akad Med Juliana Marchlewskiego Bialymstoku Supl
Roczniki Akademii Medycznej w Bialymstoku — Rocz Akad Med Bialymst
Roczniki Akademii Medycznej w Bialymstoku. Suplement — Rocz Akad Med Bialymst Supl
Roczniki Akademii Medycznej w Poznaniu — Rocz Akad Med Poznaniu
Roczniki Akademii Nauk Technicznych w Warszawie — Rocz Akad Nauk Tech Warszawie
Roczniki Akademii Rolniczej w Poznaniu — RARPC
Roczniki Akademii Rolniczej w Poznaniu [*Poland*] — Rocz Akad Roln Poznaniu
Roczniki Akademii Rolniczej w Poznaniu — Roczn Akad Roln Poznan
Roczniki Akademii Rolniczej w Poznaniu. Prace Habilitacyjne — Rocz Akad Roln Poznaniu Pr Habilitacyjne
Roczniki Akademii Rolniczej w Poznaniu. Rozprawy Naukowe — Rocz Akad Roln Poznaniu Rozpr Nauk
Roczniki Biblioteczne — Roczn Bibl
Roczniki Chemii — ROCHA
Roczniki Chemii — Rocz Chem
Roczniki Chemii — Roczn Chem
Roczniki Dziejow Spoleczno-Gospodarczych — RDSG
Roczniki Filozoficzne. Towarzystwo Naukowe Katolickiego Uniwersytetu Lubelskiego — RFKUL
Roczniki Gleboznawcze — Rocz Glebozn
Roczniki Gleboznawcze — Roczniki Glebozn
Roczniki Gleboznawcze — ROGLA
Roczniki Historyczne — RHist
Roczniki Historyczne — Rocz Hist
Roczniki Humanistyczne — RH
Roczniki Humanistyczne — Rocz Hum
Roczniki Humanistyczne — RoHum
Roczniki Humanistyczne Katolickiego Universytetu — RoczH
Roczniki Humanistyczne. Towarzystwo Naukowe Katolickiego Uniwersytetu Lubelskiego — RHKUL
Roczniki Humanistyczne Uniwersitetu Lubelskiego — RHUL
Roczniki Instytutu Handlu Wewnetrznego — Roczn Inst Handlu Wewn
Roczniki Instytutu Przemyslu Miesnego i Tluszczowego — Rocz Inst Przem Miesn Tluszczowego
Roczniki Instytutu Przemyslu Mleczarskiego [*Poland*] — Rocz Inst Przem Mlecz
Roczniki Nauk Rolniczych — Rocz Nauk Roln
Roczniki Nauk Rolniczych. A. Produkcja Roslinna — Roczn Nauk Roln A
Roczniki Nauk Rolniczych i Lesnych — Rocz Nauk Roln Les
Roczniki Nauk Rolniczych i Lesnych — Rocz Nauk Roln Lesn
Roczniki Nauk Rolniczych i Lesnych — Roczn Nauk Roln Lesn
Roczniki Nauk Rolniczych i Lesnych. Dodatek — Rocz Nauk Roln Lesn Dodatek
Roczniki Nauk Rolniczych. Seria A — Rocz Nauk Roln Ser A
Roczniki Nauk Rolniczych. Seria A. Produkcja Roslinna — Rocz Nauk Roln Ser A
Roczniki Nauk Rolniczych. Seria A. Produkcja Roslinna — Rocz Nauk Roln Ser A Prod Rosl
Roczniki Nauk Rolniczych. Seria A. Roslinna — Roczn Nauk Roln Ser A Rosl
Roczniki Nauk Rolniczych. Seria B. Zootechniczna — Rocz Nauk Roln Ser B
Roczniki Nauk Rolniczych. Seria B. Zootechniczna — Rocz Nauk Roln Ser B Zootech
Roczniki Nauk Rolniczych. Seria C. Mechznizacja Rolnictwa — Rocz Nauk Roln Ser C Mech Roln
Roczniki Nauk Rolniczych. Seria C. Technika Rolnicza — Rocz Nauk Roln Ser C
Roczniki Nauk Rolniczych. Seria C. Technika Rolnicza [*Continues Seria C. Mechznizacja Rolnictwa*] — Rocz Nauk Roln Ser C Tech Roln
Roczniki Nauk Rolniczych. Seria D. Monografie — Rocz Nauk Roln Ser D
Roczniki Nauk Rolniczych. Seria D. Monografie — Rocz Nauk Roln Ser D Monogr
Roczniki Nauk Rolniczych. Seria E. Ochrona Roslin — Rocz Nauk Roln Ser E
Roczniki Nauk Rolniczych. Seria E. Ochrona Roslin — Rocz Nauk Roln Ser E Ochr Rosl

Roczniki Nauk Rolniczych. Seria E. Weterynarii — Rocz Nauk Roln Ser E
Roczniki Nauk Rolniczych. Seria E. Weterynarii 1953-60 — Rocz Nauk Roln Ser E 1953-60
Roczniki Nauk Rolniczych. Seria F. Melioracji i Vzytkow Zielonych — Rocz Nauk Roln Ser F
Roczniki Nauk Rolniczych. Seria F. Melioracji i Vzytkow Zielonych — Rocz Nauk Roln Ser F Melio Vzytkow Zielonych
Roczniki Nauk Rolniczych. Seria H. Rybactwo — Rocz Nauk Roln Ser H
Roczniki Nauk Rolniczych. Seria H. Rybactwo — Rocz Nauk Roln Ser H Rybactwo
Roczniki Naukowe Akademii Medycznej w Lodzi — Rocz Nauk Akad Med Lodzi
Roczniki Naukowe Akademii Rolniczej w Poznaniu. Rozprawy Naukowe — Rocz Nauk Akad Roln Poznaniu Rozpr Nauk
Roczniki Naukowe. Wyzsza Szkola Wychowania Fizycznego w Gdansku — Rocz Nauk Wyzsza Szk Wychow Fiz Gdansku
Roczniki Naukowe Zootechniki — Rocz Nauk Zootech
Roczniki Naukowe Zootechniki. Monografie i Rozprawy — Rocz Nauk Zootech Monogr Rozpr
Roczniki Panstwowego Zakladu Higieny — Rocz Panstw Zakl Hig
Roczniki Panstwowego Zakladu Higieny — Roczn Panst Zakl Hig
Roczniki Panstwowego Zakladu Higieny — RPZHA
Roczniki Panstwowego Zakladu Higieny (Warszawa) — Rocz Panst Zakl Hig (Warszawa)
Roczniki Polskiego Towarzystwa Matematycznego. Seria I. Commentationes Mathematicae Prace Matematyczne — Comment Math Prace Mat
Roczniki Polskiego Towarzystwa Matematycznego. Seria II. Wiadomosci Matematyczne — Wiadom Mat 2
Roczniki Polskiego Towarzystwa Matematycznego. Seria III. Matematyka Stosowana — Mat Stos 3
Roczniki Pomorska Akademia Medyczna Imienia Generala Karola Swierczewskiego w Szczecinie — Rocz Pomor Akad Med
Roczniki Pomorska Akademia Medyczna Imienia Generala Karola Swierczewskiego w Szczecinie — Rocz Pomor Akad Med Im Gen Karola Swierczewskiego Szczecin
Roczniki Pomorska Akademia Medyczna Imienia Generala Karola Swierczewskiego w Szczecinie. Suplement — RPMSBZ
Roczniki Pomorskiej Akademii Medycznej w Szczecinie. Suplement — Rocz Pomor Akad Med Szczecinie Supl
Roczniki Technologii Chemii Zywnosci — Rocz Technol Chem Zywn
Roczniki Teologiczne Chrzescijanskiej Akademii Teologicznej — Roczn T Ch AT
Roczniki Teologiczno-Kanoniczne — Roc T Kan
Roczniki Teologiczno-Kanoniczne [*Lubin*] — RoTKan
Roczniki Teologiczno-Kanoniczne — RTK
Roczniki Teologiczno-Kanoniczne. Katolickiego Uniwersytetu Lubelskiego — RTKKUL
Roczniki Teologiczno-Kanoniczne. Katolickiego Uniwersytetu Lubelskiego — RTKL
Roczniki Towarzystwa Naukowego w Toruniu — RTNT
Roczniki Uniwersytetu Marie Curie-Sklodowskiej w Lublinie — Roczn Uniw Marie Curie Lubl
Roczniki Uniwersytetu Marii Curie-Sklodowskiej. Dzial A. Matematyka — Rocz Uniw Marii Curie Sklodowskiej Dzial A
Roczniki Uniwersytetu Marii Curie-Sklodowskiej. Dzial B. Geografia, Geologia, Mineralogia, i Petrografia — Rocz Uniw Marii Curie Sklodowskiej Dzial B
Roczniki Uniwersytetu Marii Curie-Sklodowskiej. Dzial C. Nauki Biologiczne — Rocz Uniw Marii Curie Sklodowskiej Dzial C
Roczniki Uniwersytetu Marii Curie-Sklodowskiej. Dzial C. Nauki Biologiczne. Dodatek — Rocz Uniw Marii Curie Sklodowskiej Dzial C Dodatek
Roczniki Uniwersytetu Marii Curie-Sklodowskiej. Dzial D. Nauki Lekarskie — Rocz Uniw Marii Curie Sklodowskiej Dzial D
Roczniki Uniwersytetu Marii Curie-Sklodowskiej. Dzial DD. Medycyna Weterynaryjna — Rocz Uniw Marii Curie Sklodowskiej Dzial DD
Roczniki Uniwersytetu Marii Curie-Sklodowskiej. Dzial E. Nauki Rolnicze — Rocz Uniw Marii Curie Sklodowskiej Dzial E
Roczniki Uniwersytetu Marii Curie-Sklodowskiej. Dzial E. Nauki Rolnicze. Dodatek — Rocz Uniw Marii Curie Sklodowskiej Dzial E Dodatek
Roczniki Uniwersytetu Marij Curie-Sklodowskiej. Dzial AA. Fizyka i Chemia — Rocz Uniw Marij Curi-Sklodowskiej Dzial AA
Roczniki Wyzszej Szkoly Rolniczej w Poznaniu — Rocz Wyzs Szkoly Roln Poznaniu
Roczniki Wyzszej Szkoly Rolniczej w Poznaniu — Rocz Wyzsz Roln Poznaniu
Roczniki Wyzszej Szkoly Rolniczej w Poznaniu. Prace Habilitacyjne — Rocz Wyzsz Szk Roln Poznaniu Pr Habilitacyjne
Rod and Gun and Canadian Silver Fox News — Rod and Gun and Canad Silver Fox News
Rodale's Organic Gardening — GROG
Rodd's Chemistry of Carbon Compounds [*Monograph*] — Rodds Chem Carbon Comp
Rodnoj i Russkij Jazyki v Nacional'noj Skole — RRJaNS
Rodo Kagaku — ROKAA
Rodo Kankei Minji Saibanreishu — Rominshu
Rodoeisei Kenkyujo Kenkyuhokoku — Rodo Kenky Kenky
Rodopskii Zbornik — Rodopskii Zbor
RoeFo. Fortschritte auf dem Gebiete der Roentgenstrahlen und der Nuklearmedizin — RFGND
RoeFo. Fortschritte auf dem Gebiete der Roentgenstrahlen und der Nuklearmedizin [*Germany*] — RoeFo Fortschr Geb Roentgenstr Nuklearmed
Roemische Historische Mitteilungen — RHistM
Roemische Historische Mitteilungen — RHM
Roemische Historische Mitteilungen — RoeHM
Roemische Historische Mitteilungen — Roem Hist Mitt
Roemische Limes in Oesterreich — R Li Oe
Roemische Limes in Oesterreich — RLOE
Roemische Mitteilungen — RM
Roemische [Abteilung] Mitteilungen des Deutschen Archaeologischen Instituts — Roem Mitt
Roemische Privatrecht — RPR
Roemische Quartalschrift fuer Christliche Altertumskunde und fuer Kirchengeschichte — R Q Ch A K
Roemische Quartalschrift fuer Christliche Altertumskunde und fuer Kirchengeschichte — Roe Q
Roemische Quartalschrift fuer Christliche Altertumskunde und fuer Kirchengeschichte — Roem Q
Roemische Quartalschrift fuer Christliche Altertumskunde und fuer Kirchengeschichte — Roem Q Schr
Roemische Quartalschrift fuer Christliche Altertumskunde und fuer Kirchengeschichte — Roem Qu
Roemische Quartalschrift fuer Christliche Altertumskunde und fuer Kirchengeschichte — Roemische Quartalschrift
Roemische Quartalschrift fuer Christliche Altertumskunde und fuer Kirchengeschichte — Rom Quart
Roemische Quartalschrift fuer Christliche Altertumskunde und fuer Kirchengeschichte — Rom Quartal Schrift
Roemische Quartalschrift fuer Christliche Altertumskunde und fuer Kirchengeschichte — RQ
Roemische Quartalschrift fuer Christliche Altertumskunde und fuer Kirchengeschichte — RQA
Roemische Quartalschrift fuer Christliche Altertumskunde und fuer Kirchengeschichte — RQAK
Roemische Quartalschrift fuer Christliche Altertumskunde und fuer Kirchengeschichte — RQCAK
Roemische Quartalschrift fuer Christliche Altertumskunde und fuer Kirchengeschichte — RQCAKG
Roemische Quartalschrift fuer Christliche Altertumskunde und fuer Kirchengeschichte — RQS
Roemische Quartalschrift fuer Kirchengeschichte — RQK
Roemische Quartalsschrift fuer Christliche Altertumskunde — Roem Quartschr Christl Altertskde
Roemische Quartalsschrift fuer Christliche Altertumskunde und Kirchengeschichte — Roem Quart Schr Christl Altertumskde
Roemische Rechtsgeschichte — RRG
Roemische Religionsgeschichte — RRG
Roemischen Inschriften und Bildwerke Wuertembergs — RIB Wuerttemb
Roemischen Inschriften und Bildwerke Wuertembergs — Roem Inschr Wuerttemb
Roemischen Inschriften von Tarraco — RIT
Roemischen Mosaiken in Deutschland — RMD
Roemisches Jahrbuch fuer Kunstgeschichte — Roem Jahr Kunstges
Roemisches Oesterreich — ROE
Roemisches Oesterreich. Jahresschrift der Oesterreichischen Gesellschaft fuer Archaeologie — RO
Roemisches Oesterreich. Jahresschrift der Oesterreichischen Gesellschaft fuer Archaeologie — Roem Oe
Roemisches Staatsrecht — Roem Staatsr
Roemisches Staatsrecht — Rom Staatsr
Roemisches Staatsrecht — RSR
Roemisches Staatsrecht — StR
Roemisches Strafrecht — R Str
Roemisches Strafrecht — Roem Strafr
Roemisches Strafrecht — Rom Strafr
Roemisches Zivilprozessrecht — Rz
Roemisches Zivilprozessrecht — RZPR
Roemisch-Germanische Forschungen — RGF
Roemisch-Germanische Forschungen — Roem Germ F
Roemisch-Germanische Kommission des Archaeologischen Instituts — RGKAI
Roemisch-Germanische Zentralmuseum (Mainz) — RGZM
Roemisch-Germanisches Korrespondenzblatt — RG KBl
Roemisch-Germanisches Korrespondenzblatt — RG Korr Bl
Roemisch-Germanisches Korrespondenzblatt — RG Korr Blatt
Roemisch-Germanisches Korrespondenzblatt — RGK
Roemisch-Germanisches Korrespondenzblatt — Roem Germ Korrbl
Roemisch-Germanisches Korrespondenzblatt — Rom Germ Korrbl
Roentgen Berichte — Roentgen Ber
Roentgen Laboratoriumspraxis — Roentgen Laboratoriumsprax
Roentgen Technology. Official Journal of the Indian Association of Radiological Technologists — Roentgen Technol
Roentgen-Blaetter — Roentgen-Bl
Roentgen-Blaetter. Klinik und Praxis — Roentgen Bl
Roentgenographische Duennschicht- und Oberflaechencharakterisierung — Roentgenogr Duennschicht Oberflaechencharakt
Roentgenpraxis — Roentgenprax
Roentgenpraxis — ROPXA
Roentgenstrahlen — ROEND
Roessing — RSSND
Rofo. Fortschritte auf dem Begiete der Rontgenstrahlen und der Neuen Bildgebenden Verfahren — Rofo Fortschr Beg Rontgenstr Neuen Bildgeb Verfahr
Rohm and Haas Reporter — Rohm & Haas Reptr
Rohm and Haas Reporter — Rohm Haas Rep
[*The*] **Rohmer Review** — TRR
Rohre, Rohrleitungsbau, Rohrleitungstransport — ROHRA
Rohre, Rohrleitungsbau, Rohrleitungstransport [*Germany*] — Rohre Rohrleitungsbau Rohrleitungstransp
Rohstoff und Umwelt. Vortraege des Internationalen Kongresses — Rohst Umwelt Vort Int Kongr
Rohstoff-Rundschau; Fachblatt des Gesamten Handels mit Altstoffen und Abfallstoffen, mit Ausfuehrlichen Berichten ueber die Internationalen Rohstoffmarkte und Altstoffmarkte — ALT
Rohstoffwirtschaftliche Landerberichte — Rohst Landerber

Rol Mikroelementov v Sel'skom Khozyaistve. Trudy Mezhvuzovskogo Soveshchaniya po Mikroelementam — Rol Mikroelem Selsk Khoz Tr Mezhvuz
Role of Fertilization in the Intensification of Agricultural Production. Proceedings. Congress. International Potash Institute — Role Fert Intensif Agric Prod Proc Congr Int Potash Inst
Role of Immunological Factors in Viral and Oncongenic Processes. International Symposium — Role Immunol Factors Viral Oncog Processes Int Symp
Role of Membranes in Secretory Processes. Proceedings. Meeting. International Conference on Biological Membranes — Role Membr Secretory Processes Proc Meet Int Conf Biol Membr
Role of Pharmacokinetics in Prenatal and Perinatal Toxicology. Symposium on Prenatal Development — Role Pharmacokinet Prenatal Perinat Toxicol Symp Prenatal De
Rolf Nevanlinna Institute Research Reports. A — Rolf Nevanlinna Inst Res Rep A
Rolling Stone — GROL
Rolling Stone — Roll Stone
Rolling Stone — RS
Rolling Stone — RSt
Rolnictwo a Ochrona Srodowiska Czlowieka, Materialy, z Konferencji Naukowej — Roln Ochr Srodowiska Czlowieka Mater Konf Nauk
Roma e l'Oriente — R & O
Roma Economica — Roma Econ
Roma. Rivista di Studi e di Vita Romana — RSVR
Roma Sotteranea Cristiana — RS
Roma Sotteranea Cristiana — RSC
Roma Sotterranea Cristiana — RSCr
Roma Sotterranea. Le Pitture delle Catacombe Romane — RSPCR
Romagna Medica — Romagna Med
Roman Imperial Coinage — RIC
Roman Inscriptions of Britain — RIB
Roman Republican Coin Hoards — RRCH
Roman Republican Coinage — RRC
Roman Revolution — RR
Roman Rule in Asia Minor to the End of Third Century After Christ — RRAM
Romana. Associazione Archeologica Romana — Boll Ass Arch Rom
Romana Contact — Rom Cont
Romana Contact. Organe Trimestriel de la Societe d'Archeologie — Rom Con
Romana Gens — RG
Romance Notes — Roman Note
Romance Notes — RomN
Romance Notes — RoN
Romance Philology — PRPY
Romance Philology — Roman Phil
Romance Philology — Roman Philol
Romance Philology — Romance Philol
Romance Philology — RomP
Romance Philology — RomPh
Romance Philology — ROP
Romance Philology — RP
Romance Philology — RPh
Romance Studies Presented to William Morton Day — W M Day Studies
Romania — R
Romania — Ro
Romania — Rom
Romania Comitetul de Stat al Geologiei. Institutul Geologic. Dari de Seama ale Sedintelor — Rom Com Geol Dari Seama Sedin
Romania Comitetul de Stat al Geologiei. Institutul Geologic. Studii Tehnice si Economice. Seria I. Mineralogie-Petrografie — Rom Inst Geol Stud Teh Econ Ser I
Romania Comitetul de Stat pentru Energia Nucleara. Institutul de Reactori Nucleari Energetici. Technical Report IRNE — Rom Com Stat Energ Nucl Inst React Nucl Energ Tech Rep IRNE
Romania during the 1981-1985 Development Plan — Romania P
Romania Institutul de Meteorologie si Hidrologie. Studii de Hidrogeologie — Rom Inst Meteorol Hidrol Stud Hidrogeol
Romania Institutul Geologic. Dari de Seama ale Sedintelor — Rom Inst Geol Dari Seama Sedin
Romania Institutul Geologic. Memorii — Rom Inst Geol Mem
Romania Institutul Geologic. Studii Tehnice si Economice. Seria B. Prepararea Minereurilor — Rom Inst Geol Stud Teh Econ Ser B
Romania Institutul Geologic. Studii Tehnice si Economice. Seria D. Prospectiuni Geofizice — Rom Inst Geol Stud Teh Econ Ser D
Romania Institutul Geologic. Studii Tehnice si Economice. Seria E — Rom Inst Geol Stud Teh Econ Ser E
Romania Literara — RoLit
Romania Literara [*Bucharest*] — RomLit
Romania. Oficiul de Stat pentru Inventii si Marci. Buletin de Informare pentru Inventii si Marci — Rom Of Stat Invent Marci Bul Inf Invent Marci
Romania. Oficiul de Stat pentru Inventii si Marci. Buletin pentru Inventii si Marci — Rom Of Stat Invent Marci Bul Invent Marci
Romania. Patent Document — Rom Pat Doc
Romania. Revue Consacree a l'Etude des Langues et Litteratures Romanes — Rom
Romania Today — Rom Today
Romania Today — ROTOB
Romania Viticola — Romania Vitic
Romanian Bulletin — Rom Bull
Romanian Engineering — ROW
Romanian Film — Romanian F
Romanian Foreign Trade — Rom Fgn Tr
Romanian Journal of Biophysics — Rom J Biophys
Romanian Journal of Chemistry — Rom J Chem
Romanian Journal of Endocrinology — Rom J Endocrinol
Romanian Journal of Gerontology and Geriatrics — Rom J Gerontol Geriatr
Romanian Journal of Internal Medicine — Rom J Intern Med
Romanian Journal of Medicine. Endocrinology — Rom J Med Endocrinol
Romanian Journal of Medicine. Internal Medicine — Rom J Med Intern Med
Romanian Journal of Medicine. Neurology and Psychiatry — Rom J Med Neurol Psychiatry
Romanian Journal of Medicine. Virology — Rom J Med Virol
Romanian Journal of Morphology and Embryology — Rom J Morphol Embryol
Romanian Journal of Morphology, Embryology, and Physiology — RMEPDZ
Romanian Journal of Morphology, Embryology, and Physiology. Morphology and Embryology — Rom J Morphol
Romanian Journal of Morphology, Embryology, and Physiology. Physiology — Rom J Morphol Embryol Physiol Physiol
Romanian Journal of Neurology and Psychiatry — Rom J Neurol Psychiatry
Romanian Journal of Physics — Romanian J Phys
Romanian Journal of Physiology — Rom J Physiol
Romanian Journal of Technical Sciences. Applied Mechanics — Rom J Tech Sci Appl Mech
Romanian Journal of Virology — Rom J Virol
Romanian Medical Review — Rom Med Rev
Romanian Reports in Physics — Romanian Rep Phys
Romanian Review — Romanian R
Romanian Review — RoR
Romanic Review — PROM
Romanic Review — Rom Rev
Romanic Review — Roman R
Romanic Review — Roman Rev
Romanic Review — RomR
Romanic Review — ROR
Romanic Review — RR
Romanic Review Quarterly — RRQ
Romanica Gandensia — RGand
Romanica Gandensia — Rom G
Romanica Gothoburgensia — RGo
Romanica Helvetica — RHel
Romanische Bibliothek — Roman Bibl
Romanische Bibliothek — Roman Biblioth
Romanische Forschungen — RF
Romanische Forschungen — RForsch
Romanische Forschungen — ROF
Romanische Forschungen — Rom Forsch
Romanische Forschungen — Roman Forsc
Romanische Forschungen — Roman Forsch
Romanische Forschungen — RomF
Romanische Studien — R Stud
Romanische Studien — Roman Stud
Romanische Studien — RS
Romanische Texte — Rom Texte
Romanistica Pragensia — RPrag
Romanistische Arbeitshefte — RA
Romanistische Versuche und Vorarbeiten — RVV
Romanistische Zeitschrift fuer Literaturgeschichte [*Cahiers d'Histoire des Litteratures Romanes*] — Roman Z Lit
Romanistisches Jahrbuch — RJ
Romanistisches Jahrbuch — RJb
Romanistisches Jahrbuch — ROJ
Romanistisches Jahrbuch — RomJ
Romanobarbarica — Rom Barb
Romanobarbarica. Contributi allo Studio dei Rapporti Culturali tra il Mondo Latino e Mondo Barbarico — Romanobarbar
Romano-Germanskaja Filologija — RGFil
Romanoslavica — RomSl
Romanoslavica — RSlav
Romanskoe i Germanskoe Iazykoznanie [*Minsk*] — RiGl
Romantic Movement — Romant Move
Romantic Reassessment — RcRt
Romanticism Past and Present — RP and P
Rombach Hochschul Paperback — Rombach Hochsch Paperback
Rome e l'Oriente — Re O
Rond-Point (Port-au-Prince) — Rond Point Port Au Prince
Roofing/Siding/Insulation — RSI
Roorkee University. Research Journal — Roorkee Univ Res J
Roosevelt Wild Life Bulletin — Roosevelt Wild Life Bull
Roots Digest — Roots Dig
Ropa a Uhlie — ROUHA
Rororo Science — Rororo Sci
Rosario [*Ferrara*] — Ros
Rose Annual. Royal National Rose Society — Rose Annu R Natl Rose Soc
Rose Technic. Rose Polytechnic Institute — Rose Techn
Roskill's Letter from China — Roskills Lett China
Rospravy Kralovske Ceske Spolecnosti Nauk — RKCSN
Ross Conference on Medical Research. Report — Ross Conf Med Res Rep
Ross Conference on Pediatric Research. Report — Ross Conf Pediatr Res Rep
Ross Ice Shelf Project. Technical Reports — RISPT
Rossiiskaya Akademiya Nauk. Izvestiya. Seriya Matematicheskaya — Izv Ross Akad Nauk Ser Mat
Rossija i Slavjanstvo — RiSL
Rost i Defekty Metallicheskikh Kristallov. Materialy Vsesoyuznogo Soveshchaniya po Rosty i Nesovershenstvam Metallicheskikh Kristallov — Rost Defekty Met Krist Mater Vses Soveshch
Rost i Legirovanie Poluprovodnikovykh Kristallov i Plenok. Materialy Vsesoyuznogo Simpoziuma po Protsessam Rosta i Sinteza Poluprovodnikovykh Kristallov i Plenok — Rost Legir Poluprovodn Krist Plenok Mater Vses Simp
Rost i Ustoichivost Rastenii — Rost Ustoich Rast

Rost i Ustoichivost Rastenii Respublikanskii Mezhvedomstvennyi Sbornik — Rost Ustoich Rast Respub Mezhved Sb
Rost Kristallov — RKANA
Rost Kristallov — Rost Krist
ROSTA [*Victoria. Road Safety and Traffic Authority*] **Bulletin** — ROSTA Bull
Roster of Organizations in the Field of Automatic Computing Machinery — Roster Organ Field Autom Comput Mach
Rostlinna Vyroba — Rostl Vyroba
Rostlinna Vyroba — ROVYA
Rostlinna Vyroba-Ceskoslovenska Akademie Zemedelska. Ustav Vedeckotechnickych Informaci pro Zemedelstvi — Rostl Vyroba Cesk Akad Zemed Ustav Vedeckotech Inf Zemed
Rostocker Mathematisches Kolloquium — Rostock Math Kolloq
Rostocker Physikalische Manuskripte — Rostocker Phys Manuskr
Rostovskaya Gidrometeorologicheskaya Observatoriya. Sbornik Rabot — Rostov Gidrometeorol Obs Sb Rab
Rostovskii Gosudarstvennyi Meditsinskii Institut. Sbornik Nauchnykh Trudov — Rostov Gos Med Inst Sb Nauchn Tr
Rostovskii-Na-Donu Gosudarstvennyi Pedagogiceskii Institut. Fiziko-Matematiceskii Fakultet Ucenye Zapiski — Rostov-Na Donu Gos Ped Inst Fiz Mat Fak Ucen Zap
Rostovskii-Na-Donu Gosudarstvennyi Universitet. Ucenyi Zapiski — Rostov-Na-Donu Gos Univ Ucen Zap
Rostovye Veshchestva i Rost Rastenii — Rostovye Veshchestva Rost Rast
Rotation Method in Crystallography — Rotation Method Crystallogr
Rotenburg Fermentation Symposium — Rotenburg Ferment Symp
Rotenburger Schriften — Rotenburg Schr
Rotenburger Symposium — Rotenburger Symp
Rothamsted Experimental Station. Report — Rothamsted Exp Stn Rep
Rothamsted Experimental Station. Report. Part 1 — Rothamsted Exp Stn Rep Part 1
Rothamsted Experimental Station. Report. Part 2 — Rothamsted Exp Stn Rep Part 2
Rothmill Quarterly — Rothmill Q
Roths Jahresbericht ueber die Leistungen und Fortschritte auf dem Gebiete des Militaersanitaetswesens — Jber Leistg Fortschr Milsanitw
Roths Jahresbericht ueber die Leistungen und Fortschritte auf dem Gebiete des Militaersanitaetswesens — RothsJber
Rotor and Wing International — Rotor & W
Rotterdam — RBZ
Rotterdam Europoort Delta — RBY
Rough Notes — RN
Rough Notes — RNO
Rough Times [*Formerly, Radical Therapist*] — RT
Rough Weather — RW
Roumanian Archives of Microbiology and Immunology — Roum Arch Microbiol Immunol
Roumanian Journal of Morphology and Embryology — Roum J Morphol Embryol
Roumeliotiko Hemerologio — RoH
Round Table — ROTAD
Round Table — Round Tab
Round Table [*London*] — RT
Round Table [*Australia*] — RT
Round Table Seminar. International Mineral Processing Congress — Round Table Semin Int Miner Process Congr
Roundup [*United States*] — RNDPD
Route et la Circulation Routiere — Route Circ Routiere
Roux Archiv fuer Entwicklungsmechanik der Organismen — Roux Arch Entwicklungsmech Org
Roux Archiv fuer Entwicklungsmechanik der Organismen — Roux Archiv EntwMech Organ
Roux's Archives of Developmental Biology — Roux's Arch Dev Biol
Roux's Archives of Developmental Biology — WRABDT
Rovartani Koezlemenyek — Rov Koezlem
Rovartani Lapok — Rovart Lapok
Rowett Research Institute. Annual Report. Studies in Animal Nutrition and Allied Sciences — Rowett Res Inst Annu Rep Stud Anim Nutr Allied Sci
Rowman and Allanheld Probability and Statistics Series — Rowman & Allanheld Probab Statist Ser
Rowman and Littlefield Probability and Statistics Series — Rowman & Littlefield Probab Statist Ser
Rowohlts Bildmonographien — Rowohlts Bildmonograph
Rowohlts Monographien — RM
Rowohlts's Monographien — RoMo
Royal Aeronautical Society. Journal — Roy Aeronaut Soc J
Royal Agricultural and Horticultural Society of South Australia. Proceedings — Proc R Agric Hort Soc S Aust
Royal Agricultural Society (Cairo). Bulletin. Technical Section — R Agric Soc (Cairo) Bull Tech Sect
Royal Agricultural Society of Kenya. Quarterly Journal — R Agric Soc Kenya QJ
Royal Air Force [*London*] — RAF
Royal Aircraft Establishment. List of Reports — R Aircr Establ List Reports
Royal Aircraft Establishment. Technical Report (Great Britain) — R Aircr Establ Tech Rep GB
Royal Anthropological Institute. Newsletter — RAIN
Royal Anthropological Institute of Great Britain and Ireland. Journal — Roy Anthropol Inst J
Royal Archaeological Institute — R Arch Inst
Royal Architectural Institute of Canada. Journal — Roy Arch Inst Can J
Royal Asiatic Society. Bombay Branch. Journal — RASB
Royal Asiatic Society of Great Britain and Ireland. Journal — RAS
Royal Astronomical Society. Geophysical Journal — R Astron Soc Geophys J
Royal Astronomical Society. Geophysical Journal — Royal Astron Soc Geophys Jour
Royal Astronomical Society. Memoirs — R Astron Soc Mem
Royal Astronomical Society. Memoirs — Roy Astron Soc Mem
Royal Astronomical Society. Monthly Notices. Geophysical Supplements — Royal Astron Soc Monthly Notices Geophys Supp
Royal Astronomical Society of Canada. Journal — R Astron Soc Can J
Royal Astronomical Society of Canada. Journal — Royal Astron Soc Canada Jour
Royal Astronomical Society of Canada. Selected Papers and Proceedings — R Astron Soc Can Pr
Royal Astronomical Society. Quarterly Journal — Royal Astron Soc Quart Jour
Royal Australian Air Force Reserve. Magazine — RAAF Reserve
Royal Australian Army. Educational Corps. Newsletter — RAAEC Nletter
Royal Australian Army. Educational Corps. Newsletter — Royal Aust Army Ed Corps News
Royal Australian Chemical Institute — R Aust Chem Inst
Royal Australian Chemical Institute. Journal and Proceedings — R Aust Chem Inst J Proc
Royal Australian Chemical Institute. Journal and Proceedings — Royal Aust Chem Inst J & Proc
Royal Australian Chemical Institute. Journal and Proceedings. Supplement — R Aust Chem Inst J Proc Suppl
Royal Australian Chemical Institute. Proceedings — R Aust Chem Inst Proc
Royal Australian Chemical Institute. Proceedings — Royal Aust Chem Inst Proc
Royal Australian Historical Society. Journal — Jl R Aust Hist Soc
Royal Australian Historical Society. Journal — RAHS
Royal Australian Historical Society. Journal — Roy Aust Hist J
Royal Australian Historical Society. Journal and Proceedings — J Proc R Aust Hist Soc
Royal Australian Historical Society. Journal and Proceedings — RAHSJ
Royal Australian Historical Society. Journal and Proceedings — Roy Aust Hist Soc J Proc
Royal Australian Historical Society. Journal and Proceedings — Royal Aust Hist Soc J
Royal Australian Historical Society. Journal and Proceedings — Royal Aust Hist Soc J & Proc
Royal Australian Historical Society. Newsletter — Newsletter R Aust Hist Soc
Royal Australian Planning Institute. Journal — Royal Australian Planning Inst Jnl
Royal Bank of Canada. Monthly Letter — Royal Bank Can Mo Letter
Royal Botanic Gardens (Kew). Notes from the Jodrell Laboratory — R Bot Gard (Kew) Notes Jodrell Lab
Royal Botanical Garden of Edinburgh. Notes — R Bot Garden Edinb Notes
Royal Canadian Dental Corps. Quarterly — R Can Dent Corps Q
Royal Canadian Institute. Transactions — Roy Can Inst Trans
Royal Canadian Mounted Police Quarterly — RCMPQ
Royal Canadian Navy. Monthly Review — RCNMR
Royal Central Asian Society. Journal — RCAJ
Royal College of Forestry. Department of Reforestation. Research Notes — R Coll For Dep Refor Res Notes
Royal College of General Practitioners. Journal — RCGJA
Royal College of Music. Magazine — RCM
Royal College of Obstetricians and Gynaecologists. Proceedings. Study Group — R Coll Obstet Gynaecol Proc Study Group
Royal College of Pathologists of Australia. Broadsheet — R Coll Pathol Aust Broadsheet
Royal College of Pathologists Symposia — R Coll Pathol Symp
Royal College of Physicians of London. Journal — RCPJA
Royal College of Science and Technology (Glasgow). Research Report — R Coll Sci Technol (Glasg) Res Rep
Royal College of Surgeons in Ireland. Journal — R Coll Surg Ir J
Royal Colonial Institute. Proceedings — Roy Col Inst Proc
Royal Colonial Institute Proceedings — Royal Col Inst Pr
Royal Commission on Historical Manuscripts. Reports — Hist MSS Comm Rpts
Royal Correspondence in the Hellenistic Period — RC
Royal Dublin Society. Economic Proceedings — R Dublin Soc Econ Proc
Royal Dublin Society. Journal of Life Sciences — R Dublin Soc J Life Sci
Royal Dublin Society. Journal. Scientific Proceedings — R Dublin Soc J Sc Pr
Royal Dublin Society. Report — R Dublin Soc Rep
Royal Dublin Society. Scientific Proceedings — R Dublin Soc Sci Proc
Royal Economics Society Prize Monograph — Royal Econom Soc Prize Monograph
Royal Empire Society. News — Royal Empire Soc News
Royal Engineers Journal — R Eng J
Royal Engineers Journal — REJ
Royal Engineers Journal — Roy Eng J
Royal Engineers Journal — RYEJA
Royal Entomological Society of London. Symposia — R Entomol Soc London Symp
Royal Geographical Society — RGS
Royal Geographical Society of Australasia. South Australian Branch. Proceedings — Proc S Aust Brch R Geogr Soc Australas
Royal Geographical Society of Australasia. South Australian Branch. Proceedings — RGS Austsia SA Br Proc
Royal Geographical Society of Australasia. South Australian Branch. Proceedings — Royal Geog Soc Asia SA Branch Proc
Royal Geographical Society. Proceedings — R Geog Soc Pr
Royal Geographical Society. Proceedings — Roy Geog Soc Proc
Royal Geological Society of Cornwall. Transactions — R G Soc Cornwall Tr
Royal Geological Society of Ireland. Journal — R G Soc Ireland J
Royal Geological Society of Ireland. Journal — R Geol Soc Ir J
Royal Greek Portrait Coins — RGP
Royal Greenwich Observatory. Bulletins — R Greenwich Obs Bull
Royal Historical and Archaeological Society of Ireland. Journal — R Hist Arch Soc Ir J
Royal Historical Society — R Hist Soc
Royal Historical Society of Queensland. Historical Miscellanea — Roy Hist Soc Qld Hist Misc

Royal Historical Society of Queensland. Historical Miscellanea — Royal Hist Soc Q Hist Misc
Royal Historical Society of Queensland. Journal — Jl R Hist Soc Qd
Royal Historical Society of Queensland. Journal — RHSQ
Royal Historical Society of Queensland. Journal — RHSQJ
Royal Historical Society of Queensland. Journal — Roy Hist Soc Qld J
Royal Historical Society of Queensland. Journal — Royal Hist Soc QJ
Royal Historical Society of Victoria. Newsletter — Roy Hist Soc Vic News
Royal Historical Society. Transactions — RHS
Royal Historical Society. Transactions — RHSTr
Royal Historical Society. Transactions — Roy His S
Royal Historical Society. Transactions — Roy Hist Soc Trans
Royal Historical Society. Transactions — Royal Hist Soc Trans
Royal Horticultural Society. Journal — Roy Hort Soc J
Royal Horticultural Society. Journal — Royal Hort Soc J
Royal Inscriptions from Sumer and Akkad — RISA
Royal Institute of British Architects. Journal — RIBA J
Royal Institute of British Architects. Journal — Roy Inst Brit Arch J
Royal Institute of British Architects. Transactions — Royal Inst of British Archts Trans
Royal Institute of Chemistry. Lecture Series — R Inst Chem Lect Ser
Royal Institute of Chemistry. Lectures, Monographs, and Reports — R Inst Chem Lect Monogr Rep
Royal Institute of Navigation. Journal of Navigation [*London*] — J Navigation
Royal Institute of Philosophy. Lectures — Roy Inst Ph
Royal Institute of Philosophy Supplement — Roy Inst Philos Suppl
Royal Institute of Public Health and Hygiene. Journal — R Inst Public Health Hyg J
Royal Institution of Great Britain. Proceedings — R Inst GB Proc
Royal Institution of Great Britain. Proceedings — R Inst Pr
Royal Institution of Great Britain. Proceedings — RIGB
Royal Institution of Naval Architects (London). Supplementary Papers — R Inst Nav Archit (London) Suppl Pap
Royal Institution of Naval Architects [*London*]. Quarterly Transactions — R Inst Nav Archit Q Trans
Royal Institution of Naval Architects [*London*]. Quarterly Transactions — Roy Inst Nav Architects Quart Trans
Royal Institution of Naval Architects [*London*]. Supplementary Papers — R Inst Nav Archit Suppl Pap
Royal Irish Academy. Proceedings — R Irish Ac Pr
Royal Irish Academy. Proceedings — Roy Irish Acad Proc
Royal Irish Academy. Proceedings. Section B — R Ir Acad Proc Sect B
Royal Irish Academy Transactions — R Ir Acad Trans
[*The*] **Royal Magazine** — Royal
Royal Melbourne Hospital. Clinical Reports — R Melbourne Hosp Clin Rep
Royal Meteorological Society. Quarterly Journal — Roy Meteorol Soc Q J
Royal Microscopical Society. Journal — Roy Micros Soc J
Royal Microscopical Society. Proceedings — Roy Microscop Soc Proc
Royal Microscopical Society. Proceedings — Royal Microscopical Soc Proc
Royal Military College of Canada. Civil Engineering Research Report — R Mil Coll Can Civ Eng Res Rep
Royal Military College of Canada. Civil Engineering Research Report — RCVRB
Royal Musical Association. Proceedings — RMA
Royal Musical Association. Proceedings — RMA Proc
Royal Musical Association. Research Chronicle — RMA Research
Royal Musical Association. Research Chronicle — RMARC
Royal Numismatic Society. Special Publication — R Numis Soc Spec Publ
Royal Observatory. Annals — R Obs Ann
Royal Observatory. Bulletins — R Obs Bull
Royal Ontario Museum. Division of Zoology and Palaeontology. Contributions — Royal Ontario Mus Div Zoology and Palaeontology Contr
Royal Ontario Museum. Journal — R Ont Mus J
Royal Ontario Museum. Life Sciences. Contributions — R Ont Mus Life Sci Contrib
Royal Ontario Museum. Life Sciences. Miscellaneous Publications — R Ont Mus Life Sci Misc Publ
Royal Ontario Museum. Life Sciences. Occasional Paper — R Ont Mus Life Sci Occas Pap
Royal Ontario Museum of Zoology and Paleontology. Contributions — R Ont Mus Zool Paleontol Contrib
Royal Perth Hospital. Journal — Royal Perth Hospital J
Royal Perth Hospital. Journal — RPHJ
Royal Photographic Society of Great Britain. Library Catalogue. Part 2. Subject Catalogue — RPS Subj Cat
Royal Physical Society of Edinburgh. Proceedings — R Phys Soc Edinb Pr
Royal Physical Society of Edinburgh. Proceedings — R Phys Soc Edinb Proc
Royal Prince Alfred Hospital. Journal — Royal Prince Alfred Hospital J
Royal Sanitary Institute. Journal — R San Inst Jnl
Royal Sanitary Institute. Journal — R Sanit Inst J
Royal School of Mines. Journal [*England*] — R Sch Mines J
Royal School of Mines. Journal — RSMJA
Royal Scottish Museum. Information Series. Geology — R Scott Mus Inf Ser Geol
Royal Signals and Radar Establishment. Newsletter and Research Review — R Signals Radar Establ Newsl Res Rev
Royal Society for the Promotion of Health. Health Congress. Papers — R Soc Health Health Congr Pap
Royal Society for the Promotion of Health. Journal — R Soc Promot Health J
Royal Society of Antiquaries of Ireland. Journal — R Soc Antiq Ir J
Royal Society of Arts. Journal — Roy Soc Arts J
Royal Society of Arts. Journal — Royal Soc Arts Jnl
Royal Society of Arts. Journal — RSA
Royal Society of Canada. Proceedings — R Soc Can Proc
Royal Society of Canada. Proceedings — Royal Soc Canada Proc
Royal Society of Canada. Proceedings and Transactions — R Soc Can Proc Trans
Royal Society of Canada. Proceedings and Transactions — Roy Soc Can
Royal Society of Canada. Proceedings and Transactions — Roy Soc of Canada Trans
Royal Society of Canada. Special Publications — R Soc Can Spec Publ
Royal Society of Canada. Symposium — R Soc Can Symp
Royal Society of Canada. Transactions — R Soc Can
Royal Society of Canada. Transactions — RSCT
Royal Society of Chemistry. Annual Reports. Section A. Inorganic Chemistry — R Soc Chem Annu Rep Sect A Inorg Chem
Royal Society of Chemistry. Annual Reports. Section B. Organic Chemistry — R Soc Chem Annu Rep Sect B
Royal Society of Chemistry. Annual Reports. Section C. Physical Chemistry — R Soc Chem Annu Rep Sect C
Royal Society of Chemistry. Faraday Discussions — R Soc Chem Faraday Discuss
Royal Society of Chemistry. Faraday Symposia — R Soc Chem Faraday Symp
Royal Society of Chemistry. Special Publication — R Soc Chem Spec Publ
Royal Society of Edinburgh. Communications. Physical Sciences — R Soc Edinburgh Commun Phys Sci
Royal Society of Edinburgh. Proceedings. Section A. Mathematical and Physical Sciences — R Soc Edinburgh Proc Sect A Math Phys Sci
Royal Society of Edinburgh. Proceedings. Section A. Mathematics — R Soc Edinburgh Proc Sect A Math
Royal Society of Edinburgh. Proceedings. Section B. Biology — R Soc Edinb Proc Sect B
Royal Society of Edinburgh. Proceedings. Section B. Natural Environment — R Soc Edinburgh Proc Sect B Nat Environ
Royal Society of Edinburgh. Transactions — R Soc Edinburgh Trans
Royal Society of Edinburgh. Transactions — Roy Soc Edinb Trans
Royal Society of Edinburgh. Transactions — Roy Soc of Edinburgh Trans
Royal Society of Edinburgh. Transactions. Earth Sciences — R Soc Edinburgh Trans Earth Sci
Royal Society of Health. Health Congress. Papers for Discussion — R Soc Health Health Congr Pap Discuss
Royal Society of Health. Journal — R Soc Health J
Royal Society of Health. Journal — Roy Soc Hea
Royal Society of Health. Journal — Royal Soc Hlth J
Royal Society of Health. Journal — Royal Soc of Health Jnl
Royal Society of Health. Journal — RSHEA
Royal Society of Health. Journal — RSOHJ
Royal Society of London. Philosophical Transactions — R Soc Lond Philos Trans
Royal Society of London. Philosophical Transactions — Roy Soc Lond Philos Trans
Royal Society of London. Philosophical Transactions — Roy Soc of London Philos Trans
Royal Society of London. Philosophical Transactions. Series A — R Soc Lond Philos Trans Ser A
Royal Society of London. Philosophical Transactions. Series B — R Soc Lond Philos Trans Ser B
Royal Society of London. Proceedings — R Soc London Proc
Royal Society of London. Proceedings — Roy Soc Lond Proc
Royal Society of London. Proceedings. Series A. Mathematical and Physical Sciences — R Soc London Proc A
Royal Society of London. Proceedings. Series B. Biological Sciences — R Soc Lond Proc Ser B
Royal Society of London. Proceedings. Series B. Biological Sciences — R Soc London Proc Ser B
Royal Society of Medicine. Journal — R Soc Med J
Royal Society of Medicine Services Limited International Congress and Symposium Series — R Soc Med Serv Ltd Int Congr Symp Ser
Royal Society of New South Wales. Journal — Roy Soc NSW J
Royal Society of New South Wales. Journal and Proceedings — J Roy Soc NSW
Royal Society of New South Wales. Journal and Proceedings — Roy Soc NSW J & Proc
Royal Society of New South Wales. Journal and Proceedings — Roy Soc of New South Wales Jour and Proc
Royal Society of New South Wales. Journal and Proceedings — Royal Soc NSW J & Proc
Royal Society of New South Wales. Monograph — R Soc NSW Monogr
Royal Society of New Zealand. Bulletin — R Soc NZ Bull
Royal Society of New Zealand. Bulletin — Roy Soc NZ Bull
Royal Society of New Zealand. Journal — R Soc NZJ
Royal Society of New Zealand. Journal — Roy Soc NZ J
Royal Society of New Zealand. Proceedings — R Soc NZ Proc
Royal Society of New Zealand. Proceedings — Roy Soc NZ Proc
Royal Society of New Zealand. Transactions — Roy Soc NZ Trans
Royal Society of New Zealand. Transactions and Proceedings — R Soc NZ Trans Proc
Royal Society of New Zealand. Transactions. Botany — Roy Soc NZ Trans Bot
Royal Society of New Zealand. Transactions. Earth Sciences — Roy Soc NZ Trans Earth Sci
Royal Society of New Zealand. Transactions. General — Roy Soc NZ Trans Gen
Royal Society of New Zealand. Transactions. Geology — Roy Soc NZ Trans Geol
Royal Society of New Zealand. Transactions. Zoology — Roy Soc NZ Trans Zool
Royal Society of Queensland. Proceedings — Proc Roy Soc QD
Royal Society of Queensland. Proceedings — R Soc Queensl Proc
Royal Society of Queensland. Proceedings — Roy Soc Qld Proc
Royal Society of Queensland. Proceedings — Royal Soc Q Proc
Royal Society of South Africa. Transactions — R Soc S Afr Trans
Royal Society of South Africa. Transactions — Roy Soc So Africa Trans

Royal Society of South Australia. Transactions — R Soc S Aust Trans
Royal Society of South Australia. Transactions — Roy Soc SA Trans
Royal Society of South Australia. Transactions — Royal Soc SA Trans
Royal Society of South Australia. Transactions — Trans Roy Soc S Aust
Royal Society of Tasmania. Papers and Proceedings — Pap Roy Soc Tasm
Royal Society of Tasmania. Papers and Proceedings — R Soc Tasmania Pap Proc
Royal Society of Tasmania. Papers and Proceedings — Roy Soc Tas Papers
Royal Society of Tasmania. Papers and Proceedings — Royal Soc Tas Papers & Proc
Royal Society of Tasmania. Papers and Proceedings — Royal Soc Tasmania Papers and Proc
Royal Society of Tasmania. Special Publications — Spec Pub R Soc Tasm
Royal Society of Victoria. Proceedings — Proc R Soc VIC
Royal Society of Victoria. Proceedings — Proc Roy Soc Vict
Royal Society of Victoria. Proceedings — R Soc Victoria Proc
Royal Society of Victoria. Proceedings — Roy Soc Vic Proc
Royal Society of Victoria. Proceedings — Roy Soc Victoria Proc
Royal Society of Victoria. Proceedings — Royal Soc Vic Proc
Royal Society of Victoria. Proceedings — Royal Soc Victoria Proc
Royal Society of Western Australia. Journal — J R Soc W Aust
Royal Society of Western Australia. Journal — J Roy Soc W Aust
Royal Society of Western Australia. Journal — R Soc West Aust J
Royal Society of Western Australia. Journal — Roy Soc WA J
Royal Society. Proceedings. Series A. Mathematical and Physical Sciences — PLLAA
Royal Statistical Society. Journal — Roy Stat Soc J
Royal Statistical Society. Journal — RSS
Royal Statistical Society Lecture Note Series — Roy Statist Soc Lecture Note Ser
Royal Stuart Papers — R Stuart Pap
Royal Swaziland Society of Science and Technology. Journal — R Swaziland Soc Sci Technol J
Royal Swedish Academy of Engineering Sciences. Proceedings — R Swed Acad Eng Sci Proc
Royal Swedish Institute for Engineering Research. Proceedings — R Swed Inst Eng Res Proc
Royal Technical College. Metallurgical Club. Journal — R Tech Coll Metall Club J
Royal Television Society. Journal — R Telev Soc J
Royal Television Society. Journal — Roy Telev Soc J
Royal Tombs of the First Dynasty — RT
Royal Tombs of the First Dynasty — RTD
Royal Town Planning Institute. Journal — Roy Town Plan Inst
Royal Town Planning Institute. Journal — RTPI J
Royal United Service Institution. Journal — Roy United Serv Inst J
Royal United Service Institution of India. Journal — USI
Royal Veterinary and Agricultural University. Sterility Research Institute. Annual Report — R Vet Agric Univ Steril Res Inst Annu Rep
Royal Veterinary and Agricultural University. Yearbook (Copenhagen) — R Vet Agric Univ Yearb (Copenhagen)
Royal Western Australian Historical Society. Journal — RWAHSJ
Royal Western Australian Historical Society. Journal and Proceedings — Roy West Aust Hist Soc J Proc
Royal Zoological Society of New South Wales. Proceedings — Proc Roy Zool Soc NSW
Royal Zoological Society of New South Wales. Proceedings — Roy Zool Soc NSW Proc
Royal Zoological Society of New South Wales. Proceedings — Royal Zoological Soc NSW Proc
Royalauto [*Royal Automobile Club of Victoria*] **Journal** — Royalauto
Royalton Review — Royalton R
Rozhledy v Chirurgii — ROCIA
Rozhledy v Chirurgii — Rozhl Chir
Rozhledy v Tuberkulose a v Nemocech Plicnich — Rozhl Tuberk Nemocech Plicn
Rozpravy Ceske Akademie Cisare Frantiska Josefa Pro Vedy, Slovesnost a Umeni. Trida 2. Vedy Mathematicke, Prirodni — Rozpr Ceske Acad Cisare Frantiska Josefa Vedy Tr 2 Vedy Math
Rozpravy Ceskoslovenske Akademie Ved — RCAV
Rozpravy Ceskoslovenske Akademie Ved — RCSAV
Rozpravy Ceskoslovenske Akademie Ved — Roz Cesk Akad
Rozpravy Ceskoslovenske Akademie Ved — Rozpravy CSAV
Rozpravy Ceskoslovenske Akademie Ved. Rada Matematickych a Prirodnich Ved — RCAVA
Rozpravy Ceskoslovenske Akademie Ved. Rada Matematickych a Prirodnich Ved — Rozpr Cesk Akad Ved Rada Mat Prir Ved
Rozpravy Ceskoslovenske Akademie Ved. Rada Technickych Ved — RCVTA
Rozpravy Ceskoslovenske Akademie Ved. Rada Technickych Ved [*Czechoslovakia*] — Rozpr Cesk Akad Rada Tech Ved
Rozpravy Ceskoslovenske Akademie Ved. Rada Technickych Ved — Rozpr Cesk Akad Ved Rada Tech Ved
Rozpravy Narodniho Technickeho Muzea v Praze — Roz Narod Tech Muz Praze
Rozpravy Statniho Geologickeho Ustavu Ceskoslovenske Republiky — Rozpr Statniho Geol Ustavu Cesk Repub
Rozpravy Ustredniho Ustavu Geologickeho — Rozpr Ustred Ustavu Geol
Rozprawy. Akademia Rolnicza w Szczecinie — Rozpr Akad Roln Szczecinie
Rozprawy Akademii Umiejetnosci. Wydzial Matematyczno-Przyrodniczy — Rozpr Akad Umiejetn Wydz Mat Przyr
Rozprawy Elektrotechniczne — Rozpr Elektrotech
Rozprawy Elektrotechniczne — RZETA
Rozprawy Elektrotechniczne. Polska Akademia Nauk. Instytut Technologii Elektronowej. — Rozprawy Elektrotech
Rozprawy Gdanskie Towarzystwo Naukowe. Wydzial 3. Nauk Matematyczno-Przyrodniczych — Rozpr Gdansk Tow Nauk Wydz 3
Rozprawy Hydrotechniczne — Rozpr Hydrotech
Rozprawy i Sprawozdania. Instytut Badawczy Lasow Panstwowych — Rozpr Spraw Inst Badawczy Lasow Panstw
Rozprawy i Sprawozdania. Instytut Badawczy Lesnictwa — Rozpr Spraw Inst Badawczy Lesn
Rozprawy Inzynierskie — Rozpr Inz
Rozprawy Inzynierskie — RZINA
Rozprawy Komisji Jezykowej Lodzkiego Towarzystwa Naukowego — RKJ
Rozprawy Komisji Jezykowej Lodzkiego Towarzystwa Naukowego — RKJL
Rozprawy Komisji Jezykowej Wroclawskiego Towarzystwa Naukowego — RKJW
Rozprawy Monografie — Rozpr Monogr
Rozprawy Naukowe Szkoly Glownej Gospodarstwa Wiejskiego-Akademii Rolniczej w Warszawie — Rozpr Nauk Szk Gl Gospod Wiejsk Akad Roln Warszawie
Rozprawy. Politechnika Poznanska — Rozpr Politech Poznan
Rozprawy. Politechnika Poznanska — Rozprawy Politech Poznan
Rozprawy. Politechnika Rzeszowska Imienia Ignacego Lukasiewicza — Rozpr Politech Rzeszowska Im Ignacego Lukasiewicza
Rozprawy Wydzialu 3. Nauk Matematyczno-Przyrodniczych. Gdanskie Towarzystwo Naukowe — Rozpr Wydz 3 Nauk Mat Przyr Gdansk Tow Nauk
Rozprawy Wydzialu Filologicznego Polskiej Akademyi Umiejetnosci — RWF
Rozprawy Wydzialu Lekarskiego. Polska Akademia Umiejetnosci — Rozpr Wydz Lek Pol Akad Umiejet
Rozprawy Wydzialu Matematyczno-Przyrodniczego. Polska Akademia Umiejetnosci. Dzial A. Nauki Matematyczno-Fizyczne — Rozpr Wydz Mat Przyr Pol Akad Umiejet Dzial A
Rozprawy Wydzialu Matematyczno-Przyrodniczego. Polska Akademia Umiejetnosci. Dzial B. Nauki Biologiczne — Rozpr Wydz Mat Przyr Pol Akad Umiejet Dzial B
Rozprawy Wydzialu Nauk Medycznych Polska Akademia Nauk — Rozpr Wydz Nauk Med Pol Akad Nauk
Rozprawy Wydzialu Teologiczno-Kanonicznego — RWTK
Rozprawy. Wyzsza Szkola Rolnicza w Szczecinie — Rozpr Wyzsza Szk Roln Szczecinie
RPA [*Royal Prince Alfred Hospital*] **Magazine** — RPA
RQ [*Reference Quarterly*] — IRQQ
RQ. Reference Quarterly [*American Library Association. Reference Services Division*] — RQ
RRB [*Railroad Retirement Board*] **Quarterly Review** — RRB Q Rev
RRB (Railroad Retirement Board) Quarterly Review — RRB (Railroad Retirement Bd) Q R
RRC (Report). Reactor Research Centre. Kalpakkam — RRC (Rep) React Res Cent Kalpakkam
RRIC (Rubber Research Institute of Ceylon) Bulletin — RRIC (Rubber Res Inst Ceylon) Bull
RRIM [*Rubber Research Institute of Malaysia*] **Technology Series Report** — RRIM Technol Ser Rep
RRIM [*Rubber Research Institute of Malaysia*] **Training Manual on Soils, Management of Soils, and Nutrition of Hevea** — RRIM Train Man Soils Manage Soils Nutr Hevea
RRISL [*Rubber Research Institute of Sri Lanka*] **Bulletin** — RRISL Bull
RRISL (Rubber Research Institute of Sri Lanka) Bulletin — RRI Sri Lanka Bull
RRL [*Road Research Laboratory*] **Report (UK)** — RRL Rep (UK)
RS. Kentucky Agricultural Experiment Station — RS KY Agric Exp Stn
RS. University of Kentucky. Agricultural Experiment Station — RS Univ Ky Agric Exp Stn
RSRE [*Royal Signals and RADAR Establishment*] **Newsletter and Research Review** — RSRE Newsl Res Rev
RT. Regelungstechnik [*Germany*] — RT Regelungstech
RTC [*Royal Technical College*] **Metallurgical Club. Journal** — RTC Met Cl J
RTE. Radio-TV-Electronics — RTE
RTIA. Revue Technique de l'Industrie Alimentaire — RTIA
RTN: Radio Television News — RTN
RTP. Regelungstechnische Praxis — RRPRD
RTP. Regelungstechnische Praxis — RTP Regelungstech Prax
RTSD [*Resources and Technical Services Division*] **Library Resources and Technical Services** — RTSD LRTS
RTVA. Revue Technique Veterinaire de l'Alimentation — RTVA Rev Tech Vet Aliment
Ruakura Farmers' Conference. Proceedings [*New Zealand*] — Ruakura Farm Conf Proc
Ruakura Farmers' Conference. Proceedings — Ruakura Farmers Conf Proc
Rubber Age — RUAGA
Rubber Age and Synthetics — Rubber Age Synth
Rubber Age (New York) — Rubber Age (NY)
Rubber and Plastics — Rubber Plast
Rubber and Plastics Age — Rubb Plast Age
Rubber and Plastics Age — Rubber Plast Age
Rubber and Plastics Age — RUPAA
Rubber and Plastics Fire and Flammability Bulletin — Rubb Plast Fire Flamm Bull
Rubber and Plastics News — R & P News
Rubber and Plastics News — Rubb Plast News
Rubber and Plastics News. 2 — R & P News 2
Rubber and Plastics News. 2 — Rubb Plast News 2
Rubber and Plastics Weekly — Rubber Plast Wkly
Rubber Board. Bulletin [*India*] — Rubb Board Bull
Rubber Board Bulletin (India) — Rubber Board Bull (India)
Rubber Chemistry and Technology — RCTEA
Rubber Chemistry and Technology — Rubb Chem
Rubber Chemistry and Technology — Rubber Chem & Tech
Rubber Chemistry and Technology — Rubber Chem Technol
Rubber Developments — Rubb Dev
Rubber Developments — Rubber Dev

Rubber Developments — Rubber Devs
Rubber Developments — Rubber Devts
Rubber Developments — RUDVA
Rubber Developments. Natural Rubber Producers' Research Association — Rubber Developm
Rubber Developments. Supplement — Rubber Dev Suppl
Rubber Digest (Tokyo) — Rubber Dig (Tokyo)
Rubber Division Symposia — Rubber Div Symp
Rubber (India) — Rubb (India)
Rubber Industry — Rubber Ind
Rubber Industry (London) — Rubber Ind (London)
Rubber Industry (New York) — Rubber Ind (NY)
Rubber Journal — Rubber J
Rubber Journal and International Plastics — Rubb J
Rubber Journal and International Plastics — Rubber J Int Plast
Rubber News — Rubb News
Rubber Planters' Conference. Souvenir — Rubber Plant Conf Souvenir
Rubber Research Institute of Ceylon. Advisory Circular — Rubber Res Inst Ceylon Advis Circ
Rubber Research Institute of Ceylon. Annual Report — Rubber Res Inst Ceylon Annu Rep
Rubber Research Institute of Ceylon. Annual Review — Rubber Res Inst Ceylon Annu Rev
Rubber Research Institute of Ceylon. Bulletin — Rubber Res Inst Ceylon Bull
Rubber Research Institute of Ceylon. Quarterly Circular — Rubber Res Inst Ceylon Q Circ
Rubber Research Institute of Ceylon. Quarterly Journal — Rubber Res Inst Ceylon Q J
Rubber Research Institute of Malaya. Annual Report — Rubber Res Inst Malaya Annu Rep
Rubber Research Institute of Malaya. Bulletin — Rubber Res Inst Malaya Bull
Rubber Research Institute of Malaya. Circular — Rubber Res Inst Malaya Circ
Rubber Research Institute of Malaya. Planters' Bulletin — Rubber Res Inst Malaya Plant Bull
Rubber Research Institute of Malaya. Planting Manual — Rubber Res Inst Malaya Plant Man
Rubber Research Institute of Malaya. Quarterly Journal — Rubber Res Inst Malaya Q J
Rubber Research Institute of Malaya. Report — Rubber Res Inst Malaya Rep
Rubber Research Institute of Malaysia. Annual Report — Rubber Res Inst Malays Annu Rep
Rubber Research Institute of Malaysia. Journal — Rubber Res Inst Malays J
Rubber Research Institute of Malaysia. Planters' Bulletin — Rubber Res Inst Malays Plant Bull
Rubber Research Institute of Malaysia. Planters' Conference. Proceedings — Rubber Res Inst Malays Plant Conf Proc
Rubber Research Institute of Malaysia. Technology Series Report — Rubber Res Inst Malays Technol Ser Rep
Rubber Research Institute of Sri Lanka. Advisory Circular — Rubber Res Inst Sri Lanka Advis Circ
Rubber Research Institute of Sri Lanka. Annual Review — Rubber Res Inst Sri Lanka Annu Rev
Rubber Research Institute of Sri Lanka. Bulletin — Rubber Res Inst Sri Lanka Bull
Rubber Research Institute of Sri Lanka. Journal — Rubber Res Inst Sri Lanka J
Rubber Research Institute of Sri Lanka. Quarterly Journal — Rubber Res Inst Sri Lanka Q J
Rubber Statistical Bulletin — Rubb Statist Bull
Rubber Statistical Bulletin — Rubber Bul
Rubber Technology — Rubber Technol
Rubber Trends — Rub Trends
Rubber Trends — Rubb Trends
Rubber Trends — RUT
Rubber World — IRW
Rubber World — Rubb World
Rubber World — Rubber Wld
Rubber World — RUBWA
Rubber-Stichting (Delft). Communication — Rubber Sticht (Delft) Commun
Rubey Volume — Rubey Vol
Ruch Biblijny i Liturgiczny [*Cracow*] — RuBi
Ruch Biblijny i Liturgiczny [*Cracow*] — RuchBL
Ruch Biblijny i Liturgiczny — RBL
Ruch Filozoficzny — RF
Ruch Literacki [*Krakow*] — RL
Ruch Literacki — Ruch L
Ruch Literacki [*Krakow*] — RuLit
Ruch Muzyczny — Ruch Muz
Ruch Muzyczny — RuchM
Ruch Muzyczny — RuM
Ruch Prawniczy Ekonomiczny i Socjologiczny — Ruch Prawn Ekon Socjol
Rudarski Glasnik — Rud Glas
Rudarski Glasnik — RUGLA
Rudarsko-Metalurski Zbornik — RMZBA
Rudarsko-Metalurski Zbornik — Rud-Met Zb
Rudarsko-Metalurski Zbornik — Rud-Metal Zb
Rudarstvo. Geologija i Metalurgija — Rud Geol Metal
Rudnye Mestorozhdeniya — Rudn Mestorozhd
Rudodobiv i Metalurgiya [*Bulgaria*] — Rudodob Metal
Rudodobiv i Metalurgiya — Rudodobiv Metal
Rudodobiv i Metalurgiya — RUMEA
Rudodobiv i Metalurgiya (Sofia) [*Bulgaria*] — Rudodobiv Metal (Sofia)
Rudolf Steiner Taschenbuchausgaben — Steiner Tb
Rudolstaedter Heimathefte Beitraege zur Heimatkunde des Kreises Rudolstaedt [*A publication*] — Rudolstaedter Heimath
Rudoobrazuvatelni Procesi i Mineralni Nakhodisha [*Sofia*] — Rudoobraz Procesi Miner Nakhodisha
Rudy i Metale Niezelazne — RMNZA
Rudy i Metale Niezelazne — Rudy Met Niezelaz
Rudy i Metally — Rudy Met
Rueckstands-Berichte — Rueckstands Ber
Ruf des Ostens — Ruf D Ostens
Ruimtevaart — RUIMB
Rulings Information System, Excise [*Database*] — RISE
RUM. Revue Universelle des Mines, de la Metallurgie, de la Mechanique, des Travaux Publics, des Sciences — RUM Rev Univers Mines
RUM (Revue Universelle des Mines, de la Metallurgie, de la Mechanique, des Travaux Publics, des Sciences et des Arts Appliques a l'Industrie) — RUM Rev Univers Mines Metall Mec
Rumanian Medical Review — RMERA
Rumanian Medical Review — Rum Med Rev
Rumanian Scientific Abstracts — Rum Sci Abstr
Rumen Microbial Metabolism and Ruminant Digestion — Rumen Microb Metab Ruminant Dig
Rundbrief Kraftanlagen — Rdbr Kraftanl
Rundbrief. Una Sancta — RUS
Rundbrief. Una-Sancta-Einigung — RUSE
Rundbrief zur Foerderung der Freundschaft — RFF
Rundfunk und Fernsehen — Rundfunk & F
Rundfunktechnische Mitteilungen — RUMIA
Rundfunktechnische Mitteilungen — Rundfunktech Mitt
Rundschau Deutscher Technik — Rundsch Dtsch Tech
Rundschau fuer Geologie und Verwandte Wissenschaften — Rundsch Geol Verw Wiss
Rundschau. Sammlung Gerichtlicher Entscheidungen aus dem Bezirke des Oberlandesgerichts Frankfurt am Main — Rundschau Smlg Ger Entsch Frankft
Rundschau Technischer Arbeit — Rundsch Tech Arb
Runner's World — GRUN
Runner's World — Runn World
Runner's World — RW
Running Research News — RRN
Running Times — Runn Times
Rupert-Carola — RupC
Ruperto-Carola — RC
Ruperto-Carola — RuC
Ruperto-Carola. Mitteilungen der Vereinigung der Freunde der Studentenschaft der Universitaet Heidelberg — RCMUH
Rural Advisory Leaflet. Edinburgh School of Agriculture — Rur Advis Leafl Edinb Sch Agric
Rural Africana — Rur Afr
Rural America — Rural Am
Rural Development — Rural Develop
Rural Development News — Rural Dev News
Rural Development Perspectives. RDP — Rural Dev Perspect RDP
Rural Development. Research and Education — Rural Dev Res Educ
Rural Development Research Report. United States Department of Agriculture. Economics, Statistics, and Cooperatives Service — Rural Dev Res Rep US Dep Agric Econ Stat Coop Serv
Rural Electrification News — Rural Elec N
Rural Enterprise — Rural Enterp
Rural Equipment News — REN
Rural Georgia — RUGED
Rural Georgia [*United States*] — Rural GA
Rural India — Rur Ind
Rural Libraries — Rural Libr
Rural Life Research — Rural Life Res
Rural New Yorker — Rural N Y
Rural Newsletter — Rur Newsl
Rural Newsletter. Central Coast Agricultural Research and Extension Committee — Rural Newsl
Rural Production — Rur Prod
Rural Recreation and Tourism Abstracts — Rural Recreat Tour Abstr
Rural Research — Rur Res
Rural Research — RURCA
Rural Research. A CSIRO [*Commonwealth Scientific and Industrial Research Organization*] **Quarterly** — Rural Res CSIRO Q
Rural Research. Commonwealth Scientific and Industrial Research Organisation [*A publication*] — Rur Res CSIRO
Rural Research. Commonwealth Scientific and Industrial Research Organisation [*A publication*] — Rural Res
Rural Research. Commonwealth Scientific and Industrial Research Organisation [*A publication*] — Rural Res CSIRO
Rural Research. Commonwealth Scientific and Industrial Research Organisation (Australia) — Rur Res CSIRO (Aust)
Rural Society — RS
Rural Sociologist — Rural Sociol
Rural Sociology — PRUS
Rural Sociology — RS
Rural Sociology — Rur Sociol
Rural Sociology — Rural Socio
Rural Sociology — Rural Sociol
Rural Sociology — RUSCA
Rush-Presbyterian-St. Luke's Medical Center. Bulletin — Rush-Presbyt-St Luke's Med Bull
Rush-Presbyterian-St. Luke's Medical Center. Research Report — Rush-Presbyt-St Luke's Med Cent Res Rep
Ruskin Newsletter — Rusk N
Rusky Jazyk — RJ
Rusky Jazyk — RJaz

Rusky Jazyk — RuJ
Russell-Cotes Art Gallery and Museum. Bulletin — Russell-Cotes Mus Bul
Russian Academy of Sciences. Doklady Mathematics — Russian Acad Sci Dokl Math
Russian Academy of Sciences. Izvestiya. Atmospheric and Oceanic Physics — Izv Russ Acad Sci Atmospher Ocean Phys
Russian Academy of Sciences. Izvestiya. Mathematics — Russian Acad Sci Izv Math
Russian Academy of Sciences. Sbornik. Mathematics — Russian Acad Sci Sb Math
Russian Annual of Geology and Mineralogy — Russ Annu Geol Mineral
Russian Castings Production [*English Translation*] — RCTPA
Russian Castings Production — Russ Cast Prod
Russian Castings Production (English Translation) — Russ Cast Prod Engl Transl
Russian Chemical Reviews [*English Translation*] — RCRVA
Russian Chemical Reviews — Russ Chem Rev
Russian Chemical Reviews (English Translation) — Russ Chem Rev (Engl Transl)
Russian Chemico-Pharmaceutical Journal — Russ Chem Pharm J
Russian, Croatian and Serbian, Czech and Slovak, Polish Literature — RCSCSPL
Russian Engineering Journal — RENJA
Russian Engineering Journal — Russ En J
Russian Engineering Journal — Russ Eng J
Russian Engineering Journal (English Translation) — Russ Eng J (Engl Transl)
Russian History — Russ Hist
Russian Journal of Bioorganic Chemistry (Translation of Bioorganicheskaya Khimiya) — Russ J Bioorg Chem Transl of Bioorg Khim
Russian Journal of Coordination Chemistry (Translation of Koordinatsionnaya Khimiya) — Russ J Coord Chem Transl of Koord Khim
Russian Journal of Developmental Biology (Translation of Ontogenes) — Russ J Dev Biol Transl of Ontogenes
Russian Journal of Ecology (Translation of Ekologiya) (Ekaterinburg) — Russ J Ecol Transl of Ekologiya Ekaterinburg
Russian Journal of Electrochemistry (Translation of Elektrokhimiya) — Russ J Electrochem Transl of Elektrokhimiya
Russian Journal of Genetics (Translation of Genetika) (Moscow) — Russ J Genet Transl of Genetika Moscow
Russian Journal of Inorganic Chemistry [*English Translation*] — RJICA
Russian Journal of Inorganic Chemistry — Russ J Inorg Chem
Russian Journal of Inorganic Chemistry (English Translation) — Russ J Inorg Chem (Engl Transl)
Russian Journal of Marine Biology (Translation of Biologiya Morya) (Vladivostok) — Russ J Mar Biol Transl of Biol Morya Vladivostok
Russian Journal of Mathematical Physics — Russian J Math Phys
Russian Journal of Numerical Analysis and Mathematical Modelling — Russian J Numer Anal Math Modelling
Russian Journal of Organic Chemistry (Translation of Zhurnal Organicheskoi Khimii) — Russ J Org Chem Transl of Zh Org Khim
Russian Journal of Physical Chemistry [*English Translation*] — RJPCA
Russian Journal of Physical Chemistry — Russ J Phys Chem
Russian Journal of Physical Chemistry — Russian J Physical Chem
Russian Journal of Physical Chemistry (English Translation) — Russ J Phys Chem (Engl Transl)
Russian Journal of Plant Physiology (Translation of Fiziologiya Rastenii) (Moscow) — Russ J Plant Physiol Transl of Fiziol Rast Moscow
Russian Language Journal — RLJ
Russian Linguistics — RLing
Russian Linguistics — Rus Ling
Russian Literature — RL
Russian Literature Triquarterly — RLT
Russian Literature Triquarterly — Ru L T
Russian Literature Triquarterly — Rus LT
Russian Literature Triquarterly — Russ Lit Tr
Russian Mathematical Surveys — Russ Math Surv
Russian Mathematical Surveys — Russian Math Surveys
Russian Mathematics — Russian Math
Russian Metallurgy [*English Translation*] — RUMMA
Russian Metallurgy — Russ Met
Russian Metallurgy — Russ Metall
Russian Metallurgy and Fuels — Russ Metall Fuels
Russian Metallurgy and Mining — Russ Metall Min
Russian Metallurgy (English Translation) — Russ Metall (Engl Transl)
Russian Microelectronics (Translation of Mikroelektronika) — Russ Microelectron Transl of Mikroelektronika
Russian Pharmacology and Toxicology — Russ Pharmacol Toxicol
Russian Pharmacology and Toxicology (English Translation) — Russ Pharmacol Toxicol (Engl Transl)
Russian Physics Journal — Russian Phys J
Russian Physiological Journal — Russ Physiol J
Russian Review — PRSR
Russian Review — RR
Russian Review — RusR
Russian Review — Russ R
Russian Review — Russ Rev
Russian Review — Russian R
Russian Review — Russian Rev
Russian Review (Harmondsworth) [*The Penguin Russian Review*] — Russ Rev Harmondsworth
Russian Review of Biology — Russ Rev Biol
Russian-German Herald of Science and Technology — Russ Ger Her Sci Technol
Russie et Chretiente — RChr
Russie et Chretiente — ReC
Russie et Chretiente — Rus Chr
Russie et Chretiente — Russie et Chret
Russie et Chretiente. Collection — ReCC
Russisch-Deutsche Nachrichten fuer Wissenschaft und Technik — Russ Dtsch Nachr Wiss Tech
Russische Bierbrauer — Russ Bierbrau
Russische Revue — Russ Rev
Russisches Jahrbuch der Pharmacie — Russ Jahrb Pharm
Russisches Journal fuer Experimentelle Landwirtschaft — Russ J Exp Landwirtsch
Russisch-Etymologisches Woerterbuch — REW
Russisch-Kaiserliche Mineralogische Gesellschaft zu St. Petersburg. Verhandlungen — Russ-K Min Ges St Petersburg Verh
Russkaia Literatura — Russkaia L
Russkaia Meditsina — Russk Med
Russkaja Bibliografija po Estestvoznaniju i Matematike, Sostavlennaja Sostojascim pri Imperatorskoj Akademii Nauk Sankt-Peterburgskim Bjuro Mezdunoradnoj Bibliografii — Russk Bibliogr Estestv Mat
Russkaja Demokraticeskaja Satira XVII Veka — RDS
Russkaja Filologija — RFil
Russkaja Literatura — RLit
Russkaja Literatura — RusL
Russkaja Literatura — Russ Lit
Russkaja Mysl' — RM
Russkaja Rech' — RUR
Russkaja Rech' — Rus Re
Russkaja Rech' — RusR
Russkaya Muzikal'naya Gazeta — RMG
Russkii Arkhiv Anatomii, Gistologii, i Embriologii — Russ Arkh Anat Gistol Embriol
Russkii Arkhiv Protistologii — Russk Arkh Protist
Russkii Astronomicheskii Kalendar — Russ Astron Kal
Russkii Astronomicheskii Zhurnal — Russ Astron Zh
Russkii Fiziologicheskii Zhurnal Imeni I. M. Sechenova — Russ Fiziol Zh Im I M Sechenova
Russkii Pivovar — Russ Pivovar
Russkii Pochvoved — Russ Pochvoved
Russkii Vestnik Dermatologii — Russk Vestnik Dermat
Russkii Vinograd — Russ Vinograd
Russkii Vrach — Russ Vrach
Russkii Yazyk v Shkole [*Moscow*] — RYa
Russkii Zhurnal Tropicheskoi Meditsiny — Russk Zhurnal Trop Med
Russkii Zoologicheskii Zhurnal — Russk Zool Zhurnal
Russkij Archiv — RA
Russkij Biograficeskij Slovar — RBSl
Russkij Botaniceskij Zurnal/Journal Russe de Botanique — Russk Bot Zurn
Russkij Fol'klor — RusF
Russkij Gidrobiologiceskij Zurnal/Russische Hydrobiologische Zeitschrift — Russk Gidrobiol Zurn
Russkij Jazyk v Skole — RJaS
Russkij Jazyk v Skole — RJS
Russkij Jazyk za Rubezom — RJR
Russkij Wiestnik — RW
Russko-Amerikanskij Pravoslavnyj Vestnik — RAPV
Russkoe Bogatstvo — RuB
Russkoe Entomologicheskoe Obozrenie — Russ Entomol Obozr
Russkoe Istoriceskoe Obscestvo — RIO
Russko-Germanskii Vestnik Nauki i Tekhniki — Russ Ger Vestn Nauki Tekh
Russkogo Zapadno-Evropeiskogo Patriarshego Ekzarkhata. Vestnik — RZEPEV
Rust Prevention and Control — Rust Prev Control
Rustica — RUSTA
Rutgers Byzantine Series — R By S
Rutgers Computer and Technology Law Journal — Rutgers Comput and Technol Law J
Rutgers Computer and Technology Law Journal — Rutgers Jrnl
Rutgers Journal of Computers and the Law — Rutgers J Comp & L
Rutgers Journal of Computers and the Law — Rutgers J Comput & Law
Rutgers Journal of Computers and the Law — Rutgers J Computers & Law
Rutgers Journal of Computers, Technology, and the Law — Rut J Comp L
Rutgers Journal of Computers, Technology, and the Law — Rutgers J Comput Technol and Law
Rutgers Journal of Computers, Technology, and the Law — Rutgers J Computer Tech and L
Rutgers Law Journal — Rut LJ
Rutgers Law Journal — Rutgers LJ
Rutgers Law Review — RLR
Rutgers Law Review — Rut LR
Rutgers Law Review — Rutg L Rev
Rutgers Law Review — Rutgers L Rev
Rutgers State University. College of Engineering. Engineering Research Bulletin — Rutgers State Univ Coll Eng Eng Res Bull
Rutgers State University. College of Engineering. Engineering Research Publication — Rutgers State Univ Coll Eng Eng Res Publ
Rutgers Studies in English — RSE
Rutgers University. Annual Research Conference of the Bureau of Biological Research — Rutgers Univ Annu Res Conf Bur Biol Res
Rutgers University. Bureau of Biological Research. Annual Conference on Protein Metabolism. Proceedings — Rutgers Univ Bur Biol Res Annu Conf Protein Metab Proc
Rutgers University. Bureau of Biological Research. Serological Museum. Bulletin — Rutgers Univ Bur Biol Res Serol Mus Bull
Rutgers University. Bureau of Engineering Research. Engineering Research Publication — Rutgers Univ Bur Eng Res Eng Res Publ

Rutgers University. Bureau of Mineral Research. Bulletin — Rutgers Univ Bur Miner Res Bull
Rutgers University. College of Engineering. Engineering Research Bulletin — Rutgers Univ Coll Eng Eng Res Bull
Rutgers University. Studies in English — RUSE
Rutgers-Camden Law Journal — Rut-Cam LJ
Rutgers-Camden Law Journal — Rutgers Camden L J
Rutherford Appleton Laboratory. Report RAL — Rutherford Appleton Lab Rep RAL
Rutherford Appleton Laboratory. Report RL — Rutherford Appleton Lab Rep RL
Rutherford Laboratory. Report — Rutherford Lab Rep
Rutherford Laboratory. Technical Report RL — Rutherford Lab Tech Rep RL
RV: Recreational Vehicles — RV
Ryan Advisory for Health Services Governing Boards — Ryan Advis Health Serv Gov Boards
Ryazanskii Gosudarstvennyi Pedagogicheskii Institut. Uchenye Zapiski — Ryazan Gos Pedagog Inst Uch Zap
Ryazanskii Meditsinskii Institut Imeni Akademika I. P. Pavlova. Nauchnye Trudy — Ryazan Med Inst Im Akad I P Pavlova Nauchn Tr
Rybinskii Aviatsionnyi Tekhnologicheskii Institut. Sbornik Trudov — Rybinsk Aviats Tekhnol Inst Sb Tr
Rybnaya Promyshlennost' Dal'nego Vostoka — Rybn Prom-St Dal'n Vost
Rybnaya Promyshlennost' Dal'nego Vostoka — Rybn Promst Dalnego Vostoka
Rybnoe Khozyaistvo — Ryb Khoz
Rybnoe Khozyaistvo — Rybn Khoz
Rybnoe Khozyaistvo — RYKHA
Rybnoe Khozyaistvo (Kiev) — Rybn Khoz (Kiev)
Rybnoe Khozyaistvo (Moscow) — Rybn Khoz (Moscow)
Rybnoe Khozyaistvo Respublikanskii Mezhvedomstvennyi Tematicheskii Nauchnyi Sbornik — Rybn Khoz Resp Mezhved Temat Nauchn Sb
Rybnoe Khozyaistvo SSSR — Rybn Khoz SSSR
Rybokhozyaistvennoe Izuchenie Vnutrennikh Vodoemov — Rybokhoz Izuch Vnutr Vodoemov
Rybokhozyaistvennye Issledovaniya v Basseine Baltiiskogo Morya — Rybokhoz Issled Basseine Balt Morya
Rydge's — R
Rydge's Business Journal — Rydge's
Rydge's Construction, Civil Engineering, and Mining Review — Rydge's Constr Civ Eng & Min Rev
Ryojun College of Engineering. Memoirs — Ryojun Coll Eng Mem
Ryojun College of Engineering. Publications — Ryojun Coll Eng Publ
Rythmes du Monde — Ry Mo
Rythmes du Monde — Ryth Monde
Ryukoku Daigaku Ronshu — RDR
Ryukoku Journal of Humanities and Sciences — Ryukoku J Humanit Sci
Ryukyu Daigaku Nogakubu Gakujutsu Hokoku — RDNGB
Ryukyu Mathematical Journal — Ryukyu Math J
Ryukyu Medical Journal — Ryukyu Med J
Ryusan To Kogyo — RYUSA
Ryutai Kogaku — RYKOD

S

S & P [*Standard & Poor's Corp.*] **Options Monitor Service Plus** [*Database*] — OMS
S V. Sound and Vibration — S V Sound Vib
SA [*South African*] **Archives Journal** — SA Arch J
SA [*South African*] **Cerebral Palsy Journal** — SA Cereb Palsy J
SA [*South African*] **Journal for Research in Sport. Physical Education and Recreation** — SAJ Res Sport Phys Educ Recreat
SA [*South African*] **Journal of Sports Medicine** — SA J Sports Med
SA [*South African*] **Mining and Engineering Journal** — SA Min Eng J
SA [*South African*] **Mining and Engineering Journal** — SAMEB
SA [*South Australia*] **Teachers' Journal** — SA Teachers J
SA [*South African*] **Tydskrif van Sportgeneeskunde** — SA Tydskr Sportgeneeskd
SA [*South African*] **Waterabstracts** — SA Waterabstr
SAAD [*Society for the Advancement of Anaesthesia in Dentistry*] **Digest** — SAAD Dig
Saalburg Jahrbuch. Saalburg-Museum — Saalburg Jahrb
Saalburg Jahrbuch. Saalburg-Museum — Sbg J
Saalburg-Jahrbuch — SaJ
Saalburg-Jahrbuch — SJ
Saalburg-Jahrbuch. Bericht des Saalburg-Museums — Saalb Jb
SAAS [*Southern Association of Agricultural Scientists*] **Bulletin. Biochemistry and Biotechnology** — SAAS Bull Biochem Biotechnol
Saatgut-Wirtschaft — Saatgut-Wirt
Saatgut-Wirtschaft — Saatgut-Wirtsch
Sabadellum — Sab
Sabah Forest Record — Sabah For Rec
Sabah Society. Journal — Sabah Soc J
Sabchota Meditsina — Sabchota Med
SABCO [*Society for the Areas of Biological and Chemical Overlap*] **Journal** — SABCO J
Sabouraudia — SABOA
Sabrao Newsletter — Sabrao Newslett
SABS [*South African Bureau of Standards*] **Bulletin** — SABS Bull
Saccharum — SACCD
Sachverhalte — SCHVD
Sacra Bibbia (Torino) — SBT
Sacra Doctrina — SaDo
Sacra Doctrina. Quaderni Periodici di Teologia e di Filosofia — Sac D
Sacra Dottrina — Sac Dot
Sacra Pagina — Sacra Pag
Sacra Scriptura Antiquitatibus Orientalibus Illustrata — SSAOI
Sacrae Romanae Rotae Decisiones seu Sententiae — SRRDS
Sacramentarium Veronense — Sacr Ver
Sacramento Bee — Sacramnt B
Sacramento Business — Sacramento Bus
Sacramentum Mundi [*Freiburg*] — SMD
Sacramentum Mundi [*New York*] — SME
Sacred Books of the Buddhists — SBBud
Sacred Books of the East — SBE
Sacred Books of the Hindus — SBH
Sacred Books of the Hindus. Extra Volumes — SBHE
Sacred Books of the Old and New Testaments — SBONT
Sacred Books of the Old Testament — SBOT
Sacred Music — Sac M
Sacred Music — Sacred Mus
Sacred Music — SM
Sacred Music — SMu
Sacris Erudiri. Jaarboek voor Godsdienstwetenschappen — Sac
Sacris Erudiri. Jaarboek voor Godsdienstwetenschappen — SacE
Sacris Erudiri. Jaarboek voor Godsdienstwetenschappen — SE
Sacris Erudiri. Jaarboek voor Godsdienstwetenschappen — SEJG
Sacrum Polonia Millenium — SPM
Sacrum Poloniae Millennium — Sacrum Pol Millenn
Sadivnytstvo Respublikanskyi Mizhvidomchyi Naukovo-Tematychnyi Zbirnik — Sadivn Resp Mizhvid Nauk-Temat Zb
Sado Marine Biological Station. Niigata University. Special Publication — NDRHE4
Sado Marine Biological Station. Niigata University. Special Publication — Sado Mar Biol Stn Niigata Univ Spec Publ
Sadovodstvo [*Moscow*] — SADOAJ
Sadovodstvo — Sadovod
Sadovodstvo i Vinogradarstvo Moldavii — Sadovod Vinograd Mold
Sadovodstvo i Vinogradarstvo (Moscow) — Sadovod Vinograd Moscow
Sadovodstvo i Vinogradarstvo (Tashkent) — Sadovod Vinograd (Tashkent)
Sadovodstvo Vinogradarstvo i Vinodelia Moldavii — Sadovod Vinograd Vinodel Mold
Sadtler Commercial Spectra [*United States*] — Sadtler Commer Spectra
Sadtler Commercial Spectra — SCOSA
SAE [*Society of Automotive Engineers*] **Australasia** — SAE Australas
SAE [*Society of Automotive Engineers*] **Handbook** — SAE Handb
SAE [*Society of Automotive Engineers*] **Journal** — SAE J
SAE [*Society of Automotive Engineers*] **Journal** — SAE Journ
SAE [*Society of Automotive Engineers*] **Journal** — SAEJA
SAE [*Society of Automotive Engineers*] **Journal of Automotive Engineering** — SAE J Automot Eng
Sae Mulli — NWPYA
SAE [*Society of Automotive Engineers*] **Preprints** — SAE Prepr
SAE [*Society of Automotive Engineers*] **Progress in Technology** [*United States*] — SAE Prog Technol
SAE [*Society of Automotive Engineers*] **Progress in Technology** — SAPTA
SAE [*Society of Automotive Engineers*] **Quarterly Transactions** — SAE Q Trans
SAE [*Society of Automotive Engineers*] **Quarterly Transactions** — SAE Quart Trans
SAE (Society of Automotive Engineers) Technical Papers — SAE (Soc Automot Eng) Tech Pap
SAE [*Society of Automotive Engineers*] **Special Publications** — SAE Spec Publ
SAE [*Society of Automotive Engineers*] **Special Publications** — SAESA
SAE [*Society of Automotive Engineers*] **Technical Literature Abstracts** — SAE Tech Lit Abstr
SAE [*Society of Automotive Engineers*]. Technical Paper Series — SAE Tech Pap Ser
SAE [*Society of Automotive Engineers*]. Technical Papers — SAE Tech Pap
SAE [*Society of Automotive Engineers*] **Technical Progress Series** — SAE Tech Prog Ser
SAE [*Society of Automotive Engineers*] **Technical Progress Series** — SAETB
SAE [*Society of Automotive Engineers*] **Transactions** — SAE Trans
Saechische Heimatblaetter — S Hb
Saechse Jahresschrift. Jahsesschrift fuer die Vorgeschichte der Saechsisch-Thueringischen Laender — Saechs Jahresschr
Saechsische Akademie der Wissenschaften. Philologisch-Historische Klasse. Berichte ueber die Verhandlungen — Sachs Akad d Wiss Philol-Hist Kl Ber u d Verhandl
Saechsische Akademie der Wissenschaften zu Leipzig. Philologisch-Historische Klasse — SAWPHK
Saechsische Forschungsinstitut in Leipzig — Saechs Forschungsinstitut in Leipzig
Saechsische Heimatblaetter — Saechs Heimatbl
Saechsischer Heimatschutz, Landesverein zur Pflege Heimatlicher Natur, Kunst und Bauweise/Mitteilungen des Landesvereins Saechsischer Heimatschutz — Saechs Heimatschutz Mitt Landesvereins Saechs Heimatschutz
Saechsisches Archiv fuer Deutsches Buergerliches Recht — SaechsA
Saechsisches Archiv fuer Deutsches Buergerliches Recht und Prozess — Saechs Arch Dt Buerg R
Saeculum [*Muenchen*] — Saec
Saeculum — Sm
Saeculum. Jahrbuch fuer Universalgeschichte — Saeculum
Saeculum Westgeschichte — SWG
SAED [*Societe Africaine d'Etudes et de Developpement*] **Information** — SAED Info
Saenger- und Musikantenzeitung — Saenger Musikanten Z
Saertryck. Livsmedelstekniska Forskningsinstitutet (Alnarp) — Saertr Livsmedelstek Forskningsinst (Alnarp)
Saertryck. Svenska Forskningsinstitutet foer Cement och Betong vid Kungliga Tekniska Hoegskolan i Stockholm — Saertr Sven Forskningsinst Cem Betong K Tek Hoegsk Stockholm
Saeugetierkundliche Mitteilungen — Saeugetierkd Mitt
Safety — SAFEA
Safety and Health Bulletin — Saf Hlth Bull
Safety and Health Practitioner — Saf Health Pract
Safety and Hygiene (Osaka) [*Japan*] — Saf Hyg (Osaka)
Safety Aspects of Fuel Behaviour in Off-Normal and Accident Conditions. Proceedings of a CSNI Specialist Meeting — Saf Asp Fuel Behav Off Norm Accid Cond Proc CSNI Spec Meet
Safety Digest [*Japan*] — Saf Dig
Safety Education — Safety Ed
Safety Education — Safety Educ
Safety Engineering — Saf Eng
Safety Engineering — Safety Eng
Safety, Health, and Welfare — Saf Health Welfare
Safety in Air and Ammonia Plants — Saf Air Ammonia Plants
Safety in Mines — Saf Mines

Safety in Mines Research and Testing Branch. Great Britain. Research Report — Saf Mines Res Test Branch GB Res Rep
Safety in Mines Research Establishment. Great Britain. Report — Saf Mines Res Establ GB Rep
Safety in Mines Research Establishment (Great Britain). Research Report — Saf Mines Res Establ (GB) Res Rep
Safety Maintenance — Saf Maint
Safety Maintenance — Safety Maint
Safety Maintenance and Production — Saf Maint Proc
Safety Maintenance and Production — Safety Maint & Prod
Safety Management — Saf Manage
Safety Management — Safe Manag
Safety Management Newsletter — Safety Man Newsl
Safety News Bulletin — Saf News Bull
Safety Newsletter — Saf Newsl
Safety Practitioner — Saf Pract
Safety Practitioner — SAFPD
Safety Science Abstracts Journal — Saf Sci Abstr
Safety Science Abstracts Journal — Saf Sci Abstr J
Safety Series. IAEA [*International Atomic Energy Agency*] — Saf Ser IAEA
Safety Series. IAEA [*International Atomic Energy Agency*] — SSAEA
Safety Surveyor [*United Kingdom*] — Saf Surv
Safety Surveyor — Safety Surv
SAFTTA [*South African Film and Television Technicians Association*] **Journal** — SAFTTA Jnl
Safugetierkundliche Mitteilungen — Safugetierkd Mitt
SAGA [*Sand and Gravel Association Ltd.*] **Bulletin** — SAGA Bull
Saga Daigaku Nogaku Iho — SDNIA
Saga och Sed — Saga S
Saga och Sed — SoS
Saga-Book. Viking Society for Northern Research — Saga-Book
Saga-Book. Viking Society for Northern Research — SBVS
Saga-Book. Viking Society for Northern Research — SVS
Sage Annual Reviews of Communication Research — Sage Annu R Communic Res
Sage Electoral Studies Yearbook — Sage Elect Stud Yb
Sage Family Studies Abstracts — Sage Fam Stud Abstr
Sage International Yearbook of Foreign Policy Studies — Sage Int Yb For Pol Stud
Sage Professional Papers in Comparative Politics — Sage Pap CP
Sage Public Administration Abstracts — Sage Pub Admin Abstr
Sage Public Administration Abstracts — Sage Public Adm Abstr
Sage Public Administration Abstracts — SPAA
Sage Race Relations Abstracts — SRRA
Sage University Paper Series on Quantitative Applications in the Social Sciences — Sage Univ Paper Ser Quant Appl Social Sci
Sage Urban Abstracts — Sage Urban Abs
Sage Urban Studies Abstracts — Sage Urb Stud Abstr
Sage Urban Studies Abstracts — Sage Urban Stud Abstr
Sage Urban Studies Abstracts — SUSA
Sage Yearbook in Women's Policy Studies — Sage Yb Women's Pol
Sage Yearbooks in Politics and Public Policy — Sage Yb Polit Publ Pol
Saggi di Scienze e Filosofia Naturale — Saggi Sci Filos Natur
Saggi di Umanismo Cristiano — SUC
Saggi e Memorie di Storia dell'Arte — SMSA
Saggi e Ricerche — Sag Ric
Saggi e Ricerche di Letteratura Francese — Saggi
Saggi e Ricerche di Letteratura Francese — SRLF
Saggi Fenici — Sagg Fen
Saggi Scientifici — Saggi Sci
Saggiatore — Sag
Sagkeeng News [*Fort Alexander, MB*] — SAGN
Saglik Dergisi — Saglik Derg
Saguenay Medical — Sague Med
Sahara de Demain — Sah de Dem
Said Medical Journal — Said Med J
Saiensu — SIEND
Saigai Igaku — SIGAB
Saiko Saibansho Keiji Hanreishu — Keishu
Saiko Saibansho Minji Hanreishu — Minshu
Saiko Saibansho Saibanshu — Saibanshu
Saiko To Hoan — SAHOA
Sail — GSAI
Sains Malaysiana [*Malaysia*] — Sains Malays
Saint Augustine Lecture Series — SALS
Saint Lawrence University. Geological Information and Referral Service. Bulletin — Saint Lawrence Univ Geol Inf and Referral Service Bull
Saint Louis Quarterly [*Baguio City*] — SLQ
Saint Vladimir's Theological Quarterly — St Vl Th Q
Sainte Bible. Louis Pirot et A. Clamer — SBPC
Sainte Bible Traduite en Francais sous la Direction de l'Ecole Biblique de Jerusalem — SBJ
Sairaanhoidon Vuosikirja — Sairaanh Vuosik
Sairaanhoitaja Sjukskiterskan — Sairaanhoitaja
SAIS [*School of Advanced International Studies*] **Review** — SAIS Rev
Saishin Igaku — SAIGA
SAIT [*South Australian Institute of Teachers*] **Newsletter** — SAIT News
Saitabi. Noticiario de Historia, Arte, y Arqueologia de Levante — Sait Not
Saitama Daigaku Kiyo. Kogakubu — SDKOD
Saitama Daigaku Kiyo. Shizenkagaku-Hen — SDKSB
Saitama Ika Daigaku Zasshi — SIDZD
Saitama Mathematical Journal — Saitama Math J
Saito Ho-On Kai Museum of Natural History. Research Bulletin — Saito Ho-On Kai Mus Nat Hist Res Bull
Saito Ho-On Kai Museum of Natural History. Research Bulletin — SHKBDX
Saito Ho-On Kai Museum Research Bulletin — Saito Ho-On Kai Mus Res Bull
Sakhalinskii Kompleksnyi Nauchno-Issledovatel'skii Institut. Akademiya Nauk SSSR. Trudy — Sakhalin Kompleksn Nauchno Issled Inst Akad Nauk SSSR Tr
Sakharnaya Promyshlennost — Sakh Prom
Sakharnaya Promyshlennost — Sakh Promst
Sakharnaya Promyshlennost — SAPRA
Sakharnaya Svekla — Sakh Svekla
Sakharnyi — Sakharn
Sakharthvelos SSR Mecnierebatha Akademia A. Razmadzis Sahelobis Thbilisis Mathematikis Institutis Sromebi — Sakharth SSR Mecn Akad Math Inst Srom
Sakharthvelos SSR Mecnierebatha Akademia Gamothvlithi Centris Sromebi — Sakharth SSR Mecn Akad Gamothvl Centr Srom
Sakharthvelos SSR Mecnierebatha Akademia Marthwis Sistemebis Instituti Sromebi — Sakharth SSR Mecn Akad Marthw Sistem Inst Srom
Sakharthvelos SSR Mecnierebatha Akademia Moambe — Sakharth SSR Mecn Akad Moambe
Sakharthvelos SSR Pedagogiuri Institutebis Sromebi. Phizika-Mathematikis Seria — Sakharth SSR Ped Inst Srom Phiz-Math Ser
Sakharthwelos SSR Mecnierebatha Akademiis Moambe — Sakharthw SSR Mecniereb Akad Moambe
Sakrale Kunst — Sak Ku
Sakura X-Ray Photographic Review [*Japan*] — Sakura X-Ray Photogr Rev
Sakura X-Rei Shashin Kenkyu — SXSKA
Sal Terre — Sal Ter
Saldatura Autogena — Saldat Auto
Sales and Marketing Management — SAL
Sales and Marketing Management — Sales & Mkt Mgt
Sales and Marketing Management — SLM
Sales and Marketing Management — SM
Sales and Marketing Management in Canada — SMC
Sales Catalog Index Project Input Online [*Database*] — SCIPIO
Sales Management [*Later, Sales and Marketing Management*] — Sales Mgt
Sales Management [*Later, Sales and Marketing Management*] — SM
Sales Tax Cases — Sales TC
Sales Tax Cases — STC
Salesianum — Sal
Salesianum Biblioteca [*Torino*]. — Sal B
Salesianum (Torino) — Sal T
Salisbury Medical Bulletin — Salisbury Med Bull
Salisbury Review — Salisbury Rev
Salmagundi — PSMG
Salmagundi — Salm
Salmanticensis — SAL
Salmanticensis — Salm
Salmon and Trout Magazine — Salmon Trou Mag
Salmon and Trout Magazine — Salmon Trout Mag
Salmon and Trout Magazine — STMGA
Salmon and Trout Magazine — STMGA3
Salmonsens Konversationsleksikon — SKL
Salt Lake City Tribune — Salt Lk Tr
Salt Lake Mining Review — Salt Lake M Rv
Salt Lake Mining Review — Salt Lake Min Rev
Salt Monthly (Taipei) — Salt Mon (Taipei)
Salt 'n' Pepper — SAPED
Salt Research and Industry — Salt Res Ind
Salt Research and Industry — SRSIB
Salt Research and Industry Journal — Salt Res Ind J
Salubridad y Asistencia (Mexico) — Salub Asist Mex
Salubridad y Asistencia Social (La Habana) — Salub Asist Soc Hav
Salud Ocupacional — Sal Ocup
Salud Ocupacional — Salud Ocup
Salud Publica — Sal Publ
Salud Publica de Mexico — Salud Publica Mex
Salud Publica de Mexico — SPM
Salud Publica de Mexico — SPMXA
Salute Italia Medica — Salute Italia Med
Salvador Medico — Salv Med
Salvavidas — Salvav
Salzburg Conference on Cerebral Vascular Disease — Salzburg Conf Cereb Vasc Dis
Salzburg Haus der Natur. Berichte. Abteilung B. Geologisch-Mineralogische Sammlungen — Salzburg Haus Nat Ber Abt B Geol-Mineral Samml
Salzburg Renaissance Studies — SRS
Salzburg Studies in English Literature. Elizabethan and Renaissance — SSELER
Salzburg Studies in English Literature. Romantic Reassessment — SSELRR
Salzburg Studies. Poetic Drama and Poetic Theory — SSPDPT
Salzburger Beitraege zur Paracelsusforschung — Salzburger Beitr Paracelsusforsch
Salzburger Jahrbuch fuer Philosophie — Salzburger Jrbh Phil
Salzburger Jahrbuch fuer Philosophie und Psychologie — SJP
Salzburger Kirchenblatt — SKB
Salzburger Patristische Studien — SPS
Salzburger Studien zur Anglistik und Amerikanistik — Salz St Ang
Salzburger Studien zur Anglistik und Amerikanistik — SSAA
Salzburger Studien zur Philosophie — SSPh
Salzburgische Gelehrte Unterhaltungen — Salzburg Gel Unterhalt
SAM [*Society for Advancement of Management*] **Advanced Management Journal** — AMN
SAM [*Society for Advancement of Management*] **Advanced Management Journal** — SAM
SAM [*Society for Advancement of Management*] **Advanced Management Journal** — SAM Adv Man
SAM [*Society for Advancement of Management*] **Advanced Management Journal** — SAM Advanced Mgt J

Samadhi [*Bruxelles*] — Sam
Samarkandskii Gosudarstvennyi Universitet Imeni Alishera Navoi. Trudy — Samark Gos Univ Im Alishera Navoi Tr
Samaru Agricultural Newsletter — Samaru Agr Newslett
Samaru Agricultural Newsletter — Samaru Agric Newsl
Samaru Institute for Agricultural Research. Soil Survey Bulletin — Samaru Inst Agric Res Soil Surv Bull
Samaru Miscellaneous Paper — Samaru Misc Pap
Samaru Research Bulletin — Samaru Res Bull
Sambalpur University. Journal of Science and Technology — Sambalpur Univ J Sci Technol
Same-Day Surgery — Same Day Surg
Samenvatting. Energie Studie Centrum — Samenvatting Energ Stud Cent
Samfundet St Eriks Arsbok — Samf St Eriks Arsb
Samfundets Krav — Sf K
Sami Medica. Journal. Sami Medical Association — SAMJ
Samisdat — Sam
Samiska. Journal. Indian Psychoanalytic Institute — J Indn Psychoan Inst
Samlaren — Saml
Samling af Roen Och Uptaekter, Gjorde i Senare Tider, Uti Physik, Medecin, Chirurgie, Natural-Historia, Chemie, Hushallning — Saml Roen Uptaeckter Phys
Samlingar och Studier till Svenska Kyrkans Historia — SSSKH
Samlingar Utgivna av Svenska Fornskrift-Sallskapet — SUSFS
Samlingar Utgivna av Svenska Fornskriftssallskapet — SUSF
Samlingar Utgivna av Svenska Fornskriftssallskapet (Stockholm) — SSFS
Sammelbaende der Internationalen Musikgesellschaft — Smlbde Intern Musikges
Sammelbaende. Internationale Musik Gesellschaft — SIMG
Sammelblatt der Historischer Verein Eichstatt — SHVE
Sammelblatt der Historischer Verein Freising — SHVF
Sammelblatt der Historischer Verein Ingolstadt — Sammel Bl Ingolstadt
Sammelblatt der Historischer Verein Ingolstadt — SHVI
Sammelblatt des Historischen Vereins Ingolstadt und Umgebung — Sammelbl Hist Ver Ingolstadt
Sammelbuch Griechischer Urkunden aus Aegypten — SBGU
Sammelheft. Kurznachrichten der Akademie der Wissenschaften in Goettingen — Sammelh Kurznachr Akad Wiss Goettingen
Sammelschriften Paedagogischen Fakultaet in Ostrau — Sammelschriften Paedagog Fak Ostrau
Sammendrag af Groenlands Fangstilister MV — SGFMV
Sammlung — Sam
Sammlung Auserlesener Abhandlungen zum Gebrauche Praktischer Aerzte — Samml Auserlesener Abh Gebrauche Prakt Aerzte
Sammlung Auserlesener Schriften von Staats- und Landwirthschaftlichem Inhalte — Samml Auserlesener Schriften Staats Landw Inhalt
Sammlung Ausgewaehlter Kirchen- und Dogmengeschichtlichen Quellenschriften — SKDGQ
Sammlung Ausgewaehlter Kirchen- und Dogmengeschichtlicher Quellenschriften — SQS
Sammlung Bibliothekswissenschaftlicher Arbeiten — SBWA
Sammlung Dalp — SD
Sammlung der Entscheidungen des Bayerischen Obersten Landesgerichts — BayS
Sammlung der Entscheidungen des Bayerischen Obersten Landesgerichts — Smlg Entsch Oberst Ldsger Bayern
Sammlung der Forschungsarbeiten aus der Papier- und Zellstoffindustrie — Samml Forschungsarb Pap Zellstoffind
Sammlung der Forschungsarbeiten der Landwirtschaftlichen Fakultaet. Belgrader Universitaet — Samml Forschungsarb Landwirtsch Fak Belgrader Univ
Sammlung der Griechischen Dialekinschriften — D Inschr
Sammlung der Griechischen Dialekinschriften — DI
Sammlung der Griechischen Dialekinschriften — Gr DI
Sammlung der Griechischen Dialekinschriften — SGDI
Sammlung Dialog — Sam Dial
Sammlung Dieterich — SD
Sammlung Gemeinverstaendlicher Vortraege und Schriften aus dem Gebiet der Theologie und der Religionsgeschichte — SVSThR
Sammlung Geologischer Fuehrer — Samml Geol Fuehrer
Sammlung Goeschen — Samml Goeschen
Sammlung Goeschen — SG
Sammlung Griechischer und Lateinischer Grammatiker — SGLG
Sammlung Jurisprudenz, Medizin, Philosophie, Theologie — SJMPT
Sammlung Kleiner Ausfuehrungen aus Verschiedenen Wissenschaften — Samml Kleiner Ausfuehr Verschiedenen Wiss
Sammlung Klinischer Vortraege — S Kl V
Sammlung Kurzer Grammatiken Germanischer Dialekte — SKGGD
Sammlung Kurzer Lehrbuecher der Romanischen Sprachen und Literaturen — Sammlung Kurzer Lehrbuecher d Roman Spr u Lit
Sammlung Medizin, Philosophie, Theologie — SMPT
Sammlung Metzler — SM
Sammlung Neuer und Nuetzlicher Abhandlungen und Versuche aus der Oekonomie, Mechanik und Naturlehre — Samml Neuer Nuetzl Abh Versuche Oekon
Sammlung Orientalistischer Arbeiten — S Or A
Sammlung Orientalistischer Arbeiten — SOA
Sammlung von Lehrbuechern der Praktischen Theologie in Gedraengter Darstellung — SLPT
Sammlung von Vergiftungsfaellen — Samml Vergiftungsfaellen
Sammlung Wichmann. Neue Folge — Sammlung Wichmann NF
Sammlung Wissenschaftlicher Kommentare zu Griechischen und Roemischen Schriftstellen — SWKGR
Sammlung Zwangloser Abhandlungen aus dem Gebiete der Augenheilkunde — Smlg Zwangl Abh Aughlkde
Sammlung Zwangloser Abhandlungen aus dem Gebiete der Dermatologie, der Syphilidologie und der Krankheiten des Urogenitalapparates — Samml Zwangloser Abh Dermatol
Sammlung Zwangloser Abhandlungen aus dem Gebiete der Nerven- und Geisteskrankheiten — ANGK
Sammlung Zwangloser Abhandlungen aus dem Gebiete der Psychiatrie und Neurologie — Samml Zwangl Abh Geb Psychiatr Neurol
Sammlungen Nuetzlicher und Angenehmer Gegenstaende aus Allen Theilen der Natur-Geschichte, Arzneywissenschaft und Haushaltungskunst — Samml Nuetzl Angenehmer Gegenstaende Natur-Gesch
Samoan Pacific Law Journal — Samoan Pac LJ
Samoletnoe Elektrooborudovanie — Samoletnoe Elektrooborud
Samoletostroenie i Tekhnika Vozdushnogo Flota — Samoletostr Tekh Vozdushn Flota
Samoletostroenie i Tekhnika Vozdushnogo Flota — STVFB
Samoregulyatsiya Metabolizma Rastenii. Materialy Rabochego Soveshchaniya s Kollokviumom po teme Samoregulyatsiya Metabolizma Rastenii — Samoregul Metab Rast Mater Rab Soveshch Kollok
Samostijna Ukraina [*Independent Ukraine*] — SU
Samotsvety. Materialy S'ezda MMA [*Mezhdunarodnaya Mineralogicheskaya Assotsiatsiya*] — Samotsvety Mater Sezda MMA
SAMPE [*Society for the Advancement of Material and Process Engineering*] **Journal** — SAMPE J
SAMPE [*Society for the Advancement of Material and Process Engineering*] **Quarterly** — SAMPE Q
SAMPE [*Society for the Advancement of Material and Process Engineering*] **Quarterly** — SAMPE Qtly
SAMPE [*Society for the Advancement of Material and Process Engineering*] **Quarterly** — SAMQA
Sampling and Assaying of Precious Metals. Proceedings. International Seminar — Sampling Assaying Precious Met Proc Int Semin
Samtid och Framtid — SoF
Samtiden — Sa
Samtiden — Samt
Samuel Butler Newsletter — Sam BN
Samvirke — Samv
San Antonio Executive — San Anto E
San Bernardino County Medical Society. Bulletin [*California*] — San Bernardino County Med Soc Bull
San Carlos Publications. Humanities — SCPH
San Carlos Publications. Religion — SCPR
San Diego Biomedical Symposium. Proceedings — San Diego Biomed Symp Proc
San Diego Business Journal — San Diego B
San Diego Law Review — San Diego L Rev
San Diego Law Review — San DLR
San Diego Society of Natural History. Memoirs — San Diego Soc Nat Hist Mem
San Diego Society of Natural History. Occasional Papers. Transactions — San Diego Soc Nat History Occasional Paper Trans
San Diego Society of Natural History. Transactions — San Diego Soc N H Tr
San Diego Society of Natural History. Transactions — San Diego Soc Nat History Trans
San Diego Symposium for Biomedical Engineering. Proceedings — San Diego Symp Biomed Eng Proc
San Diego Union — San Diego U
San Fernando Valley Dental Society. Bulletin [*US*] — San Fernando Val Dent Soc Bull
San Fernando Valley Law Review — San Fern Val LR
San Fernando Valley Law Review — San Fern VL Rev
San Francisco Bay Area Early Music News — SFBAEMN
San Francisco Bay Guardian — SF Bay
San Francisco Bay Guardian — SF Bay Gdn
San Francisco Business — San Francisco Bus
San Francisco Business Journal — San Fran B
San Francisco Business Journal — San Francisco Bus Jnl
San Francisco Chronicle — San Fran Cro
San Francisco Chronicle — SFC
San Francisco Examiner — SF Examiner
San Francisco Examiner and Chronicle [*This World Section*] — SFC
San Francisco Magazine — ISFM
San Francisco Magazine — SanF
San Francisco Medicine — San Francisco Med
San Francisco Microscopical Society. Transactions — San Francisco Micro Soc Tr
San Francisco Opera Magazine — San Fran Opera
San Francisco Quarterly — SFrQ
San Francisco Review — SFR
San Francisco Review of Books — SF Rev Bks
San Francisco Review of Books — SFRB
San Francisco Symphony. Program Notes — SF Sym
San Gabriel Valley Dental Society. Bulletin — San Gabriel Val Dent Soc Bull
San Jose Business Journal — San Jose Bus
San Jose Mercury News — San Jose M
San Jose Mercury News — SJMN
San Jose Studies — San Jose Stud
San Jose Studies — SJS
SAN: Journal of the Society for Ancient Numismatics — SAN
San Juan Star — SJS
SANA [*Scientists Against Nuclear Arms*] **Update Newsletter** — SANA Update Newsl
Sanat Tarihi Yilligi — ST Yill
Sanctificatio Nostra — Sanc Nost
Sanctorum Consiliorum et Decretorum Collection Nova — SCDCN
Sand Dune Research — Sand Dune Res
SAND (Sandia National Laboratories) — SAND (Sandia Natl Lab)

Sandalion. Quaderni di Cultura Classica, Cristiana, e Medievale — Sandal
Sandia National Laboratories. Technical Report SAND — Sandia Lab Tech Rep SAND
Sandia National Laboratories. Technical Report SAND — Sandia Natl Lab Tech Rep SAND
Sandia Science News — Sandia SN
Sandoz Bulletin — Sandoz Bull
Sands, Clays, and Minerals — Sands Clays Miner
Sanfujinka No Shimpo — SASHA
Sangeet Natak [*New Delhi*] — Sang Natak
Sangre — Sang
Sangre — SNGRA
Sangyo Anzen Kenkyusho Hokoku — SAKHB
Sangyo Igaku — SAIGB
Sangyo Kogai — SAKOD
Sangyo Kogai Boshi Gijutsu — SKBGD
Sangyo To Denki — SATDB
Sangyo To Kankyo — SAKAD
Sanidad Aeronautica — Sanid Aeronaut
Sanidad Militar — Sanid Mil
Sanidad y Beneficiencia Municipal — Sanid Benef Munic
Sanitaer- und Heizungstechnik — SAHEA
Sanitaer- und Heizungstechnik — Sanit Heiz Tech
Sanitaer- und Heizungstechnik [*Germany*] — Sanit Heizungstechnik
Sanitaer- und Heizungstechnik (Duesseldorf) — Sanit Heizungstech (Duesseldorf)
Sanitaere Technik (Duesseldorf) — Sanit Tech (Duesseldorf)
Sanitaer-Installateur und Heizungsbauer — SIHED
Sanitarnaya Okhrana Vodoemov ot Zagryazneniya Promyshlennymi Stochnymi Vodami — Sanit Okh Vodoemov Zagryaz Prom Stochnymi Vodami
Sanitarnaya Tekhnika — Sanit Tekh
Sanitarnaya Tekhnika — SATKB
Sanitarnaya Tekhnika. Doklady Nauchnoi Konferentsii. Leningradskii Inzhenerno-Stroitel'nyi Institut — Sanit Tekh Dokl Nauchn Konf Leningr
Sanitary and Heating Engineering — Sanitary & Heat Eng
Sanitary Engineering Papers. Colorado State University — Sanit Eng Pap Colo State Univ
Sanitary Record and Journal of Municipal Engineering — Sanit Rec J Munic Eng
Sanitary Record and Municipal Engineering — Sanit Rec Munic Eng
Sanitets Nytt — SANYD
Sanitets Nytt Utgitt av Forsvarets Sanitet — Sanit Nytt
Sanka To Fujinka — Sanka Fuji
Sanken Technical Report — Sanken Tech Rep
Sankhya — Sa
Sankhya. Series A — Sankhya Ser A
Sankhya. Series A. Indian Journal of Statistics — Sankhya A
Sankhya. Series A. Indian Journal of Statistics — Sankhya Ser A
Sankhya. Series B. Indian Journal of Statistics — SANBB
Sankhya. Series B. Indian Journal of Statistics — Sankhya B
Sankhya. Series B. Indian Journal of Statistics — Sankhya Indian J Stat Ser B
Sankhya. Series B. Indian Journal of Statistics — Sankhya Ser B
Sankhya. Series C. Indian Journal of Statistics — Sankhya C
Sankt Eriks Arsbok — Sea
Sankt-Benedikt-Stimmen — SBSt
Sankt-Gabrieler Studien — St G St
Sankt-Petersburger Medicinsche Wochenschrift — St Petersburger Med Wochenschr
Sanop Kwa Kisul — SKWKA
Sanshi Kagaku Kenkyusho Iho — SKEIA
Sanshi Kenkyu — SALEA
Sanskrittexte aus den Turfanfunden — STTF
Santa Barbara Museum of Natural History. Contributions in Science — St Barbara Mus Nat Hist Contrib Sci
Santa Barbara Museum of Natural History. Department of Geology. Bulletin — Santa Barbara Mus Nat History Dept Geology Bull
Santa Barbara Society of Natural History. Bulletin — Santa Barbara Soc N H B
Santa Clara Law Review — Sant Cl LR
Santa Clara Law Review — Santa Clara L Rev
Santa Clara Lawyer — Santa Clara L
Santa Clara Lawyer — Santa Clara Law
Santa Clara Lawyer — SCL
Santa Fe Institute Studies in the Sciences of Complexity. Lectures — Santa Fe Inst Stud Sci Complexity Lectures
Santa Fe Institute Studies in the Sciences of Complexity. Proceedings — Santa Fe Inst Stud Sci Complexity Proc
Sante Mentale au Canada — Sante
Sante Publique. Revue Internationale (Bucuresti) — Sante Publique (Bucur)
Sante Securite Sociale — Sante Secur Soc
Santiago — SO
Santo Domingo Universidad. Anales. Publicaciones — Santo Domingo Univ Anales Pub
Santo Tomas Journal of Medicine — Santo Tomas J Med
Santo Tomas Journal of Medicine — St Tomas J Med
Santo Tomas Nursing Journal — S Tomas Nurs J
Santo Tomas Nursing Journal — St Tomas Nurs J
Sanup Kwahak Gisul Yeonguso Nonmunjip [*Inha University*] — SKGND
Sanyo Gijutsu Zasshi — SGZAB
Sao Jose dos Campos. Faculdade de Odontologia. Revista — Sao Jose dos Campos Fac Odontol Rev
Sao Paulo, Brazil. Instituto de Pesquisas Tecnologicas. Boletin — Sao Paulo Brazil Inst Pesqui Tecnol Bol
Sao Paulo. Instituto Agronomico (Campinas). Boletim — Sao Paulo Inst Agron (Campinas) Bol
Sao Paulo. Instituto Agronomico (Campinas). Boletim Tecnico — Sao Paulo Inst Agron (Campinas) Bol Tec
Sao Paulo. Instituto Agronomico (Campinas). Circular — Sao Paulo Inst Agron (Campinas) Circ
Sao Paulo. Instituto Geografico e Geologico. Boletim — Sao Paulo Inst Geogr Geol Bol
Sao Paulo. Instituto Geografico e Geologico. Relatorio — Sao Paulo Inst Geogr Geol Relat
Sao Paulo Medico — Sao Paulo Med
Sao Paulo. Revista do Arquivo Municipal — SPo
Sao Paulo. Revista do Arquivo Municipal — SPRAM
Sao Paulo. Universidade. Instituto de Geociencias. Boletim — Sao Paulo Univ Inst Geocienc Bol
Sao Paulo. Universidade. Instituto de Geografia. Geografia e Planejamento — Sao Paulo Univ Inst Geogr Geogr Planejamento
Sao Paulo. Universidade. Instituto de Geografia. Geomorfologia — Sao Paulo Univ Inst Geogr Geomorfol
Sao Paulo. Universidade. Instituto de Geografia. Serie Teses e Monografias — Sao Paulo Univ Inst Geogr Ser Teses Monogr
Sapere — SAPEA
Sapientia [*La Plata*] — Sap
Sapienza. Rivista di Filosofia e di Teoogia dei Domenicani d'Italia — Sap Dom
Sapostavitelno Ezikoznanie — SEzik
Sapporo Igaku Zasshi — SIZSA
Sapporo Medical Journal — Sapporo Med J
SAR and QSAR in Environmental Research — SAR QSAR Environ Res
Sarabhai M. Chemicals. Technical News Service — Sarabhai M Chem Tech News Serv
Saratovskaya Nauchno-Issledovatel'skaya Veterinarnaya Stantsiya. Sbornik Nauchnykh Rabot — Sarat Nauchno Issled Vet Stn Sb Nauchn Rab
Saratovskii Gosudarstvennyi Meditsinskii Institut. Trudy — Sarat Gos Med Inst Tr
Saratovskii Gosudarstvennyi-Pedagogiceskii Institut. Ucenye Zapiski — Saratov Gos-Ped Inst Ucen Zap
Saratovskii Politekhnicheskii Institut. Nauchnye Trudy — Sarat Politekh Inst Nauchn Tr
Saratovskii Sel'skokhozyaistvennyi Institut. Nauchnye Trudy — Sarat Skh Inst Nauchn Tr
Saratovskii Sel'skokhozyaistvennyi Institut. Sbornik Nauchnykh Rabot — Sarat Skh Inst Sb Nauchn Rab
Saratovskii Sel'skokhozyaistvennyi Institut. Trudy — Sarat Skh Inst Tr
Saratovskoi Otdelenie Gosudarstvennogo Nauchno-Issledovatel'skogo Instituta Ozernogo i Rechnogo Rybnogo Khozyaistva. Trudy — Sarat Otd Gos Nauchno Issled Inst Ozern Rechn Rybn Khoz Tr
Sarawak Gazette [*Kuching*] — Sar Gaz
Sarawak Museum. Journal [*Kuching*] — Sar Mus J
Sarawak Museum. Journal — Sarawak Mus J
Sarawak Museum. Journal — SarawakMJ
Sarawak Museum. Journal — SMJ
Sarawak. Research Branch. Department of Agriculture. Annual Report — Sarawak Res Branch Dep Agric Annu Rep
Sarcofagi Cristiani Antichi — SCA
Sarcoidose. Rapports. Conference International — Sarcoidose Rapp Conf Int
Sarcolemma. Proceedings. Annual Meeting. International Study Group for Research in Cardiac Metabolism — Sarcolemma Proc Annu Meet Int Study Group Res Card Metab
Sardegna Economica — Sardegna Econ
Sargetia. Acta Musei Devensis — Sarget
Sargetia [*Acta Devensis*]. **Series Scientia Naturae** — Sargetia Ser Sci Nat
Sarotovskoe Otdelenie Gosudarstvennogo Nauchno-Issledovatel'skogo Instituta Ozernogo i Rechnogo Rybnogo Khozyaistva. Trudy — Sarot Otd Gos Nauchno-Issled Inst Ozern Rechn Rybn Khoz Tr
Saskatchewan Bar Review — Sask B Rev
Saskatchewan Bar Review — Sask Bar Rev
Saskatchewan Bar Review — Sask BR
Saskatchewan Bulletin — Sask Bul
Saskatchewan Business — Sask Busn
Saskatchewan. Department of Mineral Resources. Geological Sciences Branch. Precambrian Geology Division. Report — Sask Dep Miner Resour Geol Sci Br Precambrian Geol Div Rep
Saskatchewan. Department of Mineral Resources. Petroleum and Natural Gas Reservoir. Annual — Sask Dep Miner Resour Pet Natural Gas Reservoir Ann
Saskatchewan. Department of Mineral Resources. Report — Sask Dep Miner Resour Rep
Saskatchewan. Department of Natural Resources. Annual Report. Mineral Resources Branch. Miscellaneous Paper — Saskatchewan Dept Nat Res Ann Rept Mineral Res Br Misc Paper
Saskatchewan. Department of Natural Resources. Fisheries and Wildlife Branch. Fisheries Report — Sask Dep Nat Resour Fish Wildl Branch Fish Rep
Saskatchewan. Department of Natural Resources. Fisheries Branch. Fisheries Report — Sask Dep Nat Resour Fish Branch Fish Rep
Saskatchewan Education Administrator — Sask Ed Admin
Saskatchewan Gazette — Sask Gaz
Saskatchewan Geological Society. Special Publication — Sask Geol Soc Spec Publ
Saskatchewan Geological Survey. Report — Saskatchewan Geol Survey Rept
Saskatchewan History — SasH
Saskatchewan History — Sask Hist
Saskatchewan Indian — SIND
Saskatchewan Indian Federated College. Journal — SIFJ
Saskatchewan Law Review — Sask L Rev
Saskatchewan Law Review — Sask Law Rev
Saskatchewan Law Review — Sask LR
Saskatchewan Law Review — Saskatchewan L Rev
Saskatchewan Law Review — SLARD

Saskatchewan Library — Sask Libr
Saskatchewan Library Forum — Sask Lib For
Saskatchewan Mathematics Teachers' Society. Journal — SMTS Journal
Saskatchewan Medical Quarterly — Saskatch Med Quart
Saskatchewan Museums Quarterly — Sask Mus Q
Saskatchewan Native Library Services Newsletter — SNLN
Saskatchewan Power Corp. SPC Report — Sask Power Corp SPC Rep
Saskatchewan (Province). Department of Mineral Resources. Report — Sask (Prov) Dep Miner Resour Rep
Saskatchewan Research Council. Engineering Division. Report — Sask Res Counc Eng Div Rep
Saskatchewan Research Council. Engineering Division. Report E — Sask Res Counc Eng Div Rep E
Saskatchewan Research Council. Geology Division. Circular — Sask Res Counc Geol Div Circ
Saskatchewan Research Council. Geology Division. Report — Sask Res Counc Geol Div Rep
Saskatchewan Research Council. Geology Division. Report G — Sask Res Counc Geol Div Rep G
Saskatchewan Research Council. Physics Division. Report — Sask Res Counc Phys Div Rep
Saskatchewan Research Council. Publication — Sask Res Counc Publ
Saskatchewan Research Council. Report E — Sask Res Counc Rep E
Saskatchewan Research Council. Technical Report — Sask Res Counc Tech Rep
SASMIRA [*Silk and Art Silk Mills' Research Association*] **Technical Digest** — SASMIRA Tech Dig
SASMIRA's [*Silk and Art Silk Mills' Research Association*] **Bulletin** — SASMIRA's Bull
Sassar — SSARB
SASTA [*South Australian Science Teachers Association*] **Journal** — SASTAJ
Satellite Communications — Satell Commun
Satellite Communications — Satellite
Satellite Communications. Satellite Industry Directory — Satel Dir
Satellite Data Network [*Database*] — SDN
Satellite News — Satel News
Satellite Orbit International — Sat Orb Int
Satellite Science Fiction — Sat
Satellite Symposium. Congress. FIP — Satell Symp Congr FIP
Satire Newsletter — Sat NL
Satire Newsletter — Satire N
Satire Newsletter — SatireNL
Satire Newsletter — SNL
SATRA [*Shoe and Allied Trades Research Association*] **Bulletin** — SATRA Bull
Saturated Heterocyclic Chemistry — Saturated Heterocycl Chem
Saturday Evening Post — GTSE
Saturday Evening Post — Sat E P
Saturday Evening Post — Sat Eve Post
Saturday Evening Post — SEP
Saturday Night — GSAT
Saturday Night — Sat N
Saturday Night — SN
Saturday Oklahoman and Times — Sat Oklahom
Saturday Review — SaRe
Saturday Review — SARE-A
Saturday Review — Sat R
Saturday Review — Sat Rev
Saturday Review — Saturd Revw
Saturday Review — Saturday Rev
Saturday Review — SR
Saturday Review of Education — Sat R Ed
Saturday Review of Education — SRE
Saturday Review of Literature — S Rev Lit
Saturday Review of Literature — Sat R Lit
Saturday Review of Literature — SRL
Saturday Review of Politics, Literature, Science, and Art (London) — SRL
Saturday Review of Society — Sat R Soc
Saturday Review of Society — SRSD
Saturday Review of Society — SRSO
Saturday Review of Society — SR-Soc
Saturday Review of the Arts — Sat R Arts
Saturday Review of the Arts — SR Arts
Saturday Review of the Arts — SRA
Saturday Review of the Sciences — Sat R Sci
Saturday Review of the Sciences — SRSC
Saturday Review of the Sciences — SR-Sci
Saturday Review of the Sciences — SRVSB
Saturday Review/World — Sat R/World
Saturday Review/World — SR/World
Saturday Review/World — SRW
Saturn Science Fiction and Fantasy — SRN
Saudi Arabia. Directorate General of Mineral Resources. Bulletin — Saudi Arabia Dir Gen Miner Resour Bull
Saudi Arabia. Directorate General of Mineral Resources. Geologic Map — Saudi Arabia Dir Gen Miner Resour Geol Map
Saudi Arabia. Directorate General of Mineral Resources. Geologic Map GM — Saudi Arabia Dir Gen Miner Resour Geol Map GM
Saudi Arabia. Directorate General of Mineral Resources. Mineral Resources Report of Investigations — Saudi Arabia Dir Gen Miner Resour Miner Resour Rep Invest
Saudi Arabia. Directorate General of Mineral Resources. Mineral Resources Research — Saudi Arabia Dir Gen Miner Resour Miner Resour Res
Saudi Arabia Project Report. US Geological Survey — Saudi Arabia Proj Rep US Geol Surv
Saugar University. Journal. Part 2. Science — Saugar Univ J Part 2
Saugetierkundliche Mitteilungen — Saugertierkd Mitt
Saugetierkundliche Mitteilungen — Saugetierkundliche Mitt
Saugetierkundliche Mitteilungen — STKMBC
Saul Bellow Journal — SBJ
Saunders Monographs in Clinical Radiology — Saunders Monogr Clin Radiol
Saunders Monographs in Clinical Radiology — SMCRD8
Saunders Series — Saunders Ser
Savanna — Sav
Savannah State College Bulletin — SavS
Save Energy — SAEND
Savings and Development — Sav Dev
Savings and Home Financing Source Book 1984 — Home Finan
Savings and Loan News — Sav & Loan N
Savings and Loan News — Sav Loan News
Savings Bank Journal — Sav Bank J
Savings Bank Journal — Savings Bank J
Savings Bank Journal — SBJ
Savings Banks International — Savings Banks Internat
Savings Institutions — Savng Inst
Savings Institutions — SI
Savremena Poljoprivreda — SAPOA
Savremena Poljoprivreda — Savrem Poljopr
Savremena Poljoprivreda — Savrem Poljoprivreda
Savremena Poljoprivreda — Savremena Poljopr
Savremenik — Sav
Savremenna Medicina — Savrem Med
Savremenna Meditsina (Sofia) — Savrem Med (Sofia)
Savvina Kniga — Savv Kn
Savvy Woman — GSAV
SAWTRI [*South African Wool and Textile Research Institute*] **Bulletin** — SAWTRI Bull
SAWTRI [*South African Wool and Textile Research Institute*] **Digest** — SAWTRI Dig
SAWTRI (South African Wool and Textile Research Institute) Technical Report — SAWTRI Tech Rep
SAWTRI [*South African Wool and Textile Research Institute*] **Special Publication** — SAWTRI Spec Publ
Sawyer's Gas Turbine International — Sawyer's Gas Turbine Int
Sawyer's Gas Turbine International — SGTID
Saxophone Journal — SaxJ
Saxophone Journal — SJ
Saxophone Symposium — SaxS
Say It So It Makes Sense — SISIMS
Sayers Review — SRev
SB. Agricultural Experiment Station. University of Nebraska — SB Agric Exp Stn Univ Nebr
SBARMO [*Scientific Ballooning and Radiations Monitoring Organization*] **Bulletin** — SBARMO Bull
SBARMO [*Scientific Ballooning and Radiations Monitoring Organization*] **Bulletin** — SBBUD
Sbirka Pramenu Ceskeho Hnuti Nabozenskeho ve XIV. a XV. Stoleti — SPCHN
Sbirka Vynalezu — Sb Vynalezu
Sbornik. Akademiya Nauk Gruzinskoi SSR. Institut Neorganicheskoi Khimii i Elektrokhimii — Sb Akad Nauk Gruz SSR Inst Neorg Khim Elektrokhim
Sbornik Annotatsii Nauchno-Issledovatel'skikh Rabot. Tomskii Politekhnicheskii Institut — Sb Annot Nauchno Issled Rab Tomsk Politekh Inst
Sbornik Archivnich Praci — SAP
Sbornik Archivnich Praci — Sbor Arch Praci
Sbornik Aspirantskikh Rabot Kazanskii Gosudarstvennyi Universitet Estestvennye Nauki — Sb Aspir Rab Kazan Gos Univ Estest Nauki
Sbornik Aspirantskikh Rabot Kazanskii Gosudarstvennyi Universitet Estestvennye Nauki Biologiya — Sb Aspir Rab Kazan Gos Univ Estest Nauki Biol
Sbornik Aspirantskikh Rabot Kazanskii Gosudarstvennyi Universitet Tochnye Nauki Mekhanika Fizika — Sb Aspir Rab Kazan Gos Univ Tochn Nauki Mekh Fiz
Sbornik Aspirantskikh Rabot Kazanskii Khimiko Tekhnologicheskii Institut — Sb Aspir Rab Kazan Khim Tekhnol Inst
Sbornik Aspirantskikh Rabot Kazanskogo Universiteta Estestvennykh Nauk — Sb Aspir Rab Kazan Univ Estestv Nauk
Sbornik Aspirantskikh Rabot Ufimskii Neftyanoi Nauchno-Issledovatel'skii Institut — Sb Aspir Rab Ufim Neft Nauchno-Issled Inst
Sbornik Aspirantskikh Rabot Voronezhskii Lesotekhnicheskii Institut — Sb Aspir Rab Voronezh Lesotekh Inst
Sbornik Aspirantskikh Rabot Vsesoyuznyi Nauchno Issledovatel'skii Institut Zhivotnovodstva — Sb Aspir Rab Vses Nauchno Issled Inst Zhivotnovod
Sbornik Bakteriofagiya — Sb Bakteriofagiya
Sbornik. Biokhimiya Zerna. Akademiya Nauk SSSR. Institut Biokhimii Imeni A. N. Bakha — Sb Biokhim Zerna Akad Nauk SSSR Inst Biokhim A N Bakha
Sbornik Biologickych a Geologickych Ved Pedagogickych Fakulty — Sborn Biol Geol Ved Pedagog Fak
Sbornik Botanicheskikh Rabot Belorusskoe Otdelenie Vsesoyuznogo Botanicheskogo Obshchestva — Sb Bot Rab Beloruss Otd Vses Bot Ova
Sbornik Botanicheskikh Rabot Vsesoyuznogo Botanicheskogo Obshchestva. Belorusskoe Otdelenie — Sb Bot Rabot Vses Bot Obshch Beloruss Otd
Sbornik Celostatni Pracovni Konference Analytickych Chemiku — Sb Celostatni Prac Konf Anal Chem
Sbornik Ceske Akademie Zemedelske — Sb Ceske Akad Zemed
Sbornik Ceske Spolecnosti Zemevedne — Sborn Ceske Spolecn Zemevedne
Sbornik Ceskoslovenska Akademie Ved. Archeologicky Ustav — Sbornik Cesk Ak Ved Arch Ust
Sbornik Ceskoslovenska Akademie Ved. Archeologicky Ustav (Brno) — Sb (Brno)
Sbornik. Ceskoslovenska Spolecnosti Archeologicka — Sbor Brno
Sbornik. Ceskoslovenska Spolecnosti Archeologicka — Sbornik Cesk Spol Arch

Sbornik. Ceskoslovenska Spolecnosti Archeologicka — Sbornik CSSA
Sbornik. Ceskoslovenska Spolecnosti Archeologicka — SCSA
Sbornik. Ceskoslovenska Spolecnosti Archeologicka (Brno) — Sb Brno
Sbornik Ceskoslovenske Akademie Zemedelske — Sb Cesk Akad Zemed
Sbornik Ceskoslovenske Akademie Zemedelskych Ved — Sb Cesk Akad Zemed Ved
Sbornik Ceskoslovenske Akademie Zemedelskych Ved. Lesnictvi — Sb Cesk Akad Zemed Ved Lesn
Sbornik Ceskoslovenske Akademie Zemedelskych Ved. Rada A — Sb Cesk Akad Zemed Ved Rada A
Sbornik Ceskoslovenske Akademie Zemedelskych Ved. Rada B — Sb Cesk Akad Zemed Ved Rada B
Sbornik Ceskoslovenske Akademie Zemedelskych Ved. Rada B. Zemedelska Ekonomika — Sb Csl Akad Zemed Ved Zemed Ekon
Sbornik Ceskoslovenske Akademie Zemedelskych Ved. Rada C. Rostlinna Vyroba — Sb Csl Akad Zemed Ved Rostlinna Vyroba
Sbornik Ceskoslovenske Akademie Zemedelskych Ved. Rada E. Zivocisna Vyroba — Sb Csl Akad Zemed Ved Ziv Vyroba
Sbornik Ceskoslovenske Akademie Zemedelskych Ved. Rostlinna Vyroba — Sb Cesk Akad Zemed Ved Rostl Vyr
Sbornik Ceskoslovenske Akademie Zemedelskych Ved. Rostlinna Vyroba — Sb Cesk Akad Zemed Ved Rostl Vyroba
Sbornik Ceskoslovenske Akademie Zemedelskych Ved. Ser. Rostlinna Vyroba — Sborn Ceskoslov Akad Zemed Ved Rostl Vyroba
Sbornik Ceskoslovenske Akademie Zemedelskych Ved. Veterinarni Medicina — Sb Cesk Akad Zemed Ved Vet Med
Sbornik Ceskoslovenske Akademie Zemedelskych Ved. Zivocisna Vyroba — Sb Cesk Akad Zemed Ved Zivocisna Vyroba
Sbornik Ceskoslovenske Spolecnosti Zemepisne — Sborn Ceskoslov Spolecn Zemep
Sbornik Ceskoslovenske Spolecnosti Zemepisne — SCSZ
Sbornik Chekhoslovatskikh Khimicheskikh Rabot — Sb Chekh Khim Rab
Sbornik Chelyabinskii Politekhnicheskii Institut — Sb Chelyab Politekh Inst
Sbornik Dokladi. Natsionalna Konferentsiya na Mladite Nauchni Rabotnitsi i Spetsialisti Neft i Khimiya — Sb Dokl Nats Konf Mladite Nauchni Rab Spets Neft Khim
Sbornik Dokladi. Natsionalna Konferentsiya po Vodopodgotovka. Voden Rezhim i Koroziya v TETs i AETs — Sb Dokl Nats Konf Vodopodgot Voden Rezhim Koroz TETs AETs
Sbornik Dokladi. Nauchna Sesiya na Druzhestvoto po Meditsinska Khimiya — Sb Dokl Nauchna Ses Druzh Med Khim
Sbornik Dokladov Konferentsii po Poverkhnostnym Silam — Sb Dokl Konf Poverkhn Silam
Sbornik Dokladov Konferentsii po Vysokomolekularnym Soedineniyam — Sb Dokl Konf Vysokomol Soedin
Sbornik Dokladov Mezhdunarodnogo S'ezda po Obshchemu Issledovaniyu Torfov — Sb Dokl Mezhdunar Sezda Obshch Issled Torfov
Sbornik Dokladov Mezhvuzovskoi Konferentsii po Proboyu Dielektrikov i Poluprovodnikov — Sb Dokl Mezhvuz Konf Proboyu Dielektr Poluprovodn
Sbornik Dokladov na Nauchnykh Konferentsiyakh Molodykh Uchenykh TatNIPIneft — Sb Dokl Nauchn Konf Molodykh Uch TatNIPIneft
Sbornik Dokladov na Problemnom Simpoziume po Fizike Yadra — Sb Dokl Probl Simp Fiz Yadra
Sbornik Dokladov na Sibirskom Soveshchanii po Spektroskopii — Sb Dokl Sib Soveshch Spektrosk
Sbornik Dokladov na Vsesoyuznom Soveshchanii po Modelirovaniyu i Optimizatsii Kataliticheskikh Protsessov — Sb Dokl Vses Soveshch Model Optim Katal Protsessov
Sbornik Dokladov Nauchnogo Studencheskogo Obshchestva Kalininskii Gosudarstvennyi Pedagogicheskii Institut — Sb Dokl Nauchn Stud Ova Kalinin Gos Pedagog Inst
Sbornik Dokladov Nauchno-Tekhnicheskogo Soveshchaniya po Instrumental'nym Stalyam — Sb Dokl Nauchno Tekh Soveshch Instrum Stalyam
Sbornik Dokladov. Otchetnaya Nauchnaya Konferentsiya Biologicheskogo Otdela. Institut Atomnoi Energii — Sb Dokl Otchetnaya Nauchn Konf Biol Otd Inst At Energ
Sbornik Dokladov po Gidrotekhnike. Vsesoyuznyi Nauchno-Issledovatel'skii Institut Gidrotekhniki — Sb Dokl Gidrotekh Vses Nauchno Issled Inst Gidrotekh
Sbornik Dokladov Respublikanskogo S'ezda Epidemiologov. Mikrobiologov, Infektsionistov, i Gigienistov — Sb Dokl Resp Sezda Epidemiol Mikrobiol Infekts Gig
Sbornik Dokladov. Vsesoyuznaya Akusticheskaya Konferentsiya po Fizicheskoi i Tekhnicheskoi Akustike — Sb Dokl Vses Akust Konf Fiz Tekh Akust
Sbornik Dokladov Vsesoyuznogo Seminara po Prizmennym Beta-Spektrometram i Voprosam Ikh Primeneniya — Sb Dokl Vses Semin Prizmennym Beta Spektrom Vopr Ikh Primen
Sbornik Dokladov Vsesoyuznogo Shkoly po Vnutrireaktornym Metodam Issledovanii — Sb Dokl Vses Shk Vnutrireakt Metodam Issled
Sbornik Dokladov Vsesoyuznoi Konferentsii Molodykh Uchenykh po Sadovodstvu — Sb Dokl Vses Konf Molodykh Uch Sadovod
Sbornik Dokladov Vsesoyuznoi Konferentsii po Fiziologicheskim i Biokhimicheskim Osnovam Povysheniya Produktivnosti Sel'skokhozyaistvennykh Zhivotnykh — Sb Dokl Vses Konf Fiziol Biokhim Osn Povysh Prod Skh Zhivotn
Sbornik Dokladov Vsesoyuznoi Nauchnoi Konferentsii po Zhidkim Kristallam i Simpoziuma po Ikh Prakticheskomu Primeneniyu — Sb Dokl Vses Nauchn Konf Zhidk Kris Simp Ikh Prakt Primen
Sbornik Donetskii Nauchno-Issledovatel'skii Ugol'nyi Institut — Sb Donetsk Nauchno Issled Ugoln Inst
Sbornik Entomologickeho Oddeleni Narodniho Musea v Praze — Sb Ent Odd Nar Mus Praze
Sbornik Faunistickych Praci Entomologickeho Oddeleni Narodniho Musea v Praze — Sb Faun Praci Ent Odd Nar Mus Praze
Sbornik Filologicky — SF
Sbornik Filosoficke Fakulty v Bratislave — SFB
Sbornik Filozofickej Fakulty Univerzity Komenskeho — Sb Kom Fil
Sbornik Filozofickej Fakulty Univerzity Komenskeho — SFUK
Sbornik Filozofickej Fakulty Univerzity Komenskeho. Philologica — SFFUK
Sbornik Filozofickej Fakulty Univerzity P. J. Safarika — SFUS
Sbornik Filozofickej Fakulty Univerzity P. J. Safarika v Presove — SFFUP
Sbornik Geologickeho Pruzkumu Ostrava — Sb Geol Pruzkumu Ostrava
Sbornik Geologickych Ved. Antropozoikum — Sb Geol Ved Antropozoikum
Sbornik Geologickych Ved. Geologie — Sb Geol Ved Geol
Sbornik Geologickych Ved. Geologie — SGVGA
Sbornik Geologickych Ved. Hydrogeologie, Inzenyrska, Geologie — Sb Geol Ved Hydrogeol Inz Geol
Sbornik Geologickych Ved. Loziskova Geologie [*Czechoslovakia*] — Sb Geol Ved Loziskova Geol
Sbornik Geologickych Ved. Loziskova Geologie — SGVLA
Sbornik Geologickych Ved. Loziskova Geologie. Mineralogie — Sb Geol Ved Loziskova Geol Mineral
Sbornik Geologickych Ved. Paleontologie — Sb Geol Ved Paleontol
Sbornik Geologickych Ved. Rada A. Antropozoikum — Sb Geol Ved Rada A
Sbornik Geologickych Ved. Rada G. Geologie — Sb Geol Ved Rada G
Sbornik Geologickych Ved. Rada HIG. Hydrogeologie, Inzenyrska Geologie — Sb Geol Ved Rada HIG
Sbornik Geologickych Ved. Rada LG. Loziskova Geologie — Sb Geol Ved Rada LG
Sbornik Geologickych Ved. Rada Loziskova Geologie — Sb Geol Ved Rada Loziskova Geol
Sbornik Geologickych Ved. Rada P. Paleontologie — Sb Geol Ved Rada P
Sbornik Geologickych Ved. Rada P. Paleontologie — Sb Geol Ved Rada P Paleontol
Sbornik Geologickych Ved. Rada TG. Technologie, Geochemie — Sb Geol Ved Rada TG
Sbornik Geologickych Ved. Rada UG. Uzita Geofyzika — Sb Geol Ved Rada UG
Sbornik Geologickych Ved. Rada UG. Uzita Geofyzika — Sb Geol Ved Rada Uzita Geofyz
Sbornik Geologickych Ved. Technologie, Geochemie — Sb Geol Ved Technol Geochem
Sbornik Geologickych Ved. Uzita Geofyzika [*Czechoslovakia*] — Sb Geol Ved Uzita Geofyz
Sbornik Geologickych Ved. Uzita Geofyzika — SGVUA
Sbornik Geologickych Ved. Zapadne Karpaty — Sb Geol Ved Zapadne Karpaty
Sbornik Gosudarstvennogo Geologicheskogo Komiteta ChSR — Sb Gos Geol Kom ChSR
Sbornik GPO [*Geologicky Pruzkum Ostrava*] — Sb GPO
Sbornik Groznenskii Neftyanoi Institut — Sb Grozn Neft Inst
Sbornik Imperatorskogo Russkogo Istoricheskogo Obshchestva — SIRIO
Sbornik Informatsii po Obogashcheniyu i Briketirovaniyu Uglei [*Former USSR*] — Sb Inf Obogashch Briket Uglei
Sbornik Informatsii po Obogashcheniyu i Briketirovaniyu Uglei — SIOBA
Sbornik Informatsionno-Metodicheskikh Materialov. Gosudarstvennyi Nauchno-Issledovatel'skii Institut Glaznykh Boleznei — Sb Inf Metod Mater Gos Nauchno Issled Inst Glaznykh Bolezn
Sbornik Institut Neorganicheskoi Khimii i Elektrokhimii Akademiya Nauk Gruzinskoi SSR — Sb Inst Neorg Khim Elektrokhim Akad Nauk Gruz SSR
Sbornik Issledovatel'skikh Rabot po Bumage i Tsellyuloze — Sb Issled Rab Bum Tsellyul
Sbornik "Izmenenie Pochv pri Okul'turivanii, Ikh Klassifikatsiya i Diagnostika" — Sb "Izme Pochv Okul'turiv Klassifik Diagnostika"
Sbornik Jihoceskeho Muzea v Ceskych Budejovicich Prirodni Vedy — Sb Jihoceskeho Muz Cesk Budejovicich Prir Vedy
Sbornik Khimiko-Tekhnologicheskogo Instituta Praga. Protsessy i Apparaty Avtomatizatsiya — Sb Khim Tekhnol Inst Praga Protsessy Appar Avtom
Sbornik Khimiko-Tekhnologicheskogo Instituta v Prage. Neorganicheskaya i Organicheskaya Tekhnologiya — Sb Khim Tekhnol Inst Prage Neorg Org Tekhnol
Sbornik Khimiko-Tekhnologicheskogo Instituta v Prage. Neorganicheskaya Tekhnologiya — Sb Khim Tekhnol Inst Prage Neorg Tekhnol
Sbornik Khimiko-Tekhnologicheskogo Instituta v Prage. Organicheskaya Tekhnologiya — Sb Khim Tekhnol Inst Prage Org Tekhnol
Sbornik Khimiko-Tekhnologicheskogo Instituta v Prage. Tekhnologiya Vody — Sb Khim Tekhnol Inst Prage Tekhnol Vody
Sbornik Klubu Prirodovedeckeho v Brno — Sb Klubu Prirodoved Brno
Sbornik Krajskeho Muzea v Trnave. Acta Musei Tyrnaviensis — Sborn Krajsk Muz V Trnave
Sbornik Kratkie Soobshcheniya po Fizike. Akademiya Nauk SSSR. Fizicheskii Institut Imeni P. N. Lebedeva — Sb Kratk Soobshch Fiz AN SSSR Fiz Inst P N Lebedeva
Sbornik Kratkikh Soobshchenii Kazanskogo Universiteta Botanika i Pochvovedenie — Sb Kratk Soobshch Kazan Univ Bot Pochvoved
Sbornik Kratkikh Soobshchenii Kazanskogo Universiteta po Zoologii — Sb Kratk Soobshch Kazan Univ Zool
Sbornik Lekarsky — Sb Lek
Sbornik Lekarsky — Sb Lekar
Sbornik Lekarsky — SBLEA
Sbornik Lektsii. Mezhdunarodnaya Shkola po Neitronnoi Fizike — Sb Lektsii Mezhdunar Shk Neitr Fiz
Sbornik Leningradskogo Elektro-Mekhanicheskogo Instituta — Sb Leningr Elektro Mekh Inst
Sbornik Leningradskogo Industrial'nogo Instituta — Sb Leningr Ind Inst
Sbornik Leningradskogo Instituta Inzhenerov Zheleznodorozhnogo Transporta — Sb Leningr Inst Inzh Zheleznodorozhn Transp
Sbornik Leningradskogo Tekstil'nogo Instituta — Sb Leningr Tekst Inst
Sbornik Masarykovy Akademie Prace — Sb Masaryk Akad Pr

Sbornik Masarykovy Akademie Prace — Sborn Masarykovy Akad Prace
Sbornik Materialov Anapskoi Opytnoi Stantsii k Nauchno Proizvodstvennoi Konferentsii — Sb Mater Anapskoi Opytn Stn Nauchno Proizvodstvennoi Konf
Sbornik Materialov Mezhdunarodnogo Kongressa po Lugovodstvu — Sb Mater Mezhdunar Kongr Lugovod
Sbornik Materialov o Novoi Tekhnike i Peredovom Opyte v Stroitel'stve — Sb Mater Nov Tekh Peredovom Opyte Stroit
Sbornik Materialov Permskogo Nauchno-Issledovatel'skogo Ugol'nogo Instituta — Sb Mater Permsk Nauchno Issled Ugoln Inst
Sbornik Materialov po Avtomatizatsii i Dispetcherizatsii Proizvodstvennykh Protsessov — Sb Mater Avtom Dispetcher Proizvod Protsessov
Sbornik Materialov po Avtomatizatsii Proizvodstvennykh Protsessov i Dispetcherizatsii — Sb Mater Avtom Proizvod Protsessov Dispetcher
Sbornik Materialov po Geologii Tsvetnykh, Redkikh, i Bladorodnykh Metallov — Sb Mater Geol Tsvetn Redk Blagorodn Met
Sbornik Materialov po Gornomu Delu Obogashcheniyu i Metallurgii — Sb Mater Gorn Delu Obogashch Metall
Sbornik Materialov po Obmenu Opytom. Nauchnyi Institut po Udobreniyam i Insektofungitsidam — Sb Mater Obmenu Opytom Nauchn Inst Udobr Insektofungits
Sbornik Materialov po Vakuumnoi Tekhnike — Sb Mater Vak Tekh
Sbornik Matice Moravske — Sborn Matice Morav
Sbornik Mezhdunarodnogo Polyarograficheskogo S'ezda — Sb Mezhdunar Polyarogr Sezda
Sbornik Mezinarodniho Polarografickeho Sjezdu — Sb Mezinar Polarogr Sjezdu
Sbornik Mikroelementy i Produktivnost Rastenii — Sb Mikroelementy i Produktivn Rast
Sbornik Moskovskii Institut Stali — Sb Mosk Inst Stali
Sbornik Moskovskii Institut Stali Splavov [*Former USSR*] — Sb Mosk Inst Stali Splavov
Sbornik. Moskovskii Inzhenerno-Stroitel'nyi Institut Imeni V. V. Kuibysheva — Sb Mosk Inzh Stroit Inst Im V V Kuibysheva
Sbornik Muzeja Antropologii i Etnografii — Sb Muz Antropol Etnogr
Sbornik Muzeja Antropologii i Etnografii — SMAE
Sbornik na Balgarskata Akademija na Naukite — SbAk
Sbornik na Bulgarskata Akademiya na Naukite. Klon Prirodo-Matematichen — Sb Bulg Akad Nauk Klon Prir Mat
Sbornik Narodnihi Muzea v Prave Rada A. Historicky — SbNM
Sbornik Narodnihi Muzea v Prave Rada A. Historicky (Praha) — Sbornik (Praha)
Sbornik Narodniho Musea v Praze. Rada B. Prirodni Vedy (Prirodovedny). Acta Musei Nationalis Pragae. Series B. Historia Naturalis — Sborn Nar Mus V Praze Rada B Prir Vedy
Sbornik Narodniho Muzea — SNM
Sbornik Narodniho Muzea v Praze [*Acta Musei Nationalis Pragae*]. Rada A: Historia — Sbor Narod Muz Praze
Sbornik Narodniho Muzea v Praze. Rada B: Prirodni Vedy — Sb Nar Mus Praze Rada B Prir Vedy
Sbornik Nauchni Trudove — Sb Nauchni Tr
Sbornik Nauchni Trudove. Obogatyvane. NIPRORUDA [*Nauchnoizsledovatelski i Proektantski Institut za Rudodobiv i Obogatiavane*] — Sb Nauchni Tr Obogat NIPRORUDA
Sbornik Nauchni Trudove. Rudodobiv i Obogatyvane. NIPRORUDA [*Nauchnoizsledovatelski i Proektantski Institut za Rudodobiv i Obogatiavane*] — Sb Nauchni Tr Rudodobiv Obogat NIPRORUDA
Sbornik Nauchnnykh Trudov Ivanovskogo Energeticheskogo Instituta imeni V.I. Lenina — Sb Nauchn Tr Ivanov Energ Inst im V I Lenina
Sbornik Nauchnogo Studencheskogo Obshchestva Geologicheskii Fakul'tet Moskovskii Gosudarstvennyi Universitet — Sb Nauchn Stud Ova Geol Fak Mosk Gos Univ
Sbornik Nauchnogo Studencheskogo Obshchestva Geologicheskii Fakul'tet Moskovskii Gosudarstvennyi Universitet — SSGMB
Sbornik Nauchno-Issledovatel'skii Institut Gidrometeorologicheskogo Priborostroeniya — Sb Nauchno Issled Inst Gidrometeorol Priborostr
Sbornik Nauchno-Issledovatel'skii Institut Osnovanii i Podzemnykh Sooruzhenii — Sb Nauchno Issled Inst Osn Podzemn Sooruzh
Sbornik Nauchno-Issledovatel'skii Institut Sanitarnoi Tekhniki — Sb Nauchno Issled Inst Sanit Tekh
Sbornik Nauchno-Issledovatel'skii Rabot Arkhangel'skogo Lesotekhnicheskogo Instituta — Sb Nauchno Issled Rab Arkhang Lesotekh Inst
Sbornik Nauchno-Issledovatel'skikh Rabot Adygeikaya Oblast Opytnaya Stantsiya — Sb Nauchno-Issled Rab Adygeisk Oblast Opyt Sta
Sbornik Nauchno-Issledovatel'skikh Rabot Aspirantov. Altaiskii Sel'skokhozyaistvennyi Institut — Sb Nauchno Issled Rab Aspir Altai Skh Inst
Sbornik Nauchno-Issledovatel'skikh Rabot Aspirantov i Molodykh Uchenykh. Altaiskii Sel'skokhozyaistvennyi Institut — Sb Nauchno-Issled Rab Aspir Molodykh Uch Altai Skh Inst
Sbornik Nauchno-Issledovatel'skikh Rabot Azovo-Chernomorskogo Sel'skokhozyaistvennogo Instituta — Sb Nauchno-Issled Rab Azovo-Chernomorsk S-Kh Inst
Sbornik Nauchno-Issledovatel'skikh Rabot Gor'kovskoi Oblastnoi Opytnoi Stantsii Zhivotnovodstva — Sb Nauchno-Issled Rab Gor'k Obl Opytn Stn Zhivotnovod
Sbornik Nauchno-Issledovatel'skikh Rabot. Ivanovskii Tekstil'nyi Institut — Sb Nauchno Issled Rab Ivanov Tekst Inst
Sbornik Nauchno-Issledovatel'skikh Rabot. Kuibyshevskii Industrial'nyi Institut — Sb Nauchno Issled Rab Kuibyshev Ind Inst
Sbornik Nauchno-Issledovatel'skikh Rabot. Orlovskoi Gosudarstvennoi Oblastnoi Sel'skokhozyaistvennoi Opytnoi Stantsii — Sb Nauchno Issled Rab Orlov Gos Obl Skh Opytn Stn
Sbornik Nauchno-Issledovatel'skikh Rabot Orlovskoi Gosudarstvennoi Sel'skokhozyaistvennoi Opytnoi Stantsii — Sb Nauchno-Issled Rab Orlov Gos Sel'-Khoz Opyt Sta
Sbornik Nauchno-Issledovatel'skikh Rabot. Permskogo Sel'skokhozyaistvennogo Instituta — Sb Nauchno Issled Rab Permsk Skh Inst
Sbornik Nauchno-Issledovatel'skikh Rabot po Pchelovodstvu — Sb Nauchno-Issled Rab Pchel
Sbornik Nauchno-Issledovatel'skikh Rabot. Severo-Kavkazskii Zernovoi Institut — Sb Nauchno Issled Rab Sev Kavk Zernovoi Inst
Sbornik Nauchno-Issledovatel'skikh Rabot. Tashkentskii Institut Tekstil'noi i Legkoi Promyshlennosti — Sb Nauchno Issled Rab Tashk Inst Tekst Legk Promst
Sbornik Nauchno-Issledovatel'skikh Rabot Tashkentskogo Tekstil'nogo Instituta — Sb Nauchno Issled Rab Tashk Tekst Inst
Sbornik Nauchno-Issledovatel'skikh Rabot. Ul'yanovskogo Sel'skokhozyaistvennogo Instituta — Sb Nauchno Issled Rab Ulyanovsk Skh Inst
Sbornik Nauchno-Issledovatel'skikh Rabot Vsesoyuznogo Nauchno-Issledovatel'skogo Instituta Tabaka i Makhorki — Sb Nauchno-Issled Rab Vses Nauchno-Issled Inst Tab Makhorki
Sbornik Nauchno-Issledovatel'skikh Trudov Moskovskii Tekstil'nyi Institut — Sb Nauchno Issled Tr Mosk Tekst Inst
Sbornik Nauchno-Issledovatel'skikh Trudov. Moskovskogo Instituta Inzhenerov Kommunal'nogo Stroitel'stva — Sb Nauchno Issled Tr Mosk Inst Inzh Kommunaln Stroit
Sbornik Nauchno-Issledovatel'skikh Trudov. Tsentral'nyi Nauchno-Issledovatel'skii Institut Lubyanykh Volokon — Sb Nauchno Issled Tr Tsentr Nauchno Issled Inst Lub Volokon
Sbornik Nauchno-Issledovatel'skogo Instituta Fiziki OGU — Sb Nauchno Issled Inst Fiz OGU
Sbornik Nauchno-Metodicheskikh Statei po Fizike — Sb Nauchno Metod Statei Fiz
Sbornik Nauchno-Tekhnicheskoi Informatsii Vsesoyuznogo Instituta Gel'mintologii — Sb Nauchno Tekh Inf Vses Inst Gelmintol
Sbornik Nauchno-Tekhnicheskoi Statei Instituta Elektrotekhniki. Akademiya Nauk Ukrainskoi SSR — Sb Nauchno Tekh Statei Inst Elektrotekh Akad Nauk Ukr SSR
Sbornik Nauchnyk Rabot Studentov Ivanovskogo Gosudarstvennogo Meditsinskogo Instituta — Sb Nauchn Rab Stud Ivanov Gos Med Inst
Sbornik Nauchnykh i Metodicheskikh Trudov. Yaroslavskii Gosudarstvennyi Pedagogicheskii Institut Imeni K. D. Ushinskogo — Sb Nauchn Metod Tr Yarosl Gos Pedagog Inst Im K D Ushinskogo
Sbornik Nauchnykh Leningradskogo Instituta Usovershenstvovaniya Veterinarnykh Vrachei — Sb Nauch Trud Leningr Inst Usoversh Vet Vrach
Sbornik Nauchnykh Rabot. Akademiya Kommunal'nogo Khozyaistva Imeni K. D. Pamfilova — Sb Nauchn Rab Akad Kommunaln Khoz Im K D Pamfilova
Sbornik Nauchnykh Rabot. Akademiya Nauk Belorusskoi SSR. Institut Fiziko-Organicheskoi Khimii — Sb Nauchn Rab Akad Nauk B SSR Inst Fiz Org Khim
Sbornik Nauchnykh Rabot. Akademiya Nauk Belorusskoi SSR. Institut Obshchei i Neorganicheskoi Khimii — Sb Nauchn Rab Akad Nauk B SSR Inst Obshch Neorg Khim
Sbornik Nauchnykh Rabot Angarskogo Nauchno-Issledovatel'skogo Instituta Gigieny Truda i Professional'nykh Zabolevanii — Sb Nauchn Rab Angar Nauchno-Issled Inst Gig Tr Prof Zabol
Sbornik Nauchnykh Rabot. Arkhangel'skogo Oblastnogo Sanitarno-Bakteriologicheskogo Instituta — Sb Nauchn Rab Arkhang Obl Sanit Bakteriol Inst
Sbornik Nauchnykh Rabot Arkhangel'skogo Otdeleniya Vsesoyuznogo Nauchnogo Obshchestva Anatomov, Gistologov, i Embriologov — SAOAAW
Sbornik Nauchnykh Rabot Aspirantov — SNRA
Sbornik Nauchnykh Rabot Aspirantov i Molodykh Sotrudnikov Fizicheskogo Fakul'teta. Tadzhikskii Gosudarstvennyi Universitet — Sb Nauchn Rab Aspir Molodykh Sotr Fiz Fak Tadzh Gos Univ
Sbornik Nauchnykh Rabot Aspirantov Kabardino-Balkarskii Gosudarstvennyi Universitet — Sb Nauchn Rab Aspir Kabard Balkar Gos Univ
Sbornik Nauchnykh Rabot Aspirantov. L'vovskii Politekhnicheskii Institut — Sb Nauchn Rab Aspir Lvov Politekh Inst
Sbornik Nauchnykh Rabot Aspirantov Voronezhskogo Gosudarstvennogo Universiteta — Sb Nauchn Rab Aspir Voronezh Gos Univ
Sbornik Nauchnykh Rabot Aspirantov Vsesoyuznyi Nauchno-Issledovatel'skii Institut Khlopkovodstva — Sb Nauchn Rab Aspir Vses Nauchno Issled Inst Khlopkovod
Sbornik Nauchnykh Rabot. Azerbaidzhanskii Nauchno-Issledovatel'skii Oftal'mologicheskii Institut — Sb Nauchn Rab Azerb Nauchno Issled Oftalmol Inst
Sbornik Nauchnykh Rabot. Belorusskaya Sel'skokhozyaistvennaya Akademiya — Sb Nauchn Rab Beloruss Skh Akad
Sbornik Nauchnykh Rabot. Belorusskii Lesotekhnicheskii Institut — Sb Nauchn Rab Beloruss Lesotekh Inst
Sbornik Nauchnykh Rabot. Belorusskii Nauchno-Issledovatel'skii Institut Lesnogo Khozyaistvu — Sb Nauchn Rab Beloruss Nauchno Issled Inst Lesn Khoz
Sbornik Nauchnykh Rabot. Belorusskii Politekhnicheskii Institut — Sb Nauchn Rab Beloruss Politekh Inst
Sbornik Nauchnykh Rabot Belorusskii Tekhnologicheskii Institut — Sb Nauchn Rab Beloruss Tekhnol Inst
Sbornik Nauchnykh Rabot. Belorusskoe Otdelenie Vsesoyuznogo Botanicheskogo Obshchestva — Sb Nauchn Rab Beloruss Otd Vses Bot Ova
Sbornik Nauchnykh Rabot Belorusskogo Gosudarstvennogo Universiteta — Sb Nauchn Rab Beloruss Gos Univ
Sbornik Nauchnykh Rabot Belorusskogo Nauchno-Issledovatel'skogo Kozhnovenerologicheskogo Instituta — Sb Nauchn Rab Beloruss Nauchno-Issled Kozhnovenerol Inst
Sbornik Nauchnykh Rabot Checheno-Ingushskoi Nauchno-Issledovatel'skoi Veterinarnoi Stantsii — Sb Nauchn Rab Checheno Ingush Nauchno Issled Vet Stn

Sbornik Nauchnykh Rabot. Chelyabinskaya Gosudarstvennaya Sel'skokhozyaistvennaya Opytnaya Stantsiya — Sb Nauchn Rab Chelyab Gos Skh Opytn Stn
Sbornik Nauchnykh Rabot. Chernovitskogo Gosudarstvennogo Meditsinskogo Instituta — Sb Nauchn Rab Chernovits Gos Med Inst
Sbornik Nauchnykh Rabot. Chitinskii Gosudarstvennyi Meditsinskii Institut — Sb Nauchn Rab Chit Gos Med Inst
Sbornik Nauchnykh Rabot. Dagestanskii Nauchno-Issledovatel'skii Veterinarnyi Institut — Sb Nauchn Rab Dagest Nauchno Issled Vet Inst
Sbornik Nauchnykh Rabot Dal'nevostochnyi Nauchno-Issledovatel'skii Institut po Stroitel'stvu — Sb Nauchn Rab Dal'nevost Nauchno Issled Inst Stroit
Sbornik Nauchnykh Rabot Dnepropetrovskii Gosudarstvennyi Meditsinskii Institut — Sb Nauchn Rab Dnepropetr Gos Med Inst
Sbornik Nauchnykh Rabot. Dnepropetrovskii Institut Inzhenerov Zheleznodorozhnogo Transporta — Sb Nauchn Rab Dnepropetr Inst Inzh Zheleznodorozhn Transp
Sbornik Nauchnykh Rabot. Dnepropetrovskii Sel'skokhozyaistvennyi Institut — Sb Nauchn Rab Dnepropetr Skh Inst
Sbornik Nauchnykh Rabot. Farmatsevticheskii Fakul'tet. Pervyi Moskovskii Meditsinskii Institut — Sb Nauchn Rab Farm Fak Pervyi Mosk Med Inst
Sbornik Nauchnykh Rabot. Institut Fiziko-Organicheskoi Khimii. Akademiya Nauk Belorusskoi SSR — Sb Nauchn Rab Inst Fiz Org Khim Akad Nauk B SSR
Sbornik Nauchnykh Rabot. Institut Stroitel'stva i Arkhitektury. Akademiya Nauk Belorusskoi SSR — Sb Nauchn Rab Inst Stroit Arkhit Akad Nauk B SSR
Sbornik Nauchnykh Rabot. Instituta Khimii. Akademiya Nauk Belorusskoi SSR — Sb Nauchn Rab Inst Khim Akad Nauk B SSR
Sbornik Nauchnykh Rabot. Instituta Lesnogo Khozyaistva. Akademiya Sel'skokhozyaistvennykh Nauk Belorusskoi SSR — Sb Nauchn Rab Inst Lesn Khoz Akad Skh Nauk B SSR
Sbornik Nauchnykh Rabot Instituta Melioratsii. Vodnogo i Bolotnogo Khozyaistva. Akademiya Nauk Belorusskoi SSR — Sb Nauchn Rab Inst Melior Vodn Bolotnogo Khoz Akad Nauk BSSR
Sbornik Nauchnykh Rabot. Instituta Metallofiziki. Akademiya Nauk Ukrainskoi SSR — Sb Nauchn Rab Inst Metallofiz Akad Nauk Ukr SSR
Sbornik Nauchnykh Rabot. Instituta Obshchei i Neorganicheskoi Khimii. Akademiya Nauk Belorusskoi SSR — Sb Nauchn Rab Inst Obshch Neorg Khim Akad Nauk B SSR
Sbornik Nauchnykh Rabot. Institutov Okhrany Truda VTsSPS — Sb Nauchn Rab Inst Okhr Tr VTsSPS
Sbornik Nauchnykh Rabot. Irkutskii Gosudarstvennyi Meditsinskii Institut — Sb Nauchn Rab Irkutsk Gos Med Inst
Sbornik Nauchnykh Rabot Izhevskii Meditsinskii Institut — Sb Nauchn Rab Izhevsk Med Inst
Sbornik Nauchnykh Rabot Kafedry Mikrobiologii. Kirgizskii Gosudarstvennyi Meditsinskii Institut — Sb Nauchn Rab Kafedry Mikrobiol Kirg Gos Med Inst
Sbornik Nauchnykh Rabot Kafedry Otorinolaringologii Kishinevskogo Meditsinskogo Instituta Moldavskogo Nauchnogo Otorinolaringologicheskogo Obshchestva — SKOKAU
Sbornik Nauchnykh Rabot Kazanskogo Gosudarstvennogo Meditsinskogo Instituta — Sb Nauchn Rab Kazan Gos Med Inst
Sbornik Nauchnykh Rabot Khar'kovskii Institut Mekhanizatsii Sotsialisticheskogo Sel'skogo Khozyaistva — Sb Nauchn Rab Khar'k Inst Mekh Sots Sel'sk Khoz
Sbornik Nauchnykh Rabot Khar'kovskogo Gosudarstvennogo Meditsinskogo Instituta — Sb Nauchn Rab Khar'k Gos Med Inst
Sbornik Nauchnykh Rabot Khar'kovskogo Nauchno-Issledovatel'skogo Instituta Vaktsin i Syvorotok — Sb Nauchn Rab Khar'k Nauchno-Issled Inst Vaktsin Syvorot
Sbornik Nauchnykh Rabot Kievskii Voennyi Gospital — Sb Nauchn Rab Kiev Voen Gosp
Sbornik Nauchnykh Rabot Kirgizskii Meditsinskii Institut — Sb Nauchn Rab Kirg Med Inst
Sbornik Nauchnykh Rabot Kirgizskogo Gosudarstvennogo Meditsinskogo Instituta — Sb Nauchn Rab Kirg Gos Med Inst
Sbornik Nauchnykh Rabot Kirgizskogo Nauchno-Issledovatel'skogo Instituta Okhrany Materinstva i Detstva — Sb Nauchn Rab Kirg Nauchno Issled Inst Okhr Materin Det
Sbornik Nauchnykh Rabot Kirgizskogo Nauchno-Issledovatel'skogo Instituta Tuberkuleza — Sb Nauchn Rab Kirg Nauchno-Issled Inst Tuberk
Sbornik Nauchnykh Rabot Krasnoyarskogo Gosudarstvennogo Meditsinskogo Instituta — Sb Nauchn Rab Krasnoyarsk Gos Med Inst
Sbornik Nauchnykh Rabot Kurganskii Gosudarstvennyi Sel'skokhozyaistvennyi Institut — Sb Nauchn Rab Kurgan Gos S-Kh Inst
Sbornik Nauchnykh Rabot. Kurskaya Nauchno-Issledovatel'skaya Veterinarnaya Stantsiya — Sb Nauchn Rab Kursk Nauchno Issled Vet Stan
Sbornik Nauchnykh Rabot. Kurskaya Nauchno-Proizvodstvennaya Veterinarnaya Laboratoriya — Sb Nauchn Rab Kursk Nauchno Proizvod Vet Lab
Sbornik Nauchnykh Rabot. Kurskaya Oblastnaya Nauchno-Proizvodstvennaya Veterinarnaya Laboratoriya — Sb Nauchn Rab Kursk Obl Nauchno Proizvod Vet Lab
Sbornik Nauchnykh Rabot Laboratorii Metallofiziki. Akademiya Nauk Ukrainskoi SSR — Sb Nauchn Rab Lab Metallofiz Akad Nauk Ukr SSR
Sbornik Nauchnykh Rabot Leningradskii Gosudarstvennyi Institut Usovershenstvovaniya Vrachei — Sb Nauchn Rab Leningr Gos Inst Usoversh Vrachei
Sbornik Nauchnykh Rabot Leningradskii Institut Sovetskoi Torgovli — Sb Nauchn Rab Leningr Inst Sov Torg
Sbornik Nauchnykh Rabot Leningradskii Nauchno-Issledovatel'skii Institut Antibiotikov — Sb Nauchn Rab Leningr Nauchno Issled Inst Antibiot
Sbornik Nauchnykh Rabot. Leningradskii Veterinarnyi Institut — Sb Nauchn Rab Leningr Vet Inst
Sbornik Nauchnykh Rabot Leningradskogo Khimiko-Farmatsevticheskogo Instituta — Sb Nauchn Rab Leningr Khim-Farm Inst
Sbornik Nauchnykh Rabot. L'vovskii Gosudarstvennyi Meditsinskii Institut — Sb Nauchn Rab Lvov Gos Med Inst
Sbornik Nauchnykh Rabot. Magnitogorskii Gornometallurgicheskii Institut — Sb Nauchn Rab Magnitogorsk Gornometall Inst
Sbornik Nauchnykh Rabot Meditsinskogo Fakul'teta Karlova Universiteta v Gradtse Kralove — Sb Nauchn Rab Med Fak Karlova Univ Gradtse Kralove
Sbornik Nauchnykh Rabot Minskogo Gosudarstvennogo Meditsinskogo Instituta — Sb Nauchn Rab Minsk Gos Med Inst
Sbornik Nauchnykh Rabot Moldavskogo Otdeleniya Vsesoyuznogo Nauchnogo Obshchestva Mikrobiologov, Epidemiologov, i Infektsionistov — SOMIA8
Sbornik Nauchnykh Rabot Molodykh Uchenykh. Chuvashskii Sel'skokhozyaistvennyi Institut — Sb Nauchn Rab Molodykh Uch Chuv Skh Inst
Sbornik Nauchnykh Rabot. Moskovskii Gornyi Institut. Kafedra Khimii — Sb Nauchn Rab Mosk Gorn Inst Kafedra Khim
Sbornik Nauchnykh Rabot. Moskovskii Institut Narodnogo Khozyaistva — Sb Nauchn Rab Mosk Inst Nar Khoz
Sbornik Nauchnykh Rabot. Moskovskii Inzhenerno-Fizicheskii Institut — Sb Nauchn Rab Mosk Inzh Fiz Inst
Sbornik Nauchnykh Rabot Moskovskogo Farmatsevticheskogo Instituta — Sb Nauchn Rab Mosk Farm Inst
Sbornik Nauchnykh Rabot Murmanskaya Olenevodcheskaya Opytnaya Stantsiya — Sb Nauchn Rab Murm Olenevodcheskaya Opytn Stn
Sbornik Nauchnykh Rabot. Nauchno-Issledovatel'skii Institut Sadovodstva — Sb Nauchn Rab Nauchno Issled Inst Sadovod
Sbornik Nauchnykh Rabot Nauchno-Issledovatel'skogo Instituta Sadov Imeni I. V. Michurina — Sb Nauchn Rab Nauchno-Issled Inst Sadov Im I V Michurina
Sbornik Nauchnykh Rabot Nauchno-Issledovatel'skogo Instituta Stroitel'nykh Materialov (Minsk) — Sb Nauchn Rab Nauchno Issled Inst Stroit Mater (Minsk)
Sbornik Nauchnykh Rabot Novosibirskoi Nauchno-Issledovatel'skoi Veterinarnoi Stantsii — Sb Nauchn Rab Novosib Nauchno Issled Vet Stn
Sbornik Nauchnykh Rabot Omskogo Nauchno-Issledovatel'skogo Veterinarnogo Instituta — Sb Nauchn Rab Omsk Nauchno Issled Vet Inst
Sbornik Nauchnykh Rabot Pchelovodstvu — Sb Nauchn Rab Pchelovod
Sbornik Nauchnykh Rabot. Penzenskii Inzhenerno-Stroitel'nyi Institut — Sb Nauchn Rab Penz Inzh Stroit Inst
Sbornik Nauchnykh Rabot. Permskii Gosudarstvennyi Meditsinskii Institut — Sb Nauchn Rab Permsk Gos Med Inst
Sbornik Nauchnykh Rabot po Agronomicheskoi Khimii. Moskovskaya Sel'skokhozyaistvennaya Akademiya — Sb Nauchn Rab Agron Khim Mosk Skh Akad
Sbornik Nauchnykh Rabot po Lesnomu Khozyaistvu — Sb Nauchn Rab Lesn Khoz
Sbornik Nauchnykh Rabot Rizhskogo Meditsinskogo Instituta — Sb Nauchn Rab Rizh Med Inst
Sbornik Nauchnykh Rabot. Rostovskii Gosudarstvennyi Meditsinskii Institut — Sb Nauchn Rab Rostov Gos Med Inst
Sbornik Nauchnykh Rabot Rostovskogo Meditsinskogo Instituta — Sb Nauchn Rab Rostov Med Inst
Sbornik Nauchnykh Rabot. Ryazanskaya Gosudarstvennaya Sel'skokhozyaistvennaya Stantsiya — Sb Nauchn Rab Ryazan Gos Skh Stn
Sbornik Nauchnykh Rabot Ryazanskii Sel'skokhozyaistvennyi Institut — Sb Nauchn Rab Ryazan S-Kh Inst
Sbornik Nauchnykh Rabot. Ryazanskii Sel'skokhozyaistvennyi Institut Imeni Prof. P. A. Kostycheva — Sb Nauchn Rab Ryazan Skh Inst Im Prof P A Kostycheva
Sbornik Nauchnykh Rabot. Saratovskaya Nauchno-Issledovatel'skaya Veterinarnaya Stantsiya — Sb Nauchn Rab Sarat Nauchno Issled Vet Stn
Sbornik Nauchnykh Rabot. Saratovskii Institut Giproniigaz — Sb Nauchn Rab Sarat Inst Giproniigaz
Sbornik Nauchnykh Rabot Saratovskii Meditsinskii Institut — Sb Nauchn Rab Sarat Med Inst
Sbornik Nauchnykh Rabot. Saratovskii Sel'skokhozyaistvennyi Institut — Sb Nauchn Rab Sarat Skh Inst
Sbornik Nauchnykh Rabot. Severo-Osetinskii Gosudarstvennyi Meditsinskii Institut — Sb Nauchn Rab Sev Oset Gos Med Inst
Sbornik Nauchnykh Rabot. Sibirskii Nauchno-Issledovatel'skii Institut Sel'skogo Khozyaistva — Sb Nauchn Rab Sib Nauchno Issled Inst Selsk Khoz
Sbornik Nauchnykh Rabot. Sibirskii Nauchno-Issledovatel'skii Institut Zernogo Khozyaistva — Sb Nauchn Rab Sib Nauchno Issled Inst Zernogo Khoz
Sbornik Nauchnykh Rabot Sibirskogo Nauchno-Issledovatel'skogo Veterinarnogo Instituta — Sb Nauchn Rab Sib Nauchno Issled Vet Inst
Sbornik Nauchnykh Rabot Sibirskogo Zonal'nogo Nauchno-Issledovatel'skogo Veterinarnogo Instituta — Sb Nauchn Rab Sib Zon Nauchno-Issled Vet Inst
Sbornik Nauchnykh Rabot SibNIVI — Sb Nauchn Rab SibNIVI
Sbornik Nauchnykh Rabot Studentov. Donetskii Industrial'nyi Institut — Sb Nauchn Rab Stud Donetsk Ind Inst
Sbornik Nauchnykh Rabot Studentov Erevanskii Gosudarstvennyi Universitet — Sb Nauchn Rab Stud Erevan Gos Univ
Sbornik Nauchnykh Rabot Studentov i Aspirantov. Moskovskaya Veterinarnaya Akademiya — Sb Nauchn Rab Stud Aspir Mosk Vet Akad
Sbornik Nauchnykh Rabot Studentov Karelo-Finskogo Gosudarstvennogo Universiteta — Sb Nauchn Rab Stud Karelo Fin Gos Univ
Sbornik Nauchnykh Rabot Studentov Kirgizskii Gosudarstvennyi Universitet — Sb Nauchn Rab Stud Kirg Gos Univ
Sbornik Nauchnykh Rabot Studentov Leningradskogo Gornogo Instituta — Sb Nauchn Rab Stud Leningr Gorn Inst
Sbornik Nauchnykh Rabot Studentov. Moskovskaya Veterinarnaya Akademiya — Sb Nauchn Rab Stud Mosk Vet Akad
Sbornik Nauchnykh Rabot Studentov Petrozavodskogo Gosudarstvennogo Universiteta — Sb Nauchn Rab Stud Petrozavodsk Gos Univ
Sbornik Nauchnykh Rabot Studentov. Rostovskogo Gosudarstvennogo Universiteta — Sb Nauchn Rab Stud Rostov Gos Univ

Sbornik Nauchnykh Rabot Studentov Saratovskii Zootekhnichesko-Veterinarnyi Institut — Sb Nauchn Rab Stud Sarat Zootekh Vet Inst
Sbornik Nauchnykh Rabot Studentov Stalingradskogo Sel'skokhozyaistvennogo Instituta — Sb Nauchn Rab Stud Stalingr S-Kh Inst
Sbornik Nauchnykh Rabot Sverdlovskii Gosudarstvennyi Meditsinskii Institut — Sb Nauchn Rab Sverdl Gos Med Inst
Sbornik Nauchnykh Rabot Sverdlovskogo Meditsinskogo Instituta — Sb Nauchn Rab Sverdl Med Inst
Sbornik Nauchnykh Rabot Sverdlovskogo Otdeleniya Vsesoyuznogo Obshchestva Anatomov, Gistologov, i Embriologov — Sb Nauchn Rab Sverdl Otd Vses O-Va Anat Gistol Embriol
Sbornik Nauchnykh Rabot Tsentral'naya Nauchno-Issledovatel'skaya Laboratoriya Rostov'skogo Meditsinskogo Instituta — Sb Nauchn Rab Tsentr Nauchno-Issled Lab Rostov Med Inst
Sbornik Nauchnykh Rabot. Tsentral'nyi Botanicheskii Sad Akademii Nauk BSSR — Sb Nauchn Rab Tsentr Bot Sad Akad Nauk BSSR
Sbornik Nauchnykh Rabot Ukrainskii Nauchno-Issledovatel'skii Institut Sadovodstva — Sb Nauchn Rab Ukr Nauchno Issled Inst Sadovod
Sbornik Nauchnykh Rabot Vitebskogo Gosudarstvennogo Meditsinskogo Instituta — Sb Nauchn Rab Vitebsk Gos Med Inst
Sbornik Nauchnykh Rabot Vitebskogo Meditsinskogo Instituta — Sb Nauchn Rab Vitebsk Med Inst
Sbornik Nauchnykh Rabot Voenno-Meditsinskogo Fakul'teta Kuibyshevskogo Meditsinskogo Instituta — Sb Nauchn Rab Voen-Med Fak Kuibyshev Med Inst
Sbornik Nauchnykh Rabot Voenno-Meditsinskogo Fakul'teta Kuibyshevskogo Meditsinskogo Instituta [*Former USSR*] — Sb Nauchn Voen-Med Fak Kuibyshev Med Inst
Sbornik Nauchnykh Rabot Voenno-Meditsinskogo Fakul'teta Kuibyshevskogo Meditsinskogo Instituta — SNVKB
Sbornik Nauchnykh Rabot Volgogradskogo Meditsinskogo Instituta — Sb Nauchn Rab Volgogr Med Inst
Sbornik Nauchnykh Rabot Volgogradskogo Pedagogicheskogo Instituta — Sb Nauchn Rab Volgogr Pedagog Inst
Sbornik Nauchnykh Rabot Volgogradskoi Gosudarstvennyi Meditsinskii Institut — Sb Nauchn Rab Volgogr Gos Med Inst
Sbornik Nauchnykh Rabot Volgogradskoi Oblastnoi Klinicheskoi Bol'nitsy — Sb Nauchn Rab Volgogr Obl Klin Boln
Sbornik Nauchnykh Rabot. Vserossiiski Nauchno-Issledovatel'skii Institut Vinogradarstva i Vinodeliya — Sb Nauchn Rab Vseross Nauchno Issled Inst Vinograd Vinodel
Sbornik Nauchnykh Rabot Vsesoyuznogo Nauchno-Issledovatel'skogo Instituta Ovtsevodstva i Kozovodstva — Sb Nauchn Rab Vses Nauchno Issled Inst Ovtsevod Kozovod
Sbornik Nauchnykh Rabot Vsesoyuznyi Nauchno-Issledovatel'skii Institut Lekarstvennykh Rastenii — Sb Nauchn Rab Vses Nauchno-Issled Inst Lek Rast
Sbornik Nauchnykh Rabot Vsesoyuznyi Nauchno-Issledovatel'skii Institut Sadovodstva — Sb Nauchn Rab Vses Nauchno-Issled Inst Sadovod
Sbornik Nauchnykh Rabot Vsesoyuznyi Nauchno-Issledovatel'skii Institut Zhivotnovodstva — Sb Nauchn Rab Vses Nauchno-Issled Inst Zhivotnovod
Sbornik Nauchnykh Rabot. Vsesoyuznyi Nauchno-Issledovatel'skogo Institut Poligraficheskoi Promyshlennosti — Sb Nauchn Rab Vses Nauchno Issled Inst Poligr Promsti
Sbornik Nauchnykh Rabot. Vsesoyuznyi Zaochnyi Institut Sovetskoi Torgovli — Sb Nauchn Rab Vses Zaochn Inst Sov Torg
Sbornik Nauchnykh Rabot Yaroslavskogo Gorzdravotdela — Sb Nauchn Rab Yarosl Gorzdravotd
Sbornik Nauchnykh Rabot Yaroslavskogo Gorzdravotdela — Sb Nauchn Rab Yarosl Gorzdravotdela
Sbornik Nauchnykh Rabot Yaroslavskogo Meditsinskogo Instituta — Sb Nauchn Rab Yarosl Med Inst
Sbornik Nauchnykh Rabot Zaochnyi Institut Sovetskoi Torgovli — Sb Nauchn Rab Zaochn Inst Sov Torg
Sbornik Nauchnykh Rabot Zaporozhskogo Gosudarstvennogo Instituta Usovershenstvovaniya Vrachei — Sb Nauchn Rab Zaporozh Gos Inst Usoversh Vrachei
Sbornik Nauchnykh Soobshchenii Dagestanskii Gosudarstvennyi Universitet Kafedra Khimii — Sb Nauchn Soobshch Dagest Gos Univ Kafedra Khim
Sbornik Nauchnykh Soobshchenii Dagestanskogo Otdela Vsesoyuznogo Botanicheskogo Obshchestva — Sb Nauchn Soobshch Dagest Otd Vses Bot Ova
Sbornik Nauchnykh Soobshchenii Estestvennykh i Tekhnicheskikh Nauk Dagestanskogo Universitet — Sb Nauchn Soobshch Estest Tekh Nauk Dagest Univ
Sbornik Nauchnykh Soobshchenii Kafedry Arkhitektury. Odesskii Inzhenerno-Stroitel'nyi Institut — Sb Nauchn Soobshch Kafedry Arkhit Odess Inzh Stroit Inst
Sbornik Nauchnykh Soobshchenii Kafedry Organicheskoi i Fizkolloidnoi Khimii Dagestanskii Gosudarstvennyi Universitet — Sb Nauchn Soobshch Kafedry Org Fizk Khim Dagest Gos Univ
Sbornik Nauchnykh Soobshchenii Kafedry Zoologii Biologii Khimii Dagestanskogo Universiteta — Sb Nauchn Soobshch Kafedry Zool Biol Khim Dagest Univ
Sbornik Nauchnykh Soobshchenii Saratovskii Avtomobil'no Dorozhnyi Institut — Sb Nauchn Soobshch Sarat Avtomob Dorozhn Inst
Sbornik Nauchnykh Soobshchenii. Saratovskii Politekhnicheskii Institut — Sb Nauchn Soobshch Sarat Politekh Inst
Sbornik Nauchnykh Statei. Belorusskaya Sel'skokhozyaistvennaya Akademiya — Sb Nauchn Statei Beloruss Skh Akad
Sbornik Nauchnykh Statei. Institut Botaniki. Akademiya Nauk Litovskoi SSR — Sb Nauchn Statei Inst Bot Akad Nauk Lit SSR
Sbornik Nauchnykh Statei Khar'kovskogo Instituta Inzhenerov Zheleznodorozhnogo Transporta — Sb Nauchn Statei Khark Inst Inzh Zheleznodorozhn Transp
Sbornik Nauchnykh Statei. Krasnoyarskii Institut Tsvetnykh Metallov — Sb Nauchn Statei Krasnoyarsk Inst Tsvetn Met
Sbornik Nauchnykh Statei. Tashkentskii Institut Inzhenerov Zheleznodorozhnogo Transporta — Sb Nauchn Statei Tashk Inst Inzh Zheleznodorozhn Transp
Sbornik Nauchnykh Statei Vinnitskogo Gosudarstvennogo Meditsinskogo Instituta — Sb Nauchn Statei Vinnitsk Gos Med Inst
Sbornik Nauchnykh Studencheskikh Rabot Omskii Gosudarstvennyi Pedagogicheskii Institut — Sb Nauchn Stud Rab Omsk Gos Pedagog Inst
Sbornik Nauchnykh Studencheskikh Rabot Saratovskogo Zoovetinstituta — Sb Nauchn Stud Rab Sarat Zoovetinst
Sbornik Nauchnykh Trudov. Akademiya Nauk Belorusskoi SSR. Fiziko-Tekhnicheskii Institut — Sb Nauchn Tr Akad Nauk B SSR Fiz Tekh Inst
Sbornik Nauchnykh Trudov Andizhanskii Gosudarstvennyi Meditsinskii Institut — Sb Nauchn Tr Andizh Gos Med Inst
Sbornik Nauchnykh Trudov Andizhanskogo Meditsinskogo Instituta — Sb Nauchn Tr Andizh Med Inst
Sbornik Nauchnykh Trudov Armyanskii Gosudarstvennyi Pedagogicheskii Institut. Seriya Fiziko-Matematicheskaya — Sb Nauchn Tr Arm Gos Pedagog Inst Ser Fiz Mat
Sbornik Nauchnykh Trudov Armyanskogo Otdelnykh Vsesoyuznogo Botanicheskoi Obshchestva — Sb Nauchn Tr Arm Otd Vses Bot Ova
Sbornik Nauchnykh Trudov Armyanskogo Sel'skokhozyaistvennogo Instituta — Sb Nauchn Tr Arm S-Kh Inst
Sbornik Nauchnykh Trudov Azerbaidzhanskogo Nauchno-Issledovatel'skogo Instituta Gematologii i Perelivaniya Krovi — Sb Nauchn Tr Azerb Nauchno Issled Inst Gematol Pereliv Krovi
Sbornik Nauchnykh Trudov Azerbaidzhanskogo Nauchno-Issledovatel'skogo Instituta Perelivaniya Krovi — Sb Nauchn Tr Azerb Nauchno Issled Inst Perel Krovi
Sbornik Nauchnykh Trudov Azerbaidzhanskogo Nauchno-Issledovatel'skogo Instituta Perelivaniya Krovi — Sb Nauchn Tr Azerb Nauchno-Issled Inst Pereliv Krovi
Sbornik Nauchnykh Trudov Bashkirskogo Gosudarstvennogo Meditsinskogo Instituta — Sb Nauchn Tr Bashk Gos Med Inst
Sbornik Nauchnykh Trudov Bashkirskogo Meditsinskogo Instituta — Sb Nauchn Tr Bashk Med Inst
Sbornik Nauchnykh Trudov Bashkirskogo Nauchno-Issledovatel'skogo Trakhomatoznogo Instituta — Sb Nauchn Tr Bashk Nauchno-Issled Trakhomatoznogo Inst
Sbornik Nauchnykh Trudov Belorusskii Institut Mekhanizatsii Sel'skogo Khozyaistva — Sb Nauchn Tr Beloruss Inst Mekh Selsk Khoz
Sbornik Nauchnykh Trudov. Belorusskii Nauchno-Issledovatel'skii Institut Pochvovedeniya — Sb Nauchn Tr Beloruss Nauchno Issled Inst Pochvoved
Sbornik Nauchnykh Trudov Belorusskii Nauchno-Issledovatel'skii Institut Pochvovedeniya i Agrokhimii — Sb Nauchn Tr Beloruss Nauchno-Issled Inst Pochvoved Agrokhim
Sbornik Nauchnykh Trudov Belorusskii Nauchno-Issledovatel'skii Institut Zemledeliya — Sb Nauch Tr Beloruss Nauch-Issled Inst Zemled
Sbornik Nauchnykh Trudov Belorusskii Nauchno-Issledovatel'skii Institut Zemledeliya — Sb Nauchn Tr Beloruss Nauchno-Issled Inst Zemled
Sbornik Nauchnykh Trudov Belorusskii Nauchno-Issledovatel'skii Kozhno-Venerologicheskii Institut — Sb Nauchn Tr Beloruss Nauchno Issled Kozhno Venerol Inst
Sbornik Nauchnykh Trudov Belorusskii Politekhnicheskii Institut — Sb Nauchn Tr Beloruss Politekh Inst
Sbornik Nauchnykh Trudov Belorusskogo Lesotekhnicheskogo Instituta — Sb Nauchn Tr Beloruss Lesotekh Inst
Sbornik Nauchnykh Trudov Belorusskoi Sel'skokhozyaistvennoi Akademii — Sb Nauchn Tr Beloruss S-Kh Akad
Sbornik Nauchnykh Trudov Chelyabinskii Nauchno-Issledovatel'skii Institut Gornogo Dela — Sb Nauchn Tr Chelyab Nauchno Issled Inst Gorn Dela
Sbornik Nauchnykh Trudov Chelyabinskii Politekhnicheskii Institut [*Former USSR*] — Sb Nauchn Tr Chelyab Politekh Inst
Sbornik Nauchnykh Trudov Chelyabinskogo Meditsinskogo Instituta — Sb Nauchn Tr Chelyab Med Inst
Sbornik Nauchnykh Trudov Chitinskii Gosudarstvennyi Meditsinskii Institut — Sb Nauchn Tr Chit Gos Med Inst
Sbornik Nauchnykh Trudov Chuvashskogo Nauchno-Issledovatel'skogo Trakhomatoznogo Instituta — Sb Nauchn Tr Chuv Nauchno-Issled Trakhomatoznogo Inst
Sbornik Nauchnykh Trudov Dagestanskii Gosudarstvennyi Meditsinskii Institut — Sb Nauchn Tr Dagest Gos Med Inst
Sbornik Nauchnykh Trudov. Dagestanskii Nauchno-Issledovatel'skii Otdel Energetiki — Sb Nauchn Tr Dagest Nauchno Issled Otd Energ
Sbornik Nauchnykh Trudov Dnepropetrovskii Gosudarstvennyi Meditsinskii Institut — Sb Nauchn Tr Dnepropetr Gos Med Inst
Sbornik Nauchnykh Trudov Dnepropetrovskii Inzhenerno-Stroitel'nyi Institut — Sb Nauchn Tr Dnepropetr Inzh Stroit Inst
Sbornik Nauchnykh Trudov. Dnepropetrovskii Metallurgicheskii Institut — Sb Nauchn Tr Dnepropetr Metall Inst
Sbornik Nauchnykh Trudov Donskogo Sel'skokhozyaistvennogo Instituta — Sb Nauchn Tr Donskogo S-Kh Inst
Sbornik Nauchnykh Trudov Erevanskii Armyanskii Gosudarstvennyi Pedagogicheskii Institut. Khimiya — Sb Nauchn Tr Erevan Arm Gos Pedagog Inst Khim
Sbornik Nauchnykh Trudov Erevanskii Politekhnicheskii Institut [*Armenian SSR*] — Sb Nauchn Tr Erevan Politekh Inst
Sbornik Nauchnykh Trudov Estonskaya Sel'skokhozyaistvennaya Akademiya — Sb Nauchn Tr Est S-Kh Akad
Sbornik Nauchnykh Trudov. Estonskii Nauchno-Issledovatel'skii Institut Zhivotnovodstva i Veterinarii — Sb Nauchn Tr Est Nauchno Issled Inst Zhivotnovod Vet

Sbornik Nauchnykh Trudov. Estonskii Nauchno-Issledovatel'skii Institut Zhivotnovodstva i Veterinarii im A. Mel'dera — Sb Nauchn Tr Est Nauchno Issled Inst Zhivotnovod Vet im A Mel
Sbornik Nauchnykh Trudov Estonskogo Nauchnogo Instituta Zemledeliya i Melioratsii — Sb Nauch Trud Eston Nauch Inst Zeml Melior
Sbornik Nauchnykh Trudov Estonskogo Nauchno-Issledovatel'skogo Instituta Zemledeliya i Melioratsii — Sb Nauchn Tr Est Nauchno-Issled Inst Zemled Melior
Sbornik Nauchnykh Trudov Estonskoi Sel'skokhozyaistvennoi Akademii — EPSNA
Sbornik Nauchnykh Trudov Estonskoi Sel'skokhozyaistvennoi Akademii — Sb Nauch Tr Eston Sel'skokhoz Akad
Sbornik Nauchnykh Trudov Estonskoi Sel'skokhozyaistvennoi Akademii — Sb Nauch Trud Eston Sel'khoz Akad
Sbornik Nauchnykh Trudov Fiziko-Tekhnicheskii Institut Akademiya Nauk Belorusskoi SSR — Sb Nauchn Tr Fiz Tekh Inst Akad Nauk B SSR
Sbornik Nauchnykh Trudov Fiziko-Tekhnicheskii Institut Nizkikh Temperatur Akademiya Nauk Ukrainskoi SSR [*Ukrainian SSR*] — Sb Nauchn Tr Fiz Tekh Inst Nizk Temp Akad Nauk Ukr SSR
Sbornik Nauchnykh Trudov. Frunzenskogo Politekhnicheskogo Instituta — Sb Nauchn Tr Frunz Politekh Inst
Sbornik Nauchnykh Trudov Gidroproekta — Sb Nauchn Tr Gidroproekta
Sbornik Nauchnykh Trudov Glavgeologii Uzbekskoi SSR i Tashkentskogo Politekhnicheskogo Instituta — Sb Nauchn Tr Glavgeologii Uzb SSR Tashk Politekh Inst
Sbornik Nauchnykh Trudov Gosudarstvennogo Nauchno-Issledovatel'skogo Instituta Tsvetnykh Metallov — Sb Nauchn Tr Gos Nauchno-Issled Inst Tsvetn Met
Sbornik Nauchnykh Trudov Gosudarstvennogo Zaochnogo Pedagogicheskogo Instituta — Sb Nauchn Tr Arm Gos Zaochn Pedagog Inst
Sbornik Nauchnykh Trudov Gosudarstvennyi Nauchno-Issledovatel'skii i Proektnyi Institut Metallurgicheskoi Promyshlennosti — Sb Nauchn Tr Gos Nauchno Issled Proektn Inst Metall Promsti
Sbornik Nauchnykh Trudov. Gosudarstvennyi Nauchno-Issledovatel'skii i Proektnyi Institut Redkometallicheskoi Promyshlennosti — Sb Nauchn Tr Gos Nauchno Issled Proektn Inst Redkomet Promst
Sbornik Nauchnykh Trudov Gosudarstvennyi Nauchno-Issledovatel'skii Institut Elektrodnoi Promyshlennosti — Sb Nauchn Tr Gos Nauchno Issled Inst Elektrodnoi Promsti
Sbornik Nauchnykh Trudov Gosudarstvennyi Nauchno-Issledovatel'skii Institut Keramicheskoi Promyshlennosti — Sb Nauchn Tr Gos Nauchno Issled Inst Keram Promsti
Sbornik Nauchnykh Trudov Gosudarstvennyi Nauchno-Issledovatel'skii Institut po Keramzitu — Sb Nauchn Tr Gos Nauchno Issled Inst Keramzitu
Sbornik Nauchnykh Trudov. Gosudarstvennyi Nauchno-Isslovatel'skii Institut Ozernogo i Rechnogo Rybnogo Khozyaistva — Sb Nauchn Tr Gos Nauchno Issled Inst Ozern Rechn Rybn Khoz
Sbornik Nauchnykh Trudov. Gosudarstvennyi Vsesoyuznyi Nauchno-Issledovatel'skii Institut Stroitel'nykh Materialov i Konstruktsii VNIIStrom — Sb Nauchn Tr Gos Vses Nauchno Issled Inst Stroit Mater Konst
Sbornik Nauchnykh Trudov Grodnenskii Sel'skokhozyaistvennyi Institut — Sb Nauchn Tr Grodn Skh Inst
Sbornik Nauchnykh Trudov. Groznenskii Neftyanoi Nauchno-Issledovatel'skii Institut — Sb Nauchn Tr Grozn Neft Nauchno Issled Inst
Sbornik Nauchnykh Trudov Institut Biologii Akademiya Nauk Belorusskoi SSR — Sb Nauchn Tr Inst Biol Akad Nauk B SSR
Sbornik Nauchnykh Trudov. Institut Gornogo Dela Krivorozhskii Filial. Akademiya Nauk Ukrainskoi SSR — Sb Nauchn Tr Inst Gorn Dela Krivorozh Fil Akad Nauk Ukr SSR
Sbornik Nauchnykh Trudov. Institut Gornogo Dela, Sverdlovsk — Sb Nauchn Tr Inst Gorn Dela Sverdlovsk
Sbornik Nauchnykh Trudov Institut Tsvetnykh Metallov — Sb Nauchn Tr Inst Tsvetn Met
Sbornik Nauchnykh Trudov. Institut Tsvetnykh Metallov imeni M.I. Kalinina — Sb Nauchn Tr Inst Tsvetn Met im MI Kalinina
Sbornik Nauchnykh Trudov Instituta Geologii i Geofiziki Akademii Nauk Uzbekskoi SSR — Sb Nauchn Tr Inst Geol Geofiz Akad Nauk Uzb SSR
Sbornik Nauchnykh Trudov Instituta Mekhanobrchermet — Sb Nauchn Tr Inst Mekhanobrchermet
Sbornik Nauchnykh Trudov Instituta Melioratsii Vodnogo i Bolotnogo Khozyaistva Akademiya Nauk Belorusskoi SSR — Sb Nauchn Tr Inst Melior Vodn Bolotnogo Khoz Akad Nauk BSSR
Sbornik Nauchnykh Trudov Instituta Metallofiziki Akademiya Nauk Ukrainskoi SSR [*Ukrainian SSR*] — Sb Nauchn Tr Inst Metallofiz Akad Ukr SSR
Sbornik Nauchnykh Trudov. Instituta Torfa. Akademiya Nauk Belorusskoi SSR — Sb Nauchn Tr Inst Torfa Akad Nauk B SSR
Sbornik Nauchnykh Trudov Irkutskii Gosudarstvennyi Nauchno-Issledovatel'skii Institut Redkikh Metallov — Sb Nauchn Tr Irkutsk Gos Nauchno-Issled Inst Redk Met
Sbornik Nauchnykh Trudov. Irkutskii Institut Epidemiologii i Mikrobiologii — Sb Nauchn Tr Irkutsk Inst Epidemiol Mikrobiol
Sbornik Nauchnykh Trudov Ivanovskogo Energeticheskogo Instituta — Sb Nauchn Tr Ivanov Energ Inst
Sbornik Nauchnykh Trudov Ivanovskogo Energeticheskogo Instituta — SNEIA
Sbornik Nauchnykh Trudov Ivanovskogo Gosudarstvennogo Meditsinskogo Instituta — Sb Nauchn Tr Ivanov Gos Med Inst
Sbornik Nauchnykh Trudov Ivanovskogo Meditsinskogo Instituta — Sb Nauchn Tr Ivanov Med Inst
Sbornik Nauchnykh Trudov Ivanovskogo Sel'skokhozyaistvennogo Instituta — Sb Nauchn Tr Ivanov S-Kh Inst
Sbornik Nauchnykh Trudov. Kafedr Matematiki. Grafiki, Khimii i Teoreticheskoi Mekhaniki. Leningradskii Institut Tochnoi Mekhaniki i Optiki — Sb Nauchn Tr Kafedr Met Grafiki Khim Teor Mekh Leningr Inst
Sbornik Nauchnykh Trudov Kalininskaya Gosudarstvennaya Sel'skokhozyaistvennaya Opytnaya Stantsiya — Sb Nauchn Tr Kalinin Gos Skh Opytn Stant
Sbornik Nauchnykh Trudov Kalininskaya Gosudarstvennaya Sel'skokhozyaistvennaya Opytnaya Stantsiya — Sb Nauchn Tr Kalinin Gos Skh Opytn Stn
Sbornik Nauchnykh Trudov Kamenets-Podol'skogo Sel'skokhozyaistvennogo Instituta — Sb Nauchn Tr Kamenets Podolsk Skh Inst
Sbornik Nauchnykh Trudov Kazakhskii Gorno-Metallurgicheskii Institut — Sb Nauchn Tr Kaz Gorno-Metall Inst
Sbornik Nauchnykh Trudov Kazakhskii Politekhnicheskii Institut — Sb Nauchn Tr Kaz Politekh Inst
Sbornik Nauchnykh Trudov. Kazanskii Gosudarstvennyi Meditsinskii Institut — Sb Nauchn Tr Kazan Gos Med Inst
Sbornik Nauchnykh Trudov. Khabarovskii Politekhnicheskii Institut — Sb Nauchn Tr Khabar Politekh Inst
Sbornik Nauchnykh Trudov. Khar'kovskii Gornyi Institut — Sb Nauchn Tr Khark Gorn Inst
Sbornik Nauchnykh Trudov. Khar'kovskii Institut Inzhenerov Kommunal'nogo Stroitel'stva — Sb Nauchn Tr Khark Inst Inzh Kommunaln Stroit
Sbornik Nauchnykh Trudov. Khar'kovskii Inzhenerno-Stroitel'nyi Institut — Sb Nauchn Tr Khark Inzh Stroit Inst
Sbornik Nauchnykh Trudov Khar'kovskii Sel'skokhozyaistvennyi Institut Imeni V. V. Dokuchaeva — Sb Nauchn Tr Khar'k Skh Inst Im V V Dokuchaeva
Sbornik Nauchnykh Trudov Khar'kovskogo Gosudarstvennogo Meditsinskogo Instituta — Sb Nauchn Tr Kar'k Gos Med Inst
Sbornik Nauchnykh Trudov Khar'kovskogo Meditsinskogo Instituta — Sb Nauchn Tr Khar'k Med Inst
Sbornik Nauchnykh Trudov Kievskogo Instituta Inzhenerov Grazhdanskoi Aviatsii [*Ukrainian SSR*] — Sb Nauchn Tr Kiev Inst Inzh Grazhd Aviats
Sbornik Nauchnykh Trudov Kievskogo Inzhenerno-Stroitel'nogo Instituta — Sb Nauchn Tr Kiev Inzh Stroit Inst
Sbornik Nauchnykh Trudov. Kirgizskii Gosudarstvennyi Meditsinskii Institut — Sb Nauchn Tr Kirg Gos Med Inst
Sbornik Nauchnykh Trudov. Kirgizskii Nauchno-Issledovatel'skii Tekhnologicheskii Institute Pastbishch i Kormov — Sb Nauchn Tr Kirg Nauchno Issled Tekh Inst Pastbishch Kormov
Sbornik Nauchnykh Trudov Kirkizskogo Meditsinskogo Instituta — Sb Nauchn Tr Kirg Med Inst
Sbornik Nauchnykh Trudov Krasnoyarskogo Gosudarstvennogo Meditsinskogo Instituta — Sb Nauchn Tr Krasnoyarsk Gos Med Inst
Sbornik Nauchnykh Trudov Krivorozhskii Filial Instituta Gornogo Dela Akademiya Nauk Ukrainskoi SSR — Sb Nauchn Tr Krivorozh Fil Inst Gorn Dela Akad Nauk Ukr SSR
Sbornik Nauchnykh Trudov Krivorozhskii Gornorudnyi Institut — Sb Nauchn Tr Krivorozh Gornorudn Inst
Sbornik Nauchnykh Trudov Krymskogo Gosudarstvennogo Meditsinskogo Instituta — Sb Nauchn Tr Krym Gos Med Inst
Sbornik Nauchnykh Trudov Kuibyshevskii Industrial'nyi Institut — Sb Nauchn Tr Kuibyshev Ind Inst
Sbornik Nauchnykh Trudov Kuibyshevskii Inzhenerno-Stroitel'nyi Institut — Sb Nauchn Tr Kuibyshev Inzh Stroit Inst
Sbornik Nauchnykh Trudov Kuibyshevskii Nauchno-Issledovatel'skii Institut Gigeny — Sb Nauchn Tr Kuibyshev Nauchno Issled Inst Gig
Sbornik Nauchnykh Trudov Kuibyshevskogo Nauchno-Issledovatel'skogo Instituta Epidemiologii i Gigieny — Sb Nauchn Tr Kuibyshev Nauchno Issled Inst Epidemiol Gig
Sbornik Nauchnykh Trudov Kuibyshevskoi Nauchno-Issledovatel'noi Veterinarnoi Stantsii — Sb Nauchn Tr Kuibyshev Nauchno Issled Vet Stn
Sbornik Nauchnykh Trudov Kuzbasskii Politekhnicheskii Institut — Sb Nauchn Tr Kuzbasskii Politekh Inst
Sbornik Nauchnykh Trudov. Leningradskii Elektrotekhnicheskii Institut Inzhenerov Zheleznodorozhnogo Transporta — Sb Nauchn Tr Leningr Elektrotekh Inst Inzh Zheleznodorozhn T
Sbornik Nauchnykh Trudov. Leningradskii Elektrotekhnicheskii Institut Svyazi — Sb Nauchn Tr Leningr Elektrotekh Inst Svyazi
Sbornik Nauchnykh Trudov Leningradskii Farmatsevticheskii Institut — Sb Nauchn Tr Leningr Farm Inst
Sbornik Nauchnykh Trudov. Leningradskii Gosudarstvennyi Nauchno-Issledovatel'skii i Proektnyi Institut Osnovnoi Khimicheskoi Promyshlennosti — Sb Nauchn Tr Leningr Gos Inst Nauchno Issled Proektn Inst Os
Sbornik Nauchnykh Trudov Leningradskii Institut Sovetskoi Torgovli — Sb Nauchn Tr Leningr Inst Sov Torg
Sbornik Nauchnykh Trudov Leningradskii Institut Tochnoi Mekhaniki i Optiki — Sb Nauchn Tr Leningr Inst Tochn Mekh Opt
Sbornik Nauchnykh Trudov Leningradskii Inzhenerno-Stroitel'nyi Institut — Sb Nauchn Tr Leningr Inzh-Stroit Inst
Sbornik Nauchnykh Trudov Leningradskii Khimiko-Farmatsevticheskii Institut — Sb Nauchn Tr Leningr Khim Farm Inst
Sbornik Nauchnykh Trudov Leningradskii Nauchno-Issledovatel'skii Institut Antibiotikov — Sb Nauchn Tr Leningr Nauchno Issled Inst Antibiot
Sbornik Nauchnykh Trudov Leningradskii Nauchno-Issledovatel'skii Institut Lesnogo Khozyaistva — Sb Nauchn Tr Leningr Nauchno Issled Inst Lesn Khoz
Sbornik Nauchnykh Trudov. Leningradskii Sanitarno-Gigienicheskii Meditsinskii Institut — Sb Nauchn Tr Leningr Sanit Gig Med Inst
Sbornik Nauchnykh Trudov. Leningradskii Veterinarnyi Institut — Sb Nauchn Tr Leningr Vet Inst
Sbornik Nauchnykh Trudov Leningradskii Voenno-Mekhanicheskii Institut — Sb Nauchn Tr Leningr Voen Mekh Inst
Sbornik Nauchnykh Trudov Leningradskogo Instituta Usovershenstvovaniya Veterinarnykh Vrachei — Sb Nauchn Tr Leningr Inst Usoversh Vet Vrachei
Sbornik Nauchnykh Trudov Leningradskogo Instituta Usovershenstvovaniya Vrachei — Sb Nauchn Tr Leningr Inst Usoversh Vrachei

Sbornik Nauchnykh Trudov Leningradskogo Nauchno-Issledovatel'skogo Instituta Perelivanya Krovi — Sb Nauchn Tr Leningr Nauchno-Issled Inst Pereliv Krovi
Sbornik Nauchnykh Trudov. Litovskaya Sel'skokhozyaistvennaya Akademiya — Sb Nauchn Tr Litov Skh Akad
Sbornik Nauchnykh Trudov Luganskogo Sel'skokhozyaistvennogo Instituta — Sb Nauchn Tr Lugansk S-Kh Inst
Sbornik Nauchnykh Trudov L'vovskoe Nauchnoe Obshchestvo Dermato-Venerologov — Sb Nauchn Tr L'vov Nauchn Ovo Derm Venerol
Sbornik Nauchnykh Trudov Magnitogorskii Gornometallurgicheskii Institut [*Former USSR*] — Sb Nauchn Tr Magnitogorsk Gornometall Inst
Sbornik Nauchnykh Trudov. Magnitogorskii Gorno-Metallurgicheskii Institut imeni G.I. Nosova. Mezhvuzovskii Vypusk — Sb Nauchn Tr Magnitogorsk Gorno Metall Inst im G I Nosova Me
Sbornik Nauchnykh Trudov Minskii Gosudarstvennyi Meditsinskii Institut — Sb Nauchn Tr Minsk Gos Med Inst
Sbornik Nauchnykh Trudov Mogilevskaya Oblastnaya Gosudarstvennaya Sel'skokhozyaistvennaya Opytnaya Stantsiya — Sb Nauchn Tr Mogilev Obl Gos Skh Opytn Stn
Sbornik Nauchnykh Trudov Morfologicheskoi Kafedry Bashkirskogo Meditsinskogo Instituta — Sb Nauchn Tr Morfol Kafedry Bashk Med Inst
Sbornik Nauchnykh Trudov. Moskovskii Institut Inzhenerov Sel'skokhozyaistvennogo Proizvodstva — Sb Nauchn Tr Mosk Inst Inzh Skh Proizvod
Sbornik Nauchnykh Trudov. Moskovskii Institut Khimicheskogo Mashinostroeniya — Sb Nauchn Tr Mosk Inst Khim Mashinostr
Sbornik Nauchnykh Trudov Moskovskii Institut Tsvetnykh Metallov i Zolota — Sb Nauchn Tr Mosk Inst Tsvetn Met Zolota
Sbornik Nauchnykh Trudov. Moskovskii Nauchno-Issledovatel'skii Institut Gigieny — Sb Nauchn Tr Mosk Nauchno Issled Inst Gig
Sbornik Nauchnykh Trudov Moskovskii Nauchno-Issledovatel'skii Institut Gigieny Imeni F. F. Erismana — Sb Nauchn Tr Mosk Nauchno Issled Inst Gig Im F F Erismana
Sbornik Nauchnykh Trudov Moskovskii Poligraficheskii Institut — Sb Nauchn Tr Mosk Poligr Inst
Sbornik Nauchnykh Trudov Moskovskii Tekhnologicheskii Institut Pishchevoi Promyshlennosti — Sb Nauchn Tr Mosk Tekhnol Inst Pishch Promsti
Sbornik Nauchnykh Trudov Moskovskogo Gornogo Instituta — Sb Nauchn Tr Mosk Gorn Inst
Sbornik Nauchnykh Trudov Moskovskogo Oblastnogo Nauchno-Issledovatel'skogo Instituta Akusherstva i Ginekologii — Sb Nauchn Tr Mosk Obl Nauchno Issled Inst Akush Ginekol
Sbornik Nauchnykh Trudov. Nauchno-Issledovatel'skii Gornorudnyi Institut (Krivoy Rog, USSR) — Sb Nauchn Tr Nauchno Issled Gornorudn Inst Krivoy Rog USSR
Sbornik Nauchnykh Trudov. Nauchno-Issledovatel'skii i Proektno-Konstruktorskii Institut po Dobyche Poleznykh Iskopaemykh Otkrytym Sposobom — Sb Nauchn Tr Nauchno Issled Proektno Konstr Inst Dobyche Pol
Sbornik Nauchnykh Trudov. Nauchno-Issledovatel'skii i Proektnyi Institut po Obogashcheniyu i Aglomeratsii Rud Chernykh Metallov — Sb Nauchn Tr Nauchno Issled Proektn Inst Obogashch Aglom Rud
Sbornik Nauchnykh Trudov. Nauchno-Issledovatel'skii Institut Monomerov dlya Sinteticheskogo Kauchuka — Sb Nauchn Tr Nauchno Issled Inst Monomerov Sint Kauch
Sbornik Nauchnykh Trudov. Nauchno-Issledovatel'skii Institut po Ventilyatsii, Pyleulavlivaniyu i Ochistke Vozdukha na Predpriyatiyakh Metallurgicheskoi Promyshlennosti — Sb Nauchn Tr Nauchno Issled Inst Vent Pyleulavlivaniyu Ochis
Sbornik Nauchnykh Trudov. Nauchno-Issledovatel'skii Institut Veterinarii, Uzbekskaya Akademiya Sel'skokhozyaistvennykh Nauk — Sb Nauchn Tr Nauchno Issled Inst Vet Uzb Akad Skh Nauk
Sbornik Nauchnykh Trudov. Nauchno-Issledovatel'skii Institut Zemledeliya. Echmiadzin. Arfmenian SSR — Sb Nauchn Tr Nauchno Issled Inst Zemled Echmiadzin Arfmenian
Sbornik Nauchnykh Trudov Nauchno-Issledovatel'skii Institut Zemledeliya Echmiadzin (Armenian SSR) — Sb Nauchn Tr Nauchno-Issled Inst Zemled Echmiadzin (Arm SSR)
Sbornik Nauchnykh Trudov Nauchno-Issledovatel'skii Kozhno-Venerologicheskii Institut (Minsk) — Sb Nauchn Tr Nauchno Issled Kozhno Venerol Inst (Minsk)
Sbornik Nauchnykh Trudov Nauchno-Issledovatel'skogo Instituta Gematologii i Perelivaniya Krovi Armyanskoi SSR — Sb Nauchn Tr Nauchno-Issled Inst Pereliv Krovi Arm SSR
Sbornik Nauchnykh Trudov Nauchno-Issledovatel'skogo Instituta Keramzita — Sb Nauchn Tr Nauchno Issled Inst Keramzita
Sbornik Nauchnykh Trudov. Nauchno-Issledovatel'skogo Instituta Kurortologii i Fizioterapii. Yerevan — Sb Nauchn Tr Nauchno Issled Inst Kurortol Fizioter Yerevan
Sbornik Nauchnykh Trudov. Nauchno-Issledovatel'skogo Instituta Onkologii (Tbilisi) — Sb Nauchn Tr Nauchno Issled Inst Onkol (Tbilisi)
Sbornik Nauchnykh Trudov NIIKeramzita — Sb Nauchn Tr NIIKeramzita
Sbornik Nauchnykh Trudov. Novocherkasskii Nauchno-Issledovatel'skii Institut Elektrovozostroeniya — Sb Nauchn Tr Novocherk Nauchn Issled Inst Elektrovozostr
Sbornik Nauchnykh Trudov. Odesskii Inzhenerno-Stroitel'nyi Institut — Sb Nauchn Tr Odess Inzh Stroit Inst
Sbornik Nauchnykh Trudov Odesskogo Sel'skokhozyaistvennogo Instiuta — Sb Nauchn Tr Odess Skh Instiuta
Sbornik Nauchnykh Trudov Permskaya Gosudarstvennaya Sel'skokhozyaistvennaya Opytnaya Stantsiya — Sb Nauchn Tr Permsk Gos Skh Opytn Stn
Sbornik Nauchnykh Trudov Permskii Gornyi Institut — Sb Nauchn Tr Permsk Gorn Inst
Sbornik Nauchnykh Trudov Permskii Gosudarstvennyi Meditsinskii Institut — Sb Nauchn Tr Permsk Gos Med Inst
Sbornik Nauchnykh Trudov Permskij Politekhnicheskij Institut — Sb Nauchn Tr Permsk Politekh Inst
Sbornik Nauchnykh Trudov Permskogo Meditsinskogo Instituta — Sb Nauchn Tr Permsk Med Inst
Sbornik Nauchnykh Trudov po Gazovoi Khromatografii — Sb Nauchn Tr Gazov Khromatogr
Sbornik Nauchnykh Trudov po Problemam Mikroelektroniki — Sb Nauchn Tr Probl Mikroelektron
Sbornik Nauchnykh Trudov po Sanitarnoi Tekhnike — Sb Nauchn Tr Sanit Tekh
Sbornik Nauchnykh Trudov po Teploobmenu i Gidrodinamike — Sb Nauchn Tr Teploobmenu Gidrodin
Sbornik Nauchnykh Trudov Primorskogo Sel'skokhozyaistvennogo Instituta — Sb Nauchn Tr Primorsk S-Kh Inst
Sbornik Nauchnykh Trudov. Rostovskii Gosudarstvennyi Meditsinskii Institut — Sb Nauchn Tr Rostov Gos Med Inst
Sbornik Nauchnykh Trudov Rostovskii Nauchno-Issledovatel'skii Institut Akademii Kommunal'nogo Khozyaistva — Sb Nauchn Tr Rostov Nauchno-Issled Inst Akad Kommunaln Khoz
Sbornik Nauchnykh Trudov Rostovskogo-Na-Donu Gosudarstvennogo Meditsinskogo Instituta — Sb Nauchn Tr Rostov Donu Gos Med Inst
Sbornik Nauchnykh Trudov. Rostovskogo-na-Donu Instituta Inzhenerov Zheleznodorozhnogo Transporta — Sb Nauchn Tr Rostov na Donu Inst Inzh Zheleznodorozhn Transp
Sbornik Nauchnykh Trudov Ryazanskogo Meditsinskogo Instituta — Sb Nauchn Tr Ryazan Med Inst
Sbornik Nauchnykh Trudov Ryazanskogo Sel'skokhozyaistvennogo Instituta — Sb Nauchn Tr Ryazan S-Kh Inst
Sbornik Nauchnykh Trudov Samarkandskogo Gosudarstvennogo Meditsinskogo Instituta — Sb Nauchn Tr Samark Gos Med Inst
Sbornik Nauchnykh Trudov. Semipalatinskii Zootekhnichesko-Veterinarnyi Institut — Sb Nauchn Tr Semipalat Zootekh Vet Inst
Sbornik Nauchnykh Trudov Severo-Kavkazskogo Gornometallurgicheskogo Instituta — Sb Nauchn Tr Sev Kavk Gornometall Inst
Sbornik Nauchnykh Trudov Severo-Osetinskii Gosudarstvennyi Meditsinskii Institut — Sb Nauchn Tr Sev-Oset Gos Med Inst
Sbornik Nauchnykh Trudov. Sibirskii Nauchno-Issledovatel'skii Institut Geologii, Geofiziki i Mineral'nogo Syr'ya — Sb Nauchn Tr Sib Nauchno Issled Inst Geol Geofiz Miner Syrya
Sbornik Nauchnykh Trudov. Sochinskoi Nauchno-Issledovatel'skoi Opytnoi Stantsii Subtropicheskogo Lesnogo i Lesoparkovogo Khozyaistva — Sb Nauchn Tr Sochinskoi Nauchno Issled Opytn Stn Subtrop Les
Sbornik Nauchnykh Trudov Sovershenstvovanie Porod Sel'skokhozyaistvennykh Zhivotnykh — Sb Nauchn Tr Sovers Porod Skh Zhivotn
Sbornik Nauchnykh Trudov. Sredneaziatskii Nauchno-Issledovatel'skii i Proektnyi Institut Tsvetnoi Metallurgii — Sb Nauchn Tr Sredneaziat Nauchno Issled Proektn Inst Tsvetn
Sbornik Nauchnykh Trudov Stalinskii Gosudarstvennyi Meditsinskii Institut — Sb Nauchn Tr Stalinskii Gos Med Inst
Sbornik Nauchnykh Trudov Sverdlovskii Filial Moskovskogo Instituta Narodnogo Khozyaistva — Sb Nauchn Tr Sverdl Fil Mosk Inst Nar Khoz
Sbornik Nauchnykh Trudov. Tashkentskii Institut Inzhenerov Zheleznodorozhnogo Transporta — Sb Nauchn Tr Tashk Inst Inzh Zheleznodorozhn Transp
Sbornik Nauchnykh Trudov Tashkentskiy Gosudarstvennyy Universitet — Sb Nauchn Tr Tashk Gos Univ
Sbornik Nauchnykh Trudov Tashkentskogo Gosudarstvennogo Meditsinskogo Instituta — Sb Nauchn Tr Tashk Gos Med Inst
Sbornik Nauchnykh Trudov Tashkentskogo Politekhnicheskogo Instituta — Sb Nauchn Tr Tashk Politekh Inst
Sbornik Nauchnykh Trudov. Tomskii Elektromekhanicheskii Institut Inzhenerov Zheleznodorozhnogo Transporta — Sb Nauchn Tr Tomsk Elektromekh Inst Inzh Zheleznodorozhn Tra
Sbornik Nauchnykh Trudov Tomskii Inzhenerno-Stroitel'nyi Institut [*Former USSR*] — Sb Nauchn Tr Tomsk Inzh Stroit Inst
Sbornik Nauchnykh Trudov Tomskii Inzhenerno-Stroitel'nyi Institut — STISA
Sbornik Nauchnykh Trudov Tsentral'nogo Aptechnogo Nauchno-Issledovatel'skogo Instituta — Sb Nauchn Tr Tsentr Aptechn Nauchno-Issled Inst
Sbornik Nauchnykh Trudov. Tsentral'nyi Nauchno-Issledovatel'skii Aptechnyi Institut — Sb Nauchn Tr Tsentr Nauchn Issled Aptechn Inst
Sbornik Nauchnykh Trudov. Tsentral'nyi Nauchno-Issledovatel'skii Institut Mekhanicheskoi Obrabotki Drevesiny — Sb Nauchn Tr Tsentr Nauchno Issled Inst Mekh Obrab Drev
Sbornik Nauchnykh Trudov. Ukrainskii Nauchno-Issledovatel'skii Institut Eksperimental'noi Endokrinologii — Sb Nauchn Tr Ukr Nauchno Issled Inst Eksp Endokrinol
Sbornik Nauchnykh Trudov Ukrainskii Nauchno-Issledovatel'skii Institut Ogneuporov [*Ukrainian SSR*] — Sb Nauchn Tr Ukr Nauchno-Issled Inst Ogneuporov
Sbornik Nauchnykh Trudov Ukrainskii Nauchno-Issledovatel'skii Institut Ogneuporov — STUOA
Sbornik Nauchnykh Trudov Ukrainskii Nauchno-Issledovatel'skii Institut Solyanoi Promyshlennosti — Sb Nauchn Tr Ukr Nauchno Issled Inst Solyanoi Promsti
Sbornik Nauchnykh Trudov Ukrainskii Nauchno-Issledovatel'skii Uglekhimcheskii I nstitut [*Ukrainian SSR*] — Sb Nauchn Tr Ukr Nauchno-Issled Uglekhim Inst
Sbornik Nauchnykh Trudov Ukrainskogo Instituta Usovershenstvovaniy Vrachei — Sb Nauchn Tr Ukr Inst Usoversh Vrachei
Sbornik Nauchnykh Trudov. Ural'skii Politekhnicheskii Institut — Sb Nauchn Tr Ural Politekh Inst
Sbornik Nauchnykh Trudov. Uzbekskaya Akademiya Sel'skokhozyaistvennykh Nauk. Nauchno-Issledovatel'skii Institut Veterinarii — Sb Nauchn Tr Uzb Akad Skh Nauk Nauchno Issled Inst Vet

Sbornik Nauchnykh Trudov Vinnitskogo Gosudarstvennogo Meditsinskogo Instituta — Sb Nauchn Tr Vinnitsk Gos Med Inst
Sbornik Nauchnykh Trudov Vitebskogo Gosudarstvennogo Meditsinskogo Instituta — Sb Nauchn Tr Vitebsk Gos Med Inst
Sbornik Nauchnykh Trudov Vitebskogo Meditsinskogo Instituta — Sb Nauchn Tr Vitebsk Med Inst
Sbornik Nauchnykh Trudov. Vladimirskii Politekhnicheskii Institut — Sb Nauchn Tr Vladimir Politekh Inst
Sbornik Nauchnykh Trudov Vladimirskii Vechernii Politekhnicheskii Institut — Sb Nauchn Tr Vladimir Vech Politekh Inst
Sbornik Nauchnykh Trudov Vladivostokskii Meditsinskii Institut — Sb Nauchn Tr Vladivost Med Inst
Sbornik Nauchnykh Trudov VNII [*Vsesoyuznyi Nauchno-Issledovatel'skii Institut*] **Monokristallov** — Sb Nauchn Tr VNII Monokrist
Sbornik Nauchnykh Trudov VNIKhFI — Sb Nauchn Tr VNIKhFI
Sbornik Nauchnykh Trudov Voenno-Meditsinskii Fakul'tet Saratovskom Medinstitut — Sb Nauchn Tr Voen Med Fak Sarat Medinst
Sbornik Nauchnykh Trudov Voronezhskii Inzhenerno-Stroitel'nyi Institut — Sb Nauchn Tr Voronezh Inzh Stroit Inst
Sbornik Nauchnykh Trudov. Vsesoyuznogo Gosudarstvennogo Nauchno-Issledovatel'skogo i Proektnogo Instituta Khimiko-Fotograficheskoi Promyshlennosti — Sb Nauchn Tr Vses Gos Nauchno Issled Proektn Inst Khim Fotog
Sbornik Nauchnykh Trudov Vsesoyuznogo Nauchno-Issledovatel'skogo Gorno-Metallurgiceskogo Instituta Tsvetnykh Metallov [*Former USSR*] — Sb Nauchn Tr Vses Nauchno-Issled Gorno-Metall Inst Tsvet Met
Sbornik Nauchnykh Trudov. Vsesoyuznogo Nauchno-Issledovatel'skogo Instituta Mineral'nogo Syr'ya — Sb Nauchn Tr Vses Nauchno Issled Inst Miner Syrya
Sbornik Nauchnykh Trudov Vsesoyuznogo Selektsionno-Geneticheskogo Instituta — Sb Nauchn Tr Vses Sel Genet Inst
Sbornik Nauchnykh Trudov Vsesoyuznyi Nauchno-Issledovatel'skii Gornometallurgicheskii Institut Tsvetnykh Metallov — Sb Nauchn Tr Vses Nauchno Issled Gornometall Inst Tsvetn Met
Sbornik Nauchnykh Trudov. Vsesoyuznyi Nauchno-Issledovatel'skii i Tekhnologicheskii Institut Ptitsevodstva — Sb Nauchn Tr Vses Nauchno Issled Tekhnol Inst Ptitsevod
Sbornik Nauchnykh Trudov Vsesoyuznyi Nauchno-Issledovatel'skii Institut Gidrogeologii i Inzhenernoi Geologii — Sb Nauchn Tr Vses Nauchno Issled Inst Gidrogeol Inzh Geol
Sbornik Nauchnykh Trudov. Vsesoyuznyi Nauchno-Issledovatel'skii Institut Legkogo i Tekstil'nogo Mashinostroeniya — Sb Nauchn Tr Vses Nauchno Issled Inst Legk Tekst Mashinostr
Sbornik Nauchnykh Trudov Vsesoyuznyi Nauchno-Issledovatel'skii Institut Metallurgicheskoi Teplotekhniki — Sb Nauchn Tr Vses Nauchno Issled Inst Metall Teplotekh
Sbornik Nauchnykh Trudov. Vsesoyuznyi Nauchno-Issledovatel'skii Institut Ogneuporov — Sb Nauchn Tr Vses Nauchno Issled Inst Ogneuporov
Sbornik Nauchnykh Trudov. Vsesoyuznyi Nauchno-Issledovatel'skii Institut po Pererabotke Nefti — Sb Nauchn Tr Vses Nauchno Issled Inst Pererab Nefti
Sbornik Nauchnykh Trudov. Vsesoyuznyi Nauchno-Issledovatel'skii Institut Zhivotnovodstva — Sb Nauchn Tr Vses Nauchno Issled Inst Zhivotnovod
Sbornik Nauchnykh Trudov Vsesoyuznyi Neftegazovyi Nauchno-Issledovatel'skii Institut — Sb Nauchn Tr Vses Neftegazov Nauchno Issled Inst
Sbornik Nauchnykh Trudov. Vsesoyuznyi Zaochnyi Institut Pishchevoi Promyshlennosti — Sb Nauchn Tr Vses Zaochn Inst Pishch Promsti
Sbornik Nauchnykh Trudov. Yaroslavskii Politekhnicheskii Institut. Seriya Kauchuk i Rezina — Sb Nauchn Tr Yarosl Politekh Inst Ser Kauch Rezina
Sbornik Nauchnykh Trudov. Yaroslavskogo Tekhnologicheskogo Instituta — Sb Nauchn Tr Yarosl Tekhnol Inst
Sbornik Nauchnykh Trudov Zaochnyi Institut Sovetskoi Torgovli — Sb Nauchn Tr Zaochn Inst Sov Torg
Sbornik Nauchnykh Trudov Zhdanovskogo Metallurgicheskogo Instituta — Sb Nauchn Tr Zhdan Metall Inst
Sbornik Nauchnykh Trudov Zootekhnicheskogo Fakul'teta Belotserkovskii Sel'skokhozyaistvennyi Institut — Sb Nauchn Tr Zootekh Fak Belotserk Skh Inst
Sbornik Nauchnykh Vrachei Kabardino Balkarii — Sb Nauchn Vrachei Kabard Balkarii
Sbornik Naucnyh Soobscenii Dagestanskii Gosudarstvennyi Universitet Imeni V. I. Lenina — Sb Naucn Soobsc Dagestan Gos Univ
Sbornik Naucnyh Trudov Jaroslavskogo Pedagogiceskij Institut — Sb Nauc Trud Jaroslav Pedag Inst
Sbornik. Ordena Trudovogo Krasnogo Znameni Institut Fiziki. Akademiya Nauk Gruzinskoj SSR — Sb Inst Fiz Akad Nauk Gruz SSR
Sbornik ot Dokladi pred Nauchno-Metodicheska Konferentsiya po Problemite na Prepodavane vuv VUZ — Sb Dokl Nauchno Metod Konf Probl Prepod VUZ
Sbornik ot Trudov na Nauchnoizsledovatelskiya i Proektantski Institut za Rudodobiv i Obogatyavane. Obogatyavane — Sb Tr Nauchnoizsled Proekt Inst Rudodobiv Obogat Obogat
Sbornik ot Trudove na Nauchnoizsledovatelskiya i Proektantski Institut za Rudodobiv i Obogatyavane. Rudodobiv — Sb Tr Nauchnoizsled Proekt Inst Rudodobiv Obogat Rudodobiv
Sbornik ot Trudove na Nauchnoizsledovatelskiya Institut po Kauchukova i Plastmasova Promishlenost — Sb Tr Nauchnoizsled Inst Kauch Plastmasova Promst
Sbornik Pedagogicke Fakulty (Olomouci) — SPFOL
Sbornik Pedagogicke Fakulty (Ostrava) — SPFO
Sbornik Pedagogicke Fakulty v Brne — SPFB
Sbornik Pedagogicke Fakulty v Plzni. Chemie — Sb Pedagog Fak Plzni Chem
Sbornik Pedagogicke Fakulty v Plzni. Serie Chemie — Sb Pedagog Fak Plzni Ser Chem
Sbornik Pedagogickeho Institutu v Banskej Bystrici — SPIBB
Sbornik Pedagogickeho Institutu v Jihlave — Sborn Pedagog Inst V Jihlave
Sbornik Pedagogickeho Institutu v Kosiciach — Sborn Pedagog Inst V Kosiciach
Sbornik Pedagogickeho Institutu v Nitre — SPIN
Sbornik Pedagogickeho Institutu v Olomouci — SPIOL
Sbornik Pedagogickeho Institutu v Plzni — SPIP
Sbornik Pedagogickeho Institutu v Plzni — SPIPL
Sbornik Pedagogickeho Institutu v Presove — Sborn Pedagog Inst V Presove
Sbornik Pedagogickej Fakulty v Presove Univerzity P.J. Safarika v Kosiciach — Sb Pedagog Fak Presove Univ P J Safarkia Kosiciach
Sbornik po Karantinu Rastenii — Sb Karantinu Rast
Sbornik po Lesnomu Khozyaistvu i Lesokul'turam — Sb Lesn Khoz Lesokult
Sbornik Postanovlenii Plenuma Verkhovnovo Suda SSSR — Sbornik Post Plen Verkh Suda SSSR
Sbornik Prac Chemickej Fakulty Slovenskej Vysokej Skoly Technickej — Sb Prac Chem Fak SVST
Sbornik Prac Chemickotechnologickej Fakulty SVST — Sb Pr Chemickotechnol Fak SVST
Sbornik Prac Lekarskej Fakulty Univerzity P. J. Safarika v Kosiciach — Sb Pr Lek Fak Univ P J Safarika Kosiciach
Sbornik Prac Lesnickeho a Drevarskeho Muzea ve Zvolene — Sborn Prac Lesn Muz Ve Zvolene
Sbornik Praci Filosoficke Fakulty Brnenske University — Sbor Praci Filos Fak
Sbornik Praci Filosoficke Fakulty Brnenske University — SbornikP
Sbornik Praci Filosoficke Fakulty Brnenske University — SFFBU
Sbornik Praci Filosoficke Fakulty Brnenske University — SPFB
Sbornik Praci Filosoficke Fakulty Brnenske University [*Brno*] — SPFBE
Sbornik Praci Filosoficke Fakulty Brnenske University — SPFFBU
Sbornik Praci Filosoficke Fakulty Brnenske University (Brno) — Sbor (Brno)
Sbornik Praci Filosoficke Fakulty Brnenske University. Rada Hudebnevedna — Sbornik Praci Brnenske U Rada Hud
Sbornik Praci Lekarske Fakulty v Brne — Sb Pr Lek Fak Brne
Sbornik Praci Pedagogicke Faculty v Ostrave. Series A. Matematika, Fyzika — Sb Praci Ped Fak Ostrave Ser A Mat Fyz
Sbornik Praci Pedagogicke Fakulty University J.E. Purkyne v Brne — Sb Pr Pedagog Fak Univ J E Purkyne Brne
Sbornik Praci Pedagogicke Fakulty v Ostrave. Rada A. Matematika Fizika — Sb Pr Pedagog Fak Ostrave Rada A
Sbornik Praci Pedagogicke Fakulty v Ostrave. Rada A. Prirodni Vedy a Matematika — Sb Pr Pedagog Fak Ostrave Rada A Prir Vedy Mat
Sbornik Praci Pedagogicke Fakulty v Ostrave. Rada E [*Czechoslovakia*] — Sb Pr Pedagog Fak Ostrave Rada E
Sbornik Praci Pedagogicke Fakulty v Ostrave. Seria A — Sb Praci Ped Fak v Ostrave Ser A
Sbornik Praci Pedagogickeho Instituta i Ostrave Prirodni Vedy a Matematika — Sb Pr Pedagog Inst Ostrave Prir Vedy Mat
Sbornik Praci Pedagogickeho Institutu, Usti Nad Labem — SPIU
Sbornik Praci Pedagogickeho Institutu v Gottwaldove — SPIG
Sbornik Praci Pedagogickeho Institutu v Ostrave — SPIO
Sbornik Praci Prirodovedecke Fakulty University Palackeho v Olomouci — Sb Pr Prirodoved Fak Univ Palackeho Olomouci
Sbornik Praci Prirodovedecke Fakulty University Palackeho v Olomouci — Sb Praci Prirodoved Fak Univ Palackeho v Olomouci
Sbornik Praci Prirodovedecke Fakulty University Palackeho v Olomouci. Obor Chemica — Sb Praci Prirodoved Fak Univ Palackeho v Olomouci Chem
Sbornik Praci Prirodovedecke Fakulty University Palackeho v Olomouci. Obor Fyzika — Sb Praci Prirodoved Fak Univ Palackeho v Olomouci Fyz
Sbornik Praci Prirodovedecke Fakulty University Palackeho v Olomouci. Obor Matematika — Sb Praci Prirodoved Fak Univ Palackeho v Olomouci Mat
Sbornik Praci Techniku Kralovopolske Strojirny — Sb Pr Tech Kralovopolske Strojir
Sbornik Praci Ustavu pro Vyzkum Rud (Prague) — Sb Pr Ustavu Vyzk Rud (Prague)
Sbornik Praci UVP — Sb Pr UVP
Sbornik Praci VSD a VUD — Sb Pr VSD VUD
Sbornik Praci Vyzkumneho Ustavu Zelezorudnych Dolu a Hrudkoven — Sb Pr Vyzk Ustavu Zelezorudn Dolu Hrudkoven
Sbornik Praci z Vyzkumu Chemickeho Vyuziti Uhli. Dehtu a Ropy [*Czechoslovakia*] — Sb Pr Vyzk Chem Vyuziti Uhli Dehtu Ropy
Sbornik Prazhskogo Khimiko Tekhnologicheskogo Instituta Sektsiya. Protsessy i Apparaty — Sb Prazhskogo Khim Tekhnol Inst Sekts Protsessy Appar
Sbornik Prazhskogo Khimiko-Tekhnologicheskogo Instituta. B. Neorganicheskaya Khimiya i Tekhnologiya — Sb Prazhskogo Khim Tekhnol Inst B Neorg Khim Tekhnol
Sbornik Prazhskogo Khimiko-Tekhnologicheskogo Instituta. E. Pishchevye Produkty — Sb Prazhskogo Khim Tekhnol Inst E Pishch Prod
Sbornik Prazhskogo Khimiko-Tekhnologicheskogo Instituta. F. Tekhnologiya Vody i Okruzhayushchei Sredy — Sb Prazhskogo Khim Tekhnol Inst F Tekhnol Vody Okruzh Sredy
Sbornik Prazhskogo Khimiko-Tekhnologicheskogo Instituta. G. Mineralogiya — Sb Prazhskogo Khim Tekhnol Inst G Mineral
Sbornik Prazhskogo Khimiko-Tekhnologicheskogo Instituta. H. Analiticheskaya Khimiya — Sb Prazhskogo Khim Tekhnol Inst H Anal Khim
Sbornik Prazhskogo Khimiko-Tekhnologicheskogo Instituta. J. Ekonomika i Upravlenie Khimicheskoi Promyshlennost'yu — Sb Prazhskogo Khim Tekhnol Inst J Ekon Upr Khim Prom
Sbornik Prazhskogo Khimiko-Tekhnologicheskogo Instituta. L. Khimiya i Tekhnologiya Silikatov — Sb Prazhskogo Khim Tekhnol Inst L Khim Tekhnol Silik
Sbornik Prazhskogo Khimiko-Tekhnologicheskogo Instituta. N. Fizicheskaya Khimiya — Sb Prazhskogo Khim Tekhnol Inst N Fiz Khim
Sbornik Prazhskogo Khimiko-Tekhnologicheskogo Instituta. R. Avtomatizirovannye Sistemy Upravleniya i Vychislitel'nye Metody — Sb Prazhskogo Khim Tekhnol Inst R Avtom Sist Upr Vychisl Met

Sbornik Prazhskogo Khimiko-Tekhnologicheskogo Instituta. S. Polimery-Khimiya, Svoistva i Pererabotka — Sb Prazhskogo Khim Tekhnol Inst S Polim Khim Svoistva Perera
Sbornik Prazhskogo Khimiko-Tekhnologicheskogo Instituta. T. Uchebno-Vospitatel'nyi Protsess — Sb Prazhskogo Khim Tekhnol Inst T Uchebno Vospitatelnyi Prot
Sbornik Prednasek Makrotest. Celostatni Konference — Sb Prednasek Makrotest Celostatni Konf
Sbornik Prednasek Pracovniku Vyzkumneho Ustavu Tepelne Techniky — Sb Prednasek Prac Vyzk Ustavu Tepelne Tech
Sbornik Prirodovedeckeho Klubu v Kosiciach — Sborn Prir Klubu V Kosiciach
Sbornik Prirodovedecky (Prague) — Sborn Prir Prague
Sbornik pro Pathofysiologii Traveni a Vyzivy — Sb Pathofysiol Traveni Vyz
Sbornik Provozne Ekonomicke Fakulty v Ceskych Budejovicich. Zootechnicka Rada — Sb Provozne Ekon Fak Cesk Budejovicich Zootech Rada
Sbornik Provozne Ekonomicke Fakulty v Ceskych Budejovicich. Zootechnicka Rada — SPERE6
Sbornik Rabot Akademiya Nauk SSSR — Sb Akad Nauk SSSR
Sbornik Rabot Ashkhabadskoi Gidrometeorologicheskoi Observatorii — Sb Rab Ashkhab Gidrometeorol Obs
Sbornik Rabot Aspirantov Krasnodarskogo Gosudarstvennogo Pedagogicheskogo Instituta — Sb Rab Aspir Krasnodar Gos Pedagog Inst
Sbornik Rabot Aspirantov Tadzhikskii Gosudarstvennyi Universitet — Sb Rab Aspir Tadzh Gos Univ
Sbornik Rabot Aspirantov Ukrainskii Nauchno-Issledovatel'skii Institut Fiziologii Rastenii — Sb Rab Aspir Ukr Nauchno Issled Inst Fiziol Rast
Sbornik Rabot Aspirantov Voronezhskogo Gosudarstvennogo Universiteta — Sb Rab Aspir Voronezh Gos Univ
Sbornik Rabot Basseinovoi Gidrometeorologicheskoi Chernogo i Azovskogo Morei — Sb Rab Basseinovoi Gidrometeorol Obs Chern Azovskogo Morei
Sbornik Rabot Belorusskii Gosudarstvennyi Meditsinskii Institut — Sb Rab Beloruss Gos Med Inst
Sbornik Rabot Buryatskogo Otdel'nogo Vsesoyuznogo Nauchnogo Obshchestva Anatomii, Gistologii, i Embriologii — Sb Rab Buryat Otd Vses Nauchn Ova Anat Gistol Embriol
Sbornik Rabot Chuvashskoi Respublikanskoi Veterinarnoi Laboratorii — Sb Rab Chuv Resp Vet Lab
Sbornik Rabot Gor'kovskoi Volzhskoi i Rybinskoi Gidrometeorologicheskikh Observatorii — Sb Rab Gor'k Volzh Rybinsk Gidrometeorol Obs
Sbornik Rabot Gosudarstvennyi Institut Prikladnoi Khimii — Sb Rab Gos Inst Prikl Khim
Sbornik Rabot Instituta Prikladnoi Zoologii i Fitopatologii — Sb Rab Inst Prikl Zol Fitopatol
Sbornik Rabot Instituta Prikladnoi Zoologii i Fitopatologii — Sb Rab Inst Prikl Zool Fitopatol
Sbornik Rabot Instituta Tsitologii Akademii Nauk SSSR — Sb Rab Inst Tsitol Akad Nauk SSSR
Sbornik Rabot Kafedry i Fakul'tete Khirurgii Sverdlovskogo Meditsinskogo — Sb Rab Kafedry Fak Khir Sverdl Med
Sbornik Rabot Kazakhskogo Respublikanskogo Nauchnogo Obshchestva Anatomov, Gistologov, i Embriologov — Sb Rab Kaz Resp Nauchn Ova Anat Gistol Embriol
Sbornik Rabot Kurskoi Gidrometeorologicheskoi Observatorii — Sb Rab Kursk Gidrometeorol Obs
Sbornik Rabot Laboratoriya Yuzhnykh Morei Gosudarstvennyi Okeanograficheskii Institut — Sb Rab Lab Yuzhn Morei Gos Okeanogr Inst
Sbornik Rabot Leningradskii Institut Sovetskoi Torgovli — Sb Rab Leningr Inst Sov Torg
Sbornik Rabot Leningradskii Veterinarnyi Institut — Sb Rab Leningr Vet Inst
Sbornik Rabot Minskogo Meditsinskogo Instituta — Sb Rab Minsk Med Inst
Sbornik Rabot Molodykh Uchenykh Akademii Nauk Moldavskoi SSR — Sb Rab Molodykh Uch Akad Nauk Mold SSR
Sbornik Rabot Molodykh Uchenykh Gorskogo Sel'skokhozyaistvennogo Instituta — Sb Rab Molodykh Uch Gorskogo Skh Inst
Sbornik Rabot Molodykh Vsesoyuznogo Selektsii Genetiki Instituta — Sb Rab Molodykh Vses Sel Genet Inst
Sbornik Rabot Moskovskii Lesotekhnicheskii Institut — Sb Rab Mosk Lesotekh Inst
Sbornik Rabot Nauchnyi Institut po Udobreniyam i Insektofungitsidam (Moscow) — Sb Rabot Nauch Inst Udobr Insektofungits (Moscow)
Sbornik Rabot po Agronomicheskoi Fizike — Sb Rab Agron Fiz
Sbornik Rabot po Biologii. Tekhnike Rybolovstva i Tekhnologii — Sb Rab Biol Tekh Rybolov Tekhnol
Sbornik Rabot po Chistoi i Prikladnoi Khimii — Sb Rab Chist Prikl Khim
Sbornik Rabot po Gidrologii — Sb Rab Gidrol
Sbornik Rabot po Gidrologii Leningradskogo Gosudarstvennogo Gidrologicheskogo Instituta — Sb Rab Gidrol Leningr Gos Gidrol Inst
Sbornik Rabot po Ikhtiologii i Gidrobiologii — Sb Rab Ikhtiol Gidrobiol
Sbornik Rabot po Khimicheskim Istochnikam Toka — Sb Rab Khim Istochnikam Toka
Sbornik Rabot po Lesnomu Hozjajstvu. Vsesojuznyj Naucno-Issledovatel'skij Institut Lesovodstva i Mehanizacii Lesnogo Hozjajstva — Sborn Rabot Lesn Hoz Vsesojuz Nauc-Issled Inst Lesovod
Sbornik Rabot po Lesnomu Khozyaistva Moldavii Moldavskaya Lesnaya Opytnaya Stantsiya — Sb Rab Lesn Khoz Mold Mold Lesn Opytn Stn
Sbornik Rabot po Maslichnym i Efiromaslichnym Kul'turam — Sb Rab Maslichn Efiromaslichn Kul't
Sbornik Rabot po Maslichnym Kul'turam — Sb Rab Maslichn Kult
Sbornik Rabot po Mezhdunarodnomu Geofizicheskom Godu — Sb Rab Mezhdunar Geofiz Godu
Sbornik Rabot po Mikologii i Al'gologii Akademii Kirgizkoi SSR — Sb Rab Mikol Al'gol Kirg SSR
Sbornik Rabot po Mikologii i Al'gologii Akademii Kirgizskoi SSR — Sb Rab Mikol Algol Akad Kirg SSR
Sbornik Rabot po Nematodam Sel'skokhozyaistvennykh Rastenii — Sb Rab Nematodam Skh Rast
Sbornik Rabot po Silikozu — Sb Rab Silikozu
Sbornik Rabot po Silikozu Ural'skii Filial Akademii Nauk SSSR — Sb Rab Silikozu Ural Fil Akad Nauk SSSR
Sbornik Rabot po Voprosam Karantina Rastenij — Sborn Rabot Vopr Karant Rast
Sbornik Rabot po Zashchite Lesa. Moskovskii Lesotekhnicheskii Institut — Sb Rab Zashch Lesa Mosk Lesotekh Inst
Sbornik Rabot Pozharno Ispytatel'nykh Stantsii — Sb Rab Pozharno Ispyt Stn
Sbornik Rabot Rostovskoi Gidrometeorologicheskoi Observatorii — Sb Rab Rostov Gidrometeorol Obs
Sbornik Rabot Rybinskoi Gidrometeorologicheskoi Observatorii — Sb Rab Rybinsk Gidrometeorol Obs
Sbornik Rabot Studencheskogo Nauchnogo Obshchestva. Leningradskii Institut Tochnoi Mekhaniki i Optiki — Sb Rab Stud Nauchn Ova Leningr Inst Tochn Mekh Opt
Sbornik Rabot Sverdlovskii Gosudarstvennyi Meditsinskii Institut — Sb Rab Sverdl Gos Med Inst
Sbornik Rabot Sverdlovskii Nauchno-Issledovatel'skii Kozhno Venerologicheskii Institut — Sb Rab Sverdl Nauchno Issled Kozhno Venerol Inst
Sbornik Rabot Sverdlovskogo Meditsinskogo Instituta — Sb Rab Sverdl Med Inst
Sbornik Rabot Tsentral'nogo Muzeya Pochvovedeniya Imeni V. V. Dokuchaeva — Sb Rab Tsentr Muz Pochvoved Im V
Sbornik Rabot Tsentral'nogo Muzeya Pochvovedeniya Imeni V. V. Dokuchaeva — Sb Rab Tsentr Muz Pochvoved Im V V Dokuchaeva
Sbornik Rabot Tsentral'nyi Nauchno-Issledovatel'skii Institut Kozhevenno Obuvnoi Promyshlennosti — Sb Rab Tsentr Nauchno Issled Inst Kozh Obuvn Promsti
Sbornik Rabot Tsimlyanskoi Gidrometeorologicheskoi Observatorii — Sb Rab Tsiml Gidrometeorol Obs
Sbornik Rabot Ukrainskii Nauchno-Issledovatel'skii Institut Ogneuporov — Sb Rab Ukr Nauchno Issled Inst Ogneuporov
Sbornik Rabot v Pamiat Professora Ivana Mikhailovicha Sadovskago (S Peterburg) — Sborn Rabot v Pam I M Sadovskago (S Peterburg)
Sbornik Rabot Vologodskoi Nauchno-Issledovat' Skoi Veterinarnoi Opytnoi Stantsii — Sb Rab Vologod Nauchno-Issled Vet Opytn Stn
Sbornik Rabot Voprosov Proizvodstva i Primeneniya Biologicheskikh Preparatov — Sb Rab Vopr Proizvod Primen Biol Prep
Sbornik Rabot Vsesoyuznogo Nauchno-Issledovatel'skogo Instituta Agrolesomelioratsii — Sb Rab Vses Nauchno Issled Inst Agrolesomelior
Sbornik Rabot Vsesoyuznyi Nauchno-Issledovatel'skii Institut Okhrany Truda — Sb Rab Vses Nauchno Issled Inst Okhr Tr
Sbornik Rabot. Vsesoyuznyi Nauchno-Issledovatel'skii Institut Okhrany Truda imeni S. M. Kirova — Sb Rab Vses Nauchno Issled Inst Okhr Tr im SM Kirova
Sbornik Rabot Vsesoyuznyi Zaochnyi Institut Pishchevoi Promyshlennosti — Sb Rab Vses Zaochn Inst Pishch Promsti
Sbornik Rabot Vychislitel'nogo Tsentral'nogo Moskovskogo Gosudarstvennogo Universiteta — Sb Rab Vychisl Tsentra Mosk Gos Univ
Sbornik Referatov Nauchnykh Rabot. Dagestanskii Gosudarstvennyi Meditsinskii Institut — Sb Ref Nauchn Rab Dagest Gos Med Inst
Sbornik Referatov Nauchnykh Rabot. Nauchno-Issledovatel'skii Institut Okhrany Materinstva i Detstva — Sb Ref Nauchn Rab Nauchno Issled Inst Okhr Materin Det
Sbornik Referatov Nauchnykh Rabot. Vsesoyuznyi Nauchno-Issledovatel'skii Institut Maslodel'noi i Syrodel'noi Promyshlennosti — Sb Ref Nauchn Rab Vses Nauchno Issled Inst Maslodel Syrodeln
Sbornik Rost i Ustoichivost' Rastenii Akademiya Nauk Ukrainskoi SSR Respublikanskii Mezhvedomstvennyi — Sb Rost Ustoichivost Rast Akad Nauk Ukr SSR Respub Mezhved
Sbornik Rukovodyashchikh Materialov i Konsul'tatsii po Stroitel'stvu — Sb Ruk Mater Konsult Stroit
Sbornik. Service Geologique. Republique Tchecoslovaque — Sb Serv Geol Repub Tchec
Sbornik Severoceskeho Musea Prirodni Vedy Scientiae Naturales — Sb Severocesk Mus Prir Vedy Sci Nat
Sbornik Statei Aspirantov Kirgizskogo Gosudarstvennogo Universiteta — Sb Statei Aspir Kirg Gos Univ
Sbornik Statei Aspirantov Kirgizskogo Universiteta Fiziko-Matematicheskikh Estestvennykh Nauk — Sb Statei Aspir Kirg Univ Fiz-Mat Estestv Nauk
Sbornik Statei. Daugavpilsskii Pedagogicheskii Institut — Sb Statei Daugavpilsskii Pedagog Inst
Sbornik Statei. Donskoi Sel'skokhozyaistvennyi Institut — Sb Statei Donskoi Skh Inst
Sbornik Statei Erevanskii Gosudarstvennyi Universitet — Sb Statei Erevan Gos Univ
Sbornik Statei Leningradskii Institut Tochnoi Mekhaniki i Optiki — Sb Statei Leningr Inst Tochn Mekh Opt
Sbornik Statei Leningradskogo Tekhnologicheskogo Instituta Tsellyulozno-Bumazhnoi Promyshlennosti — Sb Statei Leningr Tekhnol Inst Tsellyul Bum Promsti
Sbornik Statei. Lesnomu Khozyaistvu — Sb Statei Lesn Khoz
Sbornik Statei. Magnitogorskii Gornometallurgicheskii Institut — Sb Statei Magnitogorsk Gornometall Inst
Sbornik Statei Makeevskii Nauchno Issledovatel'skii Institut Bezopasnykh Rabot Gornoi Promyshlennosti — Sb Statei Makeev Nauchno Issled Inst Bezop Rab Gorn Promsti
Sbornik Statei Molodykh Nauchnykh Rabotnikov Leningradskii Institut Vodnogo Transporta — Sb Statei Molodykh Nauchn Rab Leningr Inst Vodn Transp
Sbornik Statei Moskovskii Inzhenerno-Fizicheskii Institut [*Former USSR*] — Sb Statei Mosk Inzh-Fiz Inst

Sbornik Statei Nauchno-Issledovatel'skii Institut Organicheskikh Poluproduktov i Krasitelei — Sb Statei Nauchno Issled Inst Org Poluprod Krasitelei
Sbornik Statei Nauchnykh Sotrudnikov Leningradskikh Geologicheskikh Uchrezhdenii Akademii Nauk SSSR — Sb Statei Nauchn Sotr Leningr Geol Uchrezhd Akad Nauk SSSR
Sbornik Statei o Rabotakh Ukrainskogo Nauchno Issledovatel'skogo Instituta Maslozhirovoi Promyshlennosti — Sb Statei Rab Ukr Nauchno Issled Inst Maslozhir Promsti
Sbornik Statei po Geologii i Gidrogeologii — Sb Statei Geol Gidrogeol
Sbornik Statei po Geologii i Inzhenernoi Geologii — Sb Statei Geol Inzh Geol
Sbornik Statei po Gidrogeologii i Geotermii — Sb Statei Gidrogeol Geoterm
Sbornik Statei po Lesnomu Khozyaistvu i Lesoekspluatatsii — Sb Statei Lesn Khoz Lesoekspl
Sbornik Statei po Rezul'tatam Raboty Novgorodskoi Gosudarstvennoi Sel'skokhozyaistvennoi Opytnoi Stantsii — Sb Statei Rezult Rab Novgorod Gos Skh Opytn Stn
Sbornik Statei. Sverdlovskii Sel'skokhozyaistvennyi Institut — Sb Statei Sverdl Skh Inst
Sbornik Statei. Uralskii Politekhnicheskii Institut — Sb Statei Ural Politekh Inst
Sbornik Statei. Vsesoyuznogo Zaochnogo Politekhnicheskogo Instituta — Sb Statei Vses Zaochn Politekh Inst
Sbornik Statei. Vsesoyuznyi Nauchno-Issledovatel'skii i Konstruktorskii InstitutKhimicheskogo Mashinostroeniya — Sb Statei Vses Nauchno Issled Konstr Inst Khim Mashinostr
Sbornik Statei Vsesoyuznyi Nauchno-Issledovatel'skii Institut Khimicheskikh Reaktivov — Sb Statei Vses Nauchno Issled Inst Khim Reakt
Sbornik Statei. Vsesoyuznyi Nauchno-Issledovatel'skii Institut Transportnogo Stroitel'stva — Sb Statei Vses Nauchno Issled Inst Transp Stroit
Sbornik Statej po Obscej Chimii — Sb Stat Obsc Chim
Sbornik Statej Vsesojuznogo Zaocnogo Politechniceskogo Instituta — Sb VZPI
Sbornik Statniho Geologickeho Ustavu Ceskoslovenski Republiky — Sb Statniho Geol Ustavu Cesk Repub
Sbornik Statniho Vyzkumneho Ustavu Tepelne Techniky — Sb Statniho Vyzk Ustavu Tepelne Tech
Sbornik Studencheskikh Nauchno Issledovatel'skikh Rabot Moskovskaya Veterinarnaya Akademiya — Sb Stud Nauchn Issled Rab Mosk Vet Akad
Sbornik Studencheskikh Nauchno-Issledovatel'skikh Rabot Arkhangel'skii Lesotekhnicheskii Institut — Sb Stud Nauchn Issled Rab Arkhang Lesotekh Inst
Sbornik Studencheskikh Nauchno-Issledovatel'skikh Rabot Kirgizskogo Sel'skokhozyaistvennogo Instituta — Sb Stud Nauchno-Issled Rab Kirg S-Kh Inst
Sbornik Studencheskikh Nauchno-Issledovatel'skikh Rabot. Sibirskii Lesotekhnicheskii Institut — Sb Stud Nauchno Issled Rab Sib Lesotekh Inst
Sbornik Studencheskikh Nauchnykh Rabot Alma-Atinskogo Zooveterinarnogo Instituta — Sb Stud Nauchn Rab Alma-At Zoovet Inst
Sbornik Studencheskikh Nauchnykh Rabot Kabardino Balkarskii Gosudarstvennyi Universitet — Sb Stud Nauchn Rab Kabard Balkar Gos Univ
Sbornik Studencheskikh Nauchnykh Rabot Moskovskaya Sel'skokhozyaistvennaya Akademiya — Sb Stud Nauchn Rab Mosk Skh Akad
Sbornik Studencheskikh Nauchnykh Rabot Penzenskii Sel'skokhozyaistvennyi Institut — Sb Stud Nauchn Rab Penz Skh Inst
Sbornik Studencheskikh Nauchnykh Rabot Rostovskogo Gosudarstvennogo Universiteta — Sb Stud Nauchn Rab Rostov Gos Univ
Sbornik Studencheskikh Nauchnykh Rabot Voronezhskii Gosudarstvennyi Universitet — Sb Stud Nauchn Rab Voronezh Gos Univ
Sbornik Studencheskikh Nauchnykh Trudov Erevanskii Gosudarstvennyi Universitet — Sb Stud Nauchn Tr Erevan Gos Univ
Sbornik Studencheskikh Rabot Krasnodarskogo Gosudarstvennogo Pedagogicheskogo Instituta — Sb Stud Rab Krasnodar Gos Pedagog Inst
Sbornik Studencheskikh Rabot Moskovskogo Tekhnologicheskogo Instituta Myasnoi i Molochnoi Promyshlennosti — Sb Stud Rab Mosk Tekhnol Inst Myasn Molochn Promsti
Sbornik Studencheskikh Rabot Rostovskogo Gosudarstvennogo Universiteta — Sb Stud Rab Rostov Gos Univ
Sbornik Studencheskikh Rabot Sredneaziatskogo Gosudarstvennogo Universiteta — Sb Stud Rab Sredneaziat Gos Univ
Sbornik Studencheskikh Rabot Uzbekskogo Gosudarstvennogo Universitet — Sb Stud Rab Uzb Gos Univ
Sbornik Studencheskikh Rabot. Voronezhskii Gosudarstvennyi Universitet — Sb Stud Rab Voronezh Gos Univ
Sbornik Trudov. Abkhazskii Filial. Nauchno-Issledovatel'skii Institut Kurortologii imeni I.G. Koniashvili — Sb Tr Abkhazskii Fil Nauchno Issled Inst Kurortol im I G Kon
Sbornik Trudov Agrofizicheskii Nauchno-Issledovatel'skii Institut — Sb Tr Agrofiz Nauchno Issled Inst
Sbornik Trudov. Alma-Atinskogo Zooveterinarnogo. Seminalatinskogo Zooveterinarnogo i Omskogo Veterinarnogo Institutov — Sb Tr Alma At Zoovet Seminalat Zoovet Omsk Vet Inst
Sbornik Trudov Altaiskii Gosudarstvennyi Meditsinskii Institut — Sb Tr Altai Gos Med Inst
Sbornik Trudov Andizhanskii Gosudarstvennyi Meditsinskii Institut — Sb Tr Andizh Gos Med Inst
Sbornik Trudov Arkhangel'skii Gosudarstvennyi Meditsinskii Institut — Sb Tr Arkhang Gos Med Inst
Sbornik Trudov Arkhangel'skogo Meditsinskogo Instituta — Sb Tr Arkhang Med Inst
Sbornik Trudov. Armyanskii Nauchno-Issledovatel'skii Institut Stroitel'nykh Materialov i Sooruzhenii — Sb Tr Arm Nauchno Issled Inst Stroit Mater Sooruzh
Sbornik Trudov Armyanskoi Nauchno-Issledovatel'skoi Lesnoi Opytnoi Stantsii — Sb Tr Arm Nauchno-Issled Lesn Opytn Stn
Sbornik Trudov Aspirantov i Molodykh Nauchnykh Sotrudnikov Vsesoyuznyi Institut Rastenievodstva — Sb Tr Aspir Molodykh Nauchn Sotr Vses Inst Rastenievod
Sbornik Trudov Aspirantov i Molodykh Nauchnykh Sotrudnikov Vsesoyuznyi Nauchno-Issledovatel'skii Institut Rastenievodstva — SASRAZ
Sbornik Trudov. Aspirantov i Soiskatelei Kirgizskogo Gosudarstvennogo Universiteta — Sb Tr Aspir Soiskatelei Kirg Gos Univ
Sbornik Trudov Aspirantov Tadzhikskogo Universiteta Estestvennykh Nauk — Sb Tr Aspir Tadzh Univ Estest Nauk
Sbornik Trudov Astrakhanskoi Gosudarstvennoi Sel'skokhozyaistvennoi Opytnoi Stantsii — Sb Tr Astrakh Gos S-Kh Opytn Stn
Sbornik Trudov Astrakhanskoi Protivochumnoi Stantsii — Sb Tr Astrakh Protivochumn Stn
Sbornik Trudov. Avtomaticheskoi Svarke pod Flyusom — Sb Tr Avtom Svarke Flyusom
Sbornik Trudov Azerbaidzhanskii Gosudarstvennyi Institut Usovershenstvovaniya Vrachei — Sb Tr Azerb Gos Inst Usoversh Vrachei
Sbornik Trudov. Azerbaidzhanskii Nauchno-Issledovatel'skii Institut Neftepererabatyvayushehei Promyshlennosti — Sb Tr Azerb Nauchno Issled Inst Neftepererab Promsti
Sbornik Trudov. Azerbaidzhanskii Nauchno-Issledovatel'skii Institut Oftal'mologii — Sb Tr Azerb Nauchno Issled Inst Oftalmol
Sbornik Trudov. Azerbaidzhanskii Nauchno-Issledovatel'skii Institut po Pererabotke Nefti — Sb Tr Azerb Nauchno Issled Inst Pererab Nefti
Sbornik Trudov Azerbaidzhanskogo Gosudarstvennogo Meditsinskogo Instituta — Sb Tr Azerb Gos Med Inst
Sbornik Trudov Azerbaidzhanskogo Nauchno-Issledovatel'skogo Instituta Kurortologii i Fizicheskikh Metodov Lecheniya — Sb Tr Azerb Nauchno-Issled Inst Kurortol Fiz Metod Lech
Sbornik Trudov Bashkirskogo Zapovednika — Sb Tr Bashk Gos Zapov
Sbornik Trudov Belorusskii Gosudarstvennyi Meditsinskii Institut — Sb Tr Beloruss Gos Med Inst
Sbornik Trudov. Belorusskii Institut Mekhanizatsii Sel'skogo Khozyaistva — Sb Tr Beloruss Inst Mekh Selsk Khoz
Sbornik Trudov. Belorusskogo Lesotekhnicheskogo Instituta — Sb Tr Beloruss Lesotekh Inst
Sbornik Trudov Bryanskii Institut Transportnogo Mashinostroeniya — Sb Tr Bryansk Inst Transp Mashinostr
Sbornik Trudov Byuro Glavnoi Sudebnomeditsinskoi Ekspertizy i Kafedry Sudebnoi Meditsiny Erevanskogo Meditsinskogo Instituta — SBKMAL
Sbornik Trudov. Chelyabinskii Politekhnicheskii Institut — Sb Tr Chelyab Politekh Inst
Sbornik Trudov Chelyabinskogo Elektrometallurgicheskogo Kombinata — Sb Tr Chelyab Elektrometall Komb
Sbornik Trudov Chelyabinskogo Elektrometallurgicheskogo Kombinata [*Former USSR*] — Sb Tr Chelyabinsk Elektrometal Komb
Sbornik Trudov Dal'nevostochnyi Nauchno-Issledovatel'skii Institut Lesnogo Khozyaistva — Sb Tr Dal'nevost Nauchno-Issled Inst Lesn Khoz
Sbornik Trudov. Dnepropetrovskii Institut Inzhenerov Zheleznodorozhnogo Transporta — Sb Tr Dnepropetr Inst Inzh Zheleznodorozhn Transp
Sbornik Trudov Donetskii Nauchno-Issledovatel'skii Institut Chernoi Metallurgii [*Former USSR*] — Sb Tr Donets Nauchno-Issled Inst Chern Metall
Sbornik Trudov Donetskii Nauchno-Issledovatel'skii Institut Chernoi Metallurgii — Sb Tr Donetsk Nauchno-Issled Inst Cher Metall
Sbornik Trudov. Energeticheskii Institut imeni G.M. Krzhizhanovskogo — Sb Tr Energ Inst im G M Krzhizhanovskogo
Sbornik Trudov. Erevanskii Meditsinskii Institut — Sb Tr Erevan Med Inst
Sbornik Trudov Geobotanicheskoi Ekspeditsii L'vovskogo Universiteta — Sb Tr Geobot Eksped L'vov Univ
Sbornik Trudov. Gipronisel'prom — Sb Tr Gipronіselprom
Sbornik Trudov. GIPROSANTEKHPROM — Sb Tr GIPROSANTEKHPROM
Sbornik Trudov Glavniiproekt Energeticheskii Institut (USSR) — Sb Tr Glavniiproekt Energ Inst (USSR)
Sbornik Trudov. Gor'kovskii Gosudarstvennyi Meditsinskii Institut imeni S.M. Kirova — Sb Tr Gork Gos Med Inst im SM Kirova
Sbornik Trudov Gor'kovskogo Sel'skokhozyaistvennogo Instituta — Sb Tr Gor'k Skh Inst
Sbornik Trudov Gosudarstvennogo Instituta Prikladnoi Khimii — Sb Tr Gos Inst Prikl Khim
Sbornik Trudov Gosudarstvennogo Irkutskogo Universiteta. Recueil de Travaux de l'Universite d'Etat a Irkoutsk. Wissenschaftliche Abhandlungen der Staatsuniversitaet in Irkutsk — Sborn Trudov Gosud Irkutsk Univ
Sbornik Trudov. Gosudarstvennogo Zootekhnichesko-Veterinarnogo Institut (Tbilisi) — Sb Tr Gos Zootekh Vet Inst (Tbilisi)
Sbornik Trudov Gosudarstvennyi Institut po Proektirovaniyu Zavodov Sanitarno Tekhnicheskogo Oborudovaniya — Sb Tr Gos Inst Proekt Zavodov Sanit Tekh Oborudovaniya
Sbornik Trudov Gosudarstvennyi Nauchno-Issledovatel'skii Energeticheskii Institut Imeni G. M. Krzhizhanovskogo — Sb Tr Gos Nauchno-Issled Energ Inst Im G M Krzhizhanovskogo
Sbornik Trudov. Gosudarstvennyi Nauchno-Issledovatel'skii Institut Kurortologii i Fizioterapii (Tbilisi) — Sb Tr Gos Nauchno Issled Inst Kurortol Fizioter (Tbilisi)
Sbornik Trudov Gosudarstvennyi Nauchno-Issledovatel'skii Institut Rentgenologii i Radiologii — Sb Tr Gos Nauchno Issled Inst Rentgenol Radiol
Sbornik Trudov. Gosudarstvennyi Nauchno-Issledovatel'skii Institut Tsvetnykh Metallov — Sb Tr Gos Nauchno Issled Inst Tsvetn Met
Sbornik Trudov Gosudarstvennyi Vsesoyuznyi Nauchno-Issledovatel'skii Institut Stroitel'nykh Materialov i Konstruktsii — Sb Tr Gos Vses Nauchno-Issled Inst Stroit Mater Konstr
Sbornik Trudov Gruzinskii Zootekhnichesko Veterinarnyi Institut — Sb Tr Gruz Zootekh Vet Inst
Sbornik Trudov Gruzinskogo Zootekhnichesko-Veterinarnogo Uchebno-Issledovatel'skogo Instituta — Sb Tr Gruz Zootekh-Vet Uchebn-Issled Inst
Sbornik Trudov. Institut Avtomatiki — Sb Tr Inst Avtom

Sbornik Trudov Institut Mashinovedeniya i Avtomatizats Akademii Nauk Belorusskoi SSR — Sb Tr Inst Mashinoved Avtom Akad Nauk B SSR
Sbornik Trudov Institut Neftekhimicheskikh Protsessov Akademiya Nauk Azerbaidzhanskoi SSR — Sb Tr Inst Neftekhim Protsessov Akad Nauk Az SSR
Sbornik Trudov Institut Problem Upravlenina — Sb Trudov Inst Problem Upravlen
Sbornik Trudov Institut Stroitel'noi Mekhaniki i Seismostoikosti Akademiya Nauk Gruzinskoi SSR — Sb Tr Inst Stroit Mekh Seismostoikosti Akad Nauk Gruz SSR
Sbornik Trudov. Institut Teploenergetiki. Akademiya Nauk Ukrainskoi SSR — Sb Tr Inst Teploenerg Akad Nauk Ukr SSR
Sbornik Trudov Instituta Eksperimental'noi Patologii i Terapii Akademii Meditsinskikh Nauk SSSR — Sb Tr Inst Eksp Patol Ter Akad Med Nauk SSSR
Sbornik Trudov Instituta Elektrotekhniki Akademiya Nauk Ukrainskoi SSR — Sb Tr Inst Elektrotekh Akad Nauk Ukr SSR
Sbornik Trudov Instituta Epidemiologii i Gigieny Armyanskoi SSR — Sb Tr Inst Epidemiol Gig Arm SSR
Sbornik Trudov Instituta Gidrodinamiki. Akademiya Nauk SSSR. Sibirskoe Otdelenie — Sb Tr Inst Gidrodin Akad Nauk SSSR Sib Otd
Sbornik Trudov Instituta Gornogo Dela Akademiya Nauk Ukrainskoi SSR — Sb Tr Inst Gorn Dela Akad Nauk Ukr SSR
Sbornik Trudov Instituta. Kurortologii i Fizicheskikh Metodov Lecheniya. Yerevan — Sb Tr Inst Kurortol Fiz Metodov Lech Yerevan
Sbornik Trudov Instituta Kurortologii i Fizioterapii Yerevan — Sb Tr Inst Kurortol Fizioter Yerevan
Sbornik Trudov. Instituta Metallovedeniya i Fiziki Metallov — Sb Tr Inst Metalloved Fiz Met
Sbornik Trudov Instituta Okhrany Materinstva i Detstva — Sb Tr Inst Okhr Materin Det
Sbornik Trudov Instituta Urologii Akademii Meditsinskikh Nauk SSSR — Sb Tr Inst Urol Akad Med Nauk SSSR
Sbornik Trudov Instituta Urologii Gruzinskoi SSR — Sb Tr Inst Urol Gruz SSR
Sbornik Trudov Instituta. Vsesoyuznyi Nauchno-Issledovatel'skii Institut Prirodnykh Gazov — Sb Tr Inst Vses Nauchno Issled Inst Prir Gazov
Sbornik Trudov Ivanovskogo Meditsinskogo Instituta — Sb Tr Ivanov Med Inst
Sbornik Trudov Izhevskogo Meditsinskogo Instituta — Sb Tr Izhevsk Med Inst
Sbornik Trudov. Kafedra Yadernoi Fiziki i Radiatsionnoi Khimii. Leningradskii Tekhnolgicheskii Institut imeni Lensoveta — Sb Tr Kafedra Yad Fiz Radiats Khim Leningr Tekhnol Inst im Le
Sbornik Trudov. Kafedry Metallorezhushchie Stanki i Instrumenty Voronezhskii Politekhnicheskii Institut — Sb Tr Kafedry Metallorezhushchie Stanki Instrum Voronezh Pol
Sbornik Trudov Kafedry Mikrobiologii Orenburgskogo Meditsinskogo Instituta — Sb Tr Kafedry Mikrobiol Orenb Med Inst
Sbornik Trudov Kazanskii Gosudarstvennyi Meditsinskii Institut — Sb Tr Kazan Gos Med Inst
Sbornik Trudov. Kazanskogo Aviatsionnogo Instituta — Sb Tr Kazan Aviats Inst
Sbornik Trudov. Khabarovskii Institut Inzhenerov Zheleznodorozhnogo Transporta — Sb Tr Khabar Inst Inzh Zheleznodorozhn Transp
Sbornik Trudov Khabarovskogo Politekhnicheskogo Instituta — Sb Tr Khabar Politekh Inst
Sbornik Trudov Khar'kovskii Gidrometeorologicheskii Institut — Sb Tr Khar'k Gidrometeorol Inst
Sbornik Trudov Khar'kovskogo Avtomobil'no Dorozhnogo Instituta — Sb Tr Khar'k Avtomob Dorozhn Inst
Sbornik Trudov. Khar'kovskogo Instituta Inzhenerov Zheleznodorozhnogo Transport a — Sb Tr Khark Inst Inzh Zheleznodorozhn Transp
Sbornik Trudov Khar'kovskogo Nauchno-Issledovatel'skogo Instituta Vaktsin i Syvorotok Imeni Mechnikov — SKVSAL
Sbornik Trudov Khar'kovskogo Veterinarnogo Instituta — Sb Tr Khark Vet Inst
Sbornik Trudov. Khimiko-Tekhnologicheskii Institut — Sb Tr Khim Tekhnol Inst
Sbornik Trudov. Khimiko-Tekhnologicheskii Institut. Pardubice — Sb Tr Khim Tekhnol Inst Pardubice
Sbornik Trudov Kievskii Inzhenerno-Stroitel'nyi Institut — Sb Tr Kiev Inzh Stroit Inst
Sbornik Trudov Kievskii Stroitel'nyi Institut — Sb Tr Kiev Stroit Inst
Sbornik Trudov. Kievskii Tekhnologicheskii Institut Legkoi Promyshlennosti — Sb Tr Kiev Tekhnol Inst Legk Promsti
Sbornik Trudov Kirgizskii Nauchno-Issledovatel'skii Institut Epidemiologii, Mikrobiologii, i Gigieny — Sb Tr Kirg Nauchno-Issled Inst Epidemio! Mikrobiol Gig
Sbornik Trudov Klyuchevskogo Zavoda Ferrosplavov [*Former USSR*] — Sb Tr Klyuchevsk Zavoda Ferrosplavov
Sbornik Trudov Klyuchevskogo Zavoda Ferrosplavov — Sb Tr Klyuchevskogo Zavoda Ferrosplavov
Sbornik Trudov. Krasnoyarskii Institut Tsvetnykh Metallov — Sb Tr Krasnoyarsk Inst Tsvetn Met
Sbornik Trudov. Krivorozhskii Gornorudnyi Institut — Sb Tr Krivorozh Gornorudn Inst
Sbornik Trudov Krymskogo Gosudarstvennogo Meditsinskogo Instituta — Sb Tr Krym Gos Med Inst
Sbornik Trudov Krymskogo Meditsinskogo Instituta — Sb Tr Krym Med Inst
Sbornik Trudov Kurskii Gosudarstvennyi Meditsinskii Institut — Sb Tr Kursk Gos Med Inst
Sbornik Trudov Kurskogo Meditsinskogo Instituta — Sb Tr Kursk Med Inst
Sbornik Trudov Latviiskii Filial Vsesoyuznogo Obshchestva Pochvovedov — Sb Tr Latv Fil Vses Ova Pochvovedov
Sbornik Trudov Latviiskogo Nauchno-Issledovatel'skogo Instituta Zhivotnovodstva i Veterinarii — Sb Tr Latv Nauchno Issled Inst Zhivotnovod Vet
Sbornik Trudov. Leningradskii Gidrometeorologicheskii Institut — Sb Tr Leningr Gidrometeorol Inst
Sbornik Trudov Leningradskii Gosudarstvennyi Institut Usovershenstvaniya Vrachei — Sb Tr Leningr Gos Inst Usovérsh Vrachei
Sbornik Trudov Leningradskii Institut Inzhenerov Zheleznodorozhnogo Transporta — Sb Tr Leningr Inst Inzh Zheleznodorozhn Transp
Sbornik Trudov. Leningradskii Institut Inzhenerov Zheleznodorozhnogo Transporta imeni Akademika V. N. Obraytsova — Sb Tr Leningr Inst Inzh Zheleznodorozhn Transp im Akad V N Ob
Sbornik Trudov Leningradskii Institut Sovetskoi Torgovli — Sb Tr Leningr Inst Sov Torg
Sbornik Trudov Leningradskii Institut Usovershenstvovaniya Vrachei Imeni S. M. Kirova — Sb Tr Leningr Inst Usoversh Vrachei Im S M Kirova
Sbornik Trudov Leningradskii Inzhenerno-Stroitel'nyi Institut — Sb Tr Leningr Inzh-Stroit Inst
Sbornik Trudov Leningradskii Mekhanicheskii Institut — Sb Tr Leningr Mekh Inst
Sbornik Trudov Leningradskii Nauchno-Issledovatel'skii Institut Vaktsin i Syvorotok — Sb Tr Leningr Nauchno Issled Inst Vaktsin Syvorotok
Sbornik Trudov. Leningradskii Tekhnologicheskii Institut imeni Lensoveta. Kafedra Tekhnologii Neorganicheskikh Veshchestv — Sb Tr Leningr Tekhnol Inst im Lensoveta Kafedra Tekhnol Neor
Sbornik Trudov. Leningradskii Tekhnologicheskii Institut imeni Lensoveta. Kafedra Yadernoi Fiziki i Radiatsionnoi Khimii — Sb Tr Leningr Tekhnol Inst im Lensoveta Kafedra Yad Fiz Rad
Sbornik Trudov Leningradskogo Nauchnogo Obshchestva Nevropatologov i Psikhiatrov — Sb Tr Leningr Nauchn O-Va Nevropatol Psikhiatr
Sbornik Trudov Leningradskogo Nauchnogo Obshchestva Nevropatologov i Psikhiatrov — Sb Tr Leningr Nauchn Ova Nevropatol Psikhiatrov
Sbornik Trudov Leningradskogo Nauchno-Issledovatel'skogo Instituta Gematologii i Perelivaniya Krovi — Sb Tr Leningr Nauchno-Issled Inst Gematol Pereliv Krovi
Sbornik Trudov. Lipetskii Filial. Moskovskii Institut Stali i Splavov — Sb Tr Lipetskii Fil Mosk Inst Stali Splavov
Sbornik Trudov Meditsinskikh Uchrezhdenii Moskovsko-Oksko-Volzhskogo Vozdravotdela — Sb Tr Med Uchrezhd Mosk Oksko Volzh Vozdravotdela
Sbornik Trudov Moldavskii Nauchno-Issledovatel'skii Institut Epidemiologii, Mikrobiologii, i Gigieny — Sb Tr Mold Nauchno Issled Inst Epidemiol Mikrobiol Gig
Sbornik Trudov Moldavskoi Stantsii Vsesoyuznogo Instituta Zashchity Rastenii — Sb Tr Mold Stn Vses Inst Zashch Rast
Sbornik Trudov Molodykh Nauchnykh Rabotnikov Institut Botaniki Akademiya Nauk Gruzinskoi SSR — Sb Tr Molodykh Nauchn Rab Inst Bot Akad Nauk Gruz SSR
Sbornik Trudov Molodykh Uchenykh Kirgizskii Nauchno-Issledovatel'skii Institut Zemledeliya — Sb Tr Molodykh Uch Kirg Nauchno Issled Inst Zemled
Sbornik Trudov. Molodykh Uchenykh. Kirgizskii Nauchno-Issledovatel'skii Institut Zhivotnovodstva i Veterinarii — Sb Tr Molodykh Uch Kirg Nauchno Issled Inst Zhivotnovod Vet
Sbornik Trudov Molodykh Uchenykh. Tomskii Politekhnicheskii Institut — Sb Tr Molodykh Uch Tomsk Politekh Inst
Sbornik Trudov Molodykh Uchenykh Tselinogradskogo Meditsinskogo Instituta — Sb Tr Molodykh Uch Tselinogr Med Inst
Sbornik Trudov. Moskovskaya Sel'skokhozyaistvennaya Akademiya imeni K.A. Timiryazeva — Sb Tr Mosk Skh Akad im K A Timiryazeva
Sbornik Trudov. Moskovskii Institut Stali i Splavov. Lipetskii Filial — Sb Tr Mosk Inst Stali Splavov Lipetskii Fil
Sbornik Trudov Moskovskii Inzhenerno-Stroitel'nyi Institut — Sb Tr Mosk Inzh Stroit Inst
Sbornik Trudov Moskovskii Inzhenerno-Stroitel'nyi Institut Imeni V. V. Kuibysheva [*Former USSR*] — Sb Tr Mosk Inzh-Stroitel Inst Im V V Kuibysheva
Sbornik Trudov Moskovskii Poligraficheskii Institut — Sb Tr Mosk Poligr Inst
Sbornik Trudov Moskovskii Tekhnologicheskii Institut — Sb Tr Mosk Tekhnol Inst
Sbornik Trudov. Moskovskii Tekhnologicheskii Institut Pishchevoi Promyshlennosti — Sb Tr Mosk Tekhnol Inst Pishch Promsti
Sbornik Trudov Moskovskii Vechernii Metallurgicheskii Institut [*Former USSR*] — Sb Tr Mosk Vech Metall Inst
Sbornik Trudov Moskovskii Vechernii Metallurgicheskii Institut — SMVMA
Sbornik Trudov Moskovskii Zaochnyi Poligraficheskii Institut — Sb Tr Mosk Zaochn Poligr Inst
Sbornik Trudov Moskovskogo Nauchno-Issledovatel'skogo Instituta Kosmetologii — Sb Tr Mosk Nauchno Issled Inst Kosmetol
Sbornik Trudov Moskovskogo Oblastskogo Pedagogiceskij Institut — Sb Trud Moskov Obl Pedag Inst
Sbornik Trudov Moskovskogo Vysshego Tekhnicheskogo Uchilishcha imeni N. E. Baumana — Sb Tr Mosk Vyssh Tekh Uchil im NE Baumana
Sbornik Trudov MVTU — Sb Tr MVTU
Sbornik Trudov MVTU imeni N. E. Baumana — Sb Tr MVTU im NE Baumana
Sbornik Trudov na Nauchnoizsledovatelskiya Instituta po Trudova-Khigienna i Professionalni Bolesti — Sb Tr Nauchnoizsled Inst Tr Khig Prof Bol
Sbornik Trudov. Nauchno-Issledovatel'skii Dermato-Venerologicheskii Institut (Tbilisi) — Sb Tr Nauchno Issled Derm Venerol Inst (Tbilisi)
Sbornik Trudov. Nauchno-Issledovatel'skii Gornorudnyi Institut (Krivoy Rog, USSR) — Sb Tr Nauchno Issled Gornorudn Inst Krivoy Rog USSR
Sbornik Trudov. Nauchno-Issledovatel'skii i Proektnyi Institut Ural'skii Promstroiniiproekt — Sb Tr Nauchno Issled Proektn Inst Ural Promstroiniiproekt
Sbornik Trudov Nauchno-Issledovatel'skii Institut Akusherstva i Ginekologii (Tbilisi) — Sb Tr Nauchno Issled Inst Akush Ginekol (Tbilisi)
Sbornik Trudov Nauchno-Issledovatel'skii Institut Eksperimental'noi i Klinicheskoi Terapii — Sb Tr Nauchno-Issled Inst Eksp Klin Ter
Sbornik Trudov Nauchno-Issledovatel'skii Institut Epidemiologii, Mikrobiologii, i Gigieny — Sb Tr Nauchno Issled Inst Epidemiol Mikrobiol Gig
Sbornik Trudov Nauchno-Issledovatel'skii Institut Gematologii i Perelivaniya Krovi (Tiflis) — Sb Tr Nauchno Issled Inst Gematol Pereliv Krovi (Tiflis)

Sbornik Trudov Nauchno-Issledovatel'skii Institut Gigieny Truda i Profzabolevanii Gruzinskoi SSR — Sb Tr Nauchno-Issled Inst Gig Tr Profzabol Gruz SSR
Sbornik Trudov Nauchno-Issledovatel'skii Institut Gigieny Truda i Profzabolevanii Imeni N. I. Makhviladze — SGTPA
Sbornik Trudov Nauchno-Issledovatel'skii Institut Gigieny Truda i Profzabolevanii (Tiflis) — Sb Tr Nauchno Issled Inst Gig Tr Profzabol (Tiflis)
Sbornik Trudov Nauchno-Issledovatel'skii Institut Kurortologii i Fizioterapii Abkhazskii Filial — Sb Tr Nauchno Issled Inst Kurortol Fizioter Abkhazskii Fil
Sbornik Trudov. Nauchno-Issledovatel'skii Institut Kurortologii i Fizioterapii (Tbilisi) — Sb Tr Nauchno Issled Inst Kurortol Fizioter (Tbilisi)
Sbornik Trudov Nauchno-Issledovatel'skii Institut Kurortologii i Fizioterapii (Tiflis) — Sb Tr Nauchn Issled Inst Kurortol Fizioter (Tiflis)
Sbornik Trudov. Nauchno-Issledovatel'skii Institut Okhrany Materinstva i Detstva — Sb Tr Nauchno Issled Inst Okhr Materin Det
Sbornik Trudov. Nauchno-Issledovatel'skii Institut Osnovanii i Podzemnykh Sooruzhenii — Sb Tr Nauchno Issled Inst Osn Podzem Sooruzh
Sbornik Trudov. Nauchno-Issledovatel'skii Institut po Pererabotke Nefti — Sb Tr Nauchno Issled Inst Pererab Nefti
Sbornik Trudov Nauchno-Issledovatel'skii Institut po Probleman Kurskoi Magnitnoi Anomalii — Sb Tr Nauchn Issled Inst Probl Kursk Magn Anomalii
Sbornik Trudov. Nauchno-Issledovatel'skii Institut Promyshlennogo Stroitel'stva — Sb Tr Nauchno Issled Inst Prom Stroit
Sbornik Trudov Nauchno-Issledovatel'skii Institut Promyshlennogo Stroitel'stva Ufa — Sb Tr Nauchno Issled Inst Prom Stroit Ufa
Sbornik Trudov Nauchno-Issledovatel'skii Institut Rentgenologii i Meditsinskoi Radiologii (Tiflis) — Sb Tr Nauchno Issled Inst Rentgenol Med Radiol (Tiflis)
Sbornik Trudov. Nauchno-Issledovatel'skii Institut Sanitarii i Gigieny imeni G.M. Natadze — Sb Tr Nauchno Issled Inst Sanit Gig im GM Natadze
Sbornik Trudov Nauchno-Issledovatel'skii Institut Sanitarnoi Tekhniki — Sb Tr Nauchno Issled Inst Sanit Tekh
Sbornik Trudov. Nauchno-Issledovatel'skii Institut Sel'skogo Khozyaistva Tsentral'nykh Raionov Nechernozemnoi Zony — Sb Tr Nauchno Issled Inst Selsk Khoz Tsentr Raionov Necherno
Sbornik Trudov. Nauchno-Issledovatel'skii Institut Sinteticheskikh Spirtov i Organicheskikh Produktov — Sb Tr Nauchno Issled Inst Sint Spirtov Org Prod
Sbornik Trudov. Nauchno-Issledovatel'skii Institut Tekhniko-Ekonomicheskikh Issledovanii — Sb Tr Nauchno Issled Inst Tekh Ekon Issled
Sbornik Trudov Nauchno-Issledovatel'skii Instituta Eksperimental'noi Klinicheskoi Terapii Gruzinskoi SSR — Sb Tr Nauchno-Issled Inst Eksp Klin Ter Gruz SSR
Sbornik Trudov. Nauchno-Issledovatel'skii Kozhno-Venerologicheskii Institut (Tbilisi) — Sb Tr Nauchno Issled Kozhno Venerol Inst Tbilisi
Sbornik Trudov Nauchno-Issledovatel'skogo Institut Zashchity Rastenii Armyanskoi SSR — Sb Tr Nauchno Issled Inst Zashch Rast Arm SSR
Sbornik Trudov Nauchno-Issledovatel'skogo Instituta Gematologii i Perelivaniya Krovi Gruzinskoi SSR — Sb Tr Nauchno-Issled Inst Gematol Pereliv Krovi Gruz SSR
Sbornik Trudov Nauchno-Issledovatel'skogo Instituta Hudozestvennoj Promyshlennosti — Sb Trud Nauc-Issled Inst Hudoz Promys
Sbornik Trudov. Nauchno-Issledovatel'skogo Instituta Kurortologii i Fizioterapii. Yerevan — Sb Tr Nauchno Issled Inst Kurortol Fizioter Yerevan
Sbornik Trudov Nauchno-Issledovatel'skogo Instituta Meditsinskoi Parazitologii i Tropicheskoi Meditsiny Gruzinskoi SSR — Sb Tr Nauchno Issled Inst Med Parazitol Trop Med Gruz SSR
Sbornik Trudov Nauchno-Issledovatel'skogo Instituta po Stroitel'stvu v g. Sverdlovske — Sb Tr Nauchno Issled Inst Stroit g Sverdlovske
Sbornik Trudov Nauchno-Issledovatel'skogo Instituta Rentgenologii i Meditsinskoi Radiologii Gruzinskoi SSR — Sb Tr Nauchno-Issled Inst Rentgenol Med Radiol Gruz SSR
Sbornik Trudov Nauchno-Issledovatel'skogo Instituta Sanitarii i Gigieny Gruzinskoi SSR — Sb Tr Nauchno-Issled Inst Sanit Gig Gruz SSR
Sbornik Trudov Nauchno-Issledovatel'skogo Instituta Travmatologii i Ortopedii Gruzinskoi SSR — Sb Tr Nauchno Issled Inst Travmatol Ortop Gruz SSR
Sbornik Trudov Nauchno-Issledovatel'skogo Instituta Travmatologii i Ortopedii Gruzinskoi SSR — Sb Tr Nauchno-Issled Inst Travmatol Ortoped Gruz SSR
Sbornik Trudov Nauchno-Issledovatel'skogo Instituta Travmatologii i Ortopedii Gruzinskoi SSR — STIIBO
Sbornik Trudov Nauchno-Issledovatel'skogo Khozhno-Venerologicheskogo Instituta Gruzinskoi SSR — Sb Tr Nauchno Issled Khozhno Venerol Inst Gruz SSR
Sbornik Trudov. Nauchno-Issledovatel'skogo Tekhnokhimicheskogo Instituta Bytovogo Obsluzhivaniya — Sb Tr Nauchno Issled Tekhnokhim Inst Bytovogo Obsluzhivaniya
Sbornik Trudov Nauchno-Izsledovatelski Onkologichen Institut (Sofia) — Sb Tr Nauchno Izsled Onkol Inst (Sofia)
Sbornik Trudov. Nauchno-Tekhnicheskoe Ob'edinenie GruzNIIstrom — Sb Tr Nauchno Tekh Obedin GruzNIIstrom
Sbornik Trudov Nauchno-Tekhnicheskoi Konferentsii. Khabarovskii Politekhnicheskii Institut — Sb Tr Nauchno Tekh Konf Khabar Politekh Inst
Sbornik Trudov Novocherkasskogo Politekhnicheskogo Instituta imeni Sergo Ordzhonikidze — Sb Tr Novocherk Politekh Inst im Sergo Ordzhonikidze
Sbornik Trudov. Novorossiiskii Gosudarstvennyi Proektnyi Institut Tsementnoi Promyshlennosti — Sb Tr Novoross Gos Proektn Inst Tsem Promsti
Sbornik Trudov. Novosibirskii Institut Inzhenerov Zheleznodorozhnogo Transporta — Sb Tr Novosib Inst Inzh Zheleznodorozhn Transp
Sbornik Trudov Novosibirskogo Otdeleniya Vserossiiskogo Obshchestva Otolaringologov — Sb Tr Novosb Vseross O-Va Otolaringol
Sbornik Trudov Novosibirskogo Otdeleniya Vserossiiskogo Obshchestva Otolaringologov — Sb Tr Novosib Otd Vseross Ova Otolaringol
Sbornik Trudov Obshchetekhnicheskikh Kafedr Leningradskii Tekhnologicheskii Institut Kholodil'noi Promyshlennosti — Sb Tr Obshchetekh Kafedr Leningr Tekhnol Inst Kholod Promsti
Sbornik Trudov Odesskii Inzhenerno-Stroitel'nyi Institut — Sb Tr Odess Inzh Stroit Inst
Sbornik Trudov Odesskii Meditsinskii Institut — Sb Tr Odess Med Inst
Sbornik Trudov Odesskogo Elektrotehniceskogo Instituta Svjazi Imeni A. S. Popova — Sb Trudov Odess Elektrotehn Inst Svjazi
Sbornik Trudov Osvoeniyu Terskokumskikh Peskov — Sb Tr Osvo Terskokumskikh Peskov
Sbornik Trudov Penzenskogo Sel'skokhozyaistvennogo Instituta — Sb Tr Penz Skh Inst
Sbornik Trudov Permskoi Gorodskoi Psikhiatricheskoi Bol'nitsy — Sb Tr Permsk Gor Psikhiatr Boln
Sbornik Trudov po Agronomicheskoi Fizike — Sb Tr Agron Fiz
Sbornik Trudov po Agronomicheskoi Fizike — Sb Trud Agron Fiz
Sbornik Trudov po Agronomicheskoi Fizike — SFSLA
Sbornik Trudov po Lesnomu Khozyaistvu (Kazan) — Sb Tr Lesn Khoz (Kazan)
Sbornik Trudov po Rentgenologii — Sb Tr Rentgenol
Sbornik Trudov po Sudebnoi Meditsine i Sudebnoi Khimii — Sb Tr Sud Med Sud Khim
Sbornik Trudov Povolzhskogo Lesotekhnicheskogo Instituta — Sb Tr Povolzh Lesotekh Inst
Sbornik Trudov Proektnyi i Nauchno-Issledovatel'skii Institut "Ural'skii Promstroiniiproekt" — Sb Tr Proektn Nauchno-Issled Inst Ural Promstroiniiproekt
Sbornik Trudov Professorov i Prepodavatelej Gosudarstvennogo Irkutskogo Universiteta. Recueil des Travaux des Professeurs. Universite d'Etat a Irkoutsk — Sborn Trudov Profess Prepodav Gosud Irkutsk Univ
Sbornik Trudov Respublikanskii Nauchno-Issledovatel'skii Institut Mestnykh Stroitel'nykh Materialov — Sb Tr Resp Nauchno-Issled Inst Mestnykh Stroit Mater
Sbornik Trudov Respublikanskii Nauchno-Issledovatel'skii Institut Okhrany Materinstva Detstva — Sb Tr Resp Nauchno-Issled Inst Okhr Materin Det
Sbornik Trudov Respubliki Kostno Tuberkuleznaya Bol'nitsa Imeni Lenina — Sb Tr Resp Kostno Tuberk Bol'n Im Lenina
Sbornik Trudov Rostovskogo-na-Donu Instituta Inzhenerov Zheleznodorozhnogo Transporta — Sb Tr Rostov na Donu Inst Inzh Zheleznodorozhn Transp
Sbornik Trudov. Rybinskii Aviatsionnyi Tekhnologicheskii Institut — Sb Tr Rybinsk Aviats Tekhnol Inst
Sbornik Trudov Samarkandskogo Meditsinskogo Instituta — Sb Tr Samark Med Inst
Sbornik Trudov Sektor Radiobiologii Akademiya Nauk Armyanskoi SSR — Sb Tr Sekt Radiobiol Akad Nauk Arm SSR
Sbornik Trudov Severnyi Nauchno-Issledovatel'skii Institut Promyshlennosti — Sb Tr Sev Nauchno-Issled Inst Promsti
Sbornik Trudov Sochinskoi Nauchno-Issledovatel'skoi Opytnoi Stantsii Subtropicheskoyo Lesnogo i Lesoparkovogo Khozyaistva — Sb Tr Sochinskoi Nauchno Issled Opytn Stn Subtrop Lesn Lesopa
Sbornik Trudov Stalingradskaya Opytno-Meliorativnaya Stantsiya — Sb Tr Stalingr Opytno Melior Stn
Sbornik Trudov Stalingradskii Institut Inzhenerov Gorodskogo Khozyaistva — Sb Tr Stalingr Inst Inzh Gor Khoz
Sbornik Trudov Stalinskogo Instituta Usovershenstvovaniya Vrachei — Sb Tr Stalinskogo Inst Usoversh Vrachei
Sbornik Trudov Stavropol'skii Gosudarstvennyi Pedagogicheskii Institut — Sb Tr Stavrop Gos Pedagog Inst
Sbornik Trudov Sverdlovskii Nauchno-Issledovatel'skii Institut Pererabotki Drevesiny — Sb Tr Sverdl Nauchno Issled Inst Pererab Drev
Sbornik Trudov Sverdlovskii Nauchno-Issledovatel'skii Institut po Stroitel'stvu — Sb Tr Sverdl Nauchno-Issled Inst Stroit
Sbornik Trudov. Sverdlovskogo Gosudarstvennogo Meditsinskogo Instituta — Sb Tr Sverdl Gos Med Inst
Sbornik Trudov Sverdlovskoi Gorodskoi Klinicheskoi Bol'nitsy No. 1 — Sb Tr Sverdl Gor Klin Bol'n No 1
Sbornik Trudov Tadzhikskogo Nauchno-Issledovatel'skogo Instituta Zemledeliya — Sb Tr Tadzh Nauchno-Issled Inst Zemled
Sbornik Trudov Tbilisskii Gosudarstvennyi Nauchno-Issledovatel'skii Institut Stroitel'nykh Materialov — Sb Tr Tbilis Gos Nauchno Issled Inst Stroit Mater
Sbornik Trudov Tbilisskogo Instituta Usovershenstvovaniya Vrachei — Sb Tr Tbilis Inst Usoversh Vrachei
Sbornik Trudov Tbilisskogo Nauchno-Issledovatel'skogo Khimiko-Farmatsevticheskogo Instituta — Sb Tr Tbilis Nauchno Issled Khim Farm Inst
Sbornik Trudov. Tekhnologii i Khimii Pishchevykh Produktov — Sb Tr Tekhnol Khim Pishch Prod
Sbornik Trudov. TEPLOPROEKT — Sb Tr TEPLOPROEKT
Sbornik Trudov Tsentral'nogo Nauchno-Issledovatel'skogo Instituta Bumagi — Sb Tr Tsentr Nauchno Issled Inst Bum
Sbornik Trudov Tsentral'nogo Nauchno-Issledovatel'skogo Instituta Chernoj Metallurgii *[Former USSR]* — Sb Tr Tsent Nauchno-Issled Inst Chern Metall
Sbornik Trudov Tsentral'nogo Nauchno-Issledovatel'skogo Instituta Chernoj Metallurgii — Sb Tr Tsentr Nauchno-Issled Inst Chern Metall
Sbornik Trudov Tsentral'nyi Muzei Pochvovedeniya — Sb Tr Tsentr Muz Pochvoved
Sbornik Trudov. Tsentral'nyi Muzei Pochvovedeniya imeni V.V. Dokuchaeva — Sb Tr Tsentr Muz Pochvoved im V V Dokuchaeva
Sbornik Trudov Tsentral'nyi Nauchno-Issledovatel'skii Institut Olovyannoi Promyshlennosti — Sb Tr Tsentr Nauchno-Issled Inst Olovyannoi Promsti
Sbornik Trudov. Tsentral'nyi Nauchno-Issledovatel'skii Institut Tary i Upakovki — Sb Tr Tsentr Nauchno Issled Inst Tary Upakovki
Sbornik Trudov. Tsentral'nyi Nauchno-Issledovatel'skii Lesokhimicheskii Institut — Sb Tr Tsentr Nauchno Issled Lesokhim Inst
Sbornik Trudov Tsentral'nyi Nauchno-Issledovatel'skii Proektnyi Institut Lesokhiimicheskoi Promyshlennosti — Sb Tr Tsentr Nauchno Issled Proektn Inst Lesokhim Promsti
Sbornik Trudov Tskhaltubskii Filial Nauchno-Issledovatel'skii Institut Kurortoloogii i Fizioterapii — Sb Tr Tskhaltub Fil Nauchno Issled Inst Kurortol Fizioter
Sbornik Trudov TsNILKhI — Sb Tr TsNILKhI

Sbornik Trudov Tul'skogo Mekhanicheskogo Instituta — Sb Tr Tul Mekh Inst
Sbornik Trudov. Ufimskii Neftyanoi Nauchno-Issledovatel'skii Institut — Sb Tr Ufim Neft Nauchno Issled Inst
Sbornik Trudov Ufimskogo Neftyanogo Instituta — Sb Tr Ufim Neft Inst
Sbornik Trudov. Ukrainskii Nauchno-Issledovatel'skii Institut Kozhevenno-Obuvnoi Promyshlennosti — Sb Tr Ukr Nauchno Issled Inst Kozh Obuvn Promsti
Sbornik Trudov Ukrainskii Nauchno-Issledovatel'skii Institut Pishchevoi Promyshlennosti — Sb Tr Ukr Nauchno Issled Inst Pishch Promsti
Sbornik Trudov. Ukrainskii Nauchno-Issledovatel'skii Institut Spetsial'nykh Stalei, Splavov i Ferrosplavov — Sb Tr Ukr Nauchno Issled Inst Spets Stalei Splavov Ferrosplav
Sbornik Trudov. Ukrainskii Nauchno-Issledovatel'skii Uglekhimicheskii Institut — Sb Tr Ukr Nauchno Issled Uglekhim Inst
Sbornik Trudov Ukrainskij Nauchno-Issledovatel'skij Institut Metallov — Sb Tr Ukr Nauchno-Issled Inst Met
Sbornik Trudov Ukrainskogo Nauchno-Issledovatel'skogo Instituta Poligraficheskoi Promyshlennosti — Sb Tr Ukr Nauchno Issled Inst Poligr Promsti
Sbornik Trudov Ukrainskogo Nauchno-Issledovatel'skogo Instituta Tsellyulozno-Bumazhnoi Promyshlennosti — Sb Tr Ukr Nauchno Issled Inst Tsellyul Bum Promsti
Sbornik Trudov Ukrainskogo Tsentral'nogo Nauchno-Issledovatel'skogo Instituta Ortopedii i Travmatologii — Sb Tr Ukr Tsentr Nauchno-Issled Inst Ortop Travmatol
Sbornik Trudov. Ul'yanovskii Politekhnicheskii Institut — Sb Tr Ulyanovsk Politekh Inst
Sbornik Trudov Ural'skii Lesotekhnicheskii Institut — Sb Tr Ural Lesotekh Inst
Sbornik Trudov. Ural'skii Nauchno-Issledovatel'skii Khimicheskii Institut — Sb Tr Ural Nauchno Issled Khim Inst
Sbornik Trudov Vil'nyusskogo Gosudarstvennogo Nauchno-Issledovatel'skogo Instituta Stroitel'nykh Materialov — Sb Tr Vil'nyus Gos Nauchno Issled Inst Stroit Mater
Sbornik Trudov Vitebskogo Gosudarstvennogo Meditsinskogo Instituta — Sb Tr Vitebsk Gos Med Inst
Sbornik Trudov Vladivostokskogo Nauchno-Issledovatel'skogo Instituta Epidemiologii, Mikrobiologii, i Gigieny — Sb Tr Vladivost Nauchno Issled Inst Epidemiol Mikrobiol Gig
Sbornik Trudov VNIIB — Sb Tr VNIIB
Sbornik Trudov VNIKhFI (Vsesoiuznyi Nauchno-Issledovatel'skii Khimiko-Farmatsevticheskii Institut) — Sb Tr VNIKhFI
Sbornik Trudov. Volgogradskii Nauchno-Issledovatel'skii Institut Neftyanoi i Gazovoi Promyshlennosti — Sb Tr Volgogr Nauchno Issled Inst Neft Gazov Promsti
Sbornik Trudov Vopros Zool Kazanskii Gosudarstvennyi Pedagogicheskii Institut — Sb Trud Vopros Zool Kazansk Gos Pedagog Inst
Sbornik Trudov. Voronezhskii Gosudarstvennyi Meditsinskii Institut — Sb Tr Voronezh Gos Med Inst
Sbornik Trudov Voronezhskogo Inzhenerno-Stroitel'nogo Instituta — Sb Tr Voronezh Inzh Stroit Inst
Sbornik Trudov Voronezhskogo Otdeleniya Vsesoyuznogo Khimicheskogo Obshchestva — Sb Tr Voronezh Otd Vses Khim Ova
Sbornik Trudov Voronezhskogo Sel'skokhozyaistvennogo Instituta — Sb Tr Voronezh S-Kh
Sbornik Trudov Voronezhskogo Sel'skokhozyaistvennogo Instituta — Sb Tr Voronezh S-Kh Inst
Sbornik Trudov Vrachei Dorogi — Sb Tr Vrachei Dorogi
Sbornik Trudov Vrachei Pribaltiiskogo Zheleznodorozhiya — Sb Tr Vrachei Pribalt Zhelezn
Sbornik Trudov Vsesojuznogo Zaocnogo Politehniceskogo Instituta — Sb Trudov Vsesojuz Zaocn Politehn Inst
Sbornik Trudov Vsesoyuznogo Instituta Zashchity Rastenii — Sb Tr Vses Inst Zashch Rast
Sbornik Trudov Vsesoyuznogo Nauchno-Issledovatel'skogo Instituta po Boleznyam Ptits — Sb Tr Vses Nauchno-Issled Inst Bolezn Ptits
Sbornik Trudov Vsesoyuznogo Nauchno-Issledovatel'skogo Instituta Tsellyulozno- Bumazhnoi Promyshlennosti — Sb Tr Vses Nauchno-Issled Inst Tsellyul Bum Promsti
Sbornik Trudov Vsesoyuznogo Nauchno-Issledovatel'skogo Khimiko-Farmatsevticheskogo Instituta — Sb Tr Vses Nauchno Issled Khim Farm Inst
Sbornik Trudov Vsesoyuznogo Zaochnogo Politekhnicheskogo Instituta — Sb Tr Vses Zaochn Politekh Inst
Sbornik Trudov Vsesoyuznogo Zaochnogo Politekhnicheskogo Instituta — SBTDA
Sbornik Trudov Vsesoyuznyi Institut Rastenievodstva — Sb Tr Vses Inst Rastenievod
Sbornik Trudov. Vsesoyuznyi Nauchno-Issledovatel'skii Gornometallurgicheskii Institut Tsvetnykh Metallov — Sb Tr Vses Nauchno Issled Gornometall Inst Tsvetn Met
Sbornik Trudov Vsesoyuznyi Nauchno-Issledovatel'skii i Eksperimental'no-Konstruktorskii Institut Tary i Upakovki — Sb Tr Vses Nauchno-Issled Eksp-Konstr Inst Tary Upakovki
Sbornik Trudov. Vsesoyuznyi Nauchno-Issledovatel'skii i Proektno-Konstruktorskii Institut Yuvelirnoi Promyshlennosti — Sb Tr Vses Nauchno Issled Proektno Konstr Inst Yuvelirnoi Pr
Sbornik Trudov Vsesoyuznyi Nauchno-Issledovatel'skii i Proektnyi Institut po Teplotekhnicheskim Sooruzheniyam — Sb Tr Vses Nauchno-Issled Proektn Inst Teplotekh Sooruzh
Sbornik Trudov. Vsesoyuznyi Nauchno-Issledovatel'skii i Proektnyi Institut po Vtorichnym Metallam — Sb Tr Vses Nauchno Issled Proektn Inst Vtorichnym Met
Sbornik Trudov. Vsesoyuznyi Nauchno-Issledovatel'skii i Proektnyi Institut TEPLOPROEKT — Sb Tr Vses Nauchno Issled Proektn Inst TEPLOPROEKT
Sbornik Trudov Vsesoyuznyi Nauchno-Issledovatel'skii i Proektnyi Institut Titana — Sb Tr Vses Nauchno Issled Proektn Inst Titana
Sbornik Trudov Vsesoyuznyi Nauchno-Issledovatel'skii i Proektnyi Institut Titana [*Former USSR*] — Sb Tr Vses Nauchno-Issled Proekt Inst Titana
Sbornik Trudov. Vsesoyuznyi Nauchno-Issledovatel'skii i Proektnyi Institut Tugoplavkikh Metallov i Tverdykh Splavov — Sb Tr Vses Nauchno Issled Proektn Inst Tugoplavkikh Met Tver
Sbornik Trudov Vsesoyuznyi Nauchno-Issledovatel'skii Institut Derevoobrabatyvayuushchei Promyshlennosti — Sb Tr Vses Nauchno Issled Inst Derevoobrab Promsti
Sbornik Trudov Vsesoyuznyi Nauchno-Issledovatel'skii Institut Gidroliza Rastitel'nykh Materialov [*Former USSR*] — Sb Tr Vses Nauchno-Issled Inst Gidroliza Rastit Mater
Sbornik Trudov. Vsesoyuznyi Nauchno-Issledovatel'skii Institut Gidrotekhnicheskikh i Sanitarno-Tekhnicheskikh Rabot — Sb Tr Vses Nauchno Issled Inst Gidrotekh Sanit Tekh Rab
Sbornik Trudov Vsesoyuznyi Nauchno-Issledovatel'skii Institut "Goznaka" — Sb Tr Vses Nauchno Issled Inst "Goznaka"
Sbornik Trudov. Vsesoyuznyi Nauchno-Issledovatel'skii Institut Nerudnykh Stroitel'nykh Materialov i Gidromekhanizatsii — Sb Tr Vses Nauchno Issled Inst Nerudn Stroit Mater Gidromekh
Sbornik Trudov Vsesoyuznyi Nauchno-Issledovatel'skii Institut Novykh Stroitel'nykh Materialov [*Former USSR*] — Sb Tr Vses Nauchno-Issled Inst Nov Stroit Mater
Sbornik Trudov. Vsesoyuznyi Nauchno-Issledovatel'skii Institut Sinteticheskogo Kauchuka imeni S.V. Lebedeva — Sb Tr Vses Nauchno Issled Inst Sint Kauch im S V Lebedeva
Sbornik Trudov Vsesoyuznyi Nauchno-Issledovatel'skii Institut Stroitel'nykh Materialov i Konstruktsii — Sb Tr Vses Nauchno-Issled Inst Stroit Mater Konstr
Sbornik Trudov Vsesoyuznyi Nauchno-Issledovatel'skii Institut Tverdykh Splavov — Sb Tr Vses Nauchno Issled Inst Tverd Splavov
Sbornik Trudov. Vsesoyuznyi Neftyanoi Nauchno-Issledovatel'skii Institut — Sb Tr Vses Neft Nauchno Issled Inst
Sbornik Trudov. Vsesoyuznyi Proektnyi i Nauchno-Issledovatel'skii Institut Gipronisel'prom — Sb Tr Vses Proektn Nauchno Issled Inst Giproniselprom
Sbornik Trudov Vsesoyuznyi Zaochnyi Inzhenerno-Stroitel'nyi Institut — Sb Tr Vses Zaochn Inzh Stroit Inst
Sbornik Trudov Yuzknyi Nauchno-Issledovatel'skii Institut Promyshlennogo Stroitel'stva — Sb Tr Yuzhn Nauchno Issled Inst Prom Stroit
Sbornik Trudov Zoologicheskogo Muzeya — Sb Trud Zool Muz
Sbornik Trudov. Zoologicheskogo Muzeya MGU [*Moskovskii Gosudarstvennyi Universitet*] — Sb Tr Zool Muz MGU
Sbornik Trudov Zoologicheskogo Muzeya Moskovskogo Universiteta — Sb Tr Zool Muz Mosk Univ
Sbornik Trudove na Visshiya Meditsinski Institut I.P. Pavlov (Plovdiv, Bulgaria) — Sb Tr Vissh Med Inst I P Pavlov (Plovdiv Bulg)
Sbornik Tsentral'nogo Geologicheskogo Instituta ChSSR — Sb Tsentr Geol Inst ChSSR
Sbornik Tsentral'nyi Nauchno-Issledovatel'skii Institut Tekhnologii i Mashinostroeniya — Sb Tsentr Nauchno Issled Inst Tekhnol Mashinostr
Sbornik Uchenykh Zapisok Aspirantov. Latviiskii Nauchno-Issledovatel'skii Institut Zemledeliya — Sb Uch Zap Aspir Latv Nauchno Issled Inst Zemled
Sbornik. UNIGEO, Statni Podnik, Ostrava — Sb UNIGEO Statni Podnik Ostrava
Sbornik Ustav Vedeckotechnickych Informaci Genetika a Slechteni — Sb Ustav Vedeckotech Inf Genet Slechteni
Sbornik Ustav Vedeckotechnickych Informaci pro Zemedelstvi, Genetika, a Slechteni — Sb Ustav Vedeckotech Inf Zemed Genet Slechteni
Sbornik Ustav Vedeckotechnickych Informaci pro Zemedelstvi Rada Meliorace — Sb Ustav Vedeckotech Inf Zemed Melior
Sbornik Ustav Vedeckotechnickych Informaci. Rada Meliorace — Sb Ustav Vedeckotech Inf Melior
Sbornik Ustavu Nerostych Surovin v Kutne Hore — Sb Ustavu Nerostych Surovin Kutne Hore
Sbornik Ustavu pro Vyzkum Vyzivy Lidu v Praze — Sb Ustavu Vyzk Vyz Lidu Praze
Sbornik Ustredniho Ustavu Geologickeho — Sb Ustred Ustavu Geol
Sbornik Ustredniho Ustavu Geologickeho. Oddil Geologicky — Sb Ustred Ustavu Geol Oddil Geol
Sbornik UVTI [*Ustav Vedeckotechnickych Informaci*] **Genetika a Slechteni** — Sb UVTI Genet Slechteni
Sbornik UVTI [*Ustav Vedeckotechnickych Informaci*] **Meliorace** — Sb UVTI Melior
Sbornik UVTI [*Ustav Vedeckotechnickych Informaci*] **Ochrana Rostlin** — Sb UVTI Ochr Rostl
Sbornik UVTI (Ustav Vedeckotechnickych Informaci) Zahradnictvi — Sb UVTI (Ustav Vedeckotech Inf) Zahradnictvi
Sbornik UVTIZ [*Ustav Vedeckotechnickych Informaci Pro Zemedelstvi*]. Genetika a Slechteni — Sb UVTIZ Genet Slechteni
Sbornik UVTIZ [*Ustav Vedeckotechnickych Informaci Pro Zemedelstvi*] **Meliorace** — Sb UVTIZ Melior
Sbornik UVTIZ [*Ustav Vedeckotechnickych Informaci pro Zemedelstvi*] **Ochrana Rostlin** — SUSRD8
Sbornik UVTIZ (Ustav Vedeckotechnickych Informaci pro Zemedelstvi) Ochrana Rostlin — Sb UVTIZ (Ustav Vedeckotech Inf Zemed) Ochr Rostl
Sbornik UVTIZ (Ustav Vedeckotechnickych Informaci Pro Zemedelstvi). Potravinarske Vedy — Sb UVTIZ Potravin Vedy
Sbornik Vedeckeho Lesnickeho Ustavu Vysoke Skoly Zemedelske v Praze — Sb Ved Lesn Ustav Vys Sk Zemed Praze
Sbornik Vedeckeho Lesnickeho Ustavu Vysoke Skoly Zemedelske v Praze — Sborn Ved Lesn Ust Vysoke Skoly Zemed
Sbornik Vedeckych a Odbornych Praci. Vysoke Uceni Technicke v Brne. Fakulta Stavebni — Sb Ved Odb Praci
Sbornik Vedeckych Prac Stavebnej Fakulty Slovenskej Vysokej Skoly Technickej v Bratislave — Sb Ved Pr Stavebnej Fak Slov Vys Sk Tech Bratislave
Sbornik Vedeckych Prac Vysokej Skoly Technickej v Kosiciach — Sb Ved Pr Vys Sk Tech Kosiciach

Sbornik Vedeckych Praci Fakulty Lesnicke — Sborn Ved Praci Fak Lesn
Sbornik Vedeckych Praci Lekarske Fakulty Karlovy University v Hradci Kralove — Sb Ved Pr Lek Fak Karlovy Univ Hradci Kralove
Sbornik Vedeckych Praci Lekarske Fakulty Karlovy University v Hradci Kralove — Sb Ved Pr Lek Fak Univ Karlovy Hradci Kralove
Sbornik Vedeckych Praci Lekarske Fakulty Karlovy University v Hradci Kralove. Supplementum — Sb Ved Pr Lek Fak Karlovy Univ Hradci Kralove Suppl
Sbornik Vedeckych Praci Lekarske Fakulty Karlovy Univerzity v Hradci Kralove — Sb Ved Pr Lek Fak Karlovy Univerzity Hradci Kralove
Sbornik Vedeckych Praci Lekarske Fakulty Karlovy Univerzity v Hradci Kralove. Supplementum — Sb Ved Pr Lek Fak Karlovy Univerzity Hradci Kralove Supl
Sbornik Vedeckych Praci Ustredniho Statniho Ustavu v Praze — Sb Ved Praci Ustred Statniho Ust Praze
Sbornik Vedeckych Praci VLVDU [*Vojenskeho Lekarskeho Vyzkumneho a Doskolovaciho Ustavu*] **v Hradci Kralove** — Sb Ved Pr VLVDU Hradci Kralove
Sbornik Vedeckych Praci. Vysoka Skola Chemickotechnologicka Pardubice — Sb Ved Pr Vys Sk Chemickotechnol Pardubice
Sbornik Vedeckych Praci. Vysoka Skola Chemickotechnologicka (Pardubice) — Sb Ved Pr Vys Sk Chem-Technol (Pardubice)
Sbornik Vedeckych Praci. Vysoka Skola Chemickotechnologicka (Pardubice) — SVPVA
Sbornik Vedeckych Praci Vysoke Skoly Banske v Ostrave — Sb Ved Pr Vys Sk Banske Ostrave
Sbornik Vedeckych Praci Vysoke Skoly Banske v Ostrave — Sb Ved Pr Vys Sk Bransk Ostrave
Sbornik Vedeckych Praci Vysoke Skoly Banske v Ostrave. Rada Hornicko-Geologicka [*Czechoslovakia*] — Sb Ved Pr Vys Sk Banske Ostrave Rada Horn-Geol
Sbornik Vedeckych Praci Vysoke Skoly Banske v Ostrave. Rada Hutnicka — Sb Ved Pr Vys Banske Ostrave Rada Hutn
Sbornik Vedeckych Praci Vysoke Skoly Banske v Ostrave. Rada Hutnicka — Sb Ved Pr Vys Sk Banske Ostrave Rada Hutn
Sbornik Vedeckych Praci Vysoke Skoly Banske v Ostrave. Rada Strojnicka — Sb Ved Pr Vys Sk Banske Ostrave Rada Strojnicka
Sbornik Vedeckych Praci-Vyzkumny Ustav Vyzivy Zvirat — Sb Ved Praci Vyzk Ustav Vyz Zvirat
Sbornik Velehradsky. Archeologicky Spolek Stary Velehrad se Sidlem na Velehrade — SbV
Sbornik VIZR'a — Sb VIZRa
Sbornik Vlastivedneho Musea v Olomouci — Sborn Vlastiv Mus V Olomouci
Sbornik Vlastivednych Praci z Podblanicka — Sbor Vlast Prac Podblanicka
Sbornik "Voprosy Issledovaniya i Izpol'zovaniya Pochv Moldavii" — Sb "Vop Issled Izpol'z Pochv Moldavii"
Sbornik Vsesoyuznogo Instituta Zashchity Rastenii — Sb Vses Inst Zashch Rast
Sbornik Vsesoyuznyi Sovet Nauchno-Tekhnickeskikh Obshchestv. Komitet po Korrozi i Zashchite Metallov — Sb Vses Sov Nauchno-Tekh Obshchestv Kom Korroz Zashch Met
Sbornik Vychodoslovenskeho Muzea v Kosiciach — Sborn Vychodoslov Muz V Kosiciach
Sbornik Vyskumnych Prac z Odboru Celulozy a Papiera — Sb Vysk Pr Odboru Celul Pap
Sbornik Vyskumnych Prac z Odboru Papiera a Celulozy — Sb Vysk Pr Odboru Pap Celul
Sbornik Vysoka Skola Chemicko-Technologicka. Fakulta Potravinarske Technologie — Sb Vys Skola Chem-Technol Fak Potrav Technol
Sbornik Vysoka Skola Zemedelska v Praze Provozne Ekonomicke Fakulty v Ceskych Budejovicich Biologicka Rada — SVRBAR
Sbornik Vysoke Skoly Chemicko-Technologicke v Praze — Sb Vys Sk Chem-Technol Praze
Sbornik Vysoke Skoly Chemicko-Technologicke v Praze. A. Zpravy o Cinnosti a Jine Celoskolske Publikace — Sb Vys Sk Chem Technol Praze A
Sbornik Vysoke Skoly Chemicko-Technologicke v Praze. Analyticka Chemie — Sb Vys Sk Chem Technol Praze Anal Chem
Sbornik Vysoke Skoly Chemicko-Technologicke v Praze. Anorganicka a Organicka Technologie — Sb Vys Sk Chem Technol Praze Anorg Org Technol
Sbornik Vysoke Skoly Chemicko-Technologicke v Praze. Anorganicka Chemie a Technologie — Sb Vys Sk Chem Technol Praze Anorg Chem Technol
Sbornik Vysoke Skoly Chemicko-Technologicke v Praze. Anorganicka Chemie a Technologie — SVACB
Sbornik Vysoke Skoly Chemicko-Technologicke v Praze. Anorganicka Technologie — Sb Vys Sk Chem Technol Praze Anorg Technol
Sbornik Vysoke Skoly Chemicko-Technologicke v Praze. B. Anorganicka Chemie a Technologie — Sb Vys Sk Chem Technol Praze B Anorg Chem Technol
Sbornik Vysoke Skoly Chemicko-Technologicke v Praze. Chemicke Inzenyrstvi — Sb Vys Sk Chem Technol Praze Chem Inz
Sbornik Vysoke Skoly Chemicko-Technologicke v Praze. Chemicke Inzenyrstvi a Automatizace — Sb Vys Sk Chem Technol Praze Chem Inz Autom
Sbornik Vysoke Skoly Chemicko-Technologicke v Praze. Chemie a Technologie Silikatu — Sb Vys Sk Chem Technol Praze Chem Technol Silik
Sbornik Vysoke Skoly Chemicko-Technologicke v Praze. D. Technologie Paliv — Sb Vys Sk Chem Technol Praze D Technol Paliv
Sbornik Vysoke Skoly Chemicko-Technologicke v Praze. Ekonimika a Rizeni Chemickeho Prumyslu — Sb Vys Sk Chem Technol Praze Ekon Rizeni Chem Prum
Sbornik Vysoke Skoly Chemicko-Technologicke v Praze. Ekonomika a Rizeni Chemickeho Prumyslu — Sb Vys Chem Technol Praze Ekon Rizeni Chem Prum
Sbornik Vysoke Skoly Chemicko-Technologicke v Praze. Fysikalni Chemie — Sb Vys Sk Chem Technol Praze Fys Chem
Sbornik Vysoke Skoly Chemicko-Technologicke v Praze. Fyzika Materialu a Merici Technika — Sb Vys Sk Chem Technol Praze Fyz Mater Merici Tech
Sbornik Vysoke Skoly Chemicko-Technologicke v Praze. G. Mineralogie — Sb Vys Sk Chem Technol Praze G Miner
Sbornik Vysoke Skoly Chemicko-Technologicke v Praze. H. Analyticka Chemie — Sb Vys Sk Chem Technol Praze H Anal Chem
Sbornik Vysoke Skoly Chemicko-Technologicke v Praze. K. Chemicke Inzenyrstvi — Sb Vys Sk Chem Technol Praze K Chem Inz
Sbornik Vysoke Skoly Chemicko-Technologicke v Praze. L. Chemie a Technologie Silikatu — Sb Vys Sk Chem Technol Praze L Chem Technol Silik
Sbornik Vysoke Skoly Chemicko-Technologicke v Praze. Mineralogie — Sb Vys Sk Chem Technol Praze Mineral
Sbornik Vysoke Skoly Chemicko-Technologicke v Praze. N. Fysikalni Chemie — Sb Vys Sk Chem Technol Praze N Fys Chem
Sbornik Vysoke Skoly Chemicko-Technologicke v Praze (Oddil). Chemicke Inzenyrstvi — Sb Vysk Sk Chem-Technol Praze (Oddil) Chem Inz
Sbornik Vysoke Skoly Chemicko-Technologicke v Praze (Oddil). Chemicke Inzenyrstvi a Automatizace — Sb Vysk Sk Chem-Technol Praze (Oddil) Chem Inz Autom
Sbornik Vysoke Skoly Chemicko-Technologicke v Praze (Oddil). Fakulty Anorganicke a Organicke Technologie — Sb Vys Sk Chem Technol Praze (Oddil) Fak Anorg Technol
Sbornik Vysoke Skoly Chemicko-Technologicke v Praze (Oddil). Fakulty Poetravinarske Technologie — Sb Vys Sk Chem Technol Praze (Oddil) Fak Potravin Technol
Sbornik Vysoke Skoly Chemicko-Technologicke v Praze (Oddil). Fakulty Technologie Paliv a Vody — Sb Vys Sk Chem-Technol Praze (Oddil) Fak Technol Paliv Vody
Sbornik Vysoke Skoly Chemicko-Technologicke v Praze (Oddil). K — Sb Vysk Sk Chem Technol Praze (Oddil) K
Sbornik Vysoke Skoly Chemicko-Technologicke v Praze. Oddil Mineralogie — Sb Vys Sk Chem Technol Praze Oddil Mineral
Sbornik Vysoke Skoly Chemicko-Technologicke v Praze. Organicka Chemie a Technologie — Sb Vys Sk Chem Technol Praze Org Chem Technol
Sbornik Vysoke Skoly Chemicko-Technologicke v Praze. Organicka Technologie — Sb Vys Sk Chem Technol Praze Org Technol
Sbornik Vysoke Skoly Chemicko-Technologicke v Praze. Polymery-Chemie, Vlastnosti a Zpracovani — Sb Vys Sk Chem Technol Praze Polym Chem Vlastnosti Zprac
Sbornik Vysoke Skoly Chemicko-Technologicke v Praze, Potravinarska Technologie — Sb Vys Sk Chem Technol Praze Potravin Technol
Sbornik Vysoke Skoly Chemicko-Technologicke v Praze. Potraviny — Sb Vys Sk Chem Technol Praze Potraviny
Sbornik Vysoke Skoly Chemicko-Technologicke v Praze. Potraviny — Sb Vys Sk Chem-Technol Pr Potraviny
Sbornik Vysoke Skoly Chemicko-Technologicke v Praze. Rada B. Anorganicka Chemie a Technologie — Sb Vys Sk Chem-Technol Praze Rada B
Sbornik Vysoke Skoly Chemicko-Technologicke v Praze. Rada E. Potraviny — Sb Vys Sk Chem Technol Praze E Potraviny
Sbornik Vysoke Skoly Chemicko-Technologicke v Praze. Rada F. Technologie Vody a Prostredi — Sb Vys Sk Chem Technol Praze F Technol Vody Prostredi
Sbornik Vysoke Skoly Chemicko-Technologicke v Praze. Rada H — Sb Vys Sk Chem Technol Praze Rada H
Sbornik Vysoke Skoly Chemicko-Technologicke v Praze. S. Polymery-Chemie, Vlastnosti a Zpracovani — Sb Vys Sk Chem Technol Praze S Polym Chem Vlastnosti Zprac
Sbornik Vysoke Skoly Chemicko-Technologicke v Praze. Technologie Paliv [*Czechoslovakia*] — Sb Vys Sk Chem Technol Praze Technol Paliv
Sbornik Vysoke Skoly Chemicko-Technologicke v Praze. Technologie Vody — Sb Vys Sk Chem-Technol Praze Technol Vody
Sbornik Vysoke Skoly Chemicko-Technologicke v Praze. Technologie Vody a Prostredi — Sb Vys Sk Chem Technol Praze Technol Vody Prostredi
Sbornik Vysoke Skoly Pedagogicke v Olomouci — SVSPO
Sbornik Vysoke Skoly Pedagogicke v Olomouci. Jazyka a Literatura — SVSPO(JL)
Sbornik Vysoke Skoly Pedagogicke v Olomouci. Prirodni Vedy — Sborn Vysoke Skoly Pedagog V Olomouci Prir Vedy
Sbornik Vysoke Skoly Pedagogicke v Praze. Jazyka a Literatura — SVSPP
Sbornik Vysoke Skoly Zemedelske a Lesnicke Fakulty v Brne. Rada B. Spisy Fakulty Veterinarni — Sb Vys Sk Zemed Lesn Fak Brne B Spisy Fak Vet
Sbornik Vysoke Skoly Zemedelske a Lesnicke Fakulty v Brne. Rada B. Spisy Fakulty Veterinarni — Sb Vys Zemed Lesn Fak Brne B Spisy Fak Vet
Sbornik Vysoke Skoly Zemedelske a Lesnicke Fakulty v Brne. Rada C. Spisy Fakulty Lesnicke — Sb Vys Sk Zemed Lesn Fak Brne Rada C Spisy
Sbornik Vysoke Skoly Zemedelske a Lesnicke Fakulty v Brne. Rada C. Spisy Fakulty Lesnicke — Sb Vys Sk Zemed Lesn Fak Brne Rada C Spisy Fak Lesn
Sbornik Vysoke Skoly Zemedelske a Lesnicke v Brne. Rada C. Spisy Fakulty Lesnicke — Sb Vys Sk Zemed Lesn Brne Rada C
Sbornik Vysoke Skoly Zemedelske v Brne — Sb Vys Sk Zemed Brne
Sbornik Vysoke Skoly Zemedelske v Brne. Rada A — Sb Vys Sk Zemed v Brne A
Sbornik Vysoke Skoly Zemedelske v Brne. Rada A — Sb Vys Skoly Zemed Brne Rada A
Sbornik Vysoke Skoly Zemedelske v Brne. Rada A. Spisy Fakulty Agronomicke — Sb Vys Sk Zemed Brne Rada A
Sbornik Vysoke Skoly Zemedelske v Brne. Rada B — Sb Vys Skoly Zemed Brne Rada B
Sbornik Vysoke Skoly Zemedelske v Brne. Rada B — SSZBA
Sbornik Vysoke Skoly Zemedelske v Brne. Rada C. Spisy Fakulty Lesnicke — Sb Vys Sk Zemed Brne Rada C
Sbornik Vysoke Skoly Zemedelske v Brne. Rada C. Spisy Fakulty Lesnicke — Sb Vys Sk Zemed Brne Rada C Spisy Fak Lesn
Sbornik Vysoke Skoly Zemedelske v Praze — Sb Vys Sk Zemed Praze
Sbornik Vysoke Skoly Zemedelske v Praze — Sb Vys Skoly Zemed Praze
Sbornik Vysoke Skoly Zemedelske v Praze. Acta Universitatis Agriculturae Praha — Sborn Vysoke Skoly Zemed V Praze

Sbornik Vysoke Skoly Zemedelske v Praze. Fakulta Agronomicka — Sb Vys Sk Zemed Praze Fak Agron
Sbornik Vysoke Skoly Zemedelske v Praze. Fakulta Agronomicka. Rada A. Rostlinna Vyroba — Sb Vys Sk Zemed Praze Fak Agron Rada A
Sbornik Vysoke Skoly Zemedelske v Praze. Fakulta Agronomicka. Rada A-C. Rostlinna Vyroba-Zemedelske Meliorace a Stavby — Sb Vys Sk Zemed Praze Fak Agron Rada AC
Sbornik Vysoke Skoly Zemedelske v Praze. Fakulta Agronomicka. Rada B. Zivocisna Vyroba — Sb Vys Sk Zemed Praze Fak Agron Rada B
Sbornik Vysoke Skoly Zemedelske v Praze. Provozne Ekonomicke Fakulty v Ceskych Budejovicich. Rada Biologicka — Sb Vys Sk Zemed Praze Provozne Ekon Fak Ceskych Budejovicich
Sbornik Vysokeho Uceni Technickeho v Brne — Sb Vys Uceni Tech Brne
Sbornik Vysokeho Uceni Technickeho v Brne — Sb Vysoke Uceni Tech v Brne
Sbornik Vysokej Skoly Polnohospodarskej v Nitre Prevadzkovo-Ekonomicka Fakulta — Sb Vys Skoly Polnohospod Nitre Prevadzkovo-Ekon Fak
Sbornik Vyssej Pedagogicke Skoly v Plzni — Sborn Vyssej Pedagog Skoly V Plzni
Sbornik za Narodni Umotvorenija — SzNU
Sbornik za Narodni Umotvorenija i Narodopis — SbNU
SBPC Ciencia e Cultura — SBPC Cienc Cult
SBPR Boletin — SBPR Bol
SBZ Sanitaer-, Heizungs-, und Klimatechnik [*Germany*] — SBZ Sanit Heiz Klimatech
Scaenicorum Romanorum Fragmenta — SRF
Scandia — Sca
Scandinavian Actuarial Journal — Scand Actuar J
Scandinavian Audiology — Scand Audiol
Scandinavian Audiology. Supplement — Scand Audiol Suppl
Scandinavian Corrosion Congress. Proceedings — Scand Corros Congr Proc
Scandinavian Economic History Review — Scand Ec Hist Rev
Scandinavian Economic History Review — Scand Econ Hist Rev
Scandinavian Economic History Review — Scandinavian Econ Hist R
Scandinavian Economic History Review — SEHR
Scandinavian Economies. A Business Economic Report on Denmark, Finland, Norway, and Sweden — BDG
Scandinavian Energy — Scand Energy
Scandinavian Joint Expedition to Sudanese Nubia Publications — SJESNP
Scandinavian Journal of Behaviour Therapy — NTBEDQ
Scandinavian Journal of Behaviour Therapy — Scand J Behav Ther
Scandinavian Journal of Clinical and Laboratory Investigation — Sc J Cl Inv
Scandinavian Journal of Clinical and Laboratory Investigation — Scand J Clin Lab Inv
Scandinavian Journal of Clinical and Laboratory Investigation — Scand J Clin Lab Invest
Scandinavian Journal of Clinical and Laboratory Investigation — Scandinav J Clin Lab Invest
Scandinavian Journal of Clinical and Laboratory Investigation — SJCLA
Scandinavian Journal of Clinical and Laboratory Investigation. Supplement — Scand J Clin Lab Invest Suppl
Scandinavian Journal of Clinical and Laboratory Investigation. Supplement — SCLSA
Scandinavian Journal of Dental Research — Sc J Dent R
Scandinavian Journal of Dental Research — Scand J Dent Res
Scandinavian Journal of Economics — ETS
Scandinavian Journal of Economics — Scand J Econ
Scandinavian Journal of Economics — Scandinav J Econ
Scandinavian Journal of Educational Research — SJER
Scandinavian Journal of Forest Research — Scand J For Res
Scandinavian Journal of Forest Research — SJFRE3
Scandinavian Journal of Gastroenterology — Sc J Gastr
Scandinavian Journal of Gastroenterology — Scand J Gastroenterol
Scandinavian Journal of Gastroenterology — Scandinav J Gastroent
Scandinavian Journal of Gastroenterology — SJGRA
Scandinavian Journal of Gastroenterology. Supplement — Scand J Gastroenterol Suppl
Scandinavian Journal of Haematology — Sc J Haemat
Scandinavian Journal of Haematology — Scand J Haematol
Scandinavian Journal of Haematology — Scandinav J Haemat
Scandinavian Journal of Haematology — SJHAA
Scandinavian Journal of Haematology. Supplement — Scand J Haematol Suppl
Scandinavian Journal of Haematology. Supplement. Series Haematological — Scand J Haematol Suppl Ser Haematol
Scandinavian Journal of History — Sc J Hist
Scandinavian Journal of Immunology — Sc J Immun
Scandinavian Journal of Immunology — Scand J Immunol
Scandinavian Journal of Immunology. Supplement — Scand J Immunol Suppl
Scandinavian Journal of Infectious Diseases — Sc J In Dis
Scandinavian Journal of Infectious Diseases — Scand J Infect Dis
Scandinavian Journal of Infectious Diseases. Supplement — Scand J Infect Dis Suppl
Scandinavian Journal of Medicine & Science in Sports — SCAN J Med & Sci Sport
Scandinavian Journal of Medicine and Science in Sports — Scand J Med Sci Sports
Scandinavian Journal of Metallurgy — Scand J Metall
Scandinavian Journal of Plastic and Reconstructive Surgery — Sc J Plast
Scandinavian Journal of Plastic and Reconstructive Surgery — Scand J Plast Recon Surg
Scandinavian Journal of Plastic and Reconstructive Surgery — Scand J Plast Reconstr Surg
Scandinavian Journal of Plastic and Reconstructive Surgery — SJPRB
Scandinavian Journal of Plastic and Reconstructive Surgery and Hand Surgery — Scand J Plast Reconstr Surg Hand Surg
Scandinavian Journal of Plastic and Reconstructive Surgery and Hand Surgery. Supplementum — Scand J Plast Reconstr Surg Hand Surg Suppl
Scandinavian Journal of Plastic and Reconstructive Surgery. Supplement — Scand J Plast Reconstr Surg Suppl
Scandinavian Journal of Primary Health Care — Scand J Prim Health Care
Scandinavian Journal of Primary Health Care. Supplement — Scand J Prim Health Care Suppl
Scandinavian Journal of Psychology — Sc J Psycho
Scandinavian Journal of Psychology — Scand J Psychol
Scandinavian Journal of Psychology — SJPYA
Scandinavian Journal of Rehabilitation Medicine — Sc J Re Med
Scandinavian Journal of Rehabilitation Medicine — Scand J Rehab Med
Scandinavian Journal of Rehabilitation Medicine — Scand J Rehabil Med
Scandinavian Journal of Rehabilitation Medicine. Supplement — Scand J Rehabil Med Suppl
Scandinavian Journal of Respiratory Diseases — Sc J Resp D
Scandinavian Journal of Respiratory Diseases — Scand J Respir Dis
Scandinavian Journal of Respiratory Diseases — Scandinav J Resp Dis
Scandinavian Journal of Respiratory Diseases — SJRDA
Scandinavian Journal of Respiratory Diseases. Supplement — Scand J Respir Dis Suppl
Scandinavian Journal of Rheumatology — Sc J Rheum
Scandinavian Journal of Rheumatology — Scand J Rheumatol
Scandinavian Journal of Rheumatology. Supplement — Scand J Rheumatol Suppl
Scandinavian Journal of Social Medicine — Sc J S Med
Scandinavian Journal of Social Medicine — Scand J Soc Med
Scandinavian Journal of Social Medicine. Supplement — Scand J Soc Med Suppl
Scandinavian Journal of Sports Sciences — Scan J Sports Sci
Scandinavian Journal of Statistics — Scand J St
Scandinavian Journal of Statistics. Theory and Applications — Scan J Stat
Scandinavian Journal of Statistics. Theory and Applications — Scand J Stat Theory and Appl
Scandinavian Journal of Statistics. Theory and Applications — Scand J Statist
Scandinavian Journal of Thoracic and Cardiovascular Surgery — Sc J Thor C
Scandinavian Journal of Thoracic and Cardiovascular Surgery — Scand J Thorac Cardiovasc Surg
Scandinavian Journal of Thoracic and Cardiovascular Surgery — SJTCA
Scandinavian Journal of Thoracic and Cardiovascular Surgery. Supplement — Scand J Thorac Cardiovasc Surg Suppl
Scandinavian Journal of Urology and Nephrology — Sc J Urol N
Scandinavian Journal of Urology and Nephrology — Scand J Urol Nephrol
Scandinavian Journal of Urology and Nephrology — SJUNA
Scandinavian Journal of Urology and Nephrology. Supplement — Scand J Urol Nephrol Suppl
Scandinavian Journal of Work Environment and Health — Scand J Work Envir Hlth
Scandinavian Journal of Work Environment and Health — Scand J Work Environ Health
Scandinavian Journal of Work Environment and Health — SWEHO
Scandinavian Laundry and Dry Cleaning Journal — Scand Laundry Dry Clean J
Scandinavian Oil-Gas Magazine — Scand Oil-Gas Mag
Scandinavian Paint and Printing Ink Research Institute. Reports — Scand Paint Printing Ink Res Inst Rept
Scandinavian Periodicals Index in Economics and Business [*Database*] — SCANP
Scandinavian Political Studies — Scand Pol Stud
Scandinavian Political Studies — Scand Polit St
Scandinavian Political Studies — Scand Polit Stud
Scandinavian Public Library Quarterly — Scand Publ Libr Q
Scandinavian Public Library Quarterly — Scand Public Lib Q
Scandinavian Public Library Quarterly — Scandinavian Publ Libr Q
Scandinavian Refrigeration [*Norway*] — Scand Refrig
Scandinavian Review — GSCR
Scandinavian Review — Scan R
Scandinavian Review — Scand R
Scandinavian Review — Scandinavian R
Scandinavian Review — SCAR
Scandinavian Review — SCRE
Scandinavian Society of Forensic Odontology. Newsletter — Scan Soc Forensic Odontol Newsl
Scandinavian Studies — PSCT
Scandinavian Studies — Sc Stud
Scandinavian Studies — Scan
Scandinavian Studies — Scand Stud
Scandinavian Studies — ScSt
Scandinavian Studies — SS
Scandinavian Studies and Notes — Sc St N
Scandinavian Studies and Notes — Scand Stud No
Scandinavian Studies and Notes — ScS
Scandinavian Studies and Notes — SSN
Scandinavian Studies in Law — Sc Stud L
Scandinavian Studies in Law — Sc Stud Law
Scandinavian Studies in Law — Scand Stud in L
Scandinavian Studies in Law — Scand Stud Law
Scandinavian Symposium on Surface Chemistry — Scand Symp Surf Chem
Scandinavian University Books — ScUB
Scandinavian University Books — SUB
Scandinavian Yearbook — Scand Yb
Scandinavica — Sca
Scandinavica — Scan
Scandinavica — Scand
Scandoslavica — ScSl
Scandoslavica [*Copenhagen*] — SSL

Scanning Electron Microscopy — Scan Electron Microsc
Scanning Electron Microscopy — Scanning Electron Microsc
Scanning Microscopy — Scanning Microsc
Scanning Microscopy. Supplement — Scanning Microsc Suppl
Scanshore — CSL
Scarborough District Archaeological Society. Research Reports — Scarborough Dist Archaeol Soc Res Rep
SCB [*Statistiska Centralbyran*] **Regional Statistical Data Base** — RSDB
SCB [*Statistiska Centralbyran*] **Time Series Data Base** — TSDB
SCCWRP (Southern California Coastal Water Research Project). TR — SCCWRP TR
SCEDSIP [*Standing Conference on Educational Development Services in Polytechnics*] **Bulletin** — SCEDSIP Bull
Scelta di Opuscoli Interessanti Tradotti da Varie Lingue (Turin) — Scelta Opusc Interessanti Turin
Scenario — Scen
Scenic Trips to the Geologic Past — Scenic Trips Geol Past
Schachtgraeber von Mykenae — SGM
Schaffhauser Beitraege zur Vaterlaendischen Geschichte — SBVG
Schakels Nederlands Nieuw Guinea — SNNG
Schattauer Praxis Buecherei — Schattauer Prax Buech
Schatzkammer der Deutschen Sprachlehre. Dichtung und Geschichte — Schatzkammer
Schaulade. Unabhaengiges Internationales Fachblatt fuer Porzellan, Keramik, Glas, Geschenkartikel, und Hausrat — SLB
Schedule of Discounts, Differentials, and Service Charges Applying to Wheat — Sched Discounts Differentials Serv Charges Applying Wheat
Scheppend Ambacht. Tweemaandelijks Tijdschrift voor Toegepaste Kunst — AMD
Scherl and Roth Orchestra News — SCH
Schiff und Hafen — SCHHA
Schiffbauforschung — SCFOA
Schiffstechnik. Forschungshefte fuer Schiffbau und Schiffsmaschinenbau — Schiffstechnik
Schild von Steier. Beitraege zur Steierischen Vor- und Fruehgeschichte und Muenzkunde — Schild Steier
Schild von Steier. Beitraege zur Steirischen Vor- und Fruehgeschichte und Muenzkunde — Sch St
Schild von Steier. Beitraege zur Steirischen Vor- und Fruehgeschichte und Muenzkunde — SvS
Schildersblad. Algemeen Vakblad voor het Schildersbedrijf en Afwerkingsbedrijf — SBL
Schimmelpfeng Review — Schimmelpfeng R
Schip en Schade — S en S
Schip en Schade — SS
Schip en Werf — SCWFA
Schip en Werf. Tijdschrift Gewijd aan Scheepsbouw en Werktuigbouw, Elektrotechniek, Scheepvaart, en Aanverwante Vakken — SNW
Schippersweekblad — PHS
Schirmer News — SN
Schizophrenia Bulletin — Schizophr Bull
Schizophrenia Research — Schizophr Res
Schizophrenic Syndrome — Schizophr Syndr
Schizophrenic Syndrome: An Annual Review — Schizophr Syndr Annu Rev
Schlachtofwesen Lebensmittelueberwachung — Schlachtofwes Lebensmittelueberwach
Schleif-, Polier-, und Oberflaechentechnik — Schleif Polier Oberflaechentech
Schleif- und Poliertechnik (Hoya-Weser, Germany) — Schleif Poliertech (Hoya Weser Ger)
Schlern-Schriften — Schl Schr
Schlernschriften — Schlernschr
Schlesiens Vorzeit in Bild und Schrift — Schles Vorzeit
Schlesische Geschichtsblaetter (Breslau) — SGB
Schlesische Gesellschaft fuer Vaterlaendische Kultur. Jahres-Bericht — Schles Ges Jber
Schlesische Landwirthschaftliche Zeitschrift — Schles Landw Z
Schlesische Provinzialblaetter — Schles Provinzialbl
Schlesisches Jahrbuch fuer Deutsche Kulturarbeit im Gesamtschlesischen Raum — Schles Jb Dt Kulturarb
Schlesisches Priesterjahrbuch — SPJ
Schleswig-Holsteinische Anzeigen — Schlesw Holst Anzgn
Schleswig-Holsteinisches Aerzteblatt — Schleswig Holsteinisches Aerztebl
Schleswig-Holsteinisches Bienenzeitung — Schlesw-Holst Bienenztg
Schleswig-Holsteinisches Jahrbuch — SchHJ
Schleswig-Holsteinisches Magazin der Sammlung Vermischter Schriften zur Aufnahmeder Wissenschaften und Kuenste — Schleswig Holst Mag
Schleswig-Holstein-Lauenburgische Provinzialberichte — Schleswig Holst Lauenburg Provinzialber
Schlief- und Poliertechnik [*Germany*] — Schlief-Poliertech
(Schloemilchs) Zeitschrift feur Mathematik und Physik — Schloemilchs Zschr
Schmalenbachs Zeitschrift [feur Betriebwirtschaftliche] Forschung — Schmal Z Betriebswirtsch Forsch
Schmalenbachs Zeitschrift fuer Betriebswirtschaftliche Forschung — ZHF
Schmerz. Narkose-Anaesthesie — Schmerz Narkose Anaesth
Schmidts Jahrbuecher der In- und Auslaendischen Gesamten Medizin — Jbb In u Ausld Ges Med
Schmiedebergs Archiv — Schmiedebg Arch
Schmierstoffe und Schmierungstechnik — Schmierst Schmierungstech
Schmierstoffe und Schmierungstechnik [*Germany*] — Schmierstoffe Schmierungstech
Schmiertechnik und Tribologie — Schmiertech Tribol
Schmiertechnik und Tribologie — SCTTB
Schmollers Jahrbuch fuer Gesetzgebung, Verwaltung und Volkswirtschaft im Deutschen Reiche — Schmollers Jahrb
Schmollers Jahrbuch fuer Gesetzgebung, Verwaltung, und Volkswissenschaft im Deutschen Reich — JG
Schneeberger Heimatbuechlein — Schneeberger Hb
Schnell Informationen Hydraulik und Pneumatik — Schnell Inf Hydraul & Pneum
Schnurpfeil's Review for Glass Works — Schnurpfeils Rev Glass Works
Schoenburgische Geschichtsblaetter — Schoenburg Gesch Bl
Schoeninghs Sammlung Kirchengeschichtlicher Quellen und Darstellungen — SSKGQ
Schoenvisie. Maandblad voor de Schoenhandel en Schoenindustrie — PRA
Schoenwereld. Vakblad voor de Schoenlederbranche — SCW
Scholarly Inquiry for Nursing Practice — Sch Inq Nurs Pract
Scholarly Publishing — Scholar Pub
Scholarly Publishing — Scholarly Pub
Scholarly Publishing — SchP
Scholarly Publishing — SP
Scholars' Facsimiles and Reprints — SF & R
Scholastic Coach — ISCC
Scholastic Coach — Sch Coach
Scholastic Coach — Schol Coach
Scholastic Coach and Athletic Director — Coach & Ath Dir
Scholastic Debater — Scholastic D
Scholastic Science World — Sci World
Scholastic Teacher — Schol Teach
Scholastic Teacher. Junior/Senior High Teacher's Edition — Schol Teach JH/SH Ed
Scholastic Update. Teacher's Edition — GSUP
Scholastik — Sch
Scholastik. Vierteljahresschrift fuer Theologie und Philosophie — Schol
Scholia Satyrica — Schol S
Scholia Satyrica — ScSat
School [*Toronto*] — Sch
School Activities — Sch Activities
School and College — School & Col
School and Community — Sch & Com
School and Community News — Sch Community News
School and Home — Sch and Home
School and Home Education [*Illinois*] — Sch Ed
School and Parent — Sch & Parent
School and Society — S & S
School and Society — Sch & Soc
School and Society — School and Soc
School and Society — SS
School Arts — ISCA
School Arts Magazine — Sch Arts
School Arts Magazine — Sch Arts M
School Arts Magazine — School Arts M
School Bell — Sch Bell
School Board Gazette — SBG
School Book Review — SBR
School Counselor — Sch Counsel
School Days — Sch Days
School Dental Services Gazette (Wellington, New Zealand) — Sch Dent Serv Gaz (NZ)
School Executive — Sch Exec
School Executives Magazine — Sch Executives M
School Family — School Fam
School Foodservice Journal — Sch Foodserv J
School Foodservice Research Review — Sch Foodserv Res Rev
School Guidance Worker — Sch Guidance W
School Health Review — Sch Health Rev
School Law Bulletin — Sch L Bull
School Law Bulletin (University of North Carolina) — School Law Bul (Univ NC)
School Law Reporter. National Organization on Legal Problems in Education — School L Rep Natl Org on Legal Probs in Educ
School Librarian — Sch Lib
School Librarian — Sch Libn
School Librarian and School Library Review [*Later, School Librarian*] — Sch Librn
School Libraries — Sch Lib
School Libraries — Sch Libr
School Libraries — School Lib
School Libraries in Australia — Sch Lib Aust
School Libraries in Canada — Sch Lib Can
School Libraries in Canada — SLIC
School Library Association of California. Bulletin — Sch Lib Assn Calif Bul
School Library Bulletin — Sch Libr Bull
School Library Journal — ISCL
School Library Journal — Sch Lib J
School Library Journal — SLJ
School Library Media Quarterly — SLMQ
School Library Review and Educational Record — Sch Lib R
School Library-Media News — Sch Lib Med N
School Life — Sch Life
School Management — Sch Manag
School Management — Sch Management
School Management — Sch Mgt
School Management Bulletin — Sch Manage
School Management Bulletin — Sch Management Bul
School Media Quarterly — Sch Media Q
School Media Quarterly — SMQ
School Music — Sch Mus
School Music News [*New York*] — NY
School Musician — SchMus
School Musician — School Mus
School Musician Director and Teacher — Sch Mus Dir Teach

School Musician. Director and Teacher — SCM
School Musician. Director and Teacher — SMDTB
School of Advanced International Studies Review — Sch Adv Int Stud Rev
School of Agriculture. Aberdeen. Annual Report — Sch Agric Aberdeen Ann Rep
School of Engineering. Bulletin. North Carolina State University — Sch Eng Bull NC State Univ
School of Mines and Metallurgy. University of Missouri. Bulletin — Sch Mines Metall Univ Mo Bull
School of Mines and Metallurgy. University of Missouri. Bulletin. Technical Series — Sch Mines Metall Univ Mo Bull Tech Ser
School of Mines Quarterly — Sch Mines Q
School of Oriental and African Studies. Jordan Lectures in Comparative Religion — SOAS JLCR
School of Oriental and African Studies. University of London. London. Oriental Series — SOAS ULLOS
School of Pharmacy Bulletin. Extension Services in Pharmacy. University of Wisconsin Extension Division — Sch Pharm Bull Ext Serv Pharm Univ Wis Ext Div
School of Pharmacy. Bulletin. University of Wisconsin. Extension Division — Sch Pharm Bull Univ Wis Ext Div
School of Planning and Architecture. Journal — SPA Jnl
School Organisation and Management Abstracts — School Organ Manage Abstr
School Practices Information File [*Database*] — SPIF
School Proceedings. Winter School on Biophysics of Membrane Transport — Sch Proc Wint Sch Biophys Membr Transp
School Product News — SPN
School Psychology International — SPI
School Psychology Review — Sch Psychol R
School Psychology Review — School Psych Rev
School Review — Sch R
School Review — Sch Rev
School Review — SCLRA
School Review — SRev
School Review. A Journal of Secondary Education — School Rev
School Science — Sch Sci
School Science and Mathematics — ISSM
School Science and Mathematics — Sch Sci & Math
School Science and Mathematics — SSM
School Science Review [*England*] — Sch Sci Rev
School Science Review — SSCRA
School Shop — Sch Shop
School Technology — Sch Technol
School (Toronto) (Elementary Edition) — Sch (El Ed)
School (Toronto) (Secondary Edition) — Sch (Sec Ed)
School Trustee — Sch Trust
Schoolbestuur — SBD
Schoolmen's Week. University of Pennsylvania. Proceedings — Schoolmens W Univ PA Proc
Schopenhauer-Jahrbuch — Schopenhauer-Jahr
Schopenhauer-Jahrbuch — Schopenhauer-Jahrb
Schott Information — Schott Inf
Schouw Vakblad voor Verwarming, Sanitair, en Keukenapparatuur — MBK
Schowalter Memorial Lecture Series — SMLS
Schriften. Akademie der Wissenschaften zu Berlin — Schr Berl
Schriften aus dem Gebiet der Brennstoff-Geologie — Schr Geb Brennst Geol
Schriften der Albertus-Universitaet — SAU
Schriften der Albertus-Universitaet. Geisteswissenschaftliche Reihe — SAUG
Schriften der Baltischen Kommission zu Kiel — SBKK
Schriften der Berlinischen Gesellschaft Naturforschender Freunde — Schriften Berlin Ges Naturf Freunde
Schriften der Bremer Wissenschaftlichen Gesellschaft. Reihe B — Schr Bremer Wiss Ges Reihe B
Schriften der Duisburgischen Gelehrten Gesellschaft — Schriften Duisburg Gel Ges
Schriften der Evangelischen Studiengemeinschaft der Evangelischen Akademien — SESEA
Schriften der Finnischen Theologischen Literaturgesellschaft — SFThL
Schriften der Freien Vereinigung von Freunden der Mikroskopie — Schriften Freien Vereinigung Freunden Mikroskop
Schriften der GDMB (Gesellschaft Deutscher Metallhuetten- und Bergleute) — Schr GDMB (Ges Dtsch Metallhuetten Bergleute)
Schriften der Gesellschaft Deutscher Metallhuetten- und Bergleute — Schr Ges Dtsch Metallhuetten Bergleute
Schriften der Gesellschaft fuer Soziale Reform — Schr Ges Soz Ref
Schriften der Gesellschaft zur Foerderung der Wissenschaft des Judentums — SGFWJ
Schriften der Koenigsberger Gelehrten Gesellschaft Geisteswissenschaftliche Klasse — SGK
Schriften der Koenigsberger Gelehrten Gesellschaft. Geisteswissenschaftliche Klasse — SKGG
Schriften der Koenigsberger Gelehrten Gesellschaft. Naturwissenschaftliche Klasse — Schr Koenigsb Gelehrten Ges Naturwiss Kl
Schriften der Koenigsberger Gelehrten Gesellschaft. Naturwissenschaftliche Klasse — Schriften Koenigsberger Gel Ges Naturwiss Kl
Schriften der Koenigsberger Gelehrten Gesellschaft. Sonderreihe — SKGS
Schriften der Kurfuerstlichen Deutschen Gesellschaft in Mannheim — Schriften Kurfuerstl Deutsch Ges Mannheim
Schriften der Luther-Agricola-Gesellschaft in Finnland — SLAG
Schriften der Monumenta Germaniae Historica — SMGH
Schriften der Naturforschenden Gesellschaft zu Kopenhagen — Schriften Naturf Ges Kopenhagen
Schriften der Physikalisch-Oekonomischen Gesellschaft zu Koenigsberg — Ph Oe Schr
Schriften der Physikalisch-Oekonomischen Gesellschaft zu Koenigsberg — Schr Phys Oekon Ges Koenigsbg
Schriften der Saechsischen Kommission fuer Geschichte — SSKG
Schriften der Schweizerischen Gesellschaft fuer Volkskunde — SSGVK
Schriften der Sektion fuer Altertumswissenschaft — SAA
Schriften der Studiengemeinschaft der Evangelischen Akademien — SSEA
Schriften der Synodalkommission fuer Ostpreussische Kirchengeschichte — SSOPK
Schriften der Thueringischen Landesarbeitsgemeinschaft fuer Heilpflanzenkunde und Heilpflanzenbeschaffung Weimar — Schriften Thuering Landesarbeitsgem Heilpflanzenk Weimar
Schriften der Wiener Katholischen Akademie — SWKA
Schriften des Adam-Ries-Bundes Annaberg-Buchholz — Schrift Adam Ries Bundes Annaberg Buchholz
Schriften des Deutschen Palaestina-Instituts — SDPI
Schriften des Deutschen Schiffahrtsmuseums — Schr Deut Schiffahrtsmus
Schriften des Freien Deutschen Hochstifts — SFDH
Schriften des Hessischen Amts fuer Geschichtliche Landeskunde — SHAGL
Schriften des Instituts fuer Christliche Sozialwissenschaften — SICSW
Schriften des Instituts fuer Geschichtliche Landeskunde von Hessen-Nassau — SIGLH
Schriften des Instituts fuer Kultur- und Sozialforschung — SIKS
Schriften des Instituts Judaicum in Berlin — SIJB
Schriften des Institutum Delitzschianum zu Leipzig — SIDL
Schriften des Institutum Judaicum in Delitzschianum — SIJD
Schriften des Institutum Judaicum in Leipzig — SIJL
Schriften des Leningrader Wissenschaftlichen Forschungs-Instituts der Lebensmittelindustrie — Schr Leningr Wiss Forsch Inst Lebensmittelind
Schriften des Naturwissenschaftlichen Vereins fuer Schleswig-Holstein — Schriften Naturwiss Vereins Schleswig Holstein
Schriften des Neuen Testaments — SNT
Schriften des Oekumenischen Archivs — SOeA
Schriften des Oesterreichischen Kultur-Instituts Kairo — SOeKIK
Schriften des Reichsinstituts fuer Aeltere Deutsche Geschichtskunde — SRAeDG
Schriften des Theologischen Konvents Augsburgischen Bekenntnisses — S Th KAB
Schriften des Urchristentums — SU
Schriften des Vereins fuer die Geschichte Leipzigs — Schr Ver Gesch Leipz
Schriften des Vereins fuer die Geschichte Leipzigs — VGL
Schriften des Vereins fuer Geschichte des Bodensees und Seiner Umgebung — Schr d Bodensee V
Schriften des Vereins fuer Geschichte und Naturgeschichte der Baar und der Angrenzenden Landestheile in Donaueschingen — Schriften Vereins Gesch Baar Donaueschingen
Schriften des Vereins fuer Sozialpolitik — Schr Ver Sozialpolit
Schriften des Vereins fuer Sozialpolitik — SchrVfS
Schriften des Wissenschaftlichen Forschungs-Instituts fuer Nahrungsmittelindustrie der UdSSR — Schr Wiss Forsch Inst Nahrungsmittelind UdSSR
Schriften des Wuertembergischen Naturhistorischen Reisevereins. Enthaltend Reisebeschreibungen und Mittheilungen aus der Natur- und Voelkerkunde — Schriften Wuerttemberg Naturhist Reisevereins
Schriften des Zentralen Biochemischen Forschungs-Instituts der Nahrungs- und Genssmittelindustrie — Schr Zent Biochem Forsch Inst Nahr Genussmittelind
Schriften. Droste-Gesellschaft — SDG
Schriften far Ekonomik un Statistik — SES
Schriften. Gesellschaft fuer Theatergeschichte — SGT
Schriften. Herausgegeben von der Naturforscher-Gesellschaft bei der Universitaet Dorpat — Schriften Naturf Ges Univ Dorpat
Schriften. Koenigsberger Gelehrten-Gesellschaft — SKG
Schriften. Koenigsberger Gelehrten-Gesellschaft — SKGG
Schriften. Naturforschende Gesellschaft zu Kopenhagen — Schrift Naturf Gesellsch Kopenhagen
Schriften. Naturwissenschaftlicher Verein fuer Schleswig-Holstein — Schr Naturwiss Ver Schleswig-Holstein
Schriften. Raabe-Gesellschaft — SRG
Schriften. Strassburger Wissenschaftliche Gesellschaft in Heidelberg — SWGH
Schriften. Theodor-Storm-Gesellschaft — SSG
Schriften und Quellen der Alten Welt — SQAW
Schriften und Vortraege im Rahmen der Theologischen Fakultaet der Universitaet Graz — STFG
Schriften. Verein fuer Schleswig-Holsteinische Kirchengeschichte — SVSHKG
Schriften. Verein zur Verbreitung Naturwissenschaftlicher Kenntnisse in Wien — Schr Ver Verbr Naturwiss Kennt Wien
Schriften zur Angewandten Oekonometrie — Schrift Angew Oekonom
Schriften zur Caritaswissenschaft — SCW
Schriften zur Deutschen Literatur — SDL
Schriften zur Katechetik — SK
Schriften zur Katechetischen Unterweisung — SKU
Schriften zur Kirchen- und Rechtsgeschichte — SKRG
Schriften zur Literatur — SzL
Schriften zur Paedagogik und Katechetik — SPK
Schriften zur Rechtslehre und Politik — SRLP
Schriften zur Religionspaedagogik und Kerygmatik — SRPK
Schriften zur Religionspaedagogik und Seelsorge — SRPS
Schriften zur Religionspaedagogik und Seelsorge. Klassiker der Seelsorge und Seelenfuehrung — SRPSK
Schriften zur Theaterwissenschaft — SzT
Schriften zur Wirtschaftwissenschaftlichen Forschung — Schriften Wirtschaftwiss Forsch
Schriftenreihe. A. Stifer-Institut des Landes Oberoesterreich — SASILO
Schriftenreihe. Agrarwissenschaftliche Fakultaet. Universitaet Kiel — Schriftenr Agrarwiss Fak Univ Kiel
Schriftenreihe Arbeitsschutz — Schriftenr Arbeitsschutz

Schriftenreihe aus dem Fachgebiet Getreidetechnologie — Schriftenr Fachgeb Getreidetechnol
Schriftenreihe aus dem Gebiete des Oeffentlichen Gesundheitswesens — Schriftenr Geb Off Gesundheitswes
Schriftenreihe. Bayerisches Landesamt fuer Wasserwirtschaft — Schriftenr Bayer Landesamt Wasserwirt
Schriftenreihe. Bundesminister fuer Wissenschaftliche Forschung. Forschung und Bildung [*Germany*] — Schriftenr Bundesminist Wiss Forsch Forsch Bild
Schriftenreihe. Bundesminister fuer Wissenschaftlioho Forschung (Germany). Radionuklide — SBFRA
Schriftenreihe. Bundesminister fuer Wissenschaftliche Forschung (Germany). Strahlenschutz — SBWFA
Schriftenreihe. Bundesminister fuer Wissenschaftliche Forschung. Kernenergierecht [*Germany*] — Schriftenr Bundesminist Wiss Forsch Kernenergierecht
Schriftenreihe. Bundesminister fuer Wissenschaftliche Forschung. Strahlenschutz — Schriftenr Bundesminist Wiss Forsch Strahlenschutz
Schriftenreihe. Bundesminister fuer Wissenschaftliche Forschung (West Germany). Radionuklide — Schriftenr Bundesminist Wiss Forsch (Ger) Radionuklide
Schriftenreihe. Bundesminister fuer Wissenschaftliche Forschung (West Germany). Strahlenschutz — Schriftenr Bundesminist Wiss Forsch (Ger) Strahlenschutz
Schriftenreihe. Bundesverband der Deutschen Kalkindustrie — Schriftenr Bundesverb Dtsch Kalkind
Schriftenreihe der Aerztlichen Fortbildung — Schriftenr Aerztl Fortbild
Schriftenreihe der Bayerischen Landesapothekerkammer — Schriftenr Bayer Landesapothekerkammer
Schriftenreihe der Bundesanstalt fuer Arbeitsschutz. Gefaehrliche Arbeitsstoffe — Schriftenr Bundesanst Arbeitsschutz Gefaehrliche Arbeitsst
Schriftenreihe der Bundesapothekerkammer zur Wissenschaftlichen Fortbildung. Gelbe Reihe — Schriftenr Bundesapothekerkammer Wiss Fortbild Gelbe Reihe
Schriftenreihe der Bundesapothekerkammer zur Wissenschaftlichen Fortbildung. Weisse Reihe — Schriftenr Bundesapothekerkammer Wiss Fortbild Weisse Reihe
Schriftenreihe der Deutschen Gesellschaft fuer Atomenergie — Schriftenr Dtsch Ges Atomenerg
Schriftenreihe der Deutschen Gesellschaft fuer Technische Zusammenarbeit — Schriftenr Dtsch Ges Tech Zusammenarb
Schriftenreihe der Deutschen Phytomedizinischen Gesellschaft — Schriftenr Dtsch Phytomed Ges
Schriftenreihe der Deutschen Wollforschungsinstitutes. Technische Hochschule Aachen — Schriftenr Dtsch Wollforschungsinst Tech Hochsch Aachen
Schriftenreihe der Erdwissenschaftlichen Kommissionen. Oesterreichische Akademie der Wissenschaften — Schriftenr Erdwiss Komm Oesterr Akad Wiss
Schriftenreihe der Evangelischen Akademie — SEA
Schriftenreihe der Evangelischen Akademie Hamburg — SEAH
Schriftenreihe der Forstlichen Bundesversuchsanstalt Mariabrunn in Wien — Schriftenreihe Forstl Bundesversuchsanst Mariabrunn Wien
Schriftenreihe der GDMB — Schriftenr GDMB
Schriftenreihe der Historischen Komission bei der Bayerischen Akademie der Wissenschaften — SHKBA
Schriftenreihe der Katholischen Sozialakademie — SKSA
Schriftenreihe der Katholisch-Theologischen Fakultaet der Johannes-Gutenberg-Universitaet in Mainz — SKTFM
Schriftenreihe der Kirchlich-Theologischen Sozietaet in Wuerttemberg — SKTSW
Schriftenreihe der Landwirtschaftlichen Fakultaet der Universitaet Kiel — Schriftenreihe Landwirt Fak Univ Kiel
Schriftenreihe der Luther-Gesellschaft — SLG
Schriftenreihe der Medizinisch-Orthopaedischen Technik — Schriftenr Med Orthop Tech
Schriftenreihe der Neuen Zeitschrift fuer Missionswissenschaft — SNZM
Schriftenreihe der Oesterreichischen Computer Gesellschaft — Schriftenreihe der Oesterreich Comput Ges
Schriftenreihe der Paedagogischen Hochschule Heidelberg — Schriftenreihe Paedagog Hochsch Heidelberg
Schriftenreihe der Technischen Hochschule in Wien — Schriftenr Tech Nochsch Wien
Schriftenreihe der Universitaet Regensburg — Schriftenreihe Univ Regensburg
Schriftenreihe der Vegetationskunde. Bundesanstalt fuer Vegetationskunde, Naturschutz, und Landschaftspflege — Schriftenreihe Vegetationsk
Schriftenreihe der Wittgenstein-Gesellschaft — Schriftenreihe Wittgenstein Ges
Schriftenreihe der Zementindustrie — Schriftenr Zementind
Schriftenreihe des Arbeitskreises fuer Evangelische Kirchenmusik — SAKM
Schriftenreihe des Arbeitskreises fuer Kirchenmusik — SAKM
Schriftenreihe des Deutschen Atomforums — Schriftenr Dtsch Atomforums
Schriftenreihe des Deutschen Ausschusses fuer Stahlbeton — Schriftenr Dtsch Ausschuss Stahlbeton
Schriftenreihe des Instituts fuer Empirische Wirtschaftsforschung der Universitaet Zuerich — Schriftenreihe Inst Empirische Wirtschaftsforsch Univ Zuerich
Schriftenreihe des Instituts fuer Missionarische Seelsorge — SIMS
Schriftenreihe des Mathematischen Instituts der Universitaet Muenster. 3. Serie — Schriftenreihe Math Inst Univ Muenster 3 Ser
Schriftenreihe des Mathematischen Instituts der Universitaet Muenster. Serie 2 — Schriftenreihe Math Inst Univ Muenster Ser 2
Schriftenreihe des Mathematischen Instituts und des Graduiertenkollegs der Universitaet Muenster. 3. Serie — Schriftenreihe Math Inst Grad Univ Muenster 3 Ser
Schriftenreihe des Max-Planck-Instituts fuer Strahlenchemie — Schriftenreihe Max Planck Inst Strahlenchem
Schriftenreihe des Mennonitischen Geschichtsvereins — SMGV
Schriftenreihe des Rechenzentrums. Universitaet zu Koeln — Schriftenreihe Rechenzentrum Univ Koeln
Schriftenreihe des Studienausschusses der EKU fuer Fragen der Orthodoxen Kirche — SFOK
Schriftenreihe des Sudetendeutschen Priesterwerkes Koenigstein — SSDPW
Schriftenreihe des Theologischen Ausschusses der Evangelischen Kirche der Union — STAEKU
Schriftenreihe Didaktik der Mathematik — Schriftenreihe Didaktik Math
Schriftenreihe. Forschungsgemeinschaft Schweizerischer Lackfabrikanten — Schriftenr Forschungsgem Schweiz Lackfabr
Schriftenreihe. Forschungsinstitut fuer die Biologie Landwirtschaftlicher Nutziere — Schriftenr Forschungsinst Biol Landwirtsch Nutziere
Schriftenreihe. Forstliche Fakultaet. Universitaet Goettingen — Schrreihe Forstl Fak Univ Goettingen
Schriftenreihe. Forstliche Fakultaet. Universitaet Goettingen und Mitteilungen. Niedersaechsische Forstliche Versuchsanstalt — Schriftenr Forstl Fak Univ Goettingen
Schriftenreihe fuer Geologische Wissenschaften — Schrifter Geol Wiss
Schriftenreihe fuer Landschaftspflege und Naturschutz — Schriftenr Landschaftspflege Naturschutz
Schriftenreihe fuer Mathematik — Schriftenreihe Math
Schriftenreihe fuer Vegetationskunde — Schriftenr Vegetationskd
Schriftenreihe Intensivmedizin, Notfallmedizin, Anaesthesiologie — Schriftenr Intensivmed Notfallmed Anaesthesiol
Schriftenreihe. Internationale Gesellschaft fuer Nahrungs- und Vitalstoff-Forschung eV — Schriftenr Int Ges Nahr Vitalst Forsch eV
Schriftenreihe. Landesanstalt fuer Immissionsschutz [*Germany*] — Schriftenr Landesanst Immissionsschutz
Schriftenreihe. Lebensmittelchemie, Lebensmittelqualitaet — Schriftenr Lebensmittelchem Lebensmittelqual
Schriftenreihe. Mathematisches Institut. Universitaet Muenster — Schr Math Inst Univ Munster
Schriftenreihe. Mathematisches Institut. Universitaet Muenster — Schriftenreihe Math Inst Unlv Muenster
Schriftenreihe. Mathematisches Institut. Universitaet Muenster. 2 Serie — Schr Math Inst Univ Muenster 2
Schriftenreihe Neurologie — Schriftenr Neurol
Schriftenreihe Neurologie-Neurology Series — Schriftenr Neurol-Neurol Ser
Schriftenreihe. Oesterreichischer Wasserwirtschaftsverband — Schriftenr Oesterr Wasserwirtschaftsverb
Schriftenreihe. Otto-Graf-Institut. Universitaet Stuttgart — Schriftenr Otto Graf Inst Univ Stuttgart
Schriftenreihe Schweissen Schneiden. Bericht — Schriftenr Schweissen Schneiden Ber
Schriftenreihe Schweissen und Schneiden — Schriftenr Schweissen Schneiden
Schriftenreihe. Verein fuer Wasser, Boden, und Lufthygiene — Schriftenr Ver Wasser Boden Lufthyg
Schriftenreihe Versuchstierkunde — Schriftenr Versuchstierkd
Schriftenreihe WAR (Institut fur Wasserversorgung, Abwasserbeseitigung und Raumplanung der Technischen Hochschule Darmstadt) — Schriftenr WAR
Schriftenreihe. Wiener Internationale Akademie fuer Ganzheitsmedizin — Schriftenr Wien Int Akad Ganzheitsmed
Schriftenreihe. Zentralblatt fuer Arbeitsmedizin, Arbeitsschutz, und Prophylaxe — Schriftenr Zentralbl Arbeitsmed Arbeitsschtz Prophyl
Schriftenreihe. Zentralinstitut fuer Mathematik und Mechanik — Schriftenreihe Zentralinst Math Mech
Schriftenreihe zur Sektenkunde — SSK
Schriftenreihe zur Theorie und Praxis der Medizinischen Psychologie — Schriftenr Theor Prax Med Psychol
Schriftenreihe zur Zeitschrift Blut — Schriftenr Z Blut
Schriftenreihen der Bauforschung. Reihe Technik und Organisation — Schriftenr Bauforsch Reihe Tech Organ
Schrifttum der Agrarwirtschaft — Schrifttum Agrarwirt
Schrifttum der Bodenkultur — Schrifttum Bodenkult
Schuh Kurier. Das Wirtschaftmagazin der Schuhbranche — SRR
Schule — Sch
Schultexte aus Fara — SchF
Schwaebische Blaetter fuer Volksbildung und Heimatpflege — SBVH
Schwaebische Museum — Schwaeb Museum
Schwaebischer Imkerkalender — Schwaeb Imkerkal
Schwaebisches Archiv — Sch A
Schwedisches Magazin, oder Schriften aus der Naturforschung, Stadt- und Landwirthschaft — Schwed Mag Schriften Naturf
Schweich Lectures of the British Academy — Sch L
Schweich Lectures on Biblical Archaeology — Sch LBA
Schweiss- und Prueftechnik — Schweiss Prueftech
Schweiss- und Schneidbrenner — Schweiss Schneidbrenner
Schweissen und Schneiden — SCSCA
Schweisstechnik [*Berlin*] — SCTCA
Schweisstechnik Soudure — SCHWA
Schweisstechnik Soudure (Zurich) — Schweisstech Soudure (Zurich)
Schweisstechnische Konferenz. Vortraege — Schweisstech Konf Vortr
Schweisstechnische Praxis — Schweisstech Prax
Schweissung und Technische Gase — Schweissung Tech Gase
Schweizer Aero-Revue — Schweiz Aero Rev
Schweizer Aluminium Rundschau — SALRA
Schweizer Aluminium Rundschau — Schweiz Alum Rundsch
Schweizer Anglistische Arbeiten — SAA
Schweizer Archiv — Schweiz Arch
Schweizer Archiv fuer Angewandte Wissenschaft und Technik — SAAWA
Schweizer Archiv fuer Angewandte Wissenschaft und Technik — Schweiz Arch Angew Wiss Tech
Schweizer Archiv fuer Neurologie, Neurochirurgie, und Psychiatrie — SANNA

Schweizer Archiv fuer Neurologie, Neurochirurgie, und Psychiatrie — Schw A Neur
Schweizer Archiv fuer Neurologie, Neurochirurgie, und Psychiatrie — Schweiz Arch Neurol Neurochir Psychiatr
Schweizer Archiv fuer Neurologie und Psychiatrie — Schweiz Arch Neurol Psychiatr
Schweizer Archiv fuer Tierheilkunde — SATHA
Schweizer Archiv fuer Tierheilkunde — Schweiz Arch Tierh
Schweizer Archiv fuer Tierheilkunde — Schweiz Arch Tierheilkd
Schweizer Archiv fuer Tierheilkunde — Schweizer Arch Tierheilk
Schweizer Archiv fuer Volkskunde — SchAVk
Schweizer Archiv fuer Volkskunde — Schweizer Arch Volksk
Schweizer Beitraege zur Allgemeinen Geschichte — SBAG
Schweizer Beitraege zur Allgemeinen Geschichte — Schweiz Beitr Allg Gesch
Schweizer Beitraege zur Allgemeinen Geschichte. Etudes Suisses d'Histoire Generale — Schweiz Beitr Z Allg Gesch
Schweizer Beitrage zur Musikwissenschaft — Schweiz Beitr Musikwiss
Schweizer Blaetter fuer Wirtschafts- und Sozialpolitik — Schweiz Bll Wirtsch Polit
Schweizer Buch — SB
Schweizer Buch — SWZBA
Schweizer Buchhandel — SCU
Schweizer Buecherverzeichnis — SBV
Schweizer Bulletin des Elektrotechnischen Vereins — SchBull
Schweizer Chemiker-Zeitung Technik-Industrie — Schweiz Chem Ztg Tech Ind
Schweizer Ingenieur und Architekt — Schweiz Ing & Archit
Schweizer Landtechnik — Schweiz Landtech
Schweizer Lexikon — Schw Lex
Schweizer Maschinenmarkt — SWMCA
Schweizer Monatshefte — Sch M
Schweizer Monatshefte — Schweiz Mh
Schweizer Monatshefte — SchwM
Schweizer Monatshefte [*Zurich*] — SchwMH
Schweizer Monatshefte fuer Politik, Wirtschaft, Kultur — Schweizer Monatshefte f Polit Wirt Kult
Schweizer Monatshefte. Zeitschrift fuer Politik, Wirtschaft, Kultur — Schweiz Mhefte Pol Wirt Kultur
Schweizer Monatsschrift fuer Zahnmedizin — Schweiz Monatsschr Zahnmed
Schweizer Muenzblaetter — Schw Mbl
Schweizer Muenzblaetter [*Switzerland*] — Schweiz Muenzbl
Schweizer Muenzblaetter [*Gazette Numismatique Suisse*] — SM
Schweizer Muenzblaetter — SMB
Schweizer Musik-Zeitung — Schweiz Musikztg
Schweizer Naturschutz — Schweizer Natschutz
Schweizer Naturschutz. Protection de la Nature — Schweiz Naturschutz Prot Nat
Schweizer Textil-Zeitung — Schweiz Text Ztg
Schweizer Volkskunde — Schweiz Volkskd
Schweizer Volkskunde — SchwV
Schweizer Volkskunde — SV
Schweizer Zeitschrift fuer Vermessungswesen — SchZVermW
Schweizerische Aerztezeitung — Schweiz Aerzteztg
Schweizerische Anstalt fuer das Forstliche Versuchswesen. Mitteilungen — Schweiz Anst Forstl Versuchswes Mitt
Schweizerische Anstalt fuer das Forstliche Versuchswesen. Mitteilungen — Schweiz Anst Forstl Versuchswesen Mitt
Schweizerische Apotheker-Zeitung — Schweiz Apoth Ztg
Schweizerische Apotheker-Zeitung. Supplement — Schweiz Apoth Ztg Suppl
Schweizerische Bauzeitung — Schweiz Bauztg
Schweizerische Bauzeitung — SWBAA
Schweizerische Beitraege zur Altertumswissenschaft — SBA
Schweizerische Beitrage zur Dendrologie — Schweiz Beitr Dendrol
Schweizerische Bienen-Zeitung — Schweiz Bienen-Ztg
Schweizerische Blaetter fuer Heizung und Lueftung — SBHLA
Schweizerische Blaetter fuer Heizung und Lueftung [*Switzerland*] — Schweiz Bl Heiz Lueft
Schweizerische Brauerei-Rundschau — Schweiz Brau-Rundsch
Schweizerische Chemiker-Zeitung — Schweiz Chem Ztg
Schweizerische Chor Zeitung — SCZ
Schweizerische Elektrotechnische Zeitschrift — Schweiz Elektrotech Z
Schweizerische Gaertnerzeitung — Schweiz Gaertnerzeitung
Schweizerische Gaertnerzeitung — Schweiz Gaertnerztg
Schweizerische Gesellschaft fuer Klinische Chemie. Bulletin — Schweiz Ges Klin Chem Bull
Schweizerische Handelskammer in den Niederlanden. Mitteilungen an die Mitglieder — VNZ
Schweizerische Juristen-Zeitung — SchJZ
Schweizerische Juristen-Zeitung — Schweiz Juristenztg
Schweizerische Juristen-Zeitung — SJZ
Schweizerische Kirchenzeitung [*Lucerne*] — SchwKiZ
Schweizerische Kirchenzeitung [*Lucerne*] — SchwKZ
Schweizerische Kirchenzeitung — SKZ
Schweizerische Kreditanstalt. Bulletin — SKM
Schweizerische Landwirthschaftliche Zeitschrift Die Gruene — Schweiz Landw Z Die Gruene
Schweizerische Landwirtschaftliche Forschung — Schweiz Landw Forsch
Schweizerische Landwirtschaftliche Forschung — Schweiz Landwirtsch Forsch
Schweizerische Landwirtschaftliche Forschung — SLWFA
Schweizerische Landwirtschaftliche Forschung/La Recherche Agronomique en Suisse — Schweiz Landwirtsch Forsch Rech Agron Suisse
Schweizerische Landwirtschaftliche Monatshefte — Schweiz Landw Mh
Schweizerische Landwirtschaftliche Monatshefte — Schweiz Landwirtsch Monatsh
Schweizerische Medizinische Wochenschrift — Schw Med Wo
Schweizerische Medizinische Wochenschrift — Schweiz Med Wochenschr
Schweizerische Medizinische Wochenschrift — Schweiz Med Wschr
Schweizerische Medizinische Wochenschrift — SMWOA
Schweizerische Medizinische Wochenschrift. Supplementum — Schweiz Med Wochenschr Suppl
Schweizerische Milchwirtschaftliche Forschung — Schweiz Milchwirtsch Forsch
Schweizerische Milchzeitung — Schweiz Milchztg
Schweizerische Mineralogische und Petrographische Mitteilungen — Schweiz Mineral Petrogr Mitt
Schweizerische Mineralogische und Petrographische Mitteilungen — Schweizer Mineralog u Petrog Mitt
Schweizerische Mineralogische und Petrographische Mitteilungen — SMPTA
Schweizerische Monatsschrift fuer Offiziere aller Waffen — Schweiz Mschr Offiz
Schweizerische Monatsschrift fuer Zahnheilkunde — Schweiz Monatsschr Zahnheilkd
Schweizerische Monatsschrift fuer Zahnheilkunde — SSO
Schweizerische Monatsschrift fuer Zahnmedizin — Schweiz Monatsschr Zahnmed
Schweizerische Musikforschende Gesellschaft. Mitteilungsblatt — SMG
Schweizerische Musikpaedagogische Blaetter — SMpB
Schweizerische Musikzeitung — Sch MZ
Schweizerische Musikzeitung — Schweiz Mus
Schweizerische Musikzeitung/Revue Musicale Suisse — RM Suisse
Schweizerische Musikzeitung/Revue Musicale Suisse — S Mz
Schweizerische Musikzeitung/Revue Musicale Suisse — Schw Musikz
Schweizerische Musikzeitung und Saengerblatt — Schweizer Musikztg
Schweizerische Naturforschende Gesellschaft. Berichte der SNG zur Kernenergie — Schweiz Naturforsch Ges Ber SNG Kernenerg
Schweizerische Naturforschende Gesellschaft. Verhandlungen — Schweiz Naturf Ges Verh
Schweizerische Numismatische Rundschau — Schw NR
Schweizerische Numismatische Rundschau — SNR
Schweizerische Palaeontologische Abhandlungen — Schweiz Palaeontol Abh
Schweizerische Palaeontologische Abhandlungen. Memoires Suisses de Palaeontologie — Schweiz Palaeontol Abh-Mem Suisse Palaeontol
Schweizerische Palaeontologische Abhandlungen. Memoires Suisses de Palaeontologie — Schweizer Palaeont Abh Mem Suisses Paleontologie
Schweizerische Photorundschau — Schweiz Photorundsch
Schweizerische Photo-Zeitung — Schweiz Photo Ztg
Schweizerische Rundschau — S Rd
Schweizerische Rundschau — SchR
Schweizerische Rundschau — Schw Rd
Schweizerische Rundschau — Schweiz Rdsch
Schweizerische Rundschau — SchwRundschau
Schweizerische Rundschau — SR
Schweizerische Rundschau fuer Medizin Praxis — Schweiz Rundsch Med Prax
Schweizerische Strahler — Schweiz Strahler
Schweizerische Technikerzeitung [*Switzerland*] — Schweiz Tech
Schweizerische Technische Zeitschrift [*Switzerland*] — Schweiz Tech Z
Schweizerische Technische Zeitschrift — STZ
Schweizerische Technische Zeitschrift [*Switzerland*] — SZTZA
Schweizerische Theologische Umschau — SThU
Schweizerische Theologische Umschau — STU
Schweizerische Theologische Zeitschrift — Schweiz Theol Zs
Schweizerische Theologische Zeitschrift [*Zurich*] — SThZ
Schweizerische Tonwaren-Industrie — Schweiz Tonwaren Ind
Schweizerische Verein von Gas- und Wasserfachmaennern. Monatsbulletin [*Switzerland*] — Schweiz Ver Gas-Wasserfachmaennern Monatsbull
Schweizerische Vereinigung der Lack- und Farbenchemiker. Bulletin — Schweiz Ver Lack Farbenchem Bull
Schweizerische Vereinigung der Versicherungsmathematiker. Mitteilungen — Schweiz Verein Versicherungsmath Mitt
Schweizerische Vereinigung fuer Atomenergie. Bulletin — Schweiz Ver Atomenerg Bull
Schweizerische Vereinigung fuer Atomenergie. Bulletin — SVABB
Schweizerische Vereinigung fuer Sonnenenergie. Symposium — Schweiz Ver Sonnenenerg Symp
Schweizerische Verginigung von Faerbereifachleuten Fachorgan fuer Textilveredlung — Schw Ver Faerbereifachleuten Fachorgan Textilveredl
Schweizerische Vierteljahrsschrift fuer Kriegswissenschaft — SchVjKW
Schweizerische Wochenschrift fuer Chemie und Pharmacie — Schweiz Wochenschr Chem Pharm
Schweizerische Wochenschrift fuer Chemie und Pharmacie — Schweiz Wohnschr Chem u Pharm
Schweizerische Wochenschrift fuer Pharmacie — Schweiz Wochenschr Pharm
Schweizerische Zeitschrift fuer Allgemeine Pathologie und Bakteriologie — Schweiz Z Allg Path Bakt
Schweizerische Zeitschrift fuer Allgemeine Pathologie und Bakteriologie — Schweiz Z Allg Pathol Bakterol
Schweizerische Zeitschrift fuer Artillerie und Genie — Schweiz Zs Artill
Schweizerische Zeitschrift fuer Beurkundungs- und Grundbuchrecht — ZBGR
Schweizerische Zeitschrift fuer Biochemie — Schweiz Z Biochem
Schweizerische Zeitschrift fuer Forstwesen — Schweiz Z Forstwes
Schweizerische Zeitschrift fuer Forstwesen — SCZFA
Schweizerische Zeitschrift fuer Forstwesen — SZF
Schweizerische Zeitschrift fuer Geschichte — Schw Z f Gesch
Schweizerische Zeitschrift fuer Geschichte — Schw Z Gesc
Schweizerische Zeitschrift fuer Geschichte — Schw Zs f G
Schweizerische Zeitschrift fuer Geschichte — Schw Ztschr Ges
Schweizerische Zeitschrift fuer Geschichte — Schweiz Z Gesch
Schweizerische Zeitschrift fuer Geschichte — ScZ
Schweizerische Zeitschrift fuer Geschichte — SZG
Schweizerische Zeitschrift fuer Gynaekologie und Geburtshilfe — Schweiz Z Gynaekol Geburtshilfe
Schweizerische Zeitschrift fuer Gynaekologie und Geburtshilfe. Supplementum — Schweiz Z Gynaekol Geburtshilfe Suppl
Schweizerische Zeitschrift fuer Hydrologie — Schw Z Hydrol

Schweizerische Zeitschrift fuer Hydrologie — Schweiz Z Hydrol
Schweizerische Zeitschrift fuer Hydrologie — SZHYA
Schweizerische Zeitschrift fuer Medizin und Traumatologie — Schweiz Z Med Traumatol
Schweizerische Zeitschrift fuer Natur- und Heilkunde (C. F. von Pommer, Editor) — Pommers Zschr
Schweizerische Zeitschrift fuer Obst- und Weinbau — Schweiz Z Obst-u Weinb
Schweizerische Zeitschrift fuer Obst- und Weinbau — Schweiz Z Obst-Weinbau
Schweizerische Zeitschrift fuer Pathologie und Bakteriologie — Schweiz Z Pathol Bakteriol
Schweizerische Zeitschrift fuer Pathologie und Bakteriologie — Schwiez Z Path Bakt
Schweizerische Zeitschrift fuer Pharmacie — Schweiz Z Pharm
Schweizerische Zeitschrift fuer Pilzkunde — Schw Z Pilzk
Schweizerische Zeitschrift fuer Pilzkunde — Schweiz Z Pilzkd
Schweizerische Zeitschrift fuer Pilzkunde. Bulletin Suisse de Mycologie — Schweiz Z Pilzk
Schweizerische Zeitschrift fuer Pilzkunde. Bulletin Suisse de Mycologie — Schweiz Z Pilzkd Bull Suisse Mycol
Schweizerische Zeitschrift fuer Psychologie und Ihre Anwendungen — Schw Z Psyc
Schweizerische Zeitschrift fuer Psychologie und Ihre Anwendungen — Schw Z Psychol
Schweizerische Zeitschrift fuer Psychologie und Ihre Anwendungen — Schweiz Z Psychol Anwend
Schweizerische Zeitschrift fuer Psychologie und Ihre Anwendungen — SZPAA
Schweizerische Zeitschrift fuer Sozialversicherung — Schw Z Soz
Schweizerische Zeitschrift fuer Sozialversicherung — Schweiz Z Sozialversicherung
Schweizerische Zeitschrift fuer Sozialversicherung — SZS
Schweizerische Zeitschrift fuer Soziologie — Schweizer Z Soziol
Schweizerische Zeitschrift fuer Sportmedizin — Schw Z Sportmed
Schweizerische Zeitschrift fuer Sportmedizin — Schweiz Z Sportmed
Schweizerische Zeitschrift fuer Strafrecht — SZ Str R
Schweizerische Zeitschrift fuer Strafrecht — Z Str R
Schweizerische Zeitschrift fuer Tuberkulose — Schw Zs Tbk
Schweizerische Zeitschrift fuer Tuberkulose — Schweiz Z Tuberk
Schweizerische Zeitschrift fuer Tuberkulose und Pneumonologie — Schweiz Z Tuberk Pneumonol
Schweizerische Zeitschrift fuer Verkehrswirtschaft — Schweiz Z Verkehrswirt
Schweizerische Zeitschrift fuer Vermessung, Photogrammetrie, und Kulturtechnik — Schweiz Z Vermess Photogramm Kulturtech
Schweizerische Zeitschrift fuer Vermessungswesen — Schw Zs Vermess
Schweizerische Zeitschrift fuer Volkswirtschaft und Statistik — Schw ZV St
Schweizerische Zeitschrift fuer Volkswirtschaft und Statistik — Schweiz Z Volkswirt und Statis
Schweizerische Zeitschrift fuer Volkswirtschaft und Statistik — Schweizer Z Volkswirtsch u Statist
Schweizerische Zeitschrift fuer Volkswirtschaft und Statistik — SZ
Schweizerische Zeitschrift fuer Volkswirtschaft und Statistik — ZSV
Schweizerisches Archiv fuer Tierheilkunde und Tierzucht (Bern) — Schweiz Arch Tierh (Bern)
Schweizerisches Archiv fuer Verkehrswissenschaft und Verkehrspolitik — Schweiz Arch Verkehrswiss und Verkehrspol
Schweizerisches Archiv fuer Verkehrswissenschaft und Verkehrspolitik — Schweizer Archiv Verkehrswiss u -Polit
Schweizerisches Archiv fuer Volkskunde — SAV
Schweizerisches Archiv fuer Volkskunde — SAVK
Schweizerisches Archiv fuer Volkskunde — SchwArchV
Schweizerisches Archiv fuer Volkskunde — Schweiz Archiv f Volksk
Schweizerisches Jahrbuch fuer Musikwissenschaft — SJbMw
Schweizerisches Obligationenrecht — OR
Schweizerisches Patent-, Muster-, und Markenblatt. Ausgabe A — Schweiz Pat Muster Markenbl Ausg A
Schweizerishce Weinzeitung — Schweiz Weinztg
Schwenckfeldiana — Schwenk
Schwerpunkte Linguistik und Kommunikationswissenschaft — SLK
Schwerpunkte Linguistik und Kommunikationswissenschaft — SLKW
Schwestern Revue — Schwest Rev
SCI (Society of Chemical Industry. London) Monograph — SCI Monogr
Scienca Revuo — Sci Rev
Scienca Revuo (Belgrade) — Sci Rev (Belgrade)
Scienca Revuo. Internacia Scienca Asocio Esperantista — Sci Rev Int Sci Asoc Esperantista
Scienca Revuo (Netherlands) — Sci Rev (Neth)
Scienca Rondo — Sci Rondo
Sciencaj Komunikajoj — Sci Komun
Science — GSCI
Science — Sc
Science — SCI
Science — SCIEA
Science 80 (Eighty) — Sci 80 (Eighty)
Science Abstracts — SA
Science Abstracts — Sci Abstr
Science Abstracts — SciAb
Science Abstracts of China — Sci Abstr Ch
Science Abstracts of China. Biological Sciences — Sci Abstr China Biol Sci
Science Abstracts of China. Chemistry and Chemical Technology — Sci Abstr China Chem Chem Technol
Science Abstracts of China. Mathematical and Physical Sciences — Sci Abstr China Math Phys Sci
Science Abstracts of China. Medicine — Sci Abstr China Med
Science Abstracts of China. Technical Sciences — Sci Abstr China Tech Sci
Science Abstracts. Section A — Sci Abstr Sect A
Science Abstracts. Section A. Physics Abstracts — Sci Abstr Sect A Phys Abstr
Science Abstracts. Section B — Sci Abstr Sect B
Science Abstracts. Series C — Sci Abstr Ser C
Science Advisory Board of the Northwest Territories. Report [*Canada*] — SABNWTR
Science Advisory Board of the Northwest Territories. Research Paper [*Canada*] — SABNWTRP
Science Advisory Board of the Northwest Territories. Working Paper — SABNWTWP
Science Advocate — Sc Advocate
Science Aerienne et l'Aerotechnique — Sci Aer Aerotech
Science. American Association for the Advancement of Science — AAAS/S
Science and Appliance — Sci Appliance
Science and Archaeology — Sci & Archaeol
Science and Archaeology — SciArch
Science and Archaeology. Symposium on Archaeological Chemistry — Sci Archaeol Symp Archaeol Chem
Science and Art of Mining — Sci Art Min
Science and Australian Technology — Sci & Aust Technol
Science and Australian Technology — Sci Aust Technol
Science and Australian Technology — Sci Tech
Science and Children — Sci & Child
Science and Culture — SC
Science and Culture — Sci and Cult
Science and Culture — Sci Cult
Science and Culture — SCINA
Science and Culture. Calcutta — ScC
Science and Culture (New Delhi) — Sci Cult (New Delhi)
Science and Culture Series. Physics — Sci Cult Ser Phys
Science and Education — Sci Ed
Science and Education Administration. Agricultural Reviews and Manuals. ARM-NE — Sci Educ Adm Agric Rev Man ARM-NE
Science and Education Administration. Agricultural Reviews and Manuals. ARM-W — Sci Educ Adm Agric Rev Man ARM-W
Science and Education Administration. Agricultural Reviews and Manuals. Western Series. United States Department of Agriculture — Sci Educ Adm Agric Rev Man West Ser US Dep Agric
Science and Education Administration. North Central Region Publication — Sci Educ Adm North Cent Reg Publ
Science and Engineering — SCENA
Science and Engineering — Sci Eng
Science and Engineering Reports of Tohoku Gakuin University — Sci Eng Rep Tohoku Gakuin Univ
Science and Engineering Reports. Saitama University. Series C — Sci & Eng Rep Saitama Univ C
Science and Engineering Reports. Saitama University. Series C — Sci and Eng Rep Saitama Univ Ser C
Science and Engineering Research Council. Daresbury Laboratory. Report — Sci Eng Res Counc Daresbury Lab Rep
Science and Engineering Review. Doshisha University — Sci Eng Rev Doshisha Univ
Science and Environment — Sci Environ
Science and Government Report [*United States*] — Sci Gov Rep
Science and Government Report — Sci Govt Rep
Science and Government Report — SGR
Science and Industry — Sci Ind
Science and Industry [*Karachi*] — SINDB
Science and Industry Forum. Australian Academy of Science. Forum Report — Sci Ind Forum Aust Acad Sci Forum Rep
Science and Industry (Karachi) — Sci Ind (Karachi)
Science and Industry (Melbourne) — Sci Ind (Melbourne)
Science and Industry (Osaka) — Sci Ind (Osaka)
Science and Industry (Philips) [*The Netherlands*] — Sci Ind (Philips)
Science and its Conceptual Foundations — Sci Concept Found
Science and Justice — Sci Justice
Science and Life — Sci Life
Science and Mechanics — Sci Mech
Science and Medicine (New York) — Sci Med NY
Science and Medicine (Philadelphia) — Sci Med Philadelphia
Science and Nature — Sci Natur
Science and Practice of Clinical Medicine — Sci Pract Clin Med
Science and Practice of Surgery — Sci Pract Surg
Science and Psychoanalysis — Sci Psychoanal
Science and Public Affairs. Bulletin of the Atomic Scientists — Sci Publ Af
Science and Public Affairs. Bulletin of the Atomic Scientists — Sci Public Aff Bull At Sci
Science and Public Affairs. Bulletin of the Atomic Scientists — SPA
Science and Public Policy — Sci Pub Pol
Science and Public Policy — Sci Publ Pol
Science and Public Policy — Sci Public Policy
Science and Public Policy — SPPLB
Science and Society — PSNS
Science and Society — S & S
Science and Society — Sc
Science and Society — Sci & Scty
Science and Society — Sci & Soc
Science and Society — Sci Soc
Science and Society — ScSo
Science and Society — SS
Science and Technologies (Seoul) — Sci Technol (Seoul)
Science and Technology — Sci & Tech
Science and Technology — Sci Tech
Science and Technology — Sci Technol
Science and Technology [*New York*] — STNYA
Science and Technology Dimensions — Sci Technol Dim
Science and Technology Employment [*Database*] — STEM

Science and Technology. Engineering (Sian, China) — Sci Technol Eng Sian China
Science and Technology in China — Sci Technol China
Science and Technology in Japan — Sci Technol Japan
Science and Technology Libraries — Sci Technol Libr
Science and Technology Libraries — Science and Tech Libs
Science and Technology Libraries — STELDF
Science and Technology. Medicine — Sci Technol Med
Science and Technology (New York) — Sci Technol (NY)
Science and Technology News — Sci Tech News
Science and Technology of Environmental Protection — Sci Technol Environ Prot
Science and Technology of Japan — Sci Technol Jpn
Science and Technology of Japan — Technol Japan
Science and Technology of Nanostructured Magnetic Materials — Sci Technol Nanostruct Magn Mater
Science and Technology of Zirconia — Sci Technol Zirconia
Science and Technology. Physical Sciences (Sian, China) — Sci Technol Phys Sci Sian China
Science and Technology Quarterly — Sci Technol Quart
Science and Technology Review — Sci Technol Rev
Science and Technology (San Diego) — Sci Technol (San Diego)
Science and Technology (Surrey Hills, Australia) — Sci Technol (Surrey Hills Aust)
Science Books — SB
Science Books — Sci Bks
Science Books and Films — SB
Science Books and Films — SB & F
Science Books and Films — SBF
Science Books and Films — Sci Bk
Science Books and Films — Sci Bks & Films
Science Bulletin — Sci Bul
Science Bulletin. American-Soviet Science Society — Sci Bull Am Sov Sci Soc
Science Bulletin. College of Agriculture. University of Ryukyus. Okinawa — Sci Bull Coll Agric Univ Ryukyus Okinawa
Science Bulletin. Cotton Research Institute. Sindos — Sci Bull Cotton Res Inst Sindos
Science Bulletin. Department of Agriculture and Forestry. Union of South Africa — Sci Bull Dep Agric For Un S Afr
Science Bulletin. Department of Agriculture. New South Wales — Sci Bull Dep Agric NSW
Science Bulletin. Department of Agriculture. New South Wales — Sci Bull Dept Agr NSW
Science Bulletin. Department of Agriculture. South Africa — Sci Bull Dept Agr S Afr
Science Bulletin. Desert Botanical Garden of Arizona — Sci Bull Des Bot Gard Ariz
Science Bulletin. Faculty of Agriculture. Kyushu University — Sci Bull Fac Agr Kyushu Univ
Science Bulletin. Faculty of Agriculture. Kyushu University — Sci Bull Fac Agric Kyushu Univ
Science Bulletin. Faculty of Agriculture. University of the Ryukyus/Ryukyu Daigaku Nogakubu Gakujutsu Hokoku — Sci Bull Fac Agric Univ Ryukyus
Science Bulletin. Faculty of Education. Nagasaki University — Sci Bull Fac Ed Nagasaki Univ
Science Bulletin. Faculty of Education. Nagasaki University — Sci Bull Fac Educ Nagasaki Univ
Science Bulletin. Faculty of Liberal Arts and Education. Nagasaki University — Sci Bull Fac Lib Arts Educ Nagasaki Univ
Science Bulletin for Teachers in Secondary Schools — Sci Bul
Science Bulletin. Kansas University — Sci Bull Univ Kansas
Science Bulletin/K'o Hsueeh Hui Pao/Chinese Association for the Advancement of Science (Taipei) — Sci Bull Taipei
Science Bulletin. National Chiao-Tung University — Sci Bull Natl Chiao Tung Univ
Science Bulletin. Qatar University — Sci Bull Qatar Univ
Science Bulletin. Republic of South Africa. Department of Agricultural Technical Services — Sci Bull Repub S Afr Dept Agr Tech Serv
Science Bulletin. Science Foundation of the Philippines — Sci Bull Sci Found Philipp
Science Bulletin. South Africa. Department of Agricultural Technical Services — Sci Bull S Afr Dep Agruc Tech Serv
Science Bulletin. University of Kansas — Sci Bull Univ Kans
Science Catholique — Sc Cath
Science Chronicle (Karachi) — Sci Chron (Karachi)
Science Citation Index — SCI
Science Citation Index — Sci Cit Ind
Science Citation Index — Sci Cit Index
Science Conspectus — Sc Conspectus
Science Council of Canada. Background Study — SCCBS
Science Council of Canada. Report — SCCR
Science Council of Canada. Special Study — SCCSS
Science Council of Japan. Annual Report — Sci Counc Jap Annu Rep
Science Counselor — Sci Couns
Science Counselor. Quarterly Journal for Teachers of Science in the Catholic High Schools — Sci Counselor
Science de l'Alimentation — Sci Aliment
Science Digest [*Chicago*] — SCDIA
Science Digest — Sci Dig
Science Digest — Sci Digest
Science Diliman — Sci Diliman
Science Dimension — NRSDA
Science Dimension — Sc Dimension
Science Dimension — SCDI
Science Dimension — Sci Dimens
Science Dimension — Sci Dimension
Science du Sol — Sci Sol
Science du Sol — SCSLA
Science Education — Sci Ed
Science Education — Sci Educ
Science Education — Science Ed
Science Education Newsletter — Sci Ed News
Science Education/Rika Kyoiku (Tokyo) — Sci Educ Tokyo
Science, Engineering, Medicine, and Technology — SEMT
Science et Esprit — Sc E
Science et Esprit — ScEs
Science et Esprit — Sci Espr
Science et Esprit — Sci Esprit
Science et Esprit — SEs
Science et Humanisme — Sci Humanisme
Science et Industrie — Sci Ind
Science et Industrie. Edition Construction et Travaux Publics — Sci Ind Ed Constr Trav Publics
Science et Industrie. Edition Metallurgie. Construction, Mecaniques, Energie — Sci Ind Ed Metall Constr Mec Energ
Science et Industrie (Paris) — Sci Ind Paris
Science et Industries Photographiques — Sci Ind Phot
Science et Industries Photographiques — Sci Ind Photogr
Science et Industries Photographiques — Science et Industrie Phot
Science et Nature — Sci Nat
Science et Peche — Sci Peche
Science et Recherche — Sci Rech
Science et Recherche Odontostomatologiques — Sci Rech Odontostomatol
Science et Religion — SeR
Science et Technique du Caoutchouc — Sci Tech Caoutch
Science et Technologie Alimentaire [*People's Republic of China*] — Sci Technol Aliment
Science et Vie — Sci Vie
Science et Vie — SCVIA
Science Exploration [*Changsha*] — Sci Exploration
Science Fantasy — SCF
Science Fantasy — SFB
Science Fiction — SF
Science Fiction — SFic
Science Fiction Adventure Classics — SFAC
Science Fiction Adventure Classics — SFC
Science Fiction Adventures [*1952-1954*] — SFA
Science Fiction Adventures [*1958-1963*] — SFAB
Science Fiction Adventures [*1956-1958*] — SFAD
Science Fiction Adventures Yearbook — SAY
Science Fiction and Fantasy Book Review — SE & FBR
Science Fiction and Fantasy RoundTable [*Database*] — SFRT
Science Fiction Book Review Index [*SFBRI*] — Sci Fict Book Rev Index
Science Fiction Book Review Index — Sci Fiction Bk Rev Ind
Science Fiction Chronicle — SCC
Science Fiction Classics Annual — SCA
Science Fiction Digest — SFD
Science Fiction Monthly — SFM
Science Fiction Plus — SFP
Science Fiction Quarterly [*1951-1958*] — SFIQ
Science Fiction Quarterly [*1940-1943*] — SFQ
Science Fiction Review — S Fict R
Science Fiction Review — SFR
Science Fiction Review. Monthly — SFRM
Science Fiction. Review of Speculative Literature — SFSL
Science Fiction Stories — SFS
Science Fiction Studies — Sci Fict St
Science Fiction Studies — SFS
Science Fiction Studies — SFST
Science Fiction Times — SFTB
Science Fiction Yearbook — SFY
Science for Conservation (Tokyo) — Sci Conserv (Tokyo)
Science for People — Sc for People
Science for People — Sci Peo
Science for People — Sci Peopl
Science for People — Science
Science for People — SfP
Science for Schools [*Manila*] — SFS
Science for the Farmer — Sci Farm
Science for the Farmer — Sci Farmer
Science Forum — SCFO
Science Forum — SCFOB
Science Forum — Sci For
Science Forum — Sci Forum
Science Forum — SCIF
Science Foundation. Philippines. Science Bulletin — Sci Found Philipp Sci Bull
Science Gossip — Sc G
Science Illustrated — Sci Ilus
Science in Agriculture — Sci Agric
Science in Agriculture. Pennsylvania State University. Agricultural Experiment Station — Sci Agric PA State Univ Agric Exp Stn
Science in Alaska. Proceedings. Alaskan Science Conference — Sci Alaska Proc Alaskan Sci Conf
Science in China (Scientia Sinica). Series E — Sci China Ser E
Science in China. Series A. Mathematics, Physics, Astronomy, and Technological Sciences — Sci China A
Science in China. Series A. Mathematics, Physics, Astronomy, and Technological Sciences — Sci China Ser A
Science in China. Series B. Chemistry, Life Sciences, and Earth Sciences — Sci China B

Science in China. Series B. Chemistry, Life Sciences, and Earth Sciences — Sci China Ser B
Science in Context — Sci Context
Science in Iceland — Sci Icel
Science in Iceland — SCII
Science in Industry (London) — Sci in Ind (Lond)
Science in New Guinea — Sci New Guinea
Science in Parliament — Sc Parliament
Science in Progress (New Haven) — Sci Prog (New Haven)
Science in USSR — Sci USSR
Science Informations News. National Science Foundation — Sci Inf News
Science International (Lahore) — Sci Int (Lahore)
Science Journal — Sci J
Science Journal — Sci Jour
Science Journal Incorporating Discovery — SCJUA
Science Journal (London) — Sci J (Lond)
Science Journal (London) — Sci J London
Science Journal. Shivaji University — Sci J Shivaji Univ
Science Journal. Shivaji University — SJSUD
Science Leaflet — Sci Leafl
Science, Medicine, and Man — Sci Med Man
Science Message — Sci Message
Science Monograph SM. University of Wyoming. Agricultural Experiment Station — Sci Monogr SM Univ Wyo Agric Exp Stn
Science Monograph. University of Wyoming. Agricultural Experiment Station — Sci Monogr Univ Wyo Agric Exp Stn
Science Monograph. Wyoming Experimental Station — Sci Monogr Wyo Expl Stn
Science Monthly (Taipei) — Sci Mon Taipei
Science Museum Library. Bibliographical Series — Science Lib Bibliog Ser
Science Museum Library Bulletin — Sci Mus Lib Bull
Science Museum of Minnesota. Monograph — Sci Mus Minn Monogr
Science Networks. Historical Studies — Sci Networks Hist Stud
Science News — GSCN
Science News — Sci N
Science News — Sci News
Science News [*Washington, DC*] — SCNEB
Science News — SN
Science News/Academia Sinica/K'o Hsueh T'ung Pao (Peking) — Sci News Peking
Science News (Harmondsworth) — Sci News (Harmondsworth)
Science News Letter [*United States*] — Sci News Lett
Science News Letter — Sci NL
Science News Letter — Science N L
Science News. National Science Council (Karachi) — Sci News Karachi
Science News (Washington, D.C.) — Sci News (Washington DC)
Science of Advanced Materials and Process Engineering. Proceedings — Sci Adv Mater Process Eng Proc
Science of Advanced Materials and Process Engineering. Quarterly [*United States*] — Sci Adv Mater Process Eng Q
Science of Agriculture (Tokyo) — Sci Agric (Tokyo)
Science of Biology Journal — Sci Biol J
Science of Biology Series — Sci Biol Ser
Science of Ceramic Interfaces — Sci Ceram Interfaces
Science of Ceramics [*England*] — Sci Ceram
Science of Computer Programming — Sci Comput Program
Science of Computer Programming — Sci Comput Programming
Science of Drugs (Tokyo) — Sci Drugs (Tokyo)
Science of Food and Agriculture — Sci Food Agric
Science of Forest Products — Sci For Prod
Science of Human Life — Sci Hum Life
Science of Legumes — Sci Legumes
Science of Light — Sci Light
Science of Machine [*Japan*] — Sci Mac
Science of Man — Sci Man
Science of Man and Australasian Anthropological Journal — Sci Man
Science of Nourishment — Sci Nourishment
Science of Sintering — Sci Sinter
Science of Sintering — Sci Sintering
Science of Sintering. New Directions for Materials Processing and Microstructural Control. Proceedings. Round Table Conference on Sintering — Sci Sintering Proc Round Table Conf Sintering
Science of the Earth. Geology — Sci Earth Geol
Science of the Total Environment — Sc Total Env
Science of the Total Environment — Sci Total Environ
Science of the Total Environment — SCTE
Science on the March — Sci March
Science Paperbacks — Sci Paperbacks
Science Pictorial [*People's Republic of China*] — Sci Pict
Science Progres Decouverte — Sci Prog Decouverte
Science Progres Decouverte — Sci Progr Decouverte
Science Progres Decouverte — SPDVB
Science, Progres, la Natur (Paris) — Sci Prog Nat (Paris)
Science, Progres, la Nature — Sci Prog Nat
Science Progress — Sci Pro
Science Progress — Sci Prog
Science Progress — Sci Progr
Science Progress — Science Prog
Science Progress [*Oxford*] — SCPRA
Science Progress (London) — Sci Prog (Lond)
Science Progress (London) — Sci Prog (London)
Science Progress (Northwood, United Kingdom) — Sci Prog Northwood UK
Science Progress (Oxford) — Sci Prog (Oxf)
Science Quarterly. National University of Peking — Sci Q Natl Univ Peking
Science Record — Sci Rec
Science Record/Academia Sinica/K'o Hsueh Chi Lu (Chungking) — Sci Rec Chungking
Science Record (Chinese Edition) [*People's Republic of China*] — Sci Rec (Chin Ed)
Science Record. Otago University Science Students' Association (Dunedin) — Sci Rec Dunedin
Science Record (Peking) — Sci Rec (Peking)
Science Religieuse — Sc R
Science Report. Faculty of Liberal Arts and Education. Gifu University. Natural Science — Sci Rep Fac Liberal Art Educ Gifu Univ Natur Sci
Science Report. Gunma University. Natural Science Series/Gunma Daigaku Kiyo. Shizen Kagaku Hen — Sci Rep Gunma Univ Nat Sci Ser
Science Report. Shima Marineland — Sci Rep Shima Marinel
Science Report. Shima Marineland — SMKHDI
Science Report. Yokosuka City Museum — Sci Rep Yokosuka City Mus
Science Report. Yokosuka City Museum — Sci Rep Yokosuka Cy Mus
Science Report. Yokosuka City Museum. Natural Sciences — Sci Rep Yokosuka City Mus Nat Sci
Science Reporter — Sci Rep
Science Reporter [*New Delhi*] — SCRPA
Science Reporter (India) — Sci Rep (India)
Science Reports. Azabu Veterinary College — Sci Rep Azabu Vet Coll
Science Reports. College of General Education. Osaka University [*Japan*] — Sci Rep Coll Gen Educ Osaka Univ
Science Reports. College of General Education. Osaka University — Sci Rep College Gen Ed Osaka Univ
Science Reports. Department of Geology. Kyushu University — Sci Rep Dep Geol Kyushu Univ
Science Reports. Faculty of Agriculture. Kobe University — Sci Rep Fac Agric Kobe Univ
Science Reports. Faculty of Education. Fukushima University [*Japan*] — Sci Rep Fac Educ Fukushima Univ
Science Reports. Faculty of Education. Gifu University. Natural Science — Sci Rep Fac Ed Gifu Univ Natur Sci
Science Reports. Faculty of Education. Gunma University — Sci Rep Fac Educ Gunma Univ
Science Reports. Faculty of Literature and Science. Hirosaki University — Sci Rep Fac Lit Sci Hirosaki Univ
Science Reports. Faculty of Literature and Science. Toyama University — Sci Rep Fac Lit Sci Toyama Univ
Science Reports. Faculty of Science. Kyushu University. Geology [*Japan*] — Sci Rep Fac Sci Kyushu Univ Geol
Science Reports. Gunma Universtiy — Sci Rep Gunma Univ
Science Reports. Hirosaki University — HUSRA
Science Reports. Hirosaki University — Sci Rep Hirosaki Univ
Science Reports. Hyogo University of Agriculture — Sci Rep Hyogo Univ Agric
Science Reports. Hyogo University of Agriculture and Faculty of Agriculture. Kobe University — Sci Rep Hyogo Univ Agr Fac Agr Kobe Univ
Science Reports. Hyogo University of Agriculture and Faculty of Agriculture. Kobe University — Sci Rep Hyogo Univ Agric Fac Agric Kobe Univ
Science Reports. Hyogo University of Agriculture. Series Agricultural Chemistry — Sci Rep Hyogo Univ Agric Ser Agric Chem
Science Reports. Hyogo University of Agriculture. Series Agriculture — Sci Rep Hyogo Univ Agric Ser Agric
Science Reports. Hyogo University of Agriculture. Series Agriculture and Horticulture — Sci Rep Hyogo Univ Agric Ser Agric Hortic
Science Reports. Hyogo University of Agriculture. Series Agriculture Technology — Sci Rep Hyogo Univ Agric Ser Agric Technol
Science Reports. Hyogo University of Agriculture. Series Natural Science — Sci Rep Hyogo Univ Agric Ser Nat Sci
Science Reports. Hyogo University of Agriculture. Series Plant Protection — Sci Rep Hyogo Univ Agric Ser Plant Prot
Science Reports. Hyogo University of Agriculture. Series Zootechnical Science — Sci Rep Hyogo Univ Agric Ser Zootech Sci
Science Reports. Kagoshima University — Sci Rep Kagoshima Univ
Science Reports. Kanagawa University. Research Institute for Engineering — Sci Rep Res Inst Engrg Kanagawa Univ
Science Reports. Kanazawa University — Sci Rep Kanazawa Univ
Science Reports. Kanazawa University. Biology/Kanazawa Daigaku Rika Hokoku. Seibutsugaku — Sci Rep Kanazawa Univ Biol
Science Reports. Kanazawa University. Part II. Biology and Geology — Sci Rep Kanazawa Univ Part II Biol Geol
Science Reports. National Tsing Hua University. Series A. Mathematical, Physical, and Engineering Sciences — Sci Rep Natl Tsing Hua Univ Ser A
Science Reports. National Tsing Hua University. Series C. Geological, Geographical, and Meteorological Sciences — Sci Rep Natl Tsing Hua Univ Ser C
Science Reports. National University of Peking — Sci Rep Natl Univ Peking
Science Reports. Niigata University. Series A. Mathematics — Sci Rep Niigata Univ Ser A
Science Reports. Niigata University. Series B. Physics — Sci Rep Niigata Univ Ser B
Science Reports. Niigata University. Series C. Chemistry — Sci Rep Niigata Univ Ser C
Science Reports. Niigata University. Series D. Biology — Sci Rep Niigata Univ Ser D Biol
Science Reports. Niigata University. Series E. Geology and Mineralogy — NSEGB4
Science Reports. Niigata University. Series E. Geology and Mineralogy — Sci Rep Niigata Univ Ser E
Science Reports. Niigata University. Series F. Geology and Mineralogy — Sci Rep Niigata Univ Ser F Geol Mineral
Science Reports of National Tsing Hua University. Series B. Biological and Psychological Sciences/Kuo Li Ch'ing-Hua Ta Hsueeh Li K'o Pao Kao — Sci Rep Natl Tsing Hua Univ Ser B Biol Sci

Science Reports of South College and North College of Osaka University/ Osaka Daigaku Nanko, Hokko Rika Hokoku — Sci Rep S Coll N Coll Osaka Univ
Science Reports of the Yokohama National University. Section I. Mathematics, Physics, Chemistry — Sci Rep Yokohama Nat Univ Sect I Math Phys Chem
Science Reports. Osaka University — Sci Rep Osaka Univ
Science Reports. Research Institutes. Tohoku University — Sci Rep Res Inst Tohoku Univ
Science Reports. Research Institutes. Tohoku University. Series A. Physics, Chemistry, and Metallurgy — Sci R Toh A
Science Reports. Research Institutes. Tohoku University. Series A. Physics, Chemistry, and Metallurgy — Sci Rep Res Inst Tohoku Univ A
Science Reports. Research Institutes. Tohoku University. Series A. Physics, Chemistry, and Metallurgy — Sci Rep Res Inst Tohoku Univ Ser A
Science Reports. Research Institutes. Tohoku University. Series B. Technology — Sci Rep Res Inst Tohoku Univ Ser B
Science Reports. Research Institutes. Tohoku University. Series B. Technology. Reports. Institute of High Speed Mechanics — Sci Rep Res Inst Tohoku Univ Ser B Rep Inst High Speed Mech
Science Reports. Research Institutes. Tohoku University. Series C. Medicine — Sci Rep Res Inst Tohoku Univ Med
Science Reports. Research Institutes. Tohoku University. Series C. Medicine — Sci Rep Res Inst Tohoku Univ Ser C
Science Reports. Research Institutes. Tohoku University. Series C. Medicine — Sci Rep Res Inst Tohoku Univ Ser C Med
Science Reports. Research Institutes. Tohoku University. Series D — Sci Rep Res Inst Tohoku Univ Ser D
Science Reports. Research Institutes. Tohoku University. Series D. Agriculture — Sci Rep Res Inst Tohoku Univ Ser D Agric
Science Reports. Saitama University. Series A. Mathematics, Physics, and Chemistry — Sci Rep Saitama Univ Ser A
Science Reports. Saitama University. Series B. Biology and Earth Sciences — Sci Rep Saitama Univ Ser B Biol Earth Sci
Science Reports. Shimabara Volcano Observatory. Faculty of Science. Kyushu University — Sci Rep Shimabara Volcano Obs Fac Sci Kyushu Univ
Science Reports. Society for the Research of Physics Chemistry — Sci Rep Soc Res Phys Chem
Science Reports. Society for the Research of Theoretical Chemistry — Sci Rep Soc Res Theor Chem
Science Reports. Tohoku Imperial University. Series 1. Mathematics, Physics, Chemistry — Sci Rep Tohoku Imp Univ Ser 1
Science Reports. Tohoku Imperial University. Series 3. Mineralogy, Petrology, Economic Geology — Sci Rep Tohoku Imp Univ Ser 3
Science Reports. Tohoku Imperial University. Series 4. Biology — Sci Rep Tohoku Imp Univ Ser 4
Science Reports. Tohoku University — Sci Rep Tohoku Univ
Science Reports. Tohoku University. Eighth Series — Sci Rep Tohoku Univ 8th Series
Science Reports. Tohoku University. Eighth Series. Physics and Astronomy — Sci Rep Tohoku Univ Eighth Ser Phys and Astron
Science Reports. Tohoku University. Fifth Series — Sci Rep Tohoku Univ Fifth Ser
Science Reports. Tohoku University. Fifth Series. Geophysics — Sci Rep Tohoku Univ Fifth Ser Geophys
Science Reports. Tohoku University. Fifth Series. Geophysics [*Japan*] — Sci Rep Tohoku Univ Ser 5
Science Reports. Tohoku University. First Series [*Japan*] — Sci Rep Tohoku Univ First Ser
Science Reports. Tohoku University. First Series — Sci Rep Tohoku Univ I
Science Reports. Tohoku University. Fourth Series. Biology — Sci Rep Tohoku Univ Fourth Ser (Biol)
Science Reports. Tohoku University. Second Series. Geology — Sci Rep Tohoku Univ Second Ser (Geol)
Science Reports. Tohoku University. Series 2. Geology — Sci Rep Tohoku Univ Ser 2
Science Reports. Tohoku University. Series 8. Physics and Astronomy — Sci Rep Tohoku Univ Ser 8
Science Reports. Tohoku University. Series A — Sci Rep Tohoku Univ A
Science Reports. Tohoku University. Seventh Series [*Japan*] — Sci Rep Tohoku Univ Seventh Ser
Science Reports. Tohoku University. Seventh Series. Geography [*Japan*] — SRTG-A
Science Reports. Tohoku University. Third Series. Mineralogy, Petrology, and Economic Geology [*Japan*] — Sci Rep Tohoku Univ Third Ser
Science Reports. Tokyo Bunrika Daigaku. Section A. Mathematics, Physics, Chemistry — Sci Rep Tokyo Bunrika Daigaku Sect A
Science Reports. Tokyo Bunrika Daigaku. Section B — Sci Rep Tokyo Bunrika Daigaku Sect B
Science Reports. Tokyo Bunrika Daigaku. Section C — Sci Rep Tokyo Bunrika Daigaku Sect C
Science Reports. Tokyo Kyoiku Daigaku. Section A — Sci Rep Tokyo Kyoiku Daigaku Sect A
Science Reports. Tokyo Kyoiku Daigaku. Section B — Sci Rep Tokyo Kyoiku Daigaku Sect B
Science Reports. Tokyo Kyoiku Daigaku. Section C — Sci Rep Tokyo Kyoiku Daigaku Sect C
Science Reports. Tokyo University of Education. Section A — Sci Rep Tokyo Univ Educ Sect A
Science Reports. Tokyo University of Education. Section B — Sci Rep Tokyo Univ Educ Sect B
Science Reports. Tokyo University of Education. Section C — Sci Rep Tokyo Univ Educ Sect C
Science Reports. Tokyo University of Literature and Science. Section C. Geology — Sci Rep Tokyo Univ Let Sci Sect C
Science Reports. Tokyo Woman's Christian College — Sci Rep Tokyo Woman's Christian College
Science Reports. University of Chekiang — Sci Rep Univ Chekiang
Science Reports. Yamaguchi University — Sci Rep Yamaguchi Univ
Science Reports. Yokohama National University. Section 2. Biological and Geological Sciences — Sci Rep Yokohama Nat Univ Sect 2
Science Reports. Yokohama National University. Section I. Mathematics and Physics — Sci Rep Yokohama Nat Univ Sect I
Science Reports. Yokohama National University. Section I. Mathematics, Physics, and Chemistry — Sci Rep Yokohama Natl Univ I
Science Reports. Yokohama National University. Section I. Mathematics, Physics, and Chemistry — Sci Rep Yokohama Natl Univ Sect I
Science Reports. Yokohama National University. Section II. Biological and Geological Sciences — Sci Rep Yokohama Natl Univ Sect II Biol Geol Sci
Science Reports. Yokohama National University. Section II. Biology and Geology — Sci Rep Yokohama Natl Univ Sect II Biol Geol
Science Reports. Yokohama National University. Section II. Biology and Geology — SYUBAT
Science Research Abstracts — Sci Res Abstr
Science Research Abstracts Journal — Sci Res Abstr J
Science Research Abstracts Journal. Part A. Super Conductivity, Magnetohydrodynamics and Plasmas, Theoretical Physics — Sci Res Abstr J Part A
Science Research Abstracts Journal. Part B. Laser and Electro-Optic Reviews, Quantum Electronics, and Unconventional Energy — Sci Res Abstr J Part B
Science Research Abstracts Journal. Part B. Laser and Electro-Optic Reviews, Quantum Electronics, and Unconventional Energy Sources — Sci Res Abstr J B
Science Research Abstracts. Part A. Superconductivity, Magnetohydrodynamics, and Plasmas. Theoretical Physics — Sci Res Abstr A
Science Research News — Sci Res News
Science Research News [*Kanpur*] — SREND7
Science Research News (Kanpur) — Sci Res News (Kanpur)
Science Resource Letter — Sci Resour Lett
Science Review [*Manila*] — Sci R
Science Review — Sci Rev
Science Review [*Manila*] — SCIRA
Science Review [*Manila*] — SRe
Science Review (Manila) — Sci Rev (Manila)
Science Serves Your Farm — Sci Serves Farm
Science Sociale — Sci Sociale
Science Society of Thailand. Journal — Sci Soc Thailand J
Science Spectra — Sci Spectra
Science Stories — SST
Science Stories — STT
Science Studies — Sci Stud
Science Studies (London) — Sci Stud London
Science Studies. St. Bonaventure University — Sci Stud St Bonaventure Univ
Science Teacher — ISCT
Science Teacher — Sci Teach
Science Teacher — SCIT
Science Teacher (New Delhi) — Sci Teach (New Delhi)
Science Teachers Association of Tasmania. Newsletter — STAT News
Science Teachers News — Sci Teach News
Science, Technology, and Human Values — Sci Tech Human Values
Science, Technology, and Human Values — Sci Technol Hum Val
Science, Technology, and Human Values — STHV
Science/Technology and the Humanities — Sci Technol Humanities
Science Technology Series [*United States*] — Sci Technol Ser
Science through Experiments — Sci Exp
Science Today (Bombay) — Sci Today (Bombay)
Science Today (Bombay) — SCTYB
Science Tools — Sci Tools
Science Tools — SCTOA
Science with Soft X-Rays — Sci Soft X Rays
Science Wonder Quarterly — WQ
Science Wonder Stories — SW
Science World — ISCW
Science-Fiction Studies — PSFF
Science-Fiction Studies — Science Fiction Stud
Scienceland — Sciland
Sciences — PSCI
Sciences [*New York*] — SCNCA
Sciences Agronomiques Rennes — Sci Agron Rennes
Sciences and Technologies. Korea University [*Republic of Korea*] — Sci Technol
Sciences and Technologies. Korea University — Sci Technol Korea Univ
Sciences. Association Francaise pour l'Avancement des Sciences — Sciences Assoc Fr Av Sci
Sciences de la Terre — Sci Terre
Sciences de la Terre. Informatique Geologique — Sci Terre Inf Geol
Sciences de la Terre. Memoires — Sci Terre Mem
Sciences de l'Eau — Sci Eau
Sciences des Aliments — Sci Aliments
Sciences Ecclesiastiques — Sc Ec
Sciences Ecclesiastiques [*Montreal-Brussels*] — ScE
Sciences Ecclesiastiques — ScEccl
Sciences Ecclesiastiques — SE
Sciences et Avenir — Sci Av
Sciences et Avenir [*France*] — Sci Avenir
Sciences et Industries Spatiales [*Switzerland*] — Sci Ind Spat
Sciences et Industries Spatiales, Space Research and Engineering, Weltraumforschung und Industrie — Sci Ind Spatiales Space Res Eng Weltraumforsch Ind
Sciences et l'Enseignement des Sciences — Sci Enseign Sci

Sciences et l'Enseignement des Sciences — Sci Enseignem Sci
Sciences et Techniques de l'Armement — Sci Tech Armement
Sciences et Techniques de l'Armement. Memorial de l'Artillerie Francaise — Sci Tech Armement Meml Artillerie Fr
Sciences et Techniques de l'Eau — Sci Tech Eau
Sciences et Techniques de l'Eau — STEADG
Sciences et Techniques en Perspective — Sci Tech Persp
Sciences et Techniques en Perspective — Sci Tech Perspect
Sciences et Techniques (Paris) — Sci Tech (Paris)
Sciences et Techniques Pharmaceutiques — Sci Tech Pharm
Sciences Geologiques. Bulletin — Sci Geol Bull
Sciences Geologiques. Bulletin. Institut de Geologie. Universite Louis Pasteur de Strasbourg [*France*] — Sci Geol Bull Inst Geol Univ Louis Pasteur Strasbourg
Sciences Geologiques. Memoires — Sci Geol Mem
Sciences Humaines — Sci Hum
Sciences Medicales — Sci Med
Sciences (New York) — Sciences (NY)
Sciences. New York Academy of Sciences — Sciences NY Acad Sci
Sciences Pharmaceutiques et Biologiques de Lorraine — Sci Pharm Biol Lorraine
Sciences Philosophiques et Theologiques — SPhTh
Sciences Politiques — Sciences Pol
Sciences Religieuses — SR
Sciences. Revue de la Civilisation Scientifique — Sci Rev Civilis Sci
Sciences. Revue de l'Association Francaise pour l'Advancement des Sciences (Paris) — Sciences Paris
Sciences. Revue Francaise des Sciences et des Techniques — Sci Rev Fr Sci Tech
Sciences Sociales — Sci Soc
Sciences Sociales. Academie des Sciences de L'URSS (Moscou) — Sci Soc Moscou
Sciences, Techniques, Informations CRIAC [*Centre de Recherches Industrielles en Afrique Centrale*] — Sci Tech Inf CRIAC
Sciences Veterinaires Medecine Comparee — Sci Vet Med Comp
Sciences Veterinaires Medecine Comparee — SVMCD8
Sciencia Medica — Sciencia Med
Scientia — Sc
Scientia Agricultura Sinica — Sci Agric Sin
Scientia Agriculturae Bohemoslovaca — Sci Agric Bohemoslov
Scientia Atmospherica Sinica — Sci Atmos Sin
Scientia Canadensis. Journal of the History of Canadien Science, Technology, and Medicine — Sci Canadensis
Scientia Electrica — Sci Elec
Scientia Electrica — Sci Electr
Scientia Genetica — Sci Genet
Scientia Genetica — Scientia Genet
Scientia Geologica Sinica — Sci Geol S
Scientia Geologica Sinica — Sci Geol Sin
Scientia Horticulturae — Sci Hortic
Scientia Horticulturae (Amsterdam) — Sci Hortic (Amst)
Scientia Horticulturae (Amsterdam) — SHRTA
Scientia Islandica — Sci Isl
Scientia Islandica — Sci Island
Scientia Marina — Sci Mar
Scientia Medica Italica — Sci Med Ital
Scientia Medica Italica (English Edition) — Sci Med Ital (Engl Ed)
Scientia Nova — Sci Nova
Scientia. Organo Internazionale di Sintesi Scientifica — Sc
Scientia Orientalis — Sci Orient
Scientia Paedagogica — Sc Paed
Scientia Paedagogica Experimentalis — Sci Paed Ex
Scientia Paedagogica Experimentalis — Sci Paed Exp
Scientia Pharmaceutica — Sci Pharm
Scientia. Revista Internazionale di Sintesi Scientifica — Sci
Scientia. Rivista de Tecnica y Cultura — Sci
Scientia. Rivista Internazionale di Sintesi Scientifica — SRISS
Scientia Silvae — Sci Silvae
Scientia Silvae (Beijing) — Sci Silvae (Beijing)
Scientia Silvae Sinica — Sci Silvae Sin
Scientia Sinica — Sci Sin
Scientia Sinica — Sci Sinica
Scientia Sinica [*English Edition*] — SSINA
Scientia Sinica (Chinese Edition) — Sci Sin Chin Ed
Scientia Sinica. Series A. Mathematical, Physical, Astronomical, and Technical Sciences — Sci Sinica Ser A
Scientia Sinica. Series A. Mathematical, Physical, Astronomical, and Technical Sciences (English Edition) — Sci Sin Ser A (Engl Ed)
Scientia Sinica. Series B. Chemical, Biological, Agricultural, Medical, and Earth Sciences — Sci Sin B
Scientia Sinica. Series B. Chemical, Biological, Agricultural, Medical, and Earth Sciences — Sci Sin Ser B Chem Biol Agric Med & Earth Sci
Scientia Sinica. Series B. Chemical, Biological, Agricultural, Medical, and Earth Sciences — Sci Sinica Ser B
Scientia Sinica. Series B. Chemical, Biological, Agricultural, Medical, and Earth Sciences — SSBSEF
Scientia Sinica. Series B. Chemical, Biological, Agricultural, Medical, and Earth Sciences (English Edition) — Sci Sin Ser B (Engl Ed)
Scientia Sinica. Supplement — Sci Sinica Suppl
Scientiae Pharmaceuticae. Proceedings. Congress of Pharmaceutical Sciences — Sci Pharm Proc Congr
Scientiarum Historia — ScH
Scientiarum Historia — Sci Hist
Scientiarum Historia — Scientiarum Hist
Scientiarum Nuncius Radiophonicus — Sci Nuncius Radiophonicus
Scientific Agriculture — Sci Ag
Scientific Agriculture — Sci Agr
Scientific Agriculture — Scient Agric
Scientific Agriculture (Ottawa) — Sci Agric Ottowa
Scientific Agriculture (Taipei) — Sci Agric (Taipei)
Scientific American — GSCA
Scientific American — S Am
Scientific American — SA
Scientific American — Sc Am
Scientific American — SCAMA
Scientific American — Sci Am
Scientific American — Sci Amer
Scientific American — SciA
Scientific American — Scient Am
Scientific American — Scient Amer
Scientific American Library Paperback — Sci Amer Lib Paperback
Scientific American Monthly — Sci Am Mo
Scientific American Monthly — Sci Am Monthly
Scientific American Monthly — Sci Amer Monthly
Scientific American Science and Medicine — Sci Am Sci Med
Scientific American. Supplement — Sc Am Sup
Scientific American. Supplement — Sci Am S
Scientific American. Supplement — Scient Am Suppl
Scientific and Engineering Reports. Defense Academy — Sci and Eng Rep Def Acad
Scientific and Engineering Reports. National Defense Academy (Japanese) — Sci and Eng Rep Natl Def Acad (Jpn)
Scientific and Industrial Equipment Bulletin — Sci Ind Equip Bull
Scientific and Industrial Research Council of Alberta. Reports — Sci Ind Res Counc Alberta Rep
Scientific and Technical Aerospace Reports [*NASA*] — Sci & Tech Aerosp Reports
Scientific and Technical Aerospace Reports [*NASA*] — Sci Tech Aerosp Rep
Scientific and Technical Aerospace Reports [*NASA*] — Sci Techn Aerospace Rep
Scientific and Technical Aerospace Reports [*NASA*] [*Information service or system*] — STAR
Scientific and Technical Aerospace Reports Abstract — STA Rept Abstr
Scientific and Technical Annual Reference Review — STARR
Scientific and Technical Communications. International Congress on Glass — Sci Tech Commun Int Congr Glass
Scientific and Technical Information Processing — Sci Tech Inf Process
Scientific and Technical Information Processing (English Translation) — Sci Tech Inf Process (Engl Transl)
Scientific and Technical Information Processing (English Translation of Nauchno-Tekhnicheskaya Informatsiya Seriya I) — Sci Tech Inf Process (Eng Transl Nauchno-Tekh Inf Ser I)
Scientific and Technical Report. Soap and Detergent Association — Sci Tech Rep Soap Deterg Assoc
Scientific and Technical Reports. Mining College. Akita University — Sci Tech Rep Min Coll Akita Univ
Scientific and Technical Research Centres in Australia [*Information service or system*] — STRC
Scientific and Technical Surveys. British Food Manufacturing Industries Research Association — Sci Tech Surv Br Food Manuf Ind Res Assoc
Scientific Annals. Faculty of Physics and Mathematics. Aristotelian University of Thessaloniki — Sci Ann Fac Phys Mat Aristotelian Univ Thessaloniki
Scientific Annals. Faculty of Physics and Mathematics. Aristotelian University of Thessaloniki — Sci Ann Fac Phys Math Aristotelian Univ Thessaloniki
Scientific Asahi — Sci Asahi
Scientific Association of Trinidad. Proceedings — Sc As Trinidad Pr
Scientific Australian — SCAUA
Scientific Australian — Sci Aust
Scientific Basis for Nuclear Waste Management. Proceedings. International Symposium — Sci Basis Nucl Waste Manage
Scientific Basis for Nuclear Waste Management. Proceedings. Materials Research Society Annual Meeting — Sci Basis Nucl Waste Manage Proc Mater Res Soc Annu Meet
Scientific Basis for Nuclear Waste Management. Symposium — Sci Basis Nucl Waste Manage Symp
Scientific Basis of Medicine — Sci Basis Med
Scientific Basis of Medicine. Annual Review — Sci Bas Med Ann Rev
Scientific Basis of Psychiatry — Sci Basis Psychiatr
Scientific Bulletin. Atomic Energy and New Energies Organization — Sci Bull At Energy New Energ Organ
Scientific Bulletin. Atomic Energy Organization of Iran — Sci Bull At Energy Organ Iran
Scientific Bulletin. Canada Centre for Mineral and Energy Technology — SBCED
Scientific Bulletin. Canada Centre for Mineral and Energy Technology — Sci Bull Can Cent Miner Energy Technol
Scientific Bulletin. Polytechnic Institute of Bucharest. Chemistry and Materials Science — Sci Bull Polytech Inst Bucharest Chem Mater Sci
Scientific Bulletin. University of Agricultural Sciences — Sci Bull Univ Agric Sci
Scientific Bulletins. Academy of Mining and Metallurgy (Krakow). Ceramics — Sci Bull Acad Min Metall (Krakow) Ceram
Scientific Bulletins. Academy of Mining and Metallurgy (Krakow). Electrification and Mechanization in Mining and Metallurgy — Sci Bull Acad Min Metall (Krakow) Electrif Mech Min Metall
Scientific Bulletins. Academy of Mining and Metallurgy (Krakow). Geology — Sci Bull Acad Min Metall Krakow Geol
Scientific Bulletins. Academy of Mining and Metallurgy (Krakow). Geology — Sci Bull Academ Min Metall (Krakow) Geol
Scientific Bulletins. Academy of Mining and Metallurgy (Krakow). Mathematics, Physics, Chemistry — Sci Bull Acad Min Metall (Krakow) Math Phys Chem

Scientific Bulletins. Academy of Mining and Metallurgy (Krakow). Metallurgy and Foundry Practice — Sci Bull Acad Min Metall (Krakow) Metall Foundry Pract
Scientific Bulletins. Academy of Mining and Metallurgy (Krakow). Mining — Sci Bull Acad Min Metall (Krakow) Min
Scientific Bulletins. Academy of Mining and Metallurgy (Krakow). Special Series — Sci Bull Acad Min Metall (Krakow) Spec Ser
Scientific Bulletins. Academy of Mining and Metallurgy (Krakow). Transaction — Sci Bull Acad Min Metall Krakow Trans
Scientific Bulletins. Stanislaw Staszic Academy of Mining and Metallurgy. Chemistry — Sci Bull Stanislaw Staszic Acad Min Metall Chem
Scientific Bulletins. Stanislaw Staszic Academy of Mining and Metallurgy. Physics — Sci Bull Stanislaw Staszic Acad Min Metall Phys
Scientific Bulletins. Stanislaw Staszic University of Mining and Metallurgy. Ceramics — Sci Bull Stanislaw Staszic Univ Min Metall Ceram
Scientific Bulletins. Stanislaw Staszic University of Mining and Metallurgy. Geology — Sci Bull Stanislaw Staszic Univ Min Metall Geol
Scientific Bulletins. Stanislaw Staszic University of Mining and Metallurgy. Mathematics, Physics, Chemistry — Sci Bull Stanislaw Staszic Univ Min Metall Math Phys Chem
Scientific Bulletins. Stanislaw Staszic University of Mining and Metallurgy. Mining — Sci Bull Stanislaw Staszic Univ Min Metall Min
Scientific Bulletins. Stanislaw Staszic University of Mining and Metallurgy. Sozology and Sozotechnics — Sci Bull Stanislaw Staszic Univ Min Metall Sozol Sozotech
Scientific Bulletins. Stanislaw Staszic University of Mining and Metallurgy. Special Series — Sci Bull Stanislaw Staszic Univ Min Metall Spec Ser
Scientific Bulletins. Stanislaw Staszic University of Mining and Metallurgy. Technical and Economic Problems — Sci Bull Stanislaw Staszic Univ Min Metall Tech Econ Probl
Scientific Committee on Problems of the Environment. Report — Sci Comm Probl Environ Rep
Scientific Conference. Gesellschaft Deutscher Naturforscher und Aerzte — Sci Conf Ges Dtsch Naturforsch Aerzte
Scientific Council for Africa. Publication — Sci Counc Afr Publ
Scientific Council for Africa South of the Sahara. Publication — Sci Counc Afr South Sahara Publ
Scientific Dating Methods — Sci Dating Methods
Scientific Department Bulletin. United Planters' Association of Southern India — Sci Dep Bull United Plant Assoc South India
Scientific Detective Monthly — SD
Scientific Dissertations. Silesian Univeristy. Katowice — Sci Diss Silesian Univ Katowice
Scientific Engineering. Technical Manpower Comments — SET Manpower Comments
Scientific Film Review — Scient Film Rev
Scientific Horticulture — Sci Hort
Scientific Horticulture — Scient Hort
Scientific Horticulture (Canterbury) — Sci Hortic (Canterbury)
Scientific Information Notes — Sci Inf Notes
Scientific Information Notes — Sci Info N
Scientific Information Notes — SIN
Scientific Insect Control — Sci Ins Contr
Scientific Insect Control (Kyoto) — Sci Insect Control (Kyoto)
Scientific Instruments — Sci Instr
Scientific Instruments — Scient Instrum
Scientific Instruments. Journal of Physics. E — Sci Instr J Phys E
Scientific Investigations. Freshwater and Salmon Fisheries Research. Scottish Home Department — Sci Invest Freshw Salmon Fish Res Scott Home Dep
Scientific Investigations. Freshwater and Salmon Fisheries Research. Scottish Home Department — Sci Invest Freshwater Salmon Fish Res Scott Home Dep
Scientific Journal. Royal College of Science — Sci J R Coll Sci
Scientific Journal. Royal College of Science — Sci J Roy Coll Sci
Scientific Lubrication — Sci Lubr
Scientific Lubrication and Liquid Fuel — Sci Lubr Liq Fuel
Scientific Magazine. Chemical Catheder of Katerinoslav — Sci Mag Chem Catheder Katerinoslav
Scientific Magazine. Metallurgical Catheder at Dnepropetrovsk — Sci Mag Metall Catheder Dnepropetrovsk
Scientific Meetings — Sci Meet
Scientific Memoirs by Officers of the Medical and Sanitary Department. Government of India — Sci Mem Off Med Dept Gov India
Scientific Memoirs. Kazan State University — Sci Mem Kazan State Univ
Scientific Memoirs. M. Gor'kii University of Molotov — Sci Mem M Gorkii Univ Molotov
Scientific Memoirs. University of Perm — Sci Mem Univ Perm
Scientific Monthly — Sci Mo
Scientific Monthly — Sci Mon
Scientific Monthly — Sci Monthly
Scientific Monthly — Scient Mon
Scientific Monthly — Scient Month
Scientific Monthly — SM
Scientific Notes on the Sugar Industry — Sci Notes Sugar Ind
Scientific Opinion — Sci Opin
Scientific Papers. Cancer Research Institute. Sofia — Sci Pap Cancer Res Inst Sofia
Scientific Papers. Central Research Institute. Japan Tobacco and Salt Public Corporation — Sci Pap Cent Res Inst Jpn Tob Salt Publ Corp
Scientific Papers. Civil Veterinary Department (Madras) — Scient Papers Civil Vet Dept (Madras)
Scientific Papers. College of Arts and Sciences. University of Tokyo — Sci Pap Coll Arts Sci Univ Tokyo
Scientific Papers. College of General Education — Sci Pap Coll Ed
Scientific Papers. College of General Education. University of Tokyo — Sci Pap Coll Gen Educ Univ Tokyo
Scientific Papers. College of General Education. University of Tokyo — Sci Papers College Gen Ed Univ Tokyo
Scientific Papers. College of General Education. University of Tokyo — Scient Pap Coll Gen Educ Tokyo
Scientific Papers. College of General Education. University of Tokyo — SPUTA
Scientific Papers. College of General Education. University of Tokyo (Biological Part) — Sci Pap Coll Gen Educ Univ Tokyo (Biol Part)
Scientific Papers. Faculty of Engineering. Tokushima University — Sci Pap Fac Eng Tokushima Univ
Scientific Papers. Faculty of Engineering. University of Tokushima — Sci Pap Fac Eng Univ Tokushima
Scientific Papers. Hokkaido Fisheries Scientific Institution/Hokkaido Sui San Shikenjo Hokoku — Sci Pap Hokkaido Fish Sci Inst
Scientific Papers. Imperial Fuel Research Institute (Japan) — Sci Pap Imp Fuel Res Inst (Jpn)
Scientific Papers. Institute of Algological Research. Faculty of Science. Hokkaido University — Sci Pap Inst Algol Res Fac Sci Hokkaido Univ
Scientific Papers. Institute of Chemical Technology. Pardubice — Sci Pap Inst Chem Technol Pardubice
Scientific Papers. Institute of Chemical Technology (Prague). Chemical Engineering and Automation — Sci Pap Inst Chem Technol (Prague) Chem Eng Autom
Scientific Papers. Institute of Chemical Technology. (Prague) Faculties of Inorganic and Organic Technology — Sci Pap Inst Chem Technol Prague Fac Inorg Org Technol
Scientific Papers. Institute of Chemical Technology. (Prague). Faculty of Food Industry — Sci Pap Inst Chem Technol (Prague) Fac Food Ind
Scientific Papers. Institute of Chemical Technology. (Prague). Faculty of Fuel and Water — Sci Pap Inst Chem Technol Prague Fac Technol Fuel Water
Scientific Papers. Institute of Chemical Technology. (Prague). Inorganic Technology — Sci Pap Inst Chem Technol (Prague) Inorg Technol
Scientific Papers. Institute of Chemical Technology. (Prague). Technology of Water — Sci Pap Inst Chem Technol Prague Technol Water
Scientific Papers. Institute of Electric Machine Systems. Wroclaw Technical University — Sci Pap Inst Electr Mach Syst Wroclaw Tech Univ
Scientific Papers. Institute of Electric Power Engineering. Wroclaw Technical University — Sci Pap Inst Electr Power Eng Wroclaw Tech Univ
Scientific Papers. Institute of Organic and Physical Chemistry. Wroclaw Technical University — Sci Pap Inst Org Phys Chem Wroclaw Tech Univ
Scientific Papers. Institute of Physical and Chemical Research — Sci Pap Inst Phys and Chem Res
Scientific Papers. Institute of Physical and Chemical Research — SPIPA
Scientific Papers. Institute of Physical and Chemical Research (Japan) — Sci Pap Inst Phys Chem Res (Jpn)
Scientific Papers. Institute of Physical and Chemical Research (Tokyo) — Sci Pap Inst Phys Chem Res (Tokyo)
Scientific Papers of the College of Arts and Sciences. University of Tokyo — Sci Papers College Arts Sci Univ Tokyo
Scientific Papers of the University of Chemical Technology Prague — Sci Pap Univ Chem Technol Prague
Scientific Papers. Osaka University — Sci Pap Osaka Univ
Scientific Papers. Pasteur Institute for Veterinary Research and Biological Products (Bucharest) — Sci Pap Pasteur Inst Vet Res Biol Prod Bucharest
Scientific Papers. Prague Institute of Chemical Technology. Analytical Chemistry — Sci Pap Prague Inst Chem Technol Anal Chem
Scientific Papers. Prague Institute of Chemical Technology. C. Organic Chemistry and Technology — Sci Pap Prague Inst Chem Technol C Org Chem Technol
Scientific Papers. Prague Institute of Chemical Technology. D. Technology of Fuel — Sci Pap Prague Inst Chem Technol D Technol Fuel
Scientific Papers. Prague Institute of Chemical Technology. E. Food — Sci Pap Prague Inst Chem Technol E Food
Scientific Papers. Prague Institute of Chemical Technology. F. Technology of Water and Enviroment — Sci Pap Prague Inst Chem Technol F Technol Water Environ
Scientific Papers. Prague Institute of Chemical Technology. G. Mineralogy — Sci Pap Prague Inst Chem Technol G Mineral
Scientific Papers. Prague Institute of Chemical Technology. P. Material Science and Measurement Technique — Sci Pap Prague Inst Chem Technol P. Mater Sci Meas Tech
Scientific Papers. Prague Institute of Chemical Technology. Part C. Organic Chemistry and Technology — Sci Papers Prague ICT C
Scientific Papers. Prague Institute of Chemical Technology. S. Polymers-Chemistry, Properties, and Processing — Sci Pap Prague Inst Chem Technol S Polym Chem Prop Process
Scientific Papers. Prague Institute of Chemical Technology. Section: Chemical Engineering — Sci Pap Prague Inst Chem Technol Sect Chem Eng
Scientific Papers. Prague Institute of Chemical Technology. T. Educational Process — Sci Pap Prague Inst Chem Technol T Educ Process
Scientific Papers. University of Chemical Technology. Pardubice — Sci Pap Univ Chem Technol Pardubice
Scientific Pest Control — Sci Pest Contr
Scientific Pest Control — Sci Pest Control
Scientific Pest Control (Kyoto) — Sci Pest Control (Kyoto)
Scientific Presentations. Annual Meeting. American Animal Hospital Association — Sci Presentations Annu Meet Am Anim Hosp Assoc
Scientific Proceedings. Cardiff Medical Society — Sci Proc Cardiff Med Soc
Scientific Proceedings. Royal Dublin Society — Sci Proc Dublin Soc
Scientific Proceedings. Royal Dublin Society — Sci Proc R Dublin Soc
Scientific Proceedings. Royal Dublin Society — Sci Proc Roy Dublin Soc
Scientific Proceedings. Royal Dublin Society — Scient Proc R Dubl Soc
Scientific Proceedings. Royal Dublin Society. New Series — Sci Proc R Dublin Soc New Ser
Scientific Proceedings. Royal Dublin Society. Series A — Sci Proc R Dublin Soc A

Scientific Proceedings. Royal Dublin Society. Series A — Sci Proc R Dublin Soc Ser A
Scientific Proceedings. Royal Dublin Society. Series B — Sci Proc R Dublin Soc Ser B
Scientific Proceedings. Royal Dublin Society. Series B — Sci Proc Roy Dublin Soc Ser B
Scientific Progress [*London*] — Sci Pro
Scientific Progress (Amoy, China) — Sci Prog Amoy China
Scientific Publication. Pan American Health Organization — Sci Publ Pan Am Health Organ
Scientific Publication. Research Institute. Federal School of Physical Education. Magglingen — Sci Publ Res Inst Fed Sch Phys Educ Magglingen
Scientific Publications. Fuji Photo Film Company Limited [*Japan*] — Sci Publ Fuji Photo Film Co Ltd
Scientific Publications. Fuji Photo Film Company Ltd. — Sci Publ Fuji Photo Film C
Scientific Publications of Forestry and Timber Industry — Sci Publ For Timber Ind
Scientific Publications. Research Institute of Radiology and Radiation Hygiene [*Bulgaria*] — Sci Publ Res Inst Radiol Radiat Hyg
Scientific Publications. Science Museum of Minnesota — Sci Publ Sci Mus Minn
Scientific Publications. Science Museum of Minnesota (St. Paul) — Sci Publ Sci Mus (St Paul)
Scientific Publications. University of Forestry and Timber Industry — Sci Publ Univ For Timber Ind
Scientific Records. Gorky State University — Sci Rec Gorky State Univ
Scientific Records. Leningrad University — Sci Rec Leningrad Univ
Scientific Records. S. M. Kirov Kazakh State University — Sci Rec S M Kirov Kaz State Univ
Scientific Report. Central Research Institute. Kasauli — Sci Rep Cent Res Inst Kasauli
Scientific Report. Ehime Prefecture Paper Making Experiment Station — Sci Rep Ehime Prefect Pap Making Exp Stn
Scientific Report. Faculty of Agriculture. Ibaraki University — Sci Rep Fac Agr Ibaraki Univ
Scientific Report. Faculty of Agriculture. Okayama University — Sci Rep Fac Agr Okayama Univ
Scientific Report. Hoyo University of Agriculture — Sci Rep Hoyo Univ Agr
Scientific Report. Inter-Union Commission on Geodynamics — Sci Rep Inter-Union Comm Geodyn
Scientific Report. Kyoto Prefectural University — Sci Rep Kyoto Pref Univ
Scientific Report. Laboratory for Amphibian Biology. Hiroshima University — Sci Rep Lab Amphib Biol Hiroshima Univ
Scientific Report. Laboratory for Amphibian Biology. Hiroshima University — SRLUDT
Scientific Report. Miyagi Agricultural College — Sci Rep Miyagi Agr Coll
Scientific Report. Shiga Prefectural Junior College — Sci Rep Shiga Pref Jr Coll
Scientific Report. Tohoku University. Series IV. Biology — Sci Rep Tohoku Univ Ser IV
Scientific Report. Yerevan Physics Institute — Sci Rep Yerevan Phys Inst
Scientific Reports. Agricultural College of Norway — Sci Rep Agric Col Norw
Scientific Reports. Agricultural College of Norway — Sci Rep Agric Coll Norway
Scientific Reports. Agricultural Expedition to Cambodia — Sci Rep Agric Exped Cambodia
Scientific Reports. Agricultural University of Norway — Sci Rep Agruc Univ Norw
Scientific Reports. British Antarctic Survey — Sci Rep Br Antarct Surv
Scientific Reports. Ehime Agricultural College — Sci Rep Ehime Agric Coll
Scientific Reports. Faculty of Agriculture. Ibaraki University — Sci Rep Fac Agric Ibaraki Univ
Scientific Reports. Faculty of Agriculture. Meijo University — Sci Rep Fac Agric Meijo Univ
Scientific Reports. Faculty of Agriculture. Okayama University — Scient Rep Fac Agric Okayama Univ
Scientific Reports. Faculty of Science. Ege University — Sci Rep Fac Sci Ege Univ
Scientific Reports. Government Institute for Infectious Diseases. Tokyo Imperial University — Sci Rep Gov Inst Infect Dis Tokyo Imp Univ
Scientific Reports. Government Institute for Infectious Diseases. Tokyo Imperial University — Scient Rep Govt Inst Infect Dis Tokyo Imp Univ
Scientific Reports. Hokkaido Fisheries Experimental Station — Sci Rep Hokkaido Fish Exp Stn
Scientific Reports. Hokkaido Salmon Hatchery — Sci Rep Hokkaido Salmon Hatchery
Scientific Reports. Indian Agricultural Research Institute — Sci Rep Indian Agric Res Inst
Scientific Reports. Insitute for Atmospheric Environmental Research (Garmisch-Partenkirchen, Germany) — Sci Rep Inst Atmos Environ Res Garmisch Partenkirchen Ger
Scientific Reports. Istituto Superiore di Sanita — Sci Rep Ist Super Sanita
Scientific Reports. Kagawa Prefectural Fisheries Experimental Station — Sci Rep Kagawa Prefect Fish Exp Stn
Scientific Reports. Kazan State Universtiy — Sci Rep Karzan State Univ
Scientific Reports. Kyoto Prefectural University. Agriculture — Sci Rep Kyoto Prefect Univ Agric
Scientific Reports. Kyoto Prefectural University. Agriculture — Scient Rep Kyoto Prefect Univ Agric
Scientific Reports. Kyoto Prefectural University. Natural Science and Life Science [*Japan*] — Sci Rep Kyoto Prefect Univ Nat Sci Life Sci
Scientific Reports. Kyoto Prefectural University. Natural Science, Living Science, and Welfare Science [*Japan*] — Sci Rep Kyoto Prefect Univ Nat Sci Living Sci Welfare Sci
Scientific Reports. Matsuyama Agricultural College — Sci Rep Matsuyama Agric Coll
Scientific Reports. Meiji Seika Kaisha — Sci Rep Meiji Seika Kaisha
Scientific Reports of Shiga Agricultural Experiment Station/Shiga-Ken Nogyo Shikenjo Kenkyu Hokoku — Sci Rep Shiga Agric Exp Sta
Scientific Reports. Research Institute for Theoretical Physics. Hiroshima University [*Japan*] — Sci Rep Res Inst Theor Phys Hiroshima Univ
Scientific Reports. Saikyo University. Agriculture — Sci Rep Saikyo Univ Agric
Scientific Reports. Saitama University. Series B — Sci Rep Saitama Univ Ser B
Scientific Reports. Shiga Agricultural College — Sci Rep Shiga Agric Coll
Scientific Reports. Toyo Rayon Co., Ltd. — Sci Rep Toyo Rayon Co
Scientific Reports. University of Agricultural Sciences. Godollo, Hungary — Sci Rep Univ Agric Sci Godollo Hung
Scientific Reports. Whales Research Institute (Tokyo) — Sci Rep Whales Res Inst (Tokyo)
Scientific Research — SCREB
Scientific Research Council of Jamaica. Journal — Sci Res Counc Jam J
Scientific Research (Dacca) [*Pakistan*] — Sci Res (Dacca)
Scientific Research in British Universities and Colleges — Sci Res Br Univ Coll
Scientific Research. Natural Science Edition [*People's Republic of China*] — Sci Res Natl Sci Ed
Scientific Research (New York) — Sci Res (NY)
Scientific Researches — Sci Res
Scientific Researches (Bangladesh) — Scient Res (Bangladesh)
Scientific Researches (Dacca, Bangladesh) — Sci Res (Dacca, Bangladesh)
Scientific Review of Civil Engineering — Sci Rev Civ Eng
Scientific Roll and Magazine of Systematized Notes — Sci Roll Mag Syst Notes
Scientific Roll and Magazine of Systematized Notes. Botanical Section. Bacteria — Sci Roll Mag Syst Notes Bot Sect Bact
Scientific Serials in Australian Libraries — SSAL
Scientific Series. Inland Waters Branch. Canada — Sci Ser Inland Waters Branch Can
Scientific Series. Inland Waters Directorate (Canada) — Sci Ser Inland Waters Dir (Can)
Scientific Series. Inland Waters/Lands Directorate (Canada) — Sci Ser Inland Waters Lands Dir (Can)
Scientific Society of San Antonio. Bulletin — Sc Soc San Antonio B
Scientific South Africa — Sci S Afr
Scientific Transactions. Royal Dublin Society — Scient Trans Dubl Soc
Scientific Tree Topics — Sci Tree Top
Scientific Worker — Scient Work
Scientific Works. Agricultural College Nicolae Balcescu. Bucharest. Bucharest. Seria A. Agronomy — Sci Works Agric Coll Bucharest Ser A
Scientific Works. Agronomic Institute Nicolae Balcescu. Bucharest. Series C. Zootechny and Veterinary Science — Sci Works Agron Inst Nicolae Balcescu Bucharest Ser C
Scientific Works. Cancer Research Institute (Sofia) — Sci Works Cancer Res Inst Sofia
Scientific Works. Forest Research Institute in Zvolen — VPVLBZ
Scientific Works. Forest Research Institute (Zvolen) — Sci Works For Res Inst (Zvolen)
Scientific Works. Higher Institute of Agriculture G. Dimitrov. Zootechnical Faculty — Sci Works Higher Inst Agric Zootech Fac
Scientific Works. Higher Institute of Agriculture. Sofia. Agricultural Faculty. Series. Plant Growing — Sci Works Higher Inst Agric Sofia Agric Fac Ser Plant Grow
Scientific Works. Higher Institute of Veterinary Medicine (Sofia) — Sci Works Higher Inst Vet Med Sofia
Scientific Works. Higher Institute of Zootechnics and Veterinary Medicine. Faculty of Veterinary Medicine. Stara Zagora — Sci Works Higher Inst Zootech Vet Med Vet Med Stara Zagora
Scientific Works. Higher Medical Institute of Pleven — Sci Works High Med Inst Pleven
Scientific Works. Higher Medical Institute. Pleven — Sci Works Higher Med Inst Pleven
Scientific Works. Postgraduate Medical Institute (Sofia) — Sci Works Postgrad Med Inst (Sofia)
Scientific Works. Poultry Science. Poultry Research Institute — HYDIDH
Scientific Works. Poultry Science. Poultry Research Institute — Sci Works Poult Sci Poult Res Inst
Scientific Works. Research Institute of Animal Production at Nitra — Sci Works Res Inst Anim Prod Nitra
Scientific Works. Research Institute of Animal Production at Nitra — VPVZB9
Scientific Works. Research Institute of Epidemiology and Microbiology (Sofia) — Sci Works Res Inst Epidemiol Microbiol (Sofia)
Scientific World [*England*] — Sci World
Scientific World. Natural Science Society of China/K'o Hsueeh Shih Chieh. Chung Hua Tsu Jao K'o Hsueeh She (Chungking and Nanking) — Sci World Chunking Nanking
Scientific Yearbook. Veterinary Faculty (Thessalonica) — Sci Yearb Vet Fac (Thessalonica)
Scientifical Reports. Lithuanian Branch of All-Union Research Institute of Butter and Cheese Industries. USSR — Sci Rep Lith Branch All Union Res Inst Butter Cheese Ind USS
Scientific-Technical Conference Electrostatics in Industry. ELSTAT-80 — Sci Tech Conf Electrost Ind ELSTAT 80
Scientific-Technical Conference Glass and Fine Ceramics — Sci Tech Conf Glass Fine Ceram
Scientists and Professional Engineers Employment Registry [*Database*] — SPEER
Scientists of Our Time — Sci Our Time
Scienza del Farmaco — Sci Farm
Scienza dell'Alimentazione — Sci Aliment
Scienza dell'Alimentazione — Scienza Aliment
Scienza e Tecnica — Sci Tec
Scienza e Tecnica Lattiero-Casearia — Sci Tec Latt-Casearia
Scienza e Tecnologia degli Alimenti — Sci Tecnol Alimenti
Scienza e Tecnologia degli Alimenti — Scienza Tecnol Aliment

Scienze la Matematica e il Loro Insegnamento — Sci Mat Loro Insegnamento
Scienze Matematiche — Sci Mat
Sci-Tech News — STNWA
Scnadinavian Journal of Plastic and Reconstructive and Hand Surgery — Scand J Plst Reconstr Hand Surg
Scone and Upper Hunter Historical Society. Journal — Scone & Upper Hunter Hist Soc J
Scoops — SCP
Scotland Department of Agriculture and Fisheries. Marine Research — Scotl Dep Agric Fish Mar Res
Scotland Department of Agriculture and Fisheries. Technical Bulletin — Scotl Dep Agric Fish Tech Bull
Scots Law Times — SLT
Scots Magazine — Scots Mag
Scots Philosophical Monograph Series — Scots Philos Monograph Ser
Scotsman — SC
Scotsman Magazine — Scotsman Mag
Scott Report — Scott Rep
Scottish Agriculture — Scot Agr
Scottish Agriculture — Scott Agric
Scottish Archaeological Forum — Scot A Forum
Scottish Archaeological Forum — Scot Archaeol Forum
Scottish Art and Letters — Scot AL
Scottish Art Review — Scot Art R
Scottish Art Review — Scot Art Rev
Scottish Art Review — Scott Art Rev
Scottish Art Review — Scottish Art R
Scottish Australasian — Scott Australas
Scottish Bankers Magazine — Scott Bankers Mag
Scottish Bankers Magazine — Scottish Bankers M
Scottish Bee Journal — Scott Bee J
Scottish Beekeeper — Scott Beekeep
Scottish Beekeeper — Scott Beekpr
Scottish Birds — Scott Birds
Scottish Birds. Journal. Scottish Ornithologists' Club — Scott Birds J Scott Ornithol Club
Scottish Botanical Review — Scott Bot Rev
Scottish Economic and Social History — Scott Econ Soc Hist
Scottish Economic Bulletin — Scott Econ Bull
Scottish Economic Bulletin — Scottish Econ Bul
Scottish Educational Journal — Scottish Ednl J
Scottish Educational Review — Scott Educ Rev
Scottish Educational Studies — Scot Edu St
Scottish Educational Studies — Scottish Ednl Studies
Scottish Electrical Engineer — Scott Elect Engr
Scottish Farmer and Farming World — Scott Fmr
Scottish Field — Scott Field
Scottish Fisheries Bulletin — Scott Fish Bull
Scottish Fisheries Research Report — Scott Fish Res Rep
Scottish Forestry — Scott For
Scottish Forestry Journal — Scott For J
Scottish Gaelic Studies — ScoGaelS
Scottish Gaelic Studies — ScoGS
Scottish Gaelic Studies — SGS
Scottish Genealogist — Scott Genealog
Scottish Geographical Magazine — Scot Geog M
Scottish Geographical Magazine — Scot Geogr Mag
Scottish Geographical Magazine — Scot Geogr Mg
Scottish Geographical Magazine — Scot GM
Scottish Geographical Magazine — Scott Geogr Mag
Scottish Geographical Magazine — Scottish Geog Mag
Scottish Geographical Magazine — Scottish Geogr Mag
Scottish Geographical Magazine — SGM
Scottish Georgian Society. Bulletin — Scottish Georgian Soc Bull
Scottish Historical Review — Sc HR
Scottish Historical Review — Scot His R
Scottish Historical Review — Scot Hist R
Scottish Historical Review — Scot Hist Rev
Scottish Historical Review — Scot Hist Riv
Scottish Historical Review — Scott Hist Rev
Scottish Historical Review — SHR
Scottish Horticultural Research Institute. Annual Report — Scott Hortic Res Inst Annu Rep
Scottish Industrial History — Scott Ind Hist
Scottish Journal of Adult Education — Scott J Adult Educ
Scottish Journal of Agriculture — Scott J Agric
Scottish Journal of Geology — Scot J Geol
Scottish Journal of Geology — Scott J Geol
Scottish Journal of Physical Education — Scot J PE
Scottish Journal of Political Economy — ScJ
Scottish Journal of Political Economy — Scot J Pol Econ
Scottish Journal of Political Economy — Scot J Poli
Scottish Journal of Political Economy — Scott J Polit Econ
Scottish Journal of Political Economy — Scottish J Pol Economy
Scottish Journal of Political Economy — SJP
Scottish Journal of Political Economy — SJPE
Scottish Journal of Religious Studies — Scot J Rel
Scottish Journal of Religious Studies — Scot J Rel St
Scottish Journal of Theology — PSJT
Scottish Journal of Theology [*Edinburgh*] — ScJTh
Scottish Journal of Theology — Scot J Th
Scottish Journal of Theology — Scot J Theo
Scottish Journal of Theology — ScotJt
Scottish Journal of Theology — Scott J Theology
Scottish Journal of Theology — SJT
Scottish Journal of Theology — SJTh
Scottish Journal of Theology. Occasional Papers — SJThOP
Scottish Jurist — Scott Jur
Scottish Labour History Society Journal — Scott Labour Hist Soc J
Scottish Language — ScotL
Scottish Language — Scott Lang
Scottish Law Gazette — SLG
Scottish Law Review — Scot L Rev
Scottish Law Review — Scot LR
Scottish Life-Boat — Scott Life-Boat
Scottish Literary Journal — Sc L J
Scottish Literary Journal — Scot Lit J
Scottish Literary Journal — Scott Lit J
Scottish Marine Biological Association. Annual Report — Scott Mar Biol Assoc Annu Rep
Scottish Marxist — Scott Marxist
Scottish Medical and Surgical Journal — Scott Med Surg J
Scottish Medical Journal — Scot Med J
Scottish Medical Journal — Scott Med J
Scottish Medicine — Scott Med
Scottish Mountaineering Club Journal — Scott Mountaineering Club J
Scottish Music and Drama — Scottish Mus
Scottish National Dictionary — SND
Scottish Naturalist — Scott Nat
Scottish Naturalist (Perth) — Scott Naturalist Perth
Scottish Notes and Queries — SNQ
Scottish Opera News — Scott Opera N
Scottish Review — Scot R
Scottish Review — Scott R
Scottish Review — Scott Rev
Scottish Studies — ScoS
Scottish Studies — Scot Stud
Scottish Studies — Scott S
Scottish Studies — Scott Stud
Scottish Studies — ScS
Scottish Text Society — STS
Scottish Trade Union Review — Scott Trade Union Rev
Scottish Tradition — Scott Tradit
Scottish Universities Summer School — Scott Univ Summer Sch
Scottish Universities Summer School in Physics. Proceedings — Scott Univ Summer Sch Phys Proc
Scottish Wildlife — Scott Wildl
Scotts Turfgrass Research Conference. Proceedings — Scotts Turfgrass Res Conf Proc
Scouting in New South Wales — Scouting in NSW
SCRAM [*Scottish Campaign to Resist the Atomic Menace*] **Energy Bulletin** — SCRAM Energy Bull
Screen Education — Screen Ed
Screen Education Notes — Screen Ed Notes
Scribner's Commentator — Scrib Com
Scribner's Magazine — Scrib M
Scribner's Magazine — Scribn Mag
Scribner's Monthly — Scrib
Scrinia Florae Selectae — Scrinia Flor Sel
Scrinium — Scr
Scrinium Historiale — Scrin Hist
Scrinium Theologicum. Contributi di Scienze Religiose — Scrin Theol
Scrip. Leader in World Pharmaceutical News — SBN
Scripps Institution of Oceanography. Bulletin — Scripps Inst Oceanogr Bull
Scripps Institution of Oceanography. Contributions — Scripps Inst Oceanogr Contrib
Scripta Botanica — Scripta Bot
Scripta Botanica Musei Transsilvanici — Scripta Bot Mus Transsilv
Scripta Classica Israelica — SCI
Scripta. Computer Science and Applied Mathematics — Scripta Comput Sci Appl Math
Scripta et Documenta. Abadia de Montserrat — SDM
Scripta et Documenta. Abadia de Montserrat. Monastica — SDMM
Scripta Facultatis Scientiarum Naturalium Universita J. E. Purkyne Brunensis. Biiologia — Scr Fac Sci Nat Univ Purkynianae Bru Biol
Scripta Facultatis Scientiarum Naturalium Universita J. E. Purkyne Brunensis. Biologia — Scripta Fac Sci Natur UJEP Brunensis Biol
Scripta Facultatis Scientiarum Naturalium Universita J. E. Purkyne Brunensis. Chemia — Scripta Fac Sci Natur UJEP Brunensis Chem
Scripta Facultatis Scientiarum Naturalium Universita J. E. Purkyne Brunensis. Geologia — Scripta Fac Sci Natur UJEP Brunensis Geol
Scripta Facultatis Scientiarum Naturalium Universita J. E. Purkyne Brunensis. Mathematica — Scripta Fac Sci Natur UJEP Brunensis Math
Scripta Facultatis Scientiarum Naturalium Universita J. E. Purkyne Brunensis. Physica — Scripta Fac Sci Natur UJEP Brunensis Phys
Scripta Facultatis Scientiarum Naturalium Universitatis Purkynianae Brunensis — Scr Fac Sci Nat Univ Purkynianae Brun
Scripta Facultatis Scientiarum Naturalium Universitatis Purkynianae Brunensis — Scripta Fac Sci Natur Univ Purk Brun
Scripta Facultatis Scientiarum Naturalium Universitatis Purkynianae Brunensis. Geologia — Scr Fac Sci Nat Univ Purkynianae Brunensis Geol
Scripta Facultatis Scientiarum Naturalium Universitatis Purkynianae Brunensis. Physica — Scr Fac Sci Nat Univ Purkynianae Brunensis Phys
Scripta Geobotanica — Scr Geobot
Scripta Geographica — Scr Geogr
Scripta Geologica — Scr Geol
Scripta Geologica — Scri Geol
Scripta Geologica (Leiden) — Scr Geol (Leiden)
Scripta Hierosolymitana — Scr Hie
Scripta Hierosolymitana — Scr Hierosolymitana

Scripta Hierosolymitana — ScrH
Scripta Hierosolymitana [*Jerusalem*] — ScrHier
Scripta Hierosolymitana [*Jerusalem*] — ScrHierosol
Scripta Hierosolymitana — Script Hier
Scripta Hierosolymitana. Publications of the Hebrew University. Jerusalem — Scr Hieros
Scripta Hierosolymitana. Publications of the Hebrew University (Jerusalem) — Scr Hierosolymitana Publ Heb Univ (Jerus)
Scripta Hierosolymitana. Publications of the Hebrew University (Jerusalem) — SHPHUJ
Scripta Instituti Donneriana Aboensis — Scr I Donn
Scripta Instituti Donneriani Aboensis — SIDA
Scripta Islandica — ScI
Scripta Islandica — SIs
Scripta Judaica — Sc J
Scripta Judaica [*Oxford*] — ScrJud
Scripta Materialia — Scr Mater
Scripta Mathematica — Scr Math
Scripta Mathematica — Scripta Math
Scripta Medica (Brno) — Scr Med (Brno)
Scripta Medica Facultatis Medicae Universitatis Brunensis Purkynianae — Scr Med Fac Med Univ Brun Purkynianae
Scripta Medica. Facultatum Medicinae. Universitatum Brunensis et Olomucensis [*Czechoslovakia*] — Scr Med Fac Med Univ Brun Olomuc
Scripta Metallurgica — Scr Met
Scripta Metallurgica — Scr Metall
Scripta Metallurgica — Scrip Metal
Scripta Metallurgica et Materialia — Scr Metall Mater
Scripta Minora — SM
Scripta Minora Humanistiska Vetenskapssamfundet i Lund — SMHVL
Scripta Minora-Regiae Societatis Humaniorum Litterarum Lundensis — Scr Minora
Scripta Minores — SM
Scripta Pontificii Instituti Biblici — SPIB
Scripta Professorum Facultatis Theologicae Marianum — SPFTM
Scripta Recenter Edita — SRE
Scripta Scientifica Medica — Scr Sci Med
Scripta Scientifica Medica. Annual Scientific Papers — Scr Sci Med Annu Sci Pap
Scripta Theologica — Scr Th
Scripta Theologica [*Pamplona*] — ScrTheol
Scriptores Byzantini — Scr Byz
Scriptores Ecclesiastici Hispano-Latini Veteris et Medii Aevi — Script Eccl Hisp Lat
Scriptores Ecclesiastici Hispano-Latini Veteris et Medii Aevi — SEHL
Scriptores Latini Hiberniae — Script Lat Hib
Scriptores Latini Hiberniae — SLH
Scriptores Ordinis Praedicatorum — SOP
Scriptores Ordinis S. Benedicti — SOSB
Scriptores Rerum Hungaricarum — SRH
Scriptores Rerum Hungaricarum — SSRH
Scriptores Rerum Mythicarum Latini Tres Romae Nuper Reperti — Script Rer Myth Lat Tr Rom Nup Rep
Scriptores Rerum Prussicarum — SRP
Scriptores Rerum Suecicarum Medii Aevi — SRSMA
Scriptoria Medii Aevi Helvetica — SMAH
Scriptorium — Sc
Scriptorium [*Anvers, Belgium*] — Scr
Scriptorium — Scrip
Scriptorium — Script
Scriptorium Victoriense — Scr Vict
Scriptorum Classicorum Bibliotheca Oxoniensia — SCBO
Scriptorum Ecclestiasticorum Opuscula — SEO
Scriptura Sacra et Monumenta Orientis Antiqui — SSMOA
Scripture [*Edinburgh, Scotland*] — Scrip
Scripture — Script
Scripture Bulletin — Scr B
Scripture Bulletin — Scr Bull
Scripture Bulletin — Script B
Scritti Demolinguistici — Scr Demolinguist
Scritti Monastici — Scr Mon
Scrittori Stranieri. Il Fiore delle Varie Letterature in Traduzioni Italiane — Fiore
Scrutiny — SCR
Sculpture International — Sculp Int
Sculpture Review — Sculpt R
Scuola Cattolica — SC
Scuola Cattolica — ScCatt
Scuola Cattolica. Rivista di Scienze Religiose — Scuol C
Scuola e Citta — Scu Citta
Scuola e Cultura del Mondo — SeC
Scuola e Diritto — Scuola Dir
Scuola e Vita — SV
Scuola in Azione — Sc Azione
Scuola Italiana — SI
Scuola Positiva. Rivista di Criminologia e Diritto Criminale — Scuola Pos
Scuola Salernitana — Scu Salern
Sdelovaci Technika — Sdelovaci Tech
Se Mulli (New Physics) — Se Mulli (New Phys)
Sea Fisheries Research Station (Haifa). Bulletin — Sea Fish Res Stn (Haifa) Bull
Sea Frontiers — GSEA
Sea Frontiers — Sea Front
Sea Grant College Technical Report. University of Wisconsin — Sea Grant Coll Tech Rep Univ Wis
Sea Grant Network [*Database*] — SGNET
Sea Grant Publications Index — Sea Grant Pub Ind
Sea Technology — Sea Technol
Sea Technology — SEATA
Sea View Hospital. Bulletin — Sea View Hosp Bull
Sea Water Conversion Laboratory Report — Sea Water Convers Lab Rep
Seaby's Coin and Medal Bulletin — Coin Medal Bull
Seaby's Coin and Medal Bulletin — SCMB
Seaby's Coin and Medal Bulletin — Seabys Coin Bull
Seacoast New Hampshire. Business Digest — NH Bsns
Seafood Business — Seafood Bus
Seafood Export Journal — Seafood Export J
Seafood Merchandising — Seafood Merch
Seagoer Magazine (London) — SML
SEAISI (South East Asia Iron and Steel Institute) Quarterly — SEAISI Q
Sealift Magazine — SLM
Seamen's Journal — Seamens J
SEAN [*Scientific Event Alert Network*] **Bulletin** [*Washington, DC*] — SEAN Bull
Sean O'Casey Review — S O Rev
Sean O'Casey Review — Sean O Cas
Sean O'Casey Review — SOC Rev
Seanad Debates [*Ireland*] — Seanad Deb
Seance Publique Annuelle. Academie de Pharmacie — Seance Pub Ann Acad Pharm
Seances Generales. Societe des Lettres, Sciences, et Arts et d'Agriculture — SGSLM
Seances Publiques. Societe des Amateurs des Sciences, de l'Agriculture, et des Arts de Lille — Seances Publiques Soc Amateurs Sci Lille
Seances. Societe Belge de Biologie — Seanc Soc Belge Biol
Seances. Societe Francaise de Physique — Seanc Soc Fr Phys
Seanchas Ardhmaca — Sean Ard
Seara Medica — Seara Med
Seara Medica Neurocirurgica — Seara Med Neurocir
Seara Nova — SeN
Seara Nova — SNov
Search: Agriculture — Search Agric
Search Agriculture. Entomology (Ithaca, New York) — Search Agric Ent (Ithaca NY)
Search Agriculture (Geneva, New York) — Search Agric (Geneva NY)
Search Agriculture. New York State Agricultural Experiment Station (Ithaca) — Search Agric NY State Agric Exp Stn (Ithaca)
Search and Seizure Law Report — Search and Seizure L Rep
Search Program for Infrared Spectra [*Database*] — SPIR
Searchable Physics Information Notices [*Database*] — SPIN
Searching Together — Search Together
SEARMG [*Southeast Asian Research Materials Group*] **Newsletter** — SEARMG Newsl
Sears Foundation for Marine Research. Memoir — Sears Found Marine Research Mem
Seasoning Science — Seas Sci
Seasons. Federation of Ontario Naturalists — SEAS
Seatrade — SRA
Seatrade Business Review — Seatrade BR
Seatrade North American Yearbook — Sea Yrbk
Seatrade Week — Seatrade We
Seattle Business — Seattl Bsn
Seattle Symphony Orchestra. Program Notes — Seattle Sym
Seattle Times — Seattle T
Seaway Review — Seaway Rev
SEC [*Securities and Exchange Commission*] **Accounting Rules. Commerce Clearing House** — SEC Accounting R CCH
SEC: Bi-Monthly Magazine for Employees of the State Electricity Commission of Victoria — SEC
SEC [*Securities and Exchange Commission*] **Bulletin** [*Philippines*] — SEC Bull
SEC Magazine: Journal of the State Electricity Commission of Victoria — SEC Mag
SEC [*US Securities and Exchange Commission*] **Monthly Statistical Review** — SEC Mon Stat Rev
SEC [*US Securities and Exchange Commission*] **News Digest** — SEC News
Sechenov Journal of Physiology of the USSR — Sechenov J Physiol USSR
Sechenov. Physiological Journal of the USSR — Sechenov Physiol J USSR
Sechenov Physiological Journal of the USSR [*English translation of Fiziologicheskii Zhurnal SSSR Imeni I. M. Sechenova*] — SPJUA2
Seckauer Geschichtliche Studien — SGSt
Seckauer Hefte — SH
SECOL [*Southeastern Conference on Linguistics*] **Review** — SECOLR
SECOLAS [*Southeastern Conference on Latin American Studies*] **Annals** — SECOLAS A
Secolul XX — SXX
Second Century — Second Cent
Second City — Sec City
Second Coming — Se C
Second Cycle des Universites et Ecoles d'Ingenieurs — Second Cycle Univ Ecoles Ing
Second Opinions of Health Care Issues — Second Opin Health Care Issues
Second Wave — Sec Wave
Secondary Education — Sec Ed
Secondary Forms of Hypertension. Current Diagnosis and Management. International Symposium of Nephrology — Second Forms Hypertens Int Symp Nephrol
Secondary Industries Digest — Sec Ind Digest
Secondary Ion Mass Spectrometry. Proceedings. International Conference on Secondary Ion Mass Spectrometry — Second Ion Mass Spectrom Proc Int Conf
Secondary Learning Assistance Teachers' Association. Newsletter — SLATA
Secondary Students Information Press — SSIP
Secondary Teacher — Sec Teach

Secondary Teacher — Sec Teacher
Secondary Teacher — Secondary Teach
Second-Line Agents in the Treatment of Rheumatic Diseases — Second Line Agents Treat Rheum Dis
Secretaria de Educacion Publica [*Mexico*] — SEP
Secretaria de Industria y Comercio. Boletin (Argentina) — Secr Ind Comer Bol (Argent)
Secretariat Papers. International Wheat Council — Secr Pap Int Wheat Counc
Secretary — SEC
Secretion and Its Control. Annual Symposium — Secretion Its Control Annu Symp
Sections Romandes du Club Alpin Suisse — Sect Romandes Club Alpin Suisse
Securite et Medecine du Travail — Secur Med Trav
Securities and Federal Corporate Law Report — Sec & Fed Corp L Rep
Securities Industry Review [*Singapore*] — Sec Ind R
Securities Law Review — Sec L Rev
Securities Regulation and Law Report. Bureau of National Affairs — Sec Reg & L Rep BNA
Securities Regulation and Law Reports [*Bureau of National Affairs*] — Sec Reg & L Rep
Securities Regulation and Law Reports [*Bureau of National Affairs*] — SRLR
Securities Regulation and Law Reports (Bureau of National Affairs) — BNA Sec Reg
Securities Regulation Guide. Prentice-Hall — Sec Reg Guide P-H
Securities Regulation Law Journal — Sec Reg LJ
Securities Regulation Law Journal — Secur R Law
Securities Regulation Law Journal — SRL
Securities Regulations and Transfer Report — Sec Reg & Trans
Security Distributing and Marketing — Sec D & M
Security Forecast [*Database*] — SF
Security Industry and Product News — SIPN
Security Management — Sec Mgmt
Security Management — Sec Mgt
Security Management — Secur Manage
Security Management — SEM
Security Pacific National Bank. Quarterly Economic Report — SEJ
Security Surveyor — Security Surv
Security Systems Digest — Sec Syst Dig
Security World — Sec World
Sedalia Natural History Society. Bulletin — Sedalia N H Soc B
Sedimentary Geology — Sed Geol
Sedimentary Geology — Sediment Ge
Sedimentary Geology — Sediment Geol
Sedimentologia e Pedologia — Sedimentol Pedol
Sedimentology — Sedimentol
Seed — S
Seed and Garden Merchandising — Seed Gard Merch
Seed and Nursery Trader — Seed and Nursery Tr
Seed Bulletin — Seed Bull
Seed Research — Seed Res
Seed Research (New Delhi) — Seed Res (New Delhi)
Seed Science and Technology — Seed Sci Techn
Seed Science and Technology — Seed Sci Technol
Seed Technology in the Tropics. Papers. National Seed Symposium — Seed Technol Trop Pap Natl Seed Symp
Seed Trade Review — Seed Trade Rev
Seedlings and Horticulture/Shubyo to Engei — Seedlings Hort
Seelsorger [*Wien, Austria*] — Seels
Sefar Ha-Sana Lihude Ameriqah — SSLA
Sefarad — Sef
Segismundo — Seg
Segundo Congresso Pedagogico — SCP
Seguranca e Desenvolvimento. ADESG [*Revista da Associacao dos Diplomados da Escola Superior de Guerra*] [*Brazil*] — Seguranca Desenvolv
Seguridad Social (Buenos Aires) — Segur Soc BA
Seguridad Social Mexicana — SSM
Seguridad Social (Mexico) — Segur Soc Mex
Sei Marianna Ika Daigaku Zasshi — SMIZD
SEI (Socio-Economic Information) Ohio State University. Cooperative Extension Service — SEI Socio Econ Inf Ohio State Univ Coop Exp Serv
Seibutsu Butsuri — SEBUA
Seibutsu Butsuri Kagaku — SBBKA
Seifen Fachblatt — Seifen Fachbl
Seifen, Oele, Fette, Waechse — Seifen Ole
Seifen, Oele, Fette, Waechse. Die Internationale Fachzeitschrift — SEZ
Seifensieder-Zeitung — Seifens Zt
Seifensieder-Zeitung — Seifensieder Ztg
Seifensieder-Zeitung in Gemeinschaft auf Kriegsdauer mit Allgemeine Oel- und Fett-Zeitung — Seifensieder Ztg Allg Oel Fett Ztg
Sei-i-Kwai Medical Journal — Sei-i-Kai Med J
Seijinbyo — SEIJD
Seikagaku [*Journal of the Japanese Biochemical Society*] — Seikag
Seikei-Saigai Geka — SSGED
Seiken Ziho. Report of the Kihara Institute for Biological Research — Seik Ziho
Seishin Igaku — SEIGA
Seishin Igaku — Seish Iga
Seishin Shinkeigaku Zasshi — Seish Shink Zass
Seismic Instruments — Seism Instrum
Seismichiskie Pribory. Instrumental'naye Sredstva Seismicheskikh Nablyudenii — Seism Prib Instrum Sredstva Seism Nabl
Seismologic Series. Geological Survey (South Africa) — Seismol Ser Geol Surv (S Afr)
Seismological Bulletin — Seismol Bull
Seismological Investigations. British Association for the Advancement of Science — Seismol Invest
Seismological Series of the Earth Physics Branch — Seismol Ser Earth Phys Branch
Seismological Service of Canada. Seismological Series — Seismol Serv Can Seismol Ser
Seismological Society of America. Bulletin — Seismol Soc Am Bul
Seismology and Geology — Seismol and Geol
Seismology Society of America. Bulletin — Seismolog Soc Am Bull
Seismostoikost Sooruzhenii [*Former USSR*] — Seismostoikost Sooruzh
SEITA [*Service d'Exploitation Industrielle des Tabacs et des Allumettes*] **Annales de la Direction des Etudes de l'Equipement. Section 2** — SEITA Ann Dir Etud Equip Sect 2
Sejtosztodas Farmakologiaja — Sejtosztodas Farmakol
Sekai San Fujinka Soran. Survey of World Obstetrics and Gynaecology — Sek San Fuji Sor
Sekiyu Gakkaishi — SKGSA
Sekspirovskij Zbornik — SZ
Selecciones de Teologia — Sel Teol
Selecciones Medicas — Sel Med
Selecoes Odontologicas (Sao Paulo) — Sel Odontol (Sao Paulo)
Select Documents of the Principates of the Flavian Emperors — SDPFE
Select Journal — Select J
Select Papyri — Sel Pap
Select Papyri — SP
Selecta Chimica — Sel Chim
Selecta Mathematica. New Series — Selecta Math NS
Selecta Mathematica Sovietica — Sel Math Sov
Selecta Mathematica Sovietica — Selecta Math Soviet
Selecta Statistica Canadiana — Sel Statist Can
Selecta Statistica Canadiana — Selecta Statist Canadiana
Selected Annual Reviews of the Analytical Sciences — Sel Annu Rev Anal Sci
Selected Bibliography of Articles Dealing with the Middle East — SBAME
Selected Bibliography of Middle East Geology — Sel Bibliogr Middle East Geol
Selected Bibliography on Algae — Sel Bibliogr Algae
Selected Bibliography on Algae. Nova Scotia Research Foundation — Select Bibliogr Algae
Selected Essays. English Institute — SEEI
Selected Lectures in Mathematics. American Mathematicas Society — Sel Lecture Math
Selected Outdoor Recreation Statistics — Outdr Rec
Selected Papers. Carle Clinic and Carle Foundation — Sel Pap Carle Clin Carle Found
Selected Papers. Conference on Experimental Medicine and Surgery in Primates — Sel Pap Conf Exp Med Surg Primates
Selected Papers. Heart of America Annual Gas Compressor Institute — Sel Pap Heart Am Annu Gas Compressor Inst
Selected Papers. Heart of America Annual Gas Measurement Institute — Sel Pap Annu Gas Meas Inst
Selected Papers. Heart of America Annual Gas Measurement Institute — Sel Pap Heart Am Annu Gas Meas Inst
Selected Papers. Heart of America Annual Pipeline Operation and Maintenance Institute — Sel Pap Annu Pipeline Oper Maint Inst
Selected Papers. Institute of Human Nutrition in Prague — Sel Pap Inst Human Nutr Prague
Selected Papers. International Astronautical Congress — Sel Pap Int Astronaut Congr
Selected Papers. Israel. Environmental Protection Service — Sel Pap Isr Environ Prot Service
Selected Papers. Nuclear Engineering and Science Congress — Sel Pap Nucl Eng Sci Congr
Selected Papers of EC&M (Engineering Chemistry and Metallurgy) — Sel Pap EC&M China
Selected Papers of Engineering Chemistry and Metallurgy (China) — Sel Pap Eng Chem Metall China
Selected Papers of Italian Physicists — Select Papers Italian Phys
Selected Papers on the Environment in Israel — Sel Pap Environ Isr
Selected Papers Presented. American Chemical Society Symposium on Plastic Deformation of Polymers — Sel Pap Am Chem Soc Symp Plast Deform Plym
Selected Papers. West Virginia Shakespeare and Renaissance Association — SPWVSRA
Selected Papyri from the Archives of Zenon — Pap Zenon
Selected Philippine Periodical Index — Sel Philip Period Index
Selected Rand Abstracts — Rand
Selected Rand Abstracts — Sel Rand Abstr
Selected References on Environmental Quality — SelEnv
Selected Reports in Ethnomusicology — Selected Reports
Selected Reports: Publication of the Institute of Ethnomusicology of the University of California at Los Angeles — SRIELA
Selected Research in Microfiche — SRIM
Selected Scientific Papers. Istituto Superiore di Sanita — Sel Sci Pap Ist Super Sanita
Selected Scientific Papers. Shanghai Chiao Tung University — Sel Sci Pap Shanghai Chiao Tung Univ
Selected Scientific Papers. Shanghai Jiao Tong University — Sel Sci Pap Shanghai Jiao Tong Univ
Selected Topics in Electronics and Systems — Sel Top Electron Syst
Selected Topics in Modern Physics — Sel Top Mod Phys
Selected Topics in Solid State and Theoretical Physics. Proceedings. Latin American School of Physics — Sel Top Solid State Theor Phys Proc Lat Am Sch Phys
Selected Topics in Solid State Physics — Sel Top Solid State Phys
Selected Topics in Solid State Physics [*Elsevier Book Series*] — SSP
Selected Water Resources Abstracts — Sel Water Res Abstr
Selected Water Resources Abstracts — Sel Water Resour Abstr
Selected Water Resources Abstracts — Selec Water Resources Abstr
Selected Water Resources Abstracts — Selected Water Resources Abstr

Selected Water Resources Abstracts [*Database*] — SWRA
Selection of Greek Historical Inscriptions to the End of the Fifth Century B.C. — GHI
Selection of Greek Historical Inscriptions to the End of the Fifth Century B.C. — IGH
Selections from China Mainland Magazines [*US Consulate, Hongkong*] — SCMM
Selections from People's Republic of China Magazines [*Hong Kong*] — Sel PRC Mag
Selections from the Calcutta Review — S Cal R
Selections from the Edinburgh Review — Selec Ed R
Selections. Records of the Government (Bombay) — GRB
Selections. Records of the Government of India — SRGI
Selective Cancer Therapeutics — Sel Cancer Ther
Selective Cancer Therapeutics — Select Canc
Selective Electrode Reviews — Sel Electrode Rev
Selective Neurotoxicity — Sel Neurotoxic
Selective Organic Transformations — Sel Org Transform
Selective Soviet Annotated Bibliographies — SSAB
Selektsiya i Nasinnitstvo — Sel Nasinnitstvo
Selektsiya i Semenovodstvo — Selek Semenovod
Selektsiya i Semenovodstvo — Selekts Semenov
Selektsiya i Semenovodstvo (Kiev) — Sel Semenovod (Kiev)
Selektsiya i Semenovodstvo (Moscow) — Sel Semenovod (Mosc)
Selektsiya i Semenovodstvo Respublikanskii Mezhvedomstvennyi Tematicheskii Sbornik — Sel Semenovod Resp Mezhved Temat Sb
Selektsiya i Tekhnologiya Vozdelyvaniya Efirnomaslichnykh Kul'tur — Sel Tekhnol Vozdelyvaniya Efirnomaslichn Kul't
Selektsiya Rastenii Akklimatizatsiya i Semenovodstvo — Sel Rast Akklim Semenovod
Selektsiya, Sortoizuchenie, Agrotekhnika Plodovykh i Yagodnykh Kul'tur — Sel Sortoizuch Agrotekh Plodovykh Yagodnykh Kul't
Selenium and Tellurium Abstracts — Selenium Tellurium Abstr
Selezione Chimica Tintoria — Sel Chim Tintoria
Selezione di Tecnica Molitoria — Sel Tec Molitoria
Selezione di Tecnica Molitoria — Selez Tec Molit
Selezione Veterinaria-Istituto Zooprofilattico Sperimentale della Lombardia e dell'Emilia — Sel Vet Ist Zooprofil Sper Lomb Emilia
Self — GSEL
Self-Organization, Emerging Properties, and Learning — Self Organ Emerging Prop Learn
Self-Reliance — Self Rel
Sellowia. Anais Botanicos do Herbario Barbosa Rodriques — Sellowia Anais Bot
Selmer Bandwagon — SB
Selskab foer Nordisk Filologi Arsberetning — SNF
Selskapet for Industriell og Teknisk Forskning ved Norges Teknishki Hoegskole. Report — Selsk Ind Tek Forsk Nor Tek Hoegsk Rep
Sel'skoe Khozyaistvo — Sel'sk Khoz
Sel'skoe Khozyaistvo Belorussii — Sel'Khoz Beloruss
Sel'skoe Khozyaistvo Kazakhstana — Sel'sk Khoz Kaz
Sel'skoe Khozyaistvo Kazakstana — Sel Khoz Kazakh
Sel'skoe Khozyaistvo Kirgizii — Sel'Khoz Kirgizii
Sel'skoe Khozyaistvo Kirgizii — Sel'sk Khoz Kirg
Sel'skoe Khozyaistvo Moldavii — Sel'sk Khoz Mold
Sel'skoe Khozyaistvo Podmoskov'ya — Sel'sk Khoz Podmoskov'ya
Sel'skoe Khozyaistvo Povolzh'ya — Sel'Khoz Povol
Sel'skoe Khozyaistvo Povolzh'ya — Sel'sk Khoz Povolzh'ya
Sel'skoe Khozyaistvo Severnogo Kavkaza — Sel'Khoz Sev Kavkaz
Sel'skoe Khozyaistvo Severo-Zapadnoi Zony — Sel Khoz Sev Zap Zony
Sel'skoe Khozyaistvo Severo-Zapadnoi Zony — Sel'Khoz Sev-Zapad Zony
Sel'skoe Khozyaistvo Severo-Zapadnoi Zony — Sel'sk Khoz Sev Zapadn Zony
Sel'skoe Khozyaistvo Sibiri — Sel'Khoz Sib
Sel'skoe Khozyaistvo Tadzhikistana — Sel Khoz Tadzhik
Sel'skoe Khozyaistvo Tadzhikistana — Sel'Khoz Tadzhikistana
Sel'skoe Khozyaistvo Tadzhikistana — Sel'sk Khoz Tadzh
Sel'skoe Khozyaistvo Tatarii — Sel Khoz Tatarii
Sel'skoe Khozyaistvo Tatarii — Sel'sk Khoz Tatar
Sel'skoe Khozyaistvo Tatarii — Sel'sk Khoz Tatarii
Sel'skoe Khozyaistvo Turkmenistana — Sel Khoz Turkmen
Sel'skoe Khozyaistvo Turkmenistana — Sel'sk Khoz Turkm
Sel'skoe Khozyaistvo za Rubezhom. Rastenievodstvo — Sel'sk Khoz Rubezhom Rastenievod
Sel'skokhozyaistvennaya Biologiya — Sel'-Khoz Biol
Sel'skokhozyaistvennaya Biologiya — Sel'skokhoz Biol
Sel'skokhozyaistvennaya Biologiya — S-Kh Biol
Sel'skokhozyaistvennaya Biologiya — SSBLA
Sel'skokhozyaistvennoe Ispol'zovanie Pochv Tropikov i Subtropikov — Skh Ispolz Pochv Trop Subtrop
Sel'skokhozyaistvennoe Proizvodstvo Nechernozemnoi Zony — Sel'skokhoz Proizv Nechernozem Zony
Sel'skokhozyaistvennoe Proizvodstvo Nechernozemnoi Zony — Skh Proizvod Nechernozemn Zony
Sel'skokhozyaistvennoe Proizvodstvo Povolzh'ya — Sel'skokhoz Proizv Povol
Sel'skokhozyaistvennoe Proizvodstvo Povolzh'ya — Skh Proizvod Povolzhya
Sel'skokhozyaistvennoe Proizvodstvo Severnogo Kavkaza i TSCHO — Sel'skokhoz Proizv Sev Kavkaza TSCHO
Sel'skokhozyaistvennoe Proizvodstvo Sibiri i Dal'nego Vostoka — Sel'skokhoz Proizv Sib Dal'nego Vostoka
Sel'skokhozyaistvennoe Proizvodstvo Urala — Sel'skokhoz Proizv Urala
Sel'skokhozyaistvennoe Proizvodstvo Urala — S-Kh Proizvod Urala
Sel'skokhozyaistvo za Rubezhom Rastenievodstvo — S-Kh Rub Rastenievod
Selskostopanska Misul — Selskostop Misul
Selskostopanska Nauka — Selskostop Nauka
Selskostopanska Tekhnika — Selskostop Tekh
Seltene Assyrische Ideogramme — SAI
Seltene Metalle — Seltene Met
Selye's Guide to Stress Research — SGSRDC
Semaine dans le Monde — Sem
Semaine des Hopitaux — Sem Hop
Semaine des Hopitaux de Paris — Sem Hop Paris
Semaine des Hopitaux de Paris. Supplement. Archives d'Anatomie Pathologique — Sem Hop Paris Suppl Arch Anat Pathol
Semaine des Hopitaux de Paris. Supplement. Medecine dans le Monde — Sem Hop Paris Suppl Med Monde
Semaine des Hopitaux de Paris. Supplement. Pathologie et Biologie — Sem Hop Paris Suppl Pathol Biol
Semaine des Hopitaux de Paris. Supplement. Semaine Medicale Professionnelle et Medico-Sociale — Sem Hop Paris Suppl Sem Med Prof Med Soc
Semaine des Hopitaux. Informations — Sem Hop Inf
Semaine des Hopitaux. Supplement. Annales de Chirurgie Plastique — Sem Hop Suppl Ann Chir Plast
Semaine des Hopitaux. Supplement. Semaine Therapeutique — Sem Hop Suppl Sem Ther
Semaine des Hopitaux. Supplement. Therapeutique — Sem Hop Suppl Ther
Semaine des Hopitaux. Therapeutique — Sem Hop The
Semaine des Hopitaux. Therapeutique — Sem Hop Ther
Semaine d'Ethnologie Religieuse — SER
Semaine Judiciaire [*Switzerland*] — SJ
Semaine Juridique — Sem Jur
Semaine Medicale — Sem Med
Semaine Medicale — Semaine Med
Semaine Medicale Professionnelle et Medico-Sociale — Sem Med Prof Med Soc
Semaine Professionnelle et Medico-Sociale — Sem Prof Med Soc
Semaine Therapeutique [*France*] — Sem Ther
Semaine Veterinaire — Semaine Vet
Semana — Sem
Semana Biblica Espanola — SBE
Semana Biblica Espanola — SBEsp
Semana Biblica Espanola — Sem Bibl Esp
Semana Biblica Espanola [*Madrid*] — SemBEsp
Semana Espanola de Teologia — SET
Semana Medica — Sem Med
Semana Medica — Semana Med
Semana Medica de Mexico — Sem Med Mex
Semana Medica Espanola — Sem Med Esp
Semana Vitivinicola [*Spain*] — Sem Vitivinic
Semanario de Agricultura y Artes — Semanario Agric Artes
Semanario Judicial de la Federacion [*Mexico*] — Semanario
Semantische Hefte — SH
Sembradores de Amistad — SAm
Semeia — Se
Sementi Elette — Semen Elette
Semento Kogyo — SEMKA
Semi-Annual Progress Report. Tokai Works — Semi-Annu Prog Rep Tokai Works
Semiconductor Industry and Business Survey [*Database*] — SIBS
Semiconductor Interfaces and Microstructures — Semicond Interfaces Microstruct
Semiconductor International — Semicond Int
Semiconductor Optoelectronics — Semicond Optoelectron
Semiconductor Photonics and Technology — Semicond Photonics Technol
Semiconductor Production — Semicond Prod
Semiconductor Products — Semicond Prod
Semiconductor Products and Solid State Technology [*Later, Solid State Technology*] — Semicond Prod and Solid State Technol
Semiconductor Pure Water and Chemicals Conference — Semicond Pure Water Chem Conf
Semiconductor Science and Technology — Semicond Sci Technol
Semiconductor Silicon. International Symposium on Silicon Materials Science and Technology. Papers — Semicond Silicon Int Symp Mat Pap
Semiconductor Silicon. Papers Presented. International Symposium on Silicon Materials Science and Technology — Semicond Silicon Pap Int Symp Silicon Mater Sci Technol
Semiconductors and Insulators — Semicond and Insul
Semiconductors and Insulators — Semicond Insul
Semiconductors and Semimetals — Semicond Semimet
Semimagnetic Semiconductors and Diluted Magnetic Semiconductors — Semimagn Semicond Diluted Magn Semicond
Seminaire d'Analyse — Sem Anal
Seminaire d'Analyse Moderne — Sem Anal Moderne
Seminaire de Mathematique de Luxembourg — Sem Math Luxembourg
Seminaire de Mathematiques Superieures — Sem Math Sup
Seminaire de Mathematiques Superieures [*Montreal*] — Sem Math Superieures
Seminaire d'Enseignement. INSERM [*Institut National de la Sante et de la Recherche Medicale*] — Semin Enseign INSERM
Seminaire Lotharingien de Combinatoire — Sem Lothar Combin
Seminaire Plansee — Semin Plansee
Seminaire R & D Bioenergetique. Compte Rendu — Semin R & D Bioenerg CR
Seminaire Technologique. INSERM [*Institut National de la Sante et de la Recherche Medicale*] — Semin Technol INSERM
Seminaires de Chimie de l'Etat Solide — Semin Chim Etat Solide
Seminar — Se
Seminar — Sem
Seminar Arghiriade — Sem Arghiriade
Seminar. Fiziko-Tekhnologicheskie Voprosy Kibernetiki — Semin Fiz Tekhnol Vopr Kibern
Seminar Instituta Prikladnoi Matematiki. Annotacii Dokladov — Sem Inst Prikl Mat Annotac Dokladov

Seminar on Biomass Energy for City, Farm, and Industry — Semin Biomass Energy City Farm Ind
Seminar on Electrochemistry — Semin Electrochem
Seminar on Marine Radioecology — Semin Mar Radioecol
Seminar on Mathematical Sciences [*Yokohama*] — Sem Math Sci
Seminar on Migration and Related Social and Health Problems in New Zealand and the Pacific. Papers — Semin Migr Relat Soc Health Probl Pap
Seminar on Theoretical Physics — Semin Theor Phys
Seminar Paper. La Trobe University. School of Agriculture — Semin Pap La Trobe Univ Sch Agri
Seminar po Khimii i Tekhnicheskomu Primeneniyu Khal'kogenidov — Semin Khim Tekh Primen Khal'kogenidov
Seminar po Kraevym Zadacham. Trudy — Semin Kraev Zadacham Tr
Seminar po Problemam Upravleniya Raspredelennymi Sistemami s Podvizhnym Vozdeistviem. Materialy — Semin Probl Upr Raspred Sist Podvizhnym Vozdeistv Mater
Seminar Pokroky vo Vyrobe a Pouziti Lepidiel v Drevopriemysle. Zbornik Referatov — Semin Pokroky Vyrobe Pouziti Lepidiel Drevopriem Zb Ref
Seminar Series in Mathematics. Algebra — Sem Ser Math Algebra
Seminar Series in Mathematics. Analysis — Sem Ser Math Anal
Seminar Series. Society for Experimental Biology — Semin Ser Soc Exp Biol
Seminar. University of Singapore. Chemistry Department — Semin Univ Singapore Chem Dep
Seminare/Konferenzen [*Database*] — SEMIKON
Seminari Biologici. Facolta di Medicina e Chirurgia. Universita Cattolica del Sacro Cuore — Semin Biol Fac Med Chir Univ Cattol Sacro Cuore
Seminarie d'Analyse Convexe — Sem Anal Convexe
Seminario Conciliar — Sem
Seminario de Arte Aragones — Semin Arte Aragones
Seminario de Ensenanza de la Odontopediatria — Semin Ensen Odontopediatr
Seminario de Estudos Galegos — Semin Estud Galegos
Seminario Interno sobre Exploracion Geologico-Minera — Semin Interno Explor Geol Min
Seminario Matematico e Fisico. Universita di Modena. Atti — Semin Mat Fis Univ Modena Atti
Seminario Medico — Semin Med
Seminario sobre Amibiasis — Semin Amibiasis
Seminario sobre Evaluacion de la Contaminacion Ambiental — Semin Eval Contam Ambiental
Seminarios — SCFR
Seminarios de Estratigrafia [*Madrid*] — Semin Estratigrafia
Seminarium Kondakovianum — Sem Kond
Seminarium Kondakovianum — SK
Seminaro Nota — Sem Nota
Seminars in Anesthesia — Semin Anesth
Seminars in Arthritis and Rheumatism — Sem Arth Rh
Seminars in Arthritis and Rheumatism — Semin Arthritis Rheum
Seminars in Cancer Biology — Semin Cancer Biol
Seminars in Cell and Developmental Biology — Semin Cell Dev Biol
Seminars in Cell Biology — Semin Cell Biol
Seminars in Dermatology — SDERDN
Seminars in Dermatology — Semin Dermatol
Seminars in Developmental Biology — Semin Dev Biol
Seminars in Diagnostic Pathology — Semin Diagn Pathol
Seminars in Drug Treatment — Semin Drug Treat
Seminars in Family Medicine — Semin Fam Med
Seminars in Gastrointestinal Disease — Semin Gastrointest Dis
Seminars in Hearing — Semin Hear
Seminars in Hematology — Sem Hematol
Seminars in Hematology — Semin Hematol
Seminars in Immunology — Semin Immunol
Seminars in Infectious Disease — Sem Infect Dis
Seminars in Infectious Disease — Semin Infect Dis
Seminars in Interventional Radiology — Semin Interventional Radiol
Seminars in Liver Diseases — Semin Liver Dis
Seminars in Mathematics — Sem Math
Seminars in Mathematics. V. A. Steklov Mathematical Institute [*Leningrad*] — Sem Math V A Steklov
Seminars in Nephrology — Sem Nephrol
Seminars in Nephrology — Semin Nephrol
Seminars in Neurology — Semin Neurol
Seminars in Nuclear Medicine — Semin Nucl Med
Seminars in Nutrition — Semin Nutr
Seminars in Oncology — Semin Oncol
Seminars in Oncology Nursing — Semin Oncol Nurs
Seminars in Pediatric Neurology — Semin Pediatr Neurol
Seminars in Pediatric Surgery — Semin Pediatr Surg
Seminars in Perinatology — Semin Perinatol
Seminars in Perinatology (New York) — Semin Perinatol (NY)
Seminars in Psychiatry — Semin Psychiatry
Seminars in Reproductive Endocrinology — Semin Reprod Endocrinol
Seminars in Respiratory Infections — Semin Respir Infect
Seminars in Respiratory Medicine — Semin Respir Med
Seminars in Roentgenology — Sem Roentg
Seminars in Roentgenology — Semin Roentgenol
Seminars in Speech and Language — Semin Speech Lang
Seminars in Surgical Oncology — Semin Surg Oncol
Seminars in Thoracic and Cardiovascular Surgery — Semin Thorac Cardiovasc Surg
Seminars in Thrombosis and Hemostasis — Semin Thromb Hemost
Seminars in Thrombosis and Hemostasis — Semin Thromb Hemostas
Seminars in Thrombosis and Hemostasis — Semin Thromb Hemostasis
Seminars in Ultrasound — Sem Ultrasound
Seminars in Ultrasound [*Later, Seminars in Ultrasound, CT, and MR*] — Semin Ultrasound
Seminars in Ultrasound, CT, and MR — Semin Ultrasound CT MR
Seminars in Urologic Oncology — Semin Urol Oncol
Seminars in Urology — Semin Urol
Seminars in Vascular Surgery — Semin Vasc Surg
Seminars in Veterinary Medicine and Surgery. Small Animal — Semin Vet Med Surg Small Anim
Seminars Speech, Language, Hearing — Semin Sp Lang Hear
Seminary Quarterly — Seminary Q
Semiotic Scene — Sem S
Semiotica — Se
Semitic and Oriental Studies — SOS
Semitic Journal of Linguistics — SJL
Semitic Study Series — SSS
Semitica [*Paris*] — Sem
Semitistische Studien — Sem St
Sem'ja Skola — Sem'ja Sk
Sempaku — SMPKA
Semper Nutritionssymposium — Semper Nutritionssympo
Semper Symposium — Semper Symp
Senales-Buenos Aieres — SRB
Senckenbergiana Biologica — Senckenb Biol
Senckenbergiana Biologica — Senckenberg Biol
Senckenbergiana Biologica — Senckenbergiana Biol
Senckenbergiana Lethaea — Senckenb Lethaea
Senckenbergiana Maritima — Senckenb Marit
Senckenbergiana Maritima — Senckenberg Marit
Senckenbergiana Maritima — Senckenbergiana Marit
Senckenbergiana. Wissenschaftliche Mitteilungen der Senckenbergischen Naturforschenden Gesellschaft — Senckenbergiana Mitt Naturf
Senckenbergische Naturforschende Gesellschaft. Abhandlungen — Senckenb Naturforsch Ges Abh
Senckenbergische Naturforschende Gesellschaft in Frankfurt Am Main. Bericht — Senckenbergische Nat Ges Frankfurt Ber
Senckenbergischen Naturforschenden Gesellschaft Senckenberg-Buch — Senckenbergischen Naturf Gesell Senckenberg-Buch
Sendai Astronomiaj Raportoj — Sendai Astron Rap
Sendai Symposium on Acoustoelectronics — Sendai Symp Acoustoelectron
Sendschrift. Deutsche Orient-Gesellschaft [*Leipzig*] — SDOG
Seneca Review — Sen R
Senegal. Centre de Recherches Oceanographiques de Dakar-Thiaroye. Archive — Senegal Cent Rech Oceanogr Dakar-Thiaroye Arch
Senegal. Centre de Recherches Oceanographiques de Dakar-Thiaroye. Document Scientifique — Senegal Cent Rech Oceanogr Dakar-Thiaroye Doc Sci
Senegal. Direction des Mines et de la Geologie. Bulletin — Senegal Dir Mines Geol Bull
Senior Nurse — Sr Nurse
Senior Scholastic [*Teacher Edition*] — Scholastic
Senior Scholastic — Sen Schol
Senior Scholastic — Sr Sch
Senior Scholastic — Sr Schol
Senior Scholastic — SS
Senior Science — Sr Sci
Senpaku — SENPD
Senpaku Gijutsu Kenkyujo Hokoku — SPGKA
Sens Chretien — Sens C
Sense Processes — SENSB
Sensibilizirovannaya Fluorestsentsiya Smesej Parov Metallov — Sensibilizirovannaya Fluorests Smesej Parov Met
Sensing and Controlling Motion. Vestibular and Sensorimotor Function — Sens Controlling Motion
Sensor Fusion IV. Control Paradigms and Data Structures — Sens Fusion IV Control Paradigms Data Struct
Sensor Review — Sens Rev
Sensor Review — Sensor Rev
Sensoren. Technologie und Anwendung. Vortraege der Fachtagung — Sens Technol Anwend Vortr Fachtag
Sensornye Sistemy — Sens Sist
Sensors and Actuators — Sens and Actuators
Sensory Nerves and Neuropeptides in Gastroenterology [*Basic Science to Clincal perspectives*] — Sens Nerves Neuropept Gastroenterol
Sensory Processes — Sens Process
Sensory Processes — SEPRD
Sensory Receptors and Signal Transduction — Sens Recept Signal Transduction
Sensory Transduction — Sens Transduction
Sentencias del Tribunal Supremo de Puerto Rico — PR Sent
Seoul Journal of Medicine — Seoul J Med
Seoul National University. College of Agriculture. Bulletin — Seoul Natl Univ Coll Agric Bull
Seoul National University. Economic Review — Seoul Nat Univ Econ R
Seoul National University Engineering Report — Seoul Nat Univ Eng Rep
Seoul National University. Engineering Reports — Seoul Natl Univ Eng Rep
Seoul National University. Faculty Papers. Biology and Agriculture Series — Seoul Nat Univ Fac Pap Bio Agric Ser
Seoul National University Faculty Papers. Biology and Agriculture. Series E — Seoul Nat Univ Fac Pap Biol Agric Ser E
Seoul National University. Faculty Papers. Medicine and Pharmacy Series — Seoul Nat Univ Fac Pap Med Pharm Ser
Seoul National University. Faculty Papers. Science and Technology Series — Seoul Nat Univ Fac Pap Sci Technol Ser
Seoul National University. Journal of Agricultural Sciences — Seoul Nat Univ J Agric Sci
Seoul University. Faculty Papers. Series C. Science and Technology — Seoul Univ Fac Pap Ser C

Seoul University. Faculty Papers. Series D. Medicine and Pharmacy — Seoul Univ Fac Pap Ser D
Seoul University. Faculty Papers. Series E. Biology and Agriculture — Seoul Univ Fac Pap Ser E
Seoul University Journal. Biology and Agriculture Series/Seoul Taehak-Kyo Nonmun-Jip Soengnong-Kae — Seoul Univ J Biol Ser
Seoul University. Journal of Pharmaceutical Sciences — Seoul Univ J Pharm Sci
Seoul University. Journal of Pharmaceutical Sciences — Seoul University J Pharm Sci
Seoul University. Journal. Series A. Natural Science — Seoul Univ J Nat Sci
Seoul University. Journal. Series A. Natural Science — Seoul Univ J Nat Sci Ser A
Seoul University. Journal. Series A. Science and Technology — Seoul Univ J Sci Technol Ser A
Seoul University. Journal. Series B. Biology and Agriculture — Seoul Univ J Biol Agr Ser B
Seoul University. Journal. Series B. Biology and Agriculture — Seoul Univ J Biol Agric Ser B
Seoul University. Journal. Series B. Natural Science — Seoul Univ J Nat Sci Ser B
Seoul University. Journal. Series C. Medicine and Pharmacy — Seoul Univ J Med Pharm Ser C
Seoul University. Journal. Series C. Natural Science — Seoul Univ J Nat Sci Ser C
Separation and Purification — Sep Purif
Separation and Purification Methods — Sep Purif M
Separation and Purification Methods — Sep Purif Methods
Separation Immediate et Chromatographie. Journees Internationales d'Etude — Sep Immed Chromatogr Journ Int Etude
Separation of Hydrogen Isotopes. Symposium. Joint Conference. Chemical Institute of Canada and the American Chemical Society — Sep Hydrogen Isot Symp Jt Conf
Separation Science [*Later, Separation Science and Technology*] — Sep Sci
Separation Science [*Later, Separation Science and Technology*] — Separ Sci
Separation Science and Technology — Sep Sci Technol
Separation Science and Technology — Separation Sci Tech
Separation Science. Supplement — Sep Sci Suppl
Separation Technology. Proceedings. Engineering Foundation Conference — Sep Technol Pro Eng Found Conf
Separations Technology — Sep Technol
SEPM [*Society of Economic Paleontologists and Mineralogists*] **Short Course** — SEPM Short Course
SEPM (Society of Economic Paleontologists and Mineralogists) Field Trip Guidebook — SEPM (Soc Econ Paleontol Miner) Field Trip Guideb
Seppyo. Journal. Japanese Society of Snow and Ice — SEPP
September — S
Septentrion. Revue Archeologique Trimestrielle — Septent
Septuaginta Arbeiten — Sept Arb
Septuaginta Studien — Sept St
Sequential Analysis — Sequential Anal
Seramikkusu — SERAA
Serapeum [*Dresden*] — Ser
Serbian Academy of Sciences and Arts. Bulletin — Serb Acad Sci Arts Bull
Serbian Academy of Sciences and Arts. Glas — Serb Acad Sci Arts Glas
Serbian Academy of Sciences and Arts. Monographs. Department of Sciences — Serb Acad Sci Arts Monogr Dep Sci
Serbian Academy of Sciences and Arts. Monographs. Department of Technical Sciences — Serbian Acad Sci and Arts Monogr Dep Tech Sci
Serbian Academy of Sciences and Arts. Separate Editions. Department of Natural and Mathematical Sciences — Serb Acad Sci Arts Sep Ed Dep Nat Math Sci
Serbian Archives of General Medicine — Serb Arch Gen Med
Serbian Archives of Medicine — Serb Arch Med
Serbian Bulletin — Serb Bull
Serbian Chemical Society. Journal — Serb Chem Soc J
Serdica. Mathematical Journal — Serdica Math J
Serengeti Research Institute. Annual Report — Serengeti Res Inst Annu Rep
Seria Astronomia. Uniwersytet Imeni Adama Mickiewicza w Poznaniu — Ser Astron Uniw Adama Mickiewicza Poznaniu
Seria Biologia. Uniwersytet Imeni Adama Mickiewicza w Poznaniu — Ser Biol Uniw Adama Mickiewicza Poznaniu
Seria Chemia. Uniwersytet Imeni Adama Mickiewicza w Poznaniu — Ser Chem Uniw Adama Mickiewicza Poznaniu
Seria Filozofia i Logika — Ser Filoz Logika
Seria Fizyka. Uniwersytet Imienia Adama Mickiewicza w Poznaniu — Ser Fiz Uniw Im Adama Mickiewicza Poznaniu
Seria Matematyka — Ser Mat
Serial. Division of Industrial Chemistry. Commonwealth Scientific and Industrial Research Organisation — Ser Div Ind Chem CSIRO
Serial Handbook of Modern Psychiatry — Ser Handb Mod Psych
Serial Publication. United States Northeast Regional Plant Introduction Station — Ser Publ US Northeast Reg Plant Introd Stn
Serial Publications in Geography — Ser Publ Geogr
Serial Slants — Ser Sl
Serial Slants (Chicago) — Ser Slants Chicago
Serials in Australian Libraries: Social Sciences and Humanities — SALSSAH
Serials in Australian Libraries: Social Sciences and Humanities/Newly Reported Titles — SALSSAH/NRT
Serials in the British Lending Library — Serials BLL
Serials Librarian — SELID
Serials Librarian — Ser Lib
Serials Librarian — Ser Libr
Serials Librarian — Serials Libn
Serials Librarian — Serials Libr
Serials Review — Ser R
Serials Review — Serials R
Sericultural Research [*Japan*] — Sericult Res
Serie Bibliografia Tematica — Serie Bibliogr Temat
Serie Bibliografica — Ser Bibliogr
Serie Bibliografica. Instituto Nacional de Tecnologia Agropecuaria (Pergamino, Argentina) — Ser Bibliogr INTA (Pergamino)
Serie Cana de Azucar — Ser Cana Azucar
Serie Chimie. Universitatea din Timisoara — Ser Chim Univ Timisoara
Serie de Biologia. Monografia. Programa Regional de Desarrollo Cientifico y Tecnologico — Ser Biol Monogr Programa Reg Desarrollo Cient Tecnol
Serie de Biologia. Monografia. Programa Regional de Desenvolvimento Cientifico e Tecnologico — Ser Biol Monogr Programa Reg Desenvolvimento Cient Tecnol
Serie de Biologia. Programa Regional de Desarrollo Cientifico y Tecnologico — Ser Biol Programa Reg Desarrollo Cient Tecnol
Serie de Fisica. Monografia. Programa Regional de Desarrollo Cientifico y Tecnologico — Ser Fis Monogr Programa Reg Desarrollo Cient Tecnol
Serie de Fisica. Monografia. Programa Regional de Desenvolvimento Cientifico e Tecnologico — Ser Fis Monogr Programa Reg Desenvolvimento Cient Tecnol
Serie de Fisica. Programa Regional de Desarrollo Cientifico y Tecnologico — Ser Fis Programa Reg Desarrollo Cient Tecnol
Serie de Quimica. Monografia. Programa Regional de Desarrollo Cientifico y Tecnologico — Ser Quim Monogr Programa Reg Desarrollo Cient Tecnol
Serie de Quimica. Monografia. Programa Regional de Desenvolvimento Cientifico e Tecnologico — Ser Quim Monogr Programa Reg Desenvolvimento Cient Tecnol
Serie de Quimica. Programa Regional de Desarrollo Cientifico y Tecnologico — Ser Quim Programa Reg Desarrollo Cient Tecnol
Serie de Vocabularios y Diccionarios Indigenas — SVDI
Serie des Conferences. Union Mathematique Internationale — Ser Conf Union Math Internat
Serie di Matematica e Fisica — Ser Mat Fis
Serie Didactica. Universidad Nacional de Tucuman. Facultad de Agronomia y Zootecnia — Ser Didact Univ Nac Tucuman Fac Agronom Zooteh
Serie Divulgacao. Agronomia Angolana — Ser Divulg Agron Angolana
Serie Divulgacao. Projeto de Desenvolvimento e Pesquisa Florestal — Ser Divulg Projeto Desenvolvimento Pesqui Florestal
Serie Especial. Superintendencia do Desenvolvimento do Nordeste. Divisao de Geologia (Brazil) — Ser Espec Sup Desenvolvimento Nordeste Div Geol (Braz)
Serie Etudes sur l'Islam — SEtl
Serie Geologia Economica (Brazil). Superintendencia do Desenvolvimento do Nordeste. Divisao de Geologia — Ser Geol Econ (Braz) Sup Desenvolvimento Nordeste Div Geol
Serie Geologia Especial (Brazil). Superintendencia do Desenvolvimento do Nordeste. Divisao de Geologia — Ser Geol Espec (Braz) Supt Desenvolvimento Nordeste Div Geol
Serie Geologica. Academia de Ciencias de Cuba. Instituto de Geologia — Ser Geol Acad Cienc Cuba Inst Geol
Serie Informes de Conferencias. Cursos y Reuniones-Inter-American Institute of Agricultural Sciences — Ser Inf Conf Cursos Reun Interam Inst Agric Sci
Serie Linguistica — Ser L
Serie Linguistica Peruana — SLP
Serie Monografias. Instituto de Zootecnia — Ser Monogr Inst Zootec
Serie Notes de Recherche. Fondation Universitaire Luxembourgeoise — Ser Notes Rech Fond Univ Luxemb
Serie Orientale Roma — SOR
Serie Piper — Ser Piper
Serie Poeyana. Instituto de Biologia. Academia de Ciencias de Cuba — Ser Poeyana Inst Biol Acad Cienc Cuba
Serie Poeyana. Instituto de Zoologia. Academia de Ciencias de Cuba — Ser Poeyana Inst Zool Acad Cienc Cuba
Serie Scientifica — Ser Sci
Serie Universitaria — Ser Universitaria
Serie Universitaria. Fundacion "Juan March" — Ser Univ Fund Juan March
Series Defects in Crystalline Solids — Ser Defects Cryst Solids
Series Entomologica (The Hague) — Ser Entomol (The Hague)
Series Episcoporum Ecclesiae Catholicae — SEEC
Series Facultatis Historiae Ecclesiasticae — SFHE
Series Facultatis Juris Canonici — SFJC
Series Facultatis Missiologicae — SFM
Series Facultatis Theologicae — SFT
Series Haematologica — Ser Haematol
Series in Algebra — Ser Algebra
Series in Approximations and Decompositions — Ser Approx Decompos
Series in Computational Methods in Mechanics and Thermal Sciences — Ser Comput Methods Mech Thermal Sci
Series in Computer Science — Ser Comput Sci
Series in Food Material Science — Ser Food Mater Sci
Series in Mathematical Biology and Medicine — Ser Math Biol Med
Series in Modern Applied Mathematics — Ser Modern Appl Math
Series in Modern Condensed Matter Physics — Ser Modern Condensed Matter Phys
Series in Nonlinear Optics — Ser Nonlinear Opt
Series in Number Theory — Ser Number Theory
Series in Optics and Photonics — Ser Opt Photonics
Series in Pure Mathematics — Ser Pure Math
Series in Real Analysis — Ser Real Anal
Series in the Humanities — Ser Hum
Series in Theoretical and Applied Mechanics — Ser Theoret Appl Mech
Series of Monographs on General Physiology — Ser Monogr Gen Physiol
Series of Research Publications. Association for Research in Nervous and Mental Disease — Ser Res Publ Assoc Res Nerv Ment Dis

Series of the Centro de Estudios Cientificos de Santiago — Ser Cent Estud Cient Santiago
Series on Advances in Mathematics for Applied Sciences — Ser Adv Math Appl Sci
Series on Advances in Statistical Mechanics — Ser Adv Statist Mech
Series on Applied Mathematics — Ser Appl Math
Series on Knots and Everything — Ser Knots Everything
Series on Multivariate Analysis — Ser Multivariate Anal
Series on Mycology — Ser Mycol
Series on Optimization — Ser Optim
Series on Soviet and East European Mathematics — Ser Soviet East European Math
Series on University Mathematics — Ser Univ Math
Series on Work and Organization — Ser Work Organ
Series Paedopsychiatrica — Ser Paedopsychiatr
Seriya Astrometriya i Astrofizika — Ser Astrom Astrofiz
Seriya Eksperimental'naya Meditsina (Riga) — Ser Eksp Med (Riga)
Seriya Metallofizika — Ser Metallofiz
Seriya Molekulyarnaya Biologiya — Ser Mol Biol
Seriya Obzorov. Mezhdunarodnoe Agentstvo po Atomnoi Energii — Ser Obz Mezhdunar Agentstvo At Energ
SERL [*Sanitary Engineering Research Laboratory*] **Report** — SERL Rep
Serological Museum Bulletin — Serol Mus Bull
Serono Clinical Colloquia on Reproduction. Proceedings — Serono Clin Colloq Reprod Proc
Serono Symposia. Proceedings — Serono Symp Proc
Serono Symposia Publications from Raven Press — Serono Symp Publ Raven Press
Serono Symposia Series Advances in Experimental Medicine — Serono Symp Ser Adv Exp Med
Serotonin. Molecular Biology, Receptors, and Functional Effects — Serotonin Mol Biol Recept Funct Eff
Serra Dor — SDO
Serra d'Or — SeO
Serraika Chronika — SerrC
SERT [*Society of Electronic and Radio Technicians*] **Journal** — SERT J
Service — Ser
Service: A Review of Agricultural and Chemical Progress — Serv
Service Canadien de la Faune. Cahiers de Biologie — Serv Can Faune Cah Biol
Service Central de Protection Contre les Rayonnements Ionisants (France). Rapport d'Activite — Serv Cent Prot Rayonnem Ionis (Fr) Rapp Act
Service de Bibliographie sur l'Informatique [*Database*] — SB-I
Service de la Carte Geologique d'Alsace et de Lorraine. Bulletin — Serv Carte Geol Alsace Lorraine Bull
Service Dealer's Newsletter [*Database*] — SDN
Service d'Edition et de Vente des Publications de l'Education Nationale — SEVPEN
Service d'Exploitation Industrielle des Tabacs et des Allumettes. Annales de la Direction des Etudes et de l'Equipement — SEITA Annls
Service Employee — Ser Emp
Service Geologique de Pologne. Institut Geologique de Pologne. Bulletin — Serv Geol Pol Inst Geol Pol Bull
Service Social — Service Soc
Service Social (Bruxelles) — Serv Soc (Bruxelles)
Service Social dans le Monde — Serv Soc Monde
Service Social (Quebec) — Serv Soc (Quebec)
Service Station Merchandising — Serv Stn Merch
Service World International — Serv World
Service World International — SWI
Servicio Forestal de Investigaciones y Experiencias. Trabajos — Serv For Invest Exper Trab
Servicio Geologico de Bolivia. Boletin — Serv Geol Bolivia Bol
Servicio Nacional Minero Geologico (Argentina). Revista — Serv Nac Min Geol (Argent) Rev
Servicio Shell para el Agricultor. Serie A — Serv Shell Agric Ser A
Servicio Shell para el Agricultor. Serie A. Informe — Serv Shell Agr Ser A
Servicio Social (Lima) — Serv Soc Lima
Servicio Social (Santiago) — Serv Soc Santiago
Servico de Fomento Mineiro e Laboratorio da DGGM. Estudos. Notas e Trabalhos — Serv Fom Min Lab DGGM Estud Notas Trab
Servico Especial de Saude Publica. Revista (Brazil) — Serv Esp Saude Publica Rev (Brazil)
Servico Social de Comercio. Boletim Bibliografico — Servico Soc de Comer Bol Bibl
Servico Social e Sociedade — Servico Soc e Soc
Servico Social (Sao Paulo) — Serv Soc S Paulo
Servicos Geologicos de Portugal. Memoria — Serv Geol Port Mem
Serving Advertising in the Midwest [*Later, Adweek*] — Sam
Serving Farm, Ranch, and Home. Quarterly. University of Nebraska. College of Agriculture and Home Economics. Agricultural Experiment Station — Serv Farm Ranch Home
Servizio Geologico d'Italia Memorie Descrittive della Carta Geologica d'Italia — Serv Geol Ital Mem Descr Carta Geol Ital
SES Report. Solar Energy Studies Unit. Commonwealth Scientific and Industrial Research Organisation — SES Rep CSIRO Sol Energy Stud
SESA [*Society for Experimental Stress Analysis*] **Papers** — SESA Pap
Sesion Inaugural. Real Academia de Farmacia de Barcelona — Ses Inaug R Acad Farm Barcelona
Sesja Naukowa Instytutu Ochrony Roslin. Materialy — Ses Nauk Inst Ochr Rosl Mater
Session Cases. Court of Session [*Scotland*] — Sess Cas
Session Cases. High Court of Justiciary [*Scotland*] — Sess Cas J
Session. Comite International des Poids et Mesures. Comite Consultatif de Thermometrie — Sess Com Int Poids Mes Com Consult Thermom
Session d'Etudes Biennale de Physique Nucleaire. Comptes-Rendus — Sess Etud Bienn Phys Nucl CR
Session Laws. Arizona — Ariz Sess Laws
Session Laws. Colorado — Colo Sess Laws
Session Laws. Hawaii — Haw Sess Laws
Session Laws. Idaho — Idaho Sess Laws
Session Laws. Kansas — Kan Sess Laws
Session Laws. North Carolina — NC Sess Laws
Session Laws. Wyoming — Wyo Sess Laws
Sessioni Pubbliche dell' Ateneo Veneto — Sess Pubbliche Ateneo Veneto
Sestante Letterario — SLet
Seta Artificiale — Seta Artif
Seto Marine Biological Laboratory. Publications — Seto Mar Biol Lab Publ
Seton Hall Law Review — Set H LR
Seton Hall Law Review — Seton Hall L Rev
Seton Hall Legislative Journal — Set Hall Leg J
Seton Hall Legislative Journal — Seton Hall Leg J
Settimade di Studio. Centro Italiano di Studi sull'Alto Medioevo — SSAM
Settimana Medica [*Italy*] — Settim Med
Settimana Ospitaliera — Settim Osp
Settimane di Studio del Centro Italiano di Studi sull'Alto Medioevo — SSCISAM
Setting National Priorities. The 19-- Budget [*United States*] — Natl Prior
Setting Up a Company in the European Community [*Monograph*] — SUCEC
Set-Valued Analysis — Set Valued Anal
Seufferts Archiv fuer Entscheidungen der Obersten Gerichte in den Deutschen Staaten — Arch Entsch Oberst Gerichte
Sevcenko Gesellschaft der Wissenschaften — Sevcenko Ges Wiss
Sevcenko Societe Scientifique. Section de Chimie, de Biologie, et de Medecine — Sevcenko Soc Sci Sect Chim Biol Med
Seven — SV
Seventeen — GSEV
Seventeenth-Century News — SCN
Seventeenth-Century News — Sev Cent N
Seventeenth-Century News — Seven Ct N
Seventh-Day Adventist Periodical Index — Seventh-Day Adventist Period Index
Severni Morava Vastivedny Sbornik — Severni Morava
Severo-Osetinskii Gosudarstvennyi Meditsinskii Institut. Sbornik Nauchnykh Trudov — Sev Oset Gos Med Inst Sb Nauchn Tr
Severo-Osetinskii Gosudarstvennyi Pedagogicheskii Institut. Uchenye Zapiski — Sev-Oset Gos Pedagog Inst Uch Zap
Severo-Vostochnoe Petrograficheskoe Soveshchanie — Sev Vost Petrogr Soveshch
Severo-Vostochnyy Kompleksnyy Nauchno-Issledovatel'skiy Institut Akademiya Nauk SSSR Sibirskoye Otdeleniye — Sev-Vost Kompleks Nauch-Issled Inst Akad Nauk SSSR Sib Otd
Severo-Zapad Evropeiskoi Chasti SSSR — Sev Zapad Evr Chasti SSSR
Severo-Zapadnyi Zaochnyi Politekhnicheskii Institut Trudy — Sev Zapadn Zaochn Politekh Inst Tr
Sewage and Industrial Waste Engineering — Sewage Ind Waste Eng
Sewage and Industrial Wastes — Sewage Ind Wastes
Sewage Effluent as a Water Resource. Symposium. Report of Proceedings — Sewage Effluent Water Resour Symp Rep Proc
Sewage Purification. Land Drainage. Water and River Engineering — Sewage Purif Land Drain Water River Eng
Sewage Works Engineering and Municipal Sanitation — Sewage Works Eng Munic Sanit
Sewage Works Journal — Sewage Works J
Sewanee Review — PSEW
Sewanee Review — SeR
Sewanee Review — SeRe
Sewanee Review — Sew
Sewanee Review — Sew R
Sewanee Review — Sew Rev
Sewanee Review — Sewan R
Sewanee Review — Sewanee R
Sewanee Review — Sewanee Rev
Sewanee Review — SR
Sewanee Review — SwR
Sex Education Coalition News — SECN
Sex Over Forty — S/40
Sex Roles. A Journal of Research — ISXR
Sexual Plant Reproduction — Sex Plant R
Sexual Plant Reproduction — Sex Plant Reprod
Sexuality and Disability — SDISDC
Sexuality and Disability — Sex Disabil
Sexually Transmitted Disease Statistical Letter — STD Stat Let
Sexually Transmitted Diseases. Abstracts and Bibliography — STD Abstr Bib
Sexually-Transmitted Diseases — Sex Transm Dis
Seybold Report on Office Systems — Seybold Rep Off Systems
Seybold Report on Professional Computing — Seybold Rep Prof Comp
Seychelles Department of Agriculture. Annual Report — Seychelles Dep Agric Annu Rep
Sezatoarea. Revista de Folklor — S
S'ezd Armyanskogo Fiziologicheskogo Obshchestva — Sezd Arm Fiziol Ova
S'ezd Biokhimikov Litovskoi SSR — Sezd Biokhim Lit SSR
S'ezd Dermatologov i Venerologov BSSR — Sezd Dermatol Venerol BSSR
S'ezd Farmatsevtov Kazakhstana — Sezd Farm Kaz
S'ezd Farmatsevtov Ukrainskoi SSR — Sezd Farm Ukr SSR
S'ezd Mikrobiologov Ukrainy — Sezd Mikrobiol Ukr
S'ezd Vsesoyuznogo Fiziologicheskogo Obshchestva Imeni I. P. Pavlova — Sezd Vses Fiziol Ova Im I P Pavlova
Sezione Clinica Europea. Associazione Internazionale di Gerontologia. Congresso — Sez Clin Eur Assoc Int Gerontol Congr
Sezione Demografia e Razza — SDR
SF Commentary — SFC

SF Greats — SFG
SF Horizons — SFH
SF Impulse — SFI
SFI [*Sport Fishing Institute*] **Bulletin** — SFIB
SFPE [*Society of Fire Protection Engineers*] **Technology Report** — SFPE Technol Rep
SFRA Newsletter — SFN
SGA [*Society of Gastrointestinal Assistants*] **Journal** — SGA J
SGF [*Sveriges Gummitekniska Foerening*] **Publicerande** — SGF Publ
Shaanxi Medical Journal — Shaanxl Med J
Shadforth's Reserved Judgements — Sh
Shakaichosa-Kenkyusho Consumer Index Summary Report [*Database*] — SCI/SR
Shakespeare Association. Bulletin — SAB
Shakespeare Newsletter — ShN
Shakespeare Newsletter — SN
Shakespeare Newsletter — SNL
Shakespeare on Film Newsletter — SFNL
Shakespeare Pictorial — ShP
Shakespeare Quarterly — GSHQ
Shakespeare Quarterly — Sh Q
Shakespeare Quarterly — Shakes Q
Shakespeare Quarterly — Shakespeare Q
Shakespeare Quarterly — SQ
Shakespeare Review — ShR
Shakespeare Studies — PSHS
Shakespeare Studies — ShakS
Shakespeare Studies [*Tokyo*] — ShStud
Shakespeare Studies — SStud
Shakespeare Studies (Tokyo) — SST
Shakespeare Survey — PSHU
Shakespeare Survey — Shakes Surv
Shakespeare Survey — Shakespeare S
Shakespeare Survey — ShS
Shakespeare Survey — SS
Shakespearean Criticism — SC
Shakespearean Research Opportunities — SRO
Shakespeare-Jahrbuch — Shakes Jah
Shakespeare-Jahrbuch — Shakespeare-Jahrb
Shakespeare-Jahrbuch — Shak-Jahrb
Shakespeare-Jahrbuch — Sh-J
Shakespeare-Jahrbuch — Sh-Jb
Shakespeare-Jahrbuch — SJ
Shakespeare-Jahrbuch (Heidelberg) — SJH
Shakespeare-Jahrbuch (Weimar) — ShJW
Shakespeare-Jahrbuch (Weimar) — SJW
Shakespeare-Jahrbuch (Weimar) — SJ(Weimar)
Shakespeariana — SNA
Shakhtnoe Stroitel'stvo [*Former USSR*] — Shakhtnoe Stroit
Shakti — Sh
Shale Country — Shale Ctry
Shale Review — Shale Rev
Shane Quarterly — Shane Q
Shanghai Educational Review/Chung-Hua Chiao Yue Chieh — Shanghai Educ Rev
Shanghai Environmental Sciences — Shanghai Environ Sci
Shanghai Iron and Steel Research Institute. Technical Report [*China*] — Shanghai Iron Steel Res Inst Tech Rep
Shantung Medical Journal [*People's Republic of China*] — Shantung Med J
Shantung University Journal / Shan Tung Ta Hsueh Pao — Shantung Univ J
Shanxi Medical and Pharmaceutical Journal — Shanxi Med Pharm J
Shanxi Medical Journal — Shanxi Med J
Shanxi University Journal. Natural Science Edition — SDXKDT
Shanxi University. Journal. Natural Science Edition — Shanxi Univ J Nat Sci Ed
Shanxi-A Medicina Revuo — Shanxi A Med Rev
Sharp Technical Journal — Sharp Tech J
Sharpe's London Magazine — Sharpe
Sharpe's London Magazine — Sharpes Lond M
Shaw Bulletin — ShawB
Shaw Review — Shaw R
Shaw Review — Shaw Rev
Shchorichnyk Ukrayins'ke Botanichne Tovarystvo — Shchorichnyk Ukrayins'ke Bot Tov
Sheep and Beef Farm Survey — Sheep Beef Farm Surv
Sheep and Goat Handbook — Sheep Goat Handb
Sheep and Goat. Wool and Mohair — Sheep Goat Wool Mohair
Sheepfarming Annual — SFANA2
Sheepfarming Annual — Sheepfarm Annu
Sheepfarming Annual — Sheepfarming Annu
Sheepfarming Annual. Massey Agricultural College — Sheepfarming Annu Massey Agr Coll
Sheet Metal and Plateworking News — Sheet Met Platework News
Sheet Metal Industries — Sh Metal Inds
Sheet Metal Industries — Sheet Met Ind
Sheffield Morning Telegraph — SFT
Sheffield University. Fuel Society. Journal — Sheffield Univ Fuel Soc J
Sheffield University. Geological Society. Journal — Sheffield Univ Geol Soc J
Shelf Life of Foods and Beverages. Proceedings. International Flavor Conference — Shelf Life Foods Beverages Proc Int Flavor Conf
Shelf Paper. Alaska Outer Continental Shelf Office — SHPA
Shell Aviation News — Shell Aviat News
Shell Bitumin Review — Shell Bitum Rev
Shell Development Company. Exploration and Production Research Division. Publication — Shell Devel Co Explor and Production Research Div Pub
Shell House Journal — Shell House J
Shell in Agriculture — Shell Agric
Shell Journal — Shell J
Shell Magazine [*England*] — Shell Mag
Shell Polymers — Shell Polym
Shell Trinidad — Shell Trin
Shellfish. Market Review and Outlook — Shellfish
Shelterforce — Shelter
Shenandoah — Shen
Sheng Wu Hua Hsueh Yu Sheng Wu Wu Li Hsueh Pao — SHWPA
Shepard Commemorative Volume. Papers on Marine Geology — Shepard Commem Vol Pap Mar Geol
Sherstyanoe Delo — Sherst Delo
Shetland Times — SHT
Shield Civil Service News — Shield
Shiga University. Faculty of Education. Memoirs. Natural Science — Mem Fac Ed Shiga Univ Natur Sci
Shigaku Zasshi — SZ
Shigen — SHGNA
Shigen Gijutsu Shikenjo Hokoku — SGSHA
Shih P'in Kung Yeh — SPKYB
Shih-ta Hsueeh-pao — SH
Shih-Ta Hsueh-Pao [*Bulletin of Taiwan Normal University*] — STHP
Shih-Ta Hsueh-Pao [*Bulletin of Taiwan Normal University*] — STHPD
Shika Kiso Igakkai Zasshi — SHKKA
Shikizai Kyokaishi — SKYOA
Shikoku Acta Medica — Shikoku Acta Med
Shikoku Agricultural Research — Shikoku Agr Res
Shikoku Agricultural Research — Shikoku Agric Res
Shikoku Dental Research — Shikoku Dent Res
Shikoku Journal of Clinical Chemistry — Shikoku J Clin Chem
Shikoku Medical Journal — Shikoku Med J
Shimadzu Review — Shimadzu Rev
Shimane Daigaku Ronshu: Jinbun Kagaku [*Journal of the Shimane University: Humanistic Sciences*] — SNDR
Shimane Daigaku Ronshu: Shizen Kagaku — SDRSA
Shimane Journal of Medical Science — Shimane J Med Sci
Shimane Journal of Medical Science — SJSCDM
Shimane University. Faculty of Education. Memoirs. Natural Science — Mem Fac Ed Shimane Univ Natur Sci
Shimane University. Faculty of Science. Memoirs — Mem Fac Sci Shimane Univ
Shimizu Kensetsu Kenkyusho-Ho — SZKKB
Shin Kinzoku Kogyo — SKKOA
Shinagaku Kenkyu — SGK
Shinagawa Refractories Technical Report — Shinagawa Refract Tech Rep
Shinagawa Technical Report — Shinagawa Tech Rep
Shinko Electric Journal — Shinko Electr J
Shinshu Horticulture/Nagano Horticultural Society — Shinshu Hort
Shinshu Medical Journal [*Japan*] — Shinshu Med J
Shinshu University. Faculty of Science. Journal — Shinshu Univ Fac Sci J
Ship Abstracts — Ship Abstr
Ship and Boat — Ship Boat
Ship and Boat International — Ship and Boat
Ship and Boat International — Ship & Boat Int
Ship Research Institute (Tokyo). Papers — Ship Res Inst (Tokyo) Pap
Shipbuilder and Marine Engine Builder [*England*] — Shipbuild Mar Engine Build
Shipbuilding and Marine Engineering International — Shipbldg Mar Engng Int
Shipbuilding and Marine Engineering International — Shipbuild & Mar Engng Int
Shipbuilding and Marine Engineering International — Shipbuild Mar Eng Int
Shipbuilding and Repair — Shipbuild Rep
Shipbuilding and Shipping Record — Shipbldg Shipp Rec
Shipcare and Maritime Management — Shipcare Marit Manage
Shipping, Commerce, and Aviation of Australia — Ship Com Aviation
Shipping Regulation. Pike and Fischer — Shipping Reg P & F
Shipping Statistics — Shipping Statis
Shipping Statistics and Economics — Shipping Statis and Econ
Shipping Weekly — Shipp Weekly
Shipping World and Shipbuilder — Shipp Wld Shipbldr
Shipping World and Shipbuilder — Shipp World & Shipb
Shipping World and Shipbuilder — Shipp World & Shipbuild
Shipping World and Shipbuilder — SPW
Shire and Municipal Record — S & M Record
Shire and Municipal Record — S & MR
Shire and Municipal Record — Shire & Munic R
Shire and Municipal Record — Shire & Munic Rec
Shire and Municipal Record — Shire Munic Rec
Shire and Municipal Record — SHMRD
Shirley Institute. Bulletin — Shirley Inst Bull
Shirley Institute. Memoirs — Shirley Inst Mem
Shirley Institute Publication — Shirley Inst Publ
Shiso — Sh
Shiva Mathematics Series — Shiva Math Ser
Shivaji University. Journal — Shivaji Univ J
Shivaji University. Science Journal — Shivaji Univ Sci J
Shizenshi-Kenkyu Occasional Papers. Osaka Museum of Natural History — Shizenshi-Kenkyu Occas Pap Osaka Mus Nat Hist
Shock — SHK
Shock and Circulatory Homeostasis. Transactions of the Conference — Shock Cir Homeostasis Trans Conf
Shock and Vibration Bulletin — Shock Vib Bull
Shock and Vibration Bulletin — SVBUA
Shock and Vibration Digest — Shock Vib Dig
Shock Waves in Condensed Matter. Proceedings. American Physical Society Topical Conference on Shock Waves in Condensed Matter — Shock Waves Condens Matter Proc Am Phys Soc Top Conf
Shoe and Leather Reporter — Shoe Leather Rep

Shokubai. Supplement [*Japan*] — Shokubai Suppl
Shokubutsu Boeki/Plant Protection — Shokubutsu Boeki Plant Prot
Shokuhin Shosha — SKNSB
Shoni Geka — SHGED
Shoni Geka Naika — SGNAD
Shoni Naika — SHNAD
Shoni No Noshinkei — SHOND
Shonika — SONKA
[*The*] **Shopper Report** — TSR
Short Course Handbook. Mineralogical Association of Canada — Short Course Handb Mineral Assoc Can
Short Course Notes. Mineralogical Society of America — Short Course Notes Mineral Soc Am
Short Notes on Alaskan Geology. Alaska Department of Natural Resources. Geologic Report — SNAG
Short Report. Rhodesia Geological Survey — Short Rep Rhod Geol Surv
Short Report. Southern Rhodesia Geological Survey — Short Rep South Rhod Geol Surv
Short Story Criticism — SSC
Short Story International — SSI
Short Wave Magazine — Short Wave Mag
Shorter Encyclopaedia of Islam — SEI
Showa Densen Denran Rebyu — SDDRA
Showa Igakkai Zasshi — SIGZA
Showa Wire and Cable Review — Showa Wire and Cable Rev
Showa Wire and Cable Review [*Japan*] — Showa Wire Cable Rev
Showme [*Database*] — SME
Show-Me Libraries — Show Me Lib
Show-Me News and Views [*Missouri*] — Show-Me
Shoyakugaku Zasshi — SHZAA
Shu-Hsueh Hsueh-Pao — SHHPB
Shujutsu — SHUJA
Shuttle, Spindle, and Dyepot — Shuttle
Shuttle, Spindle, and Dyepot — Shuttle Spin and Dye
SIA [*Societe des Ingenieurs de l'Automobile*] **Journal** [*France*] — SIA J
SIA. Surface and Interface Analysis — SIA Surf Interface Anal
SIAJ: Singapore Institute of Architects. Journal — SIAJ
SIAM [*Society for Industrial and Applied Mathematics*]-AMS Proceedings [*American Mathematical Society*] — SIAM AMS Proc
SIAM [*Society for Industrial and Applied Mathematics*] **Journal on Algebraic and Discrete Methods** — SIAM J Algebraic and Discrete Methods
SIAM [*Society for Industrial and Applied Mathematics*] **Journal on Algebraic and Discrete Methods** — SIAM J Algebraic Discrete Methods
SIAM [*Society for Industrial and Applied Mathematics*] **Journal on Applied Mathematics** — SIAM J A Ma
SIAM [*Society for Industrial and Applied Mathematics*] **Journal on Applied Mathematics** — SIAM J App Math
SIAM [*Society for Industrial and Applied Mathematics*] **Journal on Applied Mathematics** — SIAM J Appl Math
SIAM [*Society for Industrial and Applied Mathematics*] **Journal on Applied Mathematics** — SMJMA
SIAM [*Society for Industrial and Applied Mathematics*] **Journal on Computing** — SIAM J Comput
SIAM [*Society for Industrial and Applied Mathematics*] **Journal on Control** — SIAM J Cont
SIAM [*Society for Industrial and Applied Mathematics*] **Journal on Control** — SIAM J Control
SIAM [*Society for Industrial and Applied Mathematics*] **Journal on Control** — SJCOA
SIAM [*Society for Industrial and Applied Mathematics*] **Journal on Control and Optimization** — SIAM J Control and Optimiz
SIAM [*Society for Industrial and Applied Mathematics*] **Journal on Control and Optimization** — SIAM J Control Optim
SIAM [*Society for Industrial and Applied Mathematics*] **Journal on Control and Optimization** — SIAM J Control Optimization
SIAM [*Society for Industrial and Applied Mathematics*] **Journal on Control and Optimization** — SJCOD
SIAM Journal on Discrete Mathematics — SIAM J Discrete Math
SIAM [*Society for Industrial and Applied Mathematics*] **Journal on Mathematical Analysis** — SIAM J Math
SIAM [*Society for Industrial and Applied Mathematics*] **Journal on Mathematical Analysis** — SIAM J Math Anal
SIAM [*Society for Industrial and Applied Mathematics*] **Journal on Mathematical Analysis** — SJMAA
SIAM Journal on Matrix Analysis and Applications — SIAM J Matrix Anal Appl
SIAM [*Society for Industrial and Applied Mathematics*] **Journal on Numerical Analysis** — SIAM J Num
SIAM [*Society for Industrial and Applied Mathematics*] **Journal on Numerical Analysis** — SIAM J Numer Anal
SIAM [*Society for Industrial and Applied Mathematics*] **Journal on Numerical Analysis** — SJNAA
SIAM Journal on Optimization — SIAM J Optim
SIAM [*Society for Industrial and Applied Mathematics*] **Journal on Scientific and Statistical Computing** — SIAM J Sci and Stat Comput
SIAM [*Society for Industrial and Applied Mathematics*] **Journal on Scientific and Statistical Computing** — SIAM J Sci Stat Comput
SIAM [*Society for Industrial and Applied Mathematics*] **Journal on Scientific and Statistical Computing** — SIAM J Sci Statist Comput
SIAM [*Society for Industrial and Applied Mathematics*] **Review** — SIAM R
SIAM [*Society for Industrial and Applied Mathematics*] **Review** — SIAM Rev
SIAM [*Society for Industrial and Applied Mathematics*] **Review** — SIREA
SIAM [*Society for Industrial and Applied Mathematics*] **Science Bulletin** — SIAM Sci Bull
SIAM [*Society for Industrial and Applied Mathematics*] **SIMS Conference Series** [*SIAM Institute for Mathematics and Society*] — SSCSDJ
SIAM (Society for Industrial and Applied Mathematics) SIMS (SIAM Institute for Mathematics and Society) Conference Series — SIAM (Soc Ind Appl Math) SIMS (SIAM Inst Math Soc) Conf Ser
SIAM [*Society for Industrial and Applied Mathematics*] **Studies in Applied Mathematics** — SIAM Stud Appl Math
SIAM [*Society for Industrial and Applied Mathematics*] **Studies in Applied Mathematics** — SIAM Studies in Appl Math
Siamese Veterinary Association. Journal — Siamese Vet Assoc J
SIAP. Revista de la Sociedad Interamericana de Planificacion [*Colombia*] — SIAP
Siauliu Pedagoginio Instituto Mokslo Darbai — SPIMD
Sibelius-Mitteilungen — Sibelius
Siberian Advances in Mathematics — Siberian Adv Math
Siberian Chemistry Journal — SCJ
Siberian Chemistry Journal — Sib Chem J
Siberian Chemistry Journal [*English Translation*] — SICJA
Siberian Chemistry Journal. English Translation — Sib Chem J Engl Transl
Siberian Journal of Biology — Sib J Biol
Siberian Journal of Chemistry — Sib J Chem
Siberian Journal of Computer Mathematics — Siberian J Comput Math
Siberian Journal of Differential Equations — Siberian J Differential Equations
Siberian Mathematical Journal — Sib Math J
Siberian Mathematical Journal — Siberian Math J
Siberian Mathematical Journal — SMJ
Siberian School of Algebra and Logic — Siberian School Algebra Logic
Siberian World — Siberian Wld
Siberskii Vestnik Sel'skokhozyaistvennoi Nauki — Sib Vest Sel'Khoz Nauki
Sibirskaia Sovetskaia Entsiklopediia — SSE
Sibirskie Ogni — SO
Sibirskii Biologicheskii Zhurnal — Sib Biol Zh
Sibirskii Fiziko-Tekhnicheskii Zhurnal — Sib Fiz Tekh Zh
Sibirskii Geograficheskii Sbornik — Sib Geogr Sb
Sibirskii Khimicheskii Zhurnal — Sib Khim Zh
Sibirskii Matematiceskii Zurnal — Sibirsk Mat Z
Sibirskii Matematiceskii Zurnal — SMZHA
Sibirskii Nauchno-Issledovatel'skii Institut Energetiki. Trudy — Sib Nauchno Issled Inst Energ Tr
Sibirskii Nauchno-Issledovatel'skii Institut Geologii. Geofiziki i Mineral'nogo Syr'ya. Trudy — Sib Nauchno Issled Inst Geol Geofiz Miner Syrya Tr
Sibirskii Nauchno-Issledovatel'skii Institut Khimizatsii Sel'skogo Khozyaistva. Nauchno-Tekhnicheskii Byulleten — Sib Nauchno Issled Inst Khim Selsk Khoz Nauchno Tekh Byull
Sibirskii Teplofizicheskii Seminar — Sib Teplofiz Semin
Sibirskiia Vrachebnyia Viedomosti — Sibirsk Vrach Viedom
Sibirskij Matematicheskij Zhurnal — Sib Mat Zh
Sibrium. Collana di Studi e Documentazioni — Sibri
Sicher Ist Sicher — SICSA
Sichere Arbeit — SICAB
Sichere Arbeit [*Austria*] — Sich Arb
Sicherheit — SICHD
Sicherheit in Chemie und Umwelt — Sicherheit Chem Umwelt
Sicherheit in Chemie und Umwelt. Zeitschrift zum Handbuch der Gefaehrlichen Gueter — Sicherh Chem Umwelt
Sicherheitsingenieur — SCIGB
Sicherheitspolitik Heute — Sicherheitspol Heute
Sicilia Archaeologica. Rassegna Periodica di Studi, Notizie e Documentazione — Sicilia Arch
Sicilia Archeologica — Sic A
Sicilia Archeologica — Sic Arch
Sicilia Archeologica — Sich Arch
Sicilia Artistica ed Archeologica — Sicil Art ed Arch
Sicilia Medica — Sicil Med
Sicilia Sacra — Sic Sac
Sicilia Sanitaria — Sicil Sanit
Siculorum Gymnasium — SG
Siculorum Gymnasium — SGym
Siculorum Gymnasium — Sic Gym
Siculorum Gymnasium — Sic Gymn
Siculorum Gymnasium — SicG
Sicurezza e l'Igiene nell'Industria — Sicurezza Ig Ind
SID [*Society for Information Display*] **Journal** — SID J
Sida Contributions to Botany — Sida Contrib Bot
Side Effects of Drugs — SEFDAO
Side Effects of Drugs — Side Eff Drugs
Side Effects of Drugs. Annual [*Elsevier Book Series*] — SEDA
Side Effects of Drugs. Annual — Side Eff Drugs Annu
Sidereal Messenger — Sid Mess
Siderurgia Latinoamericana — Sider Latinoam
Siderurgia Latinoamericana — SILAD
Sidney Newsletter — S New
Siebel Technical Review — Siebel Tech Rev
Siebenbuergische Quartalschrift — Siebenbuerg Quartalschr
Siebenbuergische Vierteljahresschrift — Sieb Vjschr
Siebenbuergische Vierteljahrsschrift — SV
Siebenbuergisches Archiv — Siebenbuerg Arch
Sieboldia Acta Biologica — SIEBA7
Sieboldia Acta Biologica — Sieboldia Acta Biol
Siedlungswasserwirtschaftliches Kolloquium — Siedlungswasserwirtsch Kolloq
Siegel aus Bogazkoy — S Bo
Siemens Components (English Edition) — Siemens Components (Engl Ed)
Siemens Electronic Components Bulletin — Siemens Electron Components Bull
Siemens Energietechnik [*Germany*] — Siemens Energietech
Siemens Forschungs- und Entwicklungsberichte — Siemens Forsch Entwicklungsber

Siemens Forschungs- und Entwicklungsberichte — Siemens Forsch- und Entwicklungsber
Siemens Forschungs- und Entwicklungsberichte. Research and Development Reports — Siemens Forsch Entwickl
Siemens Forschungs- und Entwicklungsberichte. Research and Development Reports — Siemens Forsch Entwicklungsber Res Dev Rep
Siemens Power Engineering [*Germany*] — Siemens Power Eng
Siemens Research and Development Reports — Siemens Res Dev Rep
Siemens Review — Siemens Rev
Siemens-Albis Berichte — SABRB
Siemens-Albis Berichte — Siemens-Albis Ber
Siemens-Zeitschrift — Siemens-Z
Siempre — SE
Sierra — GSIE
Sierra Club. Bulletin — SCBUB
Sierra Club. Bulletin — SCBUB8
Sierra Club. Bulletin — Sierra
Sierra Club. Bulletin — Sierra Club B
Sierra Club. Bulletin — Sierra Club Bull
Sierra Educational News — Sierra Ed News
Sierra Leona Bulletin of Religion — SLBR
Sierra Leona Studies — SLSt
Sierra Leone Agricultural Division. Ministry of Agriculture and Natural Resources. Report — Sierra Leone Agric Div Minist Agric Nat Resour Rep
Sierra Leone Bulletin of Religion — Sierra L Bull Rel
Sierra Leone Fisheries Division. Technical Paper — Sierra Leone Fish Div Tech Pap
Sierra Leone Geographical Journal — Sierra Leone Geogr J
Sierra Leone Language Review — Sierra Leone Lang R
Sierra Leone Language Review — Sierra Leone Lang Rev
Sierra Leone Language Review — SLLR
Sierra Leone. Report on the Geological Survey Division — Sierra Leone Rep Geol Surv Div
Sierra Leone Studies — Sierra Leone Stud
Sierra Leone Trade Journal — Sierra Leone Trade J
Siewernij Wiestnik — SW
Sight and Sound — GSNS
Sight and Sound — S & S
Sight and Sound — Si & So
Sight and Sound — Sight & S
Sight and Sound — SS
Sightlines — Sgtl
Sight-Saving Review — Sight-Sav R
Sight-Saving Review — Sight-Sav Rev
Sight-Saving Review — SSREA
Siglo de las Misiones — SdM
Siglo de las Misiones — Siglo Mis
Siglo Medico — Siglo Med
Sigma — SIX
Sigma. Revue du Centre d'Etudes Linguistiques d'Aix Montpellier — Sig
Sigma Series in Applied Mathematics — Sigma Ser Appl Math
Sigma Series in Pure Mathematics — Sigma Ser Pure Math
Sigma Xi Quarterly — Sigma Xi Q
Sign Language Studies — Sign Lang Stud
Sign Language Studies — SLS
Signal Processing — Signal Process
Signal Processing and Digital Filtering — Signal Process Digit Filtering
Signalman's Journal — Signalmans J
Signes du Temps — Sig T
Signes du Temps — ST
Signo-Revista para el Dialogo — SI
Signos. Estudios de Lengua y Literatura (Chile) — SSC
Signos Universitarios — SU
Signs — SIG
Signs. Journal of Women in Culture and Society — GSIG
Signs; Journal of Women in Culture and Society — Signs J Women Cult Soc
Signs. University of Chicago Press — UC/S
Sigurnost u Rudnicima — Sigurnost Rudn
SIK [*Svenska Institutet foer Konserveringsforskning*] **Publikation** — SIK Publ
SIK [*Svenska Institutet foer Konserveringsforskning*] **Rapport** — SIK Rapp
Sikh Religious Studies Information — SRSI
Sikh Review [*Calcutta*] — Sikh R
Silent Picture — Silent Pic
Silicate Conference. Proceedings — Silic Conf Proc
Silicates Industriels [*Belgium*] — SIINA
Silicates Industriels — Silic Ind
Silicates Industriels — Silicates Indus
Silicon Carbide. Proceedings. International Conference on Silicon Carbide — Silicon Carbide Proc Int Conf
Silicon for Chemical Industry. International Conference — Silicon Chem Ind Int Conf
Silicon Molecular Beam Epitaxy. Symposium — Silicon Mol Beam Epitaxy Symp
Silikat Journal — Silik J
Silikattechnik [*Germany*] — SITKA
Silikaty — SIKTA
Silikaty — Silik
Silikat-Zeitschrift — Silik Z
Silikat-Zeitschrift — Silikatzs
Silk and Artificial Silk Mercury — Silk Artif Silk Mercury
Silk and Rayon Digest — Silk Rayon Dig
Silk and Rayon Industries of India — Silk Rayon Ind India
Silk and Rayon Industries of India — SRIIA
Silk Digest Weekly — Silk Dig Wkly
Silk Journal — Silk J
Silk Journal and Rayon World — Silk J Rayon World
Silkworm Information Bulletin — Silkworm Inf Bull
Sillar-Revista Catolica de Cultura — SRA
Silliman Journal — SiJ
Silliman Journal — Silliman J
Silliman Journal — SJ
Silliman's Journal of Science — Sillimans J Sci
Silumine Fizika — Silumine Fiz
Silva Fennica — SIFEA
Silva Fennica — Silva Fenn
Silvae Genetica — SIGEA
Silvae Genetica — Silvae Gen
Silvae Genetica — Silvae Genet
Silvaecultura Tropica et Subtropica — Silvaecult Trop Subtrop
Silver Institute Letter — Silver Inst Lett
Silvicultura em Sao Paulo — Silvic Sao Paulo
Silvicultural Notes. Ontario Department of Lands and Forests — Silv Notes Ont Dep Lds For
Silviculture Research Note (Tanzania) — Silv Res Note (Tanz)
Simmons Study of Media and Markets [*Database*] — SMM
Simmons Teen-Age Research Study [*Database*] — STARS
Simon's Tax Cases [*United Kingdom*] — STC
Simon's Town Historical Society — Simon's Town Hist Soc
Simpler Nervous Systems — Simpler Nerv Syst
Simplicity Magazine — Simplicity Mag
Simposio Brasileiro de Eletroquimica e Eletroanalitica — Simp Bras Eletroquim Eletroanal
Simposio de Fermentacao — Simp Ferment
Simposio Panamericano de Farmacologia y Terapeutica — Simp Panam Farmacol Ter
Simposio Regional de Geologia — Simp Reg Geol
Simposium de Higiene Industrial — Simp Hig Ind
Simposium de Higiene Industrial. Trabajos — Simp Hig Ind Trab
Simpozion de Biodeteriorare si Climatizare. Lucrarile — Simp Biodeterior Clim Lucr
Simpozium po Otlalennoi Gibridizatsii Rastenii — Simp Otlalennoi Gibrid Rast
Simulation — SIMUA
Simulation and Games — Simul and Games
Simulation and Games — Simulat & Games
Simulation and Games — Simulat Gam
Simulation and Gaming — PSNG
Simulation Councils. Proceedings Series — Simul Counc Proc Ser
Simulation Councils. Proceedings Series — SMCPA
Simulation/Games for Learning — Simul Games Learn
Simulation Gaming News — SGN
Simulation Journal — SJ
Simulation Today — Simul Today
Simulations Councils. Proceedings — Simulations Councils Proc
SIN [*Schweizerisches Institut fuer Nuklearforschung*] **Newsletter** — SIN Newsl
Sin Nombre — SiN
Sin Nombre — Sin N
Sin Nombre — SN
Sinai Hospital. Journal — Sinai Hosp J
Sinclair Lewis Newsletter — SLN
Sinclair QL World — SQLW
Sind University Journal of Education — Sind Univ J Ed
Sind University Research Journal. Science Series — Sind Univ Res J Sci Ser
Sindar Reporter — Sindar Rep
Sinet: An Ethiopian Journal of Science — Sinet Ethiop J Sci
Sinfonian Magazine — Sinfonian Mag
Sing Out — SI
Sing Out! — SO
Singapore Business — Singapore Bus
Singapore Business — SXI
Singapore Dental Journal — Singapore Dent J
Singapore Journal of Obstetrics and Gynaecology — Singapore J Obstet Gynaecol
Singapore Journal of Physics — Singapore J Phy
Singapore Journal of Primary Industries — Singapore J Primary Ind
Singapore Journal of Tropical Geography — Singapore J Trop Geogr
Singapore Journal of Tropical Geography — SJTGD5
Singapore Law Review — Sing LR
Singapore Law Review — Singapore L Rev
Singapore Libraries — Singapore Lib
Singapore Library Journal — SLJ
Singapore Medical Journal — SIMJA
Singapore Medical Journal — Sing Med J
Singapore Medical Journal — Singapore Med J
Singapore Medical Journal — Singapore MJ
Singapore National Academy of Science. Journal — Singapore Nat Acad Sci J
Singapore National Institute of Chemistry. Bulletin — Singapore Natl Inst Chem Bull
Singapore Public Health Bulletin — Sing Pub Health B
Singapore Shipbuilding and Repairing Directory — Sing Shipbuild Rep Dir
Singapore Society for Microbiology. Congress — Singapore Soc Microbiol Congr
Singapore Statistical Bulletin — Sing Stat B
Singapore Statistical Bulletin — Singapore Statist Bull
Singapore Year Book — Sing YB
Singende Kirche — Sing Kir
Single Crystal Properties — Single Cryst Prop
Sinister Wisdom — Sinister
Sinn und Form — SuF
Sinnspruche, Aphorismen, und Lebensweisheiten [*Database*] — BONMOT
Sino-American Relations [*Taiwan*] — Sino-Am Rels
Sino-Indian Studies — SIS

Sino-Japanese Journal of Allergology and Immunology — Sino Jpn J Allergol Immunol
Sinologica [*Basel*] — Sin
Sinopse de Odontologia — Sinop Odontol
Sinte Geertruydtsbronne — SG
SINTEF [*Selskapet for Industriell og Teknisk Forskning Ved Norges Tekniske Hoegskole*] **Report** — SINTEF Rep
Sintering. Proceedings. International Symposium on the Science and Technology of Sintering — Sintering Proc Int Symp Sci Technol Sintering
Sintese Politica, Economica, Social (Rio de Janeiro) — Sint Pol Econ Soc Rio
Sintesi dell'Oriente e della Bibbia — SOB
Sintesis Economica — Sintesi Econ
Sintesis Geografica — SG
Sinteticheskie Almazy — Sint Almazy
Sinteticheskie Materialy v Meditsine — Sint Mater Med
Sinteticheskii Kauchuk — Sint Kauch
Sintez, Analiz, i Struktura Organicheskikh Soedinenii [*Former USSR*] — Sint Anal Strukt Org Soedin
Sintez i Fiziko-Khimiya Polimerov — Sint Fiz-Khim Polim
Sintez i Issledovanie Effektivnosti Khimikatov dlya Polimernykh Materialov — Sint Issled Eff Khim Polim Mater
Sintez i Issledovanie Effektivnosti Khimikatov-Dobavok dlya Polimernykh Materialov — Sint Issled Eff Khim Dobovok Polim Mater
Sintez i Issledovanie Katalizatorov Neftekhimii — Sint Issled Katal Neftekhim
Sintez i Issledovanie Svoistv Kompleksnykh Soedinenii — Sint Issled Svoistv Kompleksn Soedin
Sintez i Khimicheskie Prevrashcheniya Polimerov — Sint Khim Prevrashch Polim
Sintez-Delenie. Trudy Sovetsko-Amerikanskogo Seminara — Sint Delenie Tr Sov Am Semin
Sintezy Geterotsiklicheskikh Soedinenii — Sint Geterotsikl Soedin
Sintezy Organicheskikh Soedinenij — Sint Org Soedin
Siouan and Caddoan Linguistics — SCLing
Sipario — Sip
Sir William Jones. Bicentenary of His Birth Commemoraration Volume 1746-1946 [*Monograph*] — SWJ
SIRA Abstracts and Reviews — SIRA Abstr Rev
Sirag. Amsagir Grakanut ean ew Aruesdi — Sirag
Siriraj Hospital Gazette — SHGAB8
Siriraj Hospital Gazette — Siriraj Hosp Gaz
Sirp ja Vasar — SjV
Sirpur Industries Journal — Sirpur Ind J
Sisal Mexicano — Sisal Mex
Sisal Review — Sisal Rev
Sistema — SA
Sistema — Si
Sistema de Documentacion sobre Poblacion en America Latina [*Database*] — DOCPAL
Sistema Nervoso — Sist Nerv
Sistema Revista de Ciencias Sociales — Sistema
Sistematiceskie Zametki po Materialam Gerbarii Imeni P. N. Krylova Pri Tomskom Gosudarstvennom Universitete Imeni V. V. Kujbyseva — Sist Zametki Mater Gerb Krylova Tomsk Gosud Univ Kujbyseva
Sistemi e Automazione — Sist e Autom
Sistemnyj Metod i Sovremennaja Nauka — Sistem Metod Sovrem Nauka
Sistemy Avtomatisatsii Nauchnykh Issledovanii — Sist Avtom Nauchn Issled
Sisters Today — Sisters
Sistole. Revista Uruguaya de Cardiologia — Sistole Rev Urug Cardiol
Site Selection Handbook — Site Sel Hdbk
Site Selection Handbook — SSH
Situatia Daunatorilor Animali ai Plantelor Cultivate — Situatia Daunatorilor Anim Pl Cult
Sitzung des Arbeitskreises Rastermikroskopie in der Materialpruefung — Sitz Arbeitskreises Rastermikrosk Materialpruef
Sitzungsberichte. Akademie der Wissenschaft in Wien — SAW
Sitzungsberichte. Akademie der Wissenschaft in Wien — SAWW
Sitzungsberichte. Akademie der Wissenschaft in Wien — SBAWW
Sitzungsberichte. Akademie der Wissenschaften — Sitzungsber d Akadem d Wiss
Sitzungsberichte. Akademie der Wissenschaften der DDR. Mathematik-Naturwissenschaften-Technik — Sitzungsber Akad Wiss DDR Math Naturwiss Tech
Sitzungsberichte. Akademie der Wissenschaften der DDR. Mathematik-Naturwissenschaften-Technik. Jahrgang 1977 — Sitzungsber Akad Wiss DDR Math-Naturwiss-Tech Jahrgang 1977
Sitzungsberichte. Akademie der Wissenschaften der DDR. Mathematik-Naturwissenschaften-Technik. Jahrgang 1979 — Sitzungsber Akad Wiss DDR Math-Naturwiss Tech Jahrgang 1979
Sitzungsberichte. Akademie der Wissenschaften in Wien — Akad Wiss Wien
Sitzungsberichte. Akademie der Wissenschaften in Wien — Ber Akad Wiss Wien
Sitzungsberichte. Akademie der Wissenschaften in Wien. Mathematisch-Naturwissenschaftliche Klasse. Abteilung 2A. Mathematik, Astronomie, Physik, Meteorologie, und Technik — Sitzungsber Akad Wiss Wien Math Naturwiss Kl Abt 2A
Sitzungsberichte. Akademie der Wissenschaften in Wien. Mathematisch-Naturwissenschaftliche Klasse. Abteilung 2B. Chemie — Sitzungsber Akad Wiss Wien Math Naturwiss Kl Abt 2B
Sitzungsberichte. Akademie der Wissenschaften in Wien. Mathematisch-Naturwissenschaftliche Klasse. Abteilung 3. Anatomie und Physiologie des Menschen und der Tiere sowie Theoretische Medizin — Sitzungsber Akad Wiss Wien Math Naturwiss Kl Abt 3
Sitzungsberichte. Akademie der Wissenschaften zu Berlin — SAWB
Sitzungsberichte. Akademie der Wissenschaften zu Muenchen — SAWM
Sitzungsberichte. Bayerische Akademie der Wissenschaften [*Munich*] — SAM
Sitzungsberichte. Bayerische Akademie der Wissenschaften — SBA
Sitzungsberichte. Bayerische Akademie der Wissenschaften — SBAW
Sitzungsberichte. Bayerische Akademie der Wissenschaften — SBBAW
Sitzungsberichte. Bayerische Akademie der Wissenschaften. Mathematisch-Naturwissenschaftliche Klasse — Sitzungsber Bayer Akad Wiss Math-Naturwiss Kl
Sitzungsberichte. Bayerische Akademie der Wissenschaften zu Muenchen — Sber Bayer Akad Wiss
Sitzungsberichte. Berlinische Gesellschaft Naturforschender Freunde — Sitzungsber Berl Ges Naturforsch Freunde
Sitzungsberichte der Akademie der Wissenschaften der DDR [*Deutsche Demokratische Republik*] — Sitzungsber Akad Wiss DDR
Sitzungsberichte der Akademie der Wissenschaften in Berlin — Sitzungsber Akad Wiss Berlin
Sitzungsberichte der Akademie der Wissenschaften in Wien. Philosophisch-Historische Klasse — SAWWPH
Sitzungsberichte der Altertumsgesellschaft Prussia — Sitzgsberr Altertsges Prussia
Sitzungsberichte der Altertumsgesellschaft Prussia zu Koenigsberg — S B Prussia
Sitzungsberichte der Altertumsgesellschaft Prussia zu Koenigsberg — Sitzungsber Prussia
Sitzungsberichte der Bayerische Akademie der Wissenschaften. Mathematisch-Naturwissenschaftliche Klasse — Sitzungsber Bayer Akad Wiss Math
Sitzungsberichte der Bayerischen Akademie der Wissenschaften — Bay Sitz
Sitzungsberichte der Bayerischen Akademie der Wissenschaften — Bayer Szb
Sitzungsberichte der Bayerischen Akademie der Wissenschaften — SAB
Sitzungsberichte der Bayerischen Akademie der Wissenschaften — SB Bayer Ak
Sitzungsberichte der Bayerischen Akademie der Wissenschaften — Sb Bayern
Sitzungsberichte der Bayerischen Akademie der Wissenschaften — SBBA
Sitzungsberichte der Bayerischen Akademie der Wissenschaften — Sitz Bay Akad Wis
Sitzungsberichte der Bayerischen Akademie der Wissenschaften — Sitz Ber Bayer Akad Wiss
Sitzungsberichte der Bayerischen Akademie der Wissenschaften — Sitzungsber Bayer Akad Wiss
Sitzungsberichte der Bayerischen Akademie der Wissenschaften. Muenchen — MSB
Sitzungsberichte der Bayerischen Akademie der Wissenschaften. Muenchen — Sitzgsberr Bayer Akad Wiss
Sitzungsberichte der Bayerischen Akademie der Wissenschaften. Philosophisch-Philologisch und Historische Klasse — SBAWPPH
Sitzungsberichte der Bernischen Botanischen Gesellschaft — Sitzungsber Bern Bot Ges
Sitzungsberichte der Deutschen Akademie der Wissenschaften zu Berlin — Berl Ak Sb
Sitzungsberichte der Deutschen Akademie der Wissenschaften zu Berlin — Berl Sitz
Sitzungsberichte der Deutschen Akademie der Wissenschaften zu Berlin — Sb Berl
Sitzungsberichte der Deutschen Akademie der Wissenschaften zu Berlin — SB Deut Akad
Sitzungsberichte der Deutschen Akademie der Wissenschaften zu Berlin — Sitzgb Berlin
Sitzungsberichte der Deutschen Akademie der Wissenschaften zu Berlin. Klasse fuer Gesellschaftswissenschaften — SDAWG
Sitzungsberichte der Deutschen Akademie der Wissenschaften zu Berlin. Klasse fuer Landwirtschaftliche Wissenschaften — Sitzungsber Deutsch Akad Wiss Berlin Kl Landw Wiss
Sitzungsberichte der Finnischen Akademie der Wissenschaften — SFAW
Sitzungsberichte der Finnischen Akademie der Wissenschaften — Sitz Ber Finn Akad Wiss
Sitzungsberichte der Gelehrten Estnischen Gesellschaft — Sitzungsber Gel Estn Ges
Sitzungsberichte der Gesellschaft der Naturforschenden Freunde. Berlin — SbGNFB
Sitzungsberichte der Gesellschaft der Wissenschaften in Prag — PSB
Sitzungsberichte der Gesellschaft fuer Natur- und Heilkunde zu Dresden — Sitzungsber Ges Natur Heilk Dresden
Sitzungsberichte der Gesellschaft Naturforschender Freunde zu Berlin — Sitzungsb Gesellsch Naturf Fr Berlin
Sitzungsberichte der Gesellschaft zur Befoerderung der Gesamten Naturwissenschaft. Marburg — Sitzgsberr Ges Befoerd Ges Natwiss
Sitzungsberichte der Heidelberger Akademie der Wissenschaften. Mathematisch-Naturwissenschaftliche Klasse — Sitzungsb Heidelberger Akad Wiss Math Natur Kl
Sitzungsberichte der Heidelberger Akademie der Wissenschaften. Mathematisch-Naturwissenschaftliche Klasse — Sitzungsber Heidelberger Akad Wiss Math Naturwiss Kl
Sitzungsberichte der Heidelberger Akademie der Wissenschaften. Philosophisch-Historische Klasse — Heid Ak Sb
Sitzungsberichte der Heidelberger Akademie der Wissenschaften. Philosophisch-Historische Klasse — SB Heidelb
Sitzungsberichte der Heidelberger Akademie der Wissenschaften. Philosophisch-Historische Klasse — SHAWPH
Sitzungsberichte der Heidelberger Akademie der Wissenschaften. Philosophisch-Historische Klasse — Sitzb Heidelb Akad
Sitzungsberichte der Heidelberger Akademie der Wissenschaften. Stiftung Heinrich Lanz. Mathematisch-Naturwissenschaftliche Klasse — Sitzungsber Heidelberger Akad Wiss Stiftung Heinrich Lanz Mat
Sitzungsberichte der Kaiserlichen Akademie der Wissenschaften. Mathematisch-Naturwissenschaftliche Classe — Sitzungsber Kaiserl Akad Wiss Math Naturwiss Cl

Sitzungsberichte der Koeniglich Boehmischen Gesellschaft der Wissenschaften — Sber K Boehm Ges Wiss
Sitzungsberichte der Koenigliche Preussischen Akademie der Wissenschaften — SKPA
Sitzungsberichte der Mathematisch-Naturwissenschaftlich-Aerztlichen Sektion/ Ukrainische Sevcenko-Gesellschaft der Wissenschaften in Lemberg — Sitzungsber Math Naturwiss Aerztl Sekt
Sitzungsberichte der Mathematisch-Naturwissenschaftlichen Abteilung der Bayerischen Akademie der Wissenschaften zu Muenchen — Sitzungsber Math Naturwiss Abt Bayer Akad Wiss Muenchen
Sitzungsberichte der Mathematisch-Naturwissenschaftlichen Klasse — Sitzungsber Math Naturwiss Kl
Sitzungsberichte der Mathematisch-Naturwissenschaftlichen Klasse der Bayerischen Akademie der Wissenschaften — Sitzungsber Math Naturwiss Kl Bayer Akad Wiss
Sitzungsberichte der Mathematisch-Physikalischen Klasse der Bayerischen Akademie der Wissenschaften zu Muenchen — Sitzungsber Math Phys Kl Bayer Akad Wiss Muenchen
Sitzungsberichte der Naturforschenden Gesellschaft. Rostock — Sitzgsberr Natf Ges Rostock
Sitzungsberichte der Naturforschenden Gesellschaft zu Rostock — Sitzungsber Naturforsch Ges Rostock
Sitzungsberichte der Naturforschenden-Gesellschaft zu Leipzig — Sitzungsber Naturf Ges Leipzig
Sitzungsberichte der Naturforscher-Gesellschaft bei der Universitaet Dorpat — Sitzungsber Naturf Ges Univ Dorpat
Sitzungsberichte der Naturforscher-Gesellschaft bei der Universitaet Dorpat — Sitzungsber Naturforsch Ges Univ Dorpat
Sitzungsberichte der Naturforscher-Gesellschaft bei der Universitaet Jurjeff — Sitzungsber Naturforsch Ges Univ Jurjeff
Sitzungsberichte der Naturforscher-Gesellschaft bei der Universitaet Tartu — Sitzungsber Naturforsch Ges Univ Tartu
Sitzungsberichte der Naturforscher-Gesellschaft zu Dorpat — Sitzungsber Naturforsch Ges Dorpat
Sitzungsberichte der Oesterreichischen Akademie der Wissenschaften. Philosophisch-Historische Klasse — S Oe AW
Sitzungsberichte der Oesterreichischen Akademie der Wissenschaften. Philosophisch-Historische Klasse — SB Oe AK
Sitzungsberichte der Oesterreichischen Akademie der Wissenschaften. Philosophisch-Historische Klasse — SB Osterr
Sitzungsberichte der Oesterreichischen Akademie der Wissenschaften. Philosophisch-Historische Klasse — SOeAWPH
Sitzungsberichte der Oesterreichischen Akademie der Wissenschaften. Philosophisch-Historische Klasse (Wien) — Sb Akad (Wien)
Sitzungsberichte der Oesterreichischen Akademie der Wissenschaften. Philosophisch-Historische Klasse (Wien) — SB Wiener AK
Sitzungsberichte der Oesterreichischen Akademie der Wissenschaften. Philosophisch-Historische Klasse (Wien) — Sitz Akad Wis Wien
Sitzungsberichte der Physikalisch-Medicinischen Societaet zu Erlangen — Sitzungsber Phys Med Soc Erlangen
Sitzungsberichte der Preussischen Akademie der Wissenschaften — Sitzgsberr Preuss Akad Wiss
Sitzungsberichte der Preussischen Akademie der Wissenschaften. Philosophisch-Historische Klasse — SPAWPH
Sitzungsberichte der Preussischen Akademie der Wissenschaften zu Berlin — SBA
Sitzungsberichte der Saechischen Akademie der Wissenschaften zu Leipzig. Philologisch-Historische Klasse — SB Lpz
Sitzungsberichte der Saechischen Akademie der Wissenschaften zu Leipzig. Philologisch-Historische Klasse — SSAW
Sitzungsberichte der Saechsischen Akademie der Wissenschaften — SBdSAdW
Sitzungsberichte der Saechsischen Akademie der Wissenschaften zu Leipzig. Mathematisch-Naturwissenschaftliche Klasse — Sitzungsber Saechs Akad Wiss Leipzig Math Naturwiss Kl
Sitzungsberichte der Saechsischen Akademie der Wissenschaften zu Leipzig. Mathematisch-Naturwissenschaftliche Klasse — Sitzungsber Saechs Akas Wiss Leipzig Math Natur Kl
Sitzungsberichte der Saechsischen Akademie der Wissenschaften zu Leipzig. Philosophisch-Historische Klasse — SSAWPH
Sitzungsberichte der Wissenschaftlichen Gesellschaft an der Johann Wolfgang Goethe-Universitaet Frankfurt am Main — Sitzungsber Wiss Ges Johann Wolfgang Goethe Univ Frankfurt
Sitzungsberichte des Naturhistorischen Vereines. Bonn — SbNVB
Sitzungsberichte des Plenums und der Klassen der Akademie der Wissenschaften der DDR [*German Democratic Republic*] — Sitzungsber Plenums Kl Akad Wiss DDR
Sitzungsberichte. Deutsche Akademie der Landwirtschaftswissenschaften zu Berlin — Sber Dt Akad Landwwiss Berl
Sitzungsberichte. Deutsche Akademie der Landwirtschaftswissenschaften zu Berlin — Sitzungsber Deut Akad Landwirt Wiss Berlin
Sitzungsberichte. Deutsche Akademie der Landwirtschaftswissenschaften zu Berlin — Sitzungsber Dtsch Akad Landwirtschaftswiss Berlin
Sitzungsberichte. Deutsche Akademie der Wissenschaften zu Berlin — SDAW
Sitzungsberichte. Deutsche Akademie der Wissenschaften zu Berlin — SDAWB
Sitzungsberichte. Deutsche Akademie der Wissenschaften zu Berlin. Klasse fuer Gesellschaftswissenschaften — Sitzungsber Dtsch Akad Wiss Berlin Kl Gesellschaftswiss
Sitzungsberichte. Deutsche Akademie der Wissenschaften zu Berlin. Klasse fuer Mathematik, Physik, und Technik — Sitzungsber Deut Akad Wiss Berlin Kl Math Phys Tech
Sitzungsberichte. Deutsche Akademie der Wissenschaften zu Berlin. Klasse fuer Mathematik, Physik, und Technik — Sitzungsber Dtsch Akad Wiss Berlin Kl Math Phys Tech
Sitzungsberichte. Deutsche Akademie der Wissenschaften zu Berlin. Klasse fuer Mathematik und Allgemeine Naturwissenschaften — Sitzungsber Dtsch Akad Wiss Berlin Kl Math Allg Naturwiss
Sitzungsberichte. Deutsche Akademie der Wissenschaften zu Berlin. Klasse fuer Medizin — Sitzungsber Dtsch Akad Wiss Berlin Kl Med
Sitzungsberichte. Deutsche Akademie der Wissenschaften zu Berlin. Klasse fuer Sprachen, Literatur, und Kunst — SB Berlin
Sitzungsberichte. Deutsche Akademie der Wissenschaften zu Berlin. Klasse fuer Sprachen, Literatur, und Kunst — SBDAW
Sitzungsberichte. Deutsche Akademie der Wissenschaften zu Berlin. Klasse fuer Sprachen, Literatur, und Kunst — SBDAWB
Sitzungsberichte. Deutsche Akademie der Wissenschaften zu Berlin. Klasse fuer Technische Wissenschaften — Sitzungsber Dtsch Akad Wiss Berlin Kl Tech Wiss
Sitzungsberichte. Deutsche Akademie der Wissenschaften zu Berlin. Mathematisch-Naturwissenschaftliche Klasse — Sitzungsber Dtsch Akad Wiss Berlin Math Naturwiss Kl
Sitzungsberichte. Deutsche (Preussische) Akademie der Wissenschaften zu Berlin. Philosophisch-Historische Klasse [*Berlin*] — SAB
Sitzungsberichte. Finnische Akademie der Wissenschaften — SBFAW
Sitzungsberichte. Finnische Akademie der Wissenschaften — Sitzungsber Finn Akad Wiss
Sitzungsberichte. Gesellschaft fuer Geschichte und Altertumskunde der Ostseeprovinzen Russlands — SBGGAKOPR
Sitzungsberichte. Gesellschaft fuer Geschichte und Altertumskunde der Ostseeprovinzen Russlands — SBGGAKR
Sitzungsberichte. Gesellschaft fuer Geschichte und Altertumskunde der Ostseeprovinzen Russlands — SGAOR
Sitzungsberichte. Gesellschaft fuer Geschichte und Altertumskunde der Ostseeprovinzen Russlands — SGGAOPR
Sitzungsberichte. Gesellschaft fuer Morphologie und Physiologie in Muenchen — Sber Ges Morph Physiol Muench
Sitzungsberichte. Gesellschaft Naturforschender Freunde zu Berlin — Sber Ges Naturf Freunde Berl
Sitzungsberichte. Gesellschaft Naturforschender Freunde zu Berlin — Sitzungsber Ges Naturforsch Freunde Berlin
Sitzungsberichte. Gesellschaft zur Befoerderung der Gesamten Naturwissenschaften zu Marburg — SBGMA
Sitzungsberichte. Gesellschaft zur Befoerderung der Gesamten Naturwissenschaften zu Marburg [*Germany*] — Sitzungsber Ges Befoerd Ges Naturwiss Marburg
Sitzungsberichte. Gesellschaft zur Befoerderung der Gesamten Naturwissenschaften zu Marburg — Sitzungsber Ges Befoerd Gesamten Naturwiss Marburg
Sitzungsberichte. Heidelberg Akademie der Wissenschaft — SBHAW
Sitzungsberichte. Heidelberg Akademie der Wissenschaft — SHA
Sitzungsberichte. Heidelberg Akademie der Wissenschaft — SHAW
Sitzungsberichte. Heidelberg Akademie der Wissenschaften. Mathematisch-Naturwissenschaftliche Klasse — Sitzungsber Heidelb Akad Wiss Math-Natur Kl
Sitzungsberichte. Heidelberg Akademie der Wissenschaften. Mathematisch-Naturwissenschaftliche Klasse — Sitzungsber Heidelb Akad Wiss Math-Naturwiss Kl
Sitzungsberichte. Heidelberg Akademie der Wissenschaften. Philosophisch-Historische Klasse — S B Heidelberg
Sitzungsberichte. Heidelberg Akademie der Wissenschaften. Philosophisch-Historische Klasse — SAH
Sitzungsberichte, Herausgegeben vom Naturhistorischen Verein der Preussischen Rheinlande und Westfalens — Sitzungsber Naturhist Vereins Preuss Rheinl
Sitzungsberichte. Kaiserliche Akademie der Wissenschaften in Wien — SBKAW
Sitzungsberichte. Kaiserliche Akademie der Wissenschaften in Wien — SBKAWW
Sitzungsberichte. Kaiserliche Akademie der Wissenschaften in Wien — SKAWW
Sitzungsberichte. Kaiserliche Preussische Akademie der Wissenschaften [*Berlin*] — SBPAW
Sitzungsberichte. Kaiserliche Preussische Akademie der Wissenschaften (Berlin) — SBPAWB
Sitzungsberichte. Koeniglich-Preussische Akademie der Wissenschaften — Sber K Preuss Akad Wiss
Sitzungsberichte. Koeniglich-Preussische Akademie der Wissenschaften — Sitzungsber K Preuss Akad Wiss
Sitzungsberichte. Oesterreichische Akademie der Wissenschafte. Mathematisch-Naturwissenschaftliche Klasse. Abteilung 2. Mathematik, Astron Physik, Meteorologie und Technik — Sitzber Oesterr Akad Wiss Math
Sitzungsberichte. Oesterreichische Akademie der Wissenschaften in Wien — S B Wien
Sitzungsberichte. Oesterreichische Akademie der Wissenschaften in Wien. Philosophisch-Historische Klasse — SbOAW
Sitzungsberichte. Oesterreichische Akademie der Wissenschaften in Wien. Philosophisch-Historische Klasse — SOAW
Sitzungsberichte. Oesterreichische Akademie der Wissenschaften. Mathematisch-Naturwissenschaftliche Klasse. Abteilung 1. Biologie, Mineralogie, Erdkunde, und Verwandte Wissenschaften — Sitzungsber Oesterr Akad Wiss Math Naturwiss Kl Abt
Sitzungsberichte. Oesterreichische Akademie der Wissenschaften. Mathematisch-Naturwissenschaftliche Klasse. Abteilung 2a. Mathematik, Astronomie, Physik, Meteorologie, und Technik — Sitzungsber Oesterr Akad Wiss Math Naturwiss Kl Abt 2a
Sitzungsberichte. Oesterreichische Akademie der Wissenschaften. Mathematisch-Naturwissenschaftliche Klasse. Abteilung 2b. Chemie — Sitzungsber Oesterr Akad Wiss Math Naturwiss Kl Abt 2b

Sitzungsberichte. Oesterreichische Akademie der Wissenschaften. Mathematisch-Naturwissenschaftliche Klasse. Abteilung II. Mathematik, Astronomie, Physik, Meteorologie, und Technik — Sitzungsber Oesterr Akad Wiss Math-Naturwiss Kl Abt II
Sitzungsberichte. Preussische Akademie der Wissenschaften — Sitzungsber Preuss Akad Wiss
Sitzungsberichte. Preussische Akademie der Wissenschaften — SPA
Sitzungsberichte. Preussische Akademie der Wissenschaften — SPAW
Sitzungsberichte. Saechsische Akademie der Wissenschaften (Leipzig) — LSB
Sitzungsberichte. Saechsische Akademie der Wissenschaften (Leipzig) — SB (Leipzig)
Sitzungsberichte. Saechsische Akademie der Wissenschaften (Leipzig). Mathematisch-Naturwissenschaftliche Klasse — Sitzungber Saechs Akad Wiss (Leipzig) Math-Natur Kl
Sitzungsberichte. Saechsische Akademie der Wissenschaften (Leipzig). Philologisch-Historische Klasse — SBSAW
Sitzungsberichte. Saechsische Akademie der Wissenschaften (Leipzig). Philologisch-Historische Klasse — SBSAWL
Sitzungsberichte. Saechsische Akademie der Wissenschaften (Leipzig). Philologisch-Historische Klasse — SSAWL
Sitzungsberichte. Saechsische Gesellschaft der Wissenschaften (Leipzig) — SSGW
Sitzungsberichte und Abhandlungen der Naturforschenden Gesellschaft Isis. Dresden — Sitzgsberr Abh Natf Ges Isis
Sitzungsberichte und Abhandlungen der Naturforschenden Gesellschaft zu Rostock — Sitzungsber Abh Naturf Ges Rostock
Sitzungsberichte und Abhandlungen der Naturforschenden Gesellschaft zu Rostock — Sitzungsber Abh Naturforsch Ges Rostock
Sitzungsberichte und Mitteilungen der Braunschweigischen Wissenschaftlichen Gesellschaft — Sitzungsber Mitt Braunschw Wiss Ges
Sitzungsberichte. Welkongress der Psychiatrie — Sitzungsber Weltkongr Psychiatr
Sitzungsberichte. Wiener Akademie — SbWAk
Sitzungsberichte. Wiener Akademie — SWA
Sitzungsberichte. Wiener Akademie der Wissenschaften — SWAW
Sitzungsberichte.Deutsche Akademie der Wissenschaften zu Berlin. Klasse fuer Chemie, Geologie, und Biologie — Sitzungsber Dtsch Akad Wiss Berlin Kl Chem Geol Biol
Sivilt Beredskap — SVBSA
Sixteenth Century Journal — PSXJ
Sixteenth Century Journal — SCJ
Sixteenth Century Journal — Six Cent J
Sixteenth Century Journal — Six Ct J
Sixteenth Century Journal — Sixteen Cent J
Sixteenth Century Journal — Sixteenth Cent J
Sixth Five-Year Plan, 1983-88 (Pakistan) — Pakistn Pl
Sixth-Generation Computer Technology Series — Sixth Gener Comput Tech Ser
Sixties — Six
SJC Today. Sheldon Jackson College [*Sitka, AK*] — SJCT
Sjoehistorisk Arsbok — Sjoehist Arsb
SK and F [*Smith, Kline, and French*] **Psychiatric Reporter** — SKF Psychiatr Rep
SK. Standarti i Kachestvo — SK Stand Kach
Skandia International Symposia — Skandia Int Symp
Skandinavisk Manadsskrift foer Textilindustri — Skand Manadsskr Textilind
Skandinavisk Numismatik — Skand Numis
Skandinavisk Tidskrift foer Faerg och Lack — Skand Tidskr Faerg Lack
Skandinavisk Veterinaertidskrift foer Bakteriologi, Patologi, samt Koettoch Mjoelkhygien — Skand Vet Tidskr
Skandinaviska Banken. Quarterly Review [*Later, Skandinaviska Enskilda Banken. Quarterly Review*] — SB
Skandinaviska Enskilda Banken — Skand Bank
Skandinaviska Enskilda Banken. Quarterly Review — SKA
Skandinaviska Enskilda Banken. Quarterly Review — Skand Ensk Bank Quart R
Skandinaviska Enskilda Banken. Quarterly Review — Skandinaviska Enskilda Banken Q R
Skandinavistik — Skand
Skandinavistik — Skandinavis
Skandinavskaga Filologija — SkFi
Skandinavskij Sbornik — SkSb
Skandinavskij Sbornik — SSb
Skanes Naturskyddsfoerenings Arsberaettelse — Skanes Naturskyddsfoeren Arsberaett
Skating Magazine — Skat Mag
SKB (Svensk Kaernbraenslehantering) Technical Report — SKB Tech Rep
SKBF / KBS Teknisk Rapport — SKBF KBS Tek Repp
Skeletal Radiology — Skeletal Radiol
Skeletal Radiology — SKRAD
Skeptical Inquirer — PSKI
Skiing — GSKI
Skillings' Mining Review — Skil Mining
Skillings' Mining Review — Skillings' Min Rev
Skillings' Mining Review — SKMRA
Skin Diver — GSKD
Skin Diver Magazine — Skin Diver Mag
Skin. Drug Application and Evaluation of Environmental Hazards. OHOLO Biological Conference — Skin Drug Appl Eval Environ Hazards OHOLO Biol Conf
Skin Pharmacology — Skin Pharmacol
Skin Research — Skin Res
Skinner's Silk and Rayon Record — Skinners Silk Rayon Rec
Skipsteknikk — SKPTA
Skizuoka University Faculty of Science. Reports — Shizuoka Univ Fac Sci Rep
Sklar a Keramik — SKKEA
Sklar a Keramik — Sklar Keram
Sklarske Rozhledy — Sklarske Rozhl
Skoda Review — Skoda Rev
Skoda Works. Nuclear Power Construction Division. Information Centre. Report ZJE — Skoda Works Nucl Power Constr Div Inf Cent Rep ZJE
Skogen — Skog
Skogs- och Lantbruksakademiens Tidskrift — Skogs-Lantbruksakad Tidskr
Skogshoegskolan, Institutionen foer Skogsteknik, Rapporter och Uppsatser. Research Notes [*Sweden*] — Skogshoegsk Inst Skogstek Rapp Uppsats Res Notes
Skogstradsforadling-Institutet foer Skogsforbattring — Skogstradsforadling Inst Skogsforbattring
Skolehygiejnisk Tidsskrift — Skhy T
Skool vir Chemie in Kerntegnologie. Referate — Sk Chem Kerntegnol Ref
Skopje Univezitetot Kiril i Metodij Fakultet na Matematicka Godisen Zbornik (Skopje) — Fak Mat Univ Kiril Metodij Skopje Godisen
S-K-P (Schoenheitspflege-Kosmetik-Parfumerie) Journal — SKP J
Skrifter af Naturhistorie-Selskabet — Skr Naturhist Selsk
Skrifter av Vetenskaps-Societeten i Lund — Skr Lund
Skrifter fra Reformationstiden [*Kobenhavn, Denmark*] — SRT
Skrifter fran Mineralogisk och Paleontologisk-Geologiska Institutionerna — Skr Mineral Paleontol Geol Inst
Skrifter fran Reformationstiden. Uppsala — SRTS
Skrifter i Naturskyddsaerenden/Svenska Vetenskapsakademien — Skr Naturskyddsaerenden
Skrifter K. Norske Videnskabers Selskab — Skrifter Trondheim
Skrifter. Norges Geologiske Undersoekelse — Skr Nor Geol Unders
Skrifter. Norsk Polarinstitutt — Skr Nor Polarinst
Skrifter. Norske Videnskaps-Akademi i Oslo — SNVO
Skrifter. Norske Videnskaps-Akademi i Oslo. I. Matematisk-Naturvidenskapelig Klasse — Skr Nor Vidensk-Akad Oslo I Mat-Naturvidensk Kl
Skrifter som udi det Kiobenhavnske Selskab — SKS
Skrifter. Svenska Kyrkohistoriska Foereningen — SSKHF
Skrifter udg af Videnskabsselskabet i Kristiania — Skr Videnskabsselsk Kristiania
Skrifter Udgivet. Universitetets Zoologiske Museum (Kobenhavn) — Skr Udgivet Univ Zool Mus (Kbh)
Skrifter Utgitt av det Norske Videnskaps-Akademi i Oslo. Historisk-Filosofisk Klasse — SNVA
Skrifter Utgitt av det Norske Videnskaps-Akademi i Oslo. Historisk-Filosofisk Klasse — SNVAOHF
Skrifter Utgitt. Det Norske Videnskaps-Akademi i Oslo — SNVAO
Skrifter Utgitt. Instituttet foer Nordisk Filologi. Universitetet i Bergen — SINFUB
Skrifter Utgitt. Norske Videnskaps-Akademi i Oslo. I. Matematisk-Naturvidenskapelig Klasse — Skr Nor Vidensk-Akad Oslo I
Skrifter Utgitt. Norske Videnskaps-Akademi i Oslo. I. Matematisk-Naturvidenskapelig Klasse — Skr Norske Vid-Akad Oslo I
Skrifter utgivet av Finlands Adelsfoerbund — Skr Finl Adelsfoerb
Skrifter utgivet av Modersmalslaerarnas Foerening — MLF
Skrifter utgivet av Sjoehistoriska Samfundet — Skr Sjoehist Samf
Skrifter Utgivna av Humanistiska Vetenskapssamfundet i Lund — SHVL
Skrifter Utgivna av Humanistiska Vetenskapssamfundet i Uppsala — SHVU
Skrifter Utgivna av Kungliga. Gustav Adolfs Akademien — GAA
Skrifter Utgivna av Kungliga Humanist. Vetenskaps-Samfundet i Uppsala — Skr Uppsala
Skrifter Utgivna av Kungliga Humanistiska Vetenskapssamfundet i Lund — SKHVL
Skrifter Utgivna av Kyrkohistoriska Foereningen — SKHF
Skrifter Utgivna av Kyrkohistoriska Foereningen. Svenska Synodalakter — SKHFS
Skrifter Utgivna av Litteraturvetenskapliga Institutionen Vid. Uppsala Universitet — SULI
Skrifter Utgivna av Svenska Institutet i Athen — Acta Athen
Skrifter Utgivna av Svenska Institutet i Rom — SSIR
Skrifter Utgivna av Svenska Litteratursaellskapet i Finland — SLF
Skrifter Utgivna. Genom Landsmalsarkivet i Lund — SLL
Skrifter Utgivna. Genom Landsmals-och Folk-Minnesarkivet i Uppsala — SLFU
Skrifter Utgivna. Humanistiska Vetenskapssamfundet i Uppsala — SkHVSU
Skrifter Utgivna. Institutionen foer Nordiska Sprak Vid. Uppsala Universitet — SINSU
Skrifter Utgivna. Institutionen foer Nordiska Sprak Vid. Uppsala Universitet — SINSUU
Skrifter Utgivna. Modernsmalslararnas Forening — SMF
Skrifter Utgivna. Modernsmalslararnas Forening — SMLF
Skrifter Utgivna. Namnden foer Svensk Sprakvard — SNSS
Skrifter Utgivna. Svenska Litteratursallskapet i Finland — SSLF
Skrifter Utgivna. Svenska Litteratursallskapet Studier i Nordisk Filologi — SSLSN
Skrifter Utgivna. Vetenskaps-Societeten i Lund — Skr Lund
Skrifter Utgivna. Vetenskaps-Societeten i Lund — SUVSL
Skrifter Utgivna. Vetenskaps-Societeten i Lund — SVSL
Skrifter Uutgitt av det Norske Videnskaps-Akademi. Klasse 1. Matematisk-Naturvidenskapelig Klasse — Skr Nor Vidensk Akad Kl 1 Mat Naturvidensk Kl
Skriftserie. Roskilde Universitetsbibliotek — Skriftser Roskilde Universitetsbibl
Skriftserie. Sverige Kyrkliga Studiefoerbund — SSKSF
Skripten zur Mathematischen Statistik — Skript Math Statist
Skrivteraf Naturhistorie Selskabet Kiobenhavn — Skr Naturh Selsk Kiobenhavn
Skroty Zgloszonych Prac. Ogolnopolskie Seminarium na temat Mieszanie — Skroty Zgloszonych Pr Ogolnopol Semin Mieszanie
Skrypty Szkoly Glownej Gospodarstwa Wiejskiego-Akademii Rolniczej w Warszawie. Ogrodnictwo — Skr Szk Gl Gospod Wiejsk-Akad Roln Warszawie Ogrod
Skrypty Uczelniane — Skrypty Uczel
Skrypty Uniwersytetu Slaskiego — Skrypty Univ Slaskiego
Sky and Telescope — GSTN
Sky and Telescope — S & T

Sky and Telescope — SKTEA
Sky and Telescope — Sky & Tel
Sky and Telescope — Sky and Telesc
Sky and Telescope — Sky Telesc
Skyscraper Management — Skyscraper Mgt
Skytteanska Samfundets Handlinger — SSH
Skywriting — Sky
SLA [*Scottish Library Association*] **News** — SLA News
Slaboproudy Obzor [*Czechoslovakia*] — Slaboproudy Obz
Slaboproudy Obzor — SLOZA
Slager. Vakblad voor de Vleesspecialist — SLR
Slagersambacht — DJS
SLANT [*School Library Association of the Northern Territory*] **News** — SLANTN
Slantsevaya i Khimicheskaya Promyshlennost [*Estonian SSR*] — Slants Khim Prom-St
Slaski Kwartalnik Historyczny Sobota — SlaK
Slaski Kwartalnik Historyczny Sobotka — Slaski Kwar Hist Sobotka
Slaskie Studia Historyczno-Teologiczne — Slask STHT
Slaskie Studie Historyczno-Teologiczne — SSHT
Slave River Journal [*Fort Smith, Northwest Territory*] — SR
Slavia — S
Slavia — Sl
Slavia — Sla
Slavia — Slav
Slavia Antiqua — SlA
Slavia Antiqua — SlAnt
Slavia Antiqua — Slav Ant
Slavia Antiqua — SlavA
Slavia Antiqua — Slavia Ant
Slavia Occidentalis — Slav Occ
Slavia Occidentalis — SLOc
Slavia Occidentalis — SLOcc
Slavia Occidentalis — SO
Slavia Orientalis — Slav Or
Slavia Orientalis — SLO
Slavia Orientalis — SLOR
Slavic and East European Journal — PSEE
Slavic and East European Journal — SEEJ
Slavic and East European Journal — Slav E Eur
Slavic and East European Journal — Slavic & E Eur J
Slavic and East European Journal — Slavic E Eu
Slavic and East European Studies — SEES
Slavic and European Education Review — Slav Euro Educ Rev
Slavic Review — GSLR
Slavic Review — SlaR
Slavic Review — Slavic R
Slavic Review — Slavic Rev
Slavic Review — SlavR
Slavic Review — SR
Slavic Review — SRev
Slavic Word — SW
Slavica — SL
Slavica Gothoburgensia — Slav Goth
Slavica Helvetica — Slav Helv
Slavica Lundensia — Slav Lund
Slavica Othiniensia — SlavO
Slavica Pragensia — SlavP
Slavica Pragensia — SLPr
Slavica Slovaca — SlavS
Slavische Rundschau — Slav R
Slavische Rundschau — Slav Rdsch
Slavische Rundschau — SLR
Slavische Rundschau — SlRund
Slavistic Printings and Reprintings — SLPR
Slavistic Printings and Reprintings — SPR
Slavistica. Praci Institutu Slov'janoznavstva Ukrajins'koji Vil'noji Akademiji Nauk — Sl UVAN
Slavisticki Studii — Slav S
Slavisticna Revija — SlavR
Slavisticna Revija — SlavRev
Slavisticna Revija — SLR
Slavistische Drukken en Herdrukken — SDH
Slavjanska Lingvisticna Terminologija — SLTerm
Slavjanskaja Filologija — SlavF
Slavonic and East European Review — PSER
Slavonic and East European Review — SEER
Slavonic and East European Review — Slav East Eur Rev
Slavonic and East European Review — Slavon & E Eur R
Slavonic and East European Review — Slavon E Eu
Slavonic and East European Review — Slavonic & E Eur R
Slavonic and East European Review — Slavonic East Eur Rev
Slavonic and East European Review — SlE
Slavonic and East European Review — SLR
Slavonic and East European Review — SLRev
Slavonic Review — Slavonic R
Slavonic Review — SLAVR
Slavonic Review — SlR
Slavonic Review — SLRev
Slavonic Review — SR
Slavorum Litterae Theologicae — SLT
Slavorum Litterae Theologicae — SLTh
Sleep (New York) — Sleep NY
Sleeping Sickness Bureau. Bulletin — Sleep Sick Bureau Bull
Sleszky Numismatik — Sleszky Num
Slevarenstvi — SLEVA
Slezsky Sbornik — SlSb
Slijtersvakblad. Vakblad voor de Drankenbranche — SLY
Slitok i Svoistva Stali. Trudy Konferentsii po Fiziko-Khimicheskim Osnovam Proizvodstva Stali — Slitok Svoistva Stali Tr Konf Fiz Khim Osn Proizvod Stali
Sloan Management Review — IMW
Sloan Management Review — Sloan
Sloan Management Review — Sloan Manag
Sloan Management Review — Sloan Manage Rev
Sloan Management Review — Sloan Mgmt Rev
Sloan Management Review — Sloan Mgt R
Sloan Management Review — SMR
Sloan Management Review — SMRVA
Sloc'jans'ke Movoznavstvo — SlMov
Sloejd och Ton — SoT
Slovak Music — SloM
Slovak Musik — Slovak Mus
Slovansky Prehled — SLoP
Slovansky Prehled — Slov Preh
Slovansky Prehled — SLP
Slovansky Prehled — SP
Slovene Studies — SlovS
Slovenska Akademia Vied — SAV
Slovenska Akademia Vied. Ustav Experimentalnej Farmakologie. Zbornik Prac — Slov Akad Vied Ustav Exp Farmakol Zb Pr
Slovenska Akademija Znanosti in Umetnosti. Razred za Prirodoslovne Vede. Dela — Slov Akad Znan Umet Razred Prirodosl Vede Dela
Slovenska Archaeologia — S A
Slovenska Archeologia — SlA
Slovenska Archeologia — Slov A
Slovenska Archeologia — Slov Arch
Slovenska Archeologia — Slov Archeol
Slovenska Archeologia — Slovenska Arch
Slovenska Hudba — S H
Slovenska Hudba — Slov Hud
Slovenska Hudba — Slovenska Hud
Slovenska Literatura — SLit
Slovenska Literatura — Slov Lit
Slovenska Numizmatika — Slov Num
Slovenska Numizmatika — Slov Numiz
Slovenska Rec — SLRec
Slovenska Rec — SR
Slovenska Vysoka Skola Technicka v Bratislave. Zbornik Vedeckej Konferencie SVST — Slov Vys Sk Tech Bratislave Zb Ved Konf SVST
Slovenske Lesne a Drevarske Hospodarstvo — Slov Lesne Drev Hospod
Slovenske Odborne Nazvoslovie — SON
Slovenske. Revue Dramatickych Umeni — SDi
Slovenski Cebelar — Slov Ceb
Slovenski Etnograf — SE
Slovenski Etnograf — Slov Etnogr
Slovensky Jazyk — SJ
Slovensky Jazyk a Literatura v Skole — SJL
Slovensky Narodopis — SlovN
Slovensky Narodopis — SN
Slovensky Pohl'ady — SlovP
Slovensky Pohl'ady — SLP
Slovensky Pohl'ady — SLPo
Slovensky Pohl'ady — SLPoh
Slovensky Porocevalec — SLP
Slovensky Spisovatel — SLSp
Slovesna Veda — SV
Slovjans'ke Literaturoznavstvo i Fol'klorystyka — SLif
Slovo a Slovesnost — SaS
Slovo a Slovesnost — SS
Slovo a Tvar — ST
Slovo. Casopis Staroslavenskog Instituta — Sl
Slovo Lektora — Slo L
Slovo na Storozi — SNS
Slow Dynamics in Condensed Matter. Proceedings. Tohwa University International Symposium — Slow Dyn Condens Matter Proc Tohwa Univ Int Symp
Slow Learning Child — Slow Learn
Slow Learning Child — Slow Learn Child
Slozhnye Elektromagnitnye Polya i Elektricheskie Tsepi — Slozhnye Elektromagn Polya Elektr Tsepi
Sludge Magazine — Sludge Mag
Sludge Management Series — Sludge Manage Ser
Slupskie Prace Matematyczno-Przyrodnicze Matematyka. Fizyka — Slup Prace Mat Przyr Mat Fiz
SLZ. Schweizerische Laboratoriums-Zeitschrift — SLZ Schweiz Lab Z
SM [*Solid Mechanics*] **Archives** — SM Arch
Small and Rural Hospital Report — Small Rural Hosp Rep
Small Business Bulletin — Small Bus Bull
Small Business Computer News — Small Bus Comput News
Small Business Computers — Small Bus Comput
Small Business Computers Magazine — Small Bus Comp
Small Business Report — SBR
Small Business Report — Small Bus Rt
Small Business Report — Small Business
Small Business Reporter — Small Bus
Small Business Reporter — Small Bus Reporter
Small Business Review — Small Bus Rev
Small Computers in Libraries — SCIL
Small Computers in Libraries — Small Comput Libr
Small Farm — Sm F
Small Group Behavior — Small Gr B

Small Group Behavior — Small Group Behav
Small Industry Journal [*Quezon City*] — SIJ
Small Mammal Newsletters — Small Mamm Newsl
Small Pond — Sm Pd
Small Press Review — Sm Pr R
Small Press Review — Small Pr
Small Press Review — Small Press Rev
Small Ruminant Research — Small Ruminant Res
Small School Forum — Small Sch For
Small Stock Magazine — Small Stock Mag
Small Systems Software — Small Sys Soft
Small Systems Software — Small Syst Software
Small Systems World — Small Sys
Small Systems World — Small Syst World
Small-Scale Master Builder — Small-Scale Master Bldr
Smarandache Function Journal — Smarandache Funct Jnl
Smarandache Notions Journal — Smarandache Notions J
Smaskrift-Norway. Landbruksdepartementet. Opplysningstjenesten — Smaskrift Landbruksdep Opplysningstjenesten
SME (Society of Manufacturing Engineers) Technical Paper. Series MRR — SME Tech Pap Ser MRR
SME [*Society of Manufacturing Engineers*] **Technical Paper. Series AD. Assembly Division** — SME Tech Pap Ser AD
SME [*Society of Manufacturing Engineers*] **Technical Paper. Series IQ** — SME Tech Pap Ser IQ
SME [*Society of Manufacturing Engineers*] **Technical Paper. Series MS** — SME Tech Pap Ser MS
SMEC [*Snowy Mountains Engineering Corporation*] **Magazine** — SMEC Mag
Smelter Process Gas Handling and Treatment. Proceedings. International Symposium — Smelter Process Gas Handl Treat Proc Int Symp
Smena [*Moscow*] — Sm
SME-SPE International Solution Mining Symposium — SME SPE Int Solution Min Symp
Smith College. Museum of Art. Bulletin — Smith Coll Mus Bul
Smith College. Studies in Social Work — Smith Coll
Smith College. Studies in Social Work — Smith Coll Stud Social Work
Smith, Kline, and French. Research Symposium on New Horizons in Therapeutics — Smith Kline French Res Symp New Horiz Ther
Smith-Hurd's Illinois Annotated Statutes — Ill Ann Stat (Smith-Hurd)
Smith's Blood Diseases of Infancy and Childhood [*monograph*] — Smiths Blood Dis Infancy Child
Smithsonian — GSMI
Smithsonian — Sm
Smithsonian — Smith
Smithsonian — SMSNA
Smithsonian Annals of Flight — Smithson Ann Flight
Smithsonian Contributions to Anthropology — SCA
Smithsonian Contributions to Anthropology — Smithson Contrib Anthropol
Smithsonian Contributions to Astrophysics — SCA
Smithsonian Contributions to Astrophysics — Smithson Contrib Astrophys
Smithsonian Contributions to Botany — Smithson Contr Bot
Smithsonian Contributions to Botany — Smithson Contrib Bot
Smithsonian Contributions to Knowledge — Smithson Contrib Knowl
Smithsonian Contributions to Paleobiology — Smithson Contrib Paleobiol
Smithsonian Contributions to the Earth Sciences — SCESBH
Smithsonian Contributions to the Earth Sciences — Smithson Contrib Earth Sci
Smithsonian Contributions to the Earth Sciences — Smithson Contrib Earth Sciences
Smithsonian Contributions to the Marine Sciences — SCSCD7
Smithsonian Contributions to the Marine Sciences — Smithson Contrib Mar Sci
Smithsonian Contributions to Zoology — Smithson Contr Zool
Smithsonian Contributions to Zoology — Smithson Contrib Zool
Smithsonian Instition Miscellaneous Collection — Smithsonian Inst Misc Coll
Smithsonian Institution. Annual Report — Smithson Inst Annu Rep
Smithsonian Institution. Annual Report — Smithson Rep
Smithsonian Institution. Astrophysical Observatory — SAO
Smithsonian Institution. Center for Short-Lived Phenomena. Annual Report and Review of Events — Smithson Inst Cent Short-Lived Phenom Annu Rep Rev Events
Smithsonian Institution. Contributions — Smithson Inst Contr
Smithsonian Institution Publications. Miscellaneous Collections — Smithson Inst Publ Misc Collect
Smithsonian Institution. Report — Smithson Inst Rpt
Smithsonian Institution. Reports — Smithson Rept
Smithsonian Miscellaneous Collection — Smithson Miscell Coll
Smithsonian Miscellaneous Collections — SMC
Smithsonian Miscellaneous Collections — Smithson Misc Colins
Smithsonian Miscellaneous Collections — Smithson Misc Collect
Smithsonian Miscellaneous Collections — Smithson Misc Colln
Smithsonian Report — SR
Smithsonian Science Information Exchange [*Database*] — SSIE
Smithsonian Year — Smithson Year
Smithsonian Year — SMYRAD
Smokeless Air [*England*] — SMLAA
Smokeshop — SS
Smoking and Health Bulletin — S and H Bull
Smoking and Health Reporter — SMHR
Smolenskii Gosudarstvennyi Pedagogiceskii Institut. Ucenye Zapiski — Smolensk Gos Ped Inst Ucen Zap
SMRE [*Safety in Mines Research Establishment*] **Report** — SMRE Rep
SNA Nursery Research Journal. Southern Nurserymen's Association — SNA Nursery Res J South Nurserymen's Assoc
SNIC [*Singapore National Institute of Chemistry*] **Bulletin** — SNIC Bull
Snow Revelry — Snow Revel
Snowshoe. Newsletter. NWT [*Northwest Territories, Canada*] **Library Association** — SNWT
Soap and Chemical Specialties [*Later, Soap/Cosmetics/Chemical Specialties*] — SCHSA
Soap and Chemical Specialties [*Later, Soap/Cosmetics/Chemical Specialties*] — Soap & Chem Spec
Soap and Chemical Specialties [*Later, Soap/Cosmetics/Chemical Specialties*] — Soap Chem Spec
Soap and Sanitary Chemicals — Soap & San Chem
Soap and Sanitary Chemicals — Soap Sanit Chem
Soap/Cosmetics/Chemical Specialities — Soap/Cosmet/Chem Spec
Soap/Cosmetics/Chemical Specialties — S & C Spec
Soap/Cosmetics/Chemical Specialties — SCC Spec
Soap/Cosmetics/Chemical Specialties — Soap Cosmet
Soap Gazette and Perfumer — Soap Gaz Perfum
Soap, Perfumery, and Cosmetics — Soap Perfum Cosmet
Soap, Perfumery, and Cosmetics — Soap Prf Cos
Soap, Perfumery, and Cosmetics — SOC
Soap, Perfumery, and Cosmetics. Yearbook and Buyers' Guide — Soap Perfum Cosmet Yearb Buyers Guide
Soap, Perfumery Cosmetic Trade Review — Soap Perfum Cosmet Trade Rev
Soap Trade Review — Soap Trade Rev
Sobranie Knig Spetsial'nykh i Nauchnykh Proizvedenyi Politekhnicheskogo Instituta v Brno — Sobr Kn Spets Nauchn Proizvedenyi Politekh Inst Brno
Sobranie Spetsial'nykh i Nauchnykh Sochinenii Politekhnicheskogo Instituta. Brno. A — Sobr Spets Nauchn Sochinenii Politekh Inst g Brno A
Sobranie Spetsial'nykh i Nauchnykh Sochinenii Politekhnicheskogo Instituta v g. Brno. B — Sobr Spets Nauchn Sochinenii Politekh Inst Brno B
Sobre los Derivados de la Cana de Azucar [*Cuba*] — Sobre Deriv Cana Azucar
Soccer Journal — Soc J
Soccer Journal — Soccer J
Soccer Monthly — Soccer M
Sociaal Maandblad — SM
Sociaal Maandblad — Soc Mbl
Sociaal Maandblad Arbeid — SMA
Sociaal Maandblad Arbeid — Soc Maandbl Arb
Sociaal Maandblad Arbeid. Tijdschrift voor Sociaal Recht en Sociaal Geleid — SOM
Social Action — Soc Act
Social Action and the Law — Soc Act & L
Social Alternatives — Soc Altern
Social Alternatives [*Australia*] — Soc Alternatives
Social Anarchism — Soc Anarc
Social and Behavioral Sciences — Soc Behav Sci
Social and Economic Administration — Soc Econ Admin
Social and Economic Administration — Social and Econ Admin
Social and Economic Administration — Social Ec A
Social and Economic Commentaries on Classical Texts — SEC
Social and Economic History of the Hellenistic World — SEH
Social and Economic History of the Hellenistic World — SEHHW
Social and Economic History of the Roman Empire — SEHRE
Social and Economic Studies — SES
Social and Economic Studies — Soc & Econ Stud
Social and Economic Studies — Soc and Econ Studs
Social and Economic Studies — Soc Econ Stud
Social and Economic Studies — Social & Econ Stud
Social and Economic Studies — Social Econ
Social and Economic Studies. University of the West Indies. Institute of Social and Economic Research — UWI/SES
Social and Labour Bulletin — Scl & Lbr Bul
Social and Rehabilitation Record — Soc Rehabil Rec
Social and Rehabilitation Service. Publications — SRS
Social Behavior and Personality — Soc Beh Per
Social Behavior and Personality — Soc Behav Pers
Social Biology — PSOB
Social Biology — SOBIA
Social Biology — Soc Biol
Social Biology — Social Biol
Social Biology and Human Affairs — SBHAD7
Social Biology and Human Affairs — Soc Biol Hum Aff
Social Casework — SC
Social Casework — Soc Casework
Social Casework — Social Case
Social Casework Journal — J Soc Casework
Social Change in Sweden — SCIS
Social Choice and Welfare — Soc Choice Welf
Social Cognition — Soc Cognit
Social Cognition — SOCOEE
Social Compass — SC
Social Compass — Soc Comp
Social Compass — Soc Compass
Social Compass — Social Comp
Social Concept — Soc Con
Social Defence [*New Delhi*] — Soc Def
Social Development — Soc Dev
Social Dynamics — Soc Dyn
Social Dynamics — Soc Dynamics
Social Economist — Soc Econ
Social Education — ISED
Social Education — SE
Social Education — Soc Ed
Social Education — Soc Educ
Social Education — Social Educ
Social Forces — GSFF
Social Forces — SF

Social Forces — Soc Forces
Social Forces — Social Forc
Social Forces — SOFOA
Social History — PSOH
Social History — Soc Hist
Social History — SocH
Social History/Histoire Sociale — Soc Hist/Hist Soc
Social Hygiene — Soc Hygiene
Social Indicators Research — Soc Ind Res
Social Indicators Research — Soc Indic Res
Social Indicators Research — Soc Indicat Res
Social Indicators Research — Soc Indicators Res
Social Indicators Research — Social Ind
Social Indicators Research — Social Indicators Res
Social Insects — Soc Insects
Social Justice Review — SJR
Social Justice Review — Soc Jus R
Social Justice Review — SocJust
Social Perspectives — Soc Perspect
Social Planning, Policy, and Development Abstracts — Soc Plan Policy Dev Abstr
Social Planning/Policy and Development Abstracts — SOPODA
Social Policy — GSPO
Social Policy — SCPYB
Social Policy — Soc Pol
Social Policy — Soc Policy
Social Policy — Social Pol
Social Policy and Administration — Social Policy Admin
Social Praxis — Soc Prax
Social Praxis — Soc Praxis
Social Praxis — Social Prax
Social Problems — GSPR
Social Problems — Scl Problems
Social Problems — Soc Prob
Social Problems — Soc Probl
Social Problems — Social Prob
Social Process in Hawaii — SPH
Social Progress — Soc Pr
Social Psychiatry — Soc Psychiatry
Social Psychiatry — Social Psy
Social Psychology — Soc Psychol
Social Psychology Quarterly — PSOP
Social Psychology Quarterly — S Psy
Social Psychology Quarterly — Soc Psych Q
Social Psychology Quarterly — Soc Psychol Q
Social Psychology Quarterly — Social Psychol Q
Social Research — PSOR
Social Research — Soc R
Social Research — Soc Res
Social Research — Social Res
Social Research — SR
Social Reserve — Soc Res
Social Responsibility — Soc Resp
Social Science — Social Scie
Social Science Abstracts — SSA
Social Science and Medicine — ISMD
Social Science and Medicine — Soc Sci and Med
Social Science and Medicine — Soc Sci Med
Social Science and Medicine — Soc Sci Medic
Social Science and Medicine — Social Sc M
Social Science and Medicine (Medical Anthropology) — Soc Sci Med (Med Anthropol)
Social Science and Medicine (Medical Geography) — Soc Sci Med (Med Geogr)
Social Science and Medicine (Medical Psychology and Medical Sociology) — Soc Sci Med (Med Psychol Med Sociol)
Social Science and Medicine. Part A. Medical Psychology and Medical Sociology — Soc Sci & Med Part A Med Psychol & Med Sociol
Social Science and Medicine. Part A. Medical Psychology and Medical Sociology — SSMSDZ
Social Science and Medicine. Part A. Medical Sociology — Soc Sci & Med Part A Med Sociol
Social Science and Medicine. Part A. Medical Sociology — Soc Sci Med A
Social Science and Medicine. Part B. Medical Anthropology — Soc Sci & Med Part B Med Anthropol
Social Science and Medicine. Part B. Medical Anthropology — Soc Sci Med B
Social Science and Medicine. Part C. Medical Economics — Soc Sci & Med Part C Med Econ
Social Science and Medicine. Part C. Medical Economics — Soc Sci Med C
Social Science and Medicine. Part C. Medical Economics — Soc Sci Med Med Econ
Social Science and Medicine. Part D. Medical Geography — Soc Sci & Med Part D Med Geogr
Social Science and Medicine. Part D. Medical Geography — Soc Sci Med D
Social Science and Medicine. Part E. Medical Psychology — Soc Sci & Med Part E Med Psychol
Social Science and Medicine. Part F. Medical and Social Ethics — Soc Sci & Med Part F Med & Soc Ethics
Social Science Citation Index — Soc Sci Citation Index
Social Science History — Soc Sci Hist
Social Science Information — Soc Sci Inf
Social Science Information — Soc Sci Inform
Social Science Information — Social Sci Inf
Social Science Information — SSI
Social Science Information/Information sur les Sciences Sociales — SSI/ISS
Social Science Information Studies — Soc Sci Inf Stud
Social Science Journal — PSOS
Social Science Journal — Soc Sci J
Social Science Journal (Fort Collins) — Soc Sci J Fort Collins
Social Science Journal (Fort Collins) — Social Science J (Fort Collins)
Social Science Journal (Seoul) — Soc Sci J Seoul
Social Science Micro Review — Soc Sci Micro Rev
Social Science Monographs — Soc Sci Monographs
Social Science Newsletter — Soc Sci NL
Social Science Quarterly — GSSQ
Social Science Quarterly — Scl Sci Q
Social Science Quarterly — Soc Sci Q
Social Science Quarterly — Soc Sci Quart
Social Science Quarterly — Social Sci
Social Science Quarterly — Social Sci Q
Social Science Quarterly — Social Science Q
Social Science Quarterly — SocQ
Social Science Quarterly — SSQ
Social Science Quarterly — SSQTA
Social Science Research — PSSR
Social Science Research — Soc Sci Res
Social Science Research Council. Bulletin — Soc Sci Res Council Bull
Social Science Review [*Bangkok*] — Soc Sci R
Social Science (Winfield) — Soc Sci (Winfield)
Social Sciences — Soc Sci
Social Sciences — Soc Sciences
Social Sciences and Humanities Index — Soc Sci Humanit Index
Social Sciences and Humanities Index — SSH
Social Sciences and Humanities Index — SSHum
Social Sciences Citation Index [*Institute for Scientific Information*] [*Database*] — SSCI
Social Sciences in Canada — Soc Sci Can
Social Sciences in Mexico (Mexico) — Soc Scien Mex Mex
Social Sciences Index — Soc Sci Ind
Social Sciences Index — Soc Sci Index
Social Scientist — Soc Scientist
Social Scientist — Social Sci
Social Security Administration [*Database*] — SSA
Social Security Administration. Publications — SSA
Social Security Bulletin — Scl Sec Bul
Social Security Bulletin [*US*] — Soc Sec Bull
Social Security Bulletin — Soc Secur Bull
Social Security Bulletin [*US*] — Social Sec
Social Security Bulletin — Social Security Bul
Social Security Bulletin [*US*] — SSB
Social Security Bulletin. Annual Statistical Supplement [*US*] — Soc Secur Bull Annu Stat Suppl
Social Security Handbook — Soc Sec Handb
Social Security Reporter — Soc Sec Rep
Social Security Reporter [*Australia*] — SSR
Social Security Rulings [*on Old Age, Survivors, and Disability Insurance*] [*US*] — SSR
Social Service — Soc Serv
Social Service Delivery Systems — Soc Serv Del Syst
Social Service Quarterly — Soc Serv Q
Social Service Review — PSSV
Social Service Review — Soc Ser Rev
Social Service Review — Soc Serv R
Social Service Review — Soc Serv Rev
Social Service Review — Social Se R
Social Service Review — Social Service R
Social Service Review (Chicago) — SSRC
Social Services Abstracts — Social Services Abs
Social Services Journal — Soc Serv J
Social Services Journal — Social Services J
Social Studies — Soc St
Social Studies — Soc Stud
Social Studies — Soc Studies
Social Studies — Social Stud
Social Studies — SocS
Social Studies — SS
Social Studies of Science [*United Kingdom*] — Soc Stud Sci
Social Studies of Science — Social St S
Social Studies of Science — SSSCD
Social Survey — Soc Sur
Social Survey — Soc Surv
Social Survey — Soc Survey
Social Theory and Practice — PSTP
Social Theory and Practice — Soc Theory & Pract
Social Theory and Practice — Social Theor Pract
Social Thought — Soc Thought
Social Tidsskrift — Soc Tss
Social Trends — Soc Trends
Social Welfare — Soc Welfare
Social Welfare. Social Planning/Policy and Social Development — Soc Welf Soc Plan Policy Soc Dev
Social Work — GSWK
Social Work — Soc W
Social Work — Soc Work
Social Work — SW
Social Work (Albany) — Soc Wk (Albany)
Social Work and Christianity — SWC
Social Work in Health Care — Soc Work Health Care
Social Work in Health Care — SWHC
Social Work Lectures [*New Zealand*] — Soc Work Lect
Social Work Research and Abstracts — Soc Work Res Abstr

Social Work Research and Abstracts — SWRA
Social Work Today — Soc Work Today
Social Work Today — Social Wk Today
Social Work with Groups — SWWG
Sociale Maandstatistiek — CBE
Sociale Wetenschappen — Soc Wetensch
Sociale Wetenschappen — SWH
Sociale Zekerheidsgids — S Zek
Socialism in Yugoslav Theory and Practice — Social Yugosl Theory Pract
Socialisme en Democratie — S en D
Socialisme en Democratie — Social en Democr
Socialisme en Democratie — SOD
Socialismo y Participacion — SP
Socialist Commentary — SC
Socialist Economic Review — Soc Econ Rev
Socialist Plant Industry — Soc Plant Ind
Socialist Register — Soc Regis
Socialist Register — Social Regist
Socialist Review — ISRO
Socialist Review — Soc R
Socialist Review — Soc Rev
Socialist Review — Social R
Socialist Revolution — Soc Revol
Socialist Revolution — Social Revol
Socialist Theory and Practice — Soc Thr
Socialist Thought and Practice — SQF
Socialist Worker — Soc Workr
Socialist Worker — Socialist Wkr
Socialist Worker — SW
Socialisticeskij Trud — Soc Tr
Socialisticeskij Trud — Social Trud
Socialisticeskoe Plodoovoscnoe Hozjajstvo — Socialist Plodoovoscn Hoz
Socialisticka Ekonomicka Integrace [*Czechoslovakia*] — Soc Ekon Integrace
Socialisticke Zemedelstvi — Soc Zemed
Socialisticki Front — SF
Socialisticno Kmetifstvo in Gosudarstvo — Socialist Kmet Gos
Socialistinis Zemes Ukis — Soc Zemes Ukis
Socialistische Gids — SG
Social-Medicinsk Tidskrift — Soc Med Tidskr
Social'naja Psichologija i Filosofija — Soc Psichol Filos
Social'no-Politiceskie i Social'no-Ekonomiceskie Problemy Razvitogo Socialisticeskogo Obscestva — Soc-Polit Soc-Ekon Probl Razvit Social Obsc
Social'nye Problemy Naucno-Tehniceskogo Revoljucii — Soc Probl Nauc-Tehn Revol
Socialt Tidsskrift — Soc T
Social-Technological Bulletin [*Quezon City*] — Socio-Tech B
Sociedad Americana de Ciencias Horticolas. Region Tropical. Congreso Anual — Soc Am Cienc Hortic Reg Trop Congr Anu
Sociedad Argentina de Cancerologia. Boletines y Trabajos — Soc Argent Cancerol Bol Trab
Sociedad Argentina de Cirujanos Jornadas Quirurgicas — Soc Argent Cir Jornadas Quir
Sociedad Botanica de Mexico. Boletin — Soc Bot Mexico Bol
Sociedad Cientifica "Antonio Alzate." Memorias y Revista — Soc Cient Ant Alz Mem
Sociedad Cientifica del Paraguay. Revista — Soc Cient Parag Rev
Sociedad Cientifica y Literaria de Campeche — Soc Ci Lit Campeche
Sociedad Colombiana de Control de Malezas y Fisiologia Vegetal. Revista — Soc Colomb Control Malezas Fisiol Veg Rev
Sociedad Cubana de Historia Natural. Memorias — Soc Cubana Historia Nat Mem
Sociedad Cubana de Ingenieros. Revista — Soc Cubana Ing Rv
Sociedad Cubana de Ingenieros. Revista — Soc Cubana Ingenieros Rev
Sociedad de Biologia de Santiago de Chile. Boletin — Soc Biol Santiago de Chile Bol
Sociedad de Ciencias Naturales La Salle. Memoria — Soc Cienc Nat La Salle Mem
Sociedad de Cirugia de Buenos Aires. Boletines y Trabajos — Soc Cir Buenos Aires Bol Trab
Sociedad de Geografia y Estadistica de la Republica Mexicana. Boletin — Soc Geog Mex B
Sociedad Espanola de Historia Natural. Anales — Soc Espanola H N An
Sociedad Espanola de Historia Natural. Boletin. Seccion Geologica — Soc Espan Hist Nat Bol Secc Geol
Sociedad Espanola de Quimica Clinica. Revista — Soc Esp Quim Clin Rev
Sociedad Geografica. Boletin (Madrid) — Soc Geogr Bol (Madrid)
Sociedad Geografica de Lima. Boletin — Soc Geog Lima Bol
Sociedad Geologica Boliviana. Boletin — Soc Geol Boliv Bol
Sociedad Geologica del Peru. Boletin — Soc Geol Peru Bol
Sociedad Geologica Mexicana. Boletin — Soc G Mex B
Sociedad Geologica Mexicana. Boletin — Soc Geol Mex Bol
Sociedad Geologica Mexicana. Boletin — Soc Geol Mexicana Bol
Sociedad Malacologica. Revista — Soc Malacologica Rev
Sociedad Mexicana de Geografia y Estadistica. Boletin — Soc Mex Geog Estadistica B
Sociedad Mexicana de Geografia y Estadistica. Boletin — Soc Mexicana Geografia y Estadistica Bol
Sociedad Mexicana de Historia Natural. Revista — Soc Mexicana Historia Nat Rev
Sociedad Mexicana de Lepidopterologia. Boletin Informativo — BISLDP
Sociedad Mexicana de Lepidopterologia. Boletin Informativo — Soc Mex Lepidopterol Bol Inf
Sociedad Mexicana de Oftalmologia. Anales — Soc Mex Oftalmol An
Sociedad Numismatica de Mexico. Boletin — Soc Num Mexico Bol
Sociedad Quimica de Mexico. Revista — Soc Quim Mexico Rev
Sociedad Rural Argentina. Anales — Soc Rural Argent An
Sociedad Scientifica de Sao Paulo. Revista — Soc Sci De Sao Paulo R
Sociedad Venezolana de Ciencias Naturales. Boletin — Soc Venez Cienc Nat Bol
Sociedad Venezolana de Ciencias Naturales. Boletin — Soc Venezolana Ciencias Natur Bol
Sociedade Brasileira de Nematologia. Publicacao — PSBNDY
Sociedade Brasileira de Nematologia. Publicacao — Soc Bras Nematol Publ
Sociedade Brasileira de Zootecnia. Revista — Soc Bras Zootec Rev
Sociedade Brotheriana. Boletim — Soc Brotheriana Bol
Sociedade Cearense de Agronomia. Boletim — Soc Cear Agron Bol
Sociedade Entomologica do Brasil. Anais — Soc Entomol Bras An
Sociedade Geologica de Portugal. Boletim — Soc Geol Port Bol
Sociedade Portuguesa de Cardiologia. Boletim — Soc Port Cardiol Bol
Sociedade Portuguesa de Quimica. Boletim — Soc Port Quim Bol
Societa — So
Societa Adriatica di Scienze. Bollettino — Soc Adriat Sci Boll
Societa Alpina delle Giulie. Club Alpino Italiano. Sezione di Trieste. Commissione Grotte "Eugenio Boegan." Atti e Memorie — Soc Alp Giulie Comm Grotte Eugenio Boegan Atti Mem
Societa Astronomica Italiana. Memorie — MSATA
Societa Astronomica Italiana. Memorie — Soc Astron Ital Mem
Societa degli Alpinisti Tridentini. Annuario — Annuario Soc Alpin Trident
Societa degli Ingegneri e degli Architetti in Torino. Atti e Rassegna Tecnica — Soc Ing Archit Torino Atti Rass Tec
Societa dei Naturalisti in Napoli. Bollettino — Soc Nat Napoli Boll
Societa dell'Esplorazione Commerciale di Milano — SECM
Societa e Diritto di Roma — Soc Dir Roma
Societa e Storia — Soc Stor
Societa Geologica Italiana. Bollettino — Soc G Italiana B
Societa Geologica Italiana. Bollettino — Soc Geol Ital Boll
Societa Geologica Italiana. Memorie — Soc Geol Ital Mem
Societa Internazionale di Microbiologia. Sezione Italiana. Bollettino — Soc Int Microbiol Sez Ital Boll
Societa' Italiana di Buiatria. Atti — Soc Ital Buiatria Atti
Societa Italiana di Fisica. Atti di Conferenze — Soc Ital Fis Atti Conf
Societa Italiana di Scienza dell'Alimentazione. Rivista — Soc Ital Sci Aliment Riv
Societa Italiana di Scienze Farmaceutiche Documento — Soc Ital Sci Farm Doc
Societa Italiana di Scienze Naturali e Museo Civico di Storia Naturale di Milano. Atti — Soc Ital Sci Nat Mus Civ Stor Nat Milano Atti
Societa Italiana di Scienze Naturali e Museo Civico di Storia Naturale di Milano. Memorie — Soc Ital Sci Nat Mus Civ Stor Nat Milano Mem
Societa Italiana di Scienze Naturali in Milano. Atti — Soc Italiana Sc Nat Milano Atti
Societa Italiana per il Progresso delle Scienze. Atti della Riunione — Soc Ital Prog Sci Atti Riun
Societa Italiana per il Progresso delle Scienze. Scienze e Tecnica — Soc Ital Prog Sci Sci Tec
Societa Ligustica di Scienze Naturali e Geografiche. Atti — Soc Ligustica Sc Nat Geog Atti
Societa Medico-Chirurgica di Cremona. Bollettino — Soc Med Chir Cremona Boll
Societa Medico-Chirurgica di Modena. Bollettino — Soc Med Chir Modena Boll
Societa Nazionale di Scienze, Lettere, ed Arti in Napoli. Rendiconto dell'Accademia delle Scienze Fisiche e Matematiche. Serie 4 — Rend Accad Sci Fis Mat Napoli 4
Societa Paleontologica Italiana. Bollettino — Soc Paleontol Ital Boll
Societa Peloritana di Scienze Fisiche. Matematiche e Naturali. Atti — Soc Peloritana Sci Fis Mat Nat Atti
Societa Reale di Napoli. Accademia delle Scienze, Fisiche, e Matematiche. Atti — Soc R di Napoli Accad d Sci Fis e Mat Atti
Societa Reale di Napoli. Accademia di Archeologia, Lettere, e Belle Arti. Atti — Soc R di Nap Accad di Archeol Atti
Societa Reale di Napoli. Accademia di Archeologia, Lettere, e Belle Arti. Atti — Soc R di Napoli Accad di Archeol Atti
Societa Reale di Napoli. Accademia di Scienze Morali e Politiche. Atti — Soc R di Nap Accad di Sci Mor e Pol Atti
Societa Sismologica Italiana. Bollettino — Soc Sismol Ital Boll
Societa Svizzera di Chimica Clinica. Bulletin — Soc Svizz Chim Clin Bull
Societa Toscana di Scienze Naturali. Atti. Memorie. Serie A — Soc Toscana Sci Nat Atti Mem Ser A
Societa Veneziana di Scienze Naturali Lavori — Soc Ven Sci Nat Lav
Societas — Soc
Societas — Soct
Societas Geographica Fenniae. Acta Geographica — Soc Geog Fenniae Acta Geog
Societas Oto-Rhino-Laryngologica Latina. Conventus — Soc Oto Rhino Laryngol Lat Conv
Societas pro Fauna et Flora Fennica — SFFF
Societas pro Fauna et Flora Fennica. Flora Fennica — Soc Fauna Flora Fenn Flora Fenn
Societas pro Fauna et Flora Fennica. Memoranda — SFFFM
Societas Scientiarum Fennica. Arsbok — Soc Sci Fennica Arsb
Societas Scientiarum Fennica. Commentationes Biologicae — Soc Sci Fenn Commentat Biol
Societas Scientiarum Fennica. Commentationes Physico-Mathematicae — Soc Sci Fenn Comment Phys-Math
Societas Scientiarum Fennica. Commentationes Physico-Mathematicae — Soc Sci Fenn Commentat Phys-Math
Societas Scientiarum Fennica. Commentationes Physico-Mathematicae — Soc Sci Fennica Commentationes Phys-Math
Societas Scientiarum Fennica. Commentationes Physico-Mathematicae et Chemico-Medicae — Comment Phys Math Chem Med
Societas Scientiarum Fennicae. Arsbok-Vuosikirja — Soc Sci Fenn Arsb-Vuosik
Societas Scientiarum Fennicae. Commentationes Humanarum Litterarum — SSF CHL

Societas Scientiarum Islandica. Greinar — Soc Sci Isl Greinar
Societas Scientiarum Naturalium Croatica. Periodicum Mathematico-Physicum et Astronomicum — Soc Sci Nat Croat Period Math Phys Astron
Societas Scientiarum Stetinensis. Wydzial Nauk Lekarskich. Prace — Soc Sci Stetin Wydz Nauk Lek Pr
Societat Catalana de Biologia. Colloquis — Soc Catalana Biol Colloq
Societat Catalana de Pediatria. Butlleti — Soc Catalana Pediatr Butll
Societatea de Stiinte Geologice din Republica Socialista Romania. Buletinul — Soc Stiinte Geol Repub Soc Rom Bul
Societatea de Stiinte Matematice din RPR. Gazeta Matematica Publicatle pentru Studiul si Raspindirea Stiintelor Matematice. Seria A — Gaz Mat Ser A
Societatis Medicae Havniensis Collectanea — Soc Med Havn Collect
Societatis pro Fauna et Flora Fennica. Memoranda — Soc Fauna Flora Fenn Memo
Societatis Scientiarum Lodziensis. Acta Chimica — Soc Sci Lodz Acta Chim
Societe Agricole, Scientifique, et Litteraire des Pyrenees Orientales. Bulletin — SAPO
Societe Anatomique de Paris — Soc Anat De Paris Bul
Societe Antiesclavagiste de France. Bulletin — Soc Antiescl De France Bul
Societe Archeologique de Bruxelles. Annales — SABA
Societe Archeologique de l'Arrondissement de Nivelles. Annales — SAANAn
Societe Archeologique de Namur. Annales — SANAn
Societe Archeologique et Historique du Limousin. Bulletin — Soc Archeol & Hist Limousin Bul
Societe Arctique Francaise Bulletin — SAFB
Societe Ariegeoise des Sciences, Lettres, et Arts. Bulletin Annuel — S Ariegeoise
Societe Belge de Geographie. Bulletin — Soc Belge De Geog Bul
Societe Belge de Geologie. Bulletin — Soc Belge G B
Societe Belge de Geologie. Bulletin — Soc Belge Geol Bull
Societe Belge d'Etudes Geographiques. Bulletin — Soc Belge d'Etudes Geog Bull
Societe Belge d'Etudes Historiques et Scientifiques. Bulletin — Soc Belge D Etudes Hist Et Sci Bul
Societe Belge pour l'Etude du Petrole, de Ses Derives et Succedanes. Annales — Soc Belge Etude Pet Ses Deriv Succedanes Ann
Societe Botanique de France. Bulletin — Soc Bot France B
Societe Botanique de France. Memoires — Soc Bot Fr Mem
Societe Botanique de Geneve. Travaux — Soc Bot Geneve Trav
Societe Chimique de Tunisie. Journal — Soc Chim Tunis J
Societe Commerciale des Potasses et de l'Azote. Document Technique de la SCPA — Soc Commer Potasses Azote Doc Tech SCPA
Societe d'Anthropologie de Bruxelles. Bulletin — Soc D Anthropol De Brux Bul
Societe d'Anthropologie de Paris. Bulletin — Soc D Anthropol De Paris Bul
Societe d'Anthropologie de Paris. Bulletins et Memoires — Soc Anthropol Paris Bull Mem
Societe d'Art et d'Histoire du le Diocese de Liege. Bulletin — SAHLBull
Societe de Banque Suisse. Bulletin — Soc Banque Suisse Bul
Societe de Biologie. Comptes-Rendus (Paris) — Soc De Biol Paris Comptes Rendus
Societe de Chimie Physique. International Meeting. Proceedings — Soc Chim Phys Int Meet Proc
Societe de Geographie de Quebec. Bulletin — Soc Geog Que B
Societe de Geographie (Paris). Bulletin — Soc Geog (Paris) B
Societe de l'Ecole des Chartes — SEC
Societe de l'Histoire de France — SHF
Societe de l'Histoire de France — Soc Hist de France
Societe de l'Histoire de France. Annuaire Bulletin — SHFABull
Societe de l'Industrie Minerale. Bulletin. Comptes Rendus Mensuels des Reunions — Soc Ind Min B C R Men
Societe de l'Industrie Minerale. Congres du Centenaire — Soc l'Industrie Minerale Cong Cent
Societe de Medecine Militaire Francaise. Bulletin — Soc Med Mil Franc Bull
Societe de Microscopie du Canada. Bulletin — Soc Micros Can Bull
Societe de Pathologie Exotique. Bulletin — Soc Pathol Exot Bul
Societe de Pathologie Exotique. Bulletin — Soc Pathol Exot Bull
Societe de Pharmacie de Lille. Bulletin — Soc Pharm Lille Bull
Societe de Pharmacie de Montpellier. Travaux — Soc Pharm Montpellier Trav
Societe de Physique et d'Histoire Naturelle de Geneve. Compte Rendu des Seances — Soc Phys Hist Nat Geneve C R Seances
Societe de Physique et d'Histoire Naturelle de Geneve. Compte Rendu des Seances — Soc Physique et Histoire Nat Geneve Compte Rendu
Societe de Publications Romanes et Francaises — SPRF
Societe de Quebec pour la Protection des Plantes. Rapport — Soc Que Prot Plant Rapp
Societe de Statistique de Paris. Journal — Soc de Statist de Paris J
Societe de Statistique de Paris. Journal — Soc Statist Paris J
Societe d'Editions d'Enseignement Superieur — SEDES
Societe d'Emulation de Bruges. Annales — SEBAn
Societe d'Emulation de Cambrai. Memoires — SECMem
Societe d'Encouragement pour l'Industrie Nationale. Bulletin — Soc Encour Ind Natl Bull
Societe des Africanistes. Journal — Soc African J
Societe des Agricultures d'Algerie. Bulletin — BAALA
Societe des Agricultures d'Algerie. Bulletin [*Algeria*] — Soc Agric Alger Bull
Societe des Americanistes de Paris. Journal — Soc Amer J
Societe des Americanistes de Paris. Journal — Soc D Amer De Paris J
Societe des Americanistes de Paris. Journal — Soc d Americanistes J
Societe des Amis de la Bibliotheque de l'Ecole Polytechnique. Bulletin — Bull Soc Amis Bibl Ecole Polytech
Societe des Amis des Sciences de Poznan. Travaux. Section des Sciences Mathematiques et Naturelles — Soc Amis Sci Poznan Trav Sect Sci Math Nat
Societe des Amis des Sciences et des Lettres de Poznan. Bulletin. Serie B. Sciences Mathematiques et Naturelles — Soc Amis Sci Lett Poznan Bull Ser B
Societe des Anciens Textes Francais — SATF
Societe des Antiquaires de la Morinie. Bulletin Historique — SAMBHist
Societe des Archives Historiques du Poitou. Archives — Soc Arch Hist Poitou Arch
Societe des Etudes Indochinoises. Bulletin — Soc Etud Indochinoises Bul
Societe des Ingenieurs Civils de France. Bulletin — Soc Ing Civ Fr Bull
Societe des Ingenieurs Civils de France. Memoires — Soc Ing Civils France Mem
Societe des Ingenieurs Civils de France. Memoires ICF — Soc Ing Civ Fr Mem ICF
Societe des Naturalistes Luxembourgeois. Bulletin — Soc Nat Luxemb Bull
Societe des Oceanistes. Journal — Soc Ocean J
Societe des Recherches Congolaises. Bulletin — Soc D Rech Congol Bul
Societe des Sciences, Agriculture, et Arts de la Basse-Alsace/Gesellschaft zur Befoerderung der Wissenschaften, des Ackerbaues und der Kuenste im Unter-Elsass. Bulletin Mensuel — Soc Sci Basse Alsace Bull Mens
Societe des Sciences et des Lettres de Lodz. Bulletin. Classe 4. Sciences Medicales — Soc Sci Lett Lodz Bull Cl 4
Societe des Sciences, Lettres, et Arts de Bayonne. Bulletin — SSB
Societe des Sciences, Lettres, et Arts. Pau Bulletin — Soc Sci Lettres & Arts Pau Bul
Societe des Sciences Naturelles de l'Ouest de la France. Bulletin — Soc Sci Nat Ouest Fr Bull
Societe des Sciences Naturelles de Neuchatel. Bulletin — Soc Sc Nat Neuchatel B
Societe des Sciences Naturelles et Physiques du Maroc. Bulletin — Soc Sci Nat Phys Maroc Bull
Societe des Sciences Naturelles et Physiques du Maroc. Comptes Rendus des Seances Mensuelles — Soc Sci Nat Phys Maroc C R Seances Mens
Societe des Sciences Naturelles. Grand-Duche de Luxembourg — Soc Sci Nat Grand Duche Luxembourg
Societe des Sciences Naturelles Miscellanea Entomologia — Soc Sci Nat Misc Entomol
Societe des Textes Francais Modernes — STFM
Societe d'Etudes et d'Expansion. Revue — Soc Etud et Expansion R
Societe d'Etudes et d'Expansion. Revue — Societe d'Etudes et d'Expansion Revue
Societe d'Etudes Scientifiques d'Angers. Bulletin — Soc d'Etudes Sc d'Angers B
Societe d'Histoire et d'Archeologie de Gand. Annales — SHAGAn
Societe d'Histoire et d'Archeologie de Gand. Bulletin — SHAGBull
Societe d'Histoire et d'Archeologie de Molsheim — SoctH
Societe d'Histoire et du Musee d'Huningue et du Canton de Huningue. Bulletin — SHMH
Societe d'Histoire Naturelle de l'Afrique du Nord. Bulletin — BHNNA
Societe d'Histoire Naturelle de l'Afrique du Nord. Bulletin — Soc Hist Nat Afr Nord Bull
Societe d'Histoire Naturelle de Toulouse. Bulletin — Soc Hist Nat Toulouse Bull
Societe Entomologique du Quebec. Annales — Soc Entomol Que Ann
Societe Francaise d'Allergologie. Journees Nationales — Soc Fr Allergol Journ Natl
Societe Francaise d'Anesthesie. d'Analgesie et de Reanimation — Soc Fr Anesth Analg Reanim
Societe Francaise de Biologie Clinique. Monographie Annuelle — Soc Fr Biol Clin Monogr Annu
Societe Francaise de Dermatologie et de Syphiligraphie. Bulletin — Soc Fr Dermatol Syphiligr Bull
Societe Francaise de Gynecologie. Comptes Rendus — Soc Fr Gynecol C R
Societe Francaise de Microbiologie. Section de Microbiologie Industrielle et de Biotechnologie. Colloque — Soc Fr Microbiol Sect Microbiol Ind Biotechnol Colloq
Societe Francaise de Mineralogie. Bulletin — Soc Franc Miner B
Societe Francaise de Mineralogie et de Cristallographie. Bulletin — Soc Fr Mineral Cristallogr Bull
Societe Francaise de Mineralogie et de Cristallographie. Bulletin — Soc Francaise Mineralogie et Cristallographie Bull
Societe Francaise d'Editions Litteraires et Techniques — SFELT
Societe Fribourgeoise des Sciences Naturelles. Bulletin. Memoires — Soc Fribourgeoise Sc Nat B Mem
Societe Geographique de Liege. Bulletin [*Belgium*] — SGLI
Societe Geographique de Liege. Bulletin — Soc Geog Liege Bul
Societe Geologique de Belgique. Annales — Soc G Belgique An
Societe Geologique de Belgique. Annales — Soc Geol Belg Ann
Societe Geologique de Belgique. Annales — Soc Geol Belgique Annales
Societe Geologique de Belgique. Bulletin — Soc Geol Belg Bull
Societe Geologique de France. Bulletin — Soc Geol Fr Bull
Societe Geologique de France. Bulletin — Soc Geol France Bull
Societe Geologique de France. Bulletin. Memoires — Soc G France B Mem
Societe Geologique de France. Memoire Hors Serie — Soc Geol Fr Mem Hors Ser
Societe Geologique de France. Memoires — Soc Geol Fr Mem
Societe Geologique de Normandie. Bulletin — Soc G Normandie B
Societe Geologique de Normandie. Bulletin — Soc Geol Normandie Bull
Societe Geologique du Nord. Annales — Soc Geol Nord Ann
Societe Geologique du Nord. Annales. Memoires — Soc G Nord An Mem
Societe Geologique et Mineralogique de Bretagne. Bulletin — Soc Geol et Mineralog Bretagne Bull
Societe Geologique et Mineralogique de Bretagne. Bulletin — Soc Geol Mineral Bretagne Bull
Societe Haitienne d'Histoire de Geographie et de Geologie. Revue — Soc Haitienne Histoire Geographie Geologie Revue
Societe Historique et Archeologique dans le Duche de Limbourg. Publications — SHALPub

Societe Historique et Archeologique de Tournai. Annales — SHATAn
Societe Hongroise de Geographie. Abrege du Bulletin — Soc Hongroise Geog Abrege B
Societe Imperiale des Naturalistes de Moscou. Bulletin — Soc Imp Nat Moscou B
Societe Industrielle de Mulhouse. Bulletin — Soc Ind Mulhouse Bull
Societe Internationale de Pedodontie. Journal — Soc Int Pedod J
Societe Internationale pour l'Etude des Corps Gras. Actes du Congres Mondial — Soc Int Etude Corps Gras Actes Congr Mond
Societe Languedocienne de Geographie — Soc Languedoc Geogr
Societe Languedocienne de Geographie. Bulletin — Soc Languedocienne Geogr Bull
Societe Linneenne de Bordeaux. Bulletin — Soc Linn Bord Bull
Societe Linneenne de Lyon. Bulletin Mensuel — Soc Linn Lyon Bull
Societe Linneenne de Normandie. Bulletin — Soc Linneenne Normandie Bull
Societe Malacologique de Belgique. Annales — Soc Malac Belgique An
Societe Mathematique de France. Bulletin, Memoire — Bull Soc Math France Mem
Societe Mathematique de France. Bulletin, Supplement, Memoire — Bull Soc Math France Suppl Mem
Societe Medicale d'Afrique Noire de Langue Francaise. Bulletin — Soc Med Afr Noire Lang Fr Bull
Societe Medicale de Charleroi. Bulletin — Soc Med De Charleroi Bul
Societe Medico-Chirurgicale des Hopitaux et Formations Sanitaires des Armees — Soc Med-Chir Hop Form Sanit Armees
Societe Mineralogique de France. Bulletin — Soc Miner France
Societe Nationale des Antiquaires de France. Memoires — SAFMem
Societe Nationale des Petroles d'Aquitaine. Bulletin de Centres de Recherches de Pau — Soc Nat Pet Aquitaine Bull Cent Rech Pau
Societe Nationale des Petroles d'Aquitaine. Centre de Recherches de Pau. Bulletin. [*Later, Bulletin. Centres de Recherches Exploration-Production ELF Aquitaine*] — Cent Rech Pau Bull
Societe Nationale Elf-Aquitaine (Production). Bulletin des Centres de Recherches Exploration-Production Elf-Aquitaine — Soc Natl Elf Aquitaine Prod Bull Cent Rech Explor Prod Elf A
Societe Neuchateloise de Geographie. Bulletin — Soc Neuchat De Geog Bul
Societe Neuchateloise de Geographie. Bulletin — Soc Neuchatel Geogr Bull
Societe Paleontologique et Archeologique de l'Arrondissement Judicaire de Charleroi. Documents et Rapports — SPACDocRap
Societe pour l'Etude des Langues Romanes — Soc pour l Et des Lang Rom
Societe Prehistorique Francaise. Bulletin — Soc Prehist Fr Bull
Societe Prehistorique Francaise. Bulletin — Soc Prehist Francais Bull
Societe Prehistorique Francaise. Bulletin — Soc Prehist Francaise Bul
Societe Royale Belge de Geographie. Bulletin — Soc Roy Belge de Geog B
Societe Royale Belge de Geographie. Bulletin — Soc Roy Belge De Geog Bul
Societe Royale Belge des Electriciens. Bulletin — Soc R Belge Electr Bull
Societe Royale Belge des Ingenieurs et des Industriels. Bulletin — Soc R Belge Ing Ind Bull
Societe Royale Belge des Ingenieurs et des Industriels. Memoires — Soc R Belge Ing Ind Mem
Societe Royale Belge des Ingenieurs et des Industriels. Publications. Serie B. Memoires — Soc R Belge Ing Ind Publ Ser B
Societe Royale de Botanique de Belgique. Memoires — Soc R Bot Belg Mem
Societe Royale d'Economie Politique de Belgique — Soc Roy Econ Polit Belgique
Societe Royale d'Economie Politique de Belgique. Seances — Soc Royale Econ Pol Belgique Seance
Societe Serbe de Geographie. Memoires — Soc Serbe Geographie Mem
Societe Vaudoise des Sciences Naturelles. Bulletin — Soc Vaudoise Sci Nat Bull
Societe Zoologique de France. Bulletin — Soc Zool Fr Bull
Societe Zoologique de France. Bulletin — Soc Zool France B
Societes d'Ophtalmologie de France. Bulletin — Soc Ophtalmol Fr Bull
Society — GSOC
Society — Soc
Society — SOCYA
Society and Leisure [*Czechoslovakia*] — SCLE
Society and Leisure — Soc and Leisure
Society and Natural Resources — Soc Nat Resour
Society for Analytical Chemistry. Monograph — Soc Anal Chem Monogr
Society for Applied Bacteriology. Symposium Series — Soc Appl Bacteriol Symp Ser
Society for Applied Bacteriology. Technical Series — Soc Appl Bacteriol Tech Ser
Society for Applied Spectroscopy. Bulletin — Soc Appl Spectrosc Bull
Society for Army Historical Research. Journal — SAHR
Society for Army Historical Research. Journal [*London*] — Soc Army Hist Research Jour
Society for Developmental Biology. Symposium — Soc Dev Biol Symp
Society for Ethnomusicology Newsletter — SEMN
Society for Experimental Biology. Seminar Series — Soc Exp Biol Semin Ser
Society for Experimental Biology. Symposia — Soc for Exp Biol Symp
Society for Experimental Stress Analysis. Papers — Soc Exp Stress Anal Pap
Society for Experimental Stress Analysis. Proceedings — Soc Exp Stress Anal Proc
Society for Folk Arts Preservation. Newsletter — Soc Folk Arts Preserv Newsl
Society for General Microbiology Symposium — Soc Gen Microbiol Symp
Society for Geology Applied to Mineral Deposits. Special Publication — Soc Geol Appl Miner Deposits Spec Publ
Society for Industrial and Applied Mathematics. Journal on Applied Mathematics — Soc Ind Appl Math J Appl Math
Society for Industrial and Applied Mathematics. Journal. Series A. Control — Soc Ind Appl Math J Ser A
Society for Industrial and Applied Mathematics-American Mathematical Society Proceedings — Soc Ind Appl Math Am Math Soc Proc
Society for Information Display. Journal — Soc Inf Disp J
Society for Iranian Studies. Newsletter — SIS News
Society for Mass Media and Resource Technology. Journal — SMMART
Society for Mass Media and Resource Technology. Journal — SMMRT Journal
Society for Mass Media and Resource Technology. Journal — Soc Mass Media Resour Technol J
Society for Neuroscience. Abstracts — ASNEE5
Society for Neuroscience. Abstracts — Soc Neurosci Abstr
Society for Neuroscience. Symposia — Soc Neurosci Symp
Society for Nursing History. Gazette — Soc Nurs Hist Gaz
Society for Psychical Research. Proceedings — Soc Psych Res Proc
Society for Radiological Protection. Journal — Soc Radiol Prot J
Society for Research in Child Development. Monographs — Soc Res Child Devel Monogr
Society for Research into Higher Education. Bulletin — SRHE Bull
Society for Research into Higher Education. Newsletter — SRHE Newsl
Society for the Advancement of Electrochemical Science and Technology. Transactions — Soc Adv Electrochem Sci Technol Trans
Society for the Advancement of Material and Process Engineering. National SAMPE Symposium and Exhibition — Soc Adv Mater Process Eng Natl SAMPE Symp Exhib
Society for the Bibliography of Natural History. Journal — Soc Bibliog Nat Hist J
Society for the Promotion of Agricultural Science. Proceedings of the Annual Meeting — Soc Promotion Agr Sc Pr
Society for the Social History of Medicine. Bulletin — Soc Soc Hist Med Bull
Society for the Social History of Medicine Bulletin — Soc Social Hist Med Bull
Society for the Study of Amphibians and Reptiles. Herpetological Circular — Soc Study Amphib Reptiles Herpetol Circ
Society for the Study of Human Biology. Symposia — Soc Stud Hum Biol Symp
Society for the Study of Inborn Errors of Metabolism. Proceedings of the Symposium — Soc Study Inborn Errors Metab Proc Symp
Society for the Study of Midwestern Literature. Newsletter — SSMLN
Society for the Study of Reproduction. Annual Meeting. Abstracts — Soc Study Reprod Annu Meet Abstr
Society of Actuaries. Transactions — Soc Actuar Trans
Society of American Foresters. Proceedings — Soc Am For
Society of Architectural Historians. Journal — Soc Arch Hist J
Society of Architectural Historians. Journal — Soc Archit Hist J
Society of Architectural Historians. Journal — Soc Archtl Historians Jnl
Society of Architectural Historians. Newsletter — Soc of Archtl Historians Newsletter
Society of Arts. Journal — SOA
Society of Arts. Journal — Soc Arts J
Society of Automobile Engineers. Transactions — Soc Automob Eng Trans
Society of Automotive Engineers. Handbook — Hb SAE
Society of Automotive Engineers. Journal — Soc Auto Eng J
Society of Automotive Engineers. Journal of Automotive Engineering — Automotive Eng
Society of Automotive Engineers. Meeting. Papers — SAE Meet Pap
Society of Automotive Engineers of Australasia. Journal — J Soc Automot Engrs Australas
Society of Automotive Engineers of Japan. Review — Soc Automot Eng Jpn Rev
Society of Automotive Engineers. Proceedings — SAE Proc
Society of Automotive Engineers. Proceedings P — Soc Automot Eng Proc P
Society of Automotive Engineers. Quarterly Transactions — Soc Automot Eng Q Trans
Society of Automotive Engineers. SAE Technical Paper Series — Soc Automot Eng SAE Tech Pap Ser
Society of Automotive Engineers. Technical Paper Series — Soc Automot Eng Tech Pap Ser
Society of Automotive Engineers. Transactions — Soc Automot Eng Trans
Society of Automotive Historians. Journal — SAHJ
Society of Biblical Literature. Seminar Papers — SBL Sem Pap
Society of Chemical Industry. Journal — Soc Chem Ind J
Society of Chemical Industry. London Chemical Engineering Group. Proceedings — Soc Chem Ind London Chem Eng Group Proc
Society of Chemical Industry (London). Monograph — SCIGA
Society of Chemical Industry (London). Monograph — Soc Chem Ind (Lond) Monogr
Society of Chemical Industry Monograph — Soc Chem Ind Monogr
Society of Chemical Industry of Victoria. Proceedings — Soc Chem Ind Victoria Proc
Society of Die Casting Engineers International Die Casting Exposition and Congress — Soc Die Cast Eng Int Die Cast Expos Congr
Society of Dyers and Colourists. Journal — Soc Dyers & Col J
Society of Economic Paleontologists and Mineralogists. Core Workshop — SEPM Core Workshop
Society of Economic Paleontologists and Mineralogists. Pacific Section. Guidebooks — Soc Econ Paleontol Mineral Pac Sect Guideb
Society of Economic Paleontologists and Mineralogists. Pacific Section. Guidebooks — SPPGA
Society of Economic Paleontologists and Mineralogists. Paleontological Monograph — PMONDN
Society of Economic Paleontologists and Mineralogists. Paleontological Monograph — Soc Econ Paleontol Mineral Paleontol Monogr
Society of Economic Paleontologists and Mineralogists. Permian Basin Section. Publication — Soc Econ Paleontol Mineral Permian Basin Sect Publ
Society of Economic Paleontologists and Mineralogists. Reprint Series — Soc Econ Paleontol Mineral Repr Ser
Society of Economic Paleontologists and Mineralogists. Special Publication — Soc Econ Paleontol Mineral Spec Publ
Society of Economic Paleontologists and Mineralogists. Special Publication — Soc Econ Paleontologists and Mineralogists Spec Pub
Society of Economic Paleontologists and Mineralogists. Special Publication — Soc Econ Paleontologists and Mineralogists Special Pub
Society of Engineers (London). Journal — Soc Eng (London) J

Society of Engineers (London). Journal and Transactions — Soc Eng London J Trans
Society of Exploration Geophysicists. Annual International Meeting. Abstracts — Soc Explor Geophys Annu Int Meet Abstr
Society of Film and Television Arts. Journal — Soc F TV Arts J
Society of General Physiologists. Series — Soc Gen Physiol Ser
Society of Glass Technology. Journal — Soc Glass Technology Jour
Society of Independent Professional Earth Scientists. Bulletin — Soc Indep Prof Earth Sci Bull
Society of Leather Trades Chemists. Proceedings. Annual Convention — Soc Leather Trades Chem Proc Annu Conv
Society of Libyan Studies. Annual Report — Rep Soc Lib St
Society of Malawi. Journal — Soc Malawi J
Society of Manufacturing Engineers. Association for Finishing Processes. Technical Paper. Series FC — Soc Manuf Eng Assoc Finish Processes Tech Pap Ser FC
Society of Manufacturing Engineers. Collective Papers — SME Collect Pap
Society of Manufacturing Engineers. Creative Manufacturing Seminars. Technical Papers — SME Creative Mfg Semin Tech Pap
Society of Manufacturing Engineers. Technical Paper — SME Tech Pap
Society of Manufacturing Engineers. Technical Paper. AD — Soc Manuf Eng Tech Pap AD
Society of Manufacturing Engineers. Technical Paper. Series AD (Assembly Division) — Soc Manuf Eng Tech Pap Ser AD
Society of Manufacturing Engineers. Technical Paper. Series EE (Electrical Engineering) — SME Tech Pap Ser EE
Society of Manufacturing Engineers. Technical Paper. Series EE (Electrical Engineering) — Soc Manuf Eng Tech Pap Ser EE
Society of Manufacturing Engineers. Technical Paper. Series EM (Engineering Materials) — SME Tech Pap Ser EM
Society of Manufacturing Engineers. Technical Paper. Series EM (Engineering Materials) — Soc Manuf Eng Tech Pap Ser EM
Society of Manufacturing Engineers. Technical Paper. Series FC (Finishing and Coating) — SME Tech Pap Ser FC
Society of Manufacturing Engineers. Technical Paper. Series FC (Finishing and Coating) — Soc Manuf Eng Tech Pap Ser FC
Society of Manufacturing Engineers. Technical Paper. Series IQ (Inspection and Quality) — Soc Manuf Eng Tech Pap Ser IQ
Society of Manufacturing Engineers. Technical Paper. Series MF (Material Forming) — SME Tech Pap Ser MF
Society of Manufacturing Engineers. Technical Paper. Series MF (Material Forming) — Soc Manuf Eng Tech Pap Ser MF
Society of Manufacturing Engineers. Technical Paper. Series MR (Material Removal) — SME Tech Pap Ser MR
Society of Manufacturing Engineers. Technical Paper. Series MR (Material Removal) — Soc Manuf Eng Tech Pap Ser MR
Society of Manufacturing Engineers. Technical Paper. Series MS — Soc Manuf Eng Tech Pap Ser MS
Society of Manufacturing Engineers. Technical Paper. Series TE — Soc Manuf Eng Tech Pap Ser TE
Society of Manufacturing Engineers. Western Metal and Tool Exposition and Conference. Technical Papers — SME West Metal Tool Expos Conf Tech Pap
Society of Mass Media and Resource Technology. Journal — Soc Mass Media Res Tech Jnl
Society of Mining Engineers of AIME [*American Institute of Mining, Metallurgical, and Petroleum Engineers*] **Annual Uranium Seminar** — Soc Min Eng AIME. Annu Uranium Semin
Society of Mining Engineers of AIME [*American Institute of Mining, Metallurgical, and Petroleum Engineers*]. Transactions — Soc Min Eng AIME Trans
Society of Mining Engineers of AIME [*American Institute of Mining, Metallurgical, and Petroleum Engineers*]. Transactions — Soc Mining Engineers AIME Trans
Society of Mining Engineers. Transactions — Soc Min Eng Trans
Society of Motion Picture and Television Engineers. Journal — SMPTE J
Society of Motion Picture and Television Engineers. Journal — Soc Motion Pict Telev Eng J
Society of Naval Architects and Marine Engineers of New York. Transactions — Soc Nav Architects Mar Eng Trans
Society of Naval Architects and Marine Engineers. Technical and Research Bulletin [*New York*] — Soc Nav Architects Mar Eng Tech Res Bull
Society of Naval Architects and Marine Engineers. Transactions [*United States*] — Soc Nav Archit Mar Eng Trans
Society of Nematologists. Special Publication — Soc Nematol Spec Publ
Society of Nuclear Medicine. Southeastern Chapter. Continuing Education Lectures — Soc Nucl Med Southeast Chapter Contin Educ Lect
Society of Occupational Medicine. Journal — Soc Occup Medicine J
Society of Petroleum Engineers. American Institute of Mining, Metallurgical, and Petroleum Engineers. Improved Oil Recovery Field Reports — Soc Pet Eng AIME Improv Oil Recovery Field Rep
Society of Petroleum Engineers. American Institute of Mining, Metallurgical, and Petroleum Engineers. Journal — Soc Pet E J
Society of Petroleum Engineers. American Institute of Mining, Metallurgical, and Petroleum Engineers. Journal — Soc Pet Eng AIME J
Society of Petroleum Engineers. American Institute of Mining, Metallurgical, and Petroleum Engineers. Journal — Soc Pet Eng J
Society of Petroleum Engineers. American Institute of Mining, Metallurgical, and Petroleum Engineers. Journal — Soc Pet Engr J
Society of Petroleum Engineers. American Institute of Mining, Metallurgical, and Petroleum Engineers. Journal — Soc Pet Engrs J
Society of Petroleum Engineers. American Institute of Mining, Metallurgical, and Petroleum Engineers. Journal — Soc Petrol Eng J
Society of Petroleum Engineers. American Institute of Mining, Metallurgical, and Petroleum Engineers. Journal — Soc Petroleum Engineers Jour
Society of Petroleum Engineers. American Institute of Mining, Metallurgical, and Petroleum Engineers. Journal — SPEJ
Society of Petroleum Engineers. American Institute of Mining, Metallurgical, and Petroleum Engineers. Papers — SEAPA
Society of Petroleum Engineers. American Institute of Mining, Metallurgical, and Petroleum Engineers. Papers — Soc Pet Eng AIME Pap
Society of Petroleum Engineers. American Institute of Mining, Metallurgical, and Petroleum Engineers. Reprint Series [*United States*] — SPE Repr Ser
Society of Petroleum Engineers. American Institute of Mining, Metallurgical, and Petroleum Engineers. Transactions — Soc Pet Eng AIME Trans
Society of Petroleum Engineers. American Institute of Mining, Metallurgical, and Petroleum Engineers. Transactions — Soc Petrol Eng Trans
Society of Petroleum Engineers. American Institute of Mining, Metallurgical, and Petroleum Engineers. Transactions — Soc Potroleum Engineers AIME Trans
Society of Petroleum Engineers. Formation Evaluation — Soc Pet Eng Form Eval
Society of Petroleum Engineers. Journal — Soc Petroleum Engrs Jol
Society of Petroleum Engineers. Production Engineering — Soc Pet Eng Prod Eng
Society of Petroleum Engineers. Reservoir Engineering — Soc Pet Eng Reservoir Eng
Society of Pharmacological and Environmental Pathologists. Bulletin — Soc Pharmacol Environ Pathol Bull
Society of Photographic Instrumentation Engineers. Journal — Soc Photogr Instrum Eng J
Society of Photographic Instrumentation Engineers. Journal — SPIE Journal
Society of Photographic Instrumentation Engineers. Newsletter — Soc Phot Instr Eng Newsletter
Society of Photographic Scientists and Engineers. Annual Conference and Seminar on Quality Control. Summaries of Papers — Soc Photogr Sci Eng Annu Conf Semin Qual Control Summ Pap
Society of Photographic Scientists and Engineers. News — Soc Photogr Sci Eng News
Society of Photo-Optical Instrumentation Engineers. Annual Technical Symposium. Proceedings — Soc Photo Opt Instrum Eng Annu Tech Symp Proc
Society of Photo-Optical Instrumentation Engineers. Journal — Soc Photo Opt Instrum Eng J
Society of Photo-Optical Instrumentation Engineers. Proceedings [*United States*] — Soc Photo-Opt Instrum Eng Proc
Society of Plant Protection of North Japan. Special Report — Soc Plant Prot North Jpn Spec Rep
Society of Plastic Engineers. National Technical Conference. High Performance Plastics. Preprints — Soc Plast Eng Natl Tech Conf High Perform Plast Prepr
Society of Plastics Engineers. Divisional Technical Conference. Technical Papers — Soc Plast Eng Div Tech Conf Tech Pap
Society of Plastics Engineers European Regional Technical Conference. Plastics and Processing — Soc Plast Eng Eur Reg Tech Conf Plast Process
Society of Plastics Engineers. National Technical Conference — Soc Plast Eng Natl Tech Conf
Society of Plastics Engineers. Pacific Technical Conference. Technical Papers — Soc Plast Eng Pac Tech Conf Tech Pap
Society of Plastics Engineers. Technical Papers — Soc Plast Eng Tech Pap
Society of Plastics Engineers. Vinyl Plastics Division. Lecture Notes. Division Technical Conference — Soc Plast Eng Vinyl Plast Div Lect Notes Div Tech Conf
Society of Professional Well Log Analysts. Annual Logging Symposium. Transactions — Soc Prof Well Log Anal Annu Logging Symp Trans
Society of Rheology. Transactions — Soc Rheol Trans
Society of Soil Scientists and Fertilizer Technologists of Taiwan. Newsletter — Soc Soil Sci Fert Technol Taiwan Newsl
Society of the Plastics Industry. Cellular Plastics Division. Annual Technical Conference — Soc Plast Ind Cell Plast Div Annu Tech Conf
Society of the Plastics Industry. National Plastics Conference Proceedings — Soc Plast Ind Natl Plast Conf Proc
Society of the Plastics Industry of Canada. CanPlast — Soc Plast Ind Can CanPlast
Society of the Plastics Industry. Polyurethane Division. Proceedings. SPI Annual Technical/Marketing Conference — Soc Plast Ind Polyurethane Div Proc SPI Annu Tech Mark Conf
Society of the Plastics Industry. Structural Foam Conference. Proceedings — Soc Plast Ind Struct Foam Conf Proc
Society of Vacuum Coaters. Annual Technical Conference Proceedings — Soc Vac Coaters Annu Tech Conf Proc
Society of Vacuum Coaters. Proceedings. Annual Conference — Soc Vac Coaters Proc Annu Conf
Society of Vacuum Coaters. Proceedings. Annual Technical Conference — Soc Vac Coaters Proc Annu Tech Conf
Society of Vector Ecologists. Bulletin — Soc Vector Ecol Bull
Socijalisticko Zemjodelstvo — Soc Zemjod
Socioeconomic Issues of Health — Socioecon Issues Health
Socioeconomic Monitoring System Report — SMS Report
Socioeconomic Newsletter — Socioecon Newsletter
Socio-Economic Planning Sciences — SEPS
Socio-Economic Planning Sciences — SEPS-B
Socio-Economic Planning Sciences — Soc-Econ Plan Sci
Socio-Economic Planning Sciences — Socio-Econ
Socio-Economic Planning Sciences — Socio-Econ Plann Sci
Socio-Economic Planning Sciences — Socio-Econ Planning Sciences
Socio-Economic Planning Sciences — SOE
Socioeconomic Report. California Medical Association — Socioecon Rep
Sociolinguistics Newsletter — Socioling Newsl
Sociolinguistics Newsletter — SocN
Sociologia — SOC
Sociologia del Lavoro — Sociol Lav

Sociologia dell'Organizzazione — Sociol Org
Sociologia Internationalis — SI
Sociologia Internationalis (Berlin) — Sociol Int (Berlin)
Sociologia Neerlandica — Sociol Neer
Sociologia Religiosa — SR
Sociologia Ruralis — Sociol Rur
Sociologia Ruralis — Sociol Ruralis
Sociological Abstracts [*Sociological Abstracts, Inc.*] [*Information service or system*] — SA
Sociological Abstracts — Soc A
Sociological Abstracts — SocAb
Sociological Abstracts — Sociol Abstr
Sociological Analysis — PSGA
Sociological Analysis — SA
Sociological Analysis [*Washington, D.C*] — SAP
Sociological Analysis [*Notre Dame, Indiana*] — SAR
Sociological Analysis — Soc An
Sociological Analysis — Soc Anal
Sociological Analysis — Sociol Anal
Sociological Analysis and Theory — Sociol Anal Theory
Sociological Bulletin — Sociol Bull
Sociological Bulletin (Bombay) — Sociol B (Bombay)
Sociological Bulletin (New Delhi) — Sociol B
Sociological Focus — Sociol Focu
Sociological Inquiry — PSGI
Sociological Inquiry — Sociol Inq
Sociological Inquiry — Sociol Inquiry
Sociological Methodology — Soc Meth
Sociological Methodology — Socio Meth
Sociological Methods and Research — Sociol Meth
Sociological Methods and Research — Sociol Methods & Res
Sociological Quarterly — PSGQ
Sociological Quarterly — Sociol Q
Sociological Quarterly — Sociol Quart
Sociological Quarterly — SOLQA
Sociological Quarterly — SQ
Sociological Religiosa — Soc Rel
Sociological Review — PSGR
Sociological Review — Soc R
Sociological Review — Socio R
Sociological Review — Sociol R
Sociological Review — Sociol Rev
Sociological Review — Sociological R
Sociological Review — SR
Sociological Review. Monograph — Sociol R Mg
Sociological Review. Monograph — Sociol Rev Monogr
Sociological Review. New Series — Sociol R NS
Sociological Review (Staffordshire, England) — SRS
Sociological Studies — SS
Sociological Symposium — Sociol Symp
Sociological Theory — Soc Theory
Sociological Theory — Sociol Theory
Sociological Yearbook of Religion in Britain — Sociol Yb Relig Britain
Sociologiceskie Issledovanija (Moskva) — Sociol Issled (Moskva)
Sociologiceskie Issledovanija (Sverdlovsk) — Sociol Issled (Sverdlovsk)
Sociologicky Casopis — Sociol Cas
Sociologie Contemporaine — Sociol Contemp
Sociologie du Travail — Soc Trav
Sociologie du Travail — Soc Travail
Sociologie du Travail — Sociol Trav
Sociologie et Droit Slaves — Social Droit Slav
Sociologie et Societes — Sociol et Soc
Sociologie et Societes — Sociol et Soc
Sociologie et Societes — Sociol Soci
Sociologija Sela — Sociol Sela
Sociologisch Bulletin — SB
Sociologisch Bulletin — Soc B
Sociologische Gids — Sociol Gids
Sociologisk Forskning — Sociol Fors
Sociologiske Meddelelser — Sociol Meddel
Sociologus — Soc
Sociologus [*Berlin*] — Sociol
Sociologus. Beiheft — SocB
Sociologus Zeitschrift fuer Empirische Soziologie, Sozialpsychologische, und Ethnologische Forschung — Sociologus
Sociology — Sociol
Sociology — SY
Sociology and Economic Aspects of Medicine [*Database*] — SEAM
Sociology and Social Research — PSGH
Sociology and Social Research — Soc & Scl Res
Sociology and Social Research — Soc Soc Res
Sociology and Social Research — Sociol & Soc Res
Sociology and Social Research — Sociol & Social Res
Sociology and Social Research — Sociol Soc
Sociology and Social Research — Sociol Soc Res
Sociology and Social Research — SSR
Sociology. Journal. British Sociological Association — PSGY
Sociology of Education — Soc of Ed
Sociology of Education — Sociol Educ
Sociology of Education — Sociol of Ed
Sociology of Education Abstracts — Sociol Educ Abstr
Sociology of Health and Illness — Sociol Health Illn
Sociology of Health and Illness — Sociol Health Illness
Sociology of Law — Sociol Law
Sociology of Leisure and Sport Abstracts — Sociol Leis Sports Abstr
Sociology of Rural Life. Minnesota University. Agricultural Extension Service — Sociol Rural Life Minn Univ Agric Ext Serv
Sociology of Sport Journal — Soc Sport J
Sociology of Work and Occupations — Sociol W Oc
Sociology of Work and Occupations — Sociol Wk Occupat
Sociology of Work and Occupations — Sociol Work Occ
Sociology. Reviews of New Books — SRNB
Sociometry — Sociom
Socker Handlingar — Socker Handli
Socker. Handlingar 2. Communications from the Swedish Sugar Corporation — Socker Handl 2
Sodalitas Thomistica — Sod Thom
Sodankyla Report — Sodankyla Rep
Sodium Pump. Recent Developments. Society of General Physiologists Annual Symposium — Sodium Pump Recent Dev Soc Gen Physiol Annu Symp
Sodobnost — Sod
Soedineniya Peremennogo Sostava — Soedin Perem Sostava
Soester Zeitschrift — Soest Z
Soester Zeitschrift — Soester Z
Sofia Universitet. Geologo-Geografski Fakultet. Godishnik. Kniga 1. Geologiya — Sofia Univ Geol-Geogr Fak God Kniga 1 Geol
Sofia Universitet. Geologo-Geografski Fakultet. Godishnik. Kniga 2. Geografiya — Sofia Univ Geol-Geogr Fak God Kn 2 Geogr
Sofia Vissh Minno-Geolozhki Institut. Godishnik — Sofia Vissh Minno Geol Inst God
Sofiiski Universitet Kliment Okhridski. Biologicheski Fakultet. Godishnik — Sofii Univ Kliment Okhridski Biol Fak God
Sofiiski Universitet Kliment Okhridski. Fakultet po Matematika i Mekhanika. Godishnik — Sofii Univ Kliment Okhridski Fak Mat Mekh God
Sofiiski Universitet Kliment Okhridski. Khimicheski Fakultet. Godishnik — Sofii Univ Kliment Okhridski Khim Fak God
Sofiiskii Universitet. Matematicheski Fakultet. Godishnik — Sofii Univ Mat Fak God
Sofijskij Vremennik — Sof Vr
Soft Drinks Trade Journal — SOE
Software Abstracts for Engineers [*Database*] — SAFE
Software Development in Chemistry 4. Proceedings. Workshop Computers in Chemistry — Software Dev Chem 4 Proc Workshop Comput Chem
Software Development in Chemistry 5. Proceedings. Workshop. Computers in Chemistry — Software Dev Chem 5 Proc Workshop Comput Chem
Software Digest Ratings Newsletter — Software Dig Rat Newsl
Software Engineering Bibliographic Database — SEB
Software Engineering for Telecommunication Switching Systems. International Conference — Software Eng Telecommun Switching Syst Int Conf
Software Engineering Notes — Soft Eng Notes
Software, Environments, and Tools — Software Environ Tools
Software in Healthcare — Softw Healthc
Software Life Cycle Empirical Database — SLED
Software News — Soft News
Software News — Software N
Software Newsletter — SNUCD
Software Newsletter — Softw Newsl
Software: Practice and Experience — Software
Software: Practice and Experience — Software Pract and Exper
Software: Practice and Experience — Software Pract Exper
Software Protection — SPROE
Software Publishing Report — Software Pub Rep
Software Review — Software Rev
Software Review — SSORD
Software Theft Opposition Project [*Database*] — STOP
Software Tool Information Database — STI Database
Software Tools Communications — Software Tools Commun
Software Tools Communications — STOCD
Software World — Soft World
Software-Entwicklung in der Chemie 2. Proceedings des Workshops Computer in der Chemie — Software Entwickl Chem 2 Proc Workshops Comput Chem
Sogo Hogaku — Sogo Hog
Sogo Igaku — Sog Iga
Sogo Kyodo Kenkyusho Kiyo — Sogo Ky Kenk Kiyo
Sogo Rinsho — Sog Rinsh
Sogo Shikensho Nenpo — Sog Shik Nenpo
Sohioan — SOHID
Soil and Crop Science Society of Florida. Proceedings — Soil Crop Sci Soc Fla Proc
Soil and Fertilizer Newsletter — Soil Fert Newsl
Soil and Land-Use Surveys of the British Caribbean — Soil Ld-Use Surv Br Caribb
Soil and Plant — Soil Plant
Soil and Tillage Research — Soil Tillage Res
Soil and Water Conservation Journal — Soil and Water Conserv Jour
Soil and Water Conservation News — Soil and Water Conser News
Soil and Water Conservation News. US Department of Agriculture. Soil Conservation Service — Soil Water Conserv News US Dep Agric Soil Conserv Serv
Soil Association. Information Bulletin and Advisory Service — SAIBB
Soil Association. Information Bulletin and Advisory Service [*England*] — Soil Assoc Inf Bull Advis Serv
Soil Biochemistry — Soil Biochem
Soil Biology — Soil Biol
Soil Biology and Biochemistry — Soil Biol and Biochem
Soil Biology and Biochemistry — Soil Biol B
Soil Biology and Biochemistry — Soil Biol Biochem
Soil Biology and Microbiology — Soil Biol Microbiol

Soil Biology Section. Society for Soil Science. Hungarian Association of Agricultural Sciences. Proceedings. Meeting — Soil Biol Sect Soc Soil Sci Hung Assoc Agric Sci Proc Meet
Soil Bulletin. National Geological Survey of China — Soil Bull Natl Geol Surv China
Soil, Chemical, and Physical Sciences — Soil Chem Phys Sci
Soil Conditioners. Proceedings. Symposium — Soil Cond Proc Symp
Soil Conservation — SC
Soil Conservation — Soil Cons
Soil Conservation — Soil Conser
Soil Conservation — Soil Conserv
Soil Conservation Service of New South Wales. Journal — Soil Cons Serv NSW J
Soil Conservation Society of America. Proceedings. Annual Meeting — Soil Conserv Soc Am Proc Annu Meet
Soil Conservation. United States Soil Conservation Service — Soil Conserv US Soil Conserv Serv
Soil Cryogenesis — Soil Cryog
Soil Mechanics and Foundation Engineering — Soil Mech Found Eng
Soil Mechanics and Foundation Engineering — Soil Mech Found Engng
Soil Mechanics and Foundation Engineering (English Translation) — Soil Mech Found Eng (Engl Transl)
Soil Mechanics and Foundation Engineering. Regional Conference for Africa. Proceedings — Soil Mech Found Eng Reg Conf Afr Proc
Soil Microscopy. Proceedings. International Working-Meeting on Soil Micromorphology — Soil Microsc Proc Int Work Meet Soil Micromorphol
Soil Nitrogen as Fertilizer or Pollutant. Proceedings and Report. Research Coordination Meeting — Soil Nitrogen Fert Pollut Proc Rep Res Coord Meet
Soil Physics of Western Siberia — Soil Phys West Sib
Soil Publication. Commonwealth Scientific and Industrial Research Organisation [*Australia*] — Soil Publ
Soil Publication. Commonwealth Scientific and Industrial Research Organisation [*Australia*] — Soil Publ CSIRO
Soil Research — Soil Res
Soil Research. Supplement — Soil Res Suppl
Soil Restoration — Soil Restor
Soil Science — Soil Sci
Soil Science, Agrochemistry, and Ecology — Soil Sci Agrochem Ecol
Soil Science, Agrochemistry, and Plant Protection — Soil Sci Agrochem Plant Prot
Soil Science and Agrochemistry — Soil Sci Agrochem
Soil Science and Agronomy — Soil Sci Agron
Soil Science and Plant Nutrition — Soil Sci Pl Nutr
Soil Science and Plant Nutrition — Soil Sci Plant Nutr
Soil Science and Plant Nutrition (Tokyo) — Soil Sci Plant Nutr (Tokyo)
Soil Science Annual (Warsaw) — Soil Sci Annu Warsaw
Soil Science Society of America. Book Series — Soil Sci Soc Am Book Ser
Soil Science Society of America. Journal — Soil Sci Soc Am J
Soil Science Society of America. Journal — SSSJD
Soil Science Society of America. Proceedings — Soil Sci So
Soil Science Society of America. Proceedings — Soil Sci Soc Am Proc
Soil Science Society of America. Proceedings — Soil Sci Soc America Proc
Soil Science Society of Florida. Proceedings — Soil Sci Soc Fla Proc
Soil Series. Minnesota University. Agriculture Extension Service — Soil Ser Minn Univ Agr Ext Serv
Soil Survey Bulletin. Samaru Institute for Agricultural Research — Soil Surv Bull Samaru
Soil Survey Horizons — Soil Surv Horiz
Soil Survey Investigations. Report — Soil Surv Invest Rep
Soil Survey Papers. Netherlands Soil Survey Institute — Soil Surv Pap Neth Soil Surv Inst
Soil Survey Technical Monograph (United Kingdom) — Soil Surv Tech Monogr UK
Soil Technology — Soil Technol
Soil Testing and Plant Analysis (Revised Edition) [*Monograph*] — Soil Test Plant Anal (Revis Ed)
Soil Use and Management — Soil Use Manage
Soilless Culture — Soilless Cult
Soils and Fertilizers — SF
Soils and Fertilizers — SOIFA
Soils and Fertilizers — Soil Fert
Soils and Fertilizers — Soil Fertil
Soils and Fertilizers [*England*] — Soils Fert
Soils and Fertilizers — Soils Fertil
Soils and Fertilizers. Commonwealth Bureau of Soil Science — Soils Fert Commonw Bur Soil Sci
Soils and Fertilizers in Taiwan — Soil Fert Taiwan
Soils and Fertilizers in Taiwan — Soils Fert Taiwan
Soils and Fertilizers in Taiwan — Soils Fertil Taiwan
Soils and Foundations — Soils Found
Soils and Land Use Series. Division of Soils. Commonwealth Scientific and Industrial Research Organisation — Soils Land Use Ser Div Soils CSIRO
Soils and Land Use Series. Division of Soils. Commonwealth Scientific and Industrial Research Organisation — Soils Ld Use Ser Div Soils CSIRO
Soils Bulletin — FASBB
Soils Bulletin. Food and Agriculture Organization — Soils Bull FAO
Soils Quarterly. Geological Survey of China — Soils Quart
Soils Report. Manitoba Soil Survey — Soils Rep Manitoba Soil Surv
Soins. Cardiologie — Soins Cardiol
Soins. Chirurgie — Soins Chir
Soins. Chirurgie Generale et Specialisee — Soins Chir Gen Spec
Soins. Gynecologie, Obstetrique, Puericulture — Soins Gynecol Obst Pueric
Soins. Gynecologie, Obstetrique, Puericulture, Pediatrie — Soins Gynecol Obstet Pueric Pediatr
Soins. Pathologie Tropicale — Soins Pathol Trop
Soins. Psychiatrie — Soins Psychiatr
Sojourner — So
Sojuzot na Zdruzenijata na Farmacevtite i Farmacevtskite Tehnicari na SR Makedonija. Bilten — Sojuzot Zdruzenijata Farm Farm Teh SR Maked Bilt
Sokhrannost Radiogennogo Argona v Gornykh Porodakh — Sokhrannost Radiog Argona Gorn Porodakh
Sokolovskoe Magnetitovoe Mestorozhdenie. Geologiya, Razvedka, Perspektivy — Sokolovskoe Magnetitovoe Mestorozhd Geol Razved Perspekt
Sokrates — S
Sokrates — So
Sokrates — Sok
Solaire 1 Magazine — SMAGD
Solaire 1 Magazine [*France*] — Solaire 1 Mag
Solar Activity — Sol Act
Solar Age — SOAGD
Solar Age — Sol Age
Solar Age. A Magazine of the Sun — SAL
Solar Cells — SOCLD
Solar Cells — Sol Cells
Solar Energy — Sol Energy
Solar Energy — Solar Energ
Solar Energy Digest — Solar E D
Solar Energy Digest — Solar En D
Solar Energy Employment and Requirements, 1978-1985 — Solar 1985
Solar Energy Engineering — Sol Energy Eng
Solar Energy Intelligence Report [*Database*] — SEIR
Solar Energy Intelligence Report — Sol Energy Intel Rep
Solar Energy Intelligence Report — Sol Energy Intell Rep
Solar Energy Intelligence Report — Solar Intel
Solar Energy Materials — SOEMD
Solar Energy Materials [*Netherlands*] — Sol Energy Mater
Solar Energy Progress in Australia and New Zealand — Sol Energy Prog Aust NZ
Solar Energy R and D in the European Community. Series D — SRDDD
Solar Energy R & D in the European Community. Series D. Photochemical, Photoelectrochemical, and Photobiological Processes — Sol Energy R & D Eur Community Ser D
Solar Energy R and D [*Research and Development*] **in the European Community. Series E. Energy from Biomass** — Sol Energy R & D Eur Community Ser E Energy Biomass
Solar Energy Research and Development Report — Sol Energy Res Dev Rep
Solar Energy Research and Development Report — SRDRD
Solar Energy Research Institute. Technical Report SERI/CP — Sol Energy Res Inst Tech Rep SERI CP
Solar Energy Research Institute. Technical Report SERI/TR — Sol Energy Res Inst Tech Rep SERI TR
Solar Energy Research Report. University of Queensland — Sol Energy Res Rep Univ Queensl
Solar Energy (Seoul) — Sol Energy Seoul
Solar Energy Update — Sol Energy Update
Solar Energy Utilization — Sol Energy Util
Solar Engineering — SOEND
Solar Engineering — Sol Eng
Solar Engineering Magazine — Sol Eng Mag
Solar Flare Magnetohydrodynamics — Sol Flare Magnetohydrodyn
Solar Gamma-, X-, and EUV Radiation — Sol Gamma X EUV Radiat
Solar Heating and Cooling — SHECD
Solar Heating and Cooling — Sol Heat Cool
Solar Industry Index — Sol Ind Ind
Solar Law Reporter — Sol Law Rep
Solar Law Reporter — Solar L Rep
Solar Life — Sol Life
Solar Life — SOLID
Solar Magazine — Solar Mag
Solar Magazine — SOLMD
Solar News International [*Germany*] — Sol News Int
Solar Physics — Sol Phys
Solar Physics — Solar Phys
Solar System Research — Sol Syst Res
Solar System Research — Solar Syst Res
Solar System Research (English Translation) — Sol Syst Res (Engl Transl)
Solar Terrestrial Environmental Research in Japan — Sol Terr Environ Res Jpn
Solar Thermal Components — Sol Therm Components
Solar Thermal Energy Utilization — Sol Therm Energy Util
Solar Thermal Heating and Cooling — Sol Therm Heat Cool
Solar Thermal Power Generation — Sol Therm Power Gener
Solar Thermal Report — Sol Therm Rep
Solar Thermal Report — STHRD
Solar Times — Sol Times
Solar Times — SOTID
Solar Waerme Technik — SWTED
Solar World Congress. Proceedings. Biennial Congress. International Solar Energy Society — Sol World Congr Proc Bienn Congr Int Sol Energy Soc
Solar-Geophysical Data — SGD
Solder Mechanics. A State of the Art Assessment — Solder Mech
Soldier of Fortune — SOF
Sol-Gel Science and Technology — Sol Gel Sci Technol
Solicitor — Sol
Solicitor — Solic
Solicitors' Journal — Sol J
Solicitors' Journal — Solic J
Solicitors' Journal — Solicitors' J
Solicitors' Journal (England) — Sol Jo (Eng)
Solicitor's Quarterly — Sol Q
Solicitor's Quarterly — Solic Q

Solid Freeform Fabrication Symposium Proceedings — Solid Freeform Fabr Symp Proc
Solid Fuel Chemistry [*English Translation*] — SFCHD
Solid Fuel Chemistry [*English Translation of Khimiya Tverdogo Topliva*] — Solid Fuel Chem
Solid Fuel Chemistry (English Translation) — Solid Fuel Chem (Engl Transl)
Solid Mechanics and its Applications — Solid Mech Appl
Solid Mechanics and Its Applications — Solid Mech Its Appl
Solid Mechanics Archives — SM Arch
Solid Mechanics Archives — Solid Mech Arch
Solid State Abstracts — Solid St Abstr
Solid State Abstracts Journal — Solid State Abstr J
Solid State Chemical Sensors — Solid State Chem Sens
Solid State Communications — Sol St Comm
Solid State Communications — Solid St Commun
Solid State Communications — Solid State Commun
Solid State Devices. Invited Papers presented at the ESSDERC (European Solid State Device Research Conference) — Solid State Devices. Invited Pap ESSDERC
Solid State Devices. Papers. European Semiconductor Device Research Conference — Solid State Devices Pap Eur Semicond Device Res Conf
Solid State Ionics — SSIOD
Solid State Journal — Solid State J
Solid State Journal — SSTJA
Solid State Nuclear Magnetic Resonance — Solid State Nucl Magn Reson
Solid State Nuclear Track Detectors. Proceedings. International Conference — Solid State Nucl Track Detect Proc Int Conf
Solid State Physics — Solid State Phys
Solid State Physics — SSPHA
Solid State Physics. Advances in Research and Applications (New York) — Solid State Phys (New York)
Solid State Physics and Chemistry [*Japan*] — Solid State Phys Chem
Solid State Physics. Supplement — Solid State Phys Suppl
Solid State Physics. The Simon Fraser University Lectures — Solid State Phys Simon Fraser Univ Lect
Solid State Physics (Tokyo) — Solid State Phys (Tokyo)
Solid State Surface Science — Solid State Surf Sci
Solid State Technology — Sol St Tech
Solid State Technology — Solid Stat
Solid State Technology — Solid State Technol
Solid Waste Bulletin — Solid Waste Bull
Solid Waste Management Newsletter — Solid Waste Man Newsl
Solid Waste Systems — Solid Waste Syst
Solid Wastes Management [*World Wastes*] [*England*] [*Later,*] — Solid Wastes Manage
Solid Wastes Management [*Later, World Wastes*] — Solid Wastes Mgmt
Solid Wastes Management [*Later, World Wastes*] — Solid WM
Solid Wastes Management [*Later, World Wastes*] — SWMGA
Solid Wastes Management/Refuse Removal Journal [*Later, World Wastes*] — Solid Wastes Manage Refuse Removal J
Solidarismo y Racionalizacion (San Jose, Costa Rica) — Solidar Racional S Jose
Solidarity [*Manila*] — Sol
Solidification and Microgravity — Solidif Microgravity
Solid-State Electronics — Solid-State Electron
Solid-State Electronics — Sol-St Elec
Solnechnaya Aktivnost — Soln Akt
Solnechnye Dannye — SODAA
Solnechnye Dannye [*Former USSR*] — Soln Dannye
Solo Centro Academico "Luiz De Queiroz." Universidade de Sao Paulo — Solo Cent Acad "Luiz De Queiroz" Univ Sao Paulo
Sols Africains — Sols Afr
Solvation Phenomena. Symposium Reprints — Solvation Phenom Symp Repr
Solvent Extraction and Ion Exchange — SEIE
Solvent Extraction and Ion Exchange — Solvent Ext
Solvent Extraction and Ion Exchange — Solvent Extr Ion Exch
Solvent Extraction Research. Proceedings. International Conference on Solvent Extraction Chemistry — Solvent Extr Res Proc Int Conf Solvent Extr Chem
Solvent Extraction Reviews — Solvent Extr Rev
Solvent Substitution. Annual International Workshop on Solvent Substitution — Solvent Substitution Annu Int Workshop Solvent Substitution
Solvents Symposium for Industry — Solvents Symp Ind
Soma — SM
Somatic Cell and Molecular Genetics — Somat Cell Mol Genet
Somatic Cell and Molecular Genetics — Somatic Cell Mol Genet
Somatic Cell Genetics — Som Cell G
Somatic Cell Genetics — Somatic Cell Genet
Somatosensory and Motor Research — Somatosens Mot Res
Somatosensory Research — Somatosens Res
Some Mathematical Questions in Biology — Some Math Quest Biol
Some Oxford Papyri — P Oxf
Some Oxford Papyri — P Oxford
Some Special Aspects of Nutrition — Some Spec Aspects Nutr
Some Theoretical Problems of Catalysis. Research Reports. Soviet-Japanese Seminar on Catalysis — Some Theor Probl Catal Res Rep Sov Jpn Semin Catal
Someraj Universitataj Kursoj. Kursotekstoj — Someraj Univ Kursoj Kursotekstoj
Somerset Archaeology and Natural History — SANH
Somerset Archaeology and Natural History — Som A Natur Hist
Somerset Archaeology and Natural History — Somerset Arch Nat Hist
Somerset Archaeology and Natural History — Somerset Archaeol Natur Hist
Somerset Industrial Archaeology Society. Journal — Somerset Industrial Archaeology Soc Jnl
Somerset Levels Papers — Somerset Levels Pap
Somerset Notes and Queries — So NQ
Somersetshire Archaeological and Natural History Society. Proceedings [*Later, Somerset Archaeology and Natural History*] — So AS
Something About the Author — SA
Something About the Author. Autobiography Series — SAAAS
Somogyi Mueszaki Szemle [*Hungary*] — Somogyi Muesz Sz
Somogyi Muzeumok Koezlemenyei — SMK
Somogyi Muzeumok Koezlemenyei — Somogyi MK
Son of WSFA Journal — SWSJ
Soncino Blaetter — SB
Soncino Books of the Bible Series — SBBS
Sonderbaende des Naturwissenschaftlichen Vereins in Hamburg — Sonderb Naturwiss Ver Hamb
Sonderbaende zur Strahlentherapie — Sonderb Strahlenther
Sonderband. Der Zeitschrift Strahlentherapie und Onkologie — Sonderb Z Strahlenther Onkol
Sonderdruck aus Internistische Welt [*Germany*] — Sonderdr Internist Welt
Sonderheft. Zeitschrift fuer Pflanzenkrankheiten, Pflanzenpathologie, und Pflanzenschutz — Sonderh Z PflKrankh PflPath PflSchutz
Sonderheft zur Zeitschrift "Landwirtschaftliche Forschung" — Sonderh Landw Forsch
Sonderhefte. Bayerisches Landwirtschaftliches Jahrbuch — Sonderh Bayer Landw Jb
Sonderhefte zum Allgemeinen Statistischen Archiv — Sonderhefte zum Allgemein Statist Arch
Sonderjydsk Maanedsskrift — So M
Sonderjydsk Manedsskrift — Sonderjydsk M-Skr
Sonderjydske Aarboger — So Aa
Sonderschule — SNDSB
Song Hits Magazine — Song Hits Mag
Songklanakarin Journal of Science and Technology — Songklanakarin J Sci Technol
Songwriter Magazine — Songwriter
Songwriter's Review — Songwriters R
Songwriter's Review — SR
Sonneck Society Bulletin — SSB
Sonneck Society Bulletin for American Music — Sonneck S
Sonneck Society Newsletter — SSN
Sonnenenergie — Sonnenenerg
Sonnenenergie und Waermepumpe — Sonenergie
Sonnenenergie und Waermepumpe — Sonnenenerg Waermepumpe
Sonnenenergie und Waermepumpe — SONWD
Sonorum Speculum — Son Spec
Sonus — Son
Soobchtcheniia Russkago Palestinskago Obchtshestva — SRPO
Soobscenija Akademiji Nauk Gruzinskoj SSR — SANGruz
Soobscenija Akademiji Nauk Gruzinskoj SSR — SoANGr
Soobscenija Akademiji Nauk Gruzinskoj SSR — Soobscenija Akad Nauk Gruz SSR
Soobscenija Dal'nevostocnogo Filiala Imeni V. L. Komarova Akademii Nauk SSSR — Soobsc Dalnevost Fil Komarova Akad Nauk SSSR
Soobscenija Gosudarstvennogo Ordena Lenina Ermitaza — Soob Ermit
Soobscenija Gosudarstvennogo Russkogo Muzeja — Soobsc Gosud Russk Muz
Soobscenija Muzeja Iskusstva Narodov Vostoka — Soobsc Muz Isk Nar Vostoka
Soobscenija Otdela Machanizacii i Avtomatizacii Informacionnych Rabot — SOMA
Soobscenija po Vychislitel noi Matematike — Soobsc Vycisl Mat
Soobshcheniia Akademii Nauk Gruzinskoi SSR — Soob A N Gruz SSR
Soobshcheniia Gosudarstvennogo Ermitazha — SGE
Soobshcheniia Gosudarstvennogo Ermitazha — Soob Erm
Soobshcheniia Gosudarstvennogo Ermitazha — Soob G Ermitazh
Soobshcheniia Gosudarstvennogo Ermitazha — Soob Gos Erm
Soobshcheniia Gosudarstvennyi Muzei Izobrazitel'nykh Iskusstv Imeni A. S. Pushkina — Soob G Muz Izob Isk Pushkin
Soobshcheniia Gosudarstvennyi Muzei Izobrazitel'nykh Iskusstv imeni A.S. Pushki na — SGMII
Soobshcheniia Gosudarstvennyi Muzei Izobrazitel'nykh Iskusstv imeni A.S. Pushki na — Soob Pus
Soobshcheniia Imperatorskovo Pravoslavnovo Palestinskovo Obshchestva — SIPO
Soobshcheniia Imperialnovo Pravoslavnovo Palestinskavo Obshchestva — SoobshchIPPO
Soobshcheniia Khersonnesskogo Muzeia [*Sebastopol*] — Soob Kherson Muz
Soobshcheniya Akademii Nauk Gruzii — Soobshch Akad Nauk Gruz
Soobshcheniya Akademii Nauk Gruzinskoi SSR — Soob Gruz
Soobshcheniya Akademiya Nauk Gruzinskoi SSR — Soobshch Akad Nauk Gruzin SSR
Soobshcheniya Akademiya Nauk Gruzinskoi SSSR — Soobshch Akad Nauk Gruz SSSR
Soobshcheniya Byurakanskoi Observatorii Akademiya Nauk Armyanskoi SSR — SBOAA
Soobshcheniya Byurakanskoi Observatorii Akademiya Nauk Armyanskoi SSR — Soobshch Byurakan Obs Akad Nauk Arm SSR
Soobshcheniya Chuvashskoi Zonal'noi Agrokhimicheskoi Laboratorii — Soobshch Chuv Zon Agrokhim Lab
Soobshcheniya Dal'nevostochnogo Filiala Akademii Nauk SSSR — Soobshch Dalnevost Fil Akad Nauk SSSR
Soobshcheniya Dal'Nevostochnogo Filiala Sibirskogo Otdla Akademii Nauk SSSR — Soobshch Dal'Nevost Fil Sib Otd Aka Nauk SSSR
Soobshcheniya Gosudarstvennogo Astronomicheskogo Instituta. Moskovskii Gosudarstvennyi Universitet — Soobshch Gos Astron Inst Mosk Gos Univ
Soobshcheniya Gosudarstvennogo Ermitazha — Soob Ermit
Soobshcheniya Gosudarstvennogo Vsesoyuznogo Instituta po Proektirovaniyu Predpriyatii Koksokhimicheskoi Promyshlennosti — Soobshch Gos Vses Inst Proekt Predpr Koksokhim Promsti SSSR

Soobshcheniya Gruzinskogo Filiala Akademii Nauk SSSR — Soobshch Gruz Fil Akad Nauk SSSR
Soobshcheniya Instituta Agrokhimicheskikh Problem i Gidroponiki Akademiya Nauk Armyanskoi SSR [*Armenian SSR*] — Soobshch Inst Agrokhim Probl Gidroponiki Akad Nauk Arm SSR
Soobshcheniya Instituta Lesa Akademii Nauk SSSR — Soobshch Inst Lesa Akad Nauk SSSR
Soobshcheniya Laboratorii Agrokhimii. Akademiya Nauk Armyanskoi SSR — Soobshch Lab Agrokhim Akad Nauk Arm SSR
Soobshcheniya Laboratorii Lesovedeniya. Akademiya Nauk SSSR — Soobshch Lab Lesoved Akad Nauk SSSR
Soobshcheniya Leningradskogo Instituta Metallov — Soobshch Leningr Inst Met
Soobshcheniya Moskovskogo Otdeleniya Vsesoyuznogo Botanicheskogo Obshchestva — Soobshch Mosk Otd Vses Bot Ova
Soobshcheniya Nauchno-Issledovatel'skogo Instituta Elektronnoi Promyshlennosti KHIKI (Budapest) — Soobshch Nauchno Issled Inst Elektron Promsti KHIKI Budapest
Soobshcheniya o Nauchno-Issledovatel'skoi Rabote Kievskii Politekhnicheskii Institut — Soobshch Nauchno Issled Rab Kiev Politekh Inst
Soobshcheniya o Nauchno-Tekhnicheskikh Rabotakh. Nauchnyi Institut Udobrenii i Insektofungitsidov — Soobshch Nauchno Tekh Rab Nauchn Inst Udobr Insektofungits
Soobshcheniya Ob'edinennogo Instituta Yadernykh Issledovanii (Dubna) — Soobshch Ob'edin Inst Yad Issled (Dubna)
Soobshcheniya Obshchestvoi Laboratorii Agrokhimii Akademii Nauk Armyanskoi SSR — Soobshch Obshch Lab Agrokhim Akad Nauk Armyan SSR
Soobshcheniya Sakhalinskogo Filiala Akademii Nauk SSSR — Soobshch Sakhalin Fil Akad Nauk SSSR
Soobshcheniya Shemakhinskoi Astrofizicheskoi Observatorii. Akademiya Nauk Azerbaidzhanskoi SSR — Soobshch Shemakh Astrofiz Obs Akad Nauk Az SSR
Soobshcheniya Shemakhinskoi Astrofizicheskoi Observatorii Akademiya Nauk Azerbaidzhanskoi SSR — SSAOA
Soobshcheniya Tadzhikskogo Filiala Akademii Nauk SSSR — Soobshch Tadzh Fil Akad Nauk SSSR
Soobshcheniya Tsentral'nogo Instituta Fizicheskikh Issledovanii. Budapest — Soobshch Tsentr Inst Fiz Issled Budapest
Soobshcheniya Tsentral'nogo Instituta Metallov. Leningrad — Soobshch Tsentr Inst Met Leningrad
Soobshcheskoi Shemakhinskoi Astrofizicheskoi Observatorii Akademiya Nauk Azerbaidzhan SSR [*Azerbaidzhan SSR*] — Soobshch Shemakhinskoi Astrofiz Obs Akad Nauk Azerb SSR
Soochow Journal of Humanities [*Taipei*] — Soochow J Hum
Soochow Journal of Literature and Social Studies [*Taipei*] — Soochow J Lit Soc Stud
Soochow Journal of Mathematical and Natural Sciences [*Later, Soochow Journal of Mathematics*] — Soochow J Math Natur Sci
Soochow Journal of Mathematics [*Taipei*] — Soochow J Math
Soon Chun Hyang Journal of Medicine — SHJMD
Soon Chun Hyang Journal of Medicine [*Republic of Korea*] — Soon Chun Hyang J Med
Soon Chun Hyang Taehak Nonmunjip — SCHND
Sootnoshenie Magmatizma i Metamorfizma v Genezise Ul'trabazitov — Sootnoshenie Magmat Metamorf Genezise Ul'trabazitov
Sophia — Soph
Sophia Economic Review [*Tokyo*] — Sophia Econ R
Sophia English Studies — SES
Sophia: Studies in Western Civilization and the Cultural Interaction of East and West [*Tokyo*] — So
Sophia: Studies in Western Civilization and the Cultural Interaction of East and West (Tokyo) — Sophia:T
Sopron Muszaki Egyetemi Karok. Banyamernoki es Foldmeromernoki Karok Kozlemenyei — Soproni Musz Egy Karok Banyamern Foldmeromern Karok Kozl
Soproni Szemle — SSz
Soprotivlenie Materialov i Teoriya Sooruzhenii — Sopr Mater Teor Sooruzh
Soprotivlenie Materialov. Kaunasskii Politekhnicheskii Institut. Trudy Nauchno-Tekhicheskoi Konferentsii — Sopr Mater Kaunas Politekh Inst Tr Nauchno Tekh Konf
Sosei To Kako — SOKAB
Soshioloji — Sosh
Sosiaalinen Aikakauskirja — Sos Aikakausk
Sostav i Stroenie Osadochnykh Formatsii — Sostav Str Osad Form
Sot la Nape — SNa
Sotahistoriallisen Seuran Julkaisuja — Sotahist Seuran Julk
Sotilaslaaketieteellinen Aikakauslehti — Sotilaslaak Aikak
Sotsialisticheskaya Industriya — SOTIB
Sotsialisticheskaya Zakonnost — Sots Zak
Sotsialisticheskiy Trud — SOLTA
Sotsialisticheskiy Trud [*Former USSR*] — Sots Trud
Sotsialisticheskoe Rastenievodstvo — Sots Rastenievod
Sotsialisticheskoe Sel'skoe Khozyaistvo — Sots Selsk Khoz
Sotsialisticheskoe Sel'skoe Khozyaistvo Azerbaidzhana — Sots Sel'Khoz Azerb
Sotsialisticheskoe Sel'skoe Khozyaistvo Azerbaidzhana — Sots Sel'sk Khoz Azerb
Sotsialisticheskoe Sel'skoe Khozyaistvo Uzbekistana — Sots Sel'Khoz Uzbek
Sotsialisticheskoe Sel'skoe Khozyaistvo Uzbekistana — Sots Sel'sk Khoz Uzb
Sotsialisticheskoe Zhivotnovodstvo — Sots Zhivotnovod
Sotsialistichne Tvarinnitstvo — Sots Tvarinnit
Sotsialistik Pollumajandus — Sots Pollum
Sotsialistychne Tvarynnytstvo — Sots Tvarynnytstvo
Soudage dans le Monde — Soudage Monde
Soudage et Fusion par Faisceau d'Electrons. Colloque International — Soudage Fusion Faisceau Electrons
Soudage et Techniques Connexes — SOTCA
Soudage et Techniques Connexes — Soudage Tech Connexes
Soudni Lekarstvi — Soud Lek
Soudni Lekarstvi — Soudni Lek
Soudure et Techniques Connexes — Soudure Tech Connexes
Soul Illustrated — Soul Il
Soul Uitae Chapchi — SUICA
Soul-Taehakkyo Ronmunjip. Inmun-Sahoe-Kwahak [*Seoul University Journal. Humanities and Social Sciences*] — STR
Soumalaisen Tiedeakatemian Toimituksia — STAT
Sound and Sense [*Baguio City*] — SS
Sound and Vibration — S/V
Sound and Vibration — SFD
Sound and Vibration — Sound & Vib
Sound and Vibration — Sound Vib
Sound and Vibration — SOVIA
Sound and Vision Broadcasting — Sound Vis Broadc
Sound (Canada) — Sound (Can)
Soundboard — SB
Sounding Board — So Bod
Sounding Brass and the Conductor — SBCBA
Sounding Brass and the Conductor — Sound Brass
Soundings — So
Soundings — Soun
Soundings — Sound
Soundings. University of California. Library [*Santa Barbara*] — SCUL
Soundpost — SP
Sources and Studies for the History of the Jesuits — SSHJ
Sources and Studies in the History of Arabic Mathematics — Sources Stud Hist Arabic Math
Sources and Studies in the History of Arabic-Islamic Science. History of Mathematics Series — Sources and Stud Hist Arabic-Islamic Sci Hist of Math Ser
Sources and Studies in the History of Arabic-Islamic Science. History of Technology Series — Sources Stud Hist Arabic-Islamic Sci Hist of Tech Ser
Sources Bibliques [*Paris*] — SB
Sources Bibliques — SBi
Sources Chretiennes [*Paris*] — SC
Sources Chretiennes — SCh
Sources Chretiennes — Sources Chr
Sources Chretiennes. Serie Annexe des Textes Non-Chretiens — SCTNC
Sources de Spiritualite — SSpir
Sources for NWT [*Northwest Territory*] **History. Prince of Wales Northern Heritage Centre** [*Canada*] — SNWTH
Sources from the Ancient Near East — SANE
Sources in the History of Mathematics and Physical Sciences — Sources Hist Math Phys Sci
Sources in the History of Mathematics and Physical Sciences — Sources in Hist of Math and Phys Sci
Sources of Science — Sources Sci
Sources Orientales — SOr
Sourdough Journal. Alaska Library Association — SOUR
South Africa. Atomic Energy Board. Report PEL — S Afr At Energy Board Rep PEL
South Africa. Atomic Energy Board. Report PER — S Afr At Energy Board Rep PER
South Africa (Cape Of Good Hope) Department of Nature. Conservation Report — S Afr (Cape Good Hope) Dep Nat Conserv Rep
South Africa. Council for Scientific and Industrial Research. National Building Research Institute. Bulletin — S Afr Counc Sci Ind Res Nat Bldg Res Inst Bull
South Africa CSIR [*Council for Scientific and Industrial Research*] **Air Pollution Group. Annual Report** — S Afr CSIR Air Pollut Group Annu Rep
South Africa CSIR [*Council for Scientific and Industrial Research*] **Air Pollution Research Group. Annual Report** — S Afr CSIR Air Pollut Res Group Annu Rep
South Africa CSIR [*Council for Scientific and Industrial Research*] **Annual Report** — S Afr CSIR Annu Rep
South Africa CSIR [*Council for Scientific and Industrial Research*] **Research Report** — S Afr CSIR Res Rep
South Africa CSIR [*Council for Scientific and Industrial Research*] **Special Report** — S Afr CSIR Spec Rep
South Africa. Department of Agricultural Technical Services. Botanical Survey Memoir — S Afr Dep Agric Tech Serv Bot Surv Mem
South Africa. Department of Agricultural Technical Services. Bulletin — S Afr Dep Agric Tech Serv Bull
South Africa. Department of Agricultural Technical Services. Entomology Memoirs — S Afr Dep Agric Tech Serv Entomol Mem
South Africa. Department of Agricultural Technical Services. Pamphlet — S Afr Dep Agric Tech Serv Pam
South Africa. Department of Agricultural Technical Services. Scientific Bulletin — S Afr Dep Agric Tech Serv Sci Bull
South Africa. Department of Agricultural Technical Services. Technical Communication — S Afr Dep Agric Tech Serv Tech Commun
South Africa. Department of Agriculture and Fisheries. Entomology Memoir — S Afr Dep Agric Fish Entomol Mem
South Africa. Department of Agriculture and Fisheries. Technical Communication — S Afr Dep Agric Fish Tech Commun
South Africa. Department of Agriculture and Water Supply. Entomology Memoir — S Afr Dep Agric Water Supply Entomol Mem
South Africa. Department of Agriculture and Water Supply. Technical Communication — S Afr Dep Agric Water Supply Tech Commun
South Africa. Department of Agriculture. Entomology Memoir — RAAEAV
South Africa. Department of Agriculture. Entomology Memoir — S Afr Dep Agric Entomol Mem
South Africa. Department of Forestry. Annual Report — S Afr Dep For Annu Rep

South Africa. Department of Forestry. Bulletin — S Afr Dep For Bull
South Africa. Department of Mines. Coal Survey Memoir — S Afr Dep Mines Coal Surv Mem
South Africa. Department of Mines. Geological Survey. Annals of the Geological Survey — S Afr Dep Mines Geol Surv Ann Geol Surv
South Africa. Department of Mines. Geological Survey. Bulletin — S Afr Geol Surv Bull
South Africa. Department of Mines. Geological Survey Division. Geological Survey Memoirs — S Afr Dep Mines Geol Surv Div Geol Surv Mem
South Africa. Department of Mines. Geological Survey. Memoir — S Afr Geol Surv Mem
South Africa. Department of Mines. Quarterly Information Circular. Minerals — S Afr Dep Mines Quart Inform Circ Miner
South Africa. Division of Sea Fisheries. Annual Report — S Afr Div Sea Fish Annu Rep
South Africa. Division of Sea Fisheries. Fisheries Bulletin — S Afr Div Sea Fish Fish Bull
South Africa. Division of Sea Fisheries. Investigational Report — S Afr Div Sea Fish Invest Rep
South Africa. Geological Survey. Bibliography and Subject Index of South African Geology — S Afr Geol Surv Bibliogr Subj Index S Afr Geol
South Africa. Geological Survey. Explanation of Sheets — S Afr Geol Surv Explan Sheets
South Africa. Geological Survey. Handbook — S Afr Geol Surv Handb
South Africa. Geological Survey. Seismologic Series — S Afr Geol Surv Seismol Ser
South Africa. Geological Survey. South-West Africa Series — S Afr Geol Surv South-West Afr Ser
South Africa International — S Afr Int
South Africa International Quarterly — South Afr Int Quart
South Africa Music Teacher — SA Mus Tcr
South Africa. Nuclear Development Corporation. Report PER — S Afr Nucl Dev Corp Rep
South Africa. Patent and Trade Marks Office. Patent Journal, Including Trade Marks and Designs — S Afr Pat Trade Marks Off Pat J Incl Trade Marks Des
South Africa. Patent Document — S Afr Pat Doc
South Africa. Report of the Secretary for Water Affairs — S Afr Rep Secr Water Affairs
South Africa. Sea Fisheries Branch. Investigational Report — S Afr Sea Fish Branch Invest Rep
South Africa. Sea Fisheries Institute. Investigational Report — S Afr Sea Fish Inst Invest Rep
South Africa. Sea Fisheries Research Institute. Investigational Report — S Afr Sea Fish Res Inst Invest Rep
South African Annual Insurance Review — S Afr Annu Insur Rev
South African Archaeological Bulletin — S Afr Archaeol Bull
South African Archaeological Bulletin — SAAB
South African Archaeological Bulletin — South Afr Arch B
South African Archaeological Bulletin — South Afr Archaeol B
South African Archaeological Society. Goodwin Series — S Afr Archaeol Soc Goodwin Ser
South African Architectural Journal — S Afr Archit J
South African Architectural Record — S Afr Archit Rec
South African Archives of Ophthalmology — S Afr Arch Ophthalmol
South African Association for Marine Biological Research. Bulletin — S Afr Assoc Mar Biol Res Bull
South African Association for the Advancement of Science. Report — So African Assn Adv Sci Rpt
South African Association for the Advancement of Science. Special Publication — S Afr Assoc Adv Sci Spec Publ
South African Avifauna Series. Percy Fitzpatrick Institute of African Ornithology. University of Cape Town — SAFOAT
South African Bakery and Confectionery Review — S Afr Bakery Confect Rev
South African Bee Journal — S Afr Bee J
South African Builder — S Afr Build
South African Bureau of Standards. Bulletin — BABSD
South African Bureau of Standards. Bulletin — S Afr Bur Stand Bull
South African Cancer Bulletin — S Afr Cancer Bull
South African Chartered Accountant — S Afr Chart Account
South African Chemical Processing — S Afr Chem Process
South African Chemical Processing — SACPB
South African Chemicals — S Afr Chem
South African Citrus Journal — S Afr Citrus J
South African Construction World — S Afr Constr World
South African Corrosion Conference — S Afr Corros Conf
South African Corrosion Journal — S Afr Corros J
South African Council for Scientific and Industrial Research. Air Pollution Research Group. Report APRG — S Afr CSIR Air Pollut Res Group Rep APRG
South African Council for Scientific and Industrial Research. Report Series BOU — S Afr CSIR Rep BOU
South African Council for Scientific and Industrial Research. Special Report. Series WISK — S Afr CSIR Spec Rep WISK
South African Country Life — S African Country Life
South African Dental Journal — S Afr Dent J
South African Digest — S Afr Dig
South African Electrical Review — S Afr Electr Rev
South African Electrical Review — SAERB
South African Electrical Review and Engineer — S Afr Electr Rev Eng
South African Engineer — S Afr Eng
South African Engineer and Electrical Review — S Afr Eng Electr Rev
South African Engineer and Electrical Review — SEERB
South African Engineer and Metal Industries Review — S Afr Eng Met Ind Rev
South African Food Review — S Afr Food Rev
South African Food Review — SAFRD
South African Forestry Journal — S Afr For J
South African Forestry Journal — SAFJB
South African Friesland Journal — S Afr Friesland J
South African Geographer — S Afr Geogr
South African Geographical Journal — S Afr Geogr J
South African Geographical Journal — South Afr Geogr J
South African Historical Journal — S Afr Hist J
South African Industrial Chemist — S Afr Ind Chem
South African Institute for Medical Research. Annual Report — S Afr Inst Med Res Annu Rep
South African Institute for Medical Research. Publications — S Afr Inst Med Res Publ
South African Institute of Assayers and Analysts. Bulletin — S Afr Inst Assayers Anal Bull
South African Institute of Mining and Metallurgy. Journal — S Afr Inst Min Metall J
South African Institution of Chemical Engineers. National Meeting — S Afr Inst Chem Eng Natl Meet
South African Institution of Mechanical Engineers. Journal — S Afr Inst Mech Eng J
South African Institution of Mechanical Engineers. Journal — SAIME J
South African Insurance Magazine — S Afr Insur Mag
South African Jersey — S Afr Jersey
South African Journal for Enology and Viticulture — S Afr J Enol Vitic
South African Journal for Librarianship and Information Science — S Afr J Libr Inf Sci
South African Journal of African Affairs — S Afr J Afr Affairs
South African Journal of African Affairs — South Afr J Afr Aff
South African Journal of African Affairs — South African J African Affairs
South African Journal of Agricultural Extension — S Afr J Agric Ext
South African Journal of Agricultural Science — S Afr J Agr Sci
South African Journal of Agricultural Science — S Afr J Agric Sci
South African Journal of Animal Science — S Afr J Anim Sci
South African Journal of Animal Science — SAJAC
South African Journal of Animal Science/Suid-Afrikaanse Tydskrif vir Veekunde — S Afr J Anim Sci S Afr Tydskr Veekunde
South African Journal of Antarctic Research — S Afr J Antarct Res
South African Journal of Antarctic Research — SAJAR
South African Journal of Antarctic Research. Supplement — S Afr J Antarct Res Suppl
South African Journal of Botany — S Afr J Bot
South African Journal of Business Management — S Afr J Bus Manage
South African Journal of Chemistry — S Afr J Chem
South African Journal of Chemistry — SAJCD
South African Journal of Chemistry/Suid-Afrikaanse Tydskrif vir Chemie — S Afr J Chem/S Afr Tydskr Chem
South African Journal of Clinical Science — S Afr J Clin Sci
South African Journal of Communication Disorders — S Afr J Comm Disorders
South African Journal of Communication Disorders — S Afr J Commun Disord
South African Journal of Communication Disorders — S African J Commun Disorders
South African Journal of Continuing Medical Education — S Afr J Contin Med Educ
South African Journal of Continuing Medical Education — SACED
South African Journal of Criminal Law and Criminology — S Afr J Crim L
South African Journal of Criminal Law and Criminology — S Afr J Crim Law Criminol
South African Journal of Dairy Science — S Afr J Dairy Sci
South African Journal of Dairy Science/Suid-Afrikaanse Tydskrif vir Suiwelkunde — S Afr J Dairy Sci Suid Afr Tydskr Suiwelkunde
South African Journal of Dairy Technology — S Afr J Dairy Technol
South African Journal of Economics [*Suid-Afrikaanse Tydskrif vir Ekonomie*] — S Af J Econ
South African Journal of Economics [*Suid-Afrikaanse Tydskrif vir Ekonomie*] — S Afr J Ec
South African Journal of Economics [*Suid-Afrikaanse Tydskrif vir Ekonomie*] — S Afr J Econ
South African Journal of Economics [*Suid-Afrikaanse Tydskrif vir Ekonomie*] — SAJ
South African Journal of Economics [*Suid-Afrikaanse Tydskrif vir Ekonomie*] — SAJE
South African Journal of Economics [*Suid-Afrikaanse Tydskrif vir Ekonomie*] — South Afr J Econ
South African Journal of Economics [*Suid-Afrikaanse Tydskrif vir Ekonomie*] — South African J Econ
South African Journal of Education — S Afr J Educ
South African Journal of Ethnology — S Afr J Ethnol
South African Journal of Geology — S Afr J Geol
South African Journal of Hospital Medicine — S Afr J Hosp Med
South African Journal of Hospital Medicine — SJMED
South African Journal of Industries — S Afr J Ind
South African Journal of Industries and Labour Gazette — S Afr J Ind Labour Gaz
South African Journal of Laboratory and Clinical Medicine — S Afr J Lab Clin Med
South African Journal of Labour Relations — S Afr J Labour Relat
South African Journal of Marine Science — S Afr J Mar Sci
South African Journal of Medical Laboratory Technology — S Afr J Med Lab Technol
South African Journal of Medical Laboratory Technology — SAJTA
South African Journal of Medical Sciences — S Afr J Med Sci
South African Journal of Medical Sciences — SAJMA
South African Journal of Music Therapy — S Afr J Music Therap
South African Journal of Musicology — S Afr J Musicology
South African Journal of Musicology — SAJM

South African Journal of Musicology — SAMUS
South African Journal of Natural History — S African J Nat Hist
South African Journal of Nutrition — S Afr J Nutr
South African Journal of Nutrition/Suid-Afrikaanse Tydskrif vir Voeding — S Afr J Nutr/S Afr Tydskr Voeding
South African Journal of Obstetrics and Gynaecology — S Afr J Obstet Gynaecol
South African Journal of Occupational Therapy — S Afr J Occup Ther
South African Journal of Philosophy — S Afr J Philos
South African Journal of Photogrammetry. Remote Sensing and Cartography — S Afr J Photogramm Remote Sensing Cartogr
South African Journal of Physics — S Afr J Phys
South African Journal of Physics — SAPHD
South African Journal of Physiotherapy — S Afr J Physiother
South African Journal of Physiotherapy — SAJPA
South African Journal of Plant and Soil — S Afr J Plant Soil
South African Journal of Plant and Soil/Suid-Afrikaanse Tydskrif vir Plant en Grond — S Afr J Plant Soil S Afr Tydskr Plant Grond
South African Journal of Psychology — S Afr J Psychol
South African Journal of Psychology — S African J Psychol
South African Journal of Radiology — S Afr J Radiol
South African Journal of Radiology — SAJRA
South African Journal of Science — S Afr J Sci
South African Journal of Science — SAJSA
South African Journal of Science — So African J Sci
South African Journal of Science — South Afr J Sci
South African Journal of Science. Supplement — S Afr J Sci Suppl
South African Journal of Sociology — S Afr J Sociology
South African Journal of Sports Medicine — S Afr J Sports Med
South African Journal of Surgery — S Afr J Surg
South African Journal of Surgery — SAJSB
South African Journal of Surgery — South Afr J Surg
South African Journal of Surgery/Suid-Afrikaanse Tydskrif vir Chirurgie — S Afr J Surg/S Afr Tydskr Chir
South African Journal of Wildlife Research — S Afr J Wild Res
South African Journal of Wildlife Research — S Afr J Wildl Res
South African Journal of Zoology — S Afr J Zool
South African Journal of Zoology — SAJZD
South African Journal of Zoology/Suid-Afrikaanse Tydskrif vir Dierkunde — S Afr J Zool S Afr Tydskr Dierkd
South African Labour Bulletin — S Afr Labour Bull
South African Labour Bulletin — South African Labour Bul
South African Lapidary Magazine — S Afr Lapid Mag
South African Law Journal — S Afr Law J
South African Law Journal — S Afr LJ
South African Law Journal — SA L J
South African Law Journal — So Afr LJ
South African Law Journal — So African LJ
South African Law Journal — South Afr Law J
South African Law Journal — South Afr LJ
South African Law Reports — S Afr LR
South African Law Reports — SA
South African Law Reports — SALR
South African Law Reports — So Afr LR
South African Law Reports — So African L
South African Libraries — S Afr Libr
South African Libraries — S Afr Librs
South African Libraries — S African Lib
South African Library Quarterly Bulletin — S African Lib Q Bull
South African Machine Tool Review — S Afr Mach Tool Rev
South African Machine Tool Review — SAMRD
South African Materials Handling News — S Afr Mater Handl News
South African Mechanical Engineer — S Afr Mech Eng
South African Mechanical Engineer — S Afr Mech Engr
South African Mechanical Engineer — SAMEA
South African Medical Equipment News — MSMND
South African Medical Equipment News — S Afr Med Equip News
South African Medical Journal — S Afr Med J
South African Medical Journal — S African Med J
South African Medical Journal — SAMJA
South African Medical Journal — South African Med J
South African Medical Journal — South African MJ
South African Medical Literature [*Database*] — SAMED
South African Medical Post — S Afr Med Post
South African Medical Record — So African Med Rec
South African Medical Record — South African Med Rec
South African Medical Times — S Afr Med Tim
South African Mining and Engineering Journal — S Afr Min Eng J
South African Mining and Engineering Journal — SMIJA
South African Mining and Engineering Journal — South African Min Eng Jour
South African Mining Journal — S Afr Min J
South African Mining Review — S Afr Min Rev
South African Mining World — S Afr Min World
South African Museum. Annals — S Afr Mus Ann
South African Museum Report — S Afr Mus Rep
South African Music Teacher — S Afr Music Teach
South African Numismatic Journal — S Afr Numis J
South African Nursing Journal — S Afr Nurs J
South African Nursing Journal — SA Nurs J
South African Nursing Journal — SANJA
South African Optometrist — S Afr Optom
South African Outlook — S Afr Outl
South African Outlook — S Afr Outlook
South African Outlook — So African Outl
South African Panorama — S Afr Panorama
South African Panorama — SAPNA
South African Patent Document — S African
South African Pharmaceutical Journal — S Afr Pharm J
South African Philosophical Society. Transactions — So African Philos Soc Trans
South African Pneumoconiosis Review — S Afr Pneumoconiosis Rev
South African Poultry Bulletin — S Afr Poult Bull
South African Practitioner — S Afr Pract
South African Quarterly — So African Q
South African Radiographer — S Afr Radiogr
South African Railway. Magazine — So African Ry M
South African Railways — S Afr Railw
South African Report of Science — S African Rep Sci
South African Reserve Bank. Quarterly Bulletin — S Afr Bank
South African Science — S Afr Sci
South African Shipping News and Fishing Industry Review — S Afr Shipp News Fish Ind Rev
South African Shipping News and Fishing Industry Review — SA Shipp News
South African Shipping News and Fishing Industry Review — SASNA
South African Spectroscopy Conference. Proceedings — S Afr Spectrosc Conf Proc
South African Statistical Journal — S Afr Stat
South African Statistical Journal — S Afr Stat J
South African Statistical Journal — SoAfrStJ
South African Statistical Journal — South African Statist J
South African Sugar Association Experiment Station. Annual Report — S Afr Sugar Assoc Exp Stn Annu Rep
South African Sugar Association Experiment Station. Bulletin — S Afr Sugar Assoc Exp Stn Bull
South African Sugar Journal — S Afr Sug J
South African Sugar Journal — S Afr Sugar J
South African Sugar Journal — S African Sugar J
South African Sugar Technologists' Association. Proceedings. Annual Congress — S Afr Sugar Tehnol Assoc Proc Annu Congr
South African Sugar Year Book — S Afr Sugar Year Book
South African Survey Journal — S Afr Surv J
South African Textiles — S Afr Text
South African Transport — S Afr Transp
South African Treasurer — S Afr Treas
South African Tunnelling — S Afr Tunnel
South African Tunnelling — S Afr Tunnelling
South African Tunnelling — SATUD
South African Wool and Textile Research Institute. Annual Report — S Afr Wool Text Res Inst Annu Rep
South African Wool and Textile Research Institute. Annual Report — SAWTRI Annu Rep
South African Wool and Textile Research Institute. Bulletin — S Afr Wool Text Res Inst Bull
South African Wool and Textile Research Institute. SAWTRI Special Publication — S Afr Wool Text Res Inst SAWTRI Spec Publ
South African Wool and Textile Research Institute. Technical Report — S Afr Wool Text Res Inst Tech Rep
South African Wool Textile Research Institute. Digest — S Afr Wool Text Res Inst Dig
South African Yearbook of International Law — S Afr Yearb Int Law
South African Yearbook of International Law — S Afr YIL
South American — S Am
South American Journal of Bio-Sciences — South Am J Bio-Sci
South American Journal of Medicine — South Am J Med
South and West — S & W
South and West — SW
South Asia Papers — South Asia Pap
South Asian Affairs — SAA
South Asian Digest of Regional Writing [*Heidelberg*] — South As Dig Reg Writ
South Asian Review — S Asia R
South Asian Review — SAR
South Asian Review — SARev
South Asian Review — South Asian R
South Asian Studies [*Jaipur*] — South As Stud
South Asian Studies — South Asian Stud
South Asian Survey [*New Delhi*] — South As Surv
South Atlantic Bulletin — S Atlan Bull
South Atlantic Bulletin — SAB
South Atlantic Bulletin — So Atlan Bul
South Atlantic Bulletin — SoAB
South Atlantic Bulletin — South Atl Bull
South Atlantic Quarterly — PSAQ
South Atlantic Quarterly — S Atl Q
South Atlantic Quarterly — S Atl Quart
South Atlantic Quarterly — S Atlan Q
South Atlantic Quarterly — S Atlantic Q
South Atlantic Quarterly — SAQ
South Atlantic Quarterly — So Atl Quar
South Atlantic Quarterly — So Atlan Q
South Atlantic Quarterly — Sota
South Atlantic Quarterly — South Atl Q
South Atlantic Quarterly — South Atlan Q
South Atlantic Quarterly — South Atlantic Quart
South Atlantic Review — S Atl Rev
South Atlantic Review — SARev
South Atlantic Urban Studies — S Atl Urb Stud
South Australia. Department of Agriculture and Fisheries. Agronomy Branch. Report — South Aust Dep Agric Fish Agron Bran Rep
South Australia. Department of Agriculture and Fisheries. Agronomy Branch. Report — South Aust Dep Agric Fish Agron Branch Rep

South Australia. Department of Agriculture. Technical Bulletin — SA Dep Agric Tech Bull
South Australia. Department of Mines. Geological Survey. Bulletin — Aust South Dep Mines Geol Sur Bull
South Australia. Department of Mines. Geological Survey. Report of Investigations — Aust South Dep Mines Geol Surv Rep Invest
South Australia. Department of Mines. Mineral Resources Review — South Aust Dep Mines Miner Resour Rev
South Australia. Department of Mines. Mining Review — Aust South Dep Mines Min Rev
South Australia. Director of Mines and Government Geologist. Annual Report — S Aust Dir Mines Gov Geol Annu Rep
South Australia. Geological Survey. 1:250,000 Geological Series — S Aust Geol Surv 1:250000 Geol Ser
South Australia. Geological Survey. 1:250,000 Geological Series — South Aust Geol Surv 1:250000 Geol Ser
South Australia. Geological Survey. Atlas Series — S Aust Geol Atlas Ser
South Australia. Geological Survey. Atlas Series — SA Geol Atlas Ser
South Australia. Geological Survey. Bulletin — S Aust Geol Surv Bull
South Australia. Geological Survey. Bulletin — SA Geol Surv Bull
South Australia. Geological Survey. Bulletin — South Aust Geol Surv Bull
South Australia. Geological Survey. Geological Atlas. 1 Mile Series — SA Geol Surv Geol Atlas 1 Mile Ser
South Australia. Geological Survey. Quarterly Geological Notes — Q Geol Notes Geol Surv South Aust
South Australia. Geological Survey. Quarterly Geological Notes — S Aust Geol Surv Q Geol Notes
South Australia. Geological Survey. Quarterly Geological Notes — South Aust Geol Surv Q Geol Notes
South Australia. Geological Survey. Report of Investigations — S Aust Geol Surv Rep Invest
South Australia. Geological Survey. Report of Investigations — S Australia Geol Surv Rep Invest
South Australia. Geological Survey. Report of Investigations — SA Geol Surv Rep Invest
South Australia. Geological Survey. Report of Investigations — South Aust Geol Surv Rep Invest
South Australia Mineral Resources Review — S Aust Miner Resour Rev
South Australia. National Gallery. Bulletin — S Aus Nat Gal Bul
South Australia. Parliament. Parliamentary Debates — SA Parl Parl Deb
South Australia. Parliamentary Debates — SA Parl Deb
South Australia. Public Library. Research Service. Bibliographies — SA Res Service Bibliog
South Australia. Report of the Museum Board — S Aust Rep Mus Board
South Australia. Report of the Museum Board — South Aust Rep Mus Board
South Australia. Woods and Forests Department. Bulletin — Bull Woods For Dep South Aust
South Australia. Woods and Forests Department. Bulletin — Bull Woods Forests Dep S Aust
South Australian Advertiser Reports (Newspaper) — SA Advertiser (Newspr)
South Australian Bank Officials' Journal — SA Bank Officials J
South Australian Bank Officials' Journal — SABOJ
South Australian Clinics — S Aust Clinics
South Australian Coal Abstract Bulletin — S Aust Coal Abstr Bull
South Australian Education — SA Ed
South Australian Golfer — S Aust Golfer
South Australian Homes and Gardens — SA Homes & Gardens
South Australian Industrial Gazette — SAIG
South Australian Industrial Reports — IR
South Australian Industrial Reports — SAIR
South Australian Industrial Reports — SAR
South Australian Institutes. Journal — SA Inst J
South Australian Journal of Education Research — SA J Educ Res
South Australian Journal of Education Research — SAJER
South Australian Law Reports — LRSA
South Australian Law Reports — S Aust LR
South Australian Law Reports — S Austl LR
South Australian Law Reports — SALR
South Australian Law Reports — So Aus LR
South Australian Law Reports — So Aust LR
South Australian Law Reports — So Austr L
South Australian Law Reports — Sou Aus LR
South Australian Law Reports — South Aus LR
South Australian Law Society. Bulletin — SA Law Soc Bull
South Australian Licensing Court. Reports — SALCR
South Australian Methodist — SA Methodist
South Australian Motor — SA Motor
South Australian Motor — South Aust Mot
South Australian Museum. Records — SA Museum Rec
South Australian Naturalist — S Aust Nat
South Australian Naturalist — SA Nat
South Australian Naturalist — SA Naturalist
South Australian Naturalist — South Aust Nat
South Australian Numismatic Journal — SANJ
South Australian Ornithologist — S Aust Orn
South Australian Ornithologist — S Aust Ornithol
South Australian Ornithologist — SA Ornithol
South Australian Ornithologist — SA Ornithologist
South Australian Ornithologist — South Aust Orn
South Australian Planning Reports — SAPR
South Australian Public Service Review — SA Pub Serv R
South Australian Railways Institute. Magazine — SA Railways
South Australian Railways Institute. Magazine — SA Railways Institute Mag
South Australian Register — SA Regr
South Australian Register Reports (Newspaper) — SA Regr (Newspr)
South Australian School Post — SA Sch Post
South Australian Secrets Summary — SASS
South Australian Social Science [*Information service or system*] — SASS
South Australian State Reports — SASR
South Australian State Reports — So Austr St
South Australian Storekeepers and Grocers Journal — SA Storekeepers J
South Australian Teachers' Journal — SA Teach J
South Australiana — S Aust
South Australiana — S Australiana
South Australiana — SA
South Australiana — SotA
South Business — South Bus
South Canterbury Journal — South Cant J
South Carolina Academy of Science. Bulletin — SC Acad Sci Bull
South Carolina Academy of Science. Bulletin — South Carolina Acad Sci Bull
South Carolina. Agricultural Experiment Station. Bulletin — SC Agric Exp Stn Bull
South Carolina Agricultural Experiment Station. Bulletin SB — SC Agric Exp Stn SB
South Carolina. Agricultural Experiment Station. Circular — SC Agric Exp Stn Circ
South Carolina. Agricultural Experiment Station. Publications — SC Ag Exp
South Carolina. Agricultural Experiment Station. Technical Bulletin — SC Agric Exp Stn Tech Bull
South Carolina Agricultural Research — SC Agr Res
South Carolina Business Journal — So Car BJ
South Carolina Dental Journal — SC Dent J
South Carolina. Department of Agriculture, Commerce, and Industries. Publications — SC Ag Dept
South Carolina. Division of Geology. Bulletin — SC Div Geol Bull
South Carolina. Division of Geology. Geologic Notes — SC Div Geol Geol Notes
South Carolina. Division of Geology. Geologic Notes — South Carolina Div Geology Geol Notes
South Carolina. Division of Geology. Mineral Industries Laboratory. Monthly Bulletin — SC Div Geology Mineral Industries Lab Monthly Bull
South Carolina. Division of Geology. Mineral Resources Series — SC Div Geol Miner Resour Ser
South Carolina. Division of Geology. Miscellaneous Report — SC Div Geol Misc Rep
South Carolina. Division of Geology. Miscellaneous Report — South Carolina Div Geology Misc Rept
South Carolina Equity Reports — SC Eq
South Carolina Historical and Genealogical Magazine — SC His M
South Carolina Historical and Genealogical Magazine — SCHGM
South Carolina Historical and Genealogical Magazine — SCHM
South Carolina Historical and Genealogical Magazine — So Car Hist Mag
South Carolina Historical Association. Proceedings — SC Hist Assn Proc
South Carolina Historical Association. Proceedings — So Car Hist Assoc Proc
South Carolina Historical Magazine — SC Hist Mag
South Carolina Historical Magazine — So C Hist Mag
South Carolina Law Quarterly — SC L Q
South Carolina Law Quarterly — So Car LQ
South Carolina Law Review — SC L Rev
South Carolina Law Review — SC LR
South Carolina Law Review — So Car L Rev
South Carolina Law Review — South Carolina L Rev
South Carolina Librarian — SC Libn
South Carolina. Marine Resources Center. Technical Report — SC Mar Resour Cent Tech Rep
South Carolina. Marine Resources Center. Technical Report — SC Resour Cent Tech Rep
South Carolina Medical Association. Transactions — So Car Med Assn Trans
South Carolina Musician — SC
South Carolina Nursing — SC Nurs
South Carolina Reports — SC
South Carolina Research Planning and Development Board. Bulletin — SC Research Plan Devel Board Bull
South Carolina Review — SCR
South Carolina Review — So Ca R
South Carolina Review — SoCR
South Carolina Review — South Car R
South Carolina Review — South R
South Carolina. State Development Board. Bulletin — SC State Dev Board Bull
South Carolina State Development Board. Division of Geology. Bulletin. Geologic Notes — SC State Devel Board Div Geology Bull Geol Notes
South Carolina. State Development Board. Division of Geology. Miscellaneous Report — SC State Dev Board Div Geol Misc Rep
South Carolina State Register — SC Reg
South Carolina University. Publications. Physical Sciences Bulletin — SC Univ Pubs Phys Sci Bull
South Carolina. Water Resources Commission. Report — SC Water Resour Comm Rep
South Carolina Wildlife — SC Wildl
South Carolina Wildlife — SCWIA
South Central Bulletin — SCB
South Central Bulletin — SoCB
South China Journal of Agricultural Science — South China J Agric Sci
South China Morning Post — SCMP
South China Morning Post (Business News) — SCMPBN
South Circular — S Circular
South Dakota 4-H Doings. South Dakota State University. Cooperative Extension Service — SD 4H Doings SD State Univ Coop Ext Serv
South Dakota Academy of Science. Proceedings — S Dak Acad Sci Proc
South Dakota Agricultural Experiment Station. Agronomy Department Pamphlet — South Dakota Agric Exp Sta Agron Dept Pam

South Dakota. Agricultural Experiment Station. Bulletin — SD Agric Exp Stn Bull
South Dakota. Agricultural Experiment Station. Circular — SD Agric Exp Stn Circ
South Dakota Agricultural Experiment Station. Plant Pathology Department Pamphlet — South Dakota Agric Exp Sta Pl Pathol Dept Pam
South Dakota. Agricultural Experiment Station. Publications — SD Ag Exp
South Dakota. Agricultural Experiment Station. Technical Bulletin — S Dak Agr Expt Sta Tech Bull
South Dakota. Agricultural Experiment Station. Technical Bulletin — SD Agric Exp Stn Tech Bull
South Dakota Bird Notes — SD Bird Notes
South Dakota Black Hills Engineer — SD Black Hills Eng
South Dakota Business Review — S Dak Bus R
South Dakota Business Review — SDB
South Dakota Codified Laws Annotated — SD Codified Laws Ann
South Dakota DHIA News. South Dakota State University. Cooperative Extension Service — SD DHIA News SD State Univ Coop Ext Serv
South Dakota Farm and Home Research — S Dak Farm Home Res
South Dakota Farm and Home Research — SD Farm Home Res
South Dakota Farm and Home Research. South Dakota Agricultural Experiment Station — SD Farm Home Res SD Agric Exp Stn
South Dakota. Geological and Natural History Survey. Miscellaneous Investigations — SD Geol Nat Hist Surv Misc Invest
South Dakota Geological Survey and South Dakota Water Resources Commission. Water Resources Report — South Dakota Geol Survey Water Resources Rept
South Dakota. Geological Survey. Bulletin — S Dak Geol Surv Bull
South Dakota. Geological Survey. Bulletin — SD Geol Surv Bull
South Dakota. Geological Survey. Circular — S Dak Geol Surv Circ
South Dakota. Geological Survey. Guidebook — South Dakota Geol Survey Guidebook
South Dakota. Geological Survey. Miscellaneous Investigations — SD Geol Surv Misc Invest
South Dakota. Geological Survey. Oil and Gas Investigations Map. Report of Investigation — S Dak Geol Survey Oil and Gas Inv Map Rept Inv
South Dakota. Geological Survey. Report of Investigations — SD Geol Surv Rep Invest
South Dakota. Geological Survey. Report of Investigations — South Dakota Geol Survey Rept Inv
South Dakota. Geological Survey. Special Report — SD Geol Surv Spec Rep
South Dakota. Geological Survey. Special Report — South Dakota Geol Survey Spec Rept
South Dakota Historical Collections — So Dak Hist Coll
South Dakota Historical Review — S Dak His R
South Dakota Historical Review — S Dak HR
South Dakota Historical Review — SDHR
South Dakota History — So Dak Hist
South Dakota Journal of Medicine — S Dak J Med
South Dakota Journal of Medicine — SD J Med
South Dakota Journal of Medicine — SDMEA
South Dakota Journal of Medicine and Pharmacy — S Dak J Med Pharm
South Dakota Journal of Medicine and Pharmacy — SD J Med Pharm
South Dakota Law Review — SD L Rev
South Dakota Law Review — SD LR
South Dakota Law Review — So Dak L Rev
South Dakota Law Review — South Dak L Rev
South Dakota Law Review — South Dakota L Rev
South Dakota Library Bulletin — S Dak Lib Bull
South Dakota Library Bulletin — S Dak Libr Bull
South Dakota Library Bulletin — So Dakota Lib Bul
South Dakota Musician — SD
South Dakota Nurse — SD Nurse
South Dakota Register — SD Reg
South Dakota Reports — SD
South Dakota Review — S Dak Rev
South Dakota Review — SDR
South Dakota Review — So Dak R
South Dakota. School of Mines. Bulletin — S Dak Sch Mines B
South Dakota. School of Mines. Bulletin — SD Sch Mines Bull
South Dakota State College. Agricultural Experiment Station. Circular — SD State Coll Agric Exp Stn Circ
South Dakota State College. Agricultural Experiment Station. Technical Bulletin — SD State Coll Agric Exp Stn Tech Bull
South Dakota. State Geological Survey. Miscellaneous Investigations — SD State Geol Surv Misc Invest
South Dakota. State Geological Survey. Report of Investigations — SD State Geol Surv Rep Invest
South Dakota. State Geological Survey. Special Report — SD State Geol Surv Spec Rep
South Dakota State Geologist. Biennial Report — S Dak State Geologist Bienn Rept
South Dakota State Historical Society. Collections — S Dak His S
South Dakota State University. Agricultural Experiment Station. Bulletin — SD State Univ Agric Exp Stn Bull
South Dakota State University. Cooperative Extension Service — S Dak State Univ Coop Ext Serv
South Dakota. Water Resources Commission. Report of Investigations — SD Water Resour Comm Rep Invest
South East Asia Digest — SE Asia Dig
South East Asia Iron and Steel Institute. Quarterly — South East Asia Iron Steel Inst Q
South East Asia Journal of Theology [*Singapore*] — Se As J Theo
South East Asia Journal of Theology — SEAJT
South East Asian and Pacific Congress of Clinical Biochemistry — South East Asian Pac Congr Clin Biochem
South East Asian Review [*India*] — S E As R
South East Asian Studies [*Kyoto*] — S E As Stud
South East Asian Studies — South East Asian Stud
South Eastern Latin Americanist. Southeastern Conference on Latin American Studies — SECOLAS/SELA
South Eastern Naturalist — S E Naturalist
South Florida Business Journal — So Fla BJ
South Indian Art and Archaeological Series — S Ind Art Archaeol Ser
South Italian Vase Painting — SIV
South Italian Vase Painting — SIVP
South Lincolnshire Archaeology — S Lincolnchire Archaeol
South Magazine — South M
South Pacific — S Pac
South Pacific — S Pacific
South Pacific — South Pac
South Pacific Association for Commonwealth Literature and Language Studies. Newsletter — SPAN
South Pacific Bulletin — S Pacific Bull
South Pacific Bulletin — South Pac Bull
South Pacific Bulletin — South Pacific B
South Pacific Bulletin — South Pacific Bul
South Pacific Commission. Annual Report — S Pac Comm Ann Rep
South Pacific Commission. Handbook — South Pac Comm Handb
South Pacific Commission. Occasional Paper — S Pac Comm Occ Pap
South Pacific Journal of Education — South Pacific J Ed
South Pacific Journal of Natural Science — South Pac J Nat Sci
South Pacific Journal of Natural Science — SPJSEY
South Pacific Journal of Teacher Education — South Pac J Teach Educ
South Pacific Mail — SPM
South Pacific Marine Geological Notes [*Suva*] — South Pac Mar Geol Notes
South Texas Geological Society. Bulletin — South Texas Geol Soc Bull
South Texas Law Journal — S T LJ
South Texas Law Journal — S Tex LJ
South Texas Law Journal — S Texas LJ
South Texas Law Journal — South Texas LJ
South Texas Law Journal — STLJD
South. The Third World Magazine — SOU
South Third World Magazine — SH
South West Africa Scientific Society. Journal — South West Afr Sci Soc J
South West Pacific — SW Pacific
South Western Reporter — SW
Southeast Asia. An International Quarterly — SEAIQ
Southeast Asia Building Materials and Equipment — Southeast Asia Bldg Materials & Equipment
Southeast Asia Chronicle — Se As Chron
Southeast Asia Chronicle — SE Asia
Southeast Asia Development Advisory Group Papers — SEADAG
Southeast Asia Iron and Steel Institute Quarterly [*Singapore*] — Se As Iron Steel Inst Q
Southeast Asia Journal of Theology — SE Asia J Th
Southeast Asia Journal of Theology — Southeast Asia J Theol
Southeast Asia Petroleum Exploration Society. Proceedings — Southeast Asia Pet Explor Soc Proc
Southeast Asia Quarterly — SeAQ
Southeast Asia Treaty Organization. Medical Research Monograph — SEATO Med Res Monogr
Southeast Asian Affairs [*Singapore*] — Se As Aff
Southeast Asian Archives — SeAA
Southeast Asian Conference on Soil Engineering. Proceedings — Southeast Asian Conf Soil Eng Proc
Southeast Asian Fisheries Development Center. Aquaculture Department. Quarterly Research Report — Southeast Asian Fish Dev Cent Aquacult Dep Q Res Rep
Southeast Asian Journal of Social Science [*Singapore*] — Se As J Soc Sci
Southeast Asian Journal of Social Science — Southeast Asian J Soc Sci
Southeast Asian Journal of Sociology [*Singapore*] — SEAJS
Southeast Asian Journal of Tropical Medicine and Public Health — Southeast Asian J Trop Med Public Health
Southeast Asian Perspectives — SeAP
Southeast Asian Review of English — SARE
Southeast Conference on Application of Solar Energy. Proceedings — Southeast Conf Appl Sol Energy Proc
Southeast / East Asian English Publications in Print [*Database*] — AEPP
Southeast Region Water Resources Symposium. Proceedings — Southeast Reg Water Resour Symp Proc
Southeast Regional Conference. Kraft Mill Process and Product Engineering — Southeast Reg Conf Kraft Mill Process Prod Eng
Southeastcon Region 3 (Three) Conference Proceedings [*United States*] — Southeastcon Reg 3 (Three) Conf Proc
Southeastern Drug Journal — Southeast Drug J
Southeastern Europe — SE Eur
Southeastern Geographer — Southeast Geogr
Southeastern Geological Society. Field Conference Guidebook — Southeast Geol Soc Field Conf Guideb
Southeastern Geology [*United States*] — SOGEA
Southeastern Geology — Southeast Geol
Southeastern Geology. Special Publication — Southeast Geol Spec Publ
Southeastern Geology. Special Publication — Southeastern Geology Spec Pub
Southeastern Librarian — SE Libn
Southeastern Library Network. Newsletter — SOLINEWS
Southeastern Seminar on Thermal Sciences — Southeast Semin Therm Sci
Southeastern Seminar on Thermal Sciences. Proceedings — Southeast Semin Therm Sci Proc
Southern Africa — So Africa
Southern Africa — Sth Afr

Southern Africa Textiles — South Afr Text
Southern Africa Textiles — Sthn Afr Text
Southern African Family Practice — Sthn Afr Fam Pract
Southern Arizona Guidebook — South Ariz Guideb
Southern Association of Agriculture Scientists Bulletin Biochemistry and Biotechnology — South Assoc Agric Sci Bull Biochem Biotechnol
Southern Association Quarterly — So Assn Q
Southern Baptist Periodical Index — SBPI
Southern Baptist Periodical Index — South Bap Per Ind
Southern Baptist Periodical Index — South Baptist Period Index
Southern Beekeeper — S Beekeeper
Southern Bench and Bar Review — So Bench Bar R
Southern Birds — South Birds
Southern Birds — Sthn Birds
Southern Bivouac — So Biv
Southern Bivouac — So Bivouac
Southern California Academy of Sciences. Bulletin — S Cal Ac Sc B
Southern California Academy of Sciences. Bulletin — Southern Calif Acad Sci Bull
Southern California Business — So Cal Bsn
Southern California Coastal Water Research Project. Annual Report — South Calif Coastal Water Res Proj Annu Rep
Southern California Coastal Water Research Project. Biennial Report — South Calif Coastal Water Res Proj Bienn Rep
Southern California Crops — S Calif Crops
Southern California Law Review — S CA LR
Southern California Law Review — S Cal L Rev
Southern California Law Review — S Cal Law R
Southern California Law Review — S Calif Law Rev
Southern California Law Review — SCL
Southern California Law Review — So Cal LR
Southern California Law Review — So Calif L Rev
Southern California Law Review — South Cal Law Rev
Southern California Law Review — South Calif L Rev
Southern California Quarterly — S California Quart
Southern California Quarterly — So Calif Q
Southern California Quarterly — So Calif Quar
Southern California Quarterly — SotC
Southern California Quarterly — South Calif Q
Southern Canner and Packer — South Canner Packer
Southern Carbonator and Bottler — South Carbonator Bottler
Southern Chemical Industry — South Chem Ind
Southern Chemist — South Chem
Southern Clinic — So Clinic
Southern Communication Journal — ISCJ
Southern Conference on Gerontology. Report — South Conf Gerontol Rep
Southern Cooperative Series Bulletin — South Coop Ser Bull
Southern Corn Improvement Conference. Report — South Corn Impr Conf Rep
Southern Dairy Products Journal — South Dairy Prod J
Southern Economic Journal — S Econ J
Southern Economic Journal [*United States*] — SECJA
Southern Economic Journal — SEH
Southern Economic Journal — SEJ
Southern Economic Journal — So Econ J
Southern Economic Journal — South Econ J
Southern Economic Journal — South Econ Jour
Southern Economic Journal — Southern Econ J
Southern Economist [*Bangalore*] — South Econ
Southern Education Report — So Educ Report
Southern Exposure — So Expose
Southern Exposure [*United States*] — South Exposure
Southern Feminist — South Fem
Southern Fisherman — South Fisherman
Southern Florist and Nurseryman — S Florist Nurseryman
Southern Florist and Nurseryman [*United States*] — SFNYA
Southern Florist and Nurseryman [*United States*] — South Florist Nurseryman
Southern Folklore — South Folk
Southern Folklore Quarterly — SFQ
Southern Folklore Quarterly — So Folklore Q
Southern Folklore Quarterly — South Folk Q
Southern Folklore Quarterly — South Folkl Q
Southern Folklore Quarterly — South Folkl Quart
Southern Folklore Quarterly — Southern Folklore Q
Southern Folklore Quarterly (Gainesville, Florida) — South Folk Quart Gainesville
Southern Food Processor — South Food Process
Southern General Practitioner of Medicine and Surgery — South Gen Pract Med Surg
Southern Historical Association. Publications — So Hist Assn Publ
Southern Historical Association. Publications — South Hist Assoc Publ
Southern Historical Society — So His S
Southern Historical Society. Papers — So Hist Pap
Southern Historical Society. Papers — So Hist Soc Pap
Southern Historical Society. Papers — South Hist Soc Papers
Southern History Association. Publications — SHAssocPub
Southern Home and Garden — S Home Gard
Southern Horticulture [*New Zealand*] — South Hort
Southern Horticulture — South Hortic
Southern Hospitals — South Hosp
Southern Humanities Review — PSHR
Southern Humanities Review — S Hum Rev
Southern Humanities Review — SHR
Southern Humanities Review — SoHR
Southern Humanities Review — South Hum Rev
Southern Humanities Review — Southern H R
Southern Humanities Review — Southern Hum R
Southern Illinois Labor Tribune — South Ill Lab Trib
Southern Illinois University. Law Journal — S Ill ULJ
Southern Illinois University. Law Journal — So Ill LJ
Southern Illinois University. Law Journal — So Ill ULJ
Southern Illinois University. Law Journal — South Ill ULJ
Southern Indian Horticulture — South Indian Hortic
Southern Indian Studies — S Ind Stud
Southern Indian Studies [*United States*] — South Ind St
Southern Jeweler — South Jewel
Southern Journal of Agricultural Economics — South J Agric Econ
Southern Journal of Agricultural Economics. Southern Agricultural Economics Association — South J Agric Econ South Agric Econ Assoc
Southern Journal of Applied Forestry — South J Appl For
Southern Journal of Philosophy — S J Phil
Southern Journal of Philosophy — SJ Philos
Southern Journal of Philosophy — SJP
Southern Journal of Philosophy — Southern J Phil
Southern Journal of the Medical and Physical Sciences — Southern J Med Phys Sc
Southern Law Review — So Law R
Southern Life. Home and Garden Magazine — S Life Home Gard Mag
Southern Literary Journal — PSLJ
Southern Literary Journal — S Lit J
Southern Literary Journal — SLJ
Southern Literary Journal — So Lit J
Southern Literary Journal — SoLJ
Southern Literary Journal — South Lit J
Southern Literary Journal — Southern Lit J
Southern Literary Messenger — SLM
Southern Literary Messenger — So Lit Mess
Southern Living — GSOL
Southern Living — S Liv
Southern Living — South Liv
Southern Lumberman [*United States*] — SL
Southern Lumberman [*United States*] — SLUMA
Southern Lumberman — South Lumberman
Southern Magazine — So M
Southern Marketing Association. Proceedings — SMA
Southern Medical Association. Journal — So Med Assn J
Southern Medical Bulletin [*United States*] — SOMBA
Southern Medical Bulletin — South Med Bull
Southern Medical Journal [*United States*] — SMJOA
Southern Medical Journal — So Med J
Southern Medical Journal — South Med J
Southern Medical Journal — South MJ
Southern Medical Journal (Nashville) — S Med J Nashville
Southern Medical Reports — So Med Rpts
Southern Medicine — South Med
Southern Medicine and Surgery — South Med Surg
Southern Methodist University. Institute for the Study of Earth and Man. Reports of Investigations — South Methodist Univ Inst Stud Earth Man Rep
Southern New Jersey Business Digest — Busines NJ
Southern Pacific Commission. Technical Paper — South Pac Comm Tech Pap
Southern Patriot — S Patriot
Southern Petrochemical Industries Corp. Industrial Engineering and Training Bulletin — South Petrochem Ind Corp Ind Eng Train Bull
Southern Pharmaceutical Journal — South Pharm J
Southern Plastics and Chemicals — South Plast Chem
Southern Poetry Review — Southern P R
Southern Poetry Review — SPR
Southern Power and Industry — South Power Ind
Southern Power Journal — South Power J
Southern Practitioner — South Pract
Southern Pulp and Paper — South Pulp Pap
Southern Pulp and Paper Journal — South Pulp Pap J
Southern Pulp and Paper Manufacturer — South Pulp Pap Manuf
Southern Pulp and Paper Manufacturer — Southern Pulp Paper Mfr
Southern Pulp and Paper Manufacturer [*United States*] — SPPMA
Southern Quarterly — S Quart
Southern Quarterly — SouQ
Southern Quarterly — South Q
Southern Quarterly — South Quart
Southern Quarterly — SQ
Southern Quarterly Review — So Q
Southern Quarterly Review — So Q R
Southern Quarterly Review — South Quar
Southern Queensland Conference — South Queensl Conf
Southern Rag — South Rag
Southern Regional Beef Cow-Calf Handbook. Agricultural Extension Service. North Carolina State University — South Reg Beef Cow Calf Handb Agric Ext Serv NC State Univ
Southern Research Institute. Bulletin [*United States*] — BSRIA
Southern Research Institute. Bulletin [*United States*] — South Res Inst Bull
Southern Review — PSRV
Southern Review [*US*] — So R
Southern Review [*US*] — SouR
Southern Review — South R
Southern Review — Southern R
Southern Review — Southern Rev
Southern Review [*US*] — SR
Southern Review — Sth Rev
Southern Review (Adelaide) — S Rev (Adel)
Southern Review (Adelaide, Australia) — SoRA
Southern Review: An Australian Journal of Literary Studies — So R A

Southern Review: An Australian Journal of Literary Studies — SoR
Southern Review (Baton Rouge) — S Rev (Baton)
Southern Review: New Series [*US*] — So R NS
Southern Review of Public Administration — S Rev Pub Adm
Southern Rhodesia. Geological Survey. Bulletin — S Rhodesia Geol Surv Bull
Southern Rhodesia. Geological Survey. Bulletin — South Rhod Geol Surv Bull
Southern Rhodesia. Geological Survey. Short Report — South Rhod Geol Surv Short Rep
Southern Ruralist — So Ruralist
Southern School News — So School News
Southern Seedsman — South Seedsman
Southern Speech Communication Journal — S Speech Commun J
Southern Speech Communication Journal — South Speech Comm J
Southern Speech Communication Journal — SSCJ
Southern Speech Journal — SotS
Southern Speech Journal — SSJ
Southern Speech Journal — SSpJ
Southern Stars — South Stars
Southern States Association of Commissioners of Agriculture and Other Agricultural Workers. Proceedings — South States Assoc Comm Agric Other Agric Work Proc
Southern Studies — So St
Southern Studies — South Stud
Southern Surgeon [*United States*] — South Surg
Southern Textile Bulletin — South Text Bull
Southern University Law Review — So U L Rev
Southern University Law Review — So U LR
Southern University Law Review — So Univ L Rev
Southern University Law Review — South UL Rev
Southern University Law Review — SUL Rev
Southern Weed Science Society. Proceedings — South Weed Sci Soc Proc
Southern Workman — So Work
Southern Workman — So Workm
Southern Workman — So Workman
Southern Writers Series — SoWS
Southwest Africa Annual — Southwest Afr Ann
Southwest Agricultural Science/Hsi Nan Nung Yeh K'o Hsueeh — Southw Agric Sci
Southwest and Texas Water Works Journal — Southwest Tex Water Works J
Southwest Art — SWA
Southwest Bulletin — SNMAD
Southwest Bulletin [*United States*] — Southwest Bull
Southwest Business and Economic Review [*United States*] — Southwest Bus and Econ R
Southwest Folklore — SWF
Southwest Journal — Southwest J
Southwest Journal of Anthropology (Albuquerque, NM; Santa Fe, NM) — Southwest Jour Anthrop Albuquerque
Southwest Journal of Business and Economics — SBE
Southwest Journal of Linguistics [*US*] — SJL
Southwest Journal of Pure and Applied Mathematics — Southwest J Pure Appl Math
Southwest Museum. Papers — Southwest Mus Paper
Southwest Philosophical Studies [*United States*] — SW Phil Stud
Southwest Political Science Quarterly — Southw Pol Sci Quar
Southwest Regional Conference for Astronomy and Astrophysics. Proceedings — Southwest Reg Conf Astron Astrophys Proc
Southwest Review — PSWV
Southwest Review — Southw Rev
Southwest Review — Southwest Rev
Southwest Review — SR
Southwest Review — SRev
Southwest Review — SRv
Southwest Review — SWR
Southwest Science Bulletin — Southw Sci Bull
Southwest Water Works Journal — Southwest Water Works J
Southwest Writers Series — SWS
Southwestern American Literature — SAL
Southwestern American Literature — SwAL
Southwestern Association of Petroleum Geologists. Bulletin — Southwestern As Petroleum G B
Southwestern Entomologist — Southwest Entomol
Southwestern Entomologist — SW Entomol
Southwestern Entomologist — SWest Entomologist
Southwestern Entomologist. Supplement — Southwest Entomol Suppl
Southwestern Entomologist. Supplement — SSOED3
Southwestern Evangel — SWE
Southwestern Historical Quarterly — PSHQ
Southwestern Historical Quarterly — SHQ
Southwestern Historical Quarterly — SouH
Southwestern Historical Quarterly — Southw His Q
Southwestern Historical Quarterly — Southw Hist Quar
Southwestern Historical Quarterly [*United States*] — Southw Hist Quart
Southwestern Historical Quarterly — Southwest Hist Q
Southwestern Historical Quarterly — Southwest Hist Quart
Southwestern Historical Quarterly — SW Hist Q
Southwestern Historical Quarterly — SWHQ
Southwestern IEEE [*Institute of Electrical and Electronics Engineers*] **Conference and Exhibition. Record** — Southwest IEEE Conf Exhib Rec
Southwestern Journal of Anthropology — SJA
Southwestern Journal of Anthropology — SJAnth
Southwestern Journal of Anthropology [*United States*] — Southw J Anthrop
Southwestern Journal of Anthropology — Southwest J Anthropol
Southwestern Journal of Anthropology — Southwestern J Anthr
Southwestern Journal of Anthropology — Sthwest J Anthrop
Southwestern Journal of Anthropology — SW J Anthrop
Southwestern Journal of Anthropology — SWJA
Southwestern Journal of Anthropology. University of New Mexico — Southw J Anthropol
Southwestern Journal of Philosophy — Southw Jnl Philos
Southwestern Journal of Philosophy — Southwest J Phil
Southwestern Journal of Philosophy — SW J Phil
Southwestern Journal of Theology — SJT
Southwestern Journal of Theology [*Fort Worth, TX*] — SouthWJTh
Southwestern Journal of Theology — Sw J T
Southwestern Journal of Theology — SW J Th
Southwestern Law Journal — SLJ
Southwestern Law Journal — So West LJ
Southwestern Law Journal [*United States*] — Southw LJ
Southwestern Law Journal — Southwestern LJ
Southwestern Law Journal — SW L J
Southwestern Law Journal — SW Law J
Southwestern Legal Foundation. Institution on Oil and Gas Law and Taxation [*United States*] — Sw Legal Found Inst on Oil and Gas L and Tax
Southwestern Lore — Southw Lore
Southwestern Louisiana Journal — Southwestern LA Jour
Southwestern Medicine [*United States*] — SOMDA
Southwestern Medicine [*United States*] — Southwest Med
Southwestern Miller — Southwest Miller
Southwestern Musician — SW Musician
Southwestern Musician - Texas Music Educator — SW
Southwestern Naturalist — Southwest Nat
Southwestern Naturalist — SWest Nat
Southwestern Naturalist [*United States*] — SWNAA
Southwestern Petroleum Short Course. Proceedings of the Annual Meeting [*United States*] — Southwest Pet Short Course Proc Annu Meet
Southwestern Political and Social Science Association. Proceedings — Southw Pol Social Sci Assn Proc
Southwestern Political and Social Science Quarterly — Southw Pol and Soc Sci Q
Southwestern Review of Management and Economics [*United States*] — Southwestern R Mgt and Econ
Southwestern Social Science Quarterly — Southw Soc Sci Quar
Southwestern Social Science Quarterly — Southwest Soc Sci Quart
Southwestern Social Science Quarterly — SSSQ
Southwestern Social Science Quarterly — SW Social Sci Q
Southwestern Social Science Review — SSSR
Southwestern Studies [*University of Texas, El Paso*] — SWS
Southwestern Studies (University of Texas, El Paso) — SW St (UTEP)
Southwestern University. Law Review — Southwest UL Rev
Southwestern University. Law Review — Southwestern UL Rev
Southwestern University. Law Review — Southwestern Univ L Rev
Southwestern University. Law Review — Sw U L Rev
Southwestern University. Law Review — Sw U LR
Southwestern Veterinarian [*United States*] — Southwest Vet
Southwestern Veterinarian [*United States*] — SOVEA
Southwestern Veterinarian — SW Vet
Souvenir Nieuws — SRN
Sovershenstvovanie Agrotekhnicheskikh Priemov po Ukhodu za Sadom i Fiziologicheskie Osnovy Povysheniya Ego Produktivnosti — Soversh Agrotekh Priemov Ukhodu Sadom Fiziol Osn Povysh Ego
Sovershenstvovanie Konstruktsii i Povyshenie Effektivnosti Traktorov i Avtomobilei. Materialy Zonal'noi Konferentsii — Soversh Konstr Povysh Eff Trakt Avtomob Mater Zon Konf
Sovershenstvovanie Metodov Razrabotki Rudnykh Mestorozhdenii — Soversh Metodov Razrab Rudn Mestorozhd
Sovershenstvovanie Porod Sel'skokhozyaistvennykh Zhivotnykh — Soversh Porod Skh Zhivotn
Sovershenstvovanie Protsessov Obrabotki Metallov Rezaniem — Soversh Protsessov Obrab Met Rezaniem
Sovershenstvovanie Tekhniki i Tekhnologii Proizvodstva Kozhi, Obuvi, i Dubil'nykh Ekstraktov — Soversh Tekh Tekhnol Proizvod Kozhi Obuvi Dubilnykh Ekstr
Sovershenstvovanie Tekhnologii i Avtomatizatsii Staleplavil'nykh Protsessov — Soversh Tekhnol Avtom Staleplavil'n Protsessov
Sovershenstvovanie Tekhnologii i Kontrolya Proizvodstva Stal'noi Emalirovannoi Posudy — Soversh Tekhnol Kontrolya Proizvod Stalnoi Emal Posudy
Sovershenstvovanie Tekhnologii Pererabotki Khimicheskikh Volokon — Soversh Tekhnol Pererab Khim Volokon
Soveshchanie po Belku Sbornik Dokladov Konferentsii po Vysokomolekulyarnym Soedineniyam — Sovshch Belku Sb Dokl Konf Vysokomol Soedin
Soveshchanie po Diagnostike Vysokotemperaturnoi Plazmy. Tezisy Dokladov — Soveshch Diagn Vysokotemp Plazmy Tezisy Dokl
Soveshchanie po Dinamicheskim Effektam Rasseyaniya Rentgenovskikh Luchei i Elektronov — Soveshch Din Eff Rasseyan Rentgenovskikh Luchei Elektronov
Soveshchanie po Geologii Boksitovykh Mestorozhdenii i Proyavlenii Srednei Azii. Doklady — Soveshch Geol Boksitovykh Mestorozhd Proyavlenii Sredn Azii
Soveshchanie po Khimii i Prakticeskomu Primeneniyu Kremniiorganicheskikh Soedinenii — Soveshch Khim Prakt Primen Kremniiorg Soedin
Soveshchanie po Kinetike i Mekhanizmu Khimicheskikh Reaktsii v Tverdom Tele — Soveshch Kinet Mekh Khim Reakts Tverd Tele
Soveshchanie po Polucheniyu Profilirovannykh Kristallov i Izdelii Sposobom Stepanova i Ikh Primeneniyu v Narodnom Khozyaistve — Soveshch Poluch Profilirovannykh Krist Izdelii Sposobom Step
Soveshchanie po Spektroskopii Aktivirovannykh Kristallov — Soveshch Spektrosk Akt Krist

Soveshchanie po Teorii Liteinykh Protsessov — Soveshch Teor Liteinykh Protsessov
Soveshchanie po Voprosam Izucheniya Endogennykh Mestorozhdenii Srednei Azii. Tezisy Dokladov — Soveshch Vopr Izuch Endog Mestorozhd Sredn Azii Tezisy Dokl
Soveshchanie po Vyazkosti Zhidkostei i Kolloidnykh Rastvorov. Doklady — Soveshch Vyazkosti Zhidk Kolloidn Rastvorov Dokl
Soveshchanie po Yadernoi Spektroskopii i Strukture Atomnogo Yadra. Tezisy Dokladov — Soveshch Yad Spektrosk Strukt At Yadra Tezisy Dokl
Soveshchanie po Yadernoi Spektroskopii i Teorii Yadra. Tezisy Dokladov — Soveshch Yad Spektrosk Teor Yadra Tezisy Dokl
Soveshchanie-Seminar po Sovremennym Problemam i Metodike Prepodavaniya Kristallokhimii — Soveshch Semin Sovrem Probl Metod Prepod Kristallokhim
Soveti Krasnyi Krest [*Former USSR*] — Sov Krasnyi Krest
Sovetish Heymland — SovH
Sovetska Jazykoveda — SovJa
Sovetska Veda. Chemie — Sov Veda Chem
Sovetska Veda. Jazykoveda — SVJ
Sovetskaia Arkheologiia — Sor Ark
Sovetskaia Arkheologiia — Sov A
Sovetskaia Arkheologiia — Sovetskaja Arch
Sovetskaia Arkheologiia — Szov Arch
Sovetskaia Bibliotekovedenie — Sov Bibliotekov
Sovetskaia Etnografiia — Sov Ethnogr
Sovetskaia Istoricheskaia Entsiklopediia — SIE
Sovetskaia Vostokovedenie — SV
Sovetskaja Archeologija — Sov Arch
Sovetskaja Estonija — SE
Sovetskaja Etnografija — SE
Sovetskaja Etnografija — SEtn
Sovetskaja Etnografija — Sov Etnogr
Sovetskaja Muzyka — So M
Sovetskaja Nauka — SN
Sovetskaja Tjurkologija — Sov Tjurkolog
Sovetskaja Tjurkologija — SovT
Sovetskaya Agronomiya — Sov Agron
Sovetskaya Antarkticheskaya Ekspeditsiya. Informatsionnyi Byulleten — Sov Antarkt Eksped Inf Byull
Sovetskaya Antarkticheskaya Ekspeditsiya. Informatsionnyi Byulleten — Sov Antarkt Eksped Inform Byull
Sovetskaya Arkheologiia — Sov Arh
Sovetskaya Arkheologiya — Sov Arkheol
Sovetskaya Bibliografia — SB
Sovetskaya Bibliografia — Sov Bibliog
Sovetskaya Botanika — Sov Bot
Sovetskaya Etnografija — Sov Etnogr
Sovetskaya Etnografija — SovEt
Sovetskaya Etnografija — SovEtn
Sovetskaya Farmatsiya — Sov Farm
Sovetskaya Geologiya — Sov Geol
Sovetskaya Geologiya — Sovet Geol
Sovetskaya Geologiya — Sovet Geologiya
Sovetskaya Geologiya — SVGLA
Sovetskaya Khirurgiya — Sov Khir
Sovetskaya Kino-Fotopromyshlennost — Sov Kino Fotoprom
Sovetskaya Kino-Fotopromyshlennost — Sov Kino Fotopromst
Sovetskaya Kniga — SovKniga
Sovetskaya Latviya — SOVLA
Sovetskaya Meditsina — SOMEA
Sovetskaya Meditsina — Sov Med
Sovetskaya Metallurgiya — Sov Metall
Sovetskaya Muzyka — Sov M
Sovetskaya Muzyka — Sovet Muz
Sovetskaya Muzyka — Sovetskaya M
Sovetskaya Nauka — Sov Nauka
Sovetskaya Nevropatologiya, Psikhiatriya, i Psikhogigiena — Sov Nevropatol Psikhiatr Psikhogig
Sovetskaya Pedagogika — SP
Sovetskaya Pediatriya — Sov Pediatr
Sovetskaya Psikhonevrologiya — Sov Psikhonevrol
Sovetskaya Stomatologiya — Sov Stomatol
Sovetskaya Torgovlya — Sov Torg
Sovetskaya Torgovlya — Sub Torg
Sovetskaya Veterinariya — Sov Vet
Sovetskaya Vrachebnaya Gazeta — Sov Vrach Gaz
Sovetskaya Zolotopromyshlennost — Sov Zolotopromst
Sovetskaya Zootekhniya — Sov Zootekh
Sovetskie Arhivi — Sov Arh
Sovetskie Arkhivy — Sov Arkh
Sovetskie Subtropiki (Moscow) — Sov Subtrop (Moscow)
Sovetskie Subtropiki/Soviet Subtropics (Sukhumi) — Sovetsk Subtrop Sukhumi
Sovetskie Subtropiki (Sukhumi, USSR) — Sov Subtrop (Sukhumi USSR)
Sovetskii Kauchuk — Sov Kauch
Sovetskii Khlopok — Sov Khlopok
Sovetskii Kollektsioner — SK
Sovetskii Sakhar — Sov Sakhar
Sovetskii Shakhtior [*Former USSR*] — Sov Shakhtior
Sovetskii Shakhtior — SVSHA
Sovetskii Vestnik Oftal'mologii — Sov Vestn Oftalmol
Sovetskii Vestnik Venerologii i Dermatologii — Sov Vestn Venerol Dermatol
Sovetskii Vrachebnyi Zhurnal — Sov Vrach Zh
Sovetsko-Amerikanskaya Konferentsiya po Kosmokhimii Luny i Planet. Trudy — Sov Am Konf Kosmokhim Luny Planet Tr
Sovetsko-Amerikanskii Seminar Sintez-Delenie. Trudy — Sov Am Semin Sint Delenie Tr
Sovetsko-Amerikanskii Simpozium po Khimicheskomu Zagryazneniyu Morskoi Sredy. Trudy — Sov Am Simp Khim Zagryaz Morsk Sredy Tr
Sovetsko-Amerikanskii Simpozium po Teorii Rasseyaniya Sveta v Kondensirovannykh Sredakh — Sov Am Simp Teor Rasseyan Sveta Kondens Sredakh
Sovetsko-Amerikanskii Simpozium po Vsestoronnemu Analizu Okruzhayushchei Sredy. Trudy — Sov Am Simp Vsestoronnemu Anal Okruzh Sredy Tr
Sovetsko-Amerikanskii Simpozium Razrushenie Kompozitnykh Materialov — Sov Am Simp Razrushenie Kompoz Mater
Sovetsko-Amerikanskii Simpozium Teoreticheskie Voprosy Vochnoi Toksikologii — Sov Am Simp Teor Vopr Vodn Toksikol
Sovetsko-Bolgarskii Simpozium po Issledovaniyu Fiziko-Khimicheskikh Svoistv Prirodnykh Tseolitov. Trudy — Sov Bolg Simp Issled Fiz Khim Svoistv Prir Tseolitov Tr
Sovetskoe Bibliotekovedenie — Sovetskoe Bibl
Sovetskoe Finno-Ugrovedenie/Soviet Fenno-Ugric Studies — SFUS
Sovetskoe Foto — Sov Foto
Sovetskoe Gosudarstvo i Pravo — Sov Gos i Pravo
Sovetskoe Gosudarstvo i Pravo — Sov Gos Pravo
Sovetskoe Kotloturbostroenie — Sov Kotloturbostr
Sovetskoe Mukomol'e i Khlebopechenie — Sov Mukomole Khlebopech
Sovetskoe Slavjanovedenie — SovSlav
Sovetskoe Sudostroenie — Sov Sudostr
Sovetskoe Vostokovedenie — SV
Sovetskoe Vostokovedenie. Sbornik — Sov Vost Sb
Sovetskoe Zdravoochranenie — S Zd
Sovetskoe Zdravookhranenie — Sov Zdravookhr
Sovetskoe Zdravookhranenie — SOZDA
Sovetskoe Zdravookhranenie Kirgizii — Sov Zdravookhr Kirg
Sovetskoe Zdravookhranenie Kirgizii — SZDKA
Sovetskoe Zdravookhranenie Turkmenii — Sov Zdravookhr Turkm
Sovetsko-Frantsuzskii Seminar po Matematicheskomu Modelirovaniyu Kataliticheskikh Protsessov i Reaktorov — Sov Fr Semin Mat Model Katal Protsessov Reakt
Sovetsko-Indiiskii Simpozium po Khimii Prirodnykh Soedinenii. Tezisy Dokladov — Sov Indiiskii Simp Khim Prir Soedin Tezisy Dokl
Sovetskoje Finno-Ugrovedenie — Sov Finno-Ugroved
Sovetskoje Finno-Ugrovedenie — SovFU
Sovetskoje Vostokovedenije — SovVo
Sovetsko-Shvedskaya Kompleksnaya Ekspeditsiya v Baltiiskom More — Sov Shvedskaya Kompleksn Eksped Balt More
Sovetsko-Yaponskii Seminar po Katalizu. Sbornik Dokladov — Sov Yaponskii Semin Katal Sb Dokl
Sovetsko-Yaponskii Simpozium po Izucheniyu Stroeniya Kory i Verkhnei Mantii Zony Perekhoda ot Aziatskogo Kontinenta k Tikhomu Okeanu — Sov Yaponskii Simp Izuch Str Kory Verkhn Mantii Zony
Sovetsko-Yaponskii Simpozium po Izucheniyu Stroeniya Zemnoi Kory i Verkhnei Mantii Zony Perekhoda ot Aziatskogo Kontinenta k Tikhomu Okeanu — Sov Yaponskii Simp Izuch Str Zemnoi Kory Verkhn Mantii Zony
Soviet Aeronautics [*English Translation of Izvestiya VUZ. Aviatsionnaya Teknika*] — Sov Aeronaut
Soviet Aeronautics — Soviet Aeronaut
Soviet Agricultural Biology. Part 1. Plant Biology — Sov Agric Biol Part 1 Plant Biol
Soviet Agricultural Biology. Part 2. Animal Biology — Sov Agric Biol Part 2 Anim Biol
Soviet Agricultural Science — Soviet Agric Sci
Soviet Agricultural Sciences — Sov Agric Sci
Soviet and Eastern European Foreign Trade — SFT
Soviet and Eastern European Foreign Trade — Sov E E For
Soviet and Eastern European Foreign Trade — Sov East Europ For Trade
Soviet and Eastern European Foreign Trade — Soviet and Eastern Eur For Trade
Soviet and Eastern European Foreign Trade. A Journal of Translations — ARX
Soviet Antarctic Expedition. Information Bulletin [*English Translation*] — SAEBA
Soviet Antarctic Expedition. Information Bulletin — Sov Antarct Exped Inf Bull
Soviet Antarctic Expedition. Information Bulletin — Sov Antarct Exped Inform Bull
Soviet Antarctic Expedition. Information Bulletin (English Translation) — Sov Antarct Exped Inf Bull (Engl Transl)
Soviet Anthropology and Archaeology — SAA
Soviet Anthropology and Archeology — Sov Anthr A
Soviet Anthropology and Archeology [*New York*] — Sov Anthro Arch
Soviet Applied Mechanics [*English Translation*] — SOAMB
Soviet Applied Mechanics — Sov Appl Mech
Soviet Applied Mechanics — Soviet Appl Mech
Soviet Applied Mechanics (English Translation) — Sov Appl Mech (Engl Transl)
Soviet Astronomy [*English Translation*] — SAAJA
Soviet Astronomy — Sov Astron
Soviet Astronomy — Soviet Astronom
Soviet Astronomy (English Translation) — Sov Astron (Engl Transl)
Soviet Astronomy. Letters — Sov Astron Lett
Soviet Astronomy. Letters (English Translation) — Sov Astron Lett (Engl Transl)
Soviet Atomic Energy [*English Translation*] — SATEA
Soviet Atomic Energy — Sov At Energy
Soviet Atomic Energy — Sov Atom Energy
Soviet Atomic Energy (English Translation) — Sov At Energy (Engl Transl)
Soviet Atomic Energy (USSR) — Sov At En R
Soviet Automatic Control [*English Translation*] — SAUCB
Soviet Automatic Control — Sov Autom Control
Soviet Automatic Control — Sov Automat Contr
Soviet Automatic Control — Soviet Automat Control

Soviet Automatic Control (English Translation) — Sov Autom Control (Engl Transl)
Soviet Biotechnology — SB
Soviet Biotechnology — Sov Biotechnol
Soviet Business and Trade — Sov Bus Trade
Soviet Chemical Industry — Sov Chem Ind
Soviet Chemical Industry — Soviet Chem Ind
Soviet Chemical Industry [*English Translation*] — SVCIA
Soviet Chemical Industry (English Translation) — Sov Chem Ind (Engl Transl)
Soviet Cybernetics Review — SCR
Soviet Cybernetics Review — Sov Cybern Rev
Soviet Education — Sov Educ
Soviet Education — Soviet Ed
Soviet Electrical Engineering [*English Translation*] — SOEEA
Soviet Electrical Engineering — Sov Elec Eng
Soviet Electrical Engineering [*English Translation of Elektrotekhnika*] — Sov Electr Eng
Soviet Electrical Engineering (English Translation) — Sov Electr Eng (Engl Transl)
Soviet Electrochemistry [*English Translation*] — SOECA
Soviet Electrochemistry — Sov Electrochem
Soviet Electrochemistry (English Translation) — Sov Electrochem (Engl Transl)
Soviet Engineering Journal — Sov Eng J
Soviet Engineering Research — Sov Eng Res
Soviet Engineering Research — Sov Engng Res
Soviet Export — Sov Export
Soviet Export. Soviet Foreign Trade Bimonthly — SVD
Soviet Film — Sov Film
Soviet Film — Soviet F
Soviet Flour Milling and Baking — Sov Flour Milling Baking
Soviet Fluid Mechanics [*English Translation*] — SOFMA
Soviet Fluid Mechanics (English Translation) — Sov Fluid Mech (Engl Transl)
Soviet Genetics [*English Translation*] — SOGEB
Soviet Genetics — Sov Genet
Soviet Genetics — Soviet Genet
Soviet Genetics (English Translation) — Sov Genet (Engl Transl)
Soviet Genetics (English Translation of Genetika) — Sov Genet (Engl Transl Genetika)
Soviet Geography — ISVG
Soviet Geography. Review and Translations — SGRT
Soviet Geography. Review and Translations — Sov Geogr
Soviet Geography. Review and Translations — Sov Geogr R
Soviet Geology and Geophysics — Sov Geol and Geophys
Soviet Geology and Geophysics — Sov Geol Geophys
Soviet Geology and Geophysics (English Translation) — Sov Geol Geophys (Engl Transl)
Soviet Gold Mining Industry — Sov Gold Min Ind
Soviet Health Protection in Turkomen — Sov Health Prot Turkomen
Soviet Hydrology. Selected Papers — SHSPB
Soviet Hydrology. Selected Papers — Sov Hydrol
Soviet Hydrology. Selected Papers — Sov Hydrol Sel Pap
Soviet India Rubber — Sov India Rubber
Soviet Instrumentation and Control Journal (English Translation) — Sov Instrum Control J (Engl Transl)
Soviet Jewish Affairs — SoJA
Soviet Jewish Affairs — Sov Jew Aff
Soviet Journal of Atomic Energy — SJAEA
Soviet Journal of Atomic Energy — Sov J At
Soviet Journal of Atomic Energy — Sov J At Energy
Soviet Journal of Automation and Information Sciences — Soviet J Automat Inform Sci
Soviet Journal of Bioorganic Chemistry [*English translation of Bioorganicheskaya Khimiya*] — SJBCD5
Soviet Journal of Bioorganic Chemistry — Sov J Bioorganic Chem
Soviet Journal of Bioorganic Chemistry (English Translation of Bioorganicheskaya Khimiya) — Sov J Bioorg Chem (Engl Transl)
Soviet Journal of Bioorganic Chemistry (English Translation of Bioorganicheskaya Khimiya) — Sov J Bioorg Chem (Engl Transl Bioorg Khim)
Soviet Journal of Communications, Technology, and Electronics — Soviet J Comm Tech Electron
Soviet Journal of Computer and Systems Sciences — Soviet J Comput Systems Sci
Soviet Journal of Contemporary Mathematical Analysis — Soviet J Contemporary Math Anal
Soviet Journal of Coordination Chemistry (English Translation) — Sov J Coord Chem (Engl Transl)
Soviet Journal of Coordination Chemistry (English Translation of Koordinatsionnaya Khimiya) — Sov J Coord Chem (Engl Transl Koord Khim)
Soviet Journal of Developmental Biology — SJDBA
Soviet Journal of Developmental Biology (English Translation) — Sov J Dev Biol (Engl Transl)
Soviet Journal of Developmental Biology (English Translation of Ontogenez) — Sov J Dev Biol (Engl Transl Ontogenez)
Soviet Journal of Ecology [*English Translation*] — SJECA
Soviet Journal of Ecology — Sov J Ecol
Soviet Journal of Ecology — Soviet J Ecol
Soviet Journal of Ecology (English Translation) — Sov J Ecol (Engl Transl)
Soviet Journal of Ecology (English Translation of Ekologiya) — Sov J Ecol (Engl Transl Ekologiya)
Soviet Journal of Glass Physics and Chemistry — Sov J Glass Phys and Chem
Soviet Journal of Glass Physics and Chemistry — Sov J Glass Phys Chem
Soviet Journal of Glass Physics and Chemistry (English Translation) — Sov J Glass Phys Chem (Engl Transl)
Soviet Journal of Instrumentation and Control — Sov Instrum & Control J
Soviet Journal of Instrumentation and Control — Sov J Instrum Control
Soviet Journal of Instrumentation and Control (English Translation) — Sov J Instrum Control (Engl Transl)
Soviet Journal of Low Temperature Physics — Sov J Low Temp Phys
Soviet Journal of Low Temperature Physics (English Translation) — Sov J Low Temp Phys (Engl Transl)
Soviet Journal of Marine Biology — Sov J Mar Biol
Soviet Journal of Marine Biology (English Translation) — Sov J Mar Biol (Engl Transl)
Soviet Journal of Marine Biology (English Translation of Biologiya Morya) — Sov J Mar Biol (Engl Transl Biol Morya)
Soviet Journal of Nondestructive Testing [*English Translation*] — SJNTA
Soviet Journal of Nondestructive Testing — Sov J Nondestr Test
Soviet Journal of Nondestructive Testing — Sov J Nondestruct Test
Soviet Journal of Nondestructive Testing (English Translation) — Sov J Nondestr Test (Engl Transl)
Soviet Journal of Non-Ferrous Metals [*English Translation*] — SJFMA
Soviet Journal of Non-Ferrous Metals — Sov J Non-Ferrous Met
Soviet Journal of Nuclear Physics [*English Translation*] — SJNCA
Soviet Journal of Nuclear Physics — Sov J Nucl Phys
Soviet Journal of Nuclear Physics (English Translation) — Sov J Nucl Phys (Engl Transl)
Soviet Journal of Nuclear Physics (USSR) — Sov J Nuc R
Soviet Journal of Numerical Analysis and Mathematical Modelling — Soviet J Numer Anal Math Modelling
Soviet Journal of Optical Technology [*English Translation*] — SJOTB
Soviet Journal of Optical Technology — Sov J Opt Technol
Soviet Journal of Optical Technology (English Translation) — Sov J Opt Technol (Engl Transl)
Soviet Journal of Particles and Nuclei — SJPNA
Soviet Journal of Particles and Nuclei — Sov J Part Nucl
Soviet Journal of Particles and Nuclei — Soviet J Particles and Nuclei
Soviet Journal of Particles and Nuclei (English Translation) — Sov J Part Nucl (Engl Transl)
Soviet Journal of Plasma Physics — Sov J Plasma Phys
Soviet Journal of Plasma Physics (English Translation) — Sov J Plasma Phys (Engl Transl)
Soviet Journal of Quantum Electronics — Sov J Quant Electron
Soviet Journal of Quantum Electronics — Sov J Quantum Electron
Soviet Journal of Quantum Electronics (English Translation) — Sov J Quantum Electron (Engl Transl)
Soviet Law and Government — Sov Law & Govt
Soviet Law and Government — Sov Law Gov
Soviet Law and Government — Sov Law Gvt
Soviet Law and Government — Soviet L & Govt
Soviet Law and Government — Soviet Law and Govt
Soviet Life — GSOV
Soviet Life — SL
Soviet Life — SOLI
Soviet Literature — SL
Soviet Literature — Sov Lit
Soviet Literature — Soviet Lit
Soviet Literature — SovL
Soviet Materials Science [*English Translation*] — SOMSA
Soviet Materials Science — Sov Mater Sci
Soviet Materials Science (English Translation of Fiziko-Khimicheskaya Mekhanika Materialov) — Sov Mater Sci (Engl Transl)
Soviet Materials Science Reviews — Soviet Mat Sci Rev
Soviet Mathematics — Sov Math
Soviet Mathematics. Doklady — Soviet Math Dokl
Soviet Mathematics (English Translation) — Sov Math (Engl Transl)
Soviet Mathematics (Izvestija Vyssih Ucebnyh Zavedenii. Matematika) — Soviet Math (Iz VUZ)
Soviet Meteorology and Hydrology [*English translation of Meteorologiya i Gidrologiya*] — Sov Meteorol and Hydrol
Soviet Meteorology and Hydrology [*English translation of Meteorologiya i Gidrologiya*] — Sov Meteorol Hydrol
Soviet Meteorology and Hydrology (English Translation) — Sov Meteorol Hydrol (Engl Transl)
Soviet Microelectronics — Sov Microelectron
Soviet Military Review — Sov Ml Rev
Soviet Mining Science [*English Translation*] — SMNSA
Soviet Mining Science — Sov Min Sci
Soviet Mining Science (English Translation) — Sov Min Sci (Engl Transl)
Soviet Neurology and Psychiatry — Sov Neurol Psychiatry
Soviet Neurology and Psychiatry (USSR) — Sov Neur R
Soviet Non-Ferrous Metals Research — Sov Non-Ferrous Met Res
Soviet Non-Ferrous Metals Research (English Translation) — Sov Non-Ferrous Met Res (Engl Transl)
Soviet Oceanography — Sov Oceanogr
Soviet Panorama — SPOA
Soviet Pedagogy — Sov Pedag
Soviet Periodical Abstracts. Asia, Aftica, Latin America — SPA
Soviet Pharmacy — Sov Pharm
Soviet Physicians' Journal — Sov Physicians J
Soviet Physics. Acoustics [*English Translation*] — SOPAA
Soviet Physics. Acoustics — Sov Phys Acoust
Soviet Physics. Acoustics — Soviet Phys Acoust
Soviet Physics. Acoustics — Soviet Physics Acoust
Soviet Physics. Acoustics (English Translation) — Sov Phys Acoust (Engl Transl)
Soviet Physics. Acoustics (USSR) — Sov Ph Ac R
Soviet Physics. Collection — Sov Phys Collect
Soviet Physics. Collection [*English Translation*] — Soviet Phys Collection
Soviet Physics. Collection (English Translation) — Sov Phys Coll (Engl Transl)

Soviet Physics. Collection (English Translation) — Sov Phys Collect (Engl Transl)
Soviet Physics. Crystallography — Sov Phys Cryst
Soviet Physics. Crystallography — Sov Phys Crystallogr
Soviet Physics. Crystallography — Soviet Phys Cryst
Soviet Physics. Crystallography [*English Translation*] — SPHCA
Soviet Physics. Crystallography (English Translation) — Sov Phys Crystallogr (Engl Transl)
Soviet Physics. Doklady — Sov Phys Dokl
Soviet Physics. Doklady — Soviet Physics Dokl
Soviet Physics. Doklady [*English Translation*] — SPHDA
Soviet Physics. Doklady (English Translation) — Sov Phys Dokl (Engl Transl)
Soviet Physics. JETP [*Journal of Experimental and Theoretical Physics of the Academy of Sciences of the USSR*] — Sov Phys JETP
Soviet Physics. JETP [*Journal of Experimental and Theoretical Physics of the Academy of Sciences of the USSR*] — Soviet Phys JETP
Soviet Physics. JETP [*Journal of Experimental and Theoretical Physics of the Academy of Sciences of the USSR*] [*English Translation*] — SPHJA
Soviet Physics Journal [*English Translation*] — SOPJA
Soviet Physics Journal — Sov Phys J
Soviet Physics Journal — Soviet Phys J
Soviet Physics Journal — Soviet Physics J
Soviet Physics Journal (English Translation) — Sov Phys J (Engl Transl)
Soviet Physics. Lebedev Institute Reports [*English Translation of Sbornik Kratkie Soobshcheniya po Fizike*] — Sov Phys Lebedev Inst Rep
Soviet Physics. Lebedev Institute Reports (English Translation) — Sov Phys Lebedev Inst Rep (Engl Transl)
Soviet Physics. Semiconductors — Sov Phys Semicond
Soviet Physics. Semiconductors [*English translation*] — SPSEA
Soviet Physics. Semiconductors (English Translation) — Sov Phys Semicond (Engl Transl)
Soviet Physics. Semiconductors (USSR) — Sov Ph Se R
Soviet Physics. Solid State [*English translation of Fizika Tverdogo Tela*] — Sov Phys Solid State
Soviet Physics. Solid State (English Translation) — Sov Phys Solid State (Engl Transl)
Soviet Physics. Solid State Physics — Sov Phys Sol St
Soviet Physics. Technical Physics — Sov Phys T P
Soviet Physics. Technical Physics — Sov Phys Tech Phys
Soviet Physics. Technical Physics [*English Translation*] — SPTPA
Soviet Physics. Technical Physics (English Translation) — Sov Phys Tech Phys (Engl Transl)
Soviet Physics. Technical Physics. Letters — Sov Phys Tech Phys Lett
Soviet Physics. Uspekhi [*English Translation*] — SOPUA
Soviet Physics. Uspekhi — Sov Phys Usp
Soviet Physics. Uspekhi — Sov Phys Uspekhi
Soviet Physics. Uspekhi — Soviet Phys Uspekhi
Soviet Physics. Uspekhi (English Translation) — Sov Phys Usp (Engl Transl)
Soviet Physics. Uspeki — Soviet Phys Usp
Soviet Plant Industry Record — Sov Plant Ind Rec
Soviet Plant Physiology [*English Translation*] — SOPPA
Soviet Plant Physiology — Sov Plant Physiol
Soviet Plant Physiology — Soviet Pl Physiol
Soviet Plant Physiology — Soviet Plant Physiol
Soviet Plant Physiology (English Translation) — Sov Plant Physiol (Engl Transl)
Soviet Plant Physiology (English Translation of Fiziologiya Rastenii) — Sov Plant Physiol (Engl Transl Fiziol Rast)
Soviet Plastics [*English Translation*] — SOPLA
Soviet Plastics — Sov Plast
Soviet Plastics (English Translation) — Sov Plast (Engl Transl)
Soviet Powder Metallurgy and Metal Ceramics — Sov Powder Met Metal Ceram
Soviet Powder Metallurgy and Metal Ceramics — Sov Powder Metall and Met Ceram
Soviet Powder Metallurgy and Metal Ceramics — Sov Powder Metall Met Ceram
Soviet Powder Metallurgy and Metal Ceramics [*English Translation*] — SPMCA
Soviet Powder Metallurgy and Metal Ceramics (English Translation) — Sov Powder Metall Met Ceram (Engl Transl)
Soviet Power Engineering — Sov Power Eng
Soviet Power Engineering (English Translation of Elektricheskie Stantsii) — Sov Power Eng (Engl Transl)
Soviet Progress in Chemistry — Sov Prog Chem
Soviet Progress in Chemistry [*English Translation*] — SPCHB
Soviet Progress in Chemistry (English Translation) — Sov Prog Chem (Engl Transl)
Soviet Psychology — Sov Psychol
Soviet Psychology (USSR) — Sov Psyco R
Soviet Psychoneurology — Sov Psychoneurol
Soviet Public Health — Sov Public Health
Soviet Public Health (English Translation) — Sov Public Health (Engl Transl)
Soviet Radio Engineering — Sov Radio Eng
Soviet Radiochemistry — Sov Radiochem
Soviet Radiochemistry [*English Translation*] — SVRDA
Soviet Radiochemistry (English Translation) — Sov Radiochem (Engl Transl)
Soviet Radiophysics — Sov Radiophys
Soviet Radiophysics (English Translation of Izvestiya Vysshikh Uchebnykh Zavedenii Radiofizika) — Sov Radiophys (Engl Transl)
Soviet Research in High Energy Fission — Sov Res High Energy Fission
Soviet Research in Nuclear and Solid State Physics — Sov Res Nucl Solid State Phys
Soviet Research in Nuclear Physics — Sov Res Nucl Phys
Soviet Research in Physics — Sov Res Phys
Soviet Review — GSOR
Soviet Review — Soviet Rev
Soviet Review — SovR
Soviet Rubber Technology — Sov Rubber Technol
Soviet Rubber Technology [*English Translation*] — SRUTA
Soviet Rubber Technology (English Translation) — Sov Rubber Technol (Engl Transl)
Soviet Science — Sov Sci
Soviet Science (English Translation) — Sov Sci (Engl Transl)
Soviet Science Review [*England*] — Sov Sci Rev
Soviet Science Review — SSRWA
Soviet Scientific Reviews. Section A. Physics Reviews — Sov Sci Rev Sect A
Soviet Scientific Reviews. Section B. Chemistry Reviews — Sov Sci Rev Sect B
Soviet Scientific Reviews. Section C. Mathematical Physics Reviews — Soviet Sci Rev Sect C Math Phys Rev
Soviet Scientific Reviews. Section D. Biology Reviews — Sov Sci Rev Sect D Biol Rev
Soviet Scientific Reviews. Section D. Biology Reviews — SRSRDL
Soviet Scientific Reviews. Section E. Astrophysics and Space Physics Reviews — Sov Sci Rev Sect E
Soviet Sociology — Sov Soc
Soviet Sociology — Sov Sociol
Soviet Sociology — Soviet Sociol
Soviet Soil Science — Sov Soil Sci
Soviet Soil Science — Soviet Soil Sci
Soviet Soil Science [*English translation of Pochvovedenie*] — SSSCA
Soviet Soil Science [*English translation of Pochvovedenie*] — SSSCAE
Soviet Soil Science (English Translation of Pochvovedenie) — Sov Soil Sci (Engl Transl)
Soviet Soil Science (English Translation of Pochvovedenie) — Sov Soil Sci (Engl Transl Pochvovedenie)
Soviet Soil Science. Supplement — Sov Soil Sci Suppl
Soviet Statutes and Decisions — Sov Stat & Dec
Soviet Studies — PSVS
Soviet Studies — Sov Stud
Soviet Studies — Soviet Stud
Soviet Studies — SovS
Soviet Studies. A Quarterly Journal on the USSR and Eastern Europe — STF
Soviet Studies in History — Sov St Hist
Soviet Studies in History — Sov Stud Hist
Soviet Studies in Literature — Sov St Lit
Soviet Studies in Literature — SS Lit
Soviet Studies in Philosophy — Sov St Phil
Soviet Studies in Philosophy — Soviet Stud Phil
Soviet Sugar — Sov Sugar
Soviet Survey — SovS
Soviet Technical Physics. Letters — Sov T P Lett
Soviet Technical Physics. Letters — Sov Tech Phys Lett
Soviet Technical Physics. Letters (English Translation) — Sov Tech Phys Lett (Engl Transl)
Soviet Union — Sov Union
Soviet Union Society for Cultural Relations with Foreign Countries. Weekly News Bulletin — VOKS
Soviet Union Today — SUTD
Soviet-American Symposium on the Comprehensive Analysis of the Environment — Sov Am Symp Compr Anal Environ
Soviet-American Symposium on the Theory of Light Scattering in Solids — Sov Am Symp Theory Light Scattering Solids
Soviet-Eastern Europe-China Business and Trade — Sov East Eur China Bus Trade
Soviet-Indian Seminar on Catalysis — Sov Indian Semin Catal
Soviet-Italian Symposium on Macromolecules in the Functioning Cell — Sov Ital Symp Macromol Funct Cell
Sovietskaia Archeologiia — SA
Sovietskaya Iustitsiya — Sov Iust
Soviet-Swedish Symposium on the Pollution of the Baltic — Sov Swed Symp Pollut Balt
Sovistva Atomnykh Yader — SAYKA
Sovistva Atomnykh Yader [*Former USSR*] — Sovistva At Yader
Sovjetckaja Pecat' — So P
Sovjetskaja Rossija — SR
Sovjetunionen — Sovj
Sovmestnaya Sovetsko-Mongol'skaya Nauchno-Issledovatel'skaya Geologicheskaya Ekspeditsiya — Sovmestnaya Sov-Mong Nauchno-Issled Geol Eksped
Sovmestnaya Sovetsko-Mongol'skaya Nauchno-Issledovatel'skaya Geologicheskaya Ekspeditsiya Trudy — Sovmestnaya Sov-Mong Nauchno-Issled Geol Eksped Tr
Sovremennaya Psikhonevrologiya — Sovrem Psikhonevrol
Sovremennye Biokhimicheskie i Morfologicheskie Problemy Soedinitel'noi Tkani. Materialy Vsesoyuznogo Soveshchaniya po Soedinitel'noi Tkani — Sovrem Biokhim Morfol Probl Soedin Tkani Mater Vses Soveshch
Sovremennye Dannye po Lechebnomu Primeneniyu Vitaminov. Raboty Dolozhennye na Vsesoyuznom Soveshchani po Vitaminam — Sovrem Dannye Lech Primen Vitam Rab Vses Soveshch
Sovremennye Metody Issledovaniya — Sovrem Metody Issled
Sovremennye Metody Issledovaniya v Khimii Lignina, po Materialam Vsesoyuznogo Seminara — Sovrem Metody Issled Khim Lignina Mater Vses Semin
Sovremennye Metody YaMR [*Yadernyi Magnitnyi Rezonans*] **EPR v Khimii Tverdogo Tela. Materialy Vsesoyuznogo Koordinatsionnogo Soveshchaniya** [*Elektronnyi Paramagnitnyi Rezonans*] — Sovrem Metody YaMR EPR Khim Tverd Tela Mater Vses Koord
Sovremennye Problemy Deyatel'nosti i Stroeniya Tsentral'noe Nervnoi Sistemy — Sovrem Probl Deyat Str Tsentr Nervn Sist
Sovremennye Problemy Fizicheskoi Khimii — Sovrem Probl Fiz Khim
Sovremennye Problemy Gastroenterologii — Sovrem Probl Gastroenterol

Sovremennye Problemy Gastroenterologii Respublikanskii Mezhvedomstvennyi-Sbornik — Sovrem Probl Gastroenterol Resp Mezhved Sb
Sovremennye Problemy Gematologii i Pereliivaniya Krovi — Sovrem Probl Gematol Pereliv Krovi
Sovremennye Problemy Onkologii — Sovrem Probl Onkol
Sovremennye Problemy Organicheskoi Khimii — Sovrem Probl Org Khim
Sovremennye Problemy Organicheskoi Khimii — Sovrem Probl Organ Khim
Sovremennye Problemy Otolaringologii Respublikanskoi Mezhvedomstvennyi Sbornik — Sovrem Probl Otolaringol Resp Mezhved Sb
Sovremennye Problemy Otorinolaringologii — Sovrem Probl Otorinolaringol
Sovremennye Problemy Radiobiologii [*Former USSR*] — Sovrem Probl Radiobiol
Sovremennye Problemy Teoreticheskoi i Prikladnoi Mekhaniki. Trudy Vsesoyuznogo Sezda po Teoreticheskoi i Prikladnoi Mekhanike — Sovrem Probl Teor Prikl Mekh Tr Vses Sezda Teor Prikl Mekh
Sovremennye Psikhotropnye Sredstva — Sovrem Psikhotropnye Sredstva
Sovremennye Voprosy Endokrinologii — Sovrem Vopr Endokrinol
Sovremennye Voprosy Sudebnoi Meditsiny i Ekspertnoi Praktiki — Sovrem Vopr Sud Med Ekspertnoi Prak
Sovremennye Zadachi v Tochnykh Naukakh — Sovrem Zadachi Tochn Naukakh
Sovremennye Zapiski — SoZ
Sovremennye Zapiski — SZ
Sowjet Geologie — Sow Geol
Sowjet Kautschuk — Sow Kautsch
Sowjet Metallurgie — Sow Metall
Sowjet Pharmazie — Sow Pharm
Sowjet Studien — SSt
Sowjetliteratur. Eine Monatsschrift — So L
Sowjetrussische Aerztliche Zeitschrift — Sowjetruss Aerztl Z
Sowjetstudien — Sowjetstud
Sowjetunion Heute — SOHED
Sowjetwissenschaft — Sowjetwiss
Sowjetwissenschaft Gesellschaft — Sowjetw Ges
Soy Protein in the Prevention of Atherosclerosis. Proceedings. International Symposium — Soy Protein Prev Atheroscler Proc Int Symp
Soybean Digest — Soybean Dig
Soybean Genetics Newsletter. US Department of Agriculture. Agricultural Research Service — Soybean Genet Newsl US Dep Agric Agric Res Serv
SozEp-Berichte — SozEp Ber
Sozial- und Praeventivmedizin — Soz- Praeventivmed
Sozial- und Praeventivmedizin — SZPMA
Sozial- und Wirtschaftspolitischer Monatsspiegel aus Zeitungen und Zeitschriften — Soz und Wirtpol MSpiegel
Sozialdemokratische Pressedienst — Sozialdemokr Pressedienst
Soziale Arbeit — Soz Arbeit
Soziale Revue — SozRev
Soziale Sicherheit — Soz Sicherheit
Soziale Welt — Soz Welt
Sozialer Fortschrift — Soz Fortsch
Sozialer Fortschrift — Soz Fortschritt
Sozialgerichtsbarkeit — SZLGD
Sozialgeschichtliche Forschungen — SGF
Sozialisation und Kommunikation — Soz Kommun
Sozialistische Arbeitswissenschaft — SAW
Sozialistische Arbeitswissenschaft — Sozialistische Arbeitswiss
Sozialistische Finanzwirtschaft — Sozialistische Finwirt
Sozialistische Forstwirtschaft — SFORD
Sozialistische Forstwirtschaft — Soz Forstwirtsch
Sozialistische Forstwirtschaft — Sozial Forstw
Sozialistische Landwirtschaft von Usbekistan — Soz Landwirtsch Usb
Sozialistische Politik — Sozial Polit
Sozialistischer Wiederaufbau und Wissenschaft — Soz Wiederaufbau Wiss
Sozialmedizinische und Paedagogische Jugendkunde — Sozialmed Paedagog Jugendkd
Sozialwissenschaftliche Experten und Gutachter [*Database*] — SPEX
Sozialwissenschaftliches Jahrbuch fuer Politik — Soz Wiss Jb Polit
Sozialwissenschaftliches Literaturinformationssystem [*Database*] — SOLIS
Soziologisches Jahrbuch — Soziol Jb
SP. Nevada Agricultural Experiment Station. College of Agriculture. University of Nevada-Reno — SP Nev Agric Exp Stn Coll Agric Univ Nev Reno
Space Adventures — SPV
Space/Aeronautics — Space/Aeronaut
Space/Aeronautics — SPAEA
Space Biology and Aerospace Medicine — Space Biol Aerosp Med
Space Biology and Medicine [*English Translation*] — SBMEA
Space Biology and Medicine (English Translation) — Space Biol Med (Engl Transl)
Space Business Daily — SBD
Space City News — Space Cit
Space Commerce Bulletin — Space Comm
Space Congress — Space Congr
Space Congress. Proceedings [*United States*] — Space Congr Proc
Space Congress. Proceedings — SPCPB
Space Digest — SD
Space Economics — Space Econ
Space Electrochemical Research and Technology. Proceedings. Conference — Space Electrochem Res Technol Proc Conf
Space Industrialization — Space Ind
Space Life Sciences — Space Life Sci
Space Life Sciences — SPLSA
Space Markets — Space Marke
Space Propulsion — SP
Space Research — Space Res
Space Research and Engineering — Space Res Eng
Space Research in Bulgaria — Space Res Bulg
Space Research in Bulgaria — SRBUD
Space Science Fiction Magazine — SPF
Space Science Fiction Magazine — SSM
Space Science Instrumentation — Space Sci Instrum
Space Science Reviews — Space Sci R
Space Science Reviews — Space Sci Rev
Space Science Reviews — SPSRA
Space Simulation. Proceedings of a Symposium — Space Simul Proc Symp
Space Solar Power Review — Space Sol Power Rev
Space Solar Power Review — SSPR
Space Station Automation — Space Stn Autom
Space Stations Present and Future. Proceedings. International Astronautical Congress — Space Stn Present Future Proc Int Astronaut Congr
Space Stories — SPS
Space Travel — SPT
Space World — GSPW
Space World — Space Wld
Spacecraft Materials in Space Environment. European Symposium. Proceedings — Spacecr Mater Space Environ Eur Symp Proc
Spaceflight — SPFLA
Spaceway Science Fiction — SPW
Spain. Centro Nacional de Alimentacion y Nutricion. Boletin — Spain Cent Nac Aliment Nutr Bol
Spain. Estacion Centro de Ecologia. Boletin — Spain Estac Cent Ecol Bol
Spain. Instituto Geologico y Minero. Boletin Geologico y Minero — Spain Inst Geol Min Bol Geol Min
Spain. Instituto Geologico y Minero. Memorias — Spain Inst Geol Min Mem
Spain. Junta de Energia Nuclear. Report — Spain Junta Energ Nucl Rep
Spain. Junta de Energia Nuclear. Report JEN — Spain Junta Energ Nucl Rep JEN
Spain. Patent Document — Spain Pat Doc
Spain. Registro de la Propiedad Industrial. Boletin Oficial de la Propiedad Industrial — Spain Regist Prop Ind Bol Of Prop Ind
SPAN [*Shell Public Health and Agricultural News*] **Progress in Agriculture** — SPAN Prog Agric
SPAN. Shell Public Health and Agricultural News — SPAN
SPAN: State Planning Authority News — SPAN
Spanische Forschungen der Goerresgesellschaft — SFGG
Spanische Forschungen. Gorresgesellschaft — SFG
Spanish Economic News Service — SNS
Spanish (Patent Document) — Span
Sparkasse — SPARD
Spark's Library of American Biography — Spark's Am Biog
SPARMO [*Solar Particles and Radiation Monitoring Organization*] **Bulletin** — SPARMO Bull
SPARMO [*Solid Particles and Radiation Monitoring Organization*] **Bulletin** — SPBUA
Spatial Vision — Spat Vis
Spatial Vision — Spat Vision
Spatial Vision — SPVIEU
Spawanie i Ciecie Metali — Spawanie Ciecie Met
SPC [*South Pacific Commission*] **Handbook** — SPC Handb
SPC [*South Pacific Commission*] **Quarterly Bulletin** — SPC Quart Bull
SPC [*South Pacific Commission*] **Quarterly Bulletin** — SPCQB
SPC Report. Saskatchewan Power Corp. — SPC Rep Sask Power Corp
SPC. Soap, Perfumery, and Cosmetics — SPC Soap Perfum Cosmet
SPC [*South Pacific Commission*] **Technical Paper** — SPC Tech Pap
SPE [*Society of Petroleum Engineers*] **Formation Evaluation** — SPE Form Eval
SPE [*Society of Plastics Engineers*] **Journal** — SPE J
SPE [*Society of Plastics Engineers*] **Journal** — SPEJA
SPE [*Society of Petroleum Engineers*] **Production Engineering** — SPE Prod Eng
SPE [*Society of Plastics Engineers*] **Regional Technical Conference. Technical Papers** — SPE Reg Tech Conf Tech Pap
SPE [*Society of Petroleum Engineers*] **Reservoir Engineering** — SPE Reservoir Eng
SPE. Society of Petroleum Engineers of AIME [*American Institute of Mining, Metallurgical, and Petroleum Engineers*] **Publications** — SPE Soc Pet Eng AIME Publ
SPE [*Society of Plastics Engineers*] **Technical Papers** — SPE Tech Pap
SPE [*Society of Plastics Engineers*] **Transactions** — SPE Trans
Special Aspects of Nuclear Energy and Isotope Applications. Proceedings. International Conference on the Peaceful Uses of Atomic Energy — Spec Aspects Nucl En Isot Appl Proc Int Conf Peace Use At En
Special Bulletin. Aichi-ken Agricultural Research Center — Spec Bull Aichiken Agric Res Cent
Special Bulletin. College of Agriculture. Utsunomiya University — Spec Bull Coll Agr Utsunomiya Univ
Special Bulletin. College of Agriculture. Utsunomiya University — Spec Bull Coll Agric Utsunomiya Univ
Special Bulletin. Department of Agriculture. South Australia — Spec Bull Dep Agric S Aust
Special Bulletin. Department of Agriculture. South Australia — Spec Bull Dep Agric South Aust
Special Bulletin. First Agronomy Division. Tokai-Kinki National Agricultural Experiment Station — Spec Bull First Agron Div Tokai-Kinki Natl Agric Exp Stn
Special Bulletin. Forest Products Laboratory — Special Bull Forest Prod Lab
Special Bulletin. Fukui Agricultural Experiment Station — Spec Bull Fukui Agric Exp Stn
Special Bulletin. Fukuoka Agricultural Research Center — Spec Bull Fukuoka Agric Res Cent
Special Bulletin. Horticultural Station. Tokai Kinki Agricultural Experiment Station — Spec Bull Hortic Stn Tokai Kinki Agric Exp Stn
Special Bulletin. Horticultural Station. Tokai Kinki Agricultural Experiment Station/Tokai Kinki Nogyo Shikenjo Engei-Bu Tokubetsu Hokoku — Special Bull Hort Sta Tokai Kinki Agric Exp Sta

Special Bulletin. Michigan Agricultural Experiment Station — Spec Bull Mich Agric Exp Stn
Special Bulletin. Michigan State University. Agricultural Experiment Station — Spec Bull Mich State Univ Agr Exp Sta
Special Bulletin. Okayama Agricultural Experiment Station — Spec Bull Okayama Agr Exp Sta
Special Bulletin. Okayama Prefectural Agricultural Experiment Station — Spec Bull Okayama Prefect Agric Exp Stn
Special Bulletin. Rehovot. National and University Institute of Agriculture — Spec Bull Rehovot Nat Univ Inst Agr
Special Bulletin. Taiwan Forestry Research Institute — Spec Bull Taiwan For Res Inst
Special Bulletin. Tokai-Kinki National Agricultural Experiment Station/Norin-Sho Tokai Kinki Nogyo Shikenjo Tokubetsu Hokoku — Special Bull Tokai Kinki Natl Agric Exp Sta
Special Bulletin. Tottori Agricultural Experiment Station — Spec Bull Tottori Agric Exp Stn
Special Bulletin. University of Georgia. Cooperative Extension Service — Spec Bull Univ Ga Coop Ext Serv
Special Bulletin. University of Minnesota. Agricultural Extension Division — Special Bull Univ Minnesota Agric Exten Div
Special Care in Dentistry — Spec Care Dentist
Special Ceramics — Spec Ceram
Special Chemicals in the Oil Industry. Proceedings. Lecture Series — Spec Chem Oil Ind Proc Lect Ser
Special Circular. Massachusetts Extension Service — Spec Circ Mass Ext Serv
Special Circular. Ohio Agricultural Experiment Station — Spec Circ Ohio Agr Exp Sta
Special Circular. Ohio Agricultural Research and Development Center — Spec Circ Ohio Agric Res Dev Cent
Special Circular. Pennsylvania State University. College of Agriculture. Extension Service — Spec Circ PA State Univ Coll-Agric Ext Serv
Special Circular. University of Wisconsin. College of Agriculture. Extension Service — Spec Circ Univ Wis Coll Agr Ext Serv
Special Collections — Spec Collect
Special Contributions. Geophysical Institute. Kyoto University [*Japan*] — Spec Contrib Geophys Inst Kyoto Univ
Special Contributions. Institute of Geophysics. National Central University (Miaoli, Taiwan) — Spec Contrib Inst Geophys Natl Cent Univ (Miaoli Taiwan)
Special Contributions. Institute of Geophysics. National Central University (Taiwan) — Spec Contrib Inst Geophys Nat Cent Univ (Taiwan)
Special Discussions. Faraday Society — Spec Discuss Faraday Soc
Special Economic Series. Maine Geological Survey — Spec Econ Ser Maine Geol Surv
Special Edition. Institute for Geological, Hydrogeological, Geophysical, and Geotechnical Research — Spec Ed Inst Geol Hydrogeol Geophys Geotech Res
Special Education — Spec Educ
Special Education — Special Ed
Special Education — SPEDA
Special Education Bulletin — Spec Educ Bull
Special Education Council. Newsletter — Spec Ed Counc News
Special Education. Forward Trends — Spec Educ
Special Education. Forward Trends — Spec Educ Forward Trends
Special Education in Canada — Spec Educ Can
Special Education in Canada — Special Ed
Special Education Newsletter — Sped Newsl
Special Environmental Report — Spec Environ Rep
Special Environmental Report. World Meteorological Organization — Spec Environ Rep WMO
Special Issue. Botanical Magazine — Spec Issue Bot Mag
Special Issue of Plant and Cell Physiology — Spec Issue Plant Cell Physiol
Special Issue. Sylviculture and Education. Taiwan Forest Experiment Station/ Lin Yeh T'ui Kuang Tsuan K'an — Special Issue Sylvic Educ
Special Issues of Artificial Intelligence — Spec Issues Artificial Intelligence
Special Lectures. Aquinas Institute of Philosophy and Theology — SLAIP
Special Lectures. Institute of Spirituality — SLIS
Special Lectures. Law Society of Upper Canada — Lectures LSUC
Special Liaison Report. Commonwealth Geological Liaison Office [*London*] — Spec Liaison Rep Commonw Geol Liaison Off
Special Libraries — SL
Special Libraries — SLI
Special Libraries — Sp Lib
Special Libraries — SPE
Special Libraries — Spec Libr
Special Libraries — Spec Librs
Special Libraries — Special Lib
Special Libraries Association. Advertising and Marketing Division. Bulletin — SLA Adv & Mkt Div Bul
Special Libraries Association. Alabama Chapter. Bulletin — SLA Alabama Chap Bul
Special Libraries Association. Biological Sciences Division. Reminder — SLA Biol Sci Div Reminder
Special Libraries Association. Business and Financial Division. Bulletin — SLA Bus & Fin Div Bul
Special Libraries Association. Financial Division. Bulletin — SLA Fin Div Bul
Special Libraries Association. Geography and Map Division. Bulletin — SLA Geog & Map Div Bul
Special Libraries Association. Geography and Map Division. Bulletin — SLA Geog and Map Div Bull
Special Libraries Association. Georgia Chapter. Bulletin — SLA GA Chap Bul
Special Libraries Association. Indiana Chapter. Slant — SLA Ind Chap Slant
Special Libraries Association. Metals Division. News — SLA Metals Div News
Special Libraries Association. Michigan Chapter. Bulletin — SLA Mich Chap Bul
Special Libraries Association. Montreal Chapter. Bulletin — SLA Montreal Chap Bul
Special Libraries Association. Museum Division. Bulletin — SLA Museum Div Bul
Special Libraries Association. Picture Division. Picturescope — SLA Picture Div Picturescope
Special Libraries Association. Pittsburgh Chapter. Bulletin — SLA Pittsburgh Chap Bul
Special Libraries Association. Science-Technology Division. News — SLA Sci-Tech News
Special Libraries Association. Texas Chapter. Bulletin — SLA Texas Chap Bul
Special Libraries Association. Toronto Chapter. Bulletin — SLA Toronto Chap Bul
Special Libraries Association. Toronto Chapter. Bulletin — Spec Libr Ass Toronto Chapter Bull
Special Libraries Association. Western New York Chapter. Bulletin — SLA Western NY Chap Bul
Special Libraries Council of Philadelphia and Vicinity. Bulletin — SL Council Phila & Vicinity Bul
Special Paper. Centre for Precambrian Research. University of Adelaide — Spec Pap Cent Precambrian Res Univ Adelaide
Special Paper. Department of Natural Resources. Quebec — Spec Pap Dep Nat Resour Que
Special Paper. Geological Association of Canada — Spec Pap Geol Ass Can
Special Paper. Geological Association of Canada — Spec Pap Geol Assoc Can
Special Paper. Geological Society of America — Spec Pap Geol Soc Am
Special Paper. State of Oregon Department of Geology and Mineral Industries — Spec Pap State Ore Dep Geol Min Ind
Special Paper. University of Adelaide. Centre for Precambrian Research — Spec Pap Univ Adelaide Cent Prec Res
Special Paper. University of Adelaide. Centre for Precambrian Research — Spec Pap Univ Adelaide Cent Precambrian Res
Special Papers. Department of Natural Resources (Queensland) — Spec Pap Dep Nat Resour (Qd)
Special Papers. Geological Society of America — Special Pap Geol Soc Amer
Special Papers in Palaeontology — Spec Pap Palaeontol
Special Papers. Ohio State Academy of Sciences — Special Pap Ohio State Acad Sci
Special Programmes News — Spec Prog News
Special Publication. Academy of Natural Sciences. Philadelphia — Spec Publ Acad Nat Sci Phila
Special Publication. Agricultural Research Organization — Spec Pub Agric Res Org
Special Publication. Agricultural Research Organization. Volcani Center (Bet Dagan) — Spec Publ Agric Res Organ Volcani Cent (Bet Dagan)
Special Publication. Agronomy Society of New Zealand — Spec Publ Agron Soc NZ
Special Publication. American Concrete Institute — Spec Publ Am Concr Inst
Special Publication. American Littoral Society — Spec Publ Am Littoral Soc
Special Publication. American Society of Agronomy — Spec Publ Am Soc Agron
Special Publication. American Society of Mammalogists — Spec Publ Am Soc Mammal
Special Publication ARLCD-SP. US Army Armament Research and Development Command. Large Caliber Weapon System Laboratory — Spec Publ ARLCD SP US Army Armament Res Dev Command Large
Special Publication. Association of Exploration Geochemists — Spec Publ Assoc Explor Geochem
Special Publication. Australian Conservation Foundation — Spec Publ Aust Conserv Fdn
Special Publication. Australian Conservation Foundation — Spec Publ Aust Conserv Found
Special Publication. BCRA. British Carbonization Research Associaton — Spec Publ BCRA Br Carbonization Res Assoc
Special Publication. Biochemical Society of London — Spec Publ Biochem Soc London
Special Publication. British Carbonization Research Association — Spec Publ Br Carbonization Res Assoc
Special Publication. British Ceramics Research Association — Spec Publ Br Ceram Res Assoc
Special Publication. British Ecological Society — Spec Publ Br Ecol Soc
Special Publication. Bureau of Mines and Geology (Montana) — Spec Publ Bur Mines Geol (Mont)
Special Publication. Chemical Society — Spec Publ Chem Soc
Special Publication. College of Agriculture. National Taiwan University — Spec Publ Coll Agric Natl Taiwan Univ
Special Publication. College of Earth and Mineral Sciences. Pennsylvania State University — Spec Publ Coll Earth Miner Sci Pa State Univ
Special Publication. Colorado Geological Survey — Spec Publ Colo Geol Surv
Special Publication. Colorado Geological Survey — Spec Publ Colorado Geol Surv
Special Publication. Commonwealth Bureau of Soils — Spec Publ Commonw Bur Soils
Special Publication. Council for Agricultural Science and Technology — Spec Publ Counc Agric Sci Technol
Special Publication. Cushman Foundation for Foraminiferal Research — Spec Publ Cushman Found Foraminiferal Res
Special Publication. Ecological Society of America — Spec Publ Ecol Soc Am
Special Publication. Entomological Society of America — Spec Publ Entomol Soc Am
Special Publication. Florida Bureau of Geology — Spec Publ Fla Bur Geol
Special Publication. Forintek Canada Corporation. Eastern Laboratory — Spec Publ Forintek Can Corp East Lab
Special Publication. Geochemical Society — Spec Publ Geochem Soc
Special Publication. Geological Society of Australia — Spec Publ Geol Soc Aust

Special Publication. Geological Society of London — Spec Publ Geol Soc London
Special Publication. Geological Society of South Africa — Spec Publ Geol Soc S Afr
Special Publication. Geological Society of Zimbabwe — Spec Publ Geol Soc Zimbabwe
Special Publication. Geological Survey of Indonesia — Spec Publ Geol Surv Indones
Special Publication. IEEE Power Engineering Society — Spec Publ IEEE Power Eng Soc
Special Publication. International Association of Sedimentologists — Spec Publ Int Assoc Sedimentol
Special Publication. International Fertilizer Development Center — Spec Publ Int Fert Dev Cent
Special Publication (Israel). Agricultural Research Organization — Spec Publ (Isr) Agric Res Org
Special Publication. Kentucky Geological Survey — Spec Publ KY Geol Surv
Special Publication. Limnological Society of America — Special Publ Limnol Soc Amer
Special Publication. Montana Bureau of Mines and Geology — Spec Publ Mont Bur Mines Geol
Special Publication. Montana Bureau of Mines and Geology — Spec Publ Montana Bur Mines Geol
Special Publication. National Agricultural Research Bureau/Shih Yeh Pu Chung Yang Nung Yeh Shih Yen So K'an Mu Lu — Special Publ Natl Agric Res Bur
Special Publication. New Mexico Geological Society — Spec Publ NM Geol Soc
Special Publication. North Carolina Department of Natural and Economic Resources. Geology and Mineral Resources Section — Spec Publ NC Dep Nat Econ Resour Geol Miner Resour Sect
Special Publication. North Carolina. Geology and Mineral Resources Section — Spec Publ NC Geol Miner Resour Sect
Special Publication. Pennsylvania State University. College of Earth and Mineral Sciences — Spec Publ Pa State Univ Coll Earth Min Sci
Special Publication. Royal Numismatic Society — Spec Publ R Numis Soc
Special Publication. Royal Society of Canada — Spec Publ Roy Soc Canada
Special Publication. Royal Society of Chemistry — Spec Publ R Soc Chem
Special Publication. Sado Marine Biological Station. Niigata University — Spec Publ Sado Mar Biol Stn Niigata Univ
Special Publication. Saskatchewan Geological Society — Spec Publ Sask Geol Soc
Special Publication Series. Geological Survey of India — Spec Publ Ser Geol Surv India
Special Publication Series. International Atlantic Salmon Foundation — Spec Publ Ser Int Atl Salmon Found
Special Publication Series. Minnesota Geological Survey — Spec Publ Ser Minn Geol Surv
Special Publication Series. Soil Science Society of America — Spec Publ Ser Soil Sci Soc Amer
Special Publication. Society for Geology Applied to Mineral Deposits — Spec Publ Soc Geol Appl Miner Deposits
Special Publication. Society of Economic Paleontologists and Mineralogists — Spec Publ Soc Econ Paleontol Mineral
Special Publication. South African Association for the Advancement of Science — Spec Publ S Afr Assoc Adv Sci
Special Publication. South Australia Department of Mines and Energy — Spec Publ South Aust Dep Mines Energy
Special Publication. South Australia Department of Mines and Energy — SPSEE3
Special Publication. United States National Bureau of Standards — Spec Publ Natl Bur Stand US
Special Publication. University of New Mexico. Institute of Meteoritics — Spec Publ Univ NM Inst Meteorit
Special Publication. UNM [*University of New Mexico*] **Institute of Meteoritics** — Spec Publ UNM Inst Meteorit
Special Publication. Volcani Center (Bet Dagan) — Spec Publ Volcani Cent (Bet Dagan)
Special Publication. Western Australian Museum — Spec Publ West Aust Mus
Special Publication. World Mariculture Society — Spec Publ World Maric Soc
Special Publications. American Association of Economic Entomology — Spec Publs Am Ass Econ Ent
Special Publications. British Columbia Provincial Museum of Natural History and Anthropology — Special Publ British Columbia Prov Mus Nat Hist
Special Publications. Chicago Academy of Science — Spec Publ Chicago Acad Sci
Special Publications. College of Agriculture. National Taiwan University — Spec Publ Coll Agr Nat Taiwan U
Special Publications. Geological Survey of South Africa — Spec Publ Geol Surv S Afr
Special Publications. Indo-Pacific Fisheries Council — Special Publ Indo Pacific Fish Council
Special Publications. Museum. Texas Tech University — Spec Publ Mus Tex Tech Univ
Special Publications Series. British Ecological Society — SPBSES
Special Publications Series. British Ecological Society — Spec Publ Ser Br Ecol Soc
Special Publications. Seto Marine Biological Laboratory. Series IV — Spec Publ Seto Mar Biol Lab Ser IV
Special Publications. Seto Marine Biological Laboratory. Series IV — SPSBDR
Special Publications. Society for General Microbiology — Spec Publ Soc Gen Microbiol
Special Publications. Society for General Microbiology — SPSMDQ
Special Publications. United States Bureau of Mines — Spec Publ US Bur Mines
Special Publications. United States National Bureau of Standards — Spec Publ US Natn Bur Stand
Special Reference Briefs. National Agricultural Library (US) — Spec Ref Briefs Natl Agric Libr US
Special Report. Agricultural Experiment Station. Cooperative Extension Service. University of Arkansas — Spec Rep Agric Exp Stn Coop Ext Serv Univ Arkansas
Special Report. Agricultural Experiment Station. Oregon State University — Spec Rep Agric Exp Stn Oreg State Univ
Special Report. Alaska Division of Geological and Geophysical Surveys — Spec Rep Alaska Div Geol Geophys Surv
Special Report. Alaska. Division of Mines and Geology — Spec Rep Alaska Div Mines Geol
Special Report. APL/JHU SR. Johns Hopkins University. Applied Physics Laboratory — Spec Rep APL/JHU SR Johns Hopkins Univ Appl Phys Lab
Special Report. Arctic Institute of North America — Spec Rep Arctic Inst N Am
Special Report. Arkansas Agricultural Experiment Station — Spec Rep Ark Agr Exp Sta
Special Report. Arkansas Agricultural Experiment Station — Spec Rep Ark Agric Exp Stn
Special Report. Arkansas Agricultural Experiment Station — Spec Rep Arkansas Agric Exp Stn
Special Report. British Institute of Radiology — Spec Rep Br Inst Radiol
Special Report. British Journal of Radiology — Spec Rep Br J Radiol
Special Report. California Division of Mines and Geology — Spec Rep Calif Div Mines Geol
Special Report. Colorado Department of Game, Fish, and Parks — Spec Rep Colo Dep Game Fish Parks
Special Report. Colorado Division of Game, Fish, and Parks — Spec Rep Colo Div Game Fish Parks
Special Report. Colorado Division of Wildlife — Spec Rep Colo Div Wildl
Special Report. Commonwealth Experimental Building Station — Spec Rep Commonw Exp Bldg Stn
Special Report. Electric Power Research Institute. EPRI AF — Spec Rep Electr Power Res Inst EPRI AF
Special Report. Electric Power Research Institute. EPRI EA — Spec Rep Electr Power Res Inst EPRI EA
Special Report. Electric Power Research Institute. EPRI EL — Spec Rep Electr Power Res Inst EPRI EL
Special Report. Electric Power Research Institute. EPRI EM — Spec Rep Electr Power Res Inst EPRI EM
Special Report. Electric Power Research Institute. EPRI ER (Palo Alto, California) — Spec Rep Electr Power Res Inst EPRI ER (Palo Alto, Calif)
Special Report. Electric Power Research Institute. EPRI FP (Palo Alto, California) — Spec Rep Electr Power Res Inst EPRI FP (Palo Alto, Calif)
Special Report. Electric Power Research Institute. EPRI NP — Spec Rep Electr Power Res Inst EPRI NP
Special Report. Electric Power Research Institute. EPRI SR — Spec Rep Electr Power Res Inst EPRI SR
Special Report. Electric Power Research Institute. EPRI SR (Palo Alto, California) — Spec Rep EPRI SR Electr Power Res Inst (Palo Alto Calif)
Special Report. Fulmer Research Institute — Spec Rep Fulmer Res Inst
Special Report. Geological Survey of Japan — Spec Rep Geol Surv Jpn
Special Report. Great Britain Forest Products Research — Spec Rep GB For Prod Res
Special Report. Great Lakes Research Division. University of Michigan — Spec Rep Great Lakes Res Div Univ Mich
Special Report. Imperial Agricultural Experiment Station/Noji Shikenjo Tokubetsu Hokoku — Special Rep Imp Agric Exp Sta
Special Report. Indiana Geological Survey — Spec Rep Indiana Geol Surv
Special Report. International Council of Scientific Unions. Committee on Data for Science and Technology — Spec Rep ICSU Comm Data Sci Technol
Special Report. Iowa State University. Cooperative Extension Service — Spec Rep Iowa State Univ Coop Ext Serv
Special Report. Iron and Steel Institute of Japan — Spec Rep Iron Steel Inst Jpn
Special Report. Johns Hopkins University. Applied Physics Laboratory — Spec Rep Johns Hopkins Univ Appl Phys Lab
Special Report. Missouri. Agricultural Experiment Station — Spec Rep Mo Agric Exp Stn
Special Report. National Institute of Animal Industry — CSTHBT
Special Report. National Institute of Animal Industry — Spec Rep Natl Inst Anim Ind
Special Report. National Research Council. Highway Research Board — Spec Rep Nat Res Counc Highw Res Board
Special Report. National Research Council. Transportation Research Board — Spec Rep Nat Res Counc Transp Res Board
Special Report. National Timber Research Institute. Council for Scientific and Industrial Research (South Africa) — Spec Rep Nat Timber Res Inst CSIR(SA)
Special Report. NCASI. National Council of the Paper Industry for Air and Stream Improvement — Spec Rep NCASI Nat Counc Pap Ind Air Stream Improv
Special Report. Nebraska Agricultural Experiment Station — Spec Rep Nebr Agr Exp Sta
Special Report. New Jersey Division of Water Resources — Spec Rep NJ Div Water Resour
Special Report. New York State Agricultural Experiment Station (Geneva) — Spec Rep NY State Agric Exp Stn (Geneva)
Special Report (Oregon). Agricultural Experiment Station — Spec Rep (Oregon) Agric Exp Stn
Special Report. Oregon Forest Products Laboratory — Spec Rep Oreg For Prod Lab
Special Report. Oregon State College Agricultural Experiment Station — Spec Rep Oreg State Coll Agr Exp Sta
Special Report. Packaging Institute — Spec Rep Packag Inst
Special Report. Robert Wood Johnson Foundation — Spec Rep Robert Wood Johnson Foundation

Special Report Series. Indian Council of Medical Research — Spec Rep Ser Indian Counc Med Res
Special Report Series. Medical Research Committee (London) — Special Rep Ser Med Research Com (London)
Special Report Series. Medical Research Council (United Kingdom) — Spec Rep Ser Med Res Counc (UK)
Special Report Series. National Open Hearth Steel Committee. Iron and Steel Division. Metals Branch. American Institute of Mining, Metallurgical, and Petroleum Engineers — Spec Rep Ser Nat Open Hearth Steel Comm Iron Steel Div Met
Special Report Series. Ohio Agricultural Experiment Station — Spe Rep Ser Ohio Agr Exp Sta
Special Report. Society of Plant Protection of North Japan — Spec Rep Soc Plant Prot North Jpn
Special Report. South African Council for Scientific and Industrial Research — Spec Rep S Afr CSIR
Special Report. South Dakota Geological Survey — Spec Rep SD Geol Surv
Special Report. University of Illinois at Urbana-Champaign. Water Resources Center — Spec Rep Univ Ill Urbana Champaign Water Resour Cent
Special Report. University of Minnesota. Agricultural Extension Service — Spec Rep Univ Minn Agr Ext Serv
Special Report. University of Missouri. College of Agriculture. Experiment Station — Spec Rep Univ MO Coll Agr Exp Sta
Special Report. University of Missouri, Columbia. Agricultural Experiment Station — Spec Rep Univ MO Columbia Agric Exp Stn
Special Report. University of Wisconsin, Milwaukee. Center for Great Lakes Studies — Spec Rep Univ Wis Milwaukee Cent Great Lakes Stud
Special Report. Wood Research Laboratory. Virginia Polytechnic Institute — Spec Rep Wood Res Lab VA Polyt Inst
Special Reports. Geological Society of London — Spec Rep Geol Soc Lond
Special Reports on the Mineral Resources of Great Britain — Spec Rep Miner Resour GB
Special Research Bulletin. North China Agricultural Science Research Institute/Hua Pei Nung Yeh K'o Hsueh Yen Chiu So. Yen Chu Tsuan K'an — Special Res Bull N China Agric Sci Res Inst
Special Schools Bulletin (Northern Territory) — Special Sch Bul (NT)
Special Schools Bulletin (Queensland Department of Education) — Special Sch Bul (Qld)
Special Scientific Report. Florida Department of Natural Resources. Marine Research Laboratory — Spec Sci Rep FL Dep Nat Resour Mar Res Lab
Special Scientific Report. Wildlife. United States Fish and Wildlife Service — Spec Sci Rep Wildlife US Fish Wildlife Serv
Special Scientific Report. Wildlife. US Fish and Wildlife Service — Spec Sci Rep Wildl US Fish Wildl Serv
Special Series. Florida Department of Agriculture — Spec Ser Fla Dep Agric
Special Series. International Association of Volcanology and Chemistry of the Earth's Interior — Spec Ser Int Assoc Volcanol Chem Earths Inter
Special Session on Cotton Dust. Proceedings — Spec Sess Cotton Dust Proc
Special Session on Cotton Dust Research. Proceedings — Spec Sess Cotton Dust Res Proc
Special Steel [*Japan*] — Spec Steel
Special Steel (Tokyo) — Spec Steel (Tokyo)
Special Steels Review — Spec Steels Rev
Special Steels Technical Review — SSTRD
Special Steels Technical Review (Sheffield) — Spec Steels Tech Rev (Sheffield)
Special Studies. Utah Geological and Mineral Survey — Spec Stud Utah Geol Miner Surv
Special Symposia. American Society of Limnology and Oceanography — Spec Symp Am Soc Limnol Oceanogr
Special Symposium on Natural Radiation Environment — Spec Symp Nat Radiat Environ
Special Technical Association. Publication — Spec Tech Assoc Publ
Special Technical Association Publication. TAPPI [*Technical Association of the Pulp and Paper Industry*] — Spec Tech Assoc Publ TAPPI
Special Technical Publications. American Society for Testing Materials — Spec Tech Publs Am Soc Test Mater
Special Topics in Endocrinology and Metabolism — SEMTD8
Special Topics in Endocrinology and Metabolism — Spec Top Endocrinol Metab
Special Topics in Supercomputing — Special Topics Supercomput
Special Volume. Canadian Institute of Mining and Metallurgy — Spec Vol Can Inst Min Metall
Special Volume. Ontario Geological Survey — Spec Vol Ont Geol Surv
Specialised National Councils' Magazine (Egypt) — Specialised Nat Councils' M (Egypt)
SpeciaList — SPLID
Specialist Courses for the Food Industry — Spec Courses Fd Ind
Specialist Courses for the Food Industry [*Food Industry News*] — Spec Courses Food Ind
Specialist Periodical Reports. Alicyclic Chemistry — Spec Period Rep Alicyclic Chem
Specialist Periodical Reports. Aliphatic and Related Natural Product Chemistry — ANPCD7
Specialist Periodical Reports. Aliphatic and Related Natural Product Chemistry — Spec Period Rep Aliphatic Relat Nat Prod Chem
Specialist Periodical Reports. Aliphatic Chemistry — Spec Period Rep Aliphatic Chem
Specialist Periodical Reports. Alkaloids — Spec Period Rep Alkaloids
Specialist Periodical Reports. Amino-Acids, Peptides, and Proteins — AAPPCM
Specialist Periodical Reports. Amino-Acids, Peptides, and Proteins — Spec Period Rep Amino-Acids Pept Proteins
Specialist Periodical Reports. Amino-Acids, Peptides, and Proteins — Spec Period Rep Amino-Acids Peptides Proteins
Specialist Periodical Reports. Aromatic and Heteroaromatic Chemistry — Spec Period Rep Arom Heteroaromat Chem
Specialist Periodical Reports. Biosynthesis — Spec Period Rep Biosynth
Specialist Periodical Reports. Carbohydrate Chemistry — Spec Period Rep Carbohydr Chem
Specialist Periodical Reports. Catalysis — Spec Period Rep Catal
Specialist Periodical Reports. Chemical Physics of Solids and Their Surfaces — Spec Period Rep Chem Phys Solids Their Surf
Specialist Periodical Reports. Chemical Thermodynamics — Spec Period Rep Chem Thermodyn
Specialist Periodical Reports. Colloid Science — Spec Period Rep Colloid Sci
Specialist Periodical Reports. Dielectric and Related Molecular Processes — Spec Period Rep Dielectr Relat Mol Processes
Specialist Periodical Reports. Electrochemistry — ECHMBU
Specialist Periodical Reports. Electrochemistry — Spec Period Rep Electrochem
Specialist Periodical Reports. Electron Spin Resonance — ESRNBP
Specialist Periodical Reports. Electron Spin Resonance — Spec Period Rep Electron Spin Reson
Specialist Periodical Reports. Electronic Structure and Magnetism of Inorganic Compounds — Spec Period Rep Electron Struct Magn Inorg Compd
Specialist Periodical Reports. Environmental Chemistry — ENCHDZ
Specialist Periodical Reports. Environmental Chemistry — Spec Period Rep Environ Chem
Specialist Periodical Reports. Fluorocarbon and Related Chemistry — Spec Period Rep Fluorocarbon Relat Chem
Specialist Periodical Reports. Foreign Compound Metabolism in Mammals — Spec Period Rep Foreign Compd Metab Mamm
Specialist Periodical Reports. Gas Kinetics and Energy Transfer — Spec Period Rep Gas Kinet Energy Transfer
Specialist Periodical Reports. General and Synthetic Methods — Spec Period Rep Gen Synth Methods
Specialist Periodical Reports. Heterocyclic Chemistry — HCHED7
Specialist Periodical Reports. Heterocyclic Chemistry — Spec Period Rep Heterocycl Chem
Specialist Periodical Reports. Inorganic Biochemistry — IBIODC
Specialist Periodical Reports. Inorganic Biochemistry — Spec Period Rep Inorg Biochem
Specialist Periodical Reports. Inorganic Chemistry of the Main-Group Elements — Spec Period Rep Inorg Chem Main Group Elem
Specialist Periodical Reports. Inorganic Chemistry of the Transition Elements — IOCEB7
Specialist Periodical Reports. Inorganic Chemistry of the Transition Elements — Spec Period Rep Inorg Chem Transition Elem
Specialist Periodical Reports. Inorganic Reaction Mechanisms — IORMA3
Specialist Periodical Reports. Inorganic Reaction Mechanisms — Spec Period Rep Inorg React Mech
Specialist Periodical Reports. Macromolecular Chemistry — MCCHDC
Specialist Periodical Reports. Macromolecular Chemistry — Spec Period Rep Macromol Chem
Specialist Periodical Reports. Mass Spectrometry — MSSYBF
Specialist Periodical Reports. Mass Spectrometry — Spec Period Rep Mass Spectrom
Specialist Periodical Reports. Molecular Structure by Diffraction Methods — Spec Period Rep Mol Struct Diffr Methods
Specialist Periodical Reports. Nuclear Magnetic Resonance — NMRNBE
Specialist Periodical Reports. Nuclear Magnetic Resonance — Spec Period Rep Nucl Magn Resonance
Specialist Periodical Reports. Organic Compounds of Sulphur, Selenium, and Tellurium — OCSSB9
Specialist Periodical Reports. Organic Compounds of Sulphur, Selenium, and Tellurium — Spec Period Rep Org Compd Sulphur Selenium Tellurium
Specialist Periodical Reports. Organometallic Chemistry — OGMCAQ
Specialist Periodical Reports. Organometallic Chemistry — Spec Period Rep Organomet Chem
Specialist Periodical Reports. Organophosphorus Chemistry — OPCMAZ
Specialist Periodical Reports. Organophosphorus Chemistry — Spec Period Rep Organophosphorus Chem
Specialist Periodical Reports. Photochemistry — PHCYAQ
Specialist Periodical Reports. Photochemistry — Spec Period Rep Photochem
Specialist Periodical Reports. Radiochemistry — Spec Period Rep Radiochem
Specialist Periodical Reports. Reaction Kinetics — Spec Period Rep React Kinet
Specialist Periodical Reports. Saturated Heterocyclic Chemistry — Spec Period Rep Saturated Heterocycl Chem
Specialist Periodical Reports. Spectroscopic Properties of Inorganic and Organometallic Compounds — Spec Period Rep Spectrosc Prop Inorg Organomet Compd
Specialist Periodical Reports. Spectroscopic Properties of Inorganic and Organometallic Compounds — SPSPCY
Specialist Periodical Reports. Statistical Mechanics — Spec Period Rep Stat Mech
Specialist Periodical Reports. Surface and Defect Properties of Solids — Spec Period Rep Surf Defect Prop Solids
Specialist Periodical Reports. Terpenoids and Steroids — Spec Period Rep Terpenoids Steroids
Specialist Periodical Reports. Theoretical Chemistry — Spec Period Rep Theor Chem
Specialist Periodical Reports. Theoretical Chemistry — THCHDM
Specialists Meeting. International Combustion Institute — Spec Meet Int Combust Inst
Specialists Reports. International Congress on Reprography and Information — Spec Rep Int Congr Reprogr Inf
Speciality Chemicals — Speciality Chem
Specialized Colloque Ampere. Application of Resonance Methods in Solid State Physics — Spec Colloq Ampere Appl Reson Methods Solid State Physics
Specialized Transportation Planning and Practice — Spec Transp Plann Practice
Specialties International — Spec Int
Specialty Chemicals — Spec Chem

Specialty Conference on Atmospheric Deposition. Proceedings — Spec Conf Atmos Deposition Proc
Specialty Conference on Continuous Monitoring of Stationary Air Pollution Sources. Proceedings — Spec Conf Contin Monit Stationary Air Pollut Sources Proc
Specialty Conference on Control of Specific Toxic Pollutants. Proceedings — Spec Conf Control Specific Toxic Pollut Proc
Specialty Conference on Control Technology for Agricultural Air Pollutants — Spec Conf Control Technol Agric Air Pollut
Specialty Conference on Dredging and Its Environmental Effects. Proceedings — Spec Conf Dredging Its Environ Eff Proc
Specialty Conference on Emission Factors and Inventories. Proceedings — Spec Conf Emiss Factors Inventories Proc
Specialty Conference on Emission Inventories and Air Quality Management — Spec Conf Emiss Inventories Air Qual Manage
Specialty Conference on Long Term Maintenance of Clean Air Standards. Proceedings — Spec Conf Long Term Maint Clean Air Stand Proc
Specialty Conference on Measurement and Monitoring of Non-Criteria, Toxic Contaminants in Air — Spec Conf Meas Monit Non Criter Toxic Contam Air
Specialty Conference on Ozone/Oxidants. Interactions with the Total Environment. Proceedings — Spec Conf Ozone Oxid Interact Total Environ Proc
Specialty Conference on Quality Assurance in Air Pollution Measurement. Proceedings — Spec Conf Qual Assur Air Pollut Meas Proc
Specialty Conference on Residential Wood and Coal Combustion. Proceedings — Spec Conf Resid Wood Coal Combust Proc
Specialty Conference on the Technical Basis for a Size Specific Particulate Standard. Proceedings — Spec Conf Tech Basis Size Specific Part Stand Proc
Specialty Conference on the User and Fabric Filtration Equipment. Proceedings — Spec Conf User Fabric Filtr Equip Proc
Specialty Conference on Toxic Substances in the Air Environment. Proceedings — Spec Conf Toxic Subst Air Environ Proc
Specialty Conference on View and Visibility. Regulatory and Scientific. Proceedings — Spec Conf View Visibility Regul Sci Proc
Specialty Conference on Waste Treatment and Disposal Aspects. Combustion and Air Pollution Control Processes — Spec Conf Waste Treat Disposal Aspects Combust Air Pollut
Specialty Law Digest. Health Care Monthly — Spec Law Dig Health Care Mon
(Specification) Standards Association of Australia — ASA
Specifying Engineer — Spec Eng
Specifying Engineer — Specif Eng
Specifying Engineer — Specif Engr
Specifying Engineer — SPEND
Specimina Philologiae Slavicae — SPS
Spectateur Militaire — Spectateur Milit
Spectateur Militaire — SpM
Spectator — GSPE
Spectator — S
Spectator — Sp
Spectator — Spec
Spectator — Spect
Spectator (London) — LS
Spectator (London) — SL
Spectra Biologie — Spectra Biol
Spectral Evolution of Galaxies. Proceedings. Workshop. Advanced School of Astronomy of the "Ettore Majorana" Centre for Scientific Culture — Spectral Evol Galaxies Proc Workshop Adv Sch Astron Ettore
Spectral Line Shapes. Proceedings. International Conference — Spectral Line Shapes Proc Int Conf
Spectra-Physics Laser Technical Bulletin — Spectra Phys Laser Tech Bull
Spectrochimica Acta — SPACA
Spectrochimica Acta — Spectrochim Acta
Spectrochimica Acta. Part A. Molecular Spectroscopy — Spect Act A
Spectrochimica Acta. Part A. Molecular Spectroscopy — Spectrochim Acta A
Spectrochimica Acta. Part A. Molecular Spectroscopy — Spectrochim Acta Part A
Spectrochimica Acta. Part A. Molecular Spectroscopy — Spectrochim Acta Part A Mol Spectrosc
Spectrochimica Acta. Part B. Atomic Spectroscopy — Spect Act B
Spectrochimica Acta. Part B. Atomic Spectroscopy — Spectrochim Acta B
Spectrochimica Acta. Part B. Atomic Spectroscopy — Spectrochim Acta Part B
Spectrochimica Acta. Part B. Atomic Spectroscopy — Spectrochim Acta Part B At Spectrosc
Spectrochimica Acta. Supplement — Spectrochim Acta Suppl
Spectrometric Techniques — Spectrom Tech
Spectroscopia Molecular — Spectrosc Mol
Spectroscopic Characterization Techniques for Semiconductor Technology — Spectrosc Charact Tech Semicond Technol
Spectroscopic Properties of Inorganic and Organometallic Compounds — Spectros Prop Inorg Organomet Compd
Spectroscopy — Spectr
Spectroscopy and Spectral Analysis (Beijing) — Spectrosc Spectral Anal (Beijing)
Spectroscopy Europe — Spectrosc Eur
Spectroscopy in Science and Industry — Spectrosc Sci Ind
Spectroscopy. International Journal — Spectrosc Int J
Spectroscopy Letters — Spect Lett
Spectroscopy Letters — Spectrosc Lett
Spectroscopy Letters — SPLEB
Spectroscopy of Biological Molecules — Spectrosc Biol Mol
Spectroscopy World — Spectrosc World
Spectrum — Spec
Spectrum [*Oxford*] — SPECA
Spectrum [*Berlin*] — SPECD
Spectrum International — Spectrum Int
Speculation — Spec
Speculations in Science and Technology [*Switzerland*] — Specul Sci Technol
Speculations in Science and Technology — Speculations Sci and Technol
Speculations in Science and Technology (Complete Edition) — Speculations Sci Technol
Speculum — S
Speculum — SJMS
Speculum — Sp
Speculum — Spec
Speculum — Specu
Speculum. Journal of Medieval Studies — PSCU
Speculum. Journal of Medieval Studies — Spe
Speech Activities — SA
Speech Communication — Speech Commun
Speech Communication Abstracts — Speech Commun Abstr
Speech Foundation of America. Publication — Speech Found Am Publ
Speech Monographs — SM
Speech Monographs — Sp Mon
Speech Monographs — Speech Mon
Speech Monographs — Speech Monogr
Speech Monographs — SPMGA
Speech Pathology and Therapy — Speech Pathol Ther
Speech Teacher — Speech Teac
Speech Teacher — SpT
Speech Teacher — ST
Speech Technology — Speech Technol
Speech Transmission Laboratory. Royal Institute of Technology. Stockholm. Quarterly Progress and Status Reports — STL-QPSR
Speelgoed en Hobby. Vakblad voor de Speelgoedbranche — SMH
Speighel Historiael van de Bond van Gentse Germanisten — SH
SPEJ. Society of Petroleum Engineers [*of AIME*] **Journal** [*United States*] — SPEJ Soc Pet Eng J
Spektral'nye Elektrofotometricheskie i Radiolokatsionnye Issledovaniya Polyarnykh Siyanii i Svecheniya Nochnogo Neba — Spektr Elektrofotom Radiolokatsionnye Issled Polyarn Siyanii
Spektral'nyi Analiz v Geologii i Geokhimii. Materialy Sibirskogo Soveshchaniya po Spektroskopii — Spektr Anal Geol Geokhim Mater Sib Soveshch Spektrosk
Spektrokhimiya Vnutri- i Mezhmolekulyarnykh Vzaimodeistvii — Spektrokhim Vnutri Mezhmol Vzaimodeistvii
Spektrometertagung. Vortraege — Spektrometertag Vortr
Spektroskopi Dergisi — Spektrosk Derg
Spektroskopiya Gazorazryadnoi Plazmy — Spektrosk Gazorazryadnoi Plazmy
Spektroskopiya Kristallov. Doklady Soveshchaniya po Spektroskopii Aktivirovannykh Kristallov — Spektrosk Krist Dokl Soveshch Spektrosk Akt Krist
Spektroskopiya Kristallov. Materialy Simpoziuma po Spektroskopii Kristallov — Spektrosk Krist Mater Simp
Spektroskopiya Kristallov. Materialy Simpoziuma po Spektroskopii Kristallov Aktivirovannykh Ionami Redkozemel'nykh i Perekhodnykh Metallov — Spektrosk Krist Mater Simp Spektrosk Krist Akt Ionami
Spektroskopiya. Metody i Prilozheniya. Trudy Sibirskogo Soveshchaniya po Spektroskopii — Spektroskop Tr Sib Soveshch
Spektroskopiya Molekul i Kristallov. Materialy Respublikanskoi Shkoly-Seminara — Spektrosk Mol Krist Mater Resp Shk Semin
Spektroskopiya Svetorasseivayushchikh Sred. Doklady na Vsesoyuznom Soveshchanii — Spektrosk Svetorasseivayushchikh Sred Dokl Vses Soveshch
Spektrum der Wissenschaft [*German Federal Republic*] — Spektrum Wiss
Spekulation und Erfahrung. Abteilung II. Untersuchungen — Spekulation Erfahrung Abt II Unters
SPELD [*Societe de Promotion a l'Etranger du Livre de Droit*] **Information** — SPELD Info
Speleologia Biuletyn Speleoklubu Warszawskiego — Speleol Biul Speleoklubu Warsz
Speleological Abstracts — Speleol Abstr
Spenser Studies — Spenser St
Spenser Studies — SSt
Sperimentale — SPERA
Sperimentale. Archivio di Biologia Normale e Patologica — Sper Arch Biol Norm Patol
Sperimentale. Archivio di Biologia Normale e Patologica — Sperimentale Arch Biol Norm e Patol
Sperimentale. Sezione di Chimica Biologica — Sperimentale Sez Chim Biol
Sperry Technology — Sperry Technol
Spetsial'nye Stali i Splavy [*Former USSR*] — Spets Stali Splavy
Spettatore Internazionale — Spettatore Int
Spettatore Italiano — SI
Spettatore Italiano — SPe
Spettatore Musicale — Spettatore M
Spezielle Aspekte der Abwassertechnik. Siedlungswasserwirtschaftliches Kolloquium — Spez Aspekte Abwassertech Siedlungswasserwirtsch Kolloq
Spezielle Berichte der Keraforschungsanlage Juelich — Spez Ber Keraforschungsanlage Juelich
Sphere — Sp
Spheroid Culture in Cancer Research — Spheroid Cult Cancer Res
SPI [*Society of the Plastics Industry*] **Annual Structural Foam Conference. Proceedings** — SPI Annu Struct Foam Conf Proc
SPI [*Society of the Plastics Industry*] **Annual Technical Conference** — SPI Annu Tech Conf
SPI [*Society of the Plastics Industry*] **Annual Urethane Division Technical Conference. Proceedings** — SPI Annu Urethane Div Tech Conf Proc
SPI [*Society of the Plastics Industry*] **International Cellular Plastics Conference. Proceedings** — SPI Int Cell Plast Conf Proc
SPI [*Society of the Plastics Industry*] **International Technical/Marketing Conference** — SPI Int Tech Mark Conf

SPI [*Society of the Plastics Industry*] **Reinforced Plastics/Composites Institute. Annual Conference. Proceedings** — SPI Reinf Plast Compos Inst Annu Conf Proc
SPI [*Society of the Plastics Industry*] **Structural Foam Conference. Proceedings** — SPI Struct Foam Conf Proc
SPIC [*Southern Petrochemical Industries Corp.*] **Industrial Engineering and Training Bulletin** — SPIC Ind Eng Train Bull
Spicilegii Friburgensis Subsidia — SFS
Spicilegio Moderno — Sp M
Spicilegium Historicum Congregationis Smi Redemptoris — SHCSR
Spicilegium Pontificii Athenaei Antoniani — SPAA
Spicilegium Romanum — Spic Rom
Spicilegium Sacrum Lovaniensis — SSL
SPIE [*Society of Photo-Optical Instrumentation Engineers*] **Annual Technical Symposium. Proceedings** — SPIE Annu Tech Symp Proc
SPIE [*Society of Photo-Optical Instrumentation Engineers*] **International Society for Optical Engineering. Proceedings** — SPIE Int Soc Opt Eng Proc
SPIE [*Society of Photo-Optical Instrumentation Engineers*] **Journal** [*Optical Engineering*] [*Later,*] — SPIE J
SPIE [*Society of Photo-Optical Instrumentation Engineers*] **Newsletter** — SPIE Newsl
SPIE [*Society of Photo-Optical Instrumentation Engineers*] **Proceedings** — SPIE Proc
SPIE [*Society of Photo-Optical Instrumentation Engineers*] **Seminar Proceedings** — SPIE Semin Proc
SPIE [*Society of Photo-Optical Instrumentation Engineers*] **Volume** [*United States*] — SPIE Vol
Spiegel [*Hamburg*] — SGL
Spiegel — SPILB
Spiegel der Letteren — Spiegel Let
Spiegel der Letteren — SpL
Spiegel Historiael — SpiH
Spiegel Historiael. Maandblad voor Geschiedenis en Archaeologie — Sp Hist
Spiegel Historical — Spiegel Hist
Spielzeug. Internationales Fachblatt fuer Spielmittel, Hobby- und Modellbau-Artikel, Christbaumschmuck, Fest- und Scherzartikel, Rohstoffe, Halbteile, Werkzeuge, Maschinen, und Verpackung — SZL
SPIG [*Symposium on Physics of Ionized Gases*] **Invited Lectures** — SPIG Invited Lect
Spil. Een Progressief Onafhankelijk Maandblad voor Zelfstandigen en Werknemers in het Middenbedrijf en Kleinbedrijf — SLU
Spill Technology Newsletter — SPTN
Spinner, Weber, Textilveredlung — Spinner Weber Textilveredl
Spirit of Missions — Sp Miss
Spirit of Missions — Spirit Mis
Spirit of the Pilgrims — Spirit Pilg
Spirit That Moves Us — Spirit
Spiritual Life — Spir Life
Spiritualitas [*Roma*] — Spir
Spirituality Today — Spir Tod
Spirituosen-Verkauf — Spirit Verkauf
Spiritus-Industrie (Moscow) — Spirit Ind (Moscow)
Spirtovaya i Likero-Vodochnaya Promyshlennost. Nauchno-Tekhnicheskii Referativnyi Sbornik — Spirt Likero Vodochn Promst Nauchno Tekh Ref Sb
Spirtovaya Promyshlennost' — Spirt Prom-St'
Spirto-Vodochnaya Promyshlennost — Spirto Vodochn Promst
Spisania na Bulgarsoto Geologichesko Druzhestvo — Spis Bulg Geol Druzhu
Spisanie na Bulgarskata Akademiia na Naukite i Izkustvata — Sp BAN
Spisanie na Bulgarskata Akademiya na Naukite — SpAk
Spisanie na Bulgarskata Akademiya na Naukite — SpBA
Spisanie na Bulgarskata Akademiya na Naukite — SPBAA
Spisanie na Bulgarskata Akademiya na Naukite — SpBAN
Spisanie na Bulgarskata Akademiya na Naukite [*Bulgaria*] — Spis Bulg Akad Nauk
Spisanie na Bulgarskoto Geologichesko Druzhestvo — SBGDA
Spisanie na Bulgarskoto Geologichesko Druzhestvo — Spis Bulg Geol Druzh
Spisanie na Nauchno-Issledovatelskite Instituti pri Ministerstvata na Zemedelete i Gorite — Spis Nauchno-Issled Inst Minist Zemed Gorite
Spisanie na Nauchnoizsledovatelskite Instituti pri Ministerstvoto na Zemedelieto (Bulgaria) — Spis Nauchnoizsled Inst Minist Zemed (Bulg)
Spisanie na Zemedelskite Izpitatelni Instituti v Bulgariya — Spis Zemed Izpit Inst Bulg
Spisanie na Zemedelskite Opitni Instituti v Bulgariya — Spis Zemed Opitni Inst Bulg
Spisok Rastenij Gerbarija Flory SSSR Izdavaemogo Botaniceskim Institutom Vsesojuznogo Akademii Nauk. Schedae ad Herbarium Florae URSS ab Instituto Botanico Academiae Scientiarum URSS Editum — Spisok Rast Gerb Fl SSSR Bot Inst Vsesojuzn Akad Nauk
Spisy Lekarske Fakulty Mesarykovy University (Brno) — Spisy Lek Fak Masaryk Univ (Brno)
Spisy Lekarske Fakulty University J. E. Purkyne v Brne — Spisy Lek Fak Univ J E Purkyne Brne
Spisy Pedagogicke Fakulty v Ostrave — Spisy Pedagog Fak Ostrave
Spisy Prirodovedecke Fakulty Universita v Brne [*Czechoslovakia*] — Spisy Prir Fak Univ Brne
Spisy Prirodovedecke Fakulty Universita v Brne — Spisy Prirodoved Fak Univ Brne
Spisy Prirodovedecke Fakulty University J. E. Purkyne v Brne — Spisy Prirodoved Fak Univ JE Purkyne Brne
Spisy Prirodovedecke Fakulty University J. E. Purkyne v Brne — Spisy Priroved Fak Univ J E Purkyne Brne
Spisy University J. E. Purkyne — SUP
Spisy Vydavane Prirodovedeckou Fakultou Massarykovy University — Spisy Vydavane Prirodoved Fak Massarykovy Univ
Spixiana. Supplement (Muenchen) — Spixiana Suppl (Muench)
Spixiana. Zeitschrift fuer Zoologie — Spixiana Z Zool
Splavy Redkikh i Tugoplavkikh Metallov s Osobymi Fizicheskimi Svoistvami. Raboty Dolozhennye na Vsesoyuznom Soveshchanii po Splavam Redki Metallov — Splavy Redk Tugoplavkikh Met Osobymi Fiz Svoistvami Rab Vses
Splavy Redkikh Metallov — Splavy Redk Met
Spokane Business Examiner [*United States*] — Spokane Bs
Spoldzielczy Kwartalnik Naukomy — Spold Kwartal Nauk
Spolia Zeylanica — Spolia Zeylan
Spolia Zoologica Musei Hauniensis — Spolia Zool Mus Haun
Spomenik. Srpska Akademija Nauka i Umjetnosti — Sp
Spomenik. Srpska Akademija Nauka i Umjetnosti — Spom SANU
Spomenik. Srpska Akademija Nauka i Umjetnosti — Spomenik SAN
Spomenik Srpske Akademije Nauka — SpomSAN
Sponsa Christi — SpC
Spore Research — Spore Res
Sport — GSPM
Sport and Fitness Index — Sport Fit Ind
Sport and Leisure — Sport Leis
Sport and Recreation — Sport Rec
Sport and Recreation Index — Sport Rec Ind
Sport es Testneveles — Sport es Testn
Sport Fisheries Abstracts — Sport Fish Abstr
Sport Marketing Quarterly — Sport Market Q
Sport Science Review — Sport Sci Rev
Sport Sociology Bulletin — Sport Sociol Bul
Sportarzt Sportmedizin — Sportarzt Sportmed
Sporting News — GSPN
Sporting News — SN
Sportliteratur [*Database*] — SPOLIT
Sport-Medical Journal — Sport Med J
Sportmedizin. Aufgaben und Bedeutung fuer den Menschen in Unserer Zeit. Deutscher Sportaerztekongress — Sportmed Aufgaben Bedeutung Menschen Unserer Zeit Dsch Sport
Sportnomedicinske Objave — Sportnomed Objave
Sportologue — S
Sports Afield — ISPA
Sports Afield — SPAFA
Sports and Athletes — Sports and Ath
Sports Heritage — Sp Her
Sports History Bulletin — Sports Hist Bull
Sports Illustrated — GSPI
Sports Illustrated — SI
Sports Illustrated — SPILA
Sports Illustrated — Sports Ill
Sports Illustrated — Sports Illus
Sports Medicine — SM
Sports Medicine — Sports Med
Sports Medicine (Auckland) — Sports Med (Auckland)
Sports Medicine, Training, and Rehabilitation — Sports Med Train & Rehab
Sports 'n Spokes Magazine — Sports 'n Spokes
Sports Retailer — Sports Ret
Sports Turf Bulletin — Sports Turf Bull
Sports-Nutrition News — Sports Nutr News
Sportverletzung Sportschaden — Sportverletz Sportschaden
Sportwissenschaftliche Forschungsprojekte [*Database*] — SPOFOR
Sporulation and Germination. Proceedings. International Spore Conference — Sporulation Germination Proc Int Spore Conf
Sposoby Zapisi Informatsii na Beserebryanykh Nositelyakh — Sposoby Zap Inf Besserebr Nositelyakh
Sposoby Zapisi Informatsii na Besserebryanykh Nositelyakh — Sposoby Zapisi Inf Besserebryanykh Nositelyakh
Spotlight — SPO
Sprach der Gegenwart — SG
Sprachdienst — Sd
Sprache — Spr
Sprache der Hethiter — SH
Sprache im Technischen Zeitalter — Sprache Tech Zeit
Sprache im Technischen Zeitalter — STZ
Sprache und Datenverarbeitung — S Dv
Sprache und Datenverarbeitung — Sprache und Datenverarb
Sprache und Dichtung — SD
Sprache und Dichtung — SuD
Sprache und Gemeinschaft — SuG
Sprache und Information — S und I
Sprache und Literatur — SL
Sprache und Literatur — SuL
Sprache und Literatur. Regensburger Arbeiten zur Anglistik und Amerikanistik — SLRAA
Sprachforum — Sf
Sprachforum — Spf
Sprachkunst (Vienna) — SprV
Sprachspiegel. Schweizerische Zeitschrift fuer die Deutsche Muttersprache — SPsp
Sprague's Journal of Maine History — Sprague's J ME His
Sprak och Stil — S o S
Sprakliga Bidrag [*Lund*] — SpB
Sprakliga Bidrag — SprB
Sprakvetenskapliga Sallskapets i Uppsala Foerhandlingar — Sprakvetensk Sallsk i Uppsala Forhandl
Sprakvetenskapliga Sallskapets i Uppsala Foerhandlingar — SprSUF
Sprakvetenskapliga Sallskapets i Uppsala Foerhandlingar — SSUF
Sprawozdania — Spraw
Sprawozdania Akademii Umiejetnosci — SAU
Sprawozdania Archeologiczne — Spraw A

Sprawozdania i Prace Polskiego Towarzystwa Fizycznego — Spraw Pr Pol Tow Fiz
Sprawozdania Opolskie Towarzystwo Przyjaciol Nauk. Wydzial Nauk Medycznych — Spraw Opolskie Tow Przyj Nauk Wydz Nauk Med
Sprawozdania Panstwowego Instytutu Geologicznego — Spraw Panstw Inst Geol
Sprawozdania PMA [*Panstwowe Museum Archeologiczne*] **(Warszawa)** — Sprwoz (Warszawa)
Sprawozdania Poznanskiego Towarzystwa Przyjaciol Nauk — Spraw Poznan Tow Przyj Nauk
Sprawozdania Poznanskiego Towarzystwa Przyjaciol Nauk — SprPTPN
Sprawozdania Poznanskiego Towarzystwa Przyjaciol Nauk — SPTPN
Sprawozdania Towarzystwa Naukowego w Toruniu — Spraw Tow Nauk Toruniu
Sprawozdania Towarzystwa Naukowego w Toruniu — SprTT
Sprawozdania Towarzystwa Naukowego w Toruniu — STNT
Sprawozdania Towarzystwa Naukowego we Lwowie — Spraw Tow Nauk Lwowie
Sprawozdania Wroclawskiego Towarzystwa Naukowego — Spraw Wroclaw Tow Nauk
Sprawozdania Wroclawskiego Towarzystwa Naukowego — SWTN
Sprawozdania Wroclawskiego Towarzystwa Naukowego. Seria A — Spraw Wroclaw Tow Nauk Ser A
Sprawozdania Wroclawskiego Towarzystwa Naukowego. Seria B — Spraw Wroclaw Tow Nauk Ser B
Sprawozdania z Czynnosci i Posiedzen Lodzkiego Towarzystwa Naukowego — SprLTN
Sprawozdania z Czynnosci i Posiedzen Polskiej Akademii Umiejetnosci — SprPAUm
Sprawozdania z Czynnosci Wydawniczej i Posiedzen Naukowych Oraz Kronika Towarzystwa Naukowego Katolockiego Uniwersytetu Lubelskiego — SprKUL
Sprawozdania z Posiedzen Komisji Jezykowej Akademii Umietjetnosci — Spraw Kom Jez AU
Sprawozdania z Posiedzen Komisji Jezykowej Towarzystwa Naukowego Warszawskiego — SprKJ
Sprawozdania z Posiedzen Komisji Naukowych. Polskiej Akademii Nauk — Sprawozdania Kom Nauk PAN
Sprawozdania z Posiedzen Komisji Pan. Oddzial w Krakowie — SKPanKr
Sprawozdania z Posiedzen Towarzystwa Naukowego Warszawskiego — Spraw Posied Tow Nauk Warsz
Sprawozdania z Posiedzen Towarzystwa Naukowego Warszawskiego — Spraw TNW
Sprawozdania z Posiedzen Towarzystwa Naukowego Warszawskiego — SprTNW
Sprawozdania z Prac Panstwowego Instytutu Farmaceutycznego — Spraw Pr Panstw Inst Farm
Sprawozdanie Komisji Fizjograficznej — Spraw Komis Fizjogr
Sprawozdanie z Prac Naukowych Wydzialu Nauk Spolecznych Pan — SWNS
Sprawy Miedzynarodowe — Spr Miedzyn
Sprawy Miedzynarodowe — Spr Miedzynar
Sprechsaal fuer Keramik, Glas, Email, Silikate — SFKGA
Sprechsaal fuer Keramik, Glas, Email, Silikate — Sprechsaal Keram Glas Silik
Sprechsaal fuer Keramik, Glas, Email, Silikate. Beilage — Sprechsaal Keram Glas Email Silik Beil
Sprechsaal fuer Keramik-Glas-Email — Sprechsaal Keram Glas Email
Sprechsall fuer Keramik, Glas, Baustoffe — Sprechsaal Keram Glas Baust
Sprenger Instituut. Rapporten — Sprenger Inst Rap
Spring — SP
Springer Computer Science — Springer Comput Sci
Springer Lehrbuch Mathematik — Springer Lehrbuch Math
Springer Proceedings in Physics — Springer Proc Phys
Springer Seminars in Immunopathology — Springer Semin Immunopathol
Springer Series in Biophysics — Springer Ser Biophys
Springer Series in Chemical Physics — Springer Ser Chem Phys
Springer Series in Computational Mathematics — Springer Ser Comput Math
Springer Series in Computational Mechanics — Springer Ser Comput Mech
Springer Series in Computational Physics — Springer Ser Comput Phys
Springer Series in Electronics and Photonics — Springer Ser Electron Photonics
Springer Series in Electrophysics — Springer Ser Electrophys
Springer Series in Information Sciences — Springer Ser Inform Sci
Springer Series in Nonlinear Dynamics — Springer Ser Nonlinear Dynamics
Springer Series in Nuclear and Particle Physics — Springer Ser Nuclear Particle Phys
Springer Series in Operations Research — Springer Ser Oper Res
Springer Series in Optical Sciences — Springer Ser Opt Sci
Springer Series in Optical Sciences — Springer Ser Optical Sci
Springer Series in Solid-State Sciences — Springer Ser Solid-State Sci
Springer Series in Soviet Mathematics — Springer Ser Soviet Math
Springer Series in Statistics — Springer Ser Statist
Springer Series in Statistics. Perspectives in Statistics — Springer Ser Statist Perspect Statist
Springer Series in Statistics. Probability and its Applications — Springer Ser Statist Probab Appl
Springer Series in Surface Sciences — Springer Ser Surf Sci
Springer Series in Synergetics — Springer Ser Synergetics
Springer Series on Health Care and Society — SHCS
Springer Series on Health Care and Society — Springer Ser Health Care Soc
Springer Series on Wave Phenomena — Springer Ser Wave Phenomena
Springer Study Edition — Springer Study Ed
Springer Texts in Electrical Engineering — Springer Texts Electrical Engrg
Springer Texts in Statistics — Springer Texts Statist
Springer Tracts in Modern Physics — Springer Tracts Mod Phys
Springer Tracts in Modern Physics — Springer Tracts Modern Phys
Springer Tracts in Modern Physics — STPHB
Springer Tracts in Natural Philosophy — Springer Tracts Nat Philos
Springfield Sunday Union and Republican — SSUR
Springfielder — Spfdr
Sprog og Kultur — SOK
Sprog og Kultur — Sp o K
Sprogforeningens Aarsberetning — Sprogf Aa
Spudasmata — Spud
Spurenelement-Symposium. Arsen — Spurenelem Symp Arsen
Spurenelement-Symposium der Karl-Marx-Universitaet Leipzig und der Friedrich-Schiller-Universitaet Jena — Spurenelem Symp
Sputnik [*Moscow*] — Sp
SPWLA [*Society of Professional Well Log Analysts*] **Logging Symposium. Transactions** — SPWLA Logging Symp Trans
Squaring the Information Circle. ICSTI (International Council for Scientific and Technical Information) Symposium Proceedings — Squaring Inf Circle ICSTI Symp Proc
Squibb Abstract Bulletin — Squibb Abstr Bull
SR Science and Technology Information — SR Sci Technol Inf
SRA - Journal of the Society of Research Administrators — SRA-J Soc R
Sravnitel'naya Elektrokardiologiya. Materialy Mezhdunarodnogo Simposiuma — Sravn Elektrokardiol Mater Mezhdunar Simp
SRC [*Saskatchewan Research Council*] **Publication** — SRC Publ
SRC [*Saskatchewan Research Council*] **Report** — SRC Rep
SRC [*Saskatchewan Research Council*] **Technical Report** — SRC Tech Rep
SRDC Series. Southern Rural Development Center [*United States*] — SRDC Ser South Rural Dev Cent
Sreden Medicinski Rabotnik — Sred Med Rab
Sredneaziatskii Nauchno-Issledovatel'skii Institut Geologii i Mineral'nogo Syr'ya. Uchenye Zapiski — Sredneaziat Nauchno Issled Inst Geol Miner Syrya Uch Zap
Sredneaziatskoe Otdelenie Vsesoyuznoi Akademii Sel'skokhozyaistvennykh Nauk. Sbornik — Sredneaziat Otd Vses Akad Skh Nauk Sb
Srednee Spetsial'noe Obrazovanie [*Moscow*] — SSO
Srednie Veka. Sbornik — SV
SRI [*Stanford Research Institute*] **Journal** — SRI J
Sri Lanka Association for the Advancement of Science. Proceedings of the Annual Session — Sri Lanka Assoc Adv Sci Proc Annu Sess
Sri Lanka. Fisheries Research Station. Bulletin — Sri Lanka Fish Res Stn Bull
Sri Lanka Forester — Sri Lanka For
Sri Lanka. Geological Survey Department. Economic Bulletin — Sri Lanka Geol Surv Dep Econ Bull
Sri Lanka Journal of Humanities [*Peradeniya*] — Sri Lan J Hum
Sri Lanka Journal of the Humanities — SriLJH
Sri Lanka Labour Gazette — Sri Lanka Lab Gaz
SRI [*Stanford Research Institute*] **Pesticide Research Bulletin** — SRI Pestic Res Bull
Sri Venkateswara University. Oriental Journal — SVUOJ
Srpska Akademija Nauka i Umetnosti Odeljenje Prirodno-Matematickih Nauka (Glas) — Srp Akad Nauka Umet Od Prir-Mat Nauka (Glas)
Srpska Akademija Nauka i Umetnosti Posebna Izdanja Odeljenje Prirodno-Matematickikh Nauka — Srp Akad Nauka Umet Posebna Izdan Od Prir Mat Nauka
Srpski Arhiv za Celokupno Lekarstvo — SACLA
Srpski Arhiv za Celokupno Lekarstvo — Srp Arh Celok Lek
Srpski Arkhiv za Tselokupno Lekarstvo — Srp Arkh Tselok Lek
Srpski Dijalektoloski Zbornik — SD Zb
Srpski Dijalektoloski Zbornik — SDZ
Srpski Knjizevni Glasnik — SKG
Srpski Knjizevni Glasnik — SKGl
Srpsko Hemiskog Drustvo. Bulletin — Srpsko Hem Drus Bull
SRW [*Siemens-Reiniger-Werke*] **Nachricht** [*Germany*] — SRW Nachr
SSAL [*Scientific Serials in Australian Libraries*] **Supplement** — SSAL Suppt
SSRC [*Social Science Research Council*] **Newsletter** — SSRC Newsl
SSRF [*National Marine Fisheries Service*] [*Special Scientific Report Fisheries*] — NOAA Tech Rep NMFS SSRF
SSSA [*Soil Science Society of America*] **Special Publication** — SSSA Spec Publ
SSSA [*Soil Science Society of America*] **Special Publication Series** — SSSA Spec Publ Ser
SST. Sveriges Skogsvaardsfoerbunds Tidskrift — SST Sver Skogsvaardsfoerb Tidskr
Ssu Ch'uan Ta Hsueh Hsueh Pao - Tzu Jan K'o Hsueh — SCTHA
St. Andrews Review — St A R
St. Andrew's University. Sociological Review — St Andrew Univ Sociol R
St. Anthony Messenger — St Anth
St. Anthony's College. Far Eastern Affairs — FEA
St. Antony's Hall Publications — SAHP
St. Antony's Papers — St Antonys Pap
St. Bonaventure Science Studies — St Bonaventure Sci Stud
St. John's Law Review — SJLR
St. John's Law Review — St J LR
St. John's Law Review — St John's L Rev
St. John's University Studies — SJUS
St. John's University Studies. Theological Series — SJUST
St. Lawrence County Cooperative Extension News — St Lawrence Cty Coop Ext News
St. Louis Business Journal [*United States*] — St Louis B
St. Louis City Art Museum. Bulletin — St Louis Mus Bul
St. Louis Commerce [*United States*] — St Lou Com
St. Louis Commerce — St Louis Commer
St. Louis Druggist — St Louis Drug
St. Louis Labor Tribune — St Louis Lab Trib
St. Louis Law Review — St Louis Law R
St. Louis Manager [*United States*] — St Lou Mgr
St. Louis Metropolitan Medicine — St Louis Metropol Med
St. Louis Post-Dispatch [*United States*] — St Lou Pos
St. Louis University. Bulletin — St Louis Univ B
St. Louis University. Law Journal — Saint Louis Univ LJ

St. Louis University. Law Journal — SLULJ
St. Louis University. Law Journal — St Lou ULJ
St. Louis University. Law Journal — St Louis U L J
St. Louis University. Law Journal — St LU LJ
St. Louis University. Public Law Forum — St Louis Univ Public Law Forum
St. Louis University. Research Journal [*Baguio City*] — SLURJ
St. Louis University. Research Journal [*Baguio City*] — St Louis U Res J
St. Louis University. Research Journal. Graduate School of Arts and Sciences — SLRJ
St. Luke's Hospital Gazette — St Luke's Hosp Gaz
St. Luke's Journal of Theology — St L J Th
St. Luke's Journal of Theology — St Luke J
St. Marianna Medical Journal [*Japan*] — St Marianna Med J
St. Mark's Review — St Mark R
St. Mark's Review — St Mark Rev
St. Mark's Review — St Marks R
St. Mark's Review — St Marks Rev
St. Mary's Law Journal — SMLJ
St. Mary's Law Journal — St M LJ
St. Mary's Law Journal — St Mary's L J
St. Nicholas — St N
St. Paul Medical Journal — St Paul Med J
St. Paul's Review of Science — St Pauls Rev Sci
St. Petersburg Mathematical Journal — St Petersburg Math J
St. Petersburger Medizinische Wochenschrift — St Petersb Med Wchnschr
St. Vladimir's Seminary. Quarterly [*New York*] — StVladSemQ
St. Vladimir's Seminary Quarterly — SVSQ
St. Vladimir's Seminary. Quarterly — VSQ
St. Vladimir's Theological Quarterly — SVTQ
STAACT [*Science Teachers Association of the Australian Capital Territory*] **Journal** — STAACT J
Staat und Kirche in Katalonien und Aragon — SKKA
Staat und Recht — St u R
Staat und Recht — Staat u Recht
Staat und Selbstverwaltung — StSV
Staat und Wirtschaft in Hessen — Staat und Wirt in Hessen
Staatliche Technische Forschungsanstalt. Finnland. Publikation — Staatl Tech Forschungsanst Finnl Publ
Staatliche Zentrale fuer Strahlenschutz der DDR. Report — Staatl Zent Strahlenschutz DDR Rep
Staatliches Amt fuer Atomsicherheit und Strahlenschutz der DDR. Report — Staatl Amt Atomsicherh Strahlenschutz DDR Rep
Staats und Kommunalverwaltung — St u Komm V
Staatsanzeiger fuer Baden-Wuerttemberg — Staatsanz Baden-Wuerttemb
Staatsanzeiger fuer Rheinland-Pfalz [*German Federal Republic*] — Staatsanz Rheinl-Pfalz
Staatsblad Nederlands-Indie — SNI
Staatsblad van het Koninkrijk der Nederlanden — NS
Staatsblad van het Koninkrijk der Nederlanden — S
Staatsblad van het Koninkrijk der Nederlanden — SKH
Staatsblad van het Koninkrijk der Nederlanden — Staatsbl Koninkrijk Ned
Staatsblad van het Koninkrijk der Nederlanden — Staatsblad K Ned
Staatsblad van het Koninkrijk der Nederlanden — Stbl
Staatsblad van Indonesie — Ind S
Staatsblad van Indonesie — IS
Staatsblad van Nederlandsch Indie — Ind Stbl
Staatsbuerger-Beilage der Bayerischen Staatszeitung — Staatsbuerger-Beil Bayer Staatsztg
Staatsbuergerliches Magazin — Staatsbuergerl Mag
Staatsinstitut fuer Angewandte Botanik. Hamburg. Jahresbericht — Staatsinst Angew Bot Hamburg Jahresber
Staatskirchenrechtliche Abhandlungen — SKRA
Stability and Control. Theory, Methods, and Applications — Stability Control Theory Methods Appl
Stabilization and Solidification of Hazardous, Radioactive, and Mixed Wastes — Stab Solidif Hazard Radioact Mixed Wastes
Stable Isotopes. Proceedings. International Conference — Stable Isot Proc Int Conf
Staden-Jahrbuch — SJb
Staden-Jahrbuch — Staden-Jb
Stader Jahrbuch. Stader Geschichts- und Heimatverein — StJ
Stadion. Zeitschrift fuer Geschichte des Sports und der Koerperkultur — Stad Z
Stadler Genetics Symposia — SGSYB
Stadler Genetics Symposia — Stadler Genet Symp
Stadler Symposia — Stadler Symp
Stads- og Havneingenioren — St o H
Stadt- und Gebaeudetechnik — SGHLA
Stadt- und Gebaeudetechnik [*German Democratic Republic*] — Stadt-Gebaeudetech
Stadt- und Landesbibliothek — Stadt-LB
Stadt- und Universitaetsbibliothek — Stadt-UB
Stadtbaukunst — Stbk
Staedel-Jahrbuch — Staedel Jb
Staedtehygiene — STDHA
Staedtetag — SDTGA
Staerke — STRKA
Staff Journal (University of Reading) — Staff J (University of Reading)
Staff Paper P. Minnesota University. Department of Agricultural and Applied Economics — Staff Pap P Minn Univ Dep Agric Appl Econ
Staff Paper. University of Florida. Food and Resource Economics Department. Institute of Food and Agricultural Sciences — Staff Pap Univ Fla Food Resour Econ Dep Inst Food Agric Sci
Staff Paper. University of Florida. Food and Resources Economics Department — Staff Pap Univ Florida Food Resour Econ Dep
Staff Papers — Staff Pap
Staff Papers — STN
Staff Papers. Brookings Institution — St P Brook
Staff Papers. International Monetary Fund — IMF/SP
Staffordshire Archaeology — Staffordshire Archaeol
Stage de Biochimie. Rapport Scientifique — Stage Biochim Rapp Sci
Stahl und Eisen — STEIA
Stahl und Eisen. Beihefte — Stahl Eisen Beih
Stahl und Eisen. Zeitschrift fuer Technik und Wissenschaft der Herstellung und Verarbeitung von Eisen und Stahl — STE
Stahlbau — STAHA
Stahlbau in Technik und Wirtschaft — Stahlbau Tech Wirtsch
Stahlbau Rundschau [*Austria*] — Stahlbau Rundsch
Stahlbau-Technik — Stahlbau Tech
Stahlia Miscellaneous Papers — Stahlia Misc Pap
Stain Technology — Stain Tech
Stain Technology — Stain Technol
Stain Technology — STTEA
Stainless Steel [*South Africa*] — Stainl Steel
Stainless Steel — STASD
Stainless Steel Industry — Stainless Steel Ind
STAL. Sciences et Techniques de l'Animal de Laboratoire — STAL Sci Tech Anim Lab
Stal'e Nemetallicheskie Vklyucheniya — Stal Nemet Vklyucheniya
Staleplavil'noe Proizvodstvo — Staleplavil'n Proizvod
Staleplavil'noe Proizvodstvo (Moscow) — Staleplavil'n Proizvod (Moscow)
Stalinis Sacheolobis Tbilisis Universitatis Sromebi — Tbilisis Univ Sromebi
Stand und Leistung Agrikulturchemischer und Agrarbiologischer Forschung — Stand Leist Agrikulturchem Agrarbiol Forsch
Standaard. Dagblad voor Staatkundige, Matschappelijke, en Economische Belangen — STD
Standard and Chartered Review [*Standard Bank Review*] [*Standard Chartered Review*] [*Formerly,*] [*Later,*] — S & C Bank
Standard and Chartered Review — Stand Chartered Rev
Standard Bank Review — Stand Bank
Standard Chartered Review — SBA
Standard Chartered Review — SCR
Standard Chartered Review [*London*] — Stand Chart Rev
Standard Chartered Review — Standard Chartered R
Standard Drug File [*Database*] — SDF
Standard Federal Tax Reports. Commerce Clearing House — Stand Fed Tax Rep CCH
Standard Methods for the Examination of Dairy Products — Stand Methods Exam Dairy Prod
Standard Methods of Clinical Chemistry — Stand Methods Clin Chem
Standard of California Oil Bulletin — SCB
Standard Oiler (California) — SOC
Standard Periodical Data Base — SPD
Standard Pesticide File [*Database*] — SPF
Standard Philippine Periodicals Index — Stand Philip Per Ind
Standard Trade Index of Japan — Jpn Trade
Standardisierung und Qualitaet [*German Democratic Republic*] — Stand Qual
Standardization News — Stand News
Standardization of Physical Fitness Tests. Magglinger Symposium — Stand Phys Fitness Tests Magglinger Symp
Standards Association of Australia. Australian Standard — Stand Ass Aust Aust Stand
Standards Association of Australia. Commercial Standard — Stand Ass Aust Commercial Stand
Standards Association of Australia. Miscellaneous Publication — Stand Ass Aust Miscell Pub
Standards Referenced in Federal Legislation [*Database*] — FED-STAN
Standarti i Kachestvo (Sofia) — Stand Kach (Sofia)
Standartnye Obraztsy v Chernoi Metallurgii — Std Obraztsy Chern Metall
Standarty i Kachestvo — Stand Kach
Standarty i Kachestvo — STKAB
Standesamt — Standesa
Standeszeitung Deutscher Apotheker — Standesztg Dtsch Apoth
Stanford Campus Report — SCR
Stanford Environmental Law Annual — Stan Env't Ann
Stanford French and Italian Studies — SFIS
Stanford French Review — SFR
Stanford French Review — Stanford Fr
Stanford French Review — Stanford French Rev
Stanford German Studies — S Ger S
Stanford Honors Essays in the Humanities — SHEH
Stanford Ichthyological Bulletin — Stanford Ichthyol Bull
Stanford Italian Review — StIR
Stanford Journal of International Law — Stan J Intl L
Stanford Journal of International Law — Stanford J Internat Law
Stanford Journal of International Studies — Stan J Intl St
Stanford Journal of International Studies — Stan J Int'l Stud
Stanford Journal of International Studies — Stanf J Int
Stanford Journal of International Studies — Stanford J Int Stud
Stanford Journal of International Studies — Stanford J Internat Studies
Stanford Journal of International Studies — Stanford J Int'l Stud
Stanford Law Review — ISLV
Stanford Law Review — SLR
Stanford Law Review — Stan L Rev
Stanford Law Review — Stan LR
Stanford Law Review — Stanford L Rev
Stanford Law Review — Stanford La
Stanford Law Review — Stanford Law R
Stanford Law Review — Stanford Law Rev
Stanford Law Review — Stn L

Stanford Lawyer — Stan Law
Stanford Literature Review — Stanford Lit Rev
Stanford Medical Bulletin — Stanford M Bull
Stanford Medical Bulletin — Stanford Med Bull
Stanford Research Institute. Journal — Stanford Research Inst Jour
Stanford Research Institute. Pesticide Research Bulletin — Stanford Res Inst Pestic Res Bull
Stanford Studies in Germanics and Slavics — SSGS
Stanford Studies in Language and Literature — SSLL
Stanford Studies in Medical Sciences — Stanford Stud Med Sci
Stanford Studies in Psychology — Stanford Stud Psychol
Stanford Studies in the Civilizations of Eastern Asia — SSCES
Stanford University. Department of Civil Engineering. Technical Report — Stanford Univ Dep Civ Eng Tech Rep
Stanford University. Department of Mechanical Engineering. Technical Report — Stanford Univ Dep Mech Eng Tech Rep
Stanford University Food Research Institute Studies — FRIS
Stanford University Food Research Institute Studies in Agricultural Economics, Trade, and Development — Stud Ag Econ
Stanford University Publications in the Geological Sciences — Stanford Univ Publ Geol
Stanford University. Publications in the Geological Sciences — Stanford Univ Publ Geol Sci
Stanford University. Publications. University Series. Biological Sciences — Stanford Univ Publ Univ Ser Biol Sci
Stanford University. Publications. University Series. Engineering — Stanford Univ Publ Univ Ser Eng
Stanford University Publications. University Series. Geological Sciences — Stanford Univ Publ Univ Ser Geol Sci
Stanford University. Publications. University Series. Languages and Literatures — SUPUSLL
Stanford University. Publications. University Series. Mathematics and Astronomy — Stanford Univ Publ Univ Ser Math Astron
Stanford University. Publications. University Series. Medical Sciences — Stanford Univ Publ Univ Ser Med Sci
Stanki i Instrument — Stanki i Instrum
Stanki i Instrument — STINA
Stanki i Rezhushchie Instrumenty — Stanki Rezhushchie Instrum
Stapp Car Crash Conference. Proceedings — Stapp Car Crash Conf Proc
Star [*Johannesburg*] — St
Star Science Fiction — STR
Starch Hydrolysis Products — Starch Hydrolysis Prod
Starch/Staerke — STARD
Starchroom Laundry Journal — Starchroom Laundry J
Starinar. Organ Arheoloskog Instituta Srpska Akademija Nauk — Star
Starinar Srpskog Arkeoloskog Drustva — SSAD
Starohrvatska Prosvjeta. Muzej Hrvatskih Starina Jugoslovenske Akademij e Znanosti i Umjetnosti — SHP
Starohrvatska Prosvjeta. Muzej Hrvatskih Starina Jugoslovenske Akademij e Znanosti i Umjetnosti — Strarohrv Prosvj
Stars & Stripes — S & S
Starship. The Magazine about Science Fiction — Shp
Starship. The Magazine about Science Fiction — Star
Startling Mystery Stories — SMS
Startling Stories — SS
Startling Stories — STL
Stat. Bulletin of the Wisconsin Nurses' Association — Stat
State Agricultural College Agricultural Experiment Station Bulletin — State Agric Coll Agric Exp Sta Bull
State Agricultural College of Oregon. Engineering Experiment Station. Circular — State Agric Coll Oreg Eng Exp Stn Circ
State and Local Government Review — State and Local Govt R
State and Local Statistical Sources — SLSS
State and National Registers of Historic Places — St Nat Reg Hist Pl
State Bar of California. Journal — Calif S B
State Bar of California. Journal — Calif SBJ
State Court Journal — St Ct J
State Court Journal — State Court J
State Education Journal Index — SEJI
State Energy Data System [*Database*] — SEDS
State Fisheries Chief. Secretary's Department. New South Wales. Research Bulletin — State Fish Chief Secr Dep NSW Res Bull
State Forest Notes. California Division of Forestry — St For Note Calif Div For
State Geological and Natural History Survey of Connecticut. Report of Investigation — State Geol Nat Hist Surv Conn Rep Invest
State Geological Survey of Kansas. Bulletin — State Geol Surv Kans Bull
State Geologists Journal — State Geologists Jour
State Government — State Gov
State Government — State Govt
State Government — STG
State Government News — State Govt News
State Historical Society of North Dakota Collections — StateHSocNDColl
State Historical Society of Wisconsin. Proceedings — State Hist Soc Wis Proc
State Horticultural Association of Pennsylvania. Proceedings — State Hortic Assoc PA Proc
State Hospital Quarterly — State Hosp Q
State Institute for Technical Research. Finland. Publication — State Inst Tech Res Finl Publ
State Institute for Technical Research. Finland. Report — State Inst Tech Res Finl Rep
State Institute for Technical Research. Finland. Report. Series 2. Metals — State Inst Tech Res Finl Rep Ser 2
State Institute for Technical Research. Finland. Report. Series 3. Building — State Inst Tech Res Finl Rep Ser 3
State Legislatures — State Legis
State Librarian — State Libn
State Librarian — State Libr
State Literary and Historical Association of North Carolina. Proceedings — NC His As
State, Local, and Urban Law Newsletter — State Loc and Urb L Newsl
State, Local, and Urban Law Newsletter — State Locl & Urb L Newsl
State Mineral Profiles. United States Bureau of Mines — State Miner Profiles US Bur Mines
State Nursing Legislation. Quarterly — State Nurse Legis Q
State of Illinois. Division of the State Geological Survey. Bulletin — State Ill Div State Geol Surv Bull
State of Louisiana. Acts of the Legislature — La Acts
State of Montana. Bureau of Mines and Geology. Memoir — State Mont Bur Mines Geol Mem
State of New Jersey. Department of Conservation and Economic Development. Division of Water Policy and Supply. Special Report — New Jersey Div Water Policy and Supply Spec Rept
State of New Jersey. Department of Conservation and Economic Development. Division of Water Policy and Supply. Water Resources Circular — New Jersey Div Water Policy and Supply Water Resources Circ
State of Ohio. Legislative Acts Passed and Joint Resolutions Adopted — Ohio Laws
State of the Art Reviews. Occupational Medicine — State of the Art Rev Occup Med
State of Utah Bulletin — Utah Bull
State of Washington. Department of Fisheries. Research Division. Information Booklet — State Wash Dep Fish Res Div Inf Bkl
State of Washington. Department of Fisheries. Research Division. Information Booklet — State Wash Dep Fish Res Div Inf Booklet
State Planning and Environment Commission. Technical Bulletin — State Plann and Environ Comm Tech Bull
State Regulation Report. Toxics [*Database*] — SRR
State Report. New Hampshire Agricultural Experiment Station — State Rep NH Agric Exp Stn
State Reports (New South Wales) — SR (NSW)
State Reports (New South Wales) — St Rep (NSW)
State Reports (New South Wales). Bankruptcy and Probate — SR (NSW) B & P
State Reports (New South Wales). Equity — SR (NSW) Eq
State Reports (Queensland) — QSR
State Reports (Queensland) — SQR
State Reports (Queensland) — SRQ
State Reports (Queensland) — St R (Q)
State Reports (Queensland) — St R (Qd)
State Reports (Queensland) — St R (Queensl)
State Reports (Western Australia) — SR (WA)
State Research — State Res
State Scientific Research Institute for the Tobacco and Makhorka Industry. USSR — State Sci Res Inst Tob Makhorka Ind USSR
State Shipping Service of Western Australia. Journal — SSS Journal
State Tax Cases. Commerce Clearing House — St Tax Cas CCH
State Tax Cases Reports. Commerce Clearing House — St Tax Cas Rep CCH
State Tax Guide. Commerce Clearing House — State Tax Guide CCH
State Tax Reports. Commerce Clearing House — St Tax Rep CCH
State University College of Forestry. Syracuse University. Technical Publication — State Univ Coll For Syracuse Univ Tech Publ
State University of New York. Marine Sciences Research Center (Stony Brook). Technical Report Series — State Univ NY Mar Sci Res Cent (Stony Brook) Tech Rep Ser
State Veterinary Journal — State Vet J
State Wildlife Advisory News Service — SWANS
Staten Island Association of Arts and Sciences. Proceedings — Staten Island As Pr
Staten Island Institute of Arts and Sciences. Proceedings — Staten Island Inst Arts Sci Proc
Statens Baeginstitut (Sweden). Meddelande — Statens Vaeginst (Swed) Medd
Statens Forsoegsmejeri. Beretning — Statns Forsoegsmejeri Beret
Statens Husdjursfoersoek. Sweden. Saertryck och Foerhandsmeddelande — Statens Husdjursfoers Swed Saertr Foerhandsmedd
Statens Institut foer Byggnadsforskning. Handlingar (Translations) — Statens Inst Byggnadsforsk Handl (Trans)
Statens Institut foer Byggnadsforskning. National Swedish Building Research Document — Statens Inst Byggnadsforsk Natl Swedish Bldg Res Doc
Statens Lantbrukskemiska Kontrollanstalt. Meddelande — Statens Lantbrukskem Kontrollanst Medd
Statens Lantbrukskemiska Laboratorium. Meddelande — Statens Lantbrukskem Lab Medd
Statens Levnedsmiddelinstitut. Publikation — Statens Levnedsmiddelinst Publ
Statens Naturvetenskapliga Forskningsrad Ekologikommitter Bulletin — Statens Naturvetensk Forskningsrad Ekologikomm Bull
Statens Offentliga Utredningar — SOUTB
Statens Offentliga Utredningar — Statens Offentliga Utredn
Statens Provningsanstalt (Stockholm). Cirkulaer — Statens Provingsanst (Stockholm) Cirk
Statens Provningsanstalt (Stockholm). Meddelande — Statens Provingsanst (Stockholm) Medd
Statens Skadedyrlaboratorium Arsberetning — Statens Skadedyrlab Arsberet
Statens Tekniska Forskningsanstalt. Finland. Bericht — Statens Tek Forskningsanst Finl Ber
Statens Tekniska Forskningscentral. Forskningsrapporter — Statens Tek Forskningscent Forskningsrapp
Statens Tekniska Forskningscentral. Textillaboratoriet. Meddelande — Statens Tek Forskningscent Textillab Medd
Statens Vaeginstitut (Sweden). Rapport — Statens Vaeginst (Swed) Rapp
Statens Vaextskyddsanstalt. Flygblad — Statens Vaextskyddsanst Flygbl
Statens Vaxtskyddsanstalt Meddelanden — Statens Vaxtskyddsanst Medd

State-of-the-Art of Odor Control Technology — State-of-the-Art Odor Control Technol
Statesman and Nation — S & N
Stat'i Materialy po Bolgarskoj Dialektologii — SMBD
Static Electrification. Proceedings. Conference — Static Electrif Proc Conf
Station Bulletin. Agricultural Experiment Station. University of New Hampshire — Stn Bull New Hamps Agric Exp Stn
Station Bulletin. Department of Agricultural Economics. Agricultural Experiment Station. Purdue University — Stn Bull Dep Agri Econ Agric Exp Stn Purdue Univ
Station Bulletin. Minnesota Agricultural Experiment Station — Stn Bull Agric Exp Stn Univ Minn
Station Bulletin. Minnesota. Agricultural Experiment Station — Stn Bull Minn Agric Exp Stn
Station Bulletin. Nebraska. Agricultural Experiment Station — Stn Bull Nebr Agric Exp Stn
Station Bulletin. Oregon Agricultural Experiment Station — Stn Bull Ore Agric Exp Stn
Station Bulletin. Oregon State College. Agricultural Experiment Station — Sta Bull Oreg State Coll Agr Exp Sta
Station Bulletin. Purdue University. Agricultural Experiment Station — Stn Bull Purdue Univ Agric Exp Stn
Station Bulletin. Univerity of Minnesota. Agricultural Experiment Station — Stn Bull Univ Minn Agric Exp Stn
Station Bulletin. University of Minnesota. Agricultural Experiment Station — Sta Bull Univ Minn Agr Exp Sta
Station Circular. Oregon Agricultural Experiment Station — Stn Circ Ore Agric Exp Stn
Station Circular. Purdue University. Agricultural Experiment Station — Stn Circ Purdue Univ Agric Exp Stn
Station Circular. Washington Agricultural Experiment Station — Sta Circ Wash Agr Exp Sta
Station de Biologie Marine. Grande Riviere, Quebec. Rapport Annuel — Stn Biol Mar Grande Riviere Que Rapp Annu
Station Note. Forest, Wildlife, and Range Experiment Station (Moscow, Idaho) — Sta Note For Exp Sta (Idaho)
Station Note. University of Idaho. Forest, Wildlife, and Range Experiment Station — Stn Note Univ Idaho For Wildl Range Exp Stn
Station Paper. Forest, Wildlife, and Range Experiment Station (Moscow, Idaho) — Sta Pap For Exp Sta (Idaho)
Station Report. Horticultural Research Station (Tatura) — Stn Rep Hort Res Stn (Tatura)
Station Technical Bulletin. Oregon Agricultural Experiment Station — Stn Tech Bull Ore Agric Exp Stn
Stations Circular. Washington Agricultural Experiment Stations — Stns Circ Wash Agric Exp Stns
Stations Federales d'Essais Agricoles (Lausanne). Publication — Stn Fed Essais Agric (Lausanne) Publ
Statistica Neerlandica — SNERA
Statistica Neerlandica [*Netherlands*] — Statis Neerl
Statistica Neerlandica — Statist Neerlandica
Statistica Neerlandica — StNeerla
Statistica Neerlandica — SVS
Statistica Sinica — Statist Sinica
Statistical Abstract of Latin America — SALA
Statistical Abstract. United States — Stat Abs
Statistical Abstract. United States — Statist Abstr US
Statistical Abstracts of Israel — SAI
Statistical and Economic Information Bulletin for Africa — Statis and Econ Info Bul Africa
Statistical and Social Inquiry Society of Ireland. Journal — Stat Social Inq Soc Ir J
Statistical Bulletin. Metropolitan Insurance Companies — Stat Bull Metrop Insur Co
Statistical Bulletin. Metropolitan Life Foundation — Stat Bull Metrop Life Found
Statistical Bulletin. Metropolitan Life Insurance Company — Stat Bull
Statistical Bulletin. Metropolitan Life Insurance Company — Stat Bull Metrop Life Insur Co
Statistical Bulletin. Metropolitan Life Insurance Company — Stat Bull Metropol Life Ins Co
Statistical Bulletin. United States Department of Agriculture — Statist Bull USDA
Statistical Bulletin. United States Farm Credit Administration. Economic Analysis Division — Stat Bull US Farm Credit Admin Econ Anal Div
Statistical Distributions in Scientific Work — Statist Distributions Sci Work
Statistical Ecology Series — Statist Ecology Ser
Statistical Information System [*Database*] — STATINF
Statistical Information System of the Federal Republic [*Database*] — STATIS-BUND
Statistical Mechanics — Stat Mech
Statistical Methods in Linguistics — SMIL
Statistical Methods in Linguistics [*Stockholm*] — SML
Statistical Methods in Linguistics — St Lngst
Statistical Methods in Linguistics — Statist M L
Statistical Methods in Medical Research — Stat Methods Med Res
Statistical Modeling and Decision Science — Statist Model Decis Sci
Statistical News Letter (New Delhi) — Stat News Lett (New Delhi)
Statistical Newsletter and Abstracts. Indian Council of Agricultural Research — Statist Newslett Abstr
Statistical Notes for Health Planners — Stat Notes Health Plann
Statistical Papers — Statist Papers
Statistical Problems of Control — Statist Problems Control
Statistical Reference Index — SRI
Statistical Register of South Australia — Statistical Register of SA
Statistical Register of Western Australia — Statistical Register of WA
Statistical Report on Canada's Packaging Market — Cdn Pkg Mk
Statistical Report. Pollen and Mold Committee. American Academy of Allergy — Stat Rep Pollen Mold Comm Am Acad Allergy
Statistical Reporter [*Manila*] — SR
Statistical Reporter — SRE
Statistical Reporter — Stat Rep
Statistical Reporter — Stat Rptr
Statistical Reporter — Statis Reporter
Statistical Review of the World Oil Industry — Stat Rev Wld Oil Ind
Statistical Society Journal — Statist Soc J
Statistical Society of Australia. Newsletter — Newsl Stat Soc Aust
Statistical Summary. Canadian Gas Association — Stat Sum Can Gas Assoc
Statistical Supplement to the Engineering and Mining Journal — Stat Suppl Eng Min J
Statistical Theory and Method Abstracts — Stat Theor Meth Abstr
Statistical Theory and Method Abstracts — Stat Theory Method Abstr
Statistical Theory and Method Abstracts — Statist Theory Method Abstracts
Statistical Theory and Method Abstracts — STMA
Statistical Theory of Estimation — StTEstmatn
Statistical Yearbook of Norway — Norw Yrbk
Statistical Yearbook of the Netherlands — Neth Stat
Statistician — Ststcian
Statistick Tidskrift — Stat Tidskrift
Statisticka Revija (Beograd) — Statist R (Beograd)
Statistics and Computing — Statist Comput
Statistics and Probability Letters — Statist Probab Lett
Statistics Canada Catalogue Online [*Database*] — STATCAN
Statistics Canada. Consumption. Production Inventories of Rubber and Other Selected Sections — Statist Canad Consumpt Prodn Invent Rubb
Statistics in Medicine — STAM
Statistics in Medicine — Stat Med
Statistics of Foreign Trade. Series B. Annual. Tables by Reporting Countries — Statist Foreign Trade B
Statistics of Paper — Statist Paper
Statistics on Japanese Industries 1982 — Stat Japan
Statistics on the Use of Radiation in Japan — Stat Use Radiat Jpn
Statistics Section Paper. Forestry Commission (London) — Statist Sect Pap For Comm (Lond)
Statistics Textbooks and Monographs — Stat Textb Monogr
Statistik der Bundesrepublik Deutschland — St BRD
Statistik des Deutschen Reichs — St DR
Statistika i Elektronno-Vycislitel'naja Tehnika v Ekonomike Naucno-Issledovatel'skii Institut po Proektirovanija Vycislitel'nyh Centrov i Sistem Ekonomiceskoi Informacii CSU SSSR — Statist i Elektron-Vycisl Tehn v Ekonom
Statistique Agricole — Statis Agric
Statistique et Analyse des Donnees. Bulletin de l'Association des Statisticiens Universitaires — Statist Anal Donnees
Statistique et Decisions Economiques [*Paris*] — Statist Decisions Econom
Statistique et Developpement Pays de la Loire — Statist et Develop Loire
Statistique Generale de l'Industrie Textile Francaise — Fr Textil
Statistiques — Statis
Statistiques des Affaires Sociales — Statis Affaires Socs
Statistiques des Enseignements — Statis Enseignements
Statistiques du Commerce Exterieur. Union Economique Belgo-Luxembourgeoise — Belg Commr
Statistiques du Travail. Supplement au Bulletin Mensuel — Statist Trav Suppl B Mens
Statistiques et Etudes Financieres. Etudes Economiques (Serie Orange) — Statist Et Finance Et Econ (Ser Orange)
Statistiques et Etudes Financieres (Serie Bleue) — Statis et Etud Fins (Ser Bleue)
Statistiques et Etudes Financieres (Serie Bleue) — Statist Et Financ (Ser Bleue)
Statistiques et Etudes Financieres (Serie Orange) — Statis et Etud Fins (Ser Orange)
Statistiques et Etudes Financieres (Serie Rouge) — Statis et Etud Fins (Ser Rouge)
Statistiques et Etudes Financieres (Serie Rouge) — Statist Et Financ (Ser Rouge)
Statistiques et Etudes Midi-Pyrenees — Statis et Etud Midi Pyrenees
Statistiques et Etudes Midi-Pyrenees — Statist Et Midi-Pyrenees
Statistiques Financieres Internationales — SFI
Statistiques Judiciaires — Statis Judiciaires
Statistiques pour l'Economie Normande — Statist Econ Normande
Statistische Hefte — Statist Hefte
Statistische Hefte — StHefte
Statistische Monatshefte Rheinland-Pfalz — Statis Mhefte Rheinland-Pfalz
Statistische Nachrichten (Austria). Neue Folge — Statis Nachr (Austria) NF
Statistische Nachrichtentheorie und Ihre Anwendungen. Vortraege Gehlten auf dem Internationalen Seminar — Stat Nachrichtentheorie Ihre Anwend Vortr Int Semin
Statistische Studien (Brussels) — SEB
Statistische Vierteljahrsschrift — St Vj
Statistisches Jahrbuch Deutscher Staedte — Statist Jb Dt Staedte
Statistisches Jahrbuch fuer die Bundesrepublik Deutschland — Stat Jahr
Statistisk Manedskefte (Norway) — (Norw) Stat
Statistisk Tidskrift — Stat Tidskr
Statisztikai Szemle — Statiszt Szle
Statiunea Centrala de Apicultura si Sericicultura. Lucrari Stiintifice — Stn Cent Apic Sericic Lucr Stiint
Statni Technicka Knihovna v Praze. Vymena Zkusenosti — Statni Tech Knih Praze Vymena Zkusenosti
Statni Vyzkumny Ustav pro Stavbu Stroju. Praha-Behovice. Technicke Prirucky — Statni Vyzk Ustav Stavbu Stroju Praha Behovice Tech Prirucky

Statni Vyzkumny Ustav Sklarsky. Kradec Kralove. Informativni Prehled — Statni Vyzk Ustav Sklarsky Kradec Kralove Inf Prehl
Stato e Prospettive delle Applicazioni Industriali delle Radiazioni Nucleari. Congresso Nucleare — Stato Prospett Appl Ind Radiaz Nucl Congr Nucl
Stato Sociale — Stato Soc
Statsoekonomisk Tidsskrift — ST
Statsoekonomisk Tidsskrift — Statsokon Tss
Statsvetenskaplig Tidskrift — Statsvet Ts
Status and Future Developments in the Study of Transport Properties — Status Future Dev Study Transp Prop
Status of Differentiation Therapy in Cancer — Status Differ Ther Cancer
Statuta Capitulorum Generalium Ordinis Cisterciensis — SCGOC
Statuta Generalia de Religiosa, Clericali, Apostolica Institutione — Stat Gen
Statute Law Review — Stat LR
Statute Law Review — Statute L Rev
Statuten der Verenigingen — NSS
Statutes of Alberta — Alta Stat
Statutes of California — Cal Stat
Statutes of Nevada — Nev Stat
Statutes of Ontario [*Database*] — SO
Statutes of Practical Utility — SPU
Statutes of the Yukon Territory — Yuk Stat
Statutory Instrument (London) — Stat Instrum (Lond)
Statutory Instruments [*Ireland*] — SI
Statutory Invention Registration — Statutory Invent Regist
Statutory Orders and Regulations of Canada [*Database*] — SOR
Statutory Regulations [*New Zealand*] — SR
Statutory Rules and Orders [*London*] — SRO
Statutory Rules and Orders of Northern Ireland — Stat R & O N Ir
Statyba ir Architektura — Statyba Archit
Staub Journal — Staub J
Staub, Reinhaltung der Luft — Staub-Reinhalt Luft
Staub, Reinhaltung der Luft — STRHA
Stavanger Museums Arbok — SMA
Stavby Jadrovej Energetiky [*Supplement to Inzenyrske Stavby*] [*Czechoslovakia*] — Stavby Jadrovej Energ
Stavebnicky Casopis — Stavebnicky Cas
Stavebnicky Casopis — STVCA
Stavivo [*Czechoslovakia*] — STAVA
Stavropol'skii Sel'skokhozyaistvennyi Institut. Trudy — Stavrop Skh Inst Tr
Stazione Chimico-Agraria Sperimentale di Torino. Annuario — Stn Chim Agrar Sper Torino Annu
Stazione Sperimentale del Vetro. Revista (Murano, Italy) — Stn Sper Vetro Riv (Murano Italy)
Stazione Sperimentale di Granicoltura per la Sicilia-Catania. Pubblicazione — Stn Sper Granic Sicil Catania Pubbl
Stazione Sperimentale di Maiscoltura (Bergamo) — Sta Sper Maiscolt (Bergamo)
Stazione Sperimentale di Viticoltura e di Enologia (Conegliano, Italy). Annuario — Stn Sper Vitic Enol (Conegliano Italy) Annu
Stazione Sperimentali Agrarie Italiane — Stn Sper Agrar Ital
Stead's Review — Steads R
Steam and Fuel Users' Journal — SFUJA
Steam and Fuel Users' Journal — Steam Fuel Users J
Steam and Heating Engineer — Steam and Heat Eng
Steam and Heating Engineer — Steam Heat Eng
Steam and Heating Engineer — Steam Heat Engr
Steam and Heating Engineer — STHEA
Steam Engineer — Steam Eng
Steam Plant Engineering — Steam Plant Eng
Steam Power — Steam Pwr
Steamusers' and Fuel Users' Journal — Steamusers Fuel Users J
Steaua — Ste
Stechert-Hafner Book News — Stechert-Hafner Bk News
Steel and America — Steel Am
Steel and Materials Technology — Steel Mater Technol
Steel and Metals Magazine — Steel Met Mag
Steel Castings Research and Trade Association. Annual Conference — Steel Cast Res Trade Assoc Annu Conf
Steel Castings Research and Trade Association. Monograph — Steel Cast Res Trade Assoc Monogr
Steel Construction — Steel Const
Steel Construction — Steel Constr
Steel Fabrication Journal — Steel Fabr J
Steel Fabrication Journal — Steel Fabric J
Steel Founders' Research Journal — Steel Founders' Res J
Steel Furnace Monthly — Steel Furn Mon
Steel Horizons — Steel Horiz
Steel in the USSR — SUSRA
Steel Industry and the Energy Crisis. Proceedings. C. C. Furnas Memorial Conference — Steel Ind Energy Crisis Proc C C Furnas Meml Conf
Steel Industry and the Environment. Proceedings. C.C. Furnas Memorial Conference — Steel Ind Environ Proc CC Furnas Meml Conf
Steel Industry of Japan Annual — Steel Ind Jpn Annu
Steel International — Steel Int
Steel News — BFO
Steel Processing — Steel Process
Steel Processing — STPGA
Steel Processing and Conversion — Steel Process Convers
Steel Research — Steel Res
Steel Review — Steel Rev
Steel Statistics for Europe — Steel Stat
Steel Times — STLTA
Steel Times International [*England*] — Steel Times Int
Steel Times (Redhill) — IRC
Steel Today and Tomorrow — STJ
Steelmaking Proceedings — Steelmaking Proc
Steels and Metals International — Steel Met Int
Steiermaerkische Zeitschrift — Steiermaerk Z
Steinbeck Monograph Series — St MS
Steinbeck Monograph Series — Steinbeck M
Steinbeck Quarterly — Steinbeck Q
Steinbeck Quarterly — SteinbQ
Steinbeck Quarterly — SteiQ
Steinbeck Quarterly — StQ
Steine- und Erdengewinnung in Deutschland. Vortraege der Fachtagung — Steine Erdengewinnung Dtschl Vortr Fachtag
Steinindustrie und Steinstrassenbau — Steinind Steinstrassenbau
Stein-Industrie und -Strassenbau — Stein-Ind Strassenbau
Steinkohlenbergbauverein Kurznachrichten — KBKOD
Steinkohlenbergbauverein Kurznachrichten — Steinkohlenbergbauver Kurznachr
Steirische Beitraege zur Hydrogeologie — Steirische Beitr Hydrogeol
Steirischer Imkerbote — Steirisch Imkerbote
Steklo i Keramika — Steklo i Keram
Steklo i Keramika — Steklo Keram
Steklo i Keramika — STKRA
Steklo. Informatsionnyi Byulleten Vsesoyuznogo Nauchno-Issledovatel'skogo Instituta Stekla — Steklo Inf Byull Vses Nauchno Issled Inst Stekla
Steklo, Sitally, i Silikatnye Materialy [*Belorussian SSR*] — Steklo Sitally Silik Mater
Steklo, Sitally, i Silikaty — Steklo Sitally Silik
Steklo. Trudy Gosudarstvennogo Nauchno-Issledovatel'skogo Instituta Stekla — Steklo Tr Gos Nauchno Issled Inst Stekla
Stekloemal i Emalirovanie Metallov — Stekloemal Emal Met
Stekloobraznoe Sostoyanie. Katalizirovannaya Kristallizatsiya Stekla — Stekloobraznoe Sostoyanie Katal Krist Stekla
Stekloplastiki i Steklovolokno. Obzornaya Informatsiya — Stekloplast Steklovolokno Obz Inv
Stekol'naya i Keramicheskaya Promyshlennost — Stekolnaya Keram Promst
Stekol'naya Promyshlennost [*Former USSR*] — Stekol'naya Prom-St
Stellar Atmospheres. Beyond Classical Models — Stellar Atmos Classical Models
Stellar Evolution. Based on Lectures Given at the Summer Institute for Astronomy and Astrophysics — Stellar Evol Lect Summer Inst Astron Astrophys
Stellenbosse Student — Stellenbosse Stud
Stendhal Club — SC
Stendhal Club — SCL
Stendhal Club — Stendhal Cl
Stenografische Berichte. Fuenf Hauptversammlungen. Verband der Deutschen Juden — StB
Stenografisk Tidsskrift — Stng T
Stenoniana Catholica — Sten Cath
Stephen Crane Newsletter — SCraneN
Stephen Crane Newsletter — StCrN
Stephen Ellis — Ellis
Stephen F. Austin State College. School of Forestry. Bulletin — Stephen F Austin State Coll Sch For Bull
Stereo — ST
Stereo Review — GSTR
Stereo Review — SR
Stereo Review — St
Stereo Review — STELB
Stereo Review — Stereo
Stereo Review — Stereo R
Stereo Review — STR
Stereochemistry. Fundamentals and Methods — Stereochem Fundam Methods
Stereologia Iugoslavica — Stereol Iugosl
Stereoselective Synthesis of Natural Products. Proceedings. Workshop Conference Hoechst — Stereosel Synth Nat Prod Proc Workshop Conf Hoechst
Stereoselective Synthesis. Part B — Stereosel Synth Part B
Stereotactic and Functional Neurosurgery — Stereotactic Funct Neurosurg
Sterilization of Medical Products. Proceedings. International Kilmer Memorial Conference on the Sterilization of Medical Products — Steril Med Prod Prod Int Kilmer Meml Conf
Sterna — STER
Sterne — STNEA
Sterne und Weltraum — STUWA
Sternenbote — STRND
Steroid Hormones — Steroid Horm
Steroids — STEDA
Steroids and Lipids Research — SLPRB
Steroids and Lipids Research — Steroids Lipids Res
Steroids. Supplement — Steroids Suppl
STES [*Seasonal Thermal Energy Storage*] **Newsletter** [*United States*] — STES Newsl
Stethoscope and Virginia Medical Gazette — Stethoscope Va Med Gaz
Stetson Law Review — Stetson L Rev
Stettiner Entomologische Zeitung — Stettin Ent Ztg
Stettiner Jahrbuch — StJ
Steuer und Wirtschaft — St u W
Steuer und Wirtschaft — St u Wi
Steuer und Wirtschaft — St W
Steuer und Wirtschaft — Steuer u Wirtsch
Steuer und Zollblatt fuer Berlin — St Bl
Steuer-Archiv — StA
Steuerberater — Stb
Steuerberater-Jahrbuch — Stb Jb
Steuerberatungsgesetz — St Ber G
Steuerblatt fuer das Land Niedersachsen — St Bl Nds
Steuerblatt fuer das Land Schleswig-Holstein — St Bl Schl H

Steuerungstechnik — STEUA
Steuer-Zentralarchiv — St ZA
Stevens Indicator — Stevens Ind
Stevens Institute of Technology (Hoboken, New Jersey). Davidson Laboratory. Report — Stevens Inst Technol (Hoboken NJ) Davidson Lab Rep
STF [*Staubforschungsinstitut*] **Report** — STF Rep
Stichting Bosbouwproefstation "De Dorschkamp." Berichten — Sticht Bosbouwproefsta "Dorschkamp" Ber
Stichting Bosbouwproefstation "De Dorschkamp." Korte Mededeling — Sticht Bosbouwproefstn "De Dorschkamp" Korte Meded
Stichting Bosbouwproefstation "De Dorschkamp." Korte Mededelingen — Sticht Bosbouwproefsta "Dorschkamp" Korte Meded
Stichting Bosbouwproefstation "De Dorschkamp." Uitvoerige Verslagen — Sticht Bosbouwproefsta "Dorschkamp" Uitv Versl
Stichting Energieonderzoek Centrum Nederland. ECN Report — Sticht Energieonderz Cent Ned ECN Rep
Stichting Energieonderzoek Centrum Nederland. Report — Sticht Energieonderz Cent Ned Rep
Stichting Instituut voor Kernphysisch Onderzoek. Jaarboek — Sticht Inst Kernphys Onderz Jaarb
Stichting Instituut voor Pluimveeonderzoek "Het Spelderholt" Jaarverslag — Sticht Inst Pluimveeonderz Het Spelderholt Jaarversl
Stichting Instituut voor Pluimveeonderzoek "Het Spelderholt" Jaarverslag — Sticht Inst Pluimveeonderz Spelderholt Jaarversl
Stichting voor Coordinate van Cultuur en Onderzoek van Broodgraan Jaarboekje — Sticht Coord Cult Onderz Broodgraan Jaarb
Stichting voor Fundamenteel Onderzoek der Materie. Jaarboek — Sticht Fundam Onderz Mater Jaarb
Stichting Weg. Bulletin — SWB
Stiftelsens foer Aabo Akademi Forskningsinstitut. Meddelanden — Stiftelsens Aabo Akad Forskningsinst Medd
Stifter-Jahrbuch — Stifter Jb
Stifter-Jahrbuch — StJb
Stiinta Solului — Sti Solului
Stiinta Solului — Stiinta Sol
Stiinte si Tehnologii Alimentare — Stiinte Tehnol Aliment
Stimme der Gemeinde zum Kirchlichen Leben — SGKL
Stimme der Orthodoxie — SOrth
Stimme der Orthodoxie — Stimme D Orthodoxie
Stimmen aus Maria-Laach — SML
Stimmen der Zeit — Stimm Zeit
Stimmen der Zeit — Stimmen D Zeit
Stimmen der Zeit — STZED
Stimmen der Zeit — SZ
Stimmen des Orients — StO
Stimmwart — Stw
Stimulation Newsletter — Stimul Newsl
Stimulation Newsletter — STNLB
Stirling Engine Newsletter — Stirling E N
Stirring Science Stories — STS
Stizungsberichte der Kaiserlichen Akademie der Wissenschaften — SKAW
Stoberiet — Sto
Stochastic Modeling — Stochastic Model
Stochastic Modeling Series — Stochastic Model Ser
Stochastic Processes and Their Applications — Stoch Processes Appl
Stochastic Processes and Their Applications — Stochastic Processes Appl
Stochastic Processes and Their Applications — StocProc
Stochastics and Stochastics Reports — Stochastics Stochastics Rep
Stochastics Monographs — Stochastics Monogr
Stock Technical Analysis Reports [*Database*] — STAR
Stockholm Contributions in Geology — Stockh Contrib Geol
Stockholm Contributions in Geology — Stockholm Contrib Geol
Stockholm Papers in History and Philosophy of Technology — Stockholm Papers Hist Philos Tech
Stockholm Studies in Classical Archaeology — SSCA
Stockholm Studies in Comparative Religion — SSCR
Stockholm Studies in English Literature — SSEL
Stockholm Studies in Modern Philology — SSMP
Stockholm Studies in Russian Literature — SSRL
Stockholm Studies in Scandinavian Philology — SSSP
Stockholm. Tekniska Hogskolan. Avhandling — Stockholm Tek Hogsk Avh
Stockholm. Tekniska Hogskolan. Handlingar [*Transactions*] — Stockholm Tek Hogsk Handl
Stockholmer Germanistische Forschungen — SGF
Stockholms Historiska Bibliothek — Stockholms Hist Biblioth
Stoff- und Motivgeschichte der Deutschen Literatur — SMDL
Stoicorum Veterum Fragmenta — St VF
Stoicorum Veterum Fragmenta — SVF
Stomach and Intestine [*Japan*] — Stomach Intest
Stomach as an Endocrine Organ. Proceedings. Eric K. Fernstroem Symposium — Stomach Endocr Organ Proc Eric K Fernstroem Symp
Stomach Diseases. Current Status. Proceedings. International Congress on Stomach Diseases — Stomach Dis Curr Status Proc Int Congr
Stomatologia [*Bucharest*] — STMLA
Stomatologia Hungarica — Stomatol Hung
Stomatologia Mediterranea — Stomatol Mediterr
Stomatologica [*Genoa*] — STMTA
Stomatologicke Zpracy — Stomatol Zpr
Stomatologie der DDR [*Germany*] — Stomatol DDR
Stomatologiya — STMYA
Stomatologiya [*Moscow*] — STOAA
Stomatoloski Glasnik Srbije — SGLSA
Stomatoloski Glasnik Srbije — Stomatol Glas Srb
Stomatoloski Vjesnik [*Stomatological Review*] — Stomatol Vjesn
Stone Country — Stone C
Stone Drum — Stone D
Stone Industries — Stone Ind
Stony Hills — Stony
Stopanski Pregled — Stop Pregl
Storage, Handling and Distribution — Stor Hand Dist
Storage Handling Distribution — Storage Handl Distrib
Storefront Classroom — Storefront
Storia della Scienza — Storia Sci
Storia dell'Arte — SA
Storia dell'Arte — Stor Art
Storia dell'Arte — Stor Arte
Storia delle Letteratura di Tutto il Mondo — SLTM
Storia dell'Ebraismo in Italia. Sezione Toscana — Stor Ebr It
Storia e Critica della Psicologia — Stor Crit Psicol
Storia e Letteratura — SeL
Storia e Litteratura — SL
Storia e Litteratura — Storia e Lett
Storia e Politica — SPol
Storia e Politica — Storia e Polit
Storia e Politica Internazionale — Stor Polit Internaz
Storm — ST
Storm Data — SD
Stotz-Kontakt-Roemmler Nachrichten — Stotz-Kontakt-Roemmler Nachr
STP (Sciences Techniques et Pratiques Pharmaceutiques) Pharma Pratiques — STP Pharma Prat
Straalsaekerhetscentralen. Rapport STUK-A — Straalsaekerhetscent Rapp STUK A
Straalsaekerhetsinstitutet. Rapport STL-A — Straalsaekerhetsinst Rapp STL A
Strad — ST
Strad — Str
Strafprozessordnung [*German Democratic Republic*] — StPO
Strafvollstreckungsordnung — St VO
Strafvollstreckungsordnung — St Vollstr O
Strafwetboek — SW
Strahlenschutz in Forschung und Praxis — STFPA
Strahlenschutz in Forschung und Praxis [*Germany*] — Strahlenschutz Forsch Prax
Strahlenschutz Praxis — Strahlenschutz Prax
Strahlentherapie — STRAA
Strahlentherapie — Strahlenthe
Strahlentherapie. Sonderbaende — Strahlenther Sonderb
Strahlentherapie und Onkologie — STONE4
Strahlentherapie und Onkologie — Strahlenther Onkol
Strahltechnik. Vortraege und Posterbeitraege der Internationalen Konferenz Strahltechnik — Strahltech Vortr Posterbeitr Int Konf Strahltech
Straight Furrow — St Furrow
Strain — STRAB
Straits Times Annual [*Singapore*] — Straits Times A
Straits Times. Business Times — STBT
Stralsundisches Magazin, Oder Sammlungen Auserlesener Neuigkeiten, zur Aufnahme der Naturlehre, Arzneywissenschaft, und Haushaltungskunst — Stralsund Mag
Strand — St
Strand Magazine — STR M
Strand Magazine — Strand
Strand Magazine (London) — Strand (Lond)
Strand Magazine (New York) — Strand (NY)
Strange Adventures — STA
Strange Fantasy — STF
Strange Stories — SRS
Strange Tales of Mystery and Terror — STT
Strangest Stories Ever Told — SSE
Strannik: Dukhovnyi, Ucheno-Literaturnyi Zhurnal — St
Straphenverrkehrsgesetz — St VG
Strasbourg Medical — Strasb Med
Strassburger Post — StP
Strasse und Autobahn — Sr Autobahn
Strasse und Autobahn — St Autobahn
Strasse und Autobahn — Str Autobahn
Strasse und Verkehr — Str Verkehr
Strassen- und Tiefbau — Str Tiefbau
Strassen- und Tiefbau — STTBA
Strassenverkehrsordnung — St VO
Strassenverkehrstechnik — SVKTA
Strassenverkehrszulassungsordnung — St VZO
Strategic Analysis [*India*] — Strateg Anal
Strategic Digest — Strategic Dig
Strategic Management Journal — SMJ
Strategic Management Journal — Strateg Manage J
Strategic Planning and Energy Management — Strateg Plan Energy Manage
Strategic Review [*Washington, DC*] — Strat R
Strategic Review — Strat Rev
Strategic Review — Strategic R
Strategic Survey — Strat Svy
Strategies and Solutions — S&S
Strategies for Physical Mapping — Strategies Phys Mapp
Strategy and Tactics — S & T
Stratford Papers — Stratford Pap
Stratford Papers on Shakespeare — SPS
Stratford-On-Avon Herald — SAH
Strathclyde Bioengineering Seminars — Strathclyde Bioeng Semin
Strathclyde Education — Strathclyde Educ
Stratigraphie Comparee et Chronologie de l'Asie Occidentale — SC
Stray Feathers. Ornithological Journal — SF
Streffleurs Oesterreiche Militaerische Zeitschrift — SOMZ

Streffleurs Oesterreichische Militaerische Zeitschrift — SOeMZ
Strem Chemiker — Strem Chem
Strength and Conditioning — Strength & Con
Strength and Health — Streng and H
Strength of Materials [*English Translation*] — SMTLB
Strength of Materials — Strength Mater
Strength of Metals and Alloys. Proceedings. International Conference on Strength of Metals and Alloys — Strength Met Alloys Proc Int Conf
Strenna Bolognese — SBol
Strenna Storica Bolognese — SSB
Strenna Storica Bolognese — Strenna Stor Bolognese
Stress-Induced Phenomena in Metallization. International Workshop — Stress Induced Phenom Met Int Workshop
Strides of Medicine — Strides Med
String Education Quarterly — SEQ
Strings — Stri
Stroemungsmechanik und Stroemungsmaschinen — Stroemungsmech Stroemungsmasch
Stroenie i Fizicheskie Svoistva Veshchestva v Zhidkom Sostoyanii. Materialy Soveshchaniya — Str Fiz Svoistva Veshchestva Zhidk Sostoyanii Mater Soveshch
Stroenie, Svoistva, i Primenenie B (Beta)-Diketonatov Metallov. Materialy Vsesoyuznogo Seminara — Str Svoistva Primen Beta Diketonatov Met Mater Vses Semin
Stroezh i Funktsii na Mozuka — Stroezh Funkts Mozuka
Stroitel'naya Keramika — Stroit Keram
Stroitel'naya Mekhanika i Raschet Sooruzheniy — SMKRA
Stroitel'naya Mekhanika i Raschet Sooruzheniy [*Former USSR*] — Stroit Mekh Raschet Sooruz
Stroitel'naya Promyshlennost — Stroit Promst
Stroitelni Materiali i Silikatna Promishlenost [*Bulgaria*] — Stroit Mater Silik Prom-St
Stroitel'nye Alyuminievye Konstruktsii — Stroit Alyum Konstr
Stroitel'nye i Dorozhnye Mashiny — SDMAA
Stroitel'nye i Dorozhnye Mashiny — Stroit Dorozhn Mash
Stroitel'nye Konstruktsii — Stroit Konstr
Stroitel'nye Konstruktsii iz Alyuminievkh Splavov — Stroit Konstr Alyum Splavov
Stroitel'nye Materialy — Stroit Mater
Stroitel'nye Materialy (1929-32) — Stroit Mater (1929-32)
Stroitel'nye Materialy (1932-38) — Stroit Mater (1933-38)
Stroitel'nye Materialy. Detali i Izdeliya — Stroit Mater Detali Izdeliya
Stroitel'nye Materialy i Betony — Stroit Mater Betony
Stroitel'nye Materialy i Ikh Proizvodstvo — Stroit Mater Ikh Proizvod
Stroitel'nye Materialy i Konstruktsii — Stroit Mater Konstr
Stroitel'nye Materialy. Izdeliya i Konstruktsii — Stroit Mater Izdeliya Konstr
Stroitel'nye Materialy. Izdeliya i Sanitarnaya Tekhnika — Stroit Mater Izdeliya Sanit Tekh
Stroitel'stvo Dorog — Stroit Dorog
Stroitel'stvo i Arkhitektura — Stroit Arkhit
Stroitel'stvo i Arkhitektura Leningrada — Stroit Arkhit Leningrada
Stroitel'stvo i Arkhitektura Srednei Azii — Stroit Arkhit Sredn Azii
Stroitel'stvo i Arkhitektura Uzbekistana — SAUZA
Stroitel'stvo i Arkhitektura Uzbekistana — Stroit Arkhit Uzb
Stroitel'stvo Predpriyatii Neftyanoi Promyshlennosti — Stroit Predpr Neft Promsti
Stroitel'stvo Truboprovodov [*Former USSR*] — Stroit Truboprovodov
Stroitel'stvo Truboprovodov — STTRA
Strojirenska Vyroba — Strojir Vyroba
Strojirenstvi — STRJA
Strojnicky Casopis — STJCA
Strojnicky Casopis [*Czechoslovakia*] — Strojnicky Cas
Strojniski Vestnik — STJVA
Strojniski Vestnik — Stroj Vest
Strojniski Vestnik — Strojniski Vestn
Stroke — SJCCA
Stroke. Supplement — Stroke Suppl
Stromata — SUS
Strompraxis — Stromprax
Strucna Izdanja JUGOMA [*Jugoslavensko Drustvo za Primjenu Goriva i Maziva*] — Strucna Izd JUGOMA
Strucna Izdanja Jugoslavenskog Drustvo za Primjenu Goriva i Maziva — Strucna Izd Jugosl Drus Primjenu Goriva Maziva
Structura i Svoistva Tverdykh Tel — Strukt Svoistva Tverd Tel
Structural Analysis — Struct Anal
Structural and Phase Stability of Alloys — Struct Phase Stab Alloys
Structural Change in the United States Automobile Industry — US Auto Ind
Structural Chemistry — Struct Chem
Structural Concrete — Struct Concr
Structural Engineer — SRUEA
Structural Engineer — Struct Eng
Structural Engineer — Struct Engr
Structural Engineer. Parts A and B — Struct Engnr
Structural Engineering Practice. Analysis, Design, Management — Struct Eng Pract Anal Des Man
Structural Foam Conference. Proceedings — Struct Foam Conf Proc
Structural Mechanics in Reactor Technology — Struct Mech React Technol
Structural Mechanics of Optical Systems — Struct Mech Opt Syst
Structural Safety — Struct Saf
Structural Survey — Struct Surv
Structuralist Review — Struc Rev
Structuralist Review — Struct Rev
Structure and Bonding [*Berlin*] — STBGA
Structure and Bonding — Struct Bonding
Structure and Bonding (Berlin) — Struct Bonding Berlin
Structure and Chemistry. Part B — Struct Chem Part B
Structure and Function. Proceedings. Conversation in the Discipline Biomolecular Stereodynamics — Struct Funct Proc Conversation Discip Biomol Stereodyn
Structure and Functions of the Brain — Struct Funct Brain
Structure and Growth of Philosophic Systems from Plato to Spinoza — SGPS
Structure and Nomenclature Search System [*Database*] — SANSS
Structure Energetics and Reactivity in Chemistry Series — Struct Energ React Chem Ser
Structure of Antigens [*monograph*] — Struct Antigens
Structure of Biological Membranes — Struct Biol Membr
Structure of Glass — Struct Glass
Structure Reports — Struct Rep
Structures Report. Department of Architectural Science. University of Sydney — Struct Rep Dep Archit Sci Syd Univ
Struktura i Funktsiya Fermentov — Strukt Funkts Fermentov
Struktura i Modifikatsiya Khlopkovoi Tsellyulozy — Strukt Modif Khlopk Tsellyul
Struktura i Rol Vody v Zhivom Organizme — Strukt Rol Vody Zhivom Org
Struktura i Svoistva Kristallov — Strukt Svoistva Krist
Struktura i Svoistva Litykh Splavov — Strukt Svoistva Litykh Splavov
Struktura Organicheskikh Soedinenii i Mekhanizmy Reaktsii — Strukt Org Soedin Mekh Reakts
Strukturen Christlicher Existenz — SCE
Strukturnaja i Matematiceskaja Lingvistika — Strukturn i Mat Lingvistika
Strumenti Critici — S Cr
Strumenti Critici — Strum Crit
Strumenti per una Nuova Cultura. Guida e Manuali — Strum una Nuova Cultur Guida e Manual
Stsintillyatory i Organicheskie Lyuminofory — Stsintill Org Lyuminofory
Stsintillyatory i Stsintillyatsionnye Materialy. Materialy Koordinatsionnogo Soveshchaniya po Stsintillyatoram — Stsintill Stsintill Mater Mater Koord Soveshch
STTH. Science, Technology and the Humanities — STTH Sci Technol Hum
Studencheskie Nauchn'ie Rabot'i Kazakhskogo Un-Ta — SNRK
Studencheskie Nauchno-Issledovatel'skie Raboty. Sibirskii Tekhnologicheskii Institut — Stud Nauchno Issled Rab Sib Tekhnol Inst
Studencheskie Nauchnye Raboty. Novocherkasskii Politekhnicheskii Institut — Stud Nauchn Rab Novocherk Politekh Inst
Studencheskie Nauchnye Raboty. Universitet Druzhby Narodov — Stud Nauchn Rab Univ Druzhby Nar
Studencheskie Uchenye Zapiski. Erevanskii Gosudarstvennyi Universitet — Stud Uch Zap Erevan Gos Univ
Student Advocate — Student Adv
Student and Intellectual Observer — Stud & Intel Obs
Student and Intellectual Observer — Stud Intell Obs
Student Lawyer — St L
Student Lawyer — Student Law
Student Medicine — Stud Med
Student Monographs in Physics — Stud Monographs Phys
Student Musicologists at Minnesota — Student Musicol
Student Pharmacist — Stud Pharm
Student Services Review — Stud Serv Rev
Student und Jugendzahnarzt — Stud Jugendzahn A
Student Voice — SUVO
Student World — Stud W
Studente Veterinario — Studente Vet
Studentische Rundschau — Stud Rsch
Students' Journal. Institution of Electronics and Telecommunication Engineers — Stud J Inst Electron and Telecommun Eng
Students' Journal. Institution of Electronics and Telecommunication Engineers — Stud J Inst Electron Telecommun Eng
Students Quarterly Journal. Institution of Electrical Engineers [*England*] — Stud Q J Inst Electr Eng
Students Quarterly Journal. Institution of Electrical Engineers — Stud QJ Inst El Eng
Students'ki Naukovi Pratsi Kiivs'kii Derzhavnii Universitet — Stud Nauk Pr Kiiv Derzh Univ
Students'ki Naukovi Roboty. Kiivs'kii Derzhavnii Universitet — Stud Nauk Rob Kiiv Derzh Univ
Students'ky Naukovi Pratsi Kyyivs'kyyi Derzhavnyyi Unyversytet — Students'ky Nauk Pratsi Kyyv Derzh Unyv
Studi Americani [*Roma*] — SA
Studi Americani — Studi Am
Studi Anselmiana — StA
Studi Baltici — SB
Studi Baltici — Studi Balt
Studi Baltici. N.S. Rom — Studi Balt NS
Studi Bizantini — SB
Studi Bizantini — SBiz
Studi Bizantini e Neoellenici — SBN
Studi Bizantini e Neoellenici — StBiz
Studi Bizantini e Neoellenici — Studi Bizant Neoell
Studi Cattolici — St Catt
Studi Classici e Orientali — SCO
Studi Classici e Orientali — StClOr
Studi Classici e Orientali — Stud Cl Orient
Studi Classici e Orientali — Stud Classe Or
Studi Classici e Orientali — Studi Cl Orient
Studi Classici e Orientali — Studi Classe Orient
Studi Colombiani — SC
Studi Colombiani. Publicazioni del Civico Istituto Colombiano — Stud Colombiani
Studi Copti — St Copt
Studi Danteschi — SD
Studi Danteschi — StD
Studi de Medicina e Chirurgia dello Sport — Studi Med Chir Sport

Studi d'Economia — Studi Econ
Studi della Scuola Papirologica — SSP
Studi delle Scienze Giuridiche e Sociali — Stud Sci Giur Soc
Studi di Antichita Christiana — SAC
Studi di Antichita Cristiana — StAC
Studi di Antichita Cristiana — Stud Christ
Studi di Economia (Cagliari) — Studi Econ (Cagliari)
Studi di Filogia Italiana — SFI
Studi di Filologia Moderna — St di Filol Mod
Studi di Filologia Moderna — Studi Filol Mod
Studi di Filologia Todeska — SFT
Studi di Grammatica Italiana — SGI
Studi di Grammatica Italiana — St Gr I
Studi di Letteratura Francese — StLF
Studi di Letteratura Ispano-Americana — StLI
Studi di Litteratura Ispano-Americana — SLI
Studi di Medicina e Chirurgia dello Sport — Stud Med Chir Sport
Studi di Sociologia — Stud Sociol
Studi di Sociologia — Studi Sociol
Studi e Documenti di Storia e Diritto — SD
Studi e Documenti di Storia e Diritto — SDSD
Studi e Documenti di Storia e Diritto — Ste Doc di Stor e di Diritto
Studi e Documenti per la Storia del Palazzo Apostolico Vaticano — SSPAV
Studi e Materiali de Storia delle Religioni — St e Mat Stor Rel
Studi e Materiali de Storia delle Religioni — St Mater Stor Relig
Studi e Materiali de Storia delle Religioni — Studi Mat St Religioni
Studi e Materiali di Archeologia e Numismatica — SMAN
Studi e Materiali di Archeologia e Numismatica — St Mat An
Studi e Materiali di Archeologia e Numismatica — Studi Materiali di Arche Num
Studi e Materiali di Storia della Religioni — SMSR
Studi e Materiali di Storia della Religioni — SSR
Studi e Materiali di Storia della Religioni — St e Mat
Studi e Materiali di Storia della Religioni — Stud Mat Stor Rel
Studi e Materiali di Storia delle Religioni — StM
Studi e Materiali di Storia delle Religioni [*Rome/Bologna*] — StMSR
Studi e Problemi di Critica Testuale — SPCT
Studi e Problemi di Critica Testuale — Stud Pr Cr
Studi e Ricerche — SeR
Studi e Ricerche. Divisione Geomineraria. Comitato Nazionale per le Ricerche Nucleari — Stud Ric Div Geomineraria Com Naz Ric Nucl
Studi e Ricerche. Divisione Geomineraria. Comitato Nazionale per le Ricerche Nucleari — Studi Ric Div Geomineraria Com Naz Ric Nucl
Studi e Ricerche. Istituto di Latino. Universita di Genova — St Ric Lat
Studi e Ricerche. Istituto di Mineralogia e Petrografia. Universita di Pavia — Stud Ric Ist Mineral Petrogr Univ Pavia
Studi e Ricerche. Istituto di Mineralogia e Petrografia. Universita di Pavia — Studi Ric Ist Mineral Petrogr Univ Pavia
Studi e Richerche. Istituto di Latino — SRIL
Studi e Saggi Linguistici — SeSL
Studi e Saggi Linguistici — SSL
Studi e Testi [*Rome*] — SeT
Studi e Testi — ST
Studi e Testi. Biblioteca Apostolica Vaticana — ST
Studi e Testi. Biblioteca Apostolica Vaticana — St T
Studi e Testi. Biblioteca Apostolica Vaticana — Stud Test
Studi e Testi Francescani — STF
Studi Eblaiti — St Ebla
Studi Economici — Stud Econ
Studi Economici (Naples) — Studi Econ (Naples)
Studi Emigrazione — Stud Emigr
Studi Emigrazione — Studi Emigr
Studi Etruschi — SE
Studi Etruschi — SEt
Studi Etruschi — StE
Studi Etruschi — StEtr
Studi Etruschi — Stud Etr
Studi Filosofici — St Fil
Studi Francescani — SFran
Studi Francescani — StFr
Studi Francescani. Firenze. Biblioteca — St Fr B
Studi Francesi — S Fr
Studi Francesi — SF
Studi Francesi — Stud Fran
Studi Francesi — Stud Francesi
Studi Francesi — Studi Franc
Studi Francesi. Torino — St Fr T
Studi Genuensi — SG
Studi Genuensi — St Genuensi
Studi Germanici — SG
Studi Germanici — StG
Studi Goldoniani — SGoldoniani
Studi Goriziani — SG
Studi Goriziani — SGo
Studi Goriziani — SGor
Studi Gregoriani per la Storia di Gregorio VII — SGSG
Studi Internazionali di Filosofia — SIF
Studi Ispanici — SIs
Studi Ispanici — StI
Studi Ispanici — StIsp
Studi. Istituto Linguistico — StIL
Studi Italiana di Filologia Classica — Stud Ital Filol Class
Studi Italiani — StI
Studi Italiani di Filologia Classica — SIFC
Studi Italiani di Filologia Classica — St Fil Cl
Studi Italiani di Filologia Classica — St It
Studi Italiani di Filologia Classica — St It Fil
Studi Italiani di Filologia Classica — St Ital
Studi Italiani di Filologia Classica — StIF
Studi Italiani di Filologia Classica — Stud It
Studi Italiani di Filologia Classica — Studi Ital di Fil Cl
Studi Italiani di Filologia Classica — Studi Ital Filol Cl
Studi Italiani di Filologia Classica [*Florence*] — StudiItalFilol Class
Studi Italiani di Linguistica Teorica ed Applicata — SILTA
Studi Italici [*Kyoto*] — StIt
Studi Italici (Kyoto) — SIK
Studi Linguistici Friulani — Stud Ling Friul
Studi Linguistici Italiani — SLI
Studi Magrebini — St Magreb
Studi Magrebini — Stud Mag
Studi Magrebini — Stud Magr
Studi Medievali — SM
Studi Medievali — SMe
Studi Medievali — SMed
Studi Medievali — St Med
Studi Medievali [*Spoleto*] — StM
Studi Medievali — Stud Mediev
Studi Medievali — Stud Medievali
Studi Medievali — Studi Med
Studi Medievali — Studi Mediev
Studi Mediolatini e Volgari — SMLV
Studi Mediolatini e Volgari — SMV
Studi Micenei ed Egeo-Anatolici — SMEA
Studi Miscellanei. Seminario di Archeologia e Storia dell'Arte Greca e Romana — St Misc Rom
Studi Miscellanei, Seminario di Archeologia e Storia dell'Arte Greca e Romana dell'Universita di Roma — St Misc
Studi Musicali — Studi M
Studi Musicali — Studi Mus
Studi nelle Scienze Giuridiche e Sociali (Pavia) — Stud (Pavia)
Studi Novecenteschi — S Nov
Studi Petrarcheschi — SPetr
Studi Petrarcheschi — StP
Studi Religiosi — StR
Studi Religiosi (Roma) — SRR
Studi Romagnoli — SR
Studi Romagnoli — St Romagnoli
Studi Romagnoli — StR
Studi Romagnoli — Stud Romagn
Studi Romani [*Rome*] — SRo
Studi Romani [*Rome*] — SRom
Studi Romani — St Rom
Studi Romani [*Rome*] — StRo
Studi Romani [*Rome*] — StudRom
Studi Romani. Istituto di Studi Romani — SR
Studi Romani. Istituto di Studi Romani — SSR
Studi Romani. Istituto di Studi Romani — St Romani
Studi Romanzi [*Padua*] — StudRom
Studi Rumeni [*Rome*] — SRu
Studi Salentini — St Salent
Studi Salentini — StSa
Studi Salentini — StudSal
Studi Sardi — S Sard
Studi Sardi — SS
Studi Sardi — SSar
Studi Sardi — St Sar
Studi Sardi — St Sard
Studi Sardi — StudSard
Studi Sassaresi — Studi Sassar
Studi Sassaresi. Sezione 1 — Stud Sassar Sez 1
Studi Sassaresi. Sezione 1 — Studi Sassar Sez 1
Studi Sassaresi. Sezione 2. Archivio Bimestrale di Scienze Mediche e Naturali — SSSEAK
Studi Sassaresi. Sezione 2. Archivio Bimestrale di Scienze Mediche e Naturali — Studi Sassar Sez 2
Studi Sassaresi. Sezione 2. Archivio Bimestrale di Scienze Mediche e Naturali — Studi Sassaresi Sez 2 Arch Bimest Sci Med Nat
Studi Sassaresi. Sezione 3. Annali della Facolta di Agraria dell Universita di Sassari — Studi Sassar Sez 3
Studi Sassaresi. Sezione 3. Annali della Facolta di Agraria dell'Universita di Sassari — SSAAAK
Studi Sassaresi. Sezione 3. Annali. Facolta di Agraria. Universita di Sassari — Studi Sassar Sez 3
Studi Sassaresi. Sezione III. Annali. Facolta di Agraria. Universita di Sassari — Studi Sassar Sez III Ann Fac Agrar Univ Sassari
Studi Secenteschi — SSe
Studi Secenteschi — StSec
Studi Secenteschi — Stud Secent
Studi Semitici — SS
Studi Semitici — StSem
Studi si Cercetari de Numismatica — St C Num
Studi Storici — SS
Studi Storici — St
Studi Storici — Stud Stor
Studi Storici — Stud Storic
Studi Storici dell'Ordine dei Servi de Maria — SSOSM
Studi Storici Instituto Gramisci Editor — Studi Stor
Studi Storici per l'Antichita Classica — SSAC
Studi Storici per l'Antichita Classica — SSACl
Studi Storici per l'Antichita Classica — St St A
Studi Storici per l'Antichita Classica — Stud Stor

Studi Storici per l'Antichita Classica — Studi Stor
Studi Storico-Religioso — St Stor Rel
Studi sul Boccaccio — SBoc
Studi sul Boccaccio — StB
Studi sulla Tradizione Aristotelica nel Veneto — STAV
Studi Tassiani — ST
Studi Tassiani — StT
Studi Trentini — STr
Studi Trentini. Classe 2. Scienze Naturali ed Economiche — Studi Trentini Cl 2
Studi Trentini di Scienze Naturali — Studi Trentini Sci Nat
Studi Trentini di Scienze Naturali. Acta Biologica — STSBDL
Studi Trentini di Scienze Naturali. Acta Biologica — Studi Trentini Sci Nat Acta Biol
Studi Trentini di Scienze Naturali. Acta Geologica — STSGD2
Studi Trentini di Scienze Naturali. Acta Geologica — Studi Trentini Sci Nat Acta Geol
Studi Trentini di Scienze Naturali. Sezione A. Biologica — Studi Trentini Sci Nat Sez A
Studi Trentini di Scienze Naturali. Sezione B. Biologica — Studi Trentini Sci Nat Sez B Biol
Studi Trentini di Scienze Storiche — STr
Studi Trentini di Scienze Storiche — STSS
Studi Trentini di Scienze Storiche — Stud Trent
Studi Urbinati — St Urbin
Studi Urbinati — SU
Studi Urbinati di Scienze Giuridiche ed Economiche (Ser. A) — Stud Urb (Ser A)
Studi Urbinati di Storia, Filosofia, e Letteratura — Stud Urb
Studi Urbinati di Storia, Filosofia, e Letteratura — Stud Urb St
Studi Urbinati di Storia, Filosofia, e Letteratura — SUS
Studi Urbinati di Storia, Filosofia, e Letteratura — SUSFL
Studi Urbinati di Storia, Filosofia, e Letteratura. Nuova Serie B — Studi Urbinati NSB
Studi Urbinati. Facolta di Farmacia — Studi Urbinati Fac Farm
Studi Veneziani — Stud Ven
Studi Veneziani — Stud Venez
Studi Veneziani — Stud Veneziani
Studia [*Portugal*] — Std
Studia — Stu
Studia Academica Slovaca — SAS
Studia ad Corpus Hellenisticum Novi Testamenti — SCHNT
Studia ad Tabulas Cuneiformes Collectas a de Liagre Boehl Pertinentia — SLB
Studia Aegyptiaca — St Aeg
Studia Aegyptiaca [*Rome*] — StudAeg
Studia Albanica — SA
Studia Albanica — SALB
Studia Albanica — Stud Alb
Studia Albanica — Studia Alban
Studia Anglica Posnaniensia — SAP
Studia Anselmiana — SAns
Studia Anselmiana — St Ans
Studia Antoniana — St Ant
Studia Arabica — St Arab
Studia Archaeologica — St A
Studia Archaeologica [*Budapest*] — StA
Studia Archaeologica [*Budapest*] — Stud Arch
Studia Archaeologica [*Rome*] — Stud Arch
Studia Aristotelica — St Arist
Studia Balcanica — S Balc
Studia Balcanica — Stud Bal
Studia Biblica et Orientalia — SBO
Studia Biblica et Theologica [*New Haven, CT*] — StudBT
Studia Biologica. Academiae Scientiarum Hungaricae — Stud Biol Acad Sci Hung
Studia Biologica Hungarica — Stud Biol Hung
Studia Biophysica — St Biophys
Studia Biophysica — STBIB
Studia Biophysica — Stud Biophy
Studia Biophysica — Stud Biophys
Studia Botanica — Stud Bot
Studia Botanica Cechoslavaca — Stud Bot Cech
Studia Botanica Hungarica — Stud Bot Hung
Studia Canonica — Stud Can
Studia Canonica — Studia Can
Studia Cartesiana — St Cart
Studia Cartesiana — Stud Cartesiana
Studia Catholica — SC
Studia Catholica — SCathol
Studia Catholica — StC
Studia Catholica — StudCath
Studia Caucasia — Stud Caucasia
Studia Caucasica — SCauc
Studia Caucasica — StCau
Studia Celtica — SC
Studia Celtica — StC
Studia Celtica — Stud Celt
Studia Celtica Japonica — S C Jap
Studia Chemica. Universidad de Salamanca — Stud Chem Univ Salamanca
Studia Citrologica. Kankitsu Kenkyu. Tanaka Citrus Experiment Station — Stud Citrol
Studia Classica et Orientalia — St Class Or
Studia Comitatensia. Tanulmanyok Pest Magye Muzeumalbad — Stu Co
Studia Comitatensia. Tanulmanyok Pest Magye Muzeumalbad — Stud Com Pest
Studia Delitschiana — SD
Studia Delitzschiana — St Del
Studia Demograficzne — St Dem
Studia Demograficzne — Stud Demogr
Studia di Filologia Italiana — Stud Filol Ital
Studia Diplomatica [*Brussels*] — Stud Dipl
Studia Diplomatica — Stud Diplom
Studia Diplomatica. Institut Royal des Relations Internationales [*Bruxelles*] — IRRI/SD
Studia Doctrinae Christianae Upsaliensia — SDCU
Studia Entomologica — Stud Entomol
Studia Entomologica — Studia Ent
Studia Estetyczne — SE
Studia et Acta Ecclesiastica — SAE
Studia et Acta Orientalia — SAO
Studia et Acta Orientalia — Stud Acta Orient
Studia et Acta Orientalia — StudActOr
Studia et Documenta ad Iura Orientis — SDIO
Studia et Documenta ad Iura Orientis Antiqui Pertinenta — SDIOA
Studia et Documenta ad Iura Orientis Antiqui Pertinenta — SDIOAP
Studia et Documenta ad Iura Orientis Antiqui Pertinentia — SD
Studia et Documenta ad Iura Orientis Antiqui Pertinentia — Stud et Doca Iura Or Ant Pert
Studia et Documenta Franciscana — SDF
Studia et Documenta Historiae et Iuris — SDHI
Studia et Documenta Historiae et Iuris — St Doc
Studia et Documenta Historiae et Iuris — St Doc Hist Iur
Studia et Documenta Historiae et Iuris — Stud Doc Hist et Iuris
Studia et Documenta Historiae et Iuris — Stud Doc Hist Iur
Studia et Documenta Historiae et Juris — Stud & Doc His Jur
Studia et Documenta Orientalia — SDO
Studia et Textus Historiae Juris Canonici — STHJC
Studia Evangelica — SE
Studia Evangelica [*Berlin*] — StEv
Studia Fennica — SF
Studia Fennica — SFen
Studia Fennica — Stud Fenn
Studia Filozoficzne — SF
Studia Filozoficzne — StFil
Studia Finansowe — Stud Finans
Studia Forestalia Suecica — SFSUA
Studia Forestalia Suecica — Stud For Suec
Studia Forestalia Suecica — Studia For Suec
Studia Forestalia Suecica — Studia Forest Suecica
Studia Forestalia Suecica (Skogshogskolan) — Stud For Suec (Skogshogsk)
Studia Francisci Scholten Memoriae Dicata — SFSMD
Studia Friburgensia — SF
Studia Geographica. Ceskoslovenska Akademie Ved. Geograficky Ustav (Brno) — Stud Geogr Cesk Akad Ved Geogr Ustav (Brno)
Studia Geologica Polonica — Stud Geol Pol
Studia Geologica. Universidad de Salamanca — Stud Geol Salamanca
Studia Geologica. Universidad de Salamanca — Stud Geol Univ Salamanca
Studia Geomorphologica Carpatho-Balcanica — Stud Geomorphol Carpatho-Balcanica
Studia Geophysica et Geodaetica — SGEGA
Studia Geophysica et Geodaetica — Stud Geoph
Studia Geophysica et Geodaetica — Stud Geophys Geod
Studia Geophysica et Geodaetica (Ceskosloven-Akademie Ved) — Stud Geophys Geod (Cesk Akad Ved)
Studia Geotechnica et Mechanica — Stud Geotech Mech
Studia Geotechnica et Mechanica — Studia Geotech Mech
Studia Geotechnica. Politechnika Wroclawaka — Stud Geotech
Studia Germanica — SGer
Studia Germanica Gandensia — SGG
Studia Germanistica Upsaliensia — SGU
Studia Ghisleriana [*Pavia*] — SGh
Studia Ghisleriana — St Ghis
Studia Ghisleriana. Studi Letterari-Filosofici-Historici — St Ghis LFH
Studia Graeca Upsaliensia — SGU
Studia Grammatica — Stgr
Studia Gratiana — St Gra
Studia Hellenistica — SH
Studia Hellenistica — St Hell
Studia Helminthologica — Stud Helminthol
Studia Hibernica [*Dublin*] — SH
Studia Hibernica — SHib
Studia Hibernica — St Hib
Studia Hibernica — Stud Hib
Studia Historica Academiae Scientiarum Hungaricae — SHH
Studia Historica. Acta Societatis Historiae Oulouensis — S Hist
Studia Historico-Ecclesiastica — SHE
Studia Historico-Ecclesiastica Upsaliensia — SHEU
Studia i Materialy Oceanologiczne. Polska Akademia Nauk. Komitet Badan Morza — Stud Mater Oceanol Pol Akad Nauk Kom Badan Morza
Studia i Materialy z Dziejow Nauki Polskiej. Seria A. Historia Nauk Spolecznych — Stud Mater Dziej Nauk Pol Ser A
Studia i Materialy z Dziejow Nauki Polskiej. Seria B. Historia Nauk Biologicznych i Medycznych — Stud Mater Dziej Nauk Pol Ser B
Studia i Materialy z Dziejow Nauki Polskiej. Seria C. Historia Nauk Matematycznych, Fizykochemicznych i Geoloiczno-geograficznych — Stud Mater Dziej Nauk Pol Ser C
Studia i Materialy z Dziejow Nauki Polskiej. Seria D. Historia Techniki i Nauk Technicznych — Stud Mater Dziej Nauk Pol Ser D
Studia i Materialy z Dziejow Nauki Polskiej. Seria D. Historia Techniki i Nauk Technicznych — Stud Mater Dziejow Nauki Pol Ser D
Studia i Materialy z Dziejow Nauki Polskiej. Seria E. Zagadnienia Ogolne — Stud Mater Dziej Nauk Pol Ser E

Studia in Veteris Testamenti Pseudepigrapha — SVTP
Studia Instituti Anthropos — SIA
Studia Instituti Missiologici — SIM
Studia Iranica — Studia I
Studia Islamica — SI
Studia Islamica — SIsl
Studia Islamica [*Paris*] — StIslam
Studia Islamica — Stud Islam
Studia Islamica — Stud Islamica
Studia Islandica — StI
Studia Islandica — StIsl
Studia Judaica — SJ
Studia Judaica. Forschungen zur Wissenschaft des Judentums [*Berlin*] — StJud
Studia Laboris et Salutis — Stud Laboris Salutis
Studia Latina Stockholmiensia — SLS
Studia Latina Upsaliensia — SLatU
Studia Leibnitiana — Stud Leibn
Studia Leibnitiana — Stud Leibnit
Studia Leibnitiana — Stud Leibnitiana
Studia Leibnitiana. Supplementa — Studia Leibnitiana Suppl
Studia Linguistica [*Lund*] — SL
Studia Linguistica — StL
Studia Linguistica — StLi
Studia Linguistica — Stud Ling
Studia Linguistica et Philologica — St L P
Studia Linguistica Germanica — SLG
Studia Litteraria (University of Debrecen) — SLD
Studia Liturgica — St Lit
Studia Liturgica — Stud Lit
Studia Liturgica — Stud Liturg
Studia Logica — StLo
Studia Logica — StLog
Studia Logica — Stud Log
Studia Marina Sinica — Stud Mar Sin
Studia Mathematica — SMATA
Studia Mathematica — Stud Math
Studia Mathematica — Studia Math
Studia Mathematica/Mathematische Lehrbuecher — Studia Math/Math Lehrbuecher
Studia Mathematica/Mathematische Lehrbuecher. Taschenbuch — Studia Math/Math Lehrbuecher Taschenbuch
Studia Medica Szegedinensia — Stud Med Szeged
Studia Medica Szegedinensia — Stud Med Szegedinensia
Studia Mediewistyczne — StMed
Studia Mediewistyczne — Stud Mediew
Studia Microbiologica — Stud Microbiol
Studia Missionalia — SMiss
Studia Missionalia — St Mis
Studia Missionalia — Stud Miss
Studia Missionalia — Studia M
Studia Missionalia — Studia Mission
Studia Missionalia Upsaliensia — SMU
Studia Monastica — SMon
Studia Monastica — StM
Studia Monastica — StMon
Studia Monastica — Stu Mon
Studia Monastica — StudMon
Studia Montis Regii — SMR
Studia Musicologica [*Budapest*] — SMus
Studia Musicologica — Stud Musicol
Studia Musicologica — Studia Mus
Studia Musicologica. Academiae Scientiarum Hungaricae — S M
Studia Musicologica Norvegica — SMN
Studia Musicologica Norvegica — Stud Musicol Norvegica
Studia Musicologica Norvegica — Studia Mus Nor
Studia Mystica — SMy
Studia Mystica — St Myst
Studia Mystica — Stud Myst
Studia Nauk Politycznych — Stud Nauk Polit
Studia Neophilologica — SN
Studia Neophilologica — SNP
Studia Neophilologica — SNPh
Studia Neophilologica — St Neophil
Studia Neophilologica — Stud Neoph
Studia Neophilologica — Stud Neophilol
Studia Neophilologica — Studia Neophil
Studia Neotestamentica [*Paris/Bruges*] — StN
Studia Neotestamentica [*Paris/Bruges*] — StudNeot
Studia Oliveriana — SO
Studia Oliveriana — SOliv
Studia Oliveriana — St Oliv
Studia Oliveriana — StO
Studia Onomastica Monacensia — Stud Onomast Monacensia
Studia Onomastica Monacensia — SOnoM
Studia Orientalia — S Or
Studia Orientalia — SO
Studia Orientalia — St Or
Studia Orientalia [*Helsinki*] — Stud Orient
Studia Orientalia [*Helsinki*] — StudOr
Studia Orientalia Christiana — SOC
Studia Orientalia Christiana. Aegyptiaca — SOCAe
Studia Orientalia Christiana. Aegyptiaca. Documenti — SOCD
Studia Orientalia Christiana. Collectanea — SOC Coll
Studia Orientalia Christiana. Collectanea — SOCC
Studia Orientalia Christiana. Collectanea [*Cairo*] — StOrChrColl
Studia Orientalia. Edidit Societas Orientalis Fennica [*Helsinki*] — StOr
Studia Palmyrenskie — St Pal
Studia Palmyrenskie [*Warsaw*] — StP
Studia Papyrologica — SP
Studia Papyrologica — SPap
Studia Papyrologica [*Barcelona*] — StPapyr
Studia Papyrologica — Stud Papyrol
Studia Papyrologica — StudPap
Studia Pastristica et Liturgica — SPLi
Studia Patavina — SPat
Studia Patavina — Stu Pat
Studia Patavina. Rivista di Scienze Religiose — Stud Pat
Studia Patristica — SP
Studia Patristica — StP
Studia Patristica — StPa
Studia Patristica [*Berlin-Ost*] — StPatrist
Studia Patristica — Stud Patr
Studia Patristica et Byzantina — SPB
Studia Patristica et Byzantina — St PB
Studia Philologiae Scandinavicae Upsaliensia — SPSU
Studia Philologica Salmanticensia — S Ph S
Studia Philonica — St Philon
Studia Philosophiae Christianae — SPC
Studia Philosophiae Christiane — Stud Phil Christ
Studia Philosophica [*Basel*] — St Phil
Studia Philosophica — Stud Phil
Studia Philosophica Gandensia — SPG
Studia Philosophica (Switzerland) — Stud Phil (Switzerland)
Studia Phonetica — Stud Phonet
Studia Phonologica [*Kyoto*] — SPhon
Studia Phonologica — Stud Phonol
Studia Picena — S Picen
Studia Picena — Stud Pic
Studia Picena — Stud Picena
Studia Pneumologica et Phtiseologica Cechoslovaca — Stud Pneumol Phtiseol Cech
Studia Pohl. Pontificio Istituto Biblico — St Pohl
Studia Pontica — Stud Pont
Studia Post-Biblica [*Leiden*] — SPB
Studia Post-Biblica — StPB
Studia Prawno-Ekonomiczne — Stud Prawno-Ekon
Studia Psychologica — STPSA
Studia Psychologica — Stud Psych
Studia Psychologica [*Bratislava*] — Stud Psycho
Studia Psychologica (Bratislava) — Stud Psychol (Bratisl)
Studia Psychologiczne — Stud Psychol
Studia. Revista. Universidad del Atlantico. (Barranquilla, Colombia) — Stud Rev Univ Atl (Barranquilla Colomb)
Studia Romanica — StR
Studia Romanica — StRom
Studia Romanica et Anglica Zagrabiensia — SRAZ
Studia Romanica et Anglica Zagrabiensia — SRetA
Studia Romanica et Linguistica — SRLing
Studia Romanica Zagrabiensia — SRZ
Studia Rosenthaliana [*Assen*] — SR
Studia Rosenthaliana — Stu Ros
Studia Rossica Posnaniensia — SRP
Studia Scientiarum Mathematicarum Hungarica — SSMHA
Studia Scientiarum Mathematicarum Hungarica [*Hungary*] — Stud Sci Math Hung
Studia Scientiarum Mathematicarum Hungarica — Studia Sci Math Hungar
Studia Semitica et Orientalia — SSO
Studia Semitica Neerlandica [*Assen*] — SSN
Studia Semitica Neerlandica — St Sem
Studia Semitica Neerlandica [*Assen*] — StSemNeerl
Studia Semitica Neerlandica [*Assen*] — StudSemNeerl
Studia Semitica Upsaliensia — SSU
Studia Septentrionalia — SSept
Studia Serdicensia — SS
Studia. Series Mathematica — Studia Ser Math
Studia Slavica — StS
Studia Slavica — StSl
Studia Slavica — Stu Sl
Studia Slavica. Academiae Scientiarum Hungaricae — SSASH
Studia Slavica. Academiae Scientiarum Hungaricae — SSH
Studia Slavica. Academiae Scientiarum Hungaricae — SSlav
Studia Slavica Upsaliensia — SSIU
Studia Societatis Scientiarum Torunensis. Sectio A. Mathematica-Physica — Stud Soc Sci Torun Sect A
Studia Societatis Scientiarum Torunensis. Sectio B (Chemie) — Stud Soc Sci Torun Sect B
Studia Societatis Scientiarum Torunensis. Sectio C (Geographia et Geologia) — Stud Soc Sci Torun Sect C (Geogr Geol)
Studia Societatis Scientiarum Torunensis. Sectio D (Botanica) — Stud Soc Sci Torun Sect D (Bot)
Studia Societatis Scientiarum Torunensis. Sectio E (Zoologia) — Stud Soc Sci Torun Sect E (Zool)
Studia Societatis Scientiarum Torunensis. Sectio F (Astronomia) [*Poland*] — Stud Soc Sci Torun Sect F
Studia Societatis Scientiarum Torunensis. Sectio G (Physiologia) — Stud Soc Sci Torun Sect G (Physiol)
Studia Socjologiczne — Stud Socjol
Studia Socjologiczno-Polityczne — Stud Soc Pol
Studia Staropolskie — StuSta

Studia Taiwanica — ST
Studia Teologica — StTheol
Studia Theologica — ST
Studia Theologica — STh
Studia Theologica — StTh
Studia Theologica — Stud Th
Studia Theologica — Stud Theol
Studia Theologica Lundensia — STL
Studia Theologica Lundensia. Skrifter Utgivna av Teologiska Fakulteten i Lund — StThL
Studia Theologica Varsaviensia [*Warsaw*] — StThVars
Studia Universitatis Babes-Bolyai — Studia Univ Bab Bol
Studia Universitatis Babes-Bolyai. Series Biologia — Stud Univ Babes-Bolyai Biol
Studia Universitatis Babes-Bolyai. Series Biologia — Stud Univ Babes-Bolyai Ser Biol
Studia Universitatis Babes-Bolyai. Series Biologia — SUBBA
Studia Universitatis Babes-Bolyai. Series Chemia — Stud Univ Babes-Bolyai Chem
Studia Universitatis Babes-Bolyai. Series Chemia — Stud Univ Babes-Bolyai Ser Chem
Studia Universitatis Babes-Bolyai. Series Chemia — SUBCA
Studia Universitatis Babes-Bolyai. Series Geologia-Geographia — SBBGA
Studia Universitatis Babes-Bolyai. Series Geologia-Geographia — Stud Univ Babes-Bolyai Geol-Geogr
Studia Universitatis Babes-Bolyai. Series Geologia-Minerologia — Stud Univ Babes-Bolyai Ser Geol-Minerol
Studia Universitatis Babes-Bolyai. Series Mathematica — Stud Univ Babes-Bolyai Math
Studia Universitatis Babes-Bolyai. Series Mathematica — SUBMD
Studia Universitatis Babes-Bolyai. Series Mathematica-Mechanica — SBMMB
Studia Universitatis Babes-Bolyai. Series Mathematica-Mechanica — Studia Univ Babes-Bolyai Ser Math-Mech
Studia Universitatis Babes-Bolyai. Series Mathematica-Physica — Stud Univ Babes-Bolyai Ser Math-Phys
Studia Universitatis Babes-Bolyai. Series Mathematica-Physica — SUBPA
Studia Universitatis Babes-Bolyai. Series Philologia — SUBB
Studia Universitatis Babes-Bolyai. Series Philologia — SUBBP
Studia Universitatis Babes-Bolyai. Series Physica — SBBPA
Studia Universitatis Babes-Bolyai. Series Physica — Stud Univ Babes-Bolyai Phys
Studia Universitatis Babes-Bolyai. Series Physica — Stud Univ Babes-Bolyai Ser Phys
Studia Universitatis Babes-Bolyai. Series Physica — Studia Univ Babes-Bolyai Ser Phys
Studia z Automatiki — Studia Automat
Studia z Automatyki i Informatyki — Studia Automat Inform
Studia z Dziejow Kosciola Katolickiego — SDKK
Studia z Dziejow Kosciola Katolickiego — St Dziej Kosc Kat
Studia z Filologii Polskiej i Slowianskiej — SFPS
Studia Zoologica Regiae Scientiarum Universitatis Hungaricae Budapestensis — Studia Zool R Scient Univ Hung Budapest
Studia Zrodloznawcze. Commentationes — Stud Zrodloznawcze
Studia Zrodloznawcze. Commentationes — SZC
Studie a Prace Linguisticke — SPL
Studie Neotestamentica — SN
Studie Neotestamentica. Subsidia — SNS
Studie o Rukopisech — StR
Studie Prazskeho Linguistickeho Krouzku — SPLK
Studiea Ekonomiczne — St Ek
Studiea Phonetica — SPh
Studiecentrum TNO [*Toegepast Natuurwetenschappelijk Onderzoek*] **voor Scheepsbouw en Navigatie. Communication** — Studiecent TNO Scheepsbouw Navig Commun
Studiecentrum TNO [*Toegepast Natuurwetenschappelijk Onderzoek*] **voor Scheepsbouw en Navigatie. Report** — Studiecent TNO Scheepsbouw Navig Rep
Studien — Stud
Studien aus dem C. G. Jung-Institut — SJI
Studien aus dem Institut fuer Ost- und Suedslawische Relgions- und Kirchenkunde der Humboldt-Universitaet — SIOSR
Studien der Bibliothek Warburg — SBW
Studien der Evangelischen Geistlichen Wirtembergs — SEGW
Studien der Evangelisch-Protestantischen Geistlichen des Grossherzogtums Baden — SEPGB
Studien der Luther-Akademie — SLA
Studien des Oekumenischen Rates — SOeR
Studien des Spologetischen Seminars in Wernigerode — SASW
Studien en Bijdragen op't Gebiet der Historische Theologie — SBHT
Studien op Godsdienstig, Wetenschappelijk en Letterkundig Gebied — SGDG
Studien und Berichte der Katholischen Akademie in Bayern — SBKAB
Studien und Forschungen. Stadt- und Landkreis Offenbach Am Main — St Offenbach
Studien und Materialien zur Geschichte der Philosophie — SMGP
Studien und Materialien zur Geschichte der Philosophie — Stud Materialien Geschichte Philos
Studien und Mitteilungen aus dem Benedictiner und Cistercienser-Orden — SMBO
Studien und Mitteilungen aus dem Benediktiner- und dem Cistercienser-Orden — SMBC
Studien und Mitteilungen aus dem Benediktiner- und dem Cistercienser-Orden — SMBCO
Studien und Mitteilungen aus dem Benediktiner- und dem Cistercienser-Orden — SMBCOZ
Studien und Mitteilungen aus dem Benediktiner- und dem Cistercienser-Orden — StMBC
Studien und Mitteilungen aus dem Benediktiner- und dem Cistercienserorden — StMBCO
Studien und Mitteilungen aus dem Benediktiner- und dem Cistercienser-Orden — Stud Mitt Bened Cisterc
Studien und Mitteilungen aus dem Benediktiner- und dem Cistercienser-Orden — Studien und Mitteilungen
Studien und Mitteilungen aus dem Benediktiner- und Zisterzienser-Orden — Bened St M
Studien und Mitteilungen aus dem Kirchengeschichtlichen Seminar der Theologischen Fakultaet der Universitaet Wien — SKGSW
Studien und Mitteilungen zur Geschichte des Benediktineordens — St Mitt Gesch Benediktorden
Studien und Mitteilungen zur Geschichte des Benediktiner-Ordens — SGB
Studien und Mitteilungen zur Geschichte des Benediktiner-Ordens — StMGB
Studien und Mitteilungen zur Geschichte des Benediktiner-Ordens und Seiner Zweige — SMGB
Studien und Mitteilungen zur Geschichte des Benediktiner-Ordens und Seiner Zweige [*Salzburg*] — SMGBOZ
Studien und Mitteilungen zur Geschichte des Benediktiner-Ordens und Seiner Zweige — Stud Mitt Gesch Benediktinerorden
Studien und Mitteilungen zur Geschichte des Benediktinerordens und Seiner Zweige. Ergaenzungsheft — SMGBE
Studien und Texte zur Geistesgeschichte des Mittelalters — St und T z Geistesgesch des MA
Studien und Texte zur Geistesgeschichte des Mittelalters — STGMA
Studien und Texte zur Geistesgeschichte des Mittelalters — Stud Texte Geistesgesch Mittelalt
Studien und Versuche. Eine Anthroposophische Schriftenreihe — Stud Vers Anthropos Schriftenreihe
Studien und Voelkerkunde — St VK
Studien zu den Bogaskoey-Texten — St BT
Studien zu den Bogazkoey-Texten [*Wiesbaden*] — StBoT
Studien zu den Fundmuenzen der Antike — SFMA
Studien zu den Grundlagen der Reformation — SGR
Studien zum Achtzehnten Jahrhundert — Stud Achtzehn Jahrh
Studien zum Alten und Neuen Testament — SANT
Studien zum Alten und Neuen Testament [*Munich*] — StANT
Studien zum Alten und Neuen Testament [*Munich*] — StudzumAuNT
Studien zum Fortwirken der Antike — Stud Fort Ant
Studien zum Neuen Testament — StNT
Studien zum Neuen Testament [*Guetersloh*] — StudNT
Studien zur Algebra und Ihre Anwendungen — Stud Algebra Anwendungen
Studien zur Allgemeinen und Vergleichenden Literaturwissenschaft — SAVL
Studien zur Altaegyptischen Kultur — St Altaeg Kul
Studien zur Altbayerischen Kirchengeschichte — SABKG
Studien zur Angewandten Wirtschaftsforschung und Statistik — Stud Angew Wirtschaftsforsch Statist
Studien zur Auslandskunde — Stud Auslandskde
Studien zur Deutschen Kunstgeschichte — SDKG
Studien zur Deutschen Kunstgeschichte — St DKG
Studien zur Deutschen Literatur — SzDL
Studien zur Dogmengeschichte und Systematischen Theologie — SDGSTh
Studien zur Englischen Philologie — Stud Engl Phil
Studien zur Englischen Philologie — SzEP
Studien zur Erforschung des Christlichen Aegyptens — SECAe
Studien zur Erforschung des Christlichen Aegyptens — SFCAe
Studien zur Erforschung des Christlichen Aegyptens — SRCAe
Studien zur Evangelischen Ethik — SEE
Studien zur Evangelischen Sozialtheologie und Sozialethhik — SEST
Studien zur Germania Sacra — St GS
Studien zur Germanistik, Anglistik und Komparatistik — SGAK
Studien zur Germanistik, Anglistik und Komparatistik — StGAK
Studien zur Geschichte der Akademie der Wissenschaften der Deutsche Demokratische Republik — Stud Gesch Akad Wiss DDR
Studien zur Geschichte der Katholischen Moraltheologie — SGKMT
Studien zur Geschichte der Theologie und der Kirche — StGThK
Studien zur Geschichte der Theologie und Kirche — SGTK
Studien zur Geschichte des Neueren Protestantismus — SGNP
Studien zur Geschichte des Neueren Protestantismus. Quellenhefte — SGNPQ
Studien zur Geschichte Osteuropas — SGOE
Studien zur Geschichte und Kultur des Altertums — SGKA
Studien zur Geschichte und Kultur des Altertums — StGKA
Studien zur Geschichte und Kultur des Altertums — Stud Gesch Kult Alt
Studien zur Geschichte und Kultur des Altertums. Ergaenzungsband — SGKAE
Studien zur Geschichte und Kultur des Islamischen Orients — SGKIO
Studien zur Griechischen und Lateinischen Grammatik — SGLG
Studien zur Indologie und Iranistik — St I I
Studien zur Katholischen Bistums- und Klostergesechichte — SKBK
Studien zur Kirchengeschichte Niedersachsens — SKGNS
Studien zur Koelner Kirchengeschichte — SKKG
Studien zur Kulturkunde — Stud Kulturkunde
Studien zur Literatur der Moderne — St L M
Studien zur Medizingeschichte des Neunzehnten Jahrhunderts — Stud Medizingesch Neunzehnten Jahrhunderts
Studien zur Musikwissenschaft — S Mw
Studien zur Musikwissenschaft — StM
Studien zur Musikwissenschaft — Stud MW
Studien zur Palaeographie und Papyruskunde — SPP
Studien zur Palaeographie und Papyruskunde [*Leipzig*] — StudPal
Studien zur Philosophie und Religion — SPR
Studien zur Poetik und Geschichte der Literatur — SPGL
Studien zur Poetik und Geschichte der Literatur — Stud Poet Ges Lit

Studien zur Problemgeschichte der Antiken und Mittelalterlichen Philosophie — SPGAP
Studien zur Problemgeschichte der Antiken und Mittelalterlichen Philosophie — Stz Probl Gesch
Studien zur Rechts-und Relgionsgeschichte — SRRG
Studien zur Relgion, Geschichte, und Geisteswissenschaften — SRGG
Studien zur Religioesen Volkskunde — SRVK
Studien zur Sprache, Geschichte, und Kultur des Islamischen Orients — SSGIO
Studien zur Systematischen Theologie — SSTh
Studien zur Systematischen Theologie — St Syst Theol
Studien zur Theologie des Geistlichen Lebens — STGL
Studien zur Umwelt des Neuen Testament — St UNT
Studien zur Umwelt des Neuen Testament [*Goettingen*] — StUmwNT
Studien zur Umwelt des Neuen Testament [*Goéttingen*] — SUNT
Studien zur Vergleichenden Literaturgeschichte — SVL
Studien zur Wissenschafts-, Sozial-, und Bildungsgeschichte der Mathematik — Stud Wiss Soz Bildungsgesch Math
Studienausgaben zur Neueren Deutschen Literatur — SNDL
Studienbuecher Naturwissenschaft und Technik — Studienb Naturwiss Tech
Studiengruppe fuer Systemforschung. Heidelberg. Bericht — Studiengruppe Systemforsch Heidelberg Ber
Studienhefte der Evangelischen Akademie Rheinland-Westfalen — SEARW
Studienmaterial zur Weiterbildung Medizinisch-Technischer Assistenten — Studienmater Weiterbild Med Tech Assist
Studien-Material zur Weiterbildung Medizinisch-Technischer Laborassistenten — Stud Mater Weiterbild Med Tech Laborassistenten
Studienreihe Englisch — St E
Studienreihe Informatik — Studienreihe Inform
Studienskripten zur Soziologie — Studienskripten zur Soziol
Studien-Text. Mathematik — Stud Text Math
Studien-Texte. Physik — Stud Texte Phys
Studier fra Sprog- og Oldtidsforskning — SSO
Studier fra Sprog- og Oldtidsforskning — Stud Sprog Og Oldtidsforskn
Studier fra Sprog- og Oldtidsforskning — Stud Sprogforskn
Studier i Modern Sprakvetenskap — SiMS
Studier i Modern Sprakvetenskap — SMS
Studier i Modern Sprakvetenskap — SMSpr
Studier i Nordisk Filologi — SNF
Studier i Nordisk Filologi — SNoF
Studier i Nordisk Filologi — StNF
Studies — St
Studies — Stu
Studies — Stud
Studies: An Irish Quarterly Review of Letters, Philosophy, and Science — SIQR
Studies: An Irish Quarterly Review of Letters, Philosophy, and Science — StI
Studies: An Irish Quarterly Review of Letters, Philosophy, and Science — Stud
Studies and Documents — StD
Studies and Documents. Asian Documentation and Research Center — Stud Docum Asian Docum
Studies and Notes in Philology and Literature — Stud No Phil
Studies and Reports. Ben-Zvi Institute [*Jerusalem*] — SR
Studies and Reports in Hydrology. International Association of Hydrological Sciences - United Nations Educational, Scientific, and Cultural Organization — Stud Rep Hydrol IAHS - UNESCO
Studies and Research. Institute of Meteorology and Hydrology. Part 2. Hydrology — Stud Res Inst Meteorol Hydrol Part 2
Studies by Members of the Istanbul University English Department — SMIU
Studies. Chemotherapeutic Institute for Medical Research [*Japan*] — Stud Chemother Inst Med Res
Studies. Dutch Archaeological and Historical Society — SDAHS
Studies en Voordrachten. Faculteit der Rechtsgeleerdheid VUB [*Vrije Universiteit te Brussel*] — Stud VUB
Studies en Voordrachten. VUB [*Vrije Universiteit te Brussel*] — St Vd VUB
Studies for Trade Unionists — Stud Trade Unionists
Studies from the Geological and Mineralogical Institute. Tokyo University of Education — Stud Geol Mineral Inst Tokyo Univ Educ
Studies from the Institute of Horticulture. Kyoto University — Stud Inst Hortic Kyoto Univ
Studies from the Institute of Medical Chemistry. University of Szeged — Stud Inst Med Chem Univ Szeged
Studies in Accountancy — Stud Account
Studies in Advanced Mathematics — Stud Adv Math
Studies in African Linguistics — SAL
Studies in African Linguistics — Stud Afr Linguist
Studies in African Linguistics — Stud Afr Linguistics
Studies in African Literature — SAfrL
Studies in American Fiction — PSAF
Studies in American Fiction — SAF
Studies in American Fiction — SAmF
Studies in American Fiction — Stud Am Fic
Studies in American Humor — SAmH
Studies in American Humor — St A H
Studies in American Jewish History — SAJH
Studies in American Jewish Literature — SAJL
Studies in American Literature [*Chu Shikoku*] — SALit
Studies in American Literature [*The Hague*] — SAML
Studies in Anabaptist and Mennonite History — SAMH
Studies in Analytical Chemistry [*Elsevier Book Series*] — SACh
Studies in Ancient Civilization [*Elsevier Book Series*] — SAC
Studies in Ancient Oriental Civilization. Oriental Institute [*Chicago*] — OIS
Studies in Ancient Oriental Civilization. The Oriental Institute of the University of Chicago — SAOC
Studies in Anthropology — Stud Anthrop
Studies in Anthropology and Comparative Religion — SACR
Studies in Applied Mathematics — Stud Appl M
Studies in Applied Mathematics — Stud Appl Math
Studies in Applied Mathematics — Studies App Math
Studies in Applied Mathematics — Studies Appl Math
Studies in Applied Mechanics [*Elsevier Book Series*] — SAM
Studies in Applied Mechanics — Stud Appl Mech
Studies in Art Education — Stud Art Ed
Studies in Art Education — Stud Art Educ
Studies in Art Education — Studies in Art Ed
Studies in Ascetical Theology — SATh
Studies in Astronautics [*Elsevier Book Series*] — SA
Studies in Australian Bibliography — Studies in Aust Bibliog
Studies in Automation and Control [*Elsevier Book Series*] — SIAC
Studies in Automation and Control — Stud Automat Control
Studies in Banking and Finance — Stud Bank Fin
Studies in Bayesian Econometrics [*Elsevier Book Series*] — SIBE
Studies in Bayesian Econometrics — Stud Bayesian Econometrics
Studies in Bayesian Econometrics and Statistics — Stud Bayesian Econometrics Statist
Studies in Biblical Archaeology — SBA
Studies in Biblical Archaeology — SBAr
Studies in Biblical Theology — SBT
Studies in Biblical Theology — St Bibl Theol
Studies in Bibliography — SB
Studies in Bibliography and Booklore — SBB
Studies in Bibliography and Booklore — SBBL
Studies in Bibliography and Booklore — Stud Biblog & Bklore
Studies in Biology — Stud Biol
Studies in Black Literature — SBL
Studies in Black Literature — Stud Black Lit
Studies in Brain Function — Stud Brain Funct
Studies in British History and Culture — Stud Br His
Studies in Browning and His Circle — SBC
Studies in Browning and His Circle — SBHC
Studies in Browning and His Circle — Stud Brown
Studies in Burke and His Time — SBHT
Studies in Burke and His Time — Stud Burke Time
Studies in Canadian Literature — SCanL
Studies in Canadian Literature — SCL
Studies in Canadian Literature — St Can Lit
Studies in Canadian Literature — Studies in Can Lit
Studies in Chinese Government and Politics — Stud Ch G P
Studies in Christian Antiquity — SCA
Studies in Christian Faith and Practice — SCFP
Studies in Church History — SCH
Studies in Church History — SChH
Studies in Church History. American Society of Church History — Stud Church Hist
Studies in Church History. Institute for Dansk Church History. Kobenhaven University — SCHK
Studies in Church History (London) — SCHL
Studies in Classical Philology — SCP
Studies in Classification, Data Analysis, and Knowledge Organization — Stud Classification Data Anal Knowledge Organ
Studies in Communism, Revisionism, and Revolution — Stud Comm R
Studies in Comparative Communism — PSCC
Studies in Comparative Communism — SCC
Studies in Comparative Communism — Stud Com Co
Studies in Comparative Communism [*Los Angeles*] — Stud Comp Com
Studies in Comparative Communism — Stud Comp Commun
Studies in Comparative Communism — Stud Comp Communism
Studies in Comparative Communism. University of Southern California — USC/SCC
Studies in Comparative International Development — SCID-A
Studies in Comparative International Development — St Comp Int Devel
Studies in Comparative International Development — Stud Com I D
Studies in Comparative International Development [*New Jersey*] — Stud Comp Int Dev
Studies in Comparative International Development — Stud Comp Int Develop
Studies in Comparative International Development. Georgia Institute of Technology — GIT/SCID
Studies in Comparative Local Government — Stud Com L G
Studies in Comparative Local Government — Stud in Comp Local Govt
Studies in Comparative Religion — SCR
Studies in Comparative Religion — Stud Comp R
Studies in Comparative Religion — Stud Comp Relig
Studies in Comparative Religion — Stud Comp Religion
Studies in Computational Mathematics — Stud Comput Math
Studies in Computer Science and Artificial Intelligence — Stud Comput Sci Artif Intell
Studies in Conservation — St Cons
Studies in Conservation — Stud Conserv
Studies in Conservation — Studies Conserv
Studies in Contemporary Satire — St CS
Studies in Continuing Education — Stud in Contin Educ
Studies in Creative Criticism — SCC
Studies in Cultural Anthropology — Stud Cult Anthrop
Studies in Design Education, Craft, and Technology — Stud Design Educ Craft Technol
Studies in Development. Special Issue. Middle East Technical University — Stud Develop Special Issue
Studies in Dynamical Economic Science — Stud Dynam Econom Sci
Studies in Ecology — Stud Ecol
Studies in Economic Analysis — SEA

Studies in Economic Analysis — Studies Econ Analysis
Studies in Economic Theory — Stud Econom Theory
Studies in Education — Stud Ed
Studies in Educational Administration — SEA
Studies in Educational Evaluation — SEE
Studies in Eighteenth-Century Culture — SECC
Studies in Eighteenth-Century Culture — Stud Eight
Studies in Eighteenth-Century Culture — Stud Eighteenth-Century Cult
Studies in Electrical and Electronic Engineering [*Elsevier Book Series*] — SEEE
Studies in Electrical and Electronic Engineering — Stud Electr Electron Eng
Studies in Empirical Economics — Stud Empir Econom
Studies in English — S in Eng
Studies in English — SE
Studies in English and American — SEA
Studies in English by Members of the English Seminar of the Charles University, Prague — Prague St
Studies in English Literature — SEL
Studies in English Literature [*Japan*] — SELit
Studies in English Literature [*The Hague*] — SEngL
Studies in English Literature — St Engl Lit
Studies in English Literature — Stud Engl Lit
Studies in English Literature, 1500-1900 — GELT
Studies in English Literature, 1500-1900 — Stud Engl L
Studies in English Literature and Language [*Japan*] — SELL
Studies in English Literature (Japan) — SELJ
Studies in English Literature (Tokyo) — Stud Engl (T)
Studies in English (University of Texas) — SET
Studies in Environmental Science — SENSD
Studies in Environmental Science [*Elsevier Book Series*] — SES
Studies in Environmental Science — Stud Environ Sci
Studies in Environmental Science (Hiroshima) — Stud Environ Sci (Hiroshima)
Studies in Ethics and the Philosophy of Religion — SEPR
Studies in Ethnomethodology — Stud Ethnomethodol
Studies in Eucharistic Faith and Practice — SEFP
Studies in European Society — Stud Europ Soc
Studies in Family Planning — Stud Fam Pl
Studies in Family Planning — Stud Fam Plann
Studies in Family Planning — Stud Family Plann
Studies in Financial Economics [*Elsevier Book Series*] — SFE
Studies in Formative Spirituality — PSFS
Studies in Formative Spirituality — St Form Sp
Studies in Formative Spirituality — Stud Form Spir
Studies in French Literature — SFL
Studies in French Literature — SFrL
Studies in Fuzziness — Stud Fuzziness
Studies in General and Comparative Literature — SGCL
Studies in Genetics — Stud Genet
Studies in Geography — Stud Geogr
Studies in Geology (Tulsa, Oklahoma) — Stud Geol (Tulsa Okla)
Studies in German Literature — SGL
Studies in High Energy Physics — Stud High Energy Phys
Studies in Higher Education — Stud High Educ
Studies in Historical Theology — SHT
Studies in History and Philosophy of Science — PSHP
Studies in History and Philosophy of Science — Stud Hist P
Studies in History and Philosophy of Science — Stud Hist Phil Sci
Studies in History and Philosophy of Science — Stud Hist Philos Sci
Studies in History and Philosophy of Science. B. Studies in History and Philosophy of Modern Physics — Stud Hist Philos Sci B Stud Hist Philos Modern Phys
Studies in History and Society — Stud Hist & Soc
Studies in History and Society — StuiHS
Studies in History of Biology — Stud Hist Biol
Studies in History of Medicine — Stud Hist Med
Studies in Human Ecology — Stud Hum Ecol
Studies in Iconography — S Icon
Studies in Indo-Asian Art and Culture [*New Delhi*] — Stud Indo-As Art Cult
Studies in Indo-Muslim Mysticism — SIMM
Studies in Inorganic Chemistry [*Elsevier Book Series*] — SIC
Studies in Inorganic Chemistry — SICHEJ
Studies in Inorganic Chemistry — Stud Inorg Chem
Studies in International Economics [*Elsevier Book Series*] — SIE
Studies in Islam Series — SIS
Studies in Judaica (New York) — SJNY
Studies in Judaism in Late Antiquity — SJLA
Studies in Labour History — Stud Labour Hist
Studies in Language — S Lang
Studies in Language and Linguistics — Stud Lang Ling
Studies in Language. Companion Series — SLCS
Studies in Language. Companion Series — Stud Lang C
Studies in Language. International Journal — Stud Lang
Studies in Language Learning — SLL
Studies in Latin American Culture — SLAC
Studies in Latin American Popular Culture — SLAPC
Studies in Latin American Revolution — Stud Latin Am Rev
Studies in Law and Economic Development — Studies L & Econ Develop
Studies in Library Management — Stud Lib Man
Studies in Linguistic Analysis [*Elsevier Book Series*] — SLA
Studies in Linguistics — SIL
Studies in Linguistics — SL
Studies in Linguistics — StLing
Studies in Linguistics — Stud Ling
Studies in Linguistics and Languages Learning — Stud Ling Lang Learn
Studies in Linguistics and Philosophy — Stud Linguist Philos
Studies in Linguistics. Occasional Papers — SILOP
Studies in Literature — SLit
Studies in Literature and Philology — Studies in Lit a Philol
Studies in Logic and Computation — Stud Logic Comput
Studies in Logic and the Foundations of Mathematics [*Elsevier Book Series*] — STL
Studies in Logic and the Foundations of Mathematics — Stud Logic Foundations Math
Studies in Logic, Language, and Information — Stud Logic Lang Inform
Studies in Management Science and Systems [*Elsevier Book Series*] — SMSS
Studies in Management Science and Systems — Stud Management Sci Systems
Studies in Mathematical and Managerial Economics [*Elsevier Book Series*] — SMME
Studies in Mathematical and Managerial Economics — Stud Math Managerial Econom
Studies in Mathematical Physics — Stud Math Phys
Studies in Mathematical Thinking and Learning — Stud Math Think Learn
Studies in Mathematics and Its Applications [*Elsevier Book Series*] — SMIA
Studies in Mathematics and Its Applications — Stud Math Appl
Studies in Mathematics Education Series — Stud Math Ed Ser
Studies in Mechanical Engineering [*Elsevier Book Series*] — SIME
Studies in Medical Geography — Stud Med Geogr
Studies in Medieval and Reformation Thought — SMRT
Studies in Medieval and Renaissance History — Stud Medieval Renaiss Hist
Studies in Medieval and Renaissance Latin Language and Literature — SMRL
Studies in Medieval Culture — SMC
Studies in Medieval Culture — Stud Mediev
Studies in Medieval History — SMH
Studies in Mediterranean Archaeology — SIMA
Studies in Microbiology — Stud Microbiol
Studies in Ministry and Worship — SMW
Studies in Modern Thermodynamics [*Elsevier Book Series*] — SMT
Studies in Modern Thermodynamics — Stud Modern Thermodynamics
Studies in Monetary Economics [*Elsevier Book Series*] — SME
Studies in Music — SiM
Studies in Music — Stud M
Studies in Music — Studies Mus
Studies in Music (Australia) — S M (A)
Studies in Mycenaean Inscriptions and Dialect — SMID
Studies in Mycology — Stud Mycol
Studies in Mystical Literature — SM Lit
Studies in Natural Products Chemistry — Stud Nat Prod Chem
Studies in Natural Sciences (Portales, New Mexico) — Stud Nat Sci (Portales NM)
Studies in Neuro-Anatomy — Stud Neuro Anat
Studies in Nigerian Languages — Stud Niger Lang
Studies in Nursing Management — Stud Nurs Man
Studies in Organic Chemistry [*Elsevier Book Series*] — SOC
Studies in Organic Chemistry (Amsterdam) — Stud Org Chem Amsterdam
Studies in Pacific Languages and Cultures in Honour of Bruce Biggs — Stud Pac Lang Cult
Studies in Paint (Osaka) [*Japan*] — Stud Paint (Osaka)
Studies in Parasitology and General Zoology — Studies Parasitol and Gen Zool
Studies in Patristic Thought — SPT
Studies in Personnel Psychology — Stud Pers P
Studies in Personnel Psychology — Stud Pers Psych
Studies in Personnel Psychology — Stud Person Psychol
Studies in Philippine Linguistics — SIPL
Studies in Philippine Linguistics [*Manila*] — Stud Phil Ling
Studies in Philology — PSPH
Studies in Philology — S in Ph
Studies in Philology — SP
Studies in Philology — SPh
Studies in Philology — Stud Phil
Studies in Philology — Stud Philol
Studies in Philology — Studies Philol
Studies in Philology (Chapel Hill) — Stud Philol ChapelH
Studies in Philology. Extra Series — SPES
Studies in Philology. University of North Carolina — SPhNC
Studies in Philosophy [*The Hague*] — Stud Philos
Studies in Philosophy and Education — SPE
Studies in Philosophy and Education — Stud Phil & Ed
Studies in Philosophy and Education — Stud Phil E
Studies in Philosophy and Education — Stud Philos & Educ
Studies in Philosophy and the History of Philosophy — SPHP
Studies in Philosophy and the History of Philosophy — Stud Phil H
Studies in Philosophy and the History of Philosophy — Stud Phil Hist Phil
Studies in Philosophy of Medicine — Stud Philos Med
Studies in Physical and Theoretical Chemistry [*Elsevier Book Series*] — SPTC
Studies in Physical and Theoretical Chemistry [*Elsevier Book Series*] — SPTCDZ
Studies in Physical and Theoretical Chemistry — Stud Phys Theor Chem
Studies in Physical and Theoretical Chemistry — Stud Phys Theoret Chem
Studies in Physical Anthropology — Stud Phys Anthrop
Studies in Physical Anthropology — Stud Phys Anthropol
Studies in Plant Ecology — SPLEE2
Studies in Plant Ecology — Stud Plant Ecol
Studies in Plant Science — Stud Plant Sci
Studies in Political Economy — Studies
Studies in Political Economy — Studies Pol Economy
Studies in Polymer Science — Stud Polym Sci
Studies in Presbyterian History — SPH
Studies in Probability and Statistics — Stu Prob & St
Studies in Probability, Optimization, and Statistics — Stud Probab Optim Statist
Studies in Production and Engineering Economics [*Elsevier Book Series*] — SPEE

Studies in Production and Engineering Economics — Stud Prod Engrg Econom
Studies in Proof Theory. Lecture Notes — Stud Proof Theory Lecture Notes
Studies in Proof Theory. Monographs — Stud Proof Theory Monographs
Studies in Psychology and Psychiatry. Catholic University of America — Stud Psychol Psychiat Cath Univ Amer
Studies in Public Communication — Stud Pub Com
Studies in Public Economics [*Elsevier Book Series*] — SPE
Studies in Radiation Effects in Solids — Stud Radiat Eff Solids
Studies in Radiation Effects. Series A. Physical and Chemical — Stud Radiat Eff Ser A
Studies in Regional Science and Urban Economics [*Elsevier Book Series*] — SRSUE
Studies in Regional Science and Urban Economics — Stud Regional Sci Urban Econom
Studies in Religion — SR
Studies in Religion — SRg
Studies in Religion [*Ontario*] — Stud Rel
Studies in Religion — Stud Relig
Studies in Religion: A Canadian Journal — SRC
Studies in Religion and Culture — SRC
Studies in Religion and Culture. American Religion Series — SRCA
Studies in Religion/Sciences Religieuses — S Rel Sc Rel
Studies in Religion/Sciences Religieuses — StRel/ScRel
Studies in Romance Languages — SRL
Studies in Romanticism — PSRO
Studies in Romanticism — SIR
Studies in Romanticism — SR
Studies in Romanticism — StRom
Studies in Romanticism — Stud Roman
Studies in Romanticism — Stud Romant
Studies in Romanticism — Stud Romanticism
Studies in Sacred Theology — SST
Studies in Science Education — Stud Sci Educ
Studies in Scottish Literature — SSL
Studies in Scottish Literature — Stud Sc Lit
Studies in Scottish Literature — Stud Scott Lit
Studies in Semitic Languages and Linguistics — SSL
Studies in Semitic Languages and Linguistics — SSLI
Studies in Semitic Languages and Linguistics — StSLL
Studies in Short Fiction — GSSF
Studies in Short Fiction — SSF
Studies in Short Fiction — Stud Sh Fic
Studies in Short Fiction — Stud Short Fict
Studies in Short Fiction — Stud Short Fiction
Studies in Slavic and General Linguistics — SSGL
Studies in Social Life — Stud Soc Li
Studies in Society and History — SSH
Studies in Soviet Thought — Stud Sov Th
Studies in Soviet Thought — Stud Sov Thought
Studies in Spelaeology — Stud Spelaeol
Studies in Speleology — Stud Speleol
Studies in Speleology — Stud Speleology
Studies in Statistical Mechanics [*Elsevier Book Series*] — SSM
Studies in Statistical Mechanics — Stud Stat Mech
Studies in Statistical Mechanics — Stud Statist Mech
Studies in Surface Science and Catalysis [*Elsevier Book Series*] — SSSC
Studies in Surface Science and Catalysis [*Netherlands*] [*Elsevier Book Series*] — Stud Surf Sci Catal
Studies in the Age of Chaucer — SAC
Studies in the Age of Chaucer — Stud Age Chaucer
Studies in the American Renaissance — SAR
Studies in the American Renaissance — St Am Renaissance
Studies in the Antiquities of Stobi — Stud Stobi
Studies in the Bengal Renaissance — SBR
Studies in the Education of Adults — Stud Educ Adults
Studies in the Eighteenth Century. Papers Presented. David Nichol Smith Memorial Seminar. Canberra — Stud 18th Cent
Studies in the Foundations, Methodology, and Philosophy of Science — Stud Found Methodol Philos Sci
Studies in the Germanic Languages and Literatures — SGLL
Studies in the History and Art of the Eastern Provinces of the Roman Empire — SERP
Studies in the History of Art — Stud H Art
Studies in the History of Art — Stud Hist Art
Studies in the History of Christian Thought — SHCT
Studies in the History of Mathematics and Physical Sciences — Stud Hist Math Phys Sci
Studies in the History of Modern Science — Stud Hist Modern Sci
Studies in the History of Religions — SHR
Studies in the Humanities — SHum
Studies in the Humanities — SIH
Studies in the Humanities — St Hum
Studies in the Humanities — Studies Hum
Studies in the Learning Sciences — Stud Learn Sci
Studies in the Linguistic Sciences — SLSc
Studies in the Linguistic Sciences [*Urbana*] — Stud Ling Sci
Studies in the Literary Imagination — PSLI
Studies in the Literary Imagination — SLI
Studies in the Literary Imagination — SLitI
Studies in the Literary Imagination — Stud Lit Im
Studies in the Literary Imagination — Stud Lit Imag
Studies in the Logic of Science — Stud Logic Sci
Studies in the Management Sciences — Stud Management Sci
Studies in the Natural Sciences — Stud Nat Sci
Studies in the Natural Sciences (New York) — Stud Nat Sci NY
Studies in the Novel — PSNO
Studies in the Novel — SNovel
Studies in the Novel — Stud in the Novel
Studies in the Novel — Stud Novel
Studies in the Novel. North Texas State University — SNNTS
Studies in the Renaissance — SR
Studies in the Renaissance — SRen
Studies in the Renaissance — St Ren
Studies in the Renaissance — Stud Ren
Studies in the Renaissance — Stud Renaiss
Studies in the Renaissance — Stud Renaissance
Studies in the Renaissance — StuiR
Studies in the Twentieth Century — Stud TC
Studies in the Twentieth Century — StuTC
Studies in Third World Societies [*Williamsburg*] — Stud Third World Soc
Studies in Tropical Oceanography. Institute of Marine Science. University of Miami — Stud Trop Oceanogr Inst Mar Sci Univ Miami
Studies in Tropical Oceanography (Miami) — Stud Trop Oceanogr (Miami)
Studies in Twentieth-Century Literature — St Twen Ct
Studies in Twentieth-Century Literature — StTCL
Studies in US History and Culture — Stud US Hist Cult
Studies in Vermont Geology — Stud VT Geol
Studies in Visual Communication — Stud Vis Com
Studies in Visual Communication — Visual Com
Studies in Wind Engineering and Industrial Aerodynamics [*Elsevier Book Series*] — SWEIA
Studies in Zionism — SiZ
Studies. Institute for Medical Research (Malaya) — Stud Inst Med Res (Malaya)
Studies. Institutum Divi Thomae — SIDT
Studies. Institutum Divi Thomae — Stud Inst Divi Thomae
Studies. Nakamura Gakuin University — Stud Nakamura Gakuin Univ
Studies of Broadcasting — Stud Broadcast
Studies of Broadcasting [*Japan*] — Studies of Bcasting
Studies of Church and State — SCS
Studies of Classical India — Stud Class
Studies of Cosmic Ray [*Japan*] — Stud Cosmic Ray
Studies of High Temperature Superconductors. Advances in Research and Applications — Stud High Temp Supercond
Studies of Intellectual Precocity — Stud Intellectual Precocity
Studies of Nonlinear Phenomena in Life Science — Stud Nonlinear Phenom Life Sci
Studies of the Fauna of Suriname and Other Guyanas — Stud Fauna Suriname Other Guyanas
Studies of Vacuum Ultraviolet and X-Ray Processes — Stud Vac Ultraviolet X Ray Processes
Studies on Asia — StOA
Studies on International Relations [*Warsaw*] — STU
Studies on International Relations — Stud In Relat
Studies on International Relations — Stud Int Relat
Studies on International Relations (Warsaw) — Studies Internat Relations (Warsaw)
Studies on Social Work — Stud Soc Wk
Studies on Solid State Physics and Chemistry [*Japan*] — Stud Solid Phys Chem
Studies on the Developing Countries — Stud Developing Countries
Studies on the Fauna of Curacao and Other Caribbean Islands — Stud Fauna Curacao Other Caribb Isl
Studies on the Left — StL
Studies on the Left — Stud Left
Studies on the Neotropical Fauna [*Later, Studies on the Neotropical Fauna and Environment*] — Stud Neotrop Fauna
Studies on the Neotropical Fauna and Environment — Stud Neotrop Fauna Environ
Studies on the Soviet Union — Stud Soviet Union
Studies on the Texts of the Desert of Judah — STDJ
Studies on Voltaire and the Eighteenth Century — Stud Voltaire
Studies on Voltaire and the Eighteenth Century — Stud Voltaire 18th Cent
Studies on Voltaire and the Eighteenth Century — Stud Voltaire Eighteenth Century
Studies on Voltaire and the Eighteenth Century — StV
Studies on Voltaire and the Eighteenth Century — SVEC
Studies on Women Abstracts — Stud Women Abstr
Studies. Southern Methodist University — SSMU
Studies. Stations of the Fisheries Research Board of Canada — Stud Stn Fish Res Board Can
Studies. Tokugawa Institute — Stud Tokugawa Inst
Studies. Warburg Institute — SWI
Studies. Zoological Laboratory. University of Nebraska — Studies Zool Lab Univ Nebr
Studii Biblici Franciscani [*Jerusalem*] — StBFranc
Studii Biblici Franciscani. Liber Annus — Fran LA
Studii Biblici Franciscani. Liber Annus — SBFLA
Studii Biblici Franciscani. Liber Annus — Stud Bibl
Studii Biblici Franciscani. Liber Annuus [*Jerusalem*] — FrancLA
Studii Biblici Franciscani. Liber Annuus — SBF
Studii Biblici Franciscani. Liber Annuus [*Jerusalem*] — StBFranc LA
Studii Clasice — SC
Studii Clasice — SClas
Studii Clasice — St Cl
Studii Clasice — St Clas
Studii Clasice — Stud Cl
Studii Clasice — StudClas
Studii de Alimentari cu Apa — Stud Aliment Apa
Studii de Epurarea Apelor — Stud Epurarea Apelor
Studii de Filologia Romanza — SFR

Studii de Geotekhnica. Fundatii si Constructii Hidrotehnice — Stud Geoteh Fund Constr Hidroteh
Studii de Gramatica — SdG
Studii de Gramatica — SGr
Studii de Gramatica — SGram
Studii de Istorie Banatului — SIB
Studii de Literatura Universala [*Bucharest*] — SLU
Studii de Muzicologie — Stud Muzicol
Studii de Protectia si Epurarea Apelor — Stud Prot Epurarea Apelor
Studii Graeca Stockholmiensis — SGS
Studii Italiene — SI
Studii. Revista de Istorie — StuR
Studii si Articole de Istorie — SAI
Studii si Cercetari de Agronomie — Stud Cercet Agron
Studii si Cercetari de Agronomie. Academia Republicii Populare Romine Filiala (Cluj) — Stud Cercet Agron Acad Rep Pop Romine Fil (Cluj)
Studii si Cercetari de Antropologie — Stud Cercet Antropol
Studii si Cercetari de Astronomie — SCEAB
Studii si Cercetari de Astronomie — Stud Cercet Astron
Studii si Cercetari de Bibliologie — SCB
Studii si Cercetari de Biochimie — Stud Cercet Biochim
Studii si Cercetari de Biologie — Stud Cercet Biol
Studii si Cercetari de Biologie — Studii Cerc Biol
Studii si Cercetari de Biologie. Academia Republicii Populare Romine Filiala (Cluj) — Stud Cercet Biol Acad Rep Pop Romine Fil (Cluj)
Studii si Cercetari de Biologie. Academia Republicii Populare Romine. Seria Biologi Vegetala — Stud Cercet Biol Acad Rep Pop Romine Ser Biol Veg
Studii si Cercetari de Biologie. Etudes et Recherches de Biologie (Bucharest) — Stud Cercet Biol Bucharest
Studii si Cercetari de Biologie. Seria Biologie Animala — Stud Cercet Biol Ser Biol Anim
Studii si Cercetari de Biologie. Seria Biologie Animala — Studii Cerc Biol Biol Anim
Studii si Cercetari de Biologie. Seria Biologie Vegetala — Stud Cercet Biol Ser Biol Veg
Studii si Cercetari de Biologie. Seria Botanica — SCBOA
Studii si Cercetari de Biologie. Seria Botanica — Stud Cercet Biol Ser Bot
Studii si Cercetari de Biologie. Seria Zoologie — SCBZA
Studii si Cercetari de Biologie. Seria Zoologie — Stud Cercet Biol Ser Zool
Studii si Cercetari de Biologie. Seria Zoologie — Studii Cerc Biol Zool
Studii si Cercetari de Calcul Economic si Cibernetica Economica — Stud & Cercet Calcul Econ & Cibern Econ
Studii si Cercetari de Chimie — SCECA
Studii si Cercetari de Chimie — Stud Cercet Chim
Studii si Cercetari de Chimie — Studii Cercet Chim
Studii si Cercetari de Chimie (Cluj) — Stud Cercet Chim (Cluj)
Studii si Cercetari de Documentare — Stud & Cercet Doc
Studii si Cercetari de Documentare — Stud Cerc Docum
Studii si Cercetari de Documentare si Bibliologie — Stud Cercet Doc Bibliologie
Studii si Cercetari de Embriologie si Citologie. Seria Embriologie [*Romania*] — Stud Cercet Embriol Citol Ser Embriol
Studii si Cercetari de Endocrinologie — SCEDA
Studii si Cercetari de Endocrinologie — Stud Cercet Endocrinol
Studii si Cercetari de Energetica — Stud Cercet Energ
Studii si Cercetari de Energetica. Seria A. Energetica Generala si Electroenergetica — Stud Cercet Energ Ser A
Studii si Cercetari de Energetica. Seria B. Termoenergetica si Utilizarea Energetica a Combustibililor — Stud Cercet Energ Ser B
Studii si Cercetari de Energetica si Electrotehnica — SCEEA
Studii si Cercetari de Energetica si Electrotehnica — Stud Cercet Energ Electroteh
Studii si Cercetari de Fizica — SCEFA
Studii si Cercetari de Fizica — Stu Cer Fiz
Studii si Cercetari de Fizica — Stud Cerc Fiz
Studii si Cercetari de Fizica — Stud Cercet Fiz
Studii si Cercetari de Fiziologie — SCFZA
Studii si Cercetari de Fiziologie [*Romania*] — Stud Cercet Fiziol
Studii si Cercetari de Geofizica — Stud Cercet Geofiz
Studii si Cercetari de Geologie, Geofizica, Geografie. Geofizica — Stud Cercet Geol Geofiz Geogr Geofiz
Studii si Cercetari de Geologie, Geofizica, Geografie. Geologie — Stud Cercet Geol Geofiz Geogr Geol
Studii si Cercetari de Geologie, Geofizica, Geografie. Seria Geofizica — Stud Cercet Geol Geofiz Geogr
Studii si Cercetari de Geologie, Geofizica, si Geografie. Seria Geofizica — Stud Cercet Geol Geofiz Geogr Ser Geofiz
Studii si Cercetari de Geologie, Geofizica, si Geografie. Seria Geografie — Stud Cercet Geol Geofiz Geogr Ser Geogr
Studii si Cercetari de Geologie, Geofizica, si Geografie. Seria Geografie — Studii Cerc Geol Geofiz Geogr
Studii si Cercetari de Geologie, Geofizica, si Geografie. Seria Geologie — SCGGA
Studii si Cercetari de Geologie, Geofizica, si Geografie. Seria Geologie — Stud Cercet Geol Geofiz Geogr Ser Geol
Studii si Cercetari de Geologie-Geografie — Stud Cercet Geol Geogr
Studii si Cercetari de Igiena si Sanatate Publica — Stud Cercet Ig Sanat Publica
Studii si Cercetari de Inframicrobiologie — SCIBA
Studii si Cercetari de Inframicrobiologie — Stud Cercet Inframicrobiol
Studii si Cercetari de Inframicrobiologie, Microbiologie, si Parazitologie — Stud Cercet Inframicrobiol Microbiol Parazitol
Studii si Cercetari de Istoria Artei — Istoria Artei
Studii si Cercetari de Istoria Artei — St C Istor
Studii si Cercetari de Istoria Artei — Stud Cercetari Istoria Artei
Studii si Cercetari de Istoria Artei — Stud Istoria Artei
Studii si Cercetari de Istoria Artei. Seria Arta Plastica — SCIA
Studii si Cercetari de Istoria Artei. Seria Arta Plastica — St C Istor
Studii si Cercetari de Istoria Artei. Seria Arta Plastica — Stud Istoria Artei
Studii si Cercetari de Istorie — SCI
Studii si Cercetari de Istorie Buzoiana — Stud Cerc Buzan
Studii si Cercetari de Istorie Literara si Folclor — ILF
Studii si Cercetari de Istorie Literara si Folclor — SCILF
Studii si Cercetari de Istorie Literara si Folclor — StCILF
Studii si Cercetari de Istorie Veche [*Later, Studii si Cercetari de Istorie Veche si Arheologie*] — SCIV
Studii si Cercetari de Istorie Veche si Arheologie — SCIVA
Studii si Cercetari de Istorie Veche si Arheologie — St C Istor
Studii si Cercetari de Istorie Veche si di Archeologie — Stud Cerc Ist Veche
Studii si Cercetari de Matematica si Fizica — St Cerc Mat Fiz
Studii si Cercetari de Matematica si Fizica — Stud Cercet Mat Fiz
Studii si Cercetari de Mecanica Aplicata — SCMAA
Studii si Cercetari de Mecanica Aplicata — Stud Cerc Mec Apl
Studii si Cercetari de Mecanica Aplicata — Stud Cercet Mec Apl
Studii si Cercetari de Medicina (Cluj) — Stud Cercet Med (Cluj)
Studii si Cercetari de Medicina Interna — Stud Cercet Med Interna
Studii si Cercetari de Metalurgie [*Romania*] — Stud Cercet Metal
Studii si Cercetari de Metalurgie. Comunicari Stiintifice — Stud Cercet Metal Comun Stiint
Studii si Cercetari de Neurologie — Stud Cercet Neurol
Studii si Cercetari de Numismatica — SC Num
Studii si Cercetari de Numismatica — SCN
Studii si Cercetari de Numismatica — Stud Cerc Num
Studii si Cercetari de Silvicultura — Stud Cercet Silvic
Studii si Cercetari de Silvicultura. Institutul de Cercetari si Amenajari Silvice — Stud Cercet Silvic Inst Cercet Amenajari Silvice
Studii si Cercetari de Virusologie — Stud Cercet Virusol
Studii si Cercetari Economice — Stud Cerc Econom
Studii si Cercetari Economice — Studii Cercet Econ
Studii si Cercetari. Institutul de Cercetari Forestiere (Industrializarea Lemnului) — Stud Cerc Inst Cerc For (Industr Lemn)
Studii si Cercetari. Institutul de Cercetari Forestiere (Mecanizarea Lucrarilor Forestiere) — Stud Cerc Inst Cerc For (Mec Lucr For)
Studii si Cercetari. Institutul de Cercetari Forestiere (Silvicultura) — Stud Cerc Inst Cerc For (Silv)
Studii si Cercetari. Institutul de Cercetari Piscicole — Stud Cercet Inst Cercet Piscic
Studii si Cercetari. Institutul de Cercetari si Proiectari Piscicole — Stud Cercet Inst Cercet Proiect Piscic
Studii si Cercetari. Institutul de Meteorologie si Hidrologie. Hidrologie — Stud Cercet Inst Meteorol Hidrol Hidrol
Studii si Cercetari. Institutul de Meteorologie si Hidrologie. Partea 1. Meteorologie — Stud Cercet Inst Meteorol Hidrol Partea 1
Studii si Cercetari. Institutul de Meteorologie si Hidrologie. Partea 2. Hidrologie — Stud Cercet Inst Meteorol Hidrol Partea 2
Studii si Cercetari Lingvistice — SCL
Studii si Cercetari Lingvistice — StCL
Studii si Cercetari Matematice — Stud Cerc Mat
Studii si Cercetari Piscicole. Institutul de Cercetari si Proiectari Alimentare — Stud Cercet Piscic Inst Cercet Proiect Aliment
Studii si Cercetari Stiintifice — SC St I
Studii si Cercetari Stiintifice. Filiala Cluj. Academia Republicii Populare Romine — SCS Cluj
Studii si Cercetari Stiintifice. Filiala Cluj. Academia Republicii Populare Romine — Stud Cercet Stiint Fil Cluj Acad Repub Pop Rom
Studii si Cercetari Stiintifice. Filiala Iasi. Academia Republicii Populare Romine — Stud Cercet Stiint Fil Iasi Acad Repub Pop Rom
Studii si Cercetari Stiintifice. Filiala Iasi. Academia Republicii Populare Romine. Chimie — Stud Cercet Stiint Fil Iasi Acad Repub Pop Rom Chimie
Studii si Cercetari Stiintifice. Filiala Iasi. Academia Republicii Populare Romine. Medicina — Stud Cercet Stiint Fil Iasi Acad Repub Pop Rom. Med
Studii si Cercetari Stiintifice. Filiala Iasi. Academia Republicii Populare Romine. Seria 2. Stiinte Biologice, Medicale, si Agricole — Stud Cercet Stiint Fil Iasi Acad Repub Pop Rom Ser 2
Studii si Cercetari Stiintifice. Filiala Iasi. Academia RPR. [*Republicii Populare Romine*]. Biologice si Stiinte Agricole — Studii Cerc Stiint Iasi Biol Stiint Agric
Studii si Cercetari Stiintifice. Filologie — StCSF
Studii si Cercetari Stiintifice. Filologie (Iasi) — SCSFI
Studii si Comunicari (Brukenthal) — Stud Comun (Brukenthal)
Studii si Comunicari. Istorie, Stintele Naturii — St Com
Studii si Comunicari. Muzeul Brukenthal — St Com
Studii si Comunicari (Pitesti) — Stud Comun (Pitesti)
Studii si Comunicari (Satu Mare) — Stud Comun (Satu Mare)
Studii si Materiale de Istorie Medie — SMIM
Studii si Materiale de Istorie Medie — Stud Mat Ist Medie
Studii si Materiale de Muzeografie si Istorie Militara — SM Muz
Studii si Materiale de Muzeografie si Istorie Militara — SMIM
Studii si Materiale de Muzeografie si Istorie Militara — SMMIM
Studii si Materiale de Muzeografie si Istorie Militara — Stud Mat Muz Ist Mil
Studii si Materiale. Muzeul Judetean — SMTM
Studii si Materiale Muzeul Judetean (Suceava, Romania) — Stud Mat (Suceava)
Studii si Materiale Muzeul Judetean (Tirgu-Mures, Romania) — Stud Mat Muz (Tirgu Mures)
Studii si Materiale Privitoare la Trecutul Istorie al Judetului. Prahova, Istorie, Etnografie (Ploiesti) — St Mat (Ploiesti)
Studii Tehnice si Economice. Institutul Geologic (Romania). Seria A. Prospectiuni si Explorari Geologice — Stud Teh Econ Inst Geol (Rom) Ser A
Studii Tehnice si Economice. Institutul Geologic (Romania). Seria B. Chimie — Stud Teh Econ Inst Geol (Rom) Ser B
Studii Tehnice si Economice. Institutul Geologic (Romania). Seria C. Pedologie — Stud Teh Econ Inst Geol (Rom) Ser C

Studii Tehnice si Economice. Institutul Geologic (Romania). Seria D. Prospectiuni Geofizice — Stud Teh Econ Inst Geol (Rom) Ser D
Studii Tehnice si Economice. Institutul Geologic (Romania). Seria E. Hidrogeologie — Stud Teh Econ Inst Geol (Rom) Ser E
Studii Tehnice si Economice. Institutul Geologic (Romania). Seria E. Hidrogeologie — Stud Teh Econ Inst Geol Ser E
Studii Tehnice si Economice. Institutul Geologic (Romania). Seria F. Geologie Tehnice — Stud Teh Econ Inst Geol (Rom) Ser F
Studii Tehnice si Economice. Institutul Geologic (Romania). Seria I. Mineralogie-Petrografie — Stud Teh Econ Inst Geol Ser I
Studii Tehnice si Economice. Institutului Geologic al Romaniei — Studi Teh Econ Inst Geol Rom
Studii Tehnice si Economice. Institutului Geologic al Romaniei. Stiinta Solului — Studii Teh Econ Inst Geol Rom
Studii Tehnice si Economice. Seria A. Prospectiuni si Explorari Geologice Institut de Geologie si Geolizica. Bucharest — Stud Teh Econ Ser A Inst Geol Geofiz Bucharest
Studii Tehnice si Economice. Seria C. Pedologie. Institutul Geologic. Romania — Stud Teh Econ Ser C Inst Geol Rom
Studii Tehnice si Economice. Seria D. Prospectiuni Geofizice. Institutul de Geologie si Geofizica (Bucharest) [*Romania*] — Stud Teh Econ Ser D Inst Geol Geofiz (Bucharest)
Studii Tehnice si Economice. Seria E. Hidrogeologie. Institutul de Geologie si Geofizica — Stud Teh Econ Ser E Inst Geol Geofiz
Studii Teologice — STeol
Studii Teologice [*Bucharest*] — StTeol
Studii Teologice — Stud Teol
Studijne Zvesti Archeologickeho Ustavu Slovenskej Akademie v Nitra — Stud Zvesti
Studijne Zvesti Archeologickeho Ustavu Slovenskej Akademie v Nitra — SZAUSAV
Studijni Informace. Lesnictyi — Studijni Inform Lesnictyi
Studijni Informace. Ustav Vedeckotechnickych Informaci pro Zemedelstvi. Rostlinna Vyroba — Stud Inf Ustav Vedeckotech Inf Zemed Rostl Vyroba
Studime Filologjike — SFil
Studime Filologjike — Stud Filol
Studime Historike — S Hist
Studime Historike — Stud Hist
Studio — S
Studio International — Stud Int
Studio International — Studio
Studio International — Studio Int
Studio International — Studio Intl
Studiorum Novi Testamenti Societas. Bulletin — SNTSB
Studiorum Novi Testamenti Societas. Monograph Series — SNTSMS
Studiorum Paulinorum Congressus Internationalis Catholicus — SPCIC
Studium — St
Studium — Stu
Studium Biblicum Franciscanum — SBF
Studium Biblicum Franciscanum. Collectio Minor — SBFCMi
Studium Biblicum Franciscanum Liber Annuus — St Bi Franc
Studium Generale — SG
Studium Generale — SGen
Studium Generale [*Heidelberg*] — StG
Studium Generale — STGEA
Studium Generale — Stud Gen
Studium Generale. Zeitschrift fuer die Einheit der Wissenschaften in Zusammenhang ihrer Begriffsbildung und Forschungsmethoden — St Gen
Studium Ovetense — Stud Ov
Studium und Praxis — St u P
Studsvik Report — Studsvik Rep
Study Encounter — St Enc
Study Group. Institute for Research into Mental and Multiple Handicap [*Elsevier Book Series*] — SGMH
Study of Elementary Particles [*Japan*] — Study Elem Particles
Study of Society — Study of Soc
Study of Tea — Study Tea
Study of Tea/Chagyo Gijutsu Kenkyu. Tea Research Station. Ministry of Agriculture and Forestry — Stud Tea
Study Tour Report. Department of Primary Industries (Queensland) — Stud Tour Rep Dep Prim Ind (Queensl)
Stuekultur. Naturen og Hjemmet — Stklt
Stuttgarter Arbeiten zur Germanistik — SAG
Stuttgarter Beitraege zur Geschichte und Politik — Stuttgarter Beitraege
Stuttgarter Beitraege zur Naturkunde — Stutt Beitr Naturk
Stuttgarter Beitraege zur Naturkunde — Stuttg Beitr Naturkd
Stuttgarter Beitraege zur Naturkunde aus dem Staatlichen Museum fuer Naturkunde in Stuttgart — Stuttgarter Beitr Naturk
Stuttgarter Beitraege zur Naturkunde. Serie A (Biologie) — Stuttg Beitr Naturkd Ser A (Biol)
Stuttgarter Beitraege zur Naturkunde. Serie B (Geologie und Palaeontologie) — Stuttg Beitr Naturkd Ser B (Geol Palaeontol)
Stuttgarter Beitraege zur Naturkunde. Serie C. Allgemeinverstaendliche Aufsaetze — Stuttg Beitr Naturk Ser C Allg Aufsaetze
Stuttgarter Bibelhefte — SBh
Stuttgarter Bibelstudien — SBS
Stuttgarter Bibelstudien [*Stuttgart*] — StBSt
Stuttgarter Biblische Monographien [*Stuttgart*] — SBM
Stuttgarter Biblische Monographien — StBM
Stuttgarter Geographische Studien — Stuttg Geogr Stud
Stuttgarter Geographische Studien — Stuttgarter Geogr Stud
Stuttgartter Biblische Beitraege — SBB
STV [*Schweizerischer Technischer Verband*] **Bulletin** — STV Bull
Stvaranje — Stva
Style — PSTY
Styrelsen foer Teknisk Utveckling Informerar om Energiteknik [*Sweden*] — Styr Tek Utveckling Inf Energitek
Suara Ekonomi [*Singapore*] — Suara Ekon
Suara Universiti — Suara Univ
Sub-Cellular Biochemistry — Sub-Cell Bi
Sub-Cellular Biochemistry — Sub-Cell Biochem
Subject Index to Children's Magazines — IChildMag
Subject Index to Children's Magazines — Ind Child Mag
Subject Index to Children's Magazines — Sub Ind Child Mag
Subject Index to Children's Magazines — Subj Index Child Mag
Subject Index to Periodicals — SIP
Subject Index to Periodicals — Subj Index Period
Subject Index to Select Periodical Literature — Subj Index Sel Period Lit
Subject Index to Sources of Comparative International Statistics — SISCIS
Subject of the Day — Subj of Day
Subnuclear Series — Subnucl Ser
Subseries on Optical Science and Engineering — Subser Optical Sci Engrg
Subsidia ad Historiam SJ — SHSJ
Subsidia Diplomatica ad Selecta Juris Ecclesiastici Germaniae — SDJEG
Subsidia Hagiographica — SH
Subsidia Hagiographica — SHG
Subsidia Hagiographica — Subs Hag
Subsidia Medica — Subsidia Med
Substance and Alcohol Actions/Misuse — Subst Alcohol Actions Misuse
Substance Use and Misuse — Subst Use Misuse
Subtropicheskie Kul'tury — Subtrop Kul't
Subtropicheskie Kul'tury — SUKUA
Subtropicheskie Kul'tury. Ministerstvo Sel'skogo Khozyaistva SSSR — Subtrop Kul't Min Sel'Khoz SSSR
Suburban Life — Sub Life
Success Magazine — Success M
Successful Farming [*Iowa Edition*] — GSUF
Successful Farming — Suc Farm
Successful Farming — Success Farm
Successful Farming — Success Farming
Successful Farming — Successful F
Successful Farming in the South — Success Farm South
Successful Meetings — SMT
Successful Meetings — Success Mtg
Suck-Egg Mule — S-EM
Sucrerie Belge and Sugar Industry Abstracts — Sucr Belg Sugar Ind Abstr
Sud. Information Economique Provence-Cote D'Azur-Corse — Sud Inform Econ Provence-Cote D'Azur-Corse
Sud Medical et Chirurgical — Sud Med Chir
Sudan Agricultural Journal — Sudan Agric J
Sudan. Antiquities Service. Occasional Papers — SASOP
Sudan Engineering Society. Journal — Sudan Eng Soc J
Sudan. Geological Survey Department. Bulletin — Sudan Geol Surv Dep Bull
Sudan Journal of Economic and Social Studies — Sudan J Econ and Social Studies
Sudan Journal of Economic and Social Studies — Sudan J Econ Soc Stud
Sudan Journal of Food Science and Technology — SJFTD8
Sudan Journal of Food Science and Technology — Sudan J Food Sci Technol
Sudan Journal of Veterinary Science and Animal Husbandry — Sudan J Vet Sci Anim Husb
Sudan Medical Journal — Sud Med J
Sudan Notes and Records — SNR
Sudan Notes and Records — Sudan Notes
Sudan Notes and Records — Sudan Notes Rec
Sudan Society — Sudan Soc
Sudebno-Meditsinskaya Ekspertiza — Sudebno-Med Ekspert
Sudebno-Meditsinskaya Ekspertiza — Sud-Med Ekspert
Sudebno-Meditsinskaya Ekspertiza i Kriminalistika na Sluzhbe Sledstviya — Sud Med Ekspert Krim Sluzhbe Sledstviya
SUDENE [*Superintendencia do Desenvolvimento do Nordeste*] **Boletim do Recursos Naturais** — SUDENE Bol Recur Nat
SUDENE [*Superintendencia do Desenvolvimento do Nordeste*] **GCDP Boletim de Estudos de Pesca** [*Grupo Coordenador do Desenvolvimento da Pesca*] — BPDNA2
Sudestasie. Magazine d'Information — SUD
Sudhoffs Archiv — Sudh Arch
Sudhoffs Archiv fuer Geschichte der Medizin und der Naturwissenschaften — AGM
Sudhoffs Archiv fuer Geschichte der Medizin und der Naturwissenschaften — SAGMN
Sudhoffs Archiv fuer Geschichte der Medizin und der Naturwissenschaften — Sudhoffs Arch
Sudhoffs Archiv fuer Geschichte der Medizin und der Naturwissenschaften — Sudhoffs Arch Gesch Med Naturwiss
Sudhoffs Archiv. Zeitschrift fuer Wissenschaftsgeschichte — Sudhoffs Arch
Sudhoffs Archiv. Zeitschrift fuer Wissenschaftsgeschichte — Sudhoffs Arch Z Wissenschaftsgesch
Sudhoffs Archiv. Zeitschrift fuer Wissenschaftsgeschichte — ZWG
Sudhoffs Archiv. Zeitschrift fuer Wissenschaftsgeschichte Beihefte — Sudhoffs Arch Beih
Sudhoffs Archiv. Zeitschrift fuer Wissenschaftsgeschichte. Beihefte — Sudhoffs Arch Z Wissenschaftsgesch Beih
Sueddeutsche Apothekerzeitung — Sueddt Ap Zt
Sueddeutsche Kirchenfuehrer — SDKF
Sueddeutsche Monatshefte — SdMh
Sueddeutsche Monatshefte — Sueddt Mh
Sueddeutsche Tonindustrie- und Bauzeitung — Sueddt Tonindustrieztg
Sueddeutsche Zeitung — Sueddtsch Ztg
Sueddeutsche Zeitung — SZ
Suedostdeutsche Forschungen — Suedostdt Forsch

Suedostdeutsche Semesterblaetter — Suedostdt Semesterbl
Suedostdeutsche Vierteljahresblaetter. Suedostdeutsche Heimatblaetter — Suedostdt Vjbl
Suedostdeutsches Archiv — SO Ar
Suedostdeutsches Archiv — SODA
Suedostdeutsches Archiv — SuedA
Suedostdeutsches Archiv — SuedoA
Suedostdeutsches Archiv — Suedostdt Arch
Suedosteuropa Mitteilungen — Suedosteur Mitt
Suedosteuropa. Zeitschrift fuer Gegenwartsforschung — WDB
Suedosteuropa-Jahrbuch — SO Jb
Suedosteuropa-Jahrbuch — Suedost Eur Jb
Suedosteuropa-Jahrbuch — Suedosteur Jb
Suedost-Forschungen — SOF
Suedost-Forschungen — Suedost F
Suedostforschungen — Suedost Forsch
Suedostforschungen. Internationale Zeitschrift fuer Geschichte, Kultur, und Landeskunde Suedosteuropas — SF
Suedostforschungen. Internationale Zeitschrift fuer Geschichte, Kultur, und Landeskunde Suedosteuropas — SOF
Suedost-Forschungen. Internationale Zeitschrift fuer Geschichte, Kultur, und Landeskunde Sued-Osteuropas — Suedost-Forsch
Suedwestdeutscher Imker — Suedwestdt Imker
Suelos Ecuatoriales — Suelos Ecuat
Suesswaren. Die Fachzeitschrift der Suesswaren Industrie. Produktion, Verpackung, Verkauf — SUS
Suesswarenmarkt. Fachzeitschrift fuer Markt, Marketing, und Merchandising von Suesswaren — MLB
Suffolk Transnational Law Journal — Suff Trans LJ
Suffolk Transnational Law Journal — Suffolk Transnatl LJ
Suffolk University. Law Review — Su LR
Suffolk University. Law Review — Suff U LR
Suffolk University. Law Review — Suffolk U L Rev
Suffolk University. Law Review — Suffolk Univ L Rev
Sugaku. Mathematical Society of Japan — Sugaku
Sugar Beet Journal — Sugar Beet J
Sugar Beet Review and British Beet Grower — Sugar Beet Rev
Sugar Bulletin — Sug B
Sugar Bulletin — Sugar Bul
Sugar Bulletin [*United States*] — Sugar Bull
Sugar Industry Abstracts — Sugar Ind Abstr
Sugar Journal — Sug J
Sugar Journal — Sugar J
Sugar Molecule — Sugar Mol
Sugar Processing Research Conference. Proceedings — Sugar Process Res Conf Proc
Sugar Series [*Elsevier Book Series*] — SS
Sugar Technology Reviews — Sugar Technol Rev
Sugar y Azucar — Sug Azuc
Sugar y Azucar — Sug Azucar
Sugar y Azucar — Sugar
Sugarbeet Grower — Sugarbeet Grow
Sugarcane Breeders' Newsletter — Sugarcane Breed Newsl
Sugarcane Farmers Bulletin [*Quezon City*] — SFB
Sugarcane Variety Tests in Florida — Sugarcane Var Tests Fla
Sugarcane Variety Tests in Florida — SVTFDI
Suhrkamp Taschenbuch Wissenschaft — Suhrkamp Taschenbuch Wiss
Suicide and Life Threatening Behavior — Suicide Life Threatening Behav
Suicide and Life-Threatening Behavior — PSUI
Suicide and Life-Threatening Behavior — SLBEDP
Suicide and Life-Threatening Behavior — Suicide Life Threat Behav
Suicide Information and Education [*Database*] — SIE
Suid-Afrika. Departement van Bosbou Jaarverslag — S-Afr Dep Bosbou Jaarversl
Suid-Afrika. Departement van Landbou en Visserye. Tegniese Mededeling — S Afr Dep Landbou Viss Teg Meded
Suid-Afrika. Departement van Landbou Visserye Tegniese Mededeling — S Afr Dep Landbou Visserye Teg Meded
Suid-Afrika. Departement van Landbou-Tegniese Dienste Tegniese Mededeling — S-Afr Dep Landbou-Teg Dienste Teg Meded
Suid-Afrika. Departement van Mynwese. Geologiese Opname. Bulletin — S Afr Dep Mynwese Geol Opname Bull
Suid-Afrika. Departement van Mynwese. Geologiese Opname. Memoire — S Afr Dep Mynwese Geol Opname Mem
Suid-Afrika. Instituut Seevisserye Ondersoekverslag — S Afr Inst Seevisserye Ondersoekverslag
Suid-Afrikaanse Argief vir Oftalmologie — S-Afr Argief Oftalmol
Suid-Afrikaanse Bosbou Tydskrif — S-Afr Bosbou Tydskr
Suid-Afrikaanse Industriele Chemikus — S Afr Ind Chem
Suid-Afrikaanse Instituut van Essaieurs en Analitici. Bulletin — S Afr Inst Essaieurs Anal Bull
Suid-Afrikaanse Kankerbulletin — S Afr Kankerbull
Suid-Afrikaanse Mediese Tydskrif — S-Afr Med Tydskr
Suid-Afrikaanse Meganiese Ingenieur — S Afr Meg Ing
Suid-Afrikaanse Spektroskopiese Konferensie — S Afr Spektrosk Konf
Suid-Afrikaanse Spoorwee [*South Africa*] — S-Afr Spoorwee
Suid-Afrikaanse Spoorwee/South African Railways — SASSAR
Suid-Afrikaanse Tydskrif vir Antarktiese Navorsing — S-Afr Tydskr Antarkt Navors
Suid-Afrikaanse Tydskrif vir Antarktiese Navorsing. Supplement — S Afr Tydskr Antarkt Navors Suppl
Suid-Afrikaanse Tydskrif vir Apteekwese — S Afr Tydskr Apteekwese
Suid-Afrikaanse Tydskrif vir Chemie — S Afr Tydskr Chem
Suid-Afrikaanse Tydskrif vir Chirurgie — S-Afr Tydskr Chir
Suid-Afrikaanse Tydskrif vir Dierkunde — S Afr Tydskr Dierkd
Suid-Afrikaanse Tydskrif vir Fisika — S Afr Tydskr Fis
Suid-Afrikaanse Tydskrif vir Geneeskunde — S-Afr Tydskr Geneeskd
Suid-Afrikaanse Tydskrif vir Geneeskunde — Suid Afr Tyd Geneesk
Suid-Afrikaanse Tydskrif vir Geneeskunde — Suid-Afr Tydskr Geneesk
Suid-Afrikaanse Tydskrif vir Geologie — S Afr Tydskr Geol
Suid-Afrikaanse Tydskrif vir Kliniese Wetenskap — S Afr Tydskr Klin Wet
Suid-Afrikaanse Tydskrif vir Laboratorium en Kliniekwerk — S-Afr Tydskr Lab Kliniekwerk
Suid-Afrikaanse Tydskrif vir Landbouwetenskap — S-Afr Tydskr Landbouwet
Suid-Afrikaanse Tydskrif vir Landbouwetenskap — Suid-Afr Tydskr Landbouwetenskap
Suid-Afrikaanse Tydskrif vir Mediese Laboratorium-Tegnologie — S Afr Tydskr Med Lab Tegnol
Suid-Afrikaanse Tydskrif vir Natuurnavorsing — S Afr Tydskr Natuurnavors
Suid-Afrikaanse Tydskrif vir Natuurwetenskap en Tegnologie — S Afr Tydskr Natuurwet Tegnol
Suid-Afrikaanse Tydskrif vir Natuurwetenskap en Tegnologie — S-Afr Tydsk Natuurwet Tegnol
Suid-Afrikaanse Tydskrif vir Natuurwetenskap en Tegnologie — SATTDF
Suid-Afrikaanse Tydskrif vir Natuurwetenskap en Tegnologie — Suid-Afrikaanse Tydskr Natuurwetenskap Tegnol
Suid-Afrikaanse Tydskrif vir Navorsing in Antarktika — S Afr Tydskr Navors Antarkt
Suid-Afrikaanse Tydskrif vir Obstetrie en Ginekologie — S-Afr Tydskr Obstet Ginekol
Suid-Afrikaanse Tydskrif vir Plant en Grond — S Afr Tydskr Plant Grond
Suid-Afrikaanse Tydskrif vir Plant en Grond — SAJSEV
Suid-Afrikaanse Tydskrif vir Plantkunde — S Afr Tydskr Plantkd
Suid-Afrikaanse Tydskrif vir Plantkunde — S Afr Tydskr Plantkunde
Suid-Afrikaanse Tydskrif vir Plantkunde — SAJBDD
Suid-Afrikaanse Tydskrif vir Radiologie — S-Afr Tydskr Radiol
Suid-Afrikaanse Tydskrif vir Seewetenskap — S Afr Tydskr Seewetenskap
Suid-Afrikaanse Tydskrif vir Seewetenskap — SJMSE7
Suid-Afrikaanse Tydskrif vir Sielkunde — SJPSDL
Suid-Afrikaanse Tydskrif vir Sielkunde — Suid-Afr Tydskr Sielkd
Suid-Afrikaanse Tydskrif vir Suiweltegnologie — S-Afr Tydskr Suiweltegnol
Suid-Afrikaanse Tydskrif vir Veekunde — S-Afr Tydskr Veekd
Suid-Afrikaanse Tydskrif vir Voeding — S-Afr Tydskr Voeding
Suid-Afrikaanse Tydskrif vir Wetenskap — S-Afr Tydskr Wet
Suid-Afrikaanse Tydskrif vir Wysbegeerte — S Afr Tydskr Wysbegeerte
Suid-Afrikaanse Tydskrif vir Wysbegeerte — SAJPEM
Suid-Afrikaanse Wetenskaplike en Nywerheidnavorsingsraad. Jaarverslag — S Afr Wet Nywerheidnavorsingsraad Jaarversl
Suid-Afrikaanse Wetenskaplike en Nywerheidnavorsingsraad Navorsingsverslag — CSIRB4
Suid-Afrikaanse Wetenskaplike en Nywerheidnavorsingsraad. Navorsingsverslag — S-Afr Wet Nywerheid-Navorsingsraad Navorsingsversl
Suid-Afrikaanse Wetenskaplike en Nywerheidnavorsingsraad. Spesiale Verslag — S-Afr Wet Nywerheid-Navorsingsraad Spes Versl
Suid-Afrikaanse Woltekstiel-Navorsingsinstituut Jaarverslag — S Afr Woltekst Navorsingsinst Jaarversl
Suid-Afrikaanse Woltekstiel-Navorsingsinstituut. Technical Report — S Afr Woltekst Navorsingsinst Tech Rep
Suisse Contemporaine — S Cont
Suisse Contemporaine — SC
Suisse Primitive — SP
Sulfuric Acid and Industry [*Japan*] — Sulfuric Acid Ind
Sulphur in Agriculture — SUAGDL
Sulphur in Agriculture — Sulphur Agric
Sulphur Institute. Journal — Sulphur Inst J
Sulzer Technical Review — Sulz Tech Rev
Sulzer Technical Review — Sulzer Tech Rev
Sumarski List — Sum List
Sumarstvo — Su
Sumatra Post — SP
Sumatra Research Bulletin — Sumatra Res B
Sumer. A Journal of Archaeology and History in Iraq — Sum
Sumerian Economic Texts from the Third Ur Dynasty — SETU
Sumerischen und Akkadischen Koenigsinschriften — SAK
Sumerisches Lexikon [*Rome*] — SL
Sumitomo Bank Review — SUK
Sumitomo Bank Review — Sumitomo
Sumitomo Bank Review — Sumitomo Bank R
Sumitomo Bulletin of Industrial Health — Sumitomo Bull Ind Health
Sumitomo Electric Review [*Japan*] — Sumitomo Electr Rev
Sumitomo Electric Technical Review — Sumitomo Elec Tech Rev
Sumitomo Electric Technical Review — Sumitomo Electr Tech Rev
Sumitomo Jukikai Giho — SJGHA
Sumitomo Kikai Giho — SUKGA
Sumitomo Light Metal Technical Reports — Sumitomo Light Met Tech Rep
Sumitomo Light Metal Technical Reports — Sumitomo Light Metal Tech Rep
Sumitomo Machinery [*Japan*] — Sumitomo Mach
Sumitomo Metals — Sumitomo Met
Sumitomo Quarterly — Sumitomo Q
Summa Phytopathologica — Summa Phytopathol
Summaries of Doctoral Dissertations. Northwestern University — SDD-NU
Summaries of Doctoral Dissertations. University of Wisconsin — SDDUW
Summaries of Papers. Australian Ceramic Conference — Summ Pap Aust Ceram Conf
Summaries of Reports. Electrotechnical Laboratory (Tokyo, Japan) — Sum Rep Electrotech Lab (Tokyo Japan)
Summary of Proceedings. Soil Science Society of North Carolina — Sum Proc Soil Sci Soc NC
Summary of Proceedings. Western Cotton Production Conference — Summ Proc West Cotton Prod Conf

Summary of Progress. Geological Survey Division (Nigeria) — Summ Prog Geol Surv Div (Nigeria)
Summary of World Broadcasts. Part 1. The USSR Weekly Economic Report — Summ World Broadcasts Part 1
Summary of World Broadcasts. Part 2. Eastern Europe Weekly Economic Report — Summ World Broadcasts Part 2
Summary of World Broadcasts. Part 3. The Middle East, Africa, and Latin America Weekly Economic Report — Summ World Broadcasts Part 3
Summary Reports. Electrotechnical Laboratory [*Japan*] — Summ Rep Electrotech Lab
Summer — SM
Summer Computer Simulation Conference. Proceedings — Summer Comput Simul Conf Proc
Summer Institute on Particle Physics. Proceedings — Summer Inst Part Phys Proc
Summit Magazine — Summit Mag
Summlung Gemeinverstaendlicher Vortraege und Schriften aus dem Gebiet der Theologie und Religionsgeschichte [*Tuebingen*] — SGV
Summlung Gemeinverstaendlicher Vortraege und Schriften aus dem Gebiet der Theologie und Religionsgeschichte [*Tuebingen*] — SGVS
Sun and Moon — S & M
Sun and Moon — Sun M
Sun at Work in Britain — Sun Work Br
Sun at Work in Britain — SWBRD
Sun (Baltimore) — Baltmr Sun
Sun World — Sun Wld
Sunday Democrat and Chronicle — Sun Demo & Ch
Sunday Express [*United Kingdom*] — SE
Sunday Gazette-Mail — Sun Gaz-Ma
Sunday Gleaner (Jamaica) — SGJ
Sunday Magazine — Sund M
Sunday Magazine — Sunday M
Sunday Oklahoman — Sun Oklahom
Sunday Telegraph — ST
Sunday Telegraph [*United Kingdom*] — STEL
Sunday Telegraph (Australia) — STA
Sunday Times [*United Kingdom*] — ST
Sunday Times — Sun Times
Sunday Times — SunT
Sunday Times (London) — STL
Sunday Times Magazine — Sunday Times Mag
Sundhedsbladet — Su
Sun-Diamond Grower — Sun Diamond Grow
Sung Kyun Kwan University. Journal — Sung Kyun Kwan Univ J
Sung Studies Newsletter — Sung Stud Newsl
Sun-Herald — SH
Sun-Herald (Australia) — SHA
Sunset [*Central West edition*] — GSUN
Sunset Magazine — Sunset Mag
Sunshine State Agricultural Research Report — Sunshine St Agric Res Rep
Sunshine State Agricultural Research Report — Sunshine State Agric Res Rep
Sunshine State Agricultural Research Report. Florida University Agricultural Experiment Station — Sunshine State Agr Res Rep
SUNY Series in Ancient Greek Philosophy — SUNY Ser Anc Greek Philos
SUNY Series in Logic and Language — SUNY Ser Logic Lang
SUNY Series in Philosophy — SUNY Ser Philos
SUNY Series in Science, Technology, and Society — SUNY Ser Sci Tech Soc
Sunyatsenia. Journal. Botanical Institute. College of Agriculture. Sun Yatsen University — Sunyatsenia
Suomalainen Kirjallisuuden Seura — SKS
Suomalainen Suomi — SuSu
Suomalainen Suomi — SuSuomi
Suomalainen Suomi. Kulttuuripolittinen Aikakauskirja/Valvoja — SuSuV
Suomalaisen Tiedeakatemian Toimituksia — Suom Tiedeaka Toim
Suomalaisen Tiedeakatemian Toimituksia. Annales Academiae Scientiarum Fennicae — Annales Acad Scient Fenn
Suomalaista Psykiatriaa — Suom Psykiatr
Suomen Antropologi/Antropologi i Finland — S Ant
Suomen Elainlaakarilehti — Suom Elainlaakaril
Suomen Elainlaakarilehti. Finsk Veterinartidskrift — Suomen Elainlaakril Fin Veterinartidskr
Suomen Hammaslaakariseuran Toimituksia — Suom Hammaslaak Toim
Suomen Hammaslaakariseuran Toimituksia — Suom Hammaslaak Toimi
Suomen Historiallinen Scusa — Suomen Hist Scusa
Suomen Historian Laehteitae. Finnische Geschichtsquellen — Suom Hist Laeht
Suomen Hyonteistieteellinen Aikakauskirja — Suom Hyonteistiet Aikak
Suomen Kalatalous — Suom Kalatalous
Suomen Kemistilehti A — Suom Kemistil A
Suomen Kemistilehti A — Suomen Kemistil A
Suomen Kemistilehti A, B — Suomen Kem A B
Suomen Kemistilehti B — Suom Kemistil B
Suomen Kemistiseuran Tiedonantoja — FKAMAR
Suomen Kemistiseuran Tiedonantoja — Suom Kemistis Tied
Suomen Kemistiseuran Tiedonantoja — Suom Kemistiseuran Tied
Suomen Kirjallinen Seuran Toimituksia. Abhandlungen der Finnischen Literarischen Gesellschaft — Suom Kirj Seuran Toim
Suomen Kirkkohistoriallinen Seuran Toimituksia. Abhandlungen der Finnischen Kirchengeschichtlichen Gesellschaft — Suom Kirkkohist Seuran Toim
Suomen Laakarilehti — Suom Laakaril
Suomen Maataloustieteellinen Seura. Maataloustieteellinen Aikakauskirj — Suomen Maataloust Seura Maatalous Aikakausk
Suomen Maataloustieteellisen Seuran Julkaisuja — Suom Maatal Seur Julk
Suomen Maataloustieteellisen Seuran Julkaisuja — Suom Maataloustiet Seuran Julk
Suomen Maataloustieteellisen Seuran Julkaisuja — Suomen Maatalous Seuran Julk
Suomen Muinaismuistoyhdistyksen Aikakauskirija — SMYA
Suomen Muinaismuistoyhdistyksen Aikakauskirija — Suomen Aikakauskirija
Suomen Musukin Vuosikirja — Suomen M Vuosikirja
Suomen Naishammaslaakarit Ryhma Julkaisu — Suom Naishammaslaak Julk
Suomen Pankin Taloustieteellisen Tutkimuslaitoksen Julkaisuja — Suom Pank Tal Tutk Lait Julk
Super 8 Filmaker — S 8 Fmkr
Super Science Fiction — SSF
Super Science Stories — SSS
Superclean Rotor Steels. Workshop Proceedings — Superclean Rotor Steels. Workshop Proc
Supercomputer and Chemistry. IABG (Industrieanlangen-Betriebsgesellscha ft) Workshop — Supercomput Chem IABG Workshop
Superconducting Ceramics. Winter Meeting on Low Temperature Physics — Supercond Ceram Winter Meet Low Temp Phys
Superconductivity and Cryoelectronics. Proceedings. Symposium on Superconductivity and Cryoelectronics — Supercond Cryoelectron Proc Symp
Superconductivity. Proceedings. Italian National School on Condensed Matter Physics — Supercond Proc Ital Natl Sch Condens Matter Phys
Superconductivity. Research and Development — Supercond Res Dev
Superior Student — Sup Stud
Superlattices and Microstructures — Superlatt M
Supermagnets. Hard Magnetic Materials — Supermagnets Hard Magn Mater
Supermarket and Retailer — Supermark Retail
Supermarket Business — Super Bsns
Supermarket Business — Supermkt Bus
Supermarket News — Super News
Supermarketing — SEF
Supermarketing — Supermkt
Superphosphat-Mitteilungen — Superphosphat-Mitt
Superplasticity in Metals, Ceramics, and Intermetallics. Symposium — Superplast Met Ceram Intermet Symp
Supervision — SUP
Supervisor Nurse — Superv Nurse
Supervisory Management — SPM
Supervisory Management — Spvry Mgt
Supervisory Management — Super Mgt
Supervisory Management — Superv Manage
Supervisory Management — Supery Manage
Supervisory Management — Supvry Mgmt
Suplemento Antropologico — Supl Antropol
Suplemento Antropologico. Universidad Catolica de Nuestra Senora de la Asuncion — UCNSA/SA
Suplemento de Cuadernos de Ruedo Iberico — SCRI
Suplemento de Valencia — Suplemento Valencia
Suplemento Literario do Estado de Sao Paulo — SLESP
Supplement. Annales de Gembloux — Suppl Annls Gembloux
Supplement. Annales de l'Institut Pasteur (Paris) — Suppl Annls Inst Pasteur (Paris)
Supplement au Dictionnaire de la Bible — SDB
Supplement. Certificated Engineer — Suppl Certif Eng
Supplement. European Journal of Neuroscience — Suppl Eur J Neurosci
Supplement. Geophysics — Suppl Geophys
Supplement. Israel Journal of Botany — Suppl Israel J Bot
Supplement. Journal of the Physical Society of Japan — Suppl J Phys Soc Jap
Supplement. LC [*United States Library of Congress*] **Subject Headings** — Suppl LC Subj Head
Supplement (Massachusetts) — Mass Supp
Supplement. Popular Science Monthly — Sup Pop Sci Mo
Supplement. Progress of Theoretical Physics — Supp Pr T P
Supplement. Progress of Theoretical Physics — Suppl Prog Theor Phys
Supplement. Southwestern Entomologist — Suppl Southwest Entomol
Supplement till Naeringsforskning — Suppl Naeringsforsk
Supplement to Ancient Near Eastern Texts — SANET
Supplement to Collection of Scientific Works. Charles University Faculty of Medicine. Hradec Kralove — Suppl Collect Sci Works Charles Univ Fac Med Hradec Kralove
Supplement to Forestry. Report of the Sixth Discussion Meeting (Edinburgh) — Suppl For Rep (Sixth) Discuss Meet (Edinb)
Supplement to Social and Economic Studies — Suppl Social Econ Stud
Supplementa Entomologica — Supplta Ent
Supplementary Papers. Royal Geographical Society — Suppl Papers Roy Geogr Soc
Supplemento a la Ricerca Scientifica — Suppl Ric Sci
Supplemento alle Ricerche di Biologia della Selvaggina — Suppl Ric Biol Selvaggina
Supplements. Annales. Service des Antiquites de l'Egypt [*Cairo*] — SASAE
Supplements. Novum Testamentum [*Leiden*] — SNT
Supplements to Electroencephalography and Clinical Neurophysiology [*Elsevier Book Series*] — SECN
Supplements. Vetus Testamentum [*Leiden*] — SVT
Supplementum. Acta Universitatis Carolinae. Biologica — Suppl Acta Univ Carol Biol
Supplementum. Agrokemia es Talajtan — Suppl Agrokem Talajt
Supplementum Comicum. Commoediae Graecae Fragmenta Post Editiones Kockianam et Kaibelianam — Supp Com
Supplementum Comicum. Commoediae Graecae Fragmenta Post Editiones Kockianam et Kaibelianam — Suppl Com
Supplementum Epigraphicum Graecum — SEG
Supplementum Epigraphicum Graecum — Supp Epigr
Supplementum Epigraphicum Graecum — Suppl Epigr Gr
Supplementum Lyricis Graecis — SLG

Supplementum. Sborniku Vedeckych Praci Lekarske Fakulty University Karlovy (Hradci Kralove) — Suppl Sb Ved Pr Lek Fak Univ Karlovy (Hradci Kralove)
Supportive Care in Cancer — Support Care Cancer
Supramolecular Chemistry — Supramol Chem
Supramolecular Science — Supramol Sci
Supreme Court Almanac [*India*] — SCALE
Supreme Court Historical Society. Yearbook [*US*] — Sup Ct Hist Socy YB
Supreme Court Law Review — Sup Ct L Rev
Supreme Court Law Review — Supr Ct LR
Supreme Court Law Review — Supreme Court LR
Supreme Court of Canada Judgements [*Database*] — SCCJ
Supreme Court Reports [*New South Wales, Australia*] — SCR
Supreme Court Reports [*Database*] — SCR
Supreme Court Reports (Equity) (New South Wales) — SCR (NSW) Eq
Supreme Court Reports (Law) [*New South Wales*] — SCR (L)
Supreme Court Reports (Law) (New South Wales) — (NSW) SCR (L)
Supreme Court Reports (New Series) (New South Wales) — SCR (NS) (NSW)
Supreme Court Reports (New South Wales) — SCR (NSW)
Supreme Court Reports (New York) — NY Sup Ct
Supreme Court Researcher — Sup Ct Res
Supreme Court Review — ISCV
Supreme Court Review — S Ct Rev
Supreme Court Review — Sup Ct Rev
Supreme Court Review — Supr Court
Supreme Court Review — Supreme Court Rev
Surface Analysis Methods in Materials Science — Surf Anal Methods Mater Sci
Surface and Colloid Science — Surf Colloid Sci
Surface and Defect Properties of Solids — SPSDC
Surface and Defect Properties of Solids — Surf Defect Prop Solids
Surface and Interface Analysis — Surf and Interface Anal
Surface and Interface Analysis — Surf Interface Anal
Surface and Vacuum Physics Index — SVPIA
Surface Coatings — Surf Coat
Surface Coatings Australia — Surf Coat Aust
Surface Mining and Reclamation Symposia — Surf Min Reclam Symp
Surface Mining Law — Surf Min Law
Surface Modification Technologies 4. Proceedings. International Conference — Surf Modif Technol 4 Proc Int Conf
Surface Review and Letters — Surf Rev Lett
Surface Science — Surf Sci
Surface Science — Surface Sci
Surface Science. Lectures on Basic Concepts and Applications. Proceedings. Latin American Symposium on Surface Physics — Surf Sci Proc Lat Am Symp Surf Phys
Surface Science Reports — Surf Sci R
Surface Science Reports — Surf Sci Rep
Surface Science Spectra — Surf Sci Spectra
Surface Technology — Surf Tech
Surface Technology — Surf Technol
Surface Technology — Surface Techn
Surface Warfare — Surf Warf
Surfaces and Interfaces — Surf Interfaces
Surfacing Journal — Surf J
Surfacing Journal [*United Kingdom*] — Surfacing J
Surfactant Science Series — Surfactant Sci Ser
Surgery [*Saint Louis*] — SURGAZ
Surgery Annual — SURAB
Surgery Annual — Surg Annu
Surgery, Gynecology, and Obstetrics — SGOBA
Surgery, Gynecology, and Obstetrics — Surg Gyn Ob
Surgery, Gynecology, and Obstetrics — Surg Gynec and Obst
Surgery, Gynecology, and Obstetrics — Surg Gynecol Obstet
Surgery in Italy — Surg Ital
Surgery Today — Surg Today
Surgical and Radiologic Anatomy — Surg Radiol Anat
Surgical Business — Surg Bus
Surgical Business — Surgical
Surgical Clinics of North America — S Clin North America
Surgical Clinics of North America — Surg Cl NA
Surgical Clinics of North America — Surg Clin N Am
Surgical Clinics of North America — Surg Clin N Amer
Surgical Clinics of North America — Surg Clin North Am
Surgical Endoscopy — Surg Endosc
Surgical Forum — Surg Forum
Surgical Gastroenterology — Surg Gastroenterol
Surgical Laparoscopy and Endoscopy — Surg Laparosc Endosc
Surgical Neurology [*Tryon, NC*] — SGNRA
Surgical Neurology — Surg Neurol
Surgical Oncology — Surg Oncol
Surgical Oncology Clinics of North America — Surg Oncol Clin N Am
Surgical Technologist — Surg Technol
Surgical Therapy [*Japan*] — Surg Ther
Surimi Technology — Surimi Technol
Surinaams Juristenblad — SJB
Surinaamse Landbouw — Sur Landb
Surinaamse Landbouw — Surinaam
Surinam Agriculture — SULAAL
Surinam Agriculture — Surinam Agric
Suriname Post — SPE
Surowce Mineralne — Surowce Miner
Surrey Archaeological Collections — Surrey AC
Surrey Archaeological Collections — Surrey Arch Coll
Surrey Archaeological Collections — Surrey Archaeol Collect
Surrey Archaeological Collections — Surry A Coll
Surtsey Research Progress Report — SRPR
Surtsey Research Progress Report — Surtsey Res Prog Rep
Surveillance Technologies II — Surveill Technol II
Survey — ISVY
Survey — S
Survey and Synthesis of Pathology Research — Surv Synth Pathol Res
Survey Graphic — Surv Graphic
Survey Graphic — Survey G
Survey Notes. Utah Geological and Mineral Survey — Surv Notes Utah Geol Miner Surv
Survey of Adults and Markets of Affluence [*Database*] — SAMA
Survey of Anesthesiology — Surv Anesthesiol
Survey of Biological Progress — Surv Biol Prog
Survey of Business [*United States*] — Surv Bus
Survey of Business (University of Tennessee) — Survey Bus (Univ Tenn)
Survey of Current Affairs — SUR
Survey of Current Affairs [*London*] — Surv Curr Affairs
Survey of Current Business [*United States*] — Curr Bus
Survey of Current Business [*Washington, DC*] — SCA
Survey of Current Business [*United States*] — SCB
Survey of Current Business — Surv Cur Bus
Survey of Current Business — Surv Curr Bus
Survey of Current Business — Surv Curr Busin
Survey of Current Business — Survey Cur Bus
Survey of Current Business — Survey Current Bus
Survey of Digestive Diseases — SDDIDP
Survey of Digestive Diseases — Surv Dig Dis
Survey of Drug Research in Immunologic Disease — SDRDDC
Survey of Drug Research in Immunologic Disease — Surv Drug Res Immunol Dis
Survey of Eastern Palestine — SEP
Survey of Economic Conditions in Africa — Surv Econ Cond Afr
Survey of Economic Conditions in Japan — MAS
Survey of Economic Conditions in Japan — Surv Econ Cond Jap
Survey of English Dialects — SED
Survey of Immunologic Research — SIMRDU
Survey of Immunologic Research — Surv Immun Res
Survey of Immunologic Research — Surv Immunol Res
Survey of Ophthalmology — Surv Ophthalmol
Survey of Power Equipment Requirements of the United States Electric Utility Industry — Power Eqp
Survey of Progress in Chemistry — SPGCA
Survey of Progress in Chemistry — Surv Prog Chem
Survey of Progress in Chemistry — Survey Progr Chem
Survey of Western Palestine — SWP
Survey on Sports Attendance — Svy Sports
Survey Paper. Horace Lamb Centre for Oceanographical Research. Flinders University of South Australia — Surv Pap Horace Lamb Centre Oceanogr Res
Surveying and Mapping — Surv & Map
Surveying and Mapping — Surv Mapp
Surveying Technician — Surveying Tech
Surveyor and Municipal and County Engineer — Surv Munic Cty Eng
Surveyor-Local Government Technology — Surv-Local Gov Technol
Surveys and Bibliographies. Council for Old World Archaeology. Department of Sociology and Anthropology. Boston University — COWA
Surveys and Reference Works in Mathematics — Surveys Reference Works Math
Surveys in Applied Mathematics — Surveys Appl Math
Surveys in High Energy Physics [*Switzerland*] — Surv High Energy Phys
Surveys on Mathematics for Industry — Surveys Math Indust
Survival — Surv
Survival International Review — Survival Int Rev
Susitna Hydro Studies — SUHS
Suspect Chemicals Sourcebook [*Database*] — SCS
Suspense — SUS
Susquehanna University. Studies — SUS
Susreti — Sus
Sussex Anthropology — Sussex Anthrop
Sussex Archaeological Collections — SAC
Sussex Archaeological Collections — Sussex A Coll
Sussex Archaeological Collections — Sussex AC
Sussex Archaeological Collections — Sussex Arch Coll
Sussex Archaeological Collections Relating to the Antiquities of the County — Sussex Arch Coll
Sussex County Magazine — SCM
Sussex Essays in Anthropology — Sussex Essays In Anthrop
Sussex Notes and Queries — SNQ
Sussidi allo Studio della Antichita Cristiana — SSAC
Sustancia. Revista de Cultura Superior — SRCS
Suvaguq. Pond Inlet — SV
Suvaguuq. Pauktuutit. Inuit Women's Association of Canada. Newsletter — SUVA
Suvremenna Meditsina [*Bulgaria*] — Suvrem Med
Suvremenni Problemi na Endokrinologiyata — Suvrem Probl Endokrinol
Svarka Vzryvom i Svoistva Svarnykh Soedinenii — Svarka Vzryvom Svoistva Svarnykh Soedin
Svarochnoe Proizvodstvo — SVAPA
Svarochnoe Proizvodstvo — Svar Proizvod
Svedeniya po Zemedelieto — Sved Zemed
Svensk Artillerie Tidskrift — Svensk Artill Tidskr
Svensk Botanisk Tidskrift — SBT
Svensk Botanisk Tidskrift — Sven Bot Tidskr
Svensk Botanisk Tidskrift — Svensk Bot Tidskr
Svensk Bryggeritidskrift — Sven Bryggeritidskr
Svensk Exegetisk Arsbok — SEA

Svensk Exegetisk Arsbok — SvEA
Svensk Exegetisk Arsbok — Sven Ex Ars
Svensk Exegetisk Arsbok — SvExAb
Svensk Exegetisk Arsbok — SvExArsb
Svensk Faerg-Teknisk Tidskrift — Sven Faerg Tek Tidskr
Svensk Farmaceutisk Tidskrift — Sv Farm Tid
Svensk Farmaceutisk Tidskrift — Sven Farm Tidskr
Svensk Farmaceutisk Tidskrift. Scientific Edition — Sven Farm Tidskr Sci Ed
Svensk Foerfattningssamling — Sven Foerfattningssaml
Svensk Fotografisk Tidskrift — Sven Fotogr Tidskr
Svensk Froetidning — Sven Frotidn
Svensk Froetidning — Svensk Froetidn
Svensk Geografisk Arsbok — Svensk Geog Arsbok
Svensk Humanistisk Tidsskrift — SHT
Svensk Juristtidning — Svensk Juristtidn
Svensk Kemisk Tidskrift — SKT
Svensk Kemisk Tidskrift — Sven Kem Tidskr
Svensk Kemisk Tidskrift — Svensk Kem Tidskr
Svensk Litteraturtidskrift — SLT
Svensk Litteraturtidskrift — Svensk Litt
Svensk Missionstidskrift — SMT
Svensk Missionstidskrift — SvM
Svensk Naturvetenskap — Sven Naturvetensk
Svensk Naturvetenskap — SVNAB
Svensk Pappersfoeraedlingstidskrift — Sven Papperfoeraedlingstidskr
Svensk Pappersmassetidning — Sven Pappersmassetidn
Svensk Papperstidning — Sven Papperstidn
Svensk Papperstidning — Svensk Papperstidn
Svensk Papperstidning — SvenskPapr
Svensk Papperstidning Tidskrift — Svens Pap T
Svensk Tandlaekare Tidskrift — Sven Tandlaek Tidskr
Svensk Tandlaekare Tidskrift — Sven Tandlak Tidskr
Svensk Tandlaekareforbunds Tidning [*Sweden*] — Sven Tandlakareforb Tidn
Svensk Teologisk Kvartalskrift — STK
Svensk Teologisk Kvartalskrift — STKv
Svensk Teologisk Kvartalskrift — Svensk Teol Kvartalskr
Svensk Teologisk Kvartalskrift — SvTK
Svensk Teologisk Kvartalskrift — SvTKv
Svensk Tidskrift — ST
Svensk Tidskrift — Svensk T
Svensk Tidskrift — SvT
Svensk Tidskrift — SvTs
Svensk Tidskrift foer Musikforskning — S T Mf
Svensk Tidskrift foer Musikforskning — Sven Tids M
Svensk Tidskrift foer Musikforskning — Svensk Tid
Svensk Tidskrift foer Musikforskning — Svensk Tidskr Musikforsk
Svensk Traevaru- och Pappersmassetidning — STT
Svensk Traevaru- och Pappersmassetidning — Sv Trav Pap
Svensk Traevaru- och Pappersmassetidning — Svensk Travarutidn
Svensk Traevaru-Tidning — Sven Traevaru-Tidn
Svensk Veterinaertidning — Sven Veterinartidn
Svensk Veterinaertidskrift — Svensk Vet-Tidskr
Svenska Aeroplan Aktiebolaget [*Linkoping, Sweden*]. SAAB Technical Notes — Sv Aeroplan Ab SAAB Tech Notes
Svenska Akademiens Handlingar — SAH
Svenska Akademiens Ordbok — SAOB
Svenska Bryggarefoereningens Manadsblad — Sven Bryggarefoeren Manadsbl
Svenska Dagbladet — SKD
Svenska Dagbladet — SvD
Svenska Folkskolans Vaenner. Kalender — SFVK
Svenska Forfattare Utgivna av Svenska Vitterhetssamfundet — SFSV
Svenska Fornminnes-Foereningen Tidskrift — SvFFT
Svenska Fornminnesfoerningens. Tidskrift — Svenska Fornm Tidskr
Svenska Fornskriftssaellskapets Skrifter — SFSS
Svenska Forskningsinstitutet foer Cement och Betong vid Kungliga i Stockholm. Meddelanden Tekniska Hoegskolan [*Sweden*] — Sven Forskningsinst Cem Betong K Tek Hogsk
Svenska Forskningsinstitutet foer Cement och Betong vid Kungliga Tekniska Hoegskolan i Stockholm. Handlingar — Sven Forskningsinst Cem Betong K Tek Hoegsk Stockholm Handl
Svenska Forskningsinstitutet foer Cement och Betong vid Kungliga Tekniska Hoegskolan i Stockholm. Meddelanden — Sven Forskningsinst Cem Betong K Tek Hoegsk Stockholm Medd
Svenska Forskningsinstitutet foer Cement och Betong vid Kungliga Tekniska Hoegskolan i Stockholm. Saertryck — Sven Forskningsinst Cem Betong K Tek Hoegsk Stockholm Saertr
Svenska Forskningsinstitutet foer Cement och Betong vid Kungliga Tekniska Hoegskolan i Stockholm. Utredningar — Sven Forskningsinst Cem Betong K Tek Hoegsk Stockholm Utredn
Svenska Gasfoereningens Manadsblad — Sven Gasfoeren Manadsbl
Svenska Gasverksfoereningens Aarsbok — Sven Gasverksfoeren Aarsb
Svenska Humanistisk Tidskrift — Svenska Humanist Tidskr
Svenska Hydrografisk-Biologiska Kommissionens Skrifter. Ny Serie. Biologi — Sven Hydrogr Biol Komm Skr Ny Ser Biol
Svenska Institutet foer Konserveringsforskning. Publikation — Sven Inst Konserveringsforsk Publ
Svenska Israels-Missionens Arsbok [*Stockholm*] — SIMArsbok
Svenska Jerusalems-Foereningens Tidskrift — SJFT
Svenska Jerusalems-Foereningens Tidskrift [*Uppsala*] — SvJerTs
Svenska Kraftverksfoereningens Publikationer — Sv Kraftverksforen Publ
Svenska Kraftverksfoereningens Publikationer — Sven Kraftverksfoeren Publ
Svenska Kraftverksfoereningens Publikationer Meddelande — Sven Kraftverksfoeren Publ Medd
Svenska Kyrkans Arsbok — SKA
Svenska Kyrkans Historia — SKH
Svenska Laekaresaellskapets Foerhandlingar — Sven Laekaresaellsk Foerh
Svenska Laekartidningen — Sven Laekartidn
Svenska Laekartidningen — SVLAA
Svenska Lakare-Sallskapet. Arsberattelse — Svenska Lakare Sallsk Arsberatt
Svenska Landsmal och Svenskt Folkliv — SL
Svenska Landsmal och Svenskt Folkliv [*Uppsala*] — SLSF
Svenska Landsmal och Svenskt Folkliv — SvLm
Svenska Linne-Sallskapet Arsskrift — SLA
Svenska Linne-Sallskapet Arsskrift [*Uppsala*] — SLSA
Svenska Linne-Sallskapet Arsskrift — Sven Linne-SallskArsskr
Svenska Linnesallskapets Arsskrift — Svenska Linnesallsk Arssk
Svenska Litteratursaellskapet i Finland — SLF
Svenska Litteratursaellskapet i Uppsala — SLU
Svenska Mejeriernas Riksfoerening. Produkttekniska Avdelningen. Meddelande — Sven Mejeriernas Riksfoeren Produkttek Avd Medd
Svenska Mejeritidningen — Sven Mejeritidn
Svenska Mosskulturfoereningens Tidskrift — Sven Mosskulturfoeren Tidskr
Svenska Mosskulturforeningens Tidskrift — Svenska Mosskulturforen Tidskr
Svenska Orientsallskapets Arsbok — SOA
Svenska Skogsvardsforeningens Tidskrift — Sven Skogsvardsforen Tidskr
Svenska Texter — SvT
Svenska Turistfoereningens Arsskrift — Svenska Turistfoeren Arsskr
Svenska Vall- och Mosskulturfoereningens Meddelanden — Sven Vall Mosskulturfoeren Medd
Svenska Vattenkraftforeningens Publikationer — Sven Vattenkraftfoeren Publ
Svensklaerarfoereningens Arsskrift — SLFA
Svenskt Bibliskt Uppslagsverk — SBU
Svenskt Biografiskt Lexikon — SBL
Svenskt Gudstjaenstliv — SGGT
Svenskt Musikhistoriskt Arkiv. Bulletin — Svenskt MHistoriskt
Sverdlovskii Gosudarstvennyi Pedagogiceskii Institut. Naucnyi Trudy — Sverdlovsk God Ped Inst Naucn Trudy
Sverdlovskii Gosudarstvennyi Pedagogiceskii Institut. Ucenye Zapiski — Sverdlovsk Gos Ped Inst Ucen Zap
Sveriges Geologiska Undersoekning — SVGU
Sveriges Geologiska Undersoekning. Arsbok — Sver Geol Unders Arsb
Sveriges Geologiska Undersoekning. Arsbok. Serie C. Avhandlingar och Uppsatser — Sver Geol Unders Arsb Ser C Avh Uppsatser
Sveriges Geologiska Undersoekning. Arsbok. Serie C. Avhandlingar och Uppsatser — Sveriges Geol Unders Ser C
Sveriges Gummitekniska Foerening. Publicerande — Sver Gummitek Foren Publ
Sveriges Landbruksuniversitet Vaxtskyddsrapporter Tradgard — VATRD8
Sveriges Lantbruksuniversitet Institutionen foer Arbetsmetodik och Teknik. Rapport — Sver Lantbruksuniv Inst Arbetsmetod Tek Rapp
Sveriges Lantbruksuniversitet Institutionen foer Biometri och Skogsindelning. Rapport — Sver Lantbruksuniv Inst Biom Skogsindelning Rapp
Sveriges Lantbruksuniversitet Institutionen foer Husdjursforadling och Sjukdomsgenetik. Rapport — Sver Lantbruksuniv Inst Husdjursforadling Sjukdomsgenet Rapp
Sveriges Lantbruksuniversitet Institutionen foer Lantbrukets Byggnadsteknik. Rapport — Sver Lantbruksuniv Inst Lantbrukets Byggnadstek Rapp
Sveriges Lantbruksuniversitet Institutionen foer Lantbruksteknik. Rapport — Sver Lantbruksuniv Inst Lantbruksteknik Rapp
Sveriges Lantbruksuniversitet Institutionen foer Mikrobiologi. Rapport — Sver Lantbruksuniv Inst Mikrobiol Rapp
Sveriges Lantbruksuniversitet Institutionen foer Radiobiologi. Rapport — Sver Lantbruksuniv Inst Radiobiol Rapp
Sveriges Lantbruksuniversitet Institutionen foer Tradgardsvetenskap. Rapport — Sver Lantbruksuniv Inst Tradgardsvetensk Rapp
Sveriges Lantbruksuniversitet Institutionen foer Vaxtodling. Rapport — Sver Lantbruksuniv Inst Vaxtodling Rapp
Sveriges Lantbruksuniversitet Konsulentavdelningens Rapporter Landskap — Sver Lantbruksuniv Konsulentavd Rapp Landskap
Sveriges Lantbruksuniversitet Rapporter i Skogsekologi och Skoglig Marklara — Sver Lantbruksuniv Rapp Skogsekol Skoglig Marklara
Sveriges Lantbruksuniversitet Vaxtskyddsrapporter Avhandlingar — Sver Lantbruksuniv Vaxtskyddsrapp Avh
Sveriges Lantbruksuniversitet Vaxtskyddsrapporter Jordbruk — Sver Lantbruksuniv Vaxtskyddsrapp Jordbruk
Sveriges Lantbruksuniversitet Vaxtskyddsrapporter Tradgard — Sver Lantbruksuniv Vaxtskyddsrapp Tradg
Sveriges Mekanforbund, Mekanresultat — Sver Mekanforb Mekanresult
Sveriges Natur — Sver Nat
Sveriges Natur Arsbok — Sver Nat Arsb
Sveriges Officiella Statistik Bergshantering. Statistika Centralbyran [*Stockholm*] — Sver Off Stat Bergshantering
Sveriges Pomologiska Foerening Arsskrift — Sver Pomol Foeren Arsskr
Sveriges Pomologiska Forenings Arsskrift — Sveriges Pomol Foren Arsskr
Sveriges Riksbank. Quarterly Review — Sveriges Riksbank Q R
Sveriges Riksbank. Quarterly Review — SVI
Sveriges Runinskrifter — SRI
Sveriges Skogsvaardsfoerbunds Tidskrift — Sver Skogsvaardsfoerb Tidskr
Sveriges Skogsvardsfoerbunds Tidskrift — Sver Skogsvardsfoerbunds Tidskr
Sveriges Skogsvardsfoerbunds Tidskrift — Sver Skogsvardsforb Tidskr
Sveriges Skogsvardsforbunds Tidskrift — Sveriges Skogsvforb Tidskr
Sveriges Tandlakarforbund Tidning — Sver Tandlakarforb Tidn
Sveriges Utsaedesfoerenings Tidskrift — Sver Utsadesforen Tidskr
Sveriges Utsaedesfoerenings Tidskrift — Sver Utsaedesfoer Tidskr
Sveriges Utsaedesfoerenings Tidskrift — Sveriges Utsaedesfoer Tidskr
Sverige-Tyskland — Sverige Tyskl
Sverkhprovodimost. Issledovaniya i Razrabotki — Sverkhprovodimost Issled Razrab
Svertyvayushchaya Sistema Krovi v Akusherstve i Ginekologii — Svertyvayushchaya Sist Krovi Akush Ginekol
Sveske Fizickih Nauka — Sveske Fiz Nauka

Svetotekhnika — Svetotekh
Svetotekhnika. Svetotekhnicheskaya Komissiya Akademii Nauk SSSR — Svetotekhnika Svetotekh Kom Akad Nauk SSSR
Svetsaren: A Welding Review — Svetsaren Weld Rev
Svetsaren. Deutsche Ausgabe — Svetsaren Dtsch Ausg
Svetsaren. Edition Francaise — Svetsaren Ed Fr
SVF [*Svetstekniska Foereningen*] **Fachorgan fuer Textilveredlung** — SVF Fachorgan Textilveredl
Svinovodstvo — Svinovod
Svizzera Italiana — SI
Svizzera Italiana — SvI
Svoistva Veshchestv i Stroenie Molekul — Svoista Veshchestv Str Mol
Svojstva Atomnykh Yader — Svojstva At Yader
Swarajya. Annual Number [*Madras*] — Swarajya A
Swarthmore College Monographs on Quaker History — SCMQ
Swaziland. Annual Report. Geological Survey and Mines Department — Swaziland Annu Rep Geol Surv Mines Dep
Swaziland. Geological Survey and Mines Department. Annual Report — Swaziland Geol Surv Mines Dep Annu Rep
Swaziland National Centre Yearbook — Swaziland Natn Cent Yb
Sweden. Foersvarets Forskningsanstalt. FOA Report — Swed Foersvarets Forskningsanst FOA Rep
Sweden. Geologiska Undersoekning. Serie Ae. Geologiska Kartblad i Skala 1:50,000 — Swed Geol Unders Ser Ae Geol Kartbl 1:50000
Sweden. Geologiska Undersoekning. Serie C — Swed Geol Unders Ser C
Sweden. Geologiska Undersoekning. Serie Ca. Avhandlingar och Uppsatser — Swed Geol Unders Ser Ca Avh Uppsatser
Sweden Now — SFC
Swedish American Trade News — Swed Am TN
Swedish Budget — Swed Bud
Swedish Cypress Expedition — SCE
Swedish Deep-Sea Expedition. Reports — Swedish Deep-Sea Expedition Repts
Swedish Dental Journal — Swed Dent J
Swedish Dental Journal (Supplement) — Swed Dent J (Suppl)
Swedish Drug Information System [*Database*] — SWEDIS
Swedish Economy — Swedish Ec
Swedish Economy — Swedish Econ
Swedish Economy — SWY
Swedish Environmental Research Index [*Database*] — SERIX
Swedish Environmental Research Institute. Report B — Swed Environ Res Inst Rep B
Swedish Geotechnical Institute. Proceedings — Swed Geotech Inst Proc
Swedish Geotechnical Institute. Report — Swed Geotech Inst Rep
Swedish Historical Society. Yearbook — Swedish Hist Soc Yearbook
Swedish Institute of Agricultural Engineering. Circular — Swed Inst Agric Eng Circ
Swedish Journal of Agricultural Research — Swed J Agric Res
Swedish Journal of Economics — SJE
Swedish Journal of Economics — Swed J Econ
Swedish Journal of Economics — Swedish J Econ
Swedish Paper Journal — Swed Pap J
Swedish Pioneer Historical Quarterly — SPHQ
Swedish Pioneer Historical Quarterly — SweP
Swedish Polar Research — SWPR
Swedish State Shipbuilding Experiment Tank. Report — Swed State Shipbuild Exp Tank Report
Swedish University of Agricultural Sciences. Department of Agricultural Engineering. Report — RLITDQ
Swedish University of Agricultural Sciences. Department of Agricultural Engineering. Report — Swed Univ Agric Sci Dep Agric Eng Rep
Swedish University of Agricultural Sciences. Department of Farm Buildings. Report — RLIBD6
Swedish University of Agricultural Sciences. Department of Farm Buildings. Report — Swed Univ Agric Sci Dep Farm Build Rep
Swedish University of Agricultural Sciences. Department of Horticultural Science. Report — RSLTDM
Swedish University of Agricultural Sciences. Department of Horticultural Science. Report — Swed Univ Agric Sci Dep Hortic Sci Rep
Swedish University of Agricultural Sciences. Department of Microbiology. Report — RSLMDZ
Swedish University of Agricultural Sciences. Department of Microbiology. Report — Swed Univ Agric Sci Dep Microbiol Rep
Swedish University of Agricultural Sciences. Department of Plant Husbandry. Report — RSLVDS
Swedish University of Agricultural Sciences. Department of Plant Husbandry. Report — Swed Univ Agric Sci Dep Plant Husb Rep
Swedish University of Agricultural Sciences. Reports in Forest Ecology and Forest Soils — RSSME3
Swedish University of Agricultural Sciences. Reports in Forest Ecology and Forest Soils — Swed Univ Agric Sci Rep For Ecol For Soils
Swedish Weed Conference. Reports — Swed Weed Conf Rep
Swedish Wildlife Research (Viltrevy) — Swed Wildl Res (Viltrevy)
Swedish Wildlife Research Viltrevy — SWRVDT
Swedish-Australian and Swedish-New Zealand Trade Journal — Swedish Aust & Swedish NZ Trade J
Swim Magazine — Swim
Swimming Technique — Swimm Tech
Swimming World and Junior Swimmer — Swim Wld
Swimming World and Junior Swimmer — Swimm World Jun Swimm
Swine Day. University of California — Swine Day Univ Calif
Swine Report. University of Hawaii. Cooperative Extension Service — Swine Rep Univ Hawaii Coop Ext Serv
Swiss American Historical Society. Newsletter — SAHS
Swiss Credit Banking Bulletin — Swiss Credit Bank Bul
Swiss Economic News — Swiss News
Swiss Journal of Hydrology — Swiss J Hydrol
Swiss Review of World Affairs — Swiss R Wld Aff
Swiss Review of World Affairs. Neue Zuericher Zeitung — NZZ/SRWA
Swiss Seminars — Swiss Sem
Swiss Surgery — Swiss Surg
Swiss Surgery. Supplement — Swiss Surg Suppl
Swiss-French Studies [*Etudes Romandes*] — SFSt
Sydney Cinema Journal — SCJ
Sydney Gay Community News — Sydney GCN
Sydney Gazette — SG
Sydney Herald — SH
Sydney Jaycee — Syd Jaycee
Sydney Jewish News — Syd Jewish News
Sydney Law Review — SLR
Sydney Law Review — Syd L Rev
Sydney Law Review — Syd Law R
Sydney Law Review — Syd LR
Sydney Law Review — Sydney L Rev
Sydney Law Review — Sydney Law R
Sydney Law Review — Sydney Law Rev
Sydney Mail — SM
Sydney Morning Herald — SMH
Sydney Morning Herald — Syd Morning Her
Sydney Morning Herald — Syd Morning Herald
Sydney Morning Herald Reports (Newspaper) (New South Wales) — SMH (Newspr) (NSW)
Sydney Quarterly Magazine — Sydney Q Mag
Sydney Studies in English — SSEng
Sydney Studies in English — Syd Stud
Sydney Tourist Guide — STG
Sydney University. Gazette — Syd Univ Gaz
Sydney University. Medical Journal — Syd Univ Med J
Sydney University. Medical Journal — Sydney Univ Med J
Sydney University. School of Civil Engineering. Research Report — Sydney Univ Sch Civ Eng Res Rep
Sydney Water Board. Journal — Syd Wat Bd J
Sydney Water Board. Journal — Syd Water Bd J
Sydney Water Board. Journal — Syd Water Board J
Sydney Water Board. Journal — Sydney Water Bd J
Sydowia. Annales Mycologici — Sydowia Ann Mycol
Sydowia. Annales Mycologici. Beihefte — Sydowia Ann Mycolog Beih
Sydslesvigsk Kirkekalender — SKK
Sydsvenska Dagbladet Snaellposten — SDS
Sydsvenska Medicinhistoriska Saellskapets Arsskrift — Sydsven Medicinhist
Sydsvenska Ortnamns-Saellskapets Arsskrift — SOA
Sydsvenska Ortnamns-Saellskapets Arsskrift — SsvOA
Sydsvenska Ortnamns-Saellskapets Arsskrift — Sydsvenska Ortnamns-Sallsk Arsskr
Syesis — SYES
Sygekasse-Bladet — Sygek Bl
Sygekasse-Tidende — Sygek T
Sylloge Excerptorum e Dissertationibus ad Gradum Doctoris in Sacra Theologia — SED
Sylloge Inscriptionum Christianarum Veterum Musei Vaticani — SICV
Sylloge Inscriptionum Graecarum — SIG
Sylloge Inscriptionum Graecarum — Syll
Sylloge Inscriptionum Graecarum — Syll Inscr Gr
Sylloge Inscriptionum Oscarum — SIO
Sylloge Inscriptionum Religionis Isiacae et Serapicae — SIRIS
Sylloge Nummorum Graecarum — SNG
Syllogeus — SYLL
Syllogos. Journal de la Societe Philologique Grecque de Constantinople — Syl
Sylvatrop. The Philippine Forest Research Journal — Sylvatrop Philipp For Res J
Sylvia Porter's Personal Finance — GPEF
Symbioses — SYMBA
Symbolae Arctoae — SA
Symbolae Biblicae Upsalienses — SBU
Symbolae Biblicae Upsalienses — SyBU
Symbolae Botanicae Upsalienses — SBUPAC
Symbolae Botanicae Upsalienses — Symb Bot Ups
Symbolae Osloenses — S Osl
Symbolae Osloenses — S Oslo
Symbolae Osloenses — SO
Symbolae Osloenses — Sy Os
Symbolae Osloenses — Sy Osl
Symbolae Osloenses — Symb Oslo
Symbolae Osloenses — SymbOsl
Symbolae Osloenses. Supplement — SOS
Symbolae Philologorum Posnaniensium — SPhP
Symbolae Slavicae — SSlav
Symbolic and Numeric Computation Series — Symbol Numer Comput Ser
Symbolic Computation. Artificial Intelligence — Symbol Comput Artificial Intelligence
Symmetry. Culture and Science — Symmetry Cult Sci
Symphony — Sym
Symphony Magazine — SyM
Symphony Magazine — Sym Mag
Symphony News — Sym News
Symphony News — SyN
Symposia Angiologica Sanitoriana — Symp Angiol Sanitoriana
Symposia Biologica Hungarica — Symp Biol Hung
Symposia. British Society for Parasitology — Symp Br Soc Parasitol
Symposia. Faraday Society — Symp Faraday Soc
Symposia. Fondation Merieux [*Elsevier Book Series*] — SFM

Symposia for Cell Biology [*Japan*] — Symp Cell Biol
Symposia Gaussiana — Sympos Gaussiana
Symposia Genetica et Biologica Italica — SGBIA
Symposia Genetica et Biologica Italica — Symp Genet Biol Ital
Symposia. Giovanni Lorenzini Foundation [*Elsevier Book Series*] — SGLF
Symposia in Neuroscience — Symp Neurosci
Symposia in Neuroscience — SYNEE7
Symposia. International Society for Cell Biology — Symp Int Soc Cell Biol
Symposia Mathematica — Sympos Math
Symposia Medica Hoechst — Symp Med Hoechst
Symposia of the Giovanni Lorenzini Foundation — Symp Giovanni Lorenzini Found
Symposia on Theoretical Physics and Mathematics [*United States*] — Symp Theor Phys Math
Symposia on Theoretical Physics and Mathematics — SYMPA
Symposia. Royal Entomological Society of London — Symp R Entomol Soc Lond
Symposia. Royal Entomological Society of London — Symp R Entomol Soc London
Symposia Series. Australasian Institute of Mining and Metallurgy — Symp Ser Australas Inst Min Metall
Symposia Series in Immunobiological Standardization — Symp Ser Immunobiol Stand
Symposia. Society for Developmental Biology — Symp Soc Dev Biol
Symposia. Society for Experimental Biology — SEB Symp
Symposia. Society for Experimental Biology — Symp Soc Exp Biol
Symposia. Society for the Study of Human Biology — Symp Soc Study Hum Biol
Symposia. Swedish Nutrition Foundation — Symp Swed Nutr Found
Symposia Universitatis Upsaliensis Annum Quingentesimum Celebrantis — Sympos Univ Upsaliensis Annum Quingentesimum Celebrantis
Symposia. Zoological Society of London — Symp Zool Soc Lond
Symposium — PSYM
Symposium — S
Symposium — SM
Symposium — SY
Symposium — Sym
Symposium: A Quarterly Journal in Modern Foreign Literatures — Symposium
Symposium A1 on High Temperature Superconductor Thin Films — Symp A1 High Temp Supercond Thin Films
Symposium A2 on Solid State Ionics — Symp A2 Solid State Ionics
Symposium A4 on Composite Materials — Symp A4 Compos Mater
Symposium Brazil Gold — Symp Braz Gold
Symposium. British Ecological Society — Symp Br Ecol Soc
Symposium. British Society for Developmental Biology — SBSBDV
Symposium. British Society for Developmental Biology — Symp Br Soc Dev Biol
Symposium. Conference on Science, Philosophy, and Religion in their Relation to the Democratic Way of Life — SCSPR
Symposium de Prehistoria de la Peninsula Iberica — SPP
Symposium de Prehistoria de la Peninsula Iberica — Symp Preh
Symposium for the Salivary Gland — DASHAA
Symposium for the Salivary Gland — Symp Salivary Gland
Symposium (International) on Combustion. Proceedings — SYMCA
Symposium (International) on Combustion. Proceedings — Symp (Int) Combust Proc
Symposium. International Union of Biological Sciences. Proceedings — Symp Int Union Biol Sci Proc
Symposium. National Physical Laboratory (United Kingdom) — Symp Natl Phys Lab (UK)
Symposium of Foods — Symp Foods
Symposium of Molecular Basis of Neurological Disorders and Their Treatment — Symp Mol Basis Neurol Disord Their Treat
Symposium on Abnormal Subsurface Pressure. Proceedings — Symp Abnorm Subsurf Pressure Proc
Symposium on Advanced Oxidation Processes for the Treatment of Contaminated Water and Air — Symp Adv Oxid Processes Treat Contam Water Air
Symposium on Cell and Model Membrane Interactions — Symp Cell Model Membr Interact
Symposium on Chemically Modified Surfaces — Symp Chem Modif Surf
Symposium on Coal Management Techniques. Papers — Symp Coal Manag Tech Pap
Symposium on Coal Mine Drainage Research. Papers — Symp Coal Mine Drain Res Pap
Symposium on Coal Preparation. Papers — Symp Coal Prep Pap
Symposium on Coal Utilization. Papers — Symp Coal Util Pap
Symposium on Development and Applications of Intense Pulsed Particle Beams — Symp Dev Appl Intense Pulsed Part Beams
Symposium on Ecological Research in Humid Tropics Vegetation — Symp Ecol Res Humid Trop Vegtn
Symposium on Engineering Applications of Mechanics — Symp Eng Appl Mech
Symposium on Engineering Geology and Soils Engineering. Proceedings — Symp Eng Geol Soils Eng Proc
Symposium on Frequency Control. Proceedings — Symp Freq Control Proc
Symposium on Fundamental Cancer Research — AFCPDR
Symposium on Fundamental Cancer Research — Symp Fundam Cancer Res
Symposium on Fundamental Cancer Research. Collections of Papers — Symp Fundam Cancer Res Collect Pap
Symposium on Genetics and Breeding of Wheat. Proceedings — Symp Genet Breed Wheat Proc
Symposium on Maize Production in Southeast Asia — Symp Maize Prod Southeast Asia
Symposium on Microbial Drug Resistance — Symp Microb Drug Resist
Symposium on Mine and Preparation Plant Refuse Disposal. Papers — Symp Mine Prep Plant Refuse Disposal Pap
Symposium on Moessbauer Effect Methodology. Proceedings — Symp Moessbauer Eff Methodol Proc
Symposium on Nondestructive Evaluation and Material Properties of Advanced Materials — Symp Nondestr Eval Mater Prop Adv Mater
Symposium on Ocular Therapy — Symp Ocul Ther
Symposium on Oral Sensation and Perception — Symp Oral Sens Percept
Symposium on Particleboard. Proceedings — Symp Particleboard Proc
Symposium on Particles on Surfaces. Detection, Adhesion, and Removal — Symp Part Surf Detect Adhes Removal
Symposium on Pyrrolizidine Senecio Alkaloids. Toxicity — Symp Pyrrolizidine Senecio Alka
Symposium on Regulation of Enzyme Activity and Syntheses in Normal and Neoplastic Tissues. Proceedings — Symp Regul Enzyme Act Synth Norm Neoplast Tissues Proc
Symposium on Salt. Proceedings — SSAPD
Symposium on Superconductivity and Cryoelectronics — Symp Supercond Cryoelectron
Symposium on Surface Mining and Reclamation. Papers — Symp Surf Min Reclam Pap
Symposium on Surface Phenomena in Enhanced Oil Recovery — Symp Surf Phenom Enhanced Oil Recovery
Symposium on the Chemistry of Natural Products. Symposium Papers — Symp Chem Nat Prod Symp Pap
Symposium on the Occurrence, Prediction, and Control of Outbursts in Coal Mines — OPCOCM Symposium
Symposium on Thermophysical Properties. Proceedings — Symp Thermophys Prop Proc
Symposium on Turbulence in Liquids. Proceedings — Symp Turbul Liq Proc
Symposium on Underground Mining. Papers — Symp Underground Min Pap
Symposium Papers. Symposium on the Chemistry of Natural Products — Symp Pap Symp Chem Nat Prod
Symposium. Pharmacology, Therapeutics, and Toxicology Group. International Association for Dental Research — Symp Pharmacol Ther Toxicol Group
Symposium Photovoltaische Solarenergie — Symp Photovoltaische Solarenerg
Symposium. Private Investors Abroad — Symp Priv Invest Abroad
Symposium Proceedings. British Crop Protection Council — Symp Proc Br Crop Prot Counc
Symposium. Protein Society — Symp Protein Soc
Symposium Series. British Mycological Society — Symp Ser Br Mycol Soc
Symposium Series. Institute of Fuel (London) — Symp Ser Inst Fuel (London)
Symposium Series. Society for Applied Bacteriology — Symp Ser Soc Appl Bacteriol
Symposium. Society for General Microbiology — Symp Soc Gen Microbiol
Symposium. Society for the Study of Development and Growth — Symp Soc Study Dev Growth
Symposium. Society for the Study of Inborn Errors of Metabolism — Symp Soc Study Inborn Errors Metab
Symposium Thermische Solarenergie — Symp Therm Solarenerg
Syn og Segn — SoS
Syn og Segn — SS
Syn og Segn. Norsk-Tidsskrift — Sy S
Synaxarium Ecclesiae Constantinopolitanae — Syn CP
Synaxarium Ecclesiae Constantinopolitanae — Synax Eccl CP
Synchrotron Radiation and Dynamic Phenomena. International Meeting of Physical Chemistry — Synchrotron Radiat Dyn Phenom Int Meet Phys Chem
Syncrude Environmental Research Monograph — SERM
Synergetics [*Berlin*] — SSSYDF
Synergy. Syncrude Canada — SYNG
Synerjy — SYNED
Synodicon Oriental ou Recueil des Synodes Nestoriens — Syn Or
Synopses of the British Fauna. New Series — SBFSDH
Synopses of the British Fauna. New Series — Synop Br Fauna New Ser
Synopsis — SY
Synopsis of Swedish Building Research — Synopsis Swedish Bldg Res
Synopsis Revue — Synopsis R
Syntax and Semantics — S & S
Syntax of Classical Greek — SCG
Synthese — Synth
Synthese Historical Library — Syn Hist L
Synthese Historical Library — Synthese Hist Lib
Synthese Language Library — Synthese Language Lib
Synthese Library — Synth Libr
Synthese Library — Synthese Lib
Syntheses — Syn
Syntheses. An International Quarterly for the Logical and Psychological Study of the Foundations of the Sciences — Synth
Synthesis — SY
Synthesis and Chemistry of Agrochemicals III — Synth Chem Agrochem III
Synthesis and Reactivity in Inorganic and Metalorganic Chemistry — Syn Reac In
Synthesis and Reactivity in Inorganic and Metalorganic Chemistry — Syn Reactiv Inorg Metal Org C
Synthesis and Reactivity in Inorganic and Metalorganic Chemistry — Synth React Inorg Metorg Chem
Synthesis (Cambridge) — Synthesis (C)
Synthesis in Inorganic and Metal-Organic Chemistry [*Later, Synthesis and Reactivity in Inorganic and Metalorganic Chemistry*] — Syn Inorg Met-Org Chem
Synthetic Aperture Radar — Synth Aperture Radar
Synthetic Communications — Syn Commun
Synthetic Communications — Synth Commun
Synthetic Fuels — Synth Fuels
Synthetic Fuels Update — SFUPD

Synthetic Fuels Update — Synth Fuels Update
Synthetic Lubrication — Synth Lubr
Synthetic Metals — SYMED
Synthetic Metals [*Switzerland*] — Synth Met
Synthetic Methods of Organic Chemistry Yearbook — Synth Methods Org Chem Yearb
Synthetic Pipeline Gas Symposium. Proceedings — Synth Pipeline Gas Symp Proc
Synthetic Rubber — Synth Rubber
Synthetic Rubber Industry (Lanzhou, People's Republic of China) — Synth Rubber Ind (Lanzhou People's Repub China)
Synthetische Methoden der Organischen Chemie [*Synthetic Methods of Organic Chemistry*] — Syn Org
Syoyakugaku Zasshi. Japanese Journal of Pharmacognosy — Syoyak Zass
Syracuse Herald Journal — Syracuse HJ
Syracuse Herald-America and Post-Standard — Syracuse HA
Syracuse Journal of International Law and Commerce — Sy J Int L
Syracuse Journal of International Law and Commerce — Syr J Intl
Syracuse Journal of International Law and Commerce — Syr J Intl L & Com
Syracuse Journal of International Law and Commerce — Syracuse Int'l L & Com
Syracuse Law Review — Sy LR
Syracuse Law Review — Syr LR
Syracuse Law Review — Syrac Law R
Syracuse Law Review — Syracuse L Rev
Syria. Revue d'Art Oriental et d'Archeologie — SRA
Syria. Revue d'Art Oriental et d'Archeologie — Sy
Syria. Revue d'Art Oriental et d'Archeologie — Syr
Syria. Revue d'Art Oriental et d'Archeologie — Syria R
Syrian Journal of Stomatology — Syrian J Stomatol
Syrie et Monde Arabe [*Damascus*] — SMA
Syrie et Monde Arabe. Etude Mensuelle Economique, Politique, et Statistique — STA
Syro-Egyptian Society. Original Papers — SES
Syro-Mesopotamian Studies — SMS
Syro-Mesopotamian Studies — Syr Mesop St
System for Documentation and Information in Metallurgy [*Database*] — SDIM
System for Information on Grey Literature in Europe [*Database*] — SIGLE
System for International Literature Information on Ceramics and Glass [*Database*] — SILICA
Systema Ascomycetum — Syst Ascomycetum
Systematic and Applied Microbiology — SAMIDF
Systematic and Applied Microbiology — Syst Appl Microbiol
Systematic Biology — Syst Biol
Systematic Botany — Syst Bot
Systematic Entomology — SYENDM
Systematic Entomology — Syst Entomol
Systematic Parasitology — Syst Parasitol
Systematic Zoology — Syst Zool
Systematics Association. Publication — Syst Assoc Publ
Systematics Association. Publication — Systematics Assoc Pub
Systematics Association. Special Volume — Syst Ass Spec Vol
Systematics Association. Special Volume — Syst Assoc Spec Vol
Systematische Sammlung des Bundesrechts [*Switzerland*] — SR
Systeme Informatique pour la Conjoncture [*Database*] — SIC
Systemes de Pensee en Afrique Noire — Syst de Pensee en Afr Noire
Systemes Logiques — Syst Logiques
Systemic Autoimmunity — Syst Autoimmun
Systems — Syst
Systems Analysis Modelling Simulation — Systems Anal Modelling Simulation
Systems and Computers in Japan — Systems Comput Japan
Systems and Control — Syst & Control
Systems and Control. Foundations and Applications — Systems Control Found Appl
Systems and Control Letters — Syst and Control Lett
Systems and Control Letters — Systems Control Lett
Systems and Procedures — Sys Proced
Systems and Procedures Journal — Systems & Proc J
Systems and Software — Sys and Soft
Systems, Control, and Information — Systems Control Inform
Systems Development Corporation Magazine — SDC Mag
Systems Engineering Series — Systems Engrg Ser
Systems International — Syst Int
Systems, Objectives, Solutions — SOS
Systems, Objectives, Solutions — Syst Objectives Solutions
Systems Programming Series — Syst Program Ser
Systems Science — Syst Sci
Systems Science — Systems Sci
Systems Science and Mathematical Sciences — Systems Sci Math Sci
Systems Technology — Syst Technol
Systems Theory Research — Syst Theory Res
Systems Theory Research — Systems Theory Res
Systems User — Sys User
Systems with Fast Ionic Transport — Syst Fast Ionic Transp
Systems-Computers-Controls — Syst-Comput-Controls
Systems-Computers-Controls — Systems-Comput-Controls
Syvremenna Meditsina — Syvrem Med
Szakszervezeti Szemle — Szakszerv Szle
Szamitogepalkalmazasi Kutato Intezet. Tanulmanyok — Szamki Tanulmanyok
Szamki Koezlemenyek — Szamki Koezlem
Szamvitel es Ugyviteltechnika — Szamvit Uegyviteltech
Szazadok — Sz
Szazadok — Szaz
Szczecinskie Towarzystwo Naukowe Wydzial Nauk Przyrodniczo Rolniczych — Szczecin Tow Nauk Wydz Nauk Przyr Roln
Szegedi Varosi Muzeum Kiadvanyai — Sz VMK
Szekszardi Beri Balogh Adam Muzeum Evkonyve — Szekszardi ME
Szephalom — Szeph
Szigma. Matematikai-Koezgazdasagi Folyoirat — Szigma Mat-Koezgazdasagi Folyoirat
Szklo i Ceramika — Szklo Ceram
Szklo i Ceramika — Szklo i Ceram
Szkola Glowna Gospodarstwa Wiejskiego - Akademia Rolnicza w Warszawie. Zeszyty Naukowe. Ogrodnictwo — Szk Gl Gospod Wiejsk Akad Roln Warszawie Zesz Nauk Ogrod
Szkola Glowna Gospodarstwa Wiejskiego - Akademia Rolnicza w Warszawie. Zeszyty Naukowe. Rolnictwo — Szk Gl Gospod Wiejsk Akad Roln Warszawie Zesz Nauk Roln
Szkola Glowna Gospodarstwa Wiejskiego - Akademia Rolnicza w Warszawie. Zeszyty Naukowe. Weterynaria — Szk Gl Gospod Wiejsk Akd Roln Warszawie Zesz Nauk Weter
Szkola Glowna Gospodarstwa Wiejskiego - Akademia Rolnicza w Warszawie. Zeszyty Naukowe. Zootechnika — Szk Gl Gospod Wiejsk Akad Roln Warszawie Zesz Nauk Zootech
Szoeloeszeti, Boraszati, es Gazdasagi Lap — Szoeloesz Borasz Gazd Lap
Szoleszet es Boraszat — Szolesz Boraszat
Sztuka i Krytyka — SiK

T

T. A. Informations [*Formerly, Traduction Automatique*] — TAI
T C Series. Soil Conservation Authority (Victoria) — T C Ser Soil Conserv Auth (Vic)
T C Series. Soil Conservation Authority (Victoria) — T C Ser Soil Conserv Auth (Vict)
Taal en Tongval — Taal Tong
Taal en Tongval [*Antwerpen*] — TeT
Taal en Tongval [*Antwerpen*] — TT
TAB. Tyres, Accessories, Batteries — TAB Tyres Access Batt
Tabak Journal International — TJI
Tabak Plus — VBT
Tabak Zeitung. Fachorgan der Tabakwirtschaft — TAZ
Tabaksplant. Maandblad voor de Sigaren, Sigaretten, en Tabakshandel en Industrie — TAP
Tabaktueel Magazine — TAB
Table of Government Orders — Table Gov Order
Table Ronde — TR
Tablet. A Weekly Newspaper and Review — Tab
Tablettes Cappadociennes — TC
Tableware International — POG
Tabula Imperii Byzantini — TIB
Tabula Imperii Romani — TIR
Tabulae Biologicae — Tabul Biol
Tabulae Biologicae — Tabulae Biol
Tactical Missile Aerodynamics. General Topics — Tactical Missile Aerodyn Gen Top
Tactical Missile Aerodynamics. Prediction Methodology — Tactical Missile Aerodyn Predict Methodol
Tadzikskii Gosudarstvennyi Universitet Imeni V. I. Lenina. Trudy Mehaniko-Matematiceskogo Fakulteta — Tadzik Gos Univ Trudy Meh-Mat Fak
Tadzikskii Gosudarstvennyi Universitet Imeni V. I. Lenina. Ucenye Zapiski. Trudy Fiziko-Matematiceskogo Fakulteta. Serija Matematiceskaja — Tadzik Gos Univ Ucen Zap
Tadzikskii Sel'skohozjaistvennyi Institut i Tadzikskii Gosudarstvennyi Universitet. Trudy — Tadzik S-H Inst Trudy
TAEDA [*Technology Assessment of Energy Development in Appalachia*] **Newsletter** [*United States*] — TAEDA Newsl
Taegliche Rundschau — Taegl Rdsch
Taegliches Notizenblatt fuer die Theilnehmer an der Versammlung der Naturforscher und Aerzte zu Bonn — Taegl Notizenbl Theilnehmer Versamml Naturf Aerzte Bonn
Taehan Ankwa Hakhoe Chapchi — TAHCD
Taehan Naekwa Hakhoe Chapchi — TNHCA
Taetigkeitsbericht. Bundesanstalt fuer Geowissenschaften und Rohstoffe — Tatigkeitsber Bundesanst Geowiss Rohst
Taetigkeitsbericht. Geologisches Landesamt Nordrhein-Westfalen — Tatigkeitsber Geol Landsamt Nordrhein-Westfal
Taetigkeitsbericht. Niedersachsisches Landesamt fuer Bodenforschung — Tatigkeitsber Niedersach Landsamt Bodenforsch
TAFE [*New South Wales Department of Technical and Further Education*] **Quarterly** — TAFEQ
Tagesrundschau — Tru
Tagoro — Tag
Tagsberichte ueber die Fortschritte der Natur- und Heilkunde. Abtheilung fuer Botanik — Tagsber Fortschr Natur Heilk Abth Bot
Tagung ueber die Muellerei-Technologie. Bericht — Tag Muellerei-Technol Ber
Tagungsbericht. Akademie der Landwirtschaftswissenschaften — Tagungsber Akad Landwirtschaftswiss
Tagungsbericht. Akademie der Landwirtschaftswissenschaften der Deutschen Demokratischen Republik — Tagungsber Akad Landwirtschaftswiss DDR
Tagungsbericht. Akademie der Landwirtschaftswissenschaften der Deutschen Demokratischen Republik — Tagungsber Akad Landwirtschaftswiss Dtsch Demokr Repub
Tagungsbericht des Siemens Prozessrechner Anwenderkreises (SAK) Jahrestagung — Tagungsber Siemens Prozessrechn Anwenderkreises SAK Jahrestag
Tagungsbericht. Gesellschaft fuer Innere Medizin der DDR — Tagungsber Ges Inn Med DDR
Tagungsbericht. Jahrestagung Kerntechnik — Tagungsber Jahrestag Kerntech
Tagungsberichte. Deutsche Akademie der Landwirtschaftswissenschaften zu Berlin — Tagber Dt Akad Landw-Wiss Berl
Tagungsberichte. Deutsche Akademie der Landwirtschaftswissenschaften zu Berlin — Tagungsber Deut Akad Landwirt Wiss Berlin
Tagungsvortraege. Fachtagung Amorphe und Nanodispersive Schichsysteme — Tagungsvortr Fachtag Amorphe Nanodispersive Schichsyst
Taiga Times '71 — TT
Taika Zairyo — TKZRA
Taiki Hoshano Kansoku Seiseki — THKSA
Taikomoji Branduoline Fizika — Taikomoji Branduoline Fiz
Taisei Kensetsu Gijutsu Kenkyusho-Ho — TKGJA
Tait's Edinburgh Magazine — Tait
Taiwan Agricultural Research Journal — Taiwan Agr Res J
Taiwan Agriculture Bimonthly — Taiwan Agric Bimon
Taiwan Engineering — Taiwan Eng
Taiwan Environmental Sanitation — Taiwan Environ Sanit
Taiwan. Fisheries Research Institute. Fish Culture. Report — Taiwan Fish Res Inst Fish Cult Rep
Taiwan. Fisheries Research Institute. Laboratory of Biology. Report — Taiwan Fish Res Inst Lab Biol Rep
Taiwan. Fisheries Research Institute. Laboratory of Fishery Biology. Report — Taiwan Fish Res Inst Lab Fish Biol Rep
T'ai-Wan Huan Ching Wei Sheng — TCWSA
Taiwan Industrial Panorama — Taiw Ind
Taiwan Industrial Panorama — TAL
Taiwan Journal of Theology — Taiwan J Th
Taiwan Journal of Veterinary Medicine and Animal Husbandry — Taiwan J Vet Med Anim Husb
Taiwan Statistical Data Book — Taiw Stat
Taiwan Sugar — TWSUA
Taiwan. Sugar Experiment Station. Annual Report — Taiwan Sugar Exp Stn Annu Rep
Taiwan. Sugar Experiment Station. Research Report — Taiwan Sugar Exp Stn Res Rep
Taiwan. Sugar Research Institute. Annual Report — Taiwan Sugar Res Inst Annu Rep
Taiwan Trade Monthly — Taiwan Trade Mo
Taiwan Trade Monthly — TTM
Take One — TO
Takenaka Gijutsu Kenkyu Hokoku — TGKHA
Takenaka Technical Research Report — Takenaka Tech Res Rep
Taking Care. Newsletter of the Center for Consumer Health Education — TAKC
Talabriga — Ta
Tales of the Frightened — TOF
Tales of Tomorrow — TOT
Tales of Wonder — TOW
Taliesin [*England*] — Tal
Talisman — Tal
Talking Newspaper News — TN
Talks to Teachers of English — TTE
Tall Timbers Research Station. Miscellaneous Publication — Tall Timbers Res Stn Misc Publ
Taller Literario — TLit
Taller (Santiago, Cuba) — TallerC
Tallinna Poluetehnilise Instituudi Toimetised — Tallin Polueteh Inst Toim
Tallinna Tehnikaulikooli Toimetised — Tallinna Tehnikaulik Toim
Talouselama — Talouselam
Talouselama — TLSM
Ta-Lu Tsa-Chih [*Continent Magazine*] [*Taiwan*] — TLTC
Tamarack Review — Tamarack R
Tamarack Review [*Toronto*] — TamR
Tamarind Technical Papers — TTP
Tamil Culture — TamC
Tamil Culture — TC
Tamil Nadu Education — Tamil Nadu Ed
Tamil Nadu Journal of Co-operation — Tamil Nadu J Coop
Tamkang Journal — Tk J
Tamkang Journal of Management Sciences — Tamkang J Management Sci
Tamkang Journal of Mathematics [*Taipei*] — Tamkang J Math
Tamkang Review — Tamkang R
Tamkang Review — Tamkang Rev
Tamkang Review — TamkR
Tamkang Review — TkR
Tampa Bay Business — Tampa Bay
Tampa Tribune — Tampa Trib
Tampa Tribune and Times — Tampa Tr & Ti
TAMS [*Token and Medal Society*] **Journal** — TAMSJ
Tamsui Oxford College. Lecture Notes Series — Tamsui Oxford Coll Lecture Notes Ser
Tamsui Oxford Journal of Management Sciences — Tamsui Oxford J Management Sci
Tandlaegebladet — Tdlb
Tandplejen — Tdpl

Tanganyika Notes and Records — Tang Notes
Taniisix. Aleutian Regional School District — TNSX
Tanker and Bulk Carrier — Tanker Bulk Carr
Tanker and Bulker International [*England*] — Tanker Bulker Int
Tanker and Bulker Maritime Management [*England*] — Tank Bulk Marit Manage
Tanner Lectures on Human Values — Tan Lect HV
Tanulmanyok Magyar Tudomanyos Akademia Szamitastechnikai es Automatizalasi Kutato Intezet — Tanulmanyok Magy Tud Akad Szamitastech es Autom Kut Intez
Tanulmanyok. MTA [*Magyar Tudomanyos Akademia*] **Szamitastechnikai es Automatizalasi Kutato Intezet (Budapest)** — Tanulmanyok MTA Szamitastechn Automat Kutato Int (Budapest)
Tanzania. Ministry of Industries. Mineral Resources and Power. Annual Report of the Geological Survey Division — Tanzania Miner Resour Power Annu Rep Geol Surv Div
Tanzania Notes and Records — Tanzania Notes Recs
Tanzania Notes and Records — TNR
Tanzania. Records of the Geological Survey of Tanganyika — Tanzania Rec Geol Surv Tanganyika
Tanzania Silviculture Research Note — Tanzania Silvic Res Note
Tanzania. Silviculture Research Station. Technical Note (New Series) — Tanzania Silvic Res Stn Tech Note (New Ser)
Tap Chi Toan Hoc. Journal of Mathematics — Tap Chi Toan Hoc J Math
Tap Chi Toan Hoc. Progress of Mathematical Sciences — Tap Chi Toan Hoc
Taphikos Kyklos B ton Mykenon — TKB
TAPPI [*Technical Association of the Pulp and Paper Industry*] **Alkaline Pulping Conference Preprint** — TAPPI Alkaline Pulping Conf Prepr
TAPPI [*Technical Association of the Pulp and Paper Industry*] **Annual Meeting. Preprint** — TAPPI Annu Meet Prepr
TAPPI [*Technical Association of the Pulp and Paper Industry*] **Annual Meeting. Proceedings** [*United States*] — TAMPD
TAPPI [*Technical Association of the Pulp and Paper Industry*] **Annual Meeting. Proceedings** — TAPPI Annu Meet Proc
TAPPI [*Technical Association of the Pulp and Paper Industry*] **Bibliography of Pulp and Paper Manufacture** — TAPPI Bibl
TAPPI [*Technical Association of the Pulp and Paper Industry*] **Coating Conference. Preprint** — TAPPI Coat Conf Prepr
TAPPI [*Technical Association of the Pulp and Paper Industry*] **Environmental Conference. Proceedings** — TAPPI Environ Conf Proc
TAPPI [*Technical Association of the Pulp and Paper Industry*] **Environmental Conference. Proceedings** — TECPD
TAPPI [*Technical Association of the Pulp and Paper Industry*] **Forest Biology - Wood Chemistry Conference. Conference Papers** — TAPPI For Biol Wood Chem Conf Conf Pap
TAPPI [*Technical Association of the Pulp and Paper Industry*] **Journal** — TAPPI
Tappi Journal — Tappi J
TAPPI. Journal of the Technical Association of the Pulp and Paper Industry — TAPPI J Tech Assoc Pulp Paper Ind
TAPPI [*Technical Association of the Pulp and Paper Industry*] **Monograph Series** — TAPPI Monogr Ser
TAPPI [*Technical Association of the Pulp and Paper Industry*] **Papermakers Conference. Papers** — TAPPI Papermakers Conf Pap
TAPPI [*Technical Association of the Pulp and Paper Industry*] **Papermakers Conference. Proceedings** — TAPPI Papermakers Conf Proc
TAPPI [*Technical Association of the Pulp and Paper Industry*] **Special Reports** — TAPPI Special Rept
TAPPI [*Technical Association of the Pulp and Paper Industry*] **Special Technical Association. Publication** — TAPPI Spec Tech Assoc Publ
Tapwe — TW
Taqralik — TAQK
Taqralik [*Montreal*] — TAQL
Taqrimiut Nipingat News [*Salluit, Quebec*] — TANN
Tara. Schweizerische Fachzeitschrift fuer Moderne Verpackung — TAR
Tarbiz. Quarterly for Jewish Studies — Tarb
Target Group Index [*Database*] — TGI
Target Marketing — Target Mark
Targeted Diagnosis and Therapy — Targeted Diagn Ther
Targeted Diagnosis and Therapy Series — Targeted Diagn Ther Ser
Targets, Backgrounds, and Discrimination — Targets Backgrounds Discrim
Tarim Bakanligi. Orman Genel Mudurlugu Yayinlarindan — Tar Bak Orm Gen Mud Yay
Tarleton Term Reports — Tarl
Tarleton Term Reports — Tarl Term R
Tarsadalmi Szemle — Tarsad Szle
Tarsadalomtudomanyi Kozlemenyek — Tarsadtud Kozl
Tartu Riikliku Uelikooli Toimetised — Tartu Riikl Ul Toimetised
Tartu Riikliku Ulikooli Toimetised — Tartu Riikliku Ulik Toim
Tartu Uelikooli Juures Oleva Loodusuurijate Seltsi Kirjatoeoed. Schriften Herausgegeben von der Naturforscher-Gesellschaft bei der Universitaet Tartu — Tartu Uelik Juures Oleva Loodusuur Seltsi Kirjatoeoed
Tartu Ulikooli Toimetised — Tartu Ulik Toim
Tartu Ulikooli Toimetised. Uchenye Zapiski Tartuskogo Universiteta. Acta et Commentationes Universitatis Tartuensis — Tartu Ul Toimetised
Tarybine Mokykla — TaM
Taschenbuch fuer Gartenbesitzer und fuer Blumenfreunde — Taschenb Gartenbesitz Blumenfr
Taschenbuch fuer Kommunalpolitiker — TKP
Taschenbuch fuer Kuechen-, Garten-, Blumen-, und Landwirthschaftsfreunde — Taschenb Kuechen Landwirthschaftsfr
Taschenbuch fuer Vaterlaendische Geschichte (Von Hormayr) — Hormayrs Taschenb
Taschenbuecher fuer das Grundstudium Mathematik — Taschenbuecher Grundstud Math
Taschenkalender fuer Natur- und Gartenfreunde — Taschenkalend Natur Gartenfr
Taskentskii Gosudarstvennyi Pedagogiceskii Institut Imeni Nizami Ucenye Zapiski — Taskent Gos Ped Inst Ucen Zap
Taskentskii Gosudarstvennyi Universitet Buharskii Pedagogiceskii Institut Naucnye Trudy — Taskent Gos Univ Buharsk Ped Inst Naucn Trudy
Taskentskii Gosudarstvennyi Universitet Imeni V. I. Lenina Naucnye Trudy — Taskent Gos Univ Naucn Trudy
Taskentskii Gosudarstvennyi Universitet Sbornik Naucnyh Trudov — Taskent Gos Univ Sb Naucn Trudov
Taskentskii Institut Inzenerov Zeleznodoroznogo Transporta Trudy — Taskent Inst Inz Zeleznodoroz Transporta Trudy
Taskentskii Institut Narodnogo Hozjaistva Naucnye Zapiski — Taskent Inst Narod Hoz Naucn Zap
Taskentskii Institut Narodnogo Hozjaistva Naucnye Zapiski. Matematika v Prilozenijah — Taskent Inst Narod Hoz Naucn Zap Mat v Prilozen
Taskentskii Politehniceskii Institut Naucnye Trudy. Novaja Serija — Taskent Politehn Inst Naucn Trudy
Taskentskii Politehniceskii Institut Naucnye Trudy. Novaja Serija — Taskent Politehn Inst Naucn Trudy NS
Tasks for Vegetation Science — Tasks Veg Sci
Tasmania. Department of Agriculture. Annual Report — Tasmania Dep Agric Annu Rep
Tasmania. Department of Agriculture. Bulletin — Tasm Dep Agric Bull
Tasmania. Department of Agriculture. Research Bulletin — Tasm Dep Agric Res Bull
Tasmania. Department of Labour and Industry. Bulletin — Tas Lab & Ind Bul
Tasmania. Department of Mines. Bulletin — Tasmania Mines Dep Bull
Tasmania. Department of Mines. Geological Atlas. 1:250,000 Series SK — Tasmania Dep Mines Geol Atlas 1:250000 Ser SK
Tasmania. Department of Mines. Geological Survey. Bulletin — Tasmania Dep Mines Geol Surv Bull
Tasmania. Department of Mines. Geological Survey. Record — Tasmania Dep Mines Geol Surv Rec
Tasmania. Department of Mines. Geological Survey. Report — Tasmania Dep Mines Geol Surv Rep
Tasmania. Department of Mines. Technical Report — Tasmania Dep Mines Tech Rep
Tasmania. Department of Mines. Technical Report — Tech Rep Tasmania Dep Mines
Tasmania. Department of Mines. Underground Water Supply Paper — Tasmania Dep Mines Underground Water Supply Pap
Tasmania. Forestry Commission. Bulletin — Tasmania For Comm Bull
Tasmania. Geological Survey. Bulletin — Geol Surv Bull Tasmania
Tasmania. Geological Survey. Bulletin — Tasm Geol Surv Bull
Tasmania. Geological Survey. Bulletin — Tasmania Geol Surv Bull
Tasmania. Geological Survey. Explanatory Report — Tasmania Geol Surv Explanatory Rep
Tasmania. Geological Survey. Explanatory Report. Geological Atlas. 1 Mile Series — Tasmania Geol Surv Explan Rep Geol Atlas 1 Mile Ser
Tasmania. Geological Survey. Geological Atlas. 1 Mile Series — Tasm Geol Surv Geol Atlas 1 Mile Ser
Tasmania. Geological Survey. Record — Rec Geol Surv Tasm
Tasmania. Geological Survey. Record — Tasmania Geol Surv Rec
Tasmania. Geological Survey. Report — Tasmania Geol Surv Rep
Tasmania. Geological Survey. Underground Water Supply Paper — Tasm Geol Surv Undergr Wat Supply Pap
Tasmania. Geological Survey. Underground Water Supply Paper — Tasmania Geol Surv Underground Water Supply Pap
Tasmania. Inland Fisheries Commission. Report — Tasmania Inland Fish Comm Rep
Tasmania. Parliament. Director of Mines. Annual Report — Tasmania Parl Dir Mines Annu Rep
Tasmanian Architect — Tas Arch
Tasmanian Architect — Tas Architect
Tasmanian Association for the Teaching of English. Journal — TATEJ
Tasmanian Building Appeal Reports — Tas Bldg App R
Tasmanian Building Journal — Tasmania Build J
Tasmanian Department of Agriculture. Insect Pest Survey — Tasmanian Dep Agric Insect Pest Surv
Tasmanian Department of Agriculture. Pamphlet — Tasmanian Dep Agric Pamp
Tasmanian Education — Tas Ed
Tasmanian Education — Tas Educ
Tasmanian Education Gazette — Tas Ed Gaz
Tasmanian Farmer — Tasm Fmr
Tasmanian Fisheries Research — Tas Fish
Tasmanian Fisheries Research — Tasmanian Fis Res
Tasmanian Fisheries Research — Tasmanian Fish Res
Tasmanian Forest Commission. Bulletin — Bull Tas For Comm
Tasmanian Forestry Commission. Bulletin — Tasmanian For Comm Bull
Tasmanian Fruitgrower and Farmer — Tas Fruitgrower and Farmer
Tasmanian Fruitgrower and Farmer — Tasm Fruitgr Fmr
Tasmanian Fruitgrower and Farmer — Tasm Fruitgrow Fmr
Tasmanian Geological Survey. Geological Atlas. 1 Mile Series — Tas Geol Surv Geol Atlas 1 Mile Ser
Tasmanian Government Gazette — Tas Govt Gaz
Tasmanian Government Publications — TGP
Tasmanian Historical Research Association. Papers and Proceedings — Pap Proc Tas Hist Res Assoc
Tasmanian Historical Research Association. Papers and Proceedings — Tas Hist Research Assoc Papers & Proc
Tasmanian Historical Research Association. Papers and Proceedings — Tasm Hist Res Ass Pap Proc
Tasmanian Historical Research Association. Papers and Proceedings — THRAP
Tasmanian Hotel Review — Tas Hotel R
Tasmanian Industry — Tas Ind

Tasmanian Journal of Agriculture — Tas J Ag
Tasmanian Journal of Agriculture — Tas J Agric
Tasmanian Journal of Agriculture — Tasm J Agr
Tasmanian Journal of Agriculture — Tasm J Agric
Tasmanian Journal of Agriculture — Tasmanian J Agr
Tasmanian Journal of Agriculture — Tasmanian J Agric
Tasmanian Journal of Education — Tas J Ed
Tasmanian Law Reports — Tas LR
Tasmanian Law Reports — TLR
Tasmanian Legal Information Guide — TLIG
Tasmanian Motor News — Tas News
Tasmanian Motor Trade and Transport Journal — Tas Motor Trade & Transport J
Tasmanian Naturalist — Tas Nat
Tasmanian Naturalist — Tasm Nat
Tasmanian News Reports — Tas News
Tasmanian Nurse — Tas Nurse
Tasmanian Reports — Tas R
Tasmanian State Reports — Tas R
Tasmanian State Reports — Tas S R
Tasmanian State Reports — Tasm
Tasmanian State Reports — Tasm SR
Tasmanian State Reports — Tasm St R
Tasmanian Teacher — Tas Teach
Tasmanian Teacher — Tas Teacher
Tasmanian Trader and Successful Independent — Tas Trader
Tasmanian Tramp — Tas Tramp
Tasmanian University. Law Review — Tas Univ L Rev
Tasmanian University. Law Review — Tasm UL Rev
Tasmanian University. Law Review — Tasmanian U L Rev
Tasmanian University. Law Review — Tasmanian Univ L Rev
Tata Institute of Fundamental Research. Lectures on Mathematics and Physics — Tata Inst Fund Res Lectures on Math and Phys
Tata Institute of Fundamental Research. Studies in Mathematics — Tata Inst Fund Res Studies in Math
Tatabanyai Szenbanyak Muszaki Kozgazdasagi Kozlemenyei [*Hungary*] — Tatabanyai Szenbanyak Musz Kozgazdasagi Kozl
Tatar Tele Hem Adebijaty — TTele
Tatarskaya Neft — Tatar Neft
Tatler — Tt
Tatra Mountains Mathematical Publications — Tatra Mt Math Publ
Tatslil [*The Chord*]. Forum for Music Research and Bibliography — Tatslil
Tatsuta Technical Review — Tatsuta Tech Rev
Tatung Journal — Tatung J
Tautsaimnieciba Derigie Augi — TDAZA
Tawow. Canadian Indian Cultural Magazine — TAQO
Tax Advance Rulings [*Database*] — TAR
Tax Advisor — TAD
Tax Advisor — Tax Ad
Tax Advisor — Tax Adv
Tax Conference — Tax Conf
Tax Counselor's Quarterly — Tax Coun Q
Tax Counselor's Quarterly — TCQ
Tax Court Memorandum Decisions. Commerce Clearing House — Tax Ct Mem Dec CCH
Tax Court Memorandum Decisions. Prentice-Hall — Tax Ct Mem Dec P-H
Tax Court Reported Decisions. Prentice-Hall — Tax Ct Rep Dec P-H
Tax Court Reports. Commerce Clearing House — Tax Ct Rep CCH
Tax Executive — Tax Exec
Tax Executive — TXE
Tax Expenditures. Budget Control Options and 5-Year Projections for Fiscal Years 1983-1987 — Tax Expend
Tax, Financial, and Estate Planning for the Owner of a Closely Held Corporation — Tax Fin and Est Pl
Tax Law Review — Tax L Rev
Tax Law Review — Tax Law R
Tax Law Review — Tax LR
Tax Law Review — TLR
Tax Lawyer — T Lwyr
Tax Lawyer — Tax Law
Tax Lawyer — TLA
Tax Management International Journal — TAI
Tax Management International Journal — Tax Management Int'l
Tax Management International Journal — TMI
Tax Management Weekly Report [*Database*] — TMWR
Tax Monthly (Manila) — Tax Mo (Manila)
Tax Notes Today [*Database*] — TNT
Tax Review — Tax R
Tax Review — Tax Rev
Tax Shelter Insider [*Database*] — TSI
Taxandria — Tax
Taxation — Tax
Taxation Board of Review Decisions — TBRD
Taxation Board of Review Decisions. New Series [*Australia*] — TBRD
Taxation Board of Review Decisions (New Series) — TBRD (NS)
Taxation for Accountants — TAX
Taxation for Accountants — TFA
Taxation for Lawyers — TAL
Taxation for Lawyers — Tax for Law
Taxation in Australia — Tax in Aust
Taxation in Australia — Taxn in Aust
Taxation in Australia — TIA
Taxes. The Tax Magazine — TAM
Tax-Exempt Organizations. Prentice-Hall — Tax-Exempt Org P-H
Taxonomic Index — Taxon Index
Taxpayers' Bulletin — Taxpayers Bul
Taylor Society. Bulletin — Taylor Soc Bul
T'bilisis A. Razmadzis Saxelobis Mat'ematikis Institutis Shromebi — Tbilis A Razmadzis Saxel Mat Inst Shromebi
Tbilisskii Gosudarstvennyi Universitet Institut Prikladnoi Matematiki Trudy — Tbilis Gos Univ Inst Prikl Mat Tr
Tbilisskii Gosudarstvennyi Universitet Institut Prikladnoi Matematiki Trudy — Tbiliss Gos Univ Inst Prikl Mat Trudy
TCA [*Tissue Culture Association*] **Manual** — TCA Man
TDR. The Drama Review — GTDR
Te Reo — TeR
Te Reo. Linguistic Society of New Zealand — Reo
Tea and Coffee Trade Journal — TEA
Tea and Coffee Trade Journal — Tea & Coff
Tea Boards of Kenya, Uganda, and Tanganyika. Journal — Tea
Tea in East Africa — Tea East Afr
Tea Quarterly — Tea Q
Tea Research Association. Annual Scientific Report — Tea Res Assoc Annu Sci Rep
Tea Research Institute of Ceylon. Annual Report — Tea Res Inst Ceylon Annu Rep
Tea Research Institute of Sri Lanka. Technical Report — Tea Res Inst Sri Lanka Tech Rep
Tea Research Journal — Tea Res J
Tea Research Journal. Kyoto/Kyoto-fu Chagyo Kenkyusho Gyomu Hokokusho — Tea Res J Kyoto
Teacher — Teach
Teacher Education — TE
Teacher Education — Teach Ed
Teacher Education — Teach Educ
Teacher Education in New Countries — Teacher Ed
Teacher Feedback — Teach Feedback
Teacher of the Deaf — Teach Deaf
Teacher Today — Teach Today
Teacher-Librarian — Tea Lib
Teacher-Librarian — Teach Lib
Teacher-Librarian — Teacher Librn
Teachers College Record — GTCR
Teachers College Record — Tchr Coll Rec
Teacher's College Record — TCORA
Teacher's College Record — TCR
Teacher's College Record — Teach Col R
Teachers College Record — Teach Col Rec
Teachers College Record — Teach Coll Rec
Teachers Guild of New South Wales. Proceedings — Teach Guild NSW Proc
Teachers' Journal — Teach J
Teachers' Journal — Teachers J
Teachers' Journal and Abstract — Teach J and Abst
Teachers' Journal of Special Education — Teach J Spec Educ
Teachers' Journal (Victorian Teachers Union) — Teach J Vic
Teachers of English as an Additional Language. Occasional Papers — TEAL Occ Pap
Teachers of Home Economics Specialist Association. Newsletter — THESA N
Teacher's World — Teach W
Teaching Adults — Teach Adults
Teaching Aids News — Teach Aids News
Teaching and Learning — Teach Learn
Teaching and Training — Teach Train
Teaching at a Distance — Teach Dist
Teaching Atypical Students in Alberta — TASA
Teaching Elementary Physical Education — Teaching Elem PE
Teaching English — TEng
Teaching English to the Deaf — Teach Engl Deaf
Teaching Exceptional Children — Teach Excep Child
Teaching High School Physical Education — Teaching High Sch PE
Teaching History — Teach Hist
Teaching History — TH
Teaching Language through Literature — TLTL
Teaching London Kids — Teach Lond Kids
Teaching London Kids — TLK
Teaching Mathematics — Teach Math
Teaching Methods Page — Teach Meth Page
Teaching Middle School Physical Education — Teaching Mid Sch PE
Teaching Music — Teaching Mus
Teaching News. University of Birmingham — Teach News Birm
Teaching Newsletter — Teach Newsl
Teaching of English — Teach Eng
Teaching of English — Teach Engl
Teaching of English — Teaching Engl
Teaching Philosophy — Teach Phil
Teaching Political Science — Teach Pol S
Teaching Political Science — Teach Pol Sci
Teaching Political Science — Teaching Polit Sci
Teaching Sociology — Teach Socio
Teaching Sociology — Teach Sociol
Teatar [*Sofia*] — T
Teater SA. Quarterly for South African Theater — TSA
Teatr — T
Teatr [*Moscow*] — Te
Tebiwa Journal. Idaho Museum of Natural History — Tebiwa J Idaho Mus Nat Hist
Tebiwa Miscellaneous Papers. Idaho State University. Museum of Natural History — Tebiwa Misc Pap Idaho State Univ Mus Nat Hist
Tebtunis Papyri — PTeb
TecAd. International Journal of Technology Advances — TecAd Int J Technol Adv

Techinsches Messen-TM — Tech Mess-TM
Technic International [*Germany*] — Technic Int
Technic International — TECIB
Technica Jahrbuch — Tech Jahrb
Technical Abstract Bulletin — Tech Abstr Bull
Technical Advances in Shikoku Agriculture — Tech Adv Shikoku Agric
Technical Advisory Service for Attorneys [*Database*] — TASA
Technical Aid to the Disabled Journal — TAD J
Technical and Economical Studies. Institute of Geology and Geophysics. Series I. Mineralogy-Petrology — Tech Econ Stud Inst Geol Geophys Ser I
Technical Association Papers — Tech Assn Pa
Technical Bibliographies. Birmingham Public Libraries — Tech Bibliogr Birmingham Public Lib
Technical Bibliographies Series. Birmingham Central Libraries — Tech Bibliogr Ser Birmingham Cent Lib
Technical Bulletin. Agricultural Experiment Station. Oregon State University — Tech Bull Agric Exp Stn Ore St Univ
Technical Bulletin. Agricultural Experiment Station. South Dakota State University — TB Agric Exp Stn SD State Univ
Technical Bulletin. Agricultural Experiment Station. Washington State Institute of Agricultural Sciences — Tech Bull Agric Exp Stn Wash St
Technical Bulletin. Agricultural Research Institute — Tech Bull Agric Res Inst
Technical Bulletin. Agricultural Research Institute (Cyprus) — Tech Bull Agric Res Inst (Cyprus)
Technical Bulletin. Animal Industry and Agricultural Branch. Department of the Northern Territory — Tech Bull Anim Ind Agric Branch NT
Technical Bulletin. Animal Industry and Agriculture Branch. Northern Territory — Tech Bull Anim Ind Agric Br NT
Technical Bulletin. Arizona Agricultural Experiment Station — Tech Bull Ariz Agr Exp Sta
Technical Bulletin. Arizona Agricultural Experiment Station — Tech Bull Ariz Agric Exp Stn
Technical Bulletin. Arizona Agricultural Experiment Station. University of Arizona — Tech Bull Agric Exp Stn Univ Ariz
Technical Bulletin. Atomic Energy Organization of Iran — Tech Bull At Energy Organ Iran
Technical Bulletin. Banana Research Advisory Committee — Tech Bull Banana Res Adv Comm
Technical Bulletin. Canada Inland Waters Directorate — Tech Bull Can Inland Waters Dir
Technical Bulletin. Colorado Agricultural Experiment Station — Tech Bull Colo Agric Exp Stn
Technical Bulletin. Colorado State University. Agricultural Experiment Station — Tech Bull Colo State Univ Agr Exp Sta
Technical Bulletin. Commonwealth Institute of Biological Control — Tech Bull Commonw Inst Biol Control
Technical Bulletin. Commonwealth Institute of Biological Control — Tech Bull Commonwealth Inst Biol Contr
Technical Bulletin. Cyprus Agricultural Research Institute — Tech Bull Cyprus Agr Res Inst
Technical Bulletin. Department of Agriculture — Techn Bull Dept Agric
Technical Bulletin. Department of Agriculture (Malaysia) — Tech Bul Dep Agric (Malaysia)
Technical Bulletin. Department of Agriculture. Victoria — Tech Bull Dep Agric Vict
Technical Bulletin. Department of Agriculture. Western Australia — Tech Bull Dep Agric West Aust
Technical Bulletin. Experimental Forest. National Taiwan University — Tech Bull Exp For Taiwan Univ
Technical Bulletin. Experimental Forest of National Taiwan University — Tech Bull Exp For Natl Taiwan Univ
Technical Bulletin. Faculty of Agriculture. Kagawa University — Tech Bull Fac Agr Kagawa Univ
Technical Bulletin. Faculty of Agriculture. Kagawa University — Tech Bull Fac Agric Kagawa Univ
Technical Bulletin. Faculty of Horticulture. Chiba University — Tech Bull Fac Hort Chiba Univ
Technical Bulletin. Faculty of Horticulture. Chiba University — Tech Bull Fac Hortic Chiba Univ
Technical Bulletin. Florida Agricultural Experiment Station — Tech Bull Fla Agric Exp Stn
Technical Bulletin. Forests Products Laboratory. National Bureau of Industrial Research/Ching Chi Pu Chung Yang Kung Yeh Shih Yen So Mu To'ai Shih Yen Kuan Chuan Pao — Techn Bull Forests Prod Lab
Technical Bulletin from the Danish Government Institute of Seed Pathology for Developing Countries — Tech Bull Dan Gov Inst Seed Pathol Developing Countries
Technical Bulletin. Georgia Agricultural Experiment Stations. University of Georgia. College of Agriculture — Tech Bull GA Agr Exp Sta
Technical Bulletin. Great Britain Ministry of Agiculture, Fisheries, and Food — Tech Bull Gt Brit Min Agr Fish Food
Technical Bulletin. Harper Adams Agricultural College — Tech Bull Harper Adams Agr Coll
Technical Bulletin. Hawaii Agricultural Experiment Station — Tech Bull Hawaii Agric Exp Stn
Technical Bulletin. Hawaii Agricultural Experiment Station. University of Hawaii — Tech Bull Hawaii Agric Exp Stn Univ Hawaii
Technical Bulletin. Hokkaido Agricultural Experiment Station — Tech Bull Hokkaido Agric Exp Stn
Technical Bulletin. Institute for Land and Water Management Research — Tech Bull Inst Ld Wat Mgmt Res
Technical Bulletin. Kagawa Agricultural College — Tech Bull Kagawa Agr Coll
Technical Bulletin. Kansas Agricultural Experiment Station — Tech Bull Kans Agr Exp Sta
Technical Bulletin. Kansas Agricultural Experiment Station — Tech Bull Kans Agric Exp Stn
Technical Bulletin. Land Resources Division. Directorate of Overseas Surveys — Tech Bull Land Resour Div Dir Overseas Surv
Technical Bulletin. Life Sciences and Agriculture Experiment Station (Maine) — Tech Bull Life Sci Agric Exp Stn (Maine)
Technical Bulletin. Life Sciences and Agriculture Experiment Station. University of Maine at Orono — Tech Bull Life Sci Agric Exp Stn Univ Maine
Technical Bulletin. Michigan State College. Agricultural Experiment Station — Tech Bull Mich St Coll Agric Exp Stn
Technical Bulletin. Michigan State University. Agricultural Experiment Station — Tech Bull Mich State Univ Agr Exp Sta
Technical Bulletin. Ministry of Agriculture, Fisheries, and Food — Tech Bull Minist Agric Fish Fd
Technical Bulletin. Ministry of Agriculture, Fisheries, and Food (Great Britain) — Tech Bull Minist Agric Fish Food (GB)
Technical Bulletin. Ministry of Agriculture of Eastern Nigeria — Tech Bull Minist Agric E Niger
Technical Bulletin. Minnesota Agricultural Experiment Station — Tech Bull Minn Agric Exp Stn
Technical Bulletin. Mississippi Agricultural and Forestry Experiment Station — Tech Bull Miss Agric For Exp Stn
Technical Bulletin. Mississippi Agricultural Experiment Station — Tech Bull Miss Agr Exp Sta
Technical Bulletin. Miyagi Prefectural Agricultural Experiment Station — Tech Bull Miyagi Prefect Agr Exp Sta
Technical Bulletin. Montana Agricultural Experiment Station — Tech Bull Mont Agr Exp Sta
Technical Bulletin. North Carolina Agricultural Experiment Station — Tech Bull N Carol Agric Exp Stn
Technical Bulletin. North Carolina Agricultural Experiment Station — Tech Bull NC Agr Exp Sta
Technical Bulletin. North Carolina Agricultural Experiment Station — Tech Bull NC Agric Exp Sta
Technical Bulletin. North Carolina State College. Agricultural Experiment Station — Tech Bull N Carol St Coll Agric Exp Stn
Technical Bulletin. North Carolina State University. Agricultural Experiment Station — Tech Bull N Carol St Univ Agric Exp Stn
Technical Bulletin. Oklahoma State University. Agricultural Experiment Station — Tech Bull Okla State Univ Agr Exp Sta
Technical Bulletin. Oregon Agricultural Experiment Station — Tech Bull Ore Agric Exp Stn
Technical Bulletin. Oregon State College. Agricultural Experiment Station — Tech Bull Oreg State Coll Agr Exp Sta
Technical Bulletin. Oregon State University. Agricultural Experiment Station — Tech Bull Oreg State Univ Agric Exp Stn
Technical Bulletin. Registry of Medical Technologists — Tech Bull Regist Med Technol
Technical Bulletin. Registry of Medical Technologists — Techn Bull Reg Med Technol
Technical Bulletin. Rhodesia Agricultural Journal — Tech Bull Rhodesia Agric J
Technical Bulletin. South Carolina Agricultural Experiment Station — Tech Bull SC Agric Exp Stn
Technical Bulletin. South Dakota Agricultural Experiment Station — Tech Bull S Dak Agr Exp Sta
Technical Bulletin. Sugar Manufacturers' Association — Tech Bull Sug Manufact Ass
Technical Bulletin. Sulphur Institute — Tech Bull Sulphur Inst
Technical Bulletin. Taiwan Agricultural Research Institute — Tech Bull Taiwan Agric Res Inst
Technical Bulletin. Taiwan Fertilizer Company — Tech Bull Taiwan Fertil Co
Technical Bulletin. TARC (Tropical Agriculture Research Center) — Tech Bull TARC (Trop Agric Res Cent)
Technical Bulletin. Texas Engineering Experiment Station — Tech Bull Tex Eng Exp Stn
Technical Bulletin. Tokushima Bunri University — Tech Bull Tokushima Bunri Univ
Technical Bulletin. Tropical Agriculture Research Center — Tech Bull Trop Agric Res Cent
Technical Bulletin. United Arab Republic Ministry of Agriculture and Agrarian Reform — Tech Bull UAR Minist Agric Agrar Reform
Technical Bulletin. United States Department of Agriculture — Tech Bull US Dep Agric
Technical Bulletin. United States Department of Agriculture — Tech Bull USDA
Technical Bulletin. United States Department of Agriculture. Agricultural Research Service — Tech Bull US Dep Agric Agric Res Serv
Technical Bulletin. United States Forest Service — Tech Bull US For Serv
Technical Bulletin. University of Maine. Life Sciences and Agriculture Experiment Station — Tech Bull Univ Maine Life Sci Agric Exp Stn
Technical Bulletin. University of Minnesota. Agricultural Experiment Station — Tech Bull Minn Agric Exp Sta
Technical Bulletin. University of Minnesota. Agricultural Experiment Station — Tech Bull Univ Minn Agr Exp Sta
Technical Bulletin. University of Nevada. Agricultural Experiment Station — Tech Bull Univ Nev Agr Exp Sta
Technical Bulletin. University of the Philippines. College of Agriculture — Tech Bull Univ Philippines Coll Agr
Technical Bulletin. Victoria Country Roads Board — Tech Bull Vic Ctry Rd Bd
Technical Bulletin. Virgin Islands of the United States Agricultural Experiment Station — Tech Bul VIUS Agric Exp Stn
Technical Bulletin. Virginia Agricultural Experiment Station — Tech Bull VA Agr Exp Sta
Technical Bulletin. Washington Agricultural Experiment Station — Tech Bull Wash Agr Exp Sta

Technical Bulletin. Washington Agricultural Experiment Station — Tech Bull Wash Agric Exp Stn
Technical Bulletin. Washington State University. College of Agriculture. Research Center — Tech Bull Wash State Univ Coll Agric Res Cent
Technical Bulletin. Western Australian Department of Agriculture — Tech Bull West Aust Dep Agric
Technical Ceramics International — Tech Ceram Int
Technical Circular. Mauritius Sugar Industry Research Institute — Tech Circ Maurit Sug Ind Res Inst
Technical Communication — ITCO
Technical Communication. Bureau of Sugar Experiment Stations (Queensland) — Tech Commun Bur Sug Exp Stns (Qd)
Technical Communication. Bureau of Sugar Experiment Stations (Queensland) — Tech Commun Bur Sugar Exp Stn (Queensl)
Technical Communication. Central Information, Library, and Editorial Section. Commonwealth Scientific and Industrial Research Organisation — Tech Commun Central Inform Libr Edit Sect CSIRO
Technical Communication. Central Information, Library, and Editorial Section. Commonwealth Scientific and Industrial Research Organisation — Tech Commun CILES CSIRO
Technical Communication. Commonwealth Forestry Bureau (Oxford) — Tech Commun For Bur (Oxf)
Technical Communication. Department of Agricultural Technical Services. Republic of South Africa — Tech Commun Dept Agr Tech Serv Repub S Afr
Technical Communication. Division of Mineral Chemistry. Commonwealth Scientific and Industrial Research Organisation — Tech Commun Div Miner Chem CSIRO
Technical Communication. Division of Mineralogy. Commonwealth Scientific and Industrial Research Organisation — Tech Commun Div Miner CSIRO
Technical Communication. Minerals Research Laboratories. Commonwealth Scientific and Industrial Research Organisation — Tech Commun Miner Res Lab CSIRO
Technical Communication. Minerals Research Laboratories. Commonwealth Scientific and Industrial Research Organisation (Australia) — Tech Commun CSIRO (Aust)
Technical Communication. South Africa Department of Agriculture and Fisheries — Tech Commun S Afr Dep Agric Fish
Technical Communication. Woodland Ecology Unit. Commonwealth Scientific and Industrial Research Organisation — Tech Commun Woodld Ecol Unit CSIRO
Technical Communications — Tech Commun
Technical Communications. Royal School of Mines — Tech Commun R Sch Mines
Technical Communications. South Africa Department of Agricultural Technical Services — Tech Commun S Afr Dep Agric Tech Serv
Technical Conference Proceedings. Irrigation Association — Tech Conf Proc Irrig Assoc
Technical Cybernetics USSR — Tech Cybern USSR
Technical Data Digest — Tech Data Dig
Technical Data Digest [*United States*] — Tech Data Digest
Technical Digest — Tech Dig
Technical Digest — TEDGA
Technical Digest. International Vacuum Microelectronics Conference — Tech Dig Int Vac Microelectron Conf
Technical Digest. Symposium on Optical Fiber Measurements — Tech Dig Symp Opt Fiber Meas
Technical Document. Food and Agriculture Organization of the United Nations. Plant Protection Committee for the South East Asia and Pacific Region — Tech Doc FAO Plant Prot Comm Southeast Asia Pac Reg
Technical Education — Tech Educ
Technical Education Abstracts — Tech Educ Abstr
Technical Extracts of Traffic [*National Security Agency*] — TEXTA
Technical Forum. Society of Vacuum Coaters — Tech Forum Soc Vac Coaters
Technical Information Document — TID
Technical Information for Industry — TI
Technical Information Service — Tech Info Service
Technical Journal — Technical J
Technical Journal. Ankara Nuclear Research and Training Center — Tech J Ankara Nucl Res Train Cent
Technical Journal. Ankara Nuclear Research Center — Tech J Ankara Nucl Res Cent
Technical Journal. Japan Broadcasting Corporation — Tech J Jap Broadcast Corp
Technical Journal. Japan Broadcasting Corporation — Tech J Jpn Broadcast Corp
Technical Laboratory. Central Research Institute of the Electrical Power Industry. Report [*Japan*] — Tech Lab Cent Res Inst Electr Power Ind Rep
Technical Manpower — Tech Manpower
Technical Memoranda. Plant Protection Limited — Tech Memor Plant Protection Ltd
Technical Memorandum. California Institute of Technology. Jet Propulsion Laboratory — Tech Mem Calif Inst Technol Jet Propul Lab
Technical Memorandum. Daresbury Laboratory — Tech Memo Daresbury Lab
Technical Memorandum. Daresbury Nuclear Physics Laboratory — Tech Memo Daresbury Nucl Phys Lab
Technical Memorandum. Division of Applied Geomechanics. Commonwealth Scientific and Industrial Research Organisation — Tech Memo Div Appl Geomech CSIRO
Technical Memorandum. Division of Land Use Research. Commonwealth Scientific and Industrial Research Organisation — Tech Memo Div Land Use Res CSIRO
Technical Memorandum. Division of Wildlife Research. Commonwealth Scientific and Industrial Research Organisation — Tech Memo Div Wildl Res CSIRO
Technical Memorandum. Jet Propulsion Laboratory. California Institute of Technology — Tech Memo Jet Propul Lab Calif Inst Technol
Technical News — Tech News
Technical News Service. Sarabhai M. Chemicals — Tech News Serv Sarabhai M Chem
Technical Newsletter. Forest Products Research Institute (Kumasi, Ghana) — Tech Newslett For Prod Res Inst (Ghana)
Technical Note. Australia Defence Standards Laboratories — Tech Note Aust Def Stand Lab
Technical Note. Australia. Materials Research Laboratory — Tech Note Aust Mater Res Lab
Technical Note. Brick Manufacturers Association of New South Wales — Tech Note Brick Manuf Assoc NSW
Technical Note. Brick Manufacturers Association of New South Wales — Tech Note Brick Mf Assoc NSW
Technical Note. Bureau of Forestry and Timber — Tech Note For Timb Bur
Technical Note. Charles Kolling Research Laboratory. Department of Mechanical Engineering. University of Sydney — Tech Note Charles Kolling Res Lab
Technical Note. Department of Forest Research (Nigeria) — Tech Note Dep For Res (Nigeria)
Technical Note. East African Agriculture and Forestry Research Organization — Tech Note E Afr Agric For Res Organ
Technical Note. Forest Department (Nairobi, Kenya) — Tech Note For Dep (Kenya)
Technical Note. Forest Department (Uganda) — Tech Note For Dep (Uganda)
Technical Note. Forest Products Research and Industries Development Commission (Philippines) — Tech Note For Prod Res Ind Dev Comm (Philipp)
Technical Note. Forest Products Research Institute (Ghana) — Tech Note For Prod Res Inst (Ghana)
Technical Note. Forestry Department (British Solomon Islands Protectorate) — Tech Note For Dep (Brit Solomon Islands Protect)
Technical Note. Oji Institute for Forest Tree Improvement — Tech Note Oji Inst For Tree Impr
Technical Note. Port and Harbour Technical Research Institute. Ministry of Transportation (Japan) — Tech Note Harbour Tech Res Inst Minist Transp (Jpn)
Technical Note. Quetico-Superior Wilderness Research Center — Tech Note Quetico-Sup Wild Res Cent
Technical Note. Research Institute of Industrial Safety — Tech Note Res Inst Ind Saf
Technical Note. Solar Energy Studies. Commonwealth Scientific and Industrial Research Organisation — Tech Note Sol Energy Stud CSIRO
Technical Notes for the Rubber Industry — Tech Notes Rubb Ind
Technical Notes for the Rubber Industry — Tech Notes Rubber Ind
Technical Notes. Forestry Commission of New South Wales — Tech Notes For Comm NSW
Technical Notes on Clay Products [*Brick Development Research Institute*] — Tech Notes Clay Prod
Technical Paper. Agricultural Experiment Station (Puerto Rico) — Tech Pap Agric Exp Stn (P Rico)
Technical Paper. Animal Research Laboratories. Commonwealth Scientific and Industrial Research Organisation — Tech Pap Anim Res Lab CSIRO
Technical Paper. Animal Research Laboratories. Commonwealth Scientific and Industrial Research Organization — Tech Pap Anim Res Labs CSIRO
Technical Paper. (Australia) Commonwealth Scientific and Industrial Research Organisation. Division of Applied Geomechanics — Tech Pap (Aust) CSIRO Div Appl Geomech
Technical Paper. (Australia) Commonwealth Scientific and Industrial Research Organisation. Division of Mineragraphic Investigation — Tech Pap (Aust) CSIRO Div Mineragraphic Invest
Technical Paper. Australian Water Resources Council — Tech Pap Aust Wat Resour Coun
Technical Paper. Australian Water Resources Council — Tech Pap Aust Water Resour Coun
Technical Paper. Canadian Pulp and Paper Association — Tech Pap Canad Pulp Pap Ass
Technical Paper. Department of Forestry (Queensland) — Tech Pap Dep For (Qd)
Technical Paper. Department of Forestry (Queensland) — Tech Pap Dep For (Queensl)
Technical Paper. Division of Applied Chemistry. Commonwealth Scientific and Industrial Research Organisation — Tech Pap Div Appl Chem CSIRO
Technical Paper. Division of Applied Geomechanics. Commonwealth Scientific and Industrial Research Organisation — Tech Pap Div Appl Geomech CSIRO
Technical Paper. Division of Applied Mineralogy. Commonwealth Scientific and Industrial Research Organisation — Tech Pap Div Appl Miner CSIRO
Technical Paper. Division of Applied Organic Chemistry. Commonwealth Scientific and Industrial Research Organisation — Tech Pap Div Appl Org Chem CSIRO
Technical Paper. Division of Atmospheric Physics. Commonwealth Scientific and Industrial Research Organisation — Tech Pap Div Atmos Phys CSIRO
Technical Paper. Division of Atmospheric Physics. Commonwealth Scientific and Industrial Research Organisation — Tech Pap Div Atmosph Phys CSIRO
Technical Paper. Division of Building Research. Commonwealth Scientific and Industrial Research Organisation — Tech Pap Div Bldg Res CSIRO
Technical Paper. Division of Building Research. Commonwealth Scientific and Industrial Research Organisation — Tech Pap Div Build Res CSIRO
Technical Paper. Division of Chemical Technology. Commonwealth Scientific and Industrial Research Organisation — Tech Pap Div Chem Technol CSIRO
Technical Paper. Division of Entomology. Commonwealth Scientific and Industrial Research Organisation — Tech Pap Div Ent CSIRO
Technical Paper. Division of Fisheries and Oceanography. Commonwealth Scientific and Industrial Research Organisation — Tech Pap Div Fish Oceanogr CSIRO

Technical Paper. Division of Food Preservation. Commonwealth Scientific and Industrial Research Organisation — Tech Pap Div Fd Preserv CSIRO
Technical Paper. Division of Food Research. Commonwealth Scientific and Industrial Research Organisation — Tech Pap Div Fd Res CSIRO
Technical Paper. Division of Food Research. Commonwealth Scientific and Industrial Research Organisation — Tech Pap Div Food Res CSIRO
Technical Paper. Division of Food Research. Commonwealth Scientific and Industrial Research Organisation (Australia) — Tech Pap Div Fd Res CSIRO (Aust)
Technical Paper. Division of Land Research. Commonwealth Scientific and Industrial Research Organisation — Tech Pap Div Ld Res CSIRO
Technical Paper. Division of Land Resources Management. Commonwealth Scientific and Industrial Research Organisation — Tech Pap Div Land Resour Manage CSIRO
Technical Paper. Division of Land Use Research. Commonwealth Scientific and Industrial Research Organisation — Tech Pap Div Land Use Res CSIRO
Technical Paper. Division of Land Use Research. Commonwealth Scientific and Industrial Research Organisation — Tech Pap Div Ld Use Res CSIRO
Technical Paper. Division of Mathematical Statistics. Commonwealth Scientific and Industrial Research Organisation — Tech Pap Div Mat Statist CSIRO
Technical Paper. Division of Mathematical Statistics. Commonwealth Scientific and Industrial Research Organisation — Tech Pap Div Math Statist CSIRO
Technical Paper. Division of Mathematics and Statistics. Commonwealth Scientific and Industrial Research Organisation — Tech Pap Div Math Stat CSIRO
Technical Paper. Division of Meteorological Physics. Commonwealth Scientific and Industrial Research Organisation — Tech Pap Div Met Phys CSIRO
Technical Paper. Division of Meteorological Physics. Commonwealth Scientific and Industrial Research Organisation — Tech Pap Div Meteorol Phys CSIRO
Technical Paper. Division of Plant Industry. Commonwealth Scientific and Industrial Research Organisation — Tech Pap Div Pl Ind CSIRO
Technical Paper. Division of Plant Industry. Commonwealth Scientific and Industrial Research Organisation — Tech Pap Div Plant Ind CSIRO
Technical Paper. Division of Soil Mechanics. Commonwealth Scientific and Industrial Research Organisation — Tech Pap Div Soil Mechanics CSIRO
Technical Paper. Division of Soils. Commonwealth Scientific and Industrial Research Organisation — Tech Pap Div Soils CSIRO
Technical Paper. Division of Tropical Agronomy. Commonwealth Scientific and Industrial Research Organisation — Tech Pap Div Trop Agron CSIRO
Technical Paper. Division of Tropical Crops and Pastures. Commonwealth Scientific and Industrial Research Organisation — Tech Pap Div Trop Crops Pastures CSIRO
Technical Paper. Division of Tropical Pastures. Commonwealth Scientific and Industrial Research Organisation — Tech Pap Div Trop Pastures CSIRO
Technical Paper. Division of Wildlife Research. Commonwealth Scientific and Industrial Research Organisation — Tech Pap Div Wildl Res CSIRO
Technical Paper. Forest Research Institute. New Zealand Forest Service — Tech Pap For Res Inst NZ For Serv
Technical Paper. Forestry Commission of New South Wales — Tech Pap For Comm NSW
Technical Paper. National Measurement Laboratory. Commonwealth Scientific and Industrial Research Organisation — Tech Pap Natl Meas Lab CSIRO
Technical Paper. National Standards Laboratory. Commonwealth Scientific and Industrial Research Organisation — Tech Pap Natn Stand Lab CSIRO
Technical Paper. New York State Department of Environmental Conservation — Tech Pap NY State Dep Environ Conserv
Technical Paper. Queensland Department of Forestry — Tech Pap Queensl Dep For
Technical Paper. Society of Manufacturing Engineers. Series AD (Assembly Division) — Tech Pap Soc Manuf Eng Ser AD
Technical Paper. Society of Manufacturing Engineers. Series EE (Electrical Engineering) — Tech Pap SME Ser EE
Technical Paper. Society of Manufacturing Engineers. Series EE (Electrical Engineering) — Tech Pap Soc Manuf Eng Ser EE
Technical Paper. Society of Manufacturing Engineers. Series EM (Engineering Materials) — Tech Pap Soc Manuf Eng Ser EM
Technical Paper. Society of Manufacturing Engineers. Series FC (Finishing and Coating) — Tech Pap Soc Manuf Eng Ser FC
Technical Paper. Society of Manufacturing Engineers. Series IQ (Inspection and Quality) — Tech Pap Soc Manuf Eng Ser IQ
Technical Paper. Society of Manufacturing Engineers. Series MF (Material Forming) — Tech Pap Soc Manuf Eng Ser MF
Technical Paper. Society of Manufacturing Engineers. Series MR (Material Removal) — Tech Pap Soc Manuf Eng Ser MR
Technical Paper. University of Puerto Rico. Agricultural Experiment Station — Tech Pap Univ PR Agr Exp Sta
Technical Papers. American Pulpwood Association — Tech Pap Amer Pulpw Ass
Technical Papers. California Department of Agriculture — Tech Pap Calif Dep Agric
Technical Papers. Division of Land Research and Regional Survey. Commonwealth Scientific and Industrial Research Organisation (Australia) — Tech Pap Div Ld Res Reg Surv CSIRO (Aust)
Technical Papers. Division of Plant Industry. Commonwealth Scientific and Industrial Research Organisation (Australia) — Tech Pap Div Pl Ind CSIRO (Aust)
Technical Papers. Division of Plant Industry. C.S.I.R.O — Techn Pap Div Pl Industr CSIRO
Technical Papers. Divisional Technical Conference. Society of Plastics Engineers — Tech Pap Div Tech Conf Soc Plast Eng
Technical Papers in Hydrology — Tech Pap Hydrol
Technical Papers. Institute of Petroleum [*London*] — Tech Pap Inst Pet
Technical Papers. Intersociety Energy Conversion Engineering Conference — Tech Pap Intersoc Energy Convers Eng Conf
Technical Photography — Tech Phot
Technical Photography — Tech Photo
Technical Preprints. American Society of Lubrication Engineers — Tech Prepr Am Soc Lubr Eng
Technical Progress Report. Hawaii Agricultural Experiment Station. University of Hawaii — Tech Progr Rep Hawaii Agr Exp Sta
Technical Progress Report. United States Bureau of Mines — Tech Prog Rep US Bur Mines
Technical Progress Report. United States Bureau of Mines — XMTPB
Technical Publication. Division of Wood Technology. Forestry Commission of New South Wales — Tech Publ Div Wood Technol For Comm NSW
Technical Publication. New York State University. College of Forestry — Tech Publ NY St Coll For
Technical Publication R8-TP. US Department of Agriculture. Forest Service. Southern Region — Tech Publ R8-TP US Dep Agric For Serv South Reg
Technical Publication. State University College of Forestry. Syracuse University — Tech Publ State Univ Coll For Syracuse Univ
Technical Publications — Tech Publs
Technical Publications. Australian Society of Dairy Technology — Tech Publs Aust Soc Dairy Technol
Technical Publications. Department of Agriculture (Victoria) — Tech Publs Dep Agric (Vict)
Technical Publications. Division of Wood Technology. New South Wales Forestry Commission — Tech Publs Div Wood Technol NSW For Comm
Technical Publications. New South Wales Forestry Commission. Division of Wood Technology — Tech Publs NSW For Comm Div Wood Technol
Technical Publications. State Biological Survey of Kansas — Tech Publ State Biol Surv Kans
Technical Quarterly. Master Brewers Association of America — Tech Quart Master Brew Ass Amer
Technical Quarterly. Master Brewers Association of the Americas — Tech Q Mast Brew Assoc Am
Technical Release. American Pulpwood Association — Tech Release Amer Pulpw Ass
Technical Report. AFAPL-TR. Air Force Aero Propulsion Laboratory (United States) — Tech Rep AFAPL TR Air Force Aero Propul Lab (US)
Technical Report. AFFDL-TR. Air Force Flight Dynamics Laboratory (United States) — Tech Rep AFFDL TR Air Force Flight Dyn Lab (US)
Technical Report. AFML-TR. Air Force Materials Laboratory (United States) — Tech Rep AFML TR Air Force Mater Lab (US)
Technical Report. AFWAL-TR. United States Air Force Wright Aeronautical Laboratories — TAFSD
Technical Report. AFWAL-TR. United States Air Force Wright Aeronautical Laboratories — Tech Rep AFWAL-TR US Air Force Wright Aeronaut Lab
Technical Report. Agricultural Chemistry Branch (Queensland) — Tech Rep Agric Chem Branch (Queensl)
Technical Report. Agricultural Engineering Research Station. Ministry of Agriculture and Forestry. Series F. General [*Japan*] — Tech Rep Agric Eng Res Stn Min Agric For Ser F
Technical Report. Agricultural Land Service. Ministry of Agriculture, Fisheries, and Food — Tech Rep Agric Ld Serv Minist Agric Fish Fd
Technical Report. Australia Weapons Research Establishment — Tech Rep Aust Weapons Res Establ
Technical Report. British Electrical and Allied Industries Research Association — Techn Rep Brit El All Ind Res Ass
Technical Report. Bureau of Meteorology — Tech Rep Bur Met
Technical Report. Bureau of Meteorology — Tech Rep Bur Meteorol
Technical Report. Center for Research in Water Resources. University of Texas at Austin — Tech Rep Cent Res Water Resour Univ Tex Austin
Technical Report. Central Research Institute of the Electrical Power Industry [*Japan*] — Tech Rep Cent Res Inst Electr Power Ind
Technical Report. Construction Engineering Research Laboratory [*United States*] — Tech Rep Constr Eng Res Lab
Technical Report. Council for the Central Laboratory of the Research Councils — Tech Rep Counc Cent Lab Res Counc
Technical Report. Department of Mines. Tasmania — Tech Rep Dep Mines Tas
Technical Report. Desert Locust Control Organization for Eastern Africa — Tech Rep Desert Locust Control Organ East Afr
Technical Report. Division of Applied Geomechanics. Commonwealth Scientific and Industrial Research Organisation — Tech Rep Div Appl Geomech CSIRO
Technical Report. Division of Mechanical Engineering. Commonwealth Scientific and Industrial Research Organisation — Tech Rep Div Mech Eng CSIRO
Technical Report. Division of Mechanical Engineering. Commonwealth Scientific and Industrial Research Organisation — Tech Rep Div Mech Engng CSIRO
Technical Report. Division of Soil Mechanics. Commonwealth Scientific and Industrial Research Organisation — Tech Rep Div Soil Mech CSIRO
Technical Report. Faculty of Forestry. University of Toronto — Tech Rep Fac For Univ Toronto
Technical Report. Forest Engineering Research Institute of Canada — Tech Rep For Eng Res Inst Can
Technical Report. Grassland Research Institute — Tech Rep Grassld Res Inst
Technical Report. Hawaii University. Water Resource Research Center — Tech Rep Water Resour Res Cent Hawaii Univ
Technical Report. Institute of Printed Circuits — Tech Rep Inst Printed Circuits
Technical Report. ISSP (Institute for Solid State Physics). Series A — Tech Rep ISSP (Inst Solid State Phys) Ser A
Technical Report. Jet Propulsion Laboratory. California Institute of Technology — Tech Rep Jet Propul Lab Calif Inst Technol
Technical Report. JSS [*Japanese, Swiss, Swedish*] **Project** — Tech Rep JSS Proj
Technical Report. Nanyang University. College of Graduate Studies. Institute of Natural Sciences — Tech Rep Nanyang Univ Coll Grad Stud Inst Nat Sci
Technical Report. National Space Development Agency of Japan — Tech Rep Natl Space Dev Agency Jpn

Technical Report. Nisshin Steel Company Limited [*Japan*] — Tech Rep Nisshin Steel Co Ltd
Technical Report of Sumitomo Special Metals — Tech Rep Sumitomo Spec Met
Technical Report. Office of Naval Research (USA) — Tech Rep Off Nav Res (USA)
Technical Report on Air Pollution in Yokohama-Kawasaki Industrial Area [*Japan*] — Tech Rep Air Pollut Yokohama-Kawasaki Ind Area
Technical Report R2. US Department of Agriculture. Forest Service. Forest Pest Management — Tech Rep R2 US Dep Agric For Serv For Pest Manage
Technical Report. Regional Research Station (Samaru) — Tech Rep Reg Res Sta (Samaru)
Technical Report. School of Forest Resources. North Carolina State University — Tech Rep Sch For Resour NC St Univ
Technical Report Series: Carcinogenesis. National Cancer Institute (United States) — Tech Rep Ser Carcinog Nat Cancer Inst (US)
Technical Report Series. IAEA [*International Atomic Energy Agency*] — TRAEA
Technical Report Series. World Health Organisation — Techn Rep Ser Wld Hlth Org
Technical Report. Soil Research Institute. Ghana Academy of Sciences — Tech Rep Soil Res Inst Ghana Acad Sci
Technical Report System. American Society for Metals — Tech Rep Syst Am Soc Met
Technical Report System. American Society for Metals — Tech Rep Syst ASM
Technical Report. Tasmania Department of Mines — Tech Rep Tasm Dep Mines
Technical Report. Texas Forest Service — Tech Rep Tex For Serv
Technical Report. United States Army Engineers. Waterways Experiment Station — Tech Rep US Army Eng Waterw Exp Stn
Technical Report. University of Texas at Austin. Center for Research in Water Resources — Tech Rep Univ Tex Austin Cent Res Water Resour
Technical Report. Yale University. School of Forestry — Tech Rep Yale Sch For
Technical Reports. Engineering Research Institute. Kyoto University — Tech Rep Eng Res Inst Kyoto Univ
Technical Reports. Engineering Research Institute. Kyoto University — TREKA
Technical Reports. Institute of Atomic Energy. Kyoto University — Tech Rep Inst At Energy Kyoto Univ
Technical Reports. Institute of Atomic Energy. Kyoto University — Tech Rep Inst Atom Energy Kyoto Univ
Technical Reports Series. International Atomic Energy Agency — Tech Rep Ser Int Atom Energy Ag
Technical Reports. Sumitomo Metal Industries Ltd — Tech Rep Sumitomo Met Ind Ltd
Technical Reports. Toyo Kohan Company Limited [*Japan*] — Tech Rep Toyo Kohan Co Ltd
Technical Reprint. Graver Water Conditioning Company — Tech Repr Graver Water Cond Co
Technical Research Centre of Finland. Building Technology and Community Development Publication — Tech Res Cent Finl Build Technol Community Dev Publ
Technical Research Centre of Finland. Electrical and Nuclear Technology Publication — Tech Res Cent Finl Electr Nucl Technol Publ
Technical Research Centre of Finland. Electrical and Nuclear Technology Publication — Tech Res Cent Finland Electr and Nucl Technol Publ
Technical Research Centre of Finland. General Division Publication — Tech Res Cent Finl Gen Div Publ
Technical Research Centre of Finland. Materials and Processing Technology Publication — Tech Res Cent Finl Mater Process Technol Publ
Technical Research Centre of Finland. Materials and Processing Technology Publication — Tech Res Cent Finland Mater and Process Technol Publ
Technical Research Centre of Finland. Publications — Tech Res Cent Finl Publ
Technical Research Centre of Finland. Research Reports — Tech Res Cent Finl Res Rep
Technical Research Report. Research Institute of Industrial Science and Technology — Tech Res Rep Res Inst Ind Sci Technol
Technical Review. Mitsubishi Heavy Industries Ltd. — Tech Rev Mitsubishi Heavy Ind Ltd
Technical Review. Mitsubishi Heavy-Industries (Japanese Edition) — Tech Rev Mitsubishi Heavy-Ind (Jpn Ed)
Technical Review. Sumitomo Heavy Industries Limited — Tech Rev Sumitomo Heavy Ind Ltd
Technical Sciences. Advances in Electronics — Tech Sci Adv Electron
Technical Seminar on Chemical Spills — Tech Semin Chem Spills
Technical Series. Bureau of Entomology. United States Department of Agriculture — Tech Ser Bur Ent US
Technical Series. Florida Department of Natural Resources. Marine Research Laboratory — Tech Ser Fla Dep Nat Resour Mar Res Lab
Technical Series. Society for Applied Bacteriology — Tech Ser Soc Appl Bacteriol
Technical Services Newsletter — Tech Serv Newsl
Technical Society of the Pacific Coast. Transactions — Tech Soc Pacific Coast Tr
Technical Studies. Commonwealth Experimental Building Station — Tech Stud Common Exp Bldg Stn
Technical Studies. Commonwealth Experimental Building Station — Tech Stud Commonw Exp Bldg Stn
Technical Teacher — Tech Teach
Technical Timber Guide — Tech Timb Guide
Technical Timber Guide — Tech Timber Guide
Technical Translation Bulletin — Tech Trans Bull
Technical Translations — Tech Transl
Technical University of Poznan. Institute of Control Engineering — Inst Control Engrg
Technical World [*Chicago*] — Tech W
Technical World Magazine — Tech World
Technical-Economical Publication. Tatabanyai Szenbanyak — Tech Econ Publ Tatabanyai Szenbanyak
Technician Education Yearbook — Tech Educ Yrbk
Technicien Belge en Prothese Dentaire — Tech Belge Prothese Dent
Technicka Knihovna — Tech Knih
Technicka Knihovna — Tech Knihovna
Technicka Univerzita vo Zvolene. Drevarska Fakulta. Zbornik Vedeckych Prac — Tech Univ Zvolene Drev Fak Zb Ved Pr
Technics of Refrigeration and Air Conditioning — Tech Refrig Air Cond
Technieuws Ottawa. Korte Berichten op Technisch Wetenschappelijk Gebied — OTT
Technieuws Tokio. Korte Berichten op Technisch Wetenschappelijk Gebied — TKO
Technieuws Washington. Korte Berichten op Technisch Wetenschappelijk Gebied — WNS
Technik als Schulfach — Tech Schulfach
Technik am Bau [*Germany*] — Tech Bau
Technik Heute [*German Federal Republic*] — Tech Heute
Technik und Industrie und Schweizerische Chemiker-Zeitung — Techn u Industr
Technik und Landwirtschaft. Landtechnischer Ratgeber — Tech Landwirt
Technik und Umweltschutz [*Germany*] — Tech Umweltschutz
Technik und Wirtschaft — TuW
Technik Wlokienniczy — Tech Wlok
Technik Wlokienniczy — TWLOA
Technika Chronika — Tech Chron
Technika Chronika — Techn Chron
Technika Hronika (Greece) — TCGE-G
Technika i Gospodarka Morska [*Poland*] — Tech Gospod Morsk
Technika Lotnicza i Astronautyczna [*Poland*] — Tech Lotnicza Astronaut
Technika Motoryzacyjna — Tech Motoryzacyjna
Technika Poszukiwan — Tech Poszukiwan
Technika Poszukiwan Geologicznych — Tech Poszukiwan Geol
Technika Poszukiwan Geologicznych — TGEOD
Technika Poszukiwan Geologicznych, Geosynoptyka, i Geotermia — Tech Poszukiwan Geol Geosynoptyka Geoterm
Technika Prace [*Czechoslovakia*] — Tech Pr
Technika Radia i Telewizji — Tech Radia & Telew
Technika Skoda — Tech Skoda
Technika Smarownicza — Tech Smarownicza
Technika Smarownicza. Trybologia — Tech Smarownicza Trybol
Technika v Chemii — TCHMA
Technika v Chemii (Prague) — Tech Chem (Prague)
Technikai Kurir [*Hungary*] — Tech Kurir
Technikas Apskats — TEAPA
Technikas Apskats [*United States*] — Tech Apskats
Technikatoerteneti Szemle — Tech Szem
Techniken der Zukunft — Tech Zukunft
Technik-Geschichte — Tech Gesch
Techniki Tworczego Myslenia — Tech Tworczego Myslenia
Technik-Index ueber Plasmaphysikalische Forschung und Fusionsreaktoren [*West Germany*] — Tech-Index Plasmaphys Forsch Fusionreakt
Technik-Index ueber Plasmaphysikalische Forschung und Fusionsreaktoren — TPRRD
Technion-Israel Institute of Technology. Department of Chemical Engineering. Report CE — Technion Isr Inst Technol Dep Chem Eng Rep CE
Technique Agricole [*France*] — Tech Agri
Technique Agricole — TQAGA
Technique Agricole Internationale — Techn Agric Int
Technique de l'Eau et de l'Assainissement — Tech Eau
Technique de l'Eau et de l'Assainissement — TQE
Technique des Travaux (Liege) — Tech Trav (Liege)
Technique et Pratique Agricoles — Tech Prat Agr
Technique et Science Aeronautiques et Spatiales [*France*] — Tech Sci Aeronaut Spat
Technique et Science Informatiques — Tech et Sci Inf
Technique Meuniere — Tech Meun
Technique Moderne — Tech Mod
Technique Moderne — Techn Mod
Technique Pharmaceutique — Techn Pharm
Technique Routiere [*Belgium*] — Tech Routiere
Techniques and Instrumentation in Analytical Chemistry [*Elsevier Book Series*] — TIAC
Techniques and Methods of Polymer Evaluation — Tech Methods Polym Eval
Techniques CEM [*Compagnie Electro-Mecanique*] — Tech CEM
Techniques de Laboratoire — Techn Lab
Techniques de l'Energie — TECED
Techniques de l'Energie [*France*] — Tech Energ
Techniques de l'Energie — Tech Energie
Techniques de l'Energie (Paris) — Tech Energ (Paris)
Techniques de l'Ingenieur. Genie Chimique — Tech Ing Genie Chim
Techniques des Travaux [*Belgium*] — Tech Trav
Techniques du Petrole [*France*] — Tech Pet
Techniques du Petrole — TPETA
Techniques Electroniques - Son - Television — Tech Electron Son Telev
Techniques et Applications du Petrole [*France*] — Tech Appl Pet
Techniques et Architecture — Techn Archit
Techniques et Sciences Municipales [*France*] — Tech Sci Munic
Techniques et Sciences Municipales — Techn Sci Munic
Techniques et Sciences Municipales/l'Eau — Tech Sci Munic Eau
Techniques Hospitalieres, Medico-Sociales, et Sanitaires — Techn Hosp
Techniques in Marine Environmental Sciences — Tech Mar Environ Sci
Techniques in Protein Chemistry 2. Papers. Annual Symposium. Protein Society — Tech Protein Chem 2 Pap Annu Symp Protein Soc
Techniques in Protein Chemistry 3. Papers. Annual Symposium. Protein Society — Tech Protein Chem 3 Pap Annu Symp Protein Soc
Techniques in the Behavioral and Neural Sciences — Tech Behav Neural Sci
Techniques in the Life Sciences. Biochemistry — Tech Life Sci Biochem

Techniques of Biochemical and Biophysical Morphology — Tech Biochem Biophys Morphol
Techniques of Electrochemistry — Tech Electrochem
Techniques of Measurement in Medicine — Tech Meas Med
Techniques of Physics — Techniques Phys
Techniques of Physics Series — Tech Phys Ser
Techniques Stochastiques — Tech Stochastiques
Technisch Bericht. Stichting Nederlands Graan-Centrum — Tech Ber Sticht Nederl Graan Cont
Technisch Gemeenteblad. Officieel Orgaan van de Bond van Hoofden van Gemeentewerken en van de Hinderweten Bouwtoezichtvereniging — TG
Technisch Weekblad — BAA
Technische Berichte der C. Lorenz — Techn Ber Lorenz
Technische Gemeinschaft — Tech Gem
Technische Gemeinschaft — TEGTA
Technische Gids voor Ziekenhuis en Instelling — Tech Gids Ziekenhuis Instelling
Technische Gids voor Ziekenhuis en Instelling — TGZIA
Technische Hochschule Ilmenau. Wissenschaftliche Zeitschrift — Tech Hochsch Ilmenau Wiss Z
Technische Hochschule Koethen. Wissenschaftliche Zeitschrift — Tech Hochsch Koethen Wiss Z
Technische Hochschule Leipzig. Wissenschaftliche Zeitschrift — Tech Hochsch Leipzig Wiss Z
Technische Hogeschool Delft. Afdeling der Werktuigbouwkunde (Report) WTHD — Tech Hogesch Delft Afd Werktuigbouwkd (Rep) WTHD
Technische Hogeschool Delft. Bibliotheek. Aanwinsten — AHO
Technische Information GRW [*Geraete- und Regler Werke*] [*Germany*] — Tech Inf GRW
Technische Information GRW [*Geraete- und Regler Werke*] — TIGRB
Technische Informationen — TIFO
Technische Mitteilungen — Tech Mitt
Technische Mitteilungen — TEMIA
Technische Mitteilungen AEG- [*Allgemeine Elektrizitaets-Gesellschaft*] **Telefunken** — Tech Mitt AEG-Telefunken
Technische Mitteilungen AEG- [*Allgemeine Elektrizitaets-Gesellschaft*] **Telefunken** — TMATB
Technische Mitteilungen (Essen) — Tech Mitt (Essen)
Technische Mitteilungen Krupp [*Germany*] — Tech Mitt Krupp
Technische Mitteilungen Krupp — Techn Mitt Krupp
Technische Mitteilungen Krupp. Forschungsberichte — Tec Mit K F
Technische Mitteilungen Krupp. Forschungsberichte — Tech Mitt Krupp Forschungsber
Technische Mitteilungen Krupp. Forschungsberichte — Tech Mitteil Krupp Forschungsber
Technische Mitteilungen Krupp. Forschungsberichte — TMKFA
Technische Mitteilungen Krupp. Werksberichte — Tec Mit K W
Technische Mitteilungen Krupp. Werksberichte — Tech Mitt Krupp Werksber
Technische Mitteilungen Krupp. Werksberichte — Tech Mitteil Krupp Werksber
Technische Mitteilungen Krupp. Werksberichte — TMKWA
Technische Mitteilungen PTT — Tech Mitt PTT
Technische Mitteilungen PTT — TMPTA
Technische Mitteilungen. RFZ [*Rundfunk- und Fernsehtechnisches Zentralamt*] — Tech Mitt RFZ
Technische Rundschau — TCRUA
Technische Rundschau — Tech Rundsch
Technische Rundschau — Techn Rd
Technische Rundschau — Techn Rundschau
Technische Rundschau (Bern) [*Switzerland*] — Tech Rdsch (Bern)
Technische Rundschau Sulzer [*Switzerland*] — Tech Rundsch Sulzer
Technische Rundschau und Allgemeine Industrie- und Handelszeitung — Tech Rundsch Allg Ind Handelsz
Technische Ueberwachung [*Technological Supervising*] — Tech Ueberwach
Technische Ueberwachung — Techn Ueberw
Technische Ueberwachung [*Technological Supervising*] — TU
Technische Ueberwachung (Duesseldorf) — Tech Ueberwach Duesseldorf
Technische und Industrielle Rundschau — Techn Ind Rd
Technische Universitaet Berlin. Arbeitspapiere zur Linguistik/Working Papers in Linguistics — TUBWPL
Technische Universitaet Chemnitz-Zwickau. Wissenschaftliche Zeitschrift — Tech Univ Chemnitz Zwickau Wiss Z
Technische Universitaet Karl-Marx-Stadt. Wissenschaftliche Tagungen — Tech Univ Karl Marx Stadt Wiss Tag
Technische Universitaet Muenchen. Jahrbuch — Tech Univ Muenchen Jahrb
Technischer Bericht. Heinrich-Hertz Institut (Berlin-Charlottenburg) — Tech Ber Heinrich-Hertz Inst (Berlin-Charlottenburg)
Technisches Bulletin - Amersham Buchler — Tech Bull Amersham Buchler
Technisches Gemeindeblatt [*Germany*] — Tech Gemeindebl
Technisches Gemeindeblatt — Techn Gemeindebl
Technisches Messen ATM [*Archiv fuer Technisches Messen*] — Tech Mess ATM
Technisches Zentralblatt — Tech Zentralbl
Technisch-Physikalische Monographien — Tech-Phys Monogr
Technisch-Wirtschaftliche Zeitung fuer die Mitteleuropaeische Landwirtschaft — Techn Wirtschaftl Zeitung Mitteleurop Landw
Technisch-Wissenschaftliche Abhandlungen der Osram-Gesellschaft — Tech-Wiss Abh Osram-Ges
Technisch-Wissenschaftliche Schriftenreihe der ATV — Tech Wiss Schriftenr ATV
Technocrat. A Monthly Review of Japanese Technology and Industry — TMM
Technological Forecasting [*Later, Technological Forecasting and Social Change*] — Technol Forecast
Technological Forecasting [*Technological Forecasting and Social Change*] [*United States*] [*Later,*] — Technol Forecasting
Technological Forecasting and Social Change — Technol For
Technological Forecasting and Social Change — Technol Forecast and Soc Change
Technological Forecasting and Social Change — Technol Forecasting Soc Change
Technological Forecasting and Social Change — TEFO
Technological Forecasting and Social Change — TFS
Technological Forecasting and Social Change — TFSCB
Technological Forecasting and Social Change. An International Journal — TFR
Technological Monographs — Technol Mono
Technological Paper. Division of Forest Products. Commonwealth Scientific and Industrial Research Organisation — Technol Pap Div Forest Prod CSIRO
Technological Paper. Division of Forest Products. Commonwealth Scientific and Industrial Research Organisation — Technolog Pap Div Forest Prod CSIRO
Technological Paper. Forest Products Laboratory. Division of Applied Chemistry. Commonwealth Scientific and Industrial Research Organisation — Technol Pap For Prod Lab Div Appl Chem CSIRO
Technological Paper. Forest Products Laboratory. Division of Applied Chemistry. Commonwealth Scientific and Industrial Research Organisation — Technol Pap Forest Prod Lab Div Appl Chem CSIRO
Technological Paper. Forest Products Laboratory. Division of Building Research. Commonwealth Scientific and Industrial Research Organisation — Technol Pap For Prod Lab Div Build Res CSIRO
Technological Paper. Forest Products Laboratory. Division of Building Research. Commonwealth Scientific and Industrial Research Organisation — Technol Pap Forest Prod Lab Div Bldg Res CSIRO
Technological Review. Chonnam National University [*Republic of Korea*] — Technol Rev Chonnam Natl Univ
Technologie Respiratoire — Technol Respir
Technologie-Nachrichten. Management-Informationen [*Germany*] — Technol-Nachr Manage Inf
Technologie-Nachrichten Programm-Informationen — Technol-Nachr Programm-Inf
Technologie-Nachrichten Sonderdienst-Programme [*German Federal Republic*] — Technol-Nachr Sonderdienst-Programme
Technologies and Sciences. Chung-Ang University — Technol Sci Chung Ang Univ
Technologies Innovantes en Epuration des Eaux — Technol Innovantes Epur Eaux
Technology [*Sindri, India*] — TCNOA
Technology — Tech
Technology — Technol
Technology and Conservation — Technol Conserv
Technology and Culture — PTNC
Technology and Culture — T & C
Technology and Culture — Tech & Cult
Technology and Culture — Tech & Culture
Technology and Culture — Techn Cult
Technology and Culture — Technol Cul
Technology and Culture — Technol Cult
Technology and Environment — Tech Environ
Technology and Health Care — Technol Health Care
Technology and Information (Sapporo) — Technol Inf (Sapporo)
Technology and Learning [*Formerly, Classroom Computer Learning*] — GCCL
Technology and Programs for Radioactive Waste Management and Environmental Restoration — Technol Programs Radioact Waste Manage Environ Restor
Technology and Science of Informatics — TSI
Technology and Society — Techn Soc
Technology and Society — Technol Soc
Technology and Use of Lignite. Proceedings of a Symposium — Technol Use Lignite
Technology Assessment Database — TA
Technology Development Report EPS (Canada Environmental Protection Service) — Technol Dev Rep EPS (Can Environ Prot Serv)
Technology for Alaskan Transportation — TFAT
Technology Forecasts and Technology Surveys — Tech Fore
Technology Illustrated — Tech Illus
Technology in Education — Technol Educ
Technology in Society — Technol Soc
Technology Index for Plasmaphysics Research and Fusion Reactors [*Germany*] — Technol Index Plasmaphys Res Fusion React
Technology Information Exchange-Innovation Network [*Database*] — TIE-IN
Technology Ireland — Technol Ir
Technology Ireland — Technol Ireland
Technology Ireland — TEIRD
Technology Journal. National Science Development Board (Philippines) — Technol J Natl Sci Dev Board (Philip)
Technology News. Bureau of Mines [*United States*] — Technol News
Technology News. Bureau of Mines [*United States*] — Technol News Bur Mines
Technology Quarterly and Proceedings. Society of Arts — Tech Q
Technology Reports. Iwate University — Technol Rep Iwate Univ
Technology Reports. Kansai University — Tech Rep Kansai Univ
Technology Reports. Kansai University — Technol Rep Kansai Univ
Technology Reports. Kansai University — TRKUA
Technology Reports. Kyushu University — Technol Rep Kyushu Univ
Technology Reports. Osaka University — Tech Rep Osaka Univ
Technology Reports. Osaka University — Tech Reports Osaka Univ
Technology Reports. Osaka University — Technol Rep Osaka Univ
Technology Reports. Seikei University — Technol Rep Seikei Univ
Technology Reports. Tohoku Imperial University — Techn Rep Tohoku
Technology Reports. Tohoku University [*Sendaik, Japan*] — Technol Rep Tohoku Univ
Technology Reports. Tohoku University (Japan) — Technol Rep Tohoku Univ (Jpn)
Technology Reports. Yamaguchi University — Technol Rep Yamaguchi Univ
Technology Review — TCR

Technology Review — TDR
Technology Review — Tec R
Technology Review — Tech R
Technology Review — Tech Rev
Technology Review [*Boston*] — Technol R
Technology Review — Technol Rev
Technology Review — TEREA
Technology Review — TR
Technology (Sydney) — Technol (Syd)
Technology Transfer Times — Tech Times
Technology Utilization Program Report — Technol Utiliz Prog Rep
Technology Week — Tech W
Technology Week — Tech Wk
Technometrics — TCMTA
Technometrics — Technmcs
Technometrics — Technomet
Technos — TCNSB
Technovation [*Netherlands*] — TCH
Tecnica Agricola — Tec Agr
Tecnica Agricola (Catania) — Tec Agric (Catania)
Tecnica de la Regulacion y Mando Automatico — Tec Regul & Mando Autom
Tecnica Industrial (Madrid) — Tec Ind (Madrid)
Tecnica Italiana — Tec Ital
Tecnica Italiana — Tecn Ital
Tecnica Italiana — Tecnica Ital
Tecnica Italiana — TITLA
Tecnica (Lisbon) — TECLA
Tecnica Metalurgica [*Spain*] — Tec Metal
Tecnica Metalurgica (Barcelona) — Tec Met (Barcelona)
Tecnica Molitoria — Tec Molit
Tecnica Molitoria [*Italy*] — TEMOA
Tecnica Pecuaria en Mexico — Tec Pecu Mex
Tecnica Pecuaria en Mexico — Tec Pecuar Mex
Tecnica Pecuaria en Mexico — TPMXA
Tecnica. Rivista de Engenharia (Lisboa) — Tecnica Lisb
Tecniche dell'Automazione — Tec Autom
Tecniche e Sintesi Speciali Organiche — Tec Sint Spec Org
Tecnologia Alimentaria — Tecnol Aliment
Tecnologia, Ciencia, Educacion — Tecnol Cienc Educ
Tecnologie Elettriche — Tecnol Elettr
Tecnopolimeri e Resine — Tecnopolim Resine
Tectonophysics — TCTOA
Tectonophysics — Tectonophys
Teen — GTEE
TEES [*Texas Engineering Experiment Station*] **Technical Bulletin** — TEES Tech Bull
TEFL [*Teaching English as a Foreign Language*]/TESL Newsletter [*Teaching English as a Second Language*] — TEFL/TESL Newsl
Tegniese Mededeling. Suid Afrika Departement van Landbou en Visserye — Teg Meded S Afr Dep Landbou Viss
Tegnikon — TEGNA
Teheraner Forschungen. Deutsches Archaeologisches Institut. Abteilung Teheran — Teher Forsch
Tehnicka Fizika — Teh Fiz
Tehnika (Belgrade) — TEHBA
Tehnika Hronika — Teh Hronika
Tehnika ja Tootmine [*Estonian SSR*] — Teh Tootmine
Tehnika Rudarstvo Geologiya i Metalurgija — Teh Rud Geol Metal
Teikyo Igaku Zasshi — TIGZD
Teilhard Review [*London*] — Teilhard Rev
Teilhard Studies — Teilhard St
Teinture et Apprets — Teint Apprets
Teishin Igaku — TEIGA
Teisser's Court of Appeal. Parish of Orleans Reports — Teiss
Tejipar — TEJPA
Tekawennake. Six Nations. New Credit Reporter — TK
Tekhnicheska Mis'l — Tekh Mis'l
Tekhnicheska Misul [*Bulgaria*] — Tekh Misul
Tekhnicheska Misul — TKMSB
Tekhnicheskaya Estetika [*Former USSR*] — Tekh Estetika
Tekhnicheskaya Estetika — TKESB
Tekhnicheskaya Informatsiya. Sovet Narodnogo Khozyaistva Kuibyshevskogo Ekonomicheskogo Administrativnogo Raiona — Tekh Inf Sov Nar Khoz Kuibyshev Ekon Adm Raiona
Tekhnicheskaya Kibernetika — Tekh Kibern
Tekhnicheskie Doklady po Gidrologii — Tekh Dokl Gidrol
Tekhnicheskie Usloviya na Metody Opredeleniya Vrednykh Veshchestv v Vozdukhe — Tekh Usloviya Metody Opred Vrednykh Veshchestv Vozdukhe
Tekhnicheskiya Universitet v Plovdiv. Izvestiya. Fundamentalni Nauki i Prilozheniya — Izv Tekhn Univ Plovdiv Fund Nauk Prilozhen
Tekhnichesko Ekonomicheskie Izvestiya Tatabanyai Szenbanyak — Tekh Ekon Izv Tatabanyai Szenbanyak
Tekhnika i Vooruzhenie [*Former USSR*] — Tekh Vooruzhenie
Tekhnika Kino i Televideniya — Tekh Kino i Telev
Tekhnika Kino i Televideniya — Tekh Kino Telev
Tekhnika Kino i Televideniya — Tekn Kino Televid
Tekhnika Kino i Televideniya — TKTEA
Tekhnika Molodezhi — Tekh Molodezhi
Tekhnika (Sofia) — TEKSA
Tekhnika v Sel'skom Khozyaistve — Tekh Sel'Khoz
Tekhnika v Sel'skom Khozyaistve — TSKZA
Tekhnika Vozdushnogo Flota — Tekh Vozdushn Flota
Tekhnika Zheleznykh Dorog — Tekh Zhelezn Dorog
Tekhnologiya i Avtomatizatsiya Mashinostroeniya — Teknol Avtom Mashinostr
Tekhnologiya i Organizatsiya Proizvodstva — Tekhnol Organ Proizvod
Tekhnologiya Legkikh Splavov — Tekhnol Legk Splavov
Tekhnologiya Mashinostroeniya (Moscow) — Tekhnol Mashinostr (Moscow)
Tekhnologiya Materialov — Tekhnol Mater
Tekhnologiya Neorganicheskikh Veshchestv — Tekhnol Neorg Veshchestv
Tekhnologiya, Organizatsiya, i Mekhanizatsiya Liteinogo Proizvodstva — Tekhnol Organ Mekh Liteinogo Proizvod
Tekhnologiya Proizvodstva Sukhikh Diagnosticheskikh Pitatel'nykh Sred — Tekhnol Proizvod Sukhikh Diagn Pitatel'nykh Sred
Tekhnologiya Stroitel'nogo Proizvodstva — Tekhnol Stroit Proizvod
Teki Historyczne — TH
Tekko Rodo Eisei [*Japan*] — TROEA
Tekkokai — TEKKA
Tekniikka — TKNKB
Teknik Bulten. Petkim Petrokimya A. S. Arastirma Mudurlugu — Tek Bul Petkim Petrokimya A S Arastirma Mudurlugu
Teknik Forskningsstiftelsen Skogsarbeten — Tekn Forsknstift Skogsarb
Teknik Yayinlar. Kavakcihk Arastirma Enstitusu (Izmit, Turkey) — Tek Yay Kavak Arast Enst (Izmit)
Teknillinen Aikakauslehti — Tek Aikak
Teknillisen Kemian Aikakauslehti [*Finland*] — Tek Kem Aikak
Teknisk Information [*Sweden*] — Tek Inf
Teknisk Skoletidende — Tekn Skt
Teknisk Tidskrift — Tek Tidskr
Teknisk Tidskrift [*Sweden*] — TTIDA
Teknisk Tidsskrift for Textil og Beklaedning — Tek Tidsskr Text Beklaedning
Teknisk Ukeblad — Tek Ukebl
Teknisk Ukeblad — TUGEA
Teknisk Vetenskaplig Forskning [*Sweden*] — Tek Vetensk Forsk
Tekniska Hoegskolan Handlingar — Tek Hoegsk Handl
Tekniska Hoegskolan i Helsingfors Vetenskapliga Publikationer — Tek Hogsk Helsingfors Vetensk Publ
Tekniska Meddelanden [*Sweden*] — Tek Medd
Tekniska Samfundets Handlingar — Tek Samf Hand
Tekniske Meddelelser. Husholdningsraad (Denmark) — Tek Medd Husholdningsraad Den
Tekniskt Forum [*Finland*] — Tek Forum
Tekniskt Forum — TFORA
Tekstil — TEKTA
Tekstilna Industrija — Tekst Ind
Tekstilna Promishlennost (Sofia) — Tekst Prom (Sofia)
Tekstil'naya Promyshlennost — Tekst Prom-St
Tekstil'naya Promyshlennost — Tekstil Prom
Tekstil'naya Promyshlennost — TTLPA
Tekstil'naya Promyshlennost (Moscow) — Tekst Prom (Moscow)
Tektonika i Stratigrafiya — TKSGB
Tektonika Sibiri — Tektonika Sib
Tektonika Sibiri — TKSBB
Tel Aviv. Journal of the Tel Aviv University Institute of Archaeology — Tel Aviv J Inst A
Tel Quel — TelQ
Telcom Report — Telcom Rep
Tele (English Edition) — Tele (Engl Ed)
Tele (Swedish Edition) — Tele (Swed Ed)
Telecom Australia Research Quarterly — Telecom Aust Res Q
Telecom Market Letter — Telecom ML
Telecommunication Journal — TCJOA
Telecommunication Journal — Telecomm J
Telecommunication Journal — Telecommun J
Telecommunication Journal (English Edition) — Telecommun J (Engl Ed)
Telecommunication Journal of Australia — TCJAA
Telecommunication Journal of Australia — Telecom J
Telecommunication Journal of Australia — Telecom J Aust
Telecommunication Journal of Australia — Telecomm J Aust
Telecommunication Journal of Australia — Telecommun J Aust
Telecommunication Journal of Australia — TJA
Telecommunication Products and Technology — Telecomm Prod
Telecommunications [*English Translation*] — TCMUA
Telecommunications — Telecom
Telecommunications — Telecomm
Telecommunications [*International Edition*] — Telecomms
Telecommunications [*Dedham, MA*] — TLCOA
Telecommunications Abstracts — Telecomm Abstr
Telecommunications and Radio Engineering [*English Translation*] — TCREA
Telecommunications and Radio Engineering — Telecommun Radio Eng
Telecommunications and Radio Engineering. Part 1. Telecommunications — Telecommun and Radio Eng Part 1
Telecommunications and Radio Engineering. Part 1. Telecommunications (USSR) — Telecommun Radio Eng (USSR) Part 1
Telecommunications and Radio Engineering. Part 2. Radio Engineering — Telecommun and Radio Eng Part 2
Telecommunications and Radio Engineering (USSR) — Tel Rad E R
Telecommunications and Radio Engineering (USSR). Part 2. Radio Engineering — Telecommun Radio Eng (USSR) Part 2
Telecommunications Counselor [*Database*] — TC
Telecommunications Network Services [*Database*] — TNS
Telecommunications Policy — TEC
Telecommunications Policy — Telecomm Po
Telecommunications Policy — Telecommun Policy
Telecommunications Product Review — TPR
Telecommunications Regulatory Monitor — TRM
Telecommunications Systems and Services Directory — TSSD
TeleCommuting Report [*Database*] — TC
Telecommuting Report — Telecommut Rep
Telefon Report — Telef Rep
Telefon Report — Telefon Rep

Telefunken-Zeitschrift — TFZ
Telefunken-Zeitung [*Germany*] — Telefunken-Ztg
Telegen Abstracts — Telegen Abstr
Telegen Annual Review — Telegen Ann Rev
Telegen Document Sourcebook — Telegen Doc Sourceb
Telegraaf — TEL
Telegraaf en Telefoon — Telegr & Telef
Telegraphen- und Fernsprechtechnik — Telegr u Fernsprechtechn
Telemarketing — Telemktg
Telephone Engineer and Management [*Harcourt Brace Jovanovich Publications, Inc.*] [*Geneva, IL*] [*Information service or system*] — TE & M
Telephone Engineer and Management — Teleph Eng & Manage
Telephone Engineer and Management — Telephone
Telephone Engineer and Management — TPEMA
Telephone News — Tele News
Telephony — TPH
Telesystems Journal — Telesys J
Tele-Tech and Electronic Industries — Tele-Tech & Electronic Ind
Teleteknik. English Edition — Teleteknik Engl Ed
Telettra Review — Telettra Rev
Television — TV
Television Age — TVA
Television and Video Production — TVP
Television Digest — TVD
Television Engineering — Telev Eng
Television International — TV Int
Television. Journal of the Royal Television Society — Television JR Telev Soc
Television Quarterly — ITVQ
Television Quarterly — Telev Quart
Television Quarterly — TV Q
Television/Radio Age — TA
Television/Radio Age — Telev/Radio Age
Television/Radio Age — TRA
Television/Radio Age — TV Radio A
Television/Radio Age — TV/Radio Age
Television/Radio Age International — TV/Radio Age Int
Telex Africa — TEF
Telhan Patrica/Oilseeds Journal — Telhan Patrica Oilseeds J
Telkwa Foundation. Newsletter [*Telkwa, British Columbia*] — TKFN
Tell Edfou — Edfou
Tellus [*Sweden*] — TELLA
Tellus. Series A. Dynamic Meteorology and Oceanography — Tellus Ser A
Tellus. Series A. Dynamic Meteorology and Oceanography — Tellus Ser A Dyn Meteorol Oceanogr
Tellus. Series B. Chemical and Physical Meteorology — Tellus Ser B
Tellus. Series B. Chemical and Physical Meteorology — Tellus Ser B Chem Phys Meteorol
Tellus. Series B. Chemical and Physical Meteorology — TSBMD
Telonde [*France*] — TLNDA
Telos — GTES
Telugu Vaani [*Hyderabad*] — Tel Vaani
Temas Biblioteconomicos (Caracas) — Temas Bibliotec Caracas
Temas de Quimica y Bibliografia Quimica Argentina — Temas Quim Bibliogr Quim Argent
Temas Economicos (Caracas) — Temas Econ Caracas
Temas Odontologicos — Temas Odontol
Temas Sociales — Temas Socs
Temas Sociales (San Jose, Costa Rica) — Temas Soc S Jose
Tematicheskii Sbornik Institut Fiziologii i Biofiziki Rastenii. Akademiya Nauk Tadzhikskoi SSR — Temat Sb Inst Fiziol Biofiz Rast Akad Nauk Tadzh SSR
Tematicheskii Sbornik Nauchnykh Trudov Alma-Atinskogo i Semipalatinskogo Zooveterinarnykh Institutov — Temat Sb Nauc Trud Alma-Atin Semipalatin Zoovet Inst
Tematicheskii Sbornik Otdel Fiziologii i Biofiziki Rastenii Akademiya Nauk Tadzhikskoi SSR — Temat Sb Otd Fiziol Biofiz Rast Akad Nauk Tadzh SSR
Tematicheskii Sbornik Rabot po Gel'mintologii Sel'skokhozyaistvennykh Zhivotnykh — Temat Sb Rab Gel'mintol Skh Zhivotn
Tematicheskii Sbornik Vsesoyuznogo Nauchno-Issledovatel'skogo Instituta Gidrogeologii Inzhenerskoi Geologii — Temat Sb Vses Nauchno Issled Inst Gidrogeol Inzh Geol
Tematicheskii Sbornik Vsesoyuznyi Neftegazovyi Nauchno-Issledovatel'skii Institut — Temat Sb Vses Neftegazov Nauchno Issled Inst
Temoignage Chretien — TCh
Temoignage Chretien — Tem Chr
Temperatur Technik. Zeitschrift fuer das Gesamte Temperaturgebiet Kaltetechnik, Klimatechnik, und Heizungstechnik Einschliesslich Isolierung Lueftung, Kuehltransport, und Tiefkuehltransport — KUK
Temperature Controlled Storage and Distribution — TCS
Temperature. Its Measurement and Control in Science and Industry — TMCIA
Temple Bar — Temp Bar
Temple Dental Review — Temple Dent Rev
Temple Law Quarterly — Temp L Q
Temple Law Quarterly — Temple L Quart
Temple Law Quarterly — Temple Law
Temple Law Quarterly — TLQ
Temple University Aegean Symposium — TUAS
Tempo — Te
Tempo — Tem
Tempo Brasileiro — TB
Tempo Presente — TP
Tempo Presente — TPr
Temps Modernes — Tem
Temps Modernes — Temps Mod
Temps Modernes — TM
Temps Present — T Pr
Ten Story Fantasy — TSF
Tendance des Ventes du Vetement Masculin pour Hommes et Juniors — EVF
Tendances de la Conjoncture — Tendances Conjonct
Tendances de la Conjoncture. Graphiques Mensuels — TDN
Tendances et Politiques Actuelles dans le Domaine de l'Habitation de la Construction et de la Planification — Tendances Polit Act Dom
Tendances/Trends. Economie et Finances — Econ Trend
Tenders Electronic Daily [*Database*] — TED
Tennessee Academy of Science. Journal — Tennessee Acad Sci Jour
Tennessee Administrative Register — Tenn Admin Reg
Tennessee. Agricultural Experiment Station. Annual Report — Tenn Agric Exp Stn Annu Rep
Tennessee. Agricultural Experiment Station. Bulletin — Tenn Agric Exp Stn Bull
Tennessee. Agricultural Experiment Station. Farm Economics Bulletin — Tenn Agric Exp Stn Farm Econ Bull
Tennessee. Agricultural Experiment Station. Publications — Tenn Ag Exp
Tennessee Apiculture — Tenn Apiculture
Tennessee Appeals — Tenn App
Tennessee Bar Association. Proceedings — Tenn Bar Assn Proc
Tennessee Bar Journal — Tenn Bar J
Tennessee Bar Journal — Tenn BJ
Tennessee Code Annotated — Tenn Code Ann
Tennessee Conservationist — Tenn Conservationist
Tennessee Criminal Appeals Reports — Tenn Crim App
Tennessee. Department of Conservation. Division of Geology. Bulletin — Tenn Dep Conserv Div Geol Bull
Tennessee. Department of Conservation. Division of Geology. Information Circular — Tenn Dep Conserv Div Geol Inf Circ
Tennessee. Department of Labor. Annual Report — Tenn Dept Labor Ann Rept
Tennessee. Division of Geology. Bulletin — Tenn Div Geol Bull
Tennessee. Division of Geology. Environmental Geology Series — Tenn Div Geol Environ Geol Ser
Tennessee. Division of Geology. Geologic Map — Tennessee Div Geology Geol Map
Tennessee. Division of Geology. Information Circular — Tenn Div Geol Inf Circ
Tennessee. Division of Geology. Information Circular — Tenn Div Geol Inform Circ
Tennessee. Division of Geology. Report of Investigations — Tenn Div Geol Rep Invest
Tennessee. Division of Geology. Report of Investigations — Tennessee Div Geology Rept Inv
Tennessee. Division of Water Resources. Water Resources Series — Tenn Div Water Resour Water Resour Ser
Tennessee Engineer — Tenn Eng
Tennessee Farm and Home Science — Tenn Farm & Home Sci
Tennessee Farm and Home Science — TFHSA
Tennessee Farm and Home Science. Progress Report — Tenn Fm Home Sci Prog Rep
Tennessee Farm and Home Science. Progress Report. Tennessee Agricultural Experiment Station — Tenn Farm Home Sci Prog Rep Tenn Agric Exp Stn
Tennessee Farm and Home Science. Progress Report. University of Tennessee. Agricultural Experiment Station — Tenn Farm Home Sci Progr Rep
Tennessee Folklore Society. Bulletin — Tenn Folk S
Tennessee Folklore Society. Bulletin — TFSB
Tennessee Historical Magazine — Tenn His M
Tennessee Historical Magazine — Tenn Hist M
Tennessee Historical Quarterly — TeH
Tennessee Historical Quarterly — Tenn Hist Q
Tennessee Historical Quarterly — THQ
Tennessee Law Review — Tenn L R
Tennessee Law Review — Tenn L Rev
Tennessee Law Review — Tenn Law Rev
Tennessee Law Review — TN L
Tennessee Law Review — TN LR
Tennessee Law Review — TNLRA
Tennessee Librarian — Tenn Libn
Tennessee Librarian — Tenn Libr
Tennessee Librarian — Tenn Librn
Tennessee Magazine — Tenn Mag
Tennessee Magazine — TMAGD
Tennessee Magazine of History — Tenn Hist Mag
Tennessee Musician — TM
Tennessee Philological Bulletin — TPB
Tennessee Poetry Journal — TPJ
Tennessee Reports — Tenn
Tennessee State Board of Health. Bulletin. Report — Tenn St Bd Health B Rp
Tennessee State Geological Survey. Resources of Tennessee. Bulletin — Tenn G S Res Tenn B
Tennessee Studies in Literature — TN Stud Lit
Tennessee Studies in Literature — TSL
Tennessee Survey of Business — Tenn Surv Bus
Tennessee Survey of Business — TSBUD
Tennessee University. Engineering Experiment Station. Bulletin — Tenn Univ Eng Exp Sta Bull
Tennessee University. Water Resources Research Center. Research Report — Tenn Univ Water Resour Res Cent Res Rep
Tennessee Valley Authority. Chemical Engineering Bulletin — Tenn Val Auth Chem Eng Bul
Tennessee Valley Authority. Chemical Engineering Report — TVA Chem Eng Rept
Tennessee Valley Authority. National Fertilizer Development Center. Bulletin Y — Tenn Val Auth Natl Fert Dev Cent Bull Y
Tennessee Valley Authority. Technical Monographs — Tenn Val Auth Tech Mon
Tennessee Valley Authority. Technical Report — TVA Tech Rept

Tennessee Valley Authority. Technical Reports — Tenn Val Auth Tech Rep
Tennessee Valley Perspective — Tenn Valley Perspect
Tennessee Valley Perspective — TVPED
Tennessee Wildlife — Tenn Wildl
Tennessee's Business — Tennessees Bus
Tennis — GTEN
Tennis Magazine — Ten Mag
Tennyson Research Bulletin — TRB
Tenri Journal of Religion — TJR
Tensai Kenkyu Hokoku. Supplement [*Japan*] — Tensai Kenkyu Hokoku Suppl
Tenside [*Later, Tenside-Detergents*] — TESDA
Tenside-Detergents — Tenside
Tenside-Detergents — Tenside-Deterg
Tenside-Detergents — TSDTA
Tensile Testing — Tensile Test
Tensor — TNSRA
Tensor Club of Great Britain. Matrix and Tensor Quarterly — Matrix Tensor Quart
Teolisuuden Keskuslaboratorion Tiedonantoja — Teolisuuden Keskuslab Tied
Teollisuusliitto Tiedottaa — Teollis Tiedottaa
Teologia Espiritual — TE
Teologia Espiritual (Ecuador) — TEE
Teologia y Vida — Teol Vida
Teologia y Vida — TV
Teologinen Aikakauskirja — TA
Teologinen Aikakauskirja. Teologisk Tidskrift [*Helsinki*] — TAik
Teologisk Tidsskrift — TT
Teoreticeskaja i Matematiceskaja Fizika — Teoret Mat Fiz
Teoreticheskaya Ehlektrotekhnika — Teor Ehlektrotekh
Teoreticheskaya i Eksperimental'naya Biofizica — Teor Eksp Biofiz
Teoreticheskaya i Eksperimental'naya Khimiya — TEKHA
Teoreticheskaya i Eksperimental'naya Khimiya — Teor & Eksp Khim
Teoreticheskaya i Matematicheskaya Fizika — Teor i Mat Fiz
Teoreticheskaya i Matematicheskaya Fizika — Teor Mat Fiz
Teoreticheskaya i Matematicheskaya Fizika — TMFZA
Teoreticheskie i Prakticheskie Voprosy Mikrobiologii i Epidemiologii — Teor Prakt Vopr Mikrobiol Epidemiol
Teoreticheskie i Prakticheskie Voprosy Mikrobiologii i Epidemiologii Respublikanskii Mezhvedomstvennyi Sbornik — Teor Prakt Vopr Mikrobiol Epidemiol Resp Mezhved Sb
Teoreticheskie i Prakticheskie Voprosy Vaktsinno Syvorotochnogo Dela — Teor Prakt Vopr Vaktsinno Syvorot Dela
Teoreticheskie Osnovy Khimicheskoi Tekhnologii — Teor Osn Khim Tekhnol
Teoreticheskie Osnovy Khimicheskoi Tekhnologii — TOKTA
Teoreticheskie Voprosy Obrabotki Pochv — Teor Vopr Obrab Pochv
Teoretichna i Prilozhna Mekhanika — Teor Prilozh Mekh
Teoreticna i Prikladna Matematika — Teoret Prikl Mat
Teoreticna i Prikladna Mehanika Harkivs'kii Derzavnii Universitet Imeni O. M. Gor'kogo — Teoret i Prikladna Meh
Teoreticna i Prilozna Mehanika — Teoret i Priloz Meh
Teoria. Nuova Serie — Teoria NS
Teorie a Metoda — Teor Metod
Teorie Rozvoje Vedy — Teor Rozvoje Vedy
Teorija Verojatnostei i Matematiceskaja Statistika — Teor Verojatnost i Mat Statist
Teoriya i Praktika Fizicheskoi Kul'tury — Teor Prakt Fiz Kul't
Teoriya i Praktika Metallurgii — TPMGA
Teoriya i Praktika Metallurgii (Chelyabinsk) [*Former USSR*] — Teor Prakt Metall
Teoriya i Praktika Metallurgii (Chelyabinsk) — Teor Prakt Metall (Chelyabinsk)
Teoriya i Praktika Metallurgii (Dnepropetrovsk) — Teor Prakt Metall (Dnepropetrovsk)
Teoriya i Praktika Podgotovki i Koksovaniya Uglei — Teor Prakt Podgot Koksovaniya Uglei
Teoriya i Praktika Stomatologii — Teor Prakt Stomatol
Teoriya i Praktika Szhiganiya Gaza [*Former USSR*] — Teor Prakt Szhiganiya Gaza
Teoriya Imovirnostei ta Matematichna Statistika — Teor Imovir ta Mat Statist
Teoriya Praktika — Teor Prakt
Teoriya Verojatnostej i Matematicheskaya Statistika — Teor Verojatn Mat Stat
Teoriya Veroyatnostei i Ee Primeneniya — Teor Veroya
Teoriya Veroyatnostei i Ee Primeneniya [*Former USSR*] — Teor Veroyat Primen
Teoriya Veroyatnostei i Ee Primeneniya — Teor Veroyatn i Primen
Teoriya Veroyatnostei i Ee Primeneniya — Teor Veroyatn Primen
Teoriya Veroyatnostei i Ee Primeneniya — TVPRA
Tepatshimuwin. Journal d'Information des Attikamekes et des Montagnais — TPSM
Teploehnergetika — Teploehnerg
Teploenergetika [*Moscow*] — TPLOA
Teploenergetika Akademiya Nauk SSSR. Energeticheskii Institut — Teploenergetika Akad Nauk SSSR Energ Inst
Teplofizicheskie Kharakteristiki Veshchestv [*Former USSR*] — Teplofiz Kharakt Veshchestv
Teplofizicheskie Kharakteristiki Veshchestv — TFKVA
Teplofizicheskie Svoistva Veshchestv — Teplofiz Svoistva Veshchestv
Teplofizicheskie Svoistva Veshchestv i Materialov — Teplofiz Svoistva Veshchestv Mater
Teplofizika i Aeromekhanika — Teplofiz Aeromekh
Teplofizika i Optimizatsiya Teplovykh Protsessov — Teplofiz Optim Tepl Protsessov
Teplofizika i Teplotekhnika — Teplofiz Teplotekh
Teplofizika i Teplotekhnika — TFTTA
Teplofizika Vysokikh Temperatur — Teplofiz Vys Temp
Teplofizika Vysokikh Temperatur — TVYTA
Teploprovodnost i Diffuziya — Teploprovodnost Diffuz
Teplosilovoc Khozyaistvo — Teplosi Khoz
Teplotekhnicheskie Problemy Pryamogo Preobrazovaniya Energii [*Ukrainian SSR*] — Teplotekh Probl Pryamogo Preobraz Energ
Teplovye Napryazheniya v Elementakh Konstruktsii — Tepl Naprazh Elem Konstr
Teplovye Napryazheniya v Elementakh Konstruktsii — TNAEA
Ter Elfder Ure — TEU
Terapeutica. Revista de Medicina — Ter Rev Med
Terapevticheskaya i Ortopedicheskaya Stomatologiva — Ter Ortop Stomatol
Terapevticheskaya Stomatologiya — Ter Stomatol
Terapevticheskii Arkhiv — TEARA
Terapevticheskii Arkhiv — Ter Arkh
Terapia — TERAA
Teratogenesis, Carcinogenesis, and Mutagenesis — TCM
Teratogenesis, Carcinogenesis, and Mutagenesis — TCMUD8
Teratogenesis, Carcinogenesis, and Mutagenesis — Teratog Carcinog Mutagen
Teratogenesis, Carcinogenesis, and Mutagenesis — Teratogenesis Carcinog Mutagen
Teratology — TJADA
Tercer Mundo y Economia Mundial. Centro de Estudios Economicos y Sociales del Tercer Mundo [*Mexico*] — CEESTEM/TM
Termeloeszoevetkezetek Tanacsadoja — Termeloeszoevet Tanacsadoja
Termeszet, Gazdasagi, es Mestersegi Esmeretek Tara — Term Gazd Mest Esm Tara
Termeszettudomanyi Fuezetek — Termeszettud Fuez
Termeszettudomanyi Koezloeny — Termeszettud Koezloeny
Termicheskaya Obrabotka i Fizika Metallov — Term Obrab Fiz Met
TermNet News — TNN
Termodinamika i Fizicheskaya Kinetika Strukturoobrazovaniya i Svoistva Chuguna i Stali — Termodin Fiz Kinet Strukturoobra Svoista Chuguna Stali
Termodinamika i Fizicheskaya Kinetika Strukturoobrazovaniya i Svoistva Chuguna i Stali — Termodin Fiz Kinet Strukturoobraz Svoistva Chuguna Stali
Termodinamika i Fizicheskaya Kinetika Strukturoobrazovaniya v Stali i Chugune — Termodin Fiz Kinet Strukturoobraz Stali Chugune
Termoprochnost Materialov i Konstruktivnykh Elementov [*Former USSR*] — Termoprochn Mater Konstr Elem
Termotecnica — TERMA
Termotecnica. Supplemento [*Italy*] — Termotecnica Suppl
Terra America — Terra Amer
Terra e Sole — TESOB
Terra Lusa — TL
Terra Trentina — Terra Trent
Terrae Incognitae — Terrae Incog
Terre, Air, Mer. La Geographie — La G
Terre et la Vie. Revue d'Ecologie Appliquee — Terre Vie Rev Ecol Appl
Terre Marocaine — Terre Maroc
Terre Wallonne — TW
Terrestrial Behavior of Pesticides — Terr Behav Pestic
Terrestrial Magnetism and Atmospheric Electricity — Terr Magn
Terrestrial Magnetism and Atmospheric Electricity — Terr Magn Atmos Electr
Territorian — Territ
Territory Law Journal — Terr LJ
Terrorism — Terror
Tertiary Research Special Papers — Tertiary Res Spec Pap
Teruletrendezes [*Hungary*] — TERU
Terzake Subsidies — TZS
Terzo Congresso Geografico Italiano. Saggio di Paleogeografia — TCGI
Terzo Programma [*Roma*] — TP
Tesaur — Tes
TESL [*Teaching English as a Second Language*] **Canada Journal** — TESL Can J
Tesla Electronics — Tesla Electron
Tesla Electronics. Quarterly Review of Czechoslovak Electronics and Telecommunications — Tesla Electron Q Rev Czech Electron Telecommun
TESOL [*Teachers of English to Speakers of Other Languages*] **Quarterly** — TESOL Quart
TESOL [*Teachers of English to Speakers of Other Languages*] **Quarterly** — TESOLQ
TESOL (Teachers of English to Speakers of Other Languages) Newsletter — TESOL Newsl
Tesoro Sacro-Musical — Tesoro Sacro M
Tesoro Sacro-Musical — TSM
Test — TTW
Test Aankoop — TSF
Test Engineering and Management — Test Eng Manage
Test Memorandum. Timber Research and Development Association — Test Memor Timb Res Developm Ass
Test Record. Timber Research and Development Association — Test Rec Timb Res Developm Ass
Testimonia Linguae Etruscae — TLE
Testing, Instruments, and Controls [*Australia*] — Test Instrum Controls
Testing, Instruments, and Controls — TICOA
Testing of Polymers — Test Polym
Testing Report. Forestry Experiment Station. Ryukyu Government/Ryukyu Seifu Keizai Kyoku Ringyo Shikenjo Kenkyu Hokoku — Test Rep Forest Exp Sta Ryukyu Gov
Testing the AGN Paradigm — Test AGN Paradigm
Tests in Print — TIP
Tests of Agrochemicals and Cultivars — TACUDC
Tests of Agrochemicals and Cultivars — Tests Agrochem Cult
Tests of Agrochemicals and Cultivars — Tests Agrochem Cultiv
Tethys — TETHB
Tethys. Supplement — Tethys Suppl
Tetlit Tribune [*Fort McPherson*] — TE
Tetradi Perevodcika — TPer
Tetrahedron — TETRA
Tetrahedron Letters — TELEA

Tetrahedron Letters — Tetrahedr L
Tetrahedron Letters — Tetrahedron Lett
Tetrahedron. Supplement — Tetrahedron Suppl
Tetsu To Hagane Journal. Iron and Steel Institute of Japan — Tetsu Hagan
Tetzugaku-Kenkyu [*Tokyo*] — TK
Teubner Skripten zur Mathematischen Stochastik — Teubner Skr Math Stochastik
Teubner Skripten zur Numerik — Teubner Skr Numer
Teubner Studienbuecher Informatik — Teubner Studienbuech Inform
Teubner Studienbuecher Mathematik — Teubner Studienbuech Math
Teubner Studienbuecher Physik — Teubner Studienbuech Phys
Teubner Studienskripten — Teubner Studienskr
Teubner-Archiv zur Mathematik — Teubner Arch Math
Teubner-Texte zur Mathematik — Teubner-Texte zur Math
Teubner-Texte zur Physik — Teubner Texte Phys
Teuthonista — T
Teuthonista — Teut
Teuthonista — Teuth
Tev'a Va-Arets — TV
TEW [*Technische Edelstahlwerke*] **Technische Berichte** [*Thyssen Edelstahl Technische Berichte*] [*Later,*] — TEW Tech Ber
Texaco Star — TS
Texana — T
Texas A & M University. Department of Civil Engineering. Report — Tex A & M Univ Dep Civ Eng Rep
Texas A and M University. IUCCP Annual Symposium — Texas AM Univ IUCCP Annu Symp
Texas A and M University. IUCCP Annual Symposium on Applications of Enzyme Biotechnology — Texas AM Univ IUCCP Annu Symp Appl Enzyme Biotechnol
Texas A & M University. Oceanographic Studies — Tex A M Univ Oceanogr Stud
Texas A & M University. Sea Grant College. TAMU-SG — TAUTDV
Texas A & M University Sea Grant College. TAMU-SG — Tex A & M Univ Sea Grant Coll TAMU-SG
Texas A & M University System. Texas Agricultural Extension Service. Fish Disease Diagnostic Laboratory — Tex A & M Univ Syst Tex Agric Ext Serv Fish Dis Diagn Lab
Texas A & M University System. Texas Agricultural Extension Service. Fish Disease Diagnostic Laboratory. FDDL — Tex A M Univ Syst Tex Agric Ext Serv Fish Dis Diagn Lab FDDL
Texas A & M University. Texas Engineering Experiment Station. Technical Bulletin — Tex A & M Univ Tex Eng Exp Stn Tech Bull
Texas Academy of Sciences. Transactions — Texas Acad of Sci Trans
Texas Administrative Code — Tex Admin Code
Texas. Agricultural Experiment Station. Bulletin — Tex Agric Exp Stn Bull
Texas. Agricultural Experiment Station. Leaflet — Tex Agric Exp Stn Leafl
Texas. Agricultural Experiment Station. Miscellaneous Publication — Tex Agric Exp Stn Misc Publ
Texas. Agricultural Experiment Station. Progress Report — Tex Agric Exp Stn Prog Rep
Texas. Agricultural Experiment Station. Publications — Tex Ag Exp
Texas. Agricultural Experiment Station. Research Monograph — RMTSDH
Texas. Agricultural Experiment Station. Research Monograph — Tex Agric Exp Stn Res Monogr
Texas. Agricultural Experiment Station. Technical Monograph — Tex Agric Exp Stn Tech Monogr
Texas Agricultural Experiment Station. Technical Monograph — Texas Agric Exp Sta Techn Monogr
Texas. Agricultural Extension Service. Fish Disease Diagnostic Laboratory — Tex Agric Ext Serv Fish Dis Diagn Lab
Texas Agricultural Progress — Tex Agr Progr
Texas Agricultural Progress — Tex Agric Prog
Texas Agricultural Progress. Texas Agricultural Experiment Station — Tex Agric Prog Tex Agric Exp Stn
Texas Appeals Reports — Tex App
Texas Archaeological Society. Bulletin — TASB
Texas Archaeological Society. Papers — TASP
Texas Archeological and Paleontological Society. Bulletin — Texas Archeol Paleont Soc Bull
Texas Bankers Record — Tex Bank Rec
Texas Bar Journal — Tex B J
Texas Bar Journal — Texas BJ
Texas. Board of Water Engineers. Bulletin — Tex Board Water Eng Bull
Texas. Board of Water Engineers. Bulletin — Texas Board of Water Engineers Bull
Texas. Board of Water Engineers. Chemical Composition of Texas Surface Waters — Tex Board Water Eng Chem Compos Tex Surf Waters
Texas Business — Texas Bus
Texas Business Corporation Act Annotated (Vernon) — Tex Bus Corp Act Ann (Vernon)
Texas Business Executive — TBE
Texas Business Executive — Tex Bus Exec
Texas Business Review — Tex Bus R
Texas Business Review — Tex Bus Rev
Texas Business Review — Tex Busin Rev
Texas Business Review — Texas Bus Rev
Texas Business Review — TX Bus Rev
Texas Business Review — TXBRA
Texas Business Review — TXV
Texas Civil Appeals Reports — Tex Civ App
Texas Coach — Tex Coach
Texas Code of Criminal Procedure Annotated (Vernon) — Tex Code Crim Proc Ann (Vernon)
Texas Codes Annotated (Vernon) — Tex Code An (Vernon)
Texas Courier Record of Medicine — Texas Cour Rec Med
Texas Court of Appeals Decisions. Civil Cases — Tex Civ Cas
Texas Criminal Reports — Tex Crim
Texas Current Bibliography and Index — Tex Cur Bib Ind
Texas Dental Assistants Association. Bulletin — Tex Dent Assist Assoc Bull
Texas Dental Journal — Tex Dent J
Texas Educational Computer Courseware Database — TECC
Texas Energy — Tex Energy
Texas Energy and Mineral Resources — Tex Energy Miner Resour
Texas. Engineering Experiment Station. Bulletin — Tex Eng Exp Stn Bull
Texas Engineering Experiment Station Monograph Series — Texas Engrg Experiment Station Monograph Ser
Texas. Engineering Experiment Station. News — Tex Eng Exp Stn News
Texas. Engineering Experiment Station. Research Report — Tex Eng Exp Stn Res Rep
Texas. Engineering Experiment Station. Research Report — Texas Eng Expt Sta Research Rept
Texas Finite Element Series — Texas Finite Elem Ser
Texas Folk-lore Society. Publications — Texas Folk Lore Soc Publ
Texas Folklore Society. Publications — TFSP
Texas Forestry Paper — Tex For Pap
Texas Geographic Magazine — Tex Geogr Mag
Texas. Geological Survey. Report of Progress — Tex G S Rp Prog
Texas Health Letter — TXHL
Texas Heart Institute. Journal — Tex Heart Inst J
Texas Heart Institute. Journal — THIJDO
Texas Historical Association. Quarterly — Texas Hist Assn Q
Texas Hospitals — Tex Hosp
Texas Hospitals — Tex Hospitals
Texas Institutes — Tex Inst
Texas Insurance Code Annotated (Vernon) — Tex Ins Code Ann (Vernon)
Texas International Law Forum — Tex Int L Forum
Texas International Law Forum — Texas Internat L Forum
Texas International Law Forum — Texas Int'l LF
Texas International Law Journal — Tex Int L J
Texas International Law Journal — Tex Intl LJ
Texas International Law Journal — Texas Internat LJ
Texas International Law Journal — Texas Int'l LJ
Texas Journal — Tex J
Texas Journal of Pharmacy — Tex J Pharm
Texas Journal of Science — Tex J Sci
Texas Journal of Science — Texas J Sci
Texas Journal of Science — Texas Jour Sci
Texas Journal of Science — TJSCA
Texas Journal of Science. Special Publication — Tex J Sci Spec Publ
Texas Law Review — Tex L R
Texas Law Review — Tex L Rev
Texas Law Review — Tex Law Rev
Texas Law Review — Texas L Rev
Texas Law Review — TX L
Texas Law Review — TX LR
Texas Law Review — TXLRA
Texas Libraries — Tex Lib
Texas Libraries — Tex Libr
Texas Library Journal — Tex Lib J
Texas Medical Association. Transactions — Texas Med Assn Trans
Texas Medical Journal — Texas MJ
Texas Medicine — Tex Med
Texas Medicine — Texas Med
Texas Medicine — TXMDA
Texas Memorial Museum. Miscellaneous Papers — Tex Mem Mus Misc Pap
Texas Memorial Museum. Pearce-Sellards Series — Texas Memorial Mus Pearce-Sellards Ser
Texas Military History — TMH
Texas Monthly — ITXM
Texas Monthly — Tex Mo
Texas Monthly — Texas Mo
Texas Numismatic Association. News — TNAN
Texas Nursing — Tex Nurs
Texas Nursing — Texas Nurs
Texas Nutrition Conference. Proceedings — Tex Nutr Conf Proc
Texas Oil Journal — Texas Oil Jour
Texas Ornithological Society. Bulletin — TOS
Texas Outlook — Tex Outl
Texas Parks Wildlife — Tex Parks Wildl
Texas Petroleum Research Committee. Bulletin — Texas Petroleum Research Comm Bull
Texas Pharmacy — Tex Pharm
Texas Probate Code Annotated (Vernon) — Tex Prob Code Ann (Vernon)
Texas Quarterly — Tex Q
Texas Quarterly — Tex Quart
Texas Quarterly — TQ
Texas Register — Tex Reg
Texas Reports — Tex
Texas Reports on Biology and Medicine — Tex Rep Bio
Texas Reports on Biology and Medicine — Tex Rep Biol Med
Texas Reports on Biology and Medicine — Texas Rep Biol Med
Texas Reports on Biology and Medicine — TRBMA
Texas Review — Tex Rev
Texas Revised Civil Statutes Annotated (Vernon) — Tex Rev Civ Stat Ann (Vernon)
Texas Rules of Civil Procedure Annotated (Vernon) — Tex R Civ P Ann (Vernon)
Texas Session Law Service (Vernon) — Tex Sess Law Serv (Vernon)
Texas Southern Law Review — Tex So LR
Texas Southern University. Law Review — Tex So U L Rev

Texas Southern University. Law Review — Tex SUL Rev
Texas Southern University. Law Review — Texas South UL Rev
Texas State Historical Association. Quarterly — Tex His Q
Texas State Historical Association. Quarterly — Tex Hist Assoc Q
Texas State Historical Association. Quarterly — Tex State Hist Assoc Quar
Texas State Journal of Medicine — Tex State J Med
Texas State Journal of Medicine — Texas State J Med
Texas Studies in English — TSE
Texas Studies in English — TxSE
Texas Studies in Literature and Language — PTXS
Texas Studies in Literature and Language — Tex St Lit
Texas Studies in Literature and Language — Tex Stud Lit & Lang
Texas Studies in Literature and Language — TSLL
Texas Supreme Court Journal — Tex Sup Ct J
Texas Symposium on Relativistic Astrophysics and Cosmology — Tex Symp Relativ Astrophys Cosmol
Texas System of Natural Laboratories. Index Series — TSNL Index Series
Texas Tech Law Review — Tex Tech L Rev
Texas Tech Law Review — Tex Tech LR
Texas Tech Law Review — Texas Tech L Rev
Texas Tech University Mathematics Series — Texas Tech Univ Math Ser
Texas Transportation Researcher — Tex Transp Res
Texas University at Austin. Bureau of Economic Geology. Geological Circular — Texas Univ Austin Bur Econ Geology Geol Circ
Texas University at Austin. Bureau of Economic Geology. Guidebook — Texas Univ Austin Bur Econ Geology Guidebook
Texas University. Bulletin. Mineral Survey Bulletin — Tex Univ B Min S B
Texas University. Bureau of Economic Geology. Geological Circular — Tex Univ Bur Econ Geol Geol Circ
Texas University. Bureau of Economic Geology. Mineral Resource Circular — Tex Univ Bur Econ Geol Miner Resour Circ
Texas University. Bureau of Economic Geology. Publication — Tex Univ Bur Econ Geol Publ
Texas University. Bureau of Economic Geology. Report of Investigations — Tex Univ Bur Econ Geol Rep Invest
Texas University. Bureau of Economic Geology. Research Note — Tex Univ Bur Econ Geol Res Note
Texas University. Bureau of Engineering Research. Circular — Tex Univ Bur Eng Res Circ
Texas University. Center for Research in Water Resources. Technical Report — Tex Univ Cent Res Water Resour Tech Rep
Texas University. Publication — Tex Univ Publ
Texas University. Publication. Bureau of Economic Geology. Mineral Resource Circular. Report of Investigations — Texas Univ Pub Bur Econ Geology Mineral Res Circ Rept Inv
Texas Water Commission. Bulletin — Tex Water Comm Bull
Texas Water Commission. Circular — Tex Water Comm Circ
Texas Water Commission. Memorandum Report — Tex Water Comm Mem Rep
Texas. Water Development Board. Report — Tex Water Dev Board Rep
Texas. Water Development Board. Report — Texas Water Devel Board Rept
Texpress. Economisch en Technisch Weekblad voor de Textiel en Kledingindustrie en Handel in de Benelux — TTE
Text der Hethiter — T Heth
Text und Kontext — T und K
Text und Kontext — TeK
Text und Kritik — Text Krit
Text und Kritik — TK
Text und Kritik — TuK
Textbooks in Mathematical Sciences — Textbooks Math Sci
Texte des Spaeten Mittelalters — TSM
Texte Metzler — TexteM
Texte und Forschungen zur Byzantinisch-Neugriechischen Philologie — TF Byz Ng Phil
Texte und Untersuchungen zur Geschichte der Altchristlichen Literatur [*Berlin*] — TU
Texte und Untersuchungen zur Geschichte der Altchristlichen Literatur — TUGAL
Texte und Zeichen — TeZ
Texte und Zeichen — TuZ
Texte zur Didaktik der Mathematik — Texte Didakt Math
Texte zur Kritischen Psychologie — Texte Kritisch Psych
Texte zur Mathematisch-Naturwissenschaftlichen Forschung und Lehre — Texte Math Naturwiss Forsch Lehre
Textes Cuneiformes. Musee du Louvre. Departement des Antiquites Orientales et de la Ceramique Antique — TCL
Textes et Documents (Bruxelles) — Textes et Doc (Bruxelles)
Textes et Monuments Figures Relalifs aus Mysteres de Mithra — MMM
Textes et Monuments Figures Relalifs aus Mysteres de Mithra — TMMM
Textes et Traitement Automatique — TTrA
Textes Francais Modernes — TFM
Textes Litteraires Francais — TLF
Textes Mathematiques — Textes Math
Textes pour l'Histoire Sacree — THS
Tex-Textilis — Tex-Text
Tex-Textilis. Technisch Wetenschappelijk Maandblad voor de Benelux Textielindustrie — TEE
TextielVisie — HRH
TextielVisie. Vakblad voor de Textielbranche — TXB
Textil och Konfektion — Text Konfekt
Textil og Beklaedning — Text Beklaedning
Textil Praxis International — Text Prax Int
Textil Praxis International — Textil Prax
Textil Revue. Fachblatt fuer Textilhandel, Konfektionsindustrie, und Textilindustrie — TXV
Textil und Faerberei-Zeitung — Text Faerberei Ztg
Textil und Faserstofftechnik — Text Faserstofftech
Textil-Betrich (Poessneck, Germany) — Text Betr (Poessneck Ger)
Textilchemiker und Colorist — Textilchem Color
Textile Abstracts — Text Abstr
Textile Age — Text Age
Textile American — Text Am
Textile Analysis Bulletin Service. TABS — Text Anal Bull Serv TABS
Textile and Cordage Quarterly — Text Cordage Q
Textile Argus — Text Argus
Textile Asia — Text Asia
Textile Bulletin — Text Bull
Textile Chemist and Colorist — TCCOB
Textile Chemist and Colorist — Text Chem Color
Textile Colorist — Text Color
Textile Colorist and Converter — Text Color Converter
Textile Dyer and Printer — Text Dyer Printer
Textile History — Text Hist
Textile History — Textile Hist
Textile Horizons — Text Horiz
Textile Horizons — Text Horizons
Textile Industries — Text Ind
Textile Industries — Textil Ind
Textile Industries — Textile Ind
Textile Industries Dyegest Southern Africa — Text Ind Dyegest Sthn Afr
Textile Industries Southern Africa — Text Ind Sthn Afr
Textile Industry and Exporter — Text Ind Exporter
Textile Information Treatment Users' Service [*Database*] — TITUS
Textile Information Users Council. Proceedings of the Meeting — Text Inf Users Coun Proc Meet
Textile Institute and Industry — Text I Ind
Textile Institute and Industry — Text Inst Ind
Textile Institute and Industry — Textile Inst
Textile Institute and Industry — Textile Inst Ind
Textile Institute. Annual Report — Text Inst Ann Rep
Textile Journal of Australia — Text J Aust
Textile Journal of Australia — Textile J Aust
Textile Magazine — Text Mag
Textile Magazine. Vakblad voor de Handel in Textiel, Kleding, en Woningtextiel — TMZ
Textile Manufacturer — Text Mfr
Textile Manufacturer — Textile Mfr
Textile Manufacturer's Journal — Text Manuf J
Textile Mercury International — Text Mercury Int
Textile Month — SJR
Textile Month — Text Mon
Textile Month — Textil Mnth
Textile Museum Journal — Text MJ
Textile Museum Journal — Text Mus J
Textile Organon — Organon
Textile Patents Newsletter — Text Pat Newsl
Textile Progress — Text Prog
Textile Progress — Textile Progr
Textile Quarterly — Text Q
Textile Recorder — Text Rec
Textile Rental — Text Rent
Textile Rental — Textil Rent
Textile Research — Tex Res
Textile Research Institute. Newletter — TRI Newsl
Textile Research Journal — Tex Res J
Textile Research Journal — Text Res J
Textile Research Journal — Textile Jl
Textile Research Journal — Textile Res J
Textile Science and Technology [*Elsevier Book Series*] — TST
Textile Technology Digest — Text Tech Dig
Textile Technology Digest — Text Technol Dig
Textile Technology Digest — Textile Technol Dig
Textile Technology Digest — TTD
Textile Weekly — Text Wkly
Textile World — Text World
Textile World — Textil Wld
Textile World Buyer's Guide/Fact File — Textil Wld
Textile World Journal — Text World J
Textile World Record — Text World R
Textiles Chimiques — Text Chim
Textiles Suisses. Revue de l'Industrie Suisse des Textiles d'Habillement — TES
Textil-Forschung — Text Forsch
Textilia — MNF
Textil-Industrie (Moenchen Gladbach, Germany) — Text Ind (Moenchen Gladbach Ger)
Textil-Industrie (Munich) — Text Ind (Munich)
Textil-Industrie (Zurich) — Text Ind (Zurich)
Textil-Mitteilungen. Unabhangige Textil Zeitung fuer Handel und Industrie — TCM
Textil-Praxis [*Later, Textil Praxis International*] — Text-Prax
Textil-Ring — Text Ring
Textil-Rundschau — Text Rundsch
Textilveredelung — Textilvered
Textil-Wirtschaft — Textil-W
Textil-Wirtschaft [*Database*] — TW
Texto Critico — T Crit
Texto Critico — TC
Texto y Concreto — TYC
Textos de Matematica. Serie B — Textos Mat Ser B
Textos de Metodos Matematicos — Text Metod Mat

Textos Hispanicos Modernos — THM
Textos Universitarios — Textos Univ
Textos y Estudios del Siglo XVIII — TE (XVIII)
Texts and Monographs in Computer Science — Texts Monographs Comput Sci
Texts and Monographs in Physics — Texts Monographs Phys
Texts and Monographs in Symbolic Computation — Texts Monogr Symbol Comput
Texts and Readings in Mathematics — Texts Read Math
Texts and Studies. Contributions to Biblical and Patristic Literature — TS
Texts from Cuneiform Sources — TCS
Texts in Applied Mathematics — Texts Appl Math
Texts in Statistical Science Series — Texts Statist Sci Ser
Texts on Computational Mechanics — Texts Comput Mech
Texture of Crystalline Solids — Texture Cryst Solids
Textures and Microstructures — Textures and Microstruct
Textures and Microstructures — Textures Microstruct
Textus Minores — TM
Teylers Theologisch Tijdschrift — TTT
Tezhka Promishlenost — Tezhka Prom
Tezisy Dokladov Nauchnoi Konferentsii. Zootekhnicheskaya Sektsiya — Tez Doklad Nauch Konf Zootech Sek
Tezisy Dokladov Vsesoyuznoi Nauchno-Metodicheskoi Konferentsii Veterinarnykh Patologoanatomov — Tezisy Dokl Vses Nauchno Metod Konf Vet Patoloanat
TGA [*Toilet Goods Association*] **Cosmetic Journal** — TGAJA8
TGA (Toilet Goods Association) Cosmetic Journal — TGA (Toilet Goods Assoc) Cosmet J
TGO. Tijdschrift voor Therapie, Geneesmiddel, en Onderzoek — TGO Tijdschr Ther Geneesmiddel Onder
Thai Journal of Agricultural Science — Thai J Agric Sci
Thai Journal of Development Administration [*Bangkok*] — Thai J Dev Adm
Thai Journal of Nursing — Thai J Nurs
Thai Journal of Surgery — Thai J Surg
Thai Journal of Surgery — TJSUDJ
Thai National Scientific Papers. Fauna Series — Thai Natl Sci Pap Fauna Ser
Thai Nurses Association Journal — Thai Nurses Assoc J
Thai Science Bulletin — Thai Sci Bull
Thailand Business — TBN
Thailand. Department of Mineral Resources. Ground Water Bulletin — Thailand Dep Miner Resour Ground Water Bull
Thailand. Department of Mineral Resources. Report of Investigation — Thailand Dep Miner Resour Rep Invest
Thailand Development Report [*Bangkok*] — TDR
Thailand Plant Protection Service. Technical Bulletin — Thail Plant Prot Serv Tech Bull
Thailheimer's Synthetic Methods of Organic Chemistry Yearbook — Thailheimer's Synth Methods of Org Chem Yearb
Thailheimer's Synthetic Methods of Organic Chemistry. Yearbook — TSMYDU
Thalassia Jugoslavica — Thalassia Jugosl
Thalassia Jugoslavica — THJUA
Tharandter Forstliches Jahrbuch — Th F Jb
Tharandter Forstliches Jahrbuch — Thar Forstl Jb
Tharandter Forstliches Jahrbuch — Tharandt Forstl Jb
Tharandter Forstliches Jahrbuch — Tharandter Forstl Jahrb
Thatigkeitsbericht der Naturforschenden Gesellschaft Baselland — Thatigkeitsber Naturf Ges Baselland
Thbilisis Sahelmcipho Universiteti Gamoqenebithi Mathematikis Instituti. Sromebi — Thbilis Sahelmc Univ Gamoqeneb Math Inst Srom
Thbilisis Universitetis. Phizika-Mathematikisa de Sabunebismetqvelo Mecnierebani. Sromebi — Thbilis Univ Srom
Thbilisis Universitetis. Phizika-Mathematikisa de Sabunebismetqvelo Mecnierebani. Sromebi. A — Thbilis Univ Srom A
(The) Americas — TAM
The Arab World [*New York*] — AW
The Arab World (London) — AWL
THE [*Technological Horizons in Education*] **Journal** — THE J
THE [*Technological Horizons in Education*] **Journal** — THE Jrnl
The Mines Magazine — TMM
The Oil Weekly — TOW
The Oil Weekly. World Oil Atlas — TOWA
The Sports Network [*Database*] — TSN
Theata — THEA
Theater Arts — TAr
Theater Arts — TArts
Theater der Zeit — Th Z
Theater der Zeit — Theat Zeit
Theater Heute — Theat Heute
Theatre Annual — TA
Theatre Annual — ThA
Theatre Annual — Theat Ann
Theatre Arts — TA
Theatre Arts — ThA
Theatre Arts — ThArts
Theatre Arts Magazine — TAM
Theatre Arts Magazine — Theatre Arts M
Theatre Arts Monthly — TAM
Theatre Australia — Th Aust
Theatre Crafts — GTHC
Theatre Crafts — Theat C
Theatre Crafts — Theat Craft
Theatre Documentation — TD
Theatre/Drama Abstracts — Theatre/Drama Abstr
Theatre en Pologne - Theatre in Poland — Theatre Pol
Theatre Guild Magazine — TGM
Theatre Journal — PTJO
Theatre Journal — Theat J
Theatre Journal — Theatre J
Theatre Journal — TJ
Theatre Magazine — Theatre M
Theatre Magazine — TM
Theatre Notebook — Theat Note
Theatre Notebook — Theatre Notebk
Theatre Notebook — TN
Theatre Notebook. A Quarterly of Notes and Research — Th Nb
Theatre Quarterly — Theat Q
Theatre Quarterly — Theat Quart
Theatre Quarterly — Theatre Q
Theatre Quarterly — ThQ
Theatre Quarterly — TQ
Theatre Research — ThR
Theatre Research — TR
Theatre Research International — PTRI
Theatre Research International — Th RI
Theatre Research International — Theat Res I
Theatre Research International — Theatre Res Int
Theatre Studies — Theat Stud
Theatre Studies — Theatre S
Theatre Studies — TS
Theatre Survey — PTSU
Theatre Survey — Theat Surv
Theatre Survey — Theatre S
Theatre Survey — ThS
Theatre Survey — TS
Theban Ostraca — O Theb
Theban Ostraca — Theb Ostr
Theban Ostraca — TO
Themelios — Them
Themis. Verzameling van Bijdragen tot de Kennis van het Publiek- en Privaatrecht — T
Themis. Verzameling van Bijdragen tot de Kennis van het Publiek- en Privaatrecht — Th
Themis. Verzameling van Bijdragen tot de Kennis van het Publiek- en Privaatrecht (Den Haag) — Themis (Den Haag)
Theokratia [*Leiden/Cologne*] — Theokr
Theologia — Th
Theologia — Theol
Theologia Evangelica — Theol Evang
Theologia Practica — Th Pract
Theologia Practica — Theol Pract
Theologia Viatorum — Theol Via
Theologia Viatorum. Jahrbuch der Kirchlichen Hochschule [*Berlin*] — ThV
Theologia Viatorum. Jahrbuch der Kirchlichen Hochschule [*Berlin*] — ThViat
Theologiai Szemle — Theol Szle
Theological Abstracting and Bibliographical Services — TABS
Theological and Literary Journal — Theo & Lit J
Theological and Religious Index — Theol & Rel Ind
Theological and Religious Index — Theol Relig Index
Theological Eclectic — Theo Ecl
Theological Education — Th Ed
Theological Education — Th Educ
Theological Educator — T Ed
Theological Educator — Thol Ed
Theological Markings — Th Markings
Theological Markings — Theol Markings
Theological Monthly — Theo Mo
Theological Quarterly Review — ThQR
Theological Repository — Theo Repos
Theological Review — Theo R
Theological Review [*Princeton, NJ*] — ThR
Theological Students Fellowship. Bulletin — TSF
Theological Studies — PTHS
Theological Studies — Theol St
Theological Studies — Theol Stds
Theological Studies — Theol Stud
Theological Studies — ThS
Theological Studies — ThSt
Theological Studies — TS
Theological Studies (Baltimore) — TSB
Theologie der Gegenwart — TGegw
Theologie der Gegenwart — TGW
Theologie der Gegenwart — Theol Geg
Theologie der Gegenwart — ThG
Theologie Pastorale et Spiritualite — TPS
Theologie Pastorale et Spiritualite. Recherches et Syntheses — TPSRS
Theologie und Glaube — T Gl
Theologie und Glaube — TG
Theologie und Glaube — Th Gl
Theologie und Glaube — Theol Gl
Theologie und Glaube — ThG
Theologie und Glaube — ThuGl
Theologie und Philosophie — Th & Ph
Theologie und Philosophie — Theol Phil
Theologisch Tijdschrift — Theol Tijdschr
Theologisch Tijdschrift — ThT
Theologisch Tijdschrift — TT
Theologische Akademie — Theol Akad
Theologische Berichte — Th Ber
Theologische Blaetter [*Leipzig*] — TB
Theologische Blaetter — ThB
Theologische Existenz Heute — Th Ex H

Theologische Forschung [*Hamburg*] — ThF
Theologische Forschung Wissenschaftliche Beitraege zur Kirchlichevangelischen Lehre — TFWBKEL
Theologische Jahrbuecher — ThJ
Theologische Literaturzeitung — Th Lit
Theologische Literaturzeitung — Th Lit Z
Theologische Literaturzeitung — Theol Lit Z
Theologische Literaturzeitung — Theol Lit Ztg
Theologische Literaturzeitung — Theol Literaturzeitung
Theologische Literaturzeitung — Theol LZ
Theologische Literaturzeitung — ThLZ
Theologische Literaturzeitung — TL
Theologische Literaturzeitung — TLZ
Theologische Quartalschrift — Th QS
Theologische Quartalschrift — Theol Quart
Theologische Quartalschrift — Theol Quartschr
Theologische Quartalschrift — Theol Quart-Schrift
Theologische Quartalschrift — ThQ
Theologische Quartalschrift [*Tuebingen*] — TQ
Theologische Quartalschrift — TQS
Theologische Revue — Th Rv
Theologische Revue — Theol R
Theologische Revue — Theol Rev
Theologische Revue — ThR
Theologische Revue — ThRev
Theologische Revue [*Muenster*] — TR
Theologische Revue — TRev
Theologische Rundschau — Th Rd
Theologische Rundschau — Th Rdsch
Theologische Rundschau — Th Rdschau
Theologische Rundschau — Th Rsch
Theologische Rundschau — Theol Rdsch
Theologische Rundschau — Theol Rsch
Theologische Rundschau — Theol Ru
Theologische Rundschau — ThR
Theologische Rundschau — ThRu
Theologische Rundschau — TR
Theologische Rundschau — TRS
Theologische Rundschau [*Tuebingen*] — TRu
Theologische Rundschau. Neue Folge [*Tuebingen*] — ThRNF
Theologische Rundschau. Neue Folge — TRNF
Theologische Studien — Th St
Theologische Studien — Theol St
Theologische Studien aus Wuerttemberg — ThStW
Theologische Studien. Karl Barth — Th St B
Theologische Studien und Kritiken — Theol St Krit
Theologische Studien und Kritiken — ThS
Theologische Studien und Kritiken [*Hamburg/Berlin*] — ThSK
Theologische Studien und Kritiken [*Hamburg/Berlin*] — ThStKr
Theologische Studien und Kritiken — TSK
Theologische Versuche — ThV
Theologische Wissenschaft — Th Wiss
Theologische Zeitschrift — Theol Z
Theologische Zeitschrift — Theol Zs
Theologische Zeitschrift — ThZ
Theologische Zeitschrift — TZ
Theologische Zeitschrift aus der Schweiz — ThZSchw
Theologische Zeitschrift (Basel) — TZBas
Theologischer Jahresbericht — Theol Jber
Theologischer Jahresbericht — TJB
Theologisches Handwoerterbuch zum Alten Testament — THAT
Theologisches Jahrbuch — Th Jb
Theologisches Jahrbuch — Theol Jb
Theologisches Literaturblatt — Theol Litbl
Theologisches Literaturblatt — Theol Ltbl
Theologisches Literaturblatt [*Leipzig*] — ThL
Theologisches Literaturblatt — ThLB
Theologisches Literaturblatt [*Leipzig*] — ThLBl
Theologisches Literaturblatt [*Leipzig*] — TL
Theologisches Literaturblatt — TLB
Theologisches Literaturblatt — TLBl
Theologisches Woerterbuch zum Alten Testament — Th WAT
Theologisches Woerterbuch zum Alten Testament — Theol WB
Theologisches Woerterbuch zum Neuen Testament — Th W
Theologisches Woerterbuch zum Neuen Testament — TWNT
Theologisches Zeitblatt — Theol Zeitbl
Theologisch-Praktische Monatsschrift — ThPM
Theologisch-Praktische Quartalschrift — T P Q
Theologisch-Praktische Quartalschrift — Th P Q
Theologisch-Praktische Quartalschrift — Theol Pr Q Schr
Theologisch-Praktische Quartalschrift — Theol Pr Qu Schr
Theologisch-Praktische Quartalschrift — Theol Prakt Quart Schr
Theologisch-Praktische Quartalschrift — Theol Prakt Quartschr
Theologisch-Praktische Quartalschrift [*Linz, Austria*] — ThPrQSchr
Theologisch-Praktische Quartalschrift — TPQS
Theology — T
Theology — Th
Theology [*London*] — Theol
Theology and Life — Th Life
Theology Digest [*St. Mary's, KS*] — TD
Theology Digest [*St. Mary's, KS*] — ThD
Theology Digest [*St. Mary's, KS*] — ThDig
Theology Digest — Theol Dgst
Theology. Journal of Historic Christianity — TJHC
Theology (London) — Th (Lond)
Theology Today — GTHE
Theology Today — T Today
Theology Today — Th T
Theology Today — Th Today
Theology Today — Theo Today
Theology Today — Theol Today
Theology Today — TT
Theophrastus' Contributions to Advanced Studies in Geology — Theophrastus Contrib Adv Stud Geol
Theoretic Papers — Theoret Papers
Theoretica Chimica Acta — Theor Chim
Theoretica Chimica Acta — Theor Chim Acta
Theoretica Chimica Acta — Theoret Chim Acta
Theoretical Advanced Study Institute in Elementary Particle Physics — Theor Adv Study Inst Elem Part Phys
Theoretical and Applied Fracture Mechanics — Theor Appl Fract Mech
Theoretical and Applied Fracture Mechanics — Theoret Appl Fracture Mech
Theoretical and Applied Genetics — Theor A Gen
Theoretical and Applied Genetics — Theor Appl Genet
Theoretical and Applied Genetics — Theoret Appl Genet
Theoretical and Applied Mechanics — Theoret Appl Mech
Theoretical and Applied Mechanics (Sofia) — Theor Appl Mech (Sofia)
Theoretical and Computational Chemistry — Theor Comput Chem
Theoretical and Computational Fluid Dynamics — Theor Comput Fluid Dyn
Theoretical and Computational Models for Organic Chemistry — Theor Comput Models Org Chem
Theoretical and Experimental Biology — Theor Exp Biol
Theoretical and Experimental Biophysics — Theor Exp Biophys
Theoretical and Experimental Chemistry — Theor Exp Chem
Theoretical and Experimental Chemistry — Theor Exper Chem
Theoretical and Mathematical Physics — Theor and Math Phys
Theoretical and Mathematical Physics — Theor Math
Theoretical and Mathematical Physics — Theor Math Phys
Theoretical and Mathematical Physics — Theoret and Math Phys
Theoretical Chemical Engineering Abstracts — TCEA
Theoretical Chemical Engineering Abstracts — Theor Chem Eng Abstr
Theoretical Chemical Engineering Abstracts — Theor Chem Engng Abstr
Theoretical Chemistry — Theor Chem
Theoretical Chemistry — Theoret Chem
Theoretical Chemistry. Advances and Perspectives — Theor Chem Adv Perspect
Theoretical Chemistry (New York) — Theor Chem (NY)
Theoretical Chemistry. Periodicities in Chemistry and Biology — Theor Chem Period Chem Biol
Theoretical Computer Science — Theor Comput Sci
Theoretical Computer Science — Theoret Comput Sci
Theoretical Foundations of Chemical Engineering — Theor Found Chem Eng
Theoretical Foundations of Chemical Engineering — Theor Foundations Chem Engng
Theoretical Foundations of Chemical Engineering (Translation of Teoreticheskie Osnovy Khimicheskoi Tekhnologii) — Theor Found Chem Eng Transl of Teor Osn Khim Tekhnol
Theoretical Linguistics — Theoret Linguist
Theoretical Linguistics [*Berlin*] — TL
Theoretical Medicine — Theor Med
Theoretical Physics. Text and Exercise Books — Theoret Phys Text Exerc Books
Theoretical Population Biology — Theor Pop B
Theoretical Population Biology — Theor Popul Biol
Theoretical Population Biology — Theoret Population Biol
Theoretical Population Biology — Theoret Population Biology
Theoretical Treatment of Large Molecules and Their Interactions — Theor Treat Large Mol Their Interact
Theoretische Grundlagen der Automatischen Steuerung — Theoret Grundlagen Automat Steuerung
Theoretische und Experimentelle Methoden der Regelungstechnik — Theor Exp Methoden Regelunstech
Theoretische und Klinische Medizin in Einzeldarstellungen — Theor Klin Med Einzeldarst
Theoretische und Klinische Medizin in Einzeldarstellungen [*Germany*] — Theor Klin Med Einzeldarstell
Theoretische und Klinische Medizin in Einzeldarstellungen — TKMEB
Theoria et Historia Scientiarum — Theoria Hist Sci
Theoria to Theory — Theor Theor
Theorie en Techniek — TT
Theorie et Politique — Theorie et Polit
Theory and Applications of Categories — Theory Appl Categ
Theory and Decision — Theor Decis
Theory and Decision Library — Theory Decis Lib
Theory and Decision Library. Series B. Mathematical and Statistical Methods — Theory Decis Lib Ser B Math Statist Methods
Theory and Decision Library. Series D. System Theory, Knowledge Engineering, and Problem Solving — Theory Decis Lib Ser D Syst Theory Knowledge Engrg Probl Solv
Theory and Experiment in Exobiology — Theory Exp Exobiol
Theory and Society — Theory and Soc
Theory and Society — Theory Soc
Theory into Practice — TIP
Theory of Computation Series [*Elsevier Book Series*] — TC
Theory of Probability and Its Applications — Th Prob Ap
Theory of Probability and Its Applications — Theor Probability Appl
Theory of Probability and Its Applications — Theory Probab and Appl
Theory of Probability and Its Applications — Theory Probab Appl
Theory of Probability and Mathematical Statistics — Th Pr Ma St
Theory of Probability and Mathematical Statistics — Theory Probab Math Statist

Theory of Probability and Mathematical Statistics — Theory Probability and Math Statist
Theory of Science Development — Theory Sci Dev
Theory of Science Development — TRVED8
Theosophical Quarterly — Theos Q
Theosophy in Australia — Theosophy in Aust
Therapeutic Drug Monitoring — TDMOD
Therapeutic Drug Monitoring — Ther Drug Monit
Therapeutic Education — Therapeutic Ed
Therapeutic Gazette [*Philadelphia*] — TG
Therapeutic Gazette — Ther Gaz
Therapeutic Immunology — Ther Immunol
Therapeutic Problems of Today — Ther Probl Today
Therapeutic Recreation Journal — Ther R J
Therapeutic Recreation Journal — Ther Recr J
Therapeutic Recreation Journal — Ther Recreation J
Therapeutique. Semaine des Hopitaux — Ther Sem Hop
Therapeutische Berichte — Ther Ber
Therapeutische Halbmonatshefte — Ther Halbmonatsh
Therapeutische Halbmonatshefte — Therap Halbmonatsh
Therapeutische Monatshefte — Ther Monatsh
Therapeutische Monatshefte fuer Veterinaermedizin — Therap Monatsh Vet-Med
Therapeutische Umschau — Ther Umsch
Therapeutische Umschau und Medizinische Bibliographie — Therap Umschau
Therapia Hungarica — Ther Hung
Therapia Hungarica [*Hungarian Medical Journal*] — Therap Hung
Therapie — Therap
Therapie Bakterieller Infektionen in der Kinderklinik — Ther Bakt Infekt Kinderklin
Therapie der Gegenwart — Th d G
Therapie der Gegenwart — Th G
Therapie der Gegenwart — Ther Ggw
Therapie der Gegenwart — Therap Gegenw
Therapie der Gegenwart — Therapie Gegenw
Therapie der Gegenwart — THGEA
Therapie ueber das Nervensystem — Ther Nervensys
Therapie ueber das Nervensystem — Ther Nervensyst
Thermal Abstracts — Therm Abstr
Thermal and Nuclear Power [*Japan*] — Therm Nucl Power
Thermal Engineering — Therm Eng
Thermal Engineering — Therm Engng
Thermal Engineering — Therm Engr
Thermal Engineering (USSR) — Therm Eng (USSR)
Thermal Plasma Applications in Materials and Metallurgical Processing. Proceedings. International Symposium — Therm Plasma Appl Mater Metall Process Proc Int Symp
Thermal Power Conference. Proceedings [*United States*] — Therm Power Conf Proc
Thermal Power Generation — Therm Power Gener
Thermal Science and Engineering — Therm Sci Eng
Thermal Spray Coatings. Properties, Processes, and Applications. Proceedings. National Thermal Spray Conference — Therm Spray Coat Proc Natl Therm Spray Conf
Thermal Structures and Materials for High-Speed Flight — Therm Struct Mater High Speed Flight
Thermo- and Fluid Dynamics — Therm Fluid Dyn
Thermochimica Acta — TCA
Thermochimica Acta — Thermoc Act
Thermochimica Acta — Thermochim Acta
Thermodynamic Property Values Database — THERMO
Thermonews — Therm
Thermophilic Bacteria — Thermophilic Bact
Thesaurus — Thes
Thesaurus Graecae Linguae — TGL
Thesaurus Graecae Linguae — Th G
Thesaurus Graecae Linguae — Th Gr L
Thesaurus Linguae Latinae — Thes Li L
Thesaurus Linguae Latinae — Thes Lin Lat
Thesaurus Linguae Latinae — ThesLL
Thesaurus Linguae Latinae — ThLL
Thesaurus Linguae Latinae — TLL
These Times — T Times
Theses. Catholic Medical College — Theses Cathol Med Coll
Theses. Catholic Medical College (Seoul) — Theses Cathol Med Coll (Seoul)
Theses Collection. Incheon Junior College — Theses Collect Incheon Jr Coll
Theses Collection. Kyungnam Industrial Junior College [*Republic of Korea*] — Theses Collect Kyungnam Ind Jr Coll
Theses Collection. Kyungnam University [*Republic of Korea*] — Theses Collect Kyungnam Univ
Theses Collection of Chonnam University. Chonnam University — Theses Collect Chonnam Univ Chonnam Univ
Theses Collection. Sookmyung Women's University — Theses Collect Sookmyung Women's Univ
Theses Collection. Yeungnam University [*Republic of Korea*] — Theses Collect Yeungnam Univ
Theses Collection. Yeungnam University. Natural Sciences [*Republic of Korea*] — Theses Collect Yeungnam Univ Nat Sci
Theses de Docteur-Ingenieur. Universite de Dakar. Serie Sciences Naturelles — Theses Doct Ing Univ Dakar Ser Sci Nat
Theses of Economics and Business in Finland [*Database*] — THES
Theses Zoologicae — Theses Zool
Theses Zoologicae — THZOEN
Thesis Eleven — Thesis
Thesis Theological Cassettes — Thesis Theo Cassettes
Theskeutike kai Ethike Enkyklopaideia — ThEE
Theta News Release — Theta NR
Thiels Preussische Landwirtschaftliche Jahrbuecher — TPrLJ
Thiemig-Taschenbuecher — Thiemig Tb
Thiemig-Taschenbuecher — Thiemig-Taschenb
Thiemig-Taschenbuecher — THTAD
Thieraerztliche Mittheilungen (Carlsruhe) — Thieraerzt Mitth (Carlsruhe)
Thiermedicinische Rundschau — Thiermed Rundschau
Thin Films Science and Technology [*Elsevier Book Series*] — TFST
Thin Films. Stresses and Mechanical Properties. Symposium — Thin Films Stresses Mech Prop Symp
Thin Solid Films — Thin Sol Fi
Things — Th
Third World — Third Wld
Third World — TW
Third World Agriculture — Third Wld Agric
Third World Book Review — TWBR
Third World Forum — Third Wld
Third World Planning Review — Third World Planning R
Third World Quarterly — Third Wld Quart
Third World Quarterly — Third World Q
Third World Quarterly — Thr Wld Q
Third World Quarterly — TWQ
Third World Socialists — Third World Soc
Thirties Society. Journal — Thirties Soc Jnl
Thirty-Three/33. Magazine of the Metals Producing Industry — Thirty-Three/33 Mag Met Prod Ind
This Magazine Is about Schools [*Later, This Magazine: Education, Culture, Politics*] — This Mag
This Unrest — TU
This Week in Consumer Electronics — TWICE
Thomas Hardy Yearbook — THY
Thomas Mann-Studien — Th M S
Thomas Paine Society. Bulletin — TPSB
Thomas Say Foundation — Thomas Say Found
Thomas Say Foundation. Monographs — Thomas Say Found Monogr
Thomas Say Foundation. Monographs — TSFMES
Thomas Wolfe Newsletter — T Wolfe New
Thomas Wolfe Newsletter — TWN
Thomas Wolfe Review — T Wolfe Rev
Thomas Wolfe Review — TWR
Thomist — Thm
Thomist — Thom
Thomond Archaeological Society and Field Club — Thomond Arch Soc Fld Cl
Thompson, Yates, and Johnston Laboratories Reports — Thompson Yates and Johnston Lab Rep
Thompson-Yates Laboratories Reports — Thompson Yates Lab Rep
Thomson's Process and Chemical Engineering [*Australia*] — Thomson's Process Chem Eng
Thoracic and Cardiovascular Surgeon — Thorac Cardiovasc Surg
Thorax [*British Medical Association*] — Thor
Thoraxchirurgie und Vaskulaere Chirurgie — Thorax Chir
Thoraxchirurgie und Vaskulaere Chirurgie — Thoraxchir Vask Chir
Thoreau Journal Quarterly — Thoreau JQ
Thoreau Journal Quarterly — TJQ
Thoreau Quarterly — Thoreau Q
Thoreau Society. Booklet — T S Booklet
Thoreau Society. Bulletin — TSB
Thoroton Society. Record Series — Thoroton Soc Rec Ser
Thoth — TH
Thoth Research Journal — Thoth Res
Thought — PTHO
Thought — Th
Thought — TRCI
Thought. A Review of Culture and Idea — Tho
Thought Currents in English Literature — TCEL
Thought Patterns — TP
Threads Magazine — Threads Mag
Three Banks Review — TBR
Three Banks Review — Three Bank
Three Banks Review — Three Banks R
Three Banks Review — Three Banks Rev
Three Banks Review — TSW
Three Forks of Muddy Creek — Three Forks
Three Penny Review — TPR
Three R International [*Germany*] — Three R Int
Three Rivers Poetry Journal — Th Ri Po
Three Sigma Market Newspaper Audiences [*Database*] — SIG
TH-Report-Eindhoven University of Technology. Department of Electrical Engineering — TH Rep Eindhoven Univ Technol Dep Electr Eng
Thrill Book — TB
Thrilling Wonder Stories — TW
Thrilling Wonder Stories — TWS
Thrombosis and Haemostasis — Thromb Haemost
Thrombosis and Haemostasis — Thromb Haemostas
Thrombosis et Diathesis Haemorrhagica — Thromb Diat
Thrombosis et Diathesis Haemorrhagica — Thromb Diath Haemorrh
Thrombosis et Diathesis Haemorrhagica. Supplementum — Thromb Diath Haemorrh Suppl
Thrombosis Research — Thromb Res
Thrombosis Research. Supplement — Thromb Res Suppl
Thrust — THRU
Thrust. Journal for Employment and Training Professionals — THR
Thueringens Merkwuerdigkeiten aus dem Gebiete der Natur, der Kunst, des Menschenlebens — Thueringens Merkwuerdigk Natur
Thueringer Kirchliches Jahrbuch — ThKJ

Thueringisch-Saechsische Zeitschrift fuer Geschichte und Kunst — Thuer Saechs Zs Gesch
Thueringisch-Saechsische Zeitschrift fuer Geschichte und Kunst — Thuering Saechs Zs Gesch
Thueringisch-Saechsische Zeitschrift fuer Geschichte und Kunst — TSZGK
Thule International Symposia — Thule Int Symp
Thurgauische Beitraege zur Vaterlaendischen Geschichte — TBVG
Thurgauische Beitraege zur Vaterlaendischen Geschichte — Thurg B
Thurgood Marshall Law Journal — Thur Marsh LJ
Thymus — THYMD
Thyras Vold — Thyr V
Thyssen Edelstahl Technische Berichte — Thyssen Edelstahl Tech Ber
Thyssen Forschung. Berichte aus Forschung und Betrieb — Thyssen Forsch Ber Forsch Betr
Thyssen Technische Berichte — Thyssen Tech Ber
Ti Chih Ko Hsueh — TCKHA
Ti Ch'iu Hua Hsueh — TCHHC
TI. Technical Information for Industry [*South Africa*] — TI Tech Inf Ind
Tianjin Journal of Oncology — Tianjin J Oncol
Tianjin Medical Journal — Tianjin Med J
Tianjin Medical Journal — TIYADG
Tibet Journal [*Dharmasala*] — Tibet J
Tibet Society. Bulletin [*United States*] — Tibet Soc B
Tibetan Review [*New Delhi*] — Tibetan R
Tibetan Review — TR
Tibet-Archiv fuer Religionswissenschaft — TARW
Tidehverv — Tdhv
Tidens Tann — Tid Tann
Tidewater Virginian — Tidewtr VA
Tidning foer Byggnadskonst — Tidn Byggnadskonst
Tidschrift van de Vereniging voor Nederlandse Muziek Geschiedenis — TVNMG
Tidskrift foer Dokumentation — Tid Dok
Tidskrift foer Dokumentation — Tidsk Dokum
Tidskrift foer Dokumentation — Tidskr Dok
Tidskrift foer Hushallningssaellskapet och Skogsvardsstyrelsen i Gaevleborgs Laen — Tidskr Hushallningssaellsk Skogsvardsstyr Gaevleborgs Laen
Tidskrift foer Konstvetinskap — TfK
Tidskrift foer Lantmaen och Andelsfolk — Tidskr Lantm Andelsfolk
Tidskrift foer Lantmaen och Andelsfolk — Tidskr Lantmaen Andelsfolk
Tidskrift foer Sjukvardspedagoger — Tidskr Sjukvardspedagog
Tidskrift foer Sveriges Sjukskoterskor — Tidskr Sver Sjukskot
Tidskrift foer Teknisk-Vettenskaplig Forskning — TVF
Tidskrift foer Varme-, Ventilations-, och Sanitetsteknik [*Sweden*] — Tidskr Varme- Vent- Sanitetstek
Tidskrift for Landtman — Tidskr Landtm
Tidskrift i Militar Halsovard [*Sweden*] — Tidskr Mil Halsov
Tidskrift I Sjoevaesendet — T I Sjoevas
Tidskrift. Kungliga Krigsvetenskaps-Akademien — T Kungl Krigsvet Akad
Tidskrift. Skogs- och Lantbruksakademien — Tidskr Skog Lantbruksakad
Tidskrift Sveriges Skogsvardsforbund — Tidskr Sver Skogvardsforb
Tidskrift. Sveriges Utsaedesforeningen — Tidskr Sver Utsadesforen
Tidskrift Utgiven av Juridiska Foereningen i Finland — Ts Jur Foer Finland
Tidsskrift foer Biavl — Tidsskr Biavl
Tidsskrift foer den Norske Laegeforening — Tidsskr Nor Laegeforen
Tidsskrift foer den Norske Laegeforening — Tidsskr Norske Laegeforen
Tidsskrift foer den Norske Laegeforening — TNLAAH
Tidsskrift foer det Norske Landbruk — Tidsskr Nor Landbruk
Tidsskrift foer det Norske Landbruk — Tidsskr Norske Landbruk
Tidsskrift foer Froavl — Tidsskr Froavl
Tidsskrift foer Hermetikindustri — Tidsskr Hermetikind
Tidsskrift foer Kemi — Tidsskr Kemi
Tidsskrift foer Kemi. Farmaci og Terapi — Tidsskr Kemi Farm Ter
Tidsskrift foer Kjemi. Bergvesen og Metallurgi — Tidssk Kjemi Bergves Metall
Tidsskrift foer Kjemi. Bergvesen og Metallurgi — Tidsskr Kjemi Bergvesen Met
Tidsskrift foer Kjemi og Bergvesen — Tidsskr Kjemi Bergv
Tidsskrift foer Kjemi og Bergvesen — Tidsskr Kjemi Bergves
Tidsskrift foer Landokonomi — Tidsskr Landokon
Tidsskrift foer Norron Arkeologi — TNA
Tidsskrift foer Papirindustri — Tidsskr Papirind
Tidsskrift foer Planteavl — Tidsskr Plant
Tidsskrift foer Planteavl — Tidsskr Planteavl
Tidsskrift foer Planteavl — Tidsskr Plavl
Tidsskrift foer Planteavl — TPLAAV
Tidsskrift foer Praktiserende Tandlaeger — Tidsskr Prakt Tandlaeg
Tidsskrift foer Samfunnsforskning — Tids Samfun
Tidsskrift foer Samfunnsforskning — Tidsskr Samfunnsforskning
Tidsskrift foer Skogbruk — Tidskr Skogbruk
Tidsskrift foer Skogbruk — Tidsskr Skogbr
Tidsskrift foer Skogbruk — Tidsskr Skogbruk
Tidsskrift foer Sovaesen — T Sovaes
Tidsskrift foer Sygeplejersker — Tidsskr Sygepl
Tidsskrift foer Textilteknik — Tidsskr Textiltek
Tidsskrift foer Udenrigspolitik — T Udenrigspolitik
Tidsskrift for Biavlerforening — T Bi
Tidsskrift for Fjerkraeavlerforening — T Fjk
Tidsskrift for Froavlerforening — F Fro
Tidsskrift for Gedeavlsforeninger — T Gd
Tidsskrift for Husholnding — T Hush
Tidsskrift for Industri — T Ind
Tidsskrift for Jordemodre — T Jdm
Tidsskrift for Kaninavlerforening — T Kn
Tidsskrift for Landokonomi — T Lo
Tidsskrift for Legemsovelser — T Le
Tidsskrift for Maskinvaesen — T Msk
Tidsskrift for Planteavl — T Pla
Tidsskrift for Radio — T Rad
Tidsskrift for Rettsvitenskap — T Rtv
Tidsskrift for Sovaesen — T Sov
Tidsskrift for Sygepleje — T Sypl
Tidsskrift for Teologi og Kirke [*Oslo*] — TsTK
Tidsskrift for Teologi og Kirke [*Oslo*] — TTKi
Tidsskrift for Textilteknik — T Textilt
Tidsskrift for Udenrigspolitik — T Ud
Tiedonanto-Valtion Teknillinen Tutkimuskeskus, Poltto-, ja Voiteluainelaboratorio [*Finland*] — Tied Valt Tek Tutkimuskeskus Poltto Voiteluainelab
Tiedotus Metsateho — Tied Metsateho
Tiedotus. Valtion Teknillinen Tutkimuslaitos — Tied Valt Tekn Tutkimusl
Tien Hsia Monthly — THM
Tieraerztliche Praxis — Tieraerztl Prax
Tieraerztliche Rundschau — Tieraerztl Rd
Tieraerztliche Rundschau — Tieraerztl Rundsch
Tieraerztliche Rundschau — Tieraerztl Rundschau
Tieraerztliche Umschau — Tieraerztl Umsch
Tieraerztliche Zeitschrift — Tieraerztl Z
Tierarztliche Praxis. Supplement — Tierarztl Prax Suppl
Tierernaehrung und Fuetterung — Tierernaehr Fuetter
Tierphysiologie, Tierernaehrung, und Futtermittelkunde — Tierphysiol Tierernaehr Futtermittelk
Tierra y Sociedad — Tierra y Soc
Tiers Monde. Universite de Paris. Institut d'Etude du Developpement Economique et Social [*Paris*] — UP/TM
Tieteellisia Julkaisuja. Helsingin Teknillinen Korkeakoulu — Tiet Julk Helsingin Tek Korkeakoulu
Tietyeellisiae Tutkimuksia — Tieteel Tutk
Tiger's Eye — TE
Tihanyi Biologiai Kutatointezetenek Evkoenyve — Tihanyi Biol Kutatointezetenek Evkoen
Tijdingen. Vlaamse Chemische Vereniging — Tijd Vlaam Chem Ver
Tijdschrift Aardrijkskundig Genootschap — TAG
Tijdschrift Bataviasch Genootschap — TBG
Tijdschrift der Aardrijkskundige Genootschap — Tijdschrift Aardr Genootschap
Tijdschrift der Kantongerechten — Tijdschr d Ktg
Tijdschrift der Koninklijke Nederlandsche Heidemaatschappij — Tijdschr K Ned Heidemaatsch
Tijdschrift der Nederlandsche Dierkundige Vereniging — Tijdschr Ned Dierkd Ver
Tijdschrift der Nederlandsche Heidemaatschappij — Tijdschr Ned Heidemaatsch
Tijdschrift der Notarissen — TdN
Tijdschrift Gemeente-Financien — TGF
Tijdschrift. Koninklijk Nederlandsch Aardrijkskundig Genootschap — TsNAG
Tijdschrift. Koninklijk Nederlandsch Genootschap voor Munt en Penningkunde — TKNGMP
Tijdschrift. Koninklijk Nederlandsch Aardrijkskundig Genootschaft — TKN
Tijdschrift. Nationale Bank van Belgie — BNA
Tijdschrift over Boomteeltkunde, Bloementeelt, en Moeshovenierderij — Tijdschr Boomteeltk
Tijdschrift Primaire Energie [*Belgium*] — Tijdschr Primaire Energ
Tijdschrift ter Beoefening van het Administratief Recht — TAR
Tijdschrift van de Koninklijke Vereniging voor Nederlandse Muziekgeschiedenis — KVNM
Tijdschrift van de Nederlandse Vereniging voor Klinische Chemie — Tijdschr Ned Ver Klin Chem
Tijdschrift van de Vereeniging voor Nederlandse Muziekgeschiedenis — T Ver Nederlandse Mg
Tijdschrift van de Vereeniging voor Nederlandse Muziekgeschiedenis — VNM
Tijdschrift van de Vrederechters, Plaatsvervangers, Officieren van het Openbaar Ministerie en Griffiers — Tijdschr Vreder
Tijdschrift van de Vrige Universiteit van Brussel — TsVUB
Tijdschrift van de Vrige Universiteit van Brussel — TVUB
Tijdschrift van den Nederlandschen Werkloosheidsraad — TNW
Tijdschrift van het Bataviaasch Genootschap van Kunsten en Wetenschappen — TBGKW
Tijdschrift van het Bataviaasch Genootschap van Kunsten en Wetenschappen — Tijdschr Batav Genootsch Kunst
Tijdschrift van het Centraal Nijverheidscomite van Belgie — Tijdsch Centr Nijv Comite Belg
Tijdschrift van het Institut voor Toegepaste Linguistiek — Tijd ITL
Tijdschrift van het Institut voor Toegepaste Linguistiek [*Leuven*] — TITL
Tijdschrift van het Kon. Nederlandsche Aardrijkskundig Genootschap — T Aardrijkskundig Genoot
Tijdschrift van het (Koninklijk) Nederlandsch Aardrijkskundig Genootschap — Tijdschr Ned Aar Genoot
Tijdschrift van het Nederlands Elektronica- en Radiogenootschap — Tijdschr Ned Elektron- & Radiogenoot
Tijdschrift van het Nederlandsch Aardrijkskundig Genootschap — Tijdschr Nederld Aardrijkskd Genootsch
Tijdschrift van het Recht [*Batavia*] — T v h R
Tijdschrift van Nederlandsch-Indie — TNI
Tijdschrift voor Armwezen, Maatschappelijke Hulp en Kinderbescherming — TA
Tijdschrift voor Bestuurswetenschappen — T Best
Tijdschrift voor Bestuurswetenschappen — Tijds v Bestuursw
Tijdschrift voor Bestuurswetenschappen — Tijdschr Bestuursw
Tijdschrift voor Bestuurswetenschappen en Publiek Recht — T Best Publ R
Tijdschrift voor Bestuurswetenschappen en Publiek Recht — TB
Tijdschrift voor Bestuurswetenschappen en Publiek Recht — TBP
Tijdschrift voor Bestuurswetenschappen en Publiek Recht — Ts BW P R

Tijdschrift voor de Geschiedenis der Geneeskunde, Natuurwetenschappen, Wiskunde en Techniek — Tijdschr Gesch Geneesk Natuurwetensch Wisk Tech
Tijdschrift voor de Politie — TP
Tijdschrift voor de Studie van de Verlichting — TsSV
Tijdschrift voor Diergeneeskunde — Tijdschr Diergeneeskd
Tijdschrift voor Diergeneeskunde. Quarterly English Issue — Tijdschr Diergeneeskd Q Engl Issue
Tijdschrift voor Economic Management — Tijds Econ Manag
Tijdschrift voor Economie — Tijds Econ
Tijdschrift voor Economie — TVE
Tijdschrift voor Economie en Management — ECS
Tijdschrift voor Economische en Sociale Geografie — TEG
Tijdschrift voor Economische en Sociale Geografie — TESG
Tijdschrift voor Economische en Sociale Geografie [*Netherlands*] — TESG-A
Tijdschrift voor Economische en Sociale Geografie — Tijd Ec Soc
Tijdschrift voor Economische en Sociale Geografie — Tijd Ec Soc Geogr
Tijdschrift voor Economische en Sociale Geografie — Tijdschr Econ Soc Geogr
Tijdschrift voor Economische en Sociale Geografie — Tijdschrift voor Econ en Soc Geog
Tijdschrift voor Economische en Sociale Geographie — Tijdschr Econ Social Geogr
Tijdschrift voor Economische Geographie — Tijdschr Econ Geogr
Tijdschrift voor Effectief Directiebeleid — KOM
Tijdschrift voor Entomologie — Tijd Ent
Tijdschrift voor Entomologie — Tijdschr Ent
Tijdschrift voor Entomologie — Tijdschr Entomol
Tijdschrift voor Filosofie — TF
Tijdschrift voor Filosofie — Tijd Filos
Tijdschrift voor Filosofie — Tijdschr Filosof
Tijdschrift voor Gastro-Enterologie — Tijdschr Gastro-Enterol
Tijdschrift voor Gemeenten — Tijdschr Gemeent
Tijdschrift voor Gemeenterecht — TG
Tijdschrift voor Gemeenterecht — Tijds Gem Recht
Tijdschrift voor Geneeskunde — Tijdschr Geneeskd
Tijdschrift voor Gerontologie en Geriatrie — Tijdschr Gerontol Geriatr
Tijdschrift voor Geschiedenis — T Gesch
Tijdschrift voor Geschiedenis — Tijd Gesch
Tijdschrift voor Geschiedenis — Tijdschr Gesch
Tijdschrift voor Geschiedenis — TVG
Tijdschrift voor Geschiedenis en Folklore — TGF
Tijdschrift voor Geschiedenis. Land en Volkenkunde — TG
Tijdschrift voor Geschiedenis. Land en Volkenkunde — TGLV
Tijdschrift voor Geschiedenis Natuurwetenschap Wiskundig. Techniek — Tijdschr Geschied Natuurwet Wiskd Tec
Tijdschrift voor Geschiednis — TiG
Tijdschrift voor het Kadaster in Nederlandsch-Indie — TK
Tijdschrift voor het Notarisambt — T vh Not
Tijdschrift voor het Notarisambt. Venduwezen en Fiscaal Recht — TNVF
Tijdschrift voor Indische Taal-, Land-, en Volkenkunde — Tijd Ind TLV
Tijdschrift voor Indische Taal-, Land-, en Volkenkunde — Tijdschr Ind Taal-Land- en Volkenkunde
Tijdschrift voor Indische Taal-, Land-, en Volkenkunde — TITLV
Tijdschrift voor Indische Taal-, Land-, en Volkenkunde — TsIT
Tijdschrift voor Kadaster en Landmeetkunde — TKL
Tijdschrift voor Kadaster en Landmeetkunde — Ts Kad en Landmeetk
Tijdschrift voor Kadaster en Landmeetkunde — Ts Kad Lmk
Tijdschrift voor Kindergeneeskunde — Tijd Kindergeneeskd
Tijdschrift voor Kindergeneeskunde — Tijdschr Kindergeneeskd
Tijdschrift voor Land- en Tuinbouw en Boschkultuur — Tijdschr Land Tuinb Boschkult
Tijdschrift voor Levende Talen — Tijdschr Lev Talen
Tijdschrift voor Liturgei — TVL
Tijdschrift voor Logopedie en Audiologie — Tijd Logop Audiol
Tijdschrift voor Maatschappelijk Werk — T v M W
Tijdschrift voor Maatschappelijk Werk — TMW
Tijdschrift voor Marketing — CMQ
Tijdschrift voor Milieu en Recht — TBM
Tijdschrift voor Nederlandsche Taal- en Letterkunde — Tijd Ned T
Tijdschrift voor Nederlandsche Taal- en Letterkunde — Tijdschr Ned TL
Tijdschrift voor Nederlandsche Taal- en Letterkunde [*Leiden*] — TNTL
Tijdschrift voor Nederlandsche Taal- en Letterkunde — TsNTL
Tijdschrift voor Nederlandsche. Taalen Letterkunde — Tijdschr Ned Taalen Lettk
Tijdschrift voor Nederlandsch-Indie — Tijdschr Ned Indie
Tijdschrift voor Nederlandsch-Indie — Ts N I
Tijdschrift voor Notarissen — T Not
Tijdschrift voor Notarissen — Tijds Not
Tijdschrift voor Notarissen — Tijdschr Not
Tijdschrift voor Notarissen — TN
Tijdschrift voor Notarissen — Ts Not
Tijdschrift voor Openbaar Bestuur — TOA
Tijdschrift voor Oppervlakte Technieken van Metalen — Tijdschr Oppervlakte Tech Metal
Tijdschrift voor Oppervlaktetechnieken van Materialen — Tijdschr Oppervlaktetech Mater
Tijdschrift voor Oude Muziek — TOM
Tijdschrift voor Overheidsadministratie — Ts Ovadm
Tijdschrift voor Overheidsadministratie en Openbaar Bestuur — T v O
Tijdschrift voor Overheidsadministratie. Weekblad voor het Openbaar Bestuur — TO
Tijdschrift voor Philosophie — Tijd Phil
Tijdschrift voor Philosophie — TP
Tijdschrift voor Philosophie — TPh
Tijdschrift voor Philosophie — TsPhil
Tijdschrift voor Plantenziekten — Tijdschr Plantenz
Tijdschrift voor Plantenziekten — Tijdschr Plantenziekten
Tijdschrift voor Politicologie [*Netherlands*] — Tijdschr Polit
Tijdschrift voor Politiek — Tijdschr Polit
Tijdschrift voor Privaatrecht — Tijds Pr Recht
Tijdschrift voor Privaatrecht — Tijds Priv
Tijdschrift voor Privaatrecht — TPR
Tijdschrift voor Privaatrecht, Notariaat, en Fiscaalrecht — T v P N en F
Tijdschrift voor Privaatrecht, Notariaat, en Fiscaalrecht — TPNF
Tijdschrift voor Psychiatrie — Tijd Psych
Tijdschrift voor Rechtsgeschiedenis — T RGesch
Tijdschrift voor Rechtsgeschledenis — T v R
Tijdschrift voor Rechtsgeschiedenis — Tijd R Gesch
Tijdschrift voor Rechtsgeschiedenis — TR
Tijdschrift voor Rechtsgeschiedenis — TRG
Tijdschrift voor Rechtsgeschiedenis — TVRG
Tijdschrift voor Skandinanistiek — TS
Tijdschrift voor Sociaal Recht — Ts Soc R
Tijdschrift voor Sociaal Recht — TSR
Tijdschrift voor Sociaal Recht en van de Arbeidsgerechten — T Soc R
Tijdschrift voor Sociaal Recht en van de Arbeidsgerechten — TSRA
Tijdschrift voor Sociale Geneeskunde — Tijdschr Soc Geneeskd
Tijdschrift voor Sociale Hygiene — TSH
Tijdschrift voor Sociale Wetenschappen — Tijd Soc Wet
Tijdschrift voor Sociale Wetenschappen — Tijds Soc Wetensch
Tijdschrift voor Sociale Wetenschappen — Tijdschr Soc Wetensch
Tijdschrift voor Sociale Wetenschappen — TWA
Tijdschrift voor Strafrecht — T v S
Tijdschrift voor Strafrecht — T v Sr
Tijdschrift voor Strafrecht — Tijdschr Strafrecht
Tijdschrift voor Strafrecht — TS
Tijdschrift voor Studie. Verlichting — Tijdschr Stud Verlichting
Tijdschrift voor Taal en Letteren — Tijdschrift Taal & Lett
Tijdschrift voor Theologie [*Wageningen*] — TTh
Tijdschrift voor Theologie — TVT
Tijdschrift voor Therapie, Geneesmiddel, en Onderzoek — Tijdschr Ther Geneesmiddel Onderz
Tijdschrift voor Tuinbouw (Groningen) — Tijdschr Tuinb Groningen
Tijdschrift voor Veeartsenijkunde — Tijdschr Veeartsenijk
Tijdschrift voor Veeartsenijkunde en Veeteelt — Tijdschr Veeartsenijk en Veeteelt
Tijdschrift voor Vennootschappen, Verenigingen, en Stichtingen — TVVS
Tijdschrift voor Vervoerswetenschap — VKC
Tijdschrift voor Volkhuisvesting en Stedebouw, uitgave Nederlands Instituut voor Volkshuisvesting en Stedebouw — TVS
Tijdschrift voor Vrederechters — T Vred
Tijdschrift voor Wetenschappelijke Graphologie — W Gr
Tijdschrift voor Ziekenverpleging — Tijdschr Ziekenverpl
Tijdschriftenoverzicht — Tijdschr Ov
Tikkun — ITIK
Tilskueren — Til
Timarit Hjukrunarfelags Islands [*Reykjavik*] — Timarit Hjukrunarfel Isl
Timarit Pjooreknisfelags Islendinga 1957 — TI
Timarit Verkfraedingafelags Islands — Timarit Verkfraedingafelags Is
Timber and Plywood Annual — Timb & Plyw Ann
Timber Bulletin for Europe — Timb Bull Eur
Timber Bulletin for Europe — Timber B
Timber Bulletin for Europe. Annual Forest Products Market Review — Timber BAR
Timber Bulletin for Europe. Classification and Definitions of Forest Products — TBE Class
Timber Bulletin for Europe. Food and Agricultural Organization — Timb Bull Europe FAO
Timber Bulletin for Europe. Forest and Forest Products Country Profile (Hungary) — Timber B (Hu)
Timber Bulletin for Europe. Forest Fire Statistics — Timber BFS
Timber Bulletin for Europe. Monthly Prices for Forest Products. Supplement — Timber B Pr
Timber Bulletin for Europe. Survey of the Wood-Based Panels Industries — Timber BWP
Timber Development Association. Bulletin — TDA Bull
Timber Development Association. Information Bulletin A/IB — Timber Dev Assoc Inf Bull A/IB
Timber Development Association. Information Bulletin B/IB — Timber Dev Assoc Inf Bull B/IB
Timber Development Association. Information Bulletin G/IB — Timber Dev Assoc Inf Bull G/IB
Timber Development Association. Research Report C/RR — Timber Dev Assoc Res Rep C/RR
Timber Grower — Timb Grower
Timber Information Keyword Retrieval [*Database*] — TINKER
Timber Leaflet. Forest Department (Nairobi, Kenya) — Timb Leafl For Dep (Kenya)
Timber Leaflet. Forest Department (Uganda) — Timb Leafl For Dep (Uganda)
Timber Leaflet. Forestry Department (British Solomon Islands Protectorate) — Timb Leafl For Dep (Brit Solomon Islands Protect)
Timber Preservers' Association of Australia. Pamphlet — Timb Pres Assoc Aust
Timber Research and Development Association. Research Report C/RR — Timber Res Dev Assoc Res Rep C/RR
Timber Supply Review — Timber Supp Rev
Timber Technology — Timber Technol
Timber Trade Review [*Kuala Lumpur*] — TNS
Timber Trades Journal — Timb Tr J
Timber Trades Journal and Wood Processing — Timb Trades J Wood Process
Timber Trades Journal and Wood Processing — TTJ
Timber Trades Journal and Woodworking Machinery [*Later, Timber Trades Journal and Wood Processing*] — Timber Trades J

Timber Trades Journal and Woodworking Machinery [*Timber Trades Journal and Wood Processing*] [*London*] [*Later,*] — TJS
Timberman. An International Lumber Journal — Ti
Time — GTIM
Time — T
Time — TIM
Time — Tm
Time and Tide — T & T
Time and Tide — TT
Time (Canada) — Time (Can)
Time (New York) — Tn
Timely Turf Topics — Timely Turf Top
Times [*London*] — T
Times [*London*] — TIS
Times [*London*] — TT
Times British Colonies Review — Times Br Col R
Times British Colonies Review — Times Br Colon Rev
Times Educational Supplement — ITES
Times Educational Supplement — TES
Times Educational Supplement — Times Ednl Supp
Times Educational Supplement — Times Educ Supp
Times Health Supplement [*London*] — THS
Times Higher Education Supplement — THES
Times Higher Education Supplement — Times Higher Ed Supp
Times Higher Education Supplement — Times Higher Educ Supp
Times Higher Education Supplement — Times Higher Educ Suppl
Times Literary Supplement — GTLS
Times Literary Supplement — Times L
Times Literary Supplement — Times Lit Supp
Times Literary Supplement — Times Lit Suppl
Times Literary Supplement [*London*] — TLS
Times Literary Supplement (London) — LTimesLS
Times (London) — Times (Lond)
Times of India Annual — TIA
Times of India Annual [*Bombay*] — Times Ind A
Times of the Americas — TA
Times of Zambia — TZ
Times Review of Industry — Times R Ind
Times Review of Industry — Times Rev Ind
Times Review of Industry and Technology — Times R Ind & Tech
Times Science Review — Times Sci Rev
Times Science Review — TSRVA
Times Tribune — Times Trib
Times Weekly Edition [*London*] — TWE
Times-Picayune — Time-Picay
Timisoara. Institutul Politehnic "Traian Vuia." Buletinul Stiintific si Tehnic. Seria Chimie — Timisoara Inst Politeh Traian Vuia Bul Stiint Teh Ser Chim
Timisoara Medicala [*Romania*] — Timisoara Med
Tin and Its Uses — Tin Uses
Tin International [*London*] — TIA
Tin International — Tin Int
Tin International — Tin Inter
Tin International — Tin Intern
Tin News — TN
Tin News. Accurate Information on World Tin Production, Prices, Marketing Developments, and New Uses and Applications — TNI
Tin Research Institute (Greenford, England). Publication — Tin Res Inst (Greenford Engl) Publ
Tinbergen Institute Research Series — Tinbergen Inst Res Ser
Tingo Maria, Peru. Estacion Experimental Agricola. Boletin — Tingo Maria Peru Est Exp Agric Bol
Tin-Printer and Box Maker — Tin Print Box Mkr
TINS. Trends in Neurosciences — TINS Trends Neurosci
TINS. Trends in Neurosciences — TNSCDR
Tinsley's Magazine — Tinsley
Tip Fakultesi Mecmuasi. Istanbul Universitesi — Tip Fak Mecm
TIPRO [*Texas Independent Producers and Royalty Owners Association*] **Reporter** — TIPRO Rep
Tiraspol'skii Gosudarstvennyi Pedagogiceskii Institut Imeni T. G. Sevcenko. Ucenyi Zapiski — Tiraspol Gos Ped Inst Ucen Zap
Tire Review — Tire Rev
Tire Review. 1986 Sourcebook and Directory — Tire Rev D
Tire Science and Technology — Tire Sci Technol
Tiroler Heimat — TiH
Tiroler Heimat. Jahrbuch fuer Geschichte und Volkskunde de Tirois — TH
Tiroler Heimatblaetter — T Hbl
Tiroler Jahrbuch — TirJ
Tiroler Landwirthschaftliche Blaetter — Tiroler Landw Blaett
TISCO [*Tata Iron & Steel Company*] **Review** — TISCO Rev
TISCO [*Tata Iron & Steel Company*] **Technical Journal** — TISCO
Tishreen University Journal for Studies and Scientific Research — Tishreen Univ J Stud Sci Res
Tissue Antigens — Tissue Anti
Tissue Engineering — Tissue Eng
Tissue Reactions — IJTEDP
Tissue Reactions — Tissue React
TIT [*Tower International Technomedical*] **Journal of Life Sciences** — TIT J Lif
TIT [*Tower International Technomedical*] **Journal of Life Sciences** — TIT J Life Sci
Title News — TN
Tituli Asiae Minoris — TAM
Tituli Calymnii — Tit Calymn
Tituli Camirenses — T Camir
Tituli Camirenses — TC
Tituli Camirenses — Tit Cam
TIZ [*Tonindustrie-Zeitung*] **International** — TIZ Int
TIZ International Magazine for Powder and Bulk — TIZ Int Mag Powder Bulk
TIZ. Tonindustrie-Zeitung — TTZED
Tjurkologiceskij Sbornik — TSb
Tlalocan: A Journal of Source Materials on the Native Cultures of Mexico — TM
Tlalocan: A Journal of Source Materials on the Native Cultures of Mexico — TMS
TLS. Times Literary Supplement — Times L Suppl
TMPM. Tschermaks Mineralogische und Petrographische Mitteilungen — TMPM Tschermaks Mineral Petrogr Mitt
TNO [*Nederlands Centrale Organisatie voor Toegepast-Natuurwetenschappelijk Onderzoek*] **Division for Nutrition and Food Research TNO. Report** — TNO Div Nutr Food Res TNO Rep
TNO [*Nederlands Centrale Organisatie voor Toegepast-Natuurwetenschappelijk Onderzoek*] **Project** — TNO Proj
Tobacco — Tob
Tobacco [*New York*] — TOBAA8
Tobacco Abstracts — Tob Abstr
Tobacco Abstracts — Tob Abstracts
Tobacco Control — Tob Control
Tobacco Intelligence — TI
Tobacco International — TI
Tobacco International — Tobacco
Tobacco International (New York) — Tob Int (NY)
Tobacco Journal — Tobacco J
Tobacco Leaf — Tob Leaf
Tobacco Manufacturers' Standing Committee. Research Papers — Tob Manuf Standing Comm Res Pap
Tobacco Observer — TO
Tobacco Reporter — TR
Tobacco Research — Tob Res
Tobacco Research Board of Rhodesia. Bulletin — Tob Res Board Rhod Bull
Tobacco Research Council. Research Paper [*England*] — Tob Res Counc Res Pap
Tobacco Research Council. Research Paper — TRCRA
Tobacco Science — Tob Sci
Tobacco Science — TOSCA
Tocklai Experimental Station. Advisory Bulletin — Tocklai Exp Stn Advis Bull
Tocklai Experimental Station. Advisory Leaflet — Tocklai Exp Stn Advis Leafl
Tocnost i Nadeznost Kiberneticeskih Sistem — Tocn i Nadezn Kibernet Sistem
Tocqueville Review / Revue Tocqueville — Tocqueville Rev
Today and Tomorrow in Education — Today & Tomorrow Educ
Today for Tomorrow — Today
Today Technology — Today Technol
Today's Catholic Teacher — Tod Cath Teach
Today's Chiropractic — Todays Chiro
Today's Christian Woman — TCW
Today's Education — TE
Today's Education — Toda Educ
Today's Education — Today's Ed
Today's Education — Todays Educ
Today's Executive — Todays Exec
Today's Filmmaker — Today's Fmkr
Today's Health — TH
Today's Housing Briefs — THB
Today's Japan — TJ
Today's Ministry — Today Min
Today's Nursing Home — Todays Nurs Home
Today's Office — TOF
Today's Parish — Tod Parish
Today's Secretary — Today's Sec
Today's Speech — TS
Today's VD. Venereal Disease Control Problem — Todays VD Vener Dis Control Probl
Todd Memorial Volumes — TMV
Toelichting-Meijers — TM
Toeristenkampioen — TOK
Toertenelmi es Regeszeti Ertesitoe — Toertenelmi Regeszeti Ertes
Toertenelmi Szemle — Toert Szle
Toertenelmi Szemle — TSz
Toho Gakuho — TG
Tohoku Agricultural Research — Tohoku Agr Res
Tohoku Agriculture/Tohoku Nogyo — Tohoku Agric
Tohoku Daigaku Hisuiyoeki Kagaku Kenkyusho Hokoku — TDHYA
Tohoku Gakuin Daigaku Ronshu [*North Japan College Review: Essays and Studies in English Language and Literature*] — TGR
Tohoku Geophysical Journal. Science Reports of the Tohoku University. Fifth Series — Tohoku Geophys J Sci Rep Tohoku Univ Fifth Ser
Tohoku Imperial University Technology Reports [*Japan*] — Tohoku Imp Univ Technol Rep
Tohoku Journal of Agricultural Research — Tohoku J Agr Res
Tohoku Journal of Agricultural Research — Tohoku J Agric Res
Tohoku Journal of Experimental Medicine — TJEMA
Tohoku Journal of Experimental Medicine — Toh J Ex Me
Tohoku Journal of Experimental Medicine — Tohoku J Exp Med
Tohoku Mathematical Journal — Tohoku Math
Tohoku Mathematical Journal — Tohoku Math J
Tohoku Mathematical Journal. Second Series — Tohoku Math J 2
Tohoku Mathematical Publications — Tohoku Math Publ
Tohoku Medical Journal — Tohoku Med J
Tohoku Nogyo Shikenjo Kenkyu Hokoku — TNSKA
Tohoku Psychologica Folia — Tohoku Psychol Folia
Tohoku Psychologica Folia — TPSFA
Tohoku University. Institute for Agricultural Research. Reports — Tohoku Univ Inst Agric Res Rep

Tohoku University. Science Reports. Geology — Tohoku Univ Sci Repts Geology
Tohoku University. Science Reports. Series 2. Geology — Tohoku Univ Sci Rep Ser 2
Tohoku University. Science Reports. Series 3. Mineralogy, Petrology, and Economic Geology — Tohoku Univ Sci Rep Ser 3
Tohoku University. Science Reports. Series 5 — Tohoku Univ Sci Rep Ser 5
Toimetised. Eesti NSV Teaduste Akadeemia. Fuusika. Matemaatika — Toim Eesti NSV Tead Akad Fuus Mat
Tokai Daigaku Kiyo Kogakubu — TDKIB
Tokai Journal of Experimental and Clinical Medicine — TJEMD
Tokai Journal of Experimental and Clinical Medicine [*Japan*] — Tokai J Exp Clin Med
Tokai Technological Journal [*Japan*] — Tokai Technol J
Tokai University. Faculty of Engineering. Proceedings — Tokai Univ Fac Eng Proc
Tokai-Kinki National Agricultural Experiment Station. Research Progress Report — Tokai-Kinki Natl Agric Exp Stn Res Prog Rep
Toko-Ginecologia Practica — Tokoginecol Prac
Toko-Ginecologia Practica — Toko-Ginecol Pract
Toksikologiya Novykh Promyshlennykh Khimicheskikh Veshchestv — Toksikol Nov Prom Khim Veshchestv
Tokushima Daigaku Yakugaku Kenkyu Nempo — TDYKA
Tokushima Journal of Experimental Medicine — Tokushima J Exp Med
Tokushuko — TOKSA
Tokyo Astronomical Bulletin — Tokyo Astron Bull
Tokyo Astronomical Bulletin. Series II — Tokyo Astron Bull Ser II
Tokyo Astronomical Observatory. Kiso Information Bulletin — Tokyo Astron Obs Kiso Inf Bull
Tokyo Astronomical Observatory. Report — Tokyo Astron Obs Rep
Tokyo Astronomical Observatory. Time and Latitude Bulletins — Tokyo Astron Obs Time and Latitude Bull
Tokyo Book Development Centre. Newsletter — Tokyo Bk Dev Centre Newsl
Tokyo Conference on Advanced Catalytic Science and Technology — Tokyo Conf Adv Catal Sci Technol
Tokyo Daigaku Jishin Kenkyusho Iho — TDJKA
Tokyo Daigaku Uchu Koku Kenkyusho Hokoku — TDUKA
Tokyo Denki Daigaku Kenkyu Hokoku — RRTCD
Tokyo Denki University. Institute of Information Science and Technology. Research Reports — Res Rep Inst Inform Sci Tech Tokyo Denki Univ
Tokyo Financial Review — Tokyo Fin R
Tokyo Financial Review — WRE
Tokyo Financial Wire [*Database*] — TFW
Tokyo Gailkokugo Daigaku Ronshu [*Area and Cultural Studies*] — TGDR
Tokyo. Imperial University. Faculty of Science. Journal — Imp Univ Tokyo Fac Sci J
Tokyo Institute of Technology. Bulletin — Tokyo Inst Technol Bull
Tokyo Jikeika Medical Journal — Tokyo Jikeika Med J
Tokyo Jikeikai Ika Daigaku Zasshi — TJIDA
Tokyo Joshi Ika Daigaku Zasshi — TJIZA
Tokyo Journal of Mathematics — Tokyo J Math
Tokyo Journal of Medical Sciences — Tokyo J Med Sci
Tokyo Kyoiku Daigaku. Science Reports. Section C. Geology, Mineralogy, and Geography — Tokyo Kyoiku Daigaku Sci Rep Sec C
Tokyo Metropolitan Isotope Centre. Annual Report — Tokyo Metrop Isot Cent Annu Rep
Tokyo Metropolitan Research Institute for Environmental Protection. Annual Report. English Translation — Tokyo Metrop Res Inst Environ Prot Annu Rep Engl Transl
Tokyo Metropolitan University. Geographical Reports — Tokyo Metrop Univ Geogr Rep
Tokyo Municipal News — Tokyo Munic News
Tokyo National Science Museum. Bulletin — Tokyo Natl Sci Mus Bull
Tokyo Newsletter — TYO
Tokyo Nogyo Daigaku Nogaku Shuho — TNDNA
Tokyo Tanabe Quarterly — Tokyo Tanabe Q
Tokyo Toritsu Eisei Kenkyusho Kenkyu Hokoku — TTEKA
Tokyo Toritsu Eisei Kenkyusho Kenkyu Nempo — TRENA
Tokyo. Toyo Bunko [*Oriental Library*]. Research Department. Memoirs — MTB
Tokyo Tungsten Co., Ltd. Technical Review — Tokyo Tungsten Co Ltd Tech Rev
Tokyo University. College of General Education. Scientific Papers — Tokyo Univ Coll Gen Educ Sci Pap
Tokyo University. Earthquake Research Institute. Bulletin — Tokyo Univ Earthquake Research Inst Bull
Tokyo University. Faculty of Engineering. Journal. Series B — Tokyo Univ Fac Eng J Ser B
Tokyo University. Faculty of Science. Journal — Tokyo Univ Faculty Sci Jour
Tokyo Woman's Christian University. Science Reports — Sci Rep Tokyo Woman's Christian Univ
Tokyo-Toritsu Kogyo Shoreikan Hokoku — TTKSA
Toledo Museum of Art. Museum News — Toledo Mus N
Toledo University. Institute of Silicate Research. Information Circular — Toledo Univ Inst Silicate Research Inf Circ
Tolkien Journal — TJ
Tolva. Revista del Trigo. Harina y del Pan — Tolva
Tolvmandsbladet — Tolvmandsbl
Tombs of the Double Axes and Associated Group — TDA
Tombs of the Double Axes and Associated Group — TDoAx
Tomorrow — Tm
Tomskii Gosudarstvennyi Pedagogicheskii Institut. Uchenye Zapiski — Tomsk Gos Pedagog Inst Uch Zap
Tomskii Gosudarstvennyi Universitet Imeni V. V. Kuibyseva. Ucenye Zapiski — Tomsk Gos Univ Ucen Zap
Tonan Ajia Kenkyu [*Southeast Asia Studies*] — TAK
Tonindustrie-Zeitung — Tonind Zeitung
Tonindustrie-Zeitung und Keramische Rundschau — Tonind-Ztg Keram Rundsch
Tonindustrie-Zeitung und Keramische Rundschau — TZKRA
Tonindustrie-Zeitung und Keramische Rundschau. Zentralblatt fuer das Gesamtgebiet der Steine und Erden — TIZ
Tool and Die Journal — Tool Die J
Tool and Manufacturing Engineer — Tool & Mfg Eng
Tool and Manufacturing Engineer — Tool Mfg Eng
Tool Engineer — Tool Eng
Tooling and Production — Tool and Prod
Tooling and Production — Tool Prod
Tooling and Production — Tooling P
Tooling and Production — TOPRA
Tools and Tillage — T & T
Tools and Weapons Illustrated by the Egyptian Collection University College. London — TW
Top Management Abstracts — TMA
Top Management Abstracts — Top Manage Abstr
Top of the News — TN
Top of the News — Top News
Topical Meeting on New Horizons in Radiation Protection and Shielding — Top Meet New Horiz Radiat Prot Shielding
Topical Problems in Psychiatry and Neurology — Top Probl Psychiatry Neurol
Topical Problems of Psychotherapy — Top Probl Psychother
Topical Problems of Psychotherapy — TPPYA
Topical Report. New Brunswick Mineral Resources Branch — Top Rep NB Miner Resour Branch
Topical Reviews in Haematology — Top Rev Haematol
Topical Reviews in Haematology — TRHADS
Topics in Allergy and Clinical Immunology — Top Allerg Clin Immun
Topics in Antibiotic Chemistry — Top Antibiot Chem
Topics in Applied Physics — Top Appl Phys
Topics in Applied Physics — Topics Appl Phys
Topics in Astrophysics and Space Physics — Top Astrophys Space Phys
Topics in Automatic Chemical Analysis — Top Autom Chem Anal
Topics in Bioelectrochemistry and Bioenergetics — Top Bioelectrochem Bioenerg
Topics in Catalysis — Top Catal
Topics in Chemical Mutagenesis — TCMUE9
Topics in Chemical Mutagenesis — Top Chem Mutagen
Topics in Clinical Nursing — Top Clin Nurs
Topics in Clinical Nursing — Topics Clin Nurs
Topics in Clinical Nutrition — Top Clin Nutr
Topics in Computer Mathematics — Topics in Comput Math
Topics in Culture Learning — TICL
Topics in Current Chemistry — Top Curr Chem
Topics in Current Chemistry — TPCCA
Topics in Current Physics — Top Curr Phys
Topics in Current Physics — Topics Current Phys
Topics in Discrete Mathematics — Topics Discrete Math
Topics in Emergency Medicine — Top Emerg Med
Topics in Engineering — Topics Engrg
Topics in Environmental Health [*Elsevier Book Series*] — TEH
Topics in Environmental Health — Top Environ Health
Topics in Enzyme and Fermentation Biotechnology — Top Enzyme Ferment Biotechnol
Topics in F-Element Chemistry — Top F Elem Chem
Topics in Fluorescence Spectroscopy — Top Fluoresc Spectrosc
Topics in Gastroenterology — TOGAD2
Topics in Gastroenterology — Top Gastroenterol
Topics in Geobiology — Top Geobiol
Topics in Geriatrics — Top Geriatr
Topics in Health Care Financing — THC
Topics in Health Care Financing — THCF
Topics in Health Care Financing — Top Health Care Financ
Topics in Health Care Materials Management — THM
Topics in Health Record Management — Top Health Rec Manage
Topics in Health Record Management — TRM
Topics in Hormone Chemistry — Top Horm Chem
Topics in Hospital Pharmacy Management — Top Hosp Pharm Manage
Topics in Human Genetics — Top Hum Genet
Topics in Infectious Diseases — Top Infect Dis
Topics in Information Systems — Topics Inform Systems
Topics in Inorganic and General Chemistry [*Elsevier Book Series*] — TIGC
Topics in Lipid Chemistry — Top Lipid Chem
Topics in Magnetic Resonance Imaging — Top Magn Reson Imaging
Topics in Mathematical Physics — Top Math Phys
Topics in Medicinal Chemistry — Top Med Chem
Topics in Molecular and Structural Biology — Top Mol Struct Biol
Topics in Molecular Organization and Engineering — Top Mol Organ Eng
Topics in Molecular Pharmacology — Top Mol Pharmacol
Topics in Ocular Pharmacology and Toxicology — Top Ocular Pharmacol Toxicol
Topics in Paediatrics — Top Paediatr
Topics in Paediatrics — TPAEDP
Topics in Perinatal Medicine — Top Perinat Med
Topics in Perinatal Medicine — TPEMDZ
Topics in Pharmaceutical Sciences — Top Pharm Sci
Topics in Phosphorus Chemistry — Top Phosphorus Chem
Topics in Photosynthesis — Top Photosynth
Topics in Photosynthesis [*Elsevier Book Series*] — TP
Topics in Physical Chemistry — Top Phys Chem
Topics in Stereochemistry — Top Stereochem
Topics in Sulfur Chemistry — Top Sulfur Chem
Topics in Therapeutics — Top Therap
Topics in Vaccine Adjuvant Research — Top Vaccine Adjuvant Res

Topographical Bibliography of Ancient Egyptian Hieroglyphic Texts, Reliefs, and Paintings — TB
Topographie und Zytologie Neurosekretorischer Systeme — Topogr Zytol Neurosekretorischer Syst
Topographie und Zytologie Neurosekretorischer Systeme — TZNSDW
Topological Methods in Nonlinear Analysis — Topol Methods Nonlinear Anal
Topology and Its Applications — Topology Appl
Topology Proceedings — Topology Proc
Tops in Science Fiction — TIS
Torfnachrichten der Forschungs- und Werbestelle fuer Torf — Torfnachrichten Forsch Werbestelle Torf
Torfyanaya Promyshlennost — Torf Promst
Torfyanaya Promyshlennost — TORPA
Torfyanoe Delo — Torf Delo
Tori. Bulletin of the Ornithological Society of Japan — Tori Bull Ornithol Soc Jpn
Torino Universita. Istituto Geologico. Pubblicazioni — Torino Univ Ist Geol Pub
Toronto Life — Tor Life
Toronto Native Times — TONT
Toronto Quarterly — TQ
Toronto Stock Exchange 300 Index and Stock Statistics [*Database*] — TSE300
Toronto University. Department of Mechanical Engineering. Technical Publication Series — Toronto Univ Dep Mech Eng Tech Publ Ser
Toronto University. Institute for Aerospace Studies. UTIAS Report — Toronto Univ Inst Aerosp Stud UTIAS Rep
Toronto University. Institute for Aerospace Studies. UTIAS Review — TIRVB
Toronto University. Institute for Aerospace Studies. UTIAS Review — Toronto Univ Inst Aerosp Stud UTIAS Rev
Toronto University. Institute for Aerospace Studies. UTIAS Technical Note — Toronto Univ Inst Aerosp Stud UTIAS Tech Note
Toronto University Quarterly — Toronto Univ Qtr
Toronto University Studies. Geological Series — Toronto Univ Studies G S
Torre — Tor
Torreia Nueva Serie — Torreia Nueva Ser
Torrey Botanical Club. Bulletin — Torrey Bot Club Bull
Torry Research — Torry Res
Torry Research Station (Aberdeen, Scotland). Annual Report — Torry Res Stn (Aberdeen Scotl) Annu Rep
Torry Research Station. Annual Report on the Handling and Preservation of Fish and Fish Products — Torry Res Stn Annu Rep Handl Preserv Fish Fish Prod
Toshiba Review — TOREA
Toshiba Review [*Japan*] — Toshiba Rev
Toshiba Review (International Edition) — Toshiba Rev (Int Ed)
Toshokan Kenkyu — Tosh Kenk
Toshokan Zasshi — Tosh Zass
Toshokan-Kai — Tosh-Kai
Total Information — Total Inf
Totius Latinitatis Lexicon — TLL
Totius Latinitatis Lexicon — Tot Lat Lexikon
Toulouse. Faculte des Sciences. Annales Mathematiques. Serie 5 — Ann Fac Sci Toulouse Math Ser 5
Toulouse Faculte des Sciences. Annales. Mathematiques. Serie 6 — Ann Fac Sci Toulouse Math 6
Toulouse Medical — Toulouse Med
T'oung Pao — TP
T'oung Pao. Archives — TPA
Tour du Monde — TM
TourBase Hotel-/Unterkunftsdaten [*Database*] — TBH
TourBase Orstdaten [*Database*] — TBO
Tourbe Philosophique — Tourbe Philos
Tourism Australia — Tourism Aust
Tourism in England — Tourism Engl
Tourism Intelligence Quarterly — Tourism Intell Q
Tourism Management — TM
Tourist Information Facts and Abstracts [*Database*] — TIFA
Tours Symposium on Nuclear Physics — Tours Symp Nucl Phys
Toute l'Electronique — TOELA
Toute l'Electronique — Toute Electron
Tovaris — Tov
Tovaristvo dlya Poshirennya Politichnikh i Naukovikh Znan Ukrains'koi SSR — Tovar Poshir Polit Nauk Znan Ukr SSR
Toward Revolutionary Art — TRA
Towarzystwo Naukowe Katolickiego Uniwersytet Lubelskiego — TNKUL
Towarzystwo Naukowe Katolickiego Uniwersytet Lubelskiego. Wyklady i Przemowienia [*Lublin*] — TNKULWP
Towarzystwo Naukowe w Toruniu — TNT
Towarzystwo Naukowe w Toruniu. Prace Wydziau Filologiczno-Filosoficznego — TNT-FF
Towarzystwo Naukowe Warszawskie — TNW
Tower Hamlets Local Trade Development — Tower Hamlets Local Trade Dev
Town and Country Journal — T & CJ
Town and Country Journal — TCJ
Town and Country Monthly — ITNC
Town and Country Planning — TCPLA
Town and Country Planning — Town & Country Plan
Town and Country Planning — Town Cntry Plann
Town and Country Planning — Town Ctry Plan
Town and Country Planning — Town Ctry Plann
Town Planning and Local Government Guide — TP & LGG
Town Planning and Local Government Guide — TPG
Town Planning and Local Government Guide — TPLGG
Town Planning Institute. Journal — Town Plan Inst J
Town Planning Institute. Journal — Town Plann Inst J
Town Planning Quarterly [*New Zealand*] — Town Plann Q
Town Planning Quarterly [*New Zealand*] — TPLQ-A
Town Planning Review — Tn Plann Rev
Town Planning Review — Town Plan R
Town Planning Review — Town Plann Rev
Town Planning Review [*United Kingdom*] — Town Planning R
Town Planning Review [*United Kingdom*] — TPLR-A
Town Planning Today — Town Plann Today
Townsman — TO
Townsville Naturalist — Townsville Nat
Toxic and Hazardous Waste Disposal — Toxic Hazard Waste Disposal
Toxic Chemical Release Inventory [*Database*] — TRI
Toxic Materials Transport [*Database*] — TMT
Toxic Regulatory Listings [*Database*] — TOXLIST
Toxic Substance Mechanisms — Toxic Subst Mech
Toxic Substances Control Act Chemical Substances Inventory [*Database*] — TSCA
Toxic Substances Journal — Toxic Subst J
Toxic Substances Journal — TSJ
Toxicity Assessment — Toxicity Assess
Toxicologic Pathology — Toxicol Pathol
Toxicological and Environmental Chemistry — Toxicol Environ Chem
Toxicological and Environmental Chemistry Reviews — Toxicol Environ Chem Rev
Toxicological and Environmental Chemistry Reviews — TXECB
Toxicological European Research — Toxicol Eur Res
Toxicology — TXCYA
Toxicology and Applied Pharmacology — Tox Appl Ph
Toxicology and Applied Pharmacology — Toxic Appl Pharmac
Toxicology and Applied Pharmacology — Toxicol Appl Pharmacol
Toxicology and Applied Pharmacology — TXAPA
Toxicology and Applied Pharmacology. Supplement — Toxicol Appl Pharmacol Suppl
Toxicology and Ecotoxicology News — Toxicol Ecotoxicol News
Toxicology and Industrial Health — Toxicol Ind Health
Toxicology and Risk Assessment. Principles, Methods, and Applications [*monograph*] — Toxicol Risk Assess
Toxicology Annual — Toxicol Annu
Toxicology Letters — Toxicol Lett
Toxicology Letters (Amsterdam) — Toxicol Lett (Amst)
Toxicology Methods — Toxicol Methods
Toxicology Modeling — Toxic Model
Toxicology Modeling — Toxicol Model
Toxicon — TOXIA
Toyama Daigaku Kogakubu Kiyo — BETUA
Toyama University. Mathematics Reports — Math Rep Toyama Univ
Toyo Bungaku Kenkyu [*Studies on Oriental Literature*] — TBK
Toyo Bunka Kenkyushu Kiyo — Toyo Bunka Kenkyu Kiyo
Toyo Bunka Kenyusho Kiyo — TBKK
Toyo Daigaku Kiyo [*Bulletin. Department of Liberal Arts. Tokyo University*] — TDK
Toyo Junior College of Food Technology and Toyo Institute of Food Technology. Research Report [*Japan*] — Toyo Junior Coll Food Technol Toyo Inst Food Technol Res Rep
Toyo Ongaku Kenkyu — Toyo Ongaku
Toyo Shokuhin Kogyo Tanki Daigaku. Toyo Shokuhin Kenkyusho Kenkyu Hokokusho — TSKTA
Toyota Engineering [*Japan*] — Toyota Eng
TPI Report. Tropical Products Institute — TPI Rep Trop Prod Inst
TPI Textil Praxis International — TPI Text Prax Int
Trabajo. Laboratorio de Bioquimica y Quimica Aplicada. Instituto "Alonso Barba" — Trab Lab Bioquim Quim Apl Inst Alonso Barba
Trabajo Social (Chile) — TSC
Trabajo y Prevision Social (Mexico) — Trab Prev Soc Mex
Trabajos Cientificos de la Universidad de Cordoba — Trab Cient Univ Cordoba
Trabajos Compostelanos de Biologia — Trab Compostelanos Biol
Trabajos de Estadistica — Trabajos Estadist
Trabajos de Estadistica — TrabEsta
Trabajos de Estadistica y de Investigacion — Trab Estadistica
Trabajos de Estadistica y de Investigacion Operativa — Trabajos Estadist Investigacion Oper
Trabajos de Geologia — Trab Geol
Trabajos de Geologia. Oviedo Universidad. Facultad de Ciencias — Trab Geol Oviedo Univ Fac Cienc
Trabajos de Matematica [*Argentina*] — Trab Mat
Trabajos de Prehistoria — TP
Trabajos de Prehistoria — Trab Pr Hist
Trabajos de Prehistoria — Trab Preh
Trabajos del Laboratorio de Investigaciones Biologicas de la Universidad de Madrid — Trab Lab Invest Biol Univ Madrid
Trabajos. Departamento de Botanica y Fisiologia Vegetal. Universidad de Madrid — Trab Dep Bot Fisiol Veg Univ Madrid
Trabajos. Estacion Agricola Experimental de Leon — Trab Estac Agric Exp Leon
Trabajos. Instituto Bernardino de Sahagun — Trab Inst Bernardino Sahagun
Trabajos. Instituto Cajal de Investigaciones Biologicas — Trab Inst Cajal Invest Biol
Trabajos. Instituto de Economia y Producciones Ganaderas del Ebro — Trab Inst Econ Prod Ganad Ebro
Trabajos. Instituto de Fisiologia. Faculdade de Medicina. Universidade do Lisboa — Trab Inst Fisiol Fac Med Univ Lisboa
Trabajos. Instituto Espanol de Entomologia — Trab Inst Esp Entomol
Trabajos. Instituto Espanol de Oceanografia — Trab Inst Esp Oceanogr
Trabajos. Instituto Nacional de Ciencias Medicas (Madrid) — Trab Inst Nac Cienc Med (Madrid)
Trabajos Investigacion Operativa — Trabajos Investigacion Oper
Trabajos Presentados al Quinto Congreso Medico Latino-Americano — Trab 5 Cong Med Latino-Am
Trabajos y Comunicaciones — TrC

Trabajos y Comunicaciones (La Plata, Argentina) — Trab Comunic La Plata
Trabajos y Conferencias. Seminario de Estudios Americanistas Facultad de Filosofia y Letras — Trab Y Conf
Trabajos y Dias — TyD
Trabalho e Seguro Social (Rio de Janeiro) — Trab Segur Soc Rio
Trabalhos. Centro de Botanica. Junta de Investigacoes do Ultramar — Trab Cent Bot Junta Invest Ultramar
Trabalhos da Associacao de Filosofia Natural — TAFN
Trabalhos de Antropologia e Etnologia — TAE
Trabalhos de Antropologia e Etnologia — Trab Antropol Etnol
Trabalhos de Investigacao 79 — Trab Investigacao 79
Trabalhos de Investigacao 80 — Trab Investigacao 80
Trabalhos do Departamento de Matematica — Trab Dep Mat
Trabalhos e Pesquisas. Instituto de Nutricao. Universidade do Brasil — Trab Pesqui Inst Nutr Univ Bras
Trabalhos. Instituto Oceanografico. Universidade do Recife — Trab Inst Oceanogr Univ Recife
Trabalhos Oceanograficos. Universidade Federal de Pernambuco — Trab Oceanogr Univ Fed Pernambuco
Trabalhos. Sociedade Portuguesa de Antropologia e Etnologia — Trab Antrop Etnol
Trace Analysis — Trace Anal
Trace Elements in Medicine — Tr Elem Med
Trace Elements Science — Trace Elem Sci
Trace Metal Metabolism (Tokyo) — Trace Met Metab Tokyo
Trace Metals in the Environment — Trace Met Environ
Trace Substances in Environmental Health — PUMTA
Trace Substances in Environmental Health — Trace Subst Environ Health
Trace Substances in Environmental Health. Proceedings. University of Missouri. Annual Conference — Trace Subst Environ Health Proc Univ Mo Annu Conf
Tracer's Exogram and Oil and Gas Review — Tracers Exogram Oil Gas Rev
Track and Field Coaches Review — T & F Coaches Rev
Track and Field Quarterly Review — T and F Q Rev
Track and Field Quarterly Review — Track Field Q Rev
Track Coach — T Coach
Track Technique — Track Tech
Track Technique Annual — T Tech
Tracker — Tra
Tractatenblad — Tctbl
Tractatenblad — Trb
Tractatenblad — Trbl
Tractatenblad van het Koninkrijk der Nederlanden — T
Tractatenblad van het Koninkrijk der Nederlanden — TKN
Tractory i Sel Khozmashiny — Tract Sel Khozmashiny
Tracts in Mathematics and Natural Science — Tracts Math Nat Sci
Trade and Commerce — TCM
Trade and Commerce — Trade and Commer
Trade and Commerce — TRCO
Trade and Development — Trade Develop
Trade and Industry — Trade and Ind
Trade and Industry — Trade Ind
Trade and Industry — TRIYA
Trade and Industry Bulletin — Trade Ind Bul
Trade and Industry Index — Trade Ind Index
Trade by Commodities. Market Summaries. Series C. Exports — Trade Commod Mark Summaries C Exports
Trade by Commodities. Market Summaries. Series C. Imports — Trade Commod Mark Summaries C Imports
Trade Cases. Commerce Clearing House — Trade Cas CCH
Trade Channel — TCH
Trade Digest — Trade D
Trade Digest — Trade Dig
Trade Marks Journal — TMJ
Trade Marks Journal — Trade Mks J
Trade News North — Trade News N
Trade Opportunities in Taiwan — TBE
Trade Practices Cases — TPC
Trade Practices Commission. Decisions and Determinations — TPCD
Trade Practices Commission. Decisions and Determinations — TPCDD
Trade Practices Reporting Service — TPRS
Trade Regulation Reporter. Commerce Clearing House — Trade Reg Rep CCH
Trade Review. Swedish Chamber of Commerce for Australia — Trade R
Trade Token Topics — TTT
Trade with Greece — Trad Greec
Trade with Greece (Athens) — TGA
Trade-Mark Reporter — TM Rep
Trade-Mark Reporter — TMR
Trade-Mark Reporter — Trade-Mark Rep
Trademark Reporter — Trademark Rptr
Trades Union Digest — Trades Union D
Tradicao — T
Tradicion. Revista Peruana de Cultura — TRPC
Tradiciones de Guatemala — TDG
Traditio — T
Traditio — Trad
Traditional Kent Buildings — Traditional Kent Bldgs
Traditional Music — Tr M
Traditional Music — Trad Mus
Traditiones. Zbornik Instituta za Slovensko Narodopisje — TZI
Traduction Automatique — TA
Traduction Automatique [*The Hague*] — TrA
Traduction Automatique Informations — TA Inf
Traduction. Departement d'Exploitation et Utilisation des Bois. Universite Laval — Trad Dep Exploit Util Bois Univ Laval
Traductions de Textes Persans — Trad Textes Persans
Traduit du Russe. Biologie — Traduit Russe Biol
Traduit du Russe. Mathematiques — Traduit Russe Math
Traduit du Russe. Physique — Traduit Russe Phys
Traffic Digest and Review — Traffic Dig Rev
Traffic Education — Traff Educ
Traffic Engineering — Traff Engng
Traffic Engineering — Traffic Eng
Traffic Engineering [*United States*] — TRNGA
Traffic Engineering and Control [*England*] — TENCA
Traffic Engineering and Control — Traff Engng Control
Traffic Engineering and Control — Traffic Eng & Control
Traffic Engineering and Control — Traffic Eng Contr
Traffic Management — TM
Traffic Management — TMA
Traffic Management — Traffic Manage
Traffic Quarterly — Traff Q
Traffic Quarterly — Traffic Q
Traffic Quarterly — Traffic Qly
Traffic Quarterly — TRAQA
Traffic Safety — Traffic Saf
Traffic Safety — TSAFA
Traffic Safety Annual Report — Traffic Saf Ann Rep
Traffic Safety Research Review — Traffic Saf Res Rev
Traffic World — TRWOA
Trafik og Teknik — Traf o Tekn
Tragicorum Graecorum Fragmenta [*Goettingen*] — T Gr F
Tragicorum Graecorum Fragmenta [*Nauck*] — TGF
Tragicorum Graecorum Fragmenta [*Nauck*] — Trag Graec Frag
Tragicorum Romanorum Fragmenta — TRF
Trailer Boats — ITBO
Trailer Life — ITLI
Training — TBI
Training — TRA
Training — Train
Training and Development in Australia — Train Dev Aust
Training and Development Journal — JAE
Training and Development Journal — STD
Training and Development Journal — TDJ
Training and Development Journal — Train & Devel J
Training and Development Journal — Train Dev J
Training and Development Journal — Training & Dev J
Training and Development Organizations Directory — TDOD
Training for Agriculture and Rural Development — Train Agric Rural Dev
Training Officer — Train Off
Training School Bulletin — Train Sch B
Trains — ITRM
Traite d'Anatomie Vegetale — Traite Anat Veg
Traite des Monnaies Grecques et Romaines — TMGR
Traite des Monnaies Grecques et Romaines — Traite
Traite des Nouvelles Technologies — Traite Nouvelles Tech
Traitement Thermique — Trait Therm
Traitement Thermique — TRTHB
Traitements de Surface — Trait Surf
Traktor und die Landmaschine — Trakt Landmasch
Traktory i Sel'khozmashiny [*Former USSR*] — Trak Sel'khozmashiny
Traktory i Sel'khozmashiny — Trakt Sel'khozmash
Traktory i Sel'khozmashiny — TRASA
Transaction. Royal Society of Canada. Section 4. Geological Sciences Including Mineralogy — Trans R Soc Can Sect 4
Transaction. Royal Society of South Africa — TRSAA
Transaction. Thoroton Society of Nottinghamshire — Trans Thoroton Soc Nottinghamshire
Transaction. Worcestershire Archaeological Society — Trans Worcs Arch Soc
Transactiones Societatis Pathologicae Japonicae [*Japan*] — Trans Soc Pathol Jpn
Transactions. 8th International Congress of Soil Science — Trans 8th Int Congr Soil Sci
Transactions. Academy of Science of St. Louis — Trans Acad Sci St Louis
Transactions. Actuarial Society of Australia and New Zealand — Trans Act Soc Aust & NZ
Transactions. Actuarial Society of South Africa — Trans Actuar Soc S Afr
Transactions. Agricultural Engineering Society (Tokyo) — Trans Agric Engng Soc (Tokyo)
Transactions. AIChE [*American Institute of Chemical Engineers*] — Trans AIChE
Transactions. AIME [*American Institute of Mining, Metallurgical, and Petroleum Engineers*] **Metallurgical Society** — Trans AIME Metall Soc
Transactions. Albany Institute — Trans Albany Inst
Transactions. All-India Institute of Mental Health — Trans All-India Inst Ment Health
Transactions. All-Union Scientific Research Institute for Vegetable Oils and Margarine — Trans All Union Sci Res Inst Veg Oils Margarine
Transactions. All-Union Scientific Research Institute of the Confectionery Industry — Trans All Union Sci Res Inst Confect Ind
Transactions. American Academy of Ophthalmology and Oto-Laryngology — TAAOA
Transactions. American Academy of Ophthalmology and Otolaryngology — Tr Am Acad Ophth
Transactions. American Academy of Ophthalmology and Oto-Laryngology — Trans Am Acad Ophthalmol Oto-Laryngol
Transactions. American Academy of Ophthalmology and Otolaryngology — Trans Amer Acad Ophthalmol Otolaryngol
Transactions. American Association of Cereal Chemists — Trans Amer Ass Cereal Chem
Transactions. American Association of Cost Engineers — Trans AACE

Transactions. American Association of Cost Engineers — Trans Am Assoc Cost Eng
Transactions. American Association of Genito-Urinary Surgeons — TAAGA
Transactions. American Association of Genito-Urinary Surgeons — Tr Am Ass Genito-Urin Surg
Transactions. American Association of Genito-Urinary Surgeons — Trans Am Assoc Genito-Urin Surg
Transactions. American Association of Obstetricians and Gynecologists — Trans Am Assoc Obstet Gynecol
Transactions. American Association of Obstetricians, Gynecologists, and Abdominal Surgeons — Trans Am Assoc Obstet Gynecol Abdom Surg
Transactions. American Brewing Institute — Trans Am Brew Inst
Transactions. American Broncho-Esophagological Association — Trans Am Broncho-Esophagol Assoc
Transactions. American Ceramic Society — Trans Am Ceram Soc
Transactions. American Clinical and Climatological Association — Trans Am Clin Climatol Assoc
Transactions. American College of Cardiology — Trans Am Coll Cardiol
Transactions. American Crystallographic Association — Trans Am Crystallogr Assoc
Transactions. American Electrochemical Society — Trans Am Electroch Soc
Transactions. American Electrochemical Society — Trans Amer Electro-Chem Soc
Transactions. American Entomological Society — Trans Am Ent Soc
Transactions. American Entomological Society (Philadelphia) — Trans Am Entomol Soc (Phila)
Transactions. American Fisheries Society — T Am Fish S
Transactions. American Fisheries Society — TAFSA
Transactions. American Fisheries Society — Tr Am Fish Soc
Transactions. American Fisheries Society — Trans Am Fish Soc
Transactions. American Fisheries Society — Trans Am Fisheries Soc
Transactions. American Foundrymen's Association [*Later, American Foundrymen's Society*]. Quarterly — Trans Am Foundrymen's Assoc Q
Transactions. American Foundrymen's Society — Trans Amer Foundrymen's Soc
Transactions. American Geophysical Union — T Am Geophy
Transactions. American Geophysical Union — TAGUA
Transactions. American Geophysical Union — Trans Am Geophys Union
Transactions. American Geophysical Union — Trans Amer Geophys Union
Transactions. American Goiter Association — Trans Am Goiter Assoc
Transactions. American Gynecological Society — Trans Am Gynecol Soc
Transactions. American Institute of Chemical Engineers — Trans Am Inst Chem Eng
Transactions. American Institute of Electrical Engineers — AIEE Trans
Transactions. American Institute of Electrical Engineers — Trans Am Inst Electr Eng
Transactions. American Institute of Electrical Engineers. Part 1. Communication and Electronics — Trans Am Inst Electr Eng Part 1
Transactions. American Institute of Electrical Engineers. Part 2. Applications and Industry — Trans Am Inst Electr Eng Part 2
Transactions. American Institute of Electrical Engineers. Part 3. Power Apparatus and Systems — Trans Am Inst Electr Eng Part 3
Transactions. American Institute of Industrial Engineers — Trans Am Inst Ind Eng
Transactions. American Institute of Mining and Metallurgical Engineers — Trans Am Inst Min Metall Eng
Transactions. American Institute of Mining and Metallurgical Engineers — Trans Am Inst Min Metall Engn
Transactions. American Institute of Mining Engineers — Trans Am Inst Min Eng
Transactions. American Institute of Mining, Metallurgical, and Petroleum Engineers — Trans Am Inst Min Metall Pet Eng
Transactions. American Institution of Electrical Engineers — TrAIEE
Transactions. American Lodge of Research Free and Accepted Masons — Trans Am Res Free Acc Masons
Transactions. American Mathematical Society — T Am Math S
Transactions. American Mathematical Society — TAMTA
Transactions. American Mathematical Society — Trans Am Math Soc
Transactions. American Mathematical Society — Trans Amer Math Soc
Transactions. American Medical Association — Trans Amer Med Assoc
Transactions. American Microscopical Society — T Am Micros
Transactions. American Microscopical Society — TAMSA
Transactions. American Microscopical Society — Tr Am Micr Soc
Transactions. American Microscopical Society — Trans Am Microsc Soc
Transactions. American Microscopical Society — Trans Amer Microscop Soc
Transactions. American Neurological Association — TANAA
Transactions. American Neurological Association — Tr Am Neurol A
Transactions. American Neurological Association — Trans Am Neurol Assoc
Transactions. American Nuclear Society — T Am Nucl S
Transactions. American Nuclear Society — TANSA
Transactions. American Nuclear Society — Trans Am Nucl Soc
Transactions. American Nuclear Society — Trans Amer Nucl Soc
Transactions. American Nuclear Society. Supplement — Trans Am Nucl Soc Suppl
Transactions. American Ophthalmological Society — Tr Am Ophth Soc
Transactions. American Ophthalmological Society — Trans Am Ophthalmol Soc
Transactions. American Otological Society — Trans Am Otol Soc
Transactions. American Philological Assocation — TrAPhA
Transactions. American Philological Association — TAPHA
Transactions. American Philological Association — Trans A Ph A
Transactions. American Philological Association — Trans Act
Transactions. American Philological Association — Trans Amer Phil Ass
Transactions. American Philological Association — Trans Amer Philol Assoc
Transactions. American Philological Association — Trans APA
Transactions. American Philosophical Society — T Am Phil S
Transactions. American Philosophical Society — TA Philos Soc
Transactions. American Philosophical Society — TAPhS
Transactions. American Philosophical Society — TAPS
Transactions. American Philosophical Society — Trans Am Philos Soc
Transactions. American Society for Artificial Internal Organs — ASAIO Trans
Transactions. American Society for Artificial Internal Organs — T Am S Art
Transactions. American Society for Artificial Internal Organs — Tr Am Soc Artific Int Organs
Transactions. American Society for Artificial Internal Organs — Trans Am Soc Art Int Org
Transactions. American Society for Artificial Internal Organs — Trans Am Soc Artif Intern Organs
Transactions. American Society for Metals — Trans Am Soc Met
Transactions. American Society for Steel Treating — Trans Am Soc Steel Treat
Transactions. American Society of Agricultural Engineers — Trans Am Soc Agric Engrs
Transactions. American Society of Agricultural Engineers. General Edition — Trans Am Soc Agric Eng Gen Ed
Transactions. American Society of Agricultural Engineers. General Edition — Trans Am Soc Agric Engrs Gen Edn
Transactions. American Society of Civil Engineers — Trans Am Soc Civ Eng
Transactions. American Society of Heating and Air-Conditioning Engineers — Trans Am Soc Heat Air-Cond Eng
Transactions. American Society of Mechanical Engineers — Trans ASME
Transactions. American Society of Mechanical Engineers. Journal of Applied Mechanics — Trans ASME J Appl Mech
Transactions. American Society of Mechanical Engineers. Journal of Biomechanical Engineering — Trans ASME J Biomech Engng
Transactions. American Society of Mechanical Engineers. Journal of Dynamic Systems Measurement and Control — Trans ASME J Dyn Syst Meas & Control
Transactions. American Society of Mechanical Engineers. Journal of Energy Resources Technology — Trans ASME J Energy Resour Technol
Transactions. American Society of Mechanical Engineers. Journal of Engineering for Industry — Trans ASME J Engng Ind
Transactions. American Society of Mechanical Engineers. Journal of Engineering for Power — Trans ASME J Engng Power
Transactions. American Society of Mechanical Engineers. Journal of Engineering Materials and Technology — Trans ASME J Engng Mater & Technol
Transactions. American Society of Mechanical Engineers. Journal of Fluids Engineering — Trans ASME J Fluids Engng
Transactions. American Society of Mechanical Engineers. Journal of Heat Transfer — Trans ASME J Heat Transfer
Transactions. American Society of Mechanical Engineers. Journal of Lubrication Technology — Trans ASME J Lubr Technol
Transactions. American Society of Mechanical Engineers. Journal of Mechanical Design — Trans ASME J Mech Des
Transactions. American Society of Mechanical Engineers. Journal of Pressure Vessel Technology — Trans ASME J Pressure Vessel Technol
Transactions. American Society of Mechanical Engineers. Journal of Solar Energy Engineering — Trans ASME J Sol Energy Engng
Transactions. American Society of Ophthalmologic and Otolaryngologic Allergy — Trans Am Soc Ophthalmol Otolaryngol Allergy
Transactions. American Society of Tropical Medicine — Tr Am Soc Trop Med
Transactions. American Therapeutic Society — Trans Am Ther Soc
Transactions. American Urological Association — Trans Am Urol Assoc
Transactions. Ancient Monuments Society — Trans Ancient Monuments Soc
Transactions and Journal. British Ceramic Society — T J Br Cer
Transactions and Journal. British Ceramic Society — Trans and J Br Ceram Soc
Transactions and Journal. British Ceramic Society — Trans J Br Ceram Soc
Transactions and Journal. British Ceramic Society — Trans J Brit Ceram Soc
Transactions and Journal. Plastics Institute [*England*] — Trans J Plast Inst
Transactions and Papers. Institute of British Geographers — Trans Pap Inst Brit Geogr
Transactions and Proceedings. American Philological Association — TAA
Transactions and Proceedings. American Philological Association — TAPA
Transactions and Proceedings. American Philological Association — TAPhA
Transactions and Proceedings. American Philological Association — TP A Ph A
Transactions and Proceedings. American Philological Association — TPAPA
Transactions and Proceedings. American Philological Association — Tr A Ph A
Transactions and Proceedings. American Philological Association — Trans Proc Amer Philol Ass
Transactions and Proceedings. American Philological Association — Transact Am Phil Ass
Transactions and Proceedings. American Philological Association — Transact Proceed Amer Philol Assoc
Transactions and Proceedings. Birmingham Archaeological Society — Trans Proc Birmingham Arch Soc
Transactions and Proceedings. Botanical Society Edinburgh — Trans Proc Bot Soc Edinburgh
Transactions and Proceedings. Botanical Society of Edinburgh — Trans Bot Soc Edinb
Transactions and Proceedings. Botanical Society of Edinburgh — Trans Proc Bot Soc Edinb
Transactions and Proceedings. Geological Society of South Africa — Trans Proc Geol Soc S Afr
Transactions and Proceedings. Japan Society (London) — TPJSL
Transactions and Proceedings. Palaeontological Society of Japan — Trans Proc Palaeontol Soc Jap
Transactions and Proceedings. Palaeontological Society of Japan. New Series — Trans Proc Palaeontol Soc Japan New Ser
Transactions and Proceedings. Palaeontological Society of Japan. New Series — Trans Proc Palaeontol Soc Jpn New Ser

Transactions and Proceedings. Perthshire Society of Natural Science — Trans Proc Perthshire Soc Natur Sci
Transactions and Proceedings. Philosophical Institute of Victoria — Trans Proc Philos Inst Victoria
Transactions and Proceedings. Royal Society of Literature — TPRSL
Transactions and Proceedings. Royal Society of South Australia — Trans Proc R Soc South Aust
Transactions and Proceedings. Torquay Natural History Society — Trans Proc Torquay Natur Hist Soc
Transactions and Studies. College of Physicians of Philadelphia — Tr Coll Physicians Phila
Transactions and Studies. College of Physicians of Philadelphia — Trans Stud Coll Physicians Phila
Transactions and Studies. College of Physicians of Philadelphia — TSCPA
Transactions. Anglesey Antiquarian Society and Field Club — Trans Anglesey Antiq Soc
Transactions. Anglesey Antiquarian Society and Field Club — Trans Anglesey Antiq Soc Fld Club
Transactions. Annual Anthracite Conference of Lehigh University — Trans Ann Anthracite Conf Lehigh Univ
Transactions. Annual Conference. Canadian Nuclear Society — Trans Annu Conf Can Nucl Soc
Transactions. Annual Conference. Electric Supply Authority Engineers' Institute of New Zealand, Inc. — Trans Electr Supply Eng Inst
Transactions. Annual Meeting. Allen O. Whipple Surgical Society — Trans Annu Meet Allen O Whipple Surg Soc
Transactions. Annual Meeting. American Laryngological Association — Trans Ann Meet Am Laryngol Assoc
Transactions. Annual Technical Conference. American Society for Quality Control — Trans Annu Tech Conf Am Soc Qual Control
Transactions. Annual Technical Conference. American Society for Quality Control — Trans Annu Tech Conf ASQC
Transactions. Annual Technical Conference. Society of Vacuum Coaters — Trans Annu Tech Conf Soc Vac Coaters
Transactions. Architectural and Archaeological Society of Durham and Northumberland — Trans Architect Archaeol Soc Durham Northumberland
Transactions. Architectural Institute of Japan — Trans Architect Inst Jpn
Transactions. ASAE [*American Society of Agricultural Engineers*] — T ASAE
Transactions. ASAE [*American Society of Agricultural Engineers*] — Trans ASAE
Transactions. Ashmolean Society — Trans Ashmolean Soc
Transactions. Asiatic Society of Bengal — TASB
Transactions. Asiatic Society of Japan — TASJ
Transactions. Asiatic Society of Japan — Trans Asiat Soc Japan
Transactions. ASME [*American Society of Mechanical Engineers*] **Journal of Engineering for Gas Turbines and Power** — Trans ASME J Eng Gas Turbines Power
Transactions. ASME [*American Society of Mechanical Engineers*] **Journal of Solar Energy Engineering** — Trans ASME J Sol Energy Eng
Transactions. ASME [*American Society of Mechanical Engineers*] **Journal of Tribology** — Trans ASME J Tribol
Transactions. ASME [*American Society of Mechanical Engineers*] **Series A. Journal of Engineering for Power** — Trans ASME J Eng Power
Transactions. ASME [*American Society of Mechanical Engineers*] **Series A. Journal of Engineering for Power** — Trans ASME Ser A
Transactions. ASME [*American Society of Mechanical Engineers*] **Series A. Journal of Engineering for Power** — Trans ASME Ser A J Eng Power
Transactions. ASME [*American Society of Mechanical Engineers*] **Series B. Journal of Engineering for Industry** — Trans ASME J Eng Ind
Transactions. ASME [*American Society of Mechanical Engineers*] **Series B. Journal of Engineering for Industry** — Trans ASME Ser B
Transactions. ASME [*American Society of Mechanical Engineers*] **Series B. Journal of Engineering for Industry** — Trans ASME Ser B J Eng Ind
Transactions. ASME [*American Society of Mechanical Engineers*] **Series C. Journal of Heat Transfer** — Trans ASME Ser C
Transactions. ASME [*American Society of Mechanical Engineers*] **Series C. Journal of Heat Transfer** — Trans ASME Ser C J Heat Transfer
Transactions. ASME [*American Society of Mechanical Engineers*] **Series D** — Trans ASME Ser D
Transactions. ASME [*American Society of Mechanical Engineers*] **Series E. Journal of Applied Mechanics** — Trans ASME Ser E
Transactions. ASME [*American Society of Mechanical Engineers*] **Series E. Journal of Applied Mechanics** — Trans ASME Ser E J Appl Mech
Transactions. ASME [*American Society of Mechanical Engineers*] **Series F. Journal of Lubrication Technology** — Trans ASME Ser F
Transactions. ASME [*American Society of Mechanical Engineers*] **Series F. Journal of Lubrication Technology** — Trans ASME Ser F J Lubr Technol
Transactions. ASME [*American Society of Mechanical Engineers*] **Series G. Journal of Dynamic Systems. Measurement and Control** — Trans ASME Ser G
Transactions. ASME [*American Society of Mechanical Engineers*] **Series G. Journal of Dynamic Systems. Measurement and Control** — Trans ASME Ser G J Dyn Syst Meas and Control
Transactions. ASME [*American Society of Mechanical Engineers*] **Series G. Journal of Dynamic Systems. Measurement and Control** — Trans ASME Ser G J Dynamic Systems
Transactions. ASME [*American Society of Mechanical Engineers*] **Series G. Journal of Dynamic Systems. Measurement and Control** — Trans ASME Ser G J Dynamic Systems Measurement and Control
Transactions. ASME [*American Society of Mechanical Engineers*] **Series H. Journal of Engineering Materials and Technology** — Trans ASME J Eng Mater and Technol
Transactions. ASME [*American Society of Mechanical Engineers*] **Series H. Journal of Engineering Materials and Technology** — Trans ASME Ser H
Transactions. ASME [*American Society of Mechanical Engineers*] **Series H. Journal of Engineering Materials and Technology** — Trans ASME Ser H J Eng Mater and Technol
Transactions. ASME [*American Society of Mechanical Engineers*] **Series I. Journal of Fluids Engineering** — Trans ASME J Fluids Eng
Transactions. ASME [*American Society of Mechanical Engineers*] **Series I. Journal of Fluids Engineering** — Trans ASME Ser I
Transactions. ASME [*American Society of Mechanical Engineers*] **Series I. Journal of Fluids Engineering** — Trans ASME Ser I J Fluids Eng
Transactions. ASME [*American Society of Mechanical Engineers*] **Series J. Journal of Pressure Vessel Technology** — Trans ASME Ser J J Pressure Vessel Technol
Transactions. ASME [*American Society of Mechanical Engineers*] **Series K** — Trans ASME Ser K
Transactions. ASME [*American Society of Mechanical Engineers*] **Series K. Journal of Biomechanical Engineering** — Trans ASME J Biomech Eng
Transactions. ASME [*American Society of Mechanical Engineers*] **Series K. Journal of Biomechanical Engineering** — Trans ASME Ser K J Biomech Eng
Transactions. Association of American Physicians — TAAPA
Transactions. Association of American Physicians — Tr A Am Physicians
Transactions. Association of American Physicians — Trans Assoc Am Physicians
Transactions. Association of Industrial Medical Officers — Trans Assoc Ind Med Off
Transactions. Association of Life Insurance Medical Directors of America — TALIA
Transactions. Association of Life Insurance Medical Directors of America — Trans Assoc Life Ins Med Dir Am
Transactions. Australian College of Ophthalmologists — Trans Aust Coll Ophthalmol
Transactions. Biochemical Society — Trans Biochem Soc
Transactions. Birmingham and Midland Institute Scientific Society — Trans Birmingham Midl Inst Sci Soc
Transactions. Birmingham and Warwickshire Archaeological Society — Birm AST
Transactions. Birmingham and Warwickshire Archaeological Society — Trans B'ham Warwks Arch Soc
Transactions. Birmingham and Warwickshire Archaeological Society — Trans Birmingham Arch Soc
Transactions. Birmingham and Warwickshire Archaeological Society — Trans Birmingham Warwickshire Archaeol Soc
Transactions. Bombay Geographical Society — TBGS
Transactions. Bose Research Institute — Trans Bose Res Inst
Transactions. Bose Research Institute (Calcutta) — Trans Bose Res Inst (Calcutta)
Transactions. Bristol and Gloucestershire Archaeological Society — BGAST
Transactions. Bristol and Gloucestershire Archaeological Society — Glos Arch Soc Trans
Transactions. Bristol and Gloucestershire Archaeological Society — TBGAS
Transactions. Bristol and Gloucestershire Archaeological Society — Tr Bristol
Transactions. Bristol and Gloucestershire Archaeological Society — Trans Brist Glouces Arch Soc
Transactions. Bristol and Gloucestershire Archaeological Society — Trans Brist Gloucest Archaeol Soc
Transactions. Bristol and Gloucestershire Archaeological Society — Trans Bristol and Glos AS
Transactions. Bristol and Gloucestershire Archaeological Society — Trans Bristol Gloucestershire Arch Soc
Transactions. Bristol and Gloucestershire Archaeological Society — Trans Bristol Gloucestershire Archaeol Soc
Transactions. British Bryological Society — TBBSA
Transactions. British Bryological Society — Trans Br Bryol Soc
Transactions. British Ceramic Society — Trans Br Ceram Soc
Transactions. British Mycological Society — BMSTA
Transactions. British Mycological Society — T Br Mycol
Transactions. British Mycological Society — Trans Br Mycol Soc
Transactions. British Mycological Society — Trans Brit Mycol Soc
Transactions. British Society for the History of Pharmacy — Trans Br Soc Hist Pharm
Transactions. British Society for the History of Pharmacy — Trans Brit Soc Hist Pharm
Transactions. British Society for the Study of Orthodontics — Trans Br Soc Study Orthod
Transactions. C. S. Peirce Society — Trans C S Peirce Soc
Transactions. Caernarvonshire Historical Society — Trans Caernarvonshire Hist Soc
Transactions. Calcutta Medical Society — Trans Calcutta Med Soc
Transactions. Cambridge Bibliographical Society — TCBS
Transactions. Cambridge Philosophical Society — Trans Cambridge Philos Soc
Transactions. Canadian Institute of Mining and Metallurgy and Mining Society of Nova Scotia — Trans Can Inst Min Metall
Transactions. Canadian Institute of Mining and Metallurgy and Mining Society of Nova Scotia — Trans Can Inst Min Metall Min Soc NS
Transactions. Canadian Institute of Mining and Metallurgy and Mining Society of Nova Scotia — Trans Can Inst Mining Soc NS
Transactions. Canadian Mining Institute — Trans Can Min Inst
Transactions. Canadian Nuclear Society — Trans Can Nucl Soc
Transactions. Canadian Numismatic Research Society — TCNRS
Transactions. Canadian Society of Mechanical Engineers — Trans Can Soc Mech Eng
Transactions. Canadian Society of Mechanical Engineers — Trans Can Soc Mech Engrs
Transactions. Cardiff Naturalists Society — Trans Cardiff Nat Soc
Transactions. Cardiff Naturalists Society — Trans Cardiff Natur Soc
Transactions. Caribbean Geological Conference — TCGCB

Transactions. Carmarthenshire Antiquarian Society and Field Club — Trans Carmarthenshire Antiq Soc
Transactions. Cave Research Group of Great Britain — Trans Cave Res Group GB
Transactions. Central Scientific Research Institute of the Confectionery Industry — Trans Cent Sci Res Inst Confect Ind
Transactions. Ceylon College of Physicians — Trans Ceylon Coll
Transactions. Chalmers University of Technology [*Gothenburg, Sweden*] — TCITA
Transactions. Chalmers University of Technology (Gothenburg) [*Sweden*] — Trans Chalmers Univ Technol (Gothenburg)
Transactions. Charles S. Peirce Society — T C Peirce
Transactions. Charles S. Peirce Society — Trans C S Peirce Soc
Transactions. Charles S. Peirce Society — Trans Peirce Soc
Transactions. Chemical Division. American Society for Quality Control — Trans Chem Div Am Soc Qual Control
Transactions. Chinese Association for the Advancement of Science — Trans Chin Assoc Adv Sci
Transactions. Chosen Natural History Society/Chosen Hakubutsu Gakkai Kaiho — Trans Chosen Nat Hist Soc
Transactions. Citrus Engineering Conference — Trans Citrus Eng Conf
Transactions. College of Medicine of South Africa — Trans Coll Med S Afr
Transactions. College of Physicians of Philadelphia — TPPha
Transactions. College of Physicians of Philadelphia — Trans Coll Physicians Philadelphia
Transactions. Colonial Society of Massachusetts — TCSM
Transactions. Conference Group for Social and Administrative History — Trans Conf Group Soc Adm Hist
Transactions. Conference on Cold Injury — Trans Conf Cold Inj
Transactions. Conference on Glaucoma — Trans Conf Glaucoma
Transactions. Conference on Group Processes — Trans Conf Group Processes
Transactions. Conference on Neuropharmacology — Trans Conf Neuropharmacol
Transactions. Conference on Physiology of Prematurity — Trans Conf Physiol Prematurity
Transactions. Conference on Polysaccharides in Biology — Trans Conf Polysaccharides Biol
Transactions. Congregational Historical Society — TrCH
Transactions. Connecticut Academy of Arts and Sciences — TCAAS
Transactions. Connecticut Academy of Arts and Sciences — Trans Conn Acad Arts Sci
Transactions. Connecticut Academy of Arts and Sciences — Trans Connecticut Acad Arts Sci
Transactions. Cornish Institute of Engineers — Trans Corn Inst Eng
Transactions. Cumberland and Westmorland Antiquarian and Archaeological Society — C & W
Transactions. Cumberland and Westmorland Antiquarian and Archaeological Society — CWAT
Transactions. Cumberland and Westmorland Antiquarian and Archaeological Society — TCWA
Transactions. Cumberland and Westmorland Antiquarian and Archaeological Society — Tr Cumb
Transactions. Cumberland and Westmorland Antiquarian and Archaeological Society — Transact Cumb Ant
Transactions. Cumberland and Westmorland Antiquarian and Archaeological Society — TrCW
Transactions. Cumberland and Westmorland Antiquarian and Archaeological Society. New Series — Trans Cumberland Westmorland Antiq Archaeol Soc N Ser
Transactions. Denbighshire Historical Society — Trans Denbighshire Hist Soc
Transactions. Desert Bighorn Council — Trans Desert Bighorn Counc
Transactions. Dumfriesshire and Galloway Natural History and Antiquarian Society — D & G Trans
Transactions. Dumfriesshire and Galloway Natural History and Antiquarian Society — Trans Dumfries and Galloway NH and AS
Transactions. Dumfriesshire and Galloway Natural History and Antiquarian Society — Trans Dumfries Galloway Nat Hist Antiq Soc
Transactions. Dumfriesshire and Galloway Natural History and Antiquarian Society — Trans Dumfriesshire Galloway Natur Hist Ant Soc
Transactions. Dumfriesshire and Galloway Natural History and Antiquarian Society — Trans Dumfriesshire Galloway Natur Hist Antiq Soc
Transactions. Dumfriesshire and Galloway Natural History and Antiquarian Society — Transact Dumfries
Transactions. Dynamics of Development — Trans Dynam Dev
Transactions. East Lothian Antiquarian and Field Naturalists' Society — Trans E Lothian Antiq Fld Natur Soc
Transactions. East Lothian Antiquarian and Field Naturalists' Society — Trans East Lothian Antiq Field Nat Soc
Transactions. Edinburgh Geological Society — Trans Edinb Geol Soc
Transactions. Edinburgh Geological Society — Trans Edinburgh Geol Soc
Transactions. Electric Supply Authority Engineers' Institute of New Zealand, Inc. — Trans Electr Supply Auth Eng Inst NZ
Transactions. Electrochemical Society — Trans Electrochem Soc
Transactions. Engineering Institute of Canada — TEICA
Transactions. Engineering Institute of Canada — Trans Eng Inst Can
Transactions. English Ceramic Circle — Trans Engl Ceram Circle
Transactions. English Ceramic Society — Trans Engl Ceram Soc
Transactions. Entomological Society of London — Tr Entom Soc London
Transactions. Essex Archaeological Society — Trans Essex Arch Soc
Transactions. Essex Field Club — Trans Essex Field Club
Transactions. Estonian Agricultural Academy — Trans Est Agric Acad
Transactions. European Orthodontic Society — Trans Eur Orthod Soc
Transactions. Faculty of Horticulture. Chiba University — Trans Fac Hortic Chiba Univ
Transactions. Faraday Society — TFSOA
Transactions. Faraday Society — Trans Farady Soc
Transactions. Federal-Provincial Wildlife Conference — Trans Fed-Prov Wildl Conf
Transactions. Fifteenth International Congress on Hygiene and Demography — Tr (Fifteenth) Internat Cong Hyg and Demog
Transactions. Free Museum of Science and Art. University of Pennsylvania — TFMSA
Transactions. Gaelic Society of Glasgow — TGSG
Transactions. Gaelic Society of Inverness — TGSI
Transactions. Geological Society of Glasgow — Trans Geol Soc Glasg
Transactions. Geological Society of South Africa — Trans Geol Soc S Afr
Transactions. Georgia State Agricultural Society — Trans Georgia State Agric Soc
Transactions. Geothermal Resources Council [*United States*] — Trans Geotherm Resour Counc
Transactions. Glasgow University Oriental Society — TGUOS
Transactions. Glasgow University Oriental Society — Trans Glasgow Univ Orient Soc
Transactions. Glasgow University Oriental Society [*Hertford, England*] — TrGlasgUOrS
Transactions. Greenwich and Lewisham Antiquarian Society — Trans Greenwich Lewisham Antiq Soc
Transactions. Gulf Coast Association of Geological Societies — TGCGA
Transactions. Gulf Coast Association of Geological Societies — Trans Gulf Coast Ass Geol Soc
Transactions. Gulf Coast Association of Geological Societies — Trans Gulf Coast Assoc Geol Soc
Transactions. Gulf Coast Molecular Biology Conference — Trans Gulf Coast Mol Biol Conf
Transactions. Halifax Antiquarian Society — Trans Halifax Antiq Society
Transactions. Hawick Archaeological Society — Trans Hawick Archaeol Soc
Transactions. Hertfordshire Natural History Society and Field Club — Trans Hertfordshire Nat Hist Field Club
Transactions. Hertfordshire Natural History Society and Field Club — Trans Hertfordshire Nat Hist Soc Field Club
Transactions. Highland and Agricultural Society of Scotland — Trans Highl Agric Soc Scotl
Transactions. Historic Society of Lancashire and Cheshire — Trans Hist Soc Lancashire Cheshire
Transactions. Historical and Scientific Society of Manitoba — TrHS
Transactions. Historical Society of Ghana — Tr Hist Soc Ghana
Transactions. Historical Society of Ghana — Trans Hist Soc Ghana
Transactions. Honourable Society of Cymmrodorion — THSC
Transactions. Hull Scientific and Field Naturalists' Club — Trans Hull Sci Club
Transactions. Hunter Archaeological Society — Trans Hunter Archaeol Soc
Transactions. Hunterian Society — Trans Hunter Soc
Transactions. Illinois State Academy of Science — Trans Ill St Acad Sci
Transactions. Illinois State Academy of Science — Trans Ill State Acad Sci
Transactions. Illinois State Horticultural Society — Trans Ill St Hort Soc
Transactions. Illinois State Horticultural Society — Trans Ill State Hortic Soc
Transactions. Illinois State Horticultural Society and the Illinois Fruit Council — Trans Ill State Hortic Soc Ill Fruit Counc
Transactions. Illuminating Engineering Society — Trans Illum Eng Soc
Transactions. Illuminating Engineering Society — Trans Soc Ill Eng
Transactions. Indian Ceramic Society — Trans Indian Ceram Soc
Transactions. Indian Institute of Chemical Engineers — Trans Ind Inst Chem Eng
Transactions. Indian Institute of Chemical Engineers — Trans Indian Inst Chem Eng
Transactions. Indian Institute of Metals — Trans Indian Inst Met
Transactions. Indian Institute of Metals — Trans Indian Inst Metals
Transactions. Indian Society of Desert Technology and University Centre of Desert Studies — Trans Indian Soc Desert Technol Univ Cent Desert Stud
Transactions. Indiana Academy of Ophthalmology and Otolaryngology — TIOOA
Transactions. Indiana Academy of Ophthalmology and Otolaryngology — Trans Indiana Acad Ophthalmol Otolaryngol
Transactions. Indiana Horticultural Society — Trans Indiana Hort Soc
Transactions. Indiana State Medical Society — Tr Indiana Med Soc
Transactions. Information Processing Society of Japan — Trans Inf Process Soc Jpn
Transactions. Information Processing Society of Japan — Trans Inform Process Soc Japan
Transactions. Institute of Actuaries of Australia and New Zealand — Trans Inst Act Aust & NZ
Transactions. Institute of British Geographers — IBG/T
Transactions. Institute of British Geographers — T I Br Geog
Transactions. Institute of British Geographers — Trans Inst Brit Geogr
Transactions. Institute of British Geographers. New Series — Trans Inst Br Geogr New Ser
Transactions. Institute of Electrical Engineers of Japan — Trans Inst Electr Eng Jap
Transactions. Institute of Electrical Engineers of Japan — Trans Inst Electr Eng Jpn
Transactions. Institute of Electrical Engineers of Japan. Overseas Edition — Trans Inst Electr Eng Jap Overseas Ed
Transactions. Institute of Electrical Engineers of Japan. Part A — Trans Inst Electr Eng Jpn Part A
Transactions. Institute of Electrical Engineers of Japan. Part B — Trans Inst Electr Eng Jpn B
Transactions. Institute of Electrical Engineers of Japan. Part B — Trans Inst Electr Eng Jpn Part B
Transactions. Institute of Electrical Engineers of Japan. Part C — Trans Inst Electr Eng Jpn C

Transactions. Institute of Electrical Engineers of Japan. Part C — Trans Inst Electr Eng Jpn Part C
Transactions. Institute of Electrical Engineers of Japan. Section E — Trans Inst Electr Eng Jpn Sect E
Transactions. Institute of Electronics and Communication Engineers of Japan. Part A — Trans Inst Electron & Commun Eng Jap A
Transactions. Institute of Electronics and Communication Engineers of Japan. Part A — Trans Inst Electron and Commun Eng Jpn Part A
Transactions. Institute of Electronics and Communication Engineers of Japan. Part B — Trans Inst Electron & Commun Eng Jap B
Transactions. Institute of Electronics and Communication Engineers of Japan. Part B — Trans Inst Electron and Commun Eng Jpn Part B
Transactions. Institute of Electronics and Communication Engineers of Japan. Part B — Trans Inst Electron Commun Eng Jpn Part B
Transactions. Institute of Electronics and Communication Engineers of Japan. Part C — Trans Inst Electron & Commun Eng Jap C
Transactions. Institute of Electronics and Communication Engineers of Japan. Part C — Trans Inst Electron and Commun Eng Jpn Part C
Transactions. Institute of Electronics and Communication Engineers of Japan. Part D — Trans Inst Electron & Commun Eng Jap D
Transactions. Institute of Electronics and Communication Engineers of Japan. Part D — Trans Inst Electron and Commun Eng Jpn Part D
Transactions. Institute of Electronics and Communication Engineers of Japan. Section E — Trans Inst Electron and Commun Eng Jpn Sect E
Transactions. Institute of Electronics and Communication Engineers of Japan. Section E — Trans Inst Electron Commun Eng Jpn
Transactions. Institute of Electronics and Communication Engineers of Japan. Section E (English) — TIEED
Transactions. Institute of Electronics and Communication Engineers of Japan. Section E (English) — Trans Inst Electron Commun Eng Jpn Sect E (Engl)
Transactions. Institute of Electronics and Communication Engineers of Japan. Section J. Part A — Trans Inst Electron Commun Eng Jap Sect J Part A
Transactions. Institute of Electronics and Communication Engineers of Japan. Section J. Part C — Trans Inst Electron Commun Eng Jap Sect J Part C
Transactions. Institute of Electronics and Communication Engineers of Japan. Section J [*Japanese*] **Part D** — Trans Inst Electron Commun Eng Jap Sect J Part D
Transactions. Institute of Electronics, Information, and Communication Engineers. Section E — Trans Inst Electron Inf Commun
Transactions. Institute of Electronics, Information, and Communications Engineers. Section E. English — Trans Inst Electron Inf Commun Eng Sect E
Transactions. Institute of Engineers. Australia. Multi-Disciplinary Engineering — Trans Inst Eng Aust Multi Discip
Transactions. Institute of Marine Engineers — TIMEA
Transactions. Institute of Marine Engineers — Trans I Mar E
Transactions. Institute of Marine Engineers — Trans Inst Mar Eng
Transactions. Institute of Marine Engineers — Trans Inst Mar Engrs
Transactions. Institute of Marine Engineers — Trans Inst Marine Eng
Transactions. Institute of Marine Engineers. Conference Papers — Trans Inst Mar Eng Conf Pap
Transactions. Institute of Marine Engineers. Series C — Trans Inst Mar Eng Ser C
Transactions. Institute of Marine Engineers. Technical Meeting Papers — Trans Inst Mar Eng Tech Meet Pap
Transactions. Institute of Measurement and Control — Trans Inst Meas & Control
Transactions. Institute of Measurement and Control — Trans Inst Meas Control
Transactions. Institute of Measurement and Control — Trans Inst Measmt Control
Transactions. Institute of Metal Finishing — TIMFA
Transactions. Institute of Metal Finishing — Trans Inst Met Finish
Transactions. Institute of Mining and Metallurgy (Ostrava). Mining and Geological Series — Trans Inst Min Metall (Ostrava) Min Geol Ser
Transactions. Institute of Professional Engineers [*New Zealand*] — Trans
Transactions. Institute of Pure Chemical Reagents (Moscow) — Trans Inst Pure Chem Reagents (Moscow)
Transactions. Institute of Systems, Control, and Information Engineers — Trans Inst Systems Control Inform Engrs
Transactions. Institute of the Plastics Industry — Trans Inst Plast Ind
Transactions. Institute of Welding (London) — Trans Inst Weld (London)
Transactions. Institution of Chemical Engineers — Trans Inst Chem Eng
Transactions. Institution of Chemical Engineers — Trans Inst Chem Engrs
Transactions. Institution of Chemical Engineers — Trans Instn Chem Engrs
Transactions. Institution of Chemical Engineers and the Chemical Engineer — T I Chem En
Transactions. Institution of Chemical Engineers (London) — Trans Inst Chem Eng (London)
Transactions. Institution of Civil Engineers of Ireland — Inst Civ Eng Ir Trans
Transactions. Institution of Civil Engineers of Ireland — Trans Inst Civ Eng Ir
Transactions. Institution of Engineers and Shipbuilders in Scotland — Trans Inst Eng Shipbuilders Scot
Transactions. Institution of Engineers and Shipbuilders in Scotland — Trans Instn E Shipb Scot
Transactions. Institution of Engineers of Australia — Trans Inst Eng Aust
Transactions. Institution of Engineers of Australia. Civil Engineering — Trans Inst Eng Aust Civ Eng
Transactions. Institution of Engineers of Australia. Civil Engineering — Trans Inst Engrs Aust Civ Engng
Transactions. Institution of Engineers of Australia. Electrical Engineering — Trans Inst Eng Aust Electr Eng
Transactions. Institution of Engineers of Australia. Mechanical Engineering — Trans Inst Eng Aust Mech Eng
Transactions. Institution of Engineers of Australia. Mechanical Engineering — Trans Inst Engrs Aust Mech Engng
Transactions. Institution of Gas Engineers [*England*] — Trans Inst Gas Eng
Transactions. Institution of Mining and Metallurgy — Trans Inst Min Metall
Transactions. Institution of Mining and Metallurgy — Trans Instn Min Metall
Transactions. Institution of Mining and Metallurgy. Section A. Mining Industry — Trans Inst Min Metall Sec A
Transactions. Institution of Mining and Metallurgy. Section A. Mining Industry — Trans Inst Min Metall Sect A Min Ind
Transactions. Institution of Mining and Metallurgy. Section A. Mining Industry — Trans Inst Mining Met Sect A
Transactions. Institution of Mining and Metallurgy. Section B. Applied Earth Science — Trans Inst Min Metall Sec B
Transactions. Institution of Mining and Metallurgy. Section B. Applied Earth Science [*United Kingdom*] — Trans Inst Min Metall Sect B Appl Earth Sci
Transactions. Institution of Mining and Metallurgy. Section B. Applied Earth Science — Trans Inst Mining Met Sect B
Transactions. Institution of Mining and Metallurgy. Section C [*United Kingdom*] — Trans Inst Min Metall Sec C
Transactions. Institution of Mining and Metallurgy. Section C — Trans Inst Mining Met Sect C
Transactions. Institution of Mining Engineers — Trans Inst Min Eng
Transactions. Institution of Professional Engineers. New Zealand Civil Engineering Section — Trans Inst Prof Eng NZ
Transactions. Institution of Professional Engineers of New Zealand — Trans Inst Prof Eng
Transactions. Institution of Professional Engineers of New Zealand. Civil Engineering Section — Trans Inst Prof Eng NZ Civ Eng Sect
Transactions. Institution of Professional Engineers of New Zealand. Electrical/Mechanical/Chemical Engineering Section — Trans Inst Prof Eng NZ Electr Mech Chem Eng Sect
Transactions. Institution of Professional Engineers of New Zealand. Electrical/Mechanical/Chemical Engineering Section — Trans Inst Prof Eng NZ EMCh
Transactions. Institution of the Rubber Industry — Trans Inst Rubber Ind
Transactions. Institution of Water Engineers — Trans Inst Water Eng
Transactions. International Association for Mathematics and Computers in Simulation — Trans Int Assoc Math and Comput Simulation
Transactions. International Astronomical Union — Trans Int Astron Union
Transactions. International Ceramic Congress — Trans Int Ceram Congr
Transactions. International Conference of Orientalists in Japan — TICOJ
Transactions. International Conference of Orientalists in Japan — Trans Int Conf Or Ja
Transactions. International Conference of Soil Science — Trans Int Conf Soil Sci
Transactions. International Conference on Endodontics — Trans Int Conf Endod
Transactions. International Conference on Oral Surgery — Trans Int Conf Oral Surg
Transactions. International Congress for Agricultural Engineering — Trans Int Congr Agric Engng
Transactions. International Congress of Agricultural Engineering — Trans Int Congr Agr Eng
Transactions. International Congress of Entomology — Trans Int Congr Entomol
Transactions. International Congress of Soil Science — Trans Int Congr Soil Sci
Transactions. International Congress on the Enlightenment — Trans Int Congr Enlightenment
Transactions. International Oriental Congress (London) — TIOCL
Transactions. International Society for Geothermal Engineering — Trans Int Soc Geotherm Eng
Transactions. Inverness Gaelic Society — TIGS
Transactions. Iowa State Horticultural Society — Trans Iowa St Hort Soc
Transactions. Iowa State Horticultural Society — Trans Iowa State Hortic Soc
Transactions. Iron and Steel Institute of Japan — T Iron St I
Transactions. Iron and Steel Institute of Japan — Trans Iron Steel Inst Jap
Transactions. Iron and Steel Institute of Japan — Trans Iron Steel Inst Jpn
Transactions. Japan Institute of Metals — T Jap I Met
Transactions. Japan Institute of Metals — Trans Jap Inst Met
Transactions. Japan Institute of Metals — Trans Jap Inst Metals
Transactions. Japan Institute of Metals — Trans Jpn Inst Met
Transactions. Japan Institute of Metals. Supplement — Trans Jpn Inst Met Suppl
Transactions. Japan Society for Aeronautical and Space Sciences — TJASA
Transactions. Japan Society for Aeronautical and Space Sciences — Trans Jap Soc Aeronaut Space Sci
Transactions. Japan Society for Aeronautical and Space Sciences — Trans Jpn Soc Aeronaut and Space Sci
Transactions. Japan Society for Aeronautical and Space Sciences — Trans Jpn Soc Aeronaut Space Sci
Transactions. Japan Society for Composite Materials — Trans Japan Soc Compos Mater
Transactions. Japan Society for Composite Materials — Trans Jpn Soc Compos Mater
Transactions. Japan Society of Civil Engineers — Trans Japan Soc Civ Engrs
Transactions. Japan Society of Civil Engineers — Trans Jpn Soc Civ Eng
Transactions. Japan Society of Mechanical Engineers — Trans Jap Soc Mech Eng
Transactions. Japan Society of Mechanical Engineers. Series B — Trans Japan Soc Mech Engrs Ser B
Transactions. Japan Society of Mechanical Engineers. Series B — Trans Jpn Soc Mech Eng Ser B
Transactions. Japan Society of Mechanical Engineers. Series C — Trans Japan Soc Mech Engrs Ser C
Transactions. Japan Welding Society — Trans Jap Weld Soc
Transactions. Japan Welding Society — Trans Jpn Weld Soc
Transactions. Japanese Pathological Society — Tr Japan Path Soc
Transactions. Japanese Pathological Society — Trans Jpn Pathol Soc
Transactions. Japanese Society of Irrigation Drainage and Reclamation Engineering — Trans Jpn Soc Irrig Drain Reclam Eng
Transactions. Joint Meeting of Commissions. International Society of Soil Science — Trans Jt Mtg Comm Int Soc Soil Sci
Transactions. JWRI [*Japanese Welding Research Institute*] — Trans JWRI

Transactions. JWRI [*Japanese Welding Research Institute*] — TRJWD
Transactions. Kansai Entomological Society — Trans Kansai Ent Soc
Transactions. Kansas Academy of Science — Tr Kansas Acad Sc
Transactions. Kansas Academy of Science — Trans Kans Acad Sci
Transactions. Kentucky Academy of Science — Trans K Acad Sci
Transactions. Kentucky Academy of Science — Trans KY Acad Sci
Transactions. Kentucky State Horticultural Society — Trans Kentucky State Hort Soc
Transactions. Korean Branch. Royal Asiatic Society — TKBRAS
Transactions. Korean Branch. Royal Asiatic Society — TKRAS
Transactions. Korean Institute of Electrical Engineers — Trans Korean Inst Electr Eng
Transactions. Korean Society of Mechanical Engineers [*Republic of Korea*] — Trans Korean Soc Mech Eng
Transactions. Lancashire and Cheshire Antiquarian Society — Trans Lancashire Cheshire Antiq Soc
Transactions. Lancashire and Cheshire Antiquarian Society — Trans Lancs and Chesh Antiq Soc
Transactions. Latvian Branch. All-Union Society of Soil Science — Trans Latv Branch All Union Soc Soil Sci
Transactions. Leeds Geological Association — Trans Leeds Geol Assoc
Transactions. Leicestershire Archaeological and Historical Society — Trans Leicestershire Archaeol Hist Soc
Transactions. Lichfield and South Staffordshire Archaeological and Historical Society — Trans Lich S Staffs Arch Hist Soc
Transactions. Linnaean Society of New York — Trans Linn Soc NY
Transactions. Linnean Society of London — Trans Linn Soc Lond
Transactions. Linnean Society of London. Botany — Trans Linn Soc London Bot
Transactions. Liverpool Engineering Society — Trans Liverpool Eng Soc
Transactions. Liverpool Nautical Society — Trans Liverpool Naut Soc
Transactions. London and Middlesex Archaeological Society — Trans Lond Middx Archaeol Soc
Transactions. London and Middlesex Archaeological Society — Trans London Middlesex Archaeol Soc
Transactions. London and Middlesex Archaeological Society — Trans London M'sex Arch
Transactions. London and Middlesex Archaeological Society — Trans London Msex Arch Soc
Transactions. London and Middlesex Archaeological Society — Transact Lond
Transactions. Manchester Association of Engineers — Trans Manchester Assoc Eng
Transactions. Manchester Literary and Philosophical Society — TMLPS
Transactions. Massachusetts Horticultural Society — Trans Mass Hort Soc
Transactions. Medical and Physical Society of Bombay — Tr Med and Phys Soc Bombay
Transactions. Medical Society of London — Trans Med Soc Lond
Transactions. Medical Society of London — Trans Med Soc London
Transactions Medicales. Journal de Medecine Pratique — Trans Med
Transactions. Meeting. Japanese Forestry Society — Trans Meeting Jap Forest Soc
Transactions. Meeting of Commissions II and IV. International Society of Soil Science — Trans Meet Commns II & IV Int Soc Soil Sci
Transactions. Metal Finishers' Association of India — Trans Met Finish Assoc India
Transactions. Metallurgical Society of AIME [*American Institute of Mining, Metallurgical, and Petroleum Engineers*] — TMSAA
Transactions. Metallurgical Society of AIME [*American Institute of Mining, Metallurgical, and Petroleum Engineers*] — Trans Metall Soc AIME
Transactions. Metallurgical Society of AIME (American Institute of Mining, Metallurgical, and Petroleum Engineers) — Trans Metall Soc AIME (Am Inst Min Metall Pet Eng)
Transactions. Mining and Metallurgical Alumni Association [*Japan*] — Trans Min Metall Alumni Assoc
Transactions. Mining and Metallurgical Association (Kyoto) — Trans Min Metall Assoc (Kyoto)
Transactions. Mining, Geological, and Metallurgical Institute of India — Trans Min Geol Metall Inst India
Transactions. Mining, Geological, and Metallurgical Institute of India — Trans Mining Geol Met Inst India
Transactions. Missouri Academy of Science — MISTB
Transactions. Missouri Academy of Science — Trans MO Acad Sci
Transactions. Missouri Academy of Science — Trans MO Acad Scie
Transactions. Monumental Brass Society — Trans Monumental Brass Soc
Transactions. Morris County Research Council — Trans Morris C Res Counc
Transactions. Moscow Mathematical Society — Trans Mosc Math Soc
Transactions. Moscow Mathematical Society — Trans Moscow Math Soc
Transactions. Mycological Society of Japan — Trans Mycol Soc Jap
Transactions. Mycological Society of Japan — Trans Mycol Soc Japan
Transactions. Mycological Society of Japan — Trans Mycol Soc Jpn
Transactions. National Institute of Sciences. India — Trans Natl Inst Sci India
Transactions. National Research Institute for Metals [*Japan*] — Trans Natl Res Inst Met
Transactions. National Research Institute for Metals (Tokyo) — Trans Nat Res Inst Metals (Tokyo)
Transactions. National Research Institute for Metals (Tokyo) — Trans Natl Res Inst Met (Tokyo)
Transactions. National Safety Congress [*United States*] — Trans Natl Saf Congr
Transactions. National Vacuum Symposium — Trans Nat Vac Symp
Transactions. Natural History Society of Formosa — Trans Nat Hist Soc Formosa
Transactions. Natural History Society of Glasgow — Trans Nat Hist Soc Glasgow
Transactions. Natural History Society of Northumberland, Durham, and Newcastle-Upon-Tyne — Trans Nat Hist Northumberl Durham Newcastle Upon Tyne
Transactions. Natural History Society of Northumberland, Durham, and Newcastle-Upon-Tyne [*Later, Natural History Society of Northumbria. Transactions*] — Trans Nat Hist Soc Northumberl Durham Newcastle-Upon-Tyne
Transactions. Natural History Society of Northumbria — Trans Nat Hist Soc Northumbria
Transactions. Nebraska Academy of Sciences — Trans Nebr Acad Sci
Transactions. Nebraska Academy of Sciences and Affiliated Societies — Trans Nebr Acad Sci Affiliated Soc
Transactions. New England Obstetrical and Gynecological Society [*United States*] — Trans New Engl Obstet Gynecol Soc
Transactions. New Jersey Obstetrical and Gynecological Society — Trans NJ Obstet Gynecol Soc
Transactions. New Orleans Academy of Ophthalmology — Trans New Orleans Acad Ophthalmol
Transactions. New York Academy of Sciences — T NY Ac Sci
Transactions. New York Academy of Sciences — Tr New York Acad Sc
Transactions. New York Academy of Sciences — Trans New York Acad Sci
Transactions. New York Academy of Sciences — Trans NY Acad Sci
Transactions. New York Academy of Sciences. Series II — Trans New York Acad Sci Ser II
Transactions. New Zealand Institution of Engineers, Incorporated — Trans NZ Inst Eng
Transactions. New Zealand Institution of Engineers, Incorporated. Civil Engineering Section — Trans NZ Inst Eng CE
Transactions. New Zealand Institution of Engineers, Incorporated. Civil Engineering Section — Trans NZ Inst Eng Inc Civ Eng Sect
Transactions. New Zealand Institution of Engineers, Incorporated. Electrical/Mechanical/Chemical Engineering Section — Trans NZ Inst Eng EMCh
Transactions. New Zealand Institution of Engineers, Incorporated. Electrical/Mechanical/Chemical Engineering Section — Trans NZ Inst Eng Inc Electr Mech Chem Eng Sect
Transactions. Newbury District Field Club — Trans Newbury Dist Fld Club
Transactions. Newcomen Society — Trans Newcomen Soc
Transactions. Newcomen Society for the Study of the History of Engineering and Technology — Trans Newcomen Soc Study His Eng Technol
Transactions. North American Wildlife and Natural Resources Conference — Trans N Am Wildl Nat Resour Conf
Transactions. North American Wildlife and Natural Resources Conference — Trans N Amer Wildlife Conf
Transactions. North American Wildlife and Natural Resources Conference — Trans North Am Wildl Nat Res Conf
Transactions. North American Wildlife and Natural Resources Conference — Trans North Am Wildl Nat Resour Conf
Transactions. North American Wildlife Conference — Trans North Am Wildl Conf
Transactions. North East Coast Institution of Engineers and Shipbuilders [*British*] — Trans NE Cst Instn Engrs Shipbldrs
Transactions. North East Coast Institution of Engineers and Shipbuilders [*British*] — Trans NEC Instn E Ship
Transactions. North East Coast Institution of Engineers and Shipbuilders [*British*] — Trans North East Coast Inst Eng Shipbuild
Transactions of Metal Heat Treatment [*China*] — Trans Met Heat Treat
Transactions of Nonferrous Metals Society of China — Trans Nonferrous Met Soc China
Transactions of Royal Society of Edinburgh — TRSE
Transactions of Tallinn Technical University — Trans Tallinn Tech Univ
Transactions of the Iron and Steel Society — Trans Iron Steel Soc
Transactions of the Japan Academy — Trans Japan Acad
Transactions of the Northeast Section. Wildlife Society — Trans Northeast Sect Wildl Soc
Transactions of Tianjin University — Trans Tianjin Univ
Transactions on Office Information Systems — TOOIS
Transactions. Ophthalmological Societies of the United Kingdom — T Ophth Soc
Transactions. Ophthalmological Societies of the United Kingdom — Trans Ophthalmol Soc UK
Transactions. Ophthalmological Society of Australia — Trans Ophthal Soc Aust
Transactions. Ophthalmological Society of Australia — Trans Ophthalmol Soc Aust
Transactions. Ophthalmological Society of New Zealand — Trans Ophthalmol Soc NZ
Transactions. Optical Society — Trans Opt Soc
Transactions. Pacific Coast Obstetrical and Gynecological Society [*United States*] — Trans Pac Coast Obstet Gynecol Soc
Transactions. Pacific Coast Oto-Ophthalmological Society — Tr Pacific Coast Oto-Ophth Soc
Transactions. Pacific Coast Oto-Ophthalmological Society — Trans Pac Coast Oto-Ophthalmol Soc
Transactions. Pacific Coast Oto-Ophthalmological Society. Annual Meeting [*United States*] — Trans Pac Coast Oto-Ophthalmol Soc Annu Meet
Transactions. Pathological Society of London — Tr Path Soc London
Transactions. Peninsula Horticultural Society — Trans Peninsula Hortic Soc
Transactions. Pennsylvania Academy of Ophthalmology and Otolaryngology — Trans PA Acad Ophthalmol Otolaryngol
Transactions. Philological Society — TPhS
Transactions. Philological Society [*London*] — TPS
Transactions. Philological Society — Trans Phil Soc
Transactions. Philological Society — Trans Philol Soc
Transactions. Philological Society — Trans Philological Soc
Transactions. Philological Society. Oxford — TPhSO
Transactions. Philosophical Society [*London and Strassburg*] — TPhS
Transactions. Philosophical Society of New South Wales — Trans Philos Soc New South Wales
Transactions. Powder Metallurgy Association of India — Trans Powder Metall Assoc India

Transactions. Princeton Conference on Cerebrovascular Diseases — Trans Princeton Conf Cerebrovasc Dis
Transactions. Provincial Medical and Surgical Association — Trans Prov Med Assoc
Transactions Quarterly. American Society for Metals — Trans Q Am Soc Met
Transactions. Radnorshire Society — Trans Radnorshire Soc
Transactions. Rhodesia Scientific Association — Trans Rhod Sci Assoc
Transactions. Royal Canadian Institute — Trans R Can Inst
Transactions. Royal Entomological Society of London — T Roy Ent S
Transactions. Royal Entomological Society of London — Trans R Ent Soc Lond
Transactions. Royal Entomological Society of London — Trans R Entomol Soc Lond
Transactions. Royal Geological Society (Cornwall) — Trans R Geol Soc (Corn)
Transactions. Royal Geological Society of Cornwall — Trans Roy Geol Soc Cornwall
Transactions. Royal Highland and Agricultural Society of Scotland — Trans R Highl Agric Soc Scotl
Transactions. Royal Historical Society — Trans Roy Hist Soc
Transactions. Royal Historical Society — TRHS
Transactions. Royal Institute of Naval Architects — Trans R Inst Nav Arch
Transactions. Royal Institute of Technology (Stockholm) — Trans Roy Inst Tech (Stockholm)
Transactions. Royal Institute of Technology (Stockholm) — Trans Roy Inst Technol (Stockholm)
Transactions. Royal Institution of Naval Architects [*London*] — Trans RINA
Transactions. Royal Schools of Dentistry (Stockholm and Umea) — Trans R Sch Dent (Stockh Umea)
Transactions. Royal Society of Arts — Trans R Soc Arts
Transactions. Royal Society of Canada — T Roy Soc C
Transactions. Royal Society of Canada — Trans R Soc Can
Transactions. Royal Society of Canada — Trans Roy Soc Canada
Transactions. Royal Society of Canada — Transact Roy Soc Canada
Transactions. Royal Society of Canada — TrRS
Transactions. Royal Society of Canada — TRSC
Transactions. Royal Society of Canada — TRSCA
Transactions. Royal Society of Canada. Chemical, Mathematical, and Physical Sciences. Fourth Series — Trans Roy Soc Canada 4
Transactions. Royal Society of Canada/Memoires. Societe Royale du Canada — Trans R Soc Can Mem Soc R Can
Transactions. Royal Society of Canada. Section 1, Section 2, and Section 3 — Trans R Soc Can Sect 1 2 3
Transactions. Royal Society of Canada. Section 1, Section 2, and Section 3 — Trans Royal Soc Can Sect 1 Sect 2 and Sect 3
Transactions. Royal Society of Canada. Section 3. Chemical, Mathematical, and Physical Sciences — Trans R Soc Can Sect 3
Transactions. Royal Society of Canada. Section 5. Biological Sciences — Trans R Soc Can Sect 5
Transactions. Royal Society of Edinburgh — Tr Roy Soc Edinb
Transactions. Royal Society of Edinburgh — Trans R Soc Edinb
Transactions. Royal Society of Edinburgh — Trans R Soc Edinburgh
Transactions. Royal Society of Edinburgh — Trans Roy Soc Edinburgh
Transactions. Royal Society of Edinburgh. Earth Sciences — Trans R Soc Edinb Earth Sci
Transactions. Royal Society of Edinburgh. Earth Sciences — Trans R Soc Edinburgh Earth Sci
Transactions. Royal Society of Literature — TRSL
Transactions. Royal Society of Literature of the United Kingdom — Trans R Soc Lit
Transactions. Royal Society of New Zealand — Trans R Soc NZ
Transactions. Royal Society of New Zealand. Biological Science — Trans R Soc NZ Biol Sci
Transactions. Royal Society of New Zealand. Botany — Trans R Soc NZ Bot
Transactions. Royal Society of New Zealand. Botany — Trans Roy Soc NZ Bot
Transactions. Royal Society of New Zealand. Earth Science — Trans R Soc NZ Earth Sci
Transactions. Royal Society of New Zealand. General — Trans R Soc NZ Gen
Transactions. Royal Society of New Zealand. Geology — Trans R Soc NZ Geol
Transactions. Royal Society of New Zealand. Zoology — Trans R Soc NZ Zool
Transactions. Royal Society of South Africa — T Rs S Afr
Transactions. Royal Society of South Africa — Trans R Soc S Afr
Transactions. Royal Society of South Africa — Trans Roy Soc South Africa
Transactions. Royal Society of South Australia — Trans R Soc S Aust
Transactions. Royal Society of South Australia — Trans R Soc South Aust
Transactions. Royal Society of Tropical Medicine and Hygiene — T Rs Trop M
Transactions. Royal Society of Tropical Medicine and Hygiene — Tr Roy Soc Trop Med Hyg
Transactions. Royal Society of Tropical Medicine and Hygiene — Trans R Soc Trop Med Hyg
Transactions. Royal Society of Tropical Medicine and Hygiene — Trans Roy Soc Trop Med Hyg
Transactions. Royal Society of Tropical Medicine and Hygiene — TRSTA
Transactions. Royal Society of Tropical Medicine and Hygiene — TRSTM
Transactions. Russian Institute of Applied Chemistry — Trans Russ Inst Appl Chem
Transactions. SAEST [*Society for Advancement of Electrochemical Science and Technology*] — Trans SAEST
Transactions. Samuel Johnson Society of the Northwest — TSJSN
Transactions. Samuel Johnson Society of the Northwest — TSJSNW
Transactions. San Diego Society of Natural History — Trans San Diego Soc Nat Hist
Transactions. Science Society of China — Trans Sci Soc China
Transactions. Scientific Association — Trans Sci Assoc
Transactions. SHASE [*Society of Heating, Air Conditioning, and Sanitary Engineers*] **(Japan)** — Trans SHASE Japan
Transactions. Shikoku Entomological Society — Trans Shikoku Ent Soc
Transactions. Shikoku Entomological Society — Trans Shikoku Entomol Soc
Transactions. Shropshire Archaeological and Natural History Society — Trans Shropshire A S
Transactions. Shropshire Archaeological Society — Trans Shropshire Archaeol Soc
Transactions. Society for Advancement of Electrochemical Science and Technology — Trans Soc Adv Electrochem Sci Technol
Transactions. Society for British Entomology — Trans Soc Br Ent
Transactions. Society for British Entomology — Trans Soc Br Entomol
Transactions. Society for Mining, Metallurgy, and Exploration, Inc. — Trans Soc Min Metall Explor
Transactions. Society of Biblical Archaeology — Trans SBA
Transactions. Society of Biblical Archaeology — Trans Soc Bibl Arch
Transactions. Society of Biblical Archaeology — TSBA
Transactions. Society of Heating, Air Conditioning, and Sanitary Engineers [*Japan*] — Trans SHASE
Transactions. Society of Heating, Air Conditioning, and Sanitary Engineers of Japan — Trans Soc Heat Air Cond Sanit Eng Jpn
Transactions. Society of Instrument and Control Engineers [*Japan*] — Trans Soc Instr Control Eng
Transactions. Society of Instrument and Control Engineers — Trans Soc Instrum and Control Eng
Transactions. Society of Instrument and Control Engineers — Trans Soc Instrum Control Eng
Transactions. Society of Instrument and Control Engineers (Japan) — Trans Soc Instrum & Control Engrs (Japan)
Transactions. Society of Instrument Technology [*England*] — Trans Soc Instrum Technol
Transactions. Society of Mining Engineers. AIME [*American Institute of Mining, Metallurgical, and Petroleum Engineers*] — Trans Soc Min Eng AIME
Transactions. Society of Mining Engineers. AIME [*American Institute of Mining, Metallurgical, and Petroleum Engineers*] — Trans Soc Min Engrs AIME
Transactions. Society of Mining Engineers, Inc. — Trans Soc Min Eng
Transactions. Society of Motion Picture Engineers — Trans SMPE
Transactions. Society of Motion Picture Engineers — Trans Soc Mot Pict Eng
Transactions. Society of Motion Picture Engineers — Trans Soc Motion Pict Eng
Transactions. Society of Naval Architects and Marine Engineers — Trans Soc NAME
Transactions. Society of Naval Architects and Marine Engineers — Trans Soc Naval Architects Mar Eng
Transactions. Society of Occupational Medicine — Trans Soc Occup Med
Transactions. Society of Petroleum Engineers of AIME [*American Institute of Mining, Metallurgical, and Petroleum Engineers*] — Trans Soc Pet Eng AIME
Transactions. Society of Rheology — T Soc Rheol
Transactions. Society of Rheology — Trans Soc Rheol
Transactions. Society of Tropical Medicine and Hygiene (London) — Tr Soc Trop Med and Hyg (London)
Transactions. South African Institute of Electrical Engineers — Trans S Afr Inst Elec Eng
Transactions. South African Institute of Electrical Engineers — Trans S Afr Inst Electr Eng
Transactions. South African Institute of Electrical Engineers — TSAEA
Transactions. South African Institution of Civil Engineers — Trans S Afr Inst Civ Eng
Transactions. South African Institution of Civil Engineers — TSACA
Transactions. South Staffordshire Archaeological and Historical Society — Trans S Staffordshire Archaeol Hist Soc
Transactions. South Staffordshire Archaeological and Historical Society — Trans S Staffs Arch Hist Soc
Transactions. South Staffordshire Archaeological and Historical Society — Trans S Staffs Archaeol Hist Soc
Transactions. South Staffordshire Archaeological and Historical Society — Transact South Stafford
Transactions. Southwestern Federation of Geological Societies — Trans Southwest Fed Geol Soc
Transactions. SPWLA [*Society of Professional Well Log Analysts*] **Annual Logging Symposium** — Trans SPWLA Annu Log Symp
Transactions. St. John's Hospital Dermatological Society — Trans St John's Hosp Dermatol Soc
Transactions. State Institute of Applied Chemistry — Trans State Inst Appl Chem
Transactions. Suffolk Naturalists' Society — Trans Suffolk Natur Soc
Transactions. Technical Section. Canadian Pulp and Paper Association — Trans Tech Sect Can Pulp and Pap Assoc
Transactions. Technical Section. Canadian Pulp and Paper Association — Trans Tech Sect Can Pulp Pap Assoc
Transactions. Thoroton Society — TTS
Transactions. Thoroton Society of Nottinghamshire — Trans Thoroton Soc Notts
Transactions. Tokyo University of Fisheries — T Tokyo U F
Transactions. Tokyo University of Fisheries — Trans Tokyo Univ Fish
Transactions. Tottori Society of Agricultural Science — Trans Tottori Soc Agr Sci
Transactions. Tottori Society of Agricultural Sciences — Trans Tottori Soc Agric Sci
Transactions. Tuberculosis Society of Scotland — Trans Tuberc Soc Scotl
Transactions. Udgivet af Dansk Ingenioeren [*Denmark*] — Trans Udgivet Dan Ing
Transactions. University Centre of Desert Studies (Jodhpur, India) — Trans Univ Cent Desert Stud (Jodhpur India)
Transactions. Utah Academy of Sciences — Trans Utah Acad Sci
Transactions. Vacuum Symposium — Trans Vac Symp
Transactions. Wagner Free Institute of Science of Philadelphia — Trans Wagner Free Inst Sci Philadelphia
Transactions. Western Section of the American Urological Association — Trans West Sect Am Urol Assoc
Transactions. Western Section. Wildlife Society — Trans West Sect Wildl Soc

Transactions. Western Surgical Association — Trans West Surg Ass
Transactions. Wisconsin Academy of Science, Arts, and Letters — Trans Wisconsin Acad Sci Arts Lett
Transactions. Wisconsin Academy of Sciences, Arts, and Letters — T Wisc Ac
Transactions. Wisconsin Academy of Sciences, Arts, and Letters — Trans Wis Acad Sci
Transactions. Wisconsin Academy of Sciences, Arts, and Letters — Trans Wis Acad Sci Arts Lett
Transactions. Wisconsin Academy of Sciences, Arts, and Letters — Trans Wisc Acad Sci
Transactions. Wisconsin Academy of Sciences, Arts, and Letters — Trans Wisconsin Acad Sci
Transactions. Wisconsin Academy of Sciences, Arts, and Letters — TWA
Transactions. Woolhope Naturalists' Field Club — Trans Woolhope Natur Field Club
Transactions. Woolhope Naturalists' Field Club [*Herefordshire*] — Trans Woolhope Natur Fld Club
Transactions. Woolhope Naturalists' Field Club — Trans Woolhope Naturalists
Transactions. Worcestershire Archaeological Society — Trans Worc Arc Soc
Transactions. Worcestershire Archaeological Society — Trans Worc Arch Soc
Transactions. Worcestershire Archaeological Society — Trans Worcs Arc Soc
Transactions. Worcestershire Archaeological Society — Transact Worc
Transactions. Worcestershire Archaeological Society. Series 3 — Trans Worcestershire Archaeol Soc 3 Ser
Transactions. World Energy Conference — Trans World Energy Conf
Transactions. Yorkshire Dialect Society — TYDS
Transactions. Zimbabwe Scientific Association — Trans Zimb Sci Assoc
Transactions. Zimbabwe Scientific Association — Trans Zimbabwe Sci Assoc
Transactions. Zoological Society of London — Trans Zool Soc Lond
Transafrican Journal of History — Transafr J Hist
Transafrican Journal of History — TrsJH
Transaksies. Kollege van Geneeskunde van Suid-Afrika — Trans Koll Geneeskd S-Afr
Transatlantic Review — TR
Transatlantic Review — Trans R
Transatlantic Review — Transatl R
Transcripts of Parlibs Information Classification System [*Queensland Parliamentary Library*] — TOPICS
Transcultural Psychiatric Research Review — Transcult Psychiat Res
Transducer Technology — Transducer Technol
Transformation — TF
Transformation Groups — Transform Groups
Transformation (Supplement to La Papeterie) — Transform (Papeterie)
Transfusion [*Philadelphia*] — TRANA
Transfusion Clinique et Biologique — Transfus Clin Biol
Transfusion Medicine — Transfus Med
Transfusion Medicine Reviews — Transfus Med Rev
Transgenic Research — Transgenic Res
Transilvania University of Brasov. Bulletin. Series A. New Series — Bull Transilv Univ Brasov Ser A NS
Transilvania University of Brasov. Bulletin. Series B. New Series — Bull Transilv Univ Brasov Ser B NS
Transit Journal — Transit J
Transit Law Review — Transit L Rev
Transit Packaging — Transit Packag
Transition [*Indian and Northern Affairs, Canada*] — TRSN
Transition Metal Chemistry — TMC
Transition Metal Chemistry — TMCHD
Transition Metal Chemistry — Transition Met Chem
Transition Metal Chemistry [*New York*] — TRMCA
Transition Metal Chemistry (Weinheim, Germany) — Transit Met Chem (Weinheim Ger)
Transition Metal Coordination Chemistry — Transition Met Coord Chem
Transition Metal Nuclear Magnetic Resonance — Transition Met Nucl Magn Reson
Transkei Development Review — Transkei Dev Rev
Translantic Review (Paris) — TRP
Translated Contents Lists of Russian Periodicals — Transld Contents Lists Russ Period
Translation. Commonwealth Scientific and Industrial Research Organisation (CSIRO) (Australia) — Transl Commonw Sci Industr Res Organ (Aust)
Translation. Department of Fisheries and Forestry (Ottawa, Canada) — Transl Dep Fish For (Can)
Translation. Faculty of Forestry. University of British Columbia — Transl Fac For Univ BC
Translation. Forestry Commission (London) — Transl For Comm (Lond)
Translation Review — T Rev
Translation Review — Transl Rev
Translation. United States Forest Products Laboratory (Madison) — Transl US For Prod Lab (Madison)
Translations. Beltone Institute for Hearing Research — Transl Beltone Inst Hear Res
Translations of Mathematical Monographs — Transl Math Monographs
Translations of Mathematical Monographs. American Mathematical Society — Trans Math Monographs
Translations of Russian Game Reports — Transl Russ Game Rep
Translations on Soviet Agriculture. United States Joint Publications Research Service — Transl Soviet Agr US Joint Publ Res Serv
Translations Register-Index — Transl Reg-Index
Translations Register-Index — TRRIA
Translations Series in Mathematics and Engineering — Transl Ser Math Engrg
Translog — TRLGA
Transmission and Distribution — Transm & Distrib
Transmission and Distribution — Transm Distrib
Transmission and Distribution — TRDIA
Transnational Data Report — Transnational Data Rep
Transnational Data Report — Transnatl Data Rep
Transnational Data Report. Information Politics and Regulation — TND
Trans-Pacific — Trans-Pac
Transplant Immunology — Transpl Immunol
Transplant International — Transpl Int
Transplant International — Transplant Int
Transplantation — Transplant
Transplantation — TRPLA
Transplantation and Clinical Immunology — Transplant Clin Immunol
Transplantation Bulletin — Transplant Bull
Transplantation et Immunologie Clinique — Transplant Immunol Clin
Transplantation Proceedings — Transplan P
Transplantation Proceedings — Transplant Proc
Transplantation Proceedings — Transplantn Proc
Transplantation Proceedings — TRPPA
Transplantation Proceedings. Supplement — Transplant Proc Suppl
Transplantation Reviews — Transplan R
Transplantation Reviews — Transplant Rev
Transplantation Reviews — TRPRB
Transplantation Science — Transplant Sci
Transplantation Society. International Congress. Proceedings — Transplant Soc Int Cong Proc
Transport — TT
Transport and Communication Review — Transp Commun Rev
Transport and Communications Bulletin for Asia and the Pacific — Transport and Communications Bul Asia and Pacific
Transport and Road Research Laboratory (Great Britain). TRRL Report — Transp Road Res Lab (GB) TRRL Rep
Transport and Road Research Laboratory. Supplementary Report — TRRS
Transport and Traffic — Transp Traffic
Transport Australia — Transp Aust
Transport Digest — Transport D
Transport Echo. The Benelux Transport Magazine — BSU
Transport Economics and Operational Analysis — Trans Econ & Oper Anal
Transport en Opslag. Maandblad voor Managers en Medewerkers op het Gebied van Intern Transport, Opslag, Magazijntechniek, en Distributietechniek — TWX
Transport Engineer — TEJIA
Transport Engineer — Transp Engr
Transport Environment Circulation — TEC
Transport History — Transp Hist
Transport i Khranenie Nefti i Nefteproduktov [*Former USSR*] — Transp Khranenie Nefti Nefteprod
Transport in Porous Media — Transp Porous Media
Transport Journal — Transp J
Transport Journal of Australia — Transp J of Aust
Transport Management — Transp Manage
Transport News [*New Zealand*] — Trans News
Transport News Digest — Transp News Dig
Transport News of New Zealand — Transp News
Transport Planning and Technology — Transp Plan and Technol
Transport Policy and Decision Making — Transp Policy Decision Making
Transport Processes in Engineering — Transp Processes Eng
Transport Reviews — Transp Revs
Transport Theory and Statistical Physics — Transp Th St P
Transport Theory and Statistical Physics — Transp Theo
Transport Theory and Statistical Physics — Transp Theory Stat Phys
Transport Theory and Statistical Physics — Transport Theory Statist Phys
Transport Theory and Statistical Physics — TTSPB
Transportation — Transportat
Transportation Costing Service [*Database*] — TCS
Transportation Engineering — Transp Eng
Transportation Engineering [*Formerly, Traffic Engineering*] — Transp Engng
Transportation Engineering Journal. ASCE [*American Society of Civil Engineers*] — Transp En J
Transportation Engineering Journal. ASCE [*American Society of Civil Engineers*] — Transp Eng J ASCE
Transportation Engineering Journal. Proceedings of the American Society of Civil Engineers — Transp Engng J Proc ASCE
Transportation History — Transp His
Transportation Journal — Transp J
Transportation Journal — Transportation J
Transportation Journal — TRNJA
Transportation Law Journal — TLJ
Transportation Law Journal — Trans LJ
Transportation Law Journal — Transp L J
Transportation Legislative Data Base — TLDB
Transportation Library [*Database*] — TLIB
Transportation News Ticker [*Database*] — TNT
Transportation Planning and Technology — Transp Plann Tech
Transportation Planning and Technology — Transp Plann Technol
Transportation Planning and Technology [*London*] — Transportation Plann Tech
Transportation Proceedings — TRP
Transportation Quarterly — GTRQ
Transportation Quarterly — Transp Q
Transportation Quarterly — Transportation Q
Transportation Quarterly — TRQUD
Transportation Research — Transp Res
Transportation Research — Transportation Res
Transportation Research — TRREB
Transportation Research — TRS
Transportation Research Abstracts — Trans Res Abstr
Transportation Research Abstracts — Transp Res Abstr
Transportation Research Board. Special Report — Transp Res Board Spec Rep

Transportation Research Board. Special Report [*United States*] — TRRB
Transportation Research Board. Transportation Research Record — Transp Res Board Transp Res Rec
Transportation Research Information Service [*Database*] — TRIS
Transportation Research News — Transp Res News
Transportation Research News — TREND
Transportation Research. Part A. General — Trans Res A
Transportation Research. Part A. General — Transp Res Part A
Transportation Research. Part A. General [*England*] — Transp Res Part A Gen
Transportation Research. Part A. General — Transportation Res Part A
Transportation Research. Part B. Methodological — Trans Res B
Transportation Research. Part B. Methodological — Transp Res Part B
Transportation Research. Part B. Methodological — Transportation Res Part B
Transportation Research Record [*United States*] — Transp Res Rec
Transportation Research Record — TRRE
Transportation Research Record — TRRED
Transportation Science — TR
Transportation Science — Trans Sci
Transportation Science — Transp Sci
Transportation Science — TRSCB
Transportation USA — Tran USA
Transporter — Transp
Transportnoe Stroitel'stvo [*Former USSR*] — Transp Stroit
Transportno-Meditsinski Vesti — Transp-Med Vesti
Transunti. Accademia Nazionale dei Lincei — Acc Naz Linc Tr
Transunti. Accademia Nazionale dei Lincei — Trans Linc
Transunti. Accademia Nazionale dei Lincei — Trans Lincei
Transvaal Agricultural Journal — Transvaal Agric J
Transvaal Educational News — Tvl Educ News
Transvaal Medical Journal — Transvaal Med J
Transvaal Museum. Bulletin — Transvaal Mus Bull
Transvaal Museum. Memoirs — Transvaal Mus Mem
Transvaal Museum. Monograph — Transvaal Mus Monogr
Transvaal Museum. Report — Transvaal Mus Rep
Transvaal Nature Conservation Division. Annual Report — Transvaal Nat Conserv Div Annu Rep
Transylvania Journal of Medicine — Transylvania J Med
Trasfusione del Sangue — Trasfus Sangue
Trasporti Pubblici — Trasp Pubbl
Trasporti. Rivista di Politica, Economia, e Tecnica — Trasp
Trattamenti dei Metalli — Tratt Met
Trattamenti dei Metalli — TRMEA
Traumatology — Traumatol
Travail de l'Alphabetisation — Trav Alphabet
Travail des Metaux par Deformation — Trav Met Deform
Travail et Methodes — Trav et Meth
Travail et Methodes. Revue des Nouvelles au Service de l'Entreprise — TRG
Travail et Securite — Trav Secur
Travail et Securite — TRVSA
Travail et Societe — Trav et Soc
Travail Humain — Trav Hum
Travail Humain — Trav Humain
Travail Humain — TRHUA
Travail Quebec — Trav Quebec
Travailleur Canadien — Travailleur Can
Travail-Syndicalisme. Bibliographie — Trav-Syndicalisme Bibl
Travaux — TRAVA
Travaux. Association Henri Capitant — Trav Assoc H Capitant
Travaux. Centre de Recherches et d'Etudes Oceanographiques — Trav Cent Rech Etudes Oceanogr
Travaux. Cercle Linguistique de Copenhague — TCLC
Travaux. Cercle Linguistique de Prague — TCLP
Travaux. Classe I de Linguistique, de Litterature, et de Philosophie. Societe des Sciences et des Lettres de Lodz — TSL
Travaux. Comite d'Etudes et de Legislation de la Federation des Notaires de Belgique — Trav C Et
Travaux. Comite International pour l'Etude des Bauxites, de l'Alumine, et de l'Aluminium — Trav Com Int Etude Bauxites Alumine Alum
Travaux. Comite International pour l'Etude des Bauxites, des Oxydes, et des Hydroxydes d'Aluminium — Trav Com Int Etude Bauxites Oxydes Hydroxydes Alum
Travaux Communaux [*France*] — Trav Communaux
Travaux Communaux — TVXCA
Travaux de Chimie Alimentaire et d'Hygiene — Trav Chim Aliment Hyg
Travaux de la CCI [*Chambre de Commerce Internationale*] — Trav CCI
Travaux de la Societe d'Emulation du Departement du Jura — Trav Soc Emul Dep Jura
Travaux de Laboratoire de Geologie de la Faculte des Sciences de l'Universite de Grenoble — Trav Lab Geol Fac Sci Univ Grenoble
Travaux de l'Action Populaire — Trav Act Pop
Travaux de Linguistique — Lg
Travaux de Linguistique et de Litterature [*Strasbourg*] — TLL
Travaux de Linguistique et de Litterature — Trav Linguist Litt
Travaux de Linguistique et de Litterature. Centre de Philologie et de Litteratures Romanes. Universite de Strasbourg — Trav C Ph R
Travaux de Linguistique et de Litterature (Strasbourg) — TLLS
Travaux de Linguistique Quantitative — TLQ
Travaux de Linguistique Quebecoise — TLQue
Travaux de l'Institut d'Etudes Latino-Americaines de l'Universite de Strasbourg — Travaux Inst Etud Lat Am Univ Strasbourg
Travaux de l'Institut Francais d'Etudes Andines — Trav Inst Franc Etudes Andines
Travaux de l'Institut Francais d'Etudes Andines (Paris) — Travaux Inst Fran Etud Andines Paris
Travaux de Logique — Travaux Log
Travaux de Peinture — Trav Peint
Travaux des Jeunes Scientifiques — Trav Jeunes Sci
Travaux d'Humanisme et Renaissance — THR
Travaux d'Humanisme et Renaissance — Trav Hum Ren
Travaux du Bureau Geologique — Trav Bur Geol
Travaux du Centre de Recherches et d'Etudes Oceanographiques — Trav Centr Rech Etudes Oceanogr
Travaux du Centre de Recherches Semiologiques — Travaux Centre Rech Semiol
Travaux et Conferences. Faculte de Droit de Bruxelles — Trav Conf Brux
Travaux et Conferences. Universite Libre de Bruxelles — Tr Conf ULB
Travaux et Conferences. Universite Libre de Bruxelles. Faculte de Droit — TRAC
Travaux et Documents de Geographie Tropicale — Trav Doc Geogr Trop
Travaux et Documents. ORSTOM [*Office de la Recherche Scientifique et Technique d'Outre-Mer*] — Trav Doc ORSTOM
Travaux et Jours — Trav et Jours
Travaux et Memoires. Bureau International des Poids et Mesures — Trav Mem Bur Int Poids Mes
Travaux et Memoires. Centre de Recherche d'Histoire et Civilisation Byzantine [*Paris*] — Trav Mem
Travaux et Memoires. Centre de Recherche d'Histoire et de Civilisation Byzantines — TM
Travaux et Memoires. Centre de Recherche d'Histoire et de Civilisation Byzantines — Tr Mem
Travaux et Memoires. Centre de Recherche d'Histoire et de Civilisation Byzantines — TrM
Travaux et Notices de l'Academie d'Agriculture de France — Trav Notices Acad Agric France
Travaux et Recherches — Trav et Rech
Travaux et Recherches — Travaux Rech
Travaux et Recherches. Federation Tarnaise de Speleo-Archeologie — T & R
Travaux et Recherches. Haut Comite d'Etude et d'Information sur l'Alcoolisme — Trav Rech Haut Comite Et Inform Alcool
Travaux Geographique de Liege (Belgium) — TGGL-B
Travaux Geophysiques (Prague) — Trav Geophys (Prague)
Travaux. Institut de Geologie et d'Anthropologie Prehistorique. Faculte des Sciences de Poitiers — Trav Inst Geol Anthropol Prehist Fac Sci Poitiers
Travaux. Institut de Linguistique — TIL
Travaux. Institut de Linguistique de Lund — Trav Inst L
Travaux. Institut de Recherches Sahariennes — TIRS
Travaux. Institut de Recherches Sahariennes — Trav Inst Rech Sahar
Travaux. Institut de Speleologie "Emile Racovitza" — Trav Inst Speleo "Emile Racovitza"
Travaux. Institut d'Etudes Latino-Americaines. Universite de Strasbourg — TILAS
Travaux. Institut Francais d'Etudes Andines — Trav Inst Franc Et And
Travaux. Institut Francais d'Etudes Andines — Trav Inst Franc Et Andines
Travaux. Institut Medical Superieur — Trav Inst Med Super
Travaux. Institut Scientifique Cherifien et Faculte des Sciences de Rabat. Serie Generale — Trav Inst Sci Cherifien Fac Sci Rabat Ser Gen
Travaux. Institut Scientifique Cherifien et Faculte des Sciences. Serie: Sciences Physiques — Trav Inst Sci Cherifien Fac Sci Ser Sci Phys
Travaux. Institut Scientifique Cherifien et Faculte des Sciences. Serie Zoologie — Trav Inst Sci Cherifien Fac Sci Ser Zool
Travaux. Institut Scientifique Cherifien. Serie Botanique — Trav Inst Sci Cherifien Ser Bot
Travaux. Institut Scientifique Cherifien. Serie Botanique et Biologique Vegetale — Trav Inst Sci Cherifien Ser Bot Biol Veg
Travaux. Institut Scientifique Cherifien. Serie Geologie et Geographie Physique — Trav Inst Sci Cherifien Ser Geol Geogr Phys
Travaux. Institut Scientifique Cherifien. Serie Sciences Physiques — Trav Inst Sci Cherifien Ser Sci Phys
Travaux. Institut Scientifique Cherifien. Serie Zoologique — Trav Inst Sci Cherifien Ser Zool
Travaux. Institute d'Estudes Iboriques et Latino-Americaines — TILAS
Travaux. Laboratoire d'Anthropologie de Prehistoire et d'Ethnologie des Pays de la Mediterranee Occidentale — Trav Lab Anthropol Prehist Ethnol Pays Mediterr Occid
Travaux. Laboratoire de Geologie. Ecole Normale Superieure (Paris) — Trav Lab Geol Ec Norm Super (Paris)
Travaux. Laboratoire de Geologie. Faculte des Sciences de Grenoble — Trav Lab Geol Fac Sci Grenoble
Travaux. Laboratoire de Geologie. Faculte des Sciences de Grenoble. Memoires — Trav Lab Geol Fac Sci Grenoble Mem
Travaux. Laboratoire de Geologie. Faculte des Sciences de Lyon — Trav Lab Geol Fac Sci Lyon
Travaux. Laboratoire de Geologie. Faculte des Sciences. Universite de Bordeaux — Trav Lab Geol Fac Sci Univ Bordeaux
Travaux. Laboratoire de Geologie Historique et de Paleontologie. Centre Saint Charles. Universite de Provence — Trav Lab Geol Hist Paleontol Cent St Charles Univ Provence
Travaux. Laboratoire de Microbiologie. Faculte de Pharmacie de Nancy — Trav Lab Microbiol Fac Pharm Nancy
Travaux. Laboratoire d'Hydrobiologie et de Pisciculture. Universite de Grenoble — Trav Lab Hydrobiol Piscic Univ Grenoble
Travaux. Laboratoire d'Hydrogeologie Geochimie. Faculte des Sciences Universite de Bordeaux — Trav Lab Hydrogeol Geochim Fac Sci Univ Bordeaux
Travaux. Laboratoire Forestier de Toulouse — Trav Lab For Toulouse
Travaux. Laboratoire Forestier de Toulouse. Tome I. Articles Divers — Trav Lab For Toulouse Tome I Artic Divers
Travaux. Laboratoire Forestier de Toulouse. Tome II. Etudes Dendrologiques — Trav Lab For Toulouse Tome II Etud Dendrol

Travaux. Laboratoire Forestier de Toulouse. Tome V. Geographie Forestier du Monde — Trav Lab For Toulouse Tome V Geogr For Monde
Travaux. Laboratoire Forestier. Universite de Toulouse — Trav Lab For Univ Toulouse
Travaux. Laboratoires de Matiere Medicale et de Pharmacie Galenique. Faculte de Pharmacie (Paris) — Trav Lab Matiere Med Pharm Galenique Fac Pharm (Paris)
Travaux Linguistiques de Prague — TLP
Travaux. Musee d'Etat de l'Ermitage — TE
Travaux. Museum d'Histoire Naturelle "Grigore Antipa" — Trav Mus Hist Nat "Gr Antipa"
Travaux. Museum d'Histoire Naturelle "Grigore Antipa" — Trav Mus Hist Nat "Grigore Antipa"
Travaux Scientifiques. Centre de Recherches Scientifiques et de Projections de l'Industrie Vinicole (Sofia) — Trav Sci Cent Rech Sci Proj Ind Vini (Sofia)
Travaux Scientifiques. Chercheurs du Service de Sante des Armees — Trav Sci Chercheurs Serv Sante Armees
Travaux Scientifiques. Parc National de la Vanoise — Trav Sci Parc Natl Vanoise
Travaux. Section Scientifique et Technique. Institut Francais de Pondichery — Trav Sect Sci Tech Inst Fr Pondichery
Travaux. Section Scientifique et Technique. Institut Francais de Pondichery — Trav Sect Sci Tech Inst Franc Pondichery
Travaux. Section Scientifique et Technique. Institut Francais de Pondichery — Trav Sect Scient Tech Inst Fr Pondichery
Travaux. Seminaire d'Analyse Convexe — Travaux Sem Anal Convexe
Travaux. Societe Botanique de Geneve — Trav Soc Bot Geneve
Travaux. Societe de Pharmacie de Montpellier — Trav Soc Pharm Montp
Travaux. Societe de Pharmacie de Montpellier [*France*] — Trav Soc Pharm Montpellier
Travaux. Societe de Pharmacie de Montpellier — TSPMA
Travaux. Societe des Sciences et des Lettres de Wroclaw — Trav Soc Sci Lettres Wroclaw
Travaux. Societe Lorientaise d'Archeologie — Trav Lorient
Travaux. Station de Recherches des Eaux et Forets. Groenendaal-Hoeilaart — Trav Sta Rech Groenendaal
Travaux sur les Pecheries du Quebec — Trav Pech Que
Travaux sur Voltaire et le Dix-Huitieme Siecle — TVD
Travel — Trav
Travel and Leisure — GTNL
Travel/Holiday — Trav
Travel/Holiday — Trav/Holiday
Travel News — TN
Travel Trade Gazette UK — TTG
Travel Weekly — Travl Wkly
Travel-Holiday — GTRH
Travelling — Trav
Treaties and Other International Acts Series — TIAS
Treaties in Force. US State Department — TIF
Treating Abuse Today — TAT
Treatise on Analytical Chemistry — Treatise Anal Chem
Treatise on Materials Science and Technology — Treatise Mater Sci Technol
Treatises of the Section of Medical Sciences. Polish Academy of Sciences — Treatises Sect Med Sci Pol Acad Sci
Treatment and Use of Sewage Sludge and Liquid Agricultural Wastes. Proceedings. Symposium — Treat Use Sewage Sludge Liq Agric Wastes Proc Symp
Treaty. US State Department Series — TS
Treballs. Institut Botanic de Barcelona — Treballs Inst Bot Barc
Tree Crops Journal — Tree Crops J
Tree Physiology — Tree Physiol
Tree Planters' Notes — TPNO
Tree Planters' Notes — Tree Plant Notes
Tree Planter's Notes. United States Forest Service — Tree Plant Notes US For Serv
Tree Planters' Notes. US Department of Agriculture. Forest Service — Tree Plant Notes US Dep Agric For Serv
Tree Planters' Notes. US Forest Service — Tree Pl Notes
Tree-Ring Bulletin — Tree-Ring Bull
Trees and Natural Resources — Trees Nat Resour
Trees and Victoria's Resources — Trees Victoria's Resour
Trees in South Africa — Trees S Afr
Trees Magazine — Trees Mag
Trees on Farms. Proceedings of a Seminar on Economic and Technical Aspects of Commercial Plantations. Agro-Forestry and Shelter Belts on Farms — Tree Farm Proc
Trees. Structure and Function — Trees Struct Funct
Trefpunt — TRP
Treji Varti — TV
Trend; das Oesterreichische Wirtschaftsmagazin — OTI
Trend Prognosticke Informace — Trend Prognosticke Inf
Trends — TNDSA
Trends and Perspectives in Parasitology — TPPADK
Trends and Perspectives in Parasitology — Trends Perspect Parasitol
Trends and Perspectives in Signal Processing — Trends and Perspect Signal Process
Trends and Techniques in the Contemporary Dental Laboratory — Trends Tech Contemp Dent Lab
Trends. Financieel Economisch Magazine — TSM
Trends in Analytical Chemistry — TrAC
Trends in Analytical Chemistry — Trends Anal Chem
Trends in Analytical Chemistry — Trends Analyt Chem
Trends in Autonomic Pharmacology — TAUPDJ
Trends in Autonomic Pharmacology — Trends Auton Pharmacol
Trends in Biobmembranes and Bioenergetics — Trends Biomembr Bioenerg
Trends in Biochemical Sciences — TIBS
Trends in Biochemical Sciences — Trends Biochem Sci
Trends in Biochemical Sciences (Personal Edition) [*Netherlands*] — Trends Biochem Sci (Pers Ed)
Trends in Biochemical Sciences (Reference Edition) [*Netherlands*] — Trends Biochem Sci (Ref Ed)
Trends in Biotechnology — TBT
Trends in Biotechnology — TRBIDM
Trends in Biotechnology — Trends Biot
Trends in Biotechnology — Trends Biotechnol
Trends in Cardiovascular Medicine — Trend Card
Trends in Cardiovascular Medicine — Trends Cardiovasc Med
Trends in Cell Biology — Trends Cell Biol
Trends in Ecology and Evolution — Tr Ecol Evo
Trends in Education — Trends Ed
Trends in Education — Trends Educ
Trends in Education — Trends in Ed
Trends in Endocrinology and Metabolism — Trends Endocrinol Metab
Trends in Engineering — Trend Eng
Trends in Engineering. University of Washington — Trend Eng Univ Wash
Trends in Fluorescence — Trends Fluoresc
Trends in Genetics — Trends Gen
Trends in Genetics — Trends Genet
Trends in Genetics — TRGEE2
Trends in Glycoscience and Glycotechnology — Trends Glycoscience Glycotechnol
Trends in Haematology — Trends Haematol
Trends in History — Trends Hist
Trends in Linguistics. Studies and Monographs — Trends Linguist Stud Monogr
Trends in Microbiology — Trends Microbiol
Trends in Neurosciences — TINS
Trends in Neurosciences [*Netherlands*] — Trends Neurosci
Trends in Pharmacological Sciences — TPHSDY
Trends in Pharmacological Sciences — Trends Pharmacol Sci
Trends in Scientific Research — Trends Sci Res
Trends in Teacher Education — Trends in Teach Ed
Trends in the Hotel-Motel Industry — Tnd Hotel
Trent Law Journal — Trent LJ
Triad — TR
Trial — ITRI
Trial Diplomacy Journal — Trial Diplomacy J
Trial Diplomacy Journal — Trial Dpl J
Trial Educational Materials for Advanced Schools — Trial Ed Mater Adv Sch
Trial Lawyer's Guide — Tr Law Guide
Trial Lawyer's Guide — Trial Law G
Trial Lawyer's Guide — Trial Law Guide
Trial Lawyers Quarterly — Tr Law Q
Trial Lawyers Quarterly — Trial Law Q
Triangle [*English Edition*] — TRGLA
Triangle — TRGLB
Triangle of Mu Phi Epsilon — Tri
Tribologia e Lubrificazione — Tribol Lubrificazione
Tribologia e Lubrificazione — Tribologia & Lubr
Tribological Modeling for Mechanical Designers — Tribol Model Mech Des
Tribology International — Tribol Int
Tribology International — Tribology
Tribology International — Tribology Int
Tribology Letters — Tribol Lett
Tribology Series [*Elsevier Book Series*] — TS
Tribuna — Tri
Tribuna Farmaceutica (Curitiba) — Trib Farm (Curitiba)
Tribuna Medica — TMC
Tribuna Odontologica — Trib Odontol
Tribuna Postale e delle Telecomunicazioni — Tribuna Postale
Tribuna Romaniei — TRom
Tribune [*New York*] — Tr
Tribune. CEBEDEAU [*Centre Belge d'Etude et de Documentation des Eaux et de l'Air*] — TCEBA
Tribune. CEBEDEAU [*Centre Belge d'Etude et de Documentation des Eaux et de l'Air*] — Trib CEBEDEAU
Tribune Horticole. Societe Royale Linneenne de Bruxelles — Tribune Hort
Tribune Juive — TJ
Tribune Musical — Trib Mus
Tribus. Veroeffentlichungen des Linden-Museums. Museum fuer Laender- und Voelkerkunde — MLV/T
Tricontinental Bulletin — Tricontinental Bull
Trident (London) — TL
Trier Jahresberichte — Jahresber Trier
Trier Jahresberichte — TJ
Trier Zeitschrift fuer Geschichte und Kunst des Trierer Landes und Seiner Nachbargebiete — Tr Ztschr
Trier Zeitschrift fuer Geschichte und Kunst des Trierer Landes und Seiner Nachbargebiete — Trierer Zeitschr
Trier Zeitschrift fuer Geschichte und Kunst des Trierer Landes und Seiner Nachbargebiete — Trierer Ztschr
Trier Zeitschrift fuer Geschichte und Kunst des Trierer Landes und Seiner Nachbargebiete — TZ
Trierer Heimatbuch — THB
Trierer Studien zur Literatur — TS Lit
Trierer Theologische Zeitschrift — T Th Z
Trierer Theologische Zeitschrift [*Trier*] — TriererThZ
Trierer Theologische Zeitschrift [*Trier*] — TrierThZ
Trierer Theologische Zeitschrift — TTZ
Trierer Zeitschrift — TrZ
Trierer Zeitschrift — TZ

Trierer Zeitschrift fuer Geschichte und Kunst des Trierer Landes und Seiner Nachbargebiete — Tr Z
Trierer Zeitschrift fuer Geschichte und Kunst des Trierer Landes und Seiner Nachbargebiete — Trierer Z Gesch Kunst
Trierer Zeitschrift fuer Geschichte und Kunst des Trierer Landes und Seiner Nachbargebiete — TriererZ
Trierische Chronik — TC
Trierische Heimatblaetter — THbl
Trierisches Archiv — TA
Trierisches Archiv — Trier Archiv
Trieste Notes in Physics — Trieste Notes in Phys
Trimestre Economico — TE
Trimestre Economico — Trim Econ
Trimestre Economico — Trimes Econ
Trimestre Economico. Fondo de Cultura Economica — FCE/TE
Trimestre Politico — Trim Pol
Trinidad and Tobago Forester — Trin Tob For
Trinidad and Tobago. Ministry of Petroleum and Mines. Monthly Bulletin — Trinidad Tobago Min Petrol Mines Mon Bull
Trinity Journal — TJ
Trinity Journal — Trinity J
Trinity Seminary Review — Trinity Sem R
Trinkwasser-Verordnung — Trinkwasser-Verord
Triquarterly — PTQR
Tri-Quarterly — TQ
Tri-Quarterly — TriQ
Tri-Quarterly — Tri-Quar
Tri-Quarterly — TriQuart
Tri-State Medical Journal (Greensburo, North Carolina) — Tri State Med J (Greensburo NC)
Tri-State Medical Journal (Shreveport, Louisiana) — Tri State Med J (Shreveport LA)
Trivium — Tr
Trivium — Triv
Tromso Museums Arsberetning — Tromso Mus Arsberetning
Tromsoe Museum. Skrifter — Tromso Mus Skr
Tromura. Tromsoe Museum Rapportserie. Kulturhistorie — TMRKH
Tromura. Tromsoe Museum Rapportserie. Naturvitenskap — TMRNV
Trondheim Workingpapers — TWP
Tropenlandwirt — TROPB
Tropenlandwirtschaft (Germany, Federal Republic) — Tropenlandwirt (Germany FR)
Tropenmedizin und Parasitologie — Tropenmed P
Tropenmedizin und Parasitologie — Tropenmed Parasitol
Tropenpflanzer. Beiheft — Tropenpflanzer Beih
Trophoblast Research — Trophoblast Res
Tropical Abstracts — Trop Abstr
Tropical Agriculture — TAE
Tropical Agriculture — TAGLA
Tropical Agriculture — Trop Agr
Tropical Agriculture — Trop Agric
Tropical Agriculture Research Series — TARSD
Tropical Agriculture Research Series — Trop Agric Res Ser
Tropical Agriculture Research Series (Japan) — Trop Agric Res Ser (Japan)
Tropical Agriculture (Trinidad) — Trop Agri (Trinidad)
Tropical Agriculturist — Tropical Ag
Tropical Agriculturist and Magazine. Ceylon Agricultural Society — Trop Agricst Mag Ceylon Agric Soc
Tropical Agriculturist (Ceylon) — Trop Agr (Ceylon)
Tropical Agriculturist (Ceylon) — Trop Agri (Ceylon)
Tropical Agriculturist. Ceylon [Agricultural Society Journal] — Trop Agric Ceylon
Tropical Agriculturist (Colombo) — Trop Agric (Colombo)
Tropical and Geographical Medicine — TGMEA
Tropical and Geographical Medicine — Trop Geo Me
Tropical and Geographical Medicine — Trop Geogr Med
Tropical Animal Health and Production — Trop Anim Health Prod
Tropical Animal Production [*Dominican Republic*] — Trop Anim Prod
Tropical Building Research Notes. Division of Building Research. Commonwealth Scientific and Industrial Research Organisation — Trop Build Res Notes Div Build Res CSIRO
Tropical Dental Journal — OSTRDN
Tropical Dental Journal — Trop Dent J
Tropical Diseases Bulletin — Trop Dis Bull
Tropical Doctor — Trop Doct
Tropical Ecology — Trop Ecol
Tropical Forest Notes — Trop For Notes
Tropical Gastroenterology — Trop Gastroenterol
Tropical Grain Legume Bulletin — Trop Grain Legume Bull
Tropical Grasslands — Trop Grassl
Tropical Grasslands — Trop Grasslands
Tropical Grasslands — Trop Grasslds
Tropical Life — Trop Life
Tropical Man [*Leiden*] — Trop Man
Tropical Medicine — Trop Med
Tropical Medicine and Hygiene News — Trop Med Hyg News
Tropical Medicine and International Health — Trop Med Int Health
Tropical Medicine and Parasitology — Trop Med Parasitol
Tropical Medicine Research Studies Series — TMRSDT
Tropical Medicine Research Studies Series — Trop Med Res Stud Ser
Tropical Pest Bulletin — Trop Pest Bull
Tropical Pest Management — TPMAD5
Tropical Pest Management — Trop Pest Manage
Tropical Pesticides Research Institute. Annual Report — Trop Pestic Res Inst Annu Rep
Tropical Pesticides Research Institute. Miscellaneous Report — Trop Pestic Res Inst Misc Rep
Tropical Products Institute. Crop and Product Digest — Trop Prod Inst Crop Prod Dig
Tropical Products Institute. Report — Trop Prod Inst Rep
Tropical Science — Trop Sci
Tropical Science — TROSA
Tropical Science — TS
Tropical Scienoo Center. Occasional Paper (San Jose, Costa Rica) — Trop Sci Cent Occas Pap (San Jose Costa Rica)
Tropical Stored Products Information — Trop Stored Prod Inf
Tropical Stored Products Information — Trop Stored Prod Inform
Tropical Veterinarian — Trop Vet
Tropical Veterinarian — TRVTDJ
Tropical Veterinary Bulletin — Trop Vet Bull
Tropical Veterinary Medicine. Current Issues and Perspectives — Trop Vet Med Curr Issues Perspect
Tropical Woods — Trop Wd
Tropical Woods — Trop Woods
Tropical Woods. Yale University School of Forestry — Trop Woods Yale Univ Sch For
Tropical Zoology — Trop Zool
Tropische und Subtropische Pflanzenwelt — Trop Subtrop Pflwelt
Troquel — TL
Trouser Press — Trouser
Trouw — TRU
TRRL [*Transport and Road Research Laboratory*] **Laboratory Report** — TRRL Lab Rep
TRRL [*Transport and Road Research Laboratory*] **Report** — TRRL Rep
TRRL [*Transport and Road Research Laboratory*] **Supplementary Report** — TRRL Suppl Rep
TRRL [*Transport and Road Research Laboratory*] **Supplementary Report** — TSRLD
Trubnoe Proizvodstvo Urala — Trubn Proizvod Urala
Truck and Bus Transportation — Truck & Bus Trans
Truck and Bus Transportation — Truck & Bus Transp
Truck and Bus Transportation — Truck Bus Transpn
Truck and Off-Highway Industries [*United States*] — Truck Off-Highw Ind
Trudove na Chernomorskata Biologichna Stantsiya v Varna — Tr Chernomorsk Biol Stan Varna
Trudove na Instituta po Khigiena. Okhrana na Truda i Profesionalni Zabolyavaniya — Tr Inst Khig Okhr Tr Prof Zabol
Trudove na Minniya Nauchnoizsledovatelski i Proektno Konstruktorski Institut — Tr Minniya Nauchnoizsled Proekto Konstr Inst
Trudove na Morskata Biologichna Stantsiya v Stalin — Tr Morsk Biol Stn Stalin
Trudove na Nauchnoizsledovatelskiya Institut po Cherna Metallurgiya — Tr Nauchnoizsled Inst Cherna Metal
Trudove na Nauchnoizsledovatelskiya Institut po Vodosnabdyavane. Kanalizatsiya i Sanitarna Tekhnika [*Bulgaria*] — Tr Nauchnoizsled Inst Vodosnabdyavane Kanaliz Sanit Tekh
Trudove na Nauchnoizsledovatelskiya Instituta po Epidemiologiya i Mikrobiologiya — Tr Nauchnoizsled Inst Epidemio Mikrobiol
Trudove na Nauchnoizsledovatelskiya Instituta po Farmatsiya — Tr Nauchnoizsled Inst Farm
Trudove na Nauchnoizsledovatelskiya Instituta po Okhrana na Truda i Profesionalnite Zabolyavaniya — Tr Nauchnoizsled Inst Okhr Tr Prof Zabol
Trudove na Nauchnoizsledovatelskiya Instituta po Stroitelni Materiali (Sofia) — Tr Nauchnoizsled Inst Stroit Mater (Sofia)
Trudove na Nauchnoizsledovatelskiya Instituta po Tekstilna Promishlenost (Sofia) — Tr Nauchnoizsled Inst Tekst Promst (Sofia)
Trudove na Nauchnoizsledovatelskiya Khimiko-Farmatsevtichen Institut — Tr Nauchnoizsled Khim Farm Inst
Trudove na Nauchnoizsledovatelskiya. Proektokonstruktorski i Tekhnologicheski Institut po Tekstilna Promishlenost — Tr Nauchnoizsled Proektokonstr Tekhnol Inst Tekst Promst
Trudove na Respublikanskiya Instituta po Epidemiologiya i Mikrobiologiya — Tr Resp Inst Epidemiol Mikrobiol
Trudove na Tsentralniya Nauchnoizsledovatelski Institut po Ribovudstvo i Ribolov. Varna. Bulgarska Akademiya na Naukite — Tr Tsentr Nauchnoizsled Inst Ribovud Varna Bulg Akad Nauk
Trudove na Visshiya Institut za Narodno Stopanstvo "D. Blagoev" (Varna Bulgaria) — Tr Vissh Inst Nar Stop (Varna Bulg)
Trudove na Visshiya Pedagogicheski Institut (Plovdiv). Matematika, Fizika, Khimiya, Biologiya — Tr Vissh Pedagog Inst (Plovdiv) Mat Fiz Khim Biol
Trudove. Vissija Ikonomiceski Institut Karl Marks-Sofija — Trud Viss Ikonom Inst Karl Marks-Sofia
Trudove Vurkhu Geologiyata na Bulgariya. Seriya Geokhimaya Mineralogiya i Petrografiya — Tr Geol Bulg Ser Geokhm Mineral Petrogr
Trudove Vurkhu Geologiyata na Bulgariya. Seriya Inzhenerna Geologiya i Khidrogeologiya — Tr Geol Bulg Ser Inzh Geol Khidrogeol
Trudove Vurkhu Geologiyata na Bulgariya. Seriya Paleontologiya — Tr Geol Bulg Ser Paleonto
Trudovei na Geoloskiot Zavod na Socijalisticka Republika Makedonija — Tr Geol Zavod Soc Repub Makedonija
Trudy 1 Pervogo Moskovskogo Meditsinskogo Instituta [*Former USSR*] — Tr 1 Pervogo Mosk Med Inst
Trudy Akademii Meditsinskikh Nauk SSSR — Tr Akad Med Nauk SSSR
Trudy Akademii Nauk Gruzinskoi SSR Institut Sistem Upravleniya — Tr Akad Nauk Gruz SSR Inst Sist Upr
Trudy Akademii Nauk Latviiskoi SSR Institut Mikrobiologii — Tr Akad Nauk Latv SSR Inst Mikrobiol
Trudy Akademii Nauk Litovskoi SSR — Trudy Akad Nauk Litov SSR
Trudy Akademii Nauk Litovskoi SSR Institut Biologii — Tr Akad Nauk Litov SSR Inst Biol

Trudy Akademii Nauk Litovskoi SSR. Serija B — Trudy Akad Nauk Litov SSR Ser B
Trudy. Akademii Nauk Litovskoi SSR. Seriya B. — Trudy Akad Nauk Litovsk SSR Ser B
Trudy Akademii Nauk Litovskoi SSR. Seriya V — Tr Akad Nauk Lit SSR Ser V
Trudy Akademii Nauk Litovskoi SSR. Seriya V. Biologicheskie Nauki — Tr Akad Nauk Lit SSR Ser V Biol Nauki
Trudy Akademii Nauk Litovskoj SSR. Serija A. Obscestvennye Nauki — Trudy Akad Nauk Litov SSR Ser A Obsc Nauki
Trudy Akademii Nauk SSSR Karel'skii Filial — Tr Akad Nauk SSSR Karel Fil
Trudy Akademii Nauk Tadzhikskoi SSR — Tr Akad Nauk Tadzh SSR
Trudy Akademii Nauk Turkmenskoi SSR — Tr Akad Nauk Turkm SSR
Trudy Akademiia Nauk Kazakhskoi SSR Institut Mikrobiologii i Virusologii — Tr Akad Nauk Kaz SSR Inst Mikrobiol Virusol
Trudy Akademiia Nauk SSSR Institut Biologii Vnutrennikh Vod — Tr Akad Nauk SSSR Inst Biol Vnutr Vod
Trudy Akademiia Nauk SSSR Sibirskoe Otdelenie. Biologicheskii Institut — Tr Akad Nauk SSSR Sibirsk Otd Biol Inst
Trudy Akademiia Nauk Tadzhikskoi SSR [*Stalinabad, USSR*] — Trudy A N Tadzh
Trudy Akademiya Neftyanoi Promyslennosti — Tr Akad Neft Promsti
Trudy Akademiya Stroitel'stva i Arkhitektury SSSR Zapadno-Sibirskii Filial — Tr Akad Stroit Arkhit SSSR Zapadno Sib Fil
Trudy Alma Atinskii Gosudarstvennyi Meditsinskii Institut — Tr Alma At Gos Med Inst
Trudy Alma-Atinskogo Instituta — Tr At Zoovet Inst
Trudy Alma-Atinskogo Meditsinskogo Instituta — Tr Alma-At Med Inst
Trudy Alma-Atinskogo Nauchno-Issledovatel'skogo i Proektnogo Instituta Stroitel'nykh Materialov — Tr Alma At Nauchno Issled Proektn Inst Stroit Mater
Trudy Alma-Atinskogo Zooveterinarnogo Instituta — Tr Alma-At Zoovet Inst
Trudy Altaiskii Politehniceskii Institut Imeni I. I. Polizunova — Trudy Altai Politehn Inst
Trudy Altaiskii Politehniceskii Institut Imeni I. I. Polizunova — Trudy Altaisk Politehn Inst
Trudy Altaiskogo Gorno-Metallurgicheskogo Nauchno-Issledovatel'skogo Instituta Akademiya Nauk Kazakhskoi SSR — Tr Altai Gorno Metall Nauchno Issled Inst Akad Nauk Kaz SSR
Trudy Altaiskogo Politekhnicheskogo Instituta — Tr Altai Politekh Inst
Trudy Altaiskogo Sel'skokhozyaistvennogo Instituta — Tr Altai Skh Inst
Trudy Altaiskogo Sel'skokhozyaistvennogo Instituta — Trudy Altaisk Sel'khoz Inst
Trudy Altajskogo Politehniceskogo Instituta — Trudy Altajsk Politehn Inst
Trudy Amurskoi Sel'skokhozyaistvennoi Opytnoi Stantsii — Tr Amur Skh Opytn Stn
Trudy Andizhanskii Gosudarstvennyi Pedagogicheskii Institut — Trudy Andizhan Ped Inst
Trudy Angarskogo Filiala Irkutskogo Politekhnicheskogo Instituta — Tr Angarsk Fil Irkutsk Politekh Inst
Trudy Arhangel'skogo Lesotehniceskogo Instituta Imeni V. V. Kuibysheva — Trudy Arhangel Lesotehn Inst
Trudy Arhiva — Trudy Arh
Trudy Arkhangel'skogo Lesotekhnicheskogo Instituta — Tr Arkhang Lesotekh Inst
Trudy Arkhangel'skogo Ordena Trudovogo Kraskogo Znameni Lesotekhnicheskogo Instituta Imeni V. V. Kuibysheva — Trudy Arkhangel Lesotekh Inst Im V V Kuibysheva
Trudy Arkticheskogo i Antarkticheskogo Nauchno-Issledovatel'skogo Instituta — Tr Arkt Antarkt Nauchno-Issled Inst
Trudy Armyanskogo Geologicheskogo Upravleniya — Tr Arm Geol Upr
Trudy Armyanskogo Instituta Stroimaterialov i Sooruzhenii — Tr Arm Inst Stroim Sooruzh
Trudy Armyanskogo Nauchno-Isseldovatel'skogo Instituta Vinogradarstva Vinodeliya i Plodovodstva — Tr Arm Nauchno Issled Inst Vinograd Vinodel Plodovod
Trudy Armyanskogo Nauchno-Issledovatel'skogo Instituta Gidrotekhniki i Melioratsii — Tr Arm Nauchno Issled Inst Gidrotekh Melior
Trudy Armyanskogo Nauchno-Issledovatel'skogo Instituta Vinogradarstva Vinodeliya i Plodovodstva — Trudy Armyansk Nauchno-Issled Inst Vinograd Vinodel Plodov
Trudy Armyanskogo Nauchno-Issledovatel'skogo Instituta Zhivotnovodstva i Veterinarii — Tr Arm Nauchno-Issled Inst Zhivotnovod Vet
Trudy Armyanskogo Nauchno-Issledovatel'skogo Instituta Zhivotnovodstva i Veterinarii — Trudy Armyansk Nauchno-Issled Inst Zhivot Vet
Trudy Armyanskogo Nauchno-Issledovatel'skogo Veterinarnogo Instituta — Tr Arm Nauchno-Issled Vet Inst
Trudy Armyanskoi Protivochumnoi Stantsii — Tr Arm Protivochumn Stn
Trudy Ashkhabadskogo Nauchno-Issledovatel'skogo Instituta Epidemiologii i Gigieny — Tr Ashkhab Nauchno Issled Inst Epidemiol Gig
Trudy Aspirantov Gruzinskogo Sel'skokhozyaistvennogo Instituta — Trudy Aspirantov Gruzin Sel'-Khoz Inst
Trudy Astrakhanskogo Gosudarstvennogo Meditinskogo Instituta — Tr Astrakh Gos Med Inst
Trudy Astrakhanskogo Gosudarstvennogo Zapovednika — Tr Astrakh Gos Zapov
Trudy Astrakhanskogo Tekhnicheskogo Instituta Rybnoi Promyshlennosti i Khozyaistva — Tr Astrakh Tekh Inst Rybn Promsti Khoz
Trudy Astrofizicheskogo Instituta Akademiya Nauk Kazakhskoi SSR [*Kazakh SSR*] — Tr Astrofiz Inst Akad Nauk Kaz SSR
Trudy Astrofizicheskogo Instituta Akademiya Nauk Kazakhskoi SSR — TRAIB
Trudy Atlanticheskii Nauchno-Issledovatel'skii Institut Rybnogo Khozyaistva i Okeanografii [*Former USSR*] — Tr Atl Nauchno-Issled Inst Ryb Khoz Okeanogr
Trudy Azerbaidzhanskii Gosudarstvennyi Nauchno-Issledovatel'skii i Proektnyi Institut Neftyanoi Promyshlennosti — Tr Azerb Gos Nauchno Issled Proektn Inst Neft Promsti
Trudy Azerbaidzhanskogo Gosudarstvennogo Pedagogicheskogo Instituta — TAzerbPI
Trudy Azerbaidzhanskogo Gosudarstvennogo Pedagogicheskogo Instituta — Tr Azerb Gos Pedagog Inst
Trudy Azerbaidzhanskogo Gosudarstvennogo Universiteta. Seriya Khimicheskaya — Tr Azerb Gos Univ Ser Khim
Trudy Azerbaidzhanskogo Industrial'nogo Instituta — Tr Azerb Ind Inst
Trudy Azerbaidzhanskogo Instituta Nefti i Khimii — Tr Azerb Inst Nefti Khim
Trudy Azerbaidzhanskogo Nauchno-Issledovatel'skogo Instituta Energetiki — Tr Azerb Nauchno Issled Inst Energ
Trudy Azerbaidzhanskogo Nauchno-Issledovatel'skogo Instituta Gidrotekhniki i Melioratsii — Trudy Azerb Nauchno-Issled Inst Gidrotekh Melior
Trudy Azerbaidzhanskogo Nauchno-Issledovatel'skogo Instituta Gigieny Truda i Professional'nykh Zabolevaniya — Tr Azerb Nauchno-Issled Inst Gig Tr Prof Zabol
Trudy Azerbaidzhanskogo Nauchno-Issledovatel'skogo Instituta Lesnogo Khozyaistva i Agrolesomelioratsii — Tr Azerb Nauchno Issled Inst Lesn Khoz Agrolesomelior
Trudy Azerbaidzhanskogo Nauchno-Issledovatel'skogo Instituta Meditsinskoi Parazitologii i Trophicheskoi Meditsiny — Tr Azerb Nauchno-Issled Inst Med Parazitol Trop Med
Trudy Azerbaidzhanskogo Nauchno-Issledovatel'skogo Instituta Ovoshchevodstva — Tr Azerb Nauchno Issled Inst Ovoshchevod
Trudy Azerbaidzhanskogo Nauchno-Issledovatel'skogo Instituta po Bureniyu Neftyanykh i Gazovykh Skvazhin — Tr Azerb Nauchno Issled Inst Buren Neft Gazov Skvazhin
Trudy Azerbaidzhanskogo Nauchno-Issledovatel'skogo Instituta Virusologii Mikrobiologii i Gigieny — Tr Azerb Nauchno Issled Inst Virusol Mikrobiol Gig
Trudy Azerbaidzhanskogo Nauchno-Issledovatel'skogo Instituta Zemledeliya — Tr Azerb Nauchno Issled Inst Zemled
Trudy Azerbaidzhanskogo Nauchno-Issledovatel'skogo Instituta Zhivotnovodstva — Trudy Azerb Nauchno-Issled Inst Zhivot
Trudy Azerbaidzhanskogo Nauchno-Issledovatel'skogo Veterinarnogo Instituta — Tr Azerb Nauchno Issled Vet Inst
Trudy Azerbaidzhanskogo Nauchno-Issledovatel'skogo Veterinarnogo Instituta — Trudy Azerb Vet Inst
Trudy Azerbaidzhanskogo Neftyanogo Nauchno-Issledovatel'skogo Instituta — Tr Azerb Neft Nauchno Issled Inst
Trudy Azerbaidzhanskogo Otdeleniya Tsentral'nogo Nauchno-Issledovatel'skogo Instituta Osetrovgo Khozyaistva — Tr Azerb Otd Tsentr Nauchno Issled Inst Osetr Khoz
Trudy Azerbaidzhanskogo Politekhnicheskogo Instituta — Tr Azerb Politekh Inst
Trudy Azerbaidzhanskogo Sel'skokhozyaistvennogo Instituta — Tr Azerb Skh Inst
Trudy Azerbaidzhanskogo Veterinarnogo Nauchno-Issledovatel'skogo Instituta — Tr Azerb Vet Nauchno Issled Inst
Trudy Azerbaidzhanskoi Nauchno-Issledovatel'skoi Veterinarnoi Opytnoi Stantsii — Tr Azerb Nauchno Issled Vet Opytn Stn
Trudy Azerbajdzanskogo Opytnoj Stancii — Trudy Azerbajdzansk Opytn Sta
Trudy Azerbajdzanskoj Stancii Vsesojuznogo Instituta Zascity Rastenij — Trudy Azerbajdzansk Stancii Vsesojuzn Inst Zasc Rast
Trudy Azovsko-Chernomorskoi Nauchnoi Rybokhozyaistvennoi Stantsii — Tr Azovsko Chernomorsk Nauchn Rybokhoz Stn
Trudy Azovskogo Nauchno-Issledovatel'skogo Instituta Rybnogo Khozyaistva — Tr Azovskogo Nauchno Issled Inst Rybn Khoz
Trudy Baikal'skoi Limnologicheskoi Stantsii Akademiya Nauk SSSR Vostochno-Sibirskii Filial — Tr Baik Limnol Stn Akad Nauk SSSR Vost Sib Fil
Trudy Bakinskogo Nauchno-Issledovatel'skogo Instituta Travmatologii Ortopedii — Tr Bakinsk Nauchno-Issled Inst Travmatol Ortop
Trudy Bakinskogo Nauchno-Issledovatel'skogo Instituta Travmatologii Ortopedii — Tr Bakinskogo Nauchno Issled Inst Travmatol Ortop
Trudy Baltiiskogo Nauchno-Issledovatel'skogo Instituta Rybnogo Khozyaistva — Tr Balt Nauchno Issled Inst Rybn Khoz
Trudy Bashkirskii Gosudarstvennyi Nauchno-Issledovatel'skii i Proektnyi Institut Neftyanoi Promyshlennosti — Tr Bashk Gos Nauchno Issled Proektn Inst Neft Promsti
Trudy Bashkirskii Nauchno-Issledovatel'skii Institut po Pererabotke Nefti — TBNNA
Trudy Bashkirskii Nauchno-Issledovatel'skii Institut po Pererabotke Nefti [*Former USSR*] — Tr Bashk Nauchno-Issled Inst Pererab Nefti
Trudy Bashkirskii Nauchno-Issledovatel'skii Institut po Stroitel'stvu — Tr Bashk Nauchno Issled Inst Stroit
Trudy Bashkirskogo Gosudarstvennogo Zapovednika — Tr Bashk Gos Zapov
Trudy Bashkirskogo Nauchnogo Instituta Sel'skogo Khozyaistva — Trudy Bashkir Nauch Inst Sel Khoz
Trudy Bashkirskogo Nauchno-Issledovatel'skogo Instituta Sel'skogo Khozyaistva — Tr Bashk Nauchno Issled Inst Sel'sk Khoz
Trudy Bashkirskogo Sel'skokhozyaistvennogo Instituta — Tr Bashk S-Kh Inst
Trudy Bashkirskogo Sel'skokhozyaistvennogo Instituta — Trudy Baskir S-H Inst
Trudy Batumskogo Botanicheskogo Sada Akademii Nauk Gruzinskoi SSR — Tr Batum Bot Sada Akad Nauk Gruz SSR
Trudy Belgorodskogo Tekhnologicheskogo Instituta Stroitel'nyhmaterialov — Tr Belgorod Tekhnol Inst Stroit
Trudy Belgorodskoi Gosudarstvennoi Sel'skokhozyaistvennoi Opytnoi Stantsii — Tr Belgorod Gos Skh Opytn Stn
Trudy Belomorskoi Biologicheskoi Stantsii Moskovskogo Gosudarstvennogo Universiteta — Tr Belomorsk Biol Stn Mosk Gos Univ
Trudy Belorusskii Nauchno-Issledovatel'skii Institut Pochvovedenii — Tr Beloruss Nauchno Issled Inst Pochvoved
Trudy Belorusskii Nauchno-Issledovatel'skii Institut Promyshlennosti Prodovol'stvennykh Tovarov — Tr Beloruss Nauchno Issled Inst Promsti Prodovol Tovarov
Trudy Belorusskii Nauchno-Issledovatel'skii Institut Zhivotnovodstva — Tr Beloruss Nauchno Issled Inst Zhivotnovod
Trudy Belorusskogo Gosudarstvennogo Universiteta — TBGU

Trudy Belorusskogo Nauchno-Issledovatel'skogo Instituta Melioratsii i Vodnogo Khozyaistva — Tr Beloruss Nauchno-Issled Inst Melior Vodn Khoz
Trudy Belorusskogo Nauchno-Issledovatel'skogo Instituta Pishchevoi Promyshlennosti — Tr Beloruss Nauchno-Issled Inst Pishch Promsti
Trudy Belorusskogo Nauchno-Issledovatel'skogo Instituta Pishchevoi Promyshlennosti — Tr Beloruss Naucno-Issled Inst Pishch Prom-Sti
Trudy Belorusskogo Nauchno-Issledovatel'skogo Instituta Pochvovedeniya — Trudy Belorussk Nauchno-Issled Inst Pochv
Trudy Belorusskogo Nauchno-Issledovatel'skogo Instituta Rybnogo Khozyaistva — Tr Beloruss Nauchno Issled Inst Rybn Khoz
Trudy Belorusskoi Sel'skokhozyaistvennoi Akademii — Tr Beloruss Sel'skokhoz Akad
Trudy Belorusskoi Sel'skokhozyaistvennoi Akademii — Tr Beloruss Skh Akad
Trudy Belorusskoi Sel'skokhozyaistvennoi Akademii — Trudy Belorussk Sel'-Khoz Akad
Trudy Berdyanskii Opytnyi Neftemaslozavod — Tr Berdyanskii Opytn Neftemaslozavod
Trudy Biogeokhimicheskoi Laboratorii Akademiya Nauk SSSR — Tr Biogeokhim Lab Akad Nauk SSSR
Trudy Biologiceskogo Fakul'teta Tomskogo Gosudarstvennogo Universiteta. Wissenschaftliche Berichte der Biologischen Fakultaet der Tomsker Staats-Universitaet — Trudy Biol Fak Tomsk Gosud Univ
Trudy Biologiceskogo Naucno-Issledovatel'skogo Instituta pri Permskom Gosudarstvennom Universitete. Travaux de l'Institut des Recherches Biologiques de Perm — Trudy Biol Naucno Issl Inst Permsk Gosud Univ
Trudy Biologicheskogo Instituta Akademiya Nauk SSSR Sibirskoe Otdelenie — Tr Biol Inst Akad Nauk SSSR Sib Otd
Trudy Biologicheskogo Instituta Sibirskoe Otdelenie Akademiya Nauk SSSR — Trudy Biol Inst Sib Otd Akad Nauk SSSR
Trudy Biologicheskogo Instituta Zapadno-Sibirskogo Filiala Akademii Nauk SSSR — Tr Biol Inst Zapadno-Sib Fil Akad Nauk SSSR
Trudy Biologicheskogo Nauchno-Issledovatel'skogo Instituta i Biologicheskoi Stantsii pri Permskom Gosudarstvennom Universitete — Tr Biol Nauchno Issled Inst Biol Stn Permsk Gos Univ
Trudy Biologicheskogo Nauchno-Issledovatel'skogo Instituta pri Molotovskom Gosudarstvennom Universitete — Tr Biol Nauchno Issled Inst Molotov Gos Univ
Trudy Biologicheskoi Stantsii "Borok" Akademiya Nauk SSSR — Tr Biol Stn Borok Akad Nauk SSSR
Trudy Biologo-Pochvennogo Instituta Dal'nevostochnyi Nauchnyi Tsentr Akademiya Nauk SSSR — Tr Biol Pochv Inst Dalnevost Nauchn Tsentr Akad Nauk SSSR
Trudy Bjuro po Mikologii i Fitopatologii Ucenago Komiteta Glavnago Upravlenija Zemleustrojstva i Zemledelija — Trudy Bjuro Mikol Ucen Komiteta Glavn Upravl Zemleustr
Trudy Bjuro Prikl Bot — Bull Bur Agnew Bot
Trudy Blagoveshchenskogo Gosudarstvennogo Meditsinskogo Instituta — Tr Blagoveshch Gos Med Inst
Trudy Blagoveshchenskogo Sel'skokhozyaistvennogo Instituta — Tr Blagoveshch Skh Inst
Trudy Borodinskoj Presnovodnoj Biologiceskoj Stancii v Karelii. Berichte der Akademiker Borodin Biologischen Suesswasser Station — Trudy Borodinskoj Presnovodn Biol Stancii Karelii
Trudy Botaniceskij Institut Akademiya Nauk SSSR. Serija VI — Trudy Bot Inst Akad Nauk SSSR Ser VI
Trudy Botaniceskogo Instituta Akademii Nauk SSSR. Ser. 4. Eksperimental'naja Botanika. Acta Instituti Botanici Academiae Scientiarum URPSS. Botanica Experimentalis — Trudy Bot Inst Akad Nauk SSSR Ser 4 Eksper Bot
Trudy Botaniceskogo Instituta imeni Akademika V. L. Komarova — Trudy Bot Inst Komarova
Trudy Botaniceskogo Instituta (Tiflis) — Trudy Bot Inst Tiflis
Trudy Botaniceskogo Sada Akademii Nauk SSSR. Acta Horti Botanici Academiae Scientiarum Ante Petropolitani — Trudy Bot Sada Akad Nauk SSSR
Trudy Botaniceskogo Sada. Moskovskij Ordena Lenina Gosudarstvennyj Universitet imeni M. V. Lomonosova — Trudy Bot Sada Moskovsk Ordena Lenina Gosud Univ Lomonosova
Trudy Botanicheskikh Sadov Akademii Nauk Kazakhskoi SSR — Tr Bot Sadov Akad Nauk Kaz SSR
Trudy Botanicheskogo Instituta Akademii Nauk SSSR — Tr Bot Inst Akad Nauk SSSR
Trudy Botanicheskogo Instituta Akademii Nauk SSSR. Seriya 4 — Tr Bot Inst Akad Nauk SSSR Ser 4
Trudy Botanicheskogo Instituta Akademiya Nauk SSSR. Seriya 5. Rastitel'noe Syr'ye — Tr Bot Inst Akad Nauk SSSR Ser 5
Trudy Botanicheskogo Instituta Akademiya Nauk SSSR. Seriya 6. Introduktsiya Rastenii i Zelenoe — Tr Bot Inst Akad Nauk SSSR Ser 6
Trudy Botanicheskogo Instituta Akademiya Nauk Tadzhikskoi SSR — Tr Bot Inst Akad Nauk Tadzh SSR
Trudy Botanicheskogo Instituta Akademiya Nauk Tadzhikskoi SSR — Tr Bot Inst Akad Nauk Tadzhikskoi SSR
Trudy Botanicheskogo Instituta Azerbaidzhanskii Filial Akademii Nauk SSSR — Tr Bot Inst Azerb Fil Akad Nauk SSSR
Trudy Botanicheskogo Instituta Imeni V. L. Komarova Akademiya Nauk SSSR. Seriya VII — Tr Bot Inst V L Komarova Akad Nauk SSSR Ser VII
Trudy Botanicheskogo Sada Akademii Nauk Ukrainskoi SSR — Tr Bot Sada Akad Nauk Ukr SSR
Trudy Botanicheskogo Sada v Tashkente Akademii Nauk Uzbekskoi SSR — Tr Bot Sada Tashk Akad Nauk Uzb SSR
Trudy Botanicheskogo Sada v Tashkente Akademii Nauk Uzbekskoi SSR — Tr Bot Sada Tashkente Akad Nauk Uzb SSR
Trudy Botanicheskogo Sada Zapadno-Sibirskogo Filiala Akademii Nauk SSSR — Tr Bot Sada Zapadn-Sib Fil Akad Nauk SSSR
Trudy Botanicnogo Sadu Akademii Nauk Ukrajins'koji RSR — Trudy Bot Sadu Akad Nauk Ukrajinsk RSR
Trudy Bryanskogo Lesokhozyaistvennogo Instituta — Tr Bryansko Lesokhoz Inst
Trudy Bukharskoi Oblastnoi Opytnoi Sel'skokhozyaistvennoi Stantsii — Tr Bukhar Obl Opytn Skh Stn
Trudy Burjatskogo Instituta Obscestvennyh Nauk — Trudy Burjat Inst Obsc Nauk
Trudy Burjatskogo Komplesnogo Naucno-Issledovatel'skogo Instituta — TBurNII
Trudy Buryat-Mongol'skogo Zooveterinarnogo Instituta — Tr Buryat Mong Zoovet Inst
Trudy Buryat-Mongol'skoi Nauchno-Issledovatel'skoi Veterinarnoi Opytnoi Stantsii — Tr Buryat-Mong Nauchno-Issled Vet Opytn Stn
Trudy Buryat-Mongol'skoi Nauchno-Issledovatel'skoi Veterinarnoi Opytnoi Stantsii — Trudy Buryat Mongol Nauchno-Issled Vet Opyt Sta
Trudy Buryatskogo Instituta Estestvennykh Nauk Buryatskii Filial Sibirskoe Otdelenie Akademiya Nauk SSSR — TBBFA
Trudy Buryatskogo Instituta Estestvennykh Nauk. Buryatskii Filial. Sibirskoe Otdelenie. Akademiya Nauk SSSR — Tr Burat Inst Estest Nauk Buryat Fil Sib Otd Akad Nauk SSSR
Trudy Buryatskogo Sel'skokhozyaistvennogo Instituta — Tr Buryat S-Kh Inst
Trudy Buryatskogo Sel'skokhozyaistvennogo Instituta — Trudy Buryatsk Sel'khoz Inst
Trudy Buryatskogo Zooveterinarnogo Instituta — Tr Buryat Zoovet Inst
Trudy Chelyabinskii Gosudarstvennyi Pedagogicheskii Institut — Tr Chelyab Gos Pedagog Inst
Trudy Chelyabinskii Politekhnicheskii Institut [*Former USSR*] — Tr Chelyab Politekh Inst
Trudy Chelyabinskogo Instituta Mekhanizatsii i Elektrifikatsii Sel'skogo Khozyaistva — Tr Chelyab Inst Mekh Elektrif Selsk Khoz
Trudy Chimkentskoi Oblastnoi Sel'skokhozyaistvennoi Opytnoi Stantsii. Kazakhskaya SSR — Tr Chimkent Obl Skh Opytn Stn Kaz SSR
Trudy Chuvashskogo Sel'skokhozyaistvennogo Instituta — Tr Chuv Skh Inst
Trudy Chuvashskoi Sel'skokhozyaistvennoi Opytnoi Stantsii — Tr Chuv Skh Opytn Stn
Trudy Dagestanskogo Gosudarstvennogo Pedagogicheskogo Instituta — Tr Dagest Gos Pedagog Inst
Trudy Dagestanskogo Gosudarstvennogo Pedagogicheskogo Instituta Estestvenno-Geograficheskii Fakul'tet — Tr Dagest Gos Pedagog Inst Estestv-Geogr Fak
Trudy Dagestanskogo Nauchno-Issledovatel'skogo Instituta Sel'skogo Khozyaistva — Trudy Dagest Nauchno-Issled Inst Sel Khoz
Trudy Dagestanskogo Sel'skokhozyaistvennogo Instituta — Tr Dagest S-Kh Inst
Trudy Dal'nevostochnogo Filiala Akademii Nauk SSSR. Seriya Geologicheskaya — Tr Dalnevost Fil Akad Nauk SSSR Ser Geol
Trudy Dal'nevostochnogo Filiala Akademii Nauk SSSR. Seriya Khimicheskaya — Tr Dalnevost Fil Akad Nauk SSSR Ser Khim
Trudy Dal'nevostochnogo Geologo-Razvedochnogo Tresta — Tr Dalnevost Geol Razved Tresta
Trudy Dal'nevostochnogo Gosudarstvennogo Meditsinskogo Instituta — Tr Dal'nevost Gos Med Inst
Trudy Dal'nevostochnogo Gosudarstvennogo Universiteta — Tr Dalnevost Gos Univ
Trudy Dal'nevostochnogo Gosudarstvennogo Universiteta. Seriya 4. Lesnye Nauki — Tr Dalnevost Gos Univ Ser 4
Trudy Dal'nevostochnogo Gosudarstvennogo Universiteta. Seriya 5. Sel'skoe Khozyaistvo — Tr Dalnevost Gos Univ Ser 5
Trudy Dal'nevostochnogo Gosudarstvennogo Universiteta. Seriya 7. Fizika i Khimiya — Tr Dalnevost Gos Univ Ser 7
Trudy Dal'nevostochnogo Gosudarstvennogo Universiteta. Seriya 8. Biologiya — Tr Dalnevost Gos Univ Ser 8
Trudy Dal'nevostochnogo Gosudarstvennogo Universiteta. Seriya 11. Geologiya — Tr Dalnevost Gos Univ Ser 11
Trudy Dal'nevostochnogo Gosudarstvennogo Universiteta. Seriya 12. Gornoe Delo — Tr Dalnevost Gos Univ Ser 12
Trudy Dal'nevostochnogo Gosudarstvennogo Universiteta. Seriya 13. Tekhnika — Tr Dalnevost Gos Univ Ser 13
Trudy Dal'nevostochnogo Gosudarstvennogo Universiteta. Seriya 15. Matematika — Tr Dalnevost Gos Univ Ser 15
Trudy Dal'nevostochnogo Kraevogo Nauchno-Issledovatel'skogo Instituta — Tr Dalnevost Kraev Nauchno Issled Inst
Trudy Dal'nevostochnogo Nauchno-Issledovatel'skogo Gidrometeorologicheskogo Instituta — Tr Dalnevost Nauchno Issled Gidrometeorol Inst
Trudy Dal'nevostochnogo Nauchno-Issledovatel'skogo Veterinarnogo Instituta — Tr Dalnevost Nauchno Issled Vet Inst
Trudy Dal'nevostochnogo Politekhnicheskogo Instituta — Tr Dalnevost Politekh Inst
Trudy Dal'nevostochnogo Tekhnicheskogo Instituta Rybnoi Promyshlennosti i Khozyaistva — Tr Dalnevost Tekh Inst Rybn Promsti Khoz
Trudy Dal'nevostocnogo Filiala Akademii Nauk SSSR. Serija Botaniceskaja — Trudy Dalnevost Fil Akad Nauk SSSR Ser Bot
Trudy Darvinskogo Gosudarstvennogo Zapovednika — Tr Darvinsk Gos Zapov
Trudy Dnepropetrovskogo Instituta Inzhenerov Zheleznodorozhnogo Transporta — Tr Dnepropetr Inst Inzh Zheleznodorozhn Transp
Trudy Dnepropetrovskogo Khimiko-Tekhnologicheskogo Instituta — Tr Dnepropetr Khim Tekhnol Inst
Trudy Dnepropetrovskogo Sel'skokhozyaistvennogo Instituta — Tr Dnepropetr S-Kh Inst
Trudy Donbasskaya Nauchno-Issledovatel'skaya Laboratoriya — Tr Donbasskaya Nauchno Issled Lab
Trudy Doneckogo Politehniceskogo Instituta — Trudy Doneck Politehn Inst
Trudy Donetskogo Gosudarstvennogo Meditsinskogo Instituta — Tr Donetsk Gos Med Inst

Trudy Donetskogo Industrial'nogo Instituta [*Ukrainian SSR*] — Tr Donetsk Ind Inst
Trudy Donetskogo Politekhnicheskogo Instituta. Seriya Fiziko-Matematicheskaya — Tr Donetsk Politekh Inst Ser Fiz Mat
Trudy Donetskogo Politekhnicheskogo Instituta. Seriya Khimiko-Tekhnologicheskaya — Tr Donetsk Politekh Inst Ser Khim Tekhnol
Trudy Donetskogo Politekhnicheskogo Instituta. Seriya Metallurgicheskaya — Tr Donetsk Politekh Inst Ser Metall
Trudy Donetskogo Politekhnicheskogo Instituta. Seriya Stroitel'naya — Tr Donetsk Politekh Inst Ser Stroit
Trudy Donskogo Zonal'nogo Instituta Sel'skogo Khozyaistva — Trudy Don Zonal'Inst Sel'Khoz
Trudy Eksperimental'nyi Nauchno-Issledovatel'skii Institut Metallorezhushchikh Stankov — Tr Eksp Nauchno Issled Inst Metallorezhushchikh Stankov
Trudy Energeticheskogo Instituta Akademiya Nauk Azerbaidzhanskoi SSR — Tr Energ Inst Akad Nauk Az SSR
Trudy Energeticheskogo Instituta Azerbaidzhanskoi SSR — Tr Energ Inst Az SSR
Trudy Energeticheskogo Instituta Imeni I. G. Es'mana Akademiya Nauk Azerbaidzhanskoi SSR [*Azerbaidzhan SSR*] — Tr Energ Inst Im I G Es'mana Akad Nauk Azerb SSR
Trudy Erevanskogo Gosudarstvennogo Instituta Usovershenstvovaniya Vrachei — Tr Erevan Gos Inst Usoversh Vrachei
Trudy Erevanskogo Meditsinskogo Instituta — Tr Erevan Med Inst
Trudy Erevanskogo Zootekhnichesko-Veterinarnogo Instituta — Tr Erevan Zootekh Vet Inst
Trudy Erevanskogo Zooveterinarnogo Instituta — Tr Erevan Zoovet Inst
Trudy Estestvenno-Istoriceskago Muzeja Tavriceskago Gubernskago Zemstva — Trudy Estestv Istoric Muz Tavricesk Gub Zemstva
Trudy Estestvennonauchnogo Instituta pri Molotovskom Gosudarstvennom Universitete — Tr Estestvennonauchn Inst Molotov Gos Univ
Trudy Estestvennonauchnogo Instituta pri Permskom Gosudarstvennom Universitete — Tr Estestvennonauchn Inst Permsk Gos Univ
Trudy Estestvennonauchnogo Instituta pri Permskom Gosudarstvennom Universitete Imeni A. M. Gor'kogo Radiospektroskopiy — Tr Estestv Inst Permsk Gos Univ Radiospektrosk
Trudy Ferganskogo Politekhnicheskogo Instituta — Tr Ferg Politekh Inst
Trudy Fizicheskogo Instituta Imeni P. N. Lebedeva — Trudy Fiz Inst Lebedev
Trudy Fizicheskogo Instituta Imeni P. N. Lebedeva Akademiya Nauk SSSR — Tr Fiz Inst Akad Nauk SSSR
Trudy Fizicheskogo Instituta Imeni P. N. Lebedeva Akademiya Nauk SSSR [*Former USSR*] — Tr Fiz Inst Im P N Lebedeva Akad Nauk SSSR
Trudy Fiziko-Tekhnicheskogo Instituta Akademiya Nauk Turkmenskoi SSR — Tr Fiz Tekh Inst Akad Nauk Turkm SSR
Trudy Fiziologicheskoi Laboratorii Akademii Nauk SSSR — Tr Fiziol Lab Akad Nauk SSSR
Trudy Fiziologicheskoi Patologii Zhenshchiny — Tr Fiziol Patol Zhen
Trudy Frunzenskogo Politehniceskogo Instituta — Trudy Frunze Politehn Inst
Trudy Frunzenskogo Politekhnicheskogo Instituta — Tr Frunz Politekh Inst
Trudy Gel'mintologicheskaya Laboratoriya Akademiya Nauk SSSR — Tr Gel'mintol Lab Akad Nauk SSSR
Trudy Gel'mintologicheskoi Laboratorii — Tr Gelmintol Lab
Trudy Geofizicheskogo Instituta Akademiya Nauk SSSR — Tr Geofiz Inst Akad Nauk SSSR
Trudy Geograficheskogo Fakul'teta Kirgizskogo Universiteta — Trudy Geogr Fak Kirgiz Univ
Trudy Geologicheskogo Instituta Akademiya Nauk Gruzinskoi SSR — Tr Geol Inst Akad Nauk Gruz SSR
Trudy Geologicheskogo Instituta Akademiya Nauk Gruzinskoi SSR. Geologicheskaya Seriya — Tr Geol Inst Akad Nauk Gruz SSR Geol Ser
Trudy Geologicheskogo Instituta Akademiya Nauk Gruzinskoi SSR. Mineralogo-Petrograficheskaya Seriya — Tr Geol Inst Akad Nauk Gruz SSR Mineral Petrogr Ser
Trudy Geologicheskogo Instituta Akademiya Nauk SSSR — Tr Geol Inst Akad Nauk SSSR
Trudy Geologicheskogo Instituta (Kazan) — Tr Geol Inst (Kazan)
Trudy Geometriceskogo Seminara — Tr Geom Semin
Trudy Geometriceskogo Seminara — Trudy Geometr Sem
Trudy Geometriceskogo Seminara Kazanskii Universitet — Trudy Geom Sem Kazan Univ
Trudy GIAP — Tr GIAP
Trudy Gidrobiologicnoji Stanciji. Travaux de la Station Hydrobiologique — Trudy Gidrobiol Stanciji
Trudy Gidrometeorologicheskii Nauchno-Issledovatel'skii Tsentral'nogo SSSR — Tr Gidrometeorol Nauchno-Issled Tsentr SSSR
Trudy "Giprotsement" — Tr "Giprotsement"
Trudy Glavgeologii (Glavnoe Upravlenie Geologii i Okhrany Nedr) Uzbekskoi SSR — Tr Glavgeologii (Gl Upr Geol Okhr Nedr) Uzb SSR
Trudy Glavnogo Botanicheskogo Sada — Tr Gl Bot Sada
Trudy Glavnogo Botanicheskogo Sada — Tr Glav Bot Sada
Trudy Glavnogo Botanicheskogo Sada Akademiya Nauk SSSR — Tr Gl Bot Sada Akad Nauk SSSR
Trudy Glavnoi Geofizicheskoi Observatorii — Tr Gl Geo Obs
Trudy Glavnoi Geofizicheskoi Observatorii [*Former USSR*] — Tr Gl Geofiz Obs
Trudy Glavnoi Geofizicheskoi Observatorii Imeni A. I. Voeikova — Trudy Glav Geofiz Obs
Trudy Golovnoi Nauchno-Issledovatel'skii Institut Tsementnogo Mashinostroeniya — Tr Golovn Nauchno-Issled Inst Tsem Mashinostr
Trudy Goriiskogo Gosudarstvennogo Pedagogicheskogo Instituta — TGorPI
Trudy Goriiskogo Gosudarstvennogo Pedagogicheskogo Instituta — Tr Goriiskogo Gos Pedagog Inst
Trudy Gor'kovskii Golovnoi Sel'skokhozyaistvennyi Institut — Tr Gor'k Golovn Skh Inst
Trudy Gor'kovskii Gosudarstvennyi Nauchno-Issledovatel'skii Institut Gigieny Truda i Profboleznei — Tr Gor'k Gos Nauchno Issled Inst Gig Tr Profbolezn
Trudy Gor'kovskogo Gosudarstvennogo Meditsinskogo Instituta — Tr Gor'k Gos Med Inst
Trudy Gor'kovskogo Gosudarstvennogo Pedagogicheskogo Instituta — Tr Gork Gos Pedagog Inst
Trudy Gor'kovskogo Instituta Inzhenerov Vodnogo Transporta — Tr Gork Inst Inzh Vodn Transp
Trudy Gor'kovskogo Inzhenero-Stroitel'nogo Instituta — Tr Gork Inzh Stroit Inst
Trudy Gor'kovskogo Nauchno-Issledovatel'skogo Pediatricheskogo Instituta — Tr Gork Nauchno Issled Pediatr Inst
Trudy Gor'kovskogo Politehniceskii Institut — Trudy Gor'kov Politehn Inst
Trudy Gor'kovskogo Politekhnicheskogo Instituta — Tr Gork Politekh Inst
Trudy Gor'kovskogo Sel'skokhozyaistvennogo Instituta — Tr Gor'k S-Kh Inst
Trudy Gor'kovskogo Sel'skokhozyaistvennogo Instituta — Trudy Gor'kov Sel'-Khoz Inst
Trudy Gor'kovskoi Nauchno-Issledovatel'skoi Veterinarnoi Opytnoi Stantsii — Tr Gor'k Nauchno-Issled Vet Opytn Stn
Trudy Gorno-Geologicheskogo Instituta Akademiya Nauk SSSR Ural'skii Filial — Tr Gorno Geol Inst Akad Nauk SSSR Ural Fil
Trudy Gorno-Geologicheskogo Instituta Akademiya Nauk SSSR Zapadno-Sibirskii Filial — Tr Gorno Geol Inst Akad Nauk SSSR Zapadno Sib Fil
Trudy Gorskogo Sel'skokhozyaistvennogo Instituta — Trudy Gorsk Sel'-Khoz Inst
Trudy Gosudarstvennogo Astronomicheskogo Instituta Imeni P. K. Shternberga — Tr Gos Astron Inst Im Shternberga
Trudy Gosudarstvennogo Astronomicheskogo Instituta Moskovskii Gosudarstvennyi Universitet — Tr Gos Astron Inst Mosk Gos Univ
Trudy Gosudarstvennogo Dal'nevostocnogo Universiteta. Ser. 13. Tehnika/Memoires de l'Universite d'Etat a l'Extreme Orient. Technique/Publications. Far-Eastern State University/Veroeffentlichungen der Staatlichen Universitaet des Fernen Ostens — Trudy Gosud Dalnevost Univ Ser 13 Tehn
Trudy Gosudarstvennogo Ermitazha — TE
Trudy Gosudarstvennogo Ermitazha — Trud Erm
Trudy Gosudarstvennogo Ermitazha — Trudy Ermit
Trudy Gosudarstvennogo Ermitazha — Trudy G Ermitazh
Trudy Gosudarstvennogo Gidrologicheskogo Instituta — Tr Gos Gidrol Inst
Trudy Gosudarstvennogo Gidrologicheskogo Instituta — Trudy Gos Gidrol Inst
Trudy Gosudarstvennogo Instituta Usovershenstvovaniya Vrachei I. M. Lenina — Tr Gos Inst Usoversh Vrachei I M Lenina
Trudy Gosudarstvennogo Issledovatel'skogo Elektrokeramicheskogo Instituta [*Former USSR*] — Tr Gos Issled Elektrokeram Inst
Trudy Gosudarstvennogo Issledovatel'skogo Keramicheskogo Instituta — Tr Gos Issled Keram Inst
Trudy Gosudarstvennogo Istoriceskogo Muzeja — TGIM
Trudy Gosudarstvennogo Istorischeskogo Muzeiia — Trud Ist Muz
Trudy Gosudarstvennogo Nauchno-Eksperimental'nogo Instituta Grazhdanskikh Promyshlennykh i Inzhenernykh Sooruzhenii — Tr Gos Nauchno Eksp Inst Grazhdanskikh Prom Inzh Sooruzh
Trudy Gosudarstvennogo Nauchno-Issledovatel'skogo Elektrokeramicheskogo Instituta — Tr Gos Nauchno Issled Elektrokeram Inst
Trudy Gosudarstvennogo Nauchno-Issledovatel'skogo i Proektnogo Instituta "Gipromorneft" — Tr Gos Nauchno Issled Proektn Inst "Gipromorneft"
Trudy Gosudarstvennogo Nauchno-Issledovatel'skogo Instituta Gornokhimicheskogo Syr'ya — Tr Gos Nauchno Issled Inst Gornokhim Syr
Trudy Gosudarstvennogo Nauchno-Issledovatel'skogo Instituta Gornokhimicheskogo Syr'ya [*Former USSR*] — Tr Gos Nauchno-Issled Inst Gornokhim Syr'ya
Trudy Gosudarstvennogo Nauchno-Issledovatel'skogo Instituta Keramicheskoi Promyshlennosti — Tr Gos Nauchno Issled Inst Keram Promsti
Trudy Gosudarstvennogo Nauchno-Issledovatel'skogo Instituta Khimicheskoi Promyshlennosti — Tr Gos Nauchno Issled Inst Khim Promsti
Trudy Gosudarstvennogo Nauchno-Issledovatel'skogo Instituta po Promyshlennoi i Sanitarnoi Ochistke Gazov [*Former USSR*] — Tr Gos Nauchno-Issled Inst Prom Sanit Ochistke Gazov
Trudy Gosudarstvennogo Nauchno-Issledovatel'skogo Instituta Psikhiatrii — Tr Gos Nauchno Issled Inst Psikhiatrii
Trudy Gosudarstvennogo Nauchno-Issledovatel'skogo Instituta Ukha Gorla i Nosa — Tr Gos Nauchno-Issled Inst Ukha Gorla Nosa
Trudy Gosudarstvennogo Nauchno-Issledovatel'skogo Keramicheskogo Instituta — Tr Gos Nauchno Issled Keram Inst
Trudy Gosudarstvennogo Nauchno-Kontrol'nogo Instituta Veterinarnykh Preparatov — Tr Gos Nauchno-Kontrol'n Inst Vet Prep
Trudy. Gosudarstvennogo Nikitskogo Botaniceskogo Sada. Arbeiten aus dem Botanischen Garten Nikita, Jalta, Krim — Trudy Gosud Nikitsk Bot Sada
Trudy Gosudarstvennogo Okeanograficheskogo Instituta — Tr Gos Okeanogr Inst
Trudy Gosudarstvennogo Opticheskogo Instituta [*Former USSR*] — Tr Gos Opt Inst
Trudy Gosudarstvennogo Vsesoyuznogo Instituta po Proektirovaniyu i Nauchno-Issledovatel'skim Rabotam "Giprotsement" — Tr Gos Vses Inst Proekt Nauchno-Issled Rab Giprotsement
Trudy Gosudarstvennogo Vsesoyuznyi Instituta po Proektirovaniyu i Nauchno-Issledovatel'skim Rabotam v Tsementnoi Promyshlennosti — Tr Gos Vses Inst Proekt Nauchno-Issled Rab Tsem Promsti
Trudy Gosudarstvennyi Dorozhnyi Proektno-Izyskatel'skii i Nauchno-Issledovatel'skii Institut — Tr Gos Dorozhn Proektno Izyskatel'skii Nauchno Issled Inst
Trudy Gosudarstvennyi Institut po Proektirovaniyu i Issledovatel'skim Rabotam v Neftedobyvayushchei Promyshlennosti — TPIRA
Trudy Gosudarstvennyi Institut po Proektirovaniyu i Issledovatel'skim Rabotam v Neftedobyvayushchei Promyshlennosti [*Former USSR*] — Tr Gos Inst Proekt Issled Rab Neftedobyvayushchei Prom-Sti
Trudy Gosudarstvennyi Institut Prikladnoi Khimii — Tr Gos Inst Prikl Khim

Trudy Gosudarstvennyi Makeevski Nauchno-Issledovatel'skii Institut po Bezopasnosti Rabot v Gornoi Promyshlennosti [*Ukrainian SSR*] — Tr Gos Makeev Nauchno-Issled Inst Bezop Rab Gorn Prom-Sti
Trudy Gosudarstvennyi Nauchno-Issledovatel'skii i Proektnyi Institut Splavov i Obrabotki Tsvetnykh Metallov [*Former USSR*] — Tr Gos Nauchno-Issled Proekt Inst Splavov Obrab Tsvet Met
Trudy Gosudarstvennyi Nauchno-Issledovatel'skii Institut Stroitel'noi Keramiki [*Former USSR*] — Tr Gos Nauchno-Issled Inst Stroit Keram
Trudy Gosudarstvennyi Nauchno-Issledovatel'skii Rentgeno-Radiologicheskii Institut — Tr Gos Nauchno Issled Rentgeno Radiol Inst
Trudy Gosudarstvennyi Nikitskii Botanicheskii Sad — Tr Gos Nikitskii Bot Sad
Trudy Gosudarstvennyi Proektno-Issledovatel'skii Institut "Vostokgiprogaz" — Tr Gos Proektno Issled Inst Vostokgiprogaz
Trudy Gosudarstvennyi Proektno-Konstruktorskii i Nauchno-Issledovatel'skii Institut Morskogo Transporta — Tr Gos Proektno Konstr Nauchno Issled Inst Morsk Transp
Trudy Gosudarstvennyi Soyuznyi-Nauchno-Issledovatel'skii Traktornyi Institut — Tr Gos Soyuzn Nauchno Issled Trakt Inst
Trudy Gosudarstvennyi Tsentral'yni Nauchno-Issledovatel'skii Institut Tekhnologii i Organizatsii Proizvodstva — Tr Gos Tsentr Nauchno Issled Inst Tekhnol Organ Proizvod
Trudy Gosudarstvennyi Vsesojuznyi Central'nyi Naucno-Issledovatel'skii Institut Kompleksnoi Avtomatizacii — Trudy CNIIKA
Trudy Gosudarstvennyi Vsesoyuznyi Dorozhnyi Nauchno-Issledovatel'skii Institut — Tr Gos Vses Dorozhn Nauchno Issled Inst
Trudy Gosudarstvennyi Vsesoyuznyi Proektnyi i Nauchno-Issledovatel'skii Institut Tsementnoi Promyshlennosti [*Former USSR*] — Tr Gos Vses Proektn Nauchno-Issled Inst Tsem Prom-Sti
Trudy Gosudarstvennyj Nauchno-Issledovatel'skij i Proektnyj Institut Splavov i Obrabotki Tsvetnykh Metallov — Tr Gos Nauchno-Issled Proektn Inst Splavov Obrab Tsvetn Met
Trudy Groznenskii Neftyanoi Institut — Tr Grozn Neft Inst
Trudy Groznenskogo Neftyanogo Nauchno-Issledovatel'skogo Instituta — TNNIA
Trudy Gruzinskii Nauchno-Issledovatel'skii Institut Pishchevoi Promyshlennosti — Trudy Gruz Nauchno-Issled Pishch Prom
Trudy Gruzinskii Politekhnicheskii Institut Imeni V. I. Lenina — TGPIA
Trudy Gruzinskogo Nauchno-Issledovatel'skogo Instituta Energetiki [*Georgian SSR*] — Tr Gruz Nauchno-Issled Inst Energ
Trudy Gruzinskogo Nauchno-Issledovatel'skogo Instituta Gidrotekhniki i Melioratsii — Tr Gruz Nauchno-Issled Inst Gidrotekh Melior
Trudy Gruzinskogo Politekhnicheskogo Instituta [*Georgian SSR*] — Tr Gruz Politekh Inst
Trudy Gruzinskogo Sel'skokhozyaistvennogo Instituta — Tr Gruz S-Kh Inst
Trudy Gruzinskogo Sel'skokhozyaistvennogo Instituta Imeni L. P. Beriya — Trudy Gruz Sel'-Khoz Inst
Trudy i Materialy Donetskii Meditsinskii Institut — Tr Mater Donetsk Med Inst
Trudy i Materialy Donetskii Nauchno-Issledovatel'skii Institut Fiziologii Truda — Tr Mater Donetsk Nauchno Issled Inst Fiziol Tr
Trudy i Materialy Leningradskii Institut Organizatsii i Okhrany Truda — Tr Mater Leningr Inst Organ Okhr Tr
Trudy i Materialy Nauchno-Issledovatel'skii Institut Fiziologii Truda (Stalino) — Tr Mater Nauchno Issled Inst Fiziol Tr (Stalino)
Trudy i Materialy Pervogo Ukrainskogo Instituta Rabochei Meditsiny — Tr Mater Pervogo Ukr Inst Rab Med
Trudy i Materialy Ukrainskii Tsentral'nyi Institut Gigieny Truda i Profzabolevanii — Tr Mater Ukr Tsentr Inst Gig Tr Profzabol
Trudy i Materialy Ukrainskogo Gosudarstvennogo Instituta Patologii i Gigieny Truda — Tr Mater Ukr Gos Inst Patol Gig Tr
Trudy i Materialy Ukrainskogo Gosudarstvennogo Instituta Rabochei Meditsiny — Tr Mater Ukr Gos Inst Rab Med
Trudy Imperatorskago S.-Peterburgskago Obscestva Estestvoispytatelej. Vypusk 2. Otdelenie Botaniki. Travaux de la Societe des Naturalistes de Saint-Petersbourg. Section de Botanique — Trudy Imp S Peterburgsk Obsc Estestvoisp Vyp 2 Otd Bot
Trudy Institut Biologii Akademiya Nauk Latviiskoi SSR — Tr Inst Biol Akad Nauk Latv SSR
Trudy Institut Eksperimental'noi Meteorologii [*Former USSR*] — Tr Inst Eksp Meteorol
Trudy Institut Geologii Kori Korisnikh Koplain Akademiya Nauk Ukrains'koi RSR [*Ukrainian SSR*] — Tr Inst Geol Korisnikh Koplain Akad Nauk Ukr RSR
Trudy Institut Sistem Upravleniya Akademiya Nauk Gruzinskoj SSR — Tr Inst Sist Upr Akad Nauk Gruz SSR
Trudy Instituta Biologii Akademii Nauk Turkmenskoi SSR — Tr Inst Biol Akad Nauk Turkm SSR
Trudy Instituta Biologii Akademija Nauk SSSR. Jakutskij Filial — Trudy Inst Biol Akad Nauk SSSR Jakutsk Fil
Trudy Instituta Biologii Akademiya Nauk SSSR Ural'skii Filial [*Former USSR*] — Tr Inst Biol Akad Nauk SSSR Ural Fil
Trudy Instituta Biologii Bashkirskogo Universiteta — Tr Inst Biol Bashk Univ
Trudy Instituta Biologii Ural'skii Filial Akademiya Nauk SSSR (Sverdlovsk) — Trudy Inst Biol Ural Fil (Sverdlovsk)
Trudy Instituta Biologii Ural'skogo Filiala Akademii Nauk SSSR — Tr Inst Biol Ural Fil Akad Nauk SSSR
Trudy Instituta Biologii Vnutrennikh Vod Akademii Nauk SSSR — Tr Inst Biol Vnutr Vod Akad Nauk SSSR
Trudy Instituta Biologii Yakutskii Filial Sibirskogo Otdeleniya Akademii Nauk SSSR — Tr Inst Biol Yakutsk Fil Sib Otd Akad Nauk SSSR
Trudy Instituta Botaniki Akademii Nauk Kazakhskoi SSR — Tr Inst Bot Akad Nauk Kaz SSR
Trudy Instituta Botaniki Akademiya Nauk Azerbaidzhanskoi SSR — Tr Inst Bot Akad Nauk Azerb SSR
Trudy Instituta Botaniki Akademiya Nauk Kazakhskoi SSR — TBKZA
Trudy Instituta Botaniki Akademiya Nauk Kazakhskoi SSR — Tr Inst Bot Akad Nauk Kazakh SSR
Trudy Instituta Botaniki Akademiya Nauk Kazakhskoi SSR (Alma-Ata) — Trudy Inst Bot (Alma-Ata)
Trudy Instituta Botaniki (Ashkhabad) — Trudy Inst Bot Ashkhabad
Trudy Instituta Chistykh Khimicheskikh Reaktivov — Tr Inst Chist Khim Reakt
Trudy Instituta Ehkologii Rastenij i Zhivotnykh — Tr Inst Ehkol Rast Zhivotn
Trudy Instituta Ehlektrokhimii Akademiya Nauk SSSR Ural'skij Filial — Tr Inst Ehlektrokhim Akad Nauk SSSR Ural Fil
Trudy Instituta Ehlektrokhimii Ural'skij Nauchnyj Tsentr Akademiya Nauk SSSR — Tr Inst Ehlektrokhim Ural Nauch Tsentr Akad Nauk SSSR
Trudy Instituta Ekologii Rastenii i Zhivotnykh [*Former USSR*] — Tr Inst Ekol Rast Zhivotn
Trudy Instituta Ekologii Rastenii i Zhivotnykh Ural'skii Nauchnyi Tsentr Akademiya Nauk SSSR [*Former USSR*] — Tr Inst Ekol Rast Zhivotn Ural Nauchn Tsentr Akad Nauk SSSR
Trudy Instituta Ekologii Rastenii i Zhivotnykh Ural'skogo Filiala Akademii Nauk SSSR — Tr Inst Ekol Rast Zhivotn Ural Fil Akad Nauk SSSR
Trudy Instituta Eksperimental'noi Biologii Akademiya Nauk Estonskoi SSR — Tr Inst Eksper Biol Akad Nauk Eston SSR
Trudy Instituta Eksperimental'noi Biologii Akademiya Nauk Kazakhskoi SSR — Tr Inst Eksp Biol Akad Nauk Kaz SSR
Trudy Instituta Eksperimental'noi i Klinicheskoi Khirurgii i Gematologii — Tr Inst Eksp Klin Khir Gematol
Trudy Instituta Eksperimental'noi i Klinicheskoi Meditsiny Akademii Nauk Latviiskoi SSR — Tr Inst Eksp Klin Med Akad Nauk Latv SSR
Trudy Instituta Eksperimental'noi Klinicheskoi Onkologii Akademiya Meditsinskikh Nauk SSSR [*Former USSR*] — Tr Inst Eksp Klin Onkol Akad Med Nauk SSSR
Trudy Instituta Eksperimental'noi Meditsiny Akademii Meditsinskikh Nauk SSR — Tr Inst Eksp Med Akad Med Nauk SSR
Trudy Instituta Eksperimental'noi Meditsiny Akademii Nauk Latviiskoi SSR — Tr Inst Eksp Med Akad Nauk Latv SSR
Trudy Instituta Eksperimental'noi Meditsiny Akademii Nauk Litovskoi SSR — Tr Inst Eksp Med Akad Nauk Lit SSR
Trudy Instituta Elektrokhimii Ural'skii Nauchnyi Tsentr Akademiya Nauk SSSR [*Former USSR*] — Tr Inst Elektrokhim Ural Nauchn Tsentr Akad Nauk SSSR
Trudy Instituta Energetiki Akademiya Nauk Belorusskoi SSR [*Belorussian SSR*] — Tr Inst Energ Akad Nauk BSSR
Trudy Instituta Epidemiologii i Mikrobiologii (Frunze) — Tr Inst Epidemiol Mikrobiol (Frunze)
Trudy Instituta Etnografii — Trudy Inst Etnogr
Trudy Instituta Etnografii Imeni N. N. Miklucho Maklaja Akademija Nauk SSSR — TIEtn
Trudy Instituta Fiziki Akademii Nauk Estonskoi SSR — Tr Inst Fiz Akad Nauk Est SSR
Trudy Instituta Fiziki Akademiya Nauk Azerbaidzhanskoi SSR [*Azerbaidzhan SSR*] — Tr Inst Fiz Akad Nauk Azerb SSR
Trudy Instituta Fiziki Akademiya Nauk Gruzinskoi SSR [*Georgian SSR*] — Tr Inst Fiz Akad Nauk Gruz SSR
Trudy Instituta Fiziki i Astronomii Akademiya Nauk Ehstonskoj SSR — Tr Inst Fiz Astron Akad Nauk Ehst SSR
Trudy Instituta Fiziki Metallov Ural'skogo Nauchnogo Tsentra Akademiya Nauk SSSR [*Former USSR*] — Tr Inst Fiz Met Ural Nauchn Tsent Akad SSSR
Trudy Instituta Fiziki Vysokikh Ehnergij — Tr Inst Fiz Vys Ehnerg
Trudy Instituta Fiziki Vysokikh Energii Akademiya Nauk Kazakhskoi SSR [*Kazakh SSR*] — Tr Inst Fiz Vys Energ Akad Nauk Kaz SSR
Trudy Instituta Fiziki Zemli Akademiya Nauk SSSR [*Former USSR*] — Tr Inst Fiz Zemli Akad Nauk SSSR
Trudy Instituta Fiziologii Akademii Nauk SSSR — Tr Inst Fiziol Akad Nauk SSSR
Trudy Instituta Fiziologii Akademiya Nauk Azerbaidzhanskoi SSR (Baku) — Trudy Inst Fiziol (Baku)
Trudy Instituta Fiziologii Akademiya Nauk Gruzinskoi SSR [*Georgian SSR*] — Tr Inst Fiziol Akad Nauk Gruz SSR
Trudy Instituta Fiziologii Akademiya Nauk Kazakhskoi SSR — Tr Inst Fiziol Akad Nauk Kaz SSR
Trudy Instituta Fiziologii Imeni I. P. Pavlova Akademii Nauk SSSR — Tr Inst Fiziol Im I P Pavlova Akad Nauk SSSR
Trudy Instituta Fiziologii Imeni I. P. Pavlova Akademii Nauk SSSR — Tr Inst Fiziol Im I P Pavlova Akad SSSR
Trudy Instituta Fiziologii Imeni I. P. Pavlova Akademii Nauk SSSR — Trudy Inst Fiziol I P Pavlova
Trudy Instituta Fiziologii Rastenii Imeni K. A. Timiryazeva — Tr Inst Fiziol Rast Im K A Timiryazeva
Trudy Instituta Genetiki Akademii Nauk SSSR — Tr Inst Genet Akad Nauk SSSR
Trudy Instituta Genetiki Akademiya Nauk SSR — Trudy Inst Genet
Trudy Instituta Genetiki i Selektsii Akademii Nauk Azerbaidzhanskoi SSR — Tr Inst Genet Sel Akad Nauk Az SSR
Trudy Instituta Geofiziki Akademiya Nauk Gruzinskoi SSR [*Georgian SSR*] — Tr Inst Geofiz Akad Nauk Gruz SSR
Trudy Instituta Geografii Akademii Nauk SSSR — Tr Inst Geogr Akad Nauk SSSR
Trudy Instituta Geologiceskih Nauk. Serija Stratigrafii i Paleontologii. Trudy Instytutu Geologicnyh Nauk — Trudy Inst Geol Nauk Ser Stratigr
Trudy Instituta Geologicheskikh Nauk Akademiya Nauk Kazakhskoi SSR — TGKZA
Trudy Instituta Geologicheskikh Nauk Akademiya Nauk Kazakhskoi SSR [*Kazakh SSR*] — Tr Inst Geol Nauk Akad Nauk Kaz SSR
Trudy Instituta Geologii Akademiya Nauk Estonskoi SSR [*Estonian SSR*] — Tr Inst Geol Akad Nauk Est SSR
Trudy Instituta Geologii Akademiya Nauk Tadzhikskoi SSR — Tr Inst Geol Akad Nauk Tadzh SSR
Trudy Instituta Geologii Arktiki — Tr Inst Geol Arkt
Trudy Instituta Geologii i Geofiziki Akademiya Nauk SSSR Sibirskoe Otdelenie [*Former USSR*] — Tr Inst Geol Geofiz Akad Nauk SSSR Sib Otd
Trudy Instituta Geologii i Geofiziki (Novosibirsk) — Tr Inst Geol Geofiz Novosibirsk

Trudy Instituta "Giproninemetallorud" — Tr Inst "Giproninemetallorud"
Trudy Instituta Goryuchikh Iskopaemykh (Moscow) — Tr Inst Goryuch Iskop (Moscow)
Trudy. Instituta Imeni Pastera — Tr Inst Im Pastera
Trudy Instituta Imeni Pastera — Tr Inst Pastera
Trudy Instituta Istorii. Akademiia nauk Gruzinskoi SSR (Tbilisi) — Trud (Tbil)
Trudy Instituta Istorii, Archeologii, i Etnografii — TIIAE
Trudy Instituta Istorii, Arkheologii i Etnografii. Akademiia nauk Kasachskoi SSR (Alma-Ata) — Trudy (Alma-Ata)
Trudy Instituta Istorii Estestvoznanija i Tehniki — Trudy Inst Istor Estestvoznan Tehn
Trudy Instituta Istorii Estestvoznanija i Tehniki — Trudy Inst Istorii Estestv Tehn
Trudy Instituta Istorii Estestvoznaniya i Tekhniki Akademiya Nauk SSSR [*Former USSR*] — Tr Inst Istor Estestvozn Tekh Akad Nauk SSSR
Trudy Instituta Jazyka, Literatury, i Istorii — TJak
Trudy Instituta Jazyka, Literatury, i Istorii Komi Filiala Akademii Nauk SSSR — Trudy Inst Jaz Lit Ist Komi Fil Akad Nauk SSSR
Trudy Instituta Jazykoznanija — TIJa
Trudy Instituta Khimicheskikh Nauk Akademiya Nauk Kazakhskoi SSR — Tr Inst Khim Nauk Akad Nauk Kaz SSR
Trudy Instituta Khimii Akademiya Nauk Kirgizskoi SSR — Tr Inst Khim Akad Nauk Kirg SSR
Trudy Instituta Khimii Akademiya Nauk SSSR Ural'skii Filial [*Former USSR*] — Tr Inst Khim Akad Nauk SSSR Ural Fil
Trudy Instituta Khimii Akademiya Nauk Tadzhikskoi SSR — Tr Inst Khim Akad Nauk Tadzh SSR
Trudy Instituta Khimii Akademiya Nauk Turkmenskoi SSR — Tr Inst Khim Akad Nauk Turkm SSR
Trudy Instituta Khimii Akademiya Nauk Uzbekskoi SSR — Tr Inst Khim Akad Nauk Uzb SSR
Trudy Instituta Khimii i Metallurgii Akademiya Nauk SSSR Ural'skii Filial — Tr Inst Khim Metall Akad Nauk SSSR Ural Fil
Trudy Instituta Khimii Nefti i Prirodnykh Solei Akademiya Nauk Kazakhskoi SSSR — Tr Inst Khim Nefti Prir Solei Akad Nauk Kaz SSR
Trudy Instituta Khimii Ural'skii Nauchnyi Tsentr Akademiya Nauk SSSR — Tr Inst Khim Ural Nauchn Tsentr Akad Nauk SSSR
Trudy Instituta Klinicheskoi i Eksperimental'noi Kardiologii — Tr Inst Klin Eksp Kardiol
Trudy Instituta Klinicheskoi i Eksperimental'noi Kardiologii Akademiya Nauk Gruzinskoi SSR — Tr Inst Klin Eksp Kardiol Akad Nauk Gruz SSR
Trudy Instituta Klinicheskoi i Eksperimental'noi Khirurgii Akademii Nauk Kazakhskoi SSR — Tr Inst Klin Eksp Khir Akad Nauk Kaz SSR
Trudy Instituta Klinicheskoi i Eksperimental'noi Nevrologii Gruzinskoi SSR — Tr Inst Klin Eksp Nevrol Gruz SSR
Trudy Instituta Kraevoi Eksperimental'noi Meditsiny Akademiya Nauk Uzbekskoi SSR — Tr Inst Kraev Eksp Med Akad Nauk Uzb SSR
Trudy Instituta Kraevoi Meditsiny Akademii Nauk Kirgizskoi SSR — Tr Inst Kraev Med Akad Nauk Kirg SSR
Trudy Instituta Kraevoi Patologii Akademii Nauk Kazakhskoi SSR — Tr Inst Kraev Patol Akad Nauk Kaz SSR
Trudy Instituta Kristallografii Akademiya Nauk SSSR — Tr Inst Kristallogr Akad Nauk SSSR
Trudy Instituta Lesa Akademii Nauk Gruzinskoi SSR — Tr Inst Lesa Akad Nauk Gruz SSR
Trudy Instituta Lesa Akademii Nauk SSSR — Tr Inst Lesa Akad Nauk SSSR
Trudy Instituta Lesa Akademiya Nauk Gruzinskoi SSR — Tr Inst Lesa Akad Nauk Gruzin SSR
Trudy Instituta Lesa i Drevesiny Akademiya Nauk SSSR Sibirskoe Otdelenie — Tr Inst Lesa Drev Akad Nauk SSSR Sib Otd
Trudy Instituta Lesokhozyaistvennykh Problem i Khimii Drevesiny Akademiya Nauk Latviiskoi SSR [*Latvian SSR*] — Tr Inst Lesokhoz Probl Khim Drev Akad Nauk Latv SSR
Trudy Instituta Literatury i Jazyka Imeni Nizami — TNizam
Trudy Instituta Malyarii i Meditsinskoi Parazitologii — Tr Inst Malyarii Med Parazitol
Trudy Instituta Matematiki i Mehaniki Ural'skii Naucnyi Centr Akademija Nauk SSSR — Trudy Inst Mat i Meh Ural Naucn Centr Akad Nauk SSSR
Trudy Instituta Matematiki i Mekhaniki Akademii Nauk Azerbajdzhanskoj SSR — Tr Inst Mat Mekh Akad Nauk Az SSR
Trudy Instituta Matematiki i Mekhaniki Ural'skii Nauchnyi Tsentr Akademiya Nauk SSSR — Trudy Inst Mat i Mekh Ural Nauchn Tsentr Akad Nauk SSSR
Trudy Instituta Mekhanicheskoi Obrabotki Poleznykh Iskopaemykh — Tr Inst Mekh Obrab Polezn Iskop
Trudy Instituta Melioratsii Vodnogo i Bolotnogo Khozyaistva Akademiya Nauk Belorusskoi SSR — Tr Inst Melior Vodn Bolotnogo Khoz Akad Nauk B SSR
Trudy Instituta Merzlotovedeniya Akademiya Nauk SSSR — Tr Inst Merzlotoved Akad Nauk SSSR
Trudy Instituta Metallofiziki Metallurgii Akademiya Nauk SSSR Ural'skii Filial — Tr Inst Metallofiz Metall Akad Nauk SSSR Ural Fil
Trudy Instituta Metallov (Leningrad) — Tr Inst Met (Leningrad)
Trudy Instituta Metallurgii Akademiya Nauk SSSR — Tr Inst Metall Akad Nauk SSSR
Trudy Instituta Metallurgii Akademiya Nauk SSSR Ural'skii Nauchnyi Tsentr — Tr Inst Metall Akad Nauk SSSR Ural Nauchn Tsentr
Trudy Instituta Metallurgii i Obogashcheniya Akademiya Nauk Kazakhskoi SSR — Tr Inst Metall Obogashch Akad Nauk Kaz SSR
Trudy Instituta Metallurgii Imeni A. A. Baikova Akademiya Nauk SSSR [*Former USSR*] — Tr Inst Metall Im A A Baikova Akad Nauk SSSR
Trudy Instituta Metallurgii (Sverdlovsk) — Tr Inst Metall (Sverdlovsk)
Trudy Instituta Mikrobiologii Akademii Nauk Latviiskoi SSR — Tr Inst Mikrobiol Akad Nauk Latv SSR
Trudy Instituta Mikrobiologii Akademii Nauk SSSR — Tr Inst Mikrobiol Akad Nauk SSSR
Trudy Instituta Mikrobiologii i Virusologii Akademii Nauk Kazakhskoi SSR — Tr Inst Mikrobiol Virusol Akad Nauk Kaz SSR
Trudy Instituta Mikrobiologii (Riga) — Trudy Inst Mikrobiol Riga
Trudy Instituta Morfologii Zhivotnykh Akademii Nauk SSSR — Tr Inst Morfol Zhivotn Akad Nauk SSSR
Trudy Instituta Moskovskii Institut Tonkoi Khimicheskoi Tekhnologii — Tr Inst Mosk Inst Tonkoi Khim Tekhnol
Trudy Instituta Nefti Akademiya Nauk Azerbaidzhanskoi SSR — Tr Inst Nefti Akad Nauk Az SSR
Trudy Instituta Nefti Akademiya Nauk Kazakhoskoi SSR — Tr Inst Nefti Akad Nauk Kaz SSR
Trudy Instituta Nefti Akademiya Nauk SSSR — Tr Inst Nefti Akad Nauk SSSR
Trudy Instituta Normal'noi i Patologicheskoi Fiziologii Akademii Meditsinskikh Nauk SSSR — Tr Inst Norm Patol Fiziol Akad Med Nauk SSSR
Trudy Instituta Novogo Lubyanogo Syr'ya — Tr Inst Nov Lub Syrya
Trudy Instituta Obogashcheniya Tverdykh Goryuchikh Iskopaemykh [*Former USSR*] — Tr Inst Obogashch Tverd Goryuch Iskop
Trudy Instituta Okeanologii Akademii Nauk SSSR — Tr Inst Okeanol Akad Nauk SSSR
Trudy Instituta Okeanologii Akademiya Nauk SSSR — TIOKA
Trudy Instituta Onkologii Akademiya Meditsinskikh Nauk SSSR — Tr Inst Onkol Akad Med Nauk SSSR
Trudy Instituta Organicheskogo Kataliza i Elektrokhimii Akademiya Nauk Kazakhskoi SSR [*Kazakh SSR*] — Tr Inst Org Katal Elektrokhim Akad Nauk Kaz SSR
Trudy Instituta Pochvovedeniya Akademii Nauk Gruzinskoi SSR — Tr Inst Pochvoved Akad Nauk Gruz SSR
Trudy Instituta Pochvovedeniya Akademii Nauk Kazakhskoi SSR — Tr Inst Pochvoved Akad Nauk Kaz SSR
Trudy Instituta Pochvovedeniya i Agrokhimii Akademii Nauk Azerbaidzhanskoi SSR — Tr Inst Pochvoved Agrokhim Akad Nauk Az SSR
Trudy Instituta Pochvovedeniya i Agrokhimii Akademiya Nauk Azerbaidzhanskoi SSR (Baku) — Trudy Inst Pochv Agrokhim (Baku)
Trudy Instituta Pochvovedeniya i Agrokhimii Akademiya Nauk UzSSR — Tr Inst Pochvoved Agrokhim AN UzSSR
Trudy Instituta Pochvovedeniya (Tashkent) — Tr Inst Pochvoved (Tashkent)
Trudy Instituta Polevodstva Akademii Nauk Gruzinskoi SSR — Tr Inst Polevod Akad Nauk Gruz SSR
Trudy Instituta Poliomielita i Virusnykh Entsefalitov Akademii Meditsinskikh Nauk SSSR — Tr Inst Polio Virusn Entsefalitov Akad Med Nauk SSSR
Trudy Instituta Prikladnoi Geofiziki — TIPGA
Trudy Instituta Prikladnoi Geofiziki [*Former USSR*] — Tr Inst Prikl Geofiz
Trudy Instituta Prikladnoi Khimii i Elektrokhimii Akademiya Nauk Gruzinskoi SSR — Tr Inst Prikl Khim Elektrokhim Akad Nauk Gruz SSR
Trudy Instituta Proektnyi i Nauchno-Issledovatel'skii Institut Ural'skii Promstroiniiproekt — Tr Inst Proektn Nauchno-Issled Inst Ural Promstroiniiproekt
Trudy Instituta Razrabotki Neftyanykh i Gazovykh Mestorozhdenii Akademiya Nauk Azerbaidzhanskoi SSR — Tr Inst Razrab Neft Gazov Mestorozhd Akad Nauk Az SSR
Trudy Instituta Sadovodstva Vinogradarstva i Vinodeliya Gruzinskoi SSR — Tr Inst Sadovod Vinograd Vinodel Gruz SSR
Trudy Instituta Sadovodstva Vinogradarstva i Vinodeliya (Tiflis) — Tr Inst Sadovod Vinograd Vinodel (Tiflis)
Trudy Instituta Selektsii i Semenovodstva Khlopchatnika (Tashkent) — Tr Inst Sel Semenovod Khlop (Tashkent)
Trudy Instituta Sistem Upravleniya Akademiya Nauk Gruzinskoi SSR — Trudy Inst Sistem Upravleniya Akad Nauk Gruzin SSR
Trudy Instituta Stroitel'nogo Dela Akademiya Nauk Gruzinskoi SSR — Tr Inst Stroit Dela Akad Nauk Gruz SSR
Trudy Instituta Stroitel'noi Mekhaniki i Seismostoikosti Akademiya Nauk Gruzinskoi SSR — Tr Inst Stroit Mekh Seismostoikosti Akad Nauk Gruz SSR
Trudy Instituta Stroitel'nykh Materialov Mineral'nogo Proiskhozhdeniya i Stekla — Tr Inst Stroit Mater Miner Proiskhozhd Stekla
Trudy Instituta Stroitel'stva i Stroimaterialov Akademiya Nauk Kazakhskoi SSR — Tr Inst Stroit Stroimat Akad Nauk Kazakhskoi SSR
Trudy Instituta Teoreticeskoi Astronomii [*Former USSR*] — Tr Inst Teor Astron
Trudy Instituta Teoreticeskoi Astronomii — Trudy Inst Teoret Astronom
Trudy Instituta Teoreticheskoi Geofiziki Akademiya Nauk SSSR — Tr Inst Teor Geofiz Akad Nauk SSSR
Trudy Instituta Torfa Akademiya Nauk Belorusskoi SSR — Tr Inst Torfa Akad Nauk B SSR
Trudy Instituta Tuberkuleza Akademii Meditsinskikh Nauk SSSR — Tr Inst Tuberk Akad Med Nauk SSSR
Trudy Instituta Vinogradarstva i Vinodeliya Akademii Nauk Armyanskoi SSR — Tr Inst Vinograd Vinodel Akad Nauk Arm SSR
Trudy Instituta Vinogradarstva i Vinodeliya Akademii Nauk Gruzinskoi SSR — Tr Inst Vinograd Vinodel Akad Nauk Gruz SSR
Trudy Instituta. Vsesojuznyj Zaocnyj Finasovo-Ekonomiceskij Institut — Trudy Inst Vsesojuz Zaoc Finans Ekon Inst
Trudy Instituta. Vsesoyuznyi Nauchno-Issledovatel'skii Institut Tsellyulozno-Bumazhnoi Promyshlennosti [*Former USSR*] — Tr Inst Vses Nauchno-Issled Inst Tsellyul Bum Prom-Sti
Trudy Instituta Vulkanologii Akademiya Nauk SSSR Sibirskoe Otdelenie — Tr Inst Vulkanol Akad Nauk SSSR Sib Otd
Trudy Instituta Vychislitelnoi' Matematiki. Akademiya Nauk Gruzinskoi SSR — Trudy Inst Vychisl Mat Akad Nauk Gruzin SSR
Trudy Instituta Vysshei Nervnoi Deyatel'nosti Akademii Nauk SSSR. Seriya Fiziologicheskaya — Tr Inst Vyssh Nervn Deya Akad Nauk SSSR Fiziol
Trudy Instituta Vysshei Nervnoi Deyatel'nosti Akademii Nauk SSSR. Seriya Fiziologicheskaya — Tr Inst Vyssh Nervn Deyat Akad Nauk SSSR Ser Fiziol
Trudy Instituta Vysshei Nervnoi Deyatel'nosti. Seriya Fiziologicheskaya — Tr Inst Vyssh Nervn Deyat Ser Fiziol
Trudy Instituta Vysshei Nervnoi Deyatel'nosti. Seriya Patofiziologicheskaya — Tr Inst Vyssh Nervn Deyat Ser Patofiziol
Trudy Instituta Yadernoi Fiziki Akademiya Nauk Kazakhskoi SSR — Tr Inst Yad Fiz Akad Nauk Kaz SSR

Trudy Instituta Zashchity Rastenii Akademii Nauk Gruzinskoi SSR — Tr Inst Zashch Rast Akad Nauk Gruz SSR
Trudy Instituta Zashchity Rastenii (Tiflis) [*Georgian SSR*] — Tr Inst Zasch Rast (Tiflis)
Trudy Instituta Zashchity Rastenii (Tiflis) — Tr Inst Zashch Rast (Tiflis)
Trudy Instituta Zemledeliya Akademiya Nauk Azerbaidzhanskoi SSR — Tr Inst Zemled Akad Nauk Azerb SSR
Trudy Instituta Zemledeliya Kazakhskogo Filiala Akademii Nauk SSSR — Tr Inst Zemled Kaz Fil Akad Nauk SSSR
Trudy Instituta Zemledeliya (Leningrad). Razdel 3. Pochvovedenie — Tr Inst Zemled (Leningrad) Razdel 3
Trudy Instituta Zhivotnovodstva Akademii Nauk Turkmenskoi SSR — Tr Inst Zhivotnovod Akad Nauk Turkm SSR
Trudy Instituta Zhivotnovodstva Dagestanskogo Filiala Akademii Nauk SSSR — Tr Inst Zhivotnovod Dagest Fili Akad Nauk SSSR
Trudy Instituta Zhivotnovodstva Ministerstvo Sel'skokhozyaistva Uzbekistanskoi SSR — Tr Inst Zhivotnovod Minist Skh Uzb SSR
Trudy Instituta Zhivotnovodstva (Tashkent) — Tr Inst Zhivotnovod (Tashkent)
Trudy Instituta Zoologii Akademii Nauk Azerbaidzhanskoi SSR — Tr Inst Zool Akad Nauk Az SSR
Trudy Instituta Zoologii Akademii Nauk Gruzinskoi SSR — Tr Inst Zool Akad Nauk Gruz SSR
Trudy Instituta Zoologii Akademii Nauk Kazakhskoi SSR — Tr Inst Zool Akad Nauk Kaz SSR
Trudy Instituta Zoologii Akademii Nauk Kazakhskoi SSR — Tr Inst Zool Akad Nauk Kazakh SSR
Trudy Instituta Zoologii Akademii Nauk Ukrainskoi SSR — Tr Inst Zool Akad Nauk Ukr SSR
Trudy Instituta Zoologii i Parazitologii Akademii Nauk Uzbekskoi SSR — Tr Inst Zool Parazitol Akad Nauk Uzb SSR
Trudy Instituta Zoologii i Parazitologii Akademiya Nauk Tadzhikskoi SSR — Tr Inst Zool Parazitol Akad Nauk Tadzh SSR
Trudy Instituta Zoologii i Parazitologii Akademiya Nauk Tadzhikskoi SSR — Tr Inst Zool Parazitol Akad Tadzh SSR
Trudy Instituta Zoologii i Parazitologii Akademiya Nauk Uzbekskoi SSR (Tashkent) — Trudy Inst Zool Parazit (Tashkent)
Trudy Instituta Zoologii i Parazitologii Kirgizskogo Filiala Akademii Nauk SSR — Tr Inst Zool Parazitol Kirg Fil Akad Nauk SSR
Trudy Institute Matematiki (Novosibirsk) — Trudy Inst Mat Novosibirsk
Trudy Instituto Russkogo Jazyka — TIRJa
Trudy Institutov Komiteta Standartov Mer i Izmeritel'nykh Priborov pri Sovete Ministrov SSSR — Tr Inst Kom Stand Mer Izmer Prib Sov Minist SSSR
Trudy Instytutu Zoolohiyi ta Biolohiyi (Kiev) — Tr Inst Zool Biol (Kiev)
Trudy Introdukcionnogo Pitomnika Subtropiceskih Kul'tur — Trudy Introd Pitomn Subtrop Kult
Trudy IREA — Tr IREA
Trudy Irkutsk Nauchno-Issledovatel'skogo Instituta Epidemiologii i Mikrobiologii — Tr Irkutsk Nauchno Issled Inst Epidemiol Mikrobiol
Trudy Irkutskogo Gornometallurgicheskogo Instituta — Tr Irkutsk Gorometall Inst
Trudy Irkutskogo Gosudarstvennogo Universiteta — Tr Irkutsk Gos Univ
Trudy Irkutskogo Gosudarstvennogo Universiteta — Trudy Irkutsk Gos Univ
Trudy Irkutskogo Instituta Narodnogo Khozyaistva — Tr Irkutsk Inst Nar Khoz
Trudy Irkutskogo Politekhnicheskogo Instituta [*Former USSR*] — Tr Irkutsk Politekh Inst
Trudy Istoriko-Kraevedcheskogo Muzeia Moldavskoi SSR — Trudy Ist-Kraev Muz Mold
Trudy Iuzhno-Turkmenistanskoi Arkheologicheskoi Kompleksnoi Ekpeditsii — Trudy IUTAKE
Trudy Ivanovskogo Khimiko-Tekhnologicheskogo Instituta — Tr Ivanov Khim Tekhnol Inst
Trudy Ivanovskogo Meditsinskogo Instituta — Tr Ivanov Med Inst
Trudy Ivanovskogo Sel'skokhozyaistvennogo Instituta — Tr Ivanov Skh Inst
Trudy Izevskii Sel'skohozjaistvennyi Institut — Trudy Izevsk Sel'skohozjaistv Inst
Trudy Izhevskogo Meditsinskogo Instituta — Tr Izhevsk Med Inst
Trudy Izhevskogo Otdeleniya Vsesoyuznogo Fiziologicheskogo Obshchestva — Tr Izhevsk Otd Vses Fiziol Ova
Trudy Izhevskogo Sel'skokhoziastvennogo Instituta — Tr Izhevsk Skh Inst
Trudy Kabardino-Balkarskoi Gosudarstvennoi Sel'skokhozyaistvennoi Opytnoi Stantsii — Trudy Kabardino-Balkarsk Gos Sel'khoz Opyt Sta
Trudy Kafedry Avtomobili i Traktory Vsesoyuznyi Zaochnyi Mashinostroitel'nyi Institut — Tr Kafedry Avtomob Trakt Vses Zaochn Mashinostroit Inst
Trudy Kafedry Gospital'noi Khirugii i Lechebnogo Fakul'teta Saratovskogo Meditsinskogo Instituta — Tr Kafedry Gosp Khir Lech Fak Sarat Med Inst
Trudy Kafedry Kozhnykh i Venericheskikh Boleznei Tashkentskii Meditsinskii Institut — Tr Kafedry Kozhnykh Vener Bolezn Tashk
Trudy Kafedry Kozhnykh i Venericheskikh Boleznei Tashkentskii Meditsinskii Institut — Tr Kafedry Kozhnykh Vener Bolezn Tashk Med Inst
Trudy Kafedry Normal'noi Anatomii Saratovskogo Gosudarstvennogo Meditsinskogo Instituta — Tr Kafedry Norm Anat Sarat Gos Med Inst
Trudy Kafedry Operativnoi Khirurgii i Topograficheskoi Anatomii Tbilisskogo Gosudarstvennogo Meditsinskogo Instituta — Tr Kafedry Oper Khir Topogr Anat Tbilis Gos Med Inst
Trudy Kafedry Pochvovedeniya Biologo-Pochvennogo Fakul'teta Kazakhskii Gosudarstvennyi Universitet — Tr Kafedry Pochvoved Biol Poch Fak Kaz Gos Univ
Trudy Kafedry Pochvovedeniya Biologo-Pochvennogo Fakul'teta Kazakhskii Gosudarstvennyi Universitet — Tr Kafedry Pochvoved Biol Pochv Fak Kaz Gos Univ
Trudy Kafedry Russkogo Jazyka Vuzov Vostocnoj Sibiri i Dal'nego Vostoka — TRJaVUZ
Trudy Kafedry Teoreticheskoi i Eksperimental'noi Fiziki Kaliningradskii Gosudarstvennyi Universitet — Tr Kafedry Teor Eksp Fiz Kaliningr Gos Univ
Trudy KAI. Kazanskij Ordena Trudovogo Krasnogo Znameni Aviatsionnyj Institut Imeni A. N. Tupoleva — Tr Kazan Aviats Inst
Trudy Kaliningradskogo Tekhnicheskogo Instituta Rybnoi Promyshlennosti i Khozyaistva — Tr Kaliningr Tekh Inst Rybn Promsti Khoz
Trudy Kaliningradskoi Nauchno-Issledovatel'skoi Veterinarnoi Stantsii — Tr Kaliningr Nauchno Issled Vet Stn
Trudy Kalininskii Politekhnicheskii Institut [*Former USSR*] — Tr Kalinin Politekh Inst
Trudy Kalininskogo Gosudarstvennogo Meditsinskogo Instituta — Tr Kalinin Gos Med Inst
Trudy Kalininskogo Torfyanogo Instituta — Tr Kalinin Torf Inst
Trudy Kaluzhskoi Gosudarstvennoi Oblastnoi Sel'skokhozyaistvennoi Opytnoi Stantsii — Tr Kaluzhskoi Gos Obl Skh Opytn Stn
Trudy Kamenetsk-Podolskogo Sel'skokhozyaistvennogo Instituta — Tr Kamenetsk Podolsk Skh Inst
Trudy Kamenets-Podol'skogo Sel'skokhozyaistvennogo Instituta — Tr Kamenets Podol'sk Skh Inst
Trudy Kandalakshskogo Gosudarstvennogo Zapovednika — Tr Kandalakshskogo Gos Zapov
Trudy Karadagskoj Biologiceskoj Stancii — Trudy Karadagsk Biol Stancii
Trudy Karagandinskii Gosudarstvennyi Meditsinskii Institut — Trudy Karagand Gos Med Inst
Trudy Karagandinskogo Botanicheskogo Sada — Tr Karagandin Bot Sada
Trudy Karelo-Finskogo Filiala Akademii Nauk SSSR — Trudy Karelo Finsk Fil Akad Nauk SSSR
Trudy Karelo-Finskogo Uchitel'skogo Instituta — Tr Karelo-Fin Uchit Inst
Trudy Karel'skogo Filiala Akademii Nauk SSSR — TKar
Trudy Karel'skogo Filiala Akademii Nauk SSSR — Tr Karel Fil Akad Nauk SSSR
Trudy Karel'skogo Filiala Akademii Nauk SSSR — Trudy Karel' Fil Akad Nauk SSSR
Trudy Karel'skogo Otdeleniya Gosudarstvennogo Nauchno-Issledovatel'skogo Instituta Ozernogo i Rechnogo Rybnogo Khozyaistva — Tr Karel Otd Gos Nauchno Issled Inst Ozern Rechn Rybn Khoz
Trudy Kaspiiskii Nauchno-Issledovatel'skii Institut Rybnogo Khozyaistva — Tr Kasp Nauchno Issled Inst Rybn Khoz
Trudy Kaunasskogo Gosudarstvennogo Meditsinskogo Instituta — Tr Kaunas Gos Med Inst
Trudy Kavkazskogo Gosudarstvennogo Zapovednika — Trudy Kavkaz Gos Zapov
Trudy Kavkazskogo Instituta Mineral'nogo Syr'ya — Tr Kavk Inst Miner Syrya
Trudy Kazakhskii Institut Epidemiologii Mikrobiologii Gigieny — Tr Kaz Inst Epidemiol Mikrobiol Gig
Trudy Kazakhskogo Filiala Akademiya Stroitel'stva i Arkhitektury SSSR — Tr Kaz Fil Akad Stroit Arkhit SSSR
Trudy Kazakhskogo Gosudarstvennogo Sel'skokhozyaistvennogo Instituta — Tr Kaz Gos Skh Inst
Trudy Kazakhskogo Instituta Klinicheskoi i Eksperimental'noi Khirurgii — Tr Kaz Inst Klin Ekst Khir
Trudy Kazakhskogo Instituta Klinicheskoi i Eksperimental'noi Khirurgii Akademiya Meditsinskikh Nauk SSSR — Tr Kaz Inst Klin Eksp Khir Akad Med Nauk SSSR
Trudy Kazakhskogo Instituta Usovershenstvovaniya Vrachei Imeni V. I. Lenina — Tr Kaz Inst Usoversh Vrachei Im V I Lenina
Trudy Kazakhskogo Nauchno-Issledovatel'skogo Gidrometeorologicheskogo Instituta — Tr Kaz Nauchno-Issled Gidrometeorol Inst
Trudy Kazakhskogo Nauchno-Issledovatel'skogo Instituta Glaznykh Boleznei — Tr Kaz Nauchno Issled Inst Glaznykh Bolezn
Trudy Kazakhskogo Nauchno-Issledovatel'skogo Instituta Lesnogo Khozyaistva — Tr Kaz Nauchno-Issled Inst Lesn Khoz
Trudy Kazakhskogo Nauchno-Issledovatel'skogo Instituta Lesnogo Khozyaistva i Agrolesomelioratsii — Tr Kaz Nauchno-Issled Inst Lesn Khoz Agrolesomelior
Trudy Kazakhskogo Nauchno-Issledovatel'skogo Instituta Mineral'nogo Syr'ya — Tr Kaz Nauchno Issled Inst Miner Syrya
Trudy Kazakhskogo Nauchno-Issledovatel'skogo Instituta Onkologii i Radiologii — Tr Kaz Nauchno-Issled Inst Onkol Radiol
Trudy Kazakhskogo Nauchno-Issledovatel'skogo Instituta Tuberkuleza — Tr Kaz Nauchno-Issled Inst Tuberk
Trudy Kazakhskogo Nauchno-Issledovatel'skogo Instituta Vodnogo Khozyaistva — Tr Kaz Nauchno Issled Inst Vodn Khoz
Trudy Kazakhskogo Nauchno-Issledovatel'skogo Instituta Zashchity Rastenii — Tr Kaz Nauchno Issled Inst Zashch Rast
Trudy Kazakhskogo Nauchno-Issledovatel'skogo Instituta Zemledeliya — Tr Kaz Nauchno Issled Inst Zemled
Trudy Kazakhskogo Nauchno-Issledovatel'skogo Kozhno-Venerologicheskogo Instituta — Tr Kaz Nauchno Issled Kozhno Venerol Inst
Trudy Kazakhskogo Nauchno-Issledovatel'skogo Veterinarnogo Instituta — Tr Kaz Nauchno-Issled Vet Inst
Trudy Kazakhskogo Politekhnicheskogo Instituta [*Kazakh SSR*] — Tr Kaz Politekh Inst
Trudy Kazakhskogo Sel'skokhozyaistvennogo Instituta — Tr Kaz S-Kh Inst
Trudy Kazakhskogo Sel'skokhozyaistvennogo Instituta — Trudy Kazakh Sel'-Khoz Inst
Trudy Kazakhskogo Sel'skokhozyaistvennogo Instituta. Seriya Agronomii — Tr Kaz S-Kh Inst Ser Agron
Trudy Kazakhskoi Opytnoi Stantsii Pchelovodstva — Tr Kaz Opytn Stn Pchelovod
Trudy Kazakhskoi Opytnoi Stantsii Pchelovodstva — Trudy Kazakh Opyt Sta Pchelov
Trudy Kazanskii Gosudarstvennyi Pedagogicheskii Institut — Tr Kaz Gos Pedagog Inst
Trudy Kazanskogo Aviacionnogo Instituta. Matematika i Mehanika — Trudy Kazan Aviacion Inst
Trudy Kazanskogo Aviatsionogo Instituta. Seriya Khimicheskaya — Tr Kazan Aviats Inst Ser Khim
Trudy Kazanskogo Filiala Akademii Nauk SSSR. Seriya Geologicheskikh Nauk — Tr Kazan Fil Akad Nauk SSSR Ser Geol Nauk

Trudy Kazanskogo Filiala Akademii Nauk SSSR. Seriya Khimicheskikh Nauk — Tr Kazan Fil Akad Nauk SSSR Ser Khim Nauk
Trudy Kazanskogo Gosudarstvennogo Instituta Usovershenstvovaniya Vrachei — Tr Kazan Gos Inst Usoversh Vrachei
Trudy Kazanskogo Gosudarstvennogo Pedagogicheskogo Instituta — Trudy Kazan Gos Pedagog Inst
Trudy Kazanskogo Instituta Usovershenstvovaniya Vrachei Imeni V. I. Lenina — Tr Kazan Inst Usoversh Vrachei Im V I Lenina
Trudy Kazanskogo Inzhenerno-Stroitel'nogo Instituta — Tr Kazan Inzh Stroit Inst
Trudy Kazanskogo Khimiko-Tekhnologicheskogo Instituta — Tr Kazan Khim Tekhnol Inst
Trudy Kazanskogo Meditsinskogo Instituta — Tr Kazan Med Inst
Trudy Kazanskogo Nauchno-Issledovatel'skogo Instituta Onkologii i Radiologii — Tr Kazan Nauchno-Inst Onkol Radiol
Trudy Kazanskogo Nauchno-Issledovatel'skogo Instituta Onkologii i Radiologii — Tr Kazan Nauchno-Issled Inst Onkol Radiol
Trudy Kazanskogo Nauchno-Issledovatel'skogo Instituta Travmatologii i Ortopedii — Tr Kazan Nauchno-Issled Inst Travmatol Ortop
Trudy Kazanskogo Nauchno-Issledovatel'skogo Veterinarnogo Instituta — Tr Kazan Nauchno Issled Vet Inst
Trudy Kazanskogo Sel'skokhozyaistvennogo Instituta — Tr Kazan S-Kh Inst
Trudy Kazanskogo Sel'skokhozyaistvennogo Instituta — Trudy Kazan Sel'-Khoz Inst
Trudy Kazanskogo Sel'skokhozyaistvennogo Instituta — Trudy Kazan S-H Inst
Trudy Kazanskoi Gorodskoi Astronomiceskoi Observatorii — Trudy Kazan Gorod Astronom Observator
Trudy Kazanskoi Gorodskoi Astronomicheskoi Observatorii — Tr Kazan Gor Astron Obs
Trudy Kemerovskoi Gosudarstvennoi Sel'skokhozyaistvennoi Opytnoi Stantsii — Tr Kemer Gos Skh Opytn Stn
Trudy Kemerovskoi Gosudarstvennoi Sel'skokhozyaistvennoi Opytnoi Stantsii — Trudy Kemerov Gos Sel Khoz Opyt Sta
Trudy Kemerovskoi Oblastnoi Gosudarstvennoi Sel'skokhozyaistvennoi Opytnoi Stantsii — Tr Kemer Obl Gos S-Kh Opytn Stn
Trudy Kerchenskoi Ikhtiologicheskoi Laboratorii — Tr Kerch Ikhtiol Lab
Trudy Kerchenskoi Nauchnoi Rybokhozyaistvennoi Stantsii — Tr Kerch Nauchn Rybokhoz Stn
Trudy Khabarobskogo Politekhnicheskogo Instituta — Tr Khabar Politekh Inst
Trudy Khabarovskogo Instituta Inzhenerov Zheleznodorozhnogo Transporta — Tr Khabar Inst Inzh Zheleznodorozhn Transp
Trudy Khabarovskogo Meditsinskogo Instituta — Tr Khabar Med Inst
Trudy Khar'kovskaya Opytnaya Stantsiya Pchelovodstva — Trudy Kharkov Opyt Sta Pchelov
Trudy Khar'kovskii Gosudarstvennyi Meditsinskii Institut — Tr Khar'k Gos Med Inst
Trudy Khar'kovskii Sel'skokhozyaistvennyi Institut Imeni V. V. Dokuchaeva — Tr Khar'k Skh Inst Im V V Dokuchaeva
Trudy Khar'kovskogo Aviatsionnogo Instituta — Tr Khark Aviats Inst
Trudy Khar'kovskogo Avtodorozhnogo Instituta — Tr Khar'k Avtodorozhn Inst
Trudy Khar'kovskogo Avtomobil'no-Dorozhnogo Instituta — Tr Khar'k Avtomob Dorozhn Inst
Trudy Khar'kovskogo Avtomobil'no-Dorozhnogo Instituta — Tr Khark Avtomob Dorozhnogo Instituta
Trudy Khar'kovskogo Farmatsevticheskogo Instituta — Tr Khar'k Farm Inst
Trudy Khar'kovskogo Gosudarstvennogo Farmatsevticheskogo Instituta — Tr Khark Gos Farm Inst
Trudy Khar'kovskogo Instituta Gornogo Mashinostroeniya. Avtomatiki i Vychislitel'noi Tekhniki — Tr Khark Inst Gorn Mashinostr Avtom Vychisl Tekh
Trudy Khar'kovskogo Instituta Inzhenerov Zheleznodorozhnogo Transporta — Tr Khark Inst Inzh Zheleznodorozhn Transp
Trudy Khar'kovskogo Inzhenerno-Ekonomicheskogo Instituta — Tr Khark Inzh Ekon Inst
Trudy Khar'kovskogo Khimiko-Tekhnologicheskogo Instituta — Tr Khark Khim Tekhnol Inst
Trudy Khar'kovskogo Meditsinskogo Instituta — Tr Khar'k Med Inst
Trudy Khar'kovskogo Meditsinskogo Instituta — Tr Khar'kov Med Inst
Trudy Khar'kovskogo Nauchno-Issledovatel'skogo Khimiko-Farmatsevticheskogo Instituta — Tr Khark Nauchno Issled Khim Farm Inst
Trudy Khar'kovskogo Politekhnicheskogo Instituta — Tr Khark Politekh Inst
Trudy Khar'kovskogo Sel'skokhozyaistvennogo Instituta — TKKSA
Trudy Khar'kovskogo Sel'skokhozyaistvennogo Instituta — Tr Khar'k S-Kh Inst
Trudy Khar'kovskogo Sel'skokhozyaistvennogo Instituta — Trudy Kharkov Sel'-Khoz Inst
Trudy Khimicheskogo Instituta Imeni L. Ya. Karpova — Tr Khim Inst Im L Ya Karpova
Trudy Khimiko-Metallurgicheskogo Instituta Akademiya Nauk Kazakhskoj SSR — Tr Khim-Metall Inst Akad Nauk Kaz SSR
Trudy Khimiko-Metallurgicheskogo Instituta Akademiya Nauk SSSR Sibirskoe Otdelenie — Tr Khim Metall Inst Akad Nauk SSSR Sib Otd
Trudy Kierskoi Dukhovnoi Akademii — TKA
Trudy Kievskogo Gorodskogo Oblastnogo Nauchnogo Obshchestva Dermatologii — Tr Kiev Gor Obl Nauchn Ova Dermatol
Trudy Kievskogo Politekhnicheskogo Instituta — Tr Kiev Politekh Inst
Trudy Kievskogo Tekhnologicheskogo Instituta Pishchevoi Promyshlennosti — Tr Kiev Tekhnol Inst Pishch Promsti
Trudy Kievskogo Veterinarnogo Instituta — Tr Kiev Vet Inst
Trudy Kievskoi Dukhovnoi Akademii — TKDA
Trudy Kirgizskogo Gosudarstvennogo Meditsinskogo Instituta — Tr Kirg Gos Med Inst
Trudy Kirgizskogo Gosudarstvennogo Universiteta. Serija Matematiceskih Nauk — Trudy Kirgiz Gos Univ Ser Mat Nauk
Trudy Kirgizskogo Gosudarstvennogo Universiteta. Seriya Biologicheskikh Nauk Zoologiya-Fiziologiya — Trudy Kirgiz Gos Univ Ser Biol Nauk
Trudy Kirgizskogo Gosudarstvennogo Universiteta. Seriya Fizicheskikh Nauk — Tr Kirg Gos Univ Ser Fiz Nauk
Trudy Kirgizskogo Instituta Epidemiologii, Mikrobiologii, i Gigieny — Tr Kirg Inst Epidemiol Mikrobiol Gig
Trudy Kirgizskogo Nauchno-Issledovatel'skogo Instituta Pochvovedeniya — Tr Kirg Nauchno-Issled Inst Pochvoved
Trudy Kirgizskogo Nauchno-Issledovatel'skogo Instituta Zemledeliya — Tr Kirg Nauchno Issled Inst Zemled
Trudy Kirgizskogo Nauchno-Issledovatel'skogo Instituta Zemledeliya — Tr Kirgiz Nauch Issled Inst Zemled
Trudy Kirgizskogo Nauchno-Issledovatel'skogo Instituta Zemledeliya — Trudy Kirgiz Nauchno-Issled Inst Zeml
Trudy Kirgizskogo Nauchno-Issledovatel'skogo Instituta Zhivotnovodstva — Tr Kirg Nauchno-Issled Inst Zhivotnovod
Trudy Kirgizskogo Nauchno-Issledovatel'skogo Instituta Zhivotnovodstva i Veterinarii — Tr Kirg Nauchno-Issled Inst Zhivotnovod Vet
Trudy Kirgizskogo Nauchno-Issledovatel'skoi Instituta Onkologii i Radiologii — Tr Kirg Nauchno-Issled Inst Onkol Radiol
Trudy Kirgizskogo Sel'skokhozyaistvennogo Instituta — Tr Kirg S-Kh Inst
Trudy Kirgizskogo Sel'skokhozyaistvennogo Instituta — Trudy Kirgiz Sel'-Khoz Inst
Trudy Kirgizskogo Sel'skokhozyaistvennogo Seriya Agronomii — Tr Kirg Skh Inst Ser Agron
Trudy Kirgizskogo Universiteta Seriya Biologicheskikh Nauk — Tr Kirg Univ Ser Biol Nauk
Trudy Kirgizskoi Lesnoi Opytnoi Stantsii — Tr Kirg Lesn Opytn Stn
Trudy Kirgizskoi Opytnoi Stantsii Khlopkovodstva — Tr Kirg Opytn Stn Khlopkovod
Trudy Kirgizskoi Opytno-Selektsionnoi Stantsii po Sakharnoi Svekle — Tr Kirg Opytno-Sel Stn Sakh Svekle
Trudy Kirovskogo Oblastnogo Nauchno-Issledovatel'skogo Instituta Kraevedeniya — Tr Kirov Obl Nauchno Issled Inst Kraeved
Trudy Kirovskogo Otdeleniya Vsesoyuznogo Fiziologicheskogo Obshchestva — Tr Kirov Otd Vses Fiziol Ova
Trudy Kirovskogo Sel'skokhozyaistvennogo Instituta — Tr Kirov S-Kh Inst
Trudy Kishinevskii Politekhnicheskii Institut — Tr Kishinev Politekh Inst
Trudy Kishinevskii Sel'skokhozyaistvennyi Institut Imeni M. V. Frunze [*Former USSR*] — Tr Kishinev S-Kh Inst Im M V Frunze
Trudy Kishinevskogo Gosudarstvennogo Meditsinskogo Instituta — Tr Kishinev Gos Med Inst
Trudy Kishinevskogo Sel'skokhozyaistvennogo Instituta — Tr Kishinev S-Kh Inst
Trudy Kishinevskogo Sel'skokhozyaistvennogo Instituta — Trudy Kishinev Sel'-Khoz Inst
Trudy Klinicheskogo Otdeleniya Nauchno-Issledovatel'skogo Instituta Gigieny Truda i Profzabolevanii — Tr Klin Otd Nauchno Issled Inst Gig Tr Profzabol
Trudy Kliniki Nervnykh Boleznei Moskovskogo Oblastnogo Nauchno-Issledovatel'skogo Klinicheskogo Instituta — Tr Klin Nervn Bolezn Mosk Obl Nauchno-Issled Klin Inst
Trudy Kolomenskogo Filiala Vsesojuznyi Zaocnyi Politehniceskii Institut — Trudy Kolomen Filiala Vsesojuz Zaocn Politehn Inst
Trudy Kolomenskogo Filiala Vsesoyuznogo Zaochnogo Politekhnicheskogo Instituta — Tr Kolomenskogo Fil Vses Zaochn Politekh Inst
Trudy Komi Filiala Akademii Nauk SSSR — Tr Komi Fil Akad Nauk SSSR
Trudy Komi Filiala Akademii Nauk SSSR — Trudy Komi Fil Akad Nauk SSSR
Trudy Komi Filiala Akademii Nauk SSSR — Trudy Komi Filiala Akad Nauk SSSR
Trudy Komissii po Analiticheskoi Khimii Akademiya Nauk SSSR [*Former USSR*] — Tr Kom Anal Khim Akad Nauk SSSR
Trudy Komissii po Analiticheskoi Khimii Akademiya Nauk SSSR — Trudy Kom Analit Khim
Trudy Komissii po Bor'be s Korroziei Metallov Akademiya Nauk SSSR — Tr Kom Borbe s Korroz Met Akad Nauk SSSR
Trudy Komissii po Irrigatsii Akademiya Nauk SSSR — Tr Kom Irrig Akad Nauk SSSR
Trudy Komissii po Izuceniju Cetverticnogo Perioda — Trudy Komiss Izuc Cetvert Perioda
Trudy Komissii po Okhrane Prirody Ural'skogo Filiala Akademii Nauk SSSR — Tr Kom Okhr Prir Ural Fil Akad Nauk SSSR
Trudy Komissii po Pirometrii Vsesoyuznyi Nauchno-Issledovatel'skii Institut Metrologii — Tr Kom Pirom Vses Nauchno Issled Inst Metrol
Trudy Komissii po Spektroskopii Akademiya Nauk SSSR [*Former USSR*] — Tr Kom Spektros Akad Nauk SSSR
Trudy Kompleksnoi Ekspeditsii Dnepropetrovskogo Universiteta — Tr Kompleksn Eksped Dnepropetr Univ
Trudy Kompleksnoi Ekspeditsii Saratovskogo Universiteta po Izucheniyu Volgogradskogo i Saratovskogo Vodokhranilishch — Tr Kompleksn Eksped Sarat Univ Izuch Volgogr Sarat Vodokhran
Trudy Kompleksnoi Yuzhnoi Geologicheskoi Ekspeditsii. Akademiya Nauk SSSR — Tr Kompleksn Yuzhn Geol Eksped Akad Nauk SSSR
Trudy Konferentsiya Pochvovedov Sibiri i Dal'nego Vostoka Akademiya Nauk SSSR — Trudy Konf Pochv Sib Dal'n Vostoka Akad Nauk SSSR
Trudy Koordinatsionnykh Soveshchanyi po Gidrotekhnike — TKSGA
Trudy Koordinatsionnykh Soveshchanyi po Gidrotekhnike — Tr Koord Soveshch Gidrotekh
Trudy Kosinskoj Biologiceskog Stancii Moskovskogo Obscestva Ispytatelej Prirody. Arbeiten der Biologischen Station zu Kossino bei Moskau — Trudy Kosinsk Biol Stancii Moskovsk Obsc Isp Prir
Trudy Kostromskogo Sel'skokhozyaistvennogo Instituta "Karavaevo" — Tr Kostrom Skh Inst
Trudy Krasnodarskii Filial Vsesoyuznogo Neftegazovogo Nauchno-Issledovatel'skogo Instituta — Tr Krasnodar Fil Vses Neftegazov Nauchno Issled Inst
Trudy Krasnodarskogo Gosudarstvennogo Pedagogicheskogo Instituta — TKrasPI
Trudy Krasnodarskogo Gosudarstvennogo Pedagogicheskogo Instituta — Tr Krasnodar Gos Pedagog Inst

Trudy Krasnodarskogo Instituta Pishchevoi Promyshlennosti — Tr Krasnodar Inst Pishch Promsti
Trudy Krasnodarskogo Nauchno-Issledovatel'skogo Instituta Pischevoi Promyshlennosti — Tr Krasnodar Nauchno-Issled Inst Pishch Promsti
Trudy Krasnodarskogo Nauchno-Issledovatel'skogo Instituta Sel'skogog Khozyaistva — Tr Krasnodar Nauchno-Issled Inst Selsk Khoz
Trudy Krasnodarskogo Politekhnicheskogo Instituta — Tr Krasnodar Politekh Inst
Trudy Krasnoyarskogo Gosudarstvennogo Meditsinskogo Instituta — Tr Krasnoyarsk Gos Med Inst
Trudy Krasnoyarskogo Meditsinskogo Instituta — Tr Krasnoyarsk Med Inst
Trudy Krasnoyarskogo Nauchno-Issledovatel'skogo Instituta Sel'skogo Khozyaistva — Tr Kranoyarsk Nauchno Issled Inst Selsk Khoz
Trudy Krasnoyarskogo Nauchno-Issledovatel'skogo Instituta Sel'skogo Khozyaistva — Tr Krasnoyarsk Nauchno Issled Inst Sel'sk Khoz
Trudy Krasnoyarskogo Sel'skokhozyaistvennogo Instituta — Tr Krasnoyarsk S-Kh Inst
Trudy Krymskogo Filiala Akademiya Nauk Ukrainskoi SSR — Tr Krym Fil Akad Nauk Ukr SSR
Trudy Krymskogo Gosudarstvennogo Meditsinskogo Instituta — Tr Krym Gos Med Inst
Trudy Krymskogo Gosudarstvennogo Meditsinskogo Instituta Imeni I. V. Stalina — Tr Krym Gos Med Inst Im I V Stalina
Trudy Krymskogo Meditsinskogo Instituta — Tr Krym Med Inst
Trudy Krymskogo Sel'skokhozyaistvennogo Instituta — Tr Krym Skh Inst
Trudy Krymskogo Sel'skokhozyaistvennogo Instituta Imeni M. I. Kalinina — Tr Krym S-Kh Inst Im M I Kalinina
Trudy Krymskoi Gosudarstvennoi Sel'skokhozyaistvennoi Opytnoi Stantsii — Tr Krym Gos Skh Opytn Stn
Trudy Krymskoi Gosudarstvennoi Sel'skokhozyaistvennoi Opytnoi Stantsii — Tr Krym Gosud Sel'skokhoz Opyt Sta
Trudy Krymskoi Oblastnoi Gosudarstvennoi Sel'skokhozyaistvennoi Opytnoi Stantsii — Tr Krym Obl Gos Skh Opytn Stn
Trudy Krymskoi Opytno Selektsionnoi Stantsii VIR — Tr Krym Opytno Sel Stn VIR
Trudy Kubanskoe Otdelenie Vsesoyuznogo Obshchestva Genetikovi Selektsionerov — Tr Kuban Otd Vses Ova Genet Sel
Trudy Kubanskogo Sel'skokhozyaistvennogo Instituta — Tr Kuban S-Kh Inst
Trudy Kubanskogo Sel'skokhozyaistvennogo Instituta — Trudy Kuban Sel'-Khoz Inst
Trudy Kuibyshevskii Aviatsionnyi Institut — TKUAA
Trudy Kuibyshevskii Aviatsionnyi Institut [*Former USSR*] — Tr Kuibyshev Aviats Inst
Trudy Kuibyshevskii Gosudarstvennyi Nauchno-Issledovatel'skii Institut Neftyanoi Promyshlennosti [*Former USSR*] — Tr Kuibyshev Gos Nauchno-Issled Inst Neft Prom-Sti
Trudy Kuibyshevskii Inzhenerno-Stroitel'nyi Institut — Tr Kuibyshev Inzh-Stroit Inst
Trudy Kuibyshevskii Meditsinskii Instituta — Tr Kuibyshev Med Inst
Trudy Kuibyshevskii Nauchno-Issledovatel'skii Institut Neftyanoi Promyshlennosti — Tr Kuibyshev Nauchno-Issled Inst Neft Promsti
Trudy Kuibyshevskogo Sel'skokhozyaistvennogo Instituta — Tr Kuibyshev S-Kh Inst
Trudy (Kujbysevskij Aviacionnyj) Institut — Trudy (Kujbys Aviac) Inst
Trudy Kurganskogo Mashinostroitel'nogo Instituta — Tr Kurgan Mashinostroit Inst
Trudy Kurskogo Meditsinskogo Instituta — Tr Kursk Med Inst
Trudy Kutaisskogo Gosudarstvennogo Pedagogiceskogo Instituta — TKutPI
Trudy Kutaisskogo Sel'skokhozyaistvennogo Instituta — Tr Kutais Skh Inst
Trudy Laboratorii Biokhimii i Fiziologii Zhivotnykh Instituta Biologii Akademiya Nauk Latviiskoi SSR — Tr Lab Biokhim Fiziol Zhivotn Inst Biol Akad Nauk Latv SSR
Trudy Laboratorii Eksperimental'noi Biologii Moskovskogo Zooparka — Tr Lab Eksp Biol Mosk Zooparka
Trudy Laboratorii Elektromagnitnykh Polei Radiochastot Instituta Gigieny Truda i Professional'nykh Zabolevanii Akademii Meditsinskikh Nauk SSSR — TLEPA
Trudy Laboratorii Evolyutsionnoi i Ekologicheskoi Fiziologii Akademiya Nauk SSSR Institut Fiziologii Rastenii — Tr Lab Evol Ekol Fiziol Akad Nauk SSSR Inst Fiziol Rast
Trudy Laboratorii Fiziologii Zhivotnykh Instituta Biologii Akademii Nauk Litovskoi SSR — Tr Lab Fiziol Zhivotn Inst Biol Akad Nauk Lit SSR
Trudy Laboratorii Geologii Dokembriya Akademiya Nauk SSSR — Tr Lab Geol Dokembr Akad Nauk SSSR
Trudy Laboratorii Geologii Uglya Akademiya Nauk SSSR — Tr Lab Geol Uglya Akad Nauk SSSR
Trudy Laboratorii Gidrogeologicheskikh Problem Akademiya Nauk SSSR [*Former USSR*] — Tr Lab Gidrogeol Probl Akad Nauk SSSR
Trudy Laboratorii Lesovedeniya Akademiya Nauk SSSR — Tr Lab Lesoved Akad Nauk SSSR
Trudy Laboratorii Ozerovedeniya Leningradskii Gosudarstvennyi Universitet — Tr Lab Ozeroved Leningr Gos Univ
Trudy Laboratorii po Izucheniyu Belka Akademiya Nauk SSSR — Tr Lab Izuch Belka Akad Nauk SSSR
Trudy Laboratorii Sapropelevykh Otlozhenii Akademiya Nauk SSSR — Tr Lab Sapropelevykh Otlozh Akad Nauk SSSR
Trudy Laboratorii Vulkanologii Akademiya Nauk SSSR — Tr Lab Vulkanol Akad Nauk SSSR
Trudy Latviiskaia Sel'skokhoziaistvennaia Akademiia — Tr Latv Sel'kh Akad
Trudy Latviiskogo Instituta Eksperimental'noi i Klinicheskoi Meditsiny Akademii Meditsinskikh Nauk SSSR — Tr Latv Inst Eksp Klin Med Akad Med Nauk SSSR
Trudy Latviiskogo Nauchno-Issledovatel'skogo Instituta Gidrotekhniki i Melioratsii — Tr Latv Nauchno Issled Inst Gidrotekh Melior
Trudy Latviiskogo Nauchno-Issledovatel'skogo Instituta Zhivotnovodstva i Veterinarii — Tr Latv Nauchno-Issled Inst Zhivotnovod Vet
Trudy Latviiskogo Nauchno-Issledovatel'skogo Instituta Zhivotnovodstva i Veterinarii — Tr Latviiskogo Nauchno-Issled Inst Zhivotnovod Vet
Trudy Latviiskogo Sel'skokhozyaistvennogo Instituta — Trudy Latv Sel'-Khoz Inst
Trudy Latviiskoi Sel'skokhozyaistvennoi Akademii — Tr Latv S-Kh Akad
Trudy Leningradskii Elektrotekhnicheskii Institut Svyazi — Tr Leningr Elektrotekh Inst Svyazi
Trudy Leningradskii Gidrometeorologicheskii Institut — Tr Leningr Gidrometeorol Inst
Trudy Leningradskii Industrial'nogo Instituta — Tr Leningr Ind Inst
Trudy Leningradskii Institut Inzhenerov Kommunal'nogo Stroitel'stva — Tr Leningr Inst Inzh Kommunal'n Stroit
Trudy Leningradskii Institut Inzhenerov Zheleznodorozhnogo Transporta — Tr Leningr Inst Inzh Zheleznodorozhn Transp
Trudy Leningradskii Institut Kul'tury — Trudy Leningr Inst Kul't
Trudy Leningradskii Institut Sovetskoi Torgovli — Tr Leningr Inst Sov Torg
Trudy Leningradskii Institut Tochnoi Mekhaniki i Optiki — Tr Leningr Inst Tochn Mekh Opt
Trudy Leningradskii Inzhenerno-Ekonomicheskii Institut Imeni Pal'miro Tol'yatti — Tr Leningr Inzh Ekon Inst Im Pal'miro Tol'yatti
Trudy Leningradskii Metallicheskii Zavod — Tr Leningr Met Zavod
Trudy Leningradskii Nauchno-Issledovatel'skii i Konstruktorskii Institut Khimicheskogo Mashinostroeniya [*Former USSR*] — Tr Leningr Nauchno-Issled Konstr Inst Khim Mashinostr
Trudy Leningradskii Nauchno-Issledovatel'skii Institut Vaktsin i Syvorotok — Tr Leningr Nauchno Issled Inst Vaktsin Syvorotok
Trudy Leningradskii Voenno-Mekhanicheskii Institut — Tr Leningr Voen Mekh Inst
Trudy Leningradskogo Geologicheskogo Upravleniya — Tr Leningr Geol Upr
Trudy Leningradskogo Gidrometeorologicheskogo Instituta — Trudy Leningr Gidromet Inst
Trudy Leningradskogo Gosudarstvennogo Nauchno-Issledovatel'skogo Instituta Travmatologii i Ortopedii — Tr Leningr Gos Nauchno Issled Inst Travmatol Ortop
Trudy Leningradskogo Instituta Epidemiologii i Mikrobiologii — Tr Leningr Inst Epidemiol Mikrobiol
Trudy Leningradskogo Instituta Kinoinzhenerov — Tr Leningr Inst Kinoinzh
Trudy Leningradskogo Instituta Usovershenstvovaniya Vrachei — Tr Leningr Inst Usoversh Vrachei
Trudy Leningradskogo Instituta Vaktsin i Syvorotok — Tr Leningr Inst Vaktsin Syvorotok
Trudy Leningradskogo Instituta Vodnogo Transporta — Tr Leningr Inst Vodn Transp
Trudy Leningradskogo Inzhenerno-Ekonomicheskogo Instituta — Tr Leningr Inzh Ekon Inst
Trudy Leningradskogo Khimiko-Farmatsevticheskogo Instituta — Tr Leningr Khim-Farm Inst
Trudy Leningradskogo Khimiko-Tekhnologicheskogo Instituta — Tr Leningr Khim Tekhnol Inst
Trudy Leningradskogo Korablestroitel'nogo Instituta — Tr Leningr Korablestroit Inst
Trudy Leningradskogo Korablestroitel'nogo Instituta [*Former USSR*] — Tr Leningr Korablestroit'nogo Inst
Trudy Leningradskogo Meditsinskogo Instituta — Tr Leningr Med Inst
Trudy Leningradskogo Mekhaniko-Tekhnologicheskogo Instituta Kholodil'noi Promyshlennosti — Tr Leningr Mekh Tekhnol Inst Kholod Promsti
Trudy Leningradskogo Nauchnogo Obshchestva Patologoanatomov — Tr Leningr Nauchno Ova Patologoanat
Trudy Leningradskogo Nauchno-Issledovatel'skogo Instituta Antibiotiki — Tr Leningr Nauchno-Issled Inst Antibiot
Trudy Leningradskogo Nauchno-Issledovatel'skogo Instituta Epidemiologii i Mikrobiologii — Tr Leningr Nauchno-Issled Inst Epidemiol Mikrobiol
Trudy Leningradskogo Nauchno-Issledovatel'skogo Instituta Neirokhirurgii — Tr Leningr Nauchno Issled Inst Neirokhir
Trudy Leningradskogo Nauchno-Issledovatel'skogo Instituta Radiatsii i Gigieny — Tr Leningr Nauchno Issled Inst Radiats Gig
Trudy Leningradskogo Nauchno-Issledovatel'skogo Instituta Tuberkuleza — Tr Leningr Nauchno Issled Inst Tuberk
Trudy Leningradskogo Nauchno-Issledovatel'skogo Psikhonevrologisheskogo Instituta — Tr Leningr Nauchno Issled Psikhonevrol Inst
Trudy Leningradskogo Obshchestva Anatomov, Gistologov, i Embriologov — Tr Leningr Ova Anat Gistol Embriol
Trudy Leningradskogo Obshchestva Estestvoispytatelei — Tr Leningr O-Va Estestvoispyt
Trudy Leningradskogo Obshchestva Estestvoispytatelei — Trudy Leningr Obshch Estest
Trudy Leningradskogo Pediatricheskogo Meditsinskogo Instituta — Tr Leningr Pediatr Med Inst
Trudy Leningradskogo Politekhnicheskogo Instituta Imeni M. I. Kalinina — Tr Leningr Politekh Inst
Trudy Leningradskogo Politekhnicheskogo Instituta Imeni M. I. Kalinina [*Former USSR*] — Tr Leningr Politekh Inst Im M I Kalinina
Trudy Leningradskogo Sanitarno-Gigienicheskogo Meditsinskogo Instituta — Tr Leningr Sanit-Gig Med Inst
Trudy Leningradskogo Tehnologicheskogo Instituta Holodil'noi Promyshlennosti — Trudy Leningrad Tehnolog Inst Holod Promysl
Trudy Leningradskogo Tekhnologicheskogo Instituta [*Former USSR*] — Tr Leningr Teknol Inst
Trudy Leningradskogo Tekhnologicheskogo Instituta Imeni Lensoveta — Tr Leningr Tekhnol Inst Im Lensoveta
Trudy Leningradskogo Tekhnologicheskogo Instituta Kholodil'noi Promyshlennosti — Tr Leningr Tekhnol Inst Kholod Prom-St'

Trudy Leningradskogo Tekhnologicheskogo Instituta Pishchevoi Promyshlennosti — Tr Leningr Tekhnol Inst Pishch Prom-Sti
Trudy Leningradskogo Tekhnologicheskogo Instituta Tsellyulozno-Bumazhnoi Promyshlennosti — Tr Leningr Tekhnol Inst Tsellyul Bum Promsti
Trudy Leningradskogo Tekhnologicheskogo Instituta Tsellyulozno-Bumazhnoi Promyshlennosti — Tr Leningrad Tekhnol Inst Tsellyul-Bumazh Prom
Trudy Leningradskogo Tekstil'nogo Instituta — Tr Leningr Tekst Inst
Trudy Leningradskogo Tsentral'nogo Gosudarstvennogo Travmatologicheskogo Instituta — Tr Leningr Tsentr Gos Travmatol Inst
Trudy Leningradskoi Lesotekhnicheskoi Akademii — Tr Leningr Lesotekh Akad
Trudy Lesotekhnicheskoi Akademii — Tr Lesotekh Akad
Trudy Limnologicheskogo Instituta Siberskogo Otdeleniya. Akademii Nauk SSSR — Tr Limnol Inst Sib Otd Akad Nauk SSSR
Trudy Litovskogo Instituta Eksperimental'noi i Klinicheskoi Meditsiny Akademii Meditsinskikh Nauk SSSR — Tr Litov Inst Eksp Klin Med Akad Med Nauk SSSR
Trudy Litovskogo Instituta Eksperimental'noi Meditsiny Akademii Meditsinskikh Nauk SSSR — Tr Litov Inst Eksp Med Akad Med Nauk SSSR
Trudy Litovskogo Nauchno-Issledovatel'skogo Geologorazvedochnogo Instituta — Tr Litov Nauchno Issled Geologorazves Inst
Trudy Litovskogo Nauchno-Issledovatel'skogo Instituta Lesnogo Khozyaistva — Tr Litov Nauchno Issled Inst Lesn Khoz
Trudy Litovskogo Nauchno-Issledovatel'skogo Instituta Veterinarii — Tr Litov Nauchno Issled Inst Vet
Trudy Litovskogo Nauchno-Issledovatel'skogo Instituta Zemledeliya — Trudy Litov Nauchno-Issled Inst Zeml
Trudy LNIIA [*Leningrad Nauchno-Issledovatel'skii Institut Antibiotikov*] — Tr LNIIA
Trudy Luganskogo Sel'skokhozyaistvennoi Instituta — Tr Lugansk S-Kh Inst
Trudy Magadanskogo Zonal'nogo Nauchno-Issledovatel'skogo Instituta Sel'skogo Khozyaistva Severo-Vostoka — Tr Magadan Zon Nauchno Issled Inst Selsk Khoz Sev Vostoka
Trudy Mariiskii Gosudarstvennyi Pedagogicheskii Institut — Tr Marii Gos Pedagog Inst
Trudy Matematiceskogo Instituta Imeni V. A. Steklova — Trudy Mat Inst Steklov
Trudy Matematicheskogo Instituta Akademiya Nauk SSSR — Tr Mat Inst Akad Nauk SSSR
Trudy Metrologiceskih Institutov SSSR — Tr Metrol Inst SSSR
Trudy Metrologiceskih Institutov SSSR — Trudy Metrolog Inst SSSR
Trudy Mezhdunarodnaya Konferentsiya po Fizike Vysokikh Energii — Tr Mezhdunar Konf Fiz Vys Energ
Trudy Mezhdunarodnogo Simpoziuma po Geterogennomu Katalizu — Tr Mezhdunar Simp Geterog Katal
Trudy Mezhdunarodnogo Simpoziuma po Tsitoekologii — Tr Mezhdunar Simp Tsitoekol
Trudy Mineralogicheskogo Instituta Akademiya Nauk SSSR — Tr Mineral Inst Akad Nauk SSSR
Trudy Mineralogicheskogo Muzeya Akademiya Nauk SSSR [*Former USSR*] — Tr Mineral Muz Akad Nauk SSSR
Trudy Minskogo Gosudarstvennogo Meditsinskogo Instituta — Tr Minsk Gos Med Inst
Trudy Moldavskii Nauchno-Issledovatel'skii Institut Epidemiologii, Mikrobiologii, i Gigieny — Tr Mold Nauchno Issled Inst Epidemiol Mikrobiol Gig
Trudy Moldavskii Nauchno-Issledovatel'skii Institut Gigieny i Epidemiologii — Tr Mold Nauchno Issled Inst Gig Epidemiol
Trudy Moldavskii Nauchno-Issledovatel'skii Institut Zhivotnovodstva i Veterinarii — Tr Mold Nauchno Issled Inst Zhivotnovod Vet
Trudy Moldavskogo Nauchno-Issledovatel'nogo Instituta Tuberkuleza — Tr Mold Nauchno Issled Inst Tuberk
Trudy Moldavskogo Nauchno-Issledovatel'skogo Instituta Oroshaemogo Zemledeliya i Ovoshchevodstva — Tr Mold Nauchno Issled Inst Oroshaemogo Zemled Ovoshchevod
Trudy Moldavskogo Nauchno-Issledovatel'skogo Instituta Oroshaemogo Zemledeliya i Ovoshchevodstva — Tr Mold Nauchno-Issled Inst Orosh Zemled Ovoshchevod
Trudy Moldavskogo Nauchno-Issledovatel'skogo Instituta Oroshaemogo Zemledeliya i Ovoshchevodstva — Tr Moldav Nauch Issled Inst Orosh Zemled Ovoshchev
Trudy Moldavskogo Nauchno-Issledovatel'skogo Instituta Pishchevoi Promyshlennosti — Tr Mold Nauchno Issled Inst Pishch Promsti
Trudy Molodyh Ucenyh Kirigizskogo Universiteta — Trudy Mol Ucen Kirigiz Univ
Trudy Molodykh Uchenykh Dagestanskii Nauchno-Issledovatel'skii Institut Sel'skogo Khozyaistva — Tr Molodykh Uch Dagest Nauchno Issled Inst Selsk Khoz
Trudy Molodykh Uchenykh Spetsial'nogo Chuvashskogo Sel'skokhozyaistvennogo Instituta — Tr Molodykh Uch Spets Chuv Skh Inst
Trudy Molodykh Uchenykh Ukrainskoi Sel'skokhozyaistvennoi Akademii — Tr Molodykh Uch Ukr Skh Akad
Trudy Molodykh Uchenykh Yakutskogo Universiteta — Tr Molodykh Uch Yakutsk Univ
Trudy Molotovskogo Gosudarstvennogo Meditsinskogo Instituta — Tr Molotov Gos Med Inst
Trudy Mongol'skoj Komissii — Trudy Mongolsk Komiss
Trudy Mordovskogo Gosudarstvennogo Zapovednika Imeni P. G. Smirovicha — Tr Mord Gos Zapovednika Im P G Smirovicha
Trudy Mordovskogo Nauchno-Issledovatel'skogo Instituta Jazyka, Literatury, Istorii, i Ekonomiki — TMorNII
Trudy Morskogo Gidrofizicheskogo Instituta Akademiya Nauk Ukrainskoj SSR — Tr Morsk Gidrofiz Inst Akad Nauk Ukr SSR
Trudy Morskogo Rybnogo Instituta. Seriya A. Okeanografiya i Promyslovaya Ikhtiologiya (Gdynia, Poland) — Tr Morsk Rybn Inst Ser A (Gdynia Pol)
Trudy Morskogo Rybnogo Instituta. Seriya B (Gdynia, Poland) — Tr Morsk Rybn Inst Ser B (Gdynia Pol)
Trudy Moskovskii Fiziko-Tekhnicheskii Institut — Tr Mosk Fiz Tekh Inst
Trudy Moskovskii Gorodskoi Bakteriologicheskii Institut — Tr Mosk Gor Bakteriol Inst
Trudy Moskovskii Gorodskoi Institut Epidemiologii i Bakteriologii — Tr Mosk Gor Inst Epidemiol Bakteriol
Trudy Moskovskii Gorodskoi Nauchno-Issledovatel'skii Institut Epidemiologii i Bakteriologii — Tr Mosk Gor Nauchno Issled Inst Epidemiol Bakteriol
Trudy Moskovskii Institut Elektronnogo Mashinostroeniya — TMIEB
Trudy Moskovskii Institut Elektronnogo Mashinostroeniya [*Former USSR*] — Tr Mosk Inst Elektron Mashinostr
Trudy Moskovskii Institut Epidemiologii, Mikrobiologii, i Gigieny — Tr Mosk Inst Epidemiol Mikrobiol Gig
Trudy Moskovskii Institut Neftekhimicheskoi i Gazovoi Promyshlennosti — Tr Mosk Inst Neftekhim Gaz Promsti
Trudy Moskovskii Institut Neftekhimicheskoi i Gazovoi Promyshlennosti Imeni I. M. Gubkina [*Former USSR*] — Tr Mosk Inst Neftekhim Gazov Prom-Sti Im I M Gubkina
Trudy Moskovskii Nauchno-Issledovatel'skii Institut Epidemiologii, Mikrobiologii, i Gigieny — Tr Mosk Nauchno Issled Inst Epidemiol Mikrobiol Gig
Trudy Moskovskii Nauchno-Issledovatel'skii Institut Virusnykh Preparatov — Tr Mosk Nauchno Issled Inst Virusn Prep
Trudy Moskovskii Neftyanoi Institut — Tr Mosk Neft Inst
Trudy. Moskovskii Tekhnologicheskii Institut Pishchevoi Promyshlennosti — Tr Mosk Tekhnol Inst Pishch Promsti
Trudy Moskovskij Aviatsionnyj Institut Imeni S. Ordzhonikidze Sbornik Statei [*Former USSR*] — Tr Mosk Aviats Inst Im S Ordzhonikidze Sb Statei
Trudy Moskovskij Aviatsionnyj Tekhnologicheskij Institut — Tr Mosk Aviats Tekhnol Inst
Trudy Moskovskoe Obshchestvo Ispytatelei Prirody Otedel Biologicheskii — Tr Mosk Obshch Ispyt Prir Otedel Biol
Trudy Moskovskogo Avtomobil'no Dorozhnogo Instituta — Tr Mosk Avtomob Dorozhn Inst
Trudy Moskovskogo Elektrotehniceskogo Instituta Svjazi — Trudy Moskov Elektrotehn Inst Svjazi
Trudy Moskovskogo Energeticheskogo Instituta [*Former USSR*] — Tr Mosk Energ Inst
Trudy Moskovskogo Energeticheskogo Instituta Fizika [*Former USSR*] — Tr Mosk Energ Inst Fiz
Trudy Moskovskogo Fiziko-Tekhnicheskogo Instituta. Seriya "Obshchaya i Molekulyarnaya Fizika" — Tr MFTI Ser "Obshch Mol Fiz"
Trudy Moskovskogo Fiziko-Tekhnicheskogo Instituta. Seriya "Obshchaya i Molekulyarnaya Fizika" — Tr Mosk Fiz Tekh Inst Ser "Obshch Mol Fiz"
Trudy Moskovskogo Geologicheskogo Upravlenie — Tr Mosk Geol Upr
Trudy Moskovskogo Geologo-Razvedochnogo Instituta — Tr Mosk Geol Razved Inst
Trudy Moskovskogo Gornogo Instituta — Tr Mosk Gorn Inst
Trudy Moskovskogo Gorodskogo Nauchno-Issledovatel'skogo Instituta Skoroi Promoshchi — Tr Mosk Gor Nauchno Issled Inst Skoroi Pomoshchi
Trudy Moskovskogo Instituta Inzenernov Zeleznodoroznogo Transporta — Trudy Moskov Inst Inzen Zelezno-Doroz Transporta
Trudy Moskovskogo Instituta Inzhenerov Gorodskogo Stroitel'stva — Tr Mosk Inst Inzh Gor Stroit
Trudy Moskovskogo Instituta Inzhenerov Zheleznodorozhnogo Transporta — Tr Mosk Inst Inzh Zheleznodorozhn Transp
Trudy Moskovskogo Instituta Istoriji, Filosofiji, i Literatury — Trudy Moskov Inst Istoriji
Trudy Moskovskogo Instituta Khimicheskogo Mashinostroeniya — Tr Mosk Inst Khim Mashinostr
Trudy Moskovskogo Instituta Narodnogo Khozyaistva — Tr Mosk Inst Nar Khoz
Trudy Moskovskogo Instituta Radiotekhniki, Elektroniki, i Avtomatiki — Tr Mosk Inst Radiotekh Elektron Avtom
Trudy Moskovskogo Instituta Radiotekhniki, Elektroniki, i Avtomatiki [*Former USSR*] — Tr Mosk Radiotekh Elektron Avtomat
Trudy Moskovskogo Instituta Radiotekhniki, Elektroniki, i Avtomatiki — Trudy Moskov Inst Radiotehn Elektron i Avtomat
Trudy Moskovskogo Instituta Tonkoi Khimicheskoi Tekhnologii — Tr Mosk Inst Tonkoi Khim Tekhnol
Trudy Moskovskogo Inzhenerno-Ekonomicheskogo Instituta — Tr Mosk Inzh Ekon Inst
Trudy Moskovskogo Khimiko-Tekhnologicheskogo Instituta Imeni D. I. Mendeleeva — Tr Mosk Khim-Tekhnol Inst
Trudy Moskovskogo Matematiceskogo Obscestva — Trudy Moskov Mat Obsc
Trudy Moskovskogo Matematicheskogo Obshchestva — Tr Mosk Mat O-Va
Trudy Moskovskogo Matematicheskogo Obshchestva — Trudy Moskov Mat Obshch
Trudy Moskovskogo Meditsinskogo Stomatologichesko Instituta — Tr Mosk Med Stomatol Inst
Trudy Moskovskogo Nauchno-Issledovatel'skogo Instituta Epidemiologii i Mikrobiologii — Tr Mosk Nauchno-Issled Inst Epidemiol Mikrobiol
Trudy Moskovskogo Nauchno-Issledovatel'skogo Instituta Psikhiatrii — Tr Mosk Nauchno-Issled Inst Psikhiatr
Trudy Moskovskogo Nauchno-Issledovatel'skogo Instituta Ukha Gorla i Nosa — Tr Mosk Nauchno-Issled Inst Ukha Gorla Nosa
Trudy Moskovskogo Oblastnogo Nauchno-Issledovatel'skogo Klinicheskogo Instituta Prakticheskoi Nevropatologii — Tr Mosk Obl Nauchno Issled Klin Inst Prakt Nevropatol
Trudy Moskovskogo Obshchestva Ispytatelei Prirody [*Former USSR*] — Tr Mosk O-Va Ispyt Prir
Trudy Moskovskogo Obshchestva Ispytatelei Prirody Otdel Biologicheskii [*Former USSR*] — Tr Mosk O-Va Ispyt Prir Otd Biol
Trudy Moskovskogo Ordena Lenina Ehnergiticheskogo Instituta — Tr Mosk Ehnerg Inst
Trudy Moskovskogo Ordena Lenina Energeticeskogo Instituta — Trudy Moskov Orden Lenin Energet Inst

Trudy Moskovskogo Tekhnologicheskogo Instituta Myasnoi Molochnoi Promyshlennosti — Tr Mosk Tekhnol Inst Myasn Molochn Prom-Sti
Trudy Moskovskogo Tekhnologicheskogo Instituta Rybnoi Promyshlennosti i Khozyaistva [*Former USSR*] — Tr Mosk Tekh Inst Rybn Prom-Sti Khoz
Trudy Moskovskogo Torfyanogo Instituta — Tr Mosk Torf Inst
Trudy Moskovskogo Vysshego Tekhnicheskogo Uchilishcha [*Former USSR*] — Tr Mosk Vyssh Tekh Uchil
Trudy Moskovskoi Ordena Lenina Sel'sko-Khozyaistvennoi Akademii Imeni K. A. Timiryazeva — Trudy Mosk Ordena Lenina Sel'Khoz Akad
Trudy Moskovskoi Veterinarnoi Akademii — Tr Mosk Vet Akad
Trudy Murmanskogo Morskogo Biologicheskogo Instituta — Tr Murm Morsk Biol Inst
Trudy Murmanskoi Biologicheskoi Stantsii — Tr Murm Biol Stn
Trudy Nakhichevanskaya Kompleksnaya Zonal'naya Stantsiya — Tr Nakhich Kompleksn Zon Stn
Trudy Nakhichevanskoi Kompleksnoi Zonal'noi Opytnoi Stantsii — Tr Nakhich Kompleksn Zon Opytn Stn
Trudy Nakhichevanskoi Kompleksnoi Zonal'noi Opytnoi Stantsii — Trudy Nakhich Kompleks Zonal Opyt Sta
Trudy Nauchno Issledovatel'skogo Instituta Sel'skogo Khozyaistva Krainego Severa — Tr Nauchno-Issled Inst Sel'sk Khoz Krainego Sev
Trudy Nauchnogo Instituta po Udobreniyam i Insektofungitsidam Imeni Ya. V. Satoilova — Trudy Nauch Inst Udobr Insektofung
Trudy Nauchnogo Khimiko Farmatsevtecheskogo Instituta — Tr Nauchno Khim Farm Inst
Trudy Nauchnogo Obshchestva Studentov Erevanskii Gosudarstvennyi Universitet — Tr Nauchn Ova Stud Erevan Gos Univ
Trudy Nauchnogo Studencheskogo Obshchestva Gor'kovskii Politekhnicheskii Institut — Tr Nauchn Stud Ova Gork Politekh Inst
Trudy Nauchnoi Konferentsii Stalinskogo Gosudarstvennogo Pedagogicheskogo Instituta — Tr Nauchn Konf Stalinskogo Gos Pedagog Inst
Trudy Nauchno-Issledovatel'skaya Laboratoriya Geologii Zarubezhnykh Stran — Tr Nauchno Issled Lab Geol Zarub Stran
Trudy Nauchno-Issledovatel'skii i Proektnyi Institut Mekhanicheskoi Obrabotki Poleznykh Iskopaemykh — Tr Nauchno Issled Proektn Inst Mekh Obrab Polezn Iskop
Trudy Nauchno-Issledovatel'skii Institut Gidrometeorologicheskogo Priborostroeniya — Tr Nauchno Issled Inst Gidrometeorol Priborostr
Trudy Nauchno-Issledovatel'skii Institut Neftekhimicheskikh Proizvodstv — Tr Nauchno Issled Inst Neftekhim Proizvod
Trudy Nauchno-Issledovatel'skii Institut Onkologii (Tiflis) — Tr Nauchno Issled Inst Onkol (Tiflis)
Trudy Nauchno-Issledovatel'skii Institut po Khlopkovodstvu (Tashkent) — Tr Nauch Issled Inst Klopkovod (Tashkent)
Trudy Nauchno-Issledovatel'skii Institut po Transportu i Khraneniyu Nefti i Nefteproduktov — Tr Nauchno Issled Inst Transp Khraneniyu Nefti Nefteprod
Trudy Nauchno-Issledovatel'skii Institut po Udobreniyam i Insektofungitsidam [*Former USSR*] — Tr Nauchno-Issled Inst Udobr Insektofungits
Trudy Nauchno-Issledovatel'skii Institut Sinteticheskikh Spirtov i Organicheskikh Produktov — Tr Nauchno Issled Inst Sin Spirtov Org Prod
Trudy Nauchno-Issledovatel'skii Institut Teploenergeticheskogo Priborostroeniya — Tr Nauchno Issled Inst Teploenerg Priborostr
Trudy Nauchno-Issledovatel'skogo Dizel'nogo Instituta — Tr Nauchno Issled Dizeln Inst
Trudy Nauchno-Issledovatel'skogo Gidrometeorologicheskogo Instituta (Alma-Ata) [*Kazakh SSR*] — Tr Nauchno-Issled Gidrometerol Inst (Alma-Ata)
Trudy Nauchno-Issledovatel'skogo i Konstruktorskogo Instituta Mekhanizatsii Rybnoi Promyshlennosti — Tr Nauchno Issled Konstr Inst Mekh Rybn Prom-Sti
Trudy Nauchno-Issledovatel'skogo Instituta Betona i Zhelezobetona [*Former USSR*] — Tr Nauchno-Issled Inst Betona Zhelezobetona
Trudy Nauchno-Issledovatel'skogo Instituta Biologii i Biofiziki pri Tomskom Gosudarstvennom Universitete — Tr Nauchno Issled Inst Biol Biofiz Tomsk Gos Univ
Trudy Nauchno-Issledovatel'skogo Instituta Biologii Khar'kovskogo Gosudarstvennogo Universiteta — Tr Nauchno-Issled Inst Biol Khar'k Gos Univ
Trudy Nauchno-Issledovatel'skogo Instituta Eksperimental'noi i Klinicheskoi Terapii Gruzinskoi SSR — Tr Nauchno-Issled Inst Eksp Klin Ter Gruz SSR
Trudy Nauchno-Issledovatel'skogo Instituta Epidemiologii i Mikrobiologii — Tr Nauchno-Issled Inst Epidemiol Mikrobiol
Trudy Nauchno-Issledovatel'skogo Instituta Fiziologii — Tr Nauchno Issled Inst Fiziol
Trudy Nauchno-Issledovatel'skogo Instituta Fiziologii i Patologii Zhenshchiny — Tr Nauchno Issled Inst Fiziol Patol Zhen
Trudy Nauchno-Issledovatel'skogo Instituta Geologii Arktiki [*Former USSR*] — Tr Nauchno-Issled Inst Geol Arktiki
Trudy Nauchno-Issledovatel'skogo Instituta Geologii i Mineralogii — Tr Nauchno Issled Inst Geol Mineral
Trudy Nauchno-Issledovatel'skogo Instituta Gigieny Vodnoi Transportatsii — Tr Nauchno Issled Inst Gig Vodn Transp
Trudy Nauchno-Issledovatel'skogo Instituta Kabel'noi Promyshlennosti — Tr Nauchno Issled Inst Kabeln Prom
Trudy Nauchno-Issledovatel'skogo Instituta Kamnya i Silikatov — Tr Nauchno Issled Inst Kamnya Silik
Trudy Nauchno-Issledovatel'skogo Instituta Kartofel'nogo Khozyaistva — TIKKB8
Trudy Nauchno-Issledovatel'skogo Instituta Kartofel'nogo Khozyaistva — Tr Nauchno-Issled Inst Kartofel'n Khoz
Trudy Nauchno-Issledovatel'skogo Instituta Kartofel'nogo Khozyaistva — Tr Nauchno-Issled Inst Kartofel'nogo Khoz
Trudy Nauchno-Issledovatel'skogo Instituta Klinicheskoi i Eksperimental'noi Khirurgii — Tr Nauchno Issled Inst Klin Eksp Khir
Trudy Nauchno-Issledovatel'skogo Instituta Kraevoi Patologii [*Alma-Ata*] — TNKPB
Trudy Nauchno-Issledovatel'skogo Instituta Kraevoi Patologii (Alma-Ata) — Tr Nauchno-Issled Inst Kraev Patol (Alma-Ata)
Trudy Nauchno-Issledovatel'skogo Instituta Legkikh Metallov — Tr Nauchno-Issled Inst Legk Met
Trudy Nauchno-Issledovatel'skogo Instituta Meditsinskoi Parazitologii i Tropicheskoi Meditsiny Gruzinskoi SSR — Tr Nauchno-Issled Inst Med Parazitol Trop Med Gruz SSR
Trudy Nauchno-Issledovatel'skogo Instituta Mekhanizatsii Rybnoi Promyshlennosti — Tr Nauchno Issled Inst Mekh Rybn Promsti
Trudy Nauchno-Issledovatel'skogo Instituta Mestnoi i Toplivnoi Promyshlennosti — Tr Nauchno Issled Inst Mestnoi Topl Promsti
Trudy Nauchno-Issledovatel'skogo Instituta Ministerstvo Radiotekhnicheskoi Promyshlennosti SSSR — Tr Nauchno Issled Inst Minist Radiotekh Promsti SSSR
Trudy Nauchno-Issledovatel'skogo Instituta Okhrany Truda i Professional'nykh Zabolevanii — Tr Nauchno Issled Inst Okhr Tr Prof Zabol
Trudy Nauchno-Issledovatel'skogo Instituta Onkologii Gruzinskoi SSR — TONGA
Trudy Nauchno-Issledovatel'skogo Instituta Onkologii Gruzinskoi SSR — Tr Nauchno-Issled Inst Onkol Gruz SSR
Trudy Nauchno-Issledovatel'skogo Instituta Osnovnoi Khimii — Tr Nauchno Issled Inst Osnovnoi Khim
Trudy Nauchno-Issledovatel'skogo Instituta Pchelovodstva — Trudy Nauchno-Issled Inst Pchelov
Trudy Nauchno-Issledovatel'skogo Instituta Pishchevoi Promyshlennosti — Tr Nauchno Issled Inst Pishch Promsti
Trudy Nauchno-Issledovatel'skogo Instituta po Dobyche i Pererabotke Slantsev [*Former USSR*] — Tr Nauchno-Issled Inst Dobyche Pererab Slantsev
Trudy Nauchno-Issledovatel'skogo Instituta Pochvovedeniya Agrokhimii i Melioratsii (Tiflis) — Tr Nauchno Issled Inst Pochvoved Agrokhim Melior (Tiflis)
Trudy Nauchno-Issledovatel'skogo Instituta Pochvovedeniya i Agrokhimii Yerevan — Tr Nauchno Issled Inst Pochvoved Agrokhim Yerevan
Trudy Nauchno-Issledovatel'skogo Instituta Pochvovedeniya Tadzhikskoi SSR — Tr Nauchno Issled Inst Pochvoved Tadzh SSR
Trudy Nauchno-Issledovatel'skogo Instituta Profilaktiki i Pnevmokoniozov — Tr Nauchno-Issled Inst Profil Pnevmokoniozov
Trudy Nauchno-Issledovatel'skogo Instituta Prudovogo Rybnogo Khozyaistva — Trudy Nauchno-Issled Inst Prud Rybn Khoz
Trudy Nauchno-Issledovatel'skogo Instituta Rentgenologii Radiologii i Onkologii Azerbaidzhanskoi SSR — Tr Nauchno-Issled Inst Rentgenol Radiol Onkol Az SSR
Trudy Nauchno-Issledovatel'skogo Instituta Rezinovoi Promyshlennosti — Tr Nauchno Issled Inst Rezin Promsti
Trudy Nauchno-Issledovatel'skogo Instituta Rybnogo Khozyaistva (Riga) — Tr Nauchno Issled Inst Rybn Khoz (Riga)
Trudy Nauchno-Issledovatel'skogo Instituta Sadovodstva. Vinogradarstva i Vinodeliya (Tashkent) — Tr Nauchno Issled Inst Sadovod Vinograd Vinodel (Tashkent)
Trudy Nauchno-Issledovatel'skogo Instituta Sel'skogo Khozyaistva Krainego Severa — Tr Nauchno Issled Sel'sk Khoz Krainego Sev
Trudy Nauchno-Issledovatel'skogo Instituta Sel'skogo Khozyaistva Severnogo Zaural'ya — Trudy Nauchno-Issled Inst Sel'Khoz Severn Zaural'ya
Trudy Nauchno-Issledovatel'skogo Instituta Shinnoi Promyshlennosti — Tr Nauchno Issled Inst Shinnoi Promsti
Trudy Nauchno-Issledovatel'skogo Instituta Slantsev [*Former USSR*] — Tr Nauchno-Issled Inst Slantsev
Trudy Nauchno-Issledovatel'skogo Instituta Sociologiceskoj Kul'tury — Trudy Nauc-Issled Inst Sociol Kul't
Trudy Nauchno-Issledovatel'skogo Instituta Tuberkuleza — Tr Nauchno Issled Inst Tuberk
Trudy Nauchno-Issledovatel'skogo Instituta Virusologii Mikrobiologii Gigieny — Tr Nauchno Issled Inst Virusol Mikrobiol Gig
Trudy Nauchno-Issledovatel'skogo Instituta Zashchity Rastenii Uzbekskoi SSR — Tr Nauchno Issled Inst Zashch Rast Uzb SSR
Trudy Nauchno-Issledovatel'skogo Instituta Zhivotnovodstva (Tashkent) — Tr Nauchno Issled Inst Zhivotnovod (Tashkent)
Trudy Nauchno-Issledovatel'skogo Instituta Zhivotnovodstva. Uzbekskaya Akademiya Sel'skokhozyaistvennykh Nauk — Tr Nauchno Issled Inst Zhivotnovod Uzb Akad Skh Nauk
Trudy Nauchno-Issledovatel'skogo Khimicheskogo Instituta Moskovskii Universitet — Tr Nauchno Issled Khim Inst Mosk Univ
Trudy Nauchno-Issledovatel'skogo Protivochumnogo Instituta Kavkaza i Zakavkaz'ya — Tr Nauchno Issled Protivochumn Inst Kavk Zakavk
Trudy Nauchno-Issledovatel'skogo Sektora Moskovskogo Filiala Instituta "Orgenergostroi" — Tr Nauchno Issled Sekt Mosk Fil Inst "Orgenergostroi"
Trudy Nauchno-Issledovatel'skogo Tekhnokhimicheskogo Instituta Bytovogo Obsluzhivaniya — Tr Nauchno Issled Tekhnokhim Inst Bytovogo Obsluzhivaniya
Trudy Nauchno-Issledovatel'skogo Veterinarnogo Instituta Tadzhikskoi SSR — Tr Nauchno Issled Vet Inst Tadzh SSR
Trudy Nauchno-Proizvodstvennoi Konferentsii po Agronomii Buryatskii Zooveterinarnyi Institut — Tr Nauchno Proizvod Konf Agron Buryat Zoovet Inst
Trudy Nauchno-Tekhnicheskogo Obshchestva Chernoi Metallurgii — Tr Nauchno Tekh Ova Chern Metall
Trudy Nauchno-Tekhnicheskoi Konferentsii Leningradskogo Elektrotekhnicheskogo Instituta Svyazi — Tr Nauchno Tekh Konf Leningr Elektrotekh Inst Svyazi
Trudy Nauchno-Tekhnicheskoi Konferentsii Leningradskogo Elektro-Tekhnicheskogo Instituta Svyazi [*Former USSR*] — Tr Nauchno-Tekh Konf Leningr Elek-Tekh Inst Svyazi
Trudy Nauchnykh Korrespondentov Instituta Stroitel'nogo Dela Akademiya Nauk Gruzinskoi SSR — Tr Nauchn Korresp Inst Stroit Dela Akad Nauk Gruz SSR
Trudy Naucno-Issledovatel'skogo Instituta Botaniki. Trudy Naukova-Doslidnogo Instytutu Botaniky — Trudy Naucno Issl Inst Bot

Trudy NII [*Nauchno-Issledovatel'skogo Instituta*] **Metrologii Vysshikh Uchebnykh Zavedeniy** [*Former USSR*] — Tr NII Metrol Vyssh Uchebn Zaved
Trudy Nikitskogo Botanicheskogo Sada — Tr Nikitsk Bot Sada
Trudy Nikolaevskogo Korablestroitel'nogo Instituta — Tr Nikolaev Korablestroit Inst
Trudy NIRMMI — Tr NIRMMI
Trudy Nizhnedneprovskoi Nauchno-Issledovatel'skoi Stantsii po Obleseniyu Peskov — Tr Nizhnednepr Nauchno-Issled Stn Obleseniyu Peskov
Trudy Nizhnevolzhskogo Nauchno-Issledovatel'skogo Instituta Geologii i Geofiziki — Tr Nizhnevolzh Nauchno Issled Inst Geol Geofiz
Trudy Noril'skogo Vechernego Industrial'nogo Instituta — Tr Norilsk Vech Ind Inst
Trudy Novocherkasskogo Inzhenerno-Meliorativnogo Instituta — Tr Novocherk Inzh Melior Inst
Trudy Novocherkasskogo Inzhenerno-Meliorativnogo Instituta — Trudy Novocherk Inzh-Melior Inst
Trudy Novocherkasskogo Politekhnicheskogo Instituta — Tr Novocherk Politekh Inst
Trudy Novocherkasskogo Politekhnicheskogo Instituta [*Former USSR*] — Tr Novocherkassk Politekh Inst
Trudy Novocherkasskogo Veterinarnogo Instituta — Tr Novocherk Vet Inst
Trudy Novocherkasskogo Zootekhnichesko-Veterinarnogo Instituta — Tr Novocherk Zootekh Vet Inst
Trudy Novokuznetskogo Gosudarstvennogo Instituta Usovershenstvovaniya Vrachei — TNUVAN
Trudy Novokuznetskogo Gosudarstvennogo Instituta Usovershenstvovaniya Vrachei — Tr Novokuz Gos Inst Usoversh Vrach
Trudy Novokuznetskogo Gosudarstvennogo Instituta Usovershenstvovaniya Vrachei — Tr Novokuz Gos Inst Usoversh Vrachei
Trudy Novokuznetskogo Gosudarstvennogo Pedagogicheskogo Instituta — Tr Novokuz Gos Pedagog Inst
Trudy Novosibirskogo Gosudarstvennogo Meditsinskogo Instituta — Tr Novosib Gos Med Inst
Trudy Novosibirskogo Instituta Inzhenerov Zheleznodorozhnogo Transporta — Tr Novosib Inst Inzh Zheleznodorozhn Transp
Trudy Novosibirskogo Inzhenerno-Stroitel'nogo Instituta — Tr Novosib Inzh Stroit Inst
Trudy Novosibirskogo Sel'skokhozyaistvennogo Instituta — Tr Novosib Skh Inst
Trudy Ob'edinennogo Seminara po Gidrotekhnicheskomu i Vodokhozyaistvennomu Stroitel'stvu — Tr Obedin Semin Gidrotekh Vodokhoz Stroit
Trudy Ob'edinennoi Nauchnoi Sessii Moldavskii Filial Akademii Nauk SSR — Trudy Mold Akad Nauk
Trudy Obscestva Estestvoispytatelej i Vracej pri Imperatorskom Tomskom Universitete — Trudy Obsc Estestvoisp Imp Tomsk Univ
Trudy Obshchestva Dietskikh Vrachei v Moskve — Trudy Obsh Dietsk Vrach Moskve
Trudy Obshchestva Estestvoispytatelei pri Imperatordkom Kazanskom Universitete Kazan — Trudy Obshch Estest Imp Kazan Univ
Trudy Obshchestva Fiziologov Azerbaidzhana — Tr O-Va Fiziol Azerb
Trudy Odesskogo Gidrometeorologicheskogo Instituta — Tr Odess Gidrometeorol Inst
Trudy Odesskogo Nauchno-Issledovatel'skogo Instituta Epidemiologii i Mikrobiologii — Tr Odess Nauchno-Issled Inst Epidemiol Mikrobiol
Trudy Odesskogo Sel'skokhozyaistvennogo Instituta — Tr Odess S-Kh Inst
Trudy Odesskogo Tekhnologicheskogo Instituta — Tr Odess Tekhnol Inst
Trudy Odesskogo Tekhnologicheskogo Instituta Konservnoi Promyshlennosti — Tr Odess Tekhnol Inst Konservn Promsti
Trudy Odesskogo Tekhnologicheskogo Instituta Pishchevoi i Kholodil'noi Promyshlennosti — Tr Odess Tekhnol Inst Pishch Kholod Promsti
Trudy Okeanograficheskoi Komissii. Akademiya Nauk SSSR — Tr Okeanog Kom Akad Nauk SSSR
Trudy Omskogo Gosudarstvennogo Nauchno-Issledovatel'skogo Instituta Epidemiologii Mikrobiologii i Gigieny — Tr Omsk Gos Nauchno-Issled Inst Epidemiol Mikrobiol Gig
Trudy Omskogo Instituta Molochnogo Khozyaistva i Omskoi Zonal'noi Stantsii po Molochnomu Khozyaistvu — Tr Omsk Inst Molochn Khoz Omsk Zon Stn Molochn Khoz
Trudy Omskogo Meditsinskogo Instituta Imeni M. I. Kalinina — Tr Omsk Med Inst Im M I Kalinina
Trudy Omskogo Veterinarnogo Instituta — Trudy Omsk Vet Inst
Trudy Omskogo Vyssej Skoly Milicii — Trudy Omsk Vyss Skoly Milicii
Trudy Opytnoi Stantsii Plodovodstva Akademii Nauk Gruzinskoi SSR — Tr Opytn Stn Plodovod Akad Nauk Gruz SSR
Trudy Opytnyh Lesnicestv — Trudy Opytn Lesnic
Trudy Ordena Lenina Fizicheskogo Instituta Imeni P. N. Lebedeva — Tr Fiz Inst Im Lebedeva
Trudy Orenburgskii Nauchno-Issledovatel'skii Instituta Molochno-Myasnogo Skotovodstva — Tr Orenb Nauchno Issled Inst Molochno Myasn Skotovod
Trudy Orenburgskogo Gosudarstvennogo Meditsinskogo Instituta — Tr Orenb Gos Med Inst
Trudy Orenburgskogo Oblastnogo Otdeleniya Vserossiiskogonauchnogo Obshchestva Terapevtov — Tr Orenb Obl Otd Vseross-Nauchn O-Va Ter
Trudy Orenburgskogo Otdeleniya Vsesoyuznogo Fiziologicheskogo Obshchestva — Tr Orenb Otd Vses Fiziol Ova
Trudy Orenburgskogo Otdeleniya Vsesoyuznogo Obshchestva Fiziologov — Tr Orenb Otd Vses Ova Fiziol
Trudy Orenburgskogo Otdeleniya Vsesoyuznogo Obshchestva Fiziologov, Biokhimikov, i Farmakologov — Tr Orenb Otd Vses Ova Fiziol Biokhim Farmakol
Trudy Orenburgskogo Sel'skokhozyaistvennogo Instituta — Tr Orenb Skh Inst
Trudy Otdel Fiziologii i Biofiziki Rastenii Akademiya Nauk Tadzhikskoi SSR — Tr Otd Fiziol Biofiz Rast Akad Nauk Tadzh SSR
Trudy Otdela Drevnerusskoj Literatury — TODrL
Trudy Otdela Geologii Buryatskii Filial Sibirskoe Otdelenie Akademiya Nauk SSSR — Tr Otd Geol Buryat Fil Sib Otd Akad Nauk SSSR
Trudy Otdela Gornogo Dela i Metallurgii Akademiya Nauk Kirgizskoi SSR — Tr Otd Gorn Dela Metall Akad Nauk Kirg SSR
Trudy Otdela Istorii Iskusstva i Kul'tury Antichnogo Mira Gosudarstvennogo Ermitazha — TOAMGE
Trudy Otdela Numismatiki Gosudarstvennogo Ermitazha — TONGE
Trudy Otdela Pochvovedeniya Akademiya Nauk Kirgizskoi SSR — Tr Otd Pochvoved Akad Nauk Kirg SSR
Trudy Otdela Pochvovedeniya Dagestanskogo Filiala. Akademii Nauk SSSR — Tr Otd Pochvoved Dagest Fil Akad Nauk SSSR
Trudy Paleontologicheskogo Instituta Akademiya Nauk SSSR — Tr Paleontol Inst Akad Nauk SSSR
Trudy Pechoro-Ilychskogo Gosudarstvennogo Zapovednika — Tr Pechoro Ilychskogo Gos Zapov
Trudy Pedagogiceskih Institutov Gruzinskoi SSR. Serija Fiziki i Matematiki — Trudy Ped Inst Gruzin SSR Ser Fiz i Mat
Trudy Permskii Gosudarstvennyi Meditsinskii Institut — Tr Permsk Gos Med Inst
Trudy Permskij Gosudarstvennyj Nauchno-Issledovatel'skij i Proektnyj Institut Neftyanoj Promyshlennosti — Tr Permsk Gos Nauchno-Issled Proektn Inst Neft Prom-Sti
Trudy Permskogo Biologicheskogo Nauchno-Issledovatel'skogo Instituta — Tr Permsk Biol Nauchno Issled Inst
Trudy Permskogo Farmatseuticheskogo Instituta — Tr Permsk Farm Inst
Trudy Permskogo Gosudarstvennogo Sel'skokhozyaistvennogo Instituta — Tr Permsk Gos Skh Inst
Trudy Permskogo Nauchno-Issledovatel'skogo Instituta Vaktsin i Syvorotok — Tr Permsk Nauchno Issled Inst Vaktsin Syvorotok
Trudy Permskogo Sel'skokhozyaistvennogo Instituta — Tr Permsk S-Kh Inst
Trudy Pervogo Moskovskogo Meditsinskogo Instituta Imeni I. M. Sechenova — Tr Perv Mosk Med Inst Im I M Sechenova
Trudy Pervogo Moskovskogo Pedagogicheskogo Instituta — Tr Pervogo Mosk Pedagog Inst
Trudy Petergofskogo Biologiceskogo Instituta. Travaux de l'Institut Biologique de Peterhof — Trudy Petergofsk Biol Inst
Trudy Petergofskogo Biologicheskogo Instituta. Leningradskii Gosudarstvennyi Universitet — Tr Petergof Biol Inst Leningr Gos Univ
Trudy Petergofskogo Estestvenno-Nauchnogo Instituta — Tr Petergof Estest Nauchn Inst
Trudy Petrograficheskogo Instituta. Akademiya Nauk SSSR — Tr Petrogr Inst Akad Nauk SSSR
Trudy Plodoovoshchnogo Instituta — Tr Plodoovoshchn Inst
Trudy Plodovoshchnogo Instituta Imeni I. V. Michurina — Tr Plodovoshchn Inst Im I V Michurina
Trudy Plodovoshchnogo Instituta Imeni I. V. Michurina — Trudy Plodov Inst
Trudy Plodovo-Yagodnogo Instituta Imeni Akademika R. R. Shredera — Tr Plodovo-Yagodnogo Inst Im Akad R R Shredera
Trudy po Avtomaticheskoi Svarke pod Flyusom — Tr Avtom Svarke Flyusom
Trudy po Dinamike Razvitiya — Tr Din Raz
Trudy po Fizike Moskovskii Gornyi Institut — Tr Fiz Mosk Gorn Inst
Trudy po Fizike Poluprovodnikov — Tr Fiz Poluprovodn
Trudy po Fiziologii i Biokhimii Rastenii [*Estonian SSR*] — Tr Fiziol Biokhim Rast
Trudy po Geobotaniceskomu Obsledovaniju Pastbisc SSR Azerbajdzana. Serija A. Zimnie Pastbisca — Trudy Geobot Obsl Pastb SSR Azerbajdzana Ser A Zimn Pastb
Trudy po Izucheniyu Radiya i Radioaktivnykh Rud — Tr Izuch Radiya Radioakt Rud
Trudy po Khimii i Khimicheskoi Tekhnologii — TKKTA
Trudy po Khimii i Khimicheskoi Tekhnologii — Tr Khim Khim Tekhnol
Trudy po Khimii Prirodnykh Soedinenii — Tr Khim Prir Soedin
Trudy po Kurortologii — Tr Kurortol
Trudy po Legochnoi Patologii Institut Eksperimental'noi i Klinicheskoi Meditsiny Estonskoi SSR — Tr Legochn Patol Inst Eksp Klin Med Est SSR
Trudy po Lekarstvennym i Aromaticeskim Rastenijam — Trudy Lekarstv Aromat Rast
Trudy po Lesnomu Opytnomu Delu. Mitteilungen aus dem Forstlichen Versuchswesen (Omsk) — Trudy Lesn Opytn Delu Omsk
Trudy po Novoi Apparature i Metodikam — Tr Nov Appar Metod
Trudy po Prikladnoi Botanike Genetike i Selektsii [*Former USSR*] — Tr Prikl Bot Genet Sel
Trudy po Prikladnoi Botanike Genetike i Selektsii — Tr Prikl Bot Genet Selek
Trudy po Prikladnoi Botanike Genetike i Selektsii — Trudy Prikl Bot Genet Selek
Trudy po Prikladnoi Botanike. Genetike i Selektsii. Seriya 1. Sistematika, Geografia, i Ekologia Rastenii — Tr Prikl Bot Genet Sel Ser 1
Trudy po Prikladnoi Botanike. Genetike i Selektsii. Seriya 2. Genetika, Selektsiya, i Tsitologiya Rastenii — Tr Prikl Bot Genet Sel Ser 2
Trudy po Prikladnoi Botanike. Genetike i Selektsii. Seriya 3. Fiziologiya, Biokhimiya, i Anatomiya Rastenii — Tr Prikl Bot Genet Sel Ser 3
Trudy po Prikladnoi Botanike. Genetike i Selektsii. Seriya 4. Semenovedenie i Semennoi Kontrol — Tr Prikl Bot Genet Sel Ser 4
Trudy po Prikladnoi Botanike. Genetike i Selektsii. Seriya 5. Zernovye Kul'tury — Tr Prikl Bot Genet Sel Ser 5
Trudy po Prikladnoi Botanike. Genetike i Selektsii. Seriya 6. Ovoshchnye Kul'tury — Tr Prikl Bot Genet Sel Ser 6
Trudy po Prikladnoi Botanike. Genetike i Selektsii. Seriya 9. Tekhnicheskie Kul'tury — Tr Prikl Bot Genet Sel Ser 9
Trudy po Prikladnoi Botanike. Genetike i Selektsii. Seriya 10. Dendrologiya i Dekorativnoe Sadovodstvo — Tr Prik Bot Genet Sel Ser 10
Trudy po Prikladnoi Botanike. Genetike i Selektsii. Seriya 11. Novye Kul'tury i Voprosy Introduktsii — Tr Prikl Bot Genet Sel Ser 11
Trudy po Prikladnoi Botanike. Genetike i Selektsii. Seriya 13. Regeraty i Bibliografia — Tr Prikl Bot Genet Sel Ser 13
Trudy po Prikladnoi Botanike. Genetike i Selektsii. Seriya 14. Osvoenie Pustyn — Tr Prikl Bot Genet Sel Ser 14

Trudy po Prikladnoi Botanike. Genetike i Selektsii. Seriya 15. Severnoe (Pripolyarnoe) Zemledelie — Tr Prikl Bot Genet Sel Ser 15
Trudy po Prikladnoi Botanike. Genetike i Selektsii. Seriya A. Sotsialisticheskoe — Tr Prikl Bot Genet Sel Ser A
Trudy po Prikladnoj Botanike, Genetike, i Selekcii. Serija 1. Sistematika, Geografija, Ekologija Rastenij i Obscie Voprosy Rastenievodstva/Bulletin of Applied Botany, of Genetics, and Plant-Breeding. Systematics, Geography, Ecology of Plants, and Plant Industry in General — Trudy Prikl Bot Ser 1 Sist Rast Obscie Vopr Rasteniev
Trudy po Prikladnoj Botanike, Genetike, i Selekcii. Serija 5. Zernovye Kul'tury/ Bulletin of Applied Botany, of Genetics, and Plant-Breeding. Grain Crops — Trudy Prikl Bot Ser 5 Zernov Kult
Trudy po Prikladnoj Botanike, Genetike, i Selekcii. Serija 9. Tehniceskie Kul'tury/Bulletin of Applied Botany, of Genetics, and Plant-Breeding. Technical Plants — Trudy Prikl Bot Ser 9 Tehn Kult
Trudy po Prikladnoj Botanike, Genetike, i Selekcii. Serija 15. Problemy Severnogo Rastenievodstva/Bulletin of Applied Botany, Genetics, and Plant-Breeding. Problems of Plant Industry in the Extreme North — Trudy Prikl Bot Ser 15 Probl Severn Rasteniev
Trudy po Radiatsionnoi Gigiene — Tr Radiats Gig
Trudy po Radiatsionnoi Gigiene Leningradskii Nauchno-Issledovatel'skii Institut Radiatsionnoi Gigieny [*Former USSR*] — Tr Radiat Gig Leningr Nauchno-Issled Inst Radiats Gig
Trudy po Radiatsionnoi Gigiene Leningradskii Nauchno-Issledovatel'skii Institut Radiatsionnoi Gigieny — TRAGB
Trudy po Radiatsionnoj Gigiene Leningradskij Nauchno-Issledovatel'skij Institut Radiatsionnoj Gigieny — Tr Radiats Gig Leningr Nauchno-Issled Inst Radiats Gig
Trudy po Selektisii Agrotekhnike i Zashchite Rastenii — Tr Sel Agrotekh Zashch Rast
Trudy po Teorii Polya [*Former USSR*] — Tr Teor Polya
Trudy po Zascite Rastenij Sibiri — Trudy Zasc Rast Sibiri
Trudy Pochvennogo Instituta Imeni V. V. Dokuchaeva Akademii Nauk SSSR — Tr Pochv Inst Im V V Dokuchaeva Akad Nauk SSSR
Trudy Pochvennogo Instituta Imeni V. V. Dokuchaeva Akademiya Nauk SSSR — Tr Poch Inst V V Dokuchaeva Akad Nauk SSSR
Trudy Poljarnoj Komissii — Trudy Poljarn Komiss
Trudy Polyarnogo Nauchno-Issledovatel'skogo i Proektnogo Instituta Morskogo Rybnogo Khozyaistva i Okeanografii — TPNPAI
Trudy Polyarnyi Nauchno-Issledovatel'skii i Proektnyi Institut Morskogo Rybnogo Khozyaistva i Okeanografii [*Former USSR*] — Tr Polyar Nauchno-Issled Proekt Inst Morsk Ryb Khoz Okeanogr
Trudy Primorskogo Sel'skokhozyaistvennogo Instituta — Tr Primorsk S-Kh Inst
Trudy Prioksko-Terrasnogo Gosudarstvennogo Zapovednika — Tr Prioksko Terrasnogo Gos Zapov
Trudy Problemnoi Laboratorii Khimii Vysokomolekulyarnykh Soedinenii. Voronezhskii Gosudarstvennyi Universitet — Tr Probl Lab Khim Vysokomol Soedin Voronezh Gos Univ
Trudy Problemnoi Laboratorii Osadochnykh Formatsii i Osadochnykh Rud Tashkentskii Gosudarstvennyi Universitet — Tr Probl Lab Osad Form Osad Rud Tashk Gos Univ
Trudy Problemnoi Laboratorii Silikatnykh Materialov i Konstruktsii Voronezhskii Inzhenerno-Stroitel'nyi Institut — Tr Probl Lab Silik Mater Konstr Voronezh Inzh Stroit Inst
Trudy Problemnykh i Tematicheskikh Soveshchanii Akademiya Nauk SSSR Zoologicheskii Institut — Tr Probl Temat Soveshch Akad Nauk SSSR Zool Inst
Trudy Proizvodstvennyi i Nauchno-Issledovatel'skii Institut po Inzhenernym Izyskaniyam v Stroitel'stve — Tr Proizvod Nauchno-Issled Inst Inzh Izyskaniyam Stroit
Trudy Przeval'skogo Gosudarstvennogo Pedagogicheskogo Instituta — Trudy Przeval'sk Gos Ped Inst
Trudy Przeval'skogo Pedagogiceskogo Instituta — TPrzPI
Trudy Pskovskoi Oblastnoi Gosudarstvennoi Sel'skokhozyaistvennoi Opytnoi Stantsii — Tr Pskov Obl Gos Skh Opytn Stn
Trudy Pushkinskoi Nauchno-Issledovatel'skoi Laboratorii Razvedeniya Sel'skokhozyaistvennykh Zhivotnykh — Tr Pushkin Nauchno-Issled Lab Razvedeniya S-Kh Zhivotn
Trudy Radiatsii i Gigieny Leningradskogo Nauchno-Issledovatel'skogo Instituta Radiatsii Gigieny — Trudy Radiats Gig Leningr Nauchno-Issled Inst Radiats Gig
Trudy Radievogo Instituta Akademiya Nauk SSSR — Tr Radievogo Inst Akad Nauk SSSR
Trudy Radiotekhnicheskogo Instituta [*Former USSR*] — Tr Radiotekh Inst
Trudy Radiotekhnicheskogo Instituta Akademiya Nauk SSSR — Tr Radiotekh Inst Akad Nauk SSSR
Trudy Respublikanskogo Nauchno-Issledovatel'skogo Instituta Tuberkuleza Ministerstva Zdravookhraneniya Gruzinskoi SSR — TTZGAB
Trudy Respublikanskogo Obshchestva Ftiziatrov Nauchno-Issledovatel'skogo Instituta Tuberkuleza Kazakhskoi SSR — Tr Resp Ova Ftiziatrov Nauchno Issled Inst Tuberk Kaz SSR
Trudy Respublikanskoi Opytnoi Stantsii Kartofel'nogo i Ovoshchnogo Khozyaistva Kazakhskaya SSR — Tr Resp Opytn Stn Kartofeln Ovoshchn Khoz Kaz SSR
Trudy Respublikanskoi Stantsii Zashchity Rastenii — Tr Resp Stn Zashch Rast
Trudy Respublikanskoj Stancii Zascity Rastenij — Trudy Respubl Stancii Zasc Rast
Trudy Rizhskii Nauchno-Issledovatel'skii Institut Travmatologii i Ortopedii — Tr Rizh Nauchno Issled Inst Travmatol Ortop
Trudy Rizhskogo Instituta Inzhenerov Grazhdanskoi Aviatsii — Tr Rizh Inst Inzh Grazhdanskoi Aviats
Trudy Rjazanskogo Radiotehniceskogo Instituta — Trudy Rjazan Radiotehn Inst
Trudy Rossiiskogo Instituta Prikladnoi Khimii — Tr Ross Inst Prikl Khim
Trudy Rostovskii-Na-Donu Inzhenerno Stroitel'nyi Institut — Tr Rostov-Na-Donu Inzh Stroit Inst
Trudy Rostovskogo Gosudarstvennogo Nauchno-Issledovatel'skogo Protivochumnogo Instituta Narkomzdrava SSSR — TRPNA2
Trudy Rostovskogo-Na-Donu Instituta Inzhenerov Zheleznodorozhnogo Transporta — Tr Rostov Na Donu Inst Inzh Zheleznodorozhn Transp
Trudy Russkogo Entomologicheskogo Obshchestva — Trudy Russk Ent Obshch
Trudy Ryazanskogo Meditsinskogo Instituta — Tr Ryazan Med Inst
Trudy Ryazanskogo Radiotekhnicheskogo Instituta [*Former USSR*] — Tr Ryazan Radiotekh Inst
Trudy Sakhalinskaya Oblastnaya Stantsiya Zashchity Rastenii — Tr Sakhalin Obl Stn Zashch Rast
Trudy Samarkandskogo Gosudarstvennogo Universiteta — Tr Samark Gos Univ
Trudy Samarkandskogo Gosudarstvennogo Universiteta Imeni Alisera Navoi — Trudy Samarkand Gos Univ
Trudy Samarkandskogo Gosudarstvennogo Universiteta Imeni Alisera Navoi — TSamU
Trudy Samarkandskogo Universiteta — Trudy Samarkand Univ
Trudy Samarskogo Sel'skokhozyaistvennogo Instituta — IKSIA2
Trudy Samarskogo Sel'skokhozyaistvennogo Instituta — Tr Samar Skh Inst
Trudy Sankt-Peterburgskogo Matematicheskogo Obshchestva — Trudy S Peterburg Mat Obshch
Trudy Saratovskogo Avtomobil'no-Dorozhnogo Instituta — Tr Sarat Avtomob Dorozhn Inst
Trudy Saratovskogo Instituta Mehanizacii Sel'skogo-Hozjaistva — Trudy Saratov Inst Meh S-H
Trudy Saratovskogo Instituta Mekhanizatsii Sel'skogo Khozyaistva — Tr Sarat Inst Mekh Selsk Khoz
Trudy Saratovskogo Meditsinskogo Instituta — Tr Sarat Med Inst
Trudy Saratovskogo Obshchestva Estestvoispytatelei i Lyubitelei Estestvoznaniya — Tr Sarat Ova Estestvoispyt Lyubit Estestvozn
Trudy Saratovskogo Otdeleniya Vsesoyuznogo Nauchno-Issledovatel'skogo Instituta Ozernogo i Rechnogo Rybn Khoz — Tr Sarat Otd Vses Nauchno Issled Inst Ozern Rechn Rybn Khoz
Trudy Saratovskogo Sel'skokhozyaistvennogo Instituta — Tr Sarat S-Kh Inst
Trudy Saratovskogo Sel'skokhozyaistvennogo Instituta — Trudy Saratov Sel'-Khoz Inst
Trudy Saratovskogo Zootekhnicheskogo Veterinarnogo Instituta — Tr Sarat Zootekh Vet Inst
Trudy Saratovskogo Zootekhnicheskogo Veterinarnogo Instituta — Trudy Saratov Zootekh Vet Inst
Trudy Saratovskoi Nauchno-Issledovatel'skogo Veterinarnoi Stantsii — Tr Sarat Nauchno Issled Vet Stn
Trudy Saratovskoi Nauchno-Issledovatel'skoi Veterinarnoi Stantsii — Trudy Saratov Nauchno-Issled Vet Sta
Trudy Sary Chelekskogo Gosudarstvennogo Zapovednika — Tr Sary Chelekskogo Gos Zap
Trudy Sektora Astrobotaniki Akademiya Nauk Kazakhskoi SSR — Tr Sekt Astrobot Akad Nauk Kaz SSR
Trudy Sektora Astrobotaniki Akademiya Nauk Kazakhskoi SSR — Tr Sekt Astrobot Akad Nauk Kazakh SSR
Trudy Sektora Energetiki Azerbaidzhanskogo Filiala Akademii Nauk SSSR — Tr Sekt Energ Azerb Fil Akad Nauk SSSR
Trudy Sektora Fiziologii Akademiya Nauk Azerbaidzhanskoi SSR — Tr Sekt Fiziol Akad Nauk Az SSR
Trudy Sektora Fiziologii Zhivotnykh Instituta Biologii Akademiya Nauk Latviiskoi SSR — Tr Sekt Fiziol Zhivotn Inst Biol Akad Nauk Latv SSR
Trudy Selekcionnoj Stancii pri Moskovskom Sel'skohozjajstvennom Institute. Arbeiten der Versuchsstation fuer Pflanzenzuechtung am Moskauer Landwirtschaftlichen Institut — Trudy Selekcion Stancii Moskovsk Selskohoz Inst
Trudy Sel'skokhozyaistvennogo Samarkanskogo Instituta — Tr Skh Samarkanskogo Inst
Trudy Seminara "Bionika i Matematicheskoe Modelirovanie v Biologii" — Tr Semin "Bionika Mat Model Biol"
Trudy Seminara Imeni I. G. Petrovskogo — Trudy Sem Petrovsk
Trudy Seminara po Kraevym Zadacham — Trudy Sem Kraev Zadacham
Trudy Seminara po Matematiceskoi Fizike i Nelinienym Kolebanijam — Trudy Sem Mat Fiz Nelinien Koleban
Trudy Seminara po Vektornomu i Tenzornomu Analizu s ih Prilozenijami k Geometrii. Mehanike i Fizike — Trudy Sem Vektor Tenzor Anal
Trudy Seminara po Zharostoikim Materialam — Tr Semin Zharostoikim Mater
Trudy Semipalatinskogo Meditsinskogo Instituta — Tr Semipalat Med Inst
Trudy Semipalatinskogo Zooveterinarnogo Instituta — Tr Semipalat Zoovet Inst
Trudy Sessii Komissii po Opredeleniyu Absolyutnogo Vozrasta Geologicheskikh Formatsii Akademiya Nauk SSSR — Tr Sess Kom Opred Absol Vozrasta Geol Form Akad Nauk SSSR
Trudy Sevanskoi Gidrobiologicheskoi Stantsii — Tr Sevansk Gidrobiol Stn
Trudy Sevastopol'skoi Biologicheskoi Stantsii Akademiya Nauk Ukrainskoi SSR — Tr Sevastop Biol Stn Akad Nauk Ukr SSR
Trudy Sevastopol'skoi Biologicheskoi Stantsii Imeni A. D. Kovalenskogo Akademii Nauk Ukrainskoi SSR — Tr Sevastop Biol Stn Im A D Kovalenskogo Akad Nauk Ukr SSR
Trudy Severnyi Nauchno-Issledovatel'skii Institut Gidrotekhniki i Melioratsii — Tr Sev Nauchno Issled Inst Gidrotekh Melior
Trudy Severo. Zapadnogo Nauchno-Issledovatel'skogo Instituta Sel'skogo Khozyaistva — Tr Sev Zapadn Nauchno Issled Inst Sel'sk Khoz
Trudy Severo-Kavkazskogo Gornometallurgicheskogo Instituta — Tr Sev Kavk Gornometall Inst
Trudy Severokavkazskogo Gornometallurgicheskogo Instituta [*Former USSR*] — Tr Severokavkazskogo Gornometall Inst
Trudy Severo-Kavkazskogo Instituta Zascity Rastenij/Bulletin. North Caucasian Institute for Plant Protection — Trudy Severo Kavkazsk Inst Zasc Rast
Trudy Severo-Osetinskogo Meditsinskogo Instituta — Tr Sev-Oset Med Inst
Trudy Severo-Osetinskogo Sel'skokhozyaistvennogo Instituta — Tr Sev-Oset S-Kh Inst

Trudy Severo-Vostochnogo Kompleksnogo Instituta Dal'nevostochnyi Tsentr Akademiya Nauk SSSR — Tr Sev Vost Kompleksn Inst Dalnevost Tsentr Akad Nauk SSSR
Trudy. Severo-Zapadnyi Zaochnyi Politekhnicheskii Institut — Tr Sev Zapadn Zaochn Politekh Inst
Trudy Sibirskii Gosudarstvennyi Nauchno-Issledovatel'skii Institut Metrologii — Tr Sib Gos Nauchno Issled Inst Metrol
Trudy Sibirskii Nauchno-Issledovatel'skii Institut Energetiki — Trudy SibNIIE
Trudy Sibirskii Nauchno-Issledovatel'skii Institut Lesnoi Promyshlennosti — Tr Sib Nauchno Issled Inst Lesn Promsti
Trudy Sibirskogo Fiziko-Tehniceskogo Instituta Imeni Akademika V. D. Kuznecova — Trudy Sibirsk Fiz-Tehn Inst
Trudy Sibirskogo Fiziko-Tekhnicheskogo Instituta pri Tomskom Gosudarstvennom Universitete [*Former USSR*] — Tr Sib Fiz Tekh Inst Tomsk Gos Univ
Trudy Sibirskogo Fiziko-Tekhnicheskogo Instituta pri Tomskom Gosudarstvennom Universitete — TSFTA
Trudy Sibirskogo Lesotekhnicheskogo Instituta — Tr Sib Lesotekh Inst
Trudy Sibirskogo Metallurgicheskogo Instituta — Tr Sib Metall Inst
Trudy Sibirskogo Nauchno-Issledovatel'skogo Instituta Energetiki [*Former USSR*] — Tr Sib Nauchno-Issled Inst Energ
Trudy Sibirskogo Nauchno-Issledovatel'skogo Instituta Geologii, Geofiziki, i Mineral'nogo Syr'ya — Tr Sib Nauchno-Issled Inst Geol Geofiz Miner Syr'ya
Trudy Sibirskogo Nauchno-Issledovatel'skogo Instituta Geologii, Geofiziki, i Mineral'nogo Syr'ya — TSIGA
Trudy Sibirskogo Nauchno-Issledovatel'skogo Instituta Zhivotnovodstva — Tr Sib Nauch-Issled Inst Zhivotn
Trudy Sibirskogo Otdela Gosudarstvennogo Nauchno-Issledovatel'skogo Instituta Ozernogo i Rechnogo Rybnogo Khozyaistva — Tr Sib Otd Gos Nauchno-Issled Inst Ozern Rechn Rybn Khoz
Trudy Sibirskogo Tekhnologicheskogo Instituta — Tr Sib Tekhnol Inst
Trudy Sibirskogo Tekhnologicheskogo Instituta — TSTIA
Trudy Sikhote-Alinskogo Gosudarstvennogo Zapovednika — Tr Sikhote-Alinsk Gos Zapov
Trudy Smolenskogo Gosudarstvennogo Meditsinskogo Instituta — Tr Smolensk Gos Med Inst
Trudy Smolenskoi Nauchno-Issledovatel'skoi Veterinarnoi Stantsii — Tr Smolensk Nauchno Issled Vet Stn
Trudy Solikamskoi Sel'skokhozyaistvennoi Opytnoi Stantsii — Trudy Solikam Sel'-Khoz Opyt Sta
Trudy Solyanoi Laboratorii Vsesoyuznyi Institut Galurgii Akademiya Nauk SSSR — Tr Solyanoi Lab Vses Inst Galurgii Akad Nauk SSSR
Trudy Soveshchanii Ikhtiologicheskoi Komissii Akademii Nauk SSSR — Tr Soveshch Ikhtiol Kom Akad Nauk SSSR
Trudy Soveshchanii po Morfogenezu Rastenii — Tr Soveshch Morfogen Rast
Trudy Soveshchaniya Poliploidiya i Selektsiya Akademiya Nauk SSSR — Tr Soveshch Poliploidiya Selek Akad Nauk SSSR
Trudy Soveta po Izuceniju Prirodnyh Resursov. Serija Dal'ne-Vostocnaja — Trudy Soveta Izuc Prir Resursov Ser Dalne Vost
Trudy Sovetskoi Antarkticheskoi Ekspeditsii [*Former USSR*] — Tr Sov Antarkt Eksped
Trudy Sovetskoi Sektsii Mezhdunarodnoi Assotsiatsii Pochvovedov — Tr Sov Sekts Mezhdunar Assots Pochvovedov
Trudy Sovmestnaya Sovetsko-Mongol'skaya Nauchno-Issledovatel'skaya Geologicheskaya Ekspeditsiya — Tr Sovmestnaya Sov Mong Nauchno Issled Geol Eksped
Trudy Soyuznaya Geologopoiskovaya Kontora — Tr Soyuzn Geologopoisk Kontora
Trudy Soyuznogo Nauchno-Issledovatel'skogo Instituta Priborostroeniya [*Former USSR*] — Tr Soyuznogo Nauchno-Issled Inst Priborostr
Trudy Soyuznyi Trest Razvedochno-Burovykh Rabot — Tr Soyuzn Trest Razved Burovykh Rab
Trudy S.-Peterburgskago Obscestva Estestvoispytatelej. Otdelenie Botaniki/ Travaux de la Societe des Naturalistes de Saint-Petersbourg. Section de Botanique — Trudy S Peterburgsk Obsc Estestvoisp Otd Bot
Trudy Sredneaziat Nauchno-Issledovatel'skii Gidrometeorologicheskii Institut — Tr Sredneaziat Nauchno Issled Gidrometeorol Institut
Trudy Sredneaziatskii Nauchno-Issledovatel'skii Institut Geologii i Mineral'nogo Syr'ya — Tr Sredneaziat Nauchno Issled Inst Geol Miner Syrya
Trudy. Sredneaziatskii Nauchno-Issledovatel'skii Institut Geologii i Mineral'nogo Syr'ya — TSNGA
Trudy Sredneaziatskogo Gosudarstvennogo Universiteta — Tr Sredneaziat Gos Univ
Trudy Sredne-Aziatskogo Gosudarstvennogo Universiteta. Serija 8b. Botanika. Acta Universitatis Asiae Mediae. Botanica — Trudy Sredne Aziatsk Gosud Univ Ser 8b Bot
Trudy Sredneaziatskogo Gosudarstvennogo Universiteta. Seriya 6. Khimiya — Tr Sredneaziat Gos Univ Ser 6
Trudy Sredneaziatskogo Gosudarstvennogo Universiteta. Seriya 7a. Geologiya — Tr Sredneaziat Gos Univ Ser 7a
Trudy Sredneaziatskogo Gosudarstvennogo Universiteta. Seriya 7d. Pochvovedenie — Tr Sredneaziat Gos Univ Ser 7d
Trudy Sredneaziatskogo Gosudarstvennogo Universiteta. Seriya 8a. Zoologiya — Tr Sredneaziat Gos Univ Ser 8a
Trudy Sredneaziatskogo Gosudarstvennogo Universiteta. Seriya 8b. Botanika — Tr Sredneaziat Gos Univ Ser 8b
Trudy Sredneaziatskogo Gosudarstvennogo Universiteta. Seriya 9. Meditsina — Tr Sredneaziat Gos Univ Ser 9
Trudy Sredneaziatskogo Gosudarstvennogo Universiteta. Seriya 10. Sel'skoe Khozyaistvo — Tr Sredneaziat Gos Univ Ser 10
Trudy Sredneaziatskogo Gosudarstvennogo Universiteta. Seriya 11. Tekhnika — Tr Sredneaziat Gos Univ Ser 11
Trudy Sredneaziatskogo Gosudarstvennogo Universiteta. Seriya 13. Varia — Tr Sredneaziat Gos Univ Ser 13
Trudy Sredneaziatskogo Nauchno-Issledovatel'skogo Instituta Irrigatsii — Tr Sredneaziat Nauchno Issled Inst Irrig
Trudy Sredneaziatskogo Nauchno-Issledovatel'skogo Instituta Lesnogo Khozyaistva — Tr Sredneaziat Nauchno Issled Inst Lesn Khoz
Trudy Sredne-Aziatskogo Nauchno-Issledovatel'skogo Protivochumnogo Instituta — Tr Sredne-Aziat Nauchno-Issled Protivochumn Inst
Trudy Sredne-Volzhskogo Sel'skokhozyaistvennogo Instituta — Tr Sredne Volzh Skh Inst
Trudy Stalinabadskogo Gosudarstvennogo Meditsinskogo Instituta — Tr Stalinab Gos Med Inst
Trudy Stalinabadskoi Astronomicheskoi Observatorii — Tr Stalinab Astron Obs
Trudy Stalingradskogo Sel'skokhozyaistvennogo Instituta — Tr Stalingr S-Kh Inst
Trudy Stalinskogo Gosudarstvennogo Meditsinskogo Instituta — Tr Stalinskogo Gos Med Inst
Trudy Stalinskogo Gosudarstvennogo Pedagogicheskogo Instituta — Tr Stalinskogo Gos Pedagog Inst
Trudy Stavropol'skogo Nauchno-Issledovatel'skogo Instituta Sel'skogo Khozyaistva — Tr Stavrop Nauchno Issled Inst Selsk Khoz
Trudy Stavropol'skogo Sel'skokhozyaistvennogo Instituta — Tr Stavrop S-Kh Inst
Trudy Stavropol'skogo Sel'skokhozyaistvennogo Instituta — Tr Stavropol Sel'skokhoz Inst
Trudy Stavropol'skogo Sel'skokhozyaistvennogo Instituta — Trudy Stavropol' Sel'-Khoz Inst
Trudy Stavropol'skoi Kraevoi Nauchno-Issledovatel'skoi Veterinarnoi Stantsii — Tr Stavrop Kraev Nauchno-Issled Vet Stn
Trudy Stomatologov Litovskoi SSR — Tr Stomatol Lit SSR
Trudy Studencheskogo Nauchnogo Obshchestva Azerbaidzhanskii Gosudarstvennyi Meditsinskii Institut — Tr Stud Nauchn Ova Azerb Gos Med Inst
Trudy Studencheskogo Nauchnogo Obshchestva Khar'kovskii Politekhnicheskii Institut — Tr Stud Nauchn Ova Khark Politekh Inst
Trudy Studencheskogo Nauchno-Tekhnicheskogo Obshchestva Moskovskoe Vysshe Tekhnicheskoe Uchilishche — Tr Stud Nauchno Tekh Ova Mosk Vyssh Tekh Uchil
Trudy Sukhumskogo Botanicheskogo Sada — Tr Sukhum Bot Sada
Trudy Sukhumskoi Opytnoi Stantsii Efiromaslichnykh Kultur — Tr Sukhum Opytn Stn Efiromaslichn Kult
Trudy Sverdlovskii Nauchno-Issledovatel'skii Institut Lesnoi Promyshlennosti — Tr Sverdl Nauchno Issled Inst Lesn Promsti
Trudy Sverdlovskogo Gornogo Instituta — Tr Sverdl Gorn Inst
Trudy Sverdlovskogo Gosudarstvennogo Meditsinskogo Instituta — Tr Sverdl Gos Med Inst
Trudy Sverdlovskogo Gosudarstvennogo Meditsinskogo Instituta — TSMDAL
Trudy Sverdlovskogo Meditsinskogo Instituta — Tr Sverdl Med Inst
Trudy Sverdlovskogo Sel'skokhozyaistvennogo Instituta — Tr Sverdl Skh Inst
Trudy Sverdlovskogo Sel'skokhozyaistvennogo Instituta — Trudy Sverdlovsk Sel'-Khoz Inst
Trudy Sverdlovskoi Nauchno-Issledovatel'skoi Veterinarnoi Stantsii — Tr Sverdl Nauchno Issled Vet Stn
Trudy SZPI [*Severo-Zapadnyi Zaochnyi Politekhnicheskii Institut*] — Tr SZPI
Trudy Tadzhikskogo Gosudarstvennogo Meditsinskogo Instituta — Tr Tadzh Gos Med Inst
Trudy Tadzhikskogo Meditsinskogo Instituta — Tr Tadzh Med Inst
Trudy Tadzhikskogo Nauchno-Issledovatel'skogo Instituta Pochvovedeniya — Tr Tadzh Nauchno Issled Inst Pochvoved
Trudy Tadzhikskogo Nauchno-Issledovatel'skogo Instituta Sel'skogo Khozyaistva — Tr Tadzh Nauchno Issled Inst Selsk Khoz
Trudy Tadzhikskogo Nauchno-Issledovatel'skogo Instituta Sel'skogo Khozyaistva — Trudy Tadzhik Nauchno-Issled Inst Sel Khoz
Trudy Tadzhikskogo Nauchno-Issledovatel'skogo Instituta Zemledeliya — Tr Tadzh Nauchno-Issled Inst Zemled
Trudy Tadzhikskogo Politekhnicheskogo Instituta — Tr Tadzh Politekh Inst
Trudy Tadzhikskoi Astronomicheskoi Observatorii — Tr Tadzh Astron Obs
Trudy Tadzikistanskoj Bazy — Trudy Tadzikistansk Bazy
Trudy Tadzikskogo Politehniceskogo Instituta — Trudy Tadzik Politehn Inst
Trudy Taganrogskogo Gosudarstvennogo Pedagogiceskogo Instituta — TTagPI
Trudy Taganrogskogo Radiotekhnicheskogo Instituta — Tr Taganrog Radiotekh Inst
Trudy Tallinskogo Pedagogicheskogo Instituta [*Estonian SSR*] — Tr Tallin Pedagog Inst
Trudy Tallinskogo Politekhnicheskogo Instituta [*Estonian SSR*] — Tr Tallin Politekh Inst
Trudy Tallinskogo Politekhnicheskogo Instituta — Trudy Tallinsk Politehn Inst
Trudy Tallinskogo Politekhnicheskogo Instituta. Seriya A [*Estonian SSR*] — Tr Tallin Politekh Inst Ser A
Trudy Tallinskogo Politekhnicheskogo Instituta. Seriya B, XX — TTP
Trudy Tallinskogo Tekhnicheskogo Universiteta — Tr Tallin Tekh Univ
Trudy Tambovskogo Instituta Khimicheskogo Mashinostroeniya [*Former USSR*] — Tr Tambov Inst Khim Mashinostr
Trudy Tambovskogo Instituta Khimicheskogo Mashinostroeniya — TTKMA
Trudy Tashkentskogo Farmatsevticheskogo Instituta — Tr Tashk Farm Inst
Trudy Tashkentskogo Gosudarstvennogo Universiteta Imeni V. I. Lenina — Tr Tashk Gos Univ
Trudy Tashkentskogo Gosudarstvennogo Universiteta Imeni V. I. Lenina [*Former USSR*] — Tr Tashk Gos Univ Im V I Lenina
Trudy Tashkentskogo Instituta Inzhenerov Irrigatsii i Mekhanizatsii Sel'skogo Khozyaistva — Tr Tashk Inst Inzh Irrig Mekh Selsk Khoz
Trudy Tashkentskogo Instituta Inzhenerov Irrigatsii i Mekhanizatsii Sel'skogo Khozyaistva — TTIIA
Trudy Tashkentskogo Instituta Inzhenerov Zheleznodorozhnogo Transporta — Tr Tashk Inst Inzh Zh Zheleznodorozhn Transp

Trudy Tashkentskogo Nauchno-Issledovatel'skogo Instituta Vaktsin i Syvorotok — Tr Tashk Nauchno Issled Inst Vaktsin Syvorotok
Trudy Tashkentskogo Politekhnicheskogo Instituta — Tr Tashk Politekh Inst
Trudy Tashkentskogo Sel'skokhozyaistvennogo Instituta — Tr Tashk S-Kh Inst
Trudy Taskentskogo Gosudarstvennogo Universiteta Imeni V. I. Lenina. Matematika — Trudy Taskent Gos Univ
Trudy Tatarskii Gosudarstvennyi Nauchno-Issledovatel'skii i Proektnyi Institut Neftyanoi Promyshlennosti — Tr Tatar Gos Nauchno Issled Proektn Inst Neft Promsti
Trudy Tatarskii Nauchno-Issledovatel'skii Institut Sel'skogo Khozyaistva — Tr Tatar Nauchno Issled Inst Selsk Khoz
Trudy Tatarskii Nauchno-Issledovatel'skii Institut Sel'skogo Khozyaistva — Trudy Tatar Nauchno-Issled Inst Sel'Khoz
Trudy Tatarskii Neftyanoi Nauchno-Issledovatel'skii Institut — Tr Tatar Neft Nauchno Issled Inst
Trudy Tatarskii Respublikanskii Mezhvedomstvennyi Sbornik — Tr Tatar Resp Mezhved Sb
Trudy Tatarskogo Otdeleniya Gosudarstvennogo Nauchno-Issledovatel'skogo Instituta Ozernogo i Rechnogo Rybnogo Khozyaistva — Tr Tatar Otd Gos Nauchno Issled Inst Ozern Rechn Rybn Khoz
Trudy Tatarskoi Respublikanskoi Gosudarstvennoi Sel'skokhozyaistvennoi Opytnoi Stantsii — Tr Tatar Respub Gosud Sel'skokhoz Opyt Sta
Trudy Tatarskoi Respublikanskoi Gosudarstvennoi Sel'skokhozyaistvennoi Opytnoi Stantsii — Trudy Tatar Respub Gos Sel-Khoz Opyt Sta
Trudy Tatarskoi Respublikanskoi Sel'skokhozyaistvennoi Opytnoi Stantsii — Tr Tatar Resp Skh Opytn Stn
Trudy Tbilisskii Gosudarstvennyi Universitet Institut Prikladnoi Matematiki — Tr Tbilis Gos Univ Inst Prikl Mat
Trudy. Tbilisskii Universitet. Matematika. Mekhanika. Astronomiya — Trudy Tbiliss Univ Mat Mekh Astronom
Trudy Tbilisskogo Botaniceskogo Sada/Thbilisis Botanikuri Bagis Sromebi/Travaux du Jardin Botanique du Tibilissi — Trudy Tbilissk Bot Sada
Trudy Tbilisskogo Botanicheskogo Instituta — Tr Tbilissk Bot Inst
Trudy Tbilisskogo Botanicheskogo Instituta Akademiya Nauk Gruzinskoi SSR — Tr Tbilis Bot Inst Akad Nauk Gruz SSR
Trudy Tbilisskogo Gosudarstvennogo Meditsinskogo Instituta — Tr Tbilis Gos Med Inst
Trudy Tbilisskogo Gosudarstvennogo Pedagogiceskogo Instituta — TTPI
Trudy Tbilisskogo Gosudarstvennogo Pedagogiceskogo Instituta Imeni A. S. Pushkina — Tr Tbilis Gos Pedagog Inst
Trudy Tbilisskogo Gosudarstvennogo Universiteta — Tr Tbilis Gos Univ
Trudy Tbilisskogo Gosudarstvennogo Universiteta Imeni Stalina — Tr Tbilis Gos Univ Im Stalina
Trudy Tbilisskogo Instituta i Polikliniki Funktsional'nykh Nervnykh Zabolevanii — Tr Tbilis Inst Poliklin Funkts Nervn Zabol
Trudy Tbilisskogo Instituta Lesa — Tr Tbilis Inst Lesa
Trudy Tbilisskogo Instituta Usovershenstvovaniya Vrachei — Tr Tbilis Inst Usoversh Vrachei
Trudy Tbilisskogo Matematiceskogo Instituta Imeni A. M. Razmadze Akademija Nauk Gruzinskoi SSR — Trudy Tbiliss Mat Inst Razmadze Akad Nauk Gruzin SSR
Trudy Tbilisskogo Nauchno-Issledovatel'skogo Gidrometeorologicheskogo Instituta — Tr Tbilis Nauchno-Issled Gidrometeorol Inst
Trudy Tbilisskogo Nauchno-Issledovatel'skogo Instituta Priborostroeniya i Sredstv Avtomatizatsii — Tr Tbilis Nauchno Issled Inst Priborostr Sredstv Avtom
Trudy Tbilisskogo Ordena Trudovogo Krasnogo Znameni Matematicheskogo Instituta — Tr Tbilis Mat Inst
Trudy Tbilisskogo Pedagogiceskogo Instituta — TTb
Trudy Tbilisskogo Universiteta Fiziko-Matematiceskie i Estestvennyi Nauki — Trudy Tbilisk Univ Fiz-Mat Estestv Nauki
Trudy Tbilisskogo Universiteta Fiziko-Matematiceskie i Estestvennyi Nauki — Trudy Tbiliss Univ
Trudy Tekhnologicheskogo Instituta Pishchevoi Promyshlennosti (Kiev) — Tr Tekhnol Inst Pishch Promsti (Kiev)
Trudy Ternopol'skii Gosudarstvennyi Meditsinskii Institut — Tr Ternop Gos Med Inst
Trudy. Tomsk. Universitet — Trud Tomsk
Trudy Tomskogo Gosudarstvennogo Universiteta [*Former USSR*] — Tr Tomsk Gos Univ
Trudy Tomskogo Gosudarstvennogo Universiteta — Trudy Tomsk Gos Univ
Trudy Tomskogo Gosudarstvennogo Universiteta — TTomU
Trudy Tomskogo Gosudarstvennogo Universiteta Imeni V. V. Kuibysheva — Tr Tomsk Gos Univ Im V V Kuibysheva
Trudy Tomskogo Gosudarstvennogo Universiteta Imeni V. V. Kuibysheva. Seriya Khimicheskaya [*Former USSR*] — Tr Tomsk Gos Univ Ser Khim
Trudy Tomskogo Gosudarstvennogo Universiteta imeni V. V. Kujbyseva i Tomskogo Gosudarstvennogo Pedagogiceskogo Instituta — Trudy Tomsk Gosud Univ Kujbyseva Tomsk Gosud Pedagog Inst
Trudy Tomskogo Instituta Radioehlektroniki i Ehlektronnoj Tekhniki — Tr Tomsk Inst Radioehlektron Ehlektron Tekh
Trudy Tomskogo Meditsinskogo Instituta — Tr Tomsk Med Inst
Trudy Tomskogo Nauchno-Issledovatel'skogo Instituta Kabel'noi Promyshlennosti — Tr Tom Nauchno Issled Inst Kabeln Promsti
Trudy Tomskogo Nauchno-Issledovatel'skogo Instituta Kabel'noi Promyshlennosti — Tr Tomsk Nauchno-Issled Inst Kabel'n Promsti
Trudy Tomskogo Nauchno-Issledovatel'skogo Instituta Vaktsiny i Syvorotok — Tr Tomsk Nauchno-Issled Inst Vaksiny Syvorotok
Trudy Tomskogo Universiteta — Trudy Tomsk Univ
Trudy Transportno-Energeticheskogo Instituta Akademiya Nauk SSSR Sibirskoe Otdelenie — Tr Transp Energ Inst Akad Nauk SSSR Sib Otd
Trudy Troitskogo Veterinarnogo Instituta — Tr Troitsk Vet Inst
Trudy Tselinogradskii Gosudarstvennyi Meditsinskii Institut — Tr Tselinogr Gos Med Inst
Trudy Tselinogradskogo Meditsinskogo Instituta — Tr Tselinogr Med Inst
Trudy Tselinogradskogo Sel'skokhozyaistvennogo Instituta — Tr Tselinogr S-Kh Inst
Trudy Tselinogradskogo Sel'skokhozyaistvennogo Instituta — Tr Tselinograd Sel'skokhoz Inst
Trudy Tsentral'nogo Aptechnogo Nauchno-Issledovatel'skogo Instituta — Tr Tsentr Aptechn Nauchno-Issled Inst
Trudy Tsentral'nogo Chernozemnogo Gosudarstvennogo Zapovednika — Tr Tsentr Chernozemn Gos Zapov
Trudy Tsentral'nogo Chernozemnogo Gosudarstvennogo Zapovednika — Trudy Tsent Chernoz Gos Zapov
Trudy Tsentral'nogo Instituta Prognozov — Tr Tsentr Inst Prognozov
Trudy Tsentral'nogo Instituta Travmatologii i Ortopedii — Tr Tsentr Inst Travmatol Ortop
Trudy Tsentral'nogo Instituta Usovershenstvovaniya Vrachei — Tr Tsentr Inst Usoversh Vrachei
Trudy Tsentral'nogo Komiteta Vodookhraneniya — Tr Tsentr Kom Vodookhr
Trudy Tsentral'nogo Nauchno-Issledovatel'skogo Dezinfektsionnogo Instituta — Tr Tsentr Nauchno-Issled Dezinfekts Inst
Trudy Tsentral'nogo Nauchno-Issledovatel'skogo Dizel'nogo Instituta — Tr Tsentr Nauchno Issled Dizeln Inst
Trudy Tsentral'nogo Nauchno-Issledovatel'skogo i Proektno-Konstruktorskogo Instituta Profilaktiki Pnevmokoniozov i Tekhniki Bezopasnosti — TPIPAR
Trudy Tsentral'nogo Nauchno-Issledovatel'skogo i Proektno-Konstruktorskogo Kotloturbinnogo Instituta [*Former USSR*] — Tr Tsent Nauchno-Issled Proekt-Konst Kotloturbinnogo Inst
Trudy Tsentral'nogo Nauchno-Issledovatel'skogo Instituta Fanery i Mebeli — Tr Tsentr Nauchno Issled Inst Faner Mebeli
Trudy Tsentral'nogo Nauchno-Issledovatel'skogo Instituta Khimii Pishchevykh Sredstv — Tr Tsentr Nauchno Issled Inst Khim Pishch Sredstv
Trudy Tsentral'nogo Nauchno-Issledovatel'skogo Instituta Konditerskoi Promyshlennosti — Tr Tsentr Nauchno Issled Inst Konditer Promsti
Trudy Tsentral'nogo Nauchno-Issledovatel'skogo Instituta Kurortologii i Fizioterapii — Tr Tsentr Nauchno Issled Inst Kurortol Fizioter
Trudy Tsentral'nogo Nauchno-Issledovatel'skogo Instituta Osetrovogo Khozyaistva Nauk SSR — Tr Tsentr Nauchno Issled Inst Osetr Khoz Nauk SSR
Trudy Tsentral'nogo Nauchno-Issledovatel'skogo Instituta Rentgenologii i Radiologii — Tr Tsentr Nauchno Issled Inst Rentgenol Radiol
Trudy Tsentral'nogo Nauchno-Issledovatel'skogo Instituta Sakharnoi Promyshlennosti Moscow — Tr Tsentr Nauchno Issled Inst Sakh Promsti Moscow
Trudy Tsentral'nogo Nauchno-Issledovatel'skogo Instituta Spirtovoi i Likero-Vodochnoi Promyshlennosti [*Former USSR*] — Tr Tsentr Nauchno-Issled Inst Spirt Likero-Vodochn Prom-Sti
Trudy Tsentral'nogo Nauchno-Issledovatel'skogo Instituta Tuberkuleza — Tr Tsentr Nauchno Issled Inst Tuberk
Trudy Tsentral'nogo Nauchno-Issledovatel'skogo Rentgeno-Radiologicheskogo Instituta — Tr Tsentr Nauchno-Issled Rentgeno-Radiol Inst
Trudy Tsentral'nogo Sibirskogo Botanicheskogo Sada — Tr Tsentr Sib Bot Sada
Trudy Tsentral'nogo Sibirskogo Botanicheskogo Sada — Trudy Tsent Sib Bot Sada
Trudy Tsentral'noi Aerologicheskoi Observatorii [*Former USSR*] — Tr Tsent Aerol Obs
Trudy Tsentral'noi Aerologicheskoi Observatorii — Tr Tsentr Aerol Obs
Trudy Tsentral'noi Geneticheskoi Laboratorii Vsesoyuznaya Akademiya Sel'skokhozyaistvennykh Nauk — Tr Tsentr Genet Lab Vses Akad Skh Nauk
Trudy Tsentral'noi Genetiki Laboratorii I. V. Michurina — Tr Tsentr Genet Lab I V Michurina
Trudy Tsentral'noi Nauchno-Issledovatel'skoi Laboratorii Novosibirskogo Meditsinskogo Instituta — Tr Tsentr Nauchno Issled Lab Novosib Med Inst
Trudy Tsentral'noi Nauchno-Issledovatel'skoi Stantsii po Sel'skokhozyaistvennomu Ispol'zovaniyu Stochnykh Vod — Tr Tsentr Nauchno Issled Stn Skh Ispol'z Stochnykh Vod
Trudy Tsentral'no-Kazakhstanskogo Geologicheskogo Upravleniya — Tr Tsentr Kaz Geol Upr
Trudy Tsentral'nyi Nauchno-Issledovatel'skii Avtomobil'nyi i Avtomotornyi Institut — Tr Tsentr Nauchno Issled Avtomob Avtomot Inst
Trudy Tsentral'nyi Nauchno-Issledovatel'skii Gornorazvedochnyi Institut [*Former USSR*] — Tr Tsent Nauchno-Issled Gornorazved Inst
Trudy Tsentral'nyi Nauchno-Issledovatel'skii i Proektno-Konstruktorskii Kotloturbinnyi Institut — Tr Tsentr Nauchno Issled Proektno Konstr Kotloturbinnyi Inst
Trudy Tsentral'nyi Nauchno-Issledovatel'skii Institut Krakhmalo-Patochnoi Promyshlennosti — Tr Tsentr Nauchno Issled Inst Krakhmalo Patochn Promsti
Trudy Tsentral'nyi Nauchno-Issledovatel'skii Institut Morskogo Flota — Tr Tsentr Nauchno Issled Morsk Flota
Trudy Tsentral'nyi Nauchno-Issledovatel'skii Institut Stroitel'nykh Konstruktsii — Tr Tsentr Nauchno Issled Inst Stroit Konstr
Trudy Tsentral'nyi Nauchno-Issledovatel'skii Institut Tekhnologii i Mashinostroeniya [*Former USSR*] — Tr Tsent Nauchno-Issled Inst Tekhnol Mashinostr
Trudy Tsentral'nyi Nauchno-Issledovatel'skii Institut Tekhnologii Sudostroeniya — Tr Tsentr Nauchno Issled Inst Tekhnol Sudostr
Trudy Tsentral'nyj Nauchno-Issledovatel'skij Gornorazvedochnyj Institut — Tr Tsentr Nauchno-Issled Gornorazved Inst
Trudy Tul'skogo Mekhanicheskogo Instituta — Tr Tul Mekh Inst
Trudy Tul'skoi Gosudarstvennoi Sel'skokhozyaistvennoi Opytnoi Stantsii — Tr Tul Gos Skh Opytn Stn
Trudy Turkestanskogo Naucnogo Obscestva/Transactions. Scientific Society of Turkestan — Trudy Turkestansk Naucn Obsc
Trudy Turkmenskogo Botanicheskogo Sada Akademii Nauk Turkmenskoi SSR — Tr Turkm Bot Sada Akad Nauk Turkm SSR
Trudy Turkmenskogo Filiala Vsesoyuznogo Neftyanogo Nauchno-Issledovatel'skogo Instituta — Tr Turkm Fil Vses Neft Nauchno Issled Inst

Trudy Turkmenskogo Gosudarstvennogo Meditsinskogo Instituta — Tr Turkm Gos Med Inst
Trudy Turkmenskogo Nauchno-Issledovatel'skogo Instituta Klimatologii Kurortologii i Fizicheskikh Metodov Lecheniya — TTKLAJ
Trudy Turkmenskogo Nauchno-Issledovatel'skogo Instituta Kozhynykh Boleznei — Tr Turk Nauchno Issled Inst Kozhynykh Bolezn
Trudy Turkmenskogo Nauchno-Issledovatel'skogo Instituta Kozhynykh Boleznei — Tr Turkm Nauchno-Issled Inst Kozhynykh Bolezn
Trudy Turkmenskogo Nauchno-Issledovatel'skogo Trakhomatoznogo Instituta — Tr Turkm Nauchno Issled Trakhomatoznogo Inst
Trudy Turkmenskogo Politekhnicheskogo Instituta — Tr Turkm Politekh Inst
Trudy Turkmenskogo Sel'skokhozyaistvennogo Instituta — Tr Turkm Skh Inst
Trudy Turkmenskogo Sel'sko-Khozyaistvennogo Instituta — Trudy Turkmen Sel'Khoz Inst
Trudy Turkmenskogo Sel'skokhozyaistvennogo Instituta Imeni M. I. Kalinina — Tr Turkm S-Kh Inst Im M Kalinina
Trudy Tuvinskoi Gosudarstvennoi Sel'skokhozyaistvennoi Opytnoi Stantsii — Tr Tuvinskoi Gos Skh Opytn Stn
Trudy Tyazanskogo Radiotekhnicheskogo Instituta — Tr Tyazan Radiotekh Inst
Trudy Tyumenskogo Industrial'nogo Instituta — Tr Tyumen Ind Inst
Trudy Tyumenskogo Industrial'nogo Instituta [*Former USSR*] — Tr Tyumenskogo Ind Inst
Trudy Tyumenskogo Otdeleniya Vsesoyuznogo Nauchnogo Obshchestva Anatomov, Gistologov, i Embriologov — Tr Tyumen Otd Vses Nauchn Ova Anat Gistol Embriol
Trudy Ufimskii Neftyanoi Nauchno-Issledovatel'skii Institut — Tr Ufim Neft Naucho-Issled Inst
Trudy Ufimskogo Aviacionnogo Instituta — Trudy Ufmsk Aviac Inst
Trudy Ufimskogo Aviatsionnogo Instituta — Tr Ufim Aviats Inst
Trudy Ufimskogo Nauchno-Issledovatel'skogo Instituta Gigieny i Profzabolevanii — Tr Ufim Nauchno-Issled Inst Gig Profzabol
Trudy Ufimskogo Nauchno-Issledovatel'skogo Instituta Vaktsin i Syvorotok Imeni I. I. Mechnikova — TUVMAG
Trudy Ukrainskii Nauchno-Issledovatel'skii Geologo-Razvedochnyi Institut — Tr Ukr Nauchno Issled Geol Razved Inst
Trudy Ukrainskii Nauchno-Issledovatel'skii Geologo-Razvedochnyi Institut — TRUGA
Trudy Ukrainskii Nauchno-Issledovatel'skii Institut Pishchevoi Promyshlennosti — Tr Ukr Nauchno Issled Inst Pishch Promsti
Trudy Ukrainskii Nauchno-Issledovatel'skii Institut Prirodnykh Gazov — Tr Ukr Nauchno-Issled Inst Prir Gazov
Trudy Ukrainskii Nauchno-Issledovatel'skii Institut Spirtovoi i Likero-Vodochnoi Promyshlennosti — Tr Ukr Nauchno-Issled Inst Spirt Likero Vodochn Promsti
Trudy Ukrainskii Nauchno-Issledovatel'skii Institut Spirtovoi i Likero-Vodochnoi Promyshlennosti — TUSLA
Trudy Ukrainskogo Gidrometeorologicheskogo Instituta — Trudy Ukr Gidromet Inst
Trudy Ukrainskogo Gosudarstvennogo Nauchno-Issledovatel'skogo Instituta Prikladnoi Khimii — Tr Ukr Gos Nauchno-Issled Inst Prikl Khim
Trudy Ukrainskogo Instituta Eksperimental'noi Endokrinologii — Tr Ukr Inst Eksp Endokrinol
Trudy Ukrainskogo Nauchno-Issledovatel'skogo Gidrometeorologicheskogo Instituta — Tr Ukr Nauch-Issled Gidrometeorol Inst
Trudy Ukrainskogo Nauchno-Issledovatel'skogo Gidrometeorologicheskogo Instituta [*Ukrainian SSR*] — Tr Ukr Nauchno-Issled Gidrometeorol Inst
Trudy Ukrainskogo Nauchno-Issledovatel'skogo Instituta Klinicheskoi Meditsiny — Tr Ukr Nauchno Issled Inst Klin Med
Trudy Ukrainskogo Nauchno-Issledovatel'skogo Instituta Klinicheskoi Meditsiny — TUKMAT
Trudy Ukrainskogo Nauchno-Issledovatel'skogo Instituta Konservnoi Promyshlennosti — Tr Ukr Nauchno Issled Inst Konservn Promsti
Trudy Ukrainskogo Nauchno-Issledovatel'skogo Instituta Lesnogo Khozyaistva i Agrolesomelioratsii — Tr Ukr Nauchno-Issled Inst Lesn Khoz Agrolesomelior
Trudy Ukrainskogo Nauchno-Issledovatel'skogo Instituta Rastenievodstva Selektsii i Genetiki — Tr Ukr Nauchno-Issled Inst Rastenievod Sel Genet
Trudy Ukrainskogo Nauchno-Issledovatel'skogo Instituta Zernovogo Khozyaistva — Tr Ukr Nauchno-Issled Inst Zernovogo Khoz
Trudy Ukrainskogo Regional'nogo Nauchno-Issledovatel'skogo Instituta — Tr Ukr Reg Nauchno Issled Inst
Trudy Ukrajins'kogo Instytutu Prykladnoji Botaniky. Arbeiten des Ukrainischen Instituts fuer Angewandte Botanik — Trudy Ukrajinsk Inst Prykl Bot
Trudy Ul'yanovskaya Gosudarstvennaya Opytnaya Stantsiya Zhivotnovodstva — Tr Ul'yanovsk Gos Opytn Stn Zhivotnovod
Trudy Ul'yanovskii Politekhnicheskii Institut — Tr Ulyanovsk Politekh Inst
Trudy Ul'yanovskogo Sel'skokhozyaistvennogo Instituta — Tr Ul'yanovsk S-Kh Inst
Trudy Ul'yanovskogo Sel'skokhozyaistvennogo Instituta — Trudy Ul'yanov Sel'khoz Inst
Trudy Ul'yanovskoi Sel'skokhozyaistvennoi Opytnoi Stantsii — Tr Ul'yanovsk Skh Opytn Stn
Trudy Universiteta Druzhby Narodov — TDNLA
Trudy Universiteta Druzhby Narodov [*Former USSR*] — Tr Univ Druzhby Nar
Trudy Universiteta Druzhby Narodov. Fizika [*Former USSR*] — Tr Univ Druzhby Nar Fiz
Trudy Universiteta Druzhby Narodov Imeni Patrisa Lumumby — Tr Univ Druzhby Nar Im Patrisa Lumumby
Trudy Universiteta Druzhby Narodov Imeni Patrisa Lumumby — Trudy Univ Druzby Narod
Trudy Universiteta Druzhby Narodov Imeni Patrisa Lumumby — TUD
Trudy Universiteta Druzhby Narodov Imeni Patrisa Lumumby [*Moscow*] — TUDNL
Trudy Universiteta Druzhby Narodov Imeni Patrisa Lumumby. Seriya Fizika — Tr Univ Druzhby Nar Ser Fiz
Trudy Upravleniya Geologii i Okhrany Nedr pri Sovete Ministrov Kirgizskoi SSR — Tr Upr Geol Okhr Nedr Sov Minist Kirg SSR
Trudy Ural'skii Nauchno-Issledovatel'skii i Proektnyi Institut Mednoi Promyshlennosti [*Former USSR*] — Tr Ural Nauchno-Issled Proekt Inst Mednoi Promsti
Trudy Ural'skii Nauchno-Issledovatel'skii i Proektnyi Institut Mednoi Promyshlennosti — Tr Ural Nauchno-Issled Proektn Inst Mednoi Promsti
Trudy Ural'skii Nauchno-Issledovatel'skii i Proektnyi Institut Mednoi Promyshlennosti — TUPMA
Trudy Ural'skogo Elektromekhanicheskogo Instituta Inzhenerov Zheleznodorozhnogo Transporta — Tr Ural Elektromekh Inst Inzh Zheleznodorozhn
Trudy Ural'skogo Industrial'nogo Instituta — Tr Ural Ind Inst
Trudy Ural'skogo Lesotekhnicheskogo Instituta — Tr Ural Lesotekh Inst
Trudy Ural'skogo Nauchno-Issledovatel'skogo Instituta Chernykh Metallov — Tr Ural Nauchno-Issled Inst Chern Met
Trudy Ural'skogo Nauchno-Issledovatel'skogo Instituta Sel'skogo Khozyaistva — Tr Ural Nauchno-Issled Inst Sel'sk Khoz
Trudy Ural'skogo Nauchno-Issledovatel'skogo Khimicheskogo Instituta — Tr Ural Nauchno-Issled Khim Inst
Trudy Ural'skogo Otdeleniya Gosudarstvennyi Nauchno-Issledovatel'skii Institut Ozernogo i Rechnogo Rybnogo Khozyaistva — Tr Ural Otd Gos Nauchno-Issled Inst Ozern Rechn Rybn Khoz
Trudy Ural'skogo Otdeleniya Moskovskogo Obshchestva Ispytatelei Prirody — Tr Ural Otd Mosk Ova Ispyt Prir
Trudy Ural'skogo Otdeleniya Sibirskogo Nauchno-Issledovatel'skogo Instituta Rybnogo Khozyaistva — Tr Ural Otd Sib Nauchno-Issled Inst Rybn Khoz
Trudy Ural'skogo Politehniceskogo Instituta — Trudy Ural Politehn Inst
Trudy Ural'skogo Politekhnicheskogo Instituta Imeni S. M. Kirova — Tr Ural Politekh Inst
Trudy Ural'skogo Politekhnicheskogo Instituta Imeni S. M. Kirova [*Former USSR*] — Tr Ural Politekh Inst Im S M Kirova
Trudy Uzbekistanskogo Instituta Malyarii i Meditsinskoi Parazitologii — Tr Uzb Inst Malyarii Med Parazitol
Trudy Uzbekistanskogo Nauchno-Issledovatel'skogo Instituta Fizioterapii i Kurortologii — Tr Uzb Nauchno-Issled Inst Fizioter Kurortol
Trudy Uzbekistanskogo Nauchno-Issledovatel'skogo Instituta Ortopedii Travmatologii i Protezirovaniya — Tr Uzb Nauchno-Issled Inst Ortop Travmatol Prot
Trudy Uzbekistanskogo Nauchno-Issledovatel'skogo Instituta Ortopedii Travmatologii i Protezirovaniya — Tr Uzb Nauchno-Issled Inst Ortop Travmatol Protez
Trudy Uzbekskogo Geologicheskogo Upravlenie — Tr Uzb Geol Upr
Trudy Uzbekskogo Gosudarstvennogo Nauchno-Issledovatel'skogo i Instituta Kurortologii i Fizioterapii — Tr Uzb Gos Nauchno-Issled Inst Kurortol Fizioter
Trudy Uzbekskogo Nauchno-Issledovatel'skogo Instituta Veterinarii — Tr Uzb Nauchno-Issled Inst Vet
Trudy VAMI — Tr VAMI
Trudy Velikolukskogo Sel'skokhozyaistvennogo Instituta — Tr Velikoluk S-Kh Inst
Trudy Vinnitskogo Gosudarstvennogo Meditsinskogo Instituta — Tr Vinnitsk Gos Med Inst
Trudy Vladivostokskogo Nauchno-Issledovatel'skogo Instituta Epidemiologii, Mikrobiologii, i Gigieny — Tr Vladivost Nauchno Issled Inst Epidemiol Mikrobiol Gig
Trudy VNIGRI [*Vsesoyuznogo Neftyanogo Nauchno-Issledovatel'skogo Geologorazvedochnogo Instituta*] — Tr VNIGRI
Trudy VNIIEI [*Vsesoyuznogo Nauchno-Issledovatel'skogo i Proektno-Tekhnologicheskogo Instituta Elektrougol'nykh Izdelii*] — Tr VNIIEI
Trudy Vojennogo Instituta Inostrannykh Jazykov — TVIIJ
Trudy Vojennogo Instituta Inostrannykh Jazykov — TVIIJa
Trudy Volgogradskaya Opytno-Meliorativnaya Stantsiya — Tr Volgogr Opytno Melior Stn
Trudy Volgogradskii Gosudarstvennyi Nauchno-Issledovatel'skii i Proektnyi Institut Neftyanoi Promyshlennosti — Tr Volgogr Gos Nauchno-Issled Proektn Inst Neft Promsti
Trudy Volgogradskii Nauchno-Issledovatel'skii Institut Neftyanoi i Gazovoi Promyshlennosti — Tr Volgogr Nauchno-Issled Inst Neft Gazov Promsti
Trudy Volgogradskogo Meditsinskogo Instituta — Tr Volgogr Med Inst
Trudy Volgogradskogo Otdeleniya Gosudarstvennogo Nauchno-Issledovatel'skogo Instituta Ozernogo i Rechnogo Rybnogo Khozyaistva — Tr Volgogr Otd Gos Nauchno-Issled Inst Ozern Rechn Rybn Khoz
Trudy Volgogradskogo Sel'skokhozyaistvennogo Instituta — Tr Volgogr S-Kh Inst
Trudy Volgogradskoi Opytno-Meliorativnoi Stantsii — Trudy Volgogr Opytno-Melior Sta
Trudy Vologodskogo Molochnogo Instituta — Tr Vologod Molochn Inst
Trudy Vologodskogo Molochno-Khozyaistvennogo Instituta — Tr Vologod Molochno Khoz Inst
Trudy Vologodskogo Sel'skokhozyaistvennogo Instituta — Trudy Vologod Sel'khoz Inst
Trudy Volzhsko-Kamskogo Gosudarstvennogo Zapovednika — Tr Volzh Kamskogo Gos Zapov
Trudy Voronezhskii Gosudarstvennyi Meditsinskii Institut — Tr Voronezh Gos Med Inst
Trudy Voronezhskogo Gosudarstvennogo Universiteta — Tr Voronezh Gos Univ
Trudy Voronezhskogo Gosudarstvennogo Zapovednika — Tr Voronezh Gos Zapov
Trudy Voronezhskogo Inzhenerno-Stroitel'nogo Instituta — Tr Voronezh Inzh Stroit Inst
Trudy Voronezhskogo Khimiko-Tekhnologicheskogo Instituta — Tr Voronezh Khim Tekhnol Inst
Trudy Voronezhskogo Meditsinskogo Instituta — Tr Voronezh Med Inst

Trudy Voronezhskogo Stantsii Zashchity Rastenii — Tr Voronezh Stn Zashch Rast
Trudy Voronezhskogo Tekhnologicheskogo Instituta — Tr Voronezh Tekhnol Inst
Trudy Voronezhskogo Zooveterinarnogo Instituta — Tr Voronezh Zoovet Inst
Trudy Voronezhskogo Zooveterinarnogo Instituta — Trudy Voronezh Zoovetinst
Trudy Voronezhskoi Nauchno-Issledovatel'skoi Veterinarnoi Stantsii — Tr Voronezh Nauchno Issled Vet Stn
Trudy Voroshilovgradskogo Sel'skokhozyaistvennogo Instituta — Tr Voroshilovgr S-Kh Inst
Trudy Voroshilovskogo Gorno-Metallurgicheskogo Instituta — Tr Voroshil Gorno Metall Inst
Trudy Vostochnogo Instituta Ogneuporov [*Former USSR*] — Tr Vost Inst Ogneuporov
Trudy Vostochnogo Nauchno-Issledovatel'skogo Gornorudnogo Instituta — Tr Vost Nauchno Issled Gornorudn Inst
Trudy Vostochno-Kazakhskoi Gosudarstvennoi Sel'skokhozyaistvennoi Opytnoi Stantsii — Tr Vost Kaz Gos Skh Opytn Stn
Trudy Vostochno-Kazakhstanskaya Gosudarstvennaya Sel'skokhozyaistvennaya Opytnaya Stantsiya — Trudy Vost Kazakh Gos Opyt Sta
Trudy Vostochno-Sibirskogo Filiala Akademii Nauk SSSR — Tr Vost-Sib Fil Akad Nauk SSSR
Trudy Vostochno-Sibirskogo Geologicheskogo Instituta Akademiya Nauk SSSR Sibirskoe Otdelenie — Tr Vost Sib Geol Inst Akad Nauk SSSR Sib Otd
Trudy Vostochno-Sibirskogo Geologicheskogo Upravleniya — Tr Vost Sib Geol Upr
Trudy Vostochno-Sibirskogo Tekhnologicheskogo Instituta — Tr Vost Sib Tekhnol Inst
Trudy Vostochno-Sibirskogo Tekhnologicheskogo Instituta — Trudy Vost-Sibir Tehnol Inst
Trudy Vostocno-Sibirskogo Filiala — Trudy Vost Sibirsk Fil
Trudy Vserossiiskogo Nauchno-Issledovatel'skogo Instituta Sakharnoi Svekly i Sakhara — Tr Vseross Nauchno Issled Inst Sakh Svekly Sakhara
Trudy Vserossiiskoi Konferentsii Khirurgov po Flebologii — Tr Vseross Konf Khir Flebol
Trudy Vsesoiuznogo Nauchno-Issledovatel'skogo Instituta Iskusstvennogo Zhidkogo Topliva i Gaza [*Former USSR*] — Tr Vses Nauchno-Issled Inst Ikusstv Zhidk Topl Gaza
Trudy Vsesojuznogo Gidrobiologiceskogo Obscestva — Trudy Vsesojuzn Gidrobiol Obsc
Trudy Vsesojuznogo Nauchno-Issledovatel'skogo Instituta Sovetskogo Zakonodatel'stva — Trudy Vsesojuz Nauc-Issled Inst Sov Zakon
Trudy Vsesojuznogo Naucno-Issledovatel'skogo Instituta Elektromehaniki — Trudy Vsesojuz Naucno-Issled Inst Elektromeh
Trudy Vsesojuznogo Naucno-Issledovatel'skogo Instituta Zascity Rastenij — Trudy Vsesojuz Nauc-Issled Inst Zascity Rast
Trudy Vsesojuznogo Teplotehniceskogo Instituta — Trudy VTI
Trudy Vsesojuznogo Zaocnogo Energeticeskogo Instituta — Trudy Vsesojuz Zaocn Energet Inst
Trudy Vsesojuznoj Akademii Sel'sko-Hozjajstvennyh Nauk imeni V. I. Lenina. Serija 17. Bor'ba s Vrediteljami Sel'skohozjajstvennyh Rastenij — Trudy Vsesojuzn Akad Selsko Hoz Nauk Lenina Ser 17 Borba Vred
Trudy Vsesoyuznoe Obshchestvo Genetikov i Selektsionerov Kubanskoe Otdelenie — Tr Vses O Genet Sel Kuban Otd
Trudy Vsesoyuznogo Aerogeologicheskogo Tresta — Tr Vses Aerogeol Tresta
Trudy Vsesoyuznogo Aerogeologicheskogo Tresta — Trudy Vses Aerogeol Tresta
Trudy Vsesoyuznogo Elektrotekhnicheskogo i Instituta — Tr Vses Elektrotekh Inst
Trudy Vsesoyuznogo Entomologicheskogo Obshchestva — Tr Vses Entomol Obshch
Trudy Vsesoyuznogo Entomologicheskogo Obshchestva — Tr Vses Entomol O-Va
Trudy Vsesoyuznogo Entomologicheskogo Obshchestva — Trudy Vses Ent Obshch
Trudy Vsesoyuznogo Geologo-Razvedochnogo Ob'edineniya — Tr Vses Geol Razved Obedin
Trudy Vsesoyuznogo Gidrobiologicheskogo Obshchestva — Tr Vses Gidrobiol O-Va
Trudy Vsesoyuznogo Gosudarstvennogo Nauchno-Issledovatel'skogo Proektnogo Instituta Khimiko-Fotograficheskoi Promyshlennosti — Tr Vses Gos Nauchno Issled Proektn Inst Khim Fotogr Promsti
Trudy Vsesoyuznogo Instituta Eksperimental'noi Meditsiny — Tr Vses Inst Eksp Med
Trudy Vsesoyuznogo Instituta Eksperimental'noi Veterinarii [*Former USSR*] — Tr Vses Inst Eksp Vet
Trudy Vsesoyuznogo Instituta Rastenievodstva — Tr Vses Inst Rastenievod
Trudy Vsesoyuznogo Instituta Sodovoi Promyshlennosti — Tr Vses Inst Sodovoi Promsti
Trudy Vsesoyuznogo Instituta Zashchity Rastenii — Tr Vses Inst Zashch Rast
Trudy Vsesoyuznogo Mekhaniko-Tekhnologicheskogo Instituta Konservnoi Promyshlennosti — Tr Vses Mekh Tekhnol Inst Konservn Promsti
Trudy Vsesoyuznogo Nauchnogo Inzhenerno-Tekhnicheskogo Obshchestva Metallurgov — Tr Vses Nauchn Inzh Tekh Ova Metall
Trudy Vsesoyuznogo Nauchno-Issledovatel'skii Institut Khlopkovodstva Novykh Raionov — Tr Vses Nauchno-Issled Inst Khlopkovod Nov Raionov
Trudy Vsesoyuznogo Nauchno-Issledovatel'skogo Geologicheskogo Instituta — Tr Vses Nauchno-Issled Geol Inst
Trudy Vsesoyuznogo Nauchno-Issledovatel'skogo Geologicheskogo Instituta — Trudy Vses Nauchno-Issled Geol Inst
Trudy Vsesoyuznogo Nauchno-Issledovatel'skogo Geologorazvedochnogo Instituta — Tr Vses Nauchno Issled Geologorazved Inst
Trudy Vsesoyuznogo Nauchno-Issledovatel'skogo i Konstruktorskogo Instituta Avtogennogo Mashinostroeniya [*Former USSR*] — Tr Vses Nauchno-Issled Konstr Inst Avtog Mashinostr
Trudy Vsesoyuznogo Nauchno-Issledovatel'skogo i Proektnogo Instituta Galurgii — Tr Vses Nauchno Issled Proektn Inst Galurgii
Trudy Vsesoyuznogo Nauchno-Issledovatel'skogo Instituta Antibiotikov — Tr Vses Nauchno-Issled Inst Antibiot
Trudy Vsesoyuznogo Nauchno-Issledovatel'skogo Instituta Aviatsionnykh Materialov — Tr Vses Nauchno-Issled Inst Aviats Mater
Trudy Vsesoyuznogo Nauchno-Issledovatel'skogo Instituta Efirnomaslichnykh Kul'tur — Tr Vses Nauchno-Issled Inst Efirnomaslichn Kult
Trudy Vsesoyuznogo Nauchno-Issledovatel'skogo Instituta Elektromekhaniki — Tr Vses Nauchno-Issled Inst Elektromekh
Trudy Vsesoyuznogo Nauchno-Issledovatel'skogo Instituta Elektrotermicheskogo Oborudovaniya — Tr Vses Nauchno-Issled Inst Elektroterm Oborudovaniya
Trudy Vsesoyuznogo Nauchno-Issledovatel'skogo Instituta Fiziologii, Biokhimii, i Pitaniya Sel'skokhozyaistvennykh Zhivotnykh — Tr Vses Nauchno-Issled Inst Fiziol Biokhim Pitan Skh Zhivotn
Trudy Vsesoyuznogo Nauchno-Issledovatel'skogo Instituta Fiziologii i Biokhimii Sel'skokhozyaistvennykh Zhivotnykh — Tr Vses Nauchno-Issled Inst Fiziol Biokhim Skh Zhivotn
Trudy Vsesoyuznogo Nauchno-Issledovatel'skogo Instituta Galurgii — Tr Vses Nauchno-Issled Galurgii
Trudy Vsesoyuznogo Nauchno-Issledovatel'skogo Instituta Galurgii — Tr Vses Nauchno-Issled Inst Galurgii
Trudy Vsesoyuznogo Nauchno-Issledovatel'skogo Instituta Gidrogeologii i Inzhenernoi Geologii — Tr Vses Nauchno Issled Inst Gidrogeol Inzh Geol
Trudy Vsesoyuznogo Nauchno-Issledovatel'skogo Instituta Gidrotekhniki i Melioratsii — Tr Vses Nauchno-Issled Inst G Gidrotekh Melior
Trudy Vsesoyuznogo Nauchno-Issledovatel'skogo Instituta Gidrotekhniki i Melioratsii — Tr Vses Nauchno-Issled Inst Gidrotekh Melior
Trudy Vsesoyuznogo Nauchno-Issledovatel'skogo Instituta Iskusstvennogo Zhidkogo Topliva i Gaza — Tr Vses Nauchno Issled Inst Iskusstv Zhidk Topl Gaza
Trudy Vsesoyuznogo Nauchno-Issledovatel'skogo Instituta Karakulevodstva — Tr Vses Nauchno Issled Inst Karakulevod
Trudy Vsesoyuznogo Nauchno-Issledovatel'skogo Instituta Khimicheskikh Reaktivov — Tr Vses Nauchno-Issled Inst Khim Reakt
Trudy Vsesoyuznogo Nauchno-Issledovatel'skogo Instituta Khimicheskoi Pererabotki Gazov — Tr Vses Nauchno-Issled Inst Khim Pererab Gazov
Trudy Vsesoyuznogo Nauchno-Issledovatel'skogo Instituta Khlopkovodstva — Tr Vses Nauchno-Issled Inst Khlopkovod
Trudy Vsesoyuznogo Nauchno-Issledovatel'skogo Instituta Konditerskoi Promyshlennosti — Tr Vses Nauchno Issled Inst Konditer Promsti
Trudy Vsesoyuznogo Nauchno-Issledovatel'skogo Instituta Konservnoi i Ovoshchesushyl'noi Promyshlennosti — Tr Vses Nauchno-Issled Inst Konservn Ovoshchesush Promsti
Trudy Vsesoyuznogo Nauchno-Issledovatel'skogo Instituta Kormleniya Sel'skokhozyaistvennykh Zhivotnykh — Tr Vses Nauchno-Issled Inst Korml S-Kh Zhivotn
Trudy Vsesoyuznogo Nauchno-Issledovatel'skogo Instituta L'na — Tr Vses Nauchno-Issled Inst L'na
Trudy Vsesoyuznogo Nauchno-Issledovatel'skogo Instituta Meditsinskikh Instrumentov Oborudovaniya — Tr Vses Nauchno-Issled Inst Med Instrum Oborudovaniya
Trudy Vsesoyuznogo Nauchno-Issledovatel'skogo Instituta Meditsinskikh Priborostroenii — Tr Vses Nauchno-Issled Inst Med Priborostr
Trudy Vsesoyuznogo Nauchno-Issledovatel'skogo Instituta Metodiki i Tekhniki Razvedki — Tr Vses Nauchno Issled Inst Metod Tekh Razved
Trudy Vsesoyuznogo Nauchno-Issledovatel'skogo Instituta Molochnoi Promyshlennost — Tr Vses Nauchno-Issled Inst Molochn Prom-St
Trudy Vsesoyuznogo Nauchno-Issledovatel'skogo Instituta Morskogo Rybnogo Khozyaistva i Okeanografii [*Former USSR*] — Tr Vses Nauchno-Issled Inst Morsk Ryb Khoz Okeanogr
Trudy Vsesoyuznogo Nauchno-Issledovatel'skogo Instituta Morskogo Rybnogo Khozyaistva i Okeanografii — Tr Vses Nauchno-Issled Inst Morsk Rybn Khoz Okeanogr
Trudy Vsesoyuznogo Nauchno-Issledovatel'skogo Instituta Myasnoi Promyshlennost — Tr Vses Nauchno-Issled Inst Myasn Prom-St
Trudy Vsesoyuznogo Nauchno-Issledovatel'skogo Instituta Pererabotki i Ispol'zovaniya Topliva [*Former USSR*] — Tr Vses Nauchno-Issled Inst Pererab Ispol'z Topl
Trudy Vsesoyuznogo Nauchno-Issledovatel'skogo Instituta Pivo-Bezalkogol'noi Promyshlennosti — Tr Vses Nauchno Issled Inst Pivo Bezalkogol'n Promsti
Trudy Vsesoyuznogo Nauchno-Issledovatel'skogo Instituta po Pererabotke Slantsev [*Former USSR*] — Tr Vses Nauchno-Issled Inst Pererab Slantsev
Trudy Vsesoyuznogo Nauchno-Issledovatel'skogo Instituta Prudovogo Rybnogo Khozaistva — Tr Vses Nauchno-Issled Inst Prud Rybn Khoz
Trudy Vsesoyuznogo Nauchno-Issledovatel'skogo Instituta Ptitsevodstva — Tr Vses Nauch-Issled Inst Ptitsevod
Trudy Vsesoyuznogo Nauchno-Issledovatel'skogo Instituta Rastitel'nykh Masel i Margarina — Tr Vses Nauchno-Issled Inst Rastit Masel Margarina
Trudy Vsesoyuznogo Nauchno-Issledovatel'skogo Instituta Sakharnoi Svekly i Sakhara — Trudy Vses Nauchno-Issled Inst Sakharn Svekly Sakhara
Trudy Vsesoyuznogo Nauchno-Issledovatel'skogo Instituta Sinteticheskikh i Natural'nykh Dushistykh Veshchestv — Tr Vses Nauchno-Issled Inst Sint Nat Dushistykh Veshchestv
Trudy Vsesoyuznogo Nauchno-Issledovatel'skogo Instituta Spirtovoi i Likero-Vodochnoi Promyshlennosti [*Former USSR*] — Tr Vses Nauchn-Issled Inst Spirt Likero-Vodoch Prom
Trudy Vsesoyuznogo Nauchno-Issledovatel'skogo Instituta Spirtovoi Promyshlennosti [*Former USSR*] — Tr Vses Nauchno-Issled Inst Spirt Prom-Sti

Trudy Vsesoyuznogo Nauchno-Issledovatel'skogo Instituta Standartnykh Obraztsov i Spektral'nykh Etalonov [*Former USSR*] — Tr Vses Nauchno-Issled Inst Stand Obraztsov Spektr Etalonov
Trudy Vsesoyuznogo Nauchno-Issledovatel'skogo Instituta Steklyannogo Volokna — Tr Vses Nauchno Issled Inst Steklyannogo Volokna
Trudy Vsesoyuznogo Nauchno-Issledovatel'skogo Instituta Torfyanoi Promyshlennosti [*Former USSR*] — Tr Vses Nauchno-Issled Inst Torf Prom-Sti
Trudy Vsesoyuznogo Nauchno-Issledovatel'skogo Instituta Torfyanoi Promyshlennosti — Trudy Vses Nauchno-Issled Inst Torf Prom
Trudy Vsesoyuznogo Nauchno-Issledovatel'skogo Instituta Udobrenii Agrotekhniki i Agropochvovedeniya — Trudy Vses Nauchno-Issled Inst Udobr Agrotekh Agropochv
Trudy Vsesoyuznogo Nauchno-Issledovatel'skogo Instituta Udobrenii Agrotekhniki i Agropochvovedeniya Imeni Gedroitsa — TVUAAG
Trudy Vsesoyuznogo Nauchno-Issledovatel'skogo Instituta Udobreniya i Agropochvovedeniya — Tr Vses Nauchno-Issled Inst Udobr Agropochvoved
Trudy Vsesoyuznogo Nauchno-Issledovatel'skogo Instituta Veterinarnoi Sanitarii — Tr Vses Nauchno-Issled Inst Vet Sanit
Trudy Vsesoyuznogo Nauchno-Issledovatel'skogo Instituta Veterinarnoi Sanitarii i Ektoparazitologii — Tr Vses Nauchno-Issled Inst Vet Sanit Ektoparazitol
Trudy Vsesoyuznogo Nauchno-Issledovatel'skogo Instituta Veterinarnoi Sanitarii i Ektoparazitologii — Trudy Vses Nauchno-Issled Inst Vet Sanit Ektoparazit
Trudy Vsesoyuznogo Nauchno-Issledovatel'skogo Instituta Zashchity Rastenii — Tr Vses Nauch-Isled Inst Zashch Rast
Trudy Vsesoyuznogo Nauchno-Issledovatel'skogo Instituta Zashchity Rastenii — Tr Vses Nauchno-Issled Inst Zashch Rast
Trudy Vsesoyuznogo Nauchno-Issledovatel'skogo Instituta Zashchity Rastenii — Trudy Vses Nauchno-Issled Inst Zashch Rast
Trudy Vsesoyuznogo Nauchno-Issledovatel'skogo Instituta Zerna i Produktov Ego Pererabotki — Tr Vses Nauchno-Issled Inst Zerna Prod Pererab
Trudy Vsesoyuznogo Nauchno-Issledovatel'skogo Instituta Zheleznodorozhnogo Transporta — Tr Vses Nauchno-Issled Inst Zheleznodorozhn Transp
Trudy Vsesoyuznogo Nauchno-Issledovatel'skogo Instituta Zheleznodorozhnogo Transporta — Tr Vses Nauchno-Issled Inst Zheleznodorzhn
Trudy Vsesoyuznogo Nauchno-Issledovatel'skogo Instituta Zhivotnogo Syr'ya Pushniny — Tr Vses Nauchno-Issled Inst Zhivotn Syr'ya Pushn
Trudy Vsesoyuznogo Nauchno-Issledovatel'skogo Instituta Zolota i Redkikh Metallov [*Former USSR*] — Tr Vses Nauchno-Issled Inst Zolota Redk Met
Trudy Vsesoyuznogo Neftyanogo Nauchno-Issledovatel'skogo Geologorazvedochnogo Instituta [*Former USSR*] — Tr Vses Neft Nauchno-Issled Geologorazved Inst
Trudy Vsesoyuznogo Obshchestva Fiziologov Biokhimikov i Farmakologov — Tr Vses O-Va Fiziol Biokhim Farmakol
Trudy Vsesoyuznogo Ordena Lenina Instituta Eksperimental'noi Veterinarii — Trudy Vses Ordena Lenina Inst Eksp Vet
Trudy Vsesoyuznogo Sel'skokhozyaistvennogo Instituta Zaochnogo Obrazovaniva — Tr Vses S-Kh Inst Zaochn Obraz
Trudy Vsesoyuznogo Tsentral'nogo Nauchno-Issledovatel'skogo Instituta Zhirov — Tr Vses Tsentr Nauchno Issled Inst Zhirov
Trudy Vsesoyuznogo Zaochnogo Energeticheskogo Instituta — Tr Vses Zaochn Energ Inst
Trudy Vsesoyuznyi Alyuminievo-Magnievyi Institut — Tr Vses Alyum Magnievyi Inst
Trudy Vsesoyuznyi Institut Rastenievodstva Problema Populatsii u Vysshikh Rastenii — Tr Vses Inst Rast Prob Pop Vyssh Rast
Trudy Vsesoyuznyi Nauchno-Issledovatel'skii Alyuminievo-Magnievyi Institut — Tr Vses Nauchno Issled Alyum Magnievyi Inst
Trudy Vsesoyuznyi Nauchno-Issledovatel'skii Geologorazvedochnyi Neftyanoi Instituta — Tr Vses Nauchno-Issled Geologorazved Neft Inst
Trudy Vsesoyuznyi Nauchno-Issledovatel'skii i Eksperimental'no-Konstruktorskii Institut Prodovol'stvennogo Mashinostroeniya — Tr Vses Nauchno Issled Eksp Konstr Inst Prodovol Mashinostr
Trudy Vsesoyuznyi Nauchno-Issledovatel'skii i Konstruktorskii Institut Nauchnogo Priborostroeniya — Tr Vses Nauchno Issled Konstr Inst Nauchn Priborostr
Trudy Vsesoyuznyi Nauchno-Issledovatel'skii i Proektnyi Institut Mekhanicheskoi Obrabotki Poleznykh Iskopaemykh — Tr Vses Nauchno-Issled Proektn Inst Mekh Obrab Polezn Iskop
Trudy Vsesoyuznyi Nauchno-Issledovatel'skii Institut Abrazivov i Shlifovaniya — Tr Vses Nauchno-Issled Inst Abrazivov Shlifovaniya
Trudy Vsesoyuznyi Nauchno-Issledovatel'skii Institut Burovoi Tekhniki — Tr Vses Nauchno-Issled Inst Burovoi Tekh
Trudy Vsesoyuznyi Nauchno-Issledovatel'skii Institut Burovoi Tekhniki — TVBTA
Trudy Vsesoyuznyi Nauchno-Issledovatel'skii Institut Fermentnoi i Spirtovoi Promyshlennosti — Tr Vses Nauchno-Issled Inst Fermentn Spirt Promsti
Trudy Vsesoyuznyi Nauchno-Issledovatel'skii Institut Geofizicheskikh Metodov Razvedki — Tr Vses Nauchno Issled Inst Geofiz Metodov Razved
Trudy Vsesoyuznyi Nauchno-Issledovatel'skii Institut Khlebopekarnoi Promyshlennosti — Tr Vses Nauchno-Issled Inst Khlebopek Promsti
Trudy Vsesoyuznyi Nauchno-Issledovatel'skii Institut Krakhmaloproduktov — Tr Vses Nauchno Issled Inst Krakhmaloprod
Trudy Vsesoyuznyi Nauchno-Issledovatel'skii Institut Lubyanykh Kul'ture — Tr Vses Nauch-Issled Inst Lub Kul't
Trudy Vsesoyuznyi Nauchno-Issledovatel'skii Institut Pivovarennoi Promyshlennosti — Tr Vses Nauchno Issled Inst Pivovar Promsti
Trudy Vsesoyuznyi Nauchno-Issledovatel'skii Institut po Proizvodstvu Pishchevykh Produktov iz Kartofelya — Tr Vses Nauchno Issled Inst Proizvod Pishch Prod Kartofelya
Trudy Vsesoyuznyi Nauchno-Issledovatel'skii Institut Podzemnoi Gazifikatsii Uglei [*Former USSR*] — Tr Vses Nauchno-Issled Inst Podzemn Gazif Uglei
Trudy Vsesoyuznyi Nauchno-Issledovatel'skii Institut Prirodnykh Gazov [*Former USSR*] — Tr Vses Nauchno-Issled Inst Prir Gazov
Trudy Vsesoyuznyi Nauchno-Issledovatel'skii Institut Produktov Brozheniya [*Former USSR*] — Tr Vses Nauchno-Issled Inst Prod Brozheniya
Trudy Vsesoyuznyi Nauchno-Issledovatel'skii Institut Solvanoi Promyshlennosti — Tr Vses Nauchno Issled Inst Solvanoi Promsti
Trudy Vsesoyuznyi Nauchno-Issledovatel'skii Institut Yadernoi Geofiziki i Geokhimii [*Former USSR*] — Tr Vses Nauchno-Issled Inst Yad Geofiz Geokhim
Trudy Vsesoyuznyi Nauchno-Issledovatel'skii Institut Zerna i Produktov Ego Pererabotki — Tr Vses Nauch-Issled Inst Zerna Prod Ego Pererab
Trudy Vsesoyuznyi Nauchno-Issledovatel'skii Institut Zhirov — Tr Vses Nauchno Issled Inst Zhirov
Trudy Vsesoyuznyi Nauchno-Issledovatel'skii Institut Zhivotnovodstva — Tr Vses Nauch-Issled Inst Zhivotnovod
Trudy Vsesoyuznyi Neftegazovyi Nauchno-Issledovatel'skii Institut — Tr Vses Neftegazov Nauchno-Issled Inst
Trudy Vsesoyuznyi Neftyanoi Nauchno-Issledovatel'skii Institut po Tekhnike Bezopasnosti — Tr Vses Neft Nauchno-Issled Inst Tekh Bezop
Trudy Vsesoyuznyi Teplotekhnikii Nauchno-Issledovatel'skii Institut [*Former USSR*] — Tr Vses Teplotekh Nauchno-Issled Inst
Trudy Vsesoyuznyi Zaochnyi Institut Inzhenerov Zheleznodorozhnogo Transporta — Tr Vses Zaochn Inst Inzh Zheleznodorozhn Transp
Trudy Vsesoyuznyi Zaochnyi Institut Pishchevoi Promyshlennosti — Tr Vses Zaochn Inst Pishch Promsti
Trudy Vsesoyuznyj Nauchno-Issledovatel'skij Institut Fiziko-Tekhnicheskikh i Radiotekhnicheskikh Izmerenij — Tr VNII Fiz-Tekh Radiotekh Izmer
Trudy Vsesoyuznyj Nauchno-Issledovatel'skij Institut po Pererabotke Nefti — Tr Vses Nauchno-Issled Inst Pererab Nefti
Trudy Vsesoyuznyj Nauchno-Issledovatel'skij Institut Radiatsionnoj Tekhniki — Tr Vses Nauchno-Issled Inst Radiat Tekh
Trudy Vsesyuznogo Instituta Gel'mintologii — Tr Vses Inst Gel'mintol
Trudy VTI [*Former USSR*] — Tr VTI
Trudy Vtorogo Leningradskogo Meditsinskogo Instituta — Tr Vtorogo Leningr Med Inst
Trudy Vtorogo Moskovskogo Meditsinskogo Instituta — Tr Vtorogo Mosk Med Inst
Trudy Vychislitel'nogo Tsentra Tartuskii Gosudarstvennyi Universitet — Trudy Vychisl Tsentra Tartu Gos Univ
Trudy Vycislitel'nogo Centra Akademija Nauk Gruzinskoi SSR — Trudy Vycisl Centra Akad Nauk Gruzin SSR
Trudy Vycislitel'nogo Centra Tartuskii Gosudarstvennyi Universitet — Trudy Vycisl Centra Tartu Gos Univ
Trudy Vysokogornyj Geofizicheskij Institut — Tr Vysokogorn Geofiz Inst
Trudy Yakutskogo Filiala Akademii Nauk SSSR Seriya Geologicheskaya — Tr Yakutsk Fil Akad Nauk SSSR Ser Geol
Trudy Yakutskogo Filiala Akademiya Nauk SSSR Seriya Fizicheskaya — Tr Yakutsk Fil Akad Nauk SSSR Ser Fiz
Trudy Yakutskogo Nauchno-Issledovatel'skii Instituta Tuberkuleza — Tr Yakutsk Nauchno-Issled Inst Tuberk
Trudy Yakutskogo Nauchno-Issledovatel'skogo Instituta Sel'skogo Khozyaistva — Tr Yakutsk Nauchno-Issled Inst Selsk Khoz
Trudy Yakutskogo Otdeleniya Sibirskogo Nauchno-Issledovatel'skogo Instituta Rybnogo Khozyaistva — Tr Yakutsk Otd Sib Nauchno-Issled Inst Rybn Khoz
Trudy Yaltinskogo Nauchno-Issledovatel'nogo Instituta Fizicheskikh Metodov Lecheniya i Meditsinskoi Klimatologii — Tr Yalt Nauchno-Issled Inst Fiz Metodov Lech Med Klimatol
Trudy Yaroslavskogo Meditsinskogo Instituta — Tr Yarosl Med Inst
Trudy Yaroslavskogo Sel'skokhozyaistvennogo Instituta — Tr Yarosl Skh Inst
Trudy Zakavkazskogo Nauchno-Issledovatel'skogo Gidrometeorologicheskogo Instituta — Tr Zakavk Nauchno-Issled Gidrometeorol Inst
Trudy Zapadno-Sibirskii Filial Akademiya Stroitel'stva i Arkhitektury SSSR — Tr Zapadno Sib Fil Akad Stroit Arkhit SSSR
Trudy Zoologicheskogo Instituta Akademiya Nauk SSSR — Tr Zool Inst Akad Nauk SSSR
Trudy Zoologicheskogo Instituta Akademiya Nauk SSSR (Leningrad) — Trudy Zool Inst (Leningr)
Trugy Vychislitel'nogo Tsentra. Tartuskii Universite — Trudy Vychisl Tsentra Tartu Univ
Trust Bulletin — Trust Bull
Trust Newsletter [*National Trust of Australia*] — Trust Newsl
Trust Newsletter [*National Trust of Australia*] — Trust Nletter
Trustees for Alaska. Newsletter — TRFA
Trusts and Estates — Tr and Est
Trusts and Estates — TRE
Trusts and Estates — Tru Est
Trusts and Estates — Trusts & Es
Trusts and Estates — Trusts & Est
TRW Space Log — TRSLA
Trybuna Literacka — TL
Trybuna Spoldzielcza — Tryb Spold
TS-3 Bibliografija Informacija — TS-3 Bibliograf Informacija
TS-3 Referativnyi Sbornik — TS-3 Referativnyi Sb
Tschermaks Mineralogische und Petrographische Mitteilungen — Mineral Petrogr Mitt
Tschermaks Mineralogische und Petrographische Mitteilungen — MPMTA
Tschermaks Mineralogische und Petrographische Mitteilungen — Tsch Min Pe
Tschermaks Mineralogische und Petrographische Mitteilungen — Tschermaks Mineral Petrogr Mitt
Tschermaks Mineralogische und Petrographische Mitteilungen — Tschermaks Mineralog u Petrog Mitt
Tselliuloza, Bumaga, i Karton [*Former USSR*] — Tselliul Bum Karton
Tsementnye Rastvory dlya Krepleniya Glubokikh Skvazhin — Tsem Rastvory Krepleniya Glubokikh Skvazhin
Tsentral'nyi Nauchno-Issledovatel'skii Dizel'nyi Institut Trudy — Tsentr Nauchno Issled Dizel'n Inst Tr

Tsentral'nyi Nauchno-Issledovatel'skii Institut Bumagi Sbornik Trudov — Tsentr Nauchno-Issled Inst Bum Sbor Tr
Tsentral'nyi Nauchno-Issledovatel'skii Institut Olovyannoi Promyshlennosti Nauchnye Trudy — Tsentr Nauchno-Issled Inst Olovyannoi Promsti Nauchny Tr
Tsentral'nyi Nauchno-Issledovatel'skii Institut Tekhnologii i Mashinostroeniya Sbornik — Tsentr Nauchno-Issled Inst Tekhnol Mashinostr Sb
Tsentral'nyi Referativnyi Meditsinskii Zhurnal. Seriya A. Biologiya, Teoreticheskie Problemy Meditsiny — Tsentr Ref Med Zh Ser A
Tsentral'nyi Referativnyi Meditsinskii Zhurnal. Seriya B. Vnutrennye Bolezni — Tsentr Ref Med Zh Ser B
Tsentral'nyi Referativnyi Meditsinskii Zhurnal. Seriya G. Mikrobiologiya, Gigiena, i Sanitariya — Tsentr Ref Med Zh Ser G
Tsentral'nyi Referativnyi Meditsinskii Zhurnal. Seriya V. Khirurgiya — Tsentr Ref Med Zh Ser V
Tserkovnye Vedomosti — TsV
TSF [*Theological Students Fellowship*] **Bulletin** — TSF Bul
Tsing Hua Journal of Chinese Studies — THJCS
Tsirkulyar Shemakhinskoi Astrofizicheskoi Observatorii [*Azerbaidzhan SSR*] — Tsirk Shemakh Astrofiz Obs
Tsitittiksiny e Sovremennoi Meditsine — Tsitittiksiny Sovrem Med
Tsitologiya — TSITA
Tsitologiya — Tsitol
Tsitologiya i Genetika — TGANA
Tsitologiya i Genetika — Tsitol Genet
Tsitologiya i Genetika — Tsitologiya Genet
Tsitologiya i Genetika. Akademiya Nauk Ukrainsoi SSR — Tsitol Genet Akad Nauk Ukr SSR
Tsuchi To Kiso — TSTKA
Tsukuba Journal of Mathematics — Tsukuba J Math
Tsukuba University. Institute of Geoscience. Annual Report — Tsukuba Univ Inst Geosci Annu Rep
Tsukuba-Daigaku Shakaigaku Journal — Tsukuba-Daigaku Shakaigaku J
Tsukumo Earth Science — Tsukumo Earth Sci
Tsurumi University Dental Journal — TSHIDP
Tsurumi University. Dental Journal — Tsurumi Univ Dent J
Tsvetnaya Metallurgiya — Tsvetn Metall
Tsvetnaya Metallurgiya (Ordzhonikidze, USSR) — Tsvetn Metall (Ordzhonikidze, USSR)
Tsvetnaya Metallurgiya-Nauchno-Tekhnicheskii Byulleten — Tsvtn Metall Nauchno Tekh Byull
Tsvetnaya Metallurgiya-Nauchno-Tekhnicheskii Sbornik — Tsvetn Metall Nauchno Tekh Sb
Tsvetnye Metally — Tsvet Metal
Tsvetnye Metally — Tsvetn Met
TTAV [*Technical Teachers Association of Victoria*] **News** — TTAV
TTIS [*Translation and Technical Information Service*] **Publication** — TTIS Publ
TTUV (Technical Teachers Union of Victoria) News — TTUV News
T'u Jang Hsueh Pao — TJHPA
Tuba Journal — TJ
TUBA [Tubists Universal Brotherhood Association] Journal for Euphonium and Tuba — TUBA J
Tubercle — TUBEA
Tubercle and Lung Disease — Tuber Lung Dis
Tuberculology and Thoracic Diseases — Tuberculol Thorac Dis
Tuberculosis and Respiratory Diseases — Tuberc Respir Dis
Tuberculosis Research — KKKEA6
Tuberculosis Research — Tuberc Res
Tuberkulose Forschungsinstitut Borstel. Jahresbericht — Tuberk Forschungsinst Borstel Jahresber
Tuberkulose und Ihre Grenzgebiete in Einzeldarstellungen — Tuberk Grenzgeb Einzeldarst
Tuberkulose und Ihre Grenzgebiete in Einzeldarstellungen — Tuberk Ihre Grenzgeb Einzeldarst
Tubular Structures — Tubular Struct
Tudomany es Mezogazdasag — Tud Mezogazd
Tudomanyos Ertesito-Agrartudomanyi Egyetem Godollo — Tud Ert Agrartud Egy Godollo
Tudomanyos es Muszaki Tajekoztatas — TMT
Tudomanyos es Muszaki Tajekoztatas — Tud & Musz Tajek
Tudomanyos es Muszaki Tajekoztatas — Tudom Musz Tajek
Tudomanyszervezesi Tajekoztato — Tud-Szerv Tajekoz
Tudomanytar. Ertekezerek — Tudomanytar Ertek
Tudumanyos Ertesito-Agrartudomanyi Egyetem Godollo (Hungary) — Tud Ert Agrartud Egy Godollo (Hung)
Tuebingen Studien zur Deutschen Literatur — TSDL
Tuebinger Aegyptologische Beitraege — TAeB
Tuebinger Atlas der Vorderorients — TAVO
Tuebinger Germanistische Arbeiten — TGA
Tuebinger Theologische Quartalschrift — ThQ
Tuebinger Theologische Quartalschrift — TTQ
Tuebinger Theologische Quartalschrift (Stuttgart) — TTQS
Tuerk Arkeoloji Dergisi — Tuerk AD
Tuerk Arkeoloji Dergisi — Tuerk Ark Derg
Tuerk Etnografya Dergisi — TED
Tuerk Etnografya Dergisi — Tuerk Et Derg
Tuerk Tarih Arkeologya ve Etnografya Dergisi — Ark Derg
Tuerk Tarih Arkeologya ve Etnografya Dergisi — TT
Tuerk Tarih Arkeologya ve Etnografya Dergisi — Tuerk Ark Dergisi
Tuerk Tarih Kurumu Yalinlarinin — TTK
Tuerkische Zeitschrift fuer Hygiene und Experimentelle Biologie — Tuerk Z Hyg Exp Biol
Tuermer — T
TUeV [*Technischer Ueberwachungs-Verein*] **Mitteilungen fuer die Mitglieder. Technischer Ueberwachungs-Verein Bayern** [*German Federal Republic*] — TUeV Mitt Mitglieder Tech Ueberwach-Ver Bayern
Tufts Folia Medica — Tufts Folia Med
Tufts College Studies — Tufts Coll Studies
Tufts College Studies. Scientific Series — Tufts Coll Stud Sci Ser
Tufts Dental Outlook — Tufts Dent Outlook
Tufts Health Science Review — THSRB
Tufts Health Science Review — Tufts Health Sci Rev
Tufts University Diet and Nutrition Letter — Tufts Univ Diet Nutr Lett
Tuinderij. Vakblad voor de Intensieve Groenteteelt — TUI
Tukisiviksat — TKST
Tulane Law Review — TLR
Tulane Law Review — Tu L
Tulane Law Review — Tu LR
Tulane Law Review — Tul L Rev
Tulane Law Review — Tul LR
Tulane Law Review — Tulane L Rev
Tulane Law Review — Tulane Law R
Tulane Mineral and Tidelands Law Institute — Tul Tidelands Inst
Tulane Studies in English — TSE
Tulane Studies in English — Tulane St
Tulane Studies in English — Tulane Stud Eng
Tulane Studies in Geology — Tulane Stud Geol
Tulane Studies in Geology and Paleontology — Tulane Stud Geol Paleontol
Tulane Studies in Philosophy — TSP
Tulane Studies in Philosophy — Tulane Stud Phil
Tulane Studies in Romance Languages and Literature — TSRLL
Tulane Studies in Zoology — Tulane Stud Zool
Tulane Studies in Zoology and Botany — Tulane Stud Zool Bot
Tulane Tax Institute — TTI
Tulane Tax Institute — Tul Tax Inst
Tulane University. Bulletin — TUB
Tulane University. Studies in English — Tulane U Stud Eng
Tulsa Business Chronicle — Tulsa Bs C
Tulsa Geological Society. Digest — TGSDA
Tulsa Geological Society. Digest — Tulsa Geol Soc Dig
Tulsa Geological Society. Digest — Tulsa Geol Soc Digest
Tulsa Law Journal — Ts LJ
Tulsa Law Journal — Tulsa L J
Tulsa Medicine — Tulsa Med
Tulsa Studies in Women's Literature — PTWL
Tulsa Studies in Women's Literature — TSWL
Tulsa World — TULS
Tul'skii Gornyi Institut Nauchnye Trudy — Tul Gorn Inst Nauchn Tr
Tul'skii Gosudarstvennyi Pedagogiceskii Institut Imeni L. N. Tolstogo Ucenye Zapiski Matematiceskih Kafedr — Tul Gos Ped Inst Ucen Zap Mat Kaf
Tul'skii Gosudarstvennyi Pedagogicheskii Institut Uchenye Zapiski Fiziko-Tekhnicheskie Nauki — Tul Gos Pedagog Inst Uch Zap Fiz Tekh Nauk
Tumor Diagnostik — Tumor Diagn
Tumor Diagnostik und Therapie — Tumor Diagn Ther
Tumor Research — Tumor Res
Tumor Research — TUREA
Tumour Biology — Tumour Biol
Tundra Drums — TD
Tundra Times — TU
Tuners' Journal — Tuners JL
Tung-Hai Hsueh-Pao [*Tunghai Journal*] — THHP
Tunghai Journal — Tunghai J
Tungsram Technische Mitteilungen — TTMTA
Tungsram Technische Mitteilungen — Tungsram Tech Mitt
Tungsten and Other Advanced Metals for ULSI (Ultra Large Scale Integration) Applications in 1990. Proceedings. Workshop — Tungsten Other Adv Met ULSI Appl 1990 Proc Workshop
Tunisie Agricole — Tunis Agric
Tunisie Agricole — Tunisie Agr
Tunisie Agricole. Revue Mensuelle Illustree — TUAGAT
Tunisie Agricole. Revue Mensuelle Illustree — Tunisie Agric Rev Mens Illus
Tunisie Economique — LTE
Tunisie Economique — Tunisie Econ
Tunisie Medicale — TUMEA
Tunisie Medicale — Tunis Med
Tunneling Technology Newsletter [*United States*] — Tunn Technol Newsl
Tunneling Technology Newsletter — Tunnlg Technol Newsl
Tunneling Technology Newsletter — TUTNB
Tunnels and Tunnelling — Tunn Tunn
Tunnels and Tunnelling — Tunn Tunnlg
Tunnels and Tunnelling — Tunnels Tunnell
Tunnels and Tunnelling — TUTUB
Tunnels et Ouvrages Souterrains — TNOSA
Tunnels et Ouvrages Souterrains — Tunnels Ouvrages Souterr
Turbine Intelligence — TI
Turbomachinery International — Gas Turb
Turbomachinery International — Turbomach Int
Turbomachinery International — Turbomachinery Int
Turbomachinery International. Handbook — Gas Turb H
Turbulence Measurements in Liquids. Proceedings of Symposium — Turbul Meas Liq Proc Symp
Turcica. Revue d'Etudes Turques — Turc
Turf Bulletin — Turf Bull
Turf Culture — Turf Cult
Turin — T
Turing Institute Press Knowledge Engineering Tutorial Series — Turing Inst Press Knowledge Engrg Tutor Ser
Turistasag es Alpinismus — Turist Alpinism
Turistforeningen for Danmark. Aarbog — D Tur Aa
Turk Arkeoloji Dergisi [*Ankara*] — TAD
Turk Arkeoloji Dergisi — Turk AD

Turk Arkeoloji Dergisi — Turk Ark Derg
Turk Biologi Dergisi — Turk Biol Derg
Turk Botanik Dergisi — Turk Bot Derg
Turk Cerrahi Cemiyeti Mecmuasi — Turk Cerrahi Cemiy Mecm
Turk Fizik Dernegi Bulteni — Turk Fiz Dernegi Bul
Turk Hemsireler Dergisi — Turk Hemsire Derg
Turk Hifzissihha ve Tecrubi Biologi Mecmuasi — Turk Hifzissihha Tecr Biol Mecm
Turk Hijiyen ve Deneysel Biyoloji Dergisi — Turk Hij Deney Biyol Derg
Turk Hijiyen ve Deneysel Biyoloji Dergisi — Turk Hij Deneysel Biyol Derg
Turk Hijiyen ve Tecruby Biyoloji Dergisi — Turk Hij Tecr Biyol Derg
Turk Ljiyen ve Tecruebi Biyoloji Dergisi — Turk Ljiyen Tecruebi Biyol Dergisi
Turk Mikrobiyoloji Cemiyeti Dergisi — Turk Mikrobiyol Cemiy Derg
Turk Tarih. Arkeologya ve Etnografya Dergisi — TTAE
Turk Tarih Arkeologya ve Etnografya Dergisi — TTAED
Turk Tarih Arkeologya ve Etnografya Dergisi — Turk TAED
Turk Tarih. Arkeologya ve Etnografya Dergisi — Turk Tar Derg
Turk Tarih Kurumu — TTK
Turk Tarih Kurumu "Belleten" — TTK "Belleten"
Turk Tip Cemiyeti Mecmuasi — TTCMA
Turk Tip Dernegi Dergisi — Turk Tip Dern Derg
Turkey. Mineral Research and Exploration Institute. Bulletin — Turk Miner Res Explor Bull
Turkey Producer — Turkey Prod
Turkish Atomic Energy Commission. Ankara Nuclear Research Center. Technical Journal — Turk AEC Ankara Nucl Res Cent Tech J
Turkish Bulletin of Hygiene and Experimental Biology — Turk Bull Hyg Exp Biol
Turkish Economy — TUR
Turkish Foreign Policy Report — Turk For Pol Rep
Turkish Journal of Biology — Turk J Biol
Turkish Journal of Botany — Turk J Bot
Turkish Journal of Mathematics — Turkish J Math
Turkish Journal of Nuclear Sciences — Turk J Nucl Sci
Turkish Journal of Pediatrics — TJPDA
Turkish Journal of Pediatrics — Turk J Pediatr
Turkish Journal of Physics — Turk J Phys
Turkish Public Administration Annual — Turk Publ Adm Annu
Turkish Shipping — Turk Ship
Turkish Studies Association Bulletin — TSA Bull
Turkiyat Mecmuasi — TM
Turkiye Bitki Koruma Dergisi — Turk Bitki Koruma Derg
Turkiye Genel Kimyagerler Kurumu Dergisi-B — Turk Gen Kim Kurumu Derg B
Turkiye Jeoloji Kurumu Bulteni — Turk Jeol Kurumu Bul
Turkiye Jeomorfologlar Dernegi. Yayini — Turk Jeomorfologlar Dernegi Yayini
Turkiye Tip Akademisi Mecmuasi — Turk Tip Akad Mecm
Turkiye Tip Cemiyeti Mecmuasi [*Turkey*] — Turk Tip Cem Mecm
Turkiye Tip Cemiyeti Mecmuasi — Turk Tip Cemiy Mecm
Turkiye Tip Encumeni Arsivi — Turk Tip Encumeni Ars
Turkmenskaya Iskra [*Former USSR*] — Turkm Iskra
Turkmenskii Gosudarstvennyi Universitet Imeni A. M. Gor'kogo Ucenye Zapiski — Turkmen Gos Univ Ucen Zap
Turnbull Library Record [*New Zealand*] — Turn Rec
Turnbull Library Record — Turnbull Libr Rec
Turon Yliopiston Julkaisuja. Sarja A-II — Turon Yliopiston Julk Sar A-II
Turrialba [*Costa Rica*] — TURRA
Turrialba (Costa Rica) — TAC
Turrialba. Revista Interamericana de Ciencias Agricolas — Turrialba
Turun Historiallisen Yhdistyksen Julkaisuja — Turun Hist Yhd Julk
Turun Yliopiston Julkaisuja — Turun Yliop Julk
Tusaayaksat — TSYK
Tusculum Buecher — Tusc
Tuskegee Normal and Industrial Institute. Experiment Station. Publications — Tuskegee Exp
Tussock Grasslands and Mountain Lands Institute. Annual Report — Tussock Grassl Mt Lands Inst Annu Rep
Tutkimuksia Research Reports — Tutkimuksia Res Rep
Tutkimus ja Tekniikka — Tutkimus Tek
Tutto Musica — Tutto Mus
TV Communications — TV Commun
TV Guide — GTVG
TV Guide — TG
TV Guide — TVG
TVA Bibliography. Tennessee Valley Authority. Technical Library — TVA Bibliogr Tenn Val Auth Tech Libr
Tvaett Industrin — Tvaett Ind
Tvarinnictvo Ukraini — Tvarinnictvo Ukr
Tvarynnytstvo Ukrainy — Tvarynnytstvo Ukr
TVF. Teknisk Vetenskaplig Forskning — TVF Tek Vetensk Forsk
Tvorba — TB
Twayne's English Author Series — TEAS
Twayne's United States Authors Series — TUSAS
Twayne's World Authors Series — TWAS
Twayne's World Leaders Series — TWLS
Tweewieler — NRH
Twentienth Century Literary Criticism — TCLC
Twentieth Century — TC
Twentieth Century — TwC
Twentieth Century — Twen Cen
Twentieth Century — Twen Cent
Twentieth Century — Twent Cent
Twentieth Century — Twentieth Cent
Twentieth Century (Australia) — TCAus
Twentieth Century Fiction — TCF
Twentieth Century Interpretations — TCI
Twentieth Century Literature — TCL
Twentieth Century Literature — Twen Ct Lit
Twentieth Century Literature — Twent Century Lit
Twentieth Century Literature. A Scholarly Critical Journal — GTWC
Twentieth Century Monthly — TCM
Twentieth Century Verse — T
Twentieth Century Views — TCV
Twentieth Century Views — Twent Cen V
TWI (The Welding Institute) Journal — TWI J
Two Complete Science Adventure Books — 2CSAB
Two Complete Science Adventure Books — TSB
Tworczosc — TC
Tworczosc — Tw
Tworzywa Sztuczne'w Medycynie — Tworzywa Sztuczne Med
Two-Year College Mathematics Journal — Two-Year College Math J
Two-Year College Mathematics Journal — Two-Yr Coll Math J
Tyazhelie Mashinostroenie — Tyazh Mashinostr
Tydskrif. Suid-Afrikaanse Veterinere Vereniging — Tydskr S-Afr Vet Ver
Tydskrif. Tandheelkundige Vereniging van Suid-Afrika — Tydskr Tandheelkd Ver S-Afr
Tydskrif van die Suid-Afrikaanse Vereniging vir Spraaken Gehoorheelkunde — Tydskr S-Afr Ver Spraak Gehoorheelkd
Tydskrif vir Christelike Wetenskap — T Christ Wet
Tydskrif vir Dieetkunde en Huishoudkunde [*South Africa*] — Tydskr Dieetkd Huishoudkd
Tydskrif vir Geesteswetenskappe — T Geesteswet
Tydskrif vir Geesteswetenskappe — TsGw
Tydskrif vir Geesteswetenskappe — TvG
Tydskrif vir Hedendaagse Romeins-Hollandse Reg — T Heden Rom-Holl Reg
Tydskrif vir Letterkunde — T Letterkd
Tydskrif vir Letterkunde — TvL
Tydskrif vir Maatskaplike Navorsing — TyM
Tydskrif vir Natuurwetenskappe — Tydskr Natuurwet
Tydskrif vir Natuurwetenskappe — TYNAA
Tydskrif vir Natuurwetenskappe. Suid-Afrikaanse Akademie vir Wetenskap en Kuns — Tydskr Natuurwetenskap
Tydskrif vir Regswetenskap — T Regswet
Tydskrif vir Skoon Lug — Tydskr Skoon Lug
Tydskrif vir Volkskunde en Volkstaal — T Volkskd Volkstaal
Tydskrif vir Volkskunde en Volkstaal — TsVV
Tydskrif vir Wetenskap en Kuns — TsWK
Tydskrif vir Wetenskap en Kuns — Tydskr Wet Kuns
Tygodnik Morski — TM
Tygodnik Powszechny — TPow
Tygodnik Powszechny — TygP
Tyler's Quarterly Historical and Genealogical Magazine — TY
Tyler's Quarterly Historical and Genealogical Magazine — Tyler's
Tyler's Quarterly Historical and Genealogical Magazine — Tyler's Quar
Tyndale Bulletin — TB
Tyndale Bulletin — Tyndale Bul
Tyoevaeen Taloudellinen Tutkimuslaitos Katsaus — Tyoevaeen Taloudell Tutkimus Katsaus
Typewriting News — Typ News
Typographical Journal — Typographical J
Typographische Monatsblaetter — Typogr Monatsbl
Typological Studies in Language — TS Lang
Tyres and Accessories — Tyres & Access
TZ fuer Praktische Metallbearbeitung — TZ Prakt Metallbearb
Tzertovnyia Viedomosti — TV

U

U & S [*Urban & Schwarzenberg*] **Fachbuch** — US Fachbuch
U & S [*Urban & Schwarzenberg*] **Taschenbuecher** — US Tb
U das Technische Umweltmagazin [*Germany*] — U Tech Umweltmag
UAMR [*United Association Manufacturers' Representatives*] **Travel Newsletter** — UAMR Trav Newsl
UAS (Hebbal) Monograph Series — UAS (Hebbal) Monogr Ser
Ubersee Rundschau — URX
UC. Report FM. University of California, Berkeley. Department of Mechanical Engineering — UC Rep FM Univ Calif Berkeley Dep Mech Eng
UCD [*University of California, Davis*] **Law Review** — UCD L Rev
Ucebni Texty Vysokych Skol — UTVS
Ucenye Zapiski Adygejoskogo Naucno-Issledovatel'skogo Instituta Jazyka, Literatury, i Istorii — Uc Zap Adyg Nauc-Issled Inst Jaz Lit Ist
Ucenye Zapiski Astrachanskogo Gosudarstvennogo Pedagogiceskogo Instituta — UZAstPI
Ucenye Zapiski. Azerbajdzanskij Gosudarstvennyj Universitet. Serija Istoriceskih i Filosofskih Nauk — Ucen Zap Azerb Gosud Univ Ser Ist Filos Nauk
Ucenye Zapiski. Azerbajdzanskij Institut Narodnogo Hozjajstva. Serija Ekonomiceskih Nauk — Ucen Zap Azerb Inst Nar Hoz Ser Ekon Nauk
Ucenye Zapiski. Azerbajdzanskij Universitet. Serija Istoriceskih i Filosofskih Nauk — Ucen Zap Azerb Univ Ser Ist Filos Nauk
Ucenye Zapiski Azerbajdzanskogo Gosudarstvennogo Universiteta Imeni S. M. Kirova. Jazyk i Literatura — UZAzU
Ucenye Zapiski. Baskirskij Gosudarstvennyj Universitet. Filolog. Nauki — Uc Zap Bask Univ Filol N
Ucenye Zapiski Baskirskogo Gosudarstvennogo Universiteta. Serija Filologiceskich Nauk — UZBasU
Ucenye Zapiski Biologiceskogo Fakul'teta — Ucen Zap Biol Fak
Ucenye Zapiski Burjatskogo Gosudarstvennogo Pedagogiceskogo Instituta Imeni Dorzi Banzarova. Istoriko-Filologiceskaja Serija. Ulan-Ude — UZBurPI
Ucenye Zapiski Ceceno-Ingusskogo Pedagogiceskogo Instituta. Serija Filolo Giceskaja — UZCIngPI
Ucenye Zapiski Cerepoveckogo Gosudarstvennogo Pedagogiceskogo Instituta — UZCerepPI
Ucenye Zapiski Chabarovskogo Gosudarstvennogo Pedagogiceskogo Instituta — UZChabPI
Ucenye Zapiski Chakasskogo Naucno-Issledovatel'skogo Instituta Jazyka, Literatury, i Istorii — UZChakNII
Ucenye Zapiski Charkovskogo Universiteta Imeni A. M. Gorkogo Trudy Filologiceskogo Fakult'teta — UZCharU
Ucenye Zapiski Dagestanskogo Filiala Akademii Nauk SSSR. Serija Filologiceskaja — UZDag
Ucenye Zapiski Dagestanskogo Gosudarstvennogo Universiteta. Serija Filologiceskaja — UZDagU
Ucenye Zapiski Dal'nevostocnogo Universiteta — Ucen Zap Dal'nevost Univ
Ucenye Zapiski Dal'nevostocnogo Universiteta. Serija Filologiceskaja — UZDalU
Ucenye Zapiski. Dal'nevostocnyj Universitet — Uc Zap Dal'nevost Univ
Ucenye Zapiski. Daugavpilskij Pedagogiceskij Institut — Uc Zap Daug Ped Inst
Ucenye Zapiski Dusanbinskogo Gosudarstvennogo Pedagogiceskogo Instituta — Ucen Zap Dusan Gos Pedag Inst
Ucenye Zapiski Dusanbinskogo Gosudarstvennogo Pedagogiceskogo Instituta Imeni T. G. Seveenko Filologiceskaja Serija — UZDusPI
Ucenye Zapiski Elabuzskogo Gosudarstvennogo Pedagogiceskogo Instituta. Serija Istorii i Filologii — UZEIPI
Ucenye Zapiski Enisejskogo Gosudarstvennogo Pedagogiceskogo Instituta Kafedra Russkogo Jazyka — UZEnPI
Ucenye Zapiski Erevanskogo Gosudarstvennogo Universiteta Estestvennye Nauki — Ucen Zap Erevan Gos Univ Estestv Nauki
Ucenye Zapiski Erevanskogo Gosudarstvennogo Universiteta. Serija Filologiceskich Nauk — UZErevU
Ucenye Zapiski Gor'kovskii Gosudarstvennyi Pedagogicheskii Institut [*Gor'kii*] [*A publication*] — UZGPI
Ucenye Zapiski Gor'kovskii Pedagogicheskii Institut Inostrannykh Yazykov [*Gor'kii*] — UZGIYa
Ucenye Zapiski Gor'kovskogo Gosudarstvennogo Pedagogiceskogo Instituta Imeni M. Gor'kogo. Serija Filologiceskaja — UZGorPI
Ucenye Zapiski Gor'kovskogo Pedagogiceskogo Instituta Inostrannych Jazykov — UZGorPIIJa
Ucenye Zapiski Gor'kovskogo Universiteta Imeni N. I. Lobacevskogo. Serija Istoriko-Filologiceskaja — UZGorU
Ucenye Zapiski Gur'evskogo Gosudarstvennogo Pedagogiceskogo Instituta. Serija Istoriko-Filologiceskaja — UZGurPI
Ucenye Zapiski Hakasskogo Naucno-Issledovatel'skogo Instituta Jazyka, Literatury, i Istorii — Ucen Zap Hakas Nauc-Issled Inst Jaz Lit Ist
Ucenye Zapiski Institut Mezdunarodnych Otnosenij — Uc Zap IMO
Ucenye Zapiski Institut Mezdunarodnych Otnosenij — UZIMO
Ucenye Zapiski Instituta Istorii — UZII
Ucenye Zapiski Instituta Istorii, Jazyka, i Literatury Imeni G. Cadasy. Serija Filologiceskaja. Machackala — UZIMach
Ucenye Zapiski Instituta Slavjanovedenija — Uc Zap Inst Sl Ved
Ucenye Zapiski Instituta Slavjanovedenija — UZISL
Ucenye Zapiski Instituta Vostokovedenija Akademii Nauk Azerbajdzanskoj SSSR — UZIVAz
Ucenye Zapiski Instituta Vostokovedenija Akademija Nauk SSSR — UZIV
Ucenye Zapiski Irkutskii Pedagogicheskii Institut [*Irkutsk*] — UZIPI
Ucenye Zapiski Irkutskogo Gosudarstvennogo Pedagogiceskogo Instituta Inostrannych Jazykov — UZIrkutPI
Ucenye Zapiski Ivanovskogo Universitet — Ucen Zap Ivanov Univ
Ucenye Zapiski Kabardino-Balkarskij Naucno-Issledovatel'skij Institut pri Sovete Ministrov Kbassr — UZKBI
Ucenye Zapiski Kafedr Obscestvennykh Nauk Vuzov Goroda Leningrada Filosofskih — Ucen Zap Kaf Obsc Nauk Vuzov G Leningr Filos
Ucenye Zapiski Kafedr Obscestvennykh Nauk Vuzov Goroda Leningrada Problemy Naucnogo Kommunizma — Ucen Zap Kaf Obsc Nauk Vuzov G Leningr Probl Nauc Kommunizma
Ucenye Zapiski Kafedr Obscestvennykh Nauk Vuzov Leningrada Filosofija — Ucen Zap Kaf Obsc Nauk Leningr Filos
Ucenye Zapiski Kalininskii Gosudarstvennyi Pedagogicheskii Institut [*Kalinin*] — UZKa
Ucenye Zapiski Kalininskogo Pedagogiceskogo Instituta Imeni M. I. Kalinina. Serija Filologiceskaja — UZKalinPI
Ucenye Zapiski Kalmykskogo Naucno-Issledovatel'skogo Instituta Jazyka, Literatury, i Istorii — Ucen Zap Kalmyk Nauc-Issled Inst Jaz Lit Ist
Ucenye Zapiski Kaluzskogo Gosudarstvennogo Pedagogiceskogo Instituta — UZKAIPI
Ucenye Zapiski Karagandinskogo Pedagogiceskogo Instituta Filologiceskie Nauki — UZKaragPI
Ucenye Zapiski Karelo-Finskogo Gosudarstvennogo Universiteta — Ucen Zap Karelo Finsk Gosud Univ
Ucenye Zapiski Karel'skii Pedagogiceskii Institut. Serija Fiziko-Matematiceskih Nauk — Ucen Zap Karel Ped Inst Ser Fiz-Mat Nauk
Ucenye Zapiski Karel'skogo Pedagogiceskogo Instituta — Uc Zap Kar Ped Inst
Ucenye Zapiski Karel'skogo Pedagogiceskogo Instituta — UZKarelPI
Ucenye Zapiski Karsinskogo Gosudarstvennogo Pedagogiceskogo Instituta. Filologiceskaja Serija — UZKarPI
Ucenye Zapiski. Kazachskij Universitet — Uc Zap Kaz Univ
Ucenye Zapiski. Kazanskij Pedagogiceskij Institut — Ucen Zap Kazan Pedag Inst
Ucenye Zapiski Kazanskogo Universiteta Imeni V. I. Ul'janova'lenina — UZKazanU
Ucenye Zapiski Kemerovskogo Gosudarstvennogo Pedagogiceskogo Instituta — UZKemPI
Ucenye Zapiski Kirovabadskogo Pedagogiceskogo Instituta — UZKirovPI
Ucenye Zapiski Kishinevskii Universitet [*Kishinev*] — UZKi
Ucenye Zapiski. Kisinevskij Gosudarstvennyj Universitet — Uc Zap Kis Gos Univ
Ucenye Zapiski Kisinevskogo Gosudarstvennogo Universiteta — UZKisU
Ucenye Zapiski Kokandskogo Pedagogiceskogo Instituta Imeni Mukimi. Serija Filologiceskaja — UZKokPI
Ucenye Zapiski Kolomenskogo Gosudarstvennogo Pedagogiceskogo Instituta Istoriko-Filologiceskij Fakul'tet Kafedry Russkogo Jazyka — UZKolPI
Ucenye Zapiski Komi Gosudarstvennogo Pedagogiceskogo Instituta Kafedra Russkogo Jazyka — UZKomPI
Ucenye Zapiski Krasnodarskii Pedagogicheskii Institut [*Krasnodar*] — UZKr
Ucenye Zapiski. Krasnojarskij Gosudarstvennyj Pedagogiceskij Instituta — Ucen Zap Krasnojarsk Gosud Pedagog Inst
Ucenye Zapiski Kujbysevskogo Gosudarstvennogo Pedagogiceskogo Instituta Imeni V. V. Kujbyseva — UZKGPI
Ucenye Zapiski Kujbysevskogo Gosudarstvennogo Pedagogiceskogo Instituta Imeni V. V. Kujbyseva — UZKujPI
Ucenye Zapiski Latviiskii Gosudarstvennyi Universitet [*Riga*] — UZLa
Ucenye Zapiski. Latvijskogo Universiteta — Ucen Zap Latv Univ
Ucenye Zapiski. Leningradskij Gosudarstvennyj Pedagogiceskij Institut Imeni A. I. Gercena — Uc Zap LGPI
Ucenye Zapiski. Leningradskij Pedagogiceskij Institut — Ucen Zap Lening Pedag Inst
Ucenye Zapiski. Leningradskij Pedagogiceskij Institut Imeni Gercena — Uc Zap Leningr Ped Inst Im
Ucenye Zapiski Leningradskogo Gosudarstvennogo Ordena Lenina Universiteta Imeni A. A. Zdanova — UZLU

Ucenye Zapiski Leningradskogo Pedagogiceskogo Instituta Imeni A. I. Gercena — UZLPedI
Ucenye Zapiski Leningradskogo Pedagogiceskogo Instituta Imeni A. I. Gercena — UZLPI
Ucenye Zapiski Leningradskogo Pedagogiceskogo Instituta Imeni S. M. Kirova — UZLenPI
Ucenye Zapiski Leningradskogo Universiteta. Serija Filologiceskikh Nauk — UZLU-FN
Ucenye Zapiski l'Vovskogo Gosudarstvennogo Universiteta — UZI'VovU
Ucenye Zapiski Magnitorskogo Gosudarstvennogo Pedagogiceskogo Instituta — UZMagPI
Ucenye Zapiski. Molotovskij Gosudarstvennyj Universitet imeni A. M. Gor'kogo — Ucen Zap Molotovsk Gosud Univ Gorkogo
Ucenye Zapiski Mordovskogo Universiteta. Serija Filologiceskich Nauk — UZMorU
Ucenye Zapiski Moskovskii Gosudarstvennyi Institut Kul'tury [*Moscow*] — UZMIK
Ucenye Zapiski Moskovskii Gosudarstvennyi Pedagogicheskii Institut Imeni Lenina [*Moscow*] — UZMPI
Ucenye Zapiski Moskovskii Oblastnoi Pedagogicheskii Institut Imeni N. K. Krupskoi [*Moscow*] — UZMOPI
Ucenye Zapiski. Moskovskij Bibliotecnyj Institut — Uc Zap Mosk Bibl Inst
Ucenye Zapiski Moskovskogo Gosudarstvennogo Pedagogiceskogo Instituta — UZMPedI
Ucenye Zapiski Moskovskogo Gosudarstvennogo Pedagogiceskogo Instituta Imeni Lenina — Uc Zap MGPI
Ucenye Zapiski Moskovskogo Gosudarstvennogo Pedagogiceskogo Instituta Imeni Potemkina — UZMPI
Ucenye Zapiski Moskovskogo Gosudarstvennogo Pedagogiceskogo Instituta Inostrannych Jazykov — UZMPIIJa
Ucenye Zapiski Moskovskogo Oblastnogo Pedagogiceskogo Instituta Imeni N. K. Krupskoj — UZMKrup
Ucenye Zapiski. Moskovskogo Pedagogiceskogo Instituta — Ucen Zap Moskov Pedag Inst
Ucenye Zapiski Moskovskogo Universiteta — UZMU
Ucenye Zapiski Naucno-Issledovatel'skogo Instituta Jazyka, Literatury, Istorii, i Ekonomiki Pri Sovete Ministrov Cuvasskoj ASSR — UZCuvNII
Ucenye Zapiski Novgorodskogo Gosudarstvennogo Pedagogicesko Instituta Kafedra Russkogo Jazyka — UZNovPI
Ucenye Zapiski. Omskskij Pedagogiceskij Institut — Uc Zap Omsk Ped Inst
Ucenye Zapiski Orenburgskogo Gosudarstvennogo Pedagogiceskogo Instituta Imeni V. P. Ckalova — UZOrenPI
Ucenye Zapiski Pedagogiceskogo Instituta Jazykov Imeni M. F. Achundova. Serija Filologiceskaja — UZAzPI
Ucenye Zapiski Penzenskii Pedagogicheskii Institut [*Penza*] — UZPe
Ucenye Zapiski Permskii Universitet [*Perm'*] — UZPer
Ucenye Zapiski Permskij Gosudarstvennyj Universitet — Uc Zap Perm Gos Univ
Ucenye Zapiski Permskogo Gosudarstvennogo Universiteta Imeni A. M. Gor'kogo — UZPerm
Ucenye Zapiski Permskogo Universiteta — Ucen Zap Perm Univ
Ucenye Zapiski Petrozavodskogo Gosudarstvennogo Universiteta. Vypusk 3. Biologiceskie i Sel'skohozjajstvennye Nauki — Ucen Zap Petrozavodsk Gosud Univ Vyp 3 Biol Selskohoz Nauki
Ucenye Zapiski Petrozavodskogo Universiteta Filologiceskie Nauk — UZPU
Ucenye Zapiski Pskovskii Pedagogicheskii Institut [*Pskov*] — UZPs
Ucenye Zapiski Rjazanskogo Gosudarstvennogo Pedagogiceskogo Instituta — UZRjazPI
Ucenye Zapiski Rovenskogo Gosudarstvennogo Pedagogiceskogo Instituta Filologiceskij Fakul'tet — UZRovPI
Ucenye Zapiski Sachtinskogo Gosudarstvennogo Pedagogiceskogo Instituta — UZSachPI
Ucenye Zapiski Saratovskogo Gosudarstvennogo Pedagogiceskogo Instituta — UZSarPedI
Ucenye Zapiski Saratovskogo Gosudarstvennogo Universiteta — UZSGU
Ucenye Zapiski Smolenskogo Gosudarstvennogo Pedagogiceskogo Instituta — UZSmolPI
Ucenye Zapiski. Stavropol'skij Gosudarstvennyj Pedagogiceskij Institut — Uc Zap Stavropol Gos Pedag Inst
Ucenye Zapiski. Stavropol'skij Medicinskij Institut — Uc Zap Stavr Med Inst
Ucenye Zapiski Sterlitamakskogo Gosudarstvennogo Pedagogiceskogo Instituta. Serija Filologiceskaja — UZSterPI
Ucenye Zapiski. Tartuskij Gosudarstvennyj Universitet. Trudy po Politekonomii — Ucen Zap Tartus Gos Univ Trudy Politekon
Ucenye Zapiski Tartuskogo Gosudarstvennogo Universiteta — UZTarU
Ucenye Zapiski Tartusskii Universitet [*Tartu*] — UZTar
Ucenye Zapiski Taskentskogo Pedagogiceskogo Instituta Imeni Nizami — UZTasPINiz
Ucenye Zapiski Taskentskogo Pedagogiceskogo Instituta Inostrannych Jazykov — UZTasPIIn
Ucenye Zapiski Tikhookeanskogo Instituta — UZTI
Ucenye Zapiski Tjumenskogo Pedagogiceskogo Instituta Kafedra Russkogo Jazyka — UZTjPI
Ucenye Zapiski Tomskii Gosudarstvennyj Pedagogiceskij Institut — UZTPI
Ucenye Zapiski Tomskii Universitet [*Tomsk*] — UZToU
Ucenye Zapiski Tomskogo Universiteta Imeni V. V. Kujbyseva — UZTomU
Ucenye Zapiski. Tuvinskij Naucno-Issledovatel'skij Institut Jazyka, Literatury, Istorii — Uc Zap Tuv Nauc Issle Inst Jaz Lit Ist
Ucenye Zapiski Tuvinskogo Naucno-Issledovatel'skogo Instituta Jazyka, Literatury, i Istorii — UZTuvNII
Ucenye Zapiski Ul'janovskogo Gosudarstvennogo Pedagogiceskogo Instituta Imeni I. N. Ul'janova — UZUlPI
Ucenye Zapiski Ural'skogo Pedagogiceskogo i Ucitel'skogo Instituta Imeni Puskina — UZUPI
Ucenye Zapiski Uzbekskogo Respublikanskogo Pedagogiceskogo Instituta Kafedra Russkogo Jazyka i Literatury — UZUzPI
Ucenye Zapiski Vinnickogo Gosudarstvennogo Pedagogiceskogo Instituta Kafedra Russkogo Jazyka i Literatury — UZVinPI
Ucenye Zapiski Vologodskogo Gosudarstvennogo Pedagogiceskogo Instituta — UZVolPI
Ucenye Zapiski. Vyssaja Partijnaja Skola pri CK KPSS — Ucen Zap Vyss Part Skola CK KPSS
Ucenye Zapiskij. Tomskij Pedagogiceskij Institut — Uc Zap Tomsk Ped Inst
Ucenyi Zapiski Central'nogo Aero-Gidrodinamiceskogo Instituta — Ucen Zap CAGI
Ucenyi Zapiski po Statistike Akademija Nauk SSSR Central'nyi Ekonomiko-Matematiceskii Institut — Ucen Zap Statist
Ucenyja Zapiski. Izdavaemyja Imperatorskim Kazanskim Universitetom — Ucen Zap Imp Kazansk Univ
Ucenyje Zapiski Belorusskogo Gosudarstvennogo Universiteta — Ucenyje Zapiski Belorusskogo Gosud Univ
Ucenyje Zapiski Jaroslavskogo Universiteta — Ucenyje Zapiski Jaroslav
Ucenyje Zapiski Leningradskogo Gosudarstvennogo Pedagogiceskogo Instituta — Ucenyje Zapiski Leningrad Pedag Inst
Ucenyje Zapiski Leningradskogo Gosudarstvennogo Universiteta — Ucenyje Zapiski Leningrad
Ucenyje Zapiski Moskovskogo Gosudarstvennogo Pedagogiceskogo Instituta Inostraunych Jazykov — Ucenyje Zapiski Moskov Gosud Pedag Inst
Ucenyje Zapiski Moskovskogo Gosudarstvennogo Universiteta Imeni Lononosova — Ucenyje Zapiski Moskva
Ucenyje Zapiski Tomskogo Gosudarstvennogo Universiteta Imeni Kujbyseva (Tomsk) — Ucenyje Zapiski (Tomsk)
Uchenye Trudy Gor'kovskii Meditsinskii Institut — Uch Tr Gor'k Med Inst
Uchenye Trudy Gorkovskogo Gosudarstvennogo Meditsinskogo Instituta — Uch Tr Gork Gos Med Inst
Uchenye Zapiski Anatomov Gistologov i Embriologov Respublik Srednei Azii i Kazakhstana — Uch Zap Anat Gistol Embriol Resp Sredn Azii Kaz
Uchenye Zapiski Azerbaidzhan-Gosudarstvennogo Universiteta Imeni S. M. Kirova — Uch Zap Azerb Gos Uiv Im S M Kirova
Uchenye Zapiski Azerbaidzhanskii Gosudarstvennyi Institut Usovershenstvovaniya Vrachei — Uch Zap Azerb Gos Inst Usoversh Vrachei
Uchenye Zapiski Azerbaidzhanskii Institut Usovershenstvovaniya Vrachei — Uch Zap Azerb Inst Usoversh Vrachei
Uchenye Zapiski Azerbaidzhanskii Politekhnicheskii Institut — Uch Zap Azerb Politekh Inst
Uchenye Zapiski Azerbaidzhanskogo Gosudarstvennogo Universiteta — Uch Zap Azerb Gos Univ
Uchenye Zapiski Azerbaidzhanskogo Gosudarstvennogo Universiteta Imeni S. M. Kirova — Uch Zap Azerb Gos Univ Im S M Kirova
Uchenye Zapiski Azerbaidzhanskogo Gosudarstvennogo Universiteta Imeni S. M. Kirova. Seriya Khimicheskikh Nauk [*Azerbaidzhan SSR*] — Uch Zap Azerb Gos Univ Ser Khim Nauk
Uchenye Zapiski Azerbaidzhanskogo Gosudarstvennogo Universiteta. Seriya Biologicheskikh Nauk — Uch Zap Azerb Gos Univ Ser Biol Nauk
Uchenye Zapiski Azerbaidzhanskogo Gosudarstvennogo Universiteta. Seriya Biologicheskikh Nauk — Uchen Zap Azerb Gos Univ Ser Biol Nauk
Uchenye Zapiski Azerbaidzhanskogo Gosudarstvennogo Universiteta. Seriya Fiziko-Matematicheskikh Nauk — Uch Zap Azerb Gos Univ Ser Fiz Mat Nauk
Uchenye Zapiski Azerbaidzhanskogo Gosudarstvennogo Universiteta. Seriya Fiziko-Matematicheskikh Nauk — Uchen Zap Azerb Gos Univ Ser Fiz Mat Nauk
Uchenye Zapiski Azerbaidzhanskogo Gosudarstvennogo Universiteta. Seriya Geologo-Geograficheskikh Nauk — Uch Zap Azerb Gos Univ Ser Geol Geogr Nauk
Uchenye Zapiski Azerbaidzhanskogo Meditsinskogo Instituta — Uch Zap Azerb Med Inst
Uchenye Zapiski Azerbaidzhanskogo Meditsinskogo Instituta Klinicheskoi Meditsiny — Uch Zap Azerb Med Inst Klin Med
Uchenye Zapiski Azerbaidzhanskogo Sel'skokhozyaistvennogo Instituta — Uch Zap Azerb Skh Inst
Uchenye Zapiski Azerbaidzhanskogo Sel'skokhozyaistvennogo Instituta. Seriya Agronomii — Uch Zap Azerb Skh Inst Ser Agron
Uchenye Zapiski Azerbaidzhanskogo Sel'skokhozyaistvennogo Instituta. Seriya Veterinarii — Uch Zap Azerb S-Kh Inst Ser Vet
Uchenye Zapiski Azerbaidzhanskogo Universiteta. Seriya Biologicheskoi Nauki — Uch Zap Azerb Univ Ser Biol Nauk
Uchenye Zapiski Azerbajdzhanskij Institut Nefti i Khimii. Seriya 9 — Uch Zap Azerb Inst Nefti Khim Ser 9
Uchenye Zapiski Bashkirskogo Universiteta — Uch Zap Bashk Univ
Uchenye Zapiski Belorusskii Institut Inzhenerov Zheleznodorozhnogo Transporta — Uch Zap Beloruss Inst Inzh Zheleznodorozhn Transp
Uchenye Zapiski Belorusskogo Gosudarstvennogo Universiteta — Uch Zap Beloruss Gos Univ
Uchenye Zapiski Bel'tskii Pedagogicheskii Institut — Uch Zap Bel'tskii Pedagog Inst
Uchenye Zapiski Biologicheskogo Fakul'teta Kirgizskogo Universiteta — Uch Zap Biol Fak Kirg Univ
Uchenye Zapiski Biologicheskogo Fakul'teta Osnovnogo Gosudarstvennogo Pedagogicheskogo Instituta — Uch Zap Biol Fak Osnovn Gos Pedagog Inst
Uchenye Zapiski Birskogo Gosudarstvennogo Pedagogicheskogo Instituta — Uch Zap Birskogo Gos Pedagog Inst
Uchenye Zapiski Brestskii Gosudarstvennyi Pedagogicheskii Institut — Uch Zap Brest Gos Pedagog Inst
Uchenye Zapiski Brestskii Gosudarstvennyi Pedagogicheskii Institut — Uch Zap Brst Gos Pedagog Inst
Uchenye Zapiski Bukharskii Gosudarstvennyi Pedagogicheskii Institut — Uch Zap Bukhar Gos Pedagog Inst
Uchenye Zapiski Buryat-Mongol'skii Pedagogicheskii Institut — Uch Zap Buryat Mong Pedagog Inst
Uchenye Zapiski Buryatskii Gosudarstvennyi Pedagogicheskii Institut — Uch Zap Buryat Gos Pedagog Inst

Uchenye Zapiski Checheno-Ingushskii Gosudarstvennyi Pedagogicheskii Institut — Uch Zap Checheno Ingush Gos Pedagog Inst
Uchenye Zapiski Chelyabinskogo Gosudarstvennogo Pedagogicheskogo Instituta — Uch Zap Chelyab Gos Pedagog Inst
Uchenye Zapiski Chitinskii Gosudarstvennyi Pedagogicheskii Institut — Uch Zap Chit Gos Pedagog Inst
Uchenye Zapiski Chuvashskii Gosudarstvennyi Pedagogicheskii Institut — Uch Zap Chuv Gos Pedagog Inst
Uchenye Zapiski Dagestanskii Gosudarstvennyi Pedagogicheskii Institut — Uch Zap Dagest Gos Pedagog Inst
Uchenye Zapiski Dagestanskogo Gosudarstvennogo Universiteta — Uch Zap Dagest Gos Univ
Uchenye Zapiski Dal'nevostochnogo Universiteta — Uchen Zap Dal'nevost Univ
Uchenye Zapiski Dal'nevostochnyi Gosudarstvennyi Universitet — Uch Zap Dal'nevost Gos Univ
Uchenye Zapiski Dushanbinskii Gosudarstvennyi Pedagogicheskii Institut — Uch Zap Dushanb Gos Pedagog Inst
Uchenye Zapiski Erevanskii Gosudarstvennyi Universitet — Uch Zap Erevan Gos Univ
Uchenye Zapiski Erevanskii Universitet — Uch Zap Erevan Univ
Uchenye Zapiski Erevanskogo Universiteta Estestvennykh Nauk — Uch Zap Erevan Univ Estestv Nauk
Uchenye Zapiski Gomel'skii Gosudarstvennyi Pedagogicheskii Institut — Uch Zap Gomel Gos Pedagog Inst
Uchenye Zapiski Gomel'skogo Gosudarstvennogo Pedagogicheskogo Instituta Imeni V. P. Chkalova — Uch Zap Gomel Gos Pedagog Inst Im V P Chkalova
Uchenye Zapiski Gor'kovskogo Gosudarstvennogo Meditsinskogo Instituta Imeni S. M. Kirova — Uch Zap Gor'k Gos Med Inst Im S M Kirova
Uchenye Zapiski Gor'kovskogo Gosudarstvennogo Pedagogicheskogo Instituta — Uch Zap Gor'k Gos Pedagog Inst
Uchenye Zapiski Gor'kovskogo Gosudarstvennogo Pedagogicheskogo Instituta — Uchen Zap Gor'kov Gos Pedagog Inst
Uchenye Zapiski Gor'kovskogo Gosudarstvennogo Pedagogicheskogo Instituta Imeni A. M. Gor'kogo — Uch Zap Gor'k Gos Pedagog Inst Im A M Gor'kogo
Uchenye Zapiski Gor'kovskogo Gosudarstvennogo Universiteta — Uch Zap Gor'k Gos Univ
Uchenye Zapiski Gor'kovskogo Gosudarstvennogo Universiteta Imeni N. I. Lobachevskogo. Seriya Biologichevskaya — Uchen Zap Gor'kov Gos Univ Ser Biol
Uchenye Zapiski Gor'kovskogo Universiteta — Uch Zap Gor'k Univ
Uchenye Zapiski Gor'kovskogo Universiteta. Seriya Biologiya — Uch Zap Gor'k Univ Ser Biol
Uchenye Zapiski Gor'kovskogo Universiteta. Seriya Biologiya — Uchen Zap Gor'k Univ Ser Biol
Uchenye Zapiski Gorno-Altaiskogo Gosudarstvennogo Pedagogicheskogo Instituta — Uch Zap Gorno-Altai Gos Pedagog Inst
Uchenye Zapiski Gosudarstvennogo Instituta Fizicheskoi Kul'tury Imeni P. F. Lesgafta — Uch Zap Gos Inst Fiz Kul't Im P F Lesgafta
Uchenye Zapiski Gosudarstvennogo Nauchno-Issledovatel'skogo Instituta Glaznykh Boleznei — Uch Zap Gos Nauchno-Issled Inst Glaznykh Bolezn
Uchenye Zapiski Gosudarstvennogo Nauchno-Issledovatel'skogo Instituta Glaznykh Boleznei Imeni Gel'Mgol'Tsa — Uch Zap Gos Nauchno-Issled Inst Glazn Bolezn Im Gel'Mgol'Tsa
Uchenye Zapiski Gosudarstvennogo Pedagogicheskogo Instituta Imeni T. G. Shevchenko — Uch Zap Gos Pedagog Inst
Uchenye Zapiski Gosudarstvennogo Pedagogicheskogo Instituta Imeni T. G. Shevchenko — Uch Zap Gos Pedagog Inst Im T G Shevchenko
Uchenye Zapiski. Gosudarstvennyi Pedagogicheskii Institut. Penza — UZ Penz
Uchenye Zapiski Groznenskogo Gosudarstvennogo Pedagogicheskogo Instituta — Uch Zap Grozn Gos Pedagog Inst
Uchenye Zapiski Irkutskii Gosudarstvennyi Pedagogicheskii Institut — Uch Zap Irkutsk Gos Pedagog Inst
Uchenye Zapiski Irkutskii Institut Narodnogo Khozyaistva — Uch Zap Irkutsk Inst Nar Khoz
Uchenye Zapiski Ivanovskogo Gosudarstvennogo Pedagogicheskogo Instituta — Uch Zap Ivanov Gos Pedagog Inst
Uchenye Zapiski Kabardino-Balkarskii Gosudarstvennyi Universitet — Uch Zap Kabard Balkar Gos Univ
Uchenye Zapiski Kabardino-Balkarskogo Gosudarstvennogo Universiteta — Uchen Zap Kabardino-Balkar Gos Univ
Uchenye Zapiski Kabardino-Balkarskogo Gosudarstvennogo Universiteta — Uchen Zap Kabardino-Balkars Univ
Uchenye Zapiski Kabardino-Balkarskogo Nauchno-Issledovatel'skogo Instituta — Uch Zap Kabard-Balkar Nauchno-Issled Inst
Uchenye Zapiski Kabardinskogo Gosudarstvennogo Pedagogicheskogo Instituta — Uch Zap Kabard Gos Pedagog Inst
Uchenye Zapiski Kaliningradskii Gosudarstvennyi Universitet — Uch Zap Kaliningr Gos Univ
Uchenye Zapiski Kaliningradskogo Gosudarstvennogo Pedagogicheskogo Instituta — Uch Zap Kaliningr Gos Pedagog Inst
Uchenye Zapiski Kalininskii Gosudarstvennyi Pedagogicheskii Institut — Uch Zap Kalinin Gos Pedagog Inst
Uchenye Zapiski Karagandinskii Gosudarstvennyi Meditsinskii Institut — Uch Zap Karagand Gos Med Inst
Uchenye Zapiski Karagandinskogo Meditsinskogo Instituta — Uch Zap Karagand Med Inst
Uchenye Zapiski Karelo-Finskogo Gosudarstvennogo Universiteta Biologicheskie Nauki — Uch Zap Karelo Fin Gos Univ Biol Nauki
Uchenye Zapiski Karelo-Finskogo Gosudarstvennogo Universiteta Fiziko Matematicheskie Nauki — Uch Zap Karelo Fin Gos Univ Fiz Mat Nauki
Uchenye Zapiski Karelo-Finskogo Pedagogicheskogo Instituta — Uch Zap Karelo-Fin Pedagog Inst
Uchenye Zapiski Karel'skogo Pedagogicheskogo Instituta — Uch Zap Karel Pedagog Inst
Uchenye Zapiski Karshinskii Gosudarstvennyi Pedagogicheskii Institut — Uch Zap Karsh Gos Pedagog Inst
Uchenye Zapiski Kazakhskii Gosudarstvennyi Universitet — Uch Zap Kaz Gos Univ
Uchenye Zapiski Kazakhskogo Gosudarstvennogo Universiteta Imeni S. M. Kirova — Uch Zap Kaz Gos Uiv Im S M Kirova
Uchenye Zapiski Kazanskii Gosudarstvennyi Pedagogicheskii Institut — Uch Zap Kazan Gos Pedagog Inst
Uchenye Zapiski Kazanskii Gosudarstvennyi Universitet [*Former USSR*] — Uch Zap Kazan Gos Univ
Uchenye Zapiski Kazanskogo Gosudarstvennogo Universiteta — Uchen Zap Kazan Gos Univ
Uchenye Zapiski Kazanskogo Universiteta — Uch Zap Kazan Univ
Uchenye Zapiski Kazanskogo Veterinarnogo Instituta — Uch Zap Kazan Vet Inst
Uchenye Zapiski Kazanskogo Veterinarnogo Instituta — Uchen Zap Kazan Vet Inst
Uchenye Zapiski Kazanskogo Veterinarnogo Instituta — UZKVA
Uchenye Zapiski Kazanskogo Yuridicheskogo Instituta — Uch Zap Kazan Yuridicheskogo Inst
Uchenye Zapiski Kemerovskogo Gosudarstvennogo Pedagogicheskogo Instituta — Uch Zap Kemer Gos Pedagog Inst
Uchenye Zapiski Khabarovskii Gosudarstvennyi Pedagogicheskii Institut Biologii i Khimicheskikh Nauk — Uch Zap Khabar Gos Pedagog Inst Biol Khim Nauk
Uchenye Zapiski Khabarovskii Gosudarstvennyi Pedagogicheskii Institut. Seriya Biologiya — Uch Zap Khabar Gos Pedagog Inst Ser Biol
Uchenye Zapiski Khabarovskii Gosudarstvennyi Pedagogicheskii Institut. Seriya Estestvennykh Nauk — Uch Zap Khabar Gos Pedagog Inst Ser Estestv Nauk
Uchenye Zapiski Khabarovskogo Gosudarstvennogo Pedagogicheskogo Instituta — Uch Zap Khabar Gos Pedagog Inst
Uchenye Zapiski Khabarovskogo Nauchno-Issledovatel'skogo Instituta Epidemiologii i Mikrobiologii — Uch Zap Khabar Nauchno-Issled Inst Epidemiol Mikrobiol
Uchenye Zapiski Khar'kovskogo Universiteta Trudy Biologicheskogo Fakul'teta po Genetlike i Zoologii — Uch Zap Khar'k Univ Tr Biol Fak Genet Zool
Uchenye Zapiski Khar'kovskogo Universiteta Trudy Nauchno-Issledovatel'skogo Instituta Biologii i Biologicheskogo Fakul'teta — Uch Zap Khark Univ Tr Nauchno Issled Inst Biol Biol Fak
Uchenye Zapiski Kievskogo Nauchno-Issledovatel'skogo Rentgeno Radiologicheskogo i Onkologicheskogo Instituta — Uch Zap Kiev Nauchno-Isled Rentgeno Radiol Onkol Inst
Uchenye Zapiski Kirgizskii Zhenskii Pedagogicheskii Institut — Uch Zap Kirg Zhen Pedagog Inst
Uchenye Zapiski Kirovabadskii Pedagogicheskii Institut — Uch Zap Kirovab Pedagog Inst
Uchenye Zapiski Kirovabadskii Pedagogicheskii Institut — Uchen Zap Kirovabad Ped Inst
Uchenye Zapiski Kirovskogo Gosudarstvennogo Pedagogicheskogo Instituta — Uch Zap Kirov Gos Pedagog Inst
Uchenye Zapiski Kishinevskii Gosudarstvennyi Universitet — Uchen Zap Kishinev Univ
Uchenye Zapiski Kishinevskogo Gosudarstvennogo Universiteta — Uch Zap Kishinev Gos Univ
Uchenye Zapiski Komsomol'skogo-Na-Amure Gosudarstvennogo Pedagogicheskogo Instituta — Uch Zap Komsomol'skogo-Na-Amure Gos Pedagog Inst
Uchenye Zapiski Kostromskoi Gosudarstvennyi Pedagogicheskii Institut — Uch Zap Kostrom Gos Pedagog Inst
Uchenye Zapiski Kuibyshevskogo Gosudarstvennogo Pedagogicheskogo Instituta — Uch Zap Kuibyshev Gos Pedagog Inst
Uchenye Zapiski Kurskii Gosudarstvennyi Pedagogicheskii Institut — Uchen Zap Kursk Pedagog Inst
Uchenye Zapiski Kurskogo Gosudarstvennogo Pedagogicheskogo Instituta — Uch Zap Kursk Gos Pedagog Inst
Uchenye Zapiski Latvijskogo Gosudarstvennogo Universiteta Imeni Petra Stuchki — Uch Zap Latv Gos Univ
Uchenye Zapiski Latvijskogo Gosudarstvennogo Universiteta Imeni Petra Stuchki. Astronomiya — Uch Zap Latv Gos Univ Astron
Uchenye Zapiski Latvijskogo Universiteta — Uch Zap Latv Univ
Uchenye Zapiski Leninabadskogo Gosudarstvennogo Pedagogicheskogo Instituta — Uch Zap Leninab Gos Pedagog Inst
Uchenye Zapiski. Leningradskii Gosudarstvennii Pedagogicheskii Institut imeni A. I. Gercena — UZLGPI
Uchenye Zapiski Leningradskogo Gosudarstvennogo Instituta — Uch Zap Leningr Gos Inst
Uchenye Zapiski Leningradskogo Gosudarstvennogo Ordena Lenina Universita Imeni A. A. Zhdanova. Seriya Matematicheskikh Nauk — Uch Zap Leningr Gos Univ Ser Mat Nauk
Uchenye Zapiski Leningradskogo Gosudarstvennogo Pedagogicheskogo Instituta Gertsena — Uchen Zap Leningr Gos Pedagog Inst Gertsena
Uchenye Zapiski Leningradskogo Gosudarstvennogo Pedagogicheskogo Instituta Imeni A. I. Gertsena — Uch Zap Leningr Gos Pedagog Inst Im A I Gertsena
Uchenye Zapiski Leningradskogo Gosudarstvennogo Universiteta Imeni A. A. Zhdanova. Seriya Biologicheskikh Nauk [*Former USSR*] — Uch Zap Leningr Gos Univ Im A A Zhdanova Ser Biol Nauk
Uchenye Zapiski Leningradskogo Gosudarstvennogo Universiteta Imeni A. A. Zhdanova. Seriya Fizicheskikh Nauk [*Former USSR*] — Uch Zap Leningr Gos Univ Im A A Zhdanova Ser Fiz Nauk
Uchenye Zapiski Leningradskogo Gosudarstvennogo Universiteta Imeni A. A. Zhdanova. Seriya Geograficheskikh Nauk — Uch Zap Leningr Gos Univ Im A A Zhdanova Ser Geogr Nauk

Uchenye Zapiski Leningradskogo Gosudarstvennogo Universiteta Imeni A. A. Zhdanova. Seriya Geologicheskikh Nauk — Uch Zap Leningr Gos Univ Im A A Zhdanova Ser Geol Nauk
Uchenye Zapiski Leningradskogo Gosudarstvennogo Universiteta. Seriya Biologicheskikh Nauk — Uch Zap Leningr Gos Univ Ser Biol Nauk
Uchenye Zapiski Leningradskogo Gosudarstvennogo Universiteta. Seriya Fizicheskikh i Geologicheskikh Nauk — Uch Zap Leningr Gos Univ Ser Fiz Geol Nauk
Uchenye Zapiski Leningradskogo Gosudarstvennogo Universiteta. Seriya Fizicheskikh Nauk — Uch Zap Lenigr Gos Univ Ser Fiz Nauk
Uchenye Zapiski Leningradskogo Gosudarstvennogo Universiteta. Seriya Geograficheskikh Nauk — Uch Zap Leningr Gos Univ Ser Geogr Nauk
Uchenye Zapiski Leningradskogo Gosudarstvennogo Universiteta. Seriya Geologicheskikh Nauk — Uch Zap Leningr Gos Univ Ser Geol Nauk
Uchenye Zapiski Leningradskogo Gosudarstvennogo Universiteta. Seriya Khimicheskikh Nauk — Uch Zap Leningr Gos Univ Ser Khim Nauk
Uchenye Zapiski Leningradskogo Ordena Lenina Gosudarstvennogo Universiteta Imeni A. A. Zhdanova. Seriya Biologicheskikh Nauk — ULCBAJ
Uchenye Zapiski Mariiskii Gosudarstvennyi Pedagogicheskii Institut — Uch Zap Marii Gos Pedagog Inst
Uchenye Zapiski Michurinskii Gosudarstvennyi Pedagogicheskii Institut — Uch Zap Michurinsk Gos Pedagog Inst
Uchenye Zapiski Molotovskogo Gosudarstvennogo Universiteta Imeni A. M. Gor'kogo — Uch Zap Molotov Gos Univ Im A M Gor'kogo
Uchenye Zapiski Mordovskii Gosudarstvennyi Universitet — Uch Zap Mord Gos Univ
Uchenye Zapiski Mordovskogo Universiteta — Uch Zap Mord Univ
Uchenye Zapiski Moskovskii Gosudarstvennyi Pedagogicheskii Institut — Uch Zap Mosk Gos Pedagog Inst
Uchenye Zapiski Moskovskii Gosudarstvennyi Universitet — Uch Zap Mo Gos Univ
Uchenye Zapiski Moskovskii Gosudarstvennyi Universitet [*Former USSR*] — Uch Zap Mosk Gos Univ
Uchenye Zapiski Moskovskii Gosudarstvennyi Zaochnyi Pedagogicheskii Institut — Uch Zap Mosk Gos Zaochn Pedagog Inst
Uchenye Zapiski Moskovskii Nauchno-Issledovatel'skii Institut Gigieny — Uch Zap Mosk Nauchno-Issled Inst Gig
Uchenye Zapiski Moskovskogo Gorodskogo Pedagogicheskogo Instituta — Uch Zap Mosk Gor Pedagog Inst
Uchenye Zapiski Moskovskogo Gosudarstvennogo Pedagogicheskogo Instituta Imeni Lenina — Uch Zap Mosk Gos Pedagog Inst Im Lenina
Uchenye Zapiski Moskovskogo Gosudarstvennogo Universiteta — Uchen Zap Mosk Gos Univ
Uchenye Zapiski Moskovskogo Instituta Tonkoi Khimicheskoi Tekhnologii — Uch Zap Mosk Inst Tonkoi Khim Tekhnol
Uchenye Zapiski Moskovskogo Nauchno-Issledovatel'skogo Instituta po Glaznym Boleznam — Uch Zap Mosk Nauchno-Issled Inst Glaznym Bolezn
Uchenye Zapiski Moskovskogo Oblastnogo Pedagogicheskogo Instituta — Uch Zap Mosk Obl Pedagog Inst
Uchenye Zapiski Muromskii Gosudarstvennyi Pedagogichskii Institut — Uch Zap Murom Gos Pedagog Inst
Uchenye Zapiski Namanganskii Gosudarstvennyi Pedagogicheskii Institut — Uch Zap Namanganskii Gos Pedagog Inst
Uchenye Zapiski Nauchno-Issledovatel'skogo Instituta Geologii Arktiki Regional'naya Geologiya — Uch Zap Nauchno Issled Inst Geol Arktiki Reg Geol
Uchenye Zapiski Nauchno-Issledovatel'skogo Instituta Geologii Arktiki Regional'naya Geologiya — Uch Zap Nauchno-Issled Inst Geol Arkt Reg Geol
Uchenye Zapiski Nauchno-Issledovatel'skogo Instituta po Izucheniyu Lepry — Uch Zap Nauchno-Issled Inst Izuch Lepry
Uchenye Zapiski Novgorodskii Golovnoi Gosudarstvennyi Pedagogicheskii Institut — Uch Zap Novgorod Golovn Gos Pedagog Inst
Uchenye Zapiski Novgorodskogo Golovnogo Pedagogicheskogo Instituta — Uchen Zap Novgorod Golovn Pedagog Inst
Uchenye Zapiski Novgorodskogo Gosudarstvennogo Pedagogicheskogo Instituta — Uch Zap Novgorod Gos Pedagog
Uchenye Zapiski Novgorodskogo Gosudarstvennogo Pedagogicheskogo Instituta — Uch Zap Novgorod Gos Pedagog Inst
Uchenye Zapiski Novosibirskii Institut Sovetskoi Kooperativnoi Torgovli — Uch Zap Novosib Inst Sov Koop Torg
Uchenye Zapiski Novozybkovskii Gosudarstvennyi Pedagogicheskii Institut — Uch Zap Novozybkovskii Gos Pedagog Inst
Uchenye Zapiski Omskogo Gosudarstvennogo Pedagogicheskogo Instituta — Uch Zap Omsk Gos Pedagog Inst
Uchenye Zapiski Orenburgskii Gosudarstvennyi Pedagogicheskii Institut — Uch Zap Orenb Gos Pedagog Inst
Uchenye Zapiski Orenburgskogo Otdela Vsesoyuznogo Nauchnogo Obshchestva Anatomov, Gistologov, i Embriologov — Uch Zap Orenb Otd Vses Nauchn Ova Anat Gistol Embriol
Uchenye Zapiski Orlovskogo Gosudarstvennogo Pedagogicheskogo Instituta — Uch Zap Orlov Gos Pedagog Inst
Uchenye Zapiski Oshskii Gosudarstvennyi Pedagogicheskii Institut — Uch Zap Osh Gos Pedagog Inst
Uchenye Zapiski Penzenskogo Gosudarstvennogo Pedagogicheskogo Instituta — Uch Zap Penz Gos Pedagog Inst
Uchenye Zapiski Penzenskogo Sel'skokhozyaistvennogo Instituta — Uch Zap Penz S-Kh Inst
Uchenye Zapiski Permskii Gosudarstvennyi Pedagogicheskii Institut — Uch Zap Perm Gos Pedagog Inst
Uchenye Zapiski Permskij Gosudarstvennyj Universitet Imeni A. M. Gor'kogo — Uch Zap Perm Gos Univ
Uchenye Zapiski Permskogo Gosudarstvennogo Pedagogicheskogo Instituta — Uch Zap Permsk Gos Pedagog Inst
Uchenye Zapiski Permskogo Gosudarstvennogo Pedagogicheskogo Instituta — UPPIAI
Uchenye Zapiski Permskogo Gosudarstvennogo Universiteta — UZ Perm U
Uchenye Zapiski Permskogo Universiteta Imeni A. M. Gor'kogo — Uch Zap Perm Univ Im A M Gor'kogo
Uchenye Zapiski Permskogo Universiteta Imeni A. M. Gor'kogo — Uch Zap Permsk Univ Im A M Gor'korgo
Uchenye Zapiski Permskogo Universiteta Imeni A. M. Gor'kogo — UPGGAZ
Uchenye Zapiski Petropavlovskogo Gosudarstvennogo Instituta — Uch Zap Petropavlovsk Gos Inst
Uchenye Zapiski Petrozavodskogo Gosudarstvennogo Universiteta — Uchen Zap Petrozavodsk Gos Univ
Uchenye Zapiski Petrozavodskogo Gosudarstvennogo Universiteta Fiziko-Matematicheskie Nauki — Uch Zap Petrozavodsk Gos Univ Fiz Mat Nauki
Uchenye Zapiski Petrozavodskogo Instituta — Uch Zap Petrozavodsk Inst
Uchenye Zapiski Petrozavodskogo Universiteta — Uch Zap Petrozavodsk Univ
Uchenye Zapiski Pskovskogo Gosudarstvennogo Pedagogicheskogo Instituta — Uch Zap Pskov Gos Pedagog Inst
Uchenye Zapiski Pskovskogo Pedagogicheskogo Instituta Estestvennykh Nauk — Uch Zap Pskov Pedagog Inst Estestv Nauk
Uchenye Zapiski Pyatigorskii Farmatsevticheskii Institut — Uch Zap Pyatigorsk Farm Inst
Uchenye Zapiski Pyatigorskii Gosudarstvennyi Nauchno-Issledovatel'skii Bal'neologicheskii Institut — Uch Zap Pyatigorsk Gos Nauchno Issled Balneol Inst
Uchenye Zapiski Rizhskii Politekhnicheskii Institut — Uch Zap Rizh Politekh Inst
Uchenye Zapiski Rostovskii-Na-Donu Gosudarstvennyi Pedagogicheskii Institut Fiziko-Matematicheskii Fakul'tet — Uch Zap Rostov Na Donu Gos Pedagog Inst Fiz Mat Fak
Uchenye Zapiski Rostovskogo-Na-Donu Gosudarstvennogo Universiteta — Uch Zap Rostov Na Donu Gos Univ
Uchenye Zapiski Rostovskogo-Na-Donu Universiteta Imeni V. M. Molotova — Uch Zap Rostov Na Donu Univ V M Molotva
Uchenye Zapiski Rostovskogo-Na-Donu Universiteta Imeni V. M. Molotova — Uch Zap Rostov-Na-Donu Univ Im V M Molotova
Uchenye Zapiski Ryazanskogo Gosudarstvennogo Pedagogicheskii Instituta — Uchen Zap Ryazan Gos Pedagog Inst
Uchenye Zapiski Ryazanskogo Gosudarstvennogo Pedagogicheskogo Instituta — Uch Zap Ryazan Gos Pedagog Inst
Uchenye Zapiski Rybinskii Gosudarstvennyi Pedagogicheskii Institut — Uch Zap Rybinsk Gos Pedagog Inst
Uchenye Zapiski Saratovskogo Gosudarstvennogo Pedagogicheskogo Instituta — Uch Zap Sarat Gos Pedagog Inst
Uchenye Zapiski Saratovskogo Gosudarstvennogo Universiteta — Uch Zap Sarat Gos Univ
Uchenye Zapiski Sel'skogo Khozyaistva Dal'nogo Vostoka (Vladivostok) — Uchen Zap Sel Khoz Dal'n Vost (Vladivostok)
Uchenye Zapiski Severo-Osetinskii Gosudarstvennyi Pedagogicheskii Institut — Uch Zap Sev Oset Gos Pedagog Inst
Uchenye Zapiski Severo-Osetinskogo Gosudarstvennogo Pedagogicheskogo Instituta Imeni K. L. Khetagurova — Uch Zap Sev-Oset Gos Pedagog Inst Im K L Khetagurova
Uchenye Zapiski Smolenskogo Gosudarstvennogo Pedagogicheskogo Instituta — Uch Zap Smolensk Gos Pedagog Inst
Uchenye Zapiski Sredneaziatskii Nauchno-Issledovatel'skii Institut Geologii i Mineral'nogo Syr'ya — Uch Zap Sredneaziat Nauchno-Issled Inst Geol Miner Syr'ya
Uchenye Zapiski Stavropol'skogo Gosudarstvennogo Meditsinskogo Instituta — Uch Zap Stavrop Gos Med Inst
Uchenye Zapiski Sverdlovskii Gosudarstvennyi Pedagogicheskii Institut — Uch Zap Sverdl Gos Pedagog Inst
Uchenye Zapiski Tadzhikskogo Gosudarstvennogo Universiteta — Uch Zap Tadzh Gos Univ
Uchenye Zapiski Tartuskogo Gosudarstvennogo Universiteta [*Estonian SSR*] — Uch Zap Tartu Gos Univ
Uchenye Zapiski Tartuskogo Gosudarstvennogo Universiteta — Uchen Zap Tartu Gos Univ
Uchenye Zapiski Tashkentskii Vechernii Pedagogicheskii Institut — Uch Zap Tashk Vech Pedagog Inst
Uchenye Zapiski Tashkentskogo Gosudarstvennogo Pedagogicheskogo Instituta — Uch Zap Tashk Gos Pedagog Inst
Uchenye Zapiski Tiraspol'skii Gosudarstvennyi Pedagogicheskii Institut — Uch Zap Tirasp Gos Pedagog Inst
Uchenye Zapiski Tomskogo Gosudarstvennogo Pedagogicheskogo Instituta — Uch Zap Tomsk Gos Pedagog Inst
Uchenye Zapiski Tomskogo Gosudarstvennogo Universiteta — Uch Zap Tomsk Gos Univ
Uchenye Zapiski TsAGI [*Tsentral'nogo Aero-Gidrodinamicheskogo Instituta*] [*Former USSR*] — Uch Zap TsAGI
Uchenye Zapiski Tsentral'nogo Aero-Gidrodinamicheskogo Instituta (TsAGI) — Uchen Zap TsAGI
Uchenye Zapiski Tsentral'nyi Nauchno-Issledovatel'skii Institut Olovyannoi Promyshlennosti — Uch Zap Tsentr Nauchno-Issled Inst Olovyannoi Promsti
Uchenye Zapiski Tul'skii Gosudarstvennyi Pedagogicheskii Institut Fiziko-Tekhnicheskie Nauki [*Former USSR*] — Uch Zap Tul Gos Pedagog Inst Fiz Tekh Nauki
Uchenye Zapiski Tul'skii Gosudarstvennyi Pedagogicheskii Institut Fiziko-Tekhnicheskie Nauki — UZTFA
Uchenye Zapiski Turkmenskii Gosudarstvennyi Pedagogicheskii Institut Seriya Estestvennykh Nauk — Uch Zap Turkm Gos Pedagog Inst Ser Estest Nauk
Uchenye Zapiski Turkmenskogo Gosudarstvennogo Universiteta — Uch Zap Turkm Gos Univ
Uchenye Zapiski Tyumenskogo Gosudarstvennogo Pedagogicheskogo Instituta — Uch Zap Tyumen Gos Pedagog Inst
Uchenye Zapiski Udmurtskogo Gosudarstvennogo Pedagogicheskogo Instituta — Uch Zap Udmurt Gos Pedagog Inst

Uchenye Zapiski Udmurtskogo Pedagogicheskogo Instituta — Uch Zap Udmurt Pedagog Inst
Uchenye Zapiski Ukrainskii Institut Eksperimental'noi Endokrinologii — Uch Zap Ukr Inst Eksp Endokrinol
Uchenye Zapiski Ukrainskii Nauchno-Issledovatel'skii Institut Gigieny Truda i Profzabolevanii — Uch Zap Ukr Nauchno Issled Inst Gig Tr Profzabol
Uchenye Zapiski Ukrainskii Tsentral'nyi Institut Gigieny Truda i Profzabolevanii — Uch Zap Ukr Tsentr Inst Gig Tr Profzabol
Uchenye Zapiski Ul'yanovskii Pedagogicheskii Institut — Uch Zap Ul'yanovsk Pedagog Inst
Uchenye Zapiski Ural'skogo Gosudarstvennogo Universiteta [*Former USSR*] — Uch Zap Ural Gos Univ
Uchenye Zapiski Ural'skogo Gosudarstvennogo Universiteta Imeni A. M. Gor'kogo — Uch Zap Ural Gos Univ Im A M Gor'kogo
Uchenye Zapiski Ural'skogo Gosudarstvennogo Universiteta Imeni A. M. Gor'kogo — Uchen Zap Ural Univ
Uchenye Zapiski Ussuriiskii Gosudarstvennyi Pedagogicheskii Institut — Uch Zap Ussur Gos Pedagog Inst
Uchenye Zapiski Velikolukskii Gosudarstvennyi Pedagogicheskii Institut — Uch Zap Velikoluk Gos Pedagog Inst
Uchenye Zapiski Vitebskogo Gosudarstvennogo Pedagogicheskogo Instituta Imeni S. M. Kirova — Uch Zap Vitebsk Gos Pedagog Inst Im S M Kirova
Uchenye Zapiski Vitebskogo Veterinarnogo Instituta — Uch Zap Vitebsk Vet Inst
Uchenye Zapiski Vladimirskii Gosudarstvennyi Pedagogicheskii Institut. Seriya Fizika — Uch Zap Vladimir Gos Pedagog Inst Ser Fiz
Uchenye Zapiski Vladimirskii Gosudarstvennyi Pedagogicheskii Institut. Seriya Fiziologiya Rastenii — Uch Zap Vladimir Gos Pedagog Inst Ser Fiziol Rast
Uchenye Zapiski Vladimirskii Gosudarstvennyi Pedagogicheskii Institut. Seriya Khimiya — Uch Zap Vladimir Gos Pedagog Inst Ser Khim
Uchenye Zapiski Vladimirskogo Gosudarstvennogo Pedagogicheskogo Institut. Seriya Botanika — Uch Zap Vladimir Gos Pedagog Inst Ser Bot
Uchenye Zapiski Volgogradskogo Gosudarstvennogo Pedagogicheskogo Instituta — Uch Zap Volgogr Gos Pedagog Inst
Uchenye Zapiski Vologodskii Gosudarstvennyi Pedagogicheskii Institut — Uch Zap Vologod Gos Pedagog Inst
Uchenye Zapiski Vyborskii Gosudarstvennyi Pedagogicheskii Institut — Uch Zap Vybors Gos Pedagog Inst
Uchenye Zapiski Yakutskogo Gosudarstvennogo Universiteta — Uch Zap Yakutsk Gos Univ
Uchenye Zapiski Yakutskogo Instituta — Uch Zap Yakutsk Inst
Uchenye Zapiski Yaroslavskii Gosudarstvennyi Pedagogicheskii Institut — Uch Zap Yarosl Gos Pedagog Inst
Uchenye Zapiski Yaroslavskii Gosudarstvennyi Pedagogicheskii Institut — Uchen Zap Yaroslav Gos Pedagog Inst
Uchenye Zapiski Yaroslavskogo Tekhnologicheskogo Instituta — Uch Zap Yarosl Tekhnol Inst
Uchenyya Zapiskik Imperatorskogo Yur'evskago Universiteta — Uch Zap Imp Yur'ev Univ
Uchet i Finansy v Kolkhozakh i Sovkhozakh — Uchet Finan Kolkhoz Sovkhoz
Ucilisten Pregled — UPr
UCLA [*University of California, Los Angeles*] **Forum in Medical Sciences** — UCLA Forum Med Sci
UCLA [*University of California, Los Angeles*] **Forum in Medical Sciences** — UCMSA
UCLA [*University of California at Los Angeles*] **Historical Journal** — UCLA Hist J
UCLA [*University of California, Los Angeles*] **Law Review** — UCLA Law R
UCLA [*University of California, Los Angeles*] **Law Review** — ULA
UCLA [*University of California, Los Angeles*] **Law Review** — ULRED
UCLA [*University of California at Los Angeles*] **Slavic Studies** — UCLA Slav S
UCLA [*University of California, Los Angeles*] **Symposia on Molecular and Cellular Biology** — UCLA Symp Mol Cell Biol
UCLA (University of California at Los Angeles) Symposia on Molecular and Cellular Biology. New Series — UCLA (Univ Calif Los Ang) Symp Mol Cell Biol New Ser
UCLA (University of California, Los Angeles) Journal of Environmental Law and Policy — UCLA (Univ Cal Los Angeles) J Environmental Law and Policy
UCLA (University of California, Los Angeles) Pacific Basin Law Journal — UCLA (Univ Cal Los Angeles) Pacific Basin Law J
UCLA (University of California, Los Angeles)-Alaska Law Review — UCLA (Univ Cal Los Angeles)-Alaska Law R
UCLA [*University of California at Los Angeles*] **Working Papers in Phonetics** — WPP
Udenrigsministeriets Tidsskrift — Udm T
Udenrigspolitiske Skrifter. Serie 15 — Udenrigspolit Skr Ser 15
Udenrigspolitiske Skrifter. Serie 15 — UDSKD
Udobrenie i Urozhai — Udobr Urozhai
Udobrenie i Urozhai [*Ministerstvo Sel'skogo Khozyaistva SSSR*] — UDURA
Udobrenie i Urozhai. Komitet po Khimaisatsii Narodnogo Khozyaistva SSSR — Udobr Urozhai Kom Khim Nar Khaz SSSR
Udobrenie i Urozhai. Ministerstvo Sel'skogo Khozyaistva SSSR — Udobr Urozhai Minist Sel'sk Khoz SSSR
UE [*University of the East*] **Law Journal** [*Manila*] — UELJ
Ueber Berg und Tal — Ue Bg u Tal
Ueber das Bestehen und Wirken der Naturforschenden Gesellschaft zu Bamberg — Ueber Bestehen Wirken Naturf Ges Bamberg
Uebergaenge. Texte und Studien zu Handlung, Sprache, und Lebenswelt — Uebergaenge Texte Stud Handlung Sprache Lebenswelt
Ueberreuter Taschenbuecher — Ueberr Tb
Uebersee Rundschau — Uebersee Rdsch
Uebersicht der Neuesten Pomologischen Literatur — Uebers Neuesten Pomol Lit
UFA Revue. Union des Federations Cooperatives Agricoles de la Suisse — UFA Rev Union Fed Coop Agric Suisse
UFAW [*Universities Federation for Animal Welfare*] **Courrier** — UFAW Courr
Ufimskii Aviacionnyi Institut Imeni Ordzonikidze Trudy — Ufim Aviacion Inst Trudy
Uganda. Department of Agriculture. Annual Report — Uganda Dep Agric Annu Rep
Uganda. Department of Agriculture. Memoirs of the Research Division. Series II. Vegetation — Uganda Dep Agric Mem Res Div Ser II Veg
Uganda. Forest Department. Technical Note — Uganda For Dep Tech Note
Uganda Journal — UgandaJ
Uganda Journal — UgJ
Uganda Journal — UJ
Uganda National Parks Director's Report — Uganda Natl Parks Dir Rep
Ugarit Forschungen — Ug Fo
Ugarit Forschungen — Ugarit Forsch
Ugarit-Forschungen — UF
Ugarit-Forschungen — Ug F
Ugarit-Forschungen. Internationales Jahrbuch fuer die Altertumskunde Syrien-Palaestinas — Ugarit F
Ugaritic Handbook — Ug Hb
Ugaritic Manual — Ug Man
Ugaritic Manual — UM
Ugaritic Text — UT
Ugaritica [*Paris*] — Ug
Ugeskrift foer Agronomer og Hortonomer — Ugeskr Agron Hortonomer
Ugeskrift foer Jordbrug — Ugeskr Jordbrug
Ugeskrift foer Laeger — Ugeskr Laeg
Ugeskrift foer Laeger — UGLAA
Ugeskrift foer Landmaend — Ugeskr Landm
Ugeskrift foer Landmaend — Ugeskr Landmaend
Ugeskrift for Laeger — Ugeskr Laeger
Ugeskrift for Laeger — Ugeskr Lg
Ugeskrift for Landmaend — U Lm
Ugeskrift for Retsvaesen — U Rtv
UGGI [*Union Geodesique et Geophysique Internationale*] **Chronicle** — UGGI Chron
UGI [*Union Geographique Internationale*] **Bulletin** — UGI Bull
Ugleobogatitel'noe Oborudovanie — Ugleobogat Oborudovanie
Ugol' Ukrainy — Ugol' Ukr
Ugol' Ukrainy — UGOUA
Uhli-Rudy-Geologicky Pruzkum — Uhli Rudy Geol Pruzkum
UICC [*Union Internationale Contre le Cancer*] **Monograph Series** — UICC Monogr Ser
UICC [*Union Internationale Contre le Cancer*] **Technical Report Series** — UICC Tech Rep Ser
UIR [*University-Industry Research Program*]/Research Newsletter — UIR/Res Newsl
UIT [*Ulsan Institute of Technology*] **Report** — UIT Rep
Uitgaben Natuurwetenschappelijke Studichring voor Suriname en de Nederlandse Antillen — Uitgaben Natuurwet Stud Suriname Ned Antillen
Uitgaven der Koninklijke Vlaamse Academie voor Taal- en Letterkunde — UKVA
Uitgaven. Natuurwetenschappelijke Studiekring voor Suriname en Curacao — Uitgaven Natuurw Studiekring Suriname Curacao
Uitgaven Natuurwetenschappelijke Studiekring voor Suriname en de Nederlandse Antillen — Uitg Natuurwet Studiekring Suriname Ned Antillen
Uitgaven. Natuurwetenschappelijke Werkgroep Nederlandse Antillen (Curacao) — Uitg Natuurwet Werkgroep Ned Antillen (Curacao)
Uitgelezen — U
Uitgelezen. Documentatieoverzicht Bibliotheek en Documentatiedienst Ministerie van Sociale Zaken — UGL
Uitleg — Uit
Uitspraken van de Raad voor de Luchtvaart en Scheepvaart — NSU
Uitvaartwezen — MVW
Uitvoerige Verslagen van de Stichting Bosbouwproefstation "De Dorschkamp" — Uitvoer Versl Bosbouwproefsta
Uitvoerige Verslagen van de Stichting Bosbouwproefstation "De Dorschkamp" — Uitvoerige Versl Sticht Bosbouwproefstn De Dorschkamp
Uj Iras — UI
UJCD. Union des Jeunes Chirurgiens-Dentistes — UJCD Union Jeunes Chir Dent
UJCT [*Ulsan Junior College of Technology*] **Report** [*Republic of Korea*] — UJCT Rep
UK CEED [*Centre for Economic and Environmental Development*] **Bulletin** — UK CEED Bull
UK Trade Marks [*Database*] — UKTM
Ukalaha [*Quzinkie High School, Alaska*] — UKLA
Ukraine in Vergangenheit und Gegenwart — Ukraine Vergangenh Gegenw
Ukrainian Herald — UH
Ukrainian Journal of Biochemistry — Ukr J Biochem
Ukrainian Journal of Chemistry — Ukr J Chem
Ukrainian Mathematical Journal [*English Translation*] — UKMJB
Ukrainian Mathematical Journal — Ukr Math J
Ukrainian Mathematical Journal — Ukrainian Math J
Ukrainian Mathematical Journal — UMJ
Ukrainian Physics Journal — UKPJA
Ukrainian Physics Journal — Ukr Phys J
Ukrainian Physics Journal — Ukrain Phys J
Ukrainian Polymer Journal — Ukr Polym J
Ukrainian Quarterly — Ukr Q
Ukrainian Quarterly — Ukr Quart
Ukrainian Quarterly — Ukrain Quart
Ukrainian Quarterly — Ukrainian Q
Ukrainian Quarterly — UQ
Ukrainian Review — Ukrain Rev
Ukrainian Review — UkrR
Ukrainian Review [*London*] — UR
Ukrainica Occidentalia [*Winnipeg*] — UO
Ukrains'ka Literaturna Hazeta — ULH

Ukrains'ka Radians'ka Entsyklopediia — URE
Ukrains'ka Radjans'ka Socialistyczna Respublika — URSR
Ukrainskii Biokhimicheski Zhurnal — Ukr Biokhim
Ukrains'kii Biokhimichnii Zhurnal (1946-1977) [*Ukrainian SSR*] — Ukr Biokhim Zh (1946-1977)
Ukrainskii Fizicheskii Zhurnal — UFIZA
Ukrainskii Fizicheskii Zhurnal — Ukrain Fiz Z
Ukrainskii Fizicheskii Zhurnal (Russian Edition) — Ukr Fiz Zh Russ Ed
Ukrainskii Fizicheskii Zhurnal (Ukrainian Edition) — Ukr Fiz Zh Ukr Ed
Ukrainskii Fizichnii Zhurnal — Ukr Fiz Zh
Ukrainskii Geometriceskii Sbornik — Ukrain Geom Sb
Ukrainskii Geometriceskii Sbornik — Ukrain Geometr Sb
Ukrainskii Khimicheskii Zhurnal — Ukr Khim Zh
Ukrainskii Khimicheskii Zhurnal — UKZHA
Ukrainskii Matematicheskii Zhurnal — Ukrain Mat Z
Ukrainskii Matematicheskii Zhurnal — UMZHA
Ukrainskii Nauchno-Issledovatel'skii Institut Eksperimental'noi Veterinarii Nauchnye Trudy — Ukr Nauchno Issled Inst Eksp Vet Nauchn Tr
Ukrainskii Nauchno-Issledovatel'skii Institut Fiziologii Rastenii Nauchnye Trudy — Ukr Nauchno Issled Inst Fiziol Rast Nauchn Tr
Ukrainskii Nauchno-Issledovatel'skii Institut Pishchevoi Promyshlennosti Sbornik Trudov — Ukr Nauchno Issled Inst Pishch Promsti Sb Tr
Ukrainskii Poligraficheskii Institut Nauchnye Zapiski — Ukr Poligr Inst Nauchn Zap
Ukrains'kii Polimernii Zhurnal — Ukr Polim Zh
Ukrainskij Biokhimicheskij Zhurnal — Ukr Biokhim Zh
Ukrainskij Chimiceskij Zurnal — Ukr Chim Z
Ukrainskij Geometricheskij Sbornik — Ukr Geom Sb
Ukrainskij Matematicheskij Zhurnal — Ukr Mat Zh
Ukrainskyi Istorichnyi Zhurnal — Ukr Ist Zhurnal
Ukrains'kyi Istorychnyi Zhurnal — UkI
Ukrains'kyi Istorychnyi Zhurnal — Ukr Ist Zur
Ukrains'kyj Biochimicnyj Zurnal — Ukr Biochim Z
Ukrains'kyj Botanicnyj Zurnal — Ukr Bot Z
Ukrains'kyj Fizycnyj Zurnal — Ukr Fiz Z
Ukrajins'ka Knyha — UkrK
Ukrajins'ka Mova i Literatura v Skoli — UkrM
Ukrajins'ka Mova i Literatura v Skoli — UMLS
Ukrajins'ka Mova v Skoli — UMS
Ukrajins'ke Literaturoznavstvo — ULz
Ukrajins'ke Movnoznavstvo — Ukr Mov
Ukrajins'kyj Botanicnyj Zurnal/The Ukranian Botanical Review — Ukrajinsk Bot Zurn
Ukrajins'kyj Istoryk — UkrI
Ukrajins'kyj Samostijnyk — UkrS
Ukranian Review (London) — Ukrain Rev London
Ukrayinskyi Biokhimichnyi Zhurnal — UBZHA
Ukrayinskoyi Fizichnij Zhurnal (Ukrainian Edition) (Kiev) — Ukr Fiz Zh (Kiev)
Ukrayins'kyi Botanichnyi Zhurnal — Ukr Bot Zh
UKSTU [*United Kingdom Schmidt Telescope Unit*] **Newsletter** — UKSTU Newsl
UL [*University of Liberia*] **Science Magazine** — UL Sci Mag
Ulam Quarterly — Ulam Quart
Ulbandus Review — UlbR
ULB-VUB [*Universite Libre de Bruxelles - Vrije Universiteit Brussel*] **Inter-University Institute for High Energies. Report** — ULB-VUB Inter-Univ High Energ Rep
Ulisse — Ul
Ul'janovskii Gosudarstvennyi Pedagogiceskii Institut Imeni I. N. Ul'janova. Ucennyi Zapiski — Ul'janovsk Gos Ped Inst Ucen Zap
Ullmanns Encyklopaedie der Technischen Chemie — Ullmanns Enc Tech Chem
Ullstein Deutsche Geschichte — Ullst DG
Ullstein-Buecher. Kriminalromane — Ullst Kr
Ullstein-Kunstgeschichte — Ullst Kunst
Ulm und Oberschwaben. Zeitschrift fuer Geschichte und Kunst — U&O
Ulm-Oberschwaben — UO
Ulrich's Quarterly — Ulrich's Q
Ulrich's Quarterly — Ulrich's Qtly
Ulster Architectural Heritage Society — Ulster Arch Her Soc
Ulster Folklife [*Belfast*] — UF
Ulster Folklife — Ulster Folk
Ulster Journal of Archaeology — UJA
Ulster Journal of Archaeology — Ulster J Arch
Ulster Journal of Archaeology — Ulster Journal Arch
Ulster Journal of Archaeology. Series 3 — Ulster J Archaeol 3 Ser
Ulster Medical Journal — Ulster Med J
Ulster Medical Journal — UMJOA
Ultimate Reality and Meaning — Ult Real
Ultimate Reality and Meaning — Ultim Real Mean
Ultra Low Doses. International Congress on Ultra Low Doses — Ultra Low Doses Int Congr
Ultra Scientist of Physical Sciences — Ultra Sci Phys Sci
Ultramicroscopy — Ultramicrosc
Ultramicroscopy — ULTRD
Ultraschall in der Medizin — Ultrasc Med
Ultraschall in der Medizin — Ultraschall Med
Ultrasonic Imaging — Ultrason Imaging
Ultrasonics — ULTRA
Ultrasonics — Ultrason
Ultrasonics International. Conference Proceedings — Ultrason Int
Ultrasonics Symposium. Proceedings — ULSPD
Ultrasonics Symposium. Proceedings — Ultrason Symp Proc
Ultrasound Annual — Ultrasound Annu
Ultrasound in Medicine and Biology — Ultrasound Med & Biol
Ultrasound in Medicine and Biology — Ultrasound Med Biol
Ultrasound in Obstetrics and Gynecology — Ultrasound Obstet Gynecol
Ultrasound Teaching Cases — Ultrasound Teach Cases
Ultrastructural Pathology — Ultrastruct Pathol
Ul'trastruktura i Plastichnost Neironov — Ultrastrukt Plast Neironov
Ul'yanovskaya Sel'skokhozyaistvennaya Opytnaya Stantsiya Trudy — Ul'yanovsk Skh Opytn Stn Tr
UMBC Economic Review [*Kuala Lumpur*] — UMBC Econ R
UMEA Psychological Reports — UMEA Psychol Rep
UMEA Psychological Reports — UMEA Psychol Reports
Umform Technik — Umform Tech
Umi To Sora — UMSOA
Umjetnost Rijeci — Umjet Rij
Umjetnost Rijeci — UR
Umm el-Qura [*Mecca*] — UQ
UMRI [*University of Michigan Research Institute*] **News** — UMRI Ne
UMR-MEC [*University of Missouri, Rolla - Missouri Energy Council*] **Conference on Energy Resources. Proceedings** — UMR-MEC Conf Energy Resour Proc
Umsatzsteuergesetz — U St G
Umsatzsteuergesetz — Ums St G
Umsatzsteuer-Rundschau — U St Rd
Umschau — Um
Umschau — Umsch
Umschau in Wissenschaft und Technik — Umsch Wiss Tech
Umschau in Wissenschaft und Technik — Umsch Wiss und Tech
Umschau in Wissenschaft und Technik — Umschau
Umschau in Wissenschaft und Technik — UWTCA
Umschau ueber die Fortschritte in Wissenschaft und Technik — Umsch Fortschr Wiss Tech
Umstellungsgesetz — Umst G
UMTRI (University Michigan Transportation Research Institute) Research Review — UMTRI (Univ Mich Transportation Research Inst)
Umwandlungssteuergesetz — Umw St G
Umwelt — UMW
Umwelt — UMWTA
Umwelt. Forschung, Gestaltung, Schutz — UNL
Umwelt. Informationen des Bundesministers des Innern zur Umweltplanung und zum Umweltschutz — Umwelt Inf Bundesminist Innern
Umwelt- und Planungsrecht — Umw Planungsrecht
Umwelt Zeitschrift der Biologischen Station Wilhelminenberg — Umwelt Z Biol Stn Wilhelminenberg
Umwelt Zeitschrift der Biologischen Station Wilhelminenberg — UMWLA
Umweltforschungsdatenbank [*Database*] — UFORDAT
Umweltliteraturdatenbank [*Database*] — ULIDAT
Umweltmagazin. Fachzeitschrift fuer Umwelttechnik in Industrie und Kommune — TUF
Umweltpolitik und Umweltplanung — Umweltpolit Umweltplanung
Umwelt-Report — Umwelt-Rep
Umweltschutz. Gesundheitstechnik — Umweltschutz Gesundheitstech
Umweltschutz - Staedtereinigung — Umweltschutz - Staedtereinig
Umweltschutzdienst. Informationsdienst fuer Umweltfragen — UNE
UN Chronicle — GUNC
UN Monthly Chronicle — UN Mo Chron
UNA [*Utah Nurses Association*] **Communique** — UNA Commun
UNA [*Utah Nurses Association*] **Nursing Journal** — UNA Nurs J
UNA Nursing Journal [*Royal Victorian College of Nursing*] — UNA Nursing J
Unabashed Librarian — Unabashed Libn
Unasylva — UNASA
Unauthorized Practice News — U P News
Unauthorized Practice News — Un Prac News
Unauthorized Practice News — Unauth Prac News
Uncanny Stories — Uc
Uncanny Stories — Unc
Uncanny Tales — UnT
Uncle Remus's Magazine — Uncle Remuss M
Under Dannebrog — U Dbg
Under the Sign of Pisces — USP
Under the Sign of Pisces/Anais Nin and Her Circle — Under Sign
Undercurrents — UNDED
Undercurrents — Undercur
Undergraduate Forum — Undergrad For
Underground Engineering — Underground Eng
Underground Mining Symposia — Underground Min Symp
Underground Space — UNSPD
Underground Water Conference of Australia. Newsletter — Underground Water Conf Aust Newsl
Underground Water Supply Papers (Tasmania) — Undergr Wat Supply Pap (Tasm)
Undersea Biomedical Research — Undersea Biomed Res
Undersea Technology — Undersea Technol
Undersea Technology — UNTEA
Understanding Chemical Reactivity — Underst Chem React
Understanding Chemical Reactivity — Understanding Chem React
Understanding Natural Gas Price Control. Congressional Budget Office Study — CBO Nat Gas
Understanding the Child — Und Child
Underwater Information Bulletin — Underwater Inf Bull
Underwater Journal — Underwater J
Underwater Journal and Information Bulletin — Underw J Inf Bull
Underwater Journal and Information Bulletin — Underwater J & Inf Bull
Underwater Journal and Information Bulletin — Underwater J Inf Bull
Underwater Letter — Under Lttr
Underwater Naturalist — Underwater Nat
Underwater Science and Technology Journal — Underwater Sci Technol J
Underwater Technology Symposium — Underwater Technol Symp
Underwriters Laboratories. Bulletin of Research — Underwrit Lab Bull Res
Underwriters Laboratories. Standards — Underwriters Lab Stand

Und-Oder-Nor und Steuerungstechnik — Und-Oder-Nor & Steuerungstech
Und-Oder-Nor und Steuerungstechnik — Und-Oder-Nor Steuerungstech
UNDP [*United Nations Development Programme*]/FAO Pakistan National Forestry Research and Training Project Report [*Food and Agriculture Organization of the United Nations*] — UNDP/FAO Pakistan Nat For Res Train Proj Rep
Unearth — UNEA
Unemployment Compensation News [*Database*] — UCN
Unemployment Insurance Statistics — Unemployment Ins Statis
Unemployment Unit Bulletin and Briefing — Unempl Unit Bull Briefing
UNESCO [*United Nations Educational, Scientific, and Cultural Organization*] **Bulletin for Libraries** — UNESCO B Li
UNESCO [*United Nations Educational, Scientific, and Cultural Organization*] **Bulletin for Libraries** — UNESCO Bul Lib
UNESCO Bulletin for Libraries — UNESCO Bull For Libraries
UNESCO [*United Nations Educational, Scientific, and Cultural Organization*] **Bulletin for Libraries** — UNESCO Bull Lib
UNESCO [*United Nations Educational, Scientific, and Cultural Organization*] **Bulletin for Libraries** — UNESCO Bull Libr
UNESCO [*United Nations Educational, Scientific, and Cultural Organization*] **Chronicle** — UC
UNESCO Courier — GCUN
UNESCO [United Nations Economic, Social, and Cultural Organization] Courier — UNCo
UNESCO [*United Nations Educational, Scientific, and Cultural Organization*] **Courier** — UNCOA
UNESCO [*United Nations Educational, Scientific, and Cultural Organization*] **Courier** — UNESCO Cour
UNESCO Information Bulletin — UNESCO Inf Bul
UNESCO Information Bulletin for Reading Materials — UNESCO Inf Bul Read Mat
UNESCO [*United Nations Educational, Scientific, and Cultural Organization*] **Journal of Information Science, Librarianship, and Archives Administration** — UBU
UNESCO [*United Nations Educational, Scientific, and Cultural Organization*] **Journal of Information Science, Librarianship, and Archives Administration** — UJISLAA
UNESCO [*United Nations Educational, Scientific, and Cultural Organization*] **Journal of Information Science, Librarianship, and Archives Administration** — UNESCO J Inf Sci Librarianship and Arch Adm
UNESCO Monthly — UNESCO M
UNESCO Philippines — UNESCO Phil
UNESCO Regional Centre for Book Development in Asia — UNESCO Reg Cen Bk Dev in Asia
UNESCO [*United Nations Educational, Scientific, and Cultural Organization*] **Technical Papers in Marine Science** — UNESCO Tech Pap Mar Sci
UNESCO (United Nations Educational, Scientific, and Cultural Organization) Courier — UN (Educ Sci Cult Organ) Cour
Unesco y Cresalc — UC
Unfallchirurg — Unfallchir
Ungar Film Library — Ungar Fil L
Ungarische Forstwissenschaftliche Rundschau — Ung Forstwiss Rundsch
Ungarische Jahrbuecher — U Jb
Ungarische Jahrbuecher — UJ
Ungarische Jahrbuecher — Ung Jb
Ungarische Jahrbuecher — Ung Jhb
Ungarische Revue — Ung Rev
Ungarische Rundschau fuer Historische und Sociale Wissenschaften — Ungarische Rundschau
Ungarische Zeitschrift fuer Berg und Huettenwesen. Bergbau — Ung Z Berg Huettenwes Bergbau
Ungdomsarbejderen — Ung
Unge Paedagoger — UP
Ungerer's Bulletin — Ungerer's Bull
UNICIV [*School of Civil Engineering, University of New South Wales*] **Report** — UNICIV Rep
Unicorn Journal — Unicorn J
Unidia — UNIDA
Unified Management Corp. Database — UMC
Uniform Commercial Code Law Journal — UCC
Uniform Commercial Code Law Journal — UCCLJ
Uniform Commercial Code Law Journal — Unif C Code
Uniform Companies Act — UCA
Uniform Law Conference — Unif L Conf
UNIHI-SEAGRANT-MB. University of Hawaii. Sea Grant College Program — UNIHI SEAGRANT MB Univ Hawaii Sea Grant Coll Program
Union Agriculture — UNAGA
Union Agriculture — Union Agric
Union Apicole — Un Apic
Union Carbide Metals Review — Union Carbide Met Rev
Union Catalog of Medical Monographs and Multimedia [*Database*] — UCOM
Union Catalog of Medical Periodicals [*Database*] — ECMP
Union Catalog of Medical Periodicals — UCMP
Union College Symposium — UnC
Union der Sozialistischen Sowjetrepubliken — U d SSR
Union des Oceanographes de France [*France*] — Union Oceanogr Fr
Union des Societes Francaises d'Histoire Naturelle. Bulletin Trimestriel — Union Soc Fr Hist Nat Bull Trimest
Union Economique Benelux (The Hague) — Benelux (The Hague)
Union Internationale des Sciences Biologiques. Serie A. Generale — Union Int Sci Biol Ser A Gen
Union Internationale des Sciences Biologiques. Serie B. Colloques — Union Int Sci Biol Ser B Colloq
Union Internationale des Sciences Biologiques. Serie C. Publications Diverses — Union Int Sci Biol Ser C Publ Diverses
Union Labor Report [*Database*] — ULR
Union Labor Report. Bureau of National Affairs — Union Lab Rep BNA
Union List of Higher Degree Theses in Australian Libraries [*Database*] — HDEG
Union List of Manuscripts [*Canada (already exists in GUS II database)*] — ULM
Union List of Scientific Serials in Canadian Libraries — ULSSCL
Union List of Serials — ULS
Union List of Serials in the Social Sciences and Humanities Held by Canadian Libraries [*Database*] — ULSSSHCL
Union Medica de Mexico — Union Med Mexico
Union Medica. Sociedad del Mismo Nombre (Santiago) — Union Med Santiago
Union Medicale du Canada — UMCAA
Union Medicale du Canada — Un Med Can
Union Medicale du Canada — Union Med Can
Union Medicale (Paris) — Union Med (Paris)
Union of Burma. Journal of Life Sciences — Union Burma J Life Sci
Union of Burma. Journal of Science and Technology — UBJSA
Union of Burma. Journal of Science and Technology — Union Burma J Sci and Technol
Union of Burma. Journal of Science and Technology — Union Burma J Sci Technol
Union of International Associations. Documents — UIA
Union of South Africa. Department of Commerce and Industries. Division of Fisheries. Investigational Report — Union S Afr Dep Commer Ind Div Fish Invest Rep
Union of Soviet Socialist Republics, Komitet po Delam Izobretenii i Otkrytii, Otkrytiya, Izobreteniya — USSR Kom Delam Izobret Otkrytii Otkrytiya Izobret
Union Pacific Railroad Company — UPR Co
Union Pharmaceutique — Union Pharm
Union Recorder — Union Rec
Union Seminary. Quarterly Review — Union S Q R
Union Seminary. Quarterly Review [*New York*] — UnSemQR
Union Seminary. Quarterly Review — USQR
Union Seminary. Review — USR
Union Tank Car Company. Graver Water Conditioning Division. Technical Reprint — Union Tank Car Co Graver Water Cond Div Tech Repr
Union University. Quarterly — Union Univ Q
Unione Matematica Italiana. Bollettino. A. Serie V [*Bologna*] — Boll Un Mat Ital A V
Unione Matematica Italiana. Bollettino. A. Serie VI — Boll Un Mat Ital A VI
Unione Matematica Italiana. Bollettino. B. Serie VI — Boll Un Mat Ital B VI
Unione Matematica Italiana. Bollettino. Supplemento — Boll Un Mat Ital Suppl
UNISA [*University of South Africa*] **English Studies** — UES
UNISA [*University of South Africa*] **English Studies** — UNISA Engl Stud
UNISA [*University of South Africa*] **Psychologia** — UNISA Psychol
UNISURV G Report. School of Surveying. University of New South Wales — UNISURV G Rep
UNISURV Report. School of Surveying. University of New South Wales — UNISURV Rep
Unit Investment Trusts [*Database*] — UIT
UNITAR [*United Nations Institute for Training and Research*] **Preprints or Proceedings** — UNITAR Prepr or Proc
Unitarian Review — Unita R
Unitarian Universalist Christian — Unit Univ Chr
Unitarian Universalist World — Unitar Univ Wld
Unitarian Universalist World — UUW
Unitas [*Finland*] — UNT
Unitas. Economic Quarterly Review — NFU
Unitas. Revue Internationale — Unitas Int
Uni-Taschenbuecher — Uni-Taschenb
Uni-Taschenbuecher — Uni-TB
United Aborigines' Messenger — Unit Aborig Messenger
United Arab Republic. Geological Survey and Mineral Research Department. Papers — UAR Geol Surv Miner Res Dep Pap
United Arab Republic. Institute of Oceanography and Fisheries. Bulletin — UAR Inst Oceanogr Fish Bull
United Arab Republic. Journal of Animal Production — UARJ Anim Prod
United Arab Republic. Journal of Botany — UARJ Bot
United Arab Republic. Journal of Chemistry — UARJ Chem
United Arab Republic. Journal of Geology — UARJ Geol
United Arab Republic. Journal of Microbiology — UAR J Microbiol
United Arab Republic. Journal of Pharmaceutical Sciences — UARJ Pharm Sci
United Arab Republic. Journal of Physics — UAR J Phys
United Arab Republic. Journal of Soil Science — UARJ Soil Sci
United Arab Republic. Journal of Veterinary Science — UARJ Vet Sci
United Arab Republic. Ministry of Agriculture and Agrarian Reform. Technical Bulletin — UAR Minist Agric Agrar Reform Tech Bull
United Arab Republic. Ministry of Agriculture. Technical Bulletin — UAR Minist Agric Tech Bull
United Arab Republic (Southern Region). Ministry of Agriculture. Hydrobiological Department. Notes and Memoirs — UAR (South Reg) Minist Agric Hydrobiol Dep Notes Mem
United Asia — UA
United Bible Societies. Bulletin [*London*] — UBSB
United Bible Societies. Bulletin — Un Bi Soc Bull
United Business Education Association. Forum — UBEA Forum
United Dental Hospital of Sydney. Institute of Dental Research. Annual Report — United Dent Hosp Syd Inst Dent Res Annu Rep
United Dental Hospital of Sydney. Institute of Dental Research. Annual Report — United Dent Hosp Sydney Inst Dent Res Annu Rep
United Empire — U Empire
United Empire — UE
United Empire — United Emp
United Evangelical Action — Action
United Evangelical Action — UEA
United Fresh Fruit and Vegetable Association. Yearbook — United Fresh Fruit Veg Assoc Yearb

United Kingdom. Atomic Energy Authority. Atomic Weapons Research Establishment. Library Bibliography — UK At Energy Auth At Weapons Res Establ Lib Bibliogr
United Kingdom. Atomic Energy Authority. Atomic Weapons Research Establishment. Report. Series NR — UK At Energy Auth At Weapons Res Establ Rep Ser NR
United Kingdom. Atomic Energy Authority. Atomic Weapons Research Establishment. Report. Series O — UK At Energy Auth At Weapons Res Establ Rep Ser O
United Kingdom. Atomic Energy Authority. Atomic Weapons Research Establishment. Report. Series R — UK At Energy Auth At Weapons Res Establ Rep Ser R
United Kingdom. Atomic Energy Authority. Authority Health and Safety Branch. Memorandum — UK At Energy Auth Auth Health Saf Branch Mem
United Kingdom. Atomic Energy Authority. Authority Health and Safety Branch. Report — UK At Energy Auth Auth Health Saf Branch Rep
United Kingdom. Atomic Energy Authority. Development and Engineering Group. DEG Report — UK At Energy Auth Dev Eng Group DEG Rep
United Kingdom Atomic Energy Authority. Harwell Laboratory. Memorandum — UK At Energy Auth Harwell Lab Mem
United Kingdom Atomic Energy Authority. Harwell Laboratory. Report — UK At Energy Auth Harwell Lab Rep
United Kingdom. Atomic Energy Authority. Health and Safety Code. Authority Code — UK At Energy Auth Health Saf Code Auth Code
United Kingdom. Atomic Energy Authority. Industrial Group. IG Report — UK At Energy Auth Ind Group IG Rep
United Kingdom. Atomic Energy Authority. Production Group. PG Report — UK At Energy Auth Prod Group PG Rep
United Kingdom. Atomic Energy Authority. Radiochemical Centre. Memorandum — UK At Energy Auth Radiochem Cent Mem
United Kingdom. Atomic Energy Authority. Radiochemical Centre. Report — UK At Energy Auth Radiochem Cent Rep
United Kingdom. Atomic Energy Authority. Reactor Group. Report — UK At Energy Auth React Group Rep
United Kingdom. Atomic Energy Authority. Reactor Group. TRG Report — UK At Energy Auth React Group TRG Rep
United Kingdom. Atomic Energy Authority. Research Group. Culham Laboratory. Report — UK At Energy Auth Res Group Culham Lab Rep
United Kingdom. Atomic Energy Authority. Research Group. Culham Laboratory. Translation — UK At Energy Auth Res Group Culham Lab Transl
United Kingdom. Atomic Energy Authority. Safety and Reliability Directorate. SRD Report — UK At Energy Auth Saf Reliab Dir SRD Rep
United Kingdom. Atomic Energy Research Establishment. Analytical Method — UK At Energy Res Establ Anal Method
United Kingdom. Atomic Energy Research Establishment. Bibliography — UK At Energy Res Establ Bibliogr
United Kingdom. Atomic Energy Research Establishment. Health Physics and Medical Division. Research Progress Report — UK At Energy Res Establ Health Phys Med Div Res Prog Rep
United Kingdom. Atomic Energy Research Establishment. Lectures — UK At Energy Res Establ Lect
United Kingdom. Atomic Energy Research Establishment. Memorandum — UK At Energy Res Establ Memo
United Kingdom. Atomic Energy Research Establishment. Report — UK At Energy Res Establ Rep
United Kingdom. Atomic Energy Research Establishment. Translation — UK At Energy Res Establ Transl
United Kingdom. Joint Fire Research Organization. Fire Research Technical Paper — UK Jt Fire Res Organ Fire Res Tech Pap
United Kingdom Mineral Statistics — UK Miner Stat
United Kingdom Press Gazette — UKPG
United Methodist Periodical Index — United Methodist Period Index
United Methodist Today — UMT
United Mine Workers. Journal — UMW J
United Nations "Blue Top" — UNBT
United Nations Bulletin — UN Bul
United Nations Bulletin — UN Bull
United Nations Bulletin — UNB
United Nations Chronicle — UN Chron
United Nations Committee for Coordination of Joint Prospecting. Newsletter — UN CCOP Newslett
United Nations Documents — UN Doc
United Nations Documents. Economic and Social Council — UN Doc E
United Nations Economic Commission for Asia and the Far East. Mineral Resources Development Series — UN Econo Comm Asia Far East Miner Resour Develop Ser
United Nations Economic Commission for Asia and the Far East. Water Resources Series — UN Econ Comm Asia Far East Water Resour Ser
United Nations Economic Commission for Europe. Committee on Agricultural Problems. Working Party on Mechanization of Agriculture AGRI/WP — UN Econ Comm Eur Comm Agr Prob Work Party Mech Agr AGRI/WP
United Nations Educational, Scientific, and Cultural Organization. Natural Resources Research — UNESCO Nat Resour Res
United Nations. FAO (Food and Agriculture Organization) World Soil Resources Reports — UNFAO (Organ) World Soil Resour Rep
United Nations International Meeting on Oilfield Development Techniques — UN Int Mtg Oilfield Dev Techniques
United Nations Review — UN R
United Nations Review — UN Rev
United Nations Secretariat. Bureau of Social Affairs. Series K — UN Sec Bur Soc Aff Ser K
United Nations Symposium on the Development and Use of Geothermal Resources. Abstracts — UN Symp Dev Use Geotherm Resour Abstr
United Nations Symposium on the Development and Use of Geothermal Resources. Proceedings — UN Symp Dev Use Geotherm Resour Proc
United Nations Weekly Bulletin — UN W Bul
United Nations World — UN Wld
United Nations World — UN World
United Nations World — UNW
United Planters' Association of Southern India. Scientific Department. Bulletin — United Plant Assoc South India Sci Dep Bull
United Service Magazine — U Serv M
United Service Magazine — Un Serv M
United Service Magazine — USM
United Service (Philadelphia) — Un Serv (Phila)
United Service Quarterly — United Service Q
United Services Review — United Serv Rev
United States 1 Worksheets — US1
United States Aerospace Industry Profile — US Aeros P
United States. Aerospace Medical Research Laboratory. Technical Report. AMRL-TR — US Aerosp Med Res Lab Tech Rep AMRL-TR
United States. Aerospace Research Laboratories. Reports — US Aerosp Res Lab Rep
United States. Agricultural Research Service. Eastern Regional Research Laboratory. Publication — US Agric Res Serv East Reg Res Lab Publ
United States. Agricultural Research Service. North Central Region. Report — US Agric Res Serv North Cent Reg Rep
United States. Agriculture Marketing Service. AMS Series — US Agric Mark Serv AMS Series
United States. Air Force. Aeronautical Systems. Division Technical Note — US Air Force Aeronaut Syst Div Tech Note
United States. Air Force. Cambridge Research Laboratories. Instrumentation Papers — US Air Force Cambridge Res Lab Instrum Pap
United States. Air Force. Cambridge Research Laboratories. Physical Sciences Research Papers — US Air Force Cambridge Res Lab Phy Sci Res Pap
United States. Air Force. Human Resources Laboratory — USAF AFHRL
United States. Air Force. News Release — USAF NR
United States. Air Force. School of Aerospace Medicine. Technical Report — UAERA
United States. Air Force. Systems Command Air Force Flight Dynamics Laboratory. Technical Report — US Air Force Syst Command Air Force Flight Dyn Lab Tech Rep
United States. Air Force. Systems Command Air Force Materials Laboratory. Technical Report AFML — US Air Force Syst Command Air Force Mater Lab Tech Rep AFML
United States. Air Force. Systems Command Research and Technology Division. Technical Documentary Report. ASD — US Air Force Syst Command Res Technol Div Tech Doc Rep ASD
United States. Air Force. Technical Documentary Report — US Air Force Tech Doc Rep
United States. Air Force. Weapons Laboratory Technical Report AFWL-TR — US Air Force Weapons Lab Tech Rep AFWL-TR
United States. Air Force. Wright Air Development Center. Technical Report — US Air Force WADC Tech Rep
United States and Canadian Aviation Reports — US & C Av R
United States and Canadian Aviation Reports — US & C Avi Rep
United States and Canadian Aviation Reports — US & Can Av
United States. Argonne National Laboratory. Biological and Medical Research Division. Semiannual Report — US Argonne Nat Lab Biol Med Res Div Semiannu Rep
United States. Armed Forces Food and Container Institute. Library Bulletin — US Armed Forces Food Container Inst Libr Bull
United States. Armed Forces Medical Journal — US Armed Forc Med J
United States. Army. Behavior and Systems Research Laboratory. Technical Research Note — US Army Behav Syst Res Lab Tech Res Note
United States. Army. Behavior and Systems Research Laboratory. Technical Research Report — US Army Behav Syst Res Lab Tech Res Rep
United States. Army. Coastal Engineering Research Center. Miscellaneous Paper — US Army Coastal Eng Res Cent Misc Pap
United States. Army Corps of Engineers. Cold Regions Research and Engineering Laboratory [*Hanover, New Hampshire*]. Research Report — US Army Corps Eng Cold Reg Res Eng Lab Res Rep
United States. Army Corps of Engineers. Cold Regions Research and Engineering Laboratory [*Hanover, New Hampshire*]. Technical Report — US Army Corps Eng Cold Reg Res Eng Lab Tech Rep
United States. Army Corps of Engineers. Committee on Tidal Hydraulics. Report — US Army Corps of Engineers Comm Tidal Hydraulics Rept
United States. Army Corps of Engineers. Waterways Experiment Station. Miscellaneous Paper — US Army Corps Engineers Waterways Expt Sta Misc Paper
United States. Army Corps of Engineers. Waterways Experiment Station. Technical Report — US Army Corps Engineers Waterways Expt Sta Tech Rept
United States. Army. Diamond Ordnance Fuze Laboratories. Technical Report — US Army Diamond Ordnance Fuze Lab Tech Rep
United States. Army. Medical Research Laboratory. Report — US Army Med Res Lab Rep
United States. Atomic Energy Commission. Map. Preliminary Map — US Atomic Energy Comm Map Prelim Map
United States. Atomic Energy Commission. Report GJO — USAEC Rep GJO
United States Banker — US Banker
United States Banker — USB
United States. Beach Erosion Board. Bulletin. Technical Memorandum. Technical Report — US Beach Erosion Board Bull Tech Memo Tech Rept
United States. Bureau of Education. Bulletins — USBurEducBul
United States. Bureau of Education. Circulars — USBurEducCirc
United States. Bureau of Labor Statistics. Bulletins — US Bur Labor Bul
United States. Bureau of Labor Statistics. Monthly Labor Review — BLS Review
United States. Bureau of Labor Statistics. Producer Prices and Price Indexes — BLS PPI

United States. Bureau of Mines. Bulletin — US Bur Mines Bull
United States. Bureau of Mines. Information Circular — US Bur Mines Inform Circ
United States. Bureau of Mines. Minerals Yearbook — US Bur Mines Miner Yearb
United States. Bureau of Mines. New Publications Monthly List — US Bur Mines New Publ
United States. Bureau of Mines. Report of Investigations — US Bur Mines Rep Invest
United States. Bureau of Mines. Technical Paper — US Bur Mines Tech Pa
United States. Bureau of Mines. Technical Progress Report — US Bur Mines Tech Prog Rep
United States. Bureau of Sport Fisheries and Wildlife. Investigations in Fish Control — US Bur Sport Fish Wildl Invest Fish Control
United States. Bureau of Sport Fisheries and Wildlife. Resource Publication — US Bur Sport Fish Wildl Resour Publ
United States Catholic — US Cath
United States Catholic Historical Society — Unit Stat Cath Hist Soc
United States Catholic Historical Society. Historical Records — US Cath Hist Soc Hist Rec
United States Catholic Historical Society. Historical Records and Studies — US Cath S
United States Catholic Magazine — US Cath M
United States Cement Consumption Forecast 1981-86. Market and Economic Research — US Cem Frct
United States. Children's Bureau. Publications — US Chil Bur Pub
United States. Clearinghouse for Federal Scientific and Technical Information. AD Reports — USCFSTI AD Rep
United States. Clearinghouse for Federal Scientific and Technical Information. PB Report — USCFSTI PB Rep
United States Court of Appeals Reports (District of Columbia) — US App (DC)
United States. Department of Agriculture. Agricultural Handbook — USDA Agr Handb
United States. Department of Agriculture. Agricultural Research Service. ARS Series — US Dep Agric Agric Res Serv ARS Ser
United States. Department of Agriculture. Agricultural Research Service. Marketing Research Report — US Dep Agric Res Serv Mark Res Rep
United States. Department of Agriculture. Agricultural Research Service. Report — US Dep Agric Agric Res Serv Rep
United States. Department of Agriculture. Agricultural Research Service. Statistical Bulletin — US Dep Agric Agric Res Serv Stat Bull
United States. Department of Agriculture. Agriculture Monograph — US Dep Agric Agric Monogr
United States. Department of Agriculture. Bulletin — US Dep Agric Bull
United States Department of Agriculture Bulletin — USDA Bull
United States Department of Agriculture. Department Circular — USDA Dept Circ
United States Department of Agriculture. Division of Forestry Bulletin — USDA Div Forest Bull
United States. Department of Agriculture. Experiment Stations. Bulletin — US Dept Agric Exp St Bul
United States. Department of Agriculture. Forest Service. Forest Products Laboratory. Report — US Dep Agric For Serv For Prod Lab Rep
United States. Department of Agriculture. Forest Service. Research Note (Pacific Northwest) — US Dep Agric For Serv Res Note (PNW)
United States. Department of Agriculture. Forest Service. Research Paper NC — US Dep Agric For Serv Res Pap NC
United States. Department of Agriculture. Home Economics Research Report — US Dep Agric Home Econ Res Rep
United States. Department of Agriculture. Index-Catalogue of Medical and Veterinary Zoology. Special Publication — US Dep Agric Index-Cat Med Vet Zool Spec Publ
United States. Department of Agriculture. Index-Catalogue of Medical and Veterinary Zoology. Supplement — US Dep Agric Index-Cat Med Vet Zool Suppl
United States. Department of Agriculture. Marketing Research Report — US Dep Agric Mark Res Rep
United States. Department of Agriculture. Northeastern Forest Experiment Station. Station Paper — US Dep Agric Northeast For Exp Stn Stn Pap
United States. Department of Agriculture. PA [*Program Aid*] — USDA PA
United States Department of Agriculture Patents — US Dep Agric Pat
United States. Department of Agriculture. Production Research Report — USDA Prod Res Rep
United States. Department of Agriculture. Publications — US Agric
United States. Department of Agriculture. Soil Conservation Service. Soil Survey — US Dep Agric Soil Conserv Ser Soil Surv
United States. Department of Agriculture. Soil Survey — US Dep Agric Soil Surv
United States. Department of Agriculture. Technical Bulletin. Yearbook — US Dept Agriculture Tech Bull Yearbook
United States. Department of Agriculture. Utilization Research Report — US Dep Agric Util Res Rep
United States Department of Commerce. National Bureau of Standards. Technical Notes — NBS TN
United States. Department of Commerce. News. Office of Economic Affairs — OEA News
United States. Department of Commerce. Office of Technical Services. PB Report — US Dep Commer Off Tech Serv PB Rep
United States Department of Energy [*Database*] — USDOE
United States. Department of Energy. Indirect Liquefaction Contractors' Review Meeting — US Dep Energy Indirect Liquefaction Contract Rev Meet
United States. Department of Health, Education, and Welfare. DHEW [*Department of Health, Education, and Welfare*] **Publication. (FDA)** [*Food and Drug Administration*] — US Dep Health Educ Welfare DHEW Publ (FDA)
United States. Department of Health, Education, and Welfare. Health Services Administration. Publication HSA [*Health Services Administration*] — US Dep Health Educ Welfare Health Serv Adm Publ HSA
United States. Department of State. Bureau of Public Affairs. Background Notes — US Dep State Bur Public Aff Backgr Notes
United States. Department of the Interior. Bureau of Mines. New Publications — US Dep Inter Bur Mines New Publ
United States. Department of the Interior. Bureau of Reclamation. Division of Design [*Denver, Colorado*]. Dams Branch Report — US Bur Reclam Div Des Dams Br Rep
United States. Department of the Interior. Bureau of Reclamation. Engineering Monographs — US Bur Reclam Eng Monogr
United States. Department of the Interior. Bureau of Reclamation. Research Report — US Bur Reclam Res Rep
United States. Department of the Interior. Bureau of Reclamation. Technical Record of Design and Construction. Dams and Powerplants — US Bur Reclam Tech Rec Des Constr
United States. Department of the Interior. Fish and Wildlife Service. Research Report — US Dep Inter Fish Wildl Res Rep
United States. Department of the Interior. Geological Survey. Mineral Investigations Field Studies Map — US Geol Surv Miner Invest Field Stud Map
United States. Department of the Interior. Office of Library Services. Bibliography Series — US Dep Inter Off Libr Serv Bibliogr Ser
United States. Department of the Navy. Naval Civil Engineering Laboratory [*Port Hueneme, California*]. Technical Report — US Nav Civ Eng Lab Tech Rep
United States. Department of the Navy. Naval Ship Engineering Center. Ship Structure Committee. Report — US Nav Ship Eng Cent Ship Struct Com Rep
United States Economic Policies Affecting Industrial Trade — US Econ P
United States Egg and Poultry Magazine — US Egg
United States Embassy. Summary of Selected Japanese Magazines — SSJM
United States. Energy Research and Development Administration. Report CONF — US Energy Res Dev Adm Rep CONF
United States. Environmental Protection Agency. Environmental Monitoring — US EPA Envir Monit
United States. Environmental Protection Agency. Municipal Construction Division. Report — US Environ Prot Agency Munic Constr Div Rep
United States. Environmental Protection Agency. Office of Pesticide Programs. Report — US Environ Prot Agency Off Pestic Programs Rep
United States. Environmental Protection Agency. Office of Radiation Programs. Technical Report — US Environ Prot Agency Off Radiat Programs Tech Rep
United States. Environmental Protection Agency. Office of Research and Development. Report EPA — US Environ Prot Agency Off Res Dev Rep EPA
United States. Environmental Protection Agency. Socioeconomic Environmental Studies — US EPA Socioecon Studies
United States Executive Report — US Exec Rep
United States. Fish and Wildlife Service. Wildlife Research Report — USFWSWRR
United States. Food and Drug Administration. DHEW [*Department of Health, Education, and Welfare*] **Publication** — US Food Drug Adm DHEW Publ
United States. Forest Products Laboratory. Reports — US For Prod Lab Rep
United States. Forest Products Laboratory. Research Note FPL — US For Prod Lab Res Note FPL
United States. Forest Products Laboratory. Technical Notes — US For Prod Lab Tech Notes
United States. Forest Service. Agriculture Handbooks — US Forest Serv Agr Hdb
United States. Forest Service. Central States Forest Experiment Station. Miscellaneous Release — US For Serv Cent States For Exp Stn Misc Release
United States Forest Service. Division of Silvics. Translations — US Forest Serv Div Silvics Transl
United States. Forest Service. Forest Products Laboratory. General Technical Report FPL — US For Serv For Prod Lab Gen Tech Rep FPL
United States. Forest Service. Forest Resource Report — US For Serv For Resour Rep
United States. Forest Service. Northeastern Forest Experiment Station. Annual Report — US For Serv Northeast For Exp Stn Ann Rep
United States. Forest Service. Northeastern Forest Experiment Station. Station Paper — US For Serv Northeast For Exp Stn Stn Pap
United States. Forest Service. Pacific Northwest Forest and Range Experiment Station. Annual Report — US For Serv Pac Northwest For Range Exp Stn Ann Rep
United States. Forest Service. Pacific Northwest Forest and Range Experiment Station. Research Notes — US For Serv Pac Northwest For Range Exp Stn Res Notes
United States. Forest Service. Pacific Northwest Forest and Range Experiment Station. Research Paper — US For Serv Pac Northwest For Range Exp Stn Res Pap
United States. Forest Service. Pacific Northwest Forest and Range Experiment Station. Resource Bulletin — US For Serv Resource Bull Pacif Nthwest For Range Exp Sta
United States. Forest Service. Pacific Southwest Forest and Range Experiment Station. Miscellaneous Paper — US For Serv Pac Southwest For Range Exp Stn Misc Pap
United States. Forest Service. Research Note. Institute of Tropical Forestry — US For Serv Res Note Inst Trop For
United States. Forest Service. Research Note. Intermountain Forest and Range Experiment Station — US For Serv Res Note Intermt For Range Exp Sta
United States. Forest Service. Research Note. North Central Forest Experiment Station — US For Serv Res Note Nth Cent For Exp Sta
United States. Forest Service. Research Note. Northeastern Forest Experiment Station — US For Serv Res Note Ntheast For Exp Sta
United States. Forest Service. Research Note. Northern Forest Experiment Station — US For Serv Res Note Nth For Exp Sta

United States. Forest Service. Research Note. Pacific Northwest Forest and Range Experiment Station — US For Serv Res Note Pacif Nthwest For Range Exp Sta
United States. Forest Service. Research Note. Southern Forest Experiment Station — US For Serv Res Note Sth For Exp Sta
United States. Forest Service. Research Paper. Northern Forest Experiment Station — US For Serv Res Pap Nth For Exp Sta
United States. Forest Service. Research Paper. Rocky Mountain Forest and Range Experiment Station — US For Serv Res Pap Rocky Mt For Range Exp Sta
United States. Forest Service. Research Paper. United States Forest Products Laboratory (Madison, Wisconsin) — US For Serv Res Pap US For Prod Lab (Madison)
United States. Forest Service. Resource Bulletin. Intermountain Forest and Range Experiment Station — US For Serv Resource Bull Intermt For Range Exp Sta
United States. Forest Service. Rocky Mountain Forest and Range Experiment Station. Forest Survey Release — US For Serv Rocky Mount For Range Exp Stn For Sur Release
United States. Forest Service. Rocky Mountain Forest and Range Experiment Station. Research Notes — US For Serv Rocky Mount For Range Exp Stn Res Notes
United States. Forest Service. Rocky Mountain Forest and Range Experiment Station. Station Paper — US For Serv Rocky Mount For Range Exp Stn Stn Pap
United States. Forest Service. Southeastern Forest Experiment Station. Forest Survey Release — US For Serv Southeast For Exp Stn For Surv Release
United States. Forest Service. Southeastern Forest Experiment Station. Research Notes — US For Serv Southeast For Exp Stn Res Notes
United States. Forest Service. Southeastern Forest Experiment Station. Station Paper — US For Serv Southeast For Exp Stn Stn Pap
United States. Forest Service. Southern Forest Experiment Station. Forest Survey Release — US For Serv South For Exp Stn For Surv Release
United States Geographical and Geological Survey of the Rocky Mountain Region (Powell) — US Geog G S Rocky Mtn Reg (Powell)
United States Geological and Geographies Survey of the Territories (Hayden) — US G Geog S Terr (Hayden)
United States. Geological Survey. Annual Report — US Geol Surv Annu Rep
United States. Geological Survey. Annual Report. Professional Paper. Bulletin. Water-Supply Paper Monograph. Mineral Resources Geology Atlas — USGS An Rp PPB W-S P Mon Min Res G Atlas Top Atlas
United States. Geological Survey. Bulletin — US Geol S Bul
United States. Geological Survey. Bulletin — US Geol Surv Bull
United States. Geological Survey. Bulletin — US Geol Survey Bull
United States. Geological Survey. Bulletin — USGSB
United States. Geological Survey. Circular — US Geol Surv Circ
United States. Geological Survey. Circular — USGSC
United States. Geological Survey. Geological Quadrangle Map — US Geol Survey Geol Quad Map
United States. Geological Survey. Geophysical Investigations Map — US Geol Surv Geophys Invest Map
United States. Geological Survey. Miscellaneous Geologic Investigations Map — US Geol Surv Misc Geol Invest Map
United States. Geological Survey. Miscellaneous Geologic Investigations Map — US Geol Survey Misc Geol Inv Map
United States Geological Survey of the Territories — USGS Terr
United States. Geological Survey. Oil and Gas Investigations Map — US Geol Survey Oil and Gas Inv Map
United States. Geological Survey. Professional Paper — US Geol S Professional Pa
United States. Geological Survey. Professional Paper — US Geol Surv Prof Pap
United States. Geological Survey. Professional Paper — USGSPP
United States. Geological Survey. Trace Elements Memorandum Report — US Geol Surv Trace Elem Memo Rep
United States. Geological Survey. Water-Supply Paper — US Geol Survey Water-Supply Paper
United States. Government Printing Office. Monthly Catalog of United States Government Publications — MC
United States Government Research and Development Reports — US Govt Res Develop Rept
United States Government Research and Development Reports — US Res Developm Rep
United States Government Research Report — US Govt Res Rept
United States Gymnastic Federation. Gymnastic News — US Gym Fed Gym News
United States Industrial Outlook — US Ind Outlk
United States Industrial Outlook — US Outlook
United States Institute for Textile Research. Bulletin — US Inst Text Res Bull
United States Investor — USI
United States. Joint Publication Research Service. Translations on East European Agriculture, Forestry, and Food Industries — US Joint Publ Res Serv Transl E Eur Agr Forest Food Ind
United States Law Review — US Law R
United States Law Review — USL Rev
United States Law Review — USLR
United States Law Week. Bureau of National Affairs — USLW BNA
United States. Library of Congress. Information Bulletin — LC Inf Bul
United States Literary Gazette — US Lit Gaz
United States Lodging Industry — Lodg Ind
United States Long-Term Review — US Long Term
United States Military Posture — US Posture
United States. National Aeronautics and Space Administration. Conference Publication — USNASA Conf Publ
United States. National Bureau of Standards. Journal of Research — US Natl Bur Stand J Res
United States National Fertilizer Development Center. Bulletin Y — US Natl Fert Dev Cent Bull Y
United States National Herbarium. Contributions — US Natn Herb
United States National Laboratory (Oak Ridge, Tennessee). Review — US Natl Lab (Oak Ridge Tenn) Rev
United States National Museum. Bulletin — US Nat Mus Bull
United States National Museum. Bulletin. Proceedings — US Natl Mus Bull Proc
United States National Museum. Proceedings — US Nat Mus Proc
United States National Museum. Reports — US Nat Mus Rept
United States. National Oceanic and Atmospheric Administration. Environmental Data Service. Technical Memorandum — US Natl Oceanic Atmos Adm Environ Data Serv Tech Memo
United States. National Science Foundation. Research Applied to National Needs Report — US Natl Sci Found Res Appl Natl Needs Rep
United States. National Technical Information Service. AD Report — US NTIS AD Rep
United States. National Technical Information Service. PB Report — US NTIS PB Rep
United States. National Technical Information Service. Publication — Publ US Natl Tech Inf Serv
United States Naval Institute. Proceedings — Proc US Nav Inst
United States. Naval Institute. Proceedings — US N Inst Proc
United States Naval Institute. Proceedings — US Navl Inst Proc
United States. Naval Institute. Proceedings — USNIP
United States. Naval Institute. Proceedings — XNIPA
United States Naval Medical Bulletin — US Nav Med Bull
United States Naval Medical Bulletin — US Naval Med Bull
United States. Naval Ordnance Test Station. NAVORD Report — US Naval Ordnance Test Sta NAVORD Report
United States. Naval Postgraduate School. Technical Report/Research Paper — US Nav Postgrad Sch Tech Rep/Res Paper
United States. Naval Research Laboratories. Shock and Vibration Bulletin — US Naval Res Lab Shock Vib Bull
United States. Naval Ship Research and Development Center. Report — US Nav Ship Res Dev Cent Rep
United States. Naval Submarine Medical Center. Report — US Nav Submar Med Cent Rep
United States. Naval Submarine Medical Research Laboratory. Memorandum Report — US Nav Submar Med Res Lab Memo Rep
United States. Navy Electronics Laboratory. Report — US Navy Electronics Lab Rept
United States News and World Report — WRP
United States. Oak Ridge National Laboratory. Radiation Shielding Information Center. Report — US Oak Ridge Natl Lab Radiat Shield Inf Cent Rep
United States. Office of Education. Bulletin — US Office Ed Bul
United States Office of Education. Bulletin — USOE
United States. Office of Education. Circulars — US Office Ed Circ
United States. Office of Education. Publications — US Office Ed Pub
United States. Office of Education. Vocational Division. Bulletin — US Office Ed Voc Div Bul
United States. Office of Naval Research. Report ACR — US Off Nav Res Rep ACR
United States. Office of Saline Water Research and Development. Progress Report — US Off Saline Water Res Dev Prog Rep
United States. Office of Saline Water Research and Development. Progress Report — US Office Saline Water Research and Devel Progress Rept
United States Paper Maker — US Pap Maker
United States. Patent Office. Official Gazette — Official Gazette USPO
United States Patents Quarterly. Bureau of National Affairs — USPQ BNA
United States Political Science Documents — US Polit Sci Doc
United States Political Science Documents [*Information service or system*] — USPSD
United States. Public Health Service. Public Health Monograph — US Public Health Serv Public Health Monogr
United States Quarterly Book List — USQBL
United States Quarterly Book Review — US Q Bk R
United States Quarterly Book Review — USQ
United States Quarterly Book Review — USQBR
United States Seed Reporter — US Seed Rep
United States Service Magazine — US Serv M
United States. Ship Structure Committee. Report — US Ship Struct Com Rep
United States. Soil Conservation Service. Sedimentation Bulletin (Technical Publication) — US Soil Conserv Service Sedimentation Bull (TP)
United States Statutes at Large — Stat
United States Steel News — US Steel News
United States. Surgeon-General's Office. Bulletin — US Surg Gen Off Bul
United States. Tariff Commission. Reports — US Tariff Comm Rep
United States. Tariff Commission. TC Publication — US Tariff Comm TC Publ
United States Tax Report — US Tax Rpt
United States Tobacco and Candy Journal — USTC Jrl
United States Tobacco and Candy Journal Buyer's Guide — USTC Jl BG
United States Tobacco Journal — USTJ
United States. Veterans Administration (Washington, DC). Department of Medicine and Surgery. Bulletin of Prosthetics Research — US Veterans Adm (W) Dep Med Surg Bull Prosthet Res
United States Veterans' Bureau. Medical Bulletin — US Veterans Bur Med Bul
United States. Veterans Bureau. Medical Bulletin — US Veterans Bureau Med Bull
United States. War Department. Chief of Engineers. Annual Report — US War Dp Chief Eng An Rp
United States. Waterways Experiment Station. Contract Report — US Waterw Exp Stn Contract Rep
United States. Waterways Experiment Station. Miscellaneous Paper — US Waterw Exp Stn Misc Pap

United States. Waterways Experiment Station. Research Report — US Waterw Exp Stn Res Rep
United States. Waterways Experiment Station. Technical Report — US Waterw Exp Stn Tech Rep
United States. Waterways Experiment Station (Vicksburg, Mississippi). Miscellaneous Paper — US Waterw Exp Stn (Vicksburg Miss) Misc Pap
United States. Waterways Experiment Station (Vicksburg, Mississippi). Research Report — US Waterw Exp Stn (Vicksburg Miss) Res Rep
United States. Waterways Experiment Station (Vicksburg, Mississippi). Technical Report — US Waterw Exp Stn (Vicksburg Miss) Tech Rep
United States. Women's Bureau. Bulletin — US Women's Bur Bul
Universal Farmacia — Univers Farm
Universal Human Rights — Univ Hum Rts
Universal Human Rights — Univ Human Rights
Universal Jewish Encyclopedia — UJE
Universal Machine Language Equipment Register [*database*] — UMLER
Universal Medical Record (London) — Univ Med Rec (London)
Universal Review — Univ R
Universale Economica — UE
Universale Studium — US
Universalist Quarterly Review [*Boston*] — Univ Q
Universe Natural History Series — Universe Nat Hist Ser
Universe Science Fiction — Uni
Universidad [de Zaragoza. Revista] — Universidad
Universidad Austral de Chile. Facultad de Ciencias Agrarias. Agro Sur — Univ Austral Chile Fac Cienc Agrar Agro Sur
Universidad Autonoma de Barcelona. Colegio Universitario de Gerona. Seccion de Ciencias. Anales — Univ Auton Barcelona Col Univ Gerona Secc Cienc An
Universidad Autonoma Potosina. Instituto de Geologia y Metalurgia. Folleto Tecnico — Potosi Univ Autonoma Inst Geologia y Metalurgia Fol Tec
Universidad Autonoma Potosina. Instituto de Geologia y Metalurgia. Folleto Tecnico — Univ Auton Potosina Inst Geol Metal Foll Tec
Universidad Catolica Argentina. Facultad de Ciencias Fisicomatematicas e Ingenieria. Revista da Ingenieria — Rev Ingr
Universidad Catolica Bolivariana — Univ Catol Bolivar
Universidad Catolica Bolivariana (Medellin) — Univ Catol Bolivar Medellin
Universidad Central de Venezuela. Instituto de Materiales y Modelos Estructurales. Boletin Tecnico — Univ Cent Venez Inst Mater Modelos Estruct Bol Tec
Universidad de Antioquia [*Colombia*] — UA
Universidad de Antioquia — UAnt
Universidad de Antioquia — UDA
Universidad de Antioquia [*Colombia*] — Univ Antioquia
Universidad de Antioquia Boletin de Antropolia — BAUA
Universidad de Antioquia (Colombia) — UAC
Universidad de Antioquia Cuadernos — Univ Antioquia Cuad
Universidad de Antioquia (Medellin, Colombia) — Univ Antioq Medellin
Universidad de Buenos Aires. Facultad de Agronomia y Veterinaria. Boletin — Univ Buenos Aires Fac Agrom Vet Bol
Universidad de Buenos Aires. Instituto de Anatomia. Publicacion — Univ Buenos Aires Inst Anat Publ
Universidad de Chile. Departamento de Produccion Agricola. Publicaciones Miscelaneas Agricolas — Univ Chile Dep Prod Agric Publ Misc Agric
Universidad de Chile. Facultad de Agronomia. Departamento Sanidad Vegetal. Boletin Tecnico — Univ Chile Fac Agron Dep Sanid Veg Bol Tec
Universidad de Chile. Facultad de Agronomia. Publicaciones Miscelaneas Agricolas — Univ Chile Fac Agron Publ Misc Agric
Universidad de Chile. Facultad de Ciencias Fisicas y Matematicas. Anales — Univ Chile Fac Cienc Fis Mat An
Universidad de Chile. Facultad de Ciencias Fisicas y Matematicas. Instituto de Geologia. Publicacion — Univ Chile Fac Cienc Fis Mat Inst Geol Publ
Universidad de Chile. Facultad de Ciencias Forestales. Boletin Tecnico — Univ Chile Fac Cienc For Bol Tec
Universidad de Chile. Facultad de Ciencias Forestales. Manual — Univ Chile Fac Cienc For Manual
Universidad de Chile. Facultad de Quimica y Farmacia. Tesis de Quimicos Farmaceuticos — Univ Chile Fac Quim Farm Tesis Quim Farm
Universidad de Chile. Instituto de Chile. Instituto de Investigaciones y Ensayes de Materiales. Informe Tecnico — Univ Chile Inst Invest Ensayes Mater Inf Tec
Universidad de Honduras (Tegucigalpa) — Univ Hond Tegucigalpa
Universidad de la Habana — UdLH
Universidad de la Habana — UH
Universidad de la Habana — ULH
Universidad de la Habana — UnH
Universidad de La Habana (La Habana) — Univ Habana Hav
Universidad de la Republica del Uruguay. Facultad de Agronomia. Estacion Experimental de Paysandu Dr. Mario A. Cassinoni. Boletin Tecnico — UFBTAD
Universidad de la Republica. Facultad de Agronomia. Boletin (Montevideo) — Univ Repub Fac Agron Bol (Montev)
Universidad de la Republica (Montevideo). Facultad de Agronomia. Boletin — Univ Repub (Montevideo) Fac Agron Bol
Universidad de Madrid. Facultad de Veterinaria. Publicacion — Univ Madr Fac Vet Publ
Universidad de Medellin — UDM
Universidad de Mexico — UM
Universidad de Oriente. Instituto Oceanografico. Boletin — Univ Oriente Inst Oceanogr Bol
Universidad de Oriente. Instituto Oceanografico. Boletin Bibliografico — Univ Oriente Inst Oceanogr Bol Bibliogr
Universidad de San Carlos (Guatemala) — Univ S Carlos Guat
Universidad de San Francisco Xavier (Sucre) — Univ S Fran Xavier Sucre
Universidad de Santo Tomas — UST
Universidad de Sevilla. Publicaciones. Serie Medicina — Univ Sevilla Publ Ser Med
Universidad de Tucuman. Cuadernos de Extension Universitaria — UTCEU
Universidad de Tucuman. Publications — UNTP
Universidad de Zaragosa — UZEV
Universidad del Salvador. Anales — Univ Salvador Anal
Universidad do Rio Grande Do Sul. Escola de Geologia. Notas e Estudos — Univ Rio Grande Do Sul Esc Geol Notas Estud
Universidad Hispalense. Anales. Serie Medicina — Univ Hisp An Ser Med
Universidad Industrial de Santander. Boletin de Geologia — Univ Ind Santander Bol Geol
Universidad Libre (Bogota) — Univ Libre Bogota
Universidad. Mensual de Cultura Popular (Mexico) — Univ Mex
Universidad Michoacana (Morelia, Mexico) — Univ Michoac Morelia
Universidad (Monterrey, Mexico) — Univ Monterrey
Universidad Nacional Autonoma de Mexico — UNAM
Universidad Nacional Autonoma de Mexico. Instituto de Geologia. Anales — Univ Nac Auton Mex Inst Geol An
Universidad Nacional Autonoma de Mexico. Instituto de Geologia. Boletin — Univ Nac Auton Mex Inst Geol Bol
Universidad Nacional Autonoma de Mexico. Instituto de Geologia. Paleontologica Mexicana — Univ Nac Auton Mex Inst Geol Paleontol Mex
Universidad Nacional Autonoma de Mexico. Instituto de Geologia. Revista — Univ Nac Auton Mex Inst Geol Rev
Universidad Nacional (Bogota, Colombia) — UNB
Universidad Nacional de Colombia (Bogota) — Univ Nac Col Bogota
Universidad Nacional de Cordoba — UNC
Universidad Nacional de Cordoba. Facultad de Ciencias Medicas. Revista — Univ Nac Cordoba Fac Cienc Med Rev
Universidad Nacional de Cuyo. Facultad de Ciencias Agrarias. Boletin de Extension — Univ Nac de Cuyo Fac Cienc Agrar Bol de Ext
Universidad Nacional de Cuyo. Facultad de Ciencias Agrarias. Boletin Tecnico — Univ Nac Cuyo Fac Cien Agrar Bol Tec
Universidad Nacional de Cuyo. Facultad de Ciencias Fisico-Quimico Matematicas. Sesiones Quimicas Argentinas — Univ Nac Cuyo Fac Cienc Fis-Quim Mat Ses Quim Argent
Universidad Nacional de Cuyo. Instituto del Petroleo. Publicacion — Univ Nac Cuyo Inst Pet Publ
Universidad Nacional de Eva Peron. Facultad de Ciencias Fisicomatematicas. Publicaciones. Serie 2. Revista — Univ Nac Eva Peron Fac Cienc Fisicomat Publ Ser 2
Universidad Nacional de La Plata. Facultad de Agronomia. Laboratorio de Zoologia Agricola. Boletin — Univ Nac La Plata Fac Agron Lab Zool Agric Bol
Universidad Nacional de La Plata. Facultad de Ciencias Naturales y Museo. Serie Tecnica y Didactica — Univ Nac La Plata Fac Cienc Nat Mus Ser Tec Didact
Universidad Nacional de La Plata. Notas del Museo. Botanica — Univ Nac La Plata Notas Mus Bot
Universidad Nacional de La Plata. Notas del Museo. Geologia — Univ Nac La Plata Notas Mus Geol
Universidad Nacional de La Plata. Notas del Museo. Zoologia — Univ Nac La Plata Notas Mus Zool
Universidad Nacional de La Plata. Publicaciones. Facultad de Ciencias Fisicomatematicas — Univ Nac La Plata Publ Fac Cienc Fisicomat
Universidad Nacional de La Plata. Publicaciones. Facultad de Ciencias Fisicomatematicas. Serie 2. Revista — Univ Nac La Plata Publ Fac Cienc Fisicomat Ser 2
Universidad Nacional de Tucuman. Facultad de Agronomia. Miscelanea — Univ Nac Tucuman Fac Agron Misc
Universidad Nacional de Tucuman. Facultad de Agronomia y Zootecnia. Boletin de Divulgacion — BDUZD8
Universidad Nacional de Tucuman. Facultad de Agronomia y Zootecnia. Boletin de Divulgacion — Univ Nac Tucuman Fac Agron Zootec Bol Divulg
Universidad Nacional de Tucuman. Facultad de Agronomia y Zootecnia. Miscelanea — Univ Nac Tucuman Fac Agron Zootec Misc
Universidad Nacional de Tucuman. Facultad de Agronomia y Zootecnia. Publicacion Especial — Univ Nac Tucuman Fac Agron Zootec Publ Espec
Universidad Nacional de Tucuman. Facultad de Agronomia y Zootecnia. Serie Didactica — Univ Nac Tucuman Fac Agron Zootec Ser Didact
Universidad Nacional de Tucuman. Facultad de Ciencias Exactas y Tecnologia. Revista. Serie A. Matematicas y Fisica Teorica — Univ Nac Tucuman Rev Ser A
Universidad Nacional de Tucuman. Fundacion e Instituto Miguel Lillo. Miscelanea — Univ Nac Tucuman Fund Inst Miguel Lillo Misc
Universidad Nacional de Tucuman. Instituto de Fisica. Publicacion — Univ Nac Tucuman Inst Fis Publ
Universidad Nacional de Tucuman. Instituto de Geologia y Mineria. Revista — Univ Nac Tucuman Inst Geol Min Rev
Universidad Nacional de Tucuman. Instituto de Ingenieria Quimica. Publicacion — Univ Nac Tucuman Inst Ing Quim Pub
Universidad Nacional del Litoral — UNL
Universidad (Panama) — Univ Panama
Universidad Pontificia Bolivariana — UPB
Universidad Pontificia Bolivariana (Medellin) — Univ Pontif Bolivar Medellin
Universidad Pontificia Bolivariana. Publicacion Trimestral — Univ Pontif Bolivar Publ Trimest
Universidad Pontificia Bolivariana. Publicacion Trimestral — Univ Pontif Bolivariana Publ Trimest
Universidad (Potosi, Bolivia) — Univ Potosi
Universidad (Santa Fe, Argentina) — Univ Santa Fe
Universidad (Tarija, Bolivia) — Univ Tarija
Universidad Veracruzana (Xalapa, Mexico) — Univ Veracruz Xalapa
Universidade de Bahia. Escola de Geologia. Publicacao Avulsa — Univ Bahia Esc Geol Publ Avulsa

Universidade de Lisboa. Faculdade de Farmacia. Boletim — Univ Lisboa Fac Farm Bol

Universidade de Lisboa. Revista da Faculdade de Ciencas. 2. Serie A. Ciencias Matematicas — Univ Lisboa Revista Fac Ci A

Universidade de Lisboa. Revista da Faculdade de Ciencias. 2. Serie A. Ciencias Matematicas — Univ Lisboa Rev Fac Cienc A 2

Universidade de Sao Paulo. Escola Politecnica, Geologia, e Metalurgia. Boletim — Univ Sao Paulo Esc Politec Geol Metal Bol

Universidade de Sao Paulo. Escola Superior de Agricultura Luiz De Queiroz. Boletim Tecnico Cientifico — BTAQAO

Universidade de Sao Paulo. Escola Superior de Agricultura Luiz De Queiroz. Boletim Tecnico Cientifico — Univ Sao Paulo Esc Super Agric Luiz De Queiroz Bol Tec Cient

Universidade de Sao Paulo. Faculdade de Filosofia, Ciencias, e Letras. Boletim. Botanica — Univ Sao Paulo Fac Filos Cienc Let Bol Bot

Universidade de Sao Paulo. Faculdade de Filosofia, Ciencias, e Letras. Boletim. Geologia — Univ Sao Paulo Fac Filos Cienc Let Bol Geol

Universidade de Sao Paulo. Faculdade de Filosofia, Ciencias, e Letras. Boletim. Mineralogia — Univ Sao Paulo Fac Filos Cienc Let Bol Mineral

Universidade de Sao Paulo. Faculdade de Filosofia, Ciencias, e Letras. Boletim. Quimica — Univ Sao Paulo Fac Filos Cienc Let Bol Quim

Universidade de Sao Paulo. Instituto de Geociencias. Boletim IG [*Instituto de Geociencias*] — Univ Sao Paulo Inst Geocienc Bol IG

Universidade de Sao Paulo. Instituto de Geociencias e Astronomia. Boletim — Univ Sao Paulo Inst Geocienc Astron Bol

Universidade de Sao Paulo. Instituto de Geografia. Sedimentologia e Pedologia — Univ Sao Paulo Inst Geog Sediment Pedol

Universidade do Brasil. Centro de Estudos Zoologicos Avulso — Univ Bras Cent Estud Zool Avulso

Universidade do Rio Grande Do Sul. Escola de Geologia. Avulso — Univ Rio Grande Do Sul Esc Geol Avulso

Universidade do Rio Grande Do Sul. Escola de Geologia. Boletim — Univ Rio Grande Do Sul Esc Geol Bol

Universidade Estadual Paulista. Departamento de Educacao. Boletim — Univ Estad Paulista Dep Educ Bol

Universidade Federal de Pernambuco. Escola de Quimica. Departamento de Technologia. Publicacao Avulsa — Univ Fed Pernambuco Esc Quim Dep Technol Publ Avulsa

Universidade Federal de Pernambuco. Instituto de Biociencias. Publicacao Avulsa — Univ Fed Pernambuco Inst Biocienc Publ Avulsa

Universidade Federal de Pernambuco. Instituto de Micologia. Publicacao — Univ Fed Pernambuco Inst Micol Publ

Universidade Federal de Pernambuco. Memorias do Instituto de Biociencias — Univ Fed Pernambuco Mem Inst Biocienc

Universidade Federal de Vicosa. Biblioteca Central. Serie Bibliografias Especializadas — Univ Fed Vicosa Bibl Centr Ser Bibliogr Espec

Universidade Federal de Vicosa. Serie Tecnica. Boletin — Univ Fed Vicosa Ser Tec Bol

Universidade Federal do Parana. Centro de Estudos Portugueses. Arquivos — Univ Fed Par Cent Estud Port Arq

Universidade Federal do Rio De Janeiro. Instituto de Geociencias. Boletim Geologia — Rio De Janeiro Univ Federal Inst Geociencias Bol Geologia

Universidade Federal do Rio De Janeiro. Instituto de Geociencias. Boletim Geologia — Univ Fed Rio De J Inst Geocienc Bol Geol

Universidade Federal do Rio De Janeiro. Instituto de Geociencias. Departamento de Geologia. Contribuicao Didatica — Univ Fed Rio De J Inst Geocienc Dep Geol Contrib Dida

Universidade Federal do Rio De Janeiro. Instituto de Geociencias. Geologia. Boletim — Univ Fed Rio De Janeiro Inst Geocienc Geol Bol

Universidade Federal do Rio Grande do Sul. Faculdade de Medicina. Anais — Univ Fed Rio Grande do Sul Fac Med Anais

Universidade Federal do Rio Grande Do Sul. Instituto de Geociencias. Mapa Geologico da Folha de Morretes — Rio Grande Do Sul Inst Geocien Mapa Geol

Universidade Federal Rural do Rio Grande Do Sul. Departamento do Zootecnia. Boletin Tecnico — Univ Fed Rural Rio Grande Do Sul Dep Zootec Bol Tec

Universidade Rural de Pernambuco. Comunicado Tecnico — Univ Rural Pernambuco Comun Tec

Universidades Buenos Aires (Mexico) — Univers BA Mex

Universita Bocconi. Letterature Moderne. Rivista di Varia Umanita — Lett Mod

Universita Bocconi. Letterature Moderne. Rivista di Varia Umanita — LM

Universita degli Studi di Roma La Sapienza. Dipartimento di Metodi e Modelli Matematica per le Scienze Applicati. Pubblicaziani — Pubbl Dip Metod Model Mat Sci Appl Univ Stud Roma Quad

Universita degli Studi di Trieste. Facolta di Economia e Commercio. Istituto di Merceologia. Pubblicazione — Univ Studi Trieste Fac Econ Commer Ist Merceol Pubbl

Universita degli Studi di Trieste. Facolta di Farmacia. Istituto di Chimica, Farmaceutica, e Tossicologica. Pubblicazioni — Univ Stud Trieste Fac Farm Ist Chim Farm Tossicol Pubbl

Universita degli Studi di Trieste. Facolta di Farmacia. Istituto di Tecnica Farmaceutica. Pubblicazioni — Univ Stud Trieste Fac Farm Ist Tec Farm Pubbl

Universita degli Studi di Trieste. Facolta di Ingegneria. Istituto di Chimica Applicata. Pubblicazioni — Univ Studi Trieste Fac Ing Ist Chim App Pubbl

Universita degli Studi di Trieste. Facolta di Scienze. Istituto di Chimica. Pubblicazioni — Univ Studi Trieste Fac Sci Ist Chim Pubbl

Universita degli Studi di Trieste. Facolta di Scienze. Istituto di Geologia. Pubblicazioni — Univ Studi Triest Fac di Sci Ist Geol Pubbl

Universita degli Studi di Trieste. Facolta di Scienze. Istituto di Geologia. Pubblicazioni — Univ Studi Trieste Fac Sci Ist Geol Pubbl

Universita degli Studi di Trieste. Facolta di Scienze. Istituto di Mineralogia. Pubblicazione — Univ Studi Trieste Fac Sci Ist de Mineral Pubbl

Universita degli Studi di Trieste. Istituto di Chimica Farmaceutica e Tossicologica. Pubblicazioni — Univ Studi Trieste Ist Chim Farm Tossicol Pubbl

Universita degli Studi di Trieste. Istituto di Tecnica Farmaceutica. Pubblicazioni — Univ Stud Trieste Ist Tec Farm Pubbl

Universita di Ferrara. Annali. Sezione 6. Fisiologia e Chimica Biologica — Univ Ferrara Ann Sez 6

Universita di Ferrara. Memorie Geopaleontologiche — Univ Ferrara Mem Geopaleontol

Universita di Genova. Pubblicazioni dell'Istituto di Matematica — Univ Genova Pubbl Ist Mat

Universita di Palermo. Annali della Facolta di Economia e Commercio — Univ Palermo Ann Fac Econom Commercio

Universita di Palermo. Annali della Facolta di Economia e Commercio — Univ Palermo Ann Fac Econom e Commercio

Universita di Pavia. Istituto Geologico. Atti — Univ Pavia Ist Geol Atti

Universita di Roma. Istituto di Automatica. Notiziario — Univ Roma Ist Autom Not

Universita di Torino. Pubblicazioni della Facolta di Lettere e Filosofia — UTPLF

Universitaet Bonn. Physikalisches Institut. Technical Report — Univ Bonn Phys Inst Tech Rep

Universitaet fuer Forst- und Holzwirtschaft (Sopron). Wissenschaftliche Mitteilungen — Univ Forst Holzwirtsch (Sopron) Wiss Mitt

Universitaet Rostock. Wissenschaftliche Zeitschrift. Mathematisch-Naturwissenschaftliche Reihe — Wiss Z Univ Rostock Math-Natur Reihe

Universitaets- und Landesbibliothek — U LB

Universitaets- und Stadtbibliothek — U-Stadtbibliothek

Universitaets-Seminar fuer Wirtschaft [*Wiesbaden*] — USW

Universitaets-Taschenbuecher — UTB

Universitas — U

Universitas — Univ

Universitas — UNIVA

Universitas 2000 (Venezuela) — USV

Universitas. (Argentina) [*Texto y Contexto*] — UA

Universitas Carolina: Philologica — UCPh

Universitas Comeniana. Acta Facultatis Rerum Naturalium. Formatio et Protectio Naturae — Univ Comeniana Acta Fac Rerum Nat Form Prot Nat

Universitas Emeritensis (Merida, Venezuela) — Univ Emerit Merida

Universitas Humanistica (Colombia) — UAC

Universitas Maria Curie-Sklodowsk. Annales. Sectio B — Univ Maria Curie-Sklodowsk Ann Sect B

Universitas Pontificia Universidad Catolica Javeriana (Bogota) — Universitas (Bogota)

Universitas. Pontificia Universitates Javeriana. Facultad de Derecho y Ciencias Socioeconomicas [*Bogota*] — PUJ/U

Universitas Seoulensis. Collectio Theseon. Scientia Naturalis. Seoul Taehak-kyo Nonmun-jip. Chayon Kwahak — Univ Seoul Collect Theseon Sci Nat

Universitatea din Brasov. Lucrari Stiintifice — Univ Brasov Lucrari Stiint

Universitatea din Cluj-Napoca Gradina Botanica Contributii Botanice — Univ Cluj-Napoca Gradina Bot Contrib Bot

Universitatea din Craiova. Analele. Seria a/3. Stiinte Agricole — Univ Craiova An Ser 3

Universitatea din Craiova. Analele. Seria. Biologie, Medicina, Stiinte Agricole — Univ Craiova An Ser Biol Med Stiinte Agric

Universitatea din Craiova. Analele. Seria Chimie — Univ Craiova An Ser Chim

Universitatea din Craiova. Analele. Seria. Matematica, Fizica, Chimie, Electrotehnica — Univ Craiova An Ser Mat Fiz Chim Electroteh

Universitatea din Craiova. Analele. Seria. Matematica, Fizica-Chimie — Univ Craiova An Ser Mat Fiz Chim

Universitatea din Galati Buletinul Fascicula II Matematica Fizica. Mecanica Teoretica — Bul Univ Galati Fasc II Mat Fiz Mec Teoret

Universitatea din Timisoara. Analele. Stiinte Fizice-Chimice — Univ Timisoara An Stiinte Fiz Chim

Universitatii din Timisoara. Analele. Seria Matematica-Informatica — An Univ Timisoara Ser Mat Inform

Universitatii Tehnice din Timisoara. Buletinul Stiintific. Matematica-Fizica — Bul Stiint Univ Tehn Timosoara Mat Fiz

Universitatii Tehnice din Timisoara. Buletinul Stiintific si Tehnic. Matematica-Fizica — Bul Stiint Tehn Univ Tehn Timisoara Mat Fiz

Universitatis Babes-Bolyai. Studia. Series Mathematica — Studia Univ Babes-Bolyai Math

Universitatis Iagellonicae Acta Mathematica — Univ Iagel Acta Math

Universite Catholique de Louvain. Faculte des Sciences Agronomiques. Laboratoire de Biochimie de la Nutrition. Publication — Univ Cathol Louvain Fac Sci Agron Lab Biochim Nutr Publ

Universite Catholique de Louvain. Institut Agronomique. Memoires — Univ Cathol Louv Inst Agron Mem

Universite d'Abidjan. Departement de Geologie. Serie Documentation — Univ Abidjan Dep Geol Ser Doc

Universite d'Alger. Travaux. Institut de Recherches Sahariennes — Univ Alger Trav Inst Rech Sahariennes

Universite d'Ankara. Faculte de l'Agriculture. Publications — Univ Ankara Fac Agri Publ

Universite d'Ankara. Faculte des Sciences. Communications. Serie A. Mathematiques, Physique, et Astronomie — Univ Ankara Fac Sci Commun Ser A

Universite d'Ankara. Faculte des Sciences. Communications. Serie A2. Physique — Univ Ankara Fac Sci Commun Ser A2

Universite d'Ankara. Faculte des Sciences. Communications. Serie A3. Astronomie — Com Fac Sci Univ Ankara Ser A3 Astronom

Universite d'Ankara. Faculte des Sciences. Communications. Serie C. Sciences Naturelles — Univ Ankara Fac Sci Commun Ser C

Universite d'Ankara. Faculte des Sciences. Communications. Series B. Chemistry and Chemical Engineering — Univ Ankara Fac Sci Commun Ser B Chem Chem Eng

Universite de Bruxelles. Institut de Physique. Bulletin — Univ Bruxelles Inst Phys Bull
Universite de Grenoble. Lettres-Droit. Annales — Grenoble Univ Lett Ann
Universite de Grenoble. Sciences-Medecine. Annales — Grenoble Univ Sci Ann
Universite de Grenoble. Sciences-Medecine. Annales — Univ de Grenoble Annales n s Sci
Universite de Liege. Faculte des Sciences Appliques. Collection des Publications [*Belgium*] — Univ Liege Fac Sci Appl Coll Publ
Universite de Montreal. Chercheurs — Univ Montreal Chercheurs
Universite de Nancy. Faculte des Lettres. Annales de l'Est — Univ de Nancy Fac d Lettres Annales de l'Est
Universite de Paris. Conferences du Palais de la Decouverte. Serie A — Univ Paris Conf Palais Decouverte Ser A
Universite de Teheran. Faculte d'Agronomie. Bulletin — Univ Teheran Fac Agron Bull
Universite de Yaounde. Faculte des Sciences. Annales. Serie 3. Biologie-Biochimie — Univ Yaounde Fac Sci Ann Ser 3
Universite du Burundi. Revue — Univ Burundi Rev
Universite Forestiere et du Bois (Sopron). Publications Scientifiques — Univ For Bois (Sopron) Publ Sci
Universite Kiril et Metodij-Skopje. Faculte des Mathematiques — Univ Kiril Metodij-Skopje Fac Math
Universite Laval. Departement d'Exploitation et Utilisation des Bois. Note de Recherches — Univ Laval Dep Exploit Util Bois Note Rech
Universite Laval. Departement d'Exploitation et Utilisation des Bois. Note Technique — Univ Laval Dep Exploit Util Bois Note Tech
Universite Libre de Bruxelles. Inter-University Institute for High Energies. Report — Univ Libre Bruxelles Inter-Univ Inst High Energ Rep
Universiteit van Durban-Westville. Tydskrif — Univ Durban-Westville Tydskr
Universiteit van Stellenbosch. Annale — Univ Stellenbosch Ann
Universitet i Bergen. Arbok. Historisk-Antikvarisk Rekke — UAA
Universitet i Bergen. Arbok. Historisk-Antikvarisk Rekke — UBA
Universitet Lesnogo Khozyaistva i Derevoobrabatyvaoushchei Promyshlennosti (Sopron) Nauchnye Publikatsii — Univ Lesn Khoz Derevoobrab Prom-Sti (Sopron) Nauchn Publ
Universitetet i Bergen Arbok Medisinsk Rekke — Univ Bergen Arbok Med Rekke
Universitetet i Bergen Arbok. Naturvitenskapelig Rekke — Univ Bergen Arb Naturv R
Universitetet i Bergen Arbok. Naturvitenskapelig Rekke — Univ Bergen Arbok Naturvitensk Rekke
Universitetet i Bergen Arsmelding — Univ Bergen Arsmeld
Universitetet i Bergen Medisinske Avhandlinger — Univ Bergen Med Avh
Universitetet i Bergen Skrifter — Bergens Mus Skrifter
Universitetet i Bergen Skrifter — Univ Bergen Skr
Universitetet Oldsaksamlings Skrifter. Oslo — Univ Oldsaksaml Skrifter Oslo
Universitetsforlagets Kronikktjeneste — UFKT
Universitetsjubilaeets Danske Samfund — UJDS
Universitext. Tracts in Mathematics — Universitext Tracts Math
Universities Quarterly [*London*] — Univ Q
Universities Quarterly — Univ Quart
Universities Quarterly — Universities Q
Universities Quarterly — Univs Q
Universities Quarterly — UQ
University Affairs/Affaires Universitaires — Univ Aff/Aff Univ
University Bookman — UB
University Centre of Desert Studies. Transactions (Jodhpur, India) — Univ Cent Desert Stud Trans (Jodhpur India)
University College of Dublin. Agricultural Faculty. Report — Univ Coll Dublin Agric Fac Rep
University College of Dublin. Faculty of General Agriculture. Research Report — Univ Coll Dublin Fac Gen Agric Res Rep
University College of Swansea. Collegiate Faculty of Education. Journal — Swansea Coll Fac Ed J
University College of Wales (Aberystwyth). Memorandum — Univ Coll Wales (Aberystwyth) Memorandum
University College Quarterly — UCQ
University Debaters Annual — UDA
University Debaters' Annual — Univ Debaters Annual
University Film Association. Journal — UFAJ
University Film Study Center. Newsletter — Univ F Study
University Forum — Univ For
University Gazette [*University of Melbourne*] — Univ Gaz
University High School. Journal — Univ H Sch J
University Journal. Busan National University [*South Korea*] — Univ J Busan Natl Univ
University Journal. Busan Sanup University — Univ J Busan Sanup Univ
University Journal. Natural Sciences Series. Busan National University [*Republic of Korea*] — Univ J Nat Sci Ser
University Journal of Business — Univ J of Business
University Lecture Series — Univ Lecture Ser
University Magazine [*Montreal*] — Univ M
University Medical Magazine — Univ Med M
University Microfilms — UM
University Microfilms Publications — UM Pub
University Museum. Bulletin — Univ Mus B
University Museum. Bulletin (Philadelphia) — UMBP
University Museum Bulletin. University of Pennsylvania — UMB
University Museum. Bulletin. University of Pennsylvania — Univ Mus Bull Univ PA
University News — Univ News
University of Adelaide. Centre for Precambrian Research. Special Paper — Univ Adelaide Cent Precambrian Res Spec Pap
University of Agricultural Sciences (Bangalore). Current Research — Univ Agric Sci (Bangalore) Curr Res
University of Agricultural Sciences (Bangalore). Miscellaneous Series — Univ Agric Sci (Bangalore) Misc Ser
University of Agricultural Sciences (Bangalore). Research Series — Univ Agric Sci (Bangalore) Res Ser
University of Agricultural Sciences (Hebbal, Bangalore). Annual Report — Univ Agric Sci (Hebbal Bangalore) Annu Rep
University of Agricultural Sciences (Hebbal, Bangalore). Extension Series — Univ Agric Sci (Hebbal Bangalore) Ext Ser
University of Agricultural Sciences (Hebbal, Bangalore). Station Series — Univ Agric Sci (Hebbal Bangalore) Stn Ser
University of Agricultural Sciences (Hebbal, Bangalore). Technical Series — Univ Agric Sci (Hebbal Bangalore) Tech Ser
University of Alabama. Studies — UAS
University of Alaska. Agricultural Experiment Station. Bulletin — Univ Alaska Agric Exp Stn Bull
University of Alaska. Institute of Marine Science. Report — Univ Alaska Inst Mar Sci Rep
University of Alaska. IWR (Institute of Water Resources) Series — Univ Alaska IWR (Inst Water Resour) Ser
University of Alaska Magazine — Univ Alaska Mag
University of Alaska. Mineral Industry Research Laboratory. Report — Alaska Univ Mineral Industry Research Lab Rept
University of Alberta. Agriculture and Forestry Bulletin — Univ Alberta Agric For Bull
University of Alberta. Agriculture Bulletin — Univ Alberta Agric Bull
University of Alberta. Department of Civil Engineering. Structural Engineering Report — Univ Alberta Dep Civ Eng Struct Eng Rep
University of Alberta. Faculty of Agriculture. Bulletins — Univ Alberta Fac Agric Bull
University of Alexandria. Faculty of Engineering. Bulletin. Chemical Engineering — Univ Alexandria Fac Eng Bull Chem Eng
University of Allahabad. Studies — Univ Allahabad Stud
University of Allahabad. Studies. Biology Section — Univ Allahabad Stud Biol Sect
University of Allahabad. Studies. Botany Section — Univ Allahabad Stud Bot Sect
University of Allahabad. Studies. Chemistry Section — Univ Allahabad Stud Chem Sect
University of Allahabad. Studies. Mathematics Section — Univ Allahabad Stud Math Sect
University of Allahabad. Studies. New Series — Univ Allahabad Stud New Ser
University of Allahabad. Studies. Physics Section — Univ Allahabad Stud Phys Sect
University of Allahabad. Studies. Zoology Section — Univ Allahabad Stud Zool Sect
University of Ankara. Yearbook. Faculty of Agriculture — Univ Ankara Yearb Fac Agric
University of Arizona. Arizona Agricultural Experiment Station. Bulletin — Univ Arizona Agric Exp Sta Bull
University of Arizona. Cooperative Extension Service. Bulletin — Univ Ariz Coop Ext Serv Bull
University of Arizona. Cooperative Extension Service. Circular — Univ Ariz Coop Ext Serv Circ
University of Arizona. Cooperative Extension Service. Series P — Univ Ariz Coop Ext Serv Ser P
University of Arkansas at Little Rock. Law Journal — U Ark Little Rock LJ
University of Arkansas at Little Rock. Law Journal — UALR LJ
University of Arkansas. College of Agriculture. Arkansas Agricultural Experiment Station. Bulletin — Univ Arkansas Coll Agric Arkansas Agric Exp Sta Bull
University of Arkansas. Engineering Experiment Station. Research Report Series — Univ Arkansas Eng Exp Stn Res Rep Ser
University of Arkansas. Lecture Notes in Mathematics — Univ Arkansas Lecture Notes in Math
University of Baghdad. Natural History Research Center. Annual Report — Univ Baghdad Nat Hist Res Cent Annu Rep
University of Baghdad. Natural History Research Center. Publication — Univ Baghdad Nat Hist Res Cent Publ
University of Baltimore. Law Review — Ba LR
University of Baltimore. Law Review — U Balt L Rev
University of Baltimore. Law Review — U Balt LR
University of Baltimore. Law Review — U Baltimore L Rev
University of Baltimore. Law Review — UBLR
University of Birmingham. Historical Journal — U Birmingham Hist J
University of Birmingham. Historical Journal — UBHJ
University of Birmingham Historical Journal — UnHJ
University of Birmingham History Journal — Univ Birm Hist J
University of Botswana and Swaziland. Agricultural Research Division. Annual Report — Univ Botswana Swazil Agric Res Div Annu Rep
University of Botswana, Swaziland. Agricultural Research Division. Annual Report — Univ Botswana Swaziland Agric Res Div Annu Rep
University of Bridgeport. Law Review — U Brdgprt LR
University of Bridgeport. Law Review — U Bridgeport L Rev
University of British Columbia. Botanical Garden. Technical Bulletin — Univ BC Bot Gard Tech Bull
University of British Columbia. Law Review — U Brit Col L Rev
University of British Columbia. Law Review — U Brit Colum L Rev
University of British Columbia. Law Review — UBC L Rev
University of British Columbia. Law Review — UBC LR
University of British Columbia. Law Review — Univ British Columbia Law R
University of British Columbia. Law Review — Univ of Brit Columbia L Rev
University of British Columbia. Legal Notes — UBC Legal N
University of British Columbia. Legal Notes — UBC Legal Notes
University of British Columbia. Programme in Natural Resource Economics. Resources Paper — UBCNREP

University of British Columbia. Research Forest. Annual Report — Univ BC Res For Annu Rep
University of Buffalo. Studies — UBS
University of Calicut. Zoological Monograph — Univ Calicut Zool Monogr
University of California Agricultural Experiment Station. Reports — Univ Calif Agric Exp Sta Rep
University of California. Agricultural Extension Service — Univ Calif Agric Ext Serv
University of California (Berkeley). Publications in Agricultural Sciences — Univ Calif (Berkeley) Publ Agric Sci
University of California (Berkeley). Publications in Botany — Univ Calif (Berkeley) Publ Bot
University of California (Berkeley). Publications in Engineering — Univ Calif (Berkeley) Publ Eng
University of California (Berkeley). Publications in Entomology — Univ Calif (Berkeley) Publ Entomol
University of California (Berkeley). Publications in Pathology — Univ Calif (Berkely) Publ Pathol
University of California (Berkeley). Publications in Pharmacology — Univ Calif (Berkeley) Publ Pharmacol
University of California (Berkeley). Publications in Public Health — Univ Calif (Berkeley) Publ Health
University of California (Berkeley). Publications in Zoology — Univ Calif (Berkeley) Publ Zool
University of California (Berkeley). Sanitary Engineering Research Laboratory. Report — Univ Calif (Berkeley) Sanit Eng Res Lab Rep
University of California. Bulletin — Univ Calif Bull
University of California. Chronicle — UCC
University of California. College of Agriculture. Agricultural Experiment Station. Publications — Cal Ag Exp
University of California (Davis). Law Review — UCD
University of California (Davis). Law Review — UCD LR
University of California (Davis). Publications in English — UCDPE
University of California. Division of Agricultural Sciences. Bulletin — Univ Calif Div Agric Sci Bull
University of California. Division of Agricultural Sciences. Leaflet — Univ Calif Dlv Agric Sci Leafl
University of California. Lawrence Livermore Laboratory. Report — Univ Calif Lawrence Livermore Lab Rep
University of California Library Bulletin — Univ Cal Lib Bull
University of California (Los Angeles). Symposia on Molecular and Cellular Biology — Univ Calif (Los Angeles) Symp Mol Cell Biol
University of California Press. Publications in History — Univ Calif Press Publs Hist
University of California Publications in Agricultural Sciences — Univ Calif Publ Agric Sci
University of California. Publications in American Archaeology and Ethnology — Univ Calif Publ Am Archaeol Ethnol
University of California. Publications in Botany — Univ Calif Publ Bot
University of California. Publications in Classical Archaeology — CPCA
University of California. Publications in Classical Archaeology — UCPA
University of California. Publications in Classical Philology — CPCP
University of California. Publications in Classical Philology — UCP
University of California Publications in Classical Philology [*Berkeley and Los Angeles*] — UCPCP
University of California. Publications in Classical Philology — UCPPh
University of California. Publications in English, Linguistics, Modern Philology — Univ of Calif Publ in English Ling M Ph
University of California. Publications in English Studies — UCPES
University of California. Publications in Entomology — Univ Calif Publ Ent
University of California. Publications in Entomology — Univ Calif Publ Entomol
University of California. Publications in Entomology — Univ Calif Publs Ent
University of California. Publications in Folklore Studies — UCPFS
University of California. Publications in Geological Sciences — Univ Calif Publ Geol Sci
University of California. Publications in International Relations — Univ California Publ Internat Rel
University of California. Publications in Linguistics — UCPL
University of California. Publications in Modern Philology — UCPMP
University of California. Publications in Modern Philology — UCPMPh
University of California Publications in Modern Philology — University of Calif Publ in Mod Philol
University of California. Publications in Music — UCPM
University of California. Publications in Physiology — Univ Calif Publ Physiol
University of California. Publications in Psychology — Univ Calif Publ Psychol
University of California. Publications in Semitic Philology — UCPSP
University of California. Publications in Semitic Philology — UCPSPh
University of California. Publications in Zoology — Univ Calif Publ Zool
University of California. Publications in Zoology — Univ Calif Publications Zool
University of California. Sea Water Conversion Laboratory. Report — Univ Calif Sea Water Convers Lab Rep
University of California. Studies in Linguistics — UCSL
University of California. Studies in Modern Philology — UCSMP
University of California. University at Los Angeles. Publications in Biological Sciences — Univ Calif Univ Los Angeles Publ Biol Sci
University of California. University at Los Angeles. Publications in Mathematical and Physical Sciences — Univ Calif Univ Los Angeles Publ Math Phys Sci
University of California. Water Resources Center. Contribution — Univ Calif Water Resour Cent Contrib
University of Cambridge. Department of Applied Biology. Memoirs. Review Series — Univ Camb Dep Appl Biol Mem Rev Ser
University of Cambridge. Department of Engineering. Report. CUDE [*Cambridge University Department of Engineering*]/A-Aerodynamics — Univ Cambridge Dep Eng Rep CUDE/A-Aerodyn
University of Cambridge. Department of Engineering. Report. CUDE [*Cambridge University Department of Engineering*]/A-Thermo — Univ Cambridge Dep Eng Rep CUDE/A-Thermo
University of Cambridge. Department of Engineering. Report. CUDE [*Cambridge University Department of Engineering*]/A-Turbo — Univ Cambridge Dep Eng Rep CUDE/A-Turbo
University of Cambridge. Institute of Animal Pathology. Report of the Director — Univ Cambridge Inst Anim Pathol Rep Dir
University of Cambridge. Oriental Publications — UCOP
University of Canterbury. Publications — Univ Canterbury Publ
University of Cape Coast. English Department. Workpapers — UCCEW
University of Cape Town. Studies in English — UCTSE
University of Ceylon. Review — UCR
University of Chicago. Law Review — Ch L
University of Chicago. Law Review — Ch LR
University of Chicago. Law Review — U Chi L Rev
University of Chicago. Law Review — U Chicago L Rev
University of Chicago. Law Review — UCL
University of Chicago. Law Review — UCLR
University of Chicago. Law Review — Univ Chic L
University of Chicago Law Review — Univ Chicago Law Rev
University of Chicago. Law Review — Univ of Chi Law Rev
University of Chicago. Law Review — Univ of Chicago L Rev
University of Chicago. Law School. Conference Series — U Chi LS Conf Series
University of Chicago. Law School. Record — U Chi L Rec
University of Chicago. Law School. Record — U Chi L S Rec
University of Chicago. Law School. Record — U Chi L Sch Rec
University of Chicago Library Society Bulletin — Univ Chicago Libr Soc Bull
University of Chicago. Magazine — Univ Chic M
University of Chicago. Oriental Institute. Publications — UCOIP
University of Chicago. Publications — Univ Chicago Publ
University of Chicago. Record — Univ Chic Rec
University of Chicago. Reports — Univ Chicago Rep
University of Cincinnati. Law Review — Cin L Rev
University of Cincinnati. Law Review — Cin Law Rev
University of Cincinnati. Law Review — U Cin L Rev
University of Cincinnati. Law Review — U Cin LR
University of Cincinnati. Law Review — UCLR
University of Cincinnati. Law Review — UCR
University of Cincinnati. Law Review — Univ of Cinc Law Rev
University of Cincinnati. Law Review — Univ of Cincinnati L Rev
University of Cincinnati. Medical Bulletin — Univ Cincinnati Med Bul
University of Cincinnati. Studies — Univ Cincin Stud
University of Colorado. Engineering Experiment Station. Bulletin — Univ Col Eng Exp Stn Bull
University of Colorado. Law Review — CUR
University of Colorado. Law Review — U Colo L Rev
University of Colorado. Law Review — U Colo LR
University of Colorado. Law Review — U Color L Rev
University of Colorado. Law Review — UCLR
University of Colorado. Law Review — Univ of Colorado L Rev
University of Colorado. Studies — U Colo Stud
University of Colorado Studies — U of Col Studies
University of Colorado. Studies — Univ Col Stud
University of Colorado. Studies — Univ of Colo Studies
University of Colorado. Studies. General Series — UCSGS
University of Colorado. Studies. Series A. General Series — Univ Color Stud Ser A
University of Colorado. Studies. Series B. Studies in the Humanities — Univ Color Stud Ser B
University of Colorado. Studies. Series C. Studies in the Social Sciences — Univ Col Stud Ser C
University of Colorado. Studies. Series D. Physical and Biological Sciences — Univ Colo Stud Ser D
University of Colorado. Studies. Series in Anthropology — Univ Colo Stud Ser Anthropol
University of Colorado. Studies. Series in Biology — Univ Colo Stud Ser Biol
University of Colorado. Studies. Series in Chemistry and Pharmacy — Univ Colo Stud Ser Chem Pharm
University of Colorado. Studies. Series in Earth Sciences — Univ Colo Stud Ser Earth Sci
University of Colorado. Studies. Series in Language and Literature — UCSLL
University of Colorado. Studies. Series in Language and Literature — UCSSLL
University of Connecticut. Occasional Papers. Biological Science Series — Univ Conn Occas Pap Biol Sci Ser
University of Dayton. Law Review — U Day LR
University of Dayton. Law Review — U Dayton L Rev
University of Dayton. Review — UDR
University of Delaware Agricultural Experiment Station Bulletin — Univ Delaware Agric Exp Sta Bull
University of Delaware. Marine Laboratories. Information Series Publication — Univ Del Mar Lab Inf Ser Publ
University of Denver. Quarterly — UDQ
University of Detroit. Journal of Urban Law — U Det J Urb L
University of Detroit. Law Journal — DLJ
University of Detroit. Law Journal — U Det L J
University of Detroit. Law Journal — U Detroit LJ
University of Detroit. Law Journal — U of Detroit LJ
University of Durban-Westville. Journal — Univ Durban-Westville J
University of Durham. King's College. Department of Civil Engineering. Bulletin — Univ Durham King's Coll Dep Civ Eng Bull
University of Edinburgh. Journal — UEJ
University of Edinburgh. Journal — Univ Edinburgh J
University of Edinburgh. Pfizer Medical Monographs — Univ Edinb Pfizer Med Monogr

University of Florida. Agricultural Extension Service. Circular — Univ Fla Agric Ext Serv Circ
University of Florida. Coastal and Oceanographic Engineering Laboratory. Report. UFL/COEL/TR — Univ Fla Coastal Oceanogr Eng Lab Rep UFL COEL TR
University of Florida. Contributions. Florida State Museum. Social Sciences — Univ Fla Contrib Fla St Mus Social Sci
University of Florida. Cooperative Extension Service. Bulletin — Univ Fla Coop Ext Serv Bull
University of Florida. Institute of Food and Agricultural Sciences. Annual Research Report — Univ Fla Inst Food Agric Sci Annu Res Rep
University of Florida. Institute of Food and Agricultural Sciences. Publication — Univ Fla Inst Food Agri Sci Publ
University of Florida. Institute of Gerontology Series — Univ Fla Inst Gerontol Ser
University of Florida. Law Review — FL LR
University of Florida. Law Review — FLR
University of Florida. Law Review — U Fla L Rev
University of Florida. Law Review — U Fla LR
University of Florida. Law Review — U Florida L Rev
University of Florida. Law Review — Univ of Florida L Rev
University of Florida. Monographs. Humanities Series — UFMH
University of Florida. Publications. Biological Science Series — Univ Fla Publ Biol Sci Ser
University of Florida. Social Sciences Monograph — Univ Fl SSM
University of Florida. Water Resources Research Center. Publication — Univ Fla Water Resour Res Cent Publ
University of Forestry and Timber Industry (Sopron). Scientific Publications — Univ For Timber Ind (Sopron) Sci Publ
University of Georgia. Marine Science Center. Technical Report Series — Univ GA Mar Sci Cent Tech Rep Ser
University of Georgia. Monographs — UGM
University of Ghana. Agricultural Irrigation Research Station (Kpong). Annual Report — Univ Ghana Agric Irrig Res Stn (Kpong) Annu Rep
University of Ghana. Agricultural Research Station (Kpong). Annual Report — Univ Ghana Agric Res Stn (Kpong) Annu Rep
University of Ghana. Institute of African Studies Research Review — Univ Ghana Res Rev
University of Ghana Law Journal — UGLJ
University of Ghana Law Journal — Univ Ghana Law J
University of Hartford. Studies in Literature — U Hart St L
University of Hawaii. College of Tropical Agriculture. Departmental Paper — Univ Hawaii Coll Trop Agric Dep Pap
University of Hawaii. Cooperative Extension Service. Miscellaneous Publication — Univ Hawaii Coop Ext Ser Misc Publ
University of Hawaii. Hawaii Institute of Geophysics. Biennial Report — Univ Hawaii Hawaii Inst Geophys Bienn Rep
University of Hawaii. Hawaii Institute of Geophysics. Report HIG — Univ Hawaii Hawaii Inst Geophys Rep HIG
University of Hawaii. Law Review — U Haw LR
University of Hawaii. Law Review — U Hawaii L Rev
University of Hawaii. Occasional Papers — Univ Hawaii Occas Pap
University of Hawaii. Quarterly Bulletin — Univ Hawaii Quart Bull
University of Hawaii. Research Publications — Univ Hawaii Res Publ
University of Illinois Agricultural Experiment Station Bulletin — Univ Illinois Agric Exp Sta Bull
University of Illinois at Urbana-Champaign. Water Resources Center. Research Report — Univ Ill Urbana-Champaign Water Resour Cent Res Rep
University of Illinois at Urbana-Champaign. Water Resources Center. Special Report — Univ Ill Urbana-Champaign Water Resour Cent Spec Rep
University of Illinois. Graduate School of Library Science. Occasional Papers — Univ Ill Grad Sc Libr Sci Occas Pap
University of Illinois. Law Forum — LF
University of Illinois. Law Forum — U Ill L F
University of Illinois. Law Forum — U Ill L Forum
University of Illinois. Law Forum — Univ IL Law
University of Illinois. Law Forum — Univ Ill L Forum
University of Illinois. Law Forum — Univ of Illinois L Forum
University of Illinois. Law Review — U Ill L Rev
University of Illinois. Law Review — U Ill LR
University of Illinois. Studies in Language and Literature — UILL
University of Illinois Studies in Language and Literature — UISL
University of Illinois. Studies in Language and Literature — Univ Ill St Lang Lit
University of Indonesia. Institute of Management. Newsletter — Univ Indonesia Inst Man Newsl
University of Indore. Research Journal. Science — Univ Indore Res J Sci
University of Iowa. Monographs. Studies in Medicine — Univ Iowa Monogr Studies in Med
University of Iowa. Studies in Natural History — Univ Iowa Stud Nat Hist
University of Joensuu. Publications in Sciences — Univ Joensuu Publ Sci
University of Jordan. Dirasat — Univ Jordan Dirasat
University of Jordan. Dirasat. Series B. Pure and Applied Sciences — Univ Jordan Dirasat Ser B
University of Jyvaskyla. Studies in Sport, Physical Education, and Health — Univ Jyvaskyla Stud Sport Phys Educ Health
University of Kansas City. Law Review — Kansas City L Rev
University of Kansas City. Law Review — U Kan City L Rev
University of Kansas City. Law Review — U of Kansas City L Rev
University of Kansas City. Review — UKC
University of Kansas City. Review — UKCR
University of Kansas City. Review — UKCRv
University of Kansas City. Review — Univ KC R
University of Kansas. Law Review — U Kan L Rev
University of Kansas. Law Review — U Kan LR
University of Kansas. Museum of Natural History. Miscellaneous Publication — Univ Kans Mus Nat Hist Misc Publ
University of Kansas. Museum of Natural History. Monograph — Univ Kans Mus Nat Hist Monogr
University of Kansas. Paleontological Contributions. Article — Univ Kans Paleontol Contrib Artic
University of Kansas. Paleontological Contributions. Monograph — Univ Kans Paleontol Contrib Monogr
University of Kansas. Paleontological Contributions. Paper — Univ Kans Paleontol Contrib Pap
University of Kansas. Primary Records in Psychology. Publication — Univ Kans Primary Rec Psychol Publ
University of Kansas. Publications. Humanistic Studies — UKPHS
University of Kansas. Publications. Library Series — U Kans Publ
University of Kansas. Publications. Museum of Natural History — Univ Kans Publ Mus Nat Hist
University of Kansas. Science Bulletin — Univ Kans Sci Bull
University of Kansas. Science Bulletin — Univ Kansas Sci Bull
University of Kansas. Science Bulletin. Supplement — Univ Kans Sci Bull Suppl
University of Kentucky. College of Agriculture. Cooperative Extension Service. Report — Univ KY Coll Agric Coop Ext Ser Rep
University of Kentucky. Cooperative Extension Service. 4-H — Univ KY Coop Ext Serv 4-H
University of Kentucky. Cooperative Extension Service. Circular — Univ KY Coop Ext Serv Circ
University of Kentucky. Cooperative Extension Service. Leaflet — Univ KY Coop Ext Serv Leafl
University of Kentucky. Cooperative Extension Service. Miscellaneous — Univ KY Coop Ext Serv Misc
University of Kentucky. Engineering Experiment Station. Bulletin — Univ KY Eng Exp Stn Bull
University of Kentucky. Institute for Mining and Minerals Research. Report IMMR — Univ KY Inst Min Miner Res Rep IMMR
University of Kentucky. Institute for Mining and Minerals Research. Technical Report — Univ K Inst Min Miner Res Tech Rep
University of Kentucky. Institute for Mining and Minerals Research. Technical Report. IMMR — Univ KY Inst Min Miner Res Tech Rep IMMR
University of Kentucky. Office of Research and Engineering Services. Bulletin — Univ KY Off Res Eng Ser Bull
University of Kentucky. Publications in Anthropology and Archaeology — Univ KY Publ Anthropol Archaeol
University of Kuwait. Journal. Science — Univ Kuwait J Sci
University of Leeds. Institute of Education. Papers — Univ Leeds Inst Educ Pap
University of Leeds. Medical Journal — Univ Leeds Med J
University of Leeds. Review — ULR
University of Liverpool. Recorder — Univ Liverp Rec
University of Lodz. Department of Logic. Bulletin of the Section of Logic — Bull Sect Logic Univ Lodz
University of London. Galton Laboratory. University College Eugenics Laboratory. Memoirs — Univ London Galton Lab Univ Coll Eugen Lab Mem
University of London. Institute of Classical Studies. Bulletin — U Lond I Cl
University of London. London Oriental Series — ULLOS
University of London. University College. Galton Laboratory. Eugenics Laboratory. Memoirs — Univ Lond Univ Coll Galton Lab Eugen Lab Mem
University of Lund. Department of Anatomy. Communications — Univ Lund Dep Anat Commun
University of Maine at Orono. Life Sciences and Agriculture Experiment Station. Annual Report — Univ Maine Orono Life Sci Agric Exp Stn Annu Rep
University of Maine at Orono. Life Sciences and Agriculture Experiment Station. Technical Bulletin — Univ Maine Orono Life Sci Agric Exp Stn Tech Bull
University of Maine at Orono. Maine Agricultural Experiment Station. Annual Report — ARUSE7
University of Maine at Orono. Maine Agricultural Experiment Station. Annual Report — Univ Maine Orono Maine Agric Exp Stn Ann Rep
University of Maine. Studies — UMS
University of Maine. Studies — Univ of Maine Studies
University of Malaya. Law Review — U of Malaya L Rev
University of Malaya. Law Review — UMLR
University of Manchester. School of Education. Gazette — Manchester Sch Ed Gazette
University of Manitoba. Medical Journal — UMMJ
University of Maryland. Natural Resources Institute. Contribution — Univ MD Nat Resour Inst Contrib
University of Maryland. Sea Grant Program. Technical Report — TRMPDU
University of Maryland. Sea Grant Program. Technical Report — Univ MD Sea Grant Program Tech Rep
University of Maryland. Water Resources Research Center. Technical Report — Univ MD Water Resour Res Cent Tech Rep
University of Maryland. Water Resources Research Center. WRRC Special Report — Univ MD Water Resour Res Cent WRRC Spec Rep
University of Massachusetts. Department of Geology. Contribution — Univ Mass Dep Geol Contrib
University of Melbourne. Department of Civil Engineering. Transport Section. Bulletin — Melbourne Univ Dep Civ Eng Transp Sect Bull
University of Melbourne. Department of Civil Engineering. Transport Section. Special Report — Melbourne Univ Dep Civ Eng Transp Sect Spec Rep
University of Melbourne. Department of Electrical Engineering. Report — Melb Univ Elect Engng Dep Rep
University of Melbourne. Department of Mechanical Engineering. Human Factors Group. HF Report — Melbourne Univ Dep Mech Eng Hum Factors Group HF Rep
University of Melbourne. Gazette — Univ Melb Gaz
University of Melbourne. School of Forestry. Bulletin — Melb Univ Sch For Bull
University of Melbourne. School of Forestry. Bulletin — Univ Melb Sch For Bull

University of Mexico — UMx
University of Miami. Hispanic Studies — UMHS
University of Miami. Law Review — Mi L
University of Miami. Law Review — U Miami L Rev
University of Miami. Law Review — U Miami LR
University of Miami. Law Review — UMLR
University of Miami. Law Review — UMLRB
University of Miami. Law Review — Univ Miami Law R
University of Miami. Law Review — Univ Miami Law Rev
University of Miami. Law Review — Univ of Miami L Rev
University of Miami. Publications in English and American Literature — UMPEAL
University of Miami. Rosenstiel School of Marine and Atmospheric Science. Annual Report — Univ Miami Rosenstiel Sch Mar Atmos Sci Annu Rep
University of Miami. Rosenstiel School of Marine and Atmospheric Science. Research Review — RRUSEO
University of Miami. Rosenstiel School of Marine and Atmospheric Science. Research Review — Univ Miami Rosenstiel Sch Mar Atmos Sci Res Rev
University of Miami. Sea Grant Program. Sea Grant Field Guide Series — Univ Miami Sea Grant Program Sea Grant Field Guide Ser
University of Miami. Sea Grant Program. Sea Grant Technical Bulletin — Univ Miami Sea Grant Program Sea Grant Tech Bull
University of Michigan (Ann Arbor). Office of Research Administration. Research News — Univ Mich (Ann Arbor) Off Res Adm Res News
University of Michigan. Business Review — U Mich Bus R
University of Michigan. Business Review — Univ Mich Bus R
University of Michigan. Business Review — Univ Mich Bus Rev
University of Michigan. Contributions in Modern Philology — UMCMP
University of Michigan. Department of Naval Architecture and Marine Engineering. Report — Univ Mich Dep Nav Archit Mar Eng Rep
University of Michigan. Institute of Science and Technology. Report — Univ Mich Inst Sci Tech Rep
University of Michigan. Journal of Law Reform — U Mich J L Ref
University of Michigan. Journal of Law Reform — U Mich J Law Reform
University of Michigan. Journal of Law Reform — Univ Mich J Law Reform
University of Michigan. Journal of Law Reform — Univ of Michigan J of Law Reform
University of Michigan. Medical Bulletin — Univ Mich Med Bull
University of Michigan. Medical Center. Journal — UMCJA
University of Michigan. Medical Center. Journal — Univ Mich Med Cent J
University of Michigan. Museum of Anthropology. Technical Reports — Univ Mich Mus Anthropol Tech Rep
University of Michigan. Museum of Zoology. Circular — Univ Mich Mus Zool Circ
University of Michigan. Papers in Linguistics — Univ Mich Pap Ling
University of Michigan. Publications in Language and Literature — UMPLL
University of Michigan. Studies — UMS
University of Michigan. Studies. Humanistic Series — UMSHS
University of Michigan Studies. Scientific Series — Univ Michigan Stud Sci Ser
University of Minnesota. Agricultural Extension Service. Extension Bulletin — Univ Minn Agric Ext Serv Ext Bull
University of Minnesota. Agricultural Extension Service. Extension Folder — Univ Minn Agric Ext Serv Ext Folder
University of Minnesota. Agricultural Extension Service. Extension Pamphlet — Univ Minn Agric Ext Serv Ext Pam
University of Minnesota. Agricultural Extension Service. Miscellaneous Publications — Univ Minn Agric Ext Serv Misc
University of Minnesota. Agricultural Extension Service. Miscellaneous Publications — Univ Minn Agric Ext Serv Misc Publ
University of Minnesota. Agricultural Extension Service. Special Report — Univ Minn Agric Ext Serv Spec Rep
University of Minnesota. Continuing Medical Education — Univ Minn Contin Med Educ
University of Minnesota. Graduate School. Water Resources Research Center. Bulletin — Minnesota Univ Water Resources Research Center Bull
University of Minnesota. Medical Bulletin — Univ Minn Med Bull
University of Minnesota. Pamphlets on American Literature — UMPAL
University of Minnesota. Pamphlets on American Writers — UMPAW
University of Mississippi. Studies in English — UMSE
University of Mississippi. Studies in English — Univ Mississippi Stud Engl
University of Missouri at Kansas City. Law Review — KCR
University of Missouri at Kansas City. Law Review — U Missouri at KCL Rev
University of Missouri at Kansas City. Law Review — U MO KCL Rev
University of Missouri at Kansas City. Law Review — U MO-Kansas City L Rev
University of Missouri at Kansas City. Law Review — UMKC L Rev
University of Missouri at Kansas City. Law Review — UMKCLR
University of Missouri at Kansas City. Law Review — Univ of Missouri at Kansas City L Rev
University of Missouri. Bulletin. Engineering Experiment Station Series — Univ MO Bull Eng Exp Stn Ser
University of Missouri, Columbia. Museum of Anthropology. Annual — Univ Missouri Columbia Mus Anthrop Ann
University of Missouri. Engineering Experiment Station. Engineering Series. Bulletin — Univ MO Eng Exp Sta Eng Ser Bull
University of Missouri. School of Mines and Metallurgy. Bulletin. Technical Series — MO U Sch Mines & Met Bul Tech Ser
University of Missouri. School of Mines and Metallurgy. Bulletin. Technical Series — Univ MO Sch Mines Metall Bull Tech Ser
University of Missouri. Studies — UMoS
University of Missouri. Studies — UMS
University of Missouri. Studies — Univ Missouri Stud
University of Missouri. Studies — Univ MO Stud
University of Missouri. Studies — Univ of MO Studies
University of Natal. Wattle Research Institute. Report — Univ Natal Wattle Res Inst Rep
University of Nebraska. College of Agriculture and Home Economics. Quarterly — Univ Nebr Coll Agric Home Econ Q
University of Nebraska. Studies — UNS
University of Nevada. Mackay School of Mines. Geological and Mining Series. Bulletin — Univ Nev Mackay Sch Mines Geol Min Ser Bull
University of Nevada. Max C. Fleischmann College of Agriculture. B Series — Univ Nev Max C Fleischmann Coll Agric Ser B
University of Nevada. Max C. Fleischmann College of Agriculture. R Series — Univ Nev Max C Fleischmann Coll Agric R
University of Nevada. Max C. Fleischmann College of Agriculture. Report — Univ Nev Max C Fleischmann Coll Agric Rep
University of Nevada. Max C. Fleischmann College of Agriculture. T Series — Univ Nev Max C Fleischmann Coll Agric T Ser
University of New Brunswick. Law Journal — U New Brunswick LJ
University of New Brunswick. Law Journal — UNB L J
University of New Brunswick. Law Journal — UNB Law Journal
University of New Brunswick. Law Journal — Univ of New Brunswick LJ
University of New England. Annual Report — Univ N Engl Annu Rep
University of New England. Bulletin — Univ NE Bul
University of New England. Bulletin — Univ New Eng Bull
University of New England. Exploration Society of Australia. Report — Univ N Engl Explor Soc Aust Rep
University of New England. Exploration Society. Report — New Engl Univ Explor Soc Rep
University of New England. External Studies Gazette — NE Univ External Stud Gaz
University of New England. Union Record — NE Univ Union Rec
University of New Mexico. Bulletin. Biological Series — Univ NM Bull Biol Ser
University of New Mexico. Bulletin. Geological Series — Univ NM Bull Geol Ser
University of New Mexico. Institute of Meteoritics. Special Publication — Univ NM Inst Meteorit Spec Publ
University of New Mexico. Publication in Biology — Univ New Mexico Publ Biol
University of New Mexico. Publications in Anthropology — Univ NM Publ Anthropol
University of New Mexico. Publications in Biology — Univ NM Publ Biol
University of New Mexico. Publications in Geology — Univ NM Publ Geol
University of New Mexico. Publications in Meteoritics — Univ NM Publ Meteorit
University of New South Wales. Faculty of Engineering. Yearbook — NSW Univ Engineering Yrbk
University of New South Wales. Institute of Highway and Traffic Research. Research Note — NSW Univ Inst Highw Traff Res Res Note
University of New South Wales. Law Journal — U New S Wales LJ
University of New South Wales. Law Journal — U New South Wales LJ
University of New South Wales. Law Journal — Univ NSW LJ
University of New South Wales. Law Journal — Univ of NSW LJ
University of New South Wales. Law Journal — UNSWLJ
University of New South Wales. Occasional Papers [*Australia*] — Univ New South Wales Occas Pap
University of New South Wales. Occasional Papers — Univ NSW Occas Pap
University of New South Wales. Quarterly — Univ NSW Q
University of New South Wales. School of Civil Engineering. UNICIV Report — New South Wales Univ Sch Civ Eng UNICIV Rep
University of New South Wales. School of Civil Engineering. UNICIV Report — NSW Univ UNICIV Rep
University of New South Wales. Water Research Laboratory. Report — NSW Univ Wat Res Lab Rep
University of Newcastle. Board of Environmental Studies. Research Paper — Board Environ Stud Res Pap Univ Newcastle
University of Newcastle. Department of Physics. Research Publication — Newcastle Univ Phys Dep Res Pub
University of Newcastle. Historical Journal — UNHJ
University of Newcastle Upon Tyne. Medical Gazette — Univ Newcastle Tyne Med Gaz
University of Newcastle Upon Tyne. Report of the Dove Marine Laboratory. Third Series — Univ Newcastle Upon Tyne Rep Dove Mar Lab Third Ser
University of North Carolina News Letter — Univ No Car News Letter
University of North Carolina. Record. Research in Progress — UNCR
University of North Carolina. Studies in Comparative Literature — UNCSCL
University of North Carolina. Studies in Germanic Languages and Literatures — UNCSGL
University of North Carolina. Studies in Germanic Languages and Literatures — UNCSGLL
University of North Carolina Studies in Language and Literature — Univ of North Carolina Studies
University of North Carolina. Studies in the Romance Languages and Literatures — UNCSRL
University of North Carolina. Studies in the Romance Languages and Literatures — UNCSRLL
University of Notre Dame. Department of Theology. Studies in Christian Democracy — Univ Notre Dame Dep Theol Stud Christ Dem
University of Notre Dame. Studies in the Philosophy of Religion — U Notr D St
University of Nottingham. Department of Agriculture and Horticulture. Miscellaneous Publication — Univ Nottingham Dep Agric Hortic Misc Publ
University of Nottingham. Research Publications — UNRP
University of Oxford. Department of Engineering. Science Reports — Univ Oxford Dept Eng Sci Rep
University of Pennsylvania. Bulletin. Veterinary Extension Quarterly — Univ PA Bull Vet Ext Q
University of Pennsylvania Law Review — IUPA
University of Pennsylvania. Law Review — PA L
University of Pennsylvania. Law Review — PA L Rev
University of Pennsylvania. Law Review — U of PL Rev
University of Pennsylvania. Law Review — U of PLR
University of Pennsylvania. Law Review — U PA L Rev
University of Pennsylvania. Law Review — U PA LR

University of Pennsylvania. Law Review — Univ of Pennsylvania L Rev
University of Pennsylvania Law Review — Univ Pa Law R
University of Pennsylvania. Law Review — Univ Penn Law Rev
University of Pennsylvania. Law Review and American Law Register — U PA Law Rev
University of Pennsylvania. Library Chronicle — Univ PA Libr Chron
University of Pennsylvania. Medical Bulletin — Univ PA Med Bull
University of Pennsylvania. Monographs in Folklore and Folklife — UPMFF
University of Pennsylvania. Museum Bulletin — UMB
University of Pennsylvania. Museum Bulletin — UPMB
University of Pennsylvania. Publications in Political Economy — Univ of PA Pub Pol Econ
University of Pennsylvania. Studies in East European Languages and Literatures — UPSEELL
University of Pennsylvania Studies on South Asia — Univ Penn Stud S Asia
University of Pennsylvania. University Museum. Publications of the Babylonian Section — UMBS
University of Peshawar. Journal — Univ Peshawar J
University of Pittsburgh. Law Review — Pit L
University of Pittsburgh. Law Review — Pitts L Rev
University of Pittsburgh. Law Review — PLR
University of Pittsburgh. Law Review — U of Pitt L Rev
University of Pittsburgh. Law Review — U Pit Law
University of Pittsburgh. Law Review — U Pitt L R
University of Pittsburgh. Law Review — U Pitt L Rev
University of Pittsburgh. Law Review — Univ of Pittsburgh L Rev
University of Pittsburgh Series in the Philosophy of Science — Univ Pittsburgh Ser Philos Sci
University of Poona Science and Technology. Journal — Univ Poona Sci Tech J
University of Portland. Review — UPortR
University of Pretoria. Publications. Series 2. Natural Sciences — Univ Pretoria Publ Ser 2
University of Puget Sound. Law Review — U Puget Sound L Rev
University of Qatar. Science Bulletin — Univ Qatar Sci Bull
University of Queensland. Agriculture Department. Papers — Qd Univ Agric Dep Pap
University of Queensland. Agriculture Department. Papers — Univ Qd Agric Dep Pap
University of Queensland. Botany Department. Papers — Qd Univ Bot Dep Pap
University of Queensland. Botany Department. Papers — Univ Qd Bot Dep Pap
University of Queensland. Computer Centre. Papers — Qd Univ Comput Centre Pap
University of Queensland. Computer Centre. Papers — Univ Queensl Comput Cent Pap
University of Queensland. Department of Civil Engineering. Bulletin — Qd Univ Civ Engng Dep Bull
University of Queensland. Entomology Department. Papers — Qd Univ Ent Dep Pap
University of Queensland. Entomology Department. Papers — Univ Qd Ent Dep Pap
University of Queensland. Faculty of Veterinary Science. Papers — Qd Univ Fac Vet Sci Pap
University of Queensland. Gazette — Q Univ Gaz
University of Queensland. Gazette — Univ Q Gaz
University of Queensland. Gazette — Univ Qld Gaz
University of Queensland. Geology Department. Papers — Qd Univ Geol Dep Pap
University of Queensland. Great Barrier Reef Committee. Heron Island Research Station — Univ Queensl Great Barrier Reef Comm Heron Isl Res Stn
University of Queensland. Law Journal — Qld Univ Law J
University of Queensland. Law Journal — QU Law J
University of Queensland. Law Journal — U of Queensl LJ
University of Queensland. Law Journal — U Queens L J
University of Queensland. Law Journal — U Queensl LJ
University of Queensland. Law Journal — Univ of Queensland LJ
University of Queensland. Law Journal — Univ Q Law J
University of Queensland. Law Journal — Univ Q LJ
University of Queensland. Law Journal — Univ Qld Law J
University of Queensland. Law Journal — UQLJ
University of Queensland. Law Review — U Queens LR
University of Queensland. Law Review — Uni of Q LR
University of Queensland. Papers — UQP
University of Queensland. Papers. Department of Botany — Univ Queensl Pap Dep Bot
University of Queensland. Papers. Department of Chemistry — Univ Queensl Pap Dep Chem
University of Queensland. Papers. Department of Entomology — Univ Queensl Pap Dep Entomol
University of Queensland. Papers. Department of Geology — Univ Queensl Pap Dep Geol
University of Queensland. Papers. Department of Zoology — Univ Queensl Pap Dep Zool
University of Queensland. Papers. Faculty of Veterinary Science — Univ Queensl Pap Fac Vet Sci
University of Queensland. Papers. Social Sciences — U Qsld P SS
University of Queensland. Zoology Department. Papers — Qd Univ Pap Zool Dep
University of Queensland. Zoology Department. Papers — Qd Univ Zool Dep Pap
University of Reading. National Institute for Research in Dairying. Biennial Reviews — Univ Reading Natl Inst Res Dairy Bienn Rev
University of Reading. National Institute for Research in Dairying. Report — Univ Reading Natl Inst Res Dairy Rep
University of Rhode Island. Marine Publication Series — Univ RI Mar Publ Ser
University of Rhodesia. Faculty of Medicine. Research Lecture Series — Univ Rhod Fac Med Res Lect Ser
University of Richmond. Law Review — U Rich L Rev
University of Richmond. Law Review — U Rich LR
University of Richmond. Law Review — U Richmond L Rev
University of Richmond. Law Review — Univ of Richmond L Rev
University of Riyad. Bulletin. Faculty of Arts [*Saudi Arabia*] — URB
University of Rochester. Library Bulletin — Rochester Univ Lib Bul
University of Rochester. Library Bulletin — Univ Rochester Lib Bull
University of Rochester. Library Bulletin — Univ Rochester Libr Bull
University of Rochester. Library Bulletin — URLB
University of Roorkee. Research Journal — Univ Roorkee Res J
University of Saga. Studies in English — USSE
University of San Carlos. Series D. Occasional Monographs — Univ San Carlos. Ser D Occ Monogr
University of San Francisco. Law Review — SFLR
University of San Francisco. Law Review — U San Fran L Rev
University of San Francisco. Law Review — U San Fran LR
University of San Francisco. Law Review — U San Francisco L Rev
University of San Francisco. Law Review — Univ of San Francisco L Rev
University of San Francisco. Law Review — USF L Rev
University of San Francisco. Law Review — USFLR
University of Santa Fe — USF
University of Singapore. Chinese Society. Journal — Univ Singapore Chin Soc J
University of Singapore. School of Architecture. Journal — University of Singapore School of Archre Jnl
University of South Carolina. Business and Economic Review — U So Carol
University of South Carolina. Governmental Review — Univ SC Governmental R
University of Southern California. Abstracts of Dissertations — USCAD
University of Southern California. Allan Hancock Foundation — Univ South Calif Allan Hancock Found
University of Southern California. Institute for Marine and Coastal Studies. Sea Grant Technical Report Series — SGTADY
University of Southern California. School of Architecture. Yearbook — University of Southern Calif School of Archre Yearbook
University of Strathclyde. Annual Report — Univ Strathclyde Annu Rep
University of Strathclyde. Research Report — Univ Strathclyde Res Rep
University of Sydney. Department of Agricultural Economics. Mimeographed Report — Syd Univ Dep Agric Econ Mimeo Rep
University of Sydney. Department of Agricultural Economics. Research Bulletin — Syd Univ Ag Economics Res Bul
University of Sydney. Institute of Criminology. Proceedings [*Australia*] — Univ S Inst of Crim Proceeding
University of Sydney. Medical Journal — Univ Sydney Med J
University of Sydney. Postgraduate Committee in Medicine. Annual Postgraduate Oration — Syd Univ Post Grad Comm Med Oration
University of Sydney. Postgraduate Committee in Medicine. Bulletin — Syd Univ Post Grad Comm Med Bul
University of Sydney. Postgraduate Committee in Medicine. Bulletin — Univ Syd Post Grad Ctee Med Bull
University of Sydney. School of Agriculture. Report — Syd Univ Sch Agric Rep
University of Sydney. School of Civil Engineering. Research Report — Syd Univ Civ Engng Schl Res Rep
University of Tampa. Review — UT R
University of Tasmania. Environmental Studies. Occasional Paper — Univ Tasmania Environ Stud Occas Pap
University of Tasmania. Environmental Studies Occasional Paper — UTEPDF
University of Tasmania. Environmental Studies Working Paper — UESPDE
University of Tasmania. Environmental Studies. Working Paper — Univ Tasmania Environ Stud Work Pap
University of Tasmania. Gazette — Tas Univ Gaz
University of Tasmania. Gazette — TU Gazette
University of Tasmania. Gazette — Univ Tas Gaz
University of Tasmania. Law Review — Tas L Rev
University of Tasmania. Law Review — Tas Univ Law R
University of Tasmania. Law Review — Tas Univ Law Rev
University of Tasmania. Law Review — Tasm Univ Law Rev
University of Tasmania. Law Review — TU Law R
University of Tasmania. Law Review — U Tas LR
University of Tasmania. Law Review — U Tasm L Rev
University of Tasmania. Law Review — U Tasmania L Rev
University of Tasmania. Law Review — Uni of Tas LR
University of Tasmania. Law Review — Univ of Tas LR
University of Tasmania. Law Review — Univ of Tasmania L Rev
University of Tasmania. Law Review — Univ Tas LR
University of Tasmania. Law Review — Univ TLR
University of Tasmania. Law Review — UTLR
University of Tennessee. Record — Univ Tenn Rec
University of Tennessee. Studies in the Humanities — UTSH
University of Tennessee. Survey of Business — Univ Tenn Surv Bus
University of Texas at Austin. Bureau of Economic Geology. Geologic Quadrangle Map — Texas Univ Austin Bur Econ Geology Geol Quad Map
University of Texas at Austin. Bureau of Economic Geology. Handbook — Univ Tex Austin Bur Econ Geol Handb
University of Texas at Austin. Bureau of Economic Geology. Mineral Resource Circular — Univ Tex Austin Bur Econ Geol Miner Resour Circ
University of Texas at Austin. Bureau of Economic Geology. Report of Investigations — Texas Univ Austin Bur Econ Geology Rept Inv
University of Texas at Austin. Bureau of Economic Geology. Research Note — Univ Tex Austin Bur Econ Geol Res Note
University of Texas at Austin. Center for Highway Research. Research Report — Univ Tex Austin Cent Highw Res Res Rep
University of Texas at Austin. Center for Research in Water Resources. Technical Report — Univ Tex Austin Cent Res Water Resour Tech Rep
University of Texas. Bulletin — Univ Tex Bull

University of Texas. Bureau of Economic Geology. Publication — Univ Tex Bur Econ Geol Publ
University of Texas. Bureau of Economic Geology. Report of Investigations — Univ Tex Bur Econ Geol Rep Invest
University of Texas. Hispanic Studies — UTHS
University of Texas. M. D. Anderson Symposium on Fundamental Cancer Research — Univ Tex MD Anderson Symp Fundam Cancer Res
University of Texas. Studies in English — UTSE
University of the Orange Free State. Publication. Series C — AARCDS
University of the Orange Free State. Publication. Series C — Univ Orange Free State Publ Ser C
University of the Philippines. Natural and Applied Science Bulletin — Univ Phil Nat Appl Sci Bull
University of the Ryukyus. College of Science. Bulletin [*Naha*] — Bull College Sci Univ Ryukyus
University of the West Indies. Regional Research Centre. Soil and Land Use Surveys — Univ West Indies Reg Res Cent Soil Land Use Surv
University of the Witwatersrand. Department of Geography and Environmental Studies. Occasional Paper — Univ Witwatersrand Dep Geogr Environ Stud Occas Pap
University of Tokyo. Computer Center Report — Univ Tokyo Comp Cent Rep
University of Toledo. Law Review — To LR
University of Toledo. Law Review — Tol LR
University of Toledo. Law Review — Toledo L Rev
University of Toledo. Law Review — U Tol L Rev
University of Toledo. Law Review — U Tol Law
University of Toledo. Law Review — U Tol LR
University of Toledo. Law Review — U Toledo L Rev
University of Toledo. Law Review — Univ of Toledo L Rev
University of Toledo. Law Review — Univ Toledo Law R
University of Toronto. Biological Series — Univ Toronto Biol Ser
University of Toronto. Department of Geography. Research Publications — Univ Toronto Dep Geogr Res Publ
University of Toronto. Faculty of Forestry. Technical Report — Univ Toronto Fac For Tech Rep
University of Toronto. Faculty of Law. Review — U T Fac L Rev
University of Toronto. Faculty of Law. Review — U Tor Fac LR
University of Toronto. Faculty of Law. Review — U Toronto Fac L Rev
University of Toronto. Faculty of Law. Review — U Toronto Faculty L Rev
University of Toronto. French Series — UTFS
University of Toronto. Institute for Environmental Studies. Publication EH — Univ Toronto Inst Environ Stud Publ EH
University of Toronto. Institute of Environmental Sciences and Engineering. Publication EH — Univ Toronto Inst Environ Sci Eng Publ EH
University of Toronto. Law Journal — U Tor Law J
University of Toronto. Law Journal — U Tor LJ
University of Toronto. Law Journal — U Toronto L J
University of Toronto. Law Journal — Univ of Toronto LJ
University of Toronto. Law Journal — Univ Toronto Law J
University of Toronto. Law Journal — UTLJ
University of Toronto. Medical Journal — Univ Toronto Med J
University of Toronto Quarterly — PUTQ
University of Toronto. Quarterly — U Toronto Q
University of Toronto. Quarterly — Univ Tor Q
University of Toronto. Quarterly — Univ Toronto Q
University of Toronto Quarterly — Univ Toronto Quart
University of Toronto Quarterly — UTQ
University of Toronto. Quarterly — UTQ
University of Toronto. Studies. Biological Series — Univ Toronto Stud Biol Ser
University of Toronto. Studies. Geological Series — Univ Toronto Stud Geol Ser
University of Toronto. Studies. Papers from the Chemical Laboratories — Univ Toronto Stud Pap Chem Lab
University of Toronto. Studies. Pathological Series — Univ Toronto Stud Pathol Ser
University of Toronto. Studies. Physics Series — Univ Toronto Stud Phys Ser
University of Toronto. Studies. Physiological Series — Univ Toronto Stud Physiol Ser
University of Toronto Undergraduate Dental Journal — Univ Toronto Undergrad Dent J
University of Tripoli. Bulletin. Faculty of Engineering — Univ Tripoli Bull Fac Eng
University of Tsukuba Technical Report — Univ Tsukuba Tech Rep
University of Tulsa. Department of English. Monograph Series — UTDEMS
University of Udaipur. Research Journal — Univ Udaipur Res J
University of Udaipur. Research Studies — Univ Udaipur Res Stud
University of Ulsan. Natural Science and Engineering — Univ Ulsan Rep Natur Sci Engrg
University of Umea. Communication Research Unit. Project Report — Univ Umea Commun Res Unit Proj Rep
University of Umea. Department of Mathematics — Univ Umea Dep Math
University of Utah. Anthropological Papers — Univ Utah Anthropol Pap
University of Utah. Biological Series — Univ Utah Biol Ser
University of Virginia Alumni Bulletin — Univ Va Alumni Bul
University of Virginia. Magazine — UVM
University of Virginia. Magazine — UVMag
University of Virginia. News Letter — Univ VA News Letter
University of Warsaw. Department of Radiochemistry. Publication — Univ Warsaw Dep Radiochem Publ
University of Warwick. Occasional Papers in German Studies — UWOPGS
University of Washington. College of Fisheries. Technical Report — Univ Wash Coll Fish Tech Rep
University of Washington. Contributions. Cloud and Aerosol Research Group — UWCCARG
University of Washington. Contributions. Cloud Physics Group. Collections from Reprints — UWCCPGR
University of Washington. Contributions. Energy Transfer Group. Collections from Reprints — UWCETG
University of Washington. Engineering Experiment Station. Bulletin — Univ Wash Eng Exp Stn Bull
University of Washington. Engineering Experiment Station. Report — Univ Wash Eng Exp Stn Rep
University of Washington. Engineering Experiment Station. Technical Note — Univ Wash Eng Exp Stn Tech Note
University of Washington. Institute of Forest Products. Contributions — Univ Wash Inst For Prod Contrib
University of Washington Medicine — Univ Washington Med
University of Washington. Publications in Biology — Univ Wash Publ Biol
University of Washington. Publications in Fisheries — Univ Wash Publ Fish
University of Washington. Publications in Fisheries. New Series — Univ Wash Publ Fish New Ser
University of Washington. Publications in Fisheries. New Series — UWPFAO
University of Washington. Publications in Geology — Univ Wash Publ Geol
University of Washington. Publications in Language and Literature — UWPLL
University of Washington. Publications in Oceanography — Univ Wash Publ Oceanogr
University of Waterloo. Biology Series — Univ Waterloo Biol Ser
University of Waterloo. Faculty of Environmental Studies. Occasional Paper — Univ Waterloo Fac Environ Stud Occas Pap
University of West Los Angeles. Law Review — U West LA L Rev
University of West Los Angeles. Law Review — U West Los Angeles L Rev
University of West Los Angeles. Law Review — UWLA L Rev
University of West Los Angeles. Law Review — UWLA LR
University of Western Australia. Annual Law Review — U West Aust Ann L Rev
University of Western Australia. Annual Law Review — U Western Aust Ann L Rev
University of Western Australia. Annual Law Review — Univ WA Ann L Rev
University of Western Australia. Annual Law Review — WA Ann LR
University of Western Australia. Gazette — WA Univ Gaz
University of Western Australia. Geography Laboratory. Research Report — WA Univ Geog Lab Res Rept
University of Western Australia. Law Review — U of West Aust L Rev
University of Western Australia. Law Review — U Western Aust L Rev
University of Western Australia. Law Review — Univ of West Australia L Rev
University of Western Australia. Law Review — Univ WA L Rev
University of Western Australia. Law Review — Univ WA Law Rev
University of Western Australia. Law Review — Univ Western Australia Law R
University of Western Australia. Law Review — UNWAL Rev
University of Western Australia. Law Review — UW Austl L Rev
University of Western Australia. Law Review — UWAL Rev
University of Western Australia. Law Review — UWALR
University of Western Australia. Law Review — WALR
University of Western Australia. Law Review — WAU Law R
University of Western Australia. Law Review — West Aust L Rev
University of Western Ontario. Law Review — U Western Ont L Rev
University of Western Ontario. Law Review — UW Ont L Rev
University of Western Ontario. Law Review — UWOL Rev
University of Western Ontario. Medical Journal — Univ West Ont Med J
University of Western Ontario. Medical Journal — UWOMA6
University of Western Ontario. Series in Philosophy in Science — Univ West Ont Ser Philos Sci
University of Western Ontario. Series in Philosophy of Science — Univ Western Ontario Series in Philos Sci
University of Windsor. Review — Univ Windsor R
University of Windsor Review — UWiR
University of Windsor. Review — UWR
University of Wisconsin. College of Agricultural and Life Sciences. Research Division. Bulletin — Univ Wis Coll Agric Life Sci Res Div Bull
University of Wisconsin. College of Agricultural and Life Sciences. Research Division. Research Report — Univ Wis Coll Agric Life Sci Res Div Res Rep
University of Wisconsin. Engineering Experiment Station. Report — Univ Wis Eng Exp Stn Rep
University of Wisconsin. Sea Grant College. Technical Report — Univ Wis Sea Grant Coll Tech Rep
University of Wisconsin. Sea Grant Program. Technical Report — Univ Wis Sea Grant Program Tech Rep
University of Wisconsin Studies in Language and Literature — Univ of Wisconsin Studies in Lang and Lit
University of Wisconsin Studies in Language and Literature — WSL
University of Wisconsin. Water Resources Center. Eutrophication Information Program. Literature Review — Univ Wis Water Resour Cent Eutrophication Inf Prog Lit Rev
University of Wisconsin. Water Resources Center. Eutrophication Information Program. Literature Review — WRLRAR
University of Wisconsin. Water Resources Center. Eutrophication Information Program. Occasional Paper — WROPA2
University of Wisconsin-Madison. College of Agricultural and Life Sciences. Research Division. Research Bulletin — Univ Wis-Madison Coll Agric Life Sci Res Div Res Bull
University of Wisconsin-Madison. Mathematics Research Center. Publication — Univ Wis Madison Math Res Cent Publ
University of Wisconsin-Milwaukee. Field Stations Bulletin — Univ Wis Milw Field Stn Bull
University of Wyoming. Publications — Univ of Wyoming Publ
University of Wyoming. Publications — Univ Wyo Publ
University Perspectives — Univ Perspect
University Record — Univ Rec
University Research News — Univ Res N
University Review — Univ R
University Review — Univ Rev
University Review — UR

University Review [*Dublin*] — URev
University Series in Mathematics — Univ Ser Math
University Series in Modern Engineering — Univ Ser Modern Engrg
University Studies — US
University Studies in History — Univ Stud Hist
University Studies in History and Economics — Univ Stud
University Studies in History and Economics — Univ Stud Hist Ec
University Studies in History and Economics — Univ Studies
University Studies in Mathematics — Univ Studies Math
University Studies in Mathematics (Jaipur) — Univ Stud Math (Jaipur)
University Studies in Western Australian History — Univ Studies
University Studies. University of Nebraska — Univ Stud Univ Neb
University Vision — Univ V
Universo — Univ
Universo [*Italy*] — UNVS-A
Universum der Kunst — U d K
Univerza v Ljubljani. Tehniska Fakulteta. Acta Technica. Series Chimica — Uni Ljubljai Teh Fak Acta Tech Ser Chim
Univerzitet u Beogradu. Publikacije Elektrotehnickog Fakulteta. Serija Matematika i Fizika — Univ Beograd Publ Elektrotehn Fak Ser Mat Fiz
Univerzitet u Beogradu. Tehnicka Fizika — Univ Beograd Tehn Fiz
Univerzitet u Beogradu. Zbornik Radova Gradevinskog Fakulteta u Beogradu — Univ Beograd Zb Radova Gradevin Fak
Univerzitet u Geogradu Radovi. Zavoda za Fiziku — Univ Geograd Radovi Zavoda za Fiz
Univerzitet u Novom Sadu. Zbornik Radova Prirodno-Matematickog Fakulteta — Univ u Novom Sadu Zb Rad Prirod-Mat Fak
Univerzitet u Novom Sadu. Zbornik Radova Prirodno-Matematickog Fakulteta. Serija za Matemati — Univ u Novom Sadu Zb Rad Prirod Mat Fak Ser Mat
Univerzitet vo Skopje. Sumarski Fakultet. Godisen Zbornik — Univ Skopje Sumar Fak God Zb
Uniwersytet Gdanski Wydzial Matematyki, Fizyki, Chemii, Zeszyty Naukowe. Seria Chemia — Uniw Gdanski Wydz Mat Fiz Chem Zesz Nauk Ser Chem
Uniwersytet Imienia Adama Mickiewicza w Poznaniu — UP
Uniwersytet Imienia Adama Mickiewicza w Poznaniu. Instytut Chemii. Seria Chemia — Uniw Adama Mickiewicza Poznaniu Inst Chem Ser Chem
Uniwersytet Imienia Adama Mickiewicza w Poznaniu. Seria Astronomia — Uniw Adama Mickiewicza Poznaniu Ser Astron
Uniwersytet Imienia Adama Mickiewicza w Poznaniu. Seria Biologia — Uniw Adama Mickiewicza Poznaniu Ser Biol
Uniwersytet Imienia Adama Mickiewicza w Poznaniu. Seria Chemia — Uniw Adama Mickiewicza Poznaniu Ser Chem
Uniwersytet Imienia Adama Mickiewicza w Poznaniu. Seria Fizyka — Uniw Adama Mickiewicza w Poznaniu Ser Fiz
Uniwersytet Imienia Adama Mickiewicza w Poznaniu. Wydzial Biologii i Nauk o Ziemi. Prace. Seria Geologia — UPWBA
Uniwersytet Jagiellonski — UJ
Uniwersytet Lodzki. Acta Universitatis Lodziensis. Seria 2 — Uniw Lodz Acta Univ Lodz Ser 2
Uniwersytet Marii Curie-Sklodowskiej — UMCS
Uniwersytet Marii Curie-Sklodowskiej. Annales. Sectio AA. Physica et Chemia — Uniw Marii Curie-Sklodowskiej Ann Sect AA
Uniwersytet Opolski. Zeszyty Naukowe. Chemia — Uniw Opolski Zesz Nauk Chem
Uniwersytet Slaski w Katowicach. Prace Naukowe — Uniw Slaski w Katowicach Prace Nauk
Uniwersytet Slaski w Katowicach. Prace Naukowe — Uniw Slaski w Katowicach Prace Naukowe
Uniwersytet Slaski w Katowicach. Prace Naukowe. Prace Matematyczne — Uniw Slaski w Katowicach Prace Naukowe Prace Mat
Uniwersytet Slaski w Katowicach. Prace Naukowe. Prace Matematyczne — Uniw Slaski w Katowicach Prace Nauk-Prace Mat
Unknown — UK
Unknown Worlds — UK
Unknown Worlds — Unk
Unlisted Drugs — UD
Unmanned Systems — Unman Syst
Unmuzzled Ox — Unm Ox
Unnumbered Report. United States Department of Agriculture. Economics, Statistics, and Cooperatives Service. Statistical Research Division — Unnumbered Rep US Dep Agric Econ Stat Coop Serv Stat Res Div
Unpartizan Review — Unpartizan R
Unpopular Review — Unpop R
Unpublished Objects from Palaikastro Excavations, 1902-09 — PKU
Unreported Judgments (Supreme Court) [*India*] — UJ (SC)
Unser Sozialistisches Dorf — Unser Sozial Dorf
Unser Tsait/Unzer Tsayt — UT
Unsere Heimat. Verein fuer Landeskunde von Niederoesterreich und Wien — UH
Unsere Heimat. Zeitschrift des Vereines fuer Landeskunde von Niederoesterreich und Wien — Unsere Heim
Unsere Kunstdenkmaeler — UK
Unsteady State Processes in Catalysis. Proceedings. International Conference — Unsteady State Processes Catal Proc Int Conf
Unternehmensforschung — UNFGA
Unternehmung. Schweizerische Zeitschrift fuer Betriebswirtschaft — UNN
Unternehmung. Schweizerische Zeitschrift fuer Betriebswirtschaft — Unternehm
Unternehmungsfuehrung im Gewerbe und Gewerbliche — Unternehmungsfuehrung im Gewerbe
Unterricht Chemie — Unterr Chem
Unterricht und Forschung — U & F
Unterrichtsblaetter fuer Mathematik und Naturwissenschaften — Unterrichtsbll Math Natwiss
Unterrichtspraxis — UP
Unterrichtswissenschaft — UNWSA
Untersuchungen der Zweigstelle Kairo des Oesterreichischen Archaeologischen Institutes — Oe Al Kairo
Untersuchungen ueber Angebot und Nachfrage Mineralischer Rohstoffe — Unters Angebot Nachfrage Miner Rohst
Untersuchungen ueber die Natur des Menschen, der Thiere, und der Pflanzen — Untersuch Natur Menschen
Untersuchungen zu den Kertschen Vasen — KV
Untersuchungen zum Neuen Testament — UNT
Untersuchungen zur Antiken Literatur und Geschichte — UALG
Untersuchungen zur Assyriologie und Vorderasiatischen Archaeologie — UAVA
Untersuchungen zur Deutschen Literaturgeschichte — UDL
Untersuchungen zur Geschichte und Altertumskunde Agyptens — UGA
Untersuchungen zur Romanischen Philologie — URP
Untersuchungen zur Vergleichenden Literatur [*Hamburg*] — UVL
Uomini e Libri — U e L
Uomini e Libri — UEL
Up Here — UPHR
UP [*University of the Philippines*] **Research Digest** — UP Res Dig
UP [*University of the Philippines*] **Veterinarian** — UP Vet
Update. Clinical Immunology — Update Clin Immunol
Update in Intensive Care and Emergency Medicine — Update Intensive Care Emerg Med
Update on Law-Related Education — Update
Update Series. South Dakota Agricultural Experiment Station — Update Ser SD Agric Exp Stn
Upplands Fornminnesfoerenings Tidskrift — UFFT
Uppsala English Institute. Essays and Studies — UEIES
Uppsala Nya Tidning — UNT
Uppsala Universitets Arsskrift — Upps Arsskr
Uppsala Universitets Arsskrift — UUA
Uppsala University. Geological Institution. Bulletin — Upps Univ Geol Inst Bull
Uppsala University. Geological Institution. Bulletin — Uppsala Univ G Inst B
Upravlenie Sloznymi Sistemami. Rizskii Politekhniceskii Institut — Upravlenie Slozn Sistemami
Upravlenie Yadernymi Energeticheskimi Ustanovkami — UIEUA
Upravlenie Yadernymi Energeticheskimi Ustanovkami — Upr Yad Energ Ustanovkami
Upravlyaemye Sistemy Institut Matematiki Institut Kataliza Sibirskogo Otdeleniya Akademii Nauk SSSR — Upravlyaemye Sistemy
Upravlyayushchie Sistemy i Mashiny [*Ukrainian SSR*] — Upr Sist Mash
Uprawa Roslin i Nawozenie — Uprawa Rosl Nawozenie
Uprochnyayushchaya Termicheskaya i Termomekhanicheskaya Obrabotka Prokata — Uprochnyayushchaya Term Termomekh Obrab Prokata
Upsala Journal of Medical Sciences — Ups J Med Sci
Upsala Journal of Medical Sciences — Upsala J Med Sci
Upsala Journal of Medical Sciences. Supplement — Ups J Med Sci Suppl
Upsala Journal of Medical Sciences. Supplement — Upsala J Med Sci Suppl
Upstart Crow — UCrow
Uqaata [*Inuit Cultural Institute*] — UQTA
Ur Nutidens Musikliv — Ur Nutid Musikliv
Ur- und Fruehgeschichte Archaeologie der Schweiz — UFAS
Ural-Altaische Jahrbuecher — U Jb
Ural-Altaische Jahrbuecher — UA
Ural-Altaische Jahrbuecher — UAJ
Ural-Altaische Jahrbuecher — UAJb
Ural-Altaische Jahrbuecher — Ural Altaische Jb
Uralic and Altaic Series. Indiana University. Publications — UAS
Uralic News and Notes from the United States — UNNUS
Ural'skaya Metallurgiya — Ural Metall
Ural'skii Gosudarstvennyi Universitet Imeni A. M. Gor'kogo Ural'skoe Matematiceskoe Obscestvo Matematiceskie Zapiski — Ural Gos Univ Mat Zap
Ural'skii Politehniceskii Institut Imeni S. M. Kirova Sbornik — Ural Politehn Inst Sb
Urania [*Poland*] — URAAA
Uranium Abstracts — Uranium Abstr
Uranium Mining and Metallurgy — Uranium Min Metall
Uranium Supply and Demand. Perspectives to 1995 — Uran Supply
Urban Abstracts — Urban Abs
Urban Affairs Abstracts — Urb Aff Abstr
Urban Affairs Abstracts — Urban Aff Abs
Urban Affairs Annual Review — Urb Aff Ann R
Urban Affairs Quarterly — PUAQ
Urban Affairs Quarterly — UAQUA
Urban Affairs Quarterly — Urb Aff Q
Urban Affairs Quarterly — Urb Aff Quart
Urban Affairs Quarterly — Urban Affairs Q
Urban and Rural Planning Thought [*India*] — URPT-A
Urban and Social Change Review — Urb Soc Change R
Urban and Social Change Review — Urban Soc C
Urban Anthropology — UA
Urban Anthropology — Urb Anthrop
Urban Anthropology — Urban Anthr
Urban Anthropology — Urban Anthrop
Urban Buecher — UB
Urban Canada — Urban Can
Urban Data Service [*Database*] — UDS
Urban Data Service Report — Urban Data Service Rept
Urban Design — Urban Des
Urban Design International — Urban Des Int
Urban Design International — Urban Design Intl
Urban Design Quarterly — Urban Des Q
Urban Ecology — Urban Ecol

Urban Ecology [*Netherlands*] — URBE
Urban Ecology — URECD
Urban Education — Urban Ed
Urban Education — Urban Educ
Urban Forum — Urban For
Urban Health — Urban Hlth
Urban Health — URBH
Urban History Review [*Revue d'Histoire Urbaine*] — Urban Hist
Urban History Review — Urban Hist R
Urban History Yearbook — Urban Hist Yearb
Urban Innovation Abroad — Urban Innov Abroad
Urban Institute. Policy and Research Report — Urban Inst Policy Res Rep
Urban Land — URLAA
Urban Land Institute. Landmark Report — ULI Lm Rep
Urban Land Institute. Research Report — ULI Res Rep
Urban Land Institute. Special Report — ULI Spe Rep
Urban Law and Policy — ULPOD
Urban Law and Policy — Urb L and P
Urban Law and Policy — Urb L and Poly
Urban Law and Policy — Urb Law Pol
Urban Law Annual — Urb L Ann
Urban Law Annual — Urban L Ann
Urban Law Annual — Urban Law An
Urban Law Review — Urb L Rev
Urban Lawyer — Urb Law
Urban Lawyer — Urban Law
Urban Life — Urb Life
Urban Life and Culture [*Later, Urban Life*] — Urb Life & Cult
Urban Life and Culture [*Later, Urban Life*] — Urban Lif C
Urban Mass Transportation Research Information Service [*Database*] — UMTRIS
Urban Renewal and Low Income Housing — URLH
Urban Review — Urban R
Urban Review — Urban Rev
Urban Review — UrR
Urban Studies — PUSU
Urban Studies — Urb Stud
Urban Studies — Urban Stud
Urban Studies [*United Kingdom*] — URBS-A
Urban Systems — Urban Syst
Urban Transportation Abroad — Urban Transp Abroad
Urbanisme [*France*] — URBN-A
Urbanisme, Amenagement, Equipments et Transports [*Database*] — URBAMET
Urdmurtskogo i Glazovskogo Pedagogiceskogo Instituta Ucenye Zapiski — Urdmurt i Glazov Ped Inst Ucen Zap
Urdmurtskogo Pedagogiceskogo Instituta Ucenye Zapiski — Urdmurt Ped Inst Ucen Zap
Uremia Investigation — Uremia Invest
Urethane Plastics and Products — Urethane
Urethane Plastics and Products — Urethane Plast Prod
Urgeschichtlicher Anzeiger — UGA
Urja Oil and Gas International — Urja Oil Gas Int
Urkunden der Ptolemaeerzeit — UPZ
Urkunden der Ptolemaeerzeit — Urk
Urkunden des 18. Dynastie. Historisch-Bibliographische Urkunden — Urk
Urkunden die Aegyptischen Altertums — UAegAl
Urner Mineralien Freund — Urner Miner Freund
Urologe — URLGA
Urologe. Ausgabe A — URGAB
Urologe. Ausgabe A — Urol Ausg A
Urologe. Ausgabe A — Urologe
Urologe. Ausgabe A. Zeitschrift fuer Klinische und Praktische Urologie — Urologe A
Urologe. Ausgabe B — URLBB
Urologe. Ausgabe B — Urologe Ausg B
Urologe. Ausgabe B. Organ des Berufverbandes der Deutschen Urologen — Urologe B
Urologia Internationalis — URINA
Urologia Internationalis — Urol Int
Urologia Internationalis — Urol Intern
Urologia Internationalis — Urol Internat
Urologia Panamericana — Urol Panam
Urologia Polska — Urol Pol
Urologia. Supplemento (Treviso) — Urol Suppl (Treviso)
Urologiai es Nephrologiai Szemle [*Hungary*] — Urol Nephrol Sz
Urologic and Cutaneous Review — Urol Cutaneous Rev
Urologic Clinics of North America — Urol Clin North Am
Urologic Radiology — Urol Radiol
Urological Research — Urol Res
Urological Survey — Urol Surv
Urological Survey — URSUA
Urologiia i Nefrologiia (Moskva) — Urol Nefrol (Mosk)
Urologiya i Nefrologiya — URNEA
Urologiya i Nefrologiya — Urol i Nefrol
Urology [*Ridgewood, NJ*] — URGYA
Ur-Schweiz — Ur Schw
Us — GUSS
US Agricultural Research Service. ARS-NC — US Agric Res Serv ARS-NC
US Agricultural Research Service. ARS-NE — US Agric Res Serv ARS-NE
US Agricultural Research Service. ARS-S — US Agric Res Serv ARS-S
US Agricultural Research Service. ARS-W — US Agric Res Serv ARS-W
US Agricultural Research Service. CA — US Agric Res Serv CA
US Agricultural Research Service. Marketing Research Report — US Agric Res Serv Mark Res Rep
US Agricultural Research Service. Northeastern Region Report. ARS-NE — US Agric Res Serv Northeast Reg Rep ARS NE
US Agricultural Research Service. Southern Region Report — US Agric Res Serv South Reg Rep
US Air Force Academy. Technical Report — US Air Force Acad Tech Rep
US Air Force Academy. Technical Report — USAUD3
US Air Force. Aeronautical Systems. Division Technical Report — US Air Force Aeronaut Syst Div Tech Rep
US Air Force. Human Resources Laboratory. Technical Report AFHRL-TR — US Air Force Hum Resour Lab Tech Rep AFHRL-TR
US Air Force. Technical Documentary Report. AFSWC-TDR — US Air Force Tech Doc Rep AFSWC-TDR
US Air Force. Technical Documentary Report. AMRL-TDR — US Air Force Tech Doc Rep AMRL-TDR
US Air Force. Technical Documentary Report. ARL-TDR — US Air Force Tech Doc Rep ARL-TDR
US Air Force. Technical Documentary Report. ASD-TDR — US Air Force Tech Doc Rep ASD-TDR
US Air Force. Technical Documentary Report. RTD-TDR — US Air Force Tech Doc Rep RTD-TDR
US Air Force. Technical Documentary Report. SAM-TDR — US Air Force Tech Doc Rep SAM-TDR
US Air Force. Technical Documentary Report. SAM-TDR — XADMAY
US Air Force. Technical Documentary Report. SEG-TDR — US Air Force Tech Doc Rep SEG-TDR
US Air Force. Wright Air Development Center. Technical Notes — US Air Force Wright Air Dev Cent Tech Notes
US Air Force. Wright Air Development Center. Technical Report — US Air Force Wright Air Dev Cent Tech Rep
US Argonne National Laboratory. Report — US Argonne Natl Lab Rep
US Armed Forces. Medical Journal — US Armed Forces Med J
US Army. Armament Research and Development Command. Technical Report — US Army Armament Res Dev Command Tech Rep
US Army. Aviation Digest — Army Av D
US Army. Behavioral Science Research Laboratory. Technical Research Note — US Army Behav Sci Res Lab Tech Res Note
US Army. Coastal Engineering Research Center. Technical Memorandum — US Army Coastal Eng Res Cent Tech Memo
US Army. Diamond Ordnance Fuze Laboratories. Technical Report — US Army Diamond Ord Fuze Lab Tech Rep
US Army. Diamond Ordnance Fuze Laboratories. Technical Report — XADRAF
US Army Engineers. Waterways Experiment Station. Technical Report — US Army Eng Waterw Exp Stn Tech Rep
US Army. Natick Laboratories. Technical Report. Microbiology Series — US Army Natick Lab Tech Rep Microbiol Ser
US Atomic Energy Commission. Publication — US Atom Energy Commn Pub
US Atomic Energy Commission. Report — US Atomic Energy Comm Rept
US Atomic Energy Commission. Report. CONF — USAEC Rep CONF
US Atomic Energy Commission. Research and Development Report. AEC-TR — USAEC Res Dev Rep AEC-TR
US Atomic Energy Commission. Research and Development Report. ANL — USAEC Res Dev Rep ANL
US Atomic Energy Commission. Research and Development Report. BNL — USAEC Res Dev Rep BNL
US Atomic Energy Commission. Research and Development Report. COO — USAEC Res Dev Rep COO
US Atomic Energy Commission. Research and Development Report. HASL — USAEC Res Dev Rep HASL
US Atomic Energy Commission. Research and Development Report. HW — USAEC Res Dev Rep HW
US Atomic Energy Commission. Research and Development Report. LAMS (LA) — USAEC Res Dev Rep LAMS (LA)
US Atomic Energy Commission. Research and Development Report. LF — USAEC Res Dev Rep LF
US Atomic Energy Commission. Research and Development Report. NYO — USAEC Res Dev Rep NYO
US Atomic Energy Commission. Research and Development Report. ORINS — USAEC Res Dev Rep ORINS
US Atomic Energy Commission. Research and Development Report. ORNL — USAEC Res Dev Rep ORNL
US Atomic Energy Commission. Research and Development Report. ORO — USAEC Res Dev Rep ORO
US Atomic Energy Commission. Research and Development Report. RLO — USAEC Res Dev Rep RLO
US Atomic Energy Commission. Research and Development Report. SCR — USAEC Res Dev Rep SCR
US Atomic Energy Commission. Research and Development Report. TID — USAEC Res Dev Rep TID
US Atomic Energy Commission. Research and Development Report. UCD — USAEC Res Dev Rep UCD
US Atomic Energy Commission. Research and Development Report. UCLA — USAEC Res Dev Rep UCLA
US Atomic Energy Commission. Research and Development Report. UCRL — USAEC Res Dev Rep UCRL
US Atomic Energy Commission. Research and Development Report. UCSF — USAEC Res Dev Rep UCSF
US Atomic Energy Commission. Research and Development Report. UH — USAEC Res Dev Rep UH
US Atomic Energy Commission. Research and Development Report. UR — USAEC Res Dev Rep UR
US Atomic Energy Commission. Research and Development Report. WT — USAEC Res Dev Rep WT
US Atomic Energy Commission. Symposium Series — USAEC Symp Ser
US Bureau of American Ethnology. Bulletin — US Bur Am Ethnology Bull

US Bureau of Commercial Fisheries. Report for the Calendar Year — US Bur Commer Fish Rep Cal Year
US Bureau of Mines. Information Circular — US Bur Mines Inf Circ
US Bureau of Mines. Report of Investigations — US Bur Mines Rept Inv
US Bureau of Soils. Bulletin — US Bur Soils B
US Bureau of Sport Fisheries and Wildlife. Investigations in Fish Control — US Bureau Sport Fish Wildl Invest Fish Control
US Bureau of Sport Fisheries and Wildlife. Research Report — US Bur Sport Fish Wildl Res Rep
US Bureau of Sport Fisheries and Wildlife. Technical Papers — US Bur Sport Fish Wildl Tech Pap
US Bureau of Standards. Handbook — Bur Stand US Handb
US Bureau of Standards. Journal of Research — Bur Stand US J Res
US Catholic — GUSC
US Catholic Historical Society. Historical Records and Studies — US Cath Hist Rec
US Civil Service Commission. Annual Report — US Civil Serv Com Ann Rep
US Coast and Geodetic Survey. Publication — US Coast and Geod Survey Pub
US Commercial Newsletter [*The Hague*] — UEE
US Consulate [*Hong Kong*]. Current Background — CB
US Consumer and Marketing Service. C & MS — US Consum Marketing Serv C & MS
US Department of Agriculture. Agricultural Economic Report — USDA Agr Econ Rep
US Department of Agriculture. Agricultural Research Service. ARS — XAARAY
US Department of Agriculture. Agriculture Handbook — US Dep Agric Agric Handb
US Department of Agriculture. Agriculture Information Bulletin — US Dep Agric Agric Inf Bull
US Department of Agriculture. Bulletin — US Dp Agr B
US Department of Agriculture. Bureau of Biological Survey. Bulletin — USDA Bur Biol Surv Bull
US Department of Agriculture. Bureau of Plant Industry. Circular — USDA Bur Pl Industr Circ
US Department of Agriculture. Circular — US Dep Agric Circ
US Department of Agriculture. Conservation Research Report — US Dep Agric Conserv Res Rep
US Department of Agriculture. Division of Vegetable Pathology. Report. Chief of Division of Vegetable Pathology — USDA Div Veg Pathol Rep Chief Div Veg Pathol
US Department of Agriculture. Farmers' Bulletin — US Dep Agric Farmers' Bull
US Department of Agriculture. Fertilizer Supply — USDA Fert
US Department of Agriculture. Forest Service. Research Paper (Pacific Northwest) — US Dep Agric For Serv Res Pap (PNW)
US Department of Agriculture. Forestry Division Bulletin — USDA Forest Div Bull
US Department of Agriculture. Home and Garden Bulletin — US Dep Agric Home Gard Bull
US Department of Agriculture. Leaflet — US Dep Agric Leafl
US Department of Agriculture. Miscellaneous Publications — US Dep Agric Misc Publ
US Department of Agriculture. Office of Experiment Stations. Experiment Station Record — USDA Off Exp Sta Exp Sta Rec
US Department of Agriculture. Office of Experiment Stations. Guam Agricultural Experiment Station. Report — USDA Off Exp Sta Guam Agric Exp Sta Rep
US Department of Agriculture. Office of the Secretary. Report — USDA Off Secr Rep
US Department of Agriculture. Plant Inventory — US Dep Agric Plant Inventory
US Department of Agriculture. Plant Inventory — XACIAH
US Department of Agriculture. Production Research Report — US Dep Agric Prod Res Rep
US Department of Agriculture. Report. Pomologist — USDA Rep Pomol
US Department of Agriculture. Science and Education Administration. Agricultural Research Manual — US Dep Agric Sci Educ Adm Agric Res Man
US Department of Agriculture. Science and Education Administration. Agricultural Research Results. ARR-S — ASSUD9
US Department of Agriculture. Science and Education Administration. Agricultural Research Results. ARR-S — US Dep Agric Sci Educ Adm Agric Res Results ARR-S
US Department of Agriculture. Science and Education Administration. Agricultural Research Results. ARR-W — ARWSDG
US Department of Agriculture. Science and Education Administration. Agricultural Research Results. ARR-W — US Dep Agric Sci Educ Adm Agric Res Results ARR-W
US Department of Agriculture. Science and Education Administration. Bibliographies and Literature of Agriculture — BAUADE
US Department of Agriculture. Science and Education Administration. Bibliographies and Literature of Agriculture — US Dep Agric Sci Educ Adm Bibliogr Lit Agric
US Department of Agriculture. Soil Conservation Service. SCS-TP — US Dep Agric Soil Conserv Serv SCS-TP
US Department of Agriculture. Soil Conservation Service. SCS-TP — USASEW
US Department of Agriculture. Soil Conservation Service. Soil Survey Investigation Report — US Dep Agric Soil Conserv Serv Soil Surv Invest Rep
US Department of Agriculture. Statistical Bulletin — US Dep Agric Stat Bull
US Department of Agriculture. Technical Bulletin — US Dep Agric Tech Bull
US Department of Agriculture. Yearbook of Agriculture — US Dep Agric Yearb Agric
US Department of Commerce. Coast and Geodetic Survey. Magnetograms and Hourly Values MHV — US Coast Geod Surv Magnetograms Hourly Values MHV
US Department of Commerce. National Bureau of Standards. Technical Note — US Dep Commer Natl Bur Stand Tech Note
US Department of Commerce. National Marine Fisheries Service. Circular — US Dep Commer Natl Mar Fish Serv Circ
US Department of Commerce. National Marine Fisheries Service. Special Scientific Report. Fisheries — US Dep Commer Natl Mar Fish Serv Spec Sci Rep Fish
US Department of Energy. Bartlesville Energy Technology Center. Petroleum Product Surveys — US Dep Energy Bartlesville Energy Technol Cent Pet Prod Surv
US Department of Energy. Bartlesville Energy Technology Center. Publications — US Dep Energy Bartlesville Energy Technol Cent Publ
US Department of Energy. Environmental Measurements Laboratory. Environmental Report — US Dep Energy Environ Meas Lab Environ Rep
US Department of Health and Human Services. National Institute of Mental Health. Science Monographs — NSMOD2
US Department of Health and Human Services. National Institute of Mental Health. Science Monographs — US Dep Health Hum Serv Natl Inst Ment Health Sci Monogr
US Department of Health and Human Services. Publications — US Dept HHS Publ
US Department of Health, Education, and Welfare [*Later, US Department of Health and Human Services*] **Annual Report** — US Dep Health Educ Welfare Annu Rep
US Department of Health, Education, and Welfare [*Later, US Department of Health and Human Services*] **DHEW Publication (NIH)** — US Dep Health Educ Welfare DHEW Publ (NIH)
US Department of Health, Education, and Welfare. National Institute of Mental Health. Science Monographs — US Dep Health Educ Welfare Natl Inst Ment Health Sci Monogr
US Department of Health, Education, and Welfare [*Later, US Department of Health and Human Services*] **Publications** — US Dept HEW Publ
US Department of State. Bulletin — Dep St Bull
US Department of State Bulletin — USDS
US Department of State Dispatch — PDSD
US Department of the Interior. Conservation Yearbook — US Dep Inter Conserv Yearb
US Department of the Interior. Federal Water Pollution Control Administration. Water Pollution Control Research Series — FWPPAP
US Department of the Interior. Mining Enforcement and Safety Administration. Informational Report — US Dep Inter MESA Inf Rep
US Department of the Interior. Publication — US Dp Int
US Department of Transportation (Report). DOT/TST — US Dep Transp (Rep) DOT/TST
US Economic Outlook — US Ec Outlk
US Economic Report — US Econ Rep
US Economic Research Service. Foreign Agricultural Economic Report — US Econ Res Serv Foreign Agric Econ Rep
US Electric Utility Industry Outlook to the Year 2000 — Elec Outlk
US Energy Research and Development Administration (Report) GJO [*Grand Junction Office*] — US Energy Res Dev Adm (Rep) GJO
US Environmental Protection Agency. Ecological Research — US EPA Ecol Res
US Environmental Protection Agency. Environmental Health Effects Research — US EPA Envir Health Res
US Environmental Protection Agency. Environmental Protection Technology — US EPA Envir Prot Technol
US Environmental Protection Agency. National Environmental Research Center. Ecological Research Series — US Environ Prot Agency Natl Environ Res Cent Ecol Res Ser
US Environmental Protection Agency. Office of Air and Waste Management. EPA-450 — UEPEDY
US Environmental Protection Agency. Office of Air and Waste Management. EPA-450 — US Environ Prot Agency Off Air Waste Manage EPA-450
US Environmental Protection Agency. Office of Air Quality Planning and Standards. Technical Report — US Environ Prot Agency Off Air Qual Plann Stand Tech Rep
US Environmental Protection Agency. Office of Pesticide Programs. Substitute Chemical Program. EPA-540 — XEPPDW
US Environmental Protection Agency. Office of Radiation Programs. EPA — US Environ Prot Agency Off Radiat Programs EPA
US Environmental Protection Agency. Office of Radiation Programs. EPA-ORP — US Environ Prot Agency Off Radiat Programs EPA-ORP
US Environmental Protection Agency. Office of Radiation Programs. Technical Reports ORP-SID — US Environ Prot Agency Off Radiat Programs Tech Rep ORP-SID
US Environmental Protection Agency. Office of Research and Development. Research Reports. Ecological Research Series — US Environ Prot Agency Off Res Dev Res Rep Ecol Res Ser
US Environmental Protection Agency. Office of Research and Development. Research Reports. Ecological Research Series — XPARD6
US Environmental Protection Agency. Publication. AP Series — US Environ Prot Agency Publ AP Ser
US Farm News — US Farm
US Federal Power Commission. Annual Report — US Fed Pow Com Ann Rep
US Federal Railroad Administration. Report — US Fed Railroad Adm Rep
US Fish and Wildlife Service. Biological Report — BRUSEI
US Fish and Wildlife Service. Biological Report — US Fish Wildl Serv Biol Rep
US Fish and Wildlife Service. Biological Services Program. FWS-OBS — US Fish Wildl Serv Biol Serv Program FWS-OBS
US Fish and Wildlife Service. Biological Services Program. FWS-OBS — US Fish Wildl Serv FWS-OBS
US Fish and Wildlife Service. Biological Services Program. FWS-OBS — USFODA
US Fish and Wildlife Service. Bureau of Commercial Fisheries. Fishery Leaflet — US Fish Wildl Serv Bur Commer Fish Fish Leafl

US Fish and Wildlife Service. Bureau of Commercial Fisheries. Statistical Digest — US Fish Wildl Serv Bur Commer Fish Stat Dig
US Fish and Wildlife Service. Bureau of Sport Fisheries and Wildlife. EGL — US Fish Wildl Serv Bur Sport Fish Wildl EGL
US Fish and Wildlife Service. Circular — US Fish Wildl Serv Circ
US Fish and Wildlife Service. Fish and Wildlife Leaflet — FWLEEA
US Fish and Wildlife Service. Fish and Wildlife Leaflet — US Fish Wildl Serv Fish Wildl Leafl
US Fish and Wildlife Service. Fish Distribution Report — US Fish Wildl Serv Fish Distrib Rep
US Fish and Wildlife Service. Fishery Bulletin — US Fish and Wildlife Service Fishery Bull
US Fish and Wildlife Service. Fishery Bulletin — US Fish Wild Serv Fish Bull
US Fish and Wildlife Service. Fishery Bulletin — US Fish Wildl Serv Fish Bull
US Fish and Wildlife Service. Fishery Bulletin — XFWFA7
US Fish and Wildlife Service. FWS-OBS — USFODA
US Fish and Wildlife Service. Investigations in Fish Control — US Fish Wildl Serv Invest Fish Control
US Fish and Wildlife Service. North American Fauna — US Fish Wildl Serv N Am Fauna
US Fish and Wildlife Service. Research Report — US Fish Wildl Serv Res Rep
US Fish and Wildlife Service. Resource Publication — RPFWDE
US Fish and Wildlife Service. Resource Publication — US Fish Wildl Serv Resour Publ
US Fish and Wildlife Service. Special Scientific Report. Fisheries — US Fish Wildl Serv Spec Sci Rep Fish
US Fish and Wildlife Service. Special Scientific Report. Wildlife — US Fish Wildl Serv Spec Sci Rep Wildl
US Fish and Wildlife Service. Technical Papers — US Fish Wildl Serv Tech Pap
US Fish and Wildlife Service. Wildlife Leaflet — US Fish Wildl Serv Wildl Leafl
US Fish and Wildlife Service. Wildlife Leaflet — XFWLAP
US Fish and Wildlife Service. Wildlife Research Report — US Fish Wildl Serv Wildl Res Rep
US Foreign Trade. FT 135. General Imports. Schedule A. Commodity by Country — FT135
US Foreign Trade. FT 410. Exports. Schedule E. Commodity by Country — FT410
US Foreign Trade. FT 610. Exports SIC Based Products by World Areas — FT610
US Forest Service. AIB — US For Serv AIB
US Forest Service. Division of State and Private Forestry. Northern Region Report — US For Serv Div State Priv For North Reg Rep
US Forest Service. Forest Insect and Disease Leaflet — FIDADT
US Forest Service. Forest Insect and Disease Leaflet — US For Serv For Insect & Dis Leafl
US Forest Service. Forest Insect and Disease Management. Northern Region Report — FIDMDV
US Forest Service. Forest Insect and Disease Management. Northern Region Report — US For Serv For Insect & Dis Manage North Reg Rep
US Forest Service. Forest Pest Leaflet — US For Serv For Pest Leafl
US Forest Service. Forest Pest Management. Northern Region Report — US For Serv For Pest Manage North Reg Rep
US Forest Service. Forest Pest Management. Nothern Region Report — FPMADL
US Forest Service. Forest Products Laboratory. Annual Report — US For Serv For Prod Lab Annu Rep
US Forest Service. Forestry Research. What's New in the West — US For Serv For Res What's New West
US Forest Service. General Technical Report. INT — US For Serv Gen Tech Rep INT
US Forest Service. General Technical Report. NC — US For Serv Gen Tech Rep NC
US Forest Service. General Technical Report. NE — US For Serv Gen Tech Rep NE
US Forest Service. General Technical Report. PNW — US For Serv Gen Tech Rep PNW
US Forest Service. General Technical Report. PSW — US For Serv Gen Tech Rep PSW
US Forest Service. General Technical Report. RM — US For Serv Gen Tech Rep RM
US Forest Service. General Technical Report. SE — US For Serv Gen Tech Rep SE
US Forest Service. General Technical Report. SO — US For Serv Gen Tech Rep SO
US Forest Service. General Technical Report. WO — GTRWDF
US Forest Service. General Technical Report. WO — US For Serv Gen Tech Rep WO
US Forest Service. Northeastern Forest Experiment Station. Annual Report — US For Serv Northeast For Exp Stn Annu Rep
US Forest Service. Northern Region. Cooperative Forestry and Pest Management Report — CFPME4
US Forest Service. Northern Region. Cooperative Forestry and Pest Management Report — US For Serv North Reg Coop For Pest Manage Rep
US Forest Service. Northern Region. Forest Environmental Protection — US For Serv North Reg For Environ Prot
US Forest Service. Pacific Northwest Forest and Range Experiment Station. Annual Report — US For Serv Pac Northwest For Range Exp Stn Annu Rep
US Forest Service. Pacific Northwest Forest and Range Experiment Station. Research Paper PNW — US For Serv Pac Northwest For Range Exp Stn Res Pap PNW
US Forest Service. Pacific Northwest Forest and Range Experiment Station. Research Progress — US For Serv Pac Northwest For Range Exp Stn Res Prog
US Forest Service. Research Note. FPL — US For Serv Res Note FPL
US Forest Service. Research Note. INT — US For Serv Res Note INT
US Forest Service. Research Note. ITF — US For Serv Res Note ITF
US Forest Service. Research Note. NC — US For Serv Res Note NC
US Forest Service. Research Note. NE — US For Serv Res Note NE
US Forest Service. Research Note. Pacific Southwest Forest and Range Experiment Station — US For Serv Res Note Pacif Sthwest For Range Exp Sta
US Forest Service. Research Note. PNW — US For Serv Res Note PNW
US Forest Service. Research Note. PSW — US For Serv Res Note PSW
US Forest Service. Research Note. RM — US For Serv Res Note RM
US Forest Service. Research Note. Rocky Mountain Forest and Range Experiment Station — US For Serv Res Note Rocky Mt For Range Exp Sta
US Forest Service. Research Note. SE — US For Serv Res Note SE
US Forest Service. Research Note. SO — US For Serv Res Note SO
US Forest Service. Research Note. Southeastern Forest Experiment Station — US For Serv Res Note Stheast For Exp Sta
US Forest Service. Research Note. US Forest Products Laboratory (Madison, Wisconsin) — US For Serv Res Note US For Prod Lab (Madison)
US Forest Service. Research Notes — US Forest Serv Res Note
US Forest Service. Research Paper. FPL — US For Serv Res Pap FPL
US Forest Service. Research Paper. Institute of Tropical Forestry — US For Serv Res Pap Inst Trop For
US Forest Service. Research Paper. INT — US For Serv Res Pap INT
US Forest Service. Research Paper. Intermountain Forest and Range Experiment Station — US For Serv Res Pap Intermt For Range Exp Sta
US Forest Service. Research Paper. ITF — US For Serv Res Pap ITF
US Forest Service. Research Paper. NC — US For Serv Res Pap NC
US Forest Service. Research Paper. NE — US For Serv Res Pap NE
US Forest Service. Research Paper. North Central Forest Experiment Station — US For Serv Res Pap Nth Cent For Exp Sta
US Forest Service. Research Paper. Northeastern Forest Experiment Station — US For Serv Res Pap Ntheast For Exp Sta
US Forest Service. Research Paper. Pacific Northwest Forest and Range Experiment Station — US For Serv Res Pap Pacif Nthwest For Range Exp Sta
US Forest Service. Research Paper. Pacific Southwest Forest and Range Experiment Station — US For Serv Res Pap Pacif Sthwest For Range Exp Sta
US Forest Service. Research Paper. PNW — US For Serv Res Pap PNW
US Forest Service. Research Paper. PSW — US For Serv Res Pap PSW
US Forest Service. Research Paper. RM — US For Serv Res Pap RM
US Forest Service. Research Paper. SE — US For Serv Res Pap SE
US Forest Service. Research Paper. SO — US For Serv Res Pap SO
US Forest Service. Research Paper. Southeastern Forest Experiment Station — US For Serv Res Pap Stheast For Exp Sta
US Forest Service. Research Paper. Southern Forest Experiment Station — US For Serv Res Pap Sth For Exp Sta
US Forest Service. Research Paper. WO — US For Serv Res Pap WO
US Forest Service. Research Papers — US Forest Serv Res Paper
US Forest Service. Resource Bulletin. INT — US For Serv Resour Bull INT
US Forest Service. Resource Bulletin. NC — US For Serv Resour Bull NC
US Forest Service. Resource Bulletin. NE — US For Serv Resour Bull NE
US Forest Service. Resource Bulletin. North Central Forest Experiment Station — US For Serv Resource Bull Nth Cent For Exp Sta
US Forest Service. Resource Bulletin. Northeastern Forest Experiment Station — US For Serv Resource Bull Ntheast For Exp Sta
US Forest Service. Resource Bulletin. Northern Forest Experiment Station — US For Serv Resource Bull Nth For Exp Sta
US Forest Service. Resource Bulletin. Pacific Southwest Forest and Range Experiment Station — US For Serv Resource Bull Pacif Sthwest For Range Exp Sta
US Forest Service. Resource Bulletin. PNW — US For Serv Resour Bull PNW
US Forest Service. Resource Bulletin. PSW — US For Serv Resour Bull PSW
US Forest Service. Resource Bulletin. SE — US For Serv Resour Bull SE
US Forest Service. Resource Bulletin. SO — US For Serv Resour Bull SO
US Forest Service. Resource Bulletin. Southeastern Forest Experiment Station — US For Serv Resource Bull Stheast For Exp Sta
US Forest Service. Resource Bulletin. Southern Forest Experiment Station — US For Serv Resource Bull Sth For Exp Sta
US Forest Service. Rocky Mountain Forest and Range Experiment Station. Research Highlights. Annual Report — XRRAAH
US Forest Service. Southern Forest Experiment Station. Annual Report — US For Serv South For Exp Stn Annu Rep
US Forest Service. Technical Bulletin — US For Serv Tech Bull
US Forest Service. Tree Planters' Notes — US For Serv Tree Plant Notes
US Geological Survey. Bulletin — XDIGA
US Geological Survey. Circular — US Geol Survey Circ
US Geological Survey. Coal Investigations Map — US Geol Surv Coal Invest Map
US Geological Survey. Coal Investigations Map — US Geol Survey Coal Inv Map
US Geological Survey. Geologic Quadrangle Map — US Geol Surv Geol Quadrangle Map
US Geological Survey. Geologic Quadrangle Map — US Geol Survey Geol Quadrangle Map
US Geological Survey. Geophysical Investigations Map — US Geol Survey Geophys Inv Map
US Geological Survey. Hydrologic Investigations Atlas — US Geol Surv Hydrol Invest Atlas
US Geological Survey. Hydrologic Investigations Atlas — US Geol Survey Hydrol Inv Atlas
US Geological Survey. Index to Geologic Mapping in the United States — US Geol Survey Index Geol Mapping US
US Geological Survey. Mineral Investigations Field Studies Map — US Geol Survey Mineral Inv Field Studies Map
US Geological Survey. Mineral Investigations Resource Map — US Geol Survey Mineral Inv Res Map
US Geological Survey. Miscellaneous Field Studies Map — US Geol Surv Misc Field Stud Map

US Geological Survey. Oil and Gas Investigations Chart — US Geol Surv Oil Gas Invest Chart
US Geological Survey. Oil and Gas Investigations Chart — US Geol Survey Oil and Gas Inv Chart
US Geological Survey. Oil and Gas Investigations Map — US Geol Surv Oil Gas Invest Map
US Geological Survey. Open-File Report — US Geol Surv Open-File Rep
US Geological Survey. Professional Paper — US Geol Survey Prof Paper
US Geological Survey. Water-Resources Investigations — US Geol Surv Water-Resour Invest
US Geological Survey. Water-Supply Paper — US Geol Surv Water-Supply Pap
US Geological Survey. Water-Supply Paper — XIWSA
US Government Paper. Specification Standards — US Govt Paper Spec Std
US Government Research and Development Reports — US Gov Res Dev Rep
US Government Research and Development Reports — US Govt Res Dev Reports
US Government Research Reports — US Gov Res Rep
US Hydrographic Office — USHO
US Hydrographic Office. Publication — US Hydrog Office Pub
US Interdepartmental Committee for Atmospheric Sciences. Report — US Interdep Comm Atmos Sci Rep
US Medicine — US Med
US National Aeronautics and Space Administration. Special Publication — US Natl Aeronaut Space Admin Spec Publ
US National Bureau of Standards. Handbook — US Natl Bur Stand Handb
US National Bureau of Standards. Journal of Research. Section A — US Natl Bur Stand J Res Sec A
US National Cancer Institute. Carcinogenesis Technical Report Series — US Natl Cancer Inst Carcinog Tech Rep Ser
US National Clearinghouse for Drug Abuse Information. Report Series — NCRSAQ
US National Clearinghouse for Drug Abuse Information. Report Series — US Natl Clgh Drug Abuse Inf Rep Ser
US National Industrial Pollution Control Council. Publications — US Natl Ind Pollut Control Counc Publ
US National Institute on Drug Abuse. Research Issues — RIUPDJ
US National Institute on Drug Abuse. Research Issues — US Natl Inst Drug Abuse Res Issues
US National Institutes of Health. National Toxicology Program Technical Report Series — US Natl Inst Health Natl Toxicol Program Tech Rep Ser
US National Institutes of Health. Publication — US Natl Inst Health Publ
US National Marine Fisheries Service. Current Fisheries Statistics — US Natl Mar Fish Serv Curr Fish Stat
US National Marine Fisheries Service. Fishery Bulletin — US Natl Mar Fish Serv Fish Bull
US National Marine Fisheries Service. Fishery Facts — US Natl Mar Fish Serv Fish Facts
US National Marine Fisheries Service. Marine Fisheries Review — US Natl Mar Fish Serv Mar Fish Rev
US National Marine Fisheries Service. Report of the National Marine Fisheries Service — US Natl Mar Fish Serv Rep Natl Mar Fish Serv
US National Marine Fisheries Service. Statistical Digest — US Natl Mar Fish Serv Stat Dig
US National Museum. Bulletin — US Natl Mus Bull
US National Oceanic and Atmospheric Administration. Key to Oceanographic Records Documentation — US Natl Oceanic Atmos Adm Key Oceanogr Rec Doc
US National Oceanic and Atmospheric Administration. Northeast Fisheries Center Sandy Hook Laboratory. Technical Series Report — TSNSDH
US National Oceanographic Data Center. Publication — US Natl Oceanog Data Center Pub
US National Park Service. Ecological Services Bulletin — US Natl Park Serv Ecol Serv Bull
US National Park Service. Fauna of the National Parks of the United States. Fauna Series — US Natl Park Serv Fauna Natl Parks US Fauna Ser
US National Park Service. National Capitol Region Scientific Report — US Natl Park Serv Natl Cap Reg Sci Rep
US National Park Service. Natural History Handbook Series — US Natl Park Service Nat History Handb Ser
US National Park Service. Natural Resources Report — NRUSDD
US National Park Service. Natural Resources Report — US Natl Park Serv Nat Resour Rep
US National Park Service. Occasional Paper — US Natl Park Serv Occas Pap
US National Park Service. Scientific Monograph Series — US Natl Park Serv Sci Monogr Ser
US National Park Service. Transactions and Proceedings — PTSSD5
US Naval Aerospace Medical Institute — US Naval Aerospace Med Inst
US Naval Aerospace Medical Institute (Pensacola). Monograph — US Nav Aerosp Med Inst (Pensacola) Monogr
US Naval Aerospace Medical Institute (Pensacola). NAMI — US Nav Aerosp Med Inst (Pensacola) NAMI
US Naval Aerospace Medical Research Laboratory (Pensacola). NAMRL — US Nav Aerosp Med Res Lab (Pensacola) NAMRL
US Naval Aerospace Medical Research Laboratory (Pensacola). Special Report — US Nav Aerosp Med Res Lab (Pensacola) Spec Rep
US Naval Air Development Center. NADC — US Nav Air Dev Cent NADC
US Naval Institute. Proceedings — US Nav Inst Proc
US Naval Medical Bulletin — US Navl Med B
US Naval Medical Research Laboratory. Report — US Nav Med Res Lab Rep
US Naval Observatory Automated Data Service [*Database*] — USNO ADS
US Naval Oceanographic Office. Special Publication — US Nav Oceanogr Off Spec Publ
US Naval School of Aviation Medicine. Monograph — US Nav Sch Aviat Med Monogr
US Naval School of Aviation Medicine. Research Report — US Nav Sch Aviat Med Res Rep
US Naval Submarine Medical Center. Memorandum Report — US Nav Submar Med Cent Memo Rep
US Naval Submarine Medical Center. Report — US Naval Submar Med Cent Rep
US Naval Submarine Medical Research Laboratory. Report — US Nav Submar Med Res Lab Rep
US Navy Medicine — US Navy Med
U.S. News and World Report — GUNW
US News and World Report — US News
US News and World Report — US News World Rep
US News and World Report — USNWR
US News and World Report — XNWRA
US North Central Forest Experiment Station. Research Paper NC — US North Cent For Exp Stn Res Pap NC
US Office of Library Service. Bibliography Series — US Off Libr Serv Bibliogr Ser
US Office of Public Roads. Bulletin — US Off Pub Roads B
US Pacific Northwest Forest and Range Experiment Station. Research Note PNW — US Pac Northwest For Range Exp Stn Res Note PNW
US Patent and Trademark Office. Official Gazette of the United States Patent and Trademark Office. Patents — US Pat Trademark Off Off Gaz US Pat Trademark Off Pat
US Patent Office. Official Gazette of the United States Patent Office. Patents — US Pat Off Off Gaz US Pat Off Pat
US Pharmacist — US Pharm
US Pharmacist — USPHD5
US Public Health Report — US Publ H Rep
US Public Health Service. Radiological Health Data and Reports — US Public Health Serv Radiol Health Data Rep
US Quartermaster Food and Container Institute for the Armed Forces. Library Bulletin — US Quartermaster Food Container Inst Armed Forces Libr Bull
US Requests for Proposals [*Database*] — USRFP
US Science and Education Administration. Agricultural Research Manual — US Sci Educ Adm Agric Res Man
US Soil Conservation Service. Soil Survey — US Soil Conserv Serv Soil Surv
US Tax Cases. Commerce Clearing House — US Tax Cas CCH
US War Department. Pacific Railroad Explorations — US Pacific RR Expl
Us Wurk — UW
USA Today. The Magazine of the American Scene — GUSA
USAF [*United States Air Force*] **Nuclear Safety** — USAF Nucl Saf
US-Arab Commerce — US-Arab Commer
US-China Business Review [*Washington, DC*] — US China Bus R
USDA [*United States Department of Agriculture*]. Forest Service. General Technical Report INT-United States. Intermountain Forest and Range Experiment Station — USDA For Serv Gen Tech Rep INT Intermt For Range Exp Stn
USDA [*United States Department of Agriculture*]. Forest Service. General Technical Report NC-United States. North Central Forest Experiment Station — USDA For Serv Gen Tech Rep NC US North Cent For Exp Stn
USDA [*United States Department of Agriculture*]. Forest Service. General Technical Report NE-United States. Northeastern Forest Experiment Station — USDA For Serv Gen Tech Rep NE NE For Exp Stn
USDA [*United States Department of Agriculture*]. Forest Service. General Technical Report PSW-United States. Pacific Southwest Forest and Range Experiment Station — USDA For Serv Gen Tech Rep PSW US Pac Southwest For Exp Stn
USDA [*United States Department of Agriculture*]. Forest Service. General Technical Report SE-United States. Southeastern Forest Experiment Station — USDA For Serv Gen Tech Rep SE US Southeast For Exp Stn
USDA [*United States Department of Agriculture*]. Forest Service. Research Note FPL-United States. Forest Products Laboratory — USDA For Serv Res Note FPL US For Prod Lab
USDA [*United States Department of Agriculture*]. Forest Service. Research Note ITF-United States. Institute of Tropical Forestry — USDA For Serv Res Note ITF Inst Trop For
USDA [*United States Department of Agriculture*]. Forest Service. Research Note (Pacific Northwest) — USDA For Serv Res Note (PNW)
USDA [*United States Department of Agriculture*]. Forest Service. Research Note PSW-United States. Pacific Southwest Forest and Range Experiment Station — USDA For Serv Res Note PSW US Pac Southwest For Range Exp St
USDA [*United States Department of Agriculture*]. Forest Service. Research Note RM-United States. Rocky Mountain Forest and Range Experiment Station — USDA For Serv Res Note RM US Rocky Mt For Range Exp Stn
USDA [*United States Department of Agriculture*]. Forest Service. Research Note SE-United States. Southeastern Forest Experiment Station — USDA For Serv Res Note SE US Southeast For Exp Stn
USDA [*United States Department of Agriculture*]. Forest Service. Research Paper INT-United States. Intermountain Forest and Range Experiment Station — USDA For Serv Res Pap INT US Intermt For Range Exp Stn
USDA [*United States Department of Agriculture*]. Forest Service. Research Paper NC-United States. North Central Forest Experiment Station — USDA For Serv Res Pap NC US North Cent For Exp Stn
USDA [*United States Department of Agriculture*]. Forest Service. Research Paper NE-United States. Northeastern Forest Experiment Station — USDA For Serv Res Pap NE US Northeast For Exp Stn
USDA [*United States Department of Agriculture*]. Forest Service. Research Paper (Pacific Northwest) — USDA For Serv Res Pap (PNW)
USDA [*United States Department of Agriculture*]. Forest Service. Research Paper PSW-United States. Pacific Southwest Forest and Range Experiment Station — USDA For Ser Res Pap PSW US Pac Southwest For Range Exp Stn
USDA [*United States Department of Agriculture*]. Forest Service. Research Paper RM-United States. Rocky Mountain Forest and Range Experiment Station — USDA For Serv Res Pap RM US Rocky Mt For Range Exp Stn
USDA [*United States Department of Agriculture*]. Forest Service. Research Paper SO — USDA For Serv Res Pap SO

USDA [*United States Department of Agriculture*]. Forest Service. Resource Bulletin NC-United States. North Central Forest Experiment Station — USDA For Serv Resour Bull NC US North Cent For Exp Stn
USDA [*United States Department of Agriculture*]. Forest Service. Resource Bulletin PNW-United States. Pacific Northwest Forest and Range Experiment Station — USDA For Ser Res Bull PNW US Pac Northwest For Range Exp Stn
USDA (US Department of Agriculture) Forest Service Research Note NC. North Central Forest Experiment Station — USDA For Serv Res Note NC North Cent For Exp Stn
Use of English — UE
Use of English — Use Engl
USF Language Quarterly — USFLQ
USGA [*US Golf Association*] **Green Section Record** — USGA Green Sect Rec
USGA Green Section Record. US Golf Association — USGA Green Sect Rec US Golf Assoc
Usibelli Coal Miner [*Usibelli, AK*] — USCM
US-IBP [*International Biological Program*] **Analyses of Ecosystems Program. Interbiome Abstracts** — US-IBP Anal Ecosyst Program Interbiome Abstr
US-IBP [*International Biological Program*] **Ecosystem Analysis Studies Abstracts** — US-IBP Ecosyst Anal Stud Abstr
US-IBP [*International Biological Program*] **Synthesis Series** — US-IBP Synth Ser
Usine Nouvelle — USI
Usine Nouvelle — Usine Nouv
Usine Nouvelle — USM
Usine Nouvelle. Edition Supplementaire [*France*] — Usine Nouv Ed Suppl
Usine Nouvelle. Edition Supplementaire — Usine Nouv Suppl
Usine Nouvelle. Monthly Edition — Usine Nouv M
Using Government Publications. Volume 2. Finding Statistics and Using Special Techniques — Using Govt P
Uskoriteli. Moskovskii Inzherno-Fizicheskii Institut. Sbornik Statei [*Former USSR*] — Uskor Mosk Inzh-Fiz Inst Sb Statei
Uspechi Biologiceskoj Chimii — Usp Biol Chim
Uspechi Chimii — Usp Chim
Uspechi Fiziceskich Nauk — UFN
Uspechi Fiziceskich Nauk — Usp Fizic N
Uspechi Matematiceskich Nauk — UMN
Uspechi Sovremennoj Biologii — USB
Uspekhi Biologicheskoi Khimii — UBKHA
Uspekhi Biologicheskoi Khimii [*Former USSR*] — Usp Biol Khim
Uspekhi Fiziceskih Nauk — Uspekhi Fiz Nauk
Uspekhi Fizicheskii Nauk — Usp Fiz Nauk
Uspekhi Fizicheskikh Nauk — UFNAA
Uspekhi Fizicheskikh Nauk — Usp Fiz Nau
Uspekhi Fiziologicheskikh Nauk — Usp Fiziol Nauk
Uspekhi Fotoniki — USFOA
Uspekhi Fotoniki — Usp Foton
Uspekhi Fotoniki — Usp Fotoniki
Uspekhi Khimii — USKHA
Uspekhi Khimii — Usp Kh
Uspekhi Khimii — Usp Khim
Uspekhi Khimii Fosfororganicheskikh i Seraorganicheskikh Soedinenii — Usp Khim Fosfororg Seraorg Soedin
Uspekhi Khimii i Tekhnologii Polimerov — Usp Khim Tekhnol Polim
Uspekhi Matematicheskikh Nauk — UMANA
Uspekhi Matematicheskikh Nauk — Usp Mat Nauk
Uspekhi Matematicheskikh Nauk — Uspekhi Mat Nauk
Uspekhi Mikrobiologii — USMKA
Uspekhi Mikrobiologii — Usp Mikrobiol
Uspekhi na Molekulyarnata Biologiya — Usp Mol Biol
Uspekhi Nauchnoi Fotografii — UNFKA
Uspekhi Nauchnoi Fotografii — Usp Nauchn Fotogr
Uspekhi Sovremennoi Biologii — USBIA
Uspekhi Sovremennoi Biologii — Usp Sovrem Biol
Uspekhi Sovremennoi Genetiki — Usp Sovrem Genet
Uspekhi Sovremennoi Genetiki — USSGA
USSR. Academy of Science. Proceedings. Geographical Series — UAG
USSR Computational Mathematics and Mathematical Physics — USSR Comput Math and Math Phys
USSR Computational Mathematics and Mathematical Physics — USSR Comput Math Math Phys
USSR Computational Mathematics and Mathematical Physics — USSR Computational Math and Math Phys
USSR Report. Earth Sciences [*Arlington*] — USSR Rep Earth Sci
USSR Report. Engineering Equipment — USSR Rep Eng Equip
USSR. Union of Composers. Information Bulletin — USSR Comp Info B
UST. Journal of Graduate Research [*Philippines*] — UST J Grad Res
Ustav Jaderne Fyziky Ceskoslovenska Akademia Ved. Report — Ustav Jad Fyz Cesk Akad Ved Rep
Ustav pro Vyzkum a Vyuziti Paliv Monografie — Ustav Vyzk Vyuziti Paliv Monogr
Ustav Vedeckotechnickych Informaci. Ministerstva Zemedelstvi a Vyzivy. Rostlinna Vyroba — Ust Ved Inf MZVZ Rostl Vyroba
Ustav Vedeckotechnickych Informaci. Ministerstva Zemedelstvi. Lesniho a Vodniho Hospodarstvi. Rostlinna Vyroba — Ust Ved Inf MZLVH Rostl Vyroba
Ustav Vedeckotechnickych Informaci. Ministerstva Zemedelstvi. Rostlinna Vyroba — Ust Ved Inf MZ Rostl Vyroba
Ustav Vedeckotechnickych Informaci. MZLVH [*Ministerstva Zemedelstvi. Lesniho a Vodniho Hospodarstvi*] **Studijni Informace Pudoznalstvi a Meliorace** — Ust Ved Inf MZLVH Stud Inf Pudoz
Ustav Vedeckotechnickych Informaci pro Zemedelstvi — Ustav Vedeckotech Inf Zemed
Ustav Vedeckotechnickych Informaci pro Zemedelstvi. Sbornik UVTIZ. Rada. Meliorace — Ustav Vedeckotech Inf Zemed Sb UVTIZ Melior
Ustav Vedeckotechnickych Informaci pro Zemedelstvi Studijni Informace Ochrana Rostlin — Ustav Vedeckotech Inf Zemed Stud Inf Ochr Rostl
Ustav Vedeckotechnickych Informaci. Sbornik UVTI. Genetika a Slechteni — Ustav Vedeckotech Inf Sb UVTI Genet Slechteni
Ustav Vedeckotechnickych Informaci. Sbornik UVTI. Rada. Meliorace — Ustav Vedeckotech Inf Sb UVTI Melior
Ustredna Zidov [*Slovakia*] — UZ
Utah Academy of Sciences, Arts, and Letters. Proceedings — Utah Acad Sci Proc
Utah Academy of Sciences. Transactions — Utah Ac Sc Tr
Utah Agricultural College. Agricultural Experiment Station. Bulletin — Utah Agric Exp Sta Bull
Utah. Agricultural Experiment Station. Bulletin — Utah Agric Exp Stn Bull
Utah. Agricultural Experiment Station. Circular — Utah Agric Exp Stn Circ
Utah. Agricultural Experiment Station. Publications — Utah Ag Exp
Utah. Agricultural Experiment Station. Research Report — Utah Agric Exp Stn Res Rep
Utah. Agricultural Experiment Station. Special Report — Utah Agric Exp Stn Spec Rep
Utah. Agricultural Experiment Station. Utah Resources Series — Utah Agric Exp Stn Utah Resour Ser
Utah Bar Bulletin — Utah B Bull
Utah Bar Bulletin — Utah Bar Bull
Utah Bar Journal — UT BJ
Utah Bar Journal — Utah BJ
Utah Code Annotated — Utah Code Ann
Utah. Department of Natural Resources. Division of Water Rights. Technical Publication — Utah Dept Nat Resources Tech Pub
Utah. Department of Natural Resources. Technical Publication — Utah Dep Nat Resour Tech Publ
Utah. Department of Natural Resources. Water Circular — Utah Dep Nat Resour Water Cir
Utah. Division of Water Resources. Cooperative Investigations Report — Utah Div Water Resources Coop Inv Rept
Utah Economic and Business Review — Utah Econ and Bus R
Utah. Engineering Experiment Station. Bulletin — Utah Eng Exp Stn Bull
Utah. Engineering Experiment Station. Report — UEES Report
Utah Farm and Home Science — Utah Farm Home Sci
Utah Foreign Language Quarterly — ULQ
Utah Genealogical and Historical Magazine — Utah M
Utah. Geological and Mineralogical Survey. Bulletin — Utah Geol and Mineralog Survey Bull
Utah. Geological and Mineralogical Survey. Bulletin — Utah Geol Mineral Surv Bull
Utah. Geological and Mineralogical Survey. Circular — Utah Geol and Mineralog Survey Circ
Utah. Geological and Mineralogical Survey. Circular — Utah Geol Miner Surv Circ
Utah. Geological and Mineralogical Survey. Circular — Utah Geol Mineral Surv Circ
Utah. Geological and Mineralogical Survey. Quarterly Review — Utah Geol and Mineralog Survey Quart Rev
Utah. Geological and Mineralogical Survey. Quarterly Review — Utah Geol Miner Surv Q Rev
Utah. Geological and Mineralogical Survey. Special Studies — Utah Geol and Mineralog Survey Spec Studies
Utah. Geological and Mineralogical Survey. Special Studies — Utah Geol Mineral Surv Spec Stud
Utah. Geological and Mineralogical Survey. Survey Notes — Utah Geol Miner Surv Surv Notes
Utah. Geological and Mineralogical Survey. Water Resources Bulletin — Utah Geol and Mineralog Survey Water Resources Bull
Utah. Geological and Mineralogical Survey. Water Resources Bulletin — Utah Geol Mineral Surv Water Resour Bull
Utah Geological Association. Publication — Utah Geol Assoc Publ
Utah Geological Society. Guidebook to the Geology of Utah — Utah Geol Soc Guidebook to Geology of Utah
Utah Geology — Utah Geol
Utah Historical Quarterly — UHQ
Utah Historical Quarterly — Utah Hist Q
Utah Historical Quarterly — Utah Hist Quar
Utah Historical Quarterly — Utah Hist Quart
Utah Historical Quarterly — UtH
Utah Law Review — ULR
Utah Law Review — UT LR
Utah Law Review — Utah L Rev
Utah Law Review — Utah LR
Utah Libraries — Utah Lib
Utah Libraries — Utah Libr
Utah Library Association. Newsletter — Utah Lib Assn Newsl
Utah Medical Bulletin — Utah Med Bull
Utah Music Educator — UT
Utah Reports — Utah
Utah Resources Series. Utah Agricultural Experiment Station — Utah Resour Ser Utah Agr Exp Sta
Utah Science — Utah Sci
Utah Science — UTSCB
Utah Science. Utah Agricultural Experiment Station — Utah Sci Utah Agric Exp Stn
Utah State Engineer. Biennial Report. Technical Publications — Utah State Engineer Bienn Rept Tech Pub
Utah State Engineer. Information Bulletin — Utah State Engineer Inf Bull
Utah State Engineer. Technical Publication — Utah State Eng Tech Publ
Utah. State Engineer's Office. Basic Data Report — Utah State Eng Off Basic Data Rep
Utah State Medical Journal — Utah State Med J

Utah State University. Agricultural Experiment Station. Bulletin — Utah State Univ Agric Exp Stn Bull
Utah State University. Monograph Series — USUMS
Utah Studies in Literature and Linguistics — USLL
Utah University. Anthropological Papers. Bulletin — Utah Univ Anthropol Papers Bull
Utah University. Engineering Experiment Station. Bulletin — Utah Univ Eng Expt Sta Bull
Utah University. Engineering Experiment Station. Technical Paper — Utah Univ Eng Exp Stn Tech Pap
UTET [*Unione Tipigrafico-Editrice Torinese*] **Bollettino Editoriale** — UTET Boll Ed
Utilitas Mathematica — Utilitas Math
Utilities Law Reports. Commerce Clearing House — Util L Rep CCH
Utilization Report R8-UR. United States Department of Agriculture. Forest Service. Cooperative Forestry — Util Rep R8 UR US Dep Agric Forest Serv Coop For
UTLAS [*University of Toronto Library Automation System*] **Catalogue Support System** [*Database*] — CATSS
Utne Reader — GUTR
Utopian Eyes — Utopian E
Utrecht Micropaleontological Bulletins — Utr Micropaleontol Bull
Utrecht Micropaleontological Bulletins. Special Publication — Utr Micropaleontol Bull Spec Publ
Utrechtse Publikaties voor Algemene Literatuurwetenschap — UPAL
Utredning. Norsk Treteknisk Institutt — Utredn Norsk Tretekn Inst
Utsonomiya Daigaku Nogakubu Gakujutsu Hokoku — UDNGA
Utsunomiya Daigaku Kyoikugakubu Kiyo, Dai-2-Bu — UDKKB
Uttar Pradesh. Directorate of Geology and Mining. Monograph — Uttar Pradesh Dir Geol Min Monogr
Uttar Pradesh Historical Society. Journal — UPHS
Uttar Pradesh Journal of Zoology — Uttar Pradesh J Zool
Uttar Pradesh State Dental Journal — Uttar Pradesh State Dent J
Uttara Bharati — UB
Uusi Suomi — US
Uutuqtwa. Bristol Bay High School — UTQA
UV Spectrometry Group. Bulletin — UV Spectrom Group Bull
UVP in der Abfallwirtschaftlichen Planung. Wassertechnisches Seminar — UVP Abfallwirtsch Plan Wassertech Semin
UWD [*Umweltschutz-Dienst*] **Informationsdienst fuer Umweltfragen** — UWD
UWO [*University of Western Ontario*] **Medical Journal** — UWO Med J
UWO (University of Western Ontario) Medical Journal — UWO (Univ West Ont) Med J
Uyemura Technical Reports — Uyemury Tech Rep
Uzbekiztonda Iztimoii Fanlar — Uzbek Iztim Fanlar
Uzbekskii Biologicheskii Zhurnal — Uzb Biol Zh
Uzbekskii Biologicheskii Zhurnal — Uzbek Biol Zh
Uzbekskii Biologicheskii Zhurnal — UZBZA
Uzbekskii Geologicheskii Zhurnal — Uzbek Geol Zh
Uzbekskii Geologicheskii Zhurnal — UZGZA
Uzbekskii Khimicheskii Zhurnal — Uzb Khim Zh
Uzbekskii Khimicheskii Zhurnal — Uzbek Khim Zh
Uzbekskii Khimicheskii Zhurnal — UZKZA
Uzbekskii Matematicheskii Zhurnal — Uzbek Mat Zh
Uzbekskij Biologiceskij Zurnal — Uzbeksk Biol Zurn

V

V. A. Steklov Mathematical Institute Preprint — Steklov Math Inst Preprint
V. I. Leninis Sahelobis Sromis Citheli Drosis Ordenosani Sakharthvelos Politekhnikuri Instituti. Samecniero Sromebi — V I Lenin Sakharth Politekh Inst Samecn Srom
V Zashchitu Mira — V Zashch Mira
Vabenhuset. Kristendommen og Nutiden — Vabh
VACC [*Victorian Automobile Chamber of Commerce*] **Journal** — VACCJ
Vaccine Research — Vaccine Res
Vaccine Research and Developments — Vaccine Res Dev
Vaccines. Modern Approaches to New Vaccines Including Prevention of AIDS. Annual Meeting — Vaccines Mod Approaches New Vaccines Incl Prev AIDS Annu Meet
Vacuum — VACUA
Vacuum Chemistry [*Japan*] — Vacuum Chem
Vacuum Microbalance Techniques — Vac Microbalance Tech
Vacuum Review — Vacuum R
Vacuum Structure in Intense Fields — Vac Struct Intense Fields
Vaderland — Vd
VAE. Virginia Agricultural Economics. Virginia Polytechnic Institute and State University. Cooperative Extension Service — VAE VA Agric Econ VA Polytech Inst State Univ Coop Ext Serv
Vaeg- och Vattenbyggaren — VVTBA
Vaermlaendska Bergsmannafoereningens Annaler — Vaerml Bergsmannafoeren Ann
Vaestmanlands Fornminnesfoerenings Arsskrift — VFA
Vaextodling. Institutionen foer Vaextodlingslara. Lantbrukshoegskolan — Vaxtodling Inst Vaxtodlingslara Lantbrukshogsk
Vaextskyddsanstalt-Notiser — Vaextskyddsanst-Notiser
Vaextskyddsrapporter. Jordbruk — Vaextskyddsrapp Jordbruk
Vagabond — Vaga
Vakblad — Vbl
Vakblad voor Biologen — Vakbl Biol
Vakblad voor de Bloemisterij — VBL
Vakblad voor de Handel in Aardappelen, Groenten, en Fruit — MSA
Vakblad voor Textielreiniging — WIV
Vakbondskrant van Nederland — VBW
Vakstudie — Vk
Vakstudie-Nieuws — VN
Vakstudie-Nieuws — VStN
Vakuum in der Praxis — Vak Prax
Vakuum in Forschung und Praxis — Vak Forsch Prax
Vakuum Information — Vak Inf
Vakuum-Technik — VAKTA
Vakuum-Technik — Vak-Tech
Vakuum-Technik — Vak-Technik
Vale of Evesham Historical Society. Research Papers — Vale Evesham Hist Soc Res Pap
Valencia — V
Vallalatvezetes-Vallalatszervezes — Vallalatvez -Szerv
Valodas un Literaturas Instituta Biletens — VLIB
Valodas un Literaturas Instituta Raksti — VLIR
Valparaiso University. Law Review — Val U L Rev
Valparaiso University. Law Review — Val U LR
Valparaiso University. Law Review — Valparaiso Univ L Rev
Valparaiso University. Law Review — Valparaiso Univ Law R
Valparaiso University. Law Review — VULR
Valsalva — Valsa
Valstybine Grozines Literaturos Leidykla — VGLL
Valstybine Politines ir Mokslines Literatu — VPMLL
Valtion Maatalouskoetoiminnan Julkaisuja — Valt Maatalouskoetoiminnan Julk
Valtion Teknillinen Tutkimuskeskus. Reaktorilaboratorio. Tiedonanto — Valt Tek Tutkimuskeskus Reaktorilab Tied
Valtion Teknillinen Tutkimuslaitos. Julkaisu — Valt Tek Tutkimuslaitos Julk
Valtion Teknillinen Tutkimuslaitos. Julkaisu — VTTJA
Valtion Teknillinen Tutkimuslaitos. Tiedotus. Sarja 1. Puu — Valt Tek Tutkimuslaitos Tiedotus Sar 1 Puu
Valtion Teknillinen Tutkimuslaitos. Tiedotus. Sarja 2. Metalli — Valt Tek Tutkimuslaitos Tied Sar 2
Valtion Teknillinen Tutkimuslaitos. Tiedotus. Sarja 2. Metalli — Valt Tek Tutkimuslaitos Tiedotus Sar 2
Valtion Teknillinen Tutkimuslaitos. Tiedotus. Sarja 3. Rakennus — Valt Tek Tutkimuslaitos Tied Sar 3
Valtion Teknillinen Tutkimuslaitos. Tiedotus. Sarja 4. Kemia — Valt Tek Tutkimuslaitos Tiedotus Sar 4
Valtion Teknillinen Tutkimuslaitos Tiedotus. Sarja I. PUU — Valt Tek Tutkimuslaitos Tied Sar I PUU
Valuation — VAL
Value Engineering — Value Eng
Value Line Investment Survey — Value Line
Valvo Technische Informationen fuer die Industrie — Valvo Tech Inf Ind
Van Gorcum's Theologische Bibliotheek — GTB
Van Hanh Bulletin — VHB
Van Nostrand Reinhold Electrical/Computer Science and Engineering Series — Van Nostrand Reinhold Electric Comput Sci Engrg Ser
Van Nostrand Reinhold Mathematics Series — Van Nostrand Reinhold Math Ser
Van Zee tot Land — Van Zee Ld
Vancoram Review — Vancoram Rev
Vancouver Opera Journal — Vancouver Op Jnl
Vancouver Studies in Cognitive Science — Vancouver Stud Cogn Sci
Vanderbilt International — Vand Int
Vanderbilt Journal of Transnational Law — Vand J Trans L
Vanderbilt Journal of Transnational Law — Vand J Transnatl L
Vanderbilt Journal of Transnational Law — Vanderbilt J Transnat'l L
Vanderbilt Law Review — VAN
Vanderbilt Law Review — Vand L Rev
Vanderbilt Law Review — Vand LR
Vanderbilt Law Review — Vander Law
Vanderbilt Law Review — VLR
Vanderbilt University. Abstracts of Theses. Bulletin — Vanderbilt Univ Abs Theses Bull
Vanderbilt University Quarterly — Vanderbilt Univ Q
Vanderbilt University. Studies in the Humanities — VUSH
Vandringar Med Boeker — VMB
Vangiya Sahitya Parisat Patrika — VSPP
Vanguard Newsletter — Vanguard Newsl
Vanguard Science Fiction — Van
Vanity Fair — GVAF
Vanity Fair — Van Fair
Vara Palsdjur — Vara Palsd
Vard i Norden. Utveckling och Forskning — Vard Nord Utveckl Forsk
Varia Bio-Archaeologica — Varia Bio-Arch
Varian Instrument Applications — Varian Instrum Appl
Variegation — Vari
Varietes Scientifiques. Institut de Reboisement de Tunis — Var Sci Inst Rebois Tunis
Variety — GVAR
Variety — V
Variety — VAR
Varilna Tehnika — Varilna Teh
Various Publications Series [*Aarhus*] — Various Publ Ser
Varstvo Spomenikov — Var Spom
Varstvo Spomenikov — Varst Spom
VARTA Spezial Report [*Germany*] — VARTA Spez Rep
Vasa Supplementum — Vasa Suppl
Vasari — Va
Vascular Diseases — Vasc Dis
Vascular Surgery — Vasc Surg
Vasenlisten zur Griechischen Heldensage — Vasenlisten
Vasenlisten zur Griechischen Heldensage — VGH
Vases Sicyoniens — VS
Vasi Italioli ed Etruschi a Figure Rosse — VIE
Vassar Brothers Institute. Transactions — Vassar Bros Inst Tr
Vassar Journal of Undergraduate Studies — VJ
Vasterbottens Lans Hambygdsforenings Arsbok — Vasterbotten
Vastergotlands Fornminnesforenings Tidskrift — Vastergotlands Fornminnesforen Tidskr
Vastgoed — VAG
Vastmanlands Fornminnesforenings Arsskrift — Vastmanlands Fornminnesforen Arsskr
Vasuti Tudomanyos Kutato Intezet Evkoenyve [*Hungary*] — Vasuti Tud Kut Intez Evk
Vasvarmegyei Muzeum Termeszetrajzi Osztalyanak evi Jelentese. Annales Musei Comitati Castriferrei. Sectio Historico-Naturalis — Vasvarm Muz Term Oszt Evi Jel
Vaterlaendische Blaetter fuer den Oesterreichischen Kaiserstaat — Vaterl Blaett Oesterr Kaiserstaat
Vatican Observatory Publications. Studi Galileiani — Vatican Obs Publ Studi Galileiani
VATIS [*Victorian Association of Teachers in Independent Schools*] **Journal** — VATISJ
Vaulted Tombs of the Mesara — VT
Vaulted Tombs of the Mesara — VTM

Vaxtekologiska Studier — Vaxtekol Stud
Vaxt-Narings-Nytt — Vaxt-Nar-Nytt
Vaxtskyddsnotiser. Sveriges Lantbruksuniversitet — Vaxtskyddsnotiser Sver Lantbruksuniver
Vazduhoplovni Glasnik [*Yugoslavia*] — Vazduhoplovni Glas
Vcela Moravska — Vcela Morav
VCS [*Victorian Computer Society*] **Bulletin** — VCS Bul
VCV (Vlaamse Chemische Vereniging) Tijdingen — VCV Tijd
VDE [*Verband Deutscher Elektrotechniker*] **Fachberichte** — VDE Fachber
VDE [*Verband Deutscher Elektrotechniker*] **Fachberichte** — VDEFA
VDEW (Vereinigung Deutscher Elektrizitaetswerke) Informationsdienst (German Federal Republic) — VDEW (Ver Dtsch Elektrizitaetswerke) Informationsdienst
VDI [*Verein Deutscher Ingenieure*] **Berichte** — VDI Ber
VDI [*Verein Deutscher Ingenieure*] **Forschungsheft** — VDI Forschungsh
VDI [*Verein Deutscher Ingenieure*] **Forschungsheft** — VDIFA
VDI [*Verein Deutscher Ingenieure*] **Nachrichten** — VDNAA
VDI [*Verein Deutscher Ingenieure*] **Zeitschrift** — VDI Z
VDI [*Verein Deutscher Ingenieure*] **Zeitschriften. Fortschritt-Berichte. Reihe 5. Grund- und Werkstoffe** — VDI Z Fortschr Ber Reihe 5
VEAB Ertesitoe [*Hungary*] — VEAB Ert
Vearme- och Sanitetsteknikern — Varme- o Sanit-Tek
VEB [*Volkseigener Betrieb*] **Verlag Technik. Monthly Technical Review** — VEB Verlag Tech Mon Tech Rev
Veckans Affarer — VCK
Vecteur Environnement — Vecteur Environ
Vector — VCT
Veda a Technika Mladezi [*Czechoslovakia*] — Veda Tech Mladezi
Veda a Technika v SSSR — Veda Tech SSSR
Veda a Vyzkum v Potravinarskem Prumyslu — Veda Vyzk Potravin Prum
Veda a Vyzkum v Prumyslu Sklarskem — Veda Vyzk Prum Sklarskem
Veda a Vyzkum v Prumyslu Textilnim — Veda Vyzk Prum Text
Vedanta Kesari [*Madras*] — Ved Kes
Vedanta Kesari [*Mylapore*] — VK
Vedecke Informace CSAV [*Ceskoslovenska Akademie Ved*] — Ved Inf CSAV
Vedecke Prace Ceskoslovenskeho Zemedelskeho Muzea — Ved Pr Cesk Zemed Muz
Vedecke Prace Hydinarstvo Vyskumny Ustav Chovu a Slachtenia Hydiny — Ved Pr Hydinarstvo Vysk Ustav Chovu Slachtenia Hydiny
Vedecke Prace Laboratoria Podoznalectva v Bratislave — Ved Pr Lab Podoznalectva Bratisl
Vedecke Prace Ustavu Zelinarskeho v Olomouci — Ved Pr Ustavu Zelinarskeho Olomouci
Vedecke Prace Ustredniho Vyskumneho Ustavu Rastlinnej Vyroby CSAZV [*Ceskoslovenska Akademie Zemedelskych Ved*] **v Praze-Ruzyni** — Ved Pr Vysk Ust Rastl Vyroby Praze-Ruzyni
Vedecke Prace Ustredniho Vyskumneho Ustavu Rastlinnej Vyroby Piestanoch — Ved Pr Vysk Ust Rastl Vyroby Piestanoch
Vedecke Prace Ustredniho Vyzkumneho Ustavu Rostlinne Vyroby (Praha) — Ved Prace Ustr Vyzk Ustavu Rost Vyr (Praha)
Vedecke Prace Ustredniho Vyzkumneho Ustavu Rostlinne Vyroby v Praze-Ruzyni — Ved Pr Ustr Vyzk Ust Rostl Vyroby Praze-Ruzyni
Vedecke Prace VSCHK [*Vyzkumna Stanice pro Chov Koni*] **(Slatinany)** — Ved Pr VSCHK (Slatinany)
Vedecke Prace Vyskumneho Ustavu Kukurice v Trnave — Ved Pr Vysk Ustavu Kukurice Trnave
Vedecke Prace Vyskumneho Ustavu Kukurice v Trnave — Ved Prace Vysk Ustavu Kukurice Trnave
Vedecke Prace Vyskumneho Ustavu Lesneho Hospodarstva v Zvolene — Ved Pr Vysk Ustavu Lesn Hospod v Zvolene
Vedecke Prace Vyskumneho Ustavu Lesneho Hospodarstva v Zvolene — Ved Pr Vysk Ustavu Lesn Hospod Zvolene
Vedecke Prace Vyskumneho Ustavu Luk a Pasienkov v Banskej Bystrici — Ved Pr Vysk Ustavu Luk Pasienkov Banskej Bystrici
Vedecke Prace Vyskumneho Ustavu Ovciarskeho v Trencine — Ved Pr Vysk Ustavu Ovciar Trencine
Vedecke Prace Vyskumneho Ustavu Podoznalectva a Vyzivy Rastlin v Bratislave — Ved Pr Vysk Ustavu Podoznalectva Vyz Rastl Bratislave
Vedecke Prace Vyskumneho Ustavu Podoznalectva a Vyzivy Rastlin v Bratislave — Ved Pr Vysk Ustavu Podoznalectva Vyz Rastlin Bratisl
Vedecke Prace Vyskumneho Ustavu pro Chov Hydiny v Ivanka pri Dunaji — Ved Pr Vysk Ustavu Chov Hydiny Ivanka Dunaji
Vedecke Prace Vyskumneho Ustavu pro Chov Hydiny v Ivanka pri Dunaji — Ved Pr Vysk Ustavu pro Chov Hydiny Ivanka pri Dunaji
Vedecke Prace Vyskumneho Ustavu pro Chov Skotu Caz v Rapotine — Ved Pr Vysk Ustavu Chov Skotu Caz Rapotine
Vedecke Prace Vyskumneho Ustavu Rastlinnej Vyroby — Ved Prace Vysk Ustavu Rastlinnej Vyr
Vedecke Prace Vyskumneho Ustavu Rastlinnej Vyroby v Piestanoch — Ved Pr Vysk Ustav Rastl Vyroby Piestanoch
Vedecke Prace Vyskumneho Ustavu Rastlinnej Vyroby v Piestanoch — Ved Pr Vysk Ustavu Rastl Vyroby Piestanoch
Vedecke Prace Vyskumneho Ustavu Rastlinnej Vyroby v Piestanoch — Ved Pr Vysk Ustavu Rastlinnej Vyroby Piestanoch
Vedecke Prace Vyskumneho Ustavu Rastlinnej Vyroby v Piestanoch Krmoviny — Ved Pr Vysk Ustavu Rastl Vyroby Piestanoch Krmoviny
Vedecke Prace Vyskumneho Ustavu Zavlahoveho Hospodarstva v Bratislave — Ved Pr Vysk Ustavu Zavlahoveho Hospod Bratisl
Vedecke Prace Vyskumneho Ustavu Zavlahoveho Hospodarstva v Bratislave — Ved Prace Vysk Ustavu Zavlahov Hospod Bratislave
Vedecke Prace Vyskumneho Ustavu Zivocisnej Vyroby v Nitre — Ved Pr Vysk Ustav Zivoc Vyroby Nitre
Vedecke Prace Vyskumneho Ustavu Zivocisnej Vyroby v Nitre — Ved Pr Vysk Ustavu Zivocisnej Vyroby Nitre
Vedecke Prace Vyskumneho Ustavu Zivocisnej Vyroby v Nitre — Ved Prace Vysk Ustavu Zivoc Nitre
Vedecke Prace Vyskumny Ustav Lesneho Hospodarstva v Zvolene — Ved Prace Vyskum Ust Lesn Hosp Zvolen
Vedecke Prace Vyskumny Ustavu Zavlahoveho Hospodarstva — Ved Pr Vysk Ustav Zavlahov Hospod
Vedecke Prace Vyzkumna Stanice pro Chov Koni Slatinany — Ved Pr Vyzk Stanice Chov Koni Slatinany
Vedecke Prace Vyzkumneho Ustavu Bramborarskeho v Havlickove Brode — Ved Pr Vyzk Ustavu Bramborarskeho Havlickove Brode
Vedecke Prace Vyzkumneho Ustavu Kraivarskeho — Ved Prace Vyzk Ustavu Kraivarsk
Vedecke Prace Vyzkumneho Ustavu Krmivarskeho CSAZV [*Ceskoslovenska Akademie Zemedelskych Ved*] **v Brne** — Ved Pr Vyzk Ustavu Krmivarskeho CSAZV Brne
Vedecke Prace Vyzkumneho Ustavu Melioraci v Praze — Ved Pr Vyzk Ustavu Melior Praze
Vedecke Prace Vyzkumneho Ustavu Melioraci v Praze — VPVMA3
Vedecke Prace Vyzkumneho Ustavu Melioraci v Praze or Zbraslavi — Ved Pr Vyzk Ustavu Melior Praze Zbraslavi
Vedecke Prace Vyzkumneho Ustavu Melioraci v Zbraslavi — Ved Pr Vyzk Ustavu Melior Zbraslavi
Vedecke Prace Vyzkumneho Ustavu Melioraci v Zbraslavi — VPVMA3
Vedecke Prace Vyzkumneho Ustavu Obilnarskeho v Kromerizi — Ved Pr Vyzk Ustavu Obilnarskeho Kromerizi
Vedecke Prace Vyzkumneho Ustavu Okrasneho Zahradnictvi v Pruhonicich — Ved Pr Vyzk Ustavu Okrasneho Zahradnictvi Pruhonicich
Vedecke Prace Vyzkumneho Ustavu Ovilnarskeho v Kromerizi — Ved Pr Vyzk Ustavu Ovilnarskeho Kromerizi
Vedecke Prace Vyzkumneho Ustavu pro Chov Prasat v Kostelci Nad Orlice — Ved Pr Vyzk Ustavu Chov Prasat Kostelci Nad Orlice
Vedecke Prace Vyzkumneho Ustavu pro Chov Skotu Caz v Rapotine — Ved Pr Vyzk Ustavu Chov Skotu Caz Rapotine
Vedecke Prace Vyzkumneho Ustavu Vcelarskeho v Dole u Libcic — Ved Pr Vyzk Ust Vcelar v Dole u Libcic
Vedecke Prace Vyzkumneho Ustavu Vcelarskeho v Dole u Libcic — Ved Pr Vyzk Ustavu Vcelarskeho Dole Libcic
Vedecke Prace Vyzkumneho Ustavu Veterinarni CSAZV [*Ceskoslovenska Akademie Zemedelskych Ved*] **v Brne** — Ved Pr Vyzk Ustavu Vet CSAZV Brne
Vedecke Prace Vyzkumneho Ustavu Veterinarniho Lekarstvi v Brne [*Czechoslovakia*] — Ved Pr Vyzk Ustavu Vet Lek Brne
Vedecke Prace Vyzkumneho Ustavu Zavlahoveho Hospodarstva v Bratislave — Ved Pr Vyzk Ustavu Zavlahoveho Hospod Bratislave
Vedecke Prace Vyzkumneho Ustavu Zemedelsko-Lesnickych Melioraci CSAZV [*Ceskoslovenska Akademie Zemedelskych Ved*] **v Praze** — Ved Prace Vyzkum Ust Melior
Vedecke Prace. Vyzkumny Ustav Melioraci — Ved Pr Vyzk Ustav Melior
Vedecke Prace Vyzkumnych Ustavu Rostlinne Vyroby v Praze-Ruzyni — Ved Pr Vyzk Ustavu Rostl Vyroby Praze Ruzyni
Vedeckovyzkumny Uhelny Ustav Sbornik Vyzkumnych Praci [*Czechoslovakia*] — Vedeckovyzk Uhelny Ustav Sb Vyzk Pr
Vedecky Svet — Ved Svet
Vee en Vlees. Het Vakblad voor Handelaar en Producent — VVL
Veeartsenijkundige Bladen voor Nederlandsch-Indie — Veeartsenijk Blad Nederl-Indie
Veeteelt- en Zuivelberichten — Veeteelt Zuivelber
VEF [*Victorian Employers' Federation*] **Information Bulletin** — VEF Inf Bul
Vegetable Crops Series. California University. Department of Vegetable Crops — Veg Crops Ser Calif Univ Dept Veg Crops
Vegetable Grower — Veg Grower
Vegetable Growers News — Veg Grow News
Vegetable Situation. United States Department of Agriculture. Economic Research — Veg Situat TVS US Dep Agric Econ Res Serv
Vegetarian Monthly — Vegetarian Mo
Vegetarian Times — Veg Times
Vegyipari Kutato Intezetek Kozlemenyei — Vegyip Kut Intez Kozl
Vehicle and the Environment. Technical Papers. FISITA (Federation Internationale des Societes d'Ingenieurs des Techniques de l'Automobile) Congress — Veh Environ Tech Pap FISITA Congr
Vehicle System Dynamics — Veh Syst Dyn
Vejen Frem — Vej Fr
Vejkomiteens Skrifter — Vejkom Skr
Vejle Amts Aarbog — Vl Aa
Veldtrust [*Johannesburg*] — VLDTA8
Velhagen und Klasings Monatshefte — VKM
Veltro' — Vel
Velvet Light Trap — Vel Lt Trap
Vema Research Series — Vema Res Ser
Vendetta Agricola — Vendetta Agric
Vending International — Vend Intnl
Vending Times — Vend
Vendredi, Samedi, Dimanche — VSD
Vendsysselske Aarboger — Vds Aa
Venezolaans Nederlandse Kamer van Koophandel en Industrie. Bulletin — BVI
Venezuela. Direccion de Geologia. Boletin de Geologia — Venez Dir Geol Bol Geol
Venezuela. Direccion de Geologia. Boletin de Geologia. Publicacion Especial — Venez Dir Geol Bol Geol Publ Esp
Venezuela. Instituto Nacional de Nutricion. Publicacion — Venez Inst Nac Nutr Publ
Venezuela. Ministerio de Minas e Hidrocarburos. Direccion de Geologia. Boletin de Geologia — Venez Min Minas Hidrocarburos Dir Geol Bol Geol
Venezuela Misionera — Venez Mision
Venezuela Odontologica — Venez Odontol

Venezuela. Universidad Central. Escuela de Geologia y Minas. Laboratorio de Petrografia y Geoquimica. Informe — Venez Univ Cent Esc Geol Minas Lab Petrogr Geoquimica Inf
Venezuela Up-to-Date — Venez Up To Date
Venezuela Up-to-Date — Venez UTD
Venezuelan Economic Review — VRE
Vengarskaya Farmakoterapiya — Vengarskaya Farmakoter
Vengerskii Zhurnal Gornogo Dela i Metallurgii. Gornoe Delo — Veng Zh Gorn Dela Metall Gorn Delo
Ventana — VA
Ventilyatsiya i Konditsionirovanie Vozdukha Zdanii — Vent Kond Vozdukha Zdanii
Ventilyatsiya i Konditsionirovanie Vozdukha Zdanii Sooruzhenii — Vent Kond Vozdukha Zdanii Sooruzh
Ventilyatsiya i Ochistka Vozdukha — Vent Ochistka Vozdukha
Ventilyatsiya Shakht i Rudnikov — Vent Shakht Rudn
Vento Dell'est — VE
Venture — V
Venture — VEN
Venture Capital Investment — Vent Cap Invest
Venture Forth — Vent Forth
Venture Science Fiction — VEN
Venus: The Japanese Journal of Malacology — Venus Jpn J Malacol
Verband der Bibliotheken des Landes Nordrhein-Westfalen. Mitteilungsblatt — Ver Bibl Landes NRW Mitt
Verband der Wissenschaftler an Forschungsinstituten. Mitteilungen — Mitt VWF
Verbo — V
Verbum Caro — VC
Verbum Caro — Verb C
Verbum Domini — VD
Verbum Domino — VeDo
Verbum (Rio De Janeiro) — VeR
Verbum Salutis [*Paris*] — VS
Verbundkatalog Maschinenlesbarer Katalogdaten Deutscher Bibliotheken [*Database*] — VK
Verdad y Vida [*Milan*] — VyV
Verdens Gang — VG
Verdi Newsletter — Verdi Newsl
Verein der Freunde der Naturgeschichte in Mecklenberg. Archiv — Ver Freunde Naturg Mecklenberg Arch
Verein Deutscher Ingenieure. Nachrichten — VDI Nachr
Verein Deutscher Ingenieure. Zeitschrift — Ver Dtsch Ing Z
Verein Deutscher Ingenieure. Zeitschriften. Fortschritt-Berichte. Reihe 5. Grund- und Werkstoffe — Ver Dtsch Ing Z Fortschr Ber Reihe 5
Verein fuer das Museum Schlesischer Altertuemer — Ver Museum Schles Altert
Verein fuer die Geschichte Berlins. Schriften — Ver f d Gesch Berlins Schr
Verein fuer Erdkunde zu Dresden. Mitteilungen — Ver Erdk Dresden Mitt
Verein fuer Erdkunde zu Leipzig. Mitteilungen — Ver Erdk Leipzig Mitt
Verein fuer Geschichte Dresdens. Mitteilungen — Ver f Gesch Dresdens Mitt
Verein fuer Thueringische Geschichte und Altertumskunde. Zeitschrift — Ver f Thuer Gesch u Alt Ztsch
Verein fuer Vaterlaendische Naturkunde in Wuerttemberg. Jahreshefte — Ver Vaterl Naturk Wuerttemberg Jahresh
Verein von Freunden der Erdkunde zu Leipzig. Jahresbericht — Ver Freunden Erdk Leipzig Jber
Verein zur Verbreitung Naturwissenschaftlicher Kenntnisse in Wien. Schriften — Ver Verbr Naturwiss Kenntnisse Wien Schr
Vereinigte Destillateur-Zeitungen — Ver Destill Ztg
Vereinigung Schweizerischer Petroleum-Geologen und Ingenieure. Bulletin — Ver Schweiz Pet-Geol Ing Bull
Vereinigung Schweizerischer Petroleum-Geologen und Ingenieure. Bulletin — Ver Schweizer Petroleum-Geologen u Ingenieure Bull
Vereinigung Schweizerischer Petroleum-Geologen und Ingenieure. Bulletin — Vereinigung Schweizer Petroleum-Geologen u Ingenieure Bull
Vereinigung Schweizerischer Versicherungsmathematiker. Mitteilungen — Mitt Verein Schweiz Versicherungsmath
Vereinigung Schweizerischer Versuchs und Vermittlungstellen fuer Saatkartoffeln [*Solothurn*] — VSVVS
Vereinigung zur Foerderung des Deutschen Brandschutzes. Zeitschrift — VFDB Z
Verenigde Verzekeringspers. Wekelijks Verschijnend Vakblad voor het Verzekeringswezen in Binnenland en Buitenland — VZP
Vereniging Surinaams Bedrijfsleven. Weekbericht — WSZ
Vereniging tot Exploitatie eener Proefzuivelboerderij te Hoorn. Verslag — Ver Exploit Proefzuivelboerderij Hoorn Versl
Verfahrenstechnik International — Verfahrenstech
Verfahrenstechnik und Chemischer Apparatebau. Seminar — Verfahrenstech Chem Apparatebau Semin
Verfahrenstechnische Berichte [*Chemical and Process Engineering Abstracts*] [*Information service or system*] — VtB
Verfassung und Recht in Uebersee — Verfass Recht Uebersee
Verfassung und Recht in Uebersee — Verfassung u Recht Uebersee
Verfassung und Verfassungswirklichkeit — Verfassung u -Wirklichkeit
Verfassungsschutzgesetz — V Sch G
Verfassungsschutzgesetz — Vf Sch G
Verfinstituut TNO [*Nederlands Centrale Organisatie voor Toegepast - Natuurwetenschappelijk Onderzoek*] **Circulaire** — Verfinst TNO Circ
Verfkroniek — VER
Vergangenheit und Gegenwart — V & G
Vergangenheit und Gegenwart — Vergangenh U Gegenw
Vergangenheit und Gegenwart — VuG
Vergessenes Pompeji — VP
Verhandelingen. Afdeling Natuurkunde. Koninklijke Nederlandse Akademie van Wetenschappen. Eerste Reeks — Verh Afd Natuurkd K Ned Akad Wet Eerste Reeks
Verhandelingen der Eerste Klasse van het Koninklijk Nederlandsch Instituut van Wetenschappen, Letterkunde, en Schoone Kunsten te Amsterdam — Verh Eerste Kl Kon Ned Inst Wetensch Amsterdam
Verhandelingen der Koninklijke Akademie van Wetenschappen te Amsterdam. Afdeeling Natuurkunde — Verh Akad Wet Amsterdam Afd Natuurkd
Verhandelingen der Koninklijke Akademie van Wetenschappen te Amsterdam. Afdeeling Natuurkunde. Sectie 2 — Verh K Akad Wet Amsterdam Afd Natuurkd Sect 2
Verhandelingen der Koninklijke Nederlandse Akademie van Wetenschappen. Afdeling Letterkunde — VNAW
Verhandelingen. Instituut voor Praeventieve Geneeskunde — Verh Inst Praev Geneeskd
Verhandelingen. Koninklijke Academie voor Geneeskunde van Belgie — Verh K Acad Geneeskd Belg
Verhandelingen. Koninklijke Academie voor Wetenschappen. Letteren en Schone Kunsten van Belgie — Verh K Acad Wet Lett & Schone Kunsten Belg
Verhandelingen. Koninklijke Academie voor Wetenschappen. Letteren en Schone Kunsten van Belgie — Verh Konink Acad Wetensch Belgie
Verhandelingen. Koninklijke Academie voor Wetenschappen. Letteren en Schone Kunsten van Belgie. Klasse der Wetenschappen — Verh K Acad Wet Lett en Schone Kunsten Belg Kl Wet
Verhandelingen. Koninklijke Academie voor Wetenschappen. Letteren en Schone Kunsten van Belgie. Klasse der Wetenschappen — Verh K Acad Wet Lett Schone Kunsten Belg Kl Wet
Verhandelingen. Koninklijke Akademie van Wetenschappen — VKAW
Verhandelingen. Koninklijke Akademie van Wetenschappen. Letterkunde [*Elsevier Book Series*] — VKL
Verhandelingen. Koninklijke Akademie van Wetenschappen. Natuurkunde [*Elsevier Book Series*] — VKN
Verhandelingen. Koninklijke Akademie van Wetenschappen te Amsterdam — VAA
Verhandelingen. Koninklijke Akademie van Wetenschappen te Amsterdam. Afdeeling Natuurkunde — Verh K Akad Wet Amsterdam Afd Natuurkd
Verhandelingen. Koninklijke Nederlands Geologisch Mijnbouwkundig Genootschap — Verh K Ned Geol Mijnbouwkd Genoot
Verhandelingen. Koninklijke Nederlands Geologisch Mijnbouwkundig Genootschap. Geologische Serie — VNGGA
Verhandelingen. Koninklijke Nederlandse Akademie van Wetenschappen — VKNAW
Verhandelingen. Koninklijke Nederlandse Akademie van Wetenschappen. Afdeling Letterkunde — Verh Kon Nederl Ak Wetensch Afd Lett
Verhandelingen. Koninklijke Nederlandse Akademie van Wetenschappen. Afdeling Letterkunde — VKNA
Verhandelingen. Koninklijke Nederlandse Akademie van Wetenschappen. Afdeling Letterkunde — VKNAL
Verhandelingen. Koninklijke Nederlandse Akademie van Wetenschappen. Afdeling Natuurkunde. Reeks 1 — Verh K Ned Akad Wet Afd Natuurkd Reeks 1
Verhandelingen. Koninklijke Nederlandse Akademie van Wetenschappen. Afdeling Natuurkunde. Reeks 1 [*Netherlands*] — Verh K Ned Akad Wetensch Afd Natuurk Reeks 1
Verhandelingen. Koninklijke Nederlandse Akademie van Wetenschappen. Afdeling Natuurkunde. Reeks 2 — Verh K Ned Akad Wet Afd Natuurkd Reeks 2
Verhandelingen. Koninklijke Nederlandse Akademie van Wetenschappen. Afdeling Natuurkunde. Reeks 2 [*Netherlands*] — Verh K Ned Akad Wetensch Afd Natuurk Reeks 2
Verhandelingen. Koninklijke Nederlandse Akademie van Wetenschappen. Afdeling Natuurkunde. Tweede Reeks — Verh K Ned Akad Wet Afd Natuurkd Tweede Reeks
Verhandelingen. Koninklijke Nederlandse Geologisch Mijnbouwkundig Genootschap. Geologische Serie — Verh K Ned Geol Mijnbouwkd Genoot Geol Ser
Verhandelingen. Koninklijke Nederlandse Geologisch Mijnbouwkundig Genootschap. Mijnbouwkundige Serie — Verh K Ned Geol Mijnbouwkd Genoot Mijnbouwkd Ser
Verhandelingen. Koninklijke Vlaamse Academie voor Geneeskunde van Belgie [*Belgium*] — Verh K Vlaam Acad Geneesk Belg
Verhandelingen. Koninklijke Vlaamse Academie voor Geneeskunde van Belgie — Verh K Vlaam Acad Geneeskd Belg
Verhandelingen. Koninklijke Vlaamse Academie voor Wetenschappen, Letteren, en Schone Kunsten van Belgie. Klasse der Letteren — V Vl Ac
Verhandelingen. Koninklijke Vlaamse Academie voor Wetenschappen, Letteren, en Schone Kunsten van Belgie. Klasse der Wetenschappen — Verh K Vlaam Acad Wet Lett Schone Kunsten Belg Kl Wet
Verhandelingen. Koninklijke Vlaamse Academie voor Wetenschappen, Letteren, en Schone Kunsten van Belgie. Klasse der Wetenschappen [*Belgium*] — Verh K Vlaam Acad Wetensch Belg Kl Wetensch
Verhandelingen. Rijksinstituut voor Natuurbeheer — Verh Rijksinst Natuurbeheer
Verhandelingen Uitgegeven door het Zeeuwsch Genootschap der Wetenschappen te Vlissingen — Verh Zeeuwsch Genootsch Wetensch Vlissingen
Verhandelingen van de Natuur- en Geneeskundige Correspondentie-Societeit in de Vereenigde Nederlanden — Verh Natuur Geneesk Corresp Soc Ver Nederl
Verhandlung der Gesellschaft fuer Erdkunde zu Berlin — VGE
Verhandlung. Versammlung Deutscher Philologen — VDPh
Verhandlungen. Anatomische Gesellschaft — Verh Anat Ges
Verhandlungen. Berliner Gesellschaft fuer Anthropologie, Ethnologie, und Urgeschichte — VBGAEU
Verhandlungen. Berliner Gesellschaft fuer Anthropologie, Ethnologie, und Urgeschichte — Vh BAG

Verhandlungen. Botanischer Verein der Provinz Brandenburg — Verh Bot Ver Prov Brandenb
Verhandlungen der Allgemeinen Schweizerischen Gesellschaft fuer die Gesammten Naturwissenschaften — Verh Allg Schweiz Ges Gesammten Naturwiss
Verhandlungen der Berliner Medicinischen Gesellschaft — Verh Berliner Med Ges
Verhandlungen der Deutschen Gesellschaft fuer Chirurgie — Vhdlgg Dt Ges Chir
Verhandlungen der Deutschen Gesellschaft fuer Verdauungs- und Stoffwechselkrankheiten — Verh Dtsch Ges Verdau Stoffwechselkr
Verhandlungen der Deutschen Gesellschaft fuer Zytologie — Verh Dtsch Ges Zytol
Verhandlungen der Deutschen Physikalischen Gesellschaft — Vhdlgg Dt Physik Ges
Verhandlungen der Deutschen Roentgen-Gesellschaft — VDRG
Verhandlungen der Forstwirte in Maehren und Schlesien — Vhdlgg Forstwirte Maehren
Verhandlungen der Geologischen Bundesanstalt in Wien — VGBAW
Verhandlungen der Gesellschaft Deutscher Naturforscher und Aerzte — Verh Ges Deutsch Naturf
Verhandlungen der Gesellschaft fuer Anthropologie — VGAnthr
Verhandlungen der Gesellschaft fuer Erdkunde zu Berlin — VGEB
Verhandlungen der Gesellschaft fuer Kinderheilkunde — Vhdlgg Ges Kindheilkde
Verhandlungen der Gesellschaft zur Bekaempfung der Tuberkulose — Vhdlgg Ges Bekaempfg Tuberk
Verhandlungen der Internationalen Vereinigung fuer Theoretische und Angewandte Limnologie — Verh Int Ver Theor Angew Limnol
Verhandlungen der Internationalen Vereinigung fuer Theoretische und Angewandte Limnologie — VIVL
Verhandlungen der Kaiserlich-Koeniglichen Zoologisch-Botanischen Gesellschaft in Wien — Verh KK Zool Bot Ges Wien
Verhandlungen der Mecklenburgischen Naturforschenden Gesellschaft — Verh Mecklenburg Naturf Ges
Verhandlungen der Naturforschenden Gesellschaft. Basel — VNGB
Verhandlungen der Naturforschenden Gesellschaft in Basel — Verhandl Naturforsch Ges Basel
Verhandlungen der Ornithologischen Gesellschaft Bayern — VornGB
Verhandlungen der Pathologischen Gesellschaft. Wuerzburg — Vhdlgg Pathol Ges Wuerzbg
Verhandlungen der Versammlung Deutscher Philologen und Schulmaenner — VPS
Verhandlungen der Versammlungen Deutscher Philologen und Schulmaenner — VDP
Verhandlungen der Zoologisch-Botanischen Gesellschaft in Oesterreich — Verh Zool Bot Ges Oesterr
Verhandlungen des Berliner Botanischen Vereins — VBBVE6
Verhandlungen des Berliner Botanischen Vereins — Verh Berl Bot Ver
Verhandlungen des Botanischen Vereins der Provinz Brandenburg — VBVB
Verhandlungen des Deutschen Geographentages — VDGT
Verhandlungen des Deutschen Geographentages — Verh Deutsch Geographentages
Verhandlungen des Deutschen Juristentages — VDJT
Verhandlungen des Deutschen Juristentages — Vhdlgg Dt Juristtag
Verhandlungen des Grossherzoglich Badischen Landwirthschaftlichen Vereins zu Ettlingen und Karlsruhe — Verh Grossherzogl Bad Landw Vereins Ettlingen
Verhandlungen des Historischen Vereins fuer Niederbayern — Verhandl Hist Ver Niederbayern
Verhandlungen des Historischen Vereins fuer Niederbayern — VHVN
Verhandlungen des Internationalen Zoologenkongresses — Vhdlgg Intern Zoolkongr
Verhandlungen des Internationalen Zoologenkongresses — ViZoK
Verhandlungen des Naturforschenden Vereins zu Bruenn — VNVBr
Verhandlungen des Naturhistorischen Vereins Bonn — Vhdlgg Nathist Ver Bonn
Verhandlungen des Naturhistorischen Vereins fuer das Grossherzogthum Hessen und Umgebung — Verh Naturhist Vereins Grossherzogth Hessen
Verhandlungen des Naturhistorisch-Medicinischen Vereins zu Heidelberg — Verh Naturhist Med Vereins Heidelberg
Verhandlungen des Naturwissenschaftlichen Vereins in Hamburg — Verh Naturwiss Ver Hamb
Verhandlungen des Naturwissenschaftlichen Vereins in Hamburg — Verhandl Naturwiss Ver Hamburg
Verhandlungen des Vereins fuer Naturwissenschaftliche Heimatforschung zu Hamburg — Verh Vereins Naturwiss Heimatf Hamburg
Verhandlungen des Vereins zur Befoerderung des Gewerbefleisses — Verh Vereins Befoerd Gewerbefl
Verhandlungen. Deutsche Gesellschaft fuer Angewandte Entomologie — Verh Dt Ges Angew Ent
Verhandlungen. Deutsche Gesellschaft fuer Angewandte Entomologie — Verh Dtsch Ges Angew Entomol
Verhandlungen. Deutsche Gesellschaft fuer Experimentelle Medizin — Verh Dtsch Ges Exp Med
Verhandlungen. Deutsche Gesellschaft fuer Innere Medizin — VDGIA
Verhandlungen. Deutsche Gesellschaft fuer Innere Medizin — Verh Dtsch Ges Inn Med
Verhandlungen. Deutsche Gesellschaft fuer Kreislaufforschung — VDGKA
Verhandlungen. Deutsche Gesellschaft fuer Kreislaufforschung — Verh Dtsch Ges Kreislaufforsch
Verhandlungen. Deutsche Gesellschaft fuer Pathologie — VDGPA
Verhandlungen. Deutsche Gesellschaft fuer Pathologie — Verh Dtsch Ges Pathol
Verhandlungen. Deutsche Gesellschaft fuer Rheumatologie — VDGRA
Verhandlungen. Deutsche Gesellschaft fuer Rheumatologie — Verh Dtsch Ges Rheumatol
Verhandlungen. Deutsche Pathologische Gesellschaft — Verhandl Deutsch Path Gesellsch
Verhandlungen. Deutsche Physikalische Gesellschaft — Verh Dtsch Phys Ges
Verhandlungen. Deutsche Physikalische Gesellschaft [*Stuttgart*] — Verhandl DPG
Verhandlungen. Deutsche Zoologische Gesellschaft — Verh Dtsch Zool Ges
Verhandlungen. Deutsche Zoologische Gesellschaft — Verhandl Deutsch Zool Gesellsch
Verhandlungen. Deutsche Zoologische Gesellschaft in Bonn [*Rhein*] — Verh Dt Zool Ges Bonn
Verhandlungen. Deutsche Zoologische Gesellschaft in Erlangen — Verh Dt Zool Ges Erlangen
Verhandlungen. Deutsche Zoologische Gesellschaft in Frankfurt — Verh Dt Zool Ges Frankfurt
Verhandlungen. Deutsche Zoologische Gesellschaft in Goettingen — Verh Dt Zool Ges Goett
Verhandlungen. Deutsche Zoologische Gesellschaft in Graz — Verh Dt Zool Ges Graz
Verhandlungen. Deutsche Zoologische Gesellschaft in Hamburg — Verh Dt Zool Ges Hamburg
Verhandlungen. Deutsche Zoologische Gesellschaft in Jena — Verh Dt Zool Ges Jena
Verhandlungen. Deutsche Zoologische Gesellschaft (Kiel) — Verh Dt Zool Ges (Kiel)
Verhandlungen. Deutsche Zoologische Gesellschaft (Tuebingen) — Verh Dt Zool Ges (Tuebingen)
Verhandlungen. Deutsche Zoologische Gesellschaft (Wien) — Verh Dt Zool Ges (Wien)
Verhandlungen. Deutsche Zoologische Gesellschaft (Wilhelmshaven) — Verh Dt Zool Ges (Wilhelmshaven)
Verhandlungen. Geologische Bundesanstalt — Verh Geol Bundesanst
Verhandlungen. Geologische Bundesanstalt — Verhandl Geol Bundesanstalt
Verhandlungen. Geologische Bundesanstalt (Austria) — VGEBA
Verhandlungen. Geologische Bundesanstalt. Bundeslaenderserie — Verh Geol Bundesanst Bundeslaenderser
Verhandlungen. Gesellschaft Deutscher Naturforscher und Aerzte — Verh Ges Dsch Naturfrsch Aerzte
Verhandlungen. Gesellschaft Deutscher Naturforscher und Aerzte — Verhandl Gesellsch Deutsch Naturf u Aerzte
Verhandlungen. Historischer Verein von Niederbayern — VHVNB
Verhandlungen. Historischer Verein von Oberpfalz und Regensburg — VHVOR
Verhandlungen. Historischer Vereine von Niederbayern — Verh Hist Nied Bay
Verhandlungen. Historischer Vereine von Niederbayern — VHN
Verhandlungen. Historischer Vereine von Oberpfalz und Regensburg — Verh Hist Oberpfalz
Verhandlungen. Internationaler Psychotherapie Kongress — Verh Int Psychother Kongr
Verhandlungen. Kammer der Abgeordneten des Bayerischen Landtags. Stenographische Berichte — K d Abg Sten Ber
Verhandlungen. Naturforschende Gesellschaft in Basel — Verh Naturforsch Ges Basel
Verhandlungen. Naturforschender Verein in Bruenn — Verh Naturforsch Ver Bruenn
Verhandlungen. Naturhistorisch-Medizinischer Verein zu Heidelberg — Verh Natur-Med Ver Heidelb
Verhandlungen. Naturwissenschaftlicher Verein in Hamburg — Verhandl Naturw Ver Hamburg
Verhandlungen. Naturwissenschaftlicher Verein in Karlsruhe — Verhandl Naturw Ver Karlsruhe
Verhandlungen. Ornithologische Gesellschaft in Bayern — Verh Ornithol Ges Bayern
Verhandlungen. Physikalisch-Medizinische Gesellschaft in Wuerzburg — Verh Phys-Med Ges Wuerzb
Verhandlungen. Physikalisch-Medizinische Gesellschaft in Wuerzburg — Verh Phys-Med Ges Wuerzburg
Verhandlungen. Schweizerische Naturforschende Gesellschaft — Verh Schweiz Naturf Ges
Verhandlungen. Schweizerische Naturforschende Gesellschaft — Verh Schweiz Naturforsch Ges
Verhandlungen. Schweizerische Naturforschende Gesellschaft — Verhandl Schweiz Naturf Gesellsch
Verhandlungen. Schweizerische Naturforschende Gesellschaft. Wissenschaftlicher Teil — Verh Schweiz Naturforsch Ges Wiss Teil
Verhandlungen und Schriften der Oekonomischen Section der Schlesischen Gesellschaft fuer Vaterlaendische Cultur — Verh Schriften Oekon Sect Schles Ges Vaterl Cult
Verhandlungen. Verein der Schweizer Physiologen — Verh Ver Schweiz Physiol
Verhandlungen. Zoologisch-Botanische Gesellschaft in Wien — Verh Zool-Bot Ges Wien
Verhandlungsbericht. Deutsche Zoologische Gesellschaft — VerhBer Dt Zool Ges
Verhandlungsberichte. Kolloid-Gesellschaft — Verhandlungsber Kolloid-Ges
Veritas (Buenos Aires) — Veritas BA
Veritas (Porto Alegre, Brazil) — Veritas P Alegre
Verkeerskunde — VTA
Verkehrsmedizin und Ihre Grenzgebiete — Verkehrsmed Grenzgeb
Verkehrsmedizin und Ihre Grenzgebiete [*German Democratic Republic*] — Verkehrsmed Ihre Grenzgeb
Verksamheten. Stiftelsen foer Rasforadling av Skogstrad — Verksamheten Stift Rasforadl Skogstrad
Verkuendigung und Forschung [*Munich*] — VerkF
Verkuendigung und Forschung [*Munich*] — VF
Verkuendigung und Forschung — VuF
Vermessungs-Informationen — Vermess-Inf

Vermin and Noxious Weeds Destruction Board (Melbourne). Survey — Verm Nox Weeds Destrn Bd (Melb) Surv
Vermischte Schriften der Ackerbaugesellschaft in Tyrol — Vermischte Schriften Ackerbauges Tyrol
Vermoegensteuer- Durchfuehrungsverordnung — V St DV
Vermoegensteuergesetz — V St G
Vermont Administrative Procedures Bulletin — VT Admin Proc Bull
Vermont Administrative Procedures Compilation — VT Admin Proc Comp
Vermont. Agricultural Experiment Station. Bulletin — VT Agric Exp Stn Bull
Vermont. Agricultural Experiment Station. Publications — VT Ag Exp
Vermont Business — Vermont Bs
Vermont Farm and Home Science — VT Farm & Home Sci
Vermont Farm and Home Science — VT Farm Home Sci
Vermont Foreign Language Association. Bulletin — FLVER
Vermont. Free Public Library Commission and State Library. Bulletin — VT Bul
Vermont. Geological Survey. Bulletin — Vermont Geol Survey Bull
Vermont. Geological Survey. Bulletin — VT Geol Surv Bull
Vermont. Geological Survey. Economic Geology — VT Geol Sur Econ Geol
Vermont. Geological Survey. Water Resources Department. Environmental Geology — VT Geol Surv Water Resour Dep Environ Geol
Vermont Historical Society. Proceedings — VT His S
Vermont Historical Society. Proceedings — VtHS
Vermont History — VeH
Vermont History — VH
Vermont History — VT Hist
Vermont History. Proceedings. Vermont Historical Society — Vermont Hist
Vermont Law Review — Ver LR
Vermont Law Review — Vermont L Rev
Vermont Law Review — VT L Rev
Vermont Libraries — Vermont Lib
Vermont Libraries — VT Lib
Vermont Music Educators News — VE
Vermont Quarterly — VQ
Vermont Quarterly — VtQ
Vermont Registered Nurse — Vermont Regist Nurse
Vermont Registered Nurse — VT Regist Nurse
Vermont Reports — VT
Vermont State Agricultural College. Agricultural Experiment Station. Miscellaneous Publication — Vermont Agric Exp Sta Misc Publ
Vermont State Geologist. Report — VT St G Rp
Vermont Statutes Annotated — Vt Stat Ann
Vernacular Architecture — Vernacular Architect
Vernacular Architecture — Vernacular Archre
Vernacular Building — Vernacular Bldg
Verniciature e Decorazioni — Verniciature Decor
Vernon's Annotated Missouri Statutes — Mo Ann Stat (Vernon)
Vernon's Kansas Statutes, Annotated, Code of Civil Procedure — Kan Civ Proc Code Ann (Vernon)
Vernon's Kansas Statutes, Annotated, Code of Criminal Procedure — Kan Crim Proc Code Ann (Vernon)
Vernon's Kansas Statutes, Annotated, Corporation Code — Kan Corp Code Ann (Vernon)
Vernon's Kansas Statutes, Annotated, Criminal Code — Kan Crim Code Ann (Vernon)
Vernon's Kansas Statutes, Annotated, Probate Code — Kan Prob Code Ann (Vernon)
Vernon's Kansas Statutes Annotated (Uniform Commercial Code) — Kan UCC Ann (Vernon)
Veroeffentlichungen. Abteilung fuer Slavische Sprachen und Literaturen. Osteuropa-Institut [*Slavisches Seminar*]. Freie Universitaet Berlin — VOIB
Veroeffentlichungen. Arbeitsgemeinschaft fuer Forschung des Landes Nordrhein/Westfalen/Geisteswissenschaften [*Cologne/Opladen*] — AFLNW/G
Veroeffentlichungen aus dem Gebiete der Medizinal-Verwaltung — Veroeff Aus D Geb D Med Verwalt
Veroeffentlichungen aus dem Gebiete des Militaer-Sanitaetswesens — Veroeff Militsanitw
Veroeffentlichungen aus dem Haus der Natur in Salzburg — Veroeff Haus Natur Salzburg
Veroeffentlichungen aus dem Museum fuer Natur, Voelker- und Handelskunde Bremen. Reihe A. Naturwissenschaften — Veroeff Mus Natur Handelsk Bremen Reihe A Naturwiss
Veroeffentlichungen aus den Jahres-Veterinaer-Berichten. Beamtete Tieraerzte Preussen — Veroeffentl J-Vet-Ber Beamt Tieraerzte Preuss
Veroeffentlichungen aus der Badischen Papyrus-Sammlungen — P Baden
Veroeffentlichungen aus der Morphologischen Pathologie — Veroeff Morphol Pathol
Veroeffentlichungen aus der Pathologie — Veroeff Pathol
Veroeffentlichungen. Bundesanstalt fuer Alpine Landwirtschaft in Admont — Veroeff Bundesanst Alp Landwirtsch Admont
Veroeffentlichungen der Archenhold-Sternwarte — Veroeffentl Archenhold Sternwarte
Veroeffentlichungen der Bayerischen Kommission fuer die Internationale Erdmessung — Veroeff Bayer Komm Intern Erdmessg
Veroeffentlichungen der Forstlichen Bundesversuchsanstalt Mariabrunn in Schoenbrunn. Abteilung fuer Standortserkundung und -Kartierung — Veroeff Forstl Bundesversuchsanst Mariabrunn Schoenbrunn Abt
Veroeffentlichungen der Historischen Kommission fuer Hannover — Veroeff Hist Komm Hannov
Veroeffentlichungen der Hydrologischen Abteilung der Dortmunder Stadtwerke — Veroeff Hydrol Abt Dortm Stadtwerke
Veroeffentlichungen der Medizinisch-Naturwissenschaftlichen Gesellschaft. Muenster — VMNGM
Veroeffentlichungen der Naturwissenschaftlichen Gesellschaft Isis. Bautzen — VIsis
Veroeffentlichungen der Oesterreichischen Arbeitsgemeinschaft fuer Ur- und Fruehgeschichte — Veroeff Oe Ur Frueh Gesch
Veroeffentlichungen der Strahlenschutzkommission — Veroeff Strahlenschutzkomm
Veroeffentlichungen des Institutes fuer Geschichte der Arabisch-Islamischen Wissenschaften. Reihe B. Abteilung Mathematik — Veroeffentl Inst Gesch Arabisch Islamischen Wiss Reihe B Abt
Veroeffentlichungen des Instituts fuer Orientforschung der Deutschen Akademie der Wissenschaften (Berlin) — Veroeff IO (Berl)
Veroeffentlichungen des Instituts Wiener Kreis — Veroeffentl Inst Wiener Kreis
Veroeffentlichungen des Landesmuseums fuer Vorgeschichte in Halle — VLVH
Veroeffentlichungen des Museums fuer Ur- und Fruehgeschichte (Potsdam) — Veroeff Mus (Potsdam)
Veroeffentlichungen des Niedersaechsischen Landesverwaltungsamtes. Naturschutz und Landschaftspflege — Veroeff Niedersaechs Landesverwaltungsamtes Naturschutz Lands
Veroeffentlichungen des Provinzialmuseums Halle — Veroeff Provinzialmus Halle
Veroeffentlichungen des Tiroler Landesmuseum Ferdinandeum — Veroeff Tiroler Landesmus Ferdinandeum
Veroeffentlichungen. Deutsche Akademie fuer Sprache und Dichtung — VASD
Veroeffentlichungen. Deutsche Akademie fuer Sprache und Dichtung — VDASD
Veroeffentlichungen. Deutsche Geodaetiske Kommission. Bayerische Akademie der Wissenschaften. Reihe A [*Germany*] — Veroeff Dtsch Geod Komm Reihe A
Veroeffentlichungen. Deutsche Schillergesellschaft — VDS
Veroeffentlichungen fuer Naturschutz und Landschaftspflege in Baden-Wuerttemberg — Veroeff Naturschutz Landschaftspflege Baden Wuerttemb
Veroeffentlichungen fuer Naturschutz und Landschaftspflege in Baden-Wuerttemberg. Beihefte — Veroeff Naturschutz Landschaftspflege Baden-Wuerttemb Beih
Veroeffentlichungen. Geobotanisches Institut. Eidgenoessische Technische Hochschule Stiftung Ruebel in Zuerich — Veroeff Geobot Inst Eidg Tech Hochsch Stift Ruebel Zuer
Veroeffentlichungen. Geobotanisches Institut. Eidgenoessische Technische Hochschule Stiftung Ruebel in Zuerich — Veroeff Geobot Inst Eidg Tech Hochsch Stift Ruebel Zuerich
Veroeffentlichungen. Geobotanisches Institut Ruebel — Veroeff Geobot Inst Ruebel
Veroeffentlichungen. Grabmann Institut zur Erforschung der Mittelalterlichen Theologie und Philosophie — VGIEMTP
Veroeffentlichungen. Institut fuer Agrarmeteorologie und des Agrarmeteorologischen Observatoriums. Karl Marx-Universitaet (Leipzig) — Veroff Inst Agrarmet Univ (Leipzig)
Veroeffentlichungen. Institut fuer Deutsche Sprache und Literatur. Deutsche Akademie der Wissenschaften zu Berlin — VIDSL
Veroeffentlichungen. Institut fuer Deutsche Volkskunde. Deutsche Akademie der Wissenschaften zu Berlin — VIDV
Veroeffentlichungen. Institut fuer Meeresforschung in Bremerhaven — Veroeff Inst Meeresforsch Bremerhaven
Veroeffentlichungen. Institut fuer Meeresforschung in Bremerhaven — VIMBA
Veroeffentlichungen. Institut fuer Meeresforschung in Bremerhaven. Supplement — Veroeff Inst Meeresforsch Bremerhaven Suppl
Veroeffentlichungen. Institut fuer Orientforschung. Deutsche Akademie der Wissenschaften zu Berlin — VIO
Veroeffentlichungen. Institut fuer Romanische Sprachwissenschaft. Deutsche Akademie der Wissenschaften zu Berlin — VIRS
Veroeffentlichungen. Institut fuer Slawistik. Deutsche Akademie der Wissenschaften zu Berlin — VISI
Veroeffentlichungen. Institut fuer Slawistik. Deutsche Akademie zu Berlin — VIS
Veroeffentlichungen. Kaiser-Wilhelm-Institut fuer Silikatforschung in Berlin-Dahlem — Veroeff Kaiser Wilhelm Inst Silikatforsch Berlin Dahlem
Veroeffentlichungen. Land- und Hauswirtschaftlicher Auswertungs- und Informationsdienst — Veroff Land-Hauswirtsch Auswertungs-Informationsdienst
Veroeffentlichungen. Landwirtschaftlich-Chemische Bundesversuchsanstalt (Linz) — Veroeff Landwirtsch Chem Bundesversuchsanst (Linz)
Veroeffentlichungen. Leibniz-Archiv — Veroeffentl Leibniz-Archivs
Veroeffentlichungen. Max-Planck-Institut fuer Geschichte — Vel
Veroeffentlichungen. Meteorologischer Dienst. Deutsche Demokratische Republik — Veroeff Meteorol Dienstes DDR
Veroeffentlichungen. Meteorologischer und Hydrologischer Dienst. Deutsche Demokratische Republik — Veroeff Meterol Hydrol Dienstes DDR
Veroeffentlichungen. Naturhistorischer Museum (Basel) — Veroeff Naturhist Mus (Basel)
Veroeffentlichungen. Naturhistorischer Museum (Wien) — Veroeff Naturh Mus (Wien)
Veroeffentlichungen. Osteuropa-Institut — VOEI
Veroeffentlichungen. Reichsgesundheitsamt — Veroeff Reichsgesundheitsamts
Veroeffentlichungen. Schweizerische Gesellschaft fuer Geschichte der Medizin und der Naturwissenschaft — Veroeffentlich Schweizer Gesellsch Medizin Naturwissensch
Veroeffentlichungen. Ueberseemuseum (Bremen). Reihe A — Veroeff Ueberseemus (Bremen) Reihe A
Veroeffentlichungen. Ueberseemuseum (Bremen). Reihe E. Human-Oekologie — Veroeff Ueberseemus (Bremen) Reihe E Hum Oekol
Veroeffentlichungen. Verband Oesterreichischer Geschichts- Vereine — V Ost Geschichtsv
Veroeffentlichungen. Wissenschaftliche Photo-Laboratorien — Veroeffentl Wiss Photolab
Veroeffentlichungen. Wissenschaftliche Photo-Laboratorien (Wolfen) — Veroeff Wiss Photo Lab (Wolfen)

Veroeffentlichungen. Wissenschaftliches Zentral Laboratorium. Photographische Abteilung AGFA — Veroeff Wiss Zent Lab Photogr Abt AGFA
Veroeffentlichungen. Zentralinstitut Physik der Erde [*Czechoslovakia*] — Veroeff Zentralinst Phys Erde
Veroeffentlichungen. Zoologische Staatssammlung (Muenchen) — Veroeff Zool Staatssamml (Muench)
Veroeffentlichungen. Zoologische Staatssammlung (Muenchen) — Veroeff Zool StSamml (Muench)
Veroeffentlichungen zum Archiv fuer Voelkerkunde — VAV
Veroeffentlichungen zur Volkskunde und Kulturgeschichte Veroeffentlichungen Volkskunde Kulturgesch
Verordeningblad voor het Bezette Nederlandse Gebied — Ver Bl
Verordeningenblad — V
Verordeningenblad — Vb
Verordeningenblad Bedrijfsorganisatie — Vb Bo
Verordeningenblad Bedrijfsorganisatie — VBB
Verordeningenblad Bedrijfsorganisatie — Vbl Bedrorg
Verordeningenblad Bedrijfsorganisatie — VBo
Verordeningenblad Bedrijfsorganisatie — VRB
Verordnung ueber Orderlagerscheine — OL Sch VO
Verpackung im Chemiebetrieb — Verpack Chemiebetr
Verpackung. Schweizerische Fachzeitschrift fuer Verpackung, Technologie, Package Design, Marketing — VPA
Verpackungsberater — VPC
Verpackungs-Magazin — Verpack Mag
Verpackungs-Rundschau — Verpack-Rundsch
Verpackungs-Rundschau — VPR
Verpakken. Het Vakblad voor de Verpakkende Industrie en Verpakkingsindustrie — VEP
Verre. Bulletin d'Information — Verre Bull Inf
Verre et Silicates Industriels — Verre Silic Ind
Verre Oosten. Orgaan van de Landenkamers Verre Oosten — VEV
Verre Textile, Plastiques Renforces [*France*] — Verre Text Plast Renf
Verres et Refractaires — Verres Refract
Verres et Refractaires. Part 1. Articles Originaux — Verres Refract Part 1
Verres et Refractaires. Part 2. Documentation — Verres Refract Part 2
Verri — Ver
Verrigtinge van die Kongres van die Suid-Afrikaanse Genetiese Vereniging — Verrigt Kongr S Afr Genet Ver
Verrigtinge van die Kongres van die Suid-Afrikaanse Genetiese Vereniging — Verrigtinge Kongr S-Afr Genet Ver
Versammlungen der Freunde des Humanistischen Gymnasiums — VFHG
Verslag van de Vereeniging de Proeftuin — Verslag Ver Proeftuin
Verslagen der Vereniging van Chemisch-Technischen. Landbouwkundig Adviseurs — Versl Ver Chem Tech Landbouwkd Advis
Verslagen en Mededeelingen — VM
Verslagen en Mededeelingen der Koninklijke Akademie van Wetenschappen. Afdeeling Natuurkunde — Versl En Meded D Kon Akad V Wetensch Afd Natuurk
Verslagen en Mededeelingen. Koninklijke Akademie van Wetenschappen — VMAW
Verslagen en Mededeelingen. Koninklijke Akademie voor Nederlandse Taal- en Letterkunde — VMKA
Verslagen en Mededeelingen. Koninklijke Vlaamse Academie voor Taal- en Letterkunde — Versl Meded K Vlaam Acad Taal Lett
Verslagen en Mededeelingen. Koninklijke Vlaamse Akademie voor Taal- en Letterkunde — Versl Meded Kon Vl Ak Taal & Letterk
Verslagen en Mededeelingen. Koninklijke Vlaamse Akademie voor Taal- en Letterkunde — VMKVA
Verslagen en Mededeelingen van de Leiegouw — Leiegouw
Verslagen en Mededeelingen van de Vereeniging tot Beoefening van Overijsselsch Recht en Geschiedenis — VMVBORG
Verslagen en Mededeelingen van de Vereeniging tot Uitgaaf van der Bronnen van het Oud-Vaderlandsche Recht — VMVOVR
Verslagen en Mededelingen van het Rijkslandbouwconsulentschap Westelijk Drenthe — Versl Meded Rijkslandbouwconsul Westelijk Drenthe
Verslagen Omtrent's Rijks Oude Archieven — VROA
Verslagen. Tien-Jarenplan voor Graanonderzoek. Stichting Nederlands Graan-Centrum — Versl Tien-Jarenplan Graanonderzoek Sticht Nederl Graan-Cent
Verslagen van het Landbouwkundig Onderzoek in Nederland — Versl Landbouwk Onderz Ned
Verslagen van Interprovinciale Proeven. Proefstation voor de Akkerbouw Lelystad (Netherlands) — Versl Interprov Proeven Proefstn Akkerbouw Lelystad (Neth)
Verslagen van Interprovinciale Proeven. Proefstation voor de Akkerbouw (Wageningen) — Versl Interprov Proeven Proefstn Akkerbouw (Wageningen)
Verslagen van Landbouwkundige Onderzoekingen — Vers Landbouwkd Onderz
Verslagen van Landbouwkundige Onderzoekingen — Versl Landbouwkd Onderz
Verslagen van Landbouwkundige Onderzoekingen A. Rijkslandbouwproefstation en Bodemkundig Instituut te Groningen — Versl Landbouwkd Onderz A
Verslagen van Landbouwkundige Onderzoekingen (Agricultural Research Reports) — Versl Landbouwkd Onderz (Agric Res Rep)
Verslagen van Landbouwkundige Onderzoekingen B. Bodemikundig Instituut te Groningen — Versl Landbouwkd Onderz B
Verslagen van Landbouwkundige Onderzoekingen C. Rijkslandbouwproefstation te Hoorn — Versl Landbouwkd Onderz C
Verslagen van Landbouwkundige Onderzoekingen. Centrum voor Landbouwpublikatien en Landbouwdocumentatie — Versl Landbouwk Onderz Cent Lanbouwpubl Landbouwdoc
Verslagen van Landbouwkundige Onderzoekingen D. Rijksproefstation voor Zaadcontrole te Wageningen — Versl Landbouwkd Onderz D
Verslagen van Landbouwkundige Onderzoekingen der Rijkslandbouwproefstations — Versl Landbouwkd Onderz Rijkslandbouwproefstn
Verslagen van Landbouwkundige Onderzoekingen E. Rijkslandbouwproefstation voor Veevoederonderzoek te Wageningen — Versl Landbouwkd Onderz E
Verslagen van Landbouwkundige Onderzoekingen F. Rijkslandbouwproefstation te Maastricht — Versl Landbouwkd Onderz F
Verslagen van Landbouwkundige Onderzoekingen G. Onderzoekingen Uitgevoerd in Opdracht van den Algemeenen Nederlandschen Zuivelbond — Versl Landbouwkd Onderz G
Verstaendliche Wissenschaft — Verstaendliche Wiss
Versty — Ver
Versuche und Abhandlungen der Naturforschenden Gesellschaft in Dantzig — Versuche Abh Naturf Ges Dantzig
Versuchsergebnisse der Bundesanstalt fuer Pflanzenbau und Samenpruefung in Wien — Versuchsergeb Bundesanst Pflanzenbau Samenpruefung Wien
Versuchsgrubengesellschaft Quartalshefte [*Germany*] — Versuchsgrubenges Quartalsh
Versuchsstation fuer das Gaerungsgewerbe in Wien. Mitteilungen — Versuchsstn Gaerungsgewerbe Wien Mitt
Vertebrata Hungarica — Vertebr Hung
Vertebrata Palasiatica — Vertebr Palasiat
Vertebrata Palasiatica — Vertebr Palasiatica
Vertex — VTX
Vertical File Index — Vert File Ind
Vertical File Index — Vert File Index
Vertical Markets Information Database — VMI
Vertice (Coimbra) — VeC
Vertragshilfegesetz — VHG
Verwaltungsarchiv — VerwA
Verwaltungsfuehrung Organisation Personalwesen — VER
Verwaltungsgerichtshof — VGH
Verwaltungslexikon [*Database*] — VLON
Verwarming en Ventilatie — Verwarm Vent
Verwarming en Ventilatie. Maandblad voor Verwarming, Ventilatie, Airconditioning, en Koeling — OVC
Verzamelde Overdrukken. Plantenziektenkundige Dienst (Wageningen) — Verzam Overdruk Plantenziektenk Dienst (Wageningen)
Verzekerings-Archief — Verzekerings-Arch
Verzekeringsbode — Vb
Vesci Akademii Navuk Belaruskaj SSR. Seryja Gramadskich Navuk — VBelGrN
Vesci Akademii Navuk BSSR — VANB
Vesci Akademii Navuk BSSR — Vesci Ak BSSR
Vesci Akademii Navuk BSSR. Seryja Fizika-Matematycnyh Navuk — Vesci Akad Navuk BSSR Ser Fiz-Mat Navuk
Vesientutkimuslaitoksen Julkaisuja — Vesientutkimuslaitoksen Julk
Vesientutkimuslaitoksen Julkaisuja [*Publications. Finnish Water Research Institute*] — VSTKJ
Vesnik Vojnog Muzeja u Beogradu — VVMB
Vesnik Zavod za Geoloska i Geofizicka Istrazivanja NR Srbije — Vesn Zavod Geol Geofiz Istraz NR Srb
Vesnik Zavod za Geoloska i Geofizicka Istrazivanja. Serija A. Geologija — Vesn Zavod Geol Geofiz Istraz Ser A
Vesnik Zavod za Geoloska i Geofizicka Istrazivanja. Serija C. Priminjena Geofizika — Vesn Zavod Geol Geofiz Istraz Ser C
Vesnjani Orbriji [*Kyjiv*] — VO
Vesti. Akademiia Nauk BSSR — VAN
Vestis Latvijas Pasomju Socialistikas Republikas Zinatu Akademija [*Riga, USSR*] — Vest Latv PSR Akad
Vestlandets Forstlige Forsoksstasjon. Meddelelse — VFFM
Vestnik Akademii Meditsinskikh Nauk SSSR — Vestn Akad Med Nauk SSSR
Vestnik Akademii Nauk Belorusskoj SSR. Serija Obscestvennyh Nauk — Vestn Akad Nauk Belorussk SSR Ser Obsc Nauk
Vestnik Akademii Nauk Kazahskoj SSR — Vestn Akad Nauk Kazah SSR
Vestnik Akademii Nauk Kazahskoj SSR — Vestnik Akad Nauk Kazah SSR
Vestnik Akademii Nauk Kazakhskoi SSR — Vestn Akad Nauk Kaz SSR
Vestnik Akademii Nauk Kazakhskoi SSR — Vestnik Akad Nauk Kazakh SSR
Vestnik Akademii Nauk Kirgizskoi SSR — Ves Akad Nauk Kirg SSR
Vestnik Akademii Nauk Respubliki Kazakhstan — Vestn Akad Nauk Resp Kaz
Vestnik Akademii Nauk SSSR — VAN
Vestnik Akademii Nauk SSSR — VAN SSSR
Vestnik Akademii Nauk SSSR — Vest Ak Nauk
Vestnik Akademii Nauk SSSR — Vest Akad Nauk SSSR
Vestnik Akademii Nauk SSSR — Vestn Akad Nauk SSSR
Vestnik Akademii Nauk SSSR — Vestnik Akad Nauk SSSR
Vestnik Akademii Nauk Ukrainskoi SSR — Vestn Akad Nauk Ukr SSR
Vestnik Akademiya Nauk Kazakhskoi SSR — Vestn Akad Nauk Kazakh SSR
Vestnik. Akademiya Nauk Respubliki Kazakhstan — Vestnik Akad Nauk Respub Kazakhstan
Vestnik Belorusskogo Gosudarstvennogo Universiteta Imeni V. I. Lenina. Naucnyi Zurnal. Seriya 1. Matematika, Fizika, Mekhanika — Vestnik Beloruss Gos Univ Ser 1
Vestnik Belorusskogo Gosudarstvennogo Universiteta Imeni V. I. Lenina, Seriya 1. Fizika, Matematika, Mekhanika — Vestn Beloruss Gos Univ Im VI Lenina Ser 1
Vestnik Belorusskogo Gosudarstvennogo Universiteta Imeni V. I. Lenina. Seriya I. Fizika, Matematika, Mekhanika — Vestnik Beloruss Gos Univ Ser I Fiz Mat Mekh
Vestnik Belorusskogo Gosudarstvennogo Universiteta. Seriya 1. Matematika, Fizika, Mekhanika — Vestn Beloruss Gos Univ Ser 1
Vestnik Belorusskogo Gosudarstvennogo Universiteta. Seriya 2. Biologiya, Khimiya, Geologiya, Geografiya — Vestn Beloruss Gos Univ Ser 2 Biol Khim Geol Geogr
Vestnik Belorusskogo Universiteta — Vestn Beloruss Univ

Vestnik Ceske Akademie Ved a Umeni — VCA
Vestnik Ceskeho Geologickeho Ustavu — Vestn Cesk Geol Ustavu
Vestnik Ceskoslovenske Akademie Ved — VCA
Vestnik Ceskoslovenske Akademie Ved — VCSAV
Vestnik Ceskoslovenske Akademie Zemedelske — Vest Ces Akad Zemed
Vestnik Ceskoslovenske Akademie Zemedelske — Vestn Cesk Akad Zemed
Vestnik Ceskoslovenske Akademie Zemedelskych Ved — Vestn Cesk Akad Zemed Ved
Vestnik Ceskoslovenske Akademie Zemedelskych Ved — Vestn Ceskoslov Akad Zemed Ved
Vestnik Ceskoslovenske Spolecnosti Zoologicke — Vest Csl Spol Zool
Vestnik Ceskoslovenske Spolecnosti Zoologicke — Vestn Cesk Spol Zool
Vestnik. Chelyabinskii Universitet. Seriya 3. Matematika, Mekhanika — Vestnik Chelyabinsk Univ Ser 3 Mat Mekh
Vestnik Chkalovckogo Otdeleniya Vsesoyuznogo Khimicheskogo Obshchestva Imeni D. I. Mendeleeva — Vestn Chkal Otd Vses Khim O-Va Im D I Mendeleeva
Vestnik Dal'nevostochnogo Filiala Akademii Nauk SSSR — VDFAN
Vestnik Dal'nevostochnogo Filiala Akademii Nauk SSSR — Vest Dal'nevost Fil Akad Nauk SSSR
Vestnik Dermatologii i Venerologii — Vestn Dermatol Venerol
Vestnik Drevnei Istorii — V Dr Ist
Vestnik Drevnei Istorii — VD Ist
Vestnik Drevnei Istorii — VDI
Vestnik Drevnei Istorii — Ves Drev Ist
Vestnik Drevnei Istorii — Ves Drev Istor
Vestnik Drevnei Istorii — Vestn Drevn Ist
Vestnik Drevnej Istorii. Revue d'Histoire Ancienne — Vestn Drevnej Istor
Vestnik Elektropromyshlennosti [*Former USSR*] — Vestn Elektroprom-Sti
Vestnik Elektrotekhniki — Vestn Elektrotekh
Vestnik Estestvoznanija. Revue des Sciences Naturelles — Vestn Estestv
Vestnik Evropy — VE
Vestnik Gosudarstvennogo Muzeia Gruzii — VMG
Vestnik Gosudarstvennogo Muzeja Gruzii — Vestn Gos Muz Gruz
Vestnik Gosudarstvennogo Muzeja Gruzii Imeni Akademika S. N. Dzhanashia — Vest Gos Muz Gruz
Vestnik Gosudarstvennogo Muzeja Gruzii Imeni Akademika S. N. Dzhanashia — Vestn Gosud Muz Gruzii
Vestnik Gruzinskogo Botanicheskogo Obshchestva — Vestn Gruz Bot Ova
Vestnik Har'kovskogo Gosudarstvennogo Universiteta — Vestnik Har'kov Gos Univ
Vestnik Har'kovskogo Politehniceskogo Instituta — Vestnik Har'kov Politehn Inst
Vestnik Institut Pchelovodstva — Vest Inst Pchelovodstva
Vestnik Inzhenerov i Tekhnikov [*Former USSR*] — Vestn Inzh Tekh
Vestnik Istorii Mirovoi Kul'tury — Vest Ist Mirov Kul't
Vestnik Istorii Mirovoi Kultury — VIML
Vestnik Jaroslavskogo Universiteta — Vestn Jaroslav Univ
Vestnik Jaroslavskogo Universiteta — Vestnik Jaroslav Univ
Vestnik Kabardino-Balkarskogo Naucno-Issledovatel'skogo Instituta — Vestn Kabard Balkar Nauc-Issled Inst
Vestnik Karakalpakskogo Filiala Akademii Nauk Uzbekskoi SSR — Vestn Karakalp Fil Akad
Vestnik Karakalpakskogo Filiala Akademii Nauk Uzbekskoi SSR — Vestn Karakalp Fil Akad Nauk Uzb SSR
Vestnik Kazahskogo Filiala Akademii Nauk SSSR — Vestn Kazahsk Fil Akad Nauk SSSR
Vestnik Kazakhskogo Filiala Akademii Nauk SSSR — Vestn Kaz Fil Akad Nauk SSSR
Vestnik. Khar'kovskii Universitet — Vestnik Kharkov Univ
Vestnik Khar'kovskogo Gosudarstvennogo Universiteta. Seriya Mekhaniko-Matematicheskaya. Zapiski Mekhaniko-Matematicheskogo Fakul'teta i Khar'kovskogo Matematicheskogo Obshchestva — Vestnik Khar'kov Gos Univ
Vestnik Khar'kovskogo Politekhnicheskogo Instituta [*Ukrainian SSR*] — Vestn Khar'k Politekh Inst
Vestnik Khar'kovskogo Universiteta — Vestn Khark Univ
Vestnik Khar'kovskogo Universiteta. Astronomiya [*Ukrainian SSR*] — Vestn Khar'k Univ Astron
Vestnik Khar'kovskogo Universiteta. Geologiya i Geografiya [*Ukrainian SSR*] — Vestn Khar'k Univ Geol Geogr
Vestnik Khar'kovskogo Universiteta. Radiofizika, Elektronika [*Former USSR*] — Vest Khar'k Univ Radiofiz Elektron
Vestnik Khar'kovskogo Universiteta. Seriya Biologicheskaya — Vestn Khar'k Univ Ser Biol
Vestnik Khar'kovskogo Universiteta. Seriya Geologicheskaya [*Ukrainian SSR*] — Vestn Khar'k Univ Ser Geol
Vestnik Khar'kovskogo Universiteta. Seriya Khimicheskaya — Vestn Khar'k Univ Ser Khim
Vestnik Khar'kovskogo Universiteta. Voprosy Ehlektrokhimii — Vestn Khar'k Univ Vopr Ehlektrokhim
Vestnik Khirurgii Imeni I. I. Grekova — Vestn Khir
Vestnik Khirurgii Imeni I. I. Grekova — Vestn Khir Im I I Grek
Vestnik Khirurgii Imeni I. I. Grekova — Vestn Khir Im I I Grekova
Vestnik Kievskogo Politehniceskogo Instituta. Serija Tehniceskoi Kibernetiki — Vestnik Kiev Politehn Inst Ser Tehn Kibernet
Vestnik Kievskogo Politekhnicheskogo Instituta. Seriya Mashinostroeniya — Vestn Kiev Politekh Inst Ser Mashinostr
Vestnik Kievskogo Politekhnicheskogo Instituta. Seriya Priborostroeniya — Vestn Kiev Politekh Inst Ser Priborostr
Vestnik Kievskogo Politekhnicheskogo Instituta. Seriya Teploenergetiki — Vestn Kiev Politekh Inst Ser Teploenerg
Vestnik Kievskogo Universiteta. Modelirovanie i Optimizatsiya Slozhnykh Sistem — Vestnik Kiev Univ Model Optim Slozhn Sist
Vestnik Kralovske Ceske Spolecnosti Nauk — VKCSN
Vestnik Kralovske Ceske Spolecnosti Nauk Trida Matematicko Prirodovedecka — Vestn Kral Ceske Spol Nauk Trida Mat Prirodoved
Vestnik Kralovske Ceske Spolecnosti Nauk v Praze Trida Matematicko Prirodovedecka — Vestnik K Ceske Spolec Nauk v Praze Trida Mat Prirod
Vestnik Lavnogo Upravleniya Metallopromyshlennosti — Vestn La Upr Metallopromsti
Vestnik Leningrad University. Mathematics — Vestnik Leningrad Univ Math
Vestnik Leningradskogo Gosudarstvennogo Universiteta — Vestnik Leningr Gosud Univ
Vestnik Leningradskogo Gosudarstvennogo Universiteta — VLenU
Vestnik Leningradskogo Gosudarstvennogo Universiteta — VLU
Vestnik Leningradskogo Gosudarstvennogo Universiteta — VLUist
Vestnik Leningradskogo Gosudarstvennogo Universiteta. Seriya Biologii — Vest Leningr Gos Univ Ser Biol
Vestnik Leningradskogo Instituta — Vest Leningr Inst
Vestnik Leningradskogo Universiteta — VeL
Vestnik Leningradskogo Universiteta — Vestn Leningr Univ
Vestnik Leningradskogo Universiteta. Biologiya — Vestn Leningr Univ Biol
Vestnik Leningradskogo Universiteta. Fizika i Khimiya — Vestn Leningr Univ Fiz & Khim
Vestnik Leningradskogo Universiteta. Fizika i Khimiya — Vestnik Leningrad Univ Fiz Khim
Vestnik Leningradskogo Universiteta. Geologiya, Geografiya — Vestn Leningr Univ Geol Geogr
Vestnik Leningradskogo Universiteta. Istorija, Jazyka, i Literatury — Vestn Leningr Univ Ist Jaz Lit
Vestnik Leningradskogo Universiteta. Matematika, Mekhanika, Astronomiya — Vestn Leningr Univ Mat Mekh Astron
Vestnik Leningradskogo Universiteta. Matematika, Mekhanika, Astronomiya — Vestnik Leningrad Univ Mat Mekh Astronom
Vestnik Leningradskogo Universiteta. Serija Biologii, Geografii, i Geologii — Vestn Leningradsk Univ Ser Biol Geogr
Vestnik Leningradskogo Universiteta. Serija Ekonomiki, Filosofii, i Pravo — Vestn Leningr Univ Ser Ekon Filos Pravo
Vestnik Leningradskogo Universiteta. Seriya 3. Biologiya — Vestn Leningr Univ Ser 3 Biol
Vestnik Leningradskogo Universiteta. Seriya 7. Geologiya, Geografiya — Vestn Leningr Univ Ser 7 Geol Geogr
Vestnik Leningradskogo Universiteta. Seriya Biologii — Vestn Leningrad Univ Ser Biol
Vestnik Leningradskogo Universiteta. Seriya Biologii, Geografii, i Geologii — Vestn Lening Univ Ser Biol Geogr Geol
Vestnik Leningradskogo Universiteta. Seriya Fiziki i Khimii — V Lenin Fiz
Vestnik Leningradskogo Universiteta. Seriya Fiziki i Khimii [*Former USSR*] — Vestn Leningr Univ Ser Fiz Khim
Vestnik Leningradskogo Universiteta. Seriya Fiziki i Khimii — Vestnik Leningrad Univ Ser Fiz Khim
Vestnik Leningradskogo Universiteta. Seriya Geologii i Geografii [*Former USSR*] — Vestn Leningr Univ Ser Geol Geogr
Vestnik Leningradskogo Universiteta. Seriya Istorii, Jazyka, i Literatury — VLU
Vestnik Leningradskogo Universiteta. Seriya Matematika, Mekhanika, i Astronomiya — Vestn Leningr Univ Ser Mat Mekh & Astron
Vestnik Leningradskogo Universiteta. Seriya Matematiki, Fiziki, i Khimii — Vestn Leningr Univ Ser Mat Fiz Khim
Vestnik Leningradskogo Universiteta. Seriya Matematiki i Mekhaniki — V Lenin Mek
Vestnik L'vivs'kogo Derzhavnogo Universitetu. Seriya Fizichna [*Ukrainian SSR*] — Vestn L'viv Derzh Univ Ser Fiz
Vestnik L'vovskogo Politekhnicheskogo Instituta — Vestnik L'vov Politehn Inst
Vestnik Mashinostroeniya — Vestn Mashinostr
Vestnik Metallopromyshlennosti — Vestn Metallopromsti
Vestnik Mikrobiologii, Epidemiologii, i Parazitologii — Vest Mikrobiol Epidemiol Parazitol
Vestnik Mikrobiologii, Epidemiologii, i Parazitologii — Vestnik Mikrobiol Epidemiol i Parazitol
Vestnik Mikrobiologii i Epidemiologii — Vestnik Mikrobiol i Epidemiol
Vestnik Ministerstva Zdravotnictvi [*Czechoslovakia*] — Vestn Minist Zdrav
Vestnik Moskovskogo Gosudarstvennogo Tekhnicheskogo Universiteta. Seriya Mashinostroenie — Vestn Mosk Gos Tekh Univ Ser Mashinostr
Vestnik Moskovskogo Gosudarstvennogo Universiteta — VMU
Vestnik Moskovskogo Gosudarstvennogo Universiteta — VMUist
Vestnik Moskovskogo Gosudarstvennogo Universiteta. Seriya VI — Vest Mosk Gos Univ Ser VI
Vestnik Moskovskogo Instituta Geografii — Vest Mosk Inst Geogr
Vestnik Moskovskogo Instituta. Seriya Biologiya, Pochvovedenie — Vest Mosk Inst Biol Pochv
Vestnik Moskovskogo Universiteta — VeM
Vestnik Moskovskogo Universiteta — Vest MU
Vestnik Moskovskogo Universiteta — Vestn Mosk Univ
Vestnik Moskovskogo Universiteta. Biologiya, Pochvovedenie — Vestn Mosk Univ Biol Pochvoved
Vestnik Moskovskogo Universiteta. Ekonomika, Filosofiia — VMUE
Vestnik Moskovskogo Universiteta. Fizika, Astronomiya — Vestn Mosk Univ Fiz Astron
Vestnik Moskovskogo Universiteta. Geografiya — Vestn Mosk Univ Geogr
Vestnik Moskovskogo Universiteta. Geologiya — Vestn Mosk Univ Geol
Vestnik Moskovskogo Universiteta. Khimiya — Vestn Mosk Univ Khim
Vestnik Moskovskogo Universiteta. Matematika, Mekhanika — Vestn Mosk Univ Mat Mekh
Vestnik Moskovskogo Universiteta. Nauchnyj Zhurnal. Seriya II. Khimiya — Vestn Mosk Univ Ser II
Vestnik Moskovskogo Universiteta. Serija Ekonomika — Vestn Moskov Univ Ser Ekon
Vestnik Moskovskogo Universiteta. Serija Filosofija — Vestn Moskov Univ Ser Filos

Vestnik Moskovskogo Universiteta. Serija Geografija — Vestn Moskov Univ Ser Geogr
Vestnik Moskovskogo Universiteta. Serija I. Matematika, Mehanika — Vestnik Moskov Univ Ser I Mat Meh
Vestnik Moskovskogo Universiteta. Serija III. Fizika, Astronomija — Vestnik Moskov Univ Ser III Fiz Astronom
Vestnik Moskovskogo Universiteta. Serija Istorija — Vestn Moskov Univ Ser Ist
Vestnik Moskovskogo Universiteta. Serija Pravo — Vestn Moskov Univ Ser Pravo
Vestnik Moskovskogo Universiteta. Serija XV. Vycislitel'naja Matematika i Kibernetika — Vestnik Moskov Univ Ser XV Vycisl Mat Kibernet
Vestnik Moskovskogo Universiteta. Seriya 1. Matematika, Mekhanika — Vestn Mosk Univ Ser 1
Vestnik Moskovskogo Universiteta. Seriya 1. Matematika, Mekhanika — Vestn Mosk Univ Ser 1 Mat Mekh
Vestnik Moskovskogo Universiteta. Seriya 1. Matematika, Mekhanika — VMMMA
Vestnik Moskovskogo Universiteta. Seriya 2. Khimiya — Vestn Mosk Univ Ser 2 Khim
Vestnik Moskovskogo Universiteta. Seriya 2. Khimiya — Vestnik Mosk Univ Ser Khim
Vestnik Moskovskogo Universiteta. Seriya 2. Khimiya — VMUKA
Vestnik Moskovskogo Universiteta. Seriya 3. Fizika, Astronomiya — Vestn Mosk Univ Ser 3
Vestnik Moskovskogo Universiteta. Seriya 3. Fizika, Astronomiya — Vestn Mosk Univ Ser 3 Fiz Astron
Vestnik Moskovskogo Universiteta. Seriya 3. Fizika, Astronomiya — VMUFA
Vestnik Moskovskogo Universiteta. Seriya 4. Geologiya — Vestn Mosk Univ Ser 4 Geol
Vestnik Moskovskogo Universiteta. Seriya 4. Geologiya — VMUGA
Vestnik Moskovskogo Universiteta. Seriya 5. Geografiya — Vestn Mosk Univ Ser 5 Geogr
Vestnik Moskovskogo Universiteta. Seriya 5. Geografiya — VMOGA
Vestnik Moskovskogo Universiteta. Seriya 6 — Vestn Moskov Univ Ser 6
Vestnik Moskovskogo Universiteta. Seriya 6. Biologiya, Pochvovedenie — Vestn Mosk Univ Ser 6 Biol Pochvoved
Vestnik Moskovskogo Universiteta. Seriya 6. Biologiya, Pochvovedenie — VMUBA
Vestnik Moskovskogo Universiteta. Seriya 15. Vychislitel'naya Matematika i Kibernetika [*Former USSR*] — Vest Mosk Univ Ser 15 Vychisl Mat Kibern
Vestnik Moskovskogo Universiteta. Seriya 15. Vychislitel'naya Matematika i Kibernetika — Vestn Mosk Univ Ser 15
Vestnik Moskovskogo Universiteta. Seriya 15. Vychislitel'naya Matematika i Kibernetika — Vestn Mosk Univ Ser 15 Vychisl Mat Kibern
Vestnik Moskovskogo Universiteta. Seriya 16. Biologiya — Vestn Mosk Univ Ser 16 Biol
Vestnik Moskovskogo Universiteta. Seriya 16. Seriya Biologiia — Vestn Mosk Univ Ser 16 Ser Biol
Vestnik Moskovskogo Universiteta. Seriya 17. Pochvovedenie — Vestn Mosk Univ Ser 17 Pochvoved
Vestnik Moskovskogo Universiteta. Seriya Biologii, Pochvovedeniya, Geologii, Geografii — Vest Mosk Univ Ser Biol Pochv Geol Geogr
Vestnik Moskovskogo Universiteta. Seriya Biologii, Pochvovedeniya, Geologii, Geografii — Vestn Mosk Univ Ser Biol Pochvoved Geol Geogr
Vestnik Moskovskogo Universiteta. Seriya Fizika-Astronomiya — Vestn Moskovskogo Univ Fiz-Astron
Vestnik Moskovskogo Universiteta. Seriya Fiziki i Astronomii — V Mosk Fiz
Vestnik Moskovskogo Universiteta. Seriya Fiziko-Matematicheskikh i Estestvennykh Nauk [*Former USSR*] — Vestn Mosk Univ Ser Fiz-Mat Estestv Nauk
Vestnik Moskovskogo Universiteta. Seriya Khimiya — V Mosk U Kh
Vestnik Moskovskogo Universiteta. Seriya Khimiya — Vestn Moskovskogo Univ Khim
Vestnik Moskovskogo Universiteta. Seriya Matematiki i Mekhaniki — V Mosk Mekh
Vestnik Moskovskogo Universiteta. Seriya Matematiki, Mekhaniki, Astronomii, Fiziki, Khimii — Vestn Mosk Univ Ser Mat Mekh Astron Fiz Khim
Vestnik Moskovskogo Universiteta Teorija Naucnogo Kommunizma — Vestn Moskov Univ Teorija Nauc Kommunizma
Vestnik Moskovskogo Universiteta Zhurnalistika — VMUZh
Vestnik Nauchnoi Informatsii Zabaikal'skogo Filiala Geograficheskogo Obshchestva SSSR — Vestn Nauchn Inf Zabaik Fil Geogr Ova SSSR
Vestnik Nauchno-Issledovatel'skii Institut Pchelovodstva — Vest Nauchno-Issled Inst Pchel
Vestnik Nauchno-Issledovatel'skogo Instituta Gidrobiologii (Dnepropetrovski) — Vestn Nauchno-Issled Inst Gidrobiol (Dnepropetr)
Vestnik Obscestvennyh Nauk. Akademija Nauk Armjanskoj SSR — Vestn Obsc Nauk Akad Nauk Arm SSR
Vestnik Obshchestvennoi Veterinarii (S. Peterburg) — Vestnik Obsh Vet (S Peterburg)
Vestnik Oftal'mologii — VEOFA
Vestnik Oftal'mologii — Vestn Oftal'mol
Vestnik Oftal'mologii (Kiev) — Vest Oftal (Kiev)
Vestnik Oftal'mologii (Moskva) — Vest Oftal (Mosk)
Vestnik Otdelenija Obscestvennych Nauk. Akademija Nauk Gruzinskoj SSR — VON
Vestnik Otorinolaringologii — Vest Oto-Rino-Lar
Vestnik Oto-Rino-Laringologii — Vestn ORL
Vestnik Otorinolaringologii — Vestn Otorinolaringol
Vestnik Oto-Rino-Laringologii — VORLA
Vestnik Protivovozdushnoi Oborony — Vestn Protivovozdushnoi Oborony
Vestnik Rentgenologii i Radiologii — Vestn Rentgenol Radiol
Vestnik Rentgenologii i Radiologii — Vestnik Rentg i Radiol
Vestnik Respublikanskogo Instituta za Okhranu Prirodyi Estestvennonauchnogo Muzeya v Titograde — Vestn Respub Inst Okhr Prir Estestvennonauchn Muz Titograde
Vestnik. Rossiiskaya Akademiya Nauk. Vestnik — Vestnik Ross Akad Nauk
Vestnik Rossiiskoi Akademii Meditsinskikh Nauk — Vestn Ross Akad Med Nauk
Vestnik Rossijskago Obscestva Sadovodstva v S.-Peterburge — Vestn Rossijsk Obsc Sadov S Peterburge
Vestnik Russkogo (Studencheskogo) Khristianskogo Dvizheniia — VRKhD
Vestnik Sankt-Peterburgskogo Universiteta. Fizika. Khimiya — Vestnik S Peterburg Univ Fiz Khim
Vestnik Sankt-Peterburgskogo Universiteta. Matematika, Mekhanika, Astronomiya — Vestnik S Peterburg Univ Mat Mekh Astronom
Vestnik Sankt-Peterburgskogo Universiteta. Seriya 3. Biologiya — Vestn St Peterb Univ Ser 3 Biol
Vestnik Sankt-Peterburgskogo Universiteta. Seriya 7. Geologiya, Geografiya — Vestn St Peterb Univ Ser 7 Geol Geogr
Vestnik Sel'sko-Hozjajstvennoj Nauki — Vestn Selsk Hoz Nauki
Vestnik Sel'skokhozyaistvennoi Nauki (Alma-Ata) — Vestn Sel'skokhoz Nauki (Alma-Ata)
Vestnik Sel'skokhozyaistvennoi Nauki (Alma-Ata) [*Kazakh SSR*] — Vestn S-Kh Nauki (Alma-Ata)
Vestnik Sel'skokhozyaistvennoi Nauki (Alma-Ata). Ministerstvo Sel'skogo Khozyaistva Kazakhskoi SSR — Vest Sel'-Khoz Nauki (Alma-Ata) Minist Sel Khoz Kazakh SSR
Vestnik Sel'skokhozyaistvennoi Nauki Kazakhstana. Ezhemesiachnyi Nauchnyi Zhurnal — Vestn S-Kh Nauki Kaz
Vestnik Sel'skokhozyaistvennoi Nauki (Moscow) — Vestn Sel'skokhoz Nauki (Moscow)
Vestnik Sel'skokhozyaistvennoi Nauki (Moscow) — Vestn S-Kh Nauki (Mosc)
Vestnik Sel'skokhozyaistvennoi Nauki (Moskva) [*Former USSR*] — Vest Sel-Khoz Nauki (Mosk)
Vestnik Slovenskega Kemijskega Drustva — Vestn Slov Kem Drus
Vestnik Sotsialisticheskogo Rastenievodstva — Vestn Sots Rastenievod
Vestnik Sovremennoi Veterinarii — Vestnik Sovrem Vet
Vestnik St. Petersburg University. Mathematics — Vestnik St Petersburg Univ Math
Vestnik Standartizatsii — Vestn Stand
Vestnik Statistiki — Vestn Statis
Vestnik Statistiki — Vestn Statist
Vestnik Statistiki — Vestnik Statist
Vestnik Statniho Geologickiho Ustavu Ceskoslovenske Republiky — Vestn Statniho Geol Ustavu Cesk Repub
Vestnik Studencheskogo Nauchnogo Obshchestva Kazanskii Gosudarstvennyi Universitet Estestvennye Nauki — Vestn Stud Nauchn Ova Kazan Gos Univ Estestv Nauki
Vestnik Tbilisskogo Botanicheskogo Sada Akademii Nauk Gruzinskoi SSR — Vestn Tbilis Bot Sada Akad Nauk Gruz SSR
Vestnik Tiflisskago Botaniceskago Sada. Moniteur du Jardin Botanique de Tiflis — Vestn Tiflissk Bot Sada
Vestnik Uradu pro Vynalezy a Objevy — Vestn Uradu Vynalezy Objevy
Vestnik Uradu pro Vynalezy a Objevy. Cast A. Vynalezy — Vestn Uradu Vynalezy Objevy Cast A Vynalezy
Vestnik Uradu pro Vynalezy a Objevy. Cast B. Ochranne Znamky. Prumyslovy Vzory — Vestn Uradu Vynalezy Objevy Cast B Ochr Znamky Prum Vzory
Vestnik Uradu pro Vynalezy a Objevy. Ochranne Znamky. Prumyslovy Vzory — Vestn Uradu Vynalezy Objevy Ochr Znamky Prum Vzory
Vestnik Uradu pro Vynalezy a Objevy. Vynalezy — Vestn Uradu Vynalezy Objevy Vynalezy
Vestnik. USSR Academy of Medical Science — Vestn USSR Acad Med Sci
Vestnik Ustredniho Ustavu Geologickeho — Vest Ustred Ust Geol
Vestnik Ustredniho Ustavu Geologickeho — Vestn Ustred Ustavu Geol
Vestnik Ustredniho Ustavu Geologickeho — Vestnik Ustredniho Ustavu Geol
Vestnik Vysshei Shkoly — VVS
Vestnik Vysshej Shkoly — Vestn Vyssh Shk
Vestnik Vyzkumnych Ustavu Zemedelskych — Vestn Vyzk Ustavu Zemed
Vestnik Zapadno-Sibirskogo Geologicheskogo Upravleniya — Vestn Zapadno Sib Geol Upr
Vestnik Zapadno-Sibirskogo i Novosibirskogo Geologicheskikh Upravlenii — Vestn Zapadno Sib i Novosib Geol Upr
Vestnik Zashchity Rastenii — Vestn Zashch Rast
Vestnik Zoologii — Vest Zool
Vestnik Zoologii — Vestn Zool
Vestnik Zoologii/Zoological Record — Vestn Zool Zool Rec
Vestsi Akademii Agrarnykh Navuk Belarusi — Vestsi Akad Agrar Navuk Belarusi
Vestsi Akademii Navuk Belarusi. Seryya Fizika-Energetychnykh Navuk — Vestsi Akad Navuk Belarusi Ser Fiz Energ Navuk
Vestsi Akademii Navuk Belarusi. Seryya Fizika-Matematychnykh Navuk — Vestsi Akad Navuk Belarusi Ser Fiz Mat Navuk
Vestsi Akademii Navuk Belarusi. Seryya Khimichnykh Navuk — Vestsi Akad Navuk Belarusi Ser Khim Navuk
Vestsi Akademii Navuk Belaruskai SSR. Khimichnykh Navuk — Vestsi Akad Navuk BSSR Khim Navuk
Vestsi Akademii Navuk Belaruskai SSR. Seriya — Vestsi Akad Navuk BSSR Ser
Vestsi Akademii Navuk Belaruskai SSR. Seryya Biyalagichnykh Navuk — Vestsi Akad Navuk BSSR Ser Biyal Navuk
Vestsi Akademii Navuk Belaruskai SSR. Seryya Khimichnykh Navuk — Vestsi Akad Navuk BSSR Ser Khim Navuk
Vestsi Akademii Navuk Belaruskai SSR. Seryya Sel'skagaspadar Navuk — Vestsi Akad Navuk BSSR Ser Sel'skagas Navuk
Vestsi Akademii Navuk BSSR. Seriya Fizika-Matematicheskikh — Vestsi Akad Navuk BSSR Ser Fiz-Mat
Vestsi Akademii Navuk BSSR. Seriya Khimicheskikh [*Former USSR*] — Vestsi Akad Navuk BSSR Ser Khim
Vestsi Akademii Navuk BSSR. Seryya Biyalagichnykh Navuk — VABBA

Vestsi Akademii Navuk BSSR. Seryya Fizika-Ehnergetychnykh Navuk — Vestsi Akad Navuk BSSR Ser Fiz-Ehnerg Navuk
Vestsi Akademii Navuk BSSR. Seryya Fizika-Matematychnykh Navuk — VBSFA
Vestsi Akademii Navuk BSSR. Seryya Fizika-Matematychnykh Navuk — Vestsi Akad Navuk BSSR Ser Fiz-Mat Navuk
Vestsi Akademii Navuk BSSR. Seryya Fizika-Tekhnichnykh Navuk — VABFA
Vestsi Akademii Navuk BSSR. Seryya Fizika-Tekhnichnykh Navuk — Vestsi Akad Navuk BSSR Ser Fiz-Tekh Navuk
Vestsi Akademii Navuk BSSR. Seryya Gramadskikh Navuk [*Belorussian SSR*] — Vestsi Akad Navuk BSSR Ser Gramadskikh Navuk
Vestsi Akademii Navuk BSSR. Seryya Khimichnykh Navuk — VBSKA
Vestsi Akademii Navuk BSSR. Seryya Sel'skagaspadarchykh Navuk — Vestsi Akad Navuk BSSR Ser Selskagaspad Navuk
Vestsi Belaruskaya Akademiya Navuk. Seryya Biyalagichnykh Navuk — Vestsi Belarus Akad Navuk Ser Biyal Navuk
Vestsyi Akadehmyiyi Navuk BSSR. Seryya Fyizyika-Ehnergetychnykh Navuk — Vestsyi Akad Navuk BSSR Ser Fyiz-Ehnerg Navuk
Vestsyi Akadehmyiyi Navuk BSSR. Seryya Fyizyika-Matehmatychnykh Navuk — Vestsyi Akad Navuk BSSR Ser Fyiz-Mat Navuk
Vestsyi Akadehmyiyi Navuk BSSR. Seryya Fyizyika-Tehkhnyichnykh Navuk — Vestsyi Akad Navuk BSSR Ser Fyiz-Tehkh Navuk
Vestsyi Akadehmyiyi Navuk BSSR. Seryya Khyimyichnykh Navuk — Vestsyi Akad Navuk BSSR Ser Khyim Navuk
Veszprem Megyei Muzeumok Koezlemenyei — Veszprem Koezl
Veszprem Megyei Muzeumok Koezlemenyei — Veszprem Megyei Muz
Veszprem Megyei Muzeumok Koezlemenyei — Veszprem Megyei Muz Koezl
Veszprem Megyei Muzeumok Koezlemenyei — Veszprem Megyei Muz Koezlem
Veszprem Megyei Muzeumok Koezlemenyei — Veszprem Mk
Veszprem Megyei Muzeumok Koezlemenyei — Veszpremi Muzk
Veszprem Megyei Muzeumok Koezlemenyei — VMMK
Veszpremi Vegyipari Egyetem Kozlemenyei — Veszprmi Vegyip Egy Kozl
Veszpremi Vegyipari Egyetem Tudomanyos Ulesszakanak Eloadasai [*Hungary*] — Veszpremi Vegyip Egy Tud Ulesszakanak Eloadasai
Vetenskapliga Publikationer. Tekniska Hoegskolan i Helsingfors — Vetensk Publ Tek Hoegsk Helsingfors
Vetenskaps-Societeten i Lund — VL
Vetenskaps-Societeten i Lund — VSL
Vetenskaps-Societeten i Lund. Aarsbok — AVsLund
Vetenskaps-Societeten i Lund. Aarsbok — Vetensk Soc i Lund Arsbok
Vetenskaps-Societeten i Lund. Aarsbok — VSLA
Vetera Christianorum — V Christ
Vetera Christianorum — Vet Christ
Vetera Christianorum — VetChr
Vetera Christianorum — Vetera Chr
Veterans Jewish Legion. Bulletin — VJLB
Veterinaer- og Landbohojskole Aarskrift — Lbh Aa
Veterinaria — Vet
Veterinaria e Zootecnia — Vet Zootec
Veterinaria Espanola — Vet Espan
Veterinaria Italiana — Vet Ital
Veterinaria Mocambicana — Vet Mocambicana
Veterinaria Uruguay — Vet Urug
Veterinaria y Zootecnia Revista Peruana — Vet Zootec Rev Peru
Veterinaria y Zootecnia Revista Peruana — VZRPAS
Veterinariya [*Moscow*] — VETNAL
Veterinariya Respublikanskii Mezhvedomstvennyi Tematicheskii Nauchnyi Sbornik — Vet Resp Mezhved Temat Nauchn Sb
Veterinariya Respublikanskyu Mizhvidomchyi Tematychnyi Naukovyi Zbirnyk — Vet Resp Mizhvid Temat Nauk Zb
Veterinarna Sbirka — Vet Sbirka
Veterinarna Sbirka (Sofia) — Vet Sb (Sofia)
Veterinarna Sbirka (Sofia) — Vet Sbir (Sof)
Veterinarni Medicina — Vet Med
Veterinarni Medicina — VTMDA
Veterinarni Medicina (Prague) — Vet Med (Prague)
Veterinarni Medicina (Praha) — Vet Med (Praha)
Veterinarno Meditsinski Nauki — Vet Med Nauki
Veterinarno Meditsinski Nauki (Sofia) — Vet Med Nauki (Sofia)
Veterinarnoe Obozrienie — Vet Obozr
Veterinarnyi Zhurnal (Bratislava) — Vet Zh (Bratislava)
Veterinarski Arhiv — Vet Arh
Veterinarski Glasnik — Vet Glas
Veterinarski Glasnik — Vet Glasn
Veterinarsky Casopis — Vet Cas
Veterinarsky Casopis (Kosice) — Vet Cas (Kosice)
Veterinarsky Sbornik (Bratislava) — Vet Sb (Bratislava)
Veterinary and Comparative Orthopaedics and Traumatology. VCOT — Vet Comp Orthop Tramatol VCOT
Veterinary and Human Toxicology — Vet Hum Toxicol
Veterinary Anesthesia — Vet Anesth
Veterinary Annual — Vet Annu
Veterinary Bulletin — Vet Bull
Veterinary Bulletin (London) — Vet Bull (London)
Veterinary Bulletin (Weybridge, England) — Vet Bull (Weybridge Eng)
Veterinary Clinical Pathology — Vet Clin Pathol
Veterinary Clinics of North America — Vet Clin North Am
Veterinary Clinics of North America. Equine Practice — Vet Clin North Am Equine Pract
Veterinary Clinics of North America. Food Animal Practice — Vet Clin North Am Food Anim Pract
Veterinary Clinics of North America (Large Animal Practice) — Vet Clin North Am (Large Anim Pract)
Veterinary Clinics of North America (Small Animal Practice) — Vet Clin North Am (Small Anim Pract)
Veterinary Economics — Vet Econ
Veterinary History Bulletin. Veterinary History Society — Vet Hist
Veterinary Immunology and Immunopathology — Vet Immunol Immunopathol
Veterinary Inspector Annual. Institute of Veterinary Inspectors of New South Wales — Vet Insp Annu Inst Vet Insp NSW
Veterinary Journal — Vet J
Veterinary Journal and Annals of Comparative Pathology — Vet J and Ann Comp Path
Veterinary Journal (Bratislava) — Vet J (Bratislava)
Veterinary Literature Documentation [*Database*] — VETDOC
Veterinary Magazine — Vet Mag
Veterinary Medical Review — Vet Med Rev
Veterinary Medical Science — Vet Med Sci
Veterinary Medicine — Vet Med
Veterinary Medicine and Small Animal Clinician [*Later, Veterinary Medicine*] — Vet Med
Veterinary Medicine and Small Animal Clinician — Vet Med & Small Anim Clin
Veterinary Medicine and Small Animal Clinician — Vet Med/SAC
Veterinary Medicine and Small Animal Clinician — Vet Med Small Anim Clin
Veterinary Medicine Report — Vet Med Rep
Veterinary Microbiology [*Netherlands*] — Vet Microbiol
Veterinary News — Vet News
Veterinary Parasitology — Vet Parasitol
Veterinary Parasitology — VPARD
Veterinary Pathology — Vet Path
Veterinary Pathology — Vet Pathol
Veterinary Pathology. Supplement — Vet Pathol (Suppl)
Veterinary Professional Topics. Pets. Small Animal Professional Topics — Vet Prof Top Pets Small Anim Prof Top
Veterinary Professional Topics. Swine. Swine Professional Topics. Illinois University. Cooperative Extension Service — Vet Prof Top Swine Swine Prof Top Ill Univ Coop Ext Serv
Veterinary Quarterly — VEQUD
Veterinary Quarterly — Vet Q
Veterinary Quarterly. Quarterly Journal of Veterinary Science — Vet QQJ Vet Sci
Veterinary Radiology — VERAD9
Veterinary Radiology — Vet Radiol
Veterinary Record — Vet Rec
Veterinary Record. Journal. British Veterinary Association — Vet Rec J Br Vet Assoc
Veterinary Research — Vet Res
Veterinary Research Communications — Vet Res Commun
Veterinary Research Communications — VRCODX
Veterinary Review — Vet Rev
Veterinary Science Communications — Vet Sci Commun
Veterinary Surgery — Vet Surg
Veterinary Surgery — Vet Surgery
Veterinary Toxicology — Vet Toxicol
Veterinary World — Vet World
Vetro e Silicati — Vetro Silic
Vets Stars and Stripes for Peace — Vet Stars
Vetus Testamentum — Ve Tes
Vetus Testamentum — Vet Test
Vetus Testamentum — Vetus Test
Vetus Testamentum — VT
Vetus Testamentum. Supplementum [*Leiden*] — VTS
Vetus Testamentum. Supplementum [*Leiden*] — VTSuppl
VEV [*Vlaams Economisch Verband*] **Berichten** — VEV Ber
Vezelinstituut TNO [*Nederlands Centrale Organisatie voor Toegepast-Natuurwetenschappelijk Onderzoek*] **Delft VI Pamflet** — Vezelinst TNO Delft VI Pam
Vezetestudomany — Vezetestud
VFDB (Vereinigung zur Foerderung des Deutschen Brandschutzes eV) Zeitschrift — VFDB (Ver Foerd Dtch Brandschutzes) Z
VFDB [*Vereinigung zur Foerderung des Deutschen Brandschutzes eV*] **Zeitschrift** — VFDBA
VFW. Veterans of Foreign Wars Magazine — GVFW
VGB-Konferenz Forschung in der Kraftwerkstechnik — VGB Konf Forsch Kraftwerkstech
Viagem. Revista de Turismo, Divulgacao e Cultura — VRTDC
Viata Agricola — Viata Agric
Viata Medicala (Bucharest) — Viata Med (Buchar)
Viata Medicala. Revista a Uniunii Societatelor de Stiinte Medicale din Republica Socialista [*Romania*] — Viata Med
Viata Medicala. Revista de Informare Profesionala se Stiintifica a Cadrelor (Medii Sanitare) — Viata Med (Medii Sanit)
Viata Romaneasca [*Bucharest*] — ViR
Viata Romaneasca [*Bucharest*] — VR
Viata Romaneasca — VRo
Viator — Vi
Viator. Medieval and Renaissance Studies — Viator Med
Vibration Control in Microelectronics, Optics, and Metrology — Vib Control Microelectron Opt Metrol
Vibrational Spectra and Structure — Vib Spectra Struct
Vibrational Spectroscopy — Vib Spectr
Vic Computing — Vic Comput
Vicenza Economica — Vicenza Econ
Victimology — PVTM
Victoria. Country Roads Board. Engineering Note — Victoria Country Roads Board Eng Note
Victoria. Country Roads Board. Technical Bulletin — Victoria Country Roads Board Tech Bull
Victoria. Department of Agriculture. Research Project Series — Res Proj Ser Victoria Dep Agric

Victoria. Department of Agriculture. Research Project Series — Victoria Dep Agric Res Proj Ser
Victoria. Department of Agriculture. Technical Bulletin — Vic Dep Agric Tech Bull
Victoria. Department of Agriculture. Technical Bulletin — Victoria Dep Agric Tech Bull
Victoria. Department of Agriculture. Technical Report Series — Tech Rep Ser Victoria Dep Agric
Victoria. Department of Agriculture. Technical Report Series — Victoria Dep Agric Tech Rep Ser
Victoria. Fisheries and Wildlife Department. Fisheries Contribution — Fish Contr Vict
Victoria. Fisheries and Wildlife Department. Fisheries Contribution [*Australia*] — Victoria Fish Wildl Dep Fish Contrib
Victoria. Fisheries and Wildlife Department. Wildlife Contribution — Victoria Fish Wildl Dep Wildl Contrib
Victoria. Forests Commission. Bulletin — Vic For Comm Bull
Victoria. Forests Commission. Bulletin — Vict For Comm Bull
Victoria. Forests Commission. Forestry Technical Paper — Vict For Comm For Tech Pap
Victoria. Forests Commission. Miscellaneous Publication — Vict For Comm Misc Publ
Victoria. Geological Survey. Bulletin — Vict Geol Surv Bull
Victoria. Geological Survey. Bulletin — Victoria Geol Bull
Victoria. Geological Survey. Memoirs — Vict Geol Surv Mem
Victoria. Geological Survey. Memoirs — Victoria Geol Surv Mem
Victoria History of the Counties of England — Vict Co Hist
Victoria Institute of Colleges. Newsletter — Vic Inst Coll News
Victoria Institute of Colleges. Newsletter — VIC News
Victoria Institute or Philosophical Society of Great Britain. Journal of the Transactions — Victoria Inst Tr
Victoria Institute (Trinidad). Proceedings — Victoria Inst (Trinidad) Pr
Victoria. Mines Department. Annual Report — Victoria Mines Dep Annu Rep
Victoria. Mines Department. Groundwater Investigation Program. Report [*Australia*] — Victoria Mines Dep Groundwater Invest Program Rep
Victoria. Ministry for Conservation. Environmental Studies Program. Project Report — Proj Rep Victoria Minist Conserv Environ Stud Program
Victoria. Ministry for Conservation. Environmental Studies Program. Project Report — Victoria Minist Conserv Environ Stud Program Proj Rep
Victoria. Parliament. Parliamentary Debates — Vic Parl Parl Deb
Victoria. Soil Conservation Authority. TC Report — Vict Soil Conserv Auth TC
Victoria. Soil Conservation Authority. TC Report — Vict Soil Conserv Auth TC Rep
Victoria. State Rivers and Water Supply Commission. Annual Report — Victoria State Rivers Water Supply Comm Annu Rep
Victoria. State Rivers and Water Supply Commission. Technical Bulletin — St Riv Wat Supply Comm Tech Bull
Victoria University. College Law Review — Vict U C L Rev
Victoria University. College Law Review — VUCLR
Victoria University of Wellington. Antarctic Data Series [*New Zealand*] — Victoria Univ Antarct Data Ser
Victoria University of Wellington. Law Review — Vict U of Wellington L Rev
Victoria University of Wellington. Law Review — Vict U Well L Rev
Victoria University of Wellington. Law Review — VUWL Rev
Victoria University of Wellington. Law Review — VUWLR
Victoria Yearbook — Vic Yrbk
Victorian Adult Literacy News — VALN
Victorian Association for the Teaching of English. Journal — VATEJ
Victorian Association for the Teaching of English. Journal — Vic Assn Teach Eng J
Victorian Bar News — VBN
Victorian Bar News — Vic Bar News
Victorian Cancer News — Vict Cancer News
Victorian Chamber of Manufactures. Economic Service — Vic Chamber of Manufactures Econ Serv
Victorian Chapter Newsletter [*Australian College of Education*] — Vic Chap News
Victorian Commercial Teachers' Association. General Journal — VCTA General J
Victorian Commercial Teachers' Association. General Journal — Vic Comm Teach Assn General J
Victorian Conference of Social Welfare. Proceedings — Vic Conf Soc Welfare Proc
Victorian Conveyancing Law and Practice [*Australia*] — AVC
Victorian Creditman — Vic Creditman
Victorian Dairyfarmer — Vic Dairyfarmer
Victorian Dairyfarmer — Vict Dairyfmr
Victorian Electrical Contractor — Vic Elec Contractor
Victorian Employers' Federation. Annual Report — Vic Employers' Federation AR
Victorian Entomologist — Victorian Entomol
Victorian Federation of State Schools Mothers Clubs. Quarterly Review — VFSSMCQ
Victorian Fiction Research Guides — VFR
Victorian Geographical Journal — Vic Geogr J
Victorian Geographical Journal — Vict Geogr J
Victorian Government Gazette — Vic Govt Gaz
Victorian Government Publications — VGP
Victorian Historical Journal — VHJ
Victorian Historical Journal — Victorian Hist J
Victorian Historical Magazine [*Australia*] — VHM
Victorian Historical Magazine — Vic Hist Mag
Victorian Historical Magazine — Vict Hist Mag
Victorian Historical Magazine — Victorian Hist Mag
Victorian Horticultural Digest — Vic Hortic Dig
Victorian Horticultural Digest — Vict Hort Dig
Victorian Institute of Educational Research. Bulletin — VIER Bul
Victorian Institute of Educational Research. Bulletin — VIER Bull
Victorian Law Journal — Vict LJ
Victorian Law Reports — Vict LR
Victorian Law Reports — VLR
Victorian Law Reports (Admiralty) — VLR (Adm)
Victorian Law Reports (Equity) — VLR (E)
Victorian Law Reports (Equity) — VLR (Eq)
Victorian Law Reports (Insolvency, Probate, and Matrimonial) — VLR (IP & M)
Victorian Law Reports (Law) — VLR (L)
Victorian Law Reports (Law) — VR (Law)
Victorian Law Reports (Mining) — VLR (M)
Victorian Law Reports (Probate and Matrimonial) — VLR (P & M)
Victorian Law Times — Vict LT
Victorian Law Times — VLT
Victorian Legal Executive — Vic Legal Exec
Victorian Legal Executive — VLE
Victorian Licensing Decisions — VLD
Victorian LSA [*Limbless Soldiers' Association*] **Journal** — Vic LSAJ
Victorian National Parks Association. Journal — Victorian Natl Parks Assoc J
Victorian Naturalist — Vic Nat
Victorian Naturalist — Vic Naturalist
Victorian Naturalist — VicN
Victorian Naturalist — Vict Nat
Victorian Naturalist — Vict Naturalist
Victorian Naturalist — Victorian Nat
Victorian Newsletter — Vict Newsl
Victorian Newsletter — Victorian Newslett
Victorian Newsletter — VN
Victorian Newsletter — VNL
Victorian Parliamentary Debates — Vic Parl Deb
Victorian Periodicals Newsletter — Victorian Period Newslett
Victorian Periodicals Newsletter — VPN
Victorian Periodicals Review — Victorian Period Rev
Victorian Planning Appeal Decisions — VPA
Victorian Poetry — PVCP
Victorian Poetry — Vict Poet
Victorian Poetry — Vict Poetry
Victorian Poetry — VP
Victorian Poultry Journal — Vic Poultry J
Victorian Railways — Victorian Railw
Victorian Railways Newsletter — Vic Railways Newsletter
Victorian Railways Newsletter — VR Newsletter
Victorian Reports — Vict
Victorian Reports — Vict Rep
Victorian Reports — VR
Victorian Reports (Admiralty) — Vict Rep (Adm)
Victorian Reports (Admiralty) — VR (Adm)
Victorian Reports (Australian) — Vict Rep (Austr)
Victorian Reports (Equity) — Vict Rep (Eq)
Victorian Reports (Equity) — VR (E)
Victorian Reports (Equity) — VR (Eq)
Victorian Reports (Insolvency, Ecclesiastical, and Matrimonial) — VR (IE & M)
Victorian Reports (Law) — Vict Rep (Law)
Victorian Reports (Law) — VR (L)
Victorian Review — Vic Rev
Victorian Review — Vict Rev
Victorian Statistics Publications — Vic Stat Pub
Victorian Studies — PVCS
Victorian Studies — VicS
Victorian Studies — Vict Stud
Victorian Studies — Victorian Stud
Victorian Studies — VS
Victorian Studies Bulletin — VSB
Victorian Teachers Journal — Vic Teach J
Victorian Teachers Journal — Vic Teachers J
Victorian Town Planning Appeals Tribunal. Index of Appeals Decisions — VTPAI
Victorian Vegetable Grower — Vic Veg Grower
Victorian Veterinary Proceedings — Vic Vet Proc
Victorian Veterinary Proceedings — Victorian Vet Proc
Victoria's Resources — Vic Resour
Victoria's Resources — Vic Resources
Victoria's Resources — Vict Res
Victoria's Resources — Vict Resour
Victoria's Resources — Victoria's Resour
Victory Garden [*Database*] — VIC
Vida Agricola — Vida Agr
Vida Agricola — Vida Agric
Vida e Arte do Povo Portugues — VAPP
Vida Hispanica — VHis
Vida Literaria — VidaL
Vida Medica — Vida Med
Vida Odontologica — Vida Odontol
Vida Sobrenatural — VS
Vida Universitaria — VU
Vida Vasca — VVa
Vida y Espiritualidad (Peru) — VEP
Vide. Science, Technique et Applications — Vide Sci Tech Appl
Vide. Technique-Applications [*France*] — Vide Tech-Appl
Videnskabelige Meddelelser fra Dansk Naturhistorisk Forening — V Nh F
Videnskabelige Meddelelser fra Dansk Naturhistorisk Forening — Vidensk Medd Dan Naturhist Foren
Videnskabelige Meddelelser fra Dansk Naturhistorisk Forening i Khobenhavn — Vidensk Medd Dan Naturhist Foren Khobenhavn

Videnskabernes Selskabs Historisk-Filologiske Skrifter — VHFS
Videnskabs Selskapet Skrifter — VS
Videnskabs Selskapet Skrifter — VSS
Videnskabs Selskapet Skrifter. Forhandlingar — VSSF
Videnskabs-Selskabet i Christiania. Forhandlingar — Videnskabs-Selsk Christiana Forh
Videnskaps-Akademiets Avhandlinger — Vidensk Akad Avh
Video — GVID
Video Games Today — Vid Game T
Video Information [*Database*] — VIF
Video Marketing Newsletter — Video Mktg
Video Review — GVRE
Video Source Book — VSB
Video Systems — Video Syst
Video Systems — VSystems
Video Times — VT
Video World — Video Wld
Videotex World — VDT
Video-Tronics — Video
Vidipress Nieuwsbrief — VID
Vidya Bharati [*Bangalore*] — Vidya Bhar
Vidya. Section B. Sciences — Vidya B
Vie a la Campagne — Vie Camp
Vie Academique. Academie des Sciences (Paris) — Vie Acad Acad Sci (Paris)
Vie Agricole de la Meuse — Vie Agric Meuse
Vie Agricole et Rurale — Vie Agric et Rurale
Vie del Mondo — Vie Mondo
Vie d'Italia e del Mondo — Vie It Mondo
Vie d'Italia e dell'America Latina — Vie It Am Lat
Vie Economique (Berne) — Vie Econ (Berne)
Vie Economique. Rapports Economiques et de Statistique Sociale — VSH
Vie et Langage — V & L
Vie et Langage — VLa
Vie et Milieu. Serie A. Biologie Marine — Vie Milie A
Vie et Milieu. Serie A. Biologie Marine [*France*] — Vie Milieu Ser A
Vie et Milieu. Serie A. Biologie Marine — Vie Milieu Ser A Biol Mar
Vie et Milieu. Serie AB. Biologie Marine et Oceanographie — Vie Milieu Ser AB Biol Mar Oceanogr
Vie et Milieu. Serie AB. Biologie Marine et Oceanographie — VMSODA
Vie et Milieu. Serie B. Oceanographie — Vie Milie B
Vie et Milieu. Serie B. Oceanographie — Vie Milieu Ser B Oceanogr
Vie et Milieu. Serie C. Biologie Terrestre — Vie Milie C
Vie et Milieu. Serie C. Biologie Terrestre — Vie Milieu Ser C Biol Terr
Vie et Sciences Economiques — Vie et Sciences Econs
Vie et Sciences Economiques — Vie Sci Econ
Vie Intellectuelle — Vie Intell
Vie Medicale — Vie Med
Vie Medicale au Canada Francais — Vie Med Can Fr
Vie Musicale — Vie Mus
Vie Musicale Belge — Vie Mus Belge
Vie Musicale Belge — VMB
Vie Pedagogique — Vie Ped
Vie Sociale — Vie Soc
Vie Spirituelle. Supplement — VS Suppl
Vie Urbaine [*France*] — VURB-A
Vie Wallonne — VW
Viehbestand und Tierische Erzeugung Land und Forstwirtschaft Fischerei — Tier Erzeu
Vienna Circle Collection — Vienna Circle Coll
Viera i Razum — VR
Viere i Tzerkov — VT
Vierteljahresberichte — Vjber
Vierteljahresberichte Probleme der Entwicklungslaender — Vjhber Probl Entwicklland
Vierteljahreshefte fuer Wirtschaftsforschung — Vjh WF
Vierteljahreshefte fuer Wirtschaftsforschung — Vjh Wirtsch-Forsch
Vierteljahreshefte fuer Zeitgeschichte — V f ZG
Vierteljahreshefte fuer Zeitgeschichte — Vjh Zeitgesch
Vierteljahresschrift der Naturforschenden Gesellschaft (Zuerich) — Vj Nat Ges (Zuer)
Vierteljahresschrift fuer Schweizerische Sanitaetsoffiziere [*Switzerland*] — Vierteljahresschr Schweiz Sanitaetsoffiz
Vierteljahresschrift fuer Sozial- und Wirtschaftsgeschichte — VSU
Vierteljahresschrift fuer Sozialrecht — Vj SR
Vierteljahresschrift fuer Sozialrecht — VSSR
Vierteljahresschrift Wirtschaftsforschung [*Germany*] — Vierteljahresschr Wirtschaftsforsch
Vierteljahrschefte fuer Zeitgeschichte — VieZ
Vierteljahrschrift der Naturforschenden Gesellschaft in Zuerich — Viert Naturf Ges Zuerich
Vierteljahrschrift fuer Bibelkunde, Talmudische, und Patristische Studien — VBKTPS
Vierteljahrschrift fuer Bibelkunde, Talmudische, und Patristische Studien — VBTPS
Vierteljahrschrift fuer Bibelkunde, Talmudische, und Patristische Studien — VFB
Vierteljahrschrift fuer Forst-, Jagd- und Naturkunde — Vierteljahrschr Forst Naturk
Vierteljahrschrift fuer Gerichtliche Medizin und Oeffentliches Sanitaetswesen — Vierteljahreschr Gerichtl Med Oeff Sanitaetswes
Vierteljahrschrift fuer Praktische Pharmazie — Vierteljahrschr Prakt Pharm
Vierteljahrschrift fuer Sozial- und Wirtschaftsgeschichte — Vjschr Soz U Wirtsch Gesch
Vierteljahrschrift fuer Sozial- und Wirtschaftsgeschichte — Vjschr Soz- und Wirtschaftsgesch
Vierteljahrschrift fuer Sozial- und Wirtschaftsgeschichte — VSWS
Vierteljahrshefte fuer Zeitgeschichte — V f Z
Vierteljahrshefte fuer Zeitgeschichte — V Jh f Z
Vierteljahrshefte fuer Zeitgeschichte — V Jh ZG
Vierteljahrshefte fuer Zeitgeschichte — Vier Zeitg
Vierteljahrshefte fuer Zeitgeschichte — Vierteljahrsh Zeitgesch
Vierteljahrshefte fuer Zeitgeschichte — Vjh Zeitg
Vierteljahrshefte fuer Zeitgeschichte — Vjhefte Zeitgesch
Vierteljahrshefte fuer Zeitgeschichte — VZ
Vierteljahrshefte zur Statistik des Deutschen Reichs — Vjhh Statist Dt Reich
Vierteljahrshefte zur Wirtschaftsforschung — SIV
Vierteljahrsschrift fuer Gerichtliche und Oeffentliche Medizin — Vjschr Gerichtl Oeff Med
Vierteljahrsschrift fuer Geschichte und Landeskunde Vorarlbergs — VGLKV
Vierteljahrsschrift fuer Musikwissenschaft — V Mw
Vierteljahrsschrift fuer Musikwissenschaft — Vjschr Musikwiss
Vierteljahrsschrift fuer Sozial- und Wirtschaftsgeschichte — V f SWG
Vierteljahrsschrift fuer Sozial- und Wirtschaftsgeschichte — V Soz WG
Vierteljahrsschrift fuer Sozial- und Wirtschaftsgeschichte — VFSW
Vierteljahrsschrift fuer Sozial- und Wirtschaftsgeschichte — Vierteljahrsschr Soz Wirtschgesch
Vierteljahrsschrift fuer Sozial- und Wirtschaftsgeschichte — Vjschr Sozialgesch
Vierteljahrsschrift fuer Sozial- und Wirtschaftsgeschichte — VSG
Vierteljahrsschrift fuer Sozial- und Wirtschaftsgeschichte — VSW
Vierteljahrsschrift fuer Sozial- und Wirtschaftsgeschichte — VSWG
Vierteljahrsschrift fuer Sozial-und Wirtschaftsgeschichte — Vjhschr Soz U Wirtsch Gesch
Vierteljahrsschrift fuer Wissenschaftliche Philosophie — VJWPh
Vierteljahrsschrift fuer Wissenschaftliche Philosophie und Soziologie — Vierteljahrsschr f Wiss Philos
Vierteljahrsschrift fuer Zahnheilkunde — VjZh
Vierteljahrsschrift Herold fuer Heraldik, Sphragistik, und Genealogie — VJH
Vierteljahrsschrift. Naturforschende Gesellschaft [*Zuerich*] — Vj NGZ
Vierteljahrsschrift. Naturforschende Gesellschaft (Zuerich) — Vierteljahrsschr Naturforsch Ges (Zuer)
Vierteljahrsschrift. Naturforschende Gesellschaft (Zuerich) — Vierteljahrsschr Naturforsch Ges (Zuerich)
Vierteljahrsschrift. Naturforschende Gesellschaft (Zuerich) — Vjschr Naturf Ges (Zuerich)
Vierzehn Berliner Griechische Papyri — VBGP
Vietnam Journal of Mathematics — Vietnam J Math
Vietnamese Studies [*Hanoi*] — Viet Stud
Vietnamese Studies — VS
Vietnamica Chimica Acta — Vietnam Chim Acta
View from the Bottom — View Bot
Viewdata and Television User — Viewdata
Viewdata/Videotex Report [*Database*] — VVR
Vieweg Mathematics for Scientists and Engineers — Vieweg Math Sci Engrs
Vieweg Studium. Aufbaukurs Mathematik — Vieweg Stud Aufbaukurs Math
Vieweg Tracts in Pure and Applied Physics — Vieweg Tracts Pure Appl Phys
Viewpoint — NWU
Viewpoint — VIE
Viewpoint — VP
Viewpoint Series. Australian Conservation Foundation — Viewpoint Ser Aust Conserv Fdn
Viewpoints. Georgia Baptist History — ViGB
Viewpoints in Biology — Viewpoints Biol
Viewpoints in Teaching and Learning — Viewpoints Teach & Learn
Views and Reviews — Views & R
Vigiliae Christianae — VC
Vigiliae Christianae — VChr
Vigiliae Christianae — Vig C
Vigiliae Christianae — Vig Chr
Vigiliae Christianae — Vig Christ
Vigiliae Christianae — Vigil Chris
Viitorul Social — Viitor Soc
Vijesti Muzealaca i Konservatora (Zagreb) — Vijes (Zagreb)
Vijesti Muzealaca i Konzervatora N.R. Hrvastke — VMKH
Vijnana Parishad of India. Bulletin — Bull Vijnana Parishad India
VIK [*Vereinigung Industrielle Kraftwirtschaft*] **Mitteilungen** — VIK Mitt
Viking Fund Publication in Anthropology — Viking Fund Publ Anthropol
Viking. Norsk Arkeologisk Selskap — Vik
Vikram Mathematical Journal — Vikram Math J
Vikram. Quarterly Research Journal of Vikram University — Vikram Quart Res J Vikram University
Vilagirodalmi Figyelo — VF
Village Voice — GVIV
Village Voice — Vil V
Village Voice — Voice
Village Voice — VV
Village Voice. Literary Supplement — VLS
Villanova Law Review — Vill L Rev
Villanova Law Review — Villanova L Rev
Villanova Law Review — Vo LR
Villanova Law Review — VR
Vilniaus Pedagoginio Instituto Mokslo Darbai — VPIMD
Vilniaus Valstybinio V. Kapsuko Vardo Universiteto Mokslo Darbai — VUMD
Vilniaus Valstybinis Universitetas Mokslo Darbai — Vilniaus Valstybinis Univ Mokslo Darb
Viltrevy [*Stockholm*] — VILTAR
Vina Quarterly — Vina Q
Vinarsky Obzor — Vinar Obz
Vinculos. Revista de Antropologia. Museo Nacional de Costa Rica — MNCR/V
Vinduet — Vin

Vinea et Vino Portugaliae Documenta. Ser. II. Enologia. Centro Nacional de Estudos Vitivinicolas — Vinea Vino Portug Doc Ser 2 Enol
Vineland Historical Magazine — Vineland Hist Mag
Vingtieme Siecle Federaliste — Vingt Siecle Feder
Vini d'Italia — Vini Ital
Vinifera Wine Growers Journal — Vinifera Wine Grow J
Vinodelie i Vinogradarstvo SSSR — Vinodel Vinograd SSSR
Vinogradarstvo i Plodovodstvo (Budapest) — Vinograd Plodovod (Budapest)
Vinogradarstvo i Vinarstvo (Budapest) — Vinograd Vinar (Budapest)
Vinogradarstvo i Vinodelie — Vinograd Vinodel
Vinogradarstvo i Vinorobstvo — Vinograd Vinorobstvo
Vinyls and Polymers [*Japan*] — Vinyls Polym
Viol — VI
Viola da Gamba Society of America. Journal — VdGSA
Viola da Gamba Society of America. News — VdGSAN
Violence and Victims — Violence Vict
Violin Society of America. Journal — VSA
Violin Society of America. Newsletter — VSAJ
Violincello Society Newsletter — VcSN
Viral Gene Techniques — Viral Gene Tech
Viral Immunology — Viral Immunol
Virchows Archiv — Virchows Arch
Virchows Archiv. A. Pathological Anatomy and Histology — VAPHD
Virchows Archiv. A. Pathological Anatomy and Histology — Virc Arch A
Virchows Archiv. A. Pathological Anatomy and Histology — Virchows Arch A Pathol Anat Histol
Virchows Archiv. A. Pathological Anatomy and Histopathology — VAAHDJ
Virchows Archiv. A. Pathological Anatomy and Histopathology — Virchows Arch A Pathol Anat Histopathol
Virchows Archiv. Abteilung A. Pathologische Anatomie — Virchows Arch Abt A
Virchows Archiv. Abteilung A. Pathologische Anatomie — Virchows Arch Abt A Pathol Anat
Virchows Archiv. Abteilung B. Zellpathologie — Virchows Arch Abt B
Virchows Archiv. Abteilung B. Zellpathologie — Virchows Arch Abt B Zellpathol
Virchows Archiv. B. Cell Pathology — Virc Arch B
Virchows Archiv. B. Cell Pathology — Virchows Arch B Cell Pathol
Virchows Archiv. B. Cell Pathology Including Molecular Pathology — VABPDE
Virchows Archiv. B. Cell Pathology Including Molecular Pathology — Virchows Arch B Cell Pathol Incl Mol Pathol
Virchows Archiv fuer Pathologische Anatomie — Virchows Arch Path Anat
Virchow's Archiv fuer Pathologische Anatomie — Virchows Archiv F Pathol Anat
Virchows Archiv fuer Pathologische Anatomie und Physiologie — Arch Pathol Anat
Virchows Archiv fuer Pathologische Anatomie und Physiologie und fuer Klinische Medizin — VirchA
Virchows Archiv fuer Pathologische Anatomie und Physiologie und fuer Klinische Medizin — Virchows Arch Pathol Anat Physiol Klin Med
Virgin Island Reports — VI
Virgin Islands Bar Journal — VIBJ
Virgin Islands Code Annotated — VI Code Ann
Virgin Islands Rules and Regulations — VI R & Regs
Virgin Islands Session Laws — VI Sess Laws
Virginia. Agricultural Experiment Station. Bulletin — VA Agric Exp Stn Bull
Virginia. Agricultural Experiment Station. Technical Bulletin — VA Agric Exp Stn Tech Bull
Virginia Bar Association. Journal — VA BAJ
Virginia Cavalcade — VA Cavalcade
Virginia Cavalcade — VC
Virginia Cavalcade — VirC
Virginia Court of Appeals Reports — Va App
Virginia Dental Journal — VA Dent J
Virginia. Department of Agriculture and Immigration. Publications — VA Ag Dept
Virginia. Department of Highways. Division of Tests. Geological Yearbook — VA Dept Highways Div Tests Geol Yearbook
Virginia. Department of Labor and Industry. Annual Report — VA Dept Labor and Industry Ann Rept
Virginia. Division of Geology. Bulletin — VA Div Geol Bull
Virginia. Division of Geology. Bulletin. Reprint Series — VA Div Geology Bull Reprint Ser
Virginia. Division of Mineral Resources. Bulletin — VA Div Miner Resour Bull
Virginia. Division of Mineral Resources. Bulletin. Information Circular. Mineral Resources Circular — VA Div Mineral Res Bull Inf Circ Mineral Res Circ
Virginia. Division of Mineral Resources. Information Circular — VA Div Miner Resour Inf Cir
Virginia. Division of Mineral Resources. Mineral Resources Report — VA Div Miner Resour Miner Resour Rep
Virginia. Division of Mineral Resources. Report of Investigations — VA Div Miner Resour Rep Invest
Virginia. Division of Mineral Resources. Report of Investigations — Virginia Div Mineral Rsources Rept Inv
Virginia Farm Economics. Virginia Polytechnic Institute. Agricultural Extension Service — VA Farm Econ VA Polytech Inst Agr Ext Serv
Virginia Fisheries Laboratory. Educational Series — VA Fish Lab Educ Ser
Virginia Fruit — VA Fruit
Virginia. Geological Survey. Bulletin — VA Geol Survey Bull
Virginia. Geological Survey. Bulletin — VA GSB
Virginia. Geological Survey. Circular — VA Geol Surv Circ
Virginia. Geological Survey. Reprint Series — VA Geol Surv Repr Ser
Virginia Historical Society. Collections — VA Hist Soc Coll
Virginia Horse Industry Yearbook — VA Horse Ind Yearb
Virginia Institute of Marine Science. Special Scientific Report — VA Inst Mar Sci Spec Sci Rep
Virginia Journal of Education — VA J Ed
Virginia Journal of Education — VA J Educ
Virginia Journal of International Law — VA J Int L
Virginia Journal of International Law — VA J Intl L
Virginia Journal of International Law — Virg J Int'l L
Virginia Journal of Natural Resources Law — VA J Nat Resour Law
Virginia Journal of Natural Resources Law — VA J Nat Resources L
Virginia Journal of Science — VA J Sci
Virginia Journal of Science — VA Jour Sci
Virginia Journal of Science — Virginia J Sci
Virginia Journal of Science — Virginia Jour Sci
Virginia Kirkus' Service. Bulletin — Kirkus
Virginia Law Journal — Va Law J
Virginia Law Register — Va Law Reg
Virginia Law Review — VA L
Virginia Law Review — VA L Rev
Virginia Law Review — VA Law R
Virginia Law Review — VA Law Rev
Virginia Law Review — VA LR
Virginia Law Review — Virginia Law Rev
Virginia Law Review — VLR
Virginia Librarian — VA Libn
Virginia Library Bulletin — VA Lib Bul
Virginia Magazine of History and Biography — PVAM
Virginia Magazine of History and Biography — VA M
Virginia Magazine of History and Biography — VA Mag Hist
Virginia Magazine of History and Biography — VA Mag Hist Biog
Virginia Magazine of History and Biography — VA Mag Hist Biogr
Virginia Magazine of History and Biography — Virginia Mag Hist Biogr
Virginia Magazine of History and Biography — VirM
Virginia Magazine of History and Biography — VMHB
Virginia Medical — VA Med
Virginia Medical Monthly — Va Med Mo
Virginia Medical Monthly [*Later, Virginia Medical*] — VA Med Mon
Virginia Medical Monthly — Virginia M Month
Virginia Medical Monthly [*Later, Virginia Medical*] — Virginia Med Month
Virginia Medical Monthly [*Later, Virginia Medical*] — VMMOA
Virginia Medical Quarterly — Va Med Q
Virginia Medical Semi-Monthly — Va Med Semi Mo
Virginia Minerals — VA Miner
Virginia Minerals [*Charlottesville*] — Virginia Miner
Virginia Numismatist — VA Num
Virginia Nurse — VA Nurse
Virginia Nurse Quarterly [*Later, Virginia Nurse*] — VA Nurse Q
Virginia Polytechnic Institute. Agricultural Experiment Station. Publications — VA Ag Exp
Virginia Polytechnic Institute and State University. Research Division. Bulletin — VA Polytech Inst State Univ Res Div Bull
Virginia Polytechnic Institute and State University. Research Division. Monograph — VA Polytech Inst State Univ Res Div Monogr
Virginia Polytechnic Institute and State University. Research Division. Report — VA Polytech Inst State Univ Res Div Rep
Virginia Polytechnic Institute and State University. School of Forestry and Wildlife Resources. Publication FWS — VA Polytech Inst State Univ Sch For Wildl Resour Publ FWS
Virginia Polytechnic Institute and State University. Virginia Water Resources Research Center. Bulletin — VA Polytech Inst State Univ VA Water Resour Res Cent Bull
Virginia Polytechnic Institute and State University. Water Resources Research Center. Bulletin — VA Polytech Inst State Univ Water Resour Res Cent Bull
Virginia Polytechnic Institute. Bulletin. Engineering Experiment Station Series — VA Polytech Inst Bull Eng Expt Sta Ser
Virginia Polytechnic Institute. Engineering Extension Series. Circular — VA Polytech Inst Eng Ext Ser Cir
Virginia Polytechnic Institute. Research Division. Bulletin — VA Polytech Inst Res Div Bull
Virginia Polytechnic Institute. Research Division. Bulletin — Virginia Polytech Inst Research Div Bull
Virginia Polytechnic Institute. Research Division. Monograph — Virginia Polytech Inst Research Div Mon
Virginia Polytechnic Institute. Research Division. Wood Research and Wood Construction Laboratory [*Blacksburg*]. **Bulletin** — VA Polytech Inst Res Div Wood Res Wood Constr Lab Bull
Virginia Quarterly Review — PVAQ
Virginia Quarterly Review — VA Q R
Virginia Quarterly Review — VA Q Rev
Virginia Quarterly Review — Vir Q R
Virginia Quarterly Review — Virginia Q R
Virginia Quarterly Review — Virginia Quart Rev
Virginia Quarterly Review — VQR
Virginia Register of Regulations — Va Regs Reg
Virginia Reports — Va
Virginia Researcher — Virginia Res
Virginia Social Science Journal — VA Social Science J
Virginia State Library. Bulletin — VA State Lib Bull
Virginia Tax Review — VA Tax R
Virginia Tax Review — VTR
Virginia Teacher — VA Teach
Virginia Truck Experiment Station. Publications — VA Truck Exp
Virginia University. Bibliographical Society. Studies in Bibliography — Stud Bibliog
Virginia University. Philosophical Society. Bulletin. Scientific Series — VA Univ Ph Soc B Sc S
Virginia Water Resources Research Center. Bulletin — VA Water Resour Res Cent Bull
Virginia Wildlife — VA Wildl
Virginia Woolf Miscellany — VWM

Virginia Woolf Newsletter — VWN
Virginia Woolf Quarterly — VWQ
Virginian-Pilot — Virgin Pilo
Virginian-Pilot and Ledger-Star — Virg & Star L
Virittaja — Vir
Virology — Virol
Virology Abstracts — Virol Abstr
Virology Monographs — Virol Monogr
Virtual Laboratory — Virtual Lab
Virtuoso — VIR
Viruly's Technisch Maandblad voor de Wasindustrie — Viruly's Tech Maandbl Wasind
Virus Research — VIREDF
Virus Research — Virus Res
Virus Research. Supplement — Virus Res Suppl
VISCA Review. Visayas State College of Agriculture — VISCA Rev Visayas State Coll Agric
Vishveshvaranand Indological Journal — VIJ
Vishveshvaranand Indological Journal — VIndJ
Vishveshvaranand Indological Journal [*Hoshiarpur*] — Vish Indo J
Vishwa International Journal of Graph Theory — Vishwa Internat J Graph Theory
Visible Language — V Lang
Visible Language — Visbl Lang
Visible Language — Visible Lang
Visible Language — VisL
Visindafelag Islendinga — Visindafel Isl
Visindafelag Islendinga. Greinar — Visindafelag Isl Greinar
Visindafelag Islendinga. Rit — Visindafelag Isl Rit
Visindafelag Islendinga. Societas Scientiarum Islandica — VISSI
Vision — V
Vision — VN
Vision Index — Vis Ind
Vision Index — Vis Index
Vision of Tomorrow — VOT
Vision Research — Vision Res
Vision Research. Supplement — Vision Res Suppl
Vision Tecnologica — Vision Tecnol
Vision. The European Business Magazine — VSB
Visnik Kharkivs'kogo Universitetu. Astronomiya [*Ukrainian SSR*] — Visn Kharkiv Univ Astron
Visnik Kharkivs'kogo Universitetu. Radiofizika [*Ukrainian SSR*] — Visn Kharkiv Univ Radiofiz
Visnik Kharkivs'kogo Universitetu. Radiofizika i Elektronika [*Ukrainian SSR*] — Visn Kharkiv Univ Radiofiz Elektron
Visnik Kharkivs'koho Universytetu — VKhark
Visnik Kiivs'kogo Politekhnichnogo Institutu. Seriya Khimichnogo Mashinobuduvannya ta Tekhnologii [*Ukrainian SSR*] — Visn Kiiv Politekh Inst Ser Khim Mashinobuduv Tekhnol
Visnik Kiivs'kogo Universitetu. Serija Matematiki ta Mehaniki — Visnik Kiiv Univ Ser Mat Meh
Visnik Kiivs'kogo Universitetu. Seriya Astronomii [*Ukrainian SSR*] — Visn Kiiv Univ Ser Astron
Visnik Kiivs'kogo Universitetu. Seriya Astronomii, Fiziki, ta Khimii — Visn Kiiv Univ Ser Astron Fiz Khim
Visnik Kiivs'kogo Universitetu. Seriya Biologii [*Ukrainian SSR*] — Visn Kiiv Univ Ser Biol
Visnik Kiivs'kogo Universitetu. Seriya Fiziki — Visn Kiiv Univ Ser Fiz
Visnik Kiivs'kogo Universitetu. Seriya Fiziki ta Khimii [*Ukrainian SSR*] — Visn Kiiv Univ Ser Fiz Khim
Visnik Kiivs'kogo Universitetu. Seriya Geologii ta Geografii — Visn Kiiv Univ Ser Geol Geogr
Visnik Kiivs'kogo Universitetu. Seriya Khimii [*Ukrainian SSR*] — Visn Kiiv Univ Ser Khim
Visnik Kiivs'kogo Universitetu. Seriya Matematiki ta Mekhaniki — Visnik Kiiv Univ Ser Mat Mekh
Visnik Kiyivs'kogo Universitetu. Seriya Fizika [*Ukrainian SSR*] — Visn Kiyiv Univ Ser Fiz
Visnik L'vivs'kii Derzhavnii Universitet Imeni Ivana Franka. Seriya Fizichna [*Ukrainian SSR*] — Visn L'viv Derzh Univ Ser Fiz
Visnik. L'vivs'kii Universitet. Seriya Mekhaniko-Matematichna — Visnik Lviv Univ Ser Mekh Mat
Visnik L'vivs'kogo Derzhavnogo Universitetu Imeni Ivana Franka. Seriya Khimichna [*Ukrainian SSR*] — Visn L'viv Derzh Univ Ser Khim
Visnik L'vivs'kogo Derzhavnogo Universitetu. Seriya Biologichna — Visn L'viv Derzh Univ Ser Biol
Visnik L'vivs'kogo Derzhavnogo Universitetu. Seriya Geologichna — Visn L'viv Derzh Univ Ser Geol
Visnik L'vivs'kogo Ordena Lenina Derzavogo Universitetu Imeni Ivana Franka. Serija Mehaniko-Matematicna — Visnik L'viv Derz Univ Ser Meh-Mat
Visnik L'vivs'kogo Politehnicnogo Institutu — Visnik L'viv Politehn Inst
Visnik Odes'koi Komisii Kraezhavstva. Ukrains'kii Akademii Nauk — VOKK
Visnik Tsentral'nii Respublikans'kii Botanichnii Sad Akademiya Nauk Ukrains'koi RSR — Visn Tsentr Resp Bot Sad Akad Nauk Ukr RSR
Visnyk Akademiyi Nauk Ukrayins'koyi RSR — Visn Akad Nauk Ukr RSR
Visnyk Akademiyi Nauk Ukrayins'koyi RSR — Visnyk Akad Nauk Ukr RSR
Visnyk Kyjivs'koho Universytetu — VKyjU
Visnyk Kyyivs'koho Universytetu. Seriya Biolohiyi — Visn Kyyiv Univ Ser Biol
Visnyk L'vivs'koho Derzavnoho Universytetu — VLvivU
Visnyk L'vivs'koho Universytetu. Seriya Biolohiyi, Heohrafiyi, ta Heolohiyi — Visn L'viv Univ Ser Biol Heohr
Visnyk L'vivs'koho Universytetu. Seriya Biolohiyi, Heohrafiyi, ta Heolohiyi — Visn L'viv Univ Ser Biol Heohr Heol
Visnyk Sil's'kohospodars'koy Nauki — Visn Sil's'kohospod Nauki
Visnyk Sil's'kohospodars'koyi Nauky — Visn Sil-Hospod Nauky
Visserij. Voorlichtingsblad voor de Nederlandse Visserij — VIY
Visserijnieuws — FOV
Vissh Institut po Arkhitektura i Stroitelstvo-Sofiya. Godishnik — Vissh Inst Arkhit Stroit Sofiya God
Vistas for Volunteers — Vistas Volunt
Vistas in Astronautics — Vistas Astronaut
Vistas in Astronomy — Vistas Astron
Vistas in Botany — Vistas Bot
Visti Akademii Nauk Ukrains'koi RSR — Visti Akad Nauk Ukr RSR
Visti Institutu Fizichnoi Khimii Akademiya Nauk Ukrains'koi RSR — Visti Inst Fiz Khim Akad Nauk Ukr RSR
Visti Ukrains'kogo Naukovo Doslidchogo Institutu Fizichnoi Khimii — Visti Ukr Nauk Dosl Inst Fiz Khim
Visti Vseukrajins'koji Akademiji Nauk. Proces-verbaux de l'Academie des Sciences de l'Ukraine — Visti Vseukrajinsk Akad Nauk
Vistnyk Odes'koi Komisii Kraezhavstva. Ukrains'kii Akademii Nauk — VOKKUAN
Visual Aids News — Vis Aids News
Visual Aids Review — Vis Aids Rev
Visual Aids Review — Visual Aids R
Visual Arts — Vis Arts
Visual Arts Bulletin — Vis Arts Bul
Visual Education — Vis Educ
Visual Education — Visual Ed
Visual Flight Guide — VFG
Visual Information Processing — Visual Inf Process
Visual Medicine — Visual Med
Visual Merchandising — DIW
Visual Neuroscience — Vis Neurosci
Visual Sonic Medicine — Visual Sonic Med
Visualization of Engineering Research — Visualization Eng Res
Visva Bharati Annals — VBA
Visva Bharati Bulletin — VBB
Visva Bharati News — VBN
Visvabharati Quarterly — VBQ
Visvabharati Quarterly — VQ
Vita e Pensiero — V e P
Vita e Pensiero [*Milan*] — ViPe
Vita e Pensiero — VP
Vita e Pensiero — VPen
Vita Humana — Vita Hum
Vita International — Vita Int
Vita Italiana — Vita Ital
Vita Latina — VL
Vita Mathematica — Vita Math
Vita Monastica — Vita Mon
Vita. Revue Bimensuelle. Confederation de l'Alimentation Belge — Vita
Vital and Health Statistics. Series 1. Programs and Collection Procedures [*Unied States*] — Vital Health Stat 1
Vital and Health Statistics. Series 2. Data Evaluation and Methods Research [*United States*] — Vital Health Stat 2
Vital and Health Statistics. Series 2. Data Evaluation and Methods Research — Vital Health Statist Ser 2 Data Evaluation Methods Res
Vital and Health Statistics. Series 3. Analytical Studies [*United States*] — Vital Health Stat 3
Vital and Health Statistics. Series 4. Documents and Committee Reports [*United States*] — Vital Health Stat 4
Vital and Health Statistics. Series 10. Data from the National Health Survey [*United States*] — Vital Health Stat 10
Vital and Health Statistics. Series 11 [*United States*] — VHSKA
Vital and Health Statistics. Series 11. Data from the National Health Survey [*United States*] — Vital Health Stat 11
Vital and Health Statistics. Series 13. Data from the National Health Survey [*United States*] — Vital Health Stat 13
Vital and Health Statistics. Series 14. Data on National Health Resources [*United States*] — Vital Health Stat 14
Vital and Health Statistics. Series 20. Data from the National Vital Statistics System [*United States*] — Vital Health Stat 20
Vital and Health Statistics. Series 21. Data from the National Vital Statistics System [*United States*] — Vital Health Stat 21
Vital and Health Statistics. Series 23. Data from the National Survey of Family Growth [*United States*] — Vital Health Stat 23
Vital Christianity — Vital C
Vital Speeches — VS
Vital Speeches of the Day — VIT
Vital Speeches of the Day — Vital Speeches
Vital Speeches of the Day — Vital Speeches Day
Vital Speeches of the Day — VSP
Vital Speeches of the Day — VSpD
Vitalstoffe Zivilisationskrankheiten — Vitalst Zivilisationskr
Vitalstoffe Zivilisationskrankheiten — Vitalstoffe
Vitamin and Hormones. Advances in Research and Applications — Vitamin Horm Adv Res Appl
Vitamin D Digest — Vitam D Dig
Vitamin K in Infancy. International Symposium — Vitam K Infancy Int Symp
Vitaminnye Resursy i Ikh Ispol'zovanie — Vitam Resur Ikh Ispol'z
Vitamins and Hormones — Vitam Horm
Vitamins and Hormones — Vitams Horm
Vitaminy v Eksperimente i Klinike — Vitam Eksp Klin
Viticulture and Enology (Budapest) — Vitic Enol (Budapest)
Viticulture, Arboriculture — Vitic Arboric
Viti-Viniculture (Budapest) — Viti-Vinic (Budapest)
Vitterhets, Historie- och Antikvitets-Akademiens Handlingar — VHAAH
Vitterhets. Historie och Antiquitets Akademiens Manadsblad — VHAAM
Vivarium — Viv

Vivarium. A Journal for Mediaeval Philosophy and the Intellectual Life of the Middle Ages — Vivar
Vivienda [*Mexico*] — VIVI
Vivienda y Planificacion — Vivienda Planif
Vizantiiskii Vremenik — VizV
Vizantiiskii Vremenik — VV
Vizantiiskii Vremennik — Vizan Vrem
Vizantijskij Vremennik — Viz Vrem
Vizgazdalkodasi Tudomanyos Kutato Intezet Tanulmanyok es Kutatasi Eredmenyek — Vizgazdalkodasi Tud Kut Intez Tanulmanyok Kut Eredmenyek
Vizuegyi Koezlomonyek — Viz Koezl
Vizugyi Kozlemenyek — Vizugyi Kozl
Vizugyi Kozlemenyek — Vizugyi Kozlem
Vjesnik Arheoloskog Muzeja u Zagrebu — VAMZ
Vjesnik Arheoloskog Muzeja u Zagrebu — Vjes A Muz Zagreb
Vjesnik Bibliotekara Hrvatske — Vjesn Bibliot Hrv
Vjesnik Narodnog Fronta Hrvatske — VNFH
Vjesnik za Arheologiju i Historiju Dalmatinsku — Bull Dalm
Vjesnik za Arheologiju i Historiju Dalmatinsku — VAH Dal
Vjesnik za Arheologiju i Historiju Dalmatinsku — VAHD
Vjesnik za Arheologiju i Historiju Dalmatinsku — Vjes AH Dal
Vjesnik za Arheologiju i Historiju Dalmatinsku [*Bulletin d'Archeologie et d'Histoire Dalmates*] — Vjes Dal
Vjesnik za Arheologiju i Historiju Dalmatinsku (Split) — Vjesnik (Split)
Vlaams Diergeneeskundig Tijdschrift — Vlaams Diergeneesk Tijdschr
Vlaams Diergeneeskundig Tijdschrift — Vlaams Diergeneeskd Tijdschr
Vlaamse Chemische Vereniging. Tijdingen — Vlaam Chem Ver Tijd
Vlaamse Gids — VLG
Vladimir Nabokov Research Newletter — VNRN
Vladimirskii Gosudarstvennyi Pedagogiceskii Institut Imeni P. I. Lebedeva-Poljanskogo. Ucenyi Zapiski — Vladimir Gos Ped Inst Ucen Zap
Vladimirskii Vecernyi Politehniceskii Institut. Sbornik Naucnyh Trudov — Vladimir Vecer Politehn Inst Sb Naucn Trudov
Vladivostokskii Meditsinskii Institut. Sbornik Nauchnykh Trudov — Vladivost Med Inst Sb Nauchn Tr
Vlastivedny Obzor — Vlastiv Obzor
Vlastivedny Sbornik Vychodni Cecny — Vlastiv Sborn Vychodni Cechy
Vlastivedny Vestnik Moravsky — VLVM
Vlastivedny Vestnik Moravsky — VVM
Vlees en Vleeswaren — VKS
Vliyanie Rabochikh Sred na Svoistva Materialov — Vliyanie Rab Sred Svoistva Mater
Vlugschriften van het Instituut voor Phytopathologie — Vlugschr Inst Phytopathol
VM. Voorlichtingsblad van het Ministerie van Volksgezondheid en Milieuhygiene — VOC
VMR. Veterinary Medical Review — VMR Vet Med Rev
Vnesnjaja Torgovlja — Vnesn Torg
Vnitrni Lekarstvi — Vnitr Lek
VOC Journal of Education — Voc J Ed
Vocational Aspect of Education — Voc Aspect Ed
Vocational Aspect of Education — Vocat Asp Educ
Vocational Aspect of Education — Vocational Aspect
Vocational Education — Voc Educ
Vocational Education Curriculum Materials Database — VECM
Vocational Education Journal — IVEJ
Vocational Education Magazine — Voc Educ M
Vocational Guidance Bulletin — Voc Guidance Bul
Vocational Guidance Quarterly — VGQ
Vocational Guidance Quarterly — Voc Guid Q
Vocational Guidance Quarterly — Vocat Guid
Vocational Training — Vocat Training
Vocational Training. Bulletin — Vocat Train Bull
Vocational Training Council. Newsletter [*New Zealand*] — VTC News
Voce del Passato — VP
VocEd Business and Office Insider. Journal of the American Vocational Association — VocEd Insider
Vocero — VO
Vodni Hospodarstvi — Vodn Hospod
Vodni Hospodarstvi — Vodni Hospod
Vodni Hospodarstvi a Ochrana Osvdusi — Vod Hospod Ochr Ovzdusi
Vodni Hospodarstvi. Rada A [*Czechoslovakia*] — Vodni Hospod A
Vodni Hospodarstvi. Rada B — Vodn Hospod Rada B
Vodni Hospodarstvi. Rada B — Vodni Hospod Rada B
Vodnye Resursy [*Former USSR*] — Vodn Resur
Vodohospodarsky Casopis — Vodohospod Cas
Vodopodgotovka i Ochistka Promyshlennykh Stokov — Vodopodgot Ochistka Prom Stokov
Vodorosli i Griby Sibiri i Dal'nego Vostoka — Vodorosli Griby Sib Dal'nego Vostoka
Vodosnabzhenie i Sanitarnaya Tekhnika — Vodos Sanit Tekhn
Vodosnabzhenie i Sanitarnaya Tekhnika — Vodosnabzh Sanit Tekh
Vodosnabzhenie Kanalizatsiya Gidrotekhnicheskie Sooruzheniya — Vodosnabzh Kanaliz Gidrotekh Sooruzh
Voedingsmiddelen Technologie — NZU
Voedingsmiddelen Technologie — Voedingsmiddelen Technol
Voegel des Rheinlandes — Voegel Rheinl
Voegel des Rheinlandes — VORHDW
Voelkische Kultur — VK
Voelkischer Beobachter (Berlin) — VB (B)
Voelkischer Beobachter (Muenich) — VB (Mu)
Voenna Tekhnika [*Bulgaria*] — Voenna Tekh
Voennaya Khimiya — Voen Khim
Voenno Meditsinsko Delo — Voen Med Delo
Voenno-Istoricheskii Zhurnal — VIZ
Voenno-Istoricheskii Zhurnal — Voenno-Ist Zhurnal
Voenno-Meditsinskii Fakul'tet pri Saratovskom Medinstitute. Sbornik Nauchnykh Trudov — Voen Med Fak Sarat Medinst Sb Nauchn Tr
Voenno-Meditsinskii Zhurnal — Voen-Med Zh
Voenno-Meditsinskii Zhurnal — Voenno-Med Zh
Voenno-Meditsinskii Zhurnal (Leningrad) — Voenno Med Zhurnal (Leningrad)
Voenno-Meditsinskii Zhurnal (S. Peterburg) — Voenno-Med Zhurnal (S Peterburg)
Voenno-Sanitarnoe Delo — Voen Sanit Delo
Voennye Znaniya [*Former USSR*] — Voen Znaniya
Voennye Znaniya — VOZNA
Voennyi Vestnik [*Former USSR*] — Voen Vest
Vogelkundliche Berichte aus Niedersachsen — VBNIDQ
Vogelkundliche Berichte aus Niedersachsen — Vogelkd Ber Niedersachsen
Vogelkundliche Hefte Edertal — VHEDD8
Vogelkundliche Hefte Edertal — Vogelkd Hefte Edertal
Vogue — GVOG
Vogue Living — Vog Liv
Voice — VO
Voice of Chorus America — VCA
Voice of Chorus America — Voice Chorus Am
Voice of Missions — Vc Miss
Voice of Scotland — VS
Voice of the Lakes — VOLAD
Voice of Uganda — VU
Voice of Washington Music — WA
Voice of Youth Advocates — VOYA
Voice of Z-39 [*Later, Information Standards Quarterly*] — VOIZD
Voices — Vo
Voith Forschung und Konstruktion — Voith Forsch Konstr
Voith Research and Construction — Voith Res & Constr
Voix Dentaire — Voix Dent
Voix et Images du Pays [*University of Quebec*] — VIP
Voix et Images. Etudes Quebecoises — V & I
Vojenske Zdravotnicke Listy — Vojen Zdrav Listy
Vojenskozdravotnicka Knihovna — Vojenskozdrav Knih
Vojnoekonomski Pregled [*Yugoslavia*] — Vojnoekon Pregl
Vojnosanitetski Pregled — Vojnosanit Pregl
Vokrug Sveta — VS
Vokrug Sveta [*Moscow*] — VSv
Voks Bulletin — VB
Volcani Institute of Agricultural Research. Division of Forestry. Ilanot Leaflet — Volcani Inst Agric Res Div For Ilanot Leafl
Volcani Institute of Agricultural Research. Division of Scientific Publications. Pamphlet — Volcani Inst Agric Res Div Sci Publ Pam
Volcanological Meteorological Bulletin. Japan Meteorological Agency — Volcanol Bull Jpn Meterol Agency
Volcanological Society of Japan. Bulletin — Volcanol Soc Jap Bull
Volgogradskogo Gosudarstvennogo Pedagogiceskogo Instituta Imeni A. S. Serafimocixa Ucenye Zapiski — Volgograd Gos Ped Inst Ucen Zap
Volja Rossii — VR
Volk und Reich — Volk U Reich
Volk und Volkstum — VV
Volksforschung — Volksforsch
Volkskrant — VK
Volkskrant — VOK
Volksmusik — Volksm
Volksmusik. Zeitschrift fuer das Musikalische Laienschaffen — Volksmus
Volkstum und Kultur der Romanen — VKR
Volkstum und Landschaft. Heimatblaetter der Muensterlaendische Tageszeitung — Volkstum Landschaft
Volkswirtschaftliche Schriften — Volkswirtsch Schriften
Volleyball Magazine — Volleyball Mag
Volleyball Technical Journal — Volleyball Tech J
Vologodskii Gosudarstvennyi Pedagogiceskii Institut. Cerepoveckii Gosudarstvennyi Pedagogiceskii Institut. Ucenye Zapiski — Vologod I Cerepovec Gos Ped Inst Ucen Zap
Vologodskii Gosudarstvennyi Pedagogiceskii Institut. Ucenye Zapiski — Vologod Gos Ped Inst Ucen Zap
Volt. Electrical Trade Monthly [*Japan*] — Volt Electr Trade Mon
Volta Review — VOLRA
Volta Review — Volta R
Volume Feeding Management — Vol Feeding Mgt
Volume Retail Merchandising — Vol Ret Merch
Volumenes de Homenaje — Vol Homenaje
Voluntary Action — Volunt Action
Voluntary Action Leadership — Volunt Action Leadersh
Voluntary Action News — VAN
Voluntary Effort Quarterly — Vol Effort Q
Voluntary Forum Abstracts — Volunt Forum Abs
Voluntary Housing — Volunt Housing
Volunteer Administration — Volunt Adm
Volunteer Leader — Volunt Leader
Volzskii Matematiceskii Sbornik — Volz Mat Sb
Von Deutscher Poeterey — VDP
Von Missionsdienst der Lutherischen Kirchen — MDLK
Von Roll Mitteilungen — Von Roll Mitt
Voorlichter — VOA
Voorlichting en Onderzoek — Voorlichting Onderz
Voprosy Antropologii — Vopr Antropol
Voprosy Atomnoi Nauki i Tekhniki. Seriya Fizika Plazmy i Problemy Upravlyaemykh Termodadernykh Reaktsii [*Ukrainian SSR*] — Vopr At Nauki Tekh Ser Fiz Plazmy Probl Upr Termodad Reakts
Voprosy Atomnoi Nauki i Tekhniki. Seriya Fizika Vysokikh Energii i Atomnogo Yadra [*Ukrainian SSR*] — Vopr At Nauki Tekh Ser Fiz Vys Energ At Yadra

Voprosy Atomnoi Nauki i Tekhniki. Seriya Obshchaya i Yadernaya Fizika [*Ukrainian SSR*] — Vopr At Nauki Tekh Ser Obshch Yad Fiz
Voprosy Atomnoi Nauki i Tekhniki. Seriya Radiatsionnaya Tekhnika — Vopr At Nauki Tekh Ser Radiats Tekh
Voprosy Atomnoi Nauki i Tekhniki. Seriya Yadernye Konstanty — Vopr At Nauki Tekh Ser Yad Konstanty
Voprosy Bezopasnosti v Ugol'nykh Shakhtakh — Vopr Bezopasn Ugol'n Shakhtakh
Voprosy Biokhimii — Vopr Biokhim
Voprosy Biokhimii Mozga — Vopr Biokhim Mozga
Voprosy Biokhimii Nervnoi i Myshechnoi Sistem [*Georgian SSR*] — Vopr Biokhim Nervn Myshechnoi Sist
Voprosy Biokhimii Nervnoi Sistemy — Vopr Biokhim Nervn Sist
Voprosy Biologii — Vopr Biol
Voprosy Biologii i Kraevoi Meditsiny — Vopr Biol Kraev Med
Voprosy Biologii Semennogo Reszmnozheniya — Vopr Biol Semennogo Rezmnozheniya
Voprosy Bor'by s Silikozom v Sibiri — Vopr Bor'by Silikozom Sib
Voprosy Botaniki. Akademiya Nauk Litovskoi SSR. Institut Botaniki — Vop Bot Akad Nauk Litov SSR Inst Bot
Voprosy Botaniki. Essais de Botanique — Vopr Bot
Voprosy Cenoobrazovanija — Vopr Cenoobraz
Voprosy Chetvertechnoi Geologii — Vopr Chetvertechn Geol
Voprosy Dialektologii Tjurkskich Jazykov — VDTJ
Voprosy Dinamicheskoi Teorii Rasprostraneniya Seismicjeskikh Voln [*Former USSR*] — Vopr Din Teor Rasprostr Seism Voln
Voprosy Dinamiki i Prochnosti — Vopr Din Prochn
Voprosy Dozimetrii i Zaschity ot Izluchenii. Moskovskii Inzhenerno Fizicheskii Institut Sbornik Statei [*Former USSR*] — Vopr Dozim Zasch Izluch Mosk Inzh Fiz Inst Sb Statei
Voprosy Dozimetrii i Zashchity ot Izluchenii — Vopr Dozim Zashch Izluch
Voprosy Ekologii — Vop Ekol
Voprosy Ekologii i Biotsenologii — Vopr Ekol Biotsenol
Voprosy Ekonomiki — Vopr Ekon
Voprosy Eksperimental'noi i Klinicheskoi Radiologii [*Ukrainian SSR*] — Vopr Eksp Klin Radiol
Voprosy Eksperimental'noi Onkologii — Vopr Eksp Onkol
Voprosy Endokrinologii i Obmena Veshchestv — Vopr Endokrinol Obmena Veshchestv
Voprosy Endokrinologii Obmena Veshchestvennyi Respublikanskoi Mezhvedomstvennyi Sbornik — Vopr Endokrinol Obmena Veshchestv Resp Mezhved Sb
Voprosy Energetiki — Vopr Energ
Voprosy Erozii i Povysheniya Produktivnosti Sklonovykh Zemel' Moldavii — Vop Erozii Povysh Prod Sklon Zemel' Moldavii
Voprosy Erozii i Povysheniya Produktivnosti Sklonovykh Zemel' Moldavii — Vopr Erozii Povysh Prod Sklonovykh Zemel Mold
Voprosy Etiologii i Patogeneza Opukholei — Vopr Etiol Patog Opukholei
Voprosy Filologii — VF
Voprosy Filologii — VFil
Voprosy Filologii [*Leningrad*] — Vop Filol
Voprosy Filosofii — VF
Voprosy Filosofii [*Moscow*] — VFM
Voprosy Filosofii — Vop Fil
Voprosy Filosofii — Vop Filos
Voprosy Filosofii — Vopr Filos
Voprosy Filosofii — Voprosy Filos
Voprosy Fiziki Gornykh Porod — Vopr Fiz Gorn Porod
Voprosy Fiziki Tverdogo Tela — Vopr Fiz Tverd Tela
Voprosy Fiziki Zashchity Reaktorov [*Former USSR*] — Vopr Fiz Zasch Reaktorov
Voprosy Fiziki Zashchity Reaktorov — Vopr Fiz Zashch Reakt
Voprosy Fiziologii Akademiya Nauk Azerbaidzhanskoi SSR. Sektor Fiziologii [*Azerbaidzhan SSR*] — Vopr Fiziol Akad Nauk Azerb SSR Sekt Fiziol
Voprosy Fiziologii, Biokhimii, Zoologii, i Parazitologii — Vopr Fiziol Biokhim Zool Parazitol
Voprosy Fiziologii Cheloveka i Zhivotnykh — Vopr Fiziol Chel Zhivotn
Voprosy Fiziologii i Biokhimii Kul'turnykh Rastenii — Vopr Fiziol Biokhim Kul't Rast
Voprosy Fiziologii Rastenii i Mikrobiologii — Vopr Fiziol Rast Mikrobiol
Voprosy Fotosinteza — Vopr Fotosint
Voprosy Gazotermodinamiki Energoustanovok [*Ukrainian SSR*] — Vopr Gazotermodin Energoustanovok
Voprosy Gematologii Perelivaniya Krovi i Krovozamenitelei — Vopr Gematol Pereliv Krovi Krovozamenitelei
Voprosy Genezisa i Krypnomashtabnoi Kartirovanii Pochv Kazanskii Universitet — Vop Genez Krypnomashtabn Kartir Pochv Kazan Univ
Voprosy Geografii — Vopr Geogr
Voprosy Geografii Dal'nego Vostoka — Vopr Geogr Dal'nego Vostoka
Voprosy Geografii Kazakhstana — Vopr Geogr Kaz
Voprosy Geografii Mordovskoi ASSR — Vop Geogr Mordovsk ASSR
Voprosy Geografii Mordovskoi ASSR — Vopr Geogr Mordov ASSR
Voprosy Geokhimii i Tipomorfizm Mineralov — Vopr Geokhim Tipomorfizm Miner
Voprosy Geologii i Bureniya Neftyanykh i Gazovykh Skvazhin — Vopr Geol Buren Neft Gazov Skvazhin
Voprosy Geologii i Metallogenii Kol'skogo Poluostrova — Vopr Geol Metallog Kol'sk Poluostrova
Voprosy Geologii i Metodiki Razvedki Zolota — Vopr Geol Metod Razved Zolota
Voprosy Geologii i Mineralogii Kol'skogo Poluostrova — Vopr Geol Mineral Kolsk Poluostrova
Voprosy Geologii i Mineralogii Rudnykh Mestorozhdenii Ukrainy — Vopr Geol Mineral Rudn Mestorozhd Ukr
Voprosy Geologii i Neftegazonosnosti Uzbekistana — Vopr Geol Neftegazonsn Uzb
Voprosy Geologii i Neftenosnosti Srednego Povolzh'ya — Vopr Geol Neftenosn Sredn Povolzh'ya
Voprosy Geologii Tadzhikistana — Vopr Geol Tadzh
Voprosy Geologii Uzbekistana — Vopr Geol Uzb
Voprosy Geologii Vostochnoi Okrainy Russkoi Platformy i Yuzhnogo Urala — Vopr Geol Vost Okrainy Russ Platformy Yuzhn Urala
Voprosy Geologii Yuzhnogo Urala i Povolzh'ya — Vopr Geol Yuzhn Urala Povolzh'ya
Voprosy Geomorfologii i Geologii Bashkirii — Vopr Geomorfol Geol Bashk
Voprosy Gerontologii i Geriatrii — Vopr Gerontol Geriatr
Voprosy Gidrodinamiki i Teploobmena v Kriogennykh Sistemakh — Vopr Gidrodin Teploobmena Kriog Sist
Voprosy Gidrogeologii i Inzhenernoi Geologii Ukrainy — Vopr Gidrogeol Inzh Geol Ukr
Voprosy Gidrologii — Vopr Gidrol
Voprosy Gidrotekhniki — Vopr Gidrotekh
Voprosy Gidrotekhniki — Voprosy Gidrotekh
Voprosy Gigieny Pitaniya — Vopr Gig Pitan
Voprosy Gigieny Truda Profpatologii i Promyshlennoi Toksikologii — Vopr Gig Tr Profpatol Prom Toksikol
Voprosy Gigieny Truda v Slantsevoi Promyshlennosti Estonskoi SSR — VGTSA
Voprosy Gigieny Truda v Slantsevoi Promyshlennosti Estonskoi SSR — Vopr Gig Tr Slants Promsti Est SSR
Voprosy Iazykoznaniia. Akademiia Nauk SSSR — V Ia
Voprosy Iazykoznaniia. Akademiia Nauk SSSR — Vop Iaz
Voprosy Ikhtiologii — Vopr Ikhtiol
Voprosy Immunologii — Vopr Immunol
Voprosy Infektsionnoi Patologii i Immunologii — Vopr Infekts Patol Immunol
Voprosy Informatsionnoi Teorii i Praktiki — Vopr Inf Teor Prakt
Voprosy Introduktsii Rastenii i Zelenogo Stroitel'stva — Vopr Introd Rast Zelenogo Stroit
Voprosy Inzhenernoi Geologii i Gruntovedeniya — Vopr Inzh Geol Gruntoved
Voprosy Inzhenernoi Seismologii [*Former USSR*] — Vopr Inzh Seismol
Voprosy Issledovaniya i Ispol'zovaniya Pochvovedeniya Moldavii — Vopr Issled Ispol'z Pochv Mold
Voprosy Issledovaniya Lessovykh Gruntov Osnovanii i Fundamentov — Vopr Issled Lessovykh Gruntov Osn Fundam
Voprosy Istorii — VI
Voprosy Istorii [*Moscow*] — VIs
Voprosy Istorii — Vol
Voprosy Istorii — Vop Istor
Voprosy Istorii — VopIst
Voprosy Istorii — Vopr Ist
Voprosy Istorii — Vopr Istor
Voprosy Istorii Estestvoznaniia i Tekhniki — Vop Ist Est Tekh
Voprosy Istorii Estestvoznanija i Tehniki — Voprosy Istor Estestvoznan i Tehn
Voprosy Istorii Estestvoznaniya i Tekhniki — Vopr Istor Estestvozn Tekh
Voprosy Istorii KPSS — VolK
Voprosy Istorii KPSS [*Kommunisticheskaya Partiya Sovietskogo Soyuza*] — Vopr Ist KPSS
Voprosy Istorii (Minsk) — VI (Minsk)
Voprosy Istorii (Moscow) — V Ist
Voprosy Istorii (Moscow) — VI Moscou
Voprosy Istorii Religii i Ateizma. Sbornik Statei [*Moscow*] — VIRA
Voprosy Istorii Udmurtii — Vopr Ist Udm
Voprosy Jazyka i Literatury — VJaL
Voprosy Jazykoznanija [*Lvov*] — VJ
Voprosy Jazykoznanija [*Moscow*] — VJa
Voprosy Karstovedeniya — Vopr Karstoved
Voprosy Khimii i Biokhimii Sistem. Soderzhashchikh Marganets i Polifenoly — Vopr Khim Biokhim Sist Soderzh Marganets Polifenoly
Voprosy Khimii i Khimicheskoj Tekhnologii [*Former USSR*] — Vopr Khim Khim Tekhnol
Voprosy Kibernetiki (Moscow) — Voprosy Kibernet (Moscow)
Voprosy Kibernetiki (Tashkent) — Voprosy Kibernet (Tashkent)
Voprosy Kinetiki i Kataliza — Vopr Kinet Katal
Voprosy Klassicekoj Filologii — VKF
Voprosy Klinicheskoi i Eksperimental'noi Khirurgii — Vopr Klin Eskp Khir
Voprosy Klinicheskoi i Eksperimental'noi Onkologii — Vopr Klin Eksp Onkol
Voprosy Klinicheskoi Meditsiny — Vopr Klin Med
Voprosy Kliniki i Lecheniya Zlokachestvennykh Novoobrazovanii — Vopr Klin Lech Zlokach Novoobraz
Voprosy Kommunal'noi Gigieny — Vopr Kommunal'n Gig
Voprosy Kosmogonii — Vopr Kosmog
Voprosy Kraevoi Patologii Akademii Nauk Uzbekskoi SSR — Vopr Kraev Patol Akad Nauk Uzb SSR
Voprosy Kriogennoi Tekhniki — Vopr Kriog Tekh
Voprosy Kul'tury Reci — VKR
Voprosy Kurortologii, Fizioterapii, i Lechebnoi Fizicheskoi Kul'tury — VKFLA
Voprosy Kurortologii, Fizioterapii, i Lechebnoi Fizicheskoi Kul'tury — Vopr Kurortol Fizioter Lech Fiz Kul't
Voprosy Kurortologii i Fizioterapii (Frunze) — Vopr Kurortol Fizioter (Frunze)
Voprosy Kurortologii i Revmatologii — Vopr Kurortol Revatol
Voprosy Leikozologii — Vopr Leikozol
Voprosy Leprologii i Dermatologii — Vopr Leprol Dermatol
Voprosy Lesovedeniya — Vopr Lesoved
Voprosy Literaturovedenija i Jazykoznanija (Taskent) — VLJaTas
Voprosy Literatury — VL
Voprosy Literatury — VLit
Voprosy Litologii i Petrografii — Vopr Litol Petrogr
Voprosy Magmatizma i Metamorfizma — Vopr Magmat Metamorf
Voprosy Magmatizma i Metamorfizma [*Former USSR*] — Vopr Magmat Metamorfiz
Voprosy Magnitnoi Gidrodinamiki. Akademiya Nauk Latviiskoi SSR. Institut Fiziki [*Latvian SSR*] — Vopr Magn Gidrodin Akad Nauk Latv SSR Inst Fiz
Voprosy Marijskogo Jazykoznanija — VMarJa

Voprosy Meditsinskoi Khimii — VMDKA
Voprosy Meditsinskoi Khimii — Vop Med Kh
Voprosy Meditsinskoi Khimii — Vopr Med Khim
Voprosy Meditsinskoi Khimii Akademiya Meditsinskikh Nauk SSSR — Vopr Med Khim Akad Med Nauk SSR
Voprosy Meditsinskoi Teorii Klinicheskoi Praktiki i Kurortnogo Lecheniya — Vopr Med Teor Klin Prakt Kurortnogo Lech
Voprosy Meditsinskoi Virusologii — Vopr Med Virusol
Voprosy Mekhanika [*Former USSR*] — Vopr Mekh
Voprosy Mekhaniki Real'nogo Tverdogo Tela — Vopr Mekh Real'nogo Tverd Tela
Voprosy Metallovedeniya i Korrozii Metallov — Vopr Metalloved Korroz Met
Voprosy Metodologii Nauki — Vopr Metod Nauki
Voprosy Mikrobiologii — Vopr Mikrobiol
Voprosy Mikrobiologii. Akademiya Nauk Armyanskoi SSR — Vop Mikrobiol Akad Nauk Armyan SSR
Voprosy Mikrodozimetrii Ministerstvo Vysshego i Srednego Spetsial'nogo Obrazovaniya SSSR — Vopr Mikrodozim
Voprosy Mineralogii Osadochnykh Obrazonanii — Vopr Mineral Osad Obraz
Voprosy Nauchnogo Ateizma — VNA
Voprosy Neftekhimii — Vopr Neftekhim
Voprosy Neirokhirurgii — VONEA
Voprosy Neirokhirurgii — Vopr Neirokhir
Voprosy Obscestvennyh Nauk — Vopr Obsc Nauk
Voprosy Obshchei Khimii i Biokhimii — Vopr Obshch Khim Biokhim
Voprosy Okhrany Materinstva i Detstva — Vopr Okhr Materin Det
Voprosy Onkologii — Vopr Onkol
Voprosy Onkologii (Leningrad) — Vopr Onkol (Leningr)
Voprosy Organicheskoi Geokhimii i Gidrogeologii Neftegazonosnykh Basseinov Uzbekistana — Vopr Org Geokhim Gidrogeol Neftegazonosn Basseinov Uzb
Voprosy Patologii Krovi i Krovoobrashcheniya — Vopr Patol Krovi Krovoobrashch
Voprosy Pediatrii i Ohkrany Materinstva i Detstva — Vopr Pediatr Ohkr Materin Det
Voprosy Peredachi Informatsii [*Ukrainian SSR*] — Vopr Peredachi Inf
Voprosy Pitaniya — Vop Pitan
Voprosy Pitaniya — Vopr Pitan
Voprosy Pitaniya — VPITA
Voprosy Prikladnoi Geokhimii — Vopr Prikl Geokhim
Voprosy Prikladnoi Radiogeologii — Vopr Prikl Radiogeol
Voprosy Prochnosti i Plastichnosti Metallov — Vopr Prochn Plast Met
Voprosy Proekhitovaniya Sodovykh Zavodov — Vopr Proekt Sodovykh Zavodov
Voprosy Proizvodstva Stali — Vopr Proizvod Stali
Voprosy Proizvodstva Vaktsin i Syvorotok — Vopr Proizvod Vaktsin Syvorotok
Voprosy Psikhiatrii i Nevropatologii [*Former USSR*] — Vopr Psikhiat Nevropatol
Voprosy Psikhiatrii i Nevropatologii — Vopr Psikhiatr Nevropatol
Voprosy Psikhologii — Vop Psikhol
Voprosy Psikhologii — Vopr Psikhol
Voprosy Psikhologii — VOPSA
Voprosy Radiobiologii — Vopr Radiobiol
Voprosy Radiobiologii. Akademiya Nauk Armyanskoi SSR — Vopr Radiobiol Akad Nauk Arm SSR
Voprosy Radiobiologii i Biologicheskogo Deistviya Tsitostaticheskikh Preparatov — Vopr Radiobiol Biol Deistviya Tsitostatich Prep
Voprosy Radiobiologii i Biologicheskogo Dejstviya Tsitostaticheskikh Preparatov [*Former USSR*] — Vopr Radiobiol Biol Dejstv Tsitostatich Prep
Voprosy Radiobiologii i Klinicheskoi Radiologii — Vopr Radiobiol Klin Radiol
Voprosy Radiobiologii. Sbornik Trudov [*Armenian SSR*] — Vopr Radiobiol Sb Tr
Voprosy Radiobiologii. Sbornik Trudov — VRARA
Voprosy Radiobiologii (Yerevan) — Vopr Radiobiol (Yerevan)
Voprosy Radioelektroniki — Vopr Radioelektron
Voprosy Ratsional'nogo Pitaniya — Vopr Ratsion Pitan
Voprosy Razvedochnoi Geofiziki — Vopr Razved Geofiz
Voprosy Razvitija Licnosti — Vopr Razvit Licnosti
Voprosy Razvitiya Gazovoi Promyshlennosti Ukrainskoi SSR — Vopr Razvit Gazov Promsti Ukr SSR
Voprosy Regional'noi Geologii i Metallogenii Zabaikal'ya — Vopr Reg Geol Metallog Zabaikal'ya
Voprosy Rentgenologii i Onkologii — Vopr Rentgenol Onkol
Voprosy Revmatizma — Vopr Revm
Voprosy Rudichnogo Transporta — Vopr Rudn Transp
Voprosy Rudnoi Geofiziki [*Former USSR*] — Vopr Rud Geofiz
Voprosy Rudnoi Geofiziki — Vopr Rudn Geofiz
Voprosy Rudnoi Geofiziki. Ministerstvo Geologii i Okhrany Nedr SSSR [*Former USSR*] — Vopr Rud Geofiz Minist Geol Okhr Nedr SSSR
Voprosy Rudnoi Radiometrii — Vopr Rudn Radiom
Voprosy Russkogo Jazykoznanija — VRJa
Voprosy Russkoi Literatury. Respublikanskii Mezhvedomstvennyi Nauchnyi Sbornik — VRL
Voprosy Sel'skogo i Lesnogo Khozyaistva Dal'nego Vostoka — Vopr Sel'sk Lesn Khoz Dal'n Vost
Voprosy Sel'skogo i Lesnogo Khozyaistva Dal'nego Vostoka — Vopr Sel'sk Lesn Khoz Dal'nego Vostoka
Voprosy Slavjanskogo Jazykoznanija — V Sl Jaz
Voprosy Slavjanskogo Jazykoznanija — VSlJa
Voprosy Slavjanskogo Jazykoznanija (Lvov) — VSlJa (Lvov)
Voprosy Slavjanskogo Jazykoznanija (Moskva) — VS Ja (M)
Voprosy Slavjanskogo Jazykoznanija (Moskva) — VSlJa (Moskva)
Voprosy Sovetskogo Finno-Ugrovedenija — Vopr Sov Finno-Ugroved
Voprosy Statistiki — Vop Stat
Voprosy Stereokhimii — Vopr Stereokhim
Voprosy Stilistiki — VStil
Voprosy Strategii i Taktiki Marksistsko-Leninskih Partij — Vopr Strat Takt Marks-Lenin Partij
Voprosy Sudebnoi Meditsiny i Ekspertnoi Praktiki — Vopr Sud Med Ekspertnoi Prakt
Voprosy Sudebno-Meditsinskoi Ekspertizy — Vopr Sudebno-Med Ekspert
Voprosy Tekhnicheskoi Teplofiziki [*Ukrainian SSR*] — Vopr Tekh Teplofiz
Voprosy Tekhnologii i Tovarovedeniya Izdelii Legkoi Promyshlennosti — Vopr Tekhnol Tovaroved Izdelii Legk Promsti
Voprosy Tekhnologii Obrabotki Vody Promyshlennogo i Pit'evogo Vodosnabzheniya — Vopr Tekhnol Obrab Vody Prom Pit'evogo Vodoshnabzh
Voprosy Tekhnologii Ulavlivaniya i Pererabotki Produktov Koksovaniya — Vopr Tekhnol Ulavlivaniya Pererab Prod Koksovaniya
Voprosy Teorii Atomnykh Stolknovenii [*Former USSR*] — Vopr Teor At Stolknovenii
Voprosy Teorii i Metodiki Izucenijy Russkogo Jazyka — VTMRJa
Voprosy Teorii i Metodov Ideologiceskoj Raboty — Vopr Teorii Metod Ideol Raboty
Voprosy Teorii Plazmy — Vopr Teor Plazmy
Voprosy Teplofiziki Yadernykh Reaktorov [*Former USSR*] — Vopr Teplofiz Yad Reakt
Voprosy Teploobmena i Termodinamiki — Vopr Teploobmena Termodin
Voprosy Termodinamiki Geterogennykh Sistemi Teorii Poverkhnostnykh Yavlenii — Vopr Termodin Geterogennykh Sist Teor Poverkhn Yavlenii
Voprosy Toponomastiki — VTop
Voprosy Tuberkuleza (Riga) — Vopr Tuberk (Riga)
Voprosy Urologii — Vopr Urol
Voprosy Uzbekskogo Jazyka i Literatury — VULT
Voprosy Veterinarnoi Virusologii — Vopr Vet Virusol
Voprosy Virusologii — Vop Virus
Voprosy Virusologii — Vop Virusol
Voprosy Virusologii — Vopr Virusol
Voprosy Vodnogo Khozyaistva — Vopr Vodn Khoz
Voprosy Vychislitel'noi Matematiki i Tekhniki (Tashkent) — Vopr Vychisl Mat Tekh (Tashkent)
Voprosy Yazykoznaniya [*Moscow*] — Vya
Vor Ungdom — VU
Vor Viden — VV
Vorarbeiten zum Pommerschen Woerterbuch — VPW
Vorderasiatische Abteilung der Staatlichen Museen zu Berlin — VA
Vorderasiatische Bibliothek — VAB
Vorderasiatische Rollsiegel — VAR
Vorderasiatische Schriftdenkmaeler der Koeniglichen [*or Staatlichen*] **Museen zu Berlin** — VAS
Vorderasiatische Schriftdenkmaeler der Koeniglichen [*or Staatlichen*] **Museen zu Berlin** — VaSd
Vorderasiatische Schriftdenkmaeler der Koeniglichen Museen zu Berlin — VS
Vore Kirkegaarde — VK
Vorgeschichtliches Jahrbuch — VGJ
Vorgeschichtliches Jahrbuch fuer die Gesellschaft fuer Vorgeschichtliche Forschung — Vorgeschichtl Jb
Vorkaempfer Deutscher Freiheit. Series [*Munich*] — VDF
Vorlesungen aus dem Fachbereich Mathematik. Universitaet Essen — Vorlesungen Fachbereich Math Univ Essen
Vorlesungen der Churpfaelzischen Physicalish-Oeconomischen Gesellschaft — Vorles Churpfaelz Phys Oecon Ges
Vorlesungen. Mathematisches Institut Giessen — Vorlesungen Math Inst Giessen
Vorlesungen ueber Mathematik — Vorlesungen Math
Voronezskii Gosudarstvennyi Universitet Imeni Leninskogo Komsomola. Trudy Matematiceskogo Fakul'teta — Voronez Gos Univ Trudy Mat Fak
Voronezskii Ordena Lenina Gosudarstvennyi Universitet Imeni Leninskogo Komsomola. Trudy Naucno-Issledovatel'skogo Instituta Matematiki — Voronez Gos Univ Trudy Naucn Issled Inst Mat VGU
Voronezskii Tehnologiceskii Institut. Trudy — Voronez Tehn Inst Trudy
Vort Nordiske Modersmal — V Nord M
Vortex Science Fiction — VOR
Vortice — VE
Vortraege aus dem Gesamtgebiet der Botanik — Vortr Gesamtgeb Bot
Vortraege der Bibliothek Warburg — VBW
Vortraege der Bibliothek Warburg — Vort Warb
Vortraege fuer Pflanzenzuchter. Deutsche Landwirtschaftliche Gesellschaft Pflanzenzuchtabteilung — Vortr Pflanzenz Deut Landwirt Ges Pflanzenzuchtabt
Vortraege. Nordrhein-Westfaelische Akademie der Wissenschaften — Vortraege Nordrhein Westfaelische Akad Wiss
Vortraege und Studien. Zentrum fuer Umweltforschung der Westfaelischen Wilhelms-Universitaet — Vortr Stud Zent Umweltforsch Westfael Wilhelms Univ
Vostochnaya Neft — Vost Neft
Vostocnye Zapiski — VZ
Votes and Proceedings — V & P
Vox Evangelica — VE
Vox Guyanae — Vox Guy
Vox Medica — Vox Med
Vox Romanica — VR
Vox Sanguinis — VOSAA
Vox Sanguinis — Vox Sang
Vox Sanguinis — Vox Sanguin
Vox Theologica [*Assen*] — VoxTh
Vox Theologica [*Assen*] — VoxTheol
Voyage Archeologique en Grece et en Asie Mineure — VAGAM
Voz Farmaceutica (Lima) — Voz Farm (Lima)
Vozes Revista Catolica de Cultura — Vozes
Vozrozdenie — Vozr
Vprasanja Nasih Dni — VND
Vraag en Aanbod voor Techniek, Nijverheid, Bouwvak, en Handel — VRA
Vrachebnaia Gazeta — Vrach Gaz

Vrachebnoe Delo — Vrach Delo
Vrachebnoe Delo — VRDEA
Vrashchenie i Prilivnye Deformatsii Zemli — Vrashchenie i Prilivnye Deform Zemli
Vrednaya i Poleznaya Fauna Bespozvonochnykh Moldavii — Vrednaya Polezn Fauna Bespozvon Mold
Vremennik Glavnoi Palaty Mer i Vesov — Vremennik Gl Palaty Mer Vesov
Vremennik Puskinskogo Doma — VPD
Vrij Nederland — VNL
Vrije Universiteit Brussel. Inter-University Institute for High Energies. Report — Vrije Univ Brussel Inter-Univ Inst High Energ Rep
Vrije Volk — HVV
Vsemirnaja Istorija — VSI
Vsemirnoe Profsoiuznoe Dvizhenie — Vse Pro Dviz
Vsesojuznyi Zaocnyi Politehniceskii Institut. Sbornik Trudov — Vsesojuz Zaocn Politehn Inst Sb Trudov
Vsesojuznyj Naucno-Issledovatel'skij Geologiceskij Institut [*Moskau*] — VSEGEI
Vsesojuznyj Naucno-Issledovatel'skij Institut Lekarstvennyh Rastenij — Vsesojuzn Naucno Issl Inst Lekarstv Rast
Vsesoyuznaya Nauchno-Metod Konferentsiya Veterinarnykh Patologoanatomov — Vsesoyunaya Nauchno Metod Konf Vet Patologoanat
Vsesoyuznoe Nauchnoe Obshchestvo Neirokhirurgii — Vses Nauchn O-Vo Neirokhir
Vsesoyuznoe Paleontologicheskoe Obshchestvo Ezhegodnik — Vsesoyuznoe Paleont Obshch Ezhegodnik
Vsesoyuznoe Rabochee Soveshchanie po Primeneniyu Kompleksonov v Meditsine — Vses Rab Soveshch Primen Kompleksonov Med
Vsesoyuznoe Soveshchanie po Khimii Neorganicheskikh Gidridov — Vses Soveshch Khim Neorg Gidridov
Vsesoyuznoye Geograficheskoye Obshchestvo. Izvestiya — Vses Geogr O-Vo Izv
Vsesoyuznyi Nauchno-Issledovatel'skii Geologicheskii Institut. Informatsionnyi Sbornik — Vses Nauchno Issled Geol Inst Inf Sb
Vsesoyuznyi Nauchno-Issledovatel'skii i Proektnyi Institut Galurgii. Trudy — Vses Nauchno Issled Proektn Inst Galurgii Tr
Vsesoyuznyi Nauchno-Issledovatel'skii i Proektnyi Institut Mekhanicheskoi Obrabotki Poleznykh Iskopaemykh. Trudy — Vses Nauchno Issled Proektn Inst Mekh Obrab Polezn Iskop Tr
Vsesoyuznyi Nauchno-Issledovatel'skii Institut Eksperimental'noi Veterinarii Imeni Ya. R. Kovalenko. Byulleten — Vses Nauchno Issled Inst Eksp Vet Im Ya R Kovalenko Byull
Vsesoyuznyi Nauchno-Issledovatel'skii Institut Geofizicheskikh Metodov Razvedki. Trudy — Vses Nauchno Issled Inst Geofiz Metodov Razved Tr
Vsesoyuznyi Nauchno-Issledovatel'skii Institut Gidrogeologii i Inzhenernoi Geologii. Trudy — Vses Nauchno Issled Inst Gidrogeol Inzh Geol Tr
Vsesoyuznyi Nauchno-Issledovatel'skii Institut Khlopkovodstva. Sbornik Nauchnykh Rabot Aspirantov — Vses Nauchno Issled Inst Khlopkovod Sb Nauchn Rab Aspir
Vsesoyuznyi Nauchno-Issledovatel'skii Institut Konditerskoi Promyshlennosti. Trudy — Vses Nauchno Issled Inst Konditer Promsti Tr
Vsesoyuznyi Nauchno-Issledovatel'skii Institut Solyanoi Promyshlennosti. Trudy — Vses Nauchno Issled Inst Solyanoi Promsti Tr
Vsesoyuznyi Nauchno-Issledovatel'skii Institut Tsellyulozno-Bumazhnoi Promyshlennosti. Sbornik Trudov — Vses Nauchno Issled Inst Tsellyul Bum Promsti Sb Tr
Vsesoyuznyi Nauchno-Issledovatel'skii Institut Zhirov. Trudy — Vses Nauchno Issled Inst Zhirov Tr
Vsesoyuznyi Nauchno-Issledovatel'skii Khimiko-Farmatsevticheskii Institut. Khimiya i Meditsina — Vses Nauchno Issled Khim Farm Inst Khim Med
Vsesoyuznyi Neftyanoi Nauchno-Issledovatel'skii Geologorazvedochnyi Institut. Trudy — Vses Neft Nauchno Issled Geologorazved Inst Tr
Vsesoyuznyi Simpozium po Fotokhimicheskim Protsessam Zemnoi Atmosfery — Vses Simp Fotokhim Protsessam Zemnoi Atmos
Vsesoyuznyy Nauchno-Issledovatel'skiy Geologicheskiy Institut. Trudy — Vses Nauchno-Issled Geol Inst Tr
Vsesoyuznyy Nauchno-Issledovatel'skiy Geologorazvedochnyi Neftyanoy Institut. Trudy — Vses Nauchno-Issled Geologorazved Neft Inst Tr
Vsesvit [*Kiev*] — Vse
Vspomogatel'nye Istoricheskie Distsipliny — VID
VT. Verfahrenstechnik — VT Verfahrenstech
Vuelta (Mexico) — VUM
Vues sur l'Economie d'Aquitaine — Vues Econ Aquitaine
Vuga Gids — Vuga G
Vulkanologiya i Seismologiya — Vulkanol Seismol
Vuoriteollisuus/Bergshanteringen — VTBHA
Vuoriteollisuus/Bergshanteringen — Vuorit Bergshant
Vuoto, Scienza, e Tecnologia — VSTCB
Vuoto, Scienza, e Tecnologia — Vuoto
Vuoto, Scienza, e Tecnologia — Vuoto Sci Tecnol
Vutreshni Bolesti — Vutr Boles
VUV (Vacuum Ultraviolet) and Soft X-Ray Photoionization — VUV Soft X Ray Photoioniz
VVS och Energi — VVS Energi
VVS. Tidskrift foer Energi- och VVS [*Vaerme, Ventilation, Sanitet*]-Teknik — VVS Tidsk Energ VVS-Tek
VVS. Tidskrift foer Energi- och VVS-Teknik — VVS Tidsk Energi VVS Tek
VVS. Tidskrift foer Vaerme, Ventilation, Sanitet [*Sweden*] — VVS Tidskr Varme Vent Sanit
VVS. Tidskrift foer Vaerme, Ventilation, Sanitet, och Kylteteknik — VVS Tidskr Vaerme Vent Sanit Kyltetek
VVUU [*Vedeckovyzkumny Uhelny Ustav*] **Ostrava-Radvanice Zprava** — VVUU Zpr
Vyber Informaci z Organizacni a Vypocetni Techniky — Vyber Inf Organ Vypocetni Tech
Vychislitel'naya Seismologiya [*Former USSR*] — Vychisl Seismol
Vychislitel'naya Tekhnika i Voprosy Kibernetiki — Vychisl Tekh i Vopr Kibern
Vychislitel'naya Tekhnika. Sistemy. Upravlenie. Mezhdunarod — Vychisl Tekhn Sistemy Upravlenie
Vychislitel'nye Metody i Programmirovanie — Vychisl Metody & Program
Vychislitel'nye Metody i Programmirovanie — Vychisl Metody Progam
Vychislitel'nye Sistemy — Vychisl Sist
Vycislitel'naja i Prikladnaja Matematika (Kiev) — Vycisl Prikl Mat (Kiev)
Vycislitel'naja Matematika i Vycislitel'naja Tehnika (Kharkov) — Vycisl Mat i Vycisl Tehn (Kharkov)
Vycislitel'naja Tehnika i Voprosy Kibernetiki — Vycisl Tehn i Voprosy Kibernet
Vycislitel'nye Metody i Programmirovanie. Moskovskii Universitet. Sbornik Rabot Vycislitel'nogo Centra Moskovskogo Universiteta — Vycisl Metody i Programmirovanie
Vydavtel'stvo Slovenskej Akademie Vied — VSAV
Vyestsi Akademii Navuk BSSR. Syeryya Biyalagichnykh Navuk — Vyestsi Akad Navuk BSSR Syer Biyal Navuk
Vyestsi Akademii Navuk BSSR. Syeryya Syel' Skahaspadarchukh Navuk — Vyestsi Akad Navuk BSSR Syer Syel' Skahaspad Navuk
Vyisnik Akademyiyi Nauk Ukrayins'koyi RSR — Vyisn Akad Nauk Ukr RSR
Vyisnik Kiyivs'kogo Unyiversitetu. Seriyya Astronomii — Vyisn Kiyiv Unyiv Ser Astron
Vyisnik Kiyivs'kogo Unyiversitetu. Seriyya Fyizika [*Former USSR*] — Vyisn Kiyiv Unyiv Ser Fyiz
Vyisnik L'vyivs'kij Derzhavnij Unyiversitet Imeni I. Franka. Seriyiya Fyizichna — Vyisn L'vyiv Derzh Unyiv Ser Fyiz
Vyisnik Syil's'kogospodars'koyi Nauki — Vyisn Syil'skogospod Nauki
Vynalezy — VYNAA
Vynohradarstvo i Vynorobstvo — Vynohrad Vynorobstvo
Vyrocni Zprava Komise pro Prirodovedecke Prozkoumani Moravy — Vyr Zprava Komis Prir Prozk Moravy
Vyskumne Prace z Odboru Papiera a Celulozy — Vysk Pra Odboru Pap Celul
Vyskumne Prace z Odboru Papiera a Celulozy — Vyskum Pr Odboru Papiera Celulozy
Vyskumny Ustav Lesneho Hospodarstvavo Zvolene Lesnicke Studie — Vysk Ustav Lesn Hospod Zvolene Lesn Stud
Vyskumny Ustav Ovciarsky v Trencine. Vedecke Prace — Vysk Ustav Ovciar Trencine Ved Pr
Vysoka Skola Chemicko-Technologicka v Praze. Sbornik. E. Potraviny — Vys Sk Chem Technol Praze Sb E Potraviny
Vysoka Skola Chemicko-Technologicka v Praze. Sbornik. Oddil. Chemicke Inzenyrstvi — Vys Sk Chem-Technol Praze Sb Oddil Chem Inz
Vysoka Skola Lesnicka a Drevarska vo Zvolene. Drevarska Fakulta. Zbornik Vedeckych Prac — Vys Sk Lesn Drev Zvolene Drev Fak Zb Ved Pr
Vysoka Skola Zemedelska v Praze. Fakulta Agronomicka. Sbornik. Rada A. Rostlinna Vyroba — Vys Sk Zemed Praze Fak Agron Sb Rada A
Vysoka Skola Zemedelska v Praze Fakulta Provozne Ekonomicka v Ceskych Budejovicich Sbornik Referatu — VSSRBP
Vysokomolekulyarnye Soedineniya — VMSDA
Vysokomolekulyarnye Soedineniya — Vysokomol Soed
Vysokomolekulyarnye Soedineniya — Vysokomol Soedin
Vysokomolekulyarnye Soedineniya Geterotsepnye Vysokomolekulyarnye Soedineniya [*Former USSR*] — Vysokomol Soedin Geterotsepnye Vysokomol Soedin
Vysokomolekulyarnye Soedineniya. Seriya A — Vyso Soed A
Vysokomolekulyarnye Soedineniya. Seriya A — Vysokomol Soedin Ser A
Vysokomolekulyarnye Soedineniya. Seriya B — Vys Soed B
Vysokomolekulyarnye Soedineniya. Seriya B — Vyso Soed B
Vysokomolekulyarnye Soedineniya. Seriya B — Vysokomol Soedin Ser B
Vysokomolekulyarnye Soedineniya Vsesoyuznoe Khimicheskoe Obshchestvo — Vysokomol Soedin Vses Khim Ovo
Vysshaya Nervnaya Deyatel'nost v Norme i Patologii — Vyssh Nervn Deyat Norme Patol
Vysshoye Uchebnoye Zavedeniye. Izvestiya Geologiya i Razvedka — Vyssh Uchebn Zaved Izv Geol Razved
Vytreshni Bolesti — Vytr Boles
Vyzica a Zdravie — Vyz Zdravie
Vyziva Lidu — Vyz Lidu
Vyziva v Rodine — Vyz Rodine
Vyzkumny Ustav Vodohospodarsky. Prace a Studie — Vyzk Ustav Vodohospod Pr Stud
Vyzkumny Ustav Vodohospodarsky. Prace a Studie — Vyzk Ustav Vodohospodar Pr Stud
Vyznachnyk Prisnovodnykh Vodorostei Ukrains'koi RSR — Vyznach Prisnovod Vodor Ukr RSR
Vyzvol'nyj Sljax — VyzS
Vznik a Pocatky Slovanu [*Origine et Debuts des Slaves*] — Vznik Pocatky Slov
Vzryvnoe Delo. Nauchno-Tekhnicheskoe Gornoe Obshchestvo Sbornik [*Former USSR*] — Vzryvnoe Delo Nauchno-Tekh Gorn O-Vo Sb

W

W. J. Barrow Research Laboratory. Publication — W J Barrow Res Lab Publ
WA Education News. Education Department of Western Australia — WA Educ News
WA [*Western Australian*] **Electrical Contractor** — WA Electr Contract
WA Primary Principal. West Australian Primary Principals Association — WA Primary Princ
Wadley Medical Bulletin — Wadley Med Bull
Wadsworth and Brooks/Cole Mathematics Series — Wadsworth & Brooks Cole Math Ser
Wadsworth and Brooks/Cole Statistics/Probability Series — Wadsworth & Brooks Cole Statist Probab Ser
Wadsworth Atheneum. Bulletin — Wadsworth Ath Bul
Wadsworth Mathematics Series — Wadsworth Math Ser
Wadsworth Statistics/Probability Series — Wadsworth Statist Probab Ser
Waehrungsergaenzungsverordnung — WEVO
Waehrungsgesetz — WG
Waende Pompejis. Topographisches Verzeichnis der Bildmotive — WP
Waerme — WARMA
Waerme- und Kaeltetechnik — Waerme Kaeltetch
Waerme- und Stoffuebertragung — Waerme- Stoffuebertrag
Waerme- und Stoffuebertragung — Waerme und Stoffuebertrag
Waerme- und Stoffuebertragung — WASBB
Waerme- und Stoffuebertragung/Thermo and Fluid Dynamics — Waerme Stoffuebertrag/Thermo Fluid Dyn
Waermetechnik — Waermetech
Waffen- und Kostuemkunde — Waffen U Kostuemkde
Wage and Hour Cases. Bureau of National Affairs — Wage & Hour Cas BNA
Wage-Price Law and Economics Review — Wage-Pr L
Wage-Price Law and Economics Review — Wage-Price L & Econ Rev
Wage-Price Law and Economics Review — Wage-Price Law and Econ R
Wagga Wagga and District Historical Society. Journal — J Wagga Wagga Dist Hist Soc
Wagga Wagga and District Historical Society. Newsletter — Wagga Hist Soc News
Wagner Free Institute of Science. Bulletin. Cards — Wagner Free Inst Sci Bull Cards
Wagner Free Institute of Science [*Philadelphia*]. Transactions — Wagner Free I Sc Tr
Wahlenbergia. Scripta Botanica Umensia — WSBU
Waikato University. Antarctic Research Unit. Reports — Waikato Univ Antarct Res Unit Rep
Wakayama Igaku — WKMIA
Wakayama Medical Reports — Wakayama Med Rep
Wakayama University. Faculty of Education. Bulletin. Natural Science — Bull Fac Ed Wakayama Univ Natur Sci
Wake Forest Law Review — Wa For LR
Wake Forest Law Review — Wake For L Rev
Wake Forest Law Review — Wake Forest L Rev
Wake Forest University. Developing Nations Monograph Series. Series II. Medical Behavioral Science — Wake For Univ Dev Nations Monogr Ser Ser II Med Behav Sci
Wake Newsletter — WN
Waksman Institute of Microbiology. Rutgers University. Annual Report — Waksman Inst Microbiol Rutgers Univ Annu Rep
Wald und Holz — WH
Wales — W
Walford's Antiquarian and Bibliographer — Walford's Antiq
Walking Magazine — Walking
Wall Street Computer Review — WSC
Wall Street Journal — Wall St J
Wall Street Journal — Wall St Jnl
Wall Street Journal — Wall Str J
Wall Street Journal — WSJ
Wall Street Journal 3 Star. Eastern (Princeton, NJ) Edition — WSJ NJ
Wall Street Journal. Eastern Edition — Wall St J East Ed
Wall Street Journal. European Edition — WAI
Wall Street Journal. European Edition — WSJ Europe
Wall Street Journal Index — Wall Street J Index
Wall Street Journal. Midwest Edition — Wall St J Midwest Ed
Wall Street Journal. Three Star Eastern Edition — Wall St J Three Star East Ed
Wall Street Review of Books — Wall St R Bk
Wall Street Review of Books — WSRB
Wall Street Transcript — Wall St T
Wall Street Transcript — WSTSA
Walla Walla College. Publications — Walla Walla Coll Publ
Wallace Stevens Journal — W S Jour
Wallace Stevens Journal — Wal Steve J
Wallace Stevens Newsletter — WSN
Wallaces Farmer — Wallaces F
Wallerstein Laboratories. Communications — Wallerstein Lab Commun
Wallerstein Laboratories. Communications on the Science and Practice of Brewing — Wallerstein Lab Commun Sci Pract Brew
Wallraf-Richartz Jahrbuch — Wallraf-Richartz Jahr
Wallraf-Richartz-Jahrbuch — WRJ
Walpole Society Magazine — WSM
Walsh's American Review — Walsh's R
Walt Whitman Newsletter — WWN
Walt Whitman Review — Walt Whit R
Walt Whitman Review — WWR
Walter and Andree de Nottbeck Foundation. Scientific Reports — Walter Andree Nottbeck Found Sci Rep
Walter and Andree de Nottbeck Foundation. Scientific Reports — WANRDN
Walter Reed Army Medical Center. Progress Notes — Walter Reed Army Med Cent Prog Notes
Walter Reed General Hospital. Department of Medicine. Progress Notes — Walter Reed Gen Hosp Dep Med Prog Notes
Walters Art Gallery [*Baltimore*]. Journal — Walters J
Waman Puma — WP
WANATCA (West Australian Nut and Tree Crop Association) Yearbook — WANATCA (West Aust Nut & Tree Crop Assoc) Yearb
WANATCA [*West Australian Nut and Tree Crop Association*] **Yearbook** — WAYED5
Wanderer — WA
Wandlung — Wg
War Cry — War C
War Emergency Proceedings. Institution of Mechanical Engineers — War Emerg Proc Inst Mech Eng
War Medicine — War Med
War on Hunger — War Hung
Warburg and Courtauld Institute. Journal — Warburg & Courtauld Inst Jnl
Warburg Institute. Journal — WIJ
Warburg Institute Surveys and Texts — Warburg Inst Surveys Texts
Ward's Auto World — Ward AW
Ward's Automotive Reports — Wards Auto
Ward's Automotive Yearbook — Wards Yrbk
Ward's Bulletin — Ward's Bull
Warehousing Review — Warehousing Rev
Warehousing Supervisor's Bulletin [*United States*] — Warehousing Superv Bull
Warren Papyri — P Warren
Warsaw — Wa
Warsaw Agricultural University. SGGW-AR [*Szkola Glowna Gospodarstwa Wiejskiego - Akademia Rolnicza*] **Annals. Animal Science** — Warsaw Agric Univ SGGW-AR Ann Anim Sci
Warta Ekonomi Maritim. Facts and Analysis in Communications, Commerce, and Finance — WAD
Warta Geologi — Warta Geol
Warta Geologi (Kuala Lumpur) — Warta Geol (Kuala Lumpur)
Wascana Review — WascanaR
Waseda Daigaku Rikogaku Kenkyusho Hokoku — WDRKA
Waseda Economic Papers — WEP
Waseda Political Studies — Was Polit
Waseda Political Studies — Waseda Pol Studies
Waseda Political Studies — Waseda Polit Stud
Washburn College. Laboratory of Natural History. Bulletin — Washburn Coll Lab N H B
Washburn Law Journal — Washburn L J
Washburn Law Journal — WL Jour
Washburn Law Journal — WLJ
Washburn Law Journal — Wsb
Washington Academy of Sciences. Journal — Wash Acad Sci J
Washington Academy of Sciences. Journal — Washington Acad Sci Jour
Washington Actions on Health — Wash Actions Health
Washington Administrative Code — Wash Admin Code
Washington. Agricultural Experiment Station. Bulletin — Wash Agric Exp Stn Bull
Washington. Agricultural Experiment Station. Circular — Wash Agric Exp Stn Cir
Washington. Agricultural Experiment Station. Publications — Wash Ag Exp
Washington. Agricultural Experiment Station. Station Circular — Wash Agric Exp Stn Stn Circ
Washington. Agricultural Experiment Station. Technical Bulletin — Wash Agric Exp Stn Tech Bull

Washington and Lee Law Review — W & L
Washington and Lee Law Review — Wash & Lee L Rev
Washington and Lee Law Review — Wash and Lee LR
Washington and Lee Law Review — Washington and Lee L Rev
Washington and Lee Law Review — WLLR
Washington Appellate Reports — Wash App
Washington Association of Foreign Language Teachers. Forum — WAFLT Forum
Washington Beverage Insight [*Database*] — WBI
Washington Business Journal — Wash Bsn J
Washington Business Law Reporter — Wash Bus L Rpr
Washington. Department of Conservation. Division of Mines and Geology. Information Circular — Wash Div Mines Geol Inform Circ
Washington. Department of Conservation. Division of Mines and Geology. Report of Investigations — Wash Div Mines Geol Rep Invest
Washington. Department of Ecology. State Water Program. Biennial Report — Wash Dep Ecol State Water Program Bienn Rep
Washington. Department of Ecology. Technical Report — Wash Dep Ecol Tech Rep
Washington. Department of Ecology. Water Supply Bulletin — Wash Dep Ecol Water Supply Bull
Washington. Department of Fisheries. Annual Report — Wash Dep Fish Annu Rep
Washington. Department of Fisheries. Fisheries Research Papers — Wash Dep Fish Fish Res Pap
Washington. Department of Fisheries. Research Bulletin — Wash Dep Fish Res Bull
Washington. Department of Fisheries. Technical Report — Wash Dep Fish Tech Rep
Washington. Department of Natural Resources. Division of Mines and Geology. Bulletin — Wash Div Mines Geol Bull
Washington. Department of Natural Resources. Geology and Earth Resources Division. Bulletin — Wash Geol Earth Resour Div Bull
Washington. Department of Water Resources. Water Supply Bulletin — Wash Dep Water Resour Water Supply Bull
Washington. Department of Water Resources. Water Supply Bulletin — Washington Dept Water Resources Water Supply Bull
Washington. Division of Geology and Earth Resources. Geologic Map — Wash Div Geol Earth Resour Geol Map
Washington. Division of Geology and Earth Resources. Information Circular — Wash Div Geol Earth Resour Inf Circ
Washington. Division of Mines and Geology. Bulletin — Washington Div Mines and Geology Bull
Washington. Division of Mines and Geology. Geologic Map — Washington Div Mines and Geology Geol Map
Washington. Division of Mines and Geology. Information Circular — Washington Div Mines and Geology Inf Circ
Washington. Division of Mines and Mining. Report of Investigations — Wash Div Mines Min Rep Invest
Washington Drug Review — Wash Drug Rev
Washington Financial Reports — Wash Fin Rep
Washington. Geological Survey. Bulletin — Wash GSB
Washington Health Costs Letter — Wash Health Costs Let
Washington Historical Quarterly — Wash His Q
Washington Historical Quarterly — Wash Hist Q
Washington Journalism Review — Wash Journ Rev
Washington Journalism Review — WJR
Washington Law Review — Wa LR
Washington Law Review — Wash L Rev
Washington Law Review — Wash Law Re
Washington Law Review — Wash LR
Washington Law Review — Washington L Rev
Washington Law Review — Washington Law Rev
Washington Law Review — WLR
Washington Law Review — Wn LR
Washington Law Review — Ws L
Washington Legislative Service (West) — Wash Legis Serv (West)
Washington Medical Annals — Wash Med Ann
Washington Medical Annals — Wash Med Annals
Washington Monthly — GTWM
Washington Monthly — Wash M
Washington Monthly — Wash Mon
Washington Monthly — Washington M
Washington Monthly — WM
Washington Monthly — WSMYA
Washington News Beat — Wash News Beat
Washington Nurse — Wash Nurse
[*The*] **Washington Post** — TWP
Washington Post — Wash Post
Washington Post — WP
Washington Property Law Reporter — Wash Prop L Rpr
Washington Public Policy Notes — Wash Public Policy Notes
Washington Quarterly — Wash Q
Washington Quarterly — Washington Quart
Washington Quarterly. Georgetown University Center for Strategic and International Studies — GU/WQ
Washington Report — Wash Rep
Washington Report. News and World Report Newsletter — WR
Washington Report on Medicine and Health — Wash Rep Med Health
Washington Report on the Hemisphere — WRH
Washington Reports — Wash
Washington State Agricultural Experiment Station. Bulletin — Wash State Agric Exp Sta Bull
Washington State Agricultural Experiment Station. Station Circular — Wash State Agric Exp Sta Sta Circ
Washington State College. Research Studies — Wash State Coll Research Studies
Washington State College. Studies — WSCS
Washington State College. Washington Agricultural Experiment Station. Institute of Agricultural Sciences. Technical Bulletin — Wash State Coll Agric Exp Stn Tech Bull
Washington State. Council for Highway Research Engineering. Soils Manual — Wash State Council Highway Research Eng Soils Manual
Washington State Dental Journal — Wash State Dent J
Washington State Forest Products Institute. Bulletins. New Wood-Use Series — Wash State For Prod Inst Bull New Wood Use Ser
Washington State Genealogical and Historical Review — Wash St Geneal Hist Rev
Washington State Geologist. Annual Report — Wash St G An Rp
Washington State Historical Society. Publications — Wash His S
Washington State Institute of Technology. Bulletin — Wash State Inst Technology Bull
Washington State Institute of Technology. Circular — Wash State Inst Technol Circ
Washington State Institute of Technology. Technical Report — Wash State Inst Technol Tech Rep
Washington State Journal of Nursing — Wash State J Nurs
Washington State Nurses Association. Mini Journal — WSNA Mini J
Washington State Register — Wash St Reg
Washington State University. Agricultural Experiment Station. Institute of Agricultural Sciences. Technical Bulletin — Wash State Univ Agric Exp Stn Tech Bull
Washington State University. Agricultural Research Center. Research Bulletin — RBWCD9
Washington State University. Agricultural Research Center. Research Bulletin — Wash State Univ Agric Res Cent Res Bull
Washington State University. College of Agriculture. Research Center. Bulletin — Wash State Univ Coll Agric Res Cent Bull
Washington State University. College of Agriculture. Research Center. Technical Bulletin — Wash State Univ Coll Agric Res Cent Tech Bull
Washington State University. College of Engineering. Bulletin — Wash State Univ Coll Eng Bull
Washington State University. College of Engineering. Circular — Wash State Univ Coll Eng Circ
Washington State University. Cooperative Extension Service. Extension Bulletin — Wash State Univ Coop Ext Serv Ext Bull
Washington State University. Extension Service. EM — Wash State Univ Ext Serv EM
Washington State University. Extension Service. Extension Bulletin — Wash State Univ Ext Ser Ext Bull
Washington State University. International Symposium on Particleboard. Proceedings — Wash State Univ Int Symp Particleboard Proc
Washington State University. Publications in Geological Sciences — Wash State Univ Publ Geol Sci
Washington State University. Symposium on Particleboard. Proceedings — Wash State Univ Symp Particleboard Proc
Washington Territory Reports — Wash Terr
Washington University. Bulletin — Wash Univ Bull
Washington University. Dental Journal — Wash Univ Dent J
Washington University. Department of Geological Sciences. Abstracts of Research — Wash Univ Dep Geol Sci Abstr Res
Washington University. Law Quarterly — Wash U L Q
Washington University. Law Quarterly — Washington Univ L Quart
Washington University. Law Quarterly — WLQ
Washington University. Publications in Geology — Wash Univ Pub G
Washington University Studies — Wash Univ Studies
Washington University. Studies — WUS
Washington University. Studies. Humanistic Series — Wash Univ St Hum Ser
Washington University. Studies. Language and Literature — Wash Univ Stud Lang & Lit
Washington University. Studies. Science and Technology — Wash Univ Stud Sci & Tech
Washington University. Studies. Science and Technology. New Series — Wash Univ Stud Sci & Tech NS
Washington University. Studies. Scientific Series — Wash Univ St Sci Ser
Washington University. Studies. Social and Philosophical Sciences — Wash Univ Stud Social & Philos Sci
Washington University. Studies. Social and Philosophical Sciences. New Series — Wash Univ Stud Social & Philos Sci NS
Washingtonian — PWAS
Washington's Land and People — Wash Land People
Wasmann Journal of Biology — Wasmann J Biol
Wasser, Boden, Luft — WBOLA
Wasser, Luft, und Betrieb — Wasser Luft Betr
Wasser, Luft, und Betrieb — WSLBA
Wasser, Luft, und Betrieb. Zeitschrift fuer Umwelttechnik — WLR
Wasser und Abfall in Europa. Essener Tagung — Wasser Abfall Eur Essener Tag
Wasser- und Abfallwirtschaft in Duenn Besiedelten Gebieten. Vortraege des OWWV-Seminars — Wasser Abfallwirtsch Duenn Besiedelten Geb Vortr OWWV Semin
Wasser und Boden — WUBOA
Wasser- und Energiewirtschaft — Wasser- Energiewirt
Wasser- und Energiewirtschaft — WEW
Wasserhaushaltsgesetz — WHG
Wasserwirtschaft — WSWTA
Wasserwirtschaft-Wassertechnik — Wasserwirtsch-Wassertech
Wasserwirtschaft-Wassertechnik — Wasserwirt-Wassertech
Wasserwirtschaft-Wassertechnik — Wasswirt Wasstech
Wasserwirtschaft-Wassertechnik — WSWSA

Waste Age — WAGEA
Waste Age — WSK
Waste and Resource — Waste Resour
Waste Disposal and Recycling Bulletin — Waste Disp Recyc Bull
Waste Disposal and Water Management in Australia — Waste Dispos Water Manage Aust
Waste Disposal and Water Management in Australia — Waste Disposal & Water Manage in Aust
Waste Disposal and Water Management in Australia — Waste Disposal Water Manage Aust
Waste International — WAS
Waste Management — Waste Manage
Waste Management Information Bulletin — Waste Mgmt Inf Bull
Waste Management of Energetic Materials and Polymers — Waste Manage Energ Mater Polym
Waste Management Paper [*London*] — Waste Manage Pap
Waste Management Research — Waste Mgmt Res
Waste Management Research (Tokyo) — Waste Manage Res Tokyo
Waste Processing, Transportation, Storage, and Disposal. Technical Programs and Public Education — Waste Process Transp Storage Disposal Tech Programs Public Ed
Wastes Engineering — Wastes Eng
Wastes Management — Wastes Mgmt
WASU. Journal. West African Students Union of Great Britain — WASU
Watchmaker, Jeweller, and Silversmith — WJS
Water, Air, and Soil Pollution — WAPLA
Water, Air, and Soil Pollution — WASP
Water, Air, and Soil Pollution — Water A S P
Water, Air, and Soil Pollution — Water Air and Soil Pollut
Water, Air, and Soil Pollution — Water Air Soil Pollut
Water. American Institute of Chemical Engineers — Water Am Inst Chem Eng
Water and Electrolyte Metabolism. Proceedings of the Symposium — Water Electrolyte Metab Proc Symp
Water and Environmental Management — Water Environ Manage
Water and Pollution Control — WPOC
Water and Pollution Control (Don Mills, Canada) — Water Pollut Control (Don Mills Can)
Water and Sanitary Engineer — Water Sanit Eng
Water and Sanitation — Water and San
Water and Sanitation — Water Sanit
Water and Sewage Works — Water & Sewage Works
Water and Sewage Works — WSWOA
Water and Waste Engineering — Water & Waste Engng
Water and Waste Treatment — Wat Waste Treat
Water and Waste Treatment — Water Waste Treat
Water and Waste Treatment — WWATA
Water and Wastes Digest — Water Wastes Dig
Water and Wastes Engineering — Water Eng
Water and Wastes Engineering — Water Waste
Water and Wastes Engineering — Water Wastes Eng
Water and Wastes Engineering — WWAEA
Water and Wastes Engineering/Industrial — Water Wastes Eng Ind
Water and Wastewater Treatment Plants Operators' Newsletter — Water Wastewater Treat Plants Oper Newsl
Water and Water Engineering — Wat Wat Engng
Water and Water Engineering — Water Water Eng
Water and Water Engineering — WWENA
Water Bulletin — Wat Bull
Water Data Sources Directory [*Database*] — WDSD
Water Engineering and Management — Water E & M
Water Engineering and Management — WENMD
Water Environment and Technology — Water Environ Technol
Water in Australia — Wat Aust
Water in Biological Systems — Water Biol Syst
Water in Victoria — Wat Vict
Water Investigation. Michigan Geological Survey Division — Water Invest Mich Geol Surv Div
Water Law Newsletter [*United States*] — Water Law Newsl
Water Law Newsletter — WLNED
Water Management News — Water Manage News
Water Mineral Development — WMD
Water Pollution Abstracts — Water Poll Abstr
Water Pollution Abstracts — Water Pollut Abstr
Water Pollution Abstracts — WatPolAb
Water Pollution Control — Wat Pollut Control
Water Pollution Control — Water Pollut Control
Water Pollution Control [*Maidstone, England*] — WPOCA
Water Pollution Control Federation. Highlights — WPCF Highlights
Water Pollution Control Federation. Journal — J Water Pollut Control Fed
Water Pollution Control Federation. Journal — Water Poll Cont Fed J
Water Pollution Control Federation. Journal — Water Poll Control Fed J
Water Pollution Control Federation. Journal — Water Pollut Contr Fed J
Water Pollution Control Federation. Journal — WPCF
Water Pollution Control Federation. Journal — WPCFJ
Water Pollution Control Federation. Research Journal — Water Pollut Control Fed Res J
Water Pollution Control (London) — Water Pollut Control (London)
Water Pollution Control Research Series — Water Pollut Control Res Ser
Water Pollution. Modelling, Measuring, and Prediction. Papers. International Conference — Water Pollut Modell Meas Predict Pap Int Conf
Water Pollution Research in Canada — Water Pollut Res Can
Water Pollution Research Journal of Canada — Wat Pollut Res J Can
Water Pollution Research Journal of Canada — Water Pollut Res J Can
Water Pollution Research Journal of Canada — WRJCD9
Water Pollution Research (Stevenage) — Water Pollut Res (Stevenage)
Water Power [*England*] — WAPOA
Water Power — Wat Pwr
Water Purification and Liquid Wastes Treatment [*Japan*] — Water Purif Liquid Wastes Treat
Water Quality Instrumentation — Water Qual Instrum
Water Quality Research Journal of Canada — Water Qual Res J Can
Water Research — WARE
Water Research — Water Res
Water Research — WATRA
Water Research Centre. Notes on Water Research — NWREDP
Water Research Centre. Notes on Water Research — Water Res Cent Notes Water Res
Water Research Foundation of Australia Limited. Annual Report and Balance Sheet — Water Res Found Aust Annu Rep Balance Sheet
Water Research Foundation of Australia Limited. Annual Report and Balance Sheet — Water Res Found Aust Lted Ann Rep Balance Sheet
Water Research Foundation of Australia Limited. Bulletin — Wat Res Fdn Aust Bull
Water Research Foundation of Australia Limited. Bulletin — Water Res Found Aust Bull
Water Research Foundation of Australia Limited. Newsletter — Water Res Found of Aust Newsl
Water Research Foundation of Australia Limited. Report — Wat Res Fdn Rep
Water Research Foundation of Australia Limited. Report — Water Res Found Aust Rep
Water Research Institute. West Virginia University. Information Report — Water Res Inst W Va Univ Inf Rep
Water Research News — Water Res News
Water Resource Management Series — Water Resour Manag Ser
Water Resources — Water Resour
Water Resources Abstracts — WatResAb
Water Resources Abstracts [*Database*] — WRA
Water Resources Bulletin — WARBA
Water Resources Bulletin — Water Resour Bull
Water Resources Bulletin. Nevada Division of Water Resources — Water Resour Bull Nev Div Water Resour
Water Resources Bulletin (Puerto Rico) — Water Resour Bull (PR)
Water Resources Center. Research Report — WRC Research Report
Water Resources Circular. Arkansas Geological Commission — Water Resour Circ Arkansas Geol Comm
Water Resources (English Translation of Vodnye Resursy) — Water Resour (Engl Transl Vodnye Resursy)
Water Resources Information System. Technical Bulletin — WRIS Technical Bulletin
Water Resources Investigations — Water Resour Invest
Water Resources Investigations. United States Geological Survey — Water Resour Invest US Geol Surv
Water Resources Journal. Economic and Social Commission for Asia and the Pacific — Water Resour J Econ Soc Comm Asia Pac
Water Resources News-Clipping Service. General Issue. Water Management Service. Department of the Environment [*Ottawa*] — WG
Water Resources Newsletter — Water Resour Newsl
Water Resources. Reconnaissance Series. Nevada Division of Water Resources — Water Resour Reconnaissance Ser Nev Div Water Resour
Water Resources Report. Arizona State Land Department — Water Resour Rep Ariz State Land Dep
Water Resources Report. Ontario Ministry of the Environment. Water Resources Branch — Water Resour Rep Ont Minist Environ Water Resour Branch
Water Resources Research — WARR
Water Resources Research — Wat Resour Res
Water Resources Research — Water Res R
Water Resources Research — Water Resour Res
Water Resources Research — Water Resources Res
Water Resources Research — WRERA
Water Resources Research Center. Report (Washington) — WRRC Report (Washington)
Water Resources Research Center. Virginia Polytechnic Institute and State University. Bulletin — Water Resour Res Cent VA Polytech Inst State Univ Bull
Water Resources Review for Streamflow and Ground-Water Conditions [*United States - Canada*] — Water Resour Rev Streamflow Ground-Water Cond
Water Resources Series. Tennessee Division of Water Resources — Water Resour Ser Tenn Div Water Resour
Water Resources Symposium — Water Resour Symp
Water Resources (Translation of Vodnye Resursy) — Water Resour Transl of Vodn Resur
Water Reuse Symposium Proceedings — Water Reuse Symp Proc
Water Science and Technology — Water Sci & Technol
Water Science and Technology — WSTED
Water Science and Technology. Journal. International Association on Water Pollution Research — Water Sci Technol J Int Assoc Water Pollut Res
Water Science and Technology Library — Water Sci Technol Lib
Water Science Reviews — Water Sci Rev
Water Services — Wat Serv
Water Services — Water Serv
Water, Sewage, and Effluent — Water Sewage Effl
Water (South Africa) — Water (S Afr)
Water Spectrum — WASP
Water Spectrum — WASPB
Water Supply and Management [*England*] — Water Supply Manage
Water Supply Improvement Association. Journal — WSIA Journal
Water Supply Paper. United States Geological Survey — Water Supply Pap US Geol Surv

Water Supply Papers. Geological Survey of Great Britain. Hydrogeological Report — Water Supply Pap Geol Surv GB Hydrogeol Rep
Water Treatment and Examination — Water Treat Exam
Water Waste Treatment Journal — Water Waste Treat J
Water (Water Conservation and Irrigation Commission Staff Journal) — Water (WC and IC Staff Journal)
Water Well Journal — Water Well J
Water Well Journal — Water Well Jour
Water Well Journal — WWJOA
Water Works and Wastes Engineering — Water Works Wastes Eng
Water Works Engineering — Water Works Eng
Waterford and South-East of Ireland Archaeological Society. Journal — Waterford SE Ir Arch Soc J
Waterkampioen — WAE
Water-Resources Investigation — WRI
Waterschapsbelangen — WSR
Watersport. Maandblad voor de Zeilsport. Motorbootsport — WTS
Watson House Bulletin — Watson House Bull
Wattle Research Institute. University of Natal (South Africa). Report — Wattle Res Inst Univ Natal (S Afr) Rep
Wave Electronics — WAELD
Wave Electronics — Wave Electron
Wave Motion — WAMOD
Wave. Particle Dualism — Wave Part Dualism
Wavelet Analysis and its Applications — Wavelet Anal Appl
Wawatay News [*Sioux Lookout, Ontario*] — WN
Wawatay News Extra. Special Issues — WX
Way. Supplement — Way Suppl
Wayne Law Review — Wayne L Rev
Wayne Law Review — Wayne LR
Wayne Law Review — Wn L
Wayne Law Review — Wn LR
WEA [*Workers Educational Association*] **Bulletin** — WEA Bul
Weak Superconductivity — Weak Supercond
Wealthbuilding — WEB
Wear and Friction of Elastomers — Wear Frict Elastomers
Weather [*London*] — WTHRA
Weather and Climate — Weather and Clim
Weather, Crops, and Markets — Weather C & M
Weather Development and Research Bulletin [*Australia, Commonwealth Bureau of Meteorology*] — Weather Dev Res Bull
Weather Research Bulletin — Weather Research Bull
Weatherwise — GWEA
Weatherwise — WTHWA
Webb, A'Beckett, and Williams' Equity Reports — W A'B & W Eq
Webb, A'Beckett, and Williams' Equity Reports — Webb A'B & W Eq
Webb, A'Beckett, and Williams' Insolvency, Ecclesiastical, and Matrimonial Reports — W A'B & W IE & M
Webb, A'Beckett, and Williams' Insolvency, Ecclesiastical, and Matrimonial Reports — Webb A'B & W IE & M
Webb, A'Beckett, and Williams' Insolvency, Probate, and Matrimonial Reports — Webb A'B & W IP & M
Webb, A'Beckett, and Williams' Mining Cases — W A'B & W Min
Webb, A'Beckett, and Williams' Mining Cases — Webb A'B & W Min
Webb, A'Beckett, and Williams' Reports — W A'B & W
Webb, A'Beckett, and Williams' Reports — Webb A'B & W
Webbia; Raccolta di Scritti Botanici — Webbia Racc Scr Bot
Webster Review — Web R
Webster's New International Dictionary — WNID
Webster's New International Dictionary. 2nd Edition — W2
Webster's Third New International Dictionary — W3
WECAF (Western Central Atlantic Fishery Commission) Studies — WECAF (West Cent Atl Fish Comm) Stud
Weed Abstracts — Weed Abstr
Weed Research — Weed Res
Weed Science — Weed Sci
Weed Science — WEESA
Weed Technology. Journal. Weed Science Society of America — Weed Technol J Weed Sci Soc Am
Weeds and Weed Control — Weeds Weed Cont
Week End Review — WER
Weekberichten van de Kredietbank — Wkb Krb
Weekblad der Belastingen — WB
Weekblad der Belastingen — WdB
Weekblad der Directe Belastingen — WDB
Weekblad der Directe Belastingen, Invoerrechten en Accijnzen — DBIA
Weekblad der Directe Belastingen, Invoerrechten en Accijnzen — WDIA
Weekblad van het Recht — W
Weekblad van het Recht — W v h R
Weekblad voor de Burgerlijke Administratie — WBA
Weekblad voor de Nederlandse Bond van Gemeenteambtenaren — W v NB
Weekblad voor de Nederlandse Bond van Gemeenteambtenaren — WBGA
Weekblad voor de Nederlandse Bond van Gemeenteambtenaren — WGA
Weekblad voor de Nederlandse Bond van Gemeenteambtenaren — Wkbl Ned B Gemambt
Weekblad voor de Nederlandse Bond van Gemeenteambtenaren — WNBGA
Weekblad voor Fiscaal Recht — W v F R
Weekblad voor Fiscaal Recht — WBE
Weekblad voor Fiscaal Recht — Wbl voor Fiscaal Recht
Weekblad voor Fiscaal Recht — WFR
Weekblad voor Fiscaal Recht — Wkbl Fisc R
Weekblad voor Gemeentebelangen — GB
Weekblad voor Gemeentebelangen — Wbl v Gembel
Weekblad voor Gemeentebelangen. Orgaan van de Vereniging van Nederlandse Gemeenten — WGB
Weekblad voor het Notariaat — W v h N
Weekblad voor het Notariaat — WN
Weekblad voor Notaris-Ambt en Registratie — WNR
Weekblad voor Privaatrecht, Notariaat, en Registratie — W v Pr N en R
Weekblad voor Privaatrecht, Notariaat, en Registratie — Weekbl Priv Not en Reg
Weekblad voor Privaatrecht, Notariaat, en Registratie — WPNR
Weekblad voor Privaatrecht, Notariaat, en Registratie — WPR
Weekly Book Newsletter — WBN
Weekly Bulletin. California State Board of Health — Weekly Bull Calif State Board Health
Weekly Bulletin. Kredietbank — Kredietbnk
Weekly Coal Production — Wkly Coal
Weekly Compilation of Presidential Documents — W Comp Pres Docs
Weekly Compilation of Presidential Documents — Weekly Comp of Pres Doc
Weekly Compilation of Presidential Documents — Weekly Compilation Presidential Docum
Weekly Criminal Bulletin [*Database*] — WCB
[*The*] **Weekly Dispatch** — WD
Weekly Energy Report [*United States*] — Wkly Energy Rep
Weekly Epidemiological Record — Wkly Epidemiol Rec
Weekly Hansard - Senate — WHS
Weekly Information Bulletin — Wkly Inf Bull
Weekly Law Bulletin — W Law Bul
Weekly News Letter. United States Department of Agriculture — Weekly N L
Weekly Notes Covers (New South Wales) — WN Covers (NSW)
Weekly Notes (New South Wales) — WN (NSW)
Weekly Notes. Queensland — QWN
Weekly Observations. Royal Dublin Society — Weekly Observ Roy Dublin Soc
Weekly of Business Aviation [*Database*] — WBA
Weekly Pharmacy Reports: The Green Sheet — WPR
Weekly Record [*United States*] — Wkly Rec
Weekly Record — WR
Weekly Report (Latin American) — LAWR
Weekly Review — Review
Weekly Review — WR
Weekly Review of the Far East — W R Far East
Weekly Underwriter — W Underw
Weekly Underwriter — Weekly Underw
Weekly Underwriter — WU
Weekly Weather and Crop Bulletin — WW & CB
Weekly Women's Magazine [*Manila*] — WWM
Weerberichten. Informatiebulletin over Windenergie en Zonne-Energie — WEE
Wege der Forschung, Darmstadt, Wissenschaftliche Buchgesellschaft — WF
Wege der Forschungen — WdF
Wege zur Dichtung — WzD
Wege zur Sozialversicherung — Wege Soz Versicherung
Wegen — WEG
Wegvervoer — VYV
Wehr und Wirtschaft — Wehr und Wirt
Wehrforschung — WF
Wehrkunde — Wehrkd
Wehrmedizinische Monatsschrift — Wehrmed Monatsschr
Wehrmedizinische Monatsschrift — WEMOB
Wehrtechnik — Wehrtech
Wehrtechnik — WHTCA
Wehrwissenschaftliche Rundschau — Wehrwiss Rdsch
Weibulls Arsbok — Weibulls Arsb
Weichardts Ergebnisse der Hygiene, Bakterien-, Immunitaetsforschung, und Experimentellen Therapie — E Hy
Weichselland, Mitteilungen des Westpreussischen Geschichtsvereins — WMWG
Weight Watchers' Magazine — IWWM
Weimarer Beitraege — WB
Weinbau und Kellerwirtschaft (Budapest) — Weinbau Kellerwirtsch (Budapest)
Wein-Wissenschaft — Wein-Wiss
Weird and Occult Library — WOL
Weird Mystery — WMY
Weird Tales — WT
Weird Tales [*1973-*] — WTZ
Weird Terror Tales — WTT
Weird World — WWD
Weiterbildungszentrum fuer Mathematische Kybernetik und Rechentechnik — Weiterbildungszentrum Math Kybernet Rechentech
Weizmann Memorial Lectures — Weizmann Mem Lect
Welcome to Finland — WTF
Welcome to Greenland — WTGR
Welcome to Iceland — WTI
Welcome to the Faeroes — WTTF
Welcome to the North Atlantic — WNA
Welder [*England*] — WLDRA
Welding and Metal Fabrication — Weld and Met Fabr
Welding and Metal Fabrication — Weld Met Fabr
Welding and Metal Fabrication — Weld Metal Fab
Welding and Metal Fabrication — Weld Metal Fabr
Welding and Metal Fabrication — WLFMA
Welding Design and Fabrication — WDEFA
Welding Design and Fabrication — Weld Des and Fabr
Welding Design and Fabrication — Weld Des Fabr
Welding Design and Fabrication — Weld Dsgn
Welding Engineer — WEEGA
Welding Engineer — Weld Eng
Welding Fabrication and Design — Weld Fabr Des
Welding Fabrication and Design — Weld Fabric Design
Welding Fabrication and Design — Weld Fabrication Design
Welding in the World — WDWRA

Welding in the World — Weld World
Welding in the World/Le Soudage dans le Monde — Weld Wld
Welding in the World/Le Soudage dans le Monde — Weld World Soudage Monde
Welding Industry — Weld Ind
Welding International [*United Kingdom*] — Weld Int
Welding Journal [*Miami*] — WEJUA
Welding Journal — Weld J
Welding Journal — Weld Jrl
Welding Journal — Welding J
Welding Journal (London) — Weld J (London)
Welding Journal (Miami) — Weld J (Miami)
Welding Journal (New York) — Weld J (NY)
Welding Journal Research. Supplement — Weld J Res Suppl
Welding News — Weld News
Welding Production — Weld Prod
Welding Production [*English Translation*] — WEPRA
Welding Production (English Translation) — Weld Prod Engl Transl
Welding Production (USSR) — Weld Prod (USSR)
Welding Research Abroad — WDRAA
Welding Research Abroad — Weld Res Abroad
Welding Research Council. Bulletin — Weld Res C
Welding Research Council. Bulletin — Weld Res Counc Bull
Welding Research Council. Progress Reports — Weld Res Counc Prog Rep
Welding Research International — Weld Res Int
Welding Research (London) — Weld Res (London)
Welding Research (Miami) — Weld Res (Miami)
Welding Research (Miami, Florida) — Weld Res (Miami Fla)
Welding Research News — Weld Res News
Welding Review — Weld Rev
Welding Review — Welding Rev
Welding Review International — Weld Rev Int
Welding Technique [*Japan*] — Weld Tech
Weleda Korrespondenzblaetter fuer Aerzte — Weleda Korrespondenzbl Aerzte
Welfare Focus — Welf Focus
Welfare Reporter — Welf Reptr
Well History Control System [*Database*] — WHCS
Well Inventory Series (Metric Units). Institute of Geological Sciences — Well Inventory Ser (Metric Units) Inst Geol Sci
Well Servicing — Well Serv
Wellness Newsletter — WLNL
Wellness Perspectives — Well Perspect
Wells Fargo Bank. Business Review — Wells Frgo
Wellworthy Topics — Wellworthy Top
Welsh Bee Journal — Welsh Bee J
Welsh Beekeepers' Association. Quarterly Bulletin — Welsh Beekprs' Ass Q Bull
Welsh Historical Review — WelH
Welsh History Review — Welsh H R
Welsh History Review — Welsh Hist
Welsh History Review — Welsh Hist Rev
Welsh History Review — WHR
Welsh Journal of Agriculture — Welsh J Agric
Welsh Journal of Education — Welsh J Educ
Welsh Music — Welsh M
Welsh Plant Breeding Station (Aberystwyth) Annual Report — Welsh Plant Breed Stn (Aberystwyth) Annu Rep
Welsh Plant Breeding Station (Aberystwyth). Report — Welsh Plant Breed Stn (Aberystwyth) Rep
Welsh Plant Breeding Station (Aberystwyth). Technical Bulletin — Welsh Plant Breed Stn (Aberystwyth) Tech Bull
Welsh Plant Breeding Station. Bulletin Series — Welsh Plant Breed Stn Bull Ser
Welsh Review — WR
Welt als Geschichte — WAG
Welt Als Geschichte — Welt Als Gesch
Welt als Geschichte. Eine Zeitschrift fuer Universalgeschichte — Welt Gesch
Welt als Geschichte Zeitschrift fuer Universalgeschichtliche Forschung — WG
Welt der Bibel. Kleinkommentare zur Heiligen Schrift — KK
Welt der Slaven — WdSL
Welt der Slaven — Welt d Slaven
Welt der Slaven — WS
Welt der Slaven — WSL
Welt der Slaven — WSlav
Welt des Islams — Welt d Islam
Welt des Islams — WI
Welt des Orients — Welt D Orient
Welt des Orients — WO
Welt des Orients. Wissenschaftliche Beitraege zur Kunde des Morgenlandes [*Wuppertal/Stuttgart/Goettingen*] — WdO
Welt und Wort — WeW
Welt und Wort — WeWo
Welt und Wort — WuW
Weltliteratur der Farbenchemie — Weltlit Farbenchem
Weltraumfahrt und Raketentechnik — Weltraumfahrt Raketentech
Weltraumfahrt und Raketentechnik — WRZAA
Weltwirtschaft — Weltwirt
Weltwirtschaft — WYW
Weltwirtschaftliches Archiv — WA
Weltwirtschaftliches Archiv — WEL
Weltwirtschaftliches Archiv — Weltwir Arc
Weltwirtschaftliches Archiv — Weltwirtsch Archiv
Weltwirtschaftliches Archiv [*Kiel*] — Weltwirtschaft Archiv
Weltwirtschaftliches Archiv — WWARA
Welzijnsweekblad — TMW
WEM [*World Education Markets, Inc.*] **Newsletter** — WEM Newsl
Wen Shih Che — WSC
Wen Shih Che Hsueh-Pao [*Taiwan University*] — WSCHP
Wenner-Gren Center. International Symposium Series — Wenner-Gren Cent Int Symp Ser
Wentworth Magazine — Wentworth Mag
Wen-Tzu Kai-Ko — WTKK
Wer Informiert Woruber [*Database*] — WIW
Wereld in Ontwikkeling. Veertiendaags Overzicht van Tijdschriftartikelen en Rapporten over Problemen van de Ontwikkelingsgebieden — WOW
Wereldmarkt — EVH
Werk/Archithese — Werk
Werkgever — WEK
Werkstatt und Betrieb — Werkstatt Betr
Werkstatt und Betrieb — Werkstatt und Betr
Werkstatt und Betrieb — WKUBA
Werkstattstechnik — WERKA
Werkstattstechnik Zeitschrift fuer Industrielle Fertigung — Werkstattstech Z Ind Fertigung
Werkstattstechnik Zeitschrift fuer Industrielle Fertigung — Wt Z Ind Fe
Werkstoff und Innovation — Werkst Innov
Werkstoffe und Korrosion — Werkst Korros
Werkstoffe und Korrossion (Wernheim) — Werkst u Korrosion
Wernerian Natural History Society. Memoirs — Wernerian N H Soc Mem
Wertpapier-Mitteilungen — WM
WESCON [*Western Electronics Show and Convention*] **Conference Record** — WCRED
WESCON [*Western Electronics Show and Convention*] **Technical Papers** [*United States*] — WESCON Tech Pap
Wesley W. Spink Lectures on Comparative Medicine — Wesley W Spink Lect Comp Med
Wesleyan Advocate — W Adv
Wesleyan Theological Journal — Wesley Th J
Wesleyan Theological Journal — WyTJ
West Africa — W Afr
West Africa — W Africa
West Africa — WA
West Africa — WAF
West Africa [*London*] — West Afr
West Africa Journal of Modern Language — WAJML
West African Cocoa Research Institute. Technical Bulletin — West Afr Cocoa Res Inst Tech Bull
West African Farming and Food Processing — West African Farm Food Proc
West African Institute for Oil Palm Research. Annual Report — West Afr Inst Oil Palm Res Annu Rep
West African Institute of Social and Economic Research. Proceedings of Annual Conference — WAISER
West African Journal of Archaeology — W Afr J Arc
West African Journal of Archaeology — W Afr J Archaeol
West African Journal of Archaeology — West Afr J Archaeol
West African Journal of Biological and Applied Chemistry — West Afr J Biol Appl Chem
West African Journal of Biological Chemistry — W African J Biol Chem
West African Journal of Biological Chemistry — West Afr J Biol Chem
West African Journal of Education — WAJE
West African Journal of Education — West African J of Ed
West African Journal of Medicine — West Afr J Med
West African Journal of Modern Languages — W Afr J Mod Languages
West African Journal of Pharmacology and Drug Research — West Afr J Pharmacol Drug Res
West African Journal of Sociology and Political Science — W Afr J Sociol Polit Sci
West African Language Monograph Series — WALMS
West African Library Association. News — WALA News
West African Medical Journal — West Afr Med J
West African Medical Journal and Nigerian Medical and Dental Practitioner — West Afr Med J Niger Med Dent Pract
West African Medical Journal and Nigerian Practitioner — West Afr Med J Nigerian Pract
West African Pharmacist — West Afr Pharm
West African Religion — W Afr Relig
West African Religion — W African Rel
West American Scientist — West Am Sc
West Australian Democrat — WA Democrat
West Australian Manufacturer — WA Manuf
West Australian Manufacturer — WA Manufacturer
West Australian Mining and Commercial Review — WA Mining & Commercial R
West Australian News — WA News
West Australian Primary Principals Association — WA Primary Principal
West Canadian Journal of Anthropology — W Can J Ant
West Coast Review — WCR
West Coast Review — West Coast R
West Coast Review of Books — WCRB
West Coast Travel [*Database*] — WCT
West European Policies — W Eur Policies
West European Politics — W Eur Politics
West European Politics — West Eur Politics
West European Politics — West Europ Polit
West Georgia College. Review — WGCR
West India Committee Circular — WI Comm Circ
West Indian Bulletin — West Ind Bull
West Indian Bulletin — WIB
West Indian Digest — W Indian Dig
West Indian Economist — WI Econ
West Indian Medical Journal — W Ind Med J
West Indian Medical Journal — W Indian Med J
West Indian Medical Journal — West Indian Med J

West Indian Medical Journal — WI Med J
West Indian Review — West Ind Rev
West Indian Review — WI Rev
West Indian World — W Indian World
West Indies Chronicle — WIC
West International Law Bulletin — West Int Law Bul
West London Medical Journal — W Lond Med J
West Malaysia. Geological Survey. District Memoir — West Malays Geol Surv Dist Mem
West Malaysia. Geological Survey. Economic Bulletin — West Malays Geol Surv Econ Bull
West of Scotland Agricultural College. Research Bulletin — West Scot Agric Coll Res Bull
West of Scotland Agricultural College. Research Bulletin — West Scotl Agric Coll Res Bull
West of Scotland Iron and Steel Institute. Journal — West Scot Iron Steel Inst J
West Pakistan Journal of Agricultural Research — W Pakistan J Agr Res
West Pakistan Journal of Agricultural Research — West Pak J Agric Res
West Tennessee Historical Society. Papers — West Tenn Hist Soc Pap
West Texas Business Journal — West Tex B
West Texas Geological Society. Publication — West Texas Geol Soc Pub
West Virginia Academy of Sciences. Proceedings — W Va Acad Sci Proc
West Virginia. Agricultural and Forestry Experiment Station. Bulletin — W Va Agric For Exp Stn Bull
West Virginia. Agricultural Experiment Station. Bulletin — W Va Agric Exp Stn Bull
West Virginia. Agricultural Experiment Station. Circular — W Va Agric Exp Stn Cir
West Virginia. Agricultural Experiment Station. Circular — W Va Agric Exp Stn Circ
West Virginia. Agricultural Experiment Station. Current Report — W Va Agric Exp Stn Curr Rep
West Virginia. Agricultural Experiment Station. Miscellaneous Publication — W Va Agric Exp Stn Misc Publ
West Virginia. Agricultural Experiment Station. Publications — W Va Ag Exp
West Virginia Agriculture and Forestry — W Va Agric For
West Virginia Association for Health, Physical Education, Recreation, and Dance. Journal — WVHP
West Virginia Coal Mining Institute. Proceedings — W Va Coal Min Inst Proc
West Virginia Code — W Va Code
West Virginia Dental Journal — W Va Dent J
West Virginia. Department of Agriculture. Publications — W Va Ag Dept
West Virginia. Department of Mines. Annual Report — W Va Dep Mines Annu Rep
West Virginia Folklore — WVF
West Virginia Forestry Notes — W Va For Notes
West Virginia Forestry Notes. West Virginia University. Agricultural and Forestry Experiment Station — W Va For Notes W Va Univ Agric For Exp Stn
West Virginia. Geological and Economic Survey. Basic Data Report — W Va Geol Econ Surv Basic Data Rep
West Virginia. Geological and Economic Survey. Basic Data Report — West Virginia Geol and Econ Survey Basic Data Rept
West Virginia. Geological and Economic Survey. Bulletin — W Va Geol Econ Surv Bull
West Virginia. Geological and Economic Survey. Circular — West Virginia Geol and Econ Survey Circ
West Virginia. Geological and Economic Survey. Circular Series — W Va Geol Econ Surv Cir Ser
West Virginia. Geological and Economic Survey. Circular Series — W Va Geol Econ Surv Circ Ser
West Virginia. Geological and Economic Survey. Coal Geology Bulletin — W Va Geol Econ Surv Coal Geol Bull
West Virginia. Geological and Economic Survey. Environmental Geology Bulletin — W Va Geol Econ Surv Environ Geol Bull
West Virginia. Geological and Economic Survey. Mineral Resources Series — W Va Geol Econ Surv Miner Resour Ser
West Virginia. Geological and Economic Survey. Newsletter — W Va Geol Econ Surv Newsl
West Virginia. Geological and Economic Survey. Report of Archeological Investigations — W Va Geol Econ Surv Rep Archeol Invest
West Virginia. Geological and Economic Survey. Report of Investigations — W Va Geol Econ Surv Rep Invest
West Virginia. Geological and Economic Survey. River Basin Bulletin — W Va Geol Econ Surv River Basin Bull
West Virginia. Geological Survey — W Va G S
West Virginia. Geological Survey. Report of Investigations — W Va Geol Surv Rep Invest
West Virginia. Geological Survey. Reports — W Va Geol Surv Rep
West Virginia History — W Va His
West Virginia History — WesH
West Virginia History — West Virginia Hist
West Virginia History — WVaH
West Virginia History — WVH
West Virginia History. A Quarterly Magazine — W Va Hist
West Virginia Law Quarterly and the Bar — W Va Law Q
West Virginia Law Review — W Va L Rev
West Virginia Law Review — W Va Law R
West Virginia Law Review — W Va LR
West Virginia Law Review — West Virginia L Rev
West Virginia Law Review — WVL
West Virginia Law Review — WVLR
West Virginia Libraries — W Va Lib
West Virginia Libraries — W Va Libr
West Virginia Libraries — West Va Lib
West Virginia Medical Journal — W Va Med J
West Virginia Medical Journal — WV Med J
West Virginia Reports — W Va
West Virginia University. Agricultural and Forestry Experiment Station. Current Report — CRWSD4
West Virginia University. Agricultural and Forestry Experiment Station. Current Report — W Va Univ Agric For Exp Stn Curr Rep
West Virginia University. Agricultural Experiment Station. Bulletin — W Va Univ Agri Exp Stn Bull
West Virginia University. Agricultural Experiment Station. Current Report — W Va Univ Agric Exp Stn Curr Rep
West Virginia University. Agricultural Experiment Station. Current Report — WVARAY
West Virginia University. Agriculture and Forestry Experiment Station. Miscellaneous Publication — MPWSEX
West Virginia University. Agriculture and Forestry Experiment Station. Miscellaneous Publication — WV Univ Agric For Exp Stn Misc Publ
West Virginia University. Bulletin. Philological Studies — WVUBPL
West Virginia University. Bulletin. Proceedings. Annual Appalachian Gas Measurement Short Course — W Va Univ Bull Proc Annu Appalachian Gas Meas Short Course
West Virginia University. Business and Economic Studies — West Virginia Univ Bus Econ Stud
West Virginia University. Coal Research Bureau. School of Mines. Technical Report [*Morgantown, West Virginia*] — W Va Univ Coal Res Bur Sch Mines Tech Rep
West Virginia University. Coal Research Bureau. Technical Report — W Va Univ Coal Res Bur Tech Rep
West Virginia University. Engineering Experiment Station. Bulletin — W Va Univ Eng Exp Stn Bull
West Virginia University. Engineering Experiment Station. Research Bulletin — W Va Univ Eng Exp Stn Res Bull
West Virginia University. Engineering Experiment Station. Technical Bulletin — W Va Univ Eng Exp Sta Tech Bull
West Virginia University. Engineering Experiment Station. Technical Bulletin — W Va Univ Eng Exp Stn Tech Bull
West Virginia University. Philological Papers — W Va U Phil
West Virginia University. Philological Papers — WVUPP
West Virginia University. Report of the Board of Regents — W Va Univ Rp Bd Reg
West Vlaanderen Werkt — WVA
Westchester County Historical Society. Publications — Westchester Co Hist Soc Publ
Westchester Medical Bulletin [*New York*] — Westchester Med Bull
Westdeutsche Zeitschrift fuer Geschichte und Kunst — WdZ
Westdeutsche Zeitschrift fuer Geschichte und Kunst — Westd Zeit
Westdeutsche Zeitschrift fuer Geschichte und Kunst — Westd Zeit Gesch u Kunst
Westdeutsche Zeitschrift fuer Geschichte und Kunst — Westdt Zeitschr
Westdeutsche Zeitschrift fuer Geschichte und Kunst — WZGK
Westermanns Monatshefte — Westerm M
Westermanns Monatshefte — Westerm Monatsh
Westermanns Monatshefte — WM
Western American Literature — WAL
Western American Literature — West Am Lit
Western American Literature — Western Am Lit
Western Architect — W Arch
Western Association of Map Libraries. Information Bulletin — W Assn Map Lib Inf Bull
Western Association of Map Libraries. Information Bulletin — West Assn Map Libs Inf Bul
Western Australia. Department of Agriculture. Annual Report — West Aust Dep Agric Annu Rep
Western Australia. Department of Fisheries and Fauna. Report — West Aust Dep Fish Fauna Rep
Western Australia. Department of Fisheries and Wildlife. Report — West Aust Dep Fish Wildl Rep
Western Australia. Department of Industrial Development. Building Investment — West Aust Dep Ind Dev Build Invest
Western Australia. Department of Mines. Annual Report — West Aust Dep Mines Annu Rep
Western Australia. Department of Mines. Annual Report of the Geological Survey — Aust West Dep Mines Annu Rep Geol Surv
Western Australia. Department of Mines. Bulletin — Aust West Dep Mines Bull
Western Australia. Department of Mines. Mineral Resources of Western Australia. Bulletin — West Aust Dep Mines Min Resour West Aust Bull
Western Australia. Department of Mines. Mineral Resources of Western Australia. Bulletin — West Aust Dep Mines Miner Resour West Aust Bull
Western Australia. Department of Mines. Report of the Government Mineralogist, Analyst, and Chemist — West Aust Dep Mines Rep Gov Mineral Anal Chem
Western Australia. Egg Marketing Board. Newsletter — WA Egg Marketing Board Nletter
Western Australia Fisheries — West Aust Fish
Western Australia. Fisheries Department. Fisheries Research Bulletin — West Aust Fish Dep Fish Res Bull
Western Australia. Forests Department. Bulletin — W Aust For Dep Bull
Western Australia. Geological Survey. 1:250,000 Geological Series — W Aust Geol Surv 1:250000 Geol Ser
Western Australia. Geological Survey. 1:250,000 Geological Series — West Aust Geol Surv 1:250000 Geol Ser
Western Australia. Geological Survey. Annual Progress Report — West Aust Geol Surv Annu Prog Rep
Western Australia. Geological Survey. Annual Report — West Aust Geol Surv Annu Rep
Western Australia. Geological Survey. Bulletin — Aust West Geol Surv Bull

Western Australia. Geological Survey. Bulletin — Geol Surv West Aust Bull
Western Australia. Geological Survey. Bulletin — W Aust Geol Surv Bull
Western Australia. Geological Survey. Bulletin — West Aust Geol Surv Bull
Western Australia. Geological Survey. Geological Series. Explanatory Notes — West Aust Geol Surv Geol Ser Explan Notes
Western Australia. Geological Survey. Mineral Resources Bulletin — West Aust Geol Surv Miner Resour Bull
Western Australia. Geological Survey. Report — Rep Geol Surv West Aust
Western Australia. Geological Survey. Report — West Aust Geol Surv Rep
Western Australia. Geological Survey. Report. Government Printer — Western Australia Geol Survey Rept
Western Australia. Government Chemical Laboratories. Bulletin — Bull Gov Chem Lab West Aust
Western Australia. Government Chemical Laboratories. Bulletin — Bull Govt Chem Labs West Aust
Western Australia Government Gazette — WA Govt Gaz
Western Australia Government Gazette — WAGG
Western Australia. Main Roads Department. Technical Bulletin — Western Australia Main Roads Dep Tech Bull
Western Australia. Parliamentary Debates — WA Parl Deb
Western Australia. Report. Government Chemical Laboratories — West Aust Rep Gov Chem Lab
Western Australia SWANS [*State Wildlife Authority News Service*] — West Aust SWANS
Western Australia SWANS (State Wildlife Authority News Service) — West Aust SWANS (State Wildl Auth News Serv)
Western Australia University. Law Review — WAULR
Western Australia University. Law Review — West AULR
Western Australia Wildlife Research Centre. Wildlife Research Bulletin — West Aust Wildl Res Cent Wildl Res Bull
Western Australian Arbitration Reports — WA Arb R
Western Australian Arbitration Reports — WAAR
Western Australian Art Gallery. Bulletin — WA Art Gall Bull
Western Australian Clinical Reports — West Aust Clin Rep
Western Australian Conference. Australasian Institute of Mining and Metallurgy — West Aust Conf Australas Inst Min Metall
Western Australian Craftsman — WA Craftsman
Western Australian Fruitgrower — WA Fruitgrower
Western Australian Herbarium. Research Notes — West Aust Herb Res Notes
Western Australian Historical Society. Journal — WAHSJ
Western Australian Historical Society. Journal and Proceedings — J Proc W Aust Hist Soc
Western Australian Historical Society. Journal and Proceedings — WA Hist Soc J
Western Australian Industrial Gazette — W Austl Ind Gaz
Western Australian Industrial Gazette — WA Ind Gaz
Western Australian Industrial Gazette — WA Indus Gaz
Western Australian Industrial Gazette — WAIG
Western Australian Institute of Technology. Gazette — West Aust Inst Technol Gaz
Western Australian Law Reports — W Austl LR
Western Australian Law Reports — WALR
Western Australian Law Reports — West Austr L
Western Australian Marine Research Laboratories. Fisheries Research Bulletin — West Aust Mar Res Lab Fish Res Bull
Western Australian Museum. Special Publication — West Aust Mus Spec Publ
Western Australian Naturalist — W Aust Nat
Western Australian Naturalist — WA Nat
Western Australian Naturalist — WA Naturalist
Western Australian Naturalist — West Aust Nat
Western Australian Naturalist — West Aust Naturalist
Western Australian Nature Reserve Management Plan — West Aust Nat Reserve Manage Plan
Western Australian Nutgrowing Society. Yearbook — West Aust Nutgrow Soc Yearb
Western Australian Parent and Citizen — WA Parent & Cit
Western Australian Parent and Citizen — WA Parent & Citizen
Western Australian Reports — W Austl
Western Australian Reports — WAR
Western Australian Reports — West Austl
Western Australian School of Mines — West Aust Sch Mines
Western Australian Teachers' Journal — WA Teach J
Western Australian Teachers' Journal — WA Teachers J
Western Banker — WBK
Western Bird Bander — West Bird Bander
Western Birds — West Birds
Western Building [*United States*] — West Build
Western Business — West Bus
Western Business — Western Bs
Western Canada Beekeeper — West Can Beekpr
Western Canada Outdoors. Combining The Whooper and Defending All Outdoors — WCOD
Western Canada Water and Sewage Conference. Papers Presented at the Annual Convention — West Can Water Sewage Conf Pap Annu Conv
Western Canada Water and Sewage Conference. Proceedings of the Annual Convention — West Can Water and Sewage Conf Proc Annu Conv
Western Canadian Journal of Anthropology — WCJA
Western Canadian Journal of Anthropology — West Can J Anthropol
Western Canadian Journal of Anthropology — West Canad J Anthropol
Western Canadian Studies in Modern Languages and Literature — WCSMLL
Western Canner and Packer — West Canner Packer
Western Chapter. International Shade Tree Conference. Proceedings — West Chapter Int Shade Tree Conf Proc
Western Chemist and Metallurgist — West Chem Metall
Western City — West City
Western Construction — West Constr
Western Contractor — West Contract
Western Crops and Farm Management. Northern Edition — West Crop Farm Manage N Ed
Western Crops and Farm Management. Southern Edition — West Crop Farm Manage S Ed
Western Dental Society. Bulletin — West Dent Soc Bull
Western Druggist — West Drug
Western Economic Journal — W Econ J
Western Economic Journal — WEJ
Western Economic Journal — West Econ Jour
Western Electric Engineer — West Elec E
Western Electric Engineer — West Electr Eng
Western Electric Engineer — Western EE
Western Electric Engineer — Western Electric Eng
Western Engineering — Western Eng
Western European Education — W Europe Educ
Western European Education — West Europe Ed
Western Farmer — West Farmer
Western Feed — West Feed
Western Feed and Seed — West Feed Seed
Western Fire Journal — West Fire Jnl
Western Folklore — PWFK
Western Folklore — West Folk
Western Folklore — West Folkl
Western Folklore — WF
Western Foundation of Vertebrate Zoology. Occasional Papers — West Found Vertebr Zool Occas Pap
Western Frozen Foods — West Frozen Foods
Western Fruit Grower — West Fruit Grow
Western Gas — West Gas
Western Grower and Shipper — West Grow Ship
Western Historical Quarterly — PWHQ
Western Historical Quarterly — W Hist Q
Western Historical Quarterly — West Hist Q
Western Historical Quarterly — Western Hist Q
Western Historical Quarterly — WHQ
Western Horseman — West Horse
Western Horticultural Review — W Hort Rev
Western Humanities Review — West HR
Western Humanities Review — West Hum R
Western Humanities Review — West Hum Rev
Western Humanities Review — West Human Rev
Western Humanities Review — West Humanities Rev
Western Humanities Review — Western Hum R
Western Humanities Review — Western Hum Rev
Western Humanities Review — WHR
Western Humor and Irony Membership. Serial Yearbook [*Tempe, Arizona*] — WHIMSY
Western Illinois Regional Studies — WIRS
Western Information System for Energy Resources [*Database*] — WISER
Western Intelligence Report — WIR
Western Interstate Commission for Higher Education. Publications — WICHE Publ
Western Journal of Agricultural Economics — West J Agric Econ
Western Journal of Applied Forestry — West J Appl For
Western Journal of Medicine — West J Med
Western Journal of Medicine [*United States*] — WJMDA
Western Journal of Medicine and Surgery — West J Med Surg
Western Journal of Nursing Research — West J Nurs Res
Western Journal of Surgery, Obstetrics, and Gynecology — West J Surg
Western Journal of Surgery. Obstetrics and Gynecology — West J Surg Obstet Gynecol
Western Journal of Surgery, Obstetrics, and Gynecology — WJ Surg
Western Judean — WJ
Western Law Journal — West Law J
Western Law Journal — West LJ
Western Law Journal — WL Jour
Western Law Journal — WLJ
Western Law Journal (Ohio) — West LJ (Ohio)
Western Law Journal (Reprint) — West Law Jour
Western Law Journal (Reprint) — Western Law Jour
Western Legal Publications Database — WLP
Western Literary Journal — West Lit J
Western Livestock Journal — West Livestock J
Western Locker — West Locker
Western Machinery and Steel World — West Mach Steel World
Western Mail — W Mail
Western Mail [*British*] — WTM
Western Mail Annual — W Mail Ann
(Western Mail) Countryman's Magazine — Countryman's Mag
Western Massachusetts Business Journal — W Mass Bus
Western Medicine — West Med
Western Medicine — Western Med
Western Medicine; the Medical Journal of the West — West Med Med J West
Western Metals — West Met
Western Metalworking — West Metalwork
Western Miner — WEM
Western Miner — West Miner
Western Monthly Magazine — West M
Western Monthly Magazine and Literary Journal — W Monthly Mag
Western Monthly Review — West Mo R
Western Morning News [*United Kingdom*] — WMN
Western Naturalist — West Nat
Western New England Law Review — W N Eng LR

Western New England Law Review — W New Eng L Rev
Western New England Law Review — West New Engl L Rev
Western New York Magazine — West NY Mg
Western Oil Refining — West Oil Refin
Western Oil Reporter — West Oil Rep
Western Ontario Law Review — W Ont L Rev
Western Ontario Law Review — West Ont L Rev
Western Ontario Law Review — Western Ont L Rev
Western Paint Review — West Paint Rev
Western Pennsylvania Historical Magazine — W PA Hist Mag
Western Pennsylvania Historical Magazine — WesP
Western Pennsylvania Historical Magazine — West PA Hist Mag
Western Pennsylvania Historical Magazine — West Penn Hist Mag
Western Pennsylvania Historical Magazine — WPHM
Western Pennsylvania Hospital Medical Bulletin — West Penn Hosp Med Bull
Western Petroleum Refiners Association. Technical Publication — West Pet Refiners Assoc Tech Publ
Western Plastics — West Plast
Western Political Quarterly — PWPQ
Western Political Quarterly — W Pol Q
Western Political Quarterly — West Pol Q
Western Political Quarterly — West Polit Q
Western Political Quarterly — West Polit Quart
Western Political Quarterly — Western Pol Q
Western Political Quarterly — WPQ
Western Political Quarterly. University of Utah — UU/WPQ
Western Poultry Disease Conference — West Poult Dis Conf
Western Pulp and Paper — West Pulp Pap
Western Region Extension Publication. Cooperative Extension. United States Department of Agriculture — West Reg Ext Publ Co-Op Ext US Dep Ag
Western Regional Publication. Colorado State University. Experiment Station — West Reg Pub Colo St Univ Exp Stn
Western Regional Symposium on Mining and Mineral Processing Wastes — West Reg Symp Min Miner Process Wastes
Western Reserve Business Review — Western Res
Western Reserve Historical Society. Tracts — Western Reserve Hist Soc Tracts
Western Reserve Law Review — W Res L Rev
Western Reserve Law Review — West Res L Rev
Western Reserve Law Review — West Res Law Rev
Western Reserve Law Review — West Reserve Law Rev
Western Reserve Law Review — Western Res L Rev
Western Reserve University. Bulletin — WRU
Western Resources Conference — West Resour Conf
Western Review — West R
Western Review — WR
Western Review of Science and Industry — Western Rv Sc
Western Roads — West Roads
Western School Law Digest — West Sch Law Dig
Western Shade Tree Conference. Proceedings of the Annual Meeting — West Shade Tree Conf Proc Annu Meet
Western Snow Conference. Proceedings — WSC
Western Society of Engineers. Journal — W Soc E J
Western Society of Engineers. Journal — West Soc Eng J
Western Society of Malacologists. Annual Report — West Soc Malacol Annu Rep
Western Society of Malacologists. Occasional Paper — West Soc Malacol Occas Pap
Western Speech — WS
Western Speleological Institute. Bulletin — Western Speleol Inst Bull
Western State University. Law Review — W St UL Rev
Western State University. Law Review — West St U L Rev
Western State University. Law Review — West St U LR
Western State University. Law Review — West State UL Rev
Western States Jewish Historical Quarterly — West States Jew Hist Q
Western States Jewish Historical Quarterly — WSJHQ
Western States Section. Combustion Institute. Paper — West States Sect Combust Inst Pap
Western States Section. Combustion Institute. Paper [*United States*] — WSCPA
Western Teacher — West Teach
Western Texas Today — West Tex Today
Western Trees, Parks, and Forests — W Trees
Western Union Technical Review — West Union Tech Rev
Western Veterinarian — West Vet
Western Washington Agricultural Experiment Station. Monthly Bulletin — Western Wash Ag Exp B
Western Weekly Reports [*Database*] — WWR
Western Wildlands — West Wildlands
Western Writers Series — WWS
West-European Symposia on Clinical Chemistry — West-Eur Symp Clin Chem
Westfaelische Bienenzeitung — Westf Bienenztg
Westfaelische Bienenzeitung — Westfael Bienenztg
Westfaelische Forschungen — WF
Westfaelische Zeitschrift — WZ
Westfaelischer Anzeiger, oder Vaterlaendisches Archiv zur Befoerderung und Verbreitung des Guten und Nuetzlichen — Westfael Anz
Westfriesch Jaarboek — Westfriesch Jb
West-Frieslands Oud en Nieuw — WFON
West-Indische Gids — WIG
Westinghouse Engineer — Westinghouse Eng
Westinghouse Engineer — Westinghouse Engr
Westminister Institute Review — Westminster Inst Rev
Westminister Review — Westmin R
Westminster Review — W
Westminster Review — West Rev
Westminster Review — Westm
Westminster Review (London) — WRL
Westminster Studies in Education — Westminster Stud Educ
Westminster Theological Journal — W Th J
Westminster Theological Journal — West Th J
Westminster Theological Journal — Westm Th J
Westminster Theological Journal [*Philadelphia*] — WestTJ
Westminster Theological Journal — WTJ
West-Ost-Journal — WEO
Westpreussen-Jahrbuch — Westpreuss Jb
Westpreussischer Geschichtsverein. Zeitschrift — Westpr Geschichtsv Ztsch
West's Annotated California Code — Cal Code (West)
West's Annotated Indiana Code — Ind Code Ann (West)
West's California Reporter — Cal Rptr
West's Louisiana Civil Code, Annotated — LA Civ Code Ann (West)
West's Louisiana Code of Civil Procedure, Annotated — LA Code Civ Proc Ann (West)
West's Louisiana Code of Criminal Procedure, Annotated — LA Code Crim Proc Ann (West)
West's Louisiana Code of Juvenile Procedure, Annotated — LA Code Juv Proc Ann (West)
West's Louisiana Revised Statutes Annotated — La Rev Stat Ann (West)
West's New York Supplement — NYS
West's New York Supplement. Second Series — NYS 2d
West's Wisconsin Statutes Annotated — Wis Stat Ann (West)
Wet Ground Mica Association, Incorporated. Technical Bulletin — Wet Ground Mica Assoc Inc Tech Bull
Wetboek der Zegelrechten — W Zegel
Wetboek van Burgerlijk Procesrecht — W v B Pr
Wetboek van Burgerlijke Rechtsvordering — W v B Rv
Wetboek van de Inkomstenbelastingen — WIB
Wetboek van de met het Zegel Gelijkgestelde Taksen — W Taksen
Wetboek van Koophandel — W v K
Wetboek van Militair Strafrecht — W v M S
Wetboek van Militair Strafrecht — W v M Sr
Wetboek van Registratierechten — W Reg R
Wetboek van Strafrecht — S
Wetboek van Strafrecht — W v S
Wetboek van Strafrecht — W v Sr
Wetboek van Strafrecht — W v Str
Wetboek van Strafvordering — W v Sv
Wetboek van Successierechten — W Succ R
Wetboek voor het Koninkrijk Holland — W v K H
Wetenschap en Samenleving — Wet Samenleving
Wetenschappelijke Mededeling KNNV [*Koninklijke Nederlandse Natuurhistorische Vereniging*] — Wet Meded KNNV
Wetenschappelijke Tijdingen — WT
Wetenschappelijke Tijdingen. Vereniging voor Wetenschapp de Gent — Wet Tijd
Wetenschapsbeleid — WIB
Wetenskaplike Bydraes van die PU [*Potchefstroomse Universiteit*] **vir CHO . Reeks B: Natuurwetenskappe** [*Christelike Hoere Onderwys*] — Wet Bydraes PU CHO Reeks B Natuurwet
Wetenskaplike Studiereeks — Wetenskap Studiereeks
Wetter und Leben — Wett Leben
Wetterauer Geschichtsblaetter — Wett Gesch Bl
Wetterauer Geschichtsblaetter — WGBl
Weurman Symposium — Weurman Symp
Weyerhaeuser Science Symposium — Weyerhauser Sci Symp
Weyerhauser Forestry Paper — Weyerhauser For Pap
WFS (World Fertility Survey) Comparative Studies — WFS (World Fertil Surv) Comp Stud
Wharton Annual — Whartn Ann
Wharton Magazine — Whartn Mag
Wharton Magazine — Wharton
Wharton Magazine — Wharton M
Wharton Magazine — Wharton Mag
Wharton Quarterly — Wharton Q
What Acronym's That — WAT
What's New in Advertising and Marketing — Whats New
What's New in Building — Whats New Bldg
What's New in Computing — What's New Comput
What's New in Crops and Soils — Whats New Crops Soils
What's New in Forest Research — Whats New in For Res
What's New in Home Economics — Whats New Home Econ
What's New in Plant Physiology — Whats New Plant Physiol
What's New in Travel [*Database*] — WNT
Wheat Board Gazette — Wheat Board Gaz
Wheat Information Service — Wheat Inf Serv
Wheat Information Service — Wheat Inform Serv
Wheat Situation. Bureau of Agricultural Economics (Australia) — Wheat Situation Bur Agr Econ (Aust)
Wheat Studies. Food Research Institute — Wheat Stud Food Res Inst
Wheel Extended — WHEE
Wheel Extended — Wheel Ext
Where to Find Out More about Education — Where to Find Out More about Educ
Whetstone — Whet
Which — WHB
Which Computer — Which Comput
Which Word Processor — Which Word Process
Which Word Processor and Office System — Which Word Process and Off Syst
Whitaker's Books in Print [*Database*] — WBIP
Whitaker's Books in Print — WBP
White Cloud Journal of American Indian/Alaska Native Mental Health — WCJ
White Metal News Letter — White Met News Lett
White Paper of Japanese Economy [*English Edition*] — Japan Econ

Whitehorse Star — W
Whitman Numismatic Journal — WNJ
Whittier Law Review — Whitt L Rev
Whittier Law Review — Whittier L Rev
WHO [*World Health Organization*] **Chronicle** — WHO Chron
WHO [*World Health Organization*] **Environmental Health** — WHO Environ Health
WHO [*World Health Organization*] **Food Additives Series** — WHO Food Addit Ser
WHO [*World Health Organization*] **History of International Public Health** — WHO Hist Int Public Health
WHO [*World Health Organization*] **Library News** — WHO Libr Ne
WHO [*World Health Organization*] **Offset Publication** — WHO Offset Publ
WHO [*World Health Organization*] **Pesticide Residues Series** — WHO Pestic Residues Ser
WHO [*World Health Organization*] **Public Health Papers** — WHO Publ Hlth Pap
WHO [*World Health Organization*] **Publications** — WHO Publ
Whole Earth Catalog — WEC
Whole Earth Review — IWER
Wholesale Prices and Price Indexes. Supplement. US Bureau of Labor Statistics — BLS Whole A
Wholesale Prices and Price Indexes. US Bureau of Labor Statistics — BLS Whole
Who's Who in Germany — WWG
Who's Who in Israel — WWI
Who's Who in Japan — WWJ
Who's Who in Malaysia and Singapore — WWMS
Wiadomosci — WI
Wiadomosci Archeologiczne. Bulletin Archeologique Polonias — Wiad A
Wiadomosci Archeologicznne — W Arch
Wiadomosci Archeologicznne — WA
Wiadomosci Archeologicznne — Wiad
Wiadomosci Archeologicznne — Wiadom Arch
Wiadomosci Botaniczne — Wiad Bot
Wiadomosci Chemiczne — Wiad Chem
Wiadomosci Ekologiczne — WEKLA
Wiadomosci Ekologiczne — Wiad Ekol
Wiadomosci Elektrotechniczne — Wiad Elektrotech
Wiadomosci Gornicze [*Poland*] — Wiad Gorn
Wiadomosci Historyczne — Wiad Hist
Wiadomosci Hutnicze — Wiad Hutn
Wiadomosci. Instytut Melioracji i Uzytkow Zielonych (Warsaw) — Wiad Inst Melior Uzytkow Zielon (Warsaw)
Wiadomosci Lekarskie — Wiad Lek
Wiadomosci Matematyczne — Wiad Mat
Wiadomosci Matematyczne — Wiadom Mat
Wiadomosci Melioracyjne i Lakarskie — Wiad Melior Lak
Wiadomosci Melioracyjne i Lakarskie — Wiad Melior Lakarsk
Wiadomosci Meteorologii i Gospodarki Wodnej — Wiad Meteorol Gospod Wodnej
Wiadomosci Naftowe — Wiad Naft
Wiadomosci Numizmatyczne — WN
Wiadomosci Numizmatyczno-Archeologiczne [*Later, Wiadomosci Numizmatyczne*] — Wiad Num Arch
Wiadomosci Numizmatyczno-Archeologiczne — WNA
Wiadomosci Parazytologiczne — Wiad Parazyt
Wiadomosci Parazytologiczne — Wiad Parazytol
Wiadomosci Sluzby Hydrologicznej i Meteorologicznej — Wiad St Hydrol Met
Wiadomosci Statystyczne — Wiad Stat
Wiadomosci Statystyczne — Wiadom Statyst
Wiadomosci Telekomunikacyjne — Wiad Telekomun
Wiadomosci Zielarskie — Wiad Zielarskie
Wichita Eagle-Beacon — Wichita Eag
Wickelmannsprogramm der Archaeologischen Gesellschaft zu Berlin — B W Pr
Wide World Magazine — Wide World M
Wide World Magazine — WWM
Wieczory Teatralne — WT
Wiederbelebung. Organersatz. Intensivmedizin — Wiederbeleb Organersatz Intensivmed
Wiederherstellungschirurgie und Traumatologie — Wiederherstellungschir Traumatol
Wiedza i Zycie — WiZ
Wiedza i Zycie — WZ
Wiedza Powszechna — WP
Wien Naturhistorischer Museum. Annalen — Wien Naturh Mus Annalen
Wiener Arbeiten zur Deutschen Literatur — WADL
Wiener Archiv fuer Geschichte des Slawentums und Osteuropas — WAGSO
Wiener Archiv fuer Geschichte des Slawentums und Osteuropas — Wiener Arch Gesch Slawentum Osteur
Wiener Archiv fuer Innere Medizin — Wien Arch Innere Med
Wiener Archiv fuer Psychologie, Psychiatrie, und Neurologie — Wien Arch Psychol Psychiat Neurol
Wiener Beitraege zur Chirurgie — Wien Beitr Chir
Wiener Beitraege zur Englischen Philologie — WBEP
Wiener Beitraege zur Englischen Philologie — Wien Beitr
Wiener Beitraege zur Geschichte der Medizin — Wien Beitr Gesch Med
Wiener Beitraege zur Kulturgeschichte und Linguistik — WBKL
Wiener Blaetter fuer die Freunde der Antike — W Bl FA
Wiener Blaetter fuer die Freunde der Antike — WB
Wiener Botanische Zeitschrift — Wiener Bot Z
Wiener Byzantinistische Studien — W Byz St
Wiener Byzantinistische Studien — WBS
Wiener Chemiker Zeitung — Wien Chem Ztg
Wiener Entomologische Monatsschrift — Wien Entom Monatschr
Wiener Entomologische Rundschau — Wien Ent Rd
Wiener Ethnohistorische Blaetter — Wiener Ethnohist Bl
Wiener Geschichtsblaetter — Wien Geschichtsbl
Wiener Geschichtsblaetter — WiG
Wiener Humanistische Blaetter — WH Bl
Wiener Humanistische Blaetter — WHB
Wiener Jahrbuch fuer Kunstgeschichte — Wien Jahrb Kunstgesch
Wiener Jahrbuch fuer Kunstgeschichte — WJ f Kg
Wiener Jahrbuch fuer Kunstgeschichte — WJK
Wiener Jahrbuch fuer Kunstgeschichte — WJKG
Wiener Jahrbuch fuer Philosophie — Wiener Jahrb Phil
Wiener Jahreshefte — WJ
Wiener Jahreshefte — WJh
Wiener Juristische Blaetter — WJ Bl
Wiener Klinische Wochenschrift — W Kl Ws
Wiener Klinische Wochenschrift — W Klin Wschr
Wiener Klinische Wochenschrift — Wien Klin W
Wiener Klinische Wochenschrift — Wien Klin Wochenschr
Wiener Klinische Wochenschrift — Wien Klin Ws
Wiener Klinische Wochenschrift. Supplementum — Wien Klin Wochenschr Suppl
Wiener Klinische Wochenschrift. Supplementum (Austria) — WKWSA
Wiener Landwirtschaftliche Zeitung — Wien Landwirtsch Ztg
Wiener Library Bulletin — Wiener Libr Bull
Wiener Library Bulletin [*London*] — WLB
Wiener Linguistische Gazette — WLG
Wiener Medizinische Presse — Wien Med Presse
Wiener Medizinische Wochenschrift — Wien Med Wochenschr
Wiener Medizinische Wochenschrift — Wien Med Ws
Wiener Medizinische Wochenschrift — Wien Med Wschr
Wiener Medizinische Wochenschrift — WMWOA
Wiener Medizinische Wochenschrift (Beihefte) — Wien Med Wochenschr (Beih)
Wiener Medizinische Wochenschrift. Supplementum — Wien Med Wochenschr Suppl
Wiener Mitteilungen Photographischen Inhalts — Wien Mitt Photogr Inhalts
Wiener Mitteilungen. Wasser, Abwaesser, Gewaesser — Wien Mitt Wasser Abwasser Gewaesser
Wiener Moden-Zeitung und Zeitschrift fuer Kunst, Schoene Litteratur und Theater — Wiener Moden Zeitung Z Kunst
Wiener Pharmazeutische Wochenschrift — Wien Pharm Wochenschr
Wiener Praehistorische Zeitschrift — Wien Praeh Z
Wiener Praehistorische Zeitschrift [*Austria*] — Wien Praehist Z
Wiener Praehistorische Zeitschrift — WPZ
Wiener Slavistisches Jahrbuch — Wiener Slavist Jb
Wiener Slawistischer Almanach — W Sl A
Wiener Slawistisches Jahrbuch — WSJ
Wiener Slawistisches Jahrbuch — WSLJb
Wiener Studien — W St
Wiener Studien — Wiener Stud
Wiener Studien — WS
Wiener Studien. Zeitschrift fuer Klassische Philologie — W Studien
Wiener Studien. Zeitschrift fuer Klassische Philologie — Wien Stud
Wiener Studien. Zeitschrift fuer Klassische Philologie — Wien Stud Z Klass Philol
Wiener Studien. Zeitschrift fuer Klassische Philologie — Wiener St
Wiener Tieraerztliche Monatsschrift — Wien Tieraerztl Monatsschr
Wiener Tieraerztliche Monatsschrift — Wien Tieraerztl Mschr
Wiener Voelkerkundliche Mitteilungen — Wien Voelkerk Mitt
Wiener Voelkerkundliche Mitteilungen — Wiener Voelkerk Mitt
Wiener Voelkerkundliche Mitteilungen — Wiener Voelkerkundliche Mitt
Wiener Voelkerkundliche Mitteilungen — WVM
Wiener Vorlegeblaetter fuer Archaeologische Uebungen — Wiener Vorl Bl
Wiener Vorlegeblaetter fuer Archaeologische Uebungen — WV
Wiener Zeitschrift fuer die Kunde des Morgenlandes — W Z Morg
Wiener Zeitschrift fuer die Kunde des Morgenlandes — Wien Z Kunde Morgenlandes
Wiener Zeitschrift fuer die Kunde des Morgenlandes — Wien Zts Morg
Wiener Zeitschrift fuer die Kunde des Morgenlandes — Wiener Z Kde Morgenl
Wiener Zeitschrift fuer die Kunde des Morgenlandes — WZKM
Wiener Zeitschrift fuer die Kunde des Morgenlandes — WZM
Wiener Zeitschrift fuer die Kunde Sued- und Ostasiens und Archiv fuer Indische Philosophie — Wien Z Kunde Sued Ostasiens
Wiener Zeitschrift fuer die Kunde Sued- und Ostasiens und Archiv fuer Indische Philosophie — WZKSO
Wiener Zeitschrift fuer die Kunde Suedasiens und Archiv fuer Indische Philosophie [*Vienna*] — Wiener Z Kunde Sud
Wiener Zeitschrift fuer die Kunde Suedasiens und Archiv fuer Indische Philosophie — Wiener Z Kunde Suedasiens
Wiener Zeitschrift fuer die Kunde Suedasiens und Archiv fuer Indische Philosophie — WZKS
Wiener Zeitschrift fuer Innere Medizin und Ihre Grenzgebiete — Wien Z Inn Med Ihre Grenzgeb
Wiener Zeitschrift fuer Innere Medizin und Ihre Grenzgebiete — Wien Zs Inn Med
Wiener Zeitschrift fuer Nervenheilkunde und Deren Grenzgebiete [*Austria*] — Wien Z Nervenheilk Grenzgeb
Wiener Zeitschrift fuer Nervenheilkunde und deren Grenzgebiete — Wien Z Nervenheilkd
Wiener Zeitschrift fuer Nervenheilkunde und Deren Grenzgebiete — WZNDA
Wiener Zeitschrift fuer Volkskunde — WZV
Wiener Zeitung — Wien Zt
Wiez — Wi
Wijsgerig Perspectief op Maatschappij en Wetenschap — Wijsgerig Perspect Maatsch Wet
Wijsgerig Perspectief op Maatschappij en Wetenschap — Wijsig Perspect
Wild Barfield Heat-Treatment Journal — Wild Barfield Heat-Treat J
Wild Barfield Journal — Wild Barfield J
Wild Cat Monthly — Wild Cat
Wild Life Review — Wild Life Rev

Wildenowia Beiheft — Wildenowia Beih
Wilderness — GWIL
Wilderness Alberta — WIAB
Wilderness Camping — Wild Camp
Wildfire Statistics. United States Department of Agriculture. Forest Service — Wildfire Stat US Dep Agric For Serv
Wildfowl — WIFO
Wildlife Disease Association. Bulletin — Wildl Dis Assoc Bull
Wildlife Diseases — Wildl Dis
Wildlife in Australia — Wildl Aust
Wildlife in Australia — Wildlife
Wildlife in Australia — Wildlife A
Wildlife in Australia — Wildlife Aust
Wildlife Management Bulletin (Ottawa). Series 1 — Wildl Manage Bull (Ottawa) Ser 1
Wildlife Management Bulletin (Ottawa). Series 2 — Wildl Manage Bull (Ottawa) Ser 2
Wildlife Management News (Iceland) — WMNI
Wildlife Monographs — Wildl Monogr
Wildlife Monographs — WILM
Wildlife News — WILN
Wildlife Publications Review — Wildlife Publ Rev
Wildlife Research — Wildlif Res
Wildlife Research Quarterly — Wildl Res Q
Wildlife Review — Wildl Rev
Wildlife Review — Wildlife R
Wildlife Review. British Columbia Ministry of Environment — WIRE
Wildlife Review. New Zealand Wildlife Service — Wildl Rev NZ Wildl Serv
Wildlife Society Bulletin — Wildl SB
Wildlife Society. Bulletin — Wildl Soc Bull
Wildlife Society. Bulletin — WISB
Wildlife Society. Bulletin — WLSBA
Wildlife Working Group. Newsletter — WWGN
Wildlife-Wildlands Institute. Monograph — Wildl Wildlands Inst Monogr
Wiley Classics Library — Wiley Classics Lib
Wiley/Gauthier-Villars Series in Modern Applied Mathematics — Wiley Gauthier Villars Ser Modern Appl Math
Wiley Professional Computing — Wiley Prof Comput
Wiley Publication in Mathematical Statistics — Wiley Pub Math Statist
Wiley Series in Beam Physics and Accelerator Technology — Wiley Ser Beam Phys Accel Tech
Wiley Series in Computing — Wiley Ser Comput
Wiley Series in Nonlinear Science — Wiley Ser Nonlinear Sci
Wiley Series in Numerical Methods in Engineering — Wiley Ser Numer Methods Engrg
Wiley Series in Probability and Mathematical Statistics — Wiley Ser Probab Math Statist
Wiley Series in Probability and Mathematical Statistics. Applied Probability and Statistics — Wiley Ser Probab Math Statist Appl Probab Statist
Wiley Series in Probability and Mathematical Statistics. Probability and Mathematical Statistics — Wiley Ser Probab Math Statist Probab Math Statist
Wiley Series in Probability and Mathematical Statistics. Tracts on Probability and Statistics — Wiley Ser Probab Math Statist Tracts Probab Statist
Wiley Series in Probability and Statistics. Probability and Statistics — Wiley Ser Probab Statist Probab Statist
Wiley Series in Pure and Applied Optics — Wiley Ser Pure Appl Optics
Wiley Series on Current Topics in Reproductive Endocrinology — Wiley Ser Curr Top Reprod Endocrinol
Wiley-Interscience Librarian's Newsletter — Wiley Lib Newsl
Wiley-Interscience Publication — Wiley Intersci Publ
Wiley-Interscience Series in Discrete Mathematics — Wiley Intersci Ser Discrete Math
Wiley-Interscience Series in Discrete Mathematics and Optimization — Wiley Intersci Ser Discrete Math Optim
Wiley-Interscience Series in Systems and Optimization — Wiley Intersci Ser Systems Optim
Wiley-Tuebner Series in Computer Science — Wiley Teubner Ser Comput Sci
Wilhelm Roux' Archiv fuer Entwicklungsmechanik der Organismen [*Later, Roux' Archives of Developmental Biology*] — Wilhelm Roux' Arch
Wilhelm Roux' Archiv fuer Entwicklungsmechanik der Organismen [*Later, Roux' Archives of Developmental Biology*] — Wilhelm Roux' Arch Entwicklungsmech Org
Wilhelm Roux' Archiv fuer Entwicklungsmechanik der Organismen — Wilhelm Roux Arch EntwMech Org
Wilhelm Roux' Archives of Developmental Biology — W Roux A DB
Wilhelm Roux' Archives of Developmental Biology — Wilhelm Roux' Arch Dev Biol
Wilhelm Roux' Archives of Developmental Biology — WRABD
Wilhelm-Pieck-Universitaet Rostock. Wissenschaftliche Zeitschrift. Mathematisch-Naturwissenschaftliche Reihe — Wilhelm-Pieck Univ Rostock Wiss Z Math Naturwiss Reihe
Wilhelm-Pieck-Universitaet Rostock. Wissenschaftliche Zeitschrift. Naturwissenschaftliche Reihe — Wilhelm Pieck Univ Rostock Wiss Z Naturwiss Reihe
Willamette Law Journal — Will LJ
Willamette Law Journal — Willamette L J
Willamette Law Journal — WL Jour
Willamette Law Journal — Wm LJ
Willamette Law Journal — WML
Willamette Law Review — Will LR
Willamette Law Review — Willamette L Rev
Wildenowia Beiheft — Willdenowia Beih
Wille und Macht — Wille U Macht
Willett House Quarterly — Willett House Q
William and Mary Business Review — William and Mary Bus R
William and Mary College Quarterly — William Mary Q
William and Mary College. Quarterly — WMCQ
William and Mary Law Review — W & M
William and Mary Law Review — W & M L Rev
William and Mary Law Review — W and M LR
William and Mary Law Review — William & Mary L Rev
William and Mary Law Review — William and Mary Law R
William and Mary Law Review — Wm and Mary L Rev
William and Mary Law Review — WMLR
William and Mary Quarterly — PWMQ
William and Mary Quarterly — W & M Q
William and Mary Quarterly — William M Q
William and Mary Quarterly — William Mary Quart
William and Mary Quarterly — Wm & Mary Q
William and Mary Quarterly — Wm Mar Q
William and Mary Quarterly — WMQ
William Carlos Williams Newsletter — WCWN
William Carlos Williams Review — WCWR
William Carlos Williams Review — William Car
William Faulkner. Materials, Studies, and Criticism — WiF
William H. Roever Lectures in Geometry — William Roever Lectures Geom
William L. Hutcheson Memorial Forest. Bulletin — William L Hutcheson Mem For Bull
William Mitchell Law Review — William Mitchell L Rev
William Mitchell Law Review — Wm Mitchell L Rev
William Mitchell Law Review — WMLR
William Morris Society. Journal — WMSJ
Williston Basin Oil Review — Williston Basin Oil Rev
Wills, Estates, and Trust Service. Prentice-Hall — Wills Est & Tr Serv P-H
WILPF [*Women's International League for Peace and Freedom*]. New South Wales Branch. Monthly Bulletin — WILPFNSW Branch Monthly Bulletin
Wilson Bulletin — PWBU
Wilson Bulletin — Wilson B
Wilson Bulletin — Wilson Bull
Wilson Library Bulletin — IWLB
Wilson Library Bulletin — Wilson Lib Bul
Wilson Library Bulletin — Wilson Lib Bull
Wilson Library Bulletin — Wilson Libr Bull
Wilson Library Bulletin — WLB
Wilson Library Bulletin — WLBu
Wilson Quarterly — PWBQ
Wilson Quarterly — Wil Q
Wilson Quarterly — Wilson
Wilson Quarterly — Wilson Q
Wilson Quarterly — Wilson Quart
Wilson Quarterly — WIQUD
Wilson Quarterly — WQ
Wiltshire Archaeological and Natural History Magazine — WAM
Wiltshire Archaeological and Natural History Magazine — Wilt A Nat Hist Mag
Wiltshire Archaeological and Natural History Magazine — Wilts Arch Natur Hist Mag
Wiltshire Archaeological and Natural History Magazine — Wilts Mag
Wiltshire Archaeological and Natural History Magazine — Wiltshire Arch Natur Hist Mag
Wiltshire Archaeological and Natural History Magazine — Wiltshire Archaeol Natur Hist Mag
Wiltshire Archaeological Magazine [*Later, Wiltshire Archaeological and Natural History Magazine*] — WAM
Wiltshire Archaeological Magazine [*Later, Wiltshire Archaeological and Natural History Magazine*] — Wiltshire Arch Mag
Wiltshire Beekeepers' Gazette — Wilts Beekprs Gaz
Win Magazine — Win
Winckelmannsprogramm der Archaeologischen Gesellschaft zu Berlin — WAGB
Winckelmannsprogramm der Archaeologischen Gesellschaft zu Berlin — Winck Progr
Wind Energy Report — WIERD
Wind Energy Report — Wind En Rpt
Wind Energy Report [*United States*] — Wind Energy Rep
Wind Engineering [*England*] — Wind Eng
Wind Engineering — Wind Engng
Wind Power Digest — Wind Power Dig
Wind Quarterly — WQ
Wind Technology Journal — Wind Technol J
Windless Orchard — Wind O
Windomosci Instytutu Melioracji i Uzytkow Zielonych — Wind Inst Melior Uzytkow Zielonych
Windomosci Muzeum Ziemi — Wind Muz Ziemi
Window — WW
Window Industries — Window Inds
Windsor Magazine — Windsor
Windsor Report — Windsor R
Windsor Yearbook of Access to Justice — Windsor Yearb Access
Windspeaker — WS
Wine and Spirit — WST
Wine Marketing Handbook — Wine Hdbk
Wine Marketing Handbook — WMH
Wine Review — Wine Rev
Wine Spectator — IWIN
Wines and Vines Statistical Issue — Wine Vine
Winesburg Eagle — WE
Wing Newsletter — Wing
Wings over Africa — Wings Afr
Winnipeg Clinic. Quarterly — Winnip Clin Q
Winter — W

Winter — Win
Winter Cities Newsletter — WCNL
Winter Meeting on Statistical Physics — Winter Meet Stat Phys
Winter Soldier — Wntr Sldr
Winter's Digest — WD
Winter's Naturwissenschaftliche Taschenbuecher — Winter Tb
Wintertagung — Wintertag
Winterthur Jahrbuch — Winterthur Jb
Winterthur Jahrbuch — WJ
Winterthur Portfolio — Wih
Winterthur Portfolio — Winterthur
Winterthur Portfolio — Winterthur Port
Winthrop Studies on Major Modern Writers — Winthr St M
Wirbelsacule in Forschung und Praxis — Wirbelsacule Forsch Prax
Wire and Wire Products — Wire and Wire Prod
Wire and Wire Products — Wire Prod
Wire Industry — Wire Ind
Wire Journal — Wire J
Wire Journal International — Wire J Int
Wire Journal International — WJI
Wire Technology — Wire Technol
Wire World International — Wire World Int
Wired Librarian's Newsletter — WLN
Wireless Engineer — Wireless Eng
Wireless World — Wirel Wld
Wireless World — Wirel World
Wiring Installations and Supplies — Wiring Install and Supplies
Wirkendes Wort — WW
Wirkerei und Strickerei Technik — Wirkerei Strickerei Tech
Wirkung der Literatur — Wdl
Wirtschaft in Zahlen — Wirt in Za
Wirtschaft und Gesellschaft — Wirt und Ges
Wirtschaft und Gesellschaft — Wirtsch u Ges
Wirtschaft und Investment — Wirt und Investment
Wirtschaft und Produktivitaet — RAQ
Wirtschaft und Recht — Wirt und Recht
Wirtschaft und Recht — Wirtsch u Recht
Wirtschaft und Recht. Zeitschrift fuer Wirtschaftspolitik und Wirtschaftsrecht mit Einschluss des Sozialrechtes und Arbeidsrechtes — WUR
Wirtschaft und Statistik — Wi Stat
Wirtschaft und Statistik — Wi u Stat
Wirtschaft und Statistik — Wirt und Statis
Wirtschaft und Statistik — Wirtsch Stat
Wirtschaft und Statistik — Wirtsch u Statist
Wirtschaft und Statistik — WUS
Wirtschaft und Verwaltung [*German Federal Republic*] — Wirtsch Verwalt
Wirtschaft und Wettbewerb [*German*] — W u W
Wirtschaft und Wettbewerb — Wirt und Wettbewerb
Wirtschaft und Wettbewerb [*Germany*] — Wirtsch Wettbewerb
Wirtschaft und Wettbewerb. Zeitschrift fuer Kartellrecht, Wettbewerbsrecht, Marktorganisation — WWW
Wirtschaft und Wissen — Wirt u Wiss
Wirtschaft und Wissenschaft — WWSCA
Wirtschaftliche Lage in der Bundesrepublik Deutschland — WIL
Wirtschaftlichkeit — MUK
Wirtschafts- und Sozialwissenschaftliches Institut. Mitteilungen — Wirt und Sozwiss Inst Mitt
Wirtschaftsbericht Lateinamerika — Wirtber Lateinam
Wirtschaftsbericht ueber die Lateinamerikanischen Laender sowie Spanien und Portugal — WirtBer Lateinam Laender sowie Spanien und Port
Wirtschafts-Blaetter — Wirtschaft
Wirtschaftsdienst — Wi Di
Wirtschaftsdienst — Wirt
Wirtschaftsdienst — Wirtsch-Dienst
Wirtschaftsdienst. Wirtschaftspolitische Monatsschrift — WSD
Wirtschaftseigene Futter — Wirt Futter
Wirtschaftseigene Futter — Wirtschseig Futter
Wirtschaftsgeographisches Institut — WGI
Wirtschaftskonjunktur — Wiko
Wirtschaftskonjunktur. Analysen, Perspektiven, Indikatoren — WIA
Wirtschaftspolitische Chronik — Wi Ch
Wirtschaftspolitische Chronik — Wirtsch Polit Chronik
Wirtschaftspolitische Chronik — Wirtschaftspol Chron
Wirtschafts-Praxis — Wi Pr
Wirtschaftspruefung — WPF
Wirtschaftsrechtliche Informations-Blaetter — WI Bl
Wirtschaftsschutz und Sicherheitstechnik — Sicherheit
Wirtschaftsspiegel — Wi Spieg
Wirtschaftsstrafgesetz — Wi St G
Wirtschaftsverwaltung — Wi Verw
Wirtschaftswissenschaft — Wi Wi
Wirtschaftswissenschaft — Wi Wiss
Wirtschaftswissenschaft — Wirtschaftswiss
Wirtschaftswissenschaft — Wirtsch-Wiss
Wirtschaftswissenschaft — WSW
Wirtschaftswissenschaftliche Beitraege — Wirtschaftswiss Beitr
Wirtschaftswissenschaftliches Institut Mitteilungen — Wirt Wiss Inst Mitt
Wirtschaftswissenschaftliches Studium — Wi St
Wirtschaftswoche — WFZ
Wirtschaftswoche — Wirtswoche
Wisconsin Academy of Sciences, Arts, and Letters — Wis Acad Sci Arts Lett
Wisconsin Academy of Sciences, Arts, and Letters. Transactions — Wis Acad of Sci Trans
Wisconsin Academy of Sciences, Arts, and Letters. Transactions — Wis Acad Sci Arts Letters Trans
Wisconsin Academy of Sciences, Arts, and Letters. Transactions — Wis Acad Sciences Trans
Wisconsin Academy of Sciences, Arts, and Letters. Transactions — Wisconsin Acad Sci Arts and Letters Trans
Wisconsin Academy of Sciences, Arts, and Letters. Transactions — Wisconsin Acad Sci Arts Lett Trans
Wisconsin Academy. Review — WAR
Wisconsin Administrative Code — Wis Admin Code
Wisconsin Administrative Register — Wis Admin Reg
Wisconsin. Agricultural Experiment Station. Bulletin — Wis Agric Exp Stn Bull
Wisconsin. Agricultural Experiment Station. Bulletin — Wisconsin Agric Exp Stn Bull
Wisconsin. Agricultural Experiment Station. Publications — Wis Ag Exp
Wisconsin. Agricultural Experiment Station. Research Bulletin — Wis Agric Exp Stn Res Bull
Wisconsin. Agricultural Experiment Station. Research Report — Wis Agric Exp Stn Res Rep
Wisconsin. Agricultural Experiment Station. Special Bulletin — Wis Agric Exp Stn Spec Bull
Wisconsin Alumni Magazine — Wis Alum M
Wisconsin Archaeologist — Wis Arch
Wisconsin Bar Bulletin — Wis B Bulletin
Wisconsin Beekeeping — Wis Beekeep
Wisconsin Business — Wisc Busn
Wisconsin College of Agricultural and Life Sciences. Research Division. Research Report — Wis Coll Agric Life Sci Res Div Res Rep
Wisconsin College of Agricultural and Life Sciences. Research Division. Science Report Bulletin — Wis Coll Agric Life Sci Res Div Sci Rep Bull
Wisconsin Conservation Bulletin — Wis Conserv Bull
Wisconsin Conservation Department. Technical Bulletin — Wis Conserv Dep Tech Bull
Wisconsin Dental Association. Journal — Wis Dent Assoc J
Wisconsin. Department of Agriculture. Publications — Wis Ag Dept
Wisconsin. Department of Natural Resources. Publication — Wis Dep Nat Resour Publ
Wisconsin. Department of Natural Resources. Technical Bulletin — Wis Dep Nat Resour Tech Bull
Wisconsin. Energy Extension Service. Agricultural-Energy Transportation Digest — Wis Energy Ext Serv Agric-Energy Transp Dig
Wisconsin Engineer — Wis Eng
Wisconsin Engineer — Wis Engineer
Wisconsin. Engineering Experiment Station. Reprint — Wis Eng Exp Stn Repr
Wisconsin English Language Survey — WELS
Wisconsin. Geological and Natural History Survey — Wis G S
Wisconsin. Geological and Natural History Survey. Bulletin — Wis Geol Nat Hist Surv Bull
Wisconsin. Geological Survey. Bulletin. Information Circular — Wis Geol Survey Bull Inf Circ
Wisconsin. Geological Survey. Geology of Wisconsin. Bulletin [*Later, Wisconsin Geological and Natural History Survey*] — Wis G S G Wis B
Wisconsin Historical Society. Proceedings — Wis His Proc
Wisconsin Horticulture — Wis Hort
Wisconsin Journal of Education — Wis J Ed
Wisconsin Law Review — WI Law Rev
Wisconsin Law Review — WI LR
Wisconsin Law Review — Wis L Rev
Wisconsin Law Review — Wis Law R
Wisconsin Law Review — Wis LR
Wisconsin Law Review — Wisc LR
Wisconsin Law Review — Wisconsin L Rev
Wisconsin Law Review — Wisconsin Law Rev
Wisconsin Law Review — WLR
Wisconsin Legislative Service — Wis Legis Serv
Wisconsin Library Bulletin — Wis Lib Bul
Wisconsin Library Bulletin — Wisc LB
Wisconsin Library Bulletin — Wisc Lib Bull
Wisconsin Library Bulletin — WLB
Wisconsin Magazine of History — WiM
Wisconsin Magazine of History — Wis M
Wisconsin Magazine of History — Wis M Hist
Wisconsin Magazine of History — Wis Mag Hist
Wisconsin Magazine of History — Wisc Mag Hist
Wisconsin Magazine of History — WMH
Wisconsin Medical Journal — Wis Med J
Wisconsin Medical Journal — Wisc Med J
Wisconsin Medical Journal — Wisconsin Med J
Wisconsin Medical Journal — Wisconsin MJ
Wisconsin Natural History Society. Bulletin — Wis N H Soc B
Wisconsin Natural Resources Bulletin — Wis Nat Resour Bull
Wisconsin Paper Industry. Information Service Newsletter — Wis Paper Ind Newsl
Wisconsin Pharmacist — Wis Pharm
Wisconsin. Pharmacy Extension Bulletin — Wis Pharm Ext Bull
Wisconsin Reports — Wis
Wisconsin School Musician — WI
Wisconsin State Agricultural Experiment Station. Research Report — Wisconsin Agric Exp Sta Res Rep
Wisconsin State Cartographer's Office. Information Circular — Wis State Cartogr Off Inf Circ
Wisconsin State Historical Society. Collections — Wis His Col
Wisconsin State Historical Society. Domesday Book — Wis His S Domesday Bk
Wisconsin State Historical Society. Proceedings — Wis Hist Soc Proc
Wisconsin Statutes — Wis Stat
Wisconsin Studies in Contemporary Literature [*Later, Contemporary Literature*] — Wis Stud Contemp Lit

Wisconsin Studies in Contemporary Literature [*Later, Contemporary Literature*] — WSCL
Wisconsin Studies in Literature — WisSL
Wisconsin Then and Now — WisT
Wisconsin University. College of Engineering. Engineering Experiment Station. Report — Wis Univ Coll Eng Eng Exp Stn Rep
Wisconsin University. Department of Meteorology. Report to the Lakes and Streams Investigations Committee — Wis Univ Dept Meteorology Rept Lakes and Streams Inv Comm
Wisconsin University. Engineering Experiment Station. Bulletin — Wis Univ Eng Exp Stn Bull
Wisconsin University. Geological and Natural History Survey. Information Circular — Wis Univ Geol Natur Hist Surv Inform Circ
Wisconsin University. Geological and Natural History Survey. Special Report — Wis Univ Geol Nat Hist Surv Spec Rep
Wisconsin's Badger Bee — Wis Badger Bee
Wiseman Review — Wise Rev
Wiseman Review — WiseR
Wiseman Review — WR
WiSo-Kurzlehrbuecher. Reihe Betriebswirtschaft — WiSo Kurzlehrbuecher Reihe Betriebswirtsch
Wissen und Glauben — W & G
Wissenschaft im 20. Jahrhunders. Transdisziplinaere Reflexionen — Wiss 20 Jhd Transdiszip Reflex
Wissenschaft und Fortschritt — Wiss Fortschr
Wissenschaft und Fortschritt — Wiss Fortschritt
Wissenschaft und Gegenwart — WG
Wissenschaft und Gegenwart — Wiss Geg
Wissenschaft und Gegenwart — WuG
Wissenschaft und Kultur — Wiss Kult
Wissenschaft und Praxis in Kirche und Gesellschaft — Wiss Prax Ki Ges
Wissenschaft und Umwelt ISU [*Interdisziplinaerer Sonderbereich Umweltschutz*] [*German Federal Republic*] — Wiss Umwelt ISU
Wissenschaft und Weisheit — Wiss Weis
Wissenschaft und Weisheit — WW
Wissenschaft und Weisheit — WWe
Wissenschaft und Weltbild — Wiss U Weltbild
Wissenschaft und Weltbild — Wiss Wb
Wissenschaft und Weltbild — Wiss Welt
Wissenschaft und Weltbild — Wiss Weltb
Wissenschaft und Weltbild — WuWelt
Wissenschaft, Wirtschaft, Politik — Wiss Wirtsch Polit
Wissenschaftliche Abhandlungen der Deutschen Akademie der Landwirtschaftswissenschaften zu Berlin — Wiss Abh Dtsch Akad Landwirtschaftswiss Berlin
Wissenschaftliche Abhandlungen der Deutschen Materialpruefungsanstalten — Wiss Abh Dtsch Materialpruefungsanst
Wissenschaftliche Abhandlungen der Physikalische-Technischen Reichsanstalt — WAPRA
Wissenschaftliche Abhandlungen der Physikalische-Technischen Reichsanstalt [*West Germany*] — Wiss Abh Phys-Tech Reichsanst
Wissenschaftliche Abhandlungen der Physikalisch-Technischen Bundesanstalt — Wiss Abh Phys-Tech Bd Anst
Wissenschaftliche Abhandlungen der Physikalisch-Technischen Reichsanstalt — Abh PTRA
Wissenschaftliche Abteilungen der Arbeitsgemeinschaft fuer Forschung des Landes Nordrhein-Westfalen — WAAFLN
Wissenschaftliche Abteilungen der Arbeitsgemeinschaft fuer Forschung des Landes Nordrhein-Westfalen — WAAFLNW
Wissenschaftliche Alpenvereinshefte — Wiss Alpenvereinshefte
Wissenschaftliche Annalen — WA
Wissenschaftliche Annalen — Wiss Ann
Wissenschaftliche Annalen. Deutsche Akademie — WADA
Wissenschaftliche Arbeiten der Forschungsanstalt fuer Forstwirtschaft in Zvolen — Wiss Arb Forschungsanst Forstwirtsch Zvolen
Wissenschaftliche Beitraege — Wissensch Beitr
Wissenschaftliche Beitraege. Ingenieurhochschule Zwickau [*German Democratic Republic*] — Wiss Beitr Ingenieurhochsch Zwickau
Wissenschaftliche Beitraege. Martin Luther Universitaet (Halle-Wittenberg) — Wiss Beitr Martin Luther Univ (Halle Wittenberg)
Wissenschaftliche Beitrage. Martin Luther Universitaet (Halle-Wittenberg) — Wiss Beitr Univ (Halle)
Wissenschaftliche Beitrage. Martin Luther Universitaet (Halle-Wittenberg). Reihe M — Wiss Beitr Martin Luther Univ (Halle Wittenberg) Reihe M
Wissenschaftliche Berichte AEG-Telefunken — Wiss Ber AEG-Telefunken
Wissenschaftliche Berichte aus der Hochmagnetfeldanlage. Physikalische Institute. Technische Universitaet Braunschweig — Wiss Ber HMFA Braunschweig
Wissenschaftliche Berichte EM — Wiss Ber EM
Wissenschaftliche Berichte. Forschungszentrum Karlsruhe — Wiss Ber Forschungszent Karlsruhe
Wissenschaftliche Berichte. Zentralinstitut fuer Festkoerperphysik und Werkstofforschung — Wiss Ber Zentralinst Festkoerperphys Werkstofforsch
Wissenschaftliche Buecherei — Wiss Buecherei
Wissenschaftliche Forschungsberichte. Naturwissenschaftliche Reihe — Wiss Forschungsber Naturwiss Reihe
Wissenschaftliche Information [*Karl-Marx-Stadt*] — Wissensch Inform
Wissenschaftliche Informationen und Berichte — Wissensch Inform Ber
Wissenschaftliche Konferenz. Gesellschaft Deutscher Naturforscher und Aerzte — Wiss Konf Ges Dtsch Naturforsch Aerzte
Wissenschaftliche Meeresuntersuchungen — Wissensch Meeresuntersuch
Wissenschaftliche Mitteilungen des Bosnisch-Herzegowinischen Landesmuseums A. Archaeologie — Wiss M Bosn
Wissenschaftliche Mitteilungen fuer Forst und Holzwirtschaft — Wiss Mitt Forst Holzwirtsch
Wissenschaftliche Mitteilungen. Historiker-Gesellschaft der DDR — Wiss Mitt Historiker-Ges DDR
Wissenschaftliche Mitteilungen. Pharmazeutisches Forschungs- und Fortbildungs Institut. Oesterreichischer Apotheker-Verein — Wiss Mitt Pharm Forsch Fortbild Inst Oesterr Apoth Ver
Wissenschaftliche Mittheilungen aus Bosnien und der Herzegowina — Mitt Bosnien
Wissenschaftliche Mittheilungen aus Bosnien und der Herzegowina — Wiss Mitt Bosn u Herzeg
Wissenschaftliche Mittheilungen aus Bosnien und der Herzegowina — WM
Wissenschaftliche Mittheilungen aus Bosnien und der Herzegowina — WMBH
Wissenschaftliche Mittheilungen der Physicalisch-Medicinischen Societaet zu Erlangen — Wiss Mitth Phys Med Soc Erlangen
Wissenschaftliche Monographien zum Alten und Neuen Testament — Wiss Mon ANT
Wissenschaftliche Monographien zum Alten und Neuen Testament — WMANT
Wissenschaftliche Schriftenreihe der Technischen Hochschule Karl-Marx-Stadt — Wiss Schr Tech Hochsch Karl Marx Stadt
Wissenschaftliche Schriftenreihe. Technische Hochschule Karl-Marx-Stadt — Wiss Schriftenr Tech Hochsch Karl-Marx-Stadt
Wissenschaftliche Sitzungen zur Stochastik 80 — Wissensch Sitzungen Stochastik 80
Wissenschaftliche Sitzungen zur Stochastik 81 — Wissensch Sitzungen Stochastik 81
Wissenschaftliche Sitzungen zur Stochastik 82 — Wissensch Sitzungen Stochastik 82
Wissenschaftliche Tagungen der Technischen Universitaet Karl-Marx-Stadt — Wiss Tag Tech Univ Karl Marx Stadt
Wissenschaftliche Taschenbuecher — Wiss Taschenb
Wissenschaftliche Taschenbuecher. Reihe Mathematik/Physik — Wissensch Taschenbuecher Reihe Math Phys
Wissenschaftliche Taschenbuecher. Reihe Texte und Studien — Wissensch Taschenbuecher Reihe Texte Stud
Wissenschaftliche Untersuchungen zum Neuen Testament — Wiss Unt NT
Wissenschaftliche Untersuchungen zum Neuen Testament — WUNT
Wissenschaftliche Veroeffentlichungen aus den Siemens-Werken — Wiss Veroeff Siemens-Werken
Wissenschaftliche Veroeffentlichungen der Deutschen Orientgesellschaft — DOGWV
Wissenschaftliche Veroeffentlichungen der Deutschen Orient-Gesellschaft — VDOG
Wissenschaftliche Veroeffentlichungen der Deutschen Orient-Gesellschaft — Wiss Veroeff DOG
Wissenschaftliche Veroeffentlichungen der Deutschen Orientgesellschaft — WVDO
Wissenschaftliche Veroeffentlichungen der Deutschen Orient-Gesellschaft — WVDOG
Wissenschaftliche Veroeffentlichungen des Deutschen Instituts fuer Laenderkunde — Wiss Veroeff Dt Inst Laenderkde
Wissenschaftliche Veroeffentlichungen. Technische Hochschule (Darmstadt) — Wiss Veroeff Tech Hochsch (Darmstadt)
Wissenschaftliche Zeitschrift — Wiss Z
Wissenschaftliche Zeitschrift. Bauhaus-Universitaet Weimar — Wiss Z Bauhaus Univ Weimar
Wissenschaftliche Zeitschrift der Brandenburgischen Landeshochschule — Wiss Z Brandenburg Landeshochsch
Wissenschaftliche Zeitschrift der Elektrotechnik — Wiss Z Elektrotech
Wissenschaftliche Zeitschrift der Ernst-Moritz-Arndt Universitaet Greifswald — WisZE
Wissenschaftliche Zeitschrift der Ernst-Moritz-Arndt-Universitaet Greifswald — Wiss Z Greifswald
Wissenschaftliche Zeitschrift der Ernst-Moritz-Arndt-Universitaet Greifswald. Mathematisch-Naturwissenschaftliche Reihe — Wiss Z Ernst Moritz Arndt Univ
Wissenschaftliche Zeitschrift der Friedrich-Schiller Universitaet Jena — WisZF
Wissenschaftliche Zeitschrift der Friedrich-Schiller-Universitaet. Gesellschafts- und Sprachwissenschaftliche Reihe — Wiss Z Friedrich Schiller Univ Ges Sprachwiss Reihe
Wissenschaftliche Zeitschrift der Friedrich-Schiller-Universitaet. Jena. Mathematisch-Naturwissenschaftliche Reihe — Wiss Z Friedrich Schiller Univ Jena
Wissenschaftliche Zeitschrift der Friedrich-Schiller-Universitaet. Jena. Naturwissenschaftliche Reihe — Wiss Z Friedrich Schiller Univ Jena
Wissenschaftliche Zeitschrift der Friedrich-Schiller-Universitaet. Reihe Gesellschaft und Sprachwissenschaften — Wiss Z Jena Reihe GS
Wissenschaftliche Zeitschrift der Hochschule fuer Architektur und Bauwesen Weimar. Reihe B — Wiss Z Hochsch Archit Bauwes Weimar Reihe B
Wissenschaftliche Zeitschrift der Hochschule fuer Oekonomie Berlin — Wiss Z Hochschule Oekon Berlin
Wissenschaftliche Zeitschrift der Humboldt Universitaet Berlin — WisZH
Wissenschaftliche Zeitschrift der Humboldt Universitaet zu Berlin. Mathematisch-Naturwissenschaftliche Reihe — Wiss Z Humboldt Univ Math Naturwiss Reihe
Wissenschaftliche Zeitschrift der Humboldt-Universitaet zu Berlin. Gesellschafts- und Sprachwissenschaftliche Reihe — Wiss Z Berlin
Wissenschaftliche Zeitschrift der Humboldt-Universitaet zu Berlin. Mathematisch- Naturwissenschaftliche Reihe — Wiss Z Humboldt Univ Berl Math
Wissenschaftliche Zeitschrift der Karl-Marx Universitaet Leipzig — WisZK
Wissenschaftliche Zeitschrift der Karl-Marx-Universitaet Leipzig — Wiss Z Karl Marx Univ Leipzig
Wissenschaftliche Zeitschrift der Karl-Marx-Universitaet Leipzig. Gesellschafts- und Sprachwissenschaftliche Reihe — Wiss Z Leipzig
Wissenschaftliche Zeitschrift der Karl-Marx-Universitaet. Leipzig. Reihe Gesellschaft und Sprachwissenschaften — W Z Leipzig Reihe GS

Wissenschaftliche Zeitschrift der Martin Luther Universitaet Halle-Wittenberg — WisZM
Wissenschaftliche Zeitschrift der Martin-Luther-Universitaet. Halle-Wittenberg. Reihe Gesellschaft und Sprachwissenschaften — WZHW
Wissenschaftliche Zeitschrift der Paedagogischen Hochschule Potsdam. Gesellschafts- und Sprachwissenschaftliche Reihe — Wiss Z Paedag Hochsch Potsdam
Wissenschaftliche Zeitschrift der Technische Universitaet Dresden — WisZT
Wissenschaftliche Zeitschrift der Technischen Hochschule Dresden — Wiss Z TH Dresden
Wissenschaftliche Zeitschrift der Technischen Universitaet Chemnitz — Wiss Z Tech Univ Chemnitz
Wissenschaftliche Zeitschrift der Technischen Universitaet Karl-Marx-Stadt — Wiss Z Tech Univ Karl Marx Stadt
Wissenschaftliche Zeitschrift der Technischen Universitaet Otto von Guericke Magdeburg — Wiss Z Tech Univ Magdeburg
Wissenschaftliche Zeitschrift der Universitaet Rostock — WisZR
Wissenschaftliche Zeitschrift der Universitaet Rostock. Mathematisch-Naturwissenschaftliche Reihe — Wiss Z Univ Rostock Math Naturwiss
Wissenschaftliche Zeitschrift der Universitaet Rostock. Naturwissenschaftliche Reihe — Wiss Z Univ Rostock Naturwiss Reihe
Wissenschaftliche Zeitschrift der Universitaet Rostock. Reihe Mathematik/Naturwissenschaften — Wiss Z Univ Rostock Reihe Math
Wissenschaftliche Zeitschrift der Wilhelm-Pieck-Universitaet Rostock Mathematisch-Naturwissenschaftliche Reihe — Wiss Z Wilhelm-Pieck-Univ Rostock Math Naturwiss Reihe
Wissenschaftliche Zeitschrift der Wilhelm-Pieck-Universitaet Rostock. Naturwissenschaftliche Reihe — Wiss Z Wilhelm Pieck Univ Rostock
Wissenschaftliche Zeitschrift der Wilhelm-Pieck-Universitaet Rostock Naturwissenschaftliche Reihe — Wiss Z Wilhelm-Pieck-Univ Rostock Naturwiss Reihe
Wissenschaftliche Zeitschrift. Ernst-Moritz-Arndt-Universitaet (Greifswald) — Wiss Z Univ (Greifswald)
Wissenschaftliche Zeitschrift. Ernst-Moritz-Arndt-Universitaet (Greifswald) — WZ (Griefswald)
Wissenschaftliche Zeitschrift. Ernst-Moritz-Arndt-Universitaet (Greifswald) — WZUG
Wissenschaftliche Zeitschrift. Ernst-Moritz-Arndt-Universitaet (Greifswald). Gesellschafts- und Sprachwissenschaftliche Reihe — WZEMAUG
Wissenschaftliche Zeitschrift. Ernst-Moritz-Arndt-Universitaet (Greifswald). Mathematisch-Naturwissenschaftliche Reihe — Wiss Z Ernst Moritz Arndt Univ (Greifswald) Math Natur Reihe
Wissenschaftliche Zeitschrift. Ernst-Moritz-Arndt-Universitaet (Greifswald). Mathematisch-Naturwissenschaftliche Reihe — Wiss Z Ernst Moritz Arndt Univ Greifswald Math Naturw Reihe
Wissenschaftliche Zeitschrift. Ernst-Moritz-Arndt-Universitaet (Greifswald). Mathematisch-Naturwissenschaftliche Reihe — Wiss Z Ernst-Moritz-Arndt-Univ Greifsw Math Naturwiss Reihe
Wissenschaftliche Zeitschrift. Ernst-Moritz-Arndt-Universitaet (Greifswald). Mathematisch-Naturwissenschaftliche Reihe — Wiss Z Univ (Greifswald) Math-Naturwiss Reihe
Wissenschaftliche Zeitschrift. Friedrich-Schiller-Universitaet (Jena) — Wiss Z (Jena)
Wissenschaftliche Zeitschrift. Friedrich-Schiller-Universitaet (Jena) — WZ (Jena)
Wissenschaftliche Zeitschrift. Friedrich-Schiller-Universitaet (Jena) — WZJ
Wissenschaftliche Zeitschrift. Friedrich-Schiller-Universitaet (Jena) — WZUJ
Wissenschaftliche Zeitschrift. Friedrich-Schiller-Universitaet (Jena). Gesellschafts- und Sprachwissenschaftliche Reihe — WZFSU
Wissenschaftliche Zeitschrift. Friedrich-Schiller-Universitaet (Jena). Gesellschafts- und Sprachwissenschaftliche Reihe — WZFSUJ
Wissenschaftliche Zeitschrift. Friedrich-Schiller-Universitaet (Jena). Gesellschafts- und Sprachwissenschaftliche Reihe — WZFSUJ GSR
Wissenschaftliche Zeitschrift. Friedrich-Schiller-Universitaet (Jena). Mathematisch-Naturwissenschaftliche Reihe — Wiss Z Friedrich-Schiller-Univ (Jena) Math Naturwiss Reihe
Wissenschaftliche Zeitschrift. Friedrich-Schiller-Universitaet (Jena). Mathematisch-Naturwissenschaftliche Reihe — Wiss Z Univ (Jena) Math-Naturwiss Reihe
Wissenschaftliche Zeitschrift. Friedrich-Schiller-Universitaet (Jena). Mathematisch-Naturwissenschaftliche Reihe — WZFMA
Wissenschaftliche Zeitschrift. Hochschule fuer Architektur und Bauwesen (Weimar) — Wiss Z Hochsch Archit Bauwes (Weimar)
Wissenschaftliche Zeitschrift. Hochschule fuer Architektur und Bauwesen Weimar-Universitaet — Wiss Z Hochsch Archit Bauwesen Weimar Univ
Wissenschaftliche Zeitschrift. Hochschule fuer Bauwesen (Cottbus) — Wiss Z Hochsch Bauwes (Cottbus)
Wissenschaftliche Zeitschrift. Hochschule fuer Bauwesen (Leipzig) — Wiss Z Hochsch Bauw (Leipzig)
Wissenschaftliche Zeitschrift. Hochschule fuer Bauwesen (Leipzig) [*East Germany*] — Wiss Z Hochsch Bauwes (Leipzig)
Wissenschaftliche Zeitschrift. Hochschule fuer Elektrotechnik (Ilmenau) — Wiss Z Hochsch Elektrotech (Ilmenau)
Wissenschaftliche Zeitschrift. Hochschule fuer Landwirtschaftliche Produktionsgenossenschaften (Meissen) — Wiss Z Hochsch Landwirtsch Produktionsgenoss (Meissen)
Wissenschaftliche Zeitschrift. Hochschule fuer Maschinenbau (Karl Marx-Stadt) — Wiss Z Hochsch Maschinenbau (Karl Marx-Stadt)
Wissenschaftliche Zeitschrift. Hochschule fuer Oekonomie [*Berlin*] — Wiss Z Hochschule
Wissenschaftliche Zeitschrift. Hochschule fuer Schwermaschinenbau (Magdeburg) — Wiss Z Hochsch Schwermaschinenbau (Magdeburg)
Wissenschaftliche Zeitschrift. Hochschule fuer Verkehrswesen (Dresden) — Wiss Z Hochsch Verkehrswesen (Dresden)
Wissenschaftliche Zeitschrift. Hochschule fuer Verkehrswesen "Friedrich List" (Dresden). Die Anwendung Mathematischer Methoden im Transport- und Nachichtenwesen — Wiss Z Hochsch Verkehrswesen Friedrich List (Dresden)
Wissenschaftliche Zeitschrift. Humboldt-Universitaet (Berlin) — Wiss Z Humboldt-Univ (Berl)
Wissenschaftliche Zeitschrift. Humboldt-Universitaet (Berlin) — WZ (Berlin)
Wissenschaftliche Zeitschrift. Humboldt-Universitaet (Berlin). Gesellschafts- und Sprachwissenschaftliche Reihe — Wiss Z (Berl)
Wissenschaftliche Zeitschrift. Humboldt-Universitaet (Berlin). Gesellschafts- und Sprachwissenschaftliche Reihe — WZHU
Wissenschaftliche Zeitschrift. Humboldt-Universitaet (Berlin). Gesellschafts- und Sprachwissenschaftliche Reihe — WZHUB
Wissenschaftliche Zeitschrift. Humboldt-Universitaet (Berlin). Gesellschafts- und Sprachwissenschaftliche Reihe — WZUB
Wissenschaftliche Zeitschrift. Humboldt-Universitaet (Berlin). Mathematisch-Naturwissenschaftliche Reihe — Wiss Z Humboldt Univ (Berl) Math Naturwiss
Wissenschaftliche Zeitschrift. Humboldt-Universitaet (Berlin). Mathematisch-Naturwissenschaftliche Reihe — Wiss Z Humboldt Univ (Berlin) Math Naturwiss Reihe
Wissenschaftliche Zeitschrift. Humboldt-Universitaet (Berlin). Mathematisch-Naturwissenschaftliche Reihe — Wiss Z Humboldt-Univ (Berl) Math-Naturwiss Reihe
Wissenschaftliche Zeitschrift. Humboldt-Universitaet (Berlin). Mathematisch-Naturwissenschaftliche Reihe — Wiss Z Humboldt-Univ (Berlin) Math-Natur Reihe
Wissenschaftliche Zeitschrift. Humboldt-Universitaet (Berlin). Mathematisch-Naturwissenschaftliche Reihe — WZHMA
Wissenschaftliche Zeitschrift. Karl-Marx Universitaet. Gesellschafts- und Sprachwissenschaftliche Reihe (Leipzig) — WZULeipzig
Wissenschaftliche Zeitschrift. Karl-Marx-Universitaet — Wiss Z Karl-Marx Univ
Wissenschaftliche Zeitschrift. Karl-Marx-Universitaet [*Leipzig*] — WZKMU
Wissenschaftliche Zeitschrift. Karl-Marx-Universitaet [*Leipzig*]. Gesellschafts- und Sprachwissenschaftliche Reihe — WZMU
Wissenschaftliche Zeitschrift. Karl-Marx-Universitaet. Gesellschafts- und Sprachwissenschaftliche Reihe [*Leipzig*] — WZsl
Wissenschaftliche Zeitschrift. Karl-Marx-Universitaet (Leipzig) — WZ (Leipzig)
Wissenschaftliche Zeitschrift. Karl-Marx-Universitaet (Leipzig) — WZL
Wissenschaftliche Zeitschrift. Karl-Marx-Universitaet (Leipzig) — WZUL
Wissenschaftliche Zeitschrift. Karl-Marx-Universitaet (Leipzig). Gesellschafts- und Sprachwissenschaftliche Reihe — Wiss Z Univ (Leipzig) Ges-u Sprachwiss R
Wissenschaftliche Zeitschrift. Karl-Marx-Universitaet (Leipzig). Gesellschafts- und Sprachwissenschaftliche Reihe — WZKMUL
Wissenschaftliche Zeitschrift. Karl-Marx-Universitaet (Leipzig). Mathematisch-Naturwissenschaftliche Reihe — Wiss Z Karl-Marx-Univ (Leipz) Math-Naturwiss Reihe
Wissenschaftliche Zeitschrift. Karl-Marx-Universitaet (Leipzig). Mathematisch-Naturwissenschaftliche Reihe — Wiss Z Karl-Marx-Univ (Leipzig) Math Natur Reihe
Wissenschaftliche Zeitschrift. Karl-Marx-Universitaet (Leipzig). Mathematisch-Naturwissenschaftliche Reihe — Wiss Z Karl-Marx-Univ (Leipzig) Math-Naturwiss Reihe
Wissenschaftliche Zeitschrift. Karl-Marx-Universitaet (Leipzig). Mathematisch-Naturwissenschaftliche Reihe — Wiss Z Univ (Leipzig) Math-Naturwiss Reihe
Wissenschaftliche Zeitschrift. Martin-Luther-Universitaet — WZMLU
Wissenschaftliche Zeitschrift. Martin-Luther-Universitaet (Halle-Wittenberg) — Wiss Z (Halle)
Wissenschaftliche Zeitschrift. Martin-Luther-Universitaet (Halle-Wittenberg) — Wiss Z Martin-Luther-Univ (Halle-Wittenb)
Wissenschaftliche Zeitschrift. Martin-Luther-Universitaet (Halle-Wittenberg) — Wiss Z Martin-Luther-Univ (Halle-Wittenberg)
Wissenschaftliche Zeitschrift. Martin-Luther-Universitaet (Halle-Wittenberg) — Wiss Z Univ (Halle)
Wissenschaftliche Zeitschrift. Martin-Luther-Universitaet (Halle-Wittenberg) — WZ (Halle)
Wissenschaftliche Zeitschrift. Martin-Luther-Universitaet (Halle-Wittenberg). Gesellschafts- und Sprachwissenschaftliche Reihe — WZMLUH
Wissenschaftliche Zeitschrift. Martin-Luther-Universitaet (Halle-Wittenberg). Gesellschafts- und Sprachwissenschaftliche Reihe — WZUH
Wissenschaftliche Zeitschrift. Martin-Luther-Universitaet (Halle-Wittenberg). Gesellschafts- und Sprachwissenschaftliche Reihe — WZUHW
Wissenschaftliche Zeitschrift. Martin-Luther-Universitaet (Halle-Wittenberg). Mathematisch-Naturwissenschaftliche Reihe — Wiss Z Martin Luther Univ
Wissenschaftliche Zeitschrift. Martin-Luther-Universitaet (Halle-Wittenberg). Mathematisch-Naturwissenschaftliche Reihe — Wiss Z Martin-Luther-Univ Halle Wittenberg Math Natur Reihe
Wissenschaftliche Zeitschrift. Martin-Luther-Universitaet (Halle-Wittenberg). Mathematisch-Naturwissenschaftliche Reihe — Wiss Z Univ (Halle-Wittenberg) Math-Naturwiss Reihe
Wissenschaftliche Zeitschrift. Mathematisch-Naturwissenschaftliche Reihe. Halle Universitaet — Wiss Z Math Naturwiss Reihe Halle Univ
Wissenschaftliche Zeitschrift. Paedagogische Hochschule Karl Liebknecht (Potsdam) [*Germany*] — Wiss Z Paedag Hochsch Karl Liebknecht (Potsdam)
Wissenschaftliche Zeitschrift. Paedagogische Hochschule (Potsdam). Gesellschafts- und Sprachwissenschaftliche Reihe — WZPHP
Wissenschaftliche Zeitschrift. Technische Hochschule (Dresden) [*Germany*] [*A publication*] — Wiss Z Tech Hochsch (Dresden)
Wissenschaftliche Zeitschrift. Technische Hochschule (Dresden) — Wiss Zs TH (Dresd)
Wissenschaftliche Zeitschrift. Technische Hochschule (Dresden) — WZTDA
Wissenschaftliche Zeitschrift. Technische Hochschule fuer Chemie "Carl Schorlemmer" (Leuna-Merseburg) — Wiss Z Tech Hochsch Chem Carl Schorlemmer (Leuna-Merseburg)

Wissenschaftliche Zeitschrift. Technische Hochschule fuer Chemie "Carl Schorlemmer" (Leuna-Merseburg) — Wiss Z Tech Hochsch (Leuna-Merseburg)
Wissenschaftliche Zeitschrift. Technische Hochschule fuer Chemie (Leuna-Merseburg) — Wiss Z Tech Hochsch Chem (Leuna-Merseburg)
Wissenschaftliche Zeitschrift. Technische Hochschule fuer Chemie (Leuna-Merseburg) — Wiss Z Techn Hochsch Chem (Leuna-Merseburg)
Wissenschaftliche Zeitschrift. Technische Hochschule (Ilmenau) — Wiss Z Techn Hochsch (Ilmenau)
Wissenschaftliche Zeitschrift. Technische Hochschule (Ilmenau, West Germany) — Wiss Z Tech Hochsch (Ilmenau)
Wissenschaftliche Zeitschrift. Technische Hochschule Karl-Marx-Stadt — Wiss Z Tech Hochsch Karl-Marx-Stadt
Wissenschaftliche Zeitschrift. Technische Hochschule Karl-Marx-Stadt — Wiss Z Techn Hochsch Karl-Marx-Stadt
Wissenschaftliche Zeitschrift. Technische Hochschule Karl-Marx-Stadt — WZTKA
Wissenschaftliche Zeitschrift. Technische Hochschule Karl-Marx-Stadt. Sonderheft — Wiss Z Tech Hochsch Karl-Marx-Stadt Sonderh
Wissenschaftliche Zeitschrift. Technische Hochschule Koethen — Wiss Z Tech Hochsch Koethen
Wissenschaftliche Zeitschrift. Technische Hochschule (Leipzig) — Wiss Z Tech Hochsch (Leipzig)
Wissenschaftliche Zeitschrift. Technische Hochschule (Leuna-Merseburg) — Wiss Z Techn Hochsch (Leuna-Merseburg)
Wissenschaftliche Zeitschrift. Technische Hochschule Otto Von Guericke — Wiss Z Tech Hochsch Otto Von Guericke
Wissenschaftliche Zeitschrift. Technische Hochschule Otto Von Guericke (Magdeburg) — Wiss Z Tech Hochsch (Magdeburg)
Wissenschaftliche Zeitschrift. Technische Hochschule Otto Von Guericke (Magdeburg) — Wiss Z Tech Hochsch Otto v Guericke (Magdeburg)
Wissenschaftliche Zeitschrift. Technische Hochschule Otto Von Guericke (Magdeburg) — Wiss Z Tech Hochsch Otto von Guericke (Magdeb)
Wissenschaftliche Zeitschrift. Technische Hochschule Otto Von Guericke (Magdeburg) — Wiss Z Tech Hochsch Otto Von Guericke (Magdeburg)
Wissenschaftliche Zeitschrift. Technische Hochschule Otto Von Guericke (Magdeburg) — Wiss Z Tech Hochsch Otto von Guericke (Magdeburg)
Wissenschaftliche Zeitschrift. Technische Universitaet (Dresden) — Wiss Z Tech Univ (Dres)
Wissenschaftliche Zeitschrift. Technische Universitaet (Dresden) — Wiss Z Tech Univ (Dresden)
Wissenschaftliche Zeitschrift. Technische Universitaet (Dresden) — Wiss Z Techn Univ (Dresden)
Wissenschaftliche Zeitschrift. Universitaet Leipzig. Gesellschafts- und Sprachwissenschaftliche Reihe — WZUL
Wissenschaftliche Zeitschrift. Universitaet Rostock — Wiss Z Rostock
Wissenschaftliche Zeitschrift. Universitaet Rostock — WZ Rostock
Wissenschaftliche Zeitschrift. Universitaet Rostock — WZUR
Wissenschaftliche Zeitschrift. Universitaet Rostock. Gesellschafts- und Sprachwissenschaftliche Reihe — Wiss Z Univ Rostock Ges- & Sprachwiss Reihe
Wissenschaftliche Zeitschrift. Universitaet Rostock. Gesellschafts- und Sprachwissenschaftliche Reihe — Wiss Z Univ Rostock Ges Sprachwiss Reihe
Wissenschaftliche Zeitschrift. Universitaet Rostock. Gesellschafts- und Wissenschaftliche Reihe — Wiss Z Univ Rostock Ges-Wiss
Wissenschaftliche Zeitschrift. Universitaet Rostock. Mathematisch-Naturwissenschaftliche Reihe — Wiss Z Univ Rostock Math Naturwiss Reihe
Wissenschaftliche Zeitschrift. Universitaet Rostock. Reihe Mathematik und Naturwissenschaften — Wiss Z Univ Rostock Reihe Math Naturw
Wissenschaftliche Zeitschrift. Universitaet Wien — WZUW
Wissenschaftliche Zeitung. Humboldt-Universitaet — WissZ
Wissenschaftlicher Dienst fuer Ostmitteleuropa — Wiss Dienst Ostmitteleur
Wissenschaftlicher Dienst Suedosteuropa — Wiss Di Suedost Eur
Wissenschaftlicher Dienst Suedosteuropa — Wiss Dienst Sudosteuropa
Wissenschaftlicher Literaturanzeiger — Wiss Literaturanz
Wissenschaftlicher Literaturanzeiger — WLA
Wissenschaftliches Archiv fuer Landwirtschaft. Abteilung A. Archiv fuer Pflanzenbau — Wiss Arch Landw Abt A
Wissenschaftliches Archiv fuer Landwirtschaft. Abteilung A. Archiv fuer Pflanzenbau — Wiss Arch Landwirtsch Abt A
Wissenschaftliches Archiv fuer Landwirtschaft. Abteilung B. Archiv fuer Tierernaehrung und Teirzucht — Wiss Arch Landwirtsch Abt B
Wissenschaftlich-Technische Informationen des VEB Kombinat Automatisierungsanlagenbau — Wiss-Tech Inf VEB Kombinat Automatisierungsanlagenbau
Wissenschaftlich-Technischer Fortschrift fuer die Landwirtschaft — Wiss-Tech Fortschr Landw
Wissenschaftstheorie- Wissenschaft und Philosophie — Wissenschaftstheor Wiss Philos
Wissenschaftstheorie- Wissenschaft und Philosophie — Wissenschaftstheorie-Wissenschaft Philos
Wistar Institute. Symposium. Monograph — Wistar Inst Symp Monogr
Witchcraft and Sorcery — WAS
Wittenberg Door — WD
Witterung in Schleswig-Holstein — Witt Schlesw-Holst
Wittheit zu Bremen. Jahrbuch — Wittheit Bremen Jahrb
WJR. Washington Journalism Review — PWJR
WMO [*World Meteorological Organization*] Bulletin — WMO Bull
WMO [*World Meteorological Organization*] Bulletin — WMOBA
WMO [*World Meteorological Organization*] Publication — WMO Publ
WNNR [*Suid-Afrikaanse Wetenskaplike en Nywerheidnavorsingsraad*] Spesiale Verslag — WNNR Spes Versl
Wochenblatt der Landesbauernschaft Schleswig-Holstein — WLSH
Wochenblatt der Viehzucht — Wochenbl Viehzucht
Wochenblatt fuer Papierfabrikation — Woch Pap Fab
Wochenblatt fuer Papierfabrikation — Wochbl Papierfabr
Wochenblatt. K. K. Gesellschaft der Aerzte in Wien — Wchnbl K K Gesellsch Aerzte Wien
Wochenschrift fuer Brauerei — Wochenschr Brau
Wochenschrift fuer die Gesammte Heilkunde [*Berlin*] — Wschr Ges Hlkde
Wochenschrift fuer die Gesamte Heilkunde — Wchnschr Ges Heilk
Wochenschrift fuer Klassische Philologie — W Kl Ph
Wochenschrift fuer Klassische Philologie — WKP
Wochenschrift fuer Klassische Philologie — WKPh
Wochenschrift fuer Klassische Philologie — Woch Kl Phil
Wochenschrift fuer Klassische Philologie — Woch Kl Philol
Wochenschrift fuer Klassische Philologie — Woch Klass Philol
Wochenschrift fuer Tierheilkunde und Viehzucht — Wchnschr Tierh u Viehzucht
Woechentliche Nachrichten von Gelehrten Sachen — Woechentl Nachr Gel Sachen
Woelm Publication — Woelm Publ
Woerter und Sachen — W & S
Woerter und Sachen — Woert Sach
Woerter und Sachen — WS
Woerter und Sachen. Zeitschrift fuer Indogermanische Sprachenwissenschaft — WuS
Woerterbuch der Aegyptischen Sprache — Wb
Woerterbuch der Aegyptischen Sprache — Wort
Woerterbuch der Mythologie — Wb Myth
Woerterbuch der Mythologie — Wb Mythol
Woerterbuch der Mythologie — WbM
Woerterbuch der Ugaritische Sprache — WUS
Wohnungswirtschaftliche Informationen — WI
Wojskowy Przeglad Techniczny [*Poland*] — Wojsk Przegl Tech
Wolfenbuetteler Barock-Nachrichten — WBN
Wolfenbuetteler Beitraege — Wolfen-Buetteler B
Wolfenbuetteler Forschungen — Wolfenbuetteler Forsch
Wolfenbuetteler Studien zur Aufklaerung — Wolfenbuetteler Stud Aufklaerung
Wolfenbuetteler Studien zur Aufklarung — WSA
Wolfman Report on the Photographic Industry in the United States — Photo Ind
Wolfram-Jahrbuch — W Jb
Wolfram-Jahrbuch — WJ
Wollen- und Leinen-Industrie — Wollen- Leinen-Ind
Wollongong University College. Bulletin — Bull Wollongong Univ Coll
Woman Citizen — Woman Cit
Woman CPA — WCP
Woman Executive's Bulletin — Woman Exec Bull
Woman Physician — WOPHA
Woman's Art Journal — Woman Art J
Woman's Day — GWOD
Woman's Day — WD
Woman's Home Companion — Woman Home C
Woman's Home Companion — Woman's H C
Woman's Journal — Woman's J
Woman's World — WW
Womanspirit — Womn Sprt
Women and Environments — PWNE
Women and Health — PWNH
Women and Health — WMHE
Women and Health — WomHealth
Women and History — Women and Hist
Women and Law — Women and L
Women and Literature — W & L
Women and Literature — Women & Lit
Women and Literature — Women Lit
Women and Performance — W and P
Women and Revolution — Women Rev
Women and Therapy — Women & Ther
Women and Therapy — WOTHDJ
Women in Business — WMB
Women in Sport & Physical Activity Journal — W Sport & P Act J
Women Lawyers Journal — Women L Jour
Women Lawyers Journal — Women Law J
Women Lawyers Journal — Women Lawyers J
Women of Europe — Women of Eur
Women on the March [*New Delhi*] — Wom March
Women/Poems — Women
Women Studies Abstracts — Women Stud Abstr
Women Studies Abstracts — Women Stud Abstracts
Women Studies Abstracts — WSA
Women Workers Bulletin — Women Wkrs Bull
Women's Bureau Bulletin — Women's Bur Bull
Women's Coaching Clinic — W Coach Clinic
Women's Coaching Clinic — Women Coach Clin
Women's Health Magazine — Women Hlth Mag
Women's Law Forum — W LF
Women's Liberation — Wmn Lib
Women's Press — Womn Prss
Women's Research and Resources Centre Newsletter — WRRC
Women's Review — WR
Women's Review of Books — Women's Review
Women's Rights Law Reporter — W R LR
Women's Rights Law Reporter — Women Rights L Rep
Women's Rights Law Reporter — Women's Rights L Rep
Women's Rights Law Reporter — Women's Rights L Rptr
Women's Rights Law Reporter — Womn Rgts
Women's Rights Law Reporter. Rutgers University — Women's Rts L Rep Rutgers Univ
Women's Sports — W Sports

Women's Sports and Fitness — GWSF
Women's Studies — PWSU
Women's Studies: An Interdisciplinary Journal — Women Stud
Women's Studies: An Interdisciplinary Journal — Women's Studies
Women's Studies: An Interdisciplinary Journal — WS
Women's Studies Association. Conference Papers [*New Zealand*] — Women's Stud Assoc Conf Pap
Women's Studies Index — WSI
Women's Studies International Forum — WS
Women's Studies Newsletter — Womens Studs Newsl
Women's Studies Quarterly — GWSQ
Women's Varsity Sports — W Var Sports
Women's Wear Daily — Women Wear
Women's Wear Daily — WWD
Wonder Stories — WS
Wonder Stories Quarterly — WQ
Wonder Stories Quarterly — WSQ
Wonder Story Annual — WSA
Wonders of the Spaceways — WOS
Wonen. Vakblad voor de Woninginrichting — NBP
Woningbouwvereniging. Maandblad van de Nationale Woningraad — WBV
Woningraad. Informatiekrant voor Woningcorporaties — WBV
Woo Sok University. Medical Journal — Woo Sok Univ Med J
Wood and Fiber Science. Journal. Society of Wood Science and Technology — Wood Fiber Sci J Soc Wood Sci Technol
Wood and Wood Products — Wood & Wood Prod
Wood and Wood Products — Wood Prod
Wood and Wood Products — Wood Wood Prod
Wood Buffalo National Park. Newsletter — WBNP
Wood Industries — WI
Wood Industry — Wood Ind
Wood Preservation Report. Forest Products Research and Industries Development Commission College (Laguna, Philippines) — Wood Pres Rep For Prod Res Ind Developm Comm (Philippines)
Wood Preserving — Wood Preserv
Wood Preserving (Chicago) — Wood Preserv (Chicago)
Wood Preserving News — Wood Preserv N
Wood Preserving News — Wood Preserv News
Wood Research — WDRSA
Wood Research — Wood Res
Wood Science — Wood Sci
Wood Science and Technology — Wood Sci Te
Wood Science and Technology — Wood Sci Technol
Wood Southern Africa — Wood South Afr
Wood Southern Africa — Wood Sthn Afr
Wood Technic — Wood Tech
Woodland Research Notes. Union Camp Corporation — Woodl Res Note Union Camp Corp
Woodlands Papers. Pulp and Paper Research Institute of Canada — Woodl Pap Pulp Pap Res Inst Can
Woodlands Research Index. Pulp and Paper Research Institute of Canada — Woodlds Res Index
Woodlands Section Index. Canadian Pulp and Paper Association — Woodl Sect Index Canad Pulp Pap Ass
Woods Hole Oceanographic Institution. Annual Report — Woods Hole Oceanogr Inst Annu Rep
Woods Hole Oceanographic Institution. Annual Sea Grant Report — ASGIDF
Woods Hole Oceanographic Institution. Annual Sea Grant Report — Woods Hole Oceanogr Inst Annu Sea Grant Rep
Woods Hole Oceanographic Institution. Collected Reprints — Woods Hole Oceanogr Inst Collect Reprints
Woods Hole Oceanographic Institution. Technical Report — WHOI Technical Report
Woods Hole Oceanographic Institution. Technical Report — Woods Hole Oceanogr Inst Tech Rep
Woods Hole Oceanographic Institution. Technical Report — WOTRAC
Woodstock Papers — WP
Woodwind, Brass, and Percussion — Wood Brass Perc
Woodwind, Brass, and Percussion — Woodwind B
Woodwind Magazine — Wood Mag
Woodwind World [*Later, Woodwind World - Brass and Percussion*] — Wood World
Woodwind World - Brass and Percussion — WBP
Woodwind World - Brass and Percussion — Wood World-Brass
Woodworking Industry — Woodwkg Ind
Wool Quarterly — WQ
Wool Record — Wool Rec
Wool Record and Textile World [*Later, Wool Record*] — Wool Rec
Wool Record and Textile World — Wool Rec Text World
Wool Record and Textile World — WOR
Wool Science Review — Wool Sci Rev
Wool Technology and Sheep Breeding — Wool Tech
Wool Technology and Sheep Breeding — Wool Tech & Sheep
Wool Technology and Sheep Breeding — Wool Tech & Sheep Breeding
Wool Technology and Sheep Breeding — Wool Technol
Wool Technology and Sheep Breeding — Wool Technol Sheep Breed
Wool Technology (Sydney) — Wool Technol (Syd)
Woolworld [*New Zealand*] — Woolwld
WOPOP: Working Papers on Photography — WOPOP
Woprosy Istorii — WI
Worcester Archaeological Society. Transactions — WAS
Worcester Magazine — Worc M
Worcester, Massachusetts. Worcester Art Museum. Annual — Worcester Mus Ann
Worcester, Massachusetts. Worcester Art Museum. News Bulletin and Calendar — Worcester Mus N Bul
Worcester Medical News [*Massachusetts*] — Worcester Med News
Word — Wd
Word and Information Processing — Word and Inf Process
Word Processing and Information Systems — Word Proc
Word Processing and Information Systems — Word Process and Inf Syst
Word Processing and Information Systems — WP/IS
Word Processing Computer Information Systems — Word Process Comput Inf Systems
Word Processing Now — Word Process Now
Word Processing Systems — Word Process Syst
Word Processing World — Word Process World
Word Study — WS
Word Study — WSt
Word Watching — Word W
Word Ways — W Ways
Words — WRD
[*The*] **Wordsworth Circle** — TWC
Wordsworth Circle — WC
Wordsworth Circle — WordsC
Wordsworth Circle — Wordsworth
Work and Occupations — WAC
Work and Occupations — WOC
Work and People — WPE
Work and People (Australia) — WAP (A)
Work and Plant Maintenance — Work Plant Maint
Work in Progress — WIP
Work in Progress — Work Prog
Work in Progress — WP
Work Related Abstracts — Work Rel Abstr
Work Related Abstracts — Work Relat Abstr
Work Related Abstracts — WRA
Work Study — Wk Study
Work Study and Management Services [*Later, Management Services*] — Wk Study Mgmt Serv
Work Study and Management Services [*Later, Management Services*] — Work Study and Manage Serv
Work Study and O and M Abstracts — Work Stud Abstr
Workbasket — GWOB
Workbench — GWOR
Work-Environment-Health — WEHSA
Work-Environment-Health — Work-Environ-Health
Workers Compensation Board Decisions (Victoria) — WCB (Vic)
Workers Compensation Board Decisions (Victoria) — WCBD (Vic)
Workers Compensation Board Decisions (Western Australia) — WCBD (WA)
Workers' Compensation Cases — WCC
Workers' Compensation Reports [*New South Wales*] — WCR
Workers' Compensation Reports (New South Wales) — WCR (NSW)
Workers' Compensation Reports (Queensland) — WCR (Q)
Workers' Compensation Reports (Queensland) — WCR (Qld)
Workers' Compensation Reports (Queensland) — WCR (Qn)
Workers' Compensation Reports (Western Australia) — WCR(WA)
Workers Power — Wrk Power
Workers Vanguard — Work Vang
Workers' World — Wrk World
Working Mother — PWOM
Working Paper. Bureau of Meteorology — Work Pap Bur Meteorol
Working Paper. Giannini Foundation of Agricultural Economics. California Agricultural Experiment Station — Work Pap Giannini Found Agric Econ Calif Agric Exp Stn
Working Paper Series. California Agricultural Experiment Station. Department of Agricultural and Resource Economics — Working Pap Ser Calif Agric Exp Stn Dep Agric Resour Econ
Working Papers. Australian Arid Zone Research Conference — Work Pap Aust Arid Zone Res Conf
Working Papers. Australian Cereal and Pasture Plant Breeding Conference — Work Pap Aust Cereal Pasture Plant Breed Conf
Working Papers. Fondazione Dalle Molle — WPFDM
Working Papers for a New Society — Work Pap New Soc
Working Papers for a New Society — Working Papers
Working Papers for a New Society — Wrk Paper
Working Papers. Hebrew University of Jerusalem — WPHUJ
Working Papers in Agricultural Economics — Work Pap Agric Econ
Working Papers in Language and Linguistics — Work Pap Lang Linguist
Working Papers in Linguistics — WPL
Working Papers in Linguistics (Honolulu) — Work Pap Ling (H)
Working Papers in Linguistics (University of Hawaii) — WPLUH
Working Papers in Yiddish and East European Jewish Studies — WPYEEJS
Working Papers. Lund University. Department of Linguistics — WPLU
Working Papers Magazine — Work Papers
Working Papers on Sex, Science, and Culture — Sex Scien
Working with Girls Newsletter — Wkg Girls Newsl
Working Woman — WKW
Working Woman — Work Wom
Working Woman — WW
Working Woman — WWM
Worklife — WLF
Worklife [*Canada*] — WOL
Worklife — WORKD
Workmen's Circle Call — WCC
Workmen's Compensation Law Reports. Commerce Clearing House — Workmen's Comp L Rep CCH
Workpapers in Papua New Guinea Languages — WPNGL
Works and Plant Maintenance — Works and Plant Maint
Works and Studies. Water Research Institute Bratislava — Works Stud Water Res Inst Bratislava

Works Engineering — Wks Engng
Works Engineering [*England*] — Works Eng
Works Engineering and Factory Services — Wks Engng Fact Serv
Works Engineering and Factory Services — Works Eng Fact Serv
Works. Institute of Higher Nervous Activity. Academy of Sciences of the USSR. Pathophysiological Series — Works Inst Higher Nerv Act Acad Sci USSR Pathophysiol Ser
Works. Institute of Higher Nervous Activity. Academy of Sciences of the USSR. Physiological Series — Works Inst Higher Nerv Act Acad Sci USSR Physiol Ser
Works. Institute of Higher Nervous Activity. Pathophysiological Series — Works Inst Higher Nerv Act Pathophysiol Ser
Works. Institute of Higher Nervous Activity. Physiological Series — Works Inst Higher Nerv Act Physiol Ser
Works Management — Wks Mgmt
Works Management — WM
Works Management — WOMAA
Works. Pavlov Institute of Physiology. Academy of Sciences of the USSR — Works Pavlov Inst Physiol Acad Sci USSR
Works. Richard Hakluyt Society — WHS
Workshop Computers in Chemistry — Workshop Comput Chem
Workshop Conferences Hoechst [*Elsevier Book Series*] — WCH
Workshop Conferences Hoechst [*Elsevier Book Series*] — WCHODW
Workshop Conferences Hoechst — Workshop Conf Hoechst
Workshop Interfaces in New Materials — Workshop Interfaces New Mater
Workshop on Advanced Methods of Pharmacokinetic and Pharmacodynamic Systems Analysis — Workshop Adv Methods Pharmacokinet Pharmacodyn Syst Anal
Workshop on Failure Analysis, Corrosion Evaluation, and Metallography — Workshop Failure Anal Corros Eval Metallogr
Workshop on High Temperature Corrosion of Advanced Materials and Protective Coatings — Workshop High Temp Corros Adv Mater Prot Coat
Workshop on Materials Science and Physics of Non-Conventional Energy Sources — Workshop Mater Sci Phys Non Conv Energy Sources
Workshop on Tungsten and Other Advanced Metals for ULSI Applications — Workshop Tungsten Other Adv Met ULSI Appl
Workshop Proceedings. International Workshop on Active Matrix Liquid Crystal Displays — Workshop Proc Int Workshop Act Matrix Liq Cryst Disp
Workshop Series. Pharmacology Section. National Institute of Mental Health — Workshop Ser Pharmacol Sect Nat Inst Ment Health
Workshops in Computing — Workshops Comput
World — Wd
World Aeronautical Chart [*Air Force*] — WAC
World Aerospace System — Wld Aerospace Syst
World Affairs — PWAF
World Affairs — WA
World Affairs — Wld Aff
World Affairs — World Aff
World Affairs Journal — Wld Aff Jnl
World Affairs. Journal — World Affairs J
World Affairs Quarterly — WA
World Affairs Quarterly — Wld Aff Q
World Affairs. Quarterly — World Aff Q
World Affairs Report — WAR
World Agricultural Economics and Rural Sociology Abstracts — WAERSA
World Agricultural Economics and Rural Sociology Abstracts — WAG
World Agricultural Economics and Rural Sociology Abstracts — World Agri Econ & Rural Sociol Abstr
World Agricultural Economics and Rural Sociology Abstracts — World Agric Econ
World Agriculture — World Ag
World Agriculture — World Agr
World Agriculture — World Agric
World Air Transport Statistics — W Air Trans
World Aluminum Abstracts [*Database*] — WAA
World Aluminum Abstracts — World Alum Abstr
World and People — Wld People
World Animal Review — Wld Anim Rev
World Animal Review — World Anim Rev
World Animal Science [*Elsevier Book Series*] — WAS
World Anthropology — World Anthropol
World Archaeology — PWAR
World Archaeology — W Arch
World Archaeology — WA
World Archaeology — Wld Archaeology
World Archaeology — World A
World Archaeology — World Archa
World Archaeology — World Archaeol
World Association for Adult Education. Bulletin — World Assn for Adult Ed B
World Aviation Directory — WAD
World Bibliography of Social Security — World Bibl Social Security
World Business Weekly — WBW
World Business Weekly — World Bus W
World Cement — Wld Cem
World Cement [*London*] — World Cem
World Cement Technology [*Later, World Cement*] — Wld Cem Tech
World Cement Technology [*Later, World Cement*] — World Cem Technol
World Christian — WC
World Christian Education — Wld Chr Ed
World Coal — WOC
World Coal — WOCOD
World Coin News — WCN
World Coins — WCoins
World Commodity Report. Metals Edition — World Commod Rep Met Ed
World Conference of Psychiatry — Wld Conf Psych
World Conference on Earthquake Engineering. Proceedings — World Conf Earthquake Eng Proc
World Conference on Medical Education — Wld Conf Med Educ
World Congress of Jewish Studies — WCJS
World Congress on In Vitro Fertilization and Assisted Reproduction — World Congr In Vitro Fert Assisted Reprod
World Construction — World Constr
World Crops — Wld Crops
World Crops Production Utilization Description — WCPDD5
World Crops Production Utilization Description — World Crops Prod Util Descr
World Demand for Raw Materials in 1985 and 2000 — Wld Raw Mat
World Development — CRC
World Development — IWDV
World Development — WD
World Development — WDT
World Development — Wld Develop
World Development — WODED
World Development [*Oxford*] — World Dev
World Development — World Devel
World Development Report — Wld Dev Rpt
World Distribution — World Dist
World Dominion — WD
World Dredging and Marine Construction — World Dredging & Mar Const
World Dredging and Marine Construction — World Dredging Mar Constr
World Drinks Report - World Food Report — Wld Drink R
World Economic Outlook — WEO
World Economic Survey. Supplement — World Eco S
World Economy — WEV
World Economy — Wld Econ
World Economy — WOE
World Economy [*England*] — World Econ
World Education Reports — World Educ Rep
World Energy Conference. Transactions — World Energy Conf Trans
World Energy Industry — WEI
World Energy Outlook — Wld En Out
World Energy. The Facts and the Future — Energy F & F
World Faiths Insight — WFI
World Farming — World Farm
World Fertility Survey — World Fert Surv
World Fertility Survey. Country Reports — WFSUDO
World Fertility Survey. Country Reports — World Fertil Surv Ctry Rep
World Fertility Survey. Scientific Reports — SRWSDA
World Fertility Survey. Scientific Reports — World Fertil Surv Sci Rep
World Fisheries Abstracts — World Fish Abstr
World Fishing — Wld Fishg
World Food and Drink Report — Wld Fd & Drk
World Food Problems — Wld Fd Probl
World Food Report — Wld Food Rt
World Forestry Congress. Proceedings — Wld For Congr
World Forestry Congress. Proceedings — Wld For Congr Proc
World Forestry Series. Bulletin — World For Ser Bull
World Futures — PWFU
World Gas Report — Wld Gas Rpt
World Grain Trade Statistics — Wld Grain Tr Stat
World Health — GWOH
World Health — WOHE
World Health Organization. Chronicle — WHO Chronicle
World Health Organization. Chronicle — WHOCA
World Health Organization. Chronicle — World Health Organ Chron
World Health Organization International Agency for Research on Cancer. Annual Report — WHO Int Agency Res Cancer Annu Rep
World Health Organization. Monograph Series — WHO Monogr Ser
World Health Organization. Public Health Papers — WHO Public Health Pap
World Health Organization. Public Health Papers — WHO Public Health Papers
World Health Organization. Public Health Papers — WHOPAY
World Health Organization. Public Health Papers — Wld Hlth Org Publ Hlth Pap
World Health Organization. Technical Report Series — WHO Tech Rep Ser
World Health Organization. Technical Report Series — WHO Tech Rep Sers
World Health Organization. Technical Report Series — Wld Hlth Org Techn Rep Ser
World Health Organization. Technical Report Series — World Health Organ Tech Rep Ser
World Health Statistics. Quarterly — World Health Stat Q
World Health Statistics. Report — World Health Stat Rep
World Highways — World Highw
World Hospitals — World Hosp
World Hunger — Wld Hunger
World in the Classroom — W Class
World Jewish Congress. Annual Report [*New York*] — WJCAR
World Jewish Congress. Information Bulletin [*New York*] — WJCIB
World, Journal, and Tribune — WJT
World Journal of Surgery — WJSUD
World Journal of Surgery — World J Surg
World Journal of Urology — WJURDJ
World Journal of Urology — World J Urol
World Journal Tribune [*Defunct New York City afternoon newspaper*] — World Jnl Trib
World Justice — WJ
World Justice — World Jus
World License Review — Wld Lic Rev
World Literature Today — PWLT
World Literature Today — WLT
World Literature Today — World Lit T
World Literature Today — World Lit Today
World Literature Written in English — W Lit

World Literature Written in English — WLWE
World Magazine — IWOM
World Magazine — World
World Marxist Review — Wld Marx R
World Marxist Review — Wld Marxist Rev
World Marxist Review — WMR
World Marxist Review — World Marx R
World Marxist Review — World Marxist R
World Medical Association. Bulletin — Wld Med Ass Bull
World Medical Electronics [*England*] — World Med Electron
World Medical Instrumentation [*England*] — World Med Instrum
World Medical Journal — Wld Med J
World Medical Journal — World Med J
World Medicine — Wld Med
World Medicine — World Med
World Meetings — WM
World Meetings: Outside United States and Canada — World Meet Outs US Can
World Meetings: Outside United States and Canada — World Meet Outside US Can
World Meetings: United States and Canada — World Meet US Can
World Mental Health — Wld Ment Heal
World Metal Statistics — World Metal Statis
World Meteorological Organization. Bulletin — World Meteorol Organ Bull
World Meteorological Organization. Publications — World Meteorol Organ Publ
World Meteorological Organization. Reports on Marine Science Affairs — WMO Rep Mar Sci Aff
World Meteorological Organization. Special Environmental Report — WMO Spec Environ Rep
World Meteorological Organization. Technical Note — WMO Tech Note
World Military Expenditures and Arms Transfers — Wld Mil Ex
World Mine Production of Gold — Wld Gold
World Mineral Statistics — World Miner Stat
World Minerals and Metals — WMMTA
World Minerals and Metals — World Miner Met
World Mines Register — Wld Min Reg
World Mining — World Min
World Mining Equipment — Wld Mining
World Mining Equipment — World Min Equip
World Mining. United States Edition — World Min US Ed
World Mission — WM
World Money Outlook — Wld Money
World Monitor — PWMO
World Neurology — World Neurol
World of Banking — WOB
World of Irish Nursing — World Ir Nurs
World of Islam — WIS
World of Music [*London*] — WM
World of Music — WoM
World of Music — WOMUA
World of Music — World M
World of Music — World Mus
World of Obstetrics and Gynecology [*Japan*] — World Obstet Gynecol
World of Opera — WO
World of Steel (Japan) — World Steel (Jpn)
World of Winners — WOW
World of Work Report — Wld Work Rep
World Oil — WO
World Oil Forecast. Review Issue — World Oil
World Orchid Conference — Wld Orchid Conf
World Order — World O
World Outlook — World Outl
World Paper — World Pap
World Patent Information — World Patent Inf
World Patents Index [*Database*] — WPI
World Petrochemicals [*Database*] — WP DATA
World Petroleum — World Pet
World Petroleum — World Petrol
World Petroleum — WP
World Petroleum Availability 1980-2000 — W Petro 2000
World Petroleum Congress. Preprints — World Pet Cong Prepr
World Petroleum Congress. Proceedings — World Pet Congr Proc
World Plastics — Wld Plast
World Policy — World Pol
World Policy Journal — GWPJ
World Politics — GWPP
World Politics — Wld Polit
World Politics — Wor Pol
World Politics — World Pol
World Politics — WP
World Politics. A Quarterly Journal of International Relations — Wld Pol
World Pollen and Spore Flora — Wld Pollen Spore Flora
World Press Archives — WPA
World Press Review — GWPR
World Press Review — World Press R
World Production of Silver — Wld Silver
World Pulp and Paper Demand, Supply, and Trade — Wld P & PDem
World Pumps — Wld Pumps
World Quarterly Energy Review — Wld Qtly Energ Rev
World Refrigeration [*England*] — World Refrig
World Refrigeration and Air Conditioning — Wld Refrig Air Condit
World Report — World Rep
World Reporter — WRp
World Resources — World Resour
World Resources — WORSE9
World Review — Wld Rev
World Review — WoR
World Review — Wor R
World Review — World R
World Review — World Rev
World Review of Animal Production — World Rev Anim Prod
World Review of Nutrition and Dietetics — World Rev Nutr Diet
World Review of Pest Control — Wld Rev Pest Control
World Review of Pest Control — World R Pest Control
World Review of Pest Control — World Rev Pest Contr
World Review of Pest Control — World Rev Pest Control
World Risk Analysis Package [*Database*] — WRAP
World Science News [*India*] — World Sci News
World Science Reviews — Wld Sci Rev
World Scientific Advanced Series in Dynamical Systems — World Sci Adv Ser Dyn Syst
World Scientific Lecture Notes in Physics — World Sci Lecture Notes Phys
World Scientific Series in 20th Century Mathematics — World Sci Ser 20th Century Math
World Scientific Series in 20th Century Physics — World Sci Ser 20th Century Phys
World Scientific Series in Applicable Analysis — World Sci Ser Appl Anal
World Scientific Series in Computer Science — World Sci Ser Comput Sci
World Scientific Series in Contemporary Chemical Physics — World Sci Ser Contemp Chem Phys
World Scientific Series in Robotics and Intelligent Systems — World Sci Ser Robot Intell Systems
World Scientific Series on Directions in Condensed Matter Physics — World Sci Ser Dir Condensed Matter Phys
World Scientific Series on Nonlinear Science. Series A. Monographs and Treatises — World Sci Ser Nonlinear Sci Ser A Monogr Treatises
World Scientific Series on Nonlinear Science. Series B. Special Theme Issues and Proceedings — World Sci Ser Nonlinear Sci Ser B
World Scientific Series on Nonlinear Science. Series B. Special Theme Issues and Proceedings — World Sci Ser Nonlinear Sci Ser B Spec Theme Issues Proc
World Semiconductor Trade Statistics [*Database*] — WSTS
World Smoking and Health — WS and H
World Smoking and Health — WSAH
World Solar Markets — WSM
World Steel and Metalworking Export Manual — World Steel Metalwork Export Man
World Steel Industry. Into and Out of the 1990's — Steel Ind
World Student Christian Federation Books — WSCF Books
World Surface Coatings Abstracts — World Surf Coat
World Surface Coatings Abstracts — World Surf Coat Abstr
World Surface Coatings Abstracts — World Surface Coat Abs
World Surface Coatings Abstracts [*Paint Research Association*] [*Information service or system*] — WSCA
World Survey — Wld Surv
World Survey — World Surv
World Survey of Climatology [*Elsevier Book Series*] — WSC
World Tax Report [*London*] — WTA
World Tennis — GWOT
World Tennis — Wld Ten
World Textile Abstracts — World Text Abstr
World Textile Abstracts — World Textile Abs
World Textile Abstracts — World Textile Abstr
World Textile Abstracts [*Information service or system*] — WTA
World Tobacco — Wld Tobacco
World Tobacco — WT
World Today — IWTO
World Today — Wld Today
World Today — WT
World Today [*London*] — WTD
World Today. Royal Institute of International Affairs — RIIA/WT
World Trade. Computer Age — Wld Trade
World Trade Information — WHI
World Trade Statistics Database — TRADSTAT
World Trade Union Movement — Wld Trade Un Mov
World Travel — WTR
World Traveler — Wld Trav
World Veterinary Abstracting Journal — Wld Vet Abstr J
World Vision — WV
World Water — WWA
World Wide Web Journal of Biology [*Electronic Publication*] — World Wide Web J Biol
World Yearbook of Education — Wld Yrbk Educ
World Yearbook of Education — World Yr Bk Ed
Worlds Beyond — WB
Worlds Beyond — WBD
World's Butter Review — World's Butter Rev
World's Fair — WRD
World's Health — Wld Hlth
Worlds of Fantasy [*1968-*] — WFA
Worlds of Fantasy [*1950-1954*] — WOF
Worlds of If — WIF
Worlds of Tomorrow — WOT
World's Paper Trade Review — Wld Pap Tr Rev
World's Paper Trade Review — Wld's Pap Trade Rev
World's Paper Trade Review — World's Pap Trade Rev
World's Poultry Congress. Conference Papers. Section C — World's Poultry Cong Conf Papers Sect C
World's Poultry Science Journal — Wld Poult Sci J
World's Poultry Science Journal — World Poult
World's Poultry Science Journal — World Poultry Sci J

World's Poultry Science Journal — World's Poult Sci J
World's Poultry Science Journal — World's Poultry Sci J
World's Work — Wld Work
World's Work — WW
World's Work (London) — W Work (Lond)
Worldview — Wor
Worldview. Council on Religion and International Affairs — CRIA/W
Worldwatch Paper — Worldwatch Pap
Worldwide Abstracts — Worldwide Abstr
World-Wide Abstracts of General Medicine — Wld Wide Abstr Gen Med
Worldwide Franchise Directory — WFD
Worldwide List of Published Standards — World List Pub Stds
Worldwide List of Published Standards — Worldwide List Published Stand
World-Wide Mining Abstracts — World-Wide MinAbs
Worldwide Nuclear Power — Worldwide Nucl Power
Worm Runner's Digest — Worm Runner's Dig
Wormald Journal — Wormald J
Wormwood Review — Worm R
Wort in der Zeit — W i d Z
Wort in der Zeit — WiZ
Wort in der Zeit — WZ
Wort und Brauch — WB
Wort und Dienst — W & D
Wort und Dienst. Jahrbuch der Theologischen Schule Bethel [*Bethel Bei Bielefeld*] — WuD
Wort und Sinn — WS
Wort und Wahrheit — Wort U Wahrheit
Wort und Wahrheit — Wort Wahr
Wort und Wahrheit — Wow
Wort und Wahrheit — WoWa
Wort und Wahrheit — WuWahr
Wortkunst — W
WRAMC [*Walter Reed Army Medical Center*] **Progress Notes** — WRAMC Prog Notes
WRC [*Water Research Centre*] **Information** — WRC Inf
WREP. Western Region Extension Publication. Cooperative Extension Service — WREP West Reg Ext Publ Coop Ext Serv
Wrestling USA — Wrest
WRI [*Wattle Research Institute*] **Report** — WRI Rep
Wright Air Development Center. Technical Report — WADC Tech Rept
Writer — GTWR
Writers and Their Work — WTW
Writer's Digest — IWRD
Writers Digest — WD
Writer's Electronic Bulletin Board [*Database*] — WEBB
Writers for Young Adults. Biographies Master Index — WYA
Writers of the 21st Century. Series — Writ Cent S
Writers' Ring — Writ Ring
Writings on American History — WAH
Writings on American History — Writ Am Hist
Wroclaw — Ww
Wroclaw. Politechnika. Instytut Cybernetyki Technicznej. Prace Naukowe. Seria Konferencje — Prace Nauk Inst Cybernet Techn Politech Wroclaw Ser Konfer
Wroclaw. Politechnika. Instytut Cybernetyki Technicznej. Prace Naukowe. Seria Monografie — Prace Nauk Inst Cybernet Techn Politech Wroclaw Ser Monograf
Wroclaw. Politechnika. Instytut Cybernetyki Technicznej. Prace Naukowe. Seria Studia i Materialy — Prace Nauk Inst Cybernet Techn Wroclaw Ser Stud i Materialy
Wroclaw. Politechnika Wroclawska. Instytutu Matematyki. Prace Naukowe. Seria Konferencje — Prace Nauk Inst Mat Politech Wroclaw Ser Konfer
Wroclawskie Towarzystwo Naukowe — WTN
Wroclawskie Towarzystwo Naukowe — WTW
Wroclawskie Zapiski Numizmatyczne — Wrocl Zap Num
WRRC [*Water Resources Research Center*] **Special Report. University of Maryland** — WRRC Spec Rep Univ MD
WRRI [*Water Resources Research Institute*]. Auburn University. Bulletin — WRRI Auburn Univ Bull
WSFA [*Washington Science Fiction Association*] **Journal** — WSJ
WSI [*Wirtschafts- und Sozialwissenschaftliches Institut*] **Mitteilungen** [*German Federal Republic*] — WSI Mitt
WSIA [*Water Supply Improvement Association*] **Journal** [*United States*] — WSIA J
Wspolczesnosc — WC
Wspolczesnosc [*Warsaw*] — Wsp
WT (Werkstattstechnik). Zeitschrift fuer Industrielle Fertigung — WT (Werkstattstech) Z Ind Fertigung
WT [*Werkstattstechnik*]. Zeitschrift fuer Industrielle Fertigung — WT Z Ind Fertigung
WT [*Werkstattstechnik*]. Zeitschrift fuer Industrielle Fertigung — WTZIA
Wu Li Hsueh Pao — WLHPA
Wuerttembergische Blaetter fuer Kirchenmusik — Wuerttemberg Blaetter Km
Wuerttembergische Vierteljahresschrift fuer Landesgeschichte — WVLG
Wuerttembergisches Aerzteblatt — Wuerttemb Aerztebl
Wuerttembergisches Wochenblatt fuer Landwirtschaft — Wuerttemb Wochenbl Landwirt
Wuerttembergisch-Franken — Wuertt Franken
Wuerzburger Diozesangeschichtsblaetter — WDGB
Wuerzburger Geographische Arbeiten — Wuerzburg Geogr Arb
Wuerzburger Jahrbuecher fuer die Altertumswissenschaft — W Jbb Alt
Wuerzburger Jahrbuecher fuer die Altertumswissenschaft — WJ
Wuerzburger Jahrbuecher fuer die Altertumswissenschaft — WJA
Wuerzburger Jahrbuecher fuer die Altertumswissenschaft — Wrzb Jhrb
Wuerzburger Jahrbuecher fuer die Altertumswissenschaft — Wuerz Jb
Wuerzburger Jahrbuecher fuer die Altertumswissenschaft — Wuerzb J
Wuerzburger Jahrbuecher fuer die Altertumswissenschaft — Wuerzb Jahrb f d Alt
Wuerzburger Jahrbuecher fuer die Altertumswissenschaft — Wuerzb Jb Alt Wiss
Wuerzburger Naturwissenschaftliche Zeitschrift — Wuerzburger Naturwiss Z
Wuhan University Journal. Natural Sciences [*People's Republic of China*] — Wuhan Univ J Nat Sci
Wuyi Science Journal — WUKEE8
Wuyi Science Journal — Wuyi Sci J
WVC Documentatie. Systematisch Overzicht met Samenvattingen van Nieuwe Boeken, Tijdschriftartikelen, Parlementaire Stukken — CDX
Wyatt and Webb's Reports — WW
Wyatt and Webb's Reports — Wyatt & W
Wyatt and Webb's Reports — Wyatt & Webb
Wyatt and Webb's Reports (Equity) — W & W (E)
Wyatt and Webb's Reports (Equity) — W & W (Eq)
Wyatt and Webb's Reports (Equity) — Wyatt & W (Eq)
Wyatt and Webb's Reports (Insolvency, Ecclesiastical, and Matrimonial) — W & W (IE & M)
Wyatt and Webb's Reports (Insolvency, Ecclesiastical, and Matrimonial) — Wyatt & W (IE & M)
Wyatt and Webb's Reports (Insolvency, Probate, and Matrimonial) — Wyatt & W (IP & M)
Wyatt and Webb's Reports (Law) — W & W (L)
Wyatt and Webb's Victorian Reports — W & W
Wyatt and Webb's Victorian Reports [*1864-69*] [*Australia*] — W & W Vict
Wyatt, Webb, and A'Beckett's Reports — W & W & A'B
Wyatt, Webb, and A'Beckett's Reports — Wyatt W & A'B
Wyatt, Webb, and A'Beckett's Reports (Equity) — W & W & A'B (Eq)
Wyatt, Webb, and A'Beckett's Reports (Equity) — WW & A'B (E)
Wyatt, Webb, and A'Beckett's Reports (Equity) — Wyatt W & A'B (Eq)
Wyatt, Webb, and A'Beckett's Reports (Insolvency, Ecclesiastical, and Matrimonial) — WW & A'B (IE & M)
Wyatt, Webb, and A'Beckett's Reports (Insolvency, Ecclesiastical, and Matrimonial) — Wyatt W & A'B IE & M
Wyatt, Webb, and A'Beckett's Reports (Mining) — W & W & A'B (Min)
Wyatt, Webb, and A'Beckett's Reports (Mining) — WW & A'B (M)
Wyatt, Webb, and A'Beckett's Reports (Mining) — Wyatt W & A'B Min
Wyatt, Webb, and A'Beckett's Victorian Insolvency, Probate, and Matrimonial Reports — Wyatt W & A'B IP & M
Wyatt, Webb, and A'Beckett's Victorian Reports — WW & A'B
Wychowanie Muzyczne w Szkole — Wychowanie M Szkole
Wydawnictwa Slaskie Polskiej Akademii Umiejetnosci. Prace Jezykowe. Publications Silesiennes. Academie Polonaise des Sciences et des Lettres. Travaux Linguistiques — TLSAP
Wydawnictwo Literackie — WL
Wydawnictwo Lodzkie — WL
Wydawnictwo Lubelskie — WLub
Wydzial Matematyki Fizyki i Chemii Uniwersytet Imeni Adama Mickiewicza w Poznaniu Seria Fizyaka — Wydz Mat Fiz Chem Uniw Poznan Ser Fiz
Wye College. Department of Hop Research. Annual Report — Wye Coll Dep Hop Res Annu Rep
Wykeham Engineering and Technology Series — Wykeham Eng Technol Ser
Wykeham Science Series — Wykeham Sci Ser
Wyoming Agricultural College Agricultural Experiment Station. Mimeographed Circular — Wyoming Agric Exp Sta Mimeogr Circ
Wyoming. Agricultural Experiment Station. Bulletin — Wyo Agric Exp Stn Bull
Wyoming. Agricultural Experiment Station. Circular — Wyo Agric Exp Stn Cir
Wyoming. Agricultural Experiment Station. Publications — Wyo Ag Exp
Wyoming. Agricultural Experiment Station. Research Journal — Wyo Agric Exp Stn Res J
Wyoming. Agricultural Experiment Station. Science Monograph — Wyo Agric Exp Stn Sci Monogr
Wyoming. Agricultural Extension Service. Bulletin — Wyo Agric Ext Serv Bull
Wyoming. Energy Extension Service. Update — WY Energy Ext Serv Update
Wyoming. Game and Fish Commission. Bulletin — Wyo Game Fish Comm Bull
Wyoming Geological Association. Earth Science Bulletin — Wyo Geol Assoc Earth Sci Bull
Wyoming Geological Association. Guidebook. Annual Field Conference — Wyo Geol Assoc Guideb Ann Field Conf
Wyoming. Geological Survey. Bulletin. Report of Investigations — Wyo Geol Survey Bull Rept Inv
Wyoming. Geological Survey. Preliminary Report — Wyo Geol Surv Prelim Rep
Wyoming. Geological Survey. Preliminary Report — Wyoming Geol Survey Prelim Rept
Wyoming. Geological Survey. Report of Investigations — Wyo Geol Surv Rep Invest
Wyoming. Geologist's Office. Bulletin. Wyoming State Geologist — Wyo G Off B Wyo St G
Wyoming Historical and Geological Society. Proceedings and Collections. Publications — Wyoming Hist G Soc Pr Pub
Wyoming Issues — Wyo Issues
Wyoming Law Journal — WL Jour
Wyoming Law Journal — WLJ
Wyoming Law Journal — WY LJ
Wyoming Law Journal — Wyo L J
Wyoming Library Roundup — Wyo Lib Roundup
Wyoming Music Educator News-Letter — WY
Wyoming Nurse [*Formerly, Wyoming Nurses Newsletter*] — Wyo Nurse
Wyoming Nurses Newsletter [*Later, Wyoming Nurse*] — Wyo Nurses News
Wyoming Progress Report — Wyo Prog Rep
Wyoming Range Management — Wyo Range Manage
Wyoming Reports — Wyo
Wyoming Roundup — Wyo Roundup
Wyoming State Geologist — Wyo St G

Wyoming State Historical Department. Proceedings and Collections — Wyo His Col

Wyoming Statutes — Wyo Stat

Wyoming University. Department of Geology. Contributions to Geology — Wyo Univ Dep Geol Contrib Geol

Wyoming University. Natural Resources Institute. Information Circular — Wyo Univ Natur Resour Inst Inform Circ

Wyoming University. Natural Resources Research Institute. Bulletin — Wyo Univ Nat Resour Res Inst Bull

Wyoming University. Natural Resources Research Institute. Information Circular — Wyo Univ Nat Resour Res Inst Inf Cir

Wyoming University. School of Mines. Bulletin — Wyo Univ Sch Mines B

Wyoming University. Water Resources Research Institute. Water Resources Series — Wyo Univ Water Resour Res Inst Water Resour Ser

Wyoming Wild Life — Wyo Wild Life

Wythe County Historical Review — Wythe Cty Hist Rev

Wyzsza Szkola Pedagogiczna w Krakowie. Rocznik Naukowo-Dydaktyczny. Prace Matematyczne — Wyz Szkol Ped Krakow Rocznik Nauk-Dydakt Prace Mat

Wyzsza Szkola Pedagogiczna w Krakowie. Rocznik Naukowo-Dydaktyczny. Prace z Dydaktyki Matematyki — Wyz Szkol Ped Krakow Rocznik Nauk-Dydakt Prace Dydakt Mat

WZE. Wissenschaftliche Zeitschrift der Elektrotechnik [*Germany*] — WZE Wiss Z Elektrotech

X: A Quarterly Review — XR
Xanadu — Xa
Xavier University. Studies — XUS
X-Country Skier — X Ctry Skier
Xerogrammata Hochschulschriften — XH
Xi Psi Phi Quarterly — Xi Psi Phi Q
XIe Congres International des Sciences Historiques. Actes du Congres — Actes XIe Congr Internat Sci Hist
X-Ray Spectrometry — X-Ray Spect
X-Ray Spectrometry — X-Ray Spectrom
X-Rays in Natural Science and Medicine. Proceedings of a Symposium — X Rays Nat Sci Med Proc Symp
Xudozestvennaja Literatura — XL
Xudozestvennyj Fol'klor — XF
XVIIe Siecle — DSS
XVIIe Siecle — XVII S

Y Traethodydd — Tr
Yachting — IYAC
Yachting — Yacht
Yachting and Boating Weekly — Yacht Boat Week
Yachting World [*London*] — YW
Yacimientos Arqueologicos Espanoles [*Database*] — YAAR
Yad Vashem Studies — YVS
Yad Vashem Studies on the European Jewish Catastrophe and Resistance — Yad Vashem Stud Eur Jew Catastrophe Resist
Yadernaya Fizika — Yad Fiz
Yadernaya Geofizika — Yad Geofiz
Yadernoe Priborostroenie [*Former USSR*] — Yad Priborostr
Yadernoe Priborostroenie — YAPRA
Yaderno-Geofizicheskie Issledovaniya, Geofizicheskii Sbornik [*Former USSR*] — Yad-Geofiz Issled Geofiz Sb
Yadernye Konstanty — Yad Konstanty
Yadernyi Magnitnyi Rezonans — Yad Magn Rezon
Yadernyi Magnitnyi Rezonans v Organicheskoi Khimii — Yad Magn Rezon Org Khim
Yadrena Energiya — Yad Energ
Yakubutsu Ryoho — YKYRA
Yakugaku Kenkyu — YKKKA
Yakugaku Zasshi [*Journal of the Pharmaceutical Society of Japan*] — YKKZA
Yakugaku Zasshi/Journal of the Pharmaceutical Society of Japan — Yakugaku Zasshi J Pharmaceut Soc Jap
Yakuzaigaku — YAKUA
Yale Alumni Magazine — YaA
Yale Bicentennial Publications. Contributions to Mineralogy and Petrography — Yale Bicen Pub Contr Miner
Yale Classical Studies — Y Cl Stud
Yale Classical Studies — Yale ClSt
Yale Classical Studies — YCLS
Yale Classical Studies — YCS
Yale Classical Studies Series — Y Cl St
Yale Classical Studies Series — Yale Class Studies
Yale Divinity Quarterly [*New Haven, CT*] — Ya Div Q
Yale Divinity Quarterly — Yale Div Q
Yale Divinity Quarterly — YDQ
Yale Economic Essays — YEE
Yale French Studies — PYFS
Yale French Studies — Y Fr St
Yale French Studies — Yale Fr St
Yale French Studies — Yale Fr Stud
Yale French Studies — Yale French Stud
Yale French Studies — YFS
Yale Germanic Studies — YGS
Yale Historical Publications. Miscellaneous — Yale Hist Pub Misc
Yale Italian Studies — Y It S
Yale Italian Studies — Yale Ital S
Yale Italian Studies — Yale Ital Stud
Yale Journal of Biology and Medicine — Yale J Biol
Yale Journal of Biology and Medicine — Yale J Biol Med
Yale Journal of Criticism — IYJC
Yale Journal of World Public Order — Yale J World Pub Ord
Yale Law Journal — Yale L J
Yale Law Journal — Yale Law J
Yale Law Journal — YLJ
Yale Literary Magazine — Yale Lit Mag
Yale Literary Magazine — YLM
Yale Mathematical Monographs — Yale Math Monographs
Yale Near Eastern Researches [*New Haven/London*] — YNER
Yale Oriental Series — YOS
Yale Oriental Series — YOSR
Yale Oriental Series. Researches — YOSR
Yale Papyri in the Beinecke Rare Book and Manuscript Library — YPBRBML
Yale Poetry Review — YPR
Yale Review — GYAL
Yale Review — Yale R
Yale Review — Yale Rev
Yale Review — YR
Yale Romanic Studies — Y Rom St
Yale Romanic Studies — YRS
Yale Scientific — Yale Sci
Yale Scientific Magazine — Yale Sci Mag
Yale Scientific Magazine — Yale Scient Mag
Yale Scientific Monthly — Yale Sc Mo
Yale Studies in English — YSE
Yale Studies in World Public Order — Yale St Wld Pub Ord
Yale Studies in World Public Order — Yale Stud World PO
Yale Studies in World Public Order — Yale Stud World Pub Ord
Yale University. Art Gallery. Bulletin — Yale Art Gal Bul
Yale University. Art Gallery. Bulletin — Yale Univ Art Gal Bull
Yale University. Art Gallery. Bulletin — Yale Univ B
Yale University. Associates in Fine Arts. Bulletin — Yale Associates Bul
Yale University. Library. Gazette — Yale U Lib Gaz
Yale University. Library. Gazette — Yale U Libr
Yale University. Library. Gazette — Yale Univ Lib Gaz
Yale University. Library. Gazette — YLG
Yale University. Library. Gazette — YULG
Yale University. Peabody Museum of Natural History. Annual Report — Yale Univ Peabody Mus Nat Hist Annu Rep
Yale University. Peabody Museum of Natural History. Bulletin — Yale Univ Peabody Mus Nat Hist Bull
Yale University. Peabody Museum of Natural History. Bulletin — Yale Univ Peabody Mus Nat History Bull
Yale University. School of Forestry and Environmental Studies. Bulletin — Yale Univ Sch For Environ Stud Bull
Yale University. School of Forestry. Bulletin — Yale Forestry Bull
Yale University. School of Forestry. Bulletin — Yale Univ Sch For Bull
Yalkut Le-sivim Tekhnologyah U-Minhal Shel Tekstil — Yalkut Le-Sivim Tekhnol U-Minhal Shel Tekst
Yam (Tel Aviv) — YT
Yamaguchi Daigaku Kogakubu Kenkyu Hokoku — YDKGA
Yamaguchi Journal of Science/Yamaguchi Daigaku Rigakkai Shi — Yamaguchi J Sci
Yamaguchi Medicine [*Japan*] — Yamaguchi Med
Yankee — GYAN
Yardbird Reader — Yard R
Yarn Market News — Yarn Mark News
Yaroslavskii Gosudarstvennyi Universitet. Mezhvuzovskii Tematicheskii Sbornik — Yarosl Gos Univ Mezhvuz Temat Sb
Yawata Technical Report — Yawata Tech Rep
Year Book Australia — Year Book Aust
Year Book. Bibliographical Society. Chicago. Bibliographical Society of America — Year Book Bibliogr Soc Chicago
Year Book. Carnegie Institution of Washington — Year Book Carnegie Inst Wash
Year Book (Charleston, South Carolina) — Yr Bk (Charleston SC)
Year Book. Indian National Science Academy — Year Book Indian Nat Sci Acad
Year Book. Indian National Science Academy — Year Book Indian Natl Sci Acad
Year Book. National Auricula and Primula Society. Northern Section — Year Book Natl Auricula Primula Soc North Sec
Year Book of Diagnostic Radiology — YBDRE3
Year Book of Diagnostic Radiology — Year Book Diagn Radiol
Year Book of Endocrinology — Year Book Endocrinol
Year Book of Hand Surgery — YBHSEQ
Year Book of Hand Surgery — Year Book Hand Surg
Year Book of Nuclear Medicine [*United States*] — Year Book Nucl Med
Year Book of Obstetrics and Gynecology — Year Book Obstet Gynecol
Year Book of Obstetrics and Gynecology — YOBGAD
Year Book of Reports of Cases — YB
Year Book of World Affairs — Yearb Wld Aff
Year Book. Rhododendron Association — Year Book Rhododendron Assoc
Year Books [*Law*] [*British*] — YB
Year in Endocrinology — Year Endocrinol
Year in Immunology — Year Immunol
Year in Immunology — YEIMEY
Year in Metabolism — Year Metab
Yearbook. American Iron and Steel Institute — Yearb Am Iron Steel Inst
Yearbook. American Philosophical Society — Yearb Amer Phil Soc
Yearbook. American Pulp and Paper Mill Superintendents Association — Yearb Am Pulp Pap Mill Supt Assoc
Yearbook. Association of Pacific Coast Geographers — Yb Ass Pacif Cst Geogr
Yearbook Australia — Yrbk Austl
Yearbook. Bharat Krishak Samaj — Yearb Bharat Krishak Samaj
Yearbook. British Pirandello Society — YBPS
Yearbook. Bureau of Entomology. Hangchow/Chekiang Sheng K'un Ch'ung Chu Nien K'an — Yearb Bur Entomol Hangchow
Yearbook. Bureau of Mineral Resources. Geology and Geophysics — Yearb Bur Miner Resour Geol Geophys
Yearbook. Bureau of Mineral Resources. Geology and Geophysics (Australia) — Yearb Bur Miner Resour Geol Geo-Phys (Aus)
Yearbook. California Avocado Society — Yb Calif Avocado Soc

Yearbook. California Avocado Society — Yearb Calif Avocado Soc
Yearbook. California Macadamia Society — Yearb Calif Macad Soc
Yearbook. Canadian Society for the Study of Education — Yearb Can Soc Stud Educ
Yearbook. Carnegie Institute of Washington — Yearb Carnegie Inst Wash
Yearbook. Central Research Institute for Physics. Hungarian Academy of Sciences — Yearb Cent Res Inst Phys Hung
Yearbook. Children's Literature Association — Yearb Child Lit Assoc
Yearbook. Coke Oven Managers' Association — YCOMA
Yearbook. Coke Oven Managers' Association [*England*] — Yearb Coke Oven Managers' Assoc
Yearbook. Estonian Learned Society in America — Yearb Est Learned Soc Am
Yearbook. Estonian Learned Society in America — YTELSA
Yearbook. Faculty of Agriculture. University of Ankara — Yearb Fac Agr Univ Ankara
Yearbook for Inter-American Musical Research — Yb Inter Amer M Research
Yearbook for Traditional Music — Trad Mus Yrbk
Yearbook for Traditional Music — YTM
Yearbook. Gloucestershire Bee-Keepers Association — Yb Gloucester Beekprs Ass
Yearbook. Institute of Geochemistry. Siberian Division. Academy of Sciences (USSR) — Yearb Inst Geochem Sib Div Acad Sci (USSR)
Yearbook. International Council of Scientific Unions — YBICSU
Yearbook. International Folk Music Council — Yb Int Folk M Council
Yearbook. International Folk Music Council — Yb Int Folk Music Coun
Yearbook. International Folk Music Council — YIFMC
Yearbook. Leo Baeck Institute — Yearb Leo Baeck Inst
Yearbook. Medical Association of the Greater City of New York — Yb Med Ass Great Cy NY
Yearbook. National Farmers' Association — Yearb Nat Farmers' Ass
Yearbook. National Institute of Sciences of India — Yearb Natl Inst Sci India
Yearbook of Agricultural Cooperation — Yb Agric Coop
Yearbook of Agricultural Co-Operation — Yearb Agr Co-Op
Yearbook of Agriculture — Yearb Agric
Yearbook of Agriculture. US Department of Agriculture — Yb Agric US Dep Agric
Yearbook of Agriculture. US Department of Agriculture — Yearb Agr USDA
Yearbook of Agriculture. US Department of Agriculture — Yearb Agric US Dep Agric
Yearbook of Agriculture. Using Our Natural Resources — Yrbk Agric
Yearbook of Anesthesia — Yearb Anesth
Yearbook of Comparative and General Literature — Yb
Yearbook of Comparative and General Literature — YCGL
Yearbook of Comparative and General Literature — Yearb Comp Gen Lit
Yearbook of Comparative and General Literature — Yrbk Comp & Gen Lit
Yearbook of Comparative and General Literature — Yrbk Compar & Gen Lit
Yearbook of Comparative Criticism — YCC
Yearbook of Construction Statistics — YCS
Yearbook of Dermatology and Syphilology — Yearb Dermatol Syphilol
Yearbook of Drug Therapy — Yearb Drug Ther
Yearbook of East-European Economics — Yearbook East-Eur Econ
Yearbook of Education — Yb Educ
Yearbook of Endocrinology — Yearb Endocrinol
Yearbook of English Studies — Yearb Engl Stud
Yearbook of English Studies — YES
Yearbook of General Medicine — Yb Gen Med
Yearbook of General Surgery — Yb Gen Surg
Yearbook of General Surgery — Yearb Gen Surg
Yearbook of Higher Education — Yearb High Educ
Yearbook of Industrial and Orthopedic Surgery — Yb Ind Orthop Surg
Yearbook of Industrial Statistics — Yb Ind Stat
Yearbook of Italian Studies — YIS
Yearbook of Liturgical Studies [*Notre Dame, IN*] — YbLitgSt
Yearbook of Medicine — Yb Med
Yearbook of Medicine — Yearb Med
Yearbook of Neurology, Psychiatry, Endocrinology, and Neurosurgery — Yb Neurol Psychiat Endocr
Yearbook of Ophthalmology — Yb Ophthal
Yearbook of Pathology and Clinical Pathology — Yearb Pathol Clin Pathol
Yearbook of Pediatrics — Yb Pediat
Yearbook of Pediatrics — Yearb Pediatr
Yearbook of Pharmacy — Yearb Pharm
Yearbook of Physical Anthropology — IYPA
Yearbook of Physical Anthropology — Yearb Phys Anthropol
Yearbook of Physical Medicine and Rehabilitation — Yb Phys Med Rehabil
Yearbook of Romanian Studies — YRS
Yearbook of School Law — Yrbk Sch Law
Yearbook of Science and the Future — Yearb Sci Future
Yearbook of Social Policy in Britain — Yb Soc Pol Britain
Yearbook of Special Education — Yrbk Sp Educ
Yearbook of World Affairs — Yb Wld Aff
Yearbook of World Affairs — Yb World Aff
Yearbook of World Affairs [*London*] — Yrbk World Aff
Yearbook of World Affairs. London Institute of World Affairs — LIWA/YWA
Yearbook on International Communist Affairs — YICA
Yearbook. Ontario Rose Society — Yearb Ontario Rose Soc
Yearbook. Paper Industry Management Association — Yearb Pap Ind Manage Assoc
Yearbook. Physical Society — Yb Phys Soc
Yearbook. Royal Asiatic Society of Bengal — Yearb R Asiat Soc Bengal
Yearbook. Royal Horticulture Society — Yb R Hort Soc
Yearbook. Royal Society of London — Yb Soc
Yearbook. Royal Veterinary and Agricultural College — Yb R Vet Agric Coll
Yearbook. United States Department of Agriculture — Yb US Dep Agric
Yearbook. Yorkshire Beekeepers Association — Yb Yorks Beekprs Ass
Year's Work in Archaeology — YWA
Year's Work in Classical Studies — YW
Year's Work in Classical Studies — YWC
Year's Work in Classical Studies — YWCS
Year's Work in English Studies — Year's Work Eng Stud
Year's Work in English Studies — YW
Year's Work in English Studies — YWE
Year's Work in English Studies — YWES
Year's Work in Modern Language Studies — YWML
Year's Work in Modern Language Studies — YWMLS
Yeast Genetic Engineering — Yeast Genet Eng
Yeats Eliot Review — Yeats Eliot
Yeats Eliot Review — YER
Yeda-'am. Journal. Hebrew Folklore Society [*Tel-Aviv*] — YA
Yeda-'am. Journal. Hebrew Folklore Society [*Tel-Aviv*] — YAJ
Yellow Brick Road — Yellow B R
Yellow Pages DataSystem [*Database*] — YPD
Yellowjacket — Y
Yellowknifer — YN
Yellowstone Library and Museum Association. Yellowstone Interpretive Series — Yellowstone Libr and Mus Assoc Yellowstone Interpretive Ser
Yellowstone-Bighorn Research Project. Contribution — Yellowstone-Bighorn Research Proj Contr
Yelmo — YO
Yenching Journal of Chinese Studies — YCHP
Yenching Journal of Chinese Studies — YJCS
Yeshiva University. Information Retrieval Center on the Disadvantaged. Bulletin — IRCD Bul
Yessis Review of Soviet Physical Education and Sports — Yessis Rev
Yeung Nam University. Institute of Industrial Technology. Report — Yeung Nam Univ Inst Ind Technol Rep
Yiddishe Folk — YF
Yiddishe Kultur — YK
Yidishe Shprakh — YS
Yidishe Shprakh — YSh
Yikal Maya Than (Mexico) — YMTM
Yipster Times — Yiptime
YIVO Annual — YA
Yivo Annual of Jewish Social Science — YiA
YIVO Annual of Jewish Social Science — YIVO
YIVO Bleter [*Vilna/New York*] — YB
Yoga Journal — Yoga Jnl
Yogyo Kyokai Shi — YGKSA
Yokogawa Technical Report [*Japan*] — Yokogawa Tech Rep
Yokohama Igaku — YKIGA
Yokohama Igaku — Yoko Iga
Yokohama Mathematical Journal — Yokohama Math J
Yokohama Medical Bulletin — Yoko Med Bull
Yokohama Medical Bulletin — Yokohama Med Bull
Yokohama Medical Journal [*Japan*] — Yokohama Med J
Yokohama Shiritsu Daigaku Ronso [*Bulletin. Yokohama Municipal University Society*] — YoShiR
Yokufukai Geriatric Journal — Yokufukai Geriatr J
Yonago Acta Medica — Yon Act Med
Yonago Acta Medica — Yona Acta Med
Yonago Acta Medica — Yonago Acta Med
Yonago Igaku Zasshi — Yona Iga Zass
Yonsei Engineering Report — Yonsei Eng Rep
Yonsei Engineering Review [*South Korea*] — Yonsei Eng Rev
Yonsei Journal of Medical Science — Yonsei J Med Sci
Yonsei Medical Journal — Yonsei Med J
Yonsei Reports on Tropical Medicine — Yonsei Rep Trop Med
Yonsei Reports on Tropical Medicine — YRTMA
York County Historical Society. Papers — YorkCoHS
York Papers in Linguistics — York Papers Ling
York Papers in Linguistics — York Paps in Linguistics
York Papers in Linguistics — YPL
Yorkshire Archaeological Journal — YAJ
Yorkshire Archaeological Journal — Yorkshire A J
Yorkshire Archaeological Journal — Yorkshire Arch J
Yorkshire Archaeological Journal — Yorkshire Arch Journal
Yorkshire Archaeological Journal — Yorkshire Archaeol J
Yorkshire Architect — Yorkshire Archt
Yorkshire Beekeeper — Yorks Beekpr
Yorkshire Bulletin of Economic and Social Research — YB
Yorkshire Bulletin of Economic and Social Research — Yorks Bull Econ Soc Res
Yorkshire Celtic Studies — YCS
Yorkshire Dialect Society. Transactions — YDS
Yorkshire Geological and Polytechnic Society. Proceedings — Yorkshire G Polyt Soc Pr
Yorkshire Geological Society. Occasional Publication — Yorks Geol Soc Occas Publ
Yorkshire Geological Society. Proceedings — Yorkshire Geol Soc Proc
Yorkshire Post — YP
Young Athlete — Young Athl
Young Children — Young Child
Young Cinema and Theatre — Y C T
Young Cinema and Theatre — Young Cinema
Young Liberal — Young Lib
Young Man — YM
Young Miss Magazine — YM
Young Numismatist — YN
Young Viewers — Y Viewers
Young Woman — YW

Yo-Up Hoeji — YPHJA
Your Big Backyard — Backyard
Your Computer — Your Comput
Your Musical Cue — Your Mus Cue
Your Oklahoma Dental Association Journal — Your Okla Dent Assoc J
Your Public Lands. US Department of the Interior. Bureau of Land Mangement — YPLA
Your Radiologist — Your Radiol
Youth Aid Bulletin — Youth Aid Bull
Youth and Nation — YN
Youth and Society — PYNS
Youth and Society — Youth and Soc
Youth and Society — Youth Soc
Youth in Society — Youth in Soc
Youth Journal — YJ
Youth Quarterly — YQ
Youth Training News — Youth Train News
Yoyuen — YOYUA
Yperman. Bulletin de la Societe Belge d'Histoire de la Medecine — Yperm
Yr Haul a'r Gengell — HG
Ysgrifau Beirniadol — YB
Yuasa Technical Information [*Japan*] — Yuasa Tech Inf
Yugoslav Chemical Papers — Yugosl Chem Pap
Yugoslav Hop Symposium. Proceedings — Yugosl Hop Symp Proc
Yugoslav Journal of Operations Research — Yugosl J Oper Res
Yugoslav Law — Yugosl Law
Yugoslav Law — Yugoslav L
Yugoslav Medical Biochemistry — Yugosl Med Biochem
Yugoslav Society of Soil Science. Publication — Yug Soc Soil Sci Publ
Yugoslav Survey — YAA
Yugoslav Survey — Yug Surv
Yugoslav Survey — Yugosl Surv
Yugoslavia Export — CMF
Yugoslavia Export — Yugo Exprt
Yugoslavia Zavod za Geoloska i Geofizicka Istrazivanja. Rasprave — Yugosl Zavod Geol Geofiz Istrazivanja Raspr
Yugoslavia Zavod za Geoloska i Geofizicka Istrazivanja. Vesnik. Geologija. Serija A [*Belgrade*] — Yugosl Zavod Geol Geofiz Istrazivanja Vesn Geol
Yugoslav-Serbo-Croatian-English Contrastive Project. Reports — YSCECP Reports
Yugoslav-Serbo-Croatian-English Contrastive Project. Studies — YSCECP Studies
Yuki Gosei Kagaku Kyokaishi — YGKKA
Yukon Anniversaries Commission Newsletter — YACN
Yukon Bibliography [*Database*] — YKB
Yukon Conservation Society. Newsletter — YCSN
Yukon Economic News — YUEN
Yukon Government News Release — YGNR
Yukon Historical and Museums Association. Newsletter — YHMA
Yukon Historical and Museums Association. Newsletter — YHMAN
Yukon Indian News — YI
Yukon Indian News — YUIN
Yukon News — Y
Yukon News — YU
Yukon Reports [*Database*] — YR
Yukon Teacher — YUTR
Yukon Update — YUUD
Yukon Water Management Bulletin. Westwater Research Centre — YUWM
Yunost' [*Moscow*] — Yu
Yurosholayimer Almanakh — Y Alm
Yu-Yen Yen-Chiu [*Linguistic Researches*] — YYYC
Yu-Yen-Hsueh Lun-Ts'ung [*Essays in Linguistics*] — YLT

Z

Z Dziejow Form Artystycznych Literaturze Polskiej — ZDFALP
Z Magazine [*Zambia*] — ZMag
Z Pola Walki — Z
Z Polskich Studiow Slawistycznych — ZPSS
Za Ekonomiyu Materialov — Za Ekon Mater
Za Ekonomiyu Topliva — Za Ekon Topl
Za i Przeciw — ZiP
Za Khlopkovuyu Nezavisimost — Za Khlopk Nezavisimost
Za Ovladenie Tekhnikoi v Kamenougol'noi Promyshlennosti — Za Ovladenie Tekh Kamenougol'n Promsti
Za Progress Proizvodstva — Za Prog Proizvod
Za Rekonstruktsiyu Tekstil'noi Promyshlennosti — Za Rekonstr Tekst Promsti
Za Socialisticke Zemedelstvi — Za Soc Zemed
Za Sotsialisticheskuyu Sel'skokhozyaistvennuyu Nauku — Za Sots Sel' -Khoz Nauku
Za Sotsialisticheskuyu Sel'skokhozyaistvennuyu Nauku. Seriya A — Za Sots Sel'skokhoz Nauku Ser A
Za Tekhnicheskii Progress — ZATPA
Za Tekhnicheskii Progress (Baku) — Za Tekh Prog (Baku)
Za Tekhnicheskii Progress (Gorkiy) — Za Tekh Prog (Gorkiy)
Za Turfyanuyu Industriyu — Za Turf Ind
Zabytki Przyrody Nieozywionej Ziem Rzeczpospolitej Polskiej — Zaby Przyr Nieozyw
Zadarska Revija — Zad Rev
Zadarska Revija — ZR
ZAED [*Zentralstelle fuer Atomkernenergie-Dokumentation*] **Physik Daten** — ZAED Phys Daten
Zagadnienia Drgan Nieliniowych [*Nonlinear Vibration Problems*] — Zagadnienia Drgan Nieliniowych
Zagadnienia Ekonomiki Rolnej — Zagad Ekon Roln
Zagadnienia Ekonomiki Rolnej — Zagadn Ekon Roln
Zagadnienia Eksploatacji Maszyn [*Poland*] — Zagadn Eksploatacji Masz
Zagadnienia Rodzajow Literackich — ZRL
Zagadnienia Techniki Fal Ultradzwiekowych — Zagad Tech Fal Ultradziek
Zagadnienie Dynamiki Rozwoju Czlowieka Zeszyty Problemowe Kosmosu — Zagadnienie Dyn Rozwoju Czlowieka Zesz Probl Kosmosu
Zagreb — Z
Zagreber Germanistische Studien — Zagreber Studien
Zahn-, Mund-, und Kieferheilkunde — Zahn-Mund-Kieferheilkd
Zahn-, Mund-, und Kieferheilkunde mit Zentralblatt [*German Democratic Republic*] — Zahn- Mund- Kieferheilkd Zentralbl
Zahnaerzteblatt (Baden-Wuerttemberg) — Zahnaerztebl (Baden-Wuerttemb)
Zahnaerztliche Mitteilungen — Zahnaerztl Mitt
Zahnaerztliche Mitteilungen — ZM
Zahnaerztliche Praxis — Zahn Prax
Zahnaerztliche Praxis — Zahnaerztl Prax
Zahnaerztliche Praxisfuehrung — Zahnaerztl Praxisfuehr
Zahnaerztliche Rundschau — Zahn Rd
Zahnaerztliche Rundschau — Zahnaerztl Rundsch
Zahnaerztliche Welt — Zahnaerztl Welt
Zahnaerztliche Welt — ZAWEA
Zahnaerztliche Welt und Zahnaerztliche Reform — Zahnaerztl Welt Zahnaerztl Reform
Zahnaerztliche Welt, Zahnaerztliche Rundschau — Zahnaerztl Welt Zahnaerztl Rundsch
Zahnaerztlicher Gesundheitsdienst — Zahnaerztl Gesundheitsdienst
Zahnaerztlicher Informationsdienst — Zahn Inf Die
Zahnerhaltungskunde — Zahnerh Kd
Zahntechnik — Zahntechn
Zahntechniker — Zahntechn
Zahntechnische Nachrichten — Zahntechn Nachr
Zaire-Afrique — Z-A
Zaire-Afrique — Zaire-Afr
Zakhist Roslin — Zakhist Rosl
Zakhyst Roslyn Respublikans 'Kyi Mizhvidomchyi Tematychnyi Naukovyi Zbirnyk — Zakhyst Rosl Resp Mizhvid Temat Nauk Zb
Zaklad Narodowy Imeni Ossolinskich — ZNIO
Zakonomernosti Raspredeleniya Promesnykh Tsentrov v Ionnykh Kristallakh — Zakonomern Raspred Promesnykh Tsentrov Ionnykh Krist
Zakonomernosti Razmeshcheniya Poleznykh Iskopaemykh — Zakonomern Razmeshcheniya Polezn Iskop
Zakupki Sel'skokhozyaistvennykh Produktov — Zakupki Sel'skokhoz Prod
Zambia. Department of Game and Fisheries. Fisheries Research Bulletin — Zambia Dep Game Fish Fish Res Bull
Zambia. Department of Wildlife, Fisheries, and National Parks. Annual Report — Zambia Dep Wildl Fish Natl Parks Annu Rep
Zambia. Division of Forest Research. Annual Report — Zambia Div For Res Annu Rep
Zambia. Division of Forest Research. Research Pamphlet — Zambia Div For Res Res Pam
Zambia Forest Research Bulletin — Zambia For Res Bull
Zambia Geographical Association Magazine — Zambia Geogr Ass Mag
Zambia Geographical Association. Magazine — Zambia Geogr Assoc Mag
Zambia. Geological Survey. Annual Report — Zambia Geol Surv Annu Rep
Zambia. Geological Survey. Department Annual Report — Zambia Geol Surv Dep Annu Rep
Zambia. Geological Survey. Economic Report — Zambia Geol Surv Econ Rep
Zambia. Geological Survey. Records — Zambia Geol Surv Rec
Zambia. Geological Survey. Technical Report — Zambia Geol Surv Tech Rep
Zambia Journal of Science and Technology — Zambia J Sci Technol
Zambia Journal of Science and Technology — ZJSTD
Zambia Law Journal — Zambia Law J
Zambia Library Association Journal — Zambia Libr Assoc J
Zambia. Ministry of Lands and Mines. Geological Survey Department. Economic Report — Zambia Geol Surv Dep Econ Rep
Zambia. Ministry of Lands and Mines. Report of the Geological Survey — Zambia Rep Geol Surv
Zambia. Ministry of Lands and Natural Resources. Forest Research Bulletin — Zambia Minist Lands Nat Resour For Res Bull
Zambia. Ministry of Rural Development. Forest Research Bulletin — Zambia Minist Rural Dev For Res Bull
Zambia Nurse Journal — Zambia Nurse J
ZANCO. Scientific Journal of Sulaimaniyah University. Series A. Pure and Applied Sciences — ZANCO Ser A
ZANCO. Series A. Pure and Applied Sciences — ZANCO Ser A Pure Appl Sci
Zanzibar Protectorate. Annual Report on the Medical Department — Zanzibar Protect Ann Rep Med Dept
Zapadne Karpaty. Seria Geologia — Zapadne Karpaty Ser Geol
Zapadne Karpaty. Seria Paleontologia — Zapadn Karpaty Ser Paleontol
Zapiski Addzelu Pryrody i Narodnaj Gaspadarki — Zap Addz Pryr Nar Gasp
Zapiski Armyanskogo Otdeleniya Vsesoyuznogo Mineralogicheskogo Obshchestva — Zap Arm Otd Vses Mineral Ova
Zapiski Belorusskogo Gosudarstvennogo Instituta Sel'skogo i Lesnogo Khozyaistva — Zap Beloruss Gos Inst Sel'sk Lesn Khoz
Zapiski Central'no-Kavkazskogo Otdelenija Vsesojuznogo Botaniceskgo Obscestva — Zap Centr Kavkazsk Otd Vsesojuzn Bot Obsc
Zapiski Cukotskogo Kraevedceskogo Muzeja — Zap Cukotsk Kraeved Muz
Zapiski Dnipropetrovs'kogo Institutu Narodnoi Osviti — Z Dnipr INO
Zapiski Geograficeskogo Obscestva — Zap GO
Zapiski Gosudarstvennogo Instituta Jazyka, Literatury, i Istorii — Zap Inst Jaz Lit Ist
Zapiski Imperatorskago Russkago Arkheologicheskago Obshchestva — ZRAO
Zapiski Imperatorskago Russkago Geograficeskago Obscestva po Obscej Geografii — Zap Imp Russk Geogr Obsc Obscej Geogr
Zapiski Imperatorskoj Akademii Nauk — Zap Imp Akad Nauk
Zapiski Instituta Vostokoveden'ia Akademii Nauk SSSR — ZIVAN
Zapiski Institutu Khimii Akademiya Nauk Ukrains'koi RSR — Zap Inst Khim Akad Nauk Ukr RSR
Zapiski. Kalmyckij Naucno-Issledovatel'skij Institut Jazyka, Literatury, i Istorii — Zap Kalm Nauc Issl Inst Jaz Lit Ist
Zapiski Kavkazskogo Otdela Russkogo Geograficeskogo Obscestva — Zap KORGO
Zapiski Khar'kovskogo Sel'skokhozyaistvennogo Instituta — Zap Khar'k S-Kh Inst
Zapiski Kiivs'kogo Tovaristva Prirodoznavtsiv — Zap Kiiv Tov Prirodozn
Zapiski Kirgizskogo Otdeleniya Vsesoyuznogo Mineralogicheskogo Obshchestva — Zap Kirg Otd Vses Mineral Ova
Zapiski Komiteta Akklimatizacija, Ucrezdennago pri Imperatorskom Moskovskom Obscestve Sel'skago Hozjajstva — Zap Komiteta Akklim
Zapiski Leningradskogo Gornogo Instituta [*Former USSR*] — Zap Leningr Gorn Inst
Zapiski Leningradskogo Gornogo Instituta — ZLGIA
Zapiski Leningradskogo Sel'skokhozyaistvennogo Instituta — Zap Leningr Sel'-Khoz Inst
Zapiski Leningradskogo Sel'skokhozyaistvennogo Instituta — Zap Leningr S-Kh Inst
Zapiski Leningradskogo Sel'skokhozyaistvennogo Instituta — Zap Leningrad Sel'skokhoz Inst
Zapiski Leningradskogo Sel'skokhozyaistvennogo Instituta — ZLSIA
Zapiski Nauchnykh Seminarov — Zap Nauchn Semin

Zapiski Nauchnykh Seminarov Leningradskoe Otdelenie Matematicheskii Institut Akademia Nauk SSSR [*Former USSR*] — Zap Nauchn Semin Leningr Otd Mat Inst Akad Nauk SSSR
Zapiski Nauchnykh Seminarov Leningradskogo Otdeleniya Matematicheskogo Instituta Imeni V. A. Steklova Akademii Nauk SSSR (LOMI) — Zap Nauchn Sem Leningrad Otdel Mat Inst Steklov (LOMI)
Zapiski Naucno-Issledovatel'nogo Instituta pri Sovete Ministrov Mordovskoj ASSR — ZIMordASSR
Zapiski Naucno-Prikladnyh Otdelov Tiflisskago Botaniceskago Sada. Thbilisi Botanikur Bagis Mecnierul-Bamogenebithi Ganqophilebatha Nacerebi/ Scientific Papers. Applied Sections. Tiflis Botanical Garden — Zap Naucno Prikl Otd Tiflissk Bot Sada
Zapiski Naucnyh Seminarov Leningradskogo Otdelenija Matematiceskogo Instituta Imeni V. A. Steklova Akademii Nauk SSSR — Zap Naucn Sem Leningrad Otdel Mat Inst Steklov
Zapiski Obscestva Izucenija Amurskogo Kraja Vladivostokskogo Otdelenija Priamurskogo Otdela Russkogo Geograficeskogo Obscestva — Zap Obsc Izuc Amursk Kraja Vladivostoksk Otd Priamursk Otd Ru
Zapiski Odesskago Arkheologicheskago Obshchestva — Zapiski Odessa
Zapiski Odesskago Arkheologicheskago Obshchestva — ZOAO
Zapiski Odesskoe Arkheologicheskoe Obshchestvo [*Odessa, USSR*] — Zap Odess Ark Obshch
Zapiski Rossiiskogo Mineralogicheskogo Obshchestva — Zap Ross Mineral Ova
Zapiski Rossijskoj Akademii Nauk/Memoires de l'Academie des Sciences de Russie — Zap Rossijsk Akad Nauk
Zapiski Russkogo Naucnogo Instituta — ZRNI
Zapiski Semipalatinskago Podotdela Zapadno-Sibirskago Otdela Imperatorskago Russkago Geograficeskago Obscestva — Zap Semipalatinsk Podotd Zapadno Sibirsk Otd Imp Russk Geogr
Zapiski Severo-Dvinskogo Obscestva Izucenija Mestnogo Kraja — Z Sev-Dvin OIMK
Zapiski Severo-Kavkazskogo Kraevogo Gorskogo Naucno-Issledovatel'skogo Instituta — Zap SKK Gor NII
Zapiski Sredne-Sibirskogo Otdela Byvsego Krasnojarskogo Gosudarstvennogo Russkogo Geograficeskogo Obscestva/Memoirs. Middle-Siberian Section formerly Krasnojarsk-Section. State Russian Geographical Society — Zap Sredne Sibirsk Otd Gosud Russk Geogr Obsc
Zapiski Sverdlovskogo Otdeleniya Vsesoyuznogo Botanicheskogo Obshchestva — Zap Sverdl Otd Vses Bot Ova
Zapiski Sverdlovskogo Otdeleniya Vsesoyuznogo Botanicheskogo Obshchestva — Zap Sverdlov Otd Vsesoyuz Bot Obshch
Zapiski Tadzhikskogo Otdeleniya Vsesoyuznogo Mineralogicheskogo Obshchestva — Zap Tadzh Otd Vses Mineral Ova
Zapiski Tsentral'no-Kavkazskogo Otdeleniya Vsesoyuznogo Botanicheskogo Obshchestva — Zap Tsentr Kavk Otd Vses Bot Ova
Zapiski Ukrainskogo Otdeleniya Vsesoyuznogo Mineralogicheskogo Obshchestva — Zap Ukr Otd Vses Mineral Ova
Zapiski Ural'skago Obscestva Ljubitelej Estestvozanija/Bulletin de la Societe Ouralienne d'Amateurs des Sciences Naturelles — Zap Uralsk Obsc Ljubit Estestv
Zapiski Uzbekistanskogo Otdeleniya Vsesoyuznogo Mineralogicheskogo Obshchestva — Zap Uzb Otd Vses Mineral Ova
Zapiski Voronezhskogo Sel'skokhozyaistvennogo Instituta — Zap Voronezh Sel'-Khoz Inst
Zapiski Voronezhskogo Sel'skokhozyaistvennogo Instituta — Zap Voronezh S-Kh Inst
Zapiski Vostochno-Sibirskogo Otdeleniya Vsesoyuznogo Mineralogicheskogo Obshchestva — Zap Vost Sib Otd Vses Mineral Ova
Zapiski Vostochnovo Otdelenia — ZVO
Zapiski Vostochnovo Otdelenia Imperatorskovo Ruskavo Arkheologicheskavo Obshchestva — ZVORAO
Zapiski Vsesoyuznogo Mineralogicheskogo Obshchestva — Zap Vses Mineral Obshchest
Zapiski Vsesoyuznogo Mineralogicheskogo Obshchestva — Zap Vses Mineral O-Va
Zapiski Zabaikal'skogo Filiala Geograficheskogo Obshchestva SSSR — Zap Zabaik Fil Geogr Ova SSSR
Zapiski Zabaikal'skogo Otdela Vsesoyuznogo Geograficheskogo Obshchestva — Zap Zabaik Otd Vses Geogr O-Va
Zapiski Zapadno-Sibirskago Otdela Imperatorskago Russkago Geograficeskago Obscestva — Zap Zapadno Sibirsk Otd Imp Russk Geogr Obsc
Zapisnici Srpskog Geoloskog Drustva — Zapisnici Srp Geol Drus
Zapysky Naukovoho Tovarystva Imeny Svecenka — ZNTS
Zapysky Naukovoho Tovarystva Imeny Svecenka (Literature Series) — ZNTSL
Zaranie Slaskie — ZarSl
Zashchita Metallov — Zashch Met
Zashchita ot Korrozii v Khimicheskoi Promyshlennosti — Zashch Korroz Khim Promsti
Zashchita Rastenii (Kiev) — Zashch Rast (Kiev)
Zashchita Rastenii (Leningrad) — Zashch Rast (Leningrad)
Zashchita Rastenii (Moscow) — Zashch Rast (Mosc)
Zashchita Rastenii (Moscow) — Zashch Rast (Moscow)
Zashchita Rastenii ot Vreditelei i Boleznei — Zashch Rast Vred Bolez
Zashchita Rastenii ot Vreditelei i Boleznei — Zashch Rast Vred Bolezn
Zashchita Rastenii ot Vreditelei i Boleznei — Zashch Rast Vredit Bolez
Zashchita Truboprovodov ot Korrozii — Zashch Truboprovodov Korroz
Zashchitnye Pokrytiya na Metallakh — Zashch Pokrytiya Met
Zastita Bilja — ZABIA
Zastita Bilja — Zast Bilja
Zastita Materijala — Zast Mater
Zastosowania Matematyki — ZastMat
Zastosowania Matematyki — Zastosow Mat
Zavodskaja Laboratorija — ZL
Zavodskaya Laboratoriya — Zav Lab
Zavodskaya Laboratoriya — Zavod Lab
Zbirka Izbranih Poglavij iz Fizike — Zbirka Izbran Poglav Fiz
Zbirka Izbranih Poglavij iz Matematike — Zbirka Izbran Poglav Mat
Zbirnik Institutu Khimichnoi Tekhnologii Akademiya Nauk Ukrains'koi RSR — Zb Inst Khim Tekhnol Akad Nauk Ukr RSR
Zbirnik Naukovikh Prats Aspirantiv Kiivs'kii Inzhenerno-Budivel'nii Institut — Zb Nauk Pr Aspir Kiiv Inzh Budiv Inst
Zbirnik Naukovikh Prats Kiivs'kii Budivel'nii Institut — Zb Nauk Pr Kiiv Budiv Inst
Zbirnik Naukovikh Robit Kharkivs'kogo Derzhavnogo Medichnogo Institutu — Zb Nauk Rob Khark Derzh Med Inst
Zbirnik Prats' Institut Teploenergetiki Akademiya Nauk Ukrains'koi RSR — Zb Pr Inst Teploenerg Akad Nauk Ukr RSR
Zbirnik Prats' Ukrains'kii Derzhavnii Institut Naukovoi ta Praktichnoi Veterin arii — Zb Pr Ukr Derzh Inst Nauk Prakt Vet
Zbirnik Prats' Ukrains'kogo Institutu Eksperimental'noi Veterinarii — Zb Pr Ukr Inst Eksp Vet
Zbirnyk Biologicnogo Fakul'tetu — Zbirn Biol Fak
Zbirnyk Naukovych Prac' Aspirantiv z Filolohiji — ZbNPAF
Zbirnyk Naukovykh Prats' Aspirantiv Kyyivski Universytet Pryrodni Nauky — Zb Nauk Pr Aspir Kyyiv Univ Pryr Nauky
Zbirnyk Naukovykh Prats' Bilotserkiv'sta Doslidno-Selektvionna Statsiya — Zb Nauk Pr Bilotserk Dos Sel Statsiya
Zbirnyk Naukovykh Prats' Khimicheskoho Sil'skoho Hospodarstva Ukrayinskoyi Sil'skohospodarskoyi Akademiyi — Zb Nauk Pr Khim Sil'sk Hospod Ukr Sil'skohospod Akad
Zbirnyk Naukovykh Prats' L'viv'kyi Medychyni Instytut — Zb Nauk Pr L'viv Med Inst
Zbirnyk Naukovykh Prats' Umans'kyi Sil'skohospodarskyi Instytut — Zb Nauk Pr Umans'kyi Sil'skohospod Inst
Zbirnyk Prac' Dniprovs'koji Biologicnoji Stanciji. Travaux de la Station Biologique du Dniepre — Zbirn Prac Dniprovsk Biol Stanciji
Zbirnyk Prac' Naukovoji Sevcenkivs'koji Konferenciji — ZbirP
Zbirnyk Prat Jewrejskiej Istorychno-Arkheologichnoj Komisji [*Kiev*] — ZPJIAK
Zbirnyk Prats' Naukovodoslidnyts'koho Instytuta Fiziolohiyi Kyyivs'koho Universytetu — Zb Pr Nauk Inst Fiziol Kyyiv Univ
Zbirnyk Prats' Naukovodoslidnyts'koho Instytuta Fiziolohiyi Kyyivs'koho Universytetu — Zb Pr Naukovodosl Inst Fiziol Kyyiv Univ
Zbirnyk Prats' Zoolohichnoho Muzeyu Akademiyi Nauk Ukrayinskoyi RSR — Zb Pr Zool Muz Akad Nauk Ukr RSR
Zbirnyk Robit Aspirantiv L'Vivskij Derzavnyj Universitet — ZbRL
Zbirnyk Robit Aspirantiv L'Vivs'kyi Universytet Pryrodnykh Nauk — Zb Robit Aspir L'Viv Univ Pryr Nauk
Zbirnyk Robit Aspirantiv Romano-Germans'koji i Klazycnoji Filolohiji — ZbR
Zbornik. Arheoloski Muzej na Makedonija (Skopje) — Z (Skopje)
Zbornik Biotehniske Fakultete Univerze Edvarda Kardelja v Ljubljani. Kmetijstvo — Zb Bioteh Fak Univ Edvarda Kardelja Ljublj Kmetijstvo
Zbornik Biotehniske Fakultete Univerze Edvarda Kardelja v Ljubljani Veterinarstvo — Zb Bioteh Fak Univ Edvarda Kardelja Ljublj Vet
Zbornik Biotehniske Fakultete Univerze v Ljubljani — Zb Bioteh Fak Univ Ljubljani
Zbornik Biotehniske Fakultete Univerze v Ljubljani — Zb Biotehn Fak Univ Ljublj
Zbornik Biotehniske Fakultete Univerze v Ljubljani. Kmetijstvo — Zb Bioteh Fak Univ Ljublj Kmetijstvo
Zbornik Biotehniske Fakultete Univerze v Ljubljani. Kmetijstvo — Zborn Biotehn Fak Univ Ljublj Kmet
Zbornik Biotehniske Fakultete Univerze v Ljubljani. Veterinarstvo — Zb Bioteh Fak Univ Ljublj Vet
Zbornik Biotehniske Fakultete Univerze v Ljubljani. Veterinarstvo. Suplement — Zb Bioteh Fak Univ Ljublj Vet Supl
Zbornik Filozofickej Fakulty Univerzity Komenskeho-Philologica — ZFKPhil
Zbornik Filozofske Fakultete Ljubljana — Zbornik Ljubljana
Zbornik Filozofske Fakultete Ljubljana — ZFF
Zbornik Filozofskog Fakulteta (Belgrade) — ZFFB
Zbornik Filozofskog Fakulteta. Beograd — Zbornik Beograd
Zbornik Geologichych Vied Zapadne Karpaty — Zb Geol Vied Zapadne Karpaty
Zbornik Istorije Knijizevnosti — ZIK
Zbornik Lekarskej Fakulty (Kosice) — Zb Lek Fak (Kosice)
Zbornik Lekarskej Fakulty UPJS Kosice — Zb Lek Fak UPJS Kosice
Zbornik Matice Srpske — ZMS
Zbornik Meteoroloskih i Hidroloskih Radova [*Yugoslavia*] — Zb Meteorol Hidrol Rad
Zbornik Muzej Primenjene Umetnosti — Zbor Muz Primenjene Umet
Zbornik na Arheoloskiot Muzej — Zbor Arheol Muz
Zbornik Narodnog Muzeja [*Beograd*] — ZNM
Zbornik Narodnog Muzeja (Beograd) — Zbornik (Beograd)
Zbornik Narodnog Muzeja (Beograd) — Zbornik Nar Muz Beograd
Zbornik Narodnog Muzeja u Beogradu — Zbor Narod Muz Beogradu
Zbornik Prac Chemickotechnologickej Fakulty SVST — Zb Pr Chemickotechnol Fak SVST
Zbornik Prac Chemickotechnologickej Fakulty SVST — Zb Pr Chem-Technol Fak SVST
Zbornik Prac Chemickotechnologickej Fakulty SVST (Bratislava) — Zb Prac Chem Fak SVST (Bratislava)
Zbornik Prac Lekarskej Fakulty Univerzity P. J. Safarika v Kosiciach — Zb Pr Lek Fak Univ PJ Safarika Kosiciach
Zbornik Prats. Belaruski Dzyarzhauny Medychny Instytut — Zb Pr Belarus Dzyarzh Med Inst
Zbornik Pravnog Fakulteta u Zagreba — ZPFZ
Zbornik Pravnog Fakulteta u Zagrebu — Zb Prav Fak Zagrebu
Zbornik Rabot Belaruskaga Sel'ska-Gaspadarchaga Instytuta — Zb Rab Belarus Sel'Ska-Gaspad Inst
Zbornik Radova — Zborn Rad
Zbornik Radova. Bioloski Institut (Beograd) — Zb Rad Biol Inst (Beograd)

Zbornik Radova. Bioloski Institut N.R. Srbije. Recueil des Travaux. Institut Biologique — Zborn Rad Biol Inst Nar Republ Srbije
Zbornik Radova. Bioloski Institut NR Srbye Beograd — Zb Rad Biol Inst NR Srbye Beogr
Zbornik Radova. Filozofskog Fakulteta. Svencilista u Zagrebu — ZbRFFZ
Zbornik Radova Filozofskog Fakulteta u Nisu. Serija Matematika — Zb Rad
Zbornik Radova. Hrvatski Geoloski Kongres — Zb Rad Hrvat Geol Kongr
Zbornik Radova. Matematicki Institut (Beograd) — Zbornik Rad Mat Inst (Beograd)
Zbornik Radova. Nova Serija. Matematicki Institut (Beograd). Zbornik Radova. Nova Serija — Zb Rad Mat Inst (Beograd)
Zbornik Radova. Poljoprivredni Institut — Zb Rad Poljopr Inst
Zbornik Radova. Poljoprivredni Institut (Osijek) — Zb Rad Poljopr Inst (Osijek)
Zbornik Radova. Poljoprivrednog Fakulteta. Universitet u Beogradu — Zb Rad Poljopr Fak Univ Beogradu
Zbornik Radova. Poljoprivrednog Fakulteta. Universitet u Beogradu — Zb Rad Poljopriv Fak Univ Beogradu
Zbornik Radova. Poljoprivrednog Fakulteta. Universitet u Beogradu — Zborn Rad Poljopriv Fak Univ Beogr
Zbornik Radova. Poljoprivrednog Fakulteta. Universitet u Beogradu — ZRPBA
Zbornik Radova Prirodno-Matematichkog Fakulteta. Serija za Matematiku — Zb Rad Prirod Mat Fak Ser Mat
Zbornik Radova. Prirodno-Matematickog Fakulteta [*Yugoslavia*] — Zb Rad Prir Mat Fak
Zbornik Radova. Prirodno-Matematickog Fakulteta. Serija za Fiziku — Zb Rad Prir-Mat Fak Ser Fiz
Zbornik Radova. Prirodno-Matematickog Fakulteta Univerzitet u Novom Sadu — Zb Rad Prir-Mat Fak Univ Novom Sadu
Zbornik Radova Prirodno-Matematickog Fakulteta. Univerzitet u Novom Sadu. Serija za Hemiju — Zb Rad Prir Mat Fak Univ Nov Sadu Ser Hem
Zbornik Radova. Rudarsko-Geoloskog Fakulteta — Zb Rad Rud Geol Fak
Zbornik Radova. Srpska Akademija Nauka Geoloski Institut — Zb Rad Srp Akad Nauka Geol Inst
Zbornik Radova. Srpske Akademije Nauke — ZbSAN
Zbornik Radova. Srpske Akademije Nauke — ZRSAN
Zbornik Radova. Svenciliste u Zagrebu — ZRZ
Zbornik Radova. Sveuc. Zagrebu, Varazdin — Zb Rad Varazdin
Zbornik Radova. Univerzitet Svetozar Markovic Kragujevac. Prirodno-Matematicki Fakultet — Zb Rad Kragujevac
Zbornik Radova Vizantoloskog Instituta — ZR
Zbornik Radova Vizantoloskog Instituta — ZRVI
Zbornik Radova Vizantoloskog Instituta — ZVI
Zbornik Radova Vizantoloskog Instituta (Beograd) — Zbornik Rad (Beograd)
Zbornik Radova. Zavod za Ratarstvo (Sarajevo) — Zb Rad Zavod Ratarstvo (Sarajevo)
Zbornik Slovenskeho Narodneho Muzea — Zbor Slov Muz
Zbornik Slovenskeho Narodneho Muzea — Zbor Slov Narod Muz
Zbornik Slovenskeho Narodneho Muzea — Zbornik Slov Nar Muz
Zbornik Slovenskeho Narodneho Muzea — ZSNM
Zbornik Slovenskeho Narodneho Muzea Prirodne Vedy — Zb Slov Nar Muz Prir Vedy
Zbornik Slovenskeho Narodneho Muzea Prirodne Vedy — Zb Slov Nar Muzea Prir Vedy
Zbornik Slovenskeho Narodneho Muzea Prirodne Vedy — Zborn Slov Nar Muz Prir Vedy
Zbornik Vedeckych Prac Lesnickej Fakulty Vysokej Skoly Lesnickej a Drevarskej vo Zvolene [*Czechoslovakia*] — Zb Ved Prac Lesn Fak Vys Sk Lesn Drev Zvolene
Zbornik Vedeckych Prac. Vysokej Skoly Technickej v Kosiciach — Zb Ved Pr Vys Sk Tech Kosiciach
Zbornik Vojnomedicinske Akademije — Zb Vojnomed Akad
Zbornik Vychodoslovenskeho Muzea. Seria AB. Prirodne Vedy [*Kosice*] — Zb Vychodoslovenskeho Muzea Ser AB Prir Vedy
Zbornik Vyskumnych Prac Vyskumneho Ustavu Zvaracskeho v Bratislave — Zb Vysk Pr Vysk Ustav Zvaracskeho Bratislave
Zbornik Vyzkumnych Prac z Odboru Papiera a Celulozy — Zb Vyzk Pr Odboru Pap Celulozy
Zbornik za Filologiju i Lingvistiku — ZbFL
Zbornik za Filologiju i Lingvistiku — ZFL
Zbornik za Knjizevnost i Jezik — ZKJ
Zbornik za Likovne Umetnosti Matice Srpske — ZLUMS
Zbornik za Prirodne Nauke Matica Srpska — Zb Prir Nauke Matica Srp
Zbornik za Slavistiku — ZbS
Zbornik za Slavistiku — ZzS
Zbornik za Zgodovino Naravoslovja in Teknike — Zb Zgodovino Naravoslovja Tek
Zbraslav Research Institute for Land Reclamation and Improvement. Scientific Monograph — Zbraslav Res Inst Land Reclam Improv Sci Monogr
Zdenku Nejedlemu Ceskoslovenska Akademie Ved — ZNCAV
ZDM. Zentralblatt fuer Didaktik der Mathematik — Zentralbl Didakt Math
Zdorov'e Nauchno Populiarnyi Gigienicheskii Zhurnal — Zdorov'e Nauch Pop Gig Zhurnal
Zdravno Delo — Zdrav Delo
Zdravookhranenie Belorussii — Zdravookhr Beloruss
Zdravookhranenie Belorussii — Zdravookhr Belorussii
Zdravookhranenie Kazakhstana — ZDKAA
Zdravookhranenie Kazakhstana — Zdravookhr Kaz
Zdravookhranenie Kirgizii — Zdravookhr Kirg
Zdravookhranenie Rossiiskoi Federatsii — Zdravookhr Ross Fed
Zdravookhranenie Sovetskoi Estonii Sbornik — Zdravookhr Sov Est Sb
Zdravookhranenie Tadzhikistana — Zdravookhr Tadzh
Zdravookhranenie Turkmenistana — Zdravookhr Turkm
Zdravotni Technika a Vzduchotechnika — Zdrav Tech Vzduchotech
Zdravotni Technika a Vzduchotechnika — Zdrav Techn Vzduchotech
Zdravotnicka Pracovnice — Zdrav Prac
Zdravotnicke Aktuality — Zdrav Aktual
Zdravstveni Vestnik — Zdrav Vestn
Zdravstveni Vestnik — Zdravst Vest
Zdrowie Publiczne — Zdrow Publiczne
Ze Skarbca Kultury — ZSK
Zeeuws Fruittelersblad — Zeews Fruittelersbl
Zeichen der Zeit — Z d Z
Zeichen der Zeit — Zeich Zeit
Zeiss Information — Zeiss Inf
Zeiss Mitteilungen — Zeiss Mitt
Zeiss-Mitteilungen ueber Fortschritte der Technischen Optik — Zeiss-Mitt Fortsch Tech Optik
Zeiss-Mitteilungen ueber Fortschritte der Technischen Optik — Zeiss-Mitt Fortschr Tech Opt
Zeit. Wochenzeitung — ZEH
Zeiten und Voelker — Z & V
Zeitgemaesse Deponietechnik 4. Manuskriptsammelband zum Seminar — Zeitgemaesse Deponietech 4 Manuskriptsammelband Semin
Zeitgeschichte — Zeitgeschic
Zeitschrfit fuer Oeffentliches Recht — ZOR
Zeitschrift. Aachener Geschichtsverein — Z Aach Gesch Ver
Zeitschrift. Aachener Geschichtsverein — Z Aachener Geschichtsver
Zeitschrift. Aachener Geschichtsverein — ZAGV
Zeitschrift. Allgemeiner Deutsche Sprachverein — ZADS
Zeitschrift. Allgemeiner Oesterreichische Apotheker-Verein — Z Allg Oesterr Apoth Ver
Zeitschrift Angewandte Photographie — Zeit Angewandte Phot
Zeitschrift. Arbeitsgemeinschaft Oesterreichischer Entomologen — Z Arbeitsgem Oesterr Entomol
Zeitschrift. Bayerischer Revisions Verein — Z Bayer Revisions Ver
Zeitschrift. Bergischer Geschichtsverein — Z Berg Gesch V
Zeitschrift. Bergischer Geschichtsverein — ZBG
Zeitschrift. Bergischer Geschichtsverein — ZBGV
Zeitschrift. Bernischer Juristen-Verein — ZBJV
Zeitschrift. Dampfkesseluntersuchungs- und Versicherungs-Gesellschaft — Z Dampfkesselunters Versicher Ges
Zeitschrift der Anwaltskammer Breslau — Bresl AK
Zeitschrift der Deutschen Gemmologischen Gesellschaft (Idar-Oberstein) — Z Dtsch Gemmol Ges
Zeitschrift der Deutschen Geologischen Gesellschaft A. Abhandlungen — Z Dt Geol Ges A Abh
Zeitschrift der Deutschen Morgenlaendischen Gesellschaft — Z Deut Morgenlaend Ges
Zeitschrift der Deutschen Morgenlaendischen Gesellschaft — Z Dt Morgenl Ges
Zeitschrift der Deutschen Morgenlaendischen Gesellschaft — ZDMG
Zeitschrift der Deutschen Morgenlaendischen Gesellschaft — Zs d Deutschen Morgend Ges
Zeitschrift der Deutschen Morgenlaendischen Gesellschaft — Zs D Morg Ges
Zeitschrift der Deutschen Morgenlaendischen Gesellschaft. Supplement — ZDMG Suppl
Zeitschrift der Deutschen Mykologischen Gesellschaft — Z Deutsch Mykol Ges
Zeitschrift der Deutschen Oel- und Fett-Industrie — Z Dtsch Oel Fett Ind
Zeitschrift der Gesellschaft fuer Erdkunde — ZGE
Zeitschrift der Gesellschaft fuer Erdkunde zu Berlin — Z Ges Erdk Berl
Zeitschrift der Gesellschaft fuer Erdkunde zu Berlin — Z Ges Erdkde Berlin
Zeitschrift der Gesellschaft fuer Erdkunde zu Berlin — ZGEB
Zeitschrift der Gesellschaft fuer Schleswig-Holsteinische Geschichte — Z Ges Schleswig-Holstein Gesch
Zeitschrift der Gesellschaft fuer Schleswig-Holsteinische Geschichte — ZSHG
Zeitschrift der Savigny-Stiftung fuer Rechtsgeschichte — ZdS
Zeitschrift der Savigny-Stiftung fuer Rechtsgeschichte — ZRG
Zeitschrift der Savigny-Stiftung fuer Rechtsgeschichte — Zs Savignystiftg Rechtsgesch
Zeitschrift der Savigny-Stiftung fuer Rechtsgeschichte — ZSR
Zeitschrift der Savigny-Stiftung fuer Rechtsgeschichte — ZSRG
Zeitschrift der Savigny-Stiftung fuer Rechtsgeschichte — ZSS
Zeitschrift der Savigny-Stiftung fuer Rechtsgeschichte — ZSS f R
Zeitschrift der Savigny-Stiftung fuer Rechtsgeschichte — ZSSR
Zeitschrift der Savigny-Stiftung fuer Rechtsgeschichte. Germanistische Abteilung, Kanonistische Abteilung. Romanistische Abteilung — Z Savigny Stift Germanist Abt Kanonist Abt Romanist Abt
Zeitschrift der Savigny-Stiftung fuer Rechtsgeschichte. Romanistische Abteilung — Sav Zeitschr
Zeitschrift der Savigny-Stiftung fuer Rechtsgeschichte. Romanistische Abteilung — SZ
Zeitschrift der Savigny-Stiftung fuer Rechtsgeschichte. Romanistische Abteilung — Z Sav RGRA
Zeitschrift der Savigny-Stiftung fuer Rechtsgeschichte. Romanistische Abteilung — Zeitschr Savingy Stift
Zeitschrift der Savigny-Stiftung fuer Rechtsgeschichte. Romanistische Abteilung — Zeitschr Savingy Stiftung
Zeitschrift der Savigny-Stiftung fuer Rechtsgeschichte. Romanistische Abteilung — ZRGR
Zeitschrift der Savigny-Stiftung fuer Rechtsgeschichte. Romanistische Abteilung — ZSSR
Zeitschrift der Savigny-Stiftung fuer Rechtsgeschichte. Romanistische Abteilung — Ztschr Sav Stift
Zeitschrift des Aachener Geschichtsvereins — ZAG
Zeitschrift des Deutschen Sparkassen — Sparkasse
Zeitschrift des Deutschen Vereins fuer Kunstwissenschaft — Z Kunst W
Zeitschrift des Deutschen Vereins fuer Kunstwissenschaft — ZDVK
Zeitschrift des Gartenbau-Vereins fuer das Koenigreich Hannover — Z Gartenbau Vereins Koenigr Hannover
Zeitschrift des Geschichtsvereins. Muelheim an der Ruhr — Z Geschv Muelheim
Zeitschrift des Historischen Verein fuer Schwaben — Z Hist Ver Schwaben

Zeitschrift des Historischen Vereins fuer Niedersachsen — Zs Hist Ver Niedersachs
Zeitschrift des Historischen Vereins fuer Steiermark — ZdV
Zeitschrift des Historischen Vereins fuer Steiermark — ZHVSt
Zeitschrift des Koelner Zoo — Z Koeln Zoo
Zeitschrift des Maehrischen Landesmuseums — Z Maehr Landesmus
Zeitschrift des Oberschlesischen Berg- und Huettenmaennischen Vereins zu Katowiee — Z Oberschles Berg-Huettenmaenn Ver Kat
Zeitschrift des Oesterreichischen Ingenieur und Architekten Vereins — Z Oe IAV
Zeitschrift des Oesterreichischen Ingenieur und Architekten Vereins — Z Oesterr Ing Archit Ver
Zeitschrift des Rheinpreussischen Landwirthschaftlichen Vereins — Z Rheinpreuss Landw Vereins
Zeitschrift des Vereins Deutscher Chemiker. Teil A. Angewandte Chemie — Z Ver Dtsch Chem Teil A
Zeitschrift des Vereins fuer Hamburgische Geschichte — Z Ver Hamburg Gesch
Zeitschrift des Vereins fuer Hessische Geschichte und Landeskunde — ZVHGL
Zeitschrift des Vereins fuer Luebeckische Geschichte und Altertumskunde — Z Ver Luebeck Gesch Altertumskde
Zeitschrift des Vereins fuer Luebeckische Geschichte und Altertumskunde — ZVLGA
Zeitschrift des Vereins fuer Volkskunde — ZVS
Zeitschrift des Vereins fuer Volkskunde — ZVV
Zeitschrift des Westpreussischen Geschichtsvereins — Z Westpreuss Gesch Ver
Zeitschrift. Deutsche Geologische Gesellschaft — Z Deut Geol Ges
Zeitschrift. Deutsche Geologische Gesellschaft — Z Dt Geol Ges
Zeitschrift. Deutsche Geologische Gesellschaft — Z Dtsch Geol Ges
Zeitschrift. Deutsche Morganlaendische Gesellschaft — Z Dtsch Morgenl Ges
Zeitschrift. Deutsche Morgenlaendische Gesellschaft [*Wiesbaden*] — Z Deuts Morgen G
Zeitschrift. Deutsche Morgenlaendische Gesellschaft — Z Dtschen Morgenlaend Ges
Zeitschrift. Deutsche Morgenlaendische Gesellschaft — ZDMG
Zeitschrift. Deutschen Verein fuer Kunstwissenschaft — Z Deut Ver
Zeitschrift. Deutscher Palaestinaverein — ZDPV
Zeitschrift. Deutscher Palaestinaverein — ZPalV
Zeitschrift. Deutscher Verein fuer Buchwesen und Schrifttum — ZBS
Zeitschrift. Deutscher Verein fuer die Geschichte Maehrens und Schlesiens — ZDVGMS
Zeitschrift. Deutscher Verein fuer die Geschichte Maehrens und Schlesiens — ZVGMS
Zeitschrift. Deutscher Verein fuer Kunstwissenschaft — ZDV f Kw
Zeitschrift. Deutscher Verein fuer Kunstwissenschaft — ZDV Kw
Zeitschrift. Freiburger Geschichtsvereine — ZFGV
Zeitschrift fuer Acclimatisation — Z Acclim
Zeitschrift fuer Acker- und Pflanzenbau — Z Acker Pflanzenbau
Zeitschrift fuer Acker- und Pflanzenbau — Z Acker u Pflbau
Zeitschrift fuer Acker- und Pflanzenbau — Z Acker-Pflanzenb
Zeitschrift fuer Aegyptische Sprache und Altertumskunde — Aeg Z
Zeitschrift fuer Aegyptische Sprache und Altertumskunde — AeZ
Zeitschrift fuer Aegyptische Sprache und Altertumskunde — AgZ
Zeitschrift fuer Aegyptische Sprache und Altertumskunde — Z Ae S
Zeitschrift fuer Aegyptische Sprache und Altertumskunde — Z Aeg Spr
Zeitschrift fuer Aegyptische Sprache und Altertumskunde — Z Aegypt Sprache
Zeitschrift fuer Aegyptische Sprache und Altertumskunde — Z Aegypt Sprache Altertumskd
Zeitschrift fuer Aegyptische Sprache und Altertumskunde — ZAeg
Zeitschrift fuer Aegyptische Sprache und Altertumskunde — ZAS
Zeitschrift fuer Aegyptische Sprache und Altertumskunde — ZASA
Zeitschrift fuer Aegyptische Sprache und Altertumskunde — ZASprache
Zeitschrift fuer Aegyptische Sprache und Altertumskunde — Zeitschrift Aegypt
Zeitschrift fuer Aerosol Forschung und Therapie — Z Aerosol Forsch Ther
Zeitschrift fuer Aerztliche Fortbildung — Z Aerztl Fortbild
Zeitschrift fuer Aerztliche Fortbildung — ZAFBA
Zeitschrift fuer Aerztliche Fortbildung — Ztschr Aerztl Fortbild
Zeitschrift fuer Aerztliche Fortbildung (Jena) — Z Aerztl Fortbild (Jena)
Zeitschrift fuer Aesthetik und Allgemeine Kunstwissenschaft — Z Aes Allg Kunst
Zeitschrift fuer Aesthetik und Allgemeine Kunstwissenschaft — Z Aesth
Zeitschrift fuer Aesthetik und Allgemeine Kunstwissenschaft — ZAAK
Zeitschrift fuer Aesthetik und Kunstwissenschaft — ZAK
Zeitschrift fuer Afrikanische Sprachen — ZAS
Zeitschrift fuer Afrikanische Sprachen — Zeits F Afrikan Sp
Zeitschrift fuer Afrikanische und Oceanische Sprachen — ZAOS
Zeitschrift fuer Afrikanische und Oceanische Sprachen — Zeits F Afrikan U Ocean Sp
Zeitschrift fuer Agrargeschichte und Agrarsoziologie — A Argargesch U Sociol
Zeitschrift fuer Agrargeschichte und Agrarsoziologie — Z Agrargesch Agrarsoziol
Zeitschrift fuer Agrargeschichte und Agrarsoziologie — Z Agrargesch u -Soziol
Zeitschrift fuer Agrargeschichte und Agrarsoziologie — Z f A
Zeitschrift fuer Allgemeine Erdkunde — ZAE
Zeitschrift fuer Allgemeine Erdkunde — Zs Allg Erdk
Zeitschrift fuer Allgemeine Mikrobiologie — Z Allg Mikr
Zeitschrift fuer Allgemeine Mikrobiologie. Morphologie, Physiologie, Genetik, und Oekologie der Mikrorganismen — Z Allg Mikrobiol
Zeitschrift fuer Allgemeine Physiologie — Z Allg Physiol
Zeitschrift fuer Allgemeine Wissenschaftstheorie — Z Allg Wiss
Zeitschrift fuer Allgemeine Wissenschaftstheorie — Z Allg Wissenschaftstheor
Zeitschrift fuer Allgemeine Wissenschaftstheorie — Z Allgemeine Wissenschaftstheorie
Zeitschrift fuer Allgemeinmedizin — Z Allgemeinmed
Zeitschrift fuer Allgemeinmedizin — Z f Allg Med
Zeitschrift fuer Allgemeinmedizin der Landaerzt — Z Allg Med
Zeitschrift fuer Allgemeinmedizin (Stuttgart) — ZFA (Stuttgart)
Zeitschrift fuer Alternsforschung — Z Alternsforsch
Zeitschrift fuer Alternsforschung (Dresden) — ZFA (Dresden)
Zeitschrift fuer Analysis und Ihre Anwendungen — Z Anal Anwendungen
Zeitschrift fuer Analytische Chemie — Z Analyt Chem
Zeitschrift fuer Analytische Chemie — ZANCA
Zeitschrift fuer Anatomie und Entwicklungsgeschichte — Z Anat Entwicklungsgesch
Zeitschrift fuer Anatomie und Entwicklungsgeschichte — Z f A
Zeitschrift fuer Anatomie und Entwicklungsgeschichte — ZAEG
Zeitschrift fuer Angewandte Baeder und Klimaheilkunde — Z Angew Baeder Klimaheilkd
Zeitschrift fuer Angewandte Chemie — ZA Ch
Zeitschrift fuer Angewandte Chemie und Zentralblatt fuer Technische Chemie — Z Angew Chem
Zeitschrift fuer Angewandte Entomologie — Z Angew Entomol
Zeitschrift fuer Angewandte Geologie — Z Ang Geol
Zeitschrift fuer Angewandte Geologie — Z Angew Geol
Zeitschrift fuer Angewandte Geologie — Zeitschr Angew Geologie
Zeitschrift fuer Angewandte Ichthyologie — Z Angew Ichthyol
Zeitschrift fuer Angewandte Ichthyologie — ZAICEL
Zeitschrift fuer Angewandte Mathematik und Mechanik — Z Ang Ma Me
Zeitschrift fuer Angewandte Mathematik und Mechanik — Z Ang Math Mech
Zeitschrift fuer Angewandte Mathematik und Mechanik — Z Angew Math Mech
Zeitschrift fuer Angewandte Mathematik und Mechanik — Z Angew Math and Mech
Zeitschrift fuer Angewandte Mathematik und Mechanik — ZAMM
Zeitschrift fuer Angewandte Mathematik und Physik — Z Ang Math
Zeitschrift fuer Angewandte Mathematik und Physik — Z Ang Math Phys
Zeitschrift fuer Angewandte Mathematik und Physik — Z Angew Math Phys
Zeitschrift fuer Angewandte Mathematik und Physik — ZAMP
Zeitschrift fuer Angewandte Mechanik — ZA Mech
Zeitschrift fuer Angewandte Meteorologie — Z Angew Met
Zeitschrift fuer Angewandte Mikroskopie und Klinische Chemie — Z Angew Mikrosk Klin Chem
Zeitschrift fuer Angewandte Photographie in Wissenschaft und Technik — Z Angew Photogr Wiss Tech
Zeitschrift fuer Angewandte Physik — Z Ang Ph
Zeitschrift fuer Angewandte Physik — Z Angew Phys
Zeitschrift fuer Angewandte Psychologie und Psychologische Forschung — Z Angew Psychol
Zeitschrift fuer Angewandte Psychologie und Psychologische Forschung — Ztsch f Angew Psychol
Zeitschrift fuer Angewandte Psychologie und Psychologische Sammelforschung — Ztsch f Angew Psychol Sammelforsch
Zeitschrift fuer Angewandte Zoologie — Z Angew Zool
Zeitschrift fuer Anglistik und Amerikanistik — Z Ang & Amerik
Zeitschrift fuer Anglistik und Amerikanistik — Z Anglis Am
Zeitschrift fuer Anglistik und Amerikanistik — ZAA
Zeitschrift fuer Anorganische Chemie — Z An Ch
Zeitschrift fuer Anorganische Chemie — Z Ao Ch
Zeitschrift fuer Anorganische Chemie — ZA Ch
Zeitschrift fuer Anorganische Chemie — ZACMA
Zeitschrift fuer Anorganische Chemie — Zs Anorg Chem
Zeitschrift fuer Anorganische und Allgemeine Chemie — Z Anorg A C
Zeitschrift fuer Anorganische und Allgemeine Chemie — Z Anorg Allg Chem
Zeitschrift fuer Anorganische und Allgemeine Chemie — Z Anorg Chem
Zeitschrift fuer Anorganische und Allgemeine Chemie — Zeitschr Anorg u Allg Chemie
Zeitschrift fuer Antimikrobielle und Antineoplastiche Chemotherapie — Z Antimikrob Antineoplast Chemother
Zeitschrift fuer Arabische Linguistik — ZAL
Zeitschrift fuer Arbeitswissenschaft — Z Arbeitswiss
Zeitschrift fuer Arbeitswissenschaft — ZBA
Zeitschrift fuer Arbeitswissenschaft. Neue Folge — Z Arbeitswiss N F
Zeitschrift fuer Archaeologie — Z Arch
Zeitschrift fuer Archaeologie — Z Archaeol
Zeitschrift fuer Archaeologie — ZfA
Zeitschrift fuer Archaeologie des Mittelalters — Zeitschr Arch Mittelalter
Zeitschrift fuer Arztliche Fortbildung (Jena) — Z Arztl Fortbild Jena
Zeitschrift fuer Askese und Mystik — ZAM
Zeitschrift fuer Assyriologie — Z Assyr
Zeitschrift fuer Assyriologie [*Leipzig/Berlin*] — ZfZ
Zeitschrift fuer Assyriologie und Verwandte Gebiete — ZA
Zeitschrift fuer Assyriologie und Vorderasiatische Altertumskunde. Neue Folge — ZANF
Zeitschrift fuer Assyriologie und Vorderasiatische Archaeologie [*Berlin*] — ZA
Zeitschrift fuer Assyriologie und Vorderasiatische Archaeologie — ZAVA
Zeitschrift fuer Assyriologie und Vorderasiatische Archaeologie — Zeits f Assyr
Zeitschrift fuer Asthetik und Allgemeine Kunstwissenschaft — Z Asthet Al
Zeitschrift fuer Astrophysik [*Germany*] — Z Astrophys
Zeitschrift fuer Astrophysik — Z f A
Zeitschrift fuer Astrophysik — ZA
Zeitschrift fuer Astrophysik — ZEASA
Zeitschrift fuer Augenheilkunde — Z Augenheilkd
Zeitschrift fuer Augenheilkunde — Ztschr Augenh
Zeitschrift fuer Auslaendische Landwirtschaft — Z Auslaend Landwirtsch
Zeitschrift fuer Auslaendische Landwirtschaft — Z Ausland Landwirt
Zeitschrift fuer Auslaendisches Oeffentliches Recht und Voelkerrecht — Z Ausl Oeff R
Zeitschrift fuer Auslaendisches Oeffentliches Recht und Voelkerrecht — Z Ausl Oeff Recht Voelkerrecht
Zeitschrift fuer Auslaendisches Oeffentliches Recht und Voelkerrecht — Z Ausl Oeff RVR

Zeitschrift fuer Auslaendisches Oeffentliches Recht und Voelkerrecht — Z Auslaend Oeff Voelkerrecht
Zeitschrift fuer Auslaendisches Oeffentliches Recht und Voelkerrecht — Z f Ausl Oeff Recht u Voelkerrecht
Zeitschrift fuer Auslaendisches Oeffentliches Recht und Voelkerrecht — ZA Oe R
Zeitschrift fuer Auslaendisches Oeffentliches Recht und Voelkerrecht — ZA Oe RV
Zeitschrift fuer Auslaendisches Oeffentliches Recht und Voelkerrecht — ZAO RV
Zeitschrift fuer Auslaendisches Oeffentliches Recht und Voelkerrecht — Zschift f Ausl Offentl Recht
Zeitschrift fuer Badische Verwaltung und Verwaltungsrechtspflege — Zs Bad Verwalt
Zeitschrift fuer Balkanologie — Z Balkanol
Zeitschrift fuer Balkanologie — ZB
Zeitschrift fuer Balkanologie — ZBalk
Zeitschrift fuer Bayerische Kirchengeschichte — Z Bayer Kg
Zeitschrift fuer Bayerische Kirchengeschichte — Z Bayer Kirchengesch
Zeitschrift fuer Bayerische Kirchengeschichte — ZBKG
Zeitschrift fuer Bayerische Kirchengeschichte — ZfBK
Zeitschrift fuer Bayerische Landesgeschichte — Z Bay Land Gesch
Zeitschrift fuer Bayerische Landesgeschichte — Z Bayer Landesgesch
Zeitschrift fuer Bayerische Landesgeschichte — Z Bayer Ldg
Zeitschrift fuer Bayerische Landesgeschichte — ZBL
Zeitschrift fuer Bayerische Landesgeschichte — ZBLG
Zeitschrift fuer Bayerische Landesgeschichte — ZfBL
Zeitschrift fuer Beamtenrecht — Z Beamtenrecht
Zeitschrift fuer Beleuchtungswesen Heizungs- und Lueftungstechnik — Z Beleuchtungswes Heizungs- Lueftungstech
Zeitschrift fuer Bergrecht [*Germany*] — Z Bergrecht
Zeitschrift fuer Bergrecht — ZEBED
Zeitschrift fuer Betriebswirtschaft — Z Betriebsw
Zeitschrift fuer Betriebswirtschaft — Z Betriebswirtsch
Zeitschrift fuer Betriebswirtschaft — ZB
Zeitschrift fuer Betriebswirtschaft — ZBW
Zeitschrift fuer Betriebswirtschaftliche Forschung — ZBF
Zeitschrift fuer Bewasserungswirtschaft — Z Bewasserungswirtsch
Zeitschrift fuer Bibliothekswesen und Bibliographie — Z Bibl und Bibliog
Zeitschrift fuer Bibliothekswesen und Bibliographie — Z Bibliot u Bibliog
Zeitschrift fuer Bibliothekswesen und Bibliographie — Z Bibliothekswes Bibliogr
Zeitschrift fuer Bibliothekswesen und Bibliographie — Z Bibliothekswesen und Bibl
Zeitschrift fuer Bibliothekswesen und Bibliographie — ZBB
Zeitschrift fuer Bienenforschung — Z Bienenforsch
Zeitschrift fuer Bildende Kunst — Z Bild K
Zeitschrift fuer Bildende Kunst — Z f BK
Zeitschrift fuer Bildende Kunst — ZBK
Zeitschrift fuer Biochemie — Z Biochem
Zeitschrift fuer Biologie — Z Biol
Zeitschrift fuer Biologie — ZEBLA
Zeitschrift fuer Biologische Technik und Methodik — Z Biol Tech Method
Zeitschrift fuer Botanik — Z Bot
Zeitschrift fuer Botanik — ZB
Zeitschrift fuer Buchkunde — ZBK
Zeitschrift fuer Buecherfreunde — ZBF
Zeitschrift fuer Buecherfreunde — ZfB
Zeitschrift fuer Celtische Philologie — ZCP
Zeitschrift fuer Celtische Philologie — ZCPh
Zeitschrift fuer Celtische Philologie — Zeit Fuer Celt Philol
Zeitschrift fuer Celtische Philologie — Zft f Celt Phil
Zeitschrift fuer Celtische Philologie und Volksforschung — ZCP
Zeitschrift fuer Chemie — Z Chem
Zeitschrift fuer Chemie (Leipzig) — Z Chemie (Lpz)
Zeitschrift fuer Chemie und Industrie der Kolloide — Z Chem Ind Kolloide
Zeitschrift fuer Chemische Apparatenkunde — Z Chem Apparatenkd
Zeitschrift fuer Chemotherapie und Verwandte Gebiete. Teil 1. Originale — Z Chemother Verw Geb Teil 1
Zeitschrift fuer Chemotherapie und Verwandte Gebiete. Teil 2. Referate — Z Chemother Verw Geb Teil 2
Zeitschrift fuer Christliche Kunst — ZChK
Zeitschrift fuer Christliche Kunst — ZChrK
Zeitschrift fuer Christliche Kunst — ZCK
Zeitschrift fuer Dampfkessel und Maschinenbetrieb — Z Dampfkessel Maschinenbetr
Zeitschrift fuer das Berg-, Huetten-, und Salinenwesen — Zs Berg- Huetten- u Salinen-Wesen
Zeitschrift fuer das Berg-, Huetten-, und Salinenwesen im Deutschen Reich — Z Berg Huetten Salinenwes Dtsch Reich
Zeitschrift fuer das Gesamte Brauwesen — Z Gesamte Brauwes
Zeitschrift fuer das Gesamte Forstwesen — Z Gesamte Forstwes
Zeitschrift fuer das Gesamte Genossenschaftswesen — Z Ges Genossensch
Zeitschrift fuer das Gesamte Genossenschaftswesen — Z Gesamte Genossenschaftswes
Zeitschrift fuer das Gesamte Genossenschaftswesen — Z Gesamte Genossenschaftswesen
Zeitschrift fuer das Gesamte Genossenschaftswesen — ZGG
Zeitschrift fuer das Gesamte Getreide Muehlen- und Baeckereiwesen — Z Gesamte Getreide Muehlen Baeckereiwes
Zeitschrift fuer das Gesamte Getreidewesen — Z Gesamte Getreidewes
Zeitschrift fuer das Gesamte Handelsrecht und Wirtschaftsrecht — Z Ges Handelsrecht u Wirtsch Recht
Zeitschrift fuer das Gesamte Kreditwesen — Z Ges Kredit
Zeitschrift fuer das Gesamte Kreditwesen — Z Gesamte Kreditwesen
Zeitschrift fuer das Gesamte Kreditwesen — ZKR
Zeitschrift fuer das Gesamte Muehlenwesen — Z Gesamte Muehlenwes
Zeitschrift fuer das Gesamte Schiess- und Sprengstoffwesen — Z Gesamte Schiess Sprengstoffwes
Zeitschrift fuer das Gesamte Schiess- und Sprengstoffwesen mit der Sonderabteilung Gasschutz [*Germany*] — Z Gesamte Schiess-Sprengstoffw
Zeitschrift fuer das Gesamte Schiess- und Sprengstoffwesen mit der Sonderabteilung Gasschutz — ZGSSA
Zeitschrift fuer das Landwirtschaftliche Versuchswesen im Deutsch-Oesterreich — Z Landwirsch Versuchswes Dtsch Oesterr
Zeitschrift fuer Demographie und Statistik der Juden — ZDemogr
Zeitschrift fuer Demographie und Statistik der Juden — ZDSJ
Zeitschrift fuer Demographie und Statistik der Juden — ZDStJ
Zeitschrift fuer Demographie und Statistik der Juden — ZfDSdJ
Zeitschrift fuer den Ausbau der Entwicklungslehre — Z Ausbau Entwicklungsl
Zeitschrift fuer den Erdkundeunterricht — Z Erdk Unt
Zeitschrift fuer den Erdkundeunterricht — Z Erdkde Unterr
Zeitschrift fuer den Erdkundeunterricht — Z Erdkundeunterricht
Zeitschrift fuer den Russisch-Unterricht — ZRU
Zeitschrift fuer Desinfektions- und Gesundheitswesen — Z Desinfekt Gesundheitswes
Zeitschrift fuer Deutsche Bildung — ZDB
Zeitschrift fuer Deutsche Geistesgeschichte — ZDG
Zeitschrift fuer Deutsche Geistesgeschichte — ZDGG
Zeitschrift fuer Deutsche Geistesgeschichte — ZFDG
Zeitschrift fuer Deutsche Geisteswissenschaft — Z Dt Geisteswiss
Zeitschrift fuer Deutsche Geisteswissenschaft — ZDG
Zeitschrift fuer Deutsche Kulturphilosophie — ZDKP
Zeitschrift fuer Deutsche Mundarten — ZDM
Zeitschrift fuer Deutsche Philologie — Z Deut Phil
Zeitschrift fuer Deutsche Philologie — Z Dt Phil
Zeitschrift fuer Deutsche Philologie — Z Dtsch Philol
Zeitschrift fuer Deutsche Philologie — Z f D Phil
Zeitschrift fuer Deutsche Philologie — ZDP
Zeitschrift fuer Deutsche Philologie — ZDPh
Zeitschrift fuer Deutsche Philologie — Zeit f Deut Phil
Zeitschrift fuer Deutsche Philologie — ZFDPh
Zeitschrift fuer Deutsche Sprache — Z Dt Spr
Zeitschrift fuer Deutsche Sprache — ZDS
Zeitschrift fuer Deutsche Wortforschung — ZDW
Zeitschrift fuer Deutsche Wortforschung — ZDWF
Zeitschrift fuer Deutschen Zivilprozess (Begriff von Busch) — BuschsZ
Zeitschrift fuer Deutsches Altertum und Deutsche Literatur — Z Deut Alt
Zeitschrift fuer Deutsches Altertum und Deutsche Literatur — Z Deut Altertum Deut Llit
Zeitschrift fuer Deutsches Altertum und Deutsche Literatur — Z f D Altert
Zeitschrift fuer Deutsches Altertum und Deutsche Literatur — ZA
Zeitschrift fuer Deutsches Altertum und Deutsche Literatur — ZDA
Zeitschrift fuer Deutsches Altertum und Deutsche Literatur — ZDADL
Zeitschrift fuer Deutsches Altertum und Deutsche Literatur — ZfDA
Zeitschrift fuer Deutsches Altertum und Deutsche Literatur — Zft f D Alt
Zeitschrift fuer Deutsches Buergerliches Recht und Franzoesisches Zivilrecht — Zs Dt Buergl R Frz Zivilr
Zeitschrift fuer Deutschkunde — ZD
Zeitschrift fuer Deutschkunde — ZDK
Zeitschrift fuer Deutschkunde — Zeit f Deutk
Zeitschrift fuer Deutschlands Druckgewerbe — Z Dtschl Druckgewerbe
Zeitschrift fuer Deutschwissenschaft und Deutschunterricht — ZDWDSU
Zeitschrift fuer Dialektologie und Linguistik — ZDL
Zeitschrift fuer die Altertumswissenschaft — Z f d AW
Zeitschrift fuer die Altertumswissenschaft — Zeitschr f d Altert
Zeitschrift fuer die Alttestamentliche Wissenschaft — Z Alt Wiss
Zeitschrift fuer die Alttestamentliche Wissenschaft — Z Altt W
Zeitschrift fuer die Alttestamentliche Wissenschaft — ZATW
Zeitschrift fuer die Alttestamentliche Wissenschaft — ZAW
Zeitschrift fuer die Alttestamentliche Wissenschaft. Beihefte — ZATB
Zeitschrift fuer die Bevoelkerungswissenschaft — Z Bevoelkerungswiss
Zeitschrift fuer die Binnenfischerei der DDR — Z Binnenfisch DDR
Zeitschrift fuer die Deutsche-Oesterreichischen Gymnasien — Z fur die Oest Gym
Zeitschrift fuer die Deutsche-Oesterreichischen Gymnasien — Z Oe G
Zeitschrift fuer die Deutsche-Oesterreichischen Gymnasien — Z Oest G
Zeitschrift fuer die Deutsche-Oesterreichischen Gymnasien — Zeit f Oest Gymn
Zeitschrift fuer die Deutsche-Oesterreichischen Gymnasien — ZoG
Zeitschrift fuer die Deutsche-Oesterreichischen Gymnasien — Zost Gym
Zeitschrift fuer die Freiwillige Gerichtsbarkeit und die Gemeinderverwaltung in Wuerttemberg — Zs Frw Gerichtsbkt Wuertt
Zeitschrift fuer die Gesamte Experimentelle Medizin — Z Ges Exp Med
Zeitschrift fuer die Gesamte Experimentelle Medizin — Z Gesamte Exp Med
Zeitschrift fuer die Gesamte Experimentelle Medizin — ZGEMA
Zeitschrift fuer die Gesamte Experimentelle Medizin. Einschliesslich Experimenteller Chirurgie — Z Gesamte Exp Med Einschl Exp Chir
Zeitschrift fuer die Gesamte Giessereipraxis — Z Gesamte Giessereiprax
Zeitschrift fuer die Gesamte Hygiene und Ihre Grenzgebiete — Z Gesamte Hyg
Zeitschrift fuer die Gesamte Hygiene und Ihre Grenzgebiete — Z Gesamte Hyg Grenzgeb
Zeitschrift fuer die Gesamte Hygiene und Ihre Grenzgebiete — Z Gesamte Hyg Ihre Grenzgeb
Zeitschrift fuer die Gesamte Hygiene und Ihre Grenzgebiete — ZHYGA
Zeitschrift fuer die Gesamte Innere Medizin und Ihre Grenzgebiete — Z Ges Inn Med
Zeitschrift fuer die Gesamte Innere Medizin und Ihre Grenzgebiete — Z Gesamte Inn Med
Zeitschrift fuer die Gesamte Innere Medizin und Ihre Grenzgebiete — Z Gesamte Inn Med Grenzgeb

Zeitschrift fuer die Gesamte Innere Medizin und Ihre Grenzgebiete — Z Gesamte Inn Med Ihre Grenzgeb
Zeitschrift fuer die Gesamte Innere Medizin und Ihre Grenzgebiete. Klinik, Pathologie, Experiment — Z Gesamte Inn Med Grenzgeb Klin Pathol Exp
Zeitschrift fuer die Gesamte Innere Medizin und Ihre Grenzgebiete. Supplementum [*Germany*] — Z Gesamte Inn Med Ihre Grenzgeb Suppl
Zeitschrift fuer die Gesamte Kaelte-Industrie — Z Gesamte Kaelte Ind
Zeitschrift fuer die Gesamte Kaelte-Industrie. Beihefte. Serie 1 — Z Gesamte Kaelte Ind Beih Ser 1
Zeitschrift fuer die Gesamte Kaelte-Industrie. Beihefte. Serie 2 — Z Gesamte Kaelte Ind Beih Ser 2
Zeitschrift fuer die Gesamte Kaelte-Industrie. Beihefte. Serie 3 — Z Gesamte Kaelte-Ind Beih Ser 3
Zeitschrift fuer die Gesamte Lutherische Theologie und Kirche [*Leipzig*] — ZLThK
Zeitschrift fuer die Gesamte Naturwissenschaft — Z Gesamte Naturwiss
Zeitschrift fuer die Gesamte Nervenheilkunde und Psychotherapie [*German Democratic Republic*] — Z Gesamte Nervenheilkd Psychother
Zeitschrift fuer die Gesamte Neurologie und Psychiatrie — Z Gesamte Neurol Psychiatr
Zeitschrift fuer die Gesamte Physikalische Therapie — Z Gesamte Phys Ther
Zeitschrift fuer die Gesamte Staatswissenschaft — Z Ges Staatswiss
Zeitschrift fuer die Gesamte Staatswissenschaft — Z Gesamte Staatswiss
Zeitschrift fuer die Gesamte Staatswissenschaft — Z St W
Zeitschrift fuer die Gesamte Staatswissenschaft — Z Staatsw
Zeitschrift fuer die Gesamte Staatswissenschaft — Z Sw
Zeitschrift fuer die Gesamte Staatswissenschaft — ZGS
Zeitschrift fuer die Gesamte Staatswissenschaft — ZS
Zeitschrift fuer die Gesamte Strafrechtswissenschaft — Z St W
Zeitschrift fuer die Gesamte Strafrechtswissenschaft — Z Str W
Zeitschrift fuer die Gesamte Textilindustrie — Z Gesamte Textilind
Zeitschrift fuer die Gesamte Textil-Industrie — Z Gesamte Text-Ind
Zeitschrift fuer die Gesamte Versicherungswissenschaft — Z Gesamte Versicherungswiss
Zeitschrift fuer die Gesamten Naturwissenschaften — Zs Ges Naturw
Zeitschrift fuer die Geschichte der Juden — ZGeschJud
Zeitschrift fuer die Geschichte der Juden — ZGJ
Zeitschrift fuer die Geschichte der Juden in Deutschland [*Braunschwig/Berlin*] — ZGJD
Zeitschrift fuer die Geschichte der Saargegend — Z Gesch Saar
Zeitschrift fuer die Geschichte der Saargegend — ZGS
Zeitschrift fuer die Geschichte des Oberrheins — Z Gesch Oberrhein
Zeitschrift fuer die Geschichte des Oberrheins — Z Gesch Oberrheins
Zeitschrift fuer die Geschichte des Oberrheins — ZGO
Zeitschrift fuer die Geschichte des Oberrheins — ZGOR
Zeitschrift fuer die Geschichte des Oberrheins — ZGOrh
Zeitschrift fuer die Geschichte und Altertumskunde Ermlands — Z Gesch Altertumskde Ermland
Zeitschrift fuer die Kunde des Morgenlandes — ZKM
Zeitschrift fuer die Kunde vom Deutschtum im Ausland — Z Kde Deutschtum Ausl
Zeitschrift fuer die Landwirthschaftlichen Vereine des Grossherzogthums Hessen — Z Landw Vereine Grossherzogth Hessen
Zeitschrift fuer die Neutestamentliche Wissenschaft — Z Neut W
Zeitschrift fuer die Neutestamentliche Wissenschaft — Z Ntl W
Zeitschrift fuer die Neutestamentliche Wissenschaft — ZNTW
Zeitschrift fuer die Neutestamentliche Wissenschaft — ZNW
Zeitschrift fuer die Neutestamentliche Wissenschaft und die Kunde der Aelteren Kirche — Z Neut Wiss
Zeitschrift fuer die Neutestamentliche Wissenschaft und die Kunde der Aelteren Kirche — ZNWKAK
Zeitschrift fuer die Neutestamentliche Wissenschaft und die Kunde des Urchristentums — ZNWKU
Zeitschrift fuer die Oesterreichischen Gymnasien — ZOEG
Zeitschrift fuer die Oesterreichischen Gymnasien — ZOest G
Zeitschrift fuer die Oesterreichischen Mittelschulen — ZOEMS
Zeitschrift fuer die Ophthalmologie — Z Ophthalmol
Zeitschrift fuer die Ophthalmologie — Ztschr Ophth
Zeitschrift fuer die Organische Physik (Von C. F. Heusinger) — Heusingers Zschr
Zeitschrift fuer die Praxise des Religionsunterrichts — RU
Zeitschrift fuer die Religioesen Interessen des Judentums [*Berlin*] — ZRI
Zeitschrift fuer die Technische Ueberwachung — Z Tech Ueberwach
Zeitschrift fuer die Vereinten Nationen und Ihre Sonderorganisationen — Vereinte Nationen
Zeitschrift fuer die Zuckerindustrie — Z Zuckerind
Zeitschrift fuer die Zuckerindustrie — Z Zuckind
Zeitschrift fuer die Zuckerindustrie der Cechoslovakoschen Republik — Z Zuckerind Cech Repub
Zeitschrift fuer die Zuckerindustrie in Boehmen — Z Zuckerind Boehm
Zeitschrift fuer die Zuckerindustrie in Boehmen-Machren — Z Zuckerind Boehm Machren
Zeitschrift fuer Donauraum-Forschung — Donauraum
Zeitschrift fuer EEG-EMG [*Elektroenzephalographie, Elektromyographie, und Verwandte Gebiete*] [*German Federal Republic*] — Z EEG-EMG
Zeitschrift fuer Eingeborenen-Sprachen — ZE Spr
Zeitschrift fuer Eingeborenensprachen — Zeits F Eingeborenesp
Zeitschrift fuer Eingeboren-Sprachen — ZES
Zeitschrift fuer Eisenbahnwesen und Verkehrstechnik. Glasers. Annalen — Z Eisenbahnwes und Verkehrstech Glasers
Zeitschrift fuer Eisenbahnwesen und Verkehrstechnik. Glasers Annalen — Z Eisenbahnwes Verkehrstech
Zeitschrift fuer Eisenbahnwesen und Verkehrstechnik. Glasers. Annalen — Z Eisenbahnwes Verkehrstech Glasers Ann
Zeitschrift fuer Eis-und Kaelte-Industrie — Z Eis Kaelte Ind
Zeitschrift fuer Elektrische Informations- und Energietechnik — Z Elek Informations- und Energietech
Zeitschrift fuer Elektrische Informations- und Energietechnik [*IET*] — Z Elektr Inf & Energietech
Zeitschrift fuer Elektrische Informations- und Energietechnik — Z Elektr Inf Energietech
Zeitschrift fuer Elektrische Informations- und Energietechnik — Z Elektr Inform Energietech
Zeitschrift fuer Elektrische Informations- und Energietechnik [*IET*] — Z Elektr Informationstech Energietech
Zeitschrift fuer Elektrische Informations- und Energietechnik — ZEIZA
Zeitschrift fuer Elektrochemie — Z Elektrochem
Zeitschrift fuer Elektrochemie — ZEELA
Zeitschrift fuer Elektrochemie und Angewandte Physikalische Chemie — Z El Ch
Zeitschrift fuer Elektrochemie und Angewandte Physikalische Chemie — Z Elektrochem Angew Phy Chem
Zeitschrift fuer Elektrotechnik — Z El Techn
Zeitschrift fuer Elektrotechnik [*Germany*] — Z Elektrotech
Zeitschrift fuer Elektrotechnik — ZELTB
Zeitschrift fuer Energiewirtschaft [*German Federal Republic*] — Z Energiewirtsch
Zeitschrift fuer Entwicklungspsychologie und Paedagogische Psychologie — Z Entwick P
Zeitschrift fuer Erdkunde — Z Erdkde
Zeitschrift fuer Erkrankungen der Atmungsorgane — Z Erkr Atmungsorgane
Zeitschrift fuer Ernaehrungswissenschaft — Z Ernaehrung
Zeitschrift fuer Ernaehrungswissenschaft — Z Ernaehrungsw
Zeitschrift fuer Ernaehrungswissenschaft — Z Ernaehrungswiss
Zeitschrift fuer Ernaehrungswissenschaft. Supplementa — Z Ernaehrungswiss Suppl
Zeitschrift fuer Ernaehrungwissenschaft — Z Ernaehr Wiss
Zeitschrift fuer Erzbergbau und Metallhuettenwesen [*German Federal Republic*] — Z Erzbergbau Metallhuettenwes
Zeitschrift fuer Erzbergbau und Metallhuettenwesen — ZEMHA
Zeitschrift fuer Erziehungswissenschaftliche Forschung — ZEF
Zeitschrift fuer Ethnologie — Z Ethnol
Zeitschrift fuer Ethnologie — Z Ethnolog
Zeitschrift fuer Ethnologie — Z f Ethn
Zeitschrift fuer Ethnologie — ZE
Zeitschrift fuer Ethnologie — Zeits F Ethnol
Zeitschrift fuer Ethnologie — Zeitschr Ethn
Zeitschrift fuer Ethnologie — ZEthn
Zeitschrift fuer Ethnologie — ZfE
Zeitschrift fuer Ethnologie — Zft Ethn
Zeitschrift fuer Ethnologie — Ztschr Ethn
Zeitschrift fuer Ethnologie. Deutsche Gesellschaft fuer Voelkerkunde — DGV/ZE
Zeitschrift fuer Evangelische Ethik — Z Ev Ethik
Zeitschrift fuer Evangelische Ethik — Z Evan Eth
Zeitschrift fuer Evangelische Ethik — ZEE
Zeitschrift fuer Evangelisches Kirchenrecht — Z Ev K
Zeitschrift fuer Evangelisches Kirchenrecht — Z Ev Kr
Zeitschrift fuer Evangelisches Kirchenrecht — Z Evang Kirchenrecht
Zeitschrift fuer Evangelisches Kirchenrecht — ZEK
Zeitschrift fuer Experimentelle Chirurgie — Z Exp Chir
Zeitschrift fuer Experimentelle Chirurgie, Transplantation, und Kuenstliche Organe — Z Exp Chir Transplant Kuenstliche Organe
Zeitschrift fuer Experimentelle Chirurgie. Transplantation und Kunstliche Organe — ZECODK
Zeitschrift fuer Experimentelle Chirurgie und Chirurgische Forschung — Z Exp Chir Chir Forsch
Zeitschrift fuer Experimentelle Pathologie und Therapie — Z Exp Pathol Ther
Zeitschrift fuer Experimentelle Psychologie — Z Exp Psychol
Zeitschrift fuer Experimentelle und Angewandte Psychologie — Z Exp A Psy
Zeitschrift fuer Experimentelle und Angewandte Psychologie — Z Exp Angew Psychol
Zeitschrift fuer Experimentelle und Angewandte Psychologie — Z Exper & Angew Psychol
Zeitschrift fuer Experimentelle und Angewandte Psychologie — ZANPA
Zeitschrift fuer Familienrecht — FRZ
Zeitschrift fuer Farben Industrie — Z Farben Ind
Zeitschrift fuer Farben- und Textil-Chemie — Z Farben Text Chem
Zeitschrift fuer Fischerei und Deren Hilfswissenschaften — Z Fisch Hilfswiss
Zeitschrift fuer Fleisch- und Milchhygiene — Z Fleisch Milchhyg
Zeitschrift fuer Fleisch- und Milchhygiene — Ztschr Fleisch u Milchhyg
Zeitschrift fuer Flugwissenschaften — Z Flugwiss
Zeitschrift fuer Flugwissenschaften und Weltraumforschung — Z Flugwiss und Weltraumforsch
Zeitschrift fuer Flugwissenschaften und Weltraumforschung — Z Flugwiss Weltraumforsch
Zeitschrift fuer Forst- und Jagdwesen — Z Forst Jagdwes
Zeitschrift fuer Franzoesische Sprache und Literatur — Z Franz Spr
Zeitschrift fuer Franzoesische Sprache und Literatur — Z Franz Sprache Lit
Zeitschrift fuer Franzoesische Sprache und Literatur — Z Franzoesische Spr Lit
Zeitschrift fuer Franzoesische Sprache und Literatur — ZFrSL
Zeitschrift fuer Franzoesische Sprache und Literatur — ZFSL
Zeitschrift fuer Franzoesische Sprache und Literatur — Zft f Fr Sp u Lit
Zeitschrift fuer Franzoesische Sprache und Litteratur — ZfS
Zeitschrift fuer Franzoesische Sprache und Litteratur — Ztschr f Franz Spr u Litt
Zeitschrift fuer Franzoesischen und Englischen Unterricht — ZFEU
Zeitschrift fuer Freie Deutsche Forschung — ZFDF
Zeitschrift fuer Gaertner, Botaniker, und Blumenfreunde — Z Gaertn Bot
Zeitschrift fuer Gaerungsphysiologie — Z Gaerungsphysiol
Zeitschrift fuer Gastroenterologie — Z Gastroent
Zeitschrift fuer Gastroenterologie — Z Gastroenterol

Zeitschrift fuer Gastroenterologie. Verhandlungsband — Z Gastroenterol Verh
Zeitschrift fuer Geburtshilfe und Gynaekologie [*Later, Zeitschrift fuer Geburtshilfe und Perinatologie*] — Z Geburtshilfe Gynaekol
Zeitschrift fuer Geburtshilfe und Gynaekologie [*Later, Zeitschrift fuer Geburtshilfe und Perinatologie*] — ZGGYA
Zeitschrift fuer Geburtshilfe und Neonatologie — Z Geburtshilfe Neonatol
Zeitschrift fuer Geburtshilfe und Perinatologie — Z Geburtshilfe Perinatol
Zeitschrift fuer Genossenschaftlichen Tierversicherung — Ztschr Genossensch Tierversich
Zeitschrift fuer Geologische Wissenschaften — Z Geol Wiss
Zeitschrift fuer Geomorphologie — Z Geomorph
Zeitschrift fuer Geomorphologie — Z Geomorphol
Zeitschrift fuer Geomorphologie — Zeitschr Geomorphologie
Zeitschrift fuer Geomorphologie — ZGMPA
Zeitschrift fuer Geomorphologie. Gebrueder Borntraeger — ZG
Zeitschrift fuer Geomorphologie. Neue Folge — Zeitschr Geomorphologie Neue Folge
Zeitschrift fuer Geomorphologie. Supplementband — Z Geomorphol Suppl
Zeitschrift fuer Geophysik [*German Federal Republic*] — Z Geophys
Zeitschrift fuer Geophysik — Zeitschr Geophysik
Zeitschrift fuer Geopolitik — Gp
Zeitschrift fuer Geopolitik — Z Geopolitik
Zeitschrift fuer Geopolitik — ZG
Zeitschrift fuer Germanistik — ZG
Zeitschrift fuer Germanistische Linguistik — Z Ger Ling
Zeitschrift fuer Germanistische Linguistik — ZGL
Zeitschrift fuer Gerontologie — Z Gerontol
Zeitschrift fuer Gerontologie und Geriatrie — Z Gerontol Geriatr
Zeitschrift fuer Geschichte der Arabisch-Islamischen Wissenschaften — Z Gesch Arab Islam Wiss
Zeitschrift fuer Geschichte der Architektur — ZGdA
Zeitschrift fuer Geschichte der Erziehung und des Unterrichts — Z Gesch Erzieh u Unterr
Zeitschrift fuer Geschichte der Erziehung und des Unterrichts — ZGEU
Zeitschrift fuer Geschichte der Erziehung und des Unterrichts — Ztsch Gesch Erzieh u Unterr
Zeitschrift fuer Geschichte der Naturwissenschaften, Technik, und Medizin — Z Gesch Naturwiss
Zeitschrift fuer Geschichte der Sudetenlaender — Z Gesch Sudetenl
Zeitschrift fuer Geschichte und Altertumskunde der Ermlands — ZGAKE
Zeitschrift fuer Geschichte und Altertumskunde Ermlands — ZfgA
Zeitschrift fuer Geschichte und Landeskunde Maehrens — Z Gesch Landeskde Maehren
Zeitschrift fuer Geschichtswissenschaft — Z Geschichtsw
Zeitschrift fuer Geschichtswissenschaft — Z Gesch-Wiss
Zeitschrift fuer Geschichtswissenschaft — ZfG
Zeitschrift fuer Geschichtswissenschaft — ZG
Zeitschrift fuer Geschichtswissenschaft — ZGW
Zeitschrift fuer Gesundheitstechnik und Staedtehygiene — Z Gesundheitstech Staedtehyg
Zeitschrift fuer Gewerbe Hygiene — Ztschr Gewerbe Hyg
Zeitschrift fuer Gletscherkunde — Zs Gletscherk
Zeitschrift fuer Gletscherkunde und Glazialgeologie — Z Gletscherk Glazialgeol
Zeitschrift fuer Gletscherkunde und Glazialgeologie — Zeitschr Gletscherkunde u Glazialgeologie
Zeitschrift fuer Goldschmiede Juwelerie und Graveure — Z Godschmiede Juwelerie Graveure
Zeitschrift fuer Hals Nasen- und Ohrenheilkunde — Z Hals Nasen Ohrenheilkd
Zeitschrift fuer Haut- und Geschlechtskrankheiten — Z Haut-Geschlechtskr
Zeitschrift fuer Hautkrankheiten — Z Hautkr
Zeitschrift fuer Hebraeische Bibliographie — ZfHb
Zeitschrift fuer Hebraeische Bibliographie — ZHB
Zeitschrift fuer Heeres- und Uniformkunde — Z Heeres U Uniformkde
Zeitschrift fuer Historische Forschung — Z Hist Fors
Zeitschrift fuer Historische Theologie — ZHT
Zeitschrift fuer Historische Waffen- und Kostuemkunde — Z Hist Waffen Und Kostuemkde
Zeitschrift fuer Hygiene — Z Hyg
Zeitschrift fuer Hygiene — Ztschr Hyg
Zeitschrift fuer Hygiene und Infektionskrankheiten — Z Hyg Infekt Kr
Zeitschrift fuer Hygiene und Infektionskrankheiten — Z Hyg Infektionskr
Zeitschrift fuer Hygiene und Infektionskrankheiten — Z Hyg InfektKrankh
Zeitschrift fuer Hygiene und Infektionskrankheiten — Ztschr Hyg u Infektionskr
Zeitschrift fuer Hygienische Zoologie und Schaedlingsbekaempfung — Z Hyg Zool Schaedlingsbekaempf
Zeitschrift fuer Immunitaets- und Allergieforschung — Z Immun -Allergie-Forsch
Zeitschrift fuer Immunitaets- und Allergieforschung — Z Immunitaets-Allergieforsch
Zeitschrift fuer Immunitaets- und Allergieforschung — ZIALA
Zeitschrift fuer Immunitaetsforschung — Z Immunitaetsforsch
Zeitschrift fuer Immunitaetsforschung. Allergie und Klinische Immunologie — Z Immunitaetsforsch Allerg Klin Immunol
Zeitschrift fuer Immunitaetsforschung. Experimentelle und Klinische Immunologie — Z Immun Exp
Zeitschrift fuer Immunitaetsforschung. Experimentelle und Klinische Immunologie — Z Immunitaetsforsch Exp Klin Immunol
Zeitschrift fuer Immunitaetsforschung. Experimentelle und Klinische Immunologie. Supplemente — Z Immunitaetsforsch Exp Klin Immunol Suppl
Zeitschrift fuer Immunitaetsforschung. Immunobiology — Z Immunitaetsforsch Immunobiol
Zeitschrift fuer Immunitaetsforschung. Immunobiology. Supplemente — Z Immunitaetsforsch Immunobiol Suppl
Zeitschrift fuer Immunitaetsforschung. Supplemente — Z Immunitaetsforsch Suppl
Zeitschrift fuer Immunitaetsforschung und Experimentelle Therapie — Z ImmunForsch Exp Ther
Zeitschrift fuer Immunitaetsforschung und Experimentelle Therapie — Z Immunitaetsforsch Exp Ther
Zeitschrift fuer Immunitaetsforschung und Experimentelle Therapie — Ztschr Immunitaetsforsch u Exper Therap
Zeitschrift fuer Immunitaetsforschung und Experimentelle Therapie. 1. Abteilung Originale — Z Immunitaetsforsch Exp Ther 1 Abt Orig
Zeitschrift fuer Immunitaetsforschung und Experimentelle Therapie. 1. Originale — Z Immunitaetsforsch Exp Ther 1
Zeitschrift fuer Immunitaetsforschung und Experimentelle Therapie. 2. Referate — Z Immunitaetsforsch Exp Ther 2
Zeitschrift fuer Indologie und Iranistik [*Leipzig*] — ZII
Zeitschrift fuer Induktive Abstammungs- und Vererbungslehre — Z Indukt Abstamm u Vererblehre
Zeitschrift fuer Induktive Abstammungs- und Vererbungslehre — Z Indukt Abstammungs-Vererbungsl
Zeitschrift fuer Induktive Abstammungs- und Vererbungslehre — ZIAVA
Zeitschrift fuer Infektionskrankheiten, Parasitaere Krankheiten, und Hygiene der Haustiere — Ztschr Infektionskr Haustiere
Zeitschrift fuer Instrumentenbau — Z I
Zeitschrift fuer Instrumentenkunde [*Germany*] — Z Instrum
Zeitschrift fuer Instrumentenkunde — Z Instrumentenk
Zeitschrift fuer Instrumentenkunde — Z Instrumentenkd
Zeitschrift fuer Instrumentenkunde — ZEINA
Zeitschrift fuer Jagdwissenschaft — Z Jagdwiss
Zeitschrift fuer Journalistik — Z Journ
Zeitschrift fuer Kardiologie — Z Kardiol
Zeitschrift fuer Kardiologie. Supplementum — Z Kardiol Suppl
Zeitschrift fuer Katholische Theologie — Z Kath Theol
Zeitschrift fuer Katholische Theologie — ZKT
Zeitschrift fuer Katholische Theologie — ZKTh
Zeitschrift fuer Katholischen Religionsunterricht — ZKRU
Zeitschrift fuer Keilschriftforschung und Verwandte Gebiete — ZK
Zeitschrift fuer Keltische Philologie — ZK Ph
Zeitschrift fuer Keltische Philologie und Volksforschung — Z f K Ph
Zeitschrift fuer Keltische Philologie und Volksforschung — Zc Ph
Zeitschrift fuer Keltische Philologie und Volksforschung — ZKPVF
Zeitschrift fuer Kinder- und Jugendpsychiatrie — Z Kind Jug
Zeitschrift fuer Kinder- und Jugendpsychiatrie — Z Kinder-Jugendpsychiatr
Zeitschrift fuer Kinderchirurgie — Z Kinderchir
Zeitschrift fuer Kinderchirurgie — ZEKID8
Zeitschrift fuer Kinderchirurgie und Grenzgebiete — Z Kindch G
Zeitschrift fuer Kinderchirurgie und Grenzgebiete — Z Kinderchir Grenzgeb
Zeitschrift fuer Kinderchirurgie und Grenzgebiete — ZK Ch
Zeitschrift fuer Kinderheilkunde — Z Kinderheilkd
Zeitschrift fuer Kinderheilkunde — Zeits F Kinderheilk
Zeitschrift fuer Kinderheilkunde — ZEKIA
Zeitschrift fuer Kinderheilkunde. Referate — ZSKHA
Zeitschrift fuer Kinderpsychiatrie — Z Kinderpsychiatr
Zeitschrift fuer Kirchengeschichte — Z Kirch G
Zeitschrift fuer Kirchengeschichte — Z Kircheng
Zeitschrift fuer Kirchengeschichte — Z Kirchengesch
Zeitschrift fuer Kirchengeschichte — ZK
Zeitschrift fuer Kirchengeschichte — ZKG
Zeitschrift fuer Kirchenrecht — ZKR
Zeitschrift fuer Kirchliche Wissenschaft und Kirchliches Leben [*Leipzig*] — ZKWL
Zeitschrift fuer Klinische Chemie — Z Klin Chemie
Zeitschrift fuer Klinische Chemie — ZKLCA
Zeitschrift fuer Klinische Chemie und Klinische Biochemie — Z Klin Chem
Zeitschrift fuer Klinische Chemie und Klinische Biochemie — Z Klin Chem Klin Biochem
Zeitschrift fuer Klinische Medizin — Z Kl M
Zeitschrift fuer Klinische Medizin — Z Klin Med
Zeitschrift fuer Klinische Medizin (Berlin) — Ztschr Klin Med (Berlin)
Zeitschrift fuer Klinische Psychologie, Psychopathologie, und Psychotherapie — Z Klin Psychol Psychopathol Psychother
Zeitschrift fuer Klinische Psychologie und Psychotherapie — Z Klin Psychol Psychother
Zeitschrift fuer Kolonialsprachen — Zeits F Kolonialsp
Zeitschrift fuer Komprimierte und Fluessige Gase Sowie fuer die Pressluft-Industrie — Z Kompr Fluess Gase Pressluft-Ind
Zeitschrift fuer Krankenpflege — Z Krankenpfl
Zeitschrift fuer Krebsforschung — Z Kr F
Zeitschrift fuer Krebsforschung — Z Krebsforsch
Zeitschrift fuer Krebsforschung — Ztschr Krebsforsch
Zeitschrift fuer Krebsforschung und Klinische Onkologie — Z Krebsf Kl
Zeitschrift fuer Krebsforschung und Klinische Onkologie — Z Krebsforsch Klin Onkol
Zeitschrift fuer Kreislaufforschung — Z Kreisl Forsch
Zeitschrift fuer Kreislaufforschung — Z Kreislaufforsch
Zeitschrift fuer Kristallographie — Z Kristallogr
Zeitschrift fuer Kristallographie — Zeitschr Kristallographie
Zeitschrift fuer Kristallographie, Kristallgeometrie, Kristallphysik, Kristallchemie — Z Kr
Zeitschrift fuer Kristallographie, Kristallgeometrie, Kristallphysik, Kristallchemie — Z Krist
Zeitschrift fuer Kristallographie, Kristallgeometrie, Kristallphysik, Kristallchemie — Z Kristall
Zeitschrift fuer Kristallographie, Kristallgeometrie, Kristallphysik, Kristallchemie — Z Kristallogr Kristallgeom Kristallphys Kristallchem
Zeitschrift fuer Kristallographie und Mineralogie — Z Kristallogr Mineral
Zeitschrift fuer Krystallographie und Mineralogie — Z Kryst Miner
Zeitschrift fuer Krystallographie und Mineralogie — Zs Kryst

Zeitschrift fuer Kulturaustausch — Z f Kulturaustausch
Zeitschrift fuer Kulturaustausch — Z Kulturaustausch
Zeitschrift fuer Kulturaustausch — ZKA
Zeitschrift fuer Kulturgeschichte — Z Kult G
Zeitschrift fuer Kulturtechnik — Z Kulturtech
Zeitschrift fuer Kulturtechnik und Flurbereinigung — Z Kult-Tech Flurberein
Zeitschrift fuer Kulturtechnik und Flurbereinigung — Z Kulturtech Flurbereinig
Zeitschrift fuer Kulturtechnik und Landentwicklung — Z Kulturtech Landentwicklung
Zeitschrift fuer Kunstgeschichte — Z Kunst
Zeitschrift fuer Kunstgeschiohte — Z Kunstges
Zeitschrift fuer Kunstgeschichte — Z Kunstgesc
Zeitschrift fuer Kunstgeschichte — Z Kunstgesch
Zeitschrift fuer Kunstgeschichte — ZfK
Zeitschrift fuer Kunstgeschichte — ZfKg
Zeitschrift fuer Kunstgeschichte — ZK
Zeitschrift fuer Kunstgeschichte — ZKG
Zeitschrift fuer Kunstgeschichte — ZKuG
Zeitschrift fuer Kunstgeschichte — ZKunstG
Zeitschrift fuer Kunstwissenschaft — Z Kunstwis
Zeitschrift fuer Kunstwissenschaft — ZK
Zeitschrift fuer Kunstwissenschaft — ZKW
Zeitschrift fuer Laboratoriumsdiagnostik — Z Laboratoriumsdiagn
Zeitschrift fuer Laermbekaempfung — ZELAD
Zeitschrift fuer Landeskultur — Z Landeskult
Zeitschrift fuer Landwirtschaftliches Versuchs- und Untersuchungswesen — Z Landw Ver u Unters Wes
Zeitschrift fuer Landwirtschaftliches Versuchs- und Untersuchungswesen — Z Landwirt Vers Untersuchungsw
Zeitschrift fuer Landwirtschaftliches Versuchs- und Untersuchungswesen — Z Landwirtsch Vers Untersuchungswes
Zeitschrift fuer Landwirtschaftswissenschaften — Z Landwirtschaftswiss
Zeitschrift fuer Laryngologie, Rhinologie, Otologie — ZLROA
Zeitschrift fuer Laryngologie, Rhinologie, Otologie, und Ihre Grenzgebiete — Z Lar Rhinol Otol
Zeitschrift fuer Laryngologie, Rhinologie, Otologie, und Ihre Grenzgebiete — Z Laryngol Rhinol Otol
Zeitschrift fuer Laryngologie, Rhinologie, Otologie, und Ihre Grenzgebiete — Z Laryngol Rhinol Otol Grenzgeb
Zeitschrift fuer Laryngologie, Rhinologie, Otologie, und Ihre Grenzgebiete — Z Laryngol Rhinol Otol Ihre Grenzgeb
Zeitschrift fuer Lateinamerika (Wien). Oesterreichisches Lateinamerika Institut (Wien) — OLI/ZLW
Zeitschrift fuer Lebensmittel- Technologie und Verfahrenstechnik [*German Federal Republic*] — Z Lebensm-Technol-Verfahrenstech
Zeitschrift fuer Lebensmittel- Untersuchung und Forschung — Z Lebensmit
Zeitschrift fuer Lebensmittel- Untersuchung und Forschung — Z Lebensmitt Untersuch
Zeitschrift fuer Lebensmittel- Untersuchung und Forschung — Z Lebensmittel Untersuch Forsch
Zeitschrift fuer Lebensmittel- Untersuchung und Forschung — Z Lebensmittelunters u Forsch
Zeitschrift fuer Lebensmittel- Untersuchung und Forschung — Z Lebensm-Unters Forsch
Zeitschrift fuer Leder- und Gerberei-Chemie — Z Leder Gerberei Chem
Zeitschrift fuer Literaturwissenschaft — Z Lit Wiss
Zeitschrift fuer Literaturwissenschaft und Linguistik — LiLi
Zeitschrift fuer Literaturwissenschaft und Linguistik — Z Literaturwiss Linguist
Zeitschrift fuer Luft- und Weltraumrecht — Z Luft-Weltraumrecht
Zeitschrift fuer Luftrecht und Weltraum-Rechtsfragen — ZLW
Zeitschrift fuer Lymphologie — Z Lymphol
Zeitschrift fuer Marktforschung, Meinungsforschung, und Zukunftsforschung — Z Markt Meinungs und Zukunftsforsch
Zeitschrift fuer Marktforschung, Meinungsforschung, und Zukunftsforschung — ZMM
Zeitschrift fuer Mathematik und Physik [*Germany*] — Z Mat Phys
Zeitschrift fuer Mathematik und Physik — ZMPHA
Zeitschrift fuer Mathematische Logik und Grundlagen der Mathematik — Z Math Log
Zeitschrift fuer Mathematische Logik und Grundlagen der Mathematik — Z Math Logik Grundlag Math
Zeitschrift fuer Mathematische Logik und Grundlagen der Mathematik — Z Math Logik Grundlagen Math
Zeitschrift fuer Medizinische Chemie — Z Med Chem
Zeitschrift fuer Medizinische Isotopenforschung und Deren Grenzgebiete — Z Med Isotopenforsch Deren Grenzgeb
Zeitschrift fuer Medizinische Laboratoriumsdiagnostik — Z Med Lab Diagn
Zeitschrift fuer Medizinische Laboratoriumsdiagnostik — Z Med Laboratoriumsdiagn
Zeitschrift fuer Medizinische Laboratoriumsdiagnostik. Beilage — Z Med Laboratoriumsdiagn Beil
Zeitschrift fuer Medizinische Labortechnik — Z Med Labortech
Zeitschrift fuer Medizinische Mikrobiologie und Immunologie — Z Med Mikrobiol Immunol
Zeitschrift fuer Medizinische Mikroskopie — Z Med Mikrosk
Zeitschrift fuer Medizinstudenten und Assistenten — Med Ass
Zeitschrift fuer Menschliche Vererbungs- und Konstitutionslehre — Z Menschl Vererb-Konstitutionsl
Zeitschrift fuer Menschliche Vererbungs und Konstitutionslehre — Z Menschl Vererbungs Konstitutionsl
Zeitschrift fuer Menschliche Vererbungs- und Konstitutionslehre — ZMVKA
Zeitschrift fuer Metall- und Schmuckwaren. Fabrikation sowie Verchromung — Z Met Schmuckwaren Fabr Verchrom
Zeitschrift fuer Metallkunde — Z Metallk
Zeitschrift fuer Metallkunde — Z Metallkd
Zeitschrift fuer Metallkunde — Z Metallkun
Zeitschrift fuer Meteorologie — Z Meteorol
Zeitschrift fuer Mikroskopische Fleischschau und Populaere Mikroskopie — Ztsch Mikr Fleischschau
Zeitschrift fuer Mikroskopische-Anatomische Forschung — Z Mikrosk Anat Forsch
Zeitschrift fuer Mikroskopische-Anatomische Forschung — ZM-AF
Zeitschrift fuer Mikroskopische-Anatomische Forschung (Leipzig) — Z Mikrosk-Anat Forsch (Leipz)
Zeitschrift fuer Militaeraerzte (Tokyo) — Ztsch Militaeraerzte (Tokyo)
Zeitschrift fuer Militaergeschichte — Z Militaergesch
Zeitschrift fuer Militaergeschichte — ZM
Zeitschrift fuer Militaermedizin [*Germany*] — Z Militaermed
Zeitschrift fuer Mineralogie (By K. C. Von Leonhard) — Leonhards Zschr
Zeitschrift fuer Mineralogie (Leonhard) — Zs Miner (Leonhard)
Zeitschrift fuer Mission — Z fuer Mission
Zeitschrift fuer Missionskunde — ZM
Zeitschrift fuer Missionskunde und Religionswissenschaft — Zeits F Missionsk U Religionswis
Zeitschrift fuer Missionskunde und Religionswissenschaft — ZMK
Zeitschrift fuer Missionswissenschaft — ZMW
Zeitschrift fuer Missionswissenschaft und Religionswissenschaft — Z fuer Missionswissenschaft und Religionswissenschaft
Zeitschrift fuer Missionswissenschaft und Religionswissenschaft — Z Miss
Zeitschrift fuer Missionswissenschaft und Religionswissenschaft — Z Miss W
Zeitschrift fuer Missionswissenschaft und Religionswissenschaft — Z Missionswiss Religionswiss
Zeitschrift fuer Missionswissenschaft und Religionswissenschaft — Z Miss-u Relig Wiss
Zeitschrift fuer Missionswissenschaft und Religionswissenschaft — ZMR
Zeitschrift fuer Missionswissenschaft und Religionswissenschaft — ZMRW
Zeitschrift fuer Morphologie der Tiere — Z Morph Tie
Zeitschrift fuer Morphologie der Tiere — Z Morphol Tiere
Zeitschrift fuer Morphologie und Anthropologie — Z Morphol Anthropol
Zeitschrift fuer Morphologie und Anthropologie — Z Morphologie und Anthrop
Zeitschrift fuer Morphologie und Anthropologie — Zeits F Morphol U Anthropol
Zeitschrift fuer Morphologie und Oekologie der Tiere — Z Morph Okol Tiere
Zeitschrift fuer Morphologie und Oekologie der Tiere — Z Morphol Oekol Tiere
Zeitschrift fuer Morphologie und Oekologie der Tiere — ZMOTA
Zeitschrift fuer Morphologie und Oekologie der Tiere — Ztschr Morphol u Oekol Tiere
Zeitschrift fuer Mundartforschung — ZM
Zeitschrift fuer Mundartforschung — ZMaF
Zeitschrift fuer Mundartforschung — ZMF
Zeitschrift fuer Musik — ZFM
Zeitschrift fuer Musik — ZM
Zeitschrift fuer Musikpaedagogik — ZMP
Zeitschrift fuer Musiktheorie — Z Mth
Zeitschrift fuer Musiktheorie — Zf Mus Theorie
Zeitschrift fuer Musiktheorie — ZMtheorie
Zeitschrift fuer Musikwissenschaft — Z Mw
Zeitschrift fuer Musikwissenschaft — ZfMw
Zeitschrift fuer Mykologie — Z Mykol
Zeitschrift fuer Nahrungsmittel-Untersuchung Hygiene und Warenkunde — Z Nahrungsm Unters Hyg Warenkd
Zeitschrift fuer Namenforschung — ZN
Zeitschrift fuer Namenforschung — ZNF
Zeitschrift fuer Nationaloekonomie — Z Nationalo
Zeitschrift fuer Nationaloekonomie — Z Nationaloekon
Zeitschrift fuer Nationaloekonomie — Z Nationaloekonom
Zeitschrift fuer Nationaloekonomie — Z Nat-Oekon
Zeitschrift fuer Nationaloekonomie — ZeNo
Zeitschrift fuer Nationaloekonomie — ZN
Zeitschrift fuer Nationaloekonomie — ZNO
Zeitschrift fuer Nationaloekonomie/Journal of Economics — Z Nat Oekon
Zeitschrift fuer Natur- und Heilkunde [*Dresden*] — Zd Natkde Heilkde
Zeitschrift fuer Natur- und Heilkunde (Brosche, Editor) — Brosches Zeitschr
Zeitschrift fuer Naturforschung — Z Nat F
Zeitschrift fuer Naturforschung — Z Natforsch
Zeitschrift fuer Naturforschung — Z Naturforsch
Zeitschrift fuer Naturforschung — ZNTFA
Zeitschrift fuer Naturforschung. A — Z Naturfo A
Zeitschrift fuer Naturforschung. A. Physical Sciences — Z Natforsch A Phys Sci
Zeitschrift fuer Naturforschung. B — Z Naturfo B
Zeitschrift fuer Naturforschung. C — Z Naturfo C
Zeitschrift fuer Naturforschung. Section B. Inorganic Chemistry, Organic Chemistry — Z Naturforsch Sect B
Zeitschrift fuer Naturforschung. Section C. Biosciences — Z Naturforsch Sect C Biosci
Zeitschrift fuer Naturforschung. Section C. Journal of Biosciences — Z Naturforsch C
Zeitschrift fuer Naturforschung. Teil A — Z Naturforsch Teil A
Zeitschrift fuer Naturforschung. Teil A. Astrophysik, Physik, und Physikalische Chemie — Z Naturforsch A
Zeitschrift fuer Naturforschung. Teil A. Physik, Physikalische Chemie, Kosmophysik — Z Naturforsch A Phys Phys Chem
Zeitschrift fuer Naturforschung. Teil B — Z Naturf B
Zeitschrift fuer Naturforschung. Teil B — Z Naturforsch B
Zeitschrift fuer Naturforschung. Teil B. Anorganische Chemie, Organische Chemie — Z Naturforsch B Anorg Chem Org Chem
Zeitschrift fuer Naturforschung. Teil B. Anorganische Chemie, Organische Chemie — Z Naturforsch Teil B Anorg Chem Org Chem
Zeitschrift fuer Naturforschung. Teil B. Anorganische Chemie, Organische Chemie, Biochemie, Biophysik, Biologie [*Germany*] — Z Naturforsch B Anorg Chem Org Chem Biochem Biophys Biol

Zeitschrift fuer Naturforschung. Teil B. Anorganische Chemie, Organische Chemie, Biophysik, Biologie — Z Naturforsch B Anorg Chem Org
Zeitschrift fuer Naturforschung. Teil C. Biochemie, Biophysik, Biologie, Virologie — Z Naturf C
Zeitschrift fuer Naturforschung. Teil C. Biochemie, Biophysik, Biologie, Virologie [*Germany*] — Z Naturforsch C Biochem Biophys Biol Virol
Zeitschrift fuer Naturforschung. Teil C. Biochemie, Biophysik, Biologie, Virologie — Z Naturforsch Teil C Biochem Biophys Biol Virol
Zeitschrift fuer Naturforschung. Teil C. Biosciences [*Germany*] — Z Naturforsch C Biosci
Zeitschrift fuer Naturforschung. Teil C. Biosciences — Z Naturforsch Teil C
Zeitschrift fuer Naturheilkunde — Z Naturheilk
Zeitschrift fuer Naturwissenschaftlich-Medizinische Grundlagenforschung — Z Naturwiss-Med Grundlagenforsch
Zeitschrift fuer Neuere Sprachen — ZNS
Zeitschrift fuer Neufranzoesische Sprache und Literatur — ZNSL
Zeitschrift fuer Neurologie — Z Neurol
Zeitschrift fuer Neurologie — ZSNUA
Zeitschrift fuer Neusprachlichen Unterricht — ZFNU
Zeitschrift fuer Neusprachlichen Unterricht — ZNU
Zeitschrift fuer Numismatik — Z f Num
Zeitschrift fuer Numismatik — Zeit f Num
Zeitschrift fuer Numismatik — ZfN
Zeitschrift fuer Numismatik — Zft Num
Zeitschrift fuer Numismatik — ZN
Zeitschrift fuer Numismatik — ZNum
Zeitschrift fuer Numismatik — Ztschr Num
Zeitschrift fuer Numismatik (Berlin) — Zeitschr Num Berlin
Zeitschrift fuer Oeffentliche Chemie — Z Oeff Chem
Zeitschrift fuer Oeffentliche und Gemeinwirtschaftliche Unternehmen — Z Oeff Gem Wirtsch Unterneh
Zeitschrift fuer Oeffentliche und Gemeinwirtschaftliche Unternehmen — Z Oeff Gem Wirtsch Unternehmen
Zeitschrift fuer Oeffentliches Recht — Z Oeff Recht
Zeitschrift fuer Oesterreichisches Bibliothekswesen — ZOBW
Zeitschrift fuer Oesterreichisches Strafrecht — Zs Oester Strafr
Zeitschrift fuer Operations Research — UNK
Zeitschrift fuer Operations Research — Z Oper Res
Zeitschrift fuer Operations Research — ZOR
Zeitschrift fuer Operations Research. Mathematical Methods of Operations Research — ZOR Math Methods Oper Res
Zeitschrift fuer Operations Research. Serie A. Serie B — Z Oper Res Ser A-B
Zeitschrift fuer Operations Research. Serie A. Serie B — Z Operations Res Ser A-B
Zeitschrift fuer Operations Research. Serie A. Theorie — Z Oper Res Ser A
Zeitschrift fuer Operations Research. Serie A. Theorie — Z Operat Res Ser A
Zeitschrift fuer Operations Research. Serie B. Praxis — Z Oper Res B
Zeitschrift fuer Operations Research. Serie B. Praxis — Z Oper Res Ser B
Zeitschrift fuer Operations Research. Serie B. Praxis — Z Oper Res Ser Praxis
Zeitschrift fuer Operations Research. Serie B. Praxis — ZORPB
Zeitschrift fuer Organisation — Z Organ
Zeitschrift fuer Organisation — ZO
Zeitschrift fuer Orthopaedie und Ihre Grenzgebiete — Z Orthop
Zeitschrift fuer Orthopaedie und Ihre Grenzgebiete — Z Orthop Grenzgeb
Zeitschrift fuer Orthopaedie und Ihre Grenzgebiete — Z Orthop Ihre Grenzgeb
Zeitschrift fuer Ortsnamenforschung — ZO
Zeitschrift fuer Ortsnamenforschung — ZON
Zeitschrift fuer Osteuropaeische Geschichte — Z Osteur Gesch
Zeitschrift fuer Osteuropaeische Geschichte — ZOEG
Zeitschrift fuer Osteuropaeische Geschichte — ZOG
Zeitschrift fuer Osteuropaeisches Recht — Z Osteur Recht
Zeitschrift fuer Ostforschung — Z Ostforsch
Zeitschrift fuer Ostforschung — ZO
Zeitschrift fuer Ostforschung — ZOf
Zeitschrift fuer Ostforschung — ZOfo
Zeitschrift fuer Papier. Pappe, Zellulose, und Holzstoff — Z Pap Pappe Zellul Holzst
Zeitschrift fuer Papyrologie und Epigraphik — Z f Pap Ep
Zeitschrift fuer Papyrologie und Epigraphik — Z Papyrologie Epigraphik
Zeitschrift fuer Papyrologie und Epigraphik — Zeitschrf Pap u Epigr
Zeitschrift fuer Papyrologie und Epigraphik — ZPE
Zeitschrift fuer Parapsychologie und Grenzgebiete der Psychologie — Z Parapsych
Zeitschrift fuer Parasitenkunde — Z Parasiten
Zeitschrift fuer Parasitenkunde — Z Parasitenkd
Zeitschrift fuer Parasitenkunde — Z ParasitKde
Zeitschrift fuer Parasitenkunde (Berlin) — Ztschr Parasitenk (Berlin)
Zeitschrift fuer Parasitenkunde (Jena) — Ztschr Parasitenk (Jena)
Zeitschrift fuer Parlamentsfragen [*German Federal Republic*] — Z Parlamentsfr
Zeitschrift fuer Parlamentsfragen — Z Parlamentsfragen
Zeitschrift fuer Parlamentsfragen — ZEPAD
Zeitschrift fuer Pflanzenernaehrung, Duengung, und Bodenkunde [*Later, Zeitschrift fuer Pflanzenernaehrung und Bodenkunde*] — Z Pflanzenernaehr Dueng Bodenkd
Zeitschrift fuer Pflanzenernaehrung, Duengung, und Bodenkunde — Z Pflanzenernahr Dung Bodenkd
Zeitschrift fuer Pflanzenernaehrung, Duengung, und Bodenkunde [*Later, Zeitschrift fuer Pflanzenernaehrung und Bodenkunde*] — Z PflErnahr Dung Bodenk
Zeitschrift fuer Pflanzenernaehrung, Duengung, und Bodenkunde — ZPDBA
Zeitschrift fuer Pflanzenernaehrung, Duengung, und Bodenkunde. A. Wissenschaftlicher Teil — Z Pflanzenernaehr Duengung Bodenk A Wiss Teil
Zeitschrift fuer Pflanzenernaehrung und Bodenkunde — Z Pflanzenernaehr Bodenkd
Zeitschrift fuer Pflanzenernaehrung und Bodenkunde — Z PflErnahr Bodenk
Zeitschrift fuer Pflanzenernaehrung und Duengung — Z Pflanzenernaehr Dueng
Zeitschrift fuer Pflanzenkrankheiten — Z Pflanzenkr
Zeitschrift fuer Pflanzenkrankheiten, Pflanzenpathologie, und Pflanzenschutz — Z Pflanzenkr Pflanzenpathol Pflanzenschutz
Zeitschrift fuer Pflanzenkrankheiten, Pflanzenpathologie, und Pflanzenschutz — Z PflKrankh
Zeitschrift fuer Pflanzenkrankheiten, Pflanzenpathologie, und Pflanzenschutz. Sonderheft — Z Pflanzenkr Pflanzenpathol Pflanzenschutz Sonderh
Zeitschrift fuer Pflanzenkrankheiten und Gallenkunde — Z Pflanzenkr Gallenkd
Zeitschrift fuer Pflanzenkrankheiten und Pflanzenschutz — Z Pflanzenkr Pflanzenschutz
Zeitschrift fuer Pflanzenkrankheiten und Pflanzenschutz — Z PflKrankh PflSchutz
Zeitschrift fuer Pflanzenphysiologie — Z Pflanzenp
Zeitschrift fuer Pflanzenphysiologie — Z Pflanzenphysiol
Zeitschrift fuer Pflanzenphysiologie — Z PflPhysiol
Zeitschrift fuer Pflanzenzuechtung — Z Pflanzenz
Zeitschrift fuer Pflanzenzuechtung — Z Pflanzenzuecht
Zeitschrift fuer Pflanzenzuechtung — Z Pflzuecht
Zeitschrift fuer Philosophie und Philosophische Kritik — Z Ph Kr
Zeitschrift fuer Philosophische Forschung — Z Phil Forsch
Zeitschrift fuer Philosophische Forschung — Z Philos F
Zeitschrift fuer Philosophische Forschung — Z Philos Forsch
Zeitschrift fuer Philosophische Forschung — ZfPhF
Zeitschrift fuer Philosophische Forschung — ZPF
Zeitschrift fuer Philosophische Forschung — ZPhF
Zeitschrift fuer Phonetik — ZP
Zeitschrift fuer Phonetik, Sprachwissenschaft, und Kommunikationsforschung — Z Phon Sprachwiss Kommunikationsforsch
Zeitschrift fuer Phonetik, Sprachwissenschaft, und Kommunikationsforschung — Z Phonetik Sprachwiss Komm Forsch
Zeitschrift fuer Phonetik, Sprachwissenschaft, und Kommunikationsforschung — Z Phonetik Sprachwissenschaft und Kommunikationsforschung
Zeitschrift fuer Phonetik, Sprachwissenschaft, und Kommunikationsforschung — ZPSK
Zeitschrift fuer Phonetik und Allgemeine Sprachwissenschaft — ZPAS
Zeitschrift fuer Phonetik und Allgemeine Sprachwissenschaft — ZPhon
Zeitschrift fuer Physik — Z Phys
Zeitschrift fuer Physik — Z Physik
Zeitschrift fuer Physik — Zeit Physik
Zeitschrift fuer Physik A. Atomic Nuclei — Z Phys A At Nucl
Zeitschrift fuer Physik. A. Atomic Nuclei — Z Phys A At Nuclei
Zeitschrift fuer Physik. A. Hadrons and Nuclei — Z Phys A Hadrons Nuclei
Zeitschrift fuer Physik. B. Condensed Matter — Z Phys B Condens Mater
Zeitschrift fuer Physik. D. Atoms, Molecules, and Clusters — Z Phys D
Zeitschrift fuer Physik. Sektion A. Atoms and Nuclei — Z Phys A
Zeitschrift fuer Physik. Sektion A. Atoms and Nuclei — ZPAAD
Zeitschrift fuer Physik. Sektion B. Condensed Matter and Quanta — Z Phys B
Zeitschrift fuer Physik. Sektion B. Condensed Matter and Quanta — ZPBBD
Zeitschrift fuer Physik. Sektion C. Particles and Fields [*German Federal Republic*] — Z Phys C
Zeitschrift fuer Physikalisch-Chemische Materialforschung — Z Phys Chem Materialforsch
Zeitschrift fuer Physikalische Chemie — Z Phys Chem
Zeitschrift fuer Physikalische Chemie — Zeitschr Physikal Chemie
Zeitschrift fuer Physikalische Chemie. Abteilung A. Chemische Thermodynamik, Kinetik, Elektrochemie, Eigenschaftslehre — Z Phys Chem Abt A
Zeitschrift fuer Physikalische Chemie. Abteilung A. Chemische Thermodynamik, Kinetik, Elektrochemie, Eigenschaftslehre — ZPCAA
Zeitschrift fuer Physikalische Chemie. Abteilung B. Chemie der Elementarprozesse, Aufbau der Materie — Z Phys Chem Abt B
Zeitschrift fuer Physikalische Chemie. Abteilung B. Chemie der Elementarprozesse, Aufbau der Materie — ZPCBA
Zeitschrift fuer Physikalische Chemie (Frankfurt) — Z Phys Ch (F)
Zeitschrift fuer Physikalische Chemie (Frankfurt/Main) — Z Phys Chem (Frankfurt/Main)
Zeitschrift fuer Physikalische Chemie. Frankfurter Ausgabe. Neue Folge [*West Germany*] — Z Phys Chem Frankf Ausg Neue Folge
Zeitschrift fuer Physikalische Chemie. Frankfurter Ausgabe. Neue Folge — ZPYFA
Zeitschrift fuer Physikalische Chemie (Leipzig) — Z Phys Ch (L)
Zeitschrift fuer Physikalische Chemie (Leipzig) — Z Phys Chem (Leipzig)
Zeitschrift fuer Physikalische Chemie (Leipzig) — ZPCLA
Zeitschrift fuer Physikalische Chemie (Munich) — Z Phys Chem Munich
Zeitschrift fuer Physikalische Chemie. Neue Folge — Z Phys Chem Neue Folge
Zeitschrift fuer Physikalische Chemie. Neue Folge (Wiesbaden) — Z Phys Chem Neue Fo (Wiesbaden)
Zeitschrift fuer Physikalische Chemie, Stoechiometrie, und Verwandschaftslehre — Z Phys Chemie Stoechiom Verwandschaftsl
Zeitschrift fuer Physikalische Chemie (Wiesbaden) — Z Phys Chem (Wiesbaden)
Zeitschrift fuer Physikalische und Diaetetische Therapie — Z Phys Diaet Ther
Zeitschrift fuer Physiologie (Fr. Tiedemann and G. R. Treviranus, Editors) — Tiedemanns Zschr
Zeitschrift fuer Physiologische Chemie — Z Physiol Chem
Zeitschrift fuer Physiologische Chemie — ZPCHA
Zeitschrift fuer Physiologische Chemie — Ztschr Physiol Chem
Zeitschrift fuer Physiologische Chemie. Hoppe-Seylers [*German Federal Republic*] — Z Physiol Chem Hoppe-Seylers
Zeitschrift fuer Physiotherapie — Z Physiother
Zeitschrift fuer Pilzkunde — Z Pilzkd
Zeitschrift fuer Plastische Chirurgie — Z Plast Chir
Zeitschrift fuer Politik — Z Polit
Zeitschrift fuer Politik — Z Politik

Zeitschrift fuer Politik — Zeits F Politik
Zeitschrift fuer Politik — ZfP
Zeitschrift fuer Politik — ZP
Zeitschrift fuer Politik. Neue Folge — Z Pol N F
Zeitschrift fuer Populaere Mitteilungen aus dem Gebiete der Astronomie und Verwandter Wissenschaften — Zs Popul Mitt Astron
Zeitschrift fuer Populaere Mitteilungen aus dem Gebiete der Astronomie und Verwandter Wissenschaften (Von C. A. F. Peters) — Peters Zschr
Zeitschrift fuer Praeklinische Geriatrie — Z Praeklin Geriatr
Zeitschrift fuer Praeklinische und Klinische Geriatrie — Z Praeklin Klin Geriatr
Zeitschrift fuer Praeventivmedizin — Z Praeventivmed
Zeitschrift fuer Praeventivmedizin — Z Praventivmed
Zeitschrift fuer Praktische Anaesthesie, Wiederbelebung, und-Intensivtherapie — Z Prakt Anaesth
Zeitschrift fuer Praktische Geologie — Z Prakt Geol
Zeitschrift fuer Praktische Geologie — Zs Prak G
Zeitschrift fuer Psychische Hygiene — Z Psych Hyg
Zeitschrift fuer Psychologie — Z Psychol
Zeitschrift fuer Psychologie — Z Psycholog
Zeitschrift fuer Psychologie — ZPh
Zeitschrift fuer Psychologie — ZPs
Zeitschrift fuer Psychologie — ZTPSA
Zeitschrift fuer Psychologie mit Zeitschrift fuer Angewandte Psychologie — Z Psychol Z Angew Psychol
Zeitschrift fuer Psychologie mit Zeitschrift fuer Angewandte Psychologie und Charakterkunde — Z Psychol Z Angew Psychol Charakterkd
Zeitschrift fuer Psychologie und Physiologie der Sinnesorgane [*Germany*] — Z Psychol Physiol Sinnesorg
Zeitschrift fuer Psychologie und Physiologie der Sinnesorgane — ZPSIA
Zeitschrift fuer Psychosomatische Medizin [*Later, Zeitschrift fuer Psychosomatische Medizin und Psychoanalyse*] — Z Psychosom Med
Zeitschrift fuer Psychosomatische Medizin [*Later, Zeitschrift fuer Psychosomatische Medizin und Psychoanalyse*] — ZPSMA
Zeitschrift fuer Psychosomatische Medizin und Psychoanalyse — Z Psychos M
Zeitschrift fuer Psychosomatische Medizin und Psychoanalyse — Z Psychosom Med Psychoanal
Zeitschrift fuer Psychotherapie und Medizinische Psychologie — Z Psychot M
Zeitschrift fuer Psychotherapie und Medizinische Psychologie — Z Psychother Med Psychol
Zeitschrift fuer Psychotherapie und Medizinische Psychologie — ZPMPA
Zeitschrift fuer Rassenkunde — Z Rassk
Zeitschrift fuer Rechtsgeschichte — Zf Rechtsgesch
Zeitschrift fuer Rechtsgeschichte — Zft Rechtsg
Zeitschrift fuer Rechtsgeschichte — ZR
Zeitschrift fuer Rechtsgeschichte — ZRg
Zeitschrift fuer Rechtsmedizin [*Journal of Legal Medicine*] — Z Rechtsmed
Zeitschrift fuer Rechtspflege in Bayern — BayZ
Zeitschrift fuer Rechtspflege in Bayern — Zs Rechtspflege Bayern
Zeitschrift fuer Rechtspolitik — Z Rechtspolit
Zeitschrift fuer Rechtspolitik — ZERED
Zeitschrift fuer Reich- und Geschmackstoffe — Z Reich Geschmackstoffe
Zeitschrift fuer Religions- und Geistesgeschichte [*Koeln*] — Z Rel Geistesges
Zeitschrift fuer Religions- und Geistesgeschichte — Z Rel Gg
Zeitschrift fuer Religions- und Geistesgeschichte — Z Relig Geistesgesch
Zeitschrift fuer Religions- und Geistesgeschichte — Z Relig- u Geistesgesch
Zeitschrift fuer Religions- und Geistesgeschichte — Z Religions U Geistesgesch
Zeitschrift fuer Religions- und Geistesgeschichte — ZfRG
Zeitschrift fuer Religions- und Geistesgeschichte — ZfRuGg
Zeitschrift fuer Religions- und Geistesgeschichte — ZRG
Zeitschrift fuer Religions- und Geistesgeschichte — ZRGG
Zeitschrift fuer Religions- und Geistesgeschichte — Zs f Rel Geist Gesch
Zeitschrift fuer Religions- und Geistesgeschichte. Beihefte — ZRGGB
Zeitschrift fuer Religions- und Geistesgeschichte. Sonderhefte — ZRGGS
Zeitschrift fuer Reproduktionstechnik — Z Reproduktionstech
Zeitschrift fuer Rheumaforschung — Z Rheumaforsch
Zeitschrift fuer Rheumatologie — Z Rheumatol
Zeitschrift fuer Rheumatologie — ZRHMB
Zeitschrift fuer Rheumatologie. Supplement — Z Rheumatol Suppl
Zeitschrift fuer Romanische Philologie — Z
Zeitschrift fuer Romanische Philologie — Z Roman Ph
Zeitschrift fuer Romanische Philologie — Zeit f Rom Phil
Zeitschrift fuer Romanische Philologie — Zeitschrift f Roman Philol
Zeitschrift fuer Romanische Philologie — ZfRP
Zeitschrift fuer Romanische Philologie — ZFRPH
Zeitschrift fuer Romanische Philologie — Zft f Rom Phil
Zeitschrift fuer Romanische Philologie — ZRP
Zeitschrift fuer Romanische Philologie — ZRPH
Zeitschrift fuer Romanische Philologie — Ztschr f Roman Philol
Zeitschrift fuer Rundfunk und Fernsehen [*Database*] — RUFE
Zeitschrift fuer Saeugetierkunde — Z Saeugetierkd
Zeitschrift fuer Schweisstechnik — Z Schweisstech
Zeitschrift fuer Schweisstechnik — ZESTA
Zeitschrift fuer Schweizerische Archaeologie und Kunstgeschichte — Z Schw AKg
Zeitschrift fuer Schweizerische Archaeologie und Kunstgeschichte — Z Schw Alt
Zeitschrift fuer Schweizerische Archaeologie und Kunstgeschichte — Z Schw Arch
Zeitschrift fuer Schweizerische Archaeologie und Kunstgeschichte — Z Schweiz Arch Kunstgesch
Zeitschrift fuer Schweizerische Archaeologie und Kunstgeschichte — Z Schweiz Archaeol Kunstgesch
Zeitschrift fuer Schweizerische Archaeologie und Kunstgeschichte — Z Schweiz Kg
Zeitschrift fuer Schweizerische Archaeologie und Kunstgeschichte — ZAK
Zeitschrift fuer Schweizerische Archaeologie und Kunstgeschichte — Zeitschr Schweiz Arch Kunstgesch
Zeitschrift fuer Schweizerische Archaeologie und Kunstgeschichte — ZSAK
Zeitschrift fuer Schweizerische Archaeologie und Kunstgeschichte — ZSAKG
Zeitschrift fuer Schweizerische Geschichte — Z Sch G
Zeitschrift fuer Schweizerische Geschichte — Z Schweiz Gesch
Zeitschrift fuer Schweizerische Geschichte — ZSchwG
Zeitschrift fuer Schweizerische Geschichte — ZSG
Zeitschrift fuer Schweizerische Kirchengeschichte — Z Sch Kg
Zeitschrift fuer Schweizerische Kirchengeschichte — Z Schw KG
Zeitschrift fuer Schweizerische Kirchengeschichte — ZfSchKg
Zeitschrift fuer Schweizerische Kirchengeschichte — ZSK
Zeitschrift fuer Schweizerische Kirchengeschichte — ZSKG
Zeitschrift fuer Schweizerisches Recht — Z Sch R
Zeitschrift fuer Schweizerisches Recht — ZSR
Zeitschrift fuer Semiotik — Z Semiotik
Zeitschrift fuer Semitistik und Verwandte Gebiete — Z Sem VG
Zeitschrift fuer Semitistik und Verwandte Gebiete [*Leipzig*] — ZfS
Zeitschrift fuer Semitistik und Verwandte Gebiete [*Leipzig*] — ZS
Zeitschrift fuer Semitistik und Verwandte Gebiete [*Leipzig*] — ZSEM
Zeitschrift fuer Sinnesphysiologie [*Germany*] — Z Sinnephysiol
Zeitschrift fuer Sinnesphysiologie — ZESIA
Zeitschrift fuer Slavische Philologie — Z Slav Ph
Zeitschrift fuer Slavische Philologie — Z Slav Phil
Zeitschrift fuer Slavische Philologie — Z Slav Philol
Zeitschrift fuer Slavische Philologie — ZS Ph
Zeitschrift fuer Slavische Philologie — ZSLPh
Zeitschrift fuer Slavische Philologie — ZSP
Zeitschrift fuer Slawistik — Z Slawistik
Zeitschrift fuer Slawistik [*Berlin*] — ZS
Zeitschrift fuer Slawistik — ZSL
Zeitschrift fuer Sozialforschung — ZSF
Zeitschrift fuer Sozialpsychologie — Z Soz
Zeitschrift fuer Sozialpsychologie — Z Soz Psych
Zeitschrift fuer Sozialpsychologie — Z Soz Psychol
Zeitschrift fuer Sozialpsychologie — Z Sozialpsy
Zeitschrift fuer Sozialreform — Z Soz Ref
Zeitschrift fuer Sozialreform [*German Federal Republic*] — Z Sozialreform
Zeitschrift fuer Sozialreform — Z Sozreform
Zeitschrift fuer Sozialreform — ZSR
Zeitschrift fuer Sozialwissenschaft — ZSW
Zeitschrift fuer Soziologie — Z Soz
Zeitschrift fuer Soziologie — Z Soziol
Zeitschrift fuer Soziologie — Z Soziolog
Zeitschrift fuer Spiritusindustrie — Z Spiritusind
Zeitschrift fuer Stomatologie — Z Stomatol
Zeitschrift fuer Sudetendeutsche Geschichte — Z Sudetendt Gesch
Zeitschrift fuer Sudetendeutsche Geschichte — ZSDG
Zeitschrift fuer Systematische Theologie — ZST
Zeitschrift fuer Systematische Theologie [*Guetersloh/Berlin*] — ZSTh
Zeitschrift fuer Systematische Theologie [*Guetersloh/Berlin*] — ZSysTh
Zeitschrift fuer Technische Biologie — Z Tech Biol
Zeitschrift fuer Technische Physik — Z Tech Phys
Zeitschrift fuer Technische Physik — ZTPHA
Zeitschrift fuer Theologie und Kirche — Z Th K
Zeitschrift fuer Theologie und Kirche — Z Th Kirche
Zeitschrift fuer Theologie und Kirche — Z Theol Kir
Zeitschrift fuer Theologie und Kirche — ZTK
Zeitschrift fuer Thueringische Geschichte und Altertumskunde — ZTGAK
Zeitschrift fuer Tierernaehrung und Futtermittelkunde — Z Tierernaehr Futtermittelkd
Zeitschrift fuer Tierphysiologie, Tierernaehrung, und Futtermittelkunde — Z Tierphysiol
Zeitschrift fuer Tierphysiologie, Tierernaehrung, und Futtermittelkunde — Z Tierphysiol Tierernaehr Futtermittelk
Zeitschrift fuer Tierphysiologie, Tierernaehrung, und Futtermittelkunde — Z Tierphysiol Tiernaehr Futtermittelkd
Zeitschrift fuer Tierpsychologie — Z Tierpsychol
Zeitschrift fuer Tierpsychologie — ZT
Zeitschrift fuer Tierpsychologie. Beiheft — Z Tierpsychol Beih
Zeitschrift fuer Tierzuechtung und Zuechtungsbiologie — Z Tierz Zuechtungsbiol
Zeitschrift fuer Tierzuechtung und Zuechtungsbiologie — ZT Zue
Zeitschrift fuer Transpersonale Psychologie — Z Transp Psychol
Zeitschrift fuer Tropenmedizin und Parasitologie — Z Trop Med
Zeitschrift fuer Tropenmedizin und Parasitologie — Z Tropenmed Parasitol
Zeitschrift fuer Tuberkulose — Z Tuberk
Zeitschrift fuer Tuberkulose und Erkrankungen der Thoraxorgane — Z Tuberk Erkr Thoraxorgane
Zeitschrift fuer Tuberkulose und Erkrankungen der Thoraxorgane — Z Tuberkulose Erkr Thoraxogane
Zeitschrift fuer Tuberkulose und Erkrankungen der Thoraxorgane — ZETUA
Zeitschrift fuer Umweltpolitik — Z Umweltpolit
Zeitschrift fuer Umweltpolitik — ZEUMD
Zeitschrift fuer Unfallchirurgie und Versicherungsmedizin — Z Unfallchir Versicherungsmed
Zeitschrift fuer Unfallchirurgie, Versicherungsmedizin, und Berufskrankheiten — Z Unfallchir Versicherungsmed Berufskr
Zeitschrift fuer Unfallmedizin und Berufskrankheiten — Z Unfallmed Berufskr
Zeitschrift fuer Unternehmens- und Gesellschaftsrecht — Z Unternehmens U Ges Recht
Zeitschrift fuer Unternehmensgeschichte — Z Unternehmensgesch
Zeitschrift fuer Untersuchung der Lebensmittel — Z Unter Lebensm
Zeitschrift fuer Untersuchung der Lebensmittel — Z Unters Lebensmittel

Zeitschrift fuer Untersuchung der Nahrungs- und Genussmittel — Z Unters Nahr-u Genussmittel
Zeitschrift fuer Untersuchung der Nahrungs- und Genussmittel Sowie der Gebrauchsgegenstaende — Z Unters Nahr Genussm Gebrauchsgegenstaende
Zeitschrift fuer Urheber und Medienrecht [*Database*] — ZUM
Zeitschrift fuer Urologie [*German Democratic Republic*] — Z Urol
Zeitschrift fuer Urologie — ZEURA
Zeitschrift fuer Urologie und Nephrologie — Z Urol Nephrol
Zeitschrift fuer Urologische Chirurgie — Z Urol Chir
Zeitschrift fuer Urologische Chirurgie — ZU Ch
Zeitschrift fuer Vaterlaendische Geschichte und Altertumskunde — ZVGAK
Zeitschrift fuer Verbraucherpolitik — Z Verbraucherpol
Zeitschrift fuer Verbraucherpolitik/Journal of Consumer Policy — Z Verbraucherpolit
Zeitschrift fuer Vererbungslehre — Z Verbungsl
Zeitschrift fuer Vererbungslehre — Z Vererbungsl
Zeitschrift fuer Vererbungslehre — ZEVBA
Zeitschrift fuer Vergleichende Literaturgeschichte — ZVL
Zeitschrift fuer Vergleichende Physiologie — Z Vergl Physiol
Zeitschrift fuer Vergleichende Physiologie — Z Vgl Physiol
Zeitschrift fuer Vergleichende Physiologie — Ztschr Vergleich Physiol
Zeitschrift fuer Vergleichende Rechtswissenschaft — Zschft f Vergl Rechtswissenschaft
Zeitschrift fuer Vergleichende Rechtswissenschaft — ZVR
Zeitschrift fuer Vergleichende Rechtswissenschaft — ZVRW
Zeitschrift fuer Vergleichende Rechtswissenschaft. Einschliesslich der Ethnologischen Rechtsforschung — Z Vergl Rechtswiss
Zeitschrift fuer Vergleichende Sprachforschung — ZVS
Zeitschrift fuer Vergleichende Sprachforschung auf dem Gebiete der Indogermanischen Sprachen — Zeitschr f Vergleich Sprach
Zeitschrift fuer Vergleichende Sprachforschung auf dem Gebiete der Indogermanischen Sprachen — Zvgl Spr
Zeitschrift fuer Vergleichende Sprachforschung auf dem Gebiete der Indogermanischen Sprachen — ZVS
Zeitschrift fuer Verkehrssicherheit — Z Verkehrssicherheit
Zeitschrift fuer Verkehrswissenschaft — Z Verkehrswiss
Zeitschrift fuer Verkehrswissenschaft — ZVT
Zeitschrift fuer Vermessungswesen — Z Vermessungswes
Zeitschrift fuer Versicherung — ZV
Zeitschrift fuer Versuchstierkunde — Z Vers Kund
Zeitschrift fuer Versuchstierkunde — Z Versuchstierkd
Zeitschrift fuer Verwaltungswissenschaft — Verwaltung
Zeitschrift fuer Veterinaerkunde — Ztschr Veterinaerk
Zeitschrift fuer Vitamin-, Hormon-, und Fermentforschung — Z Vitam-Horm- u Fermentforsch
Zeitschrift fuer Vitamin-, Hormon-, und Fermentforschung — Z Vitam-Horm-Fermentforsch
Zeitschrift fuer Vitamin-, Hormon-, und Fermentforschung — ZVHFA
Zeitschrift fuer Vitaminforschung — Z VitamForsch
Zeitschrift fuer Vitaminforschung — Z Vitaminforsch
Zeitschrift fuer Voelkerpsychologie und Soziologie — Zeits F Voelkerpsychol U Soziol
Zeitschrift fuer Volksernaehrung — Z Volksernaehr
Zeitschrift fuer Volkskunde — Z Volkskde
Zeitschrift fuer Volkskunde — Z Volkskund
Zeitschrift fuer Volkskunde — Z Volkskunde
Zeitschrift fuer Volkskunde — Zeit f Volk
Zeitschrift fuer Volkskunde — ZFV
Zeitschrift fuer Volkskunde — ZV
Zeitschrift fuer Volkskunde — ZVK
Zeitschrift fuer Vulkanologie — Zs Vulkan
Zeitschrift fuer Wahrscheinlichkeitstheorie — Zeitwahr
Zeitschrift fuer Wahrscheinlichkeitstheorie und Verwandte Gebiete — Z Wahrsch V
Zeitschrift fuer Wahrscheinlichkeitstheorie und Verwandte Gebiete — Z Wahrsch Verw Gebiete
Zeitschrift fuer Wahrscheinlichkeitstheorie und Verwandte Gebiete — Z Wahrscheinlichkeitstheorie und Verw Gebiete
Zeitschrift fuer Wasser- und Abwasserforschung — Z Wasser Abwasser Forsch
Zeitschrift fuer Wasser- und Abwasserforschung — Z Wasser u Abwasserforsch
Zeitschrift fuer Wasserrecht — Z Wasserrecht
Zeitschrift fuer Wasser-Versorgung und Abwasserkunde — Z Wasser Versorg Abwasserkunde
Zeitschrift fuer Weinbau und Weinbereitung in Ungarn und Siebenbuergen, fuer Weinbergbesitzer, Winzer, Landwirthe, und Weinhaendler — Z Weinbau Weinbereitung Ungarn Siebenbuergen
Zeitschrift fuer Weltforstwirtschaft — Z Weltforstwirtsch
Zeitschrift fuer Werkstofftechnik — Z Werkstofftech
Zeitschrift fuer Werkstofftechnik/Journal of Materials Technology — Z Werkstofftech J Mater Technol
Zeitschrift fuer Wirtschaftliche Fertigung — Z Wirtsch Fertigung
Zeitschrift fuer Wirtschaftliche Fertigung und Automatisierung — Z Wirtsch Fertigung Autom
Zeitschrift fuer Wirtschafts- und Sozialwissenschaften — Z Wirt- und Sozialwiss
Zeitschrift fuer Wirtschafts- und Sozialwissenschaften — Z Wirtsch -u Soz -Wiss
Zeitschrift fuer Wirtschaftsgeographie — Z Wirtschaftsgeog
Zeitschrift fuer Wirtschaftsgeographie [*Germany*] — Z Wirtschaftsgeographie
Zeitschrift fuer Wirtschaftspolitik — Z Wirtschaftspol
Zeitschrift fuer Wirtschaftswissenschaften und Sozialwissenschaften — SJB
Zeitschrift fuer Wissenschaftliche Biologie. Abteilung A [*Germany*] — Z Wiss Biol Abt A
Zeitschrift fuer Wissenschaftliche Biologie. Abteilung A — ZWBAA
Zeitschrift fuer Wissenschaftliche Insektenbiologie — Z Wiss InsektBiol
Zeitschrift fuer Wissenschaftliche Insektenbiologie [*Germany*] — Z Wiss Insektenbiol
Zeitschrift fuer Wissenschaftliche Insektenbiologie — ZWIBA
Zeitschrift fuer Wissenschaftliche Mikroskopie — Ztschr Wissensch Mikr
Zeitschrift fuer Wissenschaftliche Mikroskopie und fuer Mikroskopische Technik — Z Wiss Mikrosk
Zeitschrift fuer Wissenschaftliche Mikroskopie und fuer Mikroskopische Technik — Z Wiss Mikrosk Mikrosk Tech
Zeitschrift fuer Wissenschaftliche Mikroskopie und fuer Mikroskopische Technik — ZWMIA
Zeitschrift fuer Wissenschaftliche Photographie, Photophysik, und Photochemie — Z Wiss Phot
Zeitschrift fuer Wissenschaftliche Photographie, Photophysik, und Photochemie — Z Wiss Photogr Photophys Photchem
Zeitschrift fuer Wissenschaftliche Photographie, Photophysik, und Photochemie [*Germany*] — Z Wiss Photogr Photophys Photochem
Zeitschrift fuer Wissenschaftliche Photographie, Photophysik, und Photochemie — ZPPA
Zeitschrift fuer Wissenschaftliche Photographie, Photophysik, und Photochemie — ZWP
Zeitschrift fuer Wissenschaftliche Theologie — ZWT
Zeitschrift fuer Wissenschaftliche Theologie — ZWTh
Zeitschrift fuer Wissenschaftliche Zoologie — Z Wiss Zool
Zeitschrift fuer Wissenschaftliche Zoologie — Ztschr Wissensch Zool
Zeitschrift fuer Wissenschaftliche Zoologie. Abteilung A — Z Wiss Zool Abt A
Zeitschrift fuer Wuerttembergische Landesgeschichte — ZfW
Zeitschrift fuer Wuerttembergische Landesgeschichte — ZWL
Zeitschrift fuer Wuerttembergische Landesgeschichte — ZWLG
Zeitschrift fuer Zellforschung und Mikroskopische Anatomie — Z Zellforsch Mikrosk Anat
Zeitschrift fuer Zellforschung und Mikroskopische Anatomie — ZZACA
Zeitschrift fuer Zellforschung und Mikroskopische Anatomie. Abteilung B. Chromosoma — Z Zellf Mikroskop Anat Abt B Chromosoma
Zeitschrift fuer Zellforschung und Mikroskopische Anatomie. Abteilung Histochemie — Z Zellforsch Mikrosk Anat Abt Histochem
Zeitschrift fuer Zoologische Systematik und Evolutionsforschung — Z Zool Syst Evolutionsforsch
Zeitschrift fuer Zuechtung. A — Z Zuecht A
Zeitschrift fuer Zuechtung. B — Z Zuecht B
Zeitschrift. Geschichtsverein Muelheim an der Ruhr (Muelheim, West Germany) — Z Geschv (Muelheim)
Zeitschrift. Gesellschaft fuer die Geschichte der Juden in der Tschechoslowakei — ZGGJT
Zeitschrift. Gesellschaft fuer die Geschichte der Juden in der Tschechoslowakei — ZGJT
Zeitschrift. Gesellschaft fuer Schleswig-Holsteinische Geschichte [*Kiel, West Germany*] — Z Schles Holst Gesch
Zeitschrift. Gesellschaft fuer Schleswig-Holsteinische Geschichte — ZGSHG
Zeitschrift. Historischer Verein fuer Niedersachsen — ZHVNS
Zeitschrift. Historischer Verein fuer Steiermark — ZHVS
Zeitschrift. Internationale Musik Gesellschaft — ZIMG
Zeitschrift. Internationaler Verein der Bohringenieure und Bohrtechniker — Z Int Ver Bohring Bohrtech
Zeitschrift. Internationales Institut fuer Zuckerruebenforschung — Z Int Inst Zuckerruebenforsch
Zeitschrift Interne Revision — Z Interne Revision
Zeitschrift Interne Revision [*Germany*] — ZIT
Zeitschrift. Museum Hildesheim — ZMH
Zeitschrift Neutralitaet — Z Neutral
Zeitschrift. Oesterreichischer Entomologe-Verein — Z Oesterr Entomol Ver
Zeitschrift. Oesterreichischer Verein fuer Bibliothekswesen — ZOVBW
Zeitschrift. Oesterreichischer Verein von Gas- und Wasserfachmaennern — Z Oesterr Ver Gas Wasserfachmaennern
Zeitschrift. Savigny-Stiftung fuer Rechtsgeschichte. Germanistische Abteilung — ZRG (GA)
Zeitschrift. Savigny-Stiftung fuer Rechtsgeschichte. Germanistische Abteilung — ZRGA
Zeitschrift. Savigny-Stiftung fuer Rechtsgeschichte. Germanistische Abteilung — Zschft Savigny-Germ
Zeitschrift. Savigny-Stiftung fuer Rechtsgeschichte. Germanistische Abteilung — ZSSGerm
Zeitschrift. Savigny-Stiftung fuer Rechtsgeschichte. Germanistische Abteilung — ZSSRGGerm
Zeitschrift. Savigny-Stiftung fuer Rechtsgeschichte. Kanonistische Abteilung — Z Savigny-Stift Rechtsgesch Kanon Abt
Zeitschrift. Savigny-Stiftung fuer Rechtsgeschichte. Kanonistische Abteilung — Zschft Savigny-Kanon
Zeitschrift. Savigny-Stiftung fuer Rechtsgeschichte. Kanonistische Abteilung — ZSRK
Zeitschrift. Savigny-Stiftung fuer Rechtsgeschichte. Kanonistische Abteilung [*Weimar*] — ZSSKanon
Zeitschrift. Savigny-Stiftung fuer Rechtsgeschichte. Kanonistische Abteilung — ZSSRGKan
Zeitschrift. Savigny-Stiftung fuer Rechtsgeschichte. Romanistische Abteilung — ZSav
Zeitschrift. Savigny-Stiftung fuer Rechtsgeschichte. Romanistische Abteilung [*Weimar*] — ZSavRG
Zeitschrift. Savigny-Stiftung fuer Rechtsgeschichte. Romanistische Abteilung — Zschft Savigny-Rom
Zeitschrift. Savigny-Stiftung fuer Rechtsgeschichte. Romanistische Abteilung — ZSSRGRom
Zeitschrift. Savigny-Stiftung fuer Rechtsgeschichte. Romanistische Abteilung — ZSSRom
Zeitschrift Technische Ueberwachung — ZTUWA
Zeitschrift. Technische Universitaet (Berlin) — Z Tech Univ (Berlin)
Zeitschrift. Technische Universitaet (Hannover) [*German Federal Republic*] — Z Tech Univ (Hannover)

Zeitschrift. Tokio Medizinischen Gesellschaft — Ztschr Tokio Med Gesellsch
Zeitschrift. Verein der Deutschen Zucker-Industrie — Z Ver Dtsch Zucker Ind
Zeitschrift. Verein der Deutschen Zucker-Industrie. Allgemeiner Teil — Z Ver Dtsch Zucker Ind Allg Teil
Zeitschrift. Verein der Deutschen Zucker-Industrie. Technischer Teil — Z Ver Dtsch Zucker Ind Tech Teil
Zeitschrift. Verein Deutscher Ingenieure — Z Ver Dtsch Ing
Zeitschrift. Verein fuer Hamburgische Geschichte — ZVHG
Zeitschrift. Verein fuer Hessische Geschichte und Landeskunde — Z Ver Hess Gesch Landesk
Zeitschrift. Verein fuer Hessische Geschichte und Landeskunde — Z Ver Hessische Gesch
Zeitschrift. Verein fuer Hessische Geschichte und Landeskunde — ZVHGLK
Zeitschrift. Verein fuer Kirchengeschichte in der Provinz Sachsen und Anhalt — ZVKPS
Zeitschrift. Verein fuer Thueringische Geschichte und Altertumskunde — ZVTGA
Zeitschrift. Verein fuer Thueringische Geschichte und Altertumskunde — ZVTGAK
Zeitschrift. Verein fuer Volkskunde — ZVV
Zeitschrift von und fuer Ungern zur Befoerderung der Vaterlaendischen Geschichte, Erdkunde, und Literatur — Z Ungern
Zeitschrift. Westpreussischer Geschichtsverein — ZWPGV
Zeitschrift. Wiener Entomologe-Verein — Z Wien Entomol Ver
Zeitschrift. Wiener Entomologische Gesellschaft — Z Wien Ent Ges
Zeitschrift. Wiener Entomologische Gesellschaft — Z Wien Entomol Ges
Zeitschrift. Wirtschaftsgruppe Zuckerindustrie — Z Wirtschaftsgruppe Zuckerind
Zeitschrift. Wirtschaftsgruppe Zuckerindustrie. Allgemeiner Teil — Z Wirtschaftsgruppe Zuckerind Allg Teil
Zeitschrift. Wirtschaftsgruppe Zuckerindustrie. Technischer Teil — Z Wirtschaftsgruppe Zuckerind Tech Teil
Zeitschrift zur Geschichte des Deutschen Judentums — ZGDJ
Zeitschriftendatenbank [*Database*] — ZDB
Zeitschriftendienst Musik — ZD Musik
Zeitschriftenkatalog der Bayerischen Staatsbibliothek, Muenchen [*Database*] — ZBSB
Zeitung fuer Gesunde — Ztg Gesunde
Zeitwende — Zeitw
Zeitwende Monatsschrift — ZW
Zelezarski Zbornik — Zelezarski Zb
Zellstoff und Papier — Zell Papier
Zellstoff und Papier — Zellst Pap
Zellstoff und Papier — ZuP
Zellstoff und Papier (Berlin) — Zellst Pap (Berlin)
Zellstoff und Papier (Leipzig) — Zellst Pap (Leipzig)
Zellstoffchemische Abhandlungen — Zellstoffchem Abh
Zellwolle und Deutsche Kunstseiden-Zeitung — Zellwolle Dtsch Kunstseiden Ztg
Zemedelstvi v Zahranici — Zemed Zahr
Zemedelska Ekonomika — Zemed Ekon
Zemedelska Technika [*Czechoslovakia*] — Zemed Tech
Zemedelska Technika. Ceskoslovenska Akademie Zemedelska Ustav Vedeckotechnickych Informaci Pro Zemedelstvi — Zemed Tech Cesk Akad Zemed Ustav Vedeckotech Inf Zemed
Zemedelsky Archiv — Zemed Arch
Zement und Beton — Zem Beton
Zement und Beton — ZMBTA
Zement-Kalk-Gips — Zem-Kalk-Gips
Zemepis ve Skole — Zem ve Sk
Zemepisny Sbornik — Zemep Sb
Zemepisny Sbornik — Zemep Sborn
Zemledel'cheskaya Mekhanika — Zemled Mekh
Zemledelie — Zemled
Zemledelie i Zhivotnovodstvo Moldavii — Zeml Zhivot Moldav
Zemledelie i Zhivotnovodstvo Moldavii — Zemled Zhivotnovod Mold
Zemlerobstvo Respublikans'kyi Mizhvidomchyi Tematychnyi Naukovyi Zbirnyk — Zemlerob Resp Mizhvid Temat Nauk Zb
Zemleustroistvo. Planirovka Sel'skikh Naselennykh Punktov i Geodeziya — Zemleustroistvo Plan Sel'sk Naselennykh Punktov Geod
Zemljiste i Biljka — Zemlj Biljka
Zemlya Sibirskaya Dal'nevostochnaya — Zemlya Sib Dal'nevost
Zenon Papyri (Cairo) — P (Cair) Zen
Zenon Papyri (Cairo) — PCZ
Zenon Papyri in the University of Michigan Collection — P Mich Zen
Zentralasiatische Studien [*Bonn*] — Z Asiat Studien
Zentralblatt der Bauverwaltung — Zentralbl Bauverwaltung
Zentralblatt der Experimentellen Medizin — Zentralbl Exp Med
Zentralblatt der Huetten- und Walzwerke — Zentralbl Huetten Walzwerke
Zentralblatt fuer Allgemeine Pathologie und Pathologische Anatomie — ZAPPA
Zentralblatt fuer Allgemeine Pathologie und Pathologische Anatomie — Zbl Allg Path
Zentralblatt fuer Allgemeine Pathologie und Pathologische Anatomie — Zentralbl Allg Pathol
Zentralblatt fuer Allgemeine Pathologie und Pathologische Anatomie — Zentralbl Allg Pathol Pathol Anat
Zentralblatt fuer Arbeitsmedizin, Arbeitsschutz, Prophylaxe, und Ergonomie [*German Federal Republic*] — Zentralbl Arbeitsmed Arbeitsschutz Prophyl Ergon
Zentralblatt fuer Arbeitsmedizin, Arbeitsschutz, und Prophylaxe [*Germany*] — Zentralbl Arbeitsmed Arbeitsschutz Prophyl
Zentralblatt fuer Arbeitsmedizin, Arbeitsschutz, und Prophylaxe — Zentralbl Arbeitsmed Arbeitsschutz Prophylaxe
Zentralblatt fuer Arbeitsmedizin und Arbeitsschutz [*Later, Zentralblatt fuer Arbeitsmedizin, Arbeitsschutz, und Prophylaxe*] — Zbl A Med
Zentralblatt fuer Arbeitsmedizin und Arbeitsschutz [*Later, Zentralblatt fuer Arbeitsmedizin, Arbeitsschutz, und Prophylaxe*] — Zentralbl Arbeitsmed
Zentralblatt fuer Arbeitsmedizin und Arbeitsschutz [*Later, Zentralblatt fuer Arbeitsmedizin, Arbeitsschutz, und Prophylaxe*] — Zentralbl Arbeitsmed Arbeitsschutz
Zentralblatt fuer Bakteriologie — Zentralbl Bakteriol
Zentralblatt fuer Bakteriologie. International Journal of Medical Microbiology — Zbl Bakt
Zentralblatt fuer Bakteriologie, Mikrobiologie, und Hugiene. 1. Abteilung. Supplemente — Zentralbl Bakteriol Mikrobiol Hyg I Abt Suppl
Zentralblatt fuer Bakteriologie, Mikrobiologie, und Hygiene. Abteilung 1. Originale A. Medizinische Mikrobiologie, Infektionskrankheiten, und Parasitologie — Zentralbl Bakteriol Mikrobiol Hyg Abt 1 Orig A
Zentralblatt fuer Bakteriologie, Mikrobiologie, und Hygiene. I Abteilung. Originale A — Zentralbl Bakteriol Mikrobiol Hyg I Abt Orig A
Zentralblatt fuer Bakteriologie, Mikrobiologie, und Hygiene. I Abteilung. Originale C — Zentralbl Bakteriol Mikrobiol Hyg I Abt Orig C
Zentralblatt fuer Bakteriologie, Mikrobiologie, und Hygiene. Serie B. Umwelthygiene, Krankenhaushygiene, Arbeitshygiene, Praeventive Medizin — Zentralbl Bakteriol Mikrobiol Hyg B
Zentralblatt fuer Bakteriologie, Mikrobiologie, und Hygiene. Serie B. Umwelthygiene, Krankenhaushygiene, Arbeitshygiene, Praeventive Medizin — Zentralbl Bakteriol Mikrobiol Hyg Ser B
Zentralblatt fuer Bakteriologie, Mikrobiologie, und Hygiene. Series A. Medical Microbiology, Infectious Diseases, Virology, Parasitology — Zentralbl Bakteriol Mikrobiol Hyg Ser A
Zentralblatt fuer Bakteriologie, Parasitenkunde, Infektionskrankheiten, und Hygiene — Zentbl Bakt ParasitKde
Zentralblatt fuer Bakteriologie, Parasitenkunde, Infektionskrankheiten, und Hygiene — Zentralbl Bakteriol Parasitenk Infektionskr Hyg
Zentralblatt fuer Bakteriologie, Parasitenkunde, Infektionskrankheiten, und Hygiene. Abteilung 1. Medizinisch-Hygienische Bakteriologie, Virusforschung, und Parasitologie. Originale — ZBPHA
Zentralblatt fuer Bakteriologie, Parasitenkunde, Infektionskrankheiten, und Hygiene. Abteilung 1. Medizinisch-Hygienische Bakteriologie, Virusforschung, und Parasitologie. Referate — Zentralbl Bakteriol Parasitenkd Infektionskr Hyg Abt 1 Ref
Zentralblatt fuer Bakteriologie, Parasitenkunde, Infektionskrankheiten, und Hygiene. Abteilung 1 or 2 — Zentbl Bakt ParasitKed Abt 1 or 2
Zentralblatt fuer Bakteriologie, Parasitenkunde, Infektionskrankheiten, und Hygiene. Abteilung 1 Originale — Zentralbl Bakteriol Parasitenkd Infektionskr Hyg Abt 1 Orig
Zentralblatt fuer Bakteriologie, Parasitenkunde, Infektionskrankheiten, und Hygiene. Abteilung 1. Supplementheft — Zentralbl Bakteriol Parasitenkd Infektionskr Hyg Abt 1 Suppl
Zentralblatt fuer Bakteriologie, Parasitenkunde, Infektionskrankheiten, und Hygiene. Abteilung 2. Allgemeine Landwirtschaftliche und Technische Mikrobiologie — Zentralbl Bakteriol Parasitenkd Infektionskr Hyg Abt 2
Zentralblatt fuer Bakteriologie, Parasitenkunde, Infektionskrankheiten, und Hygiene. Erste Abteilung. Originale Reihe A. Medizinische Mikrobiologie und Parasitologie — Zentralbl Bakteriol Orig A
Zentralblatt fuer Bakteriologie, Parasitenkunde, Infektionskrankheiten, und Hygiene. Erste Abteilung. Originale Reihe A. Medizinische Mikrobiologie und Parasitologie — ZMMPAO
Zentralblatt fuer Bakteriologie, Parasitenkunde, Infektionskrankheiten, und Hygiene. Erste Abteilung. Originale Reihe B. Hygiene, Betriebshygiene, Praeventive Medizin — Zentralbl Bakteriol (B)
Zentralblatt fuer Bakteriologie, Parasitenkunde, Infektionskrankheiten, und Hygiene. Erste Abteilung. Originale Reihe B. Hygiene, Betriebshygiene, Praeventive Medizin — Zentralbl Bakteriol (Orig B)
Zentralblatt fuer Bakteriologie, Parasitenkunde, Infektionskrankheiten, und Hygiene. Erste Abteilung. Originale Reihe B. Hygiene, Betriebshygiene, Praeventive Medizin — ZHPMA
Zentralblatt fuer Bakteriologie, Parasitenkunde, Infektionskrankheiten, und Hygiene. Erste Abteilung. Originale Reihe B. Hygiene, Betriebshygiene, Praeventive Medizin — ZHPMAT
Zentralblatt fuer Bakteriologie, Parasitenkunde, Infektionskrankheiten, und Hygiene. Naturwissenschaftliche Abteilung — Zentralbl Bakteriol Parasitenkd Infektionskrankheiten Hyg II
Zentralblatt fuer Bakteriologie, Parasitenkunde, Infektionskrankheiten, und Hygiene. Zweite Naturwissenschaftliche Abteilung. Mikrobiologie der Landwirtschaft der Technologie und des Umweltschutzes — Zentralbl Bakteriol Naturwiss
Zentralblatt fuer Bakteriologie, Parasitenkunde, und Infektionskrankheiten — Zentralb Bakteriol Parasitenkd Infektionskr
Zentralblatt fuer Bakteriologie, Parasitenkunde, und Infektionskrankheiten. Abteilung 1. Medizinische-Hygienische Bakteriologie Virusforschung und Tierische Parasitologie — Zentralbl Bakteriol Parasitenkd Infektionskr Abt 1
Zentralblatt fuer Bakteriologie. Reihe A — Zbl Bakt A
Zentralblatt fuer Bakteriologie. Reihe B — Zbl Bakt B
Zentralblatt fuer Bibliothekswesen — ZB
Zentralblatt fuer Bibliothekswesen — Zb f Bibl
Zentralblatt fuer Bibliothekswesen — ZBB
Zentralblatt fuer Bibliothekswesen — ZBBW
Zentralblatt fuer Bibliothekswesen — Zbl f Bibl
Zentralblatt fuer Bibliothekswesen — ZBW
Zentralblatt fuer Bibliothekswesen — Zentbl Biblioth
Zentralblatt fuer Bibliothekswesen — Zentr Bibl
Zentralblatt fuer Bibliothekswesen — Zentralbl Bibliothekswesen
Zentralblatt fuer Bibliothekswesen — ZfBw
Zentralblatt fuer Biochemie und Biophysik — Zentralbl Biochem Biophys
Zentralblatt fuer Biologische Aerosol-Forschung — Zentralbl Biol Aerosol-Forsch
Zentralblatt fuer Chirurgie — Zentralbl Chir
Zentralblatt fuer Chirurgie. Supplement — ZBCSA
Zentralblatt fuer Chirurgie. Supplement — Zentralbl Chir Suppl
Zentralblatt fuer das Gesamte Forstwesen — Zentralbl Gesamte Forstwes
Zentralblatt fuer das Gesamte Forstwesen — ZF

Zentralblatt fuer Didaktik der Mathematik — ZDM
Zentralblatt fuer die Gesamte Forst- und Holzwirtschaft — Zentralbl Gesamte Forst Holzw
Zentralblatt fuer die Gesamte Hygiene mit Einschluss der Bakteriologie und Immunitaetslehre — Zentralbl Gesamte Hyg Einschluss Bakteriol Immunitaetsl
Zentralblatt fuer die Gesamte Hygiene und Ihre Grenzgebiete — Zentralbl Ges Hyg
Zentralblatt fuer die Gesamte Hygiene und Ihre Grenzgebiete — Zentralbl Gesamte Hyg Ihre Grenzgeb
Zentralblatt fuer die Gesamte Physiologie und Pathologie des Stoffwechsels — Zentralbl Gesamte Physiol Pathol Stoffwechsels
Zentralblatt fuer die Gesamte Radiologie — Zentralbl Gesamte Radiol
Zentralblatt fuer die Gesamte Rechtsmedizin und Ihre Grenzgebiete — Zentralbl Gesamte Rechtsmed
Zentralblatt fuer die Gesamte Rechtsmedizin und Ihre Grenzgebiete — Zentralbl Gesamte Rechtsmed Grenzgeb
Zentralblatt fuer die Papierindustrie — Zentralbl Papierind
Zentralblatt fuer Geologie und Palaeontologie. Teil 1. Allgemeine, Angewandte, Regionale, und Historische Geologie — Zentralbl Geol Palaeontol Teil 1
Zentralblatt fuer Geologie und Palaeontologie. Teil 2. Palaeontologie — Zentralbl Geol Palaeontol Teil 2
Zentralblatt fuer Gewerbehygiene und Unfallverhuetung — Zentralbl Gewerbehyg Unfallverhuet
Zentralblatt fuer Gynaekologie — Zentralbl Gynaekol
Zentralblatt fuer Hygiene und Umweltmedizin — Zbl Hyg Umw
Zentralblatt fuer Hygiene und Umweltmedizin — Zentralbl Hyg Umweltmed
Zentralblatt fuer Industriebau — Zentralbl Industriebau
Zentralblatt fuer Innere Medizin — Zentralbl Inn Med
Zentralblatt fuer Mathematik Ihre Grenzegebiete — Zentralbl Math Ihre Grenzegeb
Zentralblatt fuer Mathematik und Ihre Grenzgebiete — Zbl
Zentralblatt fuer Mathematik und Ihre Grenzgebiete — Zbl Math
Zentralblatt fuer Mathematik und Ihre Grenzgebiete — Zent Math
Zentralblatt fuer Mathematik und Ihre Grenzgebiete — ZMG
Zentralblatt fuer Mikrobiologie — ZEMIDI
Zentralblatt fuer Mikrobiologie — Zentralbl Mikrobiol
Zentralblatt fuer Mineralogie, Geologie, und Palaeontologie — Zentralbl Mineral Geol Palaeontol
Zentralblatt fuer Mineralogie, Geologie, und Palaeontologie (Stuttgart) — ZMGPS
Zentralblatt fuer Mineralogie, Geologie, und Palaeontologie. Teil 1. Kristallographie und Mineralogie — Zentralbl Mineral Geol Palaeontol Teil 1
Zentralblatt fuer Mineralogie, Geologie, und Palaeontologie. Teil 2. Gesteinskunde, Lagerstaettenkunde, Allgemeine, und Angewandte Geologie — Zentralbl Mineral Geol Palaeontol Teil 2
Zentralblatt fuer Mineralogie, Geologie, und Palaeontologie. Teil 3. Historische und Regionale Geologie, Palaeontologie — Zentralbl Mineral Geol Palaeontol Teil 3
Zentralblatt fuer Mineralogie, Geologie, und Palaeontologie. Teil 3. Historische und Regionale Geologie, Palaeontologie — Zentralbl Mineral Teil 3 Hist Regionale Geol Palaeontol
Zentralblatt fuer Mineralogie. Teil 1. Kristallographie und Mineralogie — Zentralbl Mineral Teil 1
Zentralblatt fuer Mineralogie. Teil 2. Petrographie, Technische Mineralogie, Geochemie, und Lagerstaettenkunde — Zentralbl Mineral Teil 2
Zentralblatt fuer Neurochirurgie — Zentralbl Neurochir
Zentralblatt fuer Pathologie — Zentralbl Pathol
Zentralblatt fuer Pharmazie — Zentralbl Pharm
Zentralblatt fuer Pharmazie, Pharmakotherapie, und Laboratoriumsdiagnostik — Zentralbl Pharm Pharmakother Laboratoriumsdiagn
Zentralblatt fuer Phlebologie — Zentralbl Phlebol
Zentralblatt fuer Physiologie — Zentralbl Physiol
Zentralblatt fuer Verkehrs-Medizin, Verkehrs-Psychologie Luft-, und Raumfahrt-Medizin — Zentralbl Verkehrs-Med Verkehrs-Psychol Luft-Raumfahrt-Med
Zentralblatt fuer Veterinaermedizin — Zentralbl Veterinaermed
Zentralblatt fuer Veterinaermedizin. Beiheft — Zentralbl Veterinaermed Beih
Zentralblatt fuer Veterinaermedizin. Reihe A — Zbl Vet A
Zentralblatt fuer Veterinaermedizin. Reihe A — Zentralbl Veterinaermed Reihe A
Zentralblatt fuer Veterinaermedizin. Reihe B — Zbl Vet B
Zentralblatt fuer Veterinaermedizin. Reihe B — Zentbl Vet Med B
Zentralblatt fuer Veterinaermedizin. Reihe B — Zentralbl Veterinaermed Reihe B
Zentralblatt fuer Veterinaermedizin. Reihe C — Zentralbl Veterinaermed Reihe C
Zentralblatt fuer Veterinarmedizin. Reihe A — Zentralbl Veterinarmed A
Zentral-Europaeische Giesserei-Zeitung — Zent Eur Giesserei Ztg
Zentralinstitut fuer Kernforschung Rossendorf bei Dresden (Bericht) — Zentralinst Kernforsch Rossendorf Dresden (Ber)
Zentralinstitut fuer Versuchstierzucht. Annual Report — Zentralinst Versuchstierzucht Annu Rep
Zentralkatalog der Auslaendischen Literatur — ZKA
Zentralorgan fuer die Gesamte Chirurgie und Ihre Grenzgebiete — Zentr Org Ges Chir
Zentralstelle Dokumentation Elektrotechnik Database — ZDE
Zentral-Zeitung fuer Optik und Mechanik — Zent Ztg Opt Mech
Zentrum fuer Umweltforschung der Westfaelischen Wilhelms-Universitaet. Vortraege und Studien — Zent Umweltforsch Westfael Wilhelms Univ Vortr Stud
Zephyrus. Seminario de Arqueologia y de la Seccion Arqueologica del Centro de Estudios Salmantinos — Zeph
Zernovoe Khozyaistvo — Zernovoe Khoz
Zernovye i Maslichnye Kul'tury — Zernovye Maslichn Kul't
Zero Population Growth. National Reporter — Zero Popul Growth Natl Rep
Zero Un Hebdo — Zero Un
Zero Un Information Mensuel — Zero Un M
Zeszyt Naukowe. Politechnika Krakowska, Inzynieria, i Technologia Chemiczna — Zesz Nauk Politech Krakow Inz Technol Chem
Zeszyty Jezykoznawcze — ZJ
Zeszyty Muzeum Etnograficznego Wroclawie — Zesz Muz Etnogr Wrocl
Zeszyty Naukowe — ZN
Zeszyty Naukowe. Akademia Ekonomiczna w Krakowie — ZAEKD
Zeszyty Naukowe. Akademia Ekonomiczna w Poznaniu. Seria 2. Prace Habilitacyjne i Doktorskie — Zesz Nauk Akad Ekon Poznaniu Ser 2
Zeszyty Naukowe. Akademia Rolnicza w Szczecinie — ZARSA
Zeszyty Naukowe. Akademia Rolnicza w Szczecinie [*Poland*] — Zesz Nauk Akad Roln Szczecinie
Zeszyty Naukowe Akademii Ekonomicznej w Katowicach — Zesz Nauk Akad Ekon
Zeszyty Naukowe Akademii Ekonomicznej w Katowicach — Zesz Nauk Akad Ekon Katowic
Zeszyty Naukowe Akademii Ekonomicznej w Krakowie — Zesz Nauk Akad Ekon Krakow
Zeszyty Naukowe Akademii Ekonomicznej w Poznaniu — Zesz Nauk Akad Ekon Poznan
Zeszyty Naukowe Akademii Ekonomicznej w Wroclawiu — Zesz Nauk Akad Ekon Wroclaw
Zeszyty Naukowe Akademii Gorniczo-Hutniczej (Cracow). Elektryfikacja i Mechanizacja Gornictwa i Hutnictwa — Zesz Nauk Akad Gorn Hutn (Cracow) Eletryf Mech Gorn Hutn
Zeszyty Naukowe Akademii Gorniczo-Hutniczej (Cracow). Geologia — Zesz Nauk Akad Gorn Hutn (Cracow) Geol
Zeszyty Naukowe Akademii Gorniczo-Hutniczej (Cracow). Matematyka, Fizyka, Chemia — Zesz Nauk Akad Gorn-Hutn (Cracow) Mat Fiz Chem
Zeszyty Naukowe Akademii Gorniczo-Hutniczej (Cracow). Matematyka, Fizyka, Chemia — ZGMFA
Zeszyty Naukowe Akademii Gorniczo-Hutniczej (Cracow). Metalurgia i Odlewnictwo — Zesz Nauk Akad Gorn-Hutn (Cracow) Metal Odlew
Zeszyty Naukowe Akademii Gorniczo-Hutniczej (Cracow). Rozprawy — Zesz Nauk Akad Gorn Hutn (Cracow) Rozpr
Zeszyty Naukowe Akademii Gorniczo-Hutniczej (Cracow). Zeszyt Specjalny — ZNZSA
Zeszyty Naukowe Akademii Gorniczo-Hutniczej. Elektryfikacja i Mechanizacja Gornictwa i Hutnictwa — ZEMGA
Zeszyty Naukowe Akademii Gorniczo-Hutniczej Imienia Stanislawa Staszica. Automatyka — Zesz Nauk Akad Gorn-Hutn Stanisl Staszica Autom
Zeszyty Naukowe Akademii Gorniczo-Hutniczej Imienia Stanislawa Staszica. Ceramica — Zesz Nauk Akad Gorn-Hutn Im Stanislawa Staszica Ceram
Zeszyty Naukowe Akademii Gorniczo-Hutniczej Imienia Stanislawa Staszica. Elektryfikacja i Mechanizacja Gornictwa i Hutnictwa — ZNAHD
Zeszyty Naukowe Akademii Gorniczo-Hutniczej Imienia Stanislawa Staszica. Geologia — Zesz Nauk Akad Gorn-Hutn Im Stanislawa Staszica Geol
Zeszyty Naukowe Akademii Gorniczo-Hutniczej Imienia Stanislawa Staszica. Geologia [*Poland*] — Zesz Nauk Akad Gorn-Hutn Stanisl Staszica Geol
Zeszyty Naukowe Akademii Gorniczo-Hutniczej Imienia Stanislawa Staszica. Geologia — Zesz Nauk Akad Gorn-Hutn Stanislawa Staszica Geol
Zeszyty Naukowe Akademii Gorniczo-Hutniczej Imienia Stanislawa Staszica. Geologia — ZNAGD
Zeszyty Naukowe Akademii Gorniczo-Hutniczej Imienia Stanislawa Staszica. Gornictwo — ZAGGD
Zeszyty Naukowe Akademii Gorniczo-Hutniczej Imienia Stanislawa Staszica. Gornictwo — Zesz Nauk Akad Gorn-Hutn Im Stanislawa Staszica Gorn
Zeszyty Naukowe Akademii Gorniczo-Hutniczej Imienia Stanislawa Staszica. Gornictwo — Zesz Nauk Akad Gorn-Hutn Im Staszica Gorn
Zeszyty Naukowe Akademii Gorniczo-Hutniczej Imienia Stanislawa Staszica. Matematyka, Fizyka, Chemia — Zesz Nauk Akad Gorn-Hutn Im Stanislawa Staszica Mat Fiz Chem
Zeszyty Naukowe Akademii Gorniczo-Hutniczej Imienia Stanislawa Staszica. Matematyka, Fizyka, Chemia — Zesz Nauk Akad Gorn-Hutn Im Staszica Mat Fiz Chem
Zeszyty Naukowe Akademii Gorniczo-Hutniczej Imienia Stanislawa Staszica. Matematyka, Fizyka, Chemia — Zesz Nauk Akad Gorn-Hutn Stanisl Staszica Mat Fiz Chem
Zeszyty Naukowe Akademii Gorniczo-Hutniczej Imienia Stanislawa Staszica. Matematyka, Fizyka, Chemia — Zeszyty Nauk Akad Gorn-Hutniczej Mat Fiz Chem
Zeszyty Naukowe Akademii Gorniczo-Hutniczej Imienia Stanislawa Staszica. Matematyka, Fizyka, Chemia — ZNACD
Zeszyty Naukowe Akademii Gorniczo-Hutniczej Imienia Stanislawa Staszica. Metalurgia i Odlewnictwo — Zesz Nauk Akad Gorn-Hutn Im Stanislawa Staszica Metal Odlew
Zeszyty Naukowe Akademii Gorniczo-Hutniczej Imienia Stanislawa Staszica. Metalurgia i Odlewnictwo — Zesz Nauk Akad Gorn-Hutn Stanisl Staszica
Zeszyty Naukowe Akademii Gorniczo-Hutniczej Imienia Stanislawa Staszica. Seria Automatyka [*Poland*] — Zesz Nauk Akad Gorn-Hutn Im Stanislawa Staszica Ser Autom
Zeszyty Naukowe Akademii Gorniczo-Hutniczej Imienia Stanislawa Staszica. Zeszyt Specjalny — Zesz Nauk Akad Gorn-Hutn Im Stanislawa Staszica Zesz Spec
Zeszyty Naukowe Akademii Gorniczo-Hutniczej Imienia Stanislawa Staszica. Zeszyt Specjalny — Zesz Nauk Akad Gorn-Hutn Im Staszica Zesz Spec
Zeszyty Naukowe Akademii Gorniczo-Hutniczej (Krakow). Ceramika — Zesz Nauk Akad Gorn-Hutn (Krakow) Ceram
Zeszyty Naukowe Akademii Gorniczo-Hutniczej (Krakow). Elektryfikacja i Mechanizacja Gornictwa i Hutnictwa — Zesz Nauk Akad Gorn-Hutn (Krakow) Elektryf Mech Gorn Hutn
Zeszyty Naukowe Akademii Gorniczo-Hutniczej (Krakow). Geologia — Zesz Nauk Akad Gorn-Hutn (Krakow) Geol
Zeszyty Naukowe Akademii Gorniczo-Hutniczej (Krakow). Geologia — ZNGGA
Zeszyty Naukowe Akademii Gorniczo-Hutniczej (Krakow). Gornictwo — Zesz Nauk Akad Gorn-Hutn (Krakow) Gorn

Zeszyty Naukowe Akademii Gorniczo-Hutniczej (Krakow). Gornictwo — ZNAGB
Zeszyty Naukowe Akademii Gorniczo-Hutniczej (Krakow). Matematyka, Fizyka, Chemia — Zesz Nauk Akad Gorn-Hutn (Krakow) Mat Fiz Chem
Zeszyty Naukowe Akademii Gorniczo-Hutniczej (Krakow). Metalurgia i Odlewnictwo — Zesz Nauk Akad Gorn-Hutn (Krakow) Metal Odlew
Zeszyty Naukowe Akademii Gorniczo-Hutniczej (Krakow). Sesja Naukowa — Zesz Nauk Akad Gorn-Hutn (Krakow) Ses Nauk
Zeszyty Naukowe Akademii Gorniczo-Hutniczej (Krakow). Sozologia i Sozotechnika [*Poland*] — Zesz Nauk Akad Gorn-Hutn (Krakow) Sozologia Sozotechnika
Zeszyty Naukowe Akademii Gorniczo-Hutniczej (Krakow). Sozologia i Sozotechnika — ZNSSA
Zeszyty Naukowe Akademii Gorniczo-Hutniczej (Krakow). Zeszyty Specjalny — Zesz Nauk Akad Gorn-Hutn (Krakow) Zesz Spec
Zeszyty Naukowe Akademii Gorniczo-Hutniczej w Krakowie. Rozprawy [*Poland*] — Zesz Nauk Akad Gorn-Hutn Krakowie Rozpr
Zeszyty Naukowe Akademii Gorniczo-Hutniczej w Krakowie. Rozprawy — ZNAGA
Zeszyty Naukowe Akademii Rolniczej w Szczecinie. Seria Rybactwo Morskie [*Poland*] — Zesz Nauk Akad Roln Szczecinie Ser Rybactwo Morsk
Zeszyty Naukowe Akademii Rolniczej w Warszawie. Melioracje Rolne — Zesz Nauk Akad Roln Warszawie Melior Rolne
Zeszyty Naukowe Akademii Rolniczej w Warszawie. Ogrodnictwo — Zesz Nauk Akad Roln Warszawie Ogrod
Zeszyty Naukowe Akademii Rolniczej w Warszawie. Technologia Drewna — Zesz Nauk Akad Roln Warszawie Technol Drewna
Zeszyty Naukowe Akademii Rolniczej w Warszawie. Technologia Rolno-Spozyweza — Zesz Nauk Akad Roln Warszawie Technol Rolno Spozyw
Zeszyty Naukowe Akademii Rolniczej w Warszawie. Zootechnika — Zesz Nauk Akad Roln Warszawie Zootech
Zeszyty Naukowe Akademii Rolniczej we Wroclawiu. Melioracja — Zesz Nauk Akad Roln Wroclawiu Melior
Zeszyty Naukowe Akademii Rolniczej we Wroclawiu. Rolnictwo — Zesz Nauk Akad Roln Wroclawiu Roln
Zeszyty Naukowe Akademii Rolniczej we Wroclawiu. Weterynaria — Zesz Nauk Akad Roln Wrocl Wet
Zeszyty Naukowe Akademii Rolniczej we Wroclawiu. Weterynaria — Zesz Nauk Akad Roln Wroclawiu Weter
Zeszyty Naukowe Akademii Rolniczej we Wroclawiu. Zootechnika — Zesz Nauk Akad Roln Wroclawiu Zootech
Zeszyty Naukowe Akademii Rolniczo-Technicznej w Olsztynie — Zesz Nauk Akad Roln Tech Olsztynie
Zeszyty Naukowe Akademii Rolniczo-Technicznej w Olsztynie. Rolnictwo — Zesz Nauk Akad Roln Tech Olsztynie Roln
Zeszyty Naukowe Akademii Rolniczo-Technicznej w Olsztynie. Technologia Zywnosci — Zesz Nauk Akad Roln Tech Olsztynie Technol Zywn
Zeszyty Naukowe Akademii Rolniczo-Technicznej w Olsztynie. Technologia Zywnosci — ZNTZA
Zeszyty Naukowe Akademii Rolniczo-Technicznej w Olsztynie. Zootechnika — Zesz Nauk Akad Roln Tech Olsztynie Zootech
Zeszyty Naukowe Geometria — Zeszyty Nauk Geom
Zeszyty Naukowe Gornictwo — Zesz Nauk Gorn
Zeszyty Naukowe Instytut Ciezkiej Syntezy Organicznej w Blachowni Slaskiej — Zesz Nauk Inst Ciezkiej Synt Org Blachowni Slask
Zeszyty Naukowe, Jezykoznawstwo, Wyzsza Szkola Pedagogiczna w Opolu — ZNWSPOp
Zeszyty Naukowe Katolickiego Uniwersytetu Lubelskiego [*Lublin*] — ZeszNauKUL
Zeszyty Naukowe Katolickiego Uniwersytetu Lubelskiego — ZNKUL
Zeszyty Naukowe. Lesnictwo-Akademia Rolnicza w Warszawie — Zesz Nauk Lesn Akad Roln Warsz
Zeszyty Naukowe. Matematyka, Fizyka, Chemia [*Poland*] — Zesz Nauk Mat Fiz Chem
Zeszyty Naukowe. Matematyka, Fizyka, Chemia — ZMFWA
Zeszyty Naukowe. Mechanika i Budownictwo-Akademia Rolniczo-Techniczna w Olsztynie — Zesz Nauk Mechan Budownictwo Akad Roln-Tech Olsztyn
Zeszyty Naukowe. Melioracje Rolne-Akademia Rolnicza w Warszawie — Zesz Nauk Melior Rolne Akad Roln Warsz
Zeszyty Naukowe. Ochrona Wod i Rybactwo Srodladowe — Zesz Nauk Ochr Wod Rybactwo Srodladowe
Zeszyty Naukowe Politechnika Lodzka. Fizyka — Zesz Nauk Politech Lodz Fiz
Zeszyty Naukowe Politechnika Slaska. Energetyka — Zesz Nauk Politech Slaska Energ
Zeszyty Naukowe Politechnika Slaska. Energetyka — ZPSEA
Zeszyty Naukowe Politechniki Czestochowskiej — Zesz Nauk Politech Czestochow
Zeszyty Naukowe Politechniki Czestochowskiej. Metalurgia — Zesz Nauk Politech Czestochow Metal
Zeszyty Naukowe Politechniki Czestochowskiej. Nauki Techniczne. Hutnictwo [*Poland*] — Zesz Nauk Politech Czestochow Nauki Tech Hutn
Zeszyty Naukowe Politechniki Czestochowskiej. Nauki Techniczne. Hutnictwo — ZNTHA
Zeszyty Naukowe Politechniki Gdanskiej. Chemia — Zesz Nauk Politech Gdansk Chem
Zeszyty Naukowe Politechniki Gdanskiej. Elektryka — Zesz Nauk Politech Gdansk Elektr
Zeszyty Naukowe Politechniki Gdanskiej. Fizyka — Zesz Nauk Politech Gdansk Fiz
Zeszyty Naukowe Politechniki Gdanskiej. Matematyka — Zesz Nauk Politech Gdansk Mat
Zeszyty Naukowe Politechniki Gdanskiej. Mechanika — Zesz Nauk Politech Gdansk Mech
Zeszyty Naukowe Politechniki Krakowskiej. Chemia — Zesz Nauk Politech Krakow Chem
Zeszyty Naukowe Politechniki Krakowskiej. Mechanika — Zesz Nauk Politech Krakow Mech
Zeszyty Naukowe Politechniki Lodzkiej. Budownictwo — Zesz Nauk Politech Lod Budow
Zeszyty Naukowe Politechniki Lodzkiej. Chemia — Zesz Nauk Politech Lodz Chem
Zeszyty Naukowe Politechniki Lodzkiej. Chemia Spozywcza — Zesz Nauk Politech Lodz Chem Spozyw
Zeszyty Naukowe Politechniki Lodzkiej. Chemia Spozywcza — ZNLSA
Zeszyty Naukowe Politechniki Lodzkiej. Elektryka — Zesz Nauk Politech Lodz Elek
Zeszyty Naukowe Politechniki Lodzkiej. Elektryka — Zesz Nauk Politech Lodz Elektr
Zeszyty Naukowe Politechniki Lodzkiej. Elektryka — ZNPEA
Zeszyty Naukowe Politechniki Lodzkiej. Inzynieria Chemiczna — Zesz Nauk Politech Lodz Inz Chem
Zeszyty Naukowe Politechniki Lodzkiej. Matematyka — Zeszyty Nauk Politech Lodz Mat
Zeszyty Naukowe Politechniki Lodzkiej. Mechanika — Zesz Nauk Politech Lodz Mech
Zeszyty Naukowe Politechniki Lodzkiej. Wlokiennictwo — Zesz Nauk Politech Lodz Wlok
Zeszyty Naukowe Politechniki Poznanskiej. Chemia i Inzynieria Chemiczna — Zesz Nauk Politech Poznan Chem Inz Chem
Zeszyty Naukowe Politechniki Poznanskiej. Elektryka — Zesz Nauk Politech Poznan Elektr
Zeszyty Naukowe Politechniki Poznanskiej. Elektryka — ZNPED
Zeszyty Naukowe Politechniki Rzeszowskiej — Zesz Nauk Politech Rzeszowskiej
Zeszyty Naukowe Politechniki Rzeszowskiej. Matematyka — Zeszyty Nauk Politech Rzeszowskiej Mat
Zeszyty Naukowe Politechniki Rzeszowskiej. Matematyka i Fizyka — Zeszyty Nauk Politech Rzeszowskiej Mat Fiz
Zeszyty Naukowe Politechniki Slaskiej — Zesz Nauk Politech Slask
Zeszyty Naukowe Politechniki Slaskiej. Automatyka — Zeszyty Nauk Politech Slask Automat
Zeszyty Naukowe Politechniki Slaskiej. Chemia — Zesz Nauk Politech Slask Chem
Zeszyty Naukowe Politechniki Slaskiej. Chemia — ZNSCA
Zeszyty Naukowe Politechniki Slaskiej. Energetyka — Zesz Nauk Politech Slask Energ
Zeszyty Naukowe Politechniki Slaskiej. Gornictwo — Zesz Nauk Politech Slask Gorn
Zeszyty Naukowe Politechniki Slaskiej. Gornictwo — ZNSGA
Zeszyty Naukowe Politechniki Slaskiej. Hutnictwo — Zesz Nauk Politech Slask Hutn
Zeszyty Naukowe Politechniki Slaskiej. Inzynieria Sanitarna — Zesz Nauk Politech Slask Inz Sanit
Zeszyty Naukowe Politechniki Slaskiej. Inzynieria Sanitarna — ZSISA
Zeszyty Naukowe Politechniki Slaskiej. Seria Elektryka — Zesz Nauk Politech Slask Ser Elektr
Zeszyty Naukowe Politechniki Slaskiej. Seria Matematyka-Fizyka — Zesz Nauk Politech Slask Ser Mat-Fiz
Zeszyty Naukowe Politechniki Slaskiej. Seria Matematyka-Fizyka — Zeszyty Nauk Politech Slask Mat-Fiz
Zeszyty Naukowe Politechniki Swietokrzyska. Problemy Nauk Podstawowych — Zesz Nauk Politech Swietokrz Probl Nauk Podst
Zeszyty Naukowe Politechniki Swietokrzyskiej. Seria P. Problemy Nauk Podstawowych — ZNPPD
Zeszyty Naukowe Politechniki Szezecinskiej — Zeszyty Nauk Politech Szczecin
Zeszyty Naukowe Politechniki Szezecinskiej. Chemia — Zesz Nauk Politech Szezecin Chem
Zeszyty Naukowe Politechniki Szezecinskiej. Prace Monografiezne — Zesz Nauk Politech Szezecin Pr Monogr
Zeszyty Naukowe Politechniki Warszawskiej. Chemia — Zesz Nauk Politech Warsz Chem
Zeszyty Naukowe Politechniki Wroclawskiej. Chemia — Zesz Nauk Politech Wroclaw Chem
Zeszyty Naukowe Politechniki Wroclawskiej. Chemia — ZPWCA
Zeszyty Naukowe. Rolnictwo Akademia Rolnicza w Warszawie — Zesz Nauk Roln Akad Roln Warsz
Zeszyty Naukowe, Sekcja Jezykoznawcza, Wyzsza Szkola Pedagogiczna w Katowicach — ZNK
Zeszyty Naukowe Szkola Glowna Gospodarstwa Wiejskiego w Warszawie (Lesnictwo) — Zesz Nauk Szkol Gospod Wiejsk Warsz (Lesn)
Zeszyty Naukowe Szkola Glowna Gospodarstwa Wiejskiego w Warszawie. Technologia Drewna — Zesz Nauk Szkol Gospod Wiejsk Warsz Technol Drewna
Zeszyty Naukowe Szkoly Glownej Gospodarstwa Wiejskiego Akademii Rolniczej w Warszawie Ogrodnictwo — Zesz Nauk Szk Gl Gospod Wiejsk Akad Roln Warsz Ogrodn
Zeszyty Naukowe Szkoly Glownej Gospodarstwa Wiejskiego. Akademii Rolniczej w Warszawie. Ogrodnictwo — Zesz Nauk Szk Gl Gospod Wiejsk Akad Roln Warszawie Ogrod
Zeszyty Naukowe Szkoly Glownej Gospodarstwa Wiejskiego. Akademii Rolniczej w Warszawie. Ogrodnictwo — ZSWODE
Zeszyty Naukowe Szkoly Glownej Gospodarstwa Wiejskiego. Akademii Rolniczej w Warszawie. Weterynaria — Zesz Nauk Szk Gl Gospod Wiejsk Akad Roln Warszawie Wter
Zeszyty Naukowe Szkoly Glownej Gospodarstwa Wiejskiego. Akademii Rolniczej w Warszawie. Zootechnika — Zesz Nauk Szk Gl Gospod Wiejsk Akad Roln Warszawie Zootech
Zeszyty Naukowe Szkoly Glownej Gospodarstwa Wiejskiego w Warszawie — Zesz Nauk Szk Glow Gospod Wiejsk Warszawie
Zeszyty Naukowe Szkoly Glownej Gospodarstwa Wiejskiego w Warszawie. Lesnictwo — Zesz Nauk Szk Glo Gospod Wiejsk Warszawie Lesn

Zeszyty Naukowe Szkoly Glownej Gospodarstwa Wiejskiego w Warszawie. Melioracje Rolne — Zesz Nauk Szk Gl Gospod Wiejsk Warszawie Melior Rolne
Zeszyty Naukowe Szkoly Glownej Gospodarstwa Wiejskiego w Warszawie. Ogrodnictwo — Zesz Nauk Szk Gl Gospod Wiejsk Warszawie Ogrod
Zeszyty Naukowe Szkoly Glownej Gospodarstwa Wiejskiego w Warszawie. Rolnictwo [*Poland*] — Zesz Nauk Szk Gl Gospod Wiejsk Warszawie Roln
Zeszyty Naukowe Szkoly Glownej Gospodarstwa Wiejskiego w Warszawie. Rolnictwo — ZSWRA
Zeszyty Naukowe Szkoly Glownej Gospodarstwa Wiejskiego w Warszawie. Technologia Drewna — Zesz Nauk Szk Gl Gospod Wiejsk Warszawie Technol Drewna
Zeszyty Naukowe Szkoly Glownej Gospodarstwa Wiejskiego w Warszawie. Zootechnika — Zesz Nauk Szk Gl Gospod Wiejsk Warszawie Zootech
Zeszyty Naukowe Szkoly Glownej Planowania i Statystyki — Zesz Nauk Szk Glown Plan Statystyki
Zeszyty Naukowe Szkoly Glownej Planowania i Statystyki — Zeszyty Nauk Szkoly Glown Planowania i Statyst
Zeszyty Naukowe. Technologia Drewna-Akademia Rolnicza w Warszawie — Zesz Nauk Technol Drewna Akad Roln Warsz
Zeszyty Naukowe. Technologia Zywnosci-Akademia Rolniczo-Techniczna w Olsztynie — Zesz Nauk Technol Zywn Akad Roln-Tech Olsztynie
Zeszyty Naukowe Uniwersytet Slaski w Katowicach Sekeja Chemii — Zesz Nauk Uniw Slaski Katowicach Seke Chem
Zeszyty Naukowe Uniwersytetu Gdanskiego — ZNUG
Zeszyty Naukowe Uniwersytetu Imienia Adama Mickiewicza w Poznaniu — ZNUP
Zeszyty Naukowe Uniwersytetu Imienia Adama Mickiewicza w Poznaniu. Historia Sztuki — ZNUPHSzt
Zeszyty Naukowe Uniwersytetu Imienia Adama Mickiewicza w Poznaniu. Matematyka, Fizyka, Chemia — Zesz Nauk Uniw Poznaniu Mat Fiz Chem
Zeszyty Naukowe Uniwersytetu Imienia Adama Mickiewicza w Poznaniu. Matematyka, Fizyka, Chemia — ZNUIA
Zeszyty Naukowe Uniwersytetu Imienia Mikolaja Kopernika w Toruniu — Zesz Nauk Uniw Mikolja Kopernika Torun
Zeszyty Naukowe Uniwersytetu Jagiellonskiego — ZNUJ
Zeszyty Naukowe Uniwersytetu Jagiellonskiego. Acta Cosmologica — Zesz Nauk Uniw Jagiellon Acta Cosmol
Zeszyty Naukowe Uniwersytetu Jagiellonskiego. Prace Biologii Molekularnej [*Poland*] — Zesz Nauk Uniw Jagiellon Pr Biol Mol
Zeszyty Naukowe Uniwersytetu Jagiellonskiego. Prace Biologii Molekularnej — ZNUMD
Zeszyty Naukowe Uniwersytetu Jagiellonskiego. Prace Botaniczne — Zesz Nauk Uniw Jagiellonsk Pr Bot
Zeszyty Naukowe Uniwersytetu Jagiellonskiego. Prace Chemiczne [*Poland*] — Zesz Nauk Uniw Jagiellon Pr Chem
Zeszyty Naukowe Uniwersytetu Jagiellonskiego. Prace Chemiczne — ZUJCA
Zeszyty Naukowe Uniwersytetu Jagiellonskiego. Prace Etnograficzne — Zesz Nauk Uniw Jagiellon Pr Etnogr
Zeszyty Naukowe Uniwersytetu Jagiellonskiego. Prace Fizyczne — Zesz Nauk Uniw Jagiellon Pr Fiz
Zeszyty Naukowe Uniwersytetu Jagiellonskiego. Prace Fizyczne — Zeszyty Nauk Uniw Jagiellon Prace Fiz
Zeszyty Naukowe Uniwersytetu Jagiellonskiego. Prace Fizyczne — ZNUFA
Zeszyty Naukowe Uniwersytetu Jagiellonskiego. Prace Matematyczne — Zeszty Nauk Uniw Jagiellon Prace Mat
Zeszyty Naukowe Uniwersytetu Jagiellonskiego. Prace Zoologiczne — Zesz Nauk Uniw Jagiellon Pr Zool
Zeszyty Naukowe Uniwersytetu Jagiellonskiego. Prace Zoologiczne — Zesz Nauk Uniw Jagiellonsk Zool
Zeszyty Naukowe Uniwersytetu Jagiellonskiego. Prace Zoologiczne — ZNUZA
Zeszyty Naukowe Uniwersytetu Jagiellonskiego. Seria Nauk Matematyezno-Przyrodniczych. Matematyka, Fizyka, Chemia — Zesz Nauk Uniw Jagiellon Ser Nauk Mat Przy
Zeszyty Naukowe Uniwersytetu Jagiellonskiego. Universitatis Iagellonicae Acta Chimica — Zesz Nauk Uniw Jagiellon Univ Iagellon Acta Chim
Zeszyty Naukowe Uniwersytetu Lodzkiego — Zesz Nauk Uniw Lodz
Zeszyty Naukowe Uniwersytetu Lodzkiego — ZNUL
Zeszyty Naukowe Uniwersytetu Lodzkiego. Fizyka — Zesz Nauk Uniw Lodz Fiz
Zeszyty Naukowe Uniwersytetu Lodzkiego. Nauki Humanistyczno-Spoleczne — Zesz Nauk Uniw Lodz Nauki Humanist-Spolecz
Zeszyty Naukowe Uniwersytetu Lodzkiego. Nauki Humanistyczno-Spoleczne. Historia — ZNULHist
Zeszyty Naukowe Uniwersytetu Lodzkiego. Nauki Matematyczno-Przyrodnicze — Zesz Nauk Uniw Lodz Nauki Mat Przyr
Zeszyty Naukowe Uniwersytetu Lodzkiego. Seria II. Nauki Matematyczno-Przyrodnicze [*Poland*] — Zesz Nauk Uniw Lodz Ser II
Zeszyty Naukowe Uniwersytetu Lodzkiego. Seria III — Zesz Nauk Uniw Lodz Ser III
Zeszyty Naukowe Uniwersytetu Mikolaja Kopernika — ZNUMK
Zeszyty Naukowe Uniwersytetu Mikolaja Kopernika w Toruniu. Nauki Humanistyczno-Spoleczne — ZNUT
Zeszyty Naukowe Uniwersytetu Mikolaja Kopernika w Toruniu. Nauki Matematyczno-Przyrodniczne Biologia — ZMKBA6
Zeszyty Naukowe Uniwersytetu Opolskiego. Chemia — Zesz Nauk Uniw Opolskiego Chem
Zeszyty Naukowe Uniwersytetu Wroclawskiego — ZNUnWr
Zeszyty Naukowe Uniwersytetu Wroclawskiego Imienia B. Bieruta — ZNUW
Zeszyty Naukowe. Weterynaria-Akademia Rolnicza w Warszawie — Zesz Nauk Weter Akad Roln Warsz
Zeszyty Naukowe Wydzialu Humanistycznego, Wyzsza Szkola Pedagogiczna w Gdansku — ZNG
Zeszyty Naukowe Wydzialu Matematyki, Fizyki, Chemii. Uniwersytet Gdanski. Seria Chemia — Zesz Nauk Wydz Mat Fiz Chem Uniw Gdanski Chem
Zeszyty Naukowe Wyzsza Szkola Ekonomiczna w Poznaniu. Seria 2. Prace Habilitacyjne i Doktorskie — Zesz Nauk Wyzsza Szk Ekon Poznaniu Ser 2
Zeszyty Naukowe Wyzsza Szkola Pedagogiczna im Powstancow Slaskich w Opolu. Matematyka — Zeszyty Nauk Wyz Szkola Ped Powstancow Sl Opolu Mat
Zeszyty Naukowe Wyzsza Szkola Pedagogiczna w Katowicach — Zesz NWSP
Zeszyty Naukowe Wyzsza Szkola Rolnicza w Szczecinie — Zesz Nauk Wyzs Szk Roln Szczecinie
Zeszyty Naukowe Wyzszej Szkoly Ekonomicznej w Katowicach — Zesz Nauk Wyz Szkol Ekon
Zeszyty Naukowe Wyzszej Szkoly Ekonomicznej w Katowicach — Zesz Nauk Wyzsz Szkoly Ekon Katowic
Zeszyty Naukowe Wyzszej Szkoly Ekonomicznej w Poznaniu — Zesz Nauk Wyzs Szk Ekon Poznaniu
Zeszyty Naukowe Wyzszej Szkoly Ekonomicznej w Poznaniu — Zesz Nauk Wyzsz Szkoly Ekon Poznan
Zeszyty Naukowe Wyzszej Szkoly Inzynierskiej w Bialymstoku Matematyka, Fizyka, Chemia — Zesz Nauk Wyzsz Szk Inz Bialymstoku Mat Fiz Chem
Zeszyty Naukowe Wyzszej Szkoly Pedagogicznej (Katowice) — ZNSPK
Zeszyty Naukowe Wyzszej Szkoly Pedagogicznej (Katowice) — ZNWSPK
Zeszyty Naukowe Wyzszej Szkoly Pedagogicznej (Opole) — ZNSPO
Zeszyty Naukowe Wyzszej Szkoly Pedagogicznej (Opole) — ZNWSPO
Zeszyty Naukowe Wyzszej Szkoly Pedagogicznej w Gdansku. Matematyka, Fizyka, Chemia — Zesz Nauk Wyzsz Szk Pedagog Gdansku Mat Fiz Chem
Zeszyty Naukowe Wyzszej Szkoly Pedagogicznej w Katowicach. Sekcja Fizyki — Zesz Nauk Wyzsz Szk Pedagog Katowicach Sekc Fiz
Zeszyty Naukowe Wyzszej Szkoly Pedagogicznej w Katowicach. Sekcja Fizyki — ZNWFA
Zeszyty Naukowe Wyzszej Szkoly Pedagogicznej w Opolu. Fizyka — Zeszyty Nauk Wyz Szkoly Ped w Opolu Fiz
Zeszyty Naukowe Wyzszej Szkoly Pedagogicznej w Opolu. Matematyka — Zeszyty Nauk Wyz Szkoly Ped w Opolu Mat
Zeszyty Naukowe Wyzszej Szkoly Rolniczej w Krakowie — Zesz Nauk Wyzs Szk Roln Krakowie
Zeszyty Naukowe Wyzszej Szkoly Rolniczej w Krakowie. Zootechnika — Zesz Nauk Wyzs Szk Roln Krakowie Zootech
Zeszyty Naukowe Wyzszej Szkoly Rolniczej w Olsztynie — Zesz Nauk Wyzs Szk Roln Olsztynie
Zeszyty Naukowe Wyzszej Szkoly Rolniczej w Olsztynie — Zesz Nauk Wyzsz Szk Roln Olsztynie
Zeszyty Naukowe Wyzszej Szkoly Rolniczej w Szczecinie — Zesz Nauk Wyzsz Szk Roln Szczecinie
Zeszyty Naukowe Wyzszej Szkoly Rolniczej we Wroclawiu — Zesz Nauk Wyzs Szk Roln Wroclawiu
Zeszyty Naukowe Wyzszej Szkoly Rolniczej we Wroclawiu. Melioracja — Zesz Nauk Wyzsz Szk Roln Wrocl Melior
Zeszyty Naukowe Wyzszej Szkoly Rolniczej we Wroclawiu. Melioracja — Zesz Nauk Wyzsz Szk Roln Wroclawiu Melior
Zeszyty Naukowe Wyzszej Szkoly Rolniczej we Wroclawiu. Rolnictwo — Zesz Nauk Wyzsz Szk Roln Wrocl Roln
Zeszyty Naukowe Wyzszej Szkoly Rolniczej we Wroclawiu. Rolnictwo — Zesz Nauk Wyzsz Szk Roln Wroclawiu Roln
Zeszyty Naukowe Wyzszej Szkoly Rolniczej we Wroclawiu. Weterynaria — Zesz Nauk Wyzs Szk Roln Wroclawiu Wet
Zeszyty Naukowe Wyzszej Szkoly Rolniczej we Wroclawiu. Weterynaria — Zesz Nauk Wyzsz Szk Roln Wroclawiu Weter
Zeszyty Naukowe Wyzszej Szkoly Rolniczej we Wroclawiu. Zootechnika — Zesz Nauk Wyzsz Szk Roln Wroclawiu Zootech
Zeszyty Naukowe. Zootechnika-Akademia Rolnicza w Warszawie — Zesz Nauk Zootech Akad Roln Warsz
Zeszyty Naukowe. Zootechnika-Akademia Rolniczo-Techniczna w Olsztynie — Zesz Nauk Zootech Akad Roln-Tech Olsztyn
Zeszyty Naukowo-Techniczny Wyzsza Szkola Inzynierska w Lublinie — Zesz Nauk Tech Wyzsza Szk Inz Lublinie
Zeszyty Problemowe Gornictwa — Zesz Probl Gorn
Zeszyty Problemowe Kosmosu — Zesz Probl Kosmosu
Zeszyty Problemowe Nauki Polskiej — Zesz Probl Nauki Pol
Zeszyty Problemowe Postepow Nauk Rolniczych — Zesz Prob Postepow Nauk Roln
Zeszyty Problemowe Postepow Nauk Rolniczych — Zesz Probl Postep Nauk Roln
Zeszyty Problemowe Postepow Nauk Rolniczych — Zesz Probl Postepow Nauk Roln
Zeszyty Wroclawskie — Zesz Wrocl
Zeszyty Wroclawskie — ZYWE
Zetemata. Monographien zur Klassischen Altertumswissenschaft — Zetem
Zetetic Scholar — Zetetic Schol
Zeumer's Quellen und Studien zur Verfassungsgeschichte des Deutschen Reichs in Mittelalter und Neuzeit — Zeumer's Q St
ZEV [*Zeitschrift fuer Eisenbahnwesen und Verkehrstechnik*] **Glasers. Annalen** — ZEV Glasers Ann
ZEV. Zeitschrift fuer Eisenbahnwesen und Verkehrstecknik. Glasers Annalen — ZEV A Eisenbahnwes Verkehrstech
ZFA (Zeitschrift fuer Allgemeinmedizin) — ZAMNA
ZFI [*Zentralinstitut fuer Isotopen- und Strahlenforschung*]-Mitteilungen [*East Germany*] — ZFI-Mitt
ZFO. Zeitschrift fuer Fuehrung und Organisation — ZFO
Zgodovinski Casopis — Z Cas
Zheleznodorozhnyi Transport [*Former USSR*] — Zheleznodorozhn Transp
Zheleznye Splavy — Zhelezn Splavy
Zhelezobetonnye Konstruktsii Chelyabinsk — Zhelezobeton Konstr Chelyabinsk
Zhidkofaznoe Okislenie Nepredel'nykh Organicheskikh Soedinenii — Zhidkofazn Okislenie Nepredel'nykh Org Soedin
Zhilishchnoe i Kommunal'noe Khozyaistvo — Zhilishchnoe Kommunal'n Khoz
Zhivotnov'dni Nauki — Zhivotnov'd Nauki
Zhivotnovodstvo — Zhivotnovod
Zhivotnovodstvo i Veterinariya — Zhivotnovod Vet

Zhivotnovudni Nauki — Zhivot Nauki
Zhivotnovudni Nauki — Zhivotnovud Nauki
Zhivotnovudstvo — Zhivotnovud
Zhongguo Jiguang — ZHJID
Zhongguo Niangzao — ZHNID
Zhonghua Fangshe Yixue Yu Fanghu Zazhi — ZFYZD
Zhurnal Analiticheskoi Khimii — Zh Anal Khim
Zhurnal Analiticheskoi Khimii — Zh Analit Khim
Zhurnal Ehksperimental'noj i Teoreticheskoj Fiziki Pis'ma - Redaktsiyu [*Former USSR*] — Zh Ehksp Teor Fiz Pis'ma Red
Zhurnal Ekologicheskoi Khimii — Zh Ekol Khim
Zhurnal Eksperimental'noi Biologii i Meditsiny — Zh Eksp Biol Med
Zhurnal Eksperimentalnoi i Klinicheskoi Meditsiny — Zh Eksp Klin Med
Zhurnal Eksperimentalnoi i Teoreticheskoi Fiziki — ZETFA
Zhurnal Eksperimentalnoi i Teoreticheskoi Fiziki — Zh Eksp i Teor Fiz
Zhurnal Eksperimentalnoi i Teoreticheskoi Fiziki — Zh Eksp Teo
Zhurnal Eksperimentalnoi i Teoreticheskoi Fiziki — Zh Eksp Teor Fiz
Zhurnal Eksperimentalnoi i Teoreticheskoi Fiziki. Pis'ma — Zh Eksp Teor Fiz Pis
Zhurnal Eksperimental'noi i Teoreticheskoi Fiziki. Pis'ma — Zh Eksp Teor Fiz Pis'ma
Zhurnal Eksperimental'noi i Teoreticheskoi Fiziki. Pis'ma v Redaktsiyu — Zh Eksp and Teor Fiz Pis'ma v Red
Zhurnal Evolyutsionnoi Biokhimii i Fiziologii — ZEBFA
Zhurnal Evolyutsionnoi Biokhimii i Fiziologii — Zh Evol Biokhim Fiziol
Zhurnal Fizicheskoi Khimii — Zh Fiz Khim
Zhurnal Fizichno-Khemichnogo Tsiklu Vseukrains'ka Akademiya Nauk — Zh Fiz Khem Tsiklu Vseukr Akad Nauk
Zhurnal Geofiziki — Zh Geofiz
Zhurnal Gigieny, Epidemiologii, Mikrobiologii, i Immunologii — ZGEIA
Zhurnal Gigieny, Epidemiologii, Mikrobiologii, i Immunologii — Zh Gig Epidemiol Mikrobiol Immunol
Zhurnal Gornogo Dela i Metallurgii. Metallurgiya — Zh Gorn Dela Metall Metall
Zhurnal Khimicheskoi Promyshlennosti — Zh Khim Promsti
Zhurnal Khimicheskoi Promyshlennosti — ZHKPA
Zhurnal Khimicheskoi Termodinamiki i Termokhimii — Zh Khim Termodin Termokhim
Zhurnal Mikrobiologii — Zhurnal Mikrobiol
Zhurnal Mikrobiologii, Epidemiologii, i Immunobiologii — Zh Mikrob E
Zhurnal Mikrobiologii, Epidemiologii, i Immunobiologii — Zh Mikrobiol Epidemiol Immunobiol
Zhurnal Mikrobiologii, Epidemiologii, i Immunobiologii — ZMEIA
Zhurnal Mikrobiologii i Immunobiologii — Zh Mikrobiol Immunobiol
Zhurnal Nauchnoi i Prikladnoi Fotografii i Kinematografii — Nauchn i Prikl Fotogr i Kinematogr
Zhurnal Nauchnoi i Prikladnoi Fotografii i Kinematografii — Zh Nauch Prik Foto Kinematog
Zhurnal Nauchnoi i Prikladnoi Fotografii i Kinematografii — Zh Nauchn Prikl Fotogr Kinematogr
Zhurnal Nauchnoi i Prikladnoi Fotografii i Kinematografii — Zh Nauchnoi i Prikl Fotogr i Kinematogr
Zhurnal Nauchnoi i Prikladnoi Fotografii i Kinematografii — Zh NP Fotog
Zhurnal Neorganicheskoi Khimii — Zh Neorg Kh
Zhurnal Neorganicheskoi Khimii — Zh Neorg Khim
Zhurnal Nevropatologii i Psikhiatrii Imeni S. S. Korsakova — Zh Nevropatol Psikhiatr
Zhurnal Nevropatologii i Psikhiatrii Imeni S. S. Korsakova — Zh Nevropatol Psikhiatr Im S S Korsakova
Zhurnal Nevropatologii i Psikhiatrii Imeni S. S. Korsakova — ZNPIA
Zhurnal Obshchei Biologii — Zh Obs Biol
Zhurnal Obshchei Biologii — Zh Obshch Biol
Zhurnal Obshchei Khimii — Zh Obs Kh
Zhurnal Obshchei Khimii — Zh Obshch Khim
Zhurnal Obshchei Khimii — Zh Obshchei Khim
Zhurnal Opytnoi Agronomii — Zh Opytn Agron
Zhurnal Organicheskoi Khimii — Zh Org Kh
Zhurnal Organicheskoi Khimii — Zh Org Khim
Zhurnal po Sel'skokhozyaistvennym Naukam — Zh S'kh Nauk
Zhurnal Prikladnoi Fiziki — Zh Prikl Fiz
Zhurnal Prikladnoi Khimii — Zh Prikl Khim
Zhurnal Prikladnoi Mekhaniki i Tekhnicheskoi Fiziki — Zh Prikl Mekhan Tekh Fiz
Zhurnal Prikladnoi Mekhaniki i Tekhnicheskoi Fiziki — Zh Prikl Mekh Tekh Fiz
Zhurnal Prikladnoi Spektroskopii — Zh Prikl Spektrosk
Zhurnal Rezinovoi Promyshlennosti — Zh Rezin Promsti
Zhurnal Russkago Fiziko-Khimicheskago Obshchestva — Zh Russ Fiz-Khim Ova
Zhurnal Russkago Khimicheskago Obshchestva — Zh Russ Khim Ova
Zhurnal Russkago Khimicheskago Obshchestva i Fizicheskago Obshchestva — Zh Russ Khim Ova Fiz Ova
Zhurnal Russkogo Fiziko-Khimicheskogo Obshchestva Chast Fizicheskaya — Zh Russ Fiz-Khim Ova Chast Fiz
Zhurnal Russkogo Fiziko-Khimicheskogo Ovshchestva Chast Khimicheskaya — Zh Russ Fiz Khim Ova Chast Khim
Zhurnal Russkogo Metallurgicheskogo Obshchestva — Zh Russ Metall Ova
Zhurnal Sakharnoi Promyshlennosti — Zh Sakh Promsti
Zhurnal Strukturnoi Khimii — Zh Strukt Khim
Zhurnal Tekhnicheskoi Fiziki — Zh Tekh Fiz
Zhurnal Ushnykh Nosovykh i Gorlovykh Boleznei — Zh Ushn Nos Gorl Bolezn
Zhurnal Ushnykh Nosovykh i Gorlovykh Boleznei — Zh Ushn Nosov Gorlov Bolez
Zhurnal Ushnykh Nosovykh i Gorlovykh Boleznei — Zhu Us Nos i Gorl Bol
Zhurnal Ushnykh Nosovykh i Gorlovykh Boleznei — ZUNBA
Zhurnal Voprosy Neirokhirurgii Imeni N. N. Burdenko — Zh Vopr Neirokhir
Zhurnal Voprosy Neirokhirurgii Imeni N. N. Burdenko — Zh Vopr Neirokhir Im N N Burdenko
Zhurnal Vsesoiuznogo Khimicheskogo Obshchestva imeni D. I. Mendeleeva — Zh Vses Khim Obshchest Mendeleeva
Zhurnal Vsesoyuznogo Khimicheskogo Obshchestva — Zh Vses Khim Obshch
Zhurnal Vsesoyuznogo Khimicheskogo Obshchestva Imeni D. I. Mendeleeva — Zh Vses Khi
Zhurnal Vsesoyuznogo Khimicheskogo Obshchestva Imeni D. I. Mendeleeva — Zh Vses Khim Ova
Zhurnal Vsesoyuznogo Khimicheskogo Obshchestva Imeni D. I. Mendeleeva — Zh Vses Khim Ova Im D I Mendeleeva
Zhurnal Vsesoyuznogo Khimicheskogo Obshchestva Imeni D. I. Mendeleeva — ZVKOA
Zhurnal Vychislitel'noi Matematiki i Matematicheske Fiziki — Zh Vychisl Mat i Mat Fiz
Zhurnal Vychislitel'noi Matematiki i Matematicheske Fiziki — Zh Vychisl Mat Mat Fiz
Zhurnal Vysshei Nervnoi Deyatel'nosti — Zh Vyssh Nerv Deyat
Zhurnal Vysshei Nervnoi Deyatel'nosti Imeni I. P. Pavlova — Zh Vyss Ner
Zhurnal Vysshei Nervnoi Deyatel'nosti Imeni I. P. Pavlova — Zh Vyssh Nervn Deyat Im I P Pavlova
Zhurnal Vysshei Nervnoi Deyatel'nosti Imeni I. P. Pavlova — ZVNDA
ZI [*Ziegelindustrie*] **International** [*Germany*] — ZI Int
Ziekenhuis — ZHW
Zielsprache Deutsch — ZD
Zielsprache Spanisch — Zielspr Span
Ziemia Czestochowska — ZCzest
Ziemia i Morze — ZiM
Zig-Zag Forestiere — Zig Zag Forest
Zimbabwe Agricultural Journal — Zimb Agric J
Zimbabwe Agricultural Journal — Zimbabwe Agric J
Zimbabwe. Division of Livestock and Pastures. Annual Report — ARDSDN
Zimbabwe. Division of Livestock and Pastures. Annual Report — Zimbabwe Div Livest Pastures Annu Rep
Zimbabwe Engineer — Zimb Eng
Zimbabwe Engineer — Zimbabwe Eng
Zimbabwe Environment and Design — ZED
Zimbabwe Journal of Agricultural Research — Zimb J Agric Res
Zimbabwe Journal of Agricultural Research — Zimbabwe J Agric Res
Zimbabwe Journal of Agricultural Research — ZJARDK
Zimbabwe Journal of Economics — Zimbabwe J Econ
Zimbabwe Law Journal — Zimb Law J
Zimbabwe Librarian — Zimb Libr
Zimbabwe Review — Zimbabwe Rev
Zimbabwe Rhodesia Nurse — Zimbabwe Rhod Nurse
Zimbabwe Science News — Zimb Sci News
Zimbabwe Science News — Zimbabwe Sci News
Zimbabwe Science News — ZRSNDI
Zimbabwe Science News — ZSNED7
Zimbabwe Veterinary Journal — Zimbabwe Vet J
Zimbabwe-Rhodesia Science News — Zimbabwe Rhod Sci News
Zinatniskie Raksti. Rigas Politehniskais Instituts — Zinat Raksti Rigas Politeh Inst
Zinc Abstracts — Zinc Abstr
Zinc/Cadmium Research Digest — Zinc/Cadmium Res Dig
Zinc Research Digest — Zinc Res Dig
Zinn und Seine Verwendung — Zinn Verwend
Zionist Archives — ZA
Zionist Record — ZR
Zionist Review — ZR
ZIP Target Marketing — ZIP
Ziraat Dergisi — Ziraat Derg
Ziraat Fakultesi Dergisi Ege Universitesi — Ziraat Fak Derg Ege Univ
ZIS [*Zentralinstitut fuer Schweisstechnik*] **Mitteilungen** — ZIS Mitt
ZIS (Zentralinstitut fuer Schweisstechnik der Deutschen Demokratischen Republik) Mitteilungen — ZIS (Zentralinst Schweisstech DDR) Mitt
Zisin/Journal of the Seismological Society of Japan — Zisin J Seismol Soc Jpn
Zisin/Seismological Society of Japan. Journal — Zisin Seismol Soc Jap J
Ziva Antika — ZA
Ziva Antika — ZAnt
Ziva. Casopis pro Biologickou Praci — Ziva
Zivi Jezici — ZJ
Zivilgesetzbuch — ZGB
Zivocisna Vyroba — Zivoc Vyroba
Zivocisna Vyroba-Ceskoslovenska Akademie Zemedelska. Ustav Vedeckotechnickych Informaci pro Zemedelstvi — Zivocisna Vyroba Cesk Akad Zemed Ustav Vedeckotech Inf Zemed
Zivot — Z
Zivotne Prostredie — Zivotn Prostr
Zivotne Prostredie [*Czechoslovakia*] — ZIVP
ZM. Zahnaerztliche Mitteilungen. Ausgabe A — ZM Zahnaerztl Mitt A
Znamya [*Moscow*] — Zn
Zobozdravstveni Vestnik — Zobozdrav Vestn
Zofinger Neujahrsblatt — ZA
Zofinger Neujahrsblatt — Zof N
Zolltarifgesetz — ZTG
Zolnierz Polski [*Poland*] — Zolnierz Pol
Zolotaya Promyshlennost — Zolotaya Promst
Zona Franca — ZF
Zona Franca (Caracas) — Zona Fran Caracas
Zoning and Planning Law Report — Zoning and Plan L Rep
Zoo Biology — ZOBIDX
Zoo Biology — Zoo Biol
Zoo. Revista del Parque Zoologico de Barcelona — Zoo Rev Parque Zool Barc
Zooiatria Revista de Medicina Veterinaria y Produccion Pecuaria — Zooiatr Rev Med Vet Prod Pecu
Zoologia e Biologia Marinha — Zool Biol Mar

Zoologia e Biologia Marinha (Sao Paulo) (Nova Serie) — Zool Biol Mar (Sao Paulo) (Nova Ser)
Zoologica — ZOLGA
Zoologica Africana — Zool Afr
Zoologica Orientalis — Zool Orient
Zoologica Orientalis — ZOOREO
Zoologica Poloniae — Zool Pol
Zoologica Poloniae — Zoologica Pol
Zoologica Scripta — Zool Scr
Zoologica Scripta — Zoologica Scr
Zoologica Scripta — ZOSC
Zoological Bulletin — Zool B
Zoological Institute. Faculty of Science. University of Tokyo. Annual Report — Zool Inst Fac Sci Univ Tokyo Annu Rep
Zoological Journal. Linnean Society — Zool J Linn
Zoological Journal. Linnean Society — Zool J Linn Soc
Zoological Journal. Linnean Society of London — Zool J Linnean Soc Lond
Zoological Magazine — Zool Mag
Zoological Magazine (Tokyo) — Zool Mag (Tokyo)
Zoological Record — Zoo Rec
Zoological Record — Zool Rec
Zoological Record — ZR
Zoological Record Online — ZRO
Zoological Record Search Guide — ZRSG
Zoological Research — Zool Res
Zoological Science — Zool Sci
Zoological Science (Tokyo) — Zool Sci (Tokyo)
Zoological Society of Egypt. Bulletin — Zool Soc Egypt Bull
Zoological Society of London. Proceedings — Zool Soc London Pr
Zoological Society of London. Proceedings — Zool Soc London Proc
Zoologicheskii Zhurnal — Zool Z
Zoologicheskii Zhurnal — Zool Zh
Zoologicke a Entomologicke Listy — Zool Entomol Listy
Zoologicke Listy — Zool Listy
Zoologijas Muzeja Raksti. Invertebrata — Zool Muz Raksti Invertebrata
Zoologische Abhandlungen (Dresden) — Zool Abh (Dres)
Zoologische Annalen — Zool Ann
Zoologische Anzeiger. Supplement — Zool Anz Suppl
Zoologische Beitraege — Zool Beitr
Zoologische Bijdragen — Zool Bijdr
Zoologische Gaerten — ZOGAAV
Zoologische Gaerten — Zool Gaert
Zoologische Gaerten (Leipzig) — Zool Gart (Lpz)
Zoologische Jahrbuecher — Zool Jb
Zoologische Jahrbuecher. Abteilung fuer Allgemeine Zoologie und Physiologie der Tiere — Zool Jahrb
Zoologische Jahrbuecher. Abteilung fuer Allgemeine Zoologie und Physiologie der Tiere — Zool Jahrb Abt Allg Zool Physiol Tiere
Zoologische Jahrbuecher. Abteilung fuer Allgemeine Zoologie und Physiologie der Tiere — Zool Jb Abt Allg Zool Physiol Tiere
Zoologische Jahrbuecher. Abteilung fuer Allgemeine Zoologie und Physiologie der Tiere — Zool Jhrb Abt Allg Zool Physiol Tiere
Zoologische Jahrbuecher. Abteilung fuer Anatomie und Ontogenie der Tiere — Zool Jahrb Abt Anat Ontog Tiere
Zoologische Jahrbuecher. Abteilung fuer Systematik Oekologie und Geographie der Tiere — Zool Jahrb Abt Syst Oekol Geogr Tiere
Zoologische Jahrbuecher. Abteilung fuer Systematik Oekologie und Geographie der Tiere — Zool Jb Abt Syst Okol Geog Tiere
Zoologische Jahrbuecher. Abteilung fuer Systematik Oekologie und Geographie der Tiere (Jena) — Zool Jahrb Abt Syst (Jena)
Zoologische Mededelingen (Leiden) — Zool Meded (Leiden)
Zoologische Mededelingen. Rijks Museum van Natuurlijke Historie te Leiden — Zool Meded Rijks Mus Nat Hist Leiden
Zoologische Verhandelingen — Zool Verh
Zoologische Verhandelingen (Leiden) — Zool Verh (Leiden)
Zoologische Verhandelingen. Rijksmuseum van Natuurlijke Historie (Leiden) — Zool Verh Rijksmus Nat Hist (Leiden)
Zoologischer Anzeiger — ZA
Zoologischer Anzeiger — Zo A
Zoologischer Anzeiger — Zool Anz
Zoologischer Anzeiger — Zool Anzeiger
Zoologischer Anzeiger (Leipzig) — Zool Anz (Leipzig)
Zoologischer Bericht — Zool Ber
Zoologisches Zentralblatt — Zool Zentralbl
Zoologisk Revy — Zool Revy
Zoologiska Bidrag fran Uppsala — Zool Bidr Upps
Zoologiska Bidrag fran Uppsala — Zool Bidr Uppsala
Zoology Publications. Victoria University of Wellington — Zool Publ Victoria Univ Wellington
Zoonoses Research — Zoonoses Res
Zoophysiology and Ecology — Zoophysiol Ecol
Zootechnical Experiment Station. Research Bulletin — Zootech Experiment Stn Res Bull
Zootecnia e Vita — Zootec Vita
Zootecnica e Nutrizione Animale — ZNAND
Zootecnica e Nutrizione Animale — Zootec Nutr Anim
Zootecnica e Veterinaria — Zootec Vet
Zootecnica. Veterinaria e Agricoltura — Zootec Vet Agric
Zora — Z
Zosen — ZRI
Zprava o Cinnosti Masarykovy Akademie Prace — Zprava Cinnosti Masarykovy Akad Prace
Zpravodaj Mistopisne Komise CSAV [*Ceskoslovenske Akademie Ved*] — ZMK
Zpravodaj Mistopisne Komise CSAV [*Ceskoslovenske Akademie Ved*] — ZprMK
Zpravodajsky List Kolektivu Pocumavskych Floristu — Zprav List Kolektivu Pocumavsk Floristu
Zpravy Ceskoslovenske Keramicke a Sklarske Spolecnosti — Zpr Cesk Keram Sklarske Spol
Zpravy Ceskoslovenskeho Statniho Archeologickeho Ustavu. Praha — Zpravy Praha
Zpravy Dendrologicke Sekce Ceskoslovenske Botanicke Spolecnosti — Zpravy Dendrol Sekce Ceskoslov Bot Spolecn
Zpravy Hornickeho Ustavu CSAV [*Ceskoslovenska Akademie Ved*] — ZHUCA
Zpravy Jednoty Klasickych Filologu — ZJKF
Zpravy Jednoty Klasickych Filologu — Zpravy JKF
Zpravy Krkonosskeho Narodniho Parku — Zpravy Krkonssk Nar Parku
Zpravy Okresniho Musea v Trutnove — Zpravy Okresn Mus V Trutnove
Zpravy pro Cestinare — Zpravy
Zpravy Vlastivedneho Musea v Prostejove — Zpravy Vlastiv Mus V Prostejove
Zpravy Zemskeho Vyzkumneho Ustavu Hospodarskeho pro Pestovani Rostlin v Brne — Zpravy Zemsk Vyzk Ustavu Hospod Pestovani Rostl V Brne
Zroshuvane Zemlerobstvo — Zrosh Zemlerob
Zroshuvane Zemlerobstvo — Zroshuvane Zemlerob
Z's Briefs. CPSU [*Cooperative Park Studies Unit, University of Alaska*] **Newsletter** — ZBRS
Zubolekarski Pregled — Zubolek Pregl
Zucker Beihefte — Zucker Beih
Zucker- Frucht- und Gemueseverwertung — Zucker Frucht Gemueseverwert
Zucker Sonderbeilage — Zucker Sonderbeil
Zucker- und Suesswaren Wirtschaft — Zuck u SuesswarWirt
Zucker- und Suesswaren Wirtschaft — Zucker Suesswaren Wirtsch
Zuckerindustrie. Landwirtschaft, Technik, Chemie, Wirtschaft — DZI
Zuercher Beitraege zur Deutschen Literatur und Geistesgeschichte — ZBDLG
Zuercher Beitraege zur Deutschen Sprach- und Stilgeschichte — ZBDSS
Zuercher Beitraege zur Geschichtswissenschaft — Zuercher Beitraege
Zuercher Beitraege zur Rechtswissenschaft — Zuercher Beitraege
Zuercher Bibelkommentare — ZuB
Zuercher Denkmalpflege — ZD
Zuercher Taschenbuch — ZT
Zuercher Taschenbuch — ZTB
Zuercher-Chronik — ZC
Zuerich Universitaet. Geologisches Institut - Eidgenoessische Technische Hochschule. Geologisches Institut. Mitteilungen — Zuer Univ Geol Inst-Eidgenoss Tech Hochsch Geol Inst Mitt
Zuger Neujahrsblatt — ZN
Zuger Neujahrsblatt — ZugerNjb
Zuivelzicht — FNZ
Zunz Archive. Jewish National and University Library [*Jerusalem*] — ZA
Zur Didaktik der Physik und Chemie — Zur Didak Phys Chem
Zur Erkenntnis der Dichtung — ZED
Zur Geschichte Lateinischer Eigennamen — ZGLE
Zur Geschichte Lateinischer Eigennamen — ZGLEN
Zurnal Analiticeskoj Chimii — Z An Chim
Zurnal Analiticeskoj Chimii — Z Analit Chim
Zurnal Analiticeskoj Chimii — ZA Ch
Zurnal Ekologii i Biocenologii — Zurn Ekol Biocenol
Zurnal Eksperimental'noi i Teoreticeskoi Fiziki — Z Eksper Teoret Fiz
Zurnal Eksperimental'noi i Teoreticeskoi Fiziki — ZETF
Zurnal Eksperimental'noj i Kliniceskoj Mediciny — Z Eks Klin Med
Zurnal Ministerstva Narodnogo Prosvescenija — ZMNP
Zurnal Moskovskoi Patriarkhii [*Moscow*] — ZMP
Zurnal Neorganiceskoj Chimii — Z Neorg Chim
Zurnal Neorganiceskoj Chimii — ZN Ch
Zurnal Obscej Biologii — Z Obsc Biol
Zurnal Obscej Chimii — Z Obsc Chim
Zurnal Prikladnoi Mehaniki i Tehniceskoi Fiziki — Z Prikl Meh i Tehn Fiz
Zurnal Russkago Botaniceskago Obscestva pri Akademii Nauk. Journal de la Societe Botanique de Russie — Zurn Russk Bot Obsc Akad Nauk
Zurnal Russkago Fiziko-Himiceskago Obscestva pri Imperatorskom S.-Peterburgskom Universitete. Cast' Himiceskaja. Journal de la Societe Physico-Chemique Russe — Zurn Russk Fiz Him Obsc Imp S Peterburgsk Univ Cast Him
Zurnal Sadovodstva. Izdavaemyj Rossijskim Obscestvom Ljubitelej Sadovodstva v Moskve — Zurn Sadov
Zurnal Strukturnoi Himii. Akademija Nauk SSR. Sibirskoe Otdelenie — Z Strukturn Him
Zurnal Strukturnoj Chimii — ZS Ch
Zurnal Techniceskoj Fiziki — Z Techn Fiz
Zurnal Vycislitel'noi Matematiki i Matematiceskoi Fiziki — Z Vycisl Mat i Mat Fiz
Zurnaly Obscestva Ljubitelej Komnatnyh Rastenij i Akvariumov v S.-Peterburge — Zurn Obsc Ljubit Komnatn Rast S Peterburge
Zvaracsky Sbornik — Zvaracsky Sb
Zven'ya — Z
Zverolekarsky Obzor — Zverolek Obz
Zvezda — Zv
Zvezda Vostoka — ZvV
Zweiter Weltkongress der Musikbibliotheken — Z Weltkongress
ZWF. Zeitschrift fuer Wirtschaftliche Fertigung — ZWF Z Wirtsch Fertigung
ZWF Zeitschrift fuer Wirtschaftlichen Fabrikbetrieb — ZWF Z Wirtsch Fabrikbetr
Zwierzeta Laboratoryjne — Zwierzeta Lab
Zwingliana — Z
Zwolse Reeks van Taal- en Letterkundige Studies — ZRTLS
ZWR. Zahnaerztliche Welt, Zahnaerztliche Rundschau, Zahnaerztliche Reform — ZWR
Zycie — Z
Zycie i Mysl — ZM
Zycie Literackie — ZL
Zycie Literackie [*Krakow*] — ZLit
Zycie Nauki — ZN

Zycie Nauki — ZNa
Zycie Weterynaryjne — Zycie Weteryn
Zydowskie Towarzystwo Ochrony Sierot — ZTOS
Zydowskie Towarzystwo Opieki Spolecznej — ZTOS
Zydowskie Towarzystwo Prezeciwgruzliczego — ZTP
Zygon — PZYG
Zygon — Zy
Zygon Newsletter — Zy Newsl
Zymologica e Chemica dei Colloidi — Zymol Chem Colloidi
Zymurgy — IZYM
Zywienie Czlowieka i Metabolizm — Zywienie Czlowieka Metab
Zywnosc, Technologia, Jakosc — Zywn Technol Jakosc